Who's Who in American Law®

Who'sWho in American Law®

2003-2004

13th Edition

121 Chanlon Road
New Providence, NJ 07974 U.S.A.
www.marquiswhoswho.com

Who'sWho in American Law®

Published by Marquis Who's Who®, a member of the LexisNexis Group.

President and Chief Executive Officer John Lawler
Vice President and Chief Financial Officer Philip T. Evans
Chief Information Officer John Roney

For information, contact:
Marquis Who's Who®
121 Chanlon Road
New Providence, New Jersey 07974
1-908-673-1001
www.marquiswhoswho.com

WHO'S WHO IN AMERICAN LAW® is a registered trademark of Reed Publishing (Nederland) B.V., used under license.
Library of Congress Catalog Card Number.

International Standard Book Number 0-8379-3520-2 (Classic Edition)
0-8379-3521-0 (Deluxe Edition)

International Standard Serial Number 0083-9817

Manufactured in the United States of America.

Table of Contents

Preface

The thirteenth edition of *Who's Who in American Law* provides biographical information on close to 18,000 lawyers and professionals in law-related areas including, among others, judges, legal educators, law librarians, legal historians, and social scientists.

The biographical sketches include such information as education, vital statistics, career history, awards, publications, memberships, address(es), and more. In addition, practicing lawyers were asked to include their fields of legal expertise or interest.

In this edition, there are separate indexes for individuals involved actively in the practice of law and for other legal professionals such as judges, law librarians, and legal educators. The "Fields of Practice Index" enables *Who's Who in American Law* users to access practicing lawyers geographically by city and state within fields such as federal or state civil litigation, corporate, taxation, criminal, and approximately 70 other fields of law. The "Professional Index" lists other professionals geographically by type of career such as education, government, or judicial administration.

The selection of the law field codes for the "Fields of Practice Index" was derived from three main sources, beginning with the specialty categories described by the American Bar Association Standing Committee on Specialization. Further information was supplied by state committees and boards on specialization, outlining the specialties recognized by or certified with the respective states. These lists reflect the varying degrees of specialty certification from state to state. Finally, an acknowledged expert on specialization in the legal profession provided valuable information and recommendations for a comprehensive list of recognized areas of law.

Practicing attorneys were asked to select up to three fields that reflected personal practice or interest. The Biographees' sketches reflect these fields. The "Fields of Practice Index" lists these lawyers under their selected fields. Individualized fields not encompassed in the list and newly emerging areas with relatively few practitioners are listed by Biographee name at the end of the index under the category "Other."

As in all Marquis Who's Who biographical volumes, the principle of current reference value determines selection of Biographees. Reference interest is based either on position of responsibility or noteworthy achievement. In the editorial evaluation that resulted in the ultimate selection of the names in this directory, an individual's desire to be listed was not sufficient reason for inclusion.

Each candidate is invited to submit biographical data about his or her life and professional career. Submitted information is reviewed by the Marquis editorial staff before being written in sketch form, and a prepublication proof of the composed sketch is sent to potential Biographees for verification. Every verified sketch returned by a candidate and accepted by the editorial staff is written in the final Marquis Who's Who format. This process ensures a high degree of accuracy.

In the event that individuals of significant reference interest fail to submit biographical data, the Marquis staff compiles the information through independent research. Sketches compiled in this manner are denoted by asterisks.

Marquis Who's Who editors diligently prepare each biographical sketch for publication. Occasionally, however, errors do appear. We regret all such errors and invite Biographees to notify the publisher so that corrections can be made in a subsequent edition.

Board of Advisors

Marquis Who's Who® gratefully acknowledges the following distinguished individuals who have made themselves available for review, evaluation, and general comment with regard to the Marquis publication of the 13th edition of *Who's Who in American Law.* The advisors have enhanced the reference value of this edition by the nomination of outstanding individuals for inclusion. However, the Board of Advisors, either collectively or individually, is in no way responsible for the final selection of names appearing in this volume, nor does the Board of Advisors bear responsibility for the accuracy or comprehensiveness of the biographical information or other material contained herein.

Standards of Admission

Selection of Biographees for *Who's Who in American Law* is determined by reference interest. Such reference value is based on either of two factors: (1) incumbency in a defined position of responsibility or (2) attainment of a significant level of achievement.

Admission based on position includes the following examples:

Justices of the U.S. Supreme Court

Judges of the U.S. Circuit Courts

Judges of the U.S. District Courts

Attorney General of the United States and other high-ranking federal executive attorneys

Chief counsel of congressional committees

Justices of state and territorial courts of the highest appellate jurisdiction

State and territorial attorneys general

Chief judges of selected county courts, based on population

Deans and professors at leading law schools

General counsel of major corporations and labor unions

Officials of the American Bar Association and specialized bar groups

Officials of state and territorial bar associations

Officials of selected county and city bar associations, based on population

Highly rated lawyers in private practice

Editors of important legal journals

Admission by the factor of significant achievement is based on objective criteria for measuring accomplishments within the legal profession.

Key Information

[1] STEELE, FLETCHER DAVID, [2] mechanical engineer; **[3]** b. Normal, Ill., Jan. 20, 1939; **[4]** s. Thomas William and Susan (Shobe) S.; **[5]** m. Julie Ann Walsh, Sept. 8, 1964; **[6]** children: Honor Elizabeth Carter, Michael Thomas. **[7]** BSME, Purdue U., 1961; MS, U. Ill., 1965. **[8]** Registered profl. engr., Ill., Iowa. **[9]** Asst. engr. Kelly, Kitching, Berendes & Brault, Engrs., Chgo., 1966-67, engr., 1967-71; sr. engr. Kelly, Kitching, Berendes & Brault, Internat., Des Moines, 1971-78, mgr. fluids divsn. 1979-84, v.p. R & D, 1985-90, exec. v.p. 1990—; **[10]** lectr. Drake U., 1995-97. **[11]** Contbr. articles to Jour. Biomech. Engring., Jour. Fluids Engring. **[12]** Asst. troop leader Des Moines coun. Boy Scouts Am., 1992—. **[13]** Lt. U.S. Army, 1961-63. **[14]** Fulbright scholar, 1965. **[15]** Mem. ASME, NSPE, Iowa Mech. Engrs. Assn., Big Sand Lake Club. **[16]** Republican. **[17]** Roman Catholic. **[18]** Achievements include patent for internal piston lock for hydraulic cylinders; design of L16500 Workhorse rotar; research in linear regression analysis for large-lot engine data comparisons. **[19]** Home: 733 N Ottawa Rd Ankeny IA 50021 **[20]** Office: 1245 34th St Des Moines IA 50311

KEY

- [1] Name
- [2] Occupation
- [3] Vital statistics
- [4] Parents
- [5] Marriage
- [6] Children
- [7] Education
- [8] Professional certifications
- [9] Career
- [10] Career-related
- [11] Writings and creative works
- [12] Civic and political activities
- [13] Military
- [14] Awards and fellowships
- [15] Professional and association memberships, clubs and lodges
- [16] Political affiliation
- [17] Religion
- [18] Achievements information
- [19] Home address
- [20] Office address

Table of Abbreviations

The following abbreviations and symbols are frequently used in this book.

*An asterisk following a sketch indicates that it was researched by the Marquis Who's Who editorial staff and has not been verified by the Biographee.

A

A Associate (used with academic degrees only)
AA, A.A. Associate in Arts, Associate of Arts
AAAL American Academy of Arts and Letters
AAAS American Association for the Advancement of Science
AACD American Association for Counseling and Development
AACN American Association of Critical Care Nurses
AAHA American Academy of Health Administrators
AAHP American Association of Hospital Planners
AAHPERD American Alliance for Health, Physical Education, Recreation, and Dance
AAS Associate of Applied Science
AASL American Association of School Librarians
AASPA American Association of School Personnel Administrators
AAU Amateur Athletic Union
AAUP American Association of University Professors
AAUW American Association of University Women
AB, A.B. Arts, Bachelor of
AB Alberta
ABA American Bar Association
ABC American Broadcasting Company
AC Air Corps
acad. academy, academic
acct. accountant
acctg. accounting
ACDA Arms Control and Disarmament Agency
ACHA American College of Hospital Administrators
ACLS Advanced Cardiac Life Support
ACLU American Civil Liberties Union
ACOG American College of Ob-Gyn
ACP American College of Physicians
ACS American College of Surgeons
ADA American Dental Association
a.d.c. aide-de-camp
adj. adjunct, adjutant
adj. gen. adjutant general
adm. admiral
adminstr. administrator
adminstrn. administration
adminstrv. administrative
ADN Associate's Degree in Nursing
ADP Automatic Data Processing
adv. advocate, advisory
advt. advertising
AE, A.E. Agricultural Engineer
A.E. and P. Ambassador Extraordinary and Plenipotentiary
AEC Atomic Energy Commission
aero. aeronautical, aeronautic
aerodyn. aerodynamic
AFB Air Force Base
AFL-CIO American Federation of Labor and Congress of Industrial Organizations
AFTRA American Federation of TV and Radio Artists
AFSCME American Federation of State, County and Municipal Employees
agr. agriculture
agrl. agricultural
agt. agent
AGVA American Guild of Variety Artists
agy. agency
A&I Agricultural and Industrial
AIA American Institute of Architects
AIAA American Institute of Aeronautics and Astronautics
AIChE American Institute of Chemical Engineers
AICPA American Institute of Certified Public Accountants
AID Agency for International Development
AIDS Acquired Immune Deficiency Syndrome
AIEE American Institute of Electrical Engineers
AIM American Institute of Management
AIME American Institute of Mining, Metallurgy, and Petroleum Engineers
AK Alaska
AL Alabama
ALA American Library Association
Ala. Alabama
alt. alternate
Alta. Alberta
A&M Agricultural and Mechanical
AM, A.M. Arts, Master of
Am. American, America
AMA American Medical Association
amb. ambassador
A.M.E. African Methodist Episcopal
Amtrak National Railroad Passenger Corporation
AMVETS American Veterans of World War II, Korea, Vietnam
ANA American Nurses Association
anat. anatomical
ANCC American Nurses Credentialing Center
ann. annual
ANTA American National Theatre and Academy
anthrop. anthropological
AP Associated Press
APA American Psychological Association
APGA American Personnel Guidance Association
APHA American Public Health Association
APO Army Post Office
apptd. appointed
Apr. April
apt. apartment
AR Arkansas
ARC American Red Cross
arch. architect
archeol. archeological
archtl. architectural
Ariz. Arizona
Ark. Arkansas
ArtsD, ArtsD. Arts, Doctor of
arty. artillery
AS American Samoa
AS Associate in Science
ASCAP American Society of Composers, Authors and Publishers
ASCD Association for Supervision and Curriculum Development
ASCE American Society of Civil Engineers
ASHRAE American Society of Heating, Refrigeration, and Air Conditioning Engineers
ASME American Society of Mechanical Engineers
ASNSA American Society for Nursing Service Administrators
ASPA American Society for Public Administration
ASPCA American Society for the Prevention of Cruelty to Animals
assn. association
assoc. associate
asst. assistant
ASTD American Society for Training and Development
ASTM American Society for Testing and Materials
astron. astronomical
astrophys. astrophysical
ATLA Association of Trial Lawyers of America
ATSC Air Technical Service Command
AT&T American Telephone & Telegraph Company
atty. attorney
Aug. August
AUS Army of the United States
aux. auxiliary
Ave. Avenue
AVMA American Veterinary Medical Association
AZ Arizona
AWHONN Association of Women's Health Obstetric and Neonatal Nurses

B

B. Bachelor
b. born
BA, B.A. Bachelor of Arts
BAgr, B.Agr. Bachelor of Agriculture
Balt. Baltimore
Bapt. Baptist
BArch, B.Arch. Bachelor of Architecture

BAS, B.A.S. Bachelor of Agricultural Science
BBA, B.B.A. Bachelor of Business Administration
BBB Better Business Bureau
BBC British Broadcasting Corporation
BC, B.C. British Columbia
BCE, B.C.E. Bachelor of Civil Engineering
BChir, B.Chir. Bachelor of Surgery
BCL, B.C.L. Bachelor of Civil Law
BCLS Basic Cardiac Life Support
BCS, B.C.S. Bachelor of Commercial Science
BD, B.D. Bachelor of Divinity
bd. board
BE, B.E. Bachelor of Education
BEE, B.E.E. Bachelor of Electrical Engineering
BFA, B.F.A. Bachelor of Fine Arts
bibl. biblical
bibliog. bibliographical
biog. biographical
biol. biological
BJ, B.J. Bachelor of Journalism
Bklyn. Brooklyn
BL, B.L. Bachelor of Letters
bldg. building
BLS, B.L.S. Bachelor of Library Science
BLS Basic Life Support
Blvd. Boulevard
BMI Broadcast Music, Inc.
BMW Bavarian Motor Works (Bayerische Motoren Werke)
bn. battalion
B.&O.R.R. Baltimore & Ohio Railroad
bot. botanical
BPE, B.P.E. Bachelor of Physical Education
BPhil, B.Phil. Bachelor of Philosophy
br. branch
BRE, B.R.E. Bachelor of Religious Education
brig. gen. brigadier general
Brit. British, Brittanica
Bros. Brothers
BS, B.S. Bachelor of Science
BSA, B.S.A. Bachelor of Agricultural Science
BSBA Bachelor of Science in Business Administration
BSChemE Bachelor of Science in Chemical Engineering
BSD, B.S.D. Bachelor of Didactic Science
BSEE Bachelor of Science in Electrical Engineering
BSN Bachelor of Science in Nursing
BST, B.S.T. Bachelor of Sacred Theology
BTh, B.Th. Bachelor of Theology
bull. bulletin
bur. bureau
bus. business
B.W.I. British West Indies

C

CA California
CAA Civil Aeronautics Administration
CAB Civil Aeronautics Board
CAD-CAM Computer Aided Design–Computer Aided Model
Calif. California
C.Am. Central America
Can. Canada, Canadian
CAP Civil Air Patrol
capt. captain
cardiol. cardiological
cardiovasc. cardiovascular
CARE Cooperative American Relief Everywhere
Cath. Catholic
cav. cavalry
CBC Canadian Broadcasting Company
CBI China, Burma, India Theatre of Operations
CBS Columbia Broadcasting Company
C.C. Community College
CCC Commodity Credit Corporation
CCNY City College of New York
CCRN Critical Care Registered Nurse
CCU Cardiac Care Unit
CD Civil Defense
CE, C.E. Corps of Engineers, Civil Engineer
CEN Certified Emergency Nurse
CENTO Central Treaty Organization
CEO chief executive officer
CERN European Organization of Nuclear Research
cert. certificate, certification, certified
CETA Comprehensive Employment Training Act
CFA Chartered Financial Analyst
CFL Canadian Football League
CFO chief financial officer
CFP Certified Financial Planner
ch. church
ChD, Ch.D. Doctor of Chemistry
chem. chemical
ChemE, Chem.E. Chemical Engineer
ChFC Chartered Financial Consultant
Chgo. Chicago
chirurg. chirurgical
chmn. chairman
chpt. chapter
CIA Central Intelligence Agency
Cin. Cincinnati
cir. circle, circuit
CLE Continuing Legal Education
Cleve. Cleveland
climatol. climatological
clin. clinical
clk. clerk
C.L.U. Chartered Life Underwriter
CM, C.M. Master in Surgery
CM Northern Mariana Islands
CMA Certified Medical Assistant
cmty. community
CNA Certified Nurse's Aide
CNOR Certified Nurse (Operating Room)
C.&N.W.Ry. Chicago & North Western Railway
CO Colorado
Co. Company
COF Catholic Order of Foresters
C. of C. Chamber of Commerce
col. colonel
coll. college
Colo. Colorado
com. committee
comd. commanded
comdg. commanding
comdr. commander
comdt. commandant
comm. communications
commd. commissioned
comml. commercial
commn. commission
commr. commissioner
compt. comptroller
condr. conductor
Conf. Conference
Congl. Congregational, Congressional
Conglist. Congregationalist
Conn. Connecticut
cons. consultant, consulting
consol. consolidated
constl. constitutional
constn. constitution
constrn. construction
contbd. contributed
contbg. contributing
contbn. contribution
contbr. contributor
contr. controller
Conv. Convention
COO chief operating officer
coop. cooperative
coord. coordinator
CORDS Civil Operations and Revolutionary Development Support
CORE Congress of Racial Equality
corp. corporation, corporate
corr. correspondent, corresponding, correspondence
C.&O.Ry. Chesapeake & Ohio Railway
coun. council
CPA Certified Public Accountant
CPCU Chartered Property and Casualty Underwriter
CPH, C.P.H. Certificate of Public Health
cpl. corporal
CPR Cardio-Pulmonary Resuscitation
C.P.Ry. Canadian Pacific Railway
CRT Cathode Ray Terminal
C.S. Christian Science
CSB, C.S.B. Bachelor of Christian Science
C.S.C. Civil Service Commission
CT Connecticut
ct. court
ctr. center
ctrl. central
CWS Chemical Warfare Service
C.Z. Canal Zone

D

D. Doctor
d. daughter
DAgr, D.Agr. Doctor of Agriculture
DAR Daughters of the American Revolution
dau. daughter
DAV Disabled American Veterans
DC, D.C. District of Columbia
DCL, D.C.L. Doctor of Civil Law
DCS, D.C.S. Doctor of Commercial Science
DD, D.D. Doctor of Divinity
DDS, D.D.S. Doctor of Dental Surgery
DE Delaware

Dec. December
dec. deceased
def. defense
Del. Delaware
del. delegate, delegation
Dem. Democrat, Democratic
DEng, D.Eng. Doctor of Engineering
denom. denomination, denominational
dep. deputy
dept. department
dermatol. dermatological
desc. descendant
devel. development, developmental
DFA, D.F.A. Doctor of Fine Arts
D.F.C. Distinguished Flying Cross
DHL, D.H.L. Doctor of Hebrew Literature
dir. director
dist. district
distbg. distributing
distbn. distribution
distbr. distributor
disting. distinguished
div. division, divinity, divorce
divsn. division
DLitt, D.Litt. Doctor of Literature
DMD, D.M.D. Doctor of Dental Medicine
DMS, D.M.S. Doctor of Medical Science
DO, D.O. Doctor of Osteopathy
docs. documents
DON Director of Nursing
DPH, D.P.H. Diploma in Public Health
DPhil, D.Phil. Doctor of Philosophy
D.R. Daughters of the Revolution
Dr. Drive, Doctor
DRE, D.R.E. Doctor of Religious Education
DrPH, Dr.P.H. Doctor of Public Health, Doctor of Public Hygiene
D.S.C. Distinguished Service Cross
DSc, D.Sc. Doctor of Science
DSChemE Doctor of Science in Chemical Engineering
D.S.M. Distinguished Service Medal
DST, D.S.T. Doctor of Sacred Theology
DTM, D.T.M. Doctor of Tropical Medicine
DVM, D.V.M. Doctor of Veterinary Medicine
DVS, D.V.S. Doctor of Veterinary Surgery

E

E, E. East
ea. eastern
E. and P. Extraordinary and Plenipotentiary
Eccles. Ecclesiastical
ecol. ecological
econ. economic
ECOSOC Economic and Social Council (of the UN)
ED, E.D. Doctor of Engineering
ed. educated
EdB, Ed.B. Bachelor of Education
EdD, Ed.D. Doctor of Education
edit. edition
editl. editorial
EdM, Ed.M. Master of Education
edn. education
ednl. educational
EDP Electronic Data Processing
EdS, Ed.S. Specialist in Education
EE, E.E. Electrical Engineer
E.E. and M.P. Envoy Extraordinary and Minister Plenipotentiary
EEC European Economic Community
EEG Electroencephalogram
EEO Equal Employment Opportunity
EEOC Equal Employment Opportunity Commission
E.Ger. German Democratic Republic
EKG Electrocardiogram
elec. electrical
electrochem. electrochemical
electrophys. electrophysical
elem. elementary
EM, E.M. Engineer of Mines
EMT Emergency Medical Technician
ency. encyclopedia
Eng. England
engr. engineer
engring. engineering
entomol. entomological
environ. environmental
EPA Environmental Protection Agency
epidemiol. epidemiological
Episc. Episcopalian
ERA Equal Rights Amendment
ERDA Energy Research and Development Administration
ESEA Elementary and Secondary Education Act
ESL English as Second Language
ESPN Entertainment and Sports Programming Network
ESSA Environmental Science Services Administration
ethnol. ethnological
ETO European Theatre of Operations
Evang. Evangelical
exam. examination, examining
Exch. Exchange
exec. executive
exhbn. exhibition
expdn. expedition
expn. exposition
expt. experiment
exptl. experimental
Expy. Expressway
Ext. Extension

F

F.A. Field Artillery
FAA Federal Aviation Administration
FAO Food and Agriculture Organization (of the UN)
FBA Federal Bar Association
FBI Federal Bureau of Investigation
FCA Farm Credit Administration
FCC Federal Communications Commission
FCDA Federal Civil Defense Administration
FDA Food and Drug Administration
FDIA Federal Deposit Insurance Administration
FDIC Federal Deposit Insurance Corporation
FE, F.E. Forest Engineer
FEA Federal Energy Administration
Feb. February
fed. federal
fedn. federation
FERC Federal Energy Regulatory Commission
fgn. foreign
FHA Federal Housing Administration
fin. financial, finance
FL Florida
Fl. Floor
Fla. Florida
FMC Federal Maritime Commission
FNP Family Nurse Practitioner
FOA Foreign Operations Administration
found. foundation
FPC Federal Power Commission
FPO Fleet Post Office
frat. fraternity
FRS Federal Reserve System
FSA Federal Security Agency
Ft. Fort
FTC Federal Trade Commission
Fwy. Freeway

G

G-1 (or other number) Division of General Staff
GA, Ga. Georgia
GAO General Accounting Office
gastroent. gastroenterological
GATE Gifted and Talented Educators
GATT General Agreement on Tariffs and Trade
GE General Electric Company
gen. general
geneal. genealogical
geod. geodetic
geog. geographic, geographical
geol. geological
geophys. geophysical
geriat. geriatrics
gerontol. gerontological
G.H.Q. General Headquarters
GM General Motors Corporation
GMAC General Motors Acceptance Corporation
G.N.Ry. Great Northern Railway
gov. governor
govt. government
govtl. governmental
GPO Government Printing Office
grad. graduate, graduated
GSA General Services Administration
Gt. Great
GTE General Telephone and Electric Company
GU Guam
gynecol. gynecological

H

HBO Home Box Office
hdqs. headquarters
HEW Department of Health, Education and Welfare
HHD, H.H.D. Doctor of Humanities
HHFA Housing and Home Finance Agency
HHS Department of Health and Human Services
HI Hawaii
hist. historical, historic

HM, H.M. Master of Humanities
HMO Health Maintenance Organization
homeo. homeopathic
hon. honorary, honorable
Ho. of Dels. House of Delegates
Ho. of Reps. House of Representatives
hort. horticultural
hosp. hospital
H.S. High School
HUD Department of Housing and Urban Development
Hwy. Highway
hydrog. hydrographic

I

IA Iowa
IAEA International Atomic Energy Agency
IATSE International Alliance of Theatrical and Stage Employees and Moving Picture Operators of the United States and Canada
IBM International Business Machines Corporation
IBRD International Bank for Reconstruction and Development
ICA International Cooperation Administration
ICC Interstate Commerce Commission
ICCE International Council for Computers in Education
ICU Intensive Care Unit
ID Idaho
IEEE Institute of Electrical and Electronics Engineers
IFC International Finance Corporation
IGY International Geophysical Year
IL Illinois
Ill. Illinois
illus. illustrated
ILO International Labor Organization
IMF International Monetary Fund
IN Indiana
Inc. Incorporated
Ind. Indiana
ind. independent
Indpls. Indianapolis
indsl. industrial
inf. infantry
info. information
ins. insurance
insp. inspector
insp. gen. inspector general
inst. institute
instl. institutional
instn. institution
instr. instructor
instrn. instruction
instrnl. instructional
internat. international
intro. introduction
IRE Institute of Radio Engineers
IRS Internal Revenue Service
ITT International Telephone & Telegraph Corporation

J

JAG Judge Advocate General
JAGC Judge Advocate General Corps
Jan. January
Jaycees Junior Chamber of Commerce
JB, J.B. Jurum Baccalaureus
JCB, J.C.B. Juris Canoni Baccalaureus
JCD, J.C.D. Juris Canonici Doctor, Juris Civilis Doctor
JCL, J.C.L. Juris Canonici Licentiatus
JD, J.D. Juris Doctor
jg. junior grade
jour. journal
jr. junior
JSD, J.S.D. Juris Scientiae Doctor
JUD, J.U.D. Juris Utriusque Doctor
jud. judicial

K

Kans. Kansas
K.C. Knights of Columbus
K.P. Knights of Pythias
KS Kansas
K.T. Knight Templar
KY, Ky. Kentucky

L

LA, La. Louisiana
L.A. Los Angeles
lab. laboratory
L.Am. Latin America
lang. language
laryngol. laryngological
LB Labrador
LDS Latter Day Saints
LDS Church Church of Jesus Christ of Latter Day Saints
lectr. lecturer
legis. legislation, legislative
LHD, L.H.D. Doctor of Humane Letters
L.I. Long Island
libr. librarian, library
lic. licensed, license
L.I.R.R. Long Island Railroad
lit. literature
litig. litigation
LittB, Litt.B. Bachelor of Letters
LittD, Litt.D. Doctor of Letters
LLB, LL.B. Bachelor of Laws
LLD, L.L.D. Doctor of Laws
LLM, L.L.M. Master of Laws
Ln. Lane
L.&N.R.R. Louisville & Nashville Railroad
LPGA Ladies Professional Golf Association
LPN Licensed Practical Nurse
LS, L.S. Library Science (in degree)
lt. lieutenant
Ltd. Limited
Luth. Lutheran
LWV League of Women Voters

M

M. Master
m. married
MA, M.A. Master of Arts
MA Massachusetts
MADD Mothers Against Drunk Driving
mag. magazine
MAgr, M.Agr. Master of Agriculture
maj. major
Man. Manitoba
Mar. March
MArch, M.Arch. Master in Architecture
Mass. Massachusetts
math. mathematics, mathematical
MATS Military Air Transport Service
MB, M.B. Bachelor of Medicine
MB Manitoba
MBA, M.B.A. Master of Business Administration
MBS Mutual Broadcasting System
M.C. Medical Corps
MCE, M.C.E. Master of Civil Engineering
mcht. merchant
mcpl. municipal
MCS, M.C.S. Master of Commercial Science
MD, M.D. Doctor of Medicine
MD, Md. Maryland
MDiv Master of Divinity
MDip, M.Dip. Master in Diplomacy
mdse. merchandise
MDV, M.D.V. Doctor of Veterinary Medicine
ME, M.E. Mechanical Engineer
ME Maine
M.E.Ch. Methodist Episcopal Church
mech. mechanical
MEd., M.Ed. Master of Education
med. medical
MEE, M.E.E. Master of Electrical Engineering
mem. member
meml. memorial
merc. mercantile
met. metropolitan
metall. metallurgical
MetE, Met.E. Metallurgical Engineer
meteorol. meteorological
Meth. Methodist
Mex. Mexico
MF, M.F. Master of Forestry
MFA, M.F.A. Master of Fine Arts
mfg. manufacturing
mfr. manufacturer
mgmt. management
mgr. manager
MHA, M.H.A. Master of Hospital Administration
M.I. Military Intelligence
MI Michigan
Mich. Michigan
micros. microscopic, microscopical
mid. middle
mil. military
Milw. Milwaukee
Min. Minister
mineral. mineralogical
Minn. Minnesota
MIS Management Information Systems
Miss. Mississippi
MIT Massachusetts Institute of Technology
mktg. marketing
ML, M.L. Master of Laws
MLA Modern Language Association
M.L.D. Magister Legnum Diplomatic
MLitt, M.Litt. Master of Literature, Master of Letters
MLS, M.L.S. Master of Library Science

MME, M.M.E. Master of Mechanical Engineering
MN Minnesota
mng. managing
MO, Mo. Missouri
moblzn. mobilization
Mont. Montana
MP Northern Mariana Islands
M.P. Member of Parliament
MPA Master of Public Administration
MPE, M.P.E. Master of Physical Education
MPH, M.P.H. Master of Public Health
MPhil, M.Phil. Master of Philosophy
MPL, M.P.L. Master of Patent Law
Mpls. Minneapolis
MRE, M.R.E. Master of Religious Education
MRI Magnetic Resonance Imaging
MS, M.S. Master of Science
MS, Ms. Mississippi
MSc, M.Sc. Master of Science
MSChemE Master of Science in Chemical Engineering
MSEE Master of Science in Electrical Engineering
MSF, M.S.F. Master of Science of Forestry
MSN Master of Science in Nursing
MST, M.S.T. Master of Sacred Theology
MSW, M.S.W. Master of Social Work
MT Montana
Mt. Mount
MTO Mediterranean Theatre of Operation
MTV Music Television
mus. museum, musical
MusB, Mus.B. Bachelor of Music
MusD, Mus.D. Doctor of Music
MusM, Mus.M. Master of Music
mut. mutual
MVP Most Valuable Player
mycol. mycological

N

N. North
NAACOG Nurses Association of the American College of Obstetricians and Gynecologists
NAACP National Association for the Advancement of Colored People
NACA National Advisory Committee for Aeronautics
NACDL National Association of Criminal Defense Lawyers
NACU National Association of Colleges and Universities
NAD National Academy of Design
NAE National Academy of Engineering, National Association of Educators
NAESP National Association of Elementary School Principals
NAFE National Association of Female Executives
N.Am. North America
NAM National Association of Manufacturers
NAMH National Association for Mental Health
NAPA National Association of Performing Artists
NARAS National Academy of Recording Arts and Sciences
NAREB National Association of Real Estate Boards
NARS National Archives and Record Service
NAS National Academy of Sciences
NASA National Aeronautics and Space Administration
NASP National Association of School Psychologists
NASW National Association of Social Workers
nat. national
NATAS National Academy of Television Arts and Sciences
NATO North Atlantic Treaty Organization
NATOUSA North African Theatre of Operations, United States Army
nav. navigation
NB, N.B. New Brunswick
NBA National Basketball Association
NBC National Broadcasting Company
NC, N.C. North Carolina
NCAA National College Athletic Association
NCCJ National Conference of Christians and Jews
ND, N.D. North Dakota
NDEA National Defense Education Act
NE Nebraska
NE, N.E. Northeast
NEA National Education Association
Nebr. Nebraska
NEH National Endowment for Humanities
neurol. neurological
Nev. Nevada
NF Newfoundland
NFL National Football League
Nfld. Newfoundland
NG National Guard
NH, N.H. New Hampshire
NHL National Hockey League
NIH National Institutes of Health
NIMH National Institute of Mental Health
NJ, N.J. New Jersey
NLRB National Labor Relations Board
NM New Mexico
N.Mex. New Mexico
No. Northern
NOAA National Oceanographic and Atmospheric Administration
NORAD North America Air Defense
Nov. November
NOW National Organization for Women
N.P.Ry. Northern Pacific Railway
nr. near
NRA National Rifle Association
NRC National Research Council
NS, N.S. Nova Scotia
NSC National Security Council
NSF National Science Foundation
NSTA National Science Teachers Association
NSW New South Wales
N.T. New Testament
NT Northwest Territories
nuc. nuclear
numis. numismatic
NV Nevada
NW, N.W. Northwest
N.W.T. Northwest Territories
NY, N.Y. New York
N.Y.C. New York City
NYU New York University
N.Z. New Zealand

O

OAS Organization of American States
ob-gyn obstetrics-gynecology
obs. observatory
obstet. obstetrical
occupl. occupational
oceanog. oceanographic
Oct. October
OD, O.D. Doctor of Optometry
OECD Organization for Economic Cooperation and Development
OEEC Organization of European Economic Cooperation
OEO Office of Economic Opportunity
ofcl. official
OH Ohio
OK Oklahoma
Okla. Oklahoma
ON Ontario
Ont. Ontario
oper. operating
ophthal. ophthalmological
ops. operations
OR Oregon
orch. orchestra
Oreg. Oregon
orgn. organization
orgnl. organizational
ornithol. ornithological
orthop. orthopedic
OSHA Occupational Safety and Health Administration
OSRD Office of Scientific Research and Development
OSS Office of Strategic Services
osteo. osteopathic
otol. otological
otolaryn. otolaryngological

P

PA, Pa. Pennsylvania
P.A. Professional Association
paleontol. paleontological
path. pathological
PBS Public Broadcasting System
P.C. Professional Corporation
PE Prince Edward Island
pediat. pediatrics
P.E.I. Prince Edward Island
PEN Poets, Playwrights, Editors, Essayists and Novelists (international association)
penol. penological
P.E.O. women's organization (full name not disclosed)
pers. personnel
pfc. private first class
PGA Professional Golfers' Association of America
PHA Public Housing Administration
pharm. pharmaceutical
PharmD, Pharm.D. Doctor of Pharmacy

PharmM, Pharm.M. Master of Pharmacy
PhB, Ph.B. Bachelor of Philosophy
PhD, Ph.D. Doctor of Philosophy
PhDChemE Doctor of Science in Chemical Engineering
PhM, Ph.M. Master of Philosophy
Phila. Philadelphia
philharm. philharmonic
philol. philological
philos. philosophical
photog. photographic
phys. physical
physiol. physiological
Pitts. Pittsburgh
Pk. Park
Pky. Parkway
Pl. Place
P.&L.E.R.R. Pittsburgh & Lake Erie Railroad
Plz. Plaza
PNP Pediatric Nurse Practitioner
P.O. Post Office
PO Box Post Office Box
polit. political
poly. polytechnic, polytechnical
PQ Province of Quebec
PR, P.R. Puerto Rico
prep. preparatory
pres. president
Presbyn. Presbyterian
presdl. presidential
prin. principal
procs. proceedings
prod. produced (play production)
prodn. production
prodr. producer
prof. professor
profl. professional
prog. progressive
propr. proprietor
pros. atty. prosecuting attorney
pro tem. pro tempore
PSRO Professional Services Review Organization
psychiat. psychiatric
psychol. psychological
PTA Parent-Teachers Association
ptnr. partner
PTO Pacific Theatre of Operations, Parent Teacher Organization
pub. publisher, publishing, published
pub. public
publ. publication
pvt. private

Q

quar. quarterly
qm. quartermaster
Q.M.C. Quartermaster Corps
Que. Quebe

R

radiol. radiological
RAF Royal Air Force
RCA Radio Corporation of America
RCAF Royal Canadian Air Force
RD Rural Delivery
Rd. Road
R&D Research & Development
REA Rural Electrification Administration
rec. recording
ref. reformed
regt. regiment
regtl. regimental
rehab. rehabilitation
rels. relations
Rep. Republican
rep. representative
Res. Reserve
ret. retired
Rev. Reverend
rev. review, revised
RFC Reconstruction Finance Corporation
RFD Rural Free Delivery
rhinol. rhinological
RI, R.I. Rhode Island
RISD Rhode Island School of Design
Rlwy. Railway
Rm. Room
RN, R.N. Registered Nurse
roentgenol. roentgenological
ROTC Reserve Officers Training Corps
RR Rural Route
R.R. Railroad
rsch. research
rschr. researcher
Rt. Route

S

S. South
s. son
SAC Strategic Air Command
SAG Screen Actors Guild
SALT Strategic Arms Limitation Talks
S.Am. South America
san. sanitary
SAR Sons of the American Revolution
Sask. Saskatchewan
savs. savings
SB, S.B. Bachelor of Science
SBA Small Business Administration
SC, S.C. South Carolina
SCAP Supreme Command Allies Pacific
ScB, Sc.B. Bachelor of Science
SCD, S.C.D. Doctor of Commercial Science
ScD, Sc.D. Doctor of Science
sch. school
sci. science, scientific
SCLC Southern Christian Leadership Conference
SCV Sons of Confederate Veterans
SD, S.D. South Dakota
SE, S.E. Southeast
SEATO Southeast Asia Treaty Organization
SEC Securities and Exchange Commission
sec. secretary
sect. section
seismol. seismological
sem. seminary
Sept. September
s.g. senior grade
sgt. sergeant
SHAEF Supreme Headquarters Allied Expeditionary Forces
SHAPE Supreme Headquarters Allied Powers in Europe
S.I. Staten Island
S.J. Society of Jesus (Jesuit)
SJD Scientiae Juridicae Doctor
SK Saskatchewan
SM, S.M. Master of Science
SNP Society of Nursing Professionals
So. Southern
soc. society
sociol. sociological
S.P.Co. Southern Pacific Company
spkr. speaker
spl. special
splty. specialty
Sq. Square
S.R. Sons of the Revolution
sr. senior
S S Steamship
S S S Selective Service System
St. Saint, Street
sta. station
stats. statistics
statis. statistical
STB, S.T.B. Bachelor of Sacred Theology
stblzn. stabilization
STD, S.T.D. Doctor of Sacred Theology
std. standard
Ste. Suite
subs. subsidiary
SUNY State University of New York
supr. supervisor
supt. superintendent
surg. surgical
svc. service
SW, S.W. Southwest
sys. system

T

TAPPI Technical Association of the Pulp and Paper Industry
tb. tuberculosis
tchg. teaching
tchr. teacher
tech. technical, technology
technol. technological
tel. telephone
Tel. & Tel. Telephone & Telegraph
telecom. telecommunications
temp. temporary
Tenn. Tennessee
Ter. Territory
Ter. Terrace
TESOL Teachers of English to Speakers of Other Languages
Tex. Texas
ThD, Th.D. Doctor of Theology
theol. theological
ThM, Th.M. Master of Theology
TN Tennessee
tng. training
topog. topographical
trans. transaction, transferred
transl. translation, translated
transp. transportation
treas. treasurer
TT Trust Territory
TV television
TVA Tennessee Valley Authority

TWA Trans World Airlines
twp. township
TX Texas
typog. typographical

U

U. University
UAW United Auto Workers
UCLA University of California at Los Angeles
UDC United Daughters of the Confederacy
U.K. United Kingdom
UN United Nations
UNESCO United Nations Educational, Scientific and Cultural Organization
UNICEF United Nations International Children's Emergency Fund
univ. university
UNRRA United Nations Relief and Rehabilitation Administration
UPI United Press International
U.P.R.R. United Pacific Railroad
urol. urological
U.S. United States
U.S.A. United States of America
USAAF United States Army Air Force
USAF United States Air Force
USAFR United States Air Force Reserve
USAR United States Army Reserve
USCG United States Coast Guard
USCGR United States Coast Guard Reserve
USES United States Employment Service
USIA United States Information Agency
USMC United States Marine Corps
USMCR United States Marine Corps Reserve
USN United States Navy
USNG United States National Guard
USNR United States Naval Reserve
USO United Service Organizations
USPHS United States Public Health Service
USS United States Ship
USSR Union of the Soviet Socialist Republics
USTA United States Tennis Association
USV United States Volunteers
UT Utah

V

VA Veterans Administration
VA, Va. Virginia
vet. veteran, veterinary
VFW Veterans of Foreign Wars
VI, V.I. Virgin Islands
vice pres. vice president
vis. visiting
VISTA Volunteers in Service to America
VITA Volunteers in Technical Assistance
vocat. vocational
vol. volunteer, volume
v.p. vice president
vs. versus
VT, Vt. Vermont

W, W. West
WA Washington (state)
WAC Women's Army Corps
Wash. Washington (state)
WATS Wide Area Telecommunications Service
WAVES Women's Reserve, US Naval Reserve
WCTU Women's Christian Temperance Union
we. western
W. Ger. Germany, Federal Republic of
WHO World Health Organization
WI Wisconsin
W.I. West Indies
Wis. Wisconsin
WSB Wage Stabilization Board
WV West Virginia
W.Va. West Virginia
WWI World War I
WWII World War II
WY Wyoming
Wyo. Wyoming

X Y

YK Yukon Territory
YMCA Young Men's Christian Association
YMHA Young Men's Hebrew Association
YM & YWHA Young Men's and Young Women's Hebrew Association
yr. year
YT, Y.T. Yukon Territory
YWCA Young Women's Christian Association

Z

zool. zoological

Alphabetical Practices

Names are arranged alphabetically according to the surnames, and under identical surnames according to the first given name. If both surname and first given name are identical, names are arranged alphabetically according to the second given name.

Surnames beginning with De, Des, Du, however capitalized or spaced, are recorded with the prefix preceding the surname and arranged alphabetically under the letter D.

Surnames beginning with Mac and Mc are arranged alphabetically under M.

Surnames beginning with Saint or St. appear after names that begin Sains, and are arranged according to the second part of the name, e.g. St. Clair before Saint Dennis.

Surnames beginning with Van, Von, or von are arranged alphabetically under the letter V.

Compound surnames are arranged according to the first member of the compound.

Many hyphenated Arabic names begin Al-, El-, or al-. These names are alphabetized according to each Biographee's designation of last name. Thus Al-Bahar, Neta may be listed either under Al- or under Bahar, depending on the preference of the listee.

Also, Arabic names have a variety of possible spellings when transposed to English. Spelling of these names is always based on the practice of the Biographee. Some Biographees use a Western form of word order, while others prefer the Arabic word sequence.

Similarly, Asian names may have no comma between family and given names, but some Biographees have chosen to add the comma. In each case, punctuation follows the preference of the Biographee.

Parentheses used in connection with a name indicate which part of the full name is usually deleted in common usage. Hence Chambers, E(lizabeth) Anne indicates that the usual form of the given name is E. Anne. In such a case, the parentheses are ignored in alphabetizing and the name would be arranged as Chambers, Elizabeth Anne. However, if the name is recorded Chambers, (Elizabeth) Anne, signifying that the entire name Elizabeth is not commonly used, the alphabetizing would be arranged as though the name were Chambers, Anne. If an entire middle or last name is enclosed in parentheses, that portion of the name is used in the alphabetical arrangement. Hence Chambers, Elizabeth (Anne) would be arranged as Chambers, Elizabeth Anne.

Where more than one spelling, word order, or name of an individual is frequently encountered, the sketch has been entered under the form preferred by the Biographee, with cross-references under alternate forms.

Who'sWho in American Law®

Biographies

AARON, BENJAMIN, law educator, arbitrator; b. Chgo., Sept. 2, 1915; s. Henry Jacob and Rose (Weinstein) A.; m. Eleanor Opsahl, May 24, 1941; children: Judith, Louise. AB, U. Mich., 1937; LL.B., Harvard U., 1940; postgrad., U. Chgo., 1940-41. With Nat. War Labor Bd., 1942-45; mem. labor adv. com. to Supreme Comdr. Allied Powers, Tokyo, 1946; research assoc. Inst. Indsl. Relations; lectr. labor law, dept. econs. UCLA, 1946-51, assoc. dir., 1957-60, dir., 1960-75, prof. law, 1960-86, prof. emeritus, 1986—. Faculty mem. Salzburg (Austria) Seminar in Am. Studies, 1958, 67; arbitrator labor-mgmt. disputes, 1946— ; pub. mem. WSB, Washington, 1951-52; mem. Statutory Arbitration Bd. in R.R. Dispute, 1963-64; chmn. Calif. Farm Labor Panel, 1965-66; mem. Nat. Commn. on Tech., Automation and Economic Progress, 1965-66; pub. mem. Adv. Council on Employee Welfare and Pension Benefit Plans, 1966-68; vis. prof. Harvard U., 1972, U. Mich., 1979; mem. pub. rev. bd. U.A.W., 1975— ; mem. arbitration services adv. com. Fed. Mediation and Conciliation Service, 1974-82; mem. ILO Com. of Experts on Application of Convs. and Recommendations, 1986-94; charter emeritus fellow Coll. of Labor and Employment Lawyers, 1996—. Author: Legal Status of Employee Benefit Rights Under Private Pension Plans, 1961; Editor: The Employment Relation and The Law, 1957, Labor Courts and Grievance Settlement in Western Europe, 1970, Comparative Labor Law jour, 1979-85; co-editor: Industrial Conflict: A Comparative Legal Survey, 1972; Public-Sector Bargaining, 1979; editorial bd., Internat. Labor Law Reps., 1974— . Fellow Center for Advanced Study in Behavioral Sciences, 1966-67; vis. fellow Clare Hall, Cambridge (Eng.) U., 1973, Australian Nat. U.; named First Southwestern Legal Found. Research Fellows' Disting. Scholar in Residence, 1971; first Howard W. Wissner Meml. Lectr. Tulane U., 1971; Phi Beta Kappa vis. scholar, 1978-79 Mem. ABA (sec. sect. labor rels. law 1975-76), AAUP, Internat. Soc. Labor Law and Social Security (chmn. U.S. nat. com., internat. exec. com. 1967-83, v.p. N.Am. region 1982-85, pres. 1985-88, hon. pres. 1988—), Nat. Acad. Arbitrators (pres. 1962, bd. govs.), Indsl. Rels. Rsch. Assn. (exec. bd. 1965-68, pres. 1972, mem. CCH labor law reports panel of experts 1987-92), Am. Arbitration Assn. (mem. adv. coun. L.A. 1975-76, Disting. Svc. award 1981). Home: 316 18th St Santa Monica CA 90402-2406 Office: UCLA 405 Hilgard Ave Los Angeles CA 90095-1476

AARON, KENNETH ELLYOT, lawyer; b. Phila., Nov. 3, 1948; s. Neal L. and Dorothea G. Aaron; m. Phyllis A. Carroll, May 29, 1969; children: Seth Joel, Joshua Scott. BS in Econs., U. Pa., 1970, JD, 1973. Bar: Pa. 1973, U.S. Dist. Ct. (ea. dist.) Pa. 1973, U.S. Ct. Appeals (3d cir.) 1974, U.S. Supreme Ct. 1977, U.S. Dist. Ct. (we. and ea. dist.) Pa. 1993, Del. 2001, Fla. 2001, U.S. Dist. Ct. Del. 2001, U.S. Dist. Ct. (so. and no. dists.) Fla. 2001; cert. bus.bankruptcy law specialist Am. Bankruptcy Bd, Cert. Assoc. Astor & Weiss, Phila., 1973-76; ptnr. Casper & Davidson, P.C., Phila., 1976-80; pvt. practice Phila., 1980-83; ptnr. Garfinkel & Volpicelli, Phila., 1983-86, Mesirov, Gelman, Jaffe, Cramer & Jamieson, Phila., 1986-91, Buchanan Ingersoll P.C., Phila., 1991-2001, Weir & Ptnrs., Phila., 2001—. Mem. Ea. Dist. Pa. Bankruptcy Conf., vice chmn. edn. com. 1991, co-chmn. 1992, co-chmn. legis com., 1993; trustee Phila. Bar Found., 1997-2000. Author: Foreclosure and Repossession, 1989, (chpt.) Bus. Lawyer's Bankruptcy Guide, 1992, BNA's Environmental Due Diligence Guide, 1992, Matthew Bender's Environmental Law Practice Guide, 1992. Commr. Haverford (Pa.) Twp. Planning Bd., 1978—80; chmn. Lower Merion Zoning Bd., 1993—; planning commr. Lower Merion Twp. Planning Bd., Ardmore, Pa., 1992. Recipient Tax Writing award Nat. Assn. Accts., 1970, Am. Jr. award in Creditors' Rights, 1973. Mem.: Phila. Bar Found. (trustee 1997—2000), Phila. Bar Assn. (chmn. commn. on insolvency issues in real estate 1989—), Hias & Coun. (v.p. 1999—2002), Rotary (pres. Haverford Twp. 1982—83). Avocations: sports, camping, golfing. Bankruptcy, Commercial, contracts (including sales of goods; commercial financing), Insurance. Office: Weir & Ptnrs 1339 Chestnut St Ste 500 Philadelphia PA 19107

AARON, MERIK ROY, financial executive, educator, lawyer; b. N.Y.C., May 22, 1947; s. Harry and Gertrude S. (Scherl) A.; m. Karen M. Snyder, 1984; children: Stacey Lynn, Lauren Jill. BA, L.I. U., 1969, MA, 1971; profl. diploma, Hofstra U., 1975; EdD, Nova Southeastern U., 1982; JD, Touro Coll., 1991. Bar: N.J. 1992, U.S. Dist. Ct. N.J. 1992, Conn. 1992, U.S. Dist. Ct. (so. and ea. dists.) N.Y. 1992, D.C. 1993, Minn. 1993, N.Y. 1994, U.S. Ct. Appeals (fed. cir.) 1995, U.S. Ct. Appeals Armed Forces 1995, U.S. Ct. Claims 1995, U.S. Supreme Ct. 1995. Dist. sci. supr. Carle Place (N.Y.) Pub. Schs., 1969-80; dist. dir. sci. Lawrence (N.Y.) Pub. Schs., 1980-84; dir. curriculum Bellmore-Merrick Cen. H.S. dist., Merrick, NY, 1984—91; law clk. Liotti & Skelos, Garden City, NY, 1991—92; gen. counsel Cliff Daya Sys., Lyndhurst, N.J., 1992-94; prin. dep. town atty. Town of Hempstead, NY, 1994—. Pres. Mervic Enterprises, Smithtown, N.Y., 1980—; adj. prof. Nassau C.C., 1975—, Syracuse U., 1974-80. Trustee Carle Place Bd. Edn., 1981-86; rep. candidate of N.Y. State Assembly, 20th assembly dist., 1996, Nassau County Legislature, 2001; exec. bd. five Towns Cmty. Coun., Woodmere, N.Y., 1998-99; exec. leader North Woodmere Rep. Com., 1999—; commr. Storm Water Drainage Com., Inc., Village of Hewlett Harbor, N.Y.. Recipient Outstanding Contbrns. to Edn. award, Nassau County, 1981, Outstanding Sci. Supr. award, State of N.Y., 1986, Nation's Outstanding Sci. Supr. award, 1991. Mem. ABA, Nat. Ednl. Leadership Assn. (exec. bd. 1986), Nat. Sci. Suprs. Assn. (exec. bd. 1983-88, pres. 1986-87), N.Y. State Sci. Suprs. Assn. (pres. 1982-83), N.Y. Acad. Scis. (life), Nassau County Sci. Suprs. Assn. (pres. 1979), Am. Assn. Sex Educators, Counselors and Therapists (cert.), Bar Assn. Nassau County (chmn. fee conciliation com. 2000-02, mem. grievance com. 2002—), N.Y. State Bar Assn., Nassau Lawyers Assn. L.I. (v.p. 2003—), L.I. U./C.W. Post Campus Alumni Assn. (bd. dirs. 1997—), Phi Delta Kappa (exec. bd. 1988), Phi Alpha Delta, Civic Club, Kiwanis (pres. Westbury, N.Y. club 1982-83, Five Towns Club 1998-99), North Woodmere Rep. Club (pres. 1992-99), Woodmere Mchts. Assn. (bd. dirs. 1997-2000), Masons, Shriners. Republican. Office: Town Atty's Office 1 Washington St Hempstead NY 11550-4921

AARON, ROGER S. lawyer; b. Cleve., 1942; AB magna cum laude, Dartmouth Coll., 1964, MBA with high distinction, 1965; LLB, Yale U., 1968. Bar: N.Y. 1969. Ptnr. Skadden, Arps, Slate, Meagher & Flom, N.Y.C. Mem. ABA. Office: Skadden Arps Slate Meagher Flom 4 Times Sq New York NY 10036-6595

AARS-RYNNING, JACOB, lawyer; b. Oslo, May 9, 1940; s. Jacob and Liv Keyser (Salvesen) Aars-R.; m. Annette Kragh Aars-R; children: Jacob, Fredrik, Sven Christian. M of Law, U. Oslo, 1967. Diplomat Norwegian Fgn. Svc., 1967-85; atty. Oslo, 1985—; judge Ct. of Appeals, Oslo, 1999-2000. Bd. dirs., vice chmn. Oslo Arbeidersamfunn, 1982-85. 2d lt. Cavalry res. Avocations: human rights, international politics, international law. Immigration, naturalization, and customs, Family and matrimonial, political asylum. Home: Knud Øyensv 13C 1166 Oslo Norway Office: Skipperg 33 N-0154 Oslo Norway Fax: 47-22427879.

ABAUNZA, DONALD RICHARD, lawyer; b. New Orleans, Oct. 25, 1945; s. Alfred E. and Virginia (White) A.; m. Carolyn Thompson; 1 child, Richard. BA, Vanderbilt U., 1966; JD, Tulane U., 1969. Bar: La. 1969, U.S. Dist. Ct. (ea. dist.) La. 1969, U.S. Dist. Ct. (we. dist.) La. 1980, U.S. Supreme Ct. 1986. Ptnr. Liskow & Lewis, New Orleans, 1977—, mng. ptnr., 1996—2003. Adj. faculty Tulane Sch. Law, 1981-89. Fellow Am. Coll. Trial Lawyers; mem. La. Bar Assn. (Pres.'s award 1988). Admiralty, General civil litigation, Insurance. Office: Liskow & Lewis 1 Shell Sq 50th Fl 701 Poydras St New Orleans LA 70139-5099

ABBOTT, BARRY ALEXANDER, lawyer; b. New Haven, Aug. 20, 1950; s. Harold and Norma (Kaufman) A.; 1 child, Anne Stewart. AB, Dartmouth Coll., 1972; JD, U. Fla., 1975; MBA, Stanford U., 1977. Bar: Fla. 1975, Calif. 1976, U.S. Dist. Ct. (so. dist.) Fla. 1976, U.S. Dist. Ct. (no. dist.) Calif. 1976, U.S. Ct. Appeals (9th cir.) 1976, U.S. Supreme Ct. 1979, D.C. 1985, N.Y. 1986. Assoc. Morrison & Foerster, San Francisco, 1977-83, ptnr., 1983-94; dir. Howard Rice Nemerovski Canady Falk & Rabkin, San Francisco, 1994—. Adj. faculty mem. Boalt Hall Sch. Law, U. Calif., Berkeley, 1998; lectr. corp., comml. and fin. inst. law various orgns.; mem. Fed. Res. Bd. Consumer Adv. Coun., 1992-94, chmn. consumer credit com., 1993-94, mem. governing com. Conf. on Consumer Fin. Law; mem. Am. Coll. Consumer Fin. Svcs. Attys., 1995—, bd. regents, 1995-98, sec., 2002-. Co-author: Truth in Lending: A Comprehensive Guide; contbr. articles to profl. jours. Named One of Outstanding Young Men of Am., U.S. Jaycees, 1980. Fellow Royal Soc. Arts (Silver medal 1972); mem. ABA (chmn. young lawyers divsn. bus. law com. 1987-88, chmn. ins. products subcom. 1987-92, vice chmn. consumer fin. svcs. commn. 1995-96, active various coms.), Calif. Bar Assn. (vice chair fin. instns. com. 1991-92, chair 1992-93, mem. ins. law com. 1994-96, mem. bus. law sect. exec. com. 1996-99, treas. 1997-98, vice chair 1998-99), Fla. Bar Assn., D.C. Bar Assn., N.Y. State Bar Assn., San Francisco Bar Assn. (chmn. membership com. 1984-86, bd. dirs. 1982, 87-88, Award of Merit 1985), Barristers Club (bd. dirs. 1981-83, treas., pres. 1982), Order of Coif, Phi Beta Kappa, Phi Kappa Phi. Clubs: World Trade (San Francisco), Commonwealth (Calif.). Republican. Banking, Commercial, contracts (including sales of goods; commercial financing), Corporate, general. Office: Howard Rice 3 Embarcadero Ctr Ste 700 San Francisco CA 94111-4024 E-mail: babbott@howardrice.com.

ABBOTT, BOB, state supreme court justice; b. Kans., Nov. 1, 1932; BS, Emporia State U.; JD, Washburn U.; LLM, U. Va. Bar: Kans. 1960. Pvt. practice, Junction City, Kans., from 1960; former chief judge Kans. Ct. Appeals; justice Kans. Supreme Ct., 1990—. Office: Kansas Supreme Court 314 Kansas Judicial Ctr 301 SW 10th St Topeka KS 66612-1507

ABBOTT, CHARLES FAVOUR, lawyer; b. Sedro-Wolley, Wash., Oct. 12, 1937; s. Charles Favour and Violette Doris Abbott; m. Oranee Harward, Sept. 19, 1958; children: Patricia, Stephen, Nelson, Cynthia, Lisa, Alyson. BA in Econs., U. Wash., 1959, JD, 1962. BAr: Calif. 1962, Utah 1981. Law clk. Judge M. Oliver Koelsch, U.S. Ct. Appeals (9th cir.), San Francisco, 1963; assoc. Jones, Hatfield & Abbott, Escondido, Calif., 1964; pvt. practice Escondido, 1964-77, Provo, Utah, 1983-93; of counsel Mueller & Abbott, Escondido, 1997—; ptnr. Abbott, Thorn & Hill, Provo, 1981-83, Abbott & Abbott, Provo, 1993—. Author: How to Do Your Own Legal Work, 1976, 2d edit., 1981, How to Win in Small Claims Court, 1981, How to Be Free of Debt in 24 Hours, 1981, How to Hire the Best Lawyer at the Lowest Fee, 1981, The Lawyer's Inside Method of Making Money, 1979, The Millionaire Mindset, 1987, How to Make Big Money in the Next 30 Days, 1989, Business Legal Manual and Forms, 1990, How to Make Millions in Marketing, 1990, Telemarketing Training Course, 1990, How to Form A Corporation in Any State, 1990, The Complete Asset Protection Plan, 1990, Personal Injury and the Law, 1997, Fen-Phen Fallout--The Medical and Legal Crisis, 1998; mem. editl. bd. Wash. Law Rev. and State Bar Assn. Jour., 1961-62; bd. editors Phen-fen Litigation Strategist, 1998-2000; contbr. articles to profl. jours. Mem. ATLA, Utah Bar Assn., Calif. Bar Assn., U.S. Supreme Ct. Bar Assn. Administrative and regulatory, General civil litigation, Personal injury (including property damage). Home: 4411 N Sheffield Ct Provo UT 84058 Office: Charles F Abbott PC 3651 N 100 E Ste 300 Provo UT 84604-4521

ABBOTT, GREG WAYNE, state attorney general, former state supreme court justice; b. Wichita Falls, Tex., Nov. 13, 1957; s. Calivn Roger and Doris Lacristia (Jacks) Rowley A.; m. Cecilia Therese Phalen, Aug. 15, 1981; 1 child, Audrey. BBA, U. Tex., 1981; JD, Vanderbilt U., 1984. Bar: Tex. 1985, U.S. Dist. Ct. (so. dist.) Tex. 1985. Atty. Butler & Binion, Houston, 1984-92; judge 12th State Dist. Ct., Houston, 1992-96; justice Texas Supreme Ct., 1996—2000; partner Bracewell & Patterson, LLP; atty. gen. State of Tex., 2003—. Prof. U. Tex.; mem. com. on Pub. Trust and Confidence in Tex. Cts., Jury Task Force Implementation Project; mem. cert. bd. Tex. Ct. Reporters; exec. com. Family Law 2000 Task Force. Dir. Houston Ctr. for Barrier Free Living, 1986-87; capt. March of Dimes Team Walk, Houston, 1986-87; mem. Gov.'s Com. to Promote Adoption; bd. dirs. Tex. Inst. Rehab. and Rsch., Maywood Children and Family Svcs.; bd. trustees Goodwill Industries; adv. bd. Career and Recovery Resources Inc. Named Disabled Person of the Yr. Harris County Com. on Employment of Disabled Persons, 1985, Outstanding Young Texan Tex. Jaycees, 1995; recipient Am. Jurisprudence award Am. Jur, 1983, Named Outstanding Trial Judge, Texas Assn. of Civil Trial and Appellate Specialists, 1995. Mem. State Bar Tex. (com. on legal advt. 1988, Supreme Ct. liason for com. on jud. ethics, jud. conduct commn., code of jud. conduct), Houston Bar Assn. (Houston's Outstanding Young Lawyer 1994), Houston Young Lawyers Assn., Tex. Assn. State Judges (exec. com.). Republican. Roman Catholic. Avocations: snow-skiing, travel, swimming. Office: Capitol Station PO Box 12548 Austin TX 78711*

ABBOTT, HIRSCHEL THERON, JR., lawyer; b. Clarksdale, Miss., Jan. 11, 1942; s. Hirschel Theron Sr. and Ona Belle (Williamson) A.; m. Mimi Eugenia DuPre, June 14, 1969; children: Barkley, Chip. BBA in Acct., U. Miss., Oxford, 1964; JD, U. Va., Charlottesville, 1971. Bar: La. 1971, Miss. 1971, U.S. Dist. Ct. (ea. dist.) La. 1971, U.S. Ct. Appeals (5th cir.) 1981, U.S. Tax Ct. 1988; bd. cert. tax law specialist. Lawyer Stone Pigman Walther Wittmann LLP, New Orleans, 1971—75, ptnr., 1975—. Bd. dirs. Episcopal Housing for Srs., Inc., Lambeth House, Inc.; past trustee, sec. Preservation Resource Ctr., New Orleans; past bd. mem., chmn. Trinity Episcopal Sch. Bd. Trustees; past trustee, treas. La. Civil Svc. League; past bd. mem. Uptown Neighborhood Improvement Assn.; past mem., chmn. La. Jefferson Scholarship Selection Com. U. Va.; past regional chmn. La. U. Va. Law Sch. Annual Giving Fund; past mem. of vestry Trinity Episcopal Ch.; past mem. Adv. Bd. Jr. League New Orleans. Recipient Monte M. Lemann award, La. Civil Svc. League, 1989. Fellow Am. Coll. Trust and Estate Counsel (past mem. charitable planning and exempt orgns. com.), La. Bar Found.; mem. ABA (tax sect., bus. law sect., real property trusts probate sect.), La. Bar Assn. (past chmn. tax law specialization commn., tax sect., corp. sect., successions, donations and trusts sect.), Miss. State Bar Assn., New Orleans Estate Planning Coun., Assn. Employee Benefit Planners. Episcopalian. Corporate, general, Estate planning, Taxation, general. Office: Stone Pigman Walther et al 546 Carondelet St New Orleans LA 70130-3588 E-mail: habbott@stonepigman.com.

ABBOTT, RANDALL (LEE ABBOTT), lawyer; b. Danville, Ill., July 26, 1946; s. Kenneth D. and Lois A. (Palmer) A. AB in Latin Am. Studies, U. Ill., 1968, AB in Polit. Sci., 1968; MA, Ind. U., 1970; JD, U. Ill., 1979. Bar: Ill. 1980, U.S. Dist. Ct. (cen. dist.) Ill. 1982. Tchr. fgn. lang. Rossville (Ill.) H.S., 1971-76; asst. atty. gen. Ill. Atty. Gen., Springfield, 1980-81; legal counsel Ill. Auditor Gen., Springfield, 1981-86; pvt. practice Springfield, 1987—. Bd. dirs. 1st Fin. Ins. Co., Springfield, Guilford Ins. Co., Springfield, Alamance Reins. Co., Springfield. Past pres. Westside Neighborhood Assn., Springfield, 1985. Mem. ABA, Ill. Bar Assn., Ill. Govt. Bar Assn., Ill. Def. Trial Counsel Assn., Sangamon County Bar Assn., Phi Beta Kappa. Anglican. Avocation: numismatics. Insurance. Office: 528 S 5th St Ste 210 Springfield IL 62701-1871

ABEL, HARVEY JOSEPH, retired lawyer; b. Phila., May 3, 1928; s. Harry and Lillian (Feldman) A.; m. Marcia Koplin, June 16, 1957; children— Jonathan Stuart, Beth Karen, Saralyn. B.A., U. Ariz., 1950; LL.B., Stetson U., 1959. Bar: Fla. 1959, U.S. Dist. Ct. (mid. dist.) Fla. 1960, U.S. Ct. Appeals (5th cir.) 1960, U.S. Supreme Ct. 1967. Assoc. Paderewski & Kramer, Sarasota, Fla., 1959-89; ptnr. Abel, Band, Russell, Collier, Pitchford & Gordon, Sarasota, 1960— . Past bd. dirs. Family Service Assn. Temple Emanuel/Temple Beth Sholom, Sarasota, Sarasota Meml. Healthcare Found. Republican. Banking, Corporate, general, Property, real (including real estate development, water). Home: 340 S Palm Ave Apt 55 Sarasota FL 34236-6793 Office: Abel Band Russell Collier Pitchford & Gordon PO Box 49948 Sarasota FL 34230-6948

ABELE, ROBERT CHRISTOPHER, lawyer; b. Boonville, Mo., Mar. 24, 1958; s. William Arved and Joyce (Gowan) A. AB, U. Mo., 1980; JD, U. Mo., Kansas City, 1983. Bar: Mo. 1983, U.S. Dist. Ct. (we. dist.) Mo. 1983, U.S. Dist. Ct. Kans. 1998, U.S. Ct. Appeals (8th cir.) 1983, U.S. Ct. Appeals (10th cir.) 1985, U.S. Supreme Ct. 1991, U.S. Ct. Appeals (11th cir.) 1993. Law clk. to judge U.S. Ct. Appeals (8th cir.), 1983-85; assoc. Morrison, Hecker, Curtis, Kuder & Parrish, Kansas City, Mo., 1985-90, ptnr., 1990-91, Morrison & Hecker, Kansas City, 1991-95, Badger & Levings, Kansas City, 1995-2000; gen. atty. law dept. Sprint, Kansas City, 2001—. Adj. prof. U. Mo. Kansas City Sch. Law, 1988. Chmn. Mo. Coun. on Arts, 1989—94; trustee U. Mo.-Kansas City Law Found., 1986—99, pres., 1997—98; bd. dirs. Mid.-Am. Arts Alliance, 1989—98; treas. Nat. Assembly of State Art Agys., 1994—96; bd. dirs. SAVE, Inc., 2002—. Recipient Decade award U. Mo.-Kansas City Law Found., 1991. Mem. Kansas City Met. Bar Assn. (exec. com. 1999-2001). Republican. Avocation: classical vocal music. Federal civil litigation, Insurance, Product liability. Home: 2204 W 49th St Westwood Hills KS 66251 Office: Sprint Law Dept KSOPHN0412-4A153 6450 Sprint Pkwy Overland Park KS 66251

ABELES, CHARLES CALVERT, retired lawyer; b. Norfolk, Va., Nov. 3, 1929; s. Charles T. and Sally (Taylor) A.; m. Mehitable Mackay-Smith, Sept. 30, 1961; children— Nathaniel C., Damaris S., Jessica A.K. AB, Harvard U., 1952; JD, U. Va., 1958. Bar: Va. 1958, D.C. 1958, U.S. Dist. Ct. (D.C. dist.) 1958, U.S. Ct. Appeals 1958. Assoc. Hogan & Hartson, Washington, 1958-62; assoc. Kieffer & Moroney, Washington, 1962-64, ptnr., 1964-69, Lichtman, Abeles, Anker & Nagle, Washington, 1969-77, Wald, Harkrader & Ross, Washington, 1977-85, Piper & Marbury, Washington, 1986-95. Trustee Corina Higginson Trust. Author articles in field Served to lt. (j.g.) USN, 1952-55 Mem. D.C. Bar, Transplant Recipients Internat. Orgn. (past sec., nat. bd. dirs., past pres. local chpt.). Clubs: Metropolitan (Washington). Democrat. Corporate, general, Environmental, Securities. Home: 4339 Westover Pl NW Washington DC 20016

ABELL, RICHARD BENDER (RICHARD LON WELCH), lawyer, federal judicial official; b. Phila., Dec. 2, 1943; s. Lon Edward Welch, Jr. and Charlotte Amelia (Bender) A., stepfather Ernest George Abell; m. Lucia del Carmen Lombana-Cadavid, Dec. 2, 1968; chldren David, Christian, Rachel. BA in Internat. Affairs, George Washington U., 1966, JD, 1974. Bar: Pa. 1974. Vol. Peace Corps, Colombia, 1967-69; assoc. Reilly & Fogwell, West Chester, Pa., 1974-80; asst. dist. atty. Chester County, Pa., 1974-79; staff mem. U.S. Senator Richard Schweiker, Washington, 1979-80; dir. Office of Program Devel. Peace Corp., Washington, 1981-83; dep. asst. atty. gen. U.S. Dept. Justice, Washington, 1983-86, asst. atty. gen., 1986-90; special master U.S. Ct. Fed. Claims, 1991—. Mem. adj. faculty Del. Law Sch., Wilmington, 1975-77, West Chester State U., 1976; bd. dirs. Fed. Prison Industries, Inc., 1985-91; chmn. Nat. Crime Prevention Coalition, 1986-90; mem. adv. bd. Nat. Inst. Corrections, 1986-90; co-chmn. adv. com. Nat. Ctr. for State and Local Law Enforcement Tng., 1987-90; vice chmn. rsch. and devel. rev. bd. Dept. Justice, 1987-89; mem. nat. drug policy bd. Enforcement Coordinating Group and Coordinating Group for Drug Abuse Prevention and Health, The White House, Washington, 1988-89. Author: Peter Smith of Westmoreland County, Va. (Died 1741) and Some Descendents, 1996, Sojourns of a Patriot: Field and Prison Papers of An Unreconstructed Confederate, 1998. Chmn. Young Rep. Nat. Fedn., Washington, 1979-81; mem. exec. com. Rep. Nat. Com., 1979-81; mem. fed. coordinating coun. on Juvenile Justice and Delinquency Prevention, 1986-90; mem. Pres.'s Task Force on Adoption, 1987-88; mem. Pres.'s Commn. on Agrl. Workers, 1988-93. With U.S. Army, 1969-71. Decorated Purple Heart, Army Commendation medal for heroism, Air medal; recipient Jefferson Davis Hist. gold medal, 2000. Episcopalian. Home: 8209 Chancery Ct Alexandria VA 22308-1514

ABELMAN, ARTHUR F. lawyer; b. N.Y.C., June 12, 1933; s. Bert and Myra (Dickoff) A. AB, Harvard U., 1954, JD, 1957. Bar: N.Y. 1958, U.S. Dist. Ct. (so. and ea. dist.) N.Y. 1958, U.S. Ct. Appeals (2d cir.) 1958. Assoc. Casey Lane & Mittendorf, N.Y.C., 1957-59; counsel Am. Petroleum Inst., N.Y.C., 1959-61; corp. sec. Pocket Books, Inc., N.Y.C., 1961-65; assoc. Weil Gotshal Manges, N.Y.C., 1965-79; counsel Moses & Singer, N.Y.C., 1979—; pres. Millan House, Inc., N.Y.C., 1982—. Pres. Sculpture Ctr., Inc., N.Y.C., 1979-85, trustee, 1971-2000, exec. com., 1988-2000, treas., 1991-2000; trustee Norman Rockwell Art Collection Trust, E.E. Cummings Trust, James Beard Found. Inc., mem. exec. com., 1995—. Mem. ABA, N.Y. Bar Assn., Assn. of Bar of City of N.Y. Clubs: Harvard. Republican. Jewish. Libel, Property, real (including real estate development, water), Trademark and copyright. Home: 116 E 68th St New York NY 10021-5955 Office: Moses & Singer LLP 1301 Avenue Of The Americas New York NY 10019-6022

ABELS, JONATHAN BERLE, lawyer; b. Indpls., Feb. 22, 1944; s. Samuel and Frances (Falendar) A.; m. Linda Feiwell, May 6, 1973; children: Michelle, Ben, Matthew, Maribeth. Student, Wabash Coll., 1962-65; BA, Butler U., 1966; JD, Ind. U., 1969. Bar: Ind. 1970, U.S. Dist. Ct. 1970, U.S. Ct. Appeals 1970, U.S. Supreme Ct. 1980. Ptnr. Dann, Pecar, Newman & Kleiman, Indpls., 1976—, 1976—. Author numerous legal articles. Bd. dirs. Jewish Welfare Fedn., Indpls., 1984; pres. Jewish Community Ctr., Indpls. 1986—. Recipient Martin L. Larner award Jewish Community Ctr., 1983, L.L. Goodman award Jewish Welfare Fedn., 1984. Mem. ABA, Ind. Bar Assn., Indpls. Bar Assn., Comml. Law League Am.

Lodges: B'nai B'rith. Bankruptcy, Commercial, consumer (including collections, credit), Corporate, general. Home: 4980 Deer Ridge Cross Carmel IN 46033-8918 Office: 2300 American Sq Indianapolis IN 46282-0018

ABERNATHY, THOMAS EDWARDS, IV, lawyer; b. Chattanooga, Feb. 18, 1941; s. Edwards Selman and Elizabeth Walker (Henry) A.; 1 child, Elizabeth. B.A., Vanderbilt U., 1963, J.D., 1967; student U. Va., 1963-65. Bar: Tenn. 1967, U.S. Supreme Ct. 1970, U.S. Ct. Fed. Claims. 1970, U.S. Dist. Ct. (ea. dist.) Tenn. 1967, U.S. Dist. Ct. (no. dist.) Ga. 1972, Ga. 1972. Ptnr., Smith, Currie & Hancock, Atlanta, 1971— . Author: Construction Business Handbook, 2d edit., 1984; contbr. articles to profl. jours. Chmn. adv. bd. Met. Atlanta Area Social Services Adv. Council, Salvation Army, 1980— . Served to capt. JAGC, AUS, 1967-71. Mem. ABA (coun. mem. sect. pub. contract law 1974-78, sec. 1979-80, vice chmn. 1981-82, chmn.-elect 1982-83, chmn. 1983-84), Am. Coll. Constrn. Lawyers, State Bar Ga., Tenn. Bar Assn., Atlanta Bar Assn., Fed. Bar Assn., Lawyers Club Atlanta. Presbyterian. Contbr. articles to profl. jours. Federal civil litigation, Construction, Government contracts and claims. Office: Smith Currie & Hancock 233 Peachtree St NE Ste 2600 Atlanta GA 30303-1530

ABLAN, MICHAEL CHARLES, lawyer, law educator; b. La Crosse, Wis., Mar. 11, 1949; s. Charles J. and Joyce D. A.; m. Patti J. Severson-Langer, July 10, 1976 (div. Jan. 1984); children: Alyssa, John, Antony. BABA, Gustavus Adolphus Coll., 1971; JD, Marquette U., 1974. Bar: Wis. 1974, Minn. 1992; U.S. Dist. Ct. (ea. and we. dists.) Wis. 1973, U.S. Tax Ct. 1980, U.S. Ct. Appeals (7th cir.) 1989. Pvt. practice Michael Ablan Law Firm, La Crosse, Wis., 1974—. Adj. prof. Faculty Bus. Law and Health Care Law Viterbro U., La Crosse, 1974-2000; mem. Alternative Dispute Resolution Panl, Mpls., 1994—; pub. spkr. in field; cons. Small Bus. Devel. Ctr.; lectr. Faculty of Bus. Law, Western Wis. Tech. Coll., La Crosse, U. Wis.-LaCrosse. Bd. dirs. Fauver Hills PTO, No. Hills PTO and Hintgen Sch. PTO; mem., founder St. Elias Ch., La Crosse, 1976—; participant Big Brother/Big Sister Program, La Crosse, adv. bd. mem.; ptnr. Spl. Olympics, 1995; fund raiser, mem. Am. Heart Assn., La Crosse, 1995. Mem. State Bar of Wis. (mem. appellate practice sect., elder law sect., real property sect., probate and trust sect., taxation sect.), State Bar of Minn., Coalition of Wis. aging Groups, La Crosse Area Estate Planning Coun., Wis. Realtors Assn. (affiliate), Greater La Cross Area C. of C. (small bus. coun.), The Wilderness Soc., Friends of Hixon Forest Nature Ctr., Nat. Parks and Conservation Assn., La Crosse Nordic Ski Club, United Temple Assn., Grand Lodge Free & Accepted Masons of Wis., Wis. Bow Hunters, La Crosse Cmty. Found., La Crosse County Hist. Soc., Am. Arbitration Assn., Nat. Trust for Hist. Preservation, Native Am. Rights Fund, La Cross Riding Club, U.S. Tennis Assn., United Fund for the Arts. Avocations: tennis, scuba diving, horseback riding, golf, cross country skiing. Federal civil litigation, Corporate, general, Probate (including wills, trusts). Office: 401 King St La Crosse WI 54601-4005

ABLES, CHARLES ROBERT, lawyer, judge; b. South Pittsburg, Tenn., Sept. 13, 1930; s. William McKinley and Iva (Baldwin) A.; m. Rada B. Edmonds, May 20, 1949; children: Patricia Joan, Barbara Elain. B.S., U. Chattanooga, 1964; LL.B., U. Tenn., 1965. Bar: Tenn. 1965, U.S. Dist. Ct. (ea. dist.) Tenn. 1965, U.S. Ct. Appeals (6th cir.) 1977. Sole practice, South Pittsburg, 1971—; judge Manion County Juvenile Ct., Jasper, Tenn., 1980-90. Served with USNG, 1948-50. Mem. Lions, Masons. Republican. Presbyterian. General practice, Juvenile. Home: 105 Lee Hunt Ave South Pittsburg TN 37380-1745 Office: 320 Cedar Ave South Pittsburg TN 37380

ABNEY, FREDERICK SHERWOOD, lawyer; b. Brownwood, Tex., Dec. 2, 1919; s. DeWitt Fleetwood and Margaret (Lyles) A.; m. Jeanne Elizabeth Larson, Feb. 28, 1942; children: Stephen Frederick, James Lorntz. BA, U. Tex., Austin, 1942, LL.B., 1947. Bar: Tex. bar 1947, U.S. Supreme Ct. bar 1963. Pvt. practice, Brownwood, 1948-49, Dallas, 1949-94. Served with USAAF, 1942-45. Mem. Am., Dallas bar assns., State Bar Tex., Am. Judicature Soc., Southwestern Legal Found., Dallas Bar Found., Tex. Bar Found. (life fellow), Delta Tau Delta, Phi Delta Phi. Mem. Unity Ch. State civil litigation, Probate (including wills, trusts). Home and Office: 6730 Orchid Ln Dallas TX 75230-4137

ABRAHAM, WILLIAM JOHN, JR., lawyer; b. Jan. 17, 1948; s. William John and Constance (Dudley) A.; m. Linda Omeis, Aug. 31, 1968; children: Richard S., Heidi K. BA with honors, U. Ill., 1969; JD magna cum laude, U. Mich., Ann Arbor, 1972. Bar: Wis. 1973, U.S. Supreme Ct. 1975. Jud. clk. U.S. Ct. Appeals (D.C. cir.), Washington, 1972-73; ptnr. Foley & Lardner, Milw., 1973—. Former mem. mgmt. com., former chmn. bus. law dept; bd. dirs. The Vollrath Co., Windway Capital Corp., Phillips Plastics Corp., Quad/Graphics, Inc., Park Bank, L'eft Bank Wine Co., Ltd., TransPro, Inc.; lectr. MBA program U. Wis. Mem. Greater Milw. Open; mem. Greater Milw. Com. Children's Hosp. of Milw.; mem. adv. bd. Wis. Policy Rsch. Inst.; past bd. dirs. United Way of Greater Milw., Family Svc. of Milw., Milw. Zool. Soc.; bd. dirs., former chmn. Children's Hosp. Found. Named All-Am. Big 10 Fencing Champion, 1968—69. Mem. ABA, State Bar of Wis. (chmn. legis. com.), Milw. Bar Assn., Barristers, Tripoli Country Club (bd. dirs., pres.), Milw. Athletic Club, Milw. Club, Desert Mountain Country Club. Corporate, general, Property, real (including real estate development, water), Securities. Office: Foley & Lardner 777 E Wisconsin Ave Ste 3800 Milwaukee WI 53202-5367

ABRAHAMS, SAMUEL, writer, retired lawyer; b. N.Y.C., Dec. 3, 1923; s. Isaac and Ida (Ehrman) A.; m. Ida Savitsky, July 8, 1970. BA, Bklyn. Coll., 1945; MA, Columbia U., 1946; JD, Bklyn. Law Sch., 1956; LLM, NYU, 1961; PhD, Heed U., 1993. Bar: N.Y. 1957, U.S. Dist. Ct. (ea. and so. dists.) N.Y. 1962, U.S. Supreme Ct. 1976. Pvt. practice, Bklyn., 1958-90. Arbitrator Civil Ct. N.Y.C., 1982-87; part-time adminstrv. judge parking violations bur., 1976-88; lectr. on fgn. travel, law and politics. Author: Law in Family Conflict, 1970; contbr. articles to profl. and popular jours., newspapers. With U. S. Army, 1942-43. Mem. ABA, North Dade Profls. Jewish Fedn. Grtr. Miami, Bklyn. Coll. Alumni Assn., Internat. Assn. of Jewish Judges and Lawyers, Columbia U. Alumni Assn. Democrat. Avocation: world travel.

ABRAHAMSON, A. CRAIG, lawyer; b. Washington, May 24, 1954; s. Joseph Labe and Helen Dorothy (Selis) A.; m. Mary Ellen Bernard, Dec. 29, 1979; children: Nicholas Eric, Amy Nicole. BA, U. Minn., 1976; JD, U. Tulsa, 1979. Bar: Minn. 1979, U.S. Dist. Ct. Minn. 1979, Okla. 1982, U.S. Dist. Ct. (no. and ea. dists.) Okla. 1983, Mo. 1991. Assoc. Law Office of Joseph L. Abrahamson, Mpls., 1979-82, Freese & March, Tulsa, 1982-83, Barlow & Cox, Tulsa, 1983-86; pvt. practice Tulsa, 1986-95, 2000—; ptnr. Levinson, Smith & Abrahamson, Tulsa, 1995-2000; gen. counsel, v.p. Sandman Property Svcs., Inc. & The Sanditen Cos., 2001—. V.p. program com. Youth Svcs., Tulsa, Inc., Leadership Tulsa Class XVII, 1989-92; sec. Great Expectations Educators, Inc., 1995-99; mem. bd. trustees Am. Theatre Co., 1999—. Recipient Am. Jurisprudence Evidence award Lawyers Co-operative Pub. Co. Bancroft-Whitney Co., 1978. Mem. Okla. Bar Assn. (family law sect., real property sect.), Nat. Assn. of Indsl. and Office Properties, Tulsa County Bar Assn. (family law sect., bankruptcy sect.), Rotary Internat. Democrat. Jewish. Avocations: fishing, camping, travel, tennis. Bankruptcy, Commercial, consumer (including collections, credit), Family and matrimonial. Home: 7518 S 107th East Ave Tulsa OK 74133-2530 Office: A Craig Abrahamson 3314 E 51st St Ste 200-A Tulsa OK 74135 E-mail: craiga@abrahamsonlaw.com.

ABRAHAMSON, SHIRLEY SCHLANGER, state supreme court chief justice; b. N.Y.C., Dec. 17, 1933; d. Leo and Ceil (Sauerteig) Schlanger; m. Seymour Abrahamson, Aug. 26, 1953; 1 son, Daniel Nathan. AB, NYU, 1953; JD, Ind. U., 1956; SJD, U. Wis., 1962. Bar: Ind. 1956, N.Y. 1961, Wis. 1962. Asst. dir. Legis. Drafting Research Fund, Columbia U. Law Sch., 1957-60; since practiced in Madison, Wis., 1962-76; mem. firm LaFollette, Sinykin, Anderson & Abrahamson, 1962-76; justice Supreme Ct. Wis., Madison, 1976-96, chief justice, 1996—; prof. U. Wis. Sch. Law, 1966-92; v.p. conf. Chief Justices, 2002—. Bd. visitors Ind. U. Sch. Law, 1972—02, U. Miami Sch. Law, 1982-97, U. Chgo. Law Sch., 1988-92, Brigham Young U., Sch. Law, 1986-88, Northwestern U. Law Sch., 1989-94; chmn. Wis. Rhodes Scholarship Com., 1992-95; chmn. nat. adv. com. on ct.-adjudicated and ct.-ordered health care George Washington U. Ctr. Health Policy, Washington, 1993-95; mem. DNA adv. bd. FBI, U.S. Dept. Justice, 1995-2001; bd. dirs. Inst. Jud. Adminstrn., Inc., NYU Sch. Law; chair Nat. Inst. Justice's Commn. Future DNA Evidence, 1997-2001. Editor: Constitutions of the United States (National and State) 2 vols, 1962. Mem. study group program of rsch., mental health and the law John D. and Catherine T. MacArthur Found., 1988-96; mem. coun. fund for rsch. on dispute resolution Ford Found., 1987-91; bd. dirs. Wis. Civil Liberties Union, 1968-72; mem. ct. reform adv. panel Internat. Human Rights Law Group Cambodia Project, 1995-97. Mem. ABA (coun., sect. legal edn. and admissions to bar 1976-86, mem. commn. on undergrad. edn. in law and the humanities 1978-79, standing com. on pub. edn. 1991-95, mem. commn. on access to justice/2000 1993—02, mem. adv. bd. Ctrl. and East European law initiative 1994-99, mem. consortium on legal svcs. and the public 1995-2001, vice-chair ABA Coalition for Justice 1997-2000), Wis. Bar Assn., Dane County Bar Assn., 7th Cir. Bar Assn., Nat. Assn. Women Judges, Am. Law Inst. (mem. coun. 1985—), Am. Philos. Soc., Am. Acad. Arts and Scis. Office: Wis Supreme Ct PO Box 1688 Madison WI 53702-1688

ABRAMOWITZ, ROBERT LESLIE, lawyer; b. Phila., May 1950; s. Nathan P. and Lucille H. (Rader) A.; m. Susan Margaret Stewart, Dec. 1, 1974; children: David, Catherine. BA, Yale U., 1971; JD, Harvard U., 1974. Bar: Pa. 1974, N.J. 1975. Assoc. Ballard, Spahr, Andrews & Ingersoll, Phila., 1974-81, ptnr., 1981-90; ptrn. Morgan Lewis & Bockius, LLP, Phila., 1990—. Adj. prof. law Villanova U., 1986—2001. Trustee Moorestown (N.J.) Friends Sch., 1981-90, Rock Sch. of Pa. Ballet, 1990—; pres. Harvard Law Sch. Assn. Greater Phila., 1999-2001. Mem. ABA, Am. Coll. of Employee Benefits Counsel, Phila. Bar Assn. (exec. com. probate sect. 1982-85, pension com. 1985-94, chair 1987-89), Yale Club, Merion Cricket Club. Estate planning, Pension, profit-sharing, and employee benefits. Home: 623 Pembroke Rd Bryn Mawr PA 19010-3613 Office: Morgan Lewis & Bockius LLP 1701 Market St Philadelphia PA 19103-2903

ABRAMS, HAROLD EUGENE, lawyer; b. Pensacola, Fla., Jan. 18, 1933; s. Samuel Ralph and Sadie (Gerhardt) A.; m. Nancy Gray, June 22, 1958; children: Shari Abrams Marx, Eric Gray. BA, U. Mich., 1954; JD, Harvard U., 1957. Bar: Ga. 1958, D.C. 1976, U.S. Supreme Ct. 1970. Law clk. to presiding judge U.S. Ct. Appeals (5th cir.), Atlanta, 1957-58; assoc. Kilpatrick & Cody, Atlanta, 1958-63; ptnr. Kilpatrick Stockton, Atlanta, 1963—. Pres. Atlanta Tax Forum, 1990-91, Atlanta Estate Planning Coun., 1991-92; bd. dirs. Randall Bros., Inc., Atlanta, Selig Enterprises, Inc., Atlanta. Contbr. articles on tax and estate planning to profl. publs. Pres. Buckhead Little League, Atlanta, 1972-73; bd. dirs. Atlanta chpt. Am. Jewish Com., 1987-2001, Atlanta Jewish Fedn., 1996—; sec. Ronald McDonald's Children's Charities, Atlanta, 1988—. With U.S. Army, 1957-58. Fellow Am. Coll. Tax Counsel; mem. State Bar of Ga. (chmn. tax sect. 1964-65), So. Fed. Tax Inst. (trustee 1964-2001, pres. 1970-71, treas. 1986-95), Peachtree Club, Atlanta Lawyers Club. Avocations: tennis, travel. Corporate taxation, Estate taxation, Taxation, general. Office: Kilpatrick Stockton LLP 1100 Peachtree St NE Ste 2800 Atlanta GA 30309-4530 E-mail: habrams@kilpatrickstockton.com.

ABRAMS, LEE NORMAN, lawyer; b. Chgo., Feb. 28, 1935; s. Saul E. and Evelyn (Cohen) A.; m. Myrna Parker, Dec. 26, 1965; 1 dau., Elana Shira. AB, U. Mich., 1955, JD, 1957. Bar: Ill. 1957, U.S. Supreme Ct. 1961, U.S. Tax Ct. 1972. Assoc. firm Mayer, Brown, Rowe & Maw and predecessors, Chgo., 1957-66, ptnr., 1966—. Mem. visitors com. U. Mich. Law Sch., 1970—; bd. assocs. Nat. Coll. Edn., Chgo., 1973-80. Recipient Gold medal AICPA, 1958. Mem. ABA (coun. antitrust sect. 1975-77, fin. officer 1977-81, program chair antitrust sect. 1988-91, vice chair antitrust sect. 1991-92, chmn. forum on franchising 1982-85, chmn. antitrust com. sect. bus. law 1995-99), Chgo. Bar Assn. (antitrust law com. 1970-85), Ill. State Bar Assn. (antitrust section coun. 1994-2001), U.S. C. of C. (antitrust and trade regulation com. 1974-80), Briarwood Country Club, Royal and Ancient Golf Club of St. Andrews (Scotland). Antitrust, Federal civil litigation, Franchising. Office: Mayer Brown Rowe & Maw 190 S La Salle St Ste 3100 Chicago IL 60603-3441

ABRAMS, MARC, lawyer, state political party executive; b. N.Y.C., Mar. 23, 1957; s. Stephen Robert and Virginia Ornstein Abrams; m. Barbara Christopher, 1981; 1 child, Lawrence Christopher. BA magna cum laude, Wesleyan U., Middletown, Conn., 1978; MA, JD, U. Mich., 1981. Bar: Conn. 1982, N.Y. 1986, D.C. 1987, Pa. 1987, Oreg. 1989, U.S. Dist Ct. (so. dist.) N.Y. 1986, U.S. Dist. Co. (ea. dist.) Pa. 1988, U.S. Dist. Ct. Mont. 1989, U.S. Cir. Ct. (3d, 4th and 9th cirs.), U.S. Dist. Ct. Oreg. 1989, U.S. Supreme Ct. Asst. prof. U. Oreg., 1981-83; exec. dir. Student Press Law Ctr., 1983-85; pvt. practice, 1985—2002; sr. asst. atty. State of Oreg., 2002—. Co-author: Law of the Student Press, 1983, Confronting Wrongful Discharge Under Oregon and Washington Law, 1989. Vice chair Lane County (Oreg.) Dem. Ctrl. Com., 1981-82, Multnomah County (Oreg.) Dem. Ctrl. Com., 1991-92; mem. Oreg. Dem. State Ctrl. Com., 1981-82, 91—, Multnomah Edn. Svc. Dist. Bd., 1993-97, chmn., 1996-97; fin. chair Oreg. State Dem. Party, 1993-95, vice chair, 1994-97, chmn., 1997-99; mem. Portland Sch. Bd., 1995—, vice chair, 1998-2002; treas. Assn. State Dem. Chairs, 1998-99. Recipient Johnnie Phelps medal Vets. for Human Rights, 1995. Jewish. Office: 1753 NW Aspen Ave Portland OR 97210-1208

ABRAMS, NORMAN, law educator, university administrator; b. Chgo., July 7, 1933; s. Harry A. and Gertrude (Dick) A.; m. Toshka Alster, 1977; children: Marshall David, Julie, Hanna, Naomi. AB, U. Chgo., 1952, JD, 1955. Bar: Ill. 1956, U.S. Supreme Ct. 1967. Assoc. in law Columbia U., 1955-57; rsch. assoc. Harvard U., 1957-59; sec. Harvard-Brandeis Coop. Rsch. for Israel's Legal Devel., 1957-58, dir., 1959; mem. faculty law sch. UCLA, 1959—, prof. law, 1964—, assoc. dean law, 1989-91, vice chancellor acad. pers., 1991-2001, interim exec. v. chancellor, spring 1998, co-dir. Ctr. for internat. and strategic studies, 1982-83, chmn. steering com., 1985-87, 88-89; vis. prof. Hebrew U., 1969-70, Forchheimer vis. prof., 1986; vis. prof. Bar Ilan U., 1970-71, 78, U. So. Calif., 1972, Stanford U., 1977, U. Calif. at Berkeley, 1977, Loyola U., Los Angeles, summers 1974, 75, 76, 79; spl. asst. to U.S. atty. gen., also prof.-in-residence criminal div. Dept. Justice, 1966-67. Reporter for So. Calif. indigent accused persons study Am. Bar Found., 1963; cons. Gov. Calif. Commn. L.A. Riots, 1965, Pres.'s Commn. Law Enforcement and Adminstrn. Justice, 1966-67, Nat. Commn. on Reform of Fed. Criminal Laws, 1967-69, Rand Corp., 1968-74, Ctr. for Adminstrv. Justice, ABA, 1973-77, Nat. Adv. Commn. on Criminal Justice Stds., Organized Crime Task Force, 1976; spl. hearing officer conscientious objector cases Dept. Justice, 1967-68; vis. scholar Inst. for Advanced Studies, Hebrew U., summer, 1994. Author: (with others) Evidence, Cases and Materials, 7th edit., 1983, 8th edit., 1988, 9th edit., 1997, Federal Criminal Law and Its Enforcement, 1986, 2d and 3d edits. (with S. Beale), 1993, 2000, Anti-terrorism and Criminal Enforcement, 2003; mem. editl. bd. Criminal Law Forum, 1990—. Chmn. Jewish Conciliation Bd., L.A., 1975-81; bd. dirs. Bet Tzedek, 1975-85, L.A. Hillel Coun., 1979-82, Shalhevet High Sch., 1998—; chmn. So. Calif. region Am. Profs. for Peace in Middle East, 1981-83; bd. dirs. met. region Jewish Fedn., 1982-88, v.p. 1982-83; pres. Westwood Kehillah Congregation, 1985. Mem. Internat. Soc. for Reform of Criminal Law (mem. exec. com. 1994—), Phi Beta Kappa. Office: UCLA Law School 405 Hilgard Ave Los Angeles CA 90095-9000 E-mail: abrams@law.ucla.edu.

ABRAMS, ROBERT, lawyer, former state attorney general; b. Bronx, N.Y., July 4, 1938; s. Benjamin and Dorothy (Kaplan) A.; m. Diane B. Schulder, Sept. 15, 1974; children: Rachel Schulder, Becky Schulder. BA, Columbia U., 1960; JD, NYU, 1963; LL.D. (hon.), Hofstra U., 1979; Lugum Doctoris (hon.), Yeshiva U., 1984; LLD (hon.), L.I. U., 1989, Pace U., 1991. Mem. N.Y. State Assembly, 1965-69; pres. Borough of Bronx, 1970-78; atty. gen. State of N.Y., 1979-93; ptnr. Stroock & Stroock & Lavan, N.Y.C., 1994—. Panel mem. of disting. neutrals CPR Inst.; dir. Sterling Nat. Bank, Sterling Bancorp. Contbr. articles to profl. publs.; writer column Nat. Law Jour., N.Y. Law Jour., N.Y. Times, N.Y. Newsday, N.Y. Post, N.Y. Daily News, Buffalo News, Albany Times Union, Ganette Suburban Newspapers, The Harvard Environ. Law Rev., NYU Law Rev., Columbia Jour. Environ. Law, Pace Environ. Law Rev., Washburn Law Rev., Albany Law Rev., Pace Law Rev., The Jour. of State Gov. Pres. Citizens Union Found.; del. Dem. Nat. Conv., 1972, 76, 80, 84, mem. platform com., 1988; elector Electoral Coll., 1988; co-chair Nat. Jewish Dem. Coun., N.Y.State. Recipient Adam Clayton Powell Pub. Svc. award, Interfaith award Coun. Chs., N.Y.C., Bronx Community Coll. medallion for Svc., Scroll of Honor plaque United Jewish Appeal, Benjamin Cardozo award for legal excellence Jewish Lawyers Guild, Brotherhood award B'nai B'rith, Man of Yr. award NAACP, Alumni Achievement award NYU Sch. Law, Environmentalist of Yr. award Environ. Planning Lobby N.Y., Disting. Pub. Svc. Citation Bus. Coun. N.Y. State, N.Y. State Sheriff's Assn. award, Nat. Crime Victims award, Torch of Liberty award Anti-Defamation League, Anatoly Scharansky Freedom award N.Y. Conf. Soviet Jewry, Environmentalist of Yr. award L.I. Pine Barrens Soc., Il Leone de San Marco Hon. Italian Am. award, Cavaliere medal Pres. Italy, Pres. award Marist Coll., Hubert Humphrey Humanitarian award United Fedn. Tchrs., Law Day award N.Y. State Trial Lawyers Assn., Contbns. to Urban Law award Fordham Law Jour., Deans medal Law Sch. NYU, Margaret Sanger award N.Y. State Family Planning Advocates, Lehman/LaGuardia Civic Achievement award Anti-Defamation League B'nai B'rith and Commn. on Social Justice of the Order of Sons of Italy, Father of the Yr. award Nat. Father's Day Com., B'nai Zion Bill of Rights award, Avodah award Jewish Tchr's. Assn., Man of the Yr. award N.Y. State Consumer Assembly, Rodef Tzedek Pursuer of Justice award Restructionist Rabbinical Coll., Humanitarian award Rochester Labor and Religious Coalition, Special Recognition award Profl. Women in Construction and Allied Industries, Humanitarian award Long Island Assn. for Children with Learning Disabilities, Man of the Yr. award Mental Ilness Found., N.Y. State Ct's. Man of the Yr. award Shamrai Tzedek Soc., Grand Marshall award Schenectady Labor Coun. Labor Day Parade, Louis Brandeis award Zionist Orgn. Am., Lubavich Tzivos Hashem award, Chassidius in Am. Exemplary Leadership award Bostoner Chassidum, Recognition for Pub. Svc. award Greater Buffalo AFL-CIO Coun., Effort on Behalf of the Elderly award Workmen's Circle Home & Infirmary For the Aged, Dedication Concerning Reproductive Rights award N.Y. Coun. of Jewish Women, Citation of Appreciation N.Y. State Assn. of Architects, Pesach-Tikvah Hope Developer award, Pub. Svc. award N.Y. Soc. Clin. Psychologists, Cmty. Achievement award Am. Orthodox Fedn., State Svc. award Nat. Columbus Day Com., Environmentalist of the Yr. award Sierra Club, Svc. award N.Y. State Jewish War Veterans, Cadet award N.Y.C. Mission Soc., Disting. Achievement award AMIT Women, Man of the Yr. award Nassau County Police Res. Assn., Ann. award Lubavitch Youth Orgn., Appreciation award Japanese C. of C. of N.Y., Friend of the Cmty. award Empire State Pride Agenda, Roland Smith award Capital Region chpt. N.Y. Civil Liberties Union, Scharansky Freedom award L.I. Com. on Soviet Jewry, Cert. of Honor award N.Y. League of Histadrut, Scouting For the Handicapped Outstanding Svc. award Greater N.Y. Coun. of Boy Scouts of Am., Citizen of the Yr. award We. N.Y. Labor Coalition, Svc. award Citizen's Coun. for the Cmty. of Mentally Retarded, Rockland Hosp. Guild, Man of the Yr. award The Shield Inst. for Retarded Children, Maccabean Svc. award N.Y. Bd. of Rabbis, Thurgood Marshall award Bridge Builders Albany, Pro Choice award Naral N.Y., Dist. Humanitarian award Insts. Applied Human Dynamics, Life-Long Dedication award Holocaust Meml. Com., Disting. Cmty. Svc. award Am. Friends of Bnei Akiva; named Man of Yr. St. Patrick's Home Aged and Infirm, Man of Yr. State Israel Bonds. Mem. N.Y. State Bar Assn. (Environ. Acheivement award), Assn. Bar City of N.Y., Nat. Assn. of Attys. Gen. (pres. 1988-89, chmn. environ. protection com. 1982-85, chmn. antitrust com. 1985-88, chmn. civil rights com. 1990-92, chmn. ea. regional conf. of attys. gen. 1983-84, Wyman award for Outstanding Atty. Gen. in the Nation 1991, commn. campaign fin. reform). Democrat. Administrative and regulatory. Office: Stroock & Stroock & Lavan 180 Maiden Ln Ste 3989 New York NY 10038-4937 Office Fax: 212-806-6006.

ABRAMS, ROGER IAN, law educator, arbitrator; b. Newark, July 30, 1945; s. Avel S. and Myrna (Posner) A.; m. Frances Elise Kovitz, June 1, 1969; children: Jason, Seth. BA, Cornell U., 1967; JD, Harvard U., 1970. Bar: Mass. 1970, U.S. Dist. Ct. Mass. 1971, U.S. Ct. Appeals (1st cir.) 1971. Law clk. to Judge Frank M. Coffin U.S. Ct. Appeals (1st cir.), Boston, 1970-71; assoc. Foley, Hoag & Eliot, Boston, 1971-74; prof. law Law. Sch. Case Western Res. U., Cleve., 1974-86; dean Law Ctr. Nova U., Ft. Lauderdale, Fla., 1986-93; dean Law Sch. Rutgers U., Newark, 1993-1998; prof. law sch. Rutger U., Newark, 1993-99; Herbert J. Hannuch scholar Rutgers U., Newark, 1998-99; dean Northeastern U., Boston, 1999—2002, Richardson prof. law, 1999—. Labor arbitrator Fed. Mediation Svc., 1975—; mem. gender bias report implementation com. Fla. Supreme Ct. Author: Legal Bases: Baseball and the Law, 1998, The Money Pitch: Baseball Free Agency and Salary Arbitration, 2000, The First World Scenes and the Baseball Fanatics of 1903, 2003; contbr. articles to law jours. Bd. dirs. Inst. for Continuing Legal Edn., N.J., 1993-98. Recipient Gen. Counsel's Advocacy award NAACP, Boston, 1974; inductee Union N.J. Hall of Fame, 1995. Mem. Am. Law Inst., Am. Bar Found., Am. Arbitration Assn. (labor arbitrator). Democrat. Jewish. Avocations: swimming, distance walking, reading. Office: Northeastern Univ Sch Law 400 Huntington Ave Boston MA 02115-5005 E-mail: rabrams@neu.edu.

ABRAMS, RUTH IDA, retired state supreme court justice; b. Boston, Dec. 26, 1930; d. Samuel and Matilda A. BA, Radcliffe Coll., 1953; LLB, Harvard U., 1956; hon. degree, Mt. Holyoke Coll., 1977, Suffolk U., 1977, New Eng. Sch. Law, 1978. Bar: Mass. 1957. Ptnr. Abrams Abrams & Abrams, Boston, 1957-60; asst. dist. atty. Middlesex County, Mass., 1961-69; asst. atty. gen. Mass., chief appellate sect. criminal div., 1969-71; spl. counsel Supreme Jud. Ct. Mass., 1971-72, assoc. justice, 1977-2000; retired Supreme Jud. Ct., Boston, 2000; assoc. justice Superior Ct. Commonwealth of Mass., 1972-77. Mem. Gov.'s Commn. on Child Abuse, 1970-71, Mass. Law Revision Commn. Proposed Criminal Code for Mass., 1969-71; trustee Radcliffe Coll., from 1981 Editor: Handbook for Law Enforcement Officers, 1969-71. Recipient Radcliffe Coll. Achievement award, 1976, Radcliffe Grad. Soc. medal, 1977 Mem. ABA (com. on proposed fed. code from 1977), Mass. Bar Assn., Am. Law Inst., Am. Judicature Soc. (dir. 1978), Am. Judges Assn., Mass. Assn. Women Lawyers. Home: Supreme Jud Ct Mass 180 Beacon St Cambridge MA 02116

ABRAMS, SHERI, lawyer; b. N.Y.C. BSBA, Boston U., 1989; JD, George Washington U., 1994. Bar: Va. 1995, D.C. 1996, U.S. Dist. Ct. (ea. dist.) Va., D.C. Ct. Appeals, U.S. Ct. Appeals (4th cir.), U.S. Supreme Ct. Pvt. practice, Fairfax, Va. Mem.: ABA, Nat. Orgn. Social Security Claimants Reps., Fairfax County Bar Assn., Ctrl. Fairfax C. of C. Administrative and regulatory, Estate planning, Pension, profit-sharing, and employee benefits. Office: 4085 Chain Bridge Rd Ste 501 Fairfax VA 22030-4106 E-mail: sheri@sheriabrams.com.

ABRAMS, STANLEY DAVID, lawyer; b. Washington, Jan. 30, 1940; s. Norman J. and Sally (Taylor) A.; m. Patricia Dreisen, June 7, 1964; children: Suzanne Bari, Lori Paige. BS, U. Md., 1962, LLB, 1966, JD, 1969. Bar: Md. 1966. Trial atty. FTC, Washington, 1966-67; sr. asst. county atty. Montgomery County, Rockville, Md., 1967-71, adminstrv. hearing examiner, 1971-79; ptnr. Levitan, Ezrin, West & Kerxton, P.C., Bethesda, Md., 1979-84; city atty. City of Gaithersburg, Md., 1979—; ptnr. Abrams, West, Storm, and Diamond P.C., Bethesda, 1984—. Cons. Md. Nat. Capital Park and Planning Commn., Silver Spring, 1987, Washington Met. Transit Authority, 1985; mem. faculty ALI/ABA Land Use Inst., Phila., 1981—, Continuing Legal Edn. Inst. Md. Bar, Balt., 1980—. Author: Guide to Maryland Zoning Decisions, 1993, 4th edit., 2002, How to Win the Zoning Game, 1978; co-author: Handling the Land Use Case, 1984, Land Use Practice and Forms, 1997; contbg. author: Maryland Appellate Practice Handbook, 1977. With U.S. Army, 1958—62. Mem. Md. Bar Assn., Montgomery County Bar Assn. (sec. chmn. 1967—), Md. Bar Found., Urban Land Inst., Bethesda-Chevy Chase C. of C. (pres. 1983). Democrat. Jewish. Avocations: travel, writing, lecturing. Administrative and regulatory, Land use and zoning (including planning), Property, real (including real estate development, water). Home: 15101 Emory Ln Rockville MD 20853-1655 Office: Abrams West and Storm PC 4550 Montgomery Ave Ste 760N Bethesda MD 20814-3379 E-mail: sabrams@awsdlaw.com.

ABRAMSON, LESLIE HOPE, lawyer; b. Queens, N.Y., 1943; 1 child, Laine. Grad., Queens Coll.; JD, UCLA. Bar: Calif. 1970. Lawyer L.A. County Pub. Defender's Office, 1970—77; pvt. practice, 1977—. Recipient award for outstanding trial atty., Criminal Cts. Bar Assn., 1985. Mem.: Calif. Attys. for Criminal Justice (pres.). Office: Ste 940 4929 Wilshire Blvd Los Angeles CA 90010-3823*

ABRAVANEL, ALLAN RAY, lawyer; b. N.Y.C., Mar. 11, 1947; s. Leon and Sydelle (Berenson) A.; m. Susan Ava Paikin, Dec. 28, 1971; children: Karen, David. BA magna cum laude, Yale U., 1968; JD cum laude, Harvard U., 1971. Bar: N.Y. 1972, Oreg. 1976. Assoc. Paul, Weiss, Rifkind, Wharton & Garrison, N.Y.C., 1971-72, 74-76; fellow Internat. Legal Ctr., Lima, Peru, 1972-74; from assoc. to ptnr. Stoel, Rives, Boley, Fraser & Wyse, Portland, Oreg., 1976-83; ptnr. Perkins Coie, Portland, 1983—. Editor, pub. Abravanel Family Newsletter. Chair Oreg. Internat. Trade Com., Oreg. Dist. Export Coun. Mem. ABA, Portland Met. C. of C. Corporate, general, Private international, Municipal (including bonds). Office: Perkins Coie 1211 SW 5th Ave Portland OR 97204-3713

ABREU, LUIS ALBERTO, lawyer; b. Pinar Del Rio, Cuba, Apr. 20, 1956; came to U.S., 1961; s. Arnaldo Jesus and Justa (Villar) A.; m. Sallie Brown Shadrick, Aug. 23, 1980; children: Sarah, Maria. BA, Davidson Coll., 1978; JD, U. Fla., 1981. Bar: Va. 1981, U.S. Bankruptcy Ct. 1981, U.S. Ct. Appeals (4th cir.) 1981. From assoc. to ptnr. Clement & Wheatley, Danville, Va., 1981—. Chmn. Local Human Rights Com., Danville, Va., 1986—89; commr. Commn. Archtl. Rev.; bd. dirs., pres. YMCA, 1992; mem. planning and budget com. United Way; bd. dirs. Danville Sci. Ctr. Alex Hemby scholar Davidson Coll., 1974-78; recipient Bob Griese award Miami Touchdown Club, 1976. Mem.: ABA, Mental Health Assn. (bd. dirs.), Va. Bar Assn., Danville Mus. Fine Arts, Hist. Soc., Lions (pres. 1984—85). Republican. Roman Catholic. Avocations: racquetball, house restoration. Bankruptcy, Commercial, contracts (including sales of goods; commercial financing), Family and matrimonial. Home: 250 Shoreham Dr Danville VA 24541-5149 Office: Clement & Wheatley PO Box 8200 Danville VA 24543-8200

ABT, RALPH EDWIN, lawyer; b. Chgo., Apr. 9, 1960; s. Wendel Peter and Hedi Lucie (Wieder) A. BA, Loyola U., Chgo., 1982; JD, John Marshall Law Sch., Chgo., 1987. Bar: Ill. 1987, U.S. Dist. Ct. (no. dist.) Ill. 1987, U.S. Ct. Appeals (7th cir.) Ill. 1988. Pvt. practice, Chgo., 1987—88; staff atty. Sec. of State's Office, Chgo., 1988—95, Ill. Dept. Pub. Aid, Chgo., 1995—. Poll watcher, Chgo., 1981, 83, precinct capt., 1983, 93-2000. Mem. ABA, Ill. Bar Assn., Chgo. Bar Assn., Trade Law Assn. (charter mem., chmn. charter membership drive 1986), Phi Alpha Delta. Lutheran. Avocations: reading, tennis, bicycling, weight lifting. Home: 5067 W Balmoral Ave Chicago IL 60630-1547 Office: Ill Dept Pub Aid 32 W Randolph St Ste 1200 Chicago IL 60601-3470

ACHAMPONG, FRANCIS KOFI, law educator, consultant; b. Kumasi, Ghana, Feb. 18, 1955; came to U.S., 1981; s. John Wilberforce and Salome (Mensa) A.; m. Nicole Victoria Blache. LLB, U. Ghana, 1976; LLM, U. London, 1977, PhD, 1981; LLM, Georgetown U., 1985. Bar: N.Y. 1986, Va. 1988, U.S. Dist. Ct. (ea. dist.) Va. 1988, U.S. Ct. Appeals (4th cir.) 1988, U.S. Supreme Ct. 1990. Adj. lectr. George Washington U., Washington, 1981-82; asst. prof. Howard U., Washington, 1981-85; assoc. prof. Norfolk State U., Va., 1985—92, prof., 1992—2002, chair dept. entrepreneurial studies, 1998—2001, interim dean Sch. Bus., 2001—02; of counsel Jones, Shelton, Kmetz & Malone, P.C, Norfolk, 1998—; dir. acad. affairs Pa. State U. at Mont Alto, 2002—. Cons. Aetna Life & Casualty, Hartford, Conn., 1981-82, Profl. Ins. Assn. of Md., Pa., 1986, Shapiro, Meiselman & Greene, P.C., Rockville, Md., 1987, Crowell & Moring, Washington, 1988, Clark & Stant, Virginia Beach, Va., 1988. Author: Workplace Sexual Harassment, 1999; contbr. articles to profl. jours. Mem. Am. Risk and Ins. Assn., Acad. Legal Studies in Bus. Avocations: gospel music, exercise, reading, movies. Home: 10076 Old Forge Rd Waynesboro PA 17268- Office: Pa State Mont Alto One Campus Dr Mont Alto PA 17237 Fax: 717-749-6069. E-mail: fka3@psu.edu.

ACHELPOHL, STEVEN EDWARD, lawyer; b. Wichita, Kans., July 15, 1950; s. Ray Edward and Juanita J. (Barnes) A.; m. Shelley R. Kiel (div. Sept. 1987); m. Sara K. Nabity, Nov. 24, 1989; children: Joseph E., Samuel B., Raechel A., Ryan Sullivan, Peter Sullivan, Rebecca Sullivan. BA, U. Nebr., 1972, JD with distinction, 1975. Bar: Nebr. 1975, U.S. Dist. Ct. Nebr. 1975, U.S. Ct. Appeals (8th cir.) 1981. Law clk. hon. Donald R. Ross U.S. Ct. Appeals, Omaha, 1975-77; atty. McGrath, North, O'Mally, Kratz, Omaha, 1977-80, Dwyer, O'Leary & Martin, Omaha, 1980-83; ptnr. Schumacher & Achelpohl, Omaha, 1983-92; assoc. Smith Peterson, Omaha, 1992-93; pvt. practice Omaha, 1994—. Dir. Vis. Nurses Assn., Omaha, 1993—, fin. com., 1994—; chair, Neb. Dem. Party, 2001, 2002; fellow, Neb. State Bar Found., Am. Coll. of Trial Lawyers; mem. Democratic Nat. Com., 2001-. Democrat. Avocations: golf, baseball. General civil litigation, Criminal. Home: 6420 Underwood Ave Omaha NE 68132-1812 Office: 1823 Harney St Ste 1010 Omaha NE 68102-1900 E-mail: achelpohl@usa.net.

ACHESON, AMY J. lawyer; b. Pitts., July 16, 1963; d. Willard Phillips and Patricia Louise (Marshall) A. BA, Haverford Coll., 1984; JD cum laude, U. S.C., 1987. Bar: Pa. 1987, U.S. Dist. Ct. (we. dist.) Pa. 1987, U.S. Ct. Appeals (10th cir.) 1989, U.S. Ct. Appeals (3d cir.) 1988, U.S. Ct. Appeals (4th cir.) 1993. Atty. Reed, Smith, Shaw & McClay, Pitts., 1987—95; shareholder Berger Law Firm, Pitts., 1995—99; of counsel Ogg, Jones, Cordes & Ignelzi, Pitts., 1999—. Mem. S.C. Law Rev., 1985-87. Fin. officer Ret. Sr. Vol. Program Allegheny County, Pitts., 1990-91; treas. Parents League for Emotional Adjustments, Pitts., 1990-91; mem. adv. bd. Pa. Dept. Correction, Community Svc. Ctr. No. 1, Pitts., 1990-97; bd. mgrs. The Woodwell, Pitts., 1992-97, v.p., 1998-2000; bd. dirs. Presbyn. Seniorcare Network, Inc., 2000—; bd. trustees Shadyside Presbyn. Ch. Nursery Sch., 2001—. Mem. ABA (jud. adminstrn. div. com., chmn. subcom. on discipline of fed. judges, 1990-91), ATLA (life mem.), Allegheny County Bar Assn. (young lawyers sect. coun. 1990-91), Order of the Coif, Order of the Wig and Robe. Federal civil litigation, State civil litigation. Office: Riverview Pl 245 Fort Pitt Blvd Pittsburgh PA 15222-1511 E-mail: amyacheson@aol.com.

ACHESON, EDWIN R., JR., lawyer; b. Joplin, Mo., Sept. 14, 1955; BS in Mech. and Aerospace Engring., U. Mo., Columbia, 1977; JD, Duke U., 1980. Assoc. Frost & Jacobs, Cin., 1988-94, ptnr., 1994—. Mem. Am. Intellectual Property Law Assn., Cin. Intellectual Property Law Assn. (pres. 1997), Rotary Club. Intellectual property. Office: Frost Brown Todd LLC 201 E 5th St Ste 2500 Cincinnati OH 45202-4182

ACKER, FREDERICK GEORGE, lawyer; b. Defiance, Ohio, May 7, 1934; s. Julius William and Orah Louise (Dowler) A.; m. Cynthia Ann Wayne, Dec. 1, 1962; children: Frederick Wayne, Mary Katherine, Richard Hoghton, Jennifer Ruth. Student, Ind. U., 1952-54; BA, Valparaiso U., 1956; MA, Harvard U., 1957, JD, 1961; postgrad., U. Manchester (Eng.), 1957-58. Bar: Ill. 1961, Ind. 1961. Ptnr. Winston & Strawn, Chgo., 1961-88, McDermott, Will & Emery, Chgo., 1988—2003, counsel, 2003—. Co-chmn. Joint Prin. and Income Act. com., Chgo., 1976-81. Co-author: (portfolio) Generation-Skipping Tax, 1991; contbr. articles to profl. jours. Bd. dirs. Max McGraw Wildlife Found., Dundee, Ill., 1984-2003, chmn., pres. 1997-2001; trustee L.S. Wood Ednl. Trust, Chgo., 1975—; trustee Ill. chpt. The Nature Conservancy, Chgo., 1981-90, chmn., 1986-90. Danforth Found. fellow, 1956; Fulbright scholar, 1957. Mem. Trout Unlimited, Fulbright Assn. (bd. dirs. 1994-2000, pres. 2000), Met. Chgo. Club, Anglers Club, Chgo. Farmers Club. Lutheran. Avocations: hunting, fishing. Estate planning, Probate (including wills, trusts), Estate taxation. Home: 543 N Madison St Hinsdale IL 60521-3213 Office: McDermott Will & Emery 227 W Monroe St Ste 3100 Chicago IL 60606-5096

ACKER, WILLIAM MARSH, JR., federal judge; b. Birmingham, Ala., Oct. 25, 1927; s. William Marsh and Estelle (Lampkin) A.; m. Martha Walters, 1957; children— William Marsh III, Stacey Reed. BA, Birmingham So. Coll., 1949; LLB, Yale U., 1952. Bar: Ala. 1952. Assoc. Graham, Bibb, Wingo & Foster, Birmingham, Ala., 1952-57, Smyer, White, Reid & Acker, 1957-72, Dominick, Fletcher, Yeilding, Acker, Wood & Lloyd, Birmingham, 1972-82; judge U.S. Dist. Ct. (no. dist.) Ala., 1982-96, sr. judge, 1996—. Mem. Ala. Republican Exec. Com.; del. to Repub. Nat. Convention, 1972, 76, 80. Mem. Birmingham Bar Assn. Office: US Dist Ct 481 Hugo L Black Courthouse 1729 5th Ave N Birmingham AL 35203-2000

ACKERMAN, DAVID PAUL, lawyer; b. Chgo., June 11, 1949; s. Norman Alvin and Ruth (Renberg) A.; m. Deanna Mae Neumayer, Aug. 24, 1972; children: Paul David, Kristin Marie. AB, Princeton U., 1971; JD, Harvard U., 1974. Bar: Ill. 1974, U.S. Dist. Ct. (no. dist.) Ill. 1974. Assoc. McBride, Baker & Coles, Chgo., 1974-80, ptnr., 1980—2002; equity shareholder Jenkens & Gilchrist, Chgo., 2002—. Author various articles. Mem. ABA, Ill. Bar Assn., Chgo. Bar Assn., ESOP Assn., Nat. Ctr. for Employee Ownership, Tower Club. Mergers and acquisitions, Pension, profit-sharing, and employee benefits, Corporate taxation. Office: Jenkens & Gilchrist 225 W Washington St ste 2600 Chicago IL 60606 E-mail: dackerman@jenkens.com.

ACKERMAN, HAROLD A. federal judge; b. 1928; Student, Seton Hall U., 1945-46, 48; LL.B., Rutgers U., 1951. Bar: N.J. 1951. Adminstrv. asst. to Commr. of Labor and Industry, State of N.J., 1955-56; judge of compensation State of N.J., 1956-62, supervising judge of compensation, 1962-65; judge Union County Dist. Ct., 1965-70, presiding judge, 1966-70; judge Union County Ct., 1970-73, Superior Ct. law div., 1973-75, Superior Ct. Chancery div., 1975-79, U.S. Dist. Ct., Dist. of N.J., 1979—, now sr. judge. Mem. Supreme Ct. Com. on Revision of Rules, 1967; chmn. Supreme Ct. Com. on County Dist. Cts., 1968; mem. faculty Nat. Jud. Coll., 1978 Sgt. U.S. Army, 1946-48. Recipient Disting. Alumni award Rutgers U. Sch. Law, 1980. Fellow ABA; mem. Order of Coif. Office: US Dist Ct PO Box 999 Newark NJ 07101-0999

ACKERMAN, KENNETH EDWARD, lawyer, educator; b. Bronx, May 25, 1946; s. Kenneth L. and Anna (McCarthy) A.; m. Kathryn H. Hartnett, July 10, 1972; children: Andrew, Carl, Sheila, Edward, Daniel, Kenneth. Student, Talladega Coll., 1966; BA, Fordham Coll., 1968; JD, Cornell U., 1971. Bar: N.Y. 1972, Pa. 1994, U.S. Ct. Appeals (2d cir.) 1975, U.S. Supreme Ct. 1976; cert tchr., N.Y. State, 2002. Clk. legal dept. Port Authority N.Y. and N.J., 1969, IBM, 1970; ptnr. Mackenzie Hughes LLP, Syracuse, N.Y., 1971—. Adj. prof. banking law and negotiable instruments Am. Inst. Banking program Onondaga Community Coll., 1984—, Syracuse U. Coll., lectr.; adj. prof. white collar crime Ithaca Coll., 2002—. Author: Alcoholism-Prognosis for Recovery in the Reconstituted Soviet Republics, 1991; contbr. articles to profl. jours. Chmn. Ctrl. N.Y. chpt. March of Dimes, 1972-82; mem. A.A.-USSR Travel Group, 1987; bd. dirs. Ctrl. N.Y. Health Systems Agy., Inc., 1982-83, Syracuse Sr. Citizens Housing Corp., 1992—; trustee N.Y. State Lawyers Assistance Trust, 2003—; mem. Kaye Spl. Commn. Alcohol and Drug Abuse in the Profession, 1999-2001. Mem.: ABA, Onondaga County Bar Assn. (bd. dirs. 1990—93), N.Y. State Bar Assn. (chmn. com. lawyer alcoholism and drug abuse 1993—95). Banking, Bankruptcy, Commercial, contracts (including sales of goods; commercial financing). Office: 600 Onondaga Savs Bank Bldg Syracuse NY 13202

ACKERMANN, REUDIGER FRIEDERICH, lawyer; b. Mannheim, Germany, July 7, 1970; s. Karl Friedrich and Gisela Ackermann; m. Fides Majer, June 14, 1996. JD, U. Freiburg, 2002. Bar: Stuttgart 1998. Atty. Thuemmel, Schuetz & Ptnr., Dresden, Germany, 1998—99, Frankfurt, 1998—99, Stuttgart, 1998—99, atty., mgr. Singapore, 1999—. Pres. Struktol Corp., Stow, Ohio, 2001—. Author: The Third Party Procedure - An Economic Research, 2002. Mem.: Singapore Acad. Law, Rotary. Avocations: golf, horseback riding. Commercial, contracts (including sales of goods; commercial financing), Corporate, general, Private international. Home: 49 St Thomas Walk 15-02 The Bayron Singapore 238140 Singapore Office: Thuemmel Schutze & Ptnrs 65 Chulia St Singapore 049513 Singapore E-mail: riediger.ackermann@web.de.

ACKERT, T(ERRENCE) W(ILLIAM), lawyer; b. N.Y.C., June 8, 1946; s. T.W. and M. Ackert; m. MP. Ackert, July 4, 1970. BA in History, U. West Fla., 1969; JD, U. Fla., 1972. Bar: Fla. 1972, U.S. Dist. Ct. (mid. dist.) Fla. 1972, U.S. Supreme Ct. 1977, U.S. Ct. Appeals (fed. cir.) 1981. Pvt. practice, Orlando, Fla., 1972—; counsel Sharks Success, Inc., 1988-93, U.S. Ct. Internat. Trade, 2001—. Adj. prof. U. Cen. Fla., Orlando, 1988-93; gen. counsel (Fla.) Morgran Stiftung, Liechtenstein, 1991-95; law lectr. Profl. Skills Inst., Fla., 1981-85. Co-author: Florida Dissolution Manual, 1991; contbr. articles to profl. jours. Chmn. 9th Cir. Grievance Com., Orlando, 1989; mem. Human Svc. Planning Com., Orange County, Fla., 1984. Mem. Seminole County Bar (LAS pres. 1979, Pres. award 1980-83), Orange County Bar (LAS dir. 1980), Fla. Bar (trial lawyers sect., chmn. bar delivery of legal svc. com. 1986-88, chmn. mid-yr. conv. family law 1981, Pres.'s Svc. award 1985, 87). Avocations: pro bono service, travel. Federal civil litigation, State civil litigation, Commercial, contracts (including sales of goods; commercial financing). Office: PO Box 2548 Winter Park FL 32790-2548

ACKLEY, ROBERT O. lawyer; b. Chgo., July 24, 1952; s. William O. and Jeannette E. (Mitchell) A.; m. Patricia Ann Cerney, May 24, 1980; children: Matthew, Allison, Elizabeth, Anne, Kathryn, Kimberly. BA, No. Ill. U., 1974; MA., No. Mich. U., 1977; JD, John Marshall Law Sch., Chgo., 1988. Bar: Ill. 1988, U.S. Dist. Ct. (no. dist.) Ill. 1988, U.S. Ct. Appeals (7th cir.), 2003. Adminstrv. intern, asst. to city mgr. City of Marquette, Mich., 1976-77; adminstrv. asst. to town mgr. Town of Glastonbury, Conn., 1978; supr. Continental Bank, Chgo., 1979; chief methods analyst dept. fin. City of Chgo., 1980-81, chief supr. ops. dept. revenue, 1981-84; pres. Ackley & Assocs., Chgo., 1984-88; law clk., adminstrv. asst. to chief justice Thomas J. Moran Supreme Ct. of Ill., Lake Forest, 1988-90; atty. Cassiday, Schade & Gloor, Chgo., 1990-91; pvt. practice Chgo., 1991—2002; ptnr. Sarles & Ouimet, Chgo., 2003—, Woodstock & Dallas. Bd. dirs. Ill. Pro Bono Ctr., 1997-2002; adj. prof. Roosevelt U., Chgo., 1989-90; mem. panel arbitrators Cir. Ctr. of 19th Jud. Cir., 1991-97, Cir. Ct. Cook County, 1993-97; detention screening atty. pretrial svcs. Cir. Ct. of Cook County, 1991—; drugs panel atty. Office of State Appellate Defender, 1992—. Bd. dirs. Bryn Mawr-Broadway Ridge Mchts. Assn., Chgo., 1984-87; panel mem. Capital Resource Ctr., 1991, Community Econ. Devel. Law Project. Fellow Ill. Bar Found.; mem. Nat. Assn. Counsel Children, Ill. Bar Assn., Chgo. Bar Assn., Lake County Bar Assn. (pro bono svc. award 2000), Ill. Appellate Lawyers Assn., Acad. Polit. Sci. (life), Nat. Coun. Juvenile and Family Ct. Judges, McHenry County Bar Assn. General civil litigation, Family and matrimonial, Juvenile. Home: 606 Buckingham Pl Libertyville IL 60048-3326 Office: 500 N Lake St Ste 109 Mundelein IL 60060-1860 E-mail: roackley@calcon.net.

ACOBA, SIMEON RIVERA, JR., state supreme court justice, educator; b. Honolulu, Mar. 11, 1944; s. Simeon R. and Martina (Domingo) A.. BA, U. Hawaii, 1966; JD, Northwestern U., Chgo., 1969. Bar: Hawaii 1969, U.S. Dist. Ct. Hawaii, U.S. Ct. Appeals (9th cir.). Law clk. Hawaii Supreme Ct., Honolulu, 1969-70; housing officer U. Hawaii, Honolulu, 1970-71; dep. atty. gen. State of Hawaii, Honolulu, 1971-73; pvt. practice, Honolulu, 1973-80; judge 1st Circuit Ct. Hawaii, Honolulu, 1980-94, Intermediate Ct. Appeals Hawaii, Honolulu, 1994-2000; assoc. justice Hawaii Supreme Ct., 2000—. Instr. criminal law Hawaii Pacific U., 1992—; atty. on spl. contract divsn. OSHA, Dept. Labor, Honolulu, 1975—77, Pub. Utilities divsn., State of Hawaii, 1976—77; campaign spending com. State of Hawaii, 1976; staff atty. Hawaii State Legislature, 1975. Bd. dirs. Hawaii Mental Health Assn., 1975—77, Nuuanu YMCA, 1975—78, Hawaii Youth at Risk, 1990—91; mem. Gov.'s Conf. on Yr. 2000, Honolulu, 1970, Citizens Com. on Adminstrn. of Justice, 1972, State Drug Abuse Commn., 1975—76, Com. to Consider the Adoption of ABA Model Rules of Profl. Conduct, 1989—91; mem. Judicial Edn. Com., 1992—93, Hawaii State Bar Assn. Jud. Adminstrn. Com., 1992—94, Permanent Com. Rules Penal Procedure and Cir. Ct. Rules, 1992—96; subcom. chmn. Supreme Ct. Com. Pattern Jury Instrns., 1990—91; mem. Hawaii Supreme Ct. Ad Hoc Com. Jury Master List, 1991—92. Recipient Liberty Bell award, 1964. Mem.: Hawaii Bar Assn. (dir. young lawyers sect. 1973). Office: Hawaii Supreme Ct 417 S King St Honolulu HI 96813-2912

ACOSTA, RAYMOND LUIS, federal judge; b. N.Y.C., May 31, 1925; s. Ramon J. and Carmen J. (Acha-Jimenez) Acosta-Colon; m. Marie Hatcher, Nov. 2, 1957; children: Regina, Gregory, Ann Marie. Student, Princeton U., 1948; JD, Rutgers U., 1951. Bar: N.J. 1953, U.S. Supreme Ct. 1956, P.R. 1959. Sole practice, Hackensack, N.J., 1953-54; spl. agt. FBI, San Diego, Washington, Miami, Fla., 1954-58; asst. U.S. atty. San Juan, P.R., 1958-61; sole practice, 1961-67; trust officer Banco Credito y Ahorro Ponceno, San Juan, 1967-80; U.S. atty. Dist. P.R., Hato Rey, 1980-82; judge U.S. Dist. Ct. P.R., San Juan, 1982—. Alt. del. U.S.-P.R. Commn. on Status, 1962-63; mem. Gov.'s Spl. Com. to Study Structure and Orgn. Police Dept., P.R., 1969 Contbr. articles to profl. jours. Pres. United Fund, P.R., 1979. Served with USN, 1943-46, Normandy. Recipient Merit cert. Mayor of San Juan, 1973. Mem. Fed. Bar Assn. (pres., P.R. 1967), P.R. Bankers Assn. (chmn. trust div. 1971, 75, 77), P.R. Bar Assn., Soc. Former Spl. Agts. FBI. Office: US Courthouse & PO Bldg Ste 348 300 Recinto Sur St San Juan PR 00901

ACUFF, JOHN EDGAR, lawyer; b. Chattanooga, Tenn., July 20, 1940; s. White Hollis and Estelle (Johnson) A; m. Carolyn Howell, Sept. 6, 1963; children: John E. Jr. (dec.), William Ira Howell, Karl David. BA, David Lipscomb U., Nashville, 1962; JD, Vanderbilt U., 1969. Bar: Tenn. 1969, U.S. Dist. Ct. (mid. dist.) Tenn. 1970, U.S. Ct. Appeals (6th cir.) 1970, U.S. Supreme Ct. 1982, U.S. Ct. Claims 1986. Assoc. Cable, McDaniel, Bowie & Bond (now McGuire Battle), Balt., 1969; law clk. to chief judge Harry Phillips U.S. Ct. Appeals, Nashville, Cin., 1969-70; assoc. Crawford & Barnes, Cookeville, Tenn., 1970-71; ptnr. Barnes & Acuff, Cookeville, 1971-96; pres. Acuff & Acuff PC, Cookeville, 1996-2000, 2000—. Mem. disciplinary hearing bd. Tenn. Supreme Ct., 1978-84. Author in field; contbr. book revs. Tenn. Hist. Soc., Lawyers Weekly USA, Tenn. Bar Jour., Chattanooga News Free Press, Herald Citizen, Putnam Star, Sparta Expositor. Dir. Law Students Nixon Agnew, 1968; mem. citizens com. Gov.'s Prayer Breakfast, 1980—, chmn., 1991; elder Christ's Fellowship, Cookeville, 1981-91; bd. dirs. Dismas House, Habitat of cumberlands, Lazrus House Hospice; mem. ethics com. Cooksville Gen. Hosp., 1997-99; mem. Leadership Putnam '97, White County Libr. Found., 1999—. Lt. USNR, 1962-66, Grad Citizens Police Acad., 1998, Citizens Fire Acad.; v.p. White County Libr. Found., 1999—, Bd. Triad Youth Home, 2000—. Mem. ATLA, Tenn. Bar Assn. (house of dels. 1980-99, speaker 1995-97, bd. govs. 1995-97) Tenn. Trial Lawyers Assn. (bd. dirs. 1998), Am. Judicature Soc., Christian Legal Soc., Putnam County Bar Assn. (pres. 1984-85), Putnam County C. of C., White County C. of C., White County Garden Club, Putnam County Master Gardeners, Phi Alpha Delta, Alpha Kappa Psi. Avocations: encouraging pilgrims, gardening (Master Gardner 2000, cert. horticulture tchr.), reading, writing. Federal civil litigation, State civil litigation, Insurance. Home: Crossroads Farm 542 Almyra Rd Sparta TN 38583-5163 Office: Acuff & Acuff PC 101 S Jefferson Ave Cookeville TN 38501-3424 E-mail: acuffsbxr@blomand.net.

ADAIR, CHARLES ROBERT, JR., lawyer; b. Narrows, Va., Sept. 29, 1914; s. Charles Robert and Margaret (Davis) A.; m. Lillian Adele Duffee, Sept. 19, 1942 (dec. 1993). BS, U. Ala., 1942, LLB, 1948, JD, 1969. Bar: Ala. bar 1948. Since practiced in, Dadeville; solicitor, 1955-73. Vice chmn. Ala. Securities Commn., 1969-71; mem., chmn. Ala. Jud. Compensation Commn., 1984—; v.p., bd. dirs. Dadeville Industries, Inc.; bd. dirs. Bank of Dadeville, Ala.. Chmn. Dadeville One Drive, 1960; chmn. Horseshoe Bend Regional Library, 1960-65; mem., sec. planning commn. City of Dadeville, 1965-80; hon. life mem. Bethel Vol. Fire Dept. and Rescue Service, Jackson's Gap Vol. Fire Dept. and Rescue Service; trustee Ala. Law Inst., Ala. Bar Found. Served as officer USAAF, World War II. Mem. Ala. Bar Assn. (past v.p.), Tallapoosa Bar (past pres.), 5th Cir. Bar Assn. (past pres., named Avery Country Lawyer of 1999), Farrah Law Soc., VFW, Am. Legion, East Ala. Peace Officers Assn. (hon. life), The Club, Capital City Club, Quarterback Club (past capt.), The Denny Soc., Masons, Kiwanis, Scabbard and Blade, Omicron Delta Kappa, Delta Tau Delta, Phi Alpha Delta. Presbyterian. Banking, Corporate, general, Property, real (including real estate development, water). Home: Duffee's Hill Dadeville AL 36853 Office: Old Bank Of Dadeville Dadeville AL 36853

ADAIR, WENDELL HINTON, JR., lawyer; b. Ft. Benning, Ga., Mar. 17, 1944; s. Wendell H. Sr. and Jacqueline (Moore) A.; children: Elizabeth Carroll, John Michael, Benjamin David. BA, Emory U., 1966, postgrad., 1966-67; JD, U. Chgo., 1969. Bar: Ill. 1969, N.Y. 2000. Assoc. Ross, Hardies, O'Keefe, Babcock & Parsons, Chgo., 1969-72; ptnr. Mayer, Brown & Platt, Chgo., 1972-89, McDermott, Will & Emery, Chgo., 1989—99, Stroock & Stroock & Lowan LLP, 1999—. Editor: K & A Restructuring Register. Bd. dirs. ARC Mid-Am. chpt. 1991-99, Chgo. Opera Theatre, 1993-99; mem. Evanston Zoning Amendment Com., 1980-83. Mem. ABA (bus. sect., bcy. sect., natural resources sect., pub. utilities sect.), Ill. Bar Assn., Fed. Energy Bar Assn. (bd. dirs. 1985-87, program chmn. 1990-91), Am. Gas Assn. (bd. dirs. legal sect. 1986-89), Turnaround Mgmt. Assn. (program and publs. coms.). Clubs: Econ. (Chgo.), Chicago. Republican. Banking, Commercial, contracts (including sales of goods; commercial financing), FERC practice. Home: 5682 Sawyer Rd Sawyer MI 49125-9249 Office: Stroock Stroock & Lavan 180 Maden Ln New York NY 10038

ADAIR, WILLIAM B. (BEN ADAIR), lawyer, petroleum engineer; b. Lamesa, Tex., Sept. 12, 1927; s. Elvin Marshall and Ruth Harrell (Alldredge) A.; m. Barbara Reed, Sept. 9, 1950; children— William B., Marshall, Edward, Rebecca. Student Tex. A&M U., 1948; B.S. in Petroleum Engring., U. Tex., 1951; J.D., South Tex. Coll. Law, 1971. Bar: Tex. 1971; registered profl. engr., Tex. Various engring., cons. and sales positions with oil-related firms, 1952-72; ptnr. Brynes, Myers, Adair, Campbell & Sinex, and successor firm Adair & Myers, Houston, 1972— . Active Boy Scouts Am., Jr. Achievement; mem. Precinct Democratic Exec. Com., 1970-80. Served with AUS, 1946, to 2d lt., 1949. Mem. State Bar Tex., Houston Bar Assn., Tex. Aggie Bar Assn., South Tex. Coll. Law Alumni Assn. (past pres., chmn. bd. dirs.), Masons, Shriners, Delta Theta Phi (vice dean). Federal civil litigation, Family a[illegible] matrimonial, General practice. Home: 5242 Ariel St Houston TX 77[illegible]502 Office: 3120 Southwest Fwy Ste 320 Houston TX 77098 E-mail: wba@am-law.com.

ADAM, ANTAL, law educator; b. Janoshalma, Hungary, Feb. 14, 1930; s. Antal Adam and Franciska Faddi; m. Anna Babics, July 25, 1960; 1 child, Peter Adam. JD, U. Pecs, 1953. Asst., then asst. prof., lectr., prof. Faculty Law U. Pecs, 1953—, dean Faculty Law, 1975-78. Judge constnl. ct. Budapest, 1990-98. Author: Presidential Council of People's Republic, 1958, Associations in the System of Civil Organizations, 1964, Coordinational Activity of Council's Organs, 1974, Governmental Acitvity in Hungary, 1979, Constitutional Values and Constitutional Jurisdiction, 1998, Theory of Constitutional Law, 2001; editor-in-chief Jura, 2000–; contbr. articles to profl. jours. Mem. Internat. Assn. Constnl. Law (coun.). Avocations: music, horticulture. Office: U Pecs Faculty Law 48-as ter 1 Pecs 7622 Hungary Fax: 36/72/211-433/3226. E-mail: adamne@ajk.pte.hu.

ADAMEK, CHARLES ANDREW, lawyer; b. Chgo., Dec. 24, 1944; s. Stanley Charles and Virginia Marie (Budzban) A.; m. Lori Merriel Klein; children: Donald Steven, Elizabeth Jean. BA with honors, U. Mich., 1966, JD, 1969. Bar: Ill. 1969, Calif. 1978. Clk. U.S. Dist. Judge U.S. Fed. Cts., Chgo., 1969-71; assoc. atty. Lord Bissell & Brook, Chgo., 1971-77, ptnr., 1977-78, L.A., 1978—. Mem. ABA, Ill. State Bar Assn., State Bar Calif., Nat. Assn. Railroad Trial Counsel. Roman Catholic. Avocations: Bluegrass banjo, sr. ice hockey. General civil litigation, Insurance, Product liability. Office: Lord Bissell & Brook 300 S Grand Ave Ste 800 Los Angeles CA 90071-3119 E-mail: cadamek@lordbissell.com.

ADAMO, KENNETH R. lawyer; b. Staten Island, N.Y., Sept. 27, 1950; BS, ChE, Rensselaer Polytech. Inst., 1972; JD, Union U., Albany, 1975; LLM, John Marshall Law Sch., 1989. Bar: Ill. 1975, N.Y. 1976, Ohio 1984, Tex. 1988, U.S. Patent and Trademark Office. Ptnr. Jones, Day, Reavis & Pogue, Cleve. Mem. Internat. Bar Assn. Federal civil litigation, Intellectual property. Office: Jones Day Reavis & Pogue N Point 901 Lakeside Ave Cleveland OH 44114

ADAMS, ALBERT T. lawyer; b. Cleve., Dec. 20, 1950; BA, Harvard U., 1973, MBA, JD, Harvard U., 1977. Bar: Ohio 1977. Ptnr. Baker & Hostetler, Cleve. Office: Baker & Hostetler 3200 Nat City Ctr 1900 E 9th St Ste 3200 Cleveland OH 44114-3475

ADAMS, ALFRED GRAY, lawyer; b. Winston-Salem, N.C., Feb. 28, 1946; s. Carlton Noble and Elizabeth (Walker) A.; m. Elizabeth Lark; children: Alfred Gray Jr., Amanda Laing. BA, Wake Forest U., 1968; JD, 1973. Bar: N.C. 1973; cert. splst. bus., comml., indsl. real estate property transactions. Ptnr. Van Winkle, Buck, Wall, Starnes & Davis, P.A., Asheville, N.C., 1973-94, Kilpatrick Stockton L.L.P., Winston-Salem, 1994-2000, Womble, Carlyle, Sandridge & Rice, PLLC, Winston-Salem, 2001—. Adj. prof. law Wake Forest U., 1996—. Assoc. editor: Wake Forest Law Rev., 1972. Chmn. Buncombe County Tax. Adv. Com., Asheville, 1983; Leadership Cir. chair United Way, 2000; pres.-elect Wake Forest U. Alumni Coun., 2002; bd. dirs. Downtown Winston-Salem Devel. Found., Downtown Winston-Salem Partnership. Named among N.C. Legal Elite N.C. Mag.; James Mason scholar Wake Forest U., 1972. Mem. ABA, N.C. Bar Assn. (bd. govs. 1987-90, real property sec. vice chmn. 1982-83, chmn. 1983-84, writer, lectr. real property and future interests bar rev. course 1981-83, mem. real property curriculum adv. com. 1984-91, chmn. 1988-91, seminar planner and lectr. real property 1987-98, chmn. cont. legal edn. com. 1991-93), Am. Coll. Real Estate Lawyers, Am. Coll. Mortgage Attys. (state chair 1995—, bd. regents 1996-98, sec. 1998, pres. 2000-01), Biltmore Forest Country Club (bd. govs. 1993-94), Forsyth Country Club (bd. dirs. 2003—), Old North State Club, Rhododendron Royal Brigade of Guards (capt. Ensign Class 1986). Republican. Methodist. Banking, Property, real (including real estate development, water). Home: 115 Sullivan Way Winston Salem NC 27104-4911 Office: One W Fourth St Winston Salem NC 27101 E-mail: aadams@wcsr.com.

ADAMS, CARL DAVID, lawyer; b. Tyler, Tex., Aug. 18, 1951; s. Russell D. and Mary Elnor Adams; m. Sharon L. Cox, Feb. 9, 1983; children: Weston, Kathryn. AA, Tyler Jr. Coll., 1971; BS, North Tex. State U., 1972; JD cum laude, Baylor U., 1975. Bar: Tex. 75, U.S. Dist. Ct. (ea. dist.) Tex. 1977, U.S. Dist. Ct. (no. dist.) Tex. 1979, U.S. Ct. Appeals (5th cir.) 1985, U.S. Supreme Ct. 1980. Pvt. practice, Dallas, 1975—. Spkr., presenter in field. Contbr. articles to profl. jours. Fellow: Tex. Bar Found. Avocations: music, sports. Appellate, Professional liability, Probate (including wills, trusts). Office: 6060 N Central # 790 Dallas TX 75206 Fax: 214-691-2984.

ADAMS, CHARLES JAIRUS, lawyer; b. Randolph, Vt., Feb. 17, 1917; s. Charles B. and Jeanette E. (Metzger) A.; m. Mary E. Tobey, July 5, 1942; children: Mary Jean, Carol Ann. BS in Elec. Engring, Norwich U., 1939; LL.B., Boston U., 1951. Bar: Vt. 1951. Student engr. Gen. Electric Co., also New Eng. Power Co., 1939-41; plant supt. Demeritt Co., Waterbury, Vt., 1946-48; practiced in Montpelier and Waterbury, 1951-98; partner firm Adams, Darby & Laundon, 1980-86; of counsel Darby, Laundon, Stearns, Thorndike & Kolter, 1987-98. Treas. Vt. Bar Assn., 1951-55; atty. gen. State of Vt., 1962-63; chmn. State of Vt. Legis. Apportionment Bd., 1972-80; mem. adv. com. on civil rules Vt. Supreme Ct., 1971-82 Trustee Village of Waterbury, 1956-57, 88-90, pres., 1958; moderator Town of Waterbury, 1961; mem. Waterbury Pub. Libr. Assn., 1961-93. Mem. Am. Legion, Norwich U. Gen. Alumni Assn. (pres. 1960-61), Partridge Soc. (bd. fellows), Masons. Congregationalist. Home: 16 Harbor View Rd Apt 302 South Burlington VT 05403

ADAMS, DANIEL FENTON, law educator; b. Reading, Pa., July 29, 1922; s. Daniel Snyder and Carrie Betsy (Vought) A.; m. Eloise Williams, Sept. 6, 1968. AB, Dickinson Coll., 1947; LL.B., Dickinson Sch. Law, 1949. Bar: Pa. 1951, Ark. 1984. Prof. law Dickinson Sch. Law, Carlisle, Pa., 1949-65, asst. to dean, 1952-54, 56-60, acting dean, 1954-56, asst. dean, 1960-65; prof. Sch. Law U. Ark., Little Rock, 1965-70, 77-93, prof. emeritus, 1993—; asst. dean U. Ark. Sch. Law, Little Rock, 1966-70, acting dean, 1981-82, interim dean, 1989-91; prof. U. Miss. Sch. Law, Oxford, 1970-77. Vis. prof. Stetson U. Sch. Law, St. Petersburg, Fla., 1976-77, 99-00, U. Tenn. Coll. Law, 1993. Contbr. articles to profl. jours. Served with U.S. Army, 1943-44 Mem. ABA, Pa. Bar Assn., Ark. Bar Assn. Home: 4717 Osprey Dr Orange Beach AL 36561-5755

ADAMS, DAVID HUNTINGTON, judge; b. Cleve., May 30, 1942; s. Donald Croxton and Nancy Adams; m. Mary Watson, Dec. 4, 1982; children from previous marriage: Ann Arendell, David Huntington, Susanna Camp. AB, Washington and Lee U., 1965, JD, 1968. Bar: Va. 1968, U.S. Dist. Ct. (ea. dist.) Va. 1968, U.S. Ct. Appeals (4th cir.) 1968, U.S. Supreme Ct. 1973. Law clk. U.S. Dist. Ct., Norfolk, Va., 1968-69; assoc. law firm Willcox, Savage, Norfolk, 1969-72; ptnr. law firm Agelasto, Bernard & Adams, Norfolk, 1972-74, Taylor, Walker, Bernard & Adams, Norfolk, 1974-78, Taylor, Walker & Adams, Norfolk, 1974-87, Clark & Stant, P.C., 1987-93; judge U.S. Bankruptcy Ct. (ea. dist. Va.), 1993—. Master of the bench James Kent Am. Inn of Ct., 1994-99, pres., 1995; lectr. bankruptcy practice joint com. on cont. legal edn. Va. Bar Found., 1981, 89, 93—; adminstrv. hearing officer Commonwealth of Va., 1974-89; mem. 4th Cir. Jud. Coun., 2003—, Adminstrv. Office Bankruptcy Judges Adv. Coun., 2001—, Bankruptcy Judges Adv. Group, 2001—, Adminstrv. Office Joint Adv. Com., 2003—. Author: Virginia Landlord/Tenant Law, 1980. Bd. dirs. Heritage Mus., Norfolk, 1991-94, Virginia Beach Neptune Fest., 1997—, King Neptune XXVI; chmn. Neptune Found., 2002; pres. Bay Colony Civic League, Virginia Beach, 1978, Princess Anne Hills Civic League, Virginia Beach, 1988; mem. 4th Cir. Jud. Conf., 1974—;, 4th Cir. Jud. Coun., 2002—; mem. 2d dist. ethics com. Va. State Bar, 1983-84. Mem.: ABA, Va. Bar Assn. (bd. dirs. bankruptcy sect. 1990—93, mem. coun. jud. sect. 1995—, chmn. 1997), Virginia Beach Bar Assn., Norfolk-Portsmouth Bar Assn., Nat. Conf. Bankruptcy Judges (bd. govs. 1996—2000, sec. 2000), Am. Bankruptcy Inst., Hampton Roads Coun. Navy League U.S. (life; pres. 2000—, nat. dir. 2002—05), N.Y. Yacht Club, Cavalier Golf and Yacht Club (bd. dirs. 1993—98, commodore 1994). Episcopalian. Avocations: yachting, swimming, bicycling. Office: United States Bankruptcy Ct Walter E Hoffman US Courthouse 600 Granby St Norfolk VA 23510-1915 E-mail: david_adams@vaeb.uscourts.gov.

ADAMS, DEBORAH ROWLAND, lawyer; b. Princeton, NJ, July 28, 1952; d. Bernard S. and Natalie S. Adams; m. Charles L. Campbell, June 16, 1990. BA, Colo. Coll., Colorado Springs, 1974; JD, U. Colo., 1978. Bar: Ind. 1978, Colo. 1978, U.S. Dist. Ct. Colo. 1978. Atty. Legal Svcs. Orgn. Ind., Indpls., 1978-79, Pikes Peak Legal Svcs., Colorado Springs, 1979-80, Pub. Defender's Office, Colorado Springs, 1980-81; assoc. Ranson, Thomas, Cook and Livingston, Colorado Springs, 1982-84; pvt. practice Colorado Springs, 1985—. Mem. state Jud. Nominating Commn. for 4th Jud. Dist., 1994-99; Colo. State Grievance Com., 1997-98, Atty. Regulation Com., 1999. Bd. dirs. Domestic Violence Prevention Ctr., 1980-86, pres., 1982-84; bd. dirs. Pikes Peak Legal Svcs., 1983-88, pres., 1986-87, pro bono advocacy sch. faculty, 1990-92; co-chair Colo. Springs Devel. Com., Colo. Women's Found., 1987, grant selection com., 1988, 90; bd. dirs. Vis. Nurses Assn., 1989-91, Colo. Coll. Bus. and Cmty. Alliance Bd., 1999-2002, Citizens Project Bd., 1999-2002, CASA, 1999—, Emily Griffith Ctr., 2002–, Colo. Bar Found., 2000—, pres 2003; bd. dirs. Chins Up, 1991-97, pres., 1997-98; co-chair El Paso County sect. COLTAF Fundraising Com. for benefit of Colo. Legal Aid Found., 1991-99, chair, 1994-95; state bd. dirs. Legal Aid Found., 1994-2000, v.p., 1997-99. Recipient Pro Bono award Pikes Peak Legal Svcs., 1988; named Atty of Yr. El Paso County Legal Secs. Assn., 1990; selected to attend First Colo. Springs Leadership Class, Colorado Springs Leadership Inst., 1997. Mem. Colo. Bar Assn. (family law sect. 1991-2001, conciliation panel subcom. of profls. com. 1992, bd. govs. 1994-97, exec. com. 1995-97, nominating com. 1996), Colo. Women's Bar Assn., El Paso County Bar Assn. (pres.-elect 1994-95, pres. 1995-96, Trial Advocacy Sch. faculty 1990, 94, Moot Ct. judge 1992, 95, fee arbitration dispute com. 1995), Women Lawyer's Assn. Fourth Jud. Dist.(chairperson jud. nominating com. 1991-93, Portia award 1992), Zonta Club Colorado Springs (pres. 1989-90, co-chairperson dist. 12 regional conf. 1991-92, Zontian of Yr. 1990-91). Democrat. Avocations: reading, skiing, tennis, running, mountain biking. Family and matrimonial. Office: 2 N Cascade Ave Ste 1010 Colorado Springs CO 80903-1629

ADAMS, DEBORAH SUSAN, lawyer; b. Cin., May 17, 1955; d. Vinson and Zada Mae A.; m. Barry N. Stedman, Dec. 19, 1980; children: Kensey Alyn, Gareth Lachlan. BA, U. Cin., 1977; MA, Harvard U., 1979; JD, Harvard Law Sch., 1982. Bar: Ohio 1982, Ky. 1983, U.S. Dist. Ct. (so. dist.) Ohio 1982, U.S. Dist. Ct. (ea. dist.) Ky. 1984, U.S. Ct. Appeals (6th cir.) 1986, U.S. Ct. Appeals (4th cir.) 1999, U.S. Ct. Appeals (7th cir.) 1998, U.S. Supreme Ct. 1997. Assoc. Frost Brown Todd LLP, Cin., 1982-89, ptnr., 1989—. Trustee, chmn. nominating com. Stepping Stones Ctr. for Handicapped, Cin., 1990-96; trustee, sec. Cin. Ballet, 1984-90. Labor (including EEOC, Fair Labor Standards Act, labor-management relations, NLRB, OSHA). Office: Frost Brown Todd LLC 2200 PNC Ctr 201 E 5th St Cincinnati OH 45202 E-mail: dadams@fbtlaw.com.

ADAMS, FRANCES GRANT, II, lawyer; b. Wheeling, W.Va., Nov. 30, 1955; d. Jack Richard and Frances Irene (Grant) A. BA, W.Va. U., 1976, JD, 1979; MA, Webster U., 1983. Bar: W.Va. 1979, U.S. Dist. Ct. (so. dist.) W.Va. 1979, U.S. Ct. Mil. Appeals 1979, U.S. Supreme Ct. 1988, D.C. 1989. Asst. staff judge advocate armament divsn. USAF, Eglin AFB, Fla., 1979-82, dep. staff judge advocate Keflavik, Iceland, 1982-83, staff judge advocate 71st Air Base Group Vance AFB, Okla., 1984-86, chief gen. torts sect. claims and tort litigation staff hdqrs. Washington, 1986-88, chief mgmt. and analysis br. claims and tort litigation div. Legal Svcs. Agy., 1988-92, sr. tort atty. tort claims and litigation div. Legal Svcs. Agy., 1992-97, chief internat. torts branch, 1997—; atty. environ. law and litig. divsn., Legal Svcs. Agy. USAFR, USAF, Washington, 1992—99; chief Internat. Torts Br. Tort Claims and Litigation Divsn. USAF Legal Svcs. Agy., 1999—. Program chmn. Pentagon chpt. Fed. Bar Assn., 1989-90. Mem. DAR (chmn. procedures manual W.Va. chpt. 1989-92), Magna Carta Dames, Ancient and Honorable Arty. Co., Air Force Assn. (life), Ret. Officers Assn. (life). Avocations: photography, travel, farming, gardening.

ADAMS, GEORGE BELL, lawyer; b. NYC, Sept. 16, 1930; s. George Bell and Mary Josephine (Smith) Adams; m. Lucy Elizabeth Ahearn, Sept. 10, 1952; children: Lucy S., Marea F., George B. Adams Jr., Alison E. BA, Yale U., 1952; LLB cum laude, Harvard U., 1957. Bar: N.Y. 1957, U.S. Dist. Ct. (so. and ea. dists.) N.Y. 1965, U.S. Ct. Appeals (2d cir.) 1973. Assoc. Debevoise, Plimpton, Lyons & Gates, N.Y.C., 1957-65; ptnr. Debevoise & Plimpton, N.Y.C., 1966-97, chmn. corp. dept., 1988-93, mng. ptnr. London, 1993-96, of counsel N.Y.C., 1998—. Pres. Greater N.Y. Fund, N.Y.C., 1981—84, bd. dirs. Trustee Sarah Lawrence Coll., Bronxville, NY, 1977—, chmn. bd. trustees, 1987—91, vice chmn., chmn. exec. com., 1981—87; bd. dirs., exec. com. United Way of NYC, 1982—95, chmn. nominating com., 1985—93; bd. dirs. New Amsterdam Singers, 1997—, Lawyers Alliance for World Security, 1989—98, mem. adv. bd., 1999—; fellow Pierpont Morgan Libr., N.Y.C., 1977—, coun. of fellows, 1983—87; mem. coun. of fellows Yale U. Coun., 1983—90, chmn. Yale alumni publs., 1979—83; trustee Am. Trust for Brit. Libr., 1998—. 1st lt. U.S. Army, 1952—54. Fellow, Davenport Coll., Yale U., 1983—90. Fellow: Am. Bar Found., Royal Soc. for Arts; mem.: ABA, Assn. of Bar of City of N.Y., Am. Assn. Internat. Com. of Jurists (bd. dirs. 1998—, 1998—), Am. Arbitration Assn. (panel arbitrators), Century Assn., Pilgrim Soc., Racquet & Tennis Club, Cosmos Club. Corporate, general, Finance, Private international. Office: Debevoise & Plimpton 919 3rd Ave Fl 44 New York NY 10022-3904 E-mail: marclar@sprynet.com.

ADAMS, JO-ANN MARIE, lawyer; b. L.A., May 27, 1949; d. Joseph John and Georgia S. (Wein) A. AA, Pasadena C.C., 1968; BA, Pomona Coll., 1970; MA, Calif. State U., L.A., 1971; MBA, Pacific Luth. U., 1983; JD, Santa Clara U., 1996. cert. in telecom. and info. resource mgmt. Secondary tchr. South Pasadena (Calif.) Unified Schs., 1970-71; appraiser Riverside County (Calif.) Assessor's Office, 1972-74; systems and procedures analyst Riverside County Data Processing Dept., 1974-76, supr. systems analyst, 1976-79; systems analyst computer Boeing Computer Svcs. Co., Seattle, 1979-81; sr. systems analyst Thurston County Ctrl. Svcs., Olympia, Wash., 1981-83, data processing systems mgr., 1983-84; data processing systems engr. IBM Corp., 1984-87; realtor assoc. Dower Realty, 1987-92; corp. sales rep. UniGlobe Met. Travel, 1988-89; project mr. Servco Pacific, 1989-90, Scott Software Systems, 1990-91; systems analyst Dept. Atty. Gen., 1991-93; pvt. practice, 1986—; with Bervar & Jones, 2002—03. Cons. in field, 1993—; corp. counsel RightWorks Corp., 2000-01, Law Offices Thomas R. Hogan, 1999; instr. Riverside City Coll., 1977-79; vis. lectr. Santa Clara U., 1997-2000. Chair legis. task force Riverside/San Bernardino chpt. NOW, 1975-76, chpt. co-chair, 1978; mem. ethics com. Calif. NOW, Inc., 1978; alt. del. Calif. Dem. Caucus, 1978; del. Hawaii Dem. Caucus, 2002; mem. Gay, Lesbian, Bisexual and Transgender Caucus of Hawaii Dem. Party; bd. dirs. Honolulu Gay and Lesbian Cultural Found. Mem. ABA, NAFE, Santa Clara Calif. Bar Assn. (mem. rainbow com. 1994-2000, chair 1998, minority access com. 1 999-2000, nominating com. 2000), Pomona Coll. Alumni Assn., Santa Clara U. Alumni Assn. Estate planning. Home: 411 Hobron Ln # 801 Honolulu HI 96815-1210 Office: Seven Waterfront Plz 500 Ala Moana Blvd Ste 400 Honolulu HI 96813-4920 E-mail: jadamsesq@aol.com.

ADAMS, JOHN A. lawyer; b. Fargo, N.D., Dec. 31, 1954; BA, Brigham Young U., 1978, JD, 1981. Bar: Utah 1981, U.S. Dist. Ct. Utah 1984, Utah Ct. Appeals (D.C. cir.) 1981, U.S. Ct. Appeals (fed. cir.) 1984, U.S. Supreme Ct. 1984. Atty. Ray, Quinney & Nebeker, PC, Salt Lake City. Mem.: Utah State Bar (pres. 2002—). Environmental, Insurance, Intellectual property. Office: Ray Quinney and Nebeker PO Box 45385 36 S State St Ste 1400 Salt Lake City UT 84145-0385*

ADAMS, JOHN JILLSON, lawyer; b. Toledo, Nov. 12, 1934; s. Theodore Floyd and Esther (Jillson) A.; m. Barbara Barr, June 6, 1959; children: Leigh Ann Adams Miller, Leslie, Julie. BA, Denison U., 1956; LLB, U. Va., 1959. Bar: Va. 1959, D.C. 1967, U.S. Ct. Appeals (4th, 6th and D.C. cirs.), U.S. Supreme Ct. Assoc. Hunton & Williams, Richmond, Va., 1960-65, ptnr. Washington, 1967—; assoc. dir. Am. United for Separation of Ch. and State, Washington, 1965-66; spl. asst. U.S. State Dept., Washington, 1966-67. Served with USAR, 1959-65. Mem. ABA, Va. Bar Assn., D.C. Bar Assn. Baptist. Administrative and regulatory, Federal civil litigation, Environmental. Home: 8546 Georgetown Pike Mc Lean VA 22102-1206 Office: Hunton & Williams 1900 K St NW Washington DC 20006-1110

ADAMS, JOHN MARSHALL, lawyer; b. Columbus, Ohio, Dec. 6, 1930; s. H.F. and Ada Margaret (Gregg) A.; m. Janet Hawk, June 28, 1952; children: John Marshall, Susan Lynn, William Alfred. BA, Ohio State U., 1952; JD summa cum laude, 1954. Bar: Ohio 1954. Mem. Cowan & Adams, Columbus, 1954—55; asst. city atty. City of Columbus, 1955—56; mem. Knepper, White, Richards & Miller, 1956-63; practiced in Columbus, 1963—74; ptnr. Porter, Wright, Morris & Arthur, Columbus, 1975—91, of counsel, 1992—. Vice chmn. Ohio Bar Liability Ins. Co., 1990-93, chmn., 1994-2002, chair emeritus, 2002-; trustee Ohio Legal Ctr. Inst., 1976-81, Ohio Lawpac, 1980-89. Fellow Am. Coll. Trial Lawyers, Am. Bar Found., Ohio Bar Found. (trustee 1975-84); mem. ABA, Ohio State Bar Assn. (exec. com. 1975-80, pres. 1978-79, Ohio bar medal 1994), Columbus Bar Assn. (bd. govs. 1970-76, pres. 1974-75), Lawyers Club (pres. 1968-69), 6th Cir. Jud. Conf. (life), Order of Coif, Grey Oaks Country Club (Naples, Fla.), Scioto Country Club, Masons, Delta Upsilon, Phi Delta Phi. Republican. General civil litigation, Insurance, Personal injury (including property damage). Home: 2535 Canterbury Rd Columbus OH 43221-3081 Office: 41 S High St Columbus OH 43215-6101

ADAMS, LEE TOWNE, lawyer; b. Chatham, Ont., Can., July 12, 1922; came to U.S., 1923; s. Lee Eugene and Josephine Towne A.; m. Muriel Kathryn Stang, June 29, 1946; children: Nancy Louise, Carol Josephine, Jane Bertha. BA, U. Rochester, 1943; JD, Yale U., 1949. Atty. pvt. practice, Forestville, N.Y., 1949-72; mcpl. atty. various towns and villages, 1955-72; judge State of N.Y., Chautauqua County, 1972-93; retired, 1993—. Trustee Presbytery of Western N.Y., 1970-76; dir., vice chmn. Presbyn. Homes N.Y., 1984-90. Lt. USN, 1943-46. Mem. VFW, Am. legion, Submarine Vets. WWII, Masons, Jamestown Consistory, Ismaila Temple, Phi Beta Kappa. Republican. Avocations: gardening, reading. Home: 21 Pearl St PO Box 306 Forestville NY 14062-0306

ADAMS, NATE LAVINDER, III, lawyer; b. Camp Pendelton, Calif., July 20, 1955; s. Nate Lavinder A. AB, Coll. William & Mary, 1977; MS, Am. U., 1979; JD, Washington & Lee U., 1981. Bar: Va. 1981, D.C. 1982, U.S. Ct. Appeals (4th cir.), U.S. Dist. Ct. (ea. and we. dists.) Va., U.S. Bankruptcy Ct., U.S. Supreme Ct. Law clk. U.S. Dist. Ct., Roanoke, Va., 1981-83; assoc. Bird, Kinder & Huffman, Roanoke, Va., 1983-87; shareholder Hall, Monahan, Engle, Mahan & Mitchell, Winchester, Va., 1987-97, Adams & Kellas, Winchester, 1998—. Instr. Shenandoah U., Winchester, Va., 1996—98. Co-editor: Virginia State Bar Senior Citizens Handbook, 1993. Chmn. Winchester Bd. of Zoning Appeals; Winchester-Frederick County Econ. Planning Commn., 2002—. Winchester Planning Commn., 2002—. Mem. ABA, Va. Bar Assn., Winchester-Frederick County Bar Assn. Avocations: reading, history, travel, tennis. General civil litigation, Commercial, consumer (including collections, credit), General practice. Office: Adams & Kellas 21 S Kent St Winchester VA 22601-5049 E-mail: aklaw@ntelos.net.

ADAMS, RICHARD GLEN, lawyer; b. West Reading, Pa., Mar. 21, 1941; s. Daniel Snyder and Carrie B. (Vought) A.; m. Merrill Richards, June 13, 1964; children: Rebecca Elizabeth, Rachael Kate. AB, cert., Princeton U., 1963; LLB, MA in Econs., Yale U., 1967. Bar: Conn. 1967, U.S. Dist. Ct. Conn. 1967, U.S. Ct. Appeals (2d cir.) 1967. Assoc. Jacobs, Jacobs, Grudberg & Clifford, New Haven, 1967-72, Ribicoff & Kotkin, Hartford, 1972-73, ptnr., 1973-78; mem. Adams & Tomc, Middletown, Conn., 1978-85; pvt. practice Middletown, 1985-88; ptnr. Adams & Harding, 1988-96; pvt. practice, 1996—. Sec., dir. Lyman Farm, Inc., 1968-91; bar exam. reader and grader, 1982. Mem. bd. editors: Yale Law Jour., 1964—65. Mem. Holiday Project, 1980—95, Hunger Project, 1981—93, Conn. Legis. Task Force on Environ. Permit Streamlining, 1993—94, Middlefield Rep. town Com., 1995—, vice chair, 1998—99; bd. dirs. Camp Hazen YMCA, 1984—90; trustee Charles B. Merwin Trust, 1981—. Mem.: ABA, Middlesex County Bar Assn., Conn. Sch. Attys. Coun., Conn. Bar Assn. (chmn. adminstrv. law sect. 1998—2001), Milk Bottle Collectors Assn., Hist. Assn. of Berks County, Train Collectors Assn. Administrative and regulatory, State civil litigation, Property, real (including real estate development, water). Home: 175 Powder Hill Rd Middlefield CT 06455-1133 Office: 163 College St Middletown CT 06457-3238

ADAMS, THOMAS TILLEY, lawyer; b. Orchard Park, N.Y., Oct. 9, 1929; s. Floyd Tilley and Clara Elizabeth (Potter) A.; m. Virginia Rives Smith, Sept. 1, 1956; children: Julia, Janet, Claire, Douglas. BA, U. Buffalo, 1951; JD, Cornell U., 1957. Bar: N.Y. 1957, U.S. Ct. Appeals (2d cir.) 1962, U.S. Supreme Ct. 1962, Conn. 1964. Tchr. Lake Shore Cen. Sch., Angola, NY, 1953-54; assoc. Davies, Hardy & Schenck, N.Y.C., 1957-63; prin. Gregory & Adams P.C., Wilton, Conn., 1963—2001, of counsel, 2002—. Lectr. Cornell U. Law Sch., Ithaca, N.Y., 1962-65, emeritus mem. adv. coun., 1990—; adj. assoc. prof. law Fordham U., N.Y.C., 1973-76; adviser Dana Fund Internat. and Comparative Legal Studies, Toledo, 1976-91; assoc. bd. dirs. Union Trust Co., Stamford, Conn., 1982-94; mem. adv. bd. Norwalk Savs. Soc., 1993-97. Town atty. Town of Wilton, 1966-71; pres. Five Town Found., Norwalk, Conn., 1983-85, trustee, 1989-91; chmn. bldg. com. Wilton High Sch., 1966; bd. dirs. Woodcock Nature Ctr., Wilton-Ridgefield, Conn., 1997-99, trustee Norwalk Hosp., 1974, Wilton Library Assn., Inc., 2000-2001. Capt. USAF, 1951—53, Korea. Recipient Silver Beaver award Boy Scouts Am., 1980, Disting. Alumnus award Cornell Law Sch., 1990. Mem. ABA, Am. Judicature Soc. (dir. 1991-92), Norwalk-Wilton Bar Assn. (pres. 1990), Stamford-Norwalk Regional Bar Assn. (bd. dirs. 1991-93), Conn. Bar Assn. (ethics com. 1970-75, 92-93, mem. coun. bar pres.'s 1988-90), N.Y. Bar Assn., Assn. Bar City of N.Y., Silver Spring Country Club (gov. 1998—, asst. sec. 2003—), Cornell Club (N.Y.), Phi Delta Phi. Episcopalian. General practice, Land use and zoning (including planning), Probate (including wills, trusts). Home: 55 Deer Run Rd Wilton CT 06897-1204 also: Rogers Rock Clb Ticonderoga NY 12883 Office: Gregory & Adams PC 190 Old Ridgefield Rd Wilton CT 06897-4023 Fax: 203-834-1628.

ADAMS, THOMAS LAWRENCE, lawyer; b. Jersey City, Apr. 14, 1948; s. Lawrence Ignatius and Dorothy Tekla (Halgas) A.; m. Elizabeth Anne Russell, June 14, 1969 (div. 1981); children: Thomas, Katherine; m. Deanna Louise Mollo, July 30, 1983; stepchildren: Kathy, Kerry. BS, N.J. Inst. Tech., 1969; JD, Seton Hall U., 1975. Bar: N.J. 1975, U.S. Dist. Ct. N.J. 1975, U.S. Patent Office 1975, N.Y. 1976. Sys. engr. Grumman Aerospace, Bethpage, N.Y., 1969-71; sr. engr. Weston Instruments, Newark, 1971-74; mem. patent staff RCA, Princeton, N.J., 1974-75; corp. atty. Otis Elevator, N.Y.C., 1975-77; ptnr. Goebel & Adams, Morristown, N.J., 1978-80, Behr & Adams, Morristown and Edison, N.J., 1981—. Mem. Seton Hall Law Rev. Mem. Livingston (N.J.) Twp. Coun., 1985-88, dep. mayor, 1987; mem. Livingston Environ. Commn., 1984-87; chmn. Livingston Rep. County Com., 1992-98. Mem. N.J. Patent Law Assn., Trial Attys. N.J., N.J. Bar Assn. (chmn. patent, trademark, copyright law and unfair competiton 1991), Morris County Bar Assn., KC (grand knight 1980), Tau Beta Pi, Eta Kappa Nu. State civil litigation, Patent, Trademark and copyright. E-mail: adams@newidea.com.

ADAMS, THOMAS LYNCH, JR., lawyer; b. Fayette County, Ky., Nov. 22, 1941; s. Thomas Lynch and Amanda (Keith) A.; m. Anne Randolph, Aug. 13, 1974 (div. 1992); children: Thomas Lynch III, Randolph T., Alexander K., Andrew D. BA in History, U. Va., 1963; JD, Vanderbilt U., 1970. Bar: Ky. 1970, D.C. 1970, Tenn. 1970. Appellate atty. U.S. Dept. Justice, Washington, 1970-72; minority counsel U.S. Senate Commerce Commn., Washington, 1972-75; legal counsel SBA, Washington, 1975; asst. gen. counsel FTC, Washington, 1975-77; with govt. rels. Rep. Steel Corp., Washington, 1977-83; dep. gen. counsel U.S. EPA, Washington, 1983-86, asst. adminstr., presdl. appointee, 1986-89; ptnr. Dechert, Price & Rhoads, 1989-93; environ. dir. Internat. Paper, 1993; counsel to pres. America's Clean Water Found., 1994-95; of counsel Perkins Coie, Washington, 1995-2000; pres. Oxygenated Fuels Assn., Washington, 2000—02, sr. advisor dept. energy, asst. sec. environ. mgmt., 2002—. Lt. (j.g.) USNR, 1963-67. Mem. ABA, Ky. Bar Assn., D.C. Bar Assn., Met. Club, Beta Theta Pi. Administrative and regulatory, Environmental, Legislative.

ADAMS, THOMAS MERRITT, lawyer; b. St. Louis, Sept. 27, 1935; s. Galen Edward and Chloe (Merritt) A.; m. Sarah McCardell Davis, June 6, 1959; children: Mark Merritt, John Harrison, William Shields, Thomas Bondurant. AB, Washington U., St. Louis, 1956, JD, 1960; postgrad., London Sch. Econs., 1957; LLM, George Washington U., 1966. Bar: Mo. 1960, Calif. 1971. Atty. SEC, Washington, 1964-66; asst. dir., asst. gen. counsel Investment Bankers Assn., Washington, 1966-68; pres. Transamerica Investment Mgmt., 1969-80; ptnr. Lanning Adams & Peterson, 1980—. Author: State and Local Pension Funds, 1968; contbr. articles to profl. jours. Chmn. Salina (Kans.) Community Ambassador program, 1961. Served to capt. USAF, 1960-63. Decorated Air Force Commendation medal. Mem. Phi Beta Kappa. Episcopalian. Commercial, contracts (including sales of goods; commercial financing), Corporate, general, Securities. Office: Lanning Adams & Peterson 11777 San Vicente Blve #750 Los Angeles CA 90049-5067

ADAMS, VALEREE R. lawyer; b. Methuen, Mass., Sept. 27, 1975; m. Matthew D. Adams, July 17, 1999. BA, Catawba Coll., 1997; JD, Campbell Law Sch., 2000. Bar: NC 00. Intern Children's Law Ctr., Charlotte, NC, 1999; assoc. Tate, Young, Morphis, Bach & Taylor, Hickory, NC, 2000—. Legis. survey editor: Campbell Law Rev., 1998—2000. Chmn. children's protection policies com. New Hope Bapt. Ch., Hickory, 2002—. Mem.: ABA, Christian Legal Soc., NC Bar Assn. Baptist. Family and matrimonial, Personal injury (including property damage), General practice. Office: Tate Young Morphis Bach & Taylor PO Drawer 2428 Hickory NC 28603 Fax: 828-324-2431. E-mail: valeree@tymbt.com.

ADAMSON, TERRENCE BURDETT, lawyer; b. Floyd County, Ga., Nov. 13, 1946; s. Sollie Burdett and Lois Antoinette (Rogers) A.; m. Ede E. Holiday, June 8, 1985; children: Terrence Morgan, Kathlyn Watson Holiday, Elizabeth Rogers Holiday. BA, Emory U., 1968, JD with distinction, 1973. Bar: Ga. 1973, U.S. Supreme Ct. 1978, D.C. 1981. Reporter Atlanta Constn., 1968-70; law clk. to Hon. Griffin B. Bell U.S. Ct. Appeals (5th cir.), 1973-74; assoc. Hansell & Post, Atlanta, 1974-77; spl. asst. U.S. Atty. Gen., 1977-79; ptnr. Hansell & Post, Atlanta and Washington, 1979-86, Dow, Lohnes & Albertson, Atlanta, 1986-91, Donovan, Leisure, Rogovin & Schiller, Washington, 1991-93, Kaye, Scholer, Fierman, Hays & Handler, LLP, Washington, 1993—98; exec. v.p. Nat. Geographic Soc., 1998—. Henry Luce scholar Ishii Law Office, Tokyo, 1975-76; dir. office pub. affairs, chief spokesman U.S. Dept. Justice, Washington, 1978-79; bd. dirs. Nat. Geographic Ventures, 1996—; bd. dirs., mem. exec. com. State Justice Inst., Alexandria, Va., U.S. Presdl. appointment, 1990, 92, 94, Senate confirmed 1990, 92, 95. Contbr. articles to newspapers, mags. and law revs. Trustee Asia Found., 1984—, vice chmn. 1991-95, chmn. bd. 1995-2000; mem. steering com. Nat. Libel Def. Resource Com., 1987-91, co-chair Biennial Media Seminar, 1987-96; trustee The Nat. Faculty, 1990—; site selection com. 1988 Dem. nat. conv.; mem. U.S. Nat. Com. for Pacific Econ. Coop., 1983—, Leadership Atlanta, 1988-89, bd. trustee, exec. com., bd. councillors, gen. counsel, Carter Presdl. Ctr., Atlanta, 1983—; mem. Coun. for Excellence in Govt., 1991-94; mem. Clinton-Gore transition, 1992-93. Kennedy fellow Inst. Politics, Harvard U., 1979 Fellow Soc. Values in Edn.; mem. ABA (law and media project, conf. com. on lawyers and media 1987-90, chair defamation and media law com. 1992-93), U.S. Supreme Ct. Hist. Soc., Ga. Bar Assn., D.C. Bar Assn., Order of Coif, Order of Barristers, Omicron Delta Kappa. Democrat. Federal civil litigation, Libel, Toxic tort. Office: National Geographic Soc 1145 17th St NW Washington DC 20036-4688

ADASHEK, JAMES LEWIS, lawyer; b. Milw., July 5, 1952; s. Floyd M. and Charlotte A.; m. Vivian M., Jan. 3, 1981; children: Beth, Ben. BA in History, U. Md., 1975; JD, Vanderbilt U., 1979. Bar: U.S. Dist. Ct. (ea. dist.) Wis. 1979, (we. dist.) 1986, U.S. Ct. Appeals 7th Cir. 1986. Asst. gen. counsel Bank One Corp., Milw., 1987-97; ptnr. Quarles & Brady, Milw., 1997—. Mem. State Bar Wis., Milw. Bar Assn. Banking, Bankruptcy, Commercial, contracts (including sales of goods; commercial financing). Office: Quarles & Brady 411 E Wisconsin Ave Ste 2550 Milwaukee WI 53202-4497

ADDISON, DAVID DUNHAM, lawyer; b. Richmond, Va., Aug. 23, 1941; s. Grafton Dulany and Anne (Withers) A.; m. Marion Lee Wood, Aug. 21, 1965; children: David Dunham Jr., Marion Lee, Elizabeth Townshend. BA, Hampden-Sydney Coll., 1964; LLB, U. Va., 1967. Bar: Va. 1967. Assoc. Browder, Russell, Morris & Butcher, Richmond, 1967-72; ptnr., dir. Browder & Russell, P.C., Richmond, 1972-90; mem. firm, shareholder Williams, Mullen, Clark & Dobbins, P.C., Richmond, 1990—. Contbr. articles to profl. jours. Fellow Am. Coll. Trust and Estate Counsel (state chmn. 1986-92); mem. ABA (com. chmn. 1987-94), S.R., Va. Bar Assn., Richmond Bar Assn., Estate Planning Coun. Richmond (pres. 1987-88), Richmond Trust Adminstrs. Coun. (pres. 1986-87), Kiwanis Club of Richmond (pres. 1998-99), Country Club of Va., Commonwealth Club. Episcopalian. Avocations: travel, golf. Estate planning, Probate (including wills, trusts), Taxation, general. Office: Williams Mullen Clark & Dobbins 2 James Center 1021 E Cary St Richmond VA 23219-4000

ADDISON, LINDA LEUCHTER, lawyer, writer; b. Allentown, Pa., Nov. 25, 1951; d. Marcus and Sophie Theresa (Tisch) Leuchter; m. Max M. Addison, Sept. 10, 1977; 1 child, Alexandra Leuchter Addison. BA with honors, U. Tex., 1973, JD, 1976. Bar: Tex. 1976, U.S. Dist. Ct. (no. and so. dists.) Tex. 1977, U.S. Ct. Appeals (5th cir.) 1981. Assoc. Fulbright & Jaworski LLP, Houston, 1976—83, ptnr., 1984—, exec. com., tech. ptnr., 2002—. Expert on fed. and Tex. evidence. Author: Federal Civil Procedure and Evidence During Trial, 1997, Texas Evidence, 2002; contbr. chpt. to book; mng. editor Tex. Law Rev. 1975-76; contbr. articles to profl. jours. Trustee U. Tex. Law Sch. Found., 1994—; mem. fed. jud. evaluation com. of Sens. Hutchison and Cornyn, 1997-; exec. com. chancellor's coun., U. Tex. Sys., 1999-; bd. dirs. Holocaust Mus. Houston, 2001; mem. Commn. of 125, U. Tex., Austin, 2003—, vice chmn. task force of centennial commn., 1981-83. Named one of Am.'s Top 50 Women Litigators, Nat. Law Jour., 2001, Tex. Go To Litigators, Tex. Lawyer, 2002, Most Fascinating People in Houston, Friends of Tex. Med. Ctr. Libr., 2001, Hon. Barrister, U. Tex. Sch. Law bd. advocates, 2000, Outstanding Young Lawyer of Houston, 1984-85, Woman on the Move, Tex. Exec. Women, 2000, Woman to Watch, Jewish Women Internat., 2002; named one of Am. Bd. Trial Advs., 1986, One of Best Lawyers in Am., Woodard and White, 2003. Fellow Am. Bar Found. (life), Tex. Bar Found. (life, trustee 2003—), Houston Bar Found. (life); mem. State Bar Tex. (chmn. bar jour. com. 1988-90, 91-99, adminstrn. rules evidence com. 1988-1990), Houston Bar Assn. (chmn. continuing legal edn. com. 1981-82, mem. jud. evaluations com. 1982-83, Pres.'s award for continuing svc. 1982), Tex. Young Lawyers Assn. (bd. dirs. 1981-83), Tex. Law Rev. Ex-Editors Assn., Friar Soc, Houston Young Lawyers Assn. (chmn. continuing legal edn. com. 1977-78, bd. dirs. 1978-81, Outstanding Chmn. award), Anti-Defamation League (bd. dirs. S.W. Region 1992-94), Am. Arbitration Assn. (panel of neutrals, large complex case panel, internat. panel 1992—), Am. Intellectal Property Law Assn., World Internat. Patent Orgn. (arbitration and mediation ctr. domain name panel 2002-), Omicron Delta Kappa. Federal civil litigation, General civil litigation, State civil litigation. Office: Fulbright & Jaworski LLP 1301 McKinney St Ste 5100 Houston TX 77010-3095

ADELL, HIRSCH, lawyer; b. Novogrodek, Poland, Mar. 11, 1931; arrived in U.S., 1937; s. Nathan and Nachama (Wager) A.; m. Judith Audrey Fuss, Feb. 8, 1963; children— Jeremiah, Nikolas, Balthasar, Valentine. Student, CCNY, 1949-52; BA, UCLA, 1955, LL.B., 1963. Bar: Calif. 1963. Adminstrv. asst. to State Senator Richard Richards, 1956-60; ptnr. Warren & Adell, Los Angeles, 1963-75, Reich, Adell, Crost & Cvitan, L.A., 1975—. Gen. counsel CVT Trust, 2003—. Served with AUS, 1953-55. Mem. ABA (labor and employment law sect.) Labor (including EEOC, Fair Labor Standards Act, labor-management relations, NLRB, OSHA). Home: 545 S Norton Ave Los Angeles CA 90020-4610 Office: Reich Adell Crost & Cvitan 3550 Wilshire Blvd Ste 2000 Los Angeles CA 90010-2421

ADELMAN, DANIEL J. lawyer; b. Sacramento, Nov. 21, 1961; s. Philip J. and Hannah B. Adelman; m. Cherie B. Cohen, June 10, 1984; children: Joseph, Emily, Abby. BS in Acctg., U. Ariz., 1983; JD, Ariz. State U., 1987. Bar: Ariz. 1987, U.S. Dist. Ct. Ariz. 1987, U.S. Supreme Ct. 1991. Assoc. atty. Lewis and Roca, Phoenix, 1987—90; assoc. gen. counsel, majority Ariz. State Senate, Phoenix, 1991; assoc. atty. Begam, Lewis, Marks and Wolfe, Phoenix, 1992—95, atty., 1996—. Bd. dirs. Ariz. Ctr. Law Pub. Interest, Phoenix, 1995—; pres. Camp Swift, Phoenix, bd. dirs. Mem.: ABA, ATLA (bd. dirs. 2001—), Ariz. Trial Lawyers Assn. Avocations: guitar, harmonica, sports. Personal injury (including property damage), Product liability, Professional liability. Office: Begam Lewis Marks and Wolfe 111 W Monroe Ste 1400 Phoenix AZ 85003 Office Fax: 602-252-0042. Business E-Mail: dadelman@begamlaw.com.

ADELMAN, MICHAEL SCHWARTZ, lawyer; b. Cambridge, Mass., June 6, 1940; s. Benjamin Taft and Sally Frances (Schwartz) A.; m. Amy Kay, June 14, 1962; children: Robert, Jonathon. Student, Boston U., 1958-59; BA with honors in English, U. Mich., 1962, JD cum laude. Bar: Mich. 1968, Miss. 1974; cert. for death penalty post-conviction collateral relief cases. Assoc. Zwerdling, Miller, Klimist & Maurer, Detroit, 1968-69; ptnr. Philo, Maki, Ravitz, Glotta, Adelman, Cockrel & Robb, Detroit, 1969-70, Glotta, Adelman & Dinges, Detroit, 1970-74, Andalman, Adelman & Steiner P.A., Hattiesburg, Miss., 1974-86, Adelman & Steiner P.A., Hattiesburg, Miss., 1986—. V.p., bd. dirs. S.E. Miss. Legal Svcs., Hattiesburg. Contbr. short stories: The Deputy, The Detention Center to New Renaissance. Treas. Hattiesburg Area Equal Rights Coun.; mem. Hattiesburg Biracial Adv. Com., 1987-89, chmn., 1988-89; v.p. state bd. dirs. NAMI, 2000—. Recipient Ralph T. Abernathy award Jackson County (Miss.) So. Christian Leadership Conf., 1978. Mem.: ABA, South Ctrl. Miss. Bar Assn. (pres. 2002). Criminal, Personal injury (including property damage), Workers' compensation. Address: 33 Camellia Ct Hattiesburg MS 39402-6112 E-mail: ADELST33@aol.com.

ADELMAN, STANLEY JOSEPH, lawyer; b. Devils Lake, N.D., May 20, 1942; s. Isadore Russell Adelman and Eva Claire (Robins) Stoller; m. Mary Beth Petchaft, Jan. 30, 1972; children: Laura E., Sarah A. BS, U. Wis., 1964, JD, 1967. Bar: Ill. 1967, U.S. Dist. Ct. (no. dist.) Ill. 1967, Wis. 1968, U.S. Ct. Appeals (7th cir.), U.S. Dist. Ct. (ea. dist.) Wis. 1979, U.S. Supreme Ct. 1982, U.S. Ct. Appeals (10th cir.) 1984, U.S. Ct. Appeals (fed. cir.) 1987. Assoc. Sonnenchein, Carlin, Nath & Rosenthal, Chgo., 1967-75, ptnr., 1975-85; co-chmn. litigation dept. Rudnick & Wolfe, Chgo., 1985-91, 96-97, ptnr., 1985—, profl. responsibility ptnr., 1992-94, mem. mgmt. policy com., 1985-97, co-chmn. complex litigation practice group, 1997-98. Bd. dirs. Legal Assistance Found., Chgo., 1982—83. Fellow Nat. Inst. Trial Advocacy; mem. Chgo. Bar Assn., Chgo. Coun. Lawyers, Am. Inns of Ct. (pres. Markey/Wigmore chpt. 1998-99), Lawyers Club Chgo., Order of Coif. Jewish. Federal civil litigation, General civil litigation, State civil litigation. Home: 115 Crescent Dr Glencoe IL 60022-1303 Office: Piper Rudnick Ste 1800 203 N La Salle St Chicago IL 60601-1210 E-mail: stanley.adelman@piperrudnick.com.

ADELMAN, STEVEN HERBERT, lawyer; b. Dec. 21, 1945; s. Irving and Sylvia (Cohen) A.; m. Pamela Bernice Kozoll, June 30, 1968; children: David, Robert. BS, U. Wis., Madison, 1967; JD, DePaul U., 1970. Bar: Ill. 1970, U.S. Dist. Ct. (no. dist.) Ill. 1970, U.S. Ct. Appeals (7th cir.) 1975. Ptnr. Keck, Mahin & Cate, Chgo., 1970-93, Lord, Bissell & Brook, Chgo., 1993—. Bd. dirs. Bur. Jewish Employment Problems, Chgo., 1983—, pres. 1991, 92; employment relations com. Chgo. Assn. Commerce and Industry, 1982-90. Contbr. chpts. to books, articles to profl. jours. Fellow Coll. Labor and Employment Lawyers; mem. ABA (Silver key award 1969), Chgo. Bar Assn. (chmn. labor and employment law com. 1988-89), Ill. State Bar Assn., Chgo. Coun. Lawyers, Decalogue Soc., Leading Lawyer's Network. Labor (including EEOC, Fair Labor Standards Act, labor-management relations, NLRB, OSHA). Office: Lord Bissell & Brook 115 S La Salle St Ste 3200 Chicago IL 60603-3902 E-mail: sadelman@lordbissell.com.

ADERSON, SANFORD M. lawyer; b. Pitts., July 15, 1949; s. Sanford C. and Marjorie S. (Stern) A.; m. Leslie S. Sertner, Aug. 12, 1972; children: Benjamin, Jonathan. BSBA, Boston U., 1971, JD, 1974. Bar: Pa. 1974, U.S. Dist. Ct. (we. dist.) Pa. 1974, U.S. Tax Ct. 1978, U.S. Ct. Appeals (3d cir.) 1986. Law clk. to judge Ct. of Common Pleas, Pitts., 1974-83; with Aderson, Frank, Steiner & Blechman, Pitts., 1976-2001; of counsel Strassburger, McKenna, Gutnick & Potter, Pitts., 2000—; pres. Luttner Fin. Group, Pitts., 2001—. Bd. dirs. Jewish Cmty. Ctr. of Pitts., 1993-98, vice chair Make-A-Wish, 2000—; mem. bus. com. Pitts. Cultural Trust, 2001—. Mem.: ABA, Allegheny County Bar Assn. (bankruptcy sect. mem. of coun. 1993—98), Pa. Bar Assn., Westmoreland Country Club (bd. dirs. 1987—, pres. 2001—). Bankruptcy, Corporate, general, Mergers and acquisitions. Office: Strassburger McKenna Gurnik & Potter 244 Blvd of the Allies Pittsburgh PA 15222 E-mail: sanford_m_aderson@glic.com.

ADKISON, RON, lawyer; b. Nacogdoches, Tex., Jan. 8, 1955; s. Robert Edward and Doris Ozelle (Pollard) A.; m. Tanya Regina Williamson, June 2, 1979 (div. Dec. 1984); 1 child, Veronica Alexis Adkison; m. Donna Elaine Dennis, Apr. 1, 1990 (divorced); 1 child, Alexander Aron; m. Tamra Bryan, July 4, 2001. BA, Stephen F. Austin U., 1976; JD, Baylor U., 1978. Bar: Tex. 1979, U.S. Dist. Ct. (ea., we., so. and no. dists.) Tex., U.S. Ct. Appeals (5th cir.), U.S. Supreme Ct. Atty. Wellborn & Houston, Henderson, Tex., 1979; ptnr. Wellborn, Houston, Adkison, et al., Henderson, Tex., 1980—. Regent Stephen F. Austin State U., Nacogdoches, 1993-99; chair bd. regents, 1995-96. Fellow Am. Bd. Trial Advs., Tex. Inst. for Legal Ethics and Professionalism; mem. Coll. State Bar Tex. (Disciplinary Rev. com., Adminstrn. Rules Civil Evidence com.), Tex. Trial Lawyers Assn. (dir., chair Toxic Torts com.), Henderson Country Club (pres. 1989-94). Avocations: golf, aviation. General civil litigation, Commercial, contracts (including sales of goods; commercial financing), Environmental. Office: Wellborn Houston Adkison et al 300 W Main St Henderson TX 75652-3109

ADLER, DAVID NEIL, lawyer; b. Bklyn., Apr. 11, 1955; s. Leonard Howard and Elaine (Holder) A. Student, Colgate U., 1973-75; BA, NYU, 1977; JD, St. John's U., 1980. Bar: N.Y. 1981, U.S. Dist. Ct. (ea. and so. dists.) N.Y. 1986, U.S. Tax Ct. 1989. Pvt. practice, Kew Gardens, N.Y., 1982—. Contbr. articles to profl. jours. Mem. Queens County Bar Assn. (com. chmn. 1983—, co-editor Queens Bar Bull. 1987—, bd. mgrs. 1989—, officer 1993—, pres. 1998), N.Y. State Bar Assn. (exec. com. trusts and estates). Estate planning, Probate (including wills, trusts), Estate taxation. Office: 12510 Queens Blvd Kew Gardens NY 11415-1519

ADLER, ERWIN ELLERY, lawyer; b. Flint, Mich., July 22, 1941; s. Ben and Helen M. (Schwartz) A.; m. Stephanie Ruskin, June 8, 1967; children: Lauren, Michael, Jonathan BA, U. Mich., 1963, LL.M., 1967; JD, Harvard U., 1966. Bar: Mich. 1966, Calif. 1967. Assoc. Pillsbury, Madison & Sutro, San Francisco, 1967-73; assoc. Lawler, Felix & Hall, L.A., 1973-76, ptnr., 1977-80, Rogers & Wells, L.A., 1981-83, Richards, Watson & Gershon, L.A., 1983—. Bd. dirs. Hollywood Civic Opera Assn., 1975-76, Children's Scholarships Inc., 1979-80 Mem. ABA (vice chmn. appellate advocacy com. 1982-87), Calif. Bar Assn., Phi Beta Kappa, Phi Kappa Phi. Jewish. Appellate, Insurance, Intellectual property. Office: Richards Watson & Gershon 355 S Grand Ave Ste 4000 Los Angeles CA 90071

ADLER, FREDERICK RICHARD, lawyer, financier; b. N.Y.C., Apr. 4, 1926; s. Samuel and Rose (Axelrod) A.; m. Catherine R. George, Apr. 25, 1986; Christopher Wells, Frederick George Richard; children by previous marriage: Barbara Ilene, James Richard, Susan Ruth Chapman, Elizabeth Anne Wertheimer. BA, Bklyn. Coll., 1948; JD magna cum laude, Harvard U., 1951; Doctorate (hon.), Technion-Israel Inst. Tech., 1998. Bar: N.Y. 1952. Assoc. Reavis & McGrath, N.Y.C., 1951-58, ptnr., 1959-89, Fulbright, Jaworski, Reavis & McGrath, N.Y.C., 1989-91; ret. sr. ptnr. Fulbright & Jaworski, N.Y.C., 1991-95, of counsel, 1996—; dir., chmn. exec. com. Data Gen. Corp., Westbo, Mass., 1968-99; mng. ptnr. VENAD Assocs., Adler & Co. Bd. dirs. Sentigen Holding Corp., Colo. Trustee Tchrs. Ins. and Annuity Assn., 1977-95; bd. mgrs./overseers Meml. Sloan-Kettering Cancer Ctr.; mem. dean's adv. bd. Harvard Law Sch; trustee Horace Mann School; With U.S. Army, 1943-45. Mem. Harvard Club, Met. Club, Maroon Creek Club (Aspen, Colo.), Univ. Club (N.Y.), Atlantic Golf Club (Southampton, N.Y.), Old Oaks Country Club (Purchase, N.Y.), Palm Beach Country Club (Palm Beach, Fla.), N.Y. Athletic Club. Corporate, general. Office: 220 Sunrise Ave Palm Beach FL 33480-3869

ADLER, HOWARD, JR., lawyer; b. Chgo., Jan. 25, 1925; s. Howard and Martha (Grossman) A.; m. Mary E. Williamson, Oct. 30, 1955; children: Martine, Karla, Elizabeth. MA in Econs., JD, U. Chgo., 1951. Bar: Ill. 1952. Atty. U.S. Dept. Justice, Washington, 1952-54, law clk., 1954-55; ptnr. Bergson, Borkland, Margolis & Adler, Washington, 1956-85, Davis, Graham & Stubbs, Washington, 1986-96; of counsel Baker & McKenzie, Washington, 1996—2001, Ridberg, Press & Sherbill, LLP, Bethesda, Md., 2002—. Mediator, arbitrator, JAMS, Washington. 1st lt. USAAF, 1946, PTO. Fellow Am. Bar Found.; mem. ABA (vice chmn. coun. 1978-79, sect. on antitrust law 1973-77). Antitrust, Federal civil litigation. Home: 3711 Morrison St NW Washington DC 20015-1733 E-mail: hadler@rpslaw.com., howard3771@aol.com.

ADLER, HOWARD BRUCE, lawyer; b. N.Y.C., Apr. 29, 1951; s. Mandel and Dora (Rosenblatt) A.; m. Tanya Jean Potter; 1 child, Alexandra. BA, Johns Hopkins U., 1972; JD, NYU, 1975. Bar: N.Y. 1976, U.S. Dist. Ct. (ea. and so. dists.) N.Y. 1976, D.C. 1979, U.S. Dist. Ct. D.C., 1979, U.S. Ct. Appeals (D.C. cir.) 1979. Assoc. Shearman & Sterling, N.Y.C., 1975-79, Arnold & Porter, Washington, 1979-82; mng. counsel Mellon Bank N.A., Pitts., 1982-84; exec. v.p., gen. counsel The Riggs Nat. Bank of Wash. D.C., Riggs Nat. Corp., 1984-87; ptnr. Gibson, Dunn & Crutcher LLP, Washington, 1987—. Contbr. articles to profl. jours. Mem. ABA (banking law com.), Fed. Bar Assn. (exec. coun. banking law com. 1990-98), D.C. Bar (treas. 1996-97, steering com. corp., fin. and securities law sect., 1991-96, chmn. 1994-95, vice chmn. 1993-94, budget com. 1996-97, chmn. task force of lawyers for econ. redevel. of D.C. 1997-99), Archdiocesan Legal Network of Washington (adv. bd. 1995-2002), Congl. Country Club, Met. Club, Knights of Malta. Avocation: civil war history. Corporate, general, Mergers and acquisitions, Securities. Home: 9517 Eagle Ridge Dr Bethesda MD 20817-3916 Office: Gibson Dunn & Crutcher LLP 1050 Connecticut Ave NW Ste 900 Washington DC 20036-5306

ADLER, IRA JAY, lawyer; b. N.Y.C., Jan. 1, 1942; s. Ralph and Beatrice (Rosenblum) A.; m. Laraine Sheila Garfinkel, July 4, 1965; children: Jodi, Michael. BA, NYU, 1963, JD, 1966. Bar: N.Y. 1966. Ptnr. Certilman, Balin, Adler & Hyman, LLP, East Meadow, N.Y., 1973—. Bd. dirs. Queens County Builders and Contractors, Flushing, N.Y. Contbr. to profl. pubs. Mem. ABA, N.Y. State Bar Assn., Nassau County Bar Assn., L.I. Builders Inst. (bd. dirs. 1985—), Real Estate Inst. C.W. Post (bd. dirs. 1986—), N.Y. State Builders Assn. (bd. dirs. 1988—). Property, real (including real estate development, water). Office: Certilman Balin Adler & Hyman LLP 90 Merrick Ave East Meadow NY 11554-1571

ADLER, KENNETH, lawyer; b. Queens, N.Y., Aug. 7, 1940; s. Alfred and Florence (Resnick) A.; m. Rita Klein, June 19, 1963; children: Howard, Andrew, Samantha. B.S., L.I. U., 1962; J.D., N.Y. U., 1968. Bar: N.Y. 1969, U.S Dist. Ct. (ea. and so. dists.) N.Y. 1973, U.S. Ct. Appeals (2d cir.) 1975, U.S. Ct. Mil. Appeals, 1980, U.S. Ct. Claims, 1980, U.S. Supreme Ct. 1980. Pub. accts. J.M. Levy & Co., CPAs, N.Y.C., 1961-63, Rashbar & Pokart CPAs, N.Y.C., 1963-64; v.p. Clobar Mfgf. Co., N.Y.C., 1964-69; sr. assoc. Morris H. Halpern, Esq., N.Y.C., 1969-72; founder, sr. ptnr. Kenneth Adler & Assocs., Melville, N.Y., 1972— ; fed. ct. arbitrator. Mem., contbr. Coalition of Free Men. Recipient Am. Jurisprudence award, 1969, L.I. U. law award, 1962. Mem. Trial Lawyers Assn. Am., Nassau County Bar Assn., ABA, N.Y. State Bar Assn., Suffolk County Bar Assn., Matrimonial Bar Assn., N.Y. State Trial Lawyers Assn. Suffolk, Assn for Transp. Law Logistics and Policy. Republican. Jewish. Clubs: Hamlet Country Club, K.P. FAX: 631-424-4494. General civil litigation, Insurance, Transportation. Office: Kenneth Adler & Assocs 150 Broadhollow Rd Ste 350 Melville NY 11747-4987

ADLER, LEWIS GERARD, lawyer; b. N.Y.C., Sept. 13, 1960; s. Sherman and Esther (Weiss) A.; m. Kim Adler, Sept. 5, 1988; children: Craig, Stephanie, Katie, Samantha. AS, Vanderbilt U., 1981; JD, Rutgers U., 1985. Bar: N.J. 1986, Pa. 1985, U.S. Dist. Ct. N.J. 1986, U.S. Dist. Ct. Pa. 1990, U.S. Supreme Ct. 1990, U.S. Tax Ct. 2000, U.S. Ct. Appeals (3d cir.) 2000. Solicitor Gloucester County Constrn. Bd. Appeals, Woodbury, N.J., 1987-88; atty. Gloucester County Sr. Citizen Will Program, Woodbury,

1987-88; pvt. practice Woodbury, N.J., 1989—; spl. counsel Gloucester County, 1990—. Pub. defender Deptford Township, 1996, zoning bd. solicitor, 1997-2000. Designer computer software. Pres. Haddonfield Plays & Players, 2002—. Mem. ABA, N.J. Bar Assn., Gloucester County Bar Assn., Phila. Trial Lawyers, Pa. Bar Assn. Democrat. Avocations: water and snow skiing, spelunking, chess, bicycling, rappelling. State civil litigation, Computer, Environmental. Home: 215 Douglass Ave Haddonfield NJ 08033-1626 Office: 26 Abaston Ave Woodbury NJ 08096-4633

ADLER, MARSHALL STUART, lawyer, mediator; b. Buffalo, Feb. 28, 1956; s. Merwin Stanley and Florence (Berger) A.; m. Debra Sue Thomas, Sept. 3, 1984; children: Matthew Steven, David Scott. BA, SUNY, Buffalo, 1978; JD, Duke U., 1981. Bar: Fla. 1981, U.S. Supreme Ct. 1985, U.S. Ct. Appeals (11th cir.) 1985, U.S. Dist. Ct. (mid. dist.) Fla. 1981; cert. circuit mediator. Assoc. Akerman Law Firm, Orlando, Fla., 1981-84, Zimmerman Law Firm, Orlando, 1984-86; ptnr. Griffin, Morgan, Linder & Adler, Orlando, 1986-88, Adler & Strickland, P.A., Orlando, 1988-91; pres. Marshall S. Adler, P.A., Orlando, 1991—. Bd. dirs. Jewish Cmty. Ctr., Orlando, 1997. Mem. Orange County Bar Assn. (vice chmn. workers' compensation sect. 1987). Alternative dispute resolution, Workers' compensation. Office: 430 N Mills Ave Orlando FL 32803-5746

ADLER, SARA, arbitrator, mediator; b. Chgo., Jan. 26, 1942; d. Matthew Michael and Mildred Paula (Eckhaus) Lewison; m. James N. Adler, Aug. 19, 1967; children: Michael, Philip, Matthew. AB, U. Chgo., 1961; JD, UCLA, 1969. Bar: Calif. Cons. Inst. Criminal Justice Adminstrn. U. Calif., Davis, 1969-71; assoc. Law Office of Sara Radin, L.A., 1971-72; assoc. dir. Paralegal Tng. Inst. U. So. Calif., L.A., 1972-74; assoc. Wyman, Bautzer, et al, L.A., 1974-78; arbitrator, mediator Dispute Resolution Svcs., L.A., 1978—. Fellow: Coll. Labor and Employment Lawyers; mem.: ABA (neutral co-chair ADR in Labor/employment Law 1995—98, neutral mem. coun. Labor & Employment sect.), L.A. County Bar Assn. (chmn. labor and employment sect. 1997—98), Indsl. Rels. Rsch. Assn. (pres. so. Calif. 1991—92), Nat. Acad. Arbitrators (regional chair 1994—96, bd. govs.), Am. Arbitration Assn. (bd. dirs., exec. com., labor mgmt. law task force, employment ADR steering com.). Avocation: Avocations: travel, theater, bridge. Office: Dispute Resolution Svcs 1034 Selby Ave Los Angeles CA 90024-3106

ADLER, SIDNEY W. lawyer; b. Steubenville, Ohio, June 22, 1952; AB in Geography, Clark U., 1976; JD summa cum laude, Syracuse U., 1979. Bar: Mass. 1979, U.S. Dist. Ct. Mass. 1980. Ptnr. Morrison, Mahoney & Miller, Boston, 1979-85, Taylor, Anderson & Travers, Boston, 1985-95, Adler, Cohen, Harvey, Wakeman & Guekguezian, LLP, Boston, 1995—. General civil litigation, Health, Professional liability. Office: Adler Cohen Harvey Wakeman & Guekguezian LLP 230 Congress St Boston MA 02110-2409

AFFRONTI, FRANCIS CHRISTOPHER, lawyer; b. Rochester, N.Y., Apr. 30, 1967; s. Francis Alexander and Heather Mary Affronti; m. Lorna Rachel Stead, Jan. 11, 1997. BA, Providence Coll., 1989; JD, Union U., 1992. Bar: N.Y. 1992, U.S. Dist. Ct. (we. dist.) N.Y. 1992. Assoc. Fix Spindelman et al., Rochester, N.Y., 1993-96, Brian J. Barney, Rochester, 1996-98; ptnr. Barney & Affronti, LLP, Rochester, 1999—. Appellate, Family and matrimonial. Office: Barney & Affronti LLP 130 Linden Oaks Ste D Rochester NY 14625-2834

AGAPION, BILL, lawyer; b. Stamford, Conn., Feb. 14, 1926; s. A. Bill and Helen (Theodore) A.; m. Sophia Sitaras, Apr. 28, 1968; children—Irene, Dena, Basil, Emanuel. B.A., U. N.C., 1947, LL.B., 1952. Bar: N.C. 1952, U.S. Dist. Ct. (mid. dist.) N.C. 1952. Sole practice, Greensboro, N.C., 1952-59, 70— ; ptnr. Agapion & Agapion, Greensboro, 1960-70. Served to 2d lt. U.S. Army, 1944-46. Decorated Purple Heart (3), Combat Infantry Badge. Mem. Greensboro Bar Assn., N.C. Bar Assn. Democrat. Greek Orthodox. Insurance, Landlord-tenant, Property, real (including real estate development, water). Home: 616 Willoughby Blvd Greensboro NC 27408-3164

AGATA, BURTON C. law educator, lawyer; b. N.Y.C., Feb. 7, 1928; s. Max and Augusta (Steger) A.; m. Dale S. Granirer, Dec. 24, 1955; children: Seth Hugh, Abby Fran. AB, U. Mich., 1947, JD, 1950; LLM in Trade Regulation, NYU, 1951. Bar: N.Y. 1951. Counsel div. N.Y. State Banking Dept., 1955-59; ptnr. firm Burstein & Agata, Mineola and N.Y.C., 1959-61; prof. Mont. U., 1961-62, N.Mex. U., 1962-63, Houston U., 1963-69; counsel Nat. Commn. on Reform Fed. Criminal Laws, 1968-70; prof. law Hofstra U., 1970-2001, Max Schmertz disting. prof. law, 1982-2001, disting. prof. emeritus, 2001—, interim dean, 1989; mem. faculty Nat. Inst. Trial Advocacy, 1977-81; dir. N.E. Regional Program, 1981-84. Spl. counsel N.Y. City Charter Revision Commn., 1987-89, N.Y. State Senate Minority, 1982-87; cons. Fed. Jud. Center, 1972, Inst. Jud. Adminstrn., 1973, HEW, 1971, White House Spl. Action Office Drug Abuse Prevention, 1973, N.Y. State Temp. Com. on Constnl. Revision, 1993-95; Chmn. N.Y. State Task Force, Standards and Go als for Prosecution and Def., 1977-79; cons. Adv. Com. on Qualifications of Counsel, 2d Ct., 1977; bd. dirs. Nassau Economic Opportunity Commn., 1972-73; reporter-cons. action unit on criminal justice system N.Y. State Bar Assn., 1986-90. Contbr. articles to law jours. With JAGC U.S. Army, 1951-54. Food Law fellow NYU, 1951, fellow U. Wis., 1963. Fellow Am. Bar Found. (life); mem. Am. Law Inst. (life), ABA (state antitrust law commn. 1980-01, vice chair com. on professionalism sr. lawyers divsn. 1996-2000), N.Y. State Bar Assn. (exec. com. criminal justice sect., chmn. com. rev. of criminal law 1987—, spl. com. on pre-sentence reports 1989-2001, Donnelly Act com. 1990-2001), Assn. of Bar of City of N.Y. (criminal cts. com. 1970-73, penology com. 1973-76, criminal justice com. 1983-85, antitrust com. 1986-89), Fed. Jud. Coun., Assn. Am. Law Schs. (chmn. criminal law sect. 1973) Office: 209 Mt Merino Rd Hudson NY 12534 E-mail: vze2vnja@verizon.net.

AGEE, G. STEVEN, judge; b. Roanoke, Va., Nov. 12, 1952; BA, Bridgewater Coll.; JD, U. Va.; LLM in Taxation, NYU. Mem. 7th dist. Va. Ho. Dels., 1982—2003; justice Va. State Supreme Ct., Richmond, 2003—. Mem.: Va. Bar Assn. (mem. taxation com.), DC Bar Assn. Office: Supreme Ct Va 100 N 9th St 5th Fl Richmond VA 23219*

AGHDAMI, FARHAD, lawyer; b. Tehran, Iran, Jan. 4, 1968; came to U.S., 1971; s. Ali Asghar and Farideh H. Aghdami; m. Amanda North Jones, May 21, 1994. BA, U. Va., 1989; JD, Wake Forest U., 1992; LLM in Taxation, Georgetown U., 1995. Bar: Va. 1992, U.S. Tax Ct. 1997. Assoc. Florance, Gordon and Brown, PC, Richmond, Va., 1992-97, dir., shareholder, 1997-99; mem. Williams, Mullen, Clark & Dobbins, Richmond, 1999—. Contbr. articles to profl. jours. Mem. ABA (tax sect. fiduciary income tax com., chair 2003—). Estate planning, Probate (including wills, trusts), Estate taxation. Home: 1003 West Ave Richmond VA 23220-3717 Office: Williams Mullen Clark & Dobbins Two James Ctr PO Box 1320 1021 E Cary St Richmond VA 23218-1320 Fax: 804-783-6507. E-mail: aghdami@williamsmullen.com.

AGOGLIA, EMMET JOHN, lawyer; b. N.Y.C., Nov. 18, 1930; s. Gerard and Loretta (Clavin) A.; m. K. Carroll Wheeler, Jan. 27, 1957; children: Christine, E. Kevin, Margaret, Michael, Barbara, Elizabeth, Kathleen. BA, St. Francis Coll., 1952; LLB, St. John's Coll., 1958. Bar: N.Y. 1958, U.S. Supreme Ct.1982. Assoc. Lawless & Lynch, N.Y.C., 1959-61, Reilly & Reilly, N.Y.C., 1961-64; ptnr. Crowe, McCoy & Agoglia, Mineola, N.Y., 1964-69, McCoy & Agoglia, Mineola, N.Y., 1969-86, McCoy, Agoglia, Beckett & Fassberg, Mineola, N.Y., 1986-89, Agoglia-Fassberg-Holland & Crowe, P.C., Melville, NY. Lectr. in field. Contbr. articles to profl. publs. Fellow Am. Coll. Trial Lawyers; mem. ABA, N.Y. State Bar Assn., Am. Bd. Trial Advocates, Am. Bd. Profl. Liability Attys. (diplomate), Nassau County Bar Assn. (past bd. dirs., mem. jud. screening com.), Nassau-Suffolk Trial Lawyers, Internat. Acad. Trial Lawyers. Democrat. Roman Catholic. Federal civil litigation, Insurance, Personal injury (including property damage). Office: 535 Broadhollow Rd Ste A10 Melville NY 11747

AGOSTI, DEBORAH ANN, state supreme court chief justice; BA cum laude, U. Toledo, 1973, JD, 1976. Bar: Nev., U.S. Supreme Ct. Dep. pub. defender Montgomery County, Ohio, 1977; sr. staff atty. Sr. Citizens Legal Assistance Program, Washoe County, 1977—79; dep. dist. atty., 1979—82; justice of the peace Reno Twp., Nev., 1982—85; dist. judge 2d Jud. Dist., Reno, 1985—99; justice Nev. Supreme Court, Carson City, 1999—, now chief justice. Trustee Nat. Jud. Coll., 2001—, Pretrial Svcs. Resource Ctr., 1999—; mem. merit selection panel U.S. Dist. Ct. Nev., 2000; co-chmn. jury improvement commn. Supreme Ct. of Nev., 2001—; mem., dean's adv. bd. U. Toledo Coll. Law. Chmn. Task Force to Revitalize Interest in Attendance at Washoe County Bar Meetings, 2001—. Named Outstanding Young Woman for State of Nev., 1983, One of Am.'s 100 Young Women of Promise, Good Housekeeping mag., 1985, Reno's Outstanding Woman for 1986, One of Three Outstanding Young Nevadans, Reno Jaycees, 1986, Outstanding Women Lawyer, No. Nev. Women Lawyer's Assn., 1993, Woman of Achievement, Nev. Women's Fund, 1998, One of Nev.'s First One Hundred Women Attys.; recipient Judge of Yr., Nev. Dist. Judge's Assn., 1989. Master: Bruce Thompson Inn of Ct.; mem.: No. Nev. Women Lawyers Assn., Nat. Assn. Women Judges, Soroptimists Internat. of Truckee Meadows (life Woman of Distinction 2001). Office: Supreme Ct Nev 201 S Carson St Carson City NV 89701-4702

AGOSTINI, MASSIMO, lawyer; b. Cortona, AR., Italy, Aug. 6, 1960; s. Luigi and Bruna (Bellucci) Agostini. Lic.: Dickinson Sch. of Law (Master Comparative Law) 1989. Lt. Tax Police, Rome, 1987—88; lawyer (assoc.) Fantozzi Biscozzi, Rome, 1989—91, Gianni, Origoni, Grippo & Ptnr., Rome, 1992—98; lawyer (ptnr.) Price Waterhouse, Milan, 1998—99, Gianni, Origoni, Grippo et al, Rome, 2000—. Contbr. articles to profl. and popular jours. Office: Gianni Origoni Grippo et al Via delle Quattro Fontane 20 Rome RM 00184 Italy Office Fax: +39 06 4871101. E-mail: magostinirm@gop.it.

AGOSTO, BENNY, JR., lawyer; b. N.Y.C., Feb. 28, 1963; s. Beno Sr. and Marina A.; children: Ben III, Jon David, Victoria. BS, Houston Bapt. U., 1986; JD, So. Tex. Coll. Law, 1986. Bar: Tex. 1995, U.S. Dist. Ct. (so. dist.) Tex. 1995. Atty. Morgan & Assocs., Houston, 1995-96, Barrow & Parrott, Houston, 1996-98, Abraham, Watkins, Nichols & Friend, Houston, 1998—. Fellow Houston Bar Assn.; mem. Houston Trial Lawyers Assn., Houston Trial Lawyers Found., Houston Hispanic Bar Assn., Houston Young Lawyers Assn., Mex.-Am. Bar Assn., Alpha Tau Omega. Avocation: golf. General civil litigation, Personal injury (including property damage). Office: Abraham Watkins Nichols & Friend 800 Commerce St Houston TX 77002-1776 Fax: 713-225-0827.

AGRANOFF, GERALD NEAL, lawyer; b. Detroit, Nov. 24, 1946; s. Carl and Frances (Solomon) A.; children: Lindsay Sara, Dana Jill. BS, Wayne State U., 1969, JD, 1972; LLM, NYU, 1973. Bar: Mich. 1973, N.Y. 1975, U.S. Tax Ct. 1974, U.S. Ct. Claims 1974. Atty.-advisor U.S. Tax Ct., Washington, 1973-75; assoc. law firm Baker & McKenzie, N.Y.C., 1975-79, Baer Marks & Upham, N.Y.C., 1979-80; counsel Pryor, Cashman et al, N.Y.C., 1980-82; gen. counsel Arbitrage Securities Co., Plaza Securities Co., N.Y.C., 1982—; gen. ptnr. Edelman Securities Co., N.Y.C., 1984—. Mem. Inveraray Capital Mgmt. LLC, 2002—, Crosshaven Capital LLC, 2002—; trustee Dynacore Patent Litigation Trust; bd. dirs. Canal Capital Corp., N.Y.C., Bull Run Corp., Dynacore Holdings Corp.; adj. instr. NYU Inst. on Fed. Taxation, 1980-81. Bd. dirs. Soho Repertory Theatre, N.Y.C., 1982. Corporate taxation, Personal income taxation, State and local taxation. Office: The Edelman Cos 717 5th Ave New York NY 10022-8101 E-mail: gagranoff@edelco.com.

AGRAZ, FRANCISCO JAVIER, SR., lawyer, public affairs representative; b. Laredo, Tex., Aug. 21, 1947; s. Jose Jesus and Irene (Garcia-Gomez) A.; m. Rosalinda Varela, Aug. 23, 1969 (div. Feb. 1980); children: Francisco Javier Jr., Raquel Jeanne; m. Ruth Urquidi, Jan. 1, 1984. BA in Journalism, U. Tex. at El Paso, 1970; JD, U. Houston, 1987. Bar: Tex. 1988, U.S. Dist. Ct. (so. dist.) Tex. 1988. Anchor reporter KENS-TV, San Antonio, 1970; corr. ABC Capital Cities Comms., Chgo., Houston, N.Y., 1970-77; pub. affairs analyst Exxon Corp., Houston and Memphis, 1977-83; assoc. Wood, Burney, Cohn & Bradley, Corpus Christi, Tex., 1987-89, Redford, Wray & Woolsey, P.C., Corpus Christi, 1989-91; pres., atty. at law Francisco J. Agraz P.C., Houston, 1991—; gen. mgr. The MRAM Co., Houston, 1996-98; pub. affairs officer FBI, Houston, 1998—. Bd. govs. United Way of Coastal Bend, Corpus Christi, Tex., 1987-91. Mem. State Bar of Tex. (grievance com., pub. rels. com.). Roman Catholic. Avocation: spanish translator. Corporate, general, Private international, Other. E-mail: agrazfj@franciscoagraz.com.

AGUIGUI, IGNACIO CRUZ, lawyer; b. Agana Heights, Guam, Dec. 3, 1970; s. Joaquin Tyquiengco and Teresita Cruz Aguigui. BA magna cum laude, Yale U., 1991; JD with honors, Columbia Law Sch., 1997. Bar: Calif. 1997, U.S. Ct. Appeals (9th Cir.) 1997, U.S. Dist. Ct. (no. dist.) Calif. 1997, Guam 1999, U.S. Dist. Ct. Guam 1999, U.S. Dist. Ct. (ctrl. dist.) Calif. 2001. Spl. asst. to the gov. Office of the Gov. of Guam, Hagatna, 1993—94; extern law clk. Hon. Barrington D. Parker, Jr., U.S. Dist. Ct., So. Dist., NY, New York, 1995; atty. at law Morrison & Foerster LLP, San Francisco, 1997—98; atty. Chambers of Hon. Katherine A. Maraman, Superior Ct. of Guam, Hagatna, 1998—99, Calvo and Clark, LLP, Tamuning, 1999—2002; legal counsel Camacho/Moylan Gubernatorial Transition Com., Hagatna, 2002; mng. ptnr. Lujan, Aguigui & Perez LLP, Hagatna, 2003; counsel to gov. Office of the Gov. of Guam, Hagatna, 2003—. V.p., bd. of directors Guam Legal Services Corp., Hagatna. Mem. Rep. Party of Guam, Hagatna, 1991, Guam Election Commn., Hagatna, 2002, Guam Pub. Libr., Hagatna, 1991—92. Recipient Centennial Scholar award, NIH, 1987, U.S. Congl. award, Office of Guam's Del. to the US Ho. of Representatives, 1987, Principal's award, Inarajan H.S., Inarajan, Guam, 1987, Harlan Fiske Stone scholar, Columbia Law Sch., 1996, Achievement with Honors in Internat. & Fgn. Law, 1997, Robin Berlin Meml. prize, Yale U., 1989, Valedictorian award, Inarajan H.S., Inarajan, Guam, 1987; fellow Pub. Svc. fellow, Columbia Law Sch., 1994, Summer Rsch. fellow, U. of Calif., Berkeley, 1989, U. of Calif., San Francisco, 1990; scholar Profl./Tech. scholar, Govt. of Guam, 1994-1997, Merit Scholarship award, 1987-1991. Mem.: ABA (assoc.). R-Liberal. Roman Catholic. Avocations: travel, music, french language and culture. Private international, General civil litigation, Corporate, general. Home: 162 Western Boulevard Oka Towers 303 Tamuning GU 96913 Personal E-mail: iaguigui@aya.yale.edu. E-mail: iaguigui@aya.yale.edu.

AGUIRRE-BACA, FRANCISCO, publisher, consultant; b. León, Nicaragua, Jan. 7, 1920; came to U.S., 1947; s. Horacio and Pilar (Baca) Aguirre-Muñoz; m. Gladys Sacasa Aguirre, Dec. 27, 1941; children: Gladys, Francisco Xavier, Mariangeles, Rafael Eugenio, Guiomar, Alejandra. JD, U. Granada, Nicaragua, 1947. Various sr. positions Nicaraguan Armed Forces, 1940-47; rep., coord. numerous L.Am. newspapers and mags. Washington, 1947-53; co-founder, co-pub. Diario Las Americas, Miami, Fla., 1953—; founder Francisco Aguirre & Assocs. Latin Am. Newspapers and mag., Washington, 1960; dir. Pan Am. Divsn. Am. Road Builders Assn., Washington, 1948-53; co-founder, co-pub. Diario Las Americas, Miami, Fla., 1953; founder Francisco Aguirre & Assoc., Washington, 1960; amb. to III Summit Iberoamerican Chiefs of State Del. Dominican Republic, Salvador, Bahia, Brazil, 1993, amb. to IV Summit Iberoamerican Chiefs of State, 1994, Del. Republic Panama, Cartajena, Colombia, 1994; amb. to IV Summit Iberoamerican Pres. and Heads of States Nicaraguan Del., Santiago, Chile, 1996, amb. to official visit to His Holiness John Paul II Vatican City, Italy, 1996, amb. to Summit of the Ams. Santa Cruz, Bolivia, 1997; amb. to inauguration new Pres. Nicaragua Arnoldo Aleman Lacayo U.S. Del., Managua, Nicaragua, 1997; amb. to official visit to Republic China Nicaraguan Del., Taiwan, 1998, amb. II Summit of the Ams. Santiago, Chile, 1998, amb. XXVIII Gen. Assembly OAS Caracas, Venezuela, 1998. Internam. cons. Ambassador Extraordinary and Plenipotentiary of Nicaragua in Spl. Missions, Panama in Spl. Missions, 2002. Bd. dirs. Panamerican Divsn., Am. Rd. Builders Assn., 1948. Knight Order of St. Gregory, Sovereign Order of Malta; decorated by govts. of Argentina, Ecuador, Panama, Dominican Republic, Spain, Nicarauga, Republic of China (Taiwan). Mem. Hist. Georgetown Club, City Club, Nat. Press Club, Univ. Club, Congl. C.C. Republican. Roman Catholic. Home: 4951 Rockwood Pkwy NW Washington DC 20016-3247

AGUSTINOY GUILAYN, ALBERT, lawyer; b. Barcelona, Oct. 20, 1972; s. Fernando Agustinoy and Carmen Guilayn. Degree in law, U. Barcelona, 1995; M in European Law, Autonomous U. Barcelona, 1997; M in Internat. Law, Robert Schuman U., 1998. Parliamentary asst. European Parliament, Strasbourg, France, 1997—98; trainee Cuatrecasas, Brussels, 1998—99, assoc. Madrid, 1999—2001, Barcelona, 2001—. Lectr. U. Ramon LLull, Barcelona, 2001—, U. Navarra, Pamplona, 1999—, Internat. U. Cath. Law Sch., Barcelona, 2002; panelist UDRP procedures World Intellectual Property Orgn. Intellectual property, Computer, Trademark and copyright. Office: Cuatrecasas Paseo De Gracia 111 15th Fl 08008 Barcelona Spain Fax: +34 93 2905588. E-mail: albert.agustinoy@cuatrecasas.com.

AHLERS, GLEN-PETER, SR., law library director, educator, consultant; b. N.Y.C., Mar. 15, 1955; s. LeGrande Jacob and Joan (Stoltz) A.; m. Sondra Sue Wadley, May 17, 1987; children: Glen-Peter II, Sandia Marie, Gavin Patrick, Sierra Le Ann Rose, Stacia Camille, Sienna Catherine. BS, U. N.Mex., Albuquerque, 1979; MA, U. of South Fla., 1983; JD, Washburn U., 1987. Bar: Kans. 1987, U.S. Dist. Ct. Kans. 1987, U.S. Ct. Mil. Appeals 1988, D.C. 1990. Reference asst. U. N.Mex. Sch. Law, Albuquerque, 1979-83; asst. dir. Washburn Sch. Law Libr., Topeka, 1983-87; assoc. libr. dir. Wake Forest U., Winston-Salem, N.C., 1987-90; libr. dir., assoc. prof. D.C. Sch. Law, Washington, 1990-92, U. Ark., Fayetteville, 1992-2000, prof., 2001—02; assoc. dean info. services Barry U. Dwayne O. Andreas Sch. of Law, Orlando, Fla. Computer and libr. cons. Ctr. for R&D in Law-Related Edn., Winston-Salem, 1987-90; adj. prof. Sch. of Law Wake Forest U., Winston-Salem, N.C., 1987-90; Mid-Am. Law Sch. Libr. Consortium, 1992-02, bd. dirs. Consortium of Southestern Law Librs., 1988-90, pres. 2000-02. Author: History of Law School Libraries in the United States, 2002, Election Laws of the United States, 1995; co-author: Notary Law and Practice, 1997; editor The Maall Newsletter, 1984-87, The Scrivener, 1992—; tech. editor Washburn Law Jour., 1985-86; contbr. articles to profl. jours. Mediator N.C. Neighborhood Justice Ctr., Winston-Salem, 1989-90. Mem. ABA, ALA, Fla. Bar Assn., Am. Assn. Law Librs., Southwestern Assn. Law Librs. (pres. 1995-97), Southeastern Assn. of Law Librs., Mid Am. Assn. Law Librs. (pres. 1999-2000), Scribes (exec. dir. 1997—), Phi Kappa Phi, Kappa Delta Pi, Beta Phi Mu. Avocation: writing. Home: 1069 Winding Waters Cir Winter Springs FL 32708-6326 Office: Barry U Dwayne O Andreas Sch of Law 6441 E Colonial Dr Orlando FL 32807-3650 E-mail: gahlers@mail.barry.edu.

AHLSTROM, MICHAEL JOSEPH, lawyer; b. N.Y.C., June 1, 1953; s. Albert Warren and Bernadette Patricia (Flynn) A.; m. Mary Lou Donnelly, Apr. 19, 1980; 1 child, Courtney Leigh. BS, St. Francis Coll., 1975; JD, U. San Francisco, 1978. Bar: N.Y. 1980, U.S. Dist. Ct. (so. and ea. dists.) N.Y. 1980, Ga. 1982, U.S. Dist. Ct. (no. dist.) Ga. 1983, U.S. Ct. Appeals (11th cir.) 1984, U.S. Supreme Ct. 1987; registered neutral, arbitration, domestic mediation and early case evaluator, Ga. Counsel Gear Design, Inc., N.Y.C., 1979-80; ptnr. Ahlstrom & Ahlstrom, N.Y.C., 1981-83; gen. counsel Network Rental, Inc., Atlanta, 1984-87; assoc. John Marshall and Assocs., P.C., Atlanta, 1987; ptnr. Marshall & Ahlstrom, P.C., Atlanta, 1987-88; mng. atty. UAW-GM-Ford Chrysler Legal Plan Ga., Atlanta, 1993-96; pvt. practice, Marietta, Ga., 1988-92, 96—. Arbitrator Nat Assn. Securities Dealers, Superior Ct. Fulton County, Ga., 1987—, Ga. Lemon Law, 1991—; panel atty. Cobb County Circuit Defender; spl. master Cobb County Superior Ct., mediator, 1966-1996; mediator domestic cases Fulton County Superior Ct., 1998—, mediator juvenile cases; guardian ad litem Cobb County Superior Ct. Mem. N.Y. Bar Assn., Ga. Bar Assn. (pub. rels. com. 1989-91), Cobb County Bar Assn., Am. Corp.Counsel Assn. (program chmn. 1986-87), Am. Arbitration Assn. (comml. panel 1987—), KC, Phi Delta Phi, Alpha Kappa Psi. Republican. Roman Catholic. Avocations: fishing, hunting, tennis, golf, croquet. Commercial, contracts (including sales of goods; commercial financing), Corporate, general, General practice. Home: 613 Fairway Ct Marietta GA 30068-4159

AHMED, ATIQ RAHMAN, lawyer; b. Nagpur, Maharashtr, India, Jan. 20, 1955; came to U.S. 1974; s. Zia Rahman and Talat (Bano) A.; m. Arifa Saeed Khan, Aug. 5, 1983; children: Shafi A., Imran A., Fareed A. BBA, George Washington U., 1978, MBA, 1980; JD, Georgetown U., 1984. Bar: Md. 1985, D.C. 1985, Va. 1986, U.S. Dist. Ct. Md. 1985, U.S. Ct. Appeals (4th and D.C. cirs.) 1985, U.S. Dist. Ct. D.C. 1985, U.S. Supreme Ct. 1988. Pvt. practice, Silver Spring, Md., 1985—. Moslem. General civil litigation, Criminal, Personal injury (including property damage). Office: Ste 500 8701 Georgia Ave Silver Spring MD 20910-3723

AHRENSFELD, THOMAS FREDERICK, lawyer; b. Bklyn., June 30, 1923; s. Frederick Herman and Madeline Florence (Moffett) A.; m. Joan Ann McGowan, Mar. 17, 1944; 1 child, Thomas Frederick. AB, Bklyn. Coll., 1948; LL.B., Columbia U., 1948. Bar: N.Y. 1948. Assoc., then ptnr. Conboy, Hewitt, O'Brien & Boardman, N.Y.C., 1948-58; sec., assoc. gen. counsel Philip Morris Inc., N.Y.C., 1959-70, v.p., gen. counsel, 1970-76, sr. v.p., gen. counsel, 1976-85, Philip Morris Cos., Inc., N.Y.C., 1985-88; pvt. practice law Pleasantville, N.Y., 1988—. Trustee Trinity-Pawling Sch. Corp., 1976-98; elder Presbyn. Ch. 1st lt. USAAF, 1942-45. Decorated D.F.C., Air medal with oak leaf clusters. Mem. ABA, N.Y.C. Bar Assn., N.Y. Athletic Club, Mt. Kisco (N.Y.) Country Club, Johns Island (Fla.) Club. Corporate, general. Home and Office: 85 Nannahagan Rd Pleasantville NY 10570-2314

AH-TYE, KIRK THOMAS, lawyer; b. L.A., Mar. 31, 1951; s. Thomas and Ruth Elizabeth (Liu) Ah-T.; m. Deborah Ann Wells, Jan. 31, 1981; 1 child, Torrey Ann. BA, U. Calif., Santa Barbara, 1973; JD, Boston Coll., 1976. Bar: Calif. 1977, U.S. Dist. Ct. (cen. dist.) Calif. 1978, U.S. Dist. Ct. (ea. dist.) Calif. 1994, U.S. Ct. Appeals (9th cir.) 1978, U.S. Supreme Ct. 1981. Co-exec. dir., mng. atty. Channel Counties Legal Svcs. Assn., Santa Barbara, 1977—; directing atty. Calif. Rural Legal Assistance, Inc. Expert witness Assembly Com. on Edn., Calif. Legis., Sacramento; panelist Ctr. for the Study of Dem. Instns., Santa Barbara; panelist, instr. CLE approved classes; past legal cons. Santa Barbara chpt. calif. Assn. Bilingual Educators; inaugural prodr., moderator Santa Barbara Law, Sta. KTMS-AM, 1994—. Editor (bar newsletter) Santa Barbara Lawyer, 1992-93, (monthly legal series) Santa Barbara News-Press; contbr. articles to profl. jours. Trustee Montessori Ctr. Sch., Santa Barbara, 1991-93; bd. dirs., v.p. Santa Barbara Internat. Film Festival, 1991-93; chair adv. bd. Santa Barbara Regional Health Authority, 1985; mem. blue-ribbon com. County Bd. Suprs., Santa Barbara, 1988; chair Santa Barbara County Affirmative Action Commn., 1987-88; mem. grant-making com. Fund for Santa Barbara, 1988-92. Recipient Local Hero award Santa Barbara Ind., 1988. Master Santa Barbara Am. Inns of Ct.; mem. State Bar Calif. (state resolutions com. to state bar conf. of dels. 1994-96, exec. com. to conf. dels. 1997, ann. legal svcs. achievement award for so. Calif. 1997, Achievement award for legal svc. 1997), Santa Barbara County Bar Assn. (jud. svc. award com. 1992, chmn. pro bono com. 1993, bd. dirs., sec., CFO 1992—, pres. 1997-98),

Lawyer Referral Svc. Santa Barbara (bd. dirs., pres. 1992). Avocations: sports, film, literature, weights, tennis. General civil litigation, Education and schools, Health. Office: Calif Rural Legal Assistance Inc 324 E Carrillo St Ste B Santa Barbara CA 93101-7438

AHUKANNAH, NNENA A. lawyer; b. Port Harcourt, Nigeria; d. John and Cecilia Ahukannah. BSc, U. Nigeria, 1985, LLB, 1990; LLM, Temple U., 1999. Bar: Nigeria 1991, N.Y. 2000. Assoc. Tunde Odanye & Co, Lagos, Nigeria, 1992—93; counsel Law Offices of Lai Oshisanya & Co., Lagos, Nigeria, 1993—95; legal officer African Devel. Ins. Co., Victoria Island, Nigeria, 1995—97; in-house counsel Software Performance Systems, Inc., Arlington, Va., 2000—. Mediator Superior Ct.'s Multi-Door Dispute Resolution Program. Catechist Mother Seton Cath. Ch., Germantown, Md., 2001—02. Mem.: ABA, Nigerian Bar Assn., Global Corp. Counsel Assn., Am. Corp. Counsel Assn. Avocations: reading, travel, music. Office: Software Performance Systems Inc 2011 Crystal Dr Ste 710 Arlington VA 22202

AIBEL, HOWARD J. lawyer, arbitrator, mediator; b. N.Y.C., Mar. 24, 1929; m. Katherine Webster, June 6, 1952; children: David Webster, Daniel Walter, Jonathan Brown. AB magna cum laude, 1950; JD cum laude, Harvard U., 1951. Bar: N.Y. 1952. Assoc. White & Case, N.Y.C., 1952-57; trade regulation counsel GE, 1957-60, spl. litigation counsel elec. equipment antitrust cases, 1960-64; antitrust counsel ITT Corp., N.Y.C., 1964-66, v.p., assoc. gen. counsel, 1966-68, sr. v.p., gen. counsel, 1968-87, exec. v.p., gen. counsel, 1987-92, exec. v.p., chief legal officer, 1992-94; ptnr. LeBoeuf Lamb Greene & MacRae, N.Y.C., 1994-99, of counsel, 1999-2001. Bd. dirs. Farrel Corp., Transparancy, Internat.-USA; vice chmn. Fund for Modern Cts., 1985-95; mem. AAA/ABA/AMA Com. Health Care Dispute Resolution, 1997-2000. Mem. vis. com. Northwestern U. Law Sch., 1984—90; mem. adv. com. Corp. Counsel Ctr., chmn., 1986—87; trustee Lawyers Com. for Civil Rights, 1991—95, U. Bridgeport, 1989—91, chmn. adv. com. Sch. Law, 1987—92; cons. trustee Westport Nature Ctr. for Environ. Activities; bd. dirs. Alliance of Resident Theatres, NY, 1986—, chmn., 1989—2002, chmn. emeritus, 2002—; bd. dirs., 1st v.p. Westport Arts Ctr., 1993—96. Fellow Am. Bar Found. (life); mem. ABA (bus. law sect. corp. governance 1994-98), Am. Law Inst. (elected mem.), Am. Arbitration Assn. (chmn. exec. com. 1992-95, chmn. bd. dirs. 1995-98), Assn. Gen. Counsel, pres. Harvard Law Sch. Assn. NY, 1992-94, v.p. Harvard Law Sch. Assn., 1994-2002, Am. Judicature Soc. (bd. dirs. 1994-2001, exec. com. 1996-2001). Home and Office: 183 Steep Hill Rd Weston CT 06883-1924 E-mail: hjaibel@optonline.net.

AIDINOFF, M(ERTON) BERNARD, retired lawyer; b. Newport, R.I., Feb. 2, 1929; s. Simon and Esther (Miller) A.; m. Celia Spiro, May 30, 1956 (dec. June 28, 1984); children: Seth G., Gail M.; m. Elsie V. Newburg, Nov. 29, 1996. BA, U. Mich., 1950; LLB magna cum laude, Harvard U., 1953. Bar: D.C. 1953, N.Y. 1954. Law clk. to Judge Learned Hand, U.S. Ct. of Appeals, N.Y.C., 1955-56; with Sullivan & Cromwell, N.Y.C., 1956-63, ptnr., 1963-96, ret. ptnr., 1997. Dir. Am. Internat. Group Inc., Gibbs & Cox, Inc., Goldman Sachs Philanthropy Fund; adv. com. to IRS commr., 1979-80, 85-86. Editor in chief The Tax Lawyer, 1974-77. Trustee Spence Sch., 1971-79; mem. adv. com. Gibbs Bros. Found., 1965-94; mem. vis. com. Harvard U. Law Sch., 1976-82, 99—; adv. dir. Met. Opera Assn., 1989-2002; chmn. bd. dirs. St. Luke's Chamber Ensemble, 1988-2001, chmn. emeritus, 2001—; nat. campaign chair Campaign to Save Touro Synagogue; pres. Soc. Friends of Touro Synagogue, 2002—; 1st lt. JAGC, AUS, 1953-55. Recipient Judge Learned Hand Human Rels. award Am. Jewish Com., 1997. Mem.: ABA (vice chmn. sect. taxation 1974—77, chmn.-elect 1981—82, chmn. 1982—83, chmn. commn. taxpayer compliance 1983—88, Ho. of Dels. 1988—91, Disting. Svc. award 2003), Am. Law Inst. (cons. fed. income tax project 1974—, chmn. tax program com. 1988—, John Minor Wisdom award 1995), Assn. Bar City of N.Y. (exec. com. 1974—78, chmn. exec. com. 1977—78, v.p. 1978—79, chmn. taxation com. 1979—81, chmn. govt. ethics com. 1988—90), N.Y. State Bar Assn., The Parks Coun. (bd. dirs. 1995—97), Lawyers Com. for Human Rights (bd. dirs. 1986—, treas. 1997—2002), Coun. Fgn. Rels., East Hampton Hist. Soc. (trustee 1983—89, 1990—95), Found. for a Civil Soc. (bd. dirs. 1994—, vice chmn. 1997—98, chmn. 1999—), Guild Hall (trustee 1989—94, 1995—, treas. 1993—94, 1995—2002), Met. Club, Century Assn., India Ho., Phi Beta Kappa. Corporate taxation, Taxation, general. Home: 980 5th Ave New York NY 10021-0126 Office: Sullivan & Cromwell 125 Broad St New York NY 10004-2498 E-mail: aidinoffmb@sullcrom.com.

AIN, SANFORD KING, lawyer; b. Glen Cove, N.Y., July 24, 1947; s. Herbert and Victoria (Ben Susan) A.; m. Miriam Luskin, July 12, 1980; children: David Lloyd, Daniel Jason. BA cum laude, U. Wis., 1969; JD, Georgetown U., 1972. Bar: Va. 1972, D.C. 1973, Md. 1982. Ptnr. Sherman, Meehan, Curtin & Ain P.C., Washington, 1972—2003, Ain & Bank, P.C., Washington, 2003—. Mem. faculty continuing legal edn. program State Bar Va., D.C. Bar, Md. Bar. Fellow: Am. Acad. Matrimonial Lawyers (pres. D.C. chpt. 1991—94, 2002—, counsel 1999—2000, bd. govs. 2003—); mem.: Md. Bar Assn., Va. Trial Lawyers Assn., Am. Coll. Family Trial Lawyers. Family and matrimonial, Property, real (including real estate development, water). Office: Ain & Bank PC 1900 M St NW Ste 600 Washington DC 20036-3519

AISENBERG, IRWIN MORTON, lawyer; b. Worcester, Mass., Aug. 8, 1925; s. William and Esther (Lewis) A.; m. Lois P., Sept. 4, 1955 (div. Apr. 1986); children: Karen Sue Portner, Sondra Lee, David Craig, Steven Bennett; m. Hana Jane Barton, June 19, 1999. BS in Chem Engring., Carnegie Mellon U., 1946; JD, Georgetown U., 1957. Bar: D.C. 1958, U.S. Ct. of Customs and Patent Appeals 1958, U.S. Ct. Appeals (D.C. cir.) 1958, U.S. Supreme Ct. 1964, N.J. 1965, Va. 1969, U.S. Ct. Appeals (fed. cir.) 1982; registered profl. engr., Mass. Patent examiner U.S. Patent and Trademark Office, Washington, 1954-57; assoc. atty. Wenderoth, Lind & Ponack, Washington, 1957-63; chief patent counsel Sandoz, Inc., Hanover, N.J., 1963-67; pvt. practice Washington, 1967-75; ptnr. Berman, Aisenberg & Platt, Washington, 1975-91, mng. ptnr., 1980-85; ptnr. Jacobson Holman PLLC, Washington, 1991—. Lectr. Franklin Pierce Law Sch., Concord, N.H., 1980-88; mem. appeal bd. Nat. Register of Health Svc. Providers in Psychology, 1987-89. Mem. editl. adv. bd. IDEA, Jour. Law and Tech., 1981-95; bd. editors: Patent Strategy and Mgmt.; author: Attorney's Dictionary of Patent Claims, 1985, with yearly supplements, Patent Law Precedent, 1991, 2d edit., 1992, Modern Patent Law Precedent, 3d edit., 1997, 5th edit., 2003; contbr. articles to profl. jours.; patentee in field. Served to cpl. U.S. Army, 1950-52. Mem. ABA, Internat. Assn. Protection Indsl. Property, Am. Intellectual Property Law Assn., Am. Arbitration Assn. (mem. panel arbitrators). Clubs: Kenwood Golf and Country, Am. Contract Bridge League (life master). Jewish. Intellectual property, Patent, Trademark and copyright. Home: 8508 Meadowlark Ln Bethesda MD 20817-2921 Office: Jacobson Holman Jenifer Bldg 400 7th St NW Washington DC 20004 E-mail: iaisenberg@jhip.com.

AISON, HOWARD M. judge; b. Amsterdam, N.Y., Oct. 12, 1945; s. Nathan and Rose W. Aison; m. Margaret Halvey Aison, Aug. 12, 1979; children: Jacob J., Sarah J. BA, Syracuse U., 1967; JD, Bklyn. Law Sch., 1970. Bar: N.Y. 1972, U.S. Dist. Ct. (no. dist.) N.Y. 1974, U.S. Ct. Appeals (2d cir.) 2001. Atty. Legal Aid Soc., Amsterdam, 1973—75; dist. atty. Montgomery County, Fonda, NY, 1979—85, county judge, 1986—95; judge City of Amsterdam, 1997—. Pres. Amsterdam Ctr. for Teens, 1980—, Salamdana Park Beach and Swimming Assn., Northville, NY, 1998—. Comdr. VUV Post 401, Amsterdam, 1998—2002, Old Tryon Counties Coun. VFW, Amsterdam, Amsterdam Legion Post JF, 2000. Capt. U.S. Army, 1971—72, Vietnam. Mem.: Montgomery County Bar Assn., N.Y. State Bar Assn. Democrat. Jewish. Avocations: travel, boating, golf, tennis, camping. Home and Office: 230 Florida Ave Amsterdam NY 12010

AJALAT, SOL PETER, lawyer; b. Chgo., July 12, 1932; s. Peter S. and Tesbina (Shahadie) Ajalat; m. Lily Mary Roum, Aug. 21, 1960; children: Stephen, Gregory, Denise, Lawrence. BS, UCLA, 1958, JD, 1962. Bar: Calif. 1963, U.S. Dist. Ct. (no., cen., ea. and so. dists.) Calif. 1963, U.S. Claims Ct. 1990. Pvt. practice, L.A., 1965—. Referee Calif. State Bar Ct., 1984-90; mem. sr. lawyers com. State Bar Calif., 2002—. Pres. bd. dirs. St. Nicholas Orthodox Cath. Ch., L.A., 1976-78; pres. Toluca Lake Elem. Adv. Coun., L.A., 1979, L.A. Unified Sch. Dist. Area I Adv. Coun., 1980, Providence High Sch. Adv. Coun., L.A., 1985; bd. dirs. Med. Ctr. North Hollywood, 1991-98, Angels of the Yr. Awards, 1996—, Life Svcs., Inc., 1997-2001; mem. improvement adv. com. Burbank City media dist., 1997-2000; chmn. Toluca Lake Neighborhood Coun., 2002—. Mem. Calif. Bar Assn., L.A. County Bar Assn. (mem. L.A. Superior Ct. bench and bar com. 1987-96, chmn. mcpl. ct. com. 1985-86, trustee 1987-88), Calif. Trial Lawyers Assn., Conf. Bar Dels. (del. 1985—), L.A. County Trial Lawyers Assn., Lawyers Club L.A. County (pres. 1985-86), Toluca Lake C. of C. (pres. 1997), Wm. A. Neima Rep. Club (pres. 1978-79), Masons, Shriners, Kiwanis (pres. North Hollywood chpt. 2002-03). Eastern Orthodox. Avocation: physical fitness. State civil litigation, General practice. Office: 3800 W Alameda Ave Ste 1150 Burbank CA 91505-4304

AKEMANN, DAVID R. lawyer; b. Elgin, Ill., Oct. 31, 1951; s. Theodore H. and Lois (Marr) A.; m. Vickie C. Skala, Aug. 5, 1978; children— Carrie, Julie, Collin. B.S., Brigham Young U., 1972; J.D., Lewis U., 1978. Bar: Ill. 1978, U.S. Dist. Ct. (no. dist.) Ill. 1978, U.S. Ct. Appeals (7th cir.) 1979, U.S. Supreme Ct. 1981. Clk. States Atty. Office, Kane County, Geneva, Ill., 1977-78; asst. states atty., 1978-79, chief civil divsn., 1979—87; sole practice, Elgin, 1978—92; elected states atty., 1992-2000; asst. atty. gen., 2000-03; Apptd. commnr. Ill. Industrial Commn., 2003. Recipient Am. Jurisprudence Constn. Law award Lawyers Coop. Pub. Co., 1978. Mem. ABA, Ill. Bar Assn., Kane County Bar Assn., Ill. Pub. Employers Labor Relations Assn. (prin.). Methodist. Home: 420 Hoxie Ct Elgin IL 60123-3220

AKERMAN, NATHANIEL HOWARD, lawyer; b. Springfield, Mass., Apr. 21, 1947; s. Paul Charles and Shirley (Whitehouse) A.; m. Lisa Helmrich, Jan. 16, 1983; children: Kira Perry, Lily Farrell. BA, U. Mass., 1969; JD, Harvard U., 1972. Bar: Mass. 1972, D.C. 1975, N.Y. 1979. Staff atty. FTC, Washington, 1972-73; asst. spl. prosecutor Watergate Spl. Prosecution Force, Washington, 1973-76; asst. U.S. atty. U.S. Atty.'s Office for So. Dist. N.Y., N.Y.C., 1976-83; ptnr. Dorsey & Whitney. Mem. nat. fin. com. Dukakis for Pres., 1988. Recipient spl. commendation U.S. Dept. Justice, 1979, 81. Mem. ABA, Fed. Bar Coun., Nat. Assn. Fraud Examiners, Harvard Club. Avocations: skiing, running, photography. Home: 137 Riverside Dr Apt 11A New York NY 10024 Office: Dorsey & Whitney 250 Park Ave New York NY 10177

AKERS, SAMUEL LEE, lawyer; b. Chattanooga, Oct. 20, 1943; s. Shelby Russell and Helen Louise (Crumley) A.; m. Mercedes Lilia Vuksanovic, Mar. 13, 1967; children: Bradford Lee, Camby Leigh. BA, Berry Coll., 1966; JD, Memphis State U., 1974. Bar: Tenn. 1974, U.S. Dist. Ct. (ea. dist.) Tenn. 1976, U.S. Ct. Appeals (6th cir.) 1985, U.S. Supreme Ct. 1987, U.S. Dist. Ct. (mid. dist.) Tenn. 1989. Trust examiner Office of the Compt. of the Currency, Memphis, 1975-76; assoc. Luther, Anderson, Cleary & Ruth, Chattanooga, 1976-78, 81-84, ptnr., 1985-93, Hatfield Van Cleave & Akers, Chattanooga, 1994, Hatfield Van Cleave Akers & Adams, P.L.C., Chattanooga, 1995-96; spl. agt. FBI, Orlando, Fla., 1978-81; Clk. and Master Chancery Ct. Hamilton County, 11th Jud. Dist., Chattanooga, 1996—. Mem. comml. panel Am. Arbitration Assn., NYC, 1986—96; mem., Tenn. Judicial Info. Adv. Com., 1998; mem. nominating com. Cmty. Found. of Greater Chattanooga, Inc., 1999; treas. State Clerk's Assn. Ea divsn., 2000; mem. Estate Planning Coun. of Chattanooga, 1996—. Judge adv. Tenn. State Ct. Clk.'s Assn., 2000, County Ofcls. Assn. Tenn., 2001; County Officials Assn. of TN, Legis. Com. 2001-2003, Nominating Com. Cmty. Found. Greater Chattanooga, 1999; mem. Estate Planning Coun. Chattanooga, 1996—; asst. instr. SCUBA cert. Lt. comdr. USNR, 1967-71. Named Outstanding Young Man of Am. Jaycees, 1977. Fellow Chattanooga Bar Assn. (bd. govs. 1995-96, sec.-treas. 1997, pres.-elect 1998, pres. 1999-2000, apptd. fellow 2003); mem. Tenn. Bar Assn., Soc. Former Spl. Agts. of the FBI (chmn. Chattanooga chpt. 1987-88, 95-96), County Officials Assn. Tenn. (legis. com. 2002-2003). Republican. Roman Catholic. Avocations: jogging, bicycling, hiking, tennis, scuba diving. General civil litigation, State civil litigation, Probate (including wills, trusts). Home: 106 Westwood Dr Signal Mountain TN 37377-2525 Office: Chancery Ct Tenn 300 Courthouse Hamilton Co Chattanooga TN 37402 E-mail: leeakers@exch.hamiltontn.gov.

AKINAKA, ASA MASAYOSHI, lawyer; b. Honolulu, Jan. 19, 1938; s. Arthur Yoshinori and Misako (Miyoshi) A.; m. Betsy Yoshie Kurata, Oct. 7, 1967; children— David Asa Yoshio, Sarah Elizabeth Sachie. BA magna cum laude, Yale U., 1959; postgrad. (Rotary Found. fellow), Trinity Coll., Oxford U., 1959-60, Yale Law Sch., 1960-61; LL.B., Stanford Law Sch., 1964. Bar: Hawaii bar 1964. Research asst. U.S. Senator Oren Long, Washington, 1961-62; pvt. practice law Honolulu, 1964—. Bd. visitors Stanford Law Sch., 1971-74. Mem. Am. Bar Assn., Hawaii State Bar Assn. (pres. 1977), Nat. Conf. Bar Presidents, Pacific Club, YMCA (bd. dirs., v.p. 1970-81). Democrat. Episcopalian. Corporate, general, Property, real (including real estate development, water). Office: PO Box 1035 Honolulu HI 96808-1035

AL, MARC ANDRE, lawyer; b. Leiden, The Netherlands; came to U.S., 1991; s. Bernard P. F. Al and Toop K. Al-Duyster; m. Dawn Marie Mathson, Dec. 28, 1991; 1 child, Juliette Marieke. M in Law, Leiden U., The Netherlands, 1992; JD, William Mitchell Coll. Law, 1994. Bar: Minn. 1994, U.S. Dist. Ct. Minn., 1996, U.S. Dist. Ct. Ariz. 1999, U.S. Ct. Appeals (8th cir.) 1999, U.S. Ct. Appeals (9th cir.) 2000. Jud. law clk. to U.S. chief magistrate judge James A. Morrow, Anoka, Minn., 1994-95; jud. law clk. to Hon. Jonathan Lebedoff Mpls., 1995-97; assoc. atty. Rider, Bennett, Egan & Arundel, LLP, Mpls., 1997—2000; ptnr. Lindquist & Vennum P.L.L.P., 2000—. Legal advisor Leiden Legal Aid Found., 1990-91. Mem. ABA, Fed. Bar Assn., Fed. Cir. Bar Assn., Minn. State Bar Assn., Minn. Intellectual Property Law Assn., Hennepin County Bar Assn., Phi Delta Phi. Corporate, general, Insurance. Office: 4200 IDS Ctr Lindquist & vennum PLLP 80 S 8th St Minneapolis MN 55402 Fax: 612-371-3207. E-mail: mal@lindquist.com.

ALAIMO, ANTHONY A. federal judge; b. Sicily, Italy, Mar. 29, 1920; AB, Ohio No. U.; JD, Emory U. Bar: Ga. 1948, Ohio 1948. Assoc. Reuben A. Garland, 1949-51, 53-56; pvt. practice, Atlanta, 1967-63; ptnr. Highsmith, Highsmith, Alaimo & Knox, Brunswick, Ga., 1963-67, Cowart, Sapp, Alaimo & Gale, Brunswick, 1963-67, Alaimo, Taylor & Bishop, Brunswick, 1967-71; judge U.S. Dist. Ct. (so. dist.) Ga., Brunswick, 1971—, now sr. judge. Office: US Dist Ct PO Box 944 Brunswick GA 31521-0944

ALAN, MATTHEW W. A. lawyer; b. Cleve., Nov. 9, 1961; BA in History and Polit. Sci., Cleve. State U., 1984, JD, 1986. Bar: Ohio 1987, D.C. 1992, Pa. 1993. Sr. counsel CBS Corp., Pitts., 1993-98; sec., gen. counsel Westinghouse Safety Mgmt. Solutions, LLC, Aiken, S.C., 1998—, Safe Sites of Colo. L.L.C., Golden, 2002—, Thor Treatment Techs., LLC, Aiken, 2002—; counsel Washington Energy and Environment, 2000—. Maj. JAGC, U.S. Army, 1987-93. Corporate, general, Government contracts and claims, Private international. Office: Westinghouse Safety Mgmt Solutions LLC 2131 S Centennial Ave Aiken SC 29803-7609

ALAN, SONDRA KIRSCHNER, lawyer; b. Pitts. d. Andrew and Lora Hardy Kirschner; m. Riley L. Proffitt, July 9, 1988; children: Gregory Proffitt Alan, Victoria Jade Proffitt, Andrew Lawrence Proffitt. BA, SUNY, Buffalo, 1968; JD, Duquesne U., 1980. Bar: Pa. 1980, Va. 1983, U.S. Dist. Ct. (we. dist.) Va. 1982, U.S. Ct. Appeals (4th cir.) 1982. Art tchr. St. Gregory the Gt., Buffalo, 1966-68; mgr. visual arts lab Ind. U. Sch. of Optometry, Bloomington, 1969-71; law clk. to presiding justice Ct. Common Pleas, Waynesburg, Pa., 1979-80; assoc. Law Offices J.D. Bowie, Bristol, Va., 1980-83; pvt. practice Bristol, 1984—. Guardian ad litum for children, Va., 1995—; guardian ad litum for adults, Va., 2001—; hearing officer Va. Supreme Ct., Va., 2001—. Recipient 2d pl. award Pa. State Art Competition, 1976. Mem. Pa. Bar Assn., Va. Bar Assn., Bristol Bar Assn. (pres. 1984-85). Lutheran. Avocations: pencil sketching, stained glass, home remodeling, gardening. Family and matrimonial, General practice, Probate (including wills, trusts). Office: 923 Cumberland St Bristol VA 24201-4103

ALBAN, LUDWIG, lawyer; b. N.Y.C., Dec. 30, 1947; BS, Bradley U., 1969; JD, Tulane U., 1973. Bar: Mass. 1973. V.p. Indusco Rental Inc., N.Y.C., 1969-70; atty., treas. Feinberg & Alban P.C., Brookline, Mass., 1973—. Treas. Ferriabough Enterprises Inc. Brookline 1974-77, MVP Assocs. Inc. Brookline, 1978-84. Mem. Mass. Bar Assn., St. John's Lodge (past master), Mitzpah-Faith Lodge (past master). Estate planning, Probate (including wills, trusts), Property, real (including real estate development, water). Office: Feinberg & Alban PC 1051 Beacon St Brookline MA 02446-5685

ALBER, PHILLIP GEORGE, lawyer; b. Lansing, Mich., Dec. 10, 1948; s. Phillip Karl and Audrey Irene (Putnam) A.; m. Shari Thornton; children: Emily Nicole, Phillip George, Elisabeth Whitney, Christian Thornton. BA magna cum laude, U. Mich., 1971; JD cum laude, Wayne State U., 1974. Bar: Mich. 1975, U.S. Dist. Ct. (ea. dist.) Mich. 1975, U.S. Ct. Appeals (6th cir.) 1978, U.S. Dist. Ct. (we. dist.) Mich. 1982. Assoc. Harvey, Kruse, Westen & Milan, Detroit, 1975-79, ptnr., 1979-85, Mager, Mercer and Alber, Detroit, 1985-2000, Alber Crafton, PLLC, Troy, Mich., 2001—. Lectr. Ill. Inst. Continuing Edn., Chgo., 1980. Mem. ABA (torts ins. practice sect., vice chair fidelity and surety law com.), Detroit Bar Assn. (pub. adv. com. 1979—, cir. ct. com. 1978—), Mich. Bar Assn. (rep. assembly 1970-80), Internat. Assn. Def. Counsel (fidelity and surety com. 1984—), Surety Claims Inst., Nat. Bd. Claim Assn. (pres. 1992-94, program chair 1990—), Assn. Def. Trial Counsel, Detroit Athletic Club, Hundred Club, Goodfellows Old Newsboys Club (Detroit). Republican. Roman Catholic. Federal civil litigation, State civil litigation, Construction. Home: 673 Washington Rd Grosse Pointe Woods MI 48230-1253 Office: Alber Crafton PLLC Ste 300 2301 W Big Beaver Rd Troy MI 48084-4906 E-mail: palber@albercrafton.com.

ALBERGER, WILLIAM RELPH, lawyer, government official; b. Portland, Oreg., Oct. 11, 1945; s. Relph Griffin and Ferne (Ahlstrom) A.; children: Eric Griffin, Blake Eugene. BA, Willamette U., 1967; MBA, U. Iowa, 1971; JD, Georgetown U., 1973. Bar: D.C. 1974. Spl. asst. to U.S. Senator Bob Packwood, 1969-71; legis. asst. U.S. Rep. Al Ullman, Washington, 1972-75, adminstrv. asst., 1975-77, House Com. on Ways and Means, 1977; vice-chmn. U.S. Internat. Trade Commn., Washington, 1978-80, chmn., 1980-82; pvt. practice Washington, 1982—. Mem. ABA (chmn. standing com. customs law 1983-85), D.C. Bar Assn., Internat. Bar Assn. Democrat. Aviation, Private international, Legislative. E-mail: bill.alberger@gte.net.

ALBERT, ALAN DALE, lawyer; b. Christiansburg, Va., Feb. 6, 1956; s. Horace Wendell and Alma Juanita (Morris) A.; children: Alexander, Caroline. AB magna cum laude, Harvard Coll., 1979; MPhil, Oxford U., 1981; JD cum laude, Harvard U., 1985. Bar: Va. 1985, U.S. Dist. Ct. (ea. dist.) Va. 1989, U.S. Ct. Appeals (4th cir.) 1989, U.S. Bankruptcy Ct. (ea. dist.) Va. 1991, U.S. Ct. Appeals (fed. cir.) 2003. Instr. in legal methods, teaching fellow in fed. litigation Harvard Law Sch., 1983-85; teaching fellow faculty arts and scis. Harvard U., 1984-85; law clk. Office of the Legal Adviser U.S. Dept. State, 1984; rsch. dir., speech writer Baliles for Gov., Richmond, Va., 1985; dir. policy devel. Gov.'s Transition Office Commonwealth of Va., Richmond, 1985-86, spl. asst. to Gov. of Va., 1986-89; assoc. Mays & Valentine, Norfolk and Richmond, 1989-93, ptnr., 1994—2000, Troutman Sanders LLP, Norfolk and Richmond, Va., 2001—. Author books on environ. law, real estate and land use law, freedom of info. and pub. records access; editor Harvard Law Rev., 1983-85; contbr. articles to profl. jours. Vol. Dem. nat., state and local polit. campaigns and com. activities, 1976—; exec. dir. Va. Dems., 1988; bd. dirs. Va. Opera, 1990—; mem. Leadership Metro Richmond, 1987-88. Harvard Nat. scholar, 1974-79, George C. Marshall scholar, 1979-82, European Consortium Polit. Rsch. scholar, 1982, Pres.'s Disting. Svc. award Treas. Assn. of Va., 1995. Mem. ABA, Fed. Bar Assn., Va. Bar Assn. (sect. bd. govs. 1991-94), Va. State Bar, Tidewater Legal Aid Soc. (bd. dirs. 1990-93), Norfolk-Portsmouth Bar, Virginia Beach Bar, Town Point Club, Owl Club, Phi Beta Kappa. Legislative, Federal civil litigation, Intellectual property. Office: Troutman Sanders LLP 150 W Main St Ste 1600 Norfolk VA 23510-3338 also: NationsBank Ctr 1111 E Main St Richmond VA 23219-3531 E-mail: alan.albert@troutmansanders.com.

ALBERT, GARETT J. lawyer; b. Sept. 7, 1943; m. Eleanor Lanier Culbertson, Oct. 2, 1971. BA cum laude, Columbia U., 1965; postgrad., Harvard U. Bus. Sch., 1967-68; JD, Harvard U., 1968. Bar: D.C. 1969, N.Y. 1970. Atty. U.S. Atomic Energy Commn., 1968; assoc. Hughes Hubbard & Reed, N.Y.C., 1969-77; ptnr. Hughes Hubbard & Reed, LLP, N.Y.C., 1977—. Contbr. articles to various publs. including James Joyce Quar. Bd. dirs. Mannes Coll. Music, Nat. Acad. Design, Nat. Corp. Fund for Dance, Paul Taylor Dance Found. Winner U.S. Nat. Powerlifting Championship, Nat, Physique com., Tournament of Champions, 1996, Mr. USA, 1996, Kevin Levrone Bodybuilding Classic, 1995, and other masters powerlifting and bodybuilding championships. Mem. Union Club, Quogue (N.Y.) Field Club. Office: Hughes Hubbard & Reed LLP 1 Battery Park Plz Fl 12 New York NY 10004-1482

ALBERT, ROBERT HAMILTON, lawyer; b. Columbus, Ohio, May 25, 1931; s. Raymond Joseph Albert and Kathryn Mary (Hildebrand) Lett; m. Patricia S. Smith, June 23, 1962; children: Julie Ann Certain, Karen Marie Groeber, Robert H. Jr. BSBA, Ohio State U., 1953; LLB, Franklin U., 1960; JD, Capitol U., 1966. Bar: Ohio, 1960, U.S. Tax Ct. 1961, U.S. Dist. Ct. (so. dist.) Ohio, 1962, U.S. Ct. Appeals (6th cir.) 1966, U.S. Ct. Claims 1971, U.S. Supreme Ct. 1971. Indsl. engr. Fairmont Foods Co., Columbus, 1951-52; acct. E.C. Redmund CPA, Columbus, 1953-54; acct., contract adminstr. N.Am. Aviation, Columbus, 1956-60; ptnr. Kagay, Albert Diehl & Groeber, Columbus, 1961—. Mem. Rep. Nat. Com. Capt. USAF, 1954-56. Fellow Columbus Bar Found. (mem. legal adv. com.); mem. Ohio State Bar Assn., Columbus Bar Assn., Order of Curia, Beta Gamma Sigma, Beta Alpha Psi. Roman Catholic. Probate (including wills, trusts), Property, real (including real estate development, water), Taxation, general. Office: Kagay Albert Diehl & Groeber 6877 N High St Ste 300 Worthington OH 43085-2411

ALBERTS, BARRY S. lawyer; b. Chgo., Feb. 2, 1946; s. Irving and Evelyn Alberts; m. Susan Weinstein, Apr. 28, 1974; 1 child, Jaime Eliana. BA cum laude, Miami U., 1968; JD, U. Chgo., 1971. Bar: Ill. 1971, U.S. Dist. Ct. (no. dist.) Ill. 1971, U.S. Ct. Appeals (7th cir.) 1989, U.S. Ct.

Appeals (6th cir.) 1996, U.S. Ct. Appeals (2d cir.) 1997. Ptnr. Schiff, Hardin & Waite, Chgo. Adj. prof. law Northwestern U. Law Sch., Chgo., 1991-98; lectr. law U. Chgo. Law Sch., 1995-2003. Contbr. articles to profl. jours. Mem. bd. dirs. Chgo. Children's Choir, 2002. Mem. Am. Law Inst. (hon.), ABA (co-chair ethics and professionalism sect. litig. 1998-2002, trial evidence com., 1995-98, task force ethical guidelines settlement negotiations 2001-2002), Acad. Laureates Ill. Lawyers (hon., bd. regents), Ill. State Bar Assn. (hon.), Chgo. Bar Assn., Chgo. Coun. Lawyers, Lincoln-Am. Inn of Ct., Phi Beta Kappa. General civil litigation, Professional liability. Office: Schiff Hardin & Waite 6600 Sears Tower Chicago IL 60606-6473 Home: 200 Dempster St Evanston IL 60202-1406 Home Fax: 312-258-5600. Personal E-mail: balberts@schiffhardin.com.

ALBERTS, HAROLD, lawyer; b. San Antonio, Apr. 3, 1920; s. Bernard H. and Rose Alberts; m. Rose M. Gaskin, Mar. 25, 1945; children: Linda Rae, Barry Lawrence. LLB, U. Tex., 1942. Bar: Tex. 1943, U.S. Supreme Ct. 1950, U.S. Ct. Mil. Appeals 1959. Tchr. U. Tex., 1942, instr., 1941-42; legal officer Chase Field, 1944; sole practice Corpus Christi, Tex. Pres. Jewish Welfare Fund, Corpus Christi, 1948; chmn. S.W. Regional Anti-Defamation League, Tex. and Okla., 1970-71, chmn., 1969-72, chmn. Brotherhood Week, 1957; chmn. Nueces County (Tex.) Red Cross, 1959-61; mem. campaign exec. com., chmn. meetings United Cmty. Svcs., 1961; v.p. Little Theatre, Corpus Christi, 1964; chmn. Corpus Christi NCCJ, 1967-69, nat. dir., 1974-76; bd. dirs. Tex. State Assn. Mental Health; pres. Combined Jewish Appeal, Corpus Christi, 1974-76; moderator Friday Morning Group, 1975, 96. Served to lt. (sr. grade) USNR, 1942-46. Mem. ABA, Tex. Bar Assn., Corpus Christi Bar Assn., Kiwanis (pres. 1962), B'nai B'rith (pres. 1955), Masons (32d degree). State civil litigation, General practice, Probate (including wills, trusts). Home and Office: PO Box 271477 Corpus Christi TX 78427-1477

ALBIN, BARRY G. lawyer, rabbi; b. Wichita, Kans., Sept. 6, 1948; s. Frederick Eugene Albin and Eloise Nelda Riley; m. Marianne Kay Olish, Aug. 8, 1970 (div. Feb. 1997); children: Thomas C., Michael A., Benjamin J., Joshua S. BA, U. Kans., 1970, JD, 1973; cert. in data processing, Kansas City C.C., 1981. Bar; Kans. 1973, U.S. Dist. Ct. Kans. 1973. Staff counsel Wyandotte Legal Aid Soc., Kansas City, Kans., 1974-76; pvt. practice Kansas City, 1976-83, 85—; gen. mgr. Chameleon Dental Products, Kansas City, 1983-85; grand hierophant, CEO Modern Rite of Memphis, Inc., 2002—03. Lectr. bus. law Maple Woods C.C., Kansas City, Mo., 1978; staff counsel Kans. State Dept. Social and Rehab. Svcs., Kansas City, 1986-91; legal counsel Mid. Am. Gay Ecumenical Found., Kansas City, Mo., 1975-80, Phylaxis Soc., 1999—, N.E. Kans. Valley, AASR, Chi Rho Fraternity, Grand Tribune, 2001—; energetic healer and exorcist. Author: Climbing Jacob's Ladder, 1981, Believers Commentary on Mark, 1985, Believers Commentary on Barnabas, 1986, Catechism of Nasorean Church, 1995. Mebakker rabbi Naorean Orthodox Qahal, Kansas City, 1985—; state treas., Green Party, 2000-2002. Mem. Internat. Soc. Study of Subtle Energies and Energy Medicine, Common Cause (state sec. 1978, state v.p. 1978-79), Inst. Noetic Sci., Masons (various offices 1989—), Scottish Rite (33d degree), York Rite (Knight York Cross of Honor), Masonic Brotherhood of Blue Forget-Me-Not, Blue Lodge. Democrat. Avocations: computers, reading, hiking, teaching, scripture. Appellate, Constitutional, Criminal.

ALBIN, BARRY TODD, judge; b. Bklyn., July 7, 1952; married; 2 children. BA with high honors, Rutgers U., 1973; JD, Cornell U., 1976. Bar: N.H. 1976, U.S. Supreme Ct. 1984, U.S. Ct. Appeals (3d cir.) 1985. Dep. atty. gen. N.J. Div. Criminal Justice, Trenton, 1976-78; asst. prosecutor Passaic County, Paterson, N.J., 1978-79, Middlesex County, New Brunswick, N.J., 1979-82; assoc. Wilentz, Goldman & Spitzer, Woodbridge, N.J., 1982—; pres. NJ Assoc. of Criminal Defense Lawyers, 1999—2000; judge State Supreme Ct., 2002—. Trustee Nat. Conf. of Christians and Jews, Edison, N.J., 1986. Mem. N.J. Bar Assn., Middlesex County Bar Assn. Office: Richard J Hughes Complex PO Box 970 25 W Market St Trenton NJ 08625-0970*

ALBRIGHT, JOSEPH P. state supreme court justice; b. Parkersburg, W.Va., Nov. 8, 1938; s. M.P. and Catherine (Rathbone) A.; m. Patricia Ann Deem, 1958 (dec. 1993); children: Terri Albright Cavi, Lettie K., Joseph P. Jr., John Patrick (dec.); m. Nancie Gensert Divvens; stepchildren: Susan Divvens Bowman, Debbie Divvens Holcomb, Sandy Divvens Fox. BBA cum laude, U. Notre Dame, JD, 1962. Bar: W.Va. 1962, U.S. Dist. Ct. W.Va. 1962. Pvt. practice, Parkersburg, 1964-95; asst. prosecuting atty. Wood County, 1965-68; city atty. City of Parkersburg, W.Va., 1968; justice W.Va. Supreme Ct. of Appeals, Charleston, 1995—96, 2001—; pvt. practice Parkersburg and Charleston, 1997—2000. Former mem. W.Va. State Ethics Commn.; bd. dirs. Albrights of Belpre (Ohio), Inc. Former clk. Charter Bd. of Parkerburg; mem. W.Va. Ho. of Dels., 1970-86, mem. jud. com., chmn. com. on edn., 1977-78, chmn. com. on judiciary, 1979-84, 52d spkr. of Ho. of Dels., 1984-86; mem., former chmn. Blennerhassett Hist. Park Commn.; former co-chmn. Blennerhassett Hist. Commn.; mem. St. Francis Xavier Ch., Parkersburg, past pres. parish adv. coun. Named Freshman Legislator of Yr., Charleston Gazette, 1971. Office: WVa Supreme Ct Appeals State Capitol Complex Bldg 1 Room E308 1900 Kanawha Boulevard E Charleston WV 25305

ALBRIGHT, TERRILL D. lawyer; b. Lebanon, Ind., June 23, 1938; s. David Henry and Georgia Pauline (Doty) A.; m. Judith Ann Stoelting, June 2, 1962; children: Robert T., Elizabeth A. AB, Ind. U., 1960, JD, 1965. Bar: Ind. 1965, U.S. Dist. Ct. (so. dist.) Ind. 1965, U.S. Dist. Ct. (no. dist.) Ind. 1980, U.S. Ct. Appeals (7th cir.) 1981, U.S. Ct. Appeals (3d and D.C. cirs.) 1982, U.S. Supreme Ct. 1972; cert. arbitrator for large complex cse program constrn. and internat. commercial cases Am. Arbitration Assn., cert. mediator. Assoc. Baker and Daniels Law Firm, Indpls., 1965-72, ptnr., 1972—. Mem. panel of disting. neutrals. nat. panel for constrn. and regional comml. panel CPR Inst. for Dispute Resolution, N.Y.C. Pres. Christamore House, Indpls., 1979-86; bd. dirs. Greater Indpls. YMCA, 1980-82; chmn. Jordan YMCA, Indpls., 1982; pres. Community Ctrs. Indpls., 1987-90. 1st lt. U.S. Army, 1960—62. Fellow: Acad. Law Alumni, Ind. U. Sch. of Law (bd. dirs. 1974—80, pres. 1979—80), Am. Coll. Trial Lawyers, Indpls. Bar Found., Ind. Bar Found, Am. Bar Found.; mem.: Ind. State Bar Assn. (chmn. young lawyers sect. 1971—72, rep. 11th dist. 1983—85, bd. dirs., v.p. 1991—92, pres.-elect 1992—93, pres. 1993—94), Nat. Conf. Bar. Pres. (exec. coun. 1995—98). Democrat. Federal civil litigation, General civil litigation, Construction. Office: Baker & Daniels 300 N Meridian St Ste 2700 Indianapolis IN 46204-1782 E-mail: tdalbright@bakerd.com.

ALBRITTON, WILLIAM HAROLD, III, federal judge; b. Andalusia, Ala., Dec. 19, 1936; s. Robert Bynum and Carrie (Veal) A.; m. Jane Rollins Howard, June 2, 1958; children: William Harold IV, Benjamin Howard, Thomas Bynum. AB, U. Ala., 1959, LL.B., 1960. Bar: Ala. 1960. Assoc. firm Albrittons & Rankin, Andalusia, 1962-66, ptnr., 1966-76; ptnr. firm Albrittons & Givhan, Andalusia, 1976-86; ptnr. Albrittons, Givhan & Clifton, Andalusia, 1986-91; judge U.S. Dist. Ct. (mid. dist.) Ala., Montgomery, 1991-97, chief judge, 1998—. Mem. 11th Circuit Jud. Coun., 1998—. Pres. Ala. Law Sch. Found., 1988-91, Ala. Law Inst. Fellow Am. Coll. Trial Lawyers, Am. Bar Found.; mem. ABA, Fed. Judges Assn. (bd. dirs. 1999-2002, jud. conf. U.S. com. on ct. adminstrn. and case mgmt. 1999-), Ala. State Bar (commr. 1981-89, disciplinary commn. 1981-84, v.p. 1985-86, pres.-elect 1989-90, pres. 1990-91), Am. Judicature Soc., Am. Inns of Ct., Bluewater Bay Sailing Club, Bluewater Bay Country Club, Phi Beta Kappa, Phi Delta Phi, Omicron Delta Kappa, Alpha Tau Omega.

ALBRITTON, WILLIAM HAROLD, IV, lawyer; b. Tuscaloosa, Ala., Mar. 21, 1960; s. William Harold III and Jane Rollins (Howard) A.; m. Lucille Smith, July 23, 1983; 1 child, Elizabeth Rollins. BA, U. Ala., Tuscaloosa, 1982, JD, 1985. Ptnr. Albrittons, Clifton, Alverson, Bowden, Moody P.C., Andalusia, Ala., 1985-2001; counsel Bradley, Arant, Rose & White, Birmingham, Ala., 2001—. Bd. dirs. The Bank, Andalusia; judge Mcpl. Ct. Andalusia, 1989-2000. Bd. dirs. Covington County Arts Coun., Andalusia, 1986-90, Andalusia City Schs. Found., 1991-2001, Andalusia Area C. of C., 1986-89; elder 1st Presbyn. Ch., Andalusia, 1990—. Mem. ABA, Ala. Bar Assn. (sec. pres.'s adv. task force 1986-88, chmn. com. on local bar activities 1990, task force on minority opportunity 1990-96, character and fitness com. 1991-96, chmn. 1993-96, chmn. com. solo practitioners & small firms 1997-99), Ala. Def. Lawyers Assn. (bd. dirs. young lawyers sect. 1991-96, amicus curiae com. 1992-2002), Internat. Assn. Def. Counsel, Am. Inns of Ct., Kiwanis. Avocations: scuba diving, music, photography, sailing, motorcycling. General civil litigation, Insurance, Workers' compensation. Office: One Federal Pl 1819 Fifth Ave N Birmingham AL 35203 E-mail: halbritton@bradleyarant.com.

ALBUM, JERALD LEWIS, lawyer; b. Monroe, La., Oct. 18, 1947; s. Natt B. and Rose Marie (Pickens) A.; m. Joan Abbey Lurie, July 30, 1983; children: Nicole, Jeffrey. BS, Tulane U., 1969, JD, 1973. Bar: La. 1973, Colo. 1990, Tex. 1992, U.S. Dist. Ct. (ea. dist.) La. 1975, U.S. Dist. Ct. (mid. dist.) La. 1980, U.S. Dist. Ct. (we. dist.) La. 1983, U.S. Ct. Appeals (5th cir.) 1976. Assoc. Mmahat, Gagliano, Duffy & Giordano, Metairie, La., 1973-79; assoc. to ptnr. Lemle, Kelleher, Hunley, Moss & Frilot, New Orleans, 1980-85; shareholder Abbott Simses, Album & Knister, New Orleans, 1985-96; ptnr. Album, Stovall, Radecker & Giordano, New Orleans, Reich, Meeks & Treadaway, Metairie, La., 2001—. Mem. La. Assn. of Def. Counsel, New Orleans Bar Assn., La. State Bar Assn. Avocations: golf, volleyball, gardening. Admiralty, General civil litigation, Personal injury (including property damage). Home: 4637 Southshore Dr Metairie LA 70002-1430 Office: Reich Meeks & Treadaway 3850 N Causeway Blvd Ste 1000 Metairie LA 70002-7247

ALCOTT, COLIN C. prosecutor; b. Balt., June 26, 1945; Grad., Johns Hopkins U., 1967; grad. cum laude, Ohio State U., 1976. Bar: N.Mex. 1976, Md. 1989. Pvt. practice, 1976—91; pros., 1991—. Mem.: N.Mex. State Bar (pres. 2003). Office: 237 S Fourth St Santa Rosa NM 88435

ALCOTT, MARK HOWARD, lawyer; b. New York, Aug. 11, 1939; s. Harvey and Rose (Eigerman) A.; m. Susan M. (Bell), Sept. 3, 1961; children: Jill, Laura, Daniel, Elizabeth. AB, Harvard U., 1961, LLB, 1964. Bar: N.Y. 1965, U.S. Dist. Ct. (so. and ea. dists.) N.Y. 1966, U.S. Ct. Appeals (2d cir.) 1966, U.S. Ct. Appeals (9th and 10th cirs.) 1980, U.S. Ct. Internat. Trade 1980, U.S. Supreme Ct. 1982, U.S. Ct. Appeals (D.C. cir.) 1983, D.C. 1984, U.S. Tax Ct. 1985; U.S. Ct. Appeals (1st. cir.),2000; U.S. Ct. Appeals (11th. cir.), 2003. Assoc. Paul, Weiss, Rifkind, Wharton, and Garrison, N.Y.C., 1964-73, ptnr., 1973—. Mediator Mandatory Mediation Program, U.S Dist. Ct. (so. dist.) N.Y.; spl. master, mediator commercial divsn. N.Y. Supreme Ct.; Spl. Master Appeals Divsn. first dept. Mem. Community Planning Bd., Riverdale, N.Y., 1970-72; comr. Larchmont, N.Y. Planning Commn., 1982-94; bd. dir. Mosholu-Montefiore Community Ctr., Bronx, N.Y., 1966-77. Fellow: N.Y. Bar Found., Am. Coll. Trial Lawyers (chmn. downstate N.Y. com., 1994-1996, chmn. internat. com., 1998-2002); mem.: Fed. Bar Coun., Internat. Bar Assn. (bus. law sect., internat. litigation com.), Assn. Bar : City of N.Y. (fed. legis. com. 1970—73), N.Y. State Bar Assn. (chmn. internat. litigation com. comml. and fed. litigation sect. 1989—92, sec. exec. com., exec. vice chmn. 1992—93, sect. chmn.-elect 1993—94, sect. chmn. 1994—95, mem. ho. of dels., mem. exec. com., v.p., spl commn. on campaign finance reform, 1997—99), ABA (litigation sect. internat. litigation com.). Avocation: sailing. Federal civil litigation, General civil litigation. Office: Paul Weiss Rifkind Wharton & Garrison 1285 Ave Americas New York NY 10019-6064

ALCOX, PATRICK JOSEPH, lawyer; b. Cleve., Oct. 27, 1946; s. William B. and Helen T. Alcox; m. Karen Woelfle, Oct. 20, 1979; children: Caitlin M., Molly C. BBA, Cleve. State U., 1970; MBA, Kent State U., 1974; JD, Cleve.-Marshall Coll. Law, 1976. Bar: Ohio, 1976, U.S. Supreme Ct., 1983. Group mgr. IRS, Cleve., 1972-76; fin. account exec. Internat. Mgmt. Group, Cleve., 1976-80; pvt. practice Cleve., 1980—. Ward leader Berea (Ohio) Republican Com., 1985-97; chmn. Berea CSC, 1988-92. Personal injury (including property damage), Probate (including wills, trusts), Workers' compensation. Home: 448 Woodridge Cir Berea OH 44017-2227 Office: 75 Public Sq Ste 650 Cleveland OH 44113-2003

ALDAVE, BARBARA BADER, law educator, lawyer; b. Tacoma, Dec. 28, 1938; d. Fred A. and Patricia W. (Burns) Bader; m. Rafael Aldave, Apr. 2, 1966; children: Anna Marie, Anthony John. BS, Stanford U., 1960; JD, U. Calif.-Berkeley, 1966. Bar: Oreg. 1966, Tex. 1982. Assoc. law firm, Eugene, Oreg., 1967-70; asst. prof. U. Oreg., 1970-73, prof., 2000—; vis. prof. U. Calif., Berkeley, 1973-74; from vis. prof. to prof. U. Tex., Austin, 1974-89, co-holder James R. Dougherty chair for faculty excellence, 1981-82, Piper prof., 1982, Joe A. Worsham centennial prof., 1984-89, Liddell, Sapp, Zivley, Hill and LaBoon prof. banking financial and comml. law, 1989; dean Sch. Law, prof. St. Mary's U., San Antonio, 1989-98, Ernest W. Clemens prof. corp. law, 1996-98; Loran L. Stewart prof. corp. law, dir., Ctr. for Law and Entrepreneurship U. Oreg. Sch. Law, 2000—. Vis. prof. Northeastern U., 1985-88, 98, Boston Coll. 1999-2000, Cornell U., 2002; ABA rep. to Coun. Inter-ABA, 1995-99; NAFTA chpt. 19 panelist, 1994-96. Pres. NETWORK, 1985-89; chair Gender Bias Task Force of Supreme Ct. Tex., 1991-94; bd. dirs. Tex. Alliance Children's Rights, Lawyer's Com. for Civil Rights Under Law of Tex., 1995-2000; nat. chair Gray Panthers, 1999—. Recipient tchg. excellence award U. Tex. Student Bar Assn., 1976, Appreciation awards Thurgood Marshall Legal Soc. of U. Tex., 1979, 81, 85, 87, Tchg. Excellence award Chicano Law Students Assn. of U. Tex., 1984, Hermine Tobolowsky award Women's Law Caucus of U. Tex., 1985, Ethics award Kugle, Stewart, Dent & Frederick, 1988, Leadership award Women's Law Assn. St. Mary's U., 1989, Ann. Inspirational award Women's Advocacy Project, 1989, Appreciation award San Antonio Black Lawyers Assn., 1990, Spl. Recognition award Nat. Conv. Nat. Lawyers Guild, 1990, Spirit of the Am. Woman award J. C. Penney Co., 1992, Sarah T. Hughes award Women and the Law sect. State Bar Tex., 1994, Ann. Tchg. award Soc. Am. Law Tchrs., 1996, Legal Svcs. award Mexican-Am. Legal Def. and Ednl. Fund, 1996, Woman of Justice award NETWORK, 1997, Ann. Peacemaker award Camino a la Paz, 1997, Outstanding Profl. in the Cmty. award Dept. Pub. Justice, St. Mary's U., 1997, Charles Hamilton Houston award Black Allied Law Students Assn. St. Mary's U., 1998, Woman of Yr. award Tex. Women's Polit. Caucus, 1998, award Clin. Legal Edn. Assn., 1998, lifetime achievement award Jour. Law and Religion, 1998, Harriet Tubman award African-Am. Reflections, 2002. Mem.: ABA (com. on corp laws, sect. banking and bus. law 1982—88), Tex.-Mex. Bar Assn., Bexar County Women's Bar Assn. (Belva Lockwood Outstanding Lawyers award 1991), Stanford U. Alumni Assn., Harlan Soc., Order of Coif, Delta Theta Phi (Outstanding Law Prof award St. Mary's U. chpt. 1990, 1991), Omicron Delta Kappa, Iota Sigma Pi, Phi Delta Phi. Roman Catholic. Home: 86399 N Modesto Dr Eugene OR 97402-9031 Office: U Oreg Sch Law Eugene OR 97403-1221 E-mail: baldave@law.uoregon.edu., balaw98@aol.com.

ALDEN, STEVEN MICHAEL, lawyer; b. L.A., May 19, 1945; s. Herbert and Sylvia Zina (Hochman) A.; m. Evelyn Mae Subotky, Dec. 31, 1977; children: Carissa Louise, Bramley Marshall, Darym Alexander. AB, UCLA, 1967; JD, U. Calif., Berkeley, 1970. Bar: Calif. 1971, N.Y. 1971. Assoc. Debevoise & Plimpton, N.Y.C., 1971-78, ptnr., 1979—. Lectr., seminar panelist Practising Law Inst., N.Y.C., 1981—; panelist, lectr. N.Y. State Bar, Albany, 1984. Contbr. articles to profl. jours. Mem. ABA (real estate fin. com.), Assn. of Bar of City of N.Y. (com. real property law), Am. Land Title Assn. (assoc. lender's counsel group), Am. Coll. Real Estate Lawyers, Am. Coll. Mortgage Attys., Order of Coif, Phi Beta Kappa, Sky Club (N.Y.C.). Republican. Property, real (including real estate development, water). Office: Debevoise & Plimpton 919 3rd Ave Fl 42 New York NY 10022

ALDERMAN, SILVIA MORELL, lawyer; b. Havana, Cuba, Oct. 29, 1952; came to U.S., 1960; d. Jose and Rosa (Varona) Morell; m. Michael James Alderman, June 21, 1976; 1 child, Matthew. BS, Chadron State Coll., 1973; JD, Fla. State U., 1977. Asst. gen. counsel Dept. Environ. Regulation, Tallahassee, 1977-82, dep. gen. counsel, 1982-84; assoc., ptnr. Swann & Haddock, P.A., Tallahassee, 1984-87; ptnr. Katz, Kutter, Alderman & Bryant P.A., Tallahassee, 1987—. Adj. prof. Fla. State U. Coll. Law, 1994-95. Mem. Fla. Bar (chmn. environ. and land use law sect. 1986-87), ABA (exec. coun. adminstrv. law sect. 1993-95). Administrative and regulatory, Environmental, Land use and zoning (including planning). Office: Katz Kutter Alderman et al PA 106 E College Ave Ste 1200 Tallahassee FL 32301-7746 E-mail: silvia@katzlaw.com.

ALDISERT, RUGGERO JOHN, judge; b. Carnegie, Pa., Nov. 10, 1919; s. John S. and Elizabeth (Magnacca) Aldisert; m. Agatha Maria DeLacio, Oct. 4, 1952; children: Lisa Maria, Robert, Gregory. BA, U. Pitts., 1941, JD, 1947. Bar: Pa. 1947. Gen. practice law, Pitts., 1947—61; judge Ct. Common Pleas, Allegheny County, 1961—68, U.S. Ct. Appeals (3d cir.), Pitts., 1968—84, chief judge, 1984—87, sr. judge Pitts., Santa Barbara, Calif., 1987—. Adj. prof. law U. Pitts. Sch. Law, 1964—87; faculty Appellate Judges Seminar, NYU, 1971—85, assoc. dir., 1979—85; chmn. Fed. Appellate Judges Seminar, 1972—78; mem. Pa. Civil Procedural Rules Com., 1965—84, Jud. Conf. Com. on Adminstrn. Criminal Law, 1971—77; chmn. adv. com. on bankruptcy rules Jud. Conf. U.S., 1979—84; vis. prof. univs. in U.S. and abroad, 1965—99; intensive lectures at univs in , Italy, Germany, France, Poland, Croatia and Serbia. Author: Il Ritorno al Paese, 1966—67, The Judicial Process, Readings, Materials and Cases, 1996, 2d edit., 1996, Logic for Lawyers: A Guide to Clear Legal Thinking, 1997, 3d edit., 1997, Opinion Writing, 1990, Winning on Appeal, 1999; contbr. over 30 articles to profl. publs. Allegheny dist. chmn. Multiple Sclerosis Soc., 1961—68; pres. ISDA, Cultural Heritage Found., 1965—68; trustee U. Pitts., 1968—; mem. bd. visitors Pitts. Sch. Law, 1968—, chmn., 1969—99. Maj. reserves USMC, 1942—46. Recipient Outstanding Merit award, Allegheny County Acad. Trial Lawyers, 1964. Mem.: Am. Law Inst., Italian Sons and Daus. Am. Fraternal Assn. (nat. pres. 1960—68), Omicron Delta Kappa, Phi Alpha Delta, Phi Beta Kappa. Democrat. Roman Catholic. Office: US Ct Appeals 120 Cremona Dr Ste D Santa Barbara CA 93117-5511

ALDRICH, LOVELL W(ELD), lawyer; b. Port Chester, N.Y., Dec. 21, 1942; s. Laurence Weld and Leota A.; m. Sharon King, Aug. 20, 1966; children: Molly Colleen, Abigail Elizabeth. BBA in Fin., Tex. A&M U., 1965; JD, St. Mary's U., San Antonio, 1968. Bar: Tex. 1968, U.S. Dist. Ct. (so. dist.) Tex. 1971, U.S. Dist. Ct. (ea. dist.) Tex. 1980, U.S. Ct. Appeals (5th cir.) 1981. Assoc. Law Office of Fred Parks, Houston, 1970-72, Lloyd & Hoppess, Houston, 1972-75; pvt. practice Houston, 1975-78; ptnr. Aldrich & Buttrill, Houston, 1978-81, Aldrich, Buttrill & Kuhn, Houston, 1981-87, Lovell W. Aldrich & Assocs., A Profl. Legal Corp., Houston, 1987-98; pvt. practice Sugar Land, Tex., 1998—. Capt. U.S. Army, 1968-70, Vietnam. Mem. Tex. Bar Assn., Am. Bd. Trial Advs. Episcopalian. Avocations: travel, golf, photography, reading. General civil litigation, State civil litigation, Personal injury (including property damage). Home and Office: Lovell W Aldrich PC 1007 Horseshoe Dr Sugar Land TX 77478-0377

ALDRICH, RICHARD KINGSLEY, lawyer; b. Denver, Dec. 31, 1943; s. Harold Eugene and Mary Frances (Kingsley) A.; m. Katherine Ann Kirwan, Sept. 26, 1970; children: Amy Marie Aldrich McAffee, Lori Ann Aldrich Selwyn, Sara Kathleen. Student, Tex. Tech. U., 1962-64; BA in History, U. Mont., 1966, JD, 1969. Bar: Mont. 1969, U.S. Dist. Ct. Mont. 1969. Staff atty. Office of Field Solicitor, Dept. of Interior, Billings, Mont., 1969-85, field solicitor, supervising atty., 1985—. Bd. dirs. Billings Pub. Edn. Found., 1992-97, Mont. State U. Parent Assn., Bozeman, 1993-96, Billings Sr. Bronc Booster Club; bd. dirs., pres. Billings Sr. High Parent Adv., 1991-95. Recipient cert. of appreciation, U.S. Dept. Justice, Nat. Park Svc. and U.S. Fish and Wildlife Svc., 1994, 96, Dept. of Interior Meritorious award, 1998. Mem. ABA (spkr. panel presentation 1997, 2001, natural resources sect., environment and energy law sect., Indian law sect., sr. lawyers divsn.), Mont. State Bar, Yellostone County Bar, Phi Delta Phi, Sigma Nu. Avocations: long distance running, skiing, fly fishing, hiking, reading. Office: Dept of Interior Office of Field Solicitor 316 N 26th St Ste 3005 Billings MT 59101-1373

ALEGI, PETER CLAUDE, lawyer; b. New Haven, July 26, 1935; s. Claude D. and Margaret (Lettieri) A.; children from previous marriage: Gregory, Daniel, Peter; m. Lynda M. Martin. BA cum laude, Yale U., 1956, LL.B., 1959; postgrad. Fulbright scholar, U. Rome, Italy, 1959-60. Bar: Conn. 1959, R.I. 1962, Ill. 1965, U.S. Supreme Ct. 1965. Assoc. Hinckley, Allen, Salisbury Parsons, Providence, R.I., 1961-64, Baker & McKenzie, Chgo., 1964-65; ptnr. Milan & Rome, 1966-87; prin. Alegi & Assocs., Rome, 1987-2001; of counsel Ughi & Nunziante, Rome, 2001—. Vis. lectr. Temple U. Law Sch., Phila., 1980-81, Yale U. Law Sch., New Haven, 1981—; bd. regents Marymount Sch., Rome, 1992-98; provost Am. U. Rome, 1997-98; bd. trustees St. Thomas More Corp., Yale U. Author: Italian Income Taxation, 1988, 2d edit., 1994; contbr. articles to profl. jours. Chmn. Democrats Abroad-Italy, 1976-87, Democrats Abroad-Worldwide, 1991-95; mem. Dem. Nat. Com., 1984-95,96—, commr. Fulbright Commn., Rome, 1979-90; del. Dem. Nat. Convs., 1988, 92, 96, 2000; Rome com. U.S. C. of C. for Italy, 1994-96. Mem. ABA, Yale Law Alumni Assn. (exec. com. 1985-92, treas. 1991-92), Centro Studi Americani (v.p.), Italian Assn. Tax Advisors, Internat. Bar Assn., Internat. Fiscal Assn. Clubs: Tennis Parioli (Rome). Roman Catholic. Office: Alegi & Assocs Ughi & Nunziante Via Venti Settembre 1 00187 Rome Italy E-mail: pcalegi@tin.it., p.alegi@unlaw.

ALEKSANDER, NICHOLAS P. lawyer; b. London, May 5, 1959; m. Tobe Bendeth, Sept. 1, 1985; children: Isabelle, Abigail. MA, U. Cambridge, Eng., 1983; Law Soc. Finals, London Guildhall U., 1984. Bar: solicitor Supreme Ct. Eng. and Wales 1986. Articled clk. Bristows, Cooke & Carpmael, London, 1984-86; assoc., 1986, Travers Smith Braithwaite, London, 1986-93; ptnr., 1993-2000, Gibson, Dunn & Crutcher, London, 2001—. Contbr. articles to profl. jours., chpts. to books. Fellow Royal Soc. Arts; mem. Internat. Commn. Jurists (mem. exec. bd. Brit. sect.), Internat. Fiscal Assn., Law Soc. Eng. and Wales. Corporate taxation, Taxation, general. Office: Gibson Dunn & Crutcher 2-4 Temple Ave Telephone Ho London EC4Y OHB England Fax: 44 20 7071 4244.

ALESIA, JAMES H(ENRY), judge; b. Chgo., July 16, 1934; m. Kathryn P. Gibbons, July 8, 1961; children: Brian J., Daniel J. BS, Loyola U., Chgo., 1956; JD, Ill. Inst. Tech., Chgo., 1960; grad. Nat. Jud. Coll., U. Nev., 1976. Bar: Ill. 1960, Minn. 1970. Police officer City of Chgo., 1957-61; assoc. Law Office Anthony Scariano, Chicago Heights, Ill., 1960-61, Pretzel & Stouffer, Chgo., 1961-63; asst. gen. counsel Chgo. & North Western Transp. Co., 1963-70; assoc. Rerat Law, Mpls., 1970-71; asst. U.S. atty. No. Dist. Ill., Chgo., 1971-73; trial counsel Chessie Sys., Chgo., 1973; U.S. adminstrv. law judge Chgo., 1973-82; ptnr. Reuben & Proctor (merged with Isham, Lincoln & Beale), Chgo., 1982-87; judge U.S. Dist. Ct. for No. Dist. Ill., Chgo., 1987—. Mem. faculty Nat. Jud. Coll., U. Nev., Reno, 1979-80. Mem. FBA, Justinian Soc. Lawyers, Celtic Legal Soc. Republican. Roman Catholic. Office: US Dist Ct 219 S Dearborn St Chicago IL 60604-1800

ALESSANDRONI, VENAN JOSEPH, lawyer; b. N.Y.C., Mar. 1, 1915; s. Anthony P. and Andromeda (Rossini) A.; m. Alice Shaughnessy, Feb. 2, 1949 (dec. June 1973); m. Adelle Lincoln, Mar. 10, 1974. AB, Columbia U., 1937, JD, 1939. Bar: N.Y. 1941, also, Supreme Ct. of Korea 1946. Announcer CBS Artists Service, Inc., 1940; U.S. atty. Bd. Econ. Warfare, 1942; mem. U.S. Fgn. Econ. Adminstrn. Mission, Belgian Congo, 1943; sr. partner Wormser, Kiely, Alessandroni, Hyde & McCann (and predecessor firm), 1959—. Legal officer Mil. Govt. Korea, 1945-46; legal adviser to provincial gov. Kyunggi-Do, Korea, 1946; chief provost judge, City of Seoul, 1946; adj. prof., law sch. U. Miami, 1974— ; lectr. various tax insts., univs., profl. assns. Author: The Executor, 1963, Applied Estate Planning, 1963, also articles.; Departmental editor: Jour. Taxation, 1955-56. Recipient U.S. Army Commendation award, 1946; regional award N.Y. Times, 1932; Curtis medal Columbia, 1936 Estate planning, Probate (including wills, trusts). Home: Eggleston Ln Old Greenwich CT 06870 Office: Wormser Kiely Galef & Jacobs 825 3d Ave New York NY 10017-4014

ALESSI, ROBERT JOSEPH, lawyer, pharmacist, real estate developer; b. Rome, N.Y., Aug. 22, 1958; s. William John and Mary Jean A.; m. Ellen Mary Paczkowski, May 21, 1988; children: Laura C., Grace E. BS in Pharmacy, Union U., 1982; JD cum laude, Albany Law Sch., 1985. Bar: N.Y. 1986, U.S. Dist. Ct. (no. dist.) N.Y. 1986, U.S. Dist. Ct. (we. dist.) N.Y. 1986, U.S. Dist. Ct. (ea. dist.) N.Y. 1993, U.S. Dist. Ct. (so. dist.) N.Y. 1993, U.S. Ct. Appeals (2d cir.) 1995, U.S. Supreme Ct. 1996. Assoc. Nixon, Hargrave, Devans & Doyle, Albany, N.Y., 1985-90, LeBoeuf, Lamb, Greene & MacRae, Albany, 1990-93, ptnr., 1994—, mng. ptnr., 1999—; mng. dir. Hudson Heritage, L.L.C., 1999—. Adj. prof. law Albany Law Sch., 1989-94; town atty. Town of Bethlehem, 2001—. Co-author: Year 2000 Deskbook, 1998. Mem. master plan com. Town of Bethlehem, Delmar, N.Y., 1989-89, mem. planning bd. counsel, 1990-94. Mem. N.Y. State Bar Assn., Albany Law Sch. Environ. Alumni Group, Rockefeller Found. (advisor Pocantico roundtable consensus on brownfields). Avocations: tennis, fitness training, reading. General civil litigation, Environmental, Utilities, public. Home: 8 Partridge Rd Delmar NY 12054-3919 Office: LeBoeuf Lamb Greene & MacRae LLP One Commerce Plz Ste 2020 99 Washington Ave Albany NY 12210 Fax: 518-626-9010. E-mail: ralessi@llgm.com.

ALEXANDER, ALLISON L(ESLIE), lawyer; b. Washington; BS, Syracuse U., 1991; JD, U. Md., 1999. Bar: Md., D.C. Assoc. Piper Rudnick LLP, Washington, 1999—. Construction, Mergers and acquisitions, Finance. Office: Piper Rudnick LLP 1200 19th St NW Washington DC 20036 Office Fax: 202-223-2085.

ALEXANDER, CLIFFORD JOSEPH, lawyer; b. New Orleans, Oct. 2, 1943; s. Charles Ernest and Lois Primus (Boley) A.; m. Elizabeth McAnany, June 11, 1966; children: Brian, Heather, Rachel. AB, Rockhurst Coll., 1966; JD, Georgetown U., 1969. Bar: Mass. 1970, D.C. 1977. Mem. staff SEC, Washington, 1967-70; assoc. Gaston Snow & Ely Bartlett, Boston, 1970-75; mem. staff U.S. Senate Banking Com., Washington, 1975-77; mem. Kirkpatrick & Lockhart LLP (formerly Kirkpatrick, Lockhart, Hill, Christopher & Phillips, and predecessor), Washington, 1977—. Co-editor: Money Managers Compliance Manual. Mem. ABA (corp., banking and bus. law sect.), Boston Bar Assn., Fed. Bar Assn. (securities and banking law sects.), D.C. Bar Assn., Mass. Bar Assn., U.S. Supreme Ct. Bar. Banking, Securities, Corporate, general. Home: 8721 Bluedale St Alexandria VA 22308-2307 Office: Kirkpatrick & Lockhart 1800 Massachusetts Ave NW Fl 2 Washington DC 20036-1806

ALEXANDER, DONALD CRICHTON, lawyer; b. Pine Bluff, Ark., May 22, 1921; s. William Crichton and Ella Temple (Fox) A.; m. Margaret Louise Savage, Oct. 9, 1946; children: Robert C., James M. BA with honors, Yale U., 1942; LLB magna cum laude, Harvard U., 1948; LLD (hon.), St. Thomas Inst., 1975, Capital U., 1989. Bar: D.C. 1949, Ohio 1954, N.Y. 1978. Assoc. Covington & Burling, Washington, 1948-54, Taft, Stettinius & Hollister, Cin., 1954-56, ptnr., 1956-66, Dinsmore, Shohl, Coates & Deupree, Cin., 1966-73; commr. IRS, 1973-77; mem. Commn. on Fed. Paperwork, 1975-77; ptnr. Olwine, Connelly, Chase, O'Donnell & Weyher, N.Y.C., Washington, 1977-79, Morgan, Lewis & Bockius, N.Y.C. and Washington, 1979-85, Cadwalader, Wickersham & Taft, Washington, 1985-93, Akin, Gump, Strauss, Hauer & Feld, Washington, 1993—. Mem. adv. bd. NYU Tax Inst., 1969-73, 77-87, Tax Mgmt., Inc., 1968-73, 77—; mem. adv. Treas. Dept., 1970-72; mem. adv. group to commr. IRS, 1969-70, chmn. exempt orgns. adv. group, 1987-89; mem. adv. bd. Mertens, 1986-2002, Maxwell Macmillan fed. Taxes 2d, 1989-92; commr. Martin Luther King, Jr. Fed. Holiday Commn., 1993-96; mem. Harvard Bd. Overseers' vis. com. to law sch., 1999—; mem. com. on univ. resources Harvard U., 2002—; mem. commn. on coal leasing, 1983-84. Author: The Arkansas Plantation, 1943; contbr. more than 50 articles on fed. taxation. Co-chmn. bd. advisors NYU/IRS Continuing Profl. Edn. Program, 1982-85; dir. Treasury Hist. Assn., 1996—. Served to maj. AUS, 1942-45. Decorated Silver Star, Bronze Star. Mem. ABA (vice chmn. taxation sect. 1967-68), Am. Law Inst. (tax adv. group), U.S. C. of C. (taxation com. 1981-91, bd. dirs. 1984-89, health and employee benefit com. 1989-94, regulatory affairs com. 1993-98), Chevy Chase Club (Md.), Met. Club, Nantucket Yacht Club (Mass.), Mill Reef Club (Antigua, B.W.I.), Yale Club N.Y. Pension, profit-sharing, and employee benefits, Corporate taxation, Taxation, general. Home: 2801 New Mexico Ave NW Washington DC 20007-3921 Office: Akin Gump Strauss Hauer & Feld 1333 New Hampshire Ave NW Washington DC 20036-1564 Business E-Mail: dalexander@akingump.com.

ALEXANDER, DONALD G. state supreme court justice; Grad., Bowdoin Coll.; JD, U. Chgo. Bar: Maine. Mem. Sen. Edmund Muskie's staff; asst. Maine atty. gen., 1974-76; dep. atty. gen.; judge Dist. Ct., 1978, Maine Superior Ct., 1980-98; justice Maine Supreme Jud. Ct., 1998—. Office: Cumberland County Courthouse PO Box 368 142 Federal St Portland ME 04112-0368

ALEXANDER, FRED CALVIN, JR., lawyer; b. Abingdon, Va., Nov. 4, 1931; s. Fred C. and Mary F. (White) A.; m. Betsy Jones, May 17, 1957 (div.); children— Mitchell, Mary, Marjorie, Margaret; m. Janet Lee Hammond, Jan. 2, 1982 Student, Davidson Coll., 1950-52; BA, U. Va., 1954, LLB, 1959. Bar: Va. 1959, U.S. Dist. Ct. (ea. dist.) Va. 1959, U.S. Ct. Appeals (4th cir.) 1960. Assoc. Boothe, Prichard & Dudley, Alexandria, Va., 1959-64; ptnr. McGuire, Woods, Battle & Boothe LLP and predecessor firms, Alexandria, Va., 1964-97, ret. McLean, Va., 1997. Mem. jud. conf. U.S. Ct. Appeals (4th cir.), 1964-99; lectr. legal edn. Va. State Bar, 1970, 75-77, 89; chmn. adv. com. rules of ct. Supreme Ct. of Va., 1984-98; bd. dirs. Thomas Rutherfoord, Inc. Past bd. dirs. counsel to Alexandria Hosp., St. Stephens Sch. 1st lt. U.S. Army, 1954-56. Fellow Am. Coll. Trial Lawyers (chmn. Va. com. 1994-96), Va. Law Found.; mem. Alexandria Bar Assn. (pres. 1969-70), Va. Bar Assn. (chmn. civil litigation sect. 1989-92), Va. Assn. Def. Attys., Va. Trial Lawyers Assn., Nat. Assn. R.R. Trial Counsel, Def. Rsch. Inst. (chmn. railroad law com. 1989-92), Belle Haven Country Club (bd. dirs. 1997-2000, 2001–), Wyndemere Country Club. Episcopalian. General civil litigation, Insurance, Professional liability. Home: 1313 Gatewood Dr Alexandria VA 22307-2033 Office: McGuire Woods LLP 1750 Tysons Blvd Ste 1800 Mc Lean VA 22102-4231

ALEXANDER, GEORGE JONATHON, law educator, former dean; b. Berlin, Mar. 8, 1931; s. Walter and Sylvia (Grill) A.; m. Katharine Violet Sziklai, Sept. 6, 1958; children: Susan Katina, George Jonathon II. AB with maj. honors, U. Pa., 1953, JD cum laude, 1969; LLM, Yale U., 1965, JSD, 1969. Bar: Ill. 1960, N.Y. 1961, Calif. 1974. Instr. law, Bigelow fellow U. Chgo., 1959-60; instr. internat. relations Naval Res. Officers Sch., Forrest Park, Ill., 1959-60; prof. law Syracuse U. Coll. Law, 1960-70, assoc. dean, 1968-69; prof. law U. Santa Clara (Calif.) Law Sch., 1970—, disting. univ. prof., 1994-95, Elizabeth H. and John A. Sutro prof. law, 1995—, pres. faculty senate, 1996-97, dean, 1970-85, dir. Inst. Internat. and Comparative Law, 1986—, dir. grad. programs, 1998-2001, co-dir., 2002. Dir. summer programs at Oxford, Geneva, Strasbourg, Budapest, Tokyo, Hong Kong, Beijing, Shanghai, Ho Chi Minh City, Singapore, Bangkok, Kuala Lumpur, Seoul, Munich; vis. prof. law U. So. Calif., 1963; vis. scholar Stanford (Calif.) U. Law Sch., 1985-86, 92; cons. in field. Author: Civil Rights, U.S.A., Public Schools, 1963, Honesty and Competition, 1967, Jury Instructing on Medical Issues, 1966, Cases and Materials on Space Law, 1971, The Aged and the Need for Surrogate Management, 1972, Commercial Torts, 1973, 2d edit. 1988, U.S. Antitrust Laws, 1980, Writing A Living Will: Using a Durable Power of Attorney, 1988, (with Scheflin) Law and Mental Disabilities, 1998; author, editor: International Perspectives on Aging, 1992; also articles, chpts. in books, one film. Dir. Domestic and Internat. Bus. Problems Honors Clinic, Syracuse U., 1966-69, Regulations in Space Project, 1968-70; ednl. cons. Comptroller Gen. U.S., 1977—; mem. Nat. Sr. Citizens Law Ctr., 1983-89, pres., 1986-90. With USN, 1953-56. U.S. Navy scholar U. Pa., 1949-52; Law Bds. scholar, 1956-59; Sterling fellow Yale, 1964-65; recipient Ralph E. Kharas Civil Liberties award, Syracuse U. Sch. Law, 1970, Owens award as Alumnus of Yr., 1984, Disting. prof. Santa Clara Univ. Faculty Senate, 1994-95, 2000 award for outstanding contbns. to cause of civil liberties Freedom of Thought Found.; named Disting. Vis. Prof. Krems Danube U., Vienna, 2001. Mem. Internat. Acad. Law Mental Health (mem. sci. com. 1997-99), Calif. Bar Assn. (first chmn. com. legal problems of aging), Assn. Am. Law Schs., Soc. Am. Law Tchrs. (dir., pres. 1979, Visionary Activist for Equality, Access and Diversity Throughout Law and Soc. award 2000), AAUP (chpt. pres. 1962), N.Y. Civil Liberties Union (chpt. pres. 1965, dir., v.p. 1966-70), Am. Acad. Polit. and Social Sci., Order of Coif, Justinian Honor Soc., Phi Alpha Delta (chpt. faculty adviser 1967-70) Home: 11600 Summit Wood Ct Los Altos Hills CA 94022 Office: U Santa Clara Sch Law Santa Clara CA 95053-0001 E-mail: gjalexander@aya.yale.edu.

ALEXANDER, GERRY L. state supreme court chief justice; b. Aberdeen, Wash., Apr. 28, 1936; BA, U. Wash., 1958, JD, 1964. Bar: Wash. 1964, U.S. Supreme Ct. 2000. Pvt. practice, Olympia, Wash., 1964—73; judge Wash. Superior Ct., Olympia, 1973—85, Wash. Ct. Appeals Divsn. II, Tacoma, 1985—95; state supreme ct. justice Wash. Supreme Ct., Olympia, 1995—2000, state supreme ct. chief justice, 2000—. Lt. U.S. Army, 1958—61. Mem.: ABA, Statute Law Com., Washington Cts. Hist. Soc., Bench-Bar-Press (chair), Puget Sound Inn of Ct. (pres. 1996), Thurston-Mason County Assn. (pres. 1973), Wash. State Bar Assn., Am. Judges Assn. Office: Temple of Justice PO Box 40929 Olympia WA 98504-0929 E-mail: j_g.alexander@courts.wa.gov.

ALEXANDER, GREGORY STEWART, law educator, educator; b. 1948; BA, Ill. U., 1970; JD, Northwestern U., 1973; postgrad., U. Chgo., 1974-75. Law clk. to chief judge U.S. Ct. Appeals, 1972-74; asst. prof. law U. Ga., 1975-78, assoc. prof., 1978-84; prof. Cornell U., Ithaca, N.Y., 1984—, A. Robert Noll prof. law, 2000—. Vis. prof. Harvard Law Sch., 1997—. Bigelow fellow U. Chgo., 1974-75; fellow Max-Planck Inst. (Germany), 1995-96. Fellow Ctr. Advanced Study in Behavioral Scis.; mem. Am. Soc. Politics and Legal Philosophy, Am. Soc. Legal History. Office: Cornell U Law Sch Myron Taylor Hall Ithaca NY 14853 E-mail: gsa9@cornell.edu.

ALEXANDER, KATHARINE VIOLET, lawyer; b. N.Y.C., Nov. 19, 1934; d. George Clifford and Violet (Jambor) Sziklai; m. George Jonathon Alexander, Sept. 6, 1958; children: Susan Katina, George J. II. Student, Smith Coll., Geneva, 1954-55; BA, Goucher Coll., 1956; JD, U. Pa., 1959; student specialized courses, U. Santa Clara, 1974-76. Bar: Calif. 1974, U.S. Dist. Ct. (no. dist.) Calif. 1974, U.S. Ct. Appeals (9th cir.) 1974; cert. criminal lawyer Calif. State Bar Bd. Legal Specialization. Research dir., adminstr. Am. Bar Found., Chgo., 1959-60; lectr. law San Jose (Calif.) State U., 1972-74; sr. atty. Santa Clara County, San Jose, 1974-97, ret., 1997. Editor: Mentally Disabled and the Law, 1961; contbg. author: The Aged and the Need for Surrogate Management, 1969-70, Jury Instructions on Medical Issues, 1965-67. Community rep. Office Econ. Opportunity Com., Syracuse, N.Y., 1969-70. Mem. AAUW, Food and Wine Inst., Calif. Bar Assn., Santa Clara County Bar Assn. (trustee 1981-82), Calif. Attys. for Criminal Justice (bd. govs. 1988-92), Jr. League, Anthropology and Stanford Museum of Arts. Presbyterian. Avocations: stock market, gourmet, traveling. Home and Office: 11600 Summit Wood Ct Los Altos Hills CA 94022-4500 Fax: 650-948-7596. E-mail: Katharine_Alexander@mail.com.

ALEXANDER, KENT B. lawyer; b. Atlanta, Nov. 7, 1958; BA in Polit. Sci. magna cum laude, Tufts U., 1980; JD, U. Va., 1983. Bar: Ga. 1983. Assoc. Long & Alridge, Atlanta, 1983-85; asst. U.S. atty. for no. dist. Ga., U.S. Dept. Justice, Atlanta, 1985-92, U.S. atty., 1994-97; of counsel, ptnr. King & Spalding, Atlanta, 1992-94, ptnr., 1997-99; sr. v.p., gen. counsel Emory Univ., 2000—. Co-founder Hands On Atlanta. Office: Emory Univ 401 Administration Bldg Atlanta GA 30322-0001

ALEXANDER, LAMAR (ANDREW LAMAR ALEXANDER), senator, former secretary of education, former governor, lawyer; b. Maryville, Tenn., July 3, 1940; s. Andrew Lamar and Genevra Floreine (Rankin) A.; m. Leslee Kathryn Buhler, Jan. 4, 1969; children: Andrew, Leslee, Kathryn, Will. BA, Vanderbilt U., 1962; JD, NYU, 1965. Bar: Tenn. 1965. Law clk. to Hon. John Wisdom U.S. Ct. Appeals (5th cir.), New Orleans; assoc. Fowler, Rountree, Fowler & Robertson, Knoxville, 1965; legis. asst. to Senator Howard Baker, 1967-68; exec. asst. to Bryce Harlow, White House Congl. Liaison Office, 1969-70; ptnr. Dearborn and Ewing, Nashville, 1970-76; gov. State of Tenn., Nashville, 1979-87; chmn. Leadership Inst. Belmont Coll., Nashville, 1987-88; pres. U. Tenn., 1988-91; sec. Dept. Edn., Washington, 1991-93; counsel Baker, Donelson, Bearman & Caldwell, Nashville, 1993-98; pvt. practice Nashville, 1999—2001; U.S. senator from Tenn., 2003—. Mem. Pres.'s Task Force on Federalism; chmn. Nat. Govs. Assn., 1985-86, Pres.'s Commn. on Ams. Outdoors, 1985-87; co-director Empower Am., 1994-95; Goodman vis. prof. practice of pub. svc. Harvard U., 2001. Author: Steps Along the Way, 1986, Six Months Off, 1988, We Know What To Do, 1995; co-editor: The New Promise of American Life, 1995. Mgr. Winfield Dunn for Gov. Campaign, 1970, chief transition, 1970-71; Rep. nominee for Gov. of Tenn., 1974; chmn. Rep. Exch. Satellite Network, 1993-95; Rep. Presdl. candidate, 1995-96. Recipient Nat. Disting. Svc. to Edn. award Burger King, 1988, James B. Conant award Edn. Commn. of the States, 1988, Disting. State Leadership award Am. Assn. State Colls. and Univs., 1989, Teddy Roosevelt award Nat. Coll. Athletic Assn., 1993, honored as Silver Anniversary scholar-athlete, 1987; NYU Law Sch. Root-Tilden scholar. Fellow (sr.) Hudson Inst.; mem. Phi Beta Kappa. Republican. Presbyterian. Office: Off of Senator Alexander Dirksen 40 Ste 2 Washington DC 20510*

ALEXANDER, MILES JORDAN, lawyer; b. Reading, Pa., Nov. 20, 1931; s. Abe Alexander and Sarah (Gold) Fidlow; m. Elaine Eve Barron, May 29, 1955; children: Kent, David, Michael, Paige. BA in Polit. Sci. with honors., Emory U., 1952; LLB cum laude, Harvard U., 1955. Bar: Ga. 1955, D.C. 1977. Assoc. Kilpatrick & Stockton, Atlanta, summers 1954-55; teaching fellow Harvard U., Cambridge, 1957-58; assoc. Kilpatrick Stockton LLP, Atlanta, 1958-63; chmn. Kilpatrick & Stockton LLP, Atlanta, 1996—. Lectr. P.L.I., Internat. Trademark Assn., Am. Law Inst., ABA Internat. Franchise Assn., other seminars on trademarks and unfair competition, antitrust, franchising, dispute resolutions and litigation tactics; guest lectr. on trademark law NYU, U.Ga., Ga. State Law Sch., also bd. visitors; bd. visitors Emory U.; chmn. trademark pub. adv. com. Emory U., 2000—. Editor-in-chief: The Trademark Reporter, 1978-80; contbr. numerous articles to jours. in trademark field. Mem. City of Atlanta Ethics Bd., chmn., vice-chmn., 1980-92, Emory U. and Harvard Law Sch. Alumni Funds; legal counsel to Mayor Maynard Jackson, 1974-82, 89-93; chmn. City of Atlanta Lic. Rev. Bd., 1976-79; former pres. Am. Jewish Com.; mem. Friends of Morehouse Coll.; adv. bd. Family Outreach Ctr.; mem. adv. coun. J. Thomas McCarthy Inst. Intellectual Property and Tech. Law, 2001--. Capt. USAF, 1955-57. Recipient Human Rels. award Anti-Defamation League, 1997, Disting. Alumni award Emory U., 2000. Fellow Am. Bar Found., Am. Coll. Trial Lawyers; mem. ABA, Internat. Trademark Assn. (counsel 1997-2000, chmn. trademark pub. adv. com. 2000—), Ga. Bar Assn., Ga. State Bar Assn. (former chmn. antitrust sect., advisor to legal counsel 1997—), Atlanta Bar Assn., Lawyers Club Atlanta, Internat. Trademark Assn. (lectr., bd. dirs. 1980-82, rev. commn. 1986, legal counsel 1987-2000), Am. Law Inst. (adv. com. restatement of law of unfair competition 1986-95), J. Thomas McCarthy Inst. for Intellectual Property and Tech. Law (charter mem. adv. coun.), 191 Club (bd. dirs.), Atlanta City Club (chmn. bd.), Commerce Club, Standard Club, Old War Horse Lawyers Club , Phi Beta Kappa. Avocations: reading, sports. Antitrust, Federal civil litigation, Trademark and copyright. Office: Kilpatrick Stockton LLP 1100 Peachtree St NE Ste 2800 Atlanta GA 30309-4530

ALEXANDER, RICHARD ELMONT, lawyer; b. Yellow Springs, Ohio, Dec. 14, 1924; s. Joseph Arthur and Charlotte (Gunckel) A.; Student U. Dayton, 1942-43, Carnegie Inst. Tech., 1943-44, 46-47; J.D., U. Chgo., 1950. Bar: Ohio 1951, U.S. Ct. Customs and Patent Appeals 1955, Ill. 1956, U.S. Dist. Ct. (no. dist.) Ill. 1958, U.S. Patent Office 1958, U.S. Dist. Ct. (ea. dist.) Calif. 1968, U.S. Supreme Ct. 1971, U.S. Ct. Appeals (4th, 7th and 9th cirs.) 1975, U.S. Ct. Appeals (2d cir.) 1977, U.S. Ct. Appeals (1st cir.) 1980, U.S. Ct. Appeals (D.C. cir.) 1982. Patent atty. Gen. Motors Corp., Washington, 1953-55; assoc. Wilkinson, Huxley, Byron & Hume, Chgo., 1955-58; ptnr. Alexander & Slater, Chgo., 1958-59, Dawson, Tilton, Fallon, Lungmus & Alexander, Chgo., 1959-67, Alexander & Speckman, Chgo., 1967-74; prin. Richard E. Alexander, Chgo., 1975-81; ptnr. Alexander & Zalewa, Chgo., 1981-84, Alexander, Unikel, Bloom, Zalewa & Tenenbaum, Ltd., 1984-89, Alexander, Zalewa, Liss & Orloff, Ltd., 1989-91, Dickinson, Wright, Moon, Van Dusen & Freeman, 1991—. Bd. dirs. St. Leonard's House, Chgo., 1979-87, v.p., 1980-82; chmn. Inst. Clin. Social Work, Chgo., 1981-84; trustee Episcopal Charities, Chgo., 1982-88, v.p., 1984-88, Jo Daviess County Bd., 2002-. Served with U.S. Army, 1944-46. Decorated Purple Heart. Mem. ABA, Chgo. Bar Assn., U.S. Trademark Assn. (editorial bd. 1965-77), Chgo. Patent Law Assn., Sigma Alpha Epsilon. Episcopalian. Editor: Meditions of Andrew Morehouse, 1952. Federal civil litigation, State civil litigation, Trademark and copyright.

ALEXANDER, ROBERT GARDNER, lawyer; b. Madison, Wis., May 19, 1949; s. Charles Kohl and Jean (Gardner) A.; m. Karen Lynn Kaminski, Sept. 30, 1989; children: Elizabeth Jean, Sarah Lynn, Rebecca Ann. BA, U. Wis., 1971, JD, 1976; ML in Taxation, DePaul U., 1984. Bar: Wis. 1976, U.S. Dist. Ct. (we. dist.) Wis. 1976, U.S. Dist. Ct. (ea. dist.) Wis. 1978, U.S. Tax Ct. 1982, U.S. Ct. Appeals (7th cir.) 1983. Rsch. atty. U. Wis., Madison, 1976-77; atty. McLario Law Offices, Menomonee Falls, Wis., 1978-87, Alexander & Klemmon, S.C., Wauwatosa, Wis., 1987—. Trustee, sec. Falls Bapt. Ch., Inc., Menomonee Falls, 1987—; Preach the Word, Inc., Downers Grove, 1992—; adv. bd. Joy Bapt. Camp, Whitewater, Wis., 1992—. Mem. ABA, Nat. Acad. Elder Law Attys., Wis. State Bar, Milw. Estate Planning Counsel, Nat. Assn. Estate Planning Counselors (accredited estate planner), Ea. Wis. Planning Giving Counsel, Phi Kappa Phi. Republican. Avocations: music, art, sports. Estate planning, Probate (including wills, trusts), Estate taxation. Office: Alexander & Klemmer SC Ste 304 2675 N Mayfair Rd Wauwatosa WI 53226-1305 E-mail: alexlaw@exeepc.com.

ALEXANDER, WILLIAM BROOKS, lawyer, former state senator; b. Boyle, Miss., Dec. 23, 1921; s. William Brooks and Vivien (Beaver) A.; m. Belle McDonald, Mar. 12, 1950; children— Brooks, Becky, John, Jason, Grace. Student, Miss. Coll., 1940-42; LL.B., U. Miss., 1948. Bar: Miss. 1948. Ptnr. firm Alexander, Johnston & Alexander, Cleveland, 1948—; mem. Miss. Senate, 1960-83, past pres. pro tem. Past pres. Miss. Heart Assn.; bd. dirs. Miss. Coll. Served with AUS, 1942-46; bd. dirs. Delta Council, Miss. Econ. Council. Mem. Miss. Bar Assn. (Outstanding Legislator), Bolivar County Bar Assn., Am. Legion, VFW (past dep. comdr.) Clubs: Exchange. Lodges: Masons. Baptist. Office: PO Box 1737 Cleveland MS 38732-1737

ALEXIS, GERALDINE M. lawyer; b. N.Y.C., Nov. 3, 1948; d. William J. and Margaret Daly; m. Marcus Alexis, June 15, 1969; children: Marcus L., Hilary I., Sean C. BA, U. Rochester, 1971; MBA, JD, Northwestern U., 1976. Bar: Ill. 1976, Calif. 2001, U.S. Dist. Ct. (no. dist.): Calif. 1976, Ill. 1976, U.S. Trial Bar: 1985, U.S. Ct. Appeals (7th cir.): 1986, U.S. Ct. Appeals (5th cir.): 1996, bar: (U.S. Ct. Appeals (9th cir.)) 2002. Law clk. to Hon. John F. Grady, justice U.S. Dist. Ct. (no. dist.) Ill., Chgo., 1976-77; assoc. Sidley & Austin, Chgo., 1977-79, 81-83, ptnr., 1983-2000; advisor U.S. Dept. Justice Office Legal Counsel, Washington, 1979-81; ptnr. McCutchen, Doyle, Brown & Enersen (now Bingham McCutchen LLP), San Francisco, 2001—. Mem.: ABA (vice-chair fin. mkts. and instns. com. antitrust sect.), Bar Assn. San Francisco (chair antitrust and trade regulation sect.). Democrat. Antitrust, Federal civil litigation, Finance. Office: Bingham McCutchen LLP 3 Embarcadero Ctr San Francisco CA 94111

ALFANO, CHARLES THOMAS, SR., lawyer; b. Suffield, Conn., June 21, 1920; s. Dominick and Rosina (Dimartino) A.; m. Mary Ann Sinatro, Nov. 13, 1954; children: Diane Elizabeth, Andrea Rose, Charles Thomas Jr., Susan Marie. Student, Ill. Coll., 1939-40; BA cum laude, U. Conn., 1943; LL.B., JD, U. Mich., 1948. Bar: Conn. 1948. Since practiced in, Hartford; partner firm Alfano Halloran & Flynn; judge Town Ct. of Suffield, 1949-51, 55-59; mem. Conn. Senate, 1959-77, asst. majority leader, 1966, pres. pro tem, 1967-73, minority leader, 1973-75, v.p. pro tem, 1975-77; corp. counsel Town of Suffield, 1977-83. Dir., chmn. bd. Suffield Savs. Bank; dir. Conn. Water Co. Bd. dirs. Conn. Pub. TV. Served with USNR, 1942-47, PTO. Mem. ABA, ATLA, Conn. Bar Assn., Hartford County Bar Assn., Conn. Trial Lawyers Assn. (bd. dirs.), Hartford Club, Mystic Yacht Club, Mason's Island Yacht Club, N.Y. Athletic Club, KC, Sigma Nu. Home: 50 Marbern Dr Suffield CT 06078-1533 Office: 89 Oak St Hartford CT 06106-1515 also: 53 Mountain Rd Suffield CT 06078-2041

ALFINI, JAMES JOSEPH, dean, educator, lawyer; b. Yonkers, N.Y., Oct. 12, 1943; s. James Joseph and Olga (Genish) A.; m. Carol Miller, Dec. 23, 1966; children: David James, Michael Steven. AB, Columbia U., 1965; JD, Northwestern U., 1972. Bar: N.Y. 1973, Ill. 1976, U.S. Dist. Ct. (no. dist.) Ill. 1976, U.S. Ct. Appeals (7th cir.) 1982, U.S. Supreme Ct. 1977. Reginald Heber Smith cmty. lawyer Monroe County Legal Assistance Corp., Rochester, N.Y., 1972-73; asst. dir. research Am. Judicature Soc., Chgo., 1973-77, dir. rsch., 1977-80, asst. exec. dir. programs, 1980-85; adj. prof. law IIT Chgo.-Kent Sch. Law, 1978-85; assoc. prof. of law Fla. State U., Tallahassee, 1985-90, prof. law, 1990-91; dean, prof. No. Ill. U. Coll. Law, 1991-97, prof., 1997—. Co-author: (books) Making Jury Instructions Understandable, 1982, Judicial Conduct and Ethics, 1990, 95, 2000, Mediation Theory and Practice, 2000; mem. Christian Ch. Bd. Editors Ohio State Jour. Dispute Resolution, 1994-98. Mem. governing bd. Cook County Legal Assistance Found., 1981-83; arbitration and mediation rules com. Fla. Supreme Ct., 1988-91; mem. Ill. Jud. Ethics com., 1993-97; chmn. coord. coun. Nat. Ct. Orgns., 1982-83; bd. govs. Chgo. Coun. Lawyers. 1st lt. U.S. Army, 1965-69. Decorated Army Commendation medal. Mem. ABA (sect. dispute resolution, chair), ACLU, Am. Law Inst., Law and Soc. Assn. Democrat. E-mail: jalfini@niu.edu. Home: 525 Wing Ln Saint Charles IL 60174-2339

ALFORD, DUNCAN EARL, lawyer; b. Spartanburg, S.C., Oct. 17, 1963; s. Earl Curry and Martha Catherine (Van Ness) A.; m. Janet Lynne Gessner, Oct. 6, 1990. BA with high distinction, U. VA., 1985; postgrad., U. Calif.,

Berkeley, 1987; JD with honors, U. N.C., 1991; MLIS, U. SC, 2001. Bar: Ga. 1991, N.C. 1991, S.C. 1994. Bus. analyst McKinsey & Co., Inc., Atlanta, 1985-87; distbn. mgr. Eason Publs., Inc., Charlotte, N.C., 1988; law clk. to Hon. Burley B. Mitchell N.C. Supreme Ct., Raleigh, N.C., 1991-92; assoc. Kilpatrick & Cody, Atlanta, 1992-94; atty. Law Offices of Robert A. Hammett, Spartanburg, S.C., 1994-96; assoc. Robinson, Bradshaw & Hinson, PA, Rock Hill, S.C., 1997-2001, shareholder, 2001; reference law libr. Columbia U. Sch. Law, NYC, 2001—02; law librn. Princeton (N.J.) U., 2002—. Contbr. articles to profl. jours. Echols scholar U. Va. Mem. ABA, Phi Alpha Delta. Presbyterian. Avocations: running, golf, cycling. Corporate, general, Probate (including wills, trusts), Property, real (including real estate development, water). Home: 208 Loetscher Pl 1A Princeton NJ 08540 Office: Princeton U Firestone Libr 1 Washington Rd Princeton NJ 08544-2098

ALFORD, MARGIE SEARCY, lawyer, author; b. Tuscaloosa, Ala., Dec. 20, 1949; d. Joseph Alexander and Margaret Tyler (Zehmer) Searcy; m. Andrew Ray Alford, Sept. 4, 1992. BS, U. Ala., 1967-69, 70-71; student, U. Ams., Mexico City, 1969, Emory U., Atlanta, 1970; JD, U. Ala., 1974. Bar: Ala. 1974; U.S. Dist. Ct. (no. dist.) Ala. 1975. Assoc. univ. counsel U. Ala., Tuscaloosa, 1974-75; pvt. practice Tuscaloosa, 1975-92, Birmingham, Ala., 1992—. Editor-in-chief, prin. author: Matthew Bender's A Guide to Toxic Torts, 4 vols., 1986; contbg. author: Matthew Bender's Drug Product Liability, 4 vols.; contbr. numerous articles to legal jours., freelance writer for numerous publs. Group leader Ea. Area Diabetes Support Group, 1997—; mem. Trussville Area C. of C. Named Most Outstanding Young Career Woman in Ala. Ala. Bus. and Profl. Women, 1986. Mem. ATLA (twice nat. chair environ. and toxic tort law sect., twice nat. chair of women trial lawyers caucus), Nat. Assn. Women Bus. Owners, Bus. and Profl. Women, Ala. State Bar, Ala. Media Profls. Presbyterian. Avocations: collecting antique furniture and paintings, chow chow dog breeder, gardening, traveling. Criminal, Environmental, Personal injury (including property damage). Office: PO Box 610781 Birmingham AL 35261-0781 Fax: (205) 520-5083. E-mail: margialfor@aol.com.

ALFRED, STEPHEN JAY, retired lawyer; b. NYC, Aug. 15, 1934; s. George J. Alfred and Janet (Brenner) Miller; m. Nora Richman, June 24, 1956 (div. 1980); children: Deborah Susan, Lynda Beth, Bruce David, Julianne Richman; m. Lynne Belofsky Durchslag, Jan. 10, 1981 (div. 1992); m. Rita G. Hungate, Aug. 23, 1997. AB, Princeton U., 1956; JD, Harvard U., 1959. Bar: Ohio 1959. From assoc. to ptnr. Squire, Sanders & Dempsey, Cleve., 1959—97; councilman City of Shaker Hts., Ohio, 1972—79, 1981, mayor, 1984—91; exec. dir. Common Cause/Ga., 1998—2001; ret., 2001. Gen. chmn. Cleve. Tax Inst., 1981. Contbr. articles to profl. jours. Trustee Citizens League of Cleve., 1976-83, Com. for Sandy Springs, Atlanta, 1998-2001, vice-chair, 1999-2000; trustee Beech Brook Children's Home, Orange, Ohio, 1968-84, pres., 1971-72, treas., 1979-81; pres. Lomond Assn., Shaker Hts., 1965-67; active Peoria County Govt. Study Commn., Peoria, 2000-01; govt. vision task force Peoria Area C. of C., 2001-02; bd. dirs. Ill. Campaign for Polit. Reform, Chgo., 2000—, v.p., 2002—; bd. dirs. Mayors Vision 2020, Peoria, 2002—, Counseling and Family Svcs., Peoria, 2002—, v.p., 2003—; exec. dir. Ctrl. Ill. Biomed. Rsch. Group, 2000-02, vice-chmn., 2001-02; assoc. bd. dirs. WCBU, Peoria, 2001—, v.p., 2003—. Mem. Harvard U. Law Sch. Assn. of Cleve. (pres. 1982). Democrat. Jewish. Taxation, general. E-mail: sjalfred@aol.com.

ALHANKO, PETER, lawyer; b. Stockholm, Nov. 25, 1958; Grad. in internat. bus., Stockholm Sch. Econs., 1982; grad. in bus. law, U. Stockholm, 1984; grad. in corp. fin., Columbia U., 1987. Bar: Sweden 1992. Assoc. then ptnr. Advokatfirman Vinge, Stockholm, 1989—99; ptnr. Mannheimer Swartling Advokatbyra, 1999—. Mergers and acquisitions, Finance. Office: Mannheimer Swartling Advokatbyra Box 1711 111 87 Stockholm Sweden Fax: +46850576501. E-mail: pa@msa.se.

ALI, ARIF HYDER, lawyer; b. Chittagong, Bangladesh, June 13, 1964; , naturalized, U.S. s. Syed Hyder and Shireen Ali; m. Salma Hasan Ali, July 2, 1989; children: Saanya Syeda Hasan, Syed Zayd Akbar. BA summa cum laude, Columbia U., 1986; JD, NYU, 1990. Bar: D.C. 1991, Pa. 1990. Assoc. Shaw, Pittman, Potts & Trowbridge, Washington, 1990—91, Ackerson & Bishop, Washington, 1991—93; sect. head claims UN Compensation Commn., Geneva, 1993—96; sr. mgr. Freshfields, Bruckhaus, Derringer, Paris, 1997—99; sr. counsel World Intellectual Property Orgn. Arbitration and Mediation Ctr., Geneva, 1999—2001, Fulbright & Jaworski, Houston, 2001—. Expert UN Inst. Tng. and Rsch.; spkr. numerous internat. confs. on internat. comml. arbitration, dispute avoidance and resolution. Author: Dispute Avoidance and Resolution Best Practices for the Application Service Provider Industry, 2001; contbr. articles to profl. jours. and conf. procs. Founding mem. Digital Devel. Partnership, Global Tech. Exch., other internat. not-for-profit orgns. Recipient Order of Bahrain, King of Bahrain. Mem.: ABA (task force on E-commerce and alternative dispute resolution), Am. Soc. Internat. Law, Internat. Bar Assn., Phi Beta Kappa. Moslem. Avocations: squash, golf, cooking, travel. Alternative dispute resolution, Private international, Public international. Office: Fulbright & Jaworski 1301 McKinney Houston TX 77010 Office Fax: 713-651-5246. E-mail: aali@fulbright.com.

ALIN, ROBERT DAVID, lawyer; b. Mt. Vernon, NY, Oct. 10, 1952; s. Morris and Sylvia (Horowitz) A.; m. Arlene Susan Kerner, Feb. 14, 1988; children: Dustin, Lauren. BA in Math., U. Rochester, 1974; JD, NYU, 1977, LLM in Taxation, 1983. Bar: N.Y. Assoc. atty. Willkie Farr & Gallagher, NYC, 1977-79, Halperin Shivitz Eisenberg Schneider & Greenawalt, NYC, 1979-84, Berman Koerner Silberberg P.C., NYC, 1984-86; sr. v.p., sec., gen. counsel The Pentegra Group, White Plains, NY, 1986—. Mem. ABA, N.Y. State Bar Assn., Web Network. Democrat. Jewish. Avocations: tennis, bridge, music. Pension, profit-sharing, and employee benefits. Home: 7 Aspen Rd Scarsdale NY 10583-7301 Office: The Pentegra Group 108 Corporate Park Dr White Plains NY 10604-3805 E-mail: ralin@pentegra.com.

ALITO, SAMUEL ANTHONY, JR., federal judge; b. Trenton, N.J., Apr. 1, 1950; AB, Princeton U., 1972; JD, Yale U., 1975. Bar: NJ 1975, NY 1970. Law clk. to judge U.S. Ct. Appeals (3d cir.), Newark, 1976—77; asst. U.S. atty. U.S. Atty.'s Office, Newark, 1977—81, atty., 1987—90; asst. to solicitor gen. Office of Solicitor Gen. Dept. Justice, Washington, 1981—85; dep. asst. atty. gen. Office of Legal Counsel Dept. Justice, Washington, 1985—87; judge U.S. Ct. Appeals (3d cir.), Newark, 1990—. Office: US Courthouse PO Box 999 Newark NJ 07101-0999

ALLAN, LIONEL MANNING, lawyer; b. Detroit, Aug. 3, 1943; AB cum laude, U. Mich., 1965; JD, Stanford U., 1968; student, U. Paris. Bar: Calif. 1969, U.S. Supreme Ct. 1972. Law clk. U.S. Dist. Ct. (no. dist.) Calif., 1969—70; pres. Allan Advisors, Inc., bd. governance and legal cons. firm. Speaker and writer in field of corp. securities and pvt. internat. law; sec. adv. com. San Jose Fed. Ct., 1969-85; mem. bd. visitors Stanford Law Sch., 1985-88; mem. com. comml. code State Bar Calif., 1974-77, corps. com., 1983-86. Co-author: How to Structure the Classic Venture Capital Deal, 1983, Equity Incentives for Start-up Companies, 1985, Master Limited Partnerships, 1987. Bd. dirs. San Jose Mus. Art, 1983-87; trustee KTEH-TV Channel 54 Found., 1987—; dir. NCCJ, 1995-2001, Harker Sch., 1998—. Served to capt. JAGC, USAR, 1968-74. Mem. ABA (com. on small bus. 1980—, chmn. internat. bus. subcom. 1985-88, chmn. small bus. com. 1989-93), Santa Clara Bar Assn. (chmn. fed. ct. sect. 1971, 77), Internat. Bar Assn., San Jose C. of C. (dir.), Pi Sigma Alpha, Phi Sigma Iota, Phi Delta Phi. Corporate, general, Private international, Securities. Office: Allan Advisors Inc 18222 Seebree Ln Monte Sereno CA 95030-3135 E-mail: lonallan@attbi.com.

ALLAN, RICHMOND FREDERICK, lawyer; b. Billings, Mont., Apr. 22, 1930; s. Roy F. and Edith (Prater) A.; m. Dorothy Frost, Aug. 9, 1954; children: Richmond P., David F., Michael R. BA, U. Mont., 1954, JD, 1957; postgrad., London Sch. of Econs., 1957-58. Bar: Mont. 1957, U.S. Supreme Ct. 1961, D.C. 1965. Law clk. U.S. Ct. Appeals (9th cir.), San Francisco, 1958-59; ptnr. Kurth, Conner, Jones & Allan, Billings, 1959-61; chief asst. U.S. atty. U.S. Dept. of Justice, Billings, 1961-64; assoc. solicitor U.S. Dept. of Interior, Washington, 1965-67, dep. solicitor, 1968-69; ptnr. Weissbrodt & Weissbrodt, Washington, 1969-77, Casey, Lane & Mittendorf, Washington, 1977-78, Duncan, Weinberg, Miller & Pembroke, P.C., Washington, 1979—. Fulbright Commn. scholar, 1957. Mem. Fed. Bar Assn. (pres. Mont. chpt. 1963-65). Avocation: trap and skeet shooting. Administrative and regulatory, Oil, gas, and mineral, Property, real (including real estate development, water). Office: Duncan Weinberg Genzer & Pembroke PC 1615 M St NW Ste 800 Washington DC 20036-3219 E-mail: rfa@dwgp.com.

ALLAN, RONALD CURTIS, lawyer; b. Chgo., Oct. 5, 1937; s. Sven and Stina Allan; m. Ann Gould, Aug. 17, 1963; children: Jennifer, Katherine, Matthew. AB, U. Mich., 1959, JD, 1965. Bar: Ill. 1965, Ohio 1966; U.S. Ct. Appeals (7th cir.) 1965; U.S. Ct. Appeals (6th cir.) 1966. Assoc. Eckhart, McSwain, Hassel & Husum, Chgo., 1965-66; ptnr. Brouse & McDowell, Akron, Ohio, 1967-78; prin. Buckingham, Doolittle & Burroughs, Akron, 1979—. Sec. Yoder Bros., Inc., Barberton, Ohio, Rubber Assocs., Inc., Akron. Editor: Ohio Business Organization Laws and Rules, 4 edits., 1994-98. Trustee, sec. Akron Symphony Orch., 1975-83, Akron Art Mus., 1987-93, Akron Cmty. Found., 1990-96; trustee Akron Gen. Med. Ctr., 1990-2001; trustee Akron Gen. Med. Found., Old Trail Sch. Found., 1990-97; sec. bd. trustees Akron Rotary Found., 1996—. Capt. USNR, 1959-87. Paul Harris fellow Rotary Internat., 1990. Fellow Akron Bar Found.; mem. ABA, Ohio State Bar Assn. Avocations: classical music, opera, distance running, trout fishing. Corporate, general, Mergers and acquisitions, Non-profit and tax-exempt organizations. Office: Buckingham Doolittle & Burroughs 50 S Main St Akron OH 44308-1828

ALLAN, WALTER ROBERT, lawyer; b. Detroit, Aug. 1, 1937; s. Walter Francis and Henrietta (Fairchild) A. AB, U. Mich., 1959, JD, 1962. Bar: Calif. 1964, U.S. Ct. Appeals (9th Cir.) 1964, U.S. Supreme Ct. 1972, U.S. Ct. Appeals (D.C. cir.) 1973, U.S. Ct. Appeals (5th cir.) 1977, U.S. Ct. Appeals (3d cir.) 1988. From assoc. to ptnr. Pillsbury, Madison & Sutro, San Francisco, 1963—98; sole practitioner Tiburon, Calif., 1998—. Appellate. Office: PO Box 771 Belvedere Tiburon CA 94920-0771

ALLEGRUCCI, DONALD LEE, state supreme court justice; b. Pittsburg, Kans., Sept. 19, 1936; s. Nello and Josephine Marie (Funaro) A.; m. Joyce Ann Thompson, Nov. 30, 1963; children: Scott David, Bowen Jay. AB, Pittsburg State U., 1959; JD, Washburn U., 1963. Bar: Kans. 1963. Asst. county atty. Butler County, El Dorado, Kans., 1963-67; state senator Kans. Legislature, Topeka, 1976-80; mem. Kans. Pub. Relations Bd., 1981-82; dist. judge Kans. 11th Jud. Dist., Pittsburg, 1982-87, adminstrv. judge, 1983-87; justice Kans. Supreme Ct., Topeka, 1987—. Instr. Pittsburg State U., 1969-72; exec. dir. Mid-Kans. Community Action Program, Inc. Mem. Dem. State Com., 1974-80; candidate 5th Congl. Dist., 1978; past pres. Heart Assn.; bd. dirs. YMCA. Served with USAF, 1959-60. Mem. Kans. Bar Assn. Democrat. Office: Kansas Supreme Court 374 Kansas Judicial Ctr 301 SW 10th Ave Fl 3 Topeka KS 66612-1507

ALLEN, BRADLEY REID, SR., judge; b. Burlington, N.C., July 21, 1962; s. J.B. Allen, Jr. and Judy B. Allen; m. Dawn Michelle Donleycott, July 4, 1997; children: Kaitlyn, Zachary, Kennedy, Reid. BS Indsl. Rels and Psychology, UNC-Ch, 1985; JD, Norman Wiggins Sch. of Law, 1988. Bar: N.C. 1988. Of counsel Charles Bateman, PA, Burlington, 1988—89; asst. dist. atty. Dist. Atty. Alamance Cty., Graham, 1989—97, chief asst. dist. atty., 1997—2000; dist. ct. judge State of N.C. Dist. 15-A, 2000—. Little league coach Burlington Recreation Dept., 1991—. Mem.: Emmanuel United Methodist Ch. (life). Methodist. Office: 120 Criminal Courts Bldg 212 W Elm St Graham NC 27253-2814

ALLEN, CRAIG ADAMS, lawyer, leasing co. exec.; b. Ironton, Ohio, June 30, 1941; s. Enoch Stanley and Margaret (Adams) A.; m. Carol Linda Brewster, Aug. 15, 1964; children— Laura, Kathy. B.A. cum laude, Denison U., 1963; J.D., Ohio State U., 1966. Bar: Ohio 1966. Ptnr. Edwards, Klien, Compton & Allen, Ironton, 1966-76; sole practice, Ironton, 1976-77; ptnr. Allen & Anderson, Ironton, 1977-78, Allen, Anderson & Anderson, Ironton, 1978-82, Allen & Stillpass, Ironton, 1983-84, sole practice 1984-85, ptnr. Allen & Payne, Ironton, 1985—; dir. So. Ohio AAA. Chmn. Lawrence County (Ohio) Democratic Central Com. Served with Ohio N.G., 1966-72. Mem. Lawrence County Bar Assn., Hosp. Attys. Assn., Ironton C. of C. Episcopalian. Lodges: Lions, Elks. State civil litigation, Corporate, general, Labor (including EEOC, Fair Labor Standards Act, labor-management relations, NLRB, OSHA). Office: 311 S 3rd St Ironton OH 45638-1630

ALLEN, DAVID JAMES, lawyer; b. East Chicago, Ind. BS, Ind. U., 1957, MA, 1959, JD, 1965. Bar: Ind. 1965, U.S. Dist. Ct. (so. dist.) Ind. 1965, U.S. Ct. Appeals 1965, U.S. Tax Ct. 1965, U.S. Supreme Ct. 1965, U.S. Ct. Appeals (fed. and 7th cirs.) 1983. Of counsel Hagemier, Allen and Smith, Indpls., 1975—. Adminstrv. asst. Gov. of Ind. Mathew E. Welsh, 1961—65; counsel Ind. Gov. Roger D. Branigin, 1965—69; asst. to Gov. Edgar D. Whitcomb, 1969—70; legis. counsel Ind. Gov. Evan Bayh, 1989—90; spl. counsel Gov. Frank O'Bannon State of Ind., 1999—2002; mem. Spl. Commn. on Ind. Exec. Reorgn., 1967—69; commr. univ. counsel Ind. State U., 1969—70; commr. Ind. Utility Regulatory Commn., 1970—75; mem. Ind. Law Enforcement Acad. Bd. and Adv. Coun., 1968—85, Ind. State Police Bd., 1968—; commr. for revision Ind. Commn. Recommend Changes Ind. Legis. Process, 1990—2002; commr. Ind. Criminal Code Revision Study Commn., 1998—2002; nat. judge adv. Acacia Frat., 1980—86, 1992—2002, internat. pres., 2002—; chief counsel Ind. Ho. Reps., 1976—76, spl. counsel, 1979—89, Ind. Senate, 1990—97; adj. prof. pub. law Sch. Pub. and Environ. Affairs, Ind. U., Bloomington, 1976—. Author: (book) New Governor in Indiana: Transition to Executive Power, 1965. Mem.: ABA, Indpls. Bar Assn., Ind. State Bar Assn. (mem. adminstrv. law com. 1968—77, chmn. adminstrv. law com. 1973—76, mem. law ch. liaison com. 1977—78, criminal justice law exec. com. 1966—72). Administrative and regulatory, Legislative, Utilities, public. Office: Hagemier Allen & Smith 1170 Market Tower 10 W Market St Ste 1170 Indianapolis IN 46204-5924

ALLEN, EDWARD LEFEBVRE, lawyer; b. Richmond, Va., May 17, 1962; s. Wilbur Coleman and Frances (Gayle) A.; m. Nancy Williams, Sept. 3, 1994; children: Parker Edward, Mason Elizabeth. BA, Vanderbilt U., 1984; JD, Washington and Lee U., 1987. Bar: Va. 1987, U.S. Ct. Appeals (4th cir.) 1989, U.S. Claims Ct. 1990, U.S. Ct. Appeals (D.C. cir.) 1996. Assoc. Allen, Allen, Allen & Allen, Richmond, 1987-96, ptnr., 1996—. Mem. ABA, ATLA, Va. Trial Lawyers Assn. (bd. govs. 1999—), Va. State Bar, Fredericksburg Bar Assn. Personal injury (including property damage). Home: 401 Chamonix Dr Fredericksburg VA 22405-2029 Office: Allen Allen Allen & Allen 3405 Plank Rd Fredericksburg VA 22407-4959 E-mail: ELA@Allenandallen.com.

ALLEN, FRANK CLINTON, JR., lawyer, chemical engineer; b. New Orleans, Apr. 14, 1934; s. Frank Clinton and Lucy Charlotte (Walters) A.; m. Cynthia Ann Church, June 7, 1958; children: Frank C. III, Thomas Church, C. Ann. BSChemE, Tulane U., 1955, LLB, 1964. Registered profl. engr., La.; bar: La. 1964, Miss. 1977, Tex. 1991, U.S. Supreme Ct. 1972. Process engr. Am. Oil Co., New Orleans, 1955-60, Chevron Oil Co., New Orleans, 1960-64; atty. Jones, Walker, Waechter, New Orleans, 1964-78; v.p., gen. counsel, corp. sec. McDermott Internat., Inc., New Orleans, 1978-99; atty. Jones, Walker, Waechter, Poitevent, Carrere, Denegre, New Orleans, 1999—2002, Rushing & Guile, PLLC, Biloxi, Miss., 2002—. Mem. AIChE, ABA, La. Bar Assn., Miss. Bar Assn., Tex. Bar Assn. Avocation: sailing. Admiralty, Federal civil litigation, Corporate, general. Office: Graham, Arceneaux, & Allen, LLC 601 Poydras St Suite 2080 New Orleans LA 70112 E-mail: fallen@ametro.net., fce@gra-arc.com.

ALLEN, HARRY ROGER, lawyer; b. Memphis, June 13, 1933; s. Sam J. and Louise (Frazier) A.; children: Julie Ferriss, Steven J., Leslie Loraine Allen Anchor; m. Emily Ann Mason, May 4, 1990; 1 stepchild, Jeremy Myrick. Student, Tulane U., 1951-53; BBA, U. Miss., 1955, LLB, 1959. Bar: Miss. 1959, U.S. Dist. Ct. (so. dist.) Miss. 1961, U.S. Ct. Appeals (5th cir.) 1981, U.S. Supreme Ct. 1981. From assoc. to ptnr. Brunini Everett, Grantam & Quinn, Vicksburg, Miss., 1959-68; ptnr. Bryan, Nelson, Allen, Schroeder, Cobb & Hood, Gulfport, Miss., 1968-91; pres. Allen, Vaughn, Cobb & Hood, P.A., Gulfport, Miss., 1992—. Spl. asst. atty. gen. State of Miss., Gulfport, 1989-91. Mem. Harrison County com. region XIII commn. Mental Health and Mental Retardation, Gulfport, 1976—; fin. chmn. Miss. Rep. Party, 1982-84; Miss. Elector Bush/Quayle Ticket, Jackson, Miss., 1984; del. Rep. Nat. Conv., Dallas, 1984. Capt. USAF, 1955-58. Named to Best Lawyer in Am. publ., 1988-97. Mem. Internat. Assn. Def. Counsel, Miss. Bar Found. (former trustee), Miss. Bar Assn. (pres. Harrison County young lawyers sect. 1969-70, jud. liaison com. 1990-91), Miss. Fed. Bar Assn. (so. dist. commr. 1980-81), Miss. Bar Leadership Conf. (chmn. 1991), Harrison County Bar Assn. (pres. 1990), Lamar Order, Am. Inns of Ct. (pres. Russell 1995-96, Blass-Walker chpt. Republican. Methodist. Avocations: golf, skiing. General civil litigation, Insurance, Personal injury (including property damage). Office: Allen Vaughn Cobb & Hood P A PO Box 4108 Gulfport MS 39502-4108 E-mail: hallen@avchlaw.com.

ALLEN, HENRY SERMONES, JR., lawyer; b. Bronxville, N.Y., Aug. 26, 1947; s. Henry S. and Cecelia Marie (Chartrand) A.; m. Patricia Stromberger, Nov. 26, 1988; children: David Beckman, Amy Louise, Jeffrey Roy. AB magna cum laude, Washington U., St. Louis, 1969; MPA, Cornell U., 1973, JD, 1974. Adminstrv. resident Montefiore Hosp. and Med. Ctr., Bronx, N.Y., 1971; rsch. trainee Nat. Ctr. Health Svcs. Rsch., HEW, 1974-75; assoc. Vedder, Price, Kaufman & Kammholz, Chgo., 1975-79; pvt. practice Springfield, 1979-81; ptnr. Allen & Reed, Chgo., 1981-86, McBride, Baker & Coles, 1986—, Holland & Knight LLC. Adj. asst. prof. hosp. law Ithaca (N.Y.) Coll., 1974-75; adj. prof. Cornell U., 1995—. HUD fellow, 1969-71. Mem. Am. Health Lawyers Assn., Ill. Soc. Hosp. Attys., Nat. Health Lawyers Assn., Phi Beta Kappa, Omicron Delta Epsilon, Corneel U. of Chgo. Club. Antitrust, Federal civil litigation, Health. Office: Holland & Knight LLC Northwestern Atrium Ctr 500 W Madison St 40th Fl Chicago IL 60661

ALLEN, JEFFREY MICHAEL, lawyer; b. Chgo., Dec. 13, 1948; s. Albert A. and Miriam (Feldman) A.; m. Anne Marie Guaraglia, Aug. 9, 1975; children: Jason M., Sara M. BA in Polit. Sci. with great distinction, U. Calif., Berkeley, 1970, JD, 1973. Bar: Calif. 1973, U.S. Dist. Ct. (no. and so. dists.) Calif. 1973, U.S. Ct. Appeals (9th cir.) 1973, U.S. Dist. Ct. (ea. dist.) Calif. 1974, U.S. Dist. Ct. (cen. dist.) Calif. 1977, U.S. Dist. Ct. (so. dist.) Calif., U.S. Supreme Ct.; lic. real estate broker. Prin. Graves & Allen, Oakland, Calif., 1973—. Teaching asst. dept. polit. sci. U. Calif., Berkeley, 1970-73; lectr. St. Mary's Coll., Moraga, Calif., 1976-90; mem. faculty Oakland Coll. of Law, 1996-98; bd. dirs. Family Svcs. of the East Bay, 1987-92, 1st v.p., 1988, pres., 1988-91; mem. panel arbitrators Ala. County Superior Ct.; arbitrator comml. arbitration panel Am. Arbitration Assn. Mem. editorial bd. U. Calif. Law Rev., 1971-73, project editor, 1972-73; mem. Ecology Law Quar., 1971-72; contbr. articles to profl. jours. Mem. U.S. Youth Soccer Constl. Commn., 1997—98, U.S. Youth Soccer Bylaws Com., 1998—; mem. region 4 regional coun. U.S. Youth Soccer, 1996—99, chmn. mediation and dispute resolution com., 1999—2000; treas. Hillcrest Elem. Sch. PTA, 1984—86, pres., 1986—88; past mem. GATE adv. com., strategic planning com. on fin. and budget, dist. budget adv. com., instructional strategy counsel Oakland Unified Sch. Dist., 1986—91; mem. Oakland Met. Forum, 1987—91, Oakland Strategic Planning Com., 1988—90; mem. adv. com. St. Mary's Coll.. Paralegal Prog.; commr. Bay Oaks Youth Soccer, 1988—94; asst. dist. commr. dist. 4 Calif. Youth Soccer Assn., 1990—92, also bd. dirs., pres. dist. 4 competitive league, 1990—93, sec. bd. dirs., 1993—96, chmn. bd. dirs., 1996—99; chmn. U.S. Soccer dateabase mktg. com. Calif. Soccer Assn., 1997—99; bd. dirs. Montera Sports Complex, 1988—89, Jack London Youth Soccer League, 1988—94, Calif. Soccer Assn., 1996—99. Mem.: Rotary (bd. dirs. Oakland 1992—94), Oakland C. of C., Assn. Conflict Resolution, Calif. North Referee Assn. (referee adminstr. dist. 4 1992—96, state bd. dirs. 1996—2000), U.S. Soccer Fedn. (nat. C lic. coach and state referee, state referee instr. and state referee assessor), Calif. Scholarship Fedn., U.S. Soccer Assn. (database mktg. com., constl. commn.), Alameda County Bar Assn. (past vice chmn. com. continuing edn., exec. com. alternative dispute resolution programs, panel mediator, arbitrator), Calif. Bar Assn. (mem. ADR com. 2001—), ABA (chmn. subcom. on use of computers in real estate trans. 1985—86, chmn. real property com. gen. practice sect. 1987—91, mem. programs com. 1991—93, adv. coord. 1993—96, sect. coun. 1994—98, mktg. bd. 1996—98, mem. 1998—99, editor, columnist Tech. and Practice Guide 1998—, editl. bd. GP Solo 1999—, editor, columnist Tech. e Report 2002—). Avocations: reading, computers, photography, skiing, baseball, coaching and refereeing youth soccer. Bankruptcy, General civil litigation, Property, real (including real estate development, water). Office: Graves & Allen 436 14th St Ste 1400 Oakland CA 94612-2716 E-mail: jallenlaw@aol.com., jallenlaw@gravesandallen.com.

ALLEN, JEFFREY RODGERS, lawyer; b. West Point, N.Y., Aug. 15, 1953; s. James R. and Kathryn (Lewis) A.; m. Cynthia Lynn Colyer, Aug. 10, 1975; children: Emily Rodgers, Elizabeth Colyer, Richard Byrd. BA in History, U. Va., 1975; JD, U. Richmond, 1978. Bar: Va. 1978, U.S. Ct. Mil. Appeals 1981, U.S. Ct. Appeals (4th cir.) 1982, U.S. Supreme Ct. 1982. Trial atty. Michie, Hamlett, Donato & Lowry, Charlottesville, Va., 1982-86; chief counsel Va. Dept. Mil. Affairs, Blackstone, Va., 1986-2000; U.S. property and fiscal officer for Va. Blackstone, 2001—. Atty., advisor U.S. Army Mobile Air Surg. Transport Team, Savannah, Ga., 1980-82; steering com. X-Car Litigation Group, 1983-85; lectr., organizer Law Everyone Should Know series Piedmont (Va.) C.C., Charlottesville, 1984-86; trial atty., of counsel Thorsen, Marchant & Scher, L.L.P., Richmond, 1986-98; mem. legal adv. com. Va. Gov.'s Mil. Adv. Commn., 1987-2000, judge advocate adv. coun. N.G. Bur., 1993-96, TJAG Air N.G. judge advocate adv. coun., 1997-, coord. strategic planning com.; mem. USPFO Coun. Futures Com., 2002--. Pres. Regency Woods Condominium Assn., Richmond, 1976-78, Ashcroft Neighborhood Assn., Charlottesville, 1983-86; treas. Va. N.G. Found., 1986-2002, mem. strategic planning coun. USPFO Coun., 2002—. Capt. U.S. Army, 1978-82, lt. col. JAGC, Va. Air N.G., 1982-2000, col. USAF, 2001—. Mem. Assn. Trial Lawyers Am., Va. Trial Lawyers Assn., Richmond Bar Assn. Avocations: jogging, mountain climbing, photography, fishing, swimming. Home: 2700 Cottage Cove Dr Richmond VA 23233-3318 Office: USPFO Bldg 316 Ft Pickett Blackstone VA 23824-6316 E-mail: jeff.allen@va.ngb.army.mil.

ALLEN, JOHN THOMAS, JR., lawyer; b. St. Petersburg, Fla., Aug. 23, 1935; s. John Thomas and Mary Lita (Shields) A.; m. Joyce Ann Lindsey, June 16, 1958 (div. 1985); children: John Thomas III, Linda Joyce, Catherine Lee (dec.).; m. Janice Dearmin Hudson, Mar. 16, 1987 (div. 2002). BSBA with honors, U. Fla., 1958; JD, Stetson U., 1961. Bar: Fla. 1961, U.S. Dist. Ct. (mid. dist.) Fla. 1962, U.S. Ct. Appeals (5th cir.) 1963, U.S. Ct. Appeals (11th cir.) 1983, U.S. Supreme Ct. 1970. Assoc. Mann, Harrison, Mann & Rowe and successor Greene, Mann, Rowe, Davenport &

Stanton, St. Petersburg, 1961-67, ptnr., 1967-74; sole practice St. Petersburg, 1974-95; pvt. practice Allen & Maller, P.A., 1996-98, Gulfport, Fla., 1998—. Counsel Pinellas County Legis. Del., 1974-75; counsel for Pinellas County as spl. counsel on water matters, 1975-98. Mem. Com of 100, St. Petersburg, 1975-98. Mem. ABA, Fla. Bar Assn., St. Petersburg Bar Assn., St. Petersburg C. of C., Lions, Beta Gamma Sigma. Republican. Baptist. Appellate, General practice, General civil litigation. Home and Office: 5929 Bayview Cir S Gulfport FL 33707-3929

ALLEN, LAYMAN EDWARD, law educator, research scientist; b. Turtle Creek, Pa., June 9, 1927; s. Layman Grant and Viola Iris (Williams) A.; m. Christine R. Patmore, Mar. 29, 1950 (dec.); children: Layman G., Patricia R.; m. Emily C. Hall, Oct. 3, 1981 (div. 1992); children: Phyllip A. Hall, Kelly C. Hairston; m. Leslie A. Olsen, June 10, 1995. Student, Washington and Jefferson Coll., 1945-46; AB, Princeton U., 1951; MPub. Admnstrn., Harvard U., 1952; LLB, Yale U., 1956. Bar: Conn. 1956. Fellow Ctr. for Advanced Study in Behavioral Scis., 1961-62; sr. fellow Yale Law Sch., 1956-57, lectr., 1957-58, instr., 1958-59, asst. prof., 1959-63, assoc. prof., 1963-66; assoc. prof. law U. Mich. Law Sch., Ann Arbor, 1966-71, prof., 1971—. Chmn. bd. trustees Accelerated Learning Found., 1998—; sr. rsch. scientist Mental Health Rsch. Inst., U. Mich., 1966-99; cons. legal drafting Nat. Life Ins. Co., Mich. Blue Cross & Blue Shield (various law firms); mem. electronic data retrieval com. Am. Bar Assn.; ops. rsch. analyst McKinsey & Co.; orgn. and methods analyst Office of Sec. Air Force.; trustee Ctr. for Study of Responsive Law. Editor: Games and Simulations, Artificial Intelligence and Law Jour.; author: WFF 'N Proof: The Game of Modern Logic, 1961, latest rev. edit., 1990, (with Robin B.S. Brooks, Patricia A. James) Automatic Retrieval of Legal Literature: Why and How, 1962, WFF: The Beginner's Game of Modern Logic, 1962, latest rev. edit., 1973, Equations: The Game of Creative Mathematics, 1963, latest rev. edit., 1994, (with Mary E. Caldwell) Reflections of the Communications Sciences and Law: The Jurimetrics Conference, 1965, (with J. Ross and P. Kugel) Queries 'N Theories: The Game of Science and Language, 1970, latest rev. edit., 1973, (with F. Goodman, D. Humphrey and J. Ross), On-Words: The Game of Word Structures, 1971, rev. edit., 1973; contbr. articles to profl. jours.; co-author/designer: (with J. Ross and C. Stratton) DIG (Diagnostic Instrnl. Gaming) Math; (with C. Saxon) Normalizer Clear Legal Drafting Program, 1986, MINT System for Generating Dynamically Multiple-Interpretation Legal Decision-Assistance Systems, 1991, The Legal Argument Game of Legal Relations, 1997, (with Sandra Bartlett) LawToe: An Introduction to Resource-Allocation Games, 2003. With USNR, 1945-46. Mem. ABA (coun. sect. sci. and tech.), AAAS, ACLU, Assn. Symbolic Logic, Nat. Coun. Tchrs. Math. Democrat. Unitarian Universalist. Home: 2114 Vinewood Blvd Ann Arbor MI 48104-2726 Office: U Mich Sch Law 625 S State St Ann Arbor MI 48109-1215 E-mail: laymanal@umich.edu.

ALLEN, LEON ARTHUR, JR., lawyer; b. Springfield, Mass., July 15, 1933; s. Leon Arthur Sr. and Elsie (Shoemaker) A.; m. Patricia Mellion, June 23, 1961; 1 child, Christopher L. BEE, Cornell U., 1955; LLB, NYU, 1964. Bar: N.Y. 1964, U.S. Dist. Ct. (so. and ea. dists.) N.Y. 1965. Tech. editor McGraw Hill Pub. Co., N.Y.C., 1958-62; constrn. engr. Gilbert Assocs., N.Y.C., 1962-64; assoc. LeBoeuf, Lamb, Leiby & MacRae, N.Y.C., 1964-70; ptnr. LeBoeuf, Lamb, Leiby & MacRae (name changed to LeBoeuf, Lamb, Greene & MacRae), N.Y.C., 1971—. Served with U.S. Army, 1956-58. Mem. ABA, Assn. of Bar of City of N.Y. (chmn. adminstrv. law com. 1972-74). Clubs: Racquet & Tennis (N.Y.C.); Union (N.Y.C.), Tuxedo (Tuxedo Park, N.Y.). Administrative and regulatory, FERC practice, Private international. Home: 530 E 86th St New York NY 10028-7535 Office: LeBoeuf Lamb Greene MacRae 125 W 55th St New York NY 10019-5369 E-mail: laallen@llgm.com.

ALLEN, LYLE WALLACE, lawyer; b. Chillicothe, Ill., June 17, 1924; s. Donald M. and Mary Ellen (McEvoy) A.; m. Helen Kolar, Aug. 16, 1947; children: Mary Elizabeth Watkins, Bryan James. Student, N.C. State Coll., 1943-44; BS, Northwestern U., 1947; postgrad., Columbia Law Sch., 1947-48; JD, U. Wis., 1950. Bar: Ill. 1950, Wis. 1950. Of counsel Heyl Royster Voelker & Allen, Peoria, Ill., 1951—. Served with 87th Inf. Div. U.S. Army, World War II. Decorated Purple Heart, Bronze star. Mem. ABA, Ill. State Bar Assn. (pres. 1972-73), Assn. of Ins. Attys. (pres. 1965-66), Illinois Valley Yacht Club, Wig and Pen Club (London). Democrat. Presbyterian. Office: 124 SW Adams St Ste 600 Peoria IL 61602-1392

ALLEN, NEWTON PERKINS, lawyer; b. Memphis, Jan. 3, 1922; s. James Seddon and Sarah (Perkins) Allen; m. Malinda Lobdell Nobles, Oct. 4, 1947 (dec. Nov. 1986); children: John Lobdell, Malinda Allen Nobles, Newton Perkins, Cannon Fairfax; m. Malinda Lobdell Crutchfield, June 23, 1990. AB, Princeton, 1943; JD, U. Va., 1948. Bar: Tenn 1947, NC 1990. Assoc. Armstrong, Allen, Prewitt, Gentry, Johnston & Holmes, Memphis, 1948, ptnr., 1950-95; assoc. Dann & Allen, 1996—2001; with Newton P. Allen Law Firm, Memphis, 2001—. Contbr. articles to profl jours. Mem Chickasaw coun Boy Scouts Am, 1958—60, mem exec bd, 1961—69; trustee LeBonheur Children's Hosp, Memphis, 1964—72, vice chmn bd, 1965; mem alumni coun Princeton, 1954—64, 1990—93; chmn Greater Memphis Coun Crime and Delinquency, 1976—80; bd dirs Memphis Orchestra Soc, pres, 1979—81; pres bd trustees St Mary's Episcopal Sch, 1966—67, vpres, 1972—73; co-chmn Memphis Conf Faith at Work, 1975, bd dirs, 1976—79. Mem.: ABA (ed bd sr lawyers div 1990, pub comt chair 1993—95, coun mem 1994—95, chair travel and leisure comt 1995—96, vice chair 1996—97, chair-elect 1997—98, chair 1998—99), Princeton Alumni Asn Memphis (pres 1992), NC Bar Asn, Tenn Def Lawyers Asn, Memphis Bar Asn, Tenn Bar Asn, Am Col Trust and Estate Coun, Memphis Lions (pres 1956). General civil litigation, General practice, Probate (including wills, trusts). Office: Law Office 840 Valleybrook Dr Memphis TN 38120

ALLEN, RANDY LEE, lawyer; b. Kansas City, Kans., Oct. 19, 1963; s. William Richard and Martha Carol Allen; m. Lori B. Meendering; children: Elizabeth, Henry. BS in Petroleum Engring., Colo. Sch. Mines, 1986; JD, U. Colo., 1990. Bar: Colo. 1990, Ala. 1994. Clk. Astrella & Rice PC, Denver, 1988-90, atty., 1990-94; gen. counsel River Gas Corp., Tuscaloosa, Ala., 1994-2000; atty. Frontier Enterprises, L.L.C., Tuscaloosa, 2001—. Mem. Ind. Petroleum Assn. Am. (com. mem. 1994—), Ala. Coalbed Methane Assn. (com. mem. 1994—), Rocky Mountain Oil and Gas Assn. (com. mem. 1994—), Rocky Mountain Mineral Law Found. Corporate, general, Oil, gas, and mineral, Natural resources. Office: Frontier Enterprises LLC Ste 804 509 Energy Center Blvd Northport AL 35473 E-mail: rallen@frontier-ent.com.

ALLEN, RICHARD BLOSE, legal editor, lawyer; b. Aledo, Ill., May 10, 1919; s. James Albert and Claire (Smith) A.; m. Marion Treloar, Aug. 27, 1949; children: Penelope, Jennifer, Leslie Jean. BS, U. Ill., 1941, JD, 1947; LLD, Seton Hall U., 1977. Bar: Ill. 1947. Staff editor ABA Jour., 1947-48, 63-66, exec. editor, 1966-70, editor, 1970-83, editor, pub., 1983-86; pvt. practice Aledo, 1949-57; gen. counsel Ill. Bar Assn., 1957-63; mng. editor Def. Counsel Jour., Chgo., 1987—. Editor Sr. Lawyer, 1986-90, 94-2000. Maj. Q.M.C., AUS, 1941-46. Mem. ABA (mem. ho. of dels. 1996-99, chair sr. lawyers divsn. 2000-01), Ill. Bar Assn. (mem. assembly 1972-74), Chgo. Bar Assn., Am. Law Inst., Selden Soc., Mich. Shores Club, Kappa Tau Alpha, Phi Delta Phi, Alpha Tau Omega. Office: Def Counsel Jour 1 N Franklin St Ste 1205 Chicago IL 60606-2401 E-mail: dickall2@aol.com., rallen@iadclaw.org.

ALLEN, ROBERT DEE, lawyer; b. Tulsa, Oct. 13, 1928; s. Harve and Olive Jean (Brown) A.; m. Mary Latimer Conner, May 18, 1957; children: Scott, Randy, Blake. BA, U. Okla., 1951, LLB, 1955, JD, 1970. Bar: Okla. 1955, Ill. 1979, U.S. Dist. Ct. (we., no. and ea. dists.) Okla. 1955, U.S. Dist. Ct. (no. dist.) Ill. 1979, U.S. Ct. Appeals (10th cir.) 1956, U.S. Ct. Appeals (7th cir.) 1980, U.S. Supreme Ct. 1985. Assoc. Abernathy & Abernathy, Shawnee, Okla., 1955; law clk. to judge 10th U.S. Ct. Appeals, Denver, 1956; to judge Western Dist. Okla., 1956-57; asst. ins. commr., gen. counsel Okla. Ins. Dept., 1957-63; partner firm Quinlan, Allen & Batchelor, Oklahoma City, 1963-65, DeBois & Allen, 1965-66; counsel AT&T, Washington, 1966-67; gen. atty. Southwestern Bell Telephone Co., Okla., 1967-79; v.p., gen. counsel Ill. Bell Telephone Co., Chgo., 1979-83; sole practice law Chgo. and Oklahoma City, 1983—; mcpl. counselor Oklahoma City, 1984-89; of counsel Hartzog, Conger & Cason, 1983-90, Kimball, Wilson, Walker and Ferguson, 1990-93, Berry & Durland, 1993-94, Durland & Durland, 1994-96, White, Coffey, Galt & Fite, P.C., 1996-97, Phillips, McFall, McCaffrey, McVay & Murrah, P.C., 1997-2000; asst. general counsel Okla. Corp. Commn. Public Utilities Divsn., 2000—. Spl. counsel Okla. Mcpl. Power Authority, 1990-94, City of Altus, Okla., 1990-95; mem. Gov.'s Ad Valorem Tax Structure and Sch. Fin. Commn., 1972; bd. dirs. Taxpayers Fedn. Ill., 1980-83; adv. bd. dirs. Ctr. Am. and Internat. Law., 1985—; rsch. fellow Ctr. Am. and Internat. Law, 1994—; adj. prof. ins. law Oklahoma City U. Coll. Law, 1985—, agy. and partnership law, U. Okla. Coll. Law, 1989—; Okla. State chmn. Nat. Inst. Mcpl. Law Officers, 1984-89; apptd. mem. Legis Task Force on Okla. Adminstrv. Code, 1987; founding mem. U. Okla. Assocs., 1980. Bd. dirs. Oklahoma County Legal Aid Soc., 1973—; trustee Oklahoma City Riverfront Redevel. Authority, 1997—. With U.S. Army, 1946-48, 1st lt., 51-53; lt. col. USAR. Fellow Am. Bar Found.; mem. ABA, Fed. Bar Assn. (v.p. Okla. Chpt. 1977—), Okla. Bar Assn., Okla. County Bar Assn., Am. Judicature Soc., Okla. Assn. Mcpl. Attys. (bd. dirs. 1984-89), English Speaking Union (dir. 2001—), Order of Coif, Chgo. Club, Lions Club of Okla. City, 2000-. The Econs. Club of Okla., Oklahoma City Golf and Country Club, Phi Delta Phi, Sigma Phi Epsilon (dir.) Presbyterian. Home: 8101 Glenwood Ave Oklahoma City OK 73114-1107 E-mail: rdeeallen@aol.com.

ALLEN, ROBERT EUGENE BARTON, lawyer; b. Bloomington, Ind., Mar. 16, 1940; s. Robert Eugene Barton and Berth R. A.; m. Cecelia Ward Dooley, Sept. 23, 1960 (div. 1971); children: Victoria, Elizabeth, Robert, Charles, Suzanne, William; m. Judith Elaine Hecht, May 27, 1979 (div. 1984); m. Suzanne Nickolson, Nov. 18, 1995. BS, Columbia U., 1962; LLB, Harvard U., 1965. Bar: Ariz. 1965, U.S. Dist. Ct. Ariz. 1965, U.S. Tax Ct., 1965, U.S. Supreme Ct. 1970, U.S. Ct. Customs and Patent Appeals 1971, U.S. Dist. Ct. D.C. 1972, U.S. Ct. Appeals (9th cir.) 1974, U.S. Ct. Appeals (10th, and D.C. cirs.) 1984, U.S. Dist. Ct. N.Mex., U.S. Dist. Ct. (no. dist.) Calif., U.S. Dist. Ct. (no. dist.) Tex. 1991, U.S. Ct. Appeals (fed. cir.) 1992, U.S. Dist. Ct. (ea. dist.) Wis. 1995. Spl. asst. atty. gen., 1978; judge pro-tem Ariz. Ct. Appeals, 1984, 92, 99; Ptnr., dir. Allen, Price & Padden, Phoenix, 2000—. Nat. pres. Young Dems. Clubs Am., 1971-73; mem. exec. com. Dem. Nat. Com., 1972-73, Ariz. Gov.'s Kitchen Cabinet working on a wide range of state projects; bd. dirs. Phoenix Bapt. Hosp., 1981-83, Phoenix and Valley of the Sun Conv. and Visitors Bur., United Cerebral Palsy Ariz., 1984-89, Planned Parenthood of Ctrl. and No. Ariz., 1984-87, Internat. Coun. Ariz. Heart Inst. Found., 1998—, Cordell Hull Found. for Internat. Edn., 1996—; trustee Environ. Health Found., 1994-97, Friends of Walnut Canyon, 1991-94; bd. dirs. Ariz. Aviation Futures Task Force, chmn. Ariz. Airport Devel. Criteria Subcom.; Am. rep. exec. bd. Atlantic Alliance of Young Polit. Leaders, 1973-77, 77-80; trustee Am. Counsel of Young Polit. Leaders, 1971-76, 81-85; mem. Am. delegations to Germany, 1971, 72, 76, 79, USSR, 1971, 76, 88, France, 1974, 79, Belgium, 1974, 77, Can., 1974, Eng., 1975, 79, Norway, 1975, Denmark, 1976, Yugoslavia and Hungary, 1985; Am. observer European Parlimentary elections, Eng., France, Germany, Belgium, 1979, Moscow Congressional, Journalist delegation, 1989, NAFTA Trade Conf., Mexico City, 1993, Atlantic Assembly, Copenhagen, 1993. Contbr. articles on comml. litigation to profl. jours. Mem. ABA, Ariz. Bar Assn., Maricopa County Bar Assn., N.Mex. State Bar, D.C. Bar Assn., Am. Judicature Soc., Fed. Bar Assn., Am. Arbitration Assn., Phi Beta Kappa, Harvard Club. Democrat. Episcopalian (lay reader). Antitrust, General civil litigation, Intellectual property. Office: Allen Price & Padden 3131 E Camelback Rd Phoenix AZ 85016-4500

ALLEN, RUSSELL G. lawyer; b. Ottumwa, Iowa, Nov. 7, 1946; BA, Grinnell Coll., 1968; JD, Stanford U., 1971. Bar: Calif. 1971. Ptnr. O'Melveny & Myers LLP, Newport Beach, Calif., 1975-2001; wealth advisor J.P. Morgan Chase & Co., Newport Beach, Calif., 2001—. Trustee Grinnell Coll. Capt. JAGC, USAF, 1971-75. Fellow Am. Coll. Trust and Estate Counsel; mem. ABA (real property, probate and trust law and taxation sects.), Orange County Bar Assn. (estate planning, probate and trust sects.) Estate planning, Probate (including wills, trusts), Estate taxation. Office: JP Morgan Chase and Co Ste 200 888 San Clemente Dr Newport Beach CA 92660 E-mail: Russell.G.Allen@JPMorgan.com.

ALLEN, THOMAS DRAPER, lawyer; b. Detroit, June 25, 1926; s. Draper and Florence (Jones) A.; m. Joyce M. Johnson, July 18, 1953; children— Nancy A. Bowser, Robert D., Rebecca A. Hubbard. BS, Northwestern U., 1949; JD, U. Mich., 1952. Bar: Ill. 1952, U.S. Supreme Ct. 1971. Assoc. Kirkland & Ellis, Chgo., 1952-60, ptnr., 1961-67, Wildman, Harrold, Allen & Dixon, Chgo., 1967-96, of counsel, 1997—. Chmn. Community Caucus, Hinsdale, Ill., 1960-61; mem. Hinsdale Bd. Edn., 1965-71, pres., 1970-71; pres. West Suburban coun. Boy Scouts Am., 1980-82, mem. nat. exec. bd., 1986—, chmn. internat. com., 1995-99, mem. world program com., 1983-93; moderator Union Ch., Hinsdale, 1983-84; trustee Chgo. Theol. Sem., 1988-97, chair, 1990-96, life trustee, 1997—. With USN, 1944-46. Recipient Silver Beaver award Boy Scouts Am., 1964, Silver Buffalo award, 1997, Bronze Wolf award World Scout Orgn., 1993. Fellow Am. Coll. Trial Lawyers (state chair 1984-85, chair internat. com. 1997-99); mem. ABA, Ill. Bar Assn., Chgo. Bar Assn. (bd. of mgrs 1989-91), Law Club of Chgo., Legal Club of Chgo., Jaycees Internat. (senator, 1965), Internat. Bar Assn., Hinsdale Golf Club. Mem. United Ch. of Christ. Federal civil litigation, State civil litigation, General civil litigation. Home: 505 N Lake Shore Dr Chicago IL 60611-3427 Office: Wildman Harrold Allen & Dixon 225 W Wacker Dr Chicago IL 60606-1224

ALLEN, TONI K. lawyer; b. N.Y.C., Aug. 6, 1940; d. Irving M. and Mary (Sackler) Schoolman; m. Robert W. Clark III, July 22, 1985. AB, Wellesley Coll., 1960; LLB, NYU, 1964. Bar: N.Y. 1964, D.C. 1972. Atty. Office of Irving M. Wall, Esquire, N.Y.C., 1964-68; gen. counsel, asst. to pres. Nat. Econ. Rsch. Assocs., N.Y.C., 1968-71; atty., advisor Postal Rate Commn., Washington, 1971-72; assoc. Wald, Harkrader & Ross, Washington, 1972-73, ptnr., 1974-85, Piper & Marbury LLP, Washington, 1986-98, chmn. environ. dept., 1991-94, mem. policy and mgmt. com., 1992-94, ptnr. emeritus, 1999—; adj. sr. fellow Hudson Inst., 2001—. Adj. fellow Hudson Inst., 2001—. Trustee Levine Sch. Music, Washington, 1981—, pres., 1991-96; co-chair exec. bd. Environ. Lawyer, 1994-96, Leadership Washington, 1996-97; bd. dirs., vice chair United Way of the Nat. Capital Area, 2003—. Fellow Am. Bar Found.; mem. Order of Coif. Democrat. Avocations: sports, music, travel, cooking. E-mail: tka5640@aol.com.

ALLEN, WAYNE ALAN, lawyer, real estate and financial consultant; b. Wilmington, Del., Feb. 28, 1956; m. Andrea Joy Kershberg, June 18, 1978; children: Alison Eve, Samantha Brooke. BA summa cum laude, Syracuse U., 1978; JD magna cum laude, Boston Coll., 1981. Bar: Pa. 1981, Fla. 1989. Assoc. Wolf, Block et al, Phila., 1981-87; sr. assoc. Mesirov, Gelman, Phila., 1987-89; assoc. Hunt Cook et al, Boca Raton, Fla., 1989-91; corp. counsel Atlantic States Fin., Ft. Lauderdale, Fla., 1991-93; pres., CEO Access Fin. Svcs., Boca Raton, Fla., 1993—. Mem. ABA, Fla. Bar Assn., Palm Beach Bar Assn., Order of Coif, Phi Beta Kappa. Democrat. Avocations: computers, photography, swimming, bicycling, jogging. Banking, Corporate, general, Property, real (including real estate development, water).

ALLEN, WILLIAM HAYES, lawyer, educator; b. Palo Alto, Calif., Oct. 19, 1926; s. Ben Shannon and Victoria Rose (French) A.; m. Joan Webster Emmett, July 16, 1950; children: Edwin Hayes, Neal French, William Kent. Student, Deep Springs Coll., 1942-44; BA with gt. distinction, Stanford U., 1948, LLB, 1956. Bar: D.C. 1958. Corr. AP, Fresno, Calif., 1948-49, newsman Sacramento, 1950-53; law clk. to Chief Justice Earl Warren U.S. Supreme Ct., Washington, 1956-57; assoc. Covington & Burling, Washington, 1957-64, ptnr., 1964-92; ret., 1993—. Acting. prof. Stanford U. Law Sch., 1979; adj. prof. Howard U. Law Sch., 1981—83; lectr. George Mason U. Law Sch., 1983—86; practitioner-in-residence Cornell U. Law Sch., 1992; vis. prof. Deep Springs Coll., 1973, 96; chmn. jud. rev. com. Adminstrv. Conf. U.S., 1972—82, sr. conf. fellow, 1982—95; mem. steering com. Nat. Prison Project, 1975—93. Pres. Stanford Law Rev., vol. 8, 1955-56; contbr. articles to legal jours. Trustee Deep Springs Coll., 1984-92, chmn. bd. trustees, 1992; mem. Fair Housing Bd., Arlington County, Va., 1974-79. With U.S. Army, 1945-47. Mem. ABA (mem. coun. adminstrv. law sect. 1969-72, 79-81, chmn. 1982-83), D.C. Bar (chmn. legal ethics com. 1976-78), Am. Law Inst., Am. Acad. of Appellate Lawyers, Order of Coif, Cosmos Club. Democrat. Mem. United Ch. of Christ. Administrative and regulatory, Federal civil litigation. Office: Covington & Burling 1201 Pennsylvania Ave NW Washington DC 20004-2401 E-mail: billthedog2001@comcast.net., wallen@cov.com.

ALLENDER, JOHN ROLAND, lawyer; b. Boone, Iowa, Oct. 22, 1950; s. John S. and C. Corinne (Hayes) A.; m. Patti Allender; children: Susan A., Andrew J. BS, Iowa State U., 1972; JD, U. San Diego, 1975; LLM in Taxation, NYU, 1976. Bar: Calif. 1976, Tex. 1977, U.S. Ct. Claims 1977, U.S. Tax. Ct. 1977, U.S. Dist. Ct. (so. dist.) Tex. 1977. Assoc. Fulbright & Jaworski, Houston, 1976-83, ptnr., 1983—. Mem. adv. commn. Tex. Bd. Legal Specialization, 1986-2000. Bd. dirs. Ronald McDonald House, Houston, pres. 2003—, pres., 2002—. Mem. State Bar of Tex. (chmn. sect. taxation 1990), Houston Bar Assn. (chmn. sect. taxation 1979). Corporate, general, Corporate taxation, Taxation, general. Office: Fulbright & Jaworski 1301 Mckinney St Houston TX 77010-3031

ALLEY, JOHN-EDWARD, lawyer; b. El Dorado, Ark., Dec. 9, 1940; s. Granville Mason and Reyland (Stuppi) A.; m. Mary Elizabeth Conrad, Sept. 10, 1960 (div. 1970); 1 child, John-Edward Jr.; m. Ruth Rice, June 17, 1995. BSBA, U. Fla., 1962, JD, 1965; LLM in Labor Law, NYU, 1968. Bar: Fla. 1966, U.S. Dist. Ct. (so dist.) Fla. 1968, U.S. Supreme Ct. 1971, U.S. Ct. Appeals (5th cir.) 1972, U.S. Ct. Appeals (4th cir.) 1975, U.S. Ct. Appeals (D.C. cir.) 1975, U.S. Dist. Ct. (no. dist.) Fla. 1975, U.S. Ct. Appeals (11th cir.) 1981, U.S. Dist. Ct. (mid. dist.) Fla. 1984. Assoc. Clayton, Arnow, Duncan, Johnston, Clayton & Quincey, Gainesville, Fla., 1966-67, Bruckner & Greene, Miami, Fla., 1968; assoc., then ptnr. Paul & Thomson, Miami, 1969-74; ptnr. Alley & Alley, Chartered, Tampa, Fla., 1974-96, Alley and Alley/Ford & Harrison LLP, Tampa, 1996-98, Ford & Harrison LLP, Tampa, 1999—. Instr. U. Fla., Gainesville, 1964-66, asst. prof., 1966-67; adj. prof. Coll. Law, Stetson U., St. Petersburg, Fla., 1976-85; mem. faculty PTI Mgmt. Ctr., Houston, 1983-88. Contbr. articles to legal jours. Mem. Fla. Bus. Adv. Bd., Leading Am. Attys., Labor Lawyers Adv. Com., Coun. for Union-Free Environment. Named Leading Fla. Atty. Am. Rsch. Corp., 1996. Mem. ABA, Fla. Bar Assn. (vice chmn. continuing legal edn. com. 1984-86, 90-91, chmn. elect 1991-92, chmn. 1992-93, chmn. labor and employment law sect. 1973-74, Ralph A. Marsicano award 1988), Am. Arbitration Assn., Am. Employment Law Coun., Dade County Bar Assn., Miami City Club, Univ. Club. Avocations: flying, scuba diving, skiing, classic cars. boating. Federal civil litigation, Labor (including EEOC, Fair Labor Standards Act, labor-management relations, NLRB, OSHA), Libel. Office: Ford & Harrison LLP 101 E Kennedy Blvd Ste 900 Tampa FL 33602-5133 also: 100 SE 2d St Ste 4500 Miami FL 33131 E-mail: jalley@fordharrison.com.

ALLEY, WAYNE EDWARD, federal judge, retired army officer; b. Portland, Oreg., May 16, 1932; s. Leonard David and Hilda Myrtle (Blum) A.; m. Marie Winkelmann Dommer, Jan. 28, 1978; children: Elizabeth, David, John; stepchildren: Mark Dommer, Eric Dommer. AB, Stanford U., 1952, JD, 1957. Bar: Calif. 1957, Oreg. 1957, Okla. 1985. Ptnr. Williams & Alley, Portland, 1957-59; commd. officer JAGC, U.S. Army, advanced through grades to brig. gen., ret., 1981; dean Coll. Law, dir. Law Ctr. U. Okla., Norman, 1981-85; judge U.S. Dist. Ct. Western Dist. Okla., Oklahoma City, 1985—. Decorated D.S.M., Legion of Merit, Bronze Star Mem. Fed. Bar Assn., Oreg. Bar Assn., Okla. Bar Assn., Order of Coif, Phi Beta Kappa. Office: US Dist Ct 3102 US Courthouse 200 NW 4th St Ste 3102 Oklahoma City OK 73102-3027 Home: 1316 Brookside Dr Norman OK 73072-6348

ALLISON, JAMES PURNEY, lawyer; b. Paris, Tex., Jan. 16, 1947; s. Ardell and Billie Louise (Parker) A. BS, East Tex. State U., 1967, MS, 1968; JD, U. Tex., 1971. Bar: Tex., U.S. Dist. Ct., U.S. Ct. Appeals (5th and 11th cir.), U.S. Supreme Ct. County atty. Delta County, Cooper, Tex., 1972-79; asst. atty. gen. Atty. Gen., Austin, Tex., 1979-83; ptnr. Allison, Bass & Assocs., Austin, Tex., 1983—. Gen. counsel County Judges & Commrs. Assn. Tex., Austin, 1983—. Bd. dirs. Tex. Low-Level Radioactive Waste Disposal Authority, Austin, 1985-91; mem. Indigent Health Adv. Com., Tex. Dept. Human Resources, Austin, 1987-94. Mem. Tex. Assn. Counties (hon. life). Avocations: golf, water skiing. General civil litigation, Legislative, Personal injury (including property damage). Office: Allison Bass & Assocs 402 W 12th St Austin TX 78701-1645 E-mail: j.allison@allison-bass.com.

ALLISON, JOHN ROBERT, lawyer; b. San Antonio, Feb. 9, 1945; s. Lyle (stepfather) and Beatrice (Kaliner) Forehand; m. Rebecca M. Picard; 1 child, Katharine. BS, Stanford U., 1966; JD, U. Wash., 1969. Bar: Wash. 1969, D.C. 1973, Minn. 1994, U.S. Supreme Ct. 1973. Assoc. Garvey, Schubert & Barer, Seattle, 1969-73; ptnr., 1973-86; prin. Betts, Patterson & Mines, P.S., 1986-94; sr. counsel Minn. Mining & Mfg. Co., 1994-2000, asst. gen. counsel, 2000—. Bd. dirs. So. Minn. Regional Legal Svcs.; lectr. bus. law Seattle U., 1970, U. Wash., 1970-73; judge pro tem, King County Superior Ct., 1983-94. Mem. ABA (vice chmn. toxic and hazardous substances and environ. law com. 1986-91, chair elect 1991-92, chair 1992-93), Minn. Bar Assn., Seattle-King County Bar Assn. (chmn. jud. evaln. polling com. 1982-83), Wash. State Bar Assn. (bd. bar examiners 1984-94), D.C. Bar Assn., Nat. Inst. Pollution Liability (co-chmn. 1988), Order of the Coif. Federal civil litigation, State civil litigation, Product liability. Office: Minn Mining & Mfg Co 3 M Ctr Saint Paul MN 55144-1000 E-mail: jrallison@mmm.com.

ALLISON, RICHARD CLARK, judge; b. N.Y.C., July 10, 1924; s. Albert Fay and Anice (Clark) A.; m. Anne Elizabeth Johnston, Oct. 28, 1950; children: Anne Sidney, William Scott, Richard Clark. BA, U. Va., 1944, LLB, 1948. Bar: N.Y. 1948. Practiced in, N.Y.C., 1948-52, 54-60; with CIA, 1952—54; ptnr. Reid & Priest, 1961-87; mem. Iran-U.S. Claims Tribunal, The Hague, 1988—. Lt. (j.g.) USNR, 1942—46. Trustee, Inst. for Transnational Arbitration; fellow Southwestern Legal Found., Am. Bar Found. (life); mem. ABA (chmn. com. Latin Am. Law 1964-68, chmn. Internat. Law Sect. 1977, chmn. Nat. Inst. on Doing Bus. in Far East 1972, chmn. internat. legal exchange program 1981-85), Internat. Bar Assn. (chmn. 1986 Conf., ethics com. 1986-89), Société Internat. des Avocats, Inter-Am. Bar Assn., Am. Arbitration Assn. (internat. panel), Am. Soc. Internat. Law, Coun. on Fgn. Rels., Assn. Bar City N.Y., Raven Soc., SAR, St. Andrew's Soc. N.Y., Manhasset Bay Yacht Club, Phi Beta Kappa, Omicron Delta Kappa, Pi Kappa Alpha, Phi Delta Phi. Republican. Congregationalist. Home: 224 Circle Dr Manhasset NY 11030-1123 Office: c/o Iran-US Claims Tribunal Parkweg 13 2585 JH The Hague Netherlands

ALLRED, GLORIA RACHEL, lawyer; b. Phila., July 3, 1941; d. Morris and Stella Bloom; m. William Allred (div. Oct. 1987); 1 child, Lisa. BA, U. Pa., 1963; MA, NYU, 1966; JD, Loyola U., L.A., 1974; JD (hon.), U. West Los Angeles, 1981. Bar: Calif. 1975, U.S. Dist. Ct. (cen. dist.) Calif. 1975, U.S. Ct. Appeals (9th cir.) 1976, U.S. Supreme Ct. 1979. Ptnr. Allred, Maroko, Goldberg & Ribakoff (now Allred, Maroko & Goldberg), L.A., 1976—. Contbr. articles to profl. jours. Pres. Women's Equal Rights Legal Def. and Edn. Fund, L.A., 1978—, Women's Movement Inc., L.A. Recipient Commendation award L.A. Bd. Suprs., 1986, Mayor of L.A., 1986, Pub. Svc. award Nat. Assn. Fed. Investigators, 1986, Vol. Action award Pres. of U.S., 1986. Mem. ABA, Calif. Bar Assn., Nat. Assn. Women Lawyers, Calif. Women Lawyers Assn., Women Lawyers L.A. Assn., Friars (Beverly Hills, Calif.), Magic Castle Club (Hollywood, Calif.) Corporate, general, Family and matrimonial, Labor (including EEOC, Fair Labor Standards Act, labor-management relations, NLRB, OSHA). Office: Allred Maroko & Goldberg 6300 Wilshire Blvd Ste 1500 Los Angeles CA 90048-5217

ALLWOOD, JOSEPH CALVIN, lawyer; b. Louisiana, Mo., July 26, 1963; s. James Calvin and Judyth W. Allwood; m. Kim Marie Cardelli, Mar. 7, 1998 (div.); m. Shannon Elaine Brayton, July 6, 2002. BS in History, BA in Polit. Sci., N.E. Mo. State U., 1985; JD, U. Mo., 1992. Bar: Mo. 1992. Assoc. atty. Law Office of William W. Cheeseman, Troy, Mo., 1992-95; pvt. practice law Clarksville, Mo., 1996—. Republican. Mem. Lds Ch. Avocations: music, reading. Office: 3408 Georgia St Louisiana MO 63353 Fax: 473-242-3738. E-mail: jallwood@big-river.net.

ALOE, PAUL HUBSCHMAN, lawyer; b. Phila., Feb. 2, 1957; s. Paul Edward and Mary (Hubschman) Aloe; children: Jessica, Ryan. BA with distinction, George Washington U., 1980; JD with distinction, Hofstra U., 1983. Bar: N.J. 1983, U.S. Dist. Ct. N.J. 1983, N.Y. 1984, U.S. Dist. Ct. so. and ea. dists.) N.Y. 1985, U.S. Ct. Appeals (2d cir.) 1990, U.S. Supreme Ct. 1991, U.S. Ct. Appeals (3d cir.) 1991, Pa. 1991, U.S. Dist. Ct. (no. dist.) N.Y. 1992; U.S. Dist. Ct. (ea. dist.) Pa. 1993. Law clk. N.Y. State Third Dept., Albany, 1983-84; ptnr. RubinBaum LLP, N.Y.C., 1984—. Contbr. articles to profl. publs. Mem. ABA, N.Y. State Bar Assn. (chair com. on civil practice law and rules 1993-99), Assn. Bar City N.Y. Mem. Bankruptcy, General civil litigation, General practice. Office: RubinBaum LLP 30 Rockefeller Plz Fl 29 New York NY 10112-0093 E-mail: aloe@rubinbaum.com.

ALOI, MICHAEL JOHN, lawyer; b. Apr. 1958; BA, W.Va. Wesleyan Coll.; JD, W.Va. U. Bar: W.Va. 1983. Pntr. Manchin & Aloi, PLLC, Fairmont, W.Va. Mem.: W.Va. State Bar (pres. 2002). Address: 1543 Fairmont Ave Fairmont WV 26554*

ALPER, MICHAEL F. lawyer, political consultant; b. Irvington, N.J., Jan. 24, 1954; s. Harold and Anne (Sofman) A.; m. Meredith S. McKell, July 4, 1986 (div. May 1990). BA, Rutgers U., 1976; JD, Antioch U., 1988. Bar: N.J. 1991, U.S. Dist. Ct. N.J. 1991, U.S. Ct. Appeals (3d cir.) 1991. Atty., ptnr. Alper & Alper Esquires, Springfield, NJ, 1991—. Cons. Somerset County Dem. Orgn., Somerville, N.J., 1991—. Chmn. Bernards Twp. Dem. Com., Basking Ridge, N.J., 1992-99, Bradley Beach (N.J.) Dem. Com., 1986-89, Springfield Dem. Com., 1984-86; std. bearer Alper Civic Assn., Springfield, 1982-86; mem. Kiwanis, Springfield. Named one of Outstanding Young Men of Am., U.S. Jaycees, 1983. Mem. Fed. Bar Assn., Am. Immigration Lawyers Assn., N.J. State Bar Assn., Union County Bar Assn., Warren County Bar Assn. Democrat. Jewish. Family and matrimonial, Immigration, naturalization, and customs. Home: 14 Kenley Way Hackettstown NJ 07840

ALPERN, ANDREW, lawyer, architect, historian; b. NYC, Nov. 1, 1938; s. Dwight K. and Grace M. (Michelman) Alpern. BArch, Columbia U., 1964; DSc, London Coll. Applied Sci., 1971; JD magna cum laude, Benjamin N. Cardozo Sch. Law, 1992. Registered arch., N.Y.; bar: N.Y. 1993, U.S. Dist. Ct. (so. and ea. dists.) N.Y. 1994. With Haines Lundberg Waehler, archs., NYC, 1962—67; project dir. Saphier, Lerner, Schindler, Environetics, NYC, 1968—72; v.p., dir. arch. Environ. R&D, Inc., Space Planning & Design, NYC, 1972—75; dir. rsch. Corp. Planners & Coord., NYC, 1973—75; project mgr. Hellmuth, Obata & Kassabaum, P.C., NYC, 1977—78; mgr. real estate and facilities planning PricewaterhouseCoopers LLP, NYC, 1978—88; cons. arch., hist. arch. NYC, 1988—. Mem. adv. bd. Inst. Applied Psychotherapy, 1969—72; nat. panel arbitrators Am. Arbitration Assn., 1971—86; cons. lawyer, 1993; spl. counsel Hughes Hubbard & Reed LLP, 1994—2002; exec. v.p., counsel Peter Kimmelman Asset Mgmt. LLC, 2002—; lectr. CUNY, Inst. Architecture and Urban Studies, Grolier Club, Mcpl. Art Soc. Author: (book) Apartments for the Affluent: A Historical Survey of Buildings in New York, 1975, Garrett Ellis Winants: 1813-1890, 1976; editor-in-chief: Legal Briefs for the Cons. Industry, 1978—92; author: (book) Alpern's Architectural Aphorisms, 1979; pub.: F.M.R.A. (Edward Gorey), 1980; author: (book) Handbook of Specialty Elements in Architecture, 1981, In the Manor Housed, 1982, Holdouts!, 1983; contbg. editor: NY Habitat, 1985—92; mem. bd. adv. Profl. Office Design Mag., 1986—89; author: (book) Fifth Avenue, 1986, New York's Fabulous Luxury Apartments, 1987, Statutes of Repose and the Cons. Industry: A Proposal for New York, 1991, Luxury Apt. Houses of Manhattan: An Illus. History, 1993, Hist. Manhattan Apt. Houses, 1996, New York's Arch. Holdouts, 1997, 101 Questions About Copyright Law, 1999; contbg. columnist: Ave. Mag., 2000—02; author: (book) The New York Apartment Houses of Rosario Candela and James Carpenter, 2001. Recipient Presdl. citation, N.Y. State Assn. Archs., 1991. Mem.: AIA, Friends Cast Iron Architecture, Mcpl. Art Soc., N.Y. Hist. Soc., Bklyn. Hist. Soc., Soc. Archtl. Historians. Corporate, general.

ALPERT, LAURENT, lawyer; b. Paris, Nov. 13, 1946; arrived in U.S., 1947; s. Paul Alpert and Sophie Jaszunka; m. Johanna E. Fend, May 31, 1970. AB, Harvard Coll., 1967, JD, 1972. Bar: (N.Y.) 1973. Ptnr. Cleary Gottlieb Steen & Hamilton, N.Y.C., 1972—. Bd. dirs. Beazer Homes USA, Inc., Atlanta. Trustee, chmn. legal com. Internat. Rescue Com., N.Y.C., 1999—. Mergers and acquisitions. Office: Cleary Gottlieb Steen & Hamilton One Liberty Plz New York NY 10006 Office Fax: 212-225-3999. Business E-Mail: lalpert@cgsh.com.

ALSCHULER, ALBERT W. law educator; b. Aurora, Ill., Sept. 24, 1940; s. Sam and Winifred (King) A.; m. Louise Evans, Mar. 21, 1970 (div. 1977); 1 child, Samuel Jonathan. AB, Harvard U., 1962, LLB, 1965. Bar: Ill. 1965. Prof. law U. Tex., Austin, 1969-76, U. Colo., Boulder, 1976-84, U. Pa., Phila., 1984, U. Chgo., 1985-88, Wilson-Dickinson, 1988-2002, Julius Kreeger, 2003-. Office: U Chgo Sch Law 1111 E 60th St Chicago IL 60637-2776 Home: 1640 E 50th St Chicago IL 60615 E-mail: awaa@midway.uchicago.edu.

ALSOP, DONALD DOUGLAS, federal judge; b. Duluth, Minn., Aug. 28, 1927; s. Robert Alvin and Mathilda (Aaseng) A.; m. Jean Lois Tweeten, Aug. 16, 1952; children: David, Marcia, Robert. BS, U. Minn., 1950, LLB, 1952. Bar: Minn. 1952. Pvt. practice, New Ulm, Minn.; ptnr. Gislason, Alsop, Dosland & Hunter, 1954-75; judge U.S. Dist. Ct. Minn., St. Paul, 1975—, chief dist. judge, 1985-92, sr. dist. judge, 1992—. Mem. 8th cir. jud. coun., 1981-92, Jud. Conf. Com. to Implement Criminal Justice Act, 1979-87; mem. exec. com. Nat. Conf. Fed. Trial Judges, 1990-94. Chmn. Brown County (Minn.) Republican Com., 1960-64, 2d Congl. Dist. Rep. Com., 1968-72, Brown County chpt. ARC, 1968-74. Served with AUS, 1945-46. Mem. Minn. State Bar Assn., 8th Cir. Dist. Judges Assn. (pres. 1982-84), New Ulm C. of C. (pres. 1974-75), Order of Coif. Office: US Dist Ct 754 Fed Bldg 316 Robert St N Saint Paul MN 55101-1495

ALSTED, PETER, lawyer; b. Copenhagen, Jan. 13, 1934; s. Gunnar Alsted and Gerda (Salomonsen) Gudme; m. Alette Arntz, 1963 (div. 1981); children: Charlotte Solovej, Gregers, Michala; m. Lissi Hansen Rosendal, Oct. 21, 1982. Candidatus Juris, U. Copenhagen, 1958. Bar: Denmark, 1962. Sole practitioner law, Copenhagen, 1964—. Chmn., bd. dir. charitable founds., corps. and profl. soc.; sec.-gen. Danish Ins. Brokers Assn., 1980-89. Contbr. to Handbook on European Community Company Law (amongst others), 1997, The Holding Company and the Zero-tax Investor, 2000, The Limited Partnership in International Tax Planning, 2002, articles in field. Mem. Union Internationale des Avocats (corr.), SAME (nat. bd. dir.), Danish Bar Assn., Internat. Tax Planning Assn. Home: 13 Vilvordeparken Charlottenlund 2920 Denmark Office: Advokaterne Ret & Raad 90 Vester Voldgade Copenhagen 1552 Denmark E-mail: alsted@alsted.com.

ALTEMOSE, MARK KENNETH, lawyer; b. Easton, Pa., July 21, 1965; s. Richard and Constance Irene (Silfies) Altemose; m. Jennifer Lou Abram, Nov. 24, 1995; children: Rachel Rebecca, Meghan Grace, Abigail Lynne. BA in Econ., Lafayette Coll., 1987; JD, Villanova, 1990. Bar: Pa. 1990, N.J. 1990, U.S. Dist. Ct. N.J. 1991, U.S. Dist. Ct. (ea. dist.) Pa. 1991, U.S. Ct. Appeals (3rd cir.) 1991. Assoc. Korn, Kline & Kutner, Phila., 1990-91, Brown, Brown, Solt & Ferretti, Allentown, Pa., 1991-94, Knafo Law Offices, Allentown, Pa., 1994—. Hearing com. mem. Disciplinary Bd. Supreme Ct. of Pa., Harrisburg, 1995-2000, chmn., 1999-2000. Mem.: ATLA, Northampton County Bar Assn., Pa. Bar Assn., Pa. Trial Lawyers Assn. (bd. govs. 1998—), Lehigh County Bar Assn. (co-chmn. Law Day 1995—, bd. dirs. 2001—). Democrat. Presbyterian. Avocations: weightlifting, running, golf. Personal injury (including property damage), Product liability, Professional liability. Office: Knafo Law Offices 4201 W Tilghman St Allentown PA 18104-4448 E-mail: maltemose@knafo.com.

ALTER, ELEANOR BREITEL, lawyer; b. N.Y.C., Nov. 10, 1938; d. Charles David and Jeanne (Hollander) Breitel; children: Richard B. Zabel, David B. Zabel. BA with honors, U. Mich., 1960; postgrad., Harvard U., 1960-61; LLB, Columbia U., 1964. Bar: N.Y. 1965. Atty., office of gen. counsel, ins. dept. State of N.Y., 1964-66; assoc. Miller & Carlson, N.Y.C., 1966-68, Marshall, Bratter, Greene, Allison & Tucker, N.Y.C., 1968-74, mem. firm, 1974-82, Rosenman & Colin, 1982-97, Kasowitz, Benson, Torres & Friedman, N.Y.C., 1997—. Fellow U. Chgo. Law Sch., 1988; adj. prof. law NYU Sch. Law, 1983-87; vis. prof. law U. Chgo., 1990-91, 93; lectr. in field. Editorial bd.: N.Y. Law Jour. Contbr. articles to profl. jours. Trustee Lawyers' Fund for Client Protection of the State of N.Y., 1983—, chmn., 1985—; bd. visitors U. Chgo. Law Sch., 1984-87. Mem. Am. Law Inst., Am. Coll. Family Trial Lawyers, N.Y. State Bar Assn., Assn. of Bar of City of N.Y. (libr. com. 1978-80, com. on matrimonial law 1977-81, 87-88, 2002—, judiciary com. 1981-84, 94, 95, 96, exec. com. 1988-92), Am. Acad. Matrimonial Lawyers. Family and matrimonial. Office: Kasowitz Benson Et Al 1633 Broadway New York NY 10019

ALTERMAN, IRWIN MICHAEL, lawyer; b. Vineland, N.J., Mar. 4, 1941; s. Joseph and Rose A.; m. Susan Simon, Aug. 6, 1972 (dec. Apr. 1997); 1 son, Owen. AB, Princeton U., 1962; LLB, Columbia U., 1965. Bar: N.Y. 1966, Mich. 1967. Law clk. to chief judge Theodore Levin U.S. Dist. Ct. (ea. dist.) Mich., 1965-67; assoc. Kaye, Scholer, Fierman, Hays & Handler, N.Y.C., 1967-70, Hyman, Gurwin, Nachman, Friedman & Winkelman, Southfield, Mich., 1970-74, ptnr., 1974-88, Kaufman and Payton, Farmington Hills, Mich., 1988-89, Kemp, Klein, Umphrey, Endelman & May, Troy, Mich., 1989—. Author: Plain and Accurate Style in Court Papers, 1987; founding editor: Mich. Antitrust, 1975—92; editor: Mich. Antitrust Digest, 3d edit., 2001; contbr. articles to profl. jours. Bd. gov. Jewish Fedn. Detroit, 1990—; mem. nat. young leadership cabinet United Jewish Appeal, 1978-79, mem. nat. exec. com., 1980; past pres. Adat Shalom Synagogue, Farmington Hills, Mich. Mem. ABA, Am. Law Inst., State Bar Mich. (past chmn. com. on plain English, past. chmn. antitrust sect.), Princeton Club (past pres. Mich.). Antitrust, Federal civil litigation, Trademark and copyright. Office: Kemp Klein Umphrey & Endelman 201 W Big Beaver Rd Ste 600 Troy MI 48084-4136 E-mail: irwin.alterman@kkue.com.

ALTIERI, PETER LOUIS, lawyer; b. Norwalk, Conn., Dec. 7, 1955; s. John L. and Eileen Mary (Rudden) A.; m. Sandra Shelton White, Sept. 3, 1983; children: Brianna Burr, John Shelton. AB, Georgetown U., 1977; JD, Fordham Sch. Law, 1980. Bar: N.Y. 1981, U.S. Dist. Ct. (so. and ea. dists.) N.Y. 1981, U.S. Dist. Ct. (no. and we. dists) N.Y. 1983, U.S. Dist. Ct. Conn. 1983, U.S. Supreme Ct. 1984, U.S. Ct. Appeals (2d cir.) 1986, Conn. 1987, U.S. Ct. Appeals (6th cir.) 2001. Law clk. to judge U.S. Dist. Ct., 1978; intern U.S. Attys. Office, N.Y.C., 1978; assoc. Law Firm Malcolm A. Hoffmann, N.Y.C., 1980-87; ptnr. Epstein, Becker & Green, N.Y.C., 1987—. Mem. ABA, Conn. Bar Assn. (exec. com. antitrust sect. 1988—), Assn. Bar City N.Y. (com. uniform state laws 1985-88, com. on inter-Am. affairs 1997-99), The Patterson Club Conn., Union League Club N.Y.C. Antitrust, General civil litigation, Labor (including EEOC, Fair Labor Standards Act, labor-management relations, NLRB, OSHA). Home: 140 Burr St Fairfield CT 06824-7105 Office: Epstein Becker & Green 250 Park Ave Ste 1201 New York NY 10177-0001 E-mail: paltieri@ebglaw.com.

ALTMAN, JANE R. lawyer; b. Cambridge, Mass., Mar. 14, 1945; d. Nathan and Renee (Owlick) Rotman; m. Robert A. Altman, June 13, 1965; children: Jennifer Anne, John Scott. BA, Barnard Coll., 1966; MS, Bank Street Coll., 1967; JD, Rutgers U., 1978. Bar: N.J. 1978. Assoc. Carchman, Sochor & Carchman, Princeton, N.J., 1978-82; pvt. practice Skillman, N.J., 1982-94; ptnr. Altman & Legband Attys.-at-Law, Skillman, N.J., 1994—. Adj. prof. domestic rels. law Mercer C.C., West Windsor, N.J., 1986-90; mem. family practice com. N.J. Supreme Ct., 1998—. Mem. adv. com. Womanspace, Trenton, N.J., 1979—; trustee Millhill Child and Family Devel. Ctr., 1979-83. Mem. ABA, N.J. Bar Assn. (exec. com., family law sect.), Mercer County Bar Assn. (trustee 1983-88). Family and matrimonial. Office: Altman & Legband Attys at Law 148 Tamarack Cir Skillman NJ 08558-2021

ALTMAN, LOUIS, lawyer, author, educator; b. N.Y.C., Aug. 6, 1933; s. Benjamin and Jean (Zimmerman) A.; m. Sally J. Schlesinger, Dec. 26, 1955 (dec.); 1 child: Andrew; m. Eleanor Silver, Oct. 30, 1966; 1 child: Robert. AB, Cornell U., 1955; LLB, Harvard U., 1958. Bar: N.Y. 1959, Conn. 1970, Ill. 1973. Assoc. Amster & Levy, N.Y.C., 1958-60; patent atty. Sperry Rand, N.Y.C., 1960-63; chief patent counsel Gen. Time Corp., N.Y.C., 1963-67; ptnr. Altman & Reens, Stamford, Conn., 1967-72; chief patent counsel Baxter Labs, Deerfield, Ill., 1972-76; assoc. prof. John Marshall Law Sch., 1976-79, adj. prof., 1979-96, Loyola Law Sch., 1996-97; of counsel Gerlach, O'Brien & Kleinke, Chgo., 1981-83; ptnr. Laff, Whitesel & Saret, Chgo., 1983-2001; of counsel Michael Best & Friedrich, Chgo., 2001—. Author: Callmann on Unfair Competition, Trademarks & Monopolies, 4th edit., 1981, Business Competition Law Adviser, 1983; contbr. Construction Law, 1986, Legal Compliance Checkups, 1985, articles to legal jours. Recipient Gerald Rose Meml. award John Marshall Law Sch., 1988. Intellectual property, Patent, Trademark and copyright. Home: 3005 Manor Dr Northbrook IL 60062-6947 Office: Michael Best & Friedrich 401 N Michigan Ave Chicago IL 60611-4255 E-mail: laltman@attglobal.net.

ALTMAN, ROBERT, lawyer; b. St. Paul, Feb. 21, 1949; s. Milton and Helen (Horwitz) A.; m. Margo Geller, Mar. 28, 1998; children: (by previous marriage: Jesse, David, Aaron. BA, U. Calif., Berkeley, 1970; JD, U. Minn., 1973. Bar: Minn. 1975, Ga. 1978, U.S. Ct. Appeals (5th cir.) 1978, U.S. Ct. Appeals (11th cir.) 1981, U.S. Supreme Ct. 1981. Atty. Team Def. Project, Atlanta, 1976-77; assoc. dir. So. Prisoners Def. Com., New Orleans, 1978-79; exec. dir. Fed. Defender Program, Inc., 1980-84; pvt. practice Atlanta, 1984—; judge Mcpl. Ct. City of Atlanta, 1988-96. Pres. Fed. Defender Program, Inc., 1990-91; instr. Nat. Inst. Trial Advocacy, Emory U., Atlanta, 1983-2000; com. to rev. the criminal justice act U.S. Jud. Conf., 1991-93. Mem. Ga. Bar Assn., Atlanta Bar Assn. (Blue Ribbon commn.), Assn. Trial Lawyers Am., Ga. Trial Lawyers Assn. (chair bad faith ins. litigation group, mem. exec. com. 1999--), Ga. Assn. Criminal Def. Laywers, Phi Beta Kappa. Insurance, Personal injury (including property damage). Office: 1355 Peachtree St NE Ste 1560 Atlanta GA 30309-3275 E-mail: altlaw@mindspring.com.

ALTMAN, WILLIAM KEAN, lawyer; b. San Antonio, Feb. 18, 1944; s. Marion K. and Ruth (Nunnelee) A.; m. Doris E. Johnson, May 29, 1964; children: Brian, Brad, Blake. BBA, Tex. A&M U., 1965, MBA, 1967; JD, U. Tex., 1979. Bar: Tex. 1970, Okla. 1993, U.S. Dist. Ct. (no. and ea. dists.) Tex., U.S. Ct. Appeals (5th and 11th cirs.), U.S. Supreme Ct. Pres. Altman & Nix, Wichita Falls, Tex., 1970—. Bd. dirs. Beacon Ins. Group. Mem. Wichita Falls City Coun., 1998-2002; mayor of Wichita Falls, 2002--. Mem. ABA, Tex. Bar Assn., Assn. Trial Lawyers Am. (life) (bd. of govs. 1980-83, active coms. and sects.), Tex. Trial Lawyers Assn. (assoc. bd. dirs. 1977-78, bd. dirs. 1978—, active various coms. and sect.). Democrat. Baptist. Insurance, Personal injury (including property damage), Product liability. Office: Altman & Nix PO Box 500 Wichita Falls TX 76307-0500

ALTSCHULER, FREDRIC LAWRENCE, lawyer; b. Yonkers, N.Y., Feb. 25, 1946; s. David and Doris A.; m. Marjorie R. Olderman, Mar. 9, 1969; children: David, Elizabeth. BA, Syracuse U., 1968; JD, St. John's U., 1972. Bar: N.Y. 1972. Assoc. Milbank Tweed Hadley & McCloy, N.Y.C., 1973-81, Breed Abbott and Morgan, N.Y.C., 1981-82, ptnr., 1982-87, Spengler, Carlson, N.Y.C., 1987-92; of counsel Cadwalader, Wickersham & Taft, N.Y.C., 1992-96, ptnr., 1996—. Mem. ABA, Assn. Bar City N.Y., Urban Land Inst. Finance, Property, real (including real estate development, water). Home: 40 E 80th St New York NY 10021-0230 Office: Cadwalader Wickersham & Taft 100 Maiden Ln New York NY 10038-4818 E-mail: Fredric.altschuler@cwt.com.

ALTSHULER, KENNETH PAUL, lawyer; b. Oklahoma City, Okla., Aug. 31, 1952; s. Jerome K. and Roselyn (Weitzenhoffer) Altshuler; m. Lynn Shumans, Mar. 15, 1978 (div. July 1983); m. Lynda Ann Doyle; stepchildren: Amy Elizabeth Doyle, Chelsea Leight Doyle. BS, U. Mich., 1974; JD, U. Maine, 1985. Bar: U.S. Dist. Ct. Maine 1985, U.S. Ct. Appeals (1st cir.) 1985, Maine 1985. Ptnr. Mazziotti and Altshuler, 1985—91, Mittel, Asen, Eggert, Hunter and Altshuler, 1991—95, Altshuler Vincent and Kantz, 1995—99, Childs, Rundlett, Fifield, Shumway and Altshuler, Portland, Maine, 2000—. Instr. Franklin Pierce Coll., 1981—82; acct. Keene Acctg. Svcs., 1979—82; owner Ixtlan Bookstore, Inc., 1976—82; arbitrator Dispute Resolution Assocs., Inc., 1991—95. Bd. dirs. Resources for Divorced Families, chairperson Guardian ad Litem Task Force; bd. dirs. Vet. Ednl. Tng. Svcs., Keene NH C. of C., 1980—82; chairperson Keene Downtown Merchants Assn., 1980—82. Fellow: Am. Acad. Matrimonial Lawyers (bd. govs. Maine rep. to New Eng. chpt.); mem.: ABA (Maine reporter, Family Law sect.), Internat. Acad. Matrimonial Lawyers, Maine State Bar Assn. (chair, legis. liaison, sec. Family Law sect., lectr. Family Law sect., lectr. Pub. Affairs com.), Nat. Assn. of Counsel for Children. Family and matrimonial. Office: 257 Deering Ave Portland ME 04103

ALVAREZ-FARRÉ, EMILIO JOSÉ, lawyer; b. Havana, Cuba, Sept. 5, 1956; s. Emilio Bonifacio Alvarez and Josefina Farré; m. Martha Isabel Ona, Oct. 1, 1966; children: Nicole Sofia, Natalia Isabel. Student, Yale U., 1974-75; AB, Stanford U., 1978; postgrad., Princeton U., 1979; JD, MBA, U. Chgo., 1986. Bar: Fla. 1986. Assoc. Shutts & Bowen, Miami, Fla., 1986—88, White & Case, N.Y.C., 1988—97, ptnr., 1998—. Mem. Fla. Bar Assn., Phi Beta Kappa. Christian. Finance, Private international, Mergers and acquisitions. Office: White & Case 200 S Biscayne Blvd Ste 4900 Miami FL 33131-2352

ALVES, RODNEY ALMEIDA, lawyer, consultant; b. Sao Paulo, Brazil, Aug. 31, 1967; s. Ubirajara Maria and Marli Almeida Alves; m. Lilian Marcondes, Dec. 17, 1990; children: Giovanna M. Spirlandelli, Leonardo M. Spirlandelli. LL.B, Mackenzie Law Sch., Sao Paulo, 1994; Specialization in Antitrust with honors, Nat. Sch. Pub. Adminstrn., Brasilia, 1999; LLM in Internat. and Comparative Law, UCLA, 2003—. Bar: Sao Paulo, Brazil (Bar Assn.) 1994, Rio de Janeiro (Bar Assn.) 1997. Lawyer Interactive Televendas Brasil Ltd.., Sao Paulo, Brazil, 1994—96; sr. lawyer Villemor Amaral Law Office, Sao Paulo, Brazil, 1996—2000; mgr. lawyer Castro, Campos & Associates, Sao Paulo, Brazil, 2000—. Cons. Fênix Clinic for Drug Addicts, Peruíbe, Brazil, 2002; mem. of the bd. Seven Day Adventist Ch., Sao Paulo, Brazil, 1997—. 2nd lt. of cav. CPOR, 1987—88, Sao Paulo. Mem.: Brazilian Inst. Competition and Consumer Relationship Studies, GEDECON - Antitrust Study Group (assoc.), Landwell Network (assoc.; mem. of merger and acquisitions and antitrust groups 2002), Internat. Assn. Young Lawyers (assoc.; merger and acquisition and antitrust commns. 1999—2002). Seventh Day Adventist. Avocations: travel, football, volleyball, swimming. Mergers and acquisitions, Antitrust, Corporate, general. Office: Castro Campos & Assocs Ave Francisco Matarazzo 1400 - Milano São Paulo 05001-400 Brazil Office Fax: 55-11-3879-2801. E-mail: rodney.alves@br.pwc.com.

ALWORTH, CHARLES WESLEY, lawyer, engineer; b. Buenos Aires, Aug. 23, 1943; s. Cecil Dwight and Kathleen Mary (Whitaker) A.; m. Sally Ann Wells, Dec. 21, 1967 (div. Nov. 1981); m. Madeline E. Wilson, Feb. 14, 1983; children: Cecil Dwight II, Barbara Diane. BSEE, U. Okla., 1965, M in Elec. Engring., 1967, PhD, 1969; JD, U. Tulsa, 1992. Bar: U.S. Patent Bar Office 1989, Tex. 1993, U.S. Dist. Ct. (ea. dist.) Tex. 1993, U.S. Dist. Ct. (no. dist.) Tex. 1997, U.S. Ct. Appeals (fed. cir.) 2001; registered profl. engr., La., Okla., Tex. Tchg. asst. elec. engring. U. Okla., Norman, 1965, grad. asst. elec. engring., 1965-67, spl. instr. elec. engring., 1967-68; asst. prof. elec. engring. Tex. A&M U., College Station, Tex., 1968-74; chief, prin. cons. Conoco, Inc., Ponca City, Okla., 1974-90; rsch. assoc. profl. engr. U. Tulsa, Okla., 1990—; chief engr. Alworth Cons., Tyler, Tex., 1990—; of counsel Sefrna & Assocs., Tyler, 1993-95; prin. Charles W. Alworth Engr. & Atty. at Law; assoc. prof. and head elec. engring. U. Tex., Tyler, 1997-98. Patentee in field; contbr. articles to profl. jours. Mem. Phi Delta Phi, Tau Beta Pi, Eta Kappa Nu, Sigma Xi. Episcopalian. Avocations: aviation, woodworking, gardening. Intellectual property, Patent, Trademark and copyright. Home: 505 Cumberland Rd Tyler TX 75703-9325

AL-YAWER, RIYADH JALAL, lawyer; b. Erbil, Iraq, Sept. 25, 1940; arrived in the U.K., 1984; s. Jalal Daoud and Najia Hussein Awni (Al'Mumaiez) Al-Y.; m. Sana Muhammad Al'Dabbagh, Jan. 11, 1980; children: Farah, Hussein. BA, Baghdad (Iraq) U., 1962, MA, 1973. Solicitor Al-Yawer & Ptnrs., Baghdad, Iraq, 1962-63; mgr. in charge of studies Iraq Reinsurance Co., Baghdad, 1963; diplomat Iraqi Ministry for Fgn. Affairs, Baghdad, 1964-70; consul gen. Iraqi Embassy, London, 1966-67; mgr. legal studies and rsch. dept. Ministry of Planning, Baghdad, 1970-73; chmn., pres. Middle East Transport and Trade Co., W.L.L., Baghdad, 1973-80. Author: Fundamental Change in International Treaties, 1973. V.p. Iraqi Free Coun., London, 1991; founding mem. Iraqi Nat. Congress, Vienna, Austria, 1992; mem. exec. coun. Iraqi Nat. Congress, Salahuddin, Iraq, 1993; elected to presdl. coun. Iraqi Nat. Congress, 1999, rotating chmn. presdl. coun. Moslem. Avocations: reading, photography, boating, sports. Home and Office: 2 Greenoak Way Wimbledon London SW19 5EN England

AMABILE, JOHN LOUIS, lawyer; b. N.Y.C., Oct. 13, 1934; s. John A. and Rose (Singer) A.; m. Christina M. Leary, Nov. 23, 1963; children: Tracy Ann, John Christopher. BS cum laude, Coll. Holy Cross, 1956; LLB, St. John's Sch. Law, 1959. Bar: N.Y. 1959, U.S. Dist. Ct. (so. and ea. dists.) N.Y. 1961, U.S. Supreme Ct. 1964, U.S. Ct. Claims 1964, U.S. Ct. Appeals (2d cir.) 1970, U.S. Tax Ct. 1984, U.S. Ct. Appeals (9th cir.) 1984. Assoc.

Law Office of Allen Taylor, N.Y.C., 1959-62; assoc. Schwartz & Frohlich, N.Y.C., 1963-69, ptnr., 1969, Summit, Solomon & Feldesman (and predecessor firms), N.Y.C., 1971-93, Putney, Twombly Hall & Hirson, N.Y.C., 1993-2000, of counsel, 2001—. Faculty mem. ann. seminar Practising Law Inst., 1987-91; mediator so. dist. U.S. Dist. Ct. N.Y., comml. divsn. Supreme Ct., N.Y.; arbitrator ea. dist. U.S. Dist. Ct., Bklyn.; panel chair appellate divsn. Disciplinary Com., 1980-85, 87-92; lectr. in field. Author: Responses to Complaints: Commercial Litigation in New York State Courts, 1995, Warranties: Business and Commercial Litigation in Federal Courts, 1998, The Record of the Association of the Bar of the City of New York Vol. 54, No. 5; editor St. John Law Rev. 1958-59. Regional commr. Am. Youth Soccer Orgn., Chappaqua, N.Y., 1975-84; mem. New Castle Recreation and Parks Commn., 1984-90, chairperson, 1987-89, dir. Aiken county Coun. on Aging, 2003—. Mem. ABA, N.Y. State Bar Assn., Assn. Bar City N.Y. (mem. com. on state legis. 1971-74, chair 1975-78, com. on grievances 1979-80, com. on women in cts. 1988-94, com. on judiciary 1989-92, interim mem. 1992, 93, 94, 96, 97, 98, 99, 2000, chair com. on gender bias in fed. cts. 1991-93, coun. judicial adminstrn. 1996-2001, com. on symposium 1997-2000, chair 1998-2000), Fed. Bar Coun., Practising Law Inst. (chair winning strategies for depositions in corp. litigation 1991-92, co-chair seminars on art of taking and defending depositions in corp. litigation 1982-85). Democrat. Roman Catholic. Federal civil litigation, State civil litigation. Home: Woodside Plantation 308 Willow Lake Ct Aiken SC 29803

AMADO, HONEY KESSLER, lawyer; b. Bklyn., July 20, 1949; d. Bernard and Mildred Kessler; m. Ralph Albert Amado, Oct. 24, 1976; children: Jessica Reina, Micah Solomon, Gabrielle Beth. BA in Polit. Sci., Calif. State Coll., Long Beach, 1971; JD, Western State U., Fullerton, Calif., 1976. Bar: Calif. 1977, U.S. Dist. Ct. (ctrl. dist.) Calif. 1981, U.S. Ct. Appeals (9th cir.) 1981, U.S. Supreme Ct. 1994. Assoc. Law Offices of Jack M. Lasky, Beverly Hills, Calif., 1977-78; pvt. practice Beverly Hills, Calif., 1978—. Mem. family law exec. com. Calif. State Bar, 1987-91; lectr. in field. Contbr. articles to profl. jours.; mem. editl. bd. L.A. Lawyer mag., 1996—, articles coord., 1999-2000, chair, 2000-01. Mem. Com. Concerned Lawyers for Soviet Jewry, 1979-90; nat. v.p. Jewish Nat. Fund, 1995-97, 2002—; bd. dirs. Jewish Nat. Fund L.A., 1990-98, 2002—; mem. pres.'s coun. Am. Jewish Com., 2002—; sec. L.A. region, bd. dirs. , 1991-94, Am. Jewish Congress, Jewish Feminist Ctr., 1992-99, co-chair steering com., 1994-96; mem. Commn. on Soviet Jewry of Jewish Fedn. Coun. Greater L.A., 1977-83, chmn., 1979-81, commn. on edn., 1982-83, cmty. rels. com., 1979-83; mem. pres.'s coun. Am. Jewish Com., L.A., 2003—, bd. dirs., 2002—. Mem. Calif. Women Lawyers (bd. govs. 1988-90, 1st v.p. 1989-90, jud. evaluations co-chair 1988-90), San Fernando Valley Bar Assn. (family law mediators and arbitrators planel 1983-94, judge pro-tem panel 1987-94), Beverly Hills Bar Assn. (family law mediators panel 1985-94), L.A. County Bar Assn. (family law sect., appellate cts. com. 1987—, chmn. subcom. to examine reorgn. Calif. Supreme Ct. 1990-94, judge pro tem panel 1985-95, appellate jud. evaluations com. 1989—, editl. bd. L.A. Lawyer mag. 1996—, articles coord. 1999—, dist. 2 settlement program 1996—), Calif. State Bar, Calif. Ct. Appeal. Democrat. Jewish. Appellate, General civil litigation, Family and matrimonial. Office: 261 S Wetherly Dr Beverly Hills CA 90211-2515

AMAN, ALFRED CHARLES, JR., law educator; b. Rochester, N.Y., July 7, 1945; s. Alfred Charles Sr. and Jeannette Mary (Czebatul) Aman; m. Carol Jane Greenhouse, Sept. 23, 1976. AB, U. Rochester, 1967; JD, U. Chgo., 1970. Bar: (D.C.) 1971, Ga. 1972, N.Y. 1980. Law clk. U.S. Ct. Appeals, Atlanta, 1970—72; assoc. Sutherland, Asbill & Brennan, Atlanta, 1972—75, Washington, 1975—77; assoc. prof. Sch. Law, Cornell U., Ithaca, NY, 1977—82, prof. law, 1983—91, exec. dir. Internat. Legal Studies Program, 1988—90; dean Sch. Law, Ind. U., Bloomington, 1991—2002, prof. law, 1991—, Roscoe C. O'Byrne chair in law, 1999—, disting. Fulbright chair in comparative constitutional law, 1998; vis. prof. law U. Paris II, 1998; vis. fellow law and pub. affairs program Princton U., 2002—03. Cons. U.S. Adminstrv. Conf., Washington, 1978—80, Washington, 1986—; trustee U. Rochester, 1980—; vis. fellow Wolfson Coll., Cambridge U., 1983—84, 1990—91. Author: Energy and Natural Resources, 1983, Administrative Law in a Global Era, 1992, Administrative Law Treatise, 1992, 2d edit., 2001. Chmn. Ithaca Bd. Zoning Appeals, 1980—82. Mem.: ABA, N.Y. State Bar Assn., Ga. Bar Assn., D.C. Bar Assn., Am. Assn. Law Schs., Phi Beta Kappa. Avocations: music, jazz drumming, piano, composition and arranging. Office: Ind U Sch Law 211 S Indiana Ave Bloomington IN 47405-7001

AMAN, GEORGE MATTHIAS, III, lawyer; b. Wayne, Pa., Mar. 2, 1930; s. George Matthias and Emily (Kalbach) A.; m. Ellen McMillan, June 20, 1959; children: James E., Catherine E., Peter T. AB, Princeton U., 1952; LL.B., Harvard U., 1957. Bar: Pa. 1958. Assoc. Townsend Elliot & Munson, Phila., 1960-65; ptnr. Morgan Lewis & Bockius, Phila., 1965-93; of counsel High, Swartz, Roberts & Seidel, Norristown, Pa., 1993—. Commr. Radnor Twp., Pa., 1976-80, 86-92, planning commr., 1981-86; pres. bd. trustees Wayne Presbyn. Ch., Pa., 1981-84. Served to 1st lt. U.S. Army, 1952-54. Mem. ABA, Pa. Mcpl. Authorities Assn., Phila. Regional Mcpl. Fin. Officers Assn. (dir. 1983-87). Clubs: Merion Cricket (Haverford, Pa.); Princeton (Phila.) (dir 1977-79, treas. 1985-86). Republican. Corporate, general, Municipal (including bonds). Home: 246 Upland Way Wayne PA 19087-4859 Office: High Swartz Roberts Seidel 40 E Airy St Norristown PA 19401-4803 E-mail: george.aman@verizon.net., gaman@highswartz.com.

AMANN, LESLIE KIEFER, lawyer, educator; b. Pensacola, Fla., Dec. 21, 1955; d. Robert C. and Marilyn Joan (Franklin) K.; children: Augustus Kiefer, Nicholas Jacob. BMEd, S.W. Tex. State U., 1976; JD, U. Houston, 1987. Bar: Tex. 1987, U.S. Dist. Ct. (so. dist.) Tex. 1988, U.S. Ct. Appeals (5th cir.), 1991, U.S. Dist. Ct. (no. dist.) Tex. 1992. Legis. aide to Lindon Williams Tex. State Senate, Austin, 1977-81; tchr. The Lincoln Sch., Guadalajara, Mex., 1979-82; legal asst. Koons Rasor Fuller & McCurley, Dallas, 1983-84; clk., assoc., participating assoc. Reynolds, Allen, Cook, Reynolds & Cunningham, Houston, 1984-93; shareholder Cunningham & Amann, Houston, 1993-94; asst. gen. counsel Charter Bank, Houston, 1995-96; sr. v.p., fiduciary counsel, market trust exec. Bank of America, Houston, 1996—. Adj. faculty Law Sch., U. Houston, 1988-2000; mem. faculty Tex. Bankers Assn. Trust Sch., 1998-2003; mem. bd. dirs. U. Houston Law Alumni Assn. Contbr. articles to profl. jours. Mem. adv. bd. Probate and Trust Law Inst., South Tex. Coll. Law, Houston, 1998- 2000; vol. Annunciation Orthodox Sch., Houston, 1996-2003; vol. Greater Houston Partnership Texas Scholars, 2000-2002. Recipient Adj. Faculty award Univ. Houston Law Sch., 1999. Fellow Tex. Bar Found. (life); mem. Houston Bar Assn. (vol. lawyers in pub. schs. 1998), Tex. State Bar., Attys. in Tax and Probate, Houston Bus. and Estate Planning Coun., Houston Estate and Fin. Forum. Republican. Methodist. Avocations: writing, reading, book collecting. General civil litigation, Estate planning, Probate (including wills, trusts). Office: Bank of America PO Box 2518 700 Louisiana 6th Fl Houston TX 77252-2518

AMAON, GARY P. lawyer; b. Lubbock, Tex., Nov. 18, 1945; BS, Abilene Christian Coll., 1966; JD, U. Tex., 1969. Bar: Tex. 1969. Mem. Vinson & Elkins L.L.P., Houston. Mem. Chancellors, Order of Coif, Phi Delta Phi. Labor (including EEOC, Fair Labor Standards Act, labor-management relations, NLRB, OSHA), Pension, profit-sharing, and employee benefits. Office: Vinson & Elkins LLP 2500 First City Tower 1001 Fannin St Ste 3300 Houston TX 77002-6706 Address: 7897 Broadway, Apt #601 San Antonio TX 78209

AMBER, DOUGLAS GEORGE, lawyer; b. East Chicago, Ind., Apr. 15, 1956; s. George and Margaret (Watson) A. BA in Polit. Sci., Ind. U., 1978; JD, U. Miami, 1985. Bar: Fla. 1985, US. Ct. Claims 1986, U.S. Ct. Internat. Trade 1986, U.S. Tax Ct. 1986, U.S. Ct. Appeals (11th cir.) 1986, U.S. Dist. Ct. (mid. and so. dists.) Fla. 1987, U.S. Ct. Mil. Appeals 1987, U.S. Ct. Appeals (fed. cir.) 1987, Ind. 1988, U.S. Dist. Ct. (no. and so. dists.) Ind. 1988, U.S. Ct. Appeals (7th cir.) 1989, U.S. Supreme Ct. 1989; registered civil mediator. Dep. prosecutor 31st Jud. Cir. Ind., Crown Point, 1988-93; pvt. practice Munster, 1993—. Adj. prof. polit. sci. Purdue U., 1997—. Mem. exec. bd. dirs. Calumet coun. Boy Scouts Am., 1994-96. Mem. ABA, Acad. Legal Studies in Bus., Nat. Dist. Attys. Assn., South Lake County Bar Assn., Ind. State Bar Assn., Lake County Bar Assn. (bd. dirs. 1990-96), Ind. Trial Lawyers Assn., Audio Engring. Soc., Soc. Audio Cons. (cert. video and audio cons.), Mensa, Delta Theta Phi. Avocations: bicycling, weight training. Office: Amber Golding & Hofstetter 9250 Columbia Ave Ste E-2 Munster IN 46321-3530 E-mail: amber@calumet.purdue.edu.

AMBER, LAURIE KAUFMAN, lawyer; b. N.Y.C., Apr. 15, 1954; d. Martin and Barbara (Schiffman) Kaufman; m. Henry Michael Amber, June 18, 1977; children: Ian, Kyle. BS, Cornell U., 1974, MBA, 1975; JD, U. Miami, 1978. Bar: Fla. 1978, U.S. Dist. Ct. (so. dist.) Fla. 1978, U.S. Tax Ct. 1978, U.S. Ct. Appeals (5th cir.) 1979, U.S. Ct. Customs and Patent Appeals 1979, U.S. Customs Ct. 1979, U.S. Ct. Appeals (11th cir.) 1981, U.S. Ct. Internat. Trade 1981, U.S. Supreme Ct. 1982, U.S. Claims Ct. 1985; cert. civil circuit mediator Supreme Ct. Fla.; cert. family mediator Supreme Ct. Fla. Staff mgr. Proctor & Gamble Mfg. Co., Staten Island, N.Y., 1975; adj. asst. prof. Nova U., Fort Lauderdale, Fla., 1976-77; atty., labor arbitrator Amber & Amber, P.A., South Miami, Fla., 1978—. Arbitrator nat. labor panel Am. Arbitration Assn., Miami, 1982—, Grievance Arbitration Panel of Fla. PERC, Tallahassee, 1979—; hearing examiner pers. appeals County of Dade, Miami, 1985-91, 2000—; dir. Kids That Care Pediat. Cancer Fund, 1996—. Pres. Office Village Condominium Assn., South Miami, 1994, Children's Cancer Fund, 1996-2000; bd. dirs. Jackson Meml. Found., 1996-2000, Kids That Care Pediatric and Cancer Fund, 2000—. Named Woman of Yr. ABWA, 1983. Mem. ABA, Zonta (bd. dirs. Coral Gables, Fla. club 1988). General practice, Probate (including wills, trusts), Property, real (including real estate development, water). Office: Amber & Amber PA 7731 SW 62nd Ave Ste 202 Miami FL 33143-4908

AMBRO, THOMAS L. federal judge; b. Cambridge, Ohio, Dec. 27, 1949; BA, Georgetown U., 1971, JD, 1975. Bar: Del. 1976. Clk. Hon. Daniel L. Herrmann Del. Supreme Ct., 1975—76; assoc. Richards, Layton and Finger, 1976—82, ptnr., 1982—2000; judge U.S. Ct. Appeals (3d cir.), 2000—. Mem. State Del. Gov.'s Commn. on Mayor Comml. Litig. Reform, 1993, N.Y. TriBar Opinion Com., 1988—. Author: Third Party Legal Opinions in Asset Based Financing: A Transactional Guide, 1990; contbr. articles to profl. jours. Mem.: ABA (vice-chair com. on programs 1987—90, chair com. on meetings 1988—90, participant Silverado Conf. on Legal Opinions 1989, mem. drafting subcom. third-party legal opinion report 1989—91, chair subcom. on opinion letters 1989—95, mem. com. on comml. fin. svcs. 1989—95, chair com. on meetings 1990—94, chair or co-chair com. on publs. 1994—97, chair com. on legal opinions 1994—98, mem. coun. sect. bus. law 1994—98, editl. bd. The Bus. Lawyer 1998—99, editor The Bus. Lawyer 1999—2000, vice-chair sect. bus. law 1999—2000, sec. sect. bus. law 1998-99, 2000-01, immediate past chmn. 2002-, mem. com. on uniform comml. code, mem. com. on negotiated acquisitions, mem. bus. bankruptcy com., chair elect bus. law 2000—01, chair sec. bus. law 2001—02, immediate past chair 2002—), Am. Coll. Comml. Fin. Lawyers (bd. regents, charter), Am. Coll. Investment Counsel, Am. Coll. Bankruptcy, Del. State Bar Assn. (chmn. 1979—82, vice-chmn. 1982—83, comml. law sect., chair subcom. on uniform comml. code 1983—), Phi Beta Kappa. Office: Lockbox 32 5122 Fed Bldg 844 N King St Wilmington DE 19801

AMBROSE, ARLEN S. lawyer; b. Pueblo, Colo., Sept. 29, 1937; s. Aubrey and Harriett Ambrose; m. Janet Roseman, July 14, 1963 (div. Apr. 1979); children: David Alan, Judith Maryse; m. Ruth Lurie, July 31, 1988. BSBA, U. Colo., 1959; JD, Georgetown U., 1962. Bar: Colo. 1962, U.S. Dist. Ct. Colo. 1962, U.S. Ct. Appeals (10th cir.) 1962, U.S. Supreme Ct. 1980. Clk. Senator John A. Carroll, Washington, 1959-62; law clk. to Judge William E. Doyle U.S. Dist. Ct. Colo., Denver, 1963-64; assoc. McNichols, Wallace, Nigro & Johnson, Denver, 1964-70, Hays & Thompson, Denver, 1970-73; ptnr. Hays, Patterson & Ambrose, Denver, 1974-78; clk. U.S. Ct. Appeals (10th cir.), Denver, 1979-81; ptnr., shareholder Ambrose Porter & Higgs P.C., Englewood, Colo., 1984-88; pvt. practice Englewood, 1988—. Mem. Concerned Lawyers, Inc., Denver, 1978-85. Co-founder, officer, trustee Temple Sinai, Denver, 1967—; co-founder, pres., trustee Rocky Mountain Jewish Hist. Soc., Denver, 1976—; pres., trustee Denver Inst. Jewish Studies, 1984-89. Lt. USNR, 1973-77. Mem. Colo. Bar Assn. (com. on drugs and alcohol related problems 1978—), Arapahoe County Bar Assn., Rocky Mountain Stereo Photography Assn. (v.p. 1998—). Avocations: stereo photography, travel, genealogy, colorado history, art. Corporate, general, Family and matrimonial, Property, real (including real estate development, water). Home: 3076 S Saint Paul St Denver CO 80210-6761 Office: 3677 S Huron St Ste 105 Englewood CO 80110-3466 E-mail: leaagle@aol.com.

AMDAHL, DOUGLAS KENNETH, retired state supreme court justice; b. Mabel, Minn., Jan. 23, 1919; BBA, U. Minn., 1945; JD summa cum laude, William Mitchell Coll. Law, 1951, L.L.D. (hon.), 1987. Bar: Minn. 1951, Fed. Dist. Ct. 1952. Ptnr. Amdahl & Scott, Mpls., 1951-55; asst. county atty. Hennepin County, Minn., 1955-61; judge Mcpl. Ct., Mpls., 1961-62, Dist. Ct. 4th Dist., Minn., 1962-80, chief judge, 1973-75; assoc. justice Minn. Supreme Ct., 1980-81, chief justice, 1981-89; of counsel Rider, Bennett, Egan & Arundel, Mpls., 1989-99; ret. Asst. registrar, then registrar Mpls. Coll. Law, 1951-65; moot ct. instr. U. Minn.; faculty mem. and advisor Nat. Coll. State Judiciary; mem. Nat. Bd. Trial Advocacy; chmn. Nat. Ctr. for State Cts. Delay Reduction Adv. Com., 1986-88, Nat. Ctr. for State Cts. Coordinating Coun. on Life-Sustaining Decisionmaking by the Cts., 1989-93. Mem. ABA (chmn. com. on stds. of jud. adminstrn. 1987-96), Minn. Bar Assn., Hennepin County Bar Assn., Internat. Acad. Trial Judges, State Dist. Ct. Judges Assn. (pres. 1976-77), Conf. of Chief Judges (bd. dirs. 1987-88), Delta Theta Phi (assoc. justice supreme ct.). Home: 2322 W 53rd St Minneapolis MN 55410-2501 E-mail: dougamdahl@aol.com.

AMDUR, ARTHUR R. lawyer; b. Houston, Jan. 19, 1946; s. Paul S. and Florence Amdur; m. Dora B.; children— Josh, Jonny, Shira. B.A., 1967; J.D., 1970; LL.M., 1974. Bar: Tex. 1970, D.C. 1974; cert. immigration law Tex. Bd. Legal Specialization, 1988 . pvt. practice, Houston and Washington, 1970-76; asst. U.S. atty, Houston, 1976-82; pvt. practice, Houston, 1982—, lectr. on immigration law ; adj. prof. law South Tex. Coll. Law, Houston. Bd. dirs. YMCA Internat. Refugee Ctr., 1985—; spl. asst. to gen. counsel Republican Nat. Com., Washington, 1974. Named Adj. Law Prof. of Yr., South Tex. Coll. Law, 1983. Mem. Fed. Bar Assn. (pres. 1981), Tex. State Bar Assn., Am. Immigration Lawyers Assn., Immigration Law Examiner, State Bar Tex. (bd. legal specialization 1997—). Jewish. Club: Georgetown U. Alumni (pres. 1984) (Houston). Federal civil litigation, Immigration, naturalization, and customs, Private international. Office: Amdur Law Office 6161 Savoy Dr Ste 450 Houston TX 77036-3379

AMDUR, MARTIN BENNETT, lawyer; b. N.Y.C., Aug. 19, 1942; s. Charles and Helen (Freedman) A.; m. Shirley Bell, May 25, 1975; children: Richard J., Stephen B. AB, Cornell U., 1964; LLB, Yale U., 1967; LLM in Taxation, NYU, 1968. Bar: N.Y. 1968, U.S. Tax Ct. 1970, U.S. Dist. Ct. (so. and ea. dists.) N.Y. 1971. Assoc. Weil, Gotshal & Manges LLP, N.Y.C., 1968-75, ptnr., 1975—. Lectr. various tax insts. Contbr. articles to legal jours. Mem. ABA, Am. Coll. Tax Counsel, N.Y. State Bar Assn., Assn. Bar City N.Y. Corporate taxation, Personal income taxation. Home: 983 Park Ave Apt 6B New York NY 10028-0808 Office: Weil Gotshal & Manges LLP 767 Fifth Ave New York NY 10153-0119 Office Fax: 212-310-6891. E-mail: Martin.Amdur@Weil.com.

AMEND, JAMES MICHAEL, lawyer; b. Chgo., July 19, 1942; s. Nathan and Edith (Greenberg) A.; m. Sheila Rae Cohen, Apr. 4, 1971; children: Allison, Anthony. BSE, U. Mich., 1964, JD, 1967. Bar: Ill. 1968, U.S. Dist. Ct. (no. dist.) Ill. 1968, U.S. Ct. Appeals (7th cir.) 1969, U.S. Supreme Ct. 1970, U.S. Ct. Appeals (9th cir.) 1985. Ptnr. Kirkland & Ellis, Chgo., 1968—. Prof. Stanford U. Law Sch., 1996-97. Editor U. Mich. Law Rev., 1966, Patent Law: A Primer for Federal District Court Judges, 1998; author: Intellectual Property Law, 1982. Chmn. Chgo. Lawyers Com. for Civil Rights Under Law, 1985-86. Fulbright scholar, 1967. Mem. ABA, U.S. Trademark Assn., Mid-Am. Club (Chgo.). Jewish. Avocations: running, skiing, golf. Intellectual property, Patent, Trademark and copyright. Office: Kirkland & Ellis 200 E Randolph St Fl 54 Chicago IL 60601-6636

AMENT, MARK STEVEN, lawyer; b. Louisville, Sept. 4, 1951; s. Milton and Bernice (Rosenberg) A.; m. Elaine Sue Winkler, Dec. 28, 1976; children: Aaron Samuel, Rachel Lynn. BA, Northwestern U., 1973; JD, Duke U., 1976; LLM in Taxation, U. Miami, 1977. Bar: Ky. 1976, Fla. 1977. Assoc. Greenebaum Doll & McDonald, Louisville, 1977-82, ptnr., 1982-95; mem. Greenebaum Doll & McDonald PLLC, Louisville, 1995—, co-chair emerging techs. group, 2000—. Bd. dirs., sec. Evans Furniture Co., Louisville; lectr. in field. Commr. City of Robinswood, Ky., 1986-99; active Louisville Mayor's Task Force on Low-Income Housing, 1987; v.p. Ctrl. Agy. for Jewish Edn., 1991-94; trustee Congregation Adath Jeshurun, 1995-98; exec. com. Jewish Family and Vocat. Svc. Mem. ABA (com. on comml. fin. svcs., com. on venture capital), Ky. Bar Assn., Louisville Bar Assn., Fla. Bar Assn., Am. Health Lawyers Assn., Nat. Assn. Coll. and Univ. Attys. (mem. publs. com.), Thoroughbred Owners and Breeders Assn., Northwestern U. Alumni Assn. (bd. dirs. 2000—). Democrat. Avocations: basketball, thoroughbreds. Health, Mergers and acquisitions, Property, real (including real estate development, water). Office: Greenebaum Doll & McDonald PLLC 3300 National City Tower Louisville KY 40202 E-mail: msa@gdm.com.

AMES, GEORGE ROBERT, JR., judge; b. Westover, Md., Sept. 23, 1941; s. George Robert Ames Sr., Henrietta Lucille Ames; m. Beverly Ann Whittington, Oct. 22, 1962 (div. Oct. 1973); m. Delema Alberta Young, Apr. 10, 1976; children: Starlene, George Robert Ames III, Craig, Michael. AA in Social Sci., Chesapeake Coll., 1978, AA in Law Enforcement, 1982; AA in Ministry, Christian World Coll. of Theology, 2001. Lic. minister, cert. Christian Counselling One Christian World Coll. Theology, 2000; Criminal Justice Acad. Witness Internat. Inc., 2001. Sch. bus contractor Dorchester Md. Schs., Cambridge, 1979—2000; carrier newspaper Dorchester Md., Cambridge, 1973—2000, commr. dist. ct., 1980—89, judge orphans ct., 1994—. Notary public; judge Orphans Ct., 1994—. Contbr. Commr. Dist. Ct., 1980—89; bd. trustees Dorchester Libr. Bd., 1995—; pres. Dorchester NAACP. Airman 2d USAF, 1960—66, Vietnam. Recipient Dr. King award, TriCounty Orgn., 1987, 2000, Cmty. Svc. award, Iota Phi Lambda, Beta Epsilon chpt., 2001. Mem.: NAACP (pres. Dorchester chpt. 1987—), Dorchester Sch. Bus Contractors (pres. 1988—2000), Dorchester C. of C. (bd. dirs. 1998—), Am. Legion (life; judge advocate Cpl. Herman Hughes Post 87). Democrat. Baptist. Avocation: reading. Home: 703 High St Cambridge MD 21613

AMES, JOHN LEWIS, lawyer; b. Norfolk, Va., July 15, 1912; s. Harry Lee and Catherine I. (Betty) A.; m. Margaret Kilbon, Apr. 8, 1939 (dec. Sept. 1996); children: Margaret Lee, John Lewis. AB, Randolph-Macon Coll., 1933; JD, U. Richmond, 1937; postgrad., NYU, 1939-40. Bar: Va. 1936, N.Y. 1940. Mem. tax divsn. Home Life Ins. Co., N.Y.C., 1937-38; trial atty. Tanner, Sillocks & Friend, N.Y.C., 1938-41; house counsel Ruthrauff & Ryan, Inc., N.Y.C., 1941-42, house counsel and asst. to pres., 1945-48, sec., counsel, 1948-50, v.p., sec., 1950-55, v.p., sec., treas., 1955-57, also dir.; v.p., sec. Erwin, Wassey, Ruthrauff & Ryan, Inc., 1957-59; asst. dir. bus. affairs CBS TV Netowrk, Inc., N.Y.C., 1959-62; v.p., sec., treas. Kudner Agy., Inc., 1962-65, also dir.; sr. v.p. adminstrn. and fin. West, Weir & Bartel, Inc., N.Y.C., 1966, exec. v.p., dir., until 1968; v.p., sec. Lennen & Newell, Inc., 1968-73; v.p. bus. and legal affairs Dancer-Fitzgerald-Samplem Inc., 1973-83; legal cons. Saatchi & Saatchi DFS Inc., 1983-96. Dir. Carroll Products, Inc.; spl. agt. FBI, Washington and N.Y.C., 1942-45; spl. dept. atty. gen. N.Y. State, 1946-48; mem. Nassau County N.Y. Crime Commn., 1973-83. Trustee Randolph-Macon Coll., 1955-85, trustee emeritus, 1985—; mem. Massapequa Bd. Edn., 1952-79, pres. 1957-78; past pres. Nassau-Suffolk Sch. Bds. Assn.; past chmn. trustees Am. Assn. Advt. Agencies Group Ins.; trustee, chmn. bd. of trustees, vice chmn., chmn. adminstrv. bd. White Stone Unite Meth. Ch. Mem. N.Y. County Lawyers Assn., Am. Arbitration Assn. (mem. nat panel), Soc. Former Spl. Agts. FBI (past nat. sec.), Alumni Soc. Randolph-Macon Coll. (past pres.), Lancaster County Crime Solvers, Inc. (pres. 1991-94, 2001—), Indian Creek Yacht and Country Club, Windmill Point Yacht Club, Phi Kappa Sigma, Omicron Delta Kappa, Tau Kappa Alpha. Methodist. Home: PO Box 727 White Stone VA 22578-0727 Office: 375 Hudson St New York NY 10014-3658

AMES, MARC L. lawyer; b. Bklyn., Mar. 14, 1943; s. Arthur L. and Ray (Sardas) Ames; m. Eileen Moll, July 12, 1970 (div. Mar. 2000); children: Adam, Kimberly. JD, Bklyn. Law Sch., 1967; LLM, NYU, 1968. Bar: N.Y. 1967, U.S. Dist. Ct. (ea. and so. dist.) N.Y. 1973, U.S. Ct. Appeals (2nd cir.) 1973, U.S. Supreme Ct. 1973, U.S. Ct. Appeals (3d cir.) 1982, Pa. 1988; lic. radio amateur. Mem. faculty L.I. U., 1968-69, N.Y.C. Community Coll., 1969-70; pvt. practice, 1967—. Arbitrator U.S. Dist. Ct. (ea. dist.) N.Y. 1985, small claims divsn. N.Y.C. Civil Ct., N.Y.C. Civil Ct.; cons. disability retirement and pensions; arbitrator Am. Arbitration Assn.; bd. dirs. Internat. Comms. Concepts, Inc. Contbr. articles to profl. jours. Recipient cert. appreciation N.Y. State Trial Lawyers, commendation for disting. svc. as arbitrator. Mem. N.Y. State Trial Lawyers Assn., N.Y. County Lawyers, N.Y. State Bar Assn., Electronic Technol. Soc. N.J. Inc. Achievements include patents for bridge for billiards, storage materials for sport card collections, auto mirror, temporary replacement window with protective seat attachment primarily for use in automobiles; innovative expandable shopping cart. Administrative and regulatory, Civil rights, Labor (including EEOC, Fair Labor Standards Act, labor-management relations, NLRB, OSHA). Office: PO Box 6162 Hillsborough NJ 08844 E-mail: bestesq1@aol.com.

AMESTOY, JEFFREY LEE, state supreme court chief justice; b. Rutland, Vt., July 24, 1946; s. William Joseph and Diana (Wood) Amestoy; m. Susan Claire Lonergan, May 24, 1980; children: Katherine Leigh, Christina Elizabeth, Nancy Claire. BA, Hobart Coll., 1968; JD, U. Calif., San Francisco, 1972; MPA, Harvard U., 1982; D of Pub. Adminstrn. (hon.) , Norwich U., 1994; LLD (hon.) , Vermont Law Sch., 2002. Bar: Vt. 1973, U.S. Dist. Ct. Vt. 1973. Assoc. Mahady & Klevana, Windsor, Vt., 1973—74; legal counsel Gov.'s Justice Commn., Montpelier, Vt., 1974—77; asst. atty. gen., chief of Medicaid fraud div. State of Vt., Montpelier, 1978—81, commr. labor and industry, 1982—84, atty. gen., 1985—97; chief justice Supreme Ct. Vt., 1997—. Pres. Nat. Assn. of Attys. Gen., 1992—93. Trustee Thomas Waterman Wood Gallery, Montpelier, 1986—92. With USAR, 1968—74. Mem.: Conf. Chief Justices, Vt. Bar Assn., Kennedy Sch. Govt. Harvard U. Alumni Exec. Coun. Republican. Congregationalist. Home: 503 Loomis Hill Rd Waterbury Center VT 05677-8280

AMKRAUT, DAVID M.H. lawyer, judge; b. N.Y.C. BS, U. Calif., Santa Cruz, 1973; JD, U. Calif., Berkeley, 1987. Bar: Calif. 1987, U.S. Dist. Ct. (cen. and no. dists.) Calif. 1987, U.S. Ct. Appeals (9th cir.) 1987. Prin. Law Offices of David Amkraut, L.A., 1987—; mcpl. ct. judge, protem Glendale (Calif.), L.A. Mcpl. Cts., 1997—. Cons. various pub. and photography mags. and orgns. Contbr. various articles to profl. jours. Mem. L.A. Trial Lawyers Assn., Calif. Trial Lawyers Assn. Avocations: chess (master), writing, travelling. Office: Law Offices of David Amkraut 2272 Colorado Blvd # 1228 Los Angeles CA 90041-1143 Office Fax: 323-344-8594.

AMON, CAROL BAGLEY, federal judge; b. 1946; BS, Coll. William and Mary, 1968; JD, U. Va., 1971. Bar: Va. 1971, D.C. 1972, N.Y. 1980. Staff atty. Communications Satellite Corp., Washington, 1971-73; trial atty. U.S. Dept. Justice, Washington, 1973-74; asst. U.S. atty. Ea. Dist. N.Y., 1974-86, U.S. magistrate, 1986-90, dist. ct. judge, 1990—. Recipient John Marshall award U.S. Dept. Justice, 1983. Mem. Assn. Bar of City of N.Y., Va. State Bar Assn., D.C. Bar Assn. (chair codes of conduct com. of jud. conf. 1998-2001). Office: US District Court 225 Cadman Plz E Brooklyn NY 11201-1818

AMSTERDAM, ANTHONY GUY, law educator; b. Phila., Sept. 12, 1935; s. Gustave G. and Valla (Abel) A.; m. Lois P. Sheinfeld, Aug. 29, 1968. AB, Haverford Coll., 1957; LLB, U. Pa., 1960; LLD (hon.), John Jay Coll. Criminal Justice, 1987, Haverford Coll., 1993. Bar: D.C. 1960. Law clk. to U.S. Supreme Ct. Justice Felix Frankfurter, 1960-61; asst. U.S. atty., 1961-62; prof. law U. Pa., 1962-69, Stanford U., 1969-81, Montgomery prof. clin. legal edn., 1980-81; prof. law, dir. clin. programs and trial advocacy NYU, 1981—2001, univ. prof., 2001—. Cons. litigating atty. numerous civil rights groups; cons. govt. commns.; mem. Commn. to Study Disturbances at Columbia, 1968; trustee Death Penalty Info. Ctr., Lawyers Constl. Def. Com., NAACP Legal Def. Fund, Nat. Coalition to abolish the Death Penalty, So. Poverty Law Ctr., mem. Calif. Fed. Jud. Selection Com., 1976-80; mem. coord. coun. on lawyer competence Conf. of Chief Justices; gen. counsel N.Y. Civil Liberties Union; adv. counsel Civil Liberties Union No. Calif.; mem. ABA task force. Author: The Defensive Transfer of Civil Rights Litigation From State to Federal Courts, 1964, Trial Manual for Defense of Criminal Cases, 5th edit., 1989, (with Hertz and Guggenheim) Trial Manual for Defense Attorneys in Juvenile Court, 1991, (with Bruner) Minding the Law, 2000; editor-in-chief: U. Pa. Law Rev., 1959-60; contbr. articles to profl. jours. Named Outstanding Young Man of Year Phila. and Pa. Jaycees, 1967; recipient First Disting. Service award U. Pa. Law Sch., 1968; Haverford award Haverford Coll., 1970; Arthur V. Briesen award Nat. Legal Aid and Defender Assn., 1972, 76; named Lawyer of Year Calif. Trial Lawyers Assn., 1973; recipient 1st Earl Warren Civil Liberties award No. Calif. chpt. ACLU, 1973, Citizen of Merit award Sun Reporter, 1974, Walter J. Gores award Stanford U., 1977, William O. Douglas award Pub. Counsel, 1977, 2d ann. award Calif. Attys. Criminal Justice, 1978, award for enhancement human dignity Durfee Found., 1982, Francis Rawle award ALI-ABA, 1984, 3d ann. Civil Liberties award Pa. ACLU, 1985, clinical legal edn. award AALS Sect. on Clinical Legal Edn., 1986, August Vollmer award Am. Soc. Criminology, 1986, Disting. Tchr. award NYU, 1988, award N.Y. Criminal Bar Assn., 1989, Tchg. Achievement award Soc. Am. Law Tchrs., 1999, Kutak award ABA, 2002; named MacArthur fellow, 1989; hon. fellow for pub. interest svc. U. Pa. Law Sch., 2001. Fellow Am. Acad. Arts and Scis. Home: 68 Middle Line Hwy Southampton NY 11968-1645 Office: NYU Sch Law Clinical Ctr 161 Avenue of the Americas New York NY 10013

AMSTERDAM, MARK LEMLE, lawyer; b. N.Y.C., June 10, 1944; s. Leonard M. and Erica (Lemle) A.; children: Lauren, Matthew. AB, Columbia U., 1966, JD cum laude, 1969. Bar: N.Y. 1969, U.S. Dist. Ct. (so., ea. and no. dists.) N.Y. 1972, U.S. Dist. Ct. (no. dist.) Tex., U.S. Supreme Ct. 1973. Assoc. Fried, Frank, Harris, N.Y.C., 1969-70; staff atty. Ctr. Constl. Rights, N.Y.C., 1970-75; atty. pvt. practice, N.Y.C., 1975-76, 81—; ptnr. Rubin Hanley & Amsterdam, N.Y.C., 1976-79, Katz Amsterdam & Lewinter, N.Y.C., 1980, Amsterdam & Lewinter, N.Y.C., 1990—. Instr. N.Y. Law Sch., 1982-83. Contbr. articles to profl. jours. Fellow: N.Y. State Bar Assn.; mem.: Columbia Coll. Alumni Assn. (bd. dirs.), Columbia Law Sch. Alumni Assn. (bd. dirs.), Columbia Club, Gardeners Bay Country Club. Federal civil litigation, State civil litigation, Criminal. Home: 1220 Park Ave New York NY 10128-1733 Office: 9 E 40th St New York NY 10016-0402

AMUGHAN, KENNEDY ABBA KEDAY, lawyer; s. Activity Thompson and Juliana Omajuwatan Amughan; m. Grace Okpongu, Nov. 6, 1993; children: Ebitie Thomasina, Juliana Perebotie, Cath Tamaranpreye. LLB, U. Maiduguri, 1988. Bar: Nigeria 1990, cert.: Barrister-at-Law 1990. Tchr. State Tchg. Svc. Commn., Borno, Nigeria, 1983; sr. counsel Legal Aid Counsel, Katsina, Katsina (NYSC), Nigeria, 1989—90; dep. prin. counsel Taiwo Kupolati & Co, Lagos, Nigeria, 1990—92; prin. coun. Kennedy Amughan & Co, Lagos, 1996—. Legal cons. Savannah Bank Plc, Lagos, Nigeria, 1994—; external solicitors Union Bank PLC, Lagos, 1994—, Broad Bank PLC, Lagos, 1996—; sec., legal adviser Korea Machinery Co Ltd, Lagos, 1998—2002, head of chambers legal dept, 1998. Author: (book) Directors Under The Nigerian Companies Act 1968, 1988. Mem.: U. Maiduguri Alumu Assn. (assoc.), Nigerian Bar Assn. (exec. official 1997, Merit award 1996), Nat. Ijaw Lawyers Assn. (pres. 1997), Young Internat. Lawyers Assn. (assoc.), Internat. Bar Assn. (assoc.), U. Maidugar Alumni Assn. (sec.gen. 1994, Disting. Alumnus award 1994, Merit award 1995). Democrat-Npl. Roman Catholic. Avocations: soccer, poetry, lawn tennis, drama, reading. Commercial, consumer (including collections, credit), General practice, Property, real (including real estate development, water). Home Fax: 234-4978212, 4970911. Personal E-mail: kennedyamughan@yahoo.com.

AMZEL, VIVIANA, lawyer; b. Buenos Aires; arrived in U.S., 1969; d. David Rosenblatt and Sara Budrikier; children: Daniela, Anouk. JD, George Washington U., 1988; PhD, U. Md. Bar: Va., Pa., D.C. Ptnr. V. Amzel & Assocs., Alexandria, Va., 1990—94; counsel Ratner Prestia, Pa., 1994—97; counsel, ptnr. Arter & Hadden, L.A., 1997—2000; gen. counsel, chief intellectual property officer Epigenesis Pharms., Cranburn, NJ, 2000—. Pre-doctoral fellow, U. Md., 1975, post-doctoral fellow, Nat. Inst. Health, 1978. Mem.: LES, AIPLA, ABA. Intellectual property, Commercial, contracts (including sales of goods; commercial financing). Home: Gladwyne PA 19035 Office: Epigenesis Pharms 7 Clarke Dr Cranbury NJ 08512

ANAGNOSTOPOULOS, ILIAS, lawyer, educator; b. Athens, Greece, Jan. 1, 1956; s. Georgios and Stavroula (Toli) Anagnostopoulos; m. Persa Lampropoulou, July 20, 2002. LLM, U. Athens, 1978; JD, U. Frankfurt, 1983. Bar: Athens 1981, Supreme Ct. Greece 1990. Ptnr. Anagnostopoulos, Bazinas & Fifis, Athens, 1989—. Lectr. criminal law U. Athens Sch. Law, 1989—98, asst. prof. criminal law, 1998—; expert com. Ministry of Justice, 1990—. Author: Criminal Law in Greece, 2000; contbr. articles to profl. jours. Mem.: Nat. Assn. Criminal Def. Lawyers, European Criminal Bar Assn. (bd. dirs. 1997—), Hellenic Criminal Bar Assn. (sec. gen. 1998—, Tsirimokos prize 1987). Criminal. Office: Anagnostopoulos Bazinas & Fifis 6 Patriarchou Ioakeim 106 74 Athens Greece Office Fax: 30 2107292015. Business E-Mail: crld@abf.gr.

ANANI, TARIG, lawyer; b. Riyadh, Saudi Arabia, Jan. 22, 1965; s. Faisal Anani and Diane Katherine Hill. BA cum laude, Univ. Houston, 1988, JD, 1991; MBA, Rice Univ., 1992; MS of Jurisprudence, Stanford U., 1994. Bar: Tex. 1991, Calif. 1993, D.C. 2002, U.S. Supreme Ct. 1995. Corp. assoc. Curtis, Mallet-Prevost, Colt & Mosle, Manhattan, N.Y., 1994-97; gen. counsel SAP Arabia, Dubai, United Arab Emirates, 1998—2002; pres. internat. ops., corp. gen. counsel Petroleum Place/P2 Energy Solutions, Houston, 2002—. Bd. dirs. Mail2World, Inc., Century City, 2000—. Recipient Best Enterprise Resource Planning Solution in the Mid. East, v.p. Al Gore, 2002. Computer, Corporate, general, Private international. Home: 1300 Woodhollow Dr Apt 23202 Houston TX 77057 Office: P2 Energy Solutions 4 Houston Ctr 1221 Lamar Ste 1400 Houston TX 77010 E-mail: tanani@petroleumplace.com.

ANDERSEN, JAMES A. retired state supreme court justice; b. Auburn, Wash., Sept. 21, 1924; s. James A. and Margaret Cecelia (Norgaard) A.; m. Billiette B. Andersen; children: James Blair, Tia Louise. BA, U. Wash., 1949, JD, 1951. Bar: Wash. 1952, U.S. Dist. Ct. (we. dist.) Wash. 1957, U.S. Ct. Appeals 1957. Dep. pros. atty. King County, Seattle, 1953-57; assoc. Lycette, Diamond & Sylvester, Seattle, 1957-61; ptnr. Clinton, Andersen, Fleck & Glein, Seattle, 1961-75; judge Wash. State Ct. of Appeals, Seattle, 1975-84; justice Wash. State Supreme Ct., Olympia, 1984-92, chief justice, 1992-95; ret., 1995. Chair Legis. Ethics Bd. Mem. Wash. State Ho. of Reps., 1958-67, Wash. State Senate, 1967-72. Served with U.S. Army, 1943-45, ETO. Decorated Purple Heart; recipient Disting. Alumnus award U. Wash. Sch. of Law, 1995. Mem. ABA, Wash. State Bar Assn., Am. Judicature Soc. Home: 3008 98th Ave NE Bellevue WA 98004-1817

ANDERSEN, RICHARD ESTEN, lawyer; b. N.Y.C., Oct. 26, 1957; s. Arnold and Marianne (Singer) A.; m. Patricia Anne Woods, May 9, 1987; children: Benjamin Singer, David Woods. BA, Columbia U., 1978, JD, 1981; LLM, NYU, 1987. Bar: N.Y. 1982, U.S. Tax Ct. 1982. Ptnr. Arnold & Porter, N.Y.C. Mem. bd. advisors Jour. Internat. Taxation, Jour. Taxation Global Transactions, World Trade Exec., Tax Mgmt., Inc.; adj. prof. law grad. tax LLM program NYU. Author: Foreign Tax Credits, 1996, U.S. Income Tax Withholding (Fgn. Persons), 1997, Income Tax Treaties of the United States, revised edit., 2002. Mem.: ABA, Internat. Tax Assn. (pres. 2000—02), Internat. Fiscal Assn. (mem. USA br. coun., N.Y. exec. com.), Internat. Tax Inst., N.Y. State Bar Assn. Finance, Private international, Corporate taxation. Office: Arnold & Porter 399 Park Ave New York NY 10022 E-mail: richard_andersen@aporter.com.

ANDERSEN, ROBERT MICHAEL, lawyer; b. Council Bluffs, Iowa, June 4, 1950; s. Howard M. and Muriel Marie (Robinson) A.; m. Natalia Anne Nankovitch, May 1, 1982; children: Erica Nicole, Amelia Marie. BS, U. Iowa, 1972, JD, 1976; MPA, Harvard U., 1986. Bar: Ohio 1976, Iowa 1976, U.S. Ct. Appeals (2d, 6th, and 7th and D.C. cirs.) 1979, U.S. Supreme Ct. 1979. Assoc. Squire, Sanders & Dempsey, Cleve., 1976-78; pvt. practice Milw.; asst. regional counsel U.S. EPA, Chgo., 1980-82, assoc. regional counsel, 1982-84, dep. regional counsel, regional jud. officer, 1984-86; dep. gen. counsel NSF, Washington, 1986-90; gen. counsel Def. Nuclear Facilities Safety Bd., Washington, 1990-98; chief counsel U.S. Army Corps Engrs., 1998—. Adj. prof. lectr. waste mgmt., dept. engring. George Washington U., 1994—; lectr. internat. environ. controls for Antarctica, regulation of sci. fraud and misconduct, and waste mgmt.; mgmt. cons. in field. Articles editor Iowa U. Law Rev., 1975-76; contbr. articles to profl. jours. Recipient Bronze medal EPA, 1982, Meritorious Svc. medal NSF, 1990, Antarctic Svc. medal NSF, 1990, Antarctic medallion, NSF, 1990, Presdl. Meritorious Exec. Rank award Pres. George Bush, 1992, Predl. Disting. Exec. Rank award Pres. William Jefferson Clinton, 1995, Meritorious Svc. award Def. Nuclear Facilities Safety Bd., 1998. Roman Catholic. Avocations: mountaineering, tennis, chess, writing, mathematics. Home: 7003 Petunia St Springfield VA 22152-3428 Office: USA CE Office of Chief Counsel 441 G St NW Rm 3A29 Washington DC 20314-1000 E-mail: robert.m.andersen@usace.army.mil.

ANDERSON, ALBERT SYDNEY, III, lawyer; b. Atlanta, July 7, 1940; s. Albert S. Jr. and Constance S. (Spalding) A.; children: Judith, William. BA in Math., Emory U., 1962; MS in Physics, Stanford (Calif.) U., 1964, PhD in Physics, 1968, JD, 1977. Bar: Ga. 1978, U.S. Patent and Trademark Office 1980, U.S. Supreme Ct. 1981. Assoc. Stokes & Shapiro, Atlanta, 1978-81, Kutak, Rock & Huie, Atlanta, 1981-84; ptnr. Jones & Askew, Atlanta, 1984-96; pvt. practice Norcross, Ga., 1996—. Asst. atty. gen. State of Ga., Atlanta, 1984-88. Elder Trinity Presbyn. Ch., Atlanta, 1978-81; chmn. bd. trustees Trinity Sch., Atlanta, 1971-74. Mem. Am. Phys. Soc. Avocations: golf, hiking, music. Federal civil litigation, Patent, Trademark and copyright. Office: Patent Law Offices 35 Technology Pkwy S Ste 170 Norcross GA 30092-2928 E-mail: aanderson@andersonpatent.com.

ANDERSON, AUSTIN GOTHARD, lawyer, university administrator; b. Calumet, Minn., June 30, 1931; s. Hugo Gothard and Turna Marie (Johnson) A.; m. Catherine Antoinette Spellacy, Jan. 2. 1954; children: Todd, Susan, Timothy, Linda, Mark. BA, U. Minn., 1954, JD, 1958. Bar: Minn. 1958, Ill. 1962, Mich. 1974. Assoc. Spellacy, Spellacy, Lano & Anderson, Marble, Minn, 1958-62; dir. Ill. Inst. Continuing Legal Edn., Springfield, 1962-64; dir. dept. continuing legal edn. U. Minn., Mpls., 1964-70, assoc. dean gen. extension divsn., 1968-70; ptnr. Dorsey, Marquart, Windhorst, West & Halladay, Mpls., 1970-73; assoc. dir. Nat. Ctr. State Cts., St. Paul, 1973-74; dir. Inst. Continuing Legal Edn. U. Mich., Ann Arbor, 1973-92; dir. Inst. on Law Firm Mgmt., 1992-95; prin. Anderson-Boyer Group, Ann Arbor, 1995—; pres. Network of Leading Law Firms, 1995—. Adj. faculty U. Minn., 1974, Wayne State U., 1974-75; mem. adv. bd. Ctr. for Law Firm Mgmt. Nottingham Trent U., Eng.; draftsman ABA Guidelines for Approval of Legal Asst. Programs, 1973, Model Guidelines for Minimum Continuing Legal Edn., 1988; chair law practice mgmt. sect. State Bar Mich., 2000-2001; mem. Task Force on Court Filing, State Bar of Mich., 2000-2001; mem. Com. on Quality of Life, 2000-2001; cons. in field. Co-editor, contbg. author: Lawyer's Handbook, 1975, co-editor 3d edit., 1992; author: A Plan for Lawyer Development, 1986, Marketing Your Practice: A Practical Guide to Client Development, 1986; cons. editor, contbg. author: Webster's Legal Secretaries Handbook, 1981; cons. editor Merriam Webster's Legal Secretarial Handbook, 2d edit., 1996; co-author: The Effective Associate Training Program-Improving Firm Performance, Profits and Prospective Partners, 2000, Associate Retention: Keeping Our Best and Brightest, 2002; contbr. chpt. to book and articles to profl. jours. Chmn. City of Bloomington Park and Recreation Adv. Commn., Minn., 1970-72; chmn. Ann Arbor Citizens Recreation Adv. Com., 1981-89, Ann Arbor Parks Adv. Com., 1983-92, chair, 1991-92; rep. Class of '58 U. Minn. Law Sch., 1996-2002. Recipient Excellence award CLE sect. Assn. of Am. Law Schs., 1992. Fellow Am. Bar Found. (Mich. chmn. 2002-), State Bar Mich. Found.; mem. ABA (vice chmn. continuing legal edn. com. sect. legal edn. and admission to bar 1988-93, standing com. continuing edn. of bar 1984-90, 2000-, chmn. law practice mgmt. sect. 1981-82, Am. Law Inst.-ABA com. on continuing profl. edn. 1993-96, Am. Lw Inst.-ABA com. on continuing profl. edn. 1999—2002, spl. com. on rsch. on future of legal profession 1998-2000, sec. Coll. of Law Practice Mgmt. 1993-97, house of dels. 1993-99, comm. on lawyer advt. 1994-97, futures com., chmn. econs. of torts and ins. practice 2002—, mem. task force Lawyer Ctr. on pers. legal svcs. and client devel. 2002—, spl. advisor to standing com. on continuing edn. of the bar 2002—), Internat. Bar Assn., Mich. Bar Assn., Ill. Bar Assn., State Bar of Mich. (chair law practice mgmt. sect., 2000-2001), Minn. Bar Assn., Internat. Bar Assn., Assn. Continuing Legal Edn. Adminstrs.(pres. 1969-70), Ann Arbor Golf and Outing Club. Administrative and regulatory. Home: 4660 Bayberry Cir Ann Arbor MI 48105-9762 Office: Anderson-Boyer Group 3840 Packard St # 110 Ann Arbor MI 48108-2280 E-mail: aga@andersonboyer.com.

ANDERSON, BARBARA MCCOMAS, lawyer; b. Ft. Belvoir, Va., Dec. 18, 1950; d. Ben C. Jr. and Elsa A. McComas; m. Roy Ryden Anderson Jr., Dec. 11, 1982; 1 child, Ryden McComas Anderson. BA, Trinity U., San Antonio, 1972; JD, U. Tex., 1978. Bar: Tex. 1978; cert. in estate planning and probate Tex. Bd. Legal Specialization. From assoc. to ptnr. Locke Purnell Rain Harrell, Dallas, 1978-97; of counsel Locke Liddell & Sapp, LLP, Dallas, 1997—; pvt. practice Dallas, 1997—. Fellow: Coll. of State Bar of Tex., Tex. Bar. Found., Am. Coll. Trusts and Estates Counsel; mem.: Tex. Acad. Probate and Trust Lawyers (charter), Dallas Bar Assn., Tex. Bar Assn. (real estate, probate and trust law sect. 2003, chair 2003—). Avocations: reading mysteries, gardening. Estate planning, Probate (including wills, trusts), Estate taxation. Office: PO Box 181147 Dallas TX 75218-8147

ANDERSON, BRUCE PAIGE, lawyer; b. Albany, Ga., Mar. 5, 1952; s. Paul Macon and Ruth Alice (O'neil) A.; m. Sandra Johnston, June 30, 1973; children: Christi Lauren, Sarah Alice. AB in Econs., Ga. So. U., 1973; JD, Loyola U., New Orleans, 1977. Bar: Ga. 1977, La. 1977, Fla. 1978. Asst. atty. gen. State of La., New Orleans; pvt. practice Tallahassee, 1981—. Guest lectr. Fla. A&M U. Sch. Architecture, Tallahassee, 1984-85. Bd. dirs., past pres. Killearn Homes Assn. Mem. ABA, Fla. Bar Assn., La. Bar Assn., Ga. Bar Assn., Tallahassee Bar Assn., Jefferson County Bar Assn., Fed. Bar Assn. (past pres.). Roman Catholic. State civil litigation, Construction, General practice. Office: PO Box 10512 Tallahassee FL 32302-2512 Address: 4481 Legendary Dr Destin FL 32541

ANDERSON, CHARLES ANTHONY, lawyer; b. Ashtabula, Ohio, Nov. 21, 1945; s. Charles Lindley and Teresa (Silva) A.; m. Martha M. Bodnar, June 18, 1974; children: Charles Joshua, Kristin, Megan, Caitlin, Justin. BA, Bowling Green State U., 1967; postgrad., U. So. Calif., 1971-72; JD, U. San Francisco, 1975. Bar: Calif. 1976, Va. 1977, U.S. Ct. Appeals (D.C. cir.) 1977, U.S. Dist. Ct. (ea. dist.) Va. 1978. Staff rschr. Commn. on Fed Paperwork, Washington, 1976; com. atty. U.S. Ho. of Reps., Washington, 1977; pvt. practice Reston, Va., 1977-83; ptnr. Ralston, Redick, Norwitch, O'Connor, Craig, Anderson, Reston, 1983-88; trial atty., pvt. practice Charles A. Anderson, P.C., Reston, 1988-2000; mng. ptnr. Grenadier, Anderson, Simpson and Duffett, P.C., Reston, 2000—. Lt. USN, 1968-72. Mem. Va. Trial Lawyers' Assn. (family law exec. bd. 1990-96), KC (trustee 1993-97, Grand Knight 1994). Avocations: poker, reading, world war ii history. General civil litigation, Family and matrimonial, General practice. Home: 2657 Unicorn Ct Herndon VA 20171-2425 Office: Grenadier Anderson Simpson & Duffett Ste 130 11710 Plaza America Dr Reston VA 20190 E-mail: bxqx61a@aol.com.

ANDERSON, CHARLES HILL, lawyer; s. Ray N. and Lois M. Anderson; (div.); children: Eric S., Alicia L., Burton H. JD, U. Tenn., 1953. Bar: Tenn. 1953, U.S. Dist. Ct. Tenn. 1953, U.S. Ct. Appeals (6th cir.) 1956, U.S. Supreme Ct. 1956, U.S. Ct. Mil. 1964. Pvt. practice, Chattanooga, 1953-59, 2001—; assoc. gen. counsel Life & Casualty Ins. Co. Tenn., Nashville, 1960-69; dist. atty. U.S. Dept. Justice, Nashville, 1969-77; pvt. practice Nashville, 1977-79, 87—; asst. adj. gen. State of Tenn., Nashville, 1979-87. Mem. U.S. Atty. Gen. Adv. Com., Washington, 1973-77; del. Tenn. Constl. Conv., Nashville, 1965-66; dir. Nashville Pub. TV Coun., 1994-99; chmn. Met. Bd. of Equalization, 1998-2001. Brig. gen. AUS, ret., 1987. Mem. ABA, Tenn. Bar Assn., Nashville Bar Assn., Chattanooga Bar Assn., Fed. Bar Assn. (pres. Nashville chpt. 1972), Assn. Life Ins. Counsel, Cumberland Club (pres. 1981-82), The Federalist Soc. Presbyterian. Corporate, general, Insurance, Labor (including EEOC, Fair Labor Standards Act, labor-management relations, NLRB, OSHA). Home: 1310 Aswan Dr Signal Mountain TN 37377-2618 Office: POB 561 Signal Mountain TN 37377 E-mail: chalaw@comcast.net.

ANDERSON, CHRISTOPHER JAMES, lawyer; b. Chgo., Nov. 26, 1950; s. James M. and Margaret E. (Anderson) A.; m. Lyn R. Buckley, Jan. 3, 1976; children: Vaughn Buckley, Weston Buckley. BA, Grinnell Coll., 1972; JD with highest distinction, U. Iowa, 1975. Bar: Mo. 1975. From assoc. to ptnr. Armstrong Teasdale LLP, Kansas City, Mo., 1975—. Mem. ABA, Mo. Bar Assn., Kans. City Bar Assn., Lawyers Assn. Kansas City, Estate Planning Soc. Corporate, general, Estate planning, Personal income taxation. Office: Armstrong Teasdale, et al 2345 Grand Blvd Ste 2000 Kansas City MO 64108-2617 E-mail: canderso@armstrongteasdale.com.

ANDERSON, CRAIG EDGAR, lawyer; b. Chgo., Aug. 4, 1947; s. Edgar Warren and Arlene (Bjork) A.; m. Candace Elise Larsen, Apr. 6, 1974; 1 child, Jennifer Elise. BA, St. Olaf Coll., Northfield, Minn., 1969; JD, Loyola U., 1974. Bar: Ill. 1974, U.S. Dist. Ct. (no. dist.) Ill. 1974, U.S. Ct. Appeals (7th cir.) 1975, U.S. Supreme Ct. 1980. Ptnr. Jacobson, Brandvik and Anderson, Chgo., 1974—. Mem. ABA, Ill. Bar Assn. (bd. dirs.), Am. Counsel Assn., Nordic Law Chgo. Federal civil litigation, State civil litigation, Corporate, general. Office: Jacobson Brandvik & Anderson 20 N Wacker Dr Chicago IL 60606-2806

ANDERSON, DAMON ERNEST, lawyer; b. Minot, N.D., June 20, 1946; s. Melvin Ernest and Maxine I. (Spaulding) A.; m. Julie Kay Severson, Oct. 23, 1982; children: Joshua Daniel, Philip Kyle. BA, Dickinson State U., 1968; JD, U. N.D., 1974. Bar: N.D. 1974, Minn. 1981, U.S. Dist. Ct. N.D. 1974, U.S. Ct. Appeals (8th cir.) 1980, U.S. Supreme Ct. 1980. Pvt. practice Kessler and Anderson, Grand Forks, N.D., 1974-78, Grand Forks, N.D., 1978-98; asst. state's atty. Grand Forks County, N.D., 1978—. Past mem. divsnl. comdr. adv. coun. Salvation Army, Mpls., past mem. Salvation Army local adv. bd., Grand Forks. Sgt. U.S. Army, 1968-70. Mem. Am. Legion, Masons. Lutheran. Juvenile. Office: 151 S 4th St Ste 601 Grand Forks ND 58201-4715

ANDERSON, DORIS EHLINGER, lawyer; b. Houston; d. Joseph Otto and Cornelia Louise (Pagel) Ehlinger; m. Wiley Anderson, Jr. (dec.); children: Wiley Newton III, Joe E. BA, Rice U., 1946; permanent high sch. tchr. cert., U. Houston, 1948; JD, U. Tex., 1950; MLS in Museology, U. Okla., 1985. Bar: Tex. 1950, U.S. Supreme Ct. Assoc. Ehlinger & Anderson, Houston, 1950-52, ptnr., 1965—; assoc. Price, Guinn, Wheat & Veltmann, Houston, 1952-55, Wheat, Dyche & Thornton, Houston, 1955-65; life mem. Rice Assocs., Houston, 1984—. Hist. lectr., Harvard Negotiation Seminar, 1992 Edn. for Ministry, U of South, 1999. Editor: Houston City of Destiny, 1980; contbr. articles to hist. pubs. and to Bayou Bend. Parliamentarian Harris County Flood Control Task Force, Houston, 1975-2003; dir. Houston Bapt. Mus Am. Architecture and Decorative Arts, 1980-90, curator costume, 1980; apptd. ambassador Inst. Texan Culture U. Tex, San Antonio; past pres. gen. San Jacinto Descendants; docent Bayou Bend Mus. Fine Arts, Houston. Recipient best interpretive exhibit award Tex. Hist. Commn., 1983, Outstanding Woman of Yr. award YWCA, Houston, 1983; named adm. Tex. Navy, 1980. Mem. ABA, UDC (chaplain, pres., parliamentarian gen. Jefferson Davis chpt.), Assn. Women Attys. Houston, Houston Bar Assn., Daus. Republic Tex., Am. Mus. Soc., Harris County Heritage Soc., Kappa Beta Pi (pres. Lamda alumni). Episcopalian. Oil, gas, and mineral, Property, real (including real estate development, water). Home: 5556 Cranbrook Rd Houston TX 77056-1600 Office: Ehlinger & Anderson 5556 Sturbridge Dr Houston TX 77056-1623

ANDERSON, E. KARL, lawyer; b. Huntington, W. Va., Mar. 30, 1931; s. Earle Karl and Helen Emrie (Johnson) A.; m. Mary Elizabeth Williams, Nov. 13, 1953; children: Sharon Elizabeth, Charles Wesley. BBA, So. Methodist U., 1953, LLB, 1960. Bar: Tex. 1960, U.S. Dist. Ct. (no. dist.) Tex. 1963, U.S. Supreme Ct. 1971. Field supr. Travelers Ins. Co., Dallas, 1956-57; claim mgr. Allstate Ins. Co., Dallas, 1958-62; practiced in Dallas, 1963—; pntr. Lastelick, Anderson and Arneson, Dallas, 1968—. 1st lt. USAF, 1954—56. Fellow Tex. Bar Found.; mem. Am. Bar Assn., Dallas Assn. Trial Lawyers (dir. 1964-65, 74-75), Tex. Trial Lawyers Assn., Assn. Trial Lawyers Am., Dallas Country Club, Delta Theta Phi, Sigma Iota Epsilon, Sigma Alpha Epsilon. Presbyterian. General practice, Personal injury (including property damage), Probate (including wills, trusts). Home: 3111 Drexel Dr Dallas TX 75205-2910 Office: Univ Twr Bldg S-402 6440 N Central Expy Dallas TX 75206-4123

ANDERSON, EARL E. retired military officer, legal association administrator; b. Morgantown, W.Va., June 24, 1919; BS with acad. and mil. honors, MA, W.Va. U., 1940; JD with highest honors, George Washington U. Commd. 2d lt. USMC, 1940, advanced through grade to gen., 1972; instr. Sea Sch., Portsmouth, Va., 1941; with USS Yorktown, 1941—42, Marine Corps Base, San Diego, 2d Marine Divsn.; flight instr. U.S. Marine Corps Air Sta., Edenton, NC, 1943—44; comdr. Marine Bomber Squadron 443; exec. officer Marine Aircraft Group 61; with Office JAG; commdg. officer Marine Observation Squadron Six; asst. chief staff G-1 1st Marine Aircraft Wing; from instr. to chief air sect. Marine Corps Ednl. Ctr.; staff legal officer 3d Marine Aircraft Wing, 1960—61; comdr. Marine Aircraft Group 36, Santa Ana, Calif.; chief staff Mil. Assistance Adv. Group, 1963—64; marine tactical data sys. program coord. Hdqs. Marine Corps, 1964—66, dep. chief staff rsch., devel. and studies, 1966—67, spl. asst to chief staff, dep. dir. pers.; chief staff III Marine Amphibious Force, Vietnam, 1967—69; commdg. gen. Fleet Marine Force, Atlantic, Norfolk, Va., 1971—75; ret., 1975; bd. govs. ABA, Vienna, Va., 2001—. Bd. dirs. U.S. Olympic Com., 1970—71; mem. exec. com. Counseil Internat. du Sports Militaire. Decorated Legion of Merit with combat V and 2 gold stars, Disting. Flying Cross with one gold star, Bronze Star with combat V, Air medal with 1 silver star and 2 gold stars, Purple Heart, Nat. Order Vietnam medal 5th class, Disting. Svc. Order medal 1st class (Vietnam), Cross of Gallantry with palm (Vietnam), Chungmu Medal (Korea), Liberation Ribbon (The Philippines), others. Office: Sector Lawyers Divsn 9108 Quarter Ct Vienna VA 22182-2062 Office Fax: 703-225-0753. E-mail: genanderson@msn.com.*

ANDERSON, EDWARD RILEY, state supreme court justice; b. Chattanooga, Aug. 10, 1932; BS, U. Tenn., 1955, JD, 1957. Bar: Tenn. 1958, U.S. Dist. Ct. (ea. dist.) Tenn. 1965, U.S. Ct. Appeals (4th cir.) 1985, U.S. Ct. Appeals (6th cir.), U.S. Supreme Ct. 1988. Assoc. Joyce & Wilson, Oak Ridge, Tenn., 1957—61; ptnr. Joyce, Anderson & Meredith, Oak Ridge, 1961—87; judge Tenn. Ct. Appeals, Knoxville, 1987—90; justice Tenn. Supreme Ct., Knoxville, 1990—, chief justice, 1994—2001. Mem. Tenn. Jud. Conf., 1987—; bd. dirs. Conf. of Chief Justices, 1999-2000, vice chair children and the family com., 1998-99; chmn. Tenn. Jud. Coun., 1990-95, Select Senate/House Com. on Ct. Automation,1990-94. Past commr. Oak Ridge City Charter. Recipient Svc. award Oak Ridge Rotary Club, 2000; named Judge of Yr. Am. Bd. Trial Advocates, 1998. Fellow Am. Bar Found., Tenn. Bar Found.; mem. ABA, Am. Bd. Trial Advocates (pres. Tenn. chpt. 1987-88), Tenn. Bar Assn. (William M. Leech Jr. Pub. Svc. award 2001), Anderson County Bar Assn. (pres. 1961), Tenn. Def. Lawyers Assn. (pres. 1980-81), Am. Inns of Ct. (pres. Tenn. chpt. 1988-90). Avocations: reading, golf. Office: Tenn Supreme Ct Supreme Court Bldg 501 Main St Ste 200 Knoxville TN 37902-2512

ANDERSON, EDWARD VIRGIL, lawyer; b. San Francisco, Oct. 17, 1953; s. Virgil P and Edna Pauline (Pedersen) A.; m. Kathleen Helen Dunbar, Sept. 3, 1983; children: Elizabeth D., Hilary J. AB in Econs., Stanford U., 1975, JD, 1978. Bar: Calif. 1978. Assoc. Pillsbury Madison & Sutro, San Francisco, 1978—, ptnr., 1987-94; chmn. mng. ptnr., mem. firm mgmt. com. Skjerven Morrill LLP, San Jose, 1994—2003; ptnr. Sidley Austin Brown & Wood, San Francisco, 2003—. Editor IP Litigator, 1995—; mem. bd. editors Antitrust Law Devel., 1983-86. Trustee Lick-Wilmerding H.S., San Francisco, 1980—, pres.; trustee Santa Clara Law Found., 1995—; trustee, v.p. Hamlin Sch. for Girls, San Francisco, 1998—, v.p. Mem. ABA, Calif. Bar Assn., San Francisco Bar Assn., Santa Clara Bar Assn. (counsel), City Club San Francisco, Stanford Golf Club, Phi Beta Kappa. Republican. Episcopal. Antitrust, Intellectual property, Patent. Home: 330 Santa Clara Ave San Francisco CA 94127-2035 Office: Sidley Austin Brown & Wood Ste 5000 555 Calif St San Francisco CA 94104 E-mail: evanderson@sidley.com.

ANDERSON, ERIC SCOTT, lawyer; b. Grand Forks, N.D., Aug. 26, 1949; s. Lyle William and Norma Sylvia (Lundeby) A.; children: Peter Scott, Nathan William. BSChE, U. Wis., 1971, JD, 1977. Bar: Wis. 1977, Minn. 1977, U.S. Dist. Ct. (we. dist.) Wis. 1977, U.S. Dist. Ct. Minn. 1978. Assoc. Fredrikson & Byron, P.A., Mpls., 1977-83, shareholder, 1983—. Mem. Wis. Bar Assn., Minn. Bar Assn., Hennepin County Bar Assn., Phi Eta Sigma, Tau Beta Pi, Phi Kappa Phi, Order of Coif. Avocations: golf, running, music. Commercial, contracts (including sales of goods; commercial financing), Corporate, general, Property, real (including real estate development, water). Office: Fredrikson & Byron PA 200 S 6th St Ste 4000 Minneapolis MN 55402-1425 E-mail: eanderson@fredlaw.com.

ANDERSON, ERIC SEVERIN, lawyer; b. N.Y.C., Dec. 16, 1943; s. Edward Severin and Dorothy Elvira (Ekbloom) A. BA in History summa cum laude, St. Mary's U., San Antonio, 1968; JD cum laude, Harvard U., 1971. Bar: Tex. 1971. From assoc. to ptnr. Fulbright & Jaworski, L.L.P., Houston, 1971—. Served with USAF, 1961-65. Mem. ABA, State Bar Tex., Houston Bar Assn. Clubs: Houston Ctr., Houston City. Democrat. Avocations: classical music, theater, sports. Corporate, general, Municipal (including bonds), Securities. Home: 14 E Greenway Plz Unit 21-O Houston TX 77046-1406 Office: Fulbright & Jaworski LLP 1301 Mckinney St Houston TX 77010-3031

ANDERSON, GEOFFREY ALLEN, retired lawyer; b. Chgo., Aug. 3, 1947; s. Roger Allen and Ruth (Teninga) A. BA cum laude, Yale U., 1969; JD, Columbia U., 1972. Bar: Ill. 1972. Assoc. Isham, Lincoln & Beale, Chgo., 1972-79, ptnr., 1980-81, Reuben & Proctor, Chgo., 1981-85; dep. gen. counsel Tribune Co., Chgo., 1985-92; gen. counsel Chgo. Cubs, 1986-90, corp. counsel, 1991-92; v.p. Timber Trails Country Club, Inc., 1992—. Elder Fourth Presbyn. Ch., Chgo., chmn. worship and music com., 1990-92, trustee, 1992-95, 99-2001, v.p., 1993-94; bd. dirs. The James Chorale, Chgo., 1993-96, chmn. program com., 1994-96. Recipient Citizenship award Am. Legion, 1965. Mem. Chgo. Bar Assn. (chmn. entertainment com. 1981-82, Best Performance award 1977), Yale Club (N.Y.C.), Phi Delta Phi. Corporate, general, Securities.

ANDERSON, HERBERT HATFIELD, lawyer, farmer; b. Rainier, Oreg., Aug. 2, 1920; s. Odin A. and Mae (Hatfield) A.; m. Barbara Stuart Bastine, June 3, 1949; children— Linda, Catherine, Thomas, Amy, Elizabeth, Kenneth BA in Bus. Adminstrn., U. Oreg., 1940; JD, Yale U., 1949. Exec. trainee U.S. Steel Co., San Francisco, 1940-41; assoc. Koerner, Young, McColloch & Dezendorf, Portland, Oreg., 1949—54; ptnr. Spears, Lubersky, Bledsoe, Anderson, Young & Hilliard, 1954-90, Lane, Powell, Spears & Lubersky, Portland, 1990—. Instr. law Lewis and Clark Coll., Portland, 1950-70. Mem. planning adv. com. Yamhill County, Oreg., 1974-82; bd. dirs. Emanuel Hosp., 1967—; bd. dirs. Flyfisher Found., 1972—, pres., 1972-84; bd. dirs. Multnomah Law Library, 1958—, sec. 1962-68, 77-95, pres., 1964-74. Served to maj., parachute inf. U.S. Army, 1942-46, ETO Fellow Am. Bar Found. (chmn. Oreg. chpt. 1988—); mem. ABA (chmn. governing com. forum on health law 1984-89, chmn. standing com. on jud. selection, tenure and compensation 1978-80, Lawyer's Conf., exec. com. 1980-94, chmn. 1989-90, judicial adminstrn. divsn. coun. 1988-94, sr. lawyer's divsn. coun. 1987-89), Am. Judicature Soc. (bd. dirs. 1981-85), Soc. Law and Medicine, Nat. Health Lawyers Assn., Am. Acad. Hosp. Attys., Oreg. Soc. Hosp. Attys. (pres. 1984-85), Multnomah Bar Found. (bd. dirs. 1955—, pres. 1959-64, 87—), Nat. Bankruptcy Conf. (conferee 1964—, exec. com. 1976-79, chmn. farmer insolvency com. 1985-88), Nat. Assn. R.R. Trial Counsel, Oreg. Bar Assn. (del. to ABA 1966-68), Multnomah Bar Assn. (pres. 1955), Western States Bar Conf. (pres. 1967), Oreg. Asian Pear Coun. (pres. 1989-91), Sigma Chi. Clubs: Multnomah Athletic, Michelbook Country, Flyfishers Oreg. (pres. 1972), Willamette Amateur Field Trial (pres. 1968-72), Trial Clubs of Am. (trustee 2002-). Lodges: Masons. Democrat. Lutheran. Bankruptcy, Health, Property, real (including real estate development, water). Home: River Meadow Farm 19289 SE Neck Rd Dayton OR 97114-7815 Office: Lane Powell Spears & Lubersky 601 SW 2d Ave Ste 2100 Portland OR 97204-3158 E-mail: herband@open.org.

ANDERSON, J. TRENT, lawyer; b. Indpls., July 22, 1939; s. Robert C. and Charlotte M. (Pfeifer) A.; m. Judith J. Zimmerman, Sept. 8, 1962; children: Evan M., Molly K. BS, Purdue U., 1961; LLB, U. Va., 1964. Bar: Ill. 1965, Ind. 1965. Teaching asst. U. Cal. Law Sch., Berkeley, 1964-65; assoc. Mayer, Brown & Platt, Chgo., 1965-72; ptnr. Mayer, Brown, Rowe & Maw, Chgo., 1972—. Instr. Loyola U. Law Sch., Chgo., 1985. Mem. Law Club, Union League Club, Mich. Shores Club. Commercial, contracts (including sales of goods; commercial financing), Corporate, general, Mergers and acquisitions. Home: 3037 Iroquois Rd Wilmette IL 60091-1106 Office: Mayer Brown Rowe & Maw 190 S La Salle St Ste 3100 Chicago IL 60603-3441 E-mail: janderson@mayerbrown.com.

ANDERSON, JAMES E., JR., lawyer; AB, Stanford U., 1969, JD, 1972. Bar: Calif. 1972, Tex. 1973, Tenn. 1985. Assoc. Akin, Gump, Strauss, Hauer & Feld, 1972-74, 76-78, ptnr., 1979-83, Wald, Harkrader & Ross, 1983-84, Dearborn & Ewing, 1984-91; v.p., gen. counsel Ingram Industries Inc., 1991-96; sr. v.p., sec., gen. counsel Ingram Micro, 1996—. Office: Ingram Micro 1600 E Saint Andrew Pl Santa Ana CA 92705-4926*

ANDERSON, JAMES FRANCIS, lawyer; b. Glen Ridge, NJ, June 13, 1965; BA, Seton Hall U., 1987, JD, 1990. Bar: N.J. 1991, U.S. Supreme Ct. 1995. Pvt. practice, Spring Lake, NJ, 1991—2001; staff atty. Ocean-Monmouth Legal Svcs., Freehold, NJ, 2001—. Pro bono atty. Ocean-Monmouth Legal Svcs., Freehold, N.J., 1991-2001; mentor Manasquan (NJ) HS, 1994. Commercial, consumer (including collections, credit), Bankruptcy. Office: 65 Mechanic St Ste 201 Red Bank NJ 07701 E-mail: janderson@monmouth.com.

ANDERSON, JOHN BAYARD, lawyer, educator, former congressman; b. Rockford, Ill., Feb. 15, 1922; s. E. Albin and Mabel Edna (Ring) A.; m. Keke Machakos, Jan. 4, 1953; children: Eleanora, John Bayard, Diane, Karen, Susan Kimberly. AB, U. Ill., 1942, JD, 1946; LLM, Harvard U., 1949; hon. doctorates, No. Ill. U., Wheaton Coll., Shimer Coll., Biola Coll., Geneva Coll., North Park Coll. and Theol. Sem., Houghton Coll., Trinity Coll., Rockford Coll. Bar: Ill. 1946. Practice law Rockford, 1946-52; with U.S. Fgn. Service, 1952-55; assigned West Berlin, 1952-55; mem. 87th-95th Congresses from 16th Dist. Ill., mem. rules com.; chmn. Ho. Republican Conf., 1969-79; ind. candidate for Pres. U.S., 1980. Vis. prof. Stanford U., 1981; vis. prof. Nova-Southeastern U. Ctr. for Study Law, 1987-2003, Washington Coll. Law Am. U., 1997—; vis. prof. polit. sci. Brandeis U., 1985, Oreg. State U., 1986, U. Mass., 1985—; lectr. polit. sci. Bryn Mawr Coll., 1985. Author: Between Two Worlds: A Congressman's Choice, 1970, Vision and Betrayal in America, 1976, The American Economy We Need, 1984, A Proper Institution: Guaranteeing Televised Presidential Debates, 1988; editor: Congress and Conscience, 1970. Ind. candidate for Pres. U.S., 1980. Mem. World Federalist Assn. (pres. 1992—), Ctr. for Voting and Democracy (chmn. bd. 1996—, co-chmn. nat. adv. bd. pub. campaign for campaign fin. reform 1997—), Coun. on Fgn. Rels., Phi Beta Kappa. Mem. Evang. Free Ch. (past trustee). E-mail: jbafed@aol.com.

ANDERSON, JOHN THOMAS, lawyer; b. Gary, Ind., July 13, 1930; s. Jack and Dorothy Genevieve (Gustafson) A.; m. Marvel Nancy Filkey, Aug. 15, 1953; children: Kirsten E. Teevens, Katherine L., Eric M. AB, DePauw U., 1952; LLB, Harvard U., 1955. Bar: Ind. 1955, Ill. 1956. Assoc. Lord, Bissell & Brook, Chgo., 1958-66, ptnr., 1966-95, of counsel, 1996-98. Trustee DePauw U., Greencastle, Ind., 1982—; chmn. bd. dirs. Joyce Found., Chgo., 1979—; Lt. USNR, 1955-58. Methodist. Corporate, general, Estate planning, Securities. Home and Office: 2313 Cassia Ct Naples FL 34109-3370

ANDERSON, JON ERIC, lawyer; b. Jacksonville, N.C., Feb. 1, 1956; m. Lori Jean Schumacher, June 30, 1979; children: Andrew Jon, Elizabeth Ruth, Margaret Mary. BA, U. Wis., 1978; JD, Marquette U., 1981. Bar: Wis. 1981, U.S. Dist. Ct. (ea. and we. dists.) Wis. 1981, U.S. Ct. Appeals (7th cir.) 1996, U.S. Supreme Ct. 1988. Assoc. Mulcahy & Wherry, S.C., Milw., 1981-84, mng. atty. Sheboygan, Wis., 1984-87, Madison, 1987-90; shareholder Godfrey & Kahn, S.C., Madison, 1991-99, Lafollette, Godfrey & Kahn, S.C., 2000—. Author: (with others) Comparable Worth-A Negotiator's Guide, 1985; contbg. author Pub. Sector Labor Rels., Wis., 1988. Thomas More Soc. scholar, 1979. Mem.: ABA, Nat. Assn. Coll. and Univ. Attys., Wis. Sch. Attys. Assn. (bd. dirs. 2000—, pres.-elect 2002—03), Wis. Bar Assn. (bd. dirs. labor law sect. 1988—91), Edn. Law Assn., Madison Club, Blackhawk Country Club, Alpha Sigma Nu, Phi Delta Phi. Lutheran. Avocations: woodworking, music. Administrative and regulatory, Education and schools, Labor (including EEOC, Fair Labor Standards Act, labor-management relations, NLRB, OSHA).

ANDERSON, JON MAC, lawyer, educator; b. Rio Grande, Ohio, Jan. 10, 1937; s. Harry Rudolph and Carrie Viola (Magee) A.; m. Deborah Melton, June 1, 1961; children— Jon Gordon, Greta. AB, Ohio U., 1958; JD, Harvard Law Sch., 1961. Bar: Ohio 1961. Law clk. Hon. Kingsley A. Taft Ohio Supreme Ct., Columbus, 1961-62; assoc. Wright, Harlor, Morris & Arnold, Columbus, 1962-67, ptnr., 1968-76, Porter, Wright, Morris & Arthur, Columbus, 1977—. Adj. prof. law Ohio State U. Law Sch., Columbus, 1975-83; bar examiner State of Ohio, 1971-76, chmn., 1975-76; lectr. tax and estate planning insts.; bd. dirs. White Castle System, Inc., Columbus. Trustee Berea Coll, Ky., 1976-2000, Pro Musica Chamber Orch., Columbus, 1980-98, Opera Columbus, 1985-88, 1st Congl. Ch., Columbus, 1979-83, Greater Columbus Arts Coun., 1989-99; chmn., 1996-98; mem. adv. coun. The Textile Mus., 1996-2002. Mem. ABA, Ohio State Bar Assn., Columbus Bar Assn., The Columbus Club, Rocky Fork Hunt and Country Club. Democrat. Avocations: music, art, textiles, literature, antique collections. Corporate, general, Estate planning, Estate taxation. Office: Porter Wright Morris & Arthur 41 S High St Ste 2800 Columbus OH 43215-6194 E-mail: janderson@porterwright.com.

ANDERSON, KARL STEPHEN, editor; b. Chgo., Nov. 10, 1933; s. Karl William and Eleanore (Grell) a.; m. Saralee Hegland, Nov. 5, 1977; children by previous marriage: Matthew, Douglas, Eric. BS in Editl. Journalism, U. Ill., 1955. Successively advt. mgr., asst. to pub., plant mgr. Pioneer Press, Oak Park, St. Charles, Ill., 1955-71; asst. to pub., then pub. Crescent Newspapers, Downers Grove, Ill., 1971-73; assoc. pub., editor Chronicle Pub. Co., St. Charles, 1973-80; assoc. pub. Chgo. Daily Law Bull., 1981-88; dir. comms., editor Ill. State Bar Assn., 1988—. Past pres. Chgo. Pub. Rels. Forum. Trustee emeritus Chi Psi Ednl. Trust; trustee Leo Sowerby Found.; bd. dirs. Ill. Press Found., Chgo. Legal Svcs. Found., Swedish Am. Hist. Soc., Copley First Amendment Ctr. Recipient C.V. Amenoff award No. Ill. U. Dept. Journalism, 1976, Bd. Govs. award Ill. State Bar, 1987, Print Media Humanitarian award Coalition Sub Bar Assns., 1987, Robert C. Preble, Jr. award Chi Psi, 1991, Asian-Am. Bar Media Sensitivity award, 1991, Liberty Bell award DuPage County Bar Assn., 1993, Glass Ceiling Busters award DuPage Women Lawyers, 1993, Disting. Svc. award Chgo. Vol. Legal Svcs. Found., 1993, Gratitude award Lawyers Assistance Program, 1993, Outstanding Achievement in Comm. award Justinian Soc., 1994, Communicator of Yr. award, 1999, 3rd prize Nat. Libr. Poetry, 1995, Svc. award Women's Bar Assn. Ill., 1998, Peoria County Bar Assn., 1998. Mem. Nat. Assn. Bar Execs., Baltic Bar Assn., Chgo. Legal Sec. Assn., Chgo. Press Vets. Assn. (bd. sec.), Ill. Press assn. (Will Loomis award 1977, 80), Kane County Bar Assn., DuPage Women Lawyers Assn., West Suburban Bar Assn., N. Suburban Bar Assn. (Pub. Svc. award 1997), Bohemian Lawyers Assn. (Liberty award 1999), No. Ill. Newspaper Assn. (past pres.), Pub. Rels. Soc. Ctrl. Ill. (Master Communicator award of achievement 1997), Soc. Profl. Journalists, Headline Club (past pres.), Nordic Law Club, Nellie Fox Soc., Union League Club of Chgo., Chi Psi. Home: 3180 N Lake Shore Dr Apt 14D Chicago IL 60657-4851 Office: Ill State Bar Assn 20 S Clark St Ste 900 Chicago IL 60603-1885

ANDERSON, KATHLEEN GAY, mediator, hearing officer, arbitrator, trainer; b. Cin., July 27, 1950; d. Harold B. and Trudi L. (Chambers) Briggs; m. J.R. Carr, July 4, 1988; 1 child, Jesse J. Anderson. Student, U. Cin., 1971-72, Antioch Coll., 1973-74; cert., Nat. Jud. Coll., U. Nev., Reno, 1987, Inst. Applied Law, 1987, Acad. Family Mediators, 1991. Cert. Lemmon Mediation Inst., Acad. Family Mediators, U.S. Postal Svc. Panel, U.S. Forest Svc. Panel, Nat. Assn. Securities Panel, State of Alaska, U. Alaska, pvt. sector panels. Paralegal Lauer & Lauer, Santa Fe, 1976-79, Wilkinson, Cragun & Barker, Anchorage, 1981-82; employment law paralegal specialist Hughes, Thorsness, Gantz, Powell & Brundin, Anchorage, 1983-91; investigator, mediator Alaska State Commn. Human Rights, 1991; mediator, arbitrator, trainer The Arbitration and Mediation Group, Anchorage, 1987—; hearing officer Municipality of Anchorage, 1993-99; State of Alaska, 1994—. Mem. faculty Nat. Jud. Coll., U. Nev., Reno, 1988-89; adj. prof. U. Alaska, Anchorage, 1985-99, Alaska Pacific U., 1990-96, Chapman U., 1990; mem. Alaska Supreme Ct. Mediation Task Force, 1991-96; adv. com. Am. Arbitration Assn. for Alaska, 1995-99, ADR subcom. Supreme Ct. Civil Justice Reform task force, 1998-99; trainer, mediator. pvt. profit and nonprofit groups, pub. groups, U.S. mil., state and fed. govt.; arbitrator Anchorage Bd. Realtors, 1997-98; designer Ancients and Antiques, Trinkets and Treasures, 2000-. Author, editor: Professional Responsibility Handbook for Legal Assistants and Paralegals, 1986; contbr. articles to profl. jours. Lectr. Alaska Bar Assn., NLRB, Bus. and Profl. Women, Coun. on Edn. in Mgmt., Small Bus. Devel. Coun., various employers and bus. groups. Mem. Assn. for Conflict Resolution, Alaska Bar Assn. (assoc., alt. dispute resolution sect.), Alaska Dispute Settlement Assn. (v.p. 1992-93, chair com. on credentialing and stds. of practice, pres. 1997-98). Avocations: antiques, gourmet cooking. Home: PO Box 111517 Anchorage AK 99511-1517 Office: PO Box 240783 Anchorage AK 99524-0783 E-mail: tamg@gci.net.

ANDERSON, KEITH, retired lawyer, retired banker; b. Phoenix, June 21, 1917; s. Carl and Helen (Fairchild) A.; m. Grace R. VanDenburg, 1941 (div. 1957); m. Catherine Huber, 1960; children: Fletcher F., Warren, Nicholas H. AB, Dartmouth Coll., 1939; LLB, Harvard U., 1942. Bar: N.Y. 1942, Ariz. 1946, Colo. 1950. Ret. lawyer. Mem. Univ. Club of Denver, Cactus Club. Democrat.

ANDERSON, KIMBALL RICHARD, lawyer; b. San Antonio, Aug. 20, 1952; s. Richard John and Martha (Bishop) A.; m. Karen Gatsis, Aug. 18, 1974; children: Alexis Katrina, Melissa Martha, Sophia Diane. BA, U. Ill., 1974, JD, 1977. Bar: Ill. 1977, U.S. Ct. Appeals (7th cir.) 1979, U.S. Supreme Ct. 1987; CPA, Ill. Assoc. Winston & Strawn, Chgo., 1977-84, ptnr., 1984—, mem. exec. com., 1994—, gen. counsel. Bd. dirs. Pub. Interest Law Initiative; Disting. Neutral, CPR Inst. for Dispute Resolution. Named Person of Yr. 1996 Chgo. Lawyer. Fellow Am. Coll. Trial Lawyers; mem. ABA, Ill. Bar Assn., Chgo. Bar Assn. (bd. mgrs. 1990-92), Ill. CPA Soc., Chgo. Bar Found. Civil rights, General civil litigation, Product liability. Home: 2045 N Seminary Ave Chicago IL 60614-4109 Office: Winston & Strawn 35 W Wacker Dr Ste 4200 Chicago IL 60601-1695 E-mail: kanderson@winston.com.

ANDERSON, LAWRENCE ROBERT, JR., lawyer; b. Minden, La., Oct. 30, 1945; s. Lawrence Robert and Elnora Dale (Fincher) A.; m. Constance Lorraine Fauver, Oct. 21, 1977; children: Lauren Constance, Frank Lawrence. BS, La. State U., 1967, JD, 1971. Bar: La. 1971, U.S. Dist. Ct. (ea. dist.) La. 1971, U.S. Ct. Appeals (5th cir.) 1971, U.S. Dist. Ct. (mid. dist.) La. 1972, U.S. Dist. Ct. (we. dist.) La. 1975, U.S. Supreme Ct. 1975. Assoc. Sanders, Miller, Downing & Kean, Baton Rouge, 1971, Talley, Anthony, Hughes & Knight, Bogalusa, La., 1971-74; ptnr. Newman, Duggins, Drolla, Gamble & Anderson, Baton Rouge, 1974-76, Anderson & Roberts, Baton Rouge, 1976-79, Anderson, Anderson, Hawsey, Rainach & Stakelum, Baton Rouge, 1979-83, Anderson & Rainach, 1983-88, Anderson & Duncan, 1988-89, Seale, Smith, Zuber & Barnette, Baton Rouge, 1990—. 1st lt. U.S. Army, 1972. Mem. La. Bar Assn., Bar Assn. Fed. 5th Cir., Baton Rouge Bar Assn., Am. Bankruptcy Inst., Comml. Law League Am. Bankruptcy, Commercial, contracts (including sales of goods; commercial financing), Constitutional. Home: 11937 Lake Sherwood Ave N Baton Rouge LA 70816-4340 Office: 8550 United Plaza Blvd Ste 200 Baton Rouge LA 70809-2256 Business E-Mail: lranderson@sszblaw.com.

ANDERSON, LAWRENCE WORTHINGTON, retired lawyer; b. Dallas, Sept. 27, 1917; s. Frank William and Amelia Kathryn A.; m. Ardene Sarah Boven, June 27, 1942; children: Constance, Lawrence Jr., Carol. JD, U. Tex., 1939. Bar: Ill. 1939, Tex. 1946, U.S. Supreme Ct. 1960. Assoc. Carrington, Gowan, Dallas, 1943-48; ptnr. Harris, Anderson & Henley, Dallas, 1948-60, Anderson, Helley & Shields, Dallas, 1960-80, Ray, Anderson, Shield, Tronti, Dallas, 1980-83; of counsel Anderson, Miller & Sifford, Dallas, 1983-86, Anderson & Miller, Dallas, 1986-1990, Siffofd Anderson Vic & McFarland, Dallas, 1990—. Mem. Internat. Assn. Ins., 1960—; gen. counsel Ladies Profl. Golf Assn., 1970-78; chmn. bd. Am. Intilian Food Co., Dallas, 1978-83, Food Source, Inc., McKinney, Tex., 1985-90; mem. bd. adjustment City of Dallas, 1980-85. With USN, 1943-44. Named to Hall of Fame, Dallas Assn. Def., 1995. Mem. ABA, State Bar Tex., Dallas County Bar Assn., Smith County Bar Assn., Tex. Assn. Def., Hide-Away Lake Club. Republican. Presbyterian. Avocation: golf. Aviation, General civil litigation, Insurance. Home: 1341 Hideaway Ln W Lindale TX 75771-5115

ANDERSON, LEROY, lawyer; b. Lexington, Nebr., May 27, 1949; BS, U. Nebr. Kearney, 1971; JD, U. Nebr. Lincoln, 1973. Ptnr. Murphy Pederson Piccolo & Anderson, North Platte, Nebr., 1973—83, Roeder & Anderson, North Platte, 1983—88, Frandzel & Shore, L.A., 1988—99; litigation counsel Calif. State U., Long Beach, 1999—. Panel trustee U.S. Bankruptcy Ct., 1983—88. Office: Calif State Univ 401 Golden Shore 4th Fl Long Beach CA 90802

ANDERSON, MARY ELLEN, lawyer; b. Balt., Md., Aug. 3, 1951; AA in Nursing, Essex C.C., Balt., 1971; BS in Nursing, U. Md., 1973; MA in Psychology, Towson State U., 1976; JD, U. Md., 1994. Bar: Md. 1994; RN, Md.; lic. real estate broker, Md. Nursing asst. II Greater Balt. Med. Ctr., Towson, Md., 1970-71, staff nurse, 1971-74; clin. nurse U. Md. Hosp., Balt., 1974-76; sch. psychology intern Roanoke (Va.) City Pub. Schs., 1976; nurse clinician Walter P. Carter Ctr. Dept. Health and Mental Hygiene, Balt., 1976-79, program adminstr. mental hygiene adminstrn., 1979-86, dep. dir., 1986-88; dir. inpatient svcs. Glass Mental Health Ctrs., Inc., Balt., 1989-90; faculty assoc. mental health policy studies program U. Md. Sch. Medicine, Balt., 1988-91, sr. adminstr. dept. anesthesiology, 1991-92, sr. adminstr. dept. psychiatry, 1992-93; cons. Healthcare Cons. Svcs., 1994—; pvt. practice Phoenix, Md., 1995—. Cons. Franklin County (Ohio) Mental Health Bd., 1989, Washington County (Md.) Mental Health Authority, 1992, Liberty Inst. Cmty. Psychiatry and Behavioral Svcs., Balt., 1992-93; faculty health sci. dept. Towson State U., 1994; cons. Green Spring Health Svcs., Inc., 1993-95, Md. Medicare, 1995-96; expert witness U.S. Dept. Justice, 1989-96; mem. credit com. State Employees' Credit, Union, 1984—. Chairperson Mental Health Coalition Ctrl. Md. Health Systems Agy., 1983-84; mem. bd. dirs., treas., chair fundraising com. Md. Women's Health Coalition, 1984-86; bd. dirs. Transitional Living Coun., Inc., 1989-90; v.p. Hunter's Run Homeowner's Assn., 1988-90; bd. dirs. Ptnrs. in Progress Resource Ctr., Inc., 1996. Mem. Md. State Bar Assn. Estate planning, General practice, Health. Home: 9 Windemere Pkwy Phoenix MD 21131-2424 E-mail: mealaw@mindspring.com.

ANDERSON, MICHAEL STEVEN, lawyer; b. Mpls., May 25, 1954; s. Wesley James and Lorraine Kathrine (Sword) A.; m. Gail Karin Miller, June 18, 1977; children: Mark, Steven. BA magna cum laude, Cornell U., 1976; JD, Washington U., St. Louis, 1980. Bar: Wis. 1980, U.S. Dist. Ct. (ea. and we. dists.) Wis. 1980, U.S. Ct. Appeals (7th cir.) 1986, U.S. Supreme Ct. 1991. Ptnr. Axley Brynelson, Madison, Wis., 1980—2003, mng. ptnr., 2003—. Editor, author Washington U. Law Quarterly, 1979-80. Apptd. mem. local Bd. Attys. Profl. Responsibility, 1993—2001; preliminary rev. com. mem. Office Lawyer Regulation, 2002—. Mem.: Order of Coif. Mem. Evangelical Free Ch. Avocation: family. General civil litigation, Corporate, general, Product liability. Home: 5882 Timber Ridge Trail Madison WI 53711-5180 Office: Axley Brynelson 2 E Mifflin St Madison WI 53703-2889 E-mail: manderson@axley.com.

ANDERSON, PAUL HOLDEN, state supreme court justice; b. May 14, 1943; m. Janice M. Anderson; 2 children. BA cum laude, Macalester Coll., 1965; JD, U. Minn., 1968. Atty. Vols. in Svc. to Am., 1968—69; spl. asst. atty. gen. criminal divsn. dept. pub. safety Office Minn. Atty. Gen., 1970—71; assoc., ptnr. LeVander, Gillen & Miller, South St. Paul, Minn., 1971—92; chief judge Minn. Ct. Appeals, 1992—94; assoc. justice Minn. Supreme Ct., 1994—. Mem. PER coms. Ind. Sch. Dist. 199, 1982—84, chmn. cmty. svcs. adv. com., bd. dirs., chmn. bd.; deacon, ruling elder, clk. of session House of Hope Presbyn. Ch., St. Paul. Mem.: Dakota County Bar Assn. (bd. dirs., pres.), South St. Paul/Inver Grove Heights C. of C. (bd. dirs., exec. com.). Avocations: tennis, gourmet cooking, bike riding. Office: Minn Supreme Court 425 Saint Paul MN 55155-0001 Fax: 651-282-5115. E-mail: paul.anderson@courts.state.mn.us.

ANDERSON, PETER MACARTHUR, lawyer; b. New Castle, Ind., July 15, 1937; s. Earl Canute and Catherine Elizabeth (Schultz) A.; m. Ann Warren Gibson, Sept.1, 1962; children: David, Karen. AB, Dartmouth Coll., 1959; LLB, Stanford U., 1962. Bar: Calif. 1963, Wash. 1970. Assoc. O'Melveny & Myers, L.A., 1966-70, Bogle & Gates, Seattle, 1970-74, mem., 1974-99; ptnr. Preston Gates & Ellis, Seattle, 1999—2002, sr. counsel, 2003—. Co-chmn. equal employment law com. ABA, 1983-86. Mem. Ecumenical Commn. for Seattle Archdiocese, St. Petersburg-Seattle Sister Chs. Com. Capt. U.S. Army, 1963-65. Fellow Coll. Labor and Employment Lawyers; mem. Phi Beta Kappa. Roman Catholic. Labor (including EEOC, Fair Labor Standards Act, labor-management relations, NLRB, OSHA). Home: 9200 SE 57th St Mercer Island WA 98040-5005 Office: Preston Gates & Ellis LLP 925 4th Ave Ste 2900 Seattle WA 98104-1158

ANDERSON, PHILIP SIDNEY, lawyer; b. Little Rock, May 9, 1935; s. Philip Sidney and Frances (Walt) Anderson; m. Rosemary Gill Wright, Sept. 26, 1959; children: Sidney Walt Kenyon, Philip Wright, Catherine Gill Askew. BA, LLB, U. Ark., 1959. Bar: Ark. 1960, U.S. Supreme Ct. 1966. Assoc. Wright, Lindsey & Jennings, Little Rock, 1960—65, ptnr., 1965—88, Williams & Anderson, Little Rock, 1988—. Lectr. Ark. Law Sch., 1963—66; mem. com. on jury instrns. Ark. Supreme Ct., 1962—97; mem. panel for the 8th cir. U.S. Cir. Judge Nominating Commn., 1978—79; mem. fed. adv. com. U.S. Ct. Appeals 8th cir., 1983—88, co-chmn., 1987—88; bd. dirs. WEHCO Media, Inc., Ark. Dem.-Gazette, Inc. Co-author: Arkansas Model Jury Instructions, 1965, 1974, 1989. Pres. Friends of Little Rock Pub. Libr., 1968—69, Little Rock Unltd. Progress, Inc., 1973—74; trustee Ctrl. Ark. Libr. Sys., 1981—87, pres., 1984; trustee George W. Donaghey Found., 1976—, pres., 1979—80; trustee Ctr. for Am. and Internat. Law, 1996—, Lawyers' Com. for Civil Rights Under Law, 2001—. 2d lt. U.S. Army, 1959—60. Fellow: ABA (chair ho. of dels. 1992—94, bd. govs. 1990—94, 1997—2000, pres. 1998—99), Ark. Bar Found. (pres. 1973—74), Am. Bar Found.; mem.: Am. Law Inst. (mem. coun. 1982—), Ark. Bar Assn. (spl. award meritorious svc.). Episcopalian. Antitrust, Federal civil litigation, Corporate, general. Home: 4716 Crestwood Dr Little Rock AR 72207-5436 Office: Williams & Anderson LLP 111 Center St Ste 2200 Little Rock AR 72201-4429 E-mail: psa@wiiiamsanderson.com.

ANDERSON, RICHARD GARDINER, lawyer; b. Balt., July 3, 1936; s. Marvin Isaac and Geneva Augusta (Hauser) A.; m. Elizabeth Canfield Blessing, Aug. 17, 1957; children: Elizabeth C.B., Richard Edwin, Thomas Jonathan Jackson. AB magna cum laude, Washington and Lee U., 1957, JD, 1959. Bar: Va. 1959, Md. 1960, U.S. Ct. Mil. Appeals 1960. Ptnr. Anderson and Anderson, Annapolis, Md., 1963-82; asst. city atty. City of Annapolis, 1973-79, city atty., 1980-82; sole practice Lexington, Va., 1982—; magistrate 25th judicial dist. Commonwealth of Va., Lexington, 1986-87. Mem. trial cts. judicial nominating commn. State of Md., Annapolis, 1975-82, mem. inquiry panel and atty. grievance commn., 1978-82. Disbursing treas. New Providence Presbyn. Ch., 1986-89, elder, 1984-86, 88-90, 97-98; mem. Ctrl. Shenandoah Planning Dist. Commn., Staunton, Va., 1988-91. Capt. JAGC, U.S. Army, 1960-63. Mem. SAR (pres. Rockbridge Vols. chpt. 2001-02), Assn. Preservation of Va. Antiquities (bd. dirs. Ruth Anderson McCulloch br. 1991-96, pres. 1995-96), Rockbridge Hist. Soc. (treas. 1991-94), Brownsburg Ruritan Club (pres. 1994). Avocations: antiques, genealogy, gardening. Estate planning, Probate (including wills, trusts), Property, real (including real estate development, water). Office: 17 S Jefferson St Lexington VA 24450-2142

ANDERSON, ROBERT LANIER, III, judge; b. Macon, Ga., Nov. 12, 1936; s. Robert Lanier II and Helen Anderson; m. Nancy Briska, Aug. 18, 1962; children: Robert, William Hilliar, Browne McIntosh. AB magna cum laude, Yale U., 1958; LLB, Harvard U., 1961. Assoc. Anderson, Walkert, Reichert, Macon, Ga., 1963—79; judge U.S. Ct. Appeals (11th cir.), 1979—99, 2002—, chief judge, 1999—2002. With USAR, 1958—61, capt. U.S. Army, 1961—63. Mem.: ABA, Am. Judicature Soc., State Bar of Ga., Macon Bar Assn., Ga. Bar Assn. Office: US Ct Appeals PO Box 977 Macon GA 31202-0977

ANDERSON, ROBERT CHARLES, lawyer; b. Mt. Clemens, Mich., Nov. 24, 1951; s. Irving Rudolph and Ruth Lorraine A.; m. Sharon Melissa Schreiber, Sept. 9, 1978; children: Robert, Charles, Elizabeth, Ellen. BA, Wayne State U., 1971, U. Tenn., 1973, JD, 1977. Judge advocate USAF, Biloxi, Miss., Fairbanks, Alaska, 1978-83; asst. dist. atty. Alaska Dept. Law, Fairbanks, 1984-89, 10th Jud. Dist. Tenn., Cleveland, 1989; asst. U.S. atty. U.S. Dept. Justice (mid. dist.) Tenn., Nashville, 1989—. Instr. bus. law U. So. Miss., Gulfport, 1978, U. Alaska, Fairbanks, 1980-84. Vol. coach youth tennis, swimming and soccer. Mem. Tenn. Bar Assn. Home: 1421 Devens Dr Brentwood TN 37027 Office: US Atty's Office 110 9th Ave S Ste A961 Nashville TN 37203-3870

ANDERSON, ROBERT MONTE, lawyer; b. Logan, Utah, Feb. 19, 1938; s. E. LeRoy and Grace (Rasmussen) Anderson; m. Kathleen Hansen, Aug. 12, 1966; children: Jennifer, Katrina, Alexander. AB, Columbia Coll., 1960; LLB, U. Utah, 1963. Bar: Utah 1963, US Ct Appeals (10th cir) 1967, US Supreme Ct 1976. Assoc., shareholder, v.p. Van Cott, Bagley, Cornwall & McCarthy, Salt Lake City, 1963-82; pres., shareholder Berman & Anderson, Salt Lake City, 1982-86; v.p., shareholder Hansen & Anderson, Salt Lake City, 1986-90; pres., shareholder Anderson & Watkins, Salt Lake City, 1990-95; pres. Anderson & Smith, Salt Lake City, 1995-97; lawyer, shareholder, pres. Van Cott, Bagley Cornwall & McCarthy, Salt Lake City, 1998—. Bd dirs, mem exec comt Anderson Lumber Co, Ogden, Utah, 1982—2000. Trustee Children's Ctr., Salt Lake City, 1979—84, United Way of Salt Lake, 2002—. Mem.: ABA, Am Inns Ct, Utah State Bar Asn (cts and judges comt 1991—99), Cottonwood Club, Alta Club, Rotary. Avocations: tennis, skiing. General civil litigation, Construction, Property, real (including real estate development, water). Office: Van Cott Bagley Cornwall & McCarthy 50 S Main St Ste 1600 Salt Lake City UT 84144-2044 E-mail: randerson@vancott.com.

ANDERSON, RUSSELL A. state supreme court justice; b. Bemidji, Minn., May 28, 1942; m. Kristin Anderson; children: Rebecca, John, Sarah. BA, St. Olaf Coll., 1964; JD, U. Minn., 1968; LLM, George Washington U., 1977. Pvt. practice, 1976-82; atty. Beltrami County, 1978-82; dist. ct. judge 9th Jud. Dist., 1982-98; assoc. justice Minn. Supreme Ct., 1998—. Mem. Jud. Edn. Adv. Com., Sentencing Guidelines Commn., Supreme Ct. Adv. Com. on Rules of Criminal Procedure, Supreme Ct. Gender Fairness Implementation com., Connect U.S.-Russian Domestic Violence Delegation to Russia, 1995, 97. Lt. comdr. USN, 1968—76. Mem.: 14th Dist. Bar Assn., Minn. State Bar Assn. Office: Minn Supreme Ct 305 Minn Judicial Ctr 25 Rev Martin Luther King Jr Blvd Saint Paul MN 55155*

ANDERSON, SHERMAN LOUIS, lawyer, educator; b. Laurens, S.C., Aug. 21, 1952; s. Walter Lee and Coria Lee (Richardson) A.; 1 child, Sherman Louis II. B.A., Morehouse Coll., 1974; J.D., Case Western Res. U., 1977; MPA, Ea. Mich. U, 1993. Bar: Pa. 1978, U.S. Dist. Ct. (ea. dist.) Mich. 1982, U.S. Ct. Claims 1982, U.S. Ct. Appeals (D.C. cir.) 1982, U.S. Supreme Ct. 1982. Assoc., White, Milano & Miller, Cleve., 1977-79; county prosecutor State of Ohio, Cleve., 1980; assoc. White, Milano & Miller, Cleve., 1980; atty.-adv. Office Gen. Counsel, SBA, Washington, 1980-82; dir. legal div. Detroit Econ. Growth Corp., 1982— ; pres, Comprehensive Bus. Cons.; dir. Ednl. Opportunity Ctr., U. S.C.; instr. upward bound program Case Western Res. U.; instr. D'etre U.; guest lctr. Cleve. high schs., 1975-76. Contbr. book revs. to profl. jours. Vice chmn. bd. trustees Lexington/Richland Counties Sch. Bd. Edn. Recipient cert. U. Miami Sch. Medicine, 1972; named one of Ten Most Outstanding Young Men of Am., U.S. Jaycees, 1981. Chmn. emeritus bd. dirs. Detroit Met. Orchestra, Inc.; legal advisor Brazeal Dennard Chorale. Recipient Spirit of Detroit award, Joint REsolution State of Mich. Gen. Assembly. Mem. Pa. Bar Assn., Nat. Conf. Black Lawyers, Nat. Bar Assn., Fed. Bar Assn., Am. Soc. Public Adminstrn., Am. Polit. Sci. Assn., Conf. Minority Pub. Adminstrs., Nat. Urban League, NAACP, Columbia Urban League, Morehouse Coll. Alumni Assn., Alpha Phi Alpha, Beta Gamma Sigma, Pi Alpha Alpha, Delta Sigma Rho, Pi Sigma Alpha. Baptist. Founder, designer ofcl. coll. flag Morehouse Coll.

ANDERSON, STEPHEN HALE, federal judge; b. Salt Lake City, Jan. 12, 1932; m. Shirlee Gehring; 2 children. Student, Eastern Oreg. Coll. Edn., LaGrande, 1951, Brigham Young U., Provo, 1956; LLB, U. Utah, 1960. Bar: Utah 1960, U.S. Claims Ct. 1963, U.S. Tax Ct. 1967, U.S. Ct. Appeals (10th cir.) 1970, U.S. Supreme Ct. 1971, U.S. Ct. Appeals (9th cir.) 1972. Tchr. South H.S., Salt Lake City, 1956—57; trial atty. tax divsn. U.S. Dept. Justice, 1960—64; ptnr. Ray, Quinney & Nebeker, 1964—85; judge U.S. Ct. Appeals (10th cir.), Salt Lake City, 1985—. Spl. counsel Salt Lake County Grand Jury, 1975; chmn. fed.-state jurisdiction com. Jud. Conf. U.S., 1995—98; mem. Nat. Jud. Coun. State and Fed. Cts., 1992—96; ad hoc. com. on bankruptcy appellate panels 10th Cir. Jud. Coun., 1995—97; com. mem. U.S. Ct. Appeals (10th cir.). Editor (in chief): Utah Law Rev. With U.S. Army, 1953—55. Mem.: Am. Bar Found., Salt Lake County Bar Assn. (pres. 1977—78), Utah State Bar (pres. 1983—84), U. Utah Coll. Law Alumni Assn. (trustee 1979—83, pres. 1982—83), Salt Lake Area C. of C. (bd.govs. 1984), Order of Coif. Office: US Ct Appeals 4201 Fed Bldg 125 S State St Salt Lake City UT 84138-1102

ANDERSON, THOMAS DUNAWAY, retired lawyer; b. Oklahoma City, Mar. 9, 1912; s. Frank Ervin and Burdine (Clayton) A.; m. Helen Sharp, Feb. 21, 1938; children: Helen Shaw, Lucille Streeter, John Sharp. Student, Rice Inst., 1930-31; LLB, Washington and Lee U., 1934; LLD (hon.), Lambuth Coll., 1967. Bar: Va. 1933, Tex. 1934. Assoc. Andrews & Kurth, 1934-41, 46-47; sr. v.p., trust officer Tex. Commerce Bank, Houston, 1947-51, 60-65; co-founder Tex. Fund, 1949; pres. Tex. Fund Mgmt. Co., Houston, 1952-60; ptnr. Anderson Brown & Jones, Houston, 1965-93; ret. Trustee emeritus Washington and Lee U.; life mem., past pres. bd. visitors M.D. Anderson Cancer Ctr.; past pres., chmn. Kelsey Rsch. Fedn., Protestant Episcopal Ch. Coun., Diocese of Tex., Washington-on-Brazos State Park Assn., Mus. Fine Arts Houston, Houston Grand Opera; bd. dirs. Bayou Bend Gardens Endowment, Retina Rsch. Found., Harris County Hist. Commn. First recipient Leon Jaworski award for vol. cmty. svc., 1988. Mem. ABA, Tex. Bar Assn., Philos. Soc. Tex., Bayou, Eagle Lake Rod and Gun Club, Houston Country Club, Petroleum Club of Houston, River Oaks Garden Club (hon.), SAR, Omicron Delta Kappa, Phi Delta Phi. Episcopalian. Office: River Oaks Bank Bldg 2001 Kirby Dr Houston TX 77019-6033

ANDERSON, WARREN MATTICE, lawyer; b. Bainbridge, N.Y., Oct. 16, 1915; s. Floyd E. and Edna (Mattice) Anderson; m. Eleanor C. Sanford, June 28, 1941 (dec. Sept. 1996); children: Warren David, Lawrence, Richard, Thomas; m. Ruth W. Bennett, Aug. 25, 2001. BA, Colgate U., 1937; JD, Albany Law Sch., 1940, LLD (hon.), 1979, Hartwick Coll., 1976, Coll. of New Rochelle, 1979, Fordham U., 1980, Union Coll., 1981, Colgate U., 1982, Hamilton Coll., 1985, Clarkson U., 1987, St. Lawrence U., 1988, Elmira Coll., 1989, St. Francis Coll., 1991; LHD (hon.), Hofstra U., 1987. Bar: N.Y., 1940. Since practiced in, Binghamton; asst. county atty. Broome County, N.Y., 1940-42; assoc. Hinman, Howard & Kattell LLP, 1949-52; ptnr. Hinman, Howard & Kattell, 1952—; mem. N.Y. State Senate, 1953-88, chmn. fin. com., 1966-72, pres. pro tem, majority leader, 1973-88. Del. Rep. Nat. Conv., 1972, 76, 80, 84, 88, mem. platform com., 1972; trustee Colgate U., 1964-70, Cornell U., 1973-88, Elmira Coll., 1989-95; bd. dirs. N.Y. State Hist. Assn.; mem. N.Y. State Commn. on Jud. Nominations; mem. Hartwick Coll. Coun.; mem. adv. com. Govt. Law Ctr., Albany Law Sch.; mem. bd. overseers Nelson A. Rockefeller Inst. Govt. With AUS, 1943-45, lt. JAGD, 1945-46. Recipient Alumni award Colgate U., 1972 Fellow Am. Bar Found.; mem. ABA, Broome County Bar Assn. Clubs: Binghamton; Oteyokwa Lake (Hallstead, Pa.). Presbyterian. Probate (including wills, trusts). Home: 34 Lathrop Ave Binghamton NY 13905-4343 Office: Hinman Howard & Kattell 700 Security Mut Bldg Binghamton NY 13902-5250

ANDERSON, WILLIAM HOPPLE, lawyer; b. Cin., Feb. 28, 1926; s. Robert Waters and Anna (Hopple) A.; m. Jean Koop, Feb. 3, 1951; children: Susan Hopple, Nancy, Barbara, William Hopple Jr., Francie. Student, Carleton Coll., 1946; LL.B., U. Cin., 1952. Bar: Ohio bar 1952, U.S. Supreme Ct 1964. Mem. firm Becker, Loeb, & Becker, Cin., 1952-54; asst. pros. atty. Hamilton County, Ohio, 1953-57; of counsel Graydon, Head & Ritchey, Cin.; judge Wyoming (Ohio) Mcpl. Ct., 1960-67. Mem. Ohio Ho. of Reps., 1967-69. With USMC, 1944-46. Mem. Cin. Bar Assn. Republican. Presbyterian. Home: 297 Mount Pleasant Ave Cincinnati OH 45215-4212 Office: 511 Walnut St Cincinnati OH 45202-3115

ANDREASEN, JAMES HALLIS, retired state supreme court judge; b. Mpls., May 16, 1931; s. John A. and Alice M. Andreasen; m. Janet Andreasen, June 25, 1961 (dec. July 1985); children: Jon A., Amy E., Steven J.; m. Marilyn McGuire, May 17, 1987. BS in Commerce, U. Iowa, 1953, JD, 1958. Bar: Iowa 1958. Pvt. practice law, Algona, Iowa, 1958-75; with Algona City Coun., 1961-68; judge 3d Jud. Dist. Ct., 1975-87, Supreme Ct. Iowa, Des Moines, 1987-98, ret., sr. judge, 1998—. Lt. col. USAFR, 1954-75. Mem. ABA, Iowa State Bar Assn., Kossuth County Bar Assn. Methodist. Office: Kossuth County Courthouse Algona IA 50511

ANDREOFF, CHRISTOPHER ANDON, lawyer; b. Detroit, July 15, 1947; s. Andon Anastas and Mildred Dimitry (Kolinoff) A.; m. Nancy Anne Krochmal, Jan. 12, 1980; children: Alison Brianne, Lauren Kathleen. BA, Wayne State U., 1969; postgrad. in law, Washington U., St. Louis, 1969-70; JD, U. Detroit, 1972. Bar: Mich. 1972, U.S. Dist. Ct. (ea. dist.) Mich. 1972, U.S. Ct. Appeals (6th cir.) 1974, Fla. 1978, U.S. Supreme Ct. 1980. Legal intern Wayne County Prosecutor's Office, Detroit, 1970-72; law clk. Wayne County Cir. Ct., Detroit, 1972-73; asst. U.S. atty. U.S. Dept. Justice, Detroit, 1973-80; asst. chief criminal divsn. U.S. Atty.'s Office, 1977-80; spl. atty. organized crime and racketeering sect. U.S. Dept. Justice, 1980-84, dep. chief Detroit Organized Crime Strike Force, 1982-85, mem. narcotics adv. com., 1979-80; ptnr. Evans & Luptak, Detroit, 1985-93, Jaffe, Raitt, Heuer & Weiss, Detroit, 1995—. Lectr. U.S. Atty. Gen. Advocacy Inst., 1984. Recipient numerous spl. commendations FBI, U.S. Drug Enforcement Adminstrn., U.S. Dept. Justice, U.S. ATty. Gen. Mem. ABA, FBA (spkr. trial adv. and criminal law sect. Detroit 1983—, bd. dirs. 1989-91, chmn. criminal law sect. 1990-91), Mich. Bar Assn., Fla. Bar Assn., Nat. Assn. Criminal Def. Lawyers, Detroit Bar Assn. Greek Orthodox. Federal civil litigation, State civil litigation, Criminal. Home: 4661 Rivers Edge Dr Troy MI 48098-4161 Office: Jaffe Raitt Heuer & Weiss One Woodward Ave Ste 2400 Detroit MI 48226

ANDREOZZI, LOUIS JOSEPH, lawyer; b. N.J., 1959; m. Lisa Marie Clark, Apr. 12, 1987. BS in Bus. Adminstrn. with hons., Rutgers U., 1981; JD, Seton Hall U., 1984. Bar: N.J. 1984. Asst. gen. counsel Gordon Pub., Inc., Randolph, NJ, 1984—93; dep. gen. counsel Elsevier U.S. Holdings, Morris Plains, NJ, 1985—93; v.p., sec., gen. counsel Reed Elsevier Med. Pub., Belle Mead, NJ, 1994—95; v.p., gen. counsel, sec., head ops. support and svcs., purchasing, sales force homeworking project, customer svc. integration project Lexis-Nexis, Miamisburg, Ohio, 1994—97; pub. Martindale-Hubbell, 1996; chief legal counsel Lexis-Nexis, 1997—98; COO Martindale-Hubbell, New Providence, NJ, 1997—99, Marquis, NRP, New Providence, NJ, 1998—99; vice-chmn. Reed Tech. and Info. Svcs., Inc., 1999—2000; pres., CEO Martindale-Hubbell, Marquis, NRP, New Providence, 1999—2000, Lexis, 2000—. Mem. legal adv. bd. Lexis-Nexis, 1994—, exec. bd., 1994—; mem. Friends of the Law Libr. of Congress; bd. dirs. Am. Assn. of Pub. Named to Dept. Distinction in Bus., Rutgers U., 1981, Nat. Honor Soc. in Econs. and Bus., 1981. Mem.: ABA, N.J. Employment Law Assn., Am. Corp. Counsel Assn., Internat. Bar Assn., N.J. Bar Assn. Roman Catholic. Office: Lexis Nexis Group 9443 Springboro Pike Miamisburg OH 45342-4425

ANDRES, INGRID, lawyer; b. Offenbach, Germany, Oct. 21, 1966; d. Horst and Maria Andres. Abitur, Friedrich-Ebert-Gymnasium, Mühlheim on Main, Germany, 1986; law studies, U. Frankfurt on Main, Germany, 1986—92. Cert.: (assessor examination) 1997. Asst. U. Frankfurt, on Main, Germany, 1992—94; trainee atty. Hanau and Frankfurt on Main, Germany, 1996—97; atty. Lovells, Frankfurt on Main and Munich, Germany, 1997—. Co-author: Juristen: Ein biographisches Lexikon, 1995; author: Der Erbrechtsentcoturf von Friedrich Mommsen - Ein Beitrag zur Entstehung des BGB, 1996; co-author: Handbuch zum neuen Schuldrecht, 2002. Avocations: literature, music. Corporate, general, Mergers and acquisitions, Probate (including wills, trusts). Office: Lovells Darmstädter Landstraße 125 60598 Frankfurt on Main Germany Fax: 069 96236100. E-mail: ingrid.andres@lovells.com.

ANDRES, KENNETH G., JR., lawyer; b. Trenton, N.J., Nov. 9, 1953; s. Kenneth George and Joan Margaret (Fredericks) A. BA, Swarthmore Coll., 1975; JD, Capital U., 1978. Bar: N.J. 1978, Pa. 1978, U.S. Dist. Ct. N.J. 1978, U.S. Ct. Appeals (3rd cir.) 1981, U.S. Supreme Ct. 1994; cert. civil trial atty., N.J., cert. advocate Am. Bd. Trial Advocates. Ptnr. Andres & Berger PC, Haddonfield, N.J. Adj. prof. law Mercer County C.C., 1983-89; faculty mem. Am. Trial Lawyers Assn. - N.J., 1989—. Contbr. articles to profl. publs. Mem. N.J. Supreme Ct. Dist. III ethics com., 1994-98; mem. N.J. Supreme Ct. Civil Jury Charge Com., 1996—. Named Profl. Lawyer of Yr., N.J. Commn. Professionalism in Law, 1998. Mem. ATLA (nat. gov. 2001—), ABA, Assn. Trial Lawyers of Am.-N.J. (bd. govs. 1986-90, parliamentarian 1990-91, from asst. sec. to pres. 1990-1999, N.J. Gold Medal award 1999), Pa. State Bar Assn., N.J. State Bar Assn., Burlington County Bar Assn. (chmn. civil bench and bar com. 1992-94, trustee 1993), Mercer County Bar Assn. (trustee 1982-91). State civil litigation, Personal injury (including property damage), Product liability. Office: Andres & Berger PC 264 Kings Hwy E Haddonfield NJ 08033-1907 E-mail: kandres@andresberger.com.

ANDREU-GARCIA, JOSE ANTONIO, territory supreme court chief justice; Chief justice Supreme Ct. of P.R. Office: Supreme Ct PR PO Box 9022392 San Juan PR 00902-2392 E-mail: andreujp@tld.net., josea2@tribunales.gobierno.pr.

ANDREWS, CHERI D. lawyer; b. Oakland, Calif., May 29, 1961; m. Jay A. Andrews, 1985; children: Sarah Renee, Rachel Susanne, Rebecca Anne. BA magna cum laude, Mt. Holyoke Coll., 1983; JD, Temple U., 1987. Bar: Pa. 1987. Atty. Manning, Kinkead, Brooks & Bradbury, Norristown, Pa., 1987-96, High, Swartz, Roberts & Seidel, Norristown, 1996—. Co-author, co-editor: (manual) Montgomery County Civil Practice Manual, 1992-01 (ABA G.P. Link Project award 1995); editor: Montgomery County Law Reporter, 1994-96. Mary Lyon scholar Mt. Holyoke Coll., 1983. Mem. Montgomery Bar Assn. (bd. dirs. 1996-98, Pres.'s award 2003, co-chmn. SideBar pub., 2001-02, com. of yr. award 2002), Bucks-Mont Mothers of Multiples (sec. 1997-98). Avocations: quilting, making scrapbooks. Appellate, Trademark and copyright. Office: High Swartz Roberts & Seidel 40 E Airy St Norristown PA 19401-4803 E-mail: candrews@highswartz.com.

ANDREWS, DAVID RALPH, lawyer; b. Oakland, Calif., Jan. 4, 1942; m. Rozan McCurdy, July 1, 1962; children: David, Linda. BA, U. Calif., Berkeley, 1968; JD, U. Calif., 1971. Bar: Calif. 1971, D.C. 1986, U.S. Dist. Ct. (no. dist.) Calif. 1971, U.S. Dist. Ct. Hawaii 1991, U.S. Supreme Ct. 1980. Assoc. McCutchen, Doyle, Brown & Enersen, San Francisco, 1971-75; regional counsel Reg. IX U.S. EPA, San Francisco, 1975-77; legal counsel and spl. asst. for policy US EPA, Washington, 1977-79; dep. gen. counsel Dept. Health and Human Svcs., Washington, 1980-81; ptnr. McCutchen, Doyle, Brown & Enersen, San Francisco, 1981-97, chmn., 1991-95; legal adviser US Dept. State, Washington, 1997-2000; ptnr. McCutchen, Doyle, Brown & Enersen, San Francisco, 2000—02; sr. v.p., govt. affairs & sec. office of gen. counsel, Pepsi Co., Purchase, NY, 2002. Amb., spl. negotiator U.S./Iran Claims, 2000—; bd. dirs. Union Bank Calif., Kaiser Permanente, NetCel360 Holdings Ltd., PG&E Corp. Trustee San Francisco Mus. of Modern Art, 1988-97; bd. trustees Golden Gate Nat. Park Assn., 1992-95, Marin Cmty. Found., 1996-97; mem. U.S. Agy. for Internat. Devel. Energy Tng. Program Adv. Com. of the Inst. Internat. Edn.; mem. bd. dirs. Union Bank Calif., Kaiser Permanente and NetCel360 Holdings Ltd., 2000—. Fellow Max Planck Inst. of Pub. Internat. Law, Heidelberg, Fed. Republic of Germany, 1974. Mem. ABA (natural resources sect.), Calif. Bar Assn.), San Francisco Bar Assn. Avocations: photography, tennis, running. Administrative and regulatory, Environmental. Office: Pepsi Co Office Gen Coun 700 Anderson Hill Rd Purchase NY 10577*

ANDREWS, HORACE A. retired judge; b. Plant City, Fla., Oct. 2, 1932; s. Otis M. and Lena Taylor Andrews; m. Joan Cunningham, Aug. 2, 1953; children: H. Allan, Ashley T. BSBA, U. Fla., 1954; JD, Stetson U., 1970. Bar: Fla. 1970, U.S. Supreme Ct. 1974. Ptnr. Harris, Harris & Andrews, St. Petersburg, Fla., 1970—78, Harris, Barrett & Dew, St. Petersburg, 1978—80; county judge St. Petersburg, 1980—90; judge 6th Jud. Cir. Ct. Fla., St. Petersburg, 1991—97, sr. judge, 1997; ret. Lt. U.S. Army, 1954—58. Recipient Jud. Appreciation award, St. Petersburg Bar Assn. Baptist. Office: PO Box 15835 Saint Petersburg FL 33733 Office Fax: 727-381-9260. E-mail: haandrews@aol.com.

ANDREWS, J. DAVID, lawyer; b. Decatur, Ill., July 5, 1933; s. Jesse D. and Louise Glenna (Mason) A.; m. Helen Virginia Migely, July 12, 1958; children: Virginia, Robert, Michael, Betsy. BA magna cum laude, U. Ill., 1955, JD with honors, 1960. Bar: Wash. 1961. Ptnr. Perkins Coie, Seattle, 1960-96, counsel, 1997—. Bd. dirs., v.p. Am. Bar Ins. Plans Cons., Inc.,

1991—, also bd. dirs.; pres. Wash. Law Fund, 1997-98; bd. dirs. Cornish Inst., Seattle, 1977-83, pres. 1981-83; bd. dirs. Am. Bar Endowment, 1981-94, pres. 1985-87; bd. visitors U. Puget Sound Law Sch., 1976-94; trustee AEF Pension Fund, 1975-79. Contbr. articles to profl. jours. Bd. dirs. Leukemia Soc. Wash., 1984-99, pres. 1985-91; nat. bd. dirs. Leukemia Soc. Am., 1992-96. Capt. USAF, 1955-57. Fellow Am. Bar Found. (bd. dirs., former treas.), Am. Coll. Trial Lawyers; mem. ABA (ho. of dels. 1967-69, 75—, asst. treas. 1972-74, treas. 1975-79, bd. govs. 1975-79, fed. judiciary standing com. 1985-90), Wash. Bar Assn. (chmn. pub. rels. com. 1971-73), Seattle-King County Bar Assn., Am. Judicature Soc. (bd. dirs. 1985-89), Phi Beta Kappa, Phi Kappa Phi, Phi Eta Sigma. Federal civil litigation, State civil litigation, Labor (including EEOC, Fair Labor Standards Act, labor-management relations, NLRB, OSHA). Home: 9413 SW Quartermaster Dr Vashon WA 98070-7081 Office: Perkins Coie 1201 3rd Ave Ste 4000 Seattle WA 98101-3029 E-mail: andrj@perkinscoie.com.

ANDREWS, OAKLEY V. lawyer; b. Cleve., Apr. 15, 1940; BA, Yale U., 1962; JD, Western Reserve U., 1965. Bar: Ohio 1965, U.S. Tax Ct. 1968, U.S. Dist. Ct. (no. dist.) Ohio 1968, U.S. Ct. Appeals (6th cir.) 1968. Ptnr. Baker & Hostetler, LLP, Cleve. Fellow Am. Coll. Trust and Estate Coun.; mem. Ohio State Bar Assn., Estate Planning Coun. Cleve. (pres. 1982-83), Cleve. Bar Assn. (chmn. Estate Planning, Probate and Trust law sect. 1984-85), Phi Delta Phi Office: Baker & Hostetler LLP 3200 Nat City Ctr 1900 E 9th St Ste 3200 Cleveland OH 44114-3475 E-mail: oandrews@bakerlaw.com.

ANDREWS, RICHARD LEE, lawyer; b. Oakland, Calif., Aug. 13, 1936; s. Eugene Vernon and Ellen (Olenius) A.; m. Marjolaine Eva Tourangeau, Sept. 2, 1961 (div. July 1978); children: Christiane Marie, Paul Jonathan; m. Terry Jeanne Raymond, Aug. 13, 1978; children: Todd Raymond, Mark Richard. BA, Stanford U., 1960, JD, 1965. Bar: Calif. 1966, U.S. Dist. Ct. (no. dist.) Calif. 1966, Wash. 1979, U.S. Dist. Ct. (we. dist.) Wash. 1979, U.S. Ct. Appeals (9th cir.) 1966. Assoc. Jorgenson, Cosgrove & Flickinger, Menlo Park, Calif., 1966; ptnr. Jorgenson, Cosgrove & Andrews, Menlo Park, 1967-75; pvt. practice Menlo Park, 1975-77; ptnr. Andrews & Miller, Menlo Park, 1977-79; asst. city atty. City of Bellevue, Wash., 1980-84, city atty., 1984—. With U.S. Army, 1960. Mem. Internat. Mcpl. Lawyers Assn. (regional v.p. 1991-97, bd. dirs. 1997—), Wash. State Assn. Mcpl. Attys. (bd. dirs. 1989-95, pres. 1993-94), Calif. State Bar, Wash. State Bar, Menlo Park Rotary Club (bd. dirs. 1968-75, pres. 1973-74). Office: City of Bellevue PO Box 90012 11511 Main St Bellevue WA 98004-6404

ANDREWS, SALLY S. lawyer; BA, Duke U.; MAT, Harvard U.; MA, U. N.C.; JD, U. Tex., 1984. Bar: Tex., U.S. Tax Ct., U.S. Dist. Ct. Tex., U.S. Ct. Appeals (5th Cir.), U.S. Supreme Ct., 2003. With Rockefeller Bros. Fund; faculty assoc. Duke U. Med. Ctr., Tex. Med. Ctr. Sch. Pub. Health; pvt. practice Houston. Case ed.: journal Texas International Law Jour., 1983—84; author: (book) Elder Law Handbook Houston Bar, 2001. Advisory mem. tech. adv. com., Greater Houston YMCA, mem. endowment devel. com.; vol. Peace Corps, Ethiopia, mem. U.S. govt. selection and tng. staff. Recipient, 1996 Women on The Move Award, Houston Chronicle. Mem. Christian Legal Soc., Rotary (pres. Galleria area club 1995-96), asst. gov., 1996-98, 2001-2002, Phi Beta Kappa, Houston Bar Found.; fellow Coll. State Bar Tex., 2000-, Tex. Acad. Probate & Trust Lawyers, 1996-, Houston Bus. and Estate Coun., 2002-, Houston Estate Financial Forum, 1990-, State Bar Tex. 4-C Grievance Comm., 1991-95, chair 1994-95. Estate planning, Probate (including wills, trusts), Estate taxation. Office: 2 Bering Pk 800 Bering Dr Ste 200 Houston TX 77057-2130

ANDREWS, WILLIAM DOREY, law educator, lawyer; b. N.Y.C., Feb. 25, 1931; s. Sidney Warren and Margaret (Dorey) A.; A.B., Amherst Coll., 1952, LL.D., 1977; LL.B., Harvard U., 1955; m. Shirley May Herrman, Dec. 26, 1953; children: Helen Estelle Andrews Noble, Roy Herrman, John Frederick, Margaret Dorey Andrews Davenport, Susan Louise, Carol Mary Andrews Reid. Bar: Mass. 1959. Practice in Boston, 1959-63; assoc. Ropes & Gray, 1959-63; lectr. Harvard Law Sch., Cambridge, Mass., 1961-63, asst. prof., 1963-65, prof., 1965—, Eli Goldston prof. law, 1986— ; cons. Sullivan & Worcester, 1964—; assoc. reporter for accessions tax proposal Am. Law Inst. Fed. Estate and Gift Tax Project; gen. reporter for subchpt. C, Am. Law Inst. Fed. Income Tax Project, 1974-82, 86-93; cons. U.S. Treasury Dept., 1965-68. Mem. Zoning Bd. Appeals, Concord, 1966-73. Served to lt. USNR, 1955-58. Mem. Am. Law Inst., Am. Bar Assn. Office: Harvard U Law Sch 1545 Massachusetts Ave Cambridge MA 02138-2903

ANDRUS, ROGER DOUGLAS, lawyer; b. Floral Park, N.Y., Dec. 3, 1945; s. Winfield and Julia Margaret (Arduino) A.; m. Stephanie Andrus, Jan. 20, 1969 (div. 1983); children: Justin, Sarah; m. Patricia Ann McDonough, Oct. 4, 1986; children: Michael, David, Molly. AB cum laude, Wagner Coll., 1966; JD, NYU, 1969. Bar: N.Y. 1970, U.S. Dist. Ct. (ea. and so. dists.) 1975, U.S. Ct. Appeals 2d cir.) 1975. Assoc. Cahill Gordon & Reindel, N.Y.C., 1970-78, ptnr., 1978—. Mem. N.Y. State Bar Assn., Canoe Brook Country Club, Down Town Assn., Omicron Delta Kappa. Corporate, general, Securities. Office: Cahill Gordon & Reindel 80 Pine St New York NY 10005-1790

ANGEL, ARTHUR RONALD, lawyer, consultant; b. Long Beach, Calif., May 10, 1948; s. Morris and Betty Estelle (Unger) A.; 1 child, Jamie Kathryn. BA, U. Calif.-Berkeley, 1969; JD, Harvard U., 1972. Bar: Mass. 1972, D.C. 1975, Okla. 1979, Calif. 2001, U.S. Dist. Ct. (we. dist.) Okla. 1980, U.S. Dist. Ct. (no. dist.) Okla. 1981, U.S. Dist. Ct. (ctrl. dist.) Calif. 2001, U.S. Supreme Ct. 1983. Atty. FTC, Washington, 1972-78; pvt. practice Oklahoma City, 1978-87; ptnr. Angel & Ikard, Oklahoma City, 1987-93; of counsel Abel, Musser Sokolosky & Assoc., L.A., 1994-2000; ptnr. Carrick Law Group, L.A., 2001—02; atty. Nagler & Assocs., L.A., 2002—. Mem. adv. panel on cardiovascular devices, Washington, 1979-82; cons. FTC, 1978-79; adminstrv. law judge Okla. Dept. Labor, 1999-2000; spl. mcpl. judge City of Oklahoma City, 1999-2001. Recipient Meritorious Service award FTC, Washington, 1978. Fellow: Inst. Law and Social Scis.; mem.: Calif. Bar Assn., Mass. Bar Assn., D.C. Bar Assn., Assn. Trial Lawyers Am., Am. Arbitration Assn. Democrat. Jewish. Federal civil litigation, General practice, Personal injury (including property damage). Home: 1236 N Fairfax Ave Los Angeles CA 90046 Office: Nagler & Assocs 2300 S Sepulveda Blvd Los Angeles CA 90064 E-mail: aangel@nagler.com.

ANGEL, DENNIS, lawyer; b. Bklyn., Feb. 14, 1947; s. Morris and Rosalyn (Sobiloff) A.; m. Linda Marlene Lobel, May 15, 1977; children: Stephanie Lee, Michele Bari, Rebecca Jo. Diplome d'etudes françaises, U. Rouen, France, 1967; BA, St. Lawrence U., 1968; JD, Washington and Lee U., 1972. Cert. pratique de langue française ler Degre U. Rouen, France, 1967; bar: N.Y. 1972, U.S. Dist. Ct. (so. dist.) N.Y. 1977. Assoc. Johnson & Tannenbaum, N.Y.C., 1972-77; sole practice N.Y.C., 1978—. Contbr. articles to profl. jours. With USAR, 1969-75. Mem. ABA (subcommittee chmn. 1977-82), N.Y. State Bar Assn., Copyright Soc. U.S.A., Phi Alpha Delta. Entertainment, Trademark and copyright. Home: 8 High Point Ln Scarsdale NY 10583-3122 Office: 1075 Central Park Ave Ste 306 Scarsdale NY 10583-3232 E-mail: dangelesq@aol.com.

ANGEL, JAMES JOSEPH, lawyer; b. Racine, Wis., Apr. 1, 1956; s. William J. and Dorothy P. (Potman) A.; m. Catherine Anne Cowan, Oct. 17, 1981; children: Carter Anne, Riley James, Spenser Catherine. BA, W.Va. Wesleyan Coll., 1977; JD, U. Richmond, 1979. Dep. commonwealth atty. City of Lynchburg (Va.) Commonwealth Atty. Office, 1979-84; ptnr. Smith, Angel & Falcone, P.C., Lynchburg, 1984-87; pvt. practice Lynchburg, 1987—. Chmn. Boonsboro-Peakland Neighborhood Assn., Lynchburg, 1990-99. Mem. ATLA, Va. Trial Lawyers Assn., Va. Bar Assn., Va. Coll. Criminal Def. Attys., Lynchburg Bar Assn. (past pres. criminal law sect. 1992). Avocations: golf, whitewater rafting. Criminal, General practice, Personal injury (including property damage). Office: 725 Church St Lynchburg VA 24504-1417 also: Allied Arts Bldg PO Box 1042 Lynchburg VA 24505-1042 Office Fax: 434-528-1665.

ANGELL, M(ARY) FAITH, federal magistrate judge; b. Buffalo, May 7, 1938; d. San S. and Marie B. (Caboni) A.; m. Kenneth F. Carobus, Oct. 27, 1973; children: Andrew M. Carobus, Alexander P. Carobus. AB, Mt. Holyoke Coll., 1959; MSS, Bryn Mawr Coll., 1965; JD, Temple U., 1971. Bar: Pa. 1971, U.S. Dist. Ct. (ea. dist) Pa. 1971, U.S. Ct. Appeals (3rd cir.) Pa. 1974, U.S. Supreme Ct. 1979; Acad. Cert. Social Workers. Dir. social work, vol. svcs. Wills Eye Hosp., Phila., 1961-64, 65-69; dir. soc. work dept. juvenile divsn. Defender Assoc., Phila., 1969-71; asst. dist. atty. City of Phila., 1971-72; asst. atty. gen. Commonwealth of Pa., Phila., 1972-74, deputy atty. gen., 1974-78; regional counsel ICC, Phila., 1978-80, regional dir., 1980-88; administrv. law judge Social Security Administn., Phila., 1988-90; U.S. magistrate judge U.S. Dist. Ct. (ea. dist.) Pa., Phila., 1990—. Adj. prof. Temple U. Law Sch., Phila., 1976-94, clin. instr., 1973-76; co-chmn. Commn. on Gender, 3d Cir. Task Force on Equal Treatment in Cts., 1994—; mem. com. on racial and gender bias in the justice sys. Supreme Ct. of Pa., 2000. Federal trustee Defender Assn. Phila., 1985-90; bd. dirs. Child Welfare Adv. Bd., Phila., 1984-90, Federal Cts. 200 Adv. Bd., Phila., 1987-88, Phila. Woman's Network, 1986-88. Recipient Sr. Exec. Svc. award U.S. Govt., 1980. Mem. NASW, FBA (chair exec. com., pres. 1990-92, recognition 1992), Nat. Assn. Women Judges, Fed. Magistrate Judges Assn. (dist. dir. 1994-98), Phila. Bar Assn. (chmn. com. 1976-77), Temple Am. Inn of Cts. (master 1993-98), Third Circuit Task Force on Equal Treatment in the Courts (co-chair Commn. on Gender 1994-97), Temple Law Alumni Exec. Bd. (Women's Law Caucus Honoree 1996). Office: US District Court 601 Market St 3030 US Courthouse Philadelphia PA 19106

ANGELO, FLORENTINA DANIELA, lawyer; b. Buzău, Romania, Mar. 25, 1974; d. Florin Angelo and Georgeta Vergu. BA in Law, Law Sch., Bucharest, Romania, 1997; cert., Romanian Banking Inst., Bucharest, Romania, 2002. Jr. assoc. Dumitru Radescu Pvt. Practice, Bucharest, 1998; jr./sr. assoc. Racoti, Predoiu and Ptnrs., Bucharest, 1998—. Mem.: Bucharest Bar Assn., Romanian Lawyers Assn. Corporate, general, Commercial, contracts (including sales of goods; commercial financing), Banking. Office: Racoti Predoiu and Ptnrs Batistei 30 Bucharest Romania

ANGERS, WINSTON THOMAS, lawyer; b. Franklin, La., June 21, 1952; s. Robert John Angers, Jr. and Geraldine Beaulieu Angers; 1 child, Austen John. BA in Polit. Sci. cum laude, U. La., 1974; JD, La. State U., 1976. Bar: La. Rsch. asst. Inst. for Civil Law Studies La. State U. Law Ctr., Baton Rouge, 1975—76; law clk. 15th Jud. Dist. Ct., New Iberia, La., 1976—77; pvt. practice Lafayette, La., 1977—; pres. Beau Bayou Pub. Co., Lafayette, 1985—. Author: Cajun Cuisine, 1986; editor: History of the Louisiana Society of the Sons of the American Revolution, 1997; contbr. articles to mags. Bd. mem. Coun. for the Devel. of French in La.; past chmn. Bd. Zoning Adjustments City of Lafayette; pres. Acadiana Arts Coun., Lafayette, 1990—91; co-founder Citizens of South Lafayette; pres. Attakapas chpt. SAR, 1994; pres. Acadian Civitan Club, Lafayette, 1997—98; alt. del. Rep. Nat. Conv., Dallas, 1984, del. Houston, 1992; past chmn. by laws com. La. Rep. State Ctrl. Com.; chmn. Lafayette Parish Rep. Exec. Com., 1995—96; past chmn. Lafayette Parish Rep. Polit. Action Coun.; del.-attendee Young Rep. Nat. Fedn. Conv., 1971; del. numerous state convs. La. Rep. Party; chair U. La. at Lafayette Coll. Reps., 1971—72. Recipient Bronze Good Citizenship medal, Attakapas Chpt. SAR, 1992, Oak Leaf Cluster, 1993, Meritorious Svc. medal, 1994, Oak Leaf Cluster, 1995, Oak Leaf Cluster for Meritorious Svc. medal, La. Soc. SAR, 1996. Mem.: ABA, Civitan Internat., Rotary Internat., Phi Eta Sigma, Phi Delta Phi. Republican. Avocation: collecting rare documents and political memorabilia. Home: 116 Teche Dr Lafayette LA 70503 Office: 1126 Coolidge St Lafayette LA 70503

ANGINO, RICHARD CARMEN, lawyer; b. McKeesport, Pa., May 2, 1940; s. Carmen and Filomena (Lombardi) A.; m. Alice K. Angino, May 2, 1976; children: Elizabeth, Richard, William. BA in English, Franklin and Marshall Coll., Lancaster, Pa., 1958-62; JD, Villanova U., Pa., 1965. Bar: Pa. 1965, U.S. Supreme Ct. 1968, U.S. Ct. Appeals (3rd cir.) 1975, U.S. Dist. Ct. (ea. and cen. dist.) 1966. Ptnr., civil litigation specialist Angino & Rovner PC, Harrisburg, Pa., 1965—. Pres. Pa. Trial Lawyers Assn., Pa., 1982-83. Co-author: The Pennsylvania No-Fault Motor Vehicle Insurance Act, 1979, Pennsylvania Personal Injury Evidence, 1990. Pres. Leukemia Soc. Am., Ctrl. Pa., 1989-92; v.p. Am. Horticulture Soc., Alexandria. Va., 1990-92, Friends of Wildwood, Harrisburg, Pa., 1989-96; assoc. trustee Franklin and Marshall, 1979—; bd. cons. Villanova Univ. Sch. Law, 1994—, govs. residence preservation com., 1997-2002. Mem. Internat. Soc. Barristers, Dauphin County Bar Assn., Pa. Bar Assn., Pa. Trial Lawyers Assn., Assn. Trial Lawyers Am. Republican. Roman Catholic. Avocation: ornamental horticulture. Personal injury (including property damage), Product liability, Professional liability. Home: 2040 Fishing Creek Valley Rd Harrisburg PA 17112-9245 Office: Angino & Rovner PC 4503 N Front St Harrisburg PA 17110-1799 E-mail: rca@angino-rovner.com.

ANGIONE, HOWARD FRANCIS, lawyer, editor; b. N.Y.C., Aug. 3, 1940; s. Charles Francis Angione and Genevieve Rita (McCarthy) A.; m. Maryann Allgaier, June 24, 1971; children: Charles Francis, Mary Christine, Kathleen Elizabeth. BA in History, Holy Cross Coll., 1962; MA in Internat. Relations, Clark U., 1966; JD cum laude, St. John's U., Jamaica, N.Y., 1989. Bar: Conn. 1989, N.Y. 1990, D.C. 1991. Reporter, sci. writer Worcester Telegram, Mass., 1961-65; writer, day editor, sci. writer AP, Boston, 1965-69, editor, shift supr. Gen. Desk N.Y.C., 1969-77; tech. editor N.Y. Times, 1977-87; assoc. Weil, Gotshal & Manges, N.Y.C., 1989-93; pvt. practice, 1997—. Pub. N.Y. Region Lawyers Coop. Practice Guides, 1993-96; editor AP Stylebook, 1977; editor-in-chief N.Y. State Bar Jour., 1998—. Sec. Class of 1962 Holy Cross Coll., 1966-80. Mem. Harris Users Group (pres. 1980-84) Roman Catholic. Elder Law. Home and Office: 80-47 192d St Jamaica NY 11423-1042 E-mail: angione@nyelderlaw.com.

ANGST, GERALD L. lawyer; b. Chgo., Dec. 29, 1950; s. Gerald L. Sr. and Audrey M. (Hides) A.; m. Candace Simning, Jan. 29, 1983. BA magna cum laude, Loyola U., Chgo., 1972, JD cum laude, 1975. Assoc. Sidley Austin Brown & Wood, Chgo., 1975-82, ptnr., 1982—. Mem.: ABA (constrn. litigation com. litigation sect.), Chgo. Bar Assn. (civil practice com.). General civil litigation, Construction, Insurance. Office: Sidley Austin Brown & Wood Bank One Plz 47th Fl 10 So Dearborn St Chicago IL 60603-2000 E-mail: gangst@sidley.com.

ANGSTEAD, ROBERT KENNETH, lawyer; b. Fairfield, Iowa, Aug. 11, 1965; s. Kenneth Lee Angstead and Sherry Dee (Whitmore) Ehrhardt; m. Debra Rhey Hockanson; children: Laurel Rhey, Andrew Robert. BA, Ctrl. Methodist Coll., 1987; JD, U. Mo., 1990. Bar: Mo. 1990, U.S. Dist. Ct. (we. dist.) Mo. 1990. Law clerk Mo. Supreme Ct., Jefferson City, 1990-91; assoc. Brydon, Swearengen & England, Jefferson City, 1991-93; shareholder Newman, Comley & Ruth P.C., Jefferson City, 1993—. Author: (case notes) Jour. Dispute Resolution, 1988 (Burres award 1989), note and comment editor, 1989-90. Bd. dirs. Jefferson City Breakfast Rotary Club, 1994—; coach Ctrl. Mo. Basketball Club, Jefferson City, 1994. Mem. ABA, Mo. Bar Assn. (alternative dispute resolution com. 1993—, aviation and transp. law com. 1993—, mediator/arbitrator fee dispute resolution com. 1994, young lawyers sect. coun. 1994—), Cole County Bar Assn. (pres. 2001), Order of Barristers, Bd. of Advocates. Avocations: hunting, fishing, athletics, reading. Administrative and regulatory, General civil litigation, Insurance. Office: Newman Comley & Ruth PC 601 Monroe St Ste 301 Jefferson City MO 65102-0537 Home: 1416 Rosner Hills Rd Jefferson City MO 65109-6197

ANGUS, PATRICIA MARIE, lawyer, consultant; b. Rockville Centre, N.Y., May 13, 1964; d. John Wakefield and Patricia Gerard Angus. BA cum laude, Amherst Coll., 1986; M in Internat. Affairs, Columbia U., 1990; JD, George Washington U., 1992. Bar: N.Y. 1993. Atty. Coudert Bros., N.Y.C., 1992—96; v.p. wealth advisor JP Morgan Pvt. Bank, N.Y.C., 1996—99; ind. contractor Hughes & Whitaker/Day Berry & Howard, 2003; pres. Angus Adv. Group LLC, N.Y.C., 2003—. Presenter in field. Contbr. articles to profl. jours. Planned giving advisor N.Y. Hist. Soc., N.Y.C., 1999—; mem. advocacy coun. Citizens Com. Children N.Y., N.Y.C., 2001—; devel. com. N.Y. Women's Found., N.Y.C., 2001—. Mem.: ABA, Assn. Bar City N.Y. Estate planning, Estate taxation, Private international. Office: Angus Adv Group LLC 160 Riverside Blvd New York NY 10069

ANKER, KENT KARI, lawyer; b. N.Y.C., Apr. 10, 1969; s. Peter Louis Anker and Tiia Kari; m. Patty Chang, Nov. 21, 1992; 1 child, Grace Zhimei Chang. BA in History (with hons.), Wesleyan U., 1991; JD magna cum laude, Harvard U., 1998. Bar: (N.Y.) 1999, (U.S. Dist. Ct. (so. dist.) N.Y.) 2000. Legis. asst. United Fedn. Tchrs., N.Y.C., 1992, legis. rep., 1992—95; assoc. Willkie, Farr & Gallagher, N.Y.C., 1998—99, Boies, Schiller & Flexner, N.Y.C., 2000—02, Friedman, Kaplan, Seiler & Adelman, N.Y.C., 2002—. Del. Am. Swiss Found. Young Leaders Conf., Horgen, Switzerland, 1994. Mem.: Assn. Bar City N.Y. (mem. com. edn. and law 1999—), Phi Beta Kappa. Commercial, consumer (including collections, credit). Office: Friedman Kaplan Seiler and Adelman LP 1633 Broadway New York NY 10019 Office Fax: 212-833-1250.

ANNENBERG, NORMAN, lawyer; b. N.Y.C., Aug. 13, 1912; s. George J. and Jeannette (Lazarus) A. J.D., Harvard U., 1935. Bar: N.Y. 1936, U.S. Ct. Appeals (2d cir.) 1948, U.S. Supreme Ct., 1966. Sole practice, N.Y.C., 1936— . Mem. N.Y. County Lawyers Assn., N.Y. State Bar Assn. E-mail: anormally@aol.com. Family and matrimonial, General practice, Probate (including wills, trusts). Office: 145 W 55th St New York NY 10019-5342

ANNOTICO, RICHARD ANTHONY, legal administrator, real estate investor; b. Cleve., Sept. 17, 1930; s. Anthony and Grace (Kovarik) A. AB in Bus. with hons., Ohio U., 1953; LLB, Southwestern Law Sch., 1963; JD, UCLA, 1965. Dir. internat. sales then v.p. Liberty Records, L.A., 1957-64; real estate investment counselor Calif. Land Sales, Beverly Hills, 1964-66, R.A. Annotico & Assocs., L.A., 1966-68, real estate investor, 1969—. Spkr. in field.; mem. Bd. of Governors State Calif.; expert witness State Legis. Calif. Contbr. numerous articles to profl. jours. Commr. L.A. Transp. Commn., 1984-88, v.p. 1985-87; commr. L.A. Human Rels. Comm n., 1977-84, pres. 1983-84; mem. Calif. State Senate Small Bus. Adv. Bd., 1978-82, L.A. City County Adv. Commn. on Consolidation, 1976-77; pres. Federated Italian-Americans So. Calif., 1975-76; mem. Mayors Exec. Com. Christopher Columbus Quincentenary 1992. Lt. USAF, 1954-55. Decorated Cavaliere Ufficiale Order of Merit (Italy), Comdr. St. Lazarus Internat. Chivalric, Hospitaller and Mil. Order. Mem. Calif. State Bar Assn. (bd. govs., 1983-86, 86-89, 89-92, v.p. 1986, 89, 92). Office: Admiralty Suites 4170 Admiralty Way # 1G Marina Del Rey CA 90292

ANSARY, CYRUS A. investment company executive, lawyer; b. Shoraz, Oram, Nov. 20, 1933; s. A. R. and Jamali (Mostmand) Ansary; m. Janet C. Hodges, Aug. 1, 1970; children: Douglas C., Pary Ann, Jeffrey C., Bradley C. BS, Am. U., 1955; LLB, Columbia U., 1958. Bar: Md. 1959, D.C. 1960, Va. 1961. Pvt. practice, Washington, 1959-72; sr. ptnr. firm Ansary, Kirkpatrick and Rosse, 1964-72; chmn. bd. Industry Reports, Inc., Washington, 1960-72; organizer, 1st chmn. bd., pres. Woodland Nat. Bank, Alexandria, Va., 1963-67; lectr. Sch. Bus. Adminstrn., Am. U., 1967-71; chmn. bd. Fin. Dynamics Corp., Washington, 1967-72, Campbell Music Co., Washington, 1968-72, John L. Lindstrom and Assocs., Inc., Washington, 1962-86; pres. IK Investment A.G., Zurich, Switzerland, 1974-79, Investment Svcs. Internat. Co., Washington, 1973—; chmn. MACO Bancorp, Washington, 1988—95. Bd. dirs. Washington Mut. Investors Fund, J. P. Morgan Value Opportunities Fund, Am. Funds Tax-Exempt Series I; chmn. bd. dirs. CorPay Solutions, Inc. Trustee Am. U., 1968—96, chmn. bd., 1982—91; trustee Internat. Law Inst., 1976—88, Wolf Trap Found., Vienna, Va., 1977—82, Fried Krupp Found., Essen, Germany, 1977—79, Washington Opera Soc., 1982—89; pres. Ansary Found., Washington, 1983—; mem. Woodrow Wilson Coun., Washington, 2000—. With USMCR, 1959—64. Mem.: Nat. Press Club, Econ. Club Washington, Washington Soc. Investment Analysts, City Club, Chevy Chase Country Club (Bethesda), Met. Club (Washington), Rotary. Office: 1725 K St NW Ste 410 Washington DC 20006-1401 E-mail: cyrus817@aol.com.

ANSBACHER, BARRY BARNETT, lawyer; b. Jacksonville, Fla., Jan. 7, 1963; s. Lewis and Sybil Ansbacher; m. Elaine Kenny, Aug. 30, 1992. BA, U. Fla., 1985, JD, 1988. Bar: Fla. 1989, D.C. 1989; bd. cert. real estate atty. Fla. Atty. Ansbacher & Schneider PA, Jacksonville, 1989-97; pvt. practice law Jacksonville, 1997—. Pres. Attys. Real Property Coun. NE Fla., Inc., Jacksonville. Author: Complex Real Estate Transactions-Subdivisions, 1997, 98, Issues of Transboundary Pollution in North America, 1988. Named Outstanding Young Men of Am., 1986. Mem. Fla. Bar Assn. (environ. law sect., exec. coun. cir. rep. real property and trust law sect. 1998), Jacksonville Bar Assn. Jewish. Avocation: equestrian sports. General civil litigation, Land use and zoning (including planning), Property, real (including real estate development, water). Office: 1301 Riverplace Blvd Ste 2540 Jacksonville FL 32207-9032 E-mail: bba@ansbacher.net.

ANSBACHER, LEWIS, lawyer; b. Jacksonville, Fla., Nov. 23, 1928; s. Morris and Lillian (Pinkus) Ansbacher; m. Sybil Barnett, Oct. 27, 1957; children: Richard I., Lawrence V., Barry B. BSBA, U. Fla., 1948, JD, 1951; LLM, George Washington U., 1955. Bar: Fla. 51. Assoc. Philip Selber, Jacksonville, 1955—62; ptnr. Selber & Ansbacher, 1963—73; pvt. practice Jacksonville, 1973—80; shareholder Ansbacher & Schneider, P.A., Jacksonville, 1981—. Bd. dirs. CNB Nat. Bank, Attys.' Title Ins. Fund Inc.; trustee 4th Cir. Author (in field). Mem. planning bd. United Fund, 1965; mem. Duval County Legal Aid Assn., pres., 1964—65; mem. Gov.'s Ad Hoc Study Com. on Eminent Domain, 1984—85; v.p. Jewish Family and Children's Svc., Jacksonville, 1962—65, pres., 1965—68; v.p. Jacksonville Jewish Ctr., 1967—70. 1st lt. JAGC U.S. Army, 1952—55. Named to Hall of Fame, U. Fla. Mem.: ABA, Fla. Bar (exec. coun. real property and probate sect.). Jewish. Corporate, general, Probate (including wills, trusts), Property, real (including real estate development, water). Home: 2008 Strand St Neptune Beach FL 32266-4863 Office: 5150 Belfort Rd Bldg 100 Jacksonville FL 32256 E-mail: lewisansbacher@jaxlaw.com., sybila@bellsouth.net.

ANSELL, EDWARD ORIN, lawyer; b. Superior, Wis., Mar. 29, 1926; s. H. S. and Mollie (Rudnitzky) A.; m. Hanne B. Baer, Dec. 23, 1956; children: Deborah, William. BSEE, U. Wis., 1948; JD, George Washington U., 1955. Bar: D.C. 1955, Calif. 1960. Electronic engr. FCC, Buffalo and Washington, 1948-55; patent atty. RCA, Princeton, NJ, 1955-57; gen. mgr. AeroChem. Rsch. Labs., Princeton, 1957-58; patent atty. Aerojet-Gen. Corp., La Jolla, Calif., 1958-63, corp. patent counsel, 1963-82, asst. sec., 1970-79, sec., 1979-82, assoc. gen. counsel, 1981-82; dir. patents and licensing Calif. Inst. Tech., Pasadena, Calif., 1982-92; pvt. practice Claremont, Calif., 1992—; co-founder Gryphon Pharms., South San Francisco, 1993, Ciphergen BioSystems, Fremont, Calif., 1993. Adj. prof. U. La Verne (Calif.) Coll. Law, 1972-78; spl. advisor, task force chmn. U.S. Commn. Govt. Procurement, 1971 Editor: Intellectual Property in Academe: A Legal

Compendium, 1991; contbr. articles to profl. publs. Recipient Alumni Svc. award George Washington U., 1975. Mem. Am. Intellectual Property Law Assn., Assn. Corp. Patent Counsel, Ea. Bar Assn. Los Angeles County, L.A. Intellectual Property Law Assn., Assn. Univ. Tech. Mgrs., State Bar Calif. (exec. com. intellectual property sect. 1983-86), Athenaeum Club Pasadena, Univ. Club Claremont. Intellectual property, Patent, Trademark and copyright. Office: 427 N Yale Ave # 204 Claremont CA 91711 E-mail: anselaw@att.net.

ANSLEY, SHEPARD BRYAN, lawyer; b. July 31, 1939; s. William Bonneau and Florence Jackson (Bryan) A.; m. Boyce Lineberger, May 9, 1970; children: Anna Ansley Davis, Florence Bryan. BA, U. Ga., 1961; LLB, U. Va., 1964. Bar: Ga. 1967. Assoc. Carter & Ansley and predecessor firm Carter, Ansley, Smith & McLendon, Atlanta, 1967-73, ptnr., 1973-84, of counsel, 1984-91; with Attkisson Carter & Akers Inc., Atlanta, 1997—2000, Attkisson Carter & Co., Atlanta, 2001—. Bd. dirs. Prime Bancshares, Inc., Prime Bank, FSB; chmn. bd. dirs., pres. Sodamaster Co. Am.; exec. v.p. Woodridge Realty, Inc.; sr. v.p., ACA Consulting, Inc.; fin. cons. Attkisson, Carter & Co. Inc.; bd. dirs., sec. CRM Co., LLC, L.A. County, Calif. Vestry mem. St. Luke's Episcopal Ch., Atlanta, 1971-74; treas., exec. com., bd. dirs. Alliance Theatre Co., Atlanta, 1974-85; trustee Atlanta Music Festival Assn., Inc., 1975—; v.p., bd. dirs. Atlanta Preservation Ctr. Inc., pres., 1988-90; bd. vis. Lineberger Cancer Rsch. Ctr. U. N.C., Chapel Hill, 1987-92; pres., bd. dirs. Study Hall at Emmaus House, Inc.1988-1992, currently on bd. since 1992 ; bd. dirs. Margaret Mitchell House, Inc.; bd. govs. Ga. Pub. Policy Found., Inc., 1999-2001. Capt. U.S. Army, 1965-67. Mem. ABA, Ga. Bar Assn., Atlanta Bar Assn., Atlanta Lawyers Club 1975-1990, Am. Coll. Mortgage Attys. 1980-1990, Atlanta Jr. C. of C. (bd. dirs. 1968-72), Piedmont Driving Club. E-mail: sbansley@mindspring.com.

ANSTANDIG, MARSHALL W. lawyer, publishing executive; BA in Polit. Sci., Hope Coll., 1971; JD, Mich. State U., Detroit, 1974. Mng. ptnr. Bryan Cave, Phoenix, 1990—96; ptnr. Brown & Bain, P.A., 1996—98; v.p., sr. labor and employment counsel Knight Ridder Corp., San Jose, Calif., 1998—. Office: Knight Ridder Corp 50 W San Fernando St San Jose CA 95113-2413*

ANSTEAD, HARRY LEE, state supreme court justice; b. Jacksonville, Fla., Nov. 4, 1937; Judge, then chief judge Fla. Ct. Appeals. (4th dist.), Fla., 1976—94; justice Fla. Supreme Ct., Tallahassee, 1994—, chief justice. Office: Supreme Ct Bldg 500 S Duval St Tallahassee FL 32399-6556

ANSTINE, GLEN ROSCOE, lawyer; b. Omaha, Nebr., Sept. 23, 1952; s. Glenn D. and Phyllis M. (Pawloski) A.; m. Elizabeth Renee Fajardo, Nov. 27, 1958; children: Asia, Kali, Avalon, Sydney, Timothy, Piper, Dylan. BS, Portland State U., 1977; JD, U. Nebr., 1982. Bar: Nebr. 1983, Colo. 1984, U.S. Supreme Ct. 1990, U.S. Ct. Appeals (10th cir.) 1989. Law clk. Nebr. Supreme Ct., Lincoln, 1983-84; pvt. practice law Denver, 1985—. Panelist, trustee U.S. Trustee's Office, Denver, 1986—. Bankruptcy, Criminal. Office: 4704 Harlan St Ste 320 Denver CO 80212-7418

ANTHOINE, ROBERT, lawyer, educator; b. Portland, Maine, June 5, 1921; s. Edward S and Sara B (Pinkham) Anthoine; m. Rebecca S Rudnick, Dec. 2, 1990; children from previous marriage: Alison, Robert Neal, Nelson, Nina. AB, Duke U., 1942; JD, Columbia U., 1949. Bar: NY 1949, US Ct Appeals (2d cir) 1956, US Supreme Ct 1970. Research assoc. Am. Law Inst. fed income tax project Columbia U., N.Y.C., 1949-50; assoc. Cleary, Gottlieb, Friendly and Cox, N.Y.C., 1950-52; assoc. prof. law Columbia U., N.Y.C., 1952-56, prof. law, 1956-64, adj. prof., 1964-93; ptnr. Winthrop, Stimson, Putnam and Roberts, N.Y.C., 1963-86, sr. counsel, 1987-2000, in charge London office, 1972-76; sr. counsel Pillsbury Winthrop LLP, 2001—. Vis prof Univ Tex Law Sch, Austin, 1988, Univ NC Law Sch, Chapel Hill, 1991, Univ Pa Law Sch, Philadelphia, 1996, Seattle Univ Law Sch, 1997. Auth, ed: survey Tax Incentives for Investment in Developing Countries, 1979; contbr. articles to profl jours. Active Coun Foreign Relations; chmn. emeritus, bd. dirs. Aperture Found.; pres Lucid Art Found, S K Yee Found; dir Hazen Polsky Found; hon gov Royal Shakespeare Theatre, Stratford-upon-Avon, England; vice-chmn, bd dirs Am Friends Theater; trustee, dir Grosvenor Gallery (Fine Arts) Ltd, London; vice chair, trustee Int Photog Coun, Royal Shakespeare Theatre Trust, Sevenarts, Ltd, London; bd dirs emeritus Eric and Salome Estorick Found, Vol Lawyers Arts; bd. dirs., v.p. Morris Graves Found. Lt. USN, 1942—46. Mem.: ABA, Asn Littèraire et Artistique Int (US), Int Fiscal Asn, Asn Bar City NY, Am Law Inst (life), Queen's, Hurlingham Club (London), River Club (New York, NY), Century Asn Club. Democrat. Office: Pillsbury Winthrop LLP One Battery Park Plz New York NY 10004-1490 E-mail: robert.anthoine@pillsburywinthrop.com.

ANTHONY, ANDREW JOHN, lawyer; b. Newark, Jan. 26, 1950; s. Andrew and Mary (Norton) A.; m. Raquel Perez Montoya, Sept. 29, 1990; children: Nicholas, Natalie. BA, Kean Coll., 1973; JD cum laude, U. Miami, 1976. Bar: Fla. 1977, U.S. Dist. Ct. (so. dist.) Fla. 1977. Assoc. Knight, Peters, Hoeveler, Pickle, Niemoeller & Flynn, Miami, Fla., 1977-79, Vernis & Bowling, Miami, 1979, Ligman, Martin, Shiley & McGee, Coral Gables, Fla., 1979-86; sole practice Coral Gables, 1986—. Mem. ABA, Fla. Bar Assn. Democrat. Roman Catholic. Avocations: numismatics, fishing, reading. Personal injury (including property damage), General practice, Product liability. Home: 3703 Anderson Rd Coral Gables FL 33134-7052 Office: 866 S Dixie Hwy Coral Gables FL 33146 E-mail: ajanthony@ajalaw.com.

ANTHONY, JOAN CATON, administrative judge; b. South Bend, Ind., July 28, 1939; d. Joseph Robert and Margaret Catherine (McMeel) Caton; m. Robert Armstrong Anthony, Jan. 3, 1980; 1 child, Peter. BA, Marquette U., 1961; MA, Northwestern U., 1963; JD, Catholic U. Am., 1979. Bar: D.C. 1980, Va. 1982. Instr. English Marquette U., Milw., 1963-65, George Washington U., Washington, 1965-69, asst. prof., 1969-70; spl. asst. student affairs HEW, Washington, 1970-72; dir. Office Student and Youth Affairs U.S. Office Edn., Washington, 1972-74, legis. specialist, 1974-78; chief mgmt. ops. br. Fed. Wildlife Permit Office U.S. Fish and Wildlife Svc., Washington, 1978-81; assoc. Cate and Goodbread, Washington, 1981—85; atty., advisor office legis. counsel U.S. Dept. Interior, 1991-95; staff atty. Interior Bd. Land Appeals, 1995—2003; adminstrv. judge Def. Office of Hearings and Appeals, U.S. Dept. Def., 2003—. Mem. U.S. del. to 2d meeting Conf. Parties to Conv. on Internat. Trade in Endangered Species of Wild Fauna and Flora, San Jose, Costa Rica, 1979. Contbr. lit. revs., essays and articles on univ.-cmty. rels., western settlement and internat. negotiations to various publs. Pres. Franklin Forest Frolickers, 1985—86; den leader Cub Scouts, mem. com. Boy Scouts Am., 1990—2000; parent vol. Fairfax County Pub. Schs., 1987—2001; treas. Greater McLean Rep. Women's Club, 1987—88; bd. dirs. McLean Citizens Assn., 1982—83, Fairfax County Humane Soc., 1983. Recipient Spl. Achievement award U.S. Fish and Wildlife Svc., 1981. Mem. D.C. Bar, Va. Bar, DAR (Freedom Hill chpt.). Roman Catholic. Home: 2011 Lorraine Ave Mc Lean VA 22101-5331

ANTHONY, J(ULIAN) DANFORD, JR., lawyer; b. Boston, Oct. 23, 1935; s. Julian Danford and Eleanor Caroline (Hopkins) A.; m. Ellen Nora Brown, Apr. 8, 1961; children: Julian Danford III, Sarah Dodge, David Campbell. AB, Wesleyan U., 1957; LLB, Harvard U., 1960. Bar: Minn. 1961, Conn. 1965. Atty.-advisor U.S. Tax Ct., Washington, 1962-64; assoc. Day, Berry & Howard LLP, Hartford, Conn., 1965-70, ptnr., 1971—. Chmn. Conn. Red Cross Blood Svcs., Farmington, 1981—82; trustee J. Walton Bissell Found., Hartford, 1987—, pres., 1987—; mem. adv. bd. dirs. Salvation Army, Hartford, 1990—96; elector Wadsworth Atheneum, Hartford, 1986—95; corporator Hartford Hosp., 1988—; trustee Amistad Found., Hartford, 1997—; bd. dirs. Hartford Symphony Orch., 1993—99, Conn. Children's Med. Ctr., 1994—, chmn., 1999—2002; bd. dirs. Conn. Children's Med. Ctr. Found., 1998—, Coordinating Coun. for Founds., Hartford, 1994—99. Mem. ABA, Nat. Assn. Bond Lawyers, Nat. Assn. Coll. and Univ. Attys., Fed. Tax Inst. New Eng. (exec. com. 1987—), Conn. Bar Assn. (chmn. tax sect. 1988-91), IRS Exempt Orgns. Liaison Group, Tax Club Hartford (pres. 1970-71). Municipal (including bonds), Non-profit and tax-exempt organizations, Taxation, general. Office: Day Berry & Howard LLP Cityplace Hartford CT 06103

ANTHONY, KENNETH C., JR., lawyer; b. Spartanburg, S.C., Jan. 23, 1954; s. Kenneth C. Sr. and Carol Ferguson (Burnside) A.; m. Monta Lorraine Moody, Mar. 15, 1980; children: Jay, Mary Sullivan, Dunk, Grady. Student, Rice U., 1972-74; BA, Wofford Coll., 1975; JD, U. S.C., 1977. Bar: S.C. 1978, U.S. Dist. Ct. S.C. 1978, U.S. Ct. Appeals (4th cir.) 1988, U.S. Supreme Ct. 1996; cert. civil and family mediator; cert. civil arbitrator. Ptnr. The Anthony Law Firm, P.A., Spartanburg, 1978—. Adj. prof. Wofford Coll., Spartanburg, 1978-98; bd. advisors U. S.C. Law Sch., Columbia, 1988-92. Recipient Compleat Lawyer award, USC Law School, 2001. Fellow S.C. Bar Found. (life); mem. ABA (mem. editl. bd.ABA/BNA Lawyers; Manual on Professonal Conduct, 1995-98), S.C. Bar Assn. (ho. dels. 1985-96, chmn. Law Related Edn. Commn. 1999-2000, bd. govs. 1996-99, sec. 2000-01, treas. 2001-02, past chmn. ethic adv. com., pres. 2003—), S.C. Trial Lawyers Assn. (bd. govs. 1996-98), Am. Trial Lawyers Assn. General civil litigation, Personal injury (including property damage), Product liability. Office: The Anthony Law Firm PA 250 Magnolia St PO Box 3565 Spartanburg SC 29304-3565 Fax: 864-583-9772. E-mail: kanthony@anthonylaw.com.

ANTHONY, ROBERT ARMSTRONG, law educator; b. Washington, Dec. 28, 1931; s. Emile Peter and Martha Graham (Armstrong) Anthony; m. Ruth Grace Barrons, Feb. 7, 1959 (div.); 1 child, Graham Barrons; m. Joan Patricia Caton, Jan. 3, 1980; 1 child, Peter Christopher Caton. BA, Yale U., 1953; BA in Jurisprudence, Oxford U., 1955; JD, Stanford U., 1957. Bar: Calif. 1957, N.Y. 1971, DC 1972. Assoc. Pillsbury, Madison & Sutro, San Francisco, 1957-62, Kelso, Cotton & Ernst, San Francisco, 1962-64; assoc. prof. law Cornell U. Law Sch., 1964-68, prof., 1968-75, dir. internat. legal studies, 1964-74; chief counsel, later dir. Office Fgn. Direct Investments, Dept. Commerce, 1972-73; cons. Adminstrv. Conf. U.S., Washington, 1968-71, chmn., 1974-79; ptnr. McKenna, Conner & Cuneo, Washington, 1979-82; pvt. practice Washington, 1982-83; prof. law George Mason U., Arlington, Va., 1983—2002, prof. emeritus, 2002—. Fulbright lectr., Slovenia, 1994; lectr. Acad. Am. and Internat. Law, Southwestern Legal Found., Dallas, 1967—72; instr. Golden Gate U., 1961; cons., chmn. pubs. adv. bd. Internat. Law Inst., 1984—; cons. Inst. Pub. Adminstrn., Slovenia, 1994—. Mem. editl. adv. bd. Jour. Law and Tech., 1986—91; contbr. articles to profl. jours. Active Pres.'s Inflation Program Regulatory Coun., 1978—79; chmn. panel U.S. Dept. Edn. Appeal Bd., 1981—83; commr. Sausalito (Calif.) City Planning Commn., 1962—64; active Fairfax County (Va.) Rep. Com., 1984—86; bd. dirs. Nat. Ctr. Adminstrv. Justice, 1974—79, Marin Shakespeare Festival, San Rafael, Calif., 1961—64, Va. Assn. Scholars, 1990—98. Mem.: ABA (coun., sec. sect. adminstrv. law and regulatory practice 1988—94), Stanford U. Law Soc. Washington (pres. 1982), Am. Law Inst., Assn. Am. Rhodes Scholars, Cosmos Club. Home: 2011 Lorraine Ave Mc Lean VA 22101-5331 Office: George Mason U Law Sch 3301 N Fairfax Dr Arlington VA 22201-4426 E-mail: ranthony@gmu.edu.

ANTHONY, STEPHEN PIERCE, lawyer; b. Concord, Mass., Aug. 30, 1961; s. Reed Pierce and Barbara (Beatley) Anthony; m. Lisa Ann Battalia, June 2, 1990; children: Matthew William, Caroline Grace. AB, Dartmouth Coll., 1983; JD, Columbia U., 1988. Bar: Md. 1989, D.C. 1991, U.S. Dist. Ct. D.C. 1991, U.S. Dist. Ct. Md. 2000, U.S. Ct. Appeals (D.C. Cir.) 1991. Law clk. to Hon. Patricia M. Wald, U.S. Ct. Appeals for D.C. Cir., Washington, 1988—89; assoc. Wilmer, Cutler & Pickering, Washington, 1989—91; asst. U.S. atty. U.S. Atty.'s Office for D.C., Washington, 1991—96; trial atty. pub. integrity sect. criminal divsn. U.S. Dept. Justice, Washington, 1996—2000; with Covington & Burling, Washington, 2000—. Barrister Edward Bennett Williams Am. Inn of Ct., Washington, 1997—. Notes and comments editor Columbia Law Rev., 1987-88. Harlan Fiske Stone scholar Columbia U., 1985-86, 87-88, James Kent scholar, 1986-87. Office: Covington & Burling 1201 Pennsylvania Ave NW Washington DC 20004 E-mail: santhony@cov.com.

ANTHONY, THOMAS DALE, lawyer; b. Cleve., July 23, 1952; m. Susan Shelly; children: Lara, Elizabeth. BS, Miami U., Oxford, Ohio, 1974; JD, Case Western Res. U., 1977. Bar: Ohio 1977. Tax specialist Ernst & Young, Cleve., 1977—79; ptnr. Benesch, Friedlander, Coplan and Aronoff, Cin., 1979—89, Frost and Jacobs, Cin., 1989—98; exec. v.p., chief legal officer, sec. Choice Care, 1996—98; pres., CEO PacifiCare of Ohio, 1998—2002; counsel, vice chair corp. dept. Frost Brown Todd LLC, 2001—. Speaker various orgns. Mem. Cin. Coun. on World Affairs, 1980-82; vol. fundraising drive Sta. WVIZ, 1978-79, Sta. WCET, 1980-82; legal counsel Children's Internat. Summer Villages, 1979—; account capt. United Way of Hamilton County, 1986-88, cabinet mem., 1993; pres. State Libr. Bd., Ohio, 1987-89; mem. bus. adv. coun., subcom. ednl. legis. Mariemont City Schs. and Bd. of Edn.; bd. dirs. Greater Cin. Ctr. for Econ. Edn., Am. Heart Assn. (Cin. chpt.), Juvenile Diabetes Found. Mem. ABA (taxation sect., tax acctg. problems com., tax shelter subcom., small bus. com., mem. health law forum), Ohio State Bar Assn. (health law com., ins. sect.), Cin. Bar Assn. (chmn. tax. inst. com. 1990, adminstrn. and fin. com. 1991-93, chmn. tax sect. 1993, health law com.), Cin. C. of C., Miami U. Alumni Assn. (bd. dirs., treas. 1989-91, v.p. 1991-92), Nat. Health Lawyers Assn., Rotary (co-chair youth in city govt. program), Omicron Delta Kappa, Sigma Phi Epsilon. Corporate, general, Health. Home: 4337 Ashley Oaks Dr Cincinnati OH 45227-3947 Office: PacifiCare 11260 Chester Rd Ste 800 Cincinnati OH 45246-4096

ANTIN, MICHAEL, lawyer; b. Milw., Nov. 30, 1938; s. David Boris and Pauline (Mayer) A.; m. Evelyne Judith Hirsch, June 19, 1960; children: Stephanie, Bryan, Randall BS, Univ. Calif., 1960; JD, U. Calif., 1963. Bar: Calif. 1963; cert. tax specialist. Tax atty. Cruikshank, Antin & Grebow, Beverly Hills, Calif., 1963-81, Antin, Litz & Grebow, Beverly Hills, 1981-91, Antin & Taylor, L.A., 1993—99; sole practice L.A., 1999—. Bd. dirs. Small Bus. Counsel Am., Washington, The Group, Inc.; speaker in field; instr. Solomon S. Heubner Sch. CLU Studies, 1977-86. Author: How to Operate Your Trust or Probate, 1983; contbr. articles to profl. jours. With U.S. Air Force, 1959-67. Fellow Am. Coll. Tax Counsel, Am. Coll. of Trust and Estate Counsel, L.A. County Bowlers Assn. (bd. dirs. 1996-99). Avocations: jogging, tennis, cross country skiing, bowling. Estate planning, Probate (including wills, trusts), Taxation, general. Office: Ste 2000 1925 Century Park East Blvd Fl 20 Los Angeles CA 90067-2721

ANTOGNOLI, ANTHONY E. lawyer; b. Melrose Park, Ill., May 15, 1975; s. Edward L. and Marilyn S. Antognoli; m. Robin Ann Malinowski, Oct. 18, 2003. BS in Fin., U. Ill., 1997; JD, cert. in tax law, Loyola U., Chgo., 2000. Bar: Ill. 00. Assoc. McGuire Woods LLP, Chgo., 2000—03, Hinshaw and Culbertson, 2003—. Contbr. articles to profl.jours. Mem.: ABA, Chgo. Bar Assn. Labor (including EEOC, Fair Labor Standards Act, labor-management relations, NLRB, OSHA). Home: 401 E Ontario Unit 2904 Chicago IL 60611 Office: Hinshaw & Culbertson 222 N LaSalle St Ste 300 Chicago IL 60601-1081 Fax: 312-849-3067. E-mail: aantognoli@hinshawlaw.com.

ANTOLIN, STANISLAV, patent lawyer; b. Toronto, Ont., Can., Mar. 27, 1960; came to U.S., 1962; BS, Drexel U., 1983; MS, Carnegie Mellon U., 1985; JD, Widner U., 1994. Bar: Pa. 1994, N.C. 2000, U.S. Patent Office 1991, U.S. Dist. Ct. (we. dist.) Pa 1994. Rsch. engr. Lanxide Corp., Newark, Del., 1985-89, patent agt., 1989-94; patent counsel Kennametal Inc., Latrobe, Pa., 1994-99; assoc. Rhodes & Mason, P.L.L.C., Greensboro, N.C., 1999-2001, MacCord Mason, P.L.L.C., Greensboro, 2001—. Contbr. articles to profl. jours. Mem.: Assn. Univ. Tech. Mgrs., Nat. Assn. Patent Practitioners, N.C. Bar Assn. Intellectual property, Patent, Trademark and copyright. E-mail: santolin@maccordmason.com.

ANTON, DAVID, lawyer; b. Tampa, Fla., Nov. 25, 1958; s. Leonard Morton Anton and Joyce (Schonbrun) Hartmann. BS in Econs., U. Fla., 1981, JD, 1984. Cert. mediator; securities arbitrator Nat. Assn. Securities Dealers. Pvt. practice, Tampa. Mem. Fla. Bar Assn., Hillsborough County Bar Assn. General civil litigation, Commercial, consumer (including collections, credit), Family and matrimonial. Office: Harvey Schonbrun PA 1802 N Morgan St Tampa FL 33602-2328 E-mail: david@schonbrun.com.

ANTON, DONALD KRIS, law educator; b. St. Louis, Mar. 20, 1960; s. Donald Christian and Aurora Ida (Viglino) A.; m. Penelope Elise Mathew, Aug. 7, 1993; 1 child, Thomas Christian. BS, Ctrl. Mo. State U., 1983; JD, St. Louis U., 1986. Bar: Mo. 1986, Idaho 1988, New South Wales, Australia, 1998, Victoria, Australia, 1999. Atty. advisor Mo. Ct. Appeals, St. Louis, 1986-88; assoc. Elam, Burke & Boyd, Boise, Idaho, 1988-91; legal counsel Blake Dawson Waldron, Sydney, Australia, 1991-92; rsch. assoc. Law Sch. Columbia U., N.Y.C., 1992-94; lectr. in law U. Melbourne, Australia, 1994-97; dir. policy Environ. Defenders Office, Sydney, Australia, 1997-2000; dir. Australian Ctr. Environ. Law Australian Nat. U., 2000—. Vis. prof. law, U. Mich., 2003; chair moot ct. bd. St. Louis U., 1985-86; examiner Idaho State Bar, Boise, 1989-90; vol. advisor St. Louis Vol. Lawyers' Assn., 1987-88; rsch. fellow Environ. Defender's Office, Sydney, 1991-92; sr. lectr. in law Australian Nat. U., 2000-; presenter in field. Mem. sr. staff St. Louis Law Jour., 1986; contbr. articles to profl. publs.; book rev. editor Environ. and Planning Law Jour., 1994-2000. Mem. Environ. Law Alliance Worldwide, Eugene, Oreg., 1994; dep. election commr. St. Louis County Bd. Election Commrs.; Mo. del. Dem. Conv., 1980. Mem. ABA, Am. Soc. Internat. Law (reporter 1993), Idaho State Bar Assn., Mo. Bar Assn., Australian and New Zealand Soc. Internat. Law, Internat. Commn. Jurists, Internat. Bar Assn., Law Soc. New South Wales, Law Inst. Victoria, Nat. Environ. Law Assn., Australasian Law Tchrs. Assn. Democrat. Office: Australasian Ctr Environ Law Australian Nat U Canberra 0200 Australia

ANTON, RONALD DAVID, lawyer; b. Phila., Nov. 9, 1933; s. Emil T. Anton and Mary E. Bishara; m. Suzanne J. Winker, Aug. 19, 1976; 1 child, Ronald J. JD, U. Buffalo, 1958; LLM, U. Pa., 1959, Yale U., 1960. Bar: N.Y. 1959. Ptnr. Boniello, Anton, Conti & B., Niagara Falls, N.Y., 1960—; corp. counsel City of Niagara Falls, 2000—. Lectr. Univ. Buffalo (N.Y.) Law Sch., 1960-62; cons. N.Y. State Legis., Buffalo, Greater Buffalo (N.Y.) Devel. Found.; past pres. Niagara (N.Y.) County Legal Aid, 1966-68, Niagara Falls (N.Y.) Bar, 1968; past dist. gov. N.Y. State Trial Lawyers, 1984-88; moderator (tv show) The Law For You, N.Y., 1967. Author: Jesus, Saviour, 1992; contbr. articles to profl. jours. Rep. candidate N.Y. State Atty. Gen., 1990; trustee Stella Niagara Edn. Pk., Lewiston, N.Y., 1988—. General civil litigation. Home: 175 White Tail Run Grand Island NY 14072-3223 Office: Boniello Anton Conti & B 770 Main St Niagara Falls NY 14301-1704

ANTONE, NAHIL PETER, lawyer, civil engineer; b. Baghdad, Iraq, Jan. 17, 1952; came to U.S., 1978; s. Peter and Salima (Kammoo) A. BS in Civil Engring. with highest distinction, U. Baghdad, 1971; MS in Structural Engring., U. Surrey, 1974; JD summa cum laude, Detroit Coll. Law, 1985. Bar: Mich. 1985, U.S. Dist. Ct. (ea. dist.) Mich. 1985; registered profl. engr., Mich. Constrn. engr. Ministry Constrn., Baghdad, 1971-73; project mgr. Ministry Oil, Baghdad, 1974-78; design engr. Harley Ellington Pierce Yee, Southfield, Mich., 1978-79; v.p. Hennessey Engring. Co., Trenton, Mich., 1979-85; assoc. Bodman, Longley & Dahling, Detroit, 1985-88; owner N. Peter Antone Profl. Corp., Southfield, 1988—; ptnr. Antone & Kuhn Law Offices, Farmington Hills, Mich., 1989-93; pvt. practice Southfield, 1993—. Lectr. Detroit Coll. Law, 1986-87. Govt. of Iraq scholar, 1974; scholar Det. Coll. Law, 1982. Mem. ABA, Detroit Bar Assn., ASCE (chmn. legis. com. Southeast Mich. chpt. 1981). Avocations: tennis, swimming, exercise, travel, music. Construction, Immigration, naturalization, and customs, Public international. Office: 16445 W 12 Mile Rd Southfield MI 48076-2949 Home: 7084 Yarmouth Dr West Bloomfield MI 48322-1077

ANTONIETTI, JOAN L(YNN), lawyer; b. Great Falls, Mont., Mar. 12, 1957; d. Emmett A. and Marlene J. (Latham) Wilson; m. Daniel P. Antonietti, July 8, 1978. BA in History and Polit. Sci. cum laude, U. Mont., 1979; JD cum laude, Gonzaga U., 1983. Bar: Wash. 1983, U.S. Dist. Ct. (ea. dist.) Wash. 1985, U.S. Dist. Ct. (we. dist.) Wash. 1987, U.S. Ct. Appeals (9th cir.) 1990. Assoc. Richter Wimberley P.S., Spokane, Wash., 1984-90, ptnr., 1990-92; pvt. practice, Spokane, Wash., 1992—. Atty. Women Helping Women, 1996—; mem. Jr. League Spokane, 1985-95—, parliamentarian, 1990-91, sustaining mem., 1995—; trustee, bd. dirs., chair Vanessa Behan Crisis Nursery, Spokane, 1989-95; bd. dirs. Holy Family Hosp. Found., 2001—. Recipient Cmty. Svc. award Child Abuse and Neglect Prevention Coun., 1995, Appreciation award Vanessa Behan Crisis Nursery, 1995. Mem. ATLA, Wash. State Bar Assn. (law sch. liaison com. 1990-91, task force on professionalism 1988-90, CLE com. 1987-90), Spokane County Bar Assn., Wash. Women Lawyers (pres. Spokane chpt. 1985-86, state jud. endorsement com.), Wash. State Trial Lawyers Assn. (bd. govs. 2000-, co-chair employment law sect., 2002—), Alpha Phi Alumni (pres. 1985-87). General civil litigation, Labor (including EEOC, Fair Labor Standards Act, labor-management relations, NLRB, OSHA), Estate taxation. Office: 12402 N Division St #331 Spokane WA 99218-1930

ANTONINO, LAUREN SLEPIN, lawyer; b. Norfolk, Va., Feb. 4, 1962; d. William Raymond Slepin and Carol Mae (Gross) Levin; m. Tom L. Antonino, Aug. 18, 1990; children: Tommy, Matthew, Jamie, David. AB, Duke U., 1984; JD, U. Va., 1987. Fed. law clk. Hon. Olivia Kelsch, U.S. Ct. Appeals (9th Cir.), Seattle, 1987—88; assoc. Long, Aldridge & Norman, Atlanta, 1988—92; ptnr. Meadows Ichter & Trigg, Atlanta, 1992—2000, Chitwood & Harley, Atlanta, 2000—. Adv. bd. Atlanta Legal Aid, 1998; pres., mem. bd. Legal Aid for Homeless, Atlanta, 1992—97. Contbr. articles to profl. publs. Mem.: Am. Mensa Soc., Phi Beta Kappa. Product liability, Securities, Commercial, contracts (including sales of goods; commercial financing). Home: 1116 Santa Fe Station Dunwoody GA 30338 Office: Chitwood & Harley 1230 Peachtree St Ste 2300 Atlanta GA 30305 E-mail: lsa@classlaw.com.

ANTONUCCI, PETER A. lawyer; b. N.Y.C., Oct. 11, 1959; BA in English, U. Rochester, 1982; JD, Bklyn. Law Sch., 1990. Bar: N.Y., Conn., U.S. Dist. Ct. (ea. dist.) Wis., U.S. Dist. Ct. (so. dist.) N.Y., U.S. Dist. Ct. (ea. dist.) N.Y., U.S. Supreme Ct. Mng. clk. Martin, Clearwater & Bell, N.Y.C., 1982—87; law clk. to Chief Judge Paul P. Rao U.S. Ct. Internat. Trade, 1988; assoc. Weil, Gotshal & Manges LLP, N.Y.C., 1990—98, counsel, 1999—. Spkr. various confs. Co-author: A Punitive Damages Primer: Legal Principles and Constitutional Challenges, 1994; contbr. chapters to books; editor: numerous articles for ABA publs., 1993—; contbr. articles to profl. publs.; commentator CNN Headline News, 1996—, Fox TV Network, 1999. Pres. St. David's Sch. Alumni Assn., 1995—98; mem. exec. com. East Sixties Properties Owners' Assn., 1995—2002. Mem.: ABA (pub. rels. com. sect. tort and ins. practice 1999—2002, chair com. toxic substances and environ. law 1999—2000, mem. Yr. 2000 task force 1998—2000, co-chair subcom. on policy 1998—99, editor-in-chief newsletter 1993—98, sect. vice chair 1993—98, mem. ann. mtg. com.

1996—98, numerous other offices). Avocations: public speaking, skiing, golf, travel. Product liability, Toxic tort, Bankruptcy. Office: Weil Gotshal & Manges LLP 209 E 61st St New York NY 10021

ANZAI, EARL I. former state attorney general; b. Honolulu; Student, Emroy U., Oreg. State U.; BA, U. Hawaii, 1964, MA, 1966. Planning prog. coord. Oahu Metropolitan Planning Org., 1967—77; mgmt. analyst/investigator U.S. Gen. Accounting Office, 1968—70; sr. legislative analyst Hawaii state Office of the Legislative Auditor, 1970—75; special asst. exec. dir. Comprehensive Planning Org. San Diego, 1975—76; chief clerk/staff dir. state senate Ways and Means Com., 1979—81; com. clerk Hawaii com. on environment, agriculture, conservation and land, constitution convention of 1978, 1978; atty./chief investigator special senate com. investigating the pesticide heptachlor in milk, 1982—83; law clk. First Cir. Ct., Honolulu, 1982—83; sr. assoc. Schutter & Glickstein, 1983—88; ptnr. Anzai & Evangelista fka Anzai Ahn Holt & Evangelista fka Anzai Holt & Evangelitsta; dir. Dept. Budget and Fin., Honolulu, 1995—99; atty. gen. State Senate Hawaii, Honolulu, 1999—2002; com. clerk state senate Com. on Health, 1981—82; chief coun. com. on judiciary state senate, 1987.*

APGOOD, RICHARD D. law librarian; b. Salt Lake City, Feb. 12, 1971; s. Robert D. and Marsha F. Apgood. BA, U. Utah, 1993; MLS, Simmons Coll., 1994; JD, Am. U., 1998. Bar: Utah 1998. Gen. counsel Singlepoint Resources, Inc., Salt Lake City, 1998—2002; law libr. & adj. prof. of law U. Utah, 1999—2002; law libr. U. Washington, 2002—02. Dir. Singlepoint Resources, Inc., Salt Lake City, 1998—2002. Mem.: ABA, ALA, Utah Libr. Assn. (exhibits chair 2000—01), Am. Assn. Law Libraries (govt. rels. chair Western Pacific chpt. 2000—02), Kappa Sigma (grand master of ceremonies 1991—92). R-Liberal. Avocations: fly fishing, travel. Office: University of the District of Columbia 4200 Connecticut Ave NW Bldg39 Washington DC 20008 Office Fax: 202-274-7311. Personal E-mail: rapgood@singlepoint.net. E-mail: rapgood@singlepoint.net.

APKE, THOMAS MICHAEL, lawyer, educator; b. Santa Monica, Calif., Jan. 16, 1945; s. Edward Anthony and Harriett (Ruby) A.; m. Virginia Lee Royston, July 17, 1982; children: Daniel Edward, Sarah, Matthew. BS, Pa. State U., 1966; JD, Marquette U., 1969; LLM, U. San Diego, 1983. Bar: Calif. 1971. Assoc. Coombs & Comstock, Culver City, Calif., 1971-74; pvt. practice, Mission Viejo, Calif., 1974-84, Laguna Niguel, Calif., 1985—; prof. bus. law Calif. State U., Fullerton, 1974—. Contbr. articles on bus. law to profl. jours. Mem. Nat. Com. Recipient Disting. Faculty award Calif. State U. Fullerton Alumni Assn., 1982. Mem. Am. Bus. Law Assn., Pacific S.W. Bus. Law Assn., Pa. State U. Alumni Assn., Beta Gamma Sigma. Roman Catholic. Corporate, general, Property, real (including real estate development, water), Corporate taxation. Home: 29156 Mira Vista Laguna Niguel CA 92677-4325 E-mail: law@apke.com.

APOLINSKY, STEPHEN DOUGLAS, lawyer; b. Birmingham, Ala., Dec. 5, 1961; s. Harold Irwin and Sandra Jean (Rubenstein) A. BA, U. Mich., 1983; JD, Emory U., 1987. Bar: Ga. 1987, U.S. Dist. Ct. (no. dist.) Ga. 1987, D.C. 1989, Ala. 1994. Litigation assoc. Bentley, Karesh Seacrest Labovitz & Campbell, Atlanta, 1987-94; mem. Eastman, Stapleton & Apolinsky, LLC, Atlanta, 1995-97, Eastman & Apolinsky, L.L.P., Atlanta, 1997—. Mem. ATLA, Ga. Trial Lawyers Assn., Atlanta Bar Assn., Atlanta Claims Assn., Am.-Israel C. of C. (past bd. dirs. S.E. region), Druid Hills Civic Assn. Avocation: travel and sports. General civil litigation, Insurance, Personal injury (including property damage). Office: Eastman & Apolinsky 114 E Ponce De Leon Ave Decatur GA 30030-2526 Business E-Mail: steve@ea-law.com.

APPEL, ALBERT M. lawyer; b. N.Y.C., May 26, 1945; s. Morris and Belle (Kaplan) A.; m. Irena Uhl, June 10, 1979; 1 child, Elliott. BS in Econs., U. Pa., 1966; JD, NYU, 1969. Bar: N.Y. 1969, U.S. Dist. Ct. (so. and ea. dists.) N.Y. 1971, U.S. Ct. Appeals (2d cir.) 1974, U.S. Ct. Appeals (4th cir.) 1979, U.S. Ct. Appeals (11th Cir.) 2002. Assoc. Spear and Hill, N.Y.C., 1969-75, Webster & Sheffield, N.Y.C., 1976-80, ptnr., 1981-91; spl. counsel Stroock & Stroock & Lavan LLP, N.Y.C., 1991-97, ptnr., 1998—. Mem. ABA, Am. Health Lawyers Assn., N.Y. State Bar Assn., Assn. of Bar of City of N.Y., Beta Alpha Psi. General civil litigation, Health. Home: 670 W End Ave New York NY 10025-7313 Office: Stroock & Stroock & Lavan LLP 180 Maiden Ln New York NY 10038-4925 E-mail: aappel@stroock.com.

APPEL, NINA SCHICK, law educator, dean; b. Feb. 17, 1936; d. Leo and Nora Schick; m. Alfred Appel Jr.; children: Karen Oshman, Richard. Student, Cornell U.; JD, Columbia U., 1959. Instr. Columbia Law Sch., 1959-60; adminstr. Stanford U., mem. faculty, prof. law, 1973—, assoc. dean, 1976-83; dean Sch. Law Loyola U., 1983—. Mem. Am. Bar Found., Ill. Bar Found., Chgo. Bar Found., Chgo. Legal Club, Chgo. Network. Jewish. Office: Loyola U Sch Law 1 E Pearson St Chicago IL 60611-2055

APPEL, ROBERT EUGENE, lawyer, educator; b. Cleve., Oct. 18, 1958; s. Robert Donald and Jean Ann (Crites) Appel; m. Margaret Rose Curley, Aug. 24, 1985. BS, Cen. Conn. State U., 1980; JD, U. Bridgeport, Conn., 1982; MBA, U. Conn., 1984; LLM, Boston U., 1984. Bar: Conn. 1983. Asst. mgr. fin. services Lexington Ins. Co., Boston, 1984-85; tax. cons. Touche Ross and Co., Stamford, Conn., 1985-86; asst. dir. nat. design CIGNA Corp., Bloomfield, Conn., 1986—88, dir. nat. design, 1988—97; asst. v.p. Lincoln Nat. Life Ins. Co., Hartford, 1998—2002, 2d v.p., 2002—. Lectr. Real Estate Tng. and Ednl. Svcs., Bridgeport, 1985—88; lectr. real estate Dare Inst., Southbury, 1991—. Divsn. coord. United Way, 1988. Mem.: ABA, Conn. Bar Assn. Republican. Roman Catholic. Avocations: investing, running, weightlifting, motorcycling. Estate planning, Estate taxation, Personal income taxation. Home: 80 Kingston Dr East Hartford CT 06118-2450 Office: Lincoln Fin Group 350 Church St Hartford CT 06103-1106

APPENZELLER, PHILLIP CARL, JR., lawyer; b. Fennville, Mich., Feb. 18, 1966; s. Phillip Carl Jr. and Anna E. Appenzeller; m. Rhonda J. Brauchler, July 30, 1988; children: Brock P., Zack G. BS, Evangel Coll., Springfield, Mo., 1988; JD, U. Mo., Kansas City, 1992. Assoc. Shughart, Thomson & Kilroy, Kansas City, Mo., 1992-94, McKool Smith, Dallas, 1996—98; shareholder Munsch Hondt Kopf & Harr, 2000—. Capt. JAG, U.S. Army, 1994-96. Mem. Evangel Coll. Alumni Assn. (chmn. bd./pres. 1997—). Republican. Baptist. Avocations: weight lifting, running, basketball. General civil litigation. Office: Munsch Kopf & Harr 1445 Ross St 4000 Dallas TX 75202

APPERSON, BERNARD JAMES, lawyer; b. Washington, June 28, 1956; s. Bernard James Jr. and Ann Wentworth (Anderson) A. BA in Polit. Sci., Am. U., 1978; JD, Cumberland Sch. Law, 1981; LLM in Internat. Law, Georgetown U., 1985. Bar: Fla. 1981, Ga. 1981, D.C. 1983, U.S. Supreme Ct. 1985. Atty., U.S. trustee for so. dist. N.Y. U.S. Dept. Justice, N.Y.C., 1981; atty. EPA, Washington, 1981-83; atty. civil rights div. U.S. Dept. Justice, Washington, 1983-84, atty. office legis. affairs, 1986-87; asst. U.S. atty. Ea. Dist. Va., Alexandria, 1987-97; counsel to dir. Legal Services Corp., Washington, 1985-86; commr. U.S. Dist. Ct., Ea. Dist. Va., Alexandria, 1996-97; sr. counsel com. on govt. reform and oversight, spl. counsel subcom. Nat. Econ. Growth, Natural Resources etc. U.S. Ho. of Reps., Washington, 1997-98; assoc. ind. counsel Office of the Ind. Counsel, Washington, 1998-99, dep. ind. counsel, 1999-2000; chief counsel oversight and investigations Com. on Jud., U.S. Ho. of Reps., Washington, 2001, chief counsel subcom. on crime, terrorism & homeland security, 2001—. Instr. FBI Tng. Acad., Quantico, Va., 1990; lectr. law U. London and U. Ga., 1990. Assoc. editor Am. Jour. Trial Advocacy Cumberland Sch. Law, 1979-81. County chmn. Paula Hawkins for U.S Senate, Volusia County, Fla., 1974; nat. staff Citizens for Reagan, Fla., Kansas City, Mo., 1976; cons. Reagan for Pres., Detroit, 1980; dep. northeastern regional dir. Reagan-Bush 1984, Washington, 1984, Lawyers for Bush-Cheney, Washington, 2000. Lewis F. Powell Medal for Excellence in Advocacy Am. Coll Trial Lawyers, 1980. Mem. Federalist Soc. for Law and Pub. Policy Studies, Order of Barristers, St. Andrew's Soc. Republican. Anglican. Home: 545 E Braddock Rd Apt 704 Alexandria VA 22314-2171 Office: US Ho of Reps Jud Com Subcom Crime Terrorism and Homeland Secu 207 Cannon House Office Bld Washington DC 20515

APPLEBAUM, CHARLES, lawyer; b. Newark, May 19, 1947; s. Harry I. and Francis (Gastwirth) A.; m. Patricia (Gyurko) Applebaum; children: Matthew, David, Michael, Amanda. BA, U. Pa., 1969; JD, Rutgers U., 1973; LLM, NYU, 1978. Bar: U.S. Dist. Ct. N.J. 1973. Law clk. to Hon. Samuel A. Larner, Jersey City, 1973-74; assoc., then ptnr. Greenbaum, Rowe, Smith, Ravin, Davis & Himmel LLP, Woodbridge, N.J., 1974-89; gen. counsel Alfieri Orgn., Edison, NJ, 1989—2002, Kara Homes Inc., East Brunswick, NJ, 2002—. Adj. prof. Rutgers Law Sch., Newark, 1985-88. Co-author: New Jersey Real Estate Forms, 1988; contbr. articles to profl. jours. Mem. ABA (real property probate and trust, chmn. significant lit. and publs. 1985-97, co-editor The Acrel Papers 1992-94), Am. Coll. Real Estate Lawyers (editor publs. 1991—). Commercial, contracts (including sales of goods; commercial financing), Land use and zoning (including planning), Property, real (including real estate development, water). Office: Kara Homes Inc 197 Rte 18 Ste 101N East Brunswick NJ 08816 E-mail: capplebaum@karahomes.com.

APPLEFELD, LAURIE SUE, lawyer; b. Balt., Sept. 23, 1953; d. Leroy S. and Floraine B. (Rubin) A.; 1 child, Jordan Edward; m. Bright K. Walker, Aug. 14, 2002. BA, Boston U., 1975, MEd, 1977; JD, New Eng. Sch. L.aw, 1983. Bar: Md. 1984, U.S. Dist. Ct. Md. 1984. Pvt. practice, Balt., 1984—. Pres. Greater Balt. Savs. and Loan Assn., 1985—. Mem. Nat. Mus. Women in Arts, Washington, 1986—. Mem. ABA, Md. Bar Assn., Balt. City Bar Assn., Women's Bar Assn., Greater Balt. Bd. Realtors. Property, real (including real estate development, water). Office: PO Box 26135 Baltimore MD 21210

APPLEGATE, WILLIAM RUSSELL, lawyer; b. Columbia, S.C., Oct. 18, 1946; s. William John and Vera (Lister) Applegate; m. Jerva Ann Watson, Dec. 20, 1969; children: Jennifer Corey, Amanda Ann. AB, Wofford Coll., 1968; JD, U. S.C., 1974, MA in Criminal Justice, 1978. Bar: S.C. 1974, U.S. Dist. Ct. S.C. 1974, U.S. Supreme Ct. 1979. Assoc. E. Pickens Rish, Esquire, Lexington, SC, 1974—75; pvt. practice West Columbia, 1975—85. Judge Town of Springdale, West Columbia, 1980—90; atty. Town of Gaston, Gaston, SC, 1976—90. Vice-chmn. Episcopal Ch. Upper Diocese of S.C., Columbia, 1981—97; sr. warden St. Mary's Ch., Columbia, 1979—81. Capt. U.S. Army, 1969—71. Mem.: S.C. Bar Assn. Republican. Episcopalian. Commercial, consumer (including collections, credit), Family and matrimonial, Personal injury (including property damage). Home: 123 Woodwinds West Dr Columbia SC 29212-3629 Office: William R Applegate Esquire 1700 Sunset Blvd West Columbia SC 29169-5940

APPLEMAN, LAWRENCE JOEL, lawyer, engineer; b. Bklyn., Mar. 31, 1956; s. Sidney and Amy Stella (Poris) A.; m. Cheryl Anne Rosenberg, Aug. 16, 1992. BS, MIT, 1987; JD, New Eng. Sch. Law, 1991; MS, Boston U., 1996. Bar: Mass., 1991, Ill., 1992, D.C., 1994. Developer legal software Mirror Sys., Cambridge, Mass., 1984-87; engr. Learningways, Cambridge, 1987-91; dir. legal engring. Real World Solutions, Cambridge, 1990—92; atty. engr. LEXIS-NEXIS, Cambridge, 1992-98; project mgr. Reed-Elsevier, Cambridge, 1998—2000; devel. mgr. Reed-Elsevier, Bus. Info., Newton, 2000—. Cons. legal engring. Tech. Tng. Assocs., Cambridge, 1986-94. Tech. coord. editor New Eng. Law Rev., 1990-91; contbr. articles to profl. jours. Mem. ABA, Mass. Bar Assn., Ill. State Bar Assn., Chgo. Bar Assn., Boston Bar Assn. Jewish. Computer, Intellectual property. Home: 11 Madison Ave Cambridge MA 02140-1614 Office: Reed Bus Info 275 Washington St Newton MA 02458

APPLETON, R. O., JR., lawyer; b. San Francisco, Aug. 17, 1945; s. Robert Oser and Leslie Jeanne (Roth) A.; m. Susan Frelich, June 3, 1971; children: Jesse David, Seth Daniel. AB, Stanford U., 1967; JD, U. Calif., San Francisco, 1970; postgrad., NYU, 1971. Bar: Calif. 1971, U.S. Dist. Calif. (no. dist.) Calif. 1971, Mo. 1973, U.S. Dist. Ct. (ea. dist.) Mo. 1974, U.S. Ct. Appeals (8th cir.) 1975, U.S. Ct. Internat. Trade, 1980. Assoc. Dinkelspiel & Dinkelspiel, San Francisco, 1971-73, Schramm & Morganstern, St. Louis, 1973-75; pvt. practice, 1975-77; ptnr. Braun, Newman, Stewart & Appleton, St. Louis, 1977-82, Appleton, Newman & Kretmar, St. Louis, 1982-84, Appleton, Newman & Gerson, St. Louis, 1984-89, Appleton & Kretmar, St. Louis, 1989—, Appleton, Kretmar & Beatty. Adj. prof. pre-trial litigation Washington U. Sch. Law, St. Louis, 1985-88. Arbitrator, vol. Better Bus. Bur. of St. Louis, 1980—; St. Louis Gymnastic Centre, 1984—; bd. dirs. St. Louis Friends of Tibet, 1991-94. Mem. ABA, Calif. Bar Assn., Met. Bar Assn. of St. Louis, St. Louis County Bar Assn., Am. Arbitration Assn. (arbitrator comml. panel, arbitrator mass claims appeals com. 1999), Stanford Club (pres. 1991—). Democrat. Jewish. Avocations: jogging, swimming, cooking, model trains, reading. Corporate, general. Home: 8317 Cornell Ave Saint Louis MO 63132-5025 Office: Appleton Kretmar Beatty & Stolze 8000 Maryland Ave Ste 900 Saint Louis MO 63105-3911 E-mail: roajratty1@aol.com.

APRIL, RAND SCOTT, lawyer; b. Bklyn., Feb. 10, 1951; s. Arthur and Muriel (Marmorstein) A. BA, Northwestern U., 1972; JD, Columbia U., 1975. Bar: N.Y. 1976, U.S. Dist. Ct. (so. and ea. dists.) N.Y. 1976, Calif. 1989. Assoc. Marshall, Bratter, Greene, Allison & Tucker, N.Y.C., 1975-78, Gordon, Hurwitz, Butowsky, Baker, Weitzen & Shalov, N.Y.C., 1978-81, Skadden, Arps, Slate, Meagher & Flom, N.Y.C., 1981-83, ptnr., 1983—. Stone scholar Columbia U., 1974-75. Mem. Phi Beta Kappa. Avocation: skiing. Property, real (including real estate development, water). Office: Skadden Arps Slate Meagher & Flom 300 S Grand Ave Los Angeles CA 90071-3109

APRUZZESE, VINCENT JOHN, lawyer; b. Newark, Nov. 1, 1928; s. John and Mildred (Cerefice) A.; m. Marie A. Yeager, July 10, 1955; children: Barbara, John, Donald, Lynn, Kathy. BA, Rutgers U., 1950; LLB, U. Pa., 1953. Bar: N.J. 1954, U.S. Dist. Ct. N.J. 1954, U.S. Ct. Appeals (3d cir.) 1962, U.S. Supreme Ct. 1970, U.S. Ct. Appeals (D.C. cir. 1973), U.S. Ct. Appeals (4th cir.) 1973, D.C. 1976, N.Y. 1983. Assoc. Lum, Fairlie & Foster, Newark, 1953-54; sole practice Newark, 1954-55, 58-65; sr. ptnr. Apruzzese & McDermott, Newark, 1965-70, pres. Springfield, N.J., 1970-90, Liberty Corner and Newark. Mem. legal adv. bd. Martindale-Hubbell, 1991-98. Bd. dirs. St. Barnabas Hosp., Papermill Playhouse. With JAGC, USAF, 1956-57. Mem. ABA (mem. coun. labor and employment law sect. 1984-94, chair labor & employment law sect. 1992-93, bd. govs. 1988-91), Coll. of Labor and Employment Lawyers, Fed. Bar Assn., Internat. Labor Law Soc. (treas.), Am. Coll. Trial Lawyers, Am. Bar Found., Fed. Bar State N.J., N.J. State Bar Assn. (pres. 1982-84), Essex County Bar Assn., Somerset County Bar Assn., Baltusrol Country Club (Springfield), Chatham (Mass.) Beach and Tennis Club, Eastward Ho Country Club (Chatham). General practice, Labor (including EEOC, Fair Labor Standards Act, labor-management relations, NLRB, OSHA). Office: Apruzzese McDermott Mastro & Murphy PO Box 112 25 Independence Blvd Liberty Corner NJ 07938 E-mail: vapruzzese@excite.com.

APUZZO, ERNESTO, lawyer; b. Rome, July 1, 1971; s. Mario Oriolo Apuzzo and Cristina Haver. Trainee Insom Pamphili-Codacci Pisa New, Rome, 1995—98; jr. assoc. Simmons & Simmons, Rome, 1998—99, assoc., 2000—. Scholar Jemolo Found. scholar in law, Italy, 1997. Mergers and acquisitions, Corporate, general, Commercial, contracts (including sales of goods; commercial financing). Office: Simmons & Simmons Via Barnaba Oriani 85 00197 Rome Italy

AQUILINO, THOMAS JOSEPH, JR., federal judge, law educator; b. Mt. Kisco, N.Y., Dec. 7, 1939; s. Thomas Joseph and Virginia Burr (Doughty) A.; m. Edith Luise Berndt, Oct. 27, 1965; children: Christopher T., Philip A., Alexander B. Student, Cornell U., 1957-59, U. Munich, 1960-61; BA, Drew U., 1962; postgrad., Free U., Berlin, 1965-66; JD, Rutgers U., 1969. Bar: N.Y. 1972, U.S. Dist. Ct. (so., ea. and no. dists.) N.Y. 1973, U.S. Ct. Appeals (2nd cir.) 1973, U.S. Supreme Ct. 1976, U.S. Ct. Appeals (3rd cir.) 1977, Interstate Commerce Commn. 1978, U.S. Ct. Claims 1979, U.S. Ct. Internat. Trade 1984. Law clk. to judge U.S. Dist. Ct. (so. dist.) N.Y., N.Y.C., 1969-71; atty. Davis Polk & Wardwell, N.Y.C., 1971-85; judge U.S. Ct. Internat. Trade, N.Y.C., 1985—. Adj. prof. law Benjamin N. Cardozo Sch. of Law, 1984-95; mem. bd. visitors Drew U., 1997—. With U.S. Army, 1962-65. Mem. N.Y. State Bar Assn., Fed. Bar Coun. Roman Catholic. Avocations: sports, travel, linguistics, cinema. Office: US Ct Internat Trade 1 Federal Plz New York NY 10278-0001

AQUIRRE ANGUIANO, SERGIO SALVADOR, judge; b. Mexico, Feb. 1, 1943; Grad., U. Autonoma de Guadalajara. Councilman City of Guadalajara, 1985—86; prof. law dept. U. Panamericana, 1988—89; min. Supreme Ct. Justice, Mexico City. Office: Suprema Corte de Justicia de la Nacion Pino Suarez No 2 Col Centro 06065 Mexico City Mexico*

ARABIAN, ARMAND, arbitrator, mediator, lawyer; b. N.Y.C., Dec. 12, 1934; s. John and Aghavnie (Yalian) A.; m. Nancy Arabian, Aug. 26, 1962; children: Allison Ann, Robert Armand. BSBA, Boston U., 1956, JD, 1961; LLM, U. So. Calif., L.A., 1970; LLD (hon.) (hon.) , Southwestern Sch. Law, 1990, Pepperdine U., 1990, U. West L.A., 1994, We. State U., 1997, Thomas Jefferson Sch. of Law, 1997, Am. Coll. Law, 2001. Bar: Calif. 1962, U.S. Supreme Ct. 1966. Dep. dist. atty. L.A. County, 1962-63; pvt. practice law Van Nuys, Calif., 1963-72; judge Mcpl. Ct., L.A., 1972-73, Superior Ct., L.A., 1973-83; assoc. justice Calif. Ct. Appeal, L.A., 1983-90, Supreme Ct. Calif., San Francisco, 1990-96; ret., 1996. Adj. prof. sch. law Pepperdine U., 1996—. Contbr. 1st lt. U.S. Army, 1956-58. Recipient Stanley Lintz Meml. award San Fernando Valley Bar Assn., 1986, Lifetime Achievement award San Fernando Valley Bar Assn., 1993; Outstanding Jurist of the Yr., Malibu Bar Assn., 1996; Pappas Disting. scholar Boston U. Sch. Law, 1987; Justice Armand Arabian Resource and Comm. Ctrs. named in honor of Van Nuys and San Fernando Calif. Courthouses, 1999; Mekhitar Gosh medal Pres. of Armenia Robert Kocharian, 2001, St. James the Apostle medal Beatitude Torkom Manoogian, Jerusalem, 2001, Mesrob Mashdots medal Aram I Catholicos, Beirut, Lebanon, 1999, Mekhitar medal Brotherhood in Venice, Italy, 1999, Gold medal of honor of Peter the Great, Russian Acad. Sci., 1999, Albert Einstein Gold medal of honor, Russian Acad. Natural Scis., 2003. Republican. Office: 6259 Van Nuys Blvd Van Nuys CA 91401-2711 Fax: 818-781-6002. E-mail: honarabian@AOL.com.

ARAI, YUKI, lawyer; b. Sapporo, Japan, Aug. 23, 1976; s. Ryoichi Arai and Hideko; m. Kyoko Masuda, Mar. 21, 2002; 1 child, Kaisei. LLB, Tokyo U., 1999. Bar: Tokyo. Atty. Tokyo Eiwa Attys. at Law, 2000—. Spkr. in field. Mem.: Intellectual Property Assn. Japan. Avocations: movies, scuba diving, skiing, music, golf. Corporate taxation, Intellectual property, Product liability. Home: Nishi-Azabu 3-17-31-401 Minato ward Tokyo 106-0031 Japan Office: Tokyo Eiwa Attys at Law Shiuwakamiyacho Bldg 6F Toranomon 4-3-13 Minato ward Tokyo 105-0001 Japan Fax: +81-3-5405-7795. E-mail: ya-eiwa@bc.iij4u.or.jp.

ARAMBURU, JOHN RICHARD, lawyer; b. Spokane, Wash., Mar. 8, 1945; s. Victor B. Aramburu and Virginia (Westacott) Scarpelli; m. Lesa Rae French, Aug. 23, 1991. BA, U. Wash., 1967, JD, 1970. Bar: Wash. 1970, U.S. Dist. Ct. (we. dist.) Wash. 1970, U.S. Ct. Appeals (9th cir.) 1970, U.S. Dist. Ct. (ea. dist.) Wash. 1973. Assoc. Irving M. Clark, Jr., Seattle, 1970-78; prin. Law Offices of J. Richard Aramburu, Seattle, 1978—. Author: Real Property Deskbook, 1985, rev. edit., 1996. Bd. dirs. Allied Arts of Seattle, 1987-89; legal chair Wash. Environ. Coun., Seattle, 1982-88. Mem. Wash. State Bar (chairperson CLE com. 1977, chairperson environ. and land use law sect. 1978), Avocations: squash, skiing, river rafting. Land use and zoning (including planning), Natural resources, Property, real (including real estate development, water). Office: Law Offices of J Richard Aramburu 505 Madison St Ste 209 Seattle WA 98104-1138

ARANT, EUGENE WESLEY, lawyer; b. North Powder, Oreg., Dec. 21, 1920; s. Ernest Elbert and Wanda (Haller) A.; m. Juanita Clark Flowers, Mar. 15, 1953; children: Thomas W., Kenneth E., Richard W. BS in Elec. Engring, Oreg. State U., 1943; JD, U. So. Calif., 1949. Bar: Calif. 1950. Mem. engring. faculty U. So. Calif., 1947-51; pvt. practice L.A., 1950—51; patent atty. Hughes Aircraft Co., Culver City, Calif., 1953-56; pvt. practice L.A., 1957—2001, Lincoln City, Oreg., 2001—. Author articles. Mem. La Mirada (Calif.) City Council, 1958-60; trustee Beverly Hills Presbyn. Ch., 1976-78. Served with AUS, 1943-46, 51-53. Mem. ABA, Am. Intellectual Property Law Assn., State Bar Calif., Univ. Club Santa Barbara, Lincoln City Rotary. Democrat. Patent, Trademark and copyright. Home: 100 NE Indian Shores Lincoln City OR 97367 Office: Lincoln Tech Bldg Lincoln City OR 97367 E-mail: gwapat@wcn.net.

ARATAKE, JUNICHI, lawyer; b. Japan, Oct. 1, 1956; LLB, Keio Gijuku U., Tokyo, 1980; LLM, Columbia U., 1996. Lawyer Sakura Kyodo Law Offices, Tokyo. Author: Civil Law, 1993, Internet and Copyright, 1997, Internet Business Law, 1997. Mem.: ABA, Tokyo Bar Assn. Office: Sakura Kyodo Law Offices Yamato Seimei Bldg 16F 1-1-7 Uchisaiwaicho Chiyoda-ku Tokyo 100-0011 Japan

ARBIT, BERYL ELLEN, legal assistant; b. L.A., Aug. 16, 1949; d. Harry A. and Norma K. (Michelson) A. BA, UCLA, 1970. From legal asst. to sr. legal asst. O'Melveny & Myers, LLP, L.A., 1977—. Guest lectr. atty. asst. tng. program UCLA, 1991. Mem. UCLA Atty. Asst. Alumni Assn. (bd. dirs. 1980-82), Alpha Omicron Pi (treas. Greater L.A. alumnae chpt. 1993—), Nu Lambda (corp. bd. pres. 1978-80, chpt. adv. 1976-78). Avocations: travel, theater, needlework, bridge. Office: O'Melveny & Myers LLP 400 S Hope St Los Angeles CA 90071-2899 E-mail: barbit@omm.com.

ARBOLEYA, CARLOS JOAQUIN, lawyer, broker; b. Havana, Cuba, Aug. 16, 1958; came to U.S., 1960; s. Carlos Jose and Marta Aurora (Quintana) A. ABA, Miami Dade C.C., 1977; BBA in Fin., U. Miami, 1980, MBA in Fin., 1981, JD, 1987. Bar: Fla. 1989, U.S. Ct. Appeals (D.C. cir.) 1990. From teller to br. mgr. Barnett Bank South Fla. N.A., North Miami Beach, 1975-84; realtor, assoc. Cervera Real Estate, 1980—; pres. Owner's Box Promotions, 1993-95; owner Carlos J. Arboleya, Jr., P.A., Coconut Grove, 1988—. Adv. bd. Exec. Nat. Bank, 1994—, Linda Ray Infant Ctr., 1990—; mem 20th Anniversary Grand Prix of Miami com., 2002; bd. dirs. Pvt. Industry Coun. Jobs for Miami; Hispanic adv. com. U. Miami Sports Mktg., 1992—95. Bd. dirs. Greater Miami Tennis Found., 1995, U. Miami Ear Inst., 1993; vice chma. planning adv. bd. City of Miami, 1993-95, 98-99, chmn. 1995-98, chmn. code enforcement bd., 1990-91, vice chmn. 1989-90; asst. scoutmaster Boy Scouts Am.; participant joint civilian orientation conf. U.S. Dept. Def., 1995; pres. Cocogrove Villas Condominium Assn., 1998—; trustee United Way, Miami-Dade, 2000-01. Named One of 12 Good Men of Miami, Ronald McDonald House, 2000-01. Mem. ABA, Nat. Soc. Hispanic MBAs, Nat. Eagle Scout Assn., Cuban Am. Bar Assn., Builders Assn. South Fla., Am. Title Ins. Co., Attys. Title Ins. Fund, Inc., Fla. Bar Assn., Latin Bus. Assn., Latin Builders Assn., Hispanic Law

Students Assn., Coral Gables C. of C., Greater Miami C. of C. (sports coun., chmn., homestead motorsports complex com., 1994-97, co-chmn. existing events com., 1992-94), Leadership Miami (exec. com. 1990-93, task force 1984-88, Coconut Grove Jaycees, Phi Delta Phi, Delta Sigma Pi (Outstanding Alumni award 1982). Republican. Roman Catholic. Banking, Corporate, general, Property, real (including real estate development, water). Office: Carlos J Arboleya Jr PA 2550 S Dixie Hwy Coconut Grove FL 33133-3137

ARBUZ, JOSEPH ROBERT, lawyer; b. N.Y.C., Nov. 23, 1949; s. Jose Hernan Cortes and Rachel Dweck Arbuz; m. Millicent Luck Fornah July, 1978 (div.); 1 child, Christina. BA, Fla. State U., 1972, MS in Pub. Adminstrn., 1975; JD, Howard U., 1977; MDiv, Southwestern Bapt. Sem., 1981; postgrad. in theology, Westminster Theol. Sem., 1995; D Divinity, Cohen U. & Theol. Sem., 2000. Bar: Fla. 1978, U.S. Ct. Mil. Appeals 1983, U.S. Dist. Ct. (so. dist.) Fla. 1986, U.S. Ct. Appeals (11th cir.) 2000, U.S. Supreme Ct., 2000; lic. min. So. Bapt. Ch., 1983—. EEO investigator Smithsonian Instn., Washington, 1985; asst. atty. gen. Atty. Gen., Miami, Fla., 1986; pvt. practice Miami, Fla., 1987-90, Miami Beach, Fla., 1994—. Evangelism Gambrell St. Bapt. Ch., Ft. Worth, 1980; pastor Biscayne Bapt. Ch., Miami, 1989; choir mem. U. Bapt. Ch., Coral Gables, Fla., 1994-97; performer Miami Christmas Pageant, Miami, 1994, 96. 1st lt. Signal Corps., U.S. Army, 1972-74; capt. USAF, 1982-84. J.F.K. Tchg. scholar Miami-Dade C.C., Miami, 1969. Mem. Am. Immigration Lawyer's Assn., Atty. Title Ins. Fund, South Fla. Hispanic C. of C., Dade County Bar Assn., Lions Club, Delta Theta Phi. Democrat. Presbyterian. Avocations: exercise, theatre, reading, church activities. General practice, Immigration, naturalization, and customs, Personal injury (including property damage). Office: 80 SW 8th St Ste 2000 Miami FL 33130 Fax: 305-675-0190. E-mail: joearbuz@aol.com.

ARCHER, DENNIS WAYNE, lawyer, former mayor; b. Detroit, Jan. 1, 1942; s. Ernest James and Frances (Carroll) A.; m. Trudy Ann DunCombe, June 17, 1967; children: Dennis Wayne, Vincent DunCombe BS, Western Mich. U., 1965; JD, Detroit Coll. Law, 1970; LLD (hon.), Western Mich. U., 1987, Detroit Coll. Law, 1988, U. Detroit, 1988, John Marshall Law Sch., 1991, Gonzaga U., 1991, U. Mich., 1994; D in Pub. Svc. (hon.), Ea. Mich. U., 1994. Bar: Mich. 1970. Tchr. spl. edn. Detroit Bd. Edn., 1965-70; assoc. Gragg & Gardner, 1970-71; ptnr. Hall, Stone, Allen, Archer & Glenn, P.C., 1971-73, Charfoos, Christensen & Archer, P.C., 1973-85; assoc. justice Mich. Supreme Ct., 1986-90; ptnr. Dickinson, Wright, Moon, Van Dusen & Freeman, Detroit, 1991-93; chmn. Dickinson Wright PLLC; mayor City of Detroit, 1994—2001. Assoc. prof. Detroit Coll. Law, 1972-78; adj. prof. Wayne State U. Law Sch., Detroit, 1984-85; mem. Mich. Bd. Ethics, 1979-83; mem. adv. bd. U.S. Conf. Mayors, 1994—; bd. dirs. Nat. Conf. Black Mayors, 1994—; mem. intergovtl. policy adv. com. U.S. Trade Rep.; bd. dirs. Covisint, Compuware, Johnson Controls, Inc. Contbr. articles to legal jours. Bd. dirs. Legal Aid and Defenders Assn., Detroit, 1980-82, Nat. Conf. Black Mayors, 1994, CATCH, Henry Ford Health Sys.; co-chmn. Met. Detroit Cmty. Coalition for Dems., 1979-80; bd. trustees Olivet Coll., 1991-93; active numerous local Dem. campaigns, 1970-85; host local pub. svc. radio programs; co-chair platform com. Dem. Conv., 1996; pres. Nat. Conf. Dem. Mayors, 1996; mem. Nat. Com. on Crime Control and Prevention, 1995. Named Most Respected Judge in Mich. Mich. Lawyers Weekly Jour., 1990. Mem. ABA (ho. dels. 1979-93, chmn. drafting com. 1986-88, com. on scope and correlation of work sect. officers liaison 1987-90, chmn. gen. practice sect. 1987-88, chair commn. on opportunities for minorities in the profession 1987-91, sect. legal edn. and admissions to the bar, coun. mem. 1989-95, task force on profl. skills instrn. 1989-91, task force on law schs. and the profession, Narrowing The Gap, 1989-91, chmn. spl. com. prepaid legal svcs. 1981-83, chmn. sect. officers conf. 1988-90, resource devel. coun. 1988-91, bd. editors ABA Jour. 1988-94, bd. editors The Practical Litigator 1989-94, chmn. rules and calendar com. 1990-92, state del. 1990-96, pres. 2003), ATLA, Nat. Bar Assn. (pres. 1983-84), Am. Judicature Soc. (bd. dirs 1977-81), State Bar Mich. (pres. 1984-85), Wolverine Bar Assn. (pres. 1979-80), Detroit Bar Assn. (bd. dirs. 1973-75), Mich. Trial Lawyers Assn. (exec. bd. 1973-74), Econ. Club, Alpha Phi Alpha. Roman Catholic.

ARCHER, JAMES G. lawyer; b. San Antonio, Tex., Jan. 16, 1936; BA, U. Ill., 1957, LLB, 1959. Bar: Ill. 1960, N.Y. 1994. Ptnr. Sidley & Austin Brown & Wood, N.Y.; ret. Mem. State bd. acctg. examiners, 1976-78. Mem. Order of Coif. Private international, Mergers and acquisitions. Office: Sidley Austin Brown & Wood 10 S Dearborn St Chicago IL 60603

ARCHER, MARY ANN ELIZABETH, law librarian; b. Rochester, NY, Mar. 7, 1930; d. Samuel Colin Culley and Florence Mae Witherell; m. H. Brent Archer, Sept. 25, 1954; children: Michael, Moire, Christopher. BS magna cum laude, SUNY, Geneseo, 1953, MSLS, 1976; JD magna cum laude, William Mitchell Coll. Law, 1990. Bar: Minn. 90. Sr. info. analyst Eastman Kodak, Rochester, NY, 1967—85; county law libr. Dakota County, Hastings, Minn., 1992—2000; assoc. dir. Warren E. Burger Libr. William Mitchell Coll. Law, St. Paul, 2000—. Mem. adv. bd. Inverhills Paralegal Program, Invergrove Heights, Minn., 1996—; chmn. info. dissemination com. Counsel of Chief Judges, St. Paul, 1996—98. Mem.: Minn. State Bar Assn. (co-chmn. prose program com. 1990—2002, Law Librarianship award 2000), Am. Assn. Law Librs. Office: William Mitchell Coll Law Warren E Burger Libr 871 Summit Ave Saint Paul MN 55105 E-mail: marcher@wmitchell.edu.

ARCHER, MICHAEL DALE, lawyer; b. Marietta, Ohio, Mar. 23, 1975; s. David Michael and Arlene Marie Archer; m. Stacy Marie Handschumacher, May 5, 2001. BA summa cum laude, Marietta Coll., 1997; JD magna cum laude, U. Notre Dame, 2000. Bar: Ohio 2000. Counsel Baker & Hostetler LLP, Columbus, Ohio, 2000—. Mem.: ABA, Columbus Bar Assn., Ohio State Bar Assn. Avocation: truck and tractor pulling. Corporate, general, Mergers and acquisitions. Home: 80 Highland Hollow Dr Pataskala OH 43062 Office: Baker & Hostetler LLP 65 E State St Ste 2100 Columbus OH 43215

ARCHER, RICHARD JOSEPH, lawyer; b. Virginia, Minn., Mar. 24, 1922; s. William John and Margaret Leanore (Duff) A.; m. Kristina Hanson, Jan. 29, 1977 (dec.); children: Alison P., Cynthia J. AB, U. Mich., 1947, JD, 1948. Bar: Calif. 1949, U.S. Supreme Ct. 1962, Hawaii 1982. Partner firm Morrison and Foerster, San Francisco, 1954-71, Sullivan, Jones and Archer, San Francisco, 1971-81, Archer Rosenak & Hanson, San Francisco, 1981-85, Archer & Hanson, San Francisco, 1985—. Served with USN, 1942-45. Decorated Bronze Star. Mem. ABA, Am. Bar Found. (life), Am. Law Inst. (life). Republican. Home: 3110 Bohemian Hwy Occidental CA 95465-9113 Office: Mauka Tower Ste 2920 737 Bishop St Honolulu HI 96813-3201

ARCHIBALD, JAMES KENWAY, lawyer; b. Mass., Mar. 29, 1949; s. John Lawrence and Jean (Kenway) A.; m. Joanne Mary Ricciuti, Aug. 16, 1975; children: Kathryn, John. BA, Johns Hopkins U., 1971; JD, U. Md., 1975. Bar: Md. 1975, D.C. 1985, U.S. Dist. Ct. Md. 1976, U.S. Ct. Appeals (4th cir.) 1978, U.S. Supreme Ct. 1979, U.S. Ct. Appeals (9th cir.) 1984, Maine 1998. Assoc. Venable, Baetjer and Howard, Balt., 1975-83, ptnr., 1983—. Co-author: Pleading Causes of Action in Maryland, 1990, Model Witness Examinations, 1997. Chmn. bd. trustees Md. State Colls. and Us., 1984-86; trustee Johns Hopkins U., 1997-2000; bd. dirs. Roland Park Country Sch., Inc., Balt., 1989-94; pres. Homeland Assn., Inc., Balt., 1990. Recipient Disting. Svc. award Litigation Sect. Md. State Bar, Md., 1981. Mem. ABA (litigation sect., co-chair com. 1987-2002), Internat. Assn. Def. Counsel, Def. Rsch. Inst. (Exceptional Performance award 1989, Md. state chair 1989-93), Md. Assn. Def. Trial Counsel (pres. 1988-89), Johns Hopkins Alumni Coun. (v.p. 1996-98, pres. 1998-2000), Johns Hopkins Second Decade Soc. (nat. chair 1989-91), Am. Law Inst. General civil litigation, Personal injury (including property damage), Product liability. Home: 13037 Jerome Jay Dr Cockeysville MD 21030-1523 Office: Venable Baetjer & Howard 1800 Mercantile Bank Bldg 2 Hopkins Plz Ste 2100 Baltimore MD 21201-2982 E-mail: jkarchibald@venable.com.

ARCONTI, RICHARD DAVID, lawyer; b. Danbury, Conn., Nov. 16, 1952; s. Gino Joseph and Patricia Helen (Olmstead) A.; m. Deborah Ann Wolter, Sept. 10, 1983; children: Meghan Phelan, Richard Joseph. BA, U. Notre Dame, 1974; JD, U. Conn., 1977. Bar: Conn. 1977, U.S. Dist. Ct. Conn. 1977. Assoc. Nahley and Sullivan, Danbury, Conn., 1977-78; asst. states atty. State's Attys. Office Jud. Dist. Danbury, 1978-84; ptnr. Secor, Cassady & McPartland, P.C., Danbury, 1984; adj. prof. Western Conn. State U., Danbury, 1989—93; ptnr. Pinney, Payne, Van Lenten, Burrell, Wolfe & Dillman PC, Danbury. Chmn. West Conn. State U. Found.; dir. ARC, 1990—. Mem. ATLA, Conn. Bar Assn., Conn. Trial Lawyers Assn., Danbury Bar Assn. (pres.), Nat. Bd. Trial Adv. (diplomate 1984-94). Democrat. Roman Catholic. Avocations: baseball, golf, boating. Criminal, Personal injury (including property damage). Home: 15 Raquel Dr Danbury CT 06811-3205 Office: Pinney Payne Van Lenten Burrell Wolfe & Dillman PC 83 Wooster Heights Rd Danbury CT 06810-7538

ARCURI, SHIRLEY COPELAND, lawyer; b. Gadsden, Ala., June 25, 1949; d. Milton Wiley Jr. and Freda (White) Copeland; m. Joseph Arcuri, Mar. 11, 1973. BA, Auburn U., 1970, MA, 1972; JD, U. Va., 1977. Bar: U.S. Dist. Ct. (mid. dist.) Fla. 1979, U.S. Ct. Appeals (5th and 11th cirs.) 1979, U.S. Supreme Ct. 1988. Law clk. U.S. Bankruptcy Ct., Tampa, Fla., 1978-79; assoc. Straske, Farfante, Segall & Arcuri, Tampa, 1979-81, ptnr., 1981-90; pvt. practice Tampa, 1990—. Mem. LWV, Fla. Assn. Women Lawyers (treas. 1987-88, 91-92), Hillsborough Assn. for Women Lawyers (pres. 1983), Tampa Bay Bankruptcy Bar Assn. (dir. 1988-92, sec. 1991-92), Hillsborough County Bar Assn. (chmn. corp., banking and bus. law com. 1991-92). Democrat. Episcopalian. Avocations: travel, snow skiing. Bankruptcy. Office: Shirley C Arcuri PA 4830 W Kennedy Blvd Tampa FL 33609-2564

ARDALAN, PEZHMAN CHRISTOPHER, lawyer; b. Tehran, Iran, Aug. 26, 1973; arrived in U.S., 1977; s. Ali and Jessica Ardalan; m. Anavelle Ardalan, July 3, 1996; children: Ethan, Devin. BA cum laude, Calif. State U. Northridge, 1996; JD cum laude, Loyola Law Sch., L.A., 2000. Bar: Calif. 2000, U.S. Dist. Ct. (cen., ea., so. and no. dists) Calif. 2000, U.S. Ct. Appeals 2000. Paralegal, counsel Law Offices of Robert J. Vars, Encino, Calif., 1996—2000; counsel, pres. Vars & Ardalan PLC, Encino, 2001—02, Ardalan & Assocs. PLC, Sherman Oaks, Calif., 2002—. Commr. San Fernando Valley Pub. Safety Commn., Van Nuys, Calif., 2001—. Mem.: ATLA, ABA, Consumer Attys. Assn. L.A. Avocations: basketball, dancing, tutoring. Criminal, Family and matrimonial, Personal injury (including property damage). Office: Ardalan & Assocs PLC 15303 Ventura Blvd Ste 400 Sherman Oaks CA 91403

ARDERY, PHILIP PENDLETON, lawyer; b. Lexington, Ky., Mar. 6, 1914; s. William Breckenridge and Julia (Spencer) A.; m. Anne Stuyvesant Tweedy, Dec. 6, 1941; children: Peter Brooks (dec.), Philip Pendleton, Jr., Joseph Lord Tweedy, Julia Spencer. AB, U. Ky., 1935; JD, Harvard U., 1938; MBA, U. Louisville, 1957. Bar: Ky. 1938. Practice law, Frankfort, 1938-40, 45-50, Louisville, 1952—; ptnr. Frost Brown Todd, 1972—. Sec. Ky. Aero. Commn., 1946-48; commr. Jefferson County, 1958-61 Author: Bomber Pilot: A Memoir of World War II, 1978, Heroes and Horses, Tales of the Bluegrass, 1996; also articles. Bd. dirs. Frazier Rehab. Ctr., 1953-93, Schizophrenia Found., Ky., 1981—, Thomas D. Clark Found., 1994—, Nat. Alliance Rsch. in Schizophrenia and Depression, 1985-92, Norton Hosp. Found., 1985-94, Ky. Mental Health Assn., 1985—, Jewish Hosp. Healthcare Svcs., 1986—, Ky. Shakespeare Festival, 1989-90, Ky. Humanities Coun., 1989-94; pres. Ky. Heart Assn., 1955, chmn. bd., 1956; incorporator, dir. Ballet Español, 1984—; chmn. bd. Am. Heart Assn., 1966-69; dep. Episcopal Gen. Convs., 1970, 73, 76, 79; mem. exec. com. Ky. Hist. Soc., 1983-95; trustee U. of South, 1977-80, Episcopal Theol. Sem. in Ky., 1985-90; sec. Ky. Horse Park Found., 1985—. Col. USAAF, 1940-45, col. USAF, 1950-52, maj. gen. USAFR, ret., 1974—. Decorated Silver Star, D.F.C. (2), Air medal (4); Croix de Guerre with palm (France) Mem. ABA, Ky. Bar Assn., Louisville Bar Assn., Soc. Cin., Order First Families of Va. (Burgess), Pendennis Club, Filson Club (bd. dirs. 1986-96), Phi Beta Kappa. Democrat. Episcopalian. Home: 448 Swing Ln Louisville KY 40207-1444 Office: 3200 Providian Ctr Louisville KY 40202-2873

AREEN, JUDITH CAROL, law educator, university dean; b. Chgo., Aug. 2, 1944; d. Gordon Eric and Pauline Jeanette (Payberg) A.; m. Richard M. Cooper, Feb. 17, 1979; children: Benjamin Eric (dec.), Jonathan Gordon AB, Cornell U., 1966; JD, Yale U., 1969. Bar: Mass. 1970, D.C. 1972. Program planner for higher edn. Mayor's Office City of N.Y., 1969-70; dir. edn. voucher study Ctr. for Study Pub. Policy, Cambridge, Mass., 1970-72; mem. faculty Georgetown U., Washington, 1971—, assoc. prof. law, 1972-76, prof., 1976—, prof. cmty. and family medicine, 1980-89, assoc. dean Law Ctr., 1984-87; dean, exec. v.p. for law affairs Georgetown U, Washington, 1989—. Gen. counsel, project coord. Office Mgmt. and Budget, Washington, 1977—80; spl. counsel White House Task Force on Regulatory Reform, Washington, 1978—80; cons. NIH, 1984, NRC, 1985; bd. dirs. Kroll, Inc. Author: Youth Service Agencies, 1977, Cases and Materials on Family Law, 4th edit., 1999, Law, Science and Medicine, 1984, 2d edit., 1996. Mem. Def. Adv. Com. Women In Svcs., Washington, 1979-82; trustee Cornell Univ., 1997-2001. Woodrow Wilson Internat. Ctr. for Scholars fellow, 1988-89, Kennedy Inst. Ethics Sr. Rsch. fellow, Washington, 1982—. Mem. ABA, D.C. Bar Assn., Am. Law Inst. E-mail: areen@law.georgetown.edu.

ARENSON, GREGORY K. lawyer; b. Chgo., Feb. 11, 1949; s. Donald L. and Marcia (Terman) A.; m. Karen H. Wattel, Sept. 4, 1970; 1 child, Morgan Elizabeth. BS in Econs., MIT, 1971; JD, U. Chgo., 1975. Bar: Ill. 1975, U.S. Dist. Ct. (no. dist.) Ill. 1975, N.Y. 1978, U.S. Dist. Ct. (so. and ea. dists.) N.Y. 1978, U.S. Supreme Ct. 1985, U.S. Ct. Appeals (2nd cir.) 1987, U.S. Dist. Ct. (ctrl. dist.) Ill. 1995, U.S. Ct. Appeals (7th cir.) 1997. Assoc. Rudnick & Wolfe, Chgo., 1975-77, Schwartz, Klink & Schreiber P.C., N.Y.C., 1977-81, ptnr., 1982-87, Proskauer, Rose, Goetz & Mendelsohn, N.Y.C., 1987-93, Kaplan Fox & Kilsheimer LLP, N.Y.C., 1993—. Mediator U.S. Dist. Ct. (so. dist.) N.Y., 1993—; mem. MIT Corp., 1997—2002; mem. corp. devel. com. MIT, 1994—, mem. alumni/ae fund bd., 1989—, chair, 1994—96; mem. adv. bd. Fed. Discovery News, 1999—. Co-editor: Federal Rules of Civil Procedure, 1993 Amendments, A Practical Guide, 1994; contbr. articles to profl. jours. Mem. ABA, N.Y. State Bar Assn. (comml. and fed. litigation sect., chair com. on discovery 1989-97, chair com. fed. procedure 1997—), N.Y. Bar Found., Assn. Bar City N.Y Antitrust, Federal civil litigation, Securities. Home: 125 W 76th St Apt 2A New York NY 10023-8334 Office: Kaplan Fox & Kilsheimer LLP 805 3d Ave New York NY 10022-7513

ARENT, ALBERT EZRA, retired lawyer; b. Rochester, N.Y., Aug. 25, 1911; s. Hyman J. and Sarah (Weller) A.; m. Frances Feldman, Nov. 23, 1939; children: Stephen Weller, Margery Arent Safir. AB, Cornell U., 1932, LL.B., 1935. Bar: N.Y. 1935, D.C. 1945. Rsch. asst. N.Y. State Law Revision Commn., 1934; atty. U.S. Bur. Internal Revenue, 1935-39; spl. asst. to Atty. Gen. U.S., 1939-44; chief trial atty. Alien Property Unit, U.S. Dept. Justice, 1942-44; pvt. law practice specializing in taxation; ptnr. firm Arent, Fox, Kintner, Plotkin and Kahn and (predecessor firms), Washington, 1944-86; counsel, 1986—2003; lectr. taxation Am. U., 1948-52; prof. taxation Georgetown Law Sch., 1951-73; ret. Also lectr. tax subjects before Practising Law Inst., NYU, U. Chgo. tax insts., Am., Fed., various local and state bar assns.; prosecuted leading fgn. agt. registration act cases, World War II.; chmn. adv. coun. Cornell Law Sch., 1979-82 Contbr. articles to legal publs. Vice pres. Jewish Cmty. Coun. of Greater Washington, 1953-57, pres., 1957-61; chmn. Commn. on Social Action of Reform Judaism, 1973-77; chmn. Cornell Law Sch. Fund, 1975-77; mem. steering com. Nat. Urban Coalition, 1970-77, mem. exec. com., 1970-72; mem. governing bd. and exec. com. Common Cause, 1970-72; bd. dirs. Overseas Edn. Fund of LWV, 1961-79; vice chmn. Nat Jewish Cmty. Rels. Adv. Coun., 1967-70, chmn., 1970-73; vice chmn. Conf. Pres.'s Major Jewish Orgns., 1970-73; trustee Cornell U., 1978-83, trustee emeritus, 1983— ; 1st v.p. Washington Hebrew Congregation, 1978-80; v.p. United Jewish Appeal Fedn. Greater Washington, 1979-81. Recipient Stephen S. Wise medallion award Nat. Capital chpt. Am. Jewish Congress, 1965, Vicennial medal Georgetown U., 1971, Humanitarianism award B'nai Brith, 1975, Disting. Alumnus award Cornell U. Law Sch., 1982, award for outstanding svc. Overseas Edn. Fund, 1983, Disting. Svc. award Washington Lawyers Com. for Civil Rights Under Law, 1987, Judge Learned Hand award Am. Jewish Com., 1991. Mem. ABA, Am. Law Inst., Fed. Bar Assn., D.C. Bar Assn., Telluride Assn., Phi Beta Kappa, Phi Kappa Phi. Home: 6620 Boca Del Mar Dr Apt 608 Boca Raton FL 33433-5718

ARESTY, JEFFREY M. lawyer; b. Framingham, Mass., Dec. 31, 1951; s. Victor Joseph and Pola (Granek) A.; m. Ellen Louise Gould, Aug. 15, 1976; children: Joshua, Abigail, Joanne. BA, Johns Hopkins U., 1973; JD, Boston U., 1976, LLM in Taxation, 1978, LLM in Internat. Banking, 1993. Bar: Mass. 1977, D.C. 1982. Tax specialist Coopers & Lybrand, Boston, 1976-78; assoc. Meyers, Goldstein & Crossland, Brookline, Mass., 1978-79; ptnr. Crossland, Aresty & Levin, Boston, 1979-87, Aresty & Levin, Boston, 1987-91, Aresty Internat. Law Offices, Boston, 1992—. Cons. editor Tax Shelter Investment Rev., 1981-85. Recipient Disting. Achievement award Boston Safe Deposit and Trust, 1976, Grad. Banking Alumni Achievement award Boston U. Law Sch., 1993. Mem. ABA (membership chmn. 1981-84, coun. 1985-91, vice chmn. computer divsn. 1985-90, reporter e lawyering 1999—, chmn. internat. interest group 1992-96, chmn. internat. negotiations task force 1992-96, chmn. Mass. membership com. 1985-91, internat. law sect., chair law practice com. 1995-98, co-editor ABA Guide Internat. Bus. Negotiations 1994-2000, prodr. ABA/AT&T CD-Rom on Cross-Cultural Comm. 1997, chmn. task force on e-commerce, 2002—), Am. Bar Found. (standing com. tech. and info. systems 1998-99, pub. bd. gen. practice 1998—), Mass. Bar Assn. (bd. dels., exec. com. 1981-83, chmn. law practice sect. 1983-85), Mass. Bar Found. Alternative dispute resolution, Computer, Private international. Home: 35 Three Ponds Rd Wayland MA 01778-1732 Office: Aresty Internat Law Offices Bay 107 Union Wharf Boston MA 02109 E-mail: jaresty@abanet.org.

ARIAS, RAMON RICARDO, lawyer; b. Panama, Panama, June 8, 1963; s. Jaime Alberto Arias and Mirella Porras; m. Hildegard Vasquez, Feb. 22; children: Magdalena, Alicia. BA, Georgetown U., 1987; JD, Tulane U., 1989. Bar: Panama 1993. Assoc. Galileo Arias & Lopez, Panama, 1989—98, ptnr., 1998—. Mem. World Heritage Commn., Panama, 1995, Fundacion Chicanto, 1995—. Roman Catholic. Avocation: historic preservation. Mergers and acquisitions, Corporate, general, Commercial, contracts (including sales of goods; commercial financing). Office: Galineo Arias & Lopez PO Box 8629 Panama 5 Panama Fax: 507 263 5335. E-mail: rrarias@gala.com.pa.

ARIS, JOHN LYNNWOOD, lawyer; b. Ann Arbor, Mich., Dec. 5, 1965; s. Leslie Lynnwood and Virginia Baldwin A.; m. Lana Marie Howe, Sept. 2, 1995; children: Mark Benjamin, Amy Lynne, Ashley Marie. BA in Econs., Coll. William and Mary, 1988; JD, U. Mich., 1991. Bar: Pa. 1991, U.S. Dist. Ct. (ea. dist.) Pa. 1992, U.S. Ct. Appeals (3rd cir.) 1993. Assoc. Duane, Morris LLP, Phila., 1991—2002, Lowenthal & Abrams, P.C., Bala Cynwyd, Pa., 2002—. Mem. Vols. for Indigent, Phila., 1991-96; home meeting leader Living Word Cmty., Phila., 1994-95, 1997-99. Mem.: Pa. Trial Lawyers Assn. Avocations: Bible, tennis, softball, trumpet. General civil litigation, Insurance, Personal injury (including property damage). Office: Lowenthal & Abrams PC 555 City Line Ave Ste 440 Bala Cynwyd PA 19004

ARKIN, MICHAEL BARRY, lawyer, arbitrator, writer; b. Washington, Jan. 11, 1941; s. William Howard and Zenda Lillian (Liebermann) A.; children and stepchildren: Tracy Renee, Jeffrey Harris, Marcy Susan, Chatom Callan, Michael Edwin, Samuel Hopkins, Brandon Maddox, Jessica Remaley, Brandi Remaley, Casey Remaley; m. Laura Dorene Haynes, Aug. 16, 1998. AA, George Washington U., 1961; BA in Psychology, U. Okla., 1962, JD, 1965. Bar: Okla. 1965, U.S. Ct. Claims 1968, U.S. Supreme Ct. 1968, Calif. 1970, U.S. Tax Ct. 1970, U.S. Ct. Appeals (3d, 5th, 6th, 9th, 10th cirs.) 1970, U.S. Dist. Ct. (cen. dist.) Calif. 1970, U.S. Dist. Ct. (so. dist.) Calif. 1970, U.S. Dist. Ct. (ea. dist.) Calif. 1987. Trial atty. tax divsn. U.S. Dept. Justice, 1965-68, appellate atty., 1968-69; ptnr. Surr & Hellyer, San Bernardino, Calif., 1969-79; mng. ptnr. Wied, Granby Alford & Arkin, San Diego, 1979-82, Lorenz Alhadeff Fellmeth Arkin & Multer, San Diego, 1982, Finley, Kumble, Heine, Underberg, Manley & Casey, San Diego, 1983; pvt. practice Sacramento and San Andreas (Calif.), 1984-86; ptnr. McDonough Holland & Allen, Sacramento, 1986-87; pvt. practice San Andreas, Calif., 1987—; chief counsel Calaveras County Child Protective Svcs., 1996—2002; hearing officer Calif. Spl. Edn. Hearing Office, McGeorge Sch. Law, U. Pacific, 2002—. Judge pro-tem Calaveras County (Calif.) Consol. Cts., 1999-2002. Author: History of the Bench and Bar of Calaveras County California, 1997—. Bd. dirs. San Bernardino County Legal Aid Soc., 1971-73, sec., 1971-72, pres., 1973; mem. Calaveras County Adv. Com. on Alcohol and Drug Abuse, 1985-94, pres., 1991-92; treas. Calaveras County Legal Assistance Program, 1987—; trustee Calaveras County Law Libr., 1987-98; bd. dirs. Mark Twain Hosp. Dist., 1990-2003, treas., 1994—; mem. Calaveras County Rep. Ctrl. Com., 1990-92, 94-96; Calaveras County chmn. Wilson for Gov., 1994. Named to Hon. Order of Ky. Cols., 1967. Mem. ABA, Calif. Bar Assn. (Wiley F. Manuel pro bono pub. svc. award 1991), San Diego County Bar Assn., San Bernardino County Bar Assn. (bd. dirs., sec.-treas. 1973-75, pilot drug abuse program 1970), Calaveras County Bar Assn. (bd. dirs., v.p. 1988-90, pres. 1990-95), Am. Arbitration Assn. (arbitrator 1987—). Jewish. Corporate taxation, Estate taxation, Personal income taxation. Home: 10675 Kate Vincent Ct Nevada City CA 95959 Office: McGeorge Sch Law U of Pacific 3200 5th Ave Sacramento CA 95817 E-mail: markin2500@aol.com.

ARKIN, STANLEY S. lawyer; b. L.A., Feb. 28, 1938; s. Jerome and Lillian (Rogo) A.; m. Suzanne Arkin, Mar. 3, 1963; children: Adam Arkin, Alexander Arkin, Anthony Arkin. AB, U. So. Calif., 1959; JD cum laude, Harvard U., 1962. Bar: N.Y. 1964, Calif. 1977, D.C. 1982. Sr. ptnr. Stanley S. Arkin, P.C., N.Y.C., 1969-90, Chadbourne & Parke, N.Y.C., 1990-93, Arkin Kaplan, LLP (formerly Arkin Kaplan & Cohen LLP), N.Y.C., 1994—; chmn. Arkin Group LLC (pvt. intelligence agy.), 2000—. Author: (with Matthew Bender) Business Crime, 1982, (with Matthew Bender) Hi Tech Crimes, 1989; columnist, contbr. articles to newspapers and profl. jour. With JAGC U.S. Army, 1962—68. Fellow Am. Coll. Trial Lawyers; mem. Coun. on Fgn. Rels., Phi Beta Kappa. General civil litigation, Criminal, Securities. Office: Arkin & Kaplan LLP 590 Madison Ave 35th Fl New York NY 10022

ARKOZ, DAVID X. lawyer; b. N.Y.C., Aug. 22, 1951; s. Sherlock M. and Mycrofta (Romanov) A.; children: Jean Valjean, D'Artagnan. BA in French Lit., U. Sorbonne, Paris, 1976; BA, U. Calif., Berkeley, 1980, JD, 1986; PhD in Poetry (hon.), Harvard U., 1989. Bar: Calif. 1987, U.S. Dist. Ct. (no., ctrl., so. dists.) Calif. 1987, U.S. Ct. Appeals (9th cir.) 1987. Pvt. practice, L.A., 1987—; judge pro tem L.A., Glendale, 1996—. Contbr. articles and poetry to lit. jours. Mem. Calif. Trial Lawyers Assn., L.A. Trial

Lawyers Assn, Litigations Round Table. Constitutional, Intellectual property, Personal injury (including property damage). Address: 2272 Colorado Blvd # 1228 Los Angeles CA 90041-1143 Fax: 323-344-8594.

ARLEN, JENNIFER HALL, law educator; b. Berkeley, Calif., Jan. 7, 1959; d. Michael John and Ann (Warner) A.; m. Robert Lee Hotz, May 21, 1988; children: Michael Arlen Hotz, Robert Arlen Hotz. BA, Harvard U., 1982; JD, NYU, 1986; PhD in Econs., NYU, 1992, 1992. Bar: N.Y. 1987, U.S. Ct. Appeals (11th cir.) 1987. Summer clk. U.S. Dist. Ct. (ea. dist.) N.Y., Bklyn., 1984; summer assoc. Davis Polk & Wardwell, N.Y.C., 1985; law clk. U.S. Cir. Judge, 11th cir., Savannah, Ga., 1986-87; asst. prof. law Emory U., Atlanta, 1987-91, assoc. prof. law, 1991-93; prof. law U. So. Calif., L.A., 1994—2002, Ivadelle and Theodore Johnson prof. law and bus., 1997—2002; prof. law NYU, 2002—. Vis. prof. law U. So. Calif., 1993, Calif. Inst. Tech., winter, 2001, Yale U., 2001—02; dir. U. So. Calif. Ctr. in Law, Econs. and Orgn., 2000—02; mem. acad. bd. NYU Ctr. in Law and Bus., 2003—. Olin fellow U. Calif. Sch. Law, Berkeley, 1991. Mem. ABA, Am. Assn. Law Schs. (chair remedies sect. 1994, chair elect 1993, mem. exec. com. 1990-91, 95, chair torts sect. 1995, chair-elect 1994, treas. 1991, sec. 1992-93, exec. com. bus. assns. sect. 1995-96, 2000—, chair law and econ., sect. 1996, chair-elect law and econs. sect. 1995, chair 1996), Am. Law and Econ. Assn. (bd. dirs. 1991-93, program com. 1999), Am. Econ. Assn., Order of Coif, Am. Law Inst. Democrat. Office: NYU Law Sch 40 Washington Square S New York NY 10012

ARMBRECHT, WILLIAM HENRY, III, retired lawyer; b. Mobile, Ala., Jan. 13, 1929; s. William Henry and Katherine (Little) A.; m. Dorothy Jean Taylor, Sept. 1, 1951; children— Katherine Handley, William Taylor, Alexander Paterson. BS, U. Ala., 1950, JD, 1952. Bar: Ala. 1952, U.S. Supreme Ct. 1972. Assoc. Inge, Twitty, Armbrecht & Jackson, Mobile, 1952-56; ptnr. Armbrecht, Jackson, McConnell & DeMouy, Mobile, 1956-65, Armbrecht, Jackson & DeMouy, Mobile, 1965-75, Armbrecht, Jackson, DeMouy, Crowe, Holmes & Reeves, Mobile, 1976-94, Armbrecht, Jackson, DeMouy, Crowe, Holmes & Reeves, LLC, 1994-96. Served to 1st lt. JAGC, AUS, 1952-54. Mem. ABA, Ala. Bar Assn. (chmn. grievance com. 1973-74, chmn. sect. corp. banking and bus. law 1976-78), Mobile Bar Assn., Mobile Area C. of C. Found. (bd. dirs. 1990-92), Southeastern Corp. Law Inst. (mem. planning com. 1967-96), Phi Delta Phi, Delta Kappa Epsilon Episcopalian. Oil, gas, and mineral, Estate planning, General practice. Home: 600 Fairfax Rd E Mobile AL 36608-2931

ARMESTO, ANA, lawyer; b. Bilbao, Spain, Feb. 7, 1956; d. Ramon Armesto and Ana Campo; m. Francisco de la Peña; children: Jon, Martin. Law Degree in econ., U. Duesto, Bilbao, 1978. Bar: Vizcaya 1987, Madrid 1991. Ptnr. Garrigues Abogados y Asesores Tributarios, Bilbao, 1992—. Mem.: Asociacion de Empresarias y Directivas de Bizcaia (bd. mem. 2000—), Confederacion Española Directivos y Ejecutivos (bd. mem. 2001—), Madrid Bar Assn., Vizcaya Bar Assn., Club Financiero de Bilboa (pres. 2001—). Avocations: reading, swimming, gardening. Corporate, general, Finance, Commercial, contracts (including sales of goods; commercial financing). Office: Garrigues Abogados Rodriguez Arias P 15 4o 48008 Bilbao Spain

ARMOUR, GEORGE PORTER, lawyer; b. Bryn Mawr, Pa., June 10, 1921; s. Charles Joseph and Florence (Eagle) A.; m. Isabel Blondet, Nov. 22, 1958; children: Luis O., Carlos O. BA, Temple U., 1943, JD, 1949. Bar: Pa. 1949, N.Y. 1969, Calif. 1975. Assoc. Bennett & Bricklin, Phila., 1949-59; atty. Atlantic Richfield Co., 1959-83; gen. atty. Phila., 1965-68; assoc. gen. counsel Phila., N.Y.C., L.A., 1968-78; dep. gen. counsel L.A., 1978-83; pvt. practice law, 1983—. Chmn. Internat. and Comparative Law Ctr., Southwestern Legal Found., Dallas, 1980-82. Mem. Assocs. Calif. Inst. Tech., 1981—; mem. Soc. of Fellows Huntington Libr. and Art Gallery, San Marino, Calif., 1982—. With USAAF, 1943-46. Mem. ABA, Calif. Bar Assn., Valley Hunt Club (Pasadena). Republican. Episcopalian. Corporate, general, Oil, gas, and mineral, Private international. Home and Office: 481 S Orange Grove Blvd Apt 4 Pasadena CA 91105-1798

ARMOUR, JAMES LOTT, lawyer; b. Jackson, Tenn., May 19, 1938; s. Quintin and Frances (Breeden) A.; m. Nancy Stokes Johnson, Mar. 17, 1962; 1 son, John Lawson. BA, Vanderbilt U., 1961, LLB, 1964; LLM, So. Meth. U., 1967. Bar: Tenn. 1964, Tex. 1965, U.S. Supreme Ct. 1967, N.Y. 1969, Okla. 1972. Assoc. firm Turner Rodgers Winn Scurlock & Terry, Dallas, 1965-67; internat. atty. Mobil Corp., N.Y.C. and London, 1967-71, Phillips Petroleum Co., Bartlesville, Okla., 1971-74; asst. gen. counsel Conoco, Inc., Stamford, Conn., 1974-83; ptnr. firm Locke Liddell & Sapp LLP, Dallas, 1984-2001; pvt. practice James L. Armour Atty. at Law, Dallas, 2001—. Mem. adv. bd. oil and gas SW Legal Found., chair, 1996-99; mem. Dallas Com. on Fgn. Rels.; former mem. alumni bd. Vanderbilt Law Sch. Mem. ABA, Assn. of Bar of City of N.Y., State Bar Tex., Dallas Bar Assn., Petroleum Club, Phi Delta Phi, Kappa Sigma. Episcopalian. FERC practice, Oil, gas, and mineral, Private international. Home: 4541 Belfort Pl Dallas TX 75205-3618 Office: Law Offices of James L Armour Ste 2460 325 N St Paul St Dallas TX 75201-3864 Fax: 214 999 0603. E-mail: jlarmour@jlarmourlaw.com.

ARMSTRONG, ALAN LEIGH, lawyer; b. L.A., Apr. 25, 1945; s. Don Leigh and Barbara Caroline (Hayes) A.; m. Margie Jean Lehner, July 1, 1972; children: Don Leigh, Mark Leigh. BA, U. Calif., Riverside, 1967; JD, Western State U., Fullerton, Calif., 1984. Bar: Calif. 1984, U.S. Dist. Ct. (cen. dist.) Calif. 1985, U.S. Ct. Appeals (9th cir.) 1985, U.S. Tax Ct. 1987, U.S. Dist. Ct. (so. dist.) Calif. 1995, U.S. Dist. Ct. (no. and ea. dists.) Calif. 2002, U.S. Supreme Ct. 1988. Physicist USN, Pomona, Calif., 1967-74, engr. Seal Beach, Calif., 74-93; pvt. practice Alan Leigh Armstrong, Atty. At Law, Huntington Beach, Calif., 1985—. Adj. prof. law Trinity Law Sch., 1992—. Lay reader St. James Episcopal Ch., Newport Beach, Calif., 1991—; vestryman St. Joseph's Episcopal Ch., Buena Park, Calif., 1985-88; cubmaster Boy Scouts Am., Huntington Beach, 1988-92, asst. scoutmaster, 1992-94, com. chair, 1994-97, com. mem. 1998—. Mem. Christian Legal Soc. Republican. Avocations: sailing, automatic musical instrument collecting. Bankruptcy, Estate planning, Probate (including wills, trusts). Office: Alan Leigh Armstrong Atty At Law 18652 Florida St Ste 225 Huntington Beach CA 92648-6007 E-mail: alan@alanarmstrong.com.

ARMSTRONG, ARTHUR JOHN, lawyer; b. El Dorado, Ark., Aug. 22, 1941; s. Arthur John and Christine (Greer) Armstrong; m. Anne Alexander Armstrong, June 6, 1970; children: Katherine Reid, Ross Jefferies. BA cum laude, Vanderbilt U., 1963; JD, U. Va., 1972; LLM summa cum laude, George Washington U., 1976. Bar: Va. 1972, D.C. 1983, Marshall Islands 1984. Commd. ensign USN, 1963, advanced through grades to comdr., 1978; negotiator, counselor Exec. Office of Pres., Washington, 1977—83; ptnr. Stovall, Spradlin, Armstrong & Israel, Washington, 1983—86, Van Ness, Feldman, Sutcliffe & Curtis, 1986—89, Dorsey & Whitney, 1989—93, Armstrong PC, McLean, Va., 1993—. Legal cons. Pres.'s Com. on Marijuana and Drug Abuse, Washington, 1972—73; legal adviser Task Force on Indochinese Evacuation, Guam, 1975—76; bd. dirs. ASI, Ltd., Newgen Software Inc. Author: The Renewable Energy Policy Manual, 2000; contbr. articles to profl. jours. Vestry mem. St. Michael's Episcopal Ch., Arlington, Va., 1996—2002. Mem.: Fed. Bar Assn., Nat. Lawyers Club. Episcopalian. Corporate, general, Private international, Natural resources. Office: Armstrong et al Beverly Rd Ste 300 Mc Lean VA 22101

ARMSTRONG, EDWIN ALAN, lawyer; b. Atlanta, June 20, 1950; s. Carl Edwin and Betty (Hawkins) A.; m. Marlene Bryant, Aug. 12, 1978. BA, Berry Coll., 1972; JD, Emory U., 1976. Bar: Ga. 1976, U.S. Dist. Ct. (no. dist.) Ga. 1977, U.S. Ct. Appeals (5th cir.) 1981, U.S. Ct. Appeals (11th cir.) 1982, U.S. Supreme Ct. 1989, U.S. Dist. Ct. (so. dist.) Ga., U.S. Ct. Appeals (4th cir.), U.S. Ct. Appeals (D.C. cir.) 1992, U.S. Ct. Appeals (6th cir.) 1992, U.S. Dist. Ct. (mid. dist.) Ga 1992. Atty. Flynt Jud. Cir. Pub. Defenders Office, McDonough, Ga., 1976-77; assoc. Neely, Neely & Player, Atlanta, 1977; pvt. practice, Atlanta, 1977-79, 81—; assoc. Stolz, Shulman & Loveless, Atlanta, 1979-81. Contbr. articles to profl. jours. Mem. ABA (forum com. on air and space law, tort and ins. practice sect.), ATLA, Atlanta Bar Assn., Decatur-DeKalb Bar Assn., State Bar Ga. (chmn. aviation law sect. 1998—), Ga. Trial Lawyers Assn., Nat. Transp. Safety Bd. Bar Assn. (founding, com. legis. and regulatory activity 1989—, editor newsletter 1991-92), Lawyer-Pilots Bar Assn. Episcopalian. Avocation: flying. Aviation, Personal injury (including property damage), Product liability. Home: 4098 Northlake Creek Cv Tucker GA 30084-3416 E-mail: alan@alanarmstronglaw.com.

ARMSTRONG, JACK GILLILAND, lawyer; b. Pitts., Aug. 10, 1929; s. Hugh Collins and Mary Elizabeth (Gilliland) A.; m. Ellen Lee Gliem, June 10, 1951 (dec.); children: Thomas G., Elizabeth Armstrong Pride; m. Elizabeth Lacewell White, Mar. 27, 1993. AB, U. Mich., 1951, JD, 1956. Bar: Pa. 1956, Mich. 1956, U.S. Supreme Ct. 1968, Fla. 1981. Assoc. Buchanan, Ingersoll, Rodewald, Kyle & Buerger, Pitts., 1956-65; ptnr. Buchanan, Ingersoll, P.C., Pitts., 1965-90, counsel, 1990-94, of counsel, 1995, Rothman Gordon, P.C., 1996—. Dir. SSS Mgmt. Corp., Greer, S.C.; trustee Union Dale Cemetery, 1972—, pres., 1992-95. Dir. Sigma Nu Ednl. Found., 1998-2001. Lt. U.S. Army, 1951-53. Mem. Pa. Bar Assn. (real property, probate, and trust law sect., mem. coun. 1981-84, treas. 1985, vice chmn. probate divsn. 1986-88, chmn. 1988-89, tax law sect.), Fla. Bar (real property, probate and trust law sect., tax sect.), Allegheny County Bar Assn. (probate and trust law), Palm Beach County Bar Assn., Estate Planning Coun. Pitts., Am. Coll. Trust and Estate Counsel (Pa. state chmn. 1990-95), Am. Coll. Tax Counsel, U. Mich. Alumni Assn. (Disting. Alumni Svc. award 1981), Order of Coif, Duquesne Club, Univ. Club (pres. 1988-89), St. Clair Country Club, Town Club Jamestown, The Little Club, Delray Beach Club, Chautauqua Golf Club, Pine Tree Golf Club, Masons, Shriners, Jesters, Phi Alpha Delta, Signa Nu. Home: Dorchester # 6N 200 N Ocean Blvd Delray Beach FL 33483 E-mail: jgarmstrong@rothmangordon.com.

ARMSTRONG, REX, judge; b. Salem, Oreg., Feb. 25, 1950; s. Edwin Hamilton and Alice (McLaughlin) A.; m. Leslie McKay Roberts, Oct. 20, 1984; children: Iain McKay, Morgan McKay, Kyle MeiKai, Aeron MeiKai, Greer MeiKai. BA, U. Pa., 1974; JD, U. Oreg., 1977. Bar: Oreg. 1977, U.S. Dist. Ct. Oreg. 1978, U.S. Ct. Appeals (9th cir.) 1978, U.S. Supreme Ct. 1980. Law clk. U.S. Atty. for Oreg., Portland, 1975-77, Oreg. Supreme Ct., Salem, 1977-78; assoc. Lindsay, Hart et al., Portland, 1978-81, Kell, Alterman & Runstein, Portland, 1982-85, Bogle & Gates, Portland, 1986-94; judge Oreg. Ct. of Appeals, Salem, 1995—. Adj. prof. Northwestern Sch. Law, Portland, 1987, Willamette U. Coll. Law., Salem, Oreg., 1978; mem. Oreg. Rules of Appellate Procedure Com., Salem, 1991-94. Mem. editl. bd. Western Legal History, Pasadena, Calif., 1987-94. Recipient Hugh M. Hefner First Amendment award Playboy Found., 1988. Avocations: skiing, hiking, mountain climbing, reading. Office: Oreg Ct of Appeals 1162 Court St NE Salem OR 97301

ARMSTRONG, RICHARD CHARLES, lawyer; b. Roanoke, Va., Dec. 1, 1961; s. Charles Samuel and Mary Lee Armstrong; m. Andrea Leeds, June 27, 1993; children: Emma, Teddy. BA, U. Va., 1984, JD, 1987. Bar: NY 1987, Va. 2000, D.C. 2000. Staff atty. Legal Aid Soc., N.Y.C., 1987—97, supervising atty., 1997—2000; mem. clin. faculty U. Va. Sch. Law, Charlottesville, 2000—02; ptnr. Wyatt & Armstrong, Charlottesville, 2002—. Civil rights, Criminal, Personal injury (including property damage). Office: Wyatt & Armstrong 300 Court Sq Charlottesville VA 22902

ARMSTRONG, TIMOTHY JOSEPH, lawyer; b. Atlanta, June 17, 1945; BA, Dartmouth Coll., 1967; JD, U. Ga., 1970. Bar: Ga. 1970, Fla. 1971. Law clk. Hon. David W. Dyer, U.S. Ct. Appeals (5th cir.), Miami, 1970-71; assoc. Batchelor, Brodnax, Guthrie & Kindred, Miami, 1971-75; ptnr. Batchelor, Brodnax, Guthrie & Primm, Miami, 1975-83, Armstrong & Mejer, 1983—. Contbr. articles to profl. jours. Mem. ABA, Fed. Bar Assn., Fla. Bar Assn., Ga. Bar Assn., Dade County Bar Assn., Maritime Law Assn U.S., Am. Judicature Soc., Internat. Assn. Def. Counsel Admiralty, Appellate, Federal civil litigation. Office: Douglas Centre 2600 S Douglas Rd Miami FL 33134-6127

ARNASON, JOEL FREDERICK, lawyer; b. Grand Forks, N.D., Nov. 11, 1955; s. A. Fred and Helen M. (Rousseau) A.; m. Laurie J. Steinbar, July 30, 1983; children: Joel William, Ann Carroll, Patrick John, James Frederick. BA in Govt., Harvard U., 1978; JD, U. N.D., 1981. Bar: N.D. 1981, Minn. 1982, U.S. Dist. Ct. N.D. 1981, U.S. Ct. Appeals (8th cir.) 1988, U.S. Dist. Ct. Minn. 1992. Pvt. practice, Grand Forks, 1981—. Bd. dirs. Red River Valley chpt. ARC, 1987-93, 2000—, YMCA, Grand Forks, 1988—; mem. exec. bd. No. Lights coun. Boy Scouts Am. Mem. ABA, N.D. Bar Assn., Minn. Bar Assn., K.C., Delta Theta Phi (N.D. chancellor 1983—). Roman Catholic. Avocations: marathon running, road racing. Criminal, General practice, Personal injury (including property damage). Office: 215 S 4th St Grand Forks ND 58201-4737

ARNICK, JOHN STEPHEN, lawyer, legislator; b. Balt., Nov. 27, 1933; s. John and Josephine (Gaillardo) A. BS, U. Balt., 1956; LLD, U. Balt. Law Sch., 1961. Bar Assn. U.S. Marine Corps., 1956-59; magistrate Balt. County, 1966-67; del. Md. Gen. Assembly, Annapolis, 1967-79, 87-94, 1994—; atty. pvt. practice, Balt., Md., 1962—; del. Md. Gen. Assembly, Annapolis, 1983—. Mem. Twin Dist. Dem. Club, Battle Grove Dem. Club, Sons of Italy. Mem. Ea. Balt. C. of C., Moose Lodge, New 7th Dem. Club, South East Dem. Club. Democratic. Roman Catholic. Criminal, General practice, Personal injury (including property damage). Home: 7918 Diehlwood Rd Baltimore MD 21222-3316 Office: 6914 Holabird Ave Baltimore MD 21222-6914

ARNKRA, JOE, legal administrator, writer; b. Newark, Jan. 3, 1960; s. Sam F. and Jill E. Arnkra. BS in Fin., UCLA, 1990. Legal adminstr., Santa Monica, Calif., 1990—; writing cons., trainer, 1990—. Demorat. Roman Catholic. Avocations: freelance writing, skydiving, spelunking, cross-country and super marathon races. Office: 2272 Colorado Blvd # 1228 Los Angeles CA 90041-1143 Fax: 310-559-2603.

ARNOLD, ALANNA S. WELLING, lawyer; b. Canton, Ohio, Jan. 13, 1951; d. Coen Edward and Clara M. Welling; m. Jack Mitchell Arnold, Aug. 28, 1971; children: Cassandra L., Shanna R. BA in Sociology magna cum laude, Kent State U., 1980, MA in Applied Sociology, 1981; JD, Loyola Law Sch., New Orleans, 1991. Instr. Phillips Jr. Coll., New Orleans, 1988-90; jud. extern U.S. Ct. (ea. dist.) La., New Orleans, 1990-91; ptnr. Milling, Benson, Woodward LLP, New Orleans, 1991—2000, John Brooks Cameron & Assocs., 2000—03. Independent contractor/rschr. Case Western Reserve. Contbr. articles to profl. jours.; mem. Loyola Law rev., 1989-91. Mem. bd. Medina City YWCA, 2000-. Scholarship Gordon, Arrata McCullom, 1989-90, Outstanding scholarship Kent State U., 1980. Mem. ATLA, Ohio Assn. Trial Attys., Ohio Bar Assn., Medina City Bar Assn., Bar Applicants Admission Commn. Democrat. Avocations: painting (watercolor), reading, movies, theatre, travel. Environmental, Labor (including EEOC, Fair Labor Standards Act, labor-management relations, NLRB, OSHA), Toxic tort. Office: 200 Glenshire Ln Medina OH 44256 Business E-Mail: ASWA@earthlink.net.

ARNOLD, C. JEFFERY, judge, educator; b. Albuquerque, Dec. 16, 1943; AB, Coll. William & Mary, 1966; JD, Fla. State U., 1969. Bar: Fla. 1969, U.S. Dist. Ct. (mid. dist.) Fla. 1969, U.S. Ct. Appeals 1969, U.S. Dist. Ct. (so. dist.) Fla. 1981, U.S. Dist. Ct. (no. dist.) Fla. 1981. Law clk. to atty. gen. State of Fla., Tallahassee, 1969; assoc. Arnold, Matheny & Eagan, P.A., Orlando, Fla., 1969—70, 1972—75, ptnr., shareholder, 1975—88; ptnr. Foley & Lardner, Orlando, 1988—90; ptnr., stockholder Anderson & Rush, P.A., Orlando, 1991—94; judge Orange County 9th Jud. Cir., Orlando, 1994—. Mem. revision 7, comm. adv. group Fla. Supreme Ct., 2002—; presiding judge state finals Fla. HS Mock Trial Competition, 2002; lectr. in field. Asst. coach Winter Pk. Little League, 1975—76; mem. Brookshire Elem. Sch. PTA, 1980—88, bd. dirs., 1984—88, pres., 1993—94; participant Habitat for Humanity, 1996—; bd. dirs. Orange County Civic Facilities Authority, 1980—87; mem. DUI adv. com. Nat. Safety Coun., 1996—; bd. dirs. Waterbridge Homeowners Assn., Inc., 1984—87, pres., 1986. Capt. U.S. Army, 1970—72. Recipient Outstanding Evaluation award, Ctrl. Fla. Criminal Def. Attys. Assn., 1995—2000, Personal Committment to Victims of Crime award, Victim Svcs. Coalition Ctrl. Fla., 2001. Fellow: ATLA; mem.: Orange County Legal Aid Soc. (trustee 1984—86, teen ct. 1995—, night ct. 1996—, Dedicated Svc. award 1984), Conf. County Ct. Judges Fla. (mem. criminal law com. 1995—, mem. edn. com. 1995—, mem. delphi com. 1998—2000, bd. dirs. 1998—, rep. 9th jud. cir. 1998—2002, vice chmn. 1999—2000, chmn. 1999—2000, 1999—2000, vice chmn. 2001—02, pres. elect 2002—, Disting. Leadership award 1999, 2000, Harvey Ford award 2002), Orange County Bar Assn. (chmn. atty.'s fees com. 1979—81, sec. 1981—83, bd. dirs., mem. exec. coun. 1981—86, v.p. 1983—84, pres. 1984—85, chmn. jud. rels. com. 2001—02, award of Merit 1980, named Oustanding Com. Chmn. 1981), Fla. Bar. (vice chmn. 9th jud. cir. grievance com. 1979—82, del. All Bar Conf. 1989, chmn. voluntary bar liaison com. 1991—92, chmn. statewide law day com. 1992), Coll. William and Mary Alumni Assn. (bd. dirs. ctrl. Fla. chpt. 1990—, v.p. 1992—93), Rotary (mem. Sidewalk Art Festival 1996—, mem. Gateway Sch. Beautification Project 1997). Republican. Presbyterian. Office: Orange County Ct Ho 425 N Orange Ave Orlando FL 32801 Office Fax: 407-835-5145. Business E-Mail: ctjujaz@ocnjcc.org.

ARNOLD, FRED ENGLISH, lawyer; b. Mexico, Mo., May 10, 1938; s. Charles P. and Mary E. (Blackman) A.; m. Dorothy P. Offutt, Dec. 31, 1966 (div. Aug. 2002); children: Jane E., Charles P. III, Susan J. AB, Harvard U., 1960, LLB, 1963. Bar: Mo. 1963, U.S. Dist. Ct. (ea. dist.) Mo. 1964, U.S. Supreme Ct. 1966. Assoc. Thompson Coburn LLP, St. Louis, 1964-70, ptnr., 1971—. Trustee KETC/Channel 9, 2002—. Trustee Mary Inst., St. Louis, 1981-87, v.p., 1985-86; bd. dirs. Repertory Theatre of St. Louis, 1982-88; bd. dirs. Whitfield Sch., St. Louis, 1990-96, pres., 1991-93, Arts & Edn. Coun. Greater St. Louis, 1991-97, vice chmn., 1996-97; adv. com. Jordan Charitable Found., St. Louis, 1975—; bd. curators Ctrl. Meth. Coll., Fayette, Mo., 1997—. Mem. ABA, Am. Coll. Real Estate Lawyers, Noonday Club, (bd. govs. 2003—), The Racquet Club. Democrat. Methodist. Corporate, general, Property, real (including real estate development, water). Home: 750 S Hanley Rd Unit 190 Saint Louis MO 63105 Office: Thompson Coburn LLP One US Bank Plz Saint Louis MO 63101-1693 E-mail: farnold@thompsoncoburn.com.

ARNOLD, HARRY H., III, university adminstrator; b. Oklahoma City, Jan. 28, 1930; s. Harry H. and Lucille Lackey A.; m. Anne Morrison, Aug. 3, 1952; children— Harry H. IV, Mary Elizabeth, Daniel Steven, Tracy. B.A., U. Colo., 1952, LL.B., 1955. Bar: Colo. 1955. Staff asst. indsl. relations C F & I Steel, Pueblo, Colo., 1957-59, asst. supt., 1959-62, asst. sec., Denver, 1962-67, mgr. employee relations and communications, 1967-70, mgr. labor relations and personnel, 1970; dir. deferred giving U. Colo., Boulder, 1970-73, exec. sec. bd. regents, 1973—92, ret., 1993. Chmn., Boulder Housing Authority, 1981-82. Served to 1st lt. USMC, 1955-57. Recipient Alumni Recognition award U. Colo. Alumni Assn., 1965, Robert L. Stearns award, 1980. Republican. Presbyterian. Club: Rotary (Boulder, Colo.). Home: 260 Inca Pky Boulder CO 80303-3516

ARNOLD, JAMES MICHAEL, lawyer; b. Sikeston, Mo., Nov. 3, 1964; s. James Marion and Fleta Jo Arnold. BSBA, S.E. Mo. State, 1987; JD, U. Mo., 1991. Bar: Md. State prosecutor Jackson County, Kansas City, Mo., 1991—96; atty. Covington & Burling, Washington, 1996—2002, Dept. of Justice, Washington, 2002—. Pres. Coll. Reps., Cape Girardeau, Mo., 1986. Mem.: KC. Home: 2902 Greenwich Ct Crofton MD 21114 Office: Dept of Justice 1100 L St NW Washington DC 20005 Business E-Mail: j.michael.arnold@usdoj.gov.

ARNOLD, JOHN FOX, lawyer; b. St. Louis, Sept. 17, 1937; s. John Anderson and Mildred Chapin (Fox) A.; m. Martha Ann Freeman, June 29, 1963 (div. Oct. 1993), m. Ann Ruwitch, Mar. 3, 2003; children: Lisa A. Galena, Laura Wray, Lynne A. Binder, Lesli Johnston. AB, U. Mo., 1959, LLB, 1961. Bar: Mo. 1961, U.S. Dist. Ct. (ea. dist.) Mo. 1961, U.S. Ct. Appeals (8th cir.) 1961, U.S. Supreme Ct. 1971. Ptnr. Green, Hennings, Henry & Arnold, St. Louis, 1963-70; mem. Lashly & Baer, P.C., St. Louis, 1970—, chmn., 1987—. Mem. St. Louis County (Mo.) Charter Revision Com., 1968; chmn. St. Louis County Bd. Election Commrs., 1981—86; chmn. bd. dirs. Downtown St. Louis Inc., 1996—98, Downtown St. Louis Partnership, Inc., 1997—99; chmn. bd. overseers Lindenwood U., 1992—93, bd. dirs., 1993—95. Lt. USAR, 1961—63. Recipient citation of merit U. Mo. Law Sch., Columbia, 1984. Fellow Am. Bar Found.; mem. ABA (mem. house of dels. 1986-90), Bar Assn. Met. St. Louis (pres. 1975-76), Mo. Bar (pres. 1984-85), Nat. Conf. Commrs. on Uniform State Laws (drafting com. Securities Act, Partnership Act, article 2 sales, 2A leases and 8 investment securities of Uniform Comml. Code), Am. Law Inst. Republican. Government contracts and claims, Municipal (including bonds), Securities. Office: Lashly & Baer 714 Locust St Saint Louis MO 63101-1699 E-mail: jfarnold@lashlybaer.com.

ARNOLD, MORRIS SHEPPARD, judge; b. Texarkana, Tex., Oct. 8, 1941; BSEE, U. Ark., 1965, LLB, 1968; LLM, Harvard U., 1969, SJD, 1971; MA (hon.) , U. Pa., 1977, JD (hon.) , 1986; LLD (hon.) , U. Ark., Little Rock, 1968, U. Pa., 1985. Tchg. fellow law Harvard U., 1969-70; from asst. prof. to prof. Ind. U. Law Sch., 1971-76, prof., 1976-77, dean, 1985; prof. law, history U. Pa., 1977-81; Ben J. Altheimer disting. prof. law U. Ark., Little Rock, 1981-84; judge U.S. dist. Ct. (we. dist.) Ark., Ft. Smith, 1985-92, U.S. Cir. Ct. (8th cir.), 1992—. Vis.fellow commoner Trinity Coll., Cambridge U., 1978; v.p., dir. office of the pres. U. Pa., 1980—81; vis. prof. Stanford (Calif.) U. Law Sch., 1985. Author: Old Tenures and Natura Brevium, 1974, Yearbook 2 Richard II, 1378-79, 1975, On the Laws and Customs of England, 1980, Unequal Laws Unto a Savage Race, 1985, Select Cases of Trespass from the King's Courts, 1307-1399, 2 vols., 1985, 1987, Arkansas Colonials, 1986, Colonial Arkansas 1686-1804: A Social and Cultural History, 1991, The Rumble of a Distant Drum: Quapaws and Old World Newcomers, 1673-1804, 2000, Arkansas: A Narrative History, 2002. Chmn., Rep. party State of Ark., 1983; gen. counsel, Rep. party Ark., 1982, chmn., 1983; bd. dirs. Nature Conservancy of Ark., 1982—87, Ark. Arts Ctr., 1981—84. Decorated chevalier Ordre Palmes Acad., France; recipient Porter Literary prize, 2001, Worthen Literary prize, 2001, Ragsdale prize, 2001; Frank Knox fellow, Harvard U./U. London, 1970—71, Mus. Sci. Natural History fellow, 1986. Fellow: Am. Soc. Legal History (hon.; pres. 1981—85); mem.: Am. Antiquarian Soc., Country Club of Little Rock, Union League Club of Phila., Athenaeum Club London. Office: US Cir Judge 600 W Capital Ave Rm 208 Little Rock AR 72203-2060

ARNOLD, RICHARD SHEPPARD, federal judge; b. Texarkana, Tex., Mar. 26, 1936; s. Richard Lewis and Janet (Sheppard) Arnold; m. Gale Hussman, June 14, 1958 (div.); children: Janet Sheppard, Arnold Hart, Lydia Palmer, Arnold Turnipseed; m. Kay Kelley, Oct. 27, 1979. BA summa cum laude, Yale U., 1957; LLB magna cum laude, Harvard U., 1960; LLD, U. Ark., 1992, U. Richmond, 1998. Bar: Ark. 1960, D.C. 1961. Pvt. practice, Washington, 1961—64, Texarkana, Ark., 1964—74; law clk. to justice Brennan U.S. Supreme Ct., 1960—61; assoc. Covington & Burling,

1961—64; ptnr. Arnold & Arnold, 1964—74; legis. sec. Gov. of Ark., 1973—74, staff coord., 1974; legis. asst. Senator Bumpers of Ark., Washington, 1975—78; judge U.S. Dist. Ct. (ea. and we. dists.) Ark., 1978—80, U.S. Ct. Appeals (8th cir.), Little Rock, 1980—2001, chief judge, 1992—98; sr. judge, 2001—. Part-time instr. U. Va. Law Sch., 1962—64; mem. Ark. Constl. Revision Study Commn., 1967—68; chair spl. redaction rev. panel Jud. Conf. of the U.S., 2000—; vice chair Com. on the Jud. Br., 2001—; disting. vis. prof. law So. Meth. U. Law Sch., 2001. Case editor: Harvard Law Rev., 1959—60; contbr. articles to profl. jours. Gen. chmn. Texarkana United Way Crusade, 1969—70; pres. Texarkana Cmty. Chest, 1970—71; mem. vis. com. Harvard Law Sch., 1973—79, U. Chgo. Law Sch., 1983—86, 1994—97; mem. Com. on Legis. Orgn., 1971—72; trustee U. Ark., 1973—74; chmn. budget com. Conf. of U.S., 1987—96; del. Dem. Nat. Conv., 1968, Ark. Constl. Conv., 1969—70; candidate for Congress 4th Dist. Ark., 1966, 1972; chmn. rules com. Ark. Dem. Com., 1968—74, mem. exec. com., 1972—74. Recipient Award of the Women Lawyers' Assn. of Greater St. Louis, 1998, Edward J. Devitt Disting. Svc. to Justice award, 1999, Meador-Rosenberg award, Standing Com. on Fed. Jud. Improvements of the ABA, 1999. Fellow: Am. Bar Found.; mem.: Jud. Conf. U.S. (exec. com. 1992—98), Am. Law Inst. (coun.), Cum Laude Soc., Phi Beta Kappa. Episcopalian. Office: 600 W Capitol Ave Ste 208 Little Rock AR 72201-3321 also: Thomas F Eagleton US Cthse 111 S 10th St Rm 26 325 Saint Louis MO 63102

ARNOLD, W. H. (DUB ARNOLD), state supreme court chief justice; b. Arkadelphia, Ark., May 19, 1935; m. Betty Earlene Aud; three children. BA, Henderson State U., 1957; LLB, Ark. Law Sch., 1962. Dep. prosecuting atty. Clark County, Ark., 1965-66; prosecuting atty. 8th Jud. Dist., State of Ark., 1969-72; chmn.hief justice Ark. Workers Compensation Commn., 1973-77; prosecuting atty. 9th Jud. Dist. East, State of Ark., 1981-90; mcpl. judge Clark County, 1979-80; cir./chancery judge 9th Jud. Dist. East, State of Ark., 1991-96; chief justice Ark. Supreme Ct., 1997—. Law educator Ouachita Bapt. U., Arkadelphia, Ark., 1975-76, Ark. Law Enforcement Acad., 1990, Garland County C.C., 1993; lectr. Ark. Prosecuting Atty.'s Assn., 1988. Office: Justice Bldg 625 Marshall St, 120 Justice Building Little Rock AR 72201-1052

ARNOLD, WILLIAM MCCAULEY, lawyer; b. Waco, Tex., May 3, 1947; s. Watson Caulfield and Mary Rebecca Arnold; m. Karen Axtell, May 17, 1980; children: Margaret McCauley, William Axtell. BA, Duke U., 1969; JD, U. Tex., 1972. Bar: Tex. 1973, Va. 1975, D.C. 1977, Md. 1983, U.S. Dist. Ct. (ea. dist.) Va. 1975, U.S. Ct. Appeals (4th cir.) 1977, U.S. Ct. Claims 1977, U.S. Supreme Ct. 1978. Spl. atty. U.S. Dept. Justice, Newark, 1973-75; asst. county atty. County of Fairfax, Va., 1975-78; ptnr. Cowles, Rinaldi & Arnold, Ltd., Fairfax, 1978-95, McCandlish & Lillard, Fairfax, 1995—. Instr. No. Va. C.C., Alexandria. Pres. Clifton Betterment Assn., Va., 1979-81; chmn. Clifton Planning Commn., 1980-85, mem. Clifton Town Coun., 1985—; bd. dirs. Clifton Gentlemen's Social Club, 1981-84. Mem. ABA, Va. State Bar Assn., Fairfax County Bar Assn., Va. Trial Lawyers Assn., Associated Builders and Contractors. State civil litigation, Construction. Office: McCandlish & Lillard PC 11350 Random Hills Rd Ste 500 Fairfax VA 22030-6044 E-mail: marnold@mccandlaw.com.

ARNTSON, PETER ANDREW, lawyer; b. Washington, May 23, 1938; s. Paul Lee and Mary Ellen (Garrigan) A.; m. Colette Rousseau, July 11, 1962; 1 child, Eric Paul. BA, U. Va., 1960, JD, 1965; LLM in Taxation, Georgetown U., 1971; postgrad., U.S. Army War Coll., 1982. Bar: Va. 1965, U.S. Supreme Ct. 1973. Assoc., then ptnr. Phillips, Kendrick, Gearheart & Aylor, Arlington, Va., 1965-75; ptnr. McCandlish, Lilliard, Church & Best, Fairfax, Va., 1975-84, Miles & Stockbridge, Fairfax, 1984-95, McCandlish & Lillard, Fairfax, 1995—. Chmn. com. on taxation Va. State Bar, 1978; dep. commr. accts. County of Fairfax, 1994—. Chmn. bd. dirs. No. Va. Am. Heart Assn., 1978; bd. dirs. Benedictine Sch. Exceptional Children, Ridgely, Md., 1985—, Arlington Cmty. Found., 1992-96, No. Va. Cmty. Found., 1991—; mem. exec. coun. Nat. Capital Area coun. Boy Scouts Am., 1993—; founder, pres. Wakefield Ednl. Found., 1986—; trustee Claude Moore Charitable Found. 1st lt. U.S. Army, 1960-62, col. AUS, ret. Mem. ABA, Va. Bar Assn., Fairfax Bar Assn., Assn. U.S. Army , Rotary. Methodist. Estate planning, Probate (including wills, trusts), Estate taxation. Home: 4047 27th Rd N Arlington VA 22207-5237 Office: McCandlish & Lillard 11350 Random Hills Rd Ste 500 Fairfax VA 22030-6044

ARON, ROBERTO, lawyer, writer, educator; b. Mendoza, Argentina, Nov. 1, 1915; s. David and Catalina (Trostanetzky) A.; m. Catalina Berstein, May 1, 1940 (dec. Oct. 1965); children: Jaim, Sylvia, Daniel; m. Eva Coriat, Dec. 14, 1968; stepchildren: Sonia, Aileen (twins). BA in Law, U. Chile, 1943; LLM in Internat. Law, NYU, 1977, LLM in Corp. Law, 1979, M in Hebrew and Judaic Studies, 1995. Bar: Israel 1960. Sr. ptnr. Aron and Cia, Santiago, Chile, 1943-57, Arón, Tamir and Arón, Tel Aviv, 1960—. Adj. tchr. NYU, 1983; lectr. Tel Aviv U., 1985—, bd. govs., 1982; vis. prof. faculty of law U. Chile, 1991; bd. dirs. Otzar Itiashvut Hayeudim Bank, Tel Aviv; mem. Israeli del. to UN, 1975; participant Oxford Trial Advocacy Program. Co-author: How To Prepare Witnesses for Trial, 1985, Trial Communications Skills, 1986, Cross-Examination of Witnesses, 1989, Impeachment of Witnesses, 1990. Mem. Nat. Inst. Trial Advocacy (participant workshops on teaching trial advocacy Harvard Law Sch.), Advocates Assn., Assn. Trial Lawyers Am. Avocations: golf, pipe collecting. General civil litigation, Commercial, contracts (including sales of goods; commercial financing), Criminal. Home: 985 5th Ave Apt 12A New York NY 10021-0142 Office: Arón and Stern 7 ABA Hillel St Ramat-Gan 52522 Israel E-mail: aronbob@aol.com.

ARONOVITZ, TOD, lawyer; b. Miami, Fla., Feb. 26, 1950; AB, U. Ga., 1971; JD, U. Miami, 1974. Bar: Fla. 1974, U.S. Dist. Ct. (so. dist.) Fla. 1975, U.S. Ct. Appeals (11th cir.) 1977. Sr. ptnr. Aronovitz Trial Lawyers, Miami, Fla. Mem. Nat. Conf. Bar Presidents, So. Conf. Bar Presidents. Mem.: ABA, Dade County Bar Assn. (bd. dirs. 1976—79, 1986), Acad. Fla. Trial Lawyers, Assn. Trial lawyers Am., Am. Bd. Trial Advs., Fla. Bar (bd. govs. 1996—2001, pres.-elect 2001—02, pres. 2002—03), Soc. Bar and Gavel, Phi Delta Phi (pres. 1973). Personal injury (including property damage), General civil litigation, Aviation. Office: Aronovitz Trial Lawyers Ste 2700 Museum Tower 150 W Flagler St Miami FL 33130-1536*

ARONS, MARK DAVID, lawyer; b. Durham, N.C., Apr. 26, 1958; s. Marvin Shield Arons and Cyvia (Russian) Peters. BA, Vanderbilt U., 1980; JD, Case Western Res. U., 1983. Bar: Conn. 1983, U.S. Dist. Ct. Conn. 1983, U.S. Ct. Appeals (2d cir.) 1984, U.S. Supreme Ct. 1988; diplomate Nat. Inst. Trial Advocacy; bd. cert. civil trial lawyer Nat. Bd. Trial Advocacy. Owner The Arons Law Firm, LLC, Westport, Conn. Notes editor Case Western Res. Jour. Internat. Law, 1983. Bd. dirs. B'nai B'rith Youth Orgn., New Haven, Congregation B'nai Jacob, Woodbridge, Conn., The Children's Ctr., Hamden; past pres., bd. dirs. Coord. Coun. Children in Crisis, New Haven; mem. Jewish Fedn.-Young Leadership, New Haven, 1987-88; organizing com. Spl. Olympics World Games, New Haven, Conn., 1995. Mem. ABA, Conn. Bar Assn., Assn. Trial Lawyers Am., Conn. Trial Lawyers Assn., New Haven Young Lawyers (program chmn. 1991-92), New Haven Jaycees (bd. dirs. 1985-87), Alpha Epsilon Pi (asst. regional gov.). Democrat. General civil litigation, General practice, Personal injury (including property damage). Office: The Arrons Law Firm LLC 234 Main St Westport CT 06880 E-mail: mdalaw@netscape.net.

ARONSON, VIRGINIA L. lawyer; b. Bremerton, Wash., June 4, 1947; BA, U. Chgo., 1969, MA, 1973, JD, 1975. Bar: Ill. 1975. Ptnr. Sidley Austin Brown & Wood, Chgo. Staff mem. U. Chgo. Law Review, 1974—75; mem. exec. & mgmt. com. Sidley Austin Brown & Wood. Contbr. articles to profl. jours. Mem. Am. Coll. Real Estate Lawyers, Chgo. Mortgage Atty.'s Assn., Chgo. Fin. Exchange, The Chgo. Network (dir. Chgo. ctrl. area com., Chgo. Pub. Edn. Fund). Office: Sidley Austin Brown & Wood Bank One Plz 10 South Dearborn St Chicago IL 60603

ARONSTEIN, MARTIN JOSEPH, law educator, lawyer; b. N.Y.C., Jan. 25, 1925; s. William and Mollie (Mintz) A.; m. Sally K. Rosenau, Sept. 18, 1948 (dec.); children: Katherine Aronstein Porter, David M., James K. BE, Yale U., 1944; MBA, Harvard U., 1948; LLB, U. Pa., 1965. Bar: Pa. 1965. Bus. exec., Phila., 1948-65; assoc. firm Obermayer, Rebmann, Maxwell & Hippel, Phila., 1965-67, partner, 1968-69; assoc. prof. law U. Pa., 1969-72, prof., 1972-78; counsel firm Ballard, Spahr, Andrews & Ingersoll, Phila., 1978-80, partner, 1980-81; prof. law U. Pa., 1981-86, prof. emeritus, 1986—; of counsel firm Morgan, Lewis & Bockius, Phila., 1986-95. Contbr. articles to law revs.; mem. Permanent Editorial Bd. Uniform Comml. Code, 1978-80, counsel, 1980-87, counsel emeritus, 1987—. Served with USN, 1943-46. Mem. Am. Law Inst., ABA (reporter com. on stock certs. 1973-77, chmn. subcom. on investment securities 1982-84), Phila. Bar Assn., Order of Coif, Sigma Xi, Tau Beta Pi. Home: The Fountains at Logan Sq E Two Franklin Town Blvd 2213 Philadelphia PA 19103

AROUOFF, VERA, law librarian; b. Kiev, Ukraine, Sept. 17, 1934; arrived in U.S., 1981; d. Joseph and Khasya Davidovich; m. Leonard Arouoff, July 26, 1958; 1 child, Irene Arouoff-Kastanas. BA in Edn. with top honors, Pedagogical Inst., Nezhin, Ukraine, 1956; postgrad., Maywood Coll., 1984—86; MLS Syracuse U., 1989. Tchr. HS # 19, Kiev, 1956—61, Inst. Fgn. Langs., Kiev, 1961—79; asst. libr. Scranton (Pa.) Pub. Libr., 1981—85; rschr. Cornell U., Ithaca, NY, 1985—88; catalog libr. Loyola U. Law Sch., L.A., 1989—. Mem.: So. Calif. Assn. Law Librs., Am. Assn. Law Librs. Office: Loyola Law Sch PO Box 15019 919 S Albany St Los Angeles CA 90015-0019 Office Fax: 213-487-2204. Business E-Mail: varouoff@lls.edu.

ARQUIT, KEVIN JAMES, lawyer; b. Ithaca, N.Y., Sept. 11, 1954; s. Gordon James and Nora (Harris) A. BA cum laude, St. Lawrence U., 1975; JD cum laude, Cornell U., 1978. Bar: Ohio 1978, N.Y. 1980, U.S. Dist. Ct. (so. and ea. dists.) N.Y. 1980, U.S. Dist. Ct. (we. dist.) N.Y. 1983, U.S. Dist. Ct. (no. dist.) Calif. 1983, U.S. Ct. Appeals (3d cir.) 1983, U.S. Dist. Ct. (no. dist.) N.Y. 1985, U.S. Ct. Appeals(2d cir.) 1985, U.S. Supreme Ct. 1989. Assoc. Arter & Hadden, Cleve., 1978, Fish & Neave, N.Y.C., 1978-83, Harris, Beach & Wilcox, Rochester, N.Y., 1983-86; atty. advisor to chmn. FTC, Washington, 1986-87, chief staff, 1987-88, gen. counsel, 1988-89; dir. Bur. Competition, Washington, 1989-92; ptnr., dep. chmn., head Clifford Chance US LLP Antitrust Practice Group, N.Y.C., 1992—2002; ptnr. STB, 2003—. Republican. Roman Catholic. Antitrust. Office: Simpson Thacher & Bartlett 425 Lexington Ave New York NY 10017-3954 E-mail: karquit@stblaw.com.

ARRINGTON, JOHN LESLIE, JR., lawyer; b. Pawhuska, Okla., Oct. 15, 1931; s. John Leslie and Grace Louise (Moore) A.; m. Elizabeth Anne Waddington, 1956 (div.); children: Elizabeth Anne, John Leslie III, Winifred L., Katherine M.; m. Linda Vance, 1972. Grad., Lawrenceville Sch., 1949; AB, Princeton U., 1953; JD, Harvard U., 1956, LLM, 1957. Bar: Okla. 1956, U.S. Supreme Ct. 1960. Assoc. Arrington, Kihle, Gaberino & Dunn and predecessor firms, Tulsa, 1957-61, ptnr., 1961-93, chmn., CEO, 1994-96; gen. counsel ONEOK, Inc., 1997-98; of counsel Gable & Gotwals, Tulsa, 1998—. Chmn. bd. dirs. Woodland Bank of Tulsa, 1979-94. Prin. draftsman Okla. Supreme Ct. rules governing disciplinary proceedings, 1980-81; bd. dirs. Tulsa County Legal Aid Soc., 1965-70, pres. 1967-70; bd. dirs. Tulsa Family Mental Health Ctr., 1982-89. Named Outstanding Young Man, Tulsa Jaycees, 1963 Mem. ABA, Tulsa County Bar Assn. (Young Lawyer award 1962, pres. 1970, Pres.'s award 1984, Professionalism award 1993), Okla. Bar Assn. (mem. profl. responsiblity commn. 1977-84, vice chmn. 1983-84, Disting. svc. award 1984, Golden Gavel award 1985, Pres.'s award 1991, Masonic award for ethics 1995), So. Hills Country Club (Tulsa), Princeton Club (N.Y.C.). Republican. Episcopalian. General civil litigation, Corporate, general, Utilities, public. Home: 2300 Riverside Dr Unit 3E Tulsa OK 74114-2402 Office: 100 W 5th St Ste 1000 Tulsa OK 74103-4293

ARROWOOD, LISA GAYLE, lawyer; b. Kansas City, Mo., Aug. 7, 1956; d. Paul Miller and Catherine Margaret (Alukas) A.; m. Philip D. O'Neill, June 25, 1983; children: Alexander Edwin O'Neill, Sean Matthew O'Neill, Madeleine Clarice O'Neill. AB, Brown U., 1978; JD, Harvard U., 1982. Bar: Mass. 1982, U.S. Dist. Ct. Mass., U.S. Ct. Appeals (1st cir.). Assoc. Hale and Dorr, Boston, 1982-88, jr. ptnr., 1988-92; ptnr. Todd & Weld, Boston, 1992—. Instr. Boston U. Sch. Law, 1984-85. Fellow Am. Coll. Trial Lawyers; mem. ABA, Mass. Bar Assn., Boston Bar Assn., Phi Beta Kappa. State civil litigation, Environmental, Personal injury (including property damage). Office: Todd & Weld 28 State St 31st Fl Boston MA 02109

ARTEAGA, HAROLD AUGUSTINE, lawyer; b. San Francisco, Dec. 21, 1952; s. Augustine Jesus and Rosa Minar (Morales) A.; m. Doriliz Tovar, Sept. 3, 1967; children: Rebeca, Joshua, Michelle, Gabriel. BS in Polit. Sci., U. Santa Clara, Calif., 1976; JD, U. Calif., Berkeley, 1980; MBA in Internat. Bus., U. Miami, 1999. Atty. enforcement divsn. SEC, 1982-86; gen. counsel PAMCO Securities, Encino, Calif., 1986-88; ptnr. Casterline & Agajanian, L.A., 1988-93; sr. v.p., gen. counsel HBO Latin Am. , Caracas, Venezuela, 1993-97; exec. v.p. HBO Latin Am. Media Svcs., Miami, Fla., 1995-97; of counsel Shook, Hardy & Bacon, Miami, 1999—. Mem. Calif. State Bar, Internat. Bar Assn., Fla. State Bar Assn. Office: Shook Hardy & Bacon 201 S Biscayne Blvd Ste 2400 Miami FL 33131-4313

ARTERTON, JANET BOND, judge; b. Philadelphia, Feb. 8, 1944; m. F. Christopher Arterton; two children. BA, Mt. Holyoke Coll., 1966; JD, Northeastern U., 1977. Law clk. to Hon. Herbert J. Stern U.S. Dist. Ct. N.J., 1977-78; ptnr. Garrison & Arterton, 1978-95; judge U.S. Dist. Ct. Conn., New Haven, 1995—. Fellow Am. Bar Found., Conn. Bar Found.; mem. ATLA, Nat. Employment Lawyers Assn., Conn. Employment Lawyers Assn., Conn. State Trial Lawyers Assn. (bd. govs. 1990-95), Conn. Bar Assn. (mem. adv. com. state ct. rules 1992, mem. fed. jud. selection com. 1991-93, mem. exec. com. women and the law sect. 1990-93, chairperson fed. practice sect. 1993-95. Office: US Dist Ct Conn 141 Church St New Haven CT 06510-2030*

ARTHER, RICHARD OBERLIN, polygraphist, educator; b. Pitts., May 20, 1928; s. William Churchill Sr. and Florence Lind (Oberlin) A.; m. Mary-Esther Wuensch, Sept. 12, 1951; children: Catherine, Linda, William III. BS, Mich. State U., 1951; MA, Columbia U., 1960. Chief assoc. John E. Reid and Assocs., Chgo., 1951-53, dir. N.Y.C., 1953-58; pres. Sci. Lie Detection, Inc., N.Y.C., 1958—, Nat. Tng. Ctr. Polygraph Sci., N.Y.C., 1958—. Author: Interrogation for Investigators, 1958, The Scientific Investigator, 1964, 7th edit., Arther Polygraph Reference Guide, 1964—; editor Jour. Polygraph Sci., 1966—. Fellow Acad. Cert. Polygraphists (exec. dir. 1962—), Am. Polygraph Assn. (founding mem.), Am. Assn. Police Polygraphists (founding mem., Polygraphist of Yr. 1980), N.Y. State Polygraphists (founder), N.J. Polygraphists (founder). Office: Sci Lie Detection Inc 200 W 57th St Ste 1400 New York NY 10019-3211

ARTHUR, DAVID ANTHONY DERING, lawyer; b. England; BA with honors, U. Kent, 1975. Assoc. Barlow Lyde & Galbert, London, 1981—84, ptnr., 1984—. Mem.: Law Soc. England & Wales, Brit. Law Assn., Internat. Bar Assn. Professional liability, Transportation, Insurance. Office: Barlow Lyde & Gilbert 15 St Botolph St London EC3A 7NJ England Fax: 0044 7071 9122. E-mail: darthur@big.cc.llr.

ARTHUR, LINDSAY GRIER, retired judge, author, editor; b. Mpls., July 30, 1917; s. Hugh and Alice (Grier) A.; m. Jean Johansen, Sept. 19, 1940; children: Lindsay G., Mollie K., Julie A. AB, Princeton U., 1939; postgrad., Harvard U., 1939-40; LLB, JD, U. Minn., 1946. Bar: Minn. 1946, U.S. Dist. Ct. Minn. 1948, U.S. Supreme Ct. 1964. Lawyer Nieman, Bosard & Arthur, Mpls., 1946-54; alderman Mpls. City Coun., 1951-54; judge Mcpl. Ct., Mpls., 1954-61; chief judge juvenile divsn. Dist. Ct., Mpls., 1961-79, 87-93, judge felony, civil divsn., 1979-83, chief judge mental health divsn., 1983-87; mediator, 1987—. Arbitrator civil and family cts., 1991—. Author: Minnesota Practice, 1974, Juvenile Case Law, 1980, Twin Cities Uncovered, 1996, A Manual for Mediators, 1995; editor Digest of Juvenile and Family Law, 1983-93; contbr. articles to profl. jours. Bd. dirs. Nat. Ctr. State Cts., Williamsburg, 1974-77, Metro YMCA, Mpls. area, 1981-85; chmn. trustees Bethlehem Luth. Ch., 1979-80. Lt. USNR, 1942-45, PTO. Mem. Nat. Coun. Juvenile Ct. Judges (pres. 1972-73, Jud. scholar 1985—), ABA (disabilities com. 1984-89), Am. Law Inst. (advisor divorce law 1989-93). Avocation: writing. Home: 431 Prairie Center Dr # 323 Eden Prairie MN 55344 E-mail: lgasr@earthlink.net.

ARTHUR, MICHAEL ELBERT, lawyer, financial advisor; b. Seattle, Oct. 9, 1952; s. Theodore E. and Gladys L. (Jones) A.; m. Claire C. Meeker, Dec. 23, 1974; children: Christine, Conor, Austin. BA, U. Calif., Santa Barbara, 1974; JD, Stanford U., 1977. Ptnr. Miller Nash LLP, Portland, Oreg., 1977—2001; fin. advisor Spence Partners at UBS/Paine Webber, Portland, 2001—. Trustee Chiles Found. Banking, Corporate, general, Property, real (including real estate development, water). Home: 13535 NW Lariat Ct Portland OR 97229-7001 Office: UBS Paine Webber 805 SW Broadway Ste 2600 Portland OR 97205-3365 E-mail: mike.arthur@ubspw.com.

ARTHUR, THOMAS CARLTON, lawyer, educator; b. Roanoke, Va., July 11, 1946; s. Charles Ralph and Mary Ruth (Parker) A.; m. Carolyn Scott Fisher, June 15, 1968; children— John, David. A.B., Duke U., 1968; J.D., Yale U., 1971. Bar: D.C. 1972, Va. 1972, U.S. Ct. Appeals (D.C. cir.) 1972, U.S. Supreme Ct. 1979. Assoc. Kirkland & Ellis, Washington, 1971-77, ptnr., 1978-82; assoc. prof. Sch. Law, Emory U., Atlanta, 1982—, sr. faculty mem. Law and Econs. Ctr. 1983— ; of counsel Trotter Smith & Jacobs, Atlanta, 1984— . Contbr. to Law Rev., 1981. Pres. Falls Ch. Community Service Council, Va., 1974-75. Mem. ABA, Va. State Bar, D.C. Bar. Methodist. Office: Emory University Sch Law Gambrell Hall 1301 Clifton Rd Ste G547 Atlanta GA 30322

ARTZ, JOHN CURTIS, lawyer; b. Columbus, Ohio, Mar. 4, 1946; s. Curtis Price and Kathryn Lucille (Risley) A.; m. Nancy Eileen Jones, Apr. 5, 1969; children: John Curtis Jr., Alexander Hardie, Kathryn Cullen. BA disting. mil. grad., Allegheny Coll., 1968; JD magna cum laude, U. S.C., 1976. Bar: Pa. 1976, U.S. Dist. Ct. (we. dist.) Pa. 1976, U.S. Ct. Appeals (3d and 6th cirs.) 1996, U.S. Supreme Ct. 1980. From assoc. to ptnr. Eckert Seamans Cherin & Mellott, Pitts., 1976-94; shareholder, dir. Polito & Smock, P.C., Pitts., 1994—. Adj. asst. prof. Grad. Sch. Pub. Health U. Pitts., 1988-92; instr. Robert Morris U., Pitts., 1998—; presenter Nat. Safety Coun., Western Pa. Safety Coun., Assn. of Iron and Steel Engrs., Pa. Bar Inst., Allegheny County Bar Assn., Pitts. Human Resources Assn., Butler Human Resources Assn., Westmoreland Human Resources Assn. Inst. SMC Bus. Couns., Constrn. Fin. Mgmt. Assn., Pa. Inst. CPAs, Western Pa. Cmty. Accts., YWCA Mid-Atlantic Regional Coun. Notes editor U. S.C. Law Rev., 1975-76; contbr. articles to profl. jours. Dir. Jr. Achievement S.W. Pa., Pitts., 1994—, vice-chair adminstrn., 1998—. Capt. USAF, 1968-73. Recipient Bronze Leadership award Jr. Achievement S.W. Pa., 1993. Fellow Allegheny County Bar Found.; mem. ABA (com. on occupl. safety and health law 1981—), Soc. for Human Resource Mgmt., Pa. Bar Assn. (com. on legal ethics and profl. responsibility 1987-94), Pitts. Human Resources Assn. (treas. 1997, sr. profl. human resources 1998—), Order of Wig and Robe, Omicron Delta Kappa. Labor (including EEOC, Fair Labor Standards Act, labor-management relations, NLRB, OSHA), Workers' compensation. Office: Polito & Smock PC 444 Liberty Ave Ste 400 Pittsburgh PA 15222-1237 E-mail: jartz@politolaw.com.

ARUM, ROBERT, lawyer, sports events promoter; b. N.Y.C., Dec. 8, 1931; s. Samuel and Celia (Baumgarten) Arum; m. Barbara Mandelbaum, July 2, 1960 (div. 1977); children: John, Richard, Elizabeth; m. Sybil Ann Hamada, Dec. 18, 1977 (div. 1991); m. Lovee Hazan Du Boef, Sept. 14, 1991. BA, NYU, 1953; JD cum laude, Harvard U., 1956. Bar: NY 1956. Atty. firm Root, Barrett, Cohen, Knapp & Smith, N.Y.C., 1956—61; asst. U.S. atty., chief tax sect. U.S. Atty.'s Office, So. Dist. N.Y., 1961—64; ptnr. firm Phillips, Nizer, Benjamin, Krim & Ballon, N.Y.C., 1964—72, Arum & Katz, N.Y.C., 1972—79; chmn. Top Rank, Inc.; Promoter Ali-Frazier Super Fight II, 1974, Evel Knievel Snake River Canyon Jump, 1974, Ali-Norton World Heavyweight Championship, 1976, Monzon-Valdez World Middleweight Championships, 1976, 1977, Ali-Spinks Championships, 1978, Leonard-Duran Championships, 1980, 1989, Top Rank/ESPN Boxing Series, 1980—, Arguello-Pryor Championship, 1983, Moore-Duran Championship, 1983, Hagler-Duran Championship, 1983, Hagler-Hearns Championship, 1985, Hagler-Leonard Superfight Championship, 1987, Leonard-Hearns "The War" Championship, 1989—91, Holyfield-Foreman World Heavyweight Championship, 1991, Holyfield-Holmes World Heavyweight Championship, 1992, Foreman/Morrison Heavyweight Championship, 1993, De la Hoya/Whitaker, 1997, De la Hoya/Chavez, 1996, 1998, De la Hoya/Quartey, 1999, De la Hoya/Trinidad, 1999, De la Hoya/Mosely, 2000, Morales/Barrera, 2002, De la Hoya/Vargas, 2002. Named to Boxing Hall of Fame, 1999. Mem.: Friars Club. Home: 36 Gulf Stream Ct Las Vegas NV 89113-1354 Office: 3980 Howard Hughes Pkwy Las Vegas NV 89109-0992 E-mail: erroa@aol.com.

ARVIDSON, PER JOHAN, lawyer; b. Skovde, Sweden, Oct. 12, 1945; s. Karl Johan and Marianne (Forsberg) A.; m. Marianne Åström, July 12, 1969 (div. 1997); m. Monic Wawrzyniak, Oct. 1, 1999; 1 child, Viktor Johan. Jur. Kand., U. Uppsala, Sweden, 1971. Pvt. practice law, Uppsala, 1977—. Contbr. articles to profl. jours. 2nd lt., Swedish Navy, 1966-67, Navy Res., 1967-92. Mem. Rotary. Avocations: hunting, sailing, golf. Office: Ahlford Advokatbyra HB Fyris Torg 6 Box 1111 75141 Uppsala Sweden

ARVIN, LESTER CAVE, lawyer; b. East St. Louis, Ill., July 22, 1923; s. James B. and Beulah A. (Peery) A.; m. Kay K. Krehbiel, May 13, 1945; children— Scott B., Reed R. Student Ottawa U., 1940-42, A.B., Wichita U., 1947, J.D., Washburn U., 1949. Bar: Kans. 1949, U.S. dist. ct. Kans. 1953, U.S. Ct. Apls. (10th cir.), U.S. Sup. Ct. 1953. Dep. sheriff Sedgwick County, Kans., 1947; asst. to atty. gen. Kans., 1948; asst. to state tax atty. of Kans., 1949; csl., chief clk. PO and Civil Service Commn., U.S. Congress, 1952-53; ptnr. Mullins & Arvin, 1949-53; sr. ptnr. Arvin, Arvin & Busey and predecessor, Wichita, Kans., 1953— . Mem. Kans. Senate, 1969-72. Trustee Golden Gate Bapt. Theol. Sem. 1969, Wichita State U., Friends U.; mem. Greater Downtown Wichita; mem. planning bd. Butler County; pres. Ark. River Land Corp.; mem. Century III Found., Oak Brook, Ill. Served with M.I., U.S. Army 1943-47. Mem. ABA, Kans. Bar Assn., Sedgwick County Bar Assn., Wichita Bar Assn. (pres.' cert. of appreciation 1976), Motor Carrier's Lawyers Assn. Republican. Baptist. Club: Scottish Rite. Author: It Takes More than Eyes to See, 1955. Corporate, general, General practice, Property, real (including real estate development, water). Office: 409 Century Park Bldg Wichita KS 67202 Home: # S-157 11 Burton Hills Blvd Nashville TN 37215-6138

ASAI-SATO, CAROL YUKI, lawyer; b. Osaka, Japan, Oct. 22, 1951; came to U.S., 1953; d. Michael and Sumiko (Kamei) Asai; 1 child, Ryan Makoto Sato. BA cum laude, U. Hawaii, 1972; JD, Willamette Coll. Law, 1975. Bar: Hawaii 1975. Assoc. firm Ashford & Wriston, Honolulu, 1975-79; counsel Bank of New Eng., Boston, 1979-81; assoc. counsel

Alexander & Baldwin, Honolulu, 1981-83, sr. counsel, 1984-88; of counsel Rush, Moore, Craven, Sutton, Morry, Beh, 1988-89, ptnr., 1989-97, Alston Hunt Floyd & Ing, 1997—. Willamette Coll. Law Bd. Trustees scholar, 1972-73. Mem. ABA, Hawaii Bar Assn., Hawaii Women Lawyers, Phi Beta Kappa, Phi Kappa Phi. Democrat. Commercial, contracts (including sales of goods; commercial financing), Corporate, general, Property, real (including real estate development, water). Office: Alston Hunt Floyd & Ing Pacific Tower 18th Fl 1001 Bishop St Ste 1800 Honolulu HI 96813-3689

ASHDOWN, PHILOMENA SALDANHA, lawyer; b. Madras, India, May 29, 1958; came to U.S., 1983; d. Frederick Alexander and Dorothy Mary (D'Souza) Saldanha. BSc, U. Madras, 1978, LLB, 1984; JD, Notre Dame U., 1986. Bar: Ohio 1986, U.S. Dist. Ct. (no. dist.) Ind. 1986, U.S. Dist. Ct. (no. dist.) Ohio 1987, U.S. Ct. Appeals (7th cir.) 1987, Tamilnadu, India 1987, U.S. Ct. Appeals (6th cir.) 1988, U.S. Dist. Ct. (so. dist.) Ohio 1989, D.C. 1990. Law clk. to judge U.S. Bankruptcy Ct., South Bend, Ind., 1986-87; assoc. Thompson Hine & Flory, Cleve., 1987-95; of counsel Strauss & Troy, Cin., 1995—. Mem. Greater Cin. Women Lawyers Assn. (pres. 1995-96), Comml. Real Estate Women (pres. 1994-96), Tristate Assn. for Corporate Renewal (bd. dirs. 1999—, pres. 2000-02). Banking, Bankruptcy, Commercial, contracts (including sales of goods; commercial financing). Office: Strauss & Troy 150 E 4th St Cincinnati OH 45202-4018 E-mail: psashdown@strauss-troy.com.

ASHE, BERNARD FLEMMING, arbitrator, educator, lawyer; b. Balt., Mar. 8, 1936; s. Victor Joseph Ashe and Frances Cecelia (Johnson) Flemming; m. Grace Nannette Pegram, Mar. 23, 1963; children: Walter Joseph, David Bernard. BA, Howard U., 1956, JD, 1961. Bar: Va. 1961, D.C. 1963, Mich. 1964, N.Y. 1971. Tchr. Balt. Pub. Schs., 1956-58; atty. NLRB, Washington, 1961-63; asst. gen. counsel Internat. Union United Auto Workers, Detroit, 1963-71; gen. counsel N.Y. State United Tchrs., Albany, 1971-96, arbitrator, 1996—. Mem. adj. faculty Cornell Sch. Indsl. and Labor Rels., Albany div., 1981, 87, Fordham U. Law Sch., 1996-00, Roger Williams U. Law Sch., 1996-98. Contbr. articles on labor and constnl. law to profl. jours. Bd. dirs. Urban League Albany, 1979-85, 1st v.p., 1981-85; trustee N.Y. Lawyers Fund for Client Protection, 1981—, Adelphi Univ., Garden City, N.Y., 1997—. Recipient Nat Weinberg award, Wayne State U., Detroit, Mich., 2001. Fellow Am. Bar Found. (life), Coll. Labor and Employment Lawyers (emeritus); mem. NAACP (Thurgood Marshall Justice award 2000), ABA (chmn. sect. labor and employment law sect. 1982-83, consortium on legal svcs. and the pub. 1979-84, commn. on pub. understanding about the law 1987-91, mem. standing com. on group and prepaid legal svcs. 1996-97, ho. of dels. 1985-96, 97—, nominating com. 1988-91, chair drafting com., 1998-2000, bd. govs. 1991-94, exec. com. 1993-94, accreditation com. sect. legal edn. and admission to the bar 1994-98, chmn. standing com. on group and prepaid legal svcs. 1996-97, sr. lawyers divsn. coun. 1994-2000, standing com. on client protection 1998-2001), Am. Law Inst., Nat. Bar Assn., Am. Arbitration Assn. (bd. dirs. 1982-98, Whitney North Seymour Sr. medal 1989), N.Y. State Bar Assn., Albany County Bar Assn.

ASHER, STEVEN ALAN, lawyer; b. Phila., Mar. 7, 1947; s. Maurice and Rhea (Aranoff) A.; m. Ina Louise Elfant, May 27, 1979; children: Simma, Aviva, Jacob, Rena. BA, Johns Hopkins U., 1969; JD, NYU, 1973. Bar: N.Y. 1974, Pa. 1980. Assoc. Willkie Farr & Gallagher, N.Y.C., 1973-76, Rosenman & Colin, N.Y.C., 1976-80; ptnr. LaBrum & Doak, Phila., 1980-86; shareholder Kohn, Nast & Graf, P.C., Phila., 1987-95; ptnr. Barrack, Rodos & Bacine, 1995—2002, Fox, Rothschild LLP, Phila., 2002—. Lectr. U. Pa., others. Contbr. articles on antitrust law to legal publs. Mem. ABA (sect. on antitrust law), Phila. Bar Assn. (chmn. antitrust law com. 1989-92, mem. fed. cts. com.). Antitrust, Federal civil litigation. Home: 301 N Latches Ln Merion Station PA 19066-1728 Office: Fox Rothschild LLP 10th Fl 2000 Market St Philadelphia PA 19103 Fax: 215-299-2150. E-mail: sasher@fof.com.

ASHKIN, ROBERTA ELLEN, lawyer; b. N.Y.C., July 1, 1953; d. Sidney and Beverly Ashkin. BA magna cum laude, Hofstra U., 1975; JD, St. John's U., N.Y.C., 1978. Bar: N.Y., 1979, U.S. Dist. Ct. (ea. and so. dists.), 1980, U.S. Dist. Ct. (no. and we. dists.) 2001. Program dir. Sta. WVHC-FM, N.Y.C., 1974-75; assoc. editor Matthew Bender, N.Y.C., 1975-79; assoc. Morris & Duffy, N.Y.C., 1979-81, Lipsig, Sullivan & Liapakis, N.Y.C., 1981-84, Julien & Schlesinger, P.C., N.Y.C., 1984-89; adminstrv. law judge N.Y.C. Dept. Transp., 1988-92; ptnr. Trolman & Glaser, P.C., N.Y.C., 1991-96, Baron & Budd, P.C., N.Y.C., 1996—2002; pvt. practice, 2002—. Chmn. bd. Actor's Classical Troupe, 1987-89; bd. dirs. Daytop Village Found., 2002-03; sr. dir. Women's Policy Gephardt for Pres. 2004 Campaign. Mem.: ATLA, Trial Lawyers for Pub. Justice (bd. dirs.), N.Y. Trial Lawyers Assn. (dep. treas. 2001, bd. dirs., sec. 2002), N.Y. State Bar Assn., Phi Beta Kappa. Personal injury (including property damage), Product liability, Toxic tort.

ASHLEY, JAMES PATRICK, lawyer; b. Terre Haute, Ind., May 5, 1953; s. Cornelius Ellis and Ruth LaVerne A.; m. Lisa Ann Larsson, Aug. 2, 1975; children: Alison Elisabeth, Amanda Suzanne. BSBA, Ill. State U., 1975; JD, Drake U., 1991. Bar: Minn. 1991; U.S. Dist. Ct. Minn. 1992; U.S. Ct. Appeals (8th cir.) 1993. Claim supr., claim examiner and claim rep. Ill. Employers Ins. of Wausau, River Forest, Ill., 1976-80; casualty claim mgr. Brotherhood Mut. Ins. Co., Fort Wayne, Ind., 1980-88; law clk. Hanson, McClintock & Riley, Des Moines, 1989-91; assoc. Chadwick, Johnson & Condon, Mpls., 1991-96; shareholder Chadwick & Assocs., Chanhassen, Minn., 1996-99; trial atty. Allstate Ins. Co., Edina, Minn., 1999—. Recipient acad. scholarship Drake Law Sch., Des Moines, 1989. Roman Catholic. Avocations: reading, winemaking. General civil litigation, Insurance, Product liability. Home: 12771 Gerard Dr Eden Prairie MN 55346-3129 Office: Allstate Ins Co 7401 Metro Blvd Ste 510 Edina MN 55439-3033 E-mail: jpalal@msn.com.

ASHLEY-FARRAND, MARGALO, lawyer, mediator, private judge; b. N.Y.C., July 26, 1944; d. Joel Thomas and Margalo (Wilson) Ashley; m. Marvin H. Bennett, Mar. 5, 1964 (div. June 1974),; children: Marc, Aliza; m. Thomas Ashley-Farrand, Dec. 11, 1981. Student, UCLA, 1962-63, U. Pitts., 1972-74; BA cum laude, NYU, 1978; JD, Southwestern U., 1980. Bar: D.C. 1981, Md. 1981, Calif. 1983, U.S. Dist. Ct. (ctrl. and no. dists.) Calif. 1984; cert. family law specialist Calif. State Bar. Pvt. practice law, Washington, 1981-82; ptnr. Ashley-Farrand & Smith, Glendale, Calif., 1983-87; pvt. practice law, 1987-95; pvt. practice, 1995—; v.p. Legal Inst. Fair Elections, 1995—; settlement officer L.A. Mcpl. Ct., 1990—99. Judge pro tem L.A. Mcpl. Ct., 1989-99, L.A. Superior Ct., 1993—. Convenor, pres. East Hills chpt. NOW, 1972-74, mem. Pa. state bd., 1972-74, pres. Hollywood chpt. 1974-75, mem. bd. N.Y.C. chpt. 1975-78; convenor, coord. L.A. Women's Coalition for Better Broadcasting, 1974-75; Dem. nominee Calif. State Assembly, 1994; convenor, coord. Shades of Culture Women's Club, 2000—. Themis soc. scholar, 1980; named one of Outstanding Young Women of Am., 1980. Mem. ABA, ACLU, NOW, NWPC, League of Conservation Voters, Calif. Women Lawyers, Women Lawyers Assn. L.A., L.A. County Bar Assn., Pasadena Interracial Women's Club (pres. 1993-94). Appellate, Family and matrimonial, Probate (including wills, trusts). Office: 215 N Marengo Ave Fl 3 Pasadena CA 91101-1504

ASHMUS, KEITH ALLEN, lawyer; b. Cleve., Aug. 19, 1949; s. Richard A. and Rita (Petti) A.; m. Marie Sachiko Matsuoka, Dec. 15, 1973; children: Emmy Marie, Christopher Todd. BA in Policy Sci., Mich. State U., 1971, MA in Econs., 1972; JD, Yale U., 1974. Bar: Ohio 1974, Calif. 1991, U.S. Dist. Ct. (no. dist.) Ohio 1975, U.S. Dist. Ct. (no., so. and cen. dists.) Calif. 1991, U.S. Dist. Ct. (so. dist.) Ohio 2000, U.S. Ct. Appeals (6th cir.) 1975, U.S. Supreme Ct. 1980. Assoc. Thompson Hine & Flory LLP, Cleve., 1974-82, ptnr., 1982—2000, ptnr.-in-charge Cleve. office, 1996-99, dept. chmn., 1999-2000; founding ptnr. Frantz Ward LLP, Cleve., 2000—. Mediator/arbitrator Am. Arbitration Assn. Comml. Employment Panels, 1995—. Co-author: Public Sector Collective Bargaining: The Ohio System, 1984. Trustee community arts Baycrafters, Bay Village, Ohio, 1981-84, Hospice Council No. Ohio, 1982-84, Inst. for Personal Health Skills, Cleve. 1985-90; trustee Coun. Smaller Enterprises, 1990-96, 98—, 1st vice chmn., 2000-2001, chmn., 2001--; trustee Village Found., 1997—, Vocat. Guidance Svcs. 1999-2002, Youth Opportunities Unltd., 2000—, Cleve. Saves, 2001—; sec. George W. Codrington Charitable Found., 1994-2000; chmn. job placement for older persons Skills Available, Cleve., 1980-87; gov.'s appointee to Health Care Quality Adv. Coun., 1996; mem. adv. bd. Greater Cleve. Salvation Army, 1997—, treas., 2000-01, vice chmn., 2001—. Named one of Outstanding Vols. award Nat. Hospice Orgn., 1982, Vol. of Yr. Vocat. Guidance and Rehab. Services, 1985, 86. Mem. ABA, State Bar Calif., Ohio State Bar Assn. (coun. dels. 1995—, bd. govs. 1998-2001, pres. 2003), Cleve. Bar Assn. (trustee 1985-88, 98-2001, chmn. labor law sect. 1983-84), Def. Rsch. Inst., Pub. Sector Labor Rels. Assn. (exec. com. 1989-93). Avocations: golf, fishing. Federal civil litigation, State civil litigation, Labor (including EEOC, Fair Labor Standards Act, labor-management relations, NLRB, OSHA). Office: Frantz Ward LLP 55 Public Sq 19th Fl Cleveland OH 44113-1999 E-mail: kashmus@frantzward.com.

ASHTON, MARK RANDOLPH, lawyer; b. Abington, Pa., Sept. 10, 1955; s. Frank E. and Charlotte (Wagenbaur) A. BA in Internat. Affairs, George Washington U., 1977; JD, John Marshall U., 1980. Bar: Pa. 1980. Law clk. to Hon. Mason Avrigian Ct. of Common Pleas of Montgomery County, Norristown, Pa., 1980-81; assoc. Abrahams & Loewenstein, Norristown, 1982-87; dept. chmn. Riley, Riper, Hollin & Colagreco, 1987-90; ptnr. Fox, Rothschild, O'Brien & Frankel, Exton, Pa., 1990—. Mem. Montgomery Bar Assn. (bd. dirs. 1985-87), Chester County Bar Assn. (chmn. family law sect. 1988-90), Wissahickon Valley Hist. Soc. (former pres.), D.J. Freed Am. Inn of Ct. (pres.). Republican. Episcopalian. Family and matrimonial. Home: 413 Stratford Ave Collegeville PA 19426-2553 Office: Fox Rothschild O'Brien & Frankel 760 Constitution Dr Ste 104 Exton PA 19341-1149

ASHWORTH, BRENT FERRIN, lawyer; b. Albany, Calif., Jan. 8, 1949; s. Dell Shepherd and Bette Jean (Brailsford) Ashworth; m. Charlene Mills, Dec. 16, 1970; children: Amy, John, Matthew, Samuel(dec.) , Adam, David, Emily, Luke, Benjamin. BA, Brigham Young U., 1972; JD, U. Utah, 1975. Bar: Utah 1977. Asst. county atty. Carbon County, Price, Utah, 1975-76; assoc. atty. Frandsen & Keller, Price, Utah, 1976-77; v.p. legal affairs, sec., gen. counsel Nature's Sunshine Products, Provo, Utah, 1977—. Bd. dirs., gen. counsel Carbon County Nursing Home, Price, 1976—77; mem. Provo Landmarks Commn., 1997—2002, chmn., 2002—, co-chair sesquicentennial com., 1998—99; active Provo Libr. Bd., 2000—03, chmn., 2003—, Utah County Cancer Crusade Com., 1981—83, Provo LCOC Arts subcom., 1998—99; pres. Desert Village Spani Fork, Utah, 1988—90; gen. counsel Brigham Young Acad. Found., 1995—2001; founder, chmn. George E. Freestone Boy Scout Mus., Provo, 2000—; exec. bd. Utah Nat. Pk. coun. Boy Scouts Am., 2000—; city councilman, planning commn. Payson City, Utah, 1980—82, mayor pro tem, 1982; bd. dirs. ARC, Utah County chpt., 1988—94, Springville Mus. Art, 1998—2001, Celebration Health Found., 1999—, Provo Sch. Dist. Found., 2001—. Mem.: ATLA, SAR (pres. Utah County chpt. 1989—90, state chpts. 1st v.p. 1990—91, state soc. pres. 1991—92, chancellor 1992—94), ABA, Am. Corp. Counsel Assn. (sec. intermountain chpt. 1990—91), Utah State Bar Assn., Southeastern Utah Bar Assn. (sec. 1977), Sons Utah Pioneers, Emily Dickinson Soc. Utah (pres. 1995—97), Kiwanis Club (v.p. 1995—96, pres. 1997—98, lt. gov. Utah Idaho dist. 2001—02), Phi Eta Sigma, Phi Kappa Phi. Corporate, general, Private international. Home: 1377 Cambridge Ct Provo UT 84604-4178 Office: Natures Sunshine Products PO Box 1000 Spanish Fork UT 84660-0901

ASKEY, WILLIAM HARTMAN, US magistrate judge, lawyer; b. Williamsport, Pa., June 21, 1919; s. Charles Fisher and Marguerite Kirlin (Hartman) A.; m. Betty Arlene Moore, July 3, 1942; 1 dau., Elizabeth Powell. BA, Bucknell U., 1941; JD, U. Pitts., 1951. Bar: Lycoming County Cts., 1951, Pa. 1952, U.S. Dist. Ct. (mid. dist.) Pa. 1952, U.S. Supreme Ct. 1960. Sole practice, Williamsport, Pa., 1951—; U.S. commr. U.S. Dist. Ct. (mid. dist.) Pa., 1964-71; part-time U.S. magistrate judge, 1971—. With AAA, North Penn. Bd. dirs. Appalachia Ednl. Lab., Charleston, W.Va., 1967-85. Served to maj. USAAF, 1941-46. Mem. Lycoming Law Assn. (pres. 1968-69), Pa. Bar Assn., ABA (Nat. Conf. Spl. Ct. Judges), Fed. Bar Assn. (hon.), Fed. Magistrate Judges Assn., Charles F Greevy Jr Inn of Ct., Masons, Ross Club (Williamsport).

ASKINAZI, LISA K. mediator; d. Rena Iacono; m. Scott Edward Askinazi, Aug. 16, 1997. BA, Va. Intermont Coll., 1993; MSW, Adelphi U., 1995, postgrad., 2002. Cert. Doctoral Candidate Adelphi Univ., 2002; social worker SUNY, 1996. Clin. social work Epilepsy Found. L.I., Garden City, NY, 1995—97; grant project coord. N.Y. State Dept. Health, East Meadow, 1997; pvt. practice clin. therapy practitioner Malverne, NY, 1997—; pvt. practice divorce mediation practitioner, 1999—; family counseling and case analyst State Supreme Ct. Nassau County, Mineola, NY, 1999—. Mem.: Assn. for Conflict Resolution (assoc.). Messianic Jewish. Achievements include first to implemented and established the first social work position in the Nassau County Supreme Court; assisted over one thousand individuals in resolving contested child-based matters. Avocations: music, competitive horse show jumping. Office: State Supreme Ct Nassau County 400 County Seat Dr Mineola NY 11501

ASLAKSEN, ASLAK, lawyer; b. Oslo, Apr. 24, 1959; m. Hanne Merete Jendal; children: Mads Aslaksøn, Bård Askaksøn, Oda Aslaksdatter Jendal. Degree in Law, U. Oslo, 1985; LLM, Harvard U., 1987. With legal dept. Aker AS, Oslo, 1985; head legal dept., Borar sec. Kosmos AS, Oslo, 1987-89; assoc. IM Skaugen, Oslo, 1990-92, Law Firm Schjødt AS, Oslo, 1992-95; with Advokatfirma Lyng & Co., Oslo. Bd. dirs. numerous cos. Candidate Conservative party, Oslo, 1999—. Mem. Norwegian Bar Assn. Office: Lyng Giltun & CO Advohatjima DA Olav Vs gt 6 0280 Oslo Norway E-mail: aslak.aslaksen@lyng.giltun.no.

ASMAR, LAILA MICHELLE, lawyer; b. Laurel, Miss., July 23, 1957; d. Mitchell and Marie Jeannette Asmar. BS in BA, U. So. Miss., 1979; JD cum laude, So. Tex. Coll. Law, Houston, 1985. Bar: Tex. 1985; CPA, Tex., Miss.; bd. cert. estate planning and probate lawyer; cert. mediator; cert. arbitrator N.Y. Stock Exch. and Nat. Assn. Securities Dealers. Acct. Peat Marwick Mitchell, Jackson, Miss., 1979-80, Houston Oil Internat., Houston, 1980-81; tax analyst Tenneco Inc., Houston, 1981-84; assoc. atty. Clark Thomas Winters & Newton, Austin, Tex., 1985-87; fin. cons. Linscomb & Williams, Houston, 1988-89; pvt. practice law, Houston, 1989—. Guest expert The Ron Stone Show, Sta. KPRC-TV, Houston, 1990-92, guest reporter Morning News, 1992. Co-author of ABA pub.: Federal Income Taxation of Life Insurance, 1989; contbr. articles to profl. jours. Trustee Theater Under Stars, Houston, 1989-91. Mem. Tex. Bar Assn. Republican. Episcopalian. Estate planning, Probate (including wills, trusts), Securities.

ASPEN, MARVIN EDWARD, federal judge; b. Chgo., July 11, 1934; s. George Abraham and Helen (Adelson) A.; m. Susan Alona Tubbs, Dec. 18, 1966; children: Jennifer Marion, Jessica Maile, Andrew Joseph. BS in Sociology, Loyola Univ., 1956; JD, Northwestern U., 1958. Bar: Ill. 1958. Individual practice, Chgo., 1958-59; draftsman joint com. to draft new Ill. criminal code Chgo. Bar Assn.-Ill. Bar Assn., 1959-60; asst. state's atty. Cook County, Ill., 1960-63; asst. corp. counsel City of Chgo., 1963-71; pvt. practice law, 1971; judge Cir. Ct. Cook County, Ill., 1971-79; judge ea. divsn. U.S. Dist. Ct. (no. dist.) Ill., Chgo., 1979-95, chief judge, 1995—2002. Edward Avery Harriman adj. prof. law Northwestern U. Law Sch.; past chmn. new judges, recent devels. in criminal law, and evidence coms. Ill. Judicial Conf., past chmn., adv. bd. Inst. Criminal Justice, John Marshall Sch. Law; past mem. Ill. Law Enforcement Commn., Gov. Ill. Adv. Commn. Criminal Justice, Cook County Bd. Corrections; past chmn. assoc. rules com. Ill. Supreme Ct., com. on ordinance violation problems; past vice chmn. com. on pattern jury instrns. in criminal cases; lectr. at judicial confs. and trial advocacy programs nationally and internationally; planner, participant in legal seminars at numerous schools including Harvard U., Emory U., U. Fla., Oxford U. (Eng.), U. Bologna, Nuremberg (Germany) U., U. Cairo, Egypt, U. Zimbabwe, U. Malta, U. The Philippines, U. Madrid; past mem. Georgetown U. Law Ctr. Project on Plea Bargaining in U.S., spl. faculty NITA advanced Trial Advocacy Program introducing Brit. trial techniques to experienced Am. litigators, spl. faculty of ABA designed to acquaint Scottish lawyers with modern litigation and tech.; frequent faculty mem. Nat. Judiciary Coll., Fed. Judicial Ctr., U. Nev. (Reno), Nat. Inst. for Trial Advocacy, Colo.; bd. dir. Fed. Judicial Ctr., past chair dir. search com.; past mem. Judicial Conf. Com. on Adminstrn. of the Bankruptcy System, Trial Bar Implementation Com. on Civility of the 7th Fed. Cir.; mem. Northwestern U. Law Bd. Co-author Criminal Law for the Layman-A Citizen's Guide, 2d edit., 1977, Criminal Evidence for the Police, 1972, Protective Security Law, 1983; contbr. over two dozen articles to legal publs. Past mem. vis. com. Northwestern U. Sch. Law, chmn. adv. com. for short courses (post law sch. ednl. program), mem. law bd.; past mem. vis. com. U. Chgo. Law Sch.; mem. vis. com. No. Ill. U. Sch. Law; organizer, past pres. Northwestern Univ. Sch. of Law chpt. Amincourt Program U.S. Judicial Conf; past mem. Cook County Bd. Corrections, John Howard Assn.; active CEELI programs in Bulgaria and Yugoslavia Ford Found. Jud. Tng. Program in China. With USAF, 1958-59; trustee Am. Inns Ct. Recipient Nat. Ctr. Freedom of Info. Studies award, Ctr. for Pub. Resources award, Merit award Northwestern U. Alumni Assn., Herbert Harley award Am. Judicature Soc.; named Person of Yr. Chgo. Lawyer, 1995. Mem. Am. Bar Found. (bd. dirs.), Judicature Soc. Ill. (past chmn. coms.), Chgo. Bar Assn. (bd. mgrs. 1978-79, past chmn. criminal law com., past bd. editors Chgo. Bar Record, mem. commn. on criminal justice. coms. on cont. legal edn., devel. of law, civil disorder and others), Ill. State Bar Assn. (past chmn. pub. rels., corrections, fair trial/free press, criminal law coms., mem. others), Northwestern U. Law Alumni Assn. (past pres., Merit award), ABA (co-chair, sec. of litigation Inst. for Trial practical task force, mem. standing com. on fed. jud. improvements, pres. ABA mus., mem. bd. Am. Bar Fedn., past mem. ABA bd. govs., mem. house dels., past chmn. exec com., mem. bd. editors ABA Jour.), Nat. Conf. Fed. Trial Judges (past mem. coun. sect., past chmn. exec. com. litigation, past chmn., coun. sect. criminal justice, mem. edn. bd. sect. criminal justice mag., past co-chmn. liason jud. com. sect. litigation, mem. jury comprehension study com., ho. dels., standing com. fed. jud. improvements, co-chmn. sect. litigation Inst. Trial Practice Task Force), Am. Inns Ct. Office: US Dist Ct 2578 US Courthouse 219 S Dearborn St Chicago IL 60604-1800 E-mail: aspen@ilnd.uscourts.gov.

ASPERO, BENEDICT VINCENT, lawyer; b. Newton, N.J., Sept. 3, 1940; s. Umberto S. and Rose (Cerreta) A.; m. Sally Hennen, June 26, 1971; children: Benedict Vincent, Alexander Morgan. AB, U. Notre Dame, 1962, JD, 1966. Bar: N.J. 1970, N.Y. 1982, D.C. 1983, U.S. Dist. Ct. N.J. 1970, U.S. Supreme Ct. 1981. Assoc., then ptnr. Meyers, Lesser & Aspero, Sparta, N.J., 1971-76; atty. Benedict V. Aspero, Sparta and Morristown, N.J., 1976-82; ptnr. Broderick, Newmark, Grather & Aspero, Morristown, 1982-89, Courter, Kobert, Laufer, Purcell & Cohen, 1989-91; prin. Benedict V. Aspero, Esq., P.C., 1992—. Mem. adv. bd. Summit Bank, First Morris Bank. Trustee Harding Twp. Civic Assn., Loyola Retreat House, 1992—99, Craig Sch., 1985—, pres. bd., 1992—2002. Mem. ABA, N.J. Bar Assn., Morris County Bar Assn., Sussex County Bar Assn., Sorin Soc., Morristown Club, Essex Hunt Club. Republican. Roman Catholic. Commercial, contracts (including sales of goods; commercial financing), Corporate, general, Probate (including wills, trusts). Office: 222 Ridgedale Ave PO Box 1573 Morristown NJ 07962-1573 E-mail: bvatty@GTI.net.

ASPHAUG, ROLF GUNNAR, lawyer; b. Huntington Beach, Calif., June 14, 1958; s. Gunnar and Tulla (Mjelde) A.; m. Jane M. Asphaug; 1 child, Jonathan G. BA in History, Rice U., 1980; JD, Columbia U., 1983. Bar: Tex. 1983, Colo. 1989, U.S.Dist. Ct. (so. dist.) Tex. 1984, U.S. Dist. Ct. (ea. dist.) Tex. 1986, U.S. Dist. Ct. Colo. 1989, U.S. Ct. Appeals (5th cir.) 1984, U.S. Ct. Appeals (10th cir.) 1989, U.S. Supreme Ct. 1995. Assoc. Baker & Botts, Houston, 1983-87; law assoc. Sierra Club Legal Def. Fund, Denver, 1988-89; asst. legal counsel Regional Transp. Dist., Denver, 1989-90, acting gen. counsel, 1990-92, assoc. gen. counsel, 1992, dep. gen. counsel, 1992—. Mng. editor Columbia Jour. of Law and Social Problems, 1982-83. Sr. instr. Colo. Mountain Club, Denver, 1989-92; dir. Wilderness Trekking Sch., 1992-95. Mem. ABA, Def. Rsch. Inst., Colo. Bar Assn., Denver Bar Assn., Colo. Def. Lawyers Assn., Colo. Mountain Club (pres. 2000-01), Colo. Fourteeners Initiative (founder, bd. mem. 1997-2001), Sierra Club (life). Democrat. Avocations: hiking, backpacking, telemark skiing, photography. Office: Regional Transp Dist 1600 Blake St Denver CO 80202-1399 E-mail: rolf.asphaug@rtd-denver.com.

ASTLEFORD, PETER DAVID, lawyer; LLB, Southampton U., 1983. Solicitor of Supreme Ct., Eng. and Wales. Lawyer Linklaters, London and Brussels; group legal adviser Invesco, London; now ptnr., head fin. svcs. Dechert, London. Co-author: Starting a Hedge Fund--A European Perspective, 1999. Avocation: scuba diving. Mergers and acquisitions, Securities, Finance. Office: Dechert 2 Serjeants Inn London EC4Y 1LT England Fax: 020 7353 3683. E-mail: peter.astleford@dechert.com.

ATCHISON, RODNEY RAYMOND, retired lawyer, arbitrator; b. Hanford, Calif., Nov. 14, 1926; s. Clyde Raymond and Velma May (Watts) A.; m. Evaleen Mary McFadden, June 27, 1948; children: Cathlin Atchison, Susan Barisone, Kerry Atchison, Brian. Student, San Jose State Coll., 1946-49; JD, U. Santa Clara, 1952. Bar: Calif. 1953, U.S. Dist. Ct. (all dists.) Calif. 1953, U.S. Ct. Appeals (9th cir.) 1953, U.S. Supreme Ct. 1971. Assoc. Mullen & Filippi, Attys., San Francisco, 1953-55; dep. county counsel Santa Clara Calif. County Counsel, San Jose, 1955-57; city atty. City of Mountain View, Calif., 1957-62, City of Santa Cruz, Calif., 1962-90; pres. Atchison, Anderson, Hurley & Barisone, Profl. Law Corp., Santa Cruz, 1980-96; of counsel Atchison Barisone & Condotti, Profl. Law Corp., Santa Cruz, 1996, Law Offices of Rodney R. Atchison, 1996-2001. Arbitrator Am. Arbitration Assn., San Francisco, 1970—. Pres. Rotary Club Mountain View, Calif., 1961-62, Santa Cruz (Calif.) County Bar Assn., 1973. With USNR, 1944-46. Mem. ABA, Santa Cruz Rotary Club, Elks Lodge (life). Roman Catholic. Avocations: skiing, travel, golf. Alternative dispute resolution, Commercial, contracts (including sales of goods; commercial financing), Property, real (including real estate development, water). E-mail: r.atchison@sbcglobal.net.

ATES, J. ROBERT, lawyer; b. New Orleans, Sept. 12, 1945; s. Loten Arthur Jr. and Eugenia Lea (Carpenter) A. BA, Tulane U., 1967; JD, Loyola U., New Orleans, 1972. Bar: La. 1973, U.S. Dist. Ct. (ea., mid. and we. dists.) La., U.S. Ct. Appeals (5th cir.), U.S. Supreme Ct., Colo. 1990. Prof., chmn. sci. dept. East Jefferson High Sch., Metairie, La., 1967-72; law clk. to judge La. Ct. Appeals (4th cir.), New Orleans, 1972-73; assoc. Kierr, Gainsburgh, Benjamin, Fallon & Lewis, New Orleans, 1974-78, ptnr., 1979-87, Gainsburgh, Benjamin, Fallon, David & Ates, New Orleans, 1987-94; prin. J. Robert Ates, A Profl. Law Corp., New Orleans, 1994-95, Ates & Assocs., A Profl. Law Corp., New Orleans, 1996—. Lectr. in field; mem. adj. law faculty and skills faculty, Continuing Legal Edn. Programs, Tulane U., Loyola Law Schs. Mem. ATLA, FBA, La. Bar Assn. (vice chmn. civil law sect. 1986-87, chmn. 1987—, sec., treas. 1985—, chmn. pub. rels. and edn. com. 1987—, mem. ho. of dels. 1987-94, bd. govs. 1993—, gen. sec. and editor La. Bar Jour. 1993-95), Orleans Bar Assn., Jefferson Bar

Assn., La. Trial Lawyers Assn. (pres.'s adv. com.), Soc. Am. Law Tchrs., Am. Soc. Law and Medicine. Democrat. Baptist. Avocations: photography, snow skiing, water skiing, hunting, fishing. Admiralty, Personal injury (including property damage), Product liability. Home: 29 Turnberry Dr La Place LA 70068-1617 Office: Ates & Assocs A Profl Law Corp 4004 Magazine St Ste A New Orleans LA 70115-2762

ATKIN, GARY EUGENE, lawyer; b. Salt Lake City, Oct. 7, 1946; s. Henry Eugene and Dolores Heckman (Dykes) A.; m. Marsha Selin, June 12, 1967; children: Kathryn Dawn, Kenneth Eugene. BS in Acctg., U. Utah, 1967, JD, 1970. Bar: Utah 1970, U.S. Dist. Ct. Utah 1970, U.S. Ct. Appeals (10th cir.) 1978, U.S. Supreme Ct. 1978. Assoc. Rawlings, Roberts & Black, Salt Lake City, 1970—74; assoc. counsel Utah State Legislature, Salt Lake City, 1974—79; ptnr. Gustin, Adams, Kesting & Liapis, Salt Lake City, 1979—81, of counsel, 1981—82; ptnr. Atkin & Anderson, Salt Lake City, 1982—91; sr. ptnr. Atkin & Assocs., Salt Lake City, 1992—. Mem. Assn. Trial Lawyers Am., Fed. Bar Assn., Utah Trial Lawyers Assn. (bd. dirs. 1980-90, pres. 1984-85). Avocation: announcer. Product liability, Corporate, general, Personal injury (including property damage). Home: 4498 Adonis Dr Salt Lake City UT 84124-3923 Office: Atkin & Assocs 311 S State St Ste 380 Salt Lake City UT 84111-5215

ATKINS, PETER ALLAN, lawyer; b. N.Y.C., June 29, 1943; m. Lorraine Marilyn Feuerstadt, Apr. 3, 1966; children: Aileen Debra, Karen Jennifer. BA magna cum laude, CUNY, 1965; LLB cum laude, Harvard U., 1968. Bar: N.Y. 1969. Assoc. Skadden, Arps, Slate, Meagher & Flom LLP, N.Y.C., 1968—74, ptnr., 1975—. Mem. dean's adv. bd. Harvard Law Sch.; bd. dirs. A Better Chance, Inc. Contbr. articles to profl. jours. Mem.: ABA, Assn. of Bar of City of N.Y., N.Y. State Bar Assn. Corporate, general, Mergers and acquisitions, Securities. Office: Skadden Arps Slate Meagher & Flom LLP 4 Times Sq Fl 46 New York NY 10036-6595 E-mail: patkins@skadden.com.

ATKINS, RONALD RAYMOND, lawyer; b. Kingston, N.Y., Mar. 8, 1933; s. A. Raymond and Charlotte S. A.; m. Mary-Elizabeth Empringham, June 23, 1956; children: Peter Herrick, Timothy Barnard, Suzanne Elizabeth. BS in Econs., U. Pa., 1954; JD, Columbia U., 1959. Bar: N.Y. 1959. Assoc. Pell, Butler, Curtis & LeViness, N.Y.C., 1959-61, ptnr., 1962-67; ptnr. Bisset & Atkins, N.Y.C., 1967—, also Greenwich, Conn., 1982—; also of counsel Davidson, Dawson & Clark, LLP, N.Y.C.; mem. vis. com. Dept. Medieval Art and Cloisters, Met. Mus. Art.; mem. coun. of Friends, NYU, inst. Fine Arts; trustee Mianus Gorge Preserve, Inc., chmn., 1984-94, Westmoreland Sancutary. 1st lt. U.S. Army, 1954-56. Fellow Frick Collection, Pierpont Morgan Libr.; mem. ABA, N.Y. State Bar Assn., Assn. Bar City N.Y., Medieval Acad. Am., Coll. Art Assn., Assn. Art History, Internat. Ctr. Medieval Art. Republican. Episcopalian. Club: University (N.Y.C.), Grolier Club (N.Y.C.), Field Club (Greenwich, Conn.), U. Pa. Club (N.Y.C.), Greenwich (Conn.) Croquet. Corporate, general, Probate (including wills, trusts), Estate taxation. Home: Hobby Hill Farm Mianus River Rd Bedford NY 10506 also: 777 North St Greenwich CT 06831-3105

ATKINS, THOMAS JAY, lawyer, missionary and pastor; b. Detroit, Apr. 21, 1943; s. Robert Alfred and Dorothy Irene Atkins. BS in Applied Math. and Physics, Rensselaer Poly. Inst., 1965, MS in Engring., 1967; JD, UCLA, 1979; postgrad., Harvard Law Sch., 1979; MBA, UCLA, 1983; MDiv, MB Bibl. Sem., 2000. Bar: Calif. 1979; ordained minister Am. Bapt. Chs.-USA, 2002. Ctr. for Advanced Studies, Gen. Electric Co., Washington (DC), Santa Barbara, Calif., 1967—70; prin. Cen. Valley Distbrs., Visalia, Calif., 1970—, Thomas Jay Atkins, P.C., Sacramento, 1979—, Calif. Merc. Inc., Tulare, Calif., 1980—, United Motors, San Jose, Fresno and Sacramento, Calif., 1986—; sr. cons. ptnr. Atkins Group, LLP, L.A., N.Y.C., London, Paris, 1989—. Founder Atkins Devel. Corp. (formerly Atkins Real Estate Corp.), L.A., 1985; chmn. bd. dirs., World Parts Corp., San Francisco; chmn. bd. dirs. Students Internat., Antigua, Guatemala and Jaracoba, Dominican Republic, 1996—. Recipient rsch. commendation NASA, 1969 Mem. ABA, Am. Mgmt. Assn., UCLA Alumni Assn. (bd. dirs. 1991—), Santa Barbara Yacht Club, Visalia Country Club, Regency Club of L.A., Visalia Racquet Club Republican. Immigration, naturalization, and customs, Private international, Alternative dispute resolution. Home: Badger Hill Ranch 363 Valley View Dr Exeter CA 93221-9798 Office: PO Box 3744 Visalia CA 93278-3744 also: 969 Hilgard Ave Ste 1007 Los Angeles CA 90024-3079 E-mail: tjatkins@arilion.com.

ATKINSON, MICHAEL PEARCE, lawyer; b. Ft. Worth, Feb. 19, 1946; s. Charles Pearce and Nancy Lou (Thompson) A.; m. Melissa Jan Potter, July 17, 1976; children: Charles Travis, Kellen Elizabeth. BA, U. Okla., 1968, JD, 1972; MS, U. Tex., 1975. Bar: Okla. 1972, U.S. Dist. Ct. (we. and ea. dists.) Okla. 1972, U.S. Dist. Ct. (no. dist.) Okla. 1975, U.S. Ct. Appeals (10th cir.) 1981. Ptnr. Jones, Atkinson, Williams, Bane & Klingenberg, Enid, Okla., 1972, Best Sharp Thomas Glass & Atkinson, Tulsa, 1980-87, Thomas Glass Atkinson Haskins Nellis & Boudreaux, Tulsa, 1980-93, Atkinson Haskins Nellis Holeman Phipps Brittingham & Gladd, Tulsa, 1994—; asst. pub. defender Office of Oklahoma County Pub. Defender, Oklahoma City, 1973; asst. dist. atty. Office of Oklahoma County Dist. Atty., Oklahoma City, 1974. Asst. adj. prof. Coll. Law U. Tulsa, 1976-77. With USAR, 1970-72. Master Am. Inns of Ct. (emeritus); fellow Internat. Acad. Trial Lawyers, Am. Coll. Trial Lawyers; mem. Internat. Assn. Def. Counsel (faculty trial acad. 1986), Am. Bd. Trial Advocates (pres. Okla. chpt. 1995, diplomate). Presbyterian. Avocations: hunting, fishing, running. Insurance, Personal injury (including property damage), Product liability. Home: 2440 E 28th St Tulsa OK 74114-5611 Office: Atkinson Haskins Nellis Holeman Phipps Brittingham & Gladd 525 S Main St Tulsa OK 74103-4509 E-mail: matkinson@ahn-law.com.

ATLAS, SCOTT JEROME, lawyer; b. Austin, Tex., Jan. 15, 1950; s. Morris and Rita Jean (Willner) A.; m. Nancy Ellen Friedman, Mar. 26, 1983; 2 children. BA magna cum laude, Yale U., 1971; JD with honors, U. Tex., 1975. Bar: Tex. 1975, U.S. Dist. Ct. (so. dist.) Tex. 1976, U.S. Ct. Appeals (5th cir.) 1976, U.S. Supreme Ct. 1979, U.S. Ct. Appeals (11th cir.) 1981, U.S. Dist. Ct. (we, no. and ea. dists). Law clk. to judge U.S. Ct. Appeals (5th cir.), Austin, 1975—76; assoc. Vinson & Elkins, Houston, 1976—82, ptnr., 1982—. Mem. bd. visitors U. Tex. Law Sch., 1982-90; mem. Chancellors Coun. U. Tex., exec. com., 2001-; mem. Com. of 125, U. Tex., Austin, 2003--; lectr. numerous law schs. and legal orgns. Chancellor, Coif, editor-in-chief Tex. Law Rev.; contbr. numerous articles to profl. jours. Founding pres. Houston Shakespeare Festival, 1980-82; v.p., co-founder Tex. Lyceum Assn. Inc., 1983-85; exec. com. Alley Theatre, Houston, 1983—, ex-officio, 1989—; bd. dirs. ADL S.W. Region, 1998—, exec. com., 1999-, v.p., 2001—; past bd. dirs. Tex. Opera Theatre, Cultural Arts Coun. of Houston, Young Audiences Houston, others; county coord. U.S. Sen. Lloyd M. Bentsen, 1987-92; mem. adv. com. Law Firm Pro Bono Project, 1991-, chmn., 1997-2001. Named One of Outstanding Young Houstonians, Jaycees, 1984-85, One of Outstanding Young Tex. Exes, Tex. Ex-Students Assn., 1989, Outstanding Young Lawyer in Houston, Houston Young Lawyers Assn., 1984, Azteca Civil Rights award, Lulac Dist. XVIII, 1993, Lawyer of the Yr., Mexican-ABA Tex., 1996, spl. recognition for contbns. to cross-border relationships Tex.-Mex. Bar Assn., 1997, Pub. Interest award Tex. Law Fellowship, 1998, ADL Karen Susman Jurisprudence award, 2002. Fellow Houston Bar Found. (founder, life), Tex. Bar Found. (life), Am. Bar Found.; mem. ABA (chmn. litig. sect. 2002-03, chmn. appellate practice com. litigation sect. 1985-89, coun. mem. litigation sect. 1989-92, exec. com. 1992-96, standing com. on pro bono and pub. svc. 1995-98, co-chair strategic planning implementation task force litigation sect. 1996-97, dir. divns. litigation sect. 1997-98, co-chair fed. practice task force litigation sect. 1998-2000, liaison to civil adv. com. jud. conf. on rules of practice and procedure 1998-2000, planning com. mem. London 2000 meeting 1996-2000, working group on UCITA 2001-2002, task force on advocacy for the assn. and profession 2002-2003, Pro Bono Publico award 1986), State Bar Tex. (jud. selection funding com. 1985-87, liaison with law schs. 1988-90, legal aid to indigent com. 1986, numerous coms. 1986-87), Alliance for Jud. Funding (bd. dirs. 1992-95, 2003—), Tex. Law Rev. Assn. (past pres., bd. dirs. 1977-95, Leon Green award 1997), U. Tex. Ex-Students Assn. (exec. coun. 1992-98), Houston Bar Assn. (vol. lawyers program bd. 1998-2000), Houston U. Tex. Ex-Students Assn. (bd. dirs. 1991-92), Yale U. Alumni Club (class sec. 1991-96, coun. 1986-87, local dir. 1982-89, 90-91). Avocations: golf, books. Federal civil litigation, State civil litigation. Office: Vinson & Elkins LLP 1001 Fannin St Ste 2300 Houston TX 77002-6760 E-mail: satlas@velaw.com.

ATLASS, THEODORE BRUCE, lawyer, educator; b. Chgo., June 2, 1951; s. Ralph Louis Atlass and Opal Jeanne Collins. BSBA, U. Denver, 1972; JD, DePaul U., 1975; LLM, U. Miami, Coral Gables, Fla., 1976. Bar: Colo. 1975, U.S. Tax Ct. 1976, U.S. Supreme Ct. 1982. Shareholder Theodore B. Atlass, P.C., Denver, 1976-83, Atlass Profl. Corp., Denver, 1986—; ptnr. Welborn, Dufford, Brown & Tooley, Denver, 1983-85. Lectr. Colo. Soc. CPAs, 1977—, Coll. Law U. Denver, 1976—. Chmn. Advanced Estate Planning Symposium U. Denver, 1982—; bd. dirs. St. Joseph Hosp. Found., Denver, 1982-97, Colo. Ballet, Denver, 1985-92. Fellow Am. Coll. Tax Counsel, Am. Coll. Trust & Estate Counsel (Colo. state chair 1996-2001; fiduciary income tax com. chair 1997-2000); mem. Denver Estate Planning Coun. (pres. 1991-92), Denver Tax Assn. (pres. 1985), Centennial Estate Planning Coun. (pres. 1993-94). Republican. Presbyterian. Estate planning, Probate (including wills, trusts), Estate taxation. Office: Atlass Profl Corp Ste 100 3665 Cherry Creek North Dr Denver CO 80209-3712

ATTANASIO, JOHN BAPTIST, dean, law educator; b. Jersey City, N.J., Oct. 19, 1954; s. Gaetano and Madeline (Germinario) A.; m. Kathleen Mary Spartana, Aug. 20, 1977; children: Thomas, Michael. BA, U. Va., 1976; JD, NYU, 1979; diploma in law, Oxford U., 1982; LLM, Yale U., 1985. Bar: Md. 1979, U.S. Dist. Ct. Md. 1980, U.S. Ct. Appeals (4th cir.) 1980, U.S. Supreme Ct. 1983. Pvt. practice, Balt., 1979-81; vis. asst. prof. law U. Pitts., 1982-84; assoc. prof. law U. Notre Dame, Ind., 1985-88, prof. law, 1988-92; Regan dir. Kroc Inst. for Internat. Peace Studies, 1991-92; dean Sch. of Law St. Louis U., 1992-98; dean, William Hawley Atwell chair constnl. law So. Meth. U. Sch. Law, Dallas, 1998—. Co-author: Constitutional Law 1989. Chair adv. bd. Ctr. for Civil and Human Rights, 1990-92; mem. Fulbright awards area com., 1994-96; bd. dirs. Legal Svcs. Ea. Mo., 1996-98; bd. dirs. Ctr. for Internat. Understanding, 1993—. Recipient Legal Teaching award Sch. of Law, NYU, 1994. Mem. Ctrl. States Law Sch. Assn. (v.p. 1992-94), Phi Beta Kappa, Alpha Sigma Nu. Democrat. Roman Catholic. Office: So Meth U Dedman Sch Law PO Box 750116 3315 Daniel Ave Dallas TX 75275-0116*

ATTERBURY, LEE RICHARD, lawyer; b. Newark, Aug. 25, 1948; s. Harold Blackburn and Annabel Rose (Lee) A.; m. Sally A. Atkinson; children: Alex Blackburn, Luke Treloar, Ellen Ruth. BA cum laude, Lawrence U., 1970; JD, U. Wis., 1974. Bar: Wis. 1974, U.S. Dist. Ct. (we. dist.) Wis. 1974, U.S. Ct. Appeals (7th cir.) 1988. Cert. civil trial specialist. Assoc. Callahan & Arnold Law Office, Columbus, Wis., 1974-80; ptnr. Atterbury & Riley, S.C., Madison, Wis., 1980—. Note and comment editor U. Wis. Law Rev., 1974. Mem. Dane County Bar Assn., Assn. Trial Lawyers Am., ACLU, The Planetary Soc., Union of Concerned Scientists. Federal civil litigation, State civil litigation, Personal injury (including property damage). Home: 7873 Windermere Ct Cross Plains WI 53528

ATTOLICO, LORENZO, lawyer; b. Rome, Mar. 20, 1963; s. Giuseppe Attolico and Bianca Maria Lucherini; m. Cristiana Gellini, Jan. 15, 1994; children: Ludovica, Bianca. Law Degree, U. Rome, 1987. Bar: Italy 1990, Italian Supreme Ct. 2002. Ptnr. Studio Legale Attolico, Rome, 1987, White and Case, Rome, 2001. Intellectual property. Office: White and Case 6 Via Porta Pinciana 00187 Rome Italy

ATTRIDGE, DANIEL F. lawyer; b. Washington, Oct. 4, 1954; s. Patrick and Teresa A.; m. Anne Asbill, Aug. 23, 1980; children: James, William, and Thomas. BA magna cum laude, U. Pa., 1976; JD cum laude, Georgetown U., 1979. Bar: D.C. 1980, U.S. Dist. Ct. D.C. 1980, U.S. Ct. Appeals (D.C. cir.) 1980, U.S. Supreme Ct. 1983, U.S. Dist. Ct. Md. 1985, U.S. Ct. Appeals (fed. cir.) 1985, U.S. Ct. Appeals (2d.cir.) 1987, U.S. Ct. Claims 1988, U.S. Ct. Appeals (4th and 6th cirs.) 1990, U.S. Ct. Appeals (8th cir.) 1997, U.S. Ct. Appeals (1st cir.) 2000. Law clk. to judge Oliver Gasch U.S. Dist. Ct. D.C., Washington, 1979-80; assoc. Kirkland & Ellis, Washington, 1980-85, ptnr., 1985—. Faculty Nat. Inst. Trial Advocacy, 1991—. Exec. editor Georgetown U. Law Jour., 1978-79. Fellow Am. Bar Found.; mem. ABA (vice chmn. antitrust sect. Sherman Act sect. 2 com. 1999-2002), D.C. Bar Assn. (bd. govs. 1996-99, co-chair litigation sect. 1993-96). Roman Catholic. General civil litigation, Antitrust, Intellectual property. Home: 1249 Cherry Tree Ln Annapolis MD 21403-5023 Office: Kirkland & Ellis 655 15th St NW Fl 12 Washington DC 20005-5793 E-mail: daniel_attridge@kirkland.com.

ATTRIDGE, RICHARD BYRON, lawyer; b. Atlanta, Oct. 14, 1933; s. Archibald Angus and Katherine Elizabeth (Babb) A.; m. Florence Law, Dec. 14, 1963; children: Anne Habersham, Elizabeth Barnes, R. Byron Jr. BA, Princeton U., 1955; LLB, Emory U., 1961. Bar: Ga. 1960. Ptnr. King & Spalding, Atlanta, 1960—. Chmn. State Bd. of Bar Examiners, Ga., 1978-83. Vice chmn. Cmty. Rels. Com., Atlanta, 1968-73; various local charities; vestry Episc. Ch. 1st lt. U.S. Army, 1956-57. Fellow Am. Coll. Trial Lawyers; mem. ABA, State Bar Ga. (bd. govs. 1974-83), Atlanta Bar Assn. (pres. 1971-72), Lawyers Club Atlanta, Capital City Club (bd. dirs. 1989—), Piedmont Driving Club. Avocations: hunting, fishing, tennis. Home: 2820 Habersham Rd NW Atlanta GA 30305-2959 Office: King & Spalding 191 Peachtree St NE Ste 40 Atlanta GA 30303-1740

ATWOOD, JAMES R. lawyer; b. White Plains, N.Y., Feb. 21, 1944; s. Bernard D. and Joyce Rose Atwood; m. Wendy Fisler, Aug. 22, 1981 (div.); children: Christopher Charles, Carl Fisler; m. Nancy A. Udell, Oct. 6, 2001. BA, Yale U., 1966; JD, Stanford U., 1969. Bar: Calif. 1969, D.C. 1970. Law clk. to judge U.S. Ct. Appeals, L.A., 1969-70; law clk. to Chief Justice Warren Burger U.S. Supreme Ct., 1970-71; mem. Covington & Burling, Washington, 1971-78, ptnr., 1977-78, 81—. Dep. asst. sec. for transp. affairs U.S. Dept. State, Washington, 1978-79, dep. legal adviser, 1979-80; acting prof. Law Sch. Stanford U., 1980 Author: (with Kingman Brewster) Antitrust and American Business Abroad, 2nd edit, 1981. Mem. bd. visitors Law Sch. Stanford U., 1995-97. Mem. ABA, Am. Soc. Internat. Law, D.C. Bar Assn. Antitrust, Federal civil litigation, Private international. Home: 8020 Greentree Rd Bethesda MD 20817-1304 Office: Covington & Burling 1201 Pennsylvania Ave NW Washington DC 20004-2401

ATWOOD, ROY TRESS, lawyer; b. Streator, Ill., Sept. 21, 1957; s. Roy Crawford and June Tress A.; m. Holly Gene Beggs, Aug. 28, 1981; children: Roy Garrett, Brandon Gregory, Adam Grayson, Andrew Gerard, Amy Elizabeth. BS, U. Ill., 1979; JD cum laude, So. Meth. U., 1988. Bar: Tex. 1988. Acctg. and fin. mgr. Cargill, Inc., Ft. Worth, 1981-85; atty. Liddell, Sapp, Zivley, Hill & LaBoon, Dallas, 1988-90, Gibson, Dunn & Crutcher, Dallas, 1990-92, Herbert, Adams, Crawford & Atwood, Dallas, 1992-94, Jones Day, Dallas, 1994—. Coach nat. mock trial teams So. Meth. U., Dallas, 1992-98; mem. faculty Nat. Inst. Trial Advocacy, Dallas, 1997—. Editor-in-chief Jour. Air Law and Commerce, 1987-88 (Best article award 1987); contbr. articles to profl. jours. Mem. Carrollton Zoning Bd. Adjustment, 1995-2000; mem. Carrollton Capital Improvement Adv. Com., 2000—; trustee Spl. Care and Career Svcs., 2001—. Recipient Bell & Tucker Trial Advocacy award, 1988. Mem. Am. Inns Ct. (barrister). Republican. Methodist. Federal civil litigation, State civil litigation. Office: Jones Day 2727 N Harwood St Dallas TX 75201-1567 E-mail: royatwood@jonesday.com.

AUCHINCLOSS, JOHN WINTHROP, lawyer; s. Louis Stanton and Adele Lawrence Auchincloss; m. Tracy Pennoyer, Apr. 9, 1988; children: Emily Winthrop, James Parsons. BA, Yale U., 1980; JD, U. Va., 1983; LLM, Cambridge U., Eng., 1984. Bar: N.Y. 1984, D.C. 1985, Conn. 1995, U.S. Ct. Appeals (2d cir.) 1990, U.S. Dist. Ct. (so. and ea. dist.) N.Y. 1994. Assoc. Davis Polk & Wardwell, N.Y.C., 1984—88; asst. U.S. atty. U.S. Atty.'s Office, So. Dist. N.Y., N.Y.C., 1988—94; of counsel Levett, Rockwood & Sanders LLP, Westport, Conn., 1994—95; asst./assoc. gen. counsel Commonfund Group, Westport, Conn., 1996—2000, gen. counsel Wilton, Conn., 2000—. Notes editor (articles) Va. Law Rev. Recipient Traynor prize legal writing, U. Va. Sch. Law, 1983. Mem.: ABA, Order of the Coif. Securities, Finance, Corporate, general. Office: Commonfund Group 15 Old Danbury Rd Wilton CT 06883 Office Fax: 203-834-2670.

AUCLAIR, SUZANNE C. lawyer; AB, Brown U., 1987; JD, Boston U., 1990. Assoc. Nutter, McClennen & Fish, Boston, 1990—92, King & Spalding, Atlanta, 1992—94; assoc. counsel Met. Life Ins. Co., N.Y.C., 1994—97; first v.p. Morgan Stanley, N.Y.C., 1998—2000; assoc. gen. counsel Unilever US, Inc., N.Y.C., 2000—. Adj. prof. Benjamin N. Cardozo Sch. Law, N.Y.C., 1995—2000. Mem.: ABA. Labor (including EEOC, Fair Labor Standards Act, labor-management relations, NLRB, OSHA). Office: Unilever United States Inc 390 Park Ave New York NY 10022

AUCUTT, RONALD DAVID, lawyer; b. St. Paul, Dec. 28, 1945; s. Howard Lewis and Eleanor May (Malcolm) A.; m. Grace Diane Kok, Apr. 3, 1976; children: David Gerard, James Andrew. BA, U. Minn., 1967, JD, 1975. Bar: Minn. 1975, D.C. 1976, Va. 1978, Tex. 1999, U.S. Supreme Ct. 1978, U.S. Tax Ct. 1980, U.S. Dist. Ct. D.C. 1980, U.S. Ct. Appeals (D.C. cir.) 1980, U.S. Ct. of Claims 1980, U.S. Claims Ct. 1982, U.S. Ct. Appeals (fed. cir.) 1982, U.S. Dist. Ct. (ea. dist.) Va. 1986, U.S. Ct. Appeals (4th cir.) 1986. Assoc. Miller & Chevalier, Chartered, Washington, 1975-81, ptnr., 1982-98, McGuireWoods LLP, McLean, Va., 1998—. Mem. bd. advisors IRS Practice Alert, N.Y.C., 1987-93; adj. prof. Sch. Law U. Va., 1998—; mem. adv. com. Philip E. Heckerling Inst. on Estate Planning U. Miami, 1999—. Mem. bd. advisors Jour. Taxation Exempt Orgns., 1989-2000, Bus. Entities, N.Y.C., 1999—; mem. editl. bd. Estate Planning, N.Y.C., 1993—, mem. adv. bd. Tax Mgmt. Estates, Gifts, and Trusts Jour., 1999—; editl. adv. bd. Bus. Valuation Update, Portland, Oreg., 1999—; contbr. articles to profl. publs. Orgn. Security and Coop. in Europe internat. observer Bulgarian Parliamentary Election, 1997; sec.-treas. Miller and Chevalier Charitable Found., Washington, 1980—82, pres., 1993—97; bd. dirs. Coun. for Ct. Excellence, Washington, 1993—99, Advocates Internat., Fairfax, Va., 1997—2000, vice chmn., 1999—2000; mem. adv. bd. Trinity Law Sch., Santa Ana, Calif., 1998—2001; bd. visitors U. Minn. Law Sch., 1998—; bd. regents Trinity Internat. U., Deerfield, Ill., 2000—; bd. dirs. Evang. Free Ch. Am., Mpls., 1986—92, vice moderator, chmn. bd. dirs., 1993—95, moderator, 1995—97. Lt. USN, 1970—73. Fellow: Am. Coll. Trust and Estate Counsel (bd. regents 1996—, chmn. bus. planning com. 1997—2000, sec. 1999—2000, treas. 2000—01, v.p. 2001—02, pres.-elect 2002—03, pres. 2003—), Am. Coll. Tax Counsel, Am. Bar Found.; mem.: ABA (chair taxation sect., com. on estate and gift taxes 1986—88, vice chmn. com. on govt. submissions 1989—91, liaison to sect. real property, probate and trust law 1990—, chmn. com. on govt. submissions 1991—93, coun. 1993—97, vice chair com. ops. 1998—2000), Christian Legal Soc., Internat. Acad. Estate and Trust Law (exec. coun. 2000—, academician), U. Minn. Law Alumni Assn. (bd. dirs. 1998—), Met. Club Washington. Estate planning, Estate taxation, Taxation, general. Home: 3417 Silver Maple Pl Falls Church VA 22042-3545 Office: McGuireWoods LLP 1750 Tysons Blvd Ste 1800 Mc Lean VA 22102-4215 E-mail: raucutt@mcguirewoods.com.

AUERBACH, HILLEL JOSHUA, lawyer; b. NYC, Dec. 7, 1936; s. Philip and Bernice Lillian (Ackerman) A.; m. Sara-Ann Rosner, July 30, 1961; children-Ellen, Jonathan, Stephen. BS, MIT, 1958; LL.B., Yale U., 1961; LL.M. in Taxation, NYU, 1962. Bar: Conn. 1967, U.S. Dist. (so. and ea. dists.) N.Y. 1962, U.S. Dist. Ct. Conn. 1967, U.S. Ct. Appeals (2d cir.) 1967. Assoc. Casey Lane & Mittendorf, N.Y.C., 1962-66; ptnr. Winnick Resnik Skolnick & Auerbach, P.C., New Haven, 1966-87; solo practice, 1987—. Fellow Conn. Bar Found. (chmn. grant com. 1996-99, exec. bd. 1998-2002); mem. ABA, Conn. Bar Assn., New Haven County Bar Assn. Corporate, general, Probate (including wills, trusts), Personal income taxation. Office: Long Wharf Dr 12th Fl New Haven CT 06511 E-mail: H.Auerbach@centerprisect.com.

AUERBACH, JOSEPH, lawyer, educator, retired; b. Franklin, N.H., Dec. 3, 1916; s. Jacob and Besse Mae (Reamer) A.; m. Judith Evans, Nov. 10, 1941; children: Jonathan L., Hope B. Pym. AB, Harvard U., 1938, LLB, 1941. Bar: N.H. 1941, Mass. 1952, U.S. Ct. Appeals (1st, 2d, 3d, 5th, 7th and D.C. cirs.), U.S. Supreme Ct. 1948. Atty. SEC, Washington and Phila., 1941-43, prin. atty., 1946-49; fgn. service staff officer U.S. Dept. State, Dusseldorf, W. Ger., 1950-52; ptnr. Sullivan & Worcester, Boston, 1952-82, counsel, 1982—; lectr. Boston U. Law Sch., 1975-76, Harvard Bus. Sch., Boston, 1980-82, prof., 1982-83, Class of 1957 prof., 1983-87, prof. emeritus, 1987—; prof. Harvard Extension Sch., 1988, 91-95. Bd. dirs. Nat. Benefit Life Ins. Co., N.Y.C. Author: (with S.L. Hayes, III), Investment Banking and Diligence, 1986, Underwriting Regulation and Shelf Registration Phenomenon in Wall Street and Regulation, 1987, also chpt. to book, papers and articles in field. Trustee Mass. Eye and Ear Infirmary, Boston, 1981—, chmn. devel. com., 1985-88, chmn. nominating com., 1993-94; mem. adv. bd., former chmn. devel. com. Am. Repertory Theatre, Cambridge, Mass., 1985—; bd. dirs., past pres. Friends of Boston U. Librs., 1972—; past v.p., bd. dirs. Shakespeare Globe Ctr., N.A., 1983-90; overseer New Eng. Conservatory of Music, 1992-98, mem. fin. com.; bd. dirs. English Speaking Union, Boston, 1995-98; chair 1938 Harvard Pres. Assn.; active Harvard Coll. Fund, Harvard Law Sch. Fund. Decorated Army Commendation medal; recipient Disting. Svc. award Harvard Bus. Sch., 1996, Disting. Teaching award 1993, Exemplary Svc. award Harvard Extension Sch., 1995. Mem. ABA, Mass. Bar Assn., Boston Bar Assn., Harvard Mus. Assn., St. Botolph Club, Harvard Club N.Y.C., Shop Club, Downtown Club. Home: 300 Boylston St Apt 512 Boston MA 02116-3923 Office: Sullivan & Worcester 1 Post Office Sq Ste 2300 Boston MA 02109-2129 also: Harvard Bus Sch Cumnock Hall Rm 300 Boston MA 02163

AUERBACH, MARSHALL JAY, lawyer; b. Chgo., Sept. 5, 1932; s. Samuel M. and Sadie (Miller) A.; m. Carole Landsberg, July 3, 1960; children: Keith Alan, Michael Ward Student, U. Ill.; JD, John Marshall Law Sch., 1955. Bar: Ill. 1955. Sole practice, Evanston, Ill., 1955-72; ptnr. in charge matrimonial law sect. Jenner & Block, Chgo., 1972-80; mem. firm Marshall J. Auerbach & Assocs., Ltd., Chgo., 1980—. Mem. faculty Ill. Inst. Continuing Legal Edn. Author: Illinois Marriage and Dissolution of Marriage Act, enacted into law, 1977; Historical and Practice Notes to Illinois Marriage and Dissolution of Marriage Act, 1980-88; contbr. chpts. to Family Law, Vol. 2 Fellow Am. Acad. Matrimonial Lawyers; mem. Ill. State Bar Assn. (chmn. family law sect. 1971-72), ABA (vice-chmn. family law sect. com. for liaison with tax sect. 1974-76) Family and matrimonial. Home and Office: Marshall J Auerbach & Assoc Ltd 30 N La Salle St Ste 3400 Chicago IL 60602

AUERBACH, PAUL IRA, lawyer; b. N.Y.C., Dec. 30, 1932; s. Joseph and Fannie (Steingard) A.; children: Stuart Andrew, Beth Royce. LLB, Bklyn. Law Sch., 1954; CLU, Am. Coll., 1980, ChFC, 1982. Bar: N.Y. 1955, Fla. 1991, U.S. Dist. Ct. (so. and ea. dists.) N.Y., U.S. Dist Ct. (so. dist.) Fla.

1991. Trial counsel Cosmopolitan Mutual Ins. Corp., N.Y.C., 1955-57, Hertz Corp., N.Y.C., 1957-59; ptnr. Brent, Phillips, Auerbach & Dranoff, Rockland, N.Y., 1959-63; prin. Paul I. Auerbach, Atty. at Law, N.Y.C. and Bronx, 1963-97, Palm Beach Gardens, Fla., 1990—. Founder Young Dem. Com., Bronx, 1955-60; committeeman Rep. Com., South Orangeton, N.Y., 1970-76. Mem.: KP, Rotary (chmn. drug prevention com. 1970—74), ABA, Nat. Acad. Elder Law Attys., Internat. Assn. Fin. Planners, Planned Giving Coun. of Palm Beach County, Tax Inst. of Palm Beach County, Fla. Bar Assn., Palm Beach County Bar Assn., North Palm Beach County Bar Assn. (pres. 1999—2000), Bronx Bar Assn. (chmn. criminal law com. 1990—91), N.Y. Criminal Bar Assn., N.Y. State Bar Assn., Masons. Avocations: tennis, gourmet food, golf. Criminal, Family and matrimonial, Probate (including wills, trusts). Home: 11215 Curry Dr Palm Beach Gardens FL 33418 E-mail: piaesq@yahoo.com.

AUERBACH, SHERYL LYNN, lawyer; b. Phila., July 20, 1952; d. Nathan and Rhoda (Silverstein) A.; m. Jerome R. Richter, Nov. 5, 1977; children: Lauren, Jonathan. BA magna cum laude, Wesleyan U., 1973; JD cum laude, U. Pa., 1976. Bar: Pa. 1976 (co-chmn. moot ct. bd.), U.S. Dist. Ct. (ea. dist.) Pa. 1976, U.S. Ct. Appeals (3d cir.) 1977, U.S. Ct. Appeals (8th cir.) 1989, U.S. Supreme Ct. 1989. With Dilworth Paxson, LLP, Phila., 1977—, sr. ptnr. Bd. dirs. Atwater Kent Mus., 1989-91. Fellow Am. Bar Found.; mem. ABA, Pa. Bar Assn., Phila Bar Assn. (past chmn. State Civil Procedures Commn., past chmn. Bus. Ct. Task Force), Phi Beta Kappa. State civil litigation, Construction, Environmental. Office: Dilworth Paxson LLP 3200 Mellon Bank Ctr Philadelphia PA 19103

AUF DER MAUR, ROLF, lawyer; b. Lucerne, Switzerland, Apr. 1, 1962; JD, Zurich (Switzerland) U. Bar: Zurich. Co-founder The Portable Shop, Zurich; assoc. Bär & Karrer, Zurich; ptnr. Beglinger Holenstein, Zurich, Vischer, Zurich, Basel, Switzerland. V.p. Swiss Interactive Media and Software Assn., Zurich, Switzerland; mem. exec. bd. Internat. Assn. Entertainment Lawyers, London; chair dispute resolution com. Internat. Bar Assn., London. Mem.: Young Entrepreneurs' Orgn. (exec. bd. 1999—2002). Trademark and copyright, Patent, IT and telecommunication, Communications, Computer, Entertainment, Intellectual property. Office: Vischer Arterstrasse 24 8032 Zürich Switzerland

AUGELLO, WILLIAM JOSEPH, lawyer; b. Bklyn., Apr. 5, 1926; s. William J. and Catherine (Ehalt) A.; m. Elizabeth Deasy, July 1, 1950; children: Thomas, Charles, Patricia, William, Peggy Ann, James. LLB, Fordham U., 1950; BA, Dartmouth Coll., 1946. Bar: N.Y. 1951. Individual practice law, N.Y.C., 1953-71; mem. firm Augello, Deegan & Pezold, Huntington, N.Y., 1971-78; sr. mem. firm Augello, Pezold & Hirschmann, Huntington, 1978—98. Treas., dir. Transp. Arbitration Bd., Inc., 1978—; chmn. accreditation com. Certified Claims Profl. Accreditation Council, Inc., Washington, 1981—; exec. dir. Transp. Consumer Protection Coun. Inc., Huntington, 1974—; adv. com. pvt. internat. law study group maritime matters Dept. State; co-chmn. uniform liability regime working group Ctr. Inter-Am. Trade; adj. prof. U. Ariz.; bd. dirs. U. Denver Intermodal Transportation Inst., bd. dirs. Inst. Logistical Mgmt. Author: Freight Claims in Plain English, 1979, 82, 95, Transportation Insurance in Plain English, 1985, Defending and Avoiding Undercharge Claims and Suits, 1991, Doing Business Under the New Transportational Law: The Negotiated Rates Act of 1993, 94, How to Read Tariffs to Avoid Surprises, 1994, Shippers Domestic Truck Bill of Lading, 1996, A Guide to Transportation After the I.C.C., 1996, Protecting Shippers Interests, 1997, Corporate Procedures for Shipping and Receiving, 1998, Transportation, Logistics and the Law, 2001; co-author: Freight Claim Prevention in Plain English, 1985, Transportation Contracts in Plain English, 1991, Q & A in Plain English, 1999; author, lectr. Beginning of Freight Claims-Bill of Lading Contract, 1979, Documenting Claims, 1980, Liability Rules and Shipping/Receiving Practices Affecting Loss, Damage and Delay, 1981, Changes in Carrier Liability: Court Decisions, Statutes and Regulations, 1983, Legal Principles of Freight Claims From Claimant's Standpoint, 101 Declinations-And What To Do About Them, Differences Between Can. and U.S. Carrier Liability, Negotiating Liability in Today's Transp. Environment. Served with USN, 1944-46. Recipient Harry E. Salzberg Medallion award Syracuse U., 1994, Transp. Educator of Yr. award Operation Stimulus, 1996; named Nat. Transp. Man of Yr., Delta Nu Alpha, 1979-80. Mem. Maritime Law Assn., Transp. Lawyers Assn. (Disting. Svc. award 1988), Suffolk County Bar Assn., Assn. Transp. Law, Logistics and Policy, Indian Hills Country Club (ft. Salonga, N.Y.), El Con Conquistador Country Club (Tucson), Delta Nu Alpha. Republican. Roman Catholic. Administrative and regulatory, Transportation. Office: Augello Pezold & Hirschmann 120 Main St Huntington NY 11743-6906 also: 11520 N Palmetto Dunes Ave Tucson AZ 85737-7205 E-mail: williamaugello@att.net.

AUGUSTINI, MICHAEL CHARLES, lawyer; b. Denver, Sept. 28, 1967; m. Hope Hall, Nov. 18, 1995. BA, Bowdoin Coll., Brunswick, Maine, 1989; JD, U. Maine, 1995. Bar: Maine 1995, U.S. Ct. Appeals (1st cir.) 1996, D.C. 1996. Law clk. U.S. Ct. Appeals, 1st Cir., Bangor, Maine, 1995-96; assoc. Arnold and Porter, Washington, 1996—. Federal civil litigation, Product liability. Office: Arnold and Porter 555 12th St NW Washington DC 20004-1206

AUGUSTYN, NOEL JAMES, lawyer; b. New Castle, Pa., Dec. 25, 1946; s. Joseph Paul and Frances Elizabeth (Wilk) A.; m. Ann Marie Sweeney, Sept. 17, 1983; children: Matthew Joseph, Monica Mary, Catherine Francine. AB, Dartmouth Coll., 1968; MA, Stanford U., 1969; JD, U. Notre Dame, 1974. Bar: Mass. 1974, Pa. 1975, U.S. Dist. Ct. Mass. 1975, U.S. Ct. Appeals (1st cir.) 1975, D.C. 1976. Asst. dean, instr. Ripon (Wis.) Coll., 1969-70, Linfield Coll., McMinnville, Oreg., 1970-71; assoc. vom Baur, Coburn, Simmons & Turtle, Boston, 1974-79, Burt & Taylor, Marblehead, Mass., 1979-80; asst. prof., asst. dean Law Sch. Boston Coll., Newton, Mass., 1980-83; assoc. dir. Assn. Am. Law Schs., Washington, 1983-87; adminstrv. asst. to chief justice U.S. Supreme Ct., Washington, 1987-89; of counsel Seyfarth, Shaw, Fairweather & Geraldson, Washington, 1989-91; asst. dir. Adminstrv. Office of U.S. Cts., Washington, 1991—. Adj. prof. Georgetown U. Law Ctr., Washington, 1985-87; trustee Aquinas at Dartmouth, Inc., Hanover, N.H., 1987—. Contbr. articles to profl. jours. Trustee Supreme Ct. Hist. Soc., Washington, 1988-98. Mem. D.C. Bar Assn., Dartmouth Lawyers Assn., Thomas More Soc., John Carroll Soc., Dartmouth Club, Stanford Club. Republican. Roman Catholic. Avocations: reading, athletics, outdoor activities, piano, world travel. Office: 1 Columbus Cir NE Fl 4 Washington DC 20544-0001 E-mail: Noel_Augustyn@ao.uscourts.gov.

AUKLAND, DUNCAN DAYTON, lawyer; b. Delaware, Ohio, July 6, 1954; s. Merrill Forrest and Elva Sampson (Dayton) A.; m. Diane Sue Clevenger, Aug. 7, 1982. BA, Va. Polytech. Inst., 1978; JD, Capital U., 1982. Bar: Ohio 1982, U.S. Dist. Ct. (so. dist.) Ohio 1982. Legal intern Ohio EPA, Columbus, 1982, staff atty., 1982-83, legal cons., 1983; sole practice Columbus, 1983-90; judge adv. USNG, Columbus, 1990—. Atty. Clean Up and Recycling Backers of Clintonville, Columbus, 1983-89; deacon Overbrook Presbyn. Ch., Columbus, 1986-89. With JAGC, USAR, 1984-90. Mem. Ohio Bar Assn., Va. Poly. Alumni Assn. Cen. Ohio (pres. 1984-85), Ohio Gamma Alumni Corp. (trustee 1983-88, 91-95). Republican. Avocations: golf, home repairs. Home: 5789 Crescent Ct Worthington OH 43085-3804 Office: Ohio Adj Gen's Dept Attn: AGOH-JA 2825 W Dublin Granville Rd Columbus OH 43235-2789 E-mail: duncan.aukland@tagoh.org.

AURELL, JOHN KARL, lawyer; b. Tulsa, Sept. 26, 1935; s. George E. and Maxine (Reagor) A.; m. Jane Brevard Collins, Oct. 1, 1960; 1 child, Jane B. BA, Washington and Lee U., 1956; LLB, Yale U., 1964. Bar: Fla. 1964, D.C 1971, U.S. Dist. Ct. (no., mid. and so. dists.) Fla., U.S. Ct. Appeals (5th and 11th cirs.), U.S. Supreme Ct. Gen. counsel to Gov. State of Fla., Tallahassee, 1979-80; ptnr. Ausley & McMullen, 1994—2002, sr. counsel, 2002—. Mem. Fed. Jud. Nominating Commn. Fla.; chmn. No. Dist. Fla., 1993—97; bd. dirs. Z-Tel Techs., Inc. Mem. exec. com., v.p. Yale Law Sch. Assn., 1975-80; mem. Orange Bowl Com. 1st lt. U.S. Army, 1956-57. Fellow Am. Bar Found., Internat. Soc. Barristers, Am. Coll. Trial Lawyers; mem. ABA, Fla. Bar Assn. (bd. govs. young lawyers sect. 1966-71), Am. Law Inst., Gov.'s Club, Exch. Club, Yale Club (N.Y.C.), Econ. Club Fla. (chmn. 1997-98), Capital City Country Club. Democrat. Administrative and regulatory, Federal civil litigation, State civil litigation. Home: 1225 Live Oak Plantation Rd Tallahassee FL 32312-2509 Office: Ausley & McMullen PO Box 391 Tallahassee FL 32302-0391 E-mail: jaurell@ausley.com.

AUSHERMAN, LARRY PRICE, lawyer; b. July 1, 1952; B in Gen. Studies, U. Kans., 1974; M in Natural Resources, U. Mich., 1978; JD, U. N.Mex., 1979. Bar: N.Mex. 1979. Shareholder Modrall, Sperling, Roehl, Harris & Sisk, Albuquerque, 1979—. Mem. ABA (past chair SONREEL hard minerals com.), N.Mex. State Bar Assn. (past chair sect. natural resources, energy and environ. law), Nature Conservancy (trustee, past chmn. N.Mex. chpt.). Environmental, Natural resources. Office: Modrall Sperling Roehl Harris & Sisk 500 4th St NW Ste 1000 Albuquerque NM 87102-2186

AUSNEHMER, JOHN EDWARD, lawyer; b. Youngstown, Ohio, June 26, 1954; s. John Louis and Patricia Jean (Liguore) A.; m. Carole Marie Ausnehmer; children: Jill Ellen, Amber Layne. BS, Ohio State U., 1976; JD, U. Dayton, 1980. Bar: Ohio 1980, U.S. Dist. Ct. (no. dist.) Ohio 1981, U.S. Ct. Appeals (6th cir.) 1984, U.S. Supreme Ct. 1984. Law clk. Ohio Atty. Gen., Columbus, 1978, Green Schiavoni, Murphy, Haines & Sgambati Co., L.P.A., 1978; assoc. Dickson Law Office, Petersburg, Ohio, 1979-85; sole practice Youngstown, 1984—. Asst. pros. atty. Mahoning County, Ohio, 1986-89, 92—. Mem.: Columbiana County Bar Assn., Mahoning County Bar Assn., Cleve. Acad. Trial Attys., Ohio State Bar Assn., Ohio Acad. Trial Lawyers, Moning Valley Soccer Club (rep. 1982—84), Phi Alpha Delta. Democrat. Roman Catholic. General practice, Personal injury (including property damage), Workers' compensation. Home: 51 S Shore Dr Boardman OH 44512-5926 Office: PO Box 3965 120 Marwood Cir Youngstown OH 44513-3965

AUSTIN, ANN SHEREE, lawyer; b. Tyler, Tex., Aug. 25, 1960; d. George Patrick and Mary Jean (Brookshire) A. BA cum laude, U. Houston, 1983; JD, South Tex. Coll., 1987. Bar: Tex. 1987, U.S. Dist. Ct. (no. dist.) Tex. 1988, U.S. Ct. Appeals (5th cir.) 1989, U.S. Dist. Ct. (we. dist.) Tex. 1990, U.S. Ct. Appeals (D.C. cir.) 1992, U.S. Supreme Ct. 1992, U.S. Dist Ct. (ea. dist.) Tex. 1993. With First City Ops. Ctr., Houston, 1980-85; law clk. Lipstet, Singer, Hirsch & Wagner, Houston, 1985-86, Pizzitola, Hinton & Sussman, Houston, 1986-87; briefing atty. Hon. Hal M. Lattimore Ct. Appeals, 2d Jud. Dist., Ft. Worth, 1987-88; assoc. Cantey & Hanger, Ft. Worth and Dallas, 1988-93, Smith, Ralston & Russell, Dallas, 1993-94, Russell, Austin & Henschel, Dallas, 1994-95; pvt. practice Arlington, 1995-96; prin. Landau, Omahana & Kopka, Ltd., Dallas, 1996-97; asst. city atty. City of Dallas, 1997—2002; atty. Law Offices of W. Blake Hyde, 2002—. Tchr. Project Outreach State Bar of Tex., 1992. Author: Personnel Rules, Park & Recreation Department; co-author Annual Meeting of Invited Attorneys, Construction Law; chpt. editor: Cases and Materials on Civil Procedure, 1987. Mem. Ft. Worth Hist. Preservation Soc., com. mem., 1992; fundraiser Prevention of Child Abuse in Am., 1988—, Women's Haven. Mem. Tex. Young Lawyers Assn. (jud. rev. com. 1990, women in the profession com., profl. ethics and grievance awareness com. 1992-94), Dallas Bar Assn. (jud. com. 1992-94, ethics com. 1999—, cmty. involvement com., employment law sect. CLE com. 1999-2000), Dallas Assn. Young Lawyers, Dallas Women's Bar Assn., Ft. Worth Tarrant County Young Lawyers Assn. (treas. 1989-90, dir. 1989, Teen Ct., co-chair Adopt-A-Sch. program), Tarrant County Women's Bar Assn., Am. Inns. of Ct. Methodist. Avocations: walking, reading, sky diving. Construction, State civil litigation, Product liability. Office: Law Offices of W Blake Hyde Ste 490/LB11 1301 E Collins Blvd Richardson TX 75081

AUSTIN, ARTHUR DONALD, II, lawyer, educator; b. Staunton, Va., Dec. 2, 1932; s. George Milnes and Mae (Eichner) A.; m. Irene Clara Wittenberg, June 12, 1960; 1 son, Brian Carl. BS in Commerce, U. Va., 1958; JD, Tulane U., 1963. Bar: Va. 1964, D.C. 1970. Asst. prof. Coll. of William and Mary, Williamsburg, Va., 1963-64, Bowling Green State U., Ohio, 1964-66; asst. prof. law Cleve. State U., 1966-68; prof. law Case Western Res. U., Cleve., 1968-70, 72-78, Edgar A. Hahn prof. jurisprudence, 1978—. Atty. Dept. Justice, Washington, 1970-71 Author: Antitrust: Law, Economics, Policy, 1976, Complex Litigation Confronts the Jury System, 1984, The Empire Strikes Back: Outsiders and the Struggle Over Legal Education, 1998; contbr. articles to law revs. Served with U.S. Army, 1952-54. Decorated Bronze Star medal with V, Purple Heart. Home: 1174 Stony Hill Rd Hinckley OH 44233-9538 Office: 11075 East Blvd Cleveland OH 44106-5409

AUSTIN, DANIEL WILLIAM, lawyer; b. Springfield, Ill., Feb. 24, 1949; s. Daniel D. and Ruth A. (Ahrenkiel) A.; m. Lois Ann Austin, June 12, 1971; 1 child, Elizabeth Ann. BA, Millikin U., 1971; JD, Washington U., 1974. Bar: Ill. 1974, U.S. Dist. Ct. (cen. dist.) Ill. 1979, U.S. Ct. Appeals (7th cir.) 1980, U.S. Supreme Ct. 1980, U.S. Tax Ct. 1986. Assoc. Miley & Meyer, Taylorville, Ill., 1974-78; ptnr. Miley, Meyer & Austin, Taylorville, 1978-81; prin. Meyer, Austin & Romano P.C., Taylorville, 1981—, Meyer, Austin, Romano & Paisley, P.C., Taylorville. Pres. United Fund, Taylorville, 1980, Christian County YMCA, Taylorville, 1983-85, St. Vincent Meml. Hosp. Found., 1998—. Named one of Outstanding Young Men Am., 1985, Outstanding Citizen of City of Taylorville, 1993. Mem. ABA, Ill. Bar Assn., Christian County Bar Assn., Order of Barristers. Clubs: Taylorville Country (pres. 1985). Democrat. Presbyterian. Avocations: golf, photography. Corporate, general, Probate (including wills, trusts), Property, real (including real estate development, water). Home: 14 Westhaven Ct Taylorville IL 62568-9064 Office: Meyer Austin Romano & Paisley PC 210 S Washington St Taylorville IL 62568-2245

AUSTIN, DOUGLAS ROBERT, lawyer; b. Fairfield, Iowa, Apr. 2, 1949; s. Robert Raymond and Donna Mae (Dyson) A.; m. Dana Woodhouse, June 8, 1975; children: Amy Rebecca, Jessica Erin. BA in History and Polit. Sci., U. Mont., 1971, JD, 1975. Bar: Mont. 1975, U.S. Dist. Ct. Mont. 1975. Logger, millworker, Mineral County, Mont., 1968-75, 71-72; pvt. practice Superior and Missoula, Mont., 1975—. Mem. sch. bd. Superior (Mont.) schs., 1988-98; lay pastor The Fold of the Messiah, Superior, 1988—. Avocations: hiking, gardening, skiing, tennis, reading. General practice, Probate (including wills, trusts), Property, real (including real estate development, water). Home: 24 S Fork Nemote Cr Rd Superior MT 59872

AUSTIN, H(ARRY) GREGORY, lawyer; b. N.Y.C., Mar. 18, 1936; s. Harry Gregory and Pauline (Moore) A.; m. Deanna Ruth Anderson, Nov. 28, 1970; children: Sabrina Elizabeth, Harry Gregory III, Anne Catherine. BE, Yale U., 1957, postgrad., 1958; JD, U. Mich., 1961; LLD (hon.), Lincoln U., 1976. Bar: Colo. 1961, U.S. Supreme Ct. 1974. Assoc. Holland & Hart, Denver, 1962—73, ptnr., 1977—2001, of counsel, 2002—; gen. counsel SBA, Washington, 1973—75; solicitor, gen. counsel U.S. Dept. Interior, Washington, 1975—77. Trustee Colo. Legal Aid Found., Denver, 1984-91, chmn., 1988-91; bd. dirs. Children's Hosp., Denver, 1985-97; mem. adv. com. Colo. Sec. State, 1996—. 1st lt. USAR, 1957-64. Fellow Am. Bar Found.; mem. Am. Law Inst., Colo. Bar Assn. (chmn. bus. entities subsect. bus. law sect. 1987-89, vice chmn. bus. law sect. 1989-91, chmn. 1991-93, chmn. partnership laws com. 1993—), Denver Bar Assn., Metro Denver C. of C. (bd. dirs., sec. 1995-97). Republican. Corporate, general, Finance, Partnership. Office: Holland & Hart LLP 555 17th St Ste 2900 Denver CO 80202-3979 E-mail: gaustin@hollandhart.com.

AUSTIN, JOHN DELONG, judge; b. Cambridge, N.Y., May 31, 1935; s. John DeLong and Mabel Cowles (Bascom) A.; m. Marcia Kay Behan, Aug. 15, 1969 (dec.); children: John DeLong, Susan Behan. AB, Dartmouth Coll., 1957; postgrad., u. Minn., 1959; JD, Albany Law Sch., 1969. Bar: N.Y. 1970. Editl. dir. Glens Falls (N.Y.) Times, 1960-66; sole practice Glens Falls, 1970-79; law asst. Warren County Judge and Surrogate, 1975-79, N.Y. State Supreme Ct., 1980-84; judge Warren County Family Ct., N.Y., 1984-99, Warren County Ct. and Surrogate's Ct., 1999—. Instr. Adirondack Comm. Coll., Glens Falls. Editor New Eng. Hist. and Geneal. Register, 1970-73; contbr. hist. and geneal. articles to various periodicals. Councilman Town of Queensbury, N.Y., 1969-71, supr., 1972-74; budget officer Warren County, N.Y., 1974; mem. N.Y. State Local Govt. Records Adv. Coun. With U.S. Army, 1958-60. Recipient Adminstrv. Law prize Albany Law Sch., 1969. Fellow Am. Soc. Genealogists; mem. N.Y. State Bar Assn., Warren County Bar Assn., Mohican Grange, Elks. Republican.

AUSTIN, ROBERT EUGENE, JR., lawyer; b. Jacksonville, Fla., Oct. 10, 1937; s. Robert Eugene and Leta Fitch A.; children: Robert Eugene, George Harry Talley; m. Carolyn Rhea Songer. BA, Davidson Coll., 1959; JD, U. Fla., 1964. Bar: Fla. 1965, D.C. 1983, U.S. Supreme Ct. 1970; cert. in civil trial law Nat. Bd. Trial Advocacy. Pvt. practice law, 1965—. Asst. state atty., 1972; mem. Jud. Nominating Commn. and Grievance Com. 5th Dist. Fla.; gov. Fla. Bar, 1983; trustee U. Fla. Law Ctr.; mem. com. on std. jury instns. Fla. Supreme Ct. Chmn. Lake Dist. Boy Scouts Am.; asst. dean Leesburg Deanery Diocese Cen. Fla.; trustee Fla. House, Washington, U. Fla. Law Ctr., 1983—, chmn., 1988-90. Mem. Acad. Fla. Trial Lawyers, Am. Arbitration Assn., Am. Law Inst., Nat. Inst. Trial Advocacy, Lake County Bar Assn., Roscoe Pound Am. Trial Found., Kappa Alpha, Phi Delta Phi. Democrat. Episcopalian. General civil litigation, Personal injury (including property damage), Product liability. Home: PO Box 490200 Leesburg FL 34749-0200 Office: 1321 Citizens Blvd Ste C Leesburg FL 34748-3946 E-mail: reajr@aust-pep.com.

AVAKOFF, JOSEPH CARNEGIE, medical consultant, law consultant; b. Fairbanks, Alaska, July 15, 1936; s. Harry B. and Margaret (Adams) Avakoff; m. Teddy I. Law, May 7, 1966; children: Caroline, Joe E., John. AA, U. Calif., Berkeley, 1956, AB, 1957; MD, U. Calif., San Francisco, 1961; JD, Santa Clara U., 1985. Bar: Calif. 1987; diplomate Am. Bd. Surgery, Am. Bd. Plastic Surgery. Physicist U.S. Naval Radiol. Def. Lab., San Francisco, 1957, 59; intern So. Pacific Gen. Hosp., San Francisco, 1961-62; resident in surgery Kaiser Found. Hosp., San Francisco, 1962-66; resident in plastic surgery U. Tex. Sch. Medicine, San Antonio, 1970-72; pvt. practice specializing in surgery Sacramento, 1966-70; pvt. practice specializing in plastic surgery Los Gatos and San Jose, Calif., 1972-94; cons. to med. and legal professions, 1994—. Clin. instr. Sch. Medicine U. Calif., Davis, 1967—70; chief dept. surgery Mission Oaks Hosp., Los Gatos, 1988—90; chief divsn. plastic surgery Good Samaritan Hosp., San Jose, 1988—91; expert med. reviewer Med. Bd. Calif., 1995—2001; spl. cons. Calif. Dept. Corps., 1997—2002; presenter numerous med. orgns. Contbr. articles to profl. jours. Mem. San Jose Adv. Commn. Health, 1975—82; bd. govs. San Jose YMCA, 1977—80. Mem.: AMA, Union Am. Physicians and Dentists, Santa Clara County Med. Assn., Santa Clara County Bar Assn., Calif. Med. Assn., Phi Beta Kappa, Phi Eta Sigma. Republican. Presbyterian. Avocations: music, photography, computer programming. Home: 6832 Rockview Ct San Jose CA 95120-5607

AVALLONE, ANTHONY FRANCIS, lawyer; b. Mt. Vernon, N.Y., Nov. 5, 1926; s. Frank P. and Mary t. (Anechiarico) A.; m. Edith M. Tese; children: Mary, Camille, Elizabeth, Claire, Frank, Anthony, Michael, Joseph. LLB, Columbia U., 1952. Bar: N.Y. 1956, N.Mex. 1968, U.S. Dist. Ct. N.Y. 1960, U.S. Dist. Ct. N.Mex. 1968. Pvt. practice, Mt. Vernon, 1956-58, West Nyack, N.Y., 1958-67, 1968—99; sr. atty. Law Systems of Las Cruces, 1985—. Capt. USAR, 1947—. Mem. N.Mex. Bar Assn. Avocations: philosophy, gardening.

AVANT, GRADY, JR., lawyer; b. New Orleans, Mar. 1, 1932; s. Grady and Sarah (Rutherford) A.; m. Katherine Willis Yancey, Feb. 23, 1963; children: Grady M., Mary Willis Yancey. BA magna cum laude, Princeton U., 1954; JD, Harvard U., 1960. Bar: N.Y. 1961, Ala. 1962, Mich. 1972. Assoc. Bradley, Arant, Rose & White, Birmingham, Ala., 1961-63; assoc., ptnr. Long, Preston, Kinnaird & Avant, Detroit, 1972-87; ptnr. Dickinson, Wright, Moon, Van Dusen & Freeman, Detroit, 1988-94; sr. v.p. investment banking North Am. Capital Advisors, Inc., Bloomfield Hills, Mich., 1995-96; pvt. practice Grosse Pointe, Mich., 1996—2001, Birmingham, Ala., 2001—. Contbr. articles to legal jours. Served to lt. USMC, 1954-57. Mem. ABA (bus. law sect., fed. regulation of securities com.), State Bar of Mich. (coun. sect. antitrust law 1978-85, chmn. sect. 1983-84, bus. law sect.), Detroit Com. on Fgn. Rels. (exec. com. 1979—2001, chmn. 1986-88), Mountain Brook Club, Knickerbocker Club, Princeton Club of Mich. (pres. 1976-77, 94-95). Episcopalian. Antitrust, Corporate, general, Securities. Home and Office: 13 Cross Creek Dr Birmingham AL 35213

AVERY, BRUCE EDWARD, lawyer; b. Boonville, N.Y., Aug. 16, 1949; s. Edward Cecil and Marian Alma (Pierce) A.; m. Margaret Calvert, June 21, 1969; children: Sarah, Prudence. BA in Sociology, Polit. Sci., Hobart Coll., 1971; JD, U. Louisville, 1976. Bar: Ky. 1976, U.S. Ct. Mil. Appeals 1977, U.S. Army Ct. Mil. Rev. 1984, U.S. Supreme Ct. 1984, Md. 1992, D.C., 1993, U.S. Ct. Vet. Appeals 1992, U.S. Dist. Ct. Md. 1993. Commd. capt. U.S. Army, 1976, advanced through grades to maj., 1983; rschr. U.S. Army Rsch. Inst., Ft. Knox, Ky., 1972-76, atty., 1976-77, U.S. Army, Camp Zama, Japan, 1977-80, U.S. Army Recruiting, Ft. Meade, Md., 1980-83, U.S. Army Claims Svc., Ft. Meade, 1984-87, U.S. Armed Forces Claims Svc., Seoul, Korea, 1987-89; chief claims V Corps, Frankfort, Germany, 1989-91; pvt. practice Rockville, Md., 1991—. Mem. Ft. Knox Bd. Edn., Ky., 1975-76. Mem. ABA, ATLA, FBA, D.C. Bar, Md. State Bar., Ky. Bar Assn. Family and matrimonial. Office: 51 Monroe St Ste 1509 Rockville MD 20850-2414 E-mail: bavery@compuserve.com.

AVERY, JAMES THOMAS, III, lawyer, management consultant; b. Richmond, Va., July 21, 1945; s. James Thomas Jr. and Hester Vail (Kraemer) A.; m. Nancy Carolyn Hoag, June 22, 1968; children: James Thomas IV, Carolyn Sears, John Dolph II. AB magna cum laude, Princeton U., 1967; MBA, JD, Harvard U., 1975. Bar: Mass. 1975, U.S. Dist. Ct. Mass. 1975, U.S. Ct. Appeals (1st cir.) 1975. Assoc. Choate, Hall & Stewart, Boston, 1975-79; dir. Cambridge (Mass.) Research Inst., 1979-85; pres. The Avery Co., Boston, 1985—; prin. Symmetrix, Inc., Lexington, Mass., 1992-94; pres./CEO PHH Fantus Cons., Inc., Hunt Valley, Md., 1995-97. Bd. dirs. Boston Pub. Co. Treas. All Saints Ch., Brookline, Mass., 1976-78; vestryman Ch. of Redeemer, Chestnut Hill, Mass., 1985-89. Capt. U.S. Army, 1967-71, Vietnam. Decorated Bronze Star, Air medal. Mem. ABA, Phi Beta Kappa. Clubs: Somerset, Harvard, The Second (trustee, sec. 1980-91) (Boston); Brookline Thursday. Republican. Episcopalian. Avocations: tennis, golf, skiing.

AVERY, MELISSA J. lawyer; b. Columbus, Ohio, May 29, 1969; d. Joe Morris Toeller and Sharon Lee Parker; m. Bryan Keith Avery, Nov. 8, 1997; 1 child, Preston James. BS, Ohio U., 1991; JD, Capital U., 1994. Bar: Ohio 1995, U.S. Dist. Ct. (so. dist.) Ohio 1995, Ind. 1997, U.S. Dist. Ct. (no. and so. dists.) Ind. 1997. Assoc. Terry L. Thomas Co., LPA, Columbus, 1994—98, Phelps & Fara, Indpls., 1998—. Mem. Marion County Family Ct. Task Force, Indpls., 2000—, Marion County Family Law Rules Com., Indpls., 2002; lectr. in field. Fellow: Ind. State Bar Assn. (cert. family law specialist 2002, com. co-chair 2002); mem.: ABA (com. vice chair 2003—), Indpls. Bar Assn. (chair family law sect. 2002). Family and matrimonial. Office: Phelps & Fara 10th Fl 230 E Ohio St Indianapolis IN 46204 E-mail: mavery@phelpsandfara.com.

AVERY, PATRICIA I. lawyer; b. N.Y.C., Nov. 3, 1951; BA, NYU, 1973, JD, 1976. Bar: N.Y. 1977, U.S. Dist. Ct. (so. and ea. dists.) N.Y. 1977, U.S. Ct. Appeals (2d cir.) 1978, U.S. Dist. Ct. (no. dist.) Tex. 1979, U.S. Ct. Appeals (9th cir.) 1979, U.S. Supreme Ct. 1980, U.S. Ct. Appeals (3d and 11th cir.) 1988, U.S. Ct. Appeals (5th, 7th and 8th cirs.) 1989. Assoc. with firm, N.Y.C., 1976-82; assoc. Wolf Popper LLP, N.Y.C., 1982-85, ptnr., 1986—. Mem. ABA, N.Y. County Lawyers Assn. Avocations: zoology, travel. Federal civil litigation, State civil litigation, Securities. Office: Wolf Popper LLP 845 3rd Ave Fl 12 New York NY 10022-6662

AVERY, REIGH KESSEN, legal assistant; b. Cin., Sept. 16, 1949; d. Henry Charles and Margaret Elizabeth (Dam) Kessen; m. Gerald L. Poe, Oct. 5, 1968 (div. Nov. 1989); children: Amy Kathleen, Michael Lee; m. Melvin L. Avery, May 6, 1996. AAS, El Centro Coll., Dallas, 1988. Legal sec. Victor C. McCrea Jr. & Co., Dallas, 1983-84, legal asst., 1986-90; legal sec. Fanning, Harper & Martinson, Dallas, 1984-86, Thompson & Knight, Dallas, 1986; legal asst. Nacol, Wortham & Assocs., Dallas, 1990-91; sr. legal asst. Snelling and Snelling, Inc., Dallas, 1992-93; free-lance legal asst. Tex., 1993-95; sr. legal asst. Nationwide Mutual Ins. Co., 1995—. Chair comm. Fox Meadow Farms Homeowners Assn., Loveland, Ohio, 1972-74; pro bono vol. Child Support Clinic, Dallas, 1988, North Ctrl. Tex. Legal Svcs. Found., Inc., Dallas, 1988—; vol. Ramses The Gt. Exhbn. Dallas Mus. Nat. History Assn., 1989. Mem. Nat. Assn. Legal Assts., State Bar Tex. (legal assts. div.), Dallas Assn. Legal Assts. (litigation sect., com. nat. affairs 1988-89), Phi Theta Kappa, Phi Beta Lambda. Avocations: computers, greek mythology, logic problems, crossword puzzles. Home and Office: 725 Pinoak Dr Grand Prairie TX 75052-6522

AVERY, ROBERT DEAN, lawyer; b. Youngstown, Ohio, Apr. 23, 1944; s. Donald Carson and Alta Belle (Simon) A.; m. Ann Mitchell Lashen, May 16, 1993; 1 child from previous marriage: Benjamin Robert. BA, Northwestern U., 1966; JD, Columbia U., 1969. Bar: Ohio 1971, Calif. 1973, Ill. 2001. Law clk. to Hon. Robert P. Anderson U.S. Ct. Appeals 2d Cir., N.Y.C., 1969-70; assoc. lawyer Jones Day, Cleve., 1970-74, L.A., 1974-76, ptnr., 1977-98, adminstrv. ptnr., 1990-92, ptnr. Chgo., 1999—. Editor: Columbia Law Rev., 1968-69. Harlan Fiske Stone Scholar. Home: 45 E Division St Chicago IL 60610-2316 Office: Jones Day 77 W Wacker Dr Chicago IL 60601-1662 E-mail: rdavery@jonesday.com.

AVIL, RICHARD DANIEL, JR., lawyer; b. Phila., Nov. 28, 1948; s. Richard Daniel and Elizabeth (McGinley) A.; m. Karen Mudry, May 27, 1972; children: Sierra Soo, Brier Sung, Winston Richard. BEE, Villanova U., 1970; JD, Cornell U., 1974. Law clk. U.S. Dist. Ct. Northern Dist. N.Y., 1974-75, 75-76, U.S. Ct. Appeals Second Cir., N.Y.C., 1976-77; assoc. Jones Day, Cleve., 1977-83, ptnr., 1984-91, Washington, 1991—. Speaker in field. Mem. Energy Bar Assn. FERC practice, Oil, gas, and mineral, Utilities, public. Home: 10850 Patowmack Dr Great Falls VA 22066-3032 Office: Jones Day 51 Louisiana Ave NW Washington DC 20001-2113 E-mail: rdavil@jonesday.com.

AXE, JOHN RANDOLPH, lawyer, financial executive; b. Grand Rapids, Mich., Apr. 30, 1938; s. John Jacob and Elizabeth Katherine (Lynott) A.; m. Linda Sadlier Stroh, June 1, 1989; children from previous marriage: Catherine, Peter, Meredith, Sara, Jay, stepchildren: Suzanne Stroh, Greg Stroh. AB, U. Mich., 1960; LLB, Harvard U., 1963. Bar: Mich. 1964. Ptnr. Dickinson, Wright, McKean, Cudlip, Detroit, 1972-80, Martin, Axe, Buhl & Schwartz, Bloomfield Hills, Mich., 1981-82, Axe & Schwartz, Bloomfield Hills, 1983-85, Dykema, Gossett, Spencer, Goodnow, Detroit, 1985-89; prin. John R. Axe and Assocs., Detroit, 1989—2000; shareholder Axe & Ecklund, P.C., Detroit, 2001—. Pres. Mcpl. Fin. Cons., Inc., Detroit, 1982—; adj. prof. Wayne State U. Law Sch., 1992—. Mem. Mich. Higher Edn. Assistance Authority, Lansing, Mich., 1977-83. Served to lt. USNR, 1965-69. With USNR, 1965—69. Mem. Nat. Assn. Bond Lawyers (steering com. 1981-83, 86, bd. dirs. 1987-90), Mich. Assn. County Treas. (gen. counsel 1977-88), Downtown Assn. Club (N.Y.C.), Doubles Club (N.Y.C.), Mill Reef Club (Antigua). Office: Axe & Ecklund PC 21 Kercheval Ave Ste 360 Grosse Pointe Farms MI 48236-3633

AXE, NORMAN GOLD, lawyer; b. Phila., May 15, 1932; s. Morton and Anne Helen (Gold) Axe; m. Geraldine Schaeffer, Aug. 28, 1960 (div.); m. Eleanor Ruth Klein, Aug. 10, 1969; children— Jason, Audrey, Holly. B.S., Temple U., 1953; J.D., 1958. Bar: Pa. 1959, D.C. 1965, Calif. 1969, U.S. Supreme Ct. 1969, U.S. Ct. Appeals (9th cir.) 1970. Estate tax examiner IRS, Phila., 1959-61, lawyer, Washington, 1961-65; lawyer Am. Trucking Assn., Washington, 1965-66; assoc. various law firms, Los Angeles, 1968-70; sole practice, Santa Monica, Calif., 1970—; instr. Adult Schs., Los Angeles, 1970—, UCLA, 1979-80; referee Calif. State Bar Ct., Los Angeles, 1978-81; arbitrator Los Angeles Superior Ct., 1979—. Served to 1st lt. U.S. Army, 1953-55, col. Res. Mem. Calif. State Bar Assn. Estate planning, Probate (including wills, trusts), Personal income taxation. Home and Office: 915 Georgina Ave Santa Monica CA 90402-2023

AXELSON, JEFFREY MARK, lawyer; b. N.Y.C., Oct. 20, 1951; s. Hyman Morris and Rose (Shanes) A. AB, Colgate U., 1972; JD, Am. U., 1975. Bar: Md. 1975, D.C. 1977, U.S. Dist. Ct. D.C. 1977, U.S. Dist. Ct. Md. 1977, U.S. Ct. Appeals (D.C. cir.) 1977, U.S. Supreme Ct. 1980, Fla. 1981, U.S. Ct. Appeals (4th cir.) 1982. Assoc. Schwarzbach & Wortman, Washington, 1976-78; ptnr. Axelson & Williamowsky, Rockville, Md., 1978-80, Van Grack, Axelson & Williamowsky & Jacobs, P.C., Rockville, 1980—. Panel mem./arbitrator Commn. on Community Ownership Communities, 1991—. Mem. Homeowner Assn. task force Montgomery County Council, Rockville, 1983-85; bd. dirs. Washington Met. chpt. Community Assns. Inst., 1976-84. Mem. Md. Bar Assn., Montgomery County Bar Assn. (mem. comml. law and banking sect., taxation sect., ethics com., chmn. 1999—), Atty. Grievance Commn. of Md., Washington Bus. brokers Assn. (bd. dirs. 1992-98). Commercial, contracts (including sales of goods; commercial financing), Corporate, general, Property, real (including real estate development, water). Home: 54 Waddington Ln Rockville MD 20850 Office: Van Grack Axelson 110 N Washington St Fl 5 Rockville MD 20850-2223

AXINN, STEPHEN MARK, lawyer; b. N.Y.C., Oct. 21, 1938; s. Mack N. and Lili H. (Tannenbaum) A.; m. Stephanie Chertok, May 12, 1963; children: Audrey, David, Jill. BS, Syracuse U., 1959; LLB, Columbia U., 1962. Bar: N.Y. 1962, U.S. Supreme Ct. 1962. Assoc. Cahill & Gordon, N.Y.C., 1963-64, Malcolm A. Hoffman, N.Y.C., 1964-66, Skadden, Arps, Slate, Meagher & Flom, N.Y.C., 1966-69, ptnr., 1970-97, Axinn, Veltrop & Harkrider LLP, N.Y.C., 1997—. Lead counsel WorldCom-Spring major investigation and litigation antitrust divsn. U.S. Dept. Justice, 1999-2000; adj. prof. Law Sch. NYU, 1981-83, Law Sch. Columbia U., 1983-85. Author: Acquisitions Under H-S-R, 1980; contbr. articles to profl. jours. Chmn. lawyers div. United Jewish Appeal, N.Y.C., 1985-87; mem. exec. com., treas. Jewish Theol. Sem. Am., 1984-96; mem. bd. visitors Columbia Law Sch., 1993-98; mem. adv. panel on environ. crimes by orngs. U.S. Sentencing Commn., 1992-94. Capt. U.S. Army, 1965-68. Mem. ABA (council antitrust sect. 1983-85), N.Y. State Bar Assn. (chmn. antitrust sect. 1982-83). Antitrust, Federal civil litigation, Intellectual property. Office: Axinn Veltrop & Harkrider LLP 1370 Ave of the Americas New York NY 10019-6708 E-mail: sma@avhlaw.com.

AXTELL, CLAYTON MORGAN, JR., lawyer; b. Deposit, N.Y., Aug. 4, 1916; s. Clayton Morgan and Olive Aurora (Vosburgh) A.; m. Margaret Williamson Ritchie, Apr. 24, 1943 (dec.); children: Margaret R. Axtell Stevenson, Clayton Morgan III, Karen R. Axtell Arnold, Susan R. Axtell. AB, Cornell U., 1937, JD, 1940. Bar: N.Y. 1940, U.S. Dist. Ct. (no. dist.) N.Y. 1941, U.S. Supreme Ct. 1964. Assoc. Hinman, Howard & Kattell, Binghamton, N.Y., 1940-48, ptnr., 1948—. Former mem. adv. bd. First-City Nat. Bank, Binghamton; bd. dirs. Farmers Nat. Bank, Deposit, N.Y., First City Nat. Bank, Binghamton. Pres. N.Y. State Sch. Bd. Attys., Albany, 1962-63, Broome County Bar Assn., Binghamton, 1967-68, Conrad and Virginia Klee Found.; mem. N.Y. State Rep. Com., Binghamton, 1988-93. 1st lt. US Army, 1942-46 ETO. Decorated Bronze Star U.S. Army, 1945, Croix de Guerre, Govt. of France, 1945; recipient Disting Svc. award U.S. Jr. C. of C., 1942; named Young Man of Yr. Binghamton Jr. C. of C., 1949. Mem. ABA, N.Y. State Bar Assn., Hillcrest -Port Dick Kiwanis (past pres.), Binghamton Club. Republican. Lutheran. Home: 1338 Chenango St Binghamton NY 13901-1539 Office: Hinman Howard & Kattell 80 Exchange St Binghamton NY 13901-3490

AYALA-AGUIRRE, JOSE RAMON, lawyer; b. Mexico City, Fed. Dist., Mexico, May 8, 1976; s. Jose Ramon Ayala-Aranda and Patricia Aguirre-Moreno. LLB, U. Iberoamericana, Mex. City, Fed. Dist., 2000. Paralegal Notary Pub. No. 180, Mex. City, Mexico, 1996—98; legal clk. & assoc. Santamarina y Steta, S.C., Mex. City, 1998—. Gen. counsel (pro-bono) Found. for Children of the Street Inst. Pvt. Assistance, Mex. City, Mexico, 1999. Corporate, general, Mergers and acquisitions, Health. Office: Santamarina y Steta SC Campos Eliseos No 345-Piso 3 Fed Dist Mexico City 11560 Mexico Office Fax: (5255) 52-80-76-14. E-mail: jayala@s-s.com.mx.

AYER, DONALD BELTON, lawyer; b. San Mateo, Calif., Apr. 30, 1949; m. Anne Norton; children: Christopher, Alison BA in History with great distinction and honors, Stanford U., 1971; MA in History, Harvard U., 1973, JD cum laude, 1975. Bar: Calif. 1975, D.C. 1978. Law clk. to Judge Malcolm R. Wilkey U.S. Ct. Appeals D.C. Cir., 1975-76; law clk. to Justice William H. Rehnquist, U.S. Supreme Ct., Washington, 1976-77; asst. U.S. atty. criminal div. No. Dist. Calif., San Francisco, 1977-79, in charge San Jose office, 1978-79; assoc. Gibson Dunn & Crutcher, San Jose, Calif., 1979-81; U.S. atty. Eastern Dist. Calif., Sacramento, 1982-86; prin. dep. solicitor gen. Dept. Justice, 1986-88; ptnr. Jones, Day, Reavis & Pogue, Washington, 1988—, 1990—; dep. atty. gen. U.S. Dept. Justice, Washington, 1989-90; adminstrv. ptnr. Jones, Day, Reavis & Pogue, Washington, 1991-93, chair gov. disputes sect., 1993-96, chair. pro bono com., 2003—. Mem. Calif. State Bar Fed. Cts. Commn., 1983-86; mem. exec. com. 9th Cir. Jud. Conf., 1983-85; mem. Atty. Gen.'s Adv. Com. of U.S. Attys., 1986; publs. com. U.S. Supreme Ct. Hist. Soc., 1991—. Articles editor Harvard U. Law Rev., 1974-75; contbr. articles to legal jours. Pres. Stanford Young Reps., 1970-71; mem. vestry St. Mary's Episc. Ch., 1987-90; bd. dirs. Langley Non-Profit Housing Corp., 1990-98; mem. Fed. City Coun., 1991-93; mem. adv. com. State and Local Legal Ctr., 1992—; trustee Potomac Sch., McLean, Va., 1994-2000; bd. dirs. Am. Rivers, Inc., 1997—, treas., 1998—; bd. advisors Supreme Ct. Inst. of Georgetown U., 1999—. Fellow Am. Bar Found. (life); mem. ABA (litigation sect., task force on internat. criminal ct. 1991-94), Am. Bar Found., Am. Acad. Appellate Lawyers (mem. com. 1997-2002), Am. Law Inst., D.C. Bar Found. (adv. bd. 1992—), Calif. State Bar, D.C. Bar Assn. (ct. funding com. 2000-01), NYU Inst. Jud. Adminstrn. (bd. dirs. 2000—), Edward Coke Am. Inn of Ct. Appellate, Federal civil litigation, Constitutional. Office: Jones Day Reavis & Pogue 51 Louisiana Ave NW Washington DC 20001

AYERS, JAMES CORDON, lawyer; b. Raleigh, N.C., Aug. 2, 1934; s. Edwin White and Laura Cordon (Stedman) A.; m. Leona Bell Weston, Aug. 1, 1965; children: James Cordon Jr., Alan Andrew. BSBA, U. N.C., 1958; JD, Ohio State U., 1977. Bar: Ohio 1977, U.S. Dist. Ct. (so. dist.) 1978, U.S. Ct. Appeals (6th cir.) 1983, U.S. Supreme Ct. 1992. Dist. sales mgr. Gen. Tel. Dir. Co., 1965-71; pres. Cols. Advt. co., 1971-74; sr. v.p. Assoc. Ind. Dir., 1972-74, exec. v.p. univ. dir., 1972-74; asst. atty. gen. workers' compensation sect. State of Ohio, Columbus, 1977-79; pvt. practice James C. Ayers Law Office, Columbus, 1979—; ind. hearing examiner Ohio Dept. Pub. Safety, 1993-99. Mem. Armed Forces Disciplinary Bd., N.C. 1960; bd. dirs. Post Exch., Camp Lejeune, 1960; summary ct. martial jurisdiction USMC Camp Lejeune, 1960. Chmn. Columbus County March of Dimes, 1961; pres. SBA; jud. panelist Ohio Mock Trial, 1995—2001; trustee The Reserve, 2002—. 1st lt. USMC, 1957—60. Mem. ABA, Ohio Bar Assn., Men's Golf Assn. (dir. 1990-92, treas. 1990-91, v.p. 1992), Scarlet and Gray (dir. 1988, v.p. 1989), The Gang, Phi Delta Phi (Grad. of Yr.). Avocation: golf. General civil litigation, Personal injury (including property damage), Workers' compensation. Office: 165 N High St Columbus OH 43215-2402 Home: 8559 Stonechat Loop Dublin OH 43017-8625 E-mail: ayersj@sbcglobal.net.

AYERS, JEFFREY DAVID, lawyer; b. Grant, Nebr., Nov. 30, 1960; s. William D. and Lela R. (Gilmore) A.; m. Shelly Jo Dodds, June 11, 1988; children: Sydney Elizabeth, Bailey Anne. BS, Graceland U., 1982; MBA, JD, U. Iowa, 1985. Bar: Mo. 1985. Assoc. Stinson, Mag & Fizzell, Kansas City, Mo., 1985-88, Bryan, Cave, McPheeters & McRoberts, Kansas City, 1989-92; ptnr. Blackwell Sanders Peper Martin LLP, Kansas City, Mo., 1992-95, mng. ptnr. London, 1996-99; sr. v.p., gen. counsel and corp. sec. Aquila Mcht. Svcs., Inc., Kansas City, 1999—2002; mng. counsel Employers Reinsurance Corp., Overland Park, Kans., 2003—. Mayor City of Lake Tapawingo, Mo., 1993-96. Trustee Little Blue Valley Sewer Dist., 1994-95. Democrat. Mem. Cmtys. of Christ. Banking, Finance, Securities. Office: Employers Reinsurance Corp 5200 Metcalf PO Box 2991 Overland Park KS 66201-1391 E-mail: jayers@kc.rr.com.

AYERS, KRISTEN NESS, lawyer; b. Columbia, S.C., Nov. 5, 1973; d. Dale Sorlie and Jane (Hoover) Ness; m. Peter Garris Ayers, Aug. 18, 2001. AB in English, Duke U., 1996; postgrad., Macquarie U., 1998; JD, U. S.C., 2000. Bar: N.C. 2000, U.S. Dist. Ct. (we. dist.) N.C. 2000. Law clk. Parker Poe Adams and Bernstein LLP, Charlotte, NC, 1999, assoc., 2000—03. Adj. prof. Bus. Law Johnson C. Smith U., Charlotte, 2001; bd. dirs. Charlotte Sister Cities. Editor: S.C. Environ. Law Jour., 1999—2000. Bd. dirs. Charlotte Philharm. Orch.; vol. Aquarium Discovery Pl., Charlotte, 2002—; field rep. N.C. Earthwatch Inst., Maynard, Mass., 2001—. Mem.: ABA (Internat. Law sect.), N.C. Bar Assn. (Internat. Law sect.), Nat. Assn. Bond Lawyers. Avocations: photography, writing, scuba diving, snorkeling, marine biology. Immigration, naturalization, and customs, Environmental, Finance.

AYLING, COREY JOHN, lawyer; b. N.Y.C., Sept. 5, 1957; s. Henry F. and Julia C. Ayling; m. Teresa J. Schwarzenbart, Mar. 20, 1984 (div. Oct. 1991); children: John, Lindsay; m. Robin E. Johnson, Oct. 10, 1992; children: Blake, Claire, Alex. AB, Cornell U., 1979; MA, NYU, 1981; JD, U. Wis., 1984. Bar: Wis. 1984, Minn. 1984, U.S. Dist. Ct. (we. dist.) Wis. 1984, U.S. Dist. Ct. Minn. 1985, U.S. Dist. Ct. Ariz. 1994, U.S. Ct. Appeals (8th cir.) 1985, U.S. Ct. Appeals (9th cir.) 1996, U.S. Ct. Appeals (D.C. cir.) 1989, U.S. Supreme Ct. 1995. Law clk. U.S. Ct. Appeals-7th Cir., Chgo., 1984-85; assoc. O'Connor & Hannan, Mpls., 1985-88, ltd. ptnr., 1989-90; assoc. McGrann, Shea et al, Mpls., 1990-91, shareholder, 1992—. Mem. Fed. Pub. Defender Panel, Mpls., 1986—. Articles editor Wis. Law Rev., 1983-84; contbr. articles to profl. jours. Vol. atty. Minn. Civil Workers Union, Mpls., 1987—. General civil litigation, Criminal, Professional liability. Office: McGrann Shea et al 800 Nicollet Mall 2600 US Bancorp Ctr Minneapolis MN 55402 E-mail: cja@mcgrannshea.com.

AYRES, JEFFREY PEABODY, lawyer; b. Waltham, Mass., Sept. 23, 1952; s. John Cecil and Dora Hoxie A.; m. Janet Diehl, May 31, 1980; children: Brendan Peabody, Caroline Bradfield, Gordon Pettit. BA, Harvard U., 1974; JD, George Washington U., 1977. Bar: D.C. 1977, Md. 1978, U.S. Ct. Appeals (3d, 4th and D.C. cirs.), U.S. Dist. Ct. Md., U.S. Dist. Ct. D.C., U.S. Supreme Ct. 1985. Assoc. Arent, Fox, Kintner, Plotkin & Kahn, Washington, 1977-78, Venable, Baetjer & Howard, Balt., 1978-85, ptnr., 1986—. Contbr. articles to profl. jours. Alt., del. and parliamentarian Episcopal Diocesan Conv.; sr. warden Ch. of the Redeemer, 2002—. Mem. ABA, Md. Bar Assn., Balt. Bar Assn. (chair labor and employment sect. 1998-2000), Harvard Club Md. (pres. 1989-94, v.p. 1994-2002), Harvard Alumni Assn. (regional dir. 1995-98). Democrat. Episcopalian. Avocations: running, bicycling. Federal civil litigation, State civil litigation, Labor (including EEOC, Fair Labor Standards Act, labor-management relations, NLRB, OSHA). Home: 7120 Sheffield Rd Baltimore MD 21212-1629 Office: Venable Baetjer & Howard 1800 Mercantile Bank & Trust Blg 2 Hopkins Plz Ste 2100 Baltimore MD 21201-2982 E-mail: jpayres@venable.com.

AYRES, TED DEAN, lawyer, academic counsel; b. Hamilton, Mo., July 14, 1947; m. Marcia Sue Busselle; children: John Corbett, Jackson Frazer, Joseph Dean. BSBA, Ctrl. Mo. State Coll., 1969; JD, U. Mo., 1972. Bar: Mo. 1972, U.S. Dist. Ct. (we. dist.) Mo. 1972, U.S. Ct. Appeals (8th cir.) 1977, U.S. Supreme Ct. 1977, Colo. 1984, U.S. Dist. Ct. Colo. 1984, U.S. Ct. Appeals (10th cir.) 1984, Kans. 1987. Law clk. to presiding justice Mo. Supreme Ct., Jefferson City, 1972-73; ptnr. Stubbs & Ayres, Chillicothe, Mo., 1973-74; atty. Southwestern Bell Tel. Co., St. Louis, 1974-76; counsel U. Mo., Columbia, 1976-84; gen. counsel U. Colo., Boulder, 1984-86, Kans. Bd. Regents, Topeka, 1986-92, gen. counsel, dir. govtl. rels., 1992-96; acting pres. Pitts. State U., 1995; gen. counsel, assoc. to pres. Wichita (Kans.) State U., 1996—2002, interim dir. Edwin A. Ulrich Mus. Art, 1999-2000, v.p., gen. counsel, 2002—, dir. equal employment opportunity, 2003—. Adj. asst. prof. coll. bus. adminstrn. U. Colo., Denver, 1984-85, adj. assoc. prof., 1985-86; spl. asst. atty. gen. State of Colo., 1984-86, State of Kans., 1986—; presenter region II conf. Assn. Coll. Unions Internat., U. Mo., Rolla, 1983; spkr. Soc. Colo. Archivists, U. Colo., Boulder, 1985; adj. prof. Washburn U., Topeka, 1989; adj. prof. kinesiology and sport studies Wichita State U., 1999—. Contbr. articles to profl. jours. Active adv. com. Boone County (Mo.) Cmty. Svcs.; mem. com. social concerns Mo. United Meth. Ch., 1979-81, supervisory com. Mothers' Morning Out program, 1980-84; adminstv. bd., com. on fin. and stewardship 1st United Meth. Ch., Topeka, 1989-91, family life coun., 1994-95; trustee Mid-Mo. chpt. Nat. Multiple Sclerosis Soc., 1981-84; mem. bd. mgrs. Topeka YMCA-Downtown Br., 1991-96, fedn. coun. Indian Guides program, 1988-91; treas. pack 175 Cub Scouts, 1990-95; bd. dirs. Innovative Tech. Enterprise Corp., 1991-94, S.W. Youth Athletic Assn., Inc., 1994-96, Friends of Topeka Zoo, 1995-2000, Wichita Tech. Corp., 1997—, Wichita State U. Hist. Preservation Commn., 1998—, parents coun. Truman State U., 1997-99. Curator scholar, 1969-70, Omar E. Robinson scholar, 1970-71, John M. Dalton Ednl. Trust scholar 1971-72. Mem. Mo. Bar Assn., Nat. Assn. Coll. and Univ. Attys. (chairperson Southwestern region 1979-81, bd. dirs. 1985-88, com. mem. 1979—, del. and presenter numerous CLE workshops), U. Mo. Alumni Assn. (life). Home: 2820 Tallgrass St Wichita KS 67226-1815 Office: Wichita State Univ 203 Morrison Hall Wichita KS 67260-0001 E-mail: ted.ayres@wichita.edu.

AZEVEDO, RENATO OLIMPIO SETTE DE, lawyer; b. São Paulo, Feb. 27, 1977; s. Flávio Olimpio de Azevedo. JD, U. São Paulo, 1999. Cert.: São Paulo 2000. Trainee Flávio Olimpio de Azevedo Adv. Asst., São Paulo; ptnr. Flávio Olimpio de Azevedo Advogados Associados, São Paulo, 2000—. Corporate, general, General civil litigation, General practice. Office: Flávio Olimpio de Azevedo Advogados Assocs Rua Marques de Itu 61- 60 Andar 01223-001 São Paulo Brazil Office Fax: 551133316867. E-mail: ro7a@foaadv.com.br.

AZUELA GUITRON, MARIANO, judge; b. Mexico, Apr. 1, 1936; Grad., U. Nacional Autonoma de Mexico. Pres. Supreme Ct. Mexico, 1995—; prof. Centro U. Mexico, 1957—83, U. Iberoamericana, 1965—, U. Panamericana; min. Supreme Ct. Justice, 1984—, pres., 1995—. Office: Suprema Corte de Justicia de la Nacion Pino Suarez 2 Col Centro 06065 Mexico City Mexico*

BAADE, HANS WOLFGANG, legal educator, law expert; b. Berlin, Dec. 16, 1929; s. Fritz and Edith (Wolff) B.; m. Anne Adams Johnston; children— Friedrich James, Hans Alastair. A.B., Syracuse U., 1949; J.D., Kiel U. (Germany), 1951; LL.B., LL.M., Duke U., 1955, diploma Hague Acad. Internat. Law, 1956. Assoc. Inst. Internat. Law, Kiel, 1955-60; assoc. prof. law Duke U., 1960-64, prof. law, 1964-70; prof. law U. Toronto, 1970-71; Hugh Lamar Stone prof. civil law U. Tex., Austin, 1971— ; arbitrator internat. comml. matters; dir. Am. Soc. Comparative Law. Mem. Am. Arbitration Assn. (nat. panel arbitrators); assoc. mem. Internat. Acad. Comparative Law. Editor: Law and Comparative Problems, 1961-66; bd. editors Am. Jour. Comparative Law, 1960— ; editorial sec. German Yr. Book Internat. Law, 1956-60; contbr. numerous articles to profl. jours. Hon. fellow faculty of law U. Edinburgh (Scotland), 1997—. Home: 6002 Mountainclimb Dr Austin TX 78731-3822 Office: U Tex Sch Law Austin TX 78705

BABB, ALFRED WARD, lawyer; b. Pitts., Feb. 18, 1940; s. John Donald and Thelma Jean Babb; m. Sherie Ellen Braun, Mar. 25, 1977; children: Paul, Mitch, Michelle, David, Katie, Brandon. JD, U. Calif., San Francisco, 1972. Bar: Calif. 1972, Pa. 1975. Assoc. Bray Baldwin Egan Brietwieser, Martinez, Calif., 1972-74; gen. counsel Nat. Contractors Group, Pitts., 1974-80; ptnr. Babb, Alfred W., Pitts., 1980—; pres. Babb & Assocs., P.C., Pitts, Wexford, New Castle, 1989—. Dir. ARC Allegheny, Pitts., 1998. 1st lt. U.S. Army, 1961-63. Mem. Indsl. Sales (dir., chair 1989). Republican. Labor (including EEOC, Fair Labor Standards Act, labor-management relations, NLRB, OSHA), Personal injury (including property damage), Probate (including wills, trusts). Office: Babb & Assocs PC Ste 401 Temple Bldg New Castle PA 16101 E-mail: lawusa@stargate.net.

BABB, FRANK EDWARD, lawyer, executive; b. Maryville, Mo., Dec. 22, 1932; s. Dale Victor and Esther (Hull) B. BS, Northwest Mo. State U., Maryville, 1954; LL.B., Harvard U., 1959. Ptnr. McDermott, Will & Emery, Chgo., 1959-90, of counsel, 1991—; chmn. AF Ptnrs., Tucson, 1991—. With CIC U.S. Army, 1954-56. Mem. Univ. Club Chgo., Am. Alpine Club. Banking, Corporate, general, Securities.

BABBIN, JEFFREY R. lawyer; b. Queens, N.Y., Apr. 6, 1960; s. Saul A. Babbin and Elaine Montrose Usdane; m. Marlene B. Schwartz, May 31, 1992; children: Anna S., Charlotte N., Molly I. BS in Econs., U. Pa., 1981; JD, Stanford U., 1984. Bar: D.C. 1984, U.S. Dist. Ct. D.C. 1985, U.S. Ct. Appeals (3rd cir.) 1986, U.S. Ct. Appeals (9th cir.) 1987, U.S. Dist. Ct. Conn. 1992, Conn. 1993, U.S. Ct. Appeals (D.C., 8th and 2d cirs.) 1996, U.S. Supreme Ct. 1996. Assoc. Pierson Semmes & Finley, Washington, 1984-89, Spiegel & McDiarmid, Washington, 1989-91, Wiggin & Dana, New Haven, 1992-96, ptnr., 1997—. Co-author: Litigation Issues in the Distribution of Securities: An International Perspective, 1997. Com. chmn. Vision for Greater New Haven, 1994-96. Mem. ABA, Conn. Bar Assn. Democrat. Jewish. Administrative and regulatory, Appellate, General civil litigation. Home: 28 High St Guilford CT 06437-3410 Office: Wiggin & Dana 1 Century Tower New Haven CT 06510-7013 E-mail: jbabbin@wiggin.com.

BABBY, LON S. lawyer; b. Bklyn., Feb. 21, 1951; BA, Lehigh U., 1973; JD, Yale U., 1976. Bar: Conn. 1976, D.C. 1977, U.S. Supreme Ct. 1981, U.S. Claims Ct., 1986; cert. agt. Nat. Basketball Players Assn., Nat. Football League Players Assn. Law clk. to Hon. M. Joseph Blumenfeld

Dist. Conn., 1976-77; mem. Williams & Connolly, Washington, 1977—. Adj. faculty George Washington U. Law Sch., 1991-92. Editor Yale Law Jour., 1974-76; contbr. articles to profl. jours. Trustee Naismith Meml. Basketball Hall of Fame, 2002—. Mem. ABA, D.C. Bar, Conn. Bar Assn., Phi Beta Kappa, Omicron Delta Kappa. Commercial, contracts (including sales of goods; commercial financing), Entertainment, Sports. Office: Williams & Connolly 725 12th St NW Washington DC 20005-5901 E-mail: lbabby@wc.com.

BABCOCK, CHARLES WITTEN, JR., lawyer; b. Kansas City, Mo., Dec. 6, 1941; s. Charles W. and Esther L. (Marcy) B.; m. Sharon K. Chamberlain, June 26, 1976; children: David, William, Susan, Stephen. BA with honors, U. Mo., 1963; JD, Harvard U., 1966. Bar: Mo. 1966, Mich. 1971. Judge advocate USMC, various locations, 1966-69; assoc. Blackwell, Sanders, Kansas City, 1969-71; staff atty. Gen. Motors Corp., Detroit, 1971—. Contbr. articles to profl. jours. Bd. dirs. Mothers Against Drunk Driving, 1992-99, nat. chmn., 1996-98. Avocation: amateur radio. Administrative and regulatory, Corporate, general, Product liability. Home: 917 Grand Marais St Grosse Pointe MI 48230-1867 Office: Gen Motors Corp PO Box 33122 Detroit MI 48232-5122

BABCOCK, KEITH MOSS, lawyer; b. Camden, N.J., Aug. 5, 1951; s. William Strong Jr. and Dinah Leslie (Moss) B.; m. Jacquelyn Sue Dickman, Aug. 16, 1975; children: Michael Arthur, Max William. AB, Princeton U., 1973; JD, George Washington U., 1976. Bar: S.C. 1977, U.S. Dist. Ct. S.C. 1977, U.S. Ct. Appeals (4th cir.) 1977, U.S. Supreme Ct. 1980. Staff atty. S.C. Atty. Gen.'s Office, Columbia, 1977-78, state atty., 1978-79, asst. atty. gen., 1979-81; ptnr. Barnes & Austin, Columbia, 1981-82, Austin & Lewis, Columbia, 1982-84, Lewis, Babcock & Hawkins, Columbia, 1984—. Mem. civil justice adv. com. for dist. S.C., 1991-94; mem. S.C. Bd. Bar Examiners, 2001—. Bd. dirs. Columbia Jewish Community Pre-Sch., 1984, chmn., 1985-86; bd. dirs. Columbia Jewish Community Ctr., 1986-88. Mem. ABA, S.C. Bar Assn. (chmn. prof. resp. com. 1985-86), Richland County Bar Assn., Princeton Alumni Assn. of S.C. (v.p. 1980-86, 88-89, pres. 1990-93, 96-98), George Washington U. Law Sch. Alumni Assn. (bd. dirs. 1983-87), Summit Club, Spring Valley Country Club (Columbia). Democrat. Episcopalian. Federal civil litigation, State civil litigation, Condemnation (eminent domain). Home: 233 W Springs Rd Columbia SC 29223-6912 Office: Lewis Babcock & Hawkins 1513 Hampton St Columbia SC 29201-2928 E-mail: kmb@lbhlaw.com.

BABER, WILBUR H., JR., lawyer; b. Dec. 18, 1926; s. Wilbur H. and Martha Corinne (Allen) Baber. BA, Emory U., 1949; postgrad., U. NC, 1949—50, U. Houston, 1951—52; JD, Loyola U., New Orleans, 1965. Bar: La. 65, Tex. 66. Sole practice, Hallettsville, Tex., 1966—. Trustee Raymond Dickson Found. With U.S. Army. Mem.: ASCE, ABA, Tex. Surveyors Assn., Tex. Bar Assn., La. Bar Assn., Rotary. Methodist. State civil litigation, Oil, gas, and mineral, Probate (including wills, trusts). Office: PO Box 294 Hallettsville TX 77964-0294

BABINIEC, DENNIS HENRY, lawyer; b. Chgo., Aug. 1, 1956; s. Bruno Babiniec and Maria Johnson; m. Katherine Dowling, Mar. 14, 1981; children: Alexander Ian, Sean Michael. BS, U. Ill., 1978, JD, 1981. Bar: Ill. 1981, Colo. 1982, U.S. Dist. Ct. Colo. 1982. Assoc. Douglas S. Holden, P.C., Lakewood, Colo., 1982-85; pvt. practice Northglenn, Colo., 1985-86; prin. Dennis H. Babiniec, P.C., Northglenn, 1986—. Instr. Mile Hi Coll., Lakewood, 1983-85. Mem. Colo. Bar Assn., Colo. Bar Assn. (family law sect.), Adams County Bar Assn. Republican. Bankruptcy, State civil litigation, Family and matrimonial. Office: 10701 Melody Dr Ste 404 Denver CO 80234-4122

BABLER, WAYNE E. lawyer, retired telephone company executive; b. Orangeville, Ill., Dec. 8, 1915; s. Oscar E. and Mary (Bender) B.; m. Mary Blome, Dec. 27, 1940; children: Wayne Elroy Jr., Marilyn Anne Monson, Sally Jane Sperry. BA, Ind. Cen. Coll., 1935; JD, U. Mich., 1938; LLD, Ind. Cen. U., 1966. Bar: Mich. 1938, N.Y. 1949, Mo. 1955, Wis. 1963, U.S. Supreme Ct. 1963. Assoc. Bishop & Bishop, Detroit, 1938-42, ptnr., 1945-48; atty. AT&T, 1948-55; gen. solicitor Southwestern Bell Tel. Co., St. Louis, 1955-63, v.p., gen. counsel, sec., 1965-80, ret., 1980; v.p., gen. counsel Wis. Tel. Co., Milw., 1963-65. Bd. dirs., chmn. St. Louis Soc. Crippled Children; bd. dirs. St. Louis Symphony Soc. Mem. ABA (chmn. pub. utility sect. 1978-79), Fed. Communications Bar Assn., Mo. Bar. Assn., Delray Dunes Country Club, Ocean Club. Home: 19 Holly Dr Boynton Beach FL 33436-5534

BABLER, WAYNE E., JR., lawyer; b. Detroit, Apr. 29, 1942; s. Wayne E. and Mary E. (Blome) B.; m. Patricia A. Ward, Feb. 5, 1972; children: Dean W., Anne E. BA, Wittenberg U., 1964; JD, U. Wis., 1967. Bar: Wis. 1967, U.S. Ct. Appeals (7th cir.) 1971, U.S. Supreme Ct. 1980, U.S. Dist. Ct. (ea. and we. dists.) Wis., 1967, U.S. Dist. Ct. (ctrl. and no. dists.) Ill. 1987, U.S. Dist. Ct. (ea. and we. dists.) Mich. 1990; U.S. Ct. Appeals (9th and 10th cirs.) 1981, U.S. Ct. Appeals (D.C. cir.), 1983. Assoc. Quarles, Herriott, Clemons, Teschner & Noelke, Milw., 1971-74, Quarles & Brady, Milw., 1974-76, ptnr., 1976—. Rep. of chief justice Wis. Supreme Ct. to Wis. Jud. Compensation Com., 1983-84. Author: (with others) Business and Commercial Litigation in Federal Court, 1998; Rsch. editor Wis. Law Rev., 1966-67, Antitrust, Federal Civil Litigation, State Civil Litigation. Mem. U. Wis. Benchers Soc.; campaign cabinet United Performing Arts Fund, Inc., Milw., 1977-78; bd. dirs. Milw. Bar Found., 1976-79, treas., 1977-78; bd. dirs. Wis. Bar Found., 1983-2000, pres., 1985-87; bd. dirs. Legal Aid Soc. Milw., 1997—. With JAGC, USN, 1967-71. Fellow: Wis. Law Found., Am. Coll. Trial Lawyers (state chair 2003), Am. Bar Found.; mem.: ABA (ho. of dels. 1984—96), Bar Assn. 7th Fed. Cir., Nat. Inst. Trial Advocacy Advocates, State Bar Wis. (bd. govs. 1983—87), Milw. Bar Assn. (bd. dirs. 1976—83, pres. 1981—82), Tripoli Country Club, Univ. Club, Order of Coif. Antitrust, Federal civil litigation. Home: 1475 E Fairy Chasm Rd Milwaukee WI 53217-1433 Office: Quarles & Brady 411 E Wisconsin Ave Milwaukee WI 53202-4497 E-mail: web@quarles.com.

BABLITCH, WILLIAM A. state supreme court justice; b. Stevens Point, Wis., Mar. 1, 1941; BS, U. Wis., Madison, 1963, JD, 1968. Bar: Wis. 1968. Pvt. practice law, Stevens Point, Wis.; mem. Wis. Senate, 1972-85, senate majority leader, 1976-82; justice Wis. Supreme Ct., Madison, 1985—; dist. atty. Portage County, Wis., 1969-72. Mem. Nat. Conf. State Legislators (exec. com. 1979) Office: Wis Supreme Ct PO Box 1688 Madison WI 53702-1688

BACA, JOSEPH FRANCIS, state supreme court justice; b. Albuquerque, Oct. 1, 1936; s. Amado and Inez (Pino) B.; m. Dorothy Lee Burrow, June 28, 1969; children: Jolynn, Andrea, Anna Marie. BA in Edn., U. N.Mex., 1960; JD, George Washington U., 1964; LLM, U. Va., 1992. Asst. dist. atty. 1st Jud. Dist., Santa Fe, 1965-66; pvt. practice Albuquerque, 1966-72; dist. judge 2d Jud. Dist., Albuquerque, 1972-88; state supreme ct. justice N.Mex. Supreme Ct., Santa Fe, 1989—2002, chief justice, 1995-97; ret., 2002. Spl. asst. to atty. gen. Office of N.Mex. Atty. Gen., Albuquerque, 1966-71. Dem. precinct chmn., albuquerque, 1968; del. N.Mex. Constl. Conv., Santa Fe, 1969; bd. dirs. State Justice Inst., 1994—, V.Chmn. 1999—. Recipient Judge of Yr. award Peoples Commn. for Criminal Justice, 1989, Quincentennial Commemoration Achievement award La Hispanidad Com., 1992, Luchando por la Justicia award Mex. Am. Law Students Assn. U. N.Mex. Law Sch., 1993; J. William Fulbright Disting. Pub. Svc. award George Washington U. Alumni Assn., 1994, Recognition and Achievement award Commn. on Opportunities for Minorities in the Profession, 1992, others; named one of 100 most influential Hispanics Hispanic Bus. Mag., 1997, 98. Mem. ABA, Hispanic Nat. Bar Assn. (Lincoln-Juarez award 2000), N.Mex. Bar Assn. (outstanding jud. svc. award 1998, Disting. Jud. Svc. award 2002), Am. Law Inst., Scribes (bd. dirs. 1998—), Am. Jud. Soc. (bd. dirs. 1999—), Albuquerque Bar Assn., Santa Fe Bar Assn., N.Mex. Hispanic Bar Assn. (Outstanding Hispanic Atty. award 2000), Alumni Assn. (pres. 1980-81), Kiwanis (pres. Albuquerque chpt. 1984-85), KC (dep. grand knight 1968). Roman Catholic. Avocation: reading history. Office: Supreme Ct NMex Supreme Court Bldg PO Box 848 Santa Fe NM 87504-0848

BACH, STEVE CRAWFORD, lawyer; b. Jackson, Ky., Jan. 31, 1921; s. Bruce Grannis and Evelyn (Crawford) B.; m. Rosemary Husted, Sept. 6, 1947; children— John Crittenden, Greta Christine AB, Ind. U., 1943, JD, 1948; postgrad. Eastern studies, U. Mich., 1944, Nat. Trial Judges Coll., 1966, U. Minn. Juvenile Inst., 1967. Bar: Ky. 1948, Ind. 1948. Atty. Bach & Bach, Jackson, Ky., 1948-51; investigator U.S. CSC, Indpls., 1951-54; sole practice Mt. Vernon, Ind., 1954-65, 83—; judge 11th Jud. Circuit, Mt. Vernon, Ind., 1965-82; pres. Internat. Inst. for Youth, Inc., Mt. Vernon, 1985-90; sr. judge State of Ind., 1997—. Spl. overseas rep. Nat. Council Juvenile and Family Ct. Judges, 1983-86, bd. trustees, 1979-83; moderator Ind. Conf. Crime and Delinquency, Indpls., 1968; tchr. seminar on juvenile delinquency, Ind. Trial Judges Assn., 1969, del. Internat. Youth Magistrates Conf., Geneva, 1970, Oxford, Eng., 1974, Can., 1977; faculty adviser Criminal Law Inst., Nat. Trial Judges Coll., 1973; treas. Ind. Council Juvenile Ct. Judges, 1975, v.p., 1976, pres., 1978-79; bd. dirs. Jud. Conf., Ind. Jud. Ctr., 1978-79; faculty adviser Nat. Jud. Coll., 1978; mem. faculty Seminar for Inst. for New Judges, State of Ind., 1979. Pres. Greater Mt. Vernon Assn., 1958-59; past mem. Juvenile Justice divsn. Ind. Jud. Study Commn.; mem. Ind. Gov.'s Juvenile Justice Delinquency Prevention Adv. Bd., 1976-78, community adv. coun. Ind. U. Sch. Medicine, 1986-96. With intelligence Signal Corps, AUS, 1943-46. Mem. Nat. Coun. Juvenile Ct. Judges, Am. Legion, Ind. Bar Assn. (del.), Ind. Judges Assn. (mem. bd. mgrs. 1966-71), Masons, Elks, Kiwanis, Sigma Delta Kappa, Delta Tau Delta. Democrat. Methodist. Home and Office: 512 Walnut St Mount Vernon IN 47620-1862

BACH, THOMAS HANDFORD, lawyer, investor; b. Vineland, N.J., Dec. 25, 1928; s. Albert Ludwig and Edith May (Handford) B. AB, Rutgers U., 1950; LLB, Harvard U., 1956. Bar: N.Y. State bar 1957. Assoc. firm Hawkins, Delafield & Wood, N.Y.C., 1956—61, Reed, Hoyt, Washburn & McCarthy, N.Y.C., 1961—62; ptnr. Bach & Condren, N.Y.C., 1963—71, Bach & McAuliffe, N.Y.C., 1971—79, Stroock & Stroock & Lavan, N.Y.C., 1979—88, Sullivan & Donovan, N.Y.C., 1989—2000, of counsel, 2000—02, Sullivan, Donovan & Gentile, 2002—; arbitrator Nat. Assn of Securities Dealers Reg., 2000—. Co-counsel N.Y. State Senate Housing and Urban Devel. Com., 1971; fiscal cons. N.Y.C. Fin. Adminstrn., 1967-70; asst. counsel State Fin. Com., N.Y. State Constl. Conv. of, 1967; del. U.S./Japan Bilateral Session, 1988, Moscow Conf. on Law and Bilateral Econ. Rels., 1990; spkr. Practicing Law Inst., Mcpl. Bond Workshop, N.Y., 1995-97. Contbr. articles to profl. jours.; co-author: A Guide to Certificates of Participation, 1991, the Handbook of Municipal Bonds, 1994. Mem. N.Y. State Commn. to Study Constl. Tax Limitations, 1974-75; chmn. subcom. Pub. Securities Assn., 1990-91; dir. Citizens Union of N.Y. Served with U.S. Army, 1951-53, 1st lt. U.S. Army, 1952-53, Japan. Mem. ABA (state and local govt., dispute resolution and internat. law. sects.), N.Y. State Bar Assn., Assn. of Bar of City of N.Y., N.J. Bar Assn., N.Y. Mcpl. Analysts Group (chmn. 1973-74), Mcpl. Forum of N.Y., Market Technicians Assn. (affiliate), Internat. Fin. Svcs. Vol. Corps. Episcopalian. Finance, Securities, Alternative dispute resolution. Home: 4 E 89th St New York NY 10128-0636 also: 615 W Oak Rd Vineland NJ 08360-2262 Office: Sullivan Donovan & Gentile 20th Flr 40 Exchange Pl New York NY 10005

BACHES, SERGIO, lawyer; b. Barcelona, Dec. 4, 1970; Degree in law, U. Barcelona, 1994; LLM, Cath. U. Louvaine, Belgium, 1995; LLM in Internat. Bus. Trade Law, Fordham U., 2000. Atty. Uria & Menendez, Barcelona, 1995, Brussels, 1998—99. Asst. prof. ESADE Law Sch., Barcelona, 2001—02. Contbr. articles to profl. jours. Scholar, Fulbright Found., Madrid, 2000, Spanish Min. Edn., 1996, Catalan Regional Govt., Barcelona, 1995. Corporate, general, Antitrust, Mergers and acquisitions. Office: Uria Menendez Avda Diagonal 514 08006 Barcelona Spain Fax: 3493 4165560. E-mail: sbo@uria.com.

BACHMAN, KENNETH LEROY, JR., lawyer; b. Washington, Aug. 24, 1943; s. Kenneth Leroy and Audrey Teresa (Torrence) B.; m. Sharon Abel, June 18, 1966; children— Laura Ann, Eric Kenneth. A.B. summa cum laude, Ohio U., 1965; J.D. cum laude, Harvard U., 1968. Bar: D.C. 1968, U.S. Ct. Appeals (D.C. cir.) 1971, U.S. Supreme Ct. 1981. Law clk. to judge U.S. Dist. Ct. So. Dist. N.Y., 1968-70; assoc. Cleary, Gottlieb, Steen & Hamilton, Washington, 1970-76, ptnr., 1976— . Mem. ABA. Contbg. editor Oil and Gas Price Regulation Analyst, 1978-83, Natural Gas Journal, 1983-85; contbr. articles to profl. jours. Banking, Federal civil litigation, Public international. Home: 5332 Falmouth Rd Bethesda MD 20816-2915 Office: 1752 N St NW Washington DC 20036-2904

BACK, MICHAEL WAYNE, lawyer; b. Gary, Ind., Oct. 27, 1949; s. Virlan and Eunice Inez (Dooley) B.; m. Deborah Lynn Martinez, Oct. 1, 1988; children: Michael Christiaan, Amelia Michelle, Mark W., Hillary E. BS, Purdue U., 1976; postgrad., John Marshall Law Sch., 1979, 1979. Bar: Ind. 1979, U.S. Dist. Ct. (no. and so. dists.) Ind. 1979. Pvt. practice (atty.), Crown Point, Ind., 1979-87; hearing officer Lake County Circuit Ct., Crown Pl., 1980-87, pvt. practice, 1987--. Sargeant USAF, 1969-71. Ind. State Bar Assn., Lake County Bar Assn. (bd. dirs. 1996—), Ind. Trial Lawyers Assn. (bd. govs. 1996—), Innsbrook Country Club, Merrillville Club (sec. 1986-87, bd. dirs. 1985-93, pres. 1991-93). Democrat. Roman Catholic. Avocations: golf, tennis. Office: Lake County Circuit Ct 1 Professional Ctr Ste 204 Crown Point IN 46307-1882

BACKLAR, BYRON, lawyer; b. St. Louis, May 5, 1925; s. Joseph and Rosemary Backlar; m. Marilyn Willner, May 28, 1961 (dec. Mar. 6, 1970); children: Roger, Fredric; m. Patricia Harris, May 20, 1977. AB, Washington U., St. Louis, 1948; MS, U. Chgo., 1950; JD, Washington U., 1955. Bar: Mo. 1956, U.S. Dist. Ct. (ea. dist.) Mo. 1956. Atty. Lyng, McLeod, Abeils, and Lyng, 1953—56; atty., corp. adminstr. various indsl. cos., Los Angeles County, Calif., 1955—65; instr. ext. UCLA, 1961—67, mgr. life and health scis. office extramural support, 1965—67, asst. dir. office extramural support, 1967—70, dir. office extramural support, 1970—71, asst. dean for adminstrn. sch. medicine, 1971—84; cons. Nat. Inst. Allergy and Infectious Diseases/NIH, Rockville, Md., 1993; assoc. dean for adminstrn., assoc. prof. sch. medicine Oreg. Health Sci. U., Portland, 1984—97, assoc. dean emeritus and assoc. prof., 1997—. Mem. exec. bd. and Oreg. Health and Sci. U. rep. Puget Sound Fed. Health Coun., 1994—96; chmn. joint com. Bd. Med. Quality Assurance and Calif. Med. Schs., 1975—84; commr. Commn. on Higher Edn.'s Role in Influencing the Devel. of Fed. Rsch., Edn. and Tng. Policy of the Nat. Coun. Univ. Rsch. Adminstrs., 1971; exec. com. bd. dirs. Assoc. Western Univs., 1969—71. Chmn. adv. com. of mentally gifted minor program Santa Monica-Malibu Sch. Dist., Calif., 1976—77; chair Health Ptnrs. Coun. of Vol. Health Agencies in L.A. County, United Way, 1983—84; pres. L.A. Coastal Cities unit Am. Cancer Soc., 1979—80, pres. Oreg. divsn., 1990—92; bd. dirs. Venice (Calif.) Family Clinic, 1979—84; bd. dirs. Calif. divsn. Am. Cancer Soc., 1981—84, bd. dirs. Metro unit, 1999—2002, bd. dirs. N.W. divsn., 2001—; bd. dirs. Cascadia Behavioral Healthcare, Inc., Multnomah County, Oreg., 2002—. With USN, 1943—45, PTO. Named Vol. of the Yr., L.A. Coastal Cities unit Am. Cancer Soc., 1982; recipient Disting. Svc. award, Faculty and Profl. Staff Assn. of Harbor Gen. Hosp., 1976, Meritorious Svc. award, Rsch. and Edn. Inst., Inc. of Harbor-UCLA Med. Ctr., 1983, Leadership medal Oreg. divsn., Am. Cancer Soc., 1992. Fellow: Nat. Contract Mgmt. Assn. (Lifetime Cert. of Profl. Contract Mgmt.); mem.: Assn. of Am. Med. Colls. (mem. group on instnl. planning U.S. and Can. 1984—96, mem. group on faculty practice U.S. and Can. 1987—96, chair group on bus. affairs western region 1988—90, chair group on bus. affairs U.S. and Can. 1995—96), Portland Yacht Club, Cabrillo Beach Yacht Club, Sigma Xi, Phi Delta Phi. Avocations: sailing, reading, woodworking, photography. Home: 4160 SW Greenleaf Dr Portland OR 97221

BACKMAN, GERALD STEPHEN, lawyer; b. N.Y.C., Apr. 16, 1938; s. Morris and Marion (London) B.; m. Susan Pergament, Sept. 3, 1961 (dec. May 1978); children: Jonathan A., Kenneth S.; m. Barbara Fried Kaynes, Nov. 3, 1979 (dec. Jan. 2003); children: Jonathan J. Kaynes, Adam R. Kaynes. BA, U. Pa., 1959; LLBcum laude, Harvard U., 1962. Assoc. Weil, Gotshal & Manges LLP, N.Y.C., 1962-70, ptnr., 1970—. House counsel The Associated Merchandising Corp., N.Y.C., 1965-68; lectr. N.Y.U., 1973, Irving Trust Co., N.Y.C., 1981-88; mem. Blue Ribbon Commn. on Audit Coms. of Nat. Assn. Corp. Dirs., also chair N.Y. chpt.; adj. prof. law Fordham U. Sch. Law, N.Y.C., 2000—; mem. Tri-Bar Opinion Com., 2000—. Bd. dirs. Hewlett-East Rockaway (N.Y.) Jewish Ctr., 1976-97, chmn. legal com., 1974-85, sec., 1980-82; bd. dirs. 25 E. 86th St. Corp., N.Y.C., 1996-99. Mem.: ABA, Assn. Bar N.Y.C., N.Y. State Bar Assn. (trustee bus. law sect. 2000, chmn. securities regulation com. 2000—03), Am. Arbitration Assn. (arbitrator), Nat. Assn. Corporate Dirs. (chmn., pres. N.Y. chpt.), Masons. Republican. Jewish. Avocations: golf, skiing, tennis, fishing. Corporate, general, Mergers and acquisitions, Securities. Home: 25 E 86th St Apt 9G New York NY 10028-0553 Office: Weil Gotshal & Manges LLP 767 5th Ave New York NY 10153-0119 E-mail: Gerald.Backman@Weil.com.

BACON, BRETT KERMIT, lawyer; b. Perry, Iowa, Aug. 8, 1947; s. Royden S. and Aldeen A. (Zuker) B.; m. Bonnie Jeanne Hall; children: Jeffrey Brett, Scott Michael. BA, U. Dubuque, 1969; JD, Northwestern U., 1972. Bar: Ohio 1972, U.S. Ct. Appeals (6th cir.) 1972, U.S. Supreme Ct. 1980. Assoc. Thompson, Hine & Flory, Cleve., 1972-80, ptnr., 1980-2000; founding ptnr. Frantz Ward, Cleve., 2000—. Spkr. in field. Author: Computer Law, 1982, 84. V.p. profl. sect. United Way, Cleve., 1982-86; pres. Shaker Heights Youth Ctr., Inc., Ohio, 1984-86; elder Ch. of Western Res., 1996—. Mem. Fedn. Ins. and Corp. Counsel, Bar Assn. Greater Cleve., Cleve. Play House Club (officer 1986-94, pres. 1991-93, pres. men's com. 1993-96), Pepper Pike Civic League (trustee and treas. 1994-97). General civil litigation, Commercial, contracts (including sales of goods; commercial financing), Personal injury (including property damage). Home: 33076 Woodleigh Rd Cleveland OH 44124-5257 Office: Frantz Ward LLP Ste 1900 55 Public Sq Bldg Cleveland OH 44114

BADEL, JULIE, lawyer; b. Chgo., Sept. 14, 1946; d. Charles and Saima (Hrykas) Badel. Student, Knox Coll., 1963-65; BA, Columbia Coll., Chgo., 1967; JD, DePaul U., 1977. Bar: Ill. 1977, U.S. Dist. Ct. (no. dist.) Ill. 1977, U.S. Ct. Appeals (7th and D.C. cirs.) 1981, U.S. Supreme Ct. 1985, U.S. Dist. Ct. (ea. dist.) Mich. 1989. Hearings referee State of Ill., Chgo., 1974-78; assoc. Cohn, Lambert, Ryan & Schneider, Chgo., 1978-80, McDermott, Will & Emery, Chgo., 1980-84, ptnr., 1985-2001, Epstein, Becker & Green, PC , Chgo., 2001—. Legal counsel, mem. adv. bd. Health Evaluation Referral Svc. Chgo., 1980-89; bd. dirs. Alternatives, Inc., Chgo. chpt. Asthma and Allergy Found., 1993-94, Glenwood Sch. Author: Hospital Restructuring: Employment Law Pitfalls, 1985; editor DePaul U. Law Rev., 1976-77. Mem. ABA, Chgo. Bar Assn., Labor & Employment Alliance for Women, Columbia Coll. Alumni Assn. (1st v.p., bd. dirs. 1981-86), Pi Gamma Mu. Civil rights, Federal civil litigation, Labor (including EEOC, Fair Labor Standards Act, labor-management relations, NLRB, OSHA). Office: Epstein Becker & Green 150 N Michigan Ave Ste 420 Chicago IL 60601-7553

BADERTSCHER, DAVID GLEN, law librarian, consultant; b. Morrow, Ohio, Jan. 31, 1935; s. Glen C. and Blanche (Cluff) Badertscher; m. Betty Jo Shafer, June 25, 1965. BS, Ind. State U., 1957, MS, 1962, Rosary Coll., 1967. Tchr. Rockville HS, Ind., 1957-59, Medinah Elem. Sch., Ill., 1961-63; libr. Elgin Acad., Ill., 1963-64; tchr. Beachwood HS, Ohio, 1964-65; libr. Chgo. Pub. Libr., 1965-66; circulation, asst. reference libr. U. Chgo. Law Sch., 1966-70; libr. Schiff Hardin Waite Dorschel & Britton, Chgo., 1970-73; exec. libr. Georgetown U. Law Ctr., Washington, 1973-78; dir. libr. Milbank, Tweed, Hadley & McCloy, N.Y.C, 1978-80; prin. law libr. N.Y. Supreme Ct., N.Y.C., 1980—. Cons. Urban Rsch. Corp., Chgo., 1970—73, Herner & Co., 1977—, R. R. Bowker & Co., 1981—91, Nat. Ctr. State Cts., 1992—96; advisor Computer Law Svc., 1972—82, EIS, 1978—; adj. prof. Baruch Coll., 1982—; bd. dirs. N.Y. Met. Reference and Rsch. Libr. Agy., chmn. bd. pers. com., 1989—93; mem. judges com. automation and tech. State of N.Y. Unified Ct. Sys., 1994—96. Contbr. articles to profl. jours. Mem. corp. adv. bd. Tech. Forum Internat., 1997—. With U.S. Army, 1959—61. Mem.: ABA (assoc.; mem. com. sci. and tech. criminal justice sect. 2000—), Assn. Info. Mgrs., Am. Soc. Info. Sci. (editor SIG/Law Newsletter 1975—79), Chgo. Assn. Law Librs. (pres., conf. chmn. 1970—72, mem. com. automation and tech. judges N.Y. 1994—96), Am. Assn. Law Librs. (chmn. com. automation, sci. devel. 1970—72, chmn. state, city, and county law librs. sect. 1989—90, mem. adv. com. law libr. jour. 1989—91, conv. grantee 1970), Medinah Tchrs. Assn. (pres. 1962—63). Home: 257 Orchard St Apt 8 Westfield NJ 07090-3130 Office: NY Supreme Ct 100 Centre St New York NY 10013-4308

BADGER, DAVID HARRY, lawyer; b. Indpls., June 16, 1931; s. David Henry and Mayme Pearl (Wright) B.; m. Donna Lee Bailey, June 24, 1954; children: David Mark, Lee Ann, Steven Michael. BEE, Rose Poly. Inst., 1953; JD, Ind. U., 1964. Bar: Ind. 1964, U.S. Dist. Ct. (so and no. dists.) Ind. 1964, U.S. Patent Office 1964, U.S. Ct. Customs and Patent Appeals 1971, U.S. Ct. Appeals (fed. cir.) 1982. Engr. GE, 1953-56, Ransburg Corp., Indpls., 1956-62; chief elec. engr. Rex Metal Craft, Inc., Indpls., 1963-64; patent counsel, corp. sec. Ransburg Corp., Indpls., 1964—76; legal counsel Ball Corp., Muncie, Ind., 1976-77; ptnr. Jenkins, Coffey, Hyland, Badger & Conard, Indpls., 1977-82; mng. ptnr. Brinks, Hofer, Gilson & Lione, Indpls., 1982-98. Contbr. articles to profl. jours.; patentee in U.S. and fgn. countries. With USN, 1953-55, lt. comdr. USNR. Named Hon. Alumnus Rose Hulman Inst. Tech., 1987. Mem. ABA (various coms.), IEEE, Ind. Bar Assn. (various coms.), Am. Intellectual Property Law Assn. (various coms.), Licensing Execs. Soc. (various coms.), Indpls. Bar Assn., Internat. Assn. Intellectual Property Law, Indpls. Jazz Club (bd. dirs. 1983-85, 95-97), Junto of Indpls. (bd. dirs. 1997-99). Home: 3524 Inverness Blvd Carmel IN 46032-9379 Office: Brinks Hofer Gilson & Lione 1 Indiana Sq Ste 1600 Indianapolis IN 46204-2045 E-mail: badger938@aol.com.

BADGER, RONALD KAY, lawyer; b. Horton, Kans., Aug. 24, 1933; s. Clarence E. and Josephine L. (Rick) Badger; m. Janet L. Horner, Feb. 16, 1963; children: Hellen L. Badger Haag, Ronald K. Jr., Laura J. Badger Davis. BS in Bus., U. Kans., 1958, BS in Law, 1961, JD, 1968. Bar: Kans. 1961, U.S. Dist. Ct. Kans. 1961, U.S. Ct. Appeals (10th cir.) 1973, U.S. Supreme Ct. 1982, U.S. Ct. Claims 1990. Law clk. to Hon. Arthur J. Stanley Jr., U.S. Dist. Ct. Kans., Kansas City, 1961—62; spl. asst. to U.S. atty. for dist. of Kans., Dept. Justice, Topeka, 1962—64; assoc. Foulston & Siefkin, Wichita, Kans., 1964—66; atty. in contract adminstrn. Boeing Co., Wichita, 1966—68; pvt. practice Wichita, 1968—. Bd. dirs. Envision. Mem. bd. edtiors Kans. Bar Jour., 1966—82; contbr. articles to profl. jours. Bd. dirs. Wichita Symphony Soc., 1970—. Mem.: Fed. Bar Assn. (pres. Kans. chpt. 1978—80), Christian Legal Soc. (pres. Wichita chpt. 2001—03), Wichita Estate Planning Coun. (sec. 1996—97, pres. 1997—98), Wichita Bar Assn., Kans. Bar Assn., Lions (pres. Wichita chpt. 1984—85). Republican. Methodist. Environmental, Personal injury (including property damage), Probate (including wills, trusts). Office: 330 N Main St Wichita KS 67202

BADGEROW, JOHN NICHOLAS, lawyer; b. Macon, Mo., Apr. 7, 1951; s. Harry Leroy Badgerow and Barbara Raines (Buell) Novaria; m. Teresa Ann Zvolanek, Aug. 7, 1976; children: Anthony Thornton, Andrew Cameron, James Terrill. BA in Bus. and English with honors, Principia Coll., 1972; JD, U. Mo., Kansas City, 1975. Bar: Kans. 1976, U.S. Dist. Ct. Kans. 1976, U.S. Ct. Appeals (10th cir.) 1977, U.S. Ct. Appeals (4th cir.) 1979, U.S. Supreme Ct. 1982, U.S. Ct. Appeals (fed. cir.) 1985, U.S. Ct. Appeals (8th cir.) 1986, Mo. 1986, U.S. Dist. Ct. (we. dist.) Mo. 1986. Ptnr. McAnany, VanCleave & Phillips, P.A., Kansas City, Kans., 1975-85; ptnr.-in-charge Spencer, Fane, Britt & Browne, Kansas City, Mo. and Overland Park, Kans., 1986—. Chmn. ethics grievance com. Johnson County, 1988—; mem. Kans. Jud. Coun., 1995—, Kans. Bd. Discipline for Attys., 2000—, chmn. Ethics 2000 Commn., 2002—. Co-author: Kansas Employment Law, 1992, 2d edit., 2001; co-author, co-editor Kansas Lawyer Ethics, 1996. Co-chmn. Civil Justice Reform Act Commn., Dist. of Kans., 1995-96. Mem.: ABA, Earl O'Connor Am. Inn of Ct. (pres. 1996), Kans. Assn. Def. Counsel (age discrimination seminar), Lawyers' Assn. Kansas City, Kansas City Met. Bar Assn. (chmn. civil rights com.), Kans. Bar Assn. (employment seminar, bd. editors 1982—88, CLE com. 1989—95, ethics adv. opinion com. 1997—, Outstanding Svc. award 1995), Kans. Jud. Coun., Mission Valley Hunt Club (Stilwell, Kans.). Republican. Christian Scientist. Avocations: horseback riding, carpentry, reading. Civil rights, Federal civil litigation, General civil litigation. Office: Spencer Fane Britt & Browne 9401 Indian Creek Pkwy Ste 700 Shawnee Mission KS 66210-2038

BADR, GAMAL MOURSI, legal consultant; b. Helwan, Egypt, Feb. 8, 1924; came to U.S., 1970; s. Ahmad Moursi and Aisha Morshida (Al-Alaily) B.; m. Fatima al-Zahraa Barakat, June 18, 1950; children: Hefni, Hussein. LLB, U. Alexandria, Arab Republic of Egypt, 1944, LLD summa cum laude, 1954; diploma in econs., U. Cairo, 1945, diploma in pvt. law, 1946. Asst. dist. atty. Mixed Cts. Egypt, Alexandria, 1945-49; from assoc. to ptnr. Vatimbella, Catzeflis, Garrana & Badr, Alexandria, 1949-63; legal advisor UN Congo Operation, Kinshasa, Congo, 1963-64; justice Supreme Ct. Algeria, Algiers, 1965-69; from mem. to dep. dir. legal dept. UN Secretariat, N.Y.C., 1970-84; legal advisor Mission of Qatar to UN, N.Y.C., 1984-94; advisor Mission of Saudi Arabia to UN, N.Y.C., 1998—. Permanent bur. mem. Pan-Arab Lawyers' Fedn., Cairo, 1959-61; adj. prof. law NYU, 1982-98; lectr. The Hague Acad. Internat. Law, 1984. Author: Agency, 1980, State Immunity, 1984; gen. editor Commercial Law of the Middle East; contbr. articles to profl. jours. Mem. Internat. Law Assn. (London), Am. Soc. Internat. Law, Am. Arbitration Assn. (panel of arbitrators), Am. Fgn. Law Assn. (v.p. 1985-87, 89-92), Egyptian-Am. Assn. (pres. 1987-90), Rotary (pres. Alexandria Club 1962-63). Moslem. Home: 18 Peter Lynas Ct Tenafly NJ 07670-1115

BAE, FRANK S. H. law educator, law library administrator; b. Chung King, Szechuan, China, Dec. 19, 1941; came to U.S., 1967; s. Tse H. and Yu F. (Wang) B.; m. Anne Rita Donavan, March 15, 1975; children: Stephen, David, Marie, Elizabeth. LLB, Nat. Chung Shing U., Taipei, Taiwan, 1965; MCL, U. Miami, Fla., 1968; MS, U. Wis., 1970; JurD (hon.), New England Sch. Law, Boston, 1977. Dir. law libr. New England Sch. Law, 1970—, asst. prof. law, 1970-73, assoc. prof. law, 1973-74, prof. law, 1974—. Co-author: Searching the Law, 2nd edit., 1999. Mem. New England Law Libr. Consortium (bd. dirs.). Office: New Eng Sch Law Libr 154 Stuart St Boston MA 02116-5616

BAECHTOLD, ROBERT LOUIS, lawyer; b. Jersey City, Dec. 18, 1937; s. Fred Jacob and Catherine (Lenning) B.; m. Henrietta Thelma Hornbaker, Jan. 24, 1959; children: Kathi Ann, Christina Lee, Theresa Lynn. BS, Rutgers U., 1958; JD summa cum laude, Seton Hall U., 1966. Bar: N.Y. 1967, N.J. 1971, Pa. 1994, U.S. Dist. Ct. (so. and ea. dists.) N.Y. 1967, U.S. Ct. Appeals (fed. cir.) 1971, U.S. Ct. Appeals (2d cir.) 1967. Rsch. chemist Am. Cyanamid Co., Bound Brook, N.J., 1958-62; patent agt. M&T Chems., Inc., Rahway, N.J., 1962-65; assoc. Ward, Haselton, Orme, McElhannon, Brooks & Fitzpatrick, N.Y.C., 1965-68, ptnr., 1969-71, Fitzpatrick, Cella, Harper & Scinto, N.Y.C., 1971—. Lectr. Am. Patent Law Assn., 1979, Practising Law Inst., 1981, 88, others; mem. adv. com. to Fed. Cir. Ct. Appeals, 1991-94. Contbg. author course handbook Practising Law Inst., 1981, 88; patentee chemistry field. Mem. Cranford (N.J.) Bd. Edn., 1970-73. Nat Starch Products scholar; Leopole Schepp Found. grantee, 1954-58. Mem. ABA, Am. Intellectual Property Law Assn. (com. chmn. 1981, bd. dirs. 1987-90), Fed. Cir. Bar Assn. (bd. dirs. 1997—, pres. 2002-), N.J. Patent Law Assn. (pres. 1978-80), N.Y. Intellectual Property Law Assn., N.Y. State Bar Assn., N.J. Bar Assn. Federal civil litigation, Patent, Trademark and copyright. Office: Fitzpatrick Cella Harper & Scinto 30 Rockefeller Plz New York NY 10112 E-mail: rbaechtold@fchs.com.

BAENA, SCOTT LOUIS, lawyer; b. N.Y.C., Sept. 15, 1949; s. I. Alexander and Rose (Snofsky) B.; children: Jeffrey Lance, Brad Alexander. BBA in Acctg., Geogre Washington U., 1970, JD with honors, 1974. Bar: Fla. 1974. Ptnr. Helliwell, Melrose & DeWolf, Miami, Fla., 1974-79; mng. ptnr. Stroock & Stroock & Lavan, Miami, 1979-2000; founding ptnr. Bilzin Sumberg Baena Price & Axelrod, 2000—. Adj. prof. U. Miami Sch. of Law, 1983-89. Mem. Pres. Com. on Econ. Devel., 1970; pres. Coral Gables-Riviera Homeowners Assn., 1986; mem. Coral Gables Zoning and Planning Bd., Code Enforcement Bd., Hist. Preservation Task Force. Fellow Am. Bar Found.; mem. ABA (com. on comml. fin. svcs., corp., banking and bus. law sect. 1983—), Fla. Bar Assn. (chair bus. law sect. 1986-87, bd. govs.), Dade County Bar Assn. (bd. dirs. young lawyers div. 1977-79), Am. Law Inst. Jewish. Avocations: golf, horseback riding, woodworking. Bankruptcy, Commercial, contracts (including sales of goods; commercial financing). Office: Bilzin Sumberg et al Ste 2500 200 S Biscayne Blvd Miami FL 33131-2385 E-mail: sbaena@bilzin.com.

BAER, JOHN RICHARD FREDERICK, lawyer; b. Melrose Park, Ill., Jan. 9, 1941; s. John Richard and Zena Edith (Ostreyko) B.; m. Linda Gail Chapman, Aug. 31, 1963; children: Brett Scott, Deborah Jill. BA, U. Ill., Champaign, 1963, JD, 1966. Bar: Ill. 1966, U.S. Dist. Ct. (no. dist.) Ill. 1967, U.S. Ct. Appeals (7th cir.) 1969, U.S. Ct. Appeals (DC cir.) 1975, U.S. Ct. Appeals (9th cir.) 1979, U.S. Supreme Ct. 1975. Assoc. Keck, Mahin & Cate, Chgo., 1966-73, ptnr., 1974-97; of counsel Sonnenschein Nath & Rosenthal, Chgo., 1997-99, ptnr., 2000—. Mem. Ill. Atty. Gen.'s Franchise adv. bd., 1992-94, 96—, chair 1996—. Editor Commerce Clearing House Sales Representative Law Guide, 1998—; mem editl. bd. U. Ill. Law Forum, 1964-65, asst. editor, 1965-66; contbg. editor: Commercial Liability Risk Management and Insurance, 1978. Mem. Plan Commn., Village of Deerfield (Ill.), 1976-79, chmn., 1978-79, mem. Home Rule Study Commn., 1974-75, mem. home rule implementation com., 1975-76. Mem. ABA (topics and articles editor Franchise Law jour. 1995-96, assoc. editor 1996-99, editor-in-chief The Franchise Lawyer 1999-2002, governing com. forum on franchising 2003—), Internat. Franchise Assn. (legal/legis. com. 1990—), Inter-Pacfic Bar Assn., Ill. Bar Assn. (competition dir. region 8 nat. moot ct. 1974, profl. ethics com. 1977-84, chmn. 1982-83, spl. com. on individual lawyers advt. 1981-83, profl. responsibility com. 1983-84, standing com. on liaison with atty. registration and disciplinary commn. 1989-93, spl. com. on ethics 2000 1999—), Internat. Bar Assn. Administrative and regulatory, Commercial, contracts (including sales of goods; commercial financing), Franchising. Office: Sonnenschein Nath & Rosenthal 8000 Sears Tower 233 S Wacker Dr Chicago IL 60606-6491 E-mail: jbaer@sonnenschein.com.

BAER, TOMMY PERCY, lawyer; b. Berlin, Aug. 4, 1938; s. Bernhard and Lucie (Hirsch) B.; m. Margret A. Gogliormella, Feb. 27, 1967 (div. Feb. 1981); children: Dahlia R., Jason B.; m. Elizzbeth T. Shull, Mar. 21, 1981. BA, U. Richmond, 1960; JD, Georgetown U., 1963. Bar: Va. 1963. Law clk. U.S. Dist. Ct. (ea. dist.) Va., 1963-64, asst. U.S. Atty., 1964-67; ptnr. Horwitz, Baer & Neblett, Richmond, Va., 1974-94, Canfield, Shapiro, Baer, Heller, & Johnston, Richmond, Va., 1994—. Pres. B'nai B'rith Internat., 1994—, vice chmn. membership cabinet; mem. Gov.'s Adv. Com. on Volunteerism; mem. Henrico County Dem. Com., 1981-83; trustee World Affairs Council, 1998-, Richmond Historic Riverfront Fdn.; bd. assocs. U. Richmond, 1999-; pres. coun. Am.'s First Freedom. 2001-. Mem. Henrico County Bar Assn. (pres. 1984-85), Richmond Bar Assn. Corporate, general, Immigration, naturalization, and customs, Personal injury (including property damage). Home: 10410 Harbour Pointe Rd Midlothian VA 23112 Office: Canfield Shapiro Baer Heller & Johnston 2201 Libbie Ave Ste 200 Richmond VA 23230

BAER, ZENAS, lawyer; b. Fordville, N.D., Nov. 11, 1951; s. Allan and Edna (Brubacher) B.; m. Julia Suits, Dec. 30, 1988. BA in Polit. Scis. and German, U. Minn., 1976; JD, Hamline U., 1980. Bar: Minn. 1980, U.S. Dist. Ct. Minn. 1980, U.S. Ct. Claims, 1985, U.S. Dist. Ct. N.D. 1988, U.S. Ct. Appeals (8th cir.) 1996, U.S. Supreme Ct. 1997, White Earth Tribal Ct. 1998. Mng. ptnr. Wefald & Baer, Hawley, Minn., 1980-95; ptnr. Zenas Baer & Assocs., Hawley, 1996—. Councilman City of Hawley, 1981-89; city atty. City of Hawley, Minn, 1990—; examiner titles Clay Co., 1984—; gen. coun. for White Earth Band of Chippewa Indians; mem. Minn. Bd. Med. Practice, 1994-98. Alt. sevice as consciencious objector, 1969-72. Recipient 2 awards for excellence Lawyers Coop., Bancroft-Whitney, 1979. Mem. ABA, ATLA, Minn. Trial Lawyers Assn. (past pres.), Clay County Bar Assn., Hawley C. of C. General civil litigation, Criminal, Personal injury (including property damage). Office: Zenas Baer & Assocs 331 6th St Hawley MN 56549-4020 Home: 1715 3rd St S Moorhead MN 56560-4115 E-mail: zbaer@zbaer.com.

BAETZ, W. TIMOTHY, lawyer; b. Cin., Aug. 5, 1944; s. William G. and Virginia (Fauntleroy) Baetz. BA, Harvard U., 1966; JD, U. Mich., 1969. Bar: Ill. 1969, D.C. 1980. Assoc. McDermott, Will & Emery, Chgo., 1969-74, income ptnr., 1975-78, capital ptnr., 1979—2001. Mem. mgmt. com. McDermott, Will & Emery, 1987-92, 95-2001. With U.S. Army, 1969-75. Fellow Am. Coll. Trust and Estate Counsel. Episcopalian. Estate planning, Probate (including wills, trusts). Home: 940 Golfview Rd Glenview IL 60025-3116

BAEUMER, ULRICH J.P. lawyer; b. Luedinghausen, Germany, May 31, 1970; s. Josef and Hilde Baeumer; m. Ayuska M. Motha, Nov. 10, 1997; 1 child, Kirana. Diploma, U. Wales, 1993; Staatsexamen, U. Cologne, Germany, 1996; LLM, George Washington U., 1997; Staatsexamen, Ct. of Appeals, Darmstadt, Germany, 1999. Bar: N.Y. 1997, Frankfurt. Fgn. lawyer Berliner, Corcoran & Rowe, Washington, 1996-97; referendar Heuking, Kuhn, Dusseldorf, Germany, 1997-98, PwC Veltins, Frankfurt, Germany, 1998, GM/Opel, Frankfurt, 1999; assoc. Price Waterhouse Coopers Veltins, Frankfurt, 1999—. Editor-in-chief German Am. Law Jour., 1996-97; contbr. articles to profl. jours. Mem. ABA, DAJV. Computer, Intellectual property, General civil litigation. Home: Anf der Weide 39 65812 Bad Soden Germany Office: Pricewaterhouse Coopers Im Trutz Frankfurt 55 60322 Frankfurt Germany E-mail: ulrich.baeumer@de.pwcglobal.com.

BAFI, ALEX, lawyer; b. Mar. 16, 1965; m. Claudine Andries Bafi, Sept. 21, 2002. BS, U. Calif., Berkeley, 1985, MS, 1987, U. So. Calif., L.A., 1989; JD, NYU, 1993. Bar: N.Y. 1994. Atty. Davis Polk & Wardwell, 1993—2000; ptnr. Herbert Smith, 2001—. Mem.: ABA. Securities, Corporate, general. Office: Herbert Smith Exchange House Primrose St London EC2A 2HS England

BAGARAZZI, JAMES MICHAEL, lawyer; b. Englewood, N.J., Sept. 29, 1951; s. Michael Joseph and Dolores Marie (Barbieri) G. BS cum laude, Fairfield (Conn.) U., 1973; JD with honors, George Washington U., 1980. Bar: D.C. 1980, N.J. 1982, U.S. Ct. Appeals (Fed. cir.) 1982, S.C. 1985, U.S. Supreme Ct. 1986. Law clk. to trial judge U.S. Ct. Claims, Washington, 1980-81; assoc. Finnegan, Henderson, Farabow et al, Washington, 1981-85, Dority and Manning, P.A., Greenville, S.C., 1985-87, shareholder. Contbr. articles to profl. jours. Mem. ABA, S.C. Bar Assn., Greenville County Bar Assn., Carolina Patent Trademark and Copyright Law Assn. (pres. 1995-96). Roman Catholic. Patent, Trademark and copyright. Office: Dority and Manning PA 55 Breattie Pl Ste1600 Greenville SC 29601-3000

BAGBY, GLEN STOVALL, lawyer; b. Memphis, Sept. 1, 1944; s. Steadman Thomas and Sarah Frances (Rhodes) B.; m. Terri Stovall; children: Sarah Jane, Elizabeth Anne. AB, Transylvania U., 1966; JD, U. Ky., 1969. Bar: Ky. 1969, U.S. Ct. Claims 1975, U.S. Tax Ct. 1972, U.S. Supreme Ct. 1972. Assoc. Brock & Brock, Lexington, Ky., 1969-71; ptnr. Brock, Brock & Bagby, Lexington, Ky., 1971-98, Woodward, Hobson & Fulton, Lexington, Ky., 1999—. Chmn. Bd. Constrn. Appeals, Bd. Rev., Lexington, 1979-81. Co-author: Kentucky Probate, 2000—. Bd. dirs. Julius Marks Home for Elderly, Lexington, 1975—88; vice chmn. Good Samaritan Hosp., Lexington, 1980—92; chmn. bd. trustees Ky. Conf. United Meth. Ch., 1993—96, chancellor, 1976—2001; bd. dirs. Magee Christian Edn. Found., 1989—, pres., 2002—. Fellow: Ky. Bar Found., Am. Coll. Trust and Estate Counsel; mem.: ABA, Blue Grass Estate Planning Coun. (pres. 1987—88), Fayette County Bar Assn., Ky. Bar Assn. (probate com. 1974—2000, ho. of dels. 1985—92), U. Ky. Alumni Assn., Lexington C. of C. General civil litigation, Family and matrimonial, Probate (including wills, trusts). Office: Woodward Hobson & Fulton 200 W Vine St Fl 5 Lexington KY 40507-1720

BAGGETT, STEVEN RAY, lawyer; b. Fayetteville, Ark., July 3, 1963; s. Harold Ray and Norma June (King) B.; m. Amy Lynn Griggs, Jan. 2, 1999; 1 child, Lauren Michelle. BA, U. Ark., 1985; JD, So. Meth. U., 1988. Bar: Tex. 1988, U.S. Dist. Ct. (no. dist.) Tex. 1988, U.S. Ct. Appeals (5th cir.) 1992. Assoc. Thompson & Knight, Dallas, 1988-95, shareholder, ptnr., 1996—. Recipient Am. Jurisprudence awards Bancroft-Whitney Co., 1985-86. Mem. Tex. Bar Assn., Dallas Bar Assn. (spkrs. com. 1997—, state fair trial by jury com. 1998-2001, jud. com. 1999-2001, cmty. involvement com. 1999-2001, law in schs. and cmtys. com. 1999), Ark. U. Alumni Assn., So. Meth. U. Law Sch. Alumni Assn. (steering com.), Phi Beta Kappa. Avocations: weight training, running, ice skating, music. Federal civil litigation, General civil litigation, State civil litigation. Office: Thompson & Knight 1700 Pacific Ave Ste 3300 Dallas TX 75201-4693 E-mail: baggetts@tklaw.com.

BAGGETT, W. MIKE, lawyer; b. Waco, Tex., Nov. 8, 1946; s. Bill R. and Jenna (Robertson) B.; m. Jo Kilpatrick, May 28, 1968; children: Carl, Cary. BBA, Tex. A&M U., 1968; JD cum laude, Baylor U., 1973. Bar: Tex. 1973. Law clk. Tex. Supreme Ct., Austin, 1973—74; assoc. Winstead, Sechrest & Minick, Dallas, 1974-79, shareholder, 1979—, chmn. and chief exec. officer, 1992—. Author: Texas Foreclosure: Law & Practice, 1983, Texas Practice Series West, 2nd edit., 2001, Real Estate Litigation, Texas Practice Guide West, 2002; co-author: Lender Liability Law and Litigation, 1989. Trustee Tex. A&M Found., 1989-98, chmn., 1992-93; mem. Joint Select Com. on Judiciary, 1988; bd. dirs. Tex. Higher Edn. Coordinating Bd., 1989-95, North Tex. Commn., Dallas Citizens Coun., State Fair of Tex., Southwestern Bell-SMU Athletic Forum; chmn. Dallas Ft. Worth Regional Sports Commn.; chmn., CEO, Cotton Bowl Athletic Assn. 1st lt. U.S. Army, 1968-71, Vietnam. Decorated Bronze Star. Master: Patrick E. Higginbotham Am. Inn Ct.; fellow: Am. Bd. Trial Advocates, The Ctr. for Am. and Internat. Law, Tex. Bar Found., Am. Bar Found., Dallas Bar Found. (chmn. and trustee); mem.: Tex. Supreme Ct. Reverse Mortgage Rules Com., Tex. Supreme Ct. Home Equity Loan Foreclosures Rules Com., Dallas Bar Assn. (pres. chmn., bd. dirs.), Tex. Bar Assn. (bd. cert. civil trial com. 1983, bd. dirs., adminstn. justice com.), Baylor Law Sch. Alumni Assn. (pres., bd. dirs.), Assn. Former Students Tex. A&M U. (pres. 1988, Outstanding Alumni Coll. Bus. 1996, Disting. Alumni 1998), Ctrl. Dallas Assn. (chmn.), City Club, Royal Oaks Club. Methodist. Banking, General civil litigation, Property, real (including real estate development, water). Office: Winstead Sechrest & Minick 5400 Renaissance Tower 1201 Elm St Ste 5400 Dallas TX 75270-2199

BAGLAN, CHARLES E., JR., lawyer; b. Greenwood, Miss., Dec. 25, 1951; s. Charles E. Sr. and Mary (Smith) B.; m. Mary Katherine Hyde, Nov. 22, 1986; children: Charles Enos III, Anna Katherine. BS, Miss. State U., 1971; JD, Miss. Coll., 1978. Bar: Miss. 1978, U.S. Dist. Ct. Miss. 1978, U.S. Ct. Appeals (5th cir.) 1978. Various positions Office of the Gov., Jackson, Miss., 1978-80; ptnr. Charlie Baglan & Assoc., Batesville, Miss., 1981—, Cliff Finch & Assoc. Mem. Miss. Bar Assn., Assn. Trial Lawyers Am., Assn. Trial Lawyers Miss. General civil litigation, Personal injury (including property damage), Workers' compensation. Home: 681 Main St Courtland MS 38620-9660 Office: PO Box 1289 Batesville MS 38606-1289

BAGLEY, CHARLES FRANK, III, lawyer; b. Dec. 3, 1944; m. Kirsten L., Aug. 19, 1967; children: Charles F. IV, Gordon T. BA, Southwestern U., 1966; JD, Washington & Lee U., 1969. Judge advocates gen. ct. lt. U.S. Navy, 1969-74; ptnr. Campbell, Woods, Bagley, Emerson, McNeer & Herndon, 1974—. Pres. bd. dirs. tri state coun. Boy Scouts of Am., 1982-85; bd. dirs. Contact Huntington, Hospice Huntington, chmn. 1987-89; active Huntington Area C. of C., Enslow Park Presbyn. Ch. Fellow Internat. Soc. Barristers, West Va. Bar Found.; mem. ABA, Va. Bar Assn., W.Va. State Bar Assn. (bd. govs. 1986-93, pres. 1991-92), W.Va. Bar Assn. (exec. coun. 1986-95, pres. 1993-94), Def. Trial Coun. W.Va. (bd. govs. 1985-90), Cabell County Bar Assn. (pres. 1985-86), Internat. Assn. Ins. Coun., Def. Rsch. Inst., Inc. (state chmn. 1985-90). Alternative dispute resolution, Insurance, Toxic tort. Address: 1123 12th Ave Huntington WV 25701-3423

BAGLEY, DENNIS JOSEPH, lawyer; b. Detroit, Mar. 9, 1940; s. Harold Joseph and Mary Arzelie (Dwan) B.; m. Jacquelyn Gayle Bell, Nov. 10, 1979. BA, Sacred Heart Coll., Detroit, 1961; STB, Cath. U., Washington, 1965; MA, Cen. Mich. U., 1980; JD, Wayne State U., 1983. Bar: Mich.; U.S. dist. Ct. (ea. dist.) Mich.; U.S. Ct. Appeals (6th cir.); U.S. Supreme Ct. Assoc. Leib & Leib, Southfield, Mich., 1984-85; pvt. practice Law Offices of DJB, Madison Heights and, Farmington Hills, Mich., 1986—. Sec. Farmington Ridge Homeowners Assn., 1994-97, pres., 1997-99. Mem. West Bloomfield Optimist Club (pres. 1989-90). Republican. Roman Catholic. Criminal, Family and matrimonial, Probate (including wills, trusts). Office: 37875 W 12 Mile Rd Ste A Farmington Hills MI 48331-3043

BAGLEY, PHILIP JOSEPH, III, lawyer; b. Richmond, Va., Nov. 24, 1941; s. Philip Joseph Jr. and Louise (Bourne) B.; m. Sally Ann Twedell, Aug. 18, 1967; children: Elizabeth Bourne Faulkner, Anne Tunstall Twedell. BA, U. Richmond, 1963; LLB, U. Va., 1966. Bar: Va. 1966, U.S. Supreme Ct. 1972. Assoc. Troutman Sanders LLP, Richmond, 1970—74, ptnr., 1974—; v.p. Richmond Real Estate Group, 2002—03, pres., 2003—. Chmn. state adv. coun. Nat. Legal Svcs. Corp., Richmond, 1977-79; bd. dirs. Legal Svc. Corp. Va., 1978-86. Legal advisor Jr. League Richmond, 1977—; bd. dirs. Richmond Symphony, 1986-96, pres. 1992-94; bd. dirs. Richmond Eye and Ear Hosp., 1988—, pres. 1991-96; trustee Benedictine H.S., 1994-2002, pres., 1996-2002; bd. dirs. Carpenter Ctr. Performing Arts, 1995—, mem. exec. com., 1998—; bd. dirs., mem. exec. com. Va. Performing Arts Found., 2001—; bd. dirs. Richmond Renaissance, 2002—. Fellow Am. Law Found., Va. Bar Found.; mem. ABA (lectr. real estate financing com. 1984, title ins. com. 1987, leasing 1992, coun. real property, probate and trust law sect. 1993-98, sec. 1998-2000, vice-chair real property divsn. 2000-02, chair-elect 2002-03, chair 2003—), Am. Coll. Real Estate Lawyers (bd. govs. 1988-97, treas. 1991-93, v.p. 1993-94, pres. 1995-96), Anglo-Am. Real Property Inst. (bd. govs. 1995—), Coun. for Am.'s 1st Freedom (bd. govs. 1994-2000, pres. 1996-2000), Internat. Coun. Shopping Ctrs. (co-chair law conf. com. 1996-98), Va. Bar Assn., Richmond Bar Assn., Country Club Va., Commonwealth Club, Order of Coif, Phi Beta Kappa, Omnicron Delta Kappa. Roman Catholic. Property, real (including real estate development, water). Office: Troutman Sanders LLP 1111 E Main St Richmond VA 23219-3531

BAGSHAW, BRADLEY HOLMES, lawyer; b. Salem, Mass., Mar. 26, 1953; s. James Holmes and Hope (Bradley) Bagshaw. AB summa cum laude, Bowdoin Coll., 1975; JD cum laude, Harvard U., 1981. Bar: Wash. 1981, U.S. Dist. Ct. (we. dist.) Wash. 1981, U.S. Dist. Ct. (ea. dist.) Wash. 1989, U.S. Ct. Appeals (9th cir.) 1989. Assoc. Helsell Fetterman, Seattle, 1981-88, ptnr., 1988—, mng. ptnr., 1991-97, ptnr., 1997—. Admiralty, Federal civil litigation, State civil litigation. Office: Helsell Fetterman 1325 4th Ave Ste 1500 Seattle WA 98101-2569 E-mail: bbagshaw@helsell.com.

BAHLER, GARY M. lawyer; BA, Houghton Coll., 1973; JD, Cornell U., 1976. Bar: N.Y. 1977. Sec., dep. gen. counsel Foot Locker, Inc. (formerly Venator Group, Inc.), N.Y.C., 1991-93, v.p., gen. counsel, sec., 1993-98, sr. v.p., gen. counsel, sec., 1998—. Office: Foot Locker Inc 112 W 34th St New York NY 10120

BAHLMAN, WILLIAM THORNE, JR., retired lawyer; b. Cin., Jan. 9, 1920; s. William Thorne and Janet (Rhodes) B.; m. Nancy W. DeCamp, Mar. 21, 1953; children: Charles R., William Ward, Baker D. BA, Yale U., 1941, LL.B., 1947. Bar: Ohio 1947. Prin. Paxton & Seasongood, L.P.A., Cin., 1947-67, 73-88; ptnr. Paxton & Seasongood, Cin., 1954-67, Thompson Hine, LLP, Cin., 1989-94; prof. law U. Cin. Coll. Law, 1967-73, lectr., 1965-67, 73-77; ret., 1994. Served with USAAF, 1942-46. Mem. Am. Law Inst., ABA, Ohio State Bar Assn., Cin. Bar Assn. Estate planning, Probate (including wills, trusts), Estate taxation. Office: Thompson Hine LLP 312 Walnut St Fl 14 Cincinnati OH 45202-4024

BAHLS, STEVEN CARL, law educator, dean; b. Des Moines, Sept. 4, 1954; s. Carl Robert and Dorothy Rose (Jensen) B.; m. Jane Emily Easter, June 18, 1977; children: Daniel David, Timothy Carl, Angela Emily. BBA, U. Iowa, 1976; JD, Northwestern U., Chgo., 1979. Bar: Wis. 1979, Mont. 1979; CPA, Iowa. Assoc. Frisch, Dudek & Slattery, Milw., 1979-84, dir., 1985; assoc. dean and prof. U. Mont. Sch. of Law, Missoula, 1985-94; dean., prof. law sch. Capital U. Law Sch., Columbus, Ohio, 1994—. Coordinating exec. editor Northwestern U. Law Rev., 1979. Chair Columbus Works. Mem. ABA, Am. Agrl. Law Assn. (past pres.), Wis. Bar Assn., Mont. Bar Assn., Ohio Bar Assn., Ohio State Bar Found. (bd. govs.), Order of Coif. Avocations: photography, travel, hiking. Home: 499 N Columbia Ave Bexley OH 43209-1003 Office: Capital U Law Sch 303 E Broad St Columbus OH 43215-3200

BAHN, CHARLES FREDERICK, JR., lawyer, clergyman; b. Okinawa, Japan, Sept. 21, 1954; (parents Am. citizens); s. Charles Frederick and Betty Bowen (Morrow) B. BA in History, S.E. Mo. State U., 1977; JD, Washington and Lee U., 1981; MDiv, Tex. Christian U., 1985. Bar: Mo. 1982; ordained to ministry Christian Ch. (Disciples of Christ), 1985. Assoc. minister Webster Groves (Mo.) Christian Ch., 1985-89; assoc. area minister Ozark Lakes Area Christian Ch. (Disciples of Christ), Springfield, Mo., 1989-90; assoc. min. Nat. Ave. Christian Ch., Springfield, 1991—. Staff atty. Legal Aid S.W. Mo., 1989-92. Active Citizens for Modern Transit, Friends of Forest Park and Tower Grove Park, Landmarks Assn. St. Louis, Springfield Little Theater, Ozarks Greenways; bd. dirs. AIDS Project of the Ozarks; reading buddy Cowden Elem. Sch. Mem. Springfield Met. Bar Assn., Friends Springfield Art Mus. Bd., Ozarks Food Harvest Bd., Ministerial Alliance, Am. Guild Organists. Home: 3810 E Sunshine St Springfield MO 65809-2927

BAHNER, THOMAS MAXFIELD, lawyer; b. Little Rock, 1933; m. Sara M. Bahner; 3 children. BS, Carson-Newman Coll., 1954. JD, U. Va., 1960. Bar: Tenn. 1960, Va. 1960, U.S. Dist. Ct. (ea. dist.) Tenn. 1961, U.S. Supreme Ct. 1970, U.S. Ct. Appeals (6th cir.) 1971, U.S. Ct. Appeals (8th cir.) 1971, U.S. Ct. Appeals (4th cir.) 1975, U.S. Ct. Appeals (3d cir.) 1988, U.S. Ct. Appeals (fed. cir.) 1991, U.S. Ct. Appeals (9th cir.) 1999, U.S. Ct. Appeals (11th cir.) 1999, U.S. Dist. Ct. (we. dist.) Tenn. 2002. Assoc. Kefauver, Duggan and McDonald, Chattanooga, 1960-62; ptnr. Duggan, McDonald and Bahner, Chattanooga, 1962-64, Chambliss, Bahner, Crutchfield, Gaston and Irvine (name changed to Chambliss, Bahner & Stophel), Chattanooga, 1964—; mem., chair adv. commn. civil rules Tenn. Supreme Ct., chmn., 1982-89, mem., chair adv. com. drafting rules, 1983-89, mem. bd. profl. responsibility, 1982-85, chmn. fin. com., 1984-85; bd. commrs. Hamilton County Law Libr. Sr. contbg. editor: Evidence in America, the Federal Rules in the United States, 1987; contbr. chpts. to books. Bd. dirs. Orange Grove Ctr., Chattanooga, 1962-99, pres. 1974-75, chmn. 1976-77; bd. trustees, sec. BOTA Found., 1985--; trustee Carson-Newman Coll., Jefferson City, Tenn., 1975-2002, chmn. bd. trustees, 1983-87, 90-92, mem. pres. search com., 1977, 1999-2000; mem., dir., organizer U.S. Dist. Ct. Hist. Soc. for Ea. Dist. Tenn., v.p., 1993--; mem., organizer, bd. dirs. Tenn. Supreme Ct. Hist. Soc., pres., 1997; active Hamilton County Sch. Bd., 1970-75; bd. dirs. Chattanooga Symphony, 1980-83. Recipient Disting. Alumni award Carson-Newman Coll., 1984; bd. dirs. Chattanooga United Way, 1990-96, chmn. fund drive profl. divsn., 1992; mem. merit selection panel for Bankruptcy Judges, U.S. Dist. Ct., 1993-94, mem. Liberty Bell Award com. Fellow Am. Bar Found. (life), Tenn. Bar Found. (life, founding), Chattanooga Bar Found. (life, founding), Va. State Bar; mem. ABA (Tenn. Bar del. 1984-90, state del., mem. nominating com. 1990-99, chmn. standing com. on law and lit., bd. govs. 1999-2002, mem. exec. com. 2001-02), Tenn. Bar Assn. (bd. govs. 1975-82, pres. 1980-81), Conf. So. Bar Pres. (chmn. 1980-81), Chattanooga Bar Assn. (pres. 1969-70, med.-legal com., pres.'s award 1995, Ralph H. Kelley Humanitarian award), Am. Coll. of Trial Lawyers (state com. 1995-99, mem. profl. com. 1998--), Am. Bd. Trial Advocates, Internat. Assn. Def. Counsel, 6th Circuit Judical Conf. (life mem.), Chattanooga Trial Lawyers Assn., Tenn. Def. Lawyers Assn., Am. Judicature Soc., Estate Planning Coun. (bd. dirs. 1971-72), Mountain City Club, Walden Club, Signal Mountain Golf and Country Club, Chattanooga Rotary Club (sec. 1989-91, 1st v.p. 1997-98, pres. 2001-02), Delta Theta Phi. Baptist (deacon, former chmn., chmn. pulpit com.). Federal civil litigation, State civil litigation, Corporate, general. Home: 718 Parsons Ln Signal Mountain TN 37377-2704 Office: Chambliss Bahner & Stophel PC 1000 Tallan Bldg 2 Union Sq Ste 1000 Chattanooga TN 37402-2500 Business E-Mail: mbahner@cbslawfirm.com.

BAIER, ELIZABETH DOMSIC, lawyer; b. Chicago Heights, Ill., Aug. 4, 1954; d. Joseph Thomas and Marguerite Charlotte Domsic; m. Donald Edward Baier, June 16, 1979. BA, Ind. U., 1976, JD, 1979. Bar: Ind. 1979, U.S. Dist. Ct. (so. dist.) Ind. 1979. Pvt. practice, Mt. Vernon, Ind., 1979—; exec. dir. United Way of Posey County, Mt. Vernon, 1982—. Mem. character and fitness com. Ind. Bd. Law Examiners, Indpls., 1988—. Mem., sec. of parish coun. St. Matthew Ch., Mt. Vernon, 1987-89; bd. dirs. Mt. Vernon 175th Birthday, Inc., 1990-94, Posey County Dem. Women's Club, pres. 1991-92, 98-99, 2003—; mem. Posey County Welfare to Work Local Planning Coun., Posey County Comty. Found. Recipient Young Careerist award Bus. and Profl. Women's Club, Mt. Vernon, 1980, Woman of Yr., 1985; named to Outstanding Young Women of Am., 1983; honoree as a Sagamore of the Wabash, Gov. of Ind., 2002. Mem. Optimists (bd. dirs. Mt. Vernon chpt. 1989-92), Ind. Bar Found. (mem. pro bono com. Dist. 13, Ind. 1999—), Posey County Bar Assn. (sec./treas. 1979-80), Ind. State Bar Assn., Posey County Hist. Soc., others. Democrat. Roman Catholic. Avocations: needlepoint, gardening, reading, rose growing. Office: 128 W 3d St PO Box 367 Mount Vernon IN 47620-0367

BAILEY, BRAD DUANE, lawyer; b. Denver, Apr. 26, 1958; s. Beverly DeWayne and Carol Ann (Kettner) B.; m. Deborah Lee Jones, May 23, 1981; children: Lauren Taylor, Mackenzie Grace. BA, Colo. State U., 1980; JD, Gonzaga U., 1983. Bar: Colo., U.S. Dist. Ct. Colo., U.S. Ct. Appeals (10th cir.) 1984, U.S. Supreme Ct. 2003. Law clk. 8th Jud. Dist. Colo., Ft. Collins, 1983-85; asst. city atty. City of Longmont, Colo., 1985-88, dep. city atty., 1988-92; county atty. Clear Creek County, Georgetown, Colo., 1992-99; asst. city atty. City of Littleton, Colo., 1999—. Treas. Hist. Georgetown, Inc., 1994-97, vice-chmn., 1997-2000. Mem. ABA, Colo. Bar Assn., Arapahoe County Bar Assn., Trout Unltd., Fedn. Fly Fishers, Ducks Unltd., Longmont Optimist (pres. 1988-89, lt. gov. 1989-90). Lutheran.

BAILEY, BURCK, lawyer; b. Vinita, Okla., Aug. 22, 1934; s. Frank and Frances (Burckhalter) B.; m. Sandra Barnett, Apr. 17, 1981. BA, Westminster Coll., 1958; LLB, NYU, 1961. Bar: Mo. 1961, Okla. 1963, U.S. Supreme Ct. 1969. Assoc. Morrison, Hecker, Cozad & Morrison, Kansas City, Mo., 1961-63; asst. atty. gen. State of Okla., Oklahoma City, 1963-66; ptnr. Duval, Head, McKinney & Bailey, Oklahoma City, 1966-67, Fellers, Snider, Blankenship, Bailey & Tippens, Oklahoma City, 1967—. Fellow Am. Coll. Trial Lawyers (state chmn. 1993), Internat. Acad. Trial Lawyers, Am. Bar Found.; mem. ABA (ho. dels. 1987-88), Am. Acad. Appelate Lawyers, Okla. Bar Assn. (pres. 1988), Okla. County Bar Assn. (pres. 1983-84, mem. Okla. Jud. nominating commn. 1997-2003). General civil litigation. Office: Fellers Snider Blankenship Bailey & Tippens 100 N Broadway Ste 1700 Oklahoma City OK 73102

BAILEY, DANIEL ALLEN, lawyer; b. Pitts., Aug. 31, 1953; s. Richard A. and Virginia (Henry) B.; m. Janice Abraham, Oct. 10, 1981; children: Jeffrey, Megan. BBA, Bowling Green State U., 1975; JD, Ohio State U., 1978. Bar: Ohio 1978, U.S. Dist. Ct. (so. dist.) Ohio 1978, U.S. Tax Ct. 1979. Ptnr. Arter & Hadden, Columbus, Ohio, 1978—, chair exec. com., 2000—. Co-author: Handbook for Corporate Directors, 1985, Liability of Corporate Officers and Directors, 7th edit., 2002. Bd. dirs. Columbus Met. Community Action Orgn., 1979-80, Franklin County Head Start, Columbus, 1979-80, Faith Luth. Ch., Whitehall, Ohio, 1985-90, Luth. Social Svcs. Cen. Ohio, 1991-2000, Concorde Counseling Svcs., 2000—. Mem. ABA, Ohio Bar Assn., Columbus Bar Assn., Phi Kappa Phi, Beta Gamma Sigma, Omicron Delta Kappa. Corporate, general, Professional liability, Securities. Office: Arter & Hadden 10 W Broad St Ste 2100 Columbus OH 43215-3422

BAILEY, DANIEL B. lawyer; b. Topeka, Kans., Sept. 13, 1959; s. Daniel J. Bailey and Paula R. Upton; m. Mary Michele Hand, July 16, 1988; children: Catherine Clare, Colin Daniel. BBA, Washburn U., Topeka, 1981; JD, Washburn U., 1987. Bar: Kans. 1987, U.S. Dist. Ct. Kans. 1987, Wyo. 1993, U.S. Dist. Ct. Wyo. 1993, U.S. Ct. Appeals (10th cir.) 1993. Pres. Lubnau, Bailey & Dumbrill, P.C., Gillette, Wyo., 1991—. Mem. Moonshiner Devel., LLC, Gillette, 1999—, The Jealous Mistress, LLC, Gillette, 1991—; bd. dirs. Gillette Dental Group, PC. Mem.: Gillette Energy Rotary Club (pres. 1998—99, asst. dist. gove. dist. 5440 1999—2000). Republican. Roman Catholic. Estate planning, Personal injury (including property damage), Property, real (including real estate development, water). Home: 6000 Stone Place Ave Gillette WY 82718 Office: Lubnau Bailey & Dumbrill PC PO Box 1028 300 S Gillette Ave #2000 Gillette WY 82716 E-mail: dan@etseq.com.

BAILEY, JOHN P. lawyer; b. Wheeling, W.Va., May 2, 1951; BA, Dartmouth Coll., 1973; JD, W.Va. U., 1976. Bar: W.Va. 1976, Ohio 1981, U.S. Dist. Ct. (no. and so. dists.) W.Va. 1976, U.S. Dist. Ct. (so. dist.) Ohio 2000, U.S. Ct. Appeals (4th cir.) 1977, U.S. Supreme Ct. 1981. Law clk. to Hon. Charles H. Haden, II, U.S. Dist. Judge (no. and so. dists.) W.Va., 1976—78; asst. pros. atty., 1985—86; atty. Bailey, Riley, Buch & Harman, LC, Wheeling, W.Va. Chmn. Workers' Compensation Appeal Bd., 1985—91. Mem.: ABA, Nat. Assn. Criminal Def. Lawyers, W.Va. Trial Lawyers, W.Va. State Bar (bd. govs. 1992—95, 1998—2001, pres.-elect 2002—), Ohio County Bar Assn., W.Va. Bar Assn. (exec. coun. 1988—94, pres. 1992—93), Order of Coif, Phi Delta Phi. General civil litigation, Criminal, Administrative and regulatory. Office: Bailey Riley Buch and Harman PO Box 631 Riley Bldg 53 Fourteenth St Ste 900 Wheeling WV 26003-0081*

BAILEY, K. RONALD, lawyer; b. Sandusky, Ohio, July 30, 1947; s. Kenneth White and Virginia McClung (Sheddan) B.; m. Sara Ann Geary Bressler, Mar. 14, 1969 (div. June 1973); 1 child, Matthew Scott; m. Lynn Darlene Kammer, Aug. 31, 1973; children: Thomas Keith, Kenneth Richard. B in Liberal Studies summa cum laude, Bowling Green State U., 1979; JD, Cleveland-Marshall Law Sch., 1982; grad., Gerry Spence's Trial Lawyers Coll., 1994. Bar: Ohio 1983, U.S. Dist. Ct. (no. dist.) Ohio 1983, U.S. Dist. Ct. (D.C. cir.) 2000, U.S. Ct. Appeals (6th cir.) 1985, U.S. Supreme Ct. 1992. Tool, diemaker Gen. Motors, Sandusky, 1968-84; sole practice Huron, Ohio, 1983-87; sr. trial atty. K. Ronald Bailey & Assocs. Co., Legal Profl. Assn., Sandusky, 1987—. Chmn. Charter Rev. Com. of Huron, 1984. Mem. ATLA, ABA (criminal justice sect., white collar crimes com.), Nat. Assn. Criminal Def. Lawyers, Ohio Bar Assn. (coun. dels. 1998—, criminal justice sect., white collar crimes com., criminal law com.), Erie County Bar Assn., Ohio Assn. Criminal Def. Lawyers (bd. dirs. 1988—, v.p. publs. 1991-93, 97-98, treas. 1994, pres. 1995-96, chmn. capital litigation 1997—, Pres.'s award 1989-95, 97-98, v.p. continuing legal edn. 1997-98). Democrat. Pentecostal. Avocations: reading, photography, painting, swimming, drag racing. General civil litigation, Criminal, Personal injury (including property damage). Home: 121 Sycamore Dr Norwalk OH 44857-1914 Office: K Ronald Bailey & Assocs Co Legal Profl Assn 220 W Market St Sandusky OH 44870-2515 E-mail: krbailey@baileyandassoc.com.

BAILEY, MICHAEL KEITH, lawyer; b. Washington, Feb. 19, 1956; s. Alda Merrill and Joan (Moyers) B.; m. Linda Ann Braswell, Dec. 18, 1982; children: Julia Anne, David Allen. AB in Econs. and Polit. Sci., Coll. William and Mary, 1978; JD, Stetson U., 1981. Bar: Fla. 1981, U.S. Dist. Ct. (mid. dist.) Fla. 1982, U.S. Ct. Appeals (11th cir.) 1982, U.S. Supreme Ct. 1986. Assoc. Pitts, Eubanks, et al, Orlando, Fla., 1981-86; ptnr. Parrish, Bailey & Myers, P.A., Orlando, 1986-98, Bailey & Myers, P.A., Maitland, Fla., 1998—. Mem.: ATLA (charter, pres.'s club), ABA, Fla. Bar Bd. Ctr. (civil trial atty.), Nat. Bd. Trial Adv. (cert. civil trial advocate), Acad. Fla. Trial Lawyers (eagle patron), Orange County Bar Assn., So. Trial Lawyers Assn. Republican. Presbyterian. General civil litigation, Insurance, Personal injury (including property damage). Office: Bailey & Myers PA 100 E Sybelia Ave Ste 120 Maitland FL 32751-4777 Home: 701 Lake Sue Ave Winter Park FL 32789-5807 E-mail: mbailey@baileymyers.com.

BAILEY, R(OBERT) GREG, lawyer; b. Wichita, Kans., Mar. 11, 1954; s. Robert Earl and Joyce R. (Dudley) B. BA, U. Ill., 1976; MA, U. Mo., 1979; JD, Washington U., 1985; student, Harvard Law Sch., 1998. Bar: Mo. 1985, Ill. 1986, D.C. 1987, U.S. Dist. Ct. (ea. dist.) Mo. 1986, U.S. Dist. Ct. (so. and cen. dist.) Ill. 1991, U.S. Ct. Internat. Trade 1987, U.S. Ct. Appeals (8th cir.) 1986, U.S. Ct. Appeals (7th cir.) 1989, U.S. Supreme Ct. 1989. Staff writer Ill. Times, Springfield, 1978; reporter Collinsville (Ill.) Jour., 1980; staff mem. Ill. Ho. of Reps., Springfield, 1981; freelance writer, 1977—; corr. Chgo. Tribune, 1985-87, The Economist, London, 1981—, Time Magazine, Chgo., 1982-88; pvt. practice law St. Louis, 1985—; mem. Fgn. Press Ctr. of Japan Exch. Program, 2001. Adj. prof. Webster U., 1991, East Ctrl. Coll., 1993, McKendree Coll., 1998; freelance prodr. ABC News, 1993-2000. Bd. editors St. Louis Journalism Rev., 1987-92; editor: Entrepreneural Law, 1988; contbr. articles to profl. jours. Candidate for nomination for Mo. Ho. of Reps., 1990; Dem. nominee Mo. State Senate, 2000. Named to Govs. Followship Ill. Gov., Springfield, 1975, 100 Club, EEC Law Seminar, ULB-VUB, Brussels, 1984. Mem. Mo. Bar Assn., D.C. Bar Assn., U. Ill. Alumni Assn. Avocations: writing, auto racing. General civil litigation, Communications, Private international. Home: 2800 Black Forest Apt B Saint Louis MO 63129-4132 Office: 5541 Oakville Ctr # 103 Saint Louis MO 63129-3554 E-mail: rgbstl@aol.com.

BAILEY, ROBERT SHORT, lawyer; b. Bklyn., Oct. 17, 1931; s. Cecil Graham and Mildred (Short) B.; m. Doris Furlow, Aug. 29, 1953 (dec. 2001); children: Elizabeth Jane Goldentyer, Robert F., Barbara A. Jongbloed. AB, Wesleyan U., Middletown, Conn., 1953; JD, U. Chgo., 1956. Bar: Ill. 1965, U.S. Dist. Ct. D.C. 1956, U.S. Supreme Ct. 1960. Atty. criminal divsn. U.S. Dept. Justice, 1956-61, asst. U.S. atty. No. dist. Ill., 1961-65; ptnr. LeFevour & Bailey, Oak Park, Ill., 1965-68; pvt. practice, Chgo., 1968—. Panel atty. Fed. Defender Program, 1965—. Mem. NACDL (faculty 1976-78, legis. chmn. 1976-78). Criminal, Appellate, Labor (including EEOC, Fair Labor Standards Act, labor-management relations, NLRB, OSHA). Home: 17 Timber Trail Streamwood IL 60107-1353 Office: 53 W Jackson Blvd Ste 918 Chicago IL 60604-3607

BAILEY, RONALD E. lawyer; b. Portland, Oreg., Aug. 12, 1937; s. Thomas H. and Helen J. (Johnson) B.; m. Joanne Lee Wood, Jan. 2, 1960; children: Griffin T., Brad E. BS, U. Oreg., 1959; JD, Willamette U., 1963. Bar: Oreg. 1963, U.S. Dist. Ct. Oreg. 1963. Assoc. Bullivant, Houser, Bailey , Portland, 1963-68, ptnr., 1969—. Assoc. editor Willamette Law Rev., 1959. Pres. Metro. Business Assn., 1986; bd. visitors Willamette Coll. Law, 1980—, pres., 1986-88. Served to 1st lt. U.S. Army, 1960. Recipient Outstanding Svc. award Willamette Coll. of Law, 1989. Fellow Oreg. Law Found. (pres. 1987-88); mem. ABA, Oreg. Bar Assn. (bd. govs. 1981-84, v.p. 1983-84), Multnomah Bar Assn., Internat. Assn. Def. Counsel, Oreg. Assn. Def. Counsel (bd. dirs. 1985-91, pres. 1990). Clubs: Multnomah Athletic, Columbia Edgewater Golf and Country, Univ. (Portland). Republican. Roman Catholic. Federal civil litigation, Product liability, Toxic tort. Home: 11 SW Ridge Dr Portland OR 97219-6542 Office: Bullivant Houser Bailey et al 888 SW 5th Ave Ste 300 Portland OR 97204-2017

BAILEY, THOMAS CHARLES, lawyer; b. Rochester, N.Y., Nov. 26, 1948; s. Charles George and Teckla Barbara (Driscoll) B.; m. Rosalie Stoll, Sept. 24, 1974; children: Leah Isabelle, Molly Driscoll, Elizabeth Rose. BA, Princeton U., 1970; JD, SUNY, Buffalo, 1974. Bar: N.Y. 1975, Fla. 1977. Assoc. Little & Burt, Buffalo, 1974-78, ptnr., 1978-80, Saperston & Day, PC, Buffalo, 1980-92; pvt. practice Buffalo, 1992-97; mem. Albrecht Maguire Heffern and Gregg PC, Buffalo, 1997-2000, Phillips, Lytle, Hitchcock, Blaine & Huber, LLP, Buffalo, 2000—. Bd. dirs., sec. Buffalo Therapeutic Riding Ctr. Inc., 1999-2001. Pres. St. Thomas Moore Guild, 1981; trustee Shea's O'Connell Preservation Guild, 1986-96, chmn., 1994; bd. dirs. Opera Niagara, Ltd., 1999—, pres., 2001-. Mem. ABA, N.Y. State Bar Assn. (exec. com. of real property law sect. 1994-2000), Fla. Bar Assn., Am. Assn. Franchisees and Dealers (fair franchising standards com.), Saturn Club (dean 2000), Princeton U. Alumni Assn. Western N.Y. (pres. 1990-91), Brookhaven Trout Club. Avocations: fly fishing, boating, horses. Corporate, general, Franchising, Property, real (including real estate development, water). Office: Phillips Lytle et al 3400 HSBC Tower Buffalo NY 14203

BAILEY, TIMOTHY GORDON, lawyer; b. St. Paul, Nov. 1, 1950; s. Gordon Edward and Virginia Lois (Parlin) B.; divorced; 1 child, Amelia. BES, U. Minn., 1979, JD cum laude, 1982. Bar: Minn. 1982, U.S. Dist. Ct. Minn. 1983, U.S. Ct. Appeals (8th cir.) 1983. With Robins, Kaplan, Miller & Ciresi, Mpls.-St. Paul, 1982-98; pvt. practice Mpls., 1998—. Atty. Ramsey County Vol. Atty. Panel, St. Paul, 1983-95; mem. Minn. Civil Liberties Union, 1986-97. Mem. ABA, ATLA, Minn. Trial Lawyers Assn. (bd. govs. 1998—, chmn. publs. com. 1997-99, publs. com. 1988—, legis. com. 1987—, fin. com. 1997-99, affinity com. 1999—, co-chmn. legal tech. com. 2002—, co-chmn. elder law com. 1999—), Minn. Bar Assn. (ct. rules and procedure com. 1997-99, Ramsey County Bar Assn. (ct. rules and procedure com. 1987-97, civil litigation sect. 1997-99), Hennepin County Bar Assn. (civil litigation sect., legal-med. com.), Am. Arbitration Assn. (ins. panel arbitrator). Democrat. Roman Catholic. Personal injury (including property damage), Product liability. Office: Timothy G Bailey Attorney at Law 700 Lumber Exchange Bldg 10 S 5th St Minneapolis MN 55402-1012

BAILEY, WILLIAM SCHERER, lawyer, educator; b. St. Charles, Ill., July 28, 1948; s. Robert Wilbank and Josephine Grant (Scherer) B.; m. Sylvia Lillian Sherry, July 15, 1977; children: Robert, Mimy Ann, Lillian. BS, U. Oreg., 1970; JD, Northwestern U., 1974. Bar: Ill. 1974, U.S. Dist. Ct. (no. dist.) Ill. 1976, Wash. 1977, U.S. Dist. Ct. (we. dist.) Wash. 1977; Diplomate Am. Bd. Trial Advocates. Legal counsel govt. com. Ill. Mental Health Code, 1974-76; asst. pub. defender State of Wash., Seattle, 1976-80, asst. atty. gen., 1980-82; ptnr. Levinson, Friedman, Vhugen, Duggan, Bland & Horowitz, Seattle, 1982-87, Schroeter, Goldmark & Bender, Seattle, 1987-90; litigation cons. Office Atty Gen. State Wash., Seattle, 1987-90; ptnr. Fury Bailey, Seattle, 1991—. Adj. prof. civil trial advocacy U. Puget Sound Sch. Law, Tacoma, 1981-85, U. Wash. Sch. Law, Seattle, 1993—; judge pro tem Seattle Mcpl. Ct., 1983-89, King County Superior Ct., 1988—; arbitrator, 1985—; faculty Nat. Inst. Trial Advocacy, 1986—, Nat. Coll. Advocacy Am. Trial Lawyers Assn., 1995—. Contbr. articles to profl. jours. Mem. jud. evaluation com. Mcpl. League, Seattle, 1980-82, Mayor's Jud. Merit Selection Com., Seattle, 1981-82; legal counsel Wash. Dems., Seattle, 1985-95; candidate primary and gen. election Seattle city atty., 1989. Named Top Super Lawyer, Washington Law and Politics, 2000—02, Litigator of the Month, Nat. Law Jour., 2002; named one of Top 30 Superlawyers, Wash. Law and Politics, 2001—03. Mem. ABA, Wash. State Bar Assn. (editor jour. 1985, spl. dist. counsel, 1984-92, instr. skills tng. program 1991—, vice-chmn. disciplinary bd. 1993-94, chmn. 1994-95), Seattle-King County Bar Assn., Wash. State Trial Lawyers Assn. (Trial Lawyer of Yr. 1991), Assn. Trial Lawyers Am. (Galaxy of Rising Stars 1991), Am. Inns of Ct. (co-founder, counselor William O. Douglas chpt. 1989-92, mem. William L. Dwyer chpt. 2002-, upper level 2001-2003). Democrat. Avocations: writing, music. Personal injury (including property damage). Home: 6016 77th Ave SE Mercer Island WA 98040-4818 Office: Fury Bailey 710 Tenth Ave E Seattle WA 98102 E-mail: bill@furybailey.com.

BAILLIE, BRIGETTE ANN, lawyer; b. Johannesburg, Oct. 4, 1966; d. David Matthew and Penelope Ann (Gould) Baillie. BA, U. Cape Town, South Africa, 1989; LLM, Kings Coll., London U., 1991, U. Witwatersrand, Johannesburg, South Africa, 1998. Cert.: practicing atty., Roll, Northern Provinces 1994, practicing atty., Roll, Cape Province 1999. Candidate atty. Adams Adams, Pretoria, South Africa, 1992—93, profl. atty., 1994; assoc. Webber Wentzel Bowens, Johannesburg, 1995—96, sr. assoc., 1997—99, ptnr., 1999—. Mem.: Law Soc. Cape Province, Law Soc. Northern Provinces. Achievements include advisor on the project finance Africa Deal of the Year and the project finance EMEA Infrastructure Deal of the Year and the project finance 2003 Africa Real Estate Deal of the Year. Avocations: reading, collecting African art and African antiques. Finance, Utilities, public. Office: Webber Wentzel Bowens 10 Fricker Rd Illovo Blvd Johannesburg RSA 2196 South Africa Office Fax: 011 530 5124. Business E-Mail: brigetteb@wwb.co.za.

BAILLIE, JAMES LEONARD, lawyer; b. Mpls., Aug. 27, 1942; s. Leonard Thompson and Sylvia Alfreda (Fundberg) B.; children: Jennifer, Craig, John. AB in History, 1964; JD, U. Chgo., 1967. Bar: Minn. 1967, U.S. Dist. Ct. Minn. 1968, U.S. Ct. Appeals (8th cir.) 1969, U.S. Ct. Appeals (5th cir.) 1980. Law clk. to presiding justice U.S. Dist. Ct., Mpls., 1967-68; assoc. Fredrikson & Byron, P.A., Mpls., 1968-73, shareholder, 1973—. Mem. ABA (litigation sect. co-editor Bankruptcy Litigation 1998, bus. law sect. editl. bd. Bus. Law Today 1993-98, bus. sect. chair pro bono com. 1999—, standing com. on lawyer pub. svc. responsibility 1991-96, chmn. 1993-96, nat. pro bono award 1984, John Minor Wisdom award 1999), Minn. State Bar Assn. (chmn. bankruptcy sect. 1985-88, sec. 2000-01, treas. 2001-02, pres. 2003-), Hennepin County Bar Assn. (sec. 1992-93, treas. 1993-95, pres. 1996-97). Bankruptcy, General civil litigation, Commercial, contracts (including sales of goods; commercial financing). Office: Fredrikson & Byron PA 400 Pillsbury Ctr Minneapolis MN 55402 E-mail: jbaillie@fredlaw.com.

BAIN, C. RANDALL, lawyer; b. Greeley, Colo., Feb. 1, 1934; s. Walter Lockwood and Harriet Lucille (Stewart) B.; m. Joanne Berg, Aug. 4, 1956 (div.); children: Jennifer Harriet, Charles Alvin; m. Lois Jean Frazier, Feb. 1, 1973 (dec.); 1 child, Frazier; m. Anna Scalise, Dec. 16, 2000. BA, Yale U., 1955, LLB, 1960. Bar: Ariz. 1961, U.S. Dist. Ct. Ariz. 1961, U.S. Ct. Appeals (9th cir.) 1963, U.S. Supreme Ct. 1968, U.S. Ct. Appeals (fed. cir.) 1992. Ptnr. Brown & Bain, Phoenix, 1961—, pres., 1972-87, exec. v.p., 1987—. Bd. dirs. UDC Homes, Inc., Tempe, Ariz., 1974-95; adj. prof. of law Arizona State Univ. Sch. of Law, 2000-01. Trustee Phoenix Country Day Sch., 1983-94; chmn. bd. dirs. Ariz. Audubon, 2003—. Fellow Am. Bar Found., 2002—, mem. ABA, Ariz. Bar Assn. (chmn. fee arbitration com. 1982-86), Am. Law Inst., Yale U. Law Sch. Alumni Assn. (exec. com. 1982-85, 93-97), Audobon Soc. Ariz. (chmn. bd. dirs. 2003—). Federal civil litigation, State civil litigation, Intellectual property. Office: Brown & Bain PA 2901 N Central Ave Ste 2000 Phoenix AZ 85012-2788

BAIN, DONALD KNIGHT, lawyer; b. Denver, Jan. 28, 1935; s. Francis Marion and Jean (Knight) B.; divorced; children: Stephen A., Andrew K., William B. AB, Yale U., 1957; LLB, Harvard U., 1961. Bar: Colo. 1961. From assoc. to ptnr. Holme Roberts & Owen, Denver, 1961-93, chmn. exec. com., 1988-90; ptnr. Holme Roberts & Owen LLP, Denver, 1993—; chmn. Colo. Rep. Com., 1993-97. Bd. dirs. Fairmount Cemetery Co.; mem. grievance com. Colo. Supreme Ct., 1975-80, chmn., 1980. Trustee Denver Pub. Libr. Friends Found., 1978—96, Denver Found., 1989—95, chmn., 1993—95; trustee Berger Found., 1994—96; trustee, chmn. Colo. Coun. on Arts, 1999—; trustee Human Svcs., Inc., 1970—81, chmn., 1979—80; trustee Colo. Humanities Program, 1975—78; mem. Denver Pub. Libr. Commn., 1983—91; active Rep. Nat. Com., Washington, 1993—97; candidate for mayor City of Denver, 1987, 1991; bd. dirs. Rocky Mountain Corp. Pub. Broadcasting, 1975—83, Downtown Denver, Inc., 1977—, Denver Metro C. of C., 1998—, BigHornAction.org, 1999—2003, Auraria Found., 1986—, Legal Aid Found., Colo., 1999—, Auraria Higher Edn. Ctr., 1978—89, chmn., 1986—89. Fellow Royal Geog. Soc., Am. Coll. Trial Lawyers, Explorers Club; mem. ABA, Colo. Bar Assn., Denver Bar Assn., Colo. Yale Assn. (pres. 1974-76), Assn. Yale Alumni (bd. govs. 1982-85), Selden Soc., Am. Antiquarian Soc., Internat. Wine and Food Soc., Confrerie des Chevaliers du Tastevin, Cactus Club, Denver Country Club, Mile High Club, Denver Law Club, Grolier Club, Yale Club, Colo. Mountain Club, Capitol Hill CLub, Univ. Club (Denver). Republican. Avocations: antiquarian book collecting. Banking, Federal civil litigation, General civil litigation. Home: 1201 Williams # 13C Denver CO 80218 Office: Holme Roberts & Owen LLP 1700 Lincoln St Ste 4100 Denver CO 80203-4541 E-mail: baind@hro.com.

BAIN, DOUGLAS, lawyer, air transportation executive; b. Charlottesville, Va., Mar. 12, 1949; BA, U. Va., 1971, JD, 1974. Bar: Calif. 1974, Wash. 1982. V.p. legal, contracts, ethics and govt. rels. comml. airplanes group Boeing Co., Chgo., 1996—99, v.p., gen. counsel, 1999—2000, sr. v.p., gen. counsel, 2000—. Office: Boeing Co MC 5003-1001 100 N Riverside Chicago IL 60606-1596 Office Fax: 312-544-2828.*

BAIN, JAMES WILLIAM, lawyer; b. Suffern, N.Y., Dec. 19, 1949; s. William James and Agnes (Hoey) B.; m. Colleen K., Mar. 23, 1974; children: Rebecca, Meghan. BA, U. Conn., 1972; JD, U. Fla., 1976. Bar: Fla. 1977, U.S. Dist. Ct. (ea. dist.) Tenn. 1980, Tenn. 1984, U.S. Ct. Appeals (11th cir.) 1984, U.S. Ct. Appeals (D.C. cir.) 1984, Colo. 1986,

U.S. Dist. Ct. Colo 1986, U.S. Ct. Appeals (10th cir.) 1988, U.S. Supreme Ct. 1998. Atty. trial Tenn. Valley Authority, Knoxville, 1977-85; atty. dir. Roath & Brega, P.C., Denver, 1985-89, Brega & Winters, P.C., Denver, 1989—. Instr. U. Fla., Gainesville, 1976, U. Colo., Boulder, 1987-90; seminar chmn. Inst. for Advanced Legal Study, Denver, 1987. Contbr. articles to profl. jours.; editor constrn. law column Colo. Lawyer. Recipient Civil Litigation Writing award for 1986-87, Denver Colo. Bar Assn., 1987. Mem. ATLA, Colo. Bar Assn., Fla. Bar Assn., Am. Judicature Soc., Am. Arbitration Assn. (arbitrator 1986), Internat. Platform Assn. Avocations: soccer, skiing, biking, basketball. Federal civil litigation, State civil litigation, Construction. Office: Brega & Winters PC 1700 Lincoln St Ste 2222 Denver CO 80203-4522

BAIN, WILLIAM DONALD, JR., lawyer, chemical company executive; b. Rochelle, Ill., July 1, 1925; s. William Donald and Gretchen (Kittler) B.; m. Pauline Thomas, Jan. 14, 1950 (dec. Nov. 1991); children: Elizabeth Kittler Zibart, Anne Alexander, Nancy Hemenway Cotè; m. Barrie Feighner, Mar. 30, 1996. BS in Econs, U. Pa., 1947; JD, Washington and Lee U., 1949. Bar: S.C. 1952. Mortgage loan field rep. Travelers Ins. Co., Hartford, Conn., Cleve.; Orlando, Fla., 1949-51; with Moreland-McKesson Chem. Co., Spartanburg, S.C., 1951-83, pres., 1965-83, also dir.; v.p., gen. mgr. McKesson Chem. Corp., San Francisco, 1982-84. Bd. dirs. Cote Color & Chem. Co., Inc., Spartan Comms. Corp., Tietex Corp.; co-founder, bd. dirs. Affiliated Chem. Group, Bermuda; ptnr. Triple B Ptnrs. Mem. Spartanburg Sch. Bd., 1958—72, chmn., 1963—72; trustee Converse Coll., 1968—92, chmn. bd., 1985—92; chmn. alumni bd. Washington and Lee U., 1979—82; trustee Hollins (Va.) Coll., 1992—98; bd. dirs. Mary Black Meml. Hosp., 1975—96, chmn., 1980—82; trustee Mary Black Found., 1996—2002; trustee, former chmn. Spartanburg County Found.; bd. dirs. Spartanburg Animal Shelter, 2002—; mng. dir. Bain Found. With USAAC, 1943—45. Mem. S.C. Bar Assn., Rotary. Republican. Presbyterian.

BAINS, DAVID PAUL, lawyer; b. Shreveport, La., Oct. 9, 1950; s. John Calvin and Alice (Mixon) B.; m. A. Sue Book, Aug. 27, 1971; children: J. Ashley, D. Andrew, E. Abigail. BA, La. Coll., 1972; JD, Mercer U., 1975; LLM, Tulane U., 1982. Bar: La. 1975, Ga. 1975, U.S. Dist. Ct. (ea. dist.) La. 1975, U.S. Dist. Ct. (so. dist.) Ala. 1976, U.S. Ct. Appeals (5th cir.) 1976, U.S. Ct. Appeals (11th cir.) 1982, Fla. 1984, S.C. 1984, Miss. 1985, U.S. Dist. Ct. (we. dist.) La. 1985, U.S. Dist. Ct. (so. dist.) Miss. 1985, Ala. 1986, Ill. 1987, Tex. 1988. Assoc. Law Offices of David Vosbein, New Orleans, 1975-80; ptnr. Hilleren & Bains, New Orleans, 1980-95, Bains & Assocs., New Orleans, 1995—; asst. atty. gen. L.A. Dept. of Justice, 2001—. Mem. future studies com. Chamber New Orleans & River Region, 1983-85, The Chamber, New Orleans, 1988; bd. dirs. Church Site Corp. of La. Bapt. Conv., 1992-97, Greater New Orleans ACTS; mem. Acts com. Bapt. Assn. Greater New Orleans, 1991-2000, mem. adminstrv. com., 1989—; bd. trustees First Bapt. Ch., Kenner, 1993—, New Orleans Baptist Theo. Sem. Found. Bd., 2002- (v.p. 2003-); bd. trustees La. Baptist Found., 2003-. Mem. New Orleans Bar Assn. Admiralty, Federal civil litigation, Personal injury (including property damage). Office: Bains & Assocs 2955 Ridgelake Dr Ste 112 Metairie LA 70002-4998 Home: 2458 Lake Oaks Pkwy New Orleans LA 70122-4341

BAINTON, DENISE MARLENE, lawyer; b. Trenton, N.J., June 12, 1949; d. Milford C. and Anne M. (Docherty) Smith; m. Raymond Port McKinster, Dec. 26, 1987. MusB, U. Ariz., 1971, MusM, 1974, JD highest distinction, 1983. Bar: Ariz. 1983, U.S. Dist. Ct. Ariz. 1984, U.S. Ct. Appeals (9th cir.) 1985, U.S. Supreme Ct. 1988. Music tchr. Flowing Wells Pub. Schs., Tucson, 1971-80; piano instr. Pima Community Coll., Tucson, 1974-77; law clk. to judge U.S. Dist. Ct. Ariz., Phoenix, 1983-84; ptnr. DeConcini McDonald Yetwin & Lacy, Tucson, 1984—. Editor Ariz. Law Rev., 1982-83. Mem. Ariz. Bar Assn., Ariz. Bd. Psychol. Examiners, Pima County Bar Assn., Nat. Coun. Sch. Attys., Nat Assn. Coll. and U. Attys., Order of Coif. Civil rights, Education and schools, Labor (including EEOC, Fair Labor Standards Act, labor-management relations, NLRB, OSHA). Office: DeConcini McDonald Yetwin & Lacy 2525 E Broadway Blvd Ste 200 Tucson AZ 85716-5300

BAINTON, J(OHN) JOSEPH, lawyer; b. Long Branch, N.J., May 21, 1947; s. Robert L. and Elizabeth (Dowling) B.; 1 child, John Joseph Jr. BA, Kenyon Coll., 1969; JD, Rutgers U., Newark, 1973. Bar: N.Y. 1973. Assoc. Burke & Burke, N.Y.C., 1972-76; ptnr. Reboul, MacMurray, Hewitt, Maynard & Kristol, N.Y.C., 1976-89, Shea & Gould, N.Y.C., 1989-90, Whitman & Ransom, N.Y.C., 1991-92, Ross & Hardies, N.Y.C., 1993-98, Bainton McCarthy LLC, N.Y.C., 1998—. Contbr. articles to legal jours. Mediator Mandatory Mediation Program So. Dist. N.Y. Mem.: Nat. Inst. Trial Advocacy (faculty), Products Liability Adv. Coun., Internat. Anti-counterfeiting Coalition (bd. dirs. 1986—92), Internat. Trademark Assn. (editor The Trademark Reporter 1976). Avocation: yacht racing. General civil litigation, Product liability, Trademark and copyright. Office: Bainton McCarthy LLC 26 Broadway New York NY 10004 also: Bainton McCarthy LLC 3 Stamford Landing 46 Southfield Ave Stamford CT 06902 also: Bainton McCarthy LLC 320 Carleton Ave Central Islip NY 11722-4502

BAIR, BRUCE B. lawyer; b. St. Paul, May 26, 1928; s. Bruce B. and Emma N. (Stone) B.; m. Jane Lawler, July 19, 1952; children: Mary Jane, Thomas, Susan, Barbara, Patricia, James, Joan, Bruce, Jeffrey. BS, U. N.D., 1950, JD, 1952. Bar: N.D. 1952, U.S. Dist. Ct. N.D. 1955, U.S. Ct. Appeals (8th cir.) 1971, U.S. Supreme Ct. 1974. Assoc. Lord and Ulmer, Mandan, ND, 1955-57; ptnr. Bair, Bair, and Garrity, Mandan, 1957—2001, of counsel, 2002—. Spl. asst. atty. gen. N.D. Milk Mktg. Bd., 1967—; chmn. bd. Bank of Tioga, 1984-2003, also bd. dirs.; Rep. precinct committeeman, 1956-70, chmn. Morton County Rep. Com., 1958-62, mem. N.D. Rep. State Cen. Com., 1962-67; pres. sch. bd. St. Joseph's Cath. Ch., 1967-68; bd. dirs. Mandan Pub. Sch. Dist. #1, 1971-77; exec. com. Internat. Assn. Milk Control Agys., 1970-2000; bd. regents U. Mary, Bismarck, N.D., 1984—. 1st lt. JAG Corps USAF, 1952-55. Fellow: Am. Coll. Trust and Estate Counsel; mem.: ABA, N.D. Bar Assn., Am. Coll. Barristers (sr. counsel), Am. Legion, Elks, Rotary. Roman Catholic. General civil litigation, Estate planning, Probate (including wills, trusts). Home: 901 3rd St NW Mandan ND 58554-2537 Office: 210 1st St NW Mandan ND 58554-3115

BAIR, JOEL EVAN, lawyer; b. Mishawaka, Ind., Nov. 14, 1949; s. James E. B.; m. Susan Trimmer, June 19, 1971; children: Noelle, Jonathan, Katie. BS Ae. E., Ind. Inst. Tech., 1971; JD, U. Notre Dame, 1974, MS, 1975. Patent atty. U.S. Patent and Trademark Office. Pvt. practice, Corpus Christi, Tex., 1978-87; assoc. Varnum, Riddering, Schmidt & Howlett, LLP, Grand Rapids, 1987-93, ptnr., 1993-97, Rader, Fishman, Grauer & McGarry, Grand Rapids, 1997—2001, McGarry Bair PC, Grand Rapids, 2001—. Mem., chmn. intellectual property law sect. State Bar Mich., Lansing, 1991—. Lt. JAG USN, 1975-78; lt. USNR, 1975-78. Mem. ABA (mem. intellectual property law sect. 1989—), Internat. Trademark Assn., Am. Intellectual Property Assn., State Bar Tex., State Bar Mich. (mem. intellectual property sect., chmn. 1996-97), Grand Rapids Bar Assn. Avocations: sailing, model shipbuilding. Intellectual property. Office: McGarry Bair PC 171 Monroe Ave NW Ste 600 Grand Rapids MI 49503-2634 Fax: (616) 742-1010. E-mail: jeb@mcgarrybair.com.

BAIR, ROBERT RIPPEL, lawyer; b. New London, Conn., Nov. 24, 1925; s. Bruce Thomas and Alga (Smith) B.; m. Dorothy Burke Dorsey, June 1, 1957; c Student, Johns Hopkins U., 1943; AB summa cum laude, Brown U., 1947; JD, Harvard U., 1950. Law clk. to cir. judge U.S Ct. Appeals (4th cir.), 1950-51; atty. Bur. Legis. Reference, Md. Gen. Assembly, Annapolis, 1951-52; assoc. Venable, Baetjer and Howard, Balt., 1951-59, ptnr., 1960-89, sr. of counsel, 1990—2001. Asst. U.S. atty. U.S. Atty.'s Office, Balt., 1954—56; lectr. estate and tax planning Renaissance Inst., Coll. Notre Dame, 1991—2001. Contbr. articles to profl. jours. Chmn. Balt. City Zoning Com., 1958-61; gen. counsel Mayor's Balt. City Housing Code Com., 1962-64. Lt. SC USNR, 1946-66. Fellow Am. Coll. Trust and Estate Counsel, Md. Bar Found.; mem. ABA, Am. Judicature Soc., Md. State Bar Assn. (sec. 1965-71), Balt. City Bar Assn., Wednesday Law Club. Avocations: piano, oil and water color painting, tennis, golf, skiing. Office: Venable Baetjer & Howard 1800 Merc Bank & Trust Bldg 2 Hopkins Plz Ste 1800 Baltimore MD 21201-2982 E-mail: rrbair@venable.com.

BAIRD, BRUCE ALLEN, lawyer; b. Cin., Mar. 26, 1948; s. William Wendell and Audrey (Geignetter) B.; m. Erica Borden, July 27, 1975 (div. 1993); 1 child, Jessica; m. Nicolette Adair Heidepriem, Sept. 17, 1993; 1 child, William. BA, Cornell U., 1970; JD, NYU, 1975. Spl. asst. to dep. atty. gen. U.S. Dept. Justice, Washington, 1975-76; law clk. to presiding judge U.S. Ct. Appeals (2d cir.), Brattleboro, Vt. and N.Y.C., 1976-77; assoc. Davis, Polk & Wardwell, N.Y.C., 1977-80; asst. U.S. atty. U.S. Attys. Office (so. dist.) N.Y., N.Y.C., 1980-86, dep. chief criminal div., 1986-87, chief narcotics unit, 1987, chief securities and commodities frauds unit, 1987-89; of counsel Covington & Burling, Washington, 1989-91, ptnr., 1991—. Editor in chief NYU Law Rev., 1974-75. Mem. ABA (co-chair securities and commodities fraud subcom. of white collar crime com. of criminal justice sect. 1994—), N.Y. State Bar Assn. (profl. jud. ethics com. 1982-89), Assn. of Bar of City of N.Y. (profl. jud. ethics com. 1979-82, 86-89), Fed. Bar Council, D.C. Bar Assn. Republican. Presbyterian. Federal civil litigation, Criminal, Securities. Home: 5404 Edgemoor Ln Bethesda MD 20814-1326 E-mail: bbaird@cov.com.

BAIRD, CHARLES BRUCE, lawyer, consultant; b. DeLand, Fla., Apr. 18, 1935; s. James Turner and Ethelyn Isabelle (Williams) B.; m. Barbara Ann Fabian, June 6, 1959 (div. Dec. 1979); children: C. Bruce Jr., Robert Arthur, Bryan James; m. Byung-Ran Cho, May 23, 1982; children: Merah-Iris, Haerah Violet. BSME, U. Miami, 1958; postgrad., UCLA, 1962-64; MBA, Calif. State U., 1966; JD, Am. U., 1971. Bar: Va. 1971, U.S. Dist. Ct. (ea. dist.) Va. 1971, D.C. 1973, U.S. Dist. Ct. D.C. 1973, U.S. Ct. Appeals (4th cir.) 1974, U.S. Supreme Ct. 1975. Rsch. engr. Naval Ordnance Lab., Corona, Calif., 1961-67; aerospace engr. Naval Air Systems Command, Washington, 1967-69; cons. engr. Bird Engring. Rsch. Assts., Vienna, Va., 1969-71; prof. Def. Systems Mgmt. Coll., Ft. Belvoir, Va., 1982; spl. asst. for policy compliance USIA Voice of Am., Washington, 1983-84. Cons. Booz, Allen & Hamilton, Inc., Bethesda, 1975-82, IBM, Bethesda, Md., 1984, Logistics Mgmt. Inst., McLean, Va., 1986-98, 2002—, TelcoExchange.com, 1998-2000, 2001; adj. prof. Fla. Inst. Tech., 1988. Contbr. articles to profl. jours.; inventor computer-based comm. systems for the gravely handicapped. Bd. govs. Sch. Engring. U. Miami, 1957; trustee Galilee United Meth. Ch., Arlington, Va., 1983-87. Mem. Va. Trial Lawyers Assn., Internet. Soc., Fed. Comm. Bar Assn., United We Stand Am. (founding mem.), Sigma Alpha Epsilon. Home and Office: 5396 Gainsborough Dr Fairfax VA 22032-2744

BAIRD, DOUGLAS GORDON, law educator, dean; b. Phila., July 10, 1953; s. Henry Welles and Eleanora (Gordon) B. BA, Yale U., 1975; JD, Stanford U., 1979; LLD, U. Rochester, 1994. Law clk. U.S. Ct. Appeals (9th cir.), 1979, 80; asst. prof. law U. Chgo., 1980-83, prof. law, 1984—, assoc. dean, 1984-87, Bigelow prof. law, 1988—, dean, 1994-99. Author: (with others) Security Interests in Personal Property, 1984, 2d edit., 1987, Bankruptcy, 1985, 3d edit., 2000, Elements of Bankruptcy, 1992, 3d edit., 2001; (D. Baird, R. Gertner, R. Picker) Game Theory and the Law, 1994. Mem. AAAS, Order of Coif. Office: U Chgo Sch Law 1111 E 60th St Chicago IL 60637-2776 E-mail: Douglas_Baird@law.uchicago.edu.

BAIRD, EDWARD ROUZIE, JR., lawyer; b. Norfolk, Va., Aug. 29, 1936; s. Edward Rouzie and Eleanor Gray (Perry) B.; m. Nell McGlaughon, Oct. 8, 1967 (dec. Oct. 1973); 1 child, Eleanor Gray; m. Abby St. John Starke, Feb. 5, 1977; children: Abby St. John, Edward Rouzie V. BA, U. Va., 1960, LLB, 1967. Assoc. Baird, Creshaw & Ware, Norfolk, 1967—68; asst. dist. counsel U.S. Army C.E., Norfolk, 1968—73; asst. U.S. Atty. U.S. Atty.'s Office, Norfolk, 1973—77; sole practice Norfolk, 1977—82, 1999—; ptnr. Willcox & Baird, Norfolk, 1982—99. Served to lt. (j.g.) USN, 1960-63. Mem. Va. Bar Assn., Norfolk-Portsmouth Bar Assn., Soc. Cincinnati, Va. Club (Norfolk). Federal civil litigation, Corporate, general, Environmental. Home: 1711 Cloncurry Rd Norfolk VA 23505-1717 Office: 210 Monticello Ave Norfolk VA 23510-2301

BAIRD, KATHLEEN MARY, lawyer; b. Milw., Dec. 15, 1949; d. Paul Jerold Block and Eileen Louise Dreger; m. Brian D. Baird, Dec. 19, 1971 (div. Aug. 15, 1995); children: Brian, Stephen, Kristine. BA in Polit. Sci., U. Wis., 1972, JD. Bar: Wis. 1976, U.S. Dist. Ct. (ea. and we. dists.) Wis. 1976. Hearing examiner Dept. Industry, Labor and Human Rels., Milw., 1976—77; asst. corp. counsel Milwaukee County, Milw., 1977—83, prin. asst. corp. counsel, 1977—83, asst. family ct. commr., 1983—84; pvt. practice Milw., 1992—. Mem. Wauwatosa Sch. Bd., chair sch. referendum com.; trustee Wauwatosa (Wis.) Pub. Libr., chair bd. trustees. Mem.: Milw. Bar Assn. (chair law practice mgmt. com.), Assn. Conflict Resolution, Internat. Acad. Collaborative Profls., Collaborative Family Law Coun. Wis. (bd. dirs.), Wis. Assn. Mediators, Soc. Family Lawyers, Assn. Women Lawyers. Family and matrimonial. Office: 2300 N Mayfair Rd Ste 9070 Wauwatosa WI 53226 Office Fax: 414-774-0938. Business E-Mail: kathbair@execpc.com.

BAIRD, THOMAS BRYAN, JR., retired lawyer; b. Newport News, Va., June 21, 1931; s. Thomas Bryan and Mary Florence (Rieker) B.; m. Mildred Katherine Clark, June 23, 1956; children: Sarah, Thomas Bryan III, William, Laura. BA, U. Va., 1952; LLB, U. Tenn., 1960. Bar: Tenn. 1964, Va. 1969, U.S. Dist. Ct. (we. dist.) 1970. With Stat Farm Ins., Knoxville, Tenn., 1960-68; asst. commonwealth atty. Wytheville, Va., 1969-71; commonwealth atty. Wythe County, 1972-98; prin. Thomas B. Baird, Jr. Trustee Simmerman Home for the Aged, 1972-83. Served with U.S. Army, 1953-55. Democrat. Presbyterian. Criminal, Insurance, Property, real (including real estate development, water). Home: 875 N 18th St Wytheville VA 24382-1022

BAIRD, ZOË, foundation president, lawyer; b. Bklyn., June 20, 1952; d. Ralph Louis and Naomi (Allen) B.; m. Paul Gewirtz, June 8, 1986; 2 children. AB, U. Calif., Berkeley, 1974, JD, 1977. Bar: Washington, 1979, Calif. 1977, Conn. 1989. Law clk. Hon. Albert Wollenberg, San Francisco, 1977-78; atty., advisor Office Legal Counsel U.S. Dept. Justice, Washington, 1979-80; assoc. counsel to Pres., The White House, Washington, 1980-81; assoc., then ptnr. O'Melveny & Myers, Washington, 1981-86; counsellor, staff exec. GE, Fairfield, Conn., 1986-90; v.p., gen. counsel Aetna Life & Casualty, Hartford, 1990-93, sr. v.p., gen. counsel, 1993-96; pres. Markle Found., N.Y.C., 1998—. Bd. dirs. Chubb Corp. Bd. dirs. James A. Baker III Inst. for Pub. Policy, Lawyers for Children Am., Brookings Inst., Mexican-Am. Legal Def. and Edn. Fund, Save the Children. Mem. Am. Law Inst., Coun. on Fgn. Rels. Office: Markle Found 10 Rockefeller Plaza 16th Fl New York NY 10020-1903 E-mail: info@markle.org.*

BAIRSTOW, FRANCES KANEVSKY, arbitrator, mediator, educator; b. Racine, Wis., Feb. 19, 1920; d. William and Minnie (DuBow) Kanevsky; m. Irving P. Kaufman, Nov. 14, 1942 (div. 1949); m. David Steele Bairstow, Dec. 17, 1954; children: Dale Owen, David Anthony. Student, U. Wis., 1937-42; BS, U. Louisville, 1949; student, Oxford U., England, 1953-54; postgrad., McGill U., Montreal, Que., Can., 1958-59. Rsch. economist U.S. Senate Labor-Mgmt. Subcom., Washington, 1950-51; labor edn. specialist U. P.R., San Juan, 1951-52; chief wage data unit WSB, Washington, 1952-53; labor rsch. economist Can. Pacific Ry. Co., Montreal, Canada, 1956-58; asst. dir. indsl. rels. ctr. McGill U., 1960-66, assoc. dir., 1966-71, dir., 1971-85, lectr., indsl. rels. dept. econs., 1960-72, from asst. prof. to assoc. prof. faculty mgmt., 1972—83, prof., 1983-85; lectr. Stetson Law Sch., Fla.; spl. master Fla. Pub. Employees Rels. Commn., 1985-97. Cons. Nat. Film Bd. Can., 1965—69; arbitrator Que. Consultative Coun. Panel Arbitrators, 1968—83, Ministry Labour and Manpower, 1971—83, United Air Lines and Assn. Flight Attendants, 1990—95, Am. Airlines and Transport Workers Union, 1997—98, State U. Sys. Fla., 1990—2003, FDA, 1996—98, Social Security Adminstrn., 1996—2003, Am. Airlines, 1997—, Tampa Gen. Hosp., 1996—, Cargo Internat. Airlines, 2001, Govt. of Fla. and Fla. State Police, 2002—, Bell South and Comms. Workers, 2003—, USAF at Warner Robins and AFGE, 2003—; mediator Can. Pub. Svc. Staff Rels. Bd., 1973—85, So. Bell Tel., 1985—, AT&T and Comm. Workers Am., 1986—; cons. on collective bargaining arbitration OECD, Paris, 1979. Contbg. columnist: Montreal Star, 1971—85. Chmn. Nat. Inquiry Commn. Wider-Based Collective Bargaining, 1978; dep. commr. essential svcs. Province of Que., 1976—81. Fulbright fellow, 1953—54. Mem.: Ctrl. Fla. Indsl. Rels. Rsch. Assn. (pres. 1999), Nat. Acad. Arbitrators (bd. govs. 1977—80, program chmn. 1982—83, v.p. 1986—88, nat. coord. 1987—90), Indsl. Rels. Rsch. Assn. Am. (mem. exec. bd. 1965—68, chmn. nominating com. 1977), Can. Indsl. Rels. Rsch. Inst. (mem. exec. bd. 1965—68). Home and Office: 1430 Gulf Blvd Apt 507 Clearwater FL 33767-2856

BAIRSTOW, RICHARD RAYMOND, retired lawyer; b. Waukegan, Ill., Sept. 26, 1917; s. Fred Raymond and Mildred (Wright) B.; m. Mary Kelley, Aug. 8, 1942 (dec. June 19, 1979); children: Kathleen Bairstow Young, Suzanne Bairstow Hicks, Mary Bairstow Neely; m. Agnes Macaitis Caldwell, July 22, 1980 (dec. July 22, 1995). AB, U. Ill., 1939, JD, 1947; postgrad., George Washington U., 1939-41. Bar: Ill. 1947, U.S. Dist. Ct. (no. dist.) Ill. 1964, U.S. Ct. Mil. Appeals 1963, U.S. SUpreme Ct. 1963. Assoc. Hall, Meyer & Carey, Waukegan, 1947-49; asst. state's atty. Lake County, Waukegan, 1949-53; ptnr. McClory & Bairstow, Waukegan, 1953-60, McClory, Bairstow, Lonchar & Nordigan, Waukegan, 1960-66; prin. Richard R. Bairstow & Assocs., Waukegan, 1966-98; ret., 1998. Dist. atty. Fox Lake Fire Protection Dist., Ingleside, Ill., 1948-98; adminstrv. law judge Ill. Dept. Revenue, Chgo., 1953-87. Bd. dirs. ARC, Lake County, 1947-73; mem., pres. Salvation Army, Waukegan, 1954-66; bd. dirs. Lake County Family YMCA, 1990-91. Col. USAF, 1941-46, ETO, USAR, 1946-71, ret. U.S. Army Command and Gen. Staff Coll., 1965. Mem. ABA, Ill. Lake County Bar Assn., Assn. U.S. Army, Mil. Officers Assn. Am., Am. Legion, Glen Flora Country Club, Waukegan City Club, Elks, Delta Tau Delta, Phi Alpha Delta. Republican. Episcopalian. General practice, Probate (including wills, trusts), Property, real (including real estate development, water). Home: 2122 Ash St Waukegan IL 60087-5033

BAITY, JOHN COOLEY, lawyer; b. South Bend, Ind., June 22, 1933; s. Roscoe Flake and Gladys Paula (Kline) B.; m. Patricia Ann Bowen, Nov. 9, 1985; children: Keith F., John C. Jr., Cheryl R., Michael P., Philip J., Mark A. AB, U. Mich., 1955, JD, 1958. Bar: Ill. 1958, N.Y. 1961, Calif. 1977, D.C. 1979. Assoc. Cravath, Swaine & Moore, N.Y.C., 1960-62, Donovan Leisure Newton & Irvine, N.Y.C., 1962-65, ptnr., 1966-83, Hunton & Williams, N.Y.C., 1983-84, Baity & Joseph, Los Angeles, 1984-86, Milbank, Tweed, Hadley & McCloy LLP, N.Y.C., 1986—. Gen. counsel U.S. Golf Assn., Far Hills, NJ, 1980—85. Chmn. fin. com., mem. coun. and exec. com. Union Internationale Contre le Cancer, 1995—; trustee Nat. Hypertension Assn., N.Y.C., 1981—91; bd. dirs. Am. Cancer Soc., Atlanta, 1983—87, 1990—2002, treas., 1994—98, vice chmn., 1998—99, chmn.-elect, 1999—2000, chmn., 2000—01. Mem. N.Y. State Bar. Assn., Calif. Bar Assn., Order of Coif, Phi Beta Kappa, Phi Kappa Phi. Corporate taxation. Office: Milbank Tweed Hadley & McCloy LLP 1 Chase Manhattan Plz Fl 46 New York NY 10005-1413 E-mail: jbaity@milbank.com.

BAKALY, CHARLES GEORGE, JR., lawyer, mediator; b. Long Beach, Calif., Nov. 15, 1927; s. Charles G. Sr. and Doris (Carpenter) B.; m. Patricia Murphey, Oct. 25, 1952; children: Charles G. III, John W., Thomas B. AB, Stanford U., 1949; JD, U. S.C., 1952. Assoc. O'Melveny & Myers, L.A., 1956-63, ptnr., 1963-94; mem. JAMS, L.A., 2000—. Mem. Commn. on Calif. State Govt. Orgn. and Economy, 1991-94, President's Nat. Commn. on Employment Policy, 1992-94; mem. 9th Cir. Jud. Conf. Lawyer Del. Ch., 1984-87, mem. indigent def. panel, 1992-94; chmn. Calif. Dispute Resolution Adv. Coun., 1987-88; pres. Dispute Resolution Svcs. Bd. Dirs., Calif. Dispute Resolution Coun. Author: (with Joel M. Grossman) Modern Law of Employment Relationships, 1983, 2d edit. 1989; contbr. chpts. to books. Capt. JAG, U.S. Army, 1952-56. Fellow Am. Coll. Trial Lawyers, Coll. Labor and Employment Lawyers, Internat. Acad. Mediators; mem. ABA (chmn. sect. labor and employment law 1981-82, sect. dispute resolution), L.A. County Bar Assn. (trustee, chmn. labor law sect. 1976-77, dispute resolution sect.), Lincoln Club (pres. 1989-91), Chancery Club, Valley Hunt Club (Pasadena, Calif.), Calif. Club (L.A.), Bohemian Club (San Francisco). Federal civil litigation, State civil litigation, Labor (including EEOC, Fair Labor Standards Act, labor-management relations, NLRB, OSHA). Office: JAMS 350 S Figueroa St Ste 990 Los Angeles CA 90071-1102

BAKER, ALTHEA ROSS, court hearing officer, lawyer, mediator, arbitrator, educator; b. San Francisco, Dec. 24, 1949; d. Vernon and Ethel Ross; m. Bruce Mitchell. BA in Psychology, Pepperdine U., 1970, MA in Clin. Psychology, 1974; JD, Loyola U., L.A., 1984. Bar: Calif. 1984, U.S. Dist. Ct. (cen. dist.) Calif. 1985, U.S. Ct. Appeals (9th cir.) 1985; lic. marriage, family and child counselor, Calif. Prof., chmn. dept. L.A. Mission Coll., 1975-89; pvt. practice law L.A., 1985—93. Marriage therapist Woodland Hills, Calif., 1976-84; mediator Dispute Resolution Svcs., Santa Monica, 1987-91; referee L.A. Superior Ct., 1993; staff atty. Harriet Buhai Family Law Ctr., L.A., 1988. Trustee L.A. C.Cs., 1989-2001. Mem. Los Angeles County Bar Assn., Women Lawyers L.A., Black Women Lawyers L.A., San Fernando Valley Marriage and Family Therapists (v.p. 1978), Calif. Fedn. Tchrs. Coll. Guild (exec. bd. local 1521, 1982-89, chief negotiator collective bargaining 1988-89). Democrat. Episcopalian. Office: 1903 Parkdale Pl La Canada CA 91011 Fax: 213 255-6154.

BAKER, BERNARD ROBERT , II, lawyer; b. Toledo, Nov. 19, 1915; s. Joseph Lee and Grace (Baker) O'Neil; m. Elinor Shutts, Oct. 16, 1943; children: Bernard Robert III, Lynn Agnes. AB, Kenyon Coll., 1936; JD, Harvard U., 1941. Bar: Ohio 1946. Practice in, Toledo, 1947—95; ptnr. Brown, Baker, Schlageter & Craig and predecessor firm, 1950-91, ret. Pres. B.R. Baker Co., 1946-60; dir. emeritus First Nat. Bank Toledo, First Ohio Bankshares (now Fifth Third Bank); ret. sec., dir. Toledo Blade Co., Blade Comm., Inc. Regional vice chmn. U.S. Com. for UN, 1955-62; past pres. St. Vincent Hosp. Found., Toledo United Appeal, Toledo C. of C.; past trustee Med. Coll. Ohio at Toledo, Salvation Army, Toledo, Goodwill Industries, Toledo; trustee emeritus Rutherford B. Hayes Presdl. Ctr., Fremont, Ohio; past trustee Boys Clubs Toledo; past pres., trustee Med. Coll. Ohio Found., Toledo. Lt. comdr. USNR, 1940-45. Recipient Boys Club Bronze Keystone award, 1965, Disting. Citizen award Med. Coll. Ohio, 1986; named Toledo Outstanding Man of Year, 1948. Mem. ABA, English Speaking Union, Young Pres. Orgn., Harvard Club (N.Y.C.), Belmont Country Club, Carranor Hunt and Polo Club (Toledo), Bath and Tennis Club, Beach Club, Chevaliers du Tastevin, Old Guard Soc. (Palm Beach). Roman Catholic. Home: Apt 905 311 S Flagler Dr West Palm Beach FL 33401-5645

BAKER, BRUCE JAY, lawyer; b. Chgo., June 18, 1954; s. Kenneth and Beverly (Gould) B. Student, U. Leeds, Eng., 1974-75; BS, U. Ill., 1976; JD, Washington U., 1979. Bar: Ill. 1979, U.S. Dist. Ct. (no. dist.) Ill. 1984. Asst. atty. gen. antitrust divsn. State of Ill., Chgo., 1979-83; assoc. Mass, Miller & Josephson Ltd., Chgo., 1983-86; sr. counsel Discover Card Services Inc., Riverwoods, Ill., 1986-89; sr. legis. counsel Dean Witter Fin. Svcs. Group, Riverwoods, 1989-91; gen. counsel Ill. Commr. Banks and Trust Cos., Chgo., 1991-94; ptnr. Schiff Hardin & Waite, Chgo., 1994-99, of counsel, 1999-2001, Barak, Ferrazzano, Kirschbaum, Perlman & Nagelberg, Chgo.,

2001—; sr. v.p., gen. counsel Ill. Bankers Assn., 1999—. Gen. editor Advising Illinois Financial Institutions, 2002; contbr. articles to profl. jours. Registered lobbyist Ill. Legislature, Springfield, 1985-91, 94—. Named Ill. State scholar, 1972. Mem. ABA (antitrust com., banking com., chmn. state banking law devels. task force 1998—), Ill. State Bar Assn. (comml. banking and bankruptcy sect.), Chgo. Bar Assn. (fin. insts. com.), Ill. Bankers Assn. (legis. counsel 1985-86, gen. counsel 1994—, Disting. Bank Counsel award 1991, 97). Office: Ill Bankers Assn 111 W Jackson Blvd Ste 910 Chicago IL 60604-3502 also: Barack Ferrazzano Et Al 333 W Wacker Dr Ste 2700 Chicago IL 60606 E-mail: bbaker@ilbanker.com.

BAKER, CAMERON, lawyer; b. Chgo., Dec. 24, 1937; s. David Cameron and Marion (Fitzpatrick) B.; m. Katharine Julia Solari, Sept. 2, 1961; children: Cameron III, Ann, John. Student, U. Notre Dame, 1954-57; AB, Stanford U., 1958; LLB, U. Calif., Berkeley, 1961. Bar: Calif. 1962, U.S. Dist. Ct. (so. dist.) Calif. 1962, U.S. Dist. Ct. (no. dist.) Calif. 1963, U.S. Ct. Appeals (9th) 1963. With Adams, Duque & Hazeltine, Los Angeles, 1961-62, Pettit & Martin, San Francisco, 1962-95, mng. ptnr., 1972-81, 84-87, exec. com., 1971-82, 84-88; with Farella, Braun & Martel, San Francisco, 1995—. Mayor City of Belvedere, Calif., 1978-79; owner Larkmead Vineyards, Napa Valley, Calif. Dir. Lassen Nat. Park Found., 1992—. Mem. ABA (sects. on bus. law and internat. law and practice), Calif. Bar Assn. (sect. bus., real property and internat. law), Bar Assn. San Francisco (bd. dirs. 1966, 72-73), Boalt Hall Alumni Assn. (dir. 1982-84), Bohemian Club, Tiburon Peninsula Club. Corporate, general, Private international, Mergers and acquisitions. Home: 38 Alcatraz Ave Belvedere CA 94920-2504 Office: Farella Braun & Martel LLP 235 Montgomery St San Francisco CA 94104-2902 E-mail: cbaker@fbm.com.

BAKER, DAVID REMEMBER, lawyer; b. Durham, N.C., Jan. 17, 1932; s. Roger Denio and Eleanor Elizabeth (Ussher) B.; m. Myra Augusta Mullins, Nov. 2, 1955 PhB, U. Chgo., 1949; BA, Birmingham-So. Coll., 1951; JD, Harvard U., 1954. Bar: Ala. 1954, NY 1963, U.S. Supreme Ct. 1972. Assoc. Cabaniss & Johnston, Birmingham, Ala., 1957-62, Chadbourne, Parke, Whiteside & Wolff, N.Y.C., 1962-66, ptnr., 1967-86, Jones, Day, Reavis & Pogue, N.Y.C., 1986-93, ret. ptnr., 1993—; ptnr. Afridi, Angell & Baker, N.Y.C., 1993-96, Gersen, Baker & Wood LLP, N.Y.C., 1997-98, Baker, Johnston & Wilson LLP, Birmingham and N.Y.C., 1998—2003; of counsel Haskell Slaughter Young & Rediker, LLC, Birmingham and N.Y.C., 2003—. Gen. counsel Econ. Club N.Y., 1977—. Co-editor Due Diligence, Disclosures and Warranties in the Corporate Acquisition Practice, 1988, 2d edit., 1992; author articles and book chpts. Pres. N.Y. Legis. Svc., N.Y.C., 1975-98, chmn., 1998—; mem. adv. com. Ctr. for N.Y.C. Law, 2000—; sec., dir. Jr. Achievement of N.Y., 1973-99; dir. Jr. Achievement of Greater Birmingham, 1999—; trustee Birmingham-So. Coll., 1985—. With U.S. Army, 1954-57; dir. HiEnergy Techs., Inc., 2003-. Mem.: Musica Viva N.Y. (pres. 1994—96), Internat. Ins. Soc., N.Y. State Bar Assn. (exec. com. bus. law sect. 1987—89, exec. com. internat. law and practice sect. 1991—92, chmn. internat. investment and devel. com. 1991—92), Assn. Lloyd's Mems. (N.Am. adv. bd.), Internat. Law Assn., Internat. Bar Assn. (vice chmn. bus. orgn. com. 1986—90, rep. to U.S. mems. N.Y. area 1988—2000, chmn. com. on trusts for bus. 1990—94, prin. rep. to UN in N.Y. 1993—), Birmingham Bar Assn. (chmn. history and archives com. 2002), Ala. Bar Assn., Assn. Bar City N.Y. (chmn. com. on state legis. 1968—70), Am. Judicature Soc., Am. Fgn. Law Assn., Am. Law Inst., Am. Arbitration Assn. (nat. panel), ABA (liaison com. fin. acctg. stds. bd.), Met. Club N.Y.C., Harvard Club N.Y.C., Birmingham Athletic Club. Democrat. Unitarian Universalist. Avocation: bridge. Corporate, general, Mergers and acquisitions, Securities. Home: 1200 Beacon Pkwy E Apt 500 Birmingham AL 35209-1041 also: 315 E 72d St Apt 2-J New York NY 10021-4626 Office: Haskell Slaughter Young & Rediker LLC 1400 Park Pl Tower 2001 Park Pl N Birmingham AL 35203-2735 also: Fl 30 515 Madison Ave New York NY 10022 E-mail: drb@hsy.com.

BAKER, DONALD, lawyer, director; b. Chgo., May 28, 1929; s. Russell and Elizabeth B.; m. Gisela S. Carli, Oct. 6, 1960; children: Caryna, Andrew, Russell. Student, Deep Springs Coll., Calif., 1947-49; JDS., U. Chgo., 1954. Bar: Ill. 1955, N.Y. 1964. Ptnr. Baker & McKenzie, Chgo., 1955-94, ret., 1994; sec., gen. counsel, bd. dirs. Air South, Inc., Columbia, S.C., 1994-95. Bd. dirs. Trimedyne, Inc., Cardiomedics, Inc. Bd. dirs. exec. com. Mid-Am. Com., Chgo., 1980-94. Mem. ABA. Clubs: Michigan Shores (Wilmette, Ill.). Private international, Corporate taxation. E-mail: dbaker5727@aol.com.

BAKER, DONALD P. lawyer; b. L.A., Oct. 27, 1947; s. Albert G. and Janet C. Baker; m. Caroline E. BA magna cum laude, U. Redlands, 1970; JD, UCLA, 1973. Bar: Calif. 1973. Ptnr. Latham & Watkins, L.A., chair transp. practice group, 1991—. Dir. UCLA Pub. Interest Law Found., 1982-84, UCLA Alumni Assn., 1984-86, Japan Am. Symphony Assn. L.A., 1992-95; dir. Western Justice Ctr. Found., 1988—, pres., 1995—; trustee Claremont Grad. U., 2002—. Fellow ABA (numerous coms. and offices), Nat. Assn. Colls. and Univ. Attys., Star Bar Calif. (com. jud. nominees evaluation 1981-82), Internat. Bar Assn., L.A. County Bar Assn. (pres. 1986-87, numerous coms. and offices, Shothuck-Price Meml. award 1999), Barristers L.A. County Bar Assn. (pres. 1979-80, numerous coms. and offices), L.A. County Bar Found. (sec. 1983-84), Japan Am. Soc. So. Calif. (bd. dirs., v.p. 1992—)Chancery Club, Order of the Coif. Land use and zoning (including planning), Property, real (including real estate development, water), Transportation. Office: Latham & Watkins 633 W 5th St Ste 4000 Los Angeles CA 90071-2005

BAKER, FREDERICK MILTON, JR., lawyer; b. Flint, Mich., Nov. 2, 1949; s. Frederick Milton Baker and Mary Jean (Hallitt) Rarig; m. Irene Taylor; children: Jessica, Jordan. BA, U. Mich., 1971; JD, Washington U., St. Louis, 1975. Bar: Mich. 1975, U.S. Dist. Ct. (we. dist.) Mich. 1980, U.S. Dist. Ct. (ea. dist.) Mich. 1981, U.S. Ct. Appeals (6th cir.) 1983, U.S. Supreme Ct. 1986. Instr. law Wayne State U., Detroit, 1975-76; research atty. Mich. Ct. Appeals, Lansing, 1976-77, law clk. to chief judge, 1977; asst. prof. T.M. Cooley Law Sch., Lansing, Mich., 1978-80; ptnr. Willingham & Cote, Lansing, 1980-86, Honigman, Miller, Schwartz & Cohn, Lansing, 1986—. Adj. prof. T.M. Cooley Law Sch., 1980—86, 1995—96, Detroit Coll. Law Mich. State U., East Lansing, 2001—. Author: Michigan Bar Appeal Manual, 1982; editor Mich. Bar Jour., 1984—; contbr. articles to profl. jours. Founder, pres. Sixty Plus Law Ctr., Lansing, 1978-87, bd. dirs., 1987—; mem. community adv. bd. Lansing Jr. League, 1983-90; co-founder, dir., sec.-treas. John D. Voelker Found., 1989—; bd. dirs. Lansing chpt. ACLU, 1997—, bd. dirs. Greater Lansing chpt., 1997-99; treas. Kehillat Israel, 1996-98; trustee Thoman Found., 2000—. Recipient Disting. Brief award T.M. Cooley Law Rev., 1988, 99. Fellow Mich. State Bar Found.; mem. ABA (Outstanding Single Project award 1980), Mich. Bar Assn. (vice chmn. jour. adv. bd. 1984-87, chmn. jour. adv. bd. 1987—, young lawyers sect. coun. 1980-84, grievance com. 1982-84, John W. Cummiskey award 1984), Ingham County Bar Assn. (Disting. Vol. award 2000). Clubs: Big Oak (Baldwin, Mich.). Unitarian Universalist. Avocations: photography, fishing, running, frisbee, squash. Antitrust, Environmental, State and local taxation. Home: 5127 Barton Rd Williamston MI 48895-9304 Office: Honigman Miller Schwartz & Cohn 222 N Washington Sq Ste 400 Lansing MI 48933-1800 E-mail: fmb@honigman.com.

BAKER, JAMES P. lawyer; b. Washington, 1952; m. Elizabeth Baker. BA, U. Santa Clara, Calif., 1975, JD, 1980; LLM, Georgetown U., 1982. Bar: Calif. 1980. Ptnr. Brobeck, Phleger & Harrison, San Francisco, 1999—2003, Orrick, Herrington & Sutcliffe, LLP, San Francisco, 2003—. ERISA. Office: Orrick, Herrington & Sutcliffe LLP 400 Sansome St San Francisco CA 94111 Office Fax: 415-773-5759. Business E-Mail: jbaker@orrick.com.

BAKER, JERRY L. protective services official; m. Elaine Baker; 3 children. Student, Ind. U.; B in Criminal Justice, Ind. U.-Purdue U., 1978; grad., FBI Nat. Acad. Joined Indpls. Police Dept., 1969, sgt., 1975, comdr. auto theft br., asst. comdr. vice br., lt., comdr. Spl. Ops. and Response/SWAT Team, dep. chief West Dist., 1994—2000, chief of police, 2000—. With U.S. Army, Vietnam. Mem.: VFW, FBI Nat. Acad. Ind., Mil. Order Purple Heart, Vietnam Vets. Am., Am. Legion. Office: Inpls Police Dept Ste E211 50 N Alabama St Indianapolis IN 46204-5305*

BAKER, KEITH LEON, lawyer; b. Columbus, Ind., Jan. 22, 1950; s. Richard Leon and Sarah Elizabeth (Wisehart) B. A.B., Princeton U., 1972; J.D., Syracuse U., 1975; LL.M. with highest honors, George Washington U., 1978. Bar: N.Y. 1976, D.C. 1976, Va. 2000, U.S. Ct. Appeals (D.C. cir.) 1983, U.S. Ct. Internat. Trade 1983. Asst. bank examiner U.S. Treasury Dept., N.Y.C., 1974; law clk. U.S. Dept. of Justice, Syracuse, N.Y., 1974-75; atty.-adviser GAO, Washington, 1975-78; atty.-adviser U.S. EPA, Washington, 1978-80; pvt. practice, Washington, 1980-99; ptnr. Barton, Baker, McMahon & Tolle, 1999—. Author: Small Business Financing, 1983; contbr. articles to profl. jours. Mem. ABA, Fed. Bar Assn., Nat. Contract Mgmt. Assn. Methodist. Corporate, general, Government contracts and claims, Private international. Home: 6645 Hawthorne St Mc Lean VA 22101-4423 Office: Barton Baker McMahon & Tolle The Madison Bldg Ste 440 1320 Old Chain Bridge Rd Mc Lean VA 22101

BAKER, LINDI L. lawyer; b. San Antonio, Jan. 2, 1952; d. Louis R. and R. Jean Brandt; m. Buck N. Baker, Aug. 26, 1972. BS, S. Oreg. State U., 1974, MS, 1978; JD, U. San Francisco, 1984. Bar: Calif. 1984, Oreg. 1991. Staff atty. Calif. Supreme Ct., San Francisco, 1984-85; assoc. Heller Ehrman White & McAuliffe, San Francisco, 1985-91; of counsel Schultz Salisbury Cauble & Dole, Grants Pass, Oreg., 1997—2002; judge pro tem Circuit Ct., 2002—. Past pres. Grants Pass Mus. Art; bd. dirs. Coalition for Kids; mem. Three Rivers Sch. Dist. Site Coun. Mem. Oreg. Bar Assn., Calif. Bar Assn. General civil litigation, General practice, Property, real (including real estate development, water). Office: Josephine County Courthouse 500 NW 6th St Grants Pass OR 97526

BAKER, MARK M. lawyer, law educator; b. Long Beach, N.Y., Nov. 20, 1947; s. Barbara Baker; children: Cory M, Lindsay N. BS, Syracuse U., 1969; JD, Bklyn Law Sch., 1972. Bar: N.Y. 1973, U.S. Ct. Appeals (11th cir.) 1989, U.S. Supreme Ct. 1976, U.S. Ct. Appeals (2d cir.) 1975, U.S. Dist. Ct. (so. dist.) N.Y. 1975, U.S. Dist. Ct. (ea. dist.) N.Y. 1975, U.S. Ct. Appeals (3d cir.) 1989, U.S. Ct. Appeals (4th cir.) 1989, U.S. Ct. Appeals (5th cir.) 1989, U.S. Ct. Appeals (9th cir.) 1989. Asst. dist. atty. Kings County Dist. Atty., Bklyn., 1972—76; ptnr. Rhodes, Baker and Fisher, 1976—77; spl. asst. atty. gen. Office of Spl. State Prosecutor, N.Y.C., 1977—83; ptnr. Slotnick and Baker, 1983—94; of counsel Brafman & Ross, P.C. Adj. prof. of law Touro Coll. Law Ctr., Huntington, 2000—01. Author: (N.Y. criminal practice handbook supp) Defenses; contbr. articles to profl. jours. Mem., bd. of trustees Hebrew Inst. of Riverdale, 1975—2002, SAR Acad., 1987—90, Westchester Hebrew H.S., Mamaroneck, 1992—96; pres. River Ter. Apartments Asso., Riverdale, NY, 1980—82. Mem.: N.Y. County Lawyers Assn. (assoc.), N.Y. Coun. Def. Lawyers (assoc.), N.Y. Criminal Bar Assn. (assoc.), N.Y. State Assn. Criminal Def. Attorneys (assoc.), Nat. Assn. Criminal Def. Attorneys (assoc.), Assn of Bar City of N.Y. (assoc.). Achievements include concentrating in federal and New York criminal appeals and habeas corpus litigation. Avocations: skiing, running, reading political novels and non-fiction. Appellate, Criminal. Office: Brafman & Ross PC 767 Third Avenue - 26th Floor New York NY 10017 Office Fax: 212-750-3906. E-mail: mmbaker@brafmanross.com.

BAKER, PATRICIA (JEAN BAKER), lawyer, mediator; b. June 28, 1948; BS summa cum laude, Wright State U., Dayton, Ohio, 1973; MBA, Northeastern U., Boston, 1989; JD, Calif. Western U., San Diego, 1993. Bar: Calif. 1993; cert. mediator. With GenRad Inc., Boston, 1974-82; mktg./sales staff GE Co., Boston, 1982-84; major accounts mgr. Fluke Mfg. Co., Boston, 1984-89; pub. rels. mgr. Racal Dana, Irvine, Calif., 1989-90; legal intern Pub. Defenders Dependancy, San Diego, 1992; law clk. Civil divsn. U.S. Atty., San Diego, 1992; personal injury atty. L.H. Parker, Long Beach, Calif., 1993; mediator/atty. Baker & Assocs., San Diego, 1993-94; dir. Orange County region Am. Arbitration Assn., Irvine, 1994-97, v.p. Washington, 1997—. Mediator San Diego Mediation Ctr., 1993-97; trainer mediation skills Am. Arbitration Assn., 1994-97; adj. prof. Western State U., Irvine, 1995-96; MCLE presenter San Diego County Bar, 1994, State Bar of Calif., 1996, ABA, 1997-2003; mediator Superior Ct., San Diego, 1994-97, U.S. Bankruptcy Ct. (cen. dist.) Calif., 1995-97; adj. prof. Columbus Sch. of Law, Washington, 1997-2001; coach Georgetown Law Sch. Mediation Advocacy Team, 2003. Bd. dirs. Legal Aid Soc., San Diego, 1994, T. Homann Law Assn., San Diego, 1994, Counsel for Ct. Excellence, 2003-. Recipient Am. Jurisprudence awards, 1992/ Mem. ABA, D.C. Bar Assn., State Bar of Calif., Energy Bar Assn., Va. Bar Assn., Md. Bar Assn., Women's Bar Assn. Avocations: tennis, golf. Office: American Arbitration Assn 601 Pennsylvania Ave NW Ste 700 Washington DC 20004-2676 E-mail: BakerJ@adr.org.

BAKER, RICHARD SOUTHWORTH, lawyer; b. Lansing, Mich., Dec. 18, 1929; s. Paul Julius and Florence (Schmid) B.; m. Kathleen E. Yull, 1956 (dec. 1964); m. Marina J. Vidoli, 1965 (div. 1989); children: Garrick Richard, Lydia Joy; m. Barbara J. Walker, 1997. Student, DePauw U., 1947-49; AB cum laude, Harvard, 1951; JD, U. Mich., 1954. Bar: Ohio 1957, U.S. Dist. Ct. (no. dist.) Ohio 1958, U.S. Tax Ct. 1960, U.S. Supreme Ct. 1971, U.S. Ct. Appeals (6th cir.) 1972. Mem. firm Fuller & Henry, and predecessors, 1956-91; pvt. practice Toledo, 1991—. Chmn. nat. com. region IV Mich. Law Sch. Fund, 1967-69, mem.-at-large, 1970-85. Bd. dirs. Assn. Harvard Alumni, 1970-73. Served with AUS, 1954-56. Fellow Am. Coll. Trial Lawyers; mem. ABA, Ohio Bar Assn., Toledo Bar Assn., Toledo Club, Harvard Club (pres. Toledo chpt. 1968-77), Capital Club, Phi Delta Theta, Phi Delta Phi. General civil litigation, Federal civil litigation, State civil litigation. Office: 2819 Falmouth Rd Toledo OH 43615-2215

BAKER, ROY GORDON, JR., lawyer; b. San Antonio, June 19, 1953; s. Roy Gordon and Carolyn Blanch (Slinkert) B.; m. Cynthia Lynn Lee, July 6, 1977; children: Teri Diane, Amanda Christine. BA magna cum laude, Pepperdine U., 1974; JD, U. Calif., San Francisco, 1977; LLM in Taxation, Golden Gate U., 1989. Bar: Calif. 1977, U.S. Dist. Ct. (no. dist.) Calif. 1977, U.S. Dist. Ct. (ctrl. dist.) Calif. 1984, U.S. Ct. Appeal (9th cir.) 1977, U.S. Tax Ct. 1984; accredited estate planner. Dep. atty. gen. Calif. Dept. Justice, San Francisco, 1977-79; atty., assoc. Stark, Stewart, Wells, Rahl, Field & Schwartz, Oakland, Calif., 1979-83, atty., ptnr., 1983-85, Walnut Creek, Calif., 1985-89, Field, Baker & Richardson, Walnut Creek, 1990-94; atty., ptnr., shareholder R. Gordon Baker, Atty. At Law, P.C., Walnut Creek, 1994—. Contbr. articles to profl. jours. Participant Leadership Contra Costa, Walnut Creek C. of C., 1993. Mem. ABA (taxation sect., real property, probate and trust law sect.), State Bar Calif. (taxation sect., estate planning, trust and probate sect., bus. law sect.), Contra Costa County Bar Assn. (taxation sect., bd. dirs. 1993—, pres. 1994, 2001), Nat. Assn. Estate Planners and Counsels, Diablo Valley Estate Planning Coun. Avocations: fishing, gardening, sailing, canoeing. Corporate, general, Estate planning, Probate (including wills, trusts). Office: R Gordon Baker Atty At Law PC 2033 N Main St Ste 750 Walnut Creek CA 94596-3728 E-mail: g_baker@pacbell.net.

BAKER, THOMAS EDWARD, lawyer, accountant; b. Washington, July 24, 1923; s. John Thad and Angelina E. (Rappa) B.; m. Mildred M. Younglove, Dec. 26, 1944 (dec. May 1995); children: Jean Ann Baker Holland, Cindy Baker Goralewicz, Linda Hogan; m. Helen Draughon, Nov. 3, 1996. BS, JD, U. Okla., 1950. Bar: Okla. 1950; CPA, Okla. Pvt. practice, Oklahoma City, 1950; agt., spl. agt. IRS, 1951-53; ptnr. Shutler Baker Simpson & Logsdon, Kingfisher, Okla., 1953-79, Baker, Logsdon, Schulte & Gibson, Kingfisher, 1979—. Trustee U. Okla. Found., Inc., 1987-89. WithAUS, 1943-46. Mem. Am. Legion (past svc. officer), Elks, Rotary (pres. Kingfisher club 1957). Democrat. Mem. Christian Ch. (Disciples Of Christ). Oil, gas, and mineral, General practice, Probate (including wills, trusts). Home: 1211 Regency Ct Kingfisher OK 73750-4251 Office: Baker Logsdon Schulte & Gibson 302 N Main St Kingfisher OK 73750-2799

BAKER, THURBERT E. state attorney general; b. Rocky Mount, N.C., Dec. 16, 1952; m. Catherine Baker; children: Jocelyn, Chelsea. BA in Polit. Sci., U. N.C.; JD, Emory U., 1979. Mem. Ga. Ho. of Reps., 1988—90, asst. adminstrn. fl. leader, 1990—93, adminstrn. fl. leader, 1993—97; atty. gen. State of Ga., 1997—. Trustee Statewide Ga. Diabetes Bd., Ebenezer Bapt. Ch., Atlanta, DeKalb Coll. Found. Mem.: Nat. Med. Soc.-Emory U., DeKalb County C. of C. (bd. dirs.). Democrat. Office: Atty Gen Dept Law 40 Capitol Sq SW Atlanta GA 30334-9003

BAKER, VERNON G., II, lawyer; BA, Dartmouth Coll.; JD, Am. U. Assoc. Schnader, Harrison, Segal & Lewis; counsel Scott Paper Co.; assoc. gen. counsel Advanced Material Group; v.p., gen. counsel, Corp. Rsch. Tech. Hoechst Celanese Corp; sr. v.p., gen. counsel, sect. Meritor, 1999—2000; sr. v.p., gen. counsel ArvinMeritor, 2000—. Office: Arvin Meritor Inc 2135 W Maple Inc Troy MI 48084

BAKER, WADE FRANKLIN, retired state bar executive; b. Jackson County, Ill., Dec. 30, 1919; s. Robert David Jr. and Lillian May (Damron) B.; m. Mary Eleanor LaClair, June 29, 1947; 1 child, Denise Ann. BEd, So. Ill. U., 1941; LLB, Lincoln Coll. Law, Springfield, Ill., 1950. Bar: Ill. 1950, Mo. 1957. Asst. sec., counsel Ill. Bar Assn., 1946-57; exec. dir., sec. The Mo. Bar, Jefferson City, 1957-84; pres. B.P. & G. Adv. Svcs., Inc., Jefferson City, 1985-91; ret. Former sec. Mo. Bar Found.; former sec.-treas. Mo. Bar Research, Inc., Mo. Legal Aid Soc.; former treas., asst. sec. Mo. Press Bar Commn. Chmn. adminstrv. bd. 1st United Meth. Ch., 1981—82; dir. for life Meml. Hosp. With anti-aircraft arty. U.S. Army, 1942—46, ETO, with anti-aircraft arty. U.S. Army, 1951—52. Decorated Bronze Star; recipient Bicentennial award Mo. Bar, 1976, Fred Bolton award Nat. Assn. Bar Execs., 1978, Non-Alumni award U. Mo., 1975. Mem. Mo. Bar Assn., Jefferson City Rotary (pres. 1966-67), Jefferson City YMCA (co-founder, former bd. mem.). Home: 2505 Orchard Ln Jefferson City MO 65109-0607

BAKER, WALTER ARNOLD, lawyer; b. Columbia, Ky., Feb. 20, 1937; s. Herschel T. and Mattie B. (Barger) B.; m. Jane Stark Helm, Apr. 24, 1965; children: Thomas Herschel, Ann Tate. AB magna cum laude, Harvard U., 1958, LLB, 1961. Assoc. Brown, Ardery, Todd & Dudley, Louisville, 1961-63; ptnr. Wilson, Baker, Herbert and Garmon, Glasgow, Ky., 1963-67; pvt. practice Glasgow, 1967-81, 83—; asst. gen. counsel Office Sec. Def., Washington, 1981-83; justice Supreme Ct. of Ky., Frankfort, 1996. Rep. Ky. Ho. of Reps., 1968-71, senator State of Ky., 1972-81, 89-96; active Ky. Coun. on Postsecondary Edn., 1997—. Lt. col. USAFR. Mem. Ky. Bar Assn., Barren County Bar Assn., Glasgow Rotary, Glasgow Golf and Country Club, Phi Beta Kappa. Republican. Presbyterian. Address: 917 S Green St Glasgow KY 42141-2086 Office: 213 S Green St Glasgow KY 42141-2643

BAKER, WALTER WRAY, JR., lawyer; b. Raleigh, N.C., July 27, 1942; s. Walter Wray and Maggie Lee (Holland) B.; m. Jane Marlyn Green, June 14, 1964; children: Susan, Valerie, Walter. AA, Campbell Coll., 1962; AB, U. N.C., 1964, JD, 1966. Bar: N.C. 1966, U.S. Dist. Ct. (ea. and mid. dists.) N.C., U.S. Supreme Ct. 1974. Rsch. asst. to chief justice N.C. State Supreme Ct., Raleigh, 1966-67; pvt. practice High Point, 1967-94; ptnr. Baker & Boyan, PLLC, High Point, 1994—. Writer, lectr. continuing legal edn. personal injury & ethics; adj. prof. trial advocacy Wake Forest Sch. Law. Named among legal elite in litigation in N.C., Bus. N.C. Mag., 2002. Mem. N.C. Acad. Trial Lawyers (pres. 1985-86), High Point Bar Assn. (pres. 1985), N.C. State Bar (councillor 18th jud. dist.), Am. Bd. Trial Advocates, Joseph Br. Inn of Ct., Million Dollar Advocates Forum. Democrat. Mem. Wesleyan Ch. General civil litigation, Personal injury (including property damage). Office: Baker & Boyan PLLC 820 N Elm St High Point NC 27262-3920

BAKER, WILLIAM DUNLAP, lawyer; b. St. Louis, June 17, 1932; s. Harold Griffith and Bernice (Kraft) B.; m. Kay Stokes, May 23, 1955; children: Mark William, Kathryn X., Beth Kristie, Frederick Martin. AB, Colgate U., 1954; JD, U. Calif., Berkeley, 1960. Bar: Calif. 1961, Ariz. 1961, U.S. Supreme Ct. 1969. Practice in, Coolidge, 1961, Florence, 1961-63, Phoenix, 1963—; law clk. Stokes & Moring, 1960; spl. investigator Office Pinal County Atty., 1960-61, dep. county atty., 1961-63; partner McBryde, Vincent, Brumage & Baker, 1961-63; assoc. atty. Rawlins, Ellis, Burrus & Kiewit, 1963-65, partner, 1965-81; pres., atty. Ellis & Baker, P.C., 1981-84, Ellis, Baker, Lynch, Clark & Porter P.C., 1984-86, Ellis, Baker, Clark & Porter, P.C., 1986-89, Ellis, Baker & Porter, P.C., 1989-92, Ellis Baker & Porter Ltd., Phoenix, 1992-95, Ellis, Baker & Porter, P.C., Phoenix, 1995-99, Ellis & Baker, P.C., 1999—. Referee Juvenile Ct. Maricopa County Superior Ct., 1966-85 Contbr. articles to profl. jours. Mem. Gov.'s Adv. Coun., Phoenix, 1969-71, Ariz. Environ. Planning Commn., 1974-75; bd. dirs. Agri-Bus. Coun., 1978—, sec., 1978-82; pub. mem. State Bd. Accountancy, 1995—, sec., 1998-99, treas., 1999-2000, pres., 2000-02; pub. mem. Nat. Assn. Bds. Accountancy, litig. com., 2001-, nominating com., 2002—, Nat. Assn. State Bds. Accountancy; spl. legal counsel Ariz. Com. Rep. Party, 1965-69, mem. exec. com., 1972-78; vice-chmn. Maricopa County Rep. Com., 1968-69, chmn., 1969-71; bd. dirs. San Pablo Home for Youth, 1964-72, pres., 1971; bd. dirs. Maricopa County chpt. Nat. Found. March of Dimes, 1966-71, campaign chmn., 1970; trustee St. Luke's Hosp., 1976-85, sec., 1978-82, chmn., 1982-85; bd. dirs. Luke's Men, 1971-80, pres., 1976-77; bd. dirs. Combined Health Resources, 1982-85, St. Luke's Health Sys., 1977-95, chmn., 1985-89; bd. dirs. St. Luke's Health Initiatives, 1995—, vice chair, 2000-02; bd. dirs., v.p. Ariz. Anglican Cursillo Movement, 1982-86; Western dist. layman rep. Nat. Episcopal Cursillo Com., 1996-98; regional v.p. Colgate Alumni Corp., 1977-82; vice chancellor Episcopal Diocese Ariz., 1970-96; sr. warden Christ Ch. of Ascension, 1983-86, 2001—; ch. atty. Episc. Diocese Ariz., 1996—. Served to 1st lt. USAF, 1954-57. Mem. ABA, Nat. Water Resources Assn. (co-chmn. task force on reclamation law 1990-97, resolutions com. 1990-93, chmn. state caucus 1993-99, chair water policy task force 2000—), Ariz. Bar Assn., Calif. Bar Assn., State C. of C. (bd. dirs. 1988-92), Maricopa County Bar Assn., Nat. Assn. State Bds. Accountancy, Flagstaff Golf Assn. (bd. dirs. 1992-93, 94-96, pres. 1994-95), Phoenix Country Club, Sigma Chi, Phi Delta Phi. Episcopalian. Natural resources, Property, real (including real estate development, water), Utilities, public. Home: 1627 E Cactus Wren Dr Phoenix AZ 85020-5550 Office: Ste 320 7310 N 16th St Phoenix AZ 85020 E-mail: wdb@ellisbaker.com.

BAKER, WILLIAM PARR, lawyer; b. Balt., Sept. 5, 1946; s. George William and Jane (Parr) B.; m. Christine Corbett, Oct. 23, 1982; children: William Corbett, Brendan Parr, Laura Elizabeth. BA, St. Francis Univ., Loretto, Pa., 1968; JD, U. Md., 1971. Bar: Md. 1971, U.S. Dist. Ct. Md. 1972, U.S. Tax Ct. 1978, U.S. Supreme Ct. 1980, U.S. Ct. Appeals (4th cir.) 1982. Law clk. Md. Ct. Appeals, 1971-72; ptnr. Baker and Baker, PA and predecessors, Balt., 1972—. Civil case mediator Cir. Ct. for Balt. County; adj. prof. U. Md. Sch. Law. Contbr. articles to profl. jours. V.p. bd. dirs. Santa Claus Anonymous, 1973-76; bd. dirs. Balt. Assn. Retarded Citizens, 1981—. Mem. ABA, Md. Bar Assn., Bar Assn. Balt. City, Golfers Charitable Assn. (bd. dirs. 1989—), Am. Mensa, Balt. Country Club. Roman Catholic. Federal civil litigation, Commercial, contracts (including sales of goods; commercial financing), General practice. Office: Baker and Baker PA 1000 Mercantile Trust Bldg 409 Washington Ave Baltimore MD 21204-4920

BAKER, WILLIAM THOMPSON, JR., lawyer; b. N.Y.C., Jan. 19, 1944; s. William Thompson and Elizabeth (Baird) B.; children: Alice Whetherly, Richard Cass, Heather Thompson. BA cum laude, Yale U., 1965; JD, U. Va., 1968. Bar: N.Y. 1968, U.S. Dist. Ct. (so. and ea. dists.) N.Y. 1969, U.S. Supreme Ct. 1990, U.S. Ct. Appeals (D.C. cir.), 1992. Assoc. Thelen, Reid & Priest (formerly known as Reid & Priest), N.Y.C., 1968-74, ptnr, 1975—, mng. ptnr., 1986-87, mem. exec. com., 1980-82, 86-91, chmn. exec. com., 1990-91. Chmn. or co-chmn. Utility/Energy Svcs. Group Dept., 1991—; chmn. legal com. Edison Electric Inst., 1997-99. Trustee Episcopal Sch. in City of N.Y., 1969-71, Chase Wildlife Found., 2003—; mem. bd. govs. The Hotchkiss Sch. Alumni Assn., 2003—. Mem. ABA (chmn. subcommittee pub. utility law 1990—), New York County Lawyers Assn., Assn. Bar City N.Y., Union Club N.Y.C., Yale Club N.Y.C., N.Y. Anglers Club. Republican. Episcopalian. Avocations: fishing, fly tying, rod building, wood working. Administrative and regulatory, Corporate, general, Utilities, public.

BAKKEN, GORDON MORRIS, law educator; b. Madison, Wis., Jan. 10, 1943; s. Elwood S. and Evelyn A. H. (Anderson) B.; m. Erika Reinhardt, Mar. 24, 1943; children: Angela E., Jeffrey E. BS, U. Wis., 1966, MS, 1967, PhD, 1970, JD, 1973. From asst. to assoc. prof. history Calif. State U., Fullerton, 1969-74, prof. history, 1974—, dir. faculty affairs, 1974-86. Cons. Calif. Sch. Employees Assn., 1976-78, Calif. Bar Commn. Hist. Law., 1985—; mgmt. task force on acad. grievance procedures Calif. State Univ. and Colls. Systems, 1975; mem. Calif. Jud. Coun. Com. Trial Ct. Records Mgmt., 1992-97. Author 7 books on Am. legal history; contbr. articles to profl. jours. Placentia Jusa referee coord., 1983. Russell Sag resident fellow law, 1971-72, Am. Bar Found. fellow in legal history, 1979-80, 84-85; Am. Coun. Learned Socs. grantee-in-ai d, 1979-80. Mem. Orgn. Am. Historians, Am. Soc. Legal History, Law and Soc. Assn., Western History Assn., Calif. Supreme Ct. Hist. Soc. (v.p.), Phi Alpha Theta (v.p. 1994-95, pres. 1996-97). Democrat. Lutheran. E-mail: gbakken@fullerton.edu.

BAKKENSEN, JOHN RESER, lawyer; b. Pendleton, Oreg., Oct. 4, 1943; s. Manley John and Helen (Reser) B.; m. Ann Marie Dahlen, Sept. 30, 1978; children: Michael, Dana, Laura. AB magna cum laude, Harvard U., 1965; JD, Stanford U., 1968. Bar: Oreg. 1969, Calif. 1969, U.S. Dist. Ct. Oreg. 1969. Ptnr. Miller, Nash, Wiener, Hager & Carlsen, Portland, Oreg., 1968-99. Lawyer del. 9th Cir. Jud. Conf., San Francisco, 1980-82. Author: (with others) Advising Oregon Businesses, 1979, Arbitration and Mediation, supplement, 2000. Past bd. dirs. Assn. for Retarded Citizens, Portland; advisor Portland Youth Shelter House; mem. and counsel to bd. dirs. Friends of Pine Mountain Observatory, Portland. Mem. ABA (forum on constrn. industry), Am. Arbitration Assn., Oreg. State Bar, Oreg. Assoc. Gen. Contractors (legal com. 1991, counsel to bd. dirs. 1992), Multnomah Athletic Club. Avocation: astronomy. Alternative dispute resolution, State civil litigation, Construction.

BAKKER, THOMAS GORDON, lawyer; b. San Gabriel, Calif., Aug. 18, 1947; s. Gordon and Eva Marie (Hoekstra) B.; m. Charlotte Anne Kamstra, Aug. 1, 1969; children: Sarah, Jonathan. AB in History, Calvin Coll., Grand Rapids, Mich., 1969; JD, U. Mich., 1973. Bar: Ariz. 1973, U.S. Dist. Ct. Ariz. 1973, U.S. Ct. Appeals (9th cir.) 1973. Staff reporter Ariz. Criminal Code Revision Com., Phoenix, 1973-75; asst. atty. gen. State of Ariz., Phoenix, 1975-77; staff atty. div. 1 Ariz. Ct. Appeals, Phoenix, 1977-79; assoc. Burch, Cracchiolo et al, Phoenix, 1979-80; from assoc. to ptnr. Olson, Jantsch, Bakker , Phoenix, 1980—. Vice chmn. tort and ins. practice sect. Appellate Advocacy Commn., 1982-83; judge pro tem div. 1 Ariz. Ct. Appeals, 1985, 92. Served with U.S. Army, 1969-71. Fellow Ariz. Bar Found. (founding fellow); mem. Ariz. Bar Assn., Maricopa County Bar Assn., Am. Health Lawyers Assn., Def. Rsch. Inst., Ariz. Assn. Def. Counsel. (bd. dirs.). Mem. Christian Reformed Ch. Avocations: reading, golf, aerobics, salt water fishing. Federal civil litigation, State civil litigation, Personal injury (including property damage). Office: Olson Jantsch Bakker 7243 N 16th St Phoenix AZ 85020-5203 E-mail: TGB@OJBB.com.

BALBACH, STANLEY BYRON, lawyer; b. Normal, Ill., Dec. 26, 1919; s. Nyle Jacob and Gertrude (Cory) B.; m. Sarah Troutt Witherspoon, May 22, 1944; children: Stanley Byron Jr., Nancy Ann Fehr, Barbara Haines, Edith. BS, U. Ill., 1940, LLD, 1942. Bar: Ill. 1942, Fla. 1980, U.S. Ct. Appeals (7th cir.) 1961, U.S. Supreme Ct. 1950. Ptnr. Couchman & Balbach, Hoopeston, Ill., 1945-48, Webber & Balbach, Urbana, 1948-81, Balbach & Fehr, Urbana, 1981—. Nat. chmn. Jr. Bar Conf., 1955; bd. dirs. Atty.'s Title Guaranty Fund, Champaign, Ill. Author: Reverse Mortgages, 1997, The Lawyers Guide to Retirement: Serving a New Clientele in a Second Career in Real Estate, 1998. Capt. USAAF, 1942-45 (pilot). Mem. ABA (ho. of dels. 1956, lawyer title guaranty fund com., past mem. coun. law office practice and real property, probate and trust law sects.), LWV, Ill. State Bar Assn. (elder law com., Laureate of the Acad. Ill. Lawyers 2002), Am. Judicature Soc., Masons, Rotary, Phi Delta Phi, Alpha Kappa Lambda. General practice. Home: 1009 S Douglas Ave Urbana IL 61801-4933 Office: Balbach & Fehr Box 217 102 N Broadway Ave Urbana IL 61801-2705

BALDAUF, KENT EDWARD, lawyer; b. Pitts., Feb. 6, 1943; s. Walter William and Esther Baldauf; m. Kathleen Dian Abels, June 10, 1967; children: Kent Edward Jr., Krista K., Kara K. BS in Metall. Engring., Carnegie Mellon U., 1964; JD, Cleve. State U., 1970. Bar: Pa. 1970, U.S. Patent and Trademark Office 1971, U.S. Ct. Appeals (Fed. cir.) 1990, U.S. Supreme Ct. 1977. Shareholder, v.p., dir. Webb Law Firm, Pitts., 1988—. Mem. ABA, Pa. Bar Assn., Allegheny County Bar Assn., Am. Intellectual Property Law Assn. (pres. 1998-99), Pitts. Intellectual Property Law Assn., Valley Brook Country Club, Duquesne Club. Federal civil litigation, Patent, Trademark and copyright. Office: The Webb Law Firm 436 7th Ave Pittsburgh PA 15219-1826

BALDOCK, BOBBY RAY, judge; b. Rocky, Okla., Jan. 24, 1936; Grad., N.Mex. Mil. Inst., 1956; JD, U. Ariz., 1960. Bar: Ariz. 1960, N.Mex. 1961, U.S. Dist. Ct. N.Mex. 1965. Ptnr. Sanders, Bruin & Baldock, Roswell, N.Mex., 1960—83; adj. prof. Eastern N.Mex. U., 1962—81; judge U.S. Dist. Ct. N.Mex., Albuquerque, 1983—86, U.S. Ct. Appeals (10th cir.), 1986—2001, sr. judge, 2001—. Mem.: Chaves County Bar Assn., Ariz. Bar Assn., N.Mex. Bar Assn., Phi Alpha Delta. Office: US Ct Appeals PO Box 2388 Roswell NM 88202-2388

BALDWIN, ALLEN ADAIL, lawyer, writer; b. St. Augustine, Fla., July 15, 1939; s. Larrie Paul and Bertha Mae (Capallia) B. BA, Brigham Young U., 1969; JD, So. U., Baton Rouge, 1975. Bar: Fla. 1975. Tchr. Putnam County Sch. Bd., Palatka, Fla., 1969-71; pvt. practice, Palatka, 1975—. Author: Tricks to Make the Angels Weep, 1986, Call It Not Heaven, 1991, Redeem Us From Virtue, 1992. Mem. Latter-day Saints Ch. Avocations: reading, swimming, hiking. Family and matrimonial, General practice, Probate (including wills, trusts). Office: 308 St Johns Ave Palatka FL 32177-4723

BALDWIN, CHARLES SELDEN, IV, lawyer; b. Winston-Salem, N.C., May 30, 1968; s. Charles Selden III and Beth Dixson Baldwin; m. Devon Starr Davis, May 31, 1997; 2 children, Susanna Davis, Charles Selden V. BA in English, U. N.C., 1990; JD, Am. U., 1993, MA, 1994; LLM in Internat. Law with distinction, Georgetown U., 1996. Bar: N.C. 1993, D.C. 1994, U.S. Dist. Ct. (ea. dist.) N.C. 1996, U.S. Dist. Ct. (we. dist.) N.C. 1997, U.S. Dist. Ct. (mid. dist.) N.C. 2002, U.S. Ct. Appeals (4th cir.) 1997. Assoc. Rountree & Seagle, LLP, Wilmington, N.C., 1996-98, ptnr., 1999—. Author: International Litigation Guide to Jurisdiction Practice and Strategy, Transnational Publishers, 1998. Bd. dirs. Covenant Moravian Ch., Wilmington, 1998—; coord. Interfaith Hospitality Network, Wilmington, 1998—. Mem. N.C. Bar Assn., New Hanover County Bar Assn. Admiralty, Federal civil litigation, Private international. Office: Rountree Losee & Baldwin 2419 Market St Wilmington NC 28403-1135

BALDWIN, EDWIN STEEDMAN, lawyer; b. St. Louis, May 5, 1932; s. Richard and Almira (Steedman) B.; m. Margaret Kirkham, July 1, 1958; children: Margaret B. Dozler, Edwin S. Jr., Harold K. AB, Princeton U., 1954; LLM, Harvard U., 1957. Bar: Mo. 1957, U.S. Dist. Ct. (ea. dist.) Mo. 1957. Assoc. Teasdale, Kramer & Vaughan, St. Louis, 1957-64; ptnr. Armstrong Teasdale, LLP, St. Louis, 1965-97, of counsel, 1998—. Fellow Am. Coll. Trust and Estate Counsel, St. Louis Country Club, Noonday Club. Republican. Episcopalian. Avocations: golf, hunting, sailing. Estate planning, Probate (including wills, trusts), Estate taxation. Office: Armstrong Teasdale LLP 1 Metropolitan Sq Ste 2600 Saint Louis MO 63102-2740 E-mail: tbaldwin@armstrongteasdale.com.

BALDWIN, GORDON BREWSTER, law educator, lawyer; b. Binghamton, N.Y., Sept. 3, 1929; s. Schuyler Forbes and Doris Ambeline (Hawkins) B.; m. Helen Louise Hochgraf, Feb., 1958; children: Schuyler, Mary Page. LLB, Cornell U., 1953; BA, Haverford Coll., 1950. Bar: N.Y. 1953, Wis. 1965. Pvt. practice, Rochester and Rome, N.Y., 1953-57; prof. law U. Wis., Madison, 1957-99, Evjue-Bascom profl. law, 1991-99, emeritus prof., 1999—, assoc. dean law, 1968-70, dir. officer edn., 1972-99; of counsel Murphy & Desmond, S.C., Madison, Wis., 1986-95. Chmn. internat. law U.S. Naval War Coll., 1963-64; Fulbright prof., Cairo, 1966-67, Tehran, Iran, 1970-71; lectr. State Dept., Cyprus, 1967, 1969, 1971; counselor internat. law U.S. Dept. State, Washington, 1975-76, cons., 1976-77; vis. prof. Chuo U., Tokyo, 1984, Giessen U., Fed. Republic Germany, 1987, 92, Thommasat U., Thailand, 1997; cons. U.S. Naval War Coll., 1961-65; chmn. screening com. on law Fulbright Program, 1974; mem. constl. law com. Multi-State Bar Exam, 1972-82; chmn. State Pub. Def. Bd., 1980-83, Wis. Elections Bd., 1991-96; cons., rep. Marshall Island Constn. Conv., 1990. Mem. Wis. Bd. Elections, 1991-95, Wis. Land Coun., 1998-2002, Wis. State Ethics Bd., 2000-2003. Ford Found. fellow, 1962-63 Fellow Am. Bar Found.; mem. AAUP (nat. coun. 1975-78, pres. Wis. conf. 1986-87), Bar Assn. (vice chmn. sect. on individual rights 1973-75), Fulbright Alumni Assn. (dir. 1979-82), Am. Law Inst., Order of Coif, Madison Club, Madison Lit. Club (pres. 1985-86, 2000-03), Univ. Club, Rotary (pres. Madison 1980, dist. gov. 1999-00), Phi Beta Kappa. Home: 3958 Plymouth Cir Madison WI 53705-5212 Office: U Wis 975 Bascom Mall Sch Law Madison WI 53706-1399 E-mail: gbaldwin@facstaff.wisc.edu.

BALDWIN, JANICE MURPHY, lawyer; b. Bridgeport, Conn., July 16, 1926; d. William Henry and Josephine Gertrude (McKenna) Murphy; m. Robert Edward Baldwin, July 31, 1954; children: Jean Baldwin Grossman, Robert William, Richard Edward, Nancy Baldwin Kitsos. AB, U. Conn., 1948; MA, Mt. Holyoke Coll., 1950; postgrad., U. Manchester, Eng., 1950-51; MA, Tufts U., 1952; JD, U. Wis., 1971. Bar: Wis. 1971, U.S. Dist. Ct. (we. dist.) Wis. 1971. Staff atty. legis. coun. State of Wis., Madison, 1971-74, sr. staff atty., 1975-94; pvt. practice Madison, 1994—. Atty. adviser HUD, Washington, 1974-75, 78-79. Fulbright fellow, 1950-51. Mem. AAUW, NOW, LWV (sec. 1996-99, v.p., 1999-2001, bd. dirs. Dane County 1996—, exec. com. 1997—), U.S. and Wis. Women's Polit. Caucus, Legal Assn. for Women (chmn. Marygold Meili award com. 1997-99), Wis. Bar Assn. (pres. govt. lawyers divsn. 1985-87, bd. govs. 1985-89, treas. 1987-89, participation of women in bar com. 1987-98, professionalism com. 1990-97, bd. bar examiners rev. 1990-94, law-related edn. com. 1992-95, govt. lawyers divsn. 1981—), Dane County Bar Assn. (legis. com. 1980-81, long range planning com. 1990-97, law for the pub. com. 1993-94), Wis. Women's Network, U. Wis. Univ. League, Older Women's League, Fulbright Assn. Health, Legislative, Taxation, general. Home and Office: 125 Nautilus Dr Madison WI 53705-4329 E-mail: jbaldwin125@charter.net.

BALDWIN, JEFFREY KENTON, lawyer, educator; b. Palestine, Ill., Aug. 8, 1954; s. Howard Keith and Annabelle Lee (Kirts) B.; m. Patricia Ann Mathews, Aug. 23, 1975; children: Matthew, Katy, Timothy, Philip R. BS summa cum laude, Ball State U., 1976; JD cum laude, Ind. U., 1979. Bar: Ind. 1979, U.S. Dist. Ct. (so. dist.) Ind. 1979, U.S. Ct. Appeals (7th cir.) 1979, U.S. Dist. Ct. (no. dist.) Ind. 1984. Majority leader's staff Ind. Senate, Indpls., 1976; instr. Beer Sch. Real Estate, Indpls., 1977-78, Am. Inst. Paralegal Studies, Indpls., 1987—; dep. Office Atty. Gen., Indpls., 1979-81; mng. ptnr. Baldwin & Baldwin, Danville, Ind., 1979—. Agt. Nat. Attys. Title Assurance Fund, Vevay, Ind., 1983—; officer, bd. dirs. Baldwin Realty, Inc., Danville; conf. participant White House Conf. on Small Bus. (Ind. meeting 1994), congl. appointee, 1995; bd. dirs. Small Bus. Coun. Bd. dirs. Hendricks Civic Theatre, Inc.; organizer, Hendricks County Young Republicans, 1972; sec. Hendricks County Rep. Com., 1978-84; bd. dirs. Hendricks County Assn. for Retarded Citizens, Danville, 1982-86; cons. Hendricks County Right for Life, Brownsburg, Ind., 1984—; mem. philanthropy adv. com. Ball State U., Muncie, Ind., 1987—; judge Hendricks County unit Am. Cancer Soc., 1987; coordinator region 2 Young Leaders for Mutz, Indpls., 1987-88; cubmaster WaPaPh dist. Boy Scouts Am., 1988, S.M.E. chmn., 1988-89; steering com. Ind. Lawyers Bush/Quayle; founder, chmn. Christians for Positive Reform; candidate for Congress 7th Congl. Dist. of Ind.; del. to Annual Conf. South Ind. Conf. of United Meth. Ch., 1993, 95-98, 2000; host com. Midwest Rep. Leadership Conf., 1997; dist. coord. Hoosier Famiies for John Price for U.S. Senate; advisor John Price for Gov., 1999-2000; v.p. Danville Little League Baseball, 1998—. Recipient Presdl. award of honor Danville Jaycees, 1980; named hon. sec. State Ind., 1980. Mem. ABA, Ind. Bar Assn., Hendricks County Bar Assn., Indpls. Bar Assn., Internat. Platform Assn., Nat. Assn. Realtors, Ind. Assn. Realtors, Met. Indpls. Bd. Realtors (Hendricks County div.), Federalist Soc., Ind. Farm Bur., Nat. Fedn. Ind. Bus., Ind. C. of C., Danville C. of C. (sec. 1986), Moot Ct. Soc., Blue Key, Phi Soc. Methodist. General civil litigation, General practice, Legislative. Home: PO Box 63 Danville IN 46122-0063 E-mail: jbbfc@aol.com.

BALDWIN, JOHN, legal association administrator, lawyer; b. Salt Lake City, Feb. 9, 1954; BA, U. Utah., 1977, JD, 1980. Bar: Utah 1980, U.S. Dist. Ct. Utah 1980, U.S. Ct. Appeals (10th cir.) 1984. Assoc. Jardine, Linebaugh, Brown & Dunn, Salt Lake City, 1980-82; asst. atty. gen. Utah Atty. Gen.'s Office, Salt Lake City, 1982-85; dir. Utah Divsn. Securities, Salt Lake City, 1985-90; exec. dir. Utah State Bar, Salt Lake City, 1990—. Adj. assoc. prof. mgmt. Eccles Sch. Bus., U. Utah. Mem. N.Am. Securities Adminstrs. Assn. (bd. dirs. 1987-90, pres. 1988-89), U. Utah Young Alumni Assn. (bd. dirs. 1987-90), U. Utah Beehive Honor Soc. (bd. dirs. 1993-97), U. Utah Alumni Assn. (bd. dirs. 1995-97). Office: Utah State Bar 645 S 200 E # 310 Salt Lake City UT 84111-3837

BALDWIN, ROBERT FREDERICK, JR., lawyer; b. Syracuse, N.Y., Sept. 20, 1939; s. Robert Frederick and Marjorie Elizabeth (Thompson) Baldwin; m. Jeanella M. Mastrobattisto, Apr. 26, 1980; m. Margaret Melissa Richards, Aug. 19, 1962 (div.); children: Robert Frederick, Melissa Brooke. BSBA, Syracuse U., 1962, LLB, 1964. Bar: N.Y. 1964, U.S. Dist. Ct. (no. dist.) N.Y. 1980, Fla. 1982, U.S. Ct. Mil. Appeals 1965, U.S. Tax Ct. 1968, U.S. Ct. of Claims 1980, U.S. Supreme Ct. 1968. Assoc. Hancock, Estabrook, Ryan, Shove & Hust, Syracuse, NY, 1968—73; ptnr. Hancock, Estabrook Ryan, Shove & Hust, Syracuse, NY, 1974—84; prin. Green & Seifter, Attys, P.C., Syracuse, NY, 1984—96; ptnr. Baldwin & Sutphen, LLP, Syracuse, 1996—. Atty. Village Fayetteville, Fayetteville, 1974—94; adj. prof. law Syracuse U. Coll. Law, 1977—. Contbr. articles to profl. jours. Mem., deferred gifts com. ARC, CNY chpt., Syracuse, 1980—84; vice-chair Onondaga County Indsl. Devel. Agy., Syracuse, 1996—2002; chmn. DestiNY USA Benefits Maximization Com., Syracuse, 2002; bd. mem. Planned Parenthod CNY, Syracuse, 1978—84; trustee Fayetteville Cemetary Assn., 1974—80; bd. mem. UN Assn. CNY, Syracuse, 1971—74; trustee Fayetteville Libr. Assn., 1976—79; pres., mem. Onondaga Pastoral Counselling Ctr., Syracuse, 1994—2002; bd. govs. Citizens Found., Syracuse, 1973—76; mem. Assn. Retarded Citizens CNY, Syracuse, 1976—79; mem., steering com. Syracuse U. Tax Inst., 1980—2002. Comdr. USNR, 1965—85. Fellow: Am. Coll. Trust & Estate Counsel (chair, employee benefits com. 1997—2000); mem.: Estate Planning Coun. Ctrl. NY (pres. 1973—74), Nat. Assn. Estate Planning Couns. (pres. 1982—83), Onondaga County Bar Assn. (dir. 1976—79). Environmental, Probate (including wills, trusts), Estate taxation. Home: 5153 Burnside Dr Jamesville NY 13078 Office: Baldwin & Sutphen LLP 100 Clinton Sq Ste 320 Syracuse NY 13202 Office Fax: 315-477-5071. Personal E-mail: rbaldwin@baslaw.com.

BALDWIN, WILLIAM HOWARD, lawyer, retired foundation executive; b. Detroit, Feb. 21, 1916; s. Howard Charles and Ruth E. (Jensen) B.; m. Carol Lees, May 24, 1947; children: Susan, Jeffrey (dec.), Julie, Deborah. BA, Williams Coll., 1938; JD, U. Mich., 1941. Bar: Mich. 1941. Ptnr. Dykema Gossett, Detroit, 1970-77, of counsel, 1977—; chmn., trustee Kresge Found., Troy, Mich., 1963-87. Asst. U.S. prosecutor Nuremburg Trials, 1946. Served with USAAF, 1942-45, lt. col. (ret.). Mem. ABA, Mich. Bar Assn., Baker Hill Golf Club, Lake Sunapee Yacht Club. Republican. Episcopalian. also: PO Box 1308 New London NH 03257-1308 Home: 4620 Saint James Ave Vero Beach FL 32967-7336 E-mail: hbal@aol.com.

BALES, CANDICE MARIE, lawyer; b. Anchorage, Dec. 17, 1968; d. Clarence Sidney, Jr. and Marjorie Mae Bales. BBA in Bus. Mgmt., U. Alaska, Anchorage, 1991; JD, U. Pacific, Sacramento, 1994; LLM, Tulane U., 1995. Bar: Alaska 1994. Assoc. atty. Gorton and Assocs., Anchorage, 1996—97, Law Offices Dan Allan, Anchorage, 1998—2001; pvt. practice Palmer, Alaska, 2001—. Guest spkr. Alaska Family Resource Ctr., Palmer, 2001—. Recipient cert. of Appreciation, Alaska Family Resource Ctr., Inc., 2002. Mem.: ABA (mem. domestic violence com. 2002—), Alaska Bar Assn. Avocations: swimming, reading, logic puzzles. Family and matrimonial, Juvenile, Criminal. Office: PO Box 3722 Palmer AK 99645 Office Fax: 907-745-6924. Business E-Mail: candice@mtaonline.net.

BALES, JOHN FOSTER, III, retired lawyer; b. Springfield, Mass., July 17, 1940; s. John Foster II and Jean (Torrence) Bales; m. Jane Lee Black, Sept. 11, 1965; children: Patricia, Elizabeth, Susan. BS in Enring., Princeton U., 1962; LLB, U. Va., 1965; LLM, Georgetown U., 1972. Bar: U.S. Supreme Ct. 1972. Staff atty. U.S. SEC, Washington, 1970-72; assoc. Morgan, Lewis & Bockius, Phila., 1972-76, ptnr., 1976—2001. Bd. dirs. Ind. Publs., Inc. Trustee U.S. com. refugees, 1998—2001; vice-chmn. bd. trustees Ind. Presbyn. Med. Ctr., Phila., 1988—95, Acad. Natural Scis., Phila., 1995—; trustee Presbyn. Found., Phila., 1995—96, Immigration Refugee Svcs. Am., 1998—2001. Mem.: ABA, Colo. Bar Assn., Phila. Bar Assn., Pa. Bar Assn., Va. Bar Assn. Republican. Corporate, general, Health, Securities.

BALESTER, VIVIAN SHELTON, legal research consultant, retired lawyer; b. Pine Bluff, Ark., Dec. 10, 1931; d. Marvin W. and Mary Lena (Burke) Shelton; m. James Beverly Standerfer, Aug. 1, 1951 (dec. 1952); 1 child, Walter Eric; m. Raymond James Balester, Oct. 19, 1956; children; Carla Maria, Mark Shelton. BA cum laude, Vanderbilt U., 1955; MLS, Case Western Res. U., 1972, JD, 1975. Bar: Ohio 1975, U.S. Dist. Ct. (no. dist.) Ohio 1975. Ind. bibliographic and legal rsch. cons., Cleve., Washington, Nashville, 1959—. Head law libr. Squire, Sanders & Dempsey, Cleve., 1975-86; Ohio del. White House Conf. Librs./Info. Svcs., 1979; spkr. Law Librs. Nat. Conf., 1978, 80, 82; mem. adv. com. on profl. ethics Case Western Res. U., 1982-85. Lay reader St. Alban's Episc. Ch., 1978-2001, mem. vestry, 1977-79, 84-86, 98-2000, warden, 1979, 84; mem. coun. Diocese of Ohio, 1980-82, chmn. racial justice com., 1980-86, chmn. nominating com., 1982, del. Nat. Confs. on Faith Pub. Policy, Racism, 1982; dep. gen. Conv. of Episc. Ch. in U.S., 1985; mem. Women's Polit. Caucus, 1978-86; founder, co-chmn. Greater Cleve. Ann. Martin Luther King Celebration, 1980-86; convener AIDS Interfaith Coalition of Greater Cleve., 1987-94; mem. County Commrs. Adv. Com. on Handicapped, 1980-84; chmn. adolescent health coalition Fedn. Cmty. Planning, 1979-81, mem. health concerns commn., 1981-96, vice chairperson, 1986-96; regional chmn. alumni edn. Vanderbilt U., 1982-83; mem. cmty. adv. com. Cleve. Orch., 1983-95; bd. dirs. Hospice Coun. No. Ohio, 1979-81, vol. atty., 1982-85; bd. dirs. Interch. Coun. Greater Cleve., 1978-84, 86-88, 92, sec. bd., 1993-97, AIDS Housing Coun., 1987-94, Health Issues Task Force, 1988-94, Stopping AIDS is My Mission, 1993-96; mem. Ohio Com. Nat. Security, 1983; bd. dirs. WomenSpace, 1979-83. Recipient Merit Svc. award Cleve. Bar Assn., 1979, Outstanding Cmty. Svc. award Fedn. Cmty. Planning, 1980, Woman of Profl. Excellence award YWCA, 1983, Cleve. Mayor's award for volunteerism, 1984, Interchurch Coun. Ecumenical Adv. award, 1988, Western Res. Hist. Soc. Cmty. Leader award, 1989; NEH fellow, 1980. Democrat. Home and Office: 33227 Lakeshore Blvd Eastlake OH 44095-2408

BALICK, HELEN SHAFFER, retired judge; b. Bloomsburg, Pa. d. Walter W. and Clarissa K. (Bennett) Shaffer; m. Bernard Balick, June 29, 1967. JD, Dickinson Sch. Law, 1966, LLD, 1997. Bar: Pa. 1967, Del. 1969. Probate adminstr. Girard Trust Bank, Phila., 1966-68; pvt. practice law Wilmington, Del., 1969-74; staff atty. Legal Aid Soc. Del., Wilmington, 1969-71; master Family Ct. Del., New Castle County, 1971-74; bankruptcy judge, U.S. magistrate Dist. Del., Wilmington, 1974-80, bankruptcy judge, 1974-94, chief judge, 1994-98. Guest lectr. Dickinson Sch. Law, 1981-87; lectr. Dickinson Forum, 1982. Pres. bd. trustees Cmty. Legal Aid Soc., Inc., 1972—74; trustee Dickinson Sch. Law, 1985—2000; mem. Citizens Adv. Com., Wilmington, 1973—74, Wilmington Bd. Edn., 1974; bd. dirs. Kutz Home, 1999—2001, Jewish Hist. Soc., 1999—; active U. Del. Libr. Assocs., 1998—, sec., 2000—, v.p., 2001—02; bd. govs. The Dickinson Sch. Law, Pa. State U., 2000—. Recipient Women's Leadership award Del. State Bar Assn., 1997; named to Hall of Fame of Del. Women, 1994. Mem.: AAUW, Dickinson Sch. Law Gen. Alumni Assn. (exec. bd. 1977—80, 1987—2000, v.p. 1981—84, pres. 1984—87, Outstanding Alumni award 1991, Career Achievement award 1998), Turnaround Mgmt. Assn. (bd. dirs. 1995—97), Wilmington Women in Bus. (bd. dirs. 1980—83), Del. Alliance Profl. Women (Trailblazer award 1984), Del. Bar Assn., Am. Bankruptcy Inst., Am. Coll. Bankruptcy, Am. Judges Assn., Nat. Conf. Bankruptcy Judges (bd. govs. 1986), Fed. Bar Assn. Home: 2319 W 17th St Wilmington DE 19806-1330

BALKA, SIGMUND RONELL, lawyer; b. Phila., Aug. 1, 1935; s. I. Edwin and Jane (Chernicoff) B.; m. Elinor Bernstein, May 29, 1966. AB, Williams Coll., 1956; JD, Harvard U., 1959. Bar: Pa. and D.C. 1961, N.Y. 1969, U.S. Supreme Ct. 1966. Sr. atty. Lilco, Mineola, N.Y., 1969-70; v.p., gen. counsel Brown Boveri Corp., North Brunswick, N.J., 1970-75; asst. gen. counsel Power Authority State N.Y., N.Y.C., 1975-80; gen. counsel Krasdale Foods, Inc., N.Y.C., 1980—. Pres. Graphic Arts Coun. N.Y., 1980—. Chmn. Hunts Point Environ. Protection Coun., N.Y.C., 1980—, Soc. for a Better Bronx, 1985—; chair fellows, mem. vis. com. Williams Coll. Mus. of Art, 1996—99; exec. com. bd. trustees Queens Mus. of Art, 2001—; chmn. law com. N.Y.C. Cmty. Bd. 6, Queens, 1980—88, chmn. econ. devel. com., 1988—99; chmn. Bronx Borough Pres.'s Adv. Com. on Resource Recovery, 1988—90; bd. dirs. Bronx Arts Coun., 1981—, Greater N.Y. Met. Food Coun., 1986—, Jewish Repertory Theatre, 1987—, chmn., 2001—. Fellow Am. Bar Found.; mem. ABA (co-chmn. pro bono project corp. law dept. 1986-88, chmn. 1988-90, com. of corp. gen. counsel 1974—, planning chmn. 1994-96, membership chmn. 1996-98, pro bono chair 2000—), Am. Corp. Counsel Assn. (bd. dirs. Met. N.Y. chpt. 1987—, bd. dirs. Found. 1992-99), Assn. Bar City N.Y. Corporate, general. Office: Krasdale Foods Inc 400 Food Center Dr Bronx NY 10474-7098

BALKAN, KENNETH J. lawyer; b. N.Y.C., Oct. 18, 1948; s. Robert and Leona (Brenner) B.; m. Berta Hochman, Aug. 16, 1970; children: Richard, Lauren, Adam. BA, Fairleigh Dickinson U., 1969; JD, St. John's U., 1972. Bar: N.Y. 1973, U.S. Dist. Ct. (so. and ea. dists.) N.Y. 1974, U.S. Ct. Appeals (2d cir.) 1975, U.S. Supreme Ct. 1978. Law intern Dist. Atty.'s Office County of Queens, N.Y.C., 1971; assoc. Kroll, Edelman, Elser & Wilson, N.Y.C., 1972-77; ptnr. Wilson, Elser, Edelman & Dicker, N.Y.C., 1977-81, L'Abbate & Balkan, Garden City, N.Y., 1981-94, L'Abbate, Balkan, Colavita & Contini, L.L.P., Garden City, 1995-98, of counsel, 1999—. Mem. St. John's Law Rev., 1971-72; mediator for U.S. Dist. Ct. (ea. and so. dists.) N.Y.; adminstrv. judge Waterfront Commn. N.Y. Harbor; arbitrator, panel mem. NYSERB; arbitrator 10th Jud. Dist. Nassau County; atty. Client Fee Dispute Resolution Program; lectr. in field. Contbr. articles to profl. jours. Mem. Def. Rsch. Inst. Mem. ABA (tort and ins. practice law and litigation subcoms., nat. reporter ins. coverage, profl. officer and dirs. law com., constrn. industry com.), N.Y. State Bar Assn. (former mem. com. profl. discipline, mem. ins. negligence and compensation law com., trial lawyers com.), Nassau County Bar Assn. (coms., ins. law, fee conciliation, profl. ethics chair). General civil litigation, Insurance, Professional liability. Office: L'Abbate Balkan Colavita & Contini LLP 1050 Franklin Ave Garden City NY 11530-2929 E-mail: kbalkan@lbcclaw.com., kbalkan@aol.com.

BALKIND, BENJAMIN HART, lawyer; b. Bronx, Apr. 22, 1931; s. Max Z. Balkind and Katherine Jeanette Balking; m. Mary Josephine Lee; children: Sarah Kershaw, Benjamin Lee, Jonathan Buck. BA, Harvard U., 1953; JD, Yale U., 1957. Ptnr. Curtis Mallet Prevost et at, N.Y.C., 1959—. Judge Laurel Hollow Village. Office: Curtis Mallet Prevost et al 1564 Laurel Hollow Rd Syosset NY 11791-9636 Home: 1564 Laurel Hollow Rd Syosset NY 11791

BALKO, GEORGE ANTHONY, III, lawyer, educator; b. Bklyn., June 22, 1955; s. George Anthony Jr. and Settimia (Palumbo) B. AB, Yale U., 1977; JD, U. Calif., San Francisco, 1986. Bar: Mass. 1986, U.S. Dist. Ct. Mass. 1987, U.S. Dist. Ct. Conn. 1999, U.S. Ct. Appeals (1st cir.) 1987, D.C 1990. Assoc. Swartz & Swartz, Boston, 1986-87, Bowditch & Dewey, LLP, Worcester, Mass., 1987-95, ptnr., 1996—. Adj. prof. Anna Maria Coll., Paxton, Mass., 1988-2000, mem. paralegal studies adv. bd., 1988-95. Author: Risk Management for Nursing Homes: A Primer In Long-Term Care Adminstration Handbook, 1993, Ambulatory Care and the Law: Lien Claims Where None Exist As of Right, 1995; legal columnist Jour. of Workers Compensation, 1996-99. Mem. Rice Sch. PTA, Holden, Mass., 1989-93; bd. health Town of Holden, 1995-99, chmn. 1996-99; moderator, 1999—; pres., bd. dirs. Elm Park Ctr. for Early Childhood Edn., 1994-96, mem. 1993-97. Recipient Am. Jurisprudence award for Ins. Law Lawyers Coop. Pub. Co. and Bancroft Whitney Co., 1985. Roman Catholic. Avocations: history, travel, tennis. Insurance, Personal injury (including property damage), Product liability. Home: 4 Chestnut Hill Rd Holden MA 01520-1603 Office: Bowditch and Dewey LLP PO Box 15156 311 Main St Worcester MA 01615-0156 E-mail: gbalko@bowditch.com.

BALL, JAMES HERINGTON, retired lawyer; b. Kansas City, Mo., Sept. 20, 1942; s. James T. Jr. and Betty Sue (Herington) B.; m. Wendy Anne Wolfe, Dec. 28, 1964; children: James H. Jr., Steven Scott. AB, U. Mo., 1964; JD cum laude, St. Louis U., 1973. Bar: Mo. 1973. Asst. gen. counsel Anheuser-Busch, Inc., St. Louis, 1973-76; v.p., gen. counsel, sec. Stouffer Corp., Solon, Ohio, 1976-83; sr. v.p., gen. counsel Nestle Enterprises, Inc., Solon, 1983-91; gen. counsel, sr. v.p. Nestle USA, Inc., Glendale, Calif., 1991-99. Editor-in-chief St. Louis U. Law Jour., 1972-73. Bd. dirs. Alliance for Children's Rights, L.A., 1992-99, Am. Swiss Found., N.Y.C., 1996-99. Lt. comdr. USN, 1964-70, Vietnam. Mem. Mo. Bar Assn. Corporate, general, Mergers and acquisitions, Property, real (including real estate development, water).

BALL, MARKHAM (ROBERT BALL), lawyer, arbitrator, educator; b. Wilmington, Del., Mar. 24, 1934; s. Robert William and Helen (Slepicka) B.; m. Harriet Laura Janney, July 6, 1957; children: Laurence Markham, Richard Janney, Martha Harriet, Julia Helen. BA magna cum laude, Amherst Coll., 1956; BA with honors, Oxford (Eng.) U., 1958, MA, 1973; LLB, Harvard U., 1960. Bar: D.C. 1961, U.S. Supreme Ct. 1968. Law clk. U.S. Supreme Ct., Washington, 1960-61; assoc. Covington and Burling, Washington, 1961-64; asst. gen. counsel U.S. Office Econ. Opportunity, Washington, 1964-66; staff dir. U.S. Peace Corps, Washington, 1966-67; from assoc. to ptnr. Leva, Hawes, Symington, Martin and Oppenheimer, Washington, 1967-77; gen. counsel U.S. Agy. for Internat. Devel., Washington, 1977-79, mem. adv. com. on vol. fgn. aid, 1981-88; ptnr. Wald, Harkrader and Ross, Washington, 1980-85, Morgan, Lewis and Bockius, Washington, 1986-98, Holland and Knight, Washington, 1998—2002. Sr. fellow, dir. internat. arbitration program Internat. Law Inst., Washington, 2002—; lectr. Law Sch. U. Va., 1991—2001; adj. prof. Law Sch. Georgetown U., 2002—. Mem. adv. bd. Brasenose Coll. Charitable Found., Oxford, 1988—. Fellow Am. Bar Found.; Rhodes scholar Phi Beta Kappa, 1956-58. Mem. ABA, Internat. Bar Assn., Am. Arbitration Assn. (mem. internat. arbitration adv. panel 2002—), Alexandria Literary Soc. (sec. 1981—). Private international, Public international. Home: 7223 Stafford Rd Alexandria VA 22307-1806 Office: Internat Law Inst 1615 New Hampshire Ave Washington DC 20009 E-mail: mball@ili.org.

BALL, WILLIAM KENNETH, lawyer; b. DeQueen, Ark., Jan. 15, 1927; s. William P. and Lucille (Jeter) B.; m. Ella Hubbard Scaife, Dec. 28, 1950; children— Lucy Jane, William Ramsay, Charles Scaife. JD, U. Ark., 1953. Bar: Ark 1953, U. S. Supreme Ct., 1971. Law clk. to assoc. justice Ark. Supreme Ct., 1953-54; practice in Monticello, 1954-99; ptnr. Ball, Barton & Hoffman, 1958-99; city atty. Monticello, 1961-93; of counsel Ball, Barton & Hoffman, 1999—. Spl. justice Supreme Ct. Ark., 1975. Served with AUS, 1945-47, 50-52. Mem. Fellow Ark. Bar Found.; mem. Ark. Bar Assn., S.E. Ark. Bar Assn. (pres. 1957-58), Rotary (pres. 1962-63), Kappa Sigma, Delta Theta Phi. Presbyterian. Commercial, contracts (including sales of goods; commercial financing), General practice, Probate (including wills, trusts). Home: 104 Westminster Dr Monticello AR 71655-4814 Office: Ball Barton & Hoffman 106 W Oakland Ave Monticello AR 71655-4114

BALLANFANT, RICHARD BURTON, lawyer; b. Houston, Aug. 15, 1947; s. Richard Edward and Selma Autrey (Lewis) B.; children: Andrea Lavon, Benjamin Burton, Amy Lamer. BA, U. Tex., 1969, JD, 1972. Bar: Tex. 1972, U.S. Ct. Appeals (5th cir.) 1976, U.S. Ct. Appeals (11th cir.) 1981, U.S. Ct. Appeals (8th cir.) 1988, U.S. Dist. Ct. (so. dist.) Tex. 1974. Atty. FCC, Washington, 1973-74; asst. U.S. atty. Dept. Justice, Houston, 1974-78; sr. asst. city atty. City of Houston, 1978-80; atty. Shell Oil Co., Houston, 1980—. Mem. Citizens Adv. Bd. Met. Transit Auth., Houston, 1979-83; del. Rep. State Conv., 1978, 80, 82, 88, 90, 92, 96, del. to Rep. Nat. Conv., 1992; chmn. Personnel Bd., West University Pl., Tex., 1975-85, city councilman, 1999-2001; appt. to Battleship Tex. Adv. Bd., 1989. Capt. USAR, 1972-82. Named Outstanding Asst. U.S. Atty. Dept. Justice, 1976, 77. Mem. Houston Bar Assn., Fed. Bar Assn. (pres. 1979-80), ABA, Houston C. of C. (govt. relations com.). Episcopalian. Federal civil litigation, State civil litigation, Environmental. Home: 3123 Amherst St Houston TX 77005-3009

BALLANTINE, JOHN TILDEN, lawyer; b. Louisville, Feb. 26, 1931; s. Thomas Austin and Anna Marie (Pfeiffer) B.; m. Mary January Strode, May 15, 1954 (div. 1964); children: John T. Jr., William Clayton, Douglas C.; m. Beverley Jo Hackley, Dec. 8, 1967; 1 child, Susan Marie. BA with high distinction, U. Ky., 1952; JD, Harvard U., 1957. Bar: Ky. 1957, U.S. Ct. Appeals (6th cir.) 1958, U.S. Supreme Ct. 1982. Law clk. to presiding judge U.S. Dist Ct. (we. dist.) Ky., 1957-58; assoc. then ptnr. Ogden Newell & Welch PLLC, Louisville, 1958—. Mem. civil rules com. Ky. Supreme Ct., 1988—2002. Bd. dirs. Family and Children Agy., Louisville, 1965-75, pres., 1971-74; bd. dirs. Our Lady of Peace Hosp., Louisville, 1968-73, 88—, chmn., 1968-69, 91-93; bd. dirs. Met. United Way, Louisville, 1975-81; mem. Hist. Landmarks and Preservation Dists. Commn., Louisville, 1976-88; bd. dirs. Ky. Derby Festival, Louisville, 1975-81, v.p., 1975. 1st lt. USAF, 1952-54. Recipient Outstanding Young Man in Field of Law award Louisville Jaycees, 1966. Fellow Am. Coll. Trial Lawyers; mem. ABA, Ky. Bar Assn. (bd. govs. 1996-2002, ho. of dels. 1985-91, chmn. 1989-90, clients' security fund 1993-96, Ky. evidence rules rev. commn. 1995-2002, Outstanding Lawyer award 2003), Louisville Bar Assn. (bd. dirs. 1969-71, 88, 89, 92, 93, 96-2002, pres. 1970, profl. responsibility com. 1988-93, past chmn. physician-atty. com.), U.S. 6th Cir. Ct. Appeals Jud. Conf. (life), Fed. Def. and Corp. Counsel, Ky. Def. Counsel (pres. 1981-82), Louis D. Brandeis Am. Inn of Ct. (treas. 1997-98), Ky. Character and Fitness Com., Pendennis Club, The Law Club, Phi Beta Kappa. General civil litigation, Professional liability, Alternative dispute resolution. Office: Ogden Newell & Welch PLLC 1700 Citizens Plaza 500 W Jefferson St Ste 1700 Louisville KY 40202-2874 Business E-Mail: jballantine@ogdenlaw.com.

BALLARD, CATHERINE ANNE MARTINE, lawyer; b. Coronado, Calif., Sept. 24, 1952; d. Charles Ronald and Martine Mullaney Ballard; 1 child, Martine Alice. BA, U. Louisville, 1975; JD, Ohio State U., 1985. Bar: Ohio 1985, U.S. Ct. Appeals (6th cir.) 1988, U.S. Dist. Ct. (no. dist.) Ohio 1992. Law clk. to Hon. John D. Holschuh Fed. Dist., So. Dist. Ohio, Columbus, Ohio, 1985—87; assoc. Bricker & Eckler LLP, Columbus, 1987—94, ptnr., 1994—. Prin. Quality Mgmt. & Cons. Group, Columbus. Mem.: ABA, Soc. of Ohio Healthcare Attys. (pres. 2001—), Columbus Bar Assn., Ohio State Bar Assn. Health. Office: Bricker & Eckler LLP 100 S Third St Columbus OH 43215

BALLARD, ELIZABETH ANN, lawyer; b. Ada, Okla., Apr. 18, 1969; d. James R. and H. Arlene Treas. BS in Journalism, Okla. State U., 1991; JD, U. Okla., 1993. Bar: Okla. 1994, U.S. Dist. Ct. (ea., we. and no. dists.) Okla. 1994, U.S. Ct. Appeals (10th cir.). Assoc. Shelton Law Firm, Oklahoma City, Okla., 1994-96, Wilburn, Masterson & Smiling, Tulsa, 1997-99, Barkley, Titus, Hillis & Reynolds, Tulsa, 1999—. Pres. Tulsa Christian Legal Soc., 1998-99. Baptist. Alternative dispute resolution, Insurance, Product liability. Office: Barkley Titus Hillis & Reynolds 401 S Boston Ave Ste 2700 Tulsa OK 74103-4063

BALLMAN, B. GEORGE, lawyer; b. N.Y.C., Feb. 7, 1931; s. Bernard and Claire (Kahn) B.; m. Frances Hurst; children: Deborah, Lynda, B. George, Kimberly. AA, BS, Am. U., 1955, JD, 1957; LLM in Taxation, Georgetown U., 1980. Bar: Md. 1957, D.C. 1958, U.S. Supreme Ct. 1963. Former mng. prin. Conroy, Ballman & Dameron, Rockville, Md., 1981-97; of counsel Keegan & Sotelo PC, 2001-. Bd. dirs., treas. Bethesda-Chevy Chase Rescue Squad, 1948-50; co-founder, chancellor The Counsellors, 1963-64. Contbr. article to profl. jours. Mem. ABA, ATLA, Montgomery County Bar Assn. (treas. exec. com. 1960, chmn. law day com., 1962, pub. relations com. 1963, continuing legal edn. com. 1964, 65, 68, mem. grievance com. real estate sect. 1969-97), D.C. Bar, Montgomery County Bar Assn., Congl. Country Club. Republican. Episcopalian. Commercial, contracts (including sales of goods; commercial financing), Property, real (including real estate development, water), Estate taxation. Office: 8120 Woodmont Ave Bethesda MD 20814

BALLMAN, PATRICIA KLING, lawyer; b. Cin., May 1, 1946; d. John Joseph and Margaret Elizabeth (Stacy) Kling; children: Andrew J., Cara E. BS with honors, St. Louis U., 1967; JD with honors, Marquette U., 1977. Bar: Wisc. 1977, U.S. Dist. Ct. (ea. and we. dist Wisc.) 1980, U.S. Ct. Appeals (7th Cir.) 1983, U.S. Ct. Appeals (8th Cir.) 1986, U.S. Supreme Ct., 1986; Systems analyst Gen. Electric Co., Cin., 1967-70; lectr. computer scis. Marquette U., Milw., 1971; ptnr. Quarles & Brady, Milw., 1977—. Mem. fin. divsn., chair pers. subcom. United Way, Shorewood Bd. of Rev. Mem. ABA, Am. Acad. Matrimonial Lawyers, Wis. Bar Assn. (marital property com., specialization com., nominating com., ins. for mems. com., pres. 2002-03), Milw. Bar Assn. (chair courts com., past pres., dir., legis. com., chair ct. of appeal bench/bar com.). Appellate, General civil litigation, Family and matrimonial. Office: Quarles & Brady 411 E Wisconsin Ave #2040 Milwaukee WI 53202-4461*

BALMER, JAMES WALTER, lawyer; b. Pipestone, Minn., Sept. 26, 1948; m. Mary Beth Juntunen, 1988. BA, U. Minn., 1970, JD, 1973. Bar: Minn. 1973, Wis. 1984, U.S. Dist. Ct. Minn. 1974, U.S. Dist. Ct. (we. dist.) Wis. 1984, U.S. Ct. Appeals (7th and 8th cirs.) 1986; cert. advocate Am. Bd. Trial Advocacy, 2002—. Assoc. Donovan, McCarthy, Crassweller, Larson, Barnes & Magie, Duluth, Minn., 1973-75; ptnr. Falsani, Balmer, Berglund & Merritt, Duluth, 1975—. Chmn. 7th. Legis. Dist. Rep. Conv., 1982; active Kitchi Gammi Club. Mem. Minn. State Bar Assn. (cert. trial specialist 1988), Minn. Trial Lawyers Assn. (bd. govs. 1986-94), Duluth Trial Lawyers Assn. (sec. 1986-87, v.p. 1987-88, pres. 1988-89), Minn. Acad. Cert. Trial Lawyers, 11th Dist. Bar Assn., Am. Bd. Trial Advocacy, Nat. Bd. Trial Advocates (cert. specialist 1986, named Leading Minn. Atty. 1997—), Duluth Yacht Club (bd. dirs. 1988-90, commodore 1993-95). Roman Catholic. Avocations: sailing, jogging, downhill skiing. Insurance, Personal injury (including property damage), Workers' compensation. Office: 1200 Alworth Bldg 306 W Superior St Duluth MN 55802-1803

BALMER, THOMAS ANCIL, state supreme court justice; b. Longview, Wash., Jan. 31, 1952; s. Donald Gordon and Elisabeth Clare (Hill) B.; m. Mary Louise McClintock, Aug. 25, 1984; children: Rebecca Louise, Paul McClintock. AB, Oberlin Coll., 1974; JD, U. Chgo., 1977. Bar: Mass. 1977, D.C. 1981, U.S. Dist. Ct. Mass. 1977, Oreg. 1982, U.S. Dist. Ct. Oreg. 1982, U.S. Ct. Appeals (9th cir.) 1982, U.S. Ct. Appeals (D.C. cir.) 1983, U.S. Supreme Ct. 1987. Assoc. Choate, Hall & Stewart, Boston, 1977-79, Wald, Harkrader & Ross, Washington, 1980-82; trial atty. antitrust div. U.S. Dept. Justice, Washington, 1979-80; assoc. Lindsay, Hart, Neil & Weigler, Portland, Oreg., 1982-84, ptnr., 1985-90, Ater Wynne LLP, Portland, Oreg., 1990—93, 1997—2001; dep. atty. gen. State of Oregon, Salem, 1993-97; justice Oreg. Supreme Court, Salem, 2001—. Adj. prof. of law Northwestern Sch. Law Lewis and Clark Coll., 1983-84, 90-92. Contbr. articles to law jours. Active mission and outreach com. United Ch. of Christ, Portland, 1984-87, Met. Svc. Dist. Budget Com., Portland, 1988-90; bd. dirs. Multnomah County Legal Aid Svc., Inc., 1989-93, chair 1992-93; bd. dirs. Chamber Music Northwest, 1997—, Classroom Law Project, 2000—. Mem. ABA, Oreg. Bar Assn. (chmn. antitrust sect. 1986-87, mem. fed. practice and procedure com. 1999-2001). Home: 2521 NE 24th Ave Portland OR 97212-4831 Office: Oreg Supreme Ct Supreme Ct Bldg 1163 State St Salem OR 97310

BALTHASER, JAMES HARVEY, lawyer; b. Columbus, Ohio, Oct. 7, 1954; s. James R. and Kathryn F. (Herman) B.; m. Dianne A. Davis, June 21, 1975; 1 child, Kathryn Dee. BA, Ohio State U., 1975, JD, 1978. Bar: Ohio 1978, U.S. Tax Ct. 1984. Supr. Touche Ross & Co., Columbus, 1978-82; mem. Schwartz, Warren & Ramirez, Columbus, 1982-96; ptnr. Thompson Hine, LLP, Columbus, 1996—. Mem.: Am. Inst. CPA's, Columbus Bar Assn. Corporate, general, Estate planning, Taxation, general. Home: 9417 Avemore Ct Dublin OH 43017-9672 Office: Thompson Hine LLP 10 W Broad St Ste 700 Columbus OH 43215-3435 E-mail: jim.balthaser@thompsonhine.com.

BALVIG, FLEMMING, law educator; b. Slagelse, Denmark, Mar. 17, 1944; s. Evald and Ebba Larsen; m. Inge Leth-Sørensen, Jan. 7, 1968; children: Line, Jens Jakob. BA in Sociology, U. Copenhagen, 1966, MA in Sociology, 1972, JD, 1988. Asst. prof. Faculty of Law, U. Copenhagen, 1972—77, assoc. prof., 1977—96, prof., chmn., 1996—; dir. Inst. Legal Sci. U. Copenhagen, 1998—2002. Vis. prof. U. Oslo, 1988, 92, Calif. State U., Sacramento, 1991, U. Wuhan, China, 1997; chmn. com. for rsch. Min. of Justice, Copenhagen, 1998—; pres. The scandinavian Rsch. Coun. for Criminology, Min. of Nordic Countries, 1998—2000; bd. dirs. Criminological Sci. Coun., Coun. of Europe, Strasbourg, France, 1990—94, Ctr. of Drug Rsch., U. Aarhus, Denmark, 1997—2001. Author: Crime and Social Control, 1996, The Snow-White Image, 1988, The Violent Society, 2000, Youth at Risk, 2000. Recipient Fulbright Rsch. in the U.S. award, Fulbright Commn., 1991, Royal Danish Acad. of Sci. and Humanity, Copenhagen, 1988, Criminological Rsch. award, Coun. of Europe, 1986. Mem.: Com. for the Rsch. in Greenland, Centre Internat. de Sciences Criminelles de Paris (mem. sci. com. 1992—), Orgn. of Criminal Sci. (bd. dirs. 1997—). Home: Aakrogen 4 DK-2605 Broendby Denmark Mailing: Univ of Copenhagen Sct Peders Straede 19 DK-1453 Copenhagen Denmark

BAMBERGER, MICHAEL ALBERT, lawyer; b. Berlin, Feb. 29, 1936; s. Fritz and Kate (Schwabe) B.; m. Phylis Skloot, Dec. 19, 1965; children—Kenneth A., Richard A. AB magna cum laude, Harvard U., 1957, LLB magna cum laude, 1960. Bar: N.Y. 1960, D.C. 1982. Assoc. Proskauer Rose Goetz & Mendelsohn, N.Y.C., 1960-69, Finley, Kumble, Wagner, Heine, Underberg, Manley, Myerson & Casey, N.Y.C., 1970, ptnr., 1971-87, Sonnenschein Nath & Rosenthal, N.Y.C., 1987—. Adj. prof. Benjamin Cardozo Sch. Law, Yeshiva U., 2001—; mem. faculty various legal seminars and insts.; mem. joint editl. bd. on uninc. orgn. acts. ABA/Nat. Conf. Commrs. on Uniform State Laws, 1994—, chair, 2003—; chmn. bd. Transcontinental Music Publs., New Jewish Music Press. Author: Reckless Legislation: How Lawmakers Ignore the Constitution, 2000; co-editor: State Limited Partnership Laws, 7 vols. and supplements, 1987—, State Limited Liability Company and Partnership Laws, 5 vols. and supplements, 1993-2003; editor Harvard Law Rev., 1958-60; contbr. articles to profl. jours. Vice chair bd. overseers Hebrew Union Coll.-Jewish Inst. Religion, N.Y.C.,; v.p., bd. dirs. Leo Baeck Inst., Selfhelp Cmty. Svcs.; bd. dirs. Ctr. Jewish History. Mem. ABA (com. on ltd. partnerships 1980—, chair com. on tech. and intellectual property 1992-95, chair, ad hoc com. on security interests in intellectual property 1990-98), First Amendment Lawyers Assn., N.Y. State Bar Assn. (exec. com. comml. and fed. litigation sect. 1989-93), Assn. Bar City N.Y. (com. on fed. legislation 1979-82, com. on civil rights 1982-86, chmn. 1983-86), N.Y. County Lawyers Assn. (securities com. 1980-82). Jewish. Constitutional, Corporate, general, Libel. Home: 172 E 93d St New York NY 10128-3711 Office: Sonnenschein Nath & Rosenthal 1221 Ave of Americas New York NY 10020-1001

BAMBERGER, PHYLIS SKLOOT, judge; b. N.Y.C., May 2, 1939; d. George Joseph and Martha (Wechselblatt) S.; m. Michael A. Bamberger, Dec. 19, 1965; children: Kenneth, Richard. BA, Bklyn. Coll., 1960; LLB, NYU, 1963. Bar: N.Y. 1963, U.S. Supreme Ct. 1967, U.S. Ct. Appeals (2d cir.) 1965, U.S. Dist. Ct. (so. dist.) N.Y. 1966, U.S. Dist. Ct. (ea. dist.) N.Y. 1979. Assoc. Legal Aid Soc., N.Y.C., 1963-67; assoc.-in-charge criminal appeals Bur. Legal Aid Soc., N.Y.C., 1967-72; atty.-in-charge, fed. def. svcs. unit/appeal Legal Aid Soc., N.Y.C., 1972-88; judge N.Y. State Ct. Claims designated to sit in the N.Y. State Supreme Ct., Bronx County, 1988—. Mem. N.Y. State Chief Judge's Jury Project, 1993-94; mem. com. on alts. to incarceration Office of Ct. Adminstrn., 1994-96, mem. criminal law and procedure adv. com., 1994-98, co-chair 1998-; mem. N.Y. State Chief Judge's Commn. on the Jury, 2003-, Jury Project, Office of Ct. Adminstrn., 2003-. Author: Criminal Appeals Handbook, 1984; editor, contbr. Practice Under the Federal Sentencing Guidelines, 1988, 90, 93, 2000 (also supplements); author, compiler Recent Developments in State Constitutional Law, 1985; contbr. numerous articles to publs. Mem. ABA, N.Y. State Bar assn. (co-chair presdl. com. on problems in criminal justice sys. 1986-88, mem. com. on the future of the profession), Assn. of Bar of City of N.Y. (chair com. on provision of legal svcs. to persons of moderate means 1995-98, 21st century com. 1992-95, chair com on probation 1993-94), Phi Beta Kappa. Office: Bronx County Courthouse 851 Grand Concourse Bronx NY 10451-2937

BANCROFT, ALEXANDER CLERIHEW, lawyer; b. N.Y.C., Feb. 6, 1938; s. Harding F. and Jane (Northrop) B.; m. Margaret A. Armstrong, Mar. 14, 1964; 1 dau., Elizabeth. AB, Harvard U., 1960, LL.B., 1963. Mem. Shearman & Sterling, N.Y.C., 1964—, ptnr., 1973—. Home: 15 E 91st St New York NY 10128-0648 Office: 599 Lexington Ave New York NY 10022-6030

BANCROFT, MARGARET ARMSTRONG, lawyer; b. Mpls., May 9, 1938; d. Wallace David and Mary Elizabeth (Garland) Armstrong; m. Alexander Clerihew Bancroft, Mar. 14, 1964; 1 child, Elizabeth Armstrong. BA magna cum laude, Radcliffe Coll.-Harvard U., 1960; JD cum laude, NYU, 1969. Bar: N.Y. 1971. Reporter Mpls. Star and Tribune, 1960-61, UPI, N.Y., N.J., 1961-66; ptnr. Law Firm of Dechert LLP. Adj. prof. law NYU Sch. Law. Bd. dirs., mem. exec. com. Vis. Nurse Svc. N.Y.; pres. Vis. Nurse Svc. N.Y. Home Care, Inc. Mem. ABA (bus. law sect.), N.Y. State Bar Assn. (securities regulation com.), Assn Bar City N.Y. (com. on investment mngmt. regulation), Am. Law Inst. Corporate, general, Mergers and acquisitions, Securities. Office: Law Firm of Dechert LLP 30 Rockefeller Plz Fl 22 New York NY 10112-2200

BAND, JORDAN CLIFFORD, lawyer; b. Cleve., Aug. 15, 1923; s. Samuel Melville and Helen Rita (Krause) B.; m. Alice Jeanne Glickson, Apr. 27, 1946; children: Terril R., Stefanie Band Allweiss, Claudia Band McCord. Student, U. Ala., 1943-44; BBA, Case Western Res. U., 1947, LLB, 1948. Bar: Ohio 1948, U.S. Dist. Ct. (no. dist.) Ohio 1948. Assoc. Ulmer & Berne, Cleve., 1948-56, ptnr., 1956-94, ret., 1994—. Bd. dirs. numerous cos. Chmn. Greater Cleve. Conf. on Religion and Race, 1964-66, Greater Cleve. Project, 1978-81; nat. chmn. Nat. Jewish Community Rels. Adv. Coun., N.Y.C., 1967-70; presiding officer Cleve. Community Rels. Bd., 1970-90; nat. vice chmn. Am. Jewish Com., 1976-79; legal counsel Jewish Community Fedn. Cleve., 1984-87, also trustee, officer numerous civic and non-profit orgns. Recipient Kane Leadership award Jewish Community Fedn., 1961, Bronze medal, 1978, Cert. of Appreciation, City of Cleve., 1970-88, Cert. of Recognition, Ohio Senate, 1987. Mem. ABA, Ohio Bar Assn., Cuyahoga County Bar Assn., Cleve. Bar Assn., Order of Coif. Democrat. Avocations: community relations, civic activities, tennis. Corporate, general, Mergers and acquisitions, Property, real (including real estate development, water). Office: 18483 Parkland Dr Shaker Heights OH 44122-3450

BANDER, EDWARD JULIUS, law librarian emeritus, lawyer; b. Boston, Aug. 10, 1923; s. Abraham and Ida (Lendman) B. BA, Boston U., 1949, LLB, 1951; MLS, Simmons Coll., 1955. Bar: Mass. 1951. Asst. reference libr. Harvard U., Cambridge, Mass., 1954-55; libr. U.S. Ct. Appeals (1st cir.), Boston, 1955-60; asst. libr., asst. prof. NYU, N.Y.C., 1960-70, assoc. prof., curator, assoc. libr., 1970-78; prof., libr. Suffolk U. Law Sch., Boston, 1978-90, libr., prof. emeritus, 1991—. Author: Mr. Dooley and the Choice of Law, 1963, Mr. Dooley and Mr. Dunne, 1981, Justice Holmes Ex Cathedra, 1966, 91, Searching the Law, 1986, Shakespeare on Lawyers and the Law, 1998; co-editor bi-monthly rev. law books, 1990—. Served with USN, 1942-46. Recipient Dean Frederick A. McDermott award Suffolk U. Student Bar Assn., 1980. Mem. Assn. Am. Law Schs., New Eng. Law Libr. Democrat. Jewish. Office: 50 Church St Concord MA 01742-3050 E-mail: ebander@acad.suffolk.edu.

BANDY, JACK D. lawyer; b. Galesburg, Ill., June 19, 1932; s. Homer O. and Gladys L. (Van Winkle) B.; m. Betty McMillan, Feb. 18, 1956; children: Jean A. Bandy Abramson, D. Michael, Jeffery K. BA, Knox Coll., 1954; LLB, U. La Verne, 1967. Bar: Calif. 1972, U.S. Supreme Ct. 2000. Safety engr. Indsl. Indemnity Co., L.A., 1960-65, sr. safety engr., 1965-69, resident safety engr., 1969-72; trial atty. Employers Ins. of Wausau, L.A., 1972-79; mng. atty. Wausau Ins. Cos., L.A., 1979-92; arbitrator, mediator L.A. Superior Mcpl. Ct., 1992—. Contbr. articles to profl. jours. Youth leader YMCA, Mission Hills, Calif., 1965-72. Served with U.S. Army, 1954-56. Mem. Calif. State Bar, Am. Soc. Safety Engrs. (cert. safety profl.). Alternative dispute resolution, Insurance, Personal injury (including property damage). E-mail: bandy_jack@msn.com.

BANGS, WILL JOHNSTON, lawyer; b. N.Y.C., Oct. 7, 1923; s. Lawrence Cutler and Alma Elizabeth (Johnston) B.; m. Judith Esther Lindhal, July 27, 1957; children: Marjorie Elizabeth, Martha Ellen Alice. BA, Middlebury Coll., 1948; LLB, U. Mich., 1953. Bar: Mass. 1953, U.S. Dist. Ct. (Mass. dist.) 1955, U.S. Supreme Ct. 1973. Staff atty. Liberty-Mut. Ins. Co., Boston, 1953-56; sr. ptnr. Choate, Hall & Stewart, Boston, 1956—. Mem. fin. com., Concord, Mass., 1968-70; mem. Carlisle (Mass.) Conservation Commn., 1972-78, Carlisle Town Rep. Com., 1982-89. With U.S. Army, 1943-46. Fellow Am. Coll. Trial Lawyers; mem. ABA, Boston Bar Assn., Somerset Club, Concord Country Club. Home: 119 Bingham Rd Carlisle MA 01741-1537 Office: Exchange Pl 53 State St Boston MA 02109-2804

BANKS, EDISON G., II, lawyer; b. Whitesburg, Ky., Oct. 30, 1960; s. Edison G. Sr. and G. Sue (Flannery) B. AS, U. Ky., 1980, BA, 1982, JD, 1985. Bar: U.S. Dist. Ct. (ea. dist.) Ky., U.S. Ct. Appeals (6th cir.). Atty. Gullitt, Combs, Holliday & James, Howard, Ky., 1985-86, Wood & Banks, Whitesburg, Ky., 1987-93, Banks Law Office, Whitesburg, Ky., 1994—; from asst. commonwealth atty. to asst. county atty. 47th Jud. Cir. of Ky., Whitesburg, 1987—2000, atty., 2001—. Bd. atty. Lecher County Bd. Edn., Whitesburg, 1996-97; chmn. bd. Lether Vol. Fire and Rescue, 1992-96. Mem. ABA, Ky. Bar Assn., Whitesburg Lions Club, Ky. Trial Lawyers Assn., Am. Trial Lawyers Assn., Whitesburg Lions Club, Phi Beta Kappa, Phi Alpha Theta, Delta Theta Phi. Baptist. Office: Banks Law Office 128 W Main St Whitesburg KY 41858

BANKS, ERIC KENDALL, lawyer; b. St. Louis, Aug. 21, 1955; s. Willie James Banks Jr. and Grace (Kendall) Palmer; children: Brittany Renee, Bryson Kendall. BSBA, U. Mo., St. Louis, 1977; JD, U. Mo., Columbia, 1980. Bar: Mo. 1980, Ill. 1988, U.S. Dist. Ct. (we. dist.) Mo. 1980, U.S. Dist. Ct. (ea. dist.) Mo. 1984, U.S. Ct. Appeals (8th cir.) 1984, U.S. Ct. Appeals (D.C. cir.) 1998, U.S. Tax Ct. 1988, U.S. Supreme Ct. 1996. Asst. gen. counsel Mo. Pub. Svc. Commn., Jefferson City, 1980-84; asst. atty. Office Circuit Atty., St. Louis, 1984-87; pvt. practice, St. Louis, 1987-91, Clayton, Mo., 1991-92; corp. counsel Siegel-Robert, St. Louis, 1992-97; city counselor City of St. Louis, 1997-99; ptnr. Thompson, Coburn, 1999—, Thompson Coburn, St. Louis, 1999—. Adj. prof. civil law St. Louis U. Law Sch., 1987-92, Washington U. Sch. law, 1991; sec. bd. dirs. Black Leadership Tng. Program, St. Louis, 1975-77. Sec. bd. dirs. Wesley House Assn.; bd. trustees Mo. U. Law Sch. Found. St. Louis Met. Leadership Program fellow, 1975-77. Mem. ABA (labor and employment com.), Nat. Bar Assn., Bar Assn. Met. St. Louis, Mo. Bar Assn. (adminstrv. law com., com. counsel), Mound City Bar Assn., Bar Assn. Met. St. Louis. Clubs: Toastmasters Internat. (adminstrv. v.p. 1983, William Tellman award 1982). Lutheran. Avocations: Karate, reading, photography, public speaking, community work. Home: 2755 Russell Blvd Saint Louis MO 63104-2137 Office: Thompson Coburn One US Bank Plz Saint Louis MO 63101 Fax: (314) 552-7256. E-mail: ebanks@thompsoncoburn.com.

BANKS, FRED LEE, JR., lawyer, former state supreme court presiding justice; b. Jackson, Miss., Sept. 1, 1942; s. Fred L. and Violet (Mabry) B.; m. Taunya Lovell, June 5, 1967 (div. 1975); children: Rachel R., Jonathan L.; m. Pamela Gipson, Jan. 28, 1978; 1 child, Gabrielle G. BA, Howard U., 1965, JD cum laude, 1968. Bar: Miss. 1968, U.S. Dist. Ct. (no. and so. dists.) Miss. 1968, U.S. Ct. Appeals (5th cir.) 1968, D.C. 1969, U.S. Supreme Ct. 1971. Ptnr. Banks, Owens & Byrd and predecessor firms Anderson, Banks, Nichols & Stewart; Anderson, Banks, Nichols & Leventhal; Anderson & Banks, Jackson, 1968-85; rep. Miss. Ho. of Reps., 1975; judge Miss. 7th Cir. Ct., Hinds County and Yazoo County, 1985-91; assoc. justice Miss. Supreme Ct., Jackson, 1991—2000; presiding justice Miss. Supreme Ct., Miss., 2000—01; ptnr. Phelps Dunbar, LLP. Chair Spl. Com. on Jud. Campaign Intervention, 2002; mem. Miss. Bd. Bar Admissions, 1978-81; pres. State Mut. Fed. Savs. and Loan, Jackson, 1976-89; mem. minority adv. com. U. Miss. Sch. of Law. Bd. dirs. NAACP, 1981—; mem. Nat. Adv. Com. for the Edn. of Disadvantaged Children, 1978-80; del. Dem. Nat. Conv., 1976, 1980; co-mgr. Miss. Carter-Mondale presidl. campaign, 1976; legislator Miss. Ho. of Reps., Jackson, 1976-85; bd. visitors Miss. Coll. Sch. of Law. Mem. ABA, Magnolia Bar Assn., Nat. Bar Assn., Hinds County Bar Assn., Am. Inns of Ct., Charles Clark Inn, Miss. Bar Assn., D.C. Bar Assn., Sigma Pi Phi. Roman Catholic. Home: 976 Metairie Rd Jackson MS 39209-6948 Office: 200 S Lamar St Ste 500 Jackson MS 39201

BANKS, JOHN ROBERT, JR., lawyer; b. Balt., Mar. 15, 1958; s. John Robert and Ida Carol (Cromer) B. BA, Coll. William and Mary, Williamsburg, Va., 1980; JD, U. Houston, 1983. Bar: Tex. 1983, U.S. Dist. Ct. (so. dist.) Tex. 1983; cert. bus. bankruptcy law Tex. Bd. Legal Specialization. Assoc. Levin & Kasner, PC fka Levin, Roth & Kasner, PC, Houston, 1983-96; pvt. practice Houston, 1997; ptnr. Mason, Coplen & Banks, LLP, Houston, 1998-99; shareholder Mason, Coplen, Shuchart, Hutchins & Banks, PC, Houston, 2000—. Dir. Cmty. Assn. Inst. Greater Houston, 1995-97, chmn. amb.'s subcom., 1995-97, chmn. legal com., 1995, vice-chmn. legal com., 1994, chmn. mem. svc. com., 1998; adminstrv. bd. Chapelwood United Meth. Ch., 1997-01, trustee, 1998-01. Avocation: philately. Bankruptcy, General civil litigation, Commercial, consumer (including collections, credit). Office: Mason Coplen Shuchart Hutchins & Banks PC Attys at Law 7500 San Felipe St Ste 700 Houston TX 77063-1709 E-mail: johnbanksjr@msn.com.

BANKS, LINDA T. legal assistant, massage therapist; b. Montgomery, Ala., Apr. 23, 1948; d. Robert Tillman and Margaret (Jackson) Tanner; m. R.O. Banks, Dec. 21, 1971 (div. Apr. 1978); 1 child, Charles R. BA, Brenau Coll., Gainesville, Ga., 1970; cert., Acad. Somatic Healing Arts, Atlanta, 1998. Cert. massage therapist. Legal asst. Powell, Goldstein et al, Atlanta, 1978-81, Martin & Young, Atlanta, 1981-84; adminstrv. asst. Yokogawa Corp., Peachtree City, Ga., 1984-86; legal asst. Sanders, Mottola & Haugen, Newnan, Ga., 1986-89; flight attendant ValuJet, Atlanta, 1996-98; self-employed massage therapist, Atlanta and Newnan, 1998—; legal asst. Sutherland Asbill & Brennan, Atlanta, 1989—2002, Alston & Bird LLP, 2002—. Bd. dirs. Manget-Brannon Alliance for Arts, Newnan, 1984; mem., patron Newnan Cmty. Theatre Co., 1981—. Mem. Internat. Massage Assn., Mu Phi Epsilon. Democrat. Episcopal/Methodist. Avocations: playing keyboards in local band, acting in local theatre, tennis, volunteer work for senior citizens. Home: 27 Chestnut Dr Newnan GA 30263-2201 Office: Alston & Bird LLP 1201 W Peachtree St Atlanta GA 30309

BANKS, ROBERT SHERWOOD, lawyer; b. Newark, Mar. 28, 1934; s. Howard Douglas and Amelia Violet (Del Bagno) B.; m. Judith Lee Henry; children— Teri, William; children by previous marriage— Robert, Paul, Stephen, Roger, Gregory, Catherine. AB, Cornell U., 1956, LL.B., 1958. Bar: N.J. 1959, N.Y. 1968. Practice law, Newark, 1958-61; atty. E.I. duPont, Wilmington, Del., 1961-67; with Xerox Corp., Stamford, Conn., 1967-88, v.p., gen. counsel, 1975-88; sr. counsel Latham & Watkins, N.Y.C., 1988-89; gen. counsel Keystone Holdings, 1989-92. Bd. dirs. Cornell U. Found.; mem. panel of mediators, neutral advisors Ctr. for Pub. Resources. Mem. adv. coun. Cornell Law Sch.; past trustee U.S. Supreme Ct. Hist. Soc.; past bd. dirs. Ctr. for Pub. Resources. Mem. ABA, N.Y. Bar Assn., Am. Arbitration Assn. (panel arbitrators), Am. Judicature Soc. (exec. com., bd. dirs., pres. 1989-91), Cornell Law Assn., Am. Corp. Counsel Assn. (bd. dirs., chmn. 1982-83), Atlantic Athletic Club, Jonathan's Landing Club. Corporate, general. E-mail: RSBSR@mindspring.com.

BANNEN, CAROL, information resources director; b. St. Paul, 1951; m. John T. Bannen; children: Ryan, Kelly, Erin. BA, Coll. St. Catherine, St. Paul, 1973. Law libr. Peat Marwick & Mitchell, Mpls., 1972—75; dir. info. resources Reinhart, Boerner, Van Deuren, Milw., 1975—. Mem. Law Librs. Assn. Wis. (pres. 1987-88), Spl. Librs. Assn. (chmn. ins. and employee benefits div. 1986-87), Libr. Coun. Met. Milw., Am. Assn. Law Librs. Office: Reinhart Boerner Van Deuren 1000 N Water St Ste 2100 Milwaukee WI 53202-3197

BANOFF, SHELDON IRWIN, lawyer; b. Chgo., July 10, 1949; BSBA in Acctg., U. Ill., 1971; JD, U. Chgo., 1974. Bar: Ill. 1974, U.S. Tax Ct. 1974. Ptnr. Katten Muchin Zavis Rosenman, Chgo., 1974—. Chmn. tax conf. planning com. U. Chgo. Law Sch., 1993-94. Co-editor Jour. of Taxation, 1984—; contbr. articles to profl. jours. Mem. ABA, Chgo. Bar Assn. (fed. taxation com., mem. exec. coun. 1980—, chmn. large law firm com., 1999-2000), Am. Coll. Tax Counsel. Corporate taxation, Taxation, general, Personal income taxation. Office: Katten Muchin Zavis Rosenman 525 W Monroe St Ste 1600 Chicago IL 60661-3693 E-mail: sheldon.banoff@kmzr.com.

BANTA, DON ARTHUR, retired lawyer; b. Chgo., Mar. 10, 1926; s. George A. and Grace Regina (Donnelly) B.; m. Mickey Edwards, Mar. 31, 1951; children: Stephanie, Meredith, John, Hillary. BS, Northwestern U., 1948, LLB, 1950. Bar: Ill. 1950, U.S. Ct. Appeals (7th cir.) 1951, U.S. Dist. Ct. (no. dist.) Ill. 1953, U.S. Ct. Appeals (6th cir.) 1963, U.S. Supreme Ct. 1967, U.S. Ct. Appeals (3d cir.) 1972, U.S. Ct. Appeals (11th cir.) 1982. Assoc. Vogel & Bunge, Chgo., 1950-51; atty. Montgomery Ward & Co., Chgo., 1951-53; assoc. Pruitt & Grealis, Chgo., 1953-55; ptnr. Naphin Banta & Cox and predecessor firms, Chgo., 1956-90, Banta Hennessy & Graefe, Chgo., 1990-99, Michael Best & Friedrich, Chgo., 1999—2001; ret., 2001. Cons. Chgo. Vol. Legal Svcs. Found., 1983—, arbitrator and mediator, 2002-. Author: (with others) Labor Arbitration-A Practical Guide for Advocates. 1990, Supplement to How Arbitration Works 1985-89, 1991, How Arbitration Works, 5th edit., 1997, Discipline and Discharge in Arbitration, 1998. Bd. edn. Deerfield (Ill.) Sch. Dist., 1964-70, pres., 1968-69. With U.S. Army, 1944-46, ETO. Fellow Coll. Labor and Employment Lawyers; mem. ABA (labor sect. com. on alternative dispute resolution in labor and employment law), Ill. State Bar Assn., Chgo. Bar Assn., Phi Delta Phi, Delta Tau Delta, Union League Club. Roman Catholic. Federal civil litigation, General civil litigation, Labor (including EEOC, Fair Labor Standards Act, labor-management relations, NLRB, OSHA). Home: 1000 Lake Shore Plz 36B Chicago IL 60611-1308 E-mail: outerdrive@msn.com.

BANTON, STEPHEN CHANDLER, lawyer; b. St. Louis; s. William Conwell and Ruth (Chandler) B. AB, Bowdoin Coll., 1969; JD, Washington U., St. Louis, 1973, MBA, 1974. Bar: Mo. 1973, U.S. Dist. Ct. (ea. and we. dists.) Mo. 1973. Asst. pros. atty. St. Louis County, 1973-75; sole practice Clayton, Mo., 1975-83; ptnr. Quinn, Ground & Banton, Manchester, Mo., 1983—. Pres. Coll. for Living, 1997-98. Exploring chmn. St. Louis coun. Midland Dist. Scouts, 1975-77; pres. Am. Youth Hostels Ozarks area, 1976-80; trustee St. Louis Art Mus., 1985-94; mem. Rockwood Sch. Bd., 1997—. Served with USMC. Recipient Leadership award Lafayette Community Assn., 1983, Service award The Meramec Palisades Community Assn., 1985, Service award Profl. Remodeling Assn., 1985, Service award St. Louis Symphony Orch., 1985. Mem. ABA, Mo. Bar Assn., St. Louis County Bar Assn., Bar Assn. Met. St. Louis, Assn. Trial Lawyers Am., St. Louis County League of C. of C. (pres. 1978), West Port C. of C. (bd. dirs. 1978-81, Service award 1983), Rotary (pres. Ballwin club 1997-98), Toastmasters (adminstrv. v.p.), Lions (pres. 1977), Kiwanis (pres. West County club 2001-02), Gideons (pres. Frontenac 1999-2002). Republican. General practice, Legislative, Workers' compensation. Office: Quinn Ground & Banton 14611 Manchester Rd Ballwin MO 63011-3700 Home: 929 Saint Paul Rd Ballwin MO 63021-6061

BARACK, PETER JOSEPH, lawyer, educator; b. Cleve., Nov. 3, 1943; s. Louis Barry and Florence (Schenberg) B.; m. Elise Hoffman, June 6, 1971; children: Sarah, Jonathan, David. AB summa cum laude, Princeton U., 1965; BPhil, Oxford (Eng.) U., 1967; JD magna cum laude, Harvard U., 1970. Bar: Ill. 1970, U.S. Ct. Appeals (7th cir.) 1976, U.S. Supreme Ct. 1978. Asst. prof. bus. adminstrn. Harvard U. Grad. Sch. Bus. Adminstrn., Cambridge, Mass., 1970-72; asst. prof. law Northwestern U. Sch. Law, Chgo., 1972-74, dir. JD-MM joint degree program, 1972-80, assoc. prof., 1974-79, adj. prof. corp. law, Edward Avery Harriman lectr., 1979—, adj. prof. fin. Kellogg Grad. Sch. Mgmt., 1998—; ptnr. Levy and Erens, Chgo., 1969-74; founding, sr. ptnr. Barack, Ferrazzano, Kirschbaum Perlman & Nagelberg, LLC, Chgo., 1984—. Of counsel Mayer, Brown & Platt, Chgo., 1977-79; lectr. in field; pres. Chgo. Mgmt. Group, Inc., 1972—; bd. dirs. Christian Dior Perfumes, Inc., Duty Free Stores, Inc., Hillels of Ill. Contbr. articles to profl. jours. Pres. Highland Park (Ill.) Libr., 1982-84. Recipient Lt. John A. Larkin, Jr. Meml. prize, 1965; Marshall scholar, 1965; Nuffield scholar, 1966. Mem. ABA, Ill. State Bar Assn., Chgo. Bar Assn., Chgo. Coun. Lawyers, Assn. Marshall Scholars. Corporate, general, Private international, Securities. Home: 1379 Sheridan Rd Highland Park IL 60035-3406 Office: 333 W Wacker Dr Ste 2700 Chicago IL 60606-1227 E-mail: peter.barack@bfkpn.com.

BARAN, JAN WITOLD, lawyer, educator; b. Ingolstadt, Germany, May 14, 1948; came to U.S., 1951; s. Jerzy Leopold and Leonce Sidonie (Vanden Bussche) B.; m. Kathryn Kavanagh, June 16, 1979; children: Brendan Jerzy, Maria Leonce, Elise Jett, Anna Margaret. BA, Ohio Wesleyan U., 1970; JD, Vanderbilt U., 1973. Bar: Tenn. 1973, D.C. 1976, U.S. Dist. Ct. D.C. 1980, U.S. Ct. Appeals D.C. 1980, U.S. Ct. Appeals (10th cir.) 1994, U.S. Supreme Ct. 1980, U.S. Ct. Appeals (5th cir) 2001. Legal counsel Nat. Rep. Congl. Com., Washington, 1975-77; exec. asst. Fed. Election Commn., Washington, 1977-79; assoc. Baker & Hostetler, Washington, 1979-81, ptnr., 1981-85, Wiley, Rein & Fielding, Washington, 1985—. Gen. counsel, George Bush for Pres., Inc., 1987-88; gen. counsel, Bush-Quayle, Inc., 1988; lectr., co-chair Practicing Law Inst., Corp. Polit. Activities, Washington, 1978—. Author: The Election Law Primer for Corporations, 1984, 88, 92, 2000, 2002. Chmn. nat. adv. bd. Jour. of Law and Politics, 1983—; gen. counsel Am. bicentennial Presdl. Inaugural Inc., 1989, Rep. Nat. Com., 1989-92; mem. Pres. Commn. Fed. Ethics Law Reform; amb., head U.S. del. World Adminstrv. Radio Conf. WARC, Malaga, Spain, 1992; gen. counsel, dir. Bus.-Industry Polit. Action Com., 1996—. Patrick Wilson scholar, 1970-73. Mem. ABA (chmn. com. election law 1981-2000), D.C. Bar Assn., FBA (chmn. polit. campaign and election law com. 1981-83). Roman Catholic. Administrative and regulatory, Federal civil litigation. Home: 1608 Walleston Ct Alexandria VA 22302-3928 Office: Wiley Rein & Fielding LLP 1776 K St NW Ste 900 Washington DC 20006-2332

BARASCH, CLARENCE SYLVAN, lawyer; b. N.Y.C., May 20, 1912; s. Morris and Bertha Lydia (Herschdorfer) B.; m. Naomi Bosniak, July 1, 1957; children: Lionel, Jonathan. AB, Columbia U., 1933, JD, 1935. Bar: N.Y. 1936, U.S. Dist. Ct. (so., ea. and no. dists.) N.Y. 1936, U.S. Ct. Appeals (2d cir.) 1936. Pvt. practice, N.Y.C., 1935—. Lectr. law of real estate brokerage at various real estate bds.; faculty of N.Y. Real Estate Bd. on courses for lic. renewals required by the Dept. of State of N.Y.; chmn. Columbia U. Law Sch. Class of 1935 Ann. Fund 1965—, Columbia Coll. Class of 1933 Ann. Fund, 1977-79; decade chmn. Columbia Coll. Ann. Fund; pres. Jewish Campus Life Fund, Inc. of Columbia U., 1970-87. Author: (with Elliot L. Biskind) The Law of Real Estate Brokers, 1969; also cumulative supplements, 1971-83; contbr. articles to profl. jours. Capt. Signal Corps AUS, 1942-46. Recipient cert. of appreciation Columbia U., 1981, medal for conspicuous svc. Columbia U., 1984. Mem. ABA, N.Y. State Bar Assn. (real property com.), N.Y. County Lawyers Assn. (com. on real estate brokerage matters), Real Estate Bd. N.Y. (mem. legis and law cms., 1970—, mem. arbitration panel 1989—, rev. ann. Diary and Manual and author of summary of real estate brokerage law and related legal matters 1991— edits.), Am. Arbitration Assn. (arbitration panel 1986—), Men's Club (bd. dirs. 1972-80), Columbia U. Law Sch. Alumni Assn. (bd. dirs. 1985-89). Jewish (mem. adv. bd. to chaplain Columbia 1950-70). Federal civil litigation, General civil litigation, Property, real (including real estate development, water). Home: 1016 5th Ave New York NY 10028-0132 Office: 425 Park Ave New York NY 10022-3506

BARASCH, MAL LIVINGSTON, lawyer; b. N.Y.C., May 14, 1929; s. Joseph and Ernestine (Livingston) Barasch; m. Ann Beckley, May 19, 1962; children: Amy Pitacairn, Jody Taylor. BS in Econs. with distinction, U. Pa., 1951; LL.B., Yale U., 1954. Bar: NY 1957, US Dist Ct (so dist) NY 1960, US Tax Ct 1960. Assoc. Mudge Rose Guthrie Alexander & Ferdon, N.Y.C., 1957-62; assoc. Rosenman & Colin, N.Y.C., 1962-67; ptnr. Rosenman & Colin, LLC, 1968-2000; counsel Katten Muchin Zavis Rosenman and predecessor, 2000—. Mem exec comt, 2d vpres library NY Law Inst, 1979—2000. Treas, bd dirs Lenox Hill Neighborhood House; dist leader, mem exec comt NY County Dem Comt, 1961—65; bd dirs Visions, Servs for the Blind and Visually Impaired. With U.S. Army, 1954—56. Fellow: Am Col Trust and Estate Counsel, NY Bar Found; mem.: ABA, Int Acad Estate and Trust Law (acamedician, mem exec com.), Asn Bar City NY (chmn comt trusts, estates and surrogates cts 2000—), NY State Bar Asn, Univ Club (New York, NY), Beta Gamma Sigma. Estate planning, Probate (including wills, trusts), Estate taxation. Home: 1225 Park Ave New York NY 10128-1132 E-mail: mal.barasch@kmzr.com.

BARBADORO, PAUL JAMES, federal judge; b. Providence, June 4, 1955; s. Donald James and Elizabeth B.; m. Inez E. McDermott, Aug. 16, 1986; children: Katherine E., John James. BA cum laude, Gettysburg Coll., 1977; JD magna cum laude, Boston Coll., 1980. Bar: N.H. 1980. Asst. atty. gen. N.H. Atty. Gen., Concord, 1980-84; legal counsel U.S. Sen. Warren B. Rudman, Washington, 1984-86, Orr & Reno, Concord, 1986-87; dep. chief counsel U.S. Senate Iran-Contra Com., Washington, 1987; dir. Rath, Young, Pignatelli and Oyer, Concord, 1987-92; judge U.S. Dist. Ct., Concord, 1992-97, chief judge, 1997—. Mem. adv. group for dist. of N.H., Civil Justice Reform Act, Concord, 1992-94; mem. long range planning com. N.H. Supreme Ct., 1989-90; mem. 1st Cir. Jud. Coun., 1994-96; adj. prof. Franklin Pierce Law Ctr., 1997-98. Mem. N.H. Bar Assn. (chmn. unauthorized practice of law com. 1982-84, jud. conf. com. on automation and tech. 1996—, com. on cooperation with the cts. 1997—), U.S. Dist. Ct. N.H. Bar, 1st Cir. Ct. Appeals Bar, Order of Coif. Office: WB Rudman Courthouse 55 Pleasant St Rm 409 Concord NH 03301-3938*

BARBAGELATA, ROBERT DOMINIC, lawyer; b. San Francisco, Jan. 9, 1925; s. Dominic Joseph and Jane Zeffra (Frugoli) B.; m. Doris V. Chatfield, June 8, 1956; children: Patricia Victoria, Robert Norman, Michael Alan. BS, U. San Francisco, 1947, JD, 1950. Bar: Calif. bar 1950, U.S. Supreme Ct. bar 1964. Pvt. practice, San Francisco, 1950—; judge pro-tem San Francisco County Superior Ct., 1992-95. Lectr. U. San Francisco Law Sch., Pacific Med. Center. Contbr. to legal jours. Served with USNR, 1943-46. Mem. Calif. State Bar, Calif. Trial Lawyers Assn. (lectr., v.p.), Am. Bd. Trial Advocates (nat. pres. 1981-82, Trial Lawyer of Yr. 1986-87), Assn. Trial Lawyers Am., San Francisco Trial Lawyers Assn. (Lifetime Achievement award 2003), Am. Coll. Trial Lawyers, Internat. Soc. Barristers, San Francisco Lawyers Club. Roman Catholic. Federal civil litigation, State civil litigation, Personal injury (including property damage). Home: 819 Holly Rd Belmont CA 94002-2214 Office: 109 Geary St San Francisco CA 94108-5632

BARBEOSCH, WILLIAM PETER, bank executive, lawyer; b. N.Y.C., Nov. 25, 1954; s. Peter Joseph and Marie Delores (Slesiona) B.; m. Marta B. Varela, Sept. 6, 1986. AB magna cum laude, Brown U., 1976; JD, Columbia U., 1979; MBA, Yale U., 1989. Bar: N.Y. 1980, U.S. Tax Ct. 1985. Atty. Casey, Lane and Mittendorf (and successor firms), N.Y.C., 1979—86, Milbank, Tweed, Hadley and McCloy, N.Y.C., 1986—87; mgmt. assoc. Swiss Bank Corp., N.Y.C., 1989—90; v.p. J.P. Morgan Chase & Co. (and predecessor firms), N.Y.C., 1990—99; mng. dir. Chase Manhattan Bank & Trust Co. (Bahamas) Ltd., 1999—2002, Citigroup Trust, N.Y.C., 2002—. Bd. advisor The Chase Jour., 1997—2002. Mem. profl. adv. com. Mus. of Arts and Design, N.Y.C., 2002—. Mem. N.Y. State Bar Assn., Assn. of the Bar of City of N.Y., Brown U. Club N.Y., Stone House Club, Yale Club (N.Y.C.), Phi Kappa Psi (sec. R.I. Alpha chpt. 1974-75). Republican. Roman Catholic. Avocations: swimming, history, politics. Home: 545 W 111th St Apt 7E New York NY 10025-1965 Office: Citigroup Trust 153 E 53d St 23d Fl New York NY 10022 E-mail: williampbarbeosch@citigroup.com.

BARBER, MARK EDWARD, lawyer; b. Enumclaw, Wash., Dec. 30, 1952; s. Earl Marion Barber and Delila Mae Willis Lontz; m. Pamela Johnson, Aug. 30, 1974; 1 child, Matthew Edward. BA, U. Wash., 1975; JD, Pepperdine U., 1978. Bar: Wash. 1978, U.S. Dist. Ct. Wash. 1978, U.S. Ct. Appeals (9th cir.) 1980, U.S. Supreme Ct. 1985. Atty. Heavey & Woody, Inc. P.S., Seattle, 1978-79; sole practitioner Seattle, 1979-81; atty., prin. shareholder Warren Barber & Fontes, P.S., Renton, Wash., 1981—. Bd. dirs. Justice Polit. Action Com., Tacoma, 1993-95, Sunset Valley Farms Homeowners Assn., Issaquah, Wash., 1991-92, 95-96. Mem. ATLA, Wash. State Bar Assn., King County Bar Assn., Wash. State Trial Lawyers Assn. (pres. 1995-96). Personal injury (including property damage), Product liability, Professional liability. Office: Warren Barber et al 100 S 2nd St Renton WA 98055-2013 E-mail: mebarber@seanet.com.

BARBER, PETER EARL, lawyer; b. Dayton, Ohio, May 31, 1963; s. Russell Earl Barber and Jeannette Weiss Free; m. Anna Marie Barber, July 8, 1995; children: John Hudson, Matthew Weiss. BSME, U. of Ala., Tuscaloosa, 1986; MBA, U. of Ala., 1989, JD, 1993. Bar: Ala. 1993, U.S. Dist. Ct. (no. and mid. dist.) Ala. 1993, U.S. Patent and Trademark Office 2001. Project engr. Blount Internat., Inc., Montgomery, Ala., 1886—1989, RUST Engring., Birmingham, Ala., 1989—90; ptnr. Wallace, Jordan, Ratliff & Brandt, LLC, Birmingham, Ala., 1993—2000, 2003—; v.p. and assoc. gen. counsel Highland Capital Holding Corp., Birmingham, Ala., 2000—03. Sr. editor Ala. Law Rev., 1992. Ch. deacon Briarwood Presbyn. Ch., Birmingham, Ala., 1993—2002. Scholar Mitchell scholar, Manderson Sch. of Bus., U. of Ala., 1988, Hugo Black scholar, U. of Ala. Sch. of Law, 1990. Mem.: Tau Beta Pi. Corporate, general, Mergers and acquisitions, Intellectual property. Home: 2201 Vanessa Dr Birmingham AL 35242 Office: Wallace Jordan Ratliff & Brandt LLC 800 Shades Creek Pky Ste 400 Birmingham AL 35209 Office Fax: 205-263-4410.

BARBIN, RYTHER LYNN, lawyer; b. Port Arthur, Tex., July 15, 1943; s. L.B. and Edna Mae (Ryther) B.; m. Marla Egbert Sankey, Dec. 24, 1987; children: Jordan Ross, Gabriel, Nathaniel. BBA, Tex. Tech. U., 1966; JD, Baylor U., 1968. Bar: Tex. 1968, Hawaii 1976, U.S. Dist. Ct. Hawaii 1976; lic. realtor, Hawaii. Law clk. U.S. Dept. Justice, Washington, 1967; officer trust dept. Bank of Am., San Francisco, 1968-71; officer Investors Bank & Trust Co., Boston, 1972-74; sole practice Wailuku, Hawaii, 1974-82, 84—; ptnr. Barbin & Ball, Wailuku, 1982-84. Arbitrator Hi Supreme Ct. Bd. dirs. Maui United Way, 1980-88, v.p., 1987-88, pres., 1989-90; mem. sch. bd. Maui Dist. Sch., 1980-84; state del., dist. coun. Hawaii Dems., Wailuku,

1978-84; field rep. for U.S. Senator Daniel K. Inouye; campaign mgr. Dem. Presdl. Campaigns Maui County, 1983; vice-chmn. Maui County Dem. Party, 1986-87; chmn. Maui County Dem. Party, 1997-2000; bd. dirs. Maui Humane Soc., Maui Kokua Svc. Recipient cert. of appreciation Gov. State of Hawaii, 1981. Mem. ABA, Hawaii Bar Assn. (bd. dirs.) Maui Bar Assn. (pres. 1984-86), Upcountry Jaycees Makawao (officer 1979-83), Rotary (pres. Wailuku club 1986-87). Episcopalian. Bankruptcy, General practice, Immigration, naturalization, and customs. Home: 555 Iao Valley Rd Wailuku HI 96793-3007 Office: 24 N Church St Ste 407 Wailuku HI 96793-1608

BARBOR, JOHN HOWARD, lawyer; b. Pitts., Mar. 4, 1952; s. Thomas Sharp and Irene (Park) B.; m. Gretchen Suzanne Kunst, Mar. 20, 1982; children: Peter Howard, Katherine Suzanne. AB, Dartmouth Coll., 1974; JD, Boston Coll., 1977. Bar: Pa. 1977. Ptnr. Barbor and Barbor, Indiana, Pa., 1978-89, Barbor & Cicola, Indiana, 1989-93, Barbor, Vaporis & Sottile, P.C., Indiana, 1993—2002, Barbor Sottile & Darr, P.C., Indiana, 2003—. Bd. dirs., solicitor Indiana County YMCA, 1985-94; solicitor Indiana County Red Cross, 1979—; bd. dirs. Indiana Arts Coun., 1986-89; bd. dirs. Indiana County Zoning Appeals Bd., 1995—, chmn., 1998—. Mem. ABA, Pa. Bar Assn., Pa. Bar Inst. (bd. govs. 1995-97), Ind. County Bar Assn. (exec. bd. 1988, 95), Ind. Country Club, Phi Beta Kappa. Republican. Lutheran. State civil litigation, Probate (including wills, trusts), Property, real (including real estate development, water). Home: 217 Forest Ridge Rd Indiana PA 15701-7443 Office: Barbor Sottile & Darr PC 917 Philadelphia St Indiana PA 15701-3911

BARBOUTIS, GEORGE O. lawyer; b. Thessaloniki, Greece, Sept. 8, 1973; s. Odysseas J. Barboutis and Xanthoula J. Barbouti-Sarika. LLB, Aristotelian U. Thessaloniki, Greece, 1995; LLM, Harvard U., 1997; PhD in Fin. Law, U. London, 2000. Bar: (N.Y.) 2000. Assoc. Norton Rose, London, 1998—2000, Shearman & Sterling, London, 2000—. Contbr. articles to profl. jours. Recipient Fulbright scholarship, The Fulbright Found., 1996, Greek State scholarship award, Greek State Scholarships Found., 1996. Fellow: Soc. Advanced Legal Studies (assoc.). Office: Shearman & Sterling 9 Appold St London EC2A 2AP England Business E-Mail: gbarboutis@shearman.com.

BARCELO, JOHN JAMES, III, law educator; b. New Orleans, Sept. 23, 1940; s. John James Jr. and Elfrida Margaret (Bisso) B.; m. Lucy L. Wood, July 14, 1974; children— Lisa, Amy, Steven. BA, Tulane U., 1962, JD, 1966; S.JD, Harvard U., 1977. Bar: La. 1967, D.C. 1974, U.S. Supreme Ct. 1974, N.Y. 1975. Fulbright scholar U. Bonn, Fed. Republic Germany, 1966-67; prof. law Cornell U. Law Sch., Ithaca, N.Y., 1969—, A. Robert Noll. prof. of law, 1984-96, dir internat. legal studies, 1972-88, 90—, William Nelson Cromwell prof. internat. and comprative law, 1996—. Cons. Import Trade Adminstrn., Dept. Commerce Author: (with others) Law: Its Nature, Functions and Limits, 3rd edit., 1986, International Commercial Arbitration, 1999, 2d edit., 2003; co-editor: Lawyers' Practice and Ideals: A Comparative View, 1999, A Global Law of Jurisdiction and Judgments: Lessons from the Hague, 2002; contbr. articles to profl. jours. Mem. Am. Assn. for Comparative Study of Law (bd. dirs.), Am. Soc. Internat. Law, Am. Soc. Comparative Law, Maritime Law Assn. U.S. Office: Cornell U Law Sch Myron Taylor Hall Ithaca NY 14853

BARCLAY, H(UGH) DOUGLAS, lawyer, former state senator; b. N.Y.C., July 5, 1932; s. Hugh and Dorothy Barclay; m. Sara Seiter, Aug. 15, 1959; children: Kathryn D., David H., Dorothy G., Susan M., William A. BA, Yale U., 1955; JD, Syracuse U., 1961; LLD (hon.) , St. Lawrence U., 1980; ScD (hon.) , Clarkson Univ., 1981; LLD (hon.) , SUNY, 1990, Syracuse U., 1997. Bar: N.Y. 1962. Ptnr. Hiscock & Barclay and predecessors, Syracuse, N.Y., 1961—. Sec., gen. counsel KeyCorp and subs., Albany, N.Y., 1971-89; mem. N.Y. State Senate, 1965-84, chmn. Judiciary com., chmn. Select Task Force on Ct. Reorgn., chmn. senate codes com.; dir., chmn. bd. Syracuse Supply Co; chmn. bd. Eagle Media, Inc. Mem. N.Y. State Econ. Power Allocation Bd., N.Y. Racing Assn., bd. trustees; pres. Met. Devel. Assn.; trustee, former chmn. Syracuse U., chair chancellor search com.; vice chmn. N.Y. State George Bush for Pres., 1988; chmn. N.Y. State Bush-Quayle campaign, 1992; mem. policy coun. Gov. Pataki's Transition Team; bd. visitors Syracuse U. Coll. Law; mem. Onondaga C.C. Found.; bd. dirs. Overseas Pvt. Investment Corp., 1990-93; mem. panel of conciliators, Internat. Ctr. of Settlement of Investment Disputes, 2002. Lt. arty. U.S. Army, 1955-57, Korea. Mem. ABA, N.Y. State Bar Assn. Banking, Corporate, general. Office: Hiscock & Barclay PO Box 4878 221 S Warren St Syracuse NY 13202-1633

BARCLAY, STEVEN CALDER, lawyer; b. Phoenix, Ariz., Jan. 17, 1956; s. Leslie Calder and Ruth (Lindke) B.; m. Janice Marie Reno, Sept. 25, 1982; 1 child, Jordan Nicole. BA magna cum laude, Oral Roberts U., 1977; JD cum laude, Notre Dame U., 1980. Bar: Ariz. 1980, U.S. Dist. Ct. Ariz. 1980, U.S. Ct. Appeals (9th cir.) 1980. Assoc. Snell & Wilmer, Phoenix, 1980-83; corp. counsel S.W. divsn. CIGNA Healthplans, Inc., Phoenix, 1983-85; ptnr. Barclay & Reece, Phoenix, 1985-87; pvt. practice Phoenix, 1987-90; shareholder, pres. Barclay & Goering, PC, Phoenix, 1990-00, Steven C. Barclay, PC and Advocates West, Inc., 2001—. Mem. editl. bd. Today's Health Care Mag., 1994-96. Mem. March of Dimes (Az. chap., dir.), Project Citizen (adv. coun.); dir., counsel Ariz. Sports Coun./Grand Canyon State Games. Mem.: Pub. Affairs Profls. Ariz. (dir., pres. 1998—99), Am. Health Lawyers Assn., Ariz. Assn. Health Care Lawyers, State Bar Ariz. Republican. Avocations: camping, hiking, jogging, scuba diving, travel. Health, Insurance, Legislative. Office: Law Offices of Steven C Barclay PC PO Box 93746 Phoenix AZ 85070-3746 E-mail: scbarclay@cox.net.

BARDACKE, PAUL GREGORY, lawyer, former attorney general; b. Oakland, Calif., Dec. 16, 1944; s. Theodore Joseph and Frances (Woodward) B.; children: Julie, Brynn, Francheska, Chloe. BA cum laude, U. Calif.-Santa Barbara, 1966; JD, U. Calif.-Berkeley, 1969. Bar: Calif. 1969, N.Mex. 1970. Lawyer Legal Aid Soc., Albuquerque, 1969; assoc. firm Sutin, Thayer & Browne, Albuquerque, 1970-82; atty. gen. State of N.Mex., Santa Fe, 1982-86; ptnr. Sutin, Thayer & Browne, 1987-90, Eaves, Bardacke, Baugh, Kierst & Kiernan, P.A., 1991—2003, Eaves, Bardacke, Baugh, Kierst & Larson, 2003—. Adj. prof. N.Mex. Law Sch., Albuquerque, 1973— ; mem. faculty Nat. Inst. Trial Lawyers Advocacy, 1978— Bd. dirs. All Faiths Receiving Home, Albuquerque; bd. dirs. Friends of Art, 1974, Artspace Mag., 1979-80, Legal Aid Soc., 1970-74; bd. trustees Albuquerque Cmty. Found., 2001-. Reginald Heber Smith fellow, 1969 Fellow Am. Coll. Trial Lawyers; mem. ABA, Calif. Bar Assn., N.Mex. Bar Assn., Am. Bd. Trial Advocates (pres. N.Mex. chpt. 1992-93). Democrat. Antitrust, Federal civil litigation, State civil litigation. Office: Eaves Bardacke Baugh Kierts & Larson PO Box 35670 Albuquerque NM 87176-5670

BARDEN, ROBERT CHRISTOPHER, lawyer, psychologist, educator, legislative analyst, speaker, writer; b. Richmond, Va., June 7, 1954; s. Elliott Hatcher and Jane Elizabeth Cole (Ferris) B.; m. Robin Jones, Nov. 14, 1987. BA summa cum laude, U. Minn., 1976, PhD in Clin. Psychology, 1982; postgrad., U. Calif., Berkeley, 1977; JD cum laude, Harvard U., 1992. Lic. cons. psychologist, Minn., Tex.; diplomate Am. Bd. Forensic Examiners. Project asst. NSF, 1978-79; intern in psychology VA Med. Ctr., Stanford Med. Ctr., Palo Alto, Calif., 1979-80; dir. psychology Internat. Craniofacial Surg. Inst., Dallas, 1980-87; corp., civil litigation, family and health law atty. Lindquist and Vennum, Mpls., 1992-96; psychologist, lawyer, expert witness, pub. policy analyst R.C. Barden & Assocs., 1996—. Asst. prof. psychology So. Meth. U., Dallas, 1980—84; asst. prof., coord. child clin. psychology U. Utah, Salt Lake City, 1984—87, rsch. faculty dept. surgery, 1987—93; vis. faculty, asst. prof. psychology Gustavus Adolphus Coll., St. Peter, Minn., 1988; pres. Optimal Performance Sys., Inc., Cambridge, 1989—; mem. Minn. Bd. Psychology, 1993—97; adj. prof. law U. Minn. Law Sch., 1995—97; cons. and spkr. in field. Consulting editor Devel. Psychology, 1989; editor Harvard Jour. Law and Pub. Policy, 1990-91; contbr. to profl. publs. Project dir. ch. cmty. svc. projects, Mpls. and Cambridge, 1988—; mem. Minn. Bd. Psychology, 1993-97, Higher Edn. Coordinating Bd., 1993-94; rep. Minn. Sixth Congl. Dist. Recipient Young Scholar award Found. for Child Devel., Faculty Scholar award W.T. Grant Found., 1987-89; NSF fellow, 1978, NIMH fellow, 1976, 77. Mem. ABA, Am. Psychol. Soc., Soc. for Rsch. in Child Devel., Internat. Soc. Clin. Hypnosis, Harvard Law Sch. Soc. Law and Medicine, Lowell House Commons Rm. Harvard U., Nat.Assn. for Consumer Protection in Mental Health Practices (pres. 1995—), Sigma Xi, Phi Beta Kappa. Avocations: church and service work, tennis, martial arts, mountain climbing, music. Office: RC Barden and Assocs 1093 Duffer Ln North Salt Lake UT 84054-3313 E-mail: rcbarden@aol.com.

BARDIN, DAVID J. lawyer; b. N.Y.C., June 2, 1933; s. Shlomo and Ruth (Jonas) Bardin; m. Livia Goldeen, Mar. 12, 1961; children: Jacob, Matthew, Joseph, Sarah. AB, Columbia U., 1954, JD, 1956. Bar: N.Y. 1956, D.C. 1966, Israel 1970. Atty., dep. gen. counsel FPC, Washington, 1958-69; asst. to atty. gen. Israel, Jerusalem, 1970-72; counsel Israel Environ. Protection Svc., Jerusalem, 1973; commr. N.J. Dept. Environ. Protection, Trenton, 1974-77; dep. adminstr. FEA, Washington, 1977; adminstr. Econ. Regulatory Adminstrn., Dept. Energy, Washington, 1977-80; of counsel, mem. Arent Fox Kintner Plotkin & Kahn PLLC, Washington, 1980-2001, ret., 2001. Lectr. law Bar-Ilan U., Tel Aviv U., U. Va. Ext. Co-author: AGA Select Gas Use Handbook: Natural Gas for Environmental Control, 1985; contbr. ; author: Psychological Coercion and Human Rights, 1994. Moot ct. panel Nat. Assn. Atty. Gens.; mem. Mayor's Coun. on Environment, 1999—2001; bd. mgrs. Adas Israel Congregation, 1998—99; trustee The Found. Jewish Studies, 1991—99; trustee moot ct. panel Nat. Assn. Atty. Gens., 1993—; trustee Liberty State Pk. Devel. Corp., 1990—2000, Pinelands Preservation Alliance, 1991—99, Mental Health Liaison Group, 1993—; adv. neighborhood commr. of D.C., 1999—; mem. Mayor's Com. on Adoption Law, 2000—01; bd. dirs. D.C. Water and Sewer Authority; mem. D.C. Bldg. Code Adv. Com., 2002—. Served with U.S. Army, 1956—58. Mem.: ABA, Found. for Energy Law Jour. (bd. dirs. 1987—90), Fed. Energy Bar Assn. (bd. dirs. 1985—87), Fed. Bar Assn. Democrat. Jewish. FERC practice, Oil, gas, and mineral, Environmental. Office: Arent Fox Kintner Plotkin & Kahn 1050 Connecticut Ave NW Ste 400 Washington DC 20036-5339 E-mail: BardinD@arentfox.com.

BARENHOLTZ, CELIA GOLDWAG, lawyer; b. Washington, Dec. 11, 1955; d. Herbert and Anita Charlotte Goldwag; m. Paul K. Barenholtz, Aug. 28, 1983; children: Jeanne, Madeleine. BA, Grinnell (Iowa) Coll., 1979; JD, Columbia U., 1979. Bar: N.Y. 1980, U.S. Dist. Ct. (so. and ea. dist.) N.Y. 1980, U.S. Ct. Appeals (2d cir.) 1985, U.S. Ct. Appeals (9th cir.) 1990, U.S. Ct. Appeals (11th cir.) 1998, U.S. Ct. Appeals (7th cir.) 2000, U.S. Supreme Ct. 1992. Law clk. Hon. Eugene H. Nickerson, Bklyn., 1979-80; assoc. Paul, Weiss, Rifkind, Wharton & Garrison, N.Y.C., 1983-89; asst. U.S. atty. criminal divsn. U.S. Atty.'s Office, So. Dist. N.Y., N.Y.C., 1983-89; ptnr. Kronish Lieb Weiner & Hellman LLP, N.Y.C., 1989—. Federal civil litigation, State civil litigation, Criminal. Office: Kronish Lieb Weiner & Hellman LLP 1114 Ave of Americas New York NY 10036

BARGFREDE, JAMES ALLEN, lawyer; b. Seguin, Tex., Sept. 10, 1928; s. Herman Fred and Elsie (Vorpahl) B.; m. Virginia Felts, Nov. 27, 1970; 1 child, Charles Allen. BS, Tex. A&M U., 1950; postgrad., Ohio State U., 1952-53; JD, St. Mary's U., 1957. Bar: Tex. 1957, U.S. Patent and Trademark Office 1961; registered profl. engr., Tex. Engr. Signal Corps, San Antonio, 1950-52; elec. engr. San Antonio Pub. Svc. Bd., 1953-58; patent counsel Hubbard & Co., Chgo., 1958-59; pvt. practice law Butler, Binion, Rice, Cook & Knapp, 1960-68, 1968-74, 75—; patent and legal counsel Hydrotech Internat., Inc., 1977-81; ptnr. Bargfrede & Thompson, 1974-75. Subcom. chmn. dist. com. on admissions Supreme Ct. Tex., 1988—. Served with USAF, 1952-53. Mem. Houston Bar Assn. (chmn. automated equipment com. 1971-75), State Bar Tex., Assn. Former Students Tex. A&M U., Houston Livestock Show and Rodeo (life), Briarcroft Civic Club (pres. 1979-82), Houston A&M Club (treas. 1990, sec. 1991, v.p., 1992, pres. 1993), Delta Theta Phi. Entertainment, Patent, Trademark and copyright. Home: 5649 Piping Rock Ln Houston TX 77056-4028 Office: 5649 Piping Rock Ln Houston TX 77056-4028

BARHAM, MACK ELWIN, lawyer, educator; b. Bastrop, La., June 18, 1924; s. Henry Alfred and Lockie Izorie (Harper) B.; m. Ann LeVois, June 3, 1946; children: Bret L., Megan. JD, La. State U., 1946; postgrad., U. Colo., 1964-65. Judge City Ct., Bastrop, 1948-61, 4th Jud. Dist. Ct., Parishes of Ouachita and Morehouse, 1961-67, 2d Circuit Ct. of Appeal, 1967-68; assoc. justice La. Supreme Ct., 1968-75; prof. Sch. Law, Tulane, 1975-78; counsel Lemle, Kelleher, Kohlmeyer & Matthews, 1975-78; pres. Barham & Churchill, 1979-88; founder Barham & Arceneaux, New Orleans, 1988—. Mem. faculty Am. Acad. Jud. Edn., U. Ala., 1968-73. Chmn. Ouachita Valley council Boy Scouts Am. Recipient award Freedoms Found. at, Valley Forge, 1969; Outstanding Service award ACLU, 1976; Creative Intelligence award Am. Found. Sci., 1976 Mem. La. Juvenile Judges Assn. (past pres.), La. Law Inst. (council), Internat. Acad. Estate and Trust Law, Scribes, Kiwanis, Blue Key, Order of Coif, Omicron Delta Kappa, Lambda Chi Alpha, Phi Delta Phi, Phi Alpha Delta. General practice, Appellate. Home: 5837 Bellaire Dr New Orleans LA 70124-1103

BARIST, JEFFREY, lawyer; b. Jersey City, Dec. 29, 1941; s. Irving and Lillian (Finkelstein) B.; m. Joan Elaine Travers, Feb. 19, 1967; children: Jessica, Alexis. AB, Rutgers U., 1963; JD, Harvard U., 1966. Bar: N.Y. 1967, U.S. Ct. Appeals (2d cir.) 1968, U.S. Dist. Ct. (so. dist.) N.Y. 1969, U.S. Supreme Ct. 1975. Law sec. U.S. Dist. Judge Irving Ben Cooper, N.Y.C., 1966-67; ptnr., chmn. nat. litigation group Milbank, Tweed, Hadley & McCloy, N.Y.C., 1996—. Author: Commercial Arbitration Law and Clauses, 1994; contbr. articles to profl. jours. Bd. dirs. Lawyers Com. for Civil Rights Under Law; trustee Rutgers U. Fellow Am. Coll. Trial Lawyers, Am. Bar Found.; mem. Am. Law Inst. General civil litigation, Private international. Office: Milbank Tweed Hadley McCloy 47th Fl 1 Chase Manhattan Plz Fl 47 New York NY 10005-1413 E-mail: jbarist@milbank.com.

BARKEN, BERNARD ALLEN, lawyer; b. St. Louis, July 20, 1924; s. Gottlieb and Hattie E. (Rubin) B.; m. Jocelyn Moss Kopman, Sept. 1, 1948; children: Thomas L., Dale Susan. JD, Washington U., 1947. Bar: Mo. 1947, U.S. Dist. Ct. (ea. dist.) Mo. 1947, U.S. Ct. Appeals (8th cir.) 1954, U.S. Tax Ct. 1966, U.S. Ct. Appeals 2nd cir.) 1985, U.S. Supreme Ct. 1984. Sole practice, St. Louis, 1947-80; ptnr. Shifrin & Treiman, St. Louis, 1980-88; pres. Bernard A. Barken, St. Louis, 1988-91; ptnr. Barken & Bakewell L.L.P., St. Louis, 1991—. With USAAF, 1943-44. Mem. ABA, Bar Assn. Met. St. Louis (v.p. 1958, chmn. young lawyers 1953). Jewish. Avocations: piano, tennis, gardening. General civil litigation, Corporate, general, General practice. Home: 30 Vouga Ln Saint Louis MO 63131-2628 Office: Barken & Bakewell LLP 500 N Broadway Ste 2000 Saint Louis MO 63102-2130 Fax: 314-444-7892. E-mail: babarken@hotmail.com.

BARKER, CLAYTON ROBERT, III, lawyer; b. Statesville, N.C., Aug. 27, 1957; s. Clayton Robert Jr. and Alta Jo Barker; m. Sandra Ann Mills, June 30, 1990. AB with distinction, Stanford U., 1979; postgrad., Tufts. U., 1982; JD, U. Va., 1983. Bar: N.Y. 1984, Ga. 1995. Assoc. Shearman & Sterling, N.Y.C., 1983-85, Skadden, Arps, Slate, Meagher & Flom, N.Y.C., 1985-91; counsel The Coca-Cola Co., Atlanta, 1991-2000; ptnr. Smith Helms Mulliss & Moore, LLP, Atlanta, 2000—01, Powell, Goldstein, Frazer & Murphy, LLP, Atlanta, 2001—. Contbr. articles to profl. jours. Mem. Am. Coun. on Germany. Mem. Internat. Bar Assn., Am. Soc. Internat. Law, Nat. Assn. Corp. Dirs., N.Y. State Bar Assn. (internat. law and practice sect., fgn. investment in U.S. bus. com.), Am. Coun. on Germany (young leader 1992), Assn. for Corp. Growth (pres. Atlanta chpt. 1999-2000), Federalist Soc., Omicron Delta Kappa. Republican. Presbyterian. Corporate, general, Private international, Mergers and acquisitions. Office: Powell Goldstein Frazer & Murphy LLP Ste 1600 191 Peachtree St Atlanta GA 30303 E-mail: rbarker@pgfm.com.

BARKER, ROBERT OSBORNE (BOB BARKER), educator, mediator; b. Cleve., June 13, 1932; m. Sharon Ann (div.); children: Debra, Stephen Robert, Dawn, Michael, Colleen. Student, Henry Ford C.C., 1950; BA in Comm. Arts and Sci., Mich. State U., 1954; LLB, LaSalle U., 1969; postgrad., U. Wis., 1989, U. Fla., 1996, postgrad., 2000—03. Lic. cmty. assn. mgr. 1993-03, real estate agent; registered lobbyist Nat. Assn. Mfrs. 1972-87. With pub. rels. dept. Ford Motor Co., Dearborn, Mich., 1953; mgr. Kaiser Aluminum Co., Chgo., 1956-58; advt. mgr. Bastian Blessing Co., Chgo., 1958-59; mgr., regional tng. mgr. Sun Co., Ohio and Detroit, 1959-71; mgr. Goodyear Tire & Rubber Co., Detroit, 1971-72; mgr., v.p. Nat. Assn. Mfrs., Washington, Boston and Detroit, 1972-87; pres., CEO Barker Cons. Inc., 1987-96; mgr., v.p. seminars and materials dept. Am. Supplier Inst. (div. of FoMoCo), 1987-90; nat. mdse./mktg. mgr. Costa del Mar Sunglasses, Ormond Beach, Fla., 1990-91; resort mgr. Oceanside 99 Condo, 1992-93, Outrigger Beach Club, 1994-95. Adj. prof. pub. rels., advt., retailing, sales fundamentals, global and internat. mktg. Daytona Beach C.C., 1994—, DBCC award Bus. faculty Athletic dept., 1998; owner Dolphin Beach Club Condo, 1981-2001, bd. dirs., 1991-99; cert. and pvt. mediator (ADR Alternative Dispute Resolution), 1995—. Twp. trustee, Findlay, Ohio, 1962; lay min. Episcopal ch., 1960-85, vestry, 1981; mem. exec. bd. dirs. Volusia County Rep., 1991-2000; bd. dirs. Am. Cancer Soc., 1991—; bd. dirs. Dearborn Civic Theatre, 1980-84, Volusia Presdl. forum, 1991-99, Dearborn City Beautiful commr. emeritus, 1970-90; commr. Ormond Beach Quality of Life, Beautification and Planning bds., 1990-99; mem. adv. coun. bd. Habitat Humanity, 1995-99; res. police officer, Dearborn, 1968-88; pres. Dearborn High and Lindbergh Elem. PTA; bd. dirs. Bldg. Assn. Mgrs., 1991-95, Cmty. assoc. Inst., 1993-97, Volusia County Pers. Bd., 1991-93; mem. adv. coun. bd. Coun. of Aging, 1991-2000; mem. Fla. Police Benevolent Assn., Fla. Sheriffs Assn.; bd. dirs. Daytona and Ormond Beach Rep. Club, 1991-99, heritage mem. Ormond Meml. Art Mus., 1991-2001; amb. Daytona Internat. Airport, 1996-2002; team selection scout Fla. Citrus Sports for New Year's Bowl football game, Orlando, Fla., 1997—; mem. elder voice focus group Genesis Elder Care, 2001; asst. publicity dir. bd. dirs. Ormond Sr. Games, 1994-96. Served with USNR, 1949-58, AFROTC, 1951-54. Recipient Vol. of Yr. award Am. Cancer Soc., 1998. Mem. Advt. Fedn., Assn. Execs., Am. Heart Assn. (bd. dirs. Volusin/Flagler 2002-), Fla. Pub. Rels. Soc. (Volusia chpt., former v.p. bd. dirs. 1996-98), Am. Legion (life), Mich. State U. Alumni (life, past. pres. 4 alumni clubs), Mich. State Varsity Alumni Club (life), U. Fla. Alumni Assn. (bd. dir. 1997- Gator Club Volusia County, .v.p. edn. 1999-2002), Ormond Beach C. of C. (amb., former chmn. pub. rels., Beautification, JazzMatazz, social com. 1990-2002), Nat. Assn. Sr. Friends of Volusia/Flagler Counties (pres. 2000—), Ormond Shrine Club (pres. 1994-95), Elks, Exch. Club, Rotary (pres. 1987-88), Masons, Moose-Legion, Shriners (dir. pub. rels. 1984, provost unit, Fez on Wheels and Vets. unit), Delta Tau Delta. Home: Unit 613 229 S Ridgewood Ave Daytona Beach FL 32114-4334 E-mail: bobbarker13_99@yahoo.com., robert_barker42@falconmail.dbcc.edu.

BARKER, STEPHEN GERALD, lawyer; b. Ary, Ky., Oct. 2, 1953; s. Talmon D. and Eliza (Grigsby) B.; m. Sharon Francis, Aug. 29, 1974; children: Stephanie, Sara Kimberly, Stephen E. BS in Forestry, U. Ky., 1975, JD, 1980. Bar: Ky. 1980, U.S.Dist. Ct. (ea. dist.) Ky. 1980. News anchorman Sta. WKYH-TV, Hazard, Ky., 1972-73; dist. conservationist Soil Conservation Svs., USDA, Manchester, Ky., 1975-77; ptnr. Barker & Allen, Hazard, 1980-85; pvt. practice Hazard, 1985—; asst. gen. counsel 1st Fed. Savs., Hazard, 1981-84, gen. counsel, 1985—. Master commr. Perry Cir. Ct., hazard, 1982—; asst. gen. counsel Ky. River Coal Corp., Hazard, 1985—. Chmn. Hazard-Perry County Airport Bd., 1997—. Mem.: ABA, Soc. Am. Foresters (cert.), Ky. Bar Assn., Perry County Bar Assn. (pres. 1981—). Democrat. Baptist. Banking, General practice, Property, real (including real estate development, water). Home: Duane Mountain Bulan KY 41722 Office: 600 High St Ste 203 Hazard KY 41701-1310

BARKER, WILLIAM M. state supreme court justice; b. Chattanooga, Sept. 13, 1941; married; 3 children. BS, U. Chatanooga, 1964; JD, U. Cin., 1967. Bar: Tenn. 1967. Pvt. practice, 1967-83; cir. ct. judge, 1983-95; justice Ct. of Appeals, 1995-98, Tenn. Supreme Ct., 1998—. Adj. prof. U. Tenn., Chatanooga, 1984—. Chmn. bd. deacons 1st Presbyn. Ch. Chattanooga, 1995-97. With USAMC, 1967-69. Fellow Tenn. Bar Found., Chattanooga Bar Found.; mem. Am. Legion, Alpha Soc., U. Tenn. Chattanooga Alumni Coun., Chattanooga Rotary Club. Office: Tenn Supreme Ct 540 Mccallie Ave Ste 410 Chattanooga TN 37402-2096

BARKETT, ROSEMARY, circuit judge; b. Ciudad Victoria, Tamaulipas, Mex., Aug. 29, 1939; arrived in U.S., 1946, naturalized, 1958; BS summa cum laude, Spring Hill Coll., 1967; JD, U. Fla., 1970; LLD (hon.) , Stetson U., St. Petersburg, Fla., 1987; LHD (hon.) , Fla. Internat. U., Miami, 1987; LLD (hon.) , John Marshall Law Sch., Chgo., 1990; LHD (hon.) , U. So. Fla., Tampa, 1990; DCL (hon.) , Spring Hill Coll., Mobile, Ala., 1990; LLD (hon.) , Rollins Coll., Orlando, Fla., 1992, Nova U., Ft. Lauderdale, Fla., 1992. Bar: Fla., U.S. Dist. Ct. (so. dist.) Fla., U.S. Ct. Appeals (5th cir.), U.S. Supreme Ct. Pvt. practice, West Palm Beach, Fla., 1971—79; judge 15th Jud. Cir. Ct., Palm Beach County, Fla., 1979—82, administrative judge civil divsn., 1982—83, chief judge, 1983—84; appellate judge 4th Dist. Ct. Appeal, West Palm Beach, Fla., 1984—85; justice Supreme Ct. Fla., Tallahassee, 1985—92, chief justice, 1992—94; cir. judge U.S. Ct. Appeals (11th cir.) , Miami, 1994—. Bd. dirs. Lawyers for Children, U.S. Assn. Constl. Law; faculty U. Nev., Reno, Nat. Jud. Coll., Fla. Jud. Coll., Appellate Judges Seminar, Inst. Jud. Adminstrn., NYU; lectr. in field; vis. com. Miami U. Law Sch.; bd. visitors St. Thomas U. Mem. editl. bd.: The Florida Judges Manual. Named Women of Distinction, Crohn's & Colitis Found., 1997; named to Fla. Women's Hall of Fame, 1986, Miami Centennial Hall of Fame, 1996; recipient Woman of Achievement award, Palm Beach County Commn. on Status of Women, 1985, Hannah G. Solomon award, Nat. Coun. Jewish Women, 1991, Lifetime Achievement award, Latin Bus. Profl. Women, 1992, Breaking the Glass Ceiling award, Fla. Fedn. Bus. Profl. Women's Clubs, Inc., 1993, Disting. Jurist award, Miss. State U., 1995, Margaret Brent Women Lawyers of Achievement award, ABA Commn. Women in Profession, 1996, Harriette Glasner Freedom award, ACLU, 1999. Mem.: ABA (Minority Justice Honoree 1992), Dade Marine Inst., Fed. Judges Assn., Am. Law Inst., Assn. Trial Lawyers Am. (Achievement award 1986), Acad. Fla. Trial Lawyers (Achievement award 1988, Rosemary Barkett award named in her honor 1992), Palm Beach Marine Inst., Nat. Assn. Women Judges (Honoree of Year 1999), Fla. Assn. Women Lawyers (Judge Mattie Belle Davis award 1991, Rosemary Barkett Outstanding Achievement award named in her honor 1999), Am. Acad. Matrimonial Lawyers (award 1984), Palm Beach County Bar Assn., Fla. Bar Assn. Office: US Ct of Appeals (11th cir) Fla 99 NE 4th St Rm 1223 Miami FL 33132-2140

BARKIN, MARVIN E. lawyer; b. Winter Haven, Fla., Nov. 9, 1933; s. Isadore and Jean (Epstein) B.; m. Gertrude Parnes, Sept. 20, 1959; children: Thomas I., Michael A., Pamela L. AB, Emory U., 1955; LLB cum laude, Harvard U., 1958. Bar: Fla. 1958, U.S. Dist. Ct. (mid. and so. dists.) Fla., U.S. Ct. Appeals (5th and 11th cirs.), U.S. Supreme Ct. Research aide Dist. Ct. Appeal Fla., Third Dist., Miami, 1958-60; assoc., then ptnr. Fowler, White, Collins, Gillen, Humkey & Trenam, Tampa, 1960-69; ptnr. Trenam,

Kemker, Scharf, Barkin, Frye, O'Neill & Mullis, Tampa, 1970—; mem. Fla. Bd. Bar Examiners, 1979-84, chmn., 1982-83. Chmn. corp., banking and bus. law sect. Fla. Bar, 1974-75, chmn. appellate ct. rules subcom., 1972-73 Mem. Am. Law Inst., Am. Bar Found., Nat. Conf. Bar Examiners (bd. mgrs. 1985-95, chmn. 1993-94, 11th cir. ct. appeal com. on lawyer qualifications and conduct, chair 2001—), Fla. Bar, Omicron Delta Kappa. Democrat. Jewish. Federal civil litigation, State civil litigation, Commercial, contracts (including sales of goods; commercial financing). Home: 1605 Culbreath Isles Dr Tampa FL 33629-4824 Office: Trenam Kemker Scharf Barkin Frye O'Neill & Mullis 101 E Kennedy Blvd Tampa FL 33602-5179

BARKLEY, BRIAN EVAN, lawyer, political consultant; b. Teaneck, NJ, Jan. 30, 1945; s. Henry E. and Alice M. (Schultz) Barkley; m. Pamela A. Martin, May 5, 1979; children: Leigh Elizabeth, Christine Elizabeth, Brett Evan. BA, U. Md., 1967; JD with honors, George Washington U., 1970. Bar: Md. 1970, D.C. 1976, U.S. Dist. Ct. Md. 1973. Assoc. Everngam & Goldstein, Silver Spring, Md., 1970—72; pvt. practice Silver Spring, 1972—80, Rockville, Md., 1980—86; spl. asst. Rep. Michael Barnes, Washington, 1981—84; sr. ptnr. Barkley and Kennedy, Chartered, 1987—. Vice chmn. Nat. Capital chpt. Nat. Multiple Sclerosis Com., Washington, 1980—86, Nat. Multiple Sclerosis Soc., Washington, 1998—2001, chmn. chpt. svcs. com., 1985—2001; chmn. Montgomery County Multiple Sclerosis Com., Rockville, Md., 1980; major gifts chmn. Shady Grove Hosp., 1980; chmn. Nat. Capital chpt. Nat. Multiple Sclerosis Com., 2001—; campaign mgr. Barnes for Congress, Rockville, 1980, campaign chmn., 1982—84; campaign mgr. Montgomery County for Mondale, 1984; del. Dem. Nat. Conv., 1984; vice chmn. Montgomery County for Dukakis, 1988. Recipient Humanitarian award, Nat. Multiple Sclerosis Soc., 1989. Mem.: Montgomery County Bar Assn., Md. Bar Assn., Rockville C. of C. (pres. 1996—97), Bethesda Country Club, Masons. Democrat. Bankruptcy, General civil litigation, Family and matrimonial. Home: 12405 Copenhaver Ter Potomac MD 20854-3028 Office: 51 Monroe St Ste 1407 Rockville MD 20850-2408

BARKMAN, JON ALBERT, lawyer; b. Somerset, Pa., Oct. 8, 1947; s. Blair Albert and Billie (Dietz) B.; m. Annette E. Shaulis, Dec. 1, 1983. BA, Washington and Jefferson U., 1969; JD, Duquesne U., 1975. Bar: Pa. 1975, U.S. Dist. Ct. (we. dist.) Pa. 1975, U.S. Supreme Ct. 1984, U.S. Ct. Appeals (3rd cir.) 1989. Mem. claims dept. Liberty Mut. Ins. Co., Pitts., 1969-71; dist. justice Commonwealth of Pa., Somerset, 1973-93; pvt. practice Somerset, 1975—; pres. Barkman Realty, Inc., Somerset County Settlement and Abstract Co. Inc. Advisor Com. Against Sexual Assault, Somerset, Pa., 1984; Pa. del. Nat. Spl. Ct. Judges Conv., Honolulu, 1989, Atlanta, 1991; active Somerset County Com. for prison overcrowding, 2002-03. Paul Harris fellow, 1989. Mem. ABA, Pa. Trial Lawyers Assn., Somerset County Bar Assn. (pres. 1990—), Allegheny County Bar Assn., Elks, Rotary, Am. Legion. Republican. Methodist. Home: 388 High St Somerset PA 15501-1301 Office: 116 N Center Ave Somerset PA 15501-2027

BARKOFF, RUPERT MITCHELL, lawyer; b. New Orleans, May 7, 1948; s. Samuel and Martha B.; m. Susan Joyce Levitt, May 31, 1970; children: Stuart, Jeffrey, Lisa. BA in Econs. with high distinction, U. Mich., 1970, JD magna cum laude, 1973. Bar: Ga. 1973. Assoc. Kilpatrick Stockton LLP, Atlanta, 1973-80, ptnr., 1980—. Contbr. articles to profl. jours. Mem. ABA (bus. law sect., antitrust sect., forum on franchising, panelist ann. forums 1980-92, chmn. 1989-92, assoc. editor Franchise Law Jour. 1981-86), Ga. Bar Assn. (corp. and banking sect.), Atlanta Bar Assn., Phi Beta Kappa. Democrat. Jewish. Corporate, general, Franchising. Home: 5215 Vernon Springs Trl NW Atlanta GA 30327-4511 Office: Kilpatrick Stockton LLP 1100 Peachtree St NE Ste 2800 Atlanta GA 30309-4530 E-mail: rbarkoff@kilpatrickstockton.com.

BARKSDALE, RHESA HAWKINS, federal judge; b. Jackson, Miss., Aug. 8, 1944; s. John Woodson Jr. and Mary Bryan (Saunders) Barksdale. BS, U.S. Mil. Acad., 1966; JD, U. Miss., 1972. Law clk. to Hon. Byron R. White U.S. Supreme Ct., 1972—73; assoc., then ptnr. Butler, Snow, O'Mara, Stevens & Cannada, Jackson, 1973—90; judge U.S. Ct. Appeals (5th cir.), Jackson, 1990—. Instr. U. Miss. Sch. Law, Jackson, 1975—76, Miss. Coll. Sch. Law, Jackson, 1976. Chmn. Miss. Vietnam Vets. Leadership Program, Jackson, 1982—85; del. Rep. Nat. Conv., New Orleans, 1988; elector election of Pres. of U.S., Jackson, 1988. Capt. U.S. Army, 1966—70, Vietnam. Decorated Silver Star, Bronze Star for Valor, Purple Heart, Cross of Gallantry with silver star (Republic of Vietnam). Mem.: Phi Delta Phi (Nat. Grad. of Yr. 1972). Episcopalian. Office: US Ct Appeals 5th Cir James O Eastland Courthouse 245 E Capitol St Ste 200 Jackson MS 39201-2414*

BARLIANT, RONALD, federal judge; b. Chgo., Aug. 25, 1945; s. Lois I. Barliant; children: Claire, Anne. BA in History, Roosevelt U., Chgo., 1966; postgrad., Northwestern U., Chgo., 1966-67; JD, Stanford U., 1969. Bar: Ill. 1969, U.S. Dist. Ct. (no. dist.) Ill., U.S. Ct. Appeals (7th cir.). VISTA vol., staff atty. Cook County Legal Assistance Found., Chgo., 1969-72; assoc. Miller, Shakman, Hamilton and Kurtzon, Chgo., 1972-76, ptnr., 1976-88; judge U.S. Bankruptcy Ct. (no. dist.) Ill., Chgo., 1988—2002; pvt. practice Chgo., 2002—. Adj. prof. debtor-creditor rels. John Marshall Law Sch., 1991-92; bd. dirs. Cook County Legal Assistance Found., 1975-82; gen. counsel Chgo. Coun. Lawyers, 1983-86. Mem. Fed. Bar Assn. (bd. dirs. 1992-94), Nat. Conf. Bankruptcy Judges (bd. govs. 1997—). Avocations: opera, theatre, golf, cubs baseball.

BARLOW, WILLIAM KYLE, lawyer, state legislator; b. Smithfield, Va., Mar. 13, 1936; s. Gordon E. and Gladys (Holleman) B.; 1 child, Todd R.; m. Taylor Rowell; 1 child, Amy Elizabeth Barlow Britt. MS in Agrl. Econs. with honors, Va. Poly. Inst., 1958; LLB, U. Va., 1965. Assoc. Law Office of A. E. S. Stephens, Va., 1965-72; ptnr. Delk and Barlow, Smithfield, Va., 1972-87, Barlow, Councill & Riddick, Smithfield, Va., 1987-92; pres. Barlow & Riddick, Smithfield, Va., 1992—2002, Barlow, Riddick & Farmer, 2002—; mem. Va. Ho. of Dels., 1991—2001, mem. fin., agr., sci. & tech., general law, mem. cts. of justice, gen. laws, militia, police, pub. safety, 2001—. Past mem. PTA; past chmn. Isle of Wight County Dem. Com., past chmn. bd. selection commn., mem. C. of C.; past trustee Walter Cecil Rawls Regional Libr., Courtland Va.; mem. Smithfield Bapt. Ch., past chmn. bd. deacons, trustee, ch. moderator; former Little League baseball coach; former mem. and chmn. bd. trustees Walter Cecil Rawls Regional Libr.; mem. bd. dirs. Obici Hosp., Suffolk, Va.; legal advisor Isle of Wright County Rescue Squad. With USAF, 1958-62. Mem. Va. Tech. Alumni Assn. (past pres., bd. dirs.; mem. Peanut Alumni chpt.), Isle-Wight County-Smithfield C. of C., Rotary (past pres.), Ruritan Club, Phi Alpha Delta.

BARMANN, BERNARD CHARLES, SR., lawyer; b. Maryville, Mo., Aug. 5, 1932; s. Charles Anselm and Veronica Rose (Fisher) B.; m. Beatrice Margaret Murphy, Sept. 27, 1965; children: Bernard Charles Jr., Brigit. PhD, Stanford U., 1966; JD, U. San Diego, 1974; MPA, Calif. State U., Bakersfield. Bar: Calif. 1974, U.S. Dist. Ct. (so. dist.) Calif. 1974, U.S. Dist. Ct. (ea. dist.) Calif. 1978, U.S. Ct. Appeals (9th cir.) 1984, U.S. Supreme Ct. Asst. prof. Ohio State U., Columbus, 1966-69, U. Toronto, Ont., Can., 1969-71; dep. county counsel Kern County, Bakersfield, Calif., 1974-85, county counsel, 1985—. Adj. prof. Calif. State U., Bakersfield, 1986—. Editor: The Bottom Line, 1991-93, contbr. articles to profl. jours. Mem. exec. bd. So. Sierra coun. Boy Scouts Am., Bakersfield, 1986—; bd. dirs. Kern County Acad. Decathlon, Bakersfield, 1988—. Danforth Found. fellow, 1963-65; grantee Fulbright Found., 1963-65. Mem. Calif. Bar Assn. (law practice mgmt. sect. exec. com., jud. nominees evaluation commn. 1997-2000), County Counsel Assn. Calif. (bd. dirs. 1990—, chair 1993-94), Kern County Bar Assn. (pres. 2001), Rotary. Avocations: golf, skiing, travel, photography. Office: Kern County Office of County Counsel 1115 Truxtun Ave Bakersfield CA 93301-4639 E-mail: bbarmann@co.kern.ca.us.

BARNARD, ALLEN DONALD, lawyer; b. Williston, N.D., Feb. 22, 1944; s. Donald J. and Ruth E. (Franklin) B.; m. Andra Lynn Lebsock, Nov. 24, 1962; children: Alana, Aaron. BA in Social Scis., U. N.D., 1965; JD, U. Notre Dame, 1968. Bar: Minn. 1968, U.S. Dist. Ct. Minn. 1968, U.S. Ct. Appeals (8th cir.) 1971, U.S. Supreme Ct. 1973. Assoc. Best & Flanagan, Mpls., 1968-72, ptnr., 1972—, mng. ptnr., 1991-93. City atty. City of Golden Valley, Minn., 1988—, housing and redevel. authority atty., 1978—. Mem. ABA, Hennepin County Bar Assn., Madeline Island Yacht Club (bd. dirs. 1991-97). Avocations: sailing, skiing. General civil litigation, Condemnation (eminent domain), Land use and zoning (including planning). Office: Best & Flanagan 225 S Sixth St #4000 Minneapolis MN 55402-4331 E-mail: abarnard@bestlaw.com.

BARNARD, GEOFFREY W. judge; b. Batavia, N.Y., Apr. 4, 1945; Diploma, Univ. of Madrid, Spain, 1965; BA, Alleghany Coll., 1966; JD, Cornell Univ. Sch. of Law, Ithaca, 1969. Magistrate judge for V.I., U.S. Magistrate Ct., Charlotte Amalie, St. Thomas, 1986—. Office: US Magistrate Ct 345 US Courthouse 5500 Veterans Dr Charlotte Amalie VI 00802-6424

BARNARD, GEORGE SMITH, lawyer, former federal agency official; b. Opelika, Ala. s. George Smith and Caroline Elizabeth (Dowdell) B.; m. Muriel Elaine Outlaw, July 26, 1945; children: Elizabeth Elaine Barnard Crutcher, Charles Dowling, Beverly Laura Barnard Parker, Andrew Carey. BA, U. Ala., 1948, LLB, 1950. Bar: Fla. 1978, Ala. 1950, U.S. Tax Ct. 1950, U.S. Dist. Ct. Ala. 1950, U.S. Dist. Ct. Fla. 1978, U.S. Dist. Ct. (so. dist. trial bar) Fla. 1995, U.S. Supreme Ct. 1965, U.S. Ct. Claims 1979, U.S. Ct. Appeals (Fed. cir.) 1984, U.S. Ct. Appeals (11th cir.) 1985. Pvt. practice, Opelika, 1950-51; with IRS, 1951-78; attache, revenue service rep. Sao Paulo Brazil, S.Am. and Lesser Antilles, 1965-71, Mexico City, Bermuda Is., Bahamas, Panama, Major Antilles, C.Am., 1971-77; ptnr. Barnard, P.A., Miami, Fla., 1978-87, of counsel, 1987-91. Lectr. taxation U. Ala., 1958-60. Pres. Rocky Ridge Vol. Fire Dept., 1956-58, Rocky Ridge Civic Club, 1959, Ala. chpt. Nat. Assn. Internal Revenue Employees, 1962; commr. Rocky Ridge Civic Water Works, 1960-62; bd. dirs. S.E.Pompano Homeowners Assn., 1996-99. With USAAF, 1942-46. Recipient Albert Gallatin award U.S. Treasury Dept., 1978; named Hon. Citizen of Tex., 1979, Hon. Admiral in Tex. Navy, 1979. Mem. Fgn. Svc. Retirees Assn. of Fla. (advisor/dir. for S.E. Fla. 1987-98, dir. emeritus 1998—, original incumbent historian 1998—), Kappa Sigma. Republican. Private international, Estate taxation, Personal income taxation. Home: 671 SW 6th St Apt 602 Pompano Beach FL 33060-7739 Office: Charles D Barnard PA 3940 N Andrews Ave Fort Lauderdale FL 33309-5240 E-mail: memebarn@attbi.com.

BARNARD, MORTON JOHN, retired lawyer; b. Chgo., Mar. 22, 1905; s. Julius and Martha (Wittman) B.; m. Eleanor Spivak, Aug. 16, 1936; 1 child, James W. PhB, U. Chgo., 1926, JD, 1927. Bar: Ill. 1927, U.S. Supreme Ct. 1949, U.S. Ct. Mil. Appeals 1954, U.S. Dist. Ct. (no. dist.) Ill., U.S. Ct. Appeals (7th cir.). Ptnr. Barnard and Barnard, Chgo., 1934—85, Foss, Schuman, Drake & Barnard, Chgo., 1985-88, Gottlieb & Schwartz, Chgo., 1989-90, of counsel, 1990-93, Miller, Shakman, Hamilton, Kurtzon & Schlifke, Chgo., 1993-97; ret. practice, 2002. Adj. prof. John Marshall Law Sch., Chgo., 1947-64; pres. Ill. State Bar Assn., 1971-72; lectr. in field. Author: Contested Estates, 1985, 93; contbr. articles to profl. jours. Life mem. Chgo. Hist. Soc. Lt. col. U.S. Army, 1942-46. Recipient Certs. of Appreciation Ill. State Bar Assn., 1972, Chgo. Bar Assn., 1986, Bd. Govs.' award Ill. State Bar Assn., 1988, Austin Fleming Disting. Svc. award Chgo. Estate Planning Coun., 1993, Addis E. Hull award Ill. Inst. for Continuing Legal Edn., 1996. Fellow Am. Coll. Trust and Estate Counsel (bd. regents 1968-74), Am. Bar Found., Am. Bar Assn. (life), Ill. Bar Found., Chgo. Bar Found.; mem. Union League Club (Chgo.). Republican. Avocations: singing and acting in Bar Assn. Christmas Spirits, 1932-95.

BARNES, DONALD MICHAEL, lawyer; b. Hazleton, Pa., June 15, 1943; s. Donald A. and Margaret (Resuta) B.; m. Mary Catherine Gibbons, June 3, 1967; children: Donald M., Stephanie A., Susan E. BS in Indsl. Engring., Pa. State U., 1965; JD cum laude, George Washington U., 1970. Bar: D.C. 1970, U.S. Dist. Ct. D.C. 1970, U.S. Ct. Appeals (D.C. cir.) 1970, U.S. Ct. Appeals (5th cir.) 1980, U.S. Ct. Appeals (4th cir.) 1980, U.S. Ct. Appeals (8th cir.) 1981, U.S. Ct. Appeals (6th cir.) 1993, U.S. Supreme Ct. 1975. Assoc. Arent, Fox, Kintner, Plotkin & Kahn, Washington, 1970-78, ptnr., 1978-97; mng. shareholder Jenkens & Gilchrist, Washington, 1997-2000; ptnr. Seyfarth Shaw, Washington, 2000—02, Porter Wright Morris & Arthur, LLP, Washington, 2002—. Notes editor George Washington Law Rev., 1969-70 Mem.: ABA (criminal justice, antitrust, litigation and adminstrv. law sects.), DC Bar Assn., Order of Coif, Phi Delta Phi. Administrative and regulatory, Antitrust, Federal civil litigation. Office: Porter Wright Morris & Arthur LLP Ste 500 1919 Pennsylvania Ave NW Washington DC 20006-3434 E-mail: dbarnes@porterwright.com.

BARNES, HARRY FRANCIS, federal judge; b. Memphis, May 14, 1932; m. Mary Milburn Mann, four children. Student, Vanderbilt U., 1950-52; BS, U.S. Naval Academy, 1956; LLB, U. Ark., 1964. With Pryor & Barnes, Camden, Ark., 1964-66, Barnes & Roberts, Camden, 1966-68, Gaughan, Laney, Barnes & Roberts, Camden, 1968-78, Gaughan, Laney & Barnes, Camden, 1978-82; mcpl. judge Camden and Ouachita Counties, 1975-82; circuit judge 13th jud. dist. State of Ark., 1982-93; judge U.S. Dist. Ct. (we. dist.) Ark., 1993—. Mem. Ark. Jud. Discipline and Disability Commn. With USMC, 1956-86, col. res. ret. Named Outstanding Trial Judge in Ark., Ark. Trial Lawyers Assn., 1986, 2000. Mem. ABA, Ark. Bar Assn., Ark. Jud. Coun. (bd. dirs.). Office: US Dist Ct We Dist PO Box 1735 El Dorado AR 71731-1735

BARNES, JAMES NEIL, lawyer; b. Tulsa, June 28, 1944; s. William Harvey and Mildred E. (Norsworthy) B.; children: Deborah, Sociana; m. Anne E. Fuhrman, Dec. 18, 1992. BA, Northwestern U., 1966; JD, U. Mich., 1970. Bar: U.S. Dist. Ct. D.C. 1971, U.S. Ct. Appeals (D.C. cir.) 1973, U.S. Supreme Ct. 1977. Law clk. to judge U.S. Dist. Ct D.C., Washington, 1970-71; staff atty. Ctr. for Law and Social Policy, Washington, 1971-72, 77-81, co-dir., 1980-81; staff atty. Pub. Def. Svc., Washington, 1972-74; assoc. Hudson & Co., Port Vila, New Hebrides Islands, 1974-75; cons. Coun. for Pub. Interest Law, Washington, 1975-76; assoc. Wilmer, Cutler and Pickering, Washington, 1976-77; founder, dir. Antarctica Project, Washington, 1981-93; gen. counsel Antarctic and So. Ocean Coalition, Sydney, Wash., 1981—. East coast dir. Threshold Internat. Ctr. for Environ. Renewal, Washington, 1981-87, bd. dirs. The Antatctica Project, 1990—; sr. atty. Environ. Policy Inst. and Friends of Earth, Washington, 1987-94, head internat. dept. Friends of the Earth, 1990-94; counselor Les Amis de la Terre-France and Friends of the Earth Internat., 1994-2002; CEE Bankwatch Network, Prague, Czech Republic, 1995—, councilor and mem. statutory rev. com., 1998-2002; mem. nat. coun. Les Amis de la Terre-France, 1997-2002. Author: Let's Save Antarctica, 1982, Bankrolling Successes: A Portfolio of Sustainable Projects, 1988, 2d edit., 1995, Russian Roulette: Nuclear Power Reactors in Eastern Europe and Former Soviet Union, 1992-93, Promises, Promises: A Review of G-7 Economic Summit Declarations on Environment and Development, 1994; contbr. articles to profl. jours.; prodr.: (video) Antarctica: Soul of the Blue Planet; editor ECO, 1978—. UN rep. Greenpeace Internat., 1983-85, bd. dirs. Greenpeace USA, 1984-85; mem. State Dept. Adv. Com. on Law of the Sea, 1977-82, pub. adv. com. on Antarctica, 1978-92; mem. commn. on law and policy Internat. Union for Conservation of Nature and Natural Resources, 1980—; pres. Meridian Hill Studios Coop., 1987-90, treas., 1991-94. Recipient Golden Ark award His Royal Highness Prince Bernhard, The Netherlands, 1998; named Internat. Environmentalist of Yr., Nat. Wildlife Fedn., 1991; Ea. European projects grantee Rockefeller Bros. Fund, 1994-2002. Mem. Internat. Coun. Environ. Lawyers. Avocations: photography, guitar and harmonica, cycling. Home: 11 Ave Edouard Dupuy 24140 Villamblard Dordogne France E-mail: james.barnes@wanadoo.fr.

BARNES, JOY CHAPPELL, lawyer; b. Talladega, Ala., Aug. 24, 1950; d. George Daniel and Barbara Joyce (Riggleman) Chappell; m. L. Randolph Barnes, May 28, 1969 (dec. Mar. 1970); m. D. Gordon Lewis, Mar. 19, 1983. BA, U. Ala., Birmingham, 1980, JD, 1986. Bar: Ala. 1986, U.S. Dist. Ct. (no. dist.) Ala. 1986, U.S. Dist. Ct. (mid. dist.) Ala. 1987. Br. sec. Stromberg Time Products, Birmingham, 1970-71; sec. Hobbs Trailers/Fruehauf, Birmingham, 1971-72; office mgr. Tidwell Trailer & Equipment, Birmingham, 1972-75; asst. U. Ala., Birmingham, 1978-79; owner, operator Live Wires, Birmingham, 1979-82; assoc. Costello & Stott, Birmingham, 1986-87; ptnr. Livingston & Barnes, Birmingham, 1987-90; sole practitioner Birmingham, 1990—. Tchr. spl. studies U. Ala., Birmingham, 1988. Mem. ABA, State Bar Ala., Birmingham Bar Assn., Assn. Trial Lawyers Am., Ala. Trial Lawyers, Ala. Soc. Blue Tennie Club (pres.), Downtown Dem. Club, Sigma Delta Kappa (alumni advisor 1987-89). Democrat. Bankruptcy, Family and matrimonial, General practice. Address: 27 New Battle Garden Eskbank Midlothian EH22 3DR Scotland

BARNES, KAREN KAY, lawyer; b. June 22, 1950; d. Walter William and Vashti (Greenlee) Sessler; m. James Alan Barnes, Feb. 12, 1972; children: Timothy Matthew, Christopher Michael. BA, Valparaiso U., 1971; JD, DePaul U., 1978, LLM in Taxation, 1980. Bar: Ill. 1978, U.S. Dist. Ct. (no. dist.) Ill. 1978. Ptnr. McDermott, Will & Emery, Chgo., 1978-88; prin. William M. Mercer, Inc. and predecessor firm, Chgo., 1989-93; staff dir. legal dept. McDonald's Corp., Oak Brook, Ill., 1993-95, home office dir. legal dept., 1995-97, regulatory practice group leader and mng. counsel, 1998—. Instr. John Marshall Grad. Sch. Law, Chgo., 1986-87; mem. adv. bd. John Marshall Sch. Law, 1996—; bd. dirs. Flutes Unlimited; mem. adv. bd. dirs. Plan Sponsor Mag., 2000—. Contbr. case note to DePaul Law Rev., 1976, note and comment editor DePaul Law Rev., 1976-77, editor Taxation For Lawyers, 1986-88. Mem. Am. Coll. Employee Benefit Attys., Chgo. Bar Assn. (chair employee benefits com. 1991-92, co-chair symphony orchestra 1999—), Midwest Pension Conf. (name chged to Midwest Benefits Coun.), WEB (pres. Chgo. chpt. 1986-88, v.p. nat. bd. 1988, pres. 1989-90), Profit Sharing Coun. Am. (legal and legis. com. 1994—, bd. dirs. 1997—, 2d vice chair 1997-98, 1st vice chair 1998-2000, chair 2000—). Lutheran. Pension, profit-sharing, and employee benefits. Home: 586 Crescent Blvd # 402 Glen Ellyn IL 60137 Office: McDonald's Corp 2915 Jorie Blvd Oak Brook IL 60523 E-mail: karen.barnes@mcd.com.

BARNES, NATASHA LYNN, lawyer; b. Woodward, Okla., Aug. 24, 1971; d. Lex V. and Bonnie A. Barnes. BS, Okla. State U., 1993; JD with honors, U. Okla., 1996. Bar: Tex. 1996. Assoc. Thornton, Summers, Biechlin, Dunham and Brown, Austin, Tex., 1996-2000, Thompson, Coe, Cousins and Irons, L.L.P., Austin, 2000—. Mem. Austin Young Lawyer's Assn., Travis County Bar Assn. Insurance, Personal injury (including property damage). Office: Thompson Coe Cousins Irons 1500 Austin Ctr 701 Brazos Austin TX 78701 Fax: 512-708-8777.

BARNES, OLIVER WILLIAM ABBOTT, solicitor; b. Nov. 13, 1950; married; children: Theo, Olivia, Ottilie. BA, Trinity Hall, Cambridge U., 1972. Trainee solicitor Travers Smith Braithwaite, London, 1973-76, ptnr., 1980—. Mem. Law Soc. (co. law com. 1998-). Corporate, general, Mergers and acquisitions, Securities. Office: Travers Smith Braithwaite 10 Snow Hill London EC1A 2AL England

BARNES, PAUL MCCLUNG, lawyer; b. Phila., June 27, 1914; s. Andrew Wallace and Luella Hope (Andrew) B.; m. Elizabeth McClenahan, Dec. 28, 1940 (dec.); children: Andrew M., Margaret L. Lenart, James D., John R. (dec.). BA, Monmouth (Ill.) Coll., 1936; JD, U. Chgo., 1939. Bar: Colo. bar 1939. Assoc. Bannister & Bannister, Denver, 1939-40, Foley & Lardner, Milw., 1940-47, ptnr., 1948-88, of counsel, 1988—. Dir. Wis. Public Service Corp., 1974-77, Kickhaefer Mfg. Co., 1965-85, Attys. Liability Assurance Soc., Ltd., 1979-87; sec. Sta-Rite Industries, Inc., 1965-73 Mem. adv. bd. Milw. Protestant Home, 1975-87. Served with USNR, 1942-45. Mem. ABA, Wis. Bar Assn., Order of Coif. Corporate, general, Utilities, public. Office: Foley & Lardner 777 E Wisconsin Ave Ste 3800 Milwaukee WI 53202-5367 E-mail: pbarnes@webtv.net.

BARNES, PETER, retired lawyer; b. Cambridge, Mass., Apr. 13, 1940; s. Tracy Barnes and Janet (White) Lawrence; m. Jan Adair; children from previous marriage: K. Tracy, John E. BA magna cum laude, Yale U., 1962; LLB cum laude, Harvard U., 1965. Bar: DC 1966, Md. 1984. Assoc. Leva, Hawes, Symington, Martin & Oppenheimer, Washington, 1965-71, ptnr., 1972-83, Venable, Baetjer & Howard, Balt., 1983-86; mem., shareholder Swidler & Berlin, Chtd., Washington, 1987-98; mem. Swidler Berlin Shereff Friedman, LLP, Washington, 1998-99, counsel, 1999—2002; ret., 2002. Bd. dirs. Walker & Dunlop, Inc., Washington. Mem.: Elkridge Club, Met. Club. General civil litigation, Construction, Property, real (including real estate development, water). Home: 4 Deep Run Ct Cockeysville MD 21030-1600 E-mail: PtrBrs@aol.com.

BARNES, THOMAS G. law educator; b. 1930; AB, Harvard U., 1952; DPhil, Oxford U., 1955. From asst. prof. to assoc. prof. Lycoming Coll., Williamsport, Pa., 1956-60; from lectr. to prof. history U. Calif., Berkeley, 1960—, humanities rsch. prof., 1971-72, prof. history and law, 1974—, co-chmn. Canadian studies program, 1982—. Dir. legal history project Am. Bar Found., 1965-86; com. mem. on ct. records 9th Cir. Ct. Author: Somerset 1625-1640: A County's Government During the Personal Rule, 1961, List and Index to Star Chamber Procs., James I, 3 vols., 1975, Lawes and Libertyes of Massachusetts, 1975, Hastings College of Law: The First Century, 1978; mem. editl. bd. Gryphon Legal Classics Libr.; editor Pub. Record Office. Huntington Libr. fellow, 1960, Am. Coun. Learned Socs. fellow, 1962-63, John Simon Guggenheim Found. fellow, 1970-71. Fellow Royal Hist. Soc.; mem. Selden Soc. (councillor, state corr.), Assn. Canadian Studies (pres. 2001-). Office: U Calif Sch Law 454 Boalt Hl Berkeley CA 94720-7200

BARNES, THOMAS JOHN, lawyer; b. Grand Rapids, Mich., Apr. 1, 1943; s. James and Adeline (Molenda) B.; m. Lynn Marie Owens, Aug. 19, 1967; children: Nicolle, Cynthia. BA in Acctg., Mich. State U., 1965, BA in Polit. Sci., 1966; JD, Wayne State U., 1972. Bar: Mich. 1972, U.S. Dsit. Ct. (ea. and we. dists.) Mich. 1972, U.S. Ct. Appeals (6th cir.) 1974, U.S. Dist. Ct. (no. dist.) Ind. 1994, U.S. Ct. Appeals (7th cir.) 1995. Ptnr. Varnum, Riddering, Schmidt & Howlett, Grand Rapids, 1972—. Arbitrator Mich. Employment Rels. Commn.; spkr. in field. Editor-in-chief Wayne Law Rev.; contbr. articles to profl. jours. Fellow Coll. Labor and Employment Lawyers; mem. ABA (nat. labor rels. bd. practice and procedures com.), Am. Employment Law Coun., Mich. Bar Assn. (labor coun., sec., treas. 1987-88, chmn. 1989-90), Grand Rapids Bar Assn. (chair labor sect.) Roman Catholic. Avocations: reading, horse racing, sports. Civil rights, Labor (including EEOC, Fair Labor Standards Act, labor-management relations, NLRB, OSHA). Office: 333 Bridge St NW Grand Rapids MI 49504-5356

BARNES, TOM R., II, lawyer; b. Hays, Kans., Feb. 1, 1963; s. Tom R. and Mary C. Barnes; m. Barbara A. Robbins, Aug. 5, 1989 (div. Apr. 1998); m. Tracey A. Yahne, May 18, 2001; children: Joshua A., Joy C., Jared T. BA, Ft. Hays State U., Hays, 1985; JD, Washburn U., 1988. Bar: Kans. 1988, U.S. Dist. Ct. Kans. 1988. Sole practitioner, Hays, 1988; assoc. atty. Clinkscales & Clinkscales, Hays, 1988-89, Stumbo, Hanson & Hendricks LLP, Topeka, 1989—. Asst. city atty. Perry, Lecompton, Auburn and Silver Lake, Kans., 1989—; city atty. Harveyville, Kans., 1999—; mem. Topeka

Areawide Bankruptcy Coun., 1997-98. Mem. Kans. Bar Assn., Topeka Bar Assn. Republican. Roman Catholic. Bankruptcy, Probate (including wills, trusts), Property, real (including real estate development, water). Office: Stumbo Hanson & Hendricks 2887 SW Macvicar Ave Topeka KS 66611-1704

BARNES, WILLIE R. lawyer; b. Dallas, Dec. 9, 1931; m. Barbara Bailey; children: Michael, Sandra, Traci, Wendi, Brandi. BA, UCLA, 1953, JD, 1959. Bar: Calif. 1960, U.S. Dist. Ct. (cen. dist.) Calif. 1960. Various atty. positions Calif. Dept. of Corps., L.A., 1960-70, asst. commr. of corps., 1970-75, commr. of corps., 1975-79; ptnr., chmn. corp. dept. Manatt, Phelps, Rothenberg & Phillips, L.A., 1979-88; ptnr. Wyman, Bautzer, Kuchel & Silbert, L.A., 1989-91, Katten Muchin Zavis & Weitzman, L.A., 1991-92, Musick, Peeler & Garrett, L.A., 1992—. Chmn. svc. plan com. Knox-Keene Health Care, 1976-79; mem. securities regulatory reform com. State of Calif., 1979-81; mem. shareholders rights and securities transactions Calif. Senate Commn. on Corp. Governances, 1986—; chmn. Leveraged Real Estate Task Force, Inst. Cert. Planners, 1985-86; gen. counsel UCLA Alumni Assn., 1982-86; mem. listing qualifications panel NASDAQ. Co-mng. editor: Calif. Bus. Law Reporter, 1982-83. With U.S. Army, 1954-56. Named Law Alumnus of Year UCLA, 1976; recipient Resolution of Commendation Calif. Senate, 1979, Calif. Assembly, 1979. Mem. ABA (fed. regulation of securities and state regulation of securities coms., franchise forum, futures regulation com.), State Bar Calif. (bus. law sect. 1979, exec. com. 1983-86, vice chmn. 1985-86, com. on corps. 1982-83, ad hoc com. on corp. governance and takeovers 1986-88), Beverly Bar Assn. (corp. and comml. law sect.), L.A. Bar Assn., M.W. Securities Commrs. Assn., N.Am. Securities Assn., Ind. Commn. on L.A. Police Dept. Democrat. Avocations: tennis, basketball, photography. Corporate, general, Franchising, Securities. Office: Musick Peeler & Garrett One Wilshire Blvd Ste 2000 Los Angeles CA 90017 E-mail: w.barnes@mpglaw.com.

BARNES-BROWN, PETER NEWTON, lawyer; b. Rutland, Vt., Aug. 22, 1948; s. Rufus Enoch and Julia Pottwin (Morgan) Brown; m. Susan Linda Barnes, Aug. 11, 1974; children: Diana Morgan, David Alexander, Julia Elizabeth. AB, Brown U., 1970; JD, U. Pa., 1976. Bar: Ga. 1978, N.Y. 1979, Mass. 1985. Law clk. Assoc. Justice Alfred H. Joslin R.I. Supreme Ct., Providence, 1977-78; assoc. Olwine, Connelly, Chase, O'Donnell & Weyher, N.Y.C., 1978-84, Goodwin, Procter & Hoar, Boston, 1984-86; internat. counsel Cullinet Software, Inc., Westwood, Mass., 1986-89; co-founder, prin. Van Wert & Zimmer, P.C., Lexington, Mass., 1989-93; co-founder, mem. Morse, Barnes-Brown & Pendleton, P.C., Waltham, Mass., 1993—. Co-founding dir., clk. New Eng.-Latin Am. Bus. Coun., Inc., Boston, 1992-2000. Contbr. articles to profl. jours. Mem. ABA, Mass. Bar Assn., N.Y. State Bar Assn., State Bar Ga., Boston Bar Assn. Computer, Corporate, general, Private international. Office: Morse Barnes-Brown & Pendleton PC Reservoir Place 1601 Trapelo Rd Waltham MA 02451-7333

BARNETT, EDWARD WILLIAM, lawyer; b. New Orleans, Jan. 2, 1933; s. Phillip Nelson and Katherine (Wilkinson) B.; m. Margaret Mauk, Apr. 3, 1933; children: Margaret Barnett Stern, Edward William. BA, Rice U., 1955; LL.B., U. Tex.-Austin, 1958. Bar: Tex. 1958. Mem. Baker Botts LLP, Houston, 1958—, mng. ptnr., 1984-98, sr. counsel, 1998—. Bd. dirs., chmn. Cen. Houston, Inc., 1989-91. Trustee Rice U., Houston, 1991—, chmn. bd. trustees, 1996—; trustee Baylor Coll. Medicine, St. Luke's Episcopal Health System, Tex. Heart Inst.; life trustee U. Tex. Law Sch. Found.; bd. dirs., former chmn. Greater Houston Partnership, 1992; bd. dirs. Ctr. for Houston's Future, Reliant Resources, Inc.; chmn. bd. dirs. Houston Zoo, 2002-. Fellow Am. Coll. Trial Lawyers; mem. ABA (chmn. sect. antitrust law 1981-82), State Bar Tex., Houston Bar Assn., Coronado Club (pres. 1989), Houston Country Club, Old Baldy Club, Riverhill Country Club. Antitrust, General civil litigation. Office: Baker Botts LLP 3000 One Shell Plaza Houston TX 77002

BARNETT, GARY, lawyer; b. Chgo., Dec. 20, 1955; s. Lawrence Barnett and Deena Mae Goldberg; children: Matthew, James. BS, U. Tulsa, 1978, JD, 1981; LLM, NYU, 1986. Bar: Okla. 1981, N.Y. 1986, Calif. 1989. Legal intern Gordon & Gordon, Claremore, Okla., 1980-81; assoc. Sublett, McCormick, Andrew & Keefer, Tulsa, 1981-82; prin. Barnett & Assocs., Claremore and Tulsa, 1982-85; assoc. Cadwalader, Wickersham & Taft, N.Y.C., 1986-92, ptnr., 1993-95, O'Melveny & Myers LLP, N.Y.C., 1995-99, Shearman & Sterling, N.Y.C., 1999—. Chmn. confs. on new devel. in securitization Practising Law Inst., N.Y.C., 1995—. Contbr. articles to profl. jours. Achievements include patents in field. Finance, Securities. Office: Shearman & Sterling 599 Lexington Ave 16th Fl New York NY 10022-6030 E-mail: gbarnett@shearman.com.

BARNETT, MARK WILLIAM, former state attorney general; b. Sioux Falls, S.D., Sept. 6, 1954; s. Thomas C. and Dorothy Ann (Lievrance) Barnett; m. Deborah Ann Barnett, July 14, 1979. BS in Govt., U. S.D., 1976, JD, 1978. Bar: S.D. Pvt. practice, Sioux Falls, 1978—80; asst. atty. gen. State of S.D., Pierre, 1980—83, spl. prosecutor, 1984—90; ptnr. Schmidt, Schroyer, Colwill and Barnett, Pierre, 1984—90; atty. gen. State of S.D., Pierre, 1991—2003. Mem. S.D. Bar Commn., 1986—92, S.D. Law Enforcement Tng. Commn., 1987, S.D. Corrections Commn., 1987. Bd. dirs. D.A.R.E. Mem.: State's Atty. Assn. (bd. dirs. 1987—90), Am. Judicature Soc. (nat. bd. dirs. 1984—88), S.D. Bar Assn. (pres. young lawyers' sect. 1985). Republican. Avocations: golf, weight lifting, snowmobiling.*

BARNETT, MARTHA WALTERS, lawyer; b. Dade City, Fla., June 1, 1947; d. William Haywood and Helen (Hancock) Walters; m. Richard Rawls Barnett, Jan. 4, 1969; children: Richard Rawls, Sarah Walters. BA cum laude, Tulane U., 1969; JD cum laude, U. Fla., 1973. Bar: Fla. 1973, U.S. Dist. Ct. (mid. and so. dists.) Fla. 1973, U.S. Ct. Appeals (3d, 4th and 11th cirs.) 1975, DC 1989. Assoc. Holland & Knight LLP, Tallahassee, 1973—78, ptnr., 1979—. Bd. dirs., v.p. Fla. Lawyers Prepaid Legal Svc. Corp., 1978—80, pres., 1980—82, legis. com., 1983—84, mem. commn. on access to justice, 1984—86, exec. coun. tax sect., 1987—88, exec. coun. pub. interest. sect., 1989—91; active Fla. Commn. Ethics, 1984—87, chairperson, 1986—87, Fla. Taxation and Budget Reform Commn., 1989—; legal adv. bd. Martindale-Hubbell, 1990—; chair Ho. of Dels., 1994—96. Mem. Fla. Coun. Econ. Edn., Fla. Edn. Found.; bd. dirs. Lawyers Com. Civil Rights Under Law. Fellow: Am. Bar Found. (life); mem.: ABA (exec. coun. sect. on individual rights and responsibility 1974—86, bd. govs. 1986—89, task force on minorities in profession 1984—86, commn. on women in profession 1987—90, long range planning com. 1988—91, chair bd. govs. fin. com. 1988—89, bd. editors ABA Jour. 1990—94, exec. coun. sect. legal edn. and admission to bar 1990—94, chair commn. on pub. understanding about the law 1990—93, pres.-elect 1999—2000, pres. 2000—01, others), Tallahassee Bar Assn., Fla. Bar Assn. (exec. coun. pub. interest law sect. 1989—91), Am. Law Inst., Nat. Inst. Dispute Resolution (sec.-treas. 1988—94, bd. dirs. 1988—94, Gov. appt. Fla. Constitution revision Commn. 1997—98). Administrative and regulatory, Legislative, State and local taxation. Office: Holland & Knight LLP PO Drawer 810 Tallahassee FL 32302-0810

BARNETT, PRESTON B. lawyer, communications executive; m. Billie Barnett. BA in History, B in Bus., Birmingham-So. Coll.; JD, U. Ala. Bar: Ala., Ga. With various acctg. firms; v.p., gen. tax counsel Cox Enterprises, Atlanta, 1979—. Mem.: Tax Execs. Inst. (pres. Atlanta chpt. 1991—92, regional v.p. 1996—97), Ga. Bar Assn., Ala. Bar Assn., Birmingham-So. Coll. Nat. Alumni Assn. (pres. 2000—01). Office: Cox Enterprises 6205 Peachtree Dunwoody Rd Atlanta GA 30328*

BARNETT, ROBERT BRUCE, lawyer, educator; b. Waukegan, Ill., Aug. 26, 1946; s. Bernard and Betty Jane (Simon) Barnett; m. Rita Lynn Braver, Apr. 10, 1972; 1 child, Meredith Jane. BA, U. Wis., 1968; JD, U. Chgo., 1971. Bar: D.C. 1971. Law clk. to Hon. John Minor Wisdom U.S. Ct. Appeals (5th cir.), 1971-72; law clk. to assoc. justice Byron R. White U.S. Supreme Ct., Washington, 1972-73; legis. asst. Sen. Walter F. Mondale, Washington, 1973-75; assoc. Williams & Connolly, Washington, 1975-78, ptnr., 1979—. Adj. prof. Georgetown Law Sch., 1973—80. Trustee John F. Kennedy Ctr. for Performing Arts, 1994—; mem. bd. visitors Sanford Inst. of Pub. Policy, Duke U., 1998—2001, U. Chgo. Law Sch., 2001—. General civil litigation, Corporate, general, Entertainment. Office: Williams & Connolly LLP 725 12th St NW Washington DC 20005-5901

BARNETT, WILLIAM A. lawyer; b. Chgo., Oct. 13, 1916; s. Leo James and Anita (Olsen) B.; m. Evelyn Yates, June 23, 1945 (dec. Nov. 4, 1988); children: William, Mary Leone, Therese, Kathleen. LLB, Loyola U., Chgo., 1941. Admitted to Ill. bar, 1941. With IRS, 1948-54; atty. chief counsel's office Chgo., 1948-52; dist. counsel penal div. Detroit, 1952-54; chief tax atty. U.S. Atty's Office, Chgo., 1955-60; practitioner before the 6th Circuit Ct. Appeals, since 1954; practitioner 7th Circuit Ct. Appeals, 1955—, U.S. Supreme Ct., 1959—. Lawyer; b. Chgo., Oct. 13, 1916; s. Leo James and Anita (Olsen) B.; LL.B., Loyola U., Chgo., 1941; m. Evelyn Yates, June 23, 1945 (dec. Nov. 4, 1988); children: William, Mary Leone, Therese, Kathleen. Admitted to Ill. bar, 1941; with IRS, 1948-54, atty. chief counsel's office, Chgo., 1948-52, dist. counsel penal div., Detroit, 1952-54; chief tax atty. U.S. Atty's Office, Chgo., 1955-60; practitioner before the 6th Circuit Court of Appeals, since 1954, 7th Circuit Ct. Appeals, 1955—, U.S. Supreme Ct., 1959—. Fellow Internat. Acad. Trial Lawyers; mem. ABA, Fed. Bar Assn., Ill. Bar Assn., Nat. Assn. Criminal Def. Lawyers, Ill. Trial Lawyers Assn. Fellow Internat. Acad. Trial Lawyers; mem. ABA, Fed. Bar Assn., Ill. Bar Assn. Federal civil litigation, Criminal, Taxation, general. Home: 1448 W Norwood St Chicago IL 60660-2404 Office: 135 N La Salle St Ste 300 Chicago IL 60602 E-mail: wab144@ameritech.net.

BARNETT, WILLIAM MICHAEL, lawyer; b. New Orleans, June 15, 1925; s. Herman Lyon Barnett and Irma Samson; m. Audrey Steinert, Mar. 17, 1954 (dec. June 30, 1995); children: Robert Alan, James Michael; m. Doris Berthelot, May 4, 2002. BA, Yale U., 1950; LLB, Tulane U., 1953. Assoc. Guste, Barnett & Redmann, New Orleans, 1953-57; ptnr. Guste, Barnett & Little, New Orleans, 1957-70; mng. ptnr. Guste, Barnett & Colomb, New Orleans, 1970-75, Guste, Barnett & Shushan, New Orleans, 1975—2002. Asst. editor Tulane Law Rev., 1952-53. Pres. Madonna Manor, Jefferson Parish, La., 1964-65, Upper Audubon Assn., New Orleans, 1986-88; trustee Boy Scouts of Am., New Orleans, 1970-75, Pharm. Mus., New Orleans, 1985-93; dir. La. Civil Svc. League, New Orleans, 1985-2002, La. Landmark Soc., New Orleans, 1963-65, Continental Savs. & Loan Assn., New Orleans, 1971-82, 1st v.p. Cultural Attractions Fund, New Orleans, 1966-68; pres. New Orleans Jr. C. of C., 1960-61; chmn. New Orleans Civil Svc. Commn., City of New Orleans, 1963-75. Sgt. inf. U.S. Army, 1943-46, ETO. Decorated Bronze Star, Combat Inf. badge; recipient M.M. Lemann award City of New Orleans, 1982. Mem.: Soc. Escargot Orleanais (master chancellor 1990—92), Exeter Acad. Alumni Assn. of La. (pres. 1968—75), Yale Alumni Assn. La. (pres. 1968—70), Nat. Assn. Yale Alumni (dir. 1973—75), La. Bar Assn. (mem. ho. of dels. 1961—64), Order of the Coif, Chevaliers du Tastevin (commandeur), Omicron Delta Kappa. Republican. Unitarian Universalist. General civil litigation, Commercial, consumer (including collections, credit), Probate (including wills, trusts). Home: 7227 Benjamin St New Orleans LA 70118-3505 Office: Guste Barnett & Shushan 25th Fl 639 Loyola Ave New Orleans LA 70113-3125 E-mail: billbarney@webtv.net.

BARNETTE, CURTIS HANDLEY, steel company executive, lawyer; b. St. Albans, W.Va., Jan. 9, 1935; s. Curtis Frankin and Garnett Drucella (Robinson) Barnette; m. Loris Joan Harner, Dec. 28, 1957; children: Curtis Kevin, James David. AB with High Honors, W.Va. U., 1956; postgrad. (Fulbright scholar), U. Manchester, 1956—57; JD, Yale U., 1962; grad. advanced mgmt. program, Harvard U., 1974—75; LLD (hon.), W.Va. U., 1995, DeSales U., 1996, U. Charleston, 1998, Lehigh U., 1999, Moravian Coll., 2002. Cert. Conn., 1962, Pa., 1968, D.C., 1988, W.Va., 1990. Atty. Wiggin & Dana, New Haven, 1962—67, Bethlehem (Pa.) Steel Corp., 1967—92, sec., 1976—92, gen. counsel, 1977—92, sr. v.p., 1985—92, chmn., CEO, 1992—2000, also bd. dirs., 1986—2000; of counsel Skadden, Arps, Slate, Meagher & Flom, LLP, 2000—. Lectr. U. Md., 1958—59; law tutor Yale U., 1962—67; chmn. bd. dirs. Am. Iron and Steel Inst., 1997, dir., 1992—2000; bd. dirs. Met Life Ins. Co., Lehigh Valley Partnership; chmn. Internat. Iron and Steel Inst., 1994—95, dir., 1992—2000; comenius prof., exec. in residence Moravian Coll., 2000—. Trustee Leigh U., 1993—; Pa. Soc., 1993—; mem. Adminstrv. Conf. U.S., 1988—89; vice chmn. bd. govs. W.Va. U., 1999—; dir. W.Va. U. Found., 1982—, chair, 1987—88; mem. adv. com. Trade Policy and Negotiations, 1989—, Coal Commn., 1990, Pa. 21st Century Environ. Com., 1997—98. With Counterintelligence Corps U.S. Army, 1957—59, maj. USAR, 1959—67. Mem.: Nat. Mus. Indsl. History (chmn.), Pa. Pk. Found., Pa. Bus. Roundtable (dir. 1986—2000, chmn. 1994—95), Bus. Roundtable (policy com. 1992—2000), Bus. Coun., Pa. Chamber Bus. and Industry (dir. 1985—93), Am. Law Inst., Am. Soc. Corp. Secs. (chmn. 1986), Assn. Gen. Coun. (pres. 1988—90), W.Va. Bar Assn., D.C. Bar Assn., Northampton County Bar Assn., Conn. Bar Assn., Pa. Bar Assn., Fed. Bar Assn., ABA, Met. Club, Blooming Grove Hunting and Fishing Club, Bethlehem Club, Lobolly, Links, Saucon Valley Country Club, Yale Club of N.Y.C., Univ. Club of Washington, Phi Delta Phi, Phi Alpha Theta, Beta Theta Pi, Phi Beta Kappa. Home: 1112 Prospect Ave Bethlehem PA 18018-4914 Office: 1170 8th Ave Bethlehem PA 18016-7699 also: 1440 New York Ave NW Washington DC 20005-2111 E-mail: barnette@bethsteel.com., hbarnett@skadden.com.

BARNHARDT, ZEB ELONZO, JR., lawyer; b. Winston-Salem, N.C., Dec. 28, 1941; s. Zeb Elonzo and Katie Sue (Taylor) B.; m. Pam Hall; children: Daniel Black, Kathleen Martin. AB, Duke U., 1964; JD, Vanderbilt U., 1969. Bar: N.C. 1969; cert. mediator, N.C.. Assoc. Womble Carlyle Sandridge & Rice, PLLC, Winston-Salem, 1969-75, mem., 1975-97, of counsel, 1997-98; owner, mgr., cons. Barnhardt & Assocs., Inc., Leland, 1998—; pvt. practice law, Leland, 1998—. Bd. dirs. BarCARES of N.C., Inc., 1999—. Alumni admissions adv. com. Duke U., 1970-72; bd. dirs. Industries for Blind, Winston-Salem, 1973-85, vice chmn., 1983-84, chmn., 1985; bd. dirs. Goodwill Industries, Winston-Salem, 1973-80, BarCARES of N.C., Inc., 1999—; bd. dirs. The Little Theatre, Winston-Salem, 1979-85, asst. treas., 1980, treas., 1981-82, v.p., 1983-84, pres., 1984-85; adv. bd. Salvation Army, Winston-Salem, 1973-85, chmn., 1979-80; bd. dirs. Leadership Winston-Salem, 1984-92, v.p. adminstrn., 1988-89, pres. 1989-90; com. mem. Winston-Salem Found., 1975-84, vice chmn., 1978-80, chmn., 1983-84; trustee High Point U., 1984-96; chmn. Second Journey Inc., 2002—. With USN, 1964—66. Recipient Disting. Service award as Young Man of Yr. Winston-Salem Jaycees, 1974; Disting. Alumni award Duke U., 1979 Mem. ABA (fed. regulation securities laws com., law firms com., com. on law and acctg., bus. law sect., commn. on lawyer assistance programs), N.C. Bar Assn. (chmn. securities regulation com. 1985-87, vice chmn. bus. law sect. 1987-89, chmn. bus. law sect. 1989-91, bd. govs. 1991-94, chmn. membership recruitment and retention com. 1997-2000, chair lawyer effectiveness and quality of life com. 2001—), Winston-Salem Jaycees (life, pres. 1973-74), N.C. Jaycees (regional dir. 1974-75, legal counsel 1975-77), Greater Winston-Salem C. of C. (bd. dirs. 1973-74), Rotary. Democrat. Methodist. Corporate, general, Securities, Alternative dispute resolution. Office: Barnhardt & Assocs Inc 1158 Willow Pond Ln Leland NC 28451 E-mail: zbarnhardt@ec.rr.com.

BARNHART, KATHERINE LOUISE, lawyer; b. Detroit, Mar. 18, 1940; d. Joseph D. and Mae (MacNeill) B.; m. Feliciano Colista, Oct. 31, 1968; children: Gian A. Colista, Celia Diana Colista, Joseph Aaron Colista. BA, U. Mich., 1962; postgrad. in urban planning, Wayne State U., 1969-70, JD, 1976. Bar: Mich. 1976, U.S. Dist. Ct. (ea. dist.) Mich. 1976. Sr. social planner City of Detroit, 1964-67; sole practice Detroit, 1977—. Mem. ABA, Mich. Bar Assn. (past chair family law sect.), Detroit Bar Assn. (past chair family law com.), Women Lawyers Assn. (treas. 1978-80), Am. Acad. Matrimonial Lawyers (past chmn.). Democrat. Family and matrimonial. Office: 16824 Kercheval Pl Ste 201 Grosse Pointe MI 48230-1500

BARNHILL, CHARLES JOSEPH, JR., lawyer; b. Indpls., May 22, 1943; s. Charles J. and Phyllis (Landis) Barnhill; m. Elizabeth Louise Hayek, Aug. 14, 1971; children: Eric Charles, Colin Landis. BS in Econs., U. Pa., 1965; JD, U. Mich., 1968. Bar: Ill. 1968, U.S. Dist. Ct. (no. dist.) Ill. 1968, U.S. Ct. Appeals (7th cir.) 1969, U.S. Supreme Ct. 1972. Assoc. Kirkland & Ellis, Chgo., 1968; Reginald Heber Smith fellow Chgo. Legal Aid, 1968-69; assoc. Katz & Friedman, Chgo., 1969-72; ptnr. Davis, Miner, Barnhill & Galland, P.C. (now Miner, Barnhill & Galland), Madison, Wis., 1972—. Spl. master Fed. Dist. Ct. (no. dist.) Ill. Asst. editor: Mich. Law Rev., 1968. Chmn. Wis. Ctr. Tobacco Rsch. and Intervention, 1996; bd. dirs. Combined Health Appeal, Legal Assistance Found., Chgo., 1972—74, Old Town Triangle Assn., Chgo., 1972—75. Fellow: Am. Coll. Trial Lawyers; mem.: Order of Coif, Barristers Soc., Chgo. Coun. Lawyers (bd. dirs. 1974—76), ABA (chmn. employment litig. litig. section 1975—78). Antitrust, Civil rights. Office: Miner Barnhill & Galland 44 E Mifflin St Ste 803 Madison WI 53703-2800

BARNHILL, DAVID STAN, lawyer; b. Washington, N.C., May 10, 1949; s. Arthur David and Ida Bea (Cox) B.; m. Katherine C. Felger, July 26, 1975; children: Hannah Katherine, Mary Rachel. BS, Va. Poly. Inst., 1971, MS, 1973; doctoral studies, U. Va., 1976-79; JD magna cum laude, Washington and Lee U., 1983. Bar: Va. 1983, U.S. Ct. Appeals (4th cir.) 1983, U.S. Supreme Ct. 1990, Federal Ct. Claims 1994. Asst. prof. social sci. Va. Intermont Coll., Bristol, Va., 1973-76; soc. sci. researcher U. Va., Charlottesville, Va., 1979-80; assoc. Woods, Rogers & Hazlegrove, Roanoke, Va., 1983-88, ptnr., 1989—. Contbr. articles to profl. jours.; lead articles editor Washington & Lee Law Rev., 1982-83. Bd. dirs. Total Action Against Poverty, Roanoke, 1987-90, DePaul Children's Svcs., Roanoke, 1985-95, Legal Aid Roanoke Valley, 1990-92. Sgt. USNG, 1972-78. Named to Legal Elite litigation, Va. Bus. Mag., 2000, Legal Elite construction law, 2002. Mem.: ABA (forum on constrn. industry, civil litigation sect.), Va. Assoc. Gen. Contractors (legal affairs and contract documents coms. 1992—), Roanoke Bar Assn. (bd. dirs. 1992—94), Va. Bar Assn. (civil litigation coun. 1994—99, constrn. law coun.), Va. State Bar (chmn. 6th dist. ethics com. 1990—91, bd. govs. constrn. law sect. 1991—99, state bar coun. 1995—2001, state bar disciplinary bd. 1995—2001, vice chair bench-bar and media rels. com. 1996—2000), Va. Tech. Alumni Assn., Order of the Coif. Democrat. Baptist. Avocations: middle distance running, writing. General civil litigation, Communications, Construction. Home: 5145 Falcon Ridge Rd Roanoke VA 24014-5720 Office: Woods Rogers & Hazlegrove 10 S Jefferson St Ste 1400 Roanoke VA 24011-1319 E-mail: barnhill@woodsrogers.com.

BARNHILL, HENRY GRADY, JR., lawyer; b. Buena Vista, Ga., Aug. 24, 1930; s. Henry Grady and Imogene (Hogg) B.; m. Sarah Carolyn Haire, Oct. 29, 1953; children: Grady Michael, Stephen Drew, Kevin Scott, Carol Kelly. JD, Wake Forest U., Winston-Salem, N.C., 1958. Bar: N.C. 1958, U.S. Dist. Ct. (ea., mid. and we. dists.) N.C. 1958, U.S. Ct. Appeals (4th cir.) 1961, U.S. Supreme Ct. 1983, U.S. Ct. Appeals (fed. cir.) 1985. Assoc. Womble Carlyle Sandridge & Rice, Winston-Salem, 1958-61, ptnr., 1961—. Bd. visitors Sch. of Law Wake Forest U. Lt. USAF, 1951-55. Fellow Am. Coll. Trial Lawyers (state chmn. 1986-88); mem. Am. Bd. Trial Advs., N.C. Assn. Def. Attys., N.C. Bar Assn. (litigation sect.), 4th Cir. Jud. Conf., Forsyth County Bar (pres. 1979-80), Inns of Ct. (Chief Justice Joseph Branch). Democrat. Presbyterian. Avocation: tennis. Federal civil litigation, State civil litigation, Product liability. Home: 3121 Robinhood Rd Winston Salem NC 27106-5610 Office: Womble Carlyle Sandridge & Rice PLLC PO Drawer 84 One W 4th St Winston Salem NC 27102 E-mail: gbarnhill@wcsr.com.

BARNHILL, ROBERT EDWIN, III, lawyer; b. Lubbock, Tex., Dec. 29, 1956; s. Robert Edwin Jr. and Karen Sue (Green) B.; m. Jana Susan Barnett, Aug. 9, 1980. BBA, Tex. Tech U., 1976, MBA, JD, 1980. Bar: Tex. 1980, U.S. Dist. (no. dist.) Tex. 1980; CPA; personal fin. specialist; CFP. Staff acct. Peat, Marwick & Mitchell, Dallas, 1980-82; assoc. Blackledge Law Offices, Lubbock, 1982-83, Walters and Assocs., Lubbock, 1983-85; sole practice Lubbock, 1985—. Instr. Lubbock Christian Coll., 1982-83, So. Plains Coll., Lubbock, 1982-83, Tex. Tech. U., Lubbock, 1986—; sec., treas. Innovative Money Adv. Inc., 1985-94; pres. Live Spkrs., Inc., 1995—. Bd. dirs. So. Plains chpt. ARC, Lubbock, 1984-95, Big Bros./Big Sisters, Lubbock, 1984-95. Mem. ABA (tax sect., real estate, probate, trust), AICPAs, Tex. Bar Assn. (tax sect., real estate, probate, trust), Tex. Soc. CPAs, Fin. Planning Assn. (pres. Tex. chpt. 1988-89, pres. 2000-03), Nat. Spkrs. Assn., Toastmasters Club (dist. gov. 1986-87, sr. v.p. 1995-96, internat. pres. 1996-97, accredited spkr.). Republican. Mem. Christian Ch. Probate (including wills, trusts), Estate taxation, Personal income taxation. Home: 3311 59th St Lubbock TX 79413-5648 Office: PO Box 2583 Lubbock TX 79408-2583 E-mail: rebiii@worldnet.att.net.

BARNICK, HELEN, retired judicial clerk; b. Max, N.D., Mar. 24, 1925; d. John K. and Stacy (Kankovsky) B. BS in Music cum laude, Minot State Coll., 1954; postgrad., Am. Conservatory of Music, Chgo., 1975-76. With Epton, Bohling & Druth, Chgo., 1968-69; sec. Wildman, Harrold, Allen & Dixon, Chgo., 1969-75; part-time assignments for temporary agy. Chgo., 1975-77; sec. Friedman & Koven, Chgo., 1977-78; with Lawrence, Lawrence, Kamin & Saunders, Chgo., 1978-81; sec. Hinshaw, Culbertson et al., Chgo., 1982; sec. to magistrate judge U.S. Dist. Ct. (we. dist.) Wis., Madison, 1985-91; dep. clk., case adminstr. U.S. Bankruptcy Ct. (we. dist.) Wis., Madison, 1992-94; ret., 1994. Mem. chancel choir 1st Bapt. Ch., Mpls.; mem. choir, dir. sr. high choir Moody Ch., Chgo.; mem. chancel choir Fourth Presbyn. Ch., Chgo., Covenant Presbyn. Ch., Madison; dir. chancel choir 1st Bapt. Ch., Minot, N.D.; bd. dirs., sec.-treas. Peppertree at Tamarack Owners Assn., Inc., Wisconsin Dells, Wis.; mem. Festival Choir, Madison; mem. Madison Symphony Orch. League. Mem. Christian Bus. and Profl. Women (chmn.), Bus. and Profl. Women Assn., Participatory Learning and Tchg. Orgn., Madison Civics Club, Sigma Sigma Sigma. Home: 7364 Old Sauk Rd Madison WI 53717-1213

BARNTHOUSE, WILLIAM JOSEPH, lawyer; b. Jefferson City, Mo., Nov. 25, 1948; s. William Robison and Genevieve L.; children: Joseph, Jonathan, James. AB, Rockhurst Coll., 1970; JD, U. Mo., 1973, LLM in Trial and Criminal Law, 1976; MFA, PhD, Am. Film Conservatory. Bar: Mo. 1973, U.S. Dist. Ct. (we. dist.) Mo. 1973, U.S. Ct. Appeals (8th cir.) 1973, Colo. 1976, U.S. Dist Ct. (ea. dist.) Mo. 1976, U.S. Dist. Ct. Colo. 1976, U.S. Ct. Appeals (10th cir.) 1976, U.S. Supreme Ct. 1977. Trial clk. to presiding justice Mo. 16th Jud. Cir., Kansas City, 1972-73; pros. atty. Jackson County, Kansas City, 1973; sr. rsch. atty. Mo. Ct. Appeals, Kansas City, 1974; sr. counsel Gulf Oil Co., Denver, 1975-77; sr. regional counsel Conoco Oil Corp./Consol Coal Co./Dupont, Denver, 1978-84; gen. counsel ChemTech Corp., Denver, 1984—; pvt. practice Denver, 1984—2003. Asst. prof. fellow law U. Mo. Law Sch., Kansas City, 1974; adj. prof. U. Denver Law Sch., 1975-78; gen. counsel, chief exec. officer EnviroInc, 1984-91; gen. counsel AgriTell, Inc., 1985-91, Am. Internat. Inn Film Ltd., gen. counsel 1984-88; gen. counsel Van Schaak, 1985; gen. coun. Regency Ltd., 1991-95; bd. dirs., CEO, prodr. INN Internat. News Network, News-on-News; dean, CEO, dir. Am. Film Conservatory, 1991-2000, dir., prodr., chmn., 1992-2003; chmn dir., prodr. News-on-the-News, 1999-2002, prodr., dir., 1992-2002; prodr., dir. Caravan Europe Films, 1991-2002; dir., prodr. Am. Film Acad. Intl. Travel Network, 2003; dir. Design Props, 2003; chmn. Internat. News Network, 1992-2003; prodr., dir., actor, cinematographer Internat. Travel Network, 1992-2003; chmn., dir., prodr. Internat. Film Acad., 1992-2003, People News, 1992-2003, Real News, 1992-2003; dir. Sundance Internat. Films, 1984-2003; CEO, dir. INTL cable TV 1989-2003, Design Props 2003-; dir. News-on-the-News 1991-2003, Weather Fashions 1999-2003; CEO IFA art gallery 1989-2003. Author: International Ventures, 1973, Corporate Law Update, 1973, Media Television Law, 1976, Corporate Law, 1980, International Mergers, 1981, Media/Telephone Compliance, 1982, Internat. Media, 1983, International Contracts, 1984, International Law, 1985, Entertainment Law, 1985, Cable TV Compliance U.S. Cabinet Level Policy, 1985, General Counsel Entertainment and International Transactions, 1986, Cable TV Transactions, 1986, Media & TV Law, 1987, Sports Law, 1987, Media and Film Negotiation, 1988, Corporate Securities Law, 1989, Corporate General Counsel Liability, 1990, Film Contracts, 1991, Film & TV Law, 1991, International Transactions, 1991, International Media, 1992, General Counsel Media and TV, 1992, International Media and Film Update, 1992, Media & Television Law, 1992, International Cable TV Law, 1992, Sports Representation, 1993, International Entertainment Representation, 1994, International Cable Joint Venture, 1994, News and Media Law, 1995, Film and TV Contracts, 1995, Digital Editing, 1998, DVD and Telephony, 1999, others; dir. numerous documentaries and films. Bd. dirs. Internat. Films. Served to maj. NG, 1970-86. Nat. Inst. Trial Adv. scholar, 1974. Fellow Am. Film Conservatory; mem. ABA (comm. and media sect., vice chmn. natural resource and environ. law sect. 1980—), Colo. Bar Assn., Denver Bar Assn., Mo. Bar Assn., Colo. Trial Lawyers Assn., Rocky Mountain Mineral Law Found. Oil, gas, and mineral, Entertainment, Private international. Office: 2757 E Jamison Ave Centennial CO 80122-3323

BARNUM, CHARLES EARL, III, lawyer; b. Fargo, N.D., Apr. 10, 1951; s. Charles Earl Jr. and Margaret E. (Ebner) B.; m. Nadeen Sue Carlson, 1989; children: Aimie Joyce, Charles Earl IV. BA, U. Minn., 1974; JD, William Mitchell Coll. of Law, 1978. Pvt. practice, Crosby, Minn., 1978—2003. Mayor City of Crosby, 1988-92; firefighter Crosby Fire Dept., 1983-2003. Mem. Crosby C. of C. (pres. 1980), Lions (pres. Cuyuna Range club 1982-83), Cuyuna Country Club (sec. 1994-2002). Avocations: golf, hunting. Family and matrimonial, Probate (including wills, trusts), Property, real (including real estate development, water). Address: 15 E Main St PO Box 85 Crosby MN 56441-0085

BARNUM, JOHN WALLACE, lawyer; b. N.Y.C., Aug. 25, 1928; s. William Wallace Atterbury and Frances (Long) Barnum; m. Nancy Russell Grinnell, Sept. 13, 1958; children: Alexander Stone, Sarah Kip, Cameron Long. BA, Yale U., 1949; LLB, Inst. Derecho Internat. and Comparativo, Havana, Cuba, 1957. Bar: Conn. 1957, N.Y. 1958, D.C. 1977; on Brussels fgn. lawyer list, 1995. Adminstrn. asst. Cerro de Pasco Copper Corp., Lima, Peru, 1946; jr. asst. purser Grace Lines, 1946; analyst 1st Banking Corp., Tangier, Morocco, 1950; reg. rep. Bache & Co., London and Paris, 1951-52; assoc. Cravath, Swaine & Moore, N.Y.C., 1957-62, ptnr., 1963-71; gen. counsel U.S. Dept. Transp., Washington, 1971-73, undersec., 1973-74, dep. sec., 1974-77; resident fellow Am. Enterprise Inst. for Pub. Policy Rsch., Washington, 1977-78, vis. fellow, 1978-86; ptnr. White & Case, Washington, 1978-94, McGuireWoods, LLP, Brussels, 1995—; pres. McGuireWoods Internat. LLC, Brussels, 1999—; mng. ptnr. McGuireWoods Kazahhstan LLP, Almaty, 1999—. U.S. del. Inter Am. Comml. Arbitration Commn., 1969—71; del. NATO Com. for Challenges to Modern Soc., 1973—76; adv. mem. Coun. on Wage and Price Stability, 1974—77; mem. Coun. Adminstrv. Conf. U.S., 1973—77. Bd. editors Regulation: AEI Jour. on Govt. and Soc., 1977-86. Chmn. bd. Internat. Play Group, 1962-77; bd. dirs., mem. exec. com. N.Y C. Ctr. Music and Drama, 1969-75; trustee Washington Drama Soc. (Arena Stage), 1983-93; bd. overseers Corcoran Gallery of Art, Washington, 1994-2000; pres. U.S. Fedn. Friends Mus., 2002-. Mem.: Am. Arbitration Assn. (exec. com. 1968—72, bd. dirs. 1968—98), Nat. Def. Transp. Assn. (chmn.mil. airlift com. 1983—94, bd. dirs. 1988—94), Am. Bar Found., D.C. Bar Assn., N.Y. State Bar Assn. (exec. com., chmn. antitrust law sect. 1979—80), Internat. Bar Assn., N.Y. Yacht Club, Amateur Ski Club, Chevy Chase Club, Met. Club, Watersportvereniging Noord-Beveland, Cercle Royal Gaulois Artistique et Litteraire, Am. Club of Brussels (gov., exec. com., 1st v.p.). Antitrust, Alternative dispute resolution, Transportation. Home: 182 Ave Franklin Roosevelt 1050 Brussels Belgium also: 2029 Connecticut Ave NW Washington DC 20008-6141 Office: McGuireWoods LLP 250 Ave Louise, Bte 64 1050 Brussels Belgium E-mail: jbarnum@mcguirewoods.com.

BARON, CHARLES HILLEL, lawyer, educator; b. Phila., Aug. 18, 1936; s. Samuel A. and Rose (Bailinky) B.; m. Irma Elaine Frankel, June 15, 1958 (dec. 1985); children: Jessica Susan, Ira Benjamin, David Hume; m. Dianne M. Quartarone, Sept. 9, 1988; 1 child, Samuel Guy. AB in Philosophy with honors, U. Pa., 1958, PhD in Philosophy, 1972; LLB, Harvard U., 1961. Bar: Pa. bar 1967, U.S. Supreme Ct. bar 1970, Mass. bar 1972. Asst. prof. law U. Pa., 1965-66; assoc. firm Blank Rome Klaus & Comisky, Phila., 1966-68; chief law reform, consumer's adv. Community Legal Svcs., Inc., Phila., 1968-70; assoc. prof. law Boston Coll., 1970-74, prof., 1974—, assoc. dean, 1972-74. Exec. dir. Resource Ctr. Consumers Legal Svcs., 1975-77. Author: (with M. Saks) The Use, Nonuse, and Misuse of Applied Social Research, 1980, Droit Constitutionnel et Bioéthique: L'Expérience Americaine, 1997; contbr. articles to profl. jours. Chmn. Cheltenham Twp. (Pa.) Dem. Party, 1966-68; mem. Mass. Health Facilities Appeals Bd., 1974-75; chmn. Mass. Gov.'s Adv. Com. on Prepaid Legal Svcs., 1978-86; bd. dirs. CEPA Found., Death With Dignity Nat. Ctr., Washington, 2001—; mem. bd. overseers Mass. Supreme Jud. Ct. Hist. Soc., 1999—. Recipient various community awards; U. Pa. fellow, 1961-63 Mem. ABA, Am. Assn. Law Schs., Soc. Am. Law Tchrs., Am. Soc. Law and Medicine (bd. editors Am. Jour. Law and Medicine 1978—, bd. dirs.), Civil Liberties Union Mass. (bd. dirs., pres. 1989-91, trustee Mass. Civil Liberties Found.), ACLU. Jewish. Home: 60 Grove Hill Ave Newton MA 02460-2335 Office: Boston Coll Law Sch 885 Centre St Newton MA 02459-1148 E-mail: baron@bc.edu.

BARON, FREDERICK DAVID, lawyer; b. New Haven, Dec. 2, 1947; s. Charles Bates and Betty (Leventhal) B.; m. Kathryn Green Lazarus, Apr. 4, 1982; children: Andrew K. Lazarus, Peter D. Lazarus, Charles B. BA, Amherst Coll., 1969; JD, Stanford U., 1974. Bar: Calif. 1974, D.C. 1975, U.S. Supreme Ct. 1978, U.S. Dist. Ct. D.C. 1979, U.S. Ct. Appeals (D.C. cir.) 1979, U.S. Dist. Ct. (no. dist.) Calif. 1982, U.S. Ct. Appeals (9th cir.) 1982. Counsel select com. on intelligence U.S. Senate, Washington, 1975-76; spl. asst. to U.S. atty. gen. Washington, 1977-79; asst. U.S. atty. for D.C., 1980-82; atty. Clark, Baron & Korda, San Jose, Calif., 1982-83; ptnr. Cooley, Godward, Palo Alto, Calif., 1983—; assoc. dep. atty. gen., dir. Exec. Office for Nat. Security U.S. Dept. of Justice, 1995-96. Lectr. U.S. Info. Svc., 1979-80; pres. bd. trustees Keys Sch., Palo Alto, 1983-87; bd. dirs. Retail Resources, Inc., 1987-88; mem. bd. vis. Stanford Law Sch., 2003--. Co-author, editor U.S. Senate Select Com. on Intelligence Reports, 1975-76; also articles. Issues dir. election com. U.S. Senator Alan Cranston, 1974, Gov. Edmund G. Brown Jr., 1976; mem. transition team Pres. Carter, 1976-77, Pres. Clinton, 1992; del. Calif. Dem. Conv., 1989-90. Mem. ABA, Calif. Bar Assn., D.C. Bar Assn., Santa Clara County Bar Assn., Univ. Club. Federal civil litigation, State civil litigation. Office: Cooley Godward LLP 5 Palo Alto Sq Palo Alto CA 94306-2122

BARR, JAMES HOUSTON, III, lawyer; b. Louisville, Nov. 2, 1941; s. James Houston Jr. and Elizabeth Hamilton (Pope) Barr; m. Sarah Jane Todd, Apr. 16, 1970 (div.); 1 child, Lynn Jamison; m. Cindy Ann Jeffries, May 31, 1997; children: Worden Pope Washington, Augustine Washington Jeffries. Student, U. Va., 1960-63, U. Tenn., 1963-64; BSL, JD, U. Louisville, 1966. Bar: Ky. 1966, U.S. Ct. Appeals (6th cir.) 1969, U.S. Supreme Ct. 1971, U.S. Ct. Mil. Appeals 1978. Law clk. Ky. Ct. Appeals, Frankfort, 1966-67; asst. atty. gen. Ky. Frankfort, 1967-71, 79-82; asst. U.S. atty. U.S. Dept. Justice, Louisville, 1971-79, 83—; 1st asst. U.S. Atty., 1978-79; asst. dist. counsel U.S. Army C.E., Louisville, 1982-83. Lt. comdr. USNR, 1967-81, lt. col. USAR, 1981-91. Mem. FBA (pres. Louisville chpt. 1975-76, Younger Fed. Lawyer award 1975), Ky. Bar Assn., Louisville Bar Assn., Soc. Colonial Wars, SAR, Washington Family Soc., Pendennis Club, Louisville Boat Club, Filson Club, Delta Upsilon. Republican. Episcopalian. Home: 100 Westwind Rd Louisville KY 40207-1520 Office: US Atty 510 W Broadway Ste 1000 Louisville KY 40202-2281

BARR, JAMES NORMAN, federal judge; b. Kewanee, Ill, Oct. 21, 1940; s. James Cecil and Dorothy Evelyn (Dorsey) B.; m. Trilla Anne Reeves, Oct. 31, 1964 (div. 1979); 1 child, James N. Jr.; m. Phyllis L. DeMent, May 30, 1986; children: Renae, Michele. BS, Ill. Wesleyan U., 1962; JD, Ill. Inst. Tech., 1971. Bar: Ill. 1972, Calif. 1977. Assoc. Pretzel, Stouffer, Nolan & Rooney, Chgo., 1974-76; claims counsel Safeco Title Ins. Co., L.A., 1977-78; assoc. Kamph & Jackman, Santa Ana, Calif., 1978-80; lawyer pvt. practice Law Offices of James N. Barr, Santa Ana, 1980-86; judge U.S Bankruptcy Ct. Ctrl. Dist. Calif., Santa Anna, 1987—. Adj. prof. Chapman U. Sch. Law, 1996—. Lt. USN, 1962-67, Vietnam. Mem. Fed. Bar Assn. (Orange County chpt. bd. dirs. 1996-2000), Orange County Bar Assn. (cmty. outreach com.), Nat. Conf. Bankruptcy Judges, Orange County Bankruptcy Forum (bd. dirs. 1989—), Peter M. Elliott Inn Ct. (founder, first pres. 1990-91), Warren J. Ferguson Am. Inn of Ct. (founder). Office: US Bankruptcy Ct 411 W 4th St Santa Ana CA 92701-4500

BARR, JOHN MONTE, lawyer; b. Mt. Clemens, Mich., Jan. 1, 1935; s. Merle James and Wilhelmina Marie (Monte) B.; student Mexico City Coll., 1955; BA, Mich. State U., 1956; JD, U. Mich., 1959; m. Marlene Joy Bielenberg, Dec. 17, 1954; children: John Monte, Karl Alexander, Elizabeth Marie. Admitted to Mich. bar, 1959, since practiced in Ypsilanti; mem. Ellis B. Freatman, Jr., 1959-61; ptnr., chief trial atty. Freatman, Barr, Anhut & Moir and predecessor firm, 1961-63; pres. Barr, Anhut, Assoc. PC, 1963-01; pres. Barr, Anhut, Gilbreath, 2001—; city atty. City of Ypsilanti, 1981—, City of Belleville, 2000—. Lectr. bus. law Eastern Mich. U., 1968-70. Pres., Ypsilanti Family Service, 1967; mem. Ypsilanti Public Housing Com., 1980-84; sr. adviser Explorer law post Portage Trail council Boy Scouts Am., 1969-71, commr. Potawatomi dist., 1973-74, commr. Washtenong dist., 1974-75, dist. committeeman, 1984, wolverine coun. v.p., 1992, v.p. Great Saulk Trail coun., 1995—; bd. dirs. Mich. Mcpl. League Legal Def. Fund., pres. 1989-90, sec. High/Scope Ednl. Rsch. Found., past pres. Washtenaw 100 Club, 1980—. Served with AUS, 1959-60. Recipient Silver Beaver award Boy Scouts Am., 1992, Mich. Mcpl. League award of Merit Mcpl. League Legal Def., 1992. Mem. State Bar Mich. (grievance bd. hearing panel 1969-97, state rep. assembly 1977-82, bd. commrs. 1993—), Am., Ypsilanti, Washtenaw County (pres. 1975-76, Profl. and Civility award 1998) Bar Assns., Washtenaw County Trial Lawyers Assns., Mich. Mcpl. Attys. Assn. (pres. 1989-90, MAMA dist. mcpl. atty. award, 1993), U.S. (instr. piloting, seamanship, sail), Ann Arbor (comdr. 1972-73) power squadrons. Lutheran. Club: Washtenaw Country. Contbr. articles to boating mags. General practice. Home: 1200 Whittier Rd Ypsilanti MI 48197-2152 Office: 105 Pearl St Ypsilanti MI 48197-2611

BARR, JOHN ROBERT, retired lawyer; b. Gary, Ind., Apr. 10, 1936; s. John Andrew and Louise (Stentz) B.; m. Patricia A. Ferris, July 30, 1988; children: Mary Louise, John Mills, Jennifer Susan. BA, Grinnell Coll., 1957; LL.B. cum laude, Harvard U., 1960. Bar: Ill. 1960. Assoc. Sidley Austin Brown & Wood, Chgo., 1960—69, ptnr., 1970—99, sr. counsel, 2000—02; ret., 2002. Mem. Ill. Ho. of Reps., 1981-83, Commn. on Presdl. Scholars, Washington, 1975-77; mem. Ill. Electric Utility Property Assessment Task Force, 1998-99. Chmn. Ill. Bd. Regents, 1971-77; mem. Ill. Bd. Higher Edn., 1971-77, 87—; chmn. Ill. Student Assistance Commn., 1985—; chmn. Rep. Ctrl. Com. of Cook County, Chgo., 1978-85; mem. Rep. state ctrl. com. 9th Congl. Dist. Ill., 1986-93; trustee Grinnell Coll., 1996—, Evanston Hist. Soc., 2001—; bd. dirs. Steppenwolf Theatre Co., Chgo., 1992—. Mem. ABA (chmn. task force on utility deregulation of state and local tax coms.), Ill. State Bar Assn. (chmn. state tax sect. coun. 1986-87), Chgo. Bar Assn. (chmn. com. on state and mcpl. taxation 1974-75), Taxpayers' Fedn. Ill. (treas. 1990-92, vice chmn. 1992-95, chmn. 1995-97), The Civic Fedn. (bd. dirs. 1993-97), Selden Soc., Nat. Assn. State Bar Tax Sects. (sec.-treas. 1989-90, vice chmn. 1990-91, chmn. 1991-92), Emil Verban Soc., Lawyer's Club Chgo., Chgo. Club, Phi Beta Kappa. Episcopalian. Administrative and regulatory, Legislative, State and local taxation. Home: 1144 Asbury Ave Evanston IL 60202-1137 Office: Sidley Austin Brown & Wood Bank One Plz 10 S Dearborn Chicago IL 60603 E-mail: jrbarr@sidley.com.

BARR, JON-HENRY, lawyer; b. Livingston, N.J., Sept. 1, 1970; s. Gary and Susan Barr. BA, Lehigh U., 1992; JD, Seton Hall U., 1995. Bar: N.J. 1996, D.C. 1998, U.S. Dist. Ct. N.J. 1996, U.S. Ct. Appeals (3d cir.) 1997. Jud. law clk. Superior Ct. N.J., Freehold, N.J., 1995-96; assoc. Law Offices of Robert Blackman, Edison, N.J., 1996-98; ptnr. Barr & Canada, LLC, Clark, N.J., 1998—. Sec. Union Middlesex REACT, Woodbridge, N.J., 1989—; councilman Twp. of Clark, N.J., 1993-94; mem. Clark Rep. Civic Assn., 1996—. Named one of Outstanding Young Men of Am., 1998. Mem. N.J. State Bar Assn., Union County Bar Assn. (young lawyer trustee 2000-2001), Union County Mcpl. Prosecutors' Assn. (pres. 2001-2002). Jewish. Avocations: politics, travel. General civil litigation, Criminal, General practice. Home: 69 Fairview Rd Clark NJ 07066-2904 Office: Barr and Canada LLC 21 Brant Ave Clark NJ 07066-1512

BARR, MICHAEL CHARLES, financial journalist; b. White Plains, N.Y., Nov. 2, 1947; s. Charles Yerger and Joan Tames (Biggar) B.; m. Helen June Rumsey, Mar. 17, 1973. Student, Washington and Lee U.; BA summa cum laude, Rutgers Coll., 1969; JD, Columbia U., 1972, MBA, 1980. Bar: N.J. 1976, N.Y. 1978, U.S. Supreme Ct. 1976. Assoc. McCarter & English, Newark, 1976-77, Conboy, Hewitt, O'Brien & Boardman, N.Y.C., 1977-78; investment banker Kidder, Peabody & Co., Inc., N.Y.C., 1980-82; v.p. Mfrs. Hanover Trust Co., N.Y.C., 1982-90, A-L Assocs., N.Y.C., 1990-92; corp. sec., dir. H. Rivkin & Co., Inc., N.Y.C., 1992-93; securities analyst Standard & Poor's Corp., N.Y.C., 1993-98; Russian securities specialist H. Rivkin & Co., Inc., N.Y.C., 1998-99; emerging markets specialist HP Capital Mkts. Group, N.Y.C., 1999-2000; fin. cons. AXA Advisors, Inc., N.Y.C., 2000; corp. bond corr. Dow Jones and Co., N.Y.C., 2001—. Guest commentator on Russia, CNN, 1998-2000. Mem. adv. bd. Washington and Lee Alumni Coll., 1996-98; mem. 30th Reunion planning com. Columbia Law Sch. Class of 1972, 2002. Lt. USN, 1972-76. Recipient Loyal Son award Rutgers Alumni Assn., 1976. Mem. U.S. Polo Assn., Phi Beta Kappa.

BARR, WILLIAM PELHAM, lawyer, former attorney general of United States; b. NYC, May 23, 1950; s. Donald and Mary (Ahern) B.; m. Christine Moynihan, June 23, 1973; 3 children. AB, Columbia U., 1971, MA, 1973; JD, George Washington U., 1977. Bar: Va. 1977, D.C. 1978. Staff officer CIA, Washington, 1973-77; law clk. to presiding judge Cir. Ct., Washington, 1977-78; assoc. Shaw, Pittman, Potts & Trowbridge, Washington, 1978-82, 83-84, ptnr., 1985-89, 93-94; dep. asst. dir. domestic policy staff The White House, Washington, 1982-83; asst. atty. gen. Office Legal Counsel, U.S. Dept. Justice, Washington, 1989-90, dep. atty. gen., 1990-91, atty. gen., 1991-93; exec. v.p., gen. counsel GTE Corp., Washington; exec v.p., gen. counsel Verizon Communications, New York; vice chmn., bd. of dir. The Coll. of William & Mary. Mem. ABA, Va. State Bar Assn., D.C. Bar Assn., KC. Republican. Roman Catholic. Office: Verizon Communications Legal Dept 38th Fl 1095 Avenue of the Americas New York NY 10036*

BARRATT, JEFFREY VERNON, lawyer; b. London, Oct. 31, 1950; s. Arnold Douglas and Edith Joyce (Terry) Courtney-Lewis; m. Sharon Mary Tregaskis. LLB, Sydney U., 1973; postgrad., 1973-75. Trainee Giovanelli & Burgess, Sydney, 1971-73; asst. Mallesons, Sydney, 1973-75, Norton Rose, London, 1976-79; ptnr., 1979—. Avocations: cricket, skiing, opera, rugby. Banking, Oil, gas, and mineral. Office: Norton Rose Kempson House Camomile St EC3A 7AN London England Fax: 00442072836500.

BARRETT, BRUCE ALAN, lawyer; b. Pitts., Pa., Aug. 9, 1950; s. Hugh Horner and Ethel (McCrea) B.; m. Gayle Gray, Sept. 7, 1974; children: Eric, Sarah, Brian. BA, U. Pitts., 1972; JD, Cleve. State U., 1975. Bar: Pa. 1975, U.S. Dist. Ct. (we. dist.) Pa. 1978. Ptnr. Magee & Barrett, Meadville, Pa., 1975-79; sole practice Meadville, 1979-85; ptnr. Barrett & Dratler, Meadville, 1985—. 1st asst. pub. defender Crawford County, Meadville, 1978-2002. Chmn. parade com. Meadville Meml. Day Celebration, 1980-82. Named one of Outstanding Young Men Am., 1986. Mem. Pa. Bar Assn., Crawford County Bar Assn. (treas. 1988-91, v.p. 2003), Pa. Jaycees (parliamentarian 1988, assoc. legal counsel 1989, legal counsel 1990), Meadville Jaycees (pres. 1979-80, Amb. award 1988, Senatorship award 1990). Republican. Presbyterian. State civil litigation, Criminal, General practice. Office: Barrett & Dratler 965 S Main St Meadville PA 16335-3273

BARRETT, DAVID EUGENE, judge; b. Hiawassee, Ga., June 25, 1955; s. Homer and Laura Arispah (Wilson) B.; m. Donna L. Barrett; children: Laura Elizabeth, Thomas Jeffrey. BA summa cum laude, U. Ga., 1977, JD cum laude, 1980. Assoc. Erwin, Epting, et al, Athens, Ga., 1980-84, Blasingame, Burch, et al, Athens, 1984; pvt. practice Hiawassee, 1984-92; judge Recorders Ct., 1986-92, Superior Ct., Enotah Cir., 1992—. Counsel Towns County Humane Soc., Hiawassee, 1985-92; counselor Alzheimer Support, Hiawassee, 1985. Mem. ABA, Ga. Bar Assn., Mountain Bar Assn. (sec. 1987-88, v.p. 1988-89, pres. 1989-90), Western Bar Assn. (sec. 1983-84), Trial Lawyers Assn. Am., Towns County C. of C. (bd. dirs. 1986-87, 90-92, pres. 1988), Demosthenian Lit. Soc. (bd. dirs., sec. bd. trustees 1978-89, chmn. bd. 1986-89), Athens Jaycees (v.p. 1983-84). Home: 924 Mining Gap Ln Young Harris GA 30582-2324 Office: Superior Ct Enotah Cir 59 S Main St Ste K Cleveland GA 30528-1376

BARRETT, DAVID F. lawyer; b. L.A., Oct. 6, 1962; s. Frederick H. and E. Fern (Wagoner) Barrett; m. Teresa Lynn Emmert, Feb. 14, 1998; 1 child, Abigail Lynn. BS, Calif. State U., L.A., 1987; JD, MBA, Brigham Young U., 1992. Bar: Mo. 1993, Kans. 1993, U.S. Dist. Ct. (we. dist.) Mo. 1993, U.S. Dist. Ct. Kans. 1993. Police officer City of Alhambra, Calif., 1983-89; pvt. practice Independence, Mo., 1993—98; Joplin City prosecutor, 1998—2000; asst. atty. gen., 2001—. Editor: Trust Law, 1990, Mo. Employment Discrimination Law, 2000; author: Municipal Court Proceedings, chap. 11 of Mo. Local Govt. Law, 2002; contbr. articles to profl. jours Scholar Brigham Young U., 1990-92. Mem. Mo. Bar, Kans. Bar. Republican. Avocations: reading, racquetball. Federal civil litigation, Family and matrimonial, Labor (including EEOC, Fair Labor Standards Act, labor-management relations, NLRB, OSHA). Office: Missouri Atty Gen's Office PO Box 899 Jefferson City MO 65102

BARRETT, DAVID OLAN, lawyer; b. Indianapolis, May 25, 1970; m. Jacqueline R. Barrett. BA in Polit. Sci. and Journalism, Ind. U., 1992, JD cum laude, 1995. Bar: Ind. 1995, U.S. Dist. Ct. (no. and so. dists) Ind., 1995, U.S. Ct. Appeals (7th cir.), 1998, U.S. Supreme Ct., 1999. Assoc. Ice Miller, Indpls., 1995-99; corp. counsel Emmis Comm. Corp., Indpls., 1999—. Mem. bd. editors Ind. Law Jour.; contbr. numerous articles to lay publs. and profl. jours; presenter on topics relating to corp. and comm. law. Mem. Indpls. New Leaders Project, 1997-98; past pres., hon. v.p. No. Am. Fedn. Temple Youth (NFTY); bd. mem. Union of Am. Hebrew Congregations, 1988-89; alumni bd. dirs. Ind. U. Sch. Journalism, 2001--. Mem. ABA, Ind. State Bar Assn., Indpls. Bar Assn., Order of Barristers. General civil litigation, Communications, Corporate, general. Home: 10823 Diamond Dr Carmel IN 46032-9309 Office: Emmis Comm Corp One Emmis Plaza 40 Monument Cir Ste 700 Indianapolis IN 46204-3017 E-mail: dbarrett@emmis.com.

BARRETT, GEORGE EDWARD, lawyer; b. Nashville, Oct. 19, 1927; s. George E. and Annie (Conroy) B.; m. Eloise McBride Barrett, Sept. 14, 1957; (div. 1988); children: Anne-Louise Barrett Thompson, Mary Eloise Barrett Brewer, Kathryn Conroy Barrett Cain. BS, Spring Hill Coll., 1952; diploma, Oxford U., Eng., 1953; JD, Vanderbilt U., Nashville, 1957. Bar: Tenn., U.S. Ct. Appeals (6th cir.), U.S. Supreme Ct. Atty. Barrett, Johnston & Parsley, Nashville. Civil rights, Labor (including EEOC, Fair Labor Standards Act, labor-management relations, NLRB, OSHA). Office: Barrett Johnston & Parsley 217 2nd Ave N Nashville TN 37201-1601 E-mail: gbarrett@barrettjohnston.com.

BARRETT, JAMES EMMETT, judge; b. Lusk, Wyo., Apr. 8, 1922; s. Frank A. and Alice C. (Donoghue) Barrett; m. Carmel Ann Martinez, Oct. 8, 1949; children: Ann Catherine Barrett Sandahl, Richard James, John Donoghue. Student, U. Wyo., 1940—42, LLB, 1949; student, St. Catherine's Coll., Oxford, Eng., 1945, Cath. U. Am., 1946. Bar: Wyo. 1949. Mem. firm Barrett and Barrett, Lusk, 1949—67; atty. Niobrara Sch. Dist., 1950—64; county and pros. atty. Niobrara County, Wyo., 1951—62; atty. Town of Lusk, 1952—54; atty. gen. State of Wyo., 1967—71; judge U.S. Circuit Ct. Appeals (10th cir.), 1971—, now sr. judge. Active Boy Scouts Am.; trustee St. Joseph's Children's Home, Torrington, Wyo., 1971—85; sec.-treas. Niobrara County Rep. Ctrl. Com. Cpl. U.S. Army, 1942—45, ETO. Recipient Disting. Alumni award, U. Wyo., 1973, Coll. Law U. Wyo., 2002. Mem.: VFW, Am. Legion, Order of Coif (hon. mem. Wyo. Coll. Law/U. Wyo. chpt.).

BARRETT, JANE HAYES, lawyer; b. Dayton, Ohio, Dec. 13, 1947; d. Walter J. and Jane H. Barrett BA, Calif. State U.-Long Beach, 1969; JD, U. So. Calif., 1972. Bar: Calif. 1972, U.S. Dist. Ct. (cen. dist.) Calif. 1972, U.S. Ct. Appeals (9th cir.) 1982, U.S. Supreme Ct. Assoc. Lawler, Felix & Hall, L.A., 1972—84; ptnr. Arter & Hadden, L.A., 1984—94; mng. ptnr. Preston, Gates & Ellis, L.A., 1994—2002; ptnr. Piper Rudnick, L.A., 2002—. Lectr. bus. law Calif. State U., 1973-75. Mem. adv. bd. Harriet Buhai Legal Aid Ctr., 1991-96, mem. bd. pub. counsel, 1996-98; pres. Pilgrim Parents Orgn. 1990-91; chmn. fin. Our Mother Good Counsel Sch.; bd. regents Loyola, H.S., 2000—. Named Outstanding Grad. Calif. State U., Long Beach, 1988, Outstanding Alumnae Polit. Sci., 1993. Fellow Am. Bar Found.; mem. ABA (bd. govs. 1980-84, chmn. young lawyers divsn. 1980-81, com. on delivery of legal svcs. 1985-89, exec. coun. legal edn. and admissions sects. 1985-89, fin. sec. torts and ins. practice 1982-83, adv. mem. fed. judiciary com. 9th circuit rep. 2000—, v.p. 1997—, Am. Bar Endowment 1999, bd. dirs. 1990—, sec. 1993-95, v.p. 1998-99, pres., 1999-2000, bd. fellows young lawyers divsn. 1992—, del 9th cir. jud. conf., atty. del. U.S. Dist. Ct. ctrl. dist. Calif. Atty. Conf. 2002—), Calif. State Bar (com. adminstrn. of justice, editl. bd. Calif. Lawyers 1981-84), Legion Lex (bd. dirs. 1990-93), Los Feliz Homeowners Assn. (bd. dirs.). Democrat. Federal civil litigation, General civil litigation, Intellectual property. Office: Piper Rudnick 1999 Ave of the Stars Los Angeles CA 90067 E-mail: jane.barrett@piperrudnick.com.

BARRETT, JOHN J(AMES), JR., lawyer; b. Phila., May 19, 1948; s. John J. and Carmela (DiJohn) B.; m. Rosemary A. Campagna, Aug. 23, 1969; children: Jeffrey, Kristin, Jacqueline. BA, Temple U., 1970, JD, 1973. Bar: Pa. 1973, N.J. 1987, U.S. Dist. Ct. (ea. dist.) Pa. 1973, U.S. Ct. Appeals (3rd cir.) 1975, U.S. Dist. Ct. (mid. dist.) Pa. 1986, U.S. Supreme Ct. 1986, U.S. Dist. Ct. N.J. 1987. Assoc. Saul, Ewing, Remick & Saul, Phila.,

1973-80; ptnr. Saul Ewing LLP, 1980—. Mem. Nat. Assn. R.R. Trial Counsel, Phila. Assn. Def. Counsel. Federal civil litigation, State civil litigation, Product liability. Office: Saul Ewing LLP 3800 Centre Sq W 1500 Market St Philadelphia PA 19102

BARRETT, KAREN MOORE, lawyer; b. Pitts., Jan. 16, 1950; d. James Newton and Grace Naomi (Gigax) Moore; m. Jay Elliott Barrett, June 24, 1972; children: Catherine Grace, Elizabeth Alice. AB, Bryn Mawr Coll., 1972; JD, Harvard U., 1977. Bar: Pa. 1977, U.S. Dist. Ct. (we. dist.) Pa. 1977. Assoc. Buchanan Ingersoll Profl. Corp., Pitts., 1977-84, ptnr., 1984-89; counsel CBS Corp. (formerly Westinghouse Electric Corp.), Pitts., 1989-90, sr. counsel, 1990-93, asst. gen. counsel, 1993-2000; sr. counsel The PNC Fin. Svcs. Group, Inc., Pitts., 2000—. Bd. dirs. Planned Parenthood of Western Pa., Inc., 1983-95, v.p., 1988-92; trustee Southminster Presbyn. Ch., 1995-98. Mem. ABA, Pa. Bar Assn., Allegheny County Bar Assn., Bryn Mawr of Western Pa. (Pitts., v.p. 1984-87, pres. 1987-91). Democrat. Corporate, general, Mergers and acquisitions, Securities. Office: PNC Fin Svcs Group Inc 249 5th Ave Pittsburgh PA 15222-2707

BARRETT, MICHAEL D. lawyer; b. Bloomsberg, Pa., July 5, 1956; m. Dana M. Barrett, Nov. 13, 1982; children: Lauren, Matthew. BS cum laude, U. Minn., 1977; JD cum laude, William Mitchell Coll. of Law, St. Paul, 1987; postgrad., U. Minn., 1980—. Bar: Minn. 1987; U.S. Dist. Ct. Minn. 1987. Law clk. Cousineau, McGuire & Anderson, Mpls., 1984-87, assoc., 1987-95, officer, sr. atty., 1996—2003, shareholder, 2003—. Mem. Minn. Def. Lawyers Assn., Def. Rsch. Inst., Hennepin County Bar Assn., Minn. State Bar Assn., Casco Point Assn. (pres., co-founder 1996—). Avocations: woodworking, hunting, fishing. Insurance, Personal injury (including property damage), Workers' compensation. Office: Cousineau McGuire & Anderson 1550 Utica Ave S # 600 Minneapolis MN 55416-5318

BARRETT, PHILLIP HESTON, lawyer, director; b. Detroit, May 7, 1943; s. Richard Hamilton and Jeanne Marcille (Webb) Barrett; m. Nancy Rose Samson, June 17, 1966 (div. Aug. 1979); children: Jeffrey Adam, Douglas Austin; m. Karen Lee Hock, Jan. 10, 1981 (div. Sept. 1999); 1 child, Andrew Hamilton. BS, Ohio State U., 1965, JD, 1968. Bar: Ohio 1968, US Dist. Ct. (so. dist.) Ohio 1971, US Ct. Appeals 1982. Assoc Porter, Wright, Morris & Arthur LLP, Columbus, Ohio, 1970—74, ptnr., 1975—. Trustee United Way of Franklin County, Inc., 1985—96, chmn., 1992—95; trustee Columbus Speech & Hearing Ctr., 1972—82, chmn., 1978—80; trustee Met. Human Svcs. Commn., 1986—91, chmn., 1987—89; trustee Children's Hosp. Found., 1993—98, Children's Rsch. Inst., 1998—. Capt. Signal Corps U.S. Army, 1968—70, Vietnam, Capt. JAG Corps USNG, 1971—73. Mem.: ABA, Columbus Bar Assn., DC Bar Assn., Columbus Bar Found., Ohio Bar Assn., Capital Club (Columbus), New Albany Country Club, Ohio State U. Pres.'s Club. Avocations: squash, skiing, golf, photography. Corporate, general, Finance, Property, real (including real estate development, water). Office: Porter Wright Morris & Arthur LLP 41 S High St Ste 3100 Columbus OH 43215-6194

BARRETT, ROBERT MATTHEW, law educator, lawyer; b. Bronx, N.Y., Mar. 18, 1948; s. Harry and Rosalind B. AB summa cum laude, Georgetown U., 1976, MS in Fgn. Service, JD, 1980. Bar: Calif. 1981. Assoc. Latham & Watkins, L.A., 1980-82, Morgan, Lewis & Bockius, L.A., 1982-84, Skadden, Arps, Slate, Meagher & Flom, L.A., 1984-86, Shea & Gould, L.A., 1986-87, Donovan, Leisure, Newton & Irvine, L.A., 1988-90; ptnr. Barrett & Zipser, L.A., Calif., 1991-93; prof. law San Fernando Valley Law Sch., Woodland Hills, Calif., 1993—. Civilian vol. L.A. Sheriff's Dept., 1997-99. Mem. State Bar Calif. (standing com. on profl. responsibility and conduct 1995-99, chair 1997-98, spl. advisor 1998-99), L.A. Bar Assn. (bd. advisors vols. in parole com. 1981—). Address: 21300 Oxnard St Woodland Hills CA 91367-5058 Fax: 818-883-8142. E-mail: robertbarrett@charter.net.

BARRETT, ROGER WATSON, lawyer; b. Chgo., June 26, 1915; s. Oliver R. and Pauline S. B.; m. Nancy N. Braun, June 20, 1940; children—Victoria Barrett Bell, Holly, Oliver. AB, Princeton U., 1937; JD, Northwestern U., 1940. Bar: Ill. 1940. Mem. firm Poppenhusen, Johnson, Thompson & Raymond, Chgo., 1940-43; 45-50; charge documentary evidence Nuremberg Trial, 1944-45; regional counsel Econ. Stablzn. Agy., Chgo., 1951-52; ptnr. Mayer, Brown & Platt, Chgo., 1952-91, of counsel, 1991—. Life trustee Mus. Contemporary Art, Chgo. With AUS, 1943-45. Mem. ABA, Ill. Bar Assn., Chgo. Bar Assn., Am. Coll. Trial Lawyers, Indian Hill Club (Winnetka), Old Elm Club, Commonwealth Club (Chgo.), Caxton Club (Chgo.). Antitrust, Federal civil litigation. Home: 84 Indian Hill Rd Winnetka IL 60093-3934 Office: Mayer Brown Rowe & Maw 190 S La Salle St Chicago IL 60603-3410

BARRON, FRANCIS PATRICK, lawyer; b. Boston, Apr. 17, 1951; s. Francis P. and Audrey (Lutz) B.; m. Eve Brandis Sundelson, Sept. 13, 1981; children: Elisha Brandis, Daniel Patrick, Susanna Catherine. AB, Harvard U., 1973, JD, 1978. Bar: N.Y. 1979, U.S. Dist. Ct. (so. dist) N.Y. 1979, U.S. Dist. Ct. (ea. dists.) N.Y. 1981, U.S. Ct. Internat. Trade 1982, U.S. Ct. Appeals (2d cir.) 1981, U.S. Ct. Appeals (6th cir.) 1983, U.S. Supreme Ct. 1983. Asst. dir. film Sta. WCVB-TV, Boston, 1973-75; assoc. Cravath, Swaine & Moore, N.Y.C., 1978-85, ptnr., 1985—. Mem. Harvard Vol. Defenders, Cambridge, 1977-78. Athletic scholar Nat. Football Found. Hall of Fame, 1969. Mem. ABA, N.Y. State Bar Assn., N.Y. County Bar Assn., Assn. of Bar of City of N.Y. Antitrust, General civil litigation, Mergers and acquisitions. Office: Cravath Swaine & Moore 825 8th Ave Fl 40 New York NY 10019-7416

BARRON, HAROLD SHELDON, lawyer; b. Detroit, July 4, 1936; s. George Leslie and Rose (Weinstein) B.; m. Roberta Yellin, Nov. 17, 1963; children: Lawrence Ira, Jean Louise. AB, U. Mich., 1958, JD, 1961. Bar: N.Y. 1963, Mich. 1961, Ill. 1983, Pa. 1992. Pvt. practice, N.Y.C., 1962-68; practice in Southfield, Mich., 1968-83, Chgo., 1983-93, 1991—2002; atty. Hughes Hubbard & Reed, 1962-68; corp. counsel Bendix Corp., 1968-69, sec., assoc. gen. counsel, 1969-72, sec., gen. counsel, 1972-83, v.p., 1974-83; ptnr. Arnstein, Gluck, Lehr, Barron & Milligan, Chgo., 1983-86, Seyfarth, Shaw, Fairweather & Geraldson, Chgo., 1986-91; v.p., gen. counsel Unisys Corp., Blue Bell, Pa., 1991-92, sr. v.p., gen. counsel, 1992-94, sr. v.p., gen. counsel, sec., 1994-99, sr. v.p., gen. counsel, 1999-2001, vice chmn., 2001—02; counsel McDermott, Will & Emery, 2002—. Mem. nat. adv. coun. and faculty Practising Law Inst., N.Y.C.; bd. dirs. Royal Maccabees Life Ins. Co., Southfield, 1983-94; chmn. bd. F.A. Tucker Group, Inc., 1991-95. Editor The Business Lawyer. Com. visitors U. Mich. Law Sch.; trustee Children's Hosp. Mich., Detroit, 1976-84; mem. Census Adv. Com. on Privacy and Confidentiality, 1975-76; mem. governing bd., adv. coun. Purdue U. Info. Privacy Rsch. Ctr.; bd. dirs. Citizens Rsch. Coun. of Mich., 1982-83, Greater Phila. Econ. Devel. Coalition. Served with AUS, 1961-62. Mem. ABA (coun. bus. law sect., bus. law sect.(chair, 2002-03), editor The Bus. Lawyer, Latin Am. legal initiatives coun., chmn. com. of corp. gen. counsel, sect. bus. law coun., com. corp. law and taxation, internat. bus. law com., com. devels. in investment svcs., com. long-range issues affecting bus. law practice, com. on corp. laws), Am. Arbitration Assn., Am. Soc. Corp. Secs. (securities law com.), CPR Inst. for Dispute Resolution (exec. com.), Mich. Bar Assn., Assn. Bar City N.Y. (com. corp. law depts.), Carlton Club, Chgo. Club, Bryn Mawr Country Club (Chgo.), The Reserve (Indian Wells, Calif.). Corporate, general, Mergers and acquisitions, Securities. Office: McDermott Will & Emery 227 W Monroe Chicago IL 60606-5096*

BARRON, HOWARD ROBERT, lawyer; b. Chgo., Feb. 17, 1930; s. Irwin P. and Ada (Astrahan) B.; m. Marjorie Shapira, Aug. 12, 1953; children: Ellen Barron Feldman, Laurie A. PhB, U. Chgo., 1948; BA, Stanford U., 1950; LLB, Yale U., 1953. Bar: Ill. 1953. Assoc. Jenner & Block, Chgo., 1957-63, ptnr., 1964-97; assoc. Schiff Hardin & Waite, Chgo., 1953, of counsel, 1997—. Contbr. articles to profl. jours. and books. Mem., then pres. Lake County Sch. Dist. 107 (now Dist. 112) Bd. Edn., Highland Park, 1964-71; pres. Lake County Sch. Bd. Assn., 1970-71; mem. Lake County High Sch. Dist. 113 Bd. Edn., Highland Park, 1973-77; mem. Highland Park Zoning Bd. Appeals, 1984-89. Lt. (j.g.) USNR, 1953-57. Mem.: ABA (co-chmn. subcom. labor and employment law, com. corp. counsel litigation sect. 1983—2002), Yale Club (N.Y.C.), Met. Club, Internat. Bar Assn., Yale Law Sch. Assn. of Ill. (pres. 1962), Yale Law Sch. Assn. (v.p. 1978—81), Chgo. Bar Assn., Fed. Bar Assn., Ill. State Bar Assn. (chmn. antitrust sect. 1968—69), Standard Club. Democrat. General civil litigation, Labor (including EEOC, Fair Labor Standards Act, labor-management relations, NLRB, OSHA). Home: 1366 Sheridan Rd Highland Park IL 60035-3407 Office: Schiff Hardin & Waite 6600 Sears Tower Chicago IL 60606 E-mail: hbarron@schiffhardin.com.

BARRON, JEROME AURE, law educator; b. Tewksbury, Mass., Sept. 25, 1933; s. Henry and Sadie (Shafmaster) B.; m. Myra Hymovich, June 18, 1961; children— Jonathan Nathaniel, David Jeremiah, Jennifer Leah AB magna cum laude, Tufts Coll., 1955; JD, Yale U., 1958; LL.M., George Washington U., 1960. Bar: Mass. 1959, D.C. 1960. Law clk. to chief judge U.S. Ct. Claims, Washington, 1960-61; assoc. firm Cross, Murphy & Smith, Washington, 1961-62; asst. prof. law U. N.D., Grand Forks, 1962-64; vis. assoc. prof. U. N.Mex., Albuquerque, 1964-65; dean Syracuse U. Coll. Law, 1972-73; assoc. prof. George Washington U., from 1965, prof., 1973—, dean, 1979-88, Lyle T. Alverson prof. law, 1987-2000, Harold H. Greene prof. law, 2000—. Author: (with Donald Gillmor and Todd Simon) Mass Communication Law, Cases and Comment, 6th edit., 1998, First Amendment in a Nutshell, 2d edit. 2000, Constitutional Law: Principles and Policy, 6th edit., 2002, (with C. Thomas Dienes, Wayne McCormack and Martin Redish) Constitutional Law In A Nutshell, 5th edit., 2002; contbr. articles, chpts. to profl. publs. Served with U.S. Army, 1959-60 Mem. ABA, D.C. Bar, Cosmos Club, Phi Beta Kappa. Office: George Washington U 2000 H St NW Washington DC 20006-4234

BARRON, MYRA HYMOVICH, lawyer; b. July 5, 1938; d. Leo and Lillian Estelle (Berman) Hymovich; m. Jerome Aure Barron, June 18, 1961; children: Jonathan Nathaniel, David Jeremiah, Jennifer Leah. AB cum laude, Smith Coll., 1959; student, L'Institut des Hautes Etudes, Geneva, 1957—58; MA, Johns Hopkins U., 1961; JD, Georgetown U., 1970. Bar: Va. 70, DC 72, NY. Instr. econs. U. ND, Grand Forks, 1962—64; econ. rsch. asst. U. N.Mex., Albuquerque, 1964—65; legal aid staff atty. Fairfax County, Va., 1971—72, asst. county atty., 1974—81; assoc. Melvin & Melvin, Syracuse, NY, 1973; counsel Fairfax County Redevel. and Housing Authority, Fairfax, Va., 1981—88; ptnr. Sprenger & Lang (formerly Weissbrodt, Swiss & Mc Grew, 1989—98, Weinberg & Jacobs, Rockville, Md., 1998—2000, of counsel, 2001—. Dep. gen. counsel Housing and Devel. Law Inst., 1988—94, of counsel, 1994—2000. Editor: Jour. Affordable Housing and Cmty. Devel. Law, ABA, 1993—99; contbr. articles to housing jours.; mem.: Georgetown Law Jour., 1967—68. Recipient Samuel Bowles award, Smith Coll., 1959. Mem.: LWV (local chmn. nat. events 1962—64), ABA (mem. governing com. 1994—99, co-chmn. profit practice group 2000—03, mem. forum on affordable housing and cmty. devel. law). Home: 3231 Ellicott St NW Washington DC 20008-2061 Office: Weinberg & Jacobs LLP 11300 Rockville Pike Ste 1200 Rockville MD 20852

BARROW, BARBARA A. lawyer, educator; b. Boston, Oct. 16, 1958; d. Francis Michael and Yvette Theresa Hughes; m. Timothy Sterling Barrow, May 28, 1983; children: Jessica, Lindsay, Timothy Jr. BA, Regis Coll., 1980; MBA, Rivier Coll., 1989; JD, Roger Williams U., 1997. Bar: R.I. 1997, Mass. 1998, U.S. Dist. Ct. R.I. 1998, U.S. Supreme Ct. 2002. Atty. Updegrove & Gontarz, Ltd., Middletown, RI, 1997—. Mem. restoration adv. bd. Naval Sta., Newport, RI, 1998—. Amb. People to People, 2000—02. Mem.: ABA, Inns Ct., R.I. Trail Lawyers Assn., R.I. Bar Assn. Avocation: cello. Family and matrimonial, Education and schools, General practice. Home: 1 Wedgewood Dr Middletown RI 02842 Office: Updegrove and Gontarz Ltd 314 Oliphant Ln Middletown RI 02842

BARROW, CLISBY HALL, lawyer; b. Macon, Ga., Sept. 20, 1965; s. Fletcher Kennedy and Ann Kite Hall; children: John Costley Barrow IV. BA, Davidson Coll., 1987; JD, Vanderbilt U., 1991. Bar: Tenn. 1991, Ga. 1992. Law clk. to U.S. Dist. Judge Thomas A. Wiseman, Nashville, 1991-92; assoc. Baker, Worthington, Crossley, Stansberry & Woolf, Nashville, 1993-94, Bass, Berry & Sims, PLC, Nashville, 1994—99; ptnr. Walker, Bryant, Tipps & Malone, 2000—. Intellectual property, Personal injury (including property damage), Product liability. Office: Walker Bryant Tipps & Malone 2300 One Nashville Place 150 Fourth Ave N Nashville TN 37219

BARROWS, RONALD THOMAS, lawyer; b. Detroit, Jan. 19, 1954; s. Harland Wayne and Jeanette Edith (Authier) B. BA in English and Polit. Sci. magna cum laude, Oakland U., 1976; JD, Wayne State U., 1979. Bar: Mich. 1979, U.S. Dist. Ct. (ea. dist.) Mich. 1979, U.S. Ct. Appeals (6th cir.) 1983, U.S. Tax Ct. 1986; lic. real estate broker, Mich. Assoc. Abbott, Nicholson, Quilter, Esshaki & Youngblood, P.C., Detroit, 1979-80; counsel Lindon Land Co., Inc., Harper Woods, Mich., 1980-82; pvt. practice St. Clair Shores, Mich., 1981-87; ptnr. Barrows & Alt, P.C., Troy, Mich., 1987-90; sole practice Grosse Pointe, Mich., 1990—. Cons./counselor to corp. and pvt. real estate investors and developers; adj. prof. investment banking and venture capital formation, asset protection planning, assoc. prof. Oakland U. Paralegal Program, 1989-90. Contbr. articles to profl. jours. Mem. Mich. Comml. Investment Coun.; chmn. adv. com. Mich. chpt. Nat. Multiple Sclerosis Soc. 1996-2002, co-chair coun. adv. com., 1997-2002, mem. client programs com., 1998—. Mem. ABA, ATLA, Mich. Bar Assn. (title stds. com. 1985—, real property coun. 1987-97, treas. 1994-97, chmn. Water Law Com. 1985-90), Nat. Assn. Realtors, Mich. Assn. Realtors (sr. instr. 1980-91), Macomb County Assn. Realtors (lawyer realtor com. 1984-88), Nat. Order Barristers. Republican. Presbyterian. Avocations: sailing, billiards, theater, photography. Finance, Property, real (including real estate development, water). Office: PO Box 36958 Grosse Pointe MI 48236-0958 E-mail: baron7@comcast.net.

BARRY, DAVID EARL, lawyer; b. N.Y.C., Nov. 25, 1945; s. David J. Barry and Beatrice A. Richtmyer; m. Teresa M. Anderson, July 26, 1969; children: Andrea, David R., Kristin. BA, Coll. Holy Cross, Worcester, Mass., 1966; JD, Harvard U., 1969. Bar: N.Y. 1969, Conn. 1978. Ptnr. Kelley Drye & Warren, LLP, N.Y.C., 1969—. Mem. ABA, Univ. Club, Apawamis Club. Roman Catholic. Pension, profit-sharing, and employee benefits, Property, real (including real estate development, water). Home: 2 Puritan Rd Rye NY 10580-1931 Office: Kelley Daye & Warren LLP 101 Park Ave New York NY 10178-0002

BARRY, DAVID F. lawyer, educator; b. Marblehead, Mass., Mar. 3, 1940; s. Donald and Eileen E. (Kirchthurn) B.; m. Ann Marie Seward, June 15, 1968. BS, Salem (Mass.) State Coll., 1963; JD, Suffolk U., 1968, MBA, 1978. Bar: Mass. 1968, U.S. Dist. Ct. Mass. 1970, U.S. Ct. Appeals (3d cir.) 1978, U.S. Supreme Ct. 1979, U.S. Tax Ct. 1980. Tchr. pub. schs., Long Beach, Calif., 1963-64; pvt. practice Marblehead, 1968—. Adjudicator U.S. Govt., Boston, 1970-73; prof. bus. adminstrn. Salem (Mass.) State Coll., 1974— ; cert. mediator and arbitrator; cons. SBA, Salem, 1982— . Bd. dirs. Market Sq. Assocs., Inc., Marblehead, 1979— ; mem. U.S. Service Acad. selection com., Salem, 1983— . Mem. Mass. Bar Assn., Essex County Bar Assn., NEA. Republican. Roman Catholic. Condemnation (eminent domain), General practice, Probate (including wills, trusts). E-mail: david.barry@salemstate.edu.

BARRY, DESMOND THOMAS, JR., lawyer; b. N.Y.C., Mar. 26, 1945; s. Desmond Thomas and Kathryn (O'Connor) B.; m. Patricia Mellicker, Aug. 28, 1971; children: Kathryn, Desmond Todd. AB, Princeton U., 1967; JD, Fordham U., 1973. Bar: N.Y. 1974, U.S. Dist. Ct. (so. and ea. dist.) N.Y. 1974, U.S. Ct. Appeals (2d cir.) 1974, U.S. Ct. Appeals (9th cir.) 1980, U.S. Ct. Appeals (5th cir.) 1983, U.S. Ct. Appeals (3d cir.) 1984, U.S. Supreme Ct. 1985. Assoc. Condon & Forsyth, N.Y.C., 1973-79, ptnr., 1979—. Trustee Canterbury Sch., New Milford, Conn., 1970-80. Capt. USMC, 1967-70, Vietnam. Decorated Navy Commendation medal with combat V, Combat Action medal, 1969, Vietnamese Cross of Gallantry, 1969. Mem.: ABA (chmn. aviation and space law com. 1996—97), Internat. Assn. Def. Counsel (exec. com.), Assn. Bar City NY, NY State Bar Assn., Queenwood Golf Club (London), Hawk's Nest Golf Club (Vero Beach, Fla.), Winged Foot Golf Club (bd. govs. 1999—2001), Univ. Club N.Y.C. Republican. Roman Catholic. Aviation, Insurance. Home: 40 Charter Oak Ln New Canaan CT 06840-6705 Office: Condon & Forsyth LLP 685 3rd Ave Fl 14 New York NY 10017-4024 E-mail: dbarry@condonlaw.com.

BARRY, FRANCIS JULIAN, JR., lawyer; b. New Orleans, Oct. 7, 1949; s. Francis Julian and Bertha Anna (Lion) B.; m. Janice Leigh Gonzales, May 8, 1976; children: Francis III, Marianna. BA, Tulane U., 1970, JD, 1973. Bar: La. 1973, U.S. Dist. Ct. (ea. dist.) La. 1973, U.S. Ct. Appeals (5th cir.) 1973, U.S. Dist. Ct. (we. dist.) La. 1978, U.S. Ct. Appeals (11th cir.) 1982, U.S. Supreme Ct. 1991. Assoc. Deutsch, Kerrigan & Stiles, New Orleans, 1973-78, ptnr., 1978—. Editor Admiralty Law Inst. Symposium Tulane U., New Orleans, 1973. Adv. editor Tulane Maritime Law Jour. (formerly The Maritime Lawyer), 1975—. Served to capt. USAR. Mem. Fed. Bar Assn., La. Bar Assn., New Orleans Bar Assn., Maritime Law Assn. U.S. (proctor, carriage of goods com. 1982-87, 2000—, transp. hazardous substances com. 1987—), Admiralty Law Inst. New Orleans (mem. planning com. 1998—, mem. program com. 2000—), U.S. Naval Inst., Southeastern Admiralty Law Inst., La. Assn. Def. Counsel, Def. Rsch. Inst., Assn. Average Adjusters London, Am. Legion, Navy League U.S., Army-Navy Club (Washington), La. Landmarks Soc., Bienville Club, Univ. Club (N.Y.C.), Plimsoll Club, Mariners Club, The Round Table Club. Republican. Roman Catholic. Admiralty. Home: 4301 Dumaine St New Orleans LA 70119-3617 Office: Deutsch Kerrigan & Stiles 755 Magazine St New Orleans LA 70130-3672 E-mail: fbarry@dksno.com.

BARRY, LANCE LEONARD, judge; b. Boston, Dec. 18, 1965; s. Leonard and Theodora Ann Pawlak. BEE, Cath. U. Am., 1988; MS, Johns Hopkins U., 1991; JD, George Mason U., 1995. Bar: Va. 1995, U.S. Ct. Appeals (fed. cir.) 1995, bar: D.C. 1998. Engring. analyst RCI Internat., Vienna, Va., 1987; engring. aide MPR Assocs., Washington, 1987; engring. technician BBN Labs., Arlington, Va., 1988; cons. Booz, Allen & Hamilton, Bethesda, Md., 1988-90, sr. cons., 1990—91; patent examiner U.S. Patent and Trademark Office, Arlington, Va., 1991-95, primary examiner, 1996-99, adminstrv. patent judge, 1999—. Spkr. Va. State Bar, Richmond, 1998—; instr. U.S. Patent and Trademark Office, Arlington, 1996-97, curriculum com., 1999—; law lectr. U.S. Patent and Trademark Office, Arlington, 1997-99, EEO counselor, 1999. Pub. adv. com. mem. Lawyers Coop. Pub., Raleigh, N.C., 1995; contbr. articles to profl. jours. Head tutor St. Francis Xavier Sch., Washington, 1997-2001; cmty. svc. v.p. St. Mary's Ch., Alexandria, Va., 2001; vol. Greater D.C. Cares, Washington, 1999—; social officer Holy Trinity Ch., Washington, 1997-98; tutor kids and chemistry program Am. Chem. Soc., 2002—; lector Our Lady of Lourdes Ch., 2002—; vol. Alexandria Christmas in April, 2000—, house capt., 2003. Mem. IEEE (manuscript referee Potentials mag. 1989—), Am. Intellectual Property Law Assn., Patent and Trademark Office Soc. (rep. 1996-98), Mensa, Phi Theta Kappa, Tau Beta Pi. Avocations: volunteering, Italian, birdwatching, travel, skiing. Office: US Patent and Trademark Office 10-A12 1225 Jefferson Davis Hwy Arlington VA 22202

BARRY, MARYANNE TRUMP, federal judge; b. N.Y.C., Apr. 5, 1937; d. Fred C. and Mary Trump; m. John J. Barry, Dec. 26, 1982; 1 child, David W. Desmond. BA, Mt. Holyoke Coll., 1958; MA, Columbia U., 1962; JD, Hofstra U., 1974, LLD (hon.), Seton Hall U.; LLD (hon.), Caldwell Coll.; LLD (hon.) , Kean Coll. Bar: N.J. 1974, N.Y. 1975, U.S. Ct. Appeals (3d cir.), U.S. Supreme Ct. Asst. U.S. Atty., 1974-75; dep. chief appeals div., 1976-77; chief appeals div., 1977-82; exec. asst. U.S. Atty., 1981-82; 1st asst., 1981-83; judge U.S. Dist. Ct., N.J., 1983-99, U.S. Ct. Appeals (3d cir.), Newark, 1999—. Chmn. Com. on Criminal Law Jud. Conf. of U.S., 1994-96. Fellow Am. Bar Found.; mem. ABA, N.J. Bar Assn., Am. Judicature Soc. (bd. dirs.), Assn. Fed. Bar State of N.Y. (pres. 1982-83). Office: US Ct Appeals PO & Courthouse Bldg Rm 333 PO Box 999 Newark NJ 07101-0999*

BARRY, THOMAS JOSEPH, lawyer; b. Dallas, Dec. 20, 1955; s. James Marcellus and Marjorie (Scholl) B. BA, U. Tex., 1977, JD, 1980. Bar: Tex. 1981, U.S. Dist. Ct. (so. dist.) Tex. 1981. Legisl. aide House of Reps., Austin, Tex., 1981; assoc. Anderson, Smith, Null and Stofer, Victoria, Tex., 1981-88; prin. Law Offices Thomas J. Barry, Yorktown, Tex., 1989—. Democrat. Lutheran. Banking, Oil, gas, and mineral. Office: PO Box 546 Yorktown TX 78164-0546 Home: 10102 Brantley Bnd Austin TX 78748-1265

BARSAMIAN, J(OHN) ALBERT, lawyer, judge, educator, criminologist, arbitrator; b. Troy, N.Y., May 1, 1934; s. John and Virginia Barsamian; m. Alice Missirilan, Apr. 21, 1963; children: Bonnie, Tamara. BS in Psychology with honors, Union Coll., 1956; JD, 1968; LLB, Albany Law Sch., 1959; postgrad., SUNY, Albany, 1964, Nat. Jud. Coll., 1997. Bar: N.Y. 1961, U.S. Dist. Ct. (no. dist.) N.Y. 1961, U.S. Supreme Ct. 1967; fire tng. cert. N.Y. State Exec. Dept. Pvt. practice, 1961—; dir. criminal sci., chmn. dept. Russell Sage Coll., 1970-88, assoc. prof. criminal sci., 1977-82, prof., 1982-87, prof. emeritus, 1987—. Lectr. office local govt. divsn. criminal justice svcs. State N.Y., 1964—72, N.Y. State Police Acad., 1970; judge adminstrv. law N.Y. State Pub. Employment Rels. Bd., 1996—2001, supervising judge, asst. dir. pub. employment practice and representation, 2001—; faculty pub. affairs and policy pub. svc. tng. program Nelson A. Rockefeller Coll., 1986—91, Sch. Labor Rels. Ext. divsn. Cornell U., 1986; gaming cons. Gov's Office Indian Rels., NY, 1991—92; spl. counsel Office of Police Chief, Cohoes, NY, 1986—92, to city mgr., Troy, NY, 1993; counsel Watervliet Police Assn., 1967—74, Cohoes Police Assn., 1967—74, Colonie Police Assn., 1977—80, Troy Police Command Officers Assn., 1981—85, North Greenbush Police Assn., 1985—90, Office of the Police Chief, Syracuse, NY, 1985—90, Fire Dept. Union, Albany, NY, 1986, Shenectady Fire Fighters Union, 1992—95; gen. counsel Internat. Narcotic Enforcement Officers Assn., 1982—84, Troy Uniformed Firefighters Assn., 1977—97; spl. investigator Rensselaer County Dist. Atty., 1959—61; mem. law guardian panel N.Y. State Family Ct., 1967—77; mem. mediation panel N.Y. State Pub. Employment Rels. Bd., 1968—73; supervising judge, asst. dir. Pub. Employment Practices and Representation, 2001—. Founder, chmn. dept. police sci. Hudson Valley C.C., 1961-69; mem. adv. bd. History Ctr. Skidmore Coll., 1993—; bd. dirs. Rensselaer County ARC, 1966-70; mem. alumni coun. Union Coll., 1981-86; mem. parish coun. St. Peter Armenian Ch., Watervliet, N.Y., 1979-83, chmn., 1981-83, vice chmn., 1984; evaluator office of non-collegiate programs N.Y. State Dept. Edn., 1985—; hon. dep. sheriff St. Mary Parish (La.); mem. Rensselaer County Criminal Justice Coordinating Coun., 1976-78. Decorated chevalier, knight comdr. Sovereign Order of Cyprus; recipient Police Sci. Students award, Hudson Valley C.C., 1968, meritorious svc. to law enforcement award, Law Enforcement Officers Soc., 1969, Archbishop's cert. merit, Armenian Ch. Am., 1973, Lawyers Coop. Pub. Co. prize in criminal law, 1957, Gabrielli award, Albany Law Sch., 2002—03; scholar Tarzian, Union Coll., 1952—56, Porter, Albany Law Sch., 1954—56, Saxton, 1956—59. Mem.: Internat. Coll. Master Advocates, N.Y. State Assn. Adminstrv. Law Judges (bd. dirs. 1999, 2001), Am. Coll. Barristers,

N.Y. State Trial Lawyers Assn., Union Coll. Alumni Assn. (Silver medal 1956), Am. Assn. Criminology, Acad. Criminal Justice Scis., Am. Arbitration Assn. (svc. award 1983), Nat. Assn. Adminstrv. Law Judges, N.Y. Bar Assn. (chmn. com. on police 1970—72, trial lawyers sect. com. contg. legal edn. 1977—97, subcom. on adminstrv. law judges 2000), ABA (com. on police selection and tng. 1967—69), ATLA, N.Y. Vet. Police Assn. (life; counsel), Rose Croix (most wise master Delta chpt. 1986), Masonic Vet. Assn. Troy (life), Les Amis d'Escoffier Soc., Lambda Epsilon Chi, Alpha Phi Sigma, Phi Delta Theta. Administrative and regulatory, Criminal, Labor (including EEOC, Fair Labor Standards Act, labor-management relations, NLRB, OSHA). Home and Office: 5 Sage Hill Ln Albany NY 12204-1315

BARSKY, WAYNE MITCHELL, lawyer; b. East Meadow, N.Y., July 7, 1957; s. Murray William Barsky and Billie Joyce Luftig; m. Margaret J. Goldenhersh, Sept. 19, 1987; children: Daniel Paul, Catherine Claire. BA, SUNY, Binghamton, 1979; JD, U. Calif., Berkeley, 1983. Bar: D.C. 1984, U.S. Dist. Ct. D.C. 1984, U.S. Ct. Appeals (D.C. cir.) 1984, Calif. 1985, U.S. Dist. Ct. (cen. dist.) Calif. 1985, U.S. Ct. Appeals (9th cir.) 1985, U.S. Dist. Ct. (so., ea. and no. dists.) Calif. 1986, U.S. Ct. Appeals (fed. cir.) 1993, Mo. 1996, U.S. Dist. Ct. (ea. dist.) Mo. 1996. Assoc. Irell & Manella, LLP, L.A., 1984—89, ptnr., 1989—96; ptnr., co-chair intellectual property dept. Gibson, Dunn & Crutcher, LLP, L.A., 1997—. Bd. dirs., exec. com. Pub. Counsel Law Ctr., L.A.; commentator Intellectual Property Lawcast; co-chair Intellectual Property Inst., 1997; judge pro tem L.A. Superior Ct.; spkr. in field. Contbr. articles to profl. jours. Vol. Turning Point Shelter, Santa Monica, Calif., 1997—. Recipient Pro Bono commendation, State Bar Calif., 1986. Mem.: ABA, L.A. Intellectual Property Law Assn., Am. Intellectual Property Law Assn. Democrat. Jewish. Avocations: windsurfing, reading, running, writing. Intellectual property, Patent. Home: 17781 Camino de Yatasto Pacific Palisades CA 90272 Office: Gibson Dunn & Crutcher LLP 2029 Century Park East Los Angeles CA 90067

BARTELSTONE, TED HENRY, lawyer; b. Bronx, N.Y., Feb. 1, 1950; s. Murray J. and Janet (Rappoport) B.; m. Katherine Elizabeth Morton, Oct. 26, 1985. BS, U. Buffalo, 1972; JD, Bklyn. Law Sch., 1977. Bar: Fla. 1977, U.S. Supreme Ct. 1989, U.S. Court of Appeals 1983, Federal Circuit 2000. Atty. Sinclair, Louis, Siegel & Heath, Miami, Fla., 1977-83, Hollander & Schiffrin, Miami, 1983-87; atty./ptnr. Hollander, Schiffrin and Bartelstone, Miami, 1987-90, Hollander & Bartelstone, P.A., Miami, 1990—2001; pvt. practice Miami, 2001—. Mem. ABA, ATLA, Fla. Bar. General civil litigation, Labor (including EEOC, Fair Labor Standards Act, labor-management relations, NLRB, OSHA), Trademark and copyright. Office: Ste 2390 2 S Biscayne Blvd Miami FL 33131-1808

BARTH, KAREN ANN, lawyer; b. Dubuque, Iowa, Dec. 8, 1966; d. Henry Victor and Janet Marie Barth. BA, Colo. State U., 1989; JD, U. Calif., Davis, 1995. Bar: Calif. 1995, U.S. Dist. Ct. (cen. dist.) Calif. 1995, U.S. Dist. Ct. (so. dist.) Calif. 1999, U.S. Ct. Appeals (9th cir.) 1999. Law clk. Colo. Atty. Gen.'s Office, Denver, 1993; law clk. to Justice Davis, Calif. 3d Dist. Appellate Ct., Sacramento, 1994; legal intern Calif. Atty. Gen.'s Office, Sacramento, 1994, Sacramento Dist. Atty.'s Office, Sacramento, 1995; shareholder Baum, Hedlund, Aristei, Guilford & Schiavo and predecessor firms, L.A., 1995—. Mem. ABA, State Bar of Calif., Nat. Assn. Women Lawyers, L.A. Women Lawyers Assn., George McBurney Complex Litigation Inn of Ct. Avocations: rock climbing, diving, skiing, basketball, volleyball. Appellate, Commercial, consumer (including collections, credit), Product liability. Office: Baum Hedlund et al 12100 Wilshire Blvd Ste 950 Los Angeles CA 90025-7107 E-mail: kbarth@baumhedlundlaw.com.

BARTH, MARK HAROLD, lawyer; b. Lincoln, Ill., June 22, 1951; s. rev. Harold Julius and Maxine Virginia Barth; m. Jannette Morgan Berg, June 29, 1974; children: Katherine, Erica. BA, The Johns Hopkins U., 1973; JD, Georgetown U., 1977. Bar: N.Y. 1978. Assoc. Curtis, Mallet-Prevost, Colt & Mosle, N.Y.C., 1977-86, ptnr., 1986—, mng. ptnr. London office, 1988-92. Mem. ABA, Internat. Bar Assn., Assn. Bar City N.Y. Corporate, general, Private international, Securities. Office: Curtis Mallet-Prevost Colt & Mosle 101 Park Ave New York NY 10178-0061

BARTHOLD, WALTER, lawyer; b. Toronto, Ont., Can., June 8, 1924; came to U.S., 1924; s. Walter and Josephine (Salmon) B.; m. Denise Buffington, May 2, 1957 (div. 1996); children: Charles F., David F., Nancy L.; m. Dorothy True LaValle, Sept. 7, 1996. BS, Northwestern U., 1948; LLB, Yale U., 1951. Bar: N.Y. 1952, U.S. Supreme Ct. 1963, U.S. Ct. Appeals (2d cir.) 1955. Assoc. Arthur, Dry & Kalish, N.Y.C., 1952-60, ptnr., 1961-78, Barthold & McGuire, N.Y.C., 1978-81, Kissam, Halpin & Genovese, N.Y.C., 1981-82, Barthold & Eikenberry, N.Y.C., 1983-84; pvt. practice N.Y.C., 1984-88; counsel Leaf Sternklar & Drogin, N.Y.C., 1988-89, Ferber, Greilsheimer, Chan & Essner, 1989-92. Author: Attorney's Guide to Effective Discovery Techniques, 1965. With U.S. Army, 1943-46, ETO. Fellow Am. Coll. Trial Lawyers, Am. Bar Found., N.Y. Bar Found.; mem. ABA, Assn. Bar City N.Y., N.Y. State Bar Assn., Yale Club. Democrat. Episcopalian. Avocations: music, biking, stamp collecting. Antitrust, General civil litigation. Home: 323 Stevens Ave Ridgewood NJ 07450-5203 Office: 489 5th Ave New York NY 10017-6105

BARTKUS, ROBERT EDWARD, lawyer; b. Kearny, N.J., Sept. 30, 1946; s. Edward Charles and Dorothy Agnes (Konschott) B.; m. Mary Bartkus. BA with honors, Swarthmore Coll, 1968; JD, Stanford U., 1976. Bar: Calif. 1976, N.J. 1977, N.Y. 1977, U.S. Supreme Ct (3d, 2d cirs.), U.S. Dist. Ct. N.J., U.S. Dist. Ct. (so. and ea. dist.) N.Y. Spl. counsel Schulte, Roth & Zabel, N.Y.C., 1985-88; ptnr. Dillon, Bitar, & Luther, LLC. Tchg. asst. Stanford U. Law Sch., 1976; mem. Dist. X Ethics Com., 1992-97, chair, 2002-03; lectr. N.J. Inst. for Continuing Edn., 1988—; master John J. Gibbons Intellectual Property Inn of Ct. Articles co-editor Stanford Law Rev., 1974-76; author Innovation Competition 28 Stanford Law Rev. 1976; author, editor: New Jersey Federal Civil Practice, 1992, N.J. Federal Civil Procedure, 1999; mem. editl. bd. N.J. Law Jour. (Alfred C. Clapp award 1995). Atty. Community Law Offfice, 1976-79, Legal Aid Soc., 1979-87; mem. alumni coun. Swarthmore Coll., 1977-78. Lt. USNR, 1968-73. Mem. ABA (ethics com. Dist. X), Nat. Assn. Securities Dealers (arbitrator), N.J. Bar Assn. (chair fed. practice com.), Assn. Fed. Bar of State of N.J., Am. Arbitration Assn. (arbitrator), Delta Upsilon. Federal civil litigation, State civil litigation. Home: 6 Terrill Dr Califon NJ 07830-3443 Office: Dillon Bitar & Luther LLC 53 Maple Ave Morristown NJ 07963-0398 E-mail: rbartkus@dbl-law.com.

BARTLE, HARVEY, III, federal judge; b. Bryn Mawr, Pa., June 6, 1941; s. Harvey Jr. and Dorothy L. (Baker) B.; m. Nathalie Akin Vanderpool, June 12, 1993; 3 children, 2 stepchildren. AB in History, Princeton U., 1962; LLB, U. Pa., 1965. Bar: Pa. 1965, U.S. Dist. Ct. (ea. dist.) Pa. 1965, U.S. Ct. Appeals (3d cir.) 1969, U.S. Supreme Ct. 1978. Law clk. to Hon. John Morgan Davis U.S. Dist. Ct. (ea. dist.) Pa., 1965-67; assoc. Dechert, Price & Rhoads, 1967-73, ptnr., 1973-79, 81-91; Pa. Ins. Commr., 1979-80; Pa. Atty. Gen., 1980-81; judge U.S. Dist. Ct. (ea. dist.) Pa., 1991—. Editor Law Review U. Pa. Capt. U.S. Army Res. Mem. ABA, Phila. Bar Assn., Am. Law Inst. Episcopalian. Office: US Dist Ct 601 Market St Philadelphia PA 19106-1713

BARTLETT, CLIFFORD ADAMS, JR., lawyer; b. N.Y.C., Mar. 17, 1937; s. Clifford Adams and Frances (Burke) B.; m. Eileen Marie McCarthy; children: Elizabeth, Kathleen, Clifford III, Christopher, Karen, Charles, Eileen, Kevin, Jamison. BA, St. Francis Coll., N.Y.C., 1959; JD, St. John's U., N.Y., 1962. Bar: N.Y. 1963, U.S. Dist. Ct. (so. dist.) N.Y. 1964, U.S. Supreme Ct. 1966. Ptnr. Bartlett, McDonough, Bastone & Monaghan, Mineola, N.Y., 1992—. Mem. faculty Practicing Law Inst., N.Y., 1980—, Nassau Acad. Law, Mineola, N.Y. & N.Y.C., 1984—. Mem. ABA, N.Y. State Bar Assn., Nassau County Bar Assn., Nassau-Suffolk Trial Lawyers Assn., Suffolk County Bar Assn. Avocations: golf, skiing, swimming. General civil litigation, Personal injury (including property damage), Product liability. Office: 300 Old Country Rd Mineola NY 11501-4198 also: 237 Park Ave New York NY 10017-3140 also: 81 Main St White Plains NY 10601-1711

BARTLETT, JAMES WILSON, III, lawyer; b. Pasadena, Calif., Mar. 21, 1946; s. James Wilson Jr. and Helen (Archbold) B.; m. Jane Edmunds Graves; children: Matthew Archbold, Polly Graves. BA, Washington & Lee U., 1968; JD, Vanderbilt U., 1975. Bar: Md. 1975, U.S. Dist. Ct. Md. 1975, U.S. Dist. Ct. (no. dist.) Ohio, 1992, U.S. Ct. Claims 1984, U.S. Ct. Appeals (4th cir.) 1976, U.S. Ct. Appeals (6th cir.) 1992, U.S. Supreme Ct. 1995. Assoc. Semmes, Bowen & Semmes, Balt., 1975-85; pvt. practice Balt., 1985-86; ptnr. Kroll & Tract, Balt., 1986-87, Wilson, Elser, Moskowitz, Edelman & Dicker, Balt., 1987-98, mng. ptnr., 1998-2001; ptnr. Semmes, Bowen & Semmes, Balt., 2001—. Permanent mem. jud. conf. 4th Cir. Assoc. editor: Am. Maritime Cases, 1997—; contbr. articles to profl. jours. Chmn. law firm campaign United Fund, Balt., 1979; bd. dirs. Roland Park Civic League, 1987-90. 1st lt. U.S. Army, 1969-71. Mem.: ABA (vice chmn. 1985—88, chmn. admiralty and maritime law tort and ins. practice sect. 1990—91, vice chmn. 1992—95, chmn. admiralty and maritime litig. com. litig. sect. 1997—99, vice chmn. 1999—), Assn. Average Adjusters U.S., Assn. Average Adjusters (Eng.), Md. Def. Counsel Inc., Def. Rsch. Inst., Maritime Law Assn. U.S. (proctor, bd. dirs. 1998—2001, chair practice and proc. com. 2000—), Balt. City Bar Assn., Md. Bar Assn., St. Andrews Soc., Am. Boat and Yacht Coun., Propeller Club U.S. (gov. Balt. chpt. 1984—87, 1997—2003, v.p. 1987—88, exec. v.p. 1988—89, pres. 1989—90, nat. regional v.p. 1991—92, nat. 3d v.p. 1995—96), Md. Club. Republican. Presbyterian. Product liability, Admiralty, General civil litigation. Home: 307 Edgevale Rd Baltimore MD 21210-1913 Office: Semmes Bowen & Semmes 250 W Pratt St Baltimore MD 21201 E-mail: jbartlett@mail.semmes.com.

BARTLETT, JOSEPH WARREN, lawyer; b. Boston, June 14, 1933; s. Charles W. and Barbara (Hastings) B.; m. May Parish, Apr. 28, 1956 (div.); children: Charles, Susan, Henry; m. Barbara Bemis, Sept. 20, 1980. AB, Harvard U., 1955; LLB, Stanford U., 1960. Bar: Mass. 1962, D.C. 1969, N.Y. 1981. Law clk. Chief Justice Warren, U.S. Supreme Ct., 1960-61; pvt. practice Boston, 1961-66; ptnr. Gaston & Snow, Boston, 1966-80, Gaston & Snow (formerly Gaston Snow Beekman & Bogue), N.Y.C., 1980-90, of counsel, 1990-91; ptnr. Mayer, Brown & Platt, 1991-96, Morrison & Foerster, N.Y.C., 1996—2002; of counsel Fish & Richardson P.C., N.Y.C. Counsel Mass. Commn. Adminstrn., 1964-65; gen. counsel, under sec. Dept. Commerce, Washington, 1967-69; prin. adviser on universal social security coverage Sec. of HEW, Washington, 1978-79; acting prof. Stanford U., 1978; trustee, mem. fin. com. Montefiore Med. Ctr.; mem. Council on Fgn. Relations; adj. prof. NYU Law Sch. Served to 1st lt. U.S. Army, 1956-57. Fellow Am. Bar Found.; mem. Am. Law Inst., Am. Bar Assn., Boston Bar Assn. (pres. 1977-78) Democrat. Episcopalian. Corporate, general, Securities. Home: 200 E 71st St Apt 16C New York NY 10021-5147 Office: Fish and Richardson PC 45 Rockefeller Plaza Ste 2800 New York NY 10111 Office Fax: 212-258-2291. E-mail: joseph.bartlett@fr.com.

BARTLETT, KATHARINE TIFFANY, law educator; b. New Haven, Feb. 16, 1947; d. Edgar Parmelee and Elizabeth (Clark) B.; m. Christopher H. Schroeder, Aug. 13, 1975; children: Emily, Ted, Elizabeth. BA, Wheaton Coll., 1968; MA, Harvard U., 1969; JD, U. Calif., Berkeley, 1975. Bar: Calif. 1975, N.C. 1980, U.S. Dist. Ct. (no. dist.) Calif. 1975, U.S. Dist. Ct. (mid. dist.) N.C. Law clk. to presiding justice Calif. Supreme Ct., San Francisco, 1975-76; atty. Legal Aid Soc. of Alameda County, Oakland, Calif., 1976-79; A. Kenneth Pye prof. of law Duke U., Durham, NC, 1979—; dean, 2000—. Vis. prof. UCLA, 1985-86, Boston U., 1990. Grad. prize fellow Harvard U., 1968-69, fellow Nat. Humanities Ctr., 1992-93. Mem. Am. Law Inst., Soc. Am. Law Tchrs., N.C. Women Attys., Am. Law Inst. (reporter for principles of family dissolution), Phi Beta Kappa. Democrat. Office: Duke Univ Law Sch Sci Dr and Towerview Rd Box 90362 Durham NC 27708-0362

BARTLETT, RICHARD JAMES, lawyer, former university dean; b. Glens Falls, N.Y., Feb. 15, 1926; s. George Willard and Kathryn M. (McCarthy) B.; m. Claire E. Kennedy, Aug. 18, 1951; children: Michael, Amy. BS, Georgetown U., 1945; LLB, Harvard U., 1949; LLD (hon.), Union Coll., 1974; ScD (hon.), Albany Med. Coll., 1986. Bar: N.Y. 1949. Pvt. practice, Glens Falls, 1949-73; with Clark Bartlett & Caffry, 1962-73; justice N.Y. State Supreme Ct., 1973-79; chief adminstr. of courts N.Y. State, 1974-79; dean Albany Law Sch., Union U., Albany, 1979-86; mem. Bartlett, Pontiff, Stewart, & Rhodes P.C., Glens Falls, N.Y., 1986—. Chmn. N.Y. Bd. Law Examiners, 1998-2001, N.Y. Jud. Commn. on Justice for Children, 1988-90; bd. trustees Nat. Conf. Bar Examiners, 1987-97, pres., 1996; dir. Nat. Conf. Bar Founds., 2001—; del. N.Y. Constl. Conv., 1967. Trustee Hyde Collection, Glens Falls, 1967-98. Capt. USAF, 1951-53. Fellow Am. Bar Found.; mem. ABA (house dels. 1997-2001), N.Y. State Bar Assn. (ho. of dels. 2002—), Assn. Bar City of N.Y., Warren County Bar, N.Y. Bar Found. (bd. dirs. 1989—, pres. 2000—), Am. Law Inst. Republican. Roman Catholic. General civil litigation, General practice, Municipal (including bonds). Office: 1 Washington St PO Box 2168 Glens Falls NY 12801-2168

BARTLETT, ROBERT WILLIAM, lawyer; b. Chgo., Nov. 11, 1941; s. Robert C. and Rita E. Bartlett; m. Mary Lou Holtzman, Mar. 8, 1988; 1 child, Brooke Ann. AB, Stanford U., 1963; LLB, U. Va., 1966. Bar: Ill. 1966. Assoc. counsel U.S. League Savs. Instns., Chgo., 1970-77, assoc. gen. counsel, editor legal bull., 1977-81, sr. v.p., 1981-91; exec. editor bus. and fin. group Commerce Clearing House, Riverwoods, Ill., 1991-2000. Mem. ABA (mem. com. on savs. instns. 1973--). Roman Catholic. Avocation: running. Banking. Home: 8 Anglican Ln Lincolnshire IL 60069-3316 E-mail: bartlettrw@earthlink.net.

BARTNOFF, JUDITH, judge; b. Boston, Apr. 14, 1949; d. Shepard and Irene F. (Tennenbaum) B.; m. Eugene F. Sofer, Sept. 10, 1978; 1 child, Nelson Bartnoff Sofer. BA magna cum laude, Radcliffe Coll., 1971; JD (Harlan Fiske Stone scholar), Columbia U., 1974; LLM, Georgetown U., 1975. Bar: D.C. 1975, U.S. Dist. Ct. D.C. 1975, U.S. Ct. Appeals (D.C. cir.) 1980, U.S. Ct. Appeals (fed. cir.) 1985, U.S. Ct. Appeals (11th cir.) 1988, U.S. Ct. Appeals (3d cir.) 1989, U.S. Claims Ct. 1991. Fellow Inst. Pub. Interest Representation, Georgetown Law Ctr., Washington, 1974-75; staff atty. Coun. Pub. Interest Law, Washington, 1975-77; spl. asst. to asst. atty. gen. criminal divsn. Dept. Justice, Washington, 1977-78, assoc. dep. atty. gen., 1978-80; spl. asst. U.S. atty. Office of U.S. Atty., Washington, 1980-81, asst. U.S. atty., 1982-85; assoc. firm Patton, Boggs & Blow, 1985-87, ptnr., 1988-94, assoc. ind. counsel, 1993-94; assoc. judge Superior Ct. of D.C., Washington, 1994—. Mediator U.S. Dist. Ct. D.C., 1991-94; mem. com. on pro se litig. U.S Dist. Ct., 1991-94. Mem. D.C. Bar Task Force on Children at Risk, 1997—98, D.C. Child Support Guidelines Commn., 2003—. Fellow Am. Bar Found.; mem. Nat. Assn. Women Judges, D.C. Bar, Women's Bar Assn. Office: 500 Indiana Ave NW Washington DC 20001-2131 E-mail: bartnofj@dcsc.gov.

BARTOL, ERNEST THOMAS, lawyer; b. Mineola, N.Y., Feb. 2, 1946; s. Frank Henry and Mary Ann (Kretlein) Bartol; m. Christine Ann Pillis; children: Jacqueline Marie, Aimee Elizabeth, Suzanne Melissa. BS in Acctg., Fordham U., 1967; JD, Villanova U., 1970. Bar: N.Y. 1971, U.S. Dist. Ct. (ea. and so. dists.) N.Y. 1973, U.S. Ct. Appeals (2d cir.) 1975, U.S. Supreme Ct. 1974. Staff acct. Pustorino, Puglisi, Behan & Co., N.Y.C., 1965-70; tax specialist Arthur Young & Co., Phila., 1970; acct. Arthur Andersen & Co., N.Y.C., 1970-71; assoc. Gehrig, Ritter, Coffey et al, Hempstead, N.Y., 1971-78; founder, mng. ptnr., sr. ptnr. Murphy, Bartol & O'Brien, LLP, Mineola, 1978—. Mem. exec. com. United Cerebral Palsy Assn. Nassau County, 1978—, chmn. forget-met-not-ball, 1987—92; pres., founder cmty. adv. coun. Syosset Cmty. Hosp., 1987—92; bd. dirs. LI Children's Mus., 1996—99; exec. leader Oyster Bay Rep. Com., 1978—2003; vice chmn. Nassau County Rep. Com., 2003—; sec., mem. parish coun. and spl. sch. com. St. Edward Roman Cath. Ch., Syosset, NY, 1978—80; trustee N.Y. Inst. Tech., 1997—99; bd. dirs. LI Coalition Fair Broadcasting, Inc., 2001. Named Man of the Yr., United Cerebral Palsy Assn. Nassau County, 1993, Heart Coun. L.I., Inc., 2001. Mem.: ABA, Cath. Lawyers Guild Diocese Rockville Centre, N.Y. State Trial Lawyers Assn., Fed. Bar Coun. N.Y., Nassau Lawyers Assn. LI (bd. dirs. 1977—, chmn. 1992—93, rec. sec. 1993—94, corr. sec. 1994—95, 1st v.p. 1995—97, pres. 1997—98), Criminal Cts. Bar Assn., Nassau County Bar Assn. (estates and trusts law com. 1975—, mem. profl. ethics com. 1980—86, 1989—93), N.Y. State Bar Assn. (trusts and estates law com. 1983—, lectr. estate topics), Chaminade HS Alumni Assn. (class rep. 1971, class dir. 1971—72, 1st v.p. 1972—74, pres. 1974—76), Rotary (sec.-treas. Syosset Club 1980—90), Alpha Kappa Psi. Roman Catholic. Avocations: racquetball, tennis, fishing, softball, stamp collecting. General civil litigation, Estate planning, Probate (including wills, trusts). Office: Murphy Bartol & O'Brien LLP 22 Jericho Tpke Ste 103 Mineola NY 11501-2976 E-mail: etbartol@aol.com.

BARTOLOMEO, PAUL JOSEPH, JR., lawyer; b. Phila., Feb. 13, 1949; s. Paul Joseph and Anna (Turchi) B.; m. Patricia Anne Knopic, Jan. 30, 1982; 1 child, Julia Anne. BS, St. Joseph's U., Phila., 1970; JD, Temple U., 1974. Bar: Pa. 1974, N.J. 1995; U.S. Dist. Ct. (ea. dist.) Pa. 1976, dist. N.J. 1995. Pvt. practice, Phila., 1979—. Bd. dirs. Networks for Training and Devel., Inc., Phila., 1995— Mem. Pa. Bar Assn., Sons of Italy, Phila. Bar Assn., Justinian Soc. Democrat. Roman Catholic. Avocations: tennis, golf. Personal injury (including property damage), Probate (including wills, trusts), Workers' compensation. Office: 2401 Pennsylvania Ave Ste 1A1 Philadelphia PA 19130-3002 E-mail: pjbart1a1@aol.com.

BARTON, ALAN JOEL, lawyer; b. N.Y.C., NY, Sept. 2, 1938; s. Sidney and Claire (Greenfield) B.; m. Ann Rena Beral, Jan. 29, 1961; children: Donna Frieda Olsen, Brian Joseph. AB, U. Calif., Berkeley, 1960, JD, 1963. Assoc. Nossaman, Krueger & Mash, L.A., 1963—70, ptnr., 1970—80, Paul, Hastings, Janofsky & Walker, LLP, L.A., 1980—2002, sr. counsel, 2002—. Lectr. UCLA Sch. Law, 2001—; lectr. corp. and securities law U. Calif. Continuing Edn. Bar, 1980—; lectr. venture capital and securities law Practicing Law Inst., 1986—. Assoc. editor U. Calif. Law Rev., 1963. Dir. Ctr. for Study of Young People in Groups, L.A., 1988—, Planned Parenthood, L.A., 1999—; trustee Dubnoff Ctr. for Ednl. Therapy, North Hollywood, Calif., 1976-80. Mem. ABA (com. on fed. regulation of securities), Calif. Bar Assn. (com. on corps.), Order of Coif, The Calif. Club. Republican. Jewish. Avocations: movies, Torah study, contemporary art, tennis, travel. Mergers and acquisitions, Securities. Office: Paul Hastings Janofsky & Walker LLP 515 S Flower St Fl 25 Los Angeles CA 90071-2300

BARTON, BERNARD ALAN, JR., lawyer; b. Glens Falls, N.Y., Aug. 13, 1948; s. Bernard A. Sr. and Geraldine (Bushey) B.; children: Lindsey, Kylie. BA, U. Fla., 1969, JD, 1975, LLM, 1976. Bd. cert. tax lawyer. Ptnr. Holland & Knight, Tampa, Fla., 1976—. Editor, contbg. author Florida Taxation, State Taxation Series, 1994. Mem. ABA, Nat. Assn. Bond Attys., Fla. Bar Assn. (exec. coun. tax sect., chmn. various coms. 1980-99). Republican. Episcopalian. Corporate taxation, Taxation, general, State and local taxation. Office: Holland & Knight 400 N Ashley Dr PO Box 1288 Tampa FL 33601-1288

BARTON, DAVID JOSEPH, lawyer; b. L.A., Feb. 10, 1956; s. Joseph and Rose (Lutvack) Aguayo; m. Katheryn Eller, July 12, 1980; 1 child, Nicholas David. BA in Polit. Sci., UCLA, 1978; cert. participation, Leningrad (USSR) State U., 1978; JD, Harvard U., 1981. Bar: Calif. 1981, U.S. Dist. Ct. (ce. dist.) Calif. 1982. Assoc. Memel, Jacobs, Pierno & Gersh, L.A., 1981-85, Sachs & Phelps, L.A., 1985-86, ptnr., 1987-91; gen. counsel Sizzler Internat., Inc., L.A., 1991—97. Mem. legal com. The Nurtury, Sherman Oaks, Calif., 1988-90. Mem. Calif. State Bar Assn. (com. partnerships 1986-89, com. corps. 1989-92), L.A. Bar Assn., Beverly Hills Bar Assn. Democrat. Avocations: cross-country skiing, bird watching. Corporate, general, Franchising, Private international. Office: Pachulski Stang Ziehl Et Al 10100 Santa Monica Blvd Ste 1100 Los Angeles CA 90067-1111

BARTON, JAMES CARY, lawyer; b. Raymondville, Tex., Sept. 1, 1940; s. Dewey Albert and Dorothy Marie (Keene) B.; m. Isabel Pattee Critz, Sept. 12, 1964 (div. June 1975); children: Hamilton Keene, James Albert, John Franklin; m. Carolyn Ann Cox, Dec. 20, 1975; stepchildren: Holly Ann Adams, Laura Lee Adams, Jennifer Lynn Adams. BA, Baylor U., 1962; LLB, Harvard U., 1965. Bar: Tex. 1965, U.S. Dist. Ct. (so. dist.) Tex. 1972, U.S. Tax Ct. 1977. Trial atty. FPC, Washington, 1965-67; atty.-advisor U.S. Tax Ct., Washington, 1967-68; assoc. to ptnr. Kleberg, Mobley, Lockett & Weil, Corpus Christi, Tex., 1969-75, Brown, Maroney, Rose, Baker & Barber, Austin, Tex., 1975-82; ptnr. to of counsel Johnson & Swanson, Austin, 1982-88; dir. Smith, Barshop, Stoffer & Millsap, Inc., San Antonio, 1988-91; prin. J. Cary Barton, P.C., San Antonio, 1991-93; prin Barton & Schneider, L.L.P., San Antonio, 1993—2003, Barton, Schneider, & Russell, L.L.P., 2003—. Speaker in field. Sgt. USAF, 1968-69. Mem. ABA, State Bar Tex. (mem. coun. of real estate probate and trust law sect. 1982-85, mem. real estate forms com. 1986—), Am. Coll. Real Estate Lawyers, Tex. Bd. Legal Specialization (cert. in comml. real estate law), Tex. Coll. Real Estate Attys. Democrat. Episcopalian. Property, real (including real estate development, water). Office: Barton Schneider & Russell LLP 700 N Saint Marys St Ste 1825 San Antonio TX 78205-3596

BARTON, ROBERT LEROY, JR., judge, educator; b. Ballston Spa, N.Y., June 19, 1943; s. Robert L. Sr. and Bertha (Di Pasquale) B.; m. Jean M. Adamchic, Aug. 14, 1965; children: Robert Joseph, Katherine Anne. BA, U. Pitts., 1965; JD, Boston Coll., 1969. Bar: Mass. 1969, R.I. 1970, D.C. 1972, U.S. Ct. Appeals (1st cir.) 1970, U.S. Ct. Appeals (D.C. cir.) 1973, U.S. Dist. Ct. R.I., 1971, U.S. Dist. Ct. D.C. 1973, U.S. Dist. Ct. Md. 1973. Law clk. U.S. Dist. Ct. R.I., Providence, 1969-70; staff atty. R.I. Legal Svcs., Providence, 1970-71; spl. asst. to solicitor U.S. Dept. Labor, Washington, 1971-72; assoc. Sherman, Dunn, Cohen & Leifer, Washington, 1972-75; trial atty. FTC, Washington, 1975-88; judge Pa. Office of Hearing & Appeals, Pitts., 1988-90, Office of Hearings, Washington, 1990-95, Office of Adminstr. Law Judges, Washington, 1995—. Trial instr. Nat. Inst. Trial Advocacy, Washington, 1982-86, U.S. Dept. Justice, Washington, 1986-96. Chair com. Cath. League for Religious Rights, Milw., 1983-84. Master Am. Inn of Ct.; mem. Fed. Bar Assn. (co-chair adminstrv. jud. com.), Fed. Adminstrn. Law Judges Assn. (mem. exec. com.), Nat. Lawyers Assn. Roman Catholic. Avocations: travel tennis, swimming. Office: Office Adminstrv Law Judges 5107 Leesburg Pike Ste 1905 Falls Church VA 22041-3249 E-mail: robert.barton@usdoj.gov.

BARTON, SARAH MURIEL, lawyer; b. London, Mar. 23, 1958; d. Russell William Andrew Charles and Katherine Grizel (Maitland-Makgill-Crichton) B.; children: Daniel Russell Bernard, Caroline Sarah Katherine. BA, U. Toronto, Ont., Can., 1978; JD, Union U., Albany, 1981; LLM in Admiralty, Tulane U., 1982. Bar: N.Y. 1982, La. 1983, U.S. Dist. Ct. (ea. dist.) La. 1983, N.J. 1985, U.S. Dist. Ct. (we. dist.) La. 1985, U.S. Dist. Ct. (so. dist.) N.Y., U.S. Ct. Appeals (5th cir.) 1986. Assoc. Law Offices Frederick Gisevius, New Orleans, 1982-83, James Hanemann and Assocs.,

New Orleans, 1983-85; assoc. counsel Am. Bur. Shipping, N.Y.C. and London, 1985-96; gen. counsel ABS Group of Cos., Inc., Houston, 1997—, v.p., 1998—. Spkr. Maritime Cyprus Legal Forum, 1993, Nat. Inst. and Royal Inst. Naval Archs., London, 1994. Mem. Am. Corp. Counsel Assn., Maritime Law Assn. (proctor). Admiralty, Commercial, contracts (including sales of goods; commercial financing), Corporate, general. Home: 1511 Potomac Dr Houston TX 77057-1925 Office: ABS Group of Cos Inc 16855 Northchase Dr Houston TX 77060-6006

BARTOSIC, FLORIAN, law educator, lawyer, arbitrator; b. Danville, Pa., Sept. 15, 1926; s. Florian W. and Elsie (Woodring) B.; m. Eileen M. Payne, 1952 (div. 1969); children: Florian, Ellen, Thomas, Stephen; m. Alberta C. Chew, 1990. BA, Pontifical Coll., 1948; B.C.L., Coll. William and Mary, 1956; LL.M., Yale U., 1957. Bar: Va. 1956, U.S. Supreme Ct. 1959. Asst. instr. Yale U., 1956-57; assoc. prof. law Coll. William and Mary, 1957, Villanova U., 1957-59; atty. NLRB, Washington, 1956, 57, 59; counsel Internat. Brotherhood of Teamsters, Washington, 1959-71; prof. law Wayne State U., 1971-80, U. Calif., Davis, 1980-92; recalled to tchg., 1994-99; prof. emeritus law U. Calif., Davis, 1993—, dean law, 1980-90. Adj. prof. George Washington U., 1966-71, Cath. U. Am., 1960-71; mem. panel arbitrators Fed. Mediation and Conciliation Service, 1972— ; hearing officer Mich. Employment Relations Commn., 1972-80, Mich. Civil Rights Commn., 1974-80; bd. dirs. Mich. Legal Services Corp., 1973-80, Inst. Labor and Indsl. Relations, U. Mich., Wayne State U., 1976-80; mem. steering com. Inst. on Global Conflict and Cooperation, 1982-83; mem. adv. bd. Assn. for Union Democracy Inc., 1980—, adv. coms. Calif. Jud. Council, 1984-85, 87; vis. scholar Harvard Law Sch., 1987, Stanford Law Sch., 1987; sr. rsch. scholar ILO, 1990-91; acad. visitor Oxford U., London Sch. Econs., 1991; mem. exec. bd. Pub. Interest Clearinghouse, 1988-90. Co-author: Labor Relations Law in the Private Sector, 1977, 2d edit., 1986; contbr. articles to law jours. Mem. ABA (sec. labor rels. law sect. 1974-75), Fed. Bar Assn., Am. Law Inst. (acad. mem. labor law adv. com. on continuing profl. edn.), Soc. Profls. in Dispute Resolution (regional v.p. 1979-80), Indsl. Rels. Rsch. Assn., Internat. Soc. Labor Law and Social Legis., Internat. Indsl. Rels. Assn., Lawyers Guild, ACLU (dir. Detroit chpt. 1976-77), Order of Coif (hon.), Scribes. Home: 235 Ipanema Pl Davis CA 95616-0253 Office: U Calif Sch Law Mrak Hall Dr Davis CA 95616 E-mail: fbartosic@ucdavis.edu.

BARTUNEK, ROBERT R(ICHARD), JR., lawyer; b. Cleve., July 2, 1946; s. Robert Richard and Clare Elizabeth (Lonsway) B.; 1 child, Kathryn Elizabeth. BS, Bucknell U., 1968; MBA, Ohio State U., 1974, JD, 1975; LLM, U. Mo., Kansas City, 1986. Bar: Mo. 1975, Kans. 1997, U.S. Dist. Ct. (we. dist.) Mo. 1975, U.S. Tax Ct. 1981, U.S. Dist. Ct. Kans. 1997. Ptnr. Beckett, Lolli & Bartunek, Kansas City, 1975-96, Swanson Midgley, LLC, Kansas City, 1997—2003, Siegfreid, Bingham, Levy, Selzer & Gee, Kansas City, 2003—. Mem. Men's Sr. Baseball League. Decorated Bronze Star. Mem. ABA, Lawyers Assn. Greater Kansas City, Kansas City Met. Bar Assn. (former chmn. tax law com.). Roman Catholic. Corporate, general, Estate taxation, Commercial, contracts (including sales of goods; commercial financing). Office: Seigfried Bingham Levy Selzer & Gee 2800 Commerce Tower 911 Main St Kansas City MO 64105 Home: 10314 Howe Ln Leawood KS 66206-2517 E-mail: rbartunek@sblsg.com.

BARTZ, DAVID JOHN, lawyer; b. Appleton, Wis., Feb. 15, 1955; s. Frederick Carl and Dorothy Lucille (Weckwerth) B. BA, U. Wis., 1976; MA in Pub. Affairs, U. Minn., 1979; JD, Ariz. State U., 1985. Bar: Ariz. 1985, U.S. Dist. Ct. Ariz. 1985, U.S. Ct. Appeals (9th cir.) 1985, Wis. 1989, U.S. Dist. Ct. (we. dist.) Wis. 1996, U.S. Dist. Ct. (ea. dist.) Wis. 1997. Policy analyst Minn. Dept. Transp., St. Paul, 1978-79; office dir. Wis. Senate, Madison, 1979-82, 86; pvt. practice, Phoenix, 1985-86; adminstr. Wis. Dept. Justice, Madison, 1987-91; pvt. practice, Madison, 1991—. Mem. ASPA (sec. Wis. Capital chpt. 1981-82), Ariz. Bar Assn., Wis. Bar Assn., Dane County Bar Assn. Corporate, general, Criminal, Labor (including EEOC, Fair Labor Standards Act, labor-management relations, NLRB, OSHA).

BARUSCH, LAWRENCE ROOS, lawyer; b. Oakland, Calif., Aug. 23, 1949; s. Maurice Radston and Phyllis (Rose) B.; m. Susan Amanda Smith, Aug. 7, 1983; children: Nathaniel M., Ariana G. BA summa cum laude, Harvard U., 1971, JD cum laude, 1975. Bar: Calif. 1975. Assoc. Cotton, Seligman & Ray, San Francisco, 1975-77; gen. counsel Jones & Guerrero Co., Inc., Agana, Guam, 1977-82; ptnr. Klemm, Blair & Barusch, PC, Agana, Guam, 1982-85; assoc. Davis, Graham & Stubbs, Salt Lake City, 1986-87; counsel Parsons, Behl & Latimer, Salt Lake City, 1987-89, shareholder, 1989—; counsel Guam Tax Code Commn., 1990-94. Adj. prof. U. Utah Coll. Law, 1998-99, 2000—, vis. assoc. prof., 1999-2000; mem. com. U.S. activities of foreigners and tax treaties, tax sect. ABA, 1994—. Contbr. articles to profl. jours. including Guam Bar Jour., Utah Bar Jour., Offshore Investment and Tax Notes. Chmn. Dem. Party, Davis County, Utah, 1997-99; mem. bd. dirs. The Road Home, 2002—. Sheldon fellow Harvard U., 1971. Mem. Guam Bar Assn. (pres. 1982-84), No. Marianas Bar Assn., Utah Bar Assn. (chmn. tax sect. 1994-95), Calif. Bar Assn., Utah Tax Review Comm., Phi Beta Kappa. Estate planning, Mergers and acquisitions, Corporate taxation. Office: Parsons Behle & Latimer 201 S Main St Ste 1800 Salt Lake City UT 84111-2218 E-mail: lbarusch@pblutah.com.

BARWELL, CINDY ANN, lawyer; b. Bklyn., Aug. 3, 1957; d. Walter E. and Ingeborg (Rodenkerchen) B. BSBA, U. Denver, 1977; MBA, U. Miami, Fla., 1978; JD, U. Toledo, 1984. Bar: Fla. 1984, Colo. 1994, U.S. Dist. Ct. (so. dist.) Fla. 1987, U.S. Ct. Appeals (11th cir.) 1992, U.S. Supreme Ct. 1989. Assoc. Martz and McClure, St. Augustine, Fla., 1984-85, Novey and Mendelson, Tallahassee, Fla., 1985, Reynolds and Reynolds, Boca Raton, Fla., 1985-88; prin. Cindy A. Barwell, P.A., Boca Raton, Fla., 1988—. Traffic magistrate County of Palm Beach, Fla., 1991—; arbitrator, mediator; spl. master Collections Ct., Palm Beach County. Mem. ABA, Fla. Bar Assn. Republican. General civil litigation, General practice, Landlord-tenant. Office: Cindy A Barwell PA 1300 SW 20th St Boca Raton FL 33486-6643

BARWICK, WILLIAM D. lawyer; b. Atlanta, June 4, 1949; BA, Amherst Coll., 1971; JD, U. Ga., 1974. Bar: Ga. 1974. With Sutherland Asbill & Brennan LLP, Atlanta. Mem.: Def. Rsch. Inst., Atlanta Bar Assn. (bd. dirs. 1986—90, sec.-treas. 1990—91, pres. 1992—93), State Bar Ga. (pres. 2003, mem. young lawyers sect., exec. coun. 1980, sec. 1981—83, pres. 1984—85, sec. 2000—01, bd. govs. 1987—91, 1993—), Phi Delta Phi. Insurance, Product liability, Civil rights. Office: Sutherland Asbill & Brennan LLP 999 Peachtree St NE Atlanta GA 30309-3996*

BASHAM, W. RALPH, federal agency administrator; m. Judith A. O'Bryan; three children. BA in Bus. Adminstrn., Southeastern U. Various positions to deputy asst. dir. for trng. U.S. Secret Svc., Washington, 1993-94; spl. agent in charge Office of Investigations Washington, Louisville, 1970-74, 76-79, 86-87, 90-92; spl. agt. of Protective support Divsn. U.S. Secret Svc., Washington, 1974-76; spl. agt., asst. spl. agt. in charge Vice Presdl. Protective Svc. Washington, 1979-83; dep. chief Fin. Mgmt. Divsn. U.S. Secret Svc., Washington, 1983-85; spl. agt. in charge of Vice Presdl. Protective Svc. U.S. Svc., Washington, Cleve., 87-89, 92-93; spl. agt. in charge of Dignitary Protective Divsn. U.S. Secret Svc., Washington, 1989-90, asst. dir. for Adminstrn., 1994-98; insp. Office of Inspections Washington, 1985-86; dir. Fed. Law Enforcement Tng. Ctr. U.S. Dept. Treasury, 1998—2001; chief of staff Transp. Security Adminstrn., Washington, 2002—03; dir. US Secret Svc., Washington, 2003—. Mem. Sr. Exec. Svc. Office: US Secret Svc Comm Ctr PO Box 6500 Springfield VA 22150*

BASHWINER, STEVEN LACELLE, lawyer; b. Cin., Aug. 3, 1941; s. Carl Thomas and Ruth Marie (Burlis) B.; m. Arden J. Lang, Apr. 24, 1966 (div. 1978); children: Heather, David; m. Donna Lee Gerber, Sept. 13, 1981; children: Margaret, Matthew. AB, Holy Cross Coll., 1963; JD, U. Chgo., 1966. Bar: Ill. 1966, U.S. Dist. Ct. (no. dist.) Ill. 1967, U.S. Ct. Appeals (7th cir.) 1968, U.S. Supreme Ct. 1970, U.S. Dist. Ct. (ea. dist.) Wis. 1988, U.S. Ct. Appeals (4th cir.) 1990. Assoc. Kirkland & Ellis, Chgo., 1966-72, ptnr., 1972-76, Friedman & Koven, Chgo., 1976-86, Katten Muchin Zavis Rosenhan, Chgo., 1986—. Served to sgt. USAFR, 1966-72. Mem. ABA, 7th Cir. Bar Assn., Chgo. Bar Assn., Chgo. Inn of Ct., Lawyers Club Chgo. Federal civil litigation, Labor (including EEOC, Fair Labor Standards Act, labor-management relations, NLRB, OSHA), Securities. Home: 834 Green Bay Rd Highland Park IL 60035-4630 Office: Katten Muchin Zavis Rosenhan 525 W Monroe St Ste 1600 Chicago IL 60661-3693

BASILE, PAUL LOUIS, JR., lawyer; b. Oakland, Calif., Dec. 27, 1945; s. Paul Louis and Roma Florence (Paris) B.; m. Linda Lou Paige, June 20, 1970; m. 2d Diane Chierichetti, Sept. 2, 1977. BA, Occidental Coll., 1968; postgrad., U. Wash., 1969; JD, UCLA, 1971. Bar: Calif. 1972, U.S. Dist. Ct. (cen. dist.) Calif. 1972, U.S. Dist. Ct. (no. dist.) Calif. 1985, U.S. Ct. Appeals (9th cir.) 1972, U.S. Tax Ct. 1977, U.S. Ct. Claims. 1978, U.S. Customs Ct. 1979, U.S. Ct. Customs and Patent Appeals 1979, U.S. Ct. Internat. Trade 1981, U.S. Supreme Ct. 1977; cert. specialist in taxation law Bd. of Legal Specialization, State Bar of Calif. Assoc. Parker, Milliken, Kohlmeier, Clark & O'Hara, L.A., 1971-72; corp. counsel TFI Cos., Inc., Irvine, Calif., 1972-73; pvt. practice L.A., 1973-80, 90-96, 98-99; mem. Basile & Siener, L.A., 1980-86, Clark & Trevithick, L.A., 1986-90; ptnr. Wolf, Rifkin & Shapiro, L.A., 1990, of counsel, 1990-92; ptnr. Basile & Lane, LLP, L.A., 1996-97; of counsel Shaffer, Gold & Rubaum, L.L.P., L.A., 1996—; sr. ptnr. Basile & Assocs., L.A. and Pasadena, Calif., 1999—; pres., CEO, dir. 765 Inc., Cliffside Park, NJ, 1997—. Gen. counsel J.W. Brown, Inc., L.A., 1980—, asst. sec., 1984—92; sec., gen. counsel Souriau, Inc., Valencia, Calif., 1981—90; v.p., sec., dir., gen. counsel Pvt. Fin. Assocs., L.A., 1983—94; gen. counsel Quest Relocation Group, Toluca Lake, Calif., 1994—97, v.p. real estate, 1996—; pres., CEO, dir. 754, Inc., Cliffside Park, NJ, 1997—. Trustee, sec. Nat. Repertory Theatre Found., 1975-94, mem. exec. com., 1976-94, chmn. bd. dirs., 1991-94; mem. fin. com., bd. dirs. Calif. Music Theatre, 1988-92; bd. dirs. March of Dimes Birth Defects Found., Los Angeles County, 1982-87, mem. exec. com., 1983-86, sec., 1985-86; dist. fin. chmn. L.A. Area coun. Boy Scouts Am., 1982-83; trustee Occidental Coll., L.A., 1989-94; active L.A. Olympic Organizing Com., Ketchum Downtown YMCA, Vols. Am. L.A., others. Mem. ABA (taxation sect., corp. tax com., vice chmn. closely held bus. com. 1992-94, chair, 1994-96, chmn. subcom. on continuing legal edn. 1990-94, chmn. subcom. on estate planning 1992, sec. 1996-97, small firm lawyers com., bus. law sect., real property sect., probate and trust law sect., spl. problems of bus. owners com., estate planning and drafting, pre-death planning issues com.), State Bar Calif. (bus. law sect., nonprofit and unincorporated orgns. com. 1989-92, taxation sect., estate planning, trust and probate sect., taxation law adv. commn. 1994-97, vice chmn. 1995-96, chair 1996-97, mem. bd. legal specialization 1996-97), L.A. County Bar Assn. (taxation sect., com. on closely-held and pass-through entities, bus. and corps. law sect., sole practitioner section exec. com. 1995-99), Beverly Hills Bar Assn. (probate, trust and estate planning sect., taxation sect., vice chmn. Estate and Gift Tax Com., 1998—, law practice mgmt. sect.), Can. Calif. C. of C. (dir. 1980-89, 2d v.p. 1983-84, 1st v.p. 1984-85, pres. 1985-87), L.A.-Vancouver Sister City Assn. (dir., exec. com. 1987-92, treas. 1987-89, pres. 1989-92), French-Am. C. of C. (councilor 1979-84, v.p. 1980, 82-84), L.A. Area C. of C. (dir. 1980-81), Occidental Coll. Alumni Assn. (pres. 1979-80, v.p. 1978-79, alumni bd. govs. 1977-81, chmn. ann. fund campaign 1990-91), Grand People (bd. dirs. 1985-92, chmn. bd. 1986-92), Rotary Club of L.A. (dir. 1994-96, sergeant-at-arms 1986-87, chmn. gateway com. 1993-94, chmn. world cmty. svc. com. 1991-93, chmn. vols. Am. of L.A. com. 1988-90, chmn. golf com. 1986-87, vice-chmn. pres. com. 1985-86), Rotary Internat. (chmn. club extension com. 1995-96, cmty. svc. dir. 1993-95, chmn. gift of life com. 1992-93), Small Bus. Coun. of Am., Inc. (legal adv. bd. 1989—), The Group, Inc. (dir. 2003—), Attys. for Family Held Enterprises. Democrat. Baptist. Corporate, general, Estate planning, Taxation, general. Home: 3937 Beverly Glen Blvd Sherman Oaks CA 91423-4404 Office: Basile and Assocs 12011 San Vicente Blvd Ste 600 Los Angeles CA 90049-4948 also: 180 S Lake Ave Ste 540 Pasadena CA 91101-2666

BASILIO, ANA TEREZA PALHARES, lawyer, educator; b. Rio de Janeiro, Oct. 19, 1967; d. Francisco de Paula and Maria Regina (Palhares) B.; m. José Roberto Sampaio. LLB, Candido Mendes U., Rio de Janeiro, 1991; attended, U. Wis., 2001. Atty. Escritorio Milton Barbosa, Rio de Janeiro, 1986-88, Escritorio Sergio Bermudes, Rio de Janeiro, 1988—, Sérgio Bermudes Law Office, Rio Janeiro, 1988—98; atty., ptnr. Trench, Rossi and Watanabe (associated with Baker and McKenzie-Attys. at Law), 1998—2001; internat. ptnr. Baker and McKenzie-Attys. at Law, 2002—; tchr. Brazilian Bar Assn. Law Sch., 1993—98, PUC-Cath. U. Rio de Janeiro, 1997. Mem. Order of Lawyers of Brazil, Brazilian Bar Assn. (Rio de Janeiro chpt. 2003), Brazilian Arbitration Com., Arbitration Chamber Fedn. Industries State Rio de Janeiro (arbitrator), Brazilian Inst. Law, Comml. Assn. State Rio de Janeiro (arbitrator ctr. mediation and arbitration). Roman Catholic. Civil rights, Commercial, consumer (including collections, credit), Commercial, contracts (including sales of goods; commercial financing), Alternative dispute resolution, Bankruptcy, Insolvency & Reorganization, Property, real (including real estate development, water), Administrative and regulatory, Commercial, consumer (including collections, credit). Office: Trench Rossie Watatabe Baker & McKenzie 1-19th Fl - Sector B Ave Rio Branco 20090-003 Rio de Janeiro Brazil

BASINGER, RICHARD LEE, lawyer; b. Canton, Ohio, Nov. 24, 1941; s. Eldon R. and Alice M. (Bartholomew) B.; m. Rita Evelyn Gover, May 14, 1965; children: David A., Darron M. BA in Edn., Ariz. State U., 1963; postgrad. Macalester Coll., 1968-69; JD, U. Ariz., 1973. Bar: Ariz. 1973, U.S. Dist. Ct. Ariz. 1973, U.S. Tax Ct. 1977, U.S. Ct. Appeals (6th cir.) 1975, U.S. Ct. Appeals (9th cir.) 1976, U.S. Supreme Ct. 1977; cert. arbitrator. Assoc. law offices, Phoenix, 1973-74; pvt. practice, Scottsdale, Ariz. 1974-75; pres. Basinger & Assocs., P.C., Scottsdale, 1975—, also bd. dirs. Contbr. articles to profl. jours. Bd. dirs. Masters Trail Ventures, Scottsdale, 1984-85, Here's Life, Ariz., Scottsdale, 1976—; precinct committeeman Republican Party, Phoenix, 1983—; bd. dir. Ariz. Coll. of the Bible, 1992-93. NSF grantee, 1968-69. Mem. ABA, Ariz. Bar Assn., Maricopa County Bar Assn., Ariz. State Horseman's Assn. (bd. dirs. 1984-86, 1st v.p. 1986), Scottsdale Bar Assn., Western Saddle Club (bd. dirs. 1983-86, pres. 1985-86), Scottsdale Saddle Club, Saguaro Saddle Club. Baptist. Corporate, general, Probate (including wills, trusts), Property, real (including real estate development, water). Office: Mohave County Atty Dep County Atty Civil Divsn PO Box 7000 Kingman AZ 86402-7000

BASINSKI, ANTHONY JOSEPH, lawyer; b. Pitts., Apr. 11, 1947; s. Anthony F. and Emily C. (Klocko) B.; m. Elisabeth Fawcett, Oct. 4, 1980; children: Ann Elisabeth, Robert Anthony. BA, U. Pitts., 1969, JD, 1974. Bar: Pa. 1974, U.S. Dist. Ct. (we. dist.) Pa. 1974, U.S. Ct. Appeals (3d cir.) 1981, U.S. Ct. Appeals (4th cir.) 1992, U.S. Ct. Appeals (fed. cir.) 1995. Law clk. to presiding justice Pa. Supreme Ct., Pitts., 1974-76; ptnr. Reed, Smith, Shaw and McClay, Pitts., 1976—. Served with U.S. Army, 1969-71, Vietnam. Mem. Allegheny County Bar Assn., Am. Arbitration Assn. (arbitrator 1983—). Democratic. Roman Catholic. Federal civil litigation, State civil litigation, Securities. Home: 1749 Taper Dr Pittsburgh PA 15241-2623 Office: Reed Smith Shaw & McClay 435 6th Ave Ste 2 Pittsburgh PA 15219-1886 E-mail: abasinski@reedsmith.com.

BASKERVILL, CHARLES THORNTON, lawyer; b. South Boston, Va., May 26, 1953; s. William Nelson and Julia Alice (Moore) B.; m. Pamela Temple Shell, July 17, 1976; children: Ann Cabell, Susannah Thornton. BA, Hampden-Sydney Coll., 1975; JD, U. Richmond, 1978. Bar: Va. 1978, U.S. Dist. Ct. (ea. dist.) Va. 1978. Assoc. White, Hamilton, Wyche & Shell, P.C., Petersburg, Va., 1978-96; asst. commonwealth's atty Petersburg, Va., 1985—; assoc. Shell, Johnson, Andrews, Baskervill & Baskervill, P.C., Petersburg, Va., 1996-2001, Shell, Johnson, Andrews & Baskervill, P.C., Petersburg, Va., 2001—. Commr. of accts. City of Petersburg, Va., 1996—. Former dir. Petersburg Crime Prevention Found. Named to Athletic Hall of Fame, Hampden-Sydney Coll., 1988. Mem. Prince George County Bar Assn. (sec.-treas. 1990-91, pres. 1991-92), Petersburg Bar Assn. (pres. 2001-02). Methodist. Avocations: golf, tennis. Estate planning, Family and matrimonial, Probate (including wills, trusts). Office: Shell Johnson Andrews Baskervill PC 43 Rives Rd Petersburg VA 23805-9255

BASKINS, ANN O. lawyer, computer company executive; b. Red Bluff, Calif., Aug. 5, 1955; AB, Stanford U., 1977; JD, UCLA, 1980. Bar: Calif. 1980. Assoc. Crosby, Heafey, Roach & May, 1980—81; v.p., gen. counsel, sec. Hewlett-Packard Co., Palo Alto, Calif., 1981—. Mem.: ABA, State Bar Calif., Assn. Gen. Counsel, Am. Soc. Corp. Secs., Am. Corp. Counsel Assn. Corporate, general. Office: Hewlett Packard Co Mail Stop 1069 3000 Hanover St Palo Alto CA 94304*

BASON, GEORGE F., JR., lawyer; b. Chapel Hill, N.C., June 30, 1931; s. George Francis and Mary Isabel (Reuther) B.; m. Sheilah Margaret Weavis, Oct. 12, 1961; children— Neil William, Iain George. A.B. cum laude, Davidson Coll., 1953; J.D. cum laude, Harvard U., 1956. Bar: NC 1956, D.C. 1958, U.S. Supreme Ct. 1961, Md. 1989. Assoc. Royall, Koegel and Harris, Washington and N.Y.C., 1958-61, Martin, Whitfield and Thaler, Washington, 1962-66; asst. prof. law Am. U., 1966-69, assoc. prof., 1969-72; sole practice, Washington, 1972-78, 1988-2001; pres. George F. Bason Jr. P.C., Washington, 1978-84; judge U.S. Bankruptcy Ct. for D.C., 1984-88; of counsel Ridberg, Press & Sherbill, LLP, Bethesda, Md., 2001—; chmn. bankruptcy and reorgn. com. D.C. Bar, 1974-75; standing trustee for D.C. Wage Earner Plans Under Chapter XIII Bankruptcy Act, 1972-75. Author: Debtor and Creditor Relations, Bankruptcy and Non-bankruptcy Rights and Remedies, 1984, vols. 9, 10 and 11 West's Legal Forms 2d. Recipient Am. Bar Found. Constl. Law Essay Contest 1st prize, 1973. Mem. ABA, D.C. Bar, Md. Bar. Contbr. articles to profl. jours. Bankruptcy. Office: Ridberg Press & Sherbill LLP Ste 650 Three Bethesda Metro Center Bethesda MD 20814

BASON, GEORGE R., JR., lawyer; b. N.Y.C., 1954; AB magna cum laude, Harvard U., 1975, JDcum laude, 1978. Bar: N.Y. 1979, U.S. Dist. Ct. (so. and ea. dists.) N.Y. 1979; cert. Avocat à la Cour de Paris 1992. Assoc. Davis Polk & Wardwell, N.Y.C., 1978-85, ptnr., 1986—. Mem. ABA, Bar Assn. City N.Y., Phi Beta Kappa. Private international, Mergers and acquisitions. Office: Davis Polk & Wardwell 450 Lexington Ave New York NY 10017-3982

BASS, JAMES ORIN, lawyer; b. Sumner County, Tenn., July 12, 1910; s. Francis Marion and Sadie (Dunn) B.; m. Susanne Warner, June 9, 1937; children: James Orin, Edwin Warner, Francis Marion II, Susan Richardson. BA, U. of South, 1931; LL.B., Harvard, 1934. Bar: Tenn. 1934. Ptnr. Bass, Berry & Sims, Nashville, 1937—. Mem. Tenn. Ho. of Reps. from Davidson County, 1936-38, Tenn. Senate, 1940-42. Served to lt. col. AUS, 1942-45, ETO. Mem. ABA, Tenn. Bar Assn., Nashville Bar Assn. (pres. 1951), Am. Coll. Trial Lawyers. Presbyterian. Banking, Corporate, general, Utilities, public. Home: 4412 Georgian Pl Nashville TN 37215-4528 Office: Bass Berry & Sims PLC 315 Deaderick St Ste 2700 Nashville TN 37238-3001 E-mail: jbasssr@bassberry.com.

BASS, LEWIS, lawyer; b. Bklyn., Oct. 22, 1947; s. Alexander and Doris Bass; m. Patricia Anne Moseley; children: Scott Christopher, Stephen David, Gregory Daniel. BSME, CCNY, 1969; MS in Indsl. Engring., U. So. Calif., 1971; JD, U. Santa Clara, 1976. Bar: Calif. 1976, U.S. Dist. Ct. (no. dist.) Calif. 1976. Mech. engr. Rockwell Internat., Los Angeles, 1969-70; project engr. Aerospace Corp., Los Angeles, 1970-71; safety engr. Lockheed, Sunnyvale, Calif., 1971-77; assoc. Caputo, Liccardo, Rossi, Sturges & McNeil, San Jose, Calif., 1977-78; corp. counsel Rose Mfg. Co., Englewood, Calif., 1978-79; sole practice Campbell, Calif., 1978—. Pres. Lewis Bass Internat., Inc., Campbell, 1978—; adj. assoc. prof. safety sci. U. So. Calif., L.A., 1979—; adj. prof. U. Calif., Santa Cruz, 1991—. Author: Products Liability Design and Manufacturing Defects, 1986, 2d edit., 2001; contbr. articles to profl. jours. Named Outstanding Teaching award U. So. Calif., 1984. Mem. ABA, NFPA, Am. Soc. Quality Control, Am. Soc. Safety Engrs., Semiconductor Safety Assn. Environmental, Personal injury (including property damage), Product liability. Office: 621 E Campbell Ave Ste 11A Campbell CA 95008-2126

BASS, WILLIAM MORRIS, lawyer; b. Crowley, La., Jan. 10, 1942; s. William T. and Rebecca (Hulkahy) B.; divorced 1994; children: Aaron, Casey, James; m. Penelope McCollum, June 5, 1995. BS, La. State U., Baton Rouge, 1966; JD, Loyola U., New Orleans, 1969. Bar: La. 1969, U.S. Dist. Ct. (ea., we. and mid. dists.) 1969, U.S. Ct. Appeals (5th cir.) 1969, U.S. Superior Ct. Pvt. practice, Lafayette, La., 1969—. Mediator, 1997. Fellow La. State Bar Found.; mem. La. Bar Assn. (sect. law and medicine, 1996), Coastal Conservation Assn. (chpt. pres. 1994-96, state pres. 1998-99, nat. bd. dirs. 1995—). Republican. Episcopalian. Admiralty, Product liability, Professional liability. Office: 700 Saint John St Lafayette LA 70501-6768

BASSECHES, ROBERT TREINIS, lawyer; b. N.Y.C., Jan. 24, 1934; s. Jacob Thomas and Paula (Treinis) B.; m. Harriet Itkin, July 6, 1958; children: K.B., Joshua, Jessica. BA, Amherst Coll., 1955; LLB, Yale U., 1958. Bar: D.C. 1962, U.S. Ct. Appeals (D.C. cir.) 1962, U.S. Ct. Appeals (2d cir.) 1978, U.S. Ct. Appeals (4th cir.) 1998. Law clk. to judge David L. Bazelon U.S. Ct. Appeals (D.C. cir.), Washington, 1958-59; law clk. to justice Hugo L. Black U.S. Supreme Ct., Washington, 1959; assoc. Shea & Gardner, Washington, 1959-63, ptnr., 1963—, adminstrv. ptnr., 1980-86, chmn., exec. com., 1988-93. Trustee Green Acres Sch., Rockville, Md., 1971-76, pres., chmn. bd. trustees, 1973-75; pres. Chevy Chase (Md.) Village Citizens Assn., 1976. Mem. Maritime Adminstrv. Bar Assn. (pres. 1969-71, sec. 1967-69), Phi Beta Kappa. Administrative and regulatory, Transportation. Office: Shea & Gardner Ste 800 1800 Massachusetts Ave NW Washington DC 20036-1872

BASSEN, NED HENRY, lawyer; b. N.Y.C., June 8, 1948; s. Harold Russell and Annette (Frankfeldt) B.; m. Susan Millington Campbell, July 2, 1999; children: Amanda Lee, Susannah Spence. BS, Cornell U., 1970, JD, 1973. Bar: N.Y. 1974, U.S. Dist. Ct. (so. and ea. dists.) N.Y. 1974, U.S. Dist. Ct. (ea. dist.) Mich. 1990, U.S. Dist. Ct. (we. dist.) N.Y. 1999, U.S. Ct. Appeals (11th cir.) 1984, U.S. Ct. Appeals (2d cir.) 2001. Assoc. Baer Marks & Upham, N.Y.C., 1975-80, Kelley Drye & Warren, N.Y.C., 1973-75, 80-83, ptnr., 1983-92; ptnr., labor group head Mudge Rose Guthrie Alexander & Ferdon, N.Y.C., 1993-95; ptnr., chair labor and employment group Hughes Hubbard & Reed LLP, N.Y.C., 1995—. Note and comment editor Cornell Law Rev., 1972-73. Mem. ABA (labor and employment law sect.), U.S. Coun. for Internat. Bus., Indsl. Rels. Com., Indsl. Rels. Rsch. Assn., N.Y. State Bar Assn. (labor law sect., com. on equal employment opportunity law), N.Y. State Mgmt. Attys. Conf. Labor (including EEOC, Fair Labor Standards Act, labor-management relations, NLRB, OSHA), Alternative dispute resolution. Office: Hughes Hubbard & Reed LLP 1 Battery Park Plz Fl 12 New York NY 10004-1482

BASSETT, DEBRA LYN, lawyer, educator; b. Pleasanton, Calif., Oct. 28, 1956; d. James Arthur and Shirley Ann (Russell) Bassett. BA, U. Vt., 1977; MS, San Diego State U., 1982; JD, U. Calif., Davis, 1987. Bar: Calif. 1987, DC 1990, U.S. Dist. Ct. (no. and ea. dists.) Calif. 1988, U.S. Ct. Appeals (9th cir.) 1988, U.S. Supreme Ct. 1991. Guidance counselor Addison Cen. Supr. Union, Middlebury, Vt., 1982-83, Milton (Vt.) Elem. Sch., 1983-84; assoc. Morrison & Foerster, San Francisco, 1986; jud. clk. U.S. Ct. Appeals (9th cir.), Phoenix, 1987-88; assoc. Morrison & Foerster, San Francisco and Walnut Creek, Calif., 1988-92; sr. atty. Calif. Ct. Appeal (3d appellate dist.), Sacramento, 1992-99; assoc. prof. Mich. State U., East Lansing, 2002—. Tutor civil procedure, rsch. asst. U. Calif., Davis, 1985—87, instr., 1995—2002, lectr., 1997—2002; adj. prof. McGeorge Sch. Law, 1998—99, dir. legal process, 1999—2000, vis. prof., 2000—01. Editor: U. Calif. Law Rev., 1985—86; sr. articles editor: , 1986—87. Mem. Steiner Chorale, 2002—, Lange Singers, 2002—. Mem.: ABA (vice chmn. ethics com. young lawyers divsn. 1989—91, exec. com. labor and employment law com. 1989—90), AAUW, APA (assoc.), Scribes. Democrat. Avocations: music, tennis, travel, hiking. Home: 915 Snyder Rd East Lansing MI 48823 Office: Mich State U DCL Coll Law 417 Law Coll Bldg East Lansing MI 48824 E-mail: debbie.bassett@law.msu.edu.

BASSETT, JOHN WALDEN, JR., lawyer; b. Roswell, N.Mex., Mar. 21, 1938; s. John Walden Sr. and Evelyn (Thompson) B.; m. Patricia Lubben, May 22, 1965 (dec. Apr. 1995); children: John Walden III, Loren Patricia; m. Nolana Knight, May 2, 1998. AB in Econs., Stanford U., 1960; LLB with honors, U. Tex., 1964. Bar: Tex. 1964, N.Mex. 1964. Assoc. Atwood & Malone, Roswell, 1964-66; White House fellow, spl. asst. to U.S. Atty. Gen., Washington, 1966-67; ptnr. Atwood, Malone, Mann & Turner and predecessors, Roswell, 1967-95, Bassett & Copple, LLP, Roswell, 1995—. Bd. dirs. Belo Corp., Dallas, AMMA Found., Washington. Assoc. editor U. Tex. Law Rev., 1962. Mem. N.Mex. State Bd. Edn., 1987-91; pres., chmn. bd. United Way of Chaves County, N.Mex., 1973; bd. dirs. Ednl. Achievement Found., Roswell, 1992—, N.Mex. Bus. Roundtable for Ednl. Excellence, Albuquerque. 1st lt. U.S. Army, 1961-68. Mem. ABA, Tex. Bar Assn., N.Mex. Bar Assn., Chaves County Bar Assn., Order of Coif, Rotary (pres. 1976), N.Mex. Amigos, Phi Delta Phi. Republican. Episcopalian. General practice, Probate (including wills, trusts), Property, real (including real estate development, water). Home: 5060 Bright Sky Rd Roswell NM 88201-8800 Office: Bassett & Copple 400 N Pennsylvania Ave Ste 250 Roswell NM 88201-4788 E-mail: anabassett@aol.com.

BASSETT, WOODSON WILLIAM, JR., lawyer; b. Okmulgee, Okla., Nov. 7, 1926; s. Woodson William and Bee Irene (Knerr) B.; m. Marynm Shaw, Dec. 16, 1950; children: Woodson William III, Beverly M., Tod Corbett. JD, U. Ark., 1949. Bar: Ark. 1949. Employed in New Orleans and Monroe, La., 1949-51; claims examiner Employers Group Ins. Cos., 1949-51; mgr. Light Adjustment Co., 1951-56; v.p. legal dept. Preferred Ins. Cos., 1957-62; sr. partner Bassett Law Firm, 1962—. Spl. chief justice Ark. Supreme Ct., 1991—; mem. Ark. Bd. Law Examiners Mem. editorial staff: Ark. Law Review, 9. Pres. Sherman Lollar Boys Baseball League, 1962; v.p. Babe Ruth Baseball Assn., 1968; chmn. bd. dirs. Fayetteville Public Library, 1975-79. Served with AUS, 1950-51. Fellow Am. Coll. Trial Lawyers; mem. ABA, Ark. Bar Assn., Washington County Bar Assn. (pres. 1973-74), Am. Bd. Trial Advs., Delta Theta Phi, Kappa Sigma. Home: 2210 E Manor Dr Fayetteville AR 72701-2640 Office: Bassett Law Firm 221 N College Ave Fayetteville AR 72701-4238

BASSITT, JANET LOUISE, lawyer; b. Macomb, Ill., Oct. 8, 1941; d. James Russell Hoover and Louise Loretta (Lawrence) Hoover Reed; children: Teri Beth, William Jefferson, Margaret Louise. BA in Psychology with honors, U. Ill., Chgo., 1976; JD, John Marshall Law Sch., 1980. Bar: Ill. 1981, U.S. Dist. Ct. (no. dist.) Ill. 1982, U.S. Ct. Appeals (7th cir.) 1982, U.S. Tax Ct. 1983, U.S. Supreme Ct. 1985. Sole practice, Roselle, Ill., 1982—. Instr. Harper Coll., Palatine, Ill., 1983-88, Coll. Fin. Planning, Denver, 1985-88. Author: Attorney Conduct, 1985, Trust Yourself, 1990; contbr. articles to profl. jours. Vol. lawyer Constl. Rights Found., Chgo., 1982—; chmn. March of Dimes, Wenatchee, Wash., 1971-72; bd. dirs. United Way Schaumburg-Hoffman Estates, 1986-89; leader Wenatchee area Boy Scouts Am., 1971-72, Camp Fire Girls. Mem. ABA, Ill. Bar Assn. Health, Intellectual property. Address: PO Box 72277 Roselle IL 60172-0277

BASTARACHE, MICHEL, judge; b. June 10, 1947; s. Alfred Bastarache and Madeleine Claveau; m. Yolande Martin, 1968; children: Emilie, Jean-Françoise. BA, U. Moncton; LLL, U. Montreal; LLB, U. Ottawa; grad. degree in pub. law, U. Nice; degree (hon.) , U. Moncton, 1998, Dalhousie U., 1998, Ottawa U., 1998, U. Mt. Allison, 2001. Bar: N.B. 1980, Alta. 1985, Ont. 1986. Legal translator N.B. Govt.; v.p., dir. mktg. Assumption Life; pres., CEO Assumption Life and its subsidiaries; law prof., dean U. Moncton Law Sch., 1978—83; dir. gen. promotion of ofcl. langs. dept. sec. State of Can., 1983—84; assoc. dean common law sect. faculty law U. Ottawa, 1984—87; with Lang, Michener, Lash, Johnston, Ottawa, 1987—89, Stewart, McKelvey, Stirling, Scales, Moncton, 1994—95; apptd. mem. N.B. Ct. Appeal, 1995—97, Supreme Ct. Can., 1997—. Mem. Atlantic Provinces Econ. Coun., 1992—94, Literacy N.B., 1993—94; mem. adv. com. adminstrn. faculties U. Moncton, 1994, U. N.B., St. John, 1994. Editor, prin. author: Language Rights in Canada, 1989, Précis du droit des biens réels, 1993, editor-in-chief: Can. Bar Rev., 1998—, mem. editl. bd.: Revue générale de droit internat., Revue québécoise de droit internat., Revue générale de droit, C'est ton droit, Revue du Nouvel ONt., 1985—88; contbr. articles to profl. jours. Mem. Izaak Walton Killam Hosp. for Children Found., Halifax, 1994. Named Jurist of the Yr., Assn. des juristes francophones du Nouveau-Brunswick, 1993; recipient Ordre des francophones d'Amérique, Govt. Que., 1981, 125th Ann. medal, 1993, Prix Boréal, Fedn. des communautes francophones et acadeiennes du Can., 1995, Kavanagh award, U. Ottawa, 1998, Médaille de Commandeur de l'Ordre de la Pléiade, 1999; Goodman fellow, U. Toronto, 1999. Fellow: Am. Coll. Trial Lawyers. Office: Supreme Ct Can 301 Wellington St Ottawa ON Canada K1A 0J1

BASTIAANSE, GERARD C. lawyer; b. Holyoke, Mass., Oct. 21, 1935; s. Gerard C. and Margaret (Lally) B.; m. Paula E. Paliska, June 1, 1963; children: Elizabeth, Gerard. BSBA, Boston U., 1960; JD, U. Va., 1964. Bar: Mass. 1964, Calif. 1970. Assoc. Nutter, McClennen & Fish, Boston, 1964-65; counsel Campbell Soup Co., Camden, N.J., 1965-67; gen. counsel A&W Internat. (United Fruit Co.), Santa Monica, Calif., 1968-70; ptnr. Kindel & Anderson, Los Angeles, 1970—. Mem. ABA, Calif. Bar Assn., Mass. Bar Assn., Japan Am. Soc., Asia Soc., World Trade Ctr. Assn. Clubs: California (Los Angeles); Big Canyon Country (Newport Beach, Calif.). Corporate, general, Private international. Home: 2 San Sebastian Newport Beach CA 92660-6828 Office: Kindel & Anderson 2030 Main St Ste 1300 Irvine CA 92614-7220

BATA, RUDOLPH ANDREW, JR., lawyer; b. Akron, Ohio, Jan. 9, 1947; s. Rudolph Andrew and Margaret Eleanor (Ellis) Bata; m. Genevieve Ruth Brannan, Aug. 25, 1968 (div. May 1985); 1 child, Seth Andrew; m. Linda Lee Waldo, Apr. 7, 1985; 1 child, Sarah Ariel. BS, So. Coll., Collegedale, Tenn., 1969; JD, Emory U., 1972. Bar: D.C. 1973, N.C. 1978, U.S. Dist. Ct. N.C. 1991, U.S. Ct. Appeals (4th cir.) 1991, cert.: Adminstrv. Office of Cts. (arbitrator, mediator). Assoc. ICC, Washington, 1972-73; in house counsel B.F. Saul Real Estate Investment Trust, Chevy Chase, Md., 1973-74; staff atty. Martha, Cafferky, Powers & Jordan, Washington, 1974-75; asst. corp. counsel Hardee's Food Systems, Inc., Rocky Mount, N.C., 1975-78; ptnr. Bata & Blomeley, Murphy, N.C., 1978-87, 88-90, Bata & Sumpter, Murphy, 1987-88; sole practice, 1990—. Bd. dirs. Cherokee County United Fund, Murphy, 1981-83. Mem. ABA, N.C. Bar Assn., D.C. Bar Assn., 30th Jud. Dist. Bar Assn., So. Soc. of Adventist Attys. (pres. 1984-85), Cherokee County C. of C. (bd. dirs. 1980-82). Avocations: golf, tennis, hiking. Banking, Probate (including wills, trusts), Property, real (including real estate development, water). Office: 225 Valley River Ave Ste A Murphy NC 28906-3000 E-mail: batalaw@dnet.net.

BATCHELDER, ALICE M. federal judge; b. Aug. 15, 1944; m. William G. Batchelder III; children: William G. IV, Elisabeth. BA, Ohio Wesleyan U., 1964; JD, Akron U., 1971; LLM, U. Va., 1988. Tchr. Plain Local Sch. Dist., Franklin County, Ohio, 1965-66, Jones Jr. High Sch., 1966-67, Buckeye High Sch., Medina County, 1967-68; assoc. Williams & Batchelder, Medina, Ohio, 1971-83; judge U.S. Bankruptcy Ct., Ohio, 1983-85, U.S. Dist. Ct. (no. dist.) Ohio, Cleve., 1985-91, U.S. Ct. of Appeals (6th cir.), Cleveland, 1991—. Mem. ABA, Fed. Judge's Assn., Fed. Bar Assn., Medina County Bar Assn. Office: US Ct of Appeals (6th cir) 143 W Liberty St Medina OH 44256-2215

BATCHELOR, JAMES KENT, lawyer; b. Long Beach, Calif., Oct. 4, 1934; s. Jack Morrell and Edith Marie (Ottinger) B.; m. Jeanette Lou Dyer, Mar. 27, 1959; children: John, Suzanne; m. Susan Mary Leonard, Dec. 4, 1976. AA, Sacramento City Coll., 1954; BA, Calif. State U., Long Beach, 1956; JD, U. Calif., 1959. Bar: Calif. 1960, U.S. Dist. Ct. (cen. dist.) Calif. 1960, U.S. Supreme Ct. 1968; cert. family law specialist Calif. Bd. Legal Specialization, 1980. Dep. dist. atty., Orange County, Calif., 1960-62; assoc. Miller, Nisson, Kogler & Wenke, Santa Ana, Calif., 1962-64; ptnr. Batchelor, Cohen & Oster, Santa Ana, Calif., 1964-67, Kurilich, Ballard, Batchelor, Fullerton, Calif., 1967-72; pres. James K. Batchelor, Inc. Tchr. paralegal sect. Santa Ana City Coll.; judge pro-tem Superior Ct., 1974—; lectr. family law Calif. Continuing Edn. of Bar, 1973—. Contbr. articles to profl. jours. Named one of Best Lawyers in Am., 1989—. Fellow Am. Acad. Matrimonial Lawyers (pres. So. Calif. chpt. 1989-90); mem. ABA, Calif. State Bar (plaque chmn. family law sect. 1975-76, advisor 1976-78), Orange County Barristers (founder, pres., plaque 1963), Calif. State Barristers (plaque 1964, v.p.), Orange County Bar Assn. (plaque sec. 1977, pres. family law sect. 1968-71). Republican. Methodist. Family and matrimonial. Office: 765 The City Dr S Ste 270 Orange CA 92868-6908

BATE, DAVID SOULE, lawyer; b. Montclair, N.J., Mar. 15, 1918; s. Oscar Mortimer and Gladys (Soule) B.; m. Janet Mallon, May 29, 1942; children: Suzanne Bate Morris, David S. Jr., Nancy Bate Bayne, Catherine B. Bull. AB, Hamilton U., 1939; LLB, Harvard U., 1946. Bar: N.J. 1947, U.S. Supreme Ct. 1963. Assoc. Stryker Tams & Horner, Newark, N.J., 1946-48; ptnr. Booth Bate Grieco & Briodx, Montclair, N.J., 1948—. Atty. Borough of Essex Fells, N.J. 1966—. Trustee The Florence and John Schumann Found., Montclair, 1967—, the Internat. Found., Butler, N.J., 1984—. Served to lt. comdr. USNR, 1940-45. Mem. ABA, N.J. Bar Assn., Essex County Bar Assn., Am. Coll. Trust and Estate Counsel. Republican. Episcopalian. General practice, Probate (including wills, trusts). Home: 368 Roseland Ave Essex Fells NJ 07021-1216 Office: Booth Bate & Grieco 31 Park St Montclair NJ 07042-3407

BATEMAN, DAVID ALFRED, lawyer; b. Pitts., Jan. 28, 1946; s. Alfred V. and Ruth G. (Howe) B.; m. Trudy A. Heath, Mar. 13, 1948; children: Devin C., Mark C. AB in Geology, U. Calif., Riverside, 1966; JD, U. San Diego, 1969; LLM, Georgetown U., 1978. Bar: Calif. 1970, U.S. Dist. Ct. (so. dist.) Calif. 1970, U.S. Ct. Mil. Appeals 1972, Wash. 1973, U.S. Dist. Ct. (we. dist.) Wash. 1973, U.S. Supreme Ct. 1974, D.C. 1976, U.S. Dist. Ct. Appeals (9th cir.) 1981. Assoc. Daubney, Banche, Patterson & Nares, Oceanside, Calif., 1969-72; asst. atty. gen. State of Wash., Olympia, 1977-81; ptnr. Bateman & Woodring, Olympia, 1981-85, Woodring, Bateman & Westbrook, Olympia, 1985-89, Hanemann & Batemann, Olympia, 1989-92, Hanemann, Bateman & Jones, Olympia, 1992—. Instr. Am. Inst. Banking, San Diego, 1972, U. Puget Sound, Olympia campus, spring, 1979; assoc. broker Coldwell Banker Comml., Tacoma, Wash. Served to capt. JAGC, USAF, 1972-77; col. JAGC, USAFR, 1977-97. Mem. Calif. State Bar Assn., D.C. Bar Assn., Wash. State Bar Assn., Rotary (past chmn. internat. svcs. com.). Roman Catholic. Private international, Land use and zoning (including planning), Property, real (including real estate development, water).

BATEMAN, GREGORY ANTHONY, solicitor, lawyer; LLB, U. Sydney, 1974. Ptnr. Abbott Tout, Sydney, 1982—. Author: Company Meetings: What You Need to Know, 2001. Fellow: Chartered Inst. Co. Secs. (br. councillor 1992—2002), Australian Inst. Co. Dirs. Corporate, general, Mergers and acquisitions, Health. Office: Abbott Tout 19 Martin Pl Level 42 MLC Ctr Sydney NSW 2000 Australia

BATEMAN, HEIDI S. lawyer; b. Spokane, Wash., June 17, 1965; d. John Alan and Carole L. Havens; children: Ryan, Matthew; m. David Alan Bateman. BA with honors, Gonzaga U., 1987; JD, U. Wash., 1990. Bar: Wash. 1990, U.S. Dist. Ct. (we. dist.) Wash. 1994. Assoc. Bogle & Gates, PLLC, Seattle, 1990-96, sr. litigation atty., 1997-98; founding ptnr. Miller Bateman, LLP, Seattle, 1999—. Active Guardian Ad Litem Program, Seattle, 1990—; fund raiser U. Wash. Alumni Orgn., Seattle, 1990—. Mem. ABA (comml. and corp. litigation coms. 1998—), Wash. State Bar Assn. (legis. coms. 1995-96), King County Bar Assn. (jud. screening com. 1996-97). Federal civil litigation, State civil litigation, Property, real (including real estate development, water). Office: Miller Bateman LLP 1426 Alaskan Way Ste 301 Seattle WA 98101-2045 E-mail: hbateman@millerbateman.com.

BATEMAN, THOMAS ROBERT, lawyer; b. Winchester, Mass., Dec. 9, 1944; s. Richard Holt and Phyllis (Brown) B.; m. Katherine Elizabeth Elliott, Sept. 9, 1972; children: Kyra Elizabeth, Richard Holt, Robert Elliott. BA, Harvard U., 1967; JD, NYU, 1971. Bar: N.Y. 1972, U.S. Dist. Ct. (so. dist.) N.Y. 1973, U.S. Ct. Appeals (2d cir.) 1974, Mass. 1978, U.S. Dist. Ct. Mass. 1978, U.S. Ct. Appeals (1st cir.) 1978. Assoc. Winthrop, Stimson, Putnam & Roberts, N.Y.C., 1971-77, Skadden, Arps, Slate, Meagher & Flom, Boston, 1977-79, ptnr., 1980—. Class agent Phillips Exeter Acad., N.H., 1969—; class steering com. Harvard U., Cambridge, Mass. 1985—. Mem.: ABA, Assn. of Bar of City of N.Y., N.Y. State Bar Assn., Somerset Club, Harvard Club (Boston). Episcopalian. Corporate, general, Public international, Securities. Home: 33 Bullard Rd Weston MA 02493-2203

BATES, CHARLES WALTER, lawyer, human resources executive, politician; b. Detroit, June 28, 1953; s. E. Frederick and Virginia Marion (Nunneley) B. BA in Psychology and Econs. cum laude, Mich. State U., 1975, M in Labor and Indsl. Rels., 1977; postgrad., DePaul U., 1979-80; JD, William Mitchell Coll. Law, 1984. Bar: Wash. 1990, U.S. Dist. Ct. (we. dist.) Wash. 1992, U.S. Ct. Appeals (9th cir.) 2002; cert. sr. profl. in human resources. Job analyst Gen. Mills, Inc., Mpls., 1977-78, plant pers. asst. II Chgo., 1978-80, plant asst. pers. mgr., 1980-81, pers. mgr. consumer foods mktg. Mpls., 1981-82, pers. mgr. consumer foods mktg. divsns. and Saluto Pizza, 1982-84; human resources mgr. Western divsn. Godfather's Pizza, Inc., Costa Mesa, Calif., 1984-85, human resources mgr. western U.S. and Can. Bellevue, Wash., 1985-91; dir. human resources Royal Seafoods, Inc., Seattle, 1991-92, dir. human resources and employee rels. counsel, 1992-94, dir. human resources and counsel, 1994-95; sr. internal auditor PACCAR, Inc, Bellevue, Wash., 1995-97; dir. field human resources PACCAR Automotive, Inc., Renton, 1997, dir. human resources, 1997—2000, TransAlta Corp.-Centralia Ops., 2000—02; dir. adminstrn., corp. sec. TransAlta USA Inc., 2002—. Instr. employee labor rels. Lake Washington Tech. Coll., 1992-94; bd. dirs., TransAlta USA Inc., 2000-01, TransAlta Investments LLC, 2000-2001. Candidate for lt. gov. of Minn., 1982; mem. Sammamish Cmty. Coun., Bellevue, 1990-93; mem. Bellevue Civil Svc. Commn., 1997-2000, vice chmn., 1999, chmn., 2000; commr. Scott Lake Drainage Commn., 2002-; bd. dirs. Olympia Symphony Orch., 2001-02; asst. scoutmaster Boy Scouts Am., 1971—. Recipient Scouter's Tng. award Boy Scouts Am., 1979, Vantage Recruiting award Recruitment Today mag., 1989, Vigil Honor award Order of the Arrow, Boy Scouts Am., 1990, Dist. Award of Merit, Boy Scouts Am., 1991. Mem. ABA, Wash. State Bar Assn., Am. Soc. Corp. Secs., Soc. Human Resource Mgmt., Nat. Eagle Scout Assn. Corporate, general, Labor (including EEOC, Fair Labor Standards Act, labor-management relations, NLRB, OSHA), Pension, profit-sharing, and employee benefits. Office: TransAlta USA Inc 913 Big Hanaford Rd Centralia WA 98531-9101 E-mail: charlie_bates@hotmail.com.

BATES, JOHN CECIL, JR., lawyer; b. Buffalo, May 27, 1936; s. John C. and Geraldine K. Bates; m. Ellen Clare Eyler, June 28, 1964; children: Andrew, Jeremy, Eliot, Emily. AB magna cum laude, Harvard U., 1958; JD, U. Mich., 1961; LLM, NYU, 1962. Bar: N.Y. 1962, D.C. 1977. Assoc. Milbank, Tweed, Hadley & McCloy, N.Y.C., 1963-72; spl. asst. tax policy Treasury Dept., Washington, 1973-76; ptnr. Squire, Sanders & Dempsey, Washington, 1977-84, Reid & Priest, Washington, 1984-91, Foley & Lardner, Washington, 1992-94; tax policy advisor Dept. Treas. Tech. Assistance Program (Ctrl. and Eastern Europe), 1995-98, Deloitte Emerging Markets, 1998—99; cons. on fiscal decentralization, 2000—. Tax and fin. cons. to state local and fgn. govts., also others, 1977—; adj. prof. Fordham U. Grad. Sch. Bus. Adminstrn., 1992. Co-author: Federal Law of Public Finance, 1988; contbr. numerous articles on tax, energy and fin. to profl. jours. Fellow: Internat. Law Inst. (sr.); mem.: ABA (chmn. com. tax sect. 1981—83), D.C. Bar Assn., Harvard Club. Avocations: historic preservation, environmental protection, music. Finance, Municipal (including bonds), Corporate taxation. Home: PO Box 293 Tenants Harbor ME 04860-0293

BATES, WALTER ALAN, former lawyer; b. Wadsworth, Ohio, Oct. 27, 1925; s. Edwin Clinton and Gertrude (Connor) B.; m. Aloise Grasselli O'Brien, Feb. 9, 1957; children: Charles, Aloise, Walter Alan Jr., Thomas, David BS cum laude, Harvard U., 1945, LLB, 1950. Bar: Ohio 1950, U.S. Dist. Ct. (no. dist.) Ohio 1954, U.S. Ct. Appeals (6th cir.) 1965, U.S. Ct. Appeals (7th cir.) 1966, U.S. Dist. Ct. Conn. 1976, U.S. Ct. Appeals (2nd cir.) 1977, U.S. Dist. Ct. Minn. 1978, U.S. Ct. Appeals (8th cir.) 1980, U.S. Ct. Appeals (5th cir.) 1984, U.S. Dist. Ct. (no. dist.) Tex. 1988, U.S. Supreme Ct. 1989. Assoc. McKeehan, Merrick, Arter & Stewart, Cleve., 1950-60; ptnr. Arter & Hadden, Cleve., 1960-94; ret., 1994. Chmn. bd. trustees Cleve. Inst. Music, 1980-85, hon. trustee, 1985—; assoc. v.p., chmn. new programs com. United Way Svcs., Cleve., 1982-85, trustee, 1985-88; mem. Cleve. panel Ctr. for Pub. Resources; trustee Apollo's Fire, 1998—. Lt. USN, 1945-46, 51-53. Mem. ABA (antitrust sect.), Ohio State Bar Assn. (chmn. bd. govs. antitrust sect. 1987-91), Cleve. Bar Assn. (joint com. on bar admissions 1990-97, cert. grievance com. 1992-95). Clubs: Kirtland Country (sec., bd. dirs. 1981-86), Mentor Harbor Yachting (bd. dirs. 1980-89, commodore 1988), Tavern, Harvard (Cleve. pres. 1968-69). Republican. Roman Catholic. Avocations: sailing, traveling. Antitrust, General civil litigation, Product liability. Home: 18235 Shaker Blvd Cleveland OH 44120-1754 Office: Arter & Hadden 1100 Huntington Bldg Cleveland OH 44115 E-mail: sailor74@prodigy.net.

BATES, WILLIAM, III, lawyer; b. Phila., May 1, 1949; s. William and Elizabeth (Martin) B. BA, Yale U., 1971; JD, Stanford U., 1974. Bar: Calif. 1974, U.S. Dist. Ct. (no. dist.) Calif. 1976, U.S. Dist. Ct. (ea. dist.) Calif. 1978, U.S. Dist. Ct. (ctrl. dist.) Calif. 1984, U.S. Ct. Appeals (9th cir.) 1986, U.S. Dist. Ct. (so. dist.) Calif. 1987, U.S. Supreme Ct. Law clk. to chief judge U.S. Dist. Ct. Conn., Hartford, 1974—75; assoc. McCutchen, Doyle, Brown & Enersen, San Francisco, 1975—81; ptnr. Bingham, McCutchen (formerly McCutchen, Doyle, Brown & Enersen), 1981—. Bd. visitors Stanford Law Sch., 2003—. Mem. ABA (mem. bus. bankruptcy com.), State Bar Calif. (chair rules of ct. com. 1979-80, mem. uniform comml. code com. 1985-88, mem. debtor/creditor rels. com. 1989-92), San Francisco Bar Assn. (chair comml. law and bankruptcy sect. 1991-92). Democrat. Episcopalian. Avocations: wine tasting, bicycling, travel. Bankruptcy, General civil litigation, Intellectual property. Office: Bingham McCutchen 1900 University Ave East Palo Alto CA 94303-2223 E-mail: bill.bates@bingham.com.

BATES, WILLIAM HUBERT, lawyer; b. Lexington, Mo., Apr. 14, 1926; s. George Hubert and E. Norma (Comer) B.; m. Joy LoRue Godbehere, Oct. 20, 1956; children: William Brand, Joy Ann. BA, U. Mo., 1949; JD, U. Mich., 1952. Bar: Mo. 1952. With Lathrop & Gage L.C., Kansas City, Mo., 1952—, chmn., 1988-95. Mem., pres. bd. curators U. Mo. Multi-Campus U., 1983-89. Sgt. U.S. Army, 1943-46, ETO. Recipient Brotherhood award NCCJ, 1984; Disting. Alumni award U. Mo., 1989, Geyer award for pub. svc., 1991. Fellow Am. Bar Found. (state chmn. 1990-97); mem. ABA (ho. of dels. 1990-93), Mo. Bar Assn. (bd. dirs. 1982-91, v.p., pres. 1988-91), Kansas City Bar Assn. (pres. Found. 1985-87), Lawyers Assn. Kansas City (Charles Evans Whittaker award 1990), Mo. C. of C. (chmn., bd. dirs. 1983-85), Greater Kansas City C. of C. (bd. dirs., chmn. 1975-92), Van Guard Club, Mercury Club, Beta Theta Pi (Man of Yr. award Kansas City 1985, Oxford Cup 1996). Democrat. Methodist. Avocations: golf, swimming, music. Corporate, general, FERC practice, Legislative. Home: 310 W 49th St Apt 1002 Kansas City MO 64112-3400 Office: Lathrop & Gage L C 2345 Grand Blvd Ste 2600 Kansas City MO 64108-2617

BATLA, RAYMOND JOHN, JR., lawyer; b. Cameron, Tex., Sept. 1, 1947; s. Raymond John and Della Alvina (Jezek) B.; m. Susan Marie Clark, Oct. 1, 1983; children: Sara, Charles, Michael, Traci. BS with highest honors, U. Tex., 1970, JD with honors, 1973. Bar: Tex. 1973, D.C. 1973, U.S. Dist. Ct. (so. dist.) Tex. 1982, U.S. Ct. Appeals (D.C. cir.) 1974, U.S. Ct. Appeals (5th cir.) 1982, U.S. Ct. Appeals (10th cir.) 1978, U.S. Supreme Ct. 1977. Structural engr. Tex. Hwy. Dept., Austin, 1970; assoc. Hogan & Hatson, Washington, 1973-82, gen. ptrn., 1983—. Mem. Am. Endowment for Democracy Internat. Observer Del. to Czechoslovakia, 1990; sec. Coun. on Alt. Fuels, 1987-97. Author: Petroleum Regulation Handbook, 1980, Natural Gas Yearbook, 1991; columnist, mem. editorial bd. Natural Gas mag., 1984-91, Energy Law Jour., 1991-93; contbr. articles to profl. jours. Mem. ABA (mem. spl. com. for energy fin., vice chmn. energy com. 1981), Fed. Energy Bar Assn. (chmn. internat. energy transactions com. 1993-94), Fed. Bar Assn., D.C. Bar Assn., State Bar Tex., City Club of Wash., London Capital Club, Order of Coif, Chi Epsilon, Tau Beta Pi. Private international, Public international, Utilities, public. Home: 12406 Shari Hunt Grv Clifton VA 20124-2056 also: 5 Half Moon St London W1Y 7RA England Office: Hogan & Hartson 555 13th St NW Ste 800W Washington DC 20004-1109 also: Hogan & Hartson One Angel Ct London EC2R 7HJ England E-mail: rjbatla@hhlaw.com.

BATSON, DAVID WARREN, lawyer; b. Wichita Falls, Tex., Jan. 4, 1956; s. Warren M. Batson and Jacqueline (Latham) B. BBA, Midwestern State U., 1976; JD, U. Tex., 1979. Bar: Tex. 1980, U.S. Dist. Ct. (no. dist.) Tex. 1981, U.S. Tax Ct. 1981, U.S. Ct. Appeals (5th cir.) 1983, U.S. Ct. Appeals (D.C. cir.) 1983, U.S. Ct. Claims 1984, U.S. Supreme Ct. 1984. Atty. Arthur Andersen & Co., Ft. Worth, 1980-81; tax atty. The Western Co. of N.Am., Ft. Worth, 1981-85; sr. tax atty. Alcon Labs., Inc., Ft. Worth, 1985; gen. counsel Data Tailor, Inc., Ft. Worth, 1985-87; sr. tax atty. Arco, 1988-90; atty. pvt. practice, Wichita Falls, Tex., 1990—99; pvt. practice Stephenville, Tex., 1999—. Lectr. U. of Tex., Arlington, 1984-85; of counsel Means & Means, Corsicana, Tex., 1985-86. Contbr. articles to profl. jours. Speaker A Wish With Wings, Arlington, Tex., 1984-85, Habitat for Humanity (bd. dirs. 1999-). Fellow Tex. Bar Found.; mem. ATLA, Texas Bar Assn., Christian Legal Soc., Tex. Trial Lawyers Assn., State Bar at Tex. Coll., Phi Delta Phi. Avocations: negotiations, camping, self improvement. Commercial, contracts (including sales of goods; commercial financing), Private international, Mergers and acquisitions. Address: PO Box 585 Stephenville TX 76401-0585

BATSON, RICHARD NEAL, lawyer; b. Nashville, May 1, 1941; s. John H. and Mildred (Neal) B.; m. Jean Elizabeth Flanagan; children: John Hayes, Richard Davis. BA cum laude, Vanderbilt U., 1963, JD, 1966. Bar: Ga. 1967. Law clk. to Judge Griffin B. Bell U.S. Ct. Appeals (5th cir.), Atlanta, 1966-67; assoc. Alston & Bird (formerly Alston, Miller & Gaines), Atlanta, 1967-71, ptnr., 1971—. Spkr. Nat. Conf. Bankruptcy Judges, 1982, 86, 87, 88, 94, 96, Bank Lending Inst., 1986-87, also other instns. and assns.; adj. prof. Emory U. Sch. Law, 1994-95; co-lectr. Ga. State U., fall 1984; mem. bankruptcy rules com. Jud. Conf. U.S., 1993-99. Co-author: Problem Loan Strategies, 1985, rev. 1998; contbg. author Bankruptcy Litigation Manual, 1990—; contbg. editor Norton Bankruptcy Law and Practice, 1990—. Sgt. USAF, 1967-73. Fellow Am. Coll. Trial Lawyers, Am. Coll. Bankruptcy (bd. dirs., pres. 1997-2001, chmn. bd. dirs. 2001-03); mem. Atlanta Bar Assn. (pres. 1979-80), Am. Law Inst., Southeastern Bankruptcy Law Inst. (bd. dirs., pres. 1986-87), Nat. Bankruptcy Conf. Avocations: hiking, outdoor activities. Office: Alston & Bird One Atlantic Ctr 1201 W Peachtree St Atlanta GA 30309-3400 Home: PO Box 5201 Snowmass Village CO 81615

BATT, NICK, property and investment executive; b. Defiance, Ohio, May 6, 1952; s. Dan and Zenith (Dreher) B. BS, Purdue U., 1972; JD, U. Toledo, 1976. Asst. prosecutor Lucas County, Toledo, 1976-80, civil divsn. chief, 1980-83; village atty. Village of Holland, Ohio, 1980-91; law dir. City of Oregon, Ohio, 1984-91; spl. counsel State of Ohio, 1983-93; pres. Property & Mgmt. Connection, Inc., Toledo, 1993—2002, All Rental Property Mgmt. Co., 2002—. Mem. Maumee Valley Girl Scout Coun., Toledo, 1977-80; bd. mem. Bd. Cmty. Rels., Toledo, 1975-76; mem. Lucas County Dem. Exec. Com., 1981-83. Named One of Toledo's Outstanding Young Men, Toledo Jaycees, 1979. Mem. KC, Elks. Democrat. Roman Catholic. Office: All Rental Property Mgmt Co 1732 Arlington Ave Toledo OH 43609-3050 E-mail: NICKBATT@TOAST.NET.

BATTAGLIA, ANTHONY SYLVESTER, lawyer; b. Binghamton, N.Y., Aug. 21, 1927; s. Sylvester Anthony and Helen B.; m. Catherine Jean, Oct. 1, 1972; children: Christina, Marc Anthony; children by previous marriage— Anthony, Sandra, Brian, Brenda Lee. AA, U. Fla., 1948, BA, 1949, LL.B., 1953, JD, 1967. Bar: Fla. 1953, U.S. Dist. Ct. (mid. and so. dists.) Fla., U.S. Ct. Appeals (5th, 11th cirs.), U.S. Tax Ct., U.S. Ct. Appeals (D.C. cir.), U.S. Ct. Mil. Appeals; cert. ct. approved abritrator U.S. Dist. Ct., U.S. Supreme Ct. 1966. Asst. to U.S. dist. atty., So. Dist. Fla., 1953-56; ptnr. Parker, Parker & Battaglia, St. Petersburg, Fla., 1953-56, Parker, Battaglia & Ross, St. Petersburg, 1965-73, Parker, Battaglia, Parker, Ross & Ross, St. Petersburg, 1973-75, Battaglia, Parker, Ross, Parker & Stolba, St. Petersburg, 1975-76, Battaglia, Ross & Stolba, 1976-77, Battaglia, Ross, Stolba & Forlizzo, 1977-78, Battaglia, Ross & Forlizzo, 1978-80, Battaglia, Ross, Hastings, Dicus & Andrews, 1980-93, Battaglia, Ross, Dicus & Wein PA, 1993-2001. Mem. Fla. Pub. Svc. Commn., 1971; chmn. bd. Metrocare, Inc., 1975-78; mem. grievance com. U.S. Dist. Ct., 1985-88; pres. Asst. U.S. Attys. Assn. for Mid. Dist. Fla., 1994; guest lectr. Stetson U., 1994; bd. dirs. Intervest Bank, 1st Bankers Tampa Bay, N.A., St. Petersburg, Nat. Bank Fla., St. Petersburg, Operation PAR, Inc.; chmn. adv. bd. 1st Union Nat. Bank, South Pinellas, Fla. Republican nat. committeeman, Fla., 1956-64, bd. dirs., Tampa div.; bd. dirs. San Carlo Opera Fla., 1972-74, pres., chmn. bd. dirs., Pinellas County div., 1974-76; bd. dirs. St. Petersburg Opera Co., 1976-77; chmn. bd. Pinellas County Arthritis Found., 1985; founding sponsor Civil Justice Found.; trustee Ctr. Against Spouse Abuse, 1999. Elected to U. Fla. Hall of Fame, 1951 Master Ferguson-White Am. Inn of Ct.; fellow Am. Coll. Mortgage Attys.; mem. ABA, ATLA (sustaining), Fla. Bar Assn. (bd. govs. 1993-99), St. Petersburg Bar Assn. (pres. 1990), Fed. Bar Assn. (v.p. Mid. Fla. dist.), U.S. Attys. Assn. for Mid. Dist. Fla. (pres. 2001), Internat. Bar Assn., Hillsborough County Bar Assn., Acad. Fla. Trial Lawyers (judge student competition 1985), Am. Judicature Soc. (Supreme Ct. Hist. Soc. 1985-89), Nat. Assn. Criminal Def. Lawyers, Acad. Criminal Justice Scis., Fla. Criminal Def. Trial Lawyers, Criminal Def. Lawyers Hillsborough County, Pinellas County Trial Lawyers Assn. Roscoe Pound Am., Trial Lawyers Found. (judicial nominating com.), U. Fla. Nat. Alumni Assn., St. Petersburg C. of C. (gov.), Pinellas Inns Ct. (master bench), Herbert G. Goldberg Criminal Law Am. Inn Ct., Fla. Bar Bd. of Govs. Clubs: Treasure Island Tennis and Yacht (bd. dirs.), Suncoast Tiger Bay, St. Petersburg Yacht, Nat. Italian Am. Found., Italian-Am. Unico Internat. Lodges: K.C. Roman Catholic. Office: 980 Tyrone Blvd N Saint Petersburg FL 33710-6333

BATTAGLIA, LYNNE ANN, judge; b. Buffalo, 1946; BA Intl Relations, Amer. Univ., 1967, MA, 1968; JD, Univ. of Maryland, 1974. U.S. atty., Md., 1993-2001; chief of staff Office of U.S. Sen. Barbara A. Mikulski, 1991—93; judge Md. Ct. Appeals, 2001—. Office: Md Ct Appeals Robert C Murphy Bldg 361 Rowe Blvd Annapolis MD 21401

BATTEN, STEPHEN JOHN, lawyer; b. Williamston, N.C., Mar. 2, 1967; s. Welch Middleton and Jeanne Grogan Batten. BA, Duke U., 1989; JD, U. N.C., 1993. Bar: N.C., U.S. Dist. Ct. (ea. dist.) N.C. Assoc. Allen T. Rubeo, Miami Beach, Fla., 1993—96; solo practitioner Raleigh, NC, 1996—98; staff atty. Womble Carlyle Sandridge & Rice, PLLA, Raleigh, NC, 1998, Moore & Van Allen, PLLC, Charlotte, NC, 0998—1999; assoc. Blount Law Firm, PA, Greenville, NC, 2000—. Editl. bd. N.C. Acad. Trial Lawyers, Raleigh, 2001—. Recipient Order of Long Leaf Pine award, Gov. N.C., 1985. Mem.: ABA, Acad. Trial Lawyers of Am.., N.C. Acad. Trial Lawyers. Democrat. Episcopalian. Appellate, Personal injury (including property damage), Professional liability. Office: Blount Law Firm PA 400 W First St Greenville NC 27834 Office Fax: 252-752-2174. E-mail: stephen@theblountlawfirm.com.

BATTLE, LEONARD CARROLL, lawyer; b. Toronto, Ont., Can., Oct. 25, 1929; s. Leonard Conlon and Beatrice Hester Battle; m. Marjory Estelle Holland, Dec. 28, 1953; children: David, Tracy, Thomas, Patricia, John, Mary. AB, U. Mich., 1950; JD, Ind. U., 1958. Bar: Mich. 1961, Ind. 1961, U.S. Ct. Mil. Appeals 1964, U.S. Supreme Ct. 1964. Claims adjuster State Farm Ins. Co., 1959-61; asst. pros. atty. Midland County, Mich., 1961-67; pvt. practice, Midland, Mich., 1967—. Lt. col. JAG, USAFR, 1950-84. Mem. ATLA, Mich. Bar Assn. (mil. law com.), Midland County Bar Assn. (pres.), Air Force Ret. Judge Advs. Assn. Bankruptcy, Federal civil litigation, State civil litigation. Home: 408 Harper Ln Midland MI 48640-7321 Office: 200 E Main St Midland MI 48640-6510 E-mail: afjag05ret@webtv.net.

BATTLE, LESLIE ANNE ELIZABETH, lawyer; b. Orchard Park, N.Y. BA, Wellesley Coll., 1990, MIT, 1990; JD, Syracuse U., 1993. Bar: Mass. 1994. Counsel MetLife Auto & Home, Warwick, RI, 1994—. Andrews scholar Syracuse U. Coll. of Law, 1993, 94, 95, Dorothy Denis scholar Wellesley Coll., 1986-90, Stecher scholar, 1989. Mem. ABA, R.I. Black Lawyers Assn., R.I. In-House Counsel Assn. Corporate, general, Insurance. Office: MetLife Auto & Home 700 Quaker Ln Warwick RI 02886-6681

BATTLE, MICHAEL A. lawyer; b. 1955; Grad., Ithaca Coll., SUNY, Buffalo. Asst. U.S. atty. We. Dist. N.Y., 1985—92; asst. pub. defender Fed. Pub. Defender's Office, We. Dist. N.Y., 1992—95; asst. atty. gen. 8th Jud. Cir., N.Y. State Atty. Gen.'s Office, 1995—96; judge Erie County Family Ct., Buffalo, 1996—2002; U.S. atty. We. Dist. N.Y., 2002—. Office: 138 Delaware Ave Buffalo NY 14202*

BAUCH, THOMAS JAY, financial/investment advisor, lawyer, educator, former apparel company executive; b. Indpls., May 24, 1943; s. Thomas and Violet (Smith) B.; m. Ellen L. Burstein, Oct. 31, 1982; children: Chelsea Sara, Elizabeth Tree. BS with honors, U. Wis., 1964, JD with highest honors, 1966. Bar: Ill. 1966, Calif. 1978. Assoc. Lord, Bissell & Brook, Chgo., 1966-72; lawyer, asst. sec. Marcor-Montgomery Ward, Chgo., 1973-75; spl. asst. to solicitor Dept. Labor, Washington, 1975-77; dep. gen. counsel Levi Strauss & Co., San Francisco, 1977-81, sr. v.p., gen. counsel, 1981-96, of counsel, 1996-2000; pvt. practice, Tiburon, Calif., 1996-2000; mng. dir. Offit Hall Capital Mgmt. LLC, San Francisco, 2000—. Cons. prof. Stanford (Calif.) U. Law Sch., 1997—; ptnr. Ika Enterprises. Mem. U. Wis. Law Rev., 1964-66. Bd. dirs. Urban Sch., San Francisco, 1986-91, Gateway H.S., San Francisco, Charles Armstrong Sch., Belmont, Calif., 1998-2001, San Francisco Opera Assn., 1998-2001, Telluride Acad., 1996-2000, Corinthian Acad.; bd. visitors U. Wis. Law Sch., 1991-95. Mem. Am. Assn. Corp. Counsel (bd. dirs. 1984-87), Bay Area Gen. Counsel Assn. (chmn. 1994), Univ. Club, Villa Taverna Club, Corinthian Yacht Club, Order of Coif, San Francisco Yacht Club. Corporate, general. Office: Offit Hall Capital Mgmt One Maritime Plz Ste 500 San Francisco CA 94111 E-mail: tbauch@offithall.com.

BAUCKHAM, JOHN HENRY, lawyer; b. Royal Oak, Mich., Mar. 16, 1923; s. Henry Charles and Mabel Lillian (Stratford) B.; m. Nancy Lee Bassett, Aug. 5, 1943 (div. 1972); children: Thomas, Laura Bauckham Callander, David, Robert; m. Dorothy Ann Kobussen, Jan. 29, 1973 (div. 1988); m. Rosalie Kirklin, Feb. 14, 1993. JD, U. Mich., 1949. Bar: Mich. 1949, U.S. Dist. Ct. (we. dist.) Mich. 1953, U.S. Ct. Appeals (6th cir.) 1971, U.S. Dist. Ct. (ea. dist.) Mich. 1977, U.S. Supreme Ct. 1978. Assoc. Adams Smith & Yenner, Kalamazoo, 1949-50; ptnr. Harry F. Smith, 1950-55, Bauckham & Enslen, Kalamazoo, 1957-60, Bauckham, Reed, Lang, Shaefer & Travis, Kalamazoo, 1960-79; with Bauckham, Sparks Rolfe, Lohrstorfer & Thall PC/predecessors, 1979—, pres., 1979—. Author: Duties and Responsibilities of Michigan Townships Officials, Boards, and Commissioners, 1976, rev., through 2003. With USAF, 1943-45. Mem. ABA, Mich. Bar Assn., Kalamazoo County Bar Assn. (pres. 1966-67, chmn. state grievance panel 1982—, mem. state character and fitness com. 1987—), Elks. Republican. Episcopalian. Avocations: golf, travel, sports. Land use and zoning (including planning), Municipal (including bonds). Home: 259 Ballantrae Ct Kalamazoo MI 49006-4349 Office: Bauckham Sparks et al 458 W South St Kalamazoo MI 49007-4621 E-mail: bauckham@bsrlt.com.

BAUCOM, SIDNEY GEORGE, lawyer; b. Salt Lake City, Oct. 21, 1930; s. Sidney and Nora (Palfreyman) B.; m. Mary B., Mar. 5, 1954; children: Sidney, George, John JD, U. Utah, 1953. Bar: Utah 1953. Pvt. practice, Salt Lake City, 1953-55; asst. city atty. Salt Lake City Corp., 1955-56; asst. atty. Utah Power and Light Co., Salt Lake City, 1956-60, asst. atty., asst. sec., 1960-62, atty., asst. sec., 1962-68, v.p., gen. counsel, 1968-75, sr. v.p., gen. counsel, 1975-79, exec. v.p., gen. counsel, 1979-89, dir., 1979-89; of counsel Jones, Waldo, Holbrook & McDonough, Salt Lake City, 1989—. Past chmn. Utah Coordinating Coun. Devel. Svcs., Utah Taxpayers Assn.; past pres. Utah State Fair Found.; past dir. Utah Power & Light Co., El Paso Electric Co., vice chmn. Mem. Alta Club, Lions, Phi Delta Phi Mem. Lds Ch. Corporate, general, Utilities, public. Home: 2248 Logan Ave Salt Lake City UT 84108-2715 Office: Jones Waldo Holbrook & McDonough 1500 Wells Fargo Bank Bldg 170 S Main St Salt Lake City UT 84101-1605 E-mail: sbaucom@janeswaldo.com.

BAUER, MARVIN AGATHER, lawyer; b. Milw., June 28, 1940; m. Gray Bauer; children: Laura, Andrew. BS, U. Wis., 1962; JD, U. Chgo., 1965. Bar: Calif. 1966. Dep. atty. gen. State of Calif., Los Angeles, 1965-69; ptnr. Archbald & Spray, Santa Barbara, Calif., 1969-82, Bauer, Harris Clinkenbeard & Ramsey, Santa Barbara, 1982—. Lectr. U. Calif., 1975—77; instr. Santa Barbara Coll. Law, 2001; bd. dir. Summerland Citizens Assn. Bd. dirs. Carpinteria Valley Assn., Calif., 1980-83, Carpinteria Boys Club, 1983-84. Mem. Am. Coll. Trial Lawyers, Am. Bd. Trial Advocates, Santa Barbara Bar Assn. (pres. 1978-79, bd. dirs. 1974-80), Calif. Med.-Legal Com. (pres. 2003—), Santa Barbara Med. Legal Com. State civil litigation, Insurance, Personal injury (including property damage). Home: PO Box 1307 Summerland CA 93067-1307 Office: Bauer Harris Clinkenbeard & Ramsey 925 De La Vina St Santa Barbara CA 93101-3243

BAUER, WILLIAM JOSEPH, federal judge; b. Chgo., Sept. 15, 1926; s. William Francis and Lucille (Gleason) Bauer; m. Mary Nicol, Jan. 28, 1950; children: Patricia, Linda. AB, Elmhurst Coll., 1949, LLD, 1969; JD, DePaul U., 1952, LLD (hon.) , 1993, John Marshall Law Sch., 1987, Roosevelt U., 1994. Bar: Ill. 1951. Ptnr. Erlenborn, Bauer & Hotte, Elmhurst, Ill., 1953—64; asst. state's atty. Du Page County, Ill., 1952—56; 1st asst. state's atty., 1956—58; state's atty., 1959—64; judge 18th Jud. Cir. Ct., 1964—70; U.S. dist. atty. No. Ill. Chgo., 1970—71; judge U.S. Dist. Ct. (no. dist.), Chgo., 1971—75, U.S. Ct. Appeals (7th cir.), 1975—86, chief judge, 1986—93, senior judge, 1994—. Instr. bus law. Elmhurst Coll., 1952—59; adj. prof. law DePaul U., 1978—91; former mem. Ill. Supreme Ct. Com. on Pattern Criminal Jury Instrns.; chmn. Fed. Criminal Jury Instrn. Com. 7th Cir. Trustee Elmhurst Coll., 1979—, DePaul U., 1984—, DuPage Meml. Hosp.; bd. advisors Mercy Hosp. With U.S. Army, 1945—47. Mem.: FBA (former bd. dirs.), ABA, Chgo. Bar Assn., DuPage County Bar Assn. (past pres.), Ill. Bar Assn., Legal Club (Chgo.), Law Club, Union League Club. Roman Catholic. Office: US Ct Appeals 219 S Dearborn St Ste 2754 Chicago IL 60604

BAUERSFELD, CARL FREDERICK, lawyer; b. Balt., June 9, 1916; s. Emil George and Irene Marie (Hulse) B.; m. Ann Yancey, Mar. 3, 1944 (div.); children: Elizabeth Bauersfeld Garnett, Carl F. Student, George Washington U., 1937-42; LLB, Am. U., 1937. Bar: D.C. 1937, U.S. Dist. Ct. D.C. 1937, U.S. Ct. Appeals (D.C. cir.) 1937, U.S. Supreme Ct. 1941, U.S. Ct. Claims 1946, U.S. Tax Ct. 1946, Md. 1957, U.S. Ct. Appeals (5th cir.) 1947, (9th cir.) 1956, (3d cir.) 1958, (8th cir.) 1960, (4th cir.) 1966, (2d cir.) 1970. Practiced in, Washington, 1937—; ptnr. Bauersfeld, Burton, Hendricks & Vanderhoof, L.L.C., 1956—. Lectr. on fed. taxation at various univs. Lt. comdr. USNR, 1942-46. Mem. ABA, Md. Bar Assn., Bar Assn. D.C., Congl. Country Club, Burning Tree Club, Sigma Nu Phi, Phi Sigma Kappa. Lutheran. General civil litigation, Corporate, general, Taxation, general. Office: 7101 Wisconsin Ave Bethesda MD 20814-4805 E-mail: c.bauersfeld@bbhv.net.

BAUGHER, PETER V. lawyer; b. Chgo., Oct. 2, 1948; s. William and Marilyn (Sill) Baugher; m. Robin Stickney, Nov. 25, 1978; children: Julia Allison, Britton William Herbert. AB, Princeton U., 1970; JD, Yale U., 1973. Bar: Ill. 1974, U.S. Dist. Ct. (no. dist.) Ill. 1974, U.S. Ct. Appeals (7th cir.) 1974, U.S. Supreme Ct. 1987. Law clk. to judge U.S. Ct. Appeals (7th cir.), Chgo., 1973-74; from assoc. to ptnr. Schiff Hardin & Waite, Chgo., 1974-85; ptnr. Adams, Fox, Adelstein & Rosen, Chgo., 1985-89, Schopf & Weiss, Chgo., 1989—. Trustee Sta. WTTW Channel 11, Chgo., 1976—81, Kendall Coll., Evanston, 1980—92, WBEZ, Chgo. Pub. Radio, 1992—98, Ill. Humanities Coun., 1997—. Mem. adv. com. Rep. Nat. Conv., Detroit, 1980; bd. dirs. Protestants for the Common Good, 2001—; mem. adv. com. Northwestern U. Sch. Law Ctr. Internat. Human Rights; pres. Lincoln Inn of Ct., 1994—96. Mem.: ABA, Chgo. Coun. Fgn. Rels., Am. Law Inst., Chgo. Bar Assn. (chair internat. and fgn. law com., chair fed civil procedure com.), Ripon Soc. (chmn. 1975—76), Am. Coun. Germany, Mich. Shores Club, Econ. Club Chgo., Univ. Club. Federal civil litigation, State civil litigation, Private international. Home: 1310 Sheridan Rd Wilmette IL 60091-1834 Office: Schopf & Weiss 312 W Randolph St Chicago IL 60606-1721 E-mail: baugher@sw.com.

BAUGHMAN, R(OBERT) PATRICK, lawyer; b. Zanesville, Ohio, Nov. 18, 1938; s. Robert G. and Kathryn E. B.; m. Joyce Hall, June 17, 1959; 1 dau., Patricia. BS, Ohio State U., 1960, JD, 1963. Bar: Ohio 1963. Assoc. firm Sindell & Sindell, Cleve., 1964-71, Jones, Day, Reavis & Pogue, Cleve., 1972-73; asst. atty. gen. State of Ohio, Columbus, 1971-72; pres., prin. firm Baughman & Assocs., Cleve., 1973—. Mem. ABA, Ohio Bar Assn., Cuyahoga County Bar Assn., Nat. Council Self-Insurers, Internat. Assn. Indsl. Accident Bds. and Commns., Internat. Platform Assn. Clubs: Columbia Hills Country. Episcopalian. Admiralty, Product liability, Workers' compensation. Office: Baughman & Assocs 55 Public Sq Ste 2215 Cleveland OH 44113-1996

BAUHOF, JAMES FRANCIS, lawyer; b. Cleve., Aug. 15, 1942; s. Clarence Joseph and Eileen (Brennan) B.; Virginia Evelyn Panek, Dec. 26, 1964; children: Laura, Michael, Greg. BA, U. Dayton, 1964; JD, Ohio No. Univ., 1967. Bar: Ohio 1967, U.S. Dist. Ct. (so. dist.) Ohio 1968, U.S. Supreme Ct. 1970, Mich. 1974, U.S. Dist. Ct. (we. dist.) Mich. 1979, U.S. Ct. Appeals (6th cir.) 1979. Asst. city atty. City of Dayton (Ohio), 1967-74; asst. clk. ct. Mich. Ct. Appeals, Lansing, Mich., 1974-76; shareholder Jerkins, Plaszczak, Hurley & Bauhof, Kalamazoo, 1976-79, Plaszczak & Bauhof, P.C., Kalamazoo, 1979—. Lectr. in field, 1971—; lectr. on civil war and Abraham Lincoln. Mem. ABA, Mich. State Bar Assn., Kalamazoo County Bar Assn., Kalamazoo County Trial Lawyers Assn. (founder, pres. 1998-99, Raymond W. Fox Adv. Achievement award 1990). Roman Catholic. Avocations: lecturer on civil war and abraham lincoln, wildlife photography, cross-country skiing, historian of civil war period. Appellate, General civil litigation, Criminal. Home: 5298 Skyridge Ave Kalamazoo MI 49009-1232 Office: Plaszczak & Bauhof PC 137 N Park St Ste 203 Kalamazoo MI 49007-3769

BAULEKE, HOWARD PAUL, lawyer; b. Lawrence, Kans., Apr. 16, 1959; s. Maynard Paul and Virginia (Shirley) P. BA, U. Kans., 1981; JD, Georgetown U., 1984. Bar: Kans. 1985, D.C. 1985, U.S. Dist. Ct. Kans. 1985. Legis. asst. U.S. Rep. Jim Slattery, Washington, 1984-87, legis. dir., 1987, Washington staff dir., 1987-90, adminstrv. asst., 1991-95, U.S. Rep. Karen McCarthy, 1995; assoc. counsel U.S. House Dem. Policy Com., 1995-97; counsel U.S. House Commerce Com., 1997-99; chief of staff U.S. Rep. Dennis Moore, 1999—. Contbr. articles to profl. jours. Mem. D.C. Bar Assn., Phi Beta Kappa. Democrat. Unitarian Universalist. Home: 1840 California St NW # 10 Washington DC 20009-1822 E-mail: howard.bauleke@mail.house.gov.

BAUM, ALAN STUART, lawyer; b. Phila., Aug. 5, 1955; s. Seymour Zangwill and Harriet (Berlin) B.; m. Marjorie Fisher, May 28, 1978; children: Ryan Michael, Andrew Eric. BS in Mktg. and Real Estate with honors, Syracuse U., 1977; JD, Ohio No. U., 1980. Bar: Pa. 1980, N.J. 1981, U.S. Supreme Ct., 1995. Assoc. Zarwin & Baum, Phila., 1980-82, Grigsby, Gaca & Davies, Pitts., 1982-86, ptnr., 1987-93, Gaca, Matis, Baum & Rizza, Pitts., 1993—, mng. ptnr., 1993-98. Lectr. med. malpractice and nursing home litig. seminars; advisor Pa. Statewide Mock Trial Competition, 1991—; adj. settlement judge U.S. Dist. Ct. (we. dist.) Pa.; apptd. spl. master civil litig. Ct. Common Pleas, Allegheny County. Editor: Ohio No. U. Law Rev. Recipient Eagle Scout award Boy Scouts Am. Fellow Acad. Trial Lawyers Allegheny County; mem. Pa. Bar Assn., Allegheny County Bar Assn. (ct. rules com. players orch., civil litig. sect. counsel 1998—, officer 2002--). Avocation: tenor saxophone. General civil litigation, Insurance, Professional liability. Home: 149 Monticello Dr Monroeville PA 15146-4851 E-mail: abaum@gaca.com.

BAUM, AXEL HELMUTH, lawyer; b. Berlin, July 14, 1930; came to U.S., 1933; s. Stefan H. and Gertrud (Goette) B.; m. Elisabeth K. Nordwall, Dec. 11, 1982; children— Nicholas S., Andreas S. BA cum laude, Amherst Coll., 1952; LL.B., Yale U., 1957. Bar: Conn. 1957, N.Y. 1958, U.S. Supreme Ct. 1976; Conseil Juridique, France, 1971; Avocat à la Cour (Paris) 1972. Assoc. Hughes, Hubbard & Reed, N.Y.C., 1957-64; fgn. atty. Lovell, White & King, London, 1959-60; ptnr. Hughes, Hubbard & Reed, N.Y.C., 1964—, ptnr.-in-charge European office Paris, 1996—2002, counsel, 2002—. Lectr., spkr. various internat. forums and seminars, France, Germany, U.S., Mid. East, 1970—; arbitrator, U.S. mem. Internat. Ct. of Arbitration of ICC, Paris, 2000—; Ctr. Pub. Resources Panel of Disting. Internatl. Mediators. Mng. editor Yale Law Jour., 1957; contbr. articles to profl. jours. Bd. dirs. Am. Aid Soc., France, 1981, chmn. 1995—, Am. Ch. Com. France, 1991-96, World Monuments Fund France, 1989-; Bd. trustees, Amer. Libr. of Paris 1999-2002, Served to lt. USNR, 1952-54. Mem. ABA, Am. Arbitration Assn., U.S. Coun. Internat. Bus., ICC Commn. Internat. Arbitration, Union Internat. des Avocats, Assn. Bar N.Y.C., London Ct. Internat. Arbitration, German Inst. Arbitration, Swiss Arbitration Assn., French Comite d'Arbitrose, Internat. Arbitration Inst., Polo Club (Paris), Yacht Club France, Swedish Cruising Club, Yale Club of N.Y.C. Avocations: sailing; tennis; swimming. Commercial, contracts (including sales of goods; commercial financing), Franchising. Home: 8 Rue des Dames Augustines 92200 Neuilly Seine France Office: Hughes Hubbard & Reed 47 Ave Georges Mandel 75116 Paris France E-mail: baum@hugheshubbard.com.

BAUM, GORDON LEE, lawyer, non-profit organization administrator; b. St. Louis, Aug. 24, 1940; s. James Paul and Johnnie Thelma (Thompson) B.; m. Georgia Dee Thompson, Sept. 12, 1959 (div. 1977); children: Gordon Lee II, Mark Evans Sterling, Duane Russell Stuart; m. Linda Gaye Gulledge, Feb. 10, 1978; children: Laura Leigh, Renee Gabrielle. Grad., U. Mo., 1965; JD, St. Louis U., 1969. Bar: Mo. 1969, U.S. Dist. Ct. Mo. 1969. Sr. inspection clk. Chevrolet Divsn. GM Corp., St. Louis, 1961-65, work standards engr., 1965-69; field dir. mid-west Citizens Coun. Am., Jackson, Miss., 1969-84; pvt. practice civil law St. Louis, 1969—. Chief exec. officer, Coun. Conservative Citizens, St. Louis, 1985—, Conservative Citizens Found., St. Louis, 1985—; dir. St. Louis Met. Area Citizens Coun. Assoc. editor (newspaper) Citizens Informer, 1971—; talk show host WGNU Radio, St. Louis, 1995—. State Coord. Wallace Presdl. Campaign, Mo., 1972, 76; del. Dem. Party State Conv., 1976. Yeoman 2d class petty officer USN, 1958-61. Mem. Mo. Bar Assn., Phi Alpha Delta, MENSA, NRA, Sons of Confederate Vets., Hist. Soc. Berks County, Pa., Ger.-Am. Heritage Soc., Am. Legion. Lutheran. Avocations: politics, history, hunting, gardening, travel. Non-profit and tax-exempt organizations, Personal injury (including property damage). Home: 2412 Park Ave Saint Charles MO 63301 Office: Coun of Conservative Citizens PO Box 221683 Saint Louis MO 63122-8683 E-mail: baum@bbs.galilei.com.

BAUM, JOSEPH THOMAS, lawyer; b. Amsterdam, N.Y., May 25, 1944; s. Joseph W. and Margaret M. (Wilt) B.; children: Jason, Daniel. BA, Siena Coll., 1966; JD, Albany Law Sch., 1972. Bar: N.Y. 1973, U.S. Dist. Ct. (no. dist.) N.Y. 1973. Instr. Alfred U., N.Y., 1973-74; assigned counsel Allegany County, Belmont, N.Y., 1973-74, law sec. Family Ct., 1974; asst. atty. gen. N.Y. State, Albany, 1974-79; clin. dir. Albany Law Sch., 1981—. Town atty. Town of Sand Lake, N.Y., 1980-82, 84, 98-2000, town councilman, 1992-96; bd. dirs. YMCA, Albany, 1984-87. Recipient Disting. Pro Bono Svc. award Legal Aid Northeastern N.Y., 1987, 98. Mem. ABA, N.Y. State Bar Assn., Rensselaer County Bar Assn., Am. Assn. Law Schs. (clin. sect.), Adirondack Mountain Club. Office: Albany Law Sch 80 New Scotland Ave Albany NY 12208-3434

BAUM, LYNNE MIRIAM, lawyer; b. Waukesha, Wis., Oct. 7, 1972; d. Bernard and Julie Ann Baum. BA, U. Wis., 1994; JD, Georgetown U., 1999. Bar: NY 00, U.S. Dist. Ct. PR 01, DC 02. Law clk. to Hon. Jaime Pieras Jr. U.S. Dist. Ct. PR, San Juan, 1999—2001; assoc. Hogan & Hartson LLP, Washington, 2001—. Mem.: ABA, DC Bar Assn., NY State Bar Assn., Phi Beta Kappa. General civil litigation. Office: Hogan & Hartson LLP 555 13th St NW Washington DC 20004 Home: 1915 Kalorama Rd NW #312 Washington DC 20009

BAUM, PETER ALAN, lawyer; b. Jamaica, N.Y., Sept. 22, 1947; s. Morris and Elsa (Sturtz) B.; m. Barbara Hartman, Nov. 29, 1969; children: Benjamin, Lisa, Alexander. BA, Colgate U., 1969; JD, Syracuse U., 1972.

Bar: N.Y. 1973, U.S. Dist. Ct. (no. dist.) N.Y. 1974. House counsel William Porter Real Estate Co., Syracuse, N.Y., 1972-73; pvt. practice Syracuse, 1973-82; ptnr. DiStefano and Baum, Syracuse, 1983-85, Baum and Woodard, Syracuse, 1985-90; prin. Peter A. Baum Law Offices, Chittenango, N.Y., 1990-96; ptnr. Iaconis, Iaconis and Baum, Chittenango, 1997—. Lectr. Onondaga C.C., Syracuse, 1976-79. Chmn. bd. dirs. Syracuse Area Landmark Theater, 1982-83; bd. dirs. Syracuse Opera Co., 1979-85. Mem. N.Y. State Bar Assn. (ho. of dels. 1992-93), Madison County Bar Assn. (pres. 1993), Onondaga County Bar Assn. (continuing edn. chmn. 1977-78), Onondaga Title Assn. Landlord-tenant, Property, real (including real estate development, water). Office: Iaconis Iaconis & Baum 282 Genesee St Chittenango NY 13037-1705

BAUM, STANLEY DAVID, lawyer; b. Bklyn., Feb. 22, 1954; s. Irwin and Muriel A. (Margolis) B.; m. Ilyne Rhona Fried, June 9, 1979; children: Andrew, Miranda. BS, U. Pa., 1976, JD, 1980; LLM, NYU, 1984. Bar: N.Y. 1981, U.S. Tax Ct. 1993. Lawyer Carter, Ledyard & Milburn, N.Y.C., 1988-98; of counsel Swidler, Berlin, Shereff, Friedman, LLP, N.Y.C., 1998—. Contbr. articles to profl. jours. Mem. N.Y. State Bar Assn. (com. on employee benefits tax sect.). E-mail: sdbaum@swidlaw.com.

BAUM, STANLEY M. lawyer; b. Bronx, N.Y., Mar. 6, 1944; s. Abraham S. and Mae (Weiner) B.; m. Louise Rae Iteld, Aug. 30, 1970; children: Rachel Jennifer, Lauren Amy. BS in Commerce, Rider Coll., 1966; JD summa cum laude, John Marshall Law Sch., 1969. Bar: Ga. 1970, U.S. Dist. Ct. (no. dist.) Ga. 1970, U.S. Ct. Appeals (5th cir.) 1970, U.S. Supreme Ct. 1973, U.S. Ct. Appeals (11th cir.) 1981, U.S. Tax Ct. 1983. Law clk. to U.S. atty. No. Dist. Ga., 1969; legal aide Ga. Gen. Assembly, 1970-71; asst. U.S. atty. No. Dist. Ga., 1971-74; ptnr. Bates & Baum, 1974—. Pres. Congregation Shearith Israel, 1976-78; chmn. Rep. Party of DeKalb County, 1983-85, 4th Dist. Rep. Party, 1985-89; pres. Resurgens, Atlanta, 1987-88, Electoral Coll., 1988; del. Rep. Nat. Conv., 1992; mem. DeKalb County Bd. Ethics, 1991—, chair, 1993-95, 2001; mem. Met. Atlanta Rapid Transit Authority Bd. Ethics, 1993—. Mem. ABA (criminal justice sect. white collar com.), Ga. Bar Assn., Atlanta Bar Assn. (chmn. criminal law sect. 1985-86, bd. dirs. 1986-87), Fed. Bar Assn. (pres. Atlanta chpt. 1976-77, nat. council 1974-77), DeKalb Bar Assn. (pres. 1989-90), Am. Judicature Soc., Nat. Dist. Attys. Assn. Clubs: Atlanta Lawyers. Lodge: Masons. Office: 3151 Maple Dr NE Atlanta GA 30305-2503

BAUMAN, JOHN ANDREW, law educator; b. 1921; BSL, U. Minn., 1942, LLB, 1947; JSD, Columbia U., 1958. Bar: Wis. 1947, Minn. 1948. Assoc. prof. U. N. Mex., 1947—54; spl. fellow Columbia U., 1950—51; assoc. prof. Ind. U., 1954—59, prof., 1959—60, UCLA, 1960—91, prof. emeritus, 1991; exec. dir. Assn. Am. Law Schs., Washington, 1980—83. Author (with York): Cases and Materials on Remedies, 1967, 5th edit., 1991. Mem.: Order of Coif (sec.-treas. 1983—92). Office: UCLA Sch Law 405 Hilgard Ave Los Angeles CA 90095-9000

BAUMAN, JOHN DUANE, lawyer; b. Kaskaskia, Ill., Aug. 22, 1930; s. Louis Wells and Veronica Genevieve (Schmerbauch) B.; m. Avis Crysella Moore, Sept. 15, 1956; children: Mark Duane, Thomas Jon, Jeffery Paul. BA, S.E. Mo. U., 1952; JD, Washington U., St. Louis, 1957. Bar: Mo. 1957, Ill. 1957. Assoc. Baker, Kagy & Wagner, East Saint Louis, Ill., 1957-62; ptnr. Wagner, Bertrand, Bauman & Schmieder, Belleville, Ill., 1962-86, Hinshaw & Culbertson, Chgo. and Belleville, 1986—. Bd. dirs. Breeders Cup/Nat. Thoroughbred Racing Assn. Pres. Ill. Thoroughbred Breeders and Owners Found., 2001—; gen. counsel Okaw Valley coun. Boy Scouts Am., 1980—90. With U.S. Army, 1952—54. Mem. ABA, Ill. Bar Assn., Internat. Assn. Ins. Counsel (state membership chmn.), Assn. of Def. Trial Counsel (pres. 1975-76), St. Clair County Bar Assn. (pres. 1972-73), Horsemen's Benevolent and Protective Assn. (v.p. 1989-98), Ill. Thoroughbred Breeders and Owners Found. (bd. dirs. 1999-2002, v.p. 1996-99, sec.-treas. 1999-2000, pres. 2000—), Bradenton Country Club, St. Clair Country Club (pres. 1972-74), Paducah Country Club, Elks, Mo. Athletic Club (emeritus 1998). Roman Catholic. Avocations: horse racing, golf. General civil litigation, Personal injury (including property damage), Product liability. Office: Hinshaw & Culbertson PO Box 509 521 W Main St Belleville IL 62220-1533 E-mail: jb222555@aol.com.

BAUMANN, JULIAN HENRY, JR., lawyer; b. Ft. Leavenworth, Kans., Feb. 20, 1943; s. Julian Henry and Helene (Claiborne) B.; m. Karen Ann Hofmann, July 14, 1973; children: Andrew H., Allison C. BS, Clemson U., 1965; postgrad., U. Tenn., 1966; JD, U. S.C., 1968; LLM in Taxation, NYU, 1975. Bar: S.C. 1968, Del. 1976. Assoc. Richards, Layton & Finger, Wilmington, Del., 1975-80, dir., 1980—. Served to capt., JAGC, U.S. Army, 1969-74. Fellow Am. Coll. Tax Counsel; mem. ABA, S.C. Bar Assn., Del. State Bar (chmn., sec. taxation 1990-91), Wilmington Tax Group (chmn. 1988-89), The Com. of 100 (pres. 1994-96), Bd. of Mgrs., The Nemours Found., Wilmington Club. Democrat. Roman Catholic. Corporate taxation, Taxation, general, Personal income taxation. Home: 8 Brendle Ln Wilmington DE 19807-1300 Office: Richards Layton & Finger One Rodney Sq 10th & King Sts Wilmington DE 19801

BAUMANN, RICHARD GORDON, lawyer; b. Chgo., Apr. 7, 1938; s. Martin M. and Harriet May (Granof) B.; m. Terrie Bemel, Dec. 18, 1971; children: Michelle, Alison. BS cum laude, U. Wis., 1960, JD, 1964. Bar: Wis. 1964, Calif. 1970, U.S. Supreme Ct. 1973. Congressional intern U.S. Senator Hubert H. Humphrey, 1959; assoc. firm Kohner, Mann & Kailas, Milw., 1964-69, Sulmeyer, Kupetz & Alberts, L.A., 1969-73; mem. firm Sulmeyer, Kupetz, Baumann & Rothman, L.A., 1973—. Judge pro tem L.A. Mcpl. Ct., 1980—. Assoc. editor Comml. Law Jour., 1991—. Fellow Comml. Law Found. (bd. dirs.); mem. Nat. Inst. on Credit Mgmt. (bd. dirs.), Am. Bd. Cert. (bd. dirs.), Acad. Comml. and Bankruptcy Law Specialists (bd. dirs.), Comml. Law League (pres. 1990-91, bd. govs. 1986-92, chmn. Western Region Mem. Assn. 1982-83). State civil litigation, Commercial, consumer (including collections, credit), Commercial, contracts (including sales of goods; commercial financing). Office: 300 S Grand Ave Fl 14 Los Angeles CA 90071-3109

BAUMGARDNER, JOHN ELLWOOD, JR., lawyer; b. Balt., Jan. 6, 1951; s. John Ellwood and Nancy G. (Brandenburg) B.; m. Astrid Rehl, Sept. 7, 1974; children: Jeffrey Mark, Julia Alexis. Bar: N.Y. 1976. Assoc. Sullivan & Cromwell, N.Y.C., 1975-83, ptnr., 1983—. Supervisory dir. The Turkish Pvt. Equity Investment Co., 1991-93; trustee JPM Advisor Funds, 1996. Vice chair gen. dir.'s coun. N.Y.C. Opera. Mem.: ABA, Assn. Bar City NY (chair com. on investment mgmt. regulation), NY State Bar Assn., Nat. Dance Inst. (bd. dirs. 1988—89), Princeton Club. Corporate, general. Office: Sullivan & Cromwell LLP 125 Broad St Fl 32 New York NY 10004-2498 E-mail: baumgardnerj@sullcrom.com.

BAUMGARTEN, PAUL ANTHONY, retired lawyer; b. N.Y.C., July 31, 1934; s. Louis S. and Margaret (Karol) B.; m. Susan T., Feb. 21, 1960; children— Stephen, Michael, Lisa, Deborah BA, Swarthmore Coll., 1955; LLB, Harvard U., 1958. Bar: N.Y. Assoc. Otterbourg Steindler, Houston Rosen, N.Y.C., 1958-66; assoc. Halperin, Morris, Granett & Cowan, N.Y.C., 1960; with legal dept. Hill & Range Songs Inc., 1960-62, Warner Bros. Pictures Inc., 1962-64, Embassy Pictures Corp., 1964-70; ptnr. Krause, Hirsch & Gross, 1970-77, Rosenman & Colin, LLP, N.Y.C., 1977—2001, counsel, 2001—. Co-chmn. workshops on motion picture industry Practicing Law Inst.; trustee Copyright Soc. U.S., 1989-91. Co-author: Producing, Financing & Distributing Film (revised and expanded edition), 1992. Mem. Columbia Artists Mgmt. Inc. (dir.). Avocations: classical music, sailing, tennis. Home: 61 W Gate Blvd Plandome NY 11030-1452 Office: Katten Muchin Zavis Rosenman 575 Madison Ave New York NY 10022-2585 E-mail: paulbaumgarten@kmzr.com.

BAUMGARTEN, RONALD NEAL, lawyer; b. Chgo., May 13, 1942; s. Albert and Beatrice (Loseff) B.; m. Aloha Herman, Aug. 27, 1966; children: Brett, Reed, Jaclyn, Blake. BA, U. Ill., 1964, JD, 1966. Bar: Calif. 1970, U.S. Dist. Ct. (cen. dist.) Calif. 1970, U.S. Ct. Appeals (9th cir.) 1973, U.S. Supreme Ct. 1975. Gen. counsel, chief ops. officer Elgin Jewelry Distbrs. Inc., L.A., 1967-72, also bd. dirs.; assoc. Grobe, Rinestein, Freid & Katz P.L.C., Beverly Hills, Calif., 1972-75; ptnr. Jacobs & Baumgarten P.L.C., Beverly Hills, 1975-80, Baumgarten & Greene P.L.C., Santa Monica, Calif., 1980-88; pvt. practice law Santa Monica, 1988-89, L.A., 1989—; sr. v.p. Comml. Fin. Ctr., 1991-95, also bd. dirs.; pres. Occidental Svcs., Inc., 1992-95; pres., CEO, majority shareholder Holmby Investments, Inc., 1994—, Baumgarten Property Mgmt. Svcs., Inc., 1994—; v.p., sec. Sierra Crest Equities, LLC, 1997—, Corner Stone Real Estate Investment, Inc., 1997—; CEO Sierra Sr. Cmtys. LLC, 2001—. Chmn., bd. dirs., CEO, COO, J.D. Alexander & Assocs., Inc., L.A., 1980-92; asst. prof. law U. San Fernando Valley, Calif., 1974. Mem. L.A. World Affairs Coun., 1974—, L.A. Olympic Citizens Adv. Commn., 1982-84, Town Hall, 1983—; exec. v.p., gen. counsel, bd. dirs. Variety-The Children's Charity, 1974-2000, Variety Boy's and Girl's Club, L.A., pres., 1996-99, bd. dirs., 1981—; founder 1st Bus. Bank, L.A., 1981. Mem. ABA, Calif. Bar Assn., L.A. County Bar Assn., Beverly Hills Bar Assn., Phi Delta Phi. Commercial, contracts (including sales of goods; commercial financing), Corporate, general, Property, real (including real estate development, water). Office: 10590 Wilshire Blvd Ste 201 Los Angeles CA 90024 E-mail: rbpacpal@aol.com.

BAUMKEL, MARK S. lawyer; b. Flint, Mich., Feb. 17, 1951; s. Sherwood and Marilyn (Schiff) B.; m. Julie A. Kimbrell, Oct. 20, 1978; 1 child, Molly. BA cum laude, Oakland U., Rochester,Mich., 1973; JD cum laude, Wayne State U., 1977. Bar: Mich. 1977, U.S. Dist. Ct. Mich. 1977, U.S. Ct. Appeals (6th cir.) 1985. Assoc. dist. counsel U.S. SBA, Detroit, 1977-78; asst. pros. atty. Ingham County Prosecutor's Office, Lansing, Mich., 1978-79; assoc. atty. Shifman & Goodman, P.C., Southfield, Mich., 1979-81, Kaufman & Friedman, Southfield, 1981-84; sole practitioner Troy, Mich., 1984-94; ptnr. Provizer & Phillips, P.C., Southfield, 1994—. Mem. Assn. Trial Lawyers Am. (sustaining), Mich. Trial Lawyers Assn. (PAC contbr.), Oakland County Bar Assn., Wayne County Mediation Tribunal (mediator), Am. Arbitration Assn. (arbitrator), Oakland County Mediation (mediator). Avocations: long-distance running and biking, guitar. General civil litigation, Personal injury (including property damage), Product liability. Home: 3826 Lakecrest Dr Bloomfield Hills MI 48304-3040 Office: Provizer & Phillips PC 6785 Telegraph Rd Ste 400 Bloomfield Hills MI 48301-3149 E-mail: baumkelm@aol.com.

BAUMRIN, BERNARD STEFAN HERBERT, lawyer, educator; b. N.Y.C., Jan. 7, 1934; s. David and Regina (Zuckerburg) B.; m. Judith Anne Marti, Dec. 20, 1953; children: Seth, Jeanne, Rachel. Student, Marietta Coll., 1951-52, NYU, 1952-53; BA, Ohio State U., 1956; PhD, Johns Hopkins U., 1960; postgrad., Washington U., St. Louis, 1965-67; JD, Columbia U., 1970. Dir. forensics Johns Hopkins U., Balt., 1957—59; vis. asst. prof. philosophy Butler U., 1960—61, Antioch Coll., 1961; asst. prof. philosophy U. Del., Newark, 1961—64, Washington U., 1964—67; assoc. prof. philosophy Hunter Coll., CUNY, 1967—68, assoc. prof. philosophy Grad. Sch. and Lehman Coll., 1968—72, prof., 1972—, treas. univ. faculty senate, 1978—81, 1990, exec. com., 1976—84, bd. dirs. Research Found., 1984-91, exec. com., 1987—91, 1992—93, 1998—99, 2002—; ptnr. Baumrin, Galub & Volkomer, 1979—. Adj. prof. med. edn. Mt. Sinai Sch. of Medicine, 1988—; bd. dirs. CUNY Acad. for the Humanities and Scis. Author: Philosophy of Science, 2 vols., 1963, British Moralists, 1964, Hobbes's Leviathan, 1968, Moral Responsibility and the Professions, 1983; U.S. editor: Jour. Applied Philosophy, 1986—2001, mem. adv. bd.: Jour. Philosophy Psychiatry and Psychology, 1995—; cons. editor Metaphilosophy, 1968—; contbr. articles to profl. jours. AEC fellow, 1963, U. Del. fellow, 1962, Washington U. Forsyth fellow, 1964-67; CUNY grantee, 1968, 70, 89, 91, 93, N.Y. Council for Humanities grantee, 1976, NEH grantee, 1977-79, 91, Mellon Found. grantee, 1980-84, Am. Council Learned Socs. grantee, 1987. Mem. AAAS, AAUP, ACLU, N.Y. State Bar Assn. (chmn. ethics subcom., com. on legal edn. and admission to bar 1986—), Mind Assn., Am. Philos. Assn. (chmn. standing com. on philosophy and medicine 1988-92, chmn. standing com. on philosophy and law 1998-2001), Soc. for Philosophy and Pub. Affairs, Internat. Assn. Philosophy of Law and Social Philosophy, Conf. on Methods in Philosophy and the Scis. (chmn. 1988-90), Internat. Hobbes Assn. (exec. com. 1986—), Internat. Soc. Econs. and Philosophy (treas. 1994—). Office: CUNY Grad Sch 365 5th Ave New York NY 10016-4334 also: Lehman Coll Philosophy Dept Bronx NY 10468 E-mail: bbaumrin@tiac.net.

BAXLEY, PHILLIP KENT, lawyer; b. Sylacauga, Ala., Jan. 1, 1957; s. James Herron and Bertie Irene (Mitchell) B.; m. Mary E. Black, Feb. 22, 1986. AA in Sci., Alexander (Ala.) City Jr. Coll., 1976; BA, U. Ala., 1980, JD, 1983. Bar: Ala. 1983, U.S. Dist. Ct. (so. dist.) Ala. 1988. Spl. agent FBI, Houston, 1983-86, spl. agent N.Y.C., 1986-87; pvt. practice Mobile, Ala., 1987—. Mem. ABA, Mobile Bar Assn., Soc. Former Spl. Agts. FBI, Farrah Law Soc., Kiwanis, Phi Beta Kappa, Phi Theta Kappa, Phi Alpha Delta. Avocations: volleyball, bicycling, photography, golf. General civil litigation, General practice, Personal injury (including property damage). Office: 1115 Dauphin St Mobile AL 36604-2511

BAXTER, HOWARD H. retired lawyer; b. Cleve., July 31, 1931; s. Harold H. and Bessie (Bovee) B.; m. Ona Mae Miller, June 25, 1955; children: Kevin, Douglas, John, Susan. BS, Iowa State Coll., 1953; JD, Case Western Res. U., 1956. Bar: Ohio 1956, D.C. 1982; U.S. Dist. Ct. (no. dist.) Ohio 1962, U.S. Ct. Appeals (3rd cir.) 1978, U.S. Supreme Ct. 1978, U.S. Ct. Appeals (fed. cir.) 1982. Assoc. McNeal & Schick, Cleve., 1956-60; group counsel Harris Corp., Cleve., 1960-76; sec., gen. counsel Molins USA Inc., Richmond, Va., 1976-79; v.p., gen. counsel The Langston Co., Inc., Cherry Hill, N.J., 1976-79, Cuyahoga County Hosp. System, Cleve., 1979-81; v.p., sec., gen. counsel Macey Machine Co., Inc., Cleve., 1981-88, exec. v.p., 1988-91; ptnr. Kasdan & Baxter Co., Cleve., 1992-2000; pvt. practice Cleve., 2000—. Chmn. zoning com. Lakewood (Ohio) Rep. Club, 1959-60; vestry, sr. warden St. Stephens Episcopal Ch., Beverly, N.J., 1977-79, Lakewood, 1981—, Ch. of the Ascension, Lakewood. Mem. NRA, Ohio State Bar Assn., Cleve. Bar Assn., Great Lakes Hist. Soc. (vice chmn. 1981-88, exec. v.p. 1968-76, trustee 1968—, chmn. exec. com. 1982-94), Ohio Gun Collectors Assn., Inc., Edgewater Yacht Club. Avocations: marine history, sailing, shooting sports, scale model railroading. Commercial, contracts (including sales of goods; commercial financing), Corporate, general, Private international. Home and Office: 18107 Clifton Rd Lakewood OH 44107-1024

BAXTER, MARVIN RAY, state supreme court justice; b. Fowler, Calif., Jan. 9, 1940; m. Jane Pippert, June 22, 1963; children: Laura, Brent. BA in Econs., Calif. State U., 1962; JD, U. Calif.-Hasting Coll. Law, 1966. Bar: Calif. 1966. Appointments sec. to Gov. George Deukmejian, 1983-88; dep. dist. atty. Fresno County, Calif., 1967-68; assoc. Andrews, Andrews, Thaxter & Jones, 1968-70, ptnr., 1971-82; apptd. sec. to Gov. George Deukmejian, 1983-88; assoc. justice Calif. Ct. Appeal (5th dist.), 1988-90; state supreme ct. assoc. justice Calif. Supreme Ct., 1991—. Mem. Jud. Coun. of Calif., chmn. policy coord. and liaison com., 1996—. Mem. Fresno County Bar Assn. (bd. dirs. 1977-82, pres. 1981), Calif. Young Lawyers Assn. (bd. gov. 1973-76, sec.-treas. 1974-75), Fresno County Young Lawyers Assn. (pres. 1973-74), Fresno County Legal Svcs., Inc. (bd. dirs. 1973-74), Fresno State U. Alumni Assn. (pres. 1970-71), Fresno State U. Alumni Trust Coun. (pres. 1970-75). Office: Calif Supreme Ct 350 Mcallister St San Francisco CA 94102-4712

BAYARD, ALTON ERNEST, III, lawyer; b. New Orleans, La., Mar. 25, 1952; s. Alton Ernest Jr. and Elvy Alys (Backer) B.; m. Mary Watkins, Jan. 8, 1983; children: Andrew Ernest, David Guyton, James Christopher. BS, La. State U., 1975, JD, 1976; LLM in Taxation, So. Meth. U., 1980. Bar: La. 1977, U.S. Dist. Ct. (mid. dist.) La. 1977; cert. tax atty.; bd. cert. estate planning atty. Ptnr. Calongne & Bayard, Baton Rouge, 1977-80, Jones, Walker, 1981-85, Jones, Walker, Waechter, Poitevent, Carrere & Denegre, Baton Rouge, 1985—. Served to tech. sgt. La. Air N.G., 1970-76. Mem. ABA, La. Bar Assn., Baton Rouge Bar Assn. Avocations: family, hunting, fishing. Pension, profit-sharing, and employee benefits, Probate (including wills, trusts), Estate taxation. Office: Jones Walker Waechter Poitevent Carriere/Denegre 8555 United Plaza Blvd Fl 5 Baton Rouge LA 70809-2260

BAYERN, ARTHUR HERBERT, lawyer; b. Jan. 28, 1934; s. Henry V. and Rose (Strumer) Bayern; m. Janice O'Banion, June 10, 1961; children: William T., Robert M.(dec.). AB, Colgate U., 1954; JD, U. Tex., 1965. Bar: Tex. 1965, U.S. Dist. Ct. (we. dist.) Tex. 1966, U.S. Tax Ct. 1968, U.S. Ct. Appeals (5th cir.) 1970, U.S. Supreme Ct. 1978. Salesman IBM, Houston, 1959—62; ptnr. Remy, Bayern & Paterson, San Antonio, 1965—84, Bayern, Paterson & Aycock, San Antonio, 1984—98, Bayern & Aycock, San Antonio, 1998—. Pres. San Antonio Estate Planners Coun., 1972—73. Co-editor: (non-fiction) How to Live and Die with Texas Probate, 1983; editor (contbg.): Texas Probate System, 1974, Texas Guardianship System, 1983. Capt. USAF, 1954—57. Fellow: Am. Coll. Probate Counsel; mem.: ABA (chmn. com. on post-mortem estate and tax planning), San Antonio Bar Assn. (pres. 1980—81), State Bar Tex. (bd. dir. 1982—85, chmn. real estate, probate and trust law sect. 1981—82). Estate planning, Probate (including wills, trusts), Estate taxation. Office: Bayern & Aycock 745 E Mulberry Ave Ste 300 San Antonio TX 78212-3167

BAYKO, EMIL THOMAS, lawyer; b. Pitts., Mar. 5, 1947; s. Emil and Ruth (Alberti) B.; m. Ruth Ann Loucks, Nov. 5, 1967; children: Anthony M., Keith C., Paul S. BA in Polit. Sci., Kent State U., 1970; JD cum laude, U. Ill., Urbana-Champaign, 1973. Bar: Ill. 1973, U.S. Dist. Ct. (no. dist.) Ill. 1973, U.S. Ct. Appeals (7th cir.) 1974, D.C. 1975, N.Y. 1975, U.S. Ct. Appeals (2d cir.) 1975, U.S. Ct. Claims 1976, U.S. Dist. Ct. (so. dist.) N.Y. 1976, U.S. Ct. Appeals (D.C. cir.) 1976, U.S. Supreme Ct. 1976, U.S. Dist. Ct. (ea dist.) Pa. 1978, U.S. Ct. Appeals (3d cir.) 1978, Tex. 1980, U.S. Dist. Ct. (so. dist., no. dist., ea. dist., we. dist.) Tex. 1981, U.S. Ct. Appeals (5th cir.) 1981. Assoc. Chapman & Cutler, Chgo., 1973-74, White & Case, N.Y.C., 1975-80; ptnr. Liddell, Sapp, Zivley, Hill & LaBoon, Houston, 1981, Holtzman Urquhart Bayko & Moore, Houston, 1982-95, Bayko Gibson Carnegie & Hagan, Houston, 1995-2000, Jones Day, Houston, 2001—. Co-author: Essays on American Law, 1971, Home Rule, 1972. Harno fellow U. Ill., 1971-73. Mem. ABA, Assn. of Bar of City of N.Y., Houston Bar Assn., Chgo. Bar Assn., Tex. Bar Assn., D.C. Bar Assn., Order of Coif. Clubs: Tex., Houston. Democrat. Presbyterian. Federal civil litigation, State civil litigation, Environmental. Office: Jones Day Chase Tower 65th Fl 600 Travis St Houston TX 77002-3008 E-mail: tbayko@jonesday.com.

BAYLINSON, CHRISTOPHER MICHAEL, lawyer; b. Atlantic City, Aug. 31, 1962; s. Roy S. and Florence B.; m. Marlena, July 18, 1992; children: Christopher Stone, Jackson Graham. BA, Rollins Coll., 1984; JD, Quinnipiac Sch. Law, 1988. Bar: N.J. 1988, U.S. Dist. Ct. N.J. 1988, U.S. Ct. Appeals (3d cir.) 2000; cert. civil. trial atty. Law clk. Atlantic County Civil Divsn., Atlantic City, N.J., 1988-89; ptnr. Cooper, Perskie, April, Niedelman, Wagenheim & Levenson, Atlantic City, N.J., 1989-99, Perskie Nehmad & Perillo, Egg Harbor Twp., N.J., 1999—. Master Haneman Inns Ct., Atlantic City, 1998. Bd. dirs. Atlantic City Art Ctr. Mem. NJ State Bar Assn. (trustee 2003—), Atlantic County Bar Assn. (trustee 1997-2002, treas. 2002-03, sec. 2003-04, Outstanding Young Lawyer award 1998), Boardwalk Runners Club. Avocations: running, surfing. General civil litigation, Land use and zoning (including planning), Property, real (including real estate development, water). Office: PO Box 730 Somers Point NJ 08244-0730 E-mail: cmbaylinson@pnplaw.com.

BAYLSON, MICHAEL MORRIS, judge; b. Phila., May 29, 1939; s. Herbert and Edna Baylson; m. Frances Ruth Batzer, June 23, 1969; children: Todd, Ariella, Mira. BS in Ecnos., U. Pa., 1961, LLB, 1964. Bar: Pa. 1965. Law clk. to judge Ct. Common Pleas, Phila., 1964-65, asst. dist. atty., 1966-69, chief narcotics div., 1968, chief homicide div., 1969; ptnr. Duane, Morris , Phila., 1970—88, Duane, Morris & Heckscher, Phila., 1993—2002; U.S. atty. U.S. Dist. Ct. (ea. dist.) Pa., Phila., 1988-93, judge, 2002—. Editor: Antitrust Discovery Handbook, 1981; contbr. articles to profl. jours. Bd. dirs. Gaudenzia, Inc., 1968-94, gen. counsel, 1974-88, 93-2002; v.p. Safe Streets, 1968-78; bd. dirs. Jewish Employment and Vocat. Soc., 1975-88; treas. Arlen Specter for Senate Com., 1980-88. Mem. ABA (chmn. com on exemptions and immunities antitrust sect. 1979-82), Phila Bar Assn. (mem. fed. cts. com.). Republican. Home: 4115 Timber Ln Philadelphia PA 19144-5425

BAYLY, JOHN HENRY, JR., judge; b. Washington, Jan. 26, 1944; s. John Henry and Salome Carole (Winters) B.; m. Barbara Jean Downey, Feb. 16, 1974 (dec. Jan. 1977); 1 child, Anne Louise; m. Katherine Bridget Kenny, Dec. 1, 1979; children: Johanna, Georgia. AB, Fordham U., 1966; JD, Harvard U., 1969. Bar: U.S. Dist. Ct. D.C. 1969, U.S. Ct. Appeals (D.C. cir.) 1969, D.C. 1971, U.S. Supreme Ct. 1974. Atty., advisor FCC, Washington, 1969-71; asst. atty. Office of U.S. Atty., Washington, 1971-75, 78-85; dep. minority counsel Senate Select Com. on Intelligence, Washington, 1975-76; acting asst. gen. counsel Corp. for Pub. Broadcasting, Washington, 1976-78; gen. counsel Legal Services Corp., Washington, 1985-87, pres., 1987-88; of counsel Stein, Mitchell & Mezines, Washington, 1988-90; judge D.C. Superior Ct., 1990—. Mem. D.C. Bar Assn., John Carroll Soc., Counsellors, Bryant Inn of Ct., Lawyers Club Washington, Phi Beta Kappa. Republican. Roman Catholic. Home: 3512 Runnymede Pl NW Washington DC 20015-2420 Office: DC Superior Ct 500 Indiana Ave NW Ste 1 Washington DC 20001-2131

BAYON, ANTONIO, lawyer; b. Arecibo, PR, Aug. 13, 1972; s. Antonio Bayon and Elba Casiano; m. Jesika Planell, May 26, 2001. BSBA, U. PR, Mayaguez, 1995; JD magna cum laude, Pontifical Cath. U., Ponce, PR, 1998; LLM, Tulane U., 2001. Bar: PR 1999, U.S. Ct. Appeals (1st cir.) 1999, Fla. 2003. Clk. PR Cir. Ct. Appeals, San Juan, 1999—2000; assoc. Kurt Bosshardt and Assocs., Ft. Lauderdale, Fla., 2001—. Recipient award, PR Judiciary Assn.; Harry F. Stiles scholar, Tulane U., 2000. Roman Catholic. Avocation: offshore fishing. Admiralty, Federal civil litigation, State civil litigation. Office: Kurt Bosshard and Assocs PA 1600 SE 17th St Causeway 405 Fort Lauderdale FL 33316

BAZERMAN, STEVEN HOWARD, lawyer; b. N.Y.C., Dec. 12, 1940; s. Solomon and Miriam (Kirschenberg) B.; m. Christina Ann Gray, Aug. 28, 1981 (div. June 1988); m. Beverly Andree, Sept. 9, 2000. BS in Math., BS in Engring., U. Mich., 1962; JD, Georgetown U., 1966. Bar: D.C. 1967, N.Y. 1968, U.S. Dist. Ct. (so. dist.) N.Y. 1970, U.S. Dist. Ct. (ea. dist.) N.Y. 1973, U.S. Claims Ct. 1976, U.S. Ct. Appeals (2d cir.) 1978, U.S. Cts. Customs and Patents Appeals 1981-82, U.S. Ct. Appeals (fed. cir.) 1982. Assoc. Arthur, Dry & Kalish, N.Y.C., 1967-80, Offner & Kuhn, N.Y.C., 1980-83; ptnr., head litigation dept. Kuhn, Muller & Bazerman, N.Y.C., 1983-87; ptnr. Moore, Berson, Lifflander, Eisenberg & Mewhinney, N.Y.C., 1987-88; of counsel Lerner, David, Littenberg, Krumholz & Mentlik, Westfield, N.J., 1988, Sutton, Basseches, Magidoff & Amaral, N.Y.C., 1988-90, Graham, Campaign & McCarthy P.C., N.Y.C., 1990-96, Bazerman & Drangel, P.C., N.Y.C., 1996—. Governing counsel Community Law Offices Legal Aid Soc., N.Y.C., 1974-83, treas., 1979-82. Co-author: Guide to Registering Trademarks, 1999-2002; contbr. articles to profl. jours. Vol.

counsel community law offices Legal Aid Soc., N.Y.C., 1974-82, treas., 1979-82. Mem. Assn. of Bar of City of N.Y., Am. Intellectual Property Law Assn., N.Y. Patent, Trademark & Copyright Law Assn. Jewish. Avocation: horses. Federal civil litigation, Patent, Trademark and copyright. Office: Bazerman & Drangel PC 60 E 42nd St Rm 820 New York NY 10165-0820 E-mail: sbazerman@nyc.rr.com., bdpc@ipcounsellors.com.

BAZLER, FRANK ELLIS, retired lawyer; b. Columbus, Ohio, Jan. 17, 1930; s. Frank Hayes and Minnie Maybrum (Rucker) B.; m. Virginia Ann Hutchison, Oct. 17, 1954. BSBA, Ohio State U., 1951, JD, 1953. Bar: Ohio 1953, U.S. Dist. Ct. (we. dist.) Ohio 1956, U.S. Ct. Mil. Appeals 1957, U.S. Supreme Ct. 1957, U.S. Ct. Appeals (6th cir.) 1964. Assoc. Robert S. Miller, Atty., Troy, Ohio, 1955-57; ptnr. Miller, Bazler & Schlemmer, Troy, 1957-71; asst. corp. counsel Hobart Mfg. Co., Troy, 1971-74; corp. atty., asst. sec. Hobart Corp., Troy, 1974-95; ret., 1995; of counsel Dungan & LeFevre, Troy, 1995—. V.p. Bazler Transfer & Storage, Inc., Columbus, Ohio, 1950-58; sec., bd. dirs. Golden Triangle Farms, Inc., Troy, 1972-2001. Pres. Troy United Fund, Inc., 1960, Troy Mus. Corp., 1990; chmn. Miami County chpt. ARC, 1955-59, Miami County (Ohio) Rep. Fin. Com., 1981-84; mem. Miami County Gen. Bd. Health, 1992—, pres. pro-tem, 1998-2001, pres., 2001—; commn. on cert. of Attys. as Specialists of Supreme Ct. of Ohio, 1994-99, chmn., 1994-96. Capt. JAG, USAFR, 1953-61. Named one of Outstanding Young Men in Troy and Ohio, Troy Jaycees, 1957, Ohio Jaycees, 1961; recipient Disting. Citizen award Troy C. of C., 1985, Citizenship award Ohio State U., 1993. Fellow: Ohio State Bar Found. (pres. 1992), Am. Bar Found. (Ohio chair 1995—); mem.: ABA (mem. gen. practice sect. 1967—, coun. 1976—80, ho. of dels. 1984—2000, mem. standing com. on specialization 1999—2002), Nat. Conf. Bar Pres. (exec. coun. 1988—91), Miami County Bar Assn. (pres. 1966, Meritorious Svc. award 1985), Ohio State Bar Assn. (coun. of dels. 1979—88, pres. 1984—85, Ohio Bar medal 1990), Nat. Caucus State Bar Assns. (Ohio rep. 1993—2002, exec com. 1997—2002, pres. 2000—01), Overfield Tavern Mus. (pres. 2001—, bd. trustees 2000—), Indsl. Heritage Mus. of Miami County (trustee, sec. 1997—), Brukner Nature Ctr. (trustee 1998—, pres. 1999—2002), Kiwanis (pres. 1964), Scottish Rite, Masons. Republican. Presbyterian. Avocations: photography, travel, golf. Home: 1156 Premwood Dr Troy OH 45373-3877 Office: Dungan & LeFevre 210 W Main St Troy OH 45373-3287

BEACH, ARTHUR O'NEAL, lawyer; b. Albuquerque, Feb. 8, 1945; s. William Pearce and Vivian Lucille (Kronig) B.; m. Alex Clark Doyle, Sept. 12, 1970; 1 child, Eric Kronig. BBA, U. N.Mex., 1967, JD, 1970. Bar: N.Mex. 1970. Assoc. Smith & Ransom, Albuquerque, 1970-74, Keleher & McLeod, Albuquerque, 1974-75, ptnr., 1976-78; shareholder Keleher & McLeod, P.A., Albuquerque, 1978—. Tchg. asst. U. N.Mex., 1970. Bd. editors Natural Resources Jour., 1968-70. Mem. ABA, State Bar N.Mex. (unauthorized practice of law com., adv. opinions com., med.-legal panel, legal-dental-osteo.-podiatry com., jud. selection com., specialization bd.), Albuquerque Bar Assn. (dir. 1978-82). Democrat. Mem. Christian Sci. Ch. General civil litigation, Insurance, Personal injury (including property damage). Home: 2015 Dietz Pl NW Albuquerque NM 87107-3240 Office: Keleher & McLeod PA PO Box AA Albuquerque NM 87103

BEACH, BARBARA PURSE, lawyer; b. Washington, June 12, 1947; d. Clifford John and Lillian (Natarus) B. BA, U. Ky., 1968; MSW, U. Md., 1972; JD, Am. U., 1980. Bar: D.C. 1980, Va. 1980. Law clk. to presiding justice benefit rev. bd. U.S. Dept. Labor, Washington, 1980; asst. city atty. City of Alexandria, Va., 1981-85; atty. Ross, Marsh, Foster, Myers & Quiggle, Alexandria, 1985-90, Beach, Butt & Assocs., PC, Alexandria, 1990-92; prin. Beach & Assocs., Alexandria, 1992—; town atty. Town of Herndon, Va., 1992-94. 4th dist. com. disciplinary bd. dirs. Va. State Bd., chmn., 2000-01. Vice-chmn. Va. Health Svcs. Cost Rev. Coun., 1989-92; mem. Va. Commn. on Women and Minorities, 1990-92; bd. dirs. Am. Heart Assn., Alexandria, 1996-2000, divsn. pres., 1998-99. Alexandria Bar Assn. (pres. 1987-88), Kiwanis. Corporate, general, General practice, Land use and zoning (including planning). Office: Beach & Assocs 416 Prince St Alexandria VA 22314-3114

BEACH, STEPHEN HOLBROOK, lawyer; b. Highland Park, Mich., June 3, 1915; s. Stephen Holbrook and Katherine Jean (Campbell) B.; m. Mary Frances Mulvihill, July 6, 1951; children: Jennifer Katherine Beach Buda, Stephen Holbrook III. AB with honors in Polit. Sci, Kalamazoo Coll., 1936; LLB cum laude, U. Detroit, 1941; postgrad., Georgetown U., 1945, Columbia U., 1970. Bar: Mich. 1941, U.S. Dist. Ct. (ea. dist.) Mich., 1941, U.S. Supreme Ct. 1944, N.Y. 1947, U.S. Dist. Ct. (so. dist.) N.Y. 1947, U.S. Dist. Ct. (ea. dist.) N.Y. 1949, D.C. 1949, Conn. 1975. Assoc. Winthrop, Stimson, Putnam & Roberts, N.Y.C., 1946-48, Cann, Lamb & Kittelle, N.Y.C., 1948-56, Willkie, Farr, Gallagher, Walton and Fitzgibbon, N.Y.C., 1956-60; staff atty. IBM Corp., N.Y.C., 1960-61, of counsel supplies div. N.Y.C. and Dayton, N.J., 1961-65; v.p., gen. counsel, sec. The Svc. Bur. Corp., N.Y.C., 1965-75; v.p., gen. counsel Data Svcs. Control Data Corp., Greenwich, Conn., 1976-78, gen. counsel Computer Co. Mpls., 1979-80, v.p., assoc., gen. counsel, 1980-82, sr. v.p. telecommunications policy, corp. sec., 1983-85; of counsel Rogers, Hoge & Hills, White Plains, N.Y., 1985-86; pvt. practice law Greenwich and Stamford, Conn., 1986—. Bd. dirs., corp. sec. Dataware Techs., Inc. Editor-in-chief U. Detroit Law Jour., 1937-41. Capt. U.S. Army, 1943-46. Mem. ABA (sci. and tech. sect., banking and bus. law sect.), Conn. Bar Assn (intellectual property and computer law sects.), N.Y. State Bar Assn. (banking and bus. law sect.), D.C. Bar Assn., Assn. of Data Processing Svcs. Orgns. (v.p. govt. rels., bd. dirs. 1978-84), The Wee Burn Country Club, Ocean Club of Fla. Republican. Episcopalian. Avocation: golf. Communications, Computer, Corporate, general. Home: 52 Brushy Hill Rd Darien CT 06820-6007 Office: PO Box 1202 Darien CT 06820-1202

BEAHM, FRANKLIN D. lawyer; b. Independence, Kans., Jan. 18, 1953; s. Edgar Hiram and Dorothy S.; m. Tawny L. McIntyre, Jan. 7, 1994; children: F. David, Patrick Stuart, Kristin Sanders, Stephen McWilliams. BBA, So. Methodist U., 1975; JD, Tulane U., 1977. Bar: La. 1977, Colo. 1993, Tex. 2000, U.S. Dist. Ct. (ea. dist.) La. 1977, U.S. Dist. Ct. (mid. dist.) La. 1980, U.S. Dist. Ct. (we. dist.) La. 1985, U.S. Ct. Appeals (5th cir.), U.S. Tax Ct. 1989, U.S. Supreme Ct. 1993. Assoc. Manard & Schoenberger, New Orleans, 1977-80, Bourgeois, Bennett, Metairie, La., 1980, Hammett, Leake & Hammett, New Orleans, 1980-83, ptnr., 1983-85, Thomas, Hayes & Beahm, New Orleans, 1985-95, Chehardy, Sherman, Ellis, Breslin, Murray, Metairie, 1995-97, Beahm & Green, New Orleans, 1997—. Mem. Am. Health Lawyers Assn., Am. Soc. Law and Medicine, La. Assn. Def. Counsel, La. Bar Assn. (Interprofl. com. 1997-98, professionalism com. 1999—), La. Med. Soc. (Interprofl. com. 1997-98), La. Soc. Hosp. Attys. of the La. Hosp. Assn., Denver Bar Assn., Def. Rsch. Inst. (med. malpractice com., product liability com.), Beta Alpha Psi. Corporate, general, Health, Professional liability. Office: 145 Robert E Lee Blvd Ste 408 New Orleans LA 70124-2581 E-mail: frank@beahm.com.

BEAIRD, JAMES RALPH, law educator, dean; b. 1925. BS, U. Ala., 1949, LLB, 1951; LLM, George Washington U., 1953. Bar: Ala. 1951, D.C. 1973. Atty. U.S. Dept. Labor, 1951-56, asst. solicitor, 1956-59; assoc. gen. counsel NLRB, 1959-60; assoc. solicitor U.S. Dept. Labor, 1960-65; vis. prof. U. Ga., 1965-66, prof. law, 1967-89, prof. emeritus, dean, 1976-87, dean emeritus; John Sparkman Vis. Disting. Prof., U. Ala., 1988—; mem. Sec. Labor's Adv. Council on Welfare and Pension Plans, 1968—. Mem. adv. com. for Ga. SBA, 1969—. Mem. Farrah Order Jurisprudence. Office: U Ga Sch Law Athens GA 30602

BEAKLEY, ROBERT PAUL, lawyer; b. Millville, N.J., Sept. 29, 1946; s. John A. Jr. and Eleanor Jayne (Schanck) B.; m. Susan McClure Besinger, April 8, 1972; children: Timothy Andrew, Tara Anne. BA, W.Va. Wesleyan Coll., Buckhannon, 1969; JD, Washington & Lee U., 1972. Bar: N.J. 1972, U.S. Ct. Appeals (3d cir.) 1980. Assoc. Albert M. Ash, Ocean City, N.J., 1972-73; mgmt. trainee Coastal State Bank, Ocean City, 1973-74; staff atty. Cape-Atlantic Legal Svcs., Atlantic City, N.J., 1974-79; ptnr. Middlesworth, Beakley & Barry, Atlantic City, 1979-82; pvt. practice law Atlantic City, 1982-84, Wallen & Beakley, Atlantic City, 1984-96; pvt. practice Somers Point, N.J., 1996—. Arbitrator U.S. Dist. Ct. N.J., Superior Ct. N.J. Bd. dirs. Jr. Achievement, Cape Atlantic County, 1978; jr. warden Holy Trinity Episc. Ch., Ocean City, 1981-82; trustee Am. Diabetes Assn., Atlantic County, 1985. 1st lt. U.S. Army, 1970-78. Mem.: Atlantic County Bar Assn. Democrat. Civil rights, General practice. Home: 244 W Seaspray Rd Ocean City NJ 08226-4469 Office: Robert P Beakley Atty at Law 426 Shore Rd Somers Point NJ 08244-2698 Fax: (609) 601-0432.

BEALE, MICHAEL JOHN, lawyer; b. Rochester, NY, Apr. 18, 1964; s. Thomas Albert and Theresa Mary Beale; m. Elizabeth Louise Brabaw, Oct. 27, 1990; 1 child, Matthew Myers. BA in Acctg., Mich. State U., 1986; JD, U. Detroit Mercy, 1990. Bar: Mich. 90, U.S. Dist. Ct. (ea. and we. dists.) Mich., U.S. Ct. Appeals (6th cir.). Assoc. Plunkett & Cooney, Petoskey, Mich., 1992—95; jud. clk. Mich. Supreme Ct., Lansing, 1990—92; ptnr. Handlon Eastman, DeWitt & Beale P.C., Midland, Mich., 1995—. General practice, Personal injury (including property damage), Criminal. Home: 1307 Glendale St Midland MI 48642 Office: Handlon Eastman DeWitt & Beale PC 240 W Main St # 1100 Midland MI 48640 Fax: 989-631-1777. E-mail: TdEstmn@aol.com.

BEALES, RANDOLPH A. lawyer, former state attorney general; m. Julie Leftwich; 1 child. BA in Govt. with high honors, Coll. William and Mary; JD, U. Va. Assoc. Williams Mullen Christian & Dobbins, 1986—87; various pos. U.S. Dept. Education, 1987—92; dep. assoc. dir. policy devel. The White House, 1992—93; assoc. Peterson & Basha, P.C., 1993—94; exec. dir. Office of the Gov., State of Va., 1994—98; dep. atty. gen. Commonwealth of Va., 1998—2001, atty. gen., 2001—02; partner Christian & Barton, LLP, 2002—. Episcopalian. Office: Christian & Barton LLP 909 E Main St Richmond VA 23219*

BEAM, BETHAMY N. lawyer; b. Kingsport, Tenn., June 18, 1963; m. Paul M. Beam, Sept. 24, 1994. BA in English, U. Tenn., 1988, MA in English, 1990; JD, U. Md., 1999. Bar: Md. 1999, W.Va. 2000, D.C. 2000, U.S. Dist. Ct. Md. 2000, U.S. Dist. Ct. W.Va. 2000. Risk analyst Lockheed Martin/Oak Ridge Nat. Lab., Tenn., 1990—92, Washington, 1992—97; teaching asst., tutor U. Md. Sch. Law, Balt., 1997—99; law clk. Steptoe & Johnson, Martinsburg, W.Va., 1996—99; assoc. Miles & Stockbridge, Frederick, Md., 1999—2001, Gimmel, Weiman, Ersek & Blomberg, Gaithersburg, 2001—02, Ruble & Weaver, Frederick, 2002—. Mem.: Am. Inns of Ct., Md. Trial Lawyers Assn., D.C. Bar Assn., W.Va. State Bar Assn., Frederick County Bar Assn., Md. State Bar Assn., Phi Beta Kappa. General practice, Construction, Property, real (including real estate development, water). Home: RR 1 Box 108 Shenandoah Junction WV 25442 Office: Ruble & Weaver 1 W Church St Frederick MD 21701 Fax: 301-698-1202. E-mail: beth@ruble-weaver.com.

BEAM, CLARENCE ARLEN, judge; b. Stapleton, Nebr., Jan. 14, 1930; s. Clarence Wilson and Cecile Mary (Harvey) Beam; m. Betty Lou Fletcher, July 22, 1951; children: Randal, James, Thomas, Bradley, Gregory. BS, U. Nebr., 1951, JD, 1965. Feature writer Nebr. Farmer Mag., Lincoln, 1951; with sales dept. Steckley Seed Co., Mount Sterling, 1954—58, advt. mgr., 1958—63; from assoc. to ptnr. Chambers, Holland, Dudgeon & Knudsen, Berkheimer, Beam, et al, Lincoln, 1965—82; judge U.S. Dist. Ct. Nebr., Omaha, 1982—87, chief judge, 1986—87; cir. judge U.S. Ct. Appeals (8th cir.), 1987—. Mem. com. on lawyer discipline Nebr. Supreme Ct., 1974—82; mem. Conf. Commrs. on Uniform State Laws, 1979—, chmn. Nebr. sect., 1980—82; mem. jud. conf. com. on ct. and jud. security, 1989—93; chmn., 1992—93. Contbr. articles to profl. jours. Mem. Nebr. Rep. Ctrl. Com., 1970—78. Capt. U.S. Army, 1951—53, Korea. Scholar Regents, U. Nebr., Lincoln, 1947, Roscoe Pound scholar, 1964. Mem.: Nebr. State Bar Assn. Office: US Ct Appeals 8th Cir 435 Federal Bldg 100 Centennial Mall N Lincoln NE 68508-3859

BEAM, MARGARET ANNE RIDGEWAY, lawyer; b. Arkadelphia, Ark., Jan. 24, 1948; d. Robert Dean and Anne Spragins (Dews) Ridgeway Sr.; m. Thomas Earl Beam, Apr. 16, 1971; children: Lauren Ashley, Katherine Elizabeth, Charlotte Anne. BA, Ark. Tech. U., 1970; JD, U. Ark., Little Rock, 1982, MLS, 1989. Bar: Ark. 1984. Asst. libr. Ark. Supreme Ct. Libr., Little Rock, 1983-89; pvt. practice, Hot Springs, Ark., 1989—2001; atty. ad litem State of Ark., 2001—. Mem. ABA, Ark. Bar Assn., Garland County Bar Assn. Home: 3320 Marion Anderson Rd Hot Springs National Park AR 71913-7515 Office: 1001 W Grand Ste A Hot Springs National Park AR 71913

BEAR, JEFFREY LEWIS, lawyer; b. L.A., Apr. 16, 1947; s. Bernard and Rhoda B.; m. Linda Grodman Bear Snibbe (div.); 1 child, Ryan Steven; m. P. Renee LoCascio, Aug. 9, 1997. BA in Polit. Sci., Calif. State U., Northridge, 1968; JD, Loyola U., 1971. Bar: Calif. 1972, U.S. Dist. Ct. (cen. dist.) Calif. 1972, U.S. Ct. Appeals (9th cir.) 1972. Dep. atty. gen. Calif. Atty. Gen., L.A., 1971-73; dep. pub. defender L.A. County Pub. Defender, L.A., 1973-77; ptnr. Sommer & Bear, Beverly Hills, Calif., 1977—. Mem. arbitrator panel L.A. Superior Ct.; mem. pro tem panel L.A. Mcpl. Ct., Beverly Hills Mcpl. Ct.; spkr. in field. Co-author: Drunk Driving Trial Seminar Syllabus, 1977, 78, 79, Defense of Drunk Driving Cases, 1978—. Fellow Loyola U. Sch. Law, 1968. Mem. State Bar Calif. (mem. litig. sect.), L.A. County Bar Assn. (mem. litig. sect.), Beverly Hills Bar Assn., Consumer Attys. Assn. L.A., Porsche Club Am. (L.A. region), Profl. Assn. Diving Instrs. Criminal, Personal injury (including property damage), Product liability. Office: Sommer & Bear 9777 Wilshire Blvd Ste 512 Beverly Hills CA 90212-1905

BEARD, RONALD STRATTON, lawyer; b. Flushing, N.Y., Feb. 13, 1939; s. Charles Henry and Ethel Mary (Stratton) Beard; m. Karin Paridee, Jan. 24, 1991; children: D. Karen, Jonathan D., Dana K. BA, Denison U., 1961; LLB, Yale U., 1964. Bar: Calif. 1964, U.S. Ct. Appeals (9th cir.) 1980, U.S. Dist. Ct. (ctrl. dist.) Calif. 1964. Ptnr. Gibson, Dunn & Crutcher, LA, 1964—2001, mng. ptnr., 1991—97, chmn., 1991—2001. Trustee Denison U., Granville, Ohio, 1975—, chmn., 1998—; mem. steering com. Calif. Minority Coun. Program, 1991—2001; mem. Constl. Rights Found., 1994—, Orange County Art Mus. Mem.: ABA, LA Bar Assn., Calif. Bar Assn., Coto de Caza Golf Club, Chancery Club, City Club. Avocations: sports, travel, golf. Corporate, general, Private international. Home: 27442 Hidden Trail Rd Laguna Hills CA 92653-5876 Office: Gibson Dunn & Crutcher 4 Park Plz Ste 1700 Irvine CA 92614-8560

BEASLEY, JAMES W., JR., lawyer; b. Atlanta, July 13, 1943; s. James W. and Sara Capal (Tucker) B.; m. Elizabeth Barno Marshall-Beasley, Nov. 28, 1986. AB cum laude, Davidson Coll., 1965; LLB cum laude, Harvard U., 1968. Bar: N.Y. 1969, D.C. 1971, Fla. 1972, U.S. Supreme Ct. 1973. Assoc. Sullivan & Cromwell, N.Y.C., 1968, Wilmer, Cutler & Pickering, Washington, 1970-72; assoc., then ptnr. Paul & Thomson, Miami, Fla., 1972-78; mng. ptnr. Beasley, Olle & Downs, Miami, 1978-88; ptnr. Tew, Jordan, Schulte & Beasley, Miami, 1988-89, Cadwalader, Wickersham & Taft, Palm Beach, Fla., 1989-94, Tew & Beasley LLP, Palm Beach, 1994-97, Beasley & Hauser, P.A., Palm Beach, 1997—. Author: Florida Corporations, 1985; contbr. articles to profl. jours. Chmn. County Conv. Ctr. Adv. Bd., 1994-96. Capt. U.S. Army, 1968-70. Mem. ABA, ATLA, Fla. Bar Assn. (chmn. securities regulation com. bus. law sect. 1975-77), Acad. Fla. Trial Lawyers. General civil litigation, Appellate, Alternative dispute resolution. Office: Beasley & Hauser PA 505 S Flagler Dr West Palm Beach FL 33401-5923

BEATTIE, CHARLES ROBERT, III, lawyer; b. Red Wing, Minn., Aug. 25, 1948; s. Charles Robert Jr. and Dorothy Catherine (Shepherd) B.; m. Camilla Lawther Foot, Aug. 26, 1972; children: Virginia, Anne, Charles. BA with honors, U. Mich., 1970; JD, Yale U., 1973. Bar: Minn. 1973, U.S. Dist. Ct. Minn. 1973, U.S. Ct. Appeals (8th cir.) 1975. Assoc. Doherty, Rumble & Butler, St. Paul, 1973-78, ptnr. St. Paul and Mpls., 1978-99, chmn. dept. bus. law, 1987-89, 92-94, dir., 1989-92, 98-99; ptnr. Oppenheimer, Wolff & Donnelly, LLP, Mpls., 1999—2003, mem. mgmt. com., 2003—. Lectr. on partnerships and banking, leasing, comml. law and electronic commerce, 1983—; mem. Minn. Digital Signature Guidelines Task Force, 1997-98. Contbr. articles on ltd. partnerships and electronic commerce to profl. jours. Mem. Citizens League, St. Paul and Mpls., 1979-93; officer Leadership St. Paul, 1981-86; bd. dirs. Civic Symphony Assn., 1976-80, St. John the Evangelist Episc. Ch., St. Paul, officer, 1981-93; pres., bd. dirs. Valley Chamber Chorale, 1996-99, Afton Citizen's Forum, 2000-2003; mem. Gillette Children's Specialty Healthcare Exec. Coun., 1995—. Mem. ABA (uniform comml. code com., com. on cyberspace law 1991—, article 1 task force, subcom. sale of goods 1993—, chair 2000—, co-chair working group on electronic writings and notices 1995-97, bus. law sect. adviser NCCUSL uniform electronic transactions act drafting com. 1997-99), Minn. Bar Assn. (bus. and computer law sects.), Regional Mpls. C. of C. (bd. dirs. 1997—). Avocations: sailing, skiing, choral singing. Banking, Commercial, contracts (including sales of goods; commercial financing), Securities. E-mail: rbeattie@oppenheimer.com.

BEATTIE, RICHARD IRWIN, lawyer; b. N.Y.C., Mar. 24, 1939; s. Richard I. Beattie and Ruth (Fisher) McCarthy; m. Diana Lewis, Dec. 21, 1963; children: Lisa C., Nina M. BA, Dartmouth Coll., 1961; LLB, U. Pa., 1968; EdD, Bank Street Coll. Bar: N.Y. 1968, U.S. Dist. Ct. (so. and ea. dists.) N.Y. 1972, U.S. Ct. Appeals (2d cir.) 1975, U.S. Ct. Appeals (D.C. cir.) 1977, U.S. Supreme Ct. 1978, U.S. Ct. Appeals (5th cir.) 1979. Assoc. Simpson, Thacher & Bartlett, N.Y.C., 1968-75, ptnr., 1975-77, 80—; dep. gen. counsel U.S. Dept. Health, Edn. and Welfare, Washington, 1977-78, exec. asst. to sec., 1978-79, gen. counsel, 1978-79; spl. counsel to sec., dir. transition U.S. Dept. Edn., Washington, 1980. Teaching fellow Harvard U., 1979-81; chmn. Commn. Reorgn. of Human Resources Adminstrn., N.Y.C., 1984-85, Commn. on Spl. Edn., N.Y.C., 1984-85; Mem. Mayor's Coun. Fgn. Rels., N.Y.C. Mem. Bd. Edn., N.Y.C, 1986-87.; bd. trustees WNET/Channel 13, N.Y.C., 1983—, Natural Resources Def. Counsel, N.Y.C., 1984-86, Carnegie Corp., 1988—; chmn. fund N.Y.C. Pub. Edn, 1989—; bd. dirs. Nat. Women's Law Ctr., Am. Ditchley Found., Am. Restaurant Group, Inst. Internat. Edn., Am.-Israel Friendship League; mem. Mayor's Task Force on AIDS. Capt. USMC, 1961-65. Mem. Bar City N.Y. Avocations: skiing, mountain climbing. Corporate, general, Environmental, Health. Office: Simpson Thacher & Bartlett 425 Lexington Ave Fl 15 New York NY 10017-3954*

BEATTY, RICHARD SCRIVENER, retired lawyer; b. Washington, May 6, 1934; s. John Joseph and Helen Louise (Simpson) B.; m. Barbara Boyd, July 14, 1956; children— Charles, Alexandra, Nicholas. BA, Williams Coll., 1955; LLB, Georgetown U., 1962. Bar: D.C. 1962. Trial atty. Dept. Justice, Washington, 1962-66; assoc. chief counsel Office U.S. Comptroller of Currency, 1966-67; ptnr. firm Alston, Miller & Gaines, Washington, 1968-84; ptnr. Shaw, Pittman, Potts & Trowbridge, Washington, 1985-95, sr. counsel, 1996-99, retired, 1999. Chmn. devel. coun. Williams Coll., St. Patrick's Episcopal Day Sch., 1970—82; sr. warden, Williams Coll., St. Patrick's Episcopal Day Sch., 1980-85; trustee Mt. Vernon Coll., 1985—90; pres. Ho. of Mercy, 1999—; trustee The Key Sch., 1999—; bd. dirs. The Episc. Ch. Found., 1991—99, Sea Web, 1998—. With U.S. Army, 1956—59. Mem.: ABA, Chevy Chase Club, D.C. Bar Assn., Am. Law Inst., Order St. John of Jerusalem, Met. Club (Washington), Delta Psi. Home: 7001 Glenbrook Rd Bethesda MD 20814-1222

BEAUCHAMP, GARY FAY, lawyer; b. Waco, Tex., Oct. 21, 1951; s. Fay Harry and Mary Elva (Gaunt) B. BBA, So. Meth. U., 1975; JD, South Tex. Coll. Law, 1980. Bar: Tex. 1980, U.S.Dist. Ct (so. dist.) Tex. 1980, U.S. Supreme Ct. 1983. Pvt. practice, The Woodlands, Tex., 1980—. Scuba diving instr., profl. assoc. diving instr. Avocation: scuba diving. Criminal, General practice, Personal injury (including property damage). Office: PO Box 131225 Spring TX 77393-1225

BEAUFORT, JEAN-LOUIS, lawyer, educator; b. Nancy, France, Jan. 8, 1946; s. Abel Raoul and Raymonde Marie (Jacquemin) B.; children: Eric, Nicolas. Degree in law, U. Nancy, 1969, M in Law, 1970, cert. adminstrn. of bus., 1971, D in Law, 1978. Tchr. Ste. Elisabeth Tech. H.S., Nancy, 1971-73; asst. Law Coll. U. Nancy, 1971-78, lectr., 1979—; pvt. practice law Nancy, 1972—. Mem. RPR. Mem. RPR. Avocations: stamp collecting, fishing, skiing, walking. Home: 5 Bis rue de la gare 54950 Saint-Clement France Office: Cabinet D'Avocats 11 Ave Victor Hugo Nancy France E-mail: jlbeaufort@aol.com.

BEAUMONT, JACQUES, lawyer; b. Neuilly sur Seine, France, Sept. 29, 1964; s. Robert and Huguette (David) Beaumont; m. Anne-Marie Borrero, June 8, 1997; 1 child, Inès Eugénie. M in Bus. Law, Paris II Panthéon-Assas, 1986, degree in intellectual property, 1987; degree in European law, Paris I Panthéon-Sorbonne, 1989; LLM, London Sch. Econs., 1991. Bar: Paris 1995, qualified in trademark law: French Trademark and Patent Office 2001. Lawyer Cabinet Armengaud Lepeudry, Paris, 1991—94, Clifford Chance, Paris, 1994—96, Cabinet Lavoix, Paris, 1997, Office Blétry, Paris, 1998—2000; head trademarks dept. Deprez Dian Guignot, Paris, 2000—. Lectr. French Trademark Office, Paris, 2000—. Served with French Navy, 1988. Mem.: London Sch. Econ., LSE, Alumni in France. Avocations: history, archery. Trademark and copyright, Intellectual property. Home: 90 rue de Maubeuge 75010 Paris France Office: Deprez Dian Guignot 21 rue Clément Marot 75008 Paris France Office Fax: (331) 53238229. E-mail: beaumont@ddg.fr.

BEAUREGARD, PHILIP N. lawyer, educator; b. New Bedford, Mass., July 30, 1944; s. R. Albert Beauregard and Adrienne Champagne; m. Kate Harrison; children: Pierre, Philip, Adrienne. Student, Carnegie Inst. Tech., 1962—65; BA, U. Notre Dame, 1967; JD, Georgetown U., 1972. Assoc. Desmarais & Carey, New Bedford, Mass., 1972—76; city solicitor City of New Bedford, 1979—80; owner Beauregard Burke, New Bedford, 1980—. Adj. prof. So. New Eng. Law Sch., Dartmouth, Mass., 2003. Contbr. sects. to books. V.p. Port Soc., New Bedford, 2001—02; pres. bd. dirs. Coalition for Buzzards Bay, New Bedford, 1998—99. With U.S. Army, 1969—71. Home: One Clinton Pl New Bedford MA 02740 Office: Law Offices Beauregard Burke & Franco PO Box 952 32 William St New Bedford MA 02741 E-mail: bbf.robeson@verizon.net., andrew.robeson@verizon.net.

BEBCHICK, LEONARD NORMAN, lawyer; b. New Bedford, Mass., Dec. 11, 1932; s. Samuel and Frances (Hait) B.; m. Gabriela Meyerhoff, Aug. 31, 1968; children: Ilana, Brian. AB, Cornell U., 1955; LLB, Yale U., 1958. Bar: Mass. 1958, D.C. 1960, Md. 1989. Atty. CAB, Washington, 1958—59; assoc. Ginsburg & Leventhal, Washington, 1960-64; ptnr. Bebchick, Sher & Kushnick, Washington, 1964-74, Martin, Whitfield, Smith & Bebchick, Washington, 1974-82; pres. Leonard N. Bebchick P.C., Washington, 1982-88; ptnr. Leva, Hawes, Mason, Martin & Bebchick, Washington, 1988-89; pvt. practice as lawyer Washington, 1989—. Joint co. sec. Brit Caledonian Airways, Eng., 1963-88; bd. dirs. British Caledonian Group, Eng., 1978-88, London Transport Internat. Cons., U.S., 1990-92;

spl. counsel D.C. Pub. Svc. Commn., Washington, 1965-66, V.I. Pub. Utilities Commn., 1967-70. Bd. dirs. Jewish Found. Group Homes, 1992—; pres. Congregation Beth El of Montgomery County, 1993—95; bd. dirs. United Synagogue of Conservative Judaism, 1993—2002, Jewish Fedn. Greater Washington, 1996—2002; bd. govs. coms. Jewish Agy. Israel, 1998—2002; bd. dirs., vice chair, exec. com.. Muss H.S., Israel, 1997—; mem. nat. coun. Am. Jewish Com., 2002—. Mem.: ABA (chmn. adv. com. on aero. law 1982—83), Inst. of Dirs. (London), Internat. Assn. Jewish Lawyers and Jurists, U.S. Nat. Student Assn. (v.p. internat. affairs 1953—54). Democrat. Jewish. Administrative and regulatory, Federal civil litigation, Corporate, general. Home: 6321 Lenox Rd Bethesda MD 20817-6023 Office: 1101 Connecticut Ave NW Washington DC 20036 E-mail: beblaw@erols.com.

BEBER, ROBERT H. lawyer, financial services executive; b. N.Y.C., Aug. 17, 1933; s. Morris and Martha (Pollock) B.; m. Joan Parsons, June 14, 1957; children: Andrea, Judith, Deborah. AB in Econs, Duke U., 1955, JD, 1957. Bar: N.Y., N.C. With Everett, Everett & Everett, N.C., 1957-58; atty. SBA, Washington, 1961-63; with RCA, 1963-81; sr. v.p., gen. counsel, sec. GAF Corp., N.Y.C., 1981-83, exec. v.p., dir., 1983-84, dir. subs.; sr. v.p., gen. counsel, sec. Phlcorp, Inc. (formerly Baldwin United Corp.), Phila., 1984-88; asst. gen. counsel litigation W.R. Grace & Co., N.Y.C., 1988-89, v.p., dir. litigation, 1989-91, sr. v.p., gen. counsel, 1991-93, exec. v.p., 1993-98, ret., 1999, cons., 1999—. Bd. dirs. Advantage Bank. Bd. vis. Sch. Law, Duke U., 1996—; chmn. bd. Health Care Plan N.J., 1975-78; v.p. South Jersey C. of C., 1974-77; dir. Advantage Bank, Palm Beach, Fla., 1999—. Served with U.S. Army, 1958-61. Mem. ABA. Republican. Jewish. General civil litigation, Corporate, general. Home: 7228 Queenferry Cir Boca Raton FL 33496-5953 Office: WR Grace & Co 5400 Broken Sound Blvd NW Boca Raton FL 33487-3511

BECERRA, ROBERT JOHN, lawyer; b. Jersey City, Jan. 26, 1962; s. Joseph Hercules and Blanche (Rosado) B.; m. Christiana Marie Carroll, Oct. 30, 1993. BBA, U. Miami, 1986, JD, 1990. Bar: Fla. 1990, U.S. Dist. Ct. (so. and mid dists.) Fla. 1991, U.S. Ct. Appeals (11th cir.) 1991, U.S. Dist. Ct. (ea. dist.) Mich. 1994, U.S. Supreme Ct. 1994, U.S. Ct. Appeals (3d cir.) 1997. Assoc. Raskin & Raskin, Miami, Fla., 1990-96, ptnr., 1997—. Mem. Fed. Bar Assn., Dade County Bar Assn. (fed. cts. com., Certificate of Merit 1993), Phi Kappa Phi. Democrat. Roman Catholic. Avocations: sailplane pilot, scuba diving, boating, skiing. Aviation, Federal civil litigation, Criminal. Office: Raskin & Raskin 2937 SW 27th Ave Ste 206 Miami FL 33133-3772 E-mail: bbecerra@raskinlaw.com.

BECH, DOUGLAS YORK, lawyer, resort executive; b. Seattle, Aug. 18, 1945; s. Albert Richard and Vera Evelyn (Peterson) B.; m. Sheryl Annette Tucker, Aug. 9, 1968; children: Kristen Elizabeth, Allison York. BA, Baylor U., 1967; JD, U. Tex., 1970. Bar: Tex. 1970, N.Y. 1993. Ptnr. Andrews & Kurth, Houston, 1970-93, Akin, Gump, Strauss, Hauer & Feld, 1994-97; mng. dir. Raintree Capital Co., Houston, 1994—. Chmn., CEO Raintree Resorts Internat., Inc., Club Regina Resorts, Inc.; bd. dirs. Frontier Oil, Pride Cos., J2 Global Comm. Sgt. USAR, 1968-74. Republican. Baptist. Avocations: running, snowskiing, travel, big game hunting, golf. Corporate, general, Mergers and acquisitions, Securities. Office: Raintree Resorts Internat 10000 Memorial Dr Ste 480 Houston TX 77024-3409 E-mail: dybech@raintreeresorts.com.

BECHTEL, DEBRA NASS, lawyer; b. Oceanside, N.Y., Apr. 27, 1964; d. Rodger Burrows and Barbara Young Nass; m. H. Kenneth Bechtel, Mar. 20, 1992; children: Greg, Stephen. BA, U. Fla., 1986, JD, 1991. Bar: N.C. 1992. Asst. dist. atty. Dist. Attys. Office, Newton, NC, 1992—96; county atty. Catawba County, 1996—. Guest lectr. Wake Forest U., Winston-Salem, NC, 1992—; sec. Criminal Justice Partnership Bd., Newton, 1993—. Editor: History of State Police in U.S., 1996. Campaign cabinet mem. United Way, 2001; sec. ARC, 1995—2001. Mem.: ABA, Catawba County Bar Assn. (sec. 2002, treas. 2003), N.C. State Bar Assn. (chair Catawba County lawyers in schs. 2000—), Nat. Pub. Health Lawyers (founder), Nat. Sheriff Assn. Legal Advisors (founder), N.C. Police Attys. Assn. Republican. Mem. United Ch. Of Christ. Avocations: painting, hiking, travel, cooking. Office: Catawba County Attys Office PO Box 389 100A SW Blvd Newton NC 28658 Fax: 828-465-8465.

BECHTLE, LOUIS CHARLES, lawyer, retired federal judge; b. Phila., Dec. 14, 1927; s. Charles R. and Gladys (Kirchner) B.; m. Margaret Beck, Sept. 7, 1978; children: Barbara, Nancy, Amy; 1 stepchild, Samuel. BS, Temple U., 1951, LL.B., 1954. Bar: Pa. 1954. Asst. U.S. atty. U.S. Dept. Justice, Phila., 1957-59, U.S. atty., 1969-72; pvt. practice law Jacoby & Maxmin, Phila., 1959-62; pvt. practice Wisler, Pearlstine, Talone, Gerber, Norristown, Pa., 1962-69; U.S. dist. judge U.S. Dist. Ct., Phila., 1972—2002; sr. judge U.S. Dist. Ct. (Eastern Dist.), Phila.; atty. Conrad O'Brien Gellman & Rohn, P.C., Phila., 2002—. Adj. faculty Temple U. Law Sch., Phila., 1974-93, Villanova Law Sch., 1985-89; mem. Jud/ Panel on Multidist. Litigation, 1994—. Served with U.S. Army, 1946-47. Mem. Montgomery County Bar Assn., Fed. Bar Assn. Republican. Presbyterian. Office: Conrad O'Brien Gellman & Rohn PC 1515 Market St 16th Fl Philadelphia PA 19102 Office Fax: 215-864-9620.

BECK, ANDREW JAMES, lawyer; b. Washington, Feb. 19, 1948; s. Leonard Norman and Frances (Greif) B.; m. Carol Beck, Oct. 13, 2002; children: Carter, Lowell, Justin. BA, Carleton Coll., 1969; JD, Stanford U., 1972; MBA, Long Island U., 1975. Bar: VA. 1972, NY 1973, Pa. 1992. Assoc. Casey, Lane & Mittendorf, N.Y.C., 1972-80, ptnr., 1980-82, Haythe & Curley, N.Y.C., 1982-99, Torys LLP, N.Y.C., 1999—, exec. com., 2000—03. Trustee Bklyn. Heights Synagogue, 1980-81; trustee Bklyn. Heights Montessori Sch., 1988-92, treas., 1990-92. Mem. ABA, Va. State Bar Assn., N.Y. Stat Bar Assn., Pa. Bar Assn., Assn. of Bar of City of N.Y., Nat. Stroke Assn. (gen. counsel 1992—, sec., bd. dirs. 2000—). Avocation: bridge. Corporate, general, Securities. Home: 71 Willow St Apt 1 Brooklyn NY 11201-1657 Office: Torys LLP 237 Park Ave New York NY 10017-3142 E-mail: abeck@torys.com.

BECK, CHRISTOPHER ALAN, lawyer; b. Hartford, Conn., Feb. 24, 1953; s. Roger Seton and Ruth Virginia (Hottinger) B. BS, Allegheny Coll., 1975; JD, U. Pitts., 1978; MLLS, Duquesne U., 1999. Bar: Pa. 1978, U.S. Dist. Ct. (we. dist.) Pa. 1978, U.S. Supreme Ct. 1983, U.S. Ct. Appeals (3d cir.) 1984, U.S. Dist. Ct. (ea. and mid. dists.) Pa. 1988, W.Va. 1991, U.S. Dist. Ct. (so. dist.) W.Va. 1991, U.S. Dist. Ct. (no. dist.) W.Va. 1996, Ohio 1999. Assoc. Phillips & Galanter, Pitts., 1978—79; ptnr. Ravick, Beck & Henny (formerly McCrady, Kramer et al), Pitts., 1977—87, Riley & DeFalice, Pitts., 1988—93; assoc. Israel Wood & Puntil, Pitts., 1994—2001, Thorp Reed & Armstrong, LLP, Pitts., 2001—. Pres. King's Grant Condominium, Pitts., 1985-89; deacon Southminster Presbyn. Ch., 1992-95; sec. Pitts. Pub. Theater Assn., 1991-93; elder Southminster Presbyn. Ch., 1997-00. Mem. Pa. Bar Assn., W.Va. Bar Assn., Allegheny County Bar Assn. (vice chmn. arts and law com. 1988-89, chmn. arts and law com. 1995-96), Pa. Def. Inst., Def. Rsch. Inst., Rotary (pres. Three Rivers club 1989-90, conf. chmn. local dist. 1988-89, dist. found. chmn. 1991-92, 95-96, dist. gov. 1993-94, chmn. Youth Exch. 2001-02, dist. trainer, 2002—). Democrat. Presbyterian. Avocations: travel, photography. General civil litigation, Insurance, Product liability. Home: 281 Merion Dr Pittsburgh PA 15228-2352 Office: Thorp Reed & Armstrong LLP One Oxford Ctr 301 Grant St 14th fl Pittsburgh PA 15219-1425

BECK, EDWARD HENRY, III, lawyer; b. N.Y.C., Jan. 21, 1950; s. Edward Henry and Vera (Larkin) B.; m. Esther Troy, Oct. 11, 1975; children: Elizabeth Christiane, Emily King. BA cum laude, U. Notre Dame, 1971; JD, Fordham U., 1974. Bar: N.Y. 1975, U.S. Ct. Appeals (2d cir.) 1975, U.S. Dist. Ct. (ea. and so. dists.) N.Y. 1976, U.S. Supreme Ct. 1982, Ill. 1983, Va. 1984, U.S. Dist. Ct. (cen. dist.) Ill. 1992, U.S. Ct. Appeals (7th cir.) 1992, U.S. Ct. Appeals (4th cir.) 1993, U.S. Ct. (ea. dist.) Va. 1993, U.S. Ct. Appeals (fed. cir.) 1996. Atty. trainee N.Y. City Corp. Counsel, N.Y.C., 1974-75; asst. atty. gen. State of N.Y., N.Y.C., 1975-80; staff atty. mktg. and refining div. Mobil Oil Corp., Scarsdale, N.Y., 1980-81, Woodfield, Ill., 1982-83, Fairfax, Va., 1983-88, counsel mktg. and refining, internat. div. N.Y.C., 1988-89, sr. counsel exploration and prodn. div. Fairfax, Va., 1989-90, sr. counsel mktg. and refining div., 1990-2000, counsel litigation dept., 1996-2000; counsel fuels mktg. divsn. Exxon Mobil Corp., 2000—. Mem. ABA, Westchester County Bar Assn., Va. Bar Assn. Home: 5966 Burnside Landing Dr Burke VA 22015-2522 Office: Exxon-Mobil Corp 3225 Gallows Rd Fairfax VA 22037-0002 E-mail: edward_h_beck@email.mobil.com., ebeck@erds.com.

BECK, JAN SCOTT, lawyer; b. Newark, May 5, 1955; s. Robert William and Dorothy (Warhaftig) B.; m. Marla Terri Klein, Sept. 27, 1981; children: Jamie Kyle, Bryan Michael, Sean Jason. BA in Acctg., Rider Coll., 1977; JD, Villanova U., 1980, LLM in Taxation, 1985. Bar: N.J. 1980, U.S. Dist. Ct. N.J. 1980, N.Y. 1981, U.S. Tax Ct. 1981, D.C. 1985, U.S. Supreme Ct. 1986. Pvt. practice, Westfield, N.J., 1980-86; atty. Inspiration Resources Corp., N.Y.C., 1986-88; dir. taxation ADT Inc., Boca Raton, Fla., 1988-89, v.p., gen. counsel, 1989-96; sr. v.p., dir. ADT Security Svcs., Inc., 1996-97; mng. dir., CEO The Turbary Group, Boca Raton, Fla., 1997—2002; CFO, StarCapital Corp., 2002—. Atty. Laventhol & Horwath, Phila., 1979-80, Touche Ross & Co., N.Y.C., 1980-86; dir. taxation Inspiration Resources Corp., N.Y.C., Monsoon Internat. LLC, 2000-02. Author: The Strike: Student Involvement, 1975. Mem. ABA, N.Y. State Bar Assn., N.J. Bar Assn., AICPA, N.J. Soc. CPAs, Tax Exec. Inst., Omicron Delta Epsilon, Delta Epsilon Kappa. Avocations: camping, backpacking, mountain climbing, writing, skiing. Corporate, general, Mergers and acquisitions, Corporate taxation. Home: 20988 Solano Way Boca Raton FL 33433-1621 Office: StarCapital 3320 Fairlane Farms Rd Ste 12 Wellington FL 33414-8764 E-mail: jbeck@starcapital.net.

BECK, PHILIP S. lawyer; b. Chgo., Apr. 30, 1951; BA, U. Wis., 1973; JD, Boston U., 1976. Bar: Ill. 1977. Clerk U.S. Ct. Appeals DC Cir., 1976-77; ptnr. Bartlit Beck Herman Palenchar & Scott, Chgo. Office: Bartlit Beck Herman et al 54 W Hubbard St Chicago IL 60610-4645 E-mail: philip.beck@bartlit-beck.com.

BECK, RONALD JERRY, judge; b. Kingsport, Tenn., Sept. 22, 1941; s. Victor R. and Anna P. Beck; m. Louise Bundy, Oct. 11, 1970; children: Robyn, Gabriel. BA, Emory & Henry Coll., 1965; postgrad., Emory U., 1965-66; JD, U. Tenn., 1968. Bar: Tenn. 1969, U.S. Dist. Ct. (ea. dist.) Tenn. 1970. Ptnr. Mitchell & Beck, Kingsport, 1969-72; asst. dist. atty. Sullivan County, Offic of Dist. Atty., Blountville, Tenn., 1972-93; judge Cir. Ct., Kingsport, 1993—. Mem. Rotary, Masons. Democrat. Office: Cir Ct Panel II 200 Shelby St Kingsport TN 37660-4256

BECK, STEPHANIE G. lawyer; b. Endicott, N.Y., Jan. 10, 1964; d. Ray A. and Donna E. (Geesey) B. BA with honors, SUNY, Binghamton, 1986; JD, Syracuse U., 1989. Bar: N.Y. 1990, U.S. Dist. Ct. (no. dist.) N.Y. 1990. Atty. Young & Paniccia, Binghamton, 1990—. Advisor/vol. Drama Club for Mentally and Physically Impaired, Binghamton, 1992—96; asst. coach Boys and Girls Club, Endwell, 1986—91; mem. ch. coun. Our Saviour Luth. Ch., Endwell, NY, 1990—94, 1996, Our Savior Luth. Ch., Endwell, NY, 2003—; mem. pers. com. Broome County Coun. Chs. Mem. N.Y. State Bar Assn., Broome County Bar Assn. (bd. dirs.). Democrat. Lutheran. Avocations: softball, volleyball. Family and matrimonial, General practice, Probate (including wills, trusts). Office: Young and Paniccia 22 Riverside Dr Binghamton NY 13905-4612

BECK, STUART EDWIN, lawyer; b. Phila., Aug. 12, 1940; s. Louis M. and Anna (Cooper) B.; m. Elaine Kushner, June 20, 1964; children: Adam, Barry, Caroline. BSME, Drexel U., 1964; JD, George Washington U., 1968. Bar: Va. 1968, U.S. Dist. Ct. D.C. 1969, Pa. 1970, U.S. Dist. Ct. (ea. dist.) Pa. 1971, U.S. Ct. Appeals (3d cir.) 1971, U.S. Supreme Ct. 1980, U.S. Ct. Appeals (4th cir.) 1989, U.S. Patent and Trademark Office. Assoc. Seidel, Gonda & Goldhammer, Phila., 1969-73; atty. pvt. practice, Phila., 1974-79, 91—; ptnr. Trachman, Jacobs & Beck, Phila., 1979-88, Weinstein, Trachtman, Beck & Kimmelman, Phila., 1988-91. Adj. prof. patent law Rutgers U. Law Sch., Camden, N.J.; instr. patent, trademark and copyright law The Phila. Inst.; lectr. patent, trademark and copyright law Newmann Coll., 1999, lectr. U.S. trademark prosecution, seminar on U.S. trademark practice for paralegals, Phila., 2003. Capt. Am. Cancer Soc., 1974, 75; bd. dirs. Jewish Family and Children Svc. Phila., 1973-89, legal, fin. and budget com., 1979—, spkrs. com., 1979—, bldg. and grounds com., 1980-82, trustee, 1989; bd. dirs., by-laws revision com., bldgs. and grounds com., edn. com. Temple Beth Hillel; bd. dirs. Phila. Vol. Lawyers for Arts, 1980-84, treas., 1980-82. Mem. ABA (patent trademark and copyright law sect., litigation sect., antitrust law sect.), Am. Intellectual Property Law Assn. (com. patent contracts other than govt. 1971-75), Pa. Bar Assn., Phila. Bar Assn. (com. profl. responsibility 1975-93, com. election procedures 1976-84, com. law and arts 1976-80), Phila. Patent Law Assn. (com. ethics 1977-83, com. pub. rels. 1974-77, com. profl. responsibility 1975-79). Avocations: sailing, travel. Intellectual property, Patent, Trademark and copyright.

BECK, WILLIAM G. lawyer; b. Kansas City, Mo., Mar. 4, 1954; s. Raymond W. Beck and Wanda Williams; children: Collin M., Sergei M., Valentina M., Kseniya M. BA in Econs., U. Mo., Kansas City, 1974, JD, 1978. Bar: Mo. 1978, U.S. Dist. Ct. (we. dist.) Mo. 1978, U.S. Ct. Appeals (5th cir.) 1988, U.S. Dist. Ct. (ea. dist.) Mich. 1991, U.S. Dist. Ct. (no. dist.) Ill. 1992, U.S. Ct. Appeals (6th cir.) 1992, U.S. Dist. Ct. (ea. dist.) Wis. 1997, U.S. Ct. Appeals (2d cir.) 1997, U.S. Ct. Appeals (10th cir.) 1997, U.S. Supreme Ct. 1997, U.S. Ct. Appeals (1st cir.) 1998, U.S. Ct. Appeals (7th cir.) 1999, U.S. Dist. Ct. Colo. 2000, U.S. Dist. Ct. Rhode Island 2002, U.S. Dist. Ct. Mass. 2002. Shareholder Field, Gentry, Benjamin & Robertson, P.C., Kansas City, 1978-89; ptnr. Lathrop & Norquist, Kansas City, 1989-95, Lathrop & Gage, L.C., Kansas City, 1996—. Commr. Human Rels. Commn., Jackson County, Mo., 1985-89; chmn. Citizens Assn., Kansas City, 1991-92, 95-96; mem. Pub. Improvement Adv. Com., Kansas City, 1991-2001, vice chmn., 1995-98, chmn. 1998-2001, fin. chmn. cmty. infrastructure com., 1996-1997; mem. Waste Minimization Com., Kansas City, 1990-91. Federal civil litigation, Environmental, Toxic tort. Office: Lathrop & Gage LC 2345 Grand Blvd Ste 2800 Kansas City MO 64108-2684

BECK, WILLIAM HAROLD, JR., lawyer; b. Clarksdale, Miss., Aug. 18, 1928; s. William Harold and Mary (McGaha) B.; m. Nancy Cassity House, Jan. 30, 1954; children: Mary, Nancy, Katherine. BA, Vanderbilt U., 1950; JD, U. Miss., 1954. Bar: Miss. 1954, La. 1960. Atty., Clarksdale, 1954-57; asst. prof. Tulane U., 1957-59; ptnr. Foley & Judell, New Orleans, 1959-88, of counsel, 1988—. Capt. AUS, 1951-53. Mem. La. Bar Assn., Miss. Bar Assn., SAR, Soc. Colonial Wars, S.R., Mil and Hospitaller Order of St. Lazarus of Jerusalem, Huguenot Soc., Mil. Order Fgn. Wars. Municipal (including bonds). Office: Foley & Judell LLP 1 Canal Pl 365 Canal St Ste 2600 New Orleans LA 70130-1138 E-mail: wandnbeck@aol.com.

BECKER, DOUGLAS WESLEY, lawyer; b. St. Louis, July 12, 1950; s. Donald William and Joetta Lea (Greer) B.; m. Deborah Ackerman, June 10, 1972 (div. Oct. 1985); 1 child, Laura Marie; m. Kimberly Dinsdale, Apr. 30, 1989; children: MacKenzie Brooke, Mallory Greer. BBA, So. Meth. U., 1972, JD, 1976. Bar: Tex. 1976, U.S. Supreme Ct. 1979; cert. residential and comml. real estate law Tex. Bd. Legal Specialization. Ptnr. Gresham, Davis, Gregory, Worthy & Moore, San Antonio, 1976—82; mem. Kaufman, Becker, Reibach & Richie, Inc., San Antonio, 1983—94, Cauthorn, Hale, Hornberger, Fuller, Sheehan, Becker & Beiter, San Antonio, 1994—2003; closing atty. Chgo. Title Ins. Co., San Antonio, 2003—. Contbr. articles to profl. jours. Pres. Vis. Nurse Assn., San Antonio, 1982; trustee, chmn. San Antonio Regional Hosp., 1993-94. Staff sgt. USAR, 1971-77. Mem.: San Antonio Real Estate Coun. (chmn. govt. affairs com. 1993—94, sec. 1994—95, v.p. 1995—96, bd. dirs. 2003—), San Antonio Bd. Realtors (bd. dirs. cert. comml. investment mem. chpt. 1992—93, 1998—2002, treas. 2002—03), Am. Coll. Real Estate Lawyers, San Antonio Young Lawyers Assn. (pres. 1984), Tex. Assn. Bank Counsel, Tex. Coll. Real Estate (bd. dirs.), State Bar Tex. (coun. real estate, probate and trust law sects. 1993—97, treas. 2002—03, chmn.-elect 2003—), Oak Hills Country Club (bd. dirs. 1993—97). Avocations: golf, skiing, trivia, reading, real estate. Commercial, contracts (including sales of goods; commercial financing), Corporate, general. Office: Chgo Title Ins Co 755 E Mulberry Ste 125 San Antonio TX 78212 E-mail: beckerd@ctt.com.

BECKER, EDWARD ROY, judge; b. Phila., May 4, 1933; s. Herman A. and Jeannette (Levit) Becker; m. Flora Lyman, Aug. 11, 1957; children: James Daniel(dec.) , Jonathan Robert, Susan Rose, Charles Lyman. BA, U. Pa., 1954; LLB, Yale U., 1957; LLD (hon.) , Temple U., 2003. Bar: Pa. 1957. Ptnr. Becker, Becker & Fryman, Phila., 1957—70; U.S. Dist. Judge, 1970—82; judge U.S. Ct. Appeals (3d cir.), 1982—, chief judge, 1998—2003. Counsel Rep. City Com., Phila., 1965—70; mem. task force on implementation of new jud. article Joint State Govt. Commn., 1969; lectr. law U. Pa. Law Sch., 1978—83; mem. edn. adv. com. concerning Comprehensive Crime Control Act Fed. Jud. Ctr., 1981—90, Fed. Jud. Ctr. Com. on Sentencing, Probation and Pretrial Svcs., 1985—90; bd. dirs. Fed. Jud. Ctr., 1991—95; mem. faculty sr. appellate judges seminar Inst. Jud. Adminstrn., N.Y.C., 1992—94. Bd. editors: Manual for Complex Litigation, 1981—90; contbr. articles to profl. jours. Trustee Magna Carta Found., Phila.; vis. com. U. Chgo. Law Sch., 1988—91; chair Rhodes Scholarship Selection Com. Dist. II (Pa., N.Y., Vt., N.H.), 1996—98; bd. mem. Historic Phila., Inc., 2001—; bd. mem., adv. bd. Am. Soc. of Internat. Law, 2000. Mem.: ABA (jud. rep. antitrust sect. 1983—86), Jud. Conf. U.S. (com. on adminstrn. probation sys. 1979—87, chmn. com. on criminal law and probation adminstrn. 1987—90, com. on long range planning 1991—96, exec. com. 1998—2003), Am. Law Inst. (mem. ALI-ABA com. 1992—, chmn. program subcom. 1996—99, adv. com. restatement conflict of laws 2d), Am. Judicature Soc. (Devitt award 2001), Phila. Bar Assn., Phi Beta Kappa. Jewish. Home: 936 Herbert St Philadelphia PA 19124-2417 Office: US Ct Appeals 19613 US Courthouse 601 Market St Philadelphia PA 19106-1713

BECKER, GRACE CHUNG, lawyer; b. N.Y.C., Oct. 6, 1969; JD, Georgetown U., 1994; BA, U. Pa., 1991; BSE, U. Pa., Philadelphia, PA, 1991. Law clk. Judge Thomas Penfield Jackson, Washington, 1994—95; assoc. Williams & Connolly, Washington, 1995—96; law clk. Judge James L. Buckley, Washington, 1996—97; trial atty. Criminal Divsn. Dept. Justice, Washington, 1997—99; spl. asst. to Asst. Sec. of Army, U.S. Army, Alexandria, Va., 2000—01; asst. gen. counsel U.S. Sentencing Commn., Washington, 1999—. Bd. dirs., exec. v.p. Korean Am. Coalition, Washington, 2001—02. Office: US Sentencing Commn 1 Columbus Cir NE #2-500, South Lobby Washington DC Business E-Mail: gbecker@ussc.gov.

BECKER, NANCY ANNE, state supreme court justice; b. Las Vegas, May 23, 1955; d. Arthur William and Margaret Mary (McLoughlin) Becker. BA, U.S. Internat. U., 1976; JD, George Washington U., 1979. Bar: Nev. 1979, D.C. 1980, Md. 1982, U.S. Dist. Ct. Nev. 1987, U.S. Ct. Appeals (9th cir.) 1987. Legis. cons. D.C. Office on Aging, Washington, 1979—83; assoc. Goldstein & Ahalt, College Park, Md., 1980—82; pvt. practice Washington, 1982—83; dep. city atty., prosecutor criminal div. City of Las Vegas, 1983; judge Las Vegas Mcpl. Ct., 1987—89, Clark County Dist. Ct., Las Vegas, 1989—99; now assoc. state supreme ct. justice Nev. Supreme Ct. Cons. MADD, Las Vegas, 1983—87. Contbr. articles to profl. jours. Pres. Clark County Pro Bono Project, Las Vegas, 1984—95. Mem.: NCCJ, Am. Businesswomen's Assn. (treas. Las Vegas chpt. 1985—86), Southern Nev. Assn. Women Attys. (past officer), Soroptimist Internat., Vietnam Vets. Am., Las Vegas and Latin C. of C. Office: Nevada Supreme Court Capital Complex 316 Bridger Ave Las Vegas NV 89101-5906

BECKER, RALPH ELIHU, JR., lawyer, planner; b. Washington, May 30, 1952; s. Ralph Elihu and Ann (Watters) B.; m. Nancy Baird Hayworth, June 28, 1980; children: Derek James, William Watters. Student, Lafayette Coll., 1970-71; BA cum laude, U. Pa., 1973; JD, U. Utah, 1977, MS in Geography, 1982. Bar: Utah 1978. V.p. Bonneville Assocs., Salt Lake City, 1978-81; spl. asst. to dir. Utah Dept. Natural Resources, Salt Lake City, 1981-83; dep. dir. dept. Utah Office Planning and Budget, Salt Lake City, 1983-85, state planning coord., 1983—85; chmn., pres. Bear West, Salt Lake City, 1985—; mem. Utah Ho. of Reps., 1997—, minority whip, 1999—, minority leader, 2001—02. Adj. prof. dept. geography U. Utah, Salt Lake City, 1986—. Author, editor: Project Bold: Proposal for Utah Land Consolidation and Exchange, 1985; contbr. numerous articles to clean air, solar energy law, publ land, environmental planning to profl. jours. Mem. Greater Avenues Community Coun., Salt Lake City, 1980-84, Salt Lake City Housing Appeals and Adv. Bd., 1985-87, Salt Lake City Planning Commn., 1988-96; chair Salt Lake City Zoning Rewrite Com.; bd. dris. Policy Consensus Initiative. Recipient Outstanding Achievement award Salt Lake County Wasatch Canyon Master Plan, 1990; Flemming fellow, 2003. Fellow Am. Inst. Cert. Planners (Western Planner of Yr. 1997); mem. Utah State Bar Assn. (natural resources sect., co-chmn. pub. lands com. 1985-87), Am. Planning Assn. (mem. energy policy task force, 1990, nat.-state policy coord. com., 1990—, amicus curiae com., 1994-97, nat. awards jury, 1993), Utah Planning Assn. (chmn. legis. com. Utah chpt. 1986-88, chpt. pres. 1988-90, Outstanding Svc. to Planning Profession award 1986), Rock Mountain Land Use Inst. (regional adv. bd.). Land use and zoning (including planning), Environmental, Natural resources. Office: Bear West 145 S 400 E Salt Lake City UT 84111-2104 E-mail: rbecker@bearwest.com.

BECKER, THOMAS BAIN, lawyer; b. St. Charles, Mo., Sept. 3, 1944; s. John Bruere and Marie Louise (Denker) B.; m. Linda Ann Flynn, May 25, 1974; children: Thomas Bain Jr., Shannon Flynn. BSBA, Georgetown U., 1966; MBA, U. Mo., Columbia, 1968, JD, 1976. Bar: Mo. 1976. Acct. Kerber, Eck & Braeckel, St. Louis, 1966, Rothaus, Bartels & Earley, St. Louis, 1968; acctg. analyst U.S. Dept. Commerce, Washington, 1971-73; shareholder Stinson, Mag & Fizzell, Kansas City, 1976-98, Gilmore & Bell, P.C., Kansas City, 1998—. Bd. dirs., v.p., pres. Westport Citizens Action Coalition, Kansas City, 1987—; bd. dirs. Hist. Kansas City Found., 1981-89, Kansas City Union Sta., Inc., 1988-97; bd. commrs., vice chair Mo. Housing Devel. Commn., 1995-98; mem. task force Mayor's Odyssey 2000, Kansas City, 1993; bd. dirs., vice chmn. Citizens Assn. Kansas City, 1996—. Recipient Community Svc. award Westport Coop. Svcs., 1991. Mem. ABA, Nat. Assn. Bond Lawyers, Rockhill Tennis Club (pres., bd. govs., treas. 1999—). Democrat. Roman Catholic. Avocations: sports, politics, reading, travel. Corporate, general, Finance, Municipal (including bonds). Home: 816 Gleed Ter Kansas City MO 64109-2617 Office: Gilmore & Bell PC 2405 Grand Blvd Ste 1100 Kansas City MO 64108-2521

BECKETT, THEODORE CHARLES, lawyer; b. Boonville, Mo., May 6, 1929; s. Theodore Cooper and Gladys (Watson) B.; m. Daysie Margaret Cornwall, 1950; children: Elizabeth Gayle, Theodore Cornwall, Margaret Lynn, William Harrison, Anne Marie. BS, U. Mo., Columbia, 1950, JD, 1957. Bar: Mo. 1957. Of counsel Baker, Sterchi, Cowden & Rice, LLC; instr. polit. sci. U. Mo., Columbia, 1956-57; asst. atty. gen. State of Mo., 1961-64. Mem. City Plan Commn., Kansas City, 1976-80; bd. curators U.

Mo., 1995-2001, pres. 1998. 1st lt. U.S. Army, 1950-53. Mem. Am., Mo., Kansas City bar assns., Lawyers Assn. Kansas City, Newcomen Soc. N.Am., SAR, Order of Coif, Sigma Nu, Phi Alpha Delta. Clubs: Kansas City (Kansas City, Mo.), Blue Hills Country (Kansas City, Mo.). Presbyterian. Federal civil litigation, State civil litigation. Office: 2400 Pershing Rd Ste 500 Kansas City MO 64108

BECKEY, SYLVIA LOUISE, lawyer; b. L.A., Feb. 8, 1946; d. Andrew Gabriel and Rita Jane (Mayer) B. BA with spl. honors, U. Tex., 1968, postgrad., 1968-69; JD, Duke U., 1971; postgrad., Johns Hopkins Sch. Advanced Internat. Studies, 1973—74; LLM, NYU, 1981. Bar: D.C. 1972, N.Y. 1975, U.S. Dist. Ct. (so. and ea. dists.) N.Y. 1975, U.S. Supreme Ct. 1975, U.S. Ct. Appeals (2d cir.) 1980, U.S. Dist. Ct. (so. and we. dists) Tex. 1995. Legis. atty. Am. law div. Congl. Rsch. Svc., Libr. of Congress, Washington, 1971-74; assoc. Cole & Deitz, N.Y.C., 1975-76, Milberg, Weiss, Bershad & Specthrie, N.Y.C., 1976-78; law. clk. to Judge Mary Johnson Lowe U.S. Dist. Ct. (so. dist.) N.Y., 1979-80; asst. chief div. comml. litigation Office of Corp. Counsel of City of N.Y., 1980-86; spl. master Supreme Ct. State of N.Y./N.Y. County, 1984-86; spl. counsel-enforcement U.S. Securities and Exch. Commn., N.Y.C., 1986-89; exec. dir., counselor at law Am. Inst. Law, Econs. and Comparative Studies, N.Y., 1990—; v.p. internat., house counsel Am. Sino Trade Devel. Coun., N.Y.C., 1997—. Guest speaker U. Witwatersrand Sch. Law, Johannesburg, Republic of South Africa, 1973; guest researcher Ct. Libr., Nairobi, Kenya, 1973; pro bono Internat. League Human Rights, N.Y.C., 1974-75, 8th ann. Conf. for World Peace Through Law, Abidjan, Ivory Coast, West Africa, 1973; law instr. Baruch Coll., N.Y.C. Co-author: Handbook for Drafting Jury Instructions, U.S. Dept. Justice Civil Rights Div., 1970; assoc. editor: The Constitution of the United States of America-Analysis and Interpretation, 1972; author legis. reports on Equal Credit Opportunity Act; referee Am. Bus. Law Jour., 1980-81. Bd. dirs. Chalon Coop. Bldg., Washington, 1972-73; chmn. fine arts com., mem. bd. dirs. St. Bartholomew's Community Club, St. Bartholomew's Episcopal Ch., N.Y.C., 1982-83; mem. organizing com. Annual Clio Awards China Road Show, 1999-2001. Hinds Webbs Fund grantee, 1967. Mem. Women's Bar Assn. City of N.Y., NYU Law Alumni Assn., Duke U. Law Alumni Assn., Fed. Bar Coun., Am. Fgn. Law Assn., Consular Law Soc., Dramatists Guild, English Speaking Union, Met. Mus. Art. Democrat. E-mail: SylviaBeckey@aol.com.

BECKHAM, WALTER HULL, III, lawyer; b. Boston, Feb. 12, 1948; s. Walter Hull Beckham Jr. and Ethel Brooks (Koger) Beckham. BA, Emory U., 1970, JD, 1977; MBA, U. Mich., 1972. Bar: Ga. 1977, U.S. Dist. Ct. (no. dist.) Ga. 1978, U.S. Dist. Ct. (so. dist.) Ga. 1980, U.S. Dist. Ct. (mid. dist.) Ga. 1988, U.S. Ct. Appeals (11th cir.) 1982. Investment analyst, portfolio mgr. Life of Ga., Atlanta, 1972-74; assoc. Jessee, Ritchie & Duncan, P.C., Atlanta, 1977-81, ptnr., 1981-82; pvt. practice, Atlanta, 1982—. Bd. dirs. Cmty. Outreach YMCA, Atlanta, 1973—75; Brookhaven Boys Club Atlanta, 1976; pres. Sr. Hon. Soc. Emory U., Atlanta, 1984—85, mem. Law Sch. Coun., 1993—2001, mem. bd. govs., 2001—. Mem.: ABA (tort and ins. practice sect., long range planning com. 1986—90, chmn. satellite seminars and videotapes com. 1990—92, coun. 1990—93, chmn. pub. rels. com. 1993, com. coord. 1993, sect. chmn. 1995—96), Ga. Trial Lawyers Assn. (long range planning com. 1982—86), Internat. Acad. Trial Lawyers, Atlanta Bar Assn. (state ct. com. 1985), Ga. Bar Assn. (co-chmn. com. on professionalism 1997—2000, jud. procedure and adminstrn. com. 2000—), Kappa Alpha (Hardeman Province Ct. of Honor). Avocations: hunting, fishing, skiing. General civil litigation, Personal injury (including property damage), Securities. Home: 1208 Village Run NE Atlanta GA 30319-5303 Office: Ste 2600 75 14th St Atlanta GA 30309

BECKSTEAD, JOHN ALEXANDER, lawyer; b. Murray, Utah, July 23, 1950; s. Farol W. and Ruth I. (Elieson) B.; m. Deborah Heiner, June 28, 1972; children: Alexander, Spencer, Taylor, Christopher. BA, U. Utah, 1972, JD, 1975. Bar: Ariz. 1975, U.S. Dist. Ct. Ariz. 1975, Utah 1977, U.S. Dist. Ct. Utah 1977, U.S. Ct. Appeals (10th cir.) 1977. Dep. county atty. Maricopa County Atty.'s Office, Phoenix, 1975-77; spl. dep. county atty. Organized Crime Bur., Maricopa County (Ariz.) Atty.'s Office, Phoenix, 1977-79; mem. Callister, Nebeker & McCullough, Salt Lake City, 1977—, shareholder, dir., 1981—2001, exec. com., exec. v.p., 1991-97, adminstrv., shareholder, mng. atty., 1991-94; ptnr. Snell & Wilmer, Salt Lake City, 2001—. Trustee Utah Legal Svcs., Inc., 1994— (pres. 1998—); mentor Utah Tech. Fin. Corp., 1994-97; mem. adv. com. on rules of profl. conduct Utah Supreme Ct., 1997—. Scoutmaster Boy Scouts of Am., Salt Lake City, 1992-95. Mem. ABA (subcom. creditors rights, inventory and accounts receivable financing, factor, comml. fin. svcs. com., editl. bd. Comml. and Banking Litigation Newsletter litigation sect. 1998—), Utah Bar Assn. (sec. banking and fin. sect. 1983-84, vice chmn. 1984-85, chmn. 1985-86, chmn. subcom. on contracts/secured transactions/sales, model Utah jury instrns., sect. litigation 1989, 10th Circuit subcom. comml. bnkg. and fin. trans. com. of litigation sect. 1989-90). General civil litigation, Commercial, contracts (including sales of goods; commercial financing), Intellectual property. Office: Snell & Wilmer Gateway Tower West Ste 1200 15 W South Temple Salt Lake City UT 84101

BECKSTROM, CHARLES G. lawyer; b. Jamestown, N.Y., July 14, 1940; s. Charles Wilbert and Dorothy Helen (Carlson) B.; m. Marie Jane Trebilcock, Nov. 28, 1964; children: Kimberly Leigh, Erika Lynne, Kristyn Marie, Stephanie Rae. BA, Mich. State U., 1962; MBA, Wayne State U., 1966; JD, SUNY-Buffalo, 1969. Bar: Mich. 1969, N.Y. 1971, Pa. 1997. Ptnr. Johnson, Peterson, Tener & Anderson, Jamestown, 1970-89, Beckstrom & Plumb, Jamestown, 1989—. Fin. analyst Fisher Body div. Gen. Motors Corp., Warren, Mich., 1963-66; lawyer Ernst & Ernst, Detroit, 1969-70; town atty. Town of Ellery, N.Y., 1972-83; bd. dirs. Dowcraft Corp.,1990-2001; bd. dirs., asst. sec. Bur. Veritas Quality Internat. (N.Am.) Inc., 1995-2001; bd. dirs., sec. Ellison Bronze, Inc., 2001—. Trustee, chmn. 1st Covenant Ch. Jamestown, 1976-82; chmn., bd. pensions Evangelical Covenant Ch. Nat. Pension Plan, Chgo., 1979-84; mem. exec. bd. Evangelical Covenant Ch., 1986-92. Served with U.S. Army, 1963-64. Mem. Jamestown Bar Assn., N.Y. Assn. Sch. Attys., Jamestown Estate Planning Coun. (pres., v.p., sec.), Internat. Found. Employee Benefit Plans, Norden Club. Republican. Corporate, general, Labor (including EEOC, Fair Labor Standards Act, labor-management relations, NLRB, OSHA), Pension, profit-sharing, and employee benefits. Home: 125 Westminister Dr Jamestown NY 14701-4438 Office: PO Box 579 Jamestown NY 14702-0579 E-mail: beckplum@netsync.net., cbeck@netsync.net.

BECKWITH, EDWARD JAY, lawyer; b. Paterson, N.J., July 18, 1949; s. David and Beverly Beckwith; m. Iris Kailo; children: Jessica, Jason, Jenna. BS, Pa. State U., 1971; JD, Georgetown U., 1974, ML in Taxation, 1983. Bar: D.C., U.S. Supreme Ct., U.S. Ct. Appeals (fed. cir.), U.S. Ct. Appeals (D.C. cir.), U.S. Dist. Ct. D.C., U.S. Tax Ct., U.S. Claims Ct. Staff asst. Coun. on Environ. Quality Exec. Office of Pres., Washington, 1973; assoc. Fried, Frank, Harris, Shriver & Kampelman, Washington, 1974-82, Baker & Hostetler, Washington, 1982-83, ptnr., 1984—. Adj. prof. law Georgetown U. Law Ctr., Washington, 1984—; bd. advisors Jour. Taxation Trusts and Estates, 1989-92; mem. Greater Washington Bd. Trade. Contbr. articles to profl. publs. Mem. steering com. sect. on trusts and probate law D.C. Bar, 1985-87; chmn. planned giving adv. coun. Pa. State U., 2000—. Alumni fellow honoree Pa. State U., 1998. Fellow: Am. Bar Found., Am. Coll. Trust and Estate Counsel (state chair D.C. 1998—2003, chmn. philanthropy study com. 2000—03, chmn. charitable planning and exempt orgns. com. 2001—, regent, state chair, state chmn. D.C. 1998—2003); mem.: ABA, Am. Law Inst. (Estate Planning Coun. Washington chpt.), Pa. State U. Alumni Assn., Omicron Delta Kappa. Corporate, general, Non-profit and tax-exempt organizations, Probate (including wills, trusts). Office: Baker & Hostetler LLP 1050 Connecticut Ave NW Washington DC 20036-5304 E-mail: beckwith@bakerlaw.com.

BECKWITH, LEWIS DANIEL, lawyer; b. Indpls., Jan. 30, 1948; s. William Frederick and Helen Lorena (Smith) B.; m. Marcia Ellen Ride, June 27, 1970; children: Laura, Gregory. BA, Wabash Coll., 1970; JD, Vanderbilt U., 1973. Bar: Ind. 1973, U.S. Dist. Ct. (so. dist.) Ind. 1973. Assoc. Baker & Daniels, Indpls., 1973-80, ptnr., 1981—. Articles editor Vanderbilt Law Rev., 1972-73. Mem. ABA (assoc. editor occupational safety & health law 2002), Ind. Bar Assn., Indpls. Bar Assn., Ind. C. of C. (com. occupational safety and health law 1982—), Associated Gen. Contractors of Ind. (com. occupational safety and health 1988—, safety and health counsel), Indpls. Athletic Club, ORder of Coif, Eta Sigma Phi, Beta Theta Pi. Republican. Lutheran. Avocation: sports. Administrative and regulatory, Environmental, Labor (including EEOC, Fair Labor Standards Act, labor-management relations, NLRB, OSHA). Office: Baker & Daniels 300 N Meridian St Ste 2700 Indianapolis IN 46204-1782 E-mail: ldbeckwi@bakerd.com.

BECKWITH, SANDRA SHANK, judge; b. Norfolk, Va., Dec. 4, 1943; d. Charles Langdale and Loraine (Sterneberg) Shank; m. James Beckwith, Mar. 31, 1965 (div. June 1978); m. Thomas R. Ammann, Mar. 3, 1979. BA, U. Cin., 1965, JD, 1968. Bar: Ohio 1969, Ind. 1976, Fla. 1979, U.S. Dist. Ct. (so. dist.) Ohio 1971, U.S. Dist. Ct. Ind. 1976, U.S. Supreme Ct. 1977. Sole practice, Harrison, Ohio, 1969-77, 79-81; judge Hamilton County Mcpl. Ct., Cin., 1977-79, 81-86, commr., 1989-91; judge Ct. Common Pleas, Hamilton County Divsn. Domestic Rels., 1987-89; assoc. Graydon, Head and Ritchey, 1989-91; judge U.S. Dist. Ct. (so. dist.) Ohio, 1992—. Mem. Ohio Chief Justice's Code of Profl. Responsibility Commn., 1984, Ohio Gov.'s Com. on Prison Crowding, 1984-90, State Fed. Com. on Death Penalty Habeas Corpus, 1995—; pres. 6th Cir. Dist. Judges Assn., 1998-99; chair So. Dist. Ohio Automation Com., 1997—. Bd. dirs. Cin. chpt. ARC, 1996—, Tender Mercies. Mem. Fed. Judges Assn., Am. Judges Assn., Am. Judicature Soc., Fed. Bar Assn. (exec. com.), Fed. Cir. Bar Assn. Office: Potter Stewart US Courthouse Ste 810 Cincinnati OH 45202

BECRAFT, CHARLES D., JR., lawyer; b. Corning, N.Y., June 1, 1939; s. Charles D. and Mary A. (Szepansky) B. BS in Bus. Adminstrn., Syracuse U., 1961; LLB, JD, Union U., 1964. Bar: N.Y. 1967. Assoc. Flynn Law Offices, Bath, N.Y., 1967-68, Nasser Law Offices, Corning, N.Y., 1968-70; prin., owner Becraft Law Offices, Corning, N.Y., 1970-75, 80—; ptnr. Becraft, Knox & Kahl, Corning, N.Y., 1975-80. Asst. dist. atty. County of Steuben, N.Y., 1970-73; city judge City of Corning, 1977-80. With U.S. Army, 1965-67. Mem. N.Y. Bar Assn., Steuben County Bar Assn. (pres. 1981-83), Corning City Bar Assn., Kiwanis, Lions. Republican. Methodist. Avocations: tennis, skiing, wine making. Estate planning, General practice, Property, real (including real estate development, water). Office: 135 Cedar St Corning NY 14830-2634

BEDARD, KAMI L. law librarian; BA in Am. Lit., Middlebury Coll., 1993; M in Libr. and Info. Sci., U. S.C., 1997. Asst. libr. Pierce Atwood, Portland, Maine, 1997—99, head libr., 2000—. Mem.: New Eng. Online Users Group, Spl. Librs. Assn., Am. Assn. Law Librs. Office: Pierce Atwood One Monument Sq Portland ME 04101

BEDDALL, THOMAS HENRY, lawyer; b. Pottsville, Pa., Apr. 24, 1922; s. Thomas and Martha Roberta (Gallagher) B.; m. Priscilla Kimball, July 26, 1956 (dec.); children: Laurence, Frederic, Margaret, and Katherine; m. Catherine C. Larmore, May 2, 1994. AB, Yale U., 1943; LL.B., U. Va., 1950. Bar: N.Y. 1951, D.C. 1968. Assoc. Sullivan & Cromwell, N.Y.C., 1950-57, Paul Mellon Interests, Washington, 1957-89. Dir. Carborundum Co., Niagara Falls, N.Y., 1960-78; lectr. U. Va., 1976-79 Chmn. bd. trustees Sheridan Sch., Washington, 1972-74; trustee Va. Mus. and Fedn., 1984-99, Nat. Mus. of Racing, 1988-2001, The Textile Mus., 1990-92, Va. State Parks Found., 1992-96. Mem. Bar Assn. City N.Y., Mil. Order World Wars, Order of Coif, Raven Soc., Metropolitan Club, Phi Delta Phi, Omicron Delta Kappa, Pi Delta Epsilon, Chi Psi. Office: PO Box 914 Middleburg VA 20118-0914

BEDDOW, JOHN WARREN, lawyer; b. Washington, Apr. 8, 1952; s. Thomas John and Virginia Coleburn (Fenton) B.; m. Mary Christine Jackson, July 27, 1974; children: Blair Kristen, Christopher John. BS, U. N.C., 1974, JD, 1977. Bar: N.C. 1977, U.S. Dist. Ct. (we. dist.) N.C. 1977, U.S. Tax Ct. 1979. Assoc. Lindsey, Schrimsher, Erwin, Bernhardt & Hewitt, Charlotte, 1977-79; ptnr. Lindsey, Schrimsher, Erwin, Bernhardt, Hewitt & Beddow, Charlotte, 1979-80, Erwin & Beddow, Charlotte, 1980-85, Erwin, Beddow & Reese, Charlotte, 1985-86, Weinstein & Sturges, Charlotte, 1986-94, James, McElroy & Diehl, P.A., Charlotte, 1994—. Mem. ABA, N.C. Bar Assn. (council mem. tax sect. 1981-88), Phi Beta Kappa, Phi Eta Sigma. Clubs: Carmel Country (Charlotte). Democrat. Episcopalian. Avocations: hunting, fishing, golf. Probate (including wills, trusts), Property, real (including real estate development, water), Personal income taxation. Office: James McElroy & Diehl PA 600 S College St Charlotte NC 28202-1825

BEDDOW, RICHARD HAROLD, judge; b. Springfield, Mass., Jan. 3, 1932; s. Richard Harold and Elizabeth Christine (Geehern) B.; m. Trudy C. Howells, Jan. 14, 1967; children: Catherine Elizabeth Almand, Elissa Christine. BS, U. Mass., 1953; LLB, Boston Coll, 1959. Bar: Mass. 1960. Atty. ICC, Washington, 1959-69, mem. rev. bd., 1969-73, adminstrv. law judge, 1973-81, NLRB, Washington, 1981—2002, ret., 2002—. With USN, 1953-55. Roman Catholic. Avocation: landscape gardening. Home: 2406 Rockwood Rd Accokeek MD 20607-9584

BEDOS, JEAN-LUC, lawyer; b. France, 1956; m. Valerie d'Anglejan; children: Bastien, Théa. M, Paris Law Sch., 1979, PhD, 1984; LLM, Harvard U., 1983. Bar: Paris. Assoc. White & Case, Paris and N.Y.C., 1983—87, Slaughter and May, Paris and London, 1988—95; European counsel Proskauer Rose, Paris, 1996—98; ptnr. Lefevre Pelletier, Paris, 1999—. Prof. law Hautes Etudes Commerciales, Paris, 1985—92. Founder, chmn. Droits D'Urgence, Paris, 1995—. Mem.: Racing Club de France. Corporate, general, Mergers and acquisitions, Finance. Office: Lefevre Pelletier 136 Ave des Champs Elysees 75008 Paris France Office Fax: (33-1) 53.93.33.75. E-mail: jlbedos@lpalaw.com.

BEE, PETER ALOYSIUS, lawyer; b. Feb. 28, 1952; s. William Pelham and Jane Ann (Purcell) Bee; m. Marianne Christine Falanga; children: Elizabeth, Katharine, Victoria. BA, St. John's U., Jamaica, N.Y., 1973, JD, 1976. Bar: Fla. 1976, N.Y. 1977. Legis. aide, legal intern County of Nassau, NY, 1970—77, dep. county atty., 1977—80; ptnr. Bee Ready Fishbein Hatter & Donovan, LLP (successor to Bee, Eisman & Ready, LLP), Mineola, 1980—. Village trustee Village of Garden City, NY. Mem.: Indsl. Rels. Rsch. Assn., Nassau County Bar Assn. (labor law com.), Cherry Valley Club (Garden City). Roman Catholic. Corporate, general, General practice, Labor (including EEOC, Fair Labor Standards Act, labor-management relations, NLRB, OSHA). Home: 60 Poplar St Garden City NY 11530-6327 Office: Bee Ready Fishbein Hatter & Donovan LLP 170 Old Country Rd Mineola NY 11501-4307 E-mail: pbee@beereadylaw.com.

BEEBE, MIKE, state attorney general; b. Amagon, Ark., Dec. 28, 1946; s. Lester Kendall and Meadean Louise (Quattlebaum) B.; m. Ginger Croom, Mar. 2, 1979; 1 child, Kyle. BA, Ark. State U., 1968; JD, U. Ark., 1972. Bar: Ark. 1972. Ptnr. Lightle, Beebe, Raney, Bell & Simpson, Searcy, Ark., 1972—2003; mem. Ark. Senate, 1983—2003; pres. Ark. Senate, 2001—03; atty. gen. State of Ark., 2003—. Editor (in-Chief): U. Ark. Sch. of Law, 1972. Trustee Ark. State U., Jonesboro, 1974-79, chmn. bd. trustees, 1977-79; chmn. Ctrl. Ark. Gen. Hosp., Searcy, 1985-93. Named Outstanding Trial Lawyer, Ark., 1982. Mem. Ark. Mcpl. League (dist. svc. award 1985), Searcy C. of C. Democrat. Episcopalian. Avocation: golf. Office: Atty Gen 200 Tower Bldg 323 Center St Little Rock AR 72201

BEECH, JOHNNY GALE, lawyer; b. Chickasha, Okla., Sept. 18, 1954; s. Lovell Gale and Lucille L. (Phillips) B.; m. Judy Carol Schroeder, Dec. 31, 1977. BS, Southwestern Okla. State U., 1977; JD, U. Ark., Little Rock, 1980; LLM in Energy-Environment, Tulane U., 1985. Bar: Okla. 1980, U.S. Dist. Ct. (we. dist.) Okla. 1982, U.S. Dist. Ct. (no. dist.) Tex. 1983, U.S. Dist. Ct. (no. dist.) Okla. 1986, U.S. Dist. Ct. (ea. dist.) Okla. 1997. Assoc. Meacham, Meacham and Meacham, Clinton, Okla., 1980-84, Ford & Brown, Enid, Okla., 1985-86, Wright & Sawyer, Enid, 1986-88, Phillips, McFall, McCaffrey, McVay, Sheets and Lovelace, Oklahoma City, 1988-90; ptnr., mng. dir. Lester & Bryant, Oklahoma City, 1990-96; mgr. Beech Edwards and Percival PLLC, 1996—2001; of counsel Mulinix, Ogden, Hall, Andrews & Ludlam, PLLC, 2002—. Bd. dirs. Proserv Basketball; mcpl. judge Town of Arapaho, Okla., 1982-84; assoc. gen. counsel Proserv Basketball, 1996—. Bd. dirs. Jr. Achievement Garfield County, Enid, 1986-88; commr. Little League Baseball; bd. dirs., treas. Edmond All Sports, Inc., 1999; mem. Bus. Sch. adv. coun. Southwestern U. Mem. ABA (real property, probate and trusts sect.), ATLA, Okla. Bar Assn. (law sch. com. 1989-91, uniform laws com. 1994-96, chmn. desk manual com. young lawyers div., uniform laws com. 1994—), Okla. Assn. Def. Counsel, Garfield County Bar Assn. (treas. 1988-89), Am. Bus. Club, Southwestern Okla. State U. Alumni Assn. (pres. 1983-86, parliamentarian 1992, exec. counsel 1986—, pres. 1997—), Southwestern Sch. Bus. Alumni Assn. (v.p. 1980-92, pres. 1992-93), Jaycees, Am. Bus. Club, Phi Alpha Delta (sec. 1979). Democrat. Methodist. Avocations: reading, bike racing. Banking, State civil litigation, Sports. Home: 702 N Cook St Cordell OK 73632-3002 Office: Mulinix Ogden Hall Andrews & Ludlam 204 N Robinson Ste 3100 Oklahoma City OK 73102 E-mail: jgblaw@hotmail.com.

BEEM, JACK DARREL, lawyer; b. Chgo., Nov. 17, 1931; AB, U. Chgo., 1952, JD, 1955. Bar: Ill. 1955. Assoc. firm Wilson & McIlvaine, Chgo., 1958-63; ptnr. firm Baker & McKenzie, Chgo., 1963—. Mem. vis. com. Ctr. for East Asian Studies U. Chgo. Decorated Order of the Sacred Treasure gold rays with rosette Japan. Mem. ABA, Chgo. Bar Assn., Japan-Am. Soc. Chgo. (pres. 1988-92), Am. Fgn. Law Assn. (chmn. Chgo. br.), Univ. Club of Chgo., Tokyo Club, Tokyo Am. Club, Sons Am. Revolution, Phi Beta Kappa, Alpha Delta Phi. Private international. Home: 175 E Delaware Pl Apt 8104 Chicago IL 60611-7746 Office: Baker & McKenzie 1 Prudential Plz 130 E Randolph St Ste 3700 Chicago IL 60601-6342

BEEMER, JOHN BARRY, lawyer; b. Scranton, Pa., Sept. 4, 1941; s. Ellis and Rose Mary (Costello) B.; m. Diane Montgomery Fletcher, July 18, 1964 (dec. July 1999); children: David, Bruce. BS, U. Scranton, 1963; LL.B., George Washington U., 1966. Bar: Pa. 1966, U.S. Supreme Ct. 1980; cert. civil trial adv. Nat. Bd. Trial Advocacy. Law clk. U.S. Ct. Claims, 1966-67; clk. to judge U.S. Dist. Ct. (mid. dist.) Pa., 1967-68; assoc. Warren, Hill, Henkelman & McMenamin, Scranton, 1968-72; ptnr. Beemer, Brier, Rinaldi & Fendrick, 1972-77; pres. Beemer, Rinaldi, Fendrick & Mellody, P.C., Scranton, 1977-83; ptnr. Beemer & Beemer, Scranton, 1984—. Lectr. in law U. Scranton, 1969-70. Chmn. com. constn. and by-laws revision Lackawanna (county Pa.) United Fund., 1971; nat. chmn. U. Scranton Alumni Fund Drive, 1972. Mem. ABA, Pa. Bar Assn., Lackawanna Bar Assn. (bd. dirs. 1988—), Assn. Trial Lawyers Am., Pa. Trial Lawyers Assn., Phi Delta Phi. Federal civil litigation, State civil litigation, Criminal. Office: 114-116 N Abington Rd Clarks Summit PA 18411 E-mail: bbeemer123@aol.com.

BEER, PETER HILL, federal judge; b. New Orleans, Apr. 12, 1928; s. Mose Haas and Henret (Lowenburg) B.; children: Kimberly Beer Bailes, Kenneth, Dana Beer Long-Innes; m. Marjorie Barry, July 14, 1985. BBA, Tulane U., 1949, LLB, 1952; LLM, U. Va., 1986. Bar: La. 1952. Successively assoc., ptnr., sr. ptnr. Montgomery, Barnett, Brown & Read, New Orleans, 1955-74; judge La. Ct. Appeal, 1974-79, U.S. Dist. Ct. (ea. dist.) La., New Orleans, 1979—. Vice chmn. La. Appellate Judges Conf.; apptd. by chief justice of U.S. to state-fed. com. Jud. Conf. U.S., 1985-89; apptd. by chief justice of U.S. to Nat. Jud. Coun. State and Fed. Cts., 1993—. Mem. bd. mgrs. Touro Infirmary, New Orleans, 1969-74; mem. exec. com. Bur. Govtl. Rsch., 1965-69; chmn. profl. divsn. United Fund New Orleans, 1966-69; mem. New Orleans City Coun., 1969-74, v.p., 1972-74. Capt. USAF, 1952-55. Decorated Bronze Star. Mem. ABA (mem. ho. dels.), Am. Judicature Soc., Fed. Bar Assn., La. Bar Assn., Nat. Lawyers Club, So. Yacht Club, St. John Golf Club. Jewish. Home: 133 Bellaire Dr New Orleans LA 70124-1008 also: 204 3rd Ave Pass Christian MS 39571-3214 Office: US Dist Ct US Courthouse 500 Camp St New Orleans LA 70130-3313

BEERBOWER, CYNTHIA GIBSON, lawyer; b. Dayton, Ohio, June 25, 1949; d. Charles Augustus and Sarah (Rittenhouse) Gibson; m. John Edwin Beerbower, Aug. 28, 1971; children: John Eliot, Sarah Rittenhouse. BA, Mt. Holyoke Coll., 1971; JD, Boston U., 1974; LLB, Cambridge (Eng.) U., 1976. Bar: N.Y. 1975. Assoc. Cadwalader, Wickersham & Taft, N.Y.C., 1975-76, Simpson, Thacher & Bartlett, N.Y.C., 1977-81, ptnr., 1981-93; internat. tax counsel, dept. asst. sec. Dept. Treasury, Washington, 1993-96; chmn., CEO Reeve Ct. Ins. Ltd., 1997—2001; prin. The Quellos Group, N.Y.C., 2001—. Mem. ABA, Assn. Bar City N.Y., N.Y. State Bar Assn. (com. co-chmn. 1987-93). Presbyterian. Corporate taxation. Home: 720 Park Ave New York NY 10021-4954 Office: 667 Madison Ave New York NY 10021

BEERBOWER, JOHN EDWIN, lawyer; b. Columbus, Ohio, Jan. 7, 1948; m. Cynthia Gibson, Aug. 28, 1971; children: John Eliot, Sarah Rittenhouse. BA, Amherst Coll., 1970; JD, Harvard U., 1973; student, Trinity Coll., Cambridge (Eng.) U. Bar: N.Y. 1975. Mem. Cravath, Swaine & Moore, LLP, N.Y.C., 1980—. Bd. govs. Mannes Coll. Music, 1993—, vice chmn., 2000—02, chmn., 2002—; com. on instl. policy New Sch. U., 2003—; trustee Madison Ave. Presbyn. Ch., 1995—2001, pres. bd. trustees, 2000—01. Mem. ABA, N.Y. State Bar Assn., N.Y. Law Inst. (mem. nominating com.), Assn. of Bar of City of N.Y. (chmn. profl. and jud. ethics com. 1990-93), Soc. of Alumni Amherst Coll. (pres. 1994-95), Union Internat. Advocats, Am. Econ Assn., Phi Beta Kappa. Office: Cravath Swaine & Moore LLP Worldwide Plz 825 8th Ave Fl 40 New York NY 10019-7416

BEERS, DONALD OSBORNE, lawyer; b. Sodus, N.Y., May 28, 1949; s. John Taylor and Edna Viola (DuMond) B.; m. Deborah Constance Merkamp, Mar. 16, 1974; children: Laura DuMond, Emily Katherine, Michael Osborne, Andrew Lawrence. AB, Dartmouth Coll., 1971; JD, Columbia U., 1974. Bar: D.C. 1986, U.S. Ct. Appeals (10th cir.) 1978, U.S. Ct. Appeals (D.C. cir.) 1979, U.S. Ct. Appeals (5th cir.) 1980, U.S. Ct. Appeals (fed. cir.) 1990, U.S. Dist. Ct. D.C. 1986, U.S. Supreme Ct. 1986. Law clk. to judge U.S. Dist. Ct. (so. dist.) N.Y., N.Y.C., 1974-75; atty. office chief counsel FDA, Rockville, Md., 1975-85; of counsel McCutchen, Doyle, Brown & Enersen, Washington, 1985-87; ptnr. Arnold & Porter, 1987—. Lectr. U. Pa. Law Sch., Phila., 1982-84. Author: Generic and Innovator Drugs: A Guide to FDA Approval Requirements, 5th edit., 1999; contbr. articles to profl. jours. Mem. ABA. Democrat. Methodist. Federal civil litigation, Food and drug. Office: 555 12th St NW Washington DC 20004-1200

BEEZER, ROBERT RENAUT, federal judge; b. Seattle, July 21, 1928; s. Arnold Roswell and Josephine (May) B.; m. Hazlehurst Plant Smith, June 15, 1957; children: Robert Arnold, John Leighton, Mary Allison. Student, U. Wash., 1946-48, 51; BA, U. Va., 1951, LLB, 1956. Bar: Wash. 1956,

U.S. Supreme Ct. 1968. Ptnr. Schweppe, Krug, Tausend & Beezer, P.S., Seattle, 1956-84; judge U.S. Ct. Appeals (9th cir.), Seattle, 1984-96, sr. judge, 1996—. Alt. mem. Wash. Jud. Qualifications Commn., Olympia, 1981-84 1st lt. USMCR, 1951-53 Fellow Am. Coll. Trust and Estate Counsel, Am. Bar Found.; mem. ABA, Seattle-King County Bar Assn. (pres. 1975-76), Wash. Bar Assn. (bd. govs. 1980-83) Clubs: Rainier, Tennis (Seattle). Office: US Ct Appeals 802 US Courthouse 1010 5th Ave Seattle WA 98104-1195 E-mail: judge_beezer@ca9.uscourts.gov.

BEEZLEY, SARA S. lawyer; b. Nov. 1955; BA, So. Meth. U.; JD, Duke U. Bar: Kans. 1979. Atty., Girard, Kans. Mem.: Kans. Bar Assn. (pres.). Office: 126 S Ozark Girard KS 66743*

BEGAM, ROBERT GEORGE, lawyer; b. N.Y.C., Apr. 5, 1928; s. George and Hilda M. (Hirt) B.; m. Helen C. Clark, July 24, 1949; children—Richard, Lorinda, Michael. BA, Yale U., 1949, LL.B., 1952. Bar: N.Y. bar 1952, Ariz. bar 1956, U.S. Dist. Ct. Ariz. 1957, U.S. Ct. Appeals (9th cir.) 1958, U.S Supreme Ct. 1973. Assoc. firm Cravath, Swaine & Moore, N.Y.C., 1952-54; spl. counsel State of Ariz., Colorado River Litigation in U.S. Supreme Ct., 1956-58; pres. Begam, Lewis Marks & Wolfe, P.A., Phoenix. Author: Fireball, 1987. Pres. Ariz. Repertory Theater, 1960—66; trustee Atla Roscoe Pound Found.; bd. dirs. Boys Clubs of Met. Phoenix; bd. govs. Welzmann Inst. Sci., Rehovot, Israel; pres. Am. Com. for Welzmann Inst. of Sci., 1996—98, chmn. fin. resource devel., 2000—; bd. dirs. Phoenix Theater Ctr., 1955—60, 1987—92, Ariz. Theatre Co., 2001—, Shakespeare-Sedona Theatre Co. Fellow: Internat. Soc. Barristers; mem.: State Bar Ariz. (cert. specialist in injury and wrongful death litigation), Am. Bd. Trial Advocates (bd. dirs.), Western Trial Lawyers Assn. (pres. 1970), ATLA (pres. 1976—77, chmn. polit. action com. 1979—86), Phoenix Country Club, Yale Club (N.Y.C.). Avocations: writing, theater, golf. Personal injury (including property damage), Product liability. Office: Begam Lewis Marks & Wolfe 111 W Monroe St Ste 1400 Phoenix AZ 85003-1787 E-mail: begam@fastq.com.

BEGGS, HARRY MARK, lawyer; b. Los Angeles, Nov. 15, 1941; s. John Edgar and Agnes (Kentro) B.; m. Sandra Lynne Mikal, May 25, 1963; children: Brendan, Sean, Corey, Michael. Student, Ariz. State U., 1959-61, Phoenix Coll., 1961; LLB, U. Ariz., 1964. Bar: Ariz. 1964, U.S. Dist. Ct. Ariz. 1964, U.S. Ct. Appeals (9th cir.) 1973, U.S. Ct. Appeals (fed. cir.) 1995, U.S. Supreme Ct. 1991. Assoc. Carson Messinger Elliott Laughlin & Ragan, Phoenix, 1964-69, ptnr., 1969-93; mem., mng. lawyer Carson Messinger Elliott Laughlin & Ragan, P.L.L.C., Phoenix, 1994—. Mem. editorial bd. Ariz. Law Rev. 1963-64; contbr. articles to profl. jours. Recipient award for highest grade on state bar exam. Atty. Gen. Ariz., 1964; Fegtly Moot Ct. award, 1963, 64; Abner S. Lipscomb scholar U. Ariz. Law Sch., 1963. Fellow Ariz. Bar Found. (founder); mem. State Bar Ariz., Ariz. Acad., Maricopa County Bar Assn. Federal civil litigation, General civil litigation, State civil litigation. Office: PO Box 33907 Phoenix AZ 85067-3907 E-mail: hbeggs@carsonlaw-az.com.

BEGHE, RENATO, federal judge; b. Chgo., Mar. 12, 1933; s. Bruno and Emmavve (Frymire) B.; m. Bina House, July 10, 1954; children: Eliza Ashley, Francesca Forbes, Adam House, Jason Deneen. BA, U. Chgo., 1951, JD, 1954. Bar: N.Y. 1955. Practiced in, N.Y.C.; assoc. Carter, Ledyard & Milburn, 1954-65, ptnr., 1965-83, Morgan, Lewis & Bockius, 1983-89; judge U.S. Tax Ct., Washington, 1991—. Lectr. N.Y. U. Fed. Tax Inst., 1967, 78, U. Chgo. Fed. Tax Conf., 1974, 80, 86, also other profl. confs. Mng. editor U. Chgo. Law Rev., 1953-54; contbr. articles to profl. jours. Mem. ABA, Internat. Bar Assn., N.Y. State Bar Assn. (chmn. tax sect. 1977-78), Assn. of Bar of City of N.Y. (chmn. art law com. 1980-83), Am. Law Inst., Internat. Fiscal Assn., Am. Coll. Tax Counsel, America-Italy Soc. Inc. (bd. dirs. 1980-92), Phi Beta Kappa, Order of Coif, Phi Gamma Delta. Home: 633 E St SE Washington DC 20003-2716 Office: US Tax Ct 400 2nd St NW Washington DC 20217-0002

BEGLEITER, MARTIN DAVID, law educator, consultant; b. Middletown, Conn., Oct. 31, 1945; s. Walter and Anne Begleiter; m. Ronni Ann Frankel, Aug. 17, 1969; children: Wendy Cara, Hilary Ann. BA, U. Rochester, 1967; JD, Cornell U., 1970. Bar: N.Y. 1970, U.S. Dist. Ct. (ea. dist.) N.Y. 1971, U.S. Ct. Appeals (2d cir.) 1975. Assoc. Kelley Drye & Warren, N.Y.C., 1970—77; assoc. prof. Law Sch., Drake U., Des Moines, 1977—80, prof., 1980—87, 1993—, Richard M. and Anita Calkins disting. prof. law, 1987—93. Contbr. articles to legal jours. Mem. ABA (com. on estate and gift taxes, taxation sect. 1980—, com. malpractice, real property, probate and trust law sect. 1999—, com. on tax legislation and regulations, lifetime transfers, real property, probate and trust law sect. 1980-2002, study com. law reform 1996-2002, chmn. task force on spl. use valuation 1988-93, advisor Nat. Conf. Commns. on Uniform State Laws 1988-93), Iowa Bar Assn. (adviser, resource person, probate, trust sect. 1983-89, 93—), Am. Law Inst. (adviser restatement 3d trusts 1994—). Jewish. Avocations: science fiction, golf. Office: Drake U Sch Law 2507 University Ave Des Moines IA 50311 E-mail: martin.begleiter@drake.edu.

BEGLEY, LOUIS, novelist, lawyer; b. Stryj, Poland, Oct. 6, 1933; came to U.S., 1948, naturalized, 1953; s. Edward David Begley and Frances Hauser; m. Sally Higginson, Feb. 11, 1956 (div. May 1970); children: Peter Higginson, Amey B. Larmore, Adam C.; m. Anne Muhlstein Dujarric de la Riviere, Mar. 30, 1974. AB summa cum laude, Harvard U., 1954, LLB magna cum laude, 1959. Bar: N.Y. 1961. Assoc. Debevoise & Plimpton, N.Y.C., 1959-67, ptnr., 1968—. Author: Wartime Lies, 1991, The Man Who Was Late, 1993, As Max Saw It, 1994, About Schmidt, 1996, Mistler's Exit, 1998, Schmidt Delivered, 2000, Das Gelobte Land, 2001, Shipwreck, 2003; author: (with Anka Muhlstein) Venedig unter vier Augen, 2003; contbr. articles and revs. to newspapers and periodicals. With U.S. Army, 1954-56. Recipient Irish Times-Aer Lingus Internat. Fiction Prize, 1991, PEN/Hemingway Found. award, 1992, Prix Medicis Etranger, 1992, Harold U. Ribalow prize, 1992, award in Lit., Am. Acad. Arts and Letters, 1995, Jeanette Schocker prize, 1995, Konrad-Adenauer-Stiftung Literaturpreis, 2000, Chevalier de l'Ordre des Arts et Lettres. Mem. Am. Philos. Soc., PEN Am. Ctr. (pres. 1993-95, trustee 1995-2001), Coun. Fgn. Rels., Century Assn. Democrat. Corporate, general, Private international, Mergers and acquisitions. Office: Debevoise & Plimpton 919 3rd Ave 46th Fl New York NY 10022-3904

BEHR, RALPH STEVEN, lawyer; b. June 19, 1951; BA cum laude, SUNY, Albany, 1973; JD, Hofstra U., 1976. Bar: Oreg. 1976, N.Y. 1977, Fla. 1988, U.S.Dist. Ct. (so. dist.) Fla. 1991, U.S. Dist. Ct. (middle dist.) Fla. 1991, U.S. Dist. Ct. (we. dist.) Pa. 1991, U.S. Supreme Ct. 1991; bd. cert. criminal trial lawyer; cert. real estate broker, N.Y.; lic. commodity futures trading advisor; bd. cert. in criminal trial law Fla. Bar. Legis. clk. N.Y. State Assembly, Albany, 1971-73; dist. atty. Nassau County (N.Y.) Dist. Atty.'s Office, 1975-76; pvt. practice Portland, Oreg., 1976-77; v.p., counsel Foods Oils Corp., Carlstadt, N.J., 1977-88; pvt. practice Pvt. Label mag., Deerfield Beach, Fla., 1988—; v.p., counsel Foods Oils Corp., Carlstadt, N.J., 1977-88. Instr. legal rsch. and writing Hofstra U., 1974-76; tchg. asst. Columbia U., N.Y.C. Legal editor Pvt. Label Mag., 1978-82. Vol. atty. N.Y. Family Ct.; commr. Housing Authority Deerfield Beach, 1988—; treas. campaign Lisa G. Trachman County Ct. Judge, 1994. Goethe Inst. scholar West German Govt., 1969, N.Y. State Regents scholar, 1969. Mem. Nat. Assn. Criminal Def. Lawyers, Fla. Bar Assn. Fed. Def. Attys., Fla. Assn. Criminal Def. Lawyers, Broward Assn. Criminal Def. Lawyers (bd. dirs., mem. legis. com.), Broward County Bar Assn. (ethics com.), Pvt. Label Mfrs. Assn. (bd. dirs. 1980-83, chmn. legal affairs com. 1983-86). Avocations: sailing, golf. Corporate, general, Criminal, Public international. Office: 101 SE 10th St Fort Lauderdale FL 33316-1023 Fax: 954-761-1524. E-mail: behr@aksi.net., behr@ralphbehr.com.

BEHRENDT, JOHN THOMAS, lawyer; b. Syracuse, Kans., Oct. 26, 1945; s. Thomas Franklin Behrendt, Anna Iola (Carrithers) Behrendt; m. Theresa Ann Elmore, Oct. 27, 1985; children from previous marriage: Todd Thomas, Gretchen Jean. BA, Sterling Coll.; JD cum laude, U. Minn. Bar: Califl. 1971, Tex. 1973, N.Y. 1989. Assoc. Gibson, Dunn & Crutcher, L.A., 1970—71, sr. ptnr., 1974—. Lectr. Practicing Law Inst., Acctg. for Lawyers. Capt. JAGC U.S. Army, 1971—74. Mem.: ABA (law and acctg. com.), Order of Coif, L.A. County Bar Assn., Tuxedo Club N.Y., Union League Club N.Y., Jonathan Club L.A. Republican. Presbyterian. Federal civil litigation, Corporate, general, Private international. Office: Gibson Dunn & Crutcher 200 Park Ave Fl 47 New York NY 10166-0193

BEIHL, FREDERICK, lawyer; b. St. Joseph, Mo., Jan. 26, 1932; s. Ernst F. and Evelyn E. (Kline) B.; m. Lillis Prater, Mar. 3, 1962. AB, U. Mo., 1953, LLB, 1955. Bar: Mo. 1955, U.S. Supreme Ct. 1968. With Shook Hardy & Bacon, Kansas City, 1955-99, ptnr., 1961-99, shareholder, 1992-99. Chmn. bd. dirs. UMKC Conservatory of Music, Kansas City, 1988-91, Visiting Nurses Assn., Kansas City, 1977-79; pres. Heart of Am. Family and Children Svcs., Kansas City, 1982-84, Friends of Art Nelson Mus., Kansas City, 1979-81. Avocations: tennis, skiing, art collecting. Office: Shook Hardy & Bacon 1200 Main St Ste 3000 Kansas City MO 64105-2122 E-mail: fbeihl@shb.com.

BEIRNE, MARTIN DOUGLAS, lawyer; b. N.Y.C., Oct. 24, 1944; s. Martin Douglas and Catherine Anne Beirne; m. Kathleen Harrington; children: Martin, Shannon, Kelley. BS, Spring Hill Coll., 1966; JD with honors, St. Mary's U., 1969. Bar: Tex. 1969, U.S. Dist. Ct. (ea. dist.) Tex. 1972, U.S. Dist. Ct. (so. dist.) Tex. 1971, U.S. Dist. Ct. (no. dist.) Tex., U.S. Dist. Ct. (we. dist.) Tex., U.S. Ct. Appeals (5th and 11th cirs.) 1974, U.S. Dist. Ct. (ea. dist.) Calif., U.S. Supreme Ct. 1975. Ptnr. Fulbright & Jaworski, Houston, 1971-85; mng. ptnr. Beirne, Maynard & Parsons, Houston, 1985—. Editor-in-chief St. Mary's Law Rev. Bd. dirs. St. Thomas U., Houston Law Rev. Found., NCCJ. Capt. U.S. Army, 1969-71. Fellow Am. Bar Found., Tex. Bar Found.; mem. ABA, Tex. Bar Assn., Houston Bar Assn., Coronado Club, The Houstonian Club, Legatus-U. Houston Law Sch. Found. Roman Catholic. Federal civil litigation, State civil litigation, Corporate, general. Office: Beirne Maynard & Parsons LLP 1300 Post Oak Blvd Fl 24 Houston TX 77056-3028

BEISWANGER, GARY LEE, lawyer; b. Billings, Mont., May 31, 1938; BA in Philosophy, History-Polit. Sci., U. Mont., 1960, LLB, 1963. Bar: Mont. 1963, U.S. Dist. Ct. Mont. 1963, U.S. Ct. Appeals (9th cir.) 1987. Pvt. practice, Billings, 1965—. Mem. ABA, ATLA, State Bar Mont., Mont. Trial Lawyers Assn., Yellowstone County Bar Assn. General civil litigation, Property, real (including real estate development, water), Civil rights. Office: Rocky Village Ctr I 1500 Poly Dr Billings MT 59102-1748 E-mail: garylbeiswanger@lawyer.com.

BEITEL, BERNARD, lawyer; b. Bklyn., May 14, 1931; s. Samuel and Evelyn (Cohen) Beitel; m. Ruth B. Schneider, Feb. 15, 1959; children: Karin A., Jennifer H. Friedman, Suzanne B. Beitel-Smith. BA, Bklyn. Coll., 1952; LLB, Bklyn. Law Sch., 1954. Bar: NY 55, U.S. Dist. Ct. (so. dist.) NY 57, U.S. Tax Ct 88, U.S. Ct. Appeals 90. Law clk. Gainsburg, Gottlieb, Levitan & Cole, N.Y.C., 1953—54, assoc., 1956—64, ptnr., 1964—75, Otterbourg, Steindler, Houston & Rosen, P.C., N.Y.C., 1975—96, of counsel, 1996—. Pres., bd. dirs. Lawyers Assn. of Textile and Apparel Industries, 1980—90; arbitrator Am. Arbitration Assn., NY, 1980—90. Bd. dirs., pres. Coop.-Linden Towers Sect. II, Flushing, NY, 1963—70; trustee Temple Beth Am, Merrick, NY, 2002. Cpl. U.S. Army, 1954—56. Mem.: ABA, NY State Bar Assn., Assn. Comml. Fin. Attys. Avocation: golf. Alternative dispute resolution, Bankruptcy, General civil litigation. Office: Otterbourg Steindler Houston & Rosen PC 230 Park Ave New York NY 10169-0075 Fax: 212-682-6104. E-mail: BBeitel@oshr.com.

BEITLING, S. RICHARD, lawyer; b. Kansas CIty, Dec. 24, 1927; s. Seaman Peter and Lillian Lester Beitling; children: Richard Michael, Susan Carol Hemingway, Ann Noreen, Bridgett Careen Cool, Michael J. BA, JD, U. Mo., 1956. Bar: Mo. 1956. Asst. prosecuting atty. Jackson County, Kansas City, 1957—65; atty. pvt. practice, 1956—. Pres. Kansas City Young Dems., 1954—55. With USN, 1946—47. Mem.: Scottish Rite, Masons, Tau Kappa Epsilon, Phi Delta Phi. Democrat. Methodist. Avocations: tennis, reading, music, cooking. Criminal, Family and matrimonial, Transportation. Fax: 816-753-2441.

BEIZER, LANCE KURT, lawyer; b. Hartford, Conn., Sept. 8, 1938; s. Lawrence Sidney and Victoria Merriam (Kaplan) B. BA in Sociology, Brandeis U., 1960; MA in English, San Jose State U., 1967; JD, U. San Diego, 1975. Bar: Calif. 1975. Selective svc. affairs coord. U. Calif., 1969-73, vet. affairs coord., 1973-75; vet. outreach coord. San Diego Community Coll. Dist., 1975-76; dep. dist. atty. Santa Clara County, Calif., 1976—2002. Bd. mgrs. Santa Clara Valley S.W. YMCA, Saratoga, Calif., 1988- , chair, 1991-93; bd. dirs. The Lumen Found., San Francisco, 1985—; bd. dirs. Fedn. Cmty. Ministries, Calif., 1992—, chmn., 1996—; bd. dirs. Apostolic Cath. Orthodox Ch., 1997—. Lt. USNR, 1961-65. Mem. Nat. Assn. Counsel for Children, Am. Weil Soc., Mensa, Commonwealth Club. Republican. Episcopalian. Office: PO Box 1121 Campbell CA 95509-1121 E-mail: lbeizer@yahoo.com.

BEJARANO, DAVID, protective services official; BA in Bus. Adminstrn., Nat. U., 1983; grad., FBI Nat. Acad., 1997, FBI S.W. Command Coll., 1998. Joined San Diego Police Dept., 1979—, chief police, 1999—. U.S. marshal Calif. (so. dist.), 2003; bd. mem. Casa Familiar, Children's Initiative, Family Literacy Found. Office: US Marshals Svc 940 Front St #B-150 San Diego CA 92101

BELCHER, DENNIS IRL, lawyer; b. Wheeling, W.Va., Aug. 24, 1951; s. Finley Duncan Belcher and Ellen Jane (Huffman) Good; m. Vickie Marie Early, Aug. 2, 1975; children: Sarah Anne, Matthew Irl, Benjamin Scott. BA, Coll. William and Mary, 1973; JD, U. Richmond, 1976. Bar: Va. 1976, U.S. Tax Ct. 1978. Assoc. McGuire, Woods, Battle & Boothe, Richmond, Va., 1976-83, ptnr., 1983—, mem. exec. com., 1996—2001. Adj. prof. taxation Va. Commonwealth U., Richmond, 1985-88. Co-author: Business Tax Planning Forms for Businesses and Individuals, 1985. Chmn. Richmond chpt. Am. Heart Assn., 1984-85; trustee St. Christopher's Sch., 1993-2003. Fellow Am. Coll. Trust and Estate Counsel (bd. regents 1999—); mem. ABA (real property and probate sect., sec. 1997-98, chmn. marital deduction com., vice chmn. lifetime transfers com., ho. of dels. 1998-99, vice chair probate divsn. 1999-2001, chair 2002-03), Va. Bar Assn. (wills and trusts and taxations sects.), Bull and Bear Club, Country Club of Va., Kinloch Golf Club. Presbyterian. Avocations: golf, farming. Corporate, general, Probate (including wills, trusts), Estate taxation. Office: McGuire Woods 1 James Ctr 901 East Cary St Richmond VA 23219 E-mail: dbelcher@mcguirewoods.com.

BELDEN, H. REGINALD, JR., lawyer; b. Greensburg, Pa., Jan. 20, 1942; BA, Lafayette Coll., 1963; JD, U. Pitts., 1966. Bar: Pa. 1966. Article editor U. Pitts. Law Review, 1965—66; county solicitor, 1972—76; mng. ptnr. Belden, Belden, Persin & Johnston, Greensburg. USAR, 1966—68. Fellow: Am. Coll. Trial Lawyers, Pa. Bar Found. (life), Am. Bar Found. (life); mem.: Westmoreland County Bar Assn. (pres. 1986—87), Pa. Bar Assn. (bd. govs. 1985—88, 1995—97, pres. 2001—02), Am. Judicature Soc., ABA (ho. dels. 2000—). Professional liability, General civil litigation, Business litigation. Office: Belden Law Belden Bldg 117 N Main St Greensburg PA 15601 E-mail: RBelden@beldenlaw.com.

BELDOCK, MYRON, lawyer; b. N.Y.C., Mar. 27, 1929; s. George J. and Irene (Goldstein) B.; m. Elizabeth G. Pease, June 28, 1953 (div. 1969); children: David, Jennifer, Hannah, Benjamin, Adam Schmalholz; m. Karen L. Dippold, June 19, 1986. BA, Hamilton Coll., 1950; LLB, Harvard U., 1958. Bar: (N.Y.) 1958, N.Y. (U.S. Dist. Ct. (ea. and so. dists.)) 1960, (U.S. Ct. Appeals (2d cir.)) 1960, (U.S. Supreme Ct.) 1973. Asst. U.S. Atty. U.S. Atty's Office, Eastern Dist., N.Y., 1958-60; assoc. Geist, Netter & Marx, N.Y.C., 1960-62; sole practice N.Y.C., 1962-64; ptnr. Beldock Levine & Hoffman LLP, N.Y.C., 1964—. Bd. dirs., v.p. Brotherhood-In-Action, N.Y.C., 1972—; bd. dirs. Brookdale Revolving Fund., N.Y.C., 1973-76. Served with U.S. Army, 1951-54. Mem. Assn. of Bar of City of N.Y. (spl. com. penology 1974-80, com. on judiciary 2000-2003), N.Y. County Lawyers Assn., Bklyn. Bar Assn., Kings County Criminal Bar Assn., N.Y. County Criminal Bar Assn., N.Y. State Assn. Criminal Def. Lawyers, Nat. Assn. Criminal Def. Lawyers, Nat. Lawyers Guild. Civil rights, General civil litigation, Criminal.

BELESS, ROSEMARY JUNE, lawyer; b. Salt Lake City, July 26, 1947; d. James W. and June (Callister) B. BA, U. Utah, 1969, MA, 1972, PhD, 1977, JD, 1980. Bar: Utah 1980, U.S. Dist. Ct. Utah 1980, U.S. Ct. Appeals (10th cir.) 1997, U.S. Supreme Ct. 2000. Instr. English dept. U. Utah, Salt Lake City, 1970-77; acting editor Rocky Mt. Rev. of Lang. and Lit., Salt Lake City, 1976-77, asst. editor, 1974-78; assoc. Fabian & Clendenin, Salt Lake City, 1980-81, Hugh C. Garner & Assocs., Salt Lake City, 1981-84, Fabian & Clendenin, Salt Lake City, 1984-86, ptnr., 1986—, dir., 1992-93. Co-chmn. mining com. Utah State Bar, 1986—, chmn. title stds. subcom., 1987-88, chmn. oil and gas com., 1988—. Contbr. articles to profl. jours. William H. Leary scholar, 1980; named Lawyer of Yr. Utah State Bar energy, natural resources and environ. sect., 1989-90. Mem. ABA (natural resource sect.), Utah Bar Assn. (treas. 1991-92, sec. 1992-93, v.p. 1993-94, pres. 1994-95, energy, natural resources and environ sect., Disting. Svc. award energy, natural resources and environ. Law sect. 2000), Rocky Mt. Mineral Law Found., Salt Lake County Bar Assn., Utah Wildlife Fedn. (dir. 1988-92), Utah Mining Assn. (dir. pub. lands, environ. and legis. com.), Phi Kappa Phi. Avocation: music. Oil, gas, and mineral, Environmental, Property, real (including real estate development, water). Office: Fabian & Clendenin 12th Fl 215 S State St Fl 12 Salt Lake City UT 84111-2319

BELL, ALLEN ANDREW, JR., lawyer; b. Paris, Ill., June 23, 1951; s. Allen Andrew and Mary Elizabeth (Charley) B.; m. Carol Anne Larson, June 15, 1974; children: Sara Elizabeth, Emily Anne, David Allen, Elizabeth Anne. BA, DePauw U., 1973; JD cum laude, Ind. U. - Indpls., 1980. Bar: Ill. 1980, Ind. 1980, U.S. Dist. Ct. (so. dist.) Ind. 1980, U.S. Dist. Ct. (ctrl. dist.) Ill. 1980, (so. dist.) Ill. 1990, U.S. Ct. Appeals (7th cir.) 1988, U.S. Supreme Ct., 1994. Underwriter Am. States Ins. Co., Indpls., 1973-80; assoc. Dillavou Overaker Asher & Smith, Paris, Ill., 1980-85; ptnr. Ruff, Garst & Bell, Paris, 1985-87, Ruff & Bell, 1987-94, Jones & Jones Law Office, P.C., 1994-2000; asst. state's atty. Edgar and Clark Counties, 1987, Edgar County, 2000—; pub. defender Edgar and Clark Counties, 1982-84, 87-91; pvt. practice, 2000—. Mem. City of Paris Planning Commn., 1985-94, City of Paris Police Pension Bd., 1988-93; treas. Edgar County Hist. Soc., 1984-87; mem. Wabash Valley coun. Boy Scouts Am., 1994-2001. Mem. Ill. State Bar Assn., Ind. State Bar Assn., Edgar County Bar Assn. (pres. 1982-83, v.p. 2000, sec. 2001—), Comml. Law League, KC. Republican. Roman Catholic. Bankruptcy, Commercial, consumer (including collections, credit), General practice. Office: PO Box 725 209 N Central Paris IL 61944-0725

BELL, DERRICK ALBERT, law educator, author, lecturer; b. Pitts., Nov. 6, 1930; s. Derrick Albert and Ada Elizabeth (Childress) B.; m. Jewel Allison Hairston, June 26, 1960 (dec. Aug. 1990); m. Janet Dewart, June 28, 1992; children: Derrick Albert III, Douglass Dubois, Carter Robeson. AB, Duquesne U., 1952; LLB, U. Pitts., 1957; hon. degree in law, Toogaloo Coll., 1983, Northeastern U., 1985, Mercy Coll., 1988, Allegheny Coll., 1989, Howard U., 1995, Bates Coll., 1997, Medgar Evers Coll., 1998. Bar: D.C. 1957, Pa. 1959, N.Y. State 1966, Calif. 1969. Atty. civil rights div. Dept. Justice, Washington, 1957-59; 1st asst. counsel NAACP Legal Def. Edn. Fund, N.Y.C., 1960-66; dep. dir. Office Civil Rights, HEW, Washington, 1966-68; exec. dir. Western Ctr. on Law and Poverty, 1968-69; lectr. law Harvard U., Cambridge, Mass., 1969-71, prof. law, 1971-80, 86-92; dean U. Oreg. Law Sch., 1981-85;, 1991-93. Vis. prof. NYU Sch. Law, 1991—. Author: Race, Racism and American Law, 1973, 4th edit., 2000, Constitutional Conflicts, 1992, Shades of Brown: New Perspectives on School Desegregation, 1980, And We Are Not Saved: The Elusive Quest for Racial Justice, 1987, Faces at the Bottom of the Well: The Permanence of American Racism, 1992, Confronting Authority: Reflections of an Ardent Protester, 1994, Ethical Ambition: Living a Life of Meaning and Worth, 2002. Mem. gospel choirs Psalms of Survival in an Alien Land Called Home, 1996, Constitutional Conflicts, 1997. 1st lt. USAF, 1952-54. Grantee Ford Found., 1972, 75, 91, 93, 94-96, NEH, 1980-81. Home: 444 Central Park W Apt 14B New York NY 10025-4358 Office: NYU Sch Law 40 Washington Sq S New York NY 10012-1005

BELL, DOUGLAS MCCALL, lawyer, judge; b. Somerset, Pa., June 23, 1955; s. David McCall and Kathryn Jeannette (Countryman) B.; m. Kathleen Joan Smith; 1 child. BA cum laude, Dickinson Coll., 1978; JD, Dickinson Sch. Law, 1981. Assoc. Bruacher, Keim & Saylor, Somerset, 1981-82, Keim & Bowman, Somerset, 1982-83; assoc. counsel Somerset County Pub. Defender, 1982; assoc. Keim, Bowman & Bell, Somerset, 1983-84, ptnr., 1984-86, Bowman & Bell, Somerset, 1986; pvt. practice law Berlin, Pa., 1986-93; solicitor Somerset County Recorder of Deeds, 1992-99, Indian Lake Borough Planning Commn., 1992-99; ptnr. Bell & Dickey, 1993—. Exec. officer Somerset County (Pa.) Builders Assn., 1986—; dist. justice Somerset County, 2000—. Rep. committeeman Somerset County, 1978-80; sec. Berlin Fife and Drum Corps, 1982-92; mem. exec. com. Somerset County Single County Authority Drug and Alcohol Commn., 1984-86; pro bono counsel Berlin Area Ambulance Assn., 1984—, Berlin Vol. Fire Dept., 1984—, Miller Meml. Cmty. Ctr., 1985—; v.p. SSHared, 1987-92; mem. steering com. Berlin Borough Sesquicentennial, 1987-88; chmn. Berlin Whiskey Rebellion Celebration, 1994—; mem. local coun. Luth. Ch., 1989-91; mem. Allegheny Synod Comms. Com., 1989-91, chmn., 1991; mem. Berlin Vol. Fire Dept.; trustee Meyershale Med. Ctr., 1998—; mem. dist. com. Forbes Trail Dist. Penn's Woods coun. Boy Scouts Am. Named one of Outstanding Young Men of Am., 1985; recipient Commonwealth of Pa. DPW Sec.'s Vol. award, 1994. Mem. Pa. Bar Assn., Somerset County Bar Assn. (exec. com. 1986-89), Lions (pres. Berlin club 1989-90), NRA, Berlin Profl. Soc., Masons, Luth. Hist. Soc., Berlin Area Hist. Soc., Meyersdale Area Hist. Soc. Avocations: skiing, sailing, hunting, fishing, martial music. Home: PO Box 51 Berlin PA 15530-0051 Office: 629 Fletcher St Berlin PA 15530-1353

BELL, HARRY FULLERTON, JR., lawyer; b. Charleston, W.Va., Nov. 17, 1954; s. Harry Fullerton and Kathryn Laura (Lewis) B. BS in Econs. cum laude, W.Va. U., 1977, JD, 1980. Bar: W.Va. 1980, U.S. Dist. Ct. (so. dist.) W.Va. 1980, U.S. Dist. Ct. (no. dist.) W.Va. 1986, U.S. Ct. Appeals (4th cir.) 1986. Asst. pros. atty. Kanawha County, Charleston, 1980-82; assoc. Kay, Casto, Chaney, Love & Wise, Charleston, 1982-85, ptnr., 1986-92, Bell and Bands, PLLC, Charleston, 1992—. Instr. Marshall U., Huntington, W.Va., 1984-86. Contbr. articles to profl. jours. Pres. fireman's civil svc. commn. City of Charleston, 1985-86; mem. adminstrv. bd. Christ Meth. Ch., Charleston, 1985-87, bd. trustees, 1986-87; bd. dirs. Charleston Civic Ctr., 1987-91, 2003—, chmn., 1989-91. Mem. W.Va. Bar Assn. (vice chmn. com. on lawyers profl. liability ins. 1984-85, 90—, chmn. 1985-87, young lawyers bd. 1985, cert. merit 1985, young lawyers sect. 1985), Kanawha County Bar Assn. (chmn. courthouse renovation com. 1984-85), Def. Trial Counsel of W.Va., Def. Rsch. Inst., W.Va. U. Alumni Assn. (treas. 1985, v.p. Kanawha County chpt. 1986, pres. 1986-88), Berry Hills Country

Club, Beta Gamma Sigma, Omicron Mu Epsilon. Republican. Avocations: sports car racing, flying, golf, tennis, skiing. Federal civil litigation, State civil litigation, Insurance. Home: 1235 Upper Ridgeway Rd Charleston WV 25314-1427 Office: Bell & Bands PLLC PO Box 1723 Charleston WV 25326-1723

BELL, JASON CAMERON, lawyer; b. Danville, Ill., Dec. 14, 1963; s. Lamont Bell and Marion (Turner) Butler; m. Yolanda Scott, June 19, 1992; children: Maurice, Ricky Scott, Marcus, Charles, Natalie. BS, Fla. A&M U., 1987; JD, Ill. Inst. Tech., 1997. CPA, Ill. Dir. after-sch. program Frontline Outreach, Orlando, Fla., 1987-88; acct. Washington, Pittman & McKeever, Chgo., 1989-91; acct., founder J. Cameron Bell & Assocs., Chgo., 1991—; atty. Law Offices of Jason Bell, South Holland, Ill., 2002—. Founder East Oak Accessories, 1994—, Creative Career Design, 1999, The Everest Inst., 1999, The Fin. Freedom Forum, 1999; co-founder Adjetey & Bell, Ltd., 2000, Law Offices of Jason Bell, 2002; founder Care Med. Staffing. Bd. dirs. Black Ensemble Theatre Co., Chgo., 1991-93, Phoebe's Place Sr. Ctr., Chgo., 1994—. Named one of Outstanding Young Men Am., 1990. Mem. AICPA, Nat. Assn. Black Accts. (Outstanding Svc. award Chgo. chpt. 1990, 92), Ill. CPA Soc. Avocation: sailing. Estate planning, Property, real (including real estate development, water), Taxation, general. Office: 52 W 162nd St South Holland IL 60473

BELL, JOHN ALTON, lawyer, judge; b. Greer, S.C., Dec. 1, 1958; s. Dallas Frank Sr. and Una Merle (Gay) B.; m. Vida Ivy, June 30, 1984; children: Luke, Meredith. BA, Carson-Newman Coll., 1980; JD, Memphis State U., 1982. Bar: Tenn. 1983, U.S. Dist. Ct. (we. dist.) Tenn. 1983, U.S. Army Ct. Mil. Rev. 1984, U.S. Ct. Mil. Appeals 1987, U.S. Dist. (ea. dist.) Tenn. 1988. Assoc. Litigation Support, Inc., Memphis, 1983; officer ops. and tng. U.S. Army, Ft. Knox, Ky., 1983-84, legal assistance atty., 1984-86, defense counsel, 1986-87; assoc. King & King, Greeneville, Tenn., 1987-89; ptnr. King, King & Bell, Greeneville and Newport, Tenn., 1989-90, Bell & Bell P.C., Newport, 1990-98; judge Cocke County Sessions and Juvenile Ct., Newport, 1998—. Instr. bus. law Sullivan Jr. Coll., Ft. Knox, 1986-87; adj. prof. bus. law Walter State C.C., 1989-90, 97—. Columnist It's The Law, Newport Plain Talk, 1984-85, 89-98. Bd. dirs. Extended Sch. Program, Greeneville, 1988; co-vice chmn. Rep. Com. Cocke County, Tenn., 1989-95. Lt. comdr. USAR, 1986—. Named Ky. Col., Gov. Ky., 1986. Mem. ABA, Fed. Bar Assn., Tenn. Bar Assn., Assn. Trial Lawyers Am., Judge Advocate Gen.'s Assn. Republican. Baptist. Avocations: sports, church activities. General practice, Military, Personal injury (including property damage). Office: Cocke County Sessions Ct 111 Court Ave Newport TN 37821-3102

BELL, JONATHAN ROBERT, lawyer; b. Bklyn., Oct. 2, 1947; s. Saul A. and Hope R. (Rosenblat) B.; children: Gabriel J., Nicholas R.; m. Catherine Janow, May 5, 1989. BA, Yale U., 1969; JD, Harvard U., 1973. Bar: Mass. 1974, U.S. Tax Ct. 1977, N.Y. 1978, U.S. Dist. Ct. (so. dist.) N.Y. 1980. Assoc. Nutter, McClennen & Fish, Boston, 1973-77, Debevoise & Plimpton, N.Y.C., 1977-83, ptnr., 1984-93, Paul. Weiss, Rifkind, Wharton & Garrison, N.Y.C., 1993—2001, Duane Morris, N.Y.C., 2002—. Bd. dirs. United Way, N.Y.C., 1984-95, N.Y.C. Ballet, 1995-2003; bd. dirs. Studio in A School, 1988—, vice chair, 2003—. Fellow Am. Coll. Trust and Estate Counsel; mem. N.Y. State Bar Assn. (trusts and estates law sect.), Assn. Bar City N.Y. (chair trusts, estates and surrogate cts. com. 1995-98). Estate planning, Probate (including wills, trusts), Estate taxation. Home: 99 Jane St New York NY 10014-7221 Office: Duane Morris LLP 380 Lexington Ave New York NY 10168 E-mail: jrbell@duanemorris.com.

BELL, KEITH WHITMAN, lawyer; b. Washington, Sept. 13, 1946; s. William Eugene and Betty Brooks (Hays) B.; children: Rebecca Brooks, Sarah Elizabeth, Scott Alexander; m. Marina Balashova; 1 child, Olga Balashova. BA, Duke U., 1968; JD, U. Md., 1973. Bar: Md. 1973, Alaska 1974, U.S. Dist. Ct. Alaska 1974, U.S. Ct. Appeals (9th cir.) 1974, Wash. 1978, U.S. Supreme Ct. 1979, D.C. 1979. Asst. mcpl. atty. Municipality of Anchorage, 1974-77; ptnr. Burton, Crane & Bell, Seattle, 1978-82; pvt. practice Seattle, 1983-84, Anchorage, 1984—. Lectr. in immigration law Alaska State Bar, Wash. State Bar, Hawaii State Bar, U. Wash. Law Sch., 1981—; pro bono atty. for Cuban refugees Seattle-King County Bar Assn., 1981. Mem. Anchorage Sister Cities Commn., 1986-87. Mem. Am. Immigration Lawyers Assn. (state chmn.1980-81, 82-83), Alaska Bar Assn. (exec. com. immigration law sect. 1995—), Alaska World Affairs Coun. (v.p. 1990-96), Commonwealth N., Rotary (sec. 2000-01). Rotarian. Immigration, naturalization, and customs. E-mail: bell@ak.net.

BELL, KENNETH B. judge; m. Victoria Scherer; children: Bradley, Grace, Stephanie, Reed. Bachelor's degree, Davidson Coll., N.C.; JD cum laude, Fla. State U., 1982. Pvt. practice real estate atty.; trial judge 1st Jud. Cir. Fla.; justice Supreme Ct. Fla., Tallahassee, 2002—. Mem. cir. com. on professionalism Supreme Ct., 2000—. Founding pres. of bd. dirs. Friends of Children's Hosp. at Sacred Heart, Inc.; bd. dirs. Escambia County 4-H Found., Waterfront Rescue Mission; c-founder Yan-Bian Chinese-Korean Tech. U., China. Mem.: Escambia-Santa Rosa Bar Assn. Office: Supreme Ct Fla 500 Duval St Tallahassee FL 32399

BELL, PAMELA COLE, lawyer, educator; b. Clinton, Ill., Mar. 16, 1957; d. Grover Cleveland and Betty Mae (Quinton) Cole; m. David F. Bell, Mar. 14, 1987. BA in English, Stetson U., 1979, JD, 1982. Bar: Fla. 1983, U.S. Dist. Ct. (mid. dist.) Fla. Assoc. John D. Fernandez, P.A., Clearwater, Fla., 1983-95; pvt. practice Clearwater, 1995—2002; prof. Stetson Coll. Law, 2002—. Adj. prof. St. Petersburg Jr. Coll., 1988-94, Stetson Coll. Law, 1991-2002; trial cons. Mem. ABA. Criminal, Labor (including EEOC, Fair Labor Standards Act, labor-management relations, NLRB, OSHA), Personal injury (including property damage).

BELL, PAUL ANTHONY, II, lawyer; b. Latrobe, Pa., Mar. 12, 1954; s. Paul Anthony and Marcia Chloe (Martin) B.; m. Arlene Rotella, Aug. 19, 1978; children: Montgomery Vincent, Elyse Maureen, Alexa Marie. AB cum laude, Princeton U., 1975; JD, U. Pitts., 1978. Bar: Pa. 1978, U.S. Dist. Ct. (we. dist.) Pa. 1978. Assoc. Scales and Shaw, Greensburg, Pa., 1978, Laurel Legal Services, Indiana, Pa., 1978-81; sole practice Blairsville, Pa., 1981-88; asst. public defender Indiana County, Pa., 1982-85, asst. dist. atty., 1985-87; ptnr. Simpson, Kablack & Bell, Indiana, Pa., 1987—. Bd. dirs. Laurel Legal Services. Pres. Saints Simon and Jude Council, Blairsville, 1982-85; dir. rights com. Torrance (Pa.) State Hosp., 1984-86; dir. Blairsville-Saltburg Sch. Dist., 1996—, pres., 1997—. Mem. ABA, Pa. Bar Assn., Indiana County Bar Assn. (dir. 1995—). Lodges: Rotary. Republican. Roman Catholic. Avocations: golf, bridge, reading, basketball. Personal injury (including property damage), Probate (including wills, trusts), Property, real (including real estate development, water). Office: Simpson Kablack & Bell 834 Philadelphia St Indiana PA 15701-3908 E-mail: pbell@skblawyers.com.

BELL, PAUL BUCKNER, lawyer; b. Charlotte, N.C., July 29, 1922; s. George Fisher and Carrie (Savage) B.; m. Betty Sue Trulock, May 3, 1952; children: Paul B., Morris Trulock, Betty Fisher, Douglas Savage. BS, Wake Forest U., 1947, JD cum laude, 1948. Bar: N.C. 1948. Pres. Bell, Seltzer, Park & Gibson, Charlotte, 1948-97; of counsel Alston & Bird LLP, 1998—; dir. Southland Investors Inc., Idlewild Farms, Inc. Pres., dir. Charpat Investment Corp.; lectr. Practising Law Inst., 1974, N.C. Bar, 1985; adj. prof. patent law Wake Forest U. Sch. Law, 1974—2002; prof. patent law U. N.C. Sch. Law, 1995—2002. Trustee Mecklenburg Presbytery, Alexander Children's Ctr., Presbyn. Home of Charlotte, Mountain Retreat Assn.; chmn. Presbyn. Ch. Found. Served to 1st lt. USAAF, 1943-46. Mem. ABA, N.C. Bar Assn. (v.p. 1988—), Mecklenburg Bar Assn., Am. Intellectual Property Assn., Licensing Execs. Soc., Federation Internationale Des Conseils Propriete Industrielle (pres. U.S.A.), Charlotte City Club (past pres.), Charlotte Country Club, Charlotte Textile club (past pres.), Grandfather Golf and Country Club, Union League (N.Y.C.), Sigma Phi Epsilon, Phi Alpha Delta. Presbyterian. Federal civil litigation, Patent, Trademark and copyright. Home: 322 S Canterbury Rd Charlotte NC 28211-1838 Office: Bank of Am Plz 101 S Tryon St Ste 4000 Charlotte NC 28280-4000

BELL, RICHARD THOMAS, lawyer; b. Houston, Tex., Aug. 31, 1972; s. James Ronald Bell and Carolyn Sue Thrasher; m. Catherine Stokes, Dec. 9, 1995; 1 child, Travis Stokes. BA, Southwestern U., 1994; JD, South Tex. Coll. Law, 1997. Bar: Tex. 1997, U.S. Dist. Ct. (so. dist.) Tex. 1997, U.S. Ct. Appeals (5th cir.) 1997, Wis. 2000. Assoc. Allan A. Cease and Assocs., Sugar Land, Tex., 1995—99; ptnr. Cease and Bell, Sugar Land, 1999—. Prof. Legal Studies Alvin C.C., Alvin, Tex., 1997—. Mem. Pro Bono Coll. Tex., Austin, 2001—; bd. dirs. Fort Bend County Law Libr., Richmond, Casey Cease Outreach,Inc., Sugar Land. Mem.: ATLA, Fort Bend County Bar Assn. (pres. 2003, sec. 2001), Fort Bend County Criminal Def. Lawyers Assn., Tex. Criminal Def. Lawyers Assn. Baptist. Avocations: golf, reading, exercise, teaching Sunday school. General civil litigation. Office: Cease and Bell PLLC 2507 Williams Trace Blvd Ste 103 Sugar Land TX 77479

BELL, ROBERT CHARLES, lawyer; b. St. Paul; s. Charles N. and Esther C. (Carlsten) B.; m. Carmen Florence Anderson, Sept. 10, 1954; children: Caroline Florence Beckman, Alison McGinnity. BSc, U. Minn., 1949, LLB, 1950. Bar: Minn. 1951, U.S. Dist. Ct. Minn. 1953, U.S. Ct. Appeals (8th cir.) 1990. Ptnr. Robins, Davis & Lyons, St. Paul, 1953-61, Peterson, Bell & Converse, St. Paul, 1962-95; city atty. Roseville, Minn., 1962-95; ptnr. Jensen, Bell, Converse & Erickson, 1995—. City atty. City of Roseville, Minn., 1968—. With U.S. Army, 1944-46, PTO. Mem. ABA, Minn. State Bar Assn.; mem. Minn. Ho. of Reps., St. Paul, 1967-74. Avocations: golf, hunting, fishing, forestry. General civil litigation, Insurance, Municipal (including bonds). Home: 807 Heinel Dr Roseville MN 55113-2124 Office: Jensen Bell Converse & Erickson 30 7th St E Saint Paul MN 55101-4914

BELL, ROBERT HOLMES, district judge; b. Lansing, Mich., Apr. 19, 1944; s. Preston C. and Eileen (Holmes) B.; m. Helen Mortensen, June 28, 1968; children: Robert Holmes Jr., Ruth Eileen, Jonathan Neil. BA, Wheaton Coll., 1966; JD, Wayne State U., 1969. Bar: Mich. 1970, U.S. Dist. Ct. (we. dist.) Mich. 1970. Asst. prosecutor Ingham County Prosecutor's Office, Lansing, Mich., 1969-72; state dist. judge Mich. State Cts., 1973-78, state cir. judge, 1979-87; judge U.S. Dist. Ct. Mich., Grand Rapids, Mich., 1987-2001, chief judge, 2001—. Office: US Dist Ct 402 Fed Bldg 110 Michigan St NW Grand Rapids MI 49503-2363 E-mail: kim@miwd.uscourts.gov.

BELL, ROBERT M. state supreme court justice; b. Rocky Mount, N.C., July 6, 1943; AB with honors, Morgan State Coll., 1966; JD, Harvard U., 1969. Bar: Md. 1969. Judge Md. Dist. Ct. Dist. 1, Balt., 1975-79; former judge Cir. Ct. Md. 8th Jud. Cir.; assoc. judge Md. Ct. Spl. Appeals, 1980-91, Md. Ct. Appeals, Balt., 1991-96, chief judge, 1996—. Mem. ABA, Nat. Bar Assn., Md. State Bar Assn., Inc., Bar Assn. Balt. City, Monumental City Bar Assn. Office: Court of Appeals 634 Courthouse East 111 N Calvert St Baltimore MD 21202-1904 also: Court of Appeals 361 Rowe Blvd Annapolis MD 21401-1672

BELL, ROBERT MORRALL, lawyer; b. Graniteville, S.C., Feb. 15, 1936; s. Jonathan F. and Ruby Lee (Carpenter) B.; m. Cecelia Richardson Coker, June 11, 1965 (dec.). AB, U. S.C., 1958, LLB, 1965. Bar: S.C. 1965, U.S. Dist. Ct. S.C. 1965, U.S. Ct. Appeals (4th cir.) 1970. With Watkins, Vandiver, Kirven & Long, Anderson, S.C., 1965-67; sr. law clk. to chief judge U.S. Dist. Ct. S.C., Greenville, 1967-69; mem. Abram, Bowen & Townes, Greenville, 1969-71, Bell, Surasky and Brown, P.A., Langley, S.C., 1971-76, sr. ptnr., 1976—. County atty. Aiken County (S.C.), 1982—. Mem. S.C. Hwy Commn., 1982-86; state exec. committeeman S.C. Dem. Com., 1980-86; mem. S.C. Bd. Chiropractic Examiners, 1978-80; mem. Svc. Coun. of Aiken County, 1976-82, Aiken County Planning Commn., 1976-80; chmn. Aiken County Transp. Com., 1993-96; bd. dirs. Aiken County Crippled Children's Soc., 1976-82, Beech Island Agrl. Club, 1978-; bd. dirs. Gregg-Graniteville Found., 1984—, chmn., 1998—; bd. dirs. Beech Island Agrl. Club, 1980—; del. gen. and jurisdictional confs. United Meth. Ch., 1988-92; mem. S.C. Midlands Citizens Com. on Jud. Qualifications, 1996—. Served with USAR, 1959-60. Named to Order Ky. Cols., 1989—. Mem. ABA, ATLA, Aiken County Bar Assn., S.C. Bar Assn., S.C. Trial Lawyers Assn., Masons, Shriners, Am. Legion, Beech Island Agrl. Club, Kappa Sigma Kappa, Tau Kappa Alpha, Phi Delta Phi, Chi Psi. Democrat. Personal injury (including property damage), Workers' compensation. Office: Bell Surasky and Brown PA PO Box 1890 2625 Jefferson Davis Hwy Langley SC 29834 E-mail: psichi7@cs.com.

BELL, SAMUEL H. federal judge, educator; b. Rochester, N.Y., Dec. 31, 1925; s. Samuel H. and Marie C. (Williams) B.; m. Joyce Elaine Shaw, 1948 (dec.): children: Henry W., Steven D.; m. Jennie Lee McCall, 1983 BA, Coll. Wooster, 1947; JD, U. Akron, 1952. Pvt. practice, Cuyahoga Falls, Ohio, 1956-68; asst. pros. atty. Summit County, Ohio, 1956-58; judge Cuyahoga Falls Mcpl. Ct., Ohio, 1968-73, Ct. of Common Pleas, Akron, Ohio, 1973-77, Ohio Ct. Appeals, 9th Jud. Dist., Akron, 1977-82, U.S. Dist. Ct. (no. dist.) Ohio, Akron, 1982-2000, sr. status, 1996; sr. judge. Adj. prof. Coll. Wooster, 1987—; adj. prof., adv. bd. U. Akron Sch. Law, past trustee Dean's club; bd. dirs. Jos. R. Miller Found. Co-author: Federal Practice Guide 6th Cir., 1996. Recipient Disting. Alumni award U. Akron, 1988, St. Thomas More award, 1987. Fellow Akron Bar Found. (trustee 1989-94, pres. 1993-94); mem. Fed. Bar Assn., Akron Bar Assn., Akron U. Sch. Law Alumni Assn. (Disting. Alumni award 1983), Charles F. Scanlon Akron Inn Ct. (pres. 1990-92), Akron City Club, Masons, Phi Alpha Delta. Republican. Presbyterian. Office: US Dist Ct 433 US Court House Fed Bldg 2 S Main St Akron OH 44308-5836

BELL, STEPHEN ROBERT, lawyer; b. Menominee, Mich., July 10, 1942; s. John Martin and Catherine Irene (Goodman) B.; m. Linden Tucker, May 22, 1976. AB, Georgetown U., 1964; JD, U. Wis., 1967. Bar: D.C. 1971, Minn. 1967, Wis. 1967, U.S. Ct. Appeals (4th and 5th cirs.), U.S. Supreme Ct. Assoc. Dorsey & Whitney, Mpls., 1967-68; ptnr. Wilkinson, Cragun & Barker, Washington, 1971-82, Squire, Sanders & Dempsey, Washington, 1982-96, Willkie, Farr & Gallagher, Washington, 1996—. Contbr. article to profl. jours. Lt. USNR, 1968-71. Mem. ABA, D.C. Bar Assn., Fed. Communications Bar Assn., Computer Law Assn. (bd. dirs. 1987-93), Order of Coif. Administrative and regulatory, Communications, Computer. Office: Wilkie Farr & Gallagher Three Lafayette Ctr 1155 21st St NW Ste 600 Washington DC 20036-3384 E-mail: sbell@willkie.com.

BELL, STEWART LYNN, judge; b. L.A., Feb. 6, 1945; s. Jack C. and Kathryn Arline (Winn) B.; m. Karen Virginia Davis, Dec. 23, 1966 (div. Feb. 1974); 1 child, Linda Marie; m. Jeanne Dorothy Brick, June 8, 1974; children: Kristin Denise, Stephen Jeffrey, Gregory Matthew. BS, U. Nev., Las Vegas, 1967; JD, UCLA, 1970. Bar: Calif. 1970, Nev. 1971, U.S. Dist. Ct. Nev. 1971, U.S. Dist. Ct. (cen. dist.) Calif. 1973, U.S. Supreme Ct. 1976, U.S. Ct. Appeals (9th cir.) 1990. Legal asst. to Hon. Judge Howard W. Babcock 8th Judicial Dist. Ct., Nev., 1970-71; lawyer Clark County Pub. Defender's Office, Nev., 1971-72; sr. ptnr. Bell, Leavitt & Green, Chtd., 1974-83, Stewart L. Bell, Chtd., Las Vegas, Nev., 1983-89, Bell & Davidson, Nev., 1990-94; dist. atty. Clark County Dist. Atty. Office, Nev., 1995—2003; dist. judge U.S. Dist. Ct. (8th dist.), 2003—. Alt. judge City of North Las Vegas, 1981-88; coroner's inquest judge Clark County, 1979-94; referee Juvenile Ct., 1988-94; mental commitment judge, 1981-94; small claims judge, 1990-94; trial judge 8th Judicial Cir. Ct., 2003-. Vol. Clark Cty. Med./Legal Malpractice Screening Panel, 1974—75; vol. sec. Clark County Bar Assn., 1978, vol. v.p., 1979; vol. State Bar of Nev. Ethics and Atty. Discipline Com., 1980, Dis. court Adv. Com., 1980—82, State Bar of Nev. Bd. of Governor, 1981—92, Pro Bono Project, 1985—94. Recipient Dist. Men in Southern Nev., Asian Pacific Am. Advovate Champion of Excellence, 1995, Amigo award, Hispanics in Politics, 1996, Broche de Oro award, 1998, Stop DUI Appercation award, 1997, Families of Murder Victims award, 1997, Cir. of Excellance award, Las Vegas C. of C. Com., 1999, Louis Weiner Citizen of the Yr. award, 2001, Nat. Multiple Sclerosis Soc. Hope award for Com. Achievement, 2002. Mem. ABA, Assn. Trial Lawyers Am., Nev. Bar Assn. (bd. govs. 1981-92, v.p. 1989-90, pres. elect 1990-91, pres. 1991-92), Nev. Trial Lawyers Assn., Clark County Bar Assn. (sec. 1978, v.p. 1979, pres. 1980), State Bar Calif., Nat. Dist. Atty's Assn. (bd. dirs. 1995—, co-chair met. prosecutors com. 1996-2000, Nev. Dist. Atty's Assn. (v.p. 2000, pres. 2001), Nev. Adv. Coun. Prosecuting Atty's. Lodges: Elks. Democrat. Office: Clark County Dist Atty 200 S 3rd St #700 Las Vegas NV 89155

BELL, WILLIAM HALL, lawyer; b. Greeneville, Tenn., July 16, 1951; s. Charles B. and Peggy (Hall) B.; m. Ellen Bell, July 3, 1981; children: Burnley, Bethany. BA in Psychology, BA in Polit. Sci. with honors, U. Tenn., 1975, JD, 1978; LLM, Cambridge (Eng.) U., 1979; cert. d'Assiduite, Hague (The Netherlands) Acad. Internat. Law, 1984. Bar: Tenn 1978, U.S. Dist. Ct. Tenn. 1980. Ptnr. Bell & Mills, Greeneville, 1979—. Adv. com. Macro Engring. Group, MIT Sch. Engring.; co-counsel on Macro-Engring. Law, Internat. Law Collaborative, Cambridge, Mass.; legal advisor to solicitor-at-law in Cambridge U., Eng., 1978-79; law lectr. Cambridge Inst. Arts and Techs., 1978-79. Mem. Tenn. Trial Lawyers Assn. (bd. dirs.), Greeneville Bar Assn. (pres.). Corporate, general, Private international, Public international. Office: 102 W Mckee St Greeneville TN 37743-4814

BELL, WILLIAM WOODWARD, lawyer; b. May 15, 1938; s. Charles Smith and Janie Mae (Woodward) B.; m. Mary Elizabeth Beniteau, May 31, 1969; children: Susan Elizabeth, Carol Ann. BBA, Baylor U., 1960, JD, 1965. Bar: U.S. Dist. Ct. (we. dist.) Tex. 1967, U.S. Dist. Ct. (no. dist.) Tex. 1993, U.S. Supreme Ct. 1971. Ptnr. Sleeper, Boynton, Burleson, Williams & Johnson, Waco, Tex., 1965-68, Holloway, Slagle & Bell, Brownwood, 1968-71, Johnson, Slagle & Bell, Brownwood, 1971-74; pvt. practice Brownwood, 1974—. Capt. USMC, 1960-63. Named Vol., 1991, Developer of Yr., Tex. Indsl. Devel. Coun. Fellow Tex. Bar Found.; mem. ATLA, ABA, Tex. Bar Assn., Brown County Bar Assn., Am. Judicature Soc., Phi Alpha Delta. Baptist. State civil litigation, General practice. Home: PO Box 1564 Brownwood TX 76804-1564 Office: PO Box 1726 115 S Broadway Brownwood TX 76804-1726

BELLAH, KENNETH DAVID, lawyer; b. Aug. 17, 1955; s. Virgil and Joyce (Allen) B.; m. Dana Mills Bellah, Aug. 19, 2000. BA, Augustana Coll., 1977; JD, Chgo. Kent Coll. Law, Ill. Inst. Tech., 1980. Bar: Ill. 1980, U.S. Dist. Ct. (no. dist.) Ill. 1980, U.S. Ct. Appeals (7th cir.) 1980, Tex. 2000. Assoc. Matthias & Matthias, Chgo., 1980-83; ptnr. Matthias & Bellah, Chgo., 1983-99, Fox and Grove, Chartered, Chgo., 1999-2001; sole practice Law Offices of Kenneth D. Bellah, Chgo., 2001—. Republican. Methodist. Federal civil litigation, State civil litigation, Insurance. Office: 222 S Riverside Plz 1410 Chicago IL 60606 E-mail: KenBellah@aol.com.

BELLATTI, LAWRENCE LEE, lawyer; b. Oklahoma City, Apr. 19, 1944; s. Lawrence Fitzhugh and Esther Lee (Swank) B.; m. Barbara Gail Wolfinger, June 25, 1977; children: Julie M., Jenny E., Jill N. BS, Okla. State U., 1966; JD, Okla. U., 1969. Bar: Okla. 1969, Tex. 1974, U.S. Dist. Ct. (so. dist.) Tex. 1975, U.S. Ct. Mil. Appeals 1978, U.S. Dist. Ct. (ea. dist.) Tex. 1979, U.S. Ct. Appeals (5th cir.) 1979, U.S. Ct. Appeals (11th cir.) 1981, U.S. Ct. Appeals (10th cir.) 1982, U.S. Dist. Ct. (we. dist.) Tex. 1983, U.S Dist. Ct. (we. dist.) Okla. 1983, U.S. Dist. Ct. (no. dist.) Tex., 1984, U.S. Dist. Ct. (no. dist.) Okla., 1992, U.S. Dist. Ct. (ea. dist.) Okla. 1994. Assoc. Andrews, Kurth, Campbell & Jones, Houston, 1974-80; ptnr. Andrews & Kurth LLP, Houston, 1980—. Bd. dirs. Samaritan Counseling Ctrs., Inc., Houston, 1984—2001. Mem. Harris County Flood Control Dist. Task Force, Houston, 1984. Lt. comdr. JAGC, USNR, 1969-74. Mem. Tex. Bar Assn., Okla. Bar Assn., Houston Bar Assn., Order of Coif, Phi Kappa Phi, Sigma Chi, Phi Delta Phi. Republican. Baptist. General civil litigation, Condemnation (eminent domain), Construction. Office: Andrews & Kurth LLP 600 Travis St Ste 4200 Houston TX 77002-2910

BELLER, GARY A. lawyer, insurance company executive; b. N.Y.C., Oct. 16, 1938; s. Charles W. and Jeanne A. B.; m. Carole P. Wrubel, Nov. 22, 1967; 1 child, Jessie Melissa. BA, Cornell U., 1960; LLB, NYU, 1963, LLM, 1971. Bar: N.Y. 1963. Various positions gen. counsel's office Am. Express Co., N.Y.C., 1968-82, exec. v.p. and gen. counsel, 1983-94; exec. v.p., chief legal officer Met. Life Ins. Co., N.Y.C., 1995—. Bd. dirs. Lenox Hill Neighborhood Assn.; bd. dirs., chmn. Citizens' Crime Commn. N.Y. Mem. ABA, Assn. Bar City N.Y. Corporate, general. Office: Met Life Ins Co 1 Madison Ave # Area11G New York NY 10010-3603*

BELLER, HERBERT N. lawyer; b. Ill., 1943; BSBA, Northwestern U., 1964, JD cum laude, 1967. Bar: Ill. 1967, D.C. 1969; CPA, Ill. Law clk. to Hon. Theodore Tannenwald, Jr. U.S. Tax Ct., 1967-68; ptnr. Sutherland, Asbill & Brennan, Washington. Adj. prof. law Georgetown U., Washington, 1972-81. Editor-in-chief: The Tax Lawyer, 1993-96. Mem. ABA (mem. sect. taxation, vice chair 1993-96, chair, 2002—, mem. coun. 1989-92, liaison to AICPA tax div. 1998-2000, chmn. govt. submissions com. 1988-89, chmn. closely held corps. com. 1981-83), Am. Coll. Tax Counsel (regent), D.C. Bar Assn., Ill. State Bar Assn., Nat. Conf. Lawyers and CPAs. Office: Sutherland Asbill & Brennan LLP 1275 Pennysylvania Ave NW Washington DC 20004

BELLEVILLE, PHILIP FREDERICK, lawyer; b. Flint, Mich., Apr. 24, 1934; s. Frederick Charles and Sarah (Adelaine) B.; m. Geraldean Bickford, Sept. 2, 1953; children— Stacy L., Philip Frederick II, Jeffrey A. BA in Econs. with high distinction and honors, U. Mich., 1956, JD, 1960, MS in Psychology CCU, 1997. Bar: Calif. 1961. Assoc. Latham & Watkins, L.A., 1960-68, ptnr. L.A. and Newport Beach, Calif., 1968-98, chmn. litigation dept., 1973-80, ptnr. L.A., Newport Beach, San Diego, Washington, 1980-98, Chgo., 1983-98, N.Y.C., 1985-98, London and San Francisco, 1990-98, Moscow, 1992-98, Hong Kong, 1995-98, Tokyo, 1995-98, Singapore, 1997-98, Silicon Valley, 1997-98. Past mem. So. Calif. steering com. NAACP Legal Def. Fund, Inc.; past mem. cmty. adv. bd. San Pedro Peninsula Hosp., Calif., 1980—88; mem. Harbor Interfaith Bd. James B. Angell scholar U. Mich., 1955-56 Mem. ABA, L.A. County Bar Assn., Assn. Bus. Trial Lawyers, Order of Coif, Portuguese Bend (Calif.) Club, Palos Verdes (Calif.) Golf Club, Caballeros, Phi Beta Kappa, Phi Kappa Phi, Alpha Kappa Psi. Republican. Avocations: antique and classic autos, public service, sports, art, antiques. Antitrust, Federal civil litigation, State civil litigation.

BELLINGER, EDGAR THOMSON, lawyer; b. N.Y.C., Sept. 23, 1929; s. John and Margaret (Thomson) B.; children from previous marriage: Edgar Jr., Robert, Margaret; m. Ann Clark, Feb. 25, 1989. BA, Haverford Coll., 1951; JD with honors, George Washington U., 1955. Bar: D.C. 1955, Md. 1955. Law clk. to chief judge U.S. Dist. Ct. D.C., 1955-57; asst. U.S. aty for Washington, 1957-59; ptnr. Pope, Ballard & Loos, Washington, 1959-81, Zuckert, Scoutt and Rasenberger, Washington, 1981-94, Bellinger & Assocs., Washington and Md., 1995—. Chmn. unauthorized practice com. D.C. Ct. Appeals, 1972-78; mem. D.C. jud. conf., 1972-90; bd. mgrs. Chevy Chase Village, 1983-86. Mem. ABA (mem. fidelity and surety com., mem. forum on constrn. industry, past chmn. bonds, liens and ins. divsn.), Am. Arbitration Assn. (panel of arbitrators), D.C. Bar Assn. (D.C. Ct. Appeals orgn. com. 1972), Md. Bar Assn., Talbot County Bar Assn., Nat. Assn.

Securities Dealers (panel of arbitrators), Met. Club, Chevy Chase Club (bd. govs. 1972-77, pres. 1976-77). State civil litigation, Insurance, Probate (including wills, trusts). Home: 27497 West Point Rd Easton MD 21601-8439 Office: 888 17th St NW Washington DC 20006-3939 also: PO Box 739 Easton MD 21601-8914

BELLISARIO, DOMENIC ANTHONY, lawyer; b. Pitts., May 14, 1953; s. Domenic and Mary (Murgia) B. BA, U. Pitts., 1975, JD, 1978. Bar: Pa. 1978, U.S. Dist. Ct. (we. dist.) Pa. 1978, U.S. Dist. Ct. (no. dist.) Ohio 1999, U.S. Ct. Appeals (3d cir.) 1985, U.S. Ct. Appeals (6th cir.) 2002. Trial atty. Nat. Labor Rels. Bd., Pitts., 1978-83; human resource counsel Western Res. Care Sys., Youngstown, Ohio, 1986-89; ptnr. Bellisario & Pontier, Pitts., 1984-90; pvt. practice Pitts., 1991—. Author: Preventing and Defending Sexual Harassment Claims in Pennsylvania, 1996, Basic Wage and Hour Law in Pennsylvania, 1997. Mem. coun. Nat. Italian Am. Found., Washington, 1991. Mem. ABA, Am. Arbitration Assn. (arbitrator), Nat. Italian Am. Found., Pa. Bar Assn., Allegheny County Bar Assn., Pa. Trial Lawyers Assn., Italian Cultural Heritage Soc. West Pa. Avocations: travel, skiing. Labor (including EEOC, Fair Labor Standards Act, labor-management relations, NLRB, OSHA), Personal injury (including property damage). Office: 1000 Law & Finance Bldg Pittsburgh PA 15219 E-mail: domenic@bellisario.com.

BELLIZZI, JOHN J. law enforcement association administrator, educator, pharmacist; b. N.Y.C., July 26, 1919; s. Francis X. and Carmela (Bruno) B.; m. Celeste Morga, Sept. 1, 1942; children: John J. Jr., Robert F. PhG, St. John's U., N.Y.C., 1939; LLB, Albany Law Sch., 1960; JD, Union U., 1968; LLD, St. John's U., 1981. Pharmacist St. Luke's Hosp., N.Y.C., 1939-44; police officer N.Y.C. Police Dept., 1944-53; narcotics agt. N.Y. Bur. Narcotics Enforcement, N.Y.C., 1953-59, dir. Albany, 1959-81; exec. dir. N.Y. State Drug Abuse Commn., Albany, 1981-84, Internat. Narcotics Enforcement Assn., Albany, 1984—. Prof. pharmacy law St. John's U., N.Y.C., 1962-76; lectr. in field. Contbr. articles to profl. jours. Recipient Papal medal Vatican, 1965. Mem. Internat. Narcotics Enforcement Officers Assn. (pres. 1960-62, Anslinger medal 1979, chmn. law enforcement com. Paramount Pictures, 1972-75, Svc. award 1975), Ft. Orange Club, Albany Country Club, Univ. Club (Albany), Am. Friends of Law Enforcement Found. (bd. dirs., sec. Japanese), Phi Alpha Delta, Phi Sigma Chi (pres. 1939), Sigma Chi (fellow). Office: Internat Narcotics Enforcement Officers Assn 112 State St Albany NY 12207-2005

BELLMANN, THOMAS RICHARD, lawyer; b. Dayton, Ohio, Feb. 16, 1948; s. Bernard Robert and Joan Rita Bellmann; m. Sue Bellmann, Apr. 21, 1979 (dec. Nov. 2000); children: Max, Lacey. BA in Polit. Sci., S.W. Mo. State U., 1971; JD, U. Mo., Kansas City, 1975. Bar: Mo. 1975, U.S. Supreme Ct., U.S. Ct. Appeals (8th cir.), U.S. Dist. Ct. (we. dist.) Mo., U.S. Tax Ct.; cert. civil trial advocate Nat. Bd. Trial Advocacy. Pvt. practice, Kansas City. Mem. Jackson County Bar Assn. (spl. county counsel 1978-79), Kansas City Bar Assn. (chmn. lawyer referral 1984-86), Phi Delta Phi. Civil rights, General civil litigation, Personal injury (including property damage). Office: 9229 Ward Pkwy Ste 107 Kansas City MO 64114

BELOFF, MICHAEL JACOB, barrister; b. Adlington, Eng., Apr. 18, 1942; s. Max and Helen (Dobrin) B.; m. Judith Mary Arkinstall, Dec. 6, 1969; children:Rupert, Natasha. BA in History 1st Class, U. Oxford, 1963, BA in Jurisprudence, 1965, MA, 1967; JD (hon.) , Fairleigh Dickinson U. Bar: Eng. 1967, Queen's Counsel 1981. Recorder Crown Ct., Eng., 1984-96; dep. high ct. judge Queen's Bench Divsn., Eng., 1988-98; judge Ct. Appeals Jersey and Guernsey, Eng., 1996—; pres. Trinity Coll., Oxford, Eng., 1996—; named Master of Bench Gray's Inn, 1988. Mem. Ct. Arbitration for Sport, 1996—; vice chmn. Interception Comms. Tribunal, Guernsey, 1998-, chmn., Jersey, 2003-; dept. chmn. Data Protection Tribunal, Nat. Security, 2000—; vis. prof. Tulane Law Sch., 2001, 03; chmn. Internat. Cricket Coun. Code of Conduct Commn., 2002-. Author: The Sex Discrimination Act, 1976, Halsbury's Law, 15th edit., 1999, Sports Law, 1999; assoc. editor: Dictionary of National Biography; editor Jud. Rev., 1992—, Sweet and Maxwell Internat. Sports Law Rev., 1999—; contbr. articles to profl. jours. Fellow Inst. Advanced Legal Studies (hon.), Royal Soc. Arts; mem. Reform Club (mem. polit. com. 1963—), Royal Automobile Club (steward 1999—). Avocations: watching athletics, french films, dining in interesting company.

BELSKY, MARTIN HENRY, law educator, lawyer; b. May 29, 1944; s. Abraham and Fannie (Turnoff) Belsky; m. Kathleen Waits, Mar. 9, 1985; children: Allen Frederick, Marcia Elizabeth. BA cum laude, Temple U., 1965; JD cum laude, Columbia U., 1968; cert. of study, Hague Acad. Internat. Law, The Netherlands, 1968; diploma in Criminology, Cambridge U., England, 1969. Bar: Pa. 1969, Fla. 1983, N.Y. 1987, U.S. Dist. Ct. (ea. dist.) Pa. 1969, U.S. Ct. Appeals (3d cir.) 1970, U.S. Supreme Ct. 1973. Chief asst. dist. atty. Phila. Dist. Atty.'s Office, Pa., 1969—74; assoc. Blank, Rome, Klaus & Comisky, Phila., 1975; chief counsel U.S. Ho. of Reps., Washington, 1975—78; asst. adminstr. NOAA, Washington, 1979—82; dir. ctr. for govtl. responsibility, assoc. prof. law U. Fla. Holand Law Ctr., 1982—86; dean Albany Law Sch., 1986—91, dean emeritus, prof. law, 1991—95; dean U. Tulsa Coll. of Law, Okla., 1995—. Chmn. Select Commn. on Disabilities, NY, Spl. Commn. on Fire Svcs.; bd. advs. Ctr. Oceans Law and Policy; mem. corrections task force Pa. Gov.'s Justice Commn., 1971—75; adv. task force on cts. Nat. Adv. Commn. on Criminal Justice Standards and Goals, 1972—74; mem. com. on proposed standard jury instrns. Pa. Supreme Ct., 1974—81; lectr. in law Temple U., 1971—75; mem. faculty Pa. Coll. Judiciary, 1975—77; adj. prof. law Georgetown U., 1977—81. Author (with Steven H. Goldblatt): (non-fiction) Analysis and Commentary to the Pennsylvania Crimes Codes, 1973; author: Handbook for Trial Judges, 1976, Law and Theology, 2003, (non-fiction) Rehnquist Court: A Retrospective, 2002; editor (in chief): (jour.) Jour. Transnat. Law, Columbia Law Sch., 1968; editor: The Rehnquist Court: Farewell to the Old Order in the Court, 2002; contbr. articles to legal pubs. Chmn. N.Y. region, mem. D.C. bd. Anti-Defamation League, 1977—78, chmn. N.Y. region, mem. nat. leadership coun.; exec. v.p. Urban League Northeastern N.Y. and Tulsa Urgan League; state chair exec. com. Okla. Anti-Defamation League; pres.-elect Tulsa (Okla.) Metro. Ministry; bd. dir. Coun. on Aging & Disability; pres. Jewish Fedn.; mem. exec. com. NCCJ, Okla. Ethics Commn. Fellow Intenat., Columbia U. Law Sch.; scholar Stone. Mem.: ABA (del. young lawyers sect. exec. bd. 1973—75), Fund for Modern Cts. (bd. dirs.), Am. Law Inst., Am. Arbitration Assn. (referee N.Y. State Commn. on Jud. Discipline), Am. Soc. Internat. Law, Nat. Dist. Attys. Assn., Am. Judicature Soc., Fed. Bar Assn., Fla. Bar Assn., Pa. Bar Assn. (exec. com. young lawyers sect. 1973—75), Phila. Bar Assn. (chmn. young lawyers sect. 1974—75), Albany County Bar Assn., N.Y. State Bar Assn., United Jewish Fedn. Northeastern N.Y. (v.p., pres. elect), Cardoto Soc., B'nai B'rith (v.p. lodge 1973—75), Sword Soc., Hudson-Mohawk Assn. Coll. and Univs. (v.p.), Temple U. Liberal Arts Alumni Assn. (v.p. 1971—75). Office: U Tulsa Coll Law 3120 E 4th Pl Tulsa OK 74104-2418

BELSON, JAMES ANTHONY, judge; b. Milw., Sept. 23, 1931; s. Walter W. and Margaret (Taugher) B.; m. Rosemary P. Greenslade, Jan. 11, 1958; children: Anthony James, Marie Taylor, Elizabeth Ann, Stephen Griffin. AB cum laude, Georgetown U., 1953, JD, 1956, LLM, 1962. Bar: D.C. 1956, Md. 1962. Law clk. U.S. Ct. Appeals (D.C. cir.), 1956-57; assoc. Hogan & Hartson, Washington, 1960-67, ptnr., 1967-68; trial judge D.C. Superior Ct., 1968-81, presiding judge civil divsn., 1978-81; assoc. judge D.C. Ct. Appeals, Washington, 1981-91, sr. judge, 1991—. Faculty Nat. Jud. Coll., 1973-80; bd. dirs. Coun. for Ct. Excellence, 1981—; bencher Am. Inn of Ct. VI, 1983-90. Bd. editors Georgetown Law Jour., 1955-56. Bd. dirs. Project SHARE D.C., Inc., 1992—, chmn., 1997-99; bd. dirs. Cath. Legal Immigration Network, 1994-98. With JAGC, U.S. Army, 1957-60. Mem. ABA, Bar Assn. of D.C. (bd. dirs. 1966-67, chmn. jr. bar 1965-66), Am. Judicature Soc. (bd. dirs. 1980-85), Am. Bar Found., John Carroll Soc. (bd. govs. 1978-85, 1st v.p. 1989-91), Sovereign Mil. Order of Malta Fed. Assn. (pres. 1991-94, bd. dirs. 1988-95, 97—, chmn. task force on Cuba 1994-2000). Home: 12 W Severn Ridge Rd Annapolis MD 21401-5844 Office: DC Ct Appeals 500 Indiana Ave NW Washington DC 20001-2131 E-mail: jbelson@dcca.state.dc.us.

BELT, DAVID LEVIN, lawyer; b. Wheeling, W.Va., Jan. 13, 1944; s. David Homer and Mae Jean (Duffy) B.; m. Carolyn Emery Copeland Belt, July 22, 1967; children: David Clifford, Amy Elizabeth. BA, Yale U., 1965, LLB, 1970. Bar: Conn. 1970. Assoc. Jacobs, Grudberg, Belt & Dow, P.C., New Haven, Conn., 1970-74, mem., 1974—. Adj. faculty U. Conn. Sch. Law, 2002. Co-author: The Connecticut Unfair Trade Practices Act, 1994; contbr. articles to profl. jours. 1st lt. USAR, 1965-67, Vietnam. Fellow Conn. Bar Found. (life); mem. Conn. Bar Assn. (exec. com. antitrust and trade regulation sect. 1978—), Conn. Trial Lawyers Assn., Yale Club N.Y.C. Antitrust, Federal civil litigation, General civil litigation. Office: Jacobs Grudberg Belt & Dow PC 350 Orange St New Haven CT 06511-6415

BELTHOFF, RICHARD CHARLES, JR., lawyer; b. Denville, N.J., Jan. 28, 1958; s. Richard Charles and Barbara Ann (Erdmann) B.; m. Vicki Shannon Alligood, June 13, 1981; children: Ashley Nicole, Jason Michael. BSP, East Carolina U., 1980; JD, U. N.C., 1984. Bar: N.C. 1984, U.S. Dist. Ct. (we. dist.) N.C. 1984, U.S. Ct. Appeals (4th cir.) 1987. Assoc. Grier & Grier, Charlotte, N.C., 1984-89; ptnr. Grier Belthoff & Furr PA, Charlotte, N.C., 1989-98; chief ops. counsel, dir. real estate, asst. sec. Compass Group USA, Inc., Charlotte, NC, 1998—2002; v.p., asst. gen. counsel Wachovia Corp., Charlotte, 2002—. Contbr. articles to legal jours. Mem. N.C. State Bar, Mecklenburg County Bar Assn. Corporate, general, Environmental, Labor (including EEOC, Fair Labor Standards Act, labor-management relations, NLRB, OSHA). Home: 426 Shasta Ln Charlotte NC 28211-4054 Office: Wachovia Corp Legal Div 310 S College St NC0630 Charlotte NC 28288-0630

BELTON, JOHN THOMAS, lawyer; b. Yonkers, N.Y., Feb. 24, 1947; s. Harry James and Anne Marie (Kupko) B.; m. Linda Susanne Cheugh, jan. 6, 1973; 1 child, Joseph Timothy. BA, Ohio State U., 1972; postgrad. in bus. adminstrn., Xavier U., 1972-73; JD, Ohio No. U., 1976. Bar: Ohio 1977, U.S. Ct. of Claims. Sole practice, Columbus, Ohio, 1976-83; ptnr. Belton & Marlin, and predecessor firm Belton, Golowin & Cheugh, Columbus, 1983—; arbitrator Franklin County Ct. Common Pleas, 1983—; dir. Weeks-Finneran Inc. Rep. precinct chmn., 1983. V.p. Far Northwest Coalition, 1984. Mem. ch. coun. St. Peter's Parish, 1984—, Dublin Pub. Bd. Zoning Appeals, 1991—; pres. Dublin Youth Athletics, 1985—. With USAF, 1968-71. Mem. ABA, ATLA, Columbus Bar Assn. (com. chmn. 1976—), U.S. Dist. Ct. Fed. Bar, U.S. Supreme Ct. Bar, Ohio Bar Assn. (bd. govs. 1993—), Dublin Jr. C. of C., The Pres. Club. of Ohio State U., Ohio State Alumni, Republican Glee, Columbus Shamrock, K.C., Order of Barristers, Omicron Delta Kappa, Phi Alpha Delta (justice 1975). Roman Catholic. Avocations: reading, chess, golfing, racquetball, recreational activities. State civil litigation, Criminal, Personal injury (including property damage). Home: 8649 Dunsinane Dr Dublin OH 43017-8757 Office: Belton & Marlin 2066 Henderson Rd Columbus OH 43220-2452 E-mail: lsbjtb@cs.com.

BELTZER, HOWARD STEWART, lawyer; b. N.Y.C., Dec. 6, 1957; s. Herman Martin and Cynthia Marilyn B.; m. Alison Colette Lindsay-Beltzer, June 16, 1985; children: Clifford Benjamin, Miranda Leigh. BA magna cum laude, Harvard Coll., 1979; JD, Yale U., 1982. Ptnr., co-head fin. restructuring and insolvency group White & Case, LLP, N.Y.C., 1982—. Co-editor (with A.L. Gropper and C. Felsenfeld): International Insolvency, 2000; contbr. articles to profl. jours. Recipient Edwards Whitaker award Harvard U., 1976-79, others. Mem. Assn. of Bar of City of N.Y. (com. on bankruptcy and corp. reorganization), ABA (mem. bus. bankruptcy com.), Phi Beta Kappa. Bankruptcy. Office: White & Case LLP 1155 Avenue Of The Americas New York NY 10036-2711 E-mail: hbeltzer@whitecase.com.

BELZ, EDWIN J. lawyer; b. Latrobe, Pa., Feb. 28, 1936; s. Carl Stephen and Elizabeth Mohr B.; m. Suzanne Mary Schwarz, July 8, 1967; children: Daniel, Jeanine, Christopher, Luke. BA, St. Vincent Coll., 1958; JD, DePaul Coll., 1961. Bar: Ill. 1961, U.S. Dist. Ct. Ill. 1967. Asst. state's atty. Cook County, Chgo., 1961-64; atty. Vacarello Law Office, Chgo., 1965; ptnr. Belz & Kohl, Chgo., 1965-85, Belz & McWilliams, Chgo., 1985—. Sponsor Norwood PK. Little League, Chgo., 1973—; mem. Norwood Hist. Soc., 1980—. With U.S. Army, 1961. Mem. Chgo. Bar Assn., Northwest Bar Assn. Avocations: reading, golfing, traveling. General civil litigation. Office: Belz & McWilliams 4407 N Elston Ave Chicago IL 60630-4418

BEMBENEK, ALAN R. lawyer; b. Milw., Oct. 5, 1960; s. Walter A. and Joyce M. (Groshek) B.; m. Donna M. Potts, June 8, 1985. BS, Marquette U., 1982; JD, U. Wis., 1986. Bar: Wis. 1986, U.S. Dist. Ct. (ea. and we. dists.) Wis. 1986, U.S. Ct. Appeals (7th cir.) 1986, U.S. Ct. Claims 1996, U.S. Tax Ct. 1996. Assoc. Swarthout & Ryan, S.C., Brookfield, Wis., 1986-87; tax practitioner Arthur Andersen & Co., Milw., 1987-92; tax mgr. Gehl Co., 1992-95; assoc. Weiss Berzowski Brady & Donahue LLP, Milw., 1995—2001; corporate counsel Giles Engineering Assocs., Inc., Waukesha, 2001—. Mem. AICPA, Wis. Bar Assn., Milw. Bar Assn., Wis. Inst. Cert. Pub. Accts., Waukesha Bar Assn. Republican. Roman Catholic. Avocations: golf, mechanics. Corporate, general, Taxation, general, State and local taxation. Home: 4565 S Regal Dr New Berlin WI 53151-6735 Office: 4565 S Regal Dr New Berlin WI 53151-6735

BENAMATI, DENNIS CHARLES, librarian, editor, consultant; b. Orlando, Fla., Oct. 30, 1948; s. Thomas Guy and Ann (Clements) B.; m. Evelina Estella Lemelin, Aug. 19, 1983; children: Suzette, Alicia, Marcus. BA, St. Francis Coll., Loretto, Pa., 1970; MA, Fordham U., 1974; MLS, So. Conn. State U., 1975. Law libr. Conn. State Libr., Stamford, 1976-78; reference libr. U. Bridgeport (Conn.) Sch. Law, 1979; asst. law libr. for tech. svcs. U. Maine Sch. Law, Portland, 1979-83; asst. law libr. Aetna Life & Casualty Co., Hartford, Conn., 1983-84; head cataloging U. Conn. Sch. Law, Hartford, 1984-88; dir. The Dewey Grad. Libr. SUNY, Albany, 1988-93; adj. faculty Sch. Criminal Justice, SUNY, Albany, 1993—95; vis. elec. info. svcs. libr., instr. advanced legal rsch. U. S.C. Sch. Law, 1995—97; asst. libr. dir. Marist Coll., 1997—2002, adj. instr. criminal justice dept., interim libr. dir., adj. instr. Sch. Mgmt., 2000—02; libr. Sacred Heat U., Fairfield, Conn., 2002—. Ptnr. Lemelin & Benamati; cons., Kinderhook, N.Y., 1985—; cons. to various law firms, Lawyers Coop. Pub. Co., European Inst. for Crime Prevention and Control. Co-author: Publication Opportunities for Law Librarians, 1995, Criminal Justice Information: How to Find It, How to Use It, 1998; rapporteur World Criminal Justice Libr. Network Conf., 1997, 99, 2001; contbr. articles to profl. jours. Mem. ALA, Assn. Coll. & Rsch. Librs., Am. Assn. Law Librs., Law Librs. New England (bd. dirs. 1985-87). Roman Catholic. Home: 26 Hawthorne Dr Valatie NY 12184-5004 E-mail: benamatid@sacredheart.edu.

BENAVIDES, ALFONSO, lawyer; b. Madrid, July 19, 1965; s. Manuel Benavides and Concepcion Grases; m. Tracy Louise Clark; children: Tomas, Clara. Law degree, C.E.U. Luis Vives, Madrid, 1988; LLM, Inst. Etudes Europeens, Brussels, 1989. European Commn. trainee European Union, Brussels, 1989—90; trainee lawyer Baker & McKenzie, Madrid, 1990; lawyer Clifford Chance, Madrid, 1990—, ptnr., 1999. Lectr. real estate law Instituto de Empresa, Madrid. Avocations: racquetball, sports, swimming, running, mountain trekking. Commercial, contracts (including sales of goods; commercial financing), Property, real (including real estate development, water), hotels. Office: Clifford Chance SC Po Castellana 110 28046 Madrid Spain Office Fax: 34 91 5907575. E-mail: alfonso.benavides@cliffordchance.com.

BENAVIDES, FORTUNATO PEDRO (PETE BENAVIDES), federal judge; b. Mission, Tex., Feb. 3, 1947; BBA, U. Houston, 1968, JD, 1972. Atty. Rankin, Kern & Martinez, McAllen, Tex., 1972—74, Cisneros, Beery & Benavides, McAllen, 1974, Cisneros, Brown & Benavides, McAllen, 1975, Cisneros & Benavides, McAllen, 1976; pvt. practice McAllen, 1977; judge Hidalgo County Ct.-at-Law # 2, Edinburg, Tex., 1977—79; prin. Law Offices of Fortunato P. Benavides, McAllen, 1980—81; judge 92nd Dist. Ct. of Hidalgo County, Tex., 1981—84, 13th Ct. Appeals, Corpus Christi, Tex., 1984—91, Tex. Ct. Criminal Appeals, Austin, 1991—92; atty. Atlas & Hall, McAllen, 1993—94; judge U.S. Ct. Appeals (5th cir.), Austin, 1994—. Commr. Tex. Juvenile Probation Commn., 1983—89; vis. judge to cts. in Tex., 1993. Active Mustangs of Corpus Christi, 1990—91, hon. mem., 1992; active Mex.-Am. Dems. of Tex., 1990—92; mem. St. Michael Episc. Ch., Austin, 1992—. Mem.: ABA, Hidalgo County Bar Assn., State Bar Tex. Office: US Ct Appeals 5th Cir Homer Thornberry Judicial Bldg 903 San Jacinto Blvd Rm 450 Austin TX 78701

BENDER, CHARLES WILLIAM, lawyer; b. Cape Girardeau, Mo., Oct. 2, 1935; s. Walter William and Fern Evelyn (Stroud) Bender; m. Carolyn Percy Gavagan, June 20, 1961 (div. 1983); children: Theodore Marten, Christopher Percy; m. Betty Lou Port, May 5, 1983; stepchildren: Courtney Elizabeth, Cameron Ann. AB magna cum laude, Harvard U., 1960, LLB magna cum laude, 1963. Bar: Calif. 1965, U.S. Dist. Ct. (ctrl. dist.) Calif. 1965, U.S. Ct. Appeals (9th cir.) 1969, U.S. Supreme Ct. 1979, DC 1984. Assoc. O'Melveny & Myers, LA, 1965—71, ptnr., 1972—84, mng. ptnr., 1984—92, chmn., 1993—2001. Editor: Harvard U. Law Rev., 1961—62; articles editor: , 1962—63. Trustee LA Legal Aid Found., 1971, Lawyers' Com. for Civil Rights Under Law, Washington, 1985—2001; advisor campaign Alan Cranston for Senator, Calif., 1968, 1974, 1980; mgr. campaign Jess Unruh for Gov., Calif., 1970. Served with U.S. Army, 1956—57. Fellow Sheldon Traveling, Harvard U., 1963—64. Democrat. Administrative and regulatory, Federal civil litigation, State civil litigation. Home: 2831 The Strand Hermosa Beach CA 90254-2400 Office: O'Melveny & Myers 400 S Hope St Los Angeles CA 90071-2899

BENDER, JOEL CHARLES, lawyer; b. Bklyn., Dec. 12, 1939; s. Harry and Edna (Bogolowitz) B.; m. Terry Bender; children: Lisa, Andrew, Gary. BA, Cornell U., 1961; JD, NYU, 1964. Bar: N.Y. 1964, U.S. Supreme Ct. 1970, Fla. 1980; diplomate Am. Coll. Family Trial Lawyers. Ptnr. Bender, Jenson & Silverstein, LLP, White Plains, N.Y., 1999—. Councilman Greenburgh, N.Y. 1977-89; dep. supv., police commr. Greenburgh, 1979-89. Fellow Am. Assn. Matrimonial Lawyers, Internat. Acad. Matrimonial Lawyers; mem. ABA (mem. faculty Trial Advocacy Inst.), Am. Acad. Matrimonial Lawyers (pres. N.Y. chpt. 1999-2001, former officer, bd. mgrs.), N.Y. State Bar Assn., Fla. Bar, Westchester County Bar Assn. Democrat. State civil litigation, Corporate, general, Family and matrimonial. Office: Ste 104 120 Bloomingdale Rd White Plains NY 10605-1518 E-mail: jbender@jcbender.com.

BENDER, JOHN CHARLES, lawyer; b. N.Y.C., May 17, 1940; s. John H. and Cecilia B.; m. Helen Hadjiyannakis; 1 child, Marianna Celene. BSME, Northea. U., 1964; JD, NYU, 1968, LLM, 1971. Bar: N.Y. 1968, U.S. Dist. Ct. (so. dist.) N.Y. 1972, U.S. Supreme Ct. 1997. Atty. Marshall, Bratter, Greene, Allison and Tucker, 1968-69; asst. dir, NYU Ctr. for Internat. Studies, N.Y.C., 1969-71; atty. Poletti Freidin Prashker Feldman & Gartner, N.Y.C., 1971-75; spl. counsel Moreland Act Commn. on Nursing Homes and Residential Facilities, N.Y.C., 1975-76; gen. counsel N.Y. State Fin. Control Bd., N.Y.C., 1976-80; v.p., gen. counsel News Am. Pub. Inc., N.Y.C., 1980-85; group v.p., gen. counsel Simon & Schuster Inc., N.Y.C., 1985-90; sr. v.p., dir., gen. counsel Maxwell Macmillan Group, 1991-95; dir. Black Book Mktg. Group, Inc., 1994-96. Chmn., trustee Trust for Cultural Resources of City of N.Y., 1981-99; chmn., trustee Mary McDowell Ctr. for Learning, 1993—. Mem. ABA, Assn. of Bar of City of N.Y. (mem. com. on comm. law 1981-85, mem. spl. com. on edn. and the law 1982-85). Trademark and copyright, Corporate, general, Intellectual property. Home: 27 W 67th St New York NY 10023-6258 Office: 708 3d Ave New York NY 10017-4201

BENDER, LAURIE, lawyer; b. Seattle, July 29, 1959; d. Dean Bender and Karen Arol Bender-Evanson; m. John P. Annand, Oct. 28, 1988; children: Alexander, Quinn, Leigh. BS, We. Wash. U., 1982; JD, Lewis and Clark Coll., 1988. Bar: Oreg. Lawyer Met. Pub. Defender, Inc., Portland, Oreg., 1988-94, Bakker, Bender & Kappinski, Portland, 1994—. Coach S.E. Soccer Club, Portland, 1995—. Mem. Oreg. State Bar Assn., Multnoma Bar Assn., Oreg. Criminal Def. Lawyer Assn. Democrat. Avocations: soccer, book club, hiking. Criminal, Family and matrimonial, Juvenile. Office: Laurie Bender PC Strowbridge Bldg 735 SW First Ave 2d Fl Portland OR 97204

BENDER, MICHAEL LEE, judge; b. NYC, Jan. 7, 1942; s. Louis and Jean (Waterman) B.; m. Judith Jones, Feb. 27, 1967 (div. Mar. 1977); children: Jeremy, Aviva; m. Helen H. Hand, Sept. 10, 1977; children: Maryjean Hand-Bender, Tess Hand-Bender, Benjamin Hand-Bender. BA in Philosophy, Dartmouth Coll., 1964; JD, U. Colo., 1967. Bar: Colo. 1967, D.C. 1967, U.S. Supreme Ct. 1980. Pub. defender City and County Denver, 1968-71; assoc. regional atty. EEOC, 1974-75; supr. atty. Jefferson County Pub. Defender, 1975-77; divsn. chief Denver Pub. Defender, Denver, 1977-78; atty. Gibson, Dunn & Crutcher, L.A., 1979-80; ptnr. Bender & Treece P.C., Denver, 1983-93; pres., shareholder Michael L. Bender PC, 1993-97; justice Supreme Ct., Colo., 1997. Adj. faculty U. Denver Coll. Law, 1981-86, chair. ABA Criminal Justice sect., Washington, 1990-91, NACD Lawyers Assistant Com., 1989-90; dir. Nat. Assn. Criminal Def. Lawyers, 1984-90; mem. practitioner's adv. com. U.S. Sentencing Com., 1990-91; mem. com. for Criminal Justice Act for Dist. Colo. U.S. Dist. Ct., 1991-93, domestic rels. reform com.; liason mem. Colo. Pub. Edn. com., Ct. Svcs., 1998—, atty. regulation adv. com., 1998-99; co-chair civil justice com. Supreme Ct., 1998—. Contbr. articles to profl. jours. Bd. govs. Colo. Bar, 1989-91. Recipient Fireman award Colo. State Pub., 1990; Robert C. Heeney Meml. award Nat. Assn. Criminal Def. Lawyers, 1990; named Vol. of Yr. Denver Bar Assn., 1988. Mem. Colo. Bar Assn. (ethics com. 1980—), ABA (chair criminal justice sect. 1990-91, criminal justice standards com. 1997—). Democrat. Jewish. Avocations: aerobics, skiing, bicycling, camping. Office: Colo Supreme Ct State Jud Bldg 2 E 14th Ave Fl 4 Denver CO 80203-2115*

BENDER, PAUL, lawyer, educator; b. 1933; AB, Harvard U., 1954, LLB, 1957. Law clk. to Judge Learned Hand, 1958-59; law clk. to Justice Felix Frankfurter, U.S. Supreme Ct., 1959-60; asst. to Solicitor Gen., Dept. Justice, 1964-66; asst. prof. U. Pa. Law Sch., Phila., 1960-63, assoc. prof., 1963-66, prof., 1966-84; dean Coll. Law, Ariz. State U., Tempe, 1984-89, prof., 1989—; of counsel Meyer & Klipper, Washington D.C., 2001—. Prin. dep. solicitor gen. U.S., 1993-96; gen. counsel Nat. Commn. on Obscenity and Pornography, 1968-70; reporter UN Assn. Panel on human rights, Am. fgn. policy, 1978; justice Supreme Ct. of the Ft. MacDowell Yavapai Nation, 2000—. Author: (with Dorsen and Neuborne) Political and Civil Rights in the United States, 1976, 78. Recipient Cert. of Merit, ABA, 1973. Office: Coll Law Ariz State U Tempe AZ 85287

BENDER, PAUL EDWARD, lawyer; b. Decatur, Ill., Dec. 5, 1951; s. Kenneth Donald and Martha Rosalin (Heinzelmann) B.; m. Anne Marie Scartabello, Dec. 31, 1976 (div. 1978). BA, Millikin U., 1973; JD cum laude, Hamline U., 1976; MBA, U. Phoenix, 1997. Bar: Minn. 1976, Ill

1977, U.S. Dist Ct. (cen. dist.) Ill. 1982. Assoc. Halloran & Alfuby, Mpls., 1976-77; sole practice Bender Law Office, Arthur, Ill., 1977-79; sr. title atty Chgo. Title Ins. Co., Peoria, Ill., 1979-82; ptnr. Cordis & Bender, Princeville, Ill., 1982-84; sr. title atty. Chgo. Title Co., Champaign, Ill., 1984-88, asst. v.p., mgr., 1990-92, resident v.p., Champaign County mgr., 1992-96; mgr. McLean County Title Co., 1996—, Decatur Title, 1997—. Mem. ABA, Peoria Bar Assn. (chmn. real estate com. 1983-84, mem. continuing legal edn. 1981-83), McLean County Bar Assn., Ill. Bar Assn., Optimist Club (Peoria chpt., prs. 1981-82, lt. gov. zone 6 Ill. 1982-83), Champaign C. of C. (zoning com. 1990-96), Mason, Shriners. Republican. Methodist. Bankruptcy, Property, real (including real estate development, water). Home: 303 N Cottage Ave Normal IL 61761-4264 E-mail: benderpa@ctt.com.

BENEDICT, JAMES NELSON, lawyer; b. Norwich, N.Y., Oct. 6, 1949; s. Nelson H. and Helen (Wilson) B.; m. Janet E. Fagal, May 8, 1982. BA magna cum laude, St. Lawrence U., 1971; JD, Albany Law Sch. of Union U., 1974. Bar: N.Y. 1975, U.S. Dist. Ct. (no., ea. and so. dists.) N.Y. 1975, U.S. Ct. Appeals (2d cir.) 1975, U.S. Ct. Appeals (8th cir.) 1977, U.S. Ct. Appeals (10th cir.) 1978, U.S. Ct. Appeals (11th cir.) 1982, U.S. Supreme Ct. 1978. Assoc. Rogers & Wells, N.Y.C., 1974-82; ptnr. Clifford Chance, N.Y.C., 1982—. Mem. bd. contbg. editors and advisors The Corp. Law Rev., 1976-86; contbr. articles to profl. jours. Bd. dirs. Reece Sch., N.Y.C., 1984-89, Stanley Isaacs Neighborhood Ctr., N.Y.C., 1984-89; trustee St. Lawrence U., Canton, N.Y., 1985-91. Mem. ABA (chmn. securities litigation subcom. on 1940 Act matters 1984-86, 96—), Fed. Bar Coun. N.Y. State Bar Assn., Assn. Bar City N.Y. (com. on securities regulaton, fed. legislation com., fed. cts. com.), Am. Soc. Writers on Legal Subjects, Sky Club (N.Y.C.), Scarsdale Golf Club, Phi Beta Kappa. Federal civil litigation, State civil litigation, Securities. Home: 26 Kensington Rd Scarsdale NY 10583-2217 Office: Clifford Chance 200 Park Ave51st Fl New York NY 10166-0800

BENEDICT, MARK J. government analyst, marketing executive, lawyer, real estate investment consultant; b. San Antonio, Oct. 1, 1951; s. Irvin J and Loraine H. (Layer) B. AA cum laude, San Antonio Coll., 1970; BA summa cum laude, Trinity U., 1973; JD, U. Tex., 1977. Bar: Tex. 1978, U.S. Dist. Ct. (we. dist.) Tex. 1979, U.S. Ct. Appeals (5th cir.) 1980, U.S. Supreme Ct. 1980; lic. real estate salesperson, Tex., Va. Legis. aide Tex. State Rep., San Antonio, 1977-79; law ptnr. Nowlin and Benedict, San Antonio, 1977-79; atty., owner Law Offices of Benedict, San Antonio, 1980-86; sr. mgmt. Rasamny Group, N.Y.C., 1986-87; residential and comml. broker Shannon and Luchs, Washington, 1987-88; v.p. mktg. Microlaw/MLX, Washington, 1987-88; comml. broker Century 21 Real Estate, Fairfax, Va., 1988-91; v.p. mktg. Shared Equity Cons., Annandale, Va., 1988-91; owner, pres. PreMar Cons., Austin, Tex., 1986—, PreMar Internat., Fredericksburg, Tex., 1990—; exec. v.p. Equity Ventures Group, Inc., Washington, San Francisco, 1990-91. Cons. Resolution Trust Corp., Washington, 1989-91; mktg. aide Fairfax C. of C., 1988-91; mem. No. Va. Bd. Realtors, Fairfax, 1987—; sr. analyst U.S. Presdl. Com. for Disabled, Washington, 1991-2001; policy analyst USDA/Food Safety Inspection Svc., Washington, 2001—; v.p. programs Assoc. People with Disabilities in Agr. Rsch. editor Tex. Internat. Law Jour., 1972-73, Am. Jour. Criminal Law, 1972-73; contbr. articles to jours. and newspapers. Active Big Bros. and Sisters, San Antonio, 1979-80, Young Republicans. Benedict fellow, 1973; named one of Outstanding Young Men of Am., 1980, Top Broker, U.S. C. of C., 1979. Mem. ABA, Tex. Soc. City Attys., Tex. State Soc., Optimist Club San Antonio, Phi Beta Kappa, Phi Theta Kappa, Phi Alpha Delta, U. Tex. Ex-Student Assn. (life). Republican. Lutheran. Avocations: chess, travel, tennis, sailing, food and wine. Office: 477 Summit Cir Fredericksburg TX 78624-5042

BENEDOSSO, ANTHONY NECHOLS, lawyer; b. Bridgeport, Conn., Oct. 18, 1949; s. Tony and Sylvia (Nechols) B.; m. Michele F. Fratarcangeli, July 7, 1979; children: Anthony, Michael, Patrick. BS, Villanova U., 1971; JD, Fordham U., 1974. Bar: Conn. 1974, U.S. Dist. Ct. Conn. 1974. Asst. clk. Conn. Superior Ct., Milford, 1977-86; pvt. practice Milford. Instr. Sacred Heart U., Bridgeport, 1979. Bd. dirs. Boys Village, Milford, 1986—. Mem. Conn. Bar Assn., Milford Bar Assn. Roman Catholic. Avocation: skiing. General practice, Personal injury (including property damage), Property, real (including real estate development, water). Office: 51 Cherry St Milford CT 06460-8901

BENENSON, MARK KEITH, lawyer; b. N.Y.C., Oct. 13, 1929; s. Aaron and Luba (Stein) B.; m. Letizia Pitigliani, Dec. 29, 1959; children: Alexander, Daniela. BSS., CCNY, 1951; JD, Columbia U., 1956. Bar: N.Y. 1956. Atty. Dept. Labor, Washington, 1957-58; practiced in N.Y.C., 1958—. Bd. dirs. Amnesty Internat. U.S.A., 1966-80, sec., 1966-67, chmn., 1968-71, vice chmn., 1972-73, gen. counsel, 1972-80; pres. Vanguard Found., Inc., 1962— Contbr. articles to profl. jours., mags. and newspapers. Exec. sec. Nat. Found. for Firearms Edn., 1983-91, Pres. 1991—. With U.S. Army, 1951-53. Recipient John Amber Gun Digest Writing award, 1998. Home and Office: 585 W End Ave New York NY 10024-1715

BENESCH, KATHERINE, lawyer; b. Balt., Jan. 18, 1946; d. Isaac and Jane (Van Praag) B.; m. Thomas Romer, Oct. 21, 1977. BA, Wheaton Coll., Norton, Mass., 1968; MPH, Yale U., 1970; JD, Duquesne U., 1979. Bar: Pa., 1980, U.S. Ct. Appeals (3rd cir.) 1981, U.S. Supreme Ct. 1985, N.J. 1991, U.S. Dist. Ct. Pa. 1980, U.S. Dist. Ct. N.J. 1991, U.S. Dist. Ct. (no. dist.) N.Y., 2000, U.S. Ct. Appeals D.C. 1992. Assoc. Dickie, McCamey and Chilcote, Pitts., 1979-80; asst. exec. dir., legal counsel Presbyn. U. Hosp., Pitts., 1980-81; assoc. Specter & Buchwach PC, Pitts., 1982-84; atty. Mellon Bank Corp., Pitts., 1984-86; pvt. practice Pitts., 1986-88; prin. Katherine Benesch & Assoc., Pitts., 1989-91; ptnr. Hannoch Weisman, Trenton, N.J., 1991-93; prin. Law Offices of Katherine Benesch, Princeton, 1994-96, 98; ptnr. Benesch & Obade, Princeton, 1997, Archer & Greiner, Princeton, 1999-2001, Duane Morris LLP, Princeton, 2001—. Adj. asst. prof. anesthesiology and critical care sch. medicine U. Pitts., mem. ctr. med. ethics; advisor Princeton U. Bioethics Forum. Editor: Medicolegal Aspects of Critical Care, 1986; contbr. chpts. to books and articles to profl. jours. Fellow Am. Bar Found.; mem. ABA, ATLA, Am. Arbitration Assn., Amr. Health Lawyers Assn., Pa. Bar Assn. (del.) Allegheny County Bar Assn. (bd. govs.), Pa. Trial Lawyers Assn., N.J. Bar Assn. (health and hosp. law sect., past pres.), Mercer County Bar Assn., Princeton Bar Assn. (past pres.). General civil litigation, Health, Personal injury (including property damage). Office: Duane Morris LLP 100 College Rd W Ste 100 Princeton NJ 08540-6604

BENFIELD, ANN KOLB, lawyer; b. Reading, Pa., May 1, 1946; d. Curtis Kepler and Stella (Kolb) B. BA, George Washington U., 1969, MA, 1974; JD, U. Ky., 1983. Ky. 1983, U.S. Ct. Appeals (6th cir.) 1985, U.S. Supreme Ct. 1987; cert. mental health consumer cons./educator; cert. trained mediator. Probation officer Superior Ct. of D.C., Washington, 1973-78; jud. law clk. to chief judge U.S. Dist. Ct. (we. dist.) Ky., Louisville, 1983-86, jud. atty. to fed. sr. judge, 1989-95; trial atty. Ogden, Welsh and Newell (formerly Ogden & Robertson), Louisville, 1986-89; pvt. practice Louisville, 1995—2001; ret., 2001. Adj. prof. U. Louisville Sch. Law, 1993. Mem. exec. com., bd. dirs. Ky. chpt. ACLU, 1988-89, 91—, nat. bd. dirs., 1992-94, sec., 1995-96, treas., 1996-98; Reproductive Freedom Adv. Com., 1994-2001; mem. steering com. Fellowship Reconciliation, Louisville, 1997—; mem. governing coun. U. Louisville Women's Ctr., 1998-2001; rape crisis advocate Ctr. for Women & Families, 1997—, domestic violence advocate, 1998-; bd. dirs., gen. counsel Depressed Self-Help Svcs., Inc., 1998-2000. Fellow: Ky. Bar Found. (charter mem., bd. dirs. 1994—96); mem.: Louisville Women's Law Assn., Louisville Bar Assn., Ky. Bar Assn. (Donated Legal Svcs. Recognition award 2000, 2001), Ky. Paso Fino Horse Assn. (sec. 2000—01), Phi Beta Kappa, Order of Coif. Home and Office: 1113 Holly Springs Dr Louisville KY 40242-7762 E-mail: akbenfield@msn.com.

BENGTSON, KARL W. lawyer; b. Thibodeaux, La., Aug. 23, 1955; s. Robert W. and Bonnie Jean R. B. BA, La. State U., 1977, JD, 1980. Bar: La. 1980, U.S. Dist. Ct. (ea. dist.) La. 1980, U.S. Dist. Ct. (mid. and we. dists.) 1981, U.S. Ct. Appeals (5th cir.) 1981, U.S. Ct. Appeals (11th cir.) 1982, U.S. Supreme Ct. 1985, Tribal Cts., Coushatta, 2000, Chitimacha, 2001, Tunica-Biloxi, 2001. Tankerman Canal Barge Co., New Orleans, 1976-78; assoc. George & George, Baton Rouge, 1980-81; ptnr. Shelton & Legendre, Lafayette, La., 1981—2001; sr. mem. Bengtson Law Firm, LLC, Lafayette, 2002—. Founding sponsor Civil Justice Found. Served with USCG, 1973-76. Mem. ABA (port watch subcom., admiralty and maritime law com. 1984), ATLA (sustaining mem. Admiralty sect., vol. lawyer Trial Lawyers Care), La. Bar Assn., La. Trial Lawyers Assn. (bd. govs. 1988-92, CLE instr. 1990, 91, 97, 99-2002). Democrat. Methodist. Avocations: sailing, fishing. Admiralty, Federal civil litigation, Personal injury (including property damage). Home: 200 Idlewood Blvd Lafayette LA 70506-4913 Office: Bengtson Law Firm LLC 118 Exchange Pl Lafayette LA 70503-2510 Office Fax: 337-291-9117.

BENHAM, ROBERT, state supreme court justice; m. Nell (Dodson) B.; children: Corey Brevard, Austin Tyler. BS in Polit. Sci. with honors, Tuskegee U.; JD, U. Ga.; LLM, U. Va. Judge Ga. Ct. Appeals, Ga., 1984-89; justice Supreme Ct., State of Ga., Atlanta, 1989—, presiding justice, chief justice. Mem. adv. bd. 1st So. Bank. Chmn. Gov.'s Commn. on Drug Awareness and Prevention, State of Ga.; mem. Ga. Hist. Soc.; trustee Fa. Legal Hist. Found.; bd. dirs. Cartersville (Ga.) Devel. Authority, Cartersville-Bartow C. of C.; deacon, former Sunday Sch. supt. The Greater Mt. Olive Bapt. Ch.; notably one of first black individuals elected to a statewide position in the history of Ga. Mem Atlanta Bar Assn. (bd. dirs. jud. sect.), Ga. Bar Found., Lawyers Club Atlanta, Masons, Shriners, Elks. Office: Ga Supreme Ct 244 Washington St SW Rm 572 Atlanta GA 30334-9007 Fax: (404) 657-4329.

BENIGNO, THOMAS DANIEL, lawyer; b. Queens, N.Y., July 29, 1954; s. John Baptiste and Ernesta Mary (Yannaco) B.; m. Maria Angelica Vasquez, Jan. 26, 1980; children: Diana Maria, Laura Michelle, John Frederick. BA with honors, Hofstra U., 1976; JD, Benjamin Cardozo Law Sch., 1979. Bar: N.Y. 1981, U.S. Dist. Ct. (so. and ea. dists.) N.Y. 1985. Atty. Legal Aid Soc., Bronx, N.Y., 1979-84; ptnr. Benigno, Cassisi & Casissi, Floral Park, N.Y., 1984-87; mng. ptnr., gen. counsel Benigno/Gurrieri Real Estate Mgmt. and Devel., Bklyn., 1984-95. Pres. Gurben Properties, Inc., Floral Park, 1987-88, Movies for Kids Inc., Valley Stream, N.Y., 1989-90; gen. counsel Our Gang Assocs. Inc. (doing bus. as Thin White Line), Cedarhurst, N.Y., 1988-90. Mem. N.Y. Bar Assn., Rotary Internat. Commercial, contracts (including sales of goods; commercial financing), Construction, Property, real (including real estate development, water). Office: 269 Hempstead Ave Ste 2 Malverne NY 11565-1224

BENJAMIN, EDWARD BERNARD, JR., lawyer; b. New Orleans, Feb. 11, 1923; s. Edward Bernard and Blanche (Sternberger) B.; m. Adelaide Wisdom, May 11, 1957; children: Edward Wisdom, Mary Dabney, Ann Leith, Stuart Minor. BS, Yale U., 1944; JD, Tulane U., 1952. Bar: La. 1952. Practiced in, New Orleans, since 1952; ptnr. Jones, Walker, Waechter, Poitevent, Carrere & Denegre, New Orleans, 1967—. Pres. Am. Coll. Probate Counsel, 1986-87, Internat. Acad. Estate and Trust Law, 1976-78; vice chmn. bd. trustees Southwestern Legal Found., 1980-88, bd. dirs., 1988-90; chmn. bd. Starmount Co., Greensboro, N.C., 1968-88, chmn. emeritus, 1988—. Editor-in-chief Tulane U. Law Rev., 1951-52; mem. editl. bd. Cmty. Property Jour., 1974-89. Trustee Hollins Coll., 1966-87; chancellor Episcopal Diocese of La., 1984-2003, Trinity Episcopal Ch., New Orleans, 1974-92; mem. adv. bd. CCH Estate & Fin. Planning Svc., 1982-88; chmn. Salvation Army City Commd. Adv. Bd., 1965-68; pres. New Orleans Jr. C. of C., 1953. 1st lt., F.A. pilot, U.S. Army, 1943-46. Mem. Am. Coll. Tax Counsel, Am. Law Inst., ABA (sec. taxation sect. 1967-68, coun. 1976-79, coun. real property, probate and trust law sect. 1978-81), La. Bar Assn. (chmn. taxation sect. 1959-60), La. Law Inst., La. Bar Found. (trustee 1998-99), New Orleans Country Club, Southern Yacht Club, New Orleans Lawn Tennis Clu Estate planning, Corporate taxation, Estate taxation. Home: 1837 Palmer Ave New Orleans LA 70118-6215 Office: Jones Walker Waechter Poitevent Carrere & Denegre 201 Saint Charles Ave Fl 51 New Orleans LA 70170-1000

BENJAMIN, JAMES SCOTT, lawyer; b. Miami Beach, Fla., Aug. 28, 1954; s. Julian R. Benjamin and June Lois Garvin; m. Laura Cipolla, Mar. 5, 1989; children: Kaitlyn, Courtney. BS in Advt., U. Fla., 1976; JD, Samford U., 1979. Bar: Fla. 1980, U.S. Dist. Ct. (so. dist.) Fla. 1981, U.S. Dist. Ct. (mid. dist.) Fla. 1989, U.S. Ct. Appeals (11th cir.) 1989, U.S. Dist. Ct. (we. dist.) Tex. 1993, U.S. Supreme Ct. 1994. Asst. state atty. 17th Jud. Cir. Broward County, Ft. Lauderdale, Fla., 1981-84; shareholder Benjamin & Aaronson P.A., Ft. Lauderdale, 1984—. Presenter, lectr. in field. Author, columnist Xcitement Mag., 1990—, Screw Mag., 1998. Bd. dirs. Arthritis Found., Ft. Lauderdale, 1998, treas., 1999. Mem. Fla. Assn. Criminal Def. Attys. (bd. dirs. 1998—), Broward County Assn. Criminal Def. Lawyers (v.p. 1997-98, pres. 1998-99, bd. dirs. 1995—), First Amendment Lawyers Assn. (nat. sec. 2000—, nat. treas. 2001, v.p. 2002), Free Speech Coalition, Inns of Ct. Avocation: fly fishing. Communications, Criminal, Entertainment. Office: Benjamin & Aaronson PA Ste 1615 One Financial Plaza Fort Lauderdale FL 33394

BENJAMIN, JEFF, lawyer, pharmaceutical executive; b. Bklyn., Dec. 28, 1945; s. Haskell and Lillian (Sikofski) B.; m. Betty Gae Meckler, Mar. 21, 1971; children: Lily Meckler, Ross Meckler. BA, Cornell U., 1967; JD cum laude, NYU, 1971. Bar: N.Y. 1971, U.S. Dist. Cts. (so. and ea. dists.) N.Y. 1972. Assoc. Kronish, Lieb, Shainswit, Weiner & Hellman, N.Y.C., 1971-74; atty. Ciba-Geigy Corp., Ardsley and Tarrytown, N.Y., 1974—, counsel for regulatory affairs, 1976—, divsn. counsel, 1978—, asst. gen. counsel, 1985—, dir. legal dept., assoc. gen. counsel, 1986-89, v.p., gen. counsel, 1996-97; assoc. gen. counsel, ethics and law compliance officer Novartis Corp., N.Y.C., 1997—2001, v.p. dep. gen. counsel, ethics and law compliance officer, 2001—. Mem. adv. bd. Brennan Ctr. for Justice, 2002—; lectr. in field. Contbr. articles to law jours. Mem. Citizens Adv. Com., Ramapo, N.Y. With USAR, 1969-74. Mem. ABA, Ethics Officer Assn., Cornell U. Alumni Assn. (admissions amb.), Order of Coif. Antitrust, Corporate, general, Environmental. Home: 13 Park Ave New City NY 10956-1107 Office: Novartis Corp 608 Fifth Ave 10th Fl New York NY 10020-2305

BENJAMIN, WILLIAM CHASE, lawyer; b. Glen Cove, N.Y., Dec. 2, 1947; AB, Princeton U., 1969; postgrad., Grad. Inst. Internat. Affairs, Geneva, 1969-70; JD, Harvard U., 1973. Bar: N.Y. 1974, U.S. Tax Ct. 1978, Mass. 1983. Assoc. Cleary, Gottlieb, Steen & Hamilton, Brussels, 1975-78, N.Y.C., 1978-82; assoc. Hale and Dorr, Boston, 1982-84, jr. ptnr., 1984-86, sr. ptnr., 1986—. Fulbright scholar, 1969-70. Mem. ABA, Internat. Bar Assn., Mass. Bar Assn., Boston Bar Assn., Internat. Fiscal Assn. Avocations: skiing, tennis, swimming. sailing. Corporate, general, Private international, Corporate taxation. Office: Hale and Dorr LLP 60 State St Boston MA 02109-1816 E-mail: william.benjamin@haledorr.com.

BENKARD, JAMES W. B. lawyer; b. N.Y.C., Apr. 10, 1937; s. Franklin Bartlett and Laura Derby (Dupee) B.; m. Margaret Walker Spofford, Dec. 12, 1964; children: Andrew Minturn, James Robinson, Margaret Mercer. AB, Harvard U., 1959; LLB, Columbia U., 1963. Bar: N.Y. 1963. Assoc. Davis Polk & Wardwell, N.Y.C., 1963-73, ptnr., 1973—. Trustee Vassar Coll., Poughkeepsie, N.Y., Tchrs. Coll., N.Y.C., Environ. Def. Fund, N.Y.C., St. Mark's Sch., Southborough, Mass, Columbia Law Sch. Alumni Assn., Scenic Am. Mem. Am. Coll. Trial Lawyers, Knickerbocker Club, River Club (N.Y.C.), Fishers Island Country Club. Home: 1192 Park Ave Apt 11A New York NY 10128-1314 Office: Davis Polk & Wardwell 450 Lexington Ave Fl 31 New York NY 10017-3982

BENNETT, ALEXANDER ELLIOT, lawyer; b. Houston, Aug. 9, 1940; s. William Ernest and Verna Evelyn (Donelan) B.; m. Marilyn A. Bennett, June 6, 1960 (div. 1981); children: Andrew, Laura, Peter; m. Brooksley Born, Oct. 9, 1982; children: Nicholas Landau, Ariel Landau. BA, U. Mich., 1961, JD, 1963. Bar: D.C. 1964. Assoc. Arnold & Porter, Washington, 1966-70, ptnr., 1971—. Editor U. Mich. Law Rev., 1963. Mem. ABA, D.C. Bar Assn., Order of Coif. Democrat. Avocations: sailing, tennis. Antitrust, Federal civil litigation, Public international. Home: 2319 Tracy Pl NW Washington DC 20008-1640 Office: Arnold & Porter Thurman Arnold Bldg 555 12th St NW Washington DC 20004-1206 E-mail: alexander_bennett@aporter.com.

BENNETT, BIANCA CHERIE, lawyer; b. Washington, May 14, 1971; d. Carl Roosevelt and Barbara Jean (Pope) B. Grad., Princeton U., 1993; JD, U. Va., 1996. Bar: D.C., 1997. Assoc. Zuckert, Scoutt & Rasenberger, Washington, 1996—; mgr. Law Dept. General Dynamics Corp., Falls Church, Virginia, 1998-2000; dir. business affairs Paramount Pictures, Hollywood, Calif., 2000—02; prin. Bennett & Assoc., LA, 2003—. Mem. Washington Bar Assn., Black Entertainment and Sports Lawyers' Assn., Washington Area Lawyers for the Arts, Delta Sigma Theta Sorority, Inc. Avocations: photography, music, foreign travel, films, running. Entertainment. Office: Bennett & Assoc 4440 Finley Ave Ste 101 Los Angeles CA 90027 E-mail: Bianca.bennett@sbcglobal.net.

BENNETT, BRYCE HUGH, JR., lawyer; b. Jackson, Mich., Aug. 6, 1953; s. Bryce H. Sr. and Elizabeth Post B.; children: Carolyn, Amy, Rebecca, Molly; m. Donna Dillon, Mar. 20, 1993; children: Bryce III, Dillon, Luke. BS in Fin. with high distinction, Ind. U., 1975; JD magna cum laude, Ind. U., Indpls., 1978. Bar: Ind. 1978, U.S. Dist. Ct. (so. dist.) Ind. 1978, U.S. Ct. Appeals (7th cir.) 1981, U.S. Supreme Ct. 1991. Assoc. Callahan Riley & Hillis, Indpls., 1978-83; ptnr. Riley, Bennett & Egloff, Indpls., 1984—. Mem. ABA, Ind. State Bar Assn., Indpls. Bar Assn., Ind. Def. Lawyers Assn., Indpls. Bar Found. (pres. 2001), Indpls. Press Club, Skyline Club, Internat. Assn. Def. Counsel. Federal civil litigation, State civil litigation, Insurance. Office: Riley Bennett & Egloff 1 American Sq PO Box 82035 Indianapolis IN 46282-2035

BENNETT, EDWARD JAMES, lawyer; b. Newton, Iowa, Dec. 27, 1941; s. Erskine Francis and Malvina Esther (Goodhue) B.; m. Virginia Lee Cook, Jan. 30, 1965; children: Susan Elizabeth, Edward James. BA, U. Iowa, 1964, JD, 1966. Bar: Iowa 1966, U.S. Dist. Ct. (so. dist.) Iowa 1967. Atty. Diehl, Clayton & Cleverley, Newton, 1966-70, The Maytag Co., Newton, 1970-74, sr. atty., 1974-80, assoc. counsel, 1980-85, asst. sec., asst. gen. counsel, 1985-86, Maytag Corp. (formerly The Maytag Co.), Newton, 1986-90; sec., asst. gen. counsel Maytag Corp., Newton, 1990-99. Sec. The Hoover Co., 1990-99, Dixie-Narco Inc., 1990-99, Maytag Internat. Inc., 1990-99, Hoover Holdings Inc., 1990-99, Maytag Fin. Svcs. Corp., 1990-99, Maytag Corp. Found., 1990-99; dir. Progress Industries, 1993—, sec., 1994—. Mem. Civil Svc. Commn., Newton, 1980-86; mem. Newton Zoning Bd. Adjustment, 1978-96, chmn., 1978-85; sec., trustee Newton Cmty. Ctr., Inc., 1976-94; trustee Newton Cmty. Schs. Found., 1994-99, v.p., 1996, pres., 1997; bd. dirs. Des Moines Metro Opera, 1998—, sec. 1998-99, pres. 2001-02; bd. dirs. Des Moines Metro Opera Found., 2000—, pres. 2002—; bd. dirs. Calvin Cmty., 2002—. Mem. ABA, Iowa State Bar Assn. (mem. trade regulation com. 1981-92, 93-97, 99—), Iowa Assn. Bus. and Industry (chmn. unemployment compensation com. 1976-94), Assn. Home Appliance Mfrs. (mem. product safety com. 1975-92). Republican. Methodist. Antitrust, Corporate, general, Alternative dispute resolution. Home and Office: 203 Foster Dr Des Moines IA 50312-2539

BENNETT, FRED GILBERT, lawyer; b. May 28, 1946; HBA magna cum laude, U. Utah, 1970; JD, U. Calif., 1973. Bar: Calif. 1974. Ptnr. Gibson, Dunn & Crutcher, L.A., 1980-98; sr. ptnr. Quinn Emanuel Urquhart Oliver & Hedges, 1998—. Mem. nat. com. on arbitration U.S. Coun. for Internat. Bus., 1984—, chmn. western subcom., 1989—; comml. and constrn. arbitrator Internat. C. of C./Am. Arbitration Assn. Large Complex Case Panel; chmn. continuing edn. com. Am. Arbitration Assn. Large Complex Case Panel; bd. dirs. Am. Arbitration Assn. Mng. editor UCLA Law Rev., 1972-73. Named Outstanding U.S. Lawyer, Chambers U.S.A., 2003. Mem. ABA, Internat. Bar Assn., L.A. County Bar Assn., Phi Beta Kappa. Commercial, contracts (including sales of goods; commercial financing). Office: Quinn Emanuel Urquhart Oliver & Hedges 865 S Figueroa St Los Angeles CA 90017-2543

BENNETT, JAMES DAVISON, lawyer; b. Mineola, N.Y., Dec. 2, 1938; BA, Cornell U., 1960, JD, 1963. Bar: N.Y. 1963. Of counsel Farrell, Fritz, P.C. , Uniondale, NY, 2001—. Councilman Town of Hempstead, 1968-87, supr., 1978-87; active Nassau County Bd. Suprs., 1978-87, L.I. Power Authority, 1995-98; commr. N.Y.S. Pub. Svc. Commn., 1998—; apptd. to N.Y. State Conservation and Wildlife Fund, 1975-78; chmn. L.I. Area Devel. Agy., 1988-90, L.I. Regional Export Coun., 1988-90. Recipient citation Practising Law Inst., 1982-73, others. Mem. ABA, N.Y. State Bar Assn. (jud. conf. 1989, lectr. 1990), Nassau County Bar Assn. Corporate, general, Estate planning, Probate (including wills, trusts). Home: 34 Hilton Ave Garden City NY 11530-4414 Office: EAB Plz Uniondale NY 11556-0120 E-mail: jbennett@farrellfritz.com.

BENNETT, JAMES H. lawyer; b. Montclair, N.J., July 30, 1937; s. Richard Holcombe and Dorothea (Seller) B.; m. Mary Ellen Smith, Sept. 13, 1963 (div. Apr. 1979); children: Stephen Carroll, Kristy Lorraine; m. Lynnette Margaret Buchanan, July 14, 1979; children: John Sukwon, Margaret MiYong. AB summa cum laude, Princeton U., 1959; LLB, Stanford U., 1962. Bar: N.J. 1963, U.S. Dist. Ct. N.J. 1963, U.S. Supreme Ct. 1969, Conn. 1974, U.S. Dist. Ct. Conn. 1991. Law sec. Supreme Ct. of N.J., Newark, 1962-63; assoc. McCarter & English, Newark, 1963-66; internat. atty. Warner-Lambert, Morris Plains, N.J., 1966-68; sr. atty. internat., divsn. counsel Allied Chem. Corp., N.Y.C., 1968-70; sr. internat. atty. Richardson-Merrell Inc., Wilton, Conn., 1970-75; counsel, L.Am. bus. divsn. GE Co., Westport, Conn., 1975-78; v.p., internat. counsel Revlon Health Care Group, Tuckahoe, Tarrytown, N.Y., 1978-85; pvt. practice law New Canaan, Conn., 1985—. V.p., sec. Palladium (USA) Inc. New Canaan planning and zoning rep. Southwestern Reg. Plan Assn., 1996—; elder First Presbyn. Ch. of New Canaan, 1997—; mem. New Canaan Planning and Zoning Commn., 1985-96, chmn., 1993-96; alt. Essex county to N.J. State Rep. Com., Trenton, 1964-66; counsel, campaign mgr. Montclair Cmty. Com., 1964, 68; mem. fin. com. S.W. coun. Girl Scouts U.S.A.; treas. Presbytery of So. New Eng. Edward John Noble Found. fellow, 1959-62. Mem. Conn. Bar Assn. (chmn. exec. com. planning and zoning sect. 1988-91), Westchester-Fairfield Corp. Counsel Assn. (sec. 1984-85), Phi Beta Kappa. Republican. Avocation: swimming. Corporate, general, Private international, Property, real (including real estate development, water). Home and Office: 137 Old Kings Hwy New Canaan CT 06840-6411 E-mail: jimbennettlaw@earthlink.net.

BENNETT, JESSIE F. lawyer; b. Bridgeport, Conn. d. Cornelius T. and Jessie F. (Sutcliffe) B.; m. Ronald J. Canuel, Nov. 3, 1990. BS in Fin. with honors, Fairfield U., 1980; JD magna cum laude, Quinnipiac U., 1986. Bar: Conn., 1986; U.S. Dist. Ct. Conn., 1987, U.S. Dist. Ct. (so. and ea. dists.) N.Y. 1989, U.S. Ct. Appeals (2d cir.) 1989, D.C. Ct. of Appeals, 1989, U.S.

Supreme Ct., 1989. Jud. clk. to Judge Ellen Bree Burns U.S. Dist. Ct., New Haven, 1986; atty. Cohen & Wolf, Danbury, Conn., 1987-88, Davidson & Naylor, Norwalk, Conn., 1988-92; law clk. Jud. Dept. State of Conn., Waterbury, 1992-96; asst. state's atty. State of Conn. Divsn. Criminal Justice, 1996—. Recipient Am. Jurisprudence awards in Remedies and Family Law, Kristin Ann Carveth Meml. Scholastic award. Mem.: ATLA, ABA, D.C. Bar Assn., Conn. Trial Lawyers Assn., Nat. Dist. Attys. Assn., Conn. Bar Assn., Phi Alpha Delta (Code Enforcement Ofcl. of Yr. 1999, Pres. award 1999, Cert. of Appreciation award 1999, Svc. in Excellence award 2001, Pub. Svc. Star award 2002, Am. Registry Outstanding Profls. 2002—03), Phi Delta Phi. Roman Catholic. Avocations: exercise, music, cooking, travel. Criminal. Office: States Attys Office 80 Washington St Hartford CT 06106-4405

BENNETT, MARK J. state attorney general; m. Patricia Tomi Ohara. BA in Polit. Sci. summa cum laude, Union Coll., 1976; JD magna cum laude, Cornell U., 1979. Law clk. to Hon. Samuel P. King, Chief Judge U.S. Dist. Ct. Hawaii; asst. U.S. atty. Washington, 1980—82, Honolulu, 1982—90; atty. gen., 1991; litigation ptnr. McCorriston Miller Mukai MacKinnon LLP, Honolulu; spl. dep. atty. gen., spl. asst. proc. atty. Hawaii. Instr. criminal and civil trial advocacy Atty. Gen.'s Adv. Inst., Washington; instr. U. Hawaii Sch. Law. Republican. Office: 425 Queen St Honolulu HI 96813*

BENNETT, ROBERT LEROY, computer software development company executive; b. Salt Lake City, May 16, 1937; s. Edward L. and Helen (Hofheins) B.; m. Linda Lou Anderson, Aug. 25, 1961; children: Keri Lynn, Troy, Nicole, Jessica, Candice, Chelsea. BA, Brigham Young U., 1962; JD, UCLA, 1965. Bar: Calif. 1966, U.S. Supreme Ct. 1969. Atty., advisor CIA, Washington, 1965-70; exec. v.p., chief operating officer Mead Data Central, Inc. (now Lexis-Nexis), Washington and N.Y.C., 1970-81; assoc. Heidrick and Struggles, Inc., N.Y.C., 1982-83; pres., chief exec. officer Mirror Systems, Inc., Cambridge, Mass., 1983—93; prin. Bennett, Fisher, Giuliano and Gottsman: The Electronic Publishing Group, N.Y.C., 1993—2000. Mem.: ABA. Mem. Lds Ch. E-mail: RLBepg@earthlink.net.

BENNETT, ROBERT WILLIAM, law educator; b. Chgo., Mar. 30, 1941; s. Lewis and Henrietta (Schneider) Bennett; m. Harriet Trop, Aug. 19, 1979. BA, Harvard U., 1962, LLB, 1965. Bar: Ill. 1966. Legal asst. FCC commr. Nicholas Johnson, 1966-67; atty. Chgo. Legal Aid Bur., 1967-68; asso. firm Mayer, Brown & Platt, Chgo., 1968-69; faculty Northwestern U. Sch. Law, Chgo., 1969—, prof. law, 1974—, dean, 1985-95, Nathaniel L. Nathanson prof., 2002—. Author (with LaFrance, Schroeder and Boyd): (book) Handbook on Law of the Poor, 1973; author: Talking it Through: Puzzles of American Democracy, 2003. Knox Meml. fellow, London Sch. Econs., 1965—66. Fellow: Am. Bar Found. (pres., bd. dirs.); mem.: ABA, Am. Law Inst., Chgo. Coun. Lawyers (pres. 1971—72). Home: 2130 N Racine Ave Chicago IL 60614-4002 Office: Northwestern U Sch Law 357 E Chicago Ave Chicago IL 60611-3059

BENNETT, SCOTT LAWRENCE, lawyer; b. N.Y.C., July 8, 1949; s. Allen J. and Rhoda (Maltz) Bennett. BA with high distinction, U. Mich., 1971; JD, Cornell U., 1974. Bar: NY 1975, U.S. Ct. Appeals (2d cir.) 1975, U.S. Dist. Ct. (so. and ea. dists.) N.Y. 1975, U.S. Supreme Ct. 1976. Assoc. Donovan, Leisure, Newton & Irvine, N.Y.C., 1974—79; sr. v.p., assoc. gen. counsel, sec. The McGraw-Hill Cos., Inc., N.Y.C., 1979—. Mem.: ABA, Assn. Am. Pubs. (lawyers com.), Assn. Bar City N.Y., N.Y. State Bar Assn., Phi Beta Kappa. Corporate, general, Property, real (including real estate development, water), Securities. Office: The McGraw Hill Co Inc Fl 48 1221 Avenue Of Americas New York NY 10020-1095 E-mail: Scott_Bennett@Mcgraw-Hill.com.

BENNETT, STEVEN ALAN, lawyer; b. Rock Island, Ill., Jan. 15, 1953; s. Ralph O. and Anne E. B.; m. Jeanne Aring; children: Preston, Spencer, Hunter, Whitney. BA in Art History, U. Notre Dame, 1975; JD, U. Kans., 1982. Bar: Tex. 1983, Ohio 1995, U.S. Dist. Ct. (no. dist.) Tex. 1983, U.S. Ct. Appeals (5th cir.) 1983, U.S. Supreme Ct. 1995. Atty. Freytag, Marshall et al, Dallas, 1982-84, Baker, Mills & Glast, Dallas, 1984-87; ptnr. Shank, Irwin, Conant et al, Dallas, 1987-89; gen. counsel Bank One, Tex., N.A., Dallas, 1989-94; sr. v.p., gen. counsel, sec. Banc One Corp., Columbus, Ohio, 1994-99; exec. v.p., chief legal officer, sec. Cardinal Health, Inc., Dublin, Ohio, 1999-2001; pvt. practice Columbus, 2001—. City councilman, Mesquite, Tex., 1984-86, mayor pro tem, 1995; trustee Meadowview Sch., Mesquite, 1985-92; chair fin. com. St. Brendan Ch., Hilliard, Ohio, 1998—; pres., bd. dirs. Dallas Dem. Forum, 1993-94; bd. dirs. Ohio Hunger Task Force, Columbus; trustee Woodrow Wilson Internat. Ctr. for Scholars, Washington, 1996—, vice-chmn., 1999—; bd. dirs. Capitol U. Law Sch., Columbus, Ctr. for Thomas More Studies, Dallas. Fellow Am. Bar Found., Ohio State Bar Found.; mem. ABA, Dallas Bar Assn., Ohio State Bar Assn., Columbus Bar Assn., St. Thomas More Soc. (Dallas bd. dirs. 1990-94), Am. Corp. Counsel Assn. (sec. 1999-2000, bd. dirs. 1996-2002, chair policy com. 1997-99), Phi Beta Kappa. Avocation: landscape photography. Health, Banking, Corporate, general. E-mail: sbennett@columbus.rr.com.

BENNION, DAVID JACOBSEN, lawyer; b. Glendale, Calif., Jan. 29, 1940; s. Donald Clark and Margaret (Jacobson) B.; m. Constance Wilson, Jan. 27, 1966; children: Marian, Margaret, Elizabeth, David, Sarah, Heidi. BA, Stanford U., 1964, JD, 1966. Bar: Calif. 1966. Ptnr. Boccardo Law Firm, San Jose, Calif., 1966-79; mission pres. LDS Ch., Geneva, 1979-82; ptnr. Packard, Packard and Bennion, Palo Alto, Calif., 1982-90, Bohn, Bennion & Niland, San Jose, 1993-98; pvt. practice, San Jose, 1998—. Instr. continuing edn. of bar, personal injury trial. TMem. ABA, ATLA, Am. Bd. Trial Advs., Calif. State Bar, Am. Inns Ct. (past pres., exec. com. Santa Clara County chpt.). Republican. General civil litigation, Personal injury (including property damage), Product liability. Home: 650 Center Dr Palo Alto CA 94301 Office: 95 S Market St Ste 360 San Jose CA 95113-2301 E-mail: djb@djbennion.com.

BENOLIEL, JOEL, lawyer; b. Seattle, June 11, 1945; s. Joseph H. and Rachel (Maimon) B.; m. Maureen Alhadeff, Mar. 1971; 1 child, Joseph D. BA in Polit. Sci., U. Wash., 1967, JD, 1971. Bar: Wash., US Dist. Ct. (we. dist.) Wash., US Ct. Appeals (9th cir.), US Mil. Ct. Appeals. Assoc. atty. MacDonald, Horgue & Bayless, Seattle, 1971-73, ptnr., 1973-78; v.p., gen. counsel Jack A. Benaroya Co., Seattle, 1978-84; ptnr. Trammell Crow Co., Seattle, 1985-87, Spieker Ptnrs., Bellevue, Wash., 1987-92; sr. v.p. law and real estate, gen. counsel Price Costco, Inc., Issaquah, Wash., 1992—. Bd. dir. Overlake Sch., Redmond, Wash., 1995—, Congregation Ezra Bessaroth, Seattle, 1992-95. With US Army, 1968-74. Avocations: tennis, boating, skiing, reading fiction. Commercial, contracts (including sales of goods; commercial financing), Corporate, general, Property, real (including real estate development, water). Office: Price Costco Inc 999 Lake Dr Issaquah WA 98027-5367*

BENSON, ROBERT EUGENE, lawyer; b. Red Oak, Iowa, Apr. 7, 1940; s. Paul J. and Frances (Sever) B.; m. Ann Marie Lucke, July 20, 1968; children: Steven J., Robert J., Katherine A. BA, U. Iowa, 1962; LLB, U. Pa., 1965. Bar: Colo. 1965. Assoc. Holland & Hart, Denver, 1965-71, ptnr., 1971—. Adj. faculty U. Denver Coll. Law, 1992. Author: The Power of Arbitrators and Courts to Order Discovery in Arbitration, 1996, Application of the Pro Rata Liability, Comparative Negligence and Contribution Statues, 1994; co-author: How to Prepare For, Take and Use a Deposition, 5th edit., 1994; mng. editor: Colorado Construction Law, 1999, 2003; contbr. articles to profl. jours. Capt. USAF, 1965-73. Mem. ABA, Colo. Bar Assn., Denver Bar Assn. Avocations: golf, skiing. Home: 5454 Preserve Pky N Greenwood Village CO 80121-2185 Office: Holland & Hart LLP 555 17th St Ste 3200 Denver CO 80202-3950

BENSON, STUART WELLS, III, lawyer; b. Sewickley, Pa., Jan. 6, 1951; s. Stuart Wells and Rosalie (Sassin) B.; m. Ruthanne Ackerman, July 15, 1978; children: Kate Eileen, Laura Elizabeth, Sarah Wells. BA, Northwestern U., 1972; JD, U. Pitts., 1975. Bar: Pa. 1975, U.S. Dist. Ct. (we. dist.) Pa. 1975, U.S. Supreme Ct. 1982. Assoc. Brandt McManus Brandt & Malone, Pitts., 1975-80; ptnr. Dickie, McCamey & Chilcote, P.C., Pitts., 1980—96, Pietragallo, Bosick & Gordon, Pitts., 1996-2002, Dapper, Baldasare, Benson & Kane, PC, Pitts., 2002—. Contbr. articles to profl. jours. Bd. dirs. North Hills YMCA, Pitts., 1981-84. Mem. ABA, Am. Arbitration Assn. (Appreciation award 1980), Pa. Def. Inst., Pa. Claims Assn., Pitts. Claims Assn., Allegheny County Bar Assn., Pa. Bar Assn., Internat. Assn. Indsl. Accident Bds. and Commns., Oakmont Country Club, Wildwood Golf Club, Rotary (bd. dirs. 1979-87, pres. 1985, parliamentarian 1985—, found. chmn. 1999—) Republican. Episcopalian. Workers' compensation. Home: 2116 Grandeur Dr Gibsonia PA 15044-7498 E-mail: sbenson@dbbk.com.

BENTLEY, FRED DOUGLAS, SR., lawyer; b. Marietta, Ga., Oct. 15, 1926; s. Oscar Andrew and Ima Irene (Prather) B.; children from previous marriage: Fred Douglas, Robert Randall; m. Jane Morrill McNeel, Nov. 7, 1997. BA, Presbyn. Coll., 1949; JD, Emory U., 1948; HHD (hon.), PhD (hon.), LHD (hon.), Kennesaw State U., 2000. Bar: Ga. 1948. Sr. mem. Bentley & Dew, Marietta, 1948-51; ptnr. Bentley, Awtrey & Bartlett, Marietta, 1951-56, Edwards, Bentley, Awtrey & Parker, Marietta, 1956-75, Bentley & Schindelar, Marietta, 1975-80, Bentley, Bentley & Bentley, Marietta, 1975—. Pres. Beneficial Investment Co., Newmarket, Inc., Happy Valley, Inc., Bentley & Sons, Inc.; founder, chmn. emeritus bd. Charter Bank and Trust Co.; founder, trustee emeritus Kennesaw Coll. Mem. Ga. Ho. Reps., 1951-57, Ga. Senate, 1958; past pres. Cobb County (Ga.) C. of C.; founder, hon. curator Bentley Rare Book Galleries-Brenau U., Kennesaw State U.; mem., past chmn. Ga. Coun. Arts, 1976-89; mem. Gov.'s Fine Arts Com., 1990-92, Cummer Mus. of Art (hon. life); attache Ghana Olympic Com.; founder Cobb Emergency Svcs.; fell. U.S. Supreme Ct. Museum Acquisition Com., U.S. Constitution Museum; Served with USN. Recipient Blue Key Cmty. Svc. award, Founder's award, 1992, Clarisse Baquell award for outstanding svc., Spl. Svc. award Kennesaw State U., Robert Cleveland award for lifetime achievement in law; named Citizen of Yr., C. of C., 1951, Leader of Tomorrow, Time mag., 1953, Vol. Citizen of Yr., Atlanta Jour./Constn., 1981, Kennesaw Hist. Soc. Man of Yr., 1996, Brenau U.. Man of Yr. award, 1996, President's award Kennesaw State U., 1999, Disting. Alumna Marietta H.S., Bus. Assoc. of Yr. award ABWA, 2002, First Go to the Last Mile trphy, 2003; fellow J. Pierpont Morgan Libr., Oct. 15 Fred Bentley Day City & Coun.; Bridge named in his honor, 2000. Fellow Am. Trust Brit. Libr.; mem. Ga. Bar Assn., Ga. Mus. Art (bd. advisors, hon. life mem.), Nat. PTA (hon. life), Supreme Ct. Hist. Soc., Cobb Landmarks Soc. (founder), Kennesaw Mountain Jaycees (founder), Rotary (hon. life), Georgian Club (bd. dirs.), The Grolier Club (hon.), Fellows of Marietta Cobb Mus. of Art (founder). Republican. Presbyterian. General practice. Home: 1441 Beaumont Dr Kennesaw GA 30152-3201 Office: 241 Washington Ave NE Marietta GA 30060-1958

BENTLEY, PETER, lawyer; b. Jersey City, Sept. 1, 1915; s. Peter and Emma (Patterson) B.; m. Signe Von Krusenstierna, Apr. 15, 1944 (dec. Mar. 1984); 1 child, Frederique Bentley Boire; m. Jane Morfoot Chapman, Apr. 19, 1986. BA, Princeton U., 1938; JD, Yale U., 1941. Bar: N.Y. 1942, U.S. Ct. Appeals (2d cir.) 1943, U.S. Dist. Ct. (so. dist.) N.Y. 1944, Conn. 1952, U.S. Dist. Ct. Conn. 1954. Assoc. Simpson, Thacher & Bartlett, N.Y.C., 1941—52, Maguire, Cole, Bentley & Babson (and predecessors), Stamford, Conn., 1952—81; mem. Bentley, Mosher, Babson & Lambert, P.C. and predecessors, Stamford, 1981—99; of counsel Bentley, Mosher, Babson, & Lambert P.C., Greenwich, Conn., 1999—2002. Rep. Greenwich Town Meeting, 1966—68; bd. dirs., pres. The Carl J. Herzog Found. Inc., 1978—; bd. dirs. Feris Found. Am. Inc., 1983—90, The Royal Soc. of Medicine Found., Inc., 1991—96. Mem. ABA, Conn. Bar Assn., Stamford Bar Assn. (pres. 1971-72, bd. dirs.), Am. Skin Assn. (bd. dirs., chmn. 1988-96). Mem. Soc. Of Friends. Estate planning, General practice, Labor (including EEOC, Fair Labor Standards Act, labor-management relations, NLRB, OSHA). Home: Crawford 232 7 Riverwoods Dr Exeter NH 03833-4374 Office: Bentley Mosher Babson & Lambert PC 321 Railroad Ave Greenwich CT 06830-0788

BENTON, ANTHONY STUART, lawyer; b. Decatur, Ill., Jan. 28, 1949; s. Paul Stewart and Allene Juanita (Jones) B.; m. Peggy Ann Miller, Aug. 6, 1977; children: Allison Renee, Emily Elizabeth, Anne McKinley. BA cum laude, U. Ill., 1971; JD summa cum laude, Ind. U., 1976. Bar: Ill. 1976, Ind. 1976, U.S. Dist. Ct. (so. and no. dists.) Ind. 1976, U.S. Ct. Appeals (7th cir.) 1978, U.S. Supreme Ct. 1993. Assoc. Stuart & Branigin, Lafayette, Ind., 1976-80, ptnr., 1980—; chief legal counsel Purdue U., 2000—. Prof. in environ. Purdue U. Sch. Civil Enging., 1993-2000. Bd. dirs. Lafayette C. of C., 1993-2003, treas., 1998, chair-elect, 1999, chmn. 2000-01; bd. dirs. New Directions, Lafayette, 1978-80, Clegg Found., Lafayette, 1980-83, Wabash Ctr., Lafayette, 1984-86, Greater Lafayette CDC, 2001—, exec. com.; mem. pres. coun. Purdue U., 1990—, convocations bd. dirs., 1991-97. With USNR, 1971-77. Fellow Ind. Bar Found. (bd. dirs. 1998-02); mem. Nat. Assn. R.R. Trial Counsel, Ind. State Bar Assn. (sec. sect. on environ. law 1992), Ill. State Bar Assn., Am. Judicature Soc., Environ. Law Inst., Masons. Education and schools, Environmental, Labor (including EEOC, Fair Labor Standards Act, labor-management relations, NLRB, OSHA). Office: Stuart & Branigin PO Box 1010 Lafayette IN 47902-1010 E-mail: asb@stuartlaw.com.

BENTON, AUBURN EDGAR, lawyer; b. Colorado Springs, Colo., July 12, 1926; s. Auburn Edgar and Ella Dot (Heyer) B.; m. Stephanie Marie Jakimowitz, June 8, 1951; children— Margrit Laura, Mary Ellen BA, Colo. Coll., 1950; LLB, Yale U., 1953. Bar: Colo. 1953, U.S. Dist. Ct. Colo. 1953, U.S. Ct. Appeals (10th cir.) 1954. Assoc. Holme Roberts & Owen, Denver, 1953-57, ptnr., 1957-91, of counsel, 1992—. Mem. Bd. Edn. Denver Pub. Schs., 1961-69; mem. Colo. Commn. Higher Edn., Denver, 1975-85; mem. Colo. Bd. Ethics, Denver, 1975-98; mem. Nat. Common Cause Bd., Washington, 1975-85; dir. soc. sci. found. U. Denver. Mem. Colo. Bar Assn., Denver Bar Assn., Cactus Club (Denver), Phi Beta Kappa. Democrat. Environmental. Home: 901 Race St Denver CO 80206-3735 Office: Holme Roberts & Owen 1700 Lincoln St Ste 4100 Denver CO 80203-4541

BENTON, DONALD STEWART, publishing company executive, lawyer; b. Marlboro, N.Y., Jan. 2, 1924; s. Fred Stanton and Agnes (Townsend) B. Student, U. Leeds, Eng., 1945; BA, Columbia U., 1947, JD, 1949; LLM, NYU, 1953. Bar: N.Y. 1953. Practiced in N.Y.C., 1953-56; atty. N.Y. State Banking Dept., 1954-55; v.p. Found. Press, Inc., Bklyn., 1957-60; exec. asst. to exec. v.p. N.Y. Stock Exchange, 1960-61; dir. reference book dept. and spl. projects editor Appleton Century Crofts, N.Y.C., 1962-71; sr. editor Matthew Bender & Co., Inc., N.Y.C., 1974-77; sr. legal editor Warren, Gorham & Lamont, Inc., N.Y.C., 1977-89. Author: Thorndike Encyclopedia of Banking and Financial Tables, 3rd edit., 2000 yearbook, Federal Banking Laws, 3rd edit., 2000, Real Estate Tax Digest, 1984, Criminal Law Digest, 3rd edit., 1983, Modern Real Estate and Mortgage Checklists, 1979. Mem. Cresskill (N.J.) Zoning Bd. Adjustment, 1969-71, 82-83, 86—, Cresskill Planning Bd., 1971-74; councilman City of Cresskill, 1972-74. With AUS, 1943-46, 50-52. Decorated Bronze Star. Mem. Phi Delta Phi. Mem. Reformed Ch. in Am. Home: 117 Heatherhill Rd Cresskill NJ 07626-1020 Office: AS Pratt & Sons- Warren Gorham & Lamont 395 Hudson St New York NY 10014-3669

BENTON, LEE F. lawyer; b. Springfield, Ohio, Feb. 18, 1944; AB, Oberlin Coll., 1966; JD, U. Chgo., 1969. Bar: Calif. 1970. Mng. ptnr. Cooley Godward LLP, Palo Alto, Calif. Teaching fellow Stanford Law Sch., 1969-70. Mem. Order Coif, Phi Beta Kappa. Corporate, general, Mergers and acquisitions, Securities. Office: Cooley Godward LLP 5 Palo Alto Sq 3000 El Camino Real Palo Alto CA 94306-2120

BENTON, W. DUANE, judge; b. Springfield, Mo., Sept. 8, 1950; s. William Max and Patricia F. (Nicholson) B.; m. Sandra Snyder, Nov. 15, 1980; children: Megan Blair, William Grant. BA in Polit. Sci. summa cum laude, Northwestern U., 1972; JD, Yale U., 1975; MBA in Accounting, Memphis State U., 1979; student Inst. Jud. Adminstrn., NYU, 1992; LLD (hon.), Ctrl. Mo. State U., 1994; LLM, U. Va., 1995; LLD (hon.), Westminster Coll., 1999. Bar: Mo. 1975; CPA, Mo. Ensign USN, 1972; advanced through grades to capt., 1993; judge advocate USN, Memphis, 1975-79; chief of staff for Congressman Wendell Bailey, Washington, 1980-82; pvt. practice Jefferson City, Mo., 1983-89; dir. revenue Mo. Dept. of Revenue, Jefferson City, 1989-91; judge Mo. Supreme Ct., Jefferson City, 1991—, chief justice, 1997-99. Adj. prof. Westminster Coll., U. Mo.-Columbia Sch. Law. Contbr. articles to profl. jours.; mng. editor Yale Law Jour., 1974-75 Chmn. Multistate Tax Commn. Washington, 1990-91; chmn. Mo. State Employees Retirement System, Jefferson City, 1989-93; regent Ctrl. Mo. State U., 1987-89; dir. Coun. for Drug Free Youth, Jefferson City, 1989-97; mem. Mo. Mil. Adv. Com., 1989-91; mem. Mo. Commn. Intergovernmental Coop., Jefferson City, 1989-91; trustee, deacon 1st Bapt. Ch., Jefferson City. Danforth fellow JFK Sch. Govt. Harvard U., 1990. Mem. AICPA (tax com. 1983—), Mo. Bar Assn. (tax com. 1975—), Mo. Soc. CPA's (tax com. 1983—), Navy League, Mil. Order of World Wars, Vietnam Vets of Am., VFW, Am. Legion, Phi Beta Kappa, Beta Gamma Sigma, Rotary. Baptist. Lt. USN, 1975-80. Capt. JAGC USNR, 1993-2002. Office: Supreme Court PO Box 150 Jefferson City MO 65102-0150 E-mail: dbenton@osca.state.mo.us.

BERALL, FRANK STEWART, lawyer; b. N.Y.C., Feb. 10, 1929; s. Louis J. and Jeannette F.; m. Christiana Johnson, July 5, 1958 (dec. July 1972); children: Erik Dustin, Elissa Alexandra; m. Jenefer M. Carey, Sept. 1, 1980. BS, Yale U., 1950, JD, 1955; LLM in Tax, NYU, 1959. Bar: N.Y. 1955, Conn. 1960; accredited estate planner. Assoc. firm Mudge, Stern, Baldwin & Todd, N.Y.C., 1955-57, Townley, Updike, Carter & Rodgers, N.Y.C., 1957-60; atty. Conn. Gen. Life Ins. Co., Bloomfield, Conn., 1960-65; atty. trust dept. Hartford Nat. Bank & Trust Co., Conn., 1965-67; assoc. Cooney & Scully, Hartford, Conn., 1968-70; ptnr. Copp & Berall and predecessors, Hartford, 1970—. Asst. in instrn. Yale U. Law Sch., 1954—55; lectr. U. Conn. Sch. Ins., 1964—72, U. Conn. Law Sch., 1972—73; instr. estate planning Am. Coll. Life Ins., 1968—69; v.p., sec., gen. counsel John M. Blewer, Inc., Essex, Conn., 1969—86; counsel Conn. Gov.'s Strike Force for Full Employment, 1971—72, Conn. Gov.'s Commn. on Tax Reform, 1972—73, State Tax Commr.'s Commn., 1972—75, Com. on Tax Law Clarification, 1984—88; adj. asst. prof. grad. tax program U. Hartford, 1973—74; trustee Culver Ednl. Found., 1997—99; estate tax planning advisor; lectr., spkr. in field. Co-author: A Practitioners Guide to the Tax Reform Act of 1969, 1970, Estate Planning and the Close Cooperation, 1970, Planning Large Estates, 1970, Revocable Inter Vivos Trusts, 1985, The Migrant Client: Tax, Community Property, and Other Considerations, 1994; sr. editor Conn. Bar Jour., 1969—, mem. editl. bd. Estate Planning mag., 1973—, Practical Tax Lawyer, 1988—, Jour. Taxation of Trusts and Estates, 1988—92, Estate Tax Planning Advisor. Bd. dirs. Bloomfield Interfaith Homes, 1967—71; adv. coun. U. Hartford Tax Inst., 1970—82; trustee Culver Ednl. Found., 1997—99; co-chmn. adv. coun. Hartford Tax Inst., 1986—94; co-chmn. Notre Dame Estate Planning Inst., 1977—. 1st lt., F.A. U.S. Army, 1951—52. Fellow: Am. Coll. Trust and Estate Counsel (Conn. chpt. chmn. 1975—81, mem. editl. bd. 1975—87); mem.: ABA, Internat. Acad. Estate and Trust Law, Am. Law Inst., Hartford County Bar Assn. (chmn. com. liaison with IRS 1972—74, com. charter and by-laws 1975), Conn. Bar Assn. (chmn. tax sect. 1969—72, exec. com. 1969—, exec. com., estates and probate sect. 1973—, vice chmn. com. on specialization 1974—77, chmn. 1984—86), Am. Coll. Tax Counsel, Culver Summer Schs. Alumni Assn. (v.p. 1975—85, bd. dirs. 1985—91, 1993—, pres. 1997—99), Yale Club of Harford (dir. 1998—, pres. 1999—), Culver Club Ctrl. New Eng. (pres. 1996—), Tax Club of Hartford (pres. 1975—76). Probate (including wills, trusts), Estate taxation, State and local taxation. Home: 9 Penwood Rd Bloomfield CT 06002-1520 Office: Copp & Berall LLP 864 Wethersfield Ave Hartford CT 06114-3184

BERCH, REBECCA WHITE, state supreme court justice, lawyer; b. Phoenix, June 29, 1955; d. Robert Eugene and Janet Kay (Zimmerman) White; m. Michael Allen Berch, Mar. 9, 1981; 1 child, Jessica. BS summa cum laude, Ariz. State U., 1976, JD, 1979, MA, 1990. Bar: Ariz. 1979, U.S. Dist. Ct. Ariz., U.S. Ct. Appeals (9th cir.), U.S. Supreme Ct. Assoc., ptnr. McGroder, Tryon, Heller, Rayes & Berch, Phoenix, 1979-85; dir. legal rsch. and writing program Ariz. State U. Coll. Law, Tempe, 1986-91, 94-95; solicitor gen. State of Arizona, Phoenix, 1991-94, 1st asst. atty. gen., 1996—98; judge Ariz. Ct. Appeals, 1998—2002, Ariz. Supreme Ct., Phoenix, 2002—. Co-author: (Book) Introduction to Legal Method and Process, 1985, 2002, Teacher's Manual for Introduction to Legal Method and Process, 1992, 2002, Handling Complex Litigation, 1986; Bd. editors Jour. Legal Writing Inst., 1993—2002; contbr. articles to profl. jours. and newspapers. Bd. dirs. Tempe-Mesa chpt. ACLU, 1984—86, Homeless Legal Assistance Project , Phoenix, 1990—98. Mem. Ariz. Women Lawyer's Assn., Ariz. State Bar Assn. Republican. Methodist. Avocations: reading, travel. Office: Ariz Supreme Ct 1501 W Washington St Phoenix AZ 85009-3831

BERDON, ROBERT IRWIN, judge trial referee, retired state supreme court justice; b. New Haven, Dec. 24, 1929; s. Louis J. and Jean (Cohen) B.; m. Nancy Tarr, Aug. 30, 1964 (dec. Mar. 1992); 1 child, Peter A. BS, Duke U., 1951; JD, U. Conn., 1957; LLM in Jud. Process, U. Va., 1988. With Bank of Manhattan, 1953-54; pvt. practice New Haven, 1957-73; treas. State of Conn., 1971-73; judge Superior Ct., State of Conn., New Haven, 1973-91; justice Supreme Ct., State of Conn., 1991-99, ret., 1999—99, judge trial referee, 2000—. Adj. prof. law U. Bridgeport Sch. Law, 1986-91; lectr. in law U. Conn. Sch. of Law, 1993; assoc. fellow Saybrook Coll., Yale U., 1986—; lectr. Am. Bd. Trial Advs., 1986; mem. Conn. Bd. Pardons, 1991-92. Contbr. articles to profl. jours. Recipient Judiciary award Conn. Trial Lawyers Assn., 1976, Disting. Alumni award U. Conn., 1977, Outstanding State Trial Judge in U.S. award Assn. Trial Lawyers in Am., 1982, Pub. Svc. award U. Conn. Sch. Law Alumni Assn., 1989, Judiciary award Conn. Bar Assn., 1991, Hartford Neighborhood Housing Coalition award, 1992, RosCossi - Koskoff Justice award Conn. Trial Lawyers Assn., 1999, Jud. Recognition award Conn. Def. Lawyers Assn., 1999. Home: 245 Pleasant Point Rd Branford CT 06405-5609 Office: Superior Ct 235 Church St New Haven CT 06510

BERENATO, MARK ANTHONY, lawyer, insurance executive; b. Lansdowne, Pa., Feb. 24, 1958; s. Anthony Francis and Dena Marie (Marchione) B.; m. Linnie Louise Swineford, Sept. 9, 1989. Diploma, Episcopal Acad., 1976; BS in Acctg., Villanova U., 1980; JD, Am. U., 1983; postgrad., Temple U., 1984. Bar: Pa. 1984, U.S. Dist. Ct. (ea. dist.) Pa. 1987. Tax lawyer Deloitte, Haskins & Sells, N.Y.C., 1984-85; pvt. practice Law Offices of Mark A. Berenato, Phila., 1985—. Counsel Custom Art Metals, Inc., Barrington, N.J., 1985-91; pres. Cumberland Devel. Corp., Voorhees, N.J., 1989-95; sec., gen. counsel Sterling Metal Fabricators, Inc., Barrington, N.J., 1985-93; prin. Mark A. Berenato Ins. Agy., Glen Mills, Pa., 1993—. Mem. ABA, Pa. Bar Assn., Phila. Bar Assn., Rolling Green Golf Club, Vesper Club, Phi Alpha Delta. Republican. Roman Catholic. Avocations: golf, literature, antique collecting. General civil litigation, Corporate, general, Insurance. Home: 740 Iris Ln Media PA 19063 Office: 2 Penn Ctr Ste 200 Philadelphia PA 19102-1754 E-mail: markberenato@earthlink.net.

BERENDT, ROBERT TRYON, lawyer; b. Chgo., Mar. 8, 1939; s. Alex E. and Ethel L. (Tryon) B.; m. Sara Probert, June 15, 1963; children: David, Elizabeth, Katherine. BA, Monmouth Coll., 1961; JD with distinction, U. Iowa, 1965. Bar: Iowa 1965, Ill. 1968, U.S. Dist. Ct. (no. dist.) Ill. 1968, U.S. Ct. Appeals (7th cir.) 1968, Mo. 1979, U.S. Dist. Ct. (ea. dist.) Mo. 1979. Assoc. Schiff Hardin & Waite, Chgo., 1968-73, ptnr., 1973-78; litigation counsel Monsanto Co., St. Louis, 1978-83, asst. gen. counsel, 1983-85, assoc. gen. counsel, 1986-96; of counsel Thompson Coburn, St. Louis, 1996—. Disting. Neutral, Ctr. for Pub. Resources; editl. adv. bd. Alternatives, Inside Litigation, Product Safety and Liability Reporter-Bur. Nat. Affairs. Contbr. articles to profl. jours. Lt. USNR, 1965-68. Mem. ABA (litigation sect., coun. mem. 1993-96), Mo. Bar Assn., Ill. Bar Assn., Iowa Bar Assn., Bar Assn. Met. St. Louis, Product Liability Adv. Coun. (bd. dirs., exec. com., Inst. for the Judiciary, pres.-trustee Found. 1992-98). Avocations: golf, tennis, reading. Antitrust, General civil litigation, Environmental. Office: Thompson Coburn 1 Mercantile Ctr Ste 3400 Saint Louis MO 63101-1643

BERENS, MARK HARRY, lawyer; b. St. Paul, Aug. 4, 1928; s. Harry C. and Gertrude M. (Scherkenbach) B.; m. Barbara Jean Steichen, Nov. 20, 1954; children: Paul J., Joseph F. (dec.), John M., Stephen M., Thomas M., Michael M., Lisa B. Moran, James M., Daniel M. BS in Commerce (Acctg.) magna cum laude, U. Notre Dame, 1950, JD magna cum laude, 1951; postgrad., U. Chgo., 1951-53. Bar: Ill. 1951, D.C. 1955, U.S. Supreme Ct. 1971; CPA, Ill. Assoc. Mayer, Brown and predecessors, Chgo., 1956-61, ptnr., 1961-96; chmn., CEO Attys.' Liability Assurance Soc., Inc., Chgo., 1987-95; ptnr. Altheimer & Gray, Chgo., 1996—. Chmn. bd. dirs. Attys.' Liability Assurance Soc. (Bermuda) Ltd., 1979-95; bd. dirs. Accts. Liability Assurance Co.; nat. chmn. Nat. Assn. Law Rev. Editors, 1950-51. Editor-in-chief Notre Dame Law Rev., 1950-51; contbr. articles to profl. jours. 1st lt. JAGC U.S. Army, 1953-56. Mem. ABA, D.C. Bar Assn., Chgo. Bar Assn., Am. Law Inst., The Comml. Bar Assn. (London), Am. Assn. Atty.-CPAs, Union League Club, Lawyers Club of Chgo., Met. Club, Sunset Ridge Country Club (Northbrook). Republican. Roman Catholic. Corporate, general, Insurance, Corporate taxation. Home: 1660 North Ln Northbrook IL 60062-4708 Office: Altheimer & Gray 10 S Wacker Dr Chicago IL 60606-7482

BERENS, WILLIAM JOSEPH, lawyer; b. New Ulm, Minn., Dec. 12, 1952; s. Robert J. and Lorraine M. (O'Brien) B.; m. Janet Christiansen, June 13, 1975; children: Margaret, Elizabeth, Catherine. BA, Coll. St. Thomas, 1975; JD, U. Minn., 1978. Bar: Minn. 1978. Assoc. Dorsey & Whitney, LLP, Mpls., 1978-83, ptnr., 1984—. Adj. prof. William Mitchell Coll. of Law, St. Paul, 1981-84. Fellow: Am. Coll. Trust and Estate Counsel. Estate planning, Probate (including wills, trusts), Estate taxation. Home: 1601 Beechwood Ave Saint Paul MN 55116-2409 Office: Dorsey & Whitney LLP 50 S 6th St Minneapolis MN 55402-1498

BERENSON, AIMEE ROBIN, lawyer; b. Bronxville, N.Y., Oct. 12, 1961; d. David Alan and Joan Barbara Berenson. BA with distinction, U. Wis., 1982; JD, NYU, 1986. Bar: Minn. 1986, U.S. Dist. Ct. Minn. 1986, D.C. 1991. Fed. law clk. Fed. Dist. Judge Harry MacLaughlin, Mpls., 1986—87; family law litigator Legal Aid Soc., 1987—89; policy counsel Women's Legal Def. Fund, Washington, 1989—92; legislative counsel & dir. govtl. affairs AIDS Action Counsel, 1992—96; mng. ptnr., owner Berenson Cons. Group, 1998—. Adj. prof. law The Cath. U. Am., Washington, 1991—. Mem.: ABA, D.C. Bar Assn., Am. Soc. Law, Medicine & Ethics. Health, Alternative dispute resolution, Civil rights. Office: Berenson Cons Group 1752 Willard St NW Ste 203 Washington DC 20009 Fax: 202-986-1988.

BERENSON, WILLIAM KEITH, lawyer; b. Nashville, Nov. 23, 1954; s. Leon and Lorraine Florence (Keiles) B; m. Mara Lynn Rubinton; 1 child, Marissa Laurel. BA with honors, U. Tex., 1976; JD, So. Meth. U., 1979. Bar: Tex. 1979, U.S. Dist. Ct. (no. dist.) Tex., U.S. Ct. Appeals (5th and 11th cirs.), U.S. Supreme Ct.; cert. personal injury trial law, Tex. Bd. Legal Specialization. Mem. Supreme Ct. Jury Task Force. Author: Evaluating Settlement Offers, 1990, Texas Automobile Injury Guide, 1993, Trying the Automobile Injury Case in Texas: Plaintiff's Perspective, 1995, Automobile Injury Cases in Texas, 1996, Quantification of Personal Injury Claims, 1997; mem. editl. bd. Ins. Settlement and Litigation Reporter, Ins. Issues Annotated. Chmn. Longhorn coun. Boy Scouts Am., Ft. Worth; bd. dirs. So. Meth. U. Alumni Assn., AIDS Interfaith Network; bd. dirs. Regional Coun. Parents and Alumni, So. Meth. U.; vol. atty. Animal Rescue Orgn. Fellow Tarrant County Bar Found.; mem. ABA, ATLA (sustaining mem. pub. interest group com.), State Bar Tex., Tex. Bar Assn., Tarrant County Bar Assn. (jud. evaluation com., fee arbitration com.), Tarrant County Lawyrs Assn. (bd. dirs. 1994-2003), Tex. Trial Lawyers Assn., Coll. State Bar Tex., Nat. Coll. Advocacy, Roscoe Pound Found., Phi Alpha Delta. Avocations: golf, snow skiing. General civil litigation, Personal injury (including property damage). Office: 900 River Plaza Tower 1701 River Run Fort Worth TX 76107-6579

BERENZWEIG, JACK CHARLES, lawyer; b. Bklyn., Sept. 29, 1942; s. Sidney A. and Anne R. (Dubowe) B.; m. Susan J. Berenzweig, Aug. 8, 1968; children: Mindy, Andrew. B.E.E., Cornell U., 1964; JD, Am. U., 1968. Bar: Va. 1968, Ill. 1969. Examiner U.S. Pat. Off., Washington, 1964-66; pat. adviser U.S. Naval Air Systems Command, Washington, 1966-68; ptnr. Brinks, Hofer, Gilson & Lione and predecessor firm, Chgo., 1968—. Editorial staff Am. U. Law Rev., 1966-68; contbr. articles to profl. jours. Mem. ABA, Chgo. Bar Assn., Ill. State Bar Assn., Bar Assn. 7th Fed. Cir., Va. State Bar, Internat. Trademark Assn. (bd. dirs. 1983-85), Brand Names Edn. Found. (bd. dirs. 1993-2000), Meadow Club (Rolling Meadows, Ill.), Miramar Club (Naples, Fla.), Delta Theta Phi. Federal civil litigation, Patent, Trademark and copyright. Home: 127 W Oak St Apt A Chicago IL 60610-5422 Office: Brinks Hofer Gilson & Lione Ltd Ste 3600 455 N Cityfront Plaza Dr Chicago IL 60611-5599 E-mail: jcb@brinkshofer.com.

BEREOLOS, DEMETRIUS THEODORE, lawyer; b. Tulsa, Dec. 6, 1954; s. Theodore James and Helen Alane (Vassilou) B. BA, U. Okla., 1978, MA, 1981; JD, Gonzaga U., 1985. Bar: Okla. 1987. Dep. ct. clk. Okla. Dist. Ct., Tulsa, 1981-82; instr. Tulsa Jr. Coll., 1988—. Bd. dirs. Tulsa Region NCCJ, 1992-98, Martin Luther King Com. Soc., 1990—, Holy Trinity Greek Orthodox Parish Coun., 1990-96; mem. governing bd. Okla. chpt. Common Cause, 1988-97; regent, Gonzaga U., Spokane, Wash., 1984-85. Mem. Tulsa County Bar Assn., Soc. Profl. Journalists, Am. Hellenic Ednl. Progressive Assn.(dist. officer 1985-90, 1995—, Masons, Phi Alpha Delta. Democrat. Greek Orthodox. Avocations: golf, jogging, matchbook collecting, button collecting. Home: 1929 S Cheyenne Ave Tulsa OK 74119-5011

BERESFORD, DOUGLAS LINCOLN, lawyer; b. Washington, June 1, 1956; s. Spencer Moxon and Ann (Lincoln) B.; m. Lori Anne Mainous, Sept. 22, 1990; children: Alexander Gould, Erik Mainous. AB cum laude, Harvard U., 1978; JD, Georgetown U., 1982. Bar: D.C. 1982, U.S. Ct. Appeals (D.C. cir.) 1984, U.S. Supreme Ct. 1986. Assoc. Morgan, Lewis & Bockius, Washington, 1982-83, Newman & Holtzinger, P.C., Washington, 1983-89, ptnr., 1989-94, Long, Aldridge & Norman, Washington, 1994-2000, Hogan & Hartson LLP, Washington, 2000—. Administrative and regulatory, FERC practice, Utilities, public. Office: Hogan & Hartson LLP 555 13th St NW Ste 700E Washington DC 20004-1161 E-mail: dlberesford@hhlaw.com.

BERG, DAVID HOWARD, lawyer; b. Springfield, Ohio, Mar. 4, 1942; s. Nathan Stewart Berg and Mildred (Besser) Berg-Filion; children: Geoffrey Alan, Gabriel Adam, Caitlin Hannah; m. Kathryn Page, July 10, 1994. Student, Tulane U., 1963; BA in English, U. Houston, 1964, JD, 1967. Bar: Tex. 1967, U.S. Dist. Ct. Tex. 1967, N.Y. 1989, U.S. Dist. Ct. (so. dist.) N.Y. 1990, U.S. Ct. Appeals (2d, 4th, 5th, 8th and 11th cirs.) 1990, U.S. Supreme Ct. 1990. Law clk. NLRB, Washington, 1967-68; ptnr. David Berg & Assocs., Houston, 1968-77, Berg & Androphy, 1977—. Mem. fed. ct. lawyers adv. com. U.S. Dist. Ct. (so. dist.) Tex.; mem. U. Houston Law Found., 1996—; spl. counsel commn. on lawyer discipline, Tex. State Bar, 1996—. Contbr. articles and essays to mags. Adviser Jimmy Carter Transition Govt., Washington, 1976; adviser Mayor Kathy Whitmire campaigns, 1980-91; patron Friends of Menil Collection, 1990-91; adviser campaign Mayor Bob Lanier, 1991; chmn. City of Houston's "Imagine Houston"; mem. adv. bd. Camp for All; bd. dirs. U. Houston Law Ctr, Law Found., 1996, Houston Shakespeare Festival, 1997, Anti-Defamation League, 2002, Houston Holocaust Mus.; chmn. bd. Houston Area Water Corp., 2001--. Recipient 1st pl. for best feature article in a scholarly jour. Nat. Assn. Publ., 1991. Fellow Internat. Acad. Trial Lawyers, Houston Bar Found.; mem. ATLA, Tex. Bar Assn. (chmn. grievance com. 1984-85), Tex. Bar Found., N.Y. State Bar Assn., Tex. Trial Lawyers Assn., Houston Trial Lawyers Assn., U. Houston Law Alumni Assn. (bd. dirs. 1992-95), Am. Bd. Trial Advocates (assoc.). Democrat. Jewish. Avocations: writing, running, fishing. Criminal, Personal injury (including property damage). Home: 16 Sunset Blvd Houston TX 77005-1838 Office: Berg & Androphy 3704 Travis St Houston TX 77002-9550

BERGAN, PHILIP JAMES, lawyer; b. White Plains, N.Y., Apr. 13, 1938; s. Raymond Patrick and Marjorie (Ward) B. m. Susan Ellen Bancroft, Sept. 18, 1965; children: David Andrew, Jeffrey Matthew. AB, Holy Cross Coll., 1960; MA, Stanford U., 1963; LLB, Yale U., 1964. Bar: N.Y. 1966, U.S. Ct. Appeals (2d cir.) 1966, U.S. Supreme Ct. 1971, U.S. Dist. Ct. (so. dist.) N.Y 1973. Assoc. Shearman & Sterling, N.Y.C., Paris, London, 1964-77; gen. counsel merchant banking group Citicorp/Citibank, N.A., N.Y.C., 1978-82; v.p. gen. counsel's office Citicorp/Citibank N.A., N.Y.C., 1982-84; assoc. gen. counsel Citicorp/Citibank, N.A., N.Y.C., 1984-91; from counsel to ptnr. D'Amato & Lynch, N.Y.C., 1992—. Bd. dirs. Household Bank, Prospect Heights, Ill., 1993-2003; 1st Ctrl. Nat. Life Ins. Co. of N.Y., N.Y.C., 1998-2002. Contbr. articles to profl. jours. Mem. ABA (banking law com. bus. law sect. 1992—), N.Y. State Bar Assn., Assn. Bar City N.Y. (banking law com. 1993-96, legal history com. 1995-98), Banking, Finance, Securities. Banking, Finance, Securities. Home: 935 Park Ave New York NY 10028-0212 Office: D'Amato & Lynch 70 Pine St Fl 47 New York NY 10270-0110

BERGER, ARTHUR SEYMOUR, organization executive, city official; b. N.Y.C., Sept. 19, 1920; m. Joyce Berger. JD cum laude, NYU. Bar: N.Y. 1949. Mcpl. atty. State of N.Y., 1963-71; pres. Survival Rsch. Found., Miami, Fla., 1981—; dir. Internat. Inst. for Study of Death, 1985—; instr. Inst. for Ret. Profls., U. Miami, 1999; instr. Lifelong Learning Soc., Fla. Atlantic U.; vice mayor City of Aventura. Instr. Acad. for Lifelong Learning, Fla. Internat. U., adj. prof., 1996-97; instr. Fla. Atlantic U. Lifelong Learning Soc., Inst. for Ret. Profls., U. Miami, Nova Southeastern U.; adj. prof. Broward Coll., 1989-94, Union Inst., 1990-92; cons. Readers Digest; former commr. City of Aventura, Fla. Author: Liberation of the Person, 1964, Aristocracy of the Dead, 1987, Lives and Letters in American Parapsychology, 1988 (outstanding acad. book list), Evidence of Life After Death: Casebook for Tough-Minded, 1988, Dying and Death in Law and Medicine, 1993, When Life Ends, 1995; co-author: The Encyclopedia of Parapsychology and Physical Research, 1991, Fear of the Unknown, 1995; co-editor: Religion and Parapsychology, 1989, Perspectives in Death and Dying, 1989, To Die or Not to Die?, 1990; mem. NYU Law Rev. Mem. Aventura (Fla.) City Commn.; mem. ethics com. Columbia Aventura Hosp. and Med. Ctr.; narrator reading program for blind Libr. of Congress. 1st lt. U.S. Army, 1942-46, 50-52. Recipient Ashby Meml. award Acad. Religion, grantee, 1985, Phys. Rsch. Found., 1984, Fla. Endowment of the Arts, 1989. Mem. DAV (life), Soc. for Sci. Exploration, Am. Soc. for Psychical Rsch., Soc. for Psychical Rsch., Parapsychol. Assn. E-mail: srf5@juno.com.

BERGER, CAROLYN, judge; BA, U. Rochester, 1969; MEd, Boston U., 1971, JD, 1976. Bar: Del. 1976, U.S. Dist. Ct. Del. 1976, U.S. Ct. Appeals (3d cir.) 1981, U.S. Supreme Ct. 1981. Dep. atty. gen. Del. Dept. Justice, Wilmington, 1976-79; assoc. Prickett, Ward, Burt & Sanders, Wilmington, 1979, Skadden, Arps, Slate, Meagher & Flom, Wilmington, 1979-84; vice-chancellor Ct. of Chancery, Wilmington, 1984-94; justice Del. Supreme Ct., 1994—. Mem. ABA, Del. Bar Assn. Office: Carvel State Office Bldg 820 N French St Fl 11 Wilmington DE 19801-3509

BERGER, CHARLES LEE, lawyer; b. Evansville, Ind., Oct. 14, 1947; s. Sydney L. and Sadelle (Kaplan) B.; m. Leslie Lilly, Apr. 20, 1973; children: Sarah, Rebecca, Leah. BA, U. Evansville, 1969; JD (cum laude), Ind. U., 1972. Bar: Ind. 1972, U.S. Dist. Ct. (so. dist.) Ind. 1972, U.S. Ct. Appeals (7th cir.) 1972, U.S. Ct. Appeals D.C. 1975, U.S. Supreme Ct. 1977, U.S. Dist. Ct. (we. dist.) Ky. 1981, U.S. Ct. Appeals (6th cir.) 1984. Ptnr. Berger & Berger, Evansville, 1972—. Mem. study com. Ind. Supreme Ct. Rules of Evidence, 1993—; mem. Ind. Jud. Qualifications Disciplinary Commn., 1998—. $Den— Sarah, Rebecca, Leah. B.A., U. Evansville, 1969; J.D. cum laude, Ind. U., 1972. Bar: Ind. 1972, U.S. Dist. Ct. (so. dist.) Ind. 1972, U.S. Ct. Appeals (7th cir.) 1972, U.S. Ct. Appeals D.C. 1975, U.S. Supreme Ct. 1977, U.S. Dist. Ct. (we. dist.) Ky. 1981, U.S. Ct. Appeals (6th cir.) 1984. Ptnr., Berger & Berger, Evansville, 1972—; mem. study com. Ind. Supreme Ct. Rules of Evidence, 1993—; mem. Ind. Jud. Qualifications Disciplinary Commn., 1998—. Bd. dirs. Leadership Evansville, 1977. Fellow Ind. Bar Found.; mem. Ind. Bar Assn. (chmn. trial lawyers sect. 1982-83), Am. Bd. Trial Advocates, Ind. Trial Lawyers Assn. (bd. dirs. 1973-77, 77-84, v.p. 1984—). Bd. dirs. Leadership Evansville, 1977. Fellow Ind. Bar Found.; mem. Ind. Bar Assn. (chmn. trial lawyers sect. 1982-83), Am. Bd. Trial Advocates, Ind. Trial Lawyers Assn. (bd. dirs. 1973-77, 77-84, v.p. 1984—). Jewish. Federal civil litigation, State civil litigation, Personal injury (including property damage). Home: 7408 E Sycamore St Evansville IN 47715-3762 Office: Berger & Berger 313 Main St Evansville IN 47708-1485 E-mail: cberger@bergerlaw.com.

BERGER, DAVID, lawyer; b. Archbald, Pa., Sept. 6, 1912; s. Jonas and Anna (Raker) B.; m. Barbara Simmons Wainscott, Nov. 5, 1997; children: Jonathan, Daniel. AB cum laude, U. Pa., 1932, LLB cum laude, 1936. Bar: Pa. 1938, D.C., N.Y. Asst. to prof. U. Pa. Law Sch., Phila., 1936-38, spl. asst. to dean; law clk. Pa. Supreme Ct., Phila., 1939-40; spl. asst. to dir. enemy alien identification program U.S. Dept. Justice, Washington, 1941-42; law clk. U.S. Ct. Appeals, 1946; pvt. practice Phila., Washington and N.Y.C.; city solicitor Phila., 1956-63; founder, chmn. Berger & Montague, P.C., Phila. Former counsel Sch. Dist. Phila.; former chmn. adv. com. Pa. Superior Ct.; mem. drafting com. fed. rules evidence U.S. Supreme Ct.; lectr. on legal subjects. Author numerous articles on law. Nat. commr. Anti-Defamation League; assoc. trustee U. Pa., mem. bd. overseers Law Sch.; Presdl. appointee U.S. Holocaust Meml. Coun.; dir. Internat. Tennis Hall of Fame; bd. dirs. ARC, Palm Beach, Fla.; founder, mem. Friends of Art and Preservation in Embassies. Decorated Silver Star and Presdl. Unit Citation; Fellow Duke of Edinburgh's Award World Fellowship; David Berger chair of law for the improvement of the adminstrn. of justice established at U. Pa. Law Sch.; enshrined in U. Pa. Tennis Hall of Fame, 1997. Fellow Am. Coll. Trial Lawyers, Internat. Acad. Trial Lawyers, Internat. Soc. Barristers; mem. ABA (vice-chair tort and ins. practice sect. com. on comml. torts 1988-89), Phila. Bar Assn. (pres., bd. govs., chancellor), Phila. Bar Found. (past pres.), The Athenaeum Phila., Penn Club (N.Y.C., founder), Order of Coif, The Queens Club (London), Royal Ascot Racing Club (Ascot, Eng.). Antitrust, Bankruptcy, Federal civil litigation. Home: Elephant Walk 109 Jungle Rd Palm Beach FL 33480-4809 Office: Berger & Montague PC 1622 Locust St Philadelphia PA 19103-6305

BERGER, HAROLD, lawyer, electrical engineer; b. Archbald, Pa., June 10, 1925; s. Jonas and Anna (Raker) Berger; m. Renee Margareten, Aug. 26, 1951; children: Jill Ellen, Jonathan David. BSEE, U. Pa., 1948, JD, 1951. Bar: Pa. 1951. Practiced in Phila.; judge Ct. of Common Pleas, Phila. County, 1971-72; chmn., moderator Internat. Aerospace Meetings Princeton U., 1965-66; chmn. Western Hemisphere Internat. Law Conf., San Jose, Costa Rica, 1967; chmn. internat. Confs. on Aerospace and Internat. Law, Coll. William and Mary; permanent mem. Jud. Conf. 3d Circuit Ct. of Appeals; mem. County Bd. Law Examiners, Phila. County, 1961-71; chmn. World Conf. Internat. Law and Aerospace, Caracas, Venezuela, Internat. Conf. on Environ. and Internat. Law, U. Pa., 1974, Internat. Confs. on Global Interdependence, Princeton U., 1975, 79; mem. Pa. State Conf. Trial Judges, 1972-80, Nat. Conf. State Trial Judges, 1972—; chmn. Pa. Com. for Independent Judiciary, 1973—. Adv. coun. Biddle Law Libr. U. Pa., 1991—, mem. bd. overseers Sch. Engring. and Applied Sci., 1998—. Mem. editl. adv. bd.: Jour. Space Law, U. Miss. Sch. Law, 1973—; contbr. articles to profl. jours. Mem. We the People 200 Com. for Constn. Bicentennial, 1991. With Signal Corps, AUS, 1944—46. Recipient Alumnus of the Yr. award, Thomas McKean Law Club, U. Pa. Law Sch., 1965, Space award, GE, 1966, Nat. Disting. Achievement award, Tau Epsilon Rho, 1972, Spl. Pa. Jud. Conf. award, 1981, Special National Distinguished Svc. Award, 1978. Mem.: ABA (past chmn. aerospace law com., mem. state and fed. ct. com., nat. conf. state trial judges, Spl. Presdl. Program medal 1975), Internat. Acad. Astronautics, Assn. U.S. Mems. Internat. Inst. Space Law Internat. Astronautical Fedn. (former bd. dirs.), Phila. Bar Assn. (past chmn. jud. liaison com. 1975, chmn. internat. law com. 1977), Fed. Bar Assn. (past nat. chmn. com. aerospace law, pres. Phila. chpt. 1983—84, chmn. class action and complex litig. com. 3d cir. 1990—, nat. chmn., alt. dispute resolution com. 1992—95, pres. eastern dist. Pa. chpt. 1996—, mem. nat. exec. coun., past chmn. fed jud. com., chair spl. bench bar liason com. eastern dist. Pa. chpt. 2001—, nat. com. 1987 bi-centennial of U.S. Constn., Presdl. award 1970, Spl. Disting. Svc. award ea. dist. chapter 2002), Inter-Am. Bar Assn. (past chmn. aerospace law com.). Alternative dispute resolution, Federal civil litigation, Entertainment. Office: 1622 Locust St Philadelphia PA 19103-6305

BERGER, JOHN TORREY, JR., lawyer; b. St. Louis, Apr. 14, 1938; s. John Torrey Sr. and Maud Alice (Beattie) B.; m. Helen Lee Thompson, Aug. 26, 1961; children: John Torrey III, Helen E. JD, Washington U., 1963. Bar: Mo. 1963. Assoc. Lewis, Rice & Fingersh, L.C., St. Louis, 1963-70; mem. Lewis & Rice, St. Louis, 1971—, chmn. real estate sect. Bd. dirs. Carr Lane Mfg. Co., St. Louis, St. Louis Audubon Soc., Logos Sch., St. Louis; adv. bd. dirs. St. Louis Screw & Bolt Co. Deacon, elder, trustee Presbyn. Ch., St. Louis, 1970-75, 75—. Mem. ABA (corp. sect., real estate sect.), Mo. Bar Assn. (real estate sect., banking and securities com.), Bar Assn. Met. St. Louis, Internat. Conf. Shopping Ctrs., SAR, Phi Delta Phi. Avocations: fishing, birding, photography. Corporate, general, Mergers and acquisitions, Property, real (including real estate development, water). Home: 1257 Takara Ct Saint Louis MO 63131-1013 Office: Lewis Rice & Fingersh 500 N Broadway Ste 2000 Saint Louis MO 63102-2147 E-mail: jberger@lewisrice.com.

BERGER, LAWRENCE HOWARD, lawyer; b. Phila., May 19, 1947; s. Howard Merrill Berger and Doris Eleanor Cummins; m. Julie Mitchell Collins, Aug. 8, 1970; children: Colby Shaw, Ryan Lawrence, Lindsey Wade. BS, Mich. State U., 1969; JD, U. Va., 1972. Bar: Pa. 1972, U.S. Dist. Ct. (ea. dist.) Pa. 1973, U.S. Ct. Appeals (3d cir.) 1986. Assoc. Morgan, Lewis & Bockius LLP, Phila., 1972-79, ptnr., 1979—. Bd. dirs. US Lacrosse, 2000—, chmn., 2002—. Trustee Agnes Irwin Sch., 1984-86, 1984—86, Naomi Wood Charitable Trust-Woodford Mansion Mus., 1986—, Fairmount Park Coun. for Hist. Sites, 1989—95, Fairmont Park Hist. Trust, 1993—95; dir. Phila. Lacrosse Assn., 1992—2000. Recipient Frank Carr Community Svc. award, 1991. Fellow Am. Bar Found.; mem. ABA (sec. com. on nonprofit corps. 1980-90), Pa. Bar Assn. (chmn. com. on uniform comml. code 1978-80), Phila. Bar Assn., Pa. Bar Inst., Banking Law Inst. (lectr. 1985), Pa. Bankers Assn. (lectr. 1980, 89), Martins Dam Club, Blue Key, Omicron Delta Kappa. Banking, Corporate, general, Non-profit and tax-exempt organizations. Home: 360 Pond View Rd Devon PA 19333-1732 Office: Morgan Lewis & Bockius LLP 1701 Market St Philadelphia PA 19103-2903

BERGER, MARC JOSEPH, lawyer; b. Chgo., June 28, 1947; s. Lawrence and Esther Berger; m. Eileen Neiberg, Aug. 29, 1971. MA in Music Theory, U. Chgo., 1973; MusD, Northwestern U., 1984; JD, Southwestern U., 1989. Bar: Calif. 1989, U.S. Dist. Ct. (ctrl. dist.) Calif. 1989, U.S. Ct. Appeals (9th cir.) 1989. Prof. music Am. Conservatory Music, Chgo., 1973-79; assoc. Yusim Stein & Hanger, Encino, Calif., 1989-91, Howarth & Smith, L.A., 1991-97, Théver & Assocs., L.A., 1999—2001, Beam, Brobeck, West & Sullivan, Santa Ana, Calif., 2001—02, Michael P. Stone P.C., Pasadena, Calif., 1997-99, 2003—. Composer (opera) Der Gruftwächter, 1998. Wildman scholar Southwestern U., 1985-89. Avocations: music, theater, chess. Appellate, General civil litigation, Labor (including EEOC, Fair Labor Standards Act, labor-management relations, NLRB, OSHA).

BERGER, ROBERT BERTRAM, lawyer; b. N.Y.C., Sept. 1, 1924; s. Edward William and Sophie (Berkowitz) B.; m. Phyllis Ann Korona, June 14, 1947; children: Barry Robert, Mark Alan, Karen Elizabeth Berger Adametz, James Michael; m. 2d, Arlene Kidder Wills, Dec. 27, 1980; 1 stepchild, Kimberly Kidder Wills Campbell. BS, Georgetown U., 1948; JD, U. Conn., 1952. Bar: Conn. 1952, U.S. Dist. Ct. Conn. 1953, U.S. Tax Ct. 1967, U.S. Ct. Appeals (2d cir.) 1968. Sole practice law, 1952-56; ptnr. Berger & Alaimo, Enfield, Conn., 1956-82, Berger, Alaimo, Santy & McGuire, Enfield, Conn., 1982-91, Berger, Santy & McGuire, Enfield, 1991-94, Berger & Santy, Enfield, 1994—2001, Berger, Santy & Barbieri, Enfield, 2001—. Judge Probate Dist. of Enfield, 1989-94; dir. Enfield Vis. Nuses Assn., 1993-96; bd. dirs., mem. exec. com. Conn. Attys. Title Ins. Co., Rocky Hill. Chmn. Enfield Dem. Town Com., 1979-87, Conn. Psychiat. Security Review Bd., 1985—. Contbr. monthly polit. column Enfield Press, 1980-84. Pres. United Way North Ctrl. Conn., 1981-84; trustee St. Bernard's Roman Cath. Ch., 1977-90, 99-2000; trustee, exec. bd. mem. Johnson Meml. Hosp., Johnson Meml. Corp., Stafford, Conn.; bd. dirs. United Way of Capitol Area, 1981-85, United Way North Ctrl. Conn., 1977—. With USMCR, 1942-45. Decorated Purple Heart; recipient disting. svc. award Enfield Jr. C. of C., 1955, Clayton Frost award U.S. Jr. C. of C., 1959-60. Mem. ABA, Conn. Bar Assn., Hartford County Bar Assn., Enfield Lawyers Assn. (pres. 1973-74), Am. Judicature Soc., Enfield Rotary (pres. 1970-71, Paul Harris fellow 1984). Corporate, general, Probate (including wills, trusts), Property, real (including real estate development, water). Office: PO Box 1163 Enfield CT 06083-1163

BERGER, ROBERT MICHAEL, lawyer; b. Chgo., Jan. 29, 1942; s. David B. and Sophia (Mizock) B.; m. Joan B. Israel, Aug. 16, 1964; children: Aliza, Benjamin, David. AB, U. Mich., 1963; JD, U. Chgo., 1966. Bar: Ill. 1966, U.S. Supreme Ct. 1975. Law clk. to cir, judge Henry J. Friendly U.S. Ct. Appeals, 2d Circuit, N.Y.C., 1966-67; atty. Chgo. Legal Aid Bur. Law Reform Unit, 1967-68; mem. firm Mayer, Brown & Platt, Chgo., 1968-72, ptnr., 1972-2001; adjunct prof. Northwestern U. Law Sch., 1997—; exec. v.p., gen. counsel, sec. Capri Capital LP, 2001—; sr. counsel Krasnow, Saunders, & Cornblath, 2001—. Lectr. Northwestern U. Law Sch., 1973; adj. prof. grad. program in real estate law John Marshall Law Sch., 1995-97; summer inst. faculty mem. Nat. Inst. Law-Focused Edn., Chgo., 1969-74; mem. hearing bd. Ill. Supreme Ct. Atty. Disciplinary Sys., 1973-79; mem. Ill. Sec. State Adv. Com. on Revised Uniform Ltd. Partnership Act, 1984-88, mem. spl. tax adv. commn. to Ill. Dept. Ins., 1972; bd. dirs., legal counsel Consumer Fedn. Ill., 1967-71; mem. regional consumer adv. coun. coun. FTC, 1969; bd. dirs., chmn. program com. Legal

Assistance Found., Chgo., 1975-78; mem. Highland Park (Ill.) Zoning Bd. Appeals, 1984-86; chmn. blue ribbon com. Cook County Recorder, 1989-92; mem. real estate adv. bd. Dai-Ichi Kangyo Bank, Chgo., 1988-93; lectr. continuing legal edn. seminars. Comment editor: U. Chgo. Law Rev, 1965-66; author: Law and the Consumer, 1969, 74; author 500 page chpt. Lending, Finance and Banking, Construction Law, 1986, 92, ann. supplements; reporter Revised Uniform Ltd. Partnership Act, 1984-88; adv. com. Restatement of the Law of Property 3d-Mortgages; contbr. articles to law jours. Trustee Am. Friends of Hebrew U., bd. dirs., Primo Ctr. for Women and Children. Mem. ABA (chmn. subcom. on rev. uniform ltd. partnership act 1981-85, chmn. com. on partnerships and unincorporated bus. orgns. 1985-88), Am. Law Inst. (consultative group), Am. Coll. Real Estate Lawyers (bd. govs. 1995-98, nominating com., vice chmn. program com.), Chgo. Bar Assn. (bd. mgrs. 1970-72, chmn. com. on real estate fin. 1984-86, chmn. real property law com. 1987-88), Chgo. Coun. Lawyers (founder, bd. govs. 1969-71), Am.-Israel C. of C. (1st vice-chmn.), Order of Coif, Phi Beta Kappa, Phi Kappa Phi. Commercial, contracts (including sales of goods; commercial financing), Finance, Property, real (including real estate development, water). Office: Capri Capital LP Ste 3430 875 N Michigan Ave Chicago IL 60611 E-mail: rberger@capricap.com.

BERGER, SANFORD JASON, lawyer, securities dealer, real estate broker; b. Cleve., June 29, 1926; s. Sam and Ida (Solomon) Berger; m. Bertine Mae Benjamin, Aug. 6, 1950 (div. Dec. 1977); children: Bradley Alan, Bonnie Jean. BA, Case Western Res. U., 1950, JD, 1952. Bar: Ohio 52, U.S. Supreme Ct. 79, U.S. Ct. Appeals 81. Field examiner Ohio Dept. Taxation, Cleve., 1952; pvt. practice law Cleve., 1952—. Real estate cons., Cleve., 1960—; investment cons., Cleve., 1970—. Contbg. author Family Evaluation in Child Custody Litigation, 1982, Child Custody Litigation, 1986, The Parental Alienation Syndrome and the Differentiation Between Fabricated and Genuine Child Sex Abuse, 1987, Family Evaluation in Child Custody Mediation, Arbitration and Litigation, 1989; copyright 10 songs:. Candidate police judge, East Cleveland, 1955; mem. Bd. Edn., Beachwood, Ohio, 1963; judge ct. common pleas Cuyahoga County, Ohio, 1986; judge Ct. Appeals, 1988, 1990, 1992, 1994; mayor Beachwood, 1967. With USMC, 1944—45, PTO. Recipient Cert. Appreciation, Phi Alpha Delta, 1969, Healer award, U.S. Supreme Ct. Chief Justice Warren Burger, 1987, Outstanding Ohio Citizen award, Ohio Gen. Assembly, 1987. Mem.: B'nai B'rith (editor 1968—70). Republican. Jewish. Achievements include being a successful lawyer in U.S. Supreme Ct. Case of Cleveland Bd. of Edn. vs. Loudermill, 1985; 17 appeals to Supreme Court. Avocations: writing poetry, writing lyrics, legal writing, drag racing, scuba diving. Civil rights, Federal civil litigation, Constitutional. Home: 1032 Som Center Rd Cleveland OH 44143-3527 Office: Sanford J Berger 1836 Euclid Ave # 305 Cleveland OH 44115-2234

BERGER, STEVEN R. lawyer, state official; b. Miami, Aug. 23, 1945; s. Jerome J. and Jeanne B. B.; m. Francine Blake, Aug. 20, 1966; children: Amy, Charlie. BS, U. Ala., 1967; JD, 1969. Bar: Fla. 1969, U.S. Dist. Ct. (no. dist.) Fla. 1969, U.S. Dist. Ct. (so. dist.) Fla. 1971, U.S. Ct. Appeals (5th cir.) 1971, U.S. Supreme Ct. 1972, U.S. Ct. Claims 1977, U.S. Ct. Appeals (11th cir.) 1981, U.S. Dist. Ct. (mid. dist.) Fla. 1989, N.Y. 1990, Nev. 1991, U.S. Dist. Ct. Nev. 1991, U.S. Ct. Appeals (2nd and 9th cirs.) 1991; cert. appellate specialist Fla. Bar Bd. Assoc. W. Dexter Douglass, Tallahassee, Fla., 1969-71, William R. Dawes, Miami, 1971; ptnr. Carey, Dwyer, Cole Selwood & Bernard, Miami, 1971-81; sole practice Steven R. Berger, P.A., 1981-89; ptnr. Wolpe, Leibowitz, Berger & Brotman, 1989-94, Berger & Chafetz, 1994-99; asst. atty. gen. State of Fla., 1999—. Mem. faculty Nat. Appellate Advocacy Inst., Washington, 1980; vice chmn. bench and bar adv. com. Ct. Appeals. 4th Dist., 1986-92. Mem. steering com. Fla. Appellate Practice Manual, Fla. Bar CLE, 3d, 4th, 5th edits. Chmn. City Miramar Planning Bd., 1975-76. Mem. ABA (vice chmn. app. practice com. litigation sect. 1981-83, chmn. 5th cir. subcom. appellate practice com. 1978-81), Am. Judicature Soc., Am. Arbitration Assn., Rep. Nat. Lawyers Assn., Tallahassee Bar Assn. Appellate, General civil litigation, Criminal. Office: Office of Atty Gen 444 Brickell Ave Ste 950 Miami FL 33131-2407

BERGERSON, DAVID RAYMOND, lawyer; b. Mpls., Nov. 23, 1939; s. Raymond Kenneth and Katherine Cecille (Langworthy) Bergerson; m. Nancy Anne Heeter, Dec. 22, 1962; children: W. Thomas C., Kirsten Finch, David Raymond. BA, Yale U., 1961; JD, U. Minn., 1964. Bar: Minn. 1964. Assoc. Fredrikson Law Firm, Mpls., 1964-67; atty. Honeywell Inc., Mpls., 1967-74, asst. gen. counsel, 1974-82, v.p., asst. gen. counsel, 1983-84, v.p., gen. counsel, 1984-92; pvt. practice law Mpls., 1992-94; v.p., sec. Telcom Sys. Svcs., Inc., Plymouth, Minn., 1994-96, dir., cons., 1996-97; v.p. bd. dirs. Hogan Bergerson, Inc., Mpls., 1997—. Mem. city coun. Minnetonka Beach, Minn., 2001—; bd. dirs. Pillsbury Neighborhood Svcs., Inc., Mpls., 1983—92. Republican. Avocations: scuba diving, bird-hunting. Corporate, general, Mergers and acquisitions, Securities. Home: 2303 Huntington Point Rd E Wayzata MN 55391-9740 Office: Hogan Bergerson Inc 4040 IDS Ctr Minneapolis MN 55402 E-mail: dbergerson1@mchsi.com.

BERGHOFF, PAUL HENRY, lawyer; b. Chgo., Aug. 25, 1956; s. John Colerick Sr. and Doris Margaret (Anderson) B.; m. Kathryn Elaine Thompson, May 30, 1981. BA cum laude in Chemistry, Lawrence U., 1978; JD cum laude, U. Mich., 1981. Bars: Ill. 1981, U.S. Dist. Ct. (no. dist.) Ill. 1981, U.S. Ct. Appeals (fed. cir.) 1983, U.S. Supreme Ct. 1986. Assoc. Allegretti & Witcoff, Ltd., Chgo., 1981-85, ptnr., 1985-96; founding ptnr. McDonnell Boehnen Hulbert & Berghoff, Chgo., 1996—. Mem. Intellectual Property Owners, Am. Intellectual Property Law Assn. Mem. United Ch. of Christ. Avocation: music. Federal civil litigation, Patent, Trademark and copyright. Office: McDonnell Boehnen Hulbert & Berghoff 300 S Wacker Dr Ste 3200 Chicago IL 60606-6709 E-mail: berghoff@mbhb.com.

BERGNER, JANE COHEN, lawyer; b. Schenectady, N.Y., Apr. 6, 1943; d. Louis and Selma (Breslaw) Cohen; m. Alfred P. Bergner, May 30, 1968 (dec. Sept. 24, 2002); children: Lauren, Justin. AB, Vassar Coll., 1964; LLB, Columbia U., 1967. Bar: D.C. 1968, U.S. Dist. Ct. D.C. 1968, U.S. Ct. Appeals (D.C. cir.) 1968, U.S. Ct. Fed. Claims 1969, U.S. Ct. Appeals (fed. cir.) 1969, U.S. Tax Ct. 1979, U.S. Supreme Ct. 1992. Trial atty. tax divsn. U.S. Dept. Justice, Washington, 1967-74; assoc. Arnold & Porter, Washington, 1974-76, Rogovin, Huge & Lenzner, Washington, 1976-83; of counsel Arter & Hadden, 1983-86; ptnr. Spriggs & Hollingsworth, 1986-89, Feith & Zell, P.C., 1989-93; pvt. practice Washington, 1993—. Mem. jud. confs. U.S. Ct. Fed. Claims, U.S. Tax Ct. Author: Tax Court Practice and Court of Federal Claims Practice, West's Federal Forms, vols. 8 and 9, 2003; contbr. articles to profl. jours. Bd. dirs. Jewish Social Svc. Agy., Washington, Jewish Coun. for the Aging, Washington; former mem. cmty. adv. bd. Sta. WAMU-FM, Washington. Fellow Am. Coll. Tax Counsel; mem. ABA (sect. taxation, govt. rels. com., ct. procedure com., civil and criminal penalties com., chmn. subcom. important devels. 1991-93, chmn. regional liaison meetings com. 1993-95, sect. litigation); Vassar Coll. Class Alumnae (chair spl. gifts com. 25th reunion), D.C. Bar (chair taxation sect. 1985-90, chair tax audits and litigation com. 1990-93, Outstanding Sect. award 1986, Cmty. Outreach award 1993), Fed. Bar Assn., Women's Bar Assn. D.C., Washington Estate Planning Coun., Women's Tax Luncheon Group, Columbia U. Law Sch. Alumni Assn., Svc. Guild Washington, Vassar Club. Federal civil litigation, Estate planning, Taxation, general. Home: 5659 Bent Branch Rd Bethesda MD 20816-1049 Office: Ste 650 1615 L Street NW Washington DC 20036 E-mail: jbergnerlaw@abanet.org.

BERGQVIST, TRINE OSEN, lawyer; b. Trondheim, Norway, July 5, 1973; arrived in Sweden, 1999; d. Arve Rasch Osen and Unni Horrigmo; m. Christian Bergqvist, Sept. 30, 2000. LLM, U. Bergen, 1997, Stockholm U., 2000. Bar: Norway 1999, Sweden 2002. Atty. Notar Advokat, Trondheim, Norway, 1996—97, Vogt & Co., Oslo, 1997—99, Delphi & Co., Stockholm, 2000—. Avocations: reading, painting, diving. Antitrust, Corporate, general, Commercial, contracts (including sales of goods; commercial financing). Office: Delphi & Co Box 1432 11184 Stockholm Sweden Fax: 0046 8201884. E-mail: trine.osen-bergqvist@delphilaw.com.

BERGREN, COLLEEN DOYLE, lawyer; b. Omaha, Oct. 16, 1953; d. Robert Harold and Kathleen Clare (Hansen) Doyle; m. Randy J. Bergren, Feb. 29, 1980; children: Christine, Jacob, Katie. JD, Creighton U., 1992. Bar: Nebr. 1992, U.S. Dist. Ct. (8th cir.) 1992. Pvt. practice, Gretna, Nebr., 1992—. Atty. Sarpy County Juvenile Ct., Papillion, 1994—; mem. nominating com. 2d Jud. Dist. Nebr., Papillion, 1996—. Mem. Gretna (Nebr.) Optimists, 1993—. Mem. Nebr. Bar Assn., Sarpy County Bar Assn. Estate planning, Family and matrimonial, General practice. Office: PO Box 115 Gretna NE 68028-0115

BERGSCHNEIDER, DAVID PHILIP, legal administrator; b. Springfield, Ill., Nov. 19, 1951; s. Fred J. and Ruby A. (Martin) B.; m. Dawn E. Combes, Sept. 23, 1989; children: Alec, Bryant, Cale. Student, Bradley U., 1969-71; BA, Ill. Coll., 1973; JD, Marquette U., 1976. Bar: Ill. 1976, Wis. 1976, U.S. Ct. Appeals (7th cir.) 1990, U.S. Supreme Ct. 1980. Mem. legis. staff Ill. Gen. Assembly, Springfield, 1976-77; asst. defender Office State Appellate Defender, Springfield, 1977-93, legal dir., 1993—. Co-author: Defending Illinois Criminal Cases, 1988, 2003, Illinois Criminal Practice, 1980, Brief Writing and Oral Argument Handbook, 1988, 94, 97; author: Illinois Handbook of Criminal Law Decisions, 1993, 2d edit., 1998, supplement, 2003; also articles. Recipient Award of Excellence Ill. Pub. Defender Assn., 1989. Mem. ABA, Ill. Bar Assn. (criminal justice sect. coun. 1987-91, 94-98, sec. 1995-96, chmn. 1996-97), Ill. Attys. for Criminal Justice, Aircraft Owners and Pilots Assn. Office: Office State Appellate Def PO Box 5780 Springfield IL 62705-5780

BERGSTEDT, ANDERS SPENCER, lawyer; b. Södertälje, Sweden, May 15, 1963; came to U.S., 1965; s. Jan-Eric Oskar and Vivianne (Sanfridsson) B.; m. Brandelyn Bergstedt, 2001. BA cum laude, U. Wash., 1985, JD, 1988. Bar: Wash. 1990, U.S. Dist. Ct. (we. dist.) Wash. 1990, U.S. Dist. Ct. (ea. dist.) Wash. 2002. Exec. dir. The Tenants Union, Seattle, 1988-90; mng. atty. Hyatt Legal Svcs., Seattle, 1990-92; pvt. practice Seattle, 1992—2000; sr. ptnr. Bergstedt Wolff, PS, Seattle, 2000—. Co-founder Transgender Law and Policy Inst., 2000—. Author: Translegalities: A Legal Guide for Transsexuals, 1997. Co-founder, treas. FTM Conf. and Edn. Project, Seattle, 1996—; mem. Vol. Attys. for People with AIDS, 1992—; bd. dirs. The Pride Found, 1993-95, Internat. Conf. Transgender Law & Employment Policy, 1996—; co-chair Seattle Commn. Lesbians and Gays, 1989-91; mem. adv. bd. Office Crime Victim Advs., Olympia, Wash., 1989-92. Mem. Wash. State Bar Assn., Wash. State Trial Lawyers Assn., Golden Key, Pi Sigma Alpha, Phi Beta Kappa. Bankruptcy, Entertainment, Estate planning. Office: 2133 3rd Ave Ste 106 Seattle WA 98121-2387

BERGSTEN, WILLIAM P. lawyer; b. Tacoma, Jan. 30, 1939; s. Paul Jennings and Ethel Helena Bergsten; 1 stepchild, Gretchen A. Colwill. BA in Bus. Adminstrn., Wash. State U., 1962; JD, U. Oreg., 1967. Bar: Wash. 1968, U.S. Dist. Ct. (we. dist.) Wash. 1968, U.S. Ct. Appeals (9th cir.) 1978. Atty., trial atty. FTC, Seattle and Washington, DC, 1968—71; dep. pros. atty. Piere County Pros. Atty.'s Office, Tacoma, 1971—72; atty., former mng. ptnr. McGavick Graves, Tacoma, 1972—. Bd. trustees Pierce County Bar Assn., 1978—80; regional v.p. CLE Bd. Law Fund, 1985—87; bd. govs. Wash. State Bar, 1987—90, treas., 1990; pres. Legal Found. Wash., 1991—94; past mem. CLE Ednl. Bd. Exec. v.p. Tacoma Art Mus. Com. for Activities Coun.; bd. dirs., pres. Pantages Performing Arts, 1991—. 1st lt. U.S. Army, 1962—64, Tex., Germany. Master: Puget Sound Inns of Ct. Avocations: golf, reading, travel. Arbitration and mediation, General civil litigation. Office: McGavick Graves 1102 S Broadway Ste 500 Tacoma WA 98401

BERICK, JAMES HERSCHEL, retired lawyer; b. Cleve., Mar. 30, 1933; s. Morris and Rebecca Alice (Gerdy) B.; m. Christine Berick; children: Michael, Daniel, Robert, Joshua. AB, Columbia U., 1955; JD, Case Western Res. U., 1958. Assoc. Burke, Haber & Berick, Cleve., 1958-60, ptnr., 1960-86, mng. ptnr., 1968-83; chmn. Berick, Pearlman & Mills Co. L.P.A., 1986-99; ptnr. Squire, Sanders & Dempsey, LLP, 2000—02, ret. ptnr., 2003—. Bd. dirs. MBNA Corp., MBNA Am. Bank, N.A., MBNA Europe Bank, Ltd., The Town and Country Trust, The Town and Country Funding Corp.; sec. A. Schulman, Inc., 1973—; lectr. law Case Western Res. U., 1969—78; sec. Cleve. Browns Football Co. LLC; bd. vis. Case Western Res. U. Sch. Law, 1998—. Founding trustee Rock and Roll Hall of Fame and Mus.; mem. Shaker Heights (Ohio) Bd. Edn., 1980-83; bd. visitors Columbia Coll., 1981-87, 90-96, emeritus, 2000—; bd. dirs. Univ. Circle Inc., 1994—; trustee Arthritis Found. of N.E. Ohio, chmn. major gifts com., mem. med. and sci. com. Mem.: Soc. of Benchers, Ct. of Nisi Prius, Seagate Beach Club, Union Club (Cleve.), Hermit Club, Shoreby Club, Order of Coif. Home: 14 W Mather Ln Bratenahl OH 44108-1158 Office: Squire Sanders & Dempsey LLP 4900 Key Tower 127 Public Sq Cleveland OH 44114-1216

BERK, ALAN S. law firm executive; b. N.Y.C., May 11, 1934; s. Phil and Mae (Buchberg) B.; m. Barbara Binder, Dec. 18, 1960; children— Charles M., Peter M., Nancy M. BS in Econs., U. Pa., 1955; MS in Bus., Columbia U., 1956. CPA N.Y., 1960. Staff acct. Arthur Young & Co., N.Y.C., 1956-62, mgr., prin., 1962-67; sr. v.p. Avco Corp., Greenwich, Conn., 1967-75; dir. Arthur Young & Co., 1975—, ptnr., 1976—, chief fin. officer, 1979-89; nat. dir. fin., treas. Ernst & Young, 1989-92; exec. dir. Kelley, Drye & Warren, N.Y.C., 1993-94. Mem. nat. adv. group Nat. Tech. Inst. for the Deaf, Rochester, N.Y.; chmn. bd. dirs. Jewish Home for the Elderly of Fairfield County, Inc., 1997-99, vice chmn., 2002—; 1st v.p., treas. Bruce Mus., Greenwich, Conn.; mem. golf bd. Town of Greenwich, Conn.; commn. on aging Town of Greenwich. With U.S. Army, 1957. Mem. AICPA, N.Y. State Soc. CPAs, Fin. Execs. Inst., Landmark Club, Stockbridge (Mass.) Golf Club, Lake Dr. Homeowners Assn. (pres.), Stockbridge Bowl Assn. (1st v.p.). Home: 14 Cornelia Dr Greenwich CT 06830-3906

BERK, GREG, lawyer; Sr. ptnr. Law Offices Greg Berk, Irvine, Calif., 1999—. Immigration, naturalization, and customs. Office: 5420 Trabuco Rd Ste 150 Irvine CA 92620 Office Fax: 949-387-0155. Business E-Mail: greg@calvisa.com.

BERKERY, ROSEMARY T. lawyer, investment company executive; b. 1953; BA, Coll. Mt. St. Vincent; JD, St. John's U., Jamaica, N.Y. Bar: N.Y. 1980. Sr. v.p., assoc. gen. counsel Merrill Lynch & Co., Inc., N.Y.C., 1995—97, co-dir. global securities rsch. and econs. group, 1997—2000, sr. v.p., head U.S. pvt. client group mktg. and investment, 2000—01, exec. v.p., gen. counsel, 2001—. Office: Merrill Lynch and Co Inc 4 World Financial Ctr 32d Fl New York NY 10080*

BERKMAN, ALLEN HUGH, lawyer; b. Canton, Ohio, Jan. 7, 1912; s. Hyman and Sarah B.; m. Selma Wiener, Mar. 20, 1938 (dec. Nov. 1995); children: Barbara B. Ackerman, Susan B. Rahm, Richard L., Helen B. Habbert, James S. AB, U. Mich., 1933; JD, Harvard Law Sch., 1936; LHD (hon.), Hebrew Union Coll., 1993. Lawyer, Pitts., 1937—; founder Berkman Ruslander Pohl Lieber & Engel, Pitts., 1965-89; atty. Kirkpatrick & Lockhart, LLP, Pitts., 1989—. Trustee Pitts. Trust for Cultural Resources, 1983—, exec. com.; adb. con. Benedum Ctr. Performing Arts; bd. dirs. Bedford Internat. Festival Found., 1991—, Pitts. Symphony Soc., 1978-94, bd. dirs. 1998—; pres. Rodef Shalom Congregation, 1976-82; bd. dirs. Montefiore Found. (now Jewish Healthcare Found. Pitts.), audit fin. com. 1990—; adv. bd. The Salvation Army Pitts., 1967-82; bd. dirs. United Jewish Fedn. Greater Pitts.; nat. bd. govs. Am. Jewish Com., nat. exec. coun. (Human Rels. award Pitts. chpt., 1994); bd. dirs. Nat. Conf. for Community & Justice; trustee, chair Winchester-Thurston Sch. for Girls; bd. dirs. Am. Friends Hebrew U.; hon. mem. nat. bd. govs. Hebrew Union Coll.-Jewish Inst. Religion; dir. emeritus World Affairs Coun. Pitts. Recipient David Glick award World Affairs Coun. Pitts., 1997. Fellow Pa. Bar Found.; mem. ABA, Pa. Bar Assn., Am. Law Inst., Am. Arbitration Assn., U.S. Supreme Ct. Hist. Soc., Am. Jud. Soc., Allegheny County Bar Assn., Phi Beta Kappa. Office: Kirkpatrick & Lockhart 1500 Oliver Building Pittsburgh PA 15222-2312

BERKMAN, MICHAEL G. lawyer, chemical consultant; b. Poland, Apr. 4, 1917; came to U.S., 1921; s. Harry and Bertha (Jay) B.; m. Marjorie Edelstein, Nov. 28, 1941; children— Laurel, William BS, U. Chgo., 1937, PhD, 1941; JD, DePaul U., 1958; LLM in Intellectual Property, John Marshall Law Sch., 1962; spl. courses, Harvard U., 1943, MIT, 1943. Bar: U.S. Patent Office 1960. Research chemist Argonne Nat. Lab., 1946-51; assoc. dir., chief chemist Colburn Labs., Chgo., 1951-59; instr. chemistry Roosevelt U., Chgo., 1946-49; patent lawyer Mann, Brown & McWilliams, Chgo., 1959-63; ptnr. Kegan, Kegan & Berkman, Chgo., 1963-84, Trexler, Bushnell, Giangiorgi & Blackstone, Chgo., 1984-91; pvt. practice law Glenview, Ill., 1991—. Chem. cons.; expert witness in patent law. Contbr. articles to profl. jours. Served to 1st lt. Signal Corps, U.S. Army, 1942-46. Mem. Am. Chem. Soc., ABA, Patent Law Assn., Chgo., Sigma Xi. Home and Office: 939 Glenview Rd Glenview IL 60025-3172

BERKMAN, WILLIAM ROGER, lawyer, army reserve officer; b. Chisholm, Minn., Mar. 29, 1928; s. Carl Emil and Millie (Mikkelson) B.; m. Betty Ann Klamt, Dec. 17, 1950. AB, U. Calif., Berkeley, 1950, JD, 1957. Bar: Calif. 1957, D.C. Ct. Appeals 1957, D.C. 1957. Law clk. to judge James Alger Fee, U.S. Ct. Appeals 9th cir., 1957-58; assoc. Morrison & Foerster, San Francisco, 1958-67, mem. firm, 1967-79; comdg. gen. 351st Civil Affairs Command, Mountain View, Calif., 1975-79; chief Army Res., Dept. of Army, Washington, 1979-86; mil. exec., Res. Forces Policy Bd., Office Sec. Def. Dept. of Def., Washington, 1986-92. Mng. editor: Calif. Law Rev, 1956-57. Pres. Sausalito (Calif.) Bd. Libr. Trustees, 1976-78; pres. Civil Affairs Assn., 1979-80, 93—; bd. dirs. Army Distaff Found., 1988-92; dir. Sausalito-Marin City Sanitary Dist., pres., 2002--. Maj. gen. U.S. Army, 1979—. Decorated DSM with oak leaf cluster, Def. DSM , Def. Superior Svc. medal , S. Order of Calif., U.S. Spl. Ops. command medal U.S. Army, USN, C.G., Legion of Merit medal, Army Commendation medal; named to Hall of Fame Sr. Army Res. Comdrs. Assn.; recipient Meritorious Svc. medal, Army Outstanding Civilian Svc. medal. Mem.: ABA (chmn. standing com. on lawyers in armed svcs. 1988—91), Civil Affairs Assn. (pres. 1992—99, pres. emeritus 1999—, chief civil affairs corps), Res. Officers Assn., Assn. U.S. Army, State Bar Calif., Army and Navy Club, Lions (dir. Sausalito Marin City san. dist., pres.). Home: 33 Atwood Ave Sausalito CA 94965-2245

BERKOFF, MARK ANDREW, lawyer; b. Boston, Aug. 8, 1961; s. Marshall Richard and Bebe R. B.; m. Susan Lynn Ochalek; children: Alexander, Rachel. BA with honors, U. Wis., 1983; JD, U. Chgo., 1986. Bar: Ill. 1987, U.S. Dist. Ct. (no. dist. Ill.) 1987, U.S. Ct. Appeals (7th cir.) 1990. Ptnr. Piper Rudnick, Chgo., 1986—. Vol. Am. Cancer Soc., Chgo., 1993-96, Make-A-Wish Found. No. Ill., 1998—. Mem. ABA, Chgo. Bar Assn., Turnaround Mgmt. Assn. Avocations: sports, collecting currier & ives prints, numismatics, family. Bankruptcy, Commercial, consumer (including collections, credit). Office: Piper Rudnick 203 N LaSalle St Ste 1800 Chicago IL 60601-1210

BERKOFF, MARSHALL RICHARD, lawyer; b. Milw., Apr. 10, 1937; s. Louis S. and Edith E. (Cohen) B.; m. Bebe R. Brandwein, June 19, 1960; children: Mark Andrew, Jonathan Hale, Adam Todd. BA, U. Wis., 1959; LLB, Harvard U., 1962. Bar: Wis. 1962, U.S. Dist. Ct. (we. and ea. dists.) Wis. 1962. Ptnr. Michael, Best & Friedrich, Milw., 1962—. Co-author: Employment Law Challenges of 1987, 1987, Labor Relations: The New Rules of the Game, 1984, The Legal Issues of Managing Difficult Employees, 1987; author/editor Currier and Ives "The New Best 50", 1991. Chmn. Charles Allis and Villa Terrace Art Mus., Milw., 1983-96; chmn. Milw. County War Meml. Corp., 1989-94, bd. dirs., 1983; chmn. bd. dirs. St. Michael Hosp., Milw., 1988-89; bd. dirs. Covenant Health Care, 1993-95. Mem. ABA (labor and employment sect., hosp. and health care law sect.), Wis. Bar Assn., (chmn. labor law sect. 1977-78), Milw. Bar Assn., Am. Hist. Print Collector Soc. (pres. 1987-90, bd. dirs. 2002—). Avocations: collecting, speaking, writing, restoring and cataloguing antique Am. lithographs, fishing. Health, Labor (including EEOC, Fair Labor Standards Act, labor-management relations, NLRB, OSHA). Office: Michael Best & Friedrich 100 E Wisconsin Ave Ste 3300 Milwaukee WI 53202-4108

BERKOWITZ, HERBERT MATTIS, lawyer; b. N.Y.C., June 23, 1947; m. Gloria E. Deems, June 16, 1968; 1 child, Peter Aaron. BA, Bklyn. Coll., 1967; JD, U. Wis., 1971. Bar: Wis. 1971, Ohio 1972, Fla. 1979, U.S. Supreme Ct. 1974, U.S. Ct. Appeals (D.C. cir. 1974), U.S. Ct. Appeals (6th cir.) 1976, U.S. Ct. Appeals (5th cir.) 1981, U.S. Ct. Appeals (11th cir.) 1981. Law clk. Ohio Ct. Appeals, Cleve., 1971-73; atty. antitrust div. U.S. Dept. Justice, Cleve., 1973-74, asst. U.S. Atty., 1975-78, atty. organized crime strike force Tampa, 1978-80; assoc. Levine, Freedman, Hirsch & Levinson, Tampa, 1980-84; ptnr. Oster & Berkowitz, Tampa, 1984-90; mng. sr. ptnr. Berkowitz & Almerico, Tampa, 1990-94, Berkowitz & Assocs., Tampa, 1994-2000; of counsel Clark, Charlton & Martino, P.A., Tampa, 2000—. Mem. ABA, Fla. Bar Assn., Hillsborough County Bar Assn. (In the Trenches award 1997), ATLA (sustaining), Fla. Trial Lawyers Assn., Am. Bd. Trial Advocates, Am. Inns of Ct. General civil litigation, Insurance, Personal injury (including property damage). Office: Clark Charlton & Martino PA 3407 W Kennedy Blvd Tampa FL 33609

BERKOWITZ, LAWRENCE M. lawyer; b. Leavenworth, Kans., Nov. 29, 1941; s. Barney and Sarah (Kramer) B.; m. Ursula Lustenberger, Sept. 2, 1969; children: Lizbeth Berkowitz, Leslie Berkowitz. BA Polit. Sci., U. Mich., 1963, JD, 1966. Bar: Mo. 1966. Law clerk U.S. Dist. Ct., Kansas City, Mo., 1966-68; assoc., ptnr. Stinson, Mag & Fizzell, P.C., Kansas City, Mo., 1968-97; ptnr. Berkowitz, Stanton, et al, Kansas City, Mo., 1997—. Mng. ptnr. Stinson, Mag & Fizzell, Kansas City, 1991-92. Bd. dirs. Nelson Gallery Bus. Coun., Kansas City, 1989—, Downtown coun., Kansas City, 1992-93; trustee Kansas City Art Inst., 1994—. Fellow Am. Coll. Trial Lawyers, Am. Bar Found.; mem. ABA, Am. Judicature Soc., Kansas City Met. Bar Assn., Lawyers Assn. Kansas City, Mo. Bar Assn., Am. Coll. Trial Lawyers (state bd. 1989—). Avocations: tennis, hiking, skiing, history, reading. Office: Berkowitz Stanton et al Two Emanuel Cleaver Blvd Ste 500 Kansas City MO 64112

BERKOWSKY, PETER ARTHUR, lawyer, retired military officer; b. Cornwall, NY, Mar. 29, 1942; s. Samuel Nathan and Sydell Berkowsky; m. Dolores Ethel Finder, Aug. 3, 1980; children: Daniel Benjamin, Jesse Samuel. AB in History, Brandeis U., 1964; JD, Cornell U., 1967; grad., Air War Coll., 1992. Bar: NY, U.S. Dist. Ct. (so. and ea. dists.) NY, U.S. Ct. Appeals (2d cir. and Armed Forces), U.S. Supreme Ct. Spl. agt., Office Spl. Investigations USAF, Beale AFB, Calif., 1967-71; asst. atty. gen., Dept. Law NY State, N.Y.C., 1972-77; prin. ct. atty. Appellate Divsn. 1st dept. Supreme Ct., N.Y.C., 1977-79, 87-91, prin. law clk. to Hon. Justice Arnold L. Fein, 1979-86, prin. law clk. to Hon. Justice Richard W. Wallach, 1991—2003. Intelligence officer, USAFR, McGuire AFB, NJ, 1973-75; asst. staff judge advocate, McGuire AFB, Hanscom AFB, Mass., Pentagon, Washington, 1975-98; admissions liaison officer U.S. Air Force Acad., 1992—; mem. law dept. adv. panel for bus. sch. Baruch Coll., N.Y.C., 1998—. Founder, dir. Internat. Minyan for N.Y.C. Marathoners, 1983—. Served to col. USAF, 1967-71, USAFR, 1971-98, returned to active duty Desert Storm, 1991. Decorated Legion of Merit. Mem. Am. Assn. Jewish

Lawyers and Jurists, NY County Lawyers' Assn. (law-related edn. com.), Civil Svc. Employees Assn. (AFSCME local 1000, AFL-CIO), Cracow Soc. (2d generation), Soc. Am. Baseball Rsch., Jewish War Vets of U.S. (life mem.), NY Road Runners Club. Democrat. Jewish. Avocation: running. Home: 16 Fredon Dr Livingston NJ 07039-3136 Office: Supreme Ct Appellate Divsn 1st Dept 27 Madison Ave New York NY 10010-2201 E-mail: fud42@comcast.net.

BERKSON, JACOB BENJAMIN, lawyer, author, conservationist; b. Washington County, Md., Dec. 6, 1925; s. Meyer and Ida Evelyn (Berman) B.; m. Ann Goldstein, June 25, 1955 (div.); children: Daniel Jeremy, Susan Kay, James Meyer. BA, U. Va., 1947, LLB, 1949, JD, 1970; grad., Fed. Exec. Inst., Charlottesville, Va., 1972. Bar: Md. 1949, Va. 1949, U.S. Supreme Ct. 1965, Calif. 1975. Sole practice, Hagerstown, Md., 1949-52, 54-64; ptnr. McCauley, Cooey, Berkson & Wright, Hagerstown, 1964-70; dep. gen. counsel U.S. GSA, Washington, 1970-76; pvt. practice law Hagerstown, 1976—. Instr. Law Hagerstown Bus. Coll., 1986; trial magistrate, Hagerstown and Washington County, Md., 1951-52; mem. Legis. Coun. Md., 1955-58; del. Md. Legislature, 1955-58; trial magistrate, Hagerstown, 1958-59. Recipient commendation for svc. to U.S. Naval Acad. and pub. interest Chief of Naval Personnel, 1956. Lt. USNR, 1944-46, 52-54. Author: Shingahi Saburo and Short Stories, 1978, Comin' Home, 1993, A Canary's Tale, 1996; case editor, co-founder Va. Law Weekly, 1948; contbr. articles to profl. jours., address to Congrl. Record. Scoutmaster local coun. Boy Scouts Am.; organizer, dir. County Youth Conservation Corps; active Big Bros.; bd. dirs. Doub's Woods County Park, Devil's Backbone County Park; assisted in establishment of C&O Canal Nat. Histo. Park, 1954-70; camp sponsor YMCA; adv. Model Youth Legis.; pres. PTA; chmn. Washington County Park Commn., 1961-66; bd. dirs. Rachel Carson Coun., Inc., Chevy Chase, Md., 1996-2003. Mem. ABA, Calif. Bar Assn., Va. Bar Assn., Md. Assn. County Civil Attys. (pres., award for svc. as pres. 1966), Washington County Bar Assn. (pres.), Lile Law Soc., Am. Legion, Hagerstown Club, Lions (pres.), Speakers Soc., Elks, Torch Club (Hagerstown), Thomas Jefferson Soc. Alumni, Lile Law Soc. Republican. Jewish. Environmental, General practice, Personal injury (including property damage). Home and Office: 1419 Potomac Ave Hagerstown MD 21742-3315

BERL, JOSEPH M. lawyer; b. Bklyn., Oct. 1, 1942; AB, Columbia U., 1964; JD with honors, George Washington U., 1967. Bar: N.Y. 1968, D.C. 1972, U.S. Supreme Ct. 1972. Law clk. to Hon. Frank H. Myers D.C. Ct. Appeals, 1967-68; trial atty. Div. Trading and Markets, SEC, Washington, 1968-70, br. chief, 1970-71; ptnr. Fortas & Koven, Washington, 1971-83, Stroock and Stroock and Lavan, Washington, 1984-86, Baker & Hostetler, Washington, 1986-98, Powell, Goldstein, Frazer & Murphy LLP, Washington, 1998—. Mem. ABA (mem. corp., banking and bus. law sect.), D.C. Bar. Federal civil litigation, Corporate, general, Securities. Office: Powell Goldstein Frazer & Murphy LLP 6th Flr 1001 Pennsylvania Ave NW Fl 6 Washington DC 20004-2505 E-mail: jberl@pgfm.com.

BERLAGE, JAN INGHAM, lawyer; b. Lewiston, NY, Nov. 17, 1969; s. Jan Coxe and Gai Elizabeth (Ingham) B. BA, Wesleyan U., Middletown, Conn., 1992; postgrad., Oxford U., 1992; JD, U. Va., 1995. Law clk. to Hon. E. Stephen Derby U.S. Bankruptcy Ct. Dist. Md., Balt., 1995-96; assoc. Day, Berry & Howard, Hartford, Conn., 1996-2001, Ballard Spahr Andrews & Ingersoll, Balt., 2001—. Exec. editor Jour. Law and Politics, Charlottesville, 1994-95, mem. editl. bd., 1993-94; author: Aguilar Expression, 1990; contbr. articles to profl. jours. Deacon Avon Congl. Ch., 1997-2001; mem. Rep. Town Com., Avon, 1998-2001; mem. Avon Zoning Bd. Appeals, 1999-2001; exec. adv. bd. Heroes-Helping-Heroes, Inc., 2003—. Mem. ABA (vice chmn. young lawyers divsn. individual rights and responsibilities sect. 2001-2002, chmn. 2002—, vice chmn. young lawyers divsn. bankruptcy sect. 2002-03, chmn. 2003—), Md. State Bar Assn. (chmn. young lawyers divsn. edn. com. 2003—), Federalist Soc. (pres. U. Va. chpt. 1994-95, co-chmn. Hartford chpt. 1997-2001, bd. dirs. Chesapeake chpt. 2001—), Conn. Young Lawyers Assn. (co-chmn. comml. law and bankruptcy sect. 1997-2000, co-chmn. civil rights sect. 2000-01), N.Y. Bar Assn. (comml. law and fed. litigation sects., intellectual property subcom. 1998-2001), Jefferson Literary and Debating Soc., N.Am. Securities Adminstrn. Assn. (task force mem. 1994), Oxford U. Legal Soc., United Oxford/Cambridge U. Club, Phi Delta Phi, Psi Upsilon, Phi Beta Kappa. Bankruptcy, General civil litigation, Intellectual property. Office: Ballard Spahr Andrews & Ingersoll 300 E Lombard St Baltimore MD 21202-3268 Home: 16422 J M Pearce Rd Monkton MD 21111 E-mail: Berlageji@ballardspahr.com.

BERLAND, SUSAN AMY, lawyer; b. Jericho, N.Y., May 27, 1961; Student, Mich. State U., 1979-81; BA, SUNY, Albany, 1982; JD, Hofstra U., 1986. Bar: N.Y. 1986, Fla. 1989. Assoc. Meltzer, Lippe & Goldstein, P.C., Mineola, N.Y., 1986-87, Law Offices Russel H. Beatie, Jr., N.Y.C., 1987-89; ptnr. Berland & Winston, Albertson, N.Y., 1989-95; asst. Atty. Gen. for State of N.Y., 1989-95; ast. town atty. Town of Huntington, NY, 1996—2001, town councilwoman, 2001—. Sec., treas. Herb Winston Assocs., Inc., Jericho, 1983—. Assoc. editor Hofstra U. Labor Law Jour., l985-86. Bd. dirs. Birchwood Civic Assn., Jericho, 1982-86. Mem. N.Y. County Lawyers Assn., Assn. of Bar of City of N.Y., N.Y. State Bar Assn., Fla. Bar Assn. Democrat. Jewish. Avocations: tennis, guitar, bowling, aerobics, reading. Home: 16 Wildwood Dr Dix Hills NY 11746-6041 Office: Town of Huntington Council Office 100 Main St Huntington NY 11743-6904

BERLE, PETER ADOLF AUGUSTUS, lawyer, media director; b. N.Y.C., Dec. 8, 1937; s. Adolf Augustus and Beatrice (Bishop) B.; m. Lila Sloane Wilde, May 30, 1960; children: Adolf Augustus, Mary Alice, Beatrice Lila, Robert Thomas. BA (Knox fellow), Harvard U., 1958, LLB, 1964; LLD (hon.), Hobart Smith Coll., 1977, L.I. U., 1993, So. Vt. Coll., 1996; LLB (hon.), North Adams Tchrs. Coll., 1988. Bar: N.Y. 1964, U.S. Dist. Ct. (so. and ea. dists.) N.Y. 1966, U.S. Ct. Appeals (2d cir.) 1966, U.S. Supreme Ct. 1973. Assoc. Paul, Weiss, Rifkind, Wharton & Garrison, N.Y.C., 1964-71; ptnr. Berle, Butzel & Kass, N.Y.C., 1971-76; N.Y. state commr. environ. conservation, 1976-79; ptnr. Berle, Kass & Case, 1979-85; pres., CEO (pub. Audubon mag.) Nat. Audubon Soc., 1985-95; dir., host The Environment Show N.E. Pub. Radio, 1995—2001; trustee Twentieth Century Fund, Inc., 1971—, chmn., 1982-87. Tchg. fellow econs. Harvard Coll., Cambridge, Mass., 1963-64; assoc. adj. prof. Sch. Urban Affairs Hunter Coll., 1974, 84; vis. prof. environ. sci. and forestry SUNY, 1980. Author: Does the Citizen Stand a Chance, 1974. Mem. N.Y. State Assembly, 1968-74; chmn. N.Y. Gov.'s Transition Task Force on Environment, 1974-75; commr. N.Y. State Moreland Act Commn. on Nursing Homes, 1975-77; bd. dirs. Clean Sites, Inc., 1986-93; chmn. Commn. on the Adirondacks in the 21st Century, 1989-90; mem. EPA adv. group on biotech., 1989-92, EPA adv. grout air quality; mem. nat. com. environ., 1991-92, nat. commn. superfund, 1992-94; mem. joint pub. adv. com. N.Am. Commn. on Environ. Coop., 1994-2002; dir. N.Y. Ind. Sys. Operator, 1999—; adv. bd. Harvard U. Com. on Environment; mem. commn. internat. environ. law World Conservation Union; pres. Stockbridge Land Trust, 2001—. 1st lt. USAF, 1959-61. Decorated Commendation medal; named Outstanding Legislator Eagleton Inst. Politics, 1971 Mem. ABA, N.Y. State Bar Assn., Assn. of Bar of City of N.Y. (environ. law com., profl. responsibility com., energy policy com., internat. human rights com., internat. environ. law com.). Episcopalian. E-mail: pberle@audubon.org.

BERLEY, DAVID RICHARD, lawyer; b. Bklyn., Apr. 9, 1942; s. Alexander and Ruth (Ginsburg) B.; m. Sharon Lee Freeman, Aug. 10, 1964 (div. 1975); children: Steven N., Barbara Robin; m. Katalin Fine, Feb. 14, 1992. BS, Boston U., 1963; JD, Boston Coll., 1966. Bar: Mass. 1966, U.S. Dist. Ct. Mass. 1966, U.S. Ct. Claims 1970, Fla. 1977, U.S. Dist. Ct. (so. dist.) Fla. 1977, U.S. Tax Ct., U.S. Ct. Appeals (11th cir.). Pvt. practice, 1966-77; gen. counsel Econocar Internat. Inc., Miami, Fla., 1976-77; v.p., gen. counsel Emergency Med. Services Assn., Inc., Miami, 1977-79, pvt. practice, 1979-85; ptnr. Berley & Littman, PA, Miami, 1985-94; pvt. practice Miami, 1994—. Active Greater Miami Heart Assn., Jewish Fedn. Greater Miami, Bus. Vols. for Arts; past chmn. City of Miami Waterfront adv. bd., Coconut Grove Playhouse Soc. of Stars; mem. citizens' adv. bd. Sta.-WLRN Pub. Radio; mem. City of Miami Fin. Com. Mem. Mass. Bar Assn., Fla. Bar Assn. (grievance com.), Fla. Internat. Bankers Assn., Boston Coll. Law Sch. Alumni Assn., Greater Miami C. of C., Coconut Grove C. of C., Coconut Grove Playhouse Soc. Stars. Banking, Corporate, general, Private international. Office: 848 Brickell Ave Ste 200 Miami FL 33131-2981

BERLIN, ALAN DANIEL, lawyer, international energy and legal consultant; b. Bklyn., Oct. 20, 1939; s. Joseph Jacob and Rose (Smith) B.; m. Renee Wellinger, Dec. 22, 1962; children— Nicole Suzanne, Allison Leigh. BBA, CCNY, 1960; LLB, NYU, 1963, LLM, 1968. Bar: N.Y. 1963. Assoc. Aranow, Brodsky, Bohlinger, Einhorn & Dann, N.Y.C., 1965-68; asst. counsel Gen. Electric Co., N.Y.C., 1968-70; tax counsel Norton Simon Inc., N.Y.C., 1970-77; asst. prof. Pace U. Grad. Sch. Bus., 1977-85; pres. Belco Petroleum Corp., N.Y.C., 1977-88, The Crown Group, White Plains, N.Y., 1988-95; ptnr. Aitken Irvin Berlin & Vrooman L.L.P., 1995—. Spl. cons. to UN Dept. Tech. Cooperation for Devel., 1989—, UN Ctr. for Transnat. Corps., 1990—; hon. assoc. Ctr. for Petroleum and Mineral Law and Policy, U. Dundee, Scotland, 1993—. Author monographs on fed. income tax. With U.S. Army, 1963-65. Mem. ABA, Internat. Bar Assn., N.Y. State Bar Assn., Assn. of Bar of City of N.Y., Inter-Am. Bar Assn., Assn. Internat. Petroleum Negotiators. Lodges: Masons. Corporate, general, Oil, gas, and mineral, Taxation, general. Office: Aitken Irvin Berlin & Vrooman LLP 2 Gannett Dr White Plains NY 10604-3403 E-mail: aberlin273@aol.com., aibvlaw@yahoo.com.

BERLOW, ROBERT ALAN, lawyer; b. Detroit, Feb. 11, 1947; s. Henry and Shirley (Solovich) B.; m. Elizabeth Ann Goldin, Sept. 20, 1972; children: Stuart, Lisa. BA, U. Mich., 1968; JD, Wayne State U., 1971. Bar: Mich. 1971, U.S. Supreme Ct. 1978. Asst. to dean, instr. law sch. Wayne State U., Detroit, 1971-72; mem. Radner, Radner, Shefman, Bayer and Berlow, P.C., Southfield, Mich., 1972-78; gen. counsel Perry Drug Stores, Inc., Pontiac, Mich., 1978-80, gen. counsel, sec., 1980-82, v.p., gen. counsel, sec., 1982-88, sr. v.p., gen. counsel, sec., 1988-93, sr. v.p., chief adminstrn. officer, gen. counsel, sec., 1993-94, exec. v.p., gen. counsel, sec., 1994-95; sr. mem. Dykema Gossett, PLLC, Bloomfield Hills, Mich., 1995—, also chmn. retail practice group. Pres. Agy. for Jewish Edn., Metro Detroit, 1993-95, v.p., 1987-93; bd. dirs. Jewish Cmty. Ctr. Met. Detroit, 1989-2003, v.p., 1992-93, treas., 1996-97, sec., 1997-98. Mem. ABA, Mich. Bar Assn. (chair comml. leasing and mgmt. of real estate com. of real property law sect. 1993-98, chmn. real property law sect. 2001-2002). Avocations: sports, photography. Corporate, general, Landlord-tenant, Property, real (including real estate development, water). Office: Dykema Gossett PLLC 39577 N Woodward Ave Bloomfield Hills MI 48304-2837 E-mail: r.berlow@dykema.com.

BERMAN, BRUCE JUDSON, lawyer; b. Roslyn, N.Y., Oct. 9, 1946; s. Howard M. Berman and Soosha T. (Draizen) Hurwitz; children: Daniel H., Ann N., Andrew J., Josie A.; m. Susan Leigh Readinger, Dec. 29, 1991. BA, Williams Coll., 1968; MBA, Columbia U., 1972; JD, Boston U., 1972. Bar: Fla. 1973, U.S. Dist. Ct. (so. dist.) Fla. 1980, U.S. Dist. Ct. (mid. dist.) Fla. 1990, U.S. Ct. Appeals (5th cir.) 1980, U.S. Ct. Appeals (11th cir.) 1981, U.S. Supreme Ct. 1976. Assoc. Guggenheimer & Untermyer, N.Y.C., 1973-79; from assoc. to ptnr. Myers, Kenin, Levinson, Frank & Richards, Miami, Fla., 1979-85; ptnr. Weil, Gotshal & Manges LLP, Miami, 1985-2000, McDermott, Will & Emery, Miami, 2000—. Spl. ad hoc trial com. to Dade County (Fla.) Cir. Ct., 1988—; apptd. Fla. Supreme Ct. ct. reporter cert. planning com., 1995, Supreme Ct. Com. on Std. Jury Instrns. in Civil Cases, 2000, 03, Supreme Ct. workgroup on access to pub. records, 2000. Author: Florida Civil Procedure, 1998—99, 2001—03. Mem. New World Symphony Cmty. Bd., Miami Beach, Fla., 1991-2000; bd. dirs., Daily Bread Food Bank, 2002—. Mem. Fla. Bar (civil procedure rules com. 1984-2003, chmn. 1988-90, jud. adminstrn. rules com. 1988-2002, chmn. 1993-94), Dade County Bar. Federal civil litigation, State civil litigation, Private international. Office: McDermott Will & Emery 201 S Biscayne Blvd Miami FL 33131 E-mail: bberman@mwe.com.

BERMAN, DANIEL LEWIS, lawyer; b. Washington D.C., Dec. 14, 1934; s. Herbert A. and Ruth N. (Abramson) B.; children: Priscilla Decker, Jane, Katherine Ann, Sara Mark, Heather, Melinda. BA, Williams Coll., 1956; LLB, Columbia U., 1959. Bar: N.Y. 1960, Utah 1962. Assoc. Chadbourne, Parke, Whiteside & Wolff, N.Y.C., 1959-60; asst. prof. law U. Utah, 1960-62; pvt. practice Salt Lake City, 1962—; sr. ptnr. Berman, Tomsic & Savage, Salt Lake City, 1981—. Vis. prof. U. Utah, 1970, 74, 77; mem. Utah Coordinating Coun. Higher Edn., 1965-68, Salt Lake County Merit coun., 1974-80; mem. nominating commn. Utah Appellate Ct., 1999—. Trustee Salt Lake Art Ctr., 1978-80; Dem. candidate for U.S. Senate from Utah, 1980; mem. Utah Transit Authority, 1992-97. Mem. Am. Law Inst., Salt Lake Area C. of C. (bd. govs. 1976-79). Democrat. Jewish. Antitrust, General civil litigation, Securities. Office: Berman Tomsic & Savage 50 S Main St Ste 1250 Salt Lake City UT 84144-2073 E-mail: dlb@btslaw.net.

BERMAN, DAVID, lawyer, poet; b. N.Y.C., Sept. 11, 1934; s. Joseph and Sophie (Hersh) B. BA with honors, U. Fla., 1955; postgrad. Johns Hopkins U., 1955-56; JD, Harvard U., 1963. Bar: Mass. 1963. Teaching fellow Harvard Coll., 1962-63, 66-67; law clk. to justice Mass. Supreme Ct., 1963-64; asst. atty. gen. Commonwealth of Mass., 1964-67; assoc. Zamparelli & White, 1967, ptnr., 1968-74; pvt. practice, 1974-82, 1990—; ptnr. Berman & Moren, Medford, Mass., 1982-89. Author: Future Imperfect, 1982, Slippage, 1996, Early Mandamus in Massachusetts, Massachusetts Legal History, 1998, David Berman Greatest Hits, 1965-2002, 2003. Trustee Cantata Singers, 1981—. Mem. ABA, Mass. Bar Assn., Mass. Bar Found., Middlesex Bar Assn. (Most Outstanding Trial Lawyer Appelate award, 1998), Harvard Club (Boston), Signet Soc., Confrerie de la Chaine des Rotisseurs, Ordre Mondial, Masons. Republican. Unitarian. Land use and zoning (including planning), Appellate, Commercial, contracts (including sales of goods; commercial financing). Home: 33 Birch Hill Rd Belmont MA 02478-1729 Office: 100 George P Hassett Dr Medford MA 02155-3264

BERMAN, LEONARD KEITH, lawyer; b. Dearborn, Mich., Mar. 30, 1963; s. Hyman Jack and Doris (Grushky) B.; m. Sharon Elizabeth Williams, Oct. 8, 1988; children: Sarah, Rebbeca, Joseph. BA, Mich. State U., 1985; JD cum laude, Wayne State U., 1988. Bar: Mich. 1988, U.S. Dist. Ct. (ea. and we. dists.) Mich. 1988. Assoc. Bodman, Longley & Dahling P.C., Troy, Mich., 1987-91; staff atty. Elias Bros. Restaurants Inc., Warren, Mich., 1991-94; assoc. Hainer & Demorest P.C., Troy, 1994—96; ptnr. Hainer & Berman PC, Bingham Farms, Mich., 1996—. Of counsel Fin. Law Assocs., Troy, 1994—, Robert Riely P.C., Dearborn, 1996—. Pres. Cedar Springs Homeowners Assn., Novi, Mich., 1992—. Mem. ABA, State Bar Mich. Republican. Commercial, contracts (including sales of goods; commercial financing), General practice, Labor (including EEOC, Fair Labor Standards Act, labor-management relations, NLRB, OSHA). Office: Hainer and Berman PC 24255 W 13 Mile Rd Ste 270 Bingham Farms MI 48025-4322

BERMAN, MARK NILES, lawyer; b. Pitts., Jan. 13, 1952; s. George and Evelyn (Robin) B.; m. Beth Ann Stamell, Aug. 12, 1973; children: Lia Michelle, Daniel Scott. BA, Northwestern U., 1973; JD, Boston Coll., 1976. Bar: Mass. 1977, U.S. Dist. Ct. Mass. 1977, U.S. Ct. Appeals (1st cir.) 1985, U.S. Supreme Ct., 1985. Legal asst. Office Suffolk County Dist. Atty., Boston, 1975-76; assoc., then shareholder Widett, Slater & Goldman, P.C., Boston, 1976-88; shareholder Hutchins, Wheeler & Dittmar and predecessor firm Hutchins & Wheeler, Boston, 1988—2003; chmn. bus. dept. Hutchins, Wheeler & Dittmar, Boston, 1995—97; ptnr. Nixon Peabody LLP, Boston, 2003—. Instr. New Eng. Inst. Credit, 1989—. Chmn. Claflin Art Com., Newton, Mass., 1986-87; trustee Horace Cousens Indsl. Fund, Newton, 1987-92. Mem. ABA, Am. Bankruptcy Inst. (editl. bd. ABI World 2002, chmn. Northeast Bankruptcy Conf., 2003), Mass. Bar Assn., Boston Bar Assn. (chmn. bankruptcy law com. 1990-92, chmn. bus. law sect. 1995-97, bankruptcy sect. steering com. 1998—, legis. steering com. 2000-01), Comml. Law League Am., Clients' Security Bd. (trustee 1997-2002, sec. 2000—, vice-chair 2001); fellow Am. Coll. Bankruptcy. Bankruptcy, Commercial, contracts (including sales of goods; commercial financing), Corporate, general. Home: 98 Falmouth Rd West Newton MA 02465-1127 Office: Nixon Peabody LLP 101 Federal St Boston MA 02110-1817 E-mail: mberman@nixonpeabody.com.

BERMAN, MARSHALL FOX, lawyer; b. Portsmouth, Va., Aug. 27, 1939; s. Israel and Etta (Fox) B.; m. Barbara Pressner, Aug. 29, 1965 (dec. Feb. 1993); m. Karen Orloff Kaplan, Nov. 18, 1996; children: Richard Joseph, Deborah Lynn. BA, U. Va., 1961, postgrad. in rhetoric, 1961-62; JD, Am. U., 1967; LLM in Labor Law with highest honors, George Washington U., 1970. Bar: Va. 1967, D.C. 1971, U.S. Supreme Ct. 1971. Tchr. reading pub. schs., Washington, 1965-66; staff D.C. Minimum Wage and Indsl. Safety Bd., 1966-67; atty. NLRB, Washington, 1968-71; assoc. Gall, Lane & Powell, Washington, 1971-75; ptnr. Dow, Lohnes & Albertson, Washington, 1975-91, Epstein, Becker and Green, Washington, 1992-98, Hewes, Gelband, Lambert and Dann, Washington, 1999—2000, Ruben & Aronson, Washington, 2000—; spl. master for labor and employment cases U.S. Dist. Ct. D.C., 2001—. Co-author: Aviation Drug Testing Handbook, 1989, Aviation Drug Testing Operating Manual, 1990. Mem. ABA, Fed. Bar Assn., D.C. Bar Assn., Va. Bar Assn. Labor (including EEOC, Fair Labor Standards Act, labor-management relations, NLRB, OSHA). Home: 7732 Canal Ct Mc Lean VA 22102-1406 Office: 3299 K St NW # 403 Washington DC 20007-4415

BERMAN, MICHAEL BARRY, lawyer; b. N.Y.C., Apr. 10, 1942; s. Mark S. and Roslyn (Roberts) B.; m. Rochelle Holland, June 7, 1969 (dec. Jan. 2002); 1 child, Michele. BA, Iowa Wesleyan U., 1964; MAT, Trenton State Coll., 1973; MA in Indsl. Rels., Rutgers U., 1977; JD, Cardozo Sch. Law, N.Y.C., 1984. Bar: N.J. 1985, D.C. 1985, U.S. Ct. Appeals (3d cir.) 1985, U.S. Ct. Appeals Veterans Claims 1999, U.S. Supreme Ct. 1989. Assoc. Jerome A. Gertner, Lakewood, N.J., 1984-86; staff atty. Ocean-Monmouth Legal Svcs., Toms River, N.J., 1986-87; assoc. Cohen, Meshulam & Cohen, Verona, N.J., 1987-89, Krieger & Ferrara, Jersey City, 1989; pvt. practice Lakewood, N.J., 1989-90; ptnr. Collins & Berman, Toms River, NJ, 1990—2001; sole practitioner Toms River, 2001—. Asst. to chmn. N.J. Pub. Employment Rels. Com., Trenton, 1973-81; gen. counsel Nat. Mus. of Am. Jewish Mil. History, 1992-98, 2000--. V.p. Lakewood Cmty. Sch. Bd., 1984-87; active Lakewood Bd. Edn., 1984-87, 89, Rep. Cen. Com., Lakewood, 1987-88; pres. Lakewood Rep. Club, 1992-93; adv. bd. Ocean County Cath. Charities; pres. Congregation Ahavat Shalom, 1993-95. With U.S. Army, 1968-70. Mem. Ocean County Bar Assn., N.J. Bar Assn. (subcom. alimony support 1987), Jewish War Vets (state comdr. N.J. chpt. 1985-86, nat. com. 1985-89, nat. judge advocate 1992-98, nat. quartermaster 1996-98, nat. comdr. 1998-99), Vietnam Vets Am. (v.p. N.J. chpt. 1990-92, gen. counsel 2000--), Masons. Family and matrimonial, Labor (including EEOC, Fair Labor Standards Act, labor-management relations, NLRB, OSHA), Workers' compensation. Office: 18A Robbins St Toms River NJ 08753-7629

BERMAN, RICHARD BRUCE, lawyer; b. Freeport, N.Y., Sept. 26, 1951; s. Nathan and Helen Dorothy (Raiden) B.; m. Laurie Michael, Nov. 2, 1985. BA in Speech Communication, Am. U., 1973; JD, U. Miami, 1976. Bar: Fla. 1976, U.S. Dist. Ct. (so. dist.) Fla. 1976, D.C. 1978. Atty. Travelers Ins. Co., Ft. Lauderdale, Fla., 1977-84; assoc. Frank & Flaster P.A., Sunrise, Fla., 1984-88, DeCasare & Salerno, Ft. Lauderdale, Fla., 1988-89; pvt. practice, 1989—. Bd. dirs. Frosch Health Care Cons., Inc., Lauderhill, Employers for Ins. Reform, 2002—; mem. worker's compensation rules com. Fla. Bar, 1991-94; bd. dirs. Fla. Workers Advs., 1991—, chmn. media rels. com., 2000—. Mem. panel health care Dem. Legis. Task Force, Ft. Lauderdale, 1985-87; mem. adv. bd. Reflex Sympathetic Dystrophy Syndrome Assn. Fla., 1992—; mem. B'nai Brith; bd. dirs. Mommy & Me Enterprises, 1997—. Mem. ABA, ATLA, D.C. Bar, Fla. Bar Assn., Acad. Fla. Trial Lawyers, Broward County Trial Lawyers Assn. Avocations: writing and performing music, theatre, writing children's music. Insurance, Personal injury (including property damage), Workers' compensation. E-mail: rbberman@gate.net.

BERMAN, TONY, lawyer; b. N.Y.C., Dec. 31, 1933; s. Murray T. and Lillian L. (Levine) B.; m. Ann Rooke-Ley, 1992; children: Julie A., Nina A. JD cum laude, NYU, 1957. Bar: N.Y. 1958, U.S. Ct. Appeals (2d cir.) 1960, U.S. Dist. Ct. (so. and ea. dists.) N.Y. 1961. Asst. atty. gen. State of N.Y., N.Y.C., 1957-63; ptnr. Berman Paley Goldstein & Kannry, N.Y.C., 1963—. Co-author: Construction Business Handbook, 1978, Avoiding Liability in Architecture Design and Construction, 1983. Mem. ABA, N.Y. State Bar Assn., Assn. of Bar of City of N.Y., The Moles. Federal civil litigation, General civil litigation, Construction. Office: Berman Paley Goldstein & Kannry LLP 500 5th Ave Fl 43 New York NY 10110-0375

BERMIG, HORST DIETRICH, lawyer, consultant; b. Bad Köstritz, Germany, July 23, 1923; s. Hugo Paul and Charlotte Wilhelmine (Jaeger) B.; m. Evamarie Wenderoth; children: Stephanie, Andreas. Dr.iuris.utr., U. Heidelberg, Germany, 1949. Atty. Law Office Prof. Geiler Etc., Mannheim, Germany, 1951-52; asst. mgr. Zellstofffabrik Waldhof, Wiesbaden, Germany, 1952-56; chief solicitor Ruhrstahl AG, Witten/Ruhr, Germany, 1957-63, Rheinstahl Hüttenwerke, Essen, Germany, 1963-69; gen. atty. Rheinstahl AG, Essen, Germany, 1969-75; mng. dir. Deutscher Giessereiverband, Düsseldorf, Germany, 1976-88; pvt. practice law Essen, 1989—2001; ret., 2001. Contbr. articles to profl. jours. 1st lt. Germany Army, 1942-45. Decorated Iron Cross I. Home: Am Ruhrstein 14 D-45133 Essen Germany

BERN, AGNETA, lawyer; b. Karlshamn, Sweden, Sept. 3, 1964; LLM, U. Stockholm, 1990. Clk. Dist. Ct., Karlstad, 1990-92; assoc. Advokatfirman Delphi, Stockholm, 1992—. Mem. Swedish Bar Assn. Office: Advokatfirman Delphi & Co Box 1432 111 84 Stockholm Sweden E-mail: agneta.bern@delphilaw.com.

BERNABEI, LYNNE ANN, lawyer; b. Highland Park, Ill., Apr. 11, 1950; d. Guy and Anna (Tamarri) B. BA, Harvard U., 1972, JD, 1977. Bar: D.C. 1977, U.S. Supreme Ct. 1988, U.S. Dist. Ct. D.C. 1977, U.S. Ct. Appeals (D.C. cir.) 1979, U.S. Ct. Appeals (3d cir.) 1985, U.S. Ct. Appeals (fed. cir.) 1988, U.S. Ct. Appeals (4th cir.) 1992, U.S. Ct. Appeals (6th cir.) 1990. Clk. U.S. Dist. Ct. Judge William Bryant, Washington, 1977-78; assoc. Tigar & Buffone, Washington, 1978-80; clin. instr. Georgetown U., Washington, 1980-81; gen. counsel Govt. Accountability Project, Washington, 1981-85; ptnr. Newman, Sobol, Trister & Owens, Washington, 1985-87, Bernabei & Katz, Washington, 1987—. Co-author: The High Citadel: On the Influence of Harvard Law School, 1978; author articles. Recipient Achievement award Lambda Legal Defense and Edn. Fund, Washington, 1990. Mem. ABA, ATLA, Nat. Lawyers Guild (bd. dirs. D.C. chpt. 1992-95). Civil rights, General civil litigation, Constitutional. Office: Bernabei & Katz 1773 T St NW Ste 100 Washington DC 20009-7139 E-mail: lbernabei@aol.com.

BERNACCHI, RICHARD LLOYD, lawyer; b. Los Angeles, Dec. 15, 1938; s. Bernard and Anne B. BS with honors in Commerce (Nat. Merit Found. scholar), U. Santa Clara, 1961; LL.B. with highest honors (Legion Lex scholar, Jerry Geisler Meml. scholar), U. So. Calif., 1964. Bar: Calif. 1964. Assoc. Irell and Manella, L.A., 1964-70, ptnr., 1970—; lectr. Am. Law Inst., 1972-73; lectr. data processing contracts and law U. So. Calif., L.A., 1972, 78, 81. Co-chmn. Regional Transp. Com., 1970-72; mem. adv. bd. U. So. Calif. Computer Law Inst., 1979—, Ariz. Law and Tech. Inst., 1982-86; U. Santa Clara Computer and High Tech. Law Jour., 1982-90. Author: (with Gerald H. Larsen) Data Processing Contracts and the Law, 1974, (with Frank and Statland) Bernacchi on Computer Laaw, 1986; editor-in-chief U. So. Calif. Law Rev., 1962-64; adv. bd. Computer Negotiations Report, 1983-95, Computer and Tech. Law Jour., 1984-93, Computer Law Strategist, 1984-94. Capt. AUS, 1964-66, PTO. Mem. ABA (mem. adv. com. on edn. 1973-74, chmn. subcom. taxation computer sys. of sect. sci. and tech. 1976-78), L.A. Bar Assn., Computer Law Assn. (bd. dirs. 1973-86, chmn. preconf. symposium on law and computers 1974-75, West Coast v.p. 1976-79, sr. v.p. 1979-81, pres. 1981-83, adv. bd. 1986—), Internat. Bar Assn. (co-chmn. sect. on bus. law mem. com. on internat. tech. and e-commerce law 1995-98, steering com. 1998—), Am. Fedn. Info. Processing Socs. (mem. spl. com. electronic funds transfer sys. 1974-78), Order of Coif, Scabbard and Blade, Beta Gamma Sigma, Alpha Sigma Nu. Computer, Corporate, general, Private international. Office: Irell & Manella 1800 Avenue Of The Stars Los Angeles CA 90067-4276

BERNARD, BRUCE WILLIAM, lawyer; b. Erie, Pa., Feb. 3, 1951; s. Barney and Barbara Jean (Wurst) B.; m. Valerie Jean Noziglia, June 2, 1978 (div.); children: Elizabeth Anne, Brandon Wallace, Brittany Lynn; m. Catherine Ann Blore, May 4, 1984. BA, Case Western Res. U., Cleve., 1972; JD, Case Western Res. U., 1975. Bar: Pa. 1975, U.S. Dist. Ct. (we. dist.) Pa. 1975, U.S. Supreme Ct. 1980, U.S. Ct. Fed. Claims 1989. Assoc. Silin, Eckert & Burke, Erie, 1975-77; ptnr. Ely & Bernard, Erie, 1978-85, Bernard, Stuczynski & Bonanti, Erie, 1985—. Instr. Am. Inst. Banking, Erie, 1981-82. Bd. dirs. Erie Civic Music Assn., 1976-83, Florence Crittendon Svcs., Erie, 1978-84, Meth. Towers, Erie, 1979—. Named Vol. of Yr., Erie chpt. ARC, 1982. Mem. ATLA, Pa. Bar Assn., Pa. Trial Lawyers Assn., Erie County Bar Assn., Kiwanis (bd. dirs. 1978-81, 90-91, Disting. Svc. award 1976, 79), Phi Delta Phi. Republican. Methodist. Personal injury (including property damage), Property, real (including real estate development, water), Workers' compensation. Home: 6720 Manchester Farms Rd Fairview PA 16415-1649 Office: Bernard Stuczynski & Bonanti 234 W 6th St Erie PA 16507-1319 E-mail: bbernard@erie.net.

BERNARD, DONALD RAY, law educator, international business counselor; b. San Antonio, June 5, 1932; s. Horatio J. and Amber (McDonald) B.; children: Doren, Kevin, Koby; m. Elizabeth Priscilla Gilpin, 1986. Student, U. Mich., 1950-52; JD, U. Tex., 1958, BA, 1954, JD, 1958, LLM, 1964. Bar: Tex. 1958, U.S. Ct. Mil. Appeals, 1959, U.S. Supreme Ct. 1959; lic. comml. pilot. Commd. ensign U.S. Navy, 1954, advanced through grades to commdr., 1956-75, retired, 1975; briefing atty. Supreme Ct. Tex., Austin, 1958-59; asst. atty. gen. State of Tex., Austin, 1959-60; ptnr. Bernard & Bernard, Houston, 1960-80; pvt. practice law Houston, 1980-94; prof. internat. law U. St. Thomas, Houston, 1991-94; guest lectr. Sch. Bus. Mont. State U., 1995-96. Mem. faculty S.W. Sch. Real Estate, 1968-77. Author: Origin of the Special Verdict As Now Practiced in Texas, 1964; co-author: (novel) Bullion, 1982. Bd. dirs. Nat. Kidney Found., Houston, 1960-63; chmn. Bd. Adjustment, Hedwig Village, Houston, 1972-76; bd. regents Angeles U. Found., The Philippines; chmn. of the bd. Metro Verde Devel. Corp., The Philippines;; bd. dirs. Gloria Dei Luth. Ch., Endowment Found. Comdr. USN, 1950-92; ret., air show pilot Confederate Air Force, 1970-80. Mem. Lawyers Soc. Houston (pres. 1973-74), Houston Bd. Realtors, ABA, Inter-Am. Bar Assn., Tex. Bar Assn. (com. liaison Mex. legal profession), Houston Bar Assn. (chairperson emeritus internat. law sect.), Internat. Bar Assn. (del. to 1st seminar with Assn. Soviet Lawyers, Moscow, 1988), Assn. Soviet Lawyers , Lawyer-Pilot Bar Assn., Sons of the Republic of Tex., Lic. Execs. Soc., St. James's Club, Masons, Shriners, Alpha Tau Omega, Phi Delta Phi. Lutheran. Home: 14 Scenic Dr Whitehall MT 59759-9789 E-mail: donbernard@msn.com.

BERNARD, JAMES HARVEY, JR., lawyer; b. Kansas City, Mo., June 8, 1951; s. James and Marjorie Ann (Kirts) B.; m. Sara Fae Dickerson, Oct. 20, 1979; children: James Harvey III, Charles Andrew. BA, U. Kans., 1973; JD, Creighton U., 1976. With Slagle, Bernard & Gorman, Kansas City, Mo., 1976—, ptnr., 1981—. Pres. City of Fountains Found., 2001—; elder Second Presbyn. Ch., Kansas City, 1985—. Mem. ABA, Kansas City Bar Assn., Mo. Bar Assn., Lawyers Assn. Kansas City, Native Sons of Kansas City (v.p., pres.-elect 2002—). Avocations: travel, amateur radio. Estate planning, Property, real (including real estate development, water). Office: Slagle Bernard & Gorman 4600 Madison Ave Ste 600 Kansas City MO 64112-3031

BERNARD, JOHN MARLEY, lawyer, educator; b. Phila., Feb. 6, 1941; s. Edward and Opal (Marley) B.; children: John Marley Jr., Kendall M., Katherine M., James M.; m. Esther L. von Laue, May 31, 1986. BA, Swarthmore Coll., 1963; LLB, Harvard U., 1967. Bar: Pa. 1967. Assoc. Montgomery McCracken Walker & Rhoads, Phila., 1967-73, ptnr., 1973-86, Ballard Spahr Andrews & Ingersoll, LLP, Phila., 1986—. Lectr. Temple U. Law Sch., Phila., 1975-95; instr. Phila. Acad. for Employee Benefits Tng., 1996-99; guest instr. U.S. Dept. Labor, Washington, 1984-96; instr. U. Pa. Wharton Sch., Phila., 1989-90; bd. dirs. PENJERDEL Employee Benefits Assn., Phila. Contbg. author: Handbook of Employee Benefits, 1989. Mem. ABA, Pa. Bar Assn. Labor (including EEOC, Fair Labor Standards Act, labor-management relations, NLRB, OSHA), Pension, profit-sharing, and employee benefits, Corporate taxation. Office: Ballard Spahr Andrews & Ingersoll LLP 1735 Market St Fl 51 Philadelphia PA 19103-7599 E-mail: bernard@ballardspahr.com.

BERNARD, MICHAEL MARK, lawyer, city planning consultant; b. N.Y.C., Sept. 5, 1926; s. H.L. and Henryetta (Siegel) B.; m. Laura Jane Pincus, Aug. 28, 1958; 1 dau., Daphne Michelle. AB, U. Chgo., 1949; JD, Northwestern U., 1953; MCity Planning, Harvard U., 1959. Bar: Ill. 1952, U.S. Dist. Ct. (no. dist.) Ill. 1953, N.Y. 1955, U.S. Ct. Appeals (1st cir.) 1956. Pvt. practice law, Chgo. and N.Y.C., 1953-55; rsch. asst. Law Sch. Harvard U., 1955-56; city planning cons., atty.-adviser Puerto Rico, 1956-58; rsch. atty. Model Laws Project Am. Bar Found., 1959-60; city planner, legal adviser Chgo. Dept. City Planning, 1960-64; cons. planning and land regulation, 1964—; cons. Chgo. Area Transp. Study, 1964-65; mem. exec. faculty Boston Archtl. Ctr., 1967—. Adv. to Gov.'s Exec. Office on reorgn. Commonwealth Mass., 1968-72; chmn. 1st Nat. Transp. Needs Study Mass.; cons. A.I.A. Rsch. Corp., 1974; cons. Mass. Atty. Gen., 1981—; mem. com. urban devel. and housing World Peace Through Law Ctr., 1965—; mem. com. transp. law transp. research bd. NRC-NAS, 1966—; cons. White House Policy Adv. Com. to D.C., 1966; del. World Congress Housing and Planning, Paris, France, 1962, Tokyo, Japan, 1966; fellow Ctr. Advanced Visual Studies, M.I.T.; prin. investigator Northwestern U. Transp. Ctr.; lectr. in field; vis. prof. urban and regional planning U. Iowa, 1969-70; vis. lectr. Harvard U., MIT, U. Mich.; mem. faculty Am. Law Inst., 1978—. Author: Constitutions, Taxation and Land Policy, 2 vols., 1979-80, Airspace in Urban Development, 1963; co-editor: Policy Studies Jour.; editor, pub.: Reflections on Space; revision project mgr.: Constitutional Uniformity & Equality in State Taxation, 2 vols., 1984, Transformation of Property Rights in the "Space Age", 1993, (U.S. Govt. manual) Transportation Planning for Small Cities, 1973; spl. editor: Urban Law Ann. Washington U. Sch. Law; columnist: Jour. Real Estate Devel.; bd. editors: Real Estate Fin.; contbr. articles to profl. jours. Patron Hull House Assn., Chgo., 1965; v.p., trustee Cambridge Community Art Ctr., 1971-73; mem. standing com. Unitarian Ch.; mem. founding site com. Mus. Contemporary Art, Chgo. With USN, 1944-46. Recipient cert. of commendation for teaching Boston Archtl. Ctr., 1984; grantee NRC-NAS, 1964-66. Fellow Lincoln Inst. Land Policy; mem. ABA (land use, planning and zoning com., chmn. T.D.R. subcom. 1984-89, air and space com.), Internat. Fedn. Housing and Planning, Am. Arbitration Assn. (cert., bldg. and constrn. arbitrator),Am. Soc. Pub. Adminstrn., Policy Studies Orgn., Am. Planning Assn. (chmn. legis. com. Met. Chgo. sect. 1963-65, Mass. state reporter planning and law div. 1990—), Boston Soc. Architects (affiliate), Nat. Space Soc. (bd. dirs., space law com. Boston chpt.), Am. Underground Space Assn., Internat. Ctr. for Land Policy Studies, Urban Affairs Assn. (jour. rev. editor), Am. Crafts Coun., Mass. Assn. Craftsmen (v.p. 1975-78). Boston Visual Artists Union (hon., sec.-gen. 1971-72), New England Poetry Club (life), U. Chgo. Club Boston (bd. dirs.), Boston Athenaeum (life, dir. Poetry program). Home: 25 Stanton Ave Auburndale MA 02466-3005

BERNARD, VINCENT JACQUES NICOLAS, lawyer; b. Liège, Belgium, June 12, 1964; s. Guy Bernard and Marie-Antoinette Melon; m. Cécile Christiane Charpentier; children: Bertrand, Alix. Grad., U. Liège, 1987; postgrad., Coll. Europe, Bruges, Belgium, 1987—88. Bar: Liege Bar Assn. 1989. Asst. Backer & Mc Kenzie, Brussels, 1988—93; sr. asst. Loeff, Claeys, Verbeke, Liège, 1993—96; pvt. practice Liège, 1996—99; sr. assoc. Bogaert & Vandemeulebroeke (Landwell), Liège, 1999—. Corporate, general, Corporate taxation, Personal income taxation. Home: Rue de Liège 28 4800 Verviers Belgium Office: Bogaert & Vandemeulebroeke (Landwell) Avenue Maurice Destenay 13 4000 Liège Belgium Office Fax: 00 32 4 220 62 71. E-mail: vincent.bernard@bvlaw.be.

BERNER, FREDERIC GEORGE, JR., lawyer; b. Washington, May 7, 1943; s. Frederic George and Florence Grace (Carlton) B.; m. Lorraine Ann Ouellette, Sept. 28, 1968; children: Frederic George, III, Christina Lorraine, Jennifer Jane. BA, Middlebury Coll., 1965; MBA, Am. U., 1970; JD, George Washington U., 1973. Bar: D.C. 1973, U.S. Dist. Ct. (D.C. dist.) 1973, U.S. Ct. Appeals (D.C. cir.) 1974, U.S. Ct. Appeals (4th cir.) 1977, U.S. Ct. Appeals (11th cir.) 1984, U.S. Ct. Appeals (10th cir.) 1994, U.S. Ct. Appeals (7th cir.) 2001, U.S. Supreme Ct. 1980. Econ. intelligence officer CIA, Washington, 1965-67, 70; assoc. Sidley & Austin, Washington, 1973-80; ptnr. Sidley Austin Brown & Wood LLP, Washington, 1980—. Contbr. articles to legal publs.; bd. editl. advisors Pub. Utilities Fortnightly. Gen. counsel, bd. dirs. Washington chpt. Nat. Hemophilia Found., 1976-80. Served to 1st lt. U.S. Army, 1967-70. Mem.: ABA, D.C. Bar, Energy Bar Assn. (v.p., bd. dirs. 2003—), Order of Coif. Republican. Presbyterian. Administrative and regulatory, Antitrust, FERC practice. Home: 7605 Glenbrook Rd Bethesda MD 20814-1319 Office: Sidley Austin Brown & Wood LLP 1501 K St NW Washington DC 20005 E-mail: fberner@sidley.com.

BERNER, ROBERT LEE, JR., lawyer; b. Chgo., Dec. 9, 1931; s. Robert Lee and Mary Louise (Kenney) B.; m. Sheila Marie Reynolds, Jan. 12, 1957; children: Mary, Louise, Robert, Sheila, John. AB, U. Notre Dame, 1953; LL.B., Harvard U., 1956. Bar: Ill. 1956, NY 1989. With Petit, Olin, Overmyer & Fazio, Chgo., 1957—63, Baker & McKenzie, Chgo., 1963—; ptnr., 1964—2000; sr. counsel, 2000—. Mem. vis. com. Northwestern U. Law Sch., 1981-85; mem. legal adv. com. N.Y. Stock Exch., 1995-98. Mem. vis. com. U. Chgo. Div. Sch., 1972—, chmn., 2001—; mem. legal aid com. Metropolitan Family Svcs., Chgo., 1972—90; pres. Link Unltd., Chgo., 1991—93; mem. adv. bd. Cath. Charities, Chgo., 1971—, Loyola U., 1972—; mem. coun. Coll. Arts and Letters, U. Notre Dame, 2001—; trustee Cath. Theol. Union, Chgo., 1999—; bd. dirs., chmn. United Charities, Chgo., 1983—85; bd. dirs. Link Unltd., Chgo., 1969—; pres., bd. dirs. World Trade Ctr. of Chgo., 1990—92. Mem. ABA (chmn. bus. law sect. 1987-88), Ill. State Bar Assn., Chgo. Bar Assn., Legal Club Chgo. (pres. 1974-75), Law Club Chgo. (pres. 1991-92). Federal civil litigation, Corporate, general, Private international. Home: 932 Euclid Ave Winnetka IL 60093-1418 Office: Baker & McKenzie One Prudential Plz 130 E Randolph St Ste 3500 Chicago IL 60601-6342 E-mail: robert.l.berner@bakernet.com.

BERNHARD, ALEXANDER ALFRED, lawyer; b. New Orleans, Sept. 20, 1936; s. John Helenus and Dora (Solosko) B.; m. Martha Ruggles, Nov. 21, 1959 (div.); children: John, Jason, Frederic; m. Joyce Harrington, Dec. 30, 1976 (div.); m. Myra Mayman, Nov. 2, 1986. BS, MIT, 1957; LLB, Harvard U., 1964. Bar: Calif. 1964, Oreg. 1965, Mass. 1966, N.H. 1991. Law clk. to judge U.S. Ct. Appeals (9th cir.), 1964-65; assoc. Johnson, Johnson & Harrang, Eugene, Oreg., 1965-66, Bingham, Dana & Gould, Boston, 1966-71, Hale and Dorr, Boston, 1971-73, jr. ptnr., 1973-75, sr. ptnr., 1975—. Trustee, bd. dirs. Mass. Eye and Ear Infirmary, chmn., 1992-96, chmn. emeritus, 1996—. Lt. (submarines) USNR, 1957-61. Mem. ABA, Boston Bar Assn., Union Boat Club, Longwood Cricket Club. Democrat. Corporate, general, Private international, Corporate taxation. Office: Hale and Dorr LLP 60 State St Boston MA 02109-1803 E-mail: alexander.bernhard@haledorr.com.

BERNHARD, HERBERT ASHLEY, lawyer; b. Jersey City, Sept. 24, 1927; s. Richard C. and Amalie (Lobl) B.; m. Nancy Ellen Hirschaut, Aug. 8, 1954; children: Linda, Alison, Jordan, Melissa. Student, Mexico City Coll., 1948; BEE, N.J. Inst. Tech., 1949; MA in Math., Columbia U., 1950; JD cum laude, U. Mich., 1957. Bar: Calif. 1958, U.S. Dist. Ct. (cen. dist.) Calif. 1958, U.S. Dist. Ct. (no., ea. and so. dists.) Calif. 1963, U.S. Ct. Claims 1966, U.S. Dist. Ct. (ea. dist.) Wis. 1982, U.S. Dist. Ct. (ea. and we. dists.) Ark. 1982, U.S. Dist. Ct. Nebr. 1982, U.S. Ct. Internat. Trade 1979, U.S. Tax Ct. 1969, U.S. Ct. Appeals (2d, 3d, 4th, 5th, 7th, 8th, 9th, 10th, 11th and D.C. cirs.) 1969, U.S. Supreme Ct. 1965. Research engr. Curtis-Wright Co., Caldwell, N.J., 1950-52, Boeing Aircraft Co., Cape Canaveral, Fla., 1952-55; assoc. O'Melveny & Myers, Los Angeles, 1957-62; ptnr. Greenberg, Bernhard, et al, Los Angeles, 1962-85, Jeffer, Mangels, Butler & Marmaro, Los Angeles, 1985—. Instr. math. U. Fla., Cape Canaveral, 1952-55; instr. elec. engring. U. Mich., Ann Arbor, 1955-57; referee L.A. Superior Ct., 1985—, arbitrator, 1988—, judge pro tem, 1988—; judge pro tem L.A. Mcpl. Ct., 1985—, Beverly Hills Mcpl. Ct., 1989—, Malibu Mcpl. Ct., 1994—. Contbr. articles to profl. jours. Chmn. adv. com. Skirball Mus., 1976-98; bd. overseers Hebrew Union Coll., 1976-98. With USAF, 1946-47. Recipient Disting. Achievement award N.J. Inst. Tech., 1998. Mem. Jewish Publ. Soc. (trustee 1986-96). Antitrust, Federal civil litigation, State civil litigation. Office: Jeffer Mangels Butler & Marmaro 1900 Avenue Of The Stars Fl 7 Los Angeles CA 90067-4308

BERNICK, ALAN E. lawyer, accountant; b. St. Paul, June 20, 1958; s. Herbert Jay and Marcia Bernick; m. Elisa Kim Neff, Aug. 24, 1986; children: Joshua Norton, Daniel Noah, Matthew David. BA, U. Minn., 1980, JD, 1983. Bar: Minn. 1983, U.S. Dist. Ct. Minn. 1983, U.S. Tax Ct. 1985; CPA, Minn. Ptnr. Oppenheimer Wolff & Donnelly LLP, St. Paul, 1983-2000; v.p., gen. counsel, corp. sec. Andersen Corp., Bayport, Minn., 2000—. Mem. exec. bd. Indianhead coun. Boy Scouts Am., 1993-2002. Mem. AICPA, Minn. State Bar Assn. (chair tax sect. 1995-97), Minn. Soc. CPAs (chair 1995-96). Avocations: family, outdoor activities, golf. Corporate, general, Corporate taxation, State and local taxation. Home: 621 Hampshire Dr Mendota Heights MN 55120-1935 Office: Andersen Corp 100 4th Ave N Bayport MN 55003-1096

BERNICK, DAVID M. lawyer; b. San Francisco, June 16, 1954; s. Herman Charles and Joan (Schutz) B.; m. Christine A. Clougherty, Aug. 13, 1983; 1 child, Evan Daniel. BA, U. Chgo., 1974, JD, 1978; MA, Yale U., 1975. Bar: Ill. 1978. Ptnr. Kirkland & Ellis, Chgo., 1984—. Mem. Univ. Club, Mid-Am. Club, Phi Beta Kappa. General civil litigation. Office: Kirkland & Ellis 200 E Randolph St Fl 54 Chicago IL 60601-6636

BERNING, JESPER, lawyer; b. Copenhagen, Feb. 7, 1944; s. Sigurd Godvin and Ellen (Grum-Schwensen) B.; m. Karin Bak-Jensen, Aug. 5, 1967; children: Jakob, Christel, Emil. Grad., Gentoftestatsskole, Denmark, 1962; LLM, Copenhagen U., 1966, LLD, 1974. Bar: Denmark 1970, Supreme Ct. Denmark 1978. Law clk. B. Helmer Nielsen, Denmark, 1969-71; rsch. scholar U. Mich., Ann Arbor, 1971-72; assoc. prof. U. Copenhagen, 1972-75; ptnr. Berning Schlüter Hald, Copenhagen, 1975-98. Chmn., bd. dirs. various internat. corps. Contbr. numerous articles to profl. publs.; author legal treaties. With Danish Air Force, 1966-67. Mem. IBA, Danish Bar Assn. Avocations: tennis, golf, skiing, sailing. Finance, Mergers and acquisitions, Corporate taxation. Home: 6C Valleroedgade DK-2960 Rungsted Kyst Denmark Office: Jesper Berning Ltd 6B Valleroedgade DK-2960 Rungsted Kyst Denmark also: 10 bis rue de Chateau F 83440 Fayence France E-mail: jberning@inet.uni2.dk.

BERNING, PAUL WILSON, lawyer; b. Marceline, Mo., Apr. 22, 1948; s. Harold John and Doris (Wilson) B. BJ, U. Mo., 1970; JD with honors, U. San Francisco, 1986. Bar: Calif. 1986, U.S. Dist. Ct. (no. dist., ea. dist., so. dist.) Calif. 1986, U. S. Dist. Ct. (cen. dist.) Calif. 1989, U.S. Ct. Appeals (9th cir.) 1986, U.S. Ct. Claims 1992, U.S. Supreme Ct. 1992. Copy editor Chgo. Sun-Times, 1970-74, nat., fgn. editor, 1974-78; asst. news editor San Francisco Examiner, 1978-83; law clerk San Francisco dist. atty. Consumer Fraud Divsn., 1984; extern Calif. Supreme Ct., San Francisco, 1985, San Francisco Superior Ct., 1986; assoc. Thelen, Marrin, Johnson & Bridges, San Francisco, 1986-94, ptnr., 1995-98, Thelen Reid & Priest, San Francisco, 1998—. Co-author: (book chpt.) Proving and Pricing Construction Claims, 1990; contbr. speeches and papers to profl. confs.; editor: Construction Web Links.Com, 2000—. Mem. ABA (forum on constrn. industry 1986—), State Bar Assn. Calif., Bar Assn. San Francisco (coord. legal assistance for mil. pers. 1991-92, assoc. liaison to San Francisco lawyers com. for urban affairs 1987-92). Avocations: horseback riding, sailing, reading. Private international, Construction, Transportation. Office: Thelen Reid & Priest LLP 101 2nd St Ste 1800 San Francisco CA 94105-3601 Business E-Mail: pwberning@thelenreid.com.

BERNING, RANDALL KARL, lawyer, consultant, educator, publisher; b. Highland Park, Ill., Apr. 13, 1950; s. Karl Ives and Alpha (Mikkelsen) B.; m. Carol Ann Bublitz, Oct. 22, 1983. BA, U. Ill., 1973; JD, Golden Gate U., 1977; LLM in Health Law, Loyola U., Chgo., 1989. Bar: Ill. 1977, D.C. 1980. Asst. atty. gen. State of Ill., Chgo., 1977-79, contractural hearing officer Ill. sec. of state, 1981-83; pvt. practice law Chgo., 1979—, Washington, 1986—; pvt. practice cons. Burlingame, Calif., 1979—, Naples, Fla., 1997—. Cons. to coun. on dental practice ADA, Chgo., 1987—; clin. asst. prof., Dept. Oral Health Care Delivery, U. Md., Balt., 1992—; mem. nat. adv. coun. for nursing rsch., dept. health and human svcs., Nat. Inst. Health, 1994-98; dir. practice adminstrn., adj. prof. dental jurisprudence U. Ill. at Chgo. Coll. of Dentistry, 1993-2000; clin. instr., dept. pub. health and hygiene U. Calif. at San Francisco Sch. of Dentistry, 1992—; also affiliated with Gardner, Carton & Douglas health law dept. and Arthur Andersen LLP, higher edn. cons. practice, 1998-2001. Editl. bd. Jour. Law and Ethics in Dentistry, 1987-92; pub. The Expert Series for Dentists, The Expert Series for Physicians; originator, sponsor Ann. Dentistry and the Law Conf., 1988-94. Active Rep. Com.; vol. various civic activities; bd. deacons United Ch. of Christ, 1990-93, 2002—; mem. Boy Scouts Am. Friends of Scouting Campaign, 2003. Mem. ABA, Ill. Bar Assn., D.C. Bar Assn., Am. Health Lawyers Assn., Am. Dental Edn. Assn., Nat. Spkrs. Assn. Alternative dispute resolution, Health, Mergers and acquisitions. Home: 5850 Cloudstone Ct Naples FL 34119-4606 Office: 3400 Tamiami Trl N Ste 201 Naples FL 34103-3717 also: Ste 200 312 W Randolph St Chicago IL 60606-1758 also: Ste 700 1300 Pennsylvania Ave NW Washington DC 20004 also: Ste 200 1818 Gilbreth Rd Burlingame CA 94010 E-mail: rkberning@berning-affiliates.com.

BERNINI, GIORGIO VITTORIO, university professor, lawyer; b. Bologna, Italy, Nov. 9, 1928; m. Paola Spada; 1 daughter. JD, Bologna U., 1950; postgrad., Cambridge U., 1951; LLM, U. Mich., 1953, SJD, 1958. Bar: Italy 1950, Supreme Ct. Cassation, 1965. Prof. Ferrara and Padua Univ., 1970; prof. comml., arbitration law, pres. Inst. Arbitration Law Bologna U., 1970-99; mem. Italian Antitrust Authority, 1997-99; spl. counsel Studio Bernini Associato a Baker and McKenzie, 2002—. Min. Fgn. Trade, 1994-95; mem. chamber deps. Italian Parliament, 1994-96; bd. dirs. Italian Inst. Fgn. Trade, 1997; past vis. prof. numerous Am. and European Univs.; advisor Gen. Agreement on Trade and Tariffs, World Trade Orgn.; mem. adv. com., mem. econ. and social coun. European Cmty., counsel to Italian Min., 1997; provider testimony before U.S. Senate subcom.; counsel to Arbitral Chamber Milan C. of C.; pres. spl. com. on internat. comml. arbitration application of Geneva Conv.; hon. pres. Internat. Coun. Comml. Arbitration, 1994-; pres. Rete Ferroviaria Italiana S.p.A., 2001-. Mem. editl. bd. Italian and Fgn. Trade Arbitration Law Jour.; author treaties and monographs; contbr. articles to profl. jours. Recipient Honours Dean's medal N.Y. Law Sch., Cavalier Great Cross, Pres. Italian Republic. Mem. ABA, Internat. Bar Assn., Am. Arbitration Assn., Italian Arbitration Assn., Internat. Inst. for Promotion of Arbitration and ADR (mem. sci. com.), Assn. for Tchg. and Study of Arbitration and Internat. Trade Law (pres.), CIETAC (Beijing), Euro-Arab C. of Cs. (mem. adv. coun. sys. of conciliation, arbitration and expertise, legal practitioner, arbitrator and conciliator at nat. and internat. level in questions of antitrust, comml. indsl., internat. law, mergers and acquisitions, telecom., internet, e-commerce), Internat. C. of C. (mem. panel of arbitrators), Stockholm C. of C., Vienna C. of C., Mfrs. Assn. (v.p., Lazio region 2001-), others. Avocations: golf, skiing, motor-boating. Home: Via V Putti 15 I 40136 Bologna Italy Office: Studio Bernini Associato a Baker and McK Via Mascarella 94 I 40126 Bologna Italy E-mail: giorgio.bernini@bakernet.com., bologna.bernini@bakernet.com.

BERNS, PHILIP ALLAN, lawyer; b. N.Y.C., Mar. 18, 1933; s. Milton Benjamin and Rose (Aberman) Bernstein; m. Jane Klaw, June 7, 1959; children: David, Peter, Jay. BS in Marine Transp., N.Y. State Maritime Coll., 1955; LLB, Bklyn. Law Sch., 1960. Bar: N.Y. 1960, Calif. 1990, U.S. Ct. Appeals (2d cir.) 1962, U.S. Ct. Appeals (9th cir.) 1982. Admiralty atty. admiralty sect. U.S. Dept. Justice, N.Y.C., 1960-71, asst. atty. in charge admiralty sect., 1971-77, atty. in charge torts br. San Francisco, 1977—, rep. to Supreme Ct. subcom. on admiralty rules, 1996—. Adj. prof. McGeorge Law Sch., Sacramento, 1978-88; bd. dirs. Pacific Admiralty Seminar, San Francisco. Assoc. editor Am. Maritime Cases, 1978—; mem. bd. editors Benedict's Maritime Bull., 2002—. Chmn. exec. com. S.I. (N.Y.) Community Bds., 1969-70, 1st vice chmn. no. 3 bd., 1975-77, treas. no. 3 bd., 1973-74; chmn. 122d Precinct, Community Counsel, S.I., 1968-71; pres. Walnut Creek (Calif.) Little League, 1984-85, v.p. 1978-83; pres. Chestnut Hill Civic Assn., S.I., 1968-74, Congregation B'nai Jeshurun, S.I., 1973-76, v.p., 1971-73; cub pack leader Boy Scouts Am., S.I., 1969-70; bd. dirs. Mid-Island Little League, S.I., 1972-77, Jewish Community Ctr., S.I., 1976, Little League Dist. 4, Contra Costa (Calif.) County, 1984-90. Lt. USN, 1955-57 Named United Jewish Appeal Man of Yr., Congregation B'Nai Jeshurun, 1976. Mem. ABA (admiralty and maritime law com. 1991-94), Maritime Law Assn. U.S. (exec. com. 1991-94, vice chmn. practice and rules com. 1976-91, chmn. govt. liaison com. 1994—, mem. sec. 2002—, no. dist. Calif. admiralty rules com. 1998—). Avocations: athletics, volunteer work. Home: 3506 Sugarberry Ln Walnut Creek CA 94598-1746 Office: US Dept Justice Torts Br PO Box 36028 450 Golden Gate Ave San Francisco CA 94102-3661

BERNSTEIN, BARRY JOEL, lawyer; b. Charleston, S.C., Feb. 11, 1961; s. Charles Stanley Bernstein and Sara Blum Baumwald; m. Charlene Wilkins, May 29, 1998; children: Brandi Nichole, Alexander Nicholas. BA, U. S.C., 1983, JD, 1995; postgrad., U.S. Army Command & Gen. Staff Coll., 2001. Bar: S.C., U.S. Dist. Ct. S.C. Security mgr. Boeing, Wichita,

Kans., 1986-88; pres. Security Cons., Inc., Charleston, S.C., 1988-92; law clk. Bernstein and Bernstein, P.A., Charleston, 1992-95; ptnr. Breland and Bernstein, Greenville, S.C., 1995-97; owner, pres. Bernstein Law Firm, Greenville, 1998-2000; gen. counsel Adjutant Gen. of S.C., 2000—. Dir. Homeless Animal Res. and Placement, Greenville, 1995-2000. 1st lt. U.S. Army, 1983-86, ltc. JAG S.C. N.G., 1978—. S.C. Nat. Guard scholar U. S.C., 1980, Helen Gullickson scholar U. S.C. Sch. of Law, 1994, Claude M. Sapp scholar; named Officer of Yr. ROA, Kans.. Mem. ABA, S.C. Trial Lawyers Assn., Comml. Law League Am., Scottish Rite, Masons (past master), Phi Delta Phi (magister 1994-95, province pres. 1996-98), Zeta Beta Tau. Jewish. Home: 304 Lost Creek Columbia SC 29212 Office: Adjutant General of SC 1 National Guard Rd Columbia SC 29201-4766 E-mail: bernsteinbj@sc-arng.ngb.army.mil.

BERNSTEIN, CHARLES BERNARD, lawyer; b. Chgo., June 24, 1941; s. Norman and Adele (Shore) B.; m. Roberta Luba Lesner, Aug. 7, 1968; children: Edward Charles, Louis Charles, Henry Jacob. AB, U. Chgo., 1962; JD, DePaul U., 1965. Bar: Ill. 1965, U.S. Supreme Ct. 1972. Assoc. Axelrod, Goodman & Steiner, Chgo., 1966-67, Max & Herman Chill, Chgo., 1967-74, Bellows & Assocs., Chgo., 1974-81, Marvin Sacks Ltd., Chgo., 1981; sole practice, 1981—. Basketball press dir. U. Chgo., 1967-74. Author: (with Stuart L. Cohen) Torah and Technology: The History and Genealogy of the Anixter Family, 1986; (with Neil Rosenstein) From King David to Baron David: The Genealogical Connections Between Baron Guy de Rothschild and Baroness Alix de Rothschild, 1989; The Rothschilds of Nordstetten: Their History and Genealogy, 1989; contbr. articles to mags., profl. jours. Officer Congregation Rodfei Zedek, 1979—83, 2002—, bd. dirs., 1978—93, 2000—. Recipient Am. Jurisprudence award, 1963, My Brother's Keeper award Am. Jewish Congress, 1977, Kovod award Rodfei Zedek Men's Club, 1998; co-receipient 2d Century award Jewish Theol. Sem. Am., 1999. Mem. Chgo. Bar Assn., Ill. State Bar Assn., Chgo. Jewish Hist. Soc. (treas. 1977-79, v.p. 1979-82, dir. 1977—), Chgo. Pops Orch. Assn. (treas., exec. com. 1975-81), Am. Jewish Hist. Soc., Art Inst. of Chgo., Chgo. Hist. Soc., Jewish Geneal. Soc. (dir. 1977—), Nu Beta Epsilon, B'nai B'rith (citation meritorious svc. Dist. Grand Lodge 6 1969). General practice, Landlord-tenant, Probate (including wills, trusts). Home: 5400 S Hyde Park Blvd Unit C10 Chicago IL 60615-5828 Office: 161 N Clark St Ste 1325 Chicago IL 60601-3295 E-mail: gmn540@ameritech.net.

BERNSTEIN, DANIEL LEWIS, lawyer; b. Durham, N.C., Aug. 19, 1937; s. Edward Morris and Edith (Lewis) B.; m. Ann Lust; children: Kenneth, Margaret. AB, Amherst Coll., 1959; LLB, Harvard U., 1962. Bar: N.Y. 1962, D.C. 1976. Assoc. Law Offices of A.L. Bienstock, N.Y.C., 1962-66, Hale Russell & Gray, N.Y.C., 1966-69, ptnr., 1970-84, Reid & Priest, N.Y.C., 1984-91, mng. ptnr., 1990-91; ptnr. Mannheimer Swartling, Stockholm, Sweden, N.Y.C., 1991-93, Law Office of Daniel L. Bernstein, N.Y.C., 1994—; sr. v.p., gen. counsel Lantis Eyewear Corp., N.Y.C., 1996—; ptnr. Sussman, Sollis, Ebin, Tweedy & Wood LLP, 2001—. Trustee Georges Lurcy Charitable and Ednl. Trust, N.Y.C., 1982—. Dir. The Arts and Scis. Found. U. N.C., Chapel Hill, 1994-2000; trustee The Colleen Giblin Found. , Oradell, N.J., 1994—, Walnut Hill Sch., Natick, Mass., 1999—. Mem.: ABA, Bar Assn. of City of N.Y. Commercial, contracts (including sales of goods; commercial financing), Corporate, general, Mergers and acquisitions. Office: 461 Fifth Ave Rm 1700 New York NY 10017 E-mail: dan@bernsteinlex.com.

BERNSTEIN, DONALD SCOTT, lawyer; b. Bklyn., July 11, 1953; s. Emanuel and Shirley (Smithline) B.; m. Jo Ellen Finkel, May 31, 1987; children: Daniel Emanuel, Julia Clare. BA, Princeton U., 1975; JD, U. Chgo., 1978. Bar: N.Y. 1979, U.S. Dist. Ct. (ea. and so. dists.) N.Y. 1979. Assoc. Davis Polk & Wardwell, N.Y.C., 1978-86, ptnr., 1986—. Panelist Practicing Law Inst., N.Y.C., 1983—, Am. Law Inst., ABA, 1991—, Am. Bankruptcy Inst., 1991—; mem. vis. com. U. Chgo. Law Sch., 1995-98, chmn., 1997-98; mem. ofcl. U.S. del. Insolvency Working Group, UN Commn. on Internat. Trade Law. Contbg. author Collier on Bankruptcy, 1996—, bd. editors, 2000—. Bd. dirs. Altro Health and Rehab. Svcs., Bronx, N.Y., 1988-90, N.Y. chpt. Am. Diabetes Assn., 1992-96; mem. exec. com. bankruptcy lawyers div. United Jewish Appeal Fedn., 1985—. Mem. ABA (bus. bankruptcy com., com. on legal opinions), Am. Coll. Bankruptcy (bd. dirs., 2001—), New York County Lawyers Assn. (bd. dirs. 1992-94), Nat. Bankruptcy Conf. (exec. com. 1996-99), Am. Bankruptcy Inst., Assn. Bar City N.Y. (audit com. chmn., 2000—, com. on bankruptcy and corp. reorgn. 1979-83, 85-88, chmn. 1993-96, mem. tribar opinion com. 1988—, chmn. 1998—), Internat. Insolvency Inst. (bd. dirs.). Banking, Bankruptcy, Commercial, contracts (including sales of goods; commercial financing). Office: Davis Polk & Wardwell 450 Lexington Ave Fl 21 New York NY 10017-3982

BERNSTEIN, EDWIN S. judge; b. Long Beach, N.Y., Aug. 15, 1930; s. Harry and Lena (Strizver) B.; children: Andrea, David. BA, U. Pa., 1952; LLB, Columbia U., 1955. Bar: N.Y. 1955, U.S. Ct. Appeals (2d cir.) 1962, U.S. Dist. Ct. (ea. and so. dists.) N.Y. 1962, U.S. Tax Ct. 1962, U.S. Supreme Ct. 1964, Md. 1981, D.C. 1982. Mem. bd. contract appeals Dept. Army, Heidelberg, Fed. Republic Germany, 1968-72; regional counsel U.S. Navy, Quincy, Mass., 1972-73; adminstrv. law judge U.S. Dept. Labor, Washington, 1973-79, Fed. Mine Safety and Health Rev. Commn., Washington, 1979-81, U.S. Postal Svc., Washington, 1981-87, USDA, Washington, 1987-2000. Liaison rep. Administrv. Conf. of U.S., Washington, 1983-84; guest lectr. SUNY-Albany, 1978, U. Md., 1982, George Washington U., 1984. Author: U.S. Army Procurement Handbook, 1971; Establishing Federal Administrative Law Judges as an Independent Corps, 1984, also articles Bd. dirs. Washington Hebrew Congregation, 1985-88. Recipient Meritorious Civilian Svc. award Dept. Army, 1972. Mem. ABA, Fed. Bar Assn., D.C. Bar Assn., Fed. Adminstr. Law Judges Conf. (pres. 1983-84), Papermill Assn. (pres. 1980-81). Lodges: Masons. Avocations: golf, bridge, sailing, wines, opera. Home and Office: 7642 Elmridge Dr Boca Raton FL 33433

BERNSTEIN, ERIC MARTIN, lawyer; b. Passaic, N.J., May 5, 1957; s. Abbot Alan and Jean Hausman (Schwartz) B. BA, Drew U., 1979; JD, U. Okla., 1982; MS in Indsl. and Labor Rels., Cornell U., 1985. Bar: N.J. 1982, U.S. Dist. Ct. N.J. 1982, D.C. 1985, U.S. Ct. Appeals (3d cir.) 1985, U.S. Supreme Ct. 1986. Assoc. Mandelbaum Salsburg Gold & Lazaris, East Orange, N.J., 1982-83; pvt. practice Clifton, N.J., 1983-84; sr. assoc. Gerald L. Dorf, P.A., Rahway, N.J., 1984-87; of counsel Vaida & Vaida, P.C., Flemington, N.J., 1987-88; pvt. practice Bridgewater, Clifton and Three Bridges, N.J., 1988-92; ptnr. Weiner Lesniak, Parsippany, N.J., 1992-97, Mauro Savo Camerino & Grant, Somerville, N.J., 1998-00, Eric M. Bernstein & Assocs., LLC, Warren, N.J., 2000—. Lectr. Bur. Govt. Rsch., Rutgers U., New Brunswick, N.J., 1983—; mem. adj. faculty Raritan Valley C.C., Somerville, N.J., 1988-90; city atty. City of Passaic, N.J., 1990-92; mcpl. atty. Washington Twp.-Warren County, 1991—, Hardwick Twp.-Warren County, 1992-2001, West Windsor-Mercer County, 1993-97, North Plainfield-Somerset County, 1997—, Bethlehem Twp.-Hunterdon County, 1998-2000, Stillwater Twp.-Sussex County, 1998-2000, Paramus Borough-Bergen County, 1999-2001, Franklin Township-Hunterdon County, 1999—, Union City-Hudson County, 1999-2000, Lebanon Twp.-Hunterdon County, 2001—, High Bridge Borough, Hunterdon County, 2003—; bd. atty. Englewood Bd. Edn.-Bergen County, 1996-99, Lincoln Park Bd. Edn.-Morris County, 1997-2000; planning bd. atty. Bethlehem Twp.-Hunterdon County, 2000-02, Hillsborough Twp.-Somerset County, 2001—. Asst. editor, co-author: Governing New Jersey Municipalities, 1984, co-editor, author, 6th edit., 1995; asst. editor N.J. Mcpl. Attys. Mag., 1984-92; editor N.J. State Bar Assn. Local Govt. Law Newsletter, 1995—. Vol. atty. Lawyers for the Arts, N.J., 1986—. Mem. ABA, Fed. Bar Assn., N.J. Bar Assn. (1st vice chair local govt. law sect. 1995—), D.C. Bar Assn., Passaic County Bar Assn., Somerset County Bar Assn., Nat. Arbitration Forum (arbitrator). Republican. Jewish. Avocations: tennis, golf, stamp collecting, classical and jazz music. Education and schools, Labor (including EEOC, Fair Labor Standards Act, labor-management relations, NLRB, OSHA), Municipal (including bonds). Home: 10 Timberline Dr Bridgewater NJ 08807-1204 Office: 2 North Rd PO Box 4922 Warren NJ 07059-0922 E-mail: embernstein@embalaw.com.

BERNSTEIN, GEORGE L. lawyer, accountant; b. Phila., Feb. 22, 1932; s. Leon B. and Elizabeth (Seidman) B.; m. Phyllis Wagner, June 27, 1954; children: Harris, Lisa. BS in Econs., U. Pa., 1953, JD cum laude, 1956. Bar: Pa. 1957; CPA, Pa. Accountant Laventhol & Horwath, Phila., 1950-90, exec. ptnr., chief exec. officer, 1980-90; chief oper. officer Dilworth, Paxon, Attys., Phila., 1991-94; CFO, CAO HFA, Inc., Exec. Search Cons., Phila., 1994—2002. Nat. chmn. profl. divsn. State of Israel Bonds, 1988-90; co-chmn. bd. trustees Am. Jewish Congress, Phila., 1988-90; bd. dirs. Mann Ctr. for Performing Arts, Phila.; trustee Einstein Health Care Network, Phila. Recipient Humanitarian award State of Israel Bonds, 1989. Mem. AICPA (coun. 1976-79, 81-87, strategic planning com. 1986-90, v.p. 1986-87, bd. dirs. 1981-84, com. small and medium sized firms 1978-80, MAS exec. com. 1971-75), Pa. Inst. CPAs (pres. 1976-77, com.m on past pres., chmn. MAS com., long-range objectives com., budget and fin. com.), Locust Club (pres. 1990-92, exec. com., bd. dirs.). Democrat. Avocations: golf, walking, music, theatre.

BERNSTEIN, JACOB, lawyer; b. Glen Cove, N.Y., Dec. 23, 1932; s. David and Ida (Miller) B.; m. Eva Belle Smolokoff, June 28, 1959; children: Diane Susan, Neal Robert. AB, U. Rochester, 1954; JD, U. Mich., 1957. Bar: N.Y. 1957, U.S. Supreme Ct. Mem. Ralph J. Marino, 1959-64, Marino & Bernstein, 1964-73, Marino, Bernstein & La Marca, Oyster Bay, N.Y., 1973-99, Marino & Bernstein, 2000—. Lectr. in field. Actor Sagamore Players, 1972—. Dir. Waterfront Ctr., 2002—; mem. EPTL-SCPA adv. com. N.Y. State Legis., 1990—; foundingmem., trustee Cmty. Found., 1962—; trustee Oyster Bay Jewish Ctr., 1962—, pres., 1965—67, 2000—02; sec. bd. dirs. Oyster Bay Youth and Family Counseling Agy., 1975—2002, Oyster Bay Main St. Assn.; pres. Oyster Bay E. Norwich Youth Coun., 1976—78; bd. dirs., counsel America's Sail, 1994—; divsn. chmn. United Jewish Appeal, 1965—74. With U.S. Army, 1958—59. Named Man of Yr., Oyster Bay Jewish Ctr., 1986, 2002; recipient Award of Honor, United Jewish Appeal, 1972. Mem. ABA, N.Y. Bar Assn., U.S. Dist. Ct. Bar Assn., Nassau County Bar Assn., Nassau Lawyers Assn., North Shore Lawyers Assn., Rotary (pres. 1967-68, dist. parliamentarian 1986-87, govs. aide 1999-2000), Sagamore Yacht Club (chief legal officer 1973-99, 2001—). Republican. Estate planning, Probate (including wills, trusts), Property, real (including real estate development, water). Office: PO Box 180 Oyster Bay NY 11771-0180

BERNSTEIN, JOSEPH, lawyer; b. New Orleans, Feb. 12, 1930; s. Eugene Julian and Lola (Schlemoff) Bernstein; m. Phyllis Maxine Askanase, Sept. 4, 1955; children: Jill, Barbara, Elizabeth R., Jonathan Joseph. BS, U. Ala., 1952; LLB, Tulane U., 1957. Bar: La. 1957. Clerk to Justice E. Howard McCaleb of La. Supreme Ct., 1957; assoc. Jones, Walker, Waechter, Poitevent, Carrere & Denegre, 1957—60, ptnr., 1960—65; pvt. practice New Orleans, 1965—. Former gen. counsel Alliance for Affordable Energy. Past pres. New Orleans chpt. March of Dimes, New Orleans Jewish Cmty. Ctr.; past nat. exec. com. Am. Jewish Com.; trustee New Orleans Symphony Soc.; past mem. adv. council New Orleans Mus. Art. 2d lt. AUS, 1952—54. Mem.: ABA, La. Bar Assn., Zeta Beta Tau, Phi Delta Phi. Republican. Jewish. Corporate, general, General practice, Utilities, public. Home: 708 Explanade Ave Bay Saint Louis MS 39520 E-mail: Joelou1@bellsouth.net.

BERNSTEIN, MARK R. retired lawyer; b. York, Pa., Apr. 7, 1930; s. Phillip G. Bernstein and Evelyn (Greenfield) Spielman; m. E. Louise Bernstein, May 10, 1955; children: Phillip, Cary, Adam, Andrew, Jonathan, Evan. BA, U. Pa., 1952; JD, Yale U., 1957. Bar: N.C., U.S. Dist. Ct. (we. dist.) N.C., U.S. Ct. Appeals, U.S. Custom Ct. Atty. Kennedy, Covington, Lobdell, & Hickman, Charlotte, N.C., 1957-60, Haynes, Graham, Bernstein & Baucom, Charlotte, N.C., 1960-67, Parker, Poe, Adams & Bernstein, Charlotte, N.C., 1968-98, chmn., 1992-97. Bd. dirs. Family Dollar Stores, Inc., Nat. Welders Supply Co., Inc. Bd. dirs., past chmn. The Found. of the Carolinas, Inc., The Wildacres Found.; past pres. Charlotte Symphony Assn.; past chmn. mayor's com. for a Performing Arts Ctr., 1983-85, com. mem. Performing Arts Ctr. Task Force, 1987; past chmn. N.C. Econ. Devel. Bd.; past pres. Temple Beth El, Charlotte Jewish Cmty. Ctr., Charlotte Civitan Club, Am. Symphony Orch. League, Golden Circle Theatre, Found. of Shalom Park; past mem. exec. com. Yale Law Sch.; past mem. bd. N.C. Blumenthal Performing Arts Ctr.; co-chair Cultural Resources Master Plan. 1st lt. inf. U.S. Army, 1952—54. Recipient Disting. Svc. award Jaycees, 1961, State of Israel Humanitarian award, 1981, Charlotte Fedn. of Jewish Charities A Man of the Ages award, 1985, Silver Medallion award NCCJ, 1995, Israel Humanitarian award, The Vanguard award for personal svcs. Arts and Sci. Coun., 1998. Mem. Mecklenburg County Bar Assn. (past pres.), Charlotte City Club, The Tower Club (bd. dirs.), Olde Providence Racquet Club (past pres.). Democrat. Corporate, general, Mergers and acquisitions. Home: 5300 Hardison Rd Charlotte NC 28226-6426

BERNSTEIN, MERTON CLAY, law educator, lawyer, arbitrator; b. N.Y.C., Mar. 26, 1923; s. Benjamin and Ruth (Frederica (Kleeblatt)) B.; m. Joan Barbara Brodshaug, Dec. 17, 1955; children: Johanna Karin, Inga Saterlie, Matthew Curtis, Rachel Libby. BA, Oberlin Coll., 1943; LL.B., Columbia U., 1948. Bar: N.Y. 1948, U.S. Supreme Ct. 1952. Assoc. Schlesinger & Schlesinger, 1948; atty. NLRB, 1949-50, 50-51, Office of Solicitor, U.S. Dept. Labor, 1950; counsel Nat. Enforcement Commn., 1951, U.S. Senate Subcom. on Labor, 1952; legis. asst. to U.S. Sen. Wayne L. Morse, 1953-56; counsel U.S. Senate Com. on R.R. Retirement, 1957-58; spl. counsel U.S. Senate Subcom. on Labor, 1958; assoc. prof. law U. Nebr., 1958-59; lectr., sr. fellow Yale U. Law Sch., 1960-65; prof. law Ohio State U., 1965-75; Walter D. Coles prof. law Washington U., St. Louis, 1975-96, Walter D. Coles prof. emeritus, 1997—; mem. adv. com. to Sec. of Treas. on Coordination of Social Security and pvt. pension plans, 1967-68. Prin. cons. Nat. Commn. on Social Security Reform, 1982-83; vis. prof. Columbia U. Law Sch., 1967-68, Leiden U., 1975-76; mem. adv. com. rsch. U.S. Social Security Adminstrn., 1967-68, chmn., 1969-70; cons. Adminstrv. Conf. of the U.S., 1989, Dept. Labor, 1966-67, Russell Sage Found., 1967-68, NSF, 1970-71, Ctr. for the Study of Contemporary Problems, 1968-71. Author: The Future of Private Pensions, 1964, Private Dispute Settlement, 1969, (with Joan B. Bernstein) Social Security: The System That Works, 1988; contbr. articles to profl. jours. Mem. Bethany (Conn.) Planning and Zoning Commn., 1962-65, Ohio Retirement Study Commn., 1967-68; co-chmn. transition team for St. Louis Mayor Freeman Bosley Jr., 1993; mem. bd. of Health, City of St. Louis, 1993-2000; bd. dirs. St. Louis Theatre Project, 1981-84; pres. bd. Met. Sch. Columbus, Ohio, 1974-75; del. White House Conf. Aging, 1995; mem. Brewster (Mass.) Bd. Health, 2001- , chair, 2002—. With AUS, 1943-45. Fulbright fellow, 1975-76, Elizur Wright award, 1965. Mem. ABA (sec. sect. labor rels. law 1968-69), Internat. Assn. for Labor Law and Social Security (bd. dirs. U.S. chpt. 1973-83, 88-91), Fulbright Alumni Assn. (bd. dirs. 1976-78), Indsl. Rels. Rsch. Assn., Am. Arbitration Assn. (mem. adv. com. St. Louis region 1987—), Nat. Acad. Social Ins. (founding mem., bd. dirs. 1986-91). Democrat. Jewish. E-mail: bernstein@wulaw.wustl.edu.

BERNSTEIN, MITCHELL HARRIS, lawyer; b. N.Y.C., Sept. 19, 1949; s. Melvin and Gladys (Weissman) B.; m. Barbara Veitch, Oct. 8, 1978; children: Jonathan, Matthew, Emily. AB, U. Pa., 1970; JD, Yale U., 1973. Bar: N.Y. 1974, U.S. Ct. Appeals (2d cir.) 1974, U.S. Dist. Ct. (so. and ea. dists.) N.Y. 1974, U.S. Ct. Appeals (5th and D.C. cirs.) 1980, U.S. Supreme Ct. 1980, D.C. 1981, U.S. Ct. Appeals (4th cir.) 1981, U.S. Dist. Ct. D.C. 1982, U.S. Ct. Appeals (3d cir.) 1985. Assoc. Breed, Abbott & Morgan, N.Y.C., 1974-77; sr. atty. U.S. EPA, Washington, 1977-81; assoc. Skadden, Arps, Slate, Meagher & Flom, Washington, 1981-83, ptnr., 1983-93; mem. Van Ness Feldman, Washington, 1994—. Bd. advisors Chem. Waste Litigation Reporter, Washington, 1985—. Mem. ABA, D.C. Bar. Assn. Administrative and regulatory, Environmental. Office: Van Ness Feldman Ste 7 1050 Thomas Jefferson St NW Washington DC 20007-3837 E-mail: mhb@vnf.com.

BERNSTEIN, NADIA J. lawyer; b. Salford, Lancashire, Eng., Feb. 26, 1945; came to U.S., 1948; d. David Colin and Rose (Bolton) Cohen; m. David J. Adler, Mar. 1977 (div. 1992); m. Robert Bernstein, May, 1997. BA, CCNY, 1966; JD, NYU, 1973. Bar: N.Y. 1974, U.S. Dist. Ct. (so. and ea. dists.) N.Y. 1974, U.S. Ct. Appeals (2d cir.) 1975, U.S. Supreme Ct. 1983. Assoc. Rosenman Colin Freund Lewis & Cohen and predecessor firms, NYC, 1973-82; ptnr. Rosenman & Colin, NYC, 1983-87; v.p., gen. counsel Montefiore Med. Ctr., NYC, 1987-89, sr. v.p., gen. counsel, 1989-98; v.p., gen. counsel, corp. sec. C.R. Bard, Inc., Murray Hill, NJ, 1999—. Mem. legal affairs com. Greater N.Y. Hosp. Assn., N.Y.C., 1987-99; mem. bioethics task force, subcoms. on patient decision making, reproductive techs. and physician-assisted suicide, commn. women's equality Am. Jewish Congress, N.Y.C., 1989—; mem. bd. ethics Village Briarcliff Manor, N.Y., 1997—. Bd. dirs. Berkeley-in-Scarsdale (N.Y.) Assn., 1989-91. Mem.: ABA (forum on health care, bus. law com., law practice mgmt. com.), NJ Gen. Counsels' Group (chief legal officers 1999), Coun. Chief Legal Officers (conf. bd. 1999—), Am. Soc. Corp. Secs., Am. Corp. Coun. Assn. (law mgmt. com. 2000—), Advanced Med. Tech. Assn. (legal com. 2002—), Women Bus. Leaders U.S. Health Care Industry, Exec. Women of NJ (honoree 2000), NY State Bar Assn. (exec. com. health law sect. 1996—99, co-chair in-house counsel com. health law sect.), Am. Health Lawyers Assn., Assn. Bar of City of NY. Democrat. Administrative and regulatory, Corporate, general, Health. Office: C R Bard Inc 730 Central Ave New Providence NJ 07974-1199

BERNSTINE, DANIEL O'NEAL, law educator, university president; b. Berkeley, Calif., Sept. 7, 1947; s. Annias and Emma (Jones) B.; m. Nancy Jean Tyler, July 27, 1971 (div. Mar. 1986); children: Quincy Tyler, Justin Tyler. BA, U. Calif., Berkeley, 1969; JD, Northwestern U., Chgo., 1972; LLM, U. Wis., 1975; LLD (hon.) , Hanyang U., Seoul, Korea, 1999, Waseda U., Tokyo, Japan, 2003. Bar: D.C. 1970, Wis. 1979. Prof. law Howard U. Law Sch., Washington, 1975-78, gen. counsel, interim dean, 1987-90; prof. law U. Wis. Law Sch., Madison, 1978-97, dean, 1990-97; pres. Portland (Ore.) State Univ., 1997—. Author: Wisconsin and Federal Civil Procedure, 1986. Bd. dirs. Madison Cmty. Found., 1990-94, Portland Urban League, Legacy Health Sys., Willamette United Way, 2001—; mem. Portland Multnomah Progress Bd., 1998—, Kellogg Commn. on the Future of State and Land-Grant Univs., 1997-2000. Mem. Am. Law Inst., Portland C. of C. (bd. dirs.). Office: Portland State Univ PO Box 751 Portland OR 97207-0751

BEROLZHEIMER, KARL, lawyer; b. Chgo., Mar. 31, 1932; s. Leon J. and Rae Gloss (Lowenthal) B.; m. Diane Glick, July 10, 1954; children: Alan, Eric, Paul, Lisa. BA, U. Ill., 1953; JD, Harvard U., 1958. Bar: Ill. 1958, U.S. Ct. Appeals (7th cir.) 1964, U.S. Ct. Appeals (9th cir.) 1969, U.S. Supreme Ct. 1976. Assoc. Ross & Hardies, Chgo., 1958-66, ptnr., 1966-76, of counsel, 1993—; v.p. legal Centel Corp., Chgo., 1976-77, v.p., gen. counsel, 1977-82, sr. v.p., gen. counsel, 1982-88, sr. v.p., gen. counsel, sec., 1988-93. Nat. adv. bd. Ctr. for Informatics Law, John Marshall Law Sch., Chgo., 1988-93; mem. Corp. Counsel Ctr., Northwestern U. Law Sch., 1987-93, mem. emeritus, 1993—; mem. adv. bd. Litigation Risk Mgmt. Inst., 1989-95; bd. dirs. Milton Industries, Chgo., Devon Bank, Chgo.; cons. Mt. Pulaski Tel. and Elec. Co., Lincoln, Ill., 1981-86; sec., gen. counsel Consol. Water Co., Chgo., 1968-72; mem. human rels. task force Chgo. Cmty. Trust, 1988-90. Bd. dirs. The Nat. Conf. Commn. and Justice, Chgo., presiding co-chmn., 1987-90, mem. nat. exec. bd. dirs., 1988-98, chair investment com., 1991-94, nat. co-chair, 1992-95, pres., 1993-94, chair, 1995-98; exec. bd. Internat. Coun. Christians and Jews, 1996-2000, v.p., 1998-2000; bd. dirs. Evanston (Ill.) Mental Health, 1975-82, chair, 1978-80; dir. Evanston Cmty. Found., 1996-2003, vice chair, chair grants com., 1996-98, chair, 1999-2001; bd. dirs. Beth Emet Found., 1997; trustee Northlight Theatre, Evanston, 1992—, vice-chair, 1993-99; mem. coun. The Communitarian Network, 1993-96; trustee Beth Emet Synagogue, Evanston, 1985-87, 89, sec., 1985-89; chair Capital Campaign Plan com., 1994-97; discrimination priority com. United Way, 1990-97, vice-chair, 1993; mem. assembly Parliament of the World's Religions, 1993; mem. Ill. atty. gen.'s ad hoc com. for creation of justice commn., 1994; adv. com. Ill. Justice Commn., 1995-96; adv. bd. Nat. Underground R.R. Freedom Ctr., 1997—. 1st lt. U.S. Army, 1953-55. Fellow Am. Bar Found.; mem. ABA (chair telcom. com. bus. law sect. 1982-86, dispute resolution com. 1986-90, office com. 1991-95, mem. Coalition for Justice 1993-97, bd. editors Bus. Law Today 1995-97, co-chair conflicts of interest com. 1997-2001, past chair 2001-03), Chgo. Bar Assn. (devel. of law com. 1963-77, chair 1971-73), Chgo. Coun. Lawyers. Democrat. Home: 414 Ashland Ave Evanston IL 60202-3208 Office: Ross & Hardies 150 N Michigan Ave Ste 2500 Chicago IL 60601-7567 E-mail: dkberolz@aol.com.

BERREY, ROBERT FORREST, lawyer; b. Oak Park, Ill., Dec. 7, 1939; s. Rhodes Clay and Regina (Kasprovich) B.; m. Rebecca L. Newell, Apr. 10, 1993; children from previous marriage: Adam Forrist, Ellen Catherine, Kevin Joseph. AB, Harvard U., 1962; JD, U. Chgo., 1968. Bar: Ill. 1969, Ohio 1986. Atty. Torshen, Fortes & Eiger, Chgo., 1970-75; atty. Jewel Cos., Inc., Chgo., 1975-76, sec., 1976-80, v.p., sec., gen. counsel, 1980-85; v.p., gen. counsel Tomkins (formerly Philips) Industries, Inc., 1986-91; ptnr. Chernesky, Heyman & Kress, Dayton, Ohio, 1991-98; formerly of counsel Bieser, Greer & Landis LLP, Dayton, Ohio; pvt. practice Chapel Hill, N.C. With AUS, 1962-65. Mem. ABA, Governors Club, Old Chatham Golf Club. Antitrust, Corporate, general, Securities. E-mail: robert@berrey.org.

BERRIDGE, GEORGE BRADFORD, retired lawyer; b. Detroit, June 9, 1928; s. William Lloyd and Marjorie (George) B.; m. Mary Lee Robinson, July 6, 1957; children: George Bradford, Elizabeth A., Mary L., Robert L. AB, U. Mich., 1950, MBA, 1953, JD, 1954. Bar: N.Y. 1954. Assoc. Chadbourne & Parke, N.Y.C., 1954-61; gen. atty., v.p law Am. Airlines, Inc., N.Y.C., 1961-71; sr. v.p., gen. counsel Americana Hotels, Inc., N.Y.C., 1971-74, Nat. Westminster Bank U.S.A., N.Y.C., 1975-89, Nat. Westminster Bancorp, N.Y.C., 1989-93; ret., 1993. Contbr. articles to U. Mich. Law Rev. Served to lt. (j.g.) USN, 1951-53. Recipient Howard P. Coblentz prize U. Mich. Law Sch., 1954. Episcopalian. Administrative and regulatory, Banking, Private international. Home: 2 Circle Ave Larchmont NY 10538-4219 E-mail: gberr2@aol.com.

BERRIGAN, PATRICK JOSEPH, lawyer; b. Niagara Falls, Ont., Can., Nov. 3, 1933; came to U.S., 1950; s. Thomas Joseph and Florence Cecilia (Glynn) B.; m. Shirley Mae Snyder, July 6, 1957; children: Carolyn, Deborah, Patrick Jr., Susan, Ann, Mary, James, Tara. BA in English, Holy Cross Coll., 1954; LLB, Notre Dame U., 1957. Bar: N.Y. 1958, U.S. Dist. Ct. (we. dist.) N.Y. 1960, U.S. Dist. Ct. (we. dist.) Pa. 1976, U.S. Ct. Appeals (2d cir.) 1962, U.S. Ct. Appeals (3rd cir.) 1977. Assoc. Runals, Broderick, Shoemaker, et al, Niagara Falls, N.Y., 1959-78; pvt. practice, Niagara Falls, 1978—. Spl. investigator City of Niagara Falls, 1972; spl. dist. atty. County of Niagara N.Y., Lockport, 1974-76; mem. Judicial Conf. of the State of N.Y., 1978-80; counsel N.Y. State Assembly Com. on mortgages, Albany, 1960-63; hearing officer Com. on Jud. Conduct, 1992—. Mem. Niagara U. Adv. Bd., Lewiston, N.Y., 1978-82; bd. dirs. Nat. Conf. of Christian and Jews, Niagara Falls, 1977; mem. Youth Bd., Niagara Falls, 1965-68. Sgt. U.S. Army, 1957-59; pres. Mount St. Mary's Adv. Bd.,

1982—, bd. trustees, 1990-97; bd. dirs. Health System Niagara, 1997-99; trustee, v.p. Mount St. Mary's Hosp., 1999—. Mem. ABA (gen. practice sect. labor law 1991—), Niagara Falls Country Club (bd. govs.), Niagara Falls Bar Assn., Niagara County Bar Assn., N.Y. Bar Assn. Republican. Roman Catholic. Avocations: hockey player (old timers), golf. General civil litigation, Corporate, general, Labor (including EEOC, Fair Labor Standards Act, labor-management relations, NLRB, OSHA). Home: 790 Thornwood Dr Lewiston NY 14092-1167 Office: PO Box 712 Niagara Falls NY 14302-0712 E-mail: bpglawfirm@adelphia.net., pberrigan@adelphia.net.

BERRING, ROBERT CHARLES, JR., law educator, law librarian, former dean; b. Canton, Ohio, Nov. 20, 1949; s. Robert Charles and Rita Pauline (Franta) B.; m. Leslie Applegarth, May 20, 1998; children: Simon Robert, Daniel Fredrick. BA cum laude, Harvard U., 1971; JD, M.L.S., U. Calif.-Berkeley, 1974. Asst. prof. and reference librarian U. Ill. Law Sch., Champaign, 1974-76; assoc. librarian U. Tex. Law Sch., Austin, 1976-78; dep. librarian Harvard Law Sch., Cambridge, Mass., 1978-81; prof. law, law librarian U. Wash. Law Sch., Seattle, 1981-82, U. Calif., Boalt Hall Law Sch., Berkeley, 1982—, dean sch. library and info. scis., 1986-89, Walter Perry Johnson chair, 1998—, interim dean, 2003—. Mem. Westlaw Adv. Bd., St. Paul, 1984-91; cons. various law firms; mem. on Legal Exch. with China, 1983—, chmn., 1991-93.; vis. prof. U. Cologne, 1993. Author: How to Find the Law, 8th edit., 1984, 9th edit., 1989, Great American Law Revs., 1985, Finding the Law, 1999; co-author: Authors Guide, 1981; editor Legal Reference Svc. Quar., 1981—; author videotape series Commando Legal Rsch., 1989. Chmn. Com. Legal Ednl. Exch. with China, 1991—93. Robinson Cox fellow U. Western Australia, 1988; named West Publishing Co. Acad. Libr. of Yr., 1994. Mem. Am. Assn. Law Libraries (pres. 1985-86), Calif. Bar Assn., ABA, ALA, Am. Law Inst. Office: U Calif Law Sch Boalt Hl Rm 345 Berkeley CA 94720-0001

BERRY, ANDERS TAYLOR, lawyer; b. Hyannis, Mass., Jan. 9, 1954; s. John Raymond Jr. and Ruth (Anderson) B.; m. Barbara Sutherland, Aug. 27, 1994. BA in History, Colgate U., 1976; JD, U. Mont. Sch. Law, 1994. Bar: Mont., 1994. Supr. retail acctg. Merrill Lynch & Co., N.Y.C., 1982-89; internal auditor Gruntal & Co., Inc., N.Y.C., 1989-91; dep. county atty. Hill County, Havre, Mont., 1994-96; assoc. Smith, Walsh, Clarke & Gregoire, Great Falls, Mont., 1996-97; assoc. gen. counsel Davidson Cos., Great Falls, 1997—. Vol. Ch. of Ascension Homeless Shelter, N.Y.C., 1983-91, Poverello Ctr., Missoula, Mont., 1991-94; dir. Bear Paw Youth Guidance Home, Havre, 1994-96. Mem. ABA, Mont. Bar Assn., Cascade County Bar Assn. Republican. Episcopalian. Avocations: reading, golf, bird hunting. Corporate, general, Securities. Office: DA Davidson & Co 8 3d St N Great Falls MT 59401

BERRY, DEAN LESTER, lawyer; b. Chgo., Ill., Jan. 20, 1935; s. Ruben W. and Leonore C. (Nelson) B.; m. Donna J. Zack, Nov. 16, 1962; children: Megan, Thomas. BA with distinction, DePauw U., 1955; JD with distinction, U. Mich., 1960. Bar: Ohio 1961, U.S. Dist. Ct. (no. dist.) Ohio 1962. Assoc. Squire, Sanders & Dempsey L.L.P., Cleve., 1960-70, ptnr., 1970—2002, counsel, 2002—03. Lectr. various programs, Order of Coif. Author: Local Government in Michigan, 1960; contbr. articles to profl. jours.; participant in Quiz Kids radio program, 1945-47. Mem. council City of Rocky River, Ohio, 1967-71; mem. cen. com. Cuyahoga County Rep. Orgn., Ohio, 1963-75, mem. exec. com., 1969-2001. Served to 1st lt. USAF, 1955-57. Mem. Ohio Bar Assn., Greater Cleve. Bar Assn. (com. chmn. 1978) Soc. Profl. Journalists, Sigma Delta Chi. Methodist. Avocations: traveling, crossword puzzles. Legislative, Municipal (including bonds), Securities. Home: 478 Ravine Dr Aurora OH 44202-8236

BERRY, HENRY NEWHALL, III, lawyer; b. Boston, Sept. 25, 1930; s. Henry Newhall Jr. and Mary Antoinette Berry; m. Elizabeth Lee Kononen, Mar. 31, 1956 (div. June 1983); children: Henry, Wendy, Bethany, Melissa; m. Susan Jane Deitchman, Oct. 6, 1990. BA, U. Maine, Orono, 1955; LLB, U. Maine, Portland, 1964. Bar: Maine 1964, U.S. Dist. Ct. Maine, 1964, U.S. Ct. Appeals (1st cir.) 1969, U.S. Supreme Ct. 1967. Title atty. Maine Dept. Transp., Augusta, 1964-65; law clk. U.S. Bankruptcy Ct., Portland, 1965-66; pvt. practice Portland, 1966-72; legal aid atty. Pine Tree Legal Assistance, Portland, 1967; county atty. Cumberland County, Portland, 1973-74, dist. atty., 1975-83; pvt. practice South Portland, 1984-99, Portland, 1999—. Fed. hearing examiner U.S. Govt., Portland, 1969-70. Town councilor Cape Elizabeth (Maine) Coun., 1967-71, 97—; mem. budget com. Cumberland County, Portland, 1997—. Cpl. U.S. Army, 1952-54. Mem. Cumberland Bar Assn. Republican. Roman Catholic. General practice. Office: 1334 Washington Ave Portland ME 04103-3608

BERRY, J. MARTIN, judge; b. Mar. 26, 1946; BA, No. Ill. U., 1969, postgrad.; JD, Ill. Inst. Tech., 1974. Bar: U.S. Dist. Ct. (no. dist.) Ill. 1974. Tchr. Bro. Rice HS, 1972; asst. state atty. Cook County, Ill., 1974—80; pvt. practice, 1980—86; assoc. judge 1st Mcpl. Dist. Cook County, 1986—88, 5th Mcpl. Dist. Cook County, Bridgeview, Ill., 1988—. Co-recipient Edmund Rice award, 1997. Mem.: Bro. Rice Alumni Bar Assn., Bro. Edmund Rice Guild. Office: Cir Ct Cook County 10220 S 76th Ave Bridgeview IL 60455-2425

BERRY, JANIS MARIE, lawyer; b. Everett, Mass., Dec. 20, 1949; d. Joseph and Dorothy I. Sordillo; m. Richard G. Berry, Dec. 27, 1970; children: Alexis, Ashley, Lindsey. BA magna cum laude, Boston U., 1971, JD cum laude, 1974. Bar: Mass. 1974, U.S. Dist. Ct. Mass. 1975, U.S. Ct. Appeals (1st cir.), 1980, U.S. Supreme Ct. 1982. Law clk. Mass. Supreme Jud. Ct., Boston, 1974-75; assoc. Bingham, Dana & Gould, Boston, 1975-80; asst. U.S. atty. Boston, 1980-81; spl. atty. dept. justice N.E. Organized Crime Strike Force, Boston, 1981-84; chief atty. dept. justice N.E. Organized Crime Drug Task Force, Boston, 1984-86; ptnr. Ropes & Gray, Boston, 1986-94; pvt. practice, 1995; ptnr. Roche, Carens & DeGiacomo, 1996-97, Rubin & Rudman LLP, 1997-2001; justice Mass. Appeals Ct., 2001—. Instr. Harvard Law Sch., 1983-86, Inst. Trial Advocacy, Boston, 1984-87; lectr. Dept. Justice Advocacy Inst., 1986; mem. Mass. Bd. of Bar Overseers, 1989-93; bd. mem. Mass. Housing Fin. Agy., 1995-2001, Franciscan Children's Hosp.; chmn. merit selection panel U.S. Magistrate, 1989, Mass. Jud. Nominating Coun., 1991-92; trustee Social Law Libr., 1999-2001. Author: Defending Corporations Public Contracts Jour., (with others) Federal Criminal Practice, 1987. Candidate Mass. Atty. Gen., 1994; mem. Mass. Com. for Pub. Counsel Svcs., Boston, 1986-91; v.p. Boston Inn of Ct., 1990-91; trustee Atlanticare Hosp., 1990-94; bd. dirs. Franciscan Children's Hosp. Spl. Commendation award Dept. of Justice, Washington, 1983. Mem. Mass. Bar Assn., Boston Bar Assn., Am. Law Inst., Phi Beta Kappa. General civil litigation, Criminal, Personal injury (including property damage). Office: Mass Appeals Ct 1500 New Courthouse Boston MA 02108

BERRY, L. CLYEL, lawyer; b. Twin Falls, Idaho, July 17, 1949; s. Clyel J. and Nellie B.; m. Jill Brunzell, July 17, 1970; children: Jacob Clyel, Matthew Robert. BABA, Wash. State U., 1973; JD, U. Idaho, 1975. Bar: Idaho 1976, U.S. Dist. Ct. (dis. Idaho) 1976, U.S. Ct. Appeals (ninth cir.) 1982. Assoc. Emil F. Pike, Twin Falls, 1976-78; ptnr. Pike and Berry, Twin Falls, 1978-83; prin. Twin Falls, 1983—. Mem. Idaho State Bar Assn., Idaho Trial Lawyer Assn. (regional dir. 1981-82), Assn. Trial Lawyers of Am., Fifth Jud. Dist. Bar Assn. (sec.-treas. 1977-78). Avocations: whitewater rafting, kayaking, lic. Alaska guide, skiing, fishing, travel. General practice, Personal injury (including property damage), Workers' compensation. Office: PO Box 302 Twin Falls ID 83303-0302

BERRY, PHILLIP SAMUEL, lawyer; b. Berkeley, Calif., Jan. 30, 1937; s. Samuel Harper and Jean Mobley (Kramer) B.; children: David, Douglas, Dylan, Shane, Matthew; m. Carla Gilmer, Mar. 16, 2002. AB, Stanford U., 1958, LLB, 1961. Bar: Calif. 1962. Ptnr. Berry, Davis & McInerney, Oakland, Calif., 1968-76; owner Berry & Berry, Oakland, Calif., 1976—, pres., 1977—. Adv. com. Coll. Natural Resources, U. Calif., Berkeley; mem. Calif. State Bd. Forestry, 1974-86, vice-chmn., 1976-86. Trustee So. Calif. Ctr. for Law in Pub. Interest, 1970-87, Sierra Club Legal Def. Fund, 1975-90, Pub. Advs., 1971-86, chmn. bd., 1980-82; dir. Pacific Environment Resources Ctr., 1997—. With AUS, 1961-67. Mem. ABA, Calif. State Bar Assn., Sierra Club (nat. pres. 1969-71, 91-92, v.p. conservation law 1971—, v.p. polit. affairs 1983-85, John Muir award), Am. Alpine Club. General civil litigation, Personal injury (including property damage), Product liability. Office: 2930 Lakeshore Ave Oakland CA 94610-3614

BERRY, ROBERT WORTH, lawyer, educator, retired army officer; b. Ryderwood, Wash., Mar. 2, 1926; s. John Franklin and Anita Louise (Worth) Berry. BA in Polit. Sci., Wash. State U., 1950; JD, Harvard U., 1955; MA, John Jay Coll. Criminal Justice, 1981. Bar: D.C. 1956, U.S. Dist. Ct. (D.C.) 1956, U.S. Ct. of Appeals (D.C. cir.) 1957, U.S. Ct. Mil. Appeals 1957, Pa. 1961, U.S. Dist. Ct. (ea. dist.) Pa. 1961, U.S. Dist. Ct. (ctrl. dist.) Calif. 1967, U.S. Supreme Ct. 1961, Calif. 1967, U.S. Ct. Claims 1975, Colo. 1997, U.S. Dist. Ct. Colo. 1997, U.S. Ct. Appeals (10th cir.) 1997, U.S. Tax Ct. 1959. Research assoc. Harvard U., 1955-56; atty. Office Gen. Counsel U.S. Dept. Def., Washington, 1956-60; staff counsel Philco Ford Co., Phila., 1960-63; dir. Washington office Litton Industries, 1967-71; gen. counsel U.S. Dept. Army, Washington, 1971-74, civilian aide to sec. army, 1975-77; col. U.S. Army, 1978-87; prof., head dept. law U.S. Mil. Acad., West Point, N.Y., 1978-86; ret. as brig. gen. U.S. Army, 1987; mil. asst. to asst. sec. of army, Manpower and Res. Affairs Dept. of Army, 1986-87; asst. gen. counsel pub. affairs Litton Industries, Beverly Hills, Calif., 1963-67; chair Coun. of Def. Space Industries Assns., 1968; resident ptnr. Quarles and Brady, Washington, 1971-74; dir., corp. sec., treas., gen. counsel G.A. Wright, Inc., Denver, 1987-92, dir., 1987-2000; pvt. practice law Fort Bragg, Calif., 1993-96; spl. counsel Messner & Reeves LLC, Denver, 1997—. Bd. dirs. G.A. Wright Mktg., Inc., v.p./gen. counsel, 2001-; bd. dirs. Denver Mgmt. Svcs. Inc., v.p., gen. counsel, 2001—; foreman Mendocino County Grand Jury, 1995-96. Served with U.S. Army, 1944-46, 51-53, Korea. Decorated Bronze Star, Legion of Merit, Disting. Service Medal; recipient Disting. Civilian Service medal U.S. Dept. Army, 1973, 74, Outstanding Civilian Service medal, 1977. Mem. FBA, Bar Assn. D.C., Calif. Bar Assn., Pa. Bar Assn., Colo. State Bar Assn., Denver Bar Assn., Army-Navy Club, Army-Navy Country Club, Phi Beta Kappa, Phi Kappa Phi, Sigma Delta Chi, Lambda Chi Alpha. Protestant. Commercial, contracts (including sales of goods; commercial financing), Corporate, general, Private international. E-mail: rberry@messner.reeves.com.

BERRYMAN, RICHARD BYRON, lawyer; b. Indpls., Aug. 16, 1932; s. Herbert Byron and Ruth Katherine (Mayerhoefer) B.; m. Virginia Marie Asti, June 9, 1957; children: Steven, Susan, Kenneth. BA, Carleton Coll., 1954; JD, U. Chgo., 1957. Bar: D.C. 1957. Atty. bur. of aeronautics U.S. Dept. Navy, Washington, 1957-59, atty. office gen. counsel, 1959-62; assoc. Cox, Langford & Brown, Washington, 1962-65, ptnr., 1965-68, Fried, Frank, Harris, Shriver & Jacobson, Washington, 1968-90; pvt. practice Washington, 1990—. Mem. vis. com. Law Sch. U. Chgo., 1978-82; trustee Carleton Coll., Northfield, Minn., 1982-86; dir. Pericles Inst., Washington, 1996-2000. Mem. ABA. Administrative and regulatory, Corporate, general, Private international. Office: 6901 Old Gate Ln Rockville MD 20852 also: 1200 6 St NW Ste 800 Washington DC 20005

BERSHTEIN, HERMAN SAMMY, lawyer; b. New Haven, Sept. 2, 1925; s. William and Bessie (Burke) B.; children: Joy, Richard, Jan. BA, Yale U., 1950; LLB, U. S.C., 1954. Bar: Conn. 1954, S.C. 1954, U.S. Dist. Ct. Conn. 1955. Pvt. practice law, Hamden, Conn., 1954-69; pres. Bershtein Bershtein & Bershtein, Hamden, 1969—. Arbitrator Am. Arbitration Assn., Hamden, 1969—. Judge advocate for Jewish War Vets, Hamden, 1955-75. 2d lt. U.S. Army, 1943-46. Judge adv. Jewish War Vets., Hamden, 1955-75. Served U.S. Army, 1943—46. General civil litigation, Personal injury (including property damage), Product liability. Office: Bershtein Bershtein & Bershtein 1188 Dixwell Ave Hamden CT 06514-4732 E-mail: blawfirm@aol.com.

BERSI, ANN, lawyer; BA, MA, San Diego State U.; JD, Calif. Western Sch. of Law; PhD in Higher Edn. Adminstrn., U. Conn. Past mem. law firms Morris, Brignone & Pickering, Lionel, Sawyer & Collins, Las Vegas; dir. employee rels. State of Nev., 1981-83; exec. dir. State Bar Nev., 1983-89; dep. dist. atty. civil divsn. Clark County Dist. Atty.'s Office, Las Vegas. Past instr. pub. adminstrn. Pace U., N.Y.; legal counsel Clark County Sch. Dist. Bd. Trustees, Clark County Bd. Equalizaiton; mem. State Jud. Selection Commn., 2000—. Mem. State Bar Nev. (pres. bd. govs. 1999-2000). Office: District Attorneys Office PO Box 552215 Las Vegas NV 89155-2215

BERSIN, ALAN DOUGLAS, lawyer, school system administrator; b. Bklyn., Oct. 15, 1946; s. Arthur and Mildred (Laikin) B.; m. Elisabeth Van Aggelen, Aug. 17, 1975 (div. Dec. 1983); 1 child, Alissa Ida; m. Lisa Foster, July 20, 1991; children, Madeleine Foster, Amalia Rose. AB magna cum laude, Harvard U., 1968; student, Oxford U., 1968-71; JD, Yale U., 1974; LLD (hon.), U. San Diego, 1994, Calif. Western Sch. Law, 1996, Thomas Jefferson Sch. Law, 2000. Bar: Calif. 1975, U.S. Dist. Ct. (ctrl. dist.) Calif. 1975, U.S. Ct. Appeals (9th cir.) 1977, Alaska 1983, U.S. Dist. Ct. Alaska 1983, U.S. Dist. Ct. Hawaii 1992, U.S. Dist. Ct. (so. dist.) Calif. 1992, U.S. Supreme Ct., 1996. Exec. asst. Bd. Police Commrs., L.A., 1974-75; assoc. Munger, Tolles & Olson, L.A., 1975-77, ptnr., 1978-92; spl. dep. dist. atty. Counties of Imperial and San Diego, Calif., 1993-98; supt. pub. edn. San Diego City Schs., 1998—. Adj. prof. of law U. So. Calif. Law Ctr.; vis. prof. Sch. Law U. San Diego, 1992-93; named spl. rep. for U.S. s.w. border by U.S. Atty. Gen., 1995-98; mem. Atty Gen.'s adv. com. of U.S. Attys., 1995-98; tech. adv. panel Nat. Inst. of Justice Law Enforcement, adv. com. FCC/NTIA Pub. Safety Wireless; founder U.S./Mex. Binat. Lab. Program; chmn. bd. dirs. U.S. Border Rsch. Tech. Ctr., S.W. Border Coun.; chmn. Calif. Commn. on Tchr. Credentialing, 2000-02; mem. Nat. Bd. Profl. Tchg. Stds. Recognition, 2002; coun. visitors Calif. We. Sch. Law, 2002--. Named Rhodes scholar 1968; recipient Resolution of Merit award Mayor and City Coun. L.A., 1991, Spl. Achievement award Hispanic Urban Ctr., 1992, Peacemaker's award San Diego Mediation Assn., 1997, Morgan award San Diego LEAD, 1998, Learned Hand award, AJC, 2001, Courageous Leadership award, San Diego C. of C., 2003. Mem. Assn. Bus. Trial Lawyers (bd. govs. 1986-88), Inner City Law Ctr. (chmn. bd. dirs. 1987-90). Democrat. Jewish. Avocations: scuba diving, skiing, travel. Fax: 619-291-7182. E-mail: abersin@mail.sandi.net.

BERSTEIN-BAKER, JUDITH A. lawyer; b. N.Y.C., Sept. 27, 1945; d. Joseph Milton and Rebecca Masler Bernstein; m. Karl Baker, May 25, 1973; children: Kira Baker, Akil Baker. BA, SUNY, Binhamton, 1967; MSW, U. Pa., 1975; JD, Temple U., 1986. Bar: Pa. 1986, U.S. Ct. Appeals (3d cir.) 2002. Law clk. Ct. Common Pleas, Phila., 1986—88; atty. Support Ctr. Child Advs., Phila., 1988—90; dir. pub. svc. program U. Pa., Phila., 1990—98; atty., exec. dir. Hebrew Immigrant Aid Soc. and Coun. Migration Svc. Phila., 1998—. Group convenor Good Schs. Pa., Phila., 2001—. Recipient Equal Justice award, Cmty. Legal Svcs., 1999, cert. of Honor/Svc., Liberian Assn./African Cultural Alliance, 2002; Hon. fellow, U. Pa. Law Sch., 1998. Mem.: ABA (mem. standing com. lawyers' pub. svc. responsibilities 1992—95), Am. Immigration Lawyers Assn. (sec. Phila. chpt. 2002—). Jewish. Avocation: canoeing. Home: 154 W Hortter St Philadelphia PA 19119 Office: HIAS and Coun Migration Svc 2100 Arch St Philadelphia PA 19103-1300

BERTANI-TOMCZAK, AMY MARIE, circuit judge; b. Joliet, Ill., Apr. 1, 1957; d. Louis and Doris M. (Agazzi) Bertani; m. Jeffery J. Tomczak, July 13, 1996; children, Ursulina, Rose. BA in Polit. Sci., St. Mary's U., San Antonio, 1979; JD, Thomas M. Cooley Law Sch., 1985. Bar: Mich., 1985, Ill., 1986. Asst. state's atty. Will County State's Atty., Joliet, 1986-92; asst. atty. gen. Ill. Atty. Gen., Chgo., 1993-94; circuit judge Will County Cir. Ct., Joliet, 1994—. Mem. nominating com. Trailway coun. Girls Scouts U.S. Mem. Will County Bar Assn., Exch. Club of Joliet, Bd. Edn., Joliet Catholic Acad., 1999—. Roman Catholic. Office: Will County Ct House 14 W Jefferson St Ste 464 Joliet IL 60432-4300

BERTELSMAN, WILLIAM ODIS, federal judge; b. Cincinnati, Ohio, Jan. 31, 1936; s. Odis William and Dorothy B.; m. Margaret Ann Martin, June 13, 1959; children: Kathy, Terri, Nancy. BA, Xavier U., 1958; JD, U. Cin., 1961. Bar: Ky. 1961, Ohio 1962. Law clk. firm Taft, Stettinius & Hollister, Cin., 1960-61; mem. firm Bertelsman & Bertelsman, Newport, Ky., 1962-79; judge U.S. Dist. Ct. (ea. dist.) Ky., Covington, 1979—, chief judge, 1991-98; instr. Coll. Law U. Cin., 1965-72; city atty., prosecutor Highland Heights, Ky., 1962-69. Adj. prof. Chase Coll. of Law, 1989—. Contbr. articles to profl. jours. Served to capt. AUS, 1963-64. Mem.: U.S. Jud. Conf. (standing com. on practice and procedure 1989—95, liaison mem. adv. com. on civil rules 1989—95), Ky. Bar Assn. (bd. govs. 1978—79), ABA. Republican. Roman Catholic.

BERTHOLD, ROBERT VERNON, JR., lawyer; b. Charleston, W.Va., June 23, 1951; s. Robert V. and Betty Jeanne (Harkins) B.; m. Jacqueline G. Baisden, Aug. 9, 1976; children— Robert V., III, Matthew Chandler. B.S. cum laude, W.Va. U., 1973; J.D., 1976. Bar: W.Va. 1976, U.S. Dist. Cts. (no. and so. dists.) W.Va. 1976, U.S. Ct. Appeals (4th cir.) 1977. Assoc. Hoyer & Sergent, Charleston, W.Va., 1976-79; ptnr. Hoyer, Hoyer & Berthold, Charleston, 1979-87; pvt. practice , 1988— ; arbitrator Am. Arbitration Assn., 1978— . Mem. ABA, W.Va. Bar Assn., W.Va. Trial Lawyers Assn., (bd. dirs. 1984—), Assn. Trial Lawyers Am., Kanawha County Bar Assn. Democrat. Presbyterian. Avocation: sports. General civil litigation, Corporate, general, Personal injury (including property damage). Home: 2 Monticello Pl Charleston WV 25314-2372 Office: 208 Capitol St Charleston WV 25301-2219

BERTI-AZAR, JOSEPH, lawyer; s. Jean and Violette (Nasr) Berti-Azar. ML in French Bus. Law, La Sorbonne U. (Paris I), 2002; Lic. Lebanese Bus. Law, La Sagesse Faculty of Law, Beirut, 1997; Lic. French Bus. Law, La Sorbonne U., 1994. Bar: Beirut Bar Assn. 1998. Trainee Berti Law Firm, Beirut, 1995—96; assoc. The Law Office of Attys. Aratimos, Beirut, 1996—2001; sr. in-house legal counsel Synergy, Hospitality Svcs. & Solutions, Beirut, 2000—01; sr. legal cons. The Law Offices Of M. M. Al-Ghazali & Ptnrs., Kuwait City, Kuwait, 2001—. Banking, Corporate, general, Corporate taxation. Personal E-mail: jberti@hotmail.com.

BERTOLETTI, MARIA EDITH, lawyer; b. Rome, July 8, 1972; arrived in U.S., 1998; d. Italo and Esther Bertoletti; m. Carlos Gamboa, Aug. 19, 2001. JD summa cum laude, U. do Estado do Rio de Janeiro, Brazil, 1995; LLM, Pontifícia Universidade Católica do Rio de Janeiro, Brazil, 1996, Harvard U., 1999. Bar: NY 2000. Trainee Castro, Barros & Sobral, Rio de Janeiro, 1993—95; assoc. Xavier, Bernardes,Bragança, Rio de Janeiro, 1995—98, Shearman & Sterling, N.Y.C., 1999—2000, Sullivan & Cromwell, N.Y.C., 2000—. Avocations: running, wine, windsurfing, hiking. Office: Sullivan & Cromwell 125 Broad St New York NY 10004 Office Fax: 212-558-3588.

BERTRAM, MANYA M. retired lawyer; b. Denver; d. Samuel and Ruby (Feiner) Boran; m. Barry Bertram, June 19, 1938; children: H. Neal, Carel. JD magna cum laude, Southwestern U., 1962. Ptnr. Most and Bertram, L.A., 1963-83; of counsel Levin, Ballin, Plotkin, Zimring & Goffin, North Hollywood, Calif., 1983-92, Janice Fogg, 1993—95; ret. Former trustee Southwestern U. Sch. Law, former pres. Southwestern U. Sch. Law Alumni Assn.; former bd. advisors Whittier Coll. of Law, L.A., Beverly Coll. Law; commr. Calif. Commn. on Aging, Sacramento, 1977-82; bd. dirs. Jewish Family Svc., L.A., 1963-2001. Mem. ABA, Calif. State Bar Assn., L.A. County Bar Assn., Federacion Internac. de Abagados, Iota Tau Tau, B'nai B'rith (life mem.), Hadassah (life mem.). Avocation: geneology. Home: 440 Davis Ct #1112 San Francisco CA 94111 E-mail: manyamin@california.com.

BERTSCHY, TIMOTHY L. lawyer; b. Pekin, Ill., Nov. 12, 1952; AB magna cum laude, U. Ill., 1974; JD, George Washington U., 1977. Bar: Ill. 1977, U.S. Dist. Ct. (cen. dist.) Ill., U.S. Ct. Appeals (7th cir.) 1982, U.S. Supreme Ct. Ptnr. Heyl, Royster, Voelker & Allen, Peoria, Ill., 1977—. Editor Bus. Torts Newsletter. Fellow Ill. State Bar Found., Am. Bar Found.; mem. ABA (ho. dels. 1995—), Ill. State Bar Assn. (pres. 1998-99), Peoria County Bar Assn. General civil litigation. Office: Heyl Royster Voelker & Allen PC 124 SW Adams St Ste 600 Peoria IL 61602-1352 E-mail: tbertschy@hrva.com.

BERZ, DAVID RICHARD, lawyer; b. Chgo., May 21, 1948; m. Sherry Kirschner, Sept. 5, 1970; children: Douglas, Alexander. BA, George Washington U., 1970, JD with honors, 1973. Bar: D.C. 1973, U.S. Supreme Ct. 1977, N.Y. 1985. Mng. ptnr. Weil, Gotshal & Manges, Washington, 1985—. Author: Environmental Law in Real Estate and Business Transactions, 3 vols., 1992; mem. bd. editors Chem. Waste Litigation Reporter, 1986—; contbr. articles to profl. jours. Bd. dirs., pres. Washington Hebrew Congregation; exec. bd. mem. Am. Jewish Com.; mem. adv. bd. George Washington Univ. Nat. Law Ctr. Mem. ABA (mem. environ. controls com., corp. banking and bus. law sect., vice chmn. environ. quality control com. sect. adminstrv. law 1978-81), FBA, D.C. Bar Assn., Def. Rsch. Inst. (mem. environ. law com.), U.S. C. of C. (mem. environ. com.). Office: Weil Gotshal & Manges LLP 1501 K St NW Ste 100 Washington DC 20005-5608

BERZON, MARSHA S. federal judge; BA, Radcliffe Coll., 1966; JD, Boalt Hall Sch. Law, 1973. Bar: Calif. 1973, D.C. 1975. Clerk Judge James Browning, 9th Cir., 1973—74, Justice William Brennan, 1974—75; atty. Woll & Mayer, Washington, 1975—77, Altshuler, Berzon, Nussbaum, Berzon & Rubin, San Francisco, 1978—2000; judge U.S. Ct. Appeals 9th Cir., 2000—. Office: US Ct Appeals 9th Cir PO Box 193939 San Francisco CA 94119-3939

BERZOW, HAROLD STEVEN, lawyer; b. Bklyn., Oct. 22, 1946; s. Julius and Lillian (Hershkowitz) Brzozowsky; m. Lynore Kushner, Aug. 22, 1970; children: Alan, Jason, Rachel. BA, Bklyn. Coll., 1968; JD, Bklyn. Law Sch., 1971. Bar: N.Y. 1972, U.S. Dist. Ct. (so. and ea. dists.) N.Y. 1973, U.S. Ct. Appeals (2d cir.) 1975, U.S. Supreme Ct. 1978. Assoc. Finkel, Nadler & Goldstein, N.Y.C., 1971-77; ptnr. Finkel, Goldstein, Berzow, Rosenbloom & Nash, LLP, N.Y.C., 1977—. Mem. ABA, N.Y. County Bar Assn., N.Y. State Bar Assn., Am. Bankruptcy Inst. Jewish. Bankruptcy, Commercial, contracts (including sales of goods; commercial financing), Corporate, general. Home: 15 Acorn Ln Plainview NY 11803-1901 Office: Finkel Goldstein Berzow Rosenbloom & Nash LLP 26 Broadway New York NY 10004-1703 E-mail: hsberzow@finkgold.com.

BESEN, STEPHEN M. lawyer; b. N.Y.C., May 8, 1958; s. Stanley S. and Eleanor Besen; m. Beth Besen; children: Alex, Nicole. SB in Mgmt. and Econs., MIT, 1980; JD Harlan Fiske Stone Scholar, Columbia U., 1983. Bar: (N.Y.) 1984. Assoc. Weil, Gotshal & Manges, N.Y.C., 1983—91, ptnr., 1991—2001, Shearman & Sterling, N.Y.C., 2001—. Mergers and acquisitions, Securities. Office: Shearman & Sterling 599 Lexington Ave New York NY 10022 Office Fax: 646-848-8902. E-mail: sbesen@shearman.com.

BESHAR, ROBERT PETER, lawyer; b. N.Y.C., Mar. 3, 1928; m. Christine von Wedemeyer, Dec. 20, 1953; children: Cornelia, Jacqueline, Frederica, Peter. AB honors with exceptional distinction, Yale U., 1950,

LLB, 1953. Bar: N.Y. 1954. Asst. gen. counsel Waterfront Commn. N.Y. Harbor, 1954-55; law sec. Hon. Charles D. Breitel, Appellate div. 1st dept. N.Y. Supreme Ct., N.Y.C., 1956-58; spl. hearing officer Justice Dept., 1967-68; dep. asst. sec. Commerce; dir. Bur. Internat. Commerce; nat. export expansion coordinator Commerce Dept., Washington, 1971-72; pvt. practice, N.Y.C., 1972-2000; pres. various family enterprises, 1993—. Bd. dirs. Nat. Semicondr. Corp. (audit and dir's. affairs coms., counsel to bd. dirs. 1972-98); mem. bus. adv. panel Nat. Commn. for Rev. of Antitrust Laws, 1978-79; mem. Mcpl. Securities Rulemaking Bd., 1982-85; bd. govs. Fgn. Policy Assn., 1991—. Author: Current Legal Aspects of Doing Business With Sino-Soviet Nations, 1973; editor: Manhattan Auto Study, 1973. Trustee Westchester Coll. Found., 1992—; mem. Planning Bd. of Somers, 1984-97. Scholar of the House, Yale U., 1950. Mem. ABA (chmn. corp. and antitrust law com. 1982-85), N.Y. State Bar Assn., Elizabethan and Gypsy Trail Clubs, Phi Beta Kappa. Corporate, general, General practice. Home: 120 E End Ave New York NY 10028-7552 also: PO Box 533 Somers NY 10589-0533 E-mail: rpbeshar@netscape.net.

BESHEAR, STEVEN LYNN, lawyer; b. Dawson Springs, Ky., Sept. 21, 1944; AB, U. Ky., Lexington, 1966, JD, 1968. Bar: N.Y. 1969, Ky. 1971. Assoc. White and Case, N.Y.C., 1968-70; later ptnr. Beshear, Meng and Green, Lexington; mem. Ky. Ho. of Reps., 1974-79; atty. gen. State of Ky., Frankfort, 1979-83, lt. gov., 1983-87; ptnr. Stites & Harbison, Lexington, 1987—. Bd. editors, Ky. Law Jour., (1967-68.). Mem. Fayette County Bar Assn., Ky. Bar Assn., ABA, Order of Coif, Phi Beta Kappa, Phi Delta Phi, Omicron Delta Kappa. Administrative and regulatory, General civil litigation, Government contracts and claims. Office: Stites & Harbison Lexington Fin Ctr 250 W Main St Ste 2300 Lexington KY 40507-1758 E-mail: sbeshear@stites.com.

BESOZZI, PAUL CHARLES, lawyer; b. N.Y.C., Aug. 22, 1947; s, Alfio Joseph and Lucy Agnes (Ducibella) B.; m. Caroline Lisa Hesterberg, Oct. 7, 1978; 1 child, Christina Claire. BS cum laude in Int. Affairs, Georgetown U., 1969, JD, 1972; MBA in Bus./Govt. Rels., George Washington U., 1977. Bar: Va. 1972, D.C. 1973, U.S. Ct. Mil. Appeals 1972, U.S. Ct. Appeals (4th cir.) 1978, U.S. Ct Appeals (3d cir.) 1996, U.S. Supreme Ct. 1977. Assoc. Arnold & Porter, Washington, 1977-80; gen. counsel, minority counsel U.S. Senate Com. on Armed Svcs., Washington, 1980-84; ptnr. Hennesey, Stambler & Siebert, P.C., Washington, 1984-86, Besozzi & Gavin, Washington, 1987-93, Besozzi, Gavin & Craven, Washington, 1993-95, Besozzi, Gavin, Craven & Schmitz, Washington, 1995-96, Patton Boggs LLP, Washington, 1996—. Editor Georgetown Law Jour., 1971-72; contbr. articles and revs. to legal jours. Alumni interviewer Georgetown U. Alumni Assn., Washington, 1981—, dir. Procurement Roundtable, 1991—; mem. bd. visitors Georgetown U. Sch. Fgn. Svc. Capt. JAGC, U.S. Army, 1972-76. Mem. Fed. Comms. Bar Assn., Georgetown U. Alumni Assn. (bd. govs. 1993—), Phi Beta Kappa, Phi Alpha Theta, Pi Sigma Alpha. Communications, Legislative, Utilities, public. Office: Patton Boggs LLP 2550 M St NW Ste 400 Washington DC 20037-1301 E-mail: pbesozzi@pattonboggs.com.

BEST, FRANKLIN LUTHER, JR., lawyer; b. Lock Haven, Pa., Dec. 14, 1945; s. Franklin L. and Hazel M. (Yearick) B.; m. Kimberly R., May 1, 1982 BA, Yale U., 1967; JD, U. Pa., 1970; postgrad., Columbia U., 1994. Bar: Pa. 1970. Assoc. MacCoy, Evans & Lewis, Phila., 1970-74; asst. counsel Penn Mut. Life Ins. Co., Phila., 1974-77, asst. gen. counsel, 1978-84, assoc. gen. counsel, 1985-99, mng. corp. counsel, 1999—; counsel, asst. sec. Penn Ins. and Annuity Co., Phila., 1983-96, counsel, sec., 1996—. Lectr. Pa. Bar Inst., 1976-84. Author: Pennsylvania Insurance Law, 1991, 2d edit., 1998; contbr. articles to profl. jours. Bd. dirs. Ctr. City South Neighborhood Assn., 1979-80, pres., 1978-79; mem. Com. of Seventy, 1978-84; sec. Washington Sq. Assn., 1977-87; mem. 30th Ward Rep. Exec. Com., 1972-84, West Pikeland Twp. Open Spaces Com., 1987-99, chair, 1995-99, planning commn., 1994—, chair, 1996—. Mem.: ABA, Phila. Bar Assn., Internat. Claim Assn. (sec. 1995—2000, exec. com. 1979—81, 1985—88, 1995—, pres. 2002—03), Yale Club Phila. Baptist. General civil litigation, Insurance, Probate (including wills, trusts). Office: Penn Mut Life Ins Co 600 Dresher Rd Horsham PA 19044-2204

BEST, JUDAH, lawyer; b. N.Y.C., Sept. 4, 1932; s. Sol and Ruth (Landau) B.; m. Sally Joan Dial, June 29, 1962; 1 child, Stephen Andrew AB, Cornell U., 1954; LLB, Columbia U., 1959. Bar: N.Y. 1959, D.C. 1961, U.S. Supreme Ct. 1963. Trial atty. Solicitor's Office, U.S. Dept. Labor, Washington, 1960-61; asst. U.S. atty. for D.C., 1961-64; assoc., then ptnr. Chapman, DiSalle & Friedman, Washington, 1964-70; ptnr. Dickstein, Shapiro & Morin, Washington, 1970-80, Steptoe & Johnson, Washington, 1980-87, Debevoise & Plimpton, Washington, 1987—2002, of counsel, 2003—. Participant trial advocacy program U. Va. Sch. Law, 1981—. Contbr. articles to profl. publs. Served with U.S. Army, 1954-56 Fellow Am. Coll. Trial Lawyers; mem. ABA (coun., litigation sect. 1977-81, chmn. subcom. on litigation 1982-84, mem. fed. regulation securities com., corp. bank and bus. law sect., pub. contracts sect., vice chmn. ABA Task Force Report on RICO 1983-85, chmn. litigation sect. 1988-89, sect. del. 1989—, mem. standing com. on fed. judiciary 1990-93, chmn. 1996-97, mem. spl. com. on governance 1993-95), Fed. Bar Assn., D.C. Bar Assn., Am. Bar Found., Am. Law Inst., Cosmos Club, Washington Golf and Country Club, City Club of Washington. Federal civil litigation, Criminal. Home: 2808 Woodland Dr NW Washington DC 20008-2742 Office: Debevoise & Plimpton 555 13th St NW Ste 1100E Washington DC 20004-1163 also: 875 3rd Ave New York NY 10022-6225 E-mail: jbest@debevoise.com.

BETHEA, WILLIAM LAMAR, JR., lawyer; b. Dillon, S.C., June 2, 1940; s. William Lamar and Lillie (Hotchkiss) B.; m. Margaret McInnis, June 23, 1962 9div. Mar. 1977); children: William Lamar, Margaret Amanda; m. Paula Mikell Harper, Aug. 12, 1977. BA, Newberry Coll., 1962; JD magna cum laude, U. S.C., 1969. Bar: S.C. 1969, U.S. Dist. Ct. S.C. 1969, U.S. Ct. Appeals (4th cir.) 1974, U.S. Supreme Ct. 1981. Assoc. Harvey Battey & Bethea PA and predecessor firms, 1969-71, ptnr., 1971-81; prin. Bethea Jordan & Griffin PA, Hilton Head Island, S.C., 1981—, pres., 1981—. Chmn. Hilton Head Health Svcs. Corp., 1983-94. Trustee Hilton Head Hosp., 1974-94, chmn. 1982-94; trustee U. S.C., 1980-91, trustee emeritus, 1991—; trustee U.S.C. Bus. Partnership Found., 1983-91; trustee Newberry Coll., 1993-98, chmn., 1996-98; dir. S.C. State Port Authority, treas., 1991, vice chmn., 1992-94, chmn., 1995-99; trustee S.C. Gov.'s Sch. for Sci. and Math. Found.; bd. dirs. S.C. Coord. Coun., 1995-99; bd. dirs. Commrs. of Pilotage, Port of Charleston, S.C., 1995-99. With USMCR, 1958-62, USMC, 1962-66. Recipient Alice Glenn Doughtie Good Citizen of Yr. award Hilton Head Island, 1991. Mem. ABA, Beaufort County Bar Assn. (past pres.), Hilton Head Island Bar Assn. (past pres.), Am. Resort and Residential Devel. Assn., Communities Assn. Inst., Order Wig and Robe, Gamecock Club, U. S.C. Alumni Club, Masons, Phi Beta Kappa, Phi Alpha Delta (Outstanding Scholastic Achievement award 1969). Episcopalian. Commercial, contracts (including sales of goods; commercial financing), Private international, Property, real (including real estate development, water). Home: 14 Brams Point Rd Hilton Head Island SC 29926-2003

BETTAC, ROBERT EDWARD, lawyer; b. Ashland, Ohio, Aug. 13, 1949; s. Donald Albert and Ruth Lavina (Foos) B.; m. Suzanne Lee Shepherd, June 30, 1979; children: Jacqueline Lee, Robert Mitchell. BA in Polit. Sci., Ashland U., 1972; JD, U. Cin., 1979. Bar: U.S. Dist. Ct. (we. and so. dists.) Tex. 1983, U.S. Dist. Ct. (no. dist.) Tex. 1989, U.S. Ct. Appeals (5th and 11th cirs.) 1981, U.S. Dist. Ct. (ea. dist.) Tex. 2001. Assoc. Foster & Assocs., Inc., San Antonio, 1979-84; ptnr. Foster, Bettac & Heller, P.C., San Antonio, 1984-89, Akin Gump Strauss Hauer & Feld, San Antonio, 1989—2003. Author: (with others) Texas Practice Guide, 2d ed., 1983. Mem. Witte Mus. Coun., San Antonio, 1984—, San Antonio Public Library Found. Bd., 2003—. Labor (including EEOC, Fair Labor Standards Act, labor-management relations, NLRB, OSHA). Home: 126 Rosemary Ave San Antonio TX 78209-3841 Office: Ogletree Deakins Nash Smoak & Stewart 112 E Pecan St Ste 2600 San Antonio TX 78205 E-mail: bob.bettac@odnss.com.

BETTERIDGE, FRANCES CARPENTER, retired lawyer, mediator; b. Aug. 25, 1921; d. James Dunton and Emily (Atkinson) Carpenter; m. Albert Edwin Betteridge, Feb. 5, 1949 (div. 1975); children: Anne, Albert Edwin, James, Peter. AB, Mt. Holyoke Coll., 1942; JD, N.Y. Law Sch., 1978. Bar: Conn. 1979, Ariz. 1982. Technician in charge blood banks Roosevelt Hosp. and Mountainside Hosp., N.Y.C., Montclair, N.J., 1943-49; sub. tchr. Greenwich (Conn.) H.S., 1978-79; intern and asst. to labor contracts office Town of Greenwich, 1979-80; vol. referee Pima County Juvenile Ct., Tucson, 1981-85; sole practice immigration law Tucson, 1982-87; judge Pro Tempore Pima County Justice Cts., 1988-91. Commr. Juvenile Ct., Pima County Superior Ct., Tucson, 1985-87; hearing officer Small Claims Ct., Pima County Justice Cts., Tucson, 1982; mediator Family Crisis Svc., Tucson, 1982-85. vol. referee Pima County Superior Ct., 1981-85; lectr. Tucson Mus. Art, 1994— Pres. H.S. PTA, Greenwich, 1970, PTA Coun., 1971; mem. Greenwich Bd. Edn., 1971-76, sec. 1973-76; com. chmn. LWV Tucson, 1981, bd. dirs., 1984-85; bd. dirs., sec. Let The Sun Shine Inc., Tucson, 1981—; part time site coord. Elderhostel, Oaxaca, Mex., 1995. Mem. ABA, Conn. Bar Assn., Ariz. Bar Assn., Pima County Bar Assn., Tucson Sr. Acad., Point o'Woods Club. Republican. Avocations: imports folk art from oaxaca, mex. Home and Office: 7659 S Vivaldi Ct Tucson AZ 85747 E-mail: FMotz@aol.com.

BETTIS, BARRY PHILLIP, lawyer; b. Cumming, Ga., Nov. 11, 1954; s. W. Ruell and Mary Jo (Robbs) B.; m. Wanda Lynn Burruss, Sept. 27, 1980; children: Emily Amanda, Barry Phillip II, Spenser Roy. BBA cum laude, Mercer U., 1976; JD, Emory U., 1980. Bar: Ga. 1980, U.S. Dist. Ct. (no. dist.) Ga. 1980, U.S. Ct. Appeals (5th cir.) 1980, U.S. Ct. Appeals (11th cir.) 1982. Loan officer Fulton County Bank, Alpharetta, Ga., 1973-79; dir., officer Midway Bldg.Supply, Inc., Alpharetta, 1978—; ptnr. Boling, Rice, Bettis & Martin, Cumming, 1980—2001; atty. pvt. practice Phill Bettis, 2001—. Contbr. articles to North Ga. Jour. mag.; guest columnist Forsyth County News. Co-chmn. Cumming-Forsyth Bi-racial com., Cumming, 1987-88; chmn. Leadership Forsyth, Cumming, 1988-91; pres. Sawnee Community Ctr., Inc., Cumming, 1988-90; chmn. Cumming-Forsyth County Community Rels. Co., Cumming, 1987-88; active Leadership Ga., 1989; pres. campaign chair Forsyth County United Way, 1993-94, bd. dirs., 1993-2000; bd. trustees Forsyth County Libr., 1997—; parliamentarian Hightower Bapt. Assn., 1995-96, 2001—; trustee Lanier Tech. Coll. Mem. Ga. Bar Assn., State Bar Ga. (mem. com. on professionalism), Cumming-Forsyth County Bar Assn. (charter pres. 1984-85), Cumming C. of C. (leadership commendation 1982), Future Farmers Am. (Hon. Chpt. Farmer 1986), Kiwanis (Citizen of Yr. award 1987), Optimists (Citizen of Yr. award 1987). Baptist. Education and schools, Probate (including wills, trusts), Property, real (including real estate development, water). Home: 7411 Campground Rd Cumming GA 30040-8733 Office: Phill Bettis Atty 1080D Nine North Dr Alpharetta GA 30004

BETTS, KIRK HOWARD, lawyer; b. Jersey City, Mar. 5, 1951; s. Fred Semour and Mary Elizabeth (Morrell) B.; m. Christine Marlene Sheridan, Mar. 19, 1976; 1 child, Abigail Sheridan. BA, George Washington U., 1973; JD, Am. U., 1979. Bar: D.C. 1980, U.S. Dist. Ct. (D.C. dist.) 1980, U.S. Ct. Appeals (D.C., 5th and 11th cirs.) 1980, U.S. Supreme Ct. 1984, Md. 1986, U.S. Ct. Appeals (6th cir.) 1989, U.S. Dist. Ct. Md. 1995. Assoc. Northcutt Ely, Washington, 1979-82; mng. ptnr. Ely, Ritts, Pietrowski & Brickfield, Washington, 1982-84, Ely, Ritts, Brickfield & Betts, Washington, 1984-86; counsel Dickinson, Wright, Moon, Van Dusen & Freeman, Washington, 1986-87, ptnr., 1987-96, ptnr. in charge Washington office, 1993-95; mng. ptnr. Betts & Holt, Washington, 1996—. Asst. counsel U.S. Senate subcom. on intergovtl. rels., Washington, 1974-76; legis. aide to Hon. Wiliam V. Roth, Washington, 1973-74. Chmn. bd. mgrs. for Hallowood Conf. Ctr., St. Luke Luth. Ch., Silver Spring, Md., 1985—, ch. coun., 1987-90, 2000-02, v.p., 1989, 2000; chmn. Carl E. and Nathalia B. Rantzow Endowment for Sem. Edn., 1989—; pres.'s cabinet Luth. Theol. Sem., Gettysburg, 1995—; bd. dirs. Luth. World Relief, 1998—, sec., 2000-01, vice-chmn. 2002—; bd. dirs. Luth. Ctr. Corp., 2000—. Named to Hon. Order Ky. Cols., 1988; awarded key to City of Vanceburg, Ky., 1987. Mem. ABA (sects. on pub. utility law, law practice mgmt., trust and real property, Best Article in Series award 1980), D.C. Bar Assn., Md. State Bar Assn., Energy Bar Assn., Wash. Coll. of Law/Am. U. (alumni rels. com. 1987-88, devel. coun. 1989—, chmn. 1993-95, deans adv. coun. 1995—), Podickory Yacht Club (Annapolis, Md.) (vice commodore 1975-76). Republican. Lutheran. Avocations: sailing, woodworking, collecting lit. about Chesapeake Bay. FERC practice, Utilities, public. Home: 6412 Goldleaf Dr Bethesda MD 20817-5830 Office: Betts & Holt West Tower 10th Fl 1333 H St NW Washington DC 20005-4707 E-mail: kbetts@bettsandholt.com.

BETTS, REBECCA A. lawyer; b. Memphis, Nov. 25, 1951; BA, Dickinson Coll., 1972; JD, W.Va. U., 1976. Bar: W.Va., U.S. Dist. Ct. (so. dist.) W.Va. 1976, U.S. Ct. Appeals (4th cir.) 1978, U.S. Supreme Ct. 1984. Assoc. Spilman, Thomas, Battle & Klostermeyer, Charleston, W.Va., 1976—77; asst. U.S. atty. U.S. Atty.'s Office, 1977—81, chief civil divsn., 1979—81; founding ptnr. King, Betts & Allen, Charleston, W.Va.; U.S. atty. U.S. Dist. Ct. So. Dist., W.Va., 1994—2001; ptnr. Allen Guthrie McHugh & Thomas PLLC, 2002—. Adv. com. on rules & procedures 4th Cir. , 1995—; com. for local rules and subcom. on criminal rules So. Dist. W.Va., 1992, civil justice reform act adv. com., 91. Mem. edit. bd.: W.Va. Law Rev. Mem.: The Legal Aid Soc. of Charleston (bd. dirs.), W.Va. State Bar (past mem. com. on legal ethics), Order of the Coif. Office: Allen Guthrie McHugh & Thomas PO Box 3394 Charleston WV 25333*

BEUKEMA, JOHN FREDERICK, lawyer; b. Alpena, Mich., Jan. 30, 1947; s. Christian F. and Margaret Elizabeth (Robertson) B.; m. Cynthia Ann Parke, May 25, 1974; children: Frederick Parke, David Christian. BA, Carleton Coll., 1968; JD, U. Minn., 1971. Bar: Minn. 1971, U.S. Ct. Mil. Appeals 1974, U.S. Dist. Ct. Minn. 1975, U.S. Ct. Appeals (8th cir.) 1981, U.S. Ct. Appeals (fed. cir.) 1984, U.S. Supreme Ct. 1988, U.S. Dist. Ct. (we. dist.) Wis. 1997, U.S. Ct. Appeals (9th cir.) 1999. Assoc. Faegre & Benson, Mpls., 1971, 75-79, ptnr., 1980—. Vestryman Cathedral Ch. St. Mark, Mpls., 1983-86, 2002-; bd. dirs. Neighborhood Involvement Program, Mpls., 1986-90, pres., 1989-90; bd. dirs. Ronald McDonald House of Twin Cities, 1991-97, sec., 1995-97. Lt. JAGC, USNR, 1972-75. Mem. ABA, Minn. State Bar Assn., Hennepin County Bar Assn. Republican. Episcopalian. Antitrust, Appellate, General civil litigation. E-mail: jbeukema@faegre.com.

BEUTEL, ERNEST WILLIAM, thoracic surgeon; b. Chgo., Feb. 14, 1946; s. Ernest and Hazel Augusta (Zachow) B.; m. Anita Paulie Harrison, June 11, 1976; children: Ernest Wiley, William Andrew Harrison. BS magna cum laude, Loyola U., Chgo., 1967; MD, Loyola U., 1971, JD, 1985. Diplomate Am. Bd. Surgery and Am. Bd. Thoracic Surgery. Intern St. Joseph Hosp., Chgo., 1971-72, resident in surgery, 1972-76; resident in thoracic surgery Cook County Hosp., 1976-78; staff thoracic surgeon Naval Regional Med. Ctr., Great Lakes, 1978-80; assoc. Langston, Barker, Leininger, Inc., Chgo., 1980-84, pvt. practice thoracic surgery, 1984—; attending thoracic surgeon Resurrection Hosp., Chgo.; asst. clin. prof. Loyola U. Med. Sch. Adv. bd. Loyola U. Health Law Inst. Fellow ACS, Am. Coll. Chest Physicians, Am. Coll. Cardiology (assoc.); mem. AMA, Chgo. Surg. Soc., Ill. Bar Assn., Am. Coll. Legal Medicine, Chgo. Bar Assn., Alpha Omega Alpha, Phi Sigma Tau, Alpha Sigma Nu. Office: Taxman & Hurst Ltd 100 W Monroe St Chicago IL 60603 Home: 1481 Lawrence Ave Lake Forest IL 60045

BEUTTENMULLER, RUDOLF WILLIAM, lawyer; b. St. Louis, Dec. 20, 1953; s. Paul A. and Doris R. (Henle) B.; m. Ragina Lee Winters, July 14, 1984. AB cum laude, Princeton U., 1976; JD with distinction, Duke U., 1980. Bar: Tex. 1980, U.S. Dist. Ct. (no. dist.) Tex. 1980. Assoc. Jenkens & Gilchrist, Dallas, 1980-83; ptnr. Gregory, Self & Beuttenmuller, Dallas, 1983-88, Bradley, Bradley & Beuttenmuller, Irving, Tex., 1988-93; dir. Thomas & Self, Dallas, 1994—. Articles editor Duke Law Jour., Durham, 1979-80. Mem. Rep. Nat. Com., Washington, 1984. Mem. ABA, Dallas Bar Assn., Duke Law Alumni Assn., Princeton Alumni Assn. Banking, Corporate, general, Property, real (including real estate development, water). Home: 4428 Irvin Simmons Dr Dallas TX 75229-4247 Office: 5339 Spring Valley Rd Dallas TX 75254-3009 E-mail: rudybeutt@thomasandself.com.

BEVAN, ROBERT LEWIS, lawyer; b. Springfield, Mo., Mar. 23, 1928; s. Gene Walter and Blanche Omega (Woods) B.; m. Ronice Diane Gartin, Jan 25, 1977; children: Matthew Gene, Lisa Ann. AB, U. Mo., 1950; LLB, U. Kansas City, 1957. Bar: Mo. 1957, D.C. 1969. Adminstrv. asst. U.S. Senator T. Hennings Jr., Washington, 1957-60; legis. asst. U.S. Senator E.V. Long, Washington, 1960-69; sr. govt. relations counsel Am. Bankers Assn., Washington, 1970-84; ptnr. Hopkins & Sutter, Washington, 1984-95; of counsel Stinson, Mag and Fizzell, Kansas City, Mo., 1995-2001. Ghost author: The Intruders, 1967; contbg. editor U.S. Banker, 1985-88. Fieldman Dem. Nat. Com., 1968. Served with U.S. Army, 1946-47, 1951-53. Mem. ABA (bus. law sect., chmn. banking law com. 1988-92, commn. on IOLTA 1997-2000, co-chmn. joint banking com. 1999-2000), Echequer Club. Avocation: art and antiques. Office: 4545 Wornall Rd Ste 805 Kansas City MO 64111

BEVER, ROBERT LYNN, lawyer; b. Richmond, Ind., Apr. 30, 1953; s. Lucien C. and M. Elizabeth (Hawley) B.; m. Amy J. Chiles, July 11, 1992. BA with distinction, DePauw U., 1975; JD magna cum laude, Ind. U., Indpls., 1978. Bar: Ind. 1978, U.S. Dist. Ct. (no. and so. dists.) Ind. 1978. Assoc. Harlan, Schussler, Keller & Boston, Richmond, Ind., 1978-81; ptnr. Harlan, Schussler, Boston & Bever, Richmond, 1982-97, Boston Bever Klinge Cross & Chidester, 1998—; city atty. City of Richmond, 1996—. Chmn. Wayne County Rep. Party, 1986-89; bd. dirs., sec. Leadership Wayne County, 1978-85; bd. dirs. Wayne County Hist. Soc., 1983-88, Jr. Achievement Eastern Ind., 1984-96, pres., 1991; trustee DePauw U., 1975-78, Cen. United Meth. Ch., Richmond, 1984-87. Named one of Outstanding Young Men of Am., U.S. Jaycees, 1983. Mem. ABA, Ind. State Bar Assn. (legal edn. com. 1980-88), Ind. Trial Lawyers Assn., Richmond C. of C. (bd. dirs. 1990—), Richmond-Wayne County C. of C. (bd. dirs. 1992—). Avocations: tennis, piano, politics, reading. Banking, Commercial, contracts (including sales of goods; commercial financing), Insurance. Home: 712 Beelor Rd Richmond IN 47374-9389 Office: Boston Bever Klinge Cross & Chidester 27 N 8th St Richmond IN 47374-3028

BEYER, CLAES GUNNAR LOUIS, lawyer; b. Göteborg, Sweden, Nov. 24, 1936; s. Gunnar Robert and Kerstin (Bauer) B.; m. Anita Grönkvist, 1961 (div. 1992); 1 child, Hans; Marianne G. Lindqvist, Aug. 6, 1994. LLB, U. Lund, Sweden, 1961; LLM, U. Ill., 1962; diplomé, Inst. de Droit Comparé, Paris, 1962. Bar: Sweden. Law clk. Ct. of First Instance, Stenungsund, 1962-63; assoc. Mannheimer & Zetterlöf, Göteborg, 1963-70; ptnr. Mannheimer Swartling Advokatbyrå (merger Mannheimer & Zetterlöf and Carl Swartling), Göteborg, 1970—. Mem. Securities Coun., Sweden, 1988-2002, Swedish Industry and Commerce Stock Exch. Com., 1991—; expert Swedish Govt. Com. on Due Process in Taxation, 1993-95, Com. on the Securities, 1987-89, Com. on Reorganization Swedish Ct. Sys., 1996-98; designated by Swedish Govt. to panel of conciliators Internat. Ctr. for Settlement of Investment Disputes, 1999—; mem. disciplinary com. Swedish Securities Dealers, 2001—. Exec. bd. mem. Volvo Environment Prize Found., 1990—, Volvo Rsch. and Ednl. Founds., 1986—. Mem. Swedish Bar Assn., Assn. of the Bar of N.Y., Internat. Bar Assn. Union Internat. des Avocats. Mem. Liberal Party. Avocations: literature, sailing, tennis. Office: Mannheimer Swartling Box 2235 S-40314 Göteborg Sweden

BEYER, DANIEL G. lawyer; b. Detroit, Sept. 10, 1954; s. Herbert Albert and Barbara (Sickels) B.; m. Elaine M. Zubalik, Jan. 22, 1983; children: Laura Elaine, Anne Kathleen. BA, Albion Coll., 1976; JD, Washington and Lee U., 1979. Bar: Mich. 1979, Ohio 1998, U.S. Dist. Ct. (ea. dist.) Mich. 1979, U.S. Ct. Appeals (6th cir.) 1979, AV rating, Martindale Hubbell. Assoc. to ptnr., mem. Kerr, Russell & Weber PLC, Detroit, 1979—. Mem. ABA, Mich. Bar Assn., Detroit Bar Assn., Oakland Co. Bar Assn., Assn. Def. Trial Counsel, Mich. Def. Trial Counsel. Insurance, Labor (including EEOC, Fair Labor Standards Act, labor-management relations, NLRB, OSHA), Personal injury (including property damage). Office: Kerr Russell & Weber PLC 500 Woodward Ave Ste 2500 Detroit MI 48226-3427

BEZANSON, THOMAS EDWARD, lawyer; b. Hartford, Conn., Aug. 1, 1945; s. Philip Thomas and Lillian (Carlson) Bezanson; m. Janie H. Bezanson, Aug. 10, 1969; children: Philip, Jeffrey. BA, Grinnell, 1967; MA, Rutgers U., 1971, JD, 1974. Bar: NY 1975, U.S. Dist. Ct. (ea. and so. dists.) 1975, U.S. Ct. Appeals (2d cir.) 1975, U.S. Ct. Appeals (6th cir.) 1980, U.S. Supreme Ct. 1991. Assoc. Chadbourne & Parke, N.Y.C., 1974—81, ptnr., 1981—. Author: 42 poems, 1993. Bd. dirs. Westchester Philharm., 1992—98, NY Lawyers Pub. Interest Inc., 1997—, Legal Aid Soc., 1999—2002. With U.S. Army, 1967—69. Mem.: ABA, Asn Bar City New York, NY State Bar Assn. Federal civil litigation, State civil litigation, Product liability. Office: Chadbourne & Parke 30 Rockefeller Plz Fl 31 New York NY 10112-0129 Business E-Mail: tbezanson@chadbourne.com.

BHATNAGAR, MARY ELIZABETH, lawyer; b. Nashville, July 8, 1943; d. Thomas A. and Elizabeth D. (Levine) Kelly; m. Rajendra S. Bhatnagar, Feb. 27, 1966; children: Ranjit, Rajiv. BA, Duke U., 1965; MA, Northwestern U., 1968; JD, San Mateo Law Sch., 1979. Bar: Calif. 1979, U.S. Dist. Ct. (no. dist.) Calif. 1979. Pvt. practice, San Mateo, Calif., 1979—. Prof. bus. law Coll. San Mateo, 1979—. Bd. dirs. LWV of Cen. San Mateo county, 1989—. Mem. ABA, Calif. State Bar, San Mateo County Bar Assn. Democrat. Alternative dispute resolution, Commercial, contracts (including sales of goods; commercial financing), Estate planning. Office: Bovet Profl Ctr 177 Bovet Rd Ste 600 San Mateo CA 94402-3191

BIALKIN, KENNETH JULES, lawyer, director; b. N.Y.C., Sept. 9, 1929; s. Samuel and Lillian (Kastner) B.; m. Ann Eskind, Aug. 19, 1956; children: Lisa Beth, Johanna. AB, U. Mich., 1950; cert. of attendance, London Sch. Econ., 1952; JD, Harvard U., 1953. Bar: N.Y. 1953, U.S. Dist. Ct. (ea. dist.) N.Y. 1955, U.S. Supreme Ct. 1964, U.S. Dist. Ct. (so. dist.) N.Y. 1972, U.S. Ct. Appeals (2d cir.) 1976. Assoc. Willkie Farr & Gallagher, N.Y.C., 1953-60, ptnr., 1960-88, Skadden, Arps, Slate, Meagher & Flom, N.Y.C., 1988—. Adj. prof. law NYU, 1967-87; lectr., commentator legal and fin. symposia; mem. N.Y. Stock Exch. Legal Adv. Commn., 1983-92, 98—, chmn. internat. securities subcom., 1989-98; bd. dirs. Travelers Property and Casualty Co., 1986-2002, Mcpl. Assistance Corp. City of N.Y., Sapiens Internat., Ltd., Tecnomatix Techs., Ltd.; mem. Adminstrv. Conf. of U.S., 1987-92; chmn. Com. on Fin. Svcs.; vis. com. grad. faculty New Sch. for Social Rsch., 1992—. Editor: The Business Lawyer, 1980; bd. editors Corp. Governance Jour., 1992—; contbr. articles on corp., fin. investment law to profl. jours. Chmn. Conf. Pres. Major Am. Jewish Orgns., 1984-86; chmn. Am.-Israel Friendship League, 1995—; nat. chmn. Anti-Defamation League B'nai Brith, 1982-86; pres. Jewish Cmty. Rels. Coun. N.Y., 1989-92; vice-chmn., dir. Jerusalem Found., Inc., 1975—. Mem. ABA (chmn. fed. regulation securities com. 1974-79, chmn. com. to study fgn. investment in U.S. 1978-80, chmn. ad hoc com. on insider trading regulation 1988—, chmn. sect. corp. banking and bus. law 1981-82, 88), Am. Jewish Hist. Soc. (pres. 1997—), N.Y. County Lawyers Assn. (pres. 1986-88), Am. Bar Retirement Assn. (dir. 1981-84), Coun. Fgn. Rels., Harvard Club. Corporate, general, Mergers and acquisitions, Securities. Home: 211 Central Park

W New York NY 10024-6020 Office: Skadden Arps Slate Meagher & Flom Fl 44 4 Times Sq New York NY 10036-6595 E-mail: kbialkin@skadden.com.

BIALLA, ROWLEY, lawyer; b. N.Y.C., Aug. 13, 1914; s. Edward and Amy (Rowley) B.; m. Marian L. Dunham, Mar. 23, 1945 (div. Mar. 1951); children: Margaret L., Jean B. Murphy; m. Mary S. Wilson, Aug. 21, 1954; 1 child, Nancy R. AB, Dartmouth Coll., 1937; LLB, Yale U., 1940. Bar: N.Y. 1940; U.S. Supreme Ct. 1945. Assoc. White & Case, N.Y.C., 1940-41, 46-51; house counsel Guggenheim Interests, N.Y.C., 1952-79; pvt. practice, Northport, NY, 1979—2002. Sec. Daniel and Florence Guggenheim Found., N.Y.C., 1979-2002; sec., bd. dirs. Lavanburg Found., N.Y.C., 1981-2002. Capt. U.S. Army, 1941-45. Mem. ABA. Avocations: history, genealogy. Probate (including wills, trusts), Property, real (including real estate development, water), Estate taxation. Home and Office: Apt 7406 575 Osgood St North Andover MA 01845-1991 Fax: 978-794-8772.

BIALO, KENNETH MARC, lawyer; b. N.Y.C., Nov. 21, 1946; s. Walter and Mildred (Miller) B.; m. Katherine Ann Burghard; children: Darren Andrew, Caralyn Alyssa, Jacquelyn Anne, Matthew Joseph Geronimo, Kelsey Elizabeth Ariel. BS, U. Rochester, 1968; JD cum laude (Univ. scholar), NYU, 1971; LLM, London Sch. Econs., 1973. Bar: N.Y. 1972, U.S. Ct. Appeals (2d cir.) 1974, U.S. Ct. Appeals (fed. cir.) 1988, U.S. Supreme Ct. 1975. Law clk. Hon. L.W. Pierce U.S. Dist. Ct. (so. dist.) N.Y., 1971—72; assoc. Sullivan & Cromwell, N.Y.C., 1973—80; counsel, sr. counsel Exxon Corp., NYC, 1980—90; sr. counsel, chief litigation atty. Exxon Chem. Co., Darien, Conn., 1990—91; ptnr. Baker Botts, LLP, N.Y.C., 1992—. Lectr. Practicing Law Inst., N.Y.C., 1982, 88, N.Y. State Bar Assn., 1997; vice chmn. bd. State of N.Y. Mcpl. Bond Bank Agy., N.Y.C., 2000—; mayor Village of Larchmont, NY, 2002—. Contbg. editor: Family Legal Guide, 1974; contbr. articles to profl. jours.; note and comment editor: NYU Law Rev.; host The Larchmont Report, WVOX, Whitney Radio Group, New Rochelle, N.Y., 1995—, co-host Larchmont Today, LMC-TV, Mamaroneck, N.Y., 1995—; co-founder, prin. contbr.: Plugged In, Rep. Party Pub. Svc. Newsletter, 1996—. Trustee Village of Larchmont, N.Y., 1991-2002; mem. PLI Adv. Com. on Litig., 1994—; bd. govs., Univ. Club Larchmont, 1995-1999, pres., 1998-1999; v.p., bd. dirs. Little League, Larchmont, 1985-94, mem. recreation com., 1987-89; treas., mem. exec. com. L.I. Sound Watershed Intermcpl. Coun., Westchester County, N.Y., 2000-2002; mayor Village of Larchmont, 2002--; mem. Westchester County Legis. Stormwater Adv. Com., 2001—. Mem. ABA (litig. sect. task force on client concerns 1994-95, subcom. class action, litig. sect.), N.Y. State Bar (antitrust com., fed. and comml. litig. sect., former chmn. corp. counsel com. 1989-91), Assn. of Bar of City of N.Y. (arbitration com. 1983-85), Fed. Bar Coun. (com. 2d cir. cts. 1985-87), Am. Arbitration Assn. (mem. arbitrators panel), Order of Coif. Avocations: tennis, baseball, opera, symphony. Antitrust, Federal civil litigation. Office: Baker Botts LLP 30 Rockefeller Plaza New York NY 10112-4498

BIANCO, S. ANTHONY, lawyer; b. Bklyn., Aug. 12, 1949; s. Vincent and Rose Bianco; m. Mary Ellen Stoltz, Jan. 2, 1983; children: Anna Rose, Maria Louisa. BE in Chem. Engring., Pratt U., 1971; JD, Columbia U., 1974. Bar: N.Y. 1975, U.S. Dist. Ct. (so. dist.) 1976, U.S. Ct. Appeals (2d cir.) 1977. Assoc. Chadbourne & Park, N.Y.C., 1974-79; v.p., dep. gen. counsel Booz Allen & Hamilton Inc., N.Y.C., 1979—. Dir. Profl. Cons. Ins. Co., Burlington, Vt., 1994—. With U.S. Army, 1970-74. Mem. N.Y. Athletic Club. Commercial, contracts (including sales of goods; commercial financing), General practice, Labor (including EEOC, Fair Labor Standards Act, labor-management relations, NLRB, OSHA). Home: 25 E 86th St New York NY 10028-0553 Office: Booz Allen & Hamilton Inc 101 Park Ave Fl 21 New York NY 10178-0002

BIAS, DANA G. lawyer; b. Lexington, Ky., Mar. 12, 1959; d. Cyrus Dana and Betty Jo (Haddox) B. BA with highest honors, U. Louisville, 1981; JD magna cum laude, Boston U., 1984. Bar: Mass. 1985, N.Y. 1985, Ky. 1995, Tex. 2000, U.S. Dist. Ct. (so. and ea. dists.) N.Y. 1986, U.S. Dist. Ct. (ea. dist.) Tex. 2000. Counselor Mass. Half-Way Houses, Inc., Boston, 1982-83; sr. trial atty. Criminal Def. div. Legal Aid Soc., N.Y.C., 1984-89, mng. atty., 1989-94; sole practitioner Hauppauge, N.Y., 1995; sr. trial atty. Louisville-Jefferson County Pub. Defender Corp., 1995-97; asst. public advocate, capital trial atty. Dept. of Public Advocacy, 1997-2000; mng. atty. Lone Star Legal Aid, Nacogdoches, 2000—03, Beaumont, Tex., 2002—. Lectr. N.Y.C. Pub. Schs., 1989, AAUW, 2001. Contbr. articles to profl. jours. Mem. Nacogdoches Mayor's Com. on People with Disabilities. Mem. ABA, ACLU, N.Y. State Bar Assn., Nat. Assn. Criminal Def. Lawyers, Mass. Bar Assn., Ky. Bar Assn., Tex. Bar Assn., Jefferson County Bar Assn. (pro bono bd. dirs.), NLADA, N.Y. Civil Liberties Union, Woodcock Soc., Mortar Bd., Phi Kappa Phi, Phi Eta Sigma. Democrat. Civil rights, Appellate, Family and matrimonial. Office: Lone Star Legal Aid PO Box 2552 Beaumont TX 77704-2552 E-mail: dbias@lonestarlegal.org.

BIBIK, JACQUELINE AVIS, lawyer; b. Washington, Oct. 14, 1953; d. William Wood and Lou Emma (Ward) Grant; m. William Stanley Bibik, Dec. 2, 1994. BA cum laude, Georgetown U., 1975, JD, 1978. Bar: D.C. 1979, V.I. 1986. Atty. HUD, Washington, 1977-83, Law Office Marshall Bell, St. Thomas, V.I., 1985, Law Office of Edith Bornn, St. Thomas, 1985-86, Justice Dept. of V.I., St. Thomas, 1986-87; freelance writer Fla., 1987-92; atty. Law Office of Jacquelinea Bibik, Woodbridge, Va., 1993—. Author: Coming of Age 1953-1978, 1991. Democrat. General civil litigation, General practice, Probate (including wills, trusts). Fax: 703-583-6601. E-mail: b1114j1014@msn.com.

BICE, SCOTT HAAS, dean, lawyer, educator; b. Los Angeles, Mar. 19, 1943; s. Fred Haas and Virginia M. (Scott) B.; m. Barbara Franks, Dec. 21, 1968. BS, U. So. Calif., 1965, JD, 1968. Bar: Calif. bar 1971. Law clk. to Chief Justice Earl Warren, 1968-69; asst. prof., assoc. prof., prof. law U. So. Calif., Los Angeles, 1969—, assoc. dean, 1971-74, dean Law Sch., 1980-2000, Carl Mason Franklin prof., 1983-2000, Robert C. Packard prof. law, 2000—; CEO Five B Investment Co., 1995—. Vis. prof. polit. sci. Calif. Inst. Tech., 1977; vis. prof. U. Va., 1978-79; bd.dirs. Western Mut. Ins. Co., Residence Mut. Ins. Co., Imagine Films Entertainment Co., Jenny Craig, Inc. Mem. editl. adv. bd. Calif. Lawyer, 1989-93; contbr. articles to law jours. Bd. dirs. L.A. Family Housing Corp., 1989-93, Stone Soup Child Care Programs, 1988—, L.A. Child Guidance Clinic, 2003-; trustee Bice Passavant Found., 2000—. Affiliated scholar Am. Bar Found., 1972-74 Fellow Am. Bar Found. (life); mem. Am. Law Inst. (life), Calif. Bar, Los Angeles County Bar Assn., Am. Law Deans Assn. (pres. 1997-99), Am. Judicature Soc., Calif. Club, Chancery Club (treas. 2001-02, sec. 2002-03, v.p. 2003-), Long Beach Yacht Club, Catalina Island Yacht Club (judge adv. 2002—). Home: 787 S San Rafael Ave Pasadena CA 91105-2326 Office: U So Calif Sch Law Los Angeles CA 90089-0071 E-mail: sbice@law.usc.edu.

BICK, JOHN ALAN, lawyer; b. N.Y.C., Feb. 22, 1958; s. Alan Henry and Marie (Hensen) Bick; m. Susan Hagoort; children: Jessica, Anna. AB, Dartmouth Coll., 1980; JD, Columbia U., 1983. Bar: NY. Ptnr. Davis Polk & Wardwell, N.Y.C., 1983—. Mergers and acquisitions, Corporate, general. Office: Davis Polk & Wardwell 450 Lexington Ave New York NY 10017 E-mail: bick@dpw.com.

BICKEL, JOHN W., II, lawyer; b. Champaign, Ill., Sept. 9, 1948; s. John William and Virginia Bickel; children: Hannah, Molly, Sarah. BS, U.S. Mil. Acad., 1970; JD, So. Meth. U., 1976. Bar: N.Y. 1988, Tex. 1976, U.S. Ct. Appeals (5th and 11th cirs.) 1980, U.S. Supreme Ct. 1983. Assoc. Thompson & Knight, Dallas, 1980-83; ptnr. Brown, Thomas, Karger & Bickel, Dallas, 1983-84; co-mng., co-founder, ptnr. Bickel & Brewer, Dallas, 1984—; co-founding ptnr. Bickel & Brewer Storefront, PLLC, Dallas. Adv. mem. Tex. Supreme Ct. Jury Charge Task Force, 1992; mem. com. for qualified judiciary. Co-author: "Exhibits and other Evidence," Chpt. 13, Lawyers Cooperative Fed. Practice Guide. Mem. exec. bd. So. Meth. U. Sch. Law.; mem. Hiram A. Boaz Soc. So. Meth. U.; mem. Tex. Com.: A Time to Lead--The Campaign for So. Meth. U.; mem. adv. com. Southwestern Ball, 1997-2000, co-founder Future Leaders Program, Bickel & Brewer Nat. Pub. Policy Forum. Fellow Tex. Bar Found., Dallas Bar Found. (sustaining life); mem. ABA, State Bar Tex. (past chmn. litigation com. of environ. and natural resource law sect.), N.Y. Bar Assn., Dallas Bar Assn., Markey/Wigmore Inns of Ct. (Chgo. chpt.), West Point Assn. Grads. (trustee 1997-2000, strategic planning com. 1997—), West Point Soc. North Tex. (bd. dirs. 1992-). Federal civil litigation, General civil litigation, State civil litigation. Office: Bickel & Brewer 4800 Bank One Ctr 1717 Main St Ste 4800 Dallas TX 75201-4651 E-mail: jwb@bickelbrewer.com.

BICKFORD, NATHANIEL JUDSON, lawyer; b. N.Y.C., Jan. 6, 1940; s. Albert Conde and Esther (Horan) B.; m. Jewelle Ann Wooten, Feb. 1, 1962; children: Laura Conde, Emily Allen Lansbury. AB, Harvard U., 1961; LLB, Columbia U., 1964. Bar: N.Y. 1964. Assoc. Cahill, Gordon & Reindel, N.Y.C., 1964-70; ptnr. Lankenau, Kovner & Bickford, N.Y.C., 1970-92, Lane & Mittendorf, N.Y.C., 1993-99, Windels Marx Lane & Mittendorf, N.Y.C., 2000—. Dir. various corps. and investment groups. Mem. ABA, N.Y. State Bar Assn., N.Y.C. Bar Assn., Century Assn., Knickerbocker Club (N.Y.C.). Democrat. Episcopalian. Corporate, general, Finance, Private international. Office: Windels Marx Lane & Mittendorf 156 W 56th St Fl 22 New York NY 10019-3800 E-mail: nbickford@windelsmarx.com.

BICKS, DAVID PETER, lawyer; b. N.Y.C., Mar. 16, 1933; s. Alexander and Henrietta (Isaacson) B.; m. Marian Ruef, Aug. 24, 1957; children—John Alexander, Jennifer Williams, Caroline Todd, Edward Thomas AB, Harvard U., 1955; LL.B., Yale U., 1958. Bar: N.Y. 1959, U.S. Ct. Appeals (2d cir.) 1960, U.S. Dist. Ct. (so. dist.) N.Y. 1961. Asst. U.S. atty. U.S. Dist. Ct. (so. dist.) N.Y., N.Y.C., 1959-61; spl. counsel SEC, N.Y.C., 1961-66; ptnr. LeBoeuf, Lamb, Greene & MacRae L.L.P., N.Y.C., 1966—. Bd. editors Yale Law Jour., 1956-58 Served with U.S. Army, 1958-59 Mem. ABA, N.Y. State Bar Assn. Clubs: Castine Yacht (commodore 2000—), Castine Golf (gov. 2000—) (Maine); Harvard of N.Y. (N.Y.C.). Avocation: sailing. Corporate, general, Securities. Home: 21 E 87th St New York NY 10128-0506 Office: LeBoeuf Lamb Greene & MacRae LLP 125 W 55th St New York NY 10019-5369

BIDDLE, JOHN GARY, lawyer; b. Monterrey Park, Calif., Jan. 3, 1952; s. Walter Scott Biddle and Nancy Ann (Pellissier) Fine; m. Sandra Beth Lawson, Dec. 27, 1979; children: Jennifer, Nicholas, John. BA, U. Calif., Santa Barbara, 1973; JD, U. N.Mex., 1992. Bar: N.Mex. 1992. Jud. clk. N.Mex. Supreme Ct., Santa Fe, 1992-95; pvt. practice Santa Fe, 1995-96, 97—; staff atty. N.Mex. Ct. Appeals, Santa Fe, 1996-97. Mem. ABA, N.Mex. Trial Lawyers Assn., Phi Kappa Phi. Appellate. Home: 2 Sombra Ct Santa Fe NM 87508-8783

BIDOL, JAMES ALEXANDER, lawyer; b. Jackson, Mich., Feb. 24, 1944; s. Alexander and Helen Harriet Bidol; m. Margaret Elma Davison; children: Jonathon S., Molly J., Oliver J. AA, Jackson Jr. Coll., 1964; BA, U. Mich., 1966, JD, 1969. Bar: Mich. 1969, U.S. Dist. Ct. (we. dist.) Mich. 1970. Assoc. Lokker Boter & Dalman, Holland, Mich., 1969-70, Boter Dalman & Murphy P.C., Holland, 1970-74; ptnr. Boter Dalman Murphy & Bidol P.C., Holland, 1974-90, Cunningham Dalman P.C., Holland, 1990-99, shareholder, 1999—. Bd. dirs. Holland Cmty. Action House, 1991-96. Fellow Mich. State Bar Found.; mem. Holland Lions Club (pres. 1977-78). Avocations: michigan history, travel. Federal civil litigation, State civil litigation, Personal injury (including property damage). Home: 621 Melrose Dr Holland MI 49423-4892 Fax: 616-396-7106. E-mail: bidol@holland-law.com.

BIDWELL, JAMES TRUMAN, JR., lawyer; b. N.Y.C., Jan. 2, 1934; s. James Truman and Mary (Kane) B.; m. Gail S. Bidwell, Mar. 6, 1965 (div.); children: Hillary Day Bidwell Mackay, Kimberley Wade, Cortney E.; m. Katherine T. O'Neil, July 15, 1988. BA, Yale U., 1956; LLB, Harvard U., 1959. Bar: N.Y. 1959. Atty. USAF, Austin, Tex., 1959-62; assoc. Donovan, Leisure, Newton & Irvine, N.Y.C., 1962-68, ptnr., 1968-84, White & Case, N.Y.C., 1984-98, Thelen, Reid, Pries LLP, 2003—; sr. counsel Linklaters, N.Y.C., 1998—2003. Pres. Youth Consultation Svc., 1973-78; trustee Berkeley Divinity Sch. Mem. ABA, Fed. Bar Assn., N.Y. State Bar Assn., N.Y. County Lawyers Assn. Episcopalian. Commercial, contracts (including sales of goods; commercial financing), Corporate, general, Private international. Office: Thelen Reid & Priest LLP 875 Third Ave New York NY 10022-6225

BIEBEL, PAUL PHILIP, JR., lawyer; b. Chgo., Mar. 24, 1942; s. Paul Philip Sr. and Eleanor Mary (Sweeney) B.; divorced; children: Christine M., Brian E., Jennifer A., Susan E. AB, Marquette U., 1964; JD, Georgetown U., 1967. Bar: Ill. 1967, U.S. Dist. Ct. (no. dist.) Ill. 1967, U.S. Ct. Appeals (6th cir.) 1985, U.S. Supreme Ct. 1972. Asst. dean of men Loyola U., Chgo., 1967-69; asst. state's atty. Cook County State's Atty., Chgo., 1969-75, dep. state's atty., 1975-81; 1st asst. atty. gen. Ill. Atty. Gen., Chgo., 1981-85; pub. defender Cook County Pub. Defender, Chgo., 1986-88; ptnr. Winston & Strawn, Chgo., 1985-86, 88-94, Altheimer & Gray, Chgo., 1994-96; judge Cir. Ct. Cook County, Ill., 1996—. Contbr. articles to profl. publs. Mem. Fed. Bar Assn. (bd. dirs., pres. 1994-95), Cath. Lawyers Guild (bd. dirs., Cath. Lawyer of Yr. 1988), Ill. Judges Assn., Ill. Appellate Lawyers, 7th Cir. Bar Assn., Chgo. Bar Assn. (chmn. com. 1991-93), Georgetown Law Alumni Assn. (bd. dirs. 1991-96). Roman Catholic. Avocations: reading, golf. State civil litigation. Home: 5415 N Forest Glen Ave Chicago IL 60630-1523 Office: Presiding Judge Criminal Divsn RM 101 2600 S California Ave Chicago IL 60608

BIECK, ROBERT BARTON, JR., lawyer; b. Wiesbaden, Germany, Apr. 13, 1952; s. Robert Barton and Mary-Jean (Boeck) B.; m. Julia A. Dietz, Apr. 20, 1991. BA in Polit. Sci., U. Nebr., 1974; JD with high honors, Tex. Tech. U., 1977. Bar: Tex. 1977, La. 1977, D.C. 1992, U.S. Dist. Ct. (ea. dist.) La. 1977, U.S. Dist. Ct. (mid. dist.) La. 1978, U.S. Dist. Ct. (we. dist.) La. 1979, U.S. Dist. Ct. (no. and so. dists.) Tex. 1991, U.S. Dist. Ct. D.C. (1994, U.S. Ct. Appeals (D.C. cir.) 1992, U.S. Ct. Appeals (5th and 11th cirs.) 1981, U.S. Supreme Ct. 1980. Assoc. firm Jones, Walker, Waechter, Poitevent, Carrere & Denegre, New Orleans, 1977-82, ptnr., 1982—. Chmn. profl. liability practice group, Jones, Walker, et al. Recipient West Horn Book award West Pub. Co., 1976; Fulbright and Jaworski scholar, 1976. Mem. ABA (litigation sect., bus. law sect., federal regulation of securities com.), Securities Industry Assn., Nat. Soc. Compliance Profls., New Orleans Bar Assn., La. Bankers Assn., 5th Cir. Bar Assn., Order of Coif, Phi Kappa Phi, Phi Delta Phi. Banking, Federal civil litigation, Securities. Home: 5708 Annunciation St New Orleans LA 70115 Office: Jones Walker Waechter Poitevent Carrere & Denegre 201 Saint Charles Ave Ste 5200 New Orleans LA 70170-5100 E-mail: rbieck@joneswalker.com.

BIEHL, MICHAEL MELVIN, lawyer, author; b. Milw., Feb. 24, 1951; s. Michael Melvin Biehl and Frieda Margaret (Krieg) Davis. AB, Harvard U., 1973, JD, 1976. Bar: Wis. 1976, U.S. Dist. Ct. (ea. dist.) Wis. 1976. Assoc. Foley & Lardner, Milw., 1976-84, ptnr., 1984—. Adj. prof. law Marquette U. Law Sch., 2001—. Author: Medical Staff Legal Issues, 1990, Doctored Evidence, 2002, Lawyered to Death, 2003; editor: Physician Organizations and Medical Staff, 1996. Mem. Mt. Sinai Med. Ctr. Clin. Investigations Com., Hastings Ctr.; election monitor first multi-party elections in Rep. Ga., 1990; dir. Colorlines Found. for Arts and Culture, Inc., chmn., bd. dirs. Milw. Psychiat. Hosp. and Aurora Behavioral Health Svcs. Mem. ABA, Am. Health Lawyers Assn., Am. Coll. of Med. Quality, Am. Soc. Law and Medicine. Mem. Unitarian Ch. Health, Property, real (including real estate development, water). Home: 10315 N Versailles Ct Mequon WI 53092-5231 Office: Foley & Lardner 777 E Wisconsin Ave Ste 3800 Milwaukee WI 53202-5367

BIELENBERG, LEONARD HERMAN, lawyer; b. Genesee, Idaho, July 14, 1927; s. Herman Christian and Rosella Elizabeth (Roth) B.; m. Alta Fern Claney, Oct. 31, 1953; children: Terry, Anne, Paul, Mary. BS in Bus., U. Idaho, 1950, JD, 1952. Bar: Idaho 1952, U.S. Dist. Ct. Idaho 1952. Asst. atty. gen. State of Idaho, Boise, 1952-54; ptnr. Felton & Bielenberg, Moscow, Idaho, 1954-69; pros. atty. Latah County, Moscow, 1961-67; sr. ptnr. Felton, Bielenberg & Anderson, Moscow, 1969-73, Bielenberg & Anderson, Moscow, 1973-75, Bielenberg, Anderson & Walker, Moscow, 1975-97; ret., 1998. Lectr. U. Idaho Law Sch., Moscow, 1960-67; mem. Selective Svc. Civilian Rev. Bd. Pres. Moscow Jaycees, 1958-59; bd. dirs. Moscow Hosp. Assn., 1970-82. With USNR, 1945-46, PTO. Recipient Disting. Service award Moscow Jaycees, 1957. Mem. Idaho State Bar, Latah County Bar Assn. (exec. sec. 1964), Clearwater Bar Assn., Moscow C. of C. (bd. dirs. 1958-59), Lions (pres. Moscow 1971-72), K.C. (grand knight 1957-58), Elks, Moose. Republican. Roman Catholic. Avocations: skiing, snow and water skiing, fishing, motorcycling. Estate planning, Probate (including wills, trusts), Estate taxation. Home: 1039 Virginia Ave Moscow ID 83843-9455

BIELUCH, WILLIAM CHARLES, judge; b. Nov. 12, 1918; AB magna cum laude, Brown U., 1939; JD, Yale U., 1942. Bar: Conn. 1942. Assoc. Covington, Burling, Rublee, Acheson & Shorb, Washington, 1942-43; ptnr. Bieluch, Barry & Ramenda and predecessors, Hartford, 1946-68; judge Cir. Ct. Conn., 1968-73, Ct. Common Pleas Conn., 1973-76, Superior Ct. Conn., 1976-85, Appellate Session, 1979-83, Appellate Ct. Conn., 1985-88; ret., 1988; judge trial referee, 1988—. Trustee emeritus S. S. Cyril and Methodius Roman Cath. Ch., Hartford; corporator St. Francis Hosp. and Med. Ctr., Hartford. Lt. (j.g.) USCG, WWII. Decorated Knight St. Gregory, Pope Paul VI; recipient Merit award Polish Legion Am. Vets., 1952, Man of Yr. award United Polish Socs., 1968, Archdiocesan medal of appreciation Archbishop John F. Whealon, 1970, Disting. Grad. award Nat. Cath. Elem. Sch., 1995. Mem. Conn. Bar Assn. (chmn. Jr. Bar Sect. 1948-49), Hartford County Bar Assn., KC, Phi Beta Kappa. Republican. Office: 95 Washington St Hartford CT 06106-4431

BIENVENU, JOHN CHARLES, lawyer; b. Modesto, Calif., Sept. 11, 1957; s. Robert Charles and Martha Louise (Beard) B.; m. Sarah Luciene Brick, May 10, 1983; children: Reed Charles, Loren John. Student, U. Calif., Berkeley, 1975-78; BA summa cum laude, U. N.Mex., 1985; JD with distinction, Stanford U., 1988. Bar: Calif., 1988, N.Mex., 1990; U.S. Ct. Appeals (9th cir.) 1988, U.S. Ct. Appeals (10th cir.) 1990; U.S. Ct. Fed. Claims, 1991. Assoc. Brobeck, Phleger & Harrison, San Francisco, 1988-90, Rothstein, Walther, Donatelli, Hughes, Dahlstrom & Cron, Santa Fe, N.Mex., 1990-93; prin. Santa Fe, 1993—. Mem. ACLU (cooperating atty. N.Mex.), N.Mex. State Bar. Democrat. Civil rights, General civil litigation. Home: 1580 Cerro Gordo Rd Santa Fe NM 87501-6143 Office: PO Box 2455 310 Mckenzie St Santa Fe NM 87501-1883

BIERMACHER, KENNETH WAYNE, lawyer; b. Hartford, Conn., Oct. 15, 1953; s. Donald David and Ethel Pearl (Biermacher) Lawton; m. Joan; children; Carl Joseph II (dec.), Matthew Robert, Michelle Renee; 1 step child Brent Cohen. BS summa cum laude, U. New Haven, 1976; JD with honors, Drake U., 1979. Bar: Iowa 1980, Tex. 1985, U.S. Dist. Ct. (so. dist.) Iowa 1980, U.S. Dist. Ct. (no. dist.) Iowa, 1981, U.S. Ct. Appeals (8th cir.) 1981, U.S. Supreme Ct. 1983, U.S. Dist. Ct. (no. dist.) Tex. 1984, U.S. Dist. Ct. (so. and we. dists.) Tex. 1985, U.S. Dist. Ct. (ea. dist.) Tex. 1993, U.S. Ct. Appeals (5th cir.) 1985. Assoc. Whitfield, Musgrave, Selvy, Kelly, Eddy, Des Moines, 1980-84; shareholder Geary, Stahl & Spencer, P.C., Dallas, 1984-89, Leonard Marsh Hurt Terry & Blinn, Dallas, 1989-90; ptnr.-in-charge Dallas office Small, Craig & Werkenthin, P.C., Dallas, 1990-93; v.p., ptnr., dir. Kane, Russell, Coleman & Logan, P.C., Dallas, 1993—. Lectr. Iowa Defense Counsel Assn. Annual Meeting, 1982, Des Moines Area Community Coll. Legal Asst. Program, 1981-82, Human Resources Forum, Am. Electronics Assn., Dallas, 1986; legal research asst. Iowa State Bar Assn. Com. on Study Fed. Rules Evidence, 1982; chmn. spl. com. on Friends of Moot Ct. Drake Law Sch. Bd. Counsellors, 1983-84; founder shareholder, dir. Recruit TV, Inc., 2001—, Xlantic Records, Inc., Dallas, 2001—, Xlantic Music Pub., Inc., Dallas, 2001—, founder, pres., dir. Frontrunner Capital Corp., 1999—, CDRK, Inc., 2001--, others; bd. dirs. Retractable Techs., Inc.; bd. dirs., sec. MT Auctions.com, Inc., Dallas. Contbg. author: Understanding Iowa Law, 1984; editor: Energy and Nat. Resources Guide for Iowa, 1979; contbr. articles to law jours. Adv. U. New Haven Law Enforcement Explorers Post Boy Scouts Am., 1975; coach Johnston Sr. High Sch. Mock Trial Teams, Iowa, 1984; del. Polk County Rep. Conv., Des Moines, 1980, Iowa Rep. State Conv., 1980; deacon Canyon Creek Bapt. Ch., 1986-87; chmn. scholarship and fin. aid com. Canyon Creek Christian Acad., 1985-87; v.p., dir. Boys and Girls Clubs of Greater Dallas, Inc., 1997—, chmn. circus com., 1998—, chmn. resource devel. com., 1999—; bd. dirs. Henry C. Lee Inst. Forensic Sci., 1996—; adv. bd. Dallas Tower Club. Recipient Acad. Scholarship U. New Haven, 1973-76; semi-finalist Midwest Regional Moot Ct. Competition, 1979. Mem. ABA (subcom. on fraudulent and deceptive trade practices, sect. tort and ins. practice 1985-86, vol. atty. post-conviction death penalty representation project 1988-89), ATLA, FBA, Iowa State Bar Assn. (mem. Young Lawyer Sect. ethics com. 1981, law schs. panel com. 1982, law-related edn. com. 1983-84), Def. Rsch. Inst., Iowa Assn. Trial Lawyers (founding dir., chmn. Drake U. Law Sch. student bd. dirs. 1978-79, ex-officio mem. bd. dirs. 1978-79), Dallas Bar Assn. (mock trial com., law in changing soc. com. 1985, speech com. 1985-86, bus. litigation sect. ethic and courtesy com. 1988, qualified mediator 1989—, mem. cts. com. 1995, mem. fee dispute com. 1995), State Bar Tex. (legal assts. com. 1988-91), Dallas Assn. Young Lawyers (liaison with other profls., fed. opinions com. 1986), Order of Barristers, Atty.-Mediator Assn., Drake U. Law Sch. bd. counselors (regional v.p. for Tex. and Okla. 1986-89), Alpha Chi (vice chmn. Conn. chpt. 1975-76). Federal civil litigation, State civil litigation, Personal injury (including property damage). Home: 4324 Hollow Oak Dr Dallas TX 75287-6847 Office: Kane Russell Coleman & Logan PC 1601 Elm St Ste 3700 Dallas TX 75201-7207 E-mail: kbiermacher@krcl.com.

BIERMAN, JAMES NORMAN, lawyer; b. St. Louis, Nov. 23, 1945; s. Norman and Margaret (Loeb) B.; m. Catherine Best, Apr. 10, 1983; 1 child, James Norman. AB magna cum laude, Washington U., 1967; JD, Harvard Law Sch., 1970. Bar: D.C. 1970, U.S. Supreme Ct. 1973. Assoc. Hogan & Hartson, Washington, 1970-72; asst. dean Harvard Law Sch., Cambridge, Mass., 1973-75; assoc. Foley & Lardner, Washington, 1975-79, ptnr., 1979—, ptnr. in charge, 1985-2001, mgmt. com., 1989—98. Mem. nat. coun. Washington U. Coll. Arts and Scis., 1999—. Mng. editor Harvard Jour. Legis., 1969-70. Mem. Civil Rights Reviewing Authority HEW, Washington, 1979-80. Mem. ABA, Fed. Bar Assn., D.C. Bar Assn., Supreme Ct. Bar, Washington Lawyers Com. for Civil Rights and Urban Affairs (bd. dirs.), Phi Beta Kappa, Omicron Delta Kappa, Pi Sigma Alpha, Phi Eta Sigma, City Club (Washington). Administrative and regulatory, Private international, Mergers and acquisitions. Home: 906 Peacock Station Rd Mc Lean VA 22102-1021 Office: Foley & Lardner 3000 K St NW Fl 5 Washington DC 20007-5143 E-mail: jbierman@foleylaw.com.

BIERY, EVELYN HUDSON, lawyer; b. Lawton, Okla., Oct. 12, 1946; d. William Ray and Nellie Iris (Nunley) Hudson. BA in English and Latin summa cum laude, Abilene (Tex.) Christian U., 1968; JD, So. Meth. U., 1973. Bar: Tex. 1973, U.S. Dist. Ct. (we. dist.) Tex. 1975, U.S. Dist. Ct. (so. dist.) Tex. 1977, U.S. Dist. Ct. (no. dist.) Tex. 1979, U.S. Ct. Appeals (5th cir.) 1979, U.S. Ct. Appeals (11th cir.) 1981, U.S. Supreme Ct. 1981. Atty.

Law Offices of Bruce Waitz, San Antonio, 1973-76; mem. LeLaurin & Adams, PC, San Antonio, 1976-81; ptnr. Fulbright & Jaworski, San Antonio, 1981—, head bankruptcy, reorganization and creditors' rights sect., 1990—. Policy com. Fulbright & Jaworski, San Antonio, 1996-98; speaker on creditors' rights, bankruptcy and reorganization law; lectr. Southwestern Grad. Sch. Banking, Dallas, 1980, La. State U. Sch. Banking, 1994; presiding officer, U. Tex. Sch. of Law Bankruptcy Conf., 1976, 94, State Bar Tex. Creditors' Rights Inst., 1985, State Bar Tex. Advanced Bus. Bankruptcy Law Inst., 1985, State Bar Tex. Inst. on Advising Officers, Dirs. and Ptnrs. in Troubled Bus., 1987, State Bar Tex. Advanced Creditors Rights Inst., 1988; pres. San Antonio Young Lawyers Assn., 1979-80; mem. bankruptcy adv. com. fifth cir. jud. coun., 1979-80; vice-chmn. bankruptcy com. Comml. Law League Am., 1981-83; mem. exec. bd. So. Meth. U. Sch. Law, 1983-91. Editor: Texas Collections Manual, 1978, Creditor's Rights in Texas, 2d edit., 1981; author: (with others) Collier Bankruptcy Practice Guide, 1993. Del. to U.S./Republic of China joint session on trade, investment and econ. law , Beijing, 1987; designated mem. Bankruptcy Judge Merit Screening Com. State of Tex. by Tex. State Bar Pres., 1979-82; patron McNay Mus., San Antonio; rsch. ptnr. Mind Sci. Found., San Antonio; diplomat World Affairs Coun., San Antonio. Recipient Outstanding Young Lawyer award San Antonio Young Lawyers Assn., 1979. Fellow: Am. Coll. Bankruptcy Attys. (v.p.), Soc. Internat. Bus. Fellows (v.p.), Tex. Bar Found. (life), San Antonio Bar Found. (life); mem.: San Antonio Young Lawyers Assn. (pres. 1979—80), Tex. Assn. Bank Counsel (bd. dirs. 1988—90, 2001—02), Tex. Bar Assn. (chair bankruptcy com. 1982—83, chair corp., banking and bus. law sect. 1989—90), Zonta (Chair Z club com. 1989—90), Plaza Club San Antonio (bd. dirs. 1982—), Order of Coif. Bankruptcy, Federal civil litigation, Corporate, general. Office: Fulbright & Jaworski LLP 300 Convent St Ste 2200 San Antonio TX 78205-3720 also: 1301 Mckinney St Ste 5100 Houston TX 77010-3031

BIESTEK, JOHN PAUL, lawyer; b. Chgo., May 28, 1935; s. John P. and Selma (Glick) B.; m. Elizabeth Mary Frer, Dec. 31, 1956; children: Scott, Becky. BS, Loyola U., Chgo., 1957, JD, 1964. Bar: Ill. 1964, U.S. Dist. Ct. (no. dist.) Ill. 1964; registered investment advisor; lic. securities broker and prin. Sr. ptnr. Biestek & Facchini, Chgo., 1965-74; founding ptnr. John P. Biestek & Assocs., Ltd., Arlington Heights, Ill., 1974—; founder Profl. Retirement Specialists, Inc., 1997. Atty. Wheeling Twp. Rep. Orgn., 1978, fin. chmn., 1982-84; founder, chmn. Arlington Heights Econ. Devel. Commn., 1983-84. Mem. N.W. Suburban Bar Assn. (pres. 1977-78), Arlington Heights C. of C. (pres. 1982-84, dir. and atty. 1972-86, 91-98, Extraordinary Commitment and Leadership award 1984), Bridgeview C. of C. (pres. 1969), Rolling Green Country Club (sec. 1978-81, atty. 1980-84, 90-97, bd. dirs. 1997-98), Rotary (founder Arlington Heights chpt.). Roman Catholic. Estate planning, Probate (including wills, trusts), Estate taxation. Home: 16 Dorchester Ct Hawthorn Woods IL 60047 Office: 115 N Arlington Heights Rd Arlington Heights IL 60004-6075

BIESTERFELD, CRAIG STEWART, lawyer; b. Chicago Heights, Ill., Nov. 6, 1953; s. Howard Martin and Ula J. (Ginn) B.; m. Isabel von Phul Hall, June 6, 1981; children: Christopher, Lindsay, Samuel. BA, Westminster Coll., 1975; JD, U. Mo., 1978. Bar: Mo. 1978, Ill. 1990. Assoc. Peper, Martin, Jensen, Maichel & Hetlage, St. Louis, 1978-84, ptnr., 1985-98, Blackwell Sanders Peper Martin LLP, St. Louis, 1998—. City atty. City of Maplewood, Mo., 1988—. Mem. ABA, Mo. Bar Assn., Ill. Bar Assn., Bar Assn. Met. St. Louis. Republican. Lutheran. Land use and zoning (including planning), Municipal (including bonds), Property, real (including real estate development, water). Office: Blackwell Sanders Peper Martin LLP 720 Olive St Ste 2400 Saint Louis MO 63101-2313 E-mail: cbiesterfeld@blackwellsanders.com.

BIGELOW, ROBERT P. lawyer, arbitrator, mediator, journalist; b. N.Y.C., Jan. 17, 1927; s. Robert R.L. and Doris W.S. (Bissell) B.; m. Katharine W. MacKenty Apr. 14, 1951; children: Katharine R., Robert S., Sanford W., Edward G. AB cum laude, Harvard U., 1950, JD, 1953. Bar: Mass. 1953, N.Y. 1980. Law clk. Supreme Ct. Mass., 1953-54; assoc. Bingham Dana & Gould, Boston, 1954-56; atty., asst. counsel John Hancock Mut. Life Ins. Co., Boston, 1956-66; pvt. practice Woburn and Boston, Mass., 1966-86; of counsel Hennessy Kilburn Killgoar & Ronan, Boston, 1973-84; ptnr. Bigelow & Saltzberg, Woburn, 1980-86; counsel Warner & Stockpole, Boston, 1986-87; sole practice, 1987-91, 95-97; counsel Bird & Bird, London, 1995-97; arbitrator, mediator, 1966—. Adj. prof. Dartmouth Coll., 1982-84, Suffolk Law Sch., 1986-92; acting dir. New Eng. Law Inst., 1974-75. Author: (with Susan Nycum) Your Computer and the Law, 1975, Contracting for Computer Hardware, Software and Services, 1984-95, Computer Contracts, 1987-92; editor Law Office Econs. and Mgmt., 1969-78, Computer Law Svc., 1973-81, Computer Law and Tax Report, 1974-84, Computer Law Newsletter, 1979-87; cons. editor, 1988-91; cons. editor Bull. Computer Law Assn., 1971-97, editor, 1997-98; contbg. editor Cyberspace Lawyer, 1998—, Lawyers Competitive Edge, 1999—; mem. adv. bd. Guide to Computer Law, 1998-2001; contbr. articles to profl. jours. With U.S. Army, 1945-46, 51-64. Fellow AAAS, Brit. Computer Soc. (life, qualified arbitrator), New Zealand Computer Soc., I.S.P. Can. Info. Processing Soc., Am. Bar Found. (life), Coll. Law Practice Mgmt. (hon.); mem. ABA (editor Computers and the Law 1966, 69, 81, Jurimetrics Jour. 1971-74, Bull. Law, Sci. and Tech. 1977-800, chmn. com. law relating to computers 1979-80, briefs editor Law Practice Mgmt. 1979-91, 93-96), Mass. Bar Assn. (chmn. econs. com. 1969-73, mem. com profl. ethics 1973-79, mem. coun. law practice 1981-84, chmn. bus. law sect. 1984-85), Computer Law Assn. (pres. 1977-79, dir. 1973-84, adv. bd. 1984—), Australian Computer Soc. Alternative dispute resolution, Computer, Other. Office: 10 Mount Vernon St # 252 Winchester MA 01890-2704

BIGHAM, WILLIAM J. lawyer; b. Bryn Mawr, Pa., July 4, 1949; s. Robert H. and Regina (Schrandt) B.; m. Cindy K. Elkins, Aug. 12, 1972; children: Justin K., Joel M., Meredith E. BBA with honors, Siena Coll., 1971; JD with honors, Rutgers U., 1974. Bar: N.J. 1974, D.C. 1977, U.S. Ct. Appeals (3d cir.) 1983, U.S. Supreme Ct. 1985. Jud. law clk. to Hon. Samuel D. Lenox, Jr. Chancery Divisn. Superior Ct. of N.J., Trenton, N.J., 1974-75; mng. dir., shareholder Sterns & Weinroth, Trenton, 1975—. Mem. ABA, N.J. Bar, D.C. Bar, Mercer County Bar Assn. Roman Catholic. General civil litigation, Environmental, Labor (including EEOC, Fair Labor Standards Act, labor-management relations, NLRB, OSHA). Office: 50 W State St Ste 1400 Trenton NJ 08608-1220

BIGLOW, ROBERT ROY, lawyer; b. Ashland, Wis., June 14, 1922; s. Craque Chester and Mildred Maria (Byrne) B.; m. Genevieve Johanna Jaeger, Sept. 3, 1953; children: Michael J., Mark W., Crague C., John B., Jennifer A., Laura A., Mary, Eileen. BS, Duluth (Minn.) State U., 1942; BSL, LLB, JD, U. Minn, 1948. Bar: Minn. 1949, U.S. Dist. Ct. 1949, U.S. Ct. Appeals 1949, U.S. Supreme Ct. 1949. Pvt. practice, Mpls., 1949—. With USAAF, 1942—45, with USAAF, 1951—52, with USAAF, 1961. Avocations: music, sports, hunting, fishing. Alternative dispute resolution, Personal injury (including property damage), Probate (including wills, trusts). Home: 1621 Hillsboro Ave S Saint Louis Park MN 55426-1828 Office: 401 2d Ave S Minneapolis MN 55401

BILDERBACK, JAMES WILLIAM, II, lawyer; b. Fresno, Calif., Oct. 21, 1963; s. Dean Loy Bilderback and Florence Elizabeth (Gillmore) Ellsworth; m. Leslie Ann Reed, July 15, 1989; children: Emma Christine, Claire Elizabeth. BA, U. Calif., Berkeley, 1985; JD cum laude, U. San Francisco, 1992. Bar: Calif. 1992, U.S. Dist. Ct. (no. dist.) Calif. 1992, U.S. Dist. Ct. (ctrl. dist.) Calif. 1993, U.S. Ct. Appeals (9th cir.) 1993, U.S. Supreme Ct. 1998. Deputy atty. gen. Calif. Dept. Justice, L.A., 1992—. Mem. L.A. County Bar Assn., L.A. County Bar Assn. Barristers (pres. 1999-2000, sec. 1996-98). Office: Calif Dept Justice 300 S Spring St Fl 5 Los Angeles CA 90013-1230

BILDERSEE, ROBERT ALAN, lawyer; b. Albany, N.Y., Jan. 22, 1942; s. Max U. and Hannah (Marks) B.; m. Ellen Bernstein, June 9, 1963; 1 child, Jennifer M. BA, Columbia Coll., 1962, MA, 1964; LLB, Yale U., 1967. Assoc. Wolf Block Schorr & Solis Cohen, Phila., 1967-72; sole practice Phila., 1972-73; assoc., then ptnr. Fox Rothschild, O'Brien & Frankel, Phila., 1973-80; ptnr. Morgan Lewis & Bockius LLP, Phila., 1980-97; founding ptnr. Bildersee & Silbert, LLP, Phila., 1997—. Lectr. Temple U. Sch. Law, Phila., 1978-91; asst. in instrn. Yale U. Law Sch., New Haven, 1966. Author: Pension Regulation Manual, Pension Administrator's Forms and Checklists, 1987; contbg. author: Employee Benefits Handbook, 1982-98; editor: Beyond the Fringes; contbr. articles to profl. jours. Woodrow Wilson fellow, 1962. Mem. ABA, Pa. Bar Assn., Phila. Bar Assn. Avocation: wildlife photography. Labor (including EEOC, Fair Labor Standards Act, labor-management relations, NLRB, OSHA), Pension, profit-sharing, and employee benefits, Corporate taxation. Office: Bildersee and Silbert LLP 1617 JFK Blvd Ste 1111 Philadelphia PA 19103-1826 E-mail: erisaplus@aol.com.

BILGER, BRUCE R. lawyer; b. Balt., Feb. 27, 1952; BA, Dartmouth Coll., 1973; MBA, JD, U. Va., 1977. Bar: Tex. 1977. Mem. Vinson & Elkins, L.L.P., Houston. Mem. Phi Beta Kappa. Finance, Private international, Mergers and acquisitions. Office: Vinson & Elkins LLP 2300 First City Tower 1001 Fannin St Houston TX 77002-6760 E-mail: bbilger@velaw.com.

BILINKAS, EDWARD J. lawyer; b. Kearny, N.J., May 20, 1954; s. Edward William and Mary B.; m. Dolores D., May 6, 1984; children: Jacquline, Edward, Jennifer. BA, Ashland Coll., 1976; JD, Calif. We. Sch. Law, 1981. Bar: N.J., N.Y., U.S. Dist. Ct. N.J., U.S. Dist. Ct. (so. and ea. dists.) N.Y. Trial atty. Essex County Prosecutors Office, Newark, 1981-83; asst. U.S. atty. U.S. Attys. Office, Newark, 1983-85; 1st asst. pros. atty. Essex County Prosecutors Office, Newark, 1985-88; ptnr. Lorber, Schneider, Nuzzi, Bilinkas & Mason, Fairfield, N.J., 1988-2000; sole practitioner Randolph, N.J., 2000—. Criminal. Office: 415 Rte 10 Randolph NJ 07869

BILLINGS, FRANKLIN SWIFT, JR., federal judge; b. Woodstock, Vt., June 5, 1922; s. Franklin S. and Gertrude (Curtis) B.; m. Pauline Gillingham, Oct. 13, 1951; children: Franklin, III, Jireh Swift, Elizabeth, Ann. S.B., Harvard U., 1943; postgrad., Yale U. law Sch., 1945; JD, U. Va., 1947. Bar: Vt. 1948, U.S. Supreme Ct., 1958. With dept. electronics Gen. Electric Co., Schenectady, N.Y., 1943; bldg. dept. Vt. Marble Co., Proctor, 1945-46; pvt. practice law Woodstock, 1948-52; mem. firm Billings & Sherburne, Woodstock, 1952-66; asst. sec. Vt. Senate, 1949-55, sec., 1957-59; sec. civil and mil. affairs State of Vt., 1959-61; exec. clk. to gov., 1955-57; judge Hartford Mcpl. Ct., 1955-63; mem. Vt. Ho. of Reps., 1961-66, chmn. jud. com., 1961, speaker of ho., 1963-66; judge Vt. Superior Ct., 1966-75, assoc. justice, 1975-83, chief justice, 1983-84; judge U.S. Dist. Ct. Vt., 1984-94, chief judge, 1988-92, sr. ct. judge, 1994—. Active, Town of Woodstock, 1948-72. Served as warrant officer 1st class attached Brit. Army, 1944-45. Decorated Purple Heart; Brit. Empire medal. Mem. Vt. Bar Assn., Delta Theta Phi. Office: US Dist Ct PO Box 598 Woodstock VT 05091-0598

BILLINGSLEY, LANCE W. lawyer; b. Buffalo, Apr. 18, 1940; m. Carolyn Gouza Billingsley, Aug. 25, 1962; children: Lance II, Brant, Ashlynn. BA, U. Md., 1961; JD, U. Buffalo, 1964; state and local, Harvard U., 1988. Pntr., assoc. Nylen & Gilmore, Riverdale, Md., 1964-75; ptnr. Meyers, Billingsley, Rodbell & Rosenbaum, P.A., Riverdale, 1975-2000, Rifken, Livingston, Levitan, Silver, Greenbelt, Md., 2000—. Bd. of regents Univ. Sys. of Md., 1995-2003, chmn. 1995-99; vice-chmn. U. of Md. Found., 1985-2000; bd. dirs. U. Md. Med. Sys.; asst. atty. gen. State of Md., 1967-68; city atty. Hyattsville, Md., 1976—; chmn. Nat. Wildlife Visitors Ctr., 1989-94; chmn. bd. Prince George's county Econ. Devel. Corp., Landover, Md., 1983-92. Contbr. articles to numerous law publs. Chmn. Dem. State Cen. Com., 1970-74, Dem. Com. Prince George's County, 1974-80. Named One of Outstanding Young Men Am., 1975-80. Mem.: Md. Bar Assn., ABA (young lawyers exec. com. 1972—74, editl. bd. Barrister mag. 1973—75), U. Md. Alumni Assn. (bd. govs.), M Club, Terrapin Club (bd. dirs. 1983—2001, pres. 1998—99), Columbia Country Club (Chevy Chase, Md.), Omicron Delta Kappa. Avocations: skiing, backpacking. Municipal (including bonds), Property, real (including real estate development, water). Home: 7102 College Heights Dr Hyattsville MD 20782-1154 Office: Rifkin Livingston Levitan & Silver LLC 6305 Ivy Ln Ste 500 Greenbelt MD 20770-1405 Fax: (301) 345-1294. E-mail: billings@usmd.edu.

BILLINGSLEY, ROBERT THAINE, lawyer; b. Wichita, Kans., Jan. 9, 1954; s. Thaine Edward and Anita (Moore) B.; m. Anna Barron, Dec. 31, 1983; children: Carol Carothers, Leslie Hope. AB, Coll. of William and Mary, 1976; JD, U. Richmond, 1980. Bar: Va. 1980. Law clk. to presiding justice U.S. Dist. Ct., Roanoke, Va., 1980-81; assoc. McGuire, Woods & Battle, Richmond, Va., 1981-87, Hirschler, Fleischer, Weinberg, Cox & Allen, Richmond, Va., 1987-96; fin. advisr Kramnick & Assocs., Fredericksburg, Va., 1996—2001; rep. Northwestern Mutual Fin. Network, Fredericksburg, Va., 2001—. Bd. dirs. Make A Wish Found., Ctrl. and Western Va., 2000—. Bd. editors The Virginia Lawyer, 1984-86; mem. adv. bd. U. Richmond Law Rev., 1986-97; contbr. articles to profl. publs. Bd. dirs. Bethlehem Ctr., Richmond, 1985-89, United Meth. Found. of Va. Conf., Inc., 1993—, sec., 2000-02; bd. dirs. Hanover Indsl. Air Pk. Bus. Assn., 1994-96; mem. adminstrv. bd. Trinity United Meth. Ch., Richmond, 1986-89, trustee, 1988-96, chmn. bd. trustees, 1992-95, chmn. commitment campaign, 1995; team capt. United Way Greater Richmond, 1989, sect. chmn., 1991, divsn. chmn., 1993; team capt. Rappahannock Area United Way, 1998, divsn. chair, 1999; mem. Leadership Metro Richmond Class, 1992-93; bd. dirs. Arts Coun. of Richmond, Inc., 1994-96, exec. com., 1996; chmn. fin. com. Fredericksburg United Meth. Ch., 1999-2001; bd. dirs. College Heights Swimming Pool Assn. Mem.: ABA (litig. sect., state membership chmn., young lawyers divsn. 1985—89, state membership chmn. 1989—96), Fredericksburg Bar Assn., Richmond Bar Assn. (program com., vice chmn. 1990—91, chmn. 1991—92, adminstrn. of justice com. 1992—96), Va. State Bar Assn. (bd. govs. young lawyers conf. 1985—89, spl. com. on professionalism, legal edn., admission to bar), Va. Bar Assn. (com. on alternative dispute resolution), William and Mary Alumni Assn. (bd. dirs. Richmond chpt. 1993—95), Rotary (Rappahannock chpt. bd. dirs. 2000—, pres.-elect 2002—03, pres. 2003—), Richmond Jaycees (bd. dirs. 1984—86). Avocations: sports, travel, theatre. Federal civil litigation, General civil litigation, State civil litigation. Home: 1604 College Ave Fredericksburg VA 22401-4637 Office: Northwestern Mutual Fin Network 725 Jackson St Ste 211 Fredericksburg VA 22401

BILLINGSLEY, STANLEY MARION, judge; b. Salem, Ill., Mar. 22, 1943; s. Louis Napoleon and Christine (Stafford) Billingsley; divorced; children: Edward Bradford, Brittany Billingsley Walls; m. Gwen Rowe, May 14, 1982. Student, 1961—64; BA in History-Govt., Western Ky. U., 1964; JD, U. Ky., 1970. Pvt. practice lawyer, Carrollton, Ky., 1971—84; city atty. City of Carrollton, Ky., 1972—78; dist. judge State of Ky. 15th Jud. Dist., Carrollton, 1984—2003, sr. judge, 2003—. Ptnr. Riverhill Assocs., LLC, Carrollton, 1995—, Devpro, LLC, Carrollton, 1996—, Butler Mall, LLC, Carrollton, 1997—. Author: (book) Small Claim Court Handbook, 1989, Kentucky Driving Under the Influence Law, 1994—. Mem. Supreme Ct. Civil Rules Com., 2000—; co-chmn. Atty. Gen.'s Task Force Domestic Violence, 1998, Atty. Gen.'s Task Force Crime Against Elderly, 1999; mem. Ky. Ho. Reps. Ky. Gen. Assembly, Frankfort, 1974—75. 1st lt. USAR, 1967—73. Named Judge of the Yr., Ky. Bar Assn., 1995; named one of Top 5 Pub. Ofcls. Ky., Ky. Women's Advs., 1997. Mem.: Am. Inns Ct. Methodist. Avocation: lecturing. Office: 802 Clay St Carrollton KY 41008 Business E-Mail: Stan@Lawreader.com.

BILLINGTON, BARRY E. lawyer; b. Bruceton, Tenn., June 24, 1940; s. Charles Raymond and Edith Virginia (Bowles) B.; m. Bonnie Leslie Johnson; Oct. 16, 1971 (div. Mar. 23, 1990); children: Erin Alexis, Barry E., Jr. AB in Econs., Davidson Coll., 1964; JD, Emory U., 1968. Bar: Calif. 1969, Ga. 1971, U.S. Dist. Ct. (ctrl. dist.) Calif. 1969, U.S. Dist. Ct. (no. dist.) Ga. 1971; diplomate Nat. Assn. Coll. Advocacy Trial Lawyers. Assoc. Surr & Hellyer, San Bernardino, Calif., 1968-70; with Mfrs. Life Ins. Co., Atlanta, 1970-71; assoc. Carter, Ansley, Smith & McClendon, Atlanta, 1971-72; of counsel Raiford & Hills, Decatur, Ga., 1972-75; ptnr. Raiford, Hills, Billington & McKeithen, Atlanta, 1975-77; mem. Rich, Bass, Kidd, Witcher & Billington, Decatur, 1977-82; ptnr. Billington & Beasley, Decatur, 1982-83, Billington & Turner, Atlanta, 1983-85; owner Barry E. Billington & Assocs., Atlanta, 1985—. Editor: Ga. Rep. Party Newsletter, 1968. Rep. publicity dir. San Bernardino County Rep. Party, 1969-70, San Bernardino County for Ronald Reagan Com., 1970; alt. del. Rep. Ctrl. Com. of Calif., 1969-70; chmn. 4th dist. Conservative Caucus, 1977-79; candidate for Ga. Ho. Reps., 52nd dist., 1978, U.S. Congress, 4th dist., Ga., 1980. With U.S. Army Mil. Police Corps, 1958-60. Mem. Atlanta Bar Assn. (spkr.'s com., litigation, family law, criminal law sects. 1974-77), Decatur-DeKalb Bar Assn. (chmn. spkr.'s com. 1977-78), ABA (litigation sect. 1969-89), Ga. Trial Lawyers Assn., Assn. Trial Lawyers Am., Ga. Assn. Criminal Def. Lawyers, Nat. Assn. Criminal Def. Lawyers, Diplomat of Nat. Coll. of Advocacy Trial Advocacy Course. Criminal, Family and matrimonial, Personal injury (including property damage). Home: 7208 Peachford Circle Atlanta GA 30338 Office: 3 Dunwoody Park Ste 103 Atlanta GA 30338-6709 E-mail: bebillesq@aol.com.

BILYEAU, AMY MARIE, law librarian; BA, George Washington U., 1985; MLS, U. Mich., 1993. Paralegal CACI, Washington, 1987; legal rsch. asst. J. C. Penney Legal Dept., Washington, 1988—89; legis. specialist Wilmer, Cutler & Picking, Washington, 1990; ref. desk asst. U. Mich. Law Sch., Ann Arbor, 1992; law libr. U.S. Ct. Appeals Armed Forces, Washington, 1994—97, Exec. Office U.S. Pres., Washington, 1997—. Tutor Steps to Elevate People, Washington, 1994—95. Mem.: Law Libr. Soc. Washington, Am. Assn. Law Librs., U. Mich. Alumni Assn. (mem. scholarship com. 1998, mentor 2001—02). Avocations: softball, horseback riding, chamber music. Mailing: 2035 Georgetown Blvd Ann Arbor MI 48105-1532

BINDER, DAVID FRANKLIN, lawyer, author; b. Beaver Falls, Pa., Aug. 1, 1935; s. Walter Carl and Jessie Maivis (Bliss) B.; m. Deana Jacqueline Pines, Dec. 25, 1971; children: April, Bret. BA, Geneva Coll., 1956; JD, Harvard U., 1959. Bar: Pa. 1960, U.S. Ct. Appeals (3rd cir.) 1963, U.S. Supreme Ct. 1967. Law clk. to chief justice Pa. Supreme Ct., 1959-61; counsel Fidelity Mut. Life Ins. Co., Phila., 1964-66; ptnr. Bennett, Bricklin & Saltzburg, Phila., 1967-68; mem. Richter, Syken, Ross, and Binder, Phila., 1969-72, Raynes, McCarty, Binder, Ross and Mundy, Phila., 1972—. Mem. faculty Pa. Coll. Judiciary; judge pro tempore Phila. Common Pleas Ct., 1991-97; lectr., course planner Pa. Bar Inst.; mem. civil procedural rules com., ad hoc. com. and permanent com. on evidence Supreme Ct. Pa. Author: Hearsay Handbook, 1975, ann. supplements, 2nd edit., 1983, 3rd edit., 1991, 4th edit., 2001, Binder on Pennsylvania Evidence, 1999, 2d edit., 2001, 3d edit., 2003. Recipient Disting. Alumnus award Geneva Coll., 1981. Mem. ABA, Pa. Bar Assn., Phila. Bar Assn., Assn. Trial Lawyers Am. (lectr.), Pa. Trial Lawyers Assn., Harvard Law Sch. Assn., Am. Bd. Trial Advs., Am. Coll. Trial Lawyers, Union League. Federal civil litigation, State civil litigation, Personal injury (including property damage). Home: 1412 Flat Rock Rd Narberth PA 19072-1216 Office: Raynes McCarty Binder Ross and Mundy 1845 Walnut St Ste 2000 Philadelphia PA 19103-4767 E-mail: dfbinder@raynesmccarty.com.

BINDER, HARRY J. lawyer; b. N.Y.C., Apr. 12, 1948; m. Gloria L. Binder, May 15, 1955. BBA cum laude, CCNY, 1968; JD, Cornell U., 1971. Bar: NY, U.S. Dist. Ct. (ea. and so. dists.) NY, U.S. Dist. Ct. (so. dist.) Ala., U.S. Ct. Appeals (2d and 11th cirs.), U.S. Tax Ct., U.S. Supreme Ct. Atty. Law Offices of Jack Solerwitz, Mineola, NY, 1972—73; pvt. practice Patchogue, NY, 1973—77; sr. ptnr. Binder & Binder PC, Happauge and N.Y.C., 1978—. Trustee NY State Health Commn., Smithtown, 1976—78. Mem.: ATLA, NY State Trial Lawyers Assn., NY State Bar Assn. ERISA Disability Law, Pension, profit-sharing, and employee benefits. Office: Binder & Binder PC 1500 New York Ave Huntington Station NY 11746 Office Fax: 631-361-6475. Business E-Mail: harry@binderandbinder.com.

BINES, HARVEY ERNEST, lawyer, educator, writer; b. Winthrop, Mass., Nov. 25, 1941; s. Carl and Lillian (Cooper) B.; m. Joan Carol Paller, Dec. 27, 1964; children: Jonathan W., Joel T., Susanne R., Benjamin E. BS, MIT, 1963; JD, U. Va., 1970. Bar: Mass 1971, Va. 1971, U.S. Dist. Ct. Mass., U.S. Dist. Ct. (ea. dist.) Va., U.S. Ct. Appeals (1st, 3d, 4th, 7th and D.C. cirs.), U.S. Supreme Ct. Law clk. to hon. John D. Butzner Jr. U.S. Ct. Appeals (4th cir.), Richmond, Va., 1970-71; asst. prof. Law Sch. U. Va., Charlottesville, 1971-74, assoc. prof. Law Sch., 1974-76; assoc. Sullivan & Worcester, Boston, 1976-79, ptnr., 1980—. Adj. prof. Boston Coll. Law Sch., Chestnut Hill, Mass., 1981-88, bd. dirs., treas. Schweitzer Fellowship, Boston. Author: Law of Investment Management, 1978. Lt. USNR, 1963-67. Mem.: Boston Bar Assn., Am. Law Inst. Corporate, general, Private international, Securities. Home: 36 Clarke St Lexington MA 02421-4916 Office: Sullivan & Worcester 1 Post Office Sq Ste 2300 Boston MA 02109-2129 E-mail: hbines@sandw.com.

BING, RICHARD MCPHAIL, lawyer; b. Lewes, Del., Aug. 23, 1950; s. Arden E. and Ellen Louise (Judd) B.; m. Valerie Lynn Wasson, Dec. 18, 1971; children: Jennifer Lynn, Kristin Tyler. BA, U. Richmond, 1972, JD, 1978. Bar: Va. 1979, U.S. Dist. Ct. (ea. and we. dists.) Va. 1979, U.S. Dist. Ct. (we. dist.) Pa. 1990, U.S. Dist. Ct. (no. dist.) N.Y. 1990, U.S. Dist. Ct. (ctrl. dist.) Ill. 1996, U.S. Ct. Appeals (4th cir.) 1979, U.S. Ct. appeals (2d cir.) 1990, U.S. Supreme Ct. 1994, U.S. Dist. Ct. (ctrl. dist.) Ill. 1996. Dir. ins. Bur. of Ins., Richmond, Va., 1978-79; resident gen counsel Va. Gasoline Retailers Assn., Richmond, 1979-83; ptnr. Pearce & Bing, Richmond, 1983-93, Bing & Assocs., P.C., Richmond, 1993—. Adj. prof. law J. Sargent Reynolds Community Coll., Richmond, 1984-85. Mem. Henrico County Rep. Com; bd. dirs. Three Chopt PTA, Richmond, 1984-85. Mem. ABA, Va. Bar Assn., Va. Bar, Richmond Bar Assn., Fed. bar Assn., Assn. Trial Lawyers Am., Va. Trial Lawyers Assn., Nat. Lawyers Club, Tuckahoe Jaycees (pres. 1981-82), Bull and Bear Club, Hermitage Country Club, Tobacco Co. Club, The Spider Club (bd. dirs.), Am. Assn. of Franchisees and Dealers, Svc. Sta. Dealers of Am., Inc., Affiliate Attys. Group. Avocations: golf, bicycling, photography. Federal civil litigation, General civil litigation, Commercial, contracts (including sales of goods; commercial financing). Home: 1701 Habwood Ln Richmond VA 23233-4451 Office: Bing & Assocs PC 300 Arboretum Pl Ste 140 Richmond VA 23236-3465

BINGHAM, LISA BLOMGREN, lawyer, educator; b. Lansing, Mich., Jan. 4, 1955; d. Arthur Charles and Lola (Bonacio) Blomgren; m. Geoffrey Parker Bingham, Aug. 7, 1977. BA magna cum laude, Smith Coll., 1976; JD with high honors, U. Conn., 1979. Bar: Conn. 1979, U.S. Dist. Ct. Conn. 1980, U.S. Ct. Appeals (7th cir.) 1981. Ptnr. Shipman & Goodwin, Hartford, 1979-89; lectr.-in-law Ind. U. Sch. Law, 1989-92, assoc. prof., 1992—2003; Keller Runden prof. pub. svc. Ind. U. Sch. Pub. and Environ. Affairs, 1999—. Adj. prof. Western New Eng. Coll. Law, Springfield, Mass., 1985-87; dir. Ind. Conflict Resolution Inst., 1997—. Contbr. numerous articles to profl. jours. Dir. Nat. REDRESS Evaluation Project, U.S. Postal Svc., 1994—. Fulbright Scholar, 1983; recipient numerous rsch. and tchg. awards. Mem. ABA, Assn. for Conflict Resolution (Willoughby Abner award 2002), ASPA, LSA, IRRA, U. Conn. Law Sch. Alumni Assn. (bd. dirs. 1981-1989, pres. 1988-1989). Education and schools, Labor (including EEOC, Fair Labor Standards Act, labor-management relations, NLRB, OSHA). Home: 820 S Jordan Ave Bloomington IN 47401-5126

BINNIE, WILLIAM IAN CORNELL, judge; b. Montreal, Que., Can., Apr. 14, 1939; s. James Corneil and Phyllis (Mackenzie) Binnie; m. Susan Strickland, May 28, 1965; children: Daniel, Matthew, Alexandra, Max. BA, McGill U., 1963, LLD (hon.) , 2001; LLB, Cambridge U., 1963, LLM, 1988; LLB, U. Toronto, 1965; LLD (hon.) , Law Soc. Upper Can., 2001. Bar: English 1966, Ont. 1967, Internat. Ct. Justice 1984, Yukon Territory 1986. With Wright & McTaggart and successor firms, 1963—82; assoc. dep. min. of justice for Can., 1982—86; sr. ptnr. McCarthy Tetrault, 1986—98; justice Supreme Ct. Can., Ottawa, Canada, 1998—. Part-time lectr. on aboriginal rights Osgoode Hall Law Sch., 1975—79; commr. Internat. Commn. Jurists; lectr. in field; chmn. Ont. Rhodes Scholarship Selection Com. Contbr. articles to profl. jours. Fellow: Am. Coll. Trial Lawyers; mem.: Middle Temple Inns Ct. (Eng.). Office: Supreme Ct Can 301 Wellington St Ottawa ON Canada K1A 0J1

BINNING, J. BOYD, lawyer; b. N.Y.C., July 7, 1944; s. James Edward and Lillian (Doughty) B.; children: Peter. AA, Wesley Coll., 1964; BS cum laude, Urbana Coll., Ohio, 1970; MA in Polit. Sci., Eastern Ky. U., 1971; JD, Ohio No. U., 1974. Bar: Ohio 1976, U.S. Dist. Ct. (so. dist.) Ohio 1977, U.S. Ct. Appeals (6th cir.) 1977, U.S. Dist. Ct. (no. dist.) Ohio 1979, U.S. Supreme Ct. 1979. Dep. sheriff Miami County, Troy, Ohio, 1971-74; investigator, legal intern Miami County prosecutor's office, Troy, 1973-75; spl. counsel for the Ohio Senate Jud. Com.; instr., advisor Iowa State Law Enforcement Acad., Des Moines, 1976; pvt. practice law, Columbus, 1976—; spl. counsel jud. com. Ohio Senate; judge moot ct. Capital Law Sch., Columbus. Author: Civil Rights and the Federal Courts, 1971. Grad. scholar Eastern Ky. U., 1970-71. Mem. Ohio State Bar Assn., Columbus Bar Assn., Columbus Bar Found., Ohio Acad. Trial Lawyers, Nat. Assn. Criminal Def. Lawyers. General civil litigation, Criminal, Personal injury (including property damage). Office: 592 S 3rd St Columbus OH 43215

BINTLIFF, BARBARA ANN, law librarian, educator; b. Houston, Jan. 14, 1953; d. Donald Richard and Frances Arlene (Appling) Hay; m. Byron A. Boville, Aug. 20, 1977 (div. 1992); children: Bradley, Bruce. BA, Cen. Wash. U., 1975; JD, U. Wash., 1978, MLL, 1979. Bar: Wash. 1979, U.S. Dist. Ct. (ea. dist.) Wash. 1980, Colo. 1983, U.S. Dist. Ct. Colo. 1983. Libr. Gaddis and Fox, Seattle, 1978-79; reference libr. U. Denver Law Sch., 1979-84; assoc. libr., sr. instr. Sch. Law U. Colo., Boulder, 1984-88, assoc. prof., libr. dir., 1989—2001, prof., 2001—, Nicholas Rosenbaum prof. law, 2002—. Legal cons. Nat. Ctr. Atmospheric Rsch., Environ. and Societal Impacts Group, Boulder, 1980; vis. prof. U. Wash., Seattle, 1996, chair U. Colo. Boulder, Faculty Assembly, 2003-. Editor: A Representative Sample of Tenure Documents for Law Librarians, 1988, 2nd edit., 1994, Chapter Presidents' Handbook, 1989, Representatives Handbook, 1990; assoc. editor: Legal Reference Svcs. Quarterly, Perspectives: Teaching Legal Research and Writing; contbr. articles to profl. jours. Recipient Boulder Faculty Assembly Excellence Svc. award, 2001; named Disting. Alumnus, Ctrl. Wash. U., 2000. Mem. Am. Assn. Law Librs. (v.p./pres.-elect 2000-01, pres. 2001-02), Am. Law Inst. (elected), Colo. Bar Assn., Colo. Assn. Law Librs. (pres. 1982), Southwestern Assn. Law Librs. (pres. 1987-88, 91-92). Episcopalian. Office: U Colo Law Libr 2405 Kittredge Loop Dr Rm 190 Boulder CO 80309-0402

BIOLCHINI, ROBERT FREDRICK, lawyer; b. Detroit, Sept. 22, 1939; s. Alfred and Erma (Barbetti) Biolchini; m. Frances Lauinger, June 5, 1965; children: Robert F., Douglas C., Frances E., Tobin M., Thomas A., Christine M. BA, U. Notre Dame, 1962; LLB, George Washington U., 1965. Bar: Okla., Mich., 1965. Assoc. Doerner, Stuart, Saunders, Daniel, Anderson & Biolchini, Tulsa, Okla., 1968-71, ptnr., 1971-94, Stuart, Biolchini & Turner, Tulsa, 1994—. Pres., CEO Pennwell Corp.; chmn. bd. dirs., CEO, PennEnergy, Inc., Valley Nat. Bank, Ameritrust Holding Co., Old Faithful Underwriting Ltd.; mem. Lloyds of London, 1979—; bd. dirs. Lumen Energy Corp., Bank of The Lakes, Bank of Jackson Hole. Bd. dirs. Thomas Gilcrease Mus., past pres., chmn. bd., 1977-80, dir. emeritus, 1980—; bd. dirs., sec., legal clk. Tulsa Ballet Theatre, Inc., 1976-84; trustee Monte Cassino Endowment, 1978—; pres. Monte Cassino Sch. Bd., 1970-77; chmn. Christ the King Parish Coun., 1974-75; mem. adv. coun. U. Notre Dame Law Sch., 1982-2000, trustee U. Notre Dame, 2001—; chmn. Cath. Diocese Tulsa Fund for Future, 1998—; bd. dirs. legal counsel Tulsa Area United Way, 1986—; mem. pres.'s coun. Regis Coll., 1986—; Okla. chmn. Lawyers for Bush, 2000. Capt. U.S. Army, 1965-67. Mem. Okla. Bar Assn., Mich. Bar Assn., Met. Tulsa C. of C. (bd. dirs. 1992—), Summit Club, Southern Hills Country Club, Club Ltd., Knights of Malta, Knights of the Holy Sepulchre. Roman Catholic. Federal civil litigation, Corporate, general, Securities. Home: 1744 E 29th St Tulsa OK 74114-5402 Office: First Place Tower 15 E 5th St Ste 3300 Tulsa OK 74103-4340

BIRCH, ADOLPHO A., JR., state supreme court justice; b. Washington, Sept. 22, 1932; BA, JD, Howard U., 1956. Bar: Tenn. 1957. Pvt. practice, Nashville, 1958—66; asst. pub. defender, 1964—66; asst. dist. atty., 1966—69; judge Davidson County Gen. Sessions Ct., 1969—78, Tenn. Criminal Ct. (20th jud. dist.), 1978—87; former judge Tenn. Ct. Criminal Appeals; chief justice Tenn. Supreme Ct., Nashville, 1996—97, assoc. justice, 1997—. Assoc. prof. Nashville Sch. of Law. With USNR, 1956—58. Mem.: ABA, Napier Lobby Bar Assn. (past pres.), Nashville Bar Assn., Tenn. Bar Assn., Nat. Bar Assn. Office: 304 Supreme Court Bldg, 401 7th Ave N Nashville TN 37219-1407

BIRCH, TERRELL COLHOUN, lawyer; b. Washington, Mar. 23, 1935. B.S.E.E., George Washington U., 1959, J.D., 1963. Bar: D.C. 1964, Md. 1972, Va. 1980. Ptnr. Birch & Birch, Washington, 1964-76; ptnr. Birch, Stewart, Kolasch & Birch, Falls Church, Va., 1976— ; arbitrator Am. Arbitration Assn., Fed. Insecticide, Fungicide and Rodenticide Act, disputes Fed. Mediation and Conciliation Service. Patent, Intellectual property, Alternative dispute resolution. Office: PO Box 747 Falls Church VA 22040-0747

BIRD, WENDELL RALEIGH, lawyer; b. Atlanta, July 16, 1954; s. Raleigh Milton and R. Jean (Edwards) B. BA summa cum laude, Vanderbilt U., 1975; JD, Yale U., 1978. Bar: Ga. 1978, Ala. 1980, Calif. 1981, Fla. 1982, U.S. Ct. Appeals (2d, 3d, 4th, 5th, 6th, 7th, 8th, 9th, 10th and 11th cirs.) 1979-83, U.S. Supreme Ct. 1983. Law clk. to judge U.S. Ct. Appeals (4th cir.), Durham, N.C., 1978-79, U.S. Ct. Appeals (5th cir.), Birmingham, Ala., 1979-80; pvt. practice San Diego, 1980-82; atty. Parker, Johnson, Cook & Dunlevie, Atlanta, 1982-86; sr. ptnr. Bird & Assocs., P.C., Atlanta, 1986—. Adj. prof. Emory U. Law Sch., Atlanta, 1985—90; lectr. Washington Non-Profit Tax Conf., 1982—. Author: The Origin of Species Revisited, 2 vols., 1987; contbg. author: Federal and State Taxation of Exempt Organizations, 1994, CCH Federal Tax Service, 1988—; mem. bd. editors Yale U. Law Jour., 1977-78, others; contbr. articles to profl. jours. Recipient Egger prize Yale U., 1978, Vanderbilt U. award, 1972. Mem. ABA (litigation sect., taxation sect., com. on exempt orgns., past chmn. subcom. on religious orgns., past chmn. subcom. on state and local taxes, chmn. subcom. on charitable contbns., sect. on real property probate and trust, com. charitable gifts), Am. Law Inst., Ga. Bar Assn., Fla. Bar Assn., Calif. Bar Assn., Ala. Bar Assn., Assn. Trial Lawyers Am., Phi Beta Kappa. Republican. Avocations: science, skiing, photography, genealogy, piano, architecture. Estate planning, Non-profit and tax-exempt organizations, Federal civil litigation. Home: 92 Blackland Rd NW Atlanta GA 30342-4420 Office: Bird & Assocs PC 1150 Monarch Plz 3414 Peachtree Rd NE Atlanta GA 30326-1153

BIREN, MATTHEW BENNETT, lawyer; b. L.A., Jan. 19, 1948; s. Samuel D. and June Patricia (Dizik) B.; m. Renee L. Smith (div. 1983); children: Cary, Kelly, Adam; m. Dee Dee Lynn Deutsch, July 15, 1983; children: Andrew, Dustin. BA, UCLA, 1970; JD, Loyola U., L.A., 1973. Bar: Calif. 1973, U.S. Dist. Ct. (cen. dist.) Calif. 1974, U.S. Ct. Appeals (9th and D.C. cirs.) 1975, U.S. Supreme Ct. 1980. Assoc. Levy & Van Bourg, L.A., 1970-77; ptnr. Sroloff & Biren, L.A., 1977-81; prin. Matthew B. F. Biren & Assocs., L.A., 1981-99, Biren & Katzman, L.A., 1999—. Mem. ABA, ATLA, Trial Lawyers Pub. Justice, L.A. Bar Assn., Consumer Attys. Calif., Consumer Attys. Assn. L.A. Insurance, Personal injury (including property damage), Product liability. Office: Biren/Katzman 11911 San Vicente Blvd Ste 140 Brentwood CA 90049- Fax: 310 471-3165. E-mail: mbiren@biren.com.

BIRKBECK, A.J. KOERTS, lawyer; b. Flushing, Mich., May 31, 1960; s. Benj H. and Gretchen Anne (Gettel) B.; m. Catherine Mary Margaret Battel, Aug. 10, 1985; children: Allison, Sarah. BS, U. Mich., 1983, MBA, 1985; JD, U. Chgo., 1991. Bar: Ill. 1991; U.S. Dist. Ct. (no. dist.) Ill. 1991; MI 2001. Closing officer Great Lakes Fed. Savings, Ann Arbor, Mich., 1983-85; sr. fin. analyst Amoco Corp., Chgo., 1985-88; atty. Winston & Strawn, Chgo., 1991-93; mng. atty. Zevnik, Horton, Guibord & McGovern, Chgo., 1993-97; mng. ptnr. Fulcrum Environ. Law, Chgo., 1997-2001; mng. atty. Fulcrum Law Group, G.R., Grand Rapids, Mich., 2001—. Gen. counsel, bd. dirs. ERS Corp., 2002—; chmn., CEO Am. Brownfields Assurance Co., 1999—. Contbr. to profl. jours. Com. mem. Oak Park Energy & Environ. Commn. Ill., 1998-2001; com. mem. Barrie Park Remediation Com., Oak Park. Mem. ABA, Ill. State Bar Assn. (environ. sect. coun. 1998-2001), Lake Calumet Cluster Group, Amer. Assn. Petroleum Geologists, Chgo. Bar Assn. Presbyterian. Avocations: flying, sailing, skiing. Environmental, Property, real (including real estate development, water), Toxic tort. Home: 2093 Robinson Rd SE Grand Rapids MI 49506-1845 Fax: 616-458-9911.

BIRMINGHAM, RICHARD GREGORY, lawyer; b. Buffalo, Aug. 14, 1929; s. William Anthony and Laura Louise (Reimann) B.; m. Suzanne M. Cannon, May 20, 1961; children: Barbara A. McCarty, Maureen E., Gregory S. BA, U. Notre Dame, 1951; JD, SUNY, Buffalo, 1957. Bar: N.Y. 1957, Del. 1984, Pa. 1993. Law clk. to justices appellate div. N.Y. Supreme Ct. (4th dept.), Rochester, 1957-60; ptnr. Phillips, Lytle, Hitchcock, Blaine & Huber, Buffalo, 1960-84, 90-94, ret., 1994, ptnr. Wilmington, Del., 1984-90. Lt. comdr. USN, 1951-54, Korea. Mem. ABA, N.Y. State Bar Assn., Del. Bar Assn., Erie County Bar Assn., Rivermont Country Club. Republican. Roman Catholic. Office: 510 Shelli Ln Roswell GA 30075-2988 E-mail: rgsb510@hotmail.com.

BIRMINGHAM, RICHARD JOSEPH, lawyer; b. Seattle, Feb. 26, 1953; s. Joseph E. and Anita (Loomis) B. BA cum laude, Wash. State U., 1975; JD, Seattle U., 1978; LLM in Taxation, Boston U., 1980. Bar: Wash. 1978, Oreg. 1981, U.S. Dist. Ct. (we. dist.) Wash. 1978, U.S. Tax Ct. 1981. Ptnr. Davis Wright Tremaine, Seattle, 1982-93; shareholder Birmingham Thorson & Barnett, P.C., Seattle, 1993—. Mem. King County Bar Employee Benefit Com., Seattle, 1986, U.S. Treasury ad hoc com. employee benefits, 1988—. Contbg. editor: Compensation and Benefits Mgmt., 1985—; contbr. articles to profl. jours. Mem. ABA (employee benefits and exec. compensation com. 1982—), Wash. State Bar Assn. (speaker 1984-86, tax sect. 1982—), Oreg. State Bar Assn. (tax sect. 1982—), Western Pension Conf. (speaker 1986), Seattle Pension Round table. Democrat. Avocations: jogging, bicycling, photography. Pension, profit-sharing, and employee benefits, Personal income taxation. Home: 3820 49th Ave NE Seattle WA 98105-5234 Office: Birmingham Thorson & Barnett PC 3315 Two Union Square 601 Union St Seattle WA 98101-2341 Business E-Mail: RBirmingham@BTBPC.com.

BIRNBAUM, IRWIN MORTON, lawyer; b. Bklyn., July 15, 1935; s. Sol N. and Rose (Cohen) B.; m. Arlene R. Burrows, June 8, 1957; children: Bruce J., Leslie R. Birnbaum Ventura, Amy G. Birnbaum Heath. BS in Acctg., Bklyn. Coll., 1956; JD, NYU, 1961. Bar: N.Y. 1962. Budget officer Montefiore Med. Ctr., Bronx, N.Y., 1962-70, v.p., chief fin. officer, 1970-86; counsel Proskauer & Rose LLP, N.Y.C., 1986-89, ptnr., 1989-97; COO Yale Univ. Sch. Medicine, New Haven, Conn., 1997—. Bd. dirs. N.Y. Regional Transplant Program, N.Y.C., treas., exec. com.; chmn. bd. dirs. FFH/N.E. Ins. Com.; mem. exec. com. and chair fin. com. MCIC Vt., Inc.; adj. prof. Robert Wagner Sch. Pub. Svc., NYU; lectr. pub. health, health policy, adminstrn. Sch. Medicine Yale U.; corporator South County Hosp., South Kingstown, R.I. Editor: Health Care Law Treatise, 1990. Trustee, treas., exec. com. Malmonides Med. Ctr., Bklyn., 1988—; sec./treas., exec. com. Hosp. Trustees N.Y. State, 1990-97; bd. dirs. Jewish Home for the Aged, New Haven. Fellow N.Y. Acad. Medicine; mem. Assn. of Bar of City of N.Y. (sec. com. on medicine and law 1989-90, sec. health law com. 1995-96), Am. Acad. Hosp. Attys. (spl. com. in health care systems). Avocations: sailing, tennis, reading, travel. Health. Office: Yale Univ Sch Medicine 333 Cedar St I-209 SHM PO Box 208049 New Haven CT 06520-8049

BIRNBAUM, SHEILA L. lawyer, educator; b. 1940; BA, Hunter Coll., 1960, MA, 1962; LL.B., NYU, 1965. Bar: N.Y. 1965. Legal asst. Superior Ct., N.Y.C., 1965; assoc. Berman & Frost, N.Y.C., 1965-70, ptnr., 1970-72; prof. Fordham U., N.Y.C., 1972-78, NYU, N.Y.C., 1978-86, assoc. dean, 1982-84; ptnr. Skadden, Arps, Slate, Meagher & Flom, N.Y.C., 1984—. Author: (with Rheingold) Products Liability, Law, Practice Science, 1974. Mem. N.Y.C. Bar Assn. (mem. exec. com. 1978—, jud. com. 1977), ABA (chmn. product gen. liability, consumer land coms.), Assn. of Bar of City of N.Y. (exec. com. 1978—, 2d century com. 1984-86), Phi Beta Kappa, Phi Alpha Theta, Alpha Chi Alpha. Insurance, Product liability, Toxic tort. Office: Skadden Arps Slate Meagher & Flom 4 Times Sq Fl 24 New York NY 10036-6595 E-mail: sbirnbau@skadden.com.

BIRNE, KENNETH ANDREW, lawyer; b. Englewood, N.J., Apr. 2, 1956; s. Alvin Aaron and Rita May (Gorsky) B.; m. Pamela Beth Ross; children: Jennafer Sara, Allison Francie, Jonathan Ross. BA in Polit. Sci., Ohio State U., 1978; JD, Case Western Res. U., 1981. Bar: Ohio 1981, U.S. Dist. Ct. (no. dist.) Ohio 1981. Sole practice, Cleve., 1981-85; ptnr. Peltz & Birne, Cleve., 1985—. Instr. Am. Inst. Paralegal Studies, Cleve., 1982-93, pers. dir. Cleve. area, 1984-93; cons. in field. Mem. Ohio Bar Assn., Cleve. Bar Assn. (chmn. practice and procedure clinic 1984-86, vol. Call for Action 1986, meritorious service award 1986), Cuyahoga County Bar Assn., Phi Eta Sigma, Zeta Beta Tau, Phi Delta Phi. Lodges: Masons. State civil litigation, Personal injury (including property damage), Workers' compensation. Office: Peltz & Birne Midland Bldg Ste 1880 Cleveland OH 44115-1093

BIRNKRANT, SHERWIN MAURICE, lawyer; b. Pontiac, Mich., Dec. 20, 1927; BBA, U. Mich., 1949, MBA, 1951; JD with distinction, Wayne State U., 1954. Bar: Mich. 1955, U.S. Dist. Ct. (ea. dist.) Mich. 1960, U.S. Supreme Ct. 1960, U.S. Ct. Appeals (6th cir.) 1966. Mem. Oakland County Bd. Suprs., 1967-68; asst. atty. City of Pontiac, Mich., 1956-67, city atty., 1967-83; of counsel Schlussel, Lifton, Simon, Rands, Galvin & Jackier, Southfield, Mich., 1983-90, Sommers, Schwartz, Silver & Schwartz, Southfield, 1990-95; shareholder Birnkrant & Birnkrant P.C., Bloomfield Hills, Mich., 1995—. Mem.: ABA (Mich. chmn. pub. contract law sect. 1979—97, chmn. urban, state and local govt. law sect. 1987—88, ho. dels. 1990—93, alt. del. to ho. dels. 1993—96, vice chmn. coordinating com. model procurement code state and local 1974—), Mich. Assn. Mcpl. Attys. (pres. 1975, coun. pres. 1992—), Am. Judicature Soc., Oakland County Bar Assn. (chmn. ethics and unauthorized practices com. 1961—62), State Bar Mich. (chmn. pub. corp. law sect. 1973—74, coun. adminstrv. law sect. 1975—76). Government contracts and claims, Land use and zoning (including planning), Municipal (including bonds). Office: Birnkrant & Birnkrant PC 7 W Square Lake Rd Bloomfield Hills MI 48302

BISHOP, ALFRED CHILTON, JR., lawyer; b. Alexandria, Va., Oct. 3, 1942; s. Alfred Chilton and Margaret (Marshall) B.; divorced; 1 son, Alfred Chilton III; m. 2d Catherine Ann Keppel, May 17, 1980. B.A. with distinction, U. Va., 1965, LL.B., 1969; LL.M. in Taxation, Georgetown U., 1974. Bar: N.Y. 1970, U.S. Ct. Appeals (2d cir.), 1970, U.S. Tax Ct. 1971, U.S. Ct. Claims 1971, D.C. 1977. Assoc. Shearman and Sterling, N.Y.C., 1969-70; assoc. trial atty., Office of Chief Counsel IRS, Washington, 1970-74, sr. trial atty., 1974-80, sr. technician reviewer, 1980-81, br. chief, 1981— . Recipient Am. Jurisprudence award 1968, 1968. Mem. D.C. Bar Assn., Sr. Exec. Service Candidate Network (v.p. 1980-81, pres. 1981-82, dir. 1983), Sr. Exec. Assn., Phi Delta Phi. Episcopalian. Home: 7523 Thistledown Trl Fairfax Station VA 22039-2207

BISHOP, BRUCE TAYLOR, lawyer; b. Hartford, Conn., Sept. 13, 1951; s. Robert Wright Sr. and Barbara (Taylor) B.; m. Sarah M. Bishop, Aug. 31, 1974; children: Elizabeth, Margaret. BA in Polit. Sci., Old Dominion U., 1973; JD, U. Va., Charlottesville, 1976. Bar: Va. 1977, U.S. Supreme Ct., Va. 1976, U.S. Dist. Ct. (ea. dist.) Va., U.S. Dist. Ct. (we. dist.) Va., U.S. Ct. Appeals (4th cir.); diplomate Am. Bd. Trial Advocates. Law clk. to chief judge U.S. Dist. Ct. (ea. dist.) Va., 1976-77; assoc. Willcox & Savage, P.C., Norfolk, Va., 1977-82, ptnr., 1983—. Bd. dirs. Nautical Adventures, Inc., Norfolk FestEvents, Ltd., 1981—, pres., 1982-85; pres. Va. OpSail 2000 Found.; mem. bd. visitors Old Dominion U., 1972-83, sec., 1979-81, chmn., mem. various coms.; speaker in field. Treas. Norfolk Reps., 1978-82, also mem. numerous coms.; bd. dirs., chmn. regional Key Club campaign United Way South Hampton Roads; chmn., co-chmn. United Negro Coll. Fund, 1981, Four Cities United Way Campaign; trustee Va. Stage Co., 1982; pres. Community Promotion Corp.; commr. Norfolk Redevel. and Housing Authority, chmn., 2000—; active numerous other community orgns. Named Outstanding Young Man, Norfolk Jaycees; recipient Disting. Alumni award Old Dominion U., Dominion Vol. of Yr. award, 1993. Mem. ABA (mem. various sects.), Fed. Bar Assn. (pres. Tidewater chpt. 1980-81), Am. Bd. Trial Advocates, Va. Assn. Def. Lawyers, Va. Bar Assn., Va. Trial Lawyers Assn., Norfolk-Portsmouth Bar Assn., Def. Rsch. Inst., Internat. Assn. Def. Counsel (nat. trial acad. faculty 1997), Assn. Def. Attys., Def. Rsch. Inst., Old Dominion U. Alumni Assn. (bd. dirs. 1978-83), Old Dominion U. Ednl. Found. (bd. dirs. 1987—, sec. 2000—), Norfolk C. of C. (chmn. downtown devel. com. 1980-81), James Kent Am. Inn of Ct. (master). Avocations: basketball, tennis, gardening. Product liability, Toxic tort, Transportation. Office: Willcox & Savage PC One Commercial Place Norfolk VA 23510 E-mail: bbishop@wilsav.com.

BISHOP, DANIEL W. lawyer; b. Plainview, Tex., Jan. 11, 1957; s. J. I. and Amelia M. Bishop; m. Elayne Crump, Feb. 16, 1991; children: Alexandra, Catherine, Robert, Olivia. BA, Baylor U., 1979, JD cum laude, 1982. Bar: Tex. 1982, U.S. Dist. Ct. (so. dist.) Tex. 1987, U.S. Dist. Ct. (we. dist.) Tex. 1989, U.S. Dist. Ct. (no. dist.) Tex. 1996, U.S. Ct. Claims 1999. Briefing atty. Tex. Supreme Ct., 1982—83; atty. Scott, Douglass & Luton, 1983—95, Locke, Purnell, Rain, Harrell, 1995—98; ptnr. Watson, Bishop, London & Brophy, Austin, 1998—. Mem. Supreme Ct. Adv. Com. Evidence, 1986—88. Fellow: Tex. Bar Found.; mem.: Austin Young Lawyers Assn. (pres. 1989—90), Travis County Bar Assn., Tex. Trial Lawyers Assn., Tex. Young Lawyers Assn. (bd. dirs. 1990—92), State Bar Tex. (mem. litig. coun. 1999—2002, treas. 2002—), Am. Bd. Trial Advs. (bd. dirs. 1999—), Delta Theta Phi (dean). Personal injury (including property damage), General civil litigation. Office: Watson Bishop London and Brophy 106 E 6th St Ste 700 Austin TX 78701 Office Fax: 512-479-5939. Business E-Mail: dbishop@wblg.com.

BISHOP, JOHN MAURICE, solicitor; b. Paignton, England, June 5, 1947; s. Edwin Maurice and Joyce Emilie Bishop; m. Pauline Margaret Grogan, Apr. 18, 2002; m. Virginia Diane Welsh, Apr. 18, 1986 (div. Apr. 1999); children: Edward, Laura, Sophie, Alice, Chloe. LLB with honors, London U., 1969. Head constrn. Masons Solicitors, London, 1978—86, mng. ptnr., 1986—90, sr. ptnr., 1990—, head constrn., 2000—02. Dir. Eleco Holdings, London, 1980—93. Mem.: Chartered Inst. Arbitrators. Avocation: golf. Construction, Alternative dispute resolution. Office: Masons 30 Aylesbury St London EC1R 0ER England Fax: +44 0207 490 6311. E-mail: john.biship@masons.com.

BISKUPIC, STEVEN M. lawyer; b. Mar. 1961; BA, JD, Marquette U. Asst. U.S. atty. Ea. Dist. Wis., 1989, U.S. atty. Office: 530 Fed Bldg 517 E Wisconsin Ave Milwaukee WI 53202*

BISSELL, JOHN W. federal judge; b. Exeter, N.H., June 7, 1940; s. H. Hamilton and Sarah W. B.; m. Caroline M.; July 15, 1967; children—Megan L., Katharine W. AB, Princeton U., 1962; LLB, U. Va., 1965. Law clk. U.S. Dist. Ct., N.J., 1965-66; assoc. Pitney, Hardin & Kipp, Newark and Morristown, N.J., 1966-69, ptnr., 1972-78; asst. U.S. atty. N.J., 1969-71; judge Essex County, N.J., 1978-81, N.J. Superior Ct., 1981-82, U.S. Dist. Ct. N.J., Trenton and Newark, 1983—. Office: US Dist Ct Federal Square PO Box 999 Newark NJ 07101-0999*

BISSELL, ROLIN PLUMB, lawyer; b. Yokosuka, Japan, Sept. 19, 1960; came to U.S., 1961; s. Elliston Perot III and Edith R. Bissell; m. Avery Boling, Sept. 12, 1987. BA in Philosophy and Econs., Columbia Coll., 1982; JD, U. Va., 1985. Law clk. to Chief Justice Richard Neely Supreme Ct. of W.Va., Charleston, 1985-86; assoc. Dewey Ballantine Bushby, Palmer & Wood, N.Y.C., 1986-88, Schnader Harrison Segal & Lewis LLP, Phila., 1988-93, ptnr., 1994—. Contbr. articles to law jours. Dir. Chestnut Hill Hist. Soc., Phila., 1993-98, Landmarks Soc., Phila., 1998-2002; mem. Com. of Seventy, Phila., 1998-2002. Antitrust, Federal civil litigation, Securities. Office: Schnader Harrison Segal & Lewis 1600 Market St Fl 35 Philadelphia PA 19103-7286

BISSETTE, WINSTON LOUIS, JR., lawyer, mayor; b. Statesville, N.C., Sept. 18, 1943; s. Winston Louis and Rubye (Goode) B.; m. Sara Oliver, Aug. 21, 1965; children: W. Louis III, Thomas Anderson. BA, Wake Forest U., 1965; JD, U. N.C., Chapel Hill, 1968; MBA, U. Va., 1970. Bar: N.C. 1968. Asst. v.p. Wachovia Bank & Trust Co., Winston-Salem, N.C., 1970-74; v.p., treas. Western Carolina Bank, Asheville, N.C., 1974-76; ptnr. McGuire, Wood & Bissette, P.A., Asheville, 1976—. Mayor City of Asheville, 1985-89, mem. city coun., 1983-89; co-chmn. I-26 corridor Assn., 1987—; chmn. West N.C. Devel. Assn., 1995-98; regional adv. coun. HUD, 1986-90; mem. Gov.'s Task Force on Urban Transp., 1986, Yr. of the Mtns. Commn., 1995-97; chmn. Asheville Sports Com., 1991-97, Buncombe County Econ. Devel. Commn., 1997—; vice chmn. Asheville Cmty. Betterment Found., 1992; bd. trustees Wake Forest U., 1996—, Western Carolina U., 1995—; chmn. Advantage Asheville, 1996—; chmn. Grove Arcade Pub. Mkt. Found., 1992—; bd. dirs. Mission-St. Joseph's Health Sys., Inc., 1996-99, Mercy Svcs. Corp., Blue Ridge Pkwy. Found., vice chmn. Mem. ABA, N.C. Bar Assn., Asheville Area C. of C. (pres. 1991-92), Wake Forest U. Alumni Assn. (pres. 1992-93), Country Club of Asheville, Biltmore Forest Country Club, Civitan Club. Republican. Presbyterian. Avocations: golf, running. Corporate, general, Health. Home: 321 Old Toll Rd Asheville NC 28804-3716 Office: McGuire Wood & Bissette PA 48 Patton Ave PO Box 3180 Asheville NC 28802-3180

BISSINGER, MARK CHRISTIAN, lawyer; b. Steubenville, Ohio, June 4, 1957; s. Emerson Melvin and Nancy (Osbun) B.; m. Julie Furber, Sept. 28, 1985; children: Lucas Christian, Nathan Kenneth. BS in Civil Engring., Purdue U., 1979; JD, U. Cin., 1983. Bar: Ohio 1983, U.S. Dist. Ct. (so. dist.) Ohio 1983, U.S. Ct. Appeals (6th cir.), Ky. 1993. Assoc. Dinsmore &

Shohl, Cin., 1983-90, ptnr., 1990—. Spkr. Ohio Continuing Legal Edn., Cin., 1990—; lectr. Nat. Bus. Inst., 1990—; commn. cert. attys. as splsts. Supreme Ct. Ohio; mem. Supreme Ct. Ohio's Bd. Bar Examiners; lectr. Lorman Edn. Svcs. Pres. Ctr. for Comprehensive Alcoholism Treatment, Cin., 1989-92. Named Order of Coif, Cin., 1983; inducted class of 1999 Cin. Acad. of Leadership for Lawyers. Mem. ABA, Cin. Bar Assn., Ohio Bar Assn., No. Ky. Bar Assn., Ky. Bar Assn. Avocations: family, travel, sports. Bankruptcy, General civil litigation, Construction. Office: Dinsmore & Shohl 255 E 5th St Cincinnati OH 45202-4700

BISTLINE, F. WALTER, JR., lawyer; b. Lakeland, Fla., Sept. 30, 1950; s. Frederick Walter and Mary Carolyn (Stansell) B.; m. Rabun Huff, Mar. 18, 1972. BA, Emory U., 1972; JD, Boston U., 1975. Bar: N.Y. 1976, Tex. 1979. Assoc. firm White & Case, N.Y.C., 1975-79; assoc. Johnson & Gibbs, P.C., Dallas, 1979-81, ptnr./shareholder, 1981-95; ptnr. Porter & Hedges, L.L.P., Houston, 1995—2001, of counsel, 2001—. Lectr. So. Meth. U. Sch. of Law, 1991. Contbr. articles to profl. jours. Fellow, U. Houston, 2002—. Banking, Commercial, contracts (including sales of goods; commercial financing). Office: Porter & Hedges LLP 3500 Bank of America Ctr 700 Louisiana St Houston TX 77002-2700

BITENSKY, SUSAN HELEN, law educator; b. N.Y.C., Jan. 3, 1948; d. Reuben Bitensky; m. Elliott Lee Meyrowitz, Apr. 17, 1982; 1 child, William N. BA magna cum laude, Case Western Res. U., 1971; JD, U. Chgo., 1974. Bar: Pa. 1974, U.S. Dist. Ct. (we. dist.) Pa. 1974, U.S. Ct. Appeals (3d cir.) 1975, U.S. Ct. Appeals (2d cir.) 1977, N.Y. 1979, U.S. Dist. Ct. (so. and ea. dists.) N.Y. 1979, Mich. 1988. Asst. gen. counsel United Steelworkers Am., Pitts., 1974-77; assoc. Cohen, Weiss and Simon, N.Y.C., 1977-81; assoc. counsel N.Y.C. Bd. Edn., Bklyn., 1981-87; assoc. prof. law Mich. State U.-Detroit Coll. Law, 1988-93, prof. law, 1993—. Contbg. author: Children's Rights in America: UN Convention on the Rights of the Child Compared with U.S. Law; contbr. articles to profl. jours. Mem. ABA, Phi Beta Kappa. Office: Mich State Univ Detroit Coll Law 447 Law College Bldg East Lansing MI 48824-1300 E-mail: bitensky@msu.edu.

BITNER, JOHN HOWARD, lawyer; b. Indpls., Feb. 27, 1940; s. Harry M. Jr. and Jeanne B. (Eshelman) B.; m. Vicki Ann D'Ianni, 1961; children: Kerry, Holly, Robin. AB in English and History, Northwestern U., 1961; JD cum laude, Columbia U., 1964. Bar: Ill. 1964. Assoc. Bell, Boyd & Lloyd LLC, Chgo., 1964-71, ptnr., 1972-99, chair corp. and secs. dept., 1988-99, vice chmn. firm, 1992-99, mem., 2000—. Contbr. articles to profl. jours.; editor Columbia Law Rev. Mem. St. Gregory Episcopal Sch. Bd.; mem. bd. visitors Columbia Law Sch, tutor, GED students at Jobs for Youth Mem. ABA, Ill. Bar Assn., Chgo. Bar Assn., Union League, Mid-Day Club, Glen View Club, Lawyers Club, Delta Upsilon, Phi Delta Phi. Episcopalian. Avocations: tennis, reading, chess, golf. Corporate, general, Mergers and acquisitions, Securities. Home: 2329 Lincolnwood Dr Evanston IL 60201-2048 Office: Bell Boyd & Lloyd LLC 70 W Madison St Chicago IL 60602 Fax: (312) 827-8048. E-mail: jbitner@bellboyd.com.

BITZEGAIO, HAROLD JAMES, retired lawyer; b. Coalmont, Ind., Jan. 29, 1921; s. Nicholas Gilbert and Dora Belle (Burns) B.; m. Betty Jean Law, Apr. 15, 1950; children: Judith L. Bitzegaio Wallin, Gail Ann Bitzegaio Wright, Susan R. Bitzegaio Denyer, James R., Jane E. Disney. BS, Ind. State U., 1948; JD, Ind. U., 1953; grad., Ind. Jud. Coll., 1980. Bar: Ind. 1953, U.S. Dist. Ct. (so. dist.) Ind. 1953, U.S. Ct. Appeals (7th cir.) 1956. Sole practice, Terre Haute, Ind., 1953-58, 81-97; judge Vigo Superior Ct., Terre Haute, 1959-80; of counsel Anderson & Nichols Law Office. Editor, contbr.: Indiana Pattern Jury Instructions, 1966. Mem. Ind. Adv. Com. Civil Rights, Indpls., 1961-70, Mayor's Com. Civil Rights, Terre Haute, 1967-68; bd. dirs. Wabash Valley Council Boy Scouts Am., Terre Haute, 1960-80. Served to lt. comdr. USN, 1941-46, PTO. Decorated D.F.C. with gold star, Air medal with two gold stars, Purple Heart; named Sagamore of the Wabash, Gov. of Ind., 1990. Mem. ABA, Ind. Bar Assn., Terre Haute Bar Assn., Ind. Judges Assn. (bd. mgrs. 1961-80, pres. 1977-78), Ind. U. Law Alumni Assn. (pres. 1973-74, recipient disting. service award 1974), VFW (life), Nat. Rifle Assn. (life), Ducks Unltd. (nat. trustee, emeritus). Clubs: Terre Haute Country (bd. dirs. 1974-76). Democrat. General practice. Home and Office: 2703 E Springhill Dr Terre Haute IN 47802-8406

BIVENS, DONALD WAYNE, lawyer, judge; b. Ann Arbor, Mich., Feb. 5, 1952; s. Melvin Donley and Frances Lee (Speer) Bivens; children: Jody, Lisa, Andrew. BA magna cum laude, Yale U., 1974; JD, U. Tex., 1977. Bar: Ariz 1977, US Dist Ct Ariz 1977, US Ct Appeals (9th cir) 1977, US Ct Appeals (fed cir) 1984, US Supreme Ct 1982. Ptnr. Meyer, Hendricks & Bivens, P.A., Phoenix, 1977—. Judge pro tem Maricopa County Superior Ct, Ariz., 1987—, Ariz Ct Appeals, Phoenix, 1999—2000. Editor (note & comment ed): Tex Law Rev, 1976—77. Pres Scottsdale Men's League, 1980—82; vpres, bd dirs Phoenix Symphony Asn, 1980—86; mem adv bd Ariz Theater Co, 1987—88; pres Ariz Young Dems, 1980—82; bd dirs Scottsdale Arts Ctr Asn, 1981—84, Planned Parenthood Cent and Northern Ariz, 1989—92. Recipient Consul Award, Univ Tex Sch Law, 1977, 3 Outstanding Young Men Award, Phoenix Jaycees, 1981. Mem.: ABA (coun litigation sect 1995—98, chmn computer litigation comt 1989—92, resource develop comt litigation sect 1992—, technical task force 1998—, state del House Dels 1999—), Thurgood Marshall Inn Ct (pres 1992—93), Maricopa County Bar Asn (bd dirs, pres 1991—92, chmn Trial Adv Inst 1986—87, Mem of the Yr 1998), Ariz Trial Lawyers Asn, State Bar Ariz (bd govs 1993—2000, pres 1998—99, peer rev comt 1992—), Ariz Bar Found, Am Bar Found. Democrat. Avocations: music, theater. Federal civil litigation, Computer, Securities. Home: 6311 E Naumann Dr Paradise Valley AZ 85253-1044 Office: Meyer Hendricks & Bivens PA 3003 N Central Ave Ste 1200 Phoenix AZ 85012-2915

BIXBY, DAVID MICHAEL, lawyer; b. Pensacola, Fla., Aug. 10, 1954; s. Harry Lewellyn and Ann Olivia B.; m. Karen Louise Schroeder, Sept. 5, 1981; children: Laura, Elizabeth. BA, Harvard Coll., 1976, U. Cape Town, 1977; JD, Yale Law Sch., 1980. Bar: Ariz. 1981, U.S. Dist. Ct. Ariz. 1981, U.S. Ct. Appeals (9th cir.) 1981. Law clk. Hon. David W. Williams U.S. Dist. Ct., L.A., 1980-81; ptnr. Lewis & Roca, LLP, Phoenix, 1981-98; sr. v.p., gen. counsel Samaritan Health Sys., Phoenix, 1998—99, Banner Health Sys., Phoenix, 1999—. Mem. Assn. Am. Health Lawyers. Corporate, general, Finance, Health. Office: Banner Health Sys 1441 N 12th St Phoenix AZ 85006-2837

BIXBY, FRANK LYMAN, lawyer; b. New Richmond, Wis., May 25, 1928; s. Frank H. and Esther (Otteson) B.; m. Katharine Spence, July 7, 1951; children— Paul, Thomas, Edward, Janet. AB, Harvard U., 1950; LLB, U. Wis., 1953. Bar: Ill. 1953, Wis. 1953, Fla. 1974. Ptnr. firm Sidley Austin Brown & Wood, Chgo., 1963—97, sr. counsel, 1998—. Editor-in-chief Wis. Law Rev., 1952-53; mem. editorial bd. Chgo. Reporter, 1973-89. Trustee MacMurray Coll., Jacksonville, Ill., 1973-85; bd. dirs. Chgo. Urban League, 1962—, v.p., 1972-86, gen. counsel, 1972—, chmn. 1986-89; bd. dirs. Community Renewal Soc., 1973-86, Voices for Ill. Children, 1987-90; chmn. trustees Unitarian Ch., Evanston, Ill., 1962-63; bd. dirs. Spencer Found., 1967-2001, chmn. 1975-90; mem. dist. 202 bd. edn. Evanston Twp. High Sch., 1975-81, pres., 1977-79. Recipient Man of Year award Chgo. Urban League, 1974 Mem. ABA, Ill. Bar Assn., Chgo. Bar Assn., Chgo. Coun. Lawyers, Chgo. Coun. Fgn. Rels., Order of Coif, Harvard Club (pres. 1964-65), Mid-Day Club., Phi Beta Kappa. Estate planning, Probate (including wills, trusts), Estate taxation. Home: 505 N Lake Shore Dr Apt 4607 Chicago IL 60611-3409 Office: Sidley Austin Brown & Wood 10 S Dearborn St Chicago IL 60603-2000 E-mail: fbixby@sidley.com., kfbixby@yahoo.com.

BIZUB, JOHANNA CATHERINE, law librarian; b. Denville, N.J., Apr. 13, 1957; d. Stephen Bernard and Elizabeth Mary (Grizzle) B.; m. Scott Jeffrey Smith, 1992. BS in Criminal Justice, U. Dayton, 1979; MLS, Rutgers U., 1984. Law libr. Morris County Law Libr., 1981-83, Clapp & Eisenberg, Newark, 1984-86; dir. libr. Sills Cummis, 1986-94; libr. dir. Montville (N.J.) Twp. Pub. Libr., N.J., 1994-97; libr. dir. law dept. Prudential Ins. Co. Am., Newark, 1997—. Mem. ALA, N.J. Law Librs. Assn. (treas. 1987-89, v.p./pres.-elect 1989-90, 99-2000, pres. 1990-91, 2000-01, past pres. 1991-92, 2001-02), Am. Assn. Law Librs. (pvt. law librs. SIS, vice chair 1992-93, chair 1993-94, past chair 1994-95), N.J. Libr. Assn., Assoc. Libr. of Morris County (v.p. 1995, pres. 1996, treas. 1997-01), Spl. Libr. Assn. N.J. (treas. 1990-92), Am. Legion Aux. (treas. Rockden unit 175 1983-93). Democrat. Roman Catholic. Home: 11 Elm St Rockaway NJ 07866-3108 Office: Prudential Ins Co Am 22 Plz 751 Broad St Newark NJ 07102-3714

BJORK, ROBERT DAVID, JR., lawyer; b. Evanston, Ill., Sept. 29, 1946; s. Robert David and Lenore Evelyn (Loderhose) B.; m. Linda Louise Reese, Mar. 27, 1971; children: Heidi Lynne, Gretchen Anne. BBA, U. Wis., 1968; JD, Tulane U., 1974. Bar: La. 1974, U.S. Dist. Ct. (ea. dist.) La. 1974, U.S. Ct. Appeals (5th cir.) 1974, U.S. Dist. Ct. (mid. dist.) 1975, U.S. Supreme Ct. 1977, U.S. Dist. Ct. (we. dist.) 1978, U.S. Ct. Appeals (11th cir.) 1981, Calif. 1983, U.S. Dist. Ct. (no. dist.) Calif. 1983, U.S. Dist. Ct. (ea. dist.) Calif. 1984. Ptnr. Adams & Reese, New Orleans, 1974-83; assoc. Crosby, Heafey, Roach & May, Oakland, Calif., 1983-85; ptnr. Bjork Lawrence, Oakland, 1985—. Instr. paralegal studies Tulane U., New Orleans, 1979—82. Mem. Tulane U. Law Rev., 1973-74; editor Med. Malpractice newsletter, 1983-88. Bd. dirs. Piedmont (Calif.) Coun. Camp Fire, 1984-92, pres., 1987-89; treas. Couhig Congl. Com., New Orleans, 1980-82; bd. dirs. Camp Augusta Trust, 1990-2001. Lt. USNR, 1968-71. Mem. ABA, Internat. Assn. Def. Counsel, Calif. Bar Assn., La. Bar Assn. (chmn. young lawyers sect. 1982-83). Federal civil litigation, State civil litigation, Personal injury (including property damage). Home: 1909 Oakland Ave Piedmont CA 94611-3706 Office: Bjork Lawrence 1901 Harrison St Ste 1630 Oakland CA 94612-3501 E-mail: rbjork@bjorklaw.com.

BLACHLY, JACK LEE, lawyer; b. Dallas, Mar. 8, 1942; s. Emery Lee and Thelma Jo (Budd) B.; m. Lucy Largent Rain, Jan. 15, 1972; 1 son, Michael Talbot. BBA, So. Meth. U., 1965, JD, 1968. Bar: Tex. 1968, U.S. Ct. Appeals (5th cir.) 1969, U.S. Supreme Ct. 1975, U.S. Tax Ct. 1977. Trust officer First Nat. Bank in Dallas, 1968-70; ptnr. firm Reese & Blachly, Dallas, 1970-71; assoc. firm Rain Harrell Emery Young & Doke, Dallas, 1971-76; staff atty. Sabine Corp., Dallas, 1976-77, mgr. legal dept., 1977-80, v.p., gen. counsel, 1980-89; asst. gen. counsel Pacific Enterprises Oil Co. USA (merger Sabine Corp. and Pacific Enterprise Oil Co. USA), Dallas, 1989-90; pvt. practice Dallas, 1990—. Mem.: Dallas Bar Assn., Tex. Bar Assn., Dallas Gun Club. Baptist. Corporate, general, Oil, gas, and mineral, Securities. Office: 4409 Benton Elm Dr Plano TX 75024

BLACHMAN, MICHAEL JOEL, lawyer; b. Portsmouth, Va., Aug. 16, 1944; s. Zalmon I. and Rachel G. (Grossman) B.; m. Paula D. Levine, Nov. 23, 1969; children: Dara R., Erica Dale. BS, Am. U., 1966; JD, U. Tenn., 1969. Bar: Va. 1969, U.S. Dist. Ct. (ea. dist.) Va. 1971, U.S. Supreme Ct. 1974, U.S. Ct. Appeals (4th cir.) 1977. Asst. commonwealth's atty. Commonwealth of Va., Portsmouth, 1970-72; assoc. Bangel, Bangel & Bangel, Portsmouth, 1972-77, ptnr., 1977—. Chmn. Portsmouth Juvenile Adv. Com., 1975-78. Mem. Va. Dem. Steering Com. 1980-85; vice chmn. Indsl. Devel. Authority and Port and Indsl. Commn., Portsmouth, 1987-89, chmn. 1989-93; bd. dirs. United Jewish Fedn. Tidewater, 1980—, v.p. 1989—. With USCGR, 1966-72. Recipient Young Leadership award United Jewish Fedn. Tidewater, 1983. Mem. ABA, Assn. Trial Lawyers Am., Va. Bar Assn., Va. Trial Lawyers Assn. (v.p. 1985-88, pres. 1989-90), So. Trial Lawyers Assn. (bd. dirs. 1991—), Portsmouth Bar Assn., Portsmouth C. of C., Kiwanis (bd. dirs. Portsmouth club 1973-75), B'nai B'rith. Jewish. Avocations: tennis, travel, reading. Personal injury (including property damage). Office: # B 116 82nd St Virginia Beach VA 23451-1802

BLACK, ALLEN DECATUR, lawyer; b. Pitts., July 27, 1942; s. Gerald Richard and Amy Elizabeth (Haymaker) B. AB, Princeton U., 1963; LLB magna cum laude, U. Pa., 1966. Bar: D.C. 1967, Pa. 1971, U.S. Supreme Ct. 1975. Law clk. to Hon. John Minor Wisdom, New Orleans, 1966-67; trial atty. Dept. Justice, 1967-68; asst. prof. law U. North Dakota, Grand Forks, 1971; practice comml. and antitrust litigation law Fine, Kaplan & Black, Phila., 1975—. Lectr. in law Rutgers U., 1972-77, Temple U., 1978, U. Pa., 1985. Served with JAGC USN, 1968-71. Fellow Am. Coll. Trial Lawyers; mem. Am. Law Inst. (mem. coun.), Pa. Bar Assn., Phila. Bar Assn., Phila. Art Alliance. Republican. Episcopalian. Office: 1845 Walnut St Philadelphia PA 19103-4708

BLACK, BARBARA ARONSTEIN, legal history educator; b. Bklyn., May 6, 1933; d. Robert and Minnie (Polenberg) A.; m. Charles L. Black, Jr., Apr. 11, 1954; children— Gavin B., David A., Robin E. BA, Bklyn. Coll., 1953; LLB, Columbia U., 1955; MPhil, Yale U., 1970, PhD, 1975; LLD (hon.), N.Y. Law Sch., 1986, Marymount Manhattan Coll., 1986, Vt. Law Sch., 1987, Coll. of New Rochelle, 1987, Smith Coll., 1988, Bklyn. Coll., 1988, York U., Toronto, Can., 1990, Georgetown U., 1991. Assoc. in law Columbia U. Law Sch., N.Y.C., 1955-56; lectr. history Yale U., New Haven, 1974-76, asst. prof. history, 1976-79, assoc. prof. law, 1979-84; George Welwood Murray prof. legal history Columbia U. Law Sch., N.Y.C., 1984—, dean faculty of law, 1986-91. Editor Columbia Law Rev., 1953-55. Active N.Y. State Ethics Commn., 1992-95. Recipient Fed. Bar Assn. prize Columbia Law Sch., 1955 Mem. Am. Soc. Legal History (pres. 1986-90), Am. Acad. Arts and Scis., Am. Philos. Soc., Mass. Hist. Soc., Supreme Ct. Hist. Soc., Selden Soc., Century Assn. Office: Columbia U Sch Law 435 W 116th St New York NY 10027-7201

BLACK, BARBARA JEAN, lawyer; b. Moses Lake, Wash., Sept. 1, 1960; d. George E. and Judith C. B. BA, Wash. State U., 1982; JD, Gonzaga U. Sch. Law, 1993. Bar: Wash. 1994. Sole practice law, Moses Lake, 1994—. Mem. ABA, ATLA, Wash. State Trial Lawyers Assn., Wash. State Bar Assn., Grant County Bar Assn. Avocation: water sports. Family and matrimonial. Office: PO Box 1118 Moses Lake WA 98837-0169

BLACK, BERT, state administrator, lawyer; b. NYC, Mar. 6, 1956; s. Thomas and Evelyn Gretel (Florio) B.; m. Cynthia H. Daggett; children: Sarah, Amy. BA in Biology, SUNY, Buffalo, 1976; JD, U. Minn., 1979. Bar: Minn. 1979, U.S. Dist. Ct. Minn. 1979. Reporter Adv. Task Force on Minn. Corp. Law, Mpls., 1979-81; dir. corp. divsn. State of Minn., St. Paul, 1981-99; legal analyst Office of Sec. of State of Minn., St. Paul, 1999—2002, planning dir., 2003—. Pres. Internat. Assn. Corp. Adminstrs., 1988-89; adj. prof. U. Minn. Law Sch., 1995, William Mitchell Coll. Law, 2002; observer Revision of Revised Uniform Ltd. Partnership Act, Nat. Conf. Commrs. on Uniform State Laws; lectr. in field. Editor: Minnesota Corporations Practice Manual, 1986. Chmn. Dem.-Farmer Labor Party, 59th Dist., 1982-84, chmn. Mpls. sect., 1983-85, assoc. chair, chair 5th congl. dist., 1986-94, mem. state exec. com., 1986-2000, mem. state ctrl. com. Minn., 1982—. Jewish. Home: 3932 Harriet Ave Minneapolis MN 55409-1439 Office: Sec of State of Minn Dept Bus and Legal Analyst 180 State Office Bldg Saint Paul MN 55155-1299 E-mail: Bert.Black@state.mn.us., Bert1956@aol.com.

BLACK, FREDERICK A. b. July 2, 1949; s. John R. and Dorothy Black; m. Katie Black, Oct. 27, 1976; children: Shane, Shanthini, Sheena. BA, U. Calif., Berkeley, 1971; JD, Lewis and Clark Coll., 1975. Bar: Oreg. 1975, Guam 1976, U.S. Ct. Appeals (9th cir.) 1976. Dir. Office of Guam Pub. Defender, 1975-78; dep. dir. Office of Oreg. Fed. Defender, 1981-84; asst. U.S. atty. Dist. Guam and No. Mariana Islands, 1978-81, 84-89, 1st asst. U.S. atty., 1989-91; U.S. atty. Dept. Justice Dist. Agana, Guam and No. Mariana Islands, 1991—2003; sr. litigation counsel U.S. Attys Office, 2003—. Author: Oregon Search and Seizure Manual. Leader Boy Scouts Am. Recipient Spl. award Chief Postal Inspector, 1986, Drug Enforcement Adminstrn. award, 1986, 89. Mem. Guam Water Polo Team. Avocation: sailing. Office: US Atty's Office 108 Hernan Cortez Ave Ste 500 Hagatna GU 96910-5009

BLACK, JAMES ISAAC, III, lawyer; b. Lakeland, Fla., Oct. 26, 1951; s. James Isaac Jr. and Juanita (Feemster) B.; m. Vikki Harrison, June 15, 1973; children: Jennifer Leigh, Katharine Ann, Stephanie Marie. BA, U. Fla., 1973; JD, Harvard U., 1976. Bar: Fla. 1976, N.Y. 1977, U.S. Tax Ct. 1984. Assoc. Sullivan & Cromwell, N.Y.C., 1976-84, ptnr., 1984—. Mem. ABA, N.Y. State Bar Assn. (persons under disability com. trusts and estates law sect. 1984-90), Assn. of Bar of City of N.Y. (sec. 1980-81, trusts and estates and surrogates ct. com. 1980-83), Scarsdale Golf Club. Estate planning, Probate (including wills, trusts), Property, real (including real estate development, water). Home: 23 Chesterfield Rd Scarsdale NY 10583-2205 Office: Sullivan & Cromwell LLP 125 Broad St Fl 28 New York NY 10004-2489

BLACK, LOUIS ENGLEMAN, lawyer; b. Washington, Aug. 5, 1943; s. Fischer Sheffey and Elizabeth (Zemp) B.; m. Cecelia Whidden, Sept. 5, 1966; 1 child, Kerrison Todd. BA, NYU, 1968, JD, 1971, LLM in Taxation, 1978. Bar: N.Y. 1972. Assoc. Carter, Ledyard & Milburn, N.Y.C., 1972-79; ptnr. Van Ginkel & Benjamin, N.Y.C., 1979-83; of counsel Zimet, Haines, Moss & Friedman, N.Y.C., 1983-84, DeForest & Duer, N.Y.C., 1984-86, ptnr., 1986—2001, Black & Assocs., 2002—. Vice-chmn. bd. dirs. MacMillan Ring-Free Oil Co., Inc., 1986-87; chmn. bd. Lee's Gourmet Farms, Inc., 1993-97, United Compressor, LLC, 2002-, Kingdom Techs., LLC, 2002—; CFO, Wyzer, Inc., 2003-. Editor: NYU Jour. Internat. Law and Politics, 1970-71; author: Partnership Buy/Sell Agreements, 1977. Mem. ABA, N.Y. State Bar Assn. Computer, Corporate, general, Taxation, general. Home: 220 E 65th St Apt 24M New York NY 10021-6629 Office: Black & Assocs 20 E 46th St Ste 1401 New York NY 10017-2276 E-mail: lblack@blackesq.com.

BLACK, ROBERT ALLEN, lawyer; b. Ocala, Fla., Aug. 15, 1954; s. Allen Harrison and Rose Marie (Dupree) B. BA, U. Tex., El Paso, 1977; JD summa cum laude, Tex. Tech U., 1980. Bar: Tex. 1980, U.S. Ct. Appeals (5th and 11th cirs.) 1980, U.S. Supreme Ct. 1985. Ptnr. Mehaffy & Weber, Beaumont, Tex., 1980—, mng. ptnr., 1998—. Adj. prof. law Lamar U., Beaumont, Tex., 1981-84. Case note editor Tex. Tech Law Rev., 1979-80; editor Jefferson County Bar Jour., 1991-93. Pres. Humane Soc. S.E. Tex., Beaumont, 1983-89; bd. dirs. YMCA, Beaumont, 1985-87, Beaumont Cmty. Players, 1989-91; host TV show Pets on Parade, Beaumont, 1986-87; mem. Beaumont City Planning and Zoning Commn., 1987-90; mem. Beaumont Hist. Landmark Commn., 1989-90. Named one of Outstanding Young Men of Am., Jaycees, 1982. Fellow: Tex. Bar Found. (chair Dist. 3 nominating com.); mem.: Am. Contract Bridge League (pres. unit 201 1991—93, bd. govs. 1992—96, pres. 1994—96), Tex. Bar Assn., Jefferson County Bar Assn. (treas. 1994—95, pres.-elect 1996—97, pres. 1997—98), ABA. Democrat. Avocations: book collecting, tennis, history. Federal civil litigation, Libel, Personal injury (including property damage). Home: 601 22nd St Beaumont TX 77706-4915 Office: Mehaffy & Weber 2615 Calder St Ste 800 Beaumont TX 77702-1993 E-mail: BobBlack@mehaffyweber.com.

BLACK, ROBERT L., JR., retired judge; b. Dec. 11, 1917; s. Robert L. and Anna M. (Smith) B.; m. Helen Chatfield, July 27, 1946; children: William C., Stephen L., Luther F. AB, Yale U., 1939; LLB, Harvard U., 1942. Bar: Ohio 1946, U.S. Ct. Appeals (6th cir.) 1947, U.S. Supreme Ct. 1955. Pvt. practice, Cin., 1946-53; ptnr. Graydon, Head & Ritchey, Cin., 1953-72; judge Ct. Common Pleas, Cin., 1973-77, Ct. Appeals, Cin., 1977-89, vis. and assigned judge, 1989-92. Mem. jury instrns. com. Ohio Jud. Conf. 1973—, chmn. 1986-92. Contbr. articles on law to profl. jours. Councilman Village Indian Hill (Ohio), 1953-65, mayor, 1959-65; mem. standing com. Diocese of So. Ohio, Episcopal Ch., 1958-64, lay del. to gen. assembly, 1966, 69; vestryman, warden Indian Hill Episcopal Ch.; chmn. Cin. Human Rels. Commn., 1967-70. Served to Capt. U.S. Army, 1942-45. Decorated Bronze Star. Mem. Cin. Bar Assn., Ohio Bar Assn., ABA, Am. Judicature Soc., Nat. Legal Aid and Defender Assn., Phi Beta Kappa, Queen City Club, Camargo Club, Commonwealth (Cin.) Club. Republican. Episcopalian. Home: 5900 Drake Rd Cincinnati OH 45243-3306 E-mail: bopblack@cinci.rr.com.

BLACK, STEPHEN FRANKLIN, lawyer; b. N.Y.C., Nov. 28, 1944; s. Theodore Russel Black and Zelma Carmel Bernstein; m. Laurie N Bromberg, June 25, 1967 (div. Oct. 1988); children: Hilary F, Jane S, Katharine L; m. Anne M Richmond, Oct. 14, 1989. AB magna cum laude, Harvard U., 1965; JD magna cum laude, U. Mich., 1968; MLitt, Oxford (Eng.) U., 1970. Bar: DC 1969. Ptnr. Wilmer, Cutler & Pickering, Washington, 1970—2001. Dir Am Soc for Legal Hist, 1979—82. Author: (book) Internal Corporate Investigations, 1985, Der Zivilprozess in Den Vereinigten Staaten, 1986, Complying with Foreign Corrupt Practices Act, 1997; contbr. articles to profl jours. Trustee Shakespeare Theatre, 2001—. Mem.: Cosmos Club Washington. Bankruptcy, General civil litigation, Securities. Home: 1605 22nd St NW Washington DC 20008-1921

BLACK, WILLIAM EARL, lawyer; b. Port Arthur, Tex., Mar. 15, 1951; s. Earl Milton and Lola (Fuller) B.; m. Martha Talbot Rain, Aug. 11, 1972; children: Katherine Gano, Robert William. BA, U. Tex., 1973; JD, St. Mary's U., San Antonio, 1976. Bar: Tex.; cert. in adminstrv. law and in oil, gas, and mineral law Tex. Bd. Legal Specialization. Legal examiner R.R. Commn. of Tex., Austin, 1977-80; assoc., then ptnr. Lynch, Chappell and Alsup, Austin, 1980-91; ptnr. Hall & Black, LLP, Austin, 1991-2000; atty. pvt. practice, 2000—. Fellow Tex. Bar Found.; mem. Tex. State Bar Assn., Travis County Bar Assn., Phi Gamma Delta. Presbyterian. Avocations: music, exercise. Administrative and regulatory, Oil, gas, and mineral, Entertainment. Office: Ste 2000 100 Congress Ave Austin TX 78701

BLACK, WILLIAM REA, lawyer; b. N.Y.C., Nov. 4, 1952; s. Thomas Howard and Dorothy Chambers (Dailey) B.; m. Kathleen Jane Owen, June 24, 1978; children: William Ryan, Jonathan Wesley. BSBA, U. Denver, 1978, MBA, 1981; JD, Western State U., Fullerton, Calif., 1987. Bar: Calif., U.S. Ct. Appeals (fed. cir.), U.S. Dist. Ct.; lic. real estate broker; lic. pvt. investigator. Bus. mgr. Deere & Co., Moline, Ill., 1979-85; dir. Mgmt. Resource Svc. Co., Chgo., 1985-86; sr. v.p. Geneva Corp., Irvine, Calif., 1986-91; pvt. practice Newport Beach, Calif., 1991-92; gen. counsel Sunclipse, Inc., 1992—97; spl. counsel Amcor, Ltd., 1992—97; dir. gen. Amcor de Mex., S.A. de C.V., 1993—97; secretario KHL de Mex. S.A. de C.V., 1995—97; v.p., gen. counsel LL Knickerbocker Co., 1997-99; CEO Kuroi Kiku Corp., Kuroi Ryu Corp., First Reconnaissance Co., 1997—; v.p., gen. cousel Thales Avionics, 1999—. Mng. editor Western State U. Law Rev., Fullerton, 1984-87. Instr. Pai Lum Kung Fu Karate, Hartford, Conn., 1970-75, U.S. Judo Assn., Denver, 1975-80, United Studios Kenpo, L.A., 1995—. Recipient Am. Jurisprudence award Bancroft-Whitney Co., 1984, 85, 86; Pres.'s scholar full acad. merit scholarship, 1983. Mem. ABA, Am. Soc. Appraisers, Inst. Bus. Appraisers, Assn. Productivity Specialists, Am. Employment Law Coun., Profls. in Human Resources Assn., Am. Mgmt. Assn., Orange County Bar Assn., L.A. County Bar Assn., Mu Kappa Tau. Avocations: karate (2d degree black belt), Judo, skiing, scuba, golf. Corporate, general, Labor (including EEOC, Fair Labor Standards Act, labor-management relations, NLRB, OSHA), Mergers and acquisitions. Office: 17481 Red Hill Ave Irvine CA 92614-5630 E-mail: william.black@thales-ifs.com.

BLACKBURN, JAMES B., III, lawyer; b. Pitts., Nov. 16, 1946; s. James B. Jr. and Ethel Louise (Herrod) B.; m. Cynthia Jan Coote, Aug. 10, 1974; children: Sarah Louise, James B. IV, Natalie Alice. BA, Princeton U., 1969; MPA, N.C. State U., 1974; JD, Duke U., 1980. Bar: N.C. 1980. Staff atty. Gen. Rsch. Divsn, N.C. Gen. Assembly, Raleigh, 1980-84; gen. counsel N.C. Assn. County Commrs., Raleigh, 1984—. Sgt. U.S. Army, 1970-72. Mem. Internat. Mcpl. Lawyers Assn., N.C. Bar Assn. Home: 1100 W Forest Hills Blvd Durham NC 27707-1626 Office: NC Assn County Commrs PO Box 1488 Raleigh NC 27602-1488

BLACKBURN, JOHN D(AVID), legal educator, lawyer; b. Connersville, Ind., Dec. 19, 1949; s. James Edwin and Julia Jane (Hubbard) B.; m. Vitalia Berezina, Oct. 29, 1999; children— Jennifer Anne, Melissa Christine. B.S., Ind. State U., 1971; J.D., U. Cin., 1974. Bar: Ohio 1974. Instr. bus. adminstrn. U. Cin., 1974-75; asst. prof. bus. Ohio State U., Columbus, 1975-80, assoc. prof., 1981— ; vis. asst. prof. U. Pa., Phila., 1980-81, Ind. U., Bloomington, summer 1980; vis. assoc. prof. U. Fla., Gainesville, 2002. Author (with Elliot I. Klayman and Martin H. Malin): Legal Environment of Business, 5th edit. 1994; (with Julius Getman) Labor Relations: Law, Practice, and Policy, 1983; author (with others): Modern Business Law, 3d edit., 1990, Law and Business, 1987; (with Jack Steiber) Protecting Unorganized Employees Against Unjust Discharge, 1984; editor-in-chief: Jour. Legal Studies Edn., 1990-92, Am. Bus. Law Jour., 1986-89. Mem. Am. Bus. Law Assn. (best article award 1980). E-mail: blackburn.3@osu.edu. Home: 382 E Sycamore St Columbus OH 43206-2278 Office: Ohio State Univ 2100 Neil Ave Columbus OH 43210

BLACKBURN, RICHARD WALLACE, lawyer; b. Detroit, Mich., Apr. 21, 1942; s. Wallace Manders and E. Jean (Beetham) B.; m. Dede Frances Reid, Aug. 29, 1964; children: David Thomas, Jeffrey Manders, Megan Louise. Student, Baldwin-Wallace Coll., 1960-62; AB, Mich. State U., 1964; JD, George Washington U., 1967; grad. advanced mgmt. program, Harvard Bus. Sch., 1988. Labor atty. Chesapeake & Potomac Tele. Co., Washington, 1967-70; gen. corp. atty. Chesapeake & Potomac Telephone Co., Richmond, Va., 1970-74; regulatory atty. AT&T, NYC, 1974-76; gen. atty. New Eng. Tele. Co., Boston, 1976-81, v.p., gen. counsel, 1981—91; exec. v.p., gen. counsel, sec. Duke Energy, Charlotte, NC, 1997; sr. positions NYNEX World Wide Svc. Group, 1991; pres. and group exec. NYNEX Worldwide Comm., 1995—96. Dir. New Eng. Legal Found., 1988; mem. Concord (Mass.) Zoning Bd. Appeals, chmn., 1984, 87; trustee Mass. Eye and Ear Infirmary. Mem. Fed. Communications Bar Assn., Am. Bar Assn., Newcomen Soc. N.Am., Boston Bar Assn. Republican. Episcopalian. Office: Duke Energy Corp 526 S Church St PO Box 1006 Charlotte NC 28202-1244*

BLACKBURN, SHARON LOVELACE, federal judge; b. Pensacola, Fla., May 7, 1950; BA, U. Ala., 1973; JD, Samford U., 1977. Law clk. to Hon. Robert Varner U.S. Dist. Ct. Ala., 1977-78; staff atty. Birmingham Area Legal Svcs., 1979; asst. U.S. atty. U.S. Atty's. Office, 1979-91; judge U.S. Dist. Ct. (no. dist.) Ala., Birmingham, 1991—. Mem. Birmingham Bar Assn. Office: US Dist Ct 730 Hugo L Black US Cthouse 1729 5th Ave N Birmingham AL 35203-2000*

BLACKBURN, TERENCE LEE, dean; b. Pitts., Pa., July 13, 1948; s. Glenn E. and Ruby E. (Fornof) B.; m. Catherine T. Dwyer, Sept. 7, 1974; children: Allegra, Brandon. BA, Duquesne U., 1970; JD, Columbia U., 1973. Bar: Ohio 1973, N.Y. 1975, N.J. 1994. Asst. atty. gen. Ohio Atty. Gen. Office, Columbus, 1973-75; assoc. Aranow Brodsky et al, N.Y.C., 1975-78, Kronish Lieb et al, N.Y.C., 1978-82; v.p., gen. counsel First Nat. Properties, N.Y.C., 1982-88; prof. law Sch. Seton Hall U., Newark, 1988-97, 99-00, acting dean Sch. Diplomacy South Orange, N.J., 1997-99; dean Detroit Coll. Law Mich. State U., 2000—. Contbr. articles to profl. jours. Capt. U.S. Army, 1973. Fulbright scholar Coun. Internat. Exch. Scholars, 1995. Office: MSU Detroit Coll Law 368 Law College Bldg East Lansing MI 48824

BLACKBURN, THOMAS IRVEN, lawyer; b. Columbus, Ohio, May 4, 1949; s. Ervin C. and Dorothy E. (Wonn) B.; m. Sharon C. Mahoney, July 7, 1973; children: Ashley Anne, Christopher Ryan. BS, Ohio State U., 1972, JD, 1979. Bar: Ohio 1979, U.S. Dist. Ct. (so. dist.) Ohio 1980, U.S. Tax Ct. 1986. Computer software developer IBM, Atlantic City, 1972-76; assoc. Williams & Deeg, Columbus, 1979-81, Denmead, Gerrity & Tsitouris, Columbus, 1981-86; ptnr. Denmead, Blackburn & Brown, Columbus, 1986-92, Buckley King & Bluso, Columbus, 1992—2002, Buckley King, 2002—. Pres. Strawberry Farms Civic Assn., Columbus, 1986-87, v.p., 1984-86; mem. steering com. Westerville (Ohio) Sch. Levy Com., 1984, 88; mem. steering com. Westerville Sch. Bond Issue, 1986; trustee Newsreel Club Inc., Columbus, 1986-92. Mem. ABA, Ohio Bar Assn., Columbus Bar Assn. (admissions com. 1985—, mcpl. ct. com. 1982-85, common pleas ct. com. 1982-85, ins. com. 1987-89), Ohio Assn. Civil Trial Attys., Columbus Claims Assn. (officer, bd. dirs. 1996—, pres., 2000), Ctrl. Ohio Soccer Assn. (bd. dirs. 1997—, pres. 1999—), Def. Rsch. Inst., Athletic Club of Columbus, Rotary. Avocations: golf, running. (614) 461-5630. General civil litigation, Insurance, Product liability. Home: 888 Chelsea Ln Westerville OH 43081-2716 Office: Buckley King One Columbus 10 W Broad St Ste 1300 Columbus OH 43215-3482 E-mail: blackburn@bucklaw.com.

BLACKFORD, ROBERT NEWTON, lawyer, director; b. Cin., Feb. 5, 1937; s. Robert Criley and Virginia Pendleton (Yowell) B.; m. Margaret Ann Williams, July 22, 1961; children: William Pendleton, John Whitner. BSBA, U. Fla., 1960; JD, Emory U., 1968. Bar: Fla. 1968, Ga. 1968. Mem., dir. Maguire, Voorhis & Wells, P.A., Orlando, Fla., 1972-98, sec., treas., 1972-95; ptnr. Holland & Knight LLP, Orlando, 1998—2001. Dir. Hughes Supply, Inc., Orlando, 1970—, sec., 1972-96, asst. sec., 1996-98; dir., sec. Princeton Fin. Corp., 1987-94. Mem. Orlando Mcpl. Planning Bd., 1969-75, Orlando Downtown Devel. Bd., 1972-77, chmn., 1975-77, bd. dirs. Crime Commn., Inc., 1985-88; mem. Orange County's Refuse Disposal Citizens Coordination Com., 1988-90, Orange County Solid Waste Adv. Bd., 1992-96; mem. neighborhood concerns com. Orlando Naval Tng. Ctr. Base Closing Commn., 1994-96; trustee Chelsey G. Magruder Found., Inc., 1981—, pres., 1982-85, 92-94, 2000-02, sec./treas., 1998-2000; trustee Orlando Mus. Art, 1980-82, 85-91, pres. 1985-86, chm. bd., 1986-87, v.p. 1989-91; ruling elder First Presbyn. Ch., Orlando, 1989-2003, tchr., 1970-2000; bd. dirs. Univ. Club Orlando, 1994-97, sec., 1994-96. Mem. Fla. Bar Assn., Ga. Bar Assn., Orlando Area C. of C. (pres. 1980, chmn. bd. dirs. 1981), Orange County Hist. Soc. (bd. dirs. 1980-83), Country Club Orlando, Rotary Club Orlando (pres. 1991-92). Democrat. Corporate, general, Mergers and acquisitions, Securities. Home: 2931 Nela Ave Orlando FL 32809-6178 E-mail: rblackf398@aol.com.

BLACKMAN, JEFFREY WILLIAM, lawyer; b. L.A., Oct. 24, 1948; s. Ralph Leonard and Judith Esther (Glantz) B. BA, U. Ariz., 1970, JD, 1976. Bar: Ariz. 1976, U.S. Dist. Ct. Ariz. 1977, U.S. Ct. Appeals (9th cir.) 1980, U.S. Supreme Ct. 1980, U.S. Dist. Ct. (no. dist.) Calif. 1988. Pvt. practice, Oracle, Ariz., 1977-85; assoc. various law firms, Phoenix, Tucson, 1986-87; pvt. practice Tucson, 1988—. Participant March for the Animals, Washington, 1990, 96. 2d lt. ROTC, U.S. Army. Recipient Cert. of Appreciation, Ctr. for Environ. Protecton of the Whale Protection Fund, 1984, UNICEF, Defenders of Wildlife, Nat. Humane Edn. Soc., ASPCA, Humane Soc. of U.S., Tiger Haven, Wine Diploma, San Francisco Wine Inst. Wine Adv. Bd., 1964, Cert. of Appreciation for Service in Israel during the Gulf War, Nation of Israel; named Ptnr. for Life, Cal Farley's Boy Ranch, Amarillo, Tex., 1982. Mem. State Bar Ariz., Pima County Bar Assn., Mensa, Alliance Francaise, Animal Legal Def. Fund. Avocations: rock drummer, tennis, desert hiking, gardening, animal welfare. Criminal, General practice, Juvenile. Office: PO Box 41624 Tucson AZ 85717-1624

BLACKMAN, JOHN CALHOUN, IV, lawyer; b. Monroe, La., Dec. 13, 1944; s. John Calhoun Blackman III and Marie (Collens) Bernstein; m. Judy Swayze, Apr. 19, 1986; children: Carrie Marie, Caroline Frances, Mary Winston. BA, La. State U., 1966, JD, 1969. Bar: La. 1969, U.S. Ct. Appeals (5th cir.) 1969, U.S. Tax Ct. 1972, U.S. Supreme Ct. 1976. Ptnr. Hudson, Potts & Bernstein, Monroe, 1969-79, Blackman, Arnold & Pettway, Monroe, 1979-88, Jones, Walker, Waechter, Poitevent, Carrere & Denegre, Baton Rouge, 1988—. Adj. prof. law La. State U., Baton Rouge, 1990-93; mem. com. of 100 econ. devel., 1993—; mem. trust code com. La. State Law Inst., 1982—. Mem. La. State U. Found.; mem. adv. commn. Estate Planning and Adminstrn. Cert., 1994—99, chmn., 1998—99. Fellow Am. Bar Found., Am. Coll. Trusts and Estates Counsel (bus. planning com.), Am. Coll. Tax Counsel; mem. ABA (litigation task force, employee benefits com., taxation sect.), La. Bar Assn. (cert. tax specialist, cert. estate planning and adminstrn. specialist, chmn. taxation sect. 1976-77, chmn. liaison com. with dist. dir. IRS 1981-82, liaison com. with regional commrs. office), Estate Planning Coun. N.E. La. (pres. 1975-76), NASD (arbitrator). Republican. Episcopalian. Corporate taxation, Estate taxation, Personal income taxation. Office: Jones Walker et al 8555 United Plaza Blvd Fl 5 Baton Rouge LA 70809 E-mail: blackman@eatal.net., jblackman@joneswalker.com.

BLACKMAN, KENNETH ROBERT, lawyer; b. Providence, May 19, 1941; s. Edward and Beatrice (Wolf) B.; m. Meryl June Rosenthal, June 7, 1964; children: Michael, Susan, Kevin. AB, Brown U., 1962; LLB, MBA, Columbia U., 1965. Bar: N.Y. 1966. Law clk. to U.S. Dist. Judge, 1965-66; ptnr. Fried, Frank, Harris, Shriver & Jacobson, N.Y.C., 1966—. Mem. ABA, N.Y. Bar Assn., Assn. Bar City of N.Y., Phi Beta Kappa, Beta Gamma Sigma Bankruptcy, Corporate, general, Securities. Office: Fried Frank Harris Shriver & Jacobson 1 New York Plz Fl 22 New York NY 10004-1980

BLACKMAR, CHARLES BLAKEY, state supreme court justice; b. Kansas City, Mo., Apr. 19, 1922; s. Charles Maxwell and Eleanor (Blakey) B.; m. Ellen Day Bonnifield, July 18, 1943 (dec. 1983); children: Charles A. (dec.), Thomas J., Lucy E. Blackmar Alpaugh, Elizabeth S., George B.; m. Jeanne Stephens Lee, Oct. 5, 1984. AB summa cum laude, Princeton U., 1942; JD, U. Mich., 1948; LLD (hon.), St. Louis U., 1991. Bar: Mo. 1948. Pvt. practice law, Kansas City; ptnr. Swanson, Midgley and predecessors, 1952-66; profl. lectr. U. Mo. at Kansas City, 1949-58; prof. law St. Louis U., 1966-82, prof. emeritus; judge Supreme Ct. Mo., 1982—92, chief justice, 1989-91, sr. status, 1992; spl. asst. atty. gen. Mo., 1969-77; labor arbitrator, active sr. judge, 1992—. Chmn. Fair Pub. Accommodations Commn. Kansas City, 1964-66; mem. Commn. Human Rels. Kansas City, 1965-66. Author: (with Volz and others) Missouri Practice, 1953, West's Federal Practice Manual, 1957, 71, (with Devitt) Federal Jury Practice and Instructions, 1970, 3d edit., 1977, (with Devitt, Wolff and O'Malley) 4th edit., 1988-92; contbr. numerous articles on probate and corp. law to profl. publs. Mem. Jackson County Rep. Com., 1952-58; mem. Mo. Rep. Com., 1956-58. 1st lt., inf. AUS, 1943-46. Decorated Silver Star, Purple Heart. Mem. Am. Law Inst., Nat. Acad. Arbitrators, Mo. Bar (spl. lectr. insts.), Disciples Peace Fellowship, Scribes (pres. 1986-87), Order of Coif, Phi Beta Kappa. Mem. Christian Ch. (Disciples Of Christ). Home: 612 Hobbs Rd Jefferson City MO 65109-1075 Home (Winter): 2 Seaside Ln Apt 402 Belleair FL 33756-1989 E-mail: bcbb543@aol.com.

BLACKMON, WILLIE EDWARD BONEY, judge, military officer; b. Houston, Apr. 16, 1951; s. A. L. and Florence (Joseph) Blackmon. BBA in Mktg., Tex. A&M U., 1973; JD, Tex. Southern U., 1982. Bar: Nebr. 1984, U.S. Dist. Ct. (ea. dist.) Mich. 1984, U.S. Ct. Mil. Appeals 1984, Mich. 1985, U.S. Supreme Ct. 1987, Tex. 1989, U.S. Dist. Ct. (no. dist.) Tex. 1990, U.S. Dist. Ct. (so. dist.) Tex. 1993. Terr. sales mgr. Gillette Co., 1977-79; sales and mktg. coord. Drilco divsn. Smith Internat., 1973-77; legal intern Gulf Coast Legal Found., Houston, 1982; intern, ind. counsel City of Detroit, 1982-84; judge advocate USAF, Ellsworth AFB, Offutt AFB, S.D., 1984-89, USAFR, Reese AFB, Randolph AFB, Bergstrom AFB, Tex., 1989-94; staff judge advocate lt. col. Tex. Air N.G., Ellington Field, Tex., 1994—. Asst. criminal dist. atty. Lubbock County, Tex., 1990—91, Harris County, Tex., 1991—92; admissions liaison officer USAF Acad., 1990—; pvt. practice, Houston, 1992—97; assoc. mcpl. judge City of Houston, 1995—97, mcpl. judge, 1997—; adj. instr. Judge Adv. Gen.'s Sch. Air U., Maxwell AFB, Ala., 1996—; staff judge adv. 101st Air Refueling Wing, Pisa, Italy, 1996; internat. election supr. Orgn. Security and Coop. in Europe, Bosnia-Herzegovina, 1997; exec. dir. Assn. Minority Mil. Officers, 2000—01; lectr. in field. Bd. adv. Mickey Leland Libr. and Mus., 2003—. Decorated numerous mil. decorations; named to Tex. A&M U. Athletic Hall of Fame, 1994, Wheatley High Disting. Grad. Hall of Fame, 2002; recipient numerous awards. Mem.: NAACP (Alex award 1999), ABA, Coalition Ivorian Intellectuals Am. (adv. com.), Aggie Officers Assn., Houston Bar Assn., Mex.-Am. Bar Assn., Tex. Mcpl. Cts. Assn., Am. Judges Assn., Wolverine Bar Assn., Houston Lawyers Assn., Tex. Assn. African Am. Lawyers, Nat. Bar Assn. (Living Legend award 1990), State Bar Mich., Nebr. Bar Assn., State Bar Tex., Masons. Baptist. Avocations: scuba diving, skiing, hiking, bicycling, dancing. Home: 8766 Pattibob St Houston TX 77029-3334 Office: 1400 Lubbock St Ste 214 Houston TX 77002-1526

BLACKSHEAR, A. T., JR., lawyer; b. Dallas, July 5, 1942; s. A. T. and Janie Louise (Florey) Blackshear; m. Stuart Davis Blackshear. BBA cum laude, Baylor U., 1964, JD cum laude, 1968. CPA Tex.; bar: Tex. 1968, U.S. Ct. Appeals (5th cir.) 1970, U.S. Tax Ct. 1970. Acct. Arthur Andersen & Co., Dallas, 1964-66; assoc. Fulbright & Jaworski, Houston, 1969-75, ptnr., 1975—, chmn. exec. com., 1992—2002. Bd. dirs. Tex. Med. Ctr., Inc. Trustee Baylor Coll. Medicine; chmn. bd. Meml./Hermann Healthcare Sys.; bd. dirs. Sam Houston area coun. Boy Scouts Am.; bd. dirs. Spiritual Leadership Inst. Mem.: ABA, Houston Bar Assn., State Bar Tex., Houston Country Club, Coronado Club, Houston Ctr. Club. Baptist. Health, Corporate taxation, Personal income taxation. Office: Fulbright & Jaworski 1301 Mckinney St Fl 51 Houston TX 77010-3031

BLACKSTOCK, JERRY B. lawyer; b. Monticello, Ga., Mar. 9, 1945; s. J.B. and Eugenia (Jones) B.; m. Margaret Owen, June 10, 1967; children: Towner Anson, Michael Owen, Kendrick. BA, Davidson Coll., 1966; JD, U. Ga., 1969. Bar: Ga. 1969, U.S. Ct. Appeals (5th cir.) 1970, U.S. Supreme Ct. 1978, U.S. Ct. Appeals (11th cir.) 1981, U.S. Ct. Appeals (fed. cir.) 1984. With Powell, Goldstein, Frazer & Murphy, Atlanta, 1969—2002; chair Atlanta litigation team Hunton & Williams, 2002—. Adj. prof. law Emory U., Atlanta, 1975-81; mem. adv. bd. Jour. Intellectual Property Law, U. Ga. Sch. Law, 1992-2001; chair Ga. Jud. Qualifications Commn., 1994-2002. Author: Georgia Appellate Practice Handbook, 1977, Preparation of a Lawsuit for Trial, Pre-Trial Practice, Appellate Practice, 1980; (with others) Georgia Lawyers Basic Practice Handbook, 2d edit. Pres. parents coun. Trinity Sch. Inc., 1981-82; pres. parents club Woodward Acad. Lower Sch., 1986-88, bd. dirs., treas., Woodward Acad. Upper Sch., 1988-91, v.p., 1991-92, pres., 1992-94; chmn. Ga. Athlete Agt. Regulatory Commn., 1989-2000; chmn. bd. dirs. Pastoral Counseling Svc. Atlanta; mem. bd. visitors U. Ga. Sch. Law; bd. trustees Ga. Legal History Found.; mem. Leadership Ga., 1980; mem. Leadership Atlanta, 1990, exec. com., 1991-92; chair bd. trustees Riverside Mil. Acad., 1996—. Recipient Tradition of Excellence award for Def. Lawyer of Yr., State Bar Ga., 2002. Fellow Am. Bar Found., Am. Coll. Trial Lawyers, Internat. Acad. Trial Lawyers, Ga. Bar Assn. (editor-in-chief jour. 1984-85, bd. govs. 1982-98, exec. com. 1990-95, intellectual property law, tech. law and gen. practice and trial sects.), Ga. Bar Found.; mem. ATLA (intellectual property litig. com.), ABA (intellectual property, sci. and tech., tort and ins. practice and litig. sects.), So. Trial Lawyers Assn., Ga. Trial Lawyers Assn., Atlanta Bar Assn. (editor-in-chief Atlanta Lawyer 1972-73), Am. Law Inst., Atlanta Legal Aid Soc. (adv. bd. 1979-86), Atlanta Lawyers Club, Ga. Def. Lawyers Assn. (bd. dirs. 1989-91, dir. Trial Acad. 1987), Am. Bd. Trial Advs. (diplomate, bd. dirs. 1990—, state exec. com. 1985—), Am. Arbitration Assn. (arbitrator, comml. and constrn. panels, Ga.-Ala. adv. com. for large complex cases), Licensing Execs. Soc., Internat., Am. Intellectual Property Law Assn., Computer Law Assn., Davidson Coll. Atlanta Alumni Assn. (pres. 1982-83), Bleckley Am. Inn of Ct. (master of the bench), Commerce Club, Old War Horse Lawyers Club, Cherokee Town and Country Club, 191 Club. Methodist. Avocation: running. Federal civil litigation, General civil litigation, Intellectual property. Home: 3364 Chatham Rd NW Atlanta GA 30305-1140 Office: Hunton & Williams 4100 Bank of Am Plz 600 Peachtree St Atlanta GA 30308 Fax: 404-888-4190. E-mail: jblackstock@hunton.com.

BLACKWELL, BRUCE BEUFORD, lawyer; b. Gainesville, Fla., July 23, 1946; s. Benjamin B. and Doris Juanita (Heagy) B.; m. Julie McMillan, July 12, 1969; children: Blair Allison, Brooke McMillan. BA, Fla. State U., 1968, JD with honors, 1974. Bar: Fla. 1975, Ga. 1977, NY 1980, U.S. Supreme Ct. 1979. Atty. So. Bell Tel. & Telegraph Co., Charlotte, N.C., 1975-76, Atlanta, 1976-78; antitrust atty. AT&T, Orlando and N.Y.C., 1978-80; atty. Sun Banks, Inc., Orlando, Fla., 1980; assoc. Peed & King, P.A., Orlando, 1981-84; shareholder King & Blackwell, P.A., Orlando, 1984-97, King, Blackwell & Downs, P.A., 1997—. Counselor, master to First Ctrl. Fla. Inns of Ct., 1999—. Bd. dirs. Legal Aid Soc., Orlando, 1986-88; chmn. Winter Park (Fla.) Civil Svc. Bd., 1992-94; trustee Fla. State U. Found., 1985-86. Capt. USAF, 1968-72. Recipient award of excellence Legal Aid Soc., 1993, Judge J.C. Stone Pro Bono Disting. Svc. award, 1996, Annual Friend of FAWL award Fla. Assn. Women Lawyers, 1998. Mem. Fla. Bar (chmn. 9th cir. grievance com. 1985-87, chmn. mid-yr. meeting 1986, chmn. 9th cir. fee arbitration com. 1992-94, bd. govs. 1994-98, vice chair statewide disciplinary rev. com. 1995-96, co-chair 1997-98, vice-chmn. access to cts. com. 1995-97, chmn. annual meeting com. 1997, mem. supreme ct. spl. com. on pro bono svcs. 1996-97, mem. com. to determine need for a new DCA 1998, Fla. Bar Presidents' Pro Bono Svc. award 1997, chair spl. com. on solo/small firm practice 1997-98, mem. rules com. 1997-98, mem. edn. work force 1996-97), Fla. Bar Found. (life mem., bd. dirs. exec. com., chmn., adminstrn. justice com. 1998-2004), Orange County Bar Assn. (exec. coun. 1983-86, pres. 1987-88, co-chair fair campaign practices com. 1998-2001, William E. Trickel, Jr. Professionalism award 2003), Fla. State U. Alumni Assn. (nat. pres. 1985-86), Orlando Touchdown Club (pres. 1996-97), Gold Key, Order of Omega, Omicron Delta Kappa. Democrat. Presbyterian. Avocation: study of china. General civil litigation, Family and matrimonial, Personal injury (including property damage). Home: 1624 Roundelay Ln Winter Park FL 32789-4042 Office: PO Box 1631 Orlando FL 32802-1631

BLACKWELL, JACQUELINE MARIE, prosecutor; b. Blossburg, Pa., May 29, 1965; d. James George and Sylvia Catherine Blackwell. Student, Seton Hall Coll., 1983—86; BS, St. Vincent Coll., Latrobe, Pa., 1987; JD, Ohio No. U., 1990. Bar: Fla. 1990, Pa. 1991, U.S. Dist. Ct. (we. dist.) Pa. 1991. Instr. Mcpl. Police Acad., Indiana, 1996—. Mem.: ATLA, ABA, Indiana County Bar Assn., Pa. Bar Assn., Fla. Bar, St. Vincent Alumni Assn., Fraternal Order of Police, Fraternal Order of Eagles Ladies' Aux., Delta Theta Phi. Avocations: travel, reading. Home and Office: 370 N 8th St Indiana PA 15701 Office Fax: 724-465-2246. E-mail: jblackwell@yourinter.net.

BLACKWELL, THOMAS FRANCIS, lawyer; b. Detroit, Nov. 25, 1942; m. Sandra L. Kroczek; children: Robert T., Katherine M. BA, U. Notre Dame, Ind., 1964; JD, U. Mich., 1967. Bar: Mich and U.S. Dist. Ct. (we. and ea. dists.) Mich. 1968, U.S. Ct. Appeals (6th cir.) 1969. Assoc. Smith, Haughey, Rice & Roegge, Grand Rapids, Mich., 1967-71, ptnr., 1971—, treas., 1979-85, 89—, exec. com., 1985-89. Spl. asst. atty. gen. State of Mich., 1972-82. Fellow Mich. State Bar Found.; mem. ABA, State Bar Mich., Grand Rapids Bar Assn., FBA, Products Liability Adv. Coun., Mich. Def. Trial Attys., Peninsular, Kent Country Club. General civil litigation, Personal injury (including property damage), Product liability. Office: Smith Haughey Rice & Roegge 250 Monroe Ave NW Ste 200 Grand Rapids MI 49503-2251 E-mail: tblackwell@shrr.com.

BLADEN, EDWIN MARK, lawyer, judge; b. Detroit, Feb. 2, 1939; s. Philip and Ruth Sara (Millstein) B.; m. Paula Dee Maskin, Sept. 2, 1962; children: Philip, Sara, Jeffrey. BA, Wayne State U., 1962, JD, 1965. Asst. atty. gen. State of Mich., Lansing, 1965-86; mng. atty. Moran & Bladen, Lansing, 1987-93; pvt. practice, East Lansing, Mich., 1994-97; adminstrv. law judge USCG, 1999—. Author: Consumer Law of Michigan, 1978. Mem. Dem. Polit. Reform Comm., Mich., 1968. With U.S. Army Security, 1957-60, Korea. Recipient Alexander Freeman scholarship Wayne State U., Detroit, 1962-65. Mem. State Bar Mich. (chmn. anti-trust sect., treas./sec. 1990-94), Nat. Assn. Fraud Units (pres. 1985-86). Office: 3448 Jackson Fed Bldg 915 2nd Ave Seattle WA 98174-1009

BLAHER, NEAL JONATHAN, lawyer; b. Lowell, Mass., Nov. 6, 1960; BA in Psychology, U. Pa., 1981; JD, Villanova U., 1986. Bar: Pa. 1986, N.J. 1986, U.S. Dist. Ct. N.J. 1986, Fla. 1987, U.S. Dist. Ct. (ea. dist.) Pa. 1987, U.S. Ct. Appeals (3rd cir.) 1987, U.S. Ct. Appeals (11th cir.) 1988, U.S. Dist. Ct. (mid. dist.) Fla. 1988, U.S. Supreme Ct. 1997. Intern law clk. to presiding justice Cir. Ct., Phila., 1984-85; paralegal Fineman & Bach, Phila., 1982-83, assoc., 1986-88, Allen, Dyer, Doppelt, Milbrath & Gilchrist, P.A., Orlando, Fla., 1988-93; pvt. practice Orlando, 1993—. Mem. Fla. Bar, Orange County Bar Assn., Pub. Investors Arbitration Bar Assn. Avocation: music. Franchising, Securities, Trademark and copyright. Home and Office: PO Box 804 Orlando FL 32802-0804

BLAIN, PETER CHARLES, lawyer; b. Milw., Nov. 15, 1949; s. Emile Octave and Mary Catherine (Usalis) B.; m. Katherine Stauber, June 12, 1971; children: Thomas Peter, Timothy Charles, Katherine Elizabeth, Peter James. BS, Wis. State U., Stevens Point, 1971; JD, Georgetown U., 1978. Bar: Wis. 1978. Budget analyst VA, Washington, D.C., 1974-78; atty. Reinhart, Boerner, Van Deuren S.C. and predecessor firms, Milw., 1978—. Chmn. Wis. State Bar Insolvency Sect., 1995-97; lectr. U. Wis., Milw., 1984—. Contbr. articles to profl. jours. 2d Lt. U.S. Army, 1972-74. Listed Best Lawyers in Am., Woodward/White, 1987—. Mem. Milw. Bar Bankruptcy Sect. (prog. chmn. 1984-85, sect. chmn. 1986-87, co-chair bankruptcy sect. bench/bar com. 1998—), bankruptcy local rules com., 2002—. Democrat. Roman Catholic. Avocation: reading. Bankruptcy. Office: Reinhart Boerner Van Deuren 1000 N Water St Ste 1800 Milwaukee WI 53202-6650 E-mail: pblain@reinhartlaw.com.

BLAIN, ROBERT KRIEGER, lawyer; b. N.Y.C., July 6, 1947; s. Ewart M. and Grace M. (Krieger) B.; m. Karen M. Konrath, Mar. 4, 1978; children: Adam, Lindsay. BA, Cornell U., 1969; JD with honors, U. Ill., 1973. Bar: Ill. 1973, U.S. Dist. Ct. (no. dist.) Ill. 1973, U.S. Ct. Appeals (7th cir.) 1984, U.S. Dist. Ct. (ea. dist.) Wis. 1984. Assoc. Schiff, Hardin & Waite, Chgo., 1973-79, Lieberman, Levy, Baron, Chgo., 1979-80; ptnr. Altheimer & Gray, Chgo., 1980-91; prin. Offices Robert Blain, Chgo., 1991—. Lay min. St. Martins Ch., Des Plaines, Ill., 1996—; mem. Episcopal Lawyers Vol., Chgo., 1994—. Sgt. USMC, 1969-75. Mem. ABA, Chgo. Bar Assn., Order of Coif. Avocation: golf. Federal civil litigation, General civil litigation, State civil litigation. Office: Michael A Maciejewski Ltd 945 Oaklawn Ave Elmhurst IL 60126

BLAIR, JAMES NEWELL, lawyer; b. Washington, July 29, 1940; s. Newell and Greta (Flinterman) B.; m. Wendy Ann Miller, Apr. 22, 1978; 1 child, Hilary Ann. AB, Dartmouth Coll., 1962; JD, Harvard U., 1970. Bar: N.Y. 1971, U.S. Dist. Ct. (so. dist.) N.Y. 1974, U.S. Ct. Appeals (2d cir.) 1975. Assoc. White & Coch, N.Y.C., 1970-71, Rogers Hoge & Hills, N.Y.C., 1972-80, ptnr., 1980-86; pvt. practice N.Y.C., 1987-88; ptnr. Teitler

& Teitler, N.Y.C., 1988-91, Loselle, Greenawalt, Kaplan, Blair, N.Y.C., 1991-99, Wolman, Babitt & King, 1999—. Arbitrator small claims div. N.Y.C. Civil Ct., U.S. Dist. Ct. (ea. dist.) N.Y. Bd. dirs., treas. 600 West End Ave. Owner's Corp., N.Y.C., 1980—; mem. vestry Ch. of Christ the King, Stone Ridge, N.Y., 1991-96; mem. coun. Episcopal Diocese N.Y. Lt. USN, 1962-67. Mem. N.Y. State Bar Assn. (fed. cts. com. 1986-89, exec. com. comml. and fed. litigation sect. 1989—, chair civil practice law and rules com. 1991-95, 2000—, mem. adv. com. civil practice to chief adminstr. ctrs.), Assn. of Bar of City of N.Y. (com. on nuclear energy and the law 1989-92, others), Harvard Club of N.Y.C. Democrat. Episcopalian. Avocations: chamber music, cross-country skiing, rebuilding farmhouse. Bankruptcy, General civil litigation. Home: 600 West End Ave Apt 10A New York NY 10024-1610 Office: 521 5th Ave New York NY 10175-0003 E-mail: jblair@wbklaw.net.

BLAIR, M. WAYNE, lawyer; b. Spokane, Washington, Oct. 17, 1942; BS in Elec. Engr., U. Washington, 1965, JD, 1968. Bar: Wash. 1968. Mem. Wash. State Bd. for Jud. Adminstrn., 1995-2000. With USAF, 1968-72. Recipient Helen M. Geisness award, 1987, President's award, 1990. Mem. ABA (Ho. of Dels. 1988-91), Am. Judicature Soc., Washington State Bar Assn. (bd. govs. 1991-94, pres. 1998-99), Seattle-King County Bar Assn. (trustee 1981-83, pres. 1987-88). Alternative dispute resolution, Corporate, general, Property, real (including real estate development, water). Office: 5800 Bank of America Twr 701 5th Ave Seattle WA 98104-7097

BLAIR, RICHARD BRYSON, lawyer; b. Athens, Ohio, Oct. 1, 1945; s. Richard Holmes and Doris Ruth Blair; m. Ellen A. Riehl, Aug. 24, 1968; children: Heather Ann, Heidi Lynn, Richard Holmes II, Molly Jane. BA, Franklin and Marshall Coll., 1967; JD, Ohio Northern U., 1970. Bar: Ohio 1970, U.S. Dist. Ct. (no. dist.) Ohio 1972. Assoc. Roth and Stephens, Youngstown, Ohio, 1970-75, ptnr., 1976-77; ptnr., v.p. Roth, Stephens, Blair and Co. LPA, Youngstown, 1977—2000, Roth, Blair, Roberts, Strasfeld & Lodge Co., LPA, Youngstown, pres., 2000—. Bd. dirs. Greater Youngstown Coalition of Christians, 1994-98, co-chmn., 1996-98; trustee, mem. bd. edn. Eagle Hts. Acad. Mem. Ohio Bar Assn. (bd. dirs. potential devel. program), Mahoning County Bar Assn., Internat. Assn. Ins. Counsel, Ohio Assn. Civil Trial Attys., Def. Rsch. Inst., Nat. Assn. R.R. Trial Counsel, Christian Legal Soc. Avocations: family, church activities, golf, jogging. General civil litigation, Insurance, Personal injury (including property damage). Home: 253 Wildwood Dr Youngstown OH 44512-3340 Office: Roth Blair Roberts Strasfeld & Lodge LPA City Centre One 100 Federal Plz East Ste 600 Youngstown OH 44503

BLAIR, WILLIAM MCCORMICK, JR., lawyer; b. Chgo., Oct. 24, 1916; s. William McCormick and Helen (Bowen) B.; m. Catherine Gerlach, Sept. 9, 1961; 1 son, William McCormick III. AB, Stanford U., 1940; LL.B., U. Va., 1947. Bar: Ill. 1947, D.C. 1972. Assoc. firm Wilson & McIlvaine, Chgo., 1947-50; adminstrv. asst. to Gov. Adlai E. Stevenson of Ill., 1950-52; ptnr. firm Stevenson, Rifkind & Wirtz, Chgo., 1955-61, Paul, Weiss, Rifkind, Wharton & Garrison, N.Y.C., 1957-61; U.S. ambassador to Denmark, 1961-64, to Philippines, 1964-67; gen. dir. John F. Kennedy Ctr., 1968-72; ptnr. firm Surrey & Morse, Washington, 1978-84, of counsel, 1984-86. Bd. dirs. Am.-Scandinavian Found., N.Y.C.; v.p. bd. dirs. Albert and Mary Lasker Found., N.Y.C., 1968-98. Capt. USAAF, 1942-46. Decorated Bronze Star U.S.; officer Order of Crown, Belgium; Order of Sikatuna, Philippines; comdr. cross Order of Dannebrog 1st class, Denmark). Mem. Am. Coun. Ambs. (vice chmn., pres. 1985-89), Soc. Animal Protective Legis. (trustee), Phi Delta Phi. Office: 2510 Foxhall Rd NW Washington DC 20007-1123

BLAKE, JONATHAN DEWEY, lawyer; b. Long Branch, N.J., June 14, 1938; s. Edgar Bond and Haven (Johnstone) B.; m. Prudence Anne Rowsell, Dec. 22, 1964 (div. June 1977); children: Juliet Haven, Deborah Anne, Susanna Rowsell; m. Elizabeth L. Shriver, Dec. 9, 1977; children: Jonathan Shriver-Blake, Molly Shriver-Blake. BA magna cum laude, Yale U., 1960, LLB cum laude, 1964; BA, MA, Oxford U., Eng., 1962. Bar: D.C. 1965, U.S. Supreme Ct. 1973, U.S. Dist. Ct. D.C. 1965, U.S. Dist. Ct. Md. 1985, U.S. Ct. Appeals (D.C. cir.) 1965, U.S. Ct. Appeals (2d cir.) 1973. Assoc. Covington & Burling, Washington, 1964-72, ptnr., 1972—, chmn. mgmt. com., 1996—2002. Tchr. Howard U., Washington, 1965-70, U. Va., Charlottesville, 1965-70. Contbr. articles to profl. jours. Pres. Great Falls Citizens Assn., Va., 1967-68; exec. com., bd. dirs. Deerfield Acad, Mass., 1980-85. Rhodes scholar, 1960; recipient Gordon Brown prize, 1959. Mem. ABA (chair internat. telecomm. com. 1993-2000), Fed. Comm. Bar Assn. (pres. 1980-85). Administrative and regulatory, Communications, Private international. Home: 4926 Hillbrook Ln NW Washington DC 20016-3208 Office: Covington & Burling 1201 Pennsylvania Ave NW Washington DC 20004-7566 E-mail: jblake@cov.com.

BLAKE, WILLIAM GEORGE, lawyer; b. Lamoni, Iowa, Dec. 10, 1949; s. George Charles and Mildred Lucille (Norman) B.; m. Barbara Kay Holseid, May 28, 1972; children: Jennifer Christine, Angela Sue. BA, Graceland Coll., Lamoni, 1972; JD, U. Nebr., 1975. Bar: Nebr. 1975, U.S. Dist. Ct. Nebr. 1975. Asst. city atty. City of Lincoln (Nebr.), 1975-79, chief asst. city atty., 1979-84; assoc. Pierson, Ackerman Fitchett, Akin & Hunzeker, Lincoln, 1984-85; ptnr. Pierson, Fitchett, Hunzeker, Blake & Loftis, Lincoln, 1986—. Judge Nebr. Commn. on Indsl. Rels., 2000—. Vice chmn. Lincoln Parks and Recreation Bd., 1987-88, chmn., 1989-91; mem. Lincoln Parks and Recreation Found., bd. dirs. 1992—, chmn. 1996-97, 2001—, vice chmn., 1998-2000; judge Nebr. Commn. Indsl. Rels., 2000—. Mem. ABA, Nebr. Bar Assn., Lincoln-Lancaster County Bar Assn. Republican. Mem. Comty. of Christ. Avocation: mountaineering. General civil litigation, Condemnation (eminent domain), Property, real (including real estate development, water). Office: Pierson Fitchett Hunzeker Blake & Loftis PO Box 95109 Lincoln NE 68509-5109 E-mail: wblake@pierson-law.com.

BLAKEMAN, ROYAL EDWIN, lawyer; b. N.Y.C., June 9, 1923; s. Jesse Herbert and Edythe Roslyn (Siegel) B.; m. Edith Hughes, Sept. 1, 1945; children: Carol, Elizabeth, Forrest. BA, Hofstra Coll., 1942; LLB cum laude, NYU, 1947. Bar: N.Y. 1947, U.S. Dist. Ct. (so. dist.) N.Y. 1956, U.S. Ct. Appeals (2d cir.) 1972, Calif. 1973, U.S. Supreme Ct. 1973. Pvt. practice, Lindenhurst, N.Y., 1947-51; assoc. Jack J. Katz, N.Y.C., 1951-53, Marshall Bratter, Greene & Klein, N.Y.C., 1953-55; ptnr. Marshall, Bratter, Greene, Allison & Tucker (specializing in theatrical law), N.Y.C., 1955-81; of counsel Pryor, Cashman, Sherman & Flynn, N.Y.C., 1981-91, Robert M. Blakeman & Assocs., Valley Stream, N.Y., 1991—; gen. counsel Nat. Acad. Rec. Arts and Scis. Officer, dir. Mark Goodson Prodns. Mem. editl. bd. TV Quar. Mem. TV com. Anti Defamation League, N.Y. Served to chief petty officer U.S. Maritime Service, 1942-46. Recipient George M. Esterbrook Disting. Svc. award Hofstra Alumni Assn., 1966. Mem. Nat. Acad. TV Arts and Scis. (pres., bd. govs. N.Y.C. chpt.; past nat. pres., trustee), Nat. Youth Coun., Nat. Acad. Rec. Arts and Scis. (gen. counsel 1977-2002, Trustees award 2003), Dads Club (Long Beach) (pres. 1955). Avocations: golf, bridge, music. Home: 750105B Lido Blvd Long Beach NY 11561-5236 Office: Robert M Blakeman & Assocs 108 S Franklin Ave Valley Stream NY 11580-6105 E-mail: rmbassoc98@aol.com.

BLAKESLEE, WESLEY DANIEL, lawyer, consultant; b. Wilkes-Barre, Pa., May 28, 1947; s. Daniel Leo and Ann Blakeslee; m. Georgia Carroll Croft, July 28, 1973; children: Jaime Kiersten, Christopher Justin, Shaun Michael. BS, Pa. State U., 1969; JD, U. Md.-Balt., 1976. Bar: Md. 1976, U.S. Dist. Ct. Md. 1977, U.S. Tax Ct. 1984. Sys. analyst NASA, Greenbelt, Md., 1969-76; assoc. Semmes, Bowen & Semmes, Balt., 1976-78; pvt. practice Dulany & Davis, Westminster, Md., 1978-83; prin. Wesley D. Blakeslee, P.C., Westminster, 1984—2000; of counsel Blakeslee & Wallace PC, Westminster, 2000—. Assoc. Gen. Couns., Johns Hopkins Univ., 1999—, lectr., dir. computer devel. U. Md. Law Sch., Balt., 1984-89; dir. Union Nat. Bank, 1988-2000. Co-author, editor: Maryland District Court Practice, 1981, rev. 1983; author: Understanding Computers, 1984, 3d edit., 2003; co-author: Computers, 1984, UCITA, 2000. Bd. govs. Md. Law Sch. Fund, Balt., 1982—90. Mem. ABA, Fed. Bar Assn. (treas. Balt. chpt. 1984-90), Md. Bar Assn. (young lawyers sect. coun. 1982-84, outstanding svc. award 1984, litigation sect. coun. 1982—, chair 1995), Carroll County Bar Assn. (treas. 1984), Nat. Assn. Coll. and Univ. Attys. (co-chair intellectual property sect. 2000-01), Order of Coif, Delta Theta Phi. Roman Catholic. Commercial, contracts (including sales of goods; commercial financing), Intellectual property, Personal injury (including property damage). Home: 980 Hook Rd Westminster MD 21157-7335 Office: Johns Hopkins U 113 Garland Hall 3400 N Charles St Baltimore MD 21218 E-mail: blakesleew@jhu.edu.

BLAKLEY, BENJAMIN SPENCER, III, lawyer; b. DuBois, Pa., Sept. 1, 1952; s. Benjamin Spencer Jr. and Mary Jane (Campney) B.; m. Kathleen M. Ellermeyer, Oct. 20, 1989; children: Benjamin Spencer IV, Kevin Charles, Kyra Jane. BA, Grove City Coll., 1974; JD, Duquesne U., 1977. Bar: Pa. 1977. With Blakley & Jones, DuBois, 1977—. Pub. defender Clearfield (Pa.) County, 1977-84; instr. Pa. State U., DuBois, 1979-85; solicitor City of DuBois, 2000. Mem. adv. bd. Salvation Army Pa. Corp., DuBois, 1978-98, 2000--, chmn., 1988-91; mem. DuBois Area Youth Aid Panel, 1984-87; mem. Citizens for Effective Govt., DuBois, 1985-97; trustee DuBois Vol. Fire Dept., 1986-87, treas., 1987-90, mem., instr., 1972--; mem. DuBois Ednl. Found., 1990—, Cath. Counseling and Adoption Svcs., 1996—; bd. dirs. DuBois Sr. and Cmty. Ctr., 1992-97. Mem. Pa. Bar Assn., Clearfield County Bar Assn., DuBois Vol. Fire Dept. Relief Assn. (pres. 1998-2000). Democrat. Methodist. Criminal, Family and matrimonial, General practice, General civil litigation, Property, real (including real estate development, water). Office: Blakley & Jones 90 Beaver Dr Box 6 Du Bois PA 15801-2440 E-mail: bjmlaw@penn.com.

BLAN, OLLIE LIONEL, JR., retired lawyer; b. Ft. Smith, Ark., May 22, 1931; s. Ollie Lionel and Eva Ocie (Cross) B.; m. Allen Conner Gillon, Aug. 19, 1960; children: Bradford Lionel, Elizabeth Ann, Cynthia Gillon. AA, Ft. Smith Jr. Coll., 1951; LL.B., U. Ark., 1954. Bar: Ark. 1954, Ala. 1959, U.S. Dist. Ct. (no. dist.) Ala. 1959, U.S. Dist.Ct. (mid. and so. dist.) Ala. 1960, U.S. Ct. Appeals (5th cir.) 1960, U.S. Ct. Appeals (11th cir.) 1982, U.S. Supreme Ct. 1991. Rsch. analyst Ark. Legis. Coun., 1954-55; law clk. to judge U.S. Dist. Ct. (no. dist.) Ala., Birmingham, 1959-60; assoc. Spain, Gillon & Young, Birmingham, Ala., 1960-64; ptnr. Spain & Gillon and predecessor firms, Birmingham, Ala., 1965-2001; tchr. Am. Inst. Banking, 1965-68; ret., 2001. Speaker Ala. Inst. Continuing Edn., 1978-2001. Contbr. articles to legal jours. Treas. Jefferson County Hist. Assn., 1972-81, vice chmn., 1981-86, chmn., 1986-93; mem. Jefferson County Rep. Exec. Com., 1973-76; mem. Briarwood Sch. Bd., Birmingham, 1982-86; chmn. Here's Life Birmingham, 1986-88. Capt. USMCR, 1955-58, ret. Mem. ABA, Am. Bd. Trial Advocates, Ark. Bar Assn., Ala. Bar Assn. (com. on admissions and legal edn. 1971-74, com. jud. office 1972-76, com. ins. programs, bd. bar commrs. 1987-92, chmn. task force om. on disciplinary rules and enforcement 2001-03), Birmingham Bar Assn. (exec. com. 1986-89), Ala. Def. Lawyers Assn. (v.p. 1983-84, 91-93, bd. dirs. 1988-91, sec.-treas. 1993-94, pres. elect. 1994-95, pres. 1995-96), Am. Coun. Life Ins., Internat. Assn. Def. Counsel (chmn. accident, health and life ins. com. 1987-90, Ala. state rep. 1996-2000), Def. Rsch. Inst. (Ala. state rep. 1996-99, Louis B. Potter profl. svc. award 2000). Baptist. General civil litigation, Insurance, Personal injury (including property damage). Home: 2100 English Village Ln Birmingham AL 35223-1729

BLANCHARD, BRIAN WHEATLEY, lawyer; b. State College, Pa., Nov. 7, 1958; s. Converse Herrick and Margaret (Wheatley) B.; m. Mary Willoughby; children: Will, Ben, Allison. BA, U. Mich., 1980; JD, Northwestern U., 1989. Bar: Ill. 1989, Wis. 1997, U.S. Dist. Ct. (we. dist.) Wis., U.S. Dist. Ct. (no. dist.) Ill., U.S. Ct. Appeals (7th cir.). Reporter Miami Herald, 1980-86; law clk. Hon. Walter J. Cummings U.S. Ct. Appeals (7th cir.), Chgo., 1989-90; asst. U.S. atty. Office of the U.S. Atty., Chgo., 1990-97; assoc. Quarles & Brady, Madison, Wis., 1997-2000; dist. atty. Dane County, Wis., 2000—. Editor-in-chief Northwestern U. Law Rev. Mem. Dane County Bar Assn., Chgo. Coun. Lawyers (bd. govs. 1994-96), Order of Coif. General civil litigation, Criminal. Office: Ste 523 210 Martin Luther King Blvd Madison WI 53703-3346 E-mail: blanchard.brian@mail.da.state.wi.us.

BLANCK, LARS JAKOB, lawyer; b. Oslo, Feb. 27, 1948; s. Einar and Thale B.; m. Anne Karin, Dec. 1, 1984; children: Karianne, Fredrik. Grad., Oslo Comml. Coll., 1966; JD, U. Oslo, 1975. Rsch. asst. U. Oslo, 1972-74, rsch. scholar, 1976, asst. prof., 1976-80; cons. The Data Inspectorate, Oslo, 1980-81; assoc. judge Tromso (Norway) City Ct., 1981-82; atty. at law pvt. practice, Oslo, 1982-91; with Nyborg & Blanck, Oslo, 1992-98; advocate Sander, Truyen & Co., 1999; pres. Lindh Stabell Horten, 2000—. Author: Court Decisions Regarding Computers and Law I, 1980; editor: Data Banks and Society, 1972; contbr. articles to profl. jours. Mem. Norwegian Bar Assn., Gimle Rotary Club. Office: Haakon VIII's Gate PO Box 1364 Vika 0114 Norway E-mail: ljb@lshlaw.no.

BLANCO, RAQUEL, lawyer; b. Madrid, Apr. 10, 1966; d. Manuel Blanco and Francisca Villalba; m. Jose Dominguez, Dec. 3, 1994; children: Beatriz, Jose. Grad. with honors, Joaquin Costa Sch., Madrid, Gran Capitan; Law Degree with honors, Complutense U., Madrid, 1988; M in Co. Law, Inst. de Empresa, Madrid, 1989. Assoc. lawyer Bufete Gimenez Torres, Madrid, 1990—99; sr. assoc. lawyer Baker & McKenzie, Madrid, 1999—. Mem.: Madrid Bar Assn. Mergers and acquisitions, Construction, Commercial, contracts (including sales of goods; commercial financing). Office: Baker & McKenzie Paseo de la Castellana 33 28046 Madrid Spain

BLAND, JAMES THEODORE, JR., lawyer; b. Memphis, June 16, 1950; s. James Theodore and Martha Frances (Downen) B.; m. Pattie L. Martin, Apr. 12, 1974. BBA magna cum laude, Memphis State U., 1972, JD, 1974. Bar: Tenn. 1975, U.S. Dist. Ct. (we. dist.) Tenn. 1976, U.S. Tax Ct. 1976, U.S. Supreme Ct. 1983, U.S. Ct. Claims 1987; cert. Estate Planning specialist. Estate tax atty. IRS, Memphis, 1974-76; atty. Armstrong, Allen, Braden, Goodman, McBride & Prewitt, Memphis, 1976-91; prin. James T. Bland, Jr. and Assocs., Memphis, 1991—. Instr. in taxation, bus. law State Tchr.'s Inst., Memphis, 1975-83; bd. dirs. Thomas W. Briggs Found., Memphis. Fellow Am. Coll. Trust and Estate Counsel, Tenn. Bar Found., Memphis and Shelby County Bar Found. (pres. 1991-93); mem. ABA (legis. initiatives com., taxation sect., specialization in estate planning real property, probate and trust sect., Achievement award 1983, 85), Fed. Bar Assn. (pres. 1987-88, nat. coun. 1979—, bd. dirs. young lawyers divsn. 1979-84, pres. Memphis mid south chpt. 1979-80), Tenn. Bar Assn. (chmn. tax sect. 1984-85, bd. govs. 1984-85, 89-90, 90-91), Tenn. Young Lawyers Conf. (pres. 1985), Memphis Bar Assn. (bd. dirs. 1990-91), Tenn. Soc. CPA's. Republican. Methodist. General civil litigation, Probate (including wills, trusts), Taxation, general. Office: PO Box 770566 Memphis TN 38177-0566 E-mail: blandjr@worldnet.att.net.

BLAND, JOHN LLOYD, lawyer; b. Wichita Falls, Tex., Sept. 20, 1944; Student, Vanderbilt U.; BA, U. Tex., 1967, JD with honors, 1969. Bar: Tex. 1969. Mem. Bracewell & Patterson, LLP, Houston, 1969—. Mem. State Bar Tex., Houston Bar Assn., Phi Delta Phi. Corporate, general, Mergers and acquisitions, Securities. Office: Bracewell & Patterson LLP 2900 S Tower Pennzoil Pl 711 Louisiana St Houston TX 77002-2781 E-mail: jbland@bracepatt.com.

BLAND, J(OHN) RICHARD, lawyer; b. Denver, Oct. 30, 1946; s. Harry Edward and Julia Lenora (Bjelland) B.; m. Carole Jeanne Martin, Aug. 25, 1968. BS, Augustana Coll., 1968; JD, Drake U., 1971. Bar: Iowa 1971, Minn. 1971, U.S. Supreme Ct. 1976. Assoc. Meagher & Geer PLLP, Mpls., 1971-75, ptnr., 1975—. Lectr. Minn. Inst. of Legal Edn., Mpls., 1985—. Fellow Am. Coll. Trial Lawyers; mem. Minn. Bar Assn., Minn. Def. Lawyers Assn. (bd. dirs. 1986-88), Am. Bd. Trial Advocates. General civil litigation, Personal injury (including property damage), Professional liability. Home: 17225 5th Ave N Plymouth MN 55447-3593 Office: Meagher & Geer PLLP 33 S 6th St Ste 4200 Minneapolis MN 55402-3722 E-mail: DBland@Meagher.com.

BLANK, A(NDREW) RUSSELL, lawyer; b. Bklyn., June 13, 1945; s. Lawrence and Joan B.; children: Adam, Marisa. Student, U. N.C., 1963-64; BA, U. Fla., 1966; postgrad., Law Sch., 1966-68; JD, U. Miami, 1970. Bar: Ga. 1971, Fla. 1970; cert. civil trial advocate Nat. Bd. Trial Advocacy. Law asst. Dist. Ct. Judge, Atlanta, 1970-72; ptnr. A. Russell Blank & Assocs., PC, Atlanta, 1985—. Contbr. articles to profl. jours. Pub. adv. com. Atlanta Regional Commn., 1972-74. Recipient Merit award Ga. Bar Assn., 1981. Mem. ABA, ATLA, Atlanta Bar Assn., Ga. Bar Assn. (Merit award 1981), Ga. Trial Lawyers Assn. (officer), Lawyers Club Atlanta, Fla. Bar Assn., Am. Bd. Trial Advocates (advocate, bd. dirs. 2000—, pres. Ga. chpt.), Xenix Soc. (bd. dirs.). Federal civil litigation, State civil litigation, Personal injury (including property damage). Office: 230 Peachtree St NW Ste 2600 Atlanta GA 30303-1516

BLANKE, RICHARD BRIAN, lawyer; b. St. Louis, Oct. 28, 1954; s. Robert H. and Phyllis I. (Kessler) Schaffler. BA, U. Pa., 1977; JD, U. Mo., 1980. Bar: Mo. 1980, U.S. Dist. Ct. (ea. and we. dists.) Mo. 1980. Ptnr. Blanke & Assocs., St. Louis County, Mo., 1980-90, Uthoff, Graeber, Bobinette & Blanke, St. Louis, 1991—. Mem. ABA, ATLA, Mo. Bar Assn., Mo. Assn. Trial Attys., St. Louis Met. Bar Assn. General civil litigation, Family and matrimonial, Personal injury (including property damage). Office: Uthoff Graeber Bobinette & Blanke 906 Olive St Ste 300 Saint Louis MO 63101-1426 E-mail: rblanke@ugbblaw.com.

BLANKER, ALAN HARLOW, lawyer; b. Montague, Mass., Sept. 15, 1951; s. William Charles and Ann (Harlow) B. BA, Colby Coll., 1973; JD, Georgetown U., 1976. Bar: Mass. 1977, U.S. Dist. Ct. Mass. 1977. Ptnr. Levy, Winer, Greenfield, Mass., 1977—2002; dir., clk. Esleeck Mfg. Co., Inc., Montague, 1980—; sr. v.p., gen. counsel Greenfield Savs. Bank, 2002—. Incorporator Heritage Bank for Savs., Greenfield, 1980-86; incorporator, trustee Greenfield Savs. Bank, 1986—; trustee Greenriver Cemetery Co., 1997—. Editor Georgetown Law Jour., 1975-76. Mem. Greenfield Fin. Com., 1980-84; chmn. Greenfield Sch. Bldg. Com., 1977-81; mem. Greenfield Republican Town Com., 1976-85, Greenfield Town Coun., 1992-95, Greenfield Sch. Bldg. Com., 1996-99; incorporator Franklin Med. Ctr., 1979—, pres., treas.; bd. dirs., clk. Greenfield Area Devel. Corp.; dir. Greenfield Cmty. YMCA, 1995-2001. Mem. Franklin County C. of C. (chmn. tech. services com. 1982—), Phi Beta Kappa, Pi Sigma Alpha. Lodges: Kiwanis. Congregationalist. Banking, Corporate, general, Estate planning. Home: 840 Colrain Rd Greenfield MA 01301-9763 Office: Greenfield Savs Bank PO Box 1537 Greenfield MA 01302-1537 E-mail: ablanker@greenfieldsavings.com.

BLANTON, HOOVER CLARENCE, lawyer; b. Green Sea, S.C., Oct. 13, 1925; s. Clarence Leo and Margaret (Hoover) B.; m. Cecilia Lopez, July 31, 1949; children: Lawson Hoover, Michael Lopez. JD, U. S.C., 1953. Bar: S.C. 1953. Ordained deacon, Bapt. Ch. Assoc. Whaley & McCutchen, Columbia, SC, 1953—66; ptnr. McCutchen, Blanton, Johnson, Barvette and predecessors, Columbia, 1967—. Dir. Legal Aid Service Agy., Columbia, chmn. bd., 1972-73. Gen. counsel S.C. Rep. Conv., 1962; del. Rep. State Conv., 1962, 64, 66, 68, 70, 74; bd. dirs. Midlands Cmty. Action Agy., Columbia, vice chmn., 1972-73; bd. dirs. Wildewood Sch., 1976-78; mem. Gov.'s Legal Svcs. Adv. Coun., 1976-77, Commn. on Continuing Legal Edn. for Judiciary, 1977-84, Commn. on Continuing Lawyer Competence, 1988-92, Commn. on Continuing Legal Edn. and Specialization, 1992-2000, sec. 1995, chmn., 1996-99. Mem. ABA. S.C. Bar (ho. of dels. 1975-76, chmn. fee disputes bd. 1977-81), Richland County Bar Assn. (pres. 1980), Def. Trial Attys. (state chmn. 1971-77, 80-95, exec. coun. 1977-80), Am. Bd. Trial Advs. (pres. S.C. chpts. 1989, Trial Lawyer of Yr. 2001), Toastmasters Club (pres. 1959), Palmetto Club, Phi Delta Phi. General civil litigation, Personal injury (including property damage), Workers' compensation. Home: 3655 Deerfield Dr Columbia SC 29204-3730 Office: 1414 Lady St Columbia SC 29201-3304

BLATT, RICHARD LEE, lawyer; b. Oak Park, Ill., May 24, 1940; s. B. Lee Gray and Madelyn Gertrude (Bentley) B.; m. Carol Milner Jenkinson, May 21, 1965 (div. Dec. 1984); children: Christopher Andrew Lee, Katherine Lee, Susannah Lee; m. Carolyn Elizabeth LeBlanc, Jan. 31, 1987; 1 child, Jennifer Lee DeNux Blatt. BA, U. Ill., 1962; JD, U. Mich., 1965. Bar: Ill. 1968, U.S. Dist. Ct. (no. dist.) Ill. 1968, U.S. Ct. Appeals (7th cir.) 1968, U.S. Supreme Ct. 1974, U.S. Dist. Ct. (so. dist.) Ill. 1977, U.S. Ct. Appeals (4th cir.) 1987, N.Y. 1989, U.S. Ct. Appeals (3rd cir.) 1990, U.S. Dist. Ct. (ea. and so. dists.) N.Y. 1998. Assoc. Peterson, Lowry, Rall, Barber & Ross, Chgo., 1968-75; ptnr. Peterson, Ross, Schloeb & Seidel, Chgo., 1975-91, Peterson & Ross, Chgo., 1991-94; sr. ptnr. Blatt, Hammesfahr & Eaton, Chgo., 1994-2000; sr. mem. Cozen & O'Connor, 2000—. Rep. Disting. Neutral Ctr. Pub. Resources Inst. for Dispute Resolution; regulation bd. arbitrators NASD. Author: (with Robert G. Schloerb, Robert W. Hammesfahr, Lori S. Nugent) Punitive Damages: A Guide to the Insurability of Punitive Damages in the United States and Its Territories, 1988; (with Robert W. Hammesfahr and Lori S. Nugent) Punitive Damges: A State-by-State Guide to Law and Practice, 1991, 2002 (in Japanese 1995); co-author: At Risk-Internet and E-Commerce Insurance and Reinsurance Legal Issues, 2000, At Risk-Version 2-The Definitive Guide to Legal Issues of Insurance and Reinsurance of Internet, E-commerce and Cyber Perils, 2002. Capt. USAR, 1965—67, Korea. Fellow Chartered Inst. Arbitrators; mem. ABA (litigation sect., dispute resolution sect.), NSSAR (Ft. Dearborn chpt.), Ill. State Bar Assn., Chgo. Internat. Dispute Resolution Assn. (planning com.), Soc. Mayflower Desc. State Ill., N.Y. State Bar Assn., Chgo. Bar Assn. (alternative dispute resolution com.), Chgo. Club, Pi Kappa Alpha Ednl. Found. (trustee), Phi Beta Kappa, Phi Kappa Phi. Insurance, General civil litigation, Product liability. Home: 1415 N Dearborn Pkwy Chicago IL 60610-1559 Office: Cozen & O'Connor 222 S Riverside Plz Ste 1500 Chicago IL 60606-6000 Fax: 312-382-8910. E-mail: rblatt@earthlink.net., rblatt@cozen.com.

BLATZ, KATHLEEN ANNE, judge, state agency administrator, state legislator; BA summa cum laude, U. Notre Dame, 1976; MSW, U. Minn., 1978, JD cum laude, 1984. Psychiat. social worker, 1979—81; mem. Minn. Ho. of Reps., St. Paul, 1979—93, chmn. crime and family law, fin. instns. and ins. coms., 1985—86; judge Dist. Ct., Henne Pin County, 1993—96; justice Minn. Supreme Ct., 1996—98, chief justice, 1998—. Office: 305 Minn Judicial Ctr 25 Rev Martin Luther King Jr Blvd Saint Paul MN 55155*

BLAU, HARVEY RONALD, lawyer; b. N.Y.C., Nov. 14, 1935; s. David and Rose (Kuchinsky) B.; m. Arlene Joan Garrett, Mar. 21, 1964; children: Stephanie Elizabeth, Melissa Karen, Victoria Gayle. AB, N.Y.U., 1957, LL.M., 1965; JD, Columbia U., 1961. Bar: N.Y. 1961. Practiced in N.Y., 1961—2002; sr. ptnr. Blau, Kramer, Wactlar & Lieberman, Jericho, NY, 1966—2002; law sec. to U.S. Dist. Judge Cooper So. Dist. N.Y., 1962-63; asst. U.S. atty. So. Dist. N.Y., 1963-66; CEO Griffon Corp., 1982—. Chmn. Griffon Corp., Aeroflex Corp.; bd. dirs. Nu Horizons Electronics Corp., Benjamin N. Cardozo Sch. Law; bd. trustees Mt. Sinai Hosp., N.Y. Mayor Village of Old Westbury. Served to capt. JAGC, AUS, 1958-66. Mem. Fed.

Bar Assn., Assn. of Bar of City of N.Y., Bar Assn. of Nassau County. Home: 125 Wheatley Rd Old Westbury NY 11568-1210 Office: Griffon Corp 100 Jericho Quadrangle Jericho NY 11753-2708

BLAU, JEFFREY ALAN, lawyer; b. Havre de Grace, Md., Nov. 4, 1951; s. Theodore H. and Lili (Rosenmann) B.; m. Sherry Lynn Perez, May 2, 1987; 1 child, Joshua Ephriam BA, Case Western Res. U., 1974; JD, Calif. Western Sch. of Law, 1977. Bar: Fla. 1978, U.S. Dist. Ct. (mid. dist.) Fla. 1978, U.S. Ct. Appeals (5th cir.) 1979, U.S. Ct. Mil. Appeals 1982, U.S. Ct. Appeals (11th cir.) 1983. Assoc. Gordon & Maney, P.A., Tampa, Fla., 1978-79, James V. Caltagirone and Assocs., Tampa, 1984; asst. county atty. Hillsborough County, Tampa, 1979-83; ptnr. Crooks, Vetter, Cuellar and Blau, P.A., Tampa, 1985; pvt. practice Tampa, 1985—. Mem. Fla. Bar (chmn. consumer protection divsn. 1981-83), First Amendment Lawyers Assn., Hillsborough County Bar Assn. (Merit award 1981, Outstanding Citizen award 1981). Democrat. Jewish. Avocations: treasure salvage, biking, swimming. Constitutional, Criminal, Land use and zoning (including planning). Office: 1511 S Church Ave Tampa FL 33629-5822

BLAU, RICHARD M. lawyer; b. Tampa, Fla., Oct. 17, 1957; s. Theodore H. and Lili R. Blau; m. Valarie V. Blau, Nov. 18, 1989; children: Hannah, Jennah, Alexander. BA, Brandeis U., 1979; JD, Georgetown U., 1982. Bar: Fla., D.C., U.S. Supreme Ct., U.S. Ct. Internat. Trade, U.S. Ct. Appeals (11th and fed. cirs.), U.S. Dist. Ct. (mid. and so. dists.) Fla., U.S. Ct. Mil. Appeals. Assoc. Holland & Knight, LLP, Tampa, Fla., 1982—90, ptnr., 1990—. Spkr. in field. Author: Developments in Administrative Law and Regulatory Practice 1999-2000, 2001; editor: Annual Survey of Reported Court Decisions Affecting the Twenty-First Amendment and Related Alcohol Beverage Laws, 2001. Trustee U. Tampa, 2000—, United Way Hillsborough County, Tampa, 2000—, Fla. Holocaust Mus., St. Petersburg, 1999—2001. Mem.: ABA (chmn. com. on beverage alcohol practice 2001—), Am. Law Inst. (elected mem.), Nat. Conf. State Liquor Adminstrn. (assoc. pres.'s citation 1996), Nat. Alcohol Beverage Control Assn. (assoc.). Avocations: scuba diving, cycling, wine appreciation. Administrative and regulatory, Antitrust, General civil litigation. Office: Holland & Knight LLP 400 N Ashley Dr Ste 2300 Tampa FL 33602 Office Fax: 813-229-0134. E-mail: rblau@hklaw.com.

BLAWIE, JAMES LOUIS, law educator; b. Newark, Mar. 26, 1928; s. Louis Paul and Cecelia Ruth (Grish) B.; m. Marilyn June Beyerle, May 30, 1952; children: Elias J., Cecelia R., Christiana L. BA, U. Conn., 1950; AM, Boston U., 1951, PhD, 1959; JD, U. Chgo., 1955. Bar: Conn. 1956, Calif. 1965, U.S. Dist. Ct. (no. dist.) Calif. 1965, U.S. Ct. Appeals (9th cir.) 1967, U.S. Supreme Ct. 1968. Instr. polit. sci. Mich. State U., East Lansing, 1955; assoc. prof. U. Akron, Ohio, 1956-57, Kent State U., 1956-57; asst. prof. bus. law U. Calif., Berkeley, 1958-60; assoc. prof. law Santa Clara U., Calif., 1960-63, prof. law, 1963—; vis. prof. polit. sci. Calif. State U., Hayward, 1966-67; adminstrv. law judge U.S. Equal Employment Opportunity Commn., Washington, 1982-85. Complaints examiner U.S. Equal Employment Opportunity Agy., Office Equal Employment Opportunity; cons. in field. Author: (handbook) The Michigan Township Board, 1957; contbr. articles to profl. jours. Mem. Citizen's Adv. Com. on Capital Improvements, 1962-65; bd. dirs. Washington Hosp., 1964-68. Maj. U.S. Army, 1963-74. Boston U. Faculty fellow, 1951-53; U. Chgo. Law Sch. scholar, 1953-55; grantee Mich. State U. grantee, 1955-56, Helsinki Govt. Ministry Edn. grantee, 1980-81. Mem. ABA, Fairfield County Bar Assn., Mensa. Republican. Avocations: computers, photography, travel, rare diseases databases. Home: 41752 Marigold Dr Fremont CA 94539-4779 also: PO Box 1102 Fremont CA 94538-0110 Office: Santa Clara U Sch Law Santa Clara CA 95053-0001 E-mail: jimblawie@aol.com., macfig@aol.com.

BLAZEK-WHITE, DORIS, lawyer; b. Easton, Md., Nov. 17, 1943; d. George W. and Nola M. (Buterbaugh) Defibaugh; children: Christine T., Judson M.; m. Thacher W. White. BA, Goucher Coll., 1965; JD, Georgetown U., 1968. Bar: D.C. 1969, V.I. 1969, U.S. Ct. Appeals (3d cir. 1969), U.S. Ct. Appeals (D.C. cir.) 1971, Md. 1979. Gen. practice with Judge Warren H. Young, V.I., 1968-70; assoc. Covington & Burling, Washington, 1970-76, ptnr., 1976—. Mem. Am. Coll. Trust and Estate Counsel. Estate planning, Probate (including wills, trusts), Estate taxation. Office: Covington & Burling 1201 Pennsylvania Ave NW Washington DC 20004 E-mail: dblazek-white@cov.com.

BLAZZARD, NORSE NOVAR, lawyer; b. St. Johns, Ariz., July 8, 1937; s. Howard N. and Viola (Greer) B.; m. Mary Elizabeth Jecker, June 15, 1958; children: Howard Norse, Mary Catherine; m. Judith A. Hasenauer, July 2, 1977. AB, Stanford U., 1959; JD, U. Calif., Hastings, 1962. Bar: Calif. 1963, U.S. Dist. Ct. (no. dist.) Calif. 1966, Conn. 1974, U.S. Dist. Ct. Conn. 1975, U.S. Supreme Ct. 1975, U.S. Ct. Appeals (D.C. cir.) 1977, U.S. Ct. Appeals (2d cir.) 1978, Fla. 1993; CLU. Counsel Calif. Western Life Ins. Co., Sacramento, 1966-70; sr. v.p., gen. counsel NARE Life Svc. Co., Palo Alto, calif., 1970-74; pres. Blazzard, Grodd & Hasenauer, P.C., Westport, Conn., 1974—. Chmn. ins. products task force Fin. Products Stds. Bd., 1988-89; chmn. Nat. Assn. Variable Annuities, 1994. Bd. govs. Norwalk Symphony, 1979. Capt. JAGC, U.S. Army, 1962-66. Inductee Variable Annuity Hall of Fame, 1998. Mem. ABA, FBA, Calif. Bar Assn., Fla. Bar Assn., D.C. Bar Assn. Republican. Mem. Lds Ch. Insurance, Securities, Corporate taxation. E-mail: norse.blazzard@bghpc.com.

BLEAKLEY, PETER KIMBERLEY, lawyer; b. Franklin, Pa., Aug. 19, 1936; s. Rollin R and Marion (St James) Bleakley; m. Mary B DeRosa; children: Jennifer A, Sarah A, Nicholas D. BA, U. Va., 1958, LL.B., 1962. Bar: Va 1962, DC 1966, US Ct Appeals (2d cir), US Ct Appeals (3d cir), US Ct Appeals (5th cir), US Ct Appeals (6th cir), US Ct Appeals (7th cir), US Ct Appeals (8th cir), US Ct Appeals (9th cir), US Ct Appeals (DC cir), US Supreme Ct, US Ct Appeals (fed cir). Trial atty. Fed. Trade Commn., Washington, 1962-66; trial atty. Dept. Justice, Washington, 1966; assoc. Arnold & Porter, Washington, 1966-70, ptnr., 1971—. Fellow: Am Col Trial Lawyers; mem.: ABA. Democrat. Avocations: tennis, skiing, bicycling, golf. Antitrust, General civil litigation, Product liability. Home: 3103 Hawthorne St NW Washington DC 20008-3540 Office: Arnold & Porter 555 12th St NW Washington DC 20004-1206 E-mail: peter_bleakley@aporter.com.

BLEICH, JEFFREY LAURENCE, lawyer, law educator; b. Neubreuke, Germany, May 17, 1961; came to U.S., 1964; s. Charles Allen Bleich and Linda Sue Caplan; m. Rebecca Lee Pratt, Aug. 12, 1984; children: Jacob, Matthew, Abigail. BA in Polit. Sci., Amherst Coll., 1983; MA in Pub. Policy, Harvard U., 1986; JD, U. Calif., Berkeley, 1989. Bar: Calif. 1989, D.C. 1990, U.S. Ct. Appeals (D.C. cir.) 1990, U.S. Dist. Ct. (no. dist.) Calif. 1992, U.S. Ct. Appeals (4th cir.) 1993, U.S. Supreme Ct. 1993, U.S. Ct. Appeals (9th cir.) 1994. Law clk. U.S. Ct. Appeals, Washington, 1989-90, U.S. Supreme Ct., Washington, 1990-91; legal asst. Iran-U.S. Claims Tribunal, The Hague, 1991-92; ptnr. Munger, Tolles & Olson LLP, San Francisco, 1992—. Adj. prof. U. Calif., Berkeley, 1993—. Editor-in-chief Calif. Law Rev., Nat. Debt; columnist San Francisco Atty. Mem. adv. bd. Coalition on Homelessness, San Francisco; dir. Nat. Youth Violence Initiative, 1999—. Recipient James Madison award Soc. Profl. Journalists, 1998. Mem. ABA (chair constnl. law com., award 1996, Pro Bono Publico award 1996), Bar Assn. San Francisco (pres.), Lawyers' Com. Civil Rights of San Francisco Bay Area (co-chair), Lawyers Com. Human Rights (bd. dirs. 1998—), Legal Aid Soc. (bd. dirs. 1998—), Barristers Club San Francisco (pres.). Democrat. Avocations: short story writer, tennis, kayaking, camping. General civil litigation, Intellectual property. Office: Munger Tolles & Olson 33 New Montgomery St Fl 19 San Francisco CA 94105-4506

BLEICHER, SAMUEL ABRAM, lawyer, government official; b. Omaha, June 21, 1942; s. David Bernard and Rachael (Faigin) Bleicher; m. Beatrice Koretsky, June 16, 1965 (dec. Nov. 12, 1995); children: Leo, Zena; m. Emily Blair Chewning, May 17, 1997 (div. 2002). BA, Northwestern U., 1963; JD, Harvard U., 1966. Bar: Nebr. 1966, Ohio 1972, D.C. 1979, Va. 1989, Md. 1991. Prof. law U. Toledo Coll. Law, 1966-76; dep. dir. for regulation and enforcement Ohio EPA, 1972-75; issues generalist Carter-Mondale Presdl. Campaign, Atlanta, 1976; policy analyst Carter-Mondale Transition Planning Group, Washington, 1976-77; spl. asst. to adminstr. NOAA Dept. Commerce, Washington, 1977, dir. Office Ocean Mgmt., 1977-78, dep. asst. adminstr., 1978-80, dep. gen. counsel, 1980-81; of counsel Blank, Rome, Comisky & McCauley, Washington, 1981-85; ptnr. Frank, Bernstein, Conaway & Goldman, Tysons Corner, Va., 1985-90; prin. Miles & Stockbridge P.C., Washington, 1990—2001. Contbr. articles to profl. publs. Democrat. Jewish. Environmental, Property, real (including real estate development, water). Office: Overseas Bldg Ops Dept State Washington DC 20520 E-mail: sambleicher@comcast.net.

BLEIER, MICHAEL E. lawyer; BA, U. Tulsa, 1962; JD, Georgetown U., 1965. Bar: Pa, D.C. Atty. Office of Gen. Counsel, Bd. Govs. Fed. Reserve System, 1971-78, sr. counsel, 1979-81, asst. gen. counsel, 1981-82; mng. counsel Mellon Bank Corp., Pitts., 1982-88; asst. gen. counsel Mellon Fin. Corp., Pitts., 1989-91, dep. gen. counsel, 1991-92, gen. counsel, evp, 1992—, sr. mgmt. com. Mem. Am. Bankers Assn. (vice chmn. bank counsel com. 1996-98), Lawyers Coun. Fin. Svcs. Roundtable (chmn. 1993-98). Administrative and regulatory, Banking, Mergers and acquisitions. Office: Mellon Financial Corporation 1 Mellon Ctr Fl 19 Pittsburgh PA 15258-0001 E-mail: bleier.me@mellon.com.

BLEILER, CHARLES ARTHUR, lawyer; b. Boston, Mar. 16, 1945; s. Charles Edward and Grace Rita Bleiler; m. Joyce Ann Kohlmyer, Oct. 6, 1972; children: Charles Edward. BS, Tufts U., 1967; JD, U. San Diego, 1973. BAr: Calif. 1973, U.S. Dist. Ct. (so. dist.) Calif. 1973. Commd. ensign U.S. Navy, 1967, advanced through grades to lt. comdr., resigned, 1978; ptnr. Williams, Clodig & Bleiler, San Diego, 1974-85, Bleiler & Reiter, San Diego, 1985-91, Malowney, Chialtas & Bleiler, San Diego, 1991-93; pres. Charles A. Bleiler A.P.C., San Diego, 1987—. Lectr. San Diego Trial Lawyers Assn., 1982. Bd. dirs. Rancho Santa Fe (Calif.) Cmty. Ctr., 1990-94, pres., 1993-94; mem. San Dieguito Soccer Bd., Encinitas, Calif., 1991-92; bd. dirs. Torrey Pines H.S. Found., Del Mar, Calif., 1996-98, pres., 1997-98; founding mem., lector Nativity Ch., Rancho Santa Fe; fundraiser for charitable orgns.; bd. dirs. Rancho Santa Fe Little League, 1989-92. Mem. ATLA, Calif. State Bar, San Diego County Bar Assn., Optimist Club (charter pres. Kearny Mesa club 1987-89). Republican. Roman Catholic. Avocations: sailing, horseback riding, skiing, coaching youth baseball and soccer. Construction, Labor (including EEOC, Fair Labor Standards Act, labor-management relations, NLRB, OSHA), Personal injury (including property damage). Home: PO Box 1653 Rancho Santa Fe CA 92067-1653 Office: 12770 High Bluff Dr Ste 380 San Diego CA 92130-2060 E-mail: bleiler@worldnet.att.net.

BLENCOWE, PAUL SHERWOOD, lawyer, private investor; b. Amityville, N.Y., Feb. 10, 1953; s. Frederick Arthur and Dorothy Jeanne (Ballenger) Blencowe; m. Mary Frances Faulk, Apr. 11, 1992; children: Kristin Amanda, Alison Michelle, Caitlin Emily. BA with honors, U. Wis., 1975; MBA, U. Pa., 1976; JD, Stanford U., 1979. Bar: Tex. 1979, Calif. 1989. Assoc. Fulbright & Jaworski, Houston, 1979-86, London, 1986-87, ptnr., 1988-89, Fulbright & Jaworski L.L.P., L.A., 1989-2000, of counsel, 2000—. Editor: China's Quest for Independence: Policy Evolution in the 1970s, 1980; editor-in-chief Stanford Jour. of Internat. Law, 1978-79; contbr. articles on U.S. securities and corp. law to profl. jours. Mem. The Calif. Club, Phi Beta Kappa, Phi Kappa Phi, Beta Theta Pi. Corporate, general, Mergers and acquisitions, Securities. Office: Fulbright & Jaworski LLP 865 S Figueroa St Fl 29 Los Angeles CA 90017-2543 E-mail: pblencowe@fulbright.com.

BLENKO, WALTER JOHN, JR., lawyer; b. Pitts., June 15, 1926; s. Walter J. and Ardis Leah (Jones) B.; m. Joy Kinneman, Apr. 9, 1949; children: John W., Andrew W. BS, Carnegie-Mellon U., 1950; JD, U. Pitts., 1953. Bar: Pa. 1954. Pvt. practice law, Pitts., 1954—; ptnr. Eckert, Seamans, Cherin & Mellott, Pitts., 1984-93, of counsel, 1993—. Mem. adv. bd. dept. mech. engring. Carnegie-Mellon U., 1992—. Active Churchill Vol. Fire Co., 1970-82; charter and hon. mem. Wilkinsburg Emergency Med. Svc.; sec. Hampton Twp. Zoning Hearing Bd., 1991-92, vice-chmn., 1993; mem. Hampton Twp. Sch. Bd., 1993-97, pres. 1996; mem. Allegheny County Parks adv. bd., 2000-2002. With U.S. Army, 1944-46, ETO. Decorated Bronze Star, Combat Inf. badge; recipient Disting. Svc. award Carnegie-Mellon U. Alumni Assn., 1993, Recognition award Carnegie Mellon U. Andrew Carnegie Soc., 2002. Fellow Am. Coll. Trial Lawyers, Allegheny County Bar Found.; mem. ASME, Pa. Bar Assn., Allegheny County Bar Assn., Assn. Bar of City of N.Y., Pitts. Intellectual Property Law Assn. (pres. 1977-78), Engrs. Soc. Western Pa., Internat. Patent and Trademark Assn., Carnegie-Mellon U. Alumni Assn. (exec. bd. 1996-2001, exec. com. 1997-2001), Duquesne Club, Univ. Club, Princeton Club (N.Y.), Rolls-Royce Owners Club (bd. dirs. 1982-84, v.p. publs. 1984-87, treas. 1987-89). Avocation: old cars. Federal civil litigation, Patent, Trademark and copyright. Home: 4073 Middle Rd Allison Park PA 15101-1207 Office: Eckert Seamans Cherin & Mellott 600 Grant St Pittsburgh PA 15219-2702

BLESSING, MARIBETH, lawyer, educator, mediator, arbitrator; b. Groton, Mass., Apr. 9, 1948; d. E. James and Elizabeth A. (Woodin) Lisi; m. Joseph I. Wolfe, Dec. 27, 1969 (div. Sept. 1983); children: Gwen Elizabeth, Noel James; m. Ronald M. Blessing, Aug. 10, 1991 (dec. 1997), m. Donald Pelham, Feb. 11, 2000. BS in Elem. Edn. magna cum laude, Kutztown (Pa.) U., 1970; postgrad., U. Santa Clara, Calif., 1980; JD cum laude, Widener (Del.) U., 1991. Bar: Pa. 1991, N.J. 1992, U.S. Dist. Ct. (ea. dist.) Pa. 1992, U.S. Supreme Ct. 2003. Tchr. Chinook Elem. Sch., Anchorage, 1970-71, St. Philip Neri Sch., East Greenville, Pa., 1976-78, St. Williams Elem. Sch., Los Altos, Calif., 1978-81, Immaculate Heart of Mary Sch., Cuyahoga Falls, Ohio, 1981-83, Our Lady of Mt. Carmel Sch., Doylestown, Pa., 1983-86; hearing officer Montgomery County Domestic Rels. Office, Norristown, Pa., 1986; officer Bucks County Domestic Rels. Office, Doylestown, 1986-92; assoc. Gold-Bikin, Clifford & Young, Norristown, 1992-96; ptnr. Law Offices of Leslee Silverman Tabas, Narbeth, Pa., 1996—99; exec. dir. Ctr. Family Mediation and Arbitration, 1996—99, sole practitioner, 1999—. Co-chmn. Young Lawyers Doctor-Lawyer Project, 1994-96; instr. continuing edn. div. Pa. State U., 1994-1999; author, lectr. PBI, 1996—, chair family law sect. Montgomery, 2002-, pres. Doris Jona Freed Inn of Ct., 2003-, Mediation Adv. Panel, 1999-. Contbr. articles to legal publs. Actress Laymen Playmen, Hatfield, Pa., 1992-96. Mem. ABA, Pa. Bar Assn., Montgomery County Bar Assn. (family law support com., family law custody subcom. 1993-1995, chair divorce/equitable distbn. com. 1996, co-chair practicum com. 1998, co-chair custody com. 1998, treas., svcs. com.), Phi Kappa Phi. Republican. Roman Catholic. Family and matrimonial. Home: 24 Moredon Rd Huntingdon Valley PA 19006-7949 Office: Law Office Maribeth Blessing LLC 1494 Old York Rd Ste 200 Abington PA 19001-2616

BLEVINS, JEFFREY ALEXANDER, lawyer; b. Forest Hills, N.Y., June 18, 1955; s. William E. and Mary J. Blevins; m. Pamela A. Manos, Nov. 26, 1983 (div. Mar. 1995); 1 child, Mary Alexandria; m. Diane L. Bannon, June 12, 1999; stepchildren: Meagan Elizabeth, Laura Leigh, Jeffrey Daniel. BA, Denison U., 1977; JD, DePaul U., 1981. Bar: Ill. 1981, U.S. Dist Ct. (no. dist.) Ill. 1981, U.S. Dist. Ct. (we. dist. Wis. 1984, U.S. Ct. Appeals (7th cir.) 1984, U.S. Supreme Ct. 1990. Personnel specialist Comerica Bank, Detroit, 1979-80; assoc. Bell, Boyd & Lloyd, Chgo., 1981-88, ptnr., mem., 1988—2001; mng. atty. The Law Office of Jeffrey A. Blevins LLC, Naperville, Ill., 2001—02; pub. interest atty. Prairie State Legal Svcs., 2002—. Lectr., author Ill. Inst. Continuing Legal Edn., others; chair employment sect. Ctr. for Disability and Elder Law, 1999—. Editor in chief DePaul Law Rev., 1980. Mem. Ill. State Bar Assn. (labor and employment coun. 1992-95), Chgo. Bar Assn., Mid-day Club, Omicron Delta Epsilon. Republican. Lutheran. Federal civil litigation, State civil litigation, Labor (including EEOC, Fair Labor Standards Act, labor-management relations, NLRB, OSHA).

BLEWETT, ALEXANDER, III, lawyer; b. May 2, 1945; s. Alexander and Fern Wynnett (Foerschler) B.; m. Andrea Ann Friedl, Aug. 18, 1975; children: Anders, Drew. BS in Math., Mont. State U., 1967; JD, U. Mont., 1971. Bar: Mont. 1971, U.S. Supreme Ct., U.S. Ct. of Appeals (6th and 9th cir.). Assoc. Jardine, Stephenson, Blewett & Weaver, Great Falls, Mont., 1977-85; ptnr. Hoyt & Blewett, 1985—. Recipient Cert. of Civil Trial Advocacy, Nat. Bd. Trial Advocacy, 1983—. Mem. Am. Trial Lawyers Assn., Mont. Bar Assn., Mont. Trial Lawyers Assn., Am. Coll. Trial lawyers, Internat. Acad. Trial Lawyers, Inner Circle of Advocates (Mont. Trial Lawyer of Yr. award 1993-94), Internat. Soc. Barristers. Democrat. Federal civil litigation, Insurance, Personal injury (including property damage). Home: 1324 4th Ave N Great Falls MT 59401 Office: Hoyt & Blewett 501 2nd Ave N PO Box 2807 Great Falls MT 59403-2807 E-mail: zblewett@attbi.com., zblewett@hoytandblewett.com.

BLEWETT, ROBERT NOALL, lawyer; b. Stockton, Calif., July 12, 1915; s. Stephen Noall and Bess Errol (Simard) B.; m. Virginia Weston, Mar. 30, 1940; children: Richard Weston Blewett (dec.), Carolyn Blewett Lawrence. LLB, Stanford U., 1936, JD, 1939. Bar: Calif. 1939. Dep. dist. atty. San Joaquin County, 1942-46; practice law Stockton, 1946-98; ptnr., pres. Blewett & Allen-Garibaldi, Inc., Stockton, 1971-98. Chmn. San Joaquin County chpt. ARC, 1947-49; v.p. Goodwill Industries, 1967-68; vice chmn. Stockton Sister City Commn., 1969-70; adv. bd. bus. adminstrn. dept. U. Pacific; trustee San Joaquin Pioneer and Haggin Galleries. Fellow Am. Coll. Estate and Trust Counsel, Am. Bar Found.; mem. ABA, Am. Judicature Soc., Am. Law Inst., State Bar Calif. (mem. exec. com. on conf. of dels. 1969-72, vice chmn. 1971-72), Order of the Coif, Rotary (pres. 1987-88), Yosemite Club, San Francisco Banker's Club, Masons, Shriners, Delta Theta Phi, Theta Xi. Republican. Corporate, general, Estate planning, Probate (including wills, trusts). Office: 141 E Acacia St Stockton CA 95202-1400 E-mail: ginger21@attbi.com.

BLINDER, ALBERT ALLAN, judge; b. N.Y.C., Nov. 27, 1925; s. William and Sarah (Gold) B.; m. Meredith Zaretzki, Nov. 16, 1961 (dec.); 1 child, Adam Z.; m. Joan Goodman, Jan. 20, 1985 (dec.). AB, NYU, 1944, postgrad., 1944-45; JD, Harvard U., 1948. Bar: N.Y. 1949, U.S. Dist. Ct. (so. dist.) N.Y. 1953, U.S. Ct. Appeals (2d cir.) 1953, U.S. Supreme Ct. 1967. Asst. U.S. atty. for so. dist. N.Y., 1950-53; asst. counsel N.Y.C. Bd. High Edn., 1953-54; asst. dist. atty. County of Bronx, N.Y., 1954-60; ptnr. Saxe, Bacon & O'Shea, N.Y.C., 1960-64, Blinder, Steinhaus & Hochhauser, N.Y.C., 1965-73; judge N.Y. State Ct. Claims, 1973-96; jud. hearing officer N.Y. State Supreme Ct., 1996—. Rsch. counsel N.Y. Commn. on Law of Estates, 1965; assoc. counsel N.Y. Commn. Revision of Penal Law, 1966-70; asst. counsel N.Y. Commn. on Eminent Domain, 1970-73; rsch. asst. N.Y. Commn. State Ct. System, 1971-73. Assoc. editor Am. Criminal Law Quar., 1968-70, mem. adv. bd., 1969-70. Mem.: ABA, Am. Judges Assn., Am. Arbitration Assn. (nat. panel arbitrators 1965—73), N.Y. County Lawyers Assn., Assn. Bar City N.Y., N.Y. State Bar Assn., Internat. Bar Assn. Office: 115 Broadway Fl 15 New York NY 10006-1604 E-mail: ABLINDER@aol.com.

BLISS, DONALD TIFFANY, JR., lawyer; b. Norwalk, Conn., Nov. 24, 1941; s. Donald Tiffany and Marina (Popova) B.; m. Nancy Arnold, Sept. 14, 1974; children: Evan Hale, Bion Northam. JD, Harvard U., 1966. Bar: N.Y. 1969, D.C. 1971, U.S. Dist. Ct. D.C. 1975, U.S. Ct. Appeals (D.C. cir.) 1971, 84, U.S. Supreme Ct. 1975. Atty. Peace Corps, 1966-67; legis. counsel Congress of Micronesia, 1968; cons. judiciary, American Samoa, 1968; assoc. firm LeBoeuf, Lamb, Leiby & McCrae, N.Y.C., 1969; asst. to sec. HEW, 1969-72; spl. asst. to adminstr. EPA, 1972-73; exec. sec. AID, 1973-74; dep. gen. counsel U.S. Dept. Transp., 1975-77, acting. gen. counsel, 1976-77; ptnr. and chair, transp. practice group firm O'Melveny & Myers, Washington, 1979—. Mem. Maritime Adv. Com., 1984-85; pres. Harvard Law Sch. Assn. D.C., 1985-86; chmn. transp. sect. FBA, 1987-90; mem. interior task force Grace Commn.; nat. pres. The Ripon Soc. Author: The Law of Airline Customer Relations: Stability, Security, Safety and Service, 2002, Drug Testing and Federal Employees: Lessons from the Transportation Experience, 1988, Economic Deregulation and Safety: Are The Compatible, 1989, A Challenge to the U.S. Aviation Leadership: Launching the New Era of Global Aviation, 1991, Supreme Court Preemption Analysis: Differentiating the Hamiltonians and Jeffersonians, 1993; play The Return of Halley's Comet, 2002. Trustee Studio Theatre; trustee, 1st v.p. Arts for the Aging; pres. Dara's Canine Found., Inc. Recipient spl. citation HEW, 1972, 73, Pres.'s Cert. Exec. Mgmt., 1973, Superior Achievement award Dept. Transp., 1976. Mem. ABA (chmn. air and space law forum 1997-99), D.C. Bar Assn. (co-chmn. sect. adminstrv. law and agy. practice 1988-90), City Club D.C., Chevy Chase Club. Administrative and regulatory, Federal civil litigation. Home: 6732 Newbold Dr Bethesda MD 20817-2223 Office: O'Melveny & Myers 555 13th St NW Ste 500W Washington DC 20004-1159 E-mail: dbliss@omm.com.

BLISS, RICHARD JON, lawyer; b. Rice Lake, Wis., Apr. 27, 1951; s. Richard Burt and Lolly (Davis) B.; m. Susan Elizabeth Ramage, June 19, 1976; children: Jon, Steve, Brock. BA, Wheaton (Ill.) Coll., 1973; JD, U. Wis., 1976. Bar: Wis. 1976, U.S. Dist. Ct. (ea. dist.) Wis. 1976. Assoc. Godfrey & Kahn, S.C., Milw., 1976-82, shareholder, 1983—, mng. ptnr., pres., 1996—. Bd. dirs. Ward Adhesives, Inc., Runzheimer Internat., Inc. Note editor U. Wis. Law Rev., 1975-76. Bd. dirs. Vine and Brs. Found., Inc., Milw., 1996—, Milw. Ctr. for Independence, 1993-98, Neighborhood House, Inc., Serve Enterprises, Inc. Mem. Univ. Club of Milw., Town Club, Milw. Club. Avocations: aviation, tennis. Corporate, general, Mergers and acquisitions. Home: 706 E Lexington Blvd Whitefish Bay WI 53217-5338 Office: Godfrey & Kahn SC 780 N Water St Ste 1500 Milwaukee WI 53202-3590 E-mail: rbliss@gklaw.com.

BLISS, ROBERT HARMS, lawyer; b. Paris, Tex., Nov. 20, 1940; s. Jack Edward and Ruth Eugenia (Harms) B.; m. Juliee Dixie Fuselier, Dec. 29, 1964; 1 child, Katherine Elaine. BA, U. Colo., 1964; JD, U. Tex., 1967. Bar: Tex. 1967; cert. civil trial specialist, mediator-arbitrator, spl. master. Since practiced in, Dallas; assoc. Johnson, Bromberg, Leeds & Riggs, 1967-72; ptrn. Bliss, Danner & Bishop, 1972-74; individual practice, 1974; pres. Bliss & Hughes, P.C., Dallas, 1978-88; pvt. practice Robert Harms Bliss P.C., 1988-98; ptnr. Glast, Phillips & Murray, PC, 1998—2002; pvt. practice, 2002—. Mem. faculty advanced real estate law State Bar Tex., 1985, 92-93, 95, 97, 99, 2000, 02; mem. faculty CLE series So. Meth. U. Sch. Law, Dallas, 1989, 92, 94, 97, 98, 99, 2000; mem. faculty Mortgage Lending Inst., U. Tex. Sch. Law, 1994, 97, 98, 99, 2000, mem. faculty advanced real estate drafting course, 1995, 2000-02, course dir., 2002. Contbr. articles to profl. jours. Bd. dirs. Dallas Symphony Orch. Guild, Dallas Classic Guitar Soc.; mem. Gov.'s Task Force on Immigration, 1983-84, Tex. Real Estate Commn., 1983-87; adv. bd. Tex. Real Estate Rsch. Ctr., Tex. A&M U., 1985-87; ch. atty. Episcopal Diocese Dallas. Mem. Am. Coll. Real Estate Lawyers, State Bar Tex. (chair real estate, probate and trust sect.), Dallas Bar Assn. (past chmn. real property sect.), Tex. Coll. Real Estate Attys., Assn. Atty.-Mediators (pres.), U. Tex. Tchg. Quiz-Masters Assn., Phi Delta Phi. Home: 29 Ashton Ct Dallas TX 75230-1977 Office: PO Box 12825 Dallas TX 75225

BLISS, RONALD GLENN, lawyer; b. Buckeye, Ariz., Mar. 22, 1943; s. Glenn Francis Bliss and Jessie Marie (Waymire) Harrington; m. Charlene Wallace, Sept. 18, 1965; children: Erik, Jason. BS, USAF Acad., 1964; JD, Baylor U., 1976. Bar: Tex. 1976, U.S. Dist. Ct. (so. dist.) Tex. 1977, (no. dist.) Tex. 1981, (we. dist.) Tex. 1985, U.S. Ct. Appeals (5th cir.) 1979, (11th cir.) 1982, (D.C. cir.) 1982, U.S. Supreme Ct. 1980. Capt., fighter pilot USAF, U.S., Vietnam, 1964-74; prisoner of war Vietnam, 1966-73; assoc. Fulbright & Jaworski, Houston, 1976-84, ptnr., 1984—. Mem. adv. com. So. Dist. Tex., 1992; chmn. Tex. Aerospace Commn., 1995-96. Contbr. to profl. jours. Pres. Norchester Club Inc., 1980; bd. dirs. Athletic Club Houston, 1984-85; bd. govs. Houston Center Club, 1987—, cert. mediator. Inductee Tex. Aviation Hall of Fame. Mem.: ABA, Houston Intellectual Property Law Assn., Am. Intellectual Property Law Assn., Tex. Bar Assn., 4th Allied POW Wing. Intellectual property, Patent, Trademark and copyright. Office: Fulbright & Jaworski LLP 1301 Mckinney St Ste 5100 Houston TX 77010-3031 E-mail: rbliss@fulbright.com.

BLITZ, STEPHEN M. lawyer; b. N.Y.C., July 29, 1941; s. Leo and Dorothy B.; m. Ellen Sue Mintzer, Sept. 23, 1962; children: Catherine Denise, Thomas Joseph. BA, Columbia U., 1962, BS, 1963; LL.B., Stanford U., 1966; MS in Acctg., U. Colo., 2001. Bar: Calif. 1967, U.S. Dist. Ct. (cen. dist.) Calif. 1967, Colo. 1996. Law clk. to judge U.S. Dist. Ct. Central Dist. Calif., 1966-67; ptnr. Gibson, Dunn & Crutcher, L.A., 1967-96, Denver, 1996-2001; spl. counsel Fleishman & Shapiro, Denver, 2001—. Adj. prof. law U. West Los Angeles Sch. Law, 1978-80, dir. Pub. Counsel, 1981-83, 94-96. Bd. dirs. Colo. Preservation, Inc., 1999—. Mem. ABA, L.A. County Bar Assn. (exec. com. 1986-96, chmn. 1994-95, real property sect.), Colo. Bar Assn., Denver Bar Assn., Order of Coif, Beta Gamma Sigma. Corporate, general, Property, real (including real estate development, water). Office: Fleishman & Shapiro PC 1600 Broadway Ste 2600 Denver CO 80202-4926

BLITZER, SIDNEY MILTON, JR., lawyer; b. Baton Rouge, May 25, 1944; AB in Econs., Duke U., 1966; JD, La. State U., 1969. Bar: La. 1969; bd. cert. estate planning and adminstrn. specialist; bd. cert. tax atty. Assoc. Kantrow, Spaht, Weaver & Blitzer, Baton Rouge, 1969-72; prin. Kantrow, Spaht, Weaver & Blitzer APLC, Baton Rouge, 1972—. Spl. advisor continous revision trust com. La. Law Inst., 1975-76, mem. trust com., 1992—, mem. successions and donations com., 1990—; adj. prof. La. State U. Law Ctr., 1975-76, 83-97. Contbr. articles to profl. jours. Former bd. dirs. Baton Rouge Assn. Retarded Citizens, La. Easter Seal Soc., Baton Rouge Easter Seal Soc. Fellow Am. Coll. Trust and Estate Coun.; mem. ABA, Internat. Acad. Trust and Estate Law, La. Bar Assn. (lcetr.), Baton Rouge Bar Assn., Baton Rouge Estate and Bus. Planning Coun. Estate planning, Probate (including wills, trusts), Estate taxation. Office: Kantrow Spaht Weaver & Blitzer APLC PO Box 2997 Baton Rouge LA 70821-2997

BLIVAISS, DAVID HARVEY, lawyer, accountant; b. Chgo., Ill., May 4, 1949; s. Dr. Ben B. and Helen A. (Friedman) B.; m. Karen N. Rosenberg, Aug. 20, 1972; children: Jeffrey E., Amanda R. BSBA in Acctg., Roosevelt U., 1971; JD, Loyola U., 1974. Bar: Ill. 1974, NJ 1991; CPA Ill. 1975, NY 1984, NJ 1990. Various positions Arthur Andersen & Co., Chgo., 1974-83, ptnr. NYC, 1983-91, Eisner LLP, NYC, 1991—. Mem. AICPA, ABA, Wall Street Tax Assn. Office: Eisner LLP 750 3rd Ave New York NY 10017

BLIZMAN, PAUL JOHN, lawyer, social worker; b. Wyandotte, Mich., June 4, 1940; s. Paul J. and Olga G. (Rudenko) B.; student U. Mich., 1958-62; AB, Wayne State U., 1966, MSW, 1969; JD, Detroit Coll. Law, 1980; m. Leah Snyder, Sept. 3, 1967; 1 child, Alexis. Counselor, Reception Ctr. W.J. Maxey Sch., Whitmore Lake, Mich., 1969-71, social work supr., 1971-72, dir., 1972-74; licensing cons. Mich. Dept. Social Svcs., 1974-78; clin. social worker Health Care Inst., Detroit, 1979-80, Detroit Receiving Hosp., Univ. Health Ctr., 1980-82; pvt. practice law, 1981-83, 86—; ptnr. Melamed & Blizman, P.C., 1983-84, Melamed Blizman & Dailey, P.C., 1984-86 ; pvt. practice social work, Birmingham, Mich., 1975-85; field instr. social work Wayne State U., 1979-82. Mem. Farmington Hills Energy Commn., 1984-86; mem. Farm Hills Historic Dist. Commn., 1985—, chmn., 1988—, Farm Hills Planning Commn., 1987—. Mem. ABA, Mich. State Bar, Oakland County Bar Assn., Delta Theta Phi. General practice, Landlord-tenant, Probate (including wills, trusts). Home: 28700 Herndonwood Dr Farmington MI 48334-5235 Office: 26105 Orchard Lake Rd Ste 200 Farmington Hills MI 48334-4578

BLOCH, ALAN NEIL, federal judge; b. Pitts., Apr. 12, 1932; s. Gustave James and Molly Dorothy B.; m. Elaine Claire Amdur, Aug. 24, 1957; children: Rebecca Lee, Carolyn Jean, Evan Amdur. BS in Econs, U. Pa., 1953; JD, U. Pitts., 1958. Bar: Pa. 1959. Indsl. engr. U.S. Steel Corp., 1953; practice law Pitts., 1959-79; judge U.S. Dist. Ct. (we. dist.) Pa., Pitts., 1979-96, sr. judge, 1997—. Mem. Jud. Conf. U.S. Com. on Ct. Security, 1987-92; chmn. joint task force on death penalty representation Supreme Ct. Pa.-Ct. Appeals; past mem. Rule 11 task force Ct. Appeals (3d cir.). Contbr. articles to legal publs. Served with AUS, 1953-55. Mem. Am. Bar Assn., Acad. Trial Lawyers Allegheny County, Duquesne Club, Phi Delta Phi. Clubs: River. Jewish. Office: US Dist Ct We Dist US Post Office and Courthouse 700 Grant St Ste 837 Pittsburgh PA 15219-1934*

BLOCH, DONALD MARTIN, lawyer; b. Lynn, Mass., May 16, 1939; s. Meyer James and Bertha (Berman) B.; m. Ellen Ann Green, June 18, 1961; children: Andrew Louis, Linda Phyllis, David Michael. BA, Bowdoin Coll., 1960; LLB, Harvard U., 1963. Bar: Mass. 1963, U.S. Dist. Ct. Mass. 1974. Assoc. Lane, Altman & Owens LLP , Boston, 1966-71; ptnr. Lane, Altman & Owens LLP, Boston, 1972-2001; of counsel Posternak, Blankstein & Lund, LLP, Boston, 2001—. Mem. Framingham (Mass.) Town Meeting, 1970-95, Town Charter Commn., Framingham, 1978-79, Town Finance Com., 2002—; bd. dirs. South Middlesex Assn. for Retarded, Framingham, 1980-86, Metrowest Mental Health Assn., Framingham, 1983-95, Mary Morse Healthcare Inc., 1997—, vice chair, 2000-01, chair, 2001—; mem. Mass. Adv. Com. to U.S. Civil Rights Commn., 1991-93. Capt. U.S. Army, 1963-65. Named one of Outstanding Citizens, Greater Framingham Jewish Fedn., 1983. Mem. Harvard Club Boston, Bowdoin Club Boston (officer, bd. dirs.), Phi Beta Kappa. Republican. Corporate, general, Landlord-tenant, Property, real (including real estate development, water). Office: Posternak Blankstein & Lund LLP 100 Charles River Plz Boston MA 02114 E-mail: donmbloch@aol.com., dbloch@pbl.com.

BLOCH, FRANK SAMUEL, law educator; b. Jan. 16, 1945; s. Felix Jacob and Lore Clara (Misch) B.; m. Melissa Roth, Mar. 12, 1972; children: Julia Devi, Sara Shanti. BA, Brandeis U., 1966, MA, 1971, PhD, 1978; JD, Columbia U., 1969. Bar: Calif. 1970, Tenn. 1980, U.S. Dist. Ct. (no. dist.) Calif. 1971, U.S. Ct. Appeals (7th cir.) 1976, U.S. Dist. Ct. (mid. dist.) Tenn. 1980, U.S. Ct. Appeals (6th cir.) 1983. Assoc. atty. Calif. Rural Legal Assistance, Madera, Calif., 1971-72, directing atty., 1972-73; lectr. in law, clin. fellow U. Chgo., 1974-79; assoc. prof. law Vanderbilt U., Nashville, 1979-86, prof., 1986—, dir. clin. edn., 1979-2001. Pres. Legal Svcs. of Mid. Tenn., Inc., 1991-92, 95-96; cons. Internat. Social Security Assn., 1993-2000; cons. Adminstrv. Conf. of U.S., 1988-93. Author: Disability Determination, 1992, Bloch on Social Security Disability, 2002; editor: Who Returns to Work and Why?, 2001; contbr. articles to profl. jours. Rsch. fellow Internat. Social Security Assn., 1992-93; Fulbright grantee, 1986. Mem.: ABA, Nat. Acad. Social Ins. Democrat. Jewish. Home: 1119 Park Ridge Dr Nashville TN 37215-4515 Office: Vanderbilt U Sch Law 131 21st Ave S Nashville TN 37203-1120

BLOCK, CHERYL D. law educator; JD, SUNY, Buffalo, 1979. Bar: N.Y., U.S. Tax Ct., U.S. Dist. Ct. (so. and ea. dists.) N.Y. Law clk. Hon. Kevin Thomas Duffy, N.Y.C., 1979—80; assoc. Lord, Day & Lord, N.Y.C., 1980—82; assoc. prof. law U. Mo., Columbia, 1982—84, U. N.Mex., Albuquerque, 1984—85; prof. law George Washington U., Washington, 1985—. Author: (book) Corporate Taxation: Examples and Explanations, 1998, 2001. Co-founder, bd. dirs. Literacy Vols. of Am., Washington Capitol Area. Office: George Washington Univ School of Law 716 20th St NW Washington DC 20016

BLOCK, DENNIS JEFFREY, lawyer; b. Bronx, N.Y., Sept. 1, 1942; s. Martin and Betty (Berger) B.; m. Lauren Elizabeth Troupin, Nov. 27, 1967; children: Robert, Tracy, Meredith. BA, U. Buffalo, 1964; LLB, Bklyn. Law Sch., 1967. Bar: N.Y. 1968, U.S. Dist. Ct. (ea. dist.) N.Y., U.S. Dist. Ct. (so. dist.) N.Y., U.S. Ct. Appeals (2d, 3d, 5th, 6th, 7th, 8th, 9th, 10th and 11th cirs.), U.S. Supreme Ct. Br. chief SEC, N.Y.C., 1967-72; assoc. Weil, Gotshal & Manges, L.L.P., N.Y.C., 1972-74, ptnr., 1974-98, Cadwalader, Wickersham & Taft, LLP, N.Y.C., 1998—. Co-author: The Business Judgment Rule: Fiduciary Duties of Corporate Directors and Officers, Law & Business, Inc., 1987, 5th edit., 1998; co-editor: The Corporate Counselor's Desk Book, 1982, 5th edit., 1999; contbr. articles to profl. jours. Chmn. major gifts lawyers div., United Jewish Appeal Fedn., 1987-89, chmn. lawyers div., 1989-91. Mem. ABA (coun. litigation sect., com. on corp. laws sect. bus. law), Assn. of Bar of City of N.Y., Am. Law Inst.

BLOCK, FRANKLIN LEE, retired lawyer; b. Wilmington, N.C., Nov. 24, 1936; s. Charles Morris and Hannah (Solomon) B.; m. Wendy Barshay, June 14, 1959; children: Steven, Amy, Ellen. BS, The Citadel, 1959; JD, Wake Forest U., 1976. Bar: N.C. 1976. Pvt. practice, Wilmington, N.C., 1978-81; ptnr. Block & Trask, Wilmington, 1981-95, Block, Crouch, Keefer and Huffman, 1996-98; ret., 1998. Mem. N.C. Senate, 1987-92; U.S. magistrate (part-time) Eastern Dist. N.C., 1977-86. V.p. pres. Cape Fear United Way, Wilmington, 1982-83, pres. 1985; bd. trustees U. N.C., 1995—. Capt. U.S. Army, 1959-61. Mem. ABA, N.C. Bar Assn., N.C. Acad. Trial Lawyers, Masons. Democrat. Jewish. Address: 322 Causeway Dr Wrightsville Beach NC 28480-1911

BLOCK, MARCENE BURGESS, lawyer; b. Salina, Kans., May 15, 1954; d. Richard Benton and Marcene (Reynolds) Burgess; m. Frank Emmanuel Block Jr., Nov. 15, 1975; children: Frank Emmanuel III, Richard Burgess, John Burckhardt. Student, Smith Coll., 1972-74; BA, U. Va., Charlottesville, 1976, JD, 1979. Bar: N.C. 1980, Fla. 1984. Assoc. Everett, Creech & Hancock, Durham, N.C., 1981-82; sole practice Durham, 1982-83, Vero Beach, Fla., 1984-87. Mem. N.C. State Bar Assn., Fla. State Bar Assn. Republican. Anglican. Address: 141 El Dorado Dr Little Rock AR 72212-2763

BLOCK, NEAL JAY, lawyer; b. Chgo., Oct. 4, 1942; s. William Emanual and Dorothy (Harrison) B.; m. Frances Keer Block, Apr. 19, 1970; children: Jessica, Andrew. BS, U. Ill., 1964; JD, U. Chgo., 1967. Bar: Ill. 1967, U.S. dist. Ct. (no. dist.) Ill. 1967, U.S. Ct. Appeals (3d and 6th cirs.) 1968, U.S. Claims Ct. 1990, U.S. Ct. Appeals (Fed. cir.) 1991. Atty., advisor U.S. Tax Ct., Washington, 1967-69; assoc. Baker & McKenzie, Chgo., 1969-74, ptnr., 1974—, client credit dir., 1989—. Adj. prof. law Kent Law Sch., Ill. Inst. Tech., Chgo., 1986-90. Mem. ABA, Chgo. Bar Assn. (chmn. fed. tax com. 1983-84), Ill. State Bar Assn., AICPA (honorable mention award 1964), Ill. Soc. CPA's. (silver medal 1964, Leading Ill. Atty. 1997). Public international, Corporate taxation, Personal income taxation. Office: Baker & McKenzie 1 Prudential Pla 130 E Randolph St Ste 3500 Chicago IL 60601-6342

BLOCK, NELSON R(ICHARD), lawyer; b. San Antonio, Mar. 24, 1951; s. Norman and Ethel (Poliakoff) B. BA, Johns Hopkins U., 1973; JD, U. Tex., 1976. Bar: Tex. 1976. Law clk. 14th Ct. Appeals, Houston, 1976-77; assoc. Sheinfeld, Maley & Kay, P.C., Houston, 1977-83, shareholder, 1983-2001, Winstead Sechrest & Minick P.C., Houston, 2001—. Spkr. in field. Author: Commercial Law Manual: Ch. 40 Contractural Subordination, 1991, A Thing of the Spirit: The Life of E. Urner Goodman, 2000; pub. The Jour. of Scouting History. Mem. bd. dirs., legal counsel Sam Houston Area coun. Boy Scouts Am., 1984—, mng. trustee The Green Bar Bill Hillcourt Trust; mem. Baden-Powell World Fellowship. Fellow Gilwell (founder); mem. ABA, Tex. Bar Assn. (chmn. uniform comml. code com. 1982-84), Houston Bar Assn., Tex. Bar Found., Selden Soc. (state corr. 1978—), Houston Comml. Fin. Lawyers Forum (founder), Am. Coll. of Comml. Fin. Lawyers (regent). Avocations: camping, hiking, reading, history, sketching. Banking, Commercial, contracts (including sales of goods; commercial financing). Office: 910 Travis St Ste 2400 Houston TX 77002 E-mail: nblock@winstead.com.

BLOCK, RICHARD RAPHAEL, lawyer, arbitrator; b. Phila., Nov. 9, 1938; s. Harry and Ida (Brandes) B.; m. Joanne Kramer, July 1, 1943 (div. Jan. 1973); 1 child, Jeffrey. AB, Dickinson Coll., 1959; LLB cum laude, U. Pa., 1962. Bar: Pa. 1963, N.J. 1980, D.C. 1982. Assoc. Folz & Bard, Phila., 1963-64; ptnr. Melzer & Schiffrin, Phila., 1964-75, Beitch & Block, Phila., 1975-90; dir. community rels. Dist. Atty. of Phila., 1991-96; chief tech. officer Phila. Dept. of Commerce, 1996—. Chmn. hearing com Disciplinary Bd. Supreme Ct. Pa., 1982-90. Contbg. author: Handbook of Pennsylvania Courts, 1970, Divorce Mediation, 1985, Prenuptial Agreements, 1989, Encyclopedia on Matrimonial Practice, 1991; assoc. editor U. Pa. Law Rev.; contbr. articles to profl. jours. Vice pres. Am. Jewish Congress, Phila., 1975; campaign mgr. Elect Joan Specter to City Coun., Phila., 1978, 82, 86. Mem. Pa. Bar Assn. (arbitrator Inter-Atty. Dispute Resolution 1987—, speaker 1988) Am. Arbitration Assn., Phila. Coll. Judiciary (lectr. 1984). Republican. Avocations: horse racing, computers, music.

BLOEDE, VICTOR CARL, lawyer, academic executive; b. Woodwardville, Md., July 17, 1917; s. Carl Schon and Eleanor (Eck) B.; m. Ellen Louise Miller, May 9, 1947; children— Karl Abbott, Pamela Elena AB, Dartmouth Coll., 1940; JD cum laude, U. Md., Balt., 1950; LLM in Pub. Law, Georgetown U., 1967. Bar: Md. 1950, Fed. Hawaii 1958, U.S. Supreme Ct. 1971. Pvt. practice, Balt., 1950-64; mem. Goldman & Bloede, Balt., 1959-64; counsel Seven-Up Bottling Co., Balt., 1958-64; dep. atty. gen. Pacific Trust Ter., Honolulu, 1952-53; asst. solicitor for ters. Office of Solicitor, U.S. Dept. Interior, Washington, 1953-54; atty. U.S. Justice, Honolulu, 1955-58; assoc. gen. counsel Dept. Navy, Washington, 1960-61, 63-64; spl. legal cons. Md. Legislature, Legis. Council, 1963-64, 66-67; assoc. prof. U. Hawaii, 1961-63, dir. property mgmt., 1964-67; house counsel, dir. contracts and grants U. Hawaii System, 1967-82; house counsel U. Hawaii Research Corp., 1970-82; legal counsel Law of Sea Inst., 1978-82; legal cons. Rsch. Corp. and grad. rsch. divsn. U. Hawaii, 1982-92. Spl. counsel to Holifield Congl. Commn. on Govt. Procurement, 1970-73. Author: Hawaii Legislative Manual, 1962, Maori Affairs, New Zealand, 1964, Oceanographic Research Vessel Operations, and Liabilities, 1972, Hawaiian Archipelago, Legal Effects of a 200 Mile Territorial Sea, 1973, Copyright-Guidelines to the 1976 Act, 1977, Forms Manual, Inventions: Policy, Law and Procedure, 1982; writer, contbr. Coll. Law Digest and other publs. on legislation and pub. law. Mem. Gov.'s Task Force Hawaii and The Sea, 1969, Citizens Housing Com. Balt., 1952-64; bd. govs. Balt. Cmty. YMCA, 1954-64; bd. dirs. U. Hawaii Press, 1964-66, Coll. Housing Found., 1968-80; appointed to internat. rev. commn. Canada-France Hawaii Telescope Corp., 1973-82, chmn., 1973, 82; co-founder, incorporator First Unitarian Ch. Honolulu. Served to lt. comdr. USNR, 1942-45, PTO. Grantee ocean law studies NSF and NOAA, 1970-80. Mem. ABA, Balt. Bar Assn., Fed. Bar Assn., Am. Soc. Internat. Law, Nat. Assn. Univ. Attys. (founder & 1st chmn. patents & copyrights sect. 1974-76). Home: 635 Onaha St Honolulu HI 96816-4918

BLOM, DANIEL CHARLES, lawyer, investor; b. Portland, Oreg., Dec. 13, 1919; s. Charles D. and Anna (Reiner) B.; m. Ellen Lavon Stewart, June 28, 1952; children: Daniel Stewart (dec.), Nicole Jan Heath. BA magna cum laude, U. Wash., 1941, postgrad., 1941-42; JD, Harvard U., 1948; postgrad., U. Paris, 1954-55. Bar: Wash. 1949, U.S. Supreme Ct. 1970. Tchg. fellow speech U. Wash., 1941—42; law clk. to justice Supreme Ct. Wash., 1948—49; since practiced in Seattle; assoc. Graves, Kizer & Graves, 1949—51; gen. counsel Northwestern Life Ins. Co., 1952—54; ptnr. Case & Blom, 1952—54; assoc., ptnr., of counsel Ryan, Swanson & Cleveland, 1956—; exec. v.p., gen. counsel Family Life Ins. Co., 1964—85, spl. counsel, 1985—91. Vice chmn. Wash. Bd. Bar Examiners, 1970-72, chmn., 1972-75; mem. industry adv. com. Nat. Assn. Ins. Commrs., 1966-68; pres. Wash. Ins. Coun,, 1971-73, gen. counsel, 1975-78; mediator Arbitration Forums, Inc. Editor Wash. State Bar Jour., 1951-52; assoc. editor The Brief, 1975-76; author: Life Insurance Law of the State of Washington, 1980, Banking and Insurance, Deregulatory Cross-Currents, 1985, Hostile Insurance Company Takeovers: New Frontier of the Law, 1990, Administrative Finality Under the Washington Insurance Code, 1991, Business and Professionalism, 1994, The Civility Problem, 1995, Technics and the Civilization of Law Practice, 1997, Varieties of Regulatory Experience, 1998, Legislative Review of Administrative Rules in the State of Washington; A Light that Failed?, 2003. Chmn. jury selection Wash. Gov.'s Writer's Day Awards, 1976; bd. dirs. Crisis Clinic; trustee Bush Sch., 1971-79, v.p., 1976-77; trustee, v.p. Frye Mus., Seattle, 1976-82, World Affairs Coun. Seattle, 1972-94, Friends of Seattle Pub. Libr., 1982-87; bd. visitors U. Wash. Libr., 88-92, Friends of U. Wash. Librs., bd. dirs., 1991-95, pres., 1991-92. 2d lt. AUS, 1942-45, PTO. Decorated Bronze Star; Rhodes scholarship finalist, 1949. Fellow: Am. Bar Found.; mem.: ABA (vice chmn. com. on life ins. law, sect. tort and ins. pratice 1971—76, chmn. 1976—78, sect. program chmn. 1978—79, mem. coun. 1979—83, chmn. pub. rels. com. 1981—83, chmn. com. on profl. independence of the lawyer 1984—85, chmn. com. on scope and correlation 1985—86, chmn. com. on handbook and bylaws 1987—88, chmn. hist. com. 1991—94, del. ABA to Union Internat. des Avocats 1986—91, policy coord. tort and ins. practice sect. 1986—90), Fedn. Regulatory Counsel (dir. 1995—97, 2002—03), Found. UIA (coun. 1990—97), Am. Arbitration Assn., Am. Coun. Life Ins. (legis. com. 1982—85), Assn. Life Ins. Counsel, Am. Judicature Soc., N.Am. Found. for Internat. Legal Practice (dir. 1987—95, pres. 1987—89, chmn. 1990—95), Union Internat. des Avocats (v.p. 1987—92), Seattle Bar Assn., Wash. Bar Assn. (chmn. legal edn. liaison com. 1977—78, award of merit 1975), Harvard Assn. Seattle and Western Wash. (trustee 1976—77), Harvard Law Sch. Assn., Rainier Club, Tau Kappa Alpha, Phi Beta Kappa. Administrative and regulatory, Corporate, general, Insurance. Home: 100 Ward St # 602-3 Seattle WA 98109-5613 Office: Ryan Swanson & Cleveland 1201 3rd Ave Ste 3400 Seattle WA 98101-3034 E-mail: blom@msn.com.

BLOMBERG, ERIK BÏSON, lawyer; b. Helsingborg, Sweden, Mar. 2, 1974; Cert. of proficiency, U. Canterbury, Christchurch, New Zealand, 1998; LLM, U. Lund, Sweden, 1999, Ruprecht-Karls-U., Heidelberg, Germany, 2000. Asst. judge City Ct. Stockholm, 2000—02; assoc. Baker & McKenzie, Stockholm, 2002—. 2nd lt. Swedish Air Force Res., 1995—. Corporate, general, Mergers and acquisitions, Commercial, contracts (including sales of goods; commercial financing). Office: Baker & McKenzie Linnégatan 18 Stockholm Sweden

BLOODWORTH, A(LBERT) W(ILLIAM) FRANKLIN, lawyer; b. Atlanta, Sept. 23, 1935; s. James Morgan Bartow and Elizabeth Westfield (Dimmock) B.; m. Elizabeth Howell, Nov. 24, 1967; 1 child, Elizabeth Howell. AB in History and French, Davidson Coll., 1957; JD magna cum laude with 1st honors, U. Ga., 1963. Bar: Ga. 1962, U.S. Supreme Ct. 1971. Asst. dir. alumni and pub. relations Davidson Coll., N.C., 1959-60; assoc. Hansell & Post, Atlanta, 1963-68, ptnr., 1969-84, Bloodworth & Nix, Atlanta, 1984-95, Bloodworth & McSwain, Atlanta, 1996—. Counsel organized crime com. Met. Atlanta Commn. on Crime, 1965-67; asst. sec., counsel Met. Found. Atlanta, 1968-76. Bd. dirs. Atlanta Presbytery, 1974-78; trustee Synod of S.E., Presbyn. Ch. in U.S.A., Augusta, Ga., 1982-87; trustee Big Canoe Chapel, Ga., 1983-86, 88-91, chmn. bd. trustees, 1985-86, 90-91; mem. pres.'s adv. coun. Presbyn. Homes, 1989—; mem. president's adv. coun. Thornwell Home and Sch. for Children, 1998—. elder North Ave Presbyn. Ch., Atlanta. 1st lt. Intelligence Corps, USAR, 1957-59. Recipient Jessie Dan MacDougal Scholarship award U. Ga. Found., 1963, Outstanding Student Leadership award Student Bar Assn., U. Ga., 1963. Fellow Am. Coll. Trust and Estate Counsel; mem. ABA, State Bar Ga., Atlanta Bar Assn., Atlanta Estate Planning Coun., North Atlanta Estate Planning Coun., Capital City Club, Lawyers Club, Sphinx Club, Gridiron Club, Phi Beta Kappa, Phi Kappa Phi, Omicron Delta Kappa, Alpha Tau Omega (pres. chpt. 1957), Phi Delta Phi (grad. of yr. 1963, pres. chpt. 1963). Republican. Presbyterian. Alternative dispute resolution, Federal civil litigation, Education and schools. Home: 3784 Club Dr NE Atlanta GA 30319-1108 Office: 706 Monarch Plz 3414 Peachtree Rd NE Atlanta GA 30326-1153 Fax: 404 231-9330. E-mail: awfb@bloodworthandmcswain.com.

BLOOM, ALLEN JERRY, lawyer; b. St. Louis, May 6, 1930; d. Morris K. and Dorothy Marie (Barken) B.; m. Jeanne Akers, Nov. 23, 1960; children: Lisa S., Michael W. BSBA in Acctg., Wash. U., St. Louis, 1953; JD, St. Louis U., 1957. Bar: Mo. 1957, Ill. 1991, U.S. Dist. Ct. Mo. 1957, U.S. Dist. Ct. (so. dist.) Ill., 1990. Pvt. practice, St. Louis, 1957—. Sgt. USAF, 1948-49. Mem. ABA, Met. Bar Assn., Mo. Bar Assn. Commercial, consumer (including collections, credit), General practice, Probate (including wills, trusts). Office: 7606 Forsyth Blvd Saint Louis MO 63105 E-mail: ajbloom@anet.stl.com.

BLOOM, CHARLES JOSEPH, lawyer; b. Pitts., July 7, 1946; s. Israel C. and Ida (Lample) B.; m. Susan Halsey Potts, May 14, 1971; children: Zachary B., Amanda H., Theodore L. BA, Princeton U., 1967; JD magna cum laude, U. Pa., Phila., 1971. Bar: Pa. 1971, U.S. Dist. Ct. (ea. dist.) Pa. 1971, U.S. Ct. Appeals (3d cir.) 1972, U.S. Supreme Ct. 1978. Law clk. U.S. Ct. Appeals (3d cir.), Phila., 1971-72; assoc. Pepper, Hamilton & Scheetz, Phila., 1972-78, ptnr., 1978-80, Hunt, Kerr, Bloom & Hitchner, Phila., 1980-85, Kleinbard, Bell & Brecker, Phila., 1985-92, Stevens & Lee, P.C., Wayne, Pa., 1992—. Bd. dirs. Main Line Art Ctr., 1997—, Cloister Inn Princeton, 1980-89, chmn., 1983-85; commr. Lower Merion Twp., 1998—; v.p. Haverford (Pa.) Civic Assn., 1989—, pres., 1998. Mem. Phila. Bar Assn. (fed. cts. com. 1975—, chmn. unauthorized practice law com. 1985, bench-bar conf. com. 1985-90), Order of Coif. Avocations: numismatics, collecting antique toy trains. Federal civil litigation, Commercial, contracts (including sales of goods; commercial financing), Libel. E-mail: cjb@stevenslee.com.

BLOOM, NORMAN DOUGLAS, JR., lawyer; b. Albuquerque, Apr. 6, 1928; s. Norman Douglas and Rose (Conway) B.; m. Janet Pierce, June 11, 1949 (div. June 1970); children— Ellen Clarie, Nancy Rose, Verna Madge; m. Betty Minter, Aug. 8, 1970; children— Dorothy Jane, Norma Jo, Deborah Kay, Brenda, Nathan Dean, Norman Douglas III. B.A., U. Colo., 1952; J.D., U. N.Mex., 1966; postgrad. Nat. Dist. Attys. Coll., 1972. Bar: N.Mex. 1966, U.S. Dist. Ct. N.Mex. 1966, U.S. Ct. Appeals (10th cir.) 1975, U.S. Supreme Ct. 1977, U.S. Ct. Claims 1979. Ptnr. Fettinger, Bloom & Overstreet, Alamogordo, N.Mex., 1966-71; dist. atty. 12th Jud. Dist., Otero and Lincoln Counties, N.Mex., 1971-75; ptnr. Fettinger & Bloom, Alamogordo, 1975-94, Fettinger, Bloom & Quinlan, P.C., 1994—. Organizer, founder La Placita Children's Home, Alamogordo, 1972, pres., 1975— . Served with AUS, 1946-47; PTO. Recipient Service to Mankind awards Sertoma Club, 1978, Sertoma Internat. of South N.Mex.-S.W. Tex., 1978, Greater Rocky Mountain Region, 1978. Mem. N.Mex. State Bar Assn. Otero County Bar Assn. (sec.-treas. 1967-68, pres. 1971-72, 84-85).

Lodges: Kiwanis (bd. dirs. 1968-70, 76-78, Elks (trustee 1967-70) (Alamogordo), So. N.Mex. Am. Inns of Ct. (master bencher). State civil litigation, General practice, Juvenile. Home: 17 Indian Maid Ln Alamogordo NM 88310-9756 Office: Quinlan Bloom & Assoc PC PO Box 600 Alamogordo NM 88311

BLOOMER, HAROLD FRANKLIN, JR., retired lawyer; b. N.Y.C., Nov. 4, 1933; s. Harold Franklin and Allene (Cress) B.; m. Mary Jane Lloyd, July 16, 1955 (div. June 1976); children: Sarah Allene, Margaret Gail, Leslie Lloyd; m. Freya Donald, Nov. 30, 1985; children: Katharine Roma, Alice Donald. AB, Amherst Coll., 1956; LLB, Columbia U., 1967. Bar: Conn. 1967, N.Y. 1968, U.S. Dist. Ct. Conn. 1968, U.S. Dist. Ct. (so. and ea. dists.) N.Y. 1974, U.S. Ct. Appeals (2d cir.) 1974. Assoc. Debevoise, Plimpton, Lyons & Gates, N.Y.C., 1967-77; counsel Burlington, Underwood & Lord, Jeddah, Saudi Arabia, 1977-78; chief internat. counsel Saudi Rsch. & Devel. Corp., London, 1978-80; counsel Morgan, Lewis & Bockius LLP, London and N.Y.C., 1980-81, ptnr., 1981-2000; ret., 2000. Adj. prof. Pepperdine U. Sch. Law, London, 1985. Trustee San. Products Trust, Riverside, Conn., 1965—74; trip leader Adventure Cycling Assn., Missoula, Mont., 2000; mem. Conn. com. East Coast Greenway, 2001—; co-chmn. bd. Coastal Corridor Transp. Investment Area, State of Conn., 2001—; mem. Rep. Town Meeting, Greenwich, Conn., 1964—74, 1992—, chmn. pub. works com., 1971—74, chmn. land use com., 1998—; mem. Rep. Town Com., Greenwich, Conn., 1973—74. Lt. j.g. USNR, 1957—60. Kent scholar Columbia U., 1965-66, Stone scholar Columbia U., 1966-67. Mem. Am. Arbitration Assn. (panel of arbitrators 1990—), Riverside Yacht Club. Republican. Episcopalian. Avocations: sailing, canoeing, skiing, biking, running. Commercial, contracts (including sales of goods; commercial financing), Finance, Private international.

BLOOMFIELD, DAVID CHARLES, lawyer, educator, not-for-profit executive; b. N.Y.C., Feb. 19, 1952; BA, Brandeis U., 1975; JD, Columbia U., 1984; MPA, Princeton U., 1984. Bar: N.Y. 1984, D.C. 1985; cert. primary and elem. tchr., Mass.; cert. prin./supr., N.J.; cert. supt. N.Y. Tchr. New Lincoln Sch., N.Y.C., 1975-79; analyst Advocates for Children of N.Y., Queens, N.Y., 1979-80; law clk. to Judge Robert L. Carter U.S. Dist. Ct. (so. dist. N.Y.), N.Y.C., 1984-85; assoc. Hogan & Hartson, Washington, 1985-86; atty. N.Y.C. Law Dept., 1986-89; adminstr. N.Y.C. Bd. Edn., Bklyn., 1989-90, gen. counsel, 1990-91; gen. counsel, sr. edn. advisor Manhattan Borough Pres., N.Y.C., 1991-94; exec. dir. Partnership for Effective Edn. Mgmt., N.Y.C., 1994-96; adj. asst. prof. Tchrs. Coll. Columbia U., N.Y.C., 1996—98; assoc. prof. Bklyn. Coll., CUNY, 1999—. Head edn. adminstrn. program Bklyn. Coll. , 2001. Author: Attendance Improvement Programs in N.Y.C. Schools, 1979, African Ethnicity, 1976, Children First: N.Y.C. School Governance Legislation, 1993, Strategic Management of N.Y.C. Schools, 1997, Technology-Based Peer Education, 1999, No Child Left Behind Act, 2003, others. Recipient Paul Robeson prize Columbia U., N.Y.C., 1982, Harlan Fiske Stone scholar, 1982, Princeton (N.J.) U. fellow, 1982, African-Am. Inst. fellow, N.Y.C., 1976. E-mail: david11201@nyct.net.

BLOOMFIELD, DAVID SOLOMON, lawyer, educator; b. Dec. 13, 1944; s. Jerome P. and Anne M. (Knoll) Bloomfield; m. Sally Ward, June 4, 1969; children: David S., Paul W. BS, Ohio State U., 1966, JD, 1969; postgrad. in Law, NYU, 1969—71. Bar: Ohio 1969, U.S. Dist. Ct. (so. dist.) Ohio 1970, U.S. Dist. Ct. (no. dist.) Ohioi 1972, U.S. Ct. Appeals (6th cir.) 1973, U.S. Tax Ct. 1970, U.S. Supreme Ct. 1973. Mem. staff Lybrand Ross Bros. & Montgomery, N.Y.C., NY, 1969—70; chief tax sect. Atty. Gen. Ohio, Columbus, 1970—71; assoc., then ptnr. Ward Kaps Bainbridge Maurer Bloomfield & Melvin, and predecessor, Columbus, Ohio, 1971—92; ptnr. Bloomfield & Kempf, 1992—. Lectr. Capital U., 1972—78, Ohio Paralegal Inst., 1979; adj. prof. Capital U. Coll. Law, Columbus, 1980—, The Ohio State U., 1996—. Contbr. articles to profl. jours. Active Columbus United Way, 1979—; campaign chmn. Price for Judge, Columbus, 1980; bd. dir. N.W. Mental Health Assn., 1979—82. Recipient Merit award, Ohio Law Inst., 1975, Pub. Svc. award, U.S. Dept. Justice, 1996. Fellow: Ohio State Bar Assn.; mem.: ABA, Columbus Bar Assn. (chair coms., bd. commrs. on grievance and discipline of Supreme Ct. Ohio, client security fund Supreme Ct. Ohio), Ohio Bar Assn. (coms.), Ohio State U. Pres.'s Club (Columbus chpt.), Athletic Club. Democrat. Jewish. Avocation: woodworking. Immigration, naturalization, and customs. Home: 3741 Romnay Rd Columbus OH 43220-4877 Office: Bloomfield & Kempf 199 S 5th St Columbus OH 43215-5234 E-mail: dbloo@msn.com.

BLOOMFIELD, NEIL JON, lawyer, law educator, real estate broker; b. N.Y.C., July 25, 1945; s. Elmer Joel and Charlotte (Orlov) B.; children—Jennifer, Violet. BA cum laude, Princeton U., 1966, BA cum laude Woodrow Wilson Sch. Pub. and Internat. Affairs, 1966; cert. proficiency in pub. and internat. affairs, J.D. cum laude, Harvard U., 1969. Bar: N.Y. 1969, Calif. 1972. Assoc., Willkie, Farr & Gallagher, N.Y.C., 1969-73, ptnr. Bloomfield & Greene, 1974-80; pres. Bloomfield White & Whitney, Inc., Sausalito, Calif., 1974-77, Law Offices of Neil Jon Bloomfield, 1980—; bd. dirs. Vol. Lawyers for the Arts, N.Y.C., 1970-72; adj. prof. law U. San Francisco, 1982-83; judge pro-tem Marin Mcpl. Ct., 1983, 84; cert. expert in real estate law and trusts related to real estate Calif. Superior Ct.; spl. master, discovery referee Marin County Superior Ct., other various appts., 1987-91, 2003-. Mem. Marin County Bar Assn., San Francisco Bar Assn., Clolsrer Inn, Lincolns Inn Soc. (Cambridge). Editor: Community and Racial Crises, 1966; contbr. articles to profl. jours. including U. So. Calif. Law Rev., 1970. General civil litigation, Property, real (including real estate development, water), Taxation, general. Office: 901 E St Ste 100 San Rafael CA 94901-2928 E-mail: njb@earthlink.net.

BLOTNER, NORMAN DAVID, lawyer, real estate broker, corporate executive; b. Boston, Dec. 6, 1918; s. Leon and Sarah B.; m. Helen I. Whitman (dec.), Aug. 13, 1954; 1 son, James B. McClain (dec.). AB, Harvard U., 1940, JD, 1947. Bar: N.Y. 1948. Mem. firm Spiro, Felstiner, Prager & Treeger, N.Y.C., 1947-52; with Lane Bryant Inc., N.Y.C., 1953-82, sr. v.p., gen. counsel, sec., dir., 1968-82, ret., 1982. Bd. dirs. Better Bus. Bur. Met. N.Y., until 1982. Lt. comdr. USNR, 1941—46. Named Lacrosse All-am., 1940. Mem. Assn. of Bar of City of N.Y., Harvard Varsity Club, New Rochelle Tennis Club. Republican. Home: 140 Overlook Rd New Rochelle NY 10804-4139 also: 2784 S Ocean Blvd Palm Beach FL 33480-5506

BLOUNT, CHARLES WILLIAM, III, lawyer; b. Independence, Mo., Nov. 14, 1946; s. Charles William and Mary Marguarette (Van Trump) B.; m. Susan Penny Smith Turner, Dec. 20, 1969 (div. Nov., 1987); children: Charles William IV, Chaille Elizabeth; m. Bonnie M. Harp., Jan. 1, 1991. BS in Journalism, U. Kans., 1968; JD cum laude, U. Toledo, 1981. Bar: Mo. 1981, U.S. Dist. Ct. (we. dist.) Mo. 1981, Tex. 1985, U.S. Dist. Ct. (no. dist.) Tex. 1988, U.S. Ct. Appeals (5th cir.) 1995, U.S. Supreme Ct. 1997; cert. in civil appellate law Tex. Bd. Legal Specialization. Litigation assoc. Shugart, Thomson & Kilroy, Kansas City, Mo., 1981-84, Hughes & Luce, Dallas, 1984-87, Simpson & Dowd L.L.P., Dallas, 1987-91, ptnr., 1991-94; mem. Dowd & Blount, Dallas, 1994-99; ptnr. Perry-Miller & Blount, L.L.P., Dallas, 1999—2002; sr. counsel Smith, Underwood & Perkins, P.C., Dallas, 2002—. Mem. West Group Tex. Editl. Bd., 1999. Bd. govs. U. Toledo Coll. Law, 1980-81; trustee Episcopal Diocese We. Mo., Kansas City, 1983-84; mem., chmn. com. Boy Scouts of Am., Kansas City, 1983-84, Richardson, Tex., 1984-92. 1st lt. U.S. Army, 1968-72. Mem. Phi Kappa Phi, Phi Kappa Tau (pledge pres., social chmn., activities chmn., 1965—). Avocations: music, reading. Appellate, State civil litigation, Corporate, general. Office: Smith Underwood & Perkins PC 5420 LBJ Frwy Ste 600 Dallas TX 75240 E-mail: cblount@suplaw.com.

BLUESTEIN, EDWIN A., JR., lawyer; b. Hearne, Tex., Oct. 16, 1930; s. Edwin A. and Frances Grace (Ely) B.; m. Marsha Kay Meredith, Dec. 21, 1957; children: Boyd, Leslie. BBA, U. Tex., 1952, JD, 1958. Bar: Tex. 1957, U.S. Ct. Appeals (5th cir.) 1960, U.S. Dist. Ct. (so. dist.)Tex. 1959, U.S. Dist. Ct. (ea. dist.)Tex. 1965, U.S. Supreme Ct. 1967, U.S. Ct. Appeals (11th cir.) 1982. Law clk. U.S. Dist. Ct., Houston, 1958-59; assoc. Fulbright & Jaworski, Houston, 1959-65, participating atty., 1965-71, ptnr., 1971-97, head admiralty dept., 1984-93, sr. ptnr., 1990-97, of counsel, 1998—. Mem. permanent adv. bd. Tulane Admiralty Law Inst., New Orleans, 1983-2001; mem. planning com. Houston Marine Ins. Seminar, 1970-76; lectr. profl. seminars Assoc. editor: American Maritime Cases; contbr. articles to profl. jours. Mem. Tex. Coastal Mgmt. Adv. Com., Austin, 1975-78; bd. dirs. Barbour's Cut Seafarers Ctr., 1992—, Houston Internat. Seafarers Ctr., 1993—; chair Morgan's Point Beach Preservation Restoration Assn., 2001-. Served with U.S. Army, 1952-54. Recipient Yachtsman of Yr. award Houston Yacht Club, 1978; Eagle Scout, Boy Scouts Am., 1944. Mem. Tex. Bar Found., Maritime Law Assn. U.S. (mem. exec. com. 1980-83), Houston Maritime Arbitrators Assn. (sec.-treas. 1999—), Houston Mariners Club (pres. 1970), Southeastern Admiralty Law Inst. (dir. 1983-85, Houston C. of C. (chmn. ports and waterways com. 1978-79), Propeller Club U.S., Theta Xi (chpt. pres. 1952). Clubs: Houston Yacht (commodore 1979-80). Methodist. Admiralty, Insurance. Home: 603 Bayridge Rd La Porte TX 77571-3512 Office: Fulbright & Jaworski 1301 Mckinney St Houston TX 77010-3031

BLUESTONE, ANDREW LAVOOTT, lawyer; b. N.Y.C., Feb. 16, 1951; s. Henry Robert and Joan (Lavoott) B.; m. Janet Francesca Whelehan, May 1987; 1 child, Gabrielle. BA, Alfred U., 1973; MA, SUNY, Oswego, 1975; JD, Syracuse U., 1978. Bar: N.Y. 1979, U.S. Dist. Ct. (so. and ea. dists.) N.Y. 1979. Sr. trial asst. dist. atty. Kings County Dist. Atty., Bklyn., 1978-84; sr. assoc. Davis & Hoffman, N.Y.C., 1984-86, Donald Ayers, N.Y.C., 1986, Alexander, Ash, Schwartz & Cohen, N.Y.C., 1986-88, Trolman & Glaser, N.Y.C., 1988-89; pvt. practice, N.Y.C., 1989—. Arbitrator Small Claims Civil Ct. City of N.Y.; lectr. Practice Law Inst., N.Y. State Trial Lawyers Assn. Bd. dirs. Scandia Symphony, N.Y.C., St. Luke's AME Ch., N.Y.C. Mem. ABA, N.Y.C. Trial Lawyers Assn., Def. Assn. N.Y., Assn. Trial Lawyers Am. (lectr.), N.Y. State Trial Lawyers Assn., Bklyn. Bar Assn. General civil litigation, Commercial, contracts (including sales of goods; commercial financing), Personal injury (including property damage). Office: 233 Broadway Fl 51 New York NY 10279-5199

BLUM, HOWARD ALAN, lawyer; b. New Brunswick, N.J., Feb. 6, 1941; s. Robert Lawrence Blum and Matilda Lynn Hollander; m. Hinda Lee Funk, June 5, 1966 (div. June 11, 1983); children: Dina McCormick, Rachel Niewoehner; m. Nancy Jane Gettes, Jan. 15, 1984. BA, Bates Coll., 1963; JD, Harvard U., 1966. Lawyer Stolar Firm, St. Louis, 1966—69, Cohen, Shapiro, Polisher, et. al., Phila., 1969—95, Drinker, Biddle & Reath LLP, Phila., 1995—. Mem.: Harvard Law Sch. Assn. Greater Phila. (mem. exec. com. 1991—94). Avocations: hiking, walking, travel, historical novels. Corporate, general, Mergers and acquisitions, Securities. Office: Drinker Biddle and Reath LLP 1 Logan Sq 18th and Cherry St Philadelphia PA 19103-6996 Office Fax: 215-988-2757. Business E-Mail: howard.blum@dbr.com.

BLUMBERG, EDWARD ROBERT, lawyer; b. Phila., Feb. 15, 1951; BA in Psychology, U. Ga., 1972; JD, Coll. William and Mary, 1975. Bar: Fla., 1975, U.S. Dist. Ct. Fla. 1975, U.S. Ct. Appeals, 1975, U.S. Supreme Ct. 1979. Assoc. Knight, Peters, Hoeveler & Pickle, Miami, Fla., 1976-77; ptnr. Deutsch & Blumberg, P.A., Miami, 1978—. Adj. prof. U. Miami Sch. Paralegal Studies. Author: Proof of Negligence, Mathew Bender Florida Torts, 1988. Mem. ABA (ho. of dels. 1996-2002), ATLA, Dade County Bar Assn., Fla. State Bar (bd. govs., pres. elect 1996-97, pres. 1997-98), Acad. Fla. Trial Lawyers, Nat. Bd. Trial Advocacy (cert. civil trial adv.), Fla. Bar Found. (bd. dirs. 1996-99, bd. govs. 1996-99), Bankers Club (chmn. bd. govs. 2002-03). Personal injury (including property damage), Product liability, Professional liability. Office: Deutsch & Blumberg PA 100 Biscayne Blvd Fl 28 Miami FL 33132-2304

BLUMBERG, GERALD, lawyer; b. N.Y.C., July 25, 1911; s. Saul and Amelia (Abramowitz) B.; m. Rhoda Shapiro, Jan. 7, 1945; children: Lawrence, Rena, Alice, Leda. AB cum laude, Cornell U., 1931; JD cum laude, Harvard, 1934. Bar: Mass. 1934, N.Y. 1934. Pvt. practice, N.Y., 1934—; mem. firm Gerald & Lawrence Blumberg LLP. Instr. econs. Cornell U., 1931; mem. Harvard Legal Aid Bur., 1934. Bd. dirs., v.p., exec. com. Am. Com. Weizmann Inst. Sci.; internat. bd. govs. Weizmann Inst. Sci., 1982— . Mem. ABA, N.Y. State, Westchester, Yorktown bar assns., Phi Beta Kappa, Phi Kappa Phi. Estate planning, Probate (including wills, trusts), Estate taxation. Home: 1305 Baptist Church Rd Yorktown Heights NY 10598-5810 Office: Gerald & Lawrence Blumberg LLP 521 5th Ave New York NY 10175-0003

BLUMBERG, GRACE GANZ, law educator, lawyer; b. N.Y.C., Feb. 16, 1940; d. Samuel Gamz and Beatrice (Vinkelstein) Ganz; m. Donald R. Blumberg, Sept. 9, 1959; 1 child, Rachel. BA cum laude, U. Colo., 1960; JD summa cum laude, SUNY, 1971; LL.M., Harvard U., 1974. Bar: N.Y. 1971, Calif. 1989. Confidential law clk. Appellate Div., Supreme Ct., 4th Dept., Rochester, N.Y., 1971-72; teaching fellow Harvard Law Sch., Cambridge, Mass., 1972-74; prof. law SUNY, Buffalo, 1974-81, UCLA, 1981—. Reporter Am. Law Inst., Prins. of the Law of Family Dissolution, 2002. Author: Community Property in California, 1987, 1999, 2003, Blumberg's California Family Code Annotated; contbr. Office: UCLA Sch Law Box 951476 Los Angeles CA 90095-1476

BLUMBERG, PHILLIP IRVIN, law educator; b. Balt., Sept. 6, 1919; s. Hyman and Bess (Simons) B.; m. Janet Helen Mitchell, Nov. 17, 1945 (dec. 1976); children: William A.M., Peter M., Elizabeth B., Bruce M.; m. Ellen Ash Peters, Sept. 16, 1979. AB, Harvard U., 1939, JD, 1942; LLD (hon.), U. Conn., 1994. Bar: N.Y. 1942, Mass. 1970. Assoc. Willkie, Owen, Otis, Farr & Gallagher, N.Y.C., 1942-43, Szold, Brandwen, Meyers and Blumberg, N.Y.C., 1946-66; pres., CEO United Ventures Inc., 1962-67; pres., CEO, trustee Federated Devel. Co., N.Y.C., 1966-68, chmn. fin. com., 1968-73; prof. law Boston U., 1966-74; dean U. Conn. Sch. Law, Hartford, 1974-84, prof. law, 1984-89, dean, prof. law emeritus, 1989—. Bd. dirs. Verde Exploration Ltd.; mem. legal adv. com. to bd. dirs. N.Y. Stock Exch., 1989-93; mem. adv. com. on transnat. corps. U.S. Dept. State, 1976-79; advisor corp. governance project, restatement of suretyship and restatement of agy. Am. Law Inst.; vis. lectr. U. Brabant, Tilburg, Netherlands, 1985, U. Internat. Bus. and Econs., Beijing, 1989, U. Sydney, 1992, Jagiellonian U., Cracow, Poland, 1992. Author: Corporate Responsibility in a Changing Society, 1972, The Megacorporation in American Society, 1975, The Law of Corporate Groups: Procedure, 1983, The Law of Corporate Groups: Bankruptcy, 1985, The Law of Corporate Groups: Substantive Common Law, 1987, The Law of Corporate Groups: General Statutory Law, 1989, The Law of Corporate Groups: Specific Statutory Law, 1992, The Multinational Challenge to Corporation Law, 1993, The Law of Corporate Groups: State Statutory Law, 1995, The Law of Corporate Groups: Enterprise Liability, 1998; mem. editl. bd. Harvard Law Rev., 1940-42, treas., 1941-42; contbr. articles to profl. jours. Trustee Black Rock Forest Preserve, Inc.; trustee emeritus Conn. Bar Found. Capt. USAAF, 1943-46, ETO, maj. Res. 1946-55. Decorated Bronze Star Mem. ABA, Conn. Bar Assn., Am. Law Inst., Hartford Club, Harvard Club (Boston), Army & Navy Club (Washington), Phi Beta Kappa, Delta Upsilon. Home: 791 Prospect Ave Apt B-5 Hartford CT 06105-4224 Office: U Conn Sch Law 65 Elizabeth St Hartford CT 06105-2290 E-mail: pblumber@law.uconn.edu.

BLUME, PAUL CHIAPPE, lawyer; b. Omaha, Oct. 11, 1929; s. Herman Alexander and Marie (Simoni) B.; m. Mary Lou Higgins, June 28, 1958; children: Nancy, Julie, Paul II, William. BS in Commerce, Loyola U., Chgo.; JD. Bar: Ill. 1957. Legal sect. mgr. Aldens Inc., 1957-58; assoc. Lord, Bissell & Brook, 1959-63, of counsel, 1983—; v.p., gen. counsel Nat. Assn. Ind. Insurers, Des Plaines, Ill., 1963-83, Ill. Ins. Info. Svc., 1987-96; pres. Ins. Briefs, Inc., 1984—. Capt. U.S. Army, 1951-53. Mem. Chgo. Bar Assn., Fedn. Ins. Counsel. Office: 115 S La Salle St Chicago IL 60603-3801

BLUMENFELD, CHARLES RABAN, lawyer; b. Seattle, May 24, 1944; s. Irwin S. and Freda I. (Raban) B.; m. Karla Axell; children: David, Lisa. BA, U. Wash., JD, 1969. Bar: Wash. 1969, U.S. Dist. Ct. (we. dist.) Wash. 1969, U.S. Ct. Appeals (9th cir.) 1975, U.S. Supreme Ct. 1979, U.S. Dist. Ct. D.C. 1981, U.S. Ct. Appeals (D.C. cir.) 1981. Legis. counsel U.S. Senator Henry M. Jackson, Washington, 1969-72; ptnr. Bogle & Gates, Seattle, 1973-99, PerkinsCoie, Seattle, 1999—. Mem. ABA (sect. natural resources, energy and environment). Environmental, Land use and zoning (including planning), Legislative. Office: PerkinsCoie 1201 3rd Ave Fl 48 Seattle WA 98101-3029

BLUMENFELD, JACK BARRY, lawyer; b. Rochester, N.Y., July 31, 1952; s. Henry and Lillian (Krieger) B.; m. Jean Woodson Lodge, Feb. 28, 1982; children: Nathan, Rachel, Aaron, Mary. BA, SUNY, Albany, 1974; JD, Yale U., 1977. Bar: Del. 1979, U.S. Dist. Ct. Del. 1979, U.S. Ct. Appeals (3d cir.) 1984, U.S. Ct. Appeals (fed. cir.) 1985, U.S. Supreme Ct. 1987. Law clk. to dist. judge, Wilmington, Del., 1977-79; assoc. Morris, Nichols, Arsht & Tunnell, Wilmington, 1979-84, ptnr., 1985—. Mem. ABA, Del. State Bar Assn., Am. Intellectual Property Law Assn., N.Y. Patent Law Assn., Jewish Fedn. Del. (bd. dirs. 1985-97, officer 1988-93). Democrat. Federal civil litigation, Intellectual property, Patent. Office: Morris Nichols Arsht & Tunnell PO Box 1347 Wilmington DE 19899-1347

BLUMENFELD, JEFFREY, lawyer, educator; b. N.Y.C., May 13, 1948; s. Martin and Helen Kay (Smith) B.; m. Laura Madeline Ross, June 11, 1970; children: Jennifer Ross Blumenfeld, Joshua Ross Blumenfeld. AB in Religious Thought cum laude, Brown U., 1969; JD, U. Pa., 1973. Bar: D.C. 1973. Asst. U.S. atty. U.S. Atty. for D.C., Washington, 1975-79; trial atty. Antitrust div. U.S. Dept. of Justice, Washington, 1973-75, sr. trial atty. U.S. versus AT&T staff, 1979-82, asst. chief spl. regulated industries, 1982-84, chief U.S. versus AT&T staff, 1984, spl. counsel, 1995-97; ptnr. Blumenfeld & Cohen, Washington, 1984—2002; sr. trial counsel, antitrust divsn. U.S. Dept. Justice, 1996-97; gen. counsel, chief legal officer Rhythms Net Connections, 1997-2001; ptnr. Gray, Cary, Ware & Freidenrich, LLP, Washington, 2002—. Adj. prof. Georgetown U. Law Ctr., Washington, 1983—; spl. counsel antitrust divsn. U.S. Dept. Justice, 1995-97. Bd. dirs. Charles E. Smith Jewish Day Sch., Washington, 1991-93. Democrat. Jewish. Antitrust, Federal civil litigation, Communications. Office: Gray Cary Ware & Freidenrich LLP Ste 300 1625 Massachusetts Ave NW Washington DC 20036-2247

BLUMENTHAL, RICHARD, state attorney general; m. Cynthia Blumenthal; 4 children. BA, Harvard Coll.; JD, Yale U., 1973. Law clk. Justice Harry A. Blackmun, 1974—75; U.S. atty. State of Conn., 1977—81, former rep., 1984—87, senator, 1987—90, state atty. gen., 1990—. Sgt. USMC, Res. Democrat. Office: Atty Gen Office 55 Elm St Hartford CT 06106-1746

BLUMENTHAL, WILLIAM, lawyer; b. White Plains, N.Y., Nov. 4, 1955; s. Louis and Mary (Meyer) B.; m. Marjory Susan Spodick, Dec. 30, 1979; 1 child, Deborah Louise. AB, MA, Brown U., 1977; JD, Harvard U., 1980. Bar: D.C. 1980, U.S. Dist. Ct. D.C. 1986. Cons. Policy & Mgmt. Assocs., Inc., Boston, 1977-80; teaching fellow Harvard U., Cambridge, Mass., 1978-80; assoc. Jones, Day, Reavis & Pogue, Washington, 1980-83, Sutherland, Asbill & Brennan, Washington, 1983-87, ptnr., 1988-93, Kelley Drye & Warren, Washington, 1993-95, King & Spalding, Washington, 1995—. Editor Horizontal Mergers: Law and Policy, 1986; contbr. to book: The Merger Review Process, 1995, Mergers & Acquisitions Handbook, 1986. Harvey A. Baker fellow Brown U., 1977. Mem. ABA (chmn. Clayton Act com. 1992-94, chmn. monograph com. 1989-92, vice chmn. antitrust sect. 1997-98). Antitrust, Mergers and acquisitions. E-mail: wblumenthal@kslaw.com.

BLUMKIN, LINDA RUTH, lawyer; b. Aug. 25, 1944; d. Louis and Edith (Fortus) Blumkin. AB cum laude, Barnard Coll., 1964; LLB cum laude, Harvard U., 1967, LLM, 1973. Bar: N.Y. 1968, U.S. Dist. Ct. (so. dist.) N.Y. 1969, U.S. Ct. Appeals (2nd cir.) 1969, U.S. Supreme Ct. 1982. Assoc. Fried, Frank, Harris, Shriver & Jacobson, N.Y.C., 1967—71, ptnr., 1979—. Lectr. Boston U., 1971, asst. prof. mgmt., 1972—73; assoc. Breed, Abbott & Morgan, N.Y.C., 1973—77; asst. dir. Bur. Competition, Fed. Trade Commn., 1977—79. Mem.: ABA, N.Y.C. Bar Assn. Antitrust, Federal civil litigation. Office: Fried Frank Harris Shriver & Jacobson 1 New York Plz Fl 24 New York NY 10004-1901

BLUMSTEIN, EDWARD, lawyer; b. Phila., Aug. 24, 1933; s. Isaac and Mollye (Rodofsky) B.; m. Susan Perloff, Aug. 13, 1983; 1 child, Daniel Blumstein. BS in Econs., U. Pa., 1955; JD, Temple U., 1958. Bar: U.S. Dist. Ct. (ea. dist.) Pa. 1959, U.S. Ct. Appeals (3rd cir.) 1959. Pvt. practice, Phila., 1959-85; ptnr. Blumstein, Block & Pease, Phila., 1985—2002, Edward Blumstein, PC, Phila., 2002—. Adj. prof. Sch. Law Temple U., 1994—. Gen. Counsel to North American Ski Journalists Assn. With U.S. Army, 1958-64. Mem. ABA, Pa. Bar Assn., Phila. Bar Assn. (bd. govs. 1984-85, past chmn. family law sect. 1984), Assn. Conflict Resolution, Family Mediation Assn. Del. Valley (pres. 1990-91), B'nai B'rith. Republican. Jewish. Avocations: skiing, reading, photography. Alternative dispute resolution, Family and matrimonial, Personal injury (including property damage). Office: 1500 Walnut St Ste 1600 Philadelphia PA 19102 Fax: 215-790-1988.

BLUMSTEIN, JEFFREY PHILLIP, lawyer; b. NYC, June 27, 1947; s. Harold and Esther Blumstein; m. Vivien Verbeek, Jan. 22, 1983; children: Rene Marie, Allison. BA cum laude, Syracuse U., 1969; JD, Columbia U., 1973. Bar: N.J. 1974, U.S. Dist. Ct. N.J. 1974, U.S. Ct. Appeals (3rd cir.) 1986. Dep. atty. gen. N.J. Atty. Gen.'s Office, Trenton, 1973-77; ptnr. Szaferman, Lakind, Blumstein, Blader, Lehmann & Goldshore, PC, Lawrenceville, NJ, 1977—. Mem. Assn. Trial Lawyers N.J., Mercer County Bar Assn. Avocations: tennis, reading biographies and histories. Appellate, Federal civil litigation, State civil litigation. Office: Szaferman Lakind Blumstein Balader et al 101 Grovers Mill Rd Ste 104 Lawrenceville NJ 08648-4706

BLYTH, JOHN E. lawyer, educator; b. Rochester, N.Y., Oct. 19, 1931; s. Ray G. and Ruby Luella (Spaulding) B.; m. Joanna E. Jennings, Aug. 24, 1963; children: Geoffrey E., Jennifer E. Blyth-Schmandt, Jane Blyth Warren, James E. AB, Colgate U., 1953; LLB, NYU, 1960; JD, Goethe U., 1962. Bar: N.Y. 1961. Ptnr. Harter, Secrest & Emery, Rochester, 1961-93, Hiscock & Barclay, Rochester, 1994-95, Blyth & Lamb, Rochester, 1995-2000, Fix Spindelman Brovitz & Goldman, Rochester, NY, 2000—02; lawyer Blyth Law Offices, 2002—. Speaker in field; adj. prof. Cornell U. Law Sch., Ithaca, N.Y., 1990—; former trustee Keuka Coll., Keuka Park, N.Y., 1986—. Contbr. articles to profl. jours. Pres. Palmyra (N.Y.) Macedon Sch. Bd., 1969-72, Citizen's Tax League, Rochester, 1984-86. Sgt. U.S. Army, 1954-57, ETO. Named Internat. Exec. of Yr., Rochester C. of C., 1994. Mem. N.Y. State Bar Assn. (chair real property law sect. 1990-91), Am. Coll. Real Estate Lawyers. Avocation: organist. Private international, Property, real (including real estate development, water). Home: 1428 Hidden Pond Ln Walworth NY 14568-9538 Office: 1115 Midtown Tower Rochester NY 14604 E-mail: 2@frontiernet.net.

BLYTHE, JAMES DAVID, II, lawyer; b. Indpls., Oct. 20, 1940; s. James David and Marjorie M. (Horne) B.; m. Sara S. Frantz, Nov. 21, 1974; 1 child; Amanda Renee. BS, Butler U., 1962; JD, Ind. U., 1966. Bar: Ind. 1966, U.S. Supreme Ct. (so. dist.) Ind., 1966, U. S. Supreme Ct. 1980, U.S. Ct. Appeals (7th cir.), 1993. Diplomate, U.S. congl. staff asst. Ct. Practice Inst., 1965-69; majority atty. Ind. Ho. of Reps., 1967, 69; dep. prosecutor Marion County Prosecutor's Office, 1966, 68; pvt. practice Indpls., 1966—; sr. ptnr. Blythe & Ost, 1994—. Mem. com. on character and fitness Ind. Supreme Ct., 1974-94; host TV show Ask a Lawyer, 1977-79. Bd. dirs. Marion County chpt. Am.Cncer Soc., 1971-76 (pres. 1975-76), Cen. Ind. coun. Boy Scouts Am., 1969-72, exec. com., 1969-71, Crossroads of Am. Coun., 1972-87, executive com. 1976-84, pres., 1979-81, life mem 1987, Salvation Army, 1975—, vice chmn., 1986, chmn., 1987, 88, life mem., 2003; Ind. chmn. W.I. Amb. Exch., Jaycees, 1972-73; pres. North Ctrl. H.S. Alumni Assn., 1996-98, life mem., 2002; mem. lawyers fund raising com. Indpls. Mus. Art., 1973-74; co-membership chmn, Friends of Channel 20, 1975; hon. chmn. ann. dinner Muscular Dystrophy Family Found., 2001. Named Man of Yr., Am. Cancer Soc., 1974, Sagamore of the Wabash, 1981; named to North Ctrl. H.S. Hall of Fame, 1999; recipient cert. of merit, Am. Cancer Soc., 1971, 1974—75, Outstanding Svc. award, Indpls. br. Am. Cancer Soc., 1972—73, Richard E. Rowland award, Jaycees, 1971—72, Stanley K. Lacy Meml. award, 1974, Dist. Svc. award, Ind. Jaycees, 1974, Silver Beaver award, Boy Scouts Am., 1981, Life Mem. award, Nat. Eagle Scout Assn., 1996, commendation, Gov. State of Ind., 1973, Day named in his honor, Mayor of Indpls., 1976. Mem. Ind. Bar Assn. (legal ethics com. 1995—), Indpls. Bar Assn. (bd. mgrs. 1978-81, 89-90, chmn. grievance com. 1980-88), Kiwanis (v.p. Indpls 1986-87, pres. 1987-88, found pres. 1988-89, Indpls. Kiwanis found. 1989-99, pres. Ind. Dist. Found. 1995-98, civic award, 1991, Abe Lincoln Fellow, 1993, named Kiwanis Man of the Year, 1997), Gyro Club of Indpls. (bd. dirs. 2000-01, 03—), Kappa Sigma, Phi Delta Phi. Republican. Presbyterian. General civil litigation, Corporate, general, Family and matrimonial. Home: 11028 E Lakeshore Dr Carmel IN 46033-4402 Office: 10585 N Meridian St Ste 200 Indianapolis IN 46290-1067 E-mail: jdb2@iquest.net.

BOACKLE, K F. lawyer, writer, real estate broker; b. Jackson, Miss., Mar. 13, 1944; s. Abraham Milton and Clara Josephine Boackle; m. Sheila Marie Ashker; children: David, Paul, Mark. BBA, Loyola U., 1966; JD, Jackson Sch. Law, 1972. Real estate broker, Jackson, 1972—; pvt. law practice, 1979—. Author: Mississippi Real Estate Contracts and Closings, 1991, 2d edit., 2000, Mississippi Real Estate Foreclosure Law, 1994, 2d edit., 2001, Real Estate Closing Deskbook, 1997, 2d edit., 2003. Mem. ABA, Miss. Bar Assn., Tri-County Real Estate Attys. Assn. (pres. 1989-90), Hinds County Bar Assn, Madison County Bar Assn. General civil litigation, Personal injury (including property damage), Property, real (including real estate development, water). Office: Boackle Law Firm PLLC 1020 Northpark Dr Ste B Ridgeland MS 39157-5299

BOARDMAN, MARK SEYMOUR, lawyer; b. Birmingham, Ala., Mar. 16, 1958; s. Frank Seymour and Flora (Sarinopoulos) B.; m. Cathryn Dunkin, 1983; children:Wilson Paul, Joanna Christina. BA cum laude, U. Ala., 1979, JD, 1982. Bar: Ala. 1982, U.S. Dist. Ct. (no., so. and mid. dists.) Ala. 1982, U.S. Ct. Appeals (11th cir.) 1983, U.S. Supreme Ct. 1987. Assoc. Spain, Gillon, Riley, Tate & Etheredge, Birmingham, 1982-84; ptnr. Porterfield, Scholl, Bainbridge, Mims and Harper, P.A., Birmingham, 1984-93, Boardman Carr Weed & Hutcheson PC, Birmingham, 1993—. Pres. Holy Trinity Holy Cross Greek Orthodox Cathedral, 1991, 92, sec., 1987, asst. treas., 1986, treas., 1988, 89, v.p., 1990, 96-2003, bd. auditors, 1994; mem. coun. Greek Orthodox Diocese of Atlanta, 1992-95; mem. Shelby County (Ala.) Work Release Commn., sec., 1996; mem. ednl. adv. com. Homewood Bd. Edn., 1999-2002, strategic planning com., 2000-02; pres. Beta Theta Pi House Corp., U. Ala., 2003; bd. dirs. Ala. Coun. Sch. Sch. Bd. Attys., 2001-2003. Mem. ABA, Ala. State Bar, Ala. Workers Compensation Claims Assn., Shelby County Bar Assn. (treas. 1992-93, sec. 1994, v.p. 1995, pres. 1996), Birmingham Bar Assn. (co-chmn. econs. of law com. 1997, local bar liaison com. 1997), Ala. Def. Lawyers Assn., Def. Rsch. Inst., Ala. Claims Assn., Order of Barristers, Phi Beta Kappa, Delta Sigma Rho-Tau Kappa Alpha, Pi Sigma Alpha. Greek Orthodox. General civil litigation, Insurance, Personal injury (including property damage). Home: 1915 Wellington Rd Birmingham AL 35209-4026 Office: Boardman Carr Weed & Hutcheson PC PO Box 382886 Birmingham AL 35238-2886 also: 400 Boardman Dr Chelsea AL 35043-8211

BOAS, FRANK, retired lawyer; b. Amsterdam, North Holland, The Netherlands, July 22, 1930; came to U.S., 1940; s. Maurits Coenraad and Sophie (Brandel) B.; m. Edith Louise Bruce, June 30, 1981 (dec. July 1992); m. Jean Scripps, Aug. 6, 1993 (div. Dec. 2000). AB cum laude, Harvard U., 1951, JD, 1954. Bar: U.S. Dist. Ct. D.C. 1955, U.S. Ct. Appeals (D.C. cir.) 1955; U.S. Supreme Ct. 1958. Atty. Office of the Legal Adviser U.S. State Dept., Washington, 1957-59; pvt. practice Brussels and London, 1959-79; of counsel Patton, Boggs & Blow, Washington, 1975-80; pres. Frank Boas Found., Inc., Cambridge, Mass., 1980—. Mem. U.S. delegation to UN confs. on law of sea, Geneva, 1958, 60; vice chmn. Commn. for Ednl. Exch., Brussels, 1980-87; mem. vis. com. Harvard Law Sch., 1987-91, Ctr. for Internat. Affairs, 1988—; dir. Found. European Orgn. for Research and Treatment of Cancer, Brussels, 1978-87, Paul-Henri Spaak Found., Brussels, 1981—, East-West Ctr. Found., Honolulu, 1990-01, Law of the Sea Inst., Honolulu, 1992-97, Pacific Forum CSIS, Honolulu, 1996—, Honolulu Acad. Arts, 1997—, U. Hawaii Found., 2000—; hon. sec. Am. C. of C. in Belgium, 1966-78. With U.S. Army, 1955-57. Decorated Officer of the Order of Leopold II, comdr. Order of the Crown (Belgium), comdr. Order of Merit (Luxembourg); recipient Tribute of Appreciation award U.S. State Dept., 1981, Harvard Alumni Assn. award, 1996. Mem. ABA, Fed. D.C. Bar Assn., Pacific and Asian Affairs Coun. (pres.), Honolulu Com. Fgn. Relations, Pacific, Outrigger Canoe (Honolulu), Travellers (London), Am. and Common Market (Brussels pres. 1981-85), Honolulu Social Sci. Assn. Education and schools, Private international, Public international. Home: 4463 Aukai Ave Honolulu HI 96816-4858

BOBROW, HENRY BERNARD, lawyer; b. N.Y.C., Mar. 31, 1924; s. Jacob and Sadye (Smollen) B.; m. Phyllis-Fein, July 6, 1952; children: Joanne Schoelkopf, Richard S. BA, Johns Hopkins U., 1947; JD, Cornell U., 1952; LLM, N.Y.U. Law Sch., 1956. Bar: N.Y. 1952, U.S. Dist. Ct. (so. and ea. dists.) N.Y. 1954. Assoc. to ptnr. Carroad & Carroad, N.Y.C., 1953-58; ptnr. Bobrow, Handman & Katz, N.Y.C., 1958-69, Cutler & Cutler, N.Y.C., 1968-72, Candee, Solomon, Bobrow, Burton, Davidowitz & Distler, N.Y.C., 1972-75, Bobrow, Greenapple, Skolnik & Shakarchy (and predecessors), N.Y.C., 1975-95; of counsel Cox, Buchanan, Padmore and Shakarchy, N.Y.C., 1995-97, Roosevelt & Arfa, LLP, White Plains, N.Y., 1997-99, Bobrow & Sosis, White Plains, N.Y., 2000—. Pres. U.S. Patent Model Found., Washington, 1985-90; mem. Real Estate Bd. N.Y.C., 1987-91. Mem. Bd. Appeals, Scarsdale, N.Y., 1988-91; trustee Jewish Child Care Assn., N.Y.C., 1978—. Cpl. AUS, 1943-45, ETO. Named Outstanding Alumnus, Johns Hopkins U., 1978. Mem. ABA, Johns Hopkins Club (pres. 1966-68), Cornell Club of N.Y., B'nai B'rith (pres. 1964-66). Republican. Jewish. Avocation: tennis and swimming. Estate planning, Probate (including wills, trusts), Property, real (including real estate development, water). Office: 150 Southfield Ave Ste 2444 Stamford CT 06902 E-mail: hbbobrow@aol.com.

BOBROW, SUSAN LUKIN, lawyer; b. Cleve., Jan. 18, 1941; d. Adolph and Yetta (Babkow) Lukin; m. Martin J. Bolhower, Nov. 28, 1986 (div. Dec. 1988); children from previous marriage: Elizabeth Bobrow Pressler, Erica, David. Student, Antioch Coll., Yellow Springs, Ohio, 1958-61; BA, Antioch Coll., L.A., 1975; JD, Southwestern U., L.A., 1979. Bar: Calif. 1980. Pvt. practice, Beverly Hills, Calif., 1983-88; assoc. Schulman & Miller, Beverly Hills, 1988-89; staff counsel Fair Polit. Practices Commn., Sacramento, Calif., 1990-96; sr. counsel Calif. State Lottery, Sacramento, 1996-98; asst. gen. counsel Employment Tng. Panel, Sacramento, 1998-99, 1999—. Panel for paternity defense L.A. Superior Ct., 1984. Exhibited paintings at Death and Trasnfiguration Show, Phantom Galleries, Sacramento, 1994; exhibited photography U. Calif.-Davis Women's Art Collaborative, Phantom Galleries, Sacramento, 1997, Camera Arts, Sacramento, 1998, Viewpoint Gallery Exhibit, Sacramento, 1998. Bd. dirs. San Fernando Valley Friends of Homeless Women and Children, North Hollywood, Calif., 1985-88, Jewish Family Svcs., 1997; mem. adv. bd. Project Home, Sacramento Interfaith Svc. Coun., 1990-91; v.p. cmty. affairs B'nai Israel Sisterhood, Sacramento, 1991-93; bd. dirs. Sacramento Jewish Family Svcs., 1997-98. Recipient commendation Bd. Govs. State Bar of Calif., 1984. Mem. Inst. Noetic Scis., Sacramento Inst. Noetic Scis. (steering coun. 1994), Los Angeles County Bar Assn. (Barristers com. on adminstrn. of justice 1985), Sacramento County Bar Assn. (com. on profl. responsibility 1993-94, alt. del. to state bar conv. 1991), Sacramento Valley Photog. Arts Ctr. Democrat. Office: Employment Tng Panel 1100 J St Sacramento CA 95814-2827

BOCCIA ROSADO, ANN MARIE, paralegal; b. San Pedro, Calif., Apr. 23, 1958; d. Franklin S. and Julia (Mattera) Boccia; m. Robert Daniel Rosado. AA, Harbor Coll., 1983; paralegal cert., Continental Tech. Inst., L.A., 1986. Invoicing/sales rep. Bronson of Calif., Gardena, 1976-78; traffic mgr. GSC Athletic Equipment, San Pedro, 1978-81; exec. legal sec. Stein, Shostak, Shostak & O'Hara, L.A., 1981; office adminstr., paralegal Stolpman, Krissman, Elber & Silver LLP, Long Beach, Calif., 1981—. Cons. San Pedro Chiropractic Ctr., 1989-96; instr. Michaels Stores, Inc., 1997-2000. Recipient Presdl. award Calif. Trial Lawyers Assn., 1988; named Legal Sec. of the Yr., 1998. Mem. Nat. Paralegal Assn., Assn. Trial Lawyers Am., Consumer Attys. L.A.(formerly L.A. Trial Lawyers Assn.) (speaker 1989-92, moderator 1991, voter registration com. 1988-89, Ann. Law Day participant 1991-92, benefits 1995-2002, 2003, pres. 2000-02, gov. 2003-), L.A. Paralegal Assn., Long Beach Legal Secs. Assn. (chmn. benefits 1995-2002, chmn. day-in-ct. 1998-2000, treas. 1998, v.p. 1999, pres. 2000-02). Democrat. Roman Catholic. Avocations: cruising, walking, reading, boating, motorcycling. Office: Stolpman Krissman Elber & Silver LLP 111 W Ocean Blvd Fl 19 Long Beach CA 90802-4632 E-mail: arosado@stolpman.com.

BOCHETTO, GEORGE ALEXANDER, lawyer; b. Bklyn., Oct. 7, 1952; m. Paula Agins, Aug. 6, 1987; children: David, Evan. BA, SUNY, Albany, 1975; JD cum laude, Temple U., 1978. Bar: Pa. 1978, N.Y. 1995, U.S. Dist. Ct. (ea. dist.) Pa. 1979, U.S. Supreme Ct. 1992, U.S. Tax Ct. 1986. Pvt. practice, 1979-90; assoc. Pelino & Lentz, P.C., Phila., 1978-79, Monteverde & Hemphill, P.C., Phila., 1990-93, Bochetto & Lentz, P.C., Phila., 1993—. Contbr. articles to profl. jours. Bd. dirs. Pa. Spl. Olympics, 1986—; mem. Rep. State Com., Pa., 1992—; appt. Pa. State Athletic Commr. Gov. Ridge, 1995—. Mem. ABA, Pa. Bar Assn., Phila. Bar Assn. (subcom. chairperson profl. responsibility com. 1978—). Avocations: amateur boxing, boating, sports. General civil litigation, Commercial, contracts (including sales of goods; commercial financing), Professional liability. Office: Bochetto & Lentz PC 1524 Locust St Philadelphia PA 19102-4401

BOCHICCHIO, VITO SALVATORE, lawyer; b. Pitts. s. Richard John and Francesca (Romano) B.; m. Giovanna Febbraro, Nov. 21, 1992; children: Richard, Giosue, Francesco, Paolo. BA, MA, Duquesne U., 1984, JD, 1987. Bar: Pa. 1987, U.S. Dist. Ct. (we. dist.) Pa. 1987. Asst. dist. atty. Office Allegheny County Dist. Atty., Pitts., 1988-90; assoc. Rothman Gordon, Pitts., 1990-94; ptnr. O'Brien, Rulis & Bochicchio, Pitts., 1994—. Sec. Big Jim's Inc., Pitts., 1992—. Committeeman Allegheny County Dem. Com., Pitts., 1981—. Mem. Allegheny County Bar Assn., Small Mfrs. Coun., Calabria Club. Roman Catholic. Avocation: Karate. Insurance, Personal injury (including property damage), Workers' compensation. Office: O'Brien Rulis & Bochicchio 100 5th Ave Ste 500 Pittsburgh PA 15222-1821

BOCKEN, R. CHARLES, lawyer, arbitrator; b. Omaha, Dec. 4, 1921; s. Herman and Ann (Duffy) B.; m. Deborah Skeels Jones, July 11, 1987; children— Barbara, William, Elizabeth. B.B.A., Georgetown U., 1943; J.D., U. Nebr., 1948. Bar: Nebr., Hawaii, U.S. Ct. Appeals (9th cir.), U.S. Supreme Ct., U.S. Dist. Ct. Hawaii. Commd. 2d lt., U.S. Air Force, 1951, advanced through grades to lt. col.; judge adv., Pentagon, other locations, 1951-68; ret., 1968; assoc. Damon, Key and predecessor firms, Honolulu, 1968-71, ptnr., 1971— ; arbitrator Fed. Mediation and Conciliation Service, Honolulu, 1968— , Am. Arbitration Assn., 1968— . Bankruptcy, Federal civil litigation, Corporate, general. Office: Damon Key 1600 Pauahi Tower 1001 Bishop St Honolulu HI 96813-3429 E-mail: RCB@hawaiilawyer.com.

BOCKSTEIN, HERBERT, lawyer; b. NYC, Jan. 27, 1943; s. Stanley Joseph and Sylvia (Tannenbaum) B.; m. Bonnie Sue Ritt, Sept. 2, 1967 (div.); children: Andrew, Jana; m. Nadine Bernstein, June 27, 1988. BA, NYU, 1963, JD cum laude, 1971; MBA, Cornell U., Ithaca, N.Y., 1966. Bar: NY 1972, Mo. 1979. Assoc. Stroock & Stroock & Lavan, N.Y.C., 1971-78, Stolar, Heitzmann & Eder, St. Louis, 1978-80, Finley, Kumble, Wagner, Heine, Underberg, Manley & Casey, N.Y.C., 1980-83; ptnr. Finley, Kumble, N.Y.C., 1983-87, Myerson & Kuhn, N.Y.C., 1988-89, Ashinoff, Ross & Korff, N.Y.C., 1989-90, Newman Tannenbaum, N.Y.C., 1990—96, Blank Rome LLP, N.Y.C., 1996—. Mem. ABA, N.Y. State Bar Assn., Estate Planning Coun. N.Y.C., Order of Coif. Avocations: tennis, golf. Estate planning, Probate (including wills, trusts), Estate taxation. Home: One Scarsdale Rd Apt 41V Tuckahoe NY 10707 Office: Blank Rome LLP 405 Lexington Ave New York NY 10174-0002 E-mail: hbockstein@blankrome.com.

BÖCKSTIEGEL, KARL-HEINZ, law educator, arbitrator; b. Engers, Germany, Aug. 2, 1936; s. Heinrich and Helene (Bedbur) B.; m. Ali Kort, July 29, 1971. JD, U. Cologne, Germany, 1962. Qualification as lawyer and judge, Germany. Law clk. cts. and law firms, Germany, 1962-65; ptnr. law firm, 1965-71; prof. internat. law U. Cologne, 1971-75, chair internat. bus. law, 1975—2001, dir. Inst. Air and Space Law, 1975. Pres. Iran-U.S. Claims Tribunal, The Hague, The Netherlands, 1984-88, London Ct. Internat. Arbitration, 1993-97, German Instn. Arbitration, 1996—. Editor: (publ. series) Internat. Bus. Law, Series of the German Instn. of Arbitration, Studies in Air and Space Law, German Jour. of Air and Space Law, 1975—; author 12 books on various fields of internat. law, air and space law, internat. bus. law, and arbitration; editor 31 books on various fields of internat. law, air and space law, internat. bus. law, and arbitration; contbr. articles to profl. jours. Hon. pres. Bürgergemeinschaft Alt-Frankenforst, Bergisch Gladbach, Germany, 1997—. Mem. German Assn. Internat. Law (pres. 1994—), London Ct. of Internat. Arbiration (hon. v.p. 1998), Assn. Arbitrators (hon. v.p. 1997), Internat. Law Assn. (exec. coun. 1985—), Internat. Coun. for Comml. Arbitration, The Athenaeum Club (London). Avocations: literature (james joyce, arno schmidt), golf. Home: Parkstr 38 D-51427 Bergisch Gladbach Germany Office: U Cologne Albertus-Magnus-Platz D-50923 Cologne Germany E-mail: Sekretariat-Boeckstiegel@uni-koeln.de.

BODANSKY, ROBERT LEE, lawyer; b. N.Y.C. BA cum laude, Syracuse U., 1974; JD with honors, George Washington U., 1977; cert. postgrad. studies, Ctr. Internat. Legal Studies, Salzburg, Austria, 1978. Bar: Md. 1978, D.C. 1978, Va. 2000, U.S. Dist. Ct. Md. 1978, U.S. Ct. Appeals (D.C. cir.) 1980, U.S. Dist. Ct. D.C. 1980, U.S. Dist. Ct. (ea. dist.) Va. 2001, U.S. Ct. Appeals (4th cir.) 1981, U.S. Supreme Ct. 1982. First assoc., then ptnr. Feldman, Krieger, Goldman & Tish, Washington, 1978-83; ptnr. Feldman, Bodansky & Rubin, Washington, 1984-95; prin. Freer, McGarry, Bodansky & Rubin, P.C., Washington, 1995-97; ptnr. Nixon, Hargrave, Devans & Doyle, LLP (now Nixon Peabody LLP), Washington, 1997—. Advisor internat. bus. law and taxation programs McGeorge Sch. Law, Sacramento, Calif., 1985—. Author: Special Problems of Subcontractors and Suppliers, 1987. Legal advisor Parkwood Resident's Assn., Kensington, Md., 1984; bd. dirs. Ridgeleigh Residents' Assn., 1987-2001, Congregation Har Shalom, 1989-91, pres. 2003-; tchr. Adas Israel Congregation, Washington, 1975-91. Mem. ABA (chmn. subcom. internat. and foreign bus. law young lawyers div. 1978-80), Md. State Bar Assn., D.C. Bar Assn., Va. Bar Assn. Private international, Corporate, general, Property, real (including real estate development, water). Office: Nixon Peabody LLP 401 9th St NW Ste 900 Washington DC 20004-2134 E-mail: rbodansky@nixonpeabody.com.

BODAS, MARGIE RUTH, lawyer; b. Virginia, Minn., Mar. 15, 1954; d. William Elmer and Delia Bodas. BA in Comms., U. Minn., Duluth, 1976; JD, William Mitchell Coll. Law, St. Paul, 1986. Bar: Minn. 1986, U.S. Dist. Ct. Minn. 1986. News editor Mesabi Daily News, Virginia, 1976-80; exec. dir. Quad Cities Drug Commn., Virginia, 1980-82; with customer svc. West Pub., St. Paul, 1982-84; law clk. Hon. Hyam Segell, Ramsey County, St. Paul, 1984-86; assoc. Hanft, Friede, Swelbar & Burns, P.A., Duluth, Minn., 1986-87; lawyer, shareholder, practice mgmt. Lommen Nelson Cole & Stageberg, P.A., Mpls., 1988—. Mem. steering com. Leadership Mpls., 1997-2000, co-chair steering com., 1999-2000. Mem. ABA, Minn. Bar Assn. (chair publs. com. 1990-92), Hennepin County Bar Assn. (chair workers compensation sect. 1998-99), C. of C. Mpls. Lutheran. Avocations: photography, writing, gardening. General civil litigation, Workers' compensation. Office: Lommen Nelson Cole & Stageberg PA 1800 IDS Ctr 80 S 8th St Minneapolis MN 55402-2100 E-mail: margie@lommen.com.

BODDEN, THOMAS ANDREW, lawyer; b. Lafayette, Ind., Dec. 18, 1945; s. William A. and Dorothy B.; m. Irene Bodden; children: Wendee, Todd, Christopher. AB, Cornell U., 1968; JD, U. Miami, 1974. Bar: Hawaii 1975. Assoc. Torkildson, Katz et al, Honolulu, 1975-78, ptnr., 1978-81; pres. Bodden & Temple, LLLC, Maui and Wailuku, Hawaii, 1981—. Author: Taxation of Real Estate in Hawaii, 1979, Taxation of Real Estate in U.S., 1982, Selling DPP Programs, 1983. Pres. Kihei Community Assn., 1984-86. Served to lt. USN, 1969-72. Mem. Am. Coll. Trust and Estate Counsel, Hawaii Bar Assn., Nat. Assn. Realtors/RESSI (pres. 1987), Hawaii Assn. Realtors (pres. 1989). Estate planning, Probate (including wills, trusts), Property, real (including real estate development, water). Office: 24 N Church St Ste 200 Wailuku HI 96793-1606 E-mail: tbodden@mauiestatelaw.com.

BODDIE, REGINALD ALONZO, lawyer; b. New Haven, June 14, 1959; s. Gladys Geraldine (Harrell) B. BA, Brown U., 1981; JD, Northeastern U., 1984. Bar: N.Y., U.S. Dist. Ct. (ea. and so. dists.) N.Y. 1986, D.C. 1987, U.S. Ct. Appeals (2d cir.) 1989, U.S. Supreme Ct. 1990. Staff atty. Legal Aid Soc., N.Y.C., 1984-86, Harlem Legal Svcs., N.Y.C., 1986-88; asst. counsel Ctr. for Law and Social Justice Medgar Evers Coll. CUNY, 1988-95; pvt. practice Law Offices of Reginald A. Boddie, N.Y.C., 1995—. Arbitrator Lemon Law, N.Y. Atty. Gen. and Am. Arbitration Assn., N.Y.C., 1986-94. Founder, pres., exec. dir. United Youth Enterprises, Inc., New Haven, 1976—; founder, dir. Coll. Prep. program Ctrl. H.S., Providence, 1980-81; bd.dirs. Claremont Neighborhood Ctrs., Inc., Bronx, N.Y., 1994-96; vol. instr. ARC, New Haven, 1975-90; bd. dirs. Boys and Girls' Clubs of Union County, Union, N.J., 1996-97; vol. law edn. instr. N.Y.C. Pub. Schs., 1992—. Recipient Good Citizenship award Civitan Internat. Club, New Haven, 1977, 2 commendations Brown U., 1981, Outstanding Cmty. Svc. award New Haven Police Dept., 1984, Cmty. Svc. award Pub. Sch. 21, Bklyn., 1993, Trailblazer award for Cmty. Svc. Nat. Coun. of Negro Women, 2000, Cmty. Svc. award for Law Related Edn., Sch. Dist. 16, N.Y.C., 2000, others; named Vol. Lawyer of the Yr., N.Y.C. Civil Ct., 2000. Mem. Bklyn. Bar Assn., Optimist Internat. Club. Civil rights, General civil litigation, General practice. Office: 19 Fulton St Ste 408 New York NY 10038-2100

BODENSTEIN, IRA, lawyer; b. Atlantic City, Nov. 9, 1954; s. William and Beverly (Grossman) B.; m. Julia Elizabeth Smith, Mar. 9, 1991; children: Sarah Rose, George William, Jennie Kathryn. Student, Tel Aviv U., 1974-75; BA in Govt., Franklin & Marshall Coll., 1977; JD in Econs., U. Miami, 1980. Bar: Ill. 1980, U.S Dist Ct. (no. dist.) Ill. 1980, U.S. Ct. Appeals (7th cir.) 1982, Fla. 1983. Assoc. James S. Gordon Ltd., Chgo., 1980-85, mem., 1985-89, Portes, Sharp, Herbst & Fox, Ltd., Chgo., 1990-91; shareholder Towbin & Zazove, Ltd., Chgo., 1991-93; ptnr. D'Ancona & Pflaum, Chgo., 1993-98; U.S. Trustee Region 11, Chgo., 1998—, Region 9, Cleve., 2001—02. Pres., bd. dirs., benefit chmn. Gus Giordano Jazz Dance, Chgo., 1990—; treas. Chgo. Pub. Art Group, 1995-99. Mem. ABA (bus. law sect., rep. young lawyers divsn. dist. 15, 1986-87, ann. meeting adv. com. 1990, spkr. spring meeting 1996, 97), Chgo. Bar Assn. (bd. dirs. young lawyers sect. 1985-87, chmn.-elect 1987-88, chmn. 1988-89, antitrust com., chmn. athletics com. 1984-85, bd. mgrs. 1990-92, chmn. pub. affairs and media rels. com., chmn. assn. meetings com., memberships com. 1996, cert. of appreciation 1984-93, 96-97). Democrat. Jewish. Home: 2848 W Wilson Ave Chicago IL 60625-3743 Office: Office US Trustee 227 W Monroe St Ste 3350 Chicago IL 60606-5099 E-mail: ira.bodenstein@usdoj.gov.

BODKIN, HENRY GRATTAN, JR., lawyer; b. L.A., Dec. 8, 1921; s. Henry Grattan and Ruth May (Wallis) B.; m. Mary Louise Davis, June 28, 1943; children: Maureen L. Dixon, Sheila L. McCarthy, Timothy Grattan. BS cum laude, Loyola U., Los Angeles, 1943, JD, 1948. Bar: Calif. 1948. Pvt. practice, Los Angeles, 1948-51, 53-95; ptnr. Bodkin, McCarthy, Sargent & Smith (predecessor firms), L.A.; of counsel Sullivan, Workman & Dee, L.A., 1995—. Mem. L.A. Bd. Water and Power Commrs., 1972-74, pres., 1973-74; regent Marymount Coll., 1962-67; trustee Loyola-Marymount U., 1973-91, vice chmn., 1985-86. With USNR, 1943-45, 51-53. Fellow Am. Coll. Trial Lawyers; mem. Calif. State Bar (mem. exec. com. conf. of dels. 1968-70, vice chmn. 1969-70), California Club, Riviera Tennis Club, Tuna Club, Chancery Club (pres. 1990-91), Phi Delta Phi. Republican. Roman Catholic. Federal civil litigation, State civil litigation, Insurance. Home: 956 Linda Flora Dr Los Angeles CA 90049-1631 Office: Sullivan Workman & Dee 800 S Figueroa St Fl 12 Los Angeles CA 90017-2521

BODKIN, ROBERT THOMAS, lawyer; b. Anderson, Ind., Jan. 26, 1945; s. Robert G. and Marggie Jean (Whelchel) B.; m. Penny Ann Nichols, June 17, 1967; children: Beth Ann, Bryan Thomas. BS, Ind. U., Bloomington, 1967; JD, Ind. U., Indpls., 1973. Bar: Ind. 1973, U.S. Dist. Ct. (so. dist.) Ind. 1973, U.S. Dist. Ct. (no. dist.) Ind. 1975, U.S. Ct. Appeals (7th cir.) 1974, U.S. Supreme Ct. 1977. Law clk. U.S. Dist. Ct., Indpls., 1973-75; assoc. Bamberger Foreman Oswald & Hahn, Evansville, Ind., 1975-80, ptnr., 1980—. Town atty., Newburgh, Ind., 1984—; city atty. City of Boonville, Ind., 1988-91. Bd. dirs. Evansville Dance Theatre, 1983, Evansville Philharm. Orch., 1983-85; trustee Evansville Day Sch., 1983-86; chmn. bd. St. Mary's Warrick Hosp. Found; citizens adv. coun., IU Sch. Med. Fellow Ind. Bar Found., 1983. Fellow Am. Coll. Trial Lawyers; mem. ABA, Internat. Assn. Def. Counsel, Assn. Def. Trial Attys., Def. Rsch. Inst., Ind. Bar Assn., Evansville Bar Assn., Bar Assn. of 7th Fed. Cir., Ind. Mcpl. Lawyers Assn. (bd. dirs. 1986—), Def. Trial Counsel Ind. (dir. 1999-2002, treas. 2003—), Ind. Def. Trial Counsel (diplomat), Internat. Right-of-Way Assn. Democrat. Federal civil litigation, State civil litigation, Personal injury (including property damage). Home: # 3 100 W Water St Newburgh IN 47630-1174 Office: Bamberger Foreman Oswald & Hahn 708 Hulman Bldg Evansville IN 47708 E-mail: tbodkin@bamberger.com.

BODLE, JOHN FREDERICK, lawyer; b. Mishawaka, Ind., Dec. 14, 1924; s. Alexander Thurston and Caroline (Grimes) B.; m. Mary Alice Kayser, Jan. 13, 1951; children: David J., Thomas J., Michael J., Kathleen A., Stephen K., Caroline M. BS in Commerce magna cum laude, U. Notre

Dame, 1949, JD magna cum laude, 1950. Bar: Ind. 1950, U.s. Dist. Ct. (no. and so. dists.) Ind. 1950, U.S. Ct. Appeals (7th cir.) 1961, U.S. Supreme Ct. 1962. Assoc. Stuart & Branigin and predecessor firm, Lafayette, Ind., 1950-53, ptnr., 1953-90; dir. Gen. Telephone Co. of Ind., 1964-69; counsel to trustees Purdue U., 1977-89. Past dir., mem. Greater Lafayette C. of C.; mem. West Lafayette Bd. Zoning Appeals, 1968-83; bd. dirs. United Way, 1991-94, Greater Lafayette Cmty. Found., 1991-97. Served with USAAF, 1943-45. Mem. ABA, Ind. State Bar Assn., Tippecanoe County Bar Assn. (past pres.) Nat. Diocesan Attys. Assn., Lafayette Country Club. Roman Catholic. Federal civil litigation, State civil litigation, Corporate, general. Home: 132 Wheeler Ln West Lafayette IN 47906-2104 Office: PO Box 1010 Stuart & Branigin 8th Floor The Life Bldg Lafayette IN 47901

BODNAR, PETER O. lawyer; b. Queens, N.Y., Mar. 19, 1945; s. John and Edith (Schultz) B. BA in Govt., NYU, 1966; JD, Fordham U., 1970. Bar: N.Y. 1971, U.S. Dist. Ct. (so. dist.) N.Y. 1973. Confidential law sec. to Hon. Evans V. Brewster Family Ct. and County Ct. Westchester County, N.Y., 1970-73; pvt. practice White Plains, N.Y., 1973-77; ptnr. Bodnar & Greene, P.C., White Plains, N.Y., 1977-80, Bender & Bodnar, White Plains, N.Y., 1980-98; prin. Law Offices of Peter O. Bodnar, White Plains, N.Y., 1998-99, Bodnar & Milone LLP, White Plains, N.Y., 1999—. Pres., CEO P.A.J. Am. Ltd./The Olo Corp., 1990—97; CEO Organica, USA, Inc., 1998—; lectr. Pace U. Sch. Law Women's Justice Ctr., 2001—, Appellate Divsn. 2d Dept. Law Guardian Program, 2003—; chair Com. for Children's Right to Counsel, 2003—. Trustee Village of Ossining, N.Y., 1975-77. Fellow: Am. Acad. Matrimonial Lawyers; mem.: ABA (family law sect.), Westchester County Bar Assn. (family law sect., exec. com. 1992—, chair 2000—02), N.Y. State Bar Assn. (family law sect., exec. com. 2000—, lectr. custody and visitation 2003—). Family and matrimonial. Office: 140 Grand St White Plains NY 10601-4831 E-mail: usorganica@aol.com.

BODOFF, JOSEPH SAMUEL UBERMAN, lawyer; b. Bryn Mawr, Nov. 2, 1952; s. Bernard David and Ruth Irma (Uberman) B. BS, Pa. State U., 1974; JD, Villanova U., 1977. Bar: Pa. 1977, U.S. Dist. Ct. (ea. dist.) Pa. 1979, U.S. Ct. Appeals (3d cir.) 1980, U.S. Supreme Ct. 1988, Mass. 1987, U.S. Dist. Ct. Mass. 1988, U.S. Ct. Appeals (1st cir.) 1988, R.I. 1998, U.S. Dist. Ct. R.I. 1999. Jud. law clk. Phila. County Ct. of Common Pleas, 1977-79; assoc. Pincus, Verlin, Hahn & Reich, Phila., 1979-86; ptnr. Kaye, Fialkow, Richmond & Rothstein, Boston, 1986-91, Gaston & Snow, Boston, 1991, Warner & Stackpole, Boston, 1991-94, Hinckley, Allen & Snyder, Boston, 1994-98, Shechtman & Halperin, Boston, 1998-2000, Bodoff & Assocs., Boston, 2000—03, Bodoff & Slavitt LLP, Boston, 2003—. Dir. Am. Bankruptcy Inst., Alexandria, Va., 1995—2003, mem. exec. com., 2000—03; dir. Am. Bd. Certification, Alexandria; co-chair ABI Unsecured Trade Creditor Com., Alexandria, 1993—98, ABI Creditors' Com. Manual Task Force, 1993—94; chair ABI Task Force on Preferences, 1995—97; exec. editor ABI World, 2002—; chair NACM Bankruptcy and Insolvency Group, Portland, 1998—. Author: Cramdown: The Ultimate Chapter 11 Threat, 1992, (with others) Bankruptcy Business Acquisitions, 1998; contbr. articles to profl. publs. Mem. Mus. Coun. of Mus. of Fine Arts, Boston, 1997-99. Mem. ABA, Am. Bankruptcy Inst. (dir. 1995-2003, mem. exec. com. 2000-2003), Am. Bd. of Certification (dir. 1996-2000), Boston Bar Assn., Nat. Assn of Credit Mgmt. Avocations: skiing, tennis, wine collecting, piano. Bankruptcy, Commercial, consumer (including collections, credit), Commercial, contracts (including sales of goods; commercial financing). Home: 64 Forest St Chestnut Hill MA 02467-2930 Office: Bodoff & Slavitt LLP 77 N Washington St Boston MA 02114 E-mail: jbodoff@bodoffslavitt.com.

BODOVITZ, JAMES PHILIP, lawyer; b. Evanston, Ill., Aug. 20, 1958; s. Philip Edward and Dosha (Laurman) B. BS, U. So. Calif., 1980, JD, 1984. Bar: N.Y. 1985, D.C. 1989, Calif. 1990. Assoc. Shearman & Sterling, N.Y.C., 1984-89, San Francisco, 1989-92; br. chief divsn. broker-dealer enforcement U.S. Securities Exch. Commn., N.Y.C., 1992-96; v.p., assoc. gen. counsel law dept. The Equitable Life Assurance Soc. of U.S., N.Y.C., 1996—; sr. v.p., gen. counsel AXA Advisors, LLC, 1999—. Mem. ABA, Assn. Bar City N.Y. (Thurgood Marshall award 1998). Democrat. Federal civil litigation, General civil litigation, Securities. Office: AXA Financial Inc 12th Fl 1290 Ave of Americas New York NY 10104 E-mail: James.Bodovitz@axa-financial.com.

BODWELL, LORI, lawyer; b. Oct. 1966; AB, Bowdoin Coll., 1988; JD, Boston Coll., 1991. Bar: Alaska 1992, Maine 1993, Mass. 1992, Dist. of Alaska (US Dist. Ct.) 1994, 9th Air 1995. Mem.: Tananeu Valley Bar Assoc., Nat. Assoc. of Criminal Def. Lawyers, Alaska Bar Assn. (pres. 2002—03). Address: 712 8th Ave Fairbanks AK 99701

BOEDER, THOMAS L. lawyer; b. St. Cloud, Minn., Jan. 10, 1944; s. Oscar Morris and Eleanor (Gile) B.; m. Carol-Leigh Coombs, Apr. 6, 1968. BA, Yale U., 1965, LLB, 1968. Bar: Wash. 1970, U.S. Dist. Ct. (we. dist.) Wash. 1970, U.S. Dist. Ct. (ea. dist.) Wash. 1972, U.S. Ct. Appeals (9th cir.) 1970, U.S. Supreme Ct. 1974, U.S. Ct. Appeals (D.C. cir.) 1975, U.S. Ct. Appeals (10th cir.) 1993. Litigation atty. Wash. State Atty. Gen., Seattle, 1970-72, antitrust div. head, 1972-76, chief, consumer protection and antitrust, 1976-78, also sr. asst. atty. gen. and criminal enforcement, 1979-81; ptnr. Perkins Coie, Seattle, 1981—. Served with U.S. Army, 1968-70, Vietnam. Mem. ABA (antitrust sect.), Wash. State Bar Assn. (antitrust sect.). Lutheran. Antitrust, General civil litigation, Trade. Office: Perkins Coie 1201 3rd Ave Fl 40 Seattle WA 98101-3029

BOEHM, KENNETH, legal association administrator; 1 child, Christine. Talk show host Sta. WWDB-AM-FM, Phila.; prosecutor; adminstrv. asst. to Congressman Christopher Smith; legis. dir. Howard Jarvis' Am. Tax Reduction Movement; chmn. Nat. Legal Policy and Ctr., Falls Church, Va., 1991—. Counsel to bd. dirs. Legal Svcs. Corp. Office: Nat Legal and Policy Ctr 107 Park Washington Ct Falls Church VA 22046 Office Fax: 703-237-2090.*

BOEHM, STEVEN BRUCE, lawyer; b. N.Y.C., May 22, 1954; s. Henry and Irene (Jonas) B. BA, Rutgers U., New Brunswick, N.J., 1975; JD, Rutgers U., Newark, 1978. Bar: N.J., 1978, D.C., 1982, U.S. Dist. Ct. N.J., U.S. Dist. Ct., D.C. Enforcement atty. SEC, Washington, 1978-81, atty. office gen. counsel, 1982, counsel to the commr., 1982-83; assoc. Sutherland Asbill & Brennan, LLP, Washington, 1983-87, ptnr., 1988—. Philip J. Levin scholar Rutgers U., 1975-78. Mem. ABA (corp., banking and bus. law com.), D.C. Bar Assn., Phi Beta Kappa, Pi Sigma Alpha. Corporate, general, Insurance, Securities. Office: Sutherland Asbill & Brennan LLP 1275 Pennsylvania Ave NW Washington DC 20004-2415 E-mail: sboehm@sablaw.com.

BOEHM, THEODORE REED, judge; b. Evanston, Ill., Sept. 12, 1938; s. Hans George and Frances (Reed) B.; children from previous marriage: Elisabeth, Jennifer, Sarah, Macy; m. Margaret Stitt Harris, Jan. 27, 1985. AB summa cum laude, Brown U., 1960; JD magna cum laude, Harvard U., 1963. Bar: D.C. 1964, Ind. 1964, U.S. Supreme Ct. 1975. Law clk. to Chief Justices Warren, Reed and Burton, U.S. Supreme Ct., Washington, 1963-64; assoc. Baker & Daniels, Indpls., 1965-70, ptnr., 1970-88, 95-96, mng. ptnr., 1980-87; gen. counsel major appliances GE, Louisville, 1988-89; v.p., gen. counsel GE Aircraft Engines, Cin., 1989-91; dep. gen. counsel Eli Lilly & Co., 1991-95; justice Ind. Supreme Ct., Indpls., 1996—. Pres. Ind. Sports Corp., 1980-88; chmn. organizing com. 1987 Pan Am. Games, Indp.s. Mem. ABA, Am. Law Inst., Ind. Bar Assn., Indpls. Bar Assn. Office: Ind Supreme Ct State House Rm 324 Indianapolis IN 46204-2728 E-mail: tboehm@courts.state.in.us.

BOEHMER, RICHARD A. lawyer; b. St. Louis, June 26, 1951; BA, Harvey Mudd Coll. and U. So. Calif., 1973; JD, Loyola U., L.A., 1976. Bar: Calif. 1976. With O'Melveny & Myers, L.A. Recipient Acad. scholarship Loyola U. Sch. Law, 1974, 75. Mem. ABA, L.A. County Bar Assn., Phi Beta Kappa, Phi Kappa Phi. Corporate, general, Mergers and acquisitions, Securities. Office: O'Melveny & Myers 400 S Hope St Los Angeles CA 90071-2899

BOEHNEN, DANIEL A. lawyer; b. Mitchell, S.D., Aug. 5, 1950; s. Lloyd and Mary Elizabeth (Buche) B.; m. Joan Bensing, May 22, 1976; children: Christopher, Lindsey. BS in Chem. Engring. cum laude, Notre Dame U., 1973; JD, Cornell U., 1976. Bar: Ill, U.S. Dist. Ct. (no. dist.) Ill., U.S. Ct. Appeals (7th and fed. cirs.), U.S. Supreme Ct. Atty. Allegretti, Newitt, Witcoff & McAndrews Ltd., Chgo., 1976—, assoc., 1982—; ptnr., exec. officer Allegretti & Witcoff, Ltd., Chgo., 1986—, bd. dirs., 1993—95; founder, mng. ptnr. McDonnell Boehnen Hulbert & Berghoff, Chgo., 1996—. Bd. dirs. Mitchell (S.D.) Prehist. Indian Village Soc., 1983—; commr. Northbrook Planning Commn., 1993—. Mem. ABA, AIPLA, Cornell Law Assn. Chg. (chmn.), Fed. Cir. Bar Assn. (bd. dirs.), Assn. Patent Law Firms (pres., bd. dirs.). Avocations: skiing, photography, scuba diving. Federal civil litigation, Patent, Trademark and copyright. Office: McDonnell Boehnen Hulbert & Berghoff 300 S Wacker Dr Chicago IL 60606-6709 Office Fax: 312-913-0002.

BOEHNEN, DAVID LEO, lawyer; b. Mitchell, S.D., Dec. 3, 1946; s. Lloyd L. Boehnen and Mary Elizabeth (Buche) Roby; m. Shari A. Bauhs, Sept. 9, 1969; children: Lesley, Michelle, Heather. AB, U. Notre Dame, 1968; JD with honors, Cornell U., 1971. Bar: Minn. 1971. Assoc. Dorsey & Whitney, Mpls., 1971—76, ptnr., 1977—89; sr. v.p. law and external rels. Supervalu Inc., Mpls., 1991—97, exec. v.p., 1997—. Vis. prof. law Cornell U. Law Sch., Ithaca, NY, 1982. Bd. dirs. ATM Med. Inc.; mem. adv. coun. on arts and letters U. Notre Dame, 1993—; mem. adv. coun. Cornell U. Law Sch., 1983—92, chmn. coun., 1986—90. Mem.: Greater Mpls. C. of C. (bd. dirs. 1988—90), Minn. Bar Assn. (chmn. bus. law sect. 1986), Spring Hill Golf Club, Minikahda Club (Mpls.). Roman Cath. Home: 71 Otis Ln Saint Paul MN 55104-5645 E-mail: david.boehnen@supervalu.com.

BOEHNER, LEONARD BRUCE, lawyer; b. Council Bluffs, Iowa, Apr. 19, 1930; s. Bruce and Flora (Kruse) B. AB, Harvard U., 1952, JD, 1955. Bar: N.Y. 1956, U.S. Dist. Ct. (so. dist.) N.Y. 1963, U.S. Ct. Appeals (2d cir.) 1963, U.S. Supreme Ct. 1964. Assoc. Dewey, Ballantine, Bushby, Palmer & Wood, N.Y.C., 1959-66; ptnr. Clare & Whitehead, N.Y.C., 1966-73, Morris & McVeigh LLP, N.Y.C. 1973—. Served to lt. USN, 1955-59. Mem. Assn. Bar City N.Y. Club: Union (N.Y.C.). Corporate, general, Estate planning, Securities. Office: Morris & McVeigh 767 3rd Ave New York NY 10017-2023

BOELTER, PHILIP FLOYD, real estate company officer, mortgage company executive; b. Independence, Iowa, Mar. 25, 1943; s. Floyd Joseph and Eileen R. (Wilson) B.; m. Linda Lee Franck, June 7, 1964; children: Carrie Lynn, John Philip. BS in Indsl. Engring., Iowa State U., 1965; JD, U. Iowa, 1968. Ptnr. Dorsey & Whitney, Mpls., 1968—2002; exec. v.p., chief oper. officer Kraus-Anderson Cos., Inc., Mpls., 2002—. Trustee Gustavus Adolphus Coll., 1996—; bd. dir. Jr. Achievement of the Upper Midwest, 2003—. Mem. Mpls. Athletic Club (treas. 1992, sec. 1993, v.p. 1994, pres. 1995). Lutheran. Avocations: landscape gardening, skiing, golfing, reading, volleyball. Office: Kraus-Anderson 525 S 8th St Minneapolis MN 55404 E-mail: pboelter.phil@k-a-c.com.

BOENSCH, ARTHUR CRANWELL, retired lawyer; b. Charleston, S.C., Nov. 9, 1933; s. Frank Neville and Mary Alice (Cranwell) B.; m. Katherine Hume Lucas, June 16, 1956; children: Arthur Cranwell, Katherine Breland, Alice Metzendorf, Frances Murdaugh, Benjamin; m. 2d, Annelle Yvonne Beach, July 27, 1979. BS in Gen. Engring., U.S. Naval Acad., 1956; JD, U. S.C., 1970. Bar: S.C. 1970, U.S. Dist. Ct. (so. dist.) Ga. 1970, U.S. Dist. Ct. S.C. 1971. Ptnr. Ackerman & Boensch, Walterboro, S.C., 1970-73, Bogoslow & Boensch, Walterboro, S.C., 1973-75; pvt. practice Walterboro, SC, 1976—2002; ret., 2002. City recorder, mcpl. ct. judge, Walterboro, 1973-78. Chmn. Colleton County Alcohol and Drug Abuse Commn., 1991-96; dist. chmn. Boy Scouts Am., 1988-95, mem. exec. bd. Coastal Carolina coun., 1978—; vestryman, jr. warden St. Jude's Episcopal Ch.; lay rector Cursillo Episcopal Diocese of S.C., 1989; del. Episcopal conv. Diocese of S.C., 1995-96, 98-99, mem. standing com., 1997-99; mem. nat. bd. Faith Alive Movement, Episcopal Ch. Lt. comdr. USN, 1956-57. Recipient Silver Beaver award and Dist. Merit award Boy Scouts Am., 1982; James West fellow, 1996. Mem. S.C. Bar Assn. (chmn. lawyers caring about lawyers com. 1989-91), Rotary, Phi Alpha Delta. General practice.

BOETTCHER, ARMIN SCHLICK, lawyer, banker; b. East Bernard, Tex., Apr. 12, 1941; s. Clem C. and Frances Helene (Schlick) B.; m. Virginia Nan Barkley, Apr. 13, 1963; children: Lynn Frances, Laura Anne. BBA, U. Tex., Austin, 1963, JD, 1967. Various positions personal trust dept. Republic Bank Houston, 1967-75, sr. v.p., trust officer, head trust dept., 1975-82; exec. v.p., dir. Union State Bank, East Bernard, 1988-98; exec. v.p. Prosperity Bank, East Bernard, 1998—. Bd. dirs. Whispering Oaks Civic Club, 1980-85, pres., 1981. Mem. Houston Bus. and Estate Planning Coun., U. Tex. Ex-Students Assn. (life), Meml. Forest Club (dir. 1981-83), Clubs of Lakeway, Sigma Chi. Methodist. Estate planning, Probate (including wills, trusts). Office: Prosperity Bank Bldg PO Box 40 East Bernard TX 77435-0040

BOETTICHER, HELENE, lawyer; b. Syracuse, N.Y., Mar. 26, 1920; d. Ford and Emily (Bennett) Zogg; m. William Donald Boetticher, Oct. 18, 1958 (dec. July 1990); children: John, Amy, Sally. BA, U. Wis., 1941, LLB, 1943. Bar: Wis., Ill. Atty. NLRB, Chgo., 1951—57, OSHA Rev., Washington, 1972—73, Dept. Labor, 1973—95, counsel for litigation, 1978—95. Contbr. articles to profl. jours. Democrat. Episcopalian. Avocation: travel. Home: 15204 Carrollton Rd Rockville MD 20853 E-mail: hzb3099@aol.com.

BOGAARD, JONATHAN HARVEY, lawyer; b. Humboldt, Iowa, Mar. 25, 1957; m. Milena B. Vujovich, Nov. 26, 1983; children: Joseph Daniel, Jonathan Thomas. BBA in Acctg., U. Iowa, 1978, MA in Acctg., JD, U. Iowa, 1981. Bar: Ill. 1981, Iowa 1981, U.S. Dist. Ct. (no. dist.) Ill. 1978, U.S. Tax Ct. 1983. Assoc. McDermott, Will & Emery, Chgo., 1981—86, ptnr., 1986—91, Vedder Price, Chgo., 1991—. Bd. dirs. North Suburban YMCA, Northbrook, Ill., 1997—2002. Corporate taxation, Corporate, general, Aviation, Equipment Finance. Office: Vedder Price 222 N LaSalle Ste 2600 Chicago IL 60601-1003 Office Fax: 312-609-5005. Business E-Mail: jbogaard@vedderprice.com.

BOGAARD, WILLIAM JOSEPH, mayor, lawyer, educator; b. Sioux City, Iowa, Jan. 18, 1938; s. Joseph and Irene Marie (Hensing) B.; m. Claire Marie Whalen, Jan. 28, 1961; children: Michele, Jeannine, Joseph, Matthew. BS, Loyola Marymount U., L.A., 1959; JD with honors, U. Mich., 1965. Bar: Calif. 1966, U.S. Dist. Ct. (ctrl. dist.) Calif. 1966. Ptnr. Agnew, Miller & Carlson, L.A., 1970-82; exec. v.p., gen. counsel 1st Interstate Bancorp, L.A., 1982-96; vis. prof. securities regulation and banking Mich. Law Sch., Ann Arbor, 1996-97; lectr. securities regulation and corps. U. So. Calif. Law Sch., L.A., 1997—; mayor Pasadena, Calif., 1999—. Mem. Calif. Commn. on Jud. Nominees Evaluation, 1997-99. Mem. city coun., mayor City of Pasadena, Calif., 1978-86. Capt. USAF, 1959-62. Mem. Calif. State Bar, Los Angeles County Bar Assn. (Corp. Counsel of Yr. award 1988). Avocations: jogging, french and spanish languages, hiking. Office: 100 N Garfield Ave Pasadena CA 91101-1726 E-mail: bbogaard@ci.pasadena.ca.us.

BOGARD, LAWRENCE JOSEPH, lawyer; b. Champaign, Ill., July 12, 1952; s. Morris Ray and Norma Jean (Shingleton) B.; m. Rebecca Lynn Jackson, May 6, 1978; children: Caitlyn Elizabeth, Peter Jackson. AB, Vassar Coll., Poughkeepsie, N.Y., 1974; JD, Georgetown U., 1977. Bar: D.C. 1977. Atty. U.S. Customs Svc., Washington, 1977-80; assoc. Cladouhos & Brashares, Washington, 1980-84; atty. U.S. Dept. Commerce, Washington, 1984; ptnr. Rose, Schmidt, Hasley & Disalle, Washington, 1984-88, McKenna & Cuneo, Washington, 1988-98, Neville Peterson LLP, Washington, 1998—. Faculty Practicing Law Inst., 1984, 92; mem. U.S.-Can. Free Trade Agreement Ch. 19 Dispute Resolution Roster, 1991-94, panelist, 1992, panel chair 1993; mem. NAFTA Dispute Resolution Roster, 1994—, panel chair, 2001. Author: (with others) Commerce Speaks on Antidumping, 1984, Treatment of Non-Market Economies Under U.S. Antidumping and Countervailing Duty Law: A Petitioner's Perspective, 1992, (with others) Transnational Contracts, 2000—; supervisory editor Customs Law and Administration, 1998—. Mem. ABA, D.C. Bar Assn., Ct. Internat. Trade Bar Assn. Democrat. Presbyterian. Administrative and regulatory, Private international. Office: Neville Peterson LLP 1900 M St NW Ste 850 Washington DC 20036 E-mail: lbogard@npwdc.com.

BOGART, JEFFREY B. lawyer, educator; b. N.Y.C., July 18, 1947; s. Robert and Corinee Bogart; m. Christine C. Bogart; children: Jaclyn, Courtney, Noah, Alexis, John Davis. BS, Bradley U., 1969; JD, U. Toledo, 1972. Bar: N.Y. 1972, Ga. 1976. Asst. dist. atty., NY, 1973—76; asst. U.S. atty., 1976—77; spl. prosecutor State Bar Ga., 1977—79, 1985—87. Instr. Emory Law Sch., NITA, 1985—2002, ICLE. Contbr. articles to legal jours. Mem.: ABA (white collar crime com. 1988—91), Ga. Trial Lawyers Assn. (chmn. family law 2000—01), Nat. Assn. Criminal Def. Lawyers (sentencing com.), State Bar Ga. (bench and bar com. 1982—83, 1990—92), Atlanta Bar Assn. (instr. issues and devels. in family law 1991, chmn. family law sect. 1987—88), Lawyers Club Atlanta. Family and matrimonial, Criminal, General practice. Office: Bogart & Bogart PC Ste 175 6640 Powers Ferry Rd Atlanta GA 30339

BOGART, WILLIAM HARRY, lawyer; b. Sayre, Pa., Mar. 5, 1931; s. Harry M. and Luella C. Bogart; m. Karin Rudolph, Dec. 12, 1962 (div. Dec. 1987); children: Barbara, Silke. AB, Duke U., 1953; AAA, The Hague Acad. Internat. Law, 1962; JD, Syracuse U., 1963. Bar: N.Y. 1964. Mem. Ali, Gerber, Parr & Bogart, Syracuse, N.Y., 1966-67, Bogart & Andrews, Syracuse, 1967-77, Bogart & Assocs., P.C., Syracuse, 1977—. Cons. in field to various govts, fin. instns., ednl. instns.; lectr. in field; active with Acad. Scis. and Russian Govt. drawing comml., ins. and banking laws. Contbr. articles to profl. jours.; drafted civil rights laws for Czechoslovak constn. Mem. missionary com. Presbyn. Ch., 1974-77. With USMC, 1951-52. Mem. ABA, Am. Arbitration Assn., N.Y. State Bar Assn., N.Y. State Trial Lawyers Assn., Onandaga County Bar Assn., Assn. Attenders and Alumni, Lawyers Intergroups, World Ct., Assn. Atty. and Advocates, UN Assn., Witte Soc., Univ. Club, Army and Navy Club, The Hague Club, Masons (32d degree). Democrat. Commercial, contracts (including sales of goods; commercial financing), Private international, Personal injury (including property damage). Home: 110 E Lake Rd - 9 Day Ln Skaneateles NY 13152-9110 Office: 1600 State Tower Bldg 109 S Warren St Syracuse NY 13202-1798 E-mail: bogart@dreamscape.com.

BOGDEN, DANIEL G. prosecutor; Grad., Ashland U.; JD, U. Toledo. Dep. dist. atty. Washoe County, 1987—90; asst. U.S. atty. U.S. Dept. Justice, Nev., 1990—2001, U.S. atty., 2001—. Office: Lloyd George Fed Bldg 333 S Las Vegas Blvd Las Vegas NV 89101*

BOGENSCHUTZ, J. DAVID, lawyer; b. Covington, Ky., May 15, 1944; s. John Francis and Virginia Margaret (Dugan) B.; m. Mary H. McCleary, Oct. 24, 1981; children: Kathleen, Emily. BA, Miami U., Oxford, Ohio, 1966; JD, U. Cin., 1969. Bar: Ohio 1969, U.S. Dist. Ct. (so. dist.) Ohio 1970, U.S. Ct. Appeals (6th cir.) 1971, Fla. 1971, U.S. Dist. Ct. (so. dist.) Fla. 1972, U.S. Ct. Appeals (5th cir.) 1980, U.S. Dist. Ct. (mid. dist.) Fla. 1981, U.S. Ct. Appeals (4th and 11th cirs.) 1981, U.S. Dist. Ct. (ea. dist.) Wis. 1989, U.S. Ct. Appeals (3d cir.) 1999. Instr. Criminal Justice Inst. Nova U., 1977; instr. Broward County Criminal Justice Inst., 1972; asst. solicitor County of Broward, 1971, chief asst. state's atty., 1974-77; ptnr. Bogenschutz & Dutko, P.A., Ft. Lauderdale, Fla. Mem. Gov.'s Com. on Criminal Justice Standards and Goals, 1975-76; mem. bench bar liaison com. U.S. Dist. Ct. (so. dist.) Fla., 1985—. Mem. ATLA, NACDL, Broward County Bar Assn. (criminal law sect. chmn. 1980-81, exec. com. 1981-86, sec., treas. 1985-86), Ohio Bar Assn., Fla. Bar Assn. (criminal law sect., grievance com. 17th jud. cir. 1982-84), Fed. Bar Assn., Greene County Bar Assn., Fla. Pros. Atty.'s Assn., Nat. Dist. Atty.'s Assn., Nat. Assn. Criminal Def. Attys. Democrat. Roman Catholic. Appellate, Criminal. Office: Bogenschutz & Dutko PA 600 S Andrews Ave Ste 500 Fort Lauderdale FL 33301-2851

BOGGIO, MIRIAM ALTAGRACIA, lawyer; b. NYC, July 28, 1952; d. Marco Antonio and Estella (Tejeda) B.; children: Andrew P. Boggio-Dandry, Edward M. Boggio-Dandry, Gregory A. Boggio-Dandry. BA in Polit. Sci. with honors, CUNY, 1973; JD, St. Johns U., 1976; AA in Fashion Design, Fashion Inst. Tech., 1984. Bar: N.Y. 1977, Fla. 1977, U.S. Dist. Ct. (ea. and so. dists.) N.Y. 1978, U.S. Tax Ct. 1982, U.S. Supreme Ct. 1982. Assoc. Schwartzman, Weinstock, Garelik & Mann PC, N.Y.C., 1977-84; counsel N.Y. Assembly Judiciary Com., Albany, 1977-84; dep. supt. N.Y. State Ins. Dept., N.Y.C., 1984-97; counsel govt. affairs, asst. corp. sec. Group Health Inc., N.Y.C., 1997-99; prin. ct. atty. N.Y. State Supreme Ct., N.Y.C., 2000—. SEEK scholar, 1973; recipient SEEK honors, 1973. Mem. Fla. Bar Assn., NY Co. Lawyers' Bar Assn., Phi Beta Kappa. Democrat. Roman Catholic. Office: NY State Supreme Ct 60 Centre St New York NY 10007

BOGGS, BETH CLEMENS, lawyer; b. Dubuque, Iowa, July 28, 1967; d. Theodore Alan and Mary Ann (Fleckenstein) Clemens; m. T. Darin Boggs, Mar. 9, 1991. BA, Govs. State U., 1987; JD, So. Ill. U., 1991. Bar: Ill. 1991, Mo. 1992, U.S. Dist. Ct. (so. dist.) Ill. 1991, U.S. Dist. Ct. (ea. dist.) Mo. 1992, U.S. Dist. Ct. (we. dist.) Mo. 2002, U.S. Dist. Ct. (cen. dist.) Ill. 1997. Clk. R. Courtney Hughes & Assocs., Carbondale, Ill., 1990-91; lawyer Sandberg Phoenix & von Gontard, St. Louis, 1991-93; assoc. LaTourette, Schlueter & Byrne, St. Louis, 1993-95; mng. ptnr. Landau, Omahana & Kopka, P.C., St. Louis, 1995-99; mng. and founding ptnr. Boggs, Backer & Bates, LLC, St. Louis, 1999—. Adj. faculty Webster U., 1995—. Editor student articles So. Ill. U. Law Jour., 1991; contbr. articles to profl. jours. Mem. Young Lawyers divsn. of ABA (vice chair corp. counsel com. 1991-92, editor Corp. Counsel Newsletter 1991-92), Bus. Women St. Louis, Women Lawyers Assn., Lawyers Assn. St. Louis, Def. Rsch. inst., Mo. Orgn. Def. Lawyers. Avocations: tennis, softball, golf. General civil litigation, Corporate, general, Insurance. Office: BBB 7912 Bonhomme Ave Ste 400 Saint Louis MO 63105-3512 E-mail: bbblawyers@aol.com.

BOGGS, DANNY JULIAN, judge; b. Havana, Cuba, Oct. 23, 1944; s. Robert Lilburn and Yolanda (Pereda) Boggs; m. Judith Susan Solow, Dec. 23, 1967; children: Rebecca, David, Jonathan. AB cum laude, Harvard Coll., Cambridge, Mass., 1965; JD, U. Chgo., 1968; LLD (hon.) , U. Detroit Mercy, 1994. Dep. commr. Ky. Dept. Econ. Security, 1969—70; legal counsel, adminstrv. asst. Gov. Ky., 1970—71; legis. counsel to Rep. legislators Ky. Gen. Assembly, 1972; asst. to solicitor gen. U.S. Dept. Justice, Washington, 1973—75; asst. to chmn. FPC, Washington, 1975—77; dep. minority counsel Senate Energy Com., Washington, 1977—79; of counsel Bushnell, Gage, et al., Washington, 1979—80; spl. asst. to Pres. White House, Washington, 1981—83; dep. sec. U.S. Dept. Energy, Washington, 1983—86; judge U.S. Ct. Appeals (6th cir.), Cin., 1986—. Mem. adv. com. on appellate rules Jud. Conf. U.S., 1991—94, com. on automation and tech., 1994—2000. Mem. vis. com. U. Chgo. Law

Sch., 1984—87, 1999—2002; trustee Lexington Sch., 1999—; del. Rep. Nat. Conv., 1972; staff dir. energy subcom. Rep. Platform Com., 1980. Mem.: ABA (chair appellate judges conf. 2001—02), Mont Pelerin Soc., Ky. Bar Assn., Phila. Soc., Phi Delta Phi, Order of Coif. Office: US Ct Appeals US Courthouse 601 W Broadway Ste 220 Louisville KY 40202-2227

BOGGS, JAMES DOTSON, lawyer; b. Kansas City, Mo., Aug. 31, 1949; s. William C. and Helen C. (Harbison) B.; m. Vickie R. Boggs, May 27, 1972; children: William Christian, Meghan Raye. BA, U. Mo., Columbia, 1971; JD, U. Mo., Kansas City, 1975. Bar: Mo. 1975, U.S. Dist. Ct. (we. dist.) Mo., U.S. Ct. Appeals (8th cir.), U.S. Supreme Ct. Assoc. Witt and Shafer, Platte City, Mo., 1975-78; ptnr. Witt and Boggs, Platte City, Mo., 1979-81, Witt, Boggs & Shaw, Platte City, Mo., 1982-85, Witt, Boggs, Shaw & Van Amburg, Platte City, Mo., 1985-87; pvt. practice Kansas City, Mo., 1987—. Chmn. Platte County Dem. PArty, 1985-86; commr. Platte County Jud. Commn., 1987-93, 93—. Mem. Mo. Bar Assn. (gov. 1992-97), Mo. Assn. Trial Attys. (govs., 1985—, exec. com. 1994—, v.p. 2000, pres. 2002), Reach Out Am. (dir. 1994—). Office: 6406 N Cosby Ave Kansas City MO 64151-2377

BOGGS, JUDITH SUSAN, lawyer, health policy expert; b. Bklyn., Feb. 11, 1946; d. Robert Henry and Ethel (Shapiro) Solow; m. Danny Julian Boggs; children: Rebecca, David, Jonathan. BA cum laude, Bklyn. Coll., 1966; JD, U. Chgo., 1969. Bar: Ky. 1970. Human rights rep. Ky. Human Rights Commn., Frankfort, Ky., 1969; legal counsel Ky. Dept. Mental Health, Frankfort, 1970-73; sr. legal advisor Social and Rehabilitation Service, Washington, 1973-77; dir., health systems div. Health Care Fin. Adminstrn., Washington, 1978-82, special asst. to assoc. adminstr. for policy, 1982-86, spl. asst. to adminstr., 1986-87; sr. policy analyst The White House, Washington, 1987-89; of counsel Alagia, Day, Trautwein & Smith, Louisville, 1989-93; sr. v.p., gen. counsel Ky. Hosp. Assn., 1993-94; pvt. practice, 1994—2002; mem. (judge) Adminstrv. Rev. Bd. U.S. Dept. Labor, 2002—. Apptd. mem. Ky. Registry Election Fin., 2001—02. Mem. ABA, Ky. Bar Assn., Am. Health Lawyers Assn., Louisville Bar Assn. Administrative and regulatory, Health. Office: 200 Constitution Ave NW Washington DC

BOGGS, RALPH STUART, retired lawyer; b. Toledo, June 6, 1917; s. Nolan and Sarah (MacPhie) B.; m. Mary Frances Sharp Wiggins, Sept. 7, 1940; children: Sally Ann Boggs Bashore, William S., Robert A. AB, Denison U., 1939; LL.B., U. Mich., 1942. Bar: Ohio 1942, U.S. Supreme Ct. 1960. Spl. agt. FBI, 1942-45; practiced in Toledo, 1946-99; ptnr. Boggs, Boggs & Boggs (P.A.), 1946-87; of counsel Eastman and Smith, 1987-98; ret. Mem. Maumee Bd. Edn., 1953-69, Maumee Recreation Com., 1954-69; life mem. Toledo adv. com. Salvation Army, pres., 1981-83; pres. Maumee Men's Rep. Club, 1947-48; former chmn. bd. trustees Presbytery of Maumee, Inc.; trustee, sec. Masonic Toledo Trust, 1986-97; trustee Stranahan Theatre Trust, 1997—, sec., 1997-98; asst. sec. Otis Avery Browning Masonic Meml. Fund, 1987-97. Named to Toledo H.S. Athletes Hall of Fame, 1995. Mem. ABA, Ex-FBI Agts. Soc., Ohio Bar Assn., Lucas County Bar Assn., Toledo Bar Assn., Masons (33 degree), Shriners, Heather Downs Country Club (Toledo) (past pres., dir.), Sigma Chi (life). Presbyterian (elder). Home: 5916 Cresthaven Ln Apt B416 Toledo OH 43614-1200

BOGGS, STEVEN EUGENE, real estate broker, lawyer; b. Santa Monica, Calif., Apr. 28, 1947; s. Eugene W. and Annie (Happe) B. BA in Econ., U. Calif., Santa Barbara, 1969; D of Chiropractic summa cum laude, Cleveland Chiropractic, L.A., 1974; PhD in Fin. Planning, Columbia Pacific U., 1986; JD in Law, U. So. Calif., 1990. Bar: Calif. 1990, U.S. Dist. Ct. (cen. dist.) Calif. 1990, Hawaii 1991, U.S. Ct. Appeals (9th cir.), Colo. 1999; CFP; lic. chiropractor Hawaii, Calif.; lic. radiography X-ray supr. and operator; real estate broker, Colo. Faculty mem. Cleveland Chiropractic Coll., 1972-74; pres. clinic dir. Hawaii Chiropratic Clinic, Inc., Aiea, 1974-87; pvt. practice Honolulu, 1991-99; mem. faculty Hawaii Pacific U., 1997-99; broker, dir. REO/asset mgmt. team (bank foreclosures) Coldwell Banker Walker & Co., 2000—02, RE/MAX Properties, Inc., 2002—. Cons. in field; seminar presenter 1990—. Contbr. articles to profl. jours. Recipient Cert. Appreciation State of Hawaii, 1981-84. Fellow Internat. Coll. of Chiropractic; mem. ABA, Am. Trial Lawyers Assn., Consumer Lawyers of Hawaii, Am. Chriopractic Assn., Hawaii State Chiropractic Assn. (pres. 1978, 85, 86, v.p. 1977, sec. 1979-84, treas. 1976, other coms., Valuable Svc. award 1984, Cert. Appreciation 1986, Cert. Achievement 1986, Chiropractor of Yr. 1986, Outstanding Achievement award 1991), Consumer Lawyers of Hawaii (bd. dirs.). Republican. Avocations: bicycling, car racing. Office: 19050 Archers Dr Monument CO 80132-2807 E-mail: steve@steveboggs.com., boggs@iglide.net.

BOGREN, BENGT HJALMAR, lawyer; b. Göteborg, Sweden, Aug. 14, 1938; s. Hjalmar and Astrid (Settergren) B.; m. Märta-Stina Croona, May 28, 1966; children: Johan, Fredrik, Lotta. LLB, U. Lund, Sweden, 1963. Clk. Dist. Ct., Skene, Sweden, 1963-65, County Adminstrv. Bd., Göteborg, 1965-67, Law Office, Borås, Sweden, 1967-70; atty. at law Göteborg, 1970—. Pres. Lions, Lerum, Sweden, 1980. Office: Östra Hamngatan 29 S 41110 Goteborg Sweden Personal E-mail: bengt.bogren@swipnet.se. Business E-Mail: bengt.bogren@delphilaw.com.

BOGUS, CARL THOMAS, law educator; b. Fall River, Mass., May 14, 1948; s. Isidore E. and Carolyn (Dashoff) B.; m. Dale Shepard, Sept. 5, 1970 (div. 1987); children: Elizabeth Carol, Ian Troy; m. Cynthia J. Giles, Nov. 5, 1988; 1 child, Zoe Churchill. AB, Syracuse U., 1970, JD, 1972. Bar: Pa. 1973, U.S. Dist. Ct. (ea. dist.) Pa. 1973, U.S. Ct. Appeals (3d cir.) 1976, U.S. Supreme Ct. 1977. Assoc. Steinberg, Greenstein, Gorelick & Price, Phila., 1973-79, ptnr., 1979-83; assoc. Mesirov, Gelman, Jaffe, Cramer & Jamieson, Phila., 1983-84, ptnr., 1985-91; assoc. prof. Roger Williams U. Sch. Law, Bristol, RI, 1996—2002, prof., 2002—. Vis. prof. Rutgers U. Sch. Law, Camden, 1992—96; mem. bd. visitors Coll. Law, Syracuse (N.Y.) U., 1976—2001; mem. Nat. adv. panel Violence Policy Ctr., 1993—. Author: Why Lawyers Are Good for America: Disciplined Democracy, Big Business and the Common Law, 2001; editor: The Second Amendment in Law and History, 2001; contbr. articles to profl. jours. Bd. dirs. Handgun Control, Inc., 1987-89, bd. govs., 1992-93; bd. dirs. Ctr. to Prevent Handgun Violence, 1989-92, Lawyers Alliance for Nuclear Arms Control, 1987-89; mem. state governing bd. Common Cause R.I., 1999-2001. Mem. ABA (Ross Essay award 1991), Syracuse Law Coll. Assn. (exec. sec. 1979-83, 2d v.p. 1983-85). Democrat. Mem. Soc. Of Friends. Office: Roger William U Sch Law 10 Metacom Ave Bristol RI 02809-5103 E-mail: cbogus@law.rwu.edu.

BOGUTZ, JEROME EDWIN, lawyer, educator; b. Bridgeton, N.J., June 7, 1935; s. Charles and Gertrude (Lahn) B.; m. Helene Carole Ross, Nov. 20, 1960; children: Marc Lahn, Tami Lynne BS in Fin., Pa. State U., 1957; JD, Villanova U., 1962. Bar: Pa., U.S. Dist. Ct. (ea. dist.) Pa., U.S. Ct. Appeals (3d cir.), U.S. Supreme Ct. Assoc. Dash & Levy, Phila., 1962—63, Abrahams & Loewenstein, Phila., 1963—64; dep. dir., chief of litigation Community Legal Svcs., Phila., 1964—68, dir., 1968—78; emeritus, 1978—; pvt. practice law, 1968—71; ptnr. Bogutz & Mazer, Phila., 1971—81, Fox Rothschild O'Brien & Frankel, Phila., 1981—98; judge Pro Tem Phila. Ct. Common Pleas, 1992—; ptnr. Christie, Pabarue, Mortensen & Young, P.C., Phila., 1998—. Adj. clin. prof. law Villanova (Pa.) U., 1969-72, lectr., 1987—, bd. consultors Law Sch., 1983—; pres. Internat. Mobile Machines, Phila., 1980-81, Interdigital Comm., 1980-81, also bd. dirs. ABA-JAD Lawyers Conf., 1987-92, mem. exec. coun., 1986-92, vice chmn., 1987-88, chmn., 1989-90, chmn. nominating com., 1989-90, mem. long range planning com., 1989-90; mem. adv. bd. Pa. Med. Profl. Liability Catastrophe Loss Fund, 2000—; bd. dirs. Jefferson Park Hosp., Phila. Bd. dirs. Am. Friends of Hebrew U., 1988-93, chmn. exec. com., 1991-93, pres., 1993-95, chmn. bd. 1995-98, chair steering com., pres. Pa. Futures Commn. on Justice in the 21st Century, 1993—, chmn. of bd., 1993-97. With USAR, 1956-60. Fellow Am. Bar Found. (life), Pa. Bar Found. (life, pres. 1986-88, bd. dirs. 1983—, lifetime dir. 1991—), Am. Judicature Soc. (life, bd. dirs. 1990—); mem. ABA (ho. of dels. 1980-84, 86-96, credentials and admissions com. 1987-88, nominating com. 1992, 93, chair ABA/JAD bench bar com., vice chmn. lawyer's conf. 1987-89, chair 1988-90, co-chair mid-yr. meeting com. 1987-88, planning com., conf. sect. officers, 1988-90, bd. mem. consortium on legal svcs. and pub. 1987-91, mem. disaster relief task force, bd. dirs., commr., chmn. ABA Commn. on Advt. 1988-91, adv. coun. ABA Commn. Responsibility 1999—), Pa. Bar Assn. (pres. 1985-86, bd. dirs. 1983-90, chair Governance Com., 1996-98), Phila. Bar Found. (pres. 1981), Phila. Bar Assn. (v.p. 1978, pres.-elect 1979, chancellor 1980, sec. 1975-78, trustee 1979—), Pa. Bar Trust (life mem., chmn. 1993-2001, chmn. emeritus 2001—), Pa. House of Dels. (life; chair governance com. 1996-98), Nat. Met. Bar Leaders (founder, pres. 1979-82, pres. emeritus 1983—), Nat. Conf. Bar Pres. (exec. coun. 1981-84), Phila. C. of C. (bd. dirs. 1980-83). Republican. Jewish. Avocations: golf, sailing. Corporate, general, Insurance, Professional liability. Home: Apt 6B 1901 Walnut St Philadelphia PA 19103 Office: Christie Pabarue Mortensen & Young 1880 JFK Blvd Fl 10 Philadelphia PA 19103-7424

BOHAN, THOMAS LYNCH, physicist, lawyer; b. Terre Haute, Ind., Feb. 12, 1938; s. Richard Timothy and Anna Elizabeth (Lynch) B.; m. Linda Ann Sian, Nov. 26, 1960 (div. Dec. 1981); children: Richard Michael, Cecilia Anne, John Charles; m. Rhonda Beth Berg, July 4, 1987. BS in Physics, U. Chgo., 1960; MS in Physics, U. Ill., 1964, PhD in Physics, 1968; JD, Franklin Pierce Law Ctr., 1980. Bar: Maine 1980, Mass. 1980, U.S. Dist. Ct. Maine 1980, U.S. Patent Office 1980, U.S. Ct. Appeals (1st cir.) 1992, U.S. Ct. Appeals (2nd cir.) 1994, U.S. Supreme Ct., 1996. Rsch. assoc. U. Ill., Urbana, 1968—69; asst. prof. physics Bowdoin Coll., Brunswick, Maine, 1969—76; assoc. Sunenblick, Fontaine and Reben, Portland, Maine, 1980—81; ptnr. Med. and Tech. Cons. (now MTC Forensics), Portland, 1982—86, sole propr., 1986—; propr. Thomas L. Bohan & Assoc., Portland, 1985—2001, Bohan Mathers & Assocs., Portland, 2002, of counsel, 2003—. Editor (with A. Damask) Forensic Accident Investigation: Motor Vehicles-1, 1995; editor Forensic Accident Investigation: Motor Vehicles-2, 1997; contbr. articles to profl. jours. Chmn. Community Devel. Com., Brunswick, 1976-78; organizer, treas., pres. Peaks Island Land Preserve, Inc., 1994-97. Research grantee Am. Heart Assn., 1970-76, The Research Corp., 1972-74, NSF/NATO, 1967; fellow Tex. Instruments, 1965; Fulbright scholar, Peru, 1972-73. Fellow: Am. Acad. Forensic Sci. (chair engrng. sci. sect. 1997—98, bd. dirs. 1999—, exec. com. bd. dirs. 2000—); mem.: AAAS, Nat. Assn. Patent Practitioners, Maine Patent Practitioners Group, Maine Trial Lawyers Assn., Cumberland County Bar Assn., Am. Phys. Soc., Sigma Xi. Home: 54 Pleasant Ave Peaks Island ME 04108-1188 Office: MTC-Forensics and Bohan Mathers & Assoc 371 Fore St Portland ME 04101-5010 E-mail: tbohan2@maine.rr.com., tlb@bohanlaw.com., tlb@mtcforensics.com.

BOHANNON, CHARLES TAD, lawyer; b. Dallas, June 25, 1964; s. Charles Spencer and Donna Pauline (Smith) B.; m. Gayle Renee Alston, July 26, 1986. BA, Hendrix Coll., 1986; JD, U. Ark., Little Rock, 1992; LLM, Washington U., St. Louis, 1993. Bar: Ark. 1992, Tex. 1993, U.S. Dist. Ct. (ea. and we. dists.) Ark. 1992, U.S. Dist. Ct. (no. dist.) Tex. 1994, U.S. Ct. Appeals (5th and 8th cirs.) 1994, U.S. Tax Ct. 1994. Staff atty. U.S. Ct. Appeals (8th cir.), St. Louis, 1992-94; assoc. Gill Law Firm, Little Rock, 1994-98; ptnr. Wright, Lindsey & Jennings, LLP, Little Rock, 1998—. Contbr. articles to profl. jours. Mem. ABA, Ark. Bar Assn., Pulaski County Bar Assn., Nat. Transp. Safety Bd., Bar Assn. State Bar of Tex., Nat. Assn. Bond Lawyers, Aircraft Owners and Pilots Assn. Avocations: soccer (player, referee, coach), flying, fly fishing, home renovation. Aviation, Municipal (including bonds), Taxation, general. Office: Wright Lindsey & Jennings 200 W Capitol Ave Ste 2300 Little Rock AR 72201-3699 E-mail: ctbohannon@wlj.com.

BOHANON, LUTHER L. federal judge; b. Ft. Smith, Ark., Aug. 9, 1901; s. William Joseph and Artelia (Campbell) B.; m. Marie Swatek, July 17, 1933; 1 son, Richard L. LLB, U. Okla., 1927; LLD (hon.), Oklahoma City U., 1991. Bar: Okla. 1927, U.S. Supreme Ct. 1937. Gen. practice law, Seminole, Okla. and Oklahoma City, 1927-61; judge U.S. Dist. Ct. Okla. (no., ea., and we. dists.), 1961-74, sr. judge, 1974—. Mem. platform com. Democratic Nat. Conv., 1940. Served to maj. USAAF, 1942-45. Recipient citations and awards including citation from Okla. Senate and Ho. of Reps., 1979, Okla. County Bar Assn. and Jour. Record award, 1987, Humanitarian award NCCJ, 1991; Luther Bohanon Am. Inn of Ct. named in his honor Am. Inn of Ct. XXIII/U. Okla., 1991. Mem. U.S. Dist. Judges Assn. (10th cir.), Fed. Judges Assn., Okla. Bar Assn., Oklahoma County Bar Assn., Oklahoma City C. of C., Sigma Nu, Phi Alpha Delta. Clubs: Mason (Shriner, 32 deg.), K.T, Jester, Kiwanis, Com.of 100, Men's Dinner Club. Methodist. Office: US Dist Ct PO Box 1514 Oklahoma City OK 73102-3028

BOHLENDER, HUGH DARROW, lawyer; b. Sacramento, Oct. 27, 1951; s. Hugh S. and Dorothy Elrene (Darrow) B.; m. Eliese Susanna Wagenseil, June 9, 1973 (div. Feb. 1982); children: Philip Edward, Karen Leslie; m. Ingrid Elizabeth Rieck, Dec. 27, 1997. BS, U.S. Mil. Acad., 1973; MA, Northwestern U., 1982, JD, 1986, postgrad. Bar: Ill. 1986, U.S. Dist. Ct. (no dist.) Ill. 1986. Commd. 2nd lt. U.S. Army, 1975, advanced through grades to capt., 1977, resigned, 1981; lectr. Northwestern U., Evanston, Ill., 1984-85; assoc. Lord Bissell & Brook, Chgo., 1986-90; of counsel Allstate Ins. Co., 1990—. Dir. Ala. Ins. Guaranty Assn., 1992-93. Vice chmn. Northbrook (Ill.) Evang. Covenant Ch., 1988-91. Maj. USAR, 1986-93; ret. Mem. ABA, Ill. Bar Assn. Republican. Avocations: running, cycling, camping, photography, computers. Administrative and regulatory, Corporate, general, Trademark and copyright. Office: Allstate Ins Co Allstate Plz N Northbrook IL 60062

BOHM, JACK NELSON, retired lawyer; b. Sharon, Pa., July 5, 1924; s. Joseph and Irene (Bohm) B.; m. Elizabeth Viscofsky, Sept. 27, 1947; children: Robert Mark, Richard Darrell, Lorie Joyce Klumb. Student, U. Pa., 1942-43, U. Ga., 1943-44; JD, Washington U., St. Louis, 1948. Bar: Mo. 1948, U.S Dist. Ct. (we. dist.) Mo. 1948, U.S. Ct. of Mil. Appeals 1955, U.S. Supreme Ct. 1955, U.S. Ct. of Appeals (8th Cir.) 1960, Kans. 1985, U.S. Dist. Ct. Kans. 1985. Assoc. Hall Bresler & Cohn, Kansas City, Mo., 1948—61; ptnr. Glass Bohm & Hirschman, Kansas City, Mo., 1961—71, Stoup & Bohm, Kansas City, Mo., 1971—81; chmn. bd. Buck Bohm & Stein, P.C., Kansas City/Leawood, Kans., 1981—97; sr. counsel Morrison & Hecker LLP, Overland Park, Kans., 1997—99, ret., 1999. Chief judge U.S. Army Ct. of Mil. Appeals, 1977-80, Mobilization Designation. Editor: State Variations of Commercial Law, 1985. Pres. Dist. 2 B'nai B'rith, 1964; co-chmn., NCCJ, Kansas City, 1968-71. With U.S. Army 1943-46, USAR, 1948-84, brigadier gen. AUS, ret. 1977-84. Legion of Merit U.S. Army, 1984. Mem. ABA, Mo. Bar Assn. (chmn. commr. law com. 1977-79), Kans. Bar Assn., Meadowbrook Country Club, Phi Alpha Delta. Bankruptcy, Corporate, general, Probate (including wills, trusts). Home: 11300 Fontana St Leawood KS 66211-1751 E-mail: brgen@aol.com.

BOHN, ROBERT HERBERT, lawyer; b. Austin, Tex., Sept. 2, 1935; s. Herbert and Alice B.; m. Gay P. Maloy, June 4, 1957; children: Rebecca Shoemaker, Katherine Bernat, Robert H., Jr.. BBA, U. Tex., 1957, LLB, 1963. Bar: Tex. 1963, Calif. 1965. Ptnr. Boccardo Law Firm, San Jose, Calif., 1965-87, Alexander & Bohn, San Jose, 1987-91; Bohn, Bennion & Niland, 1992-97; Bohn & Bohn, 1998—. Spkr. Calif. Continuing Edn. of Bar; judge pro tem Superior Ct. of Calif., San Jose, 1975-96. Mem. ATLA, Am. Coll. Barristers, Consumer Attys. Calif., Am. Bd. Trial Advocates, Santa Clara County Bar Assn., Calif. State Bar Assn., Santa Clara County Trial Lawyers Assn. (pres. 1999, Trial Lawyer of Yr. 2000), Trial Lawyers Pub. Justice, Roscoe Pound Found., Million Dollar Advocates Forum, Silicon Valley Capital Club, Texas Cowboys Assn., Phi Gamma Delta. Alternative dispute resolution, General civil litigation, Personal injury (including property damage). Office: 152 N 3rd St Ste 200 San Jose CA 95112-5515 E-mail: bbohn@bohnlaw.com.

BOHNEN, MICHAEL J. lawyer; b. Buffalo, N.Y., Mar. 9, 1947; s. Joyce B. Oppenheim, June 19, 1969; children: Sharon, Deborah. BA, Harvard U., 1968, JD, 1972. Bar: Mass. 1972. Assoc. Nutter, McClennen & Fish, LLP, Boston, 1972-80, ptnr., 1980—. Lectr. Boston U. Law Sch., 1981—2001. Co-author: Mass. Corporate Forms, 1990-2002. Pres. Solomon Schechter Day Sch., Newton, 1980—82; chmn. Jewish Coun. for Pub. Affairs, 2002—03; trustee United Jewish Cmtys., 1999—; pres. Jewish Cmty. Rels. Coun., Boston, 1991—93; chmn. Combined Jewish Philanthropies, 1993—95, New Jewish H.S., 1995—. Mem. Boston Bar Assn. (chmn. corp. law com. 1997-99). Corporate, general, Mergers and acquisitions, Securities. Home: 60 Nathan Rd Newton MA 02459-1105 Office: Nutter McClennen & Fish LLP World Trade Center West Boston MA 02210

BOHNHOFF, HENRY M. lawyer; b. Albuquerque, Dec. 25, 1956; s. Herman Carl William and Lois Marie (Jacobsen) B.; m. Jennifer Lynn Swedberg, June 7, 1980; children: H. Matthew, J. Christopher, J. Thomas. BS with honors, Stanford U., 1978; JD, Columbia U., 1982. Bar: N.Mex. 1982, U.S. Dist. Ct. N.Mex. 1983, U.S. Ct. Appeals (10th cir.) 1983, U.S. Supreme Ct. 1987. Law clk. to chief judge U.S. Dist. Ct. N.Mex., Albuquerque, 1982-83; assoc. Rodey, Dickason, Sloan, Akin & Robb, Albuquerque, 1983-87; chief asst. atty. gen. N.Mex. Atty. Gen.'s Office, Santa Fe, 1987-88; dept. atty. gen. N.Mex. Atty. Gen., Santa Fe, 1988-89; ptnr. Rodey, Dickason, Sloan, Akin & Robb, Albuquerque, 1989—. Exec. editor Columbia Jour. Environ. Law, 1981-82. Mem. ABA, N.Mex. Bar Assn., Phi Beta Kappa. Republican. Avocations: rock climbing, woodworking, sailing, tennis. Federal civil litigation, Construction, Professional liability. Office: Rodey Dickason Sloan Akin Robb PA 200 3rd St NW Ste 2200 Albuquerque NM 87102-3334 E-mail: hmbohnho@rodey.com.

BOHREN, MICHAEL OSCAR, lawyer; b. Appleton, Wis., Feb. 27, 1947; s. Oscar Robert and Martha (Anderson) B.; m. Mary Joset Morse, Nov. 26, 1977; children: Juliana Rose, Katherine Elizabeth. AB, Ripon Coll., 1969; JD, Marquette U., 1975. Bar: Wis. 1978, U.S. Dist. Ct. (ea. and we. dists.) Wis. 1975, U.S. Ct. Appeals (5th and 7th cirs.) 1976, U.S. Supreme Ct. 1978. Atty. USDA, Washington, 1975; gen. counsel Aries Ltd., Milw., 1975—78; atty. Marola & Bohren, Milw., 1978—2000; cir. ct. judge br. I Waukesha County, 2000—; presiding judge Criminal Traffic divsn. Waukesha County, 2002—. Bd. dirs. Kettle Moraine Sch. Dist., Wales, Wis., 1982-2000, pres., 1986-94, 96-99; bd. dirs. Waukesha (Wis.) Symphony, 1997—; v.p. Greenfield (Wis.) Sch. Dist., 1977-81. Mem. ABA, ATLA, Wis. Bar Assn., Wis. Trial Lawyers Assn., Masons, Kiwanis (mem. exec. bd.). Avocations: geology, politics, reading. Civil rights, General civil litigation, Criminal. Home: W315 W496 Christopher Way Delafield WI 53018 Office: Waukesha County Courthouse Waukesha WI 53187 E-mail: moblawgo@execpc.com.

BOIES, DAVID, lawyer; b. Sycamore, Ill., Mar. 11, 1941; BS, U. Redlands, Northwestern U., 1964; LLB, Yale U., 1966. Chief counsel, staff dir. Senate Antitrust Subcom., 1978, Sen. Judiciary Com., 1979; mem. Cravath, Swaine & Moore, N.Y., 1966—77; partner Boies, Schiller, & Flexner, Armonk, NY, 1997—. Mem. ABA, N.Y. State Bar Assn., Assn. of Bar of City of N.Y. Office: Boies Schiller & Flexner 570 Lexington Ave New York NY 10022*

BOIES, WILBER H. lawyer; b. Bloomington, Ill., Mar. 15, 1944; s. W. H. and Martha Jane (Hutchison) B.; m. Victoria Joan Steinitz, Sept. 17, 1966; children: Andrew Charles, Carolyn Ursula. AB, Brown U., 1965; JD, U. Chgo., 1968. Bar: Ill. 1968, U.S. Dist. Ct. (no. dist.) Ill. 1968, U.S. Dist. Ct. (ea. dist.) Wis. 1973, U.S. Ct. Appeals (7th cir.) 1974, U.S. Ct. Appeals (5th cir.) 1975, U.S. Ct. Appeals (3d cir.) 1977, U.S. Supreme Ct. 1978, U.S. Ct. Appeals (8th cir.) 1994, U.S. Ct. Appeals (9th cir.) 1995. Assoc. Altheimer & Gray, Chgo., 1968-71; ptnr. McDermott, Will & Emery, Chgo., 1971—. Contbr. articles to profl. jours. Active CPR Inst. for Dispute Resolution. Mem. ABA, Bar Assn. 7th Fed. Cir., Chgo. Bar Assn. (chmn. class litigation com. 1991-92), Chgo. Coun. Lawyers, Lawyers Club Chgo., Met. Club, Chgo. Bar Found.(dir.). Alternative dispute resolution, Federal civil litigation, State civil litigation. Office: McDermott Will & Emery 227 W Monroe St Ste 4400 Chicago IL 60606-5096 E-mail: bboies@mwe.com.

BOIRON, JEAN-ERIC, lawyer; b. Limoges, France, Dec. 27, 1960; s. Jean-Francois Boiron and Marie-Josephe Laproste; m. Claire Desportes, June 25, 1987 (div. June 10, 1991); 1 child, Edouard; m. Marie-Claire Coudy-Boiron, July 8, 1994. Lic. droit, U. Paris II, 1982, M, 1983. Bar: Paris 1985. Assoc. Gide Lourette Novel, Paris, 1985—89; ptnr. Martinet Bataillon, Paris, 1990—91; sr. assoc. Linklaters, Paris and London, 1991—96; ptnr. Landwell & Assocs., Paris, 1997—. Exec. dir. COMILOG, France, Gabon. Co-author: European Restructuring and Insolvency Guide 2002/2003; contbr. articles to profl. jours. Served with French mil., 1983—84. Mergers and acquisitions, Bankruptcy, Banking. Office: Landwell & Assocs 32 Rue Guersant 75017 Paris France Office Fax: (33-1) 56-57-70-44. E-mail: jean-eric.boiron@fr.landwellglobal.com.

BOK, JOHN FAIRFIELD, lawyer; b. Boston, Aug. 30, 1930; AB magna cum laude, Harvard U., 1952, LLB magna cum laude, 1955. Bar: Mass. 1955, N.Y. 1982, Pa. 1984. Assoc. firm Ropes & Gray, Boston, 1957-62, 64-69; counsel to devel. adminstr. Boston Redevel. Authority, 1962-64; ptnr. firm Csaplar & Bok, Boston, 1969-90, Gaston & Snow, Boston, 1990-91; of counsel Foley, Hoag & Eliot, Boston, 1991-2000. Instr. law Boston Coll. Law Sch., part-time 1974-75; lectr. Practicing Law Inst., 1974, New Eng. Law Inst., 1973 Editor Harvard Law Rev., 1954-55. Pres. Cambridge St. Comty. Devel. Corp., 1972-75, Citizens Housing and Planning Assn., 1968-70, Met. Cultural Alliance, 1973-75, Beacon Hill Civic Assn., 1959-61, Beacon Hill Nursery Sch., 1964-65, Peddock's Island Trust, 1982-85, Mus. Wharf, 1989-94, Boston Ballet, 1991-94, Peter Faneuil Devel. Group, Inc., 1992—, Mass. Hort. Soc., 1995-98; v.p. The Cmty. Builders, Inc., 1969-97, pres. or chmn., 1998—; chmn. Boston Children's Mus., 1976-78, Mass. Housing Partnership, 1985-92, Social Policy Rsch. Group Inc., 1985-92, Boston Mcpl. Rsch. Bur., 1979-81, bd. dirs. and/or officer Boston Neighborhood Housing Svcs., 1974-76, Boston Waterfront Devel. Corp., 1970-85, Archtl. Conservation Trust for Mass., 1978-92, Wheelock Coll., 1980-95, Strawberry Banke, Inc., 1981-86, Met. Boston Housing Partnership, Inc., 1984-95, Cambridge Coll., 1984-95, Boston Housing Authority monitoring com., 1984-90, The Boston Harbor Assn., 1984-92, Back Bay Assn., 1988-92, Hist. Mass., 1989—, African Am. Meeting House, 1993—; mem. Boston Archives and Records Advt. Commn., 1988-95, Cmty. Music Ctr., 1995—, Island Alliance, 1995—, Light Boston!, 1995—. Fulbright-Hays scholar, 1976 Mem. ABA, Mass. Bar Assn., Boston Bar Assn. (chmn. land use com. 1971-74), Phi Beta Kappa. Home: 53 Pinckney St Boston MA 02114-4801

BÖKWALL, CARL, lawyer; b. Malmö, Sweden, Oct. 9, 1970; s. Christer and Ulla Bökwall; m. Ewa Jansson; 1 child, Sofie. LLB, U. Lund, Sweden, 1996; LLM, U. Lund, 1997. Bar: Sweden 2002. Trainee Tisell & Co. Solicitors, Stockholm, 1997—98; jr. judge City Ct. Stockholm, 1998—99; assoc. Baker & McKenzie, Stockholm, 1999—. Contbr. , articles to profl. jours. 2nd lt. Swedish Army, 1990—91. Avocations: skiing, scuba diving, hiking, literature, cooking. Antitrust, Mergers and acquisitions, Intellectual property. Office: Baker & McKenzie Linnégatan 18 Stockholm Sweden

BOLAND, CHRISTOPHER THOMAS, II, lawyer; b. Scranton, Pa., June 10, 1915; s. Patrick J. and Sarah (Jennings) B.; m. Nora Cusick, Jan. 23, 1943; m. Cornelia Bingham, Mar. 1, 1980. BSS cum laude, Georgetown U., 1937; LL.B., Harvard, 1940. Staff dir. Spl. Senate Com. on Atomic Energy, 1945—47; staff dir., counsel Joint Senate-House Com. on Atomic Energy, 1947; pvt. practice Washington, 1947—; sr. ptnr. Gallagher Boland & Meiburger, Washington, 1955—93, sr. counsel, 1994—. Utility specialist Dept. Energy. Served to lt. col., intelligence USAAF, 1941-45. Mem. ABA, D.C. Bar Assn., Fed. Energy Bar Assn. (pres. 1970), Congressional Country Club (pres. 1974), Harvard Club (Washington), Burning Tree Club (Bethesda, Md.), Rehoboth Beach (Del.) Country Club. Administrative and regulatory, FERC practice. Home: 5309 Cardinal Ct Spring Hill Bethesda MD 20816 Office: 1023 15th St NW Ste 900 Washington DC 20005-2627 E-mail: cboland@gbmdc.com.

BOLANTE, RODELLE BAROÑA, lawyer; b. Bangued, Philippines, Sept. 13, 1968; s. Roderick Alcantara Bolante and Lea Aspacio Baroña; m. Beatriz Pauline Obliga Bolante, Oct. 9, 1993; children: Jose Ramon A., Jose Rodrigo A., Jose Ricardo A. AB in Philippine Studies, U. Philippines, 1990, LLB, 1996. Bar: Philippines 1997. Legal officer and asst. corp. sec. Radio Philippines Network, Inc., Quezon City, Philippines, 1996—99; U. legal counsel U. Philippines, Quezon City, 1998—99; sr. assoc. SyCip Salazar Hernandez & Gatmaitan, Makati City, Philippines, 1999—. Mem. editl. staff: Philippine Law Jour., 1993—94. Mem.: Immigration Lawyers Assn. of Philippines, Philippine Bar Assn., Integrated Bar of Philippines, Rotary Club Marikina West (dir. 2002—). Roman Catholic. Labor (including EEOC, Fair Labor Standards Act, labor-management relations, NLRB, OSHA), Immigration, naturalization, and customs. Home: 103 Bluebird St Marikina Philippines Office: SyCip Salazar Hernandez & Gatmaitan 105 Paseo de Roxas Makati 1200 Philippines Fax: 632 817-3896. E-mail: rbbolante@syciplaw.com.

BOLDT, MICHAEL HERBERT, lawyer; b. Detroit, Oct. 11, 1950; s. Herbert M. and Mary Therese (Fitzgerald) B.; m. Margaret E. Clarke, May 25, 1974; children: Timothy (dec.), Matthew. Student, U. Detroit, 1968-70; BA, Wayne State U., 1972; JD, U. Mich., 1975. Bar: Ind. 1975, U.S. Dist. Ct. (so. dist.) Ind. 1975, U.S. Ct. Appeals (7th cir.) 1979, U.S. Supreme Ct. 1980, U.S. Ct. Appeals (D.C. cir.) 1983. Assoc. Ice Miller, Indpls., 1975-81, ptnr., 1982—. Bd. dirs. Brooke's Place for Grieving Young People, Inc. Contbr. articles to profl. jours. Mem. Ind. State Bar Assn., Indpls. Bar Assn., Highland Golf and Country Club (bd. dirs.). Labor (including EEOC, Fair Labor Standards Act, labor-management relations, NLRB, OSHA), Pension, profit-sharing, and employee benefits. Office: Ice Miller Box 82001 1 American Sq Indianapolis IN 46282-0002 E-mail: Michael.Boldt@icemiller.com.

BOLLA, WILLIAM JOSEPH, lawyer; b. Chester, Pa., Aug. 2, 1947; s. William Andrew and Margaret Mary (Campbell) B.; divorced; children: Christopher Campbell, Gregory Gibson. BS in Psychology, Pa. State U., 1969; JD, Dickinson Sch. Law, 1972. Bar: Pa. 1972, U.S. Supreme Ct. 1986. Assoc. McGavin DeSantis & Koch, Reading, Pa., 1973; asst. dist. atty. Bucks County, Doylestown, Pa., 1973-76; ptnr. Heckler & Bolla, Doylestown, 1976-85, McNamara, Heckler & Bolla, Doylestown, 1986-98, McNamara, Bolla & Williams, Doylestown, 1998—. Bd. dirs. Bucks County chpt. Am. Cancer Soc., Doylestown, v.p., 1991—92, pres., 1993—95; bd. dirs. Bucks County Symphony Soc., 1995—96, Doylestown Twp. Pks. and Recreation Bd., 1992—95, Bucks County Writers' Rm., 2003—; founder, pres. Bucks County Challenger Baseball Program for Handicapped Children, 1994—99; mem. adv. bd. Big Bros./Big Sisters Bucks County, Doylestown, 1987—93; chair Ctrl. Bucks Teen Ctr. Bldg. Com., 2000—01; mem. Doylestown Borough Revitalization Com., 2000—; minority counsel state govt. com. Pa. Senate, Harrisburg, 1976—77, mem. fin. com., 1978—81. Mem. Pa. Bar Assn. (ho. dels. 1997-98), Bucks County Bar Assn. (bd. dirs., chmn. young lawyers com. 1976-77, chmn. real estate sect. 1987-88, chmn. merit selection of judges 1984-85, chmn. bench and bar com. 1992-95, chmn. realtor legal com. 1991—, v.p./pres.-elect 1995-96, pres. 1996-97). Republican. Avocations: Civil war, travel. E-mail address. Family and matrimonial, Property, real (including real estate development, water), Land use and zoning (including planning). Office: McNamara Bolla Williams & Panzer 122 E Court St Doylestown PA 18901-4321 E-mail: wjbolla@mbwplaw.com.

BOLLER, MATTHEW HUBLY, lawyer; b. Fairbanks, Alaska, Nov. 15, 1967; s. Max Alfred and Jane Marie Boller; m. Kathleen Muranaka George, Nov. 24, 1995; children: Emma Muranaka, Olivia Satori. BA, De Pauw U., 1990; JD, D.C. Sch. Law, 1994. Bar: Fla. 94, DC, Wis. 99. Asst. pub. defender Dade County Pub. Defender's Office, Miami, Fla., 1994—96; assoc. Stephen, Lynn, Klein & McNicholas, West Palm Beach, Fla., 1996—99; ptnr. Murphy, Vaughan, Boller & Pressentin, Monona, Wis., 2000—. Mayoral appointe Cmty. Svc. Commn., Madison, Wis., 2001—; asst. prof. Madison Area Tech. Coll., 2002. Mem.: ATLA, Wis. Acad. Trial Lawyers. Personal injury (including property damage), Insurance. Office: Murphy Vaughan Boller & Pressentin 708 River Pl Monona WI 53716 Fax: 608-222-7089.

BOLLES, DONALD SCOTT, lawyer; b. Buffalo, Dec. 17, 1936; s. Theodore H. and Marie (Heth) B.; m. Jean Waytulonis Oct. 12, 1963 (dec. May 1983); children: Scott, Matthew; m. Geraldine Novinger, Feb. 14, 1988. BA, Alfred U., 1960; JD cum laude, U. San Diego Sch. Law, 1970. Bar: Calif. 1971, U.S. Dist. Ct. (so. and no. dists.) Calif. 1971. Ptnr. Hutton, Foley, Anderson & Bolles, Inc., King City, Calif., 1971-95, Anderson & Bolles, Inc., King City, Calif., 1995-99. Editor lead articles San Diego Law Rev., 1969-70. Chmn. King City Recreation Commn., 1974—77; candidate mcpl. judge primary and gen. election Monterey County, Calif., 1986; trustee Mee Meml. Hosp., King City, 1974—78, chmn., 1978—80; sec., founding mem. bd. dirs. Project Teen Ctr. Inc., 1986—90; bd. dirs. Sun St. Ctrs., 1991—99, Monterey Coll. Law, 1995—2002, pres., 2000—01; pres. Corral de Tierra Homeowners Assn., 1996—98, pres., 2001—; mem. Camerata Singers, 2000—. Decorated Combat Infantryman's badge, Army Commendation medal. Mem. Monterey County Bar Assn. (exec. com. 1985-86). Clubs: Toastmasters (King City) (pres. 1972-74). Lodges: Lions (pres. 1975-76, sec. 1984-86 King City club). Republican. Avocations: application of computer science to practice of law, tennis, golf, bridge, choir. State civil litigation, Family and matrimonial, General practice. Home: 23799-18 Monterey Salinas Hwy Salinas CA 93908-9328 E-mail: dsbolles@aol.com.

BOLT, THOMAS ALVIN WALDREP, lawyer; b. Anderson, S.C., Dec. 1, 1956; s. Thomas Alvin Waldrep Jr. and Jane Gray Sullivan; m. Jenifer Smith, Sept. 2, 1989; 1 stepchild, Royce Stevenson Ward. BA in Govt. and English, Wofford Coll., 1978; postgrad., U. S.C., 1980-81, JD, 1982. Bar: V.I., 1983. Asst. to Gov. Exec. Office of Gov., Columbia, S.C., 1979; exec. asst. S.C. Senate, Columbia, 1979-80; legal clk. S.C. Pub. Svc. Commn., Columbia, 1981; legis. asst. S.C. Ho. of Reps., Columbia, 1981-82; asst. to atty. gen. Office of Atty. Gen., Columbia, 1982; legis. counsel Legis. of V.I., St. Thomas, V.I., 1983-87, counsel to pres., 1987, counsel to the majority, 1987-88; exec. dir., counsel to the commn. V.I. Law Revision Commn., St. Thomas, 1988-91; pvt. practice Tom Bolt & Assocs. P.C., St. Thomas, V.I., 1991—. Intern UN, N.Y.C., 1976; commr. Nat. Conf. Commrs. on Uniform State Laws, Chgo., 1988—, chmn. drafting com. on Uniform Money Svcs. Act, 1996—; prof. law U. V.I., St. Thomas; tchr. history All Saints Cathedral Sch., 1983; mem. bd. advisors V.I. Bus. Jour., 1994-98; mem. V.I. Law Revision Commn., 2001—. Editor: Revised United States Virgin Islands Criminal Code, 1988-91. Mem. Friends of Denmark LWV, St. Thomas Arts Coun., V.I. Youth Multi-Svc. Ctr.; treas. Coun. on Alcoholism, St. Thomas-St. John, 1992—93; sec. St. Thomas Hist. Trust, 1987—88; pres. Blackbeard's Hill Neighborhood Assn., 1988—95; state committeeman S.C. Dem. Com., Columbia, 1980—83, vice chmn., 1980—82; territorial committeeman V.I. Dem. Com., St. Thomas, 1988—92; bd. dirs. Friends of Baa Pub. Libr., 1994—2001, pres., 1995—2002. Frank Hoke Leadership scholar Delta Sigma Phi, 1976, Am. Legion scholar, 1978-82. Mem.: ABA (ho. of dels. 1989—, membership com. 1989—, vice chmn. state adminstrv. law com. 1990—, sect. on internat. law and practice Caribbean law com. 1990—, drafting com. 1992—96, ho. com. state and local bar assns. 1996—98, select com. 1998—2000, Am. Law Inst.-ABA com. on continuing profl. edn. 1999—, sect. on gen. practice, solo and small firm, real estate interest group sect. on law practice mgmt., sect. on state and local govt., young lawyers divsn., exec. subcom., govt. lawyers com., vice chmn. cmty. law week com., govt. ops. com., sect. gen. practice, sect. on adminstrv. law and regulatory practice, chmn. liaison com. 2003—), Am. Law Inst., V.I. Bar Assn. (chmn. com. legis. and law reform 1987—93, bd. govs. 1988, 1990—, pres. 2002—03, Pres.'s award 2000), Am. Law Network (bd. dirs. 1992—95, 1999—), Attys. Liability Protection Soc. (bd. dirs. 1995—), Am. Law Inst.-ABA In-House, St. Thomas-St. John C. of C., Rotary (bd. dirs. St. Thomas II chpt. 1987—89, 1990—92, sgt. arms 1991—92, clk. consistory bd. dirs. 1991—93, bd. dirs. St. Thomas II chpt. 1998—, sgt. arms 1999—2000, pres. 2002—03). Mem. Reformed Ch. Am. Avocations: travel, sailing, hist. preservation. Finance, Legislative, Property, real (including real estate development, water). Home: Morning Star Beach St Thomas VI 00802 Office: Corporate Pl Royal Dane Mall Charlotte Amalie VI 00802-6410 E-mail: tbolt@vilaw.com.

BOLTON, DAVID, lawyer, educator; b. N.Y.C., Nov. 12, 1912; s. Samuel Bolton, Annie (Danziger) Bolton; m. Ruth Davega (div.); children: Mickey, David Becker, Bert Gunn; m. Roxcy O'Neal; children: Bonnie, David, Baron. BS, Columbia U., 1933, LLB, 1936. Bar: N.Y., S.C., Tex., Fla., U.S. Supreme Ct. Counsel Com. on Interstate Commerce U.S. Senate, Washington, 1936—38; counsel Bd. Econ. Def., Washington, 1941—42, USN, 1942—64; spl. asst. atty. gen. State of Fla., Tallahassee, 1965—66; dir. legal clinic So. Meth. U., Dallas, 1966—. Chief prosecutor WWII USN War Crimes, 1947—49; vis. prof. law So. Meth U., Dallas, U. Miami, Fla. Author: Manuel for Legal Clinics, 1967, Manuel for Criminal trial Advocacy, 1967, Commentary on Handling Divorce, 1967. Spl. rep. Amb. to Japan, 1960—63. Comdr. USN, 1942—64. Recipient Letter of Commendation, USN, 1964, Outstanding Social Work award, Japanese Govt., 1963; grantee Dallas Legal Svcs. Project, Fed. Govt., 1966. Mem.: ABA, Am. Trial Lawyers Assn., Delta Theta Phi (life). Democrat. Jewish. Achievements include Inaugerated Seagoville Project by Fed. Bur. Prisons. Avocation: writing. Home: 124 Cadima Ave Coral Gables FL 33134

BOLTON, TERRELL, protective services official; Sgt. Dallas Police Dept., 1984, dep. chief, 1988, two-star asst. chief, 1991, chief police, 1999—. Office: Dallas Police Dept 6th Fl 1400 S Lamar St Dallas TX 75201-5203

BOLTZ, GERALD EDMUND, lawyer; b. Dennison, Ohio, June 1, 1931; s. Harold E. and Margaret Eve (Hecky) B.; m. Janet Ruth Scott, Sept. 19, 1959; children: Gretchen Boltz Fields, Eric Scott, Jill Marie. BA, Ohio No. U., 1953, JD, 1955. Bar: Ohio 1955, U.S. Supreme Ct. 1964, Calif. 1978, U.S. Dist. Ct. (cen. dist.) Calif. 1978. Asst. atty. gen. State of Ohio, 1958; atty. spl. investigations unit SEC, 1959-60, legal asst. to commr., 1960-61, sr. trial and spl. counsel, 1961-66, regional adminstr. Ft. Worth, 1967-71, regional adminstr. and mng. ptnr. L.A., 1972-78; ptnr. Fine, Perzik& Friedman, L.A., 1979-83, Rogers & Wells, L.A., 1983-92, Bryan Cave, L.A., 1992—. Co-author: Securities Law Techniques. Served with U.S. Army, 1955-57. Mem. ABA, Fed. Bar Assn., L.A. Bar Assn., Ohio Bar Assn., Calif. Bar Assn., Bel Air Bay Club. Republican. Presbyn. (elder). Avocations: sailing, piano. Corporate, general. Home: 1105 Centinela Ave Santa Monica CA 90403-2316 Office: Bryan Cave 120 Broadway Ste 300 Santa Monica CA 90401-2386 E-mail: geboltz@bryancave.com.

BOMAN, MARC ALLEN, lawyer; b. Cleve., Sept. 4, 1948; s. David S. and Shirley T. (Freier) B.; m. Leah Eilenberg, June 10, 1984; children: Autumn, Heidi, Jane, David. Student, Purdue U., 1966-68; BA, Case Western Res. U., 1971, JD, 1974. Bar: Ohio 1974, Wash. 1978, D.C. 1978, U.S. Dist. Ct. (we. dist.) Wash. 1980, U.S. Ct. Appeals (9th cir.), U.S. Dist. Ct. (ea. dist.) Wash. 1985, U.S. Ct. Appeals (fed. cir.) 1986. Atty.-advisor Office of Gen. Counsel U.S. Gen. Acctg. Office, Washington, 1974-78; dep. prosecuting atty. Office of Prosecuting Atty., King County, Wash., 1978-81; assoc. Perkins Coie, Seattle, 1981-86, ptnr., 1986—. Spl. ind. dep. prosecutor ethics investigation of county execs., 1994; mem. Seattle Ethics and Elections Commn., 1995-98; spkr. in field, spl. ind. prosecutor to Met. King Cty. State v. Ridgway capital murder case, 2002. Bd. dirs. Perkins Coie Cmty. Svcs. Fellowship, 1987-97, co-chmn., 1994-97; former bd. dirs. Totem coun. Girl Scouts U.S., Seattle Day Ctr. for Adults, Madrona Neighborhood Coun.; trustee Herzl-Ner Tamid Congregation, 1987-98, pres., 1994-96; mem. Leadership Tomorrow, United Way King County-Seattle C. of C., 1987-88; trustee King County Bar Found., 1995-2000, v.p., 1997-98, pres., 1998-99. Recipient Pres.'s award King County Bar Assn., 1999; Mayoral proclamation declaring Marc Boman Day named in honor of contbn. to citizens of Seattle, 1998. Mem. Seattle King Bar Assn. (trustee 1986-89, chmn. divsn. young lawyers 1984-85), Wash. State Bar Assn. (co-chair Blue Ribbon Panel on Criminal Def. 2003). General civil litigation, Construction, Government contracts and claims. Office: Perkins Coie 1201 3rd Ave Fl 40 Seattle WA 98101-3029

BOMCHIL, MAXIMO LUIS, lawyer; b. Buenos Aires, May 13, 1950; s. Máximo Bomchil and Sara Lydia (Garcia) Martin; m. Ana Lucrecia de Las Carreras, Nov. 24, 1982; children: Máximo José, Miguel, Martin. LLB, Univ. Catolica, Argentina, 1973; JD, U. Munich, Germany, 1976; M of Laws, London U., 1977. Mng. ptnr. M. & M. Bomchil, Buenos Aires, 1973—. Contbr. articles to profl. jours. Decorated Nat. Order of Merit French Govt. Mem.: ABA, Internat. Bar Assn., Circulo de Armas, Jockey Club, Golf Club Argentino. Office: M&M Bomchil Suipacha 268 Piso 12 1355 Buenos Aires Argentina

BONAPART, ALAN DAVID, lawyer; b. San Francisco, Aug. 4, 1930; s. Benjamin and Rose B.; m. Helen Sennett, Aug. 20, 1955; children— Paul S., Andrew D. AB with honors, U. Calif., Berkeley, 1951, JD, 1954. Bar: Calif. 1955, U.S. Tax Ct. 1965, U.S. Supreme Ct. 1971. Assoc. Bancroft & McAlister (formerly Bancroft, Avery & McAlister), San Francisco, 1959-62; ptnr. Bancroft & McAlister, San Francisco, 1962-93, Bancroft & McAlister, A Profl. Corp., 1993-99, Bancroft & McAlister LLP, 1999—. Past trustee Bancroft and McAlister Found.; mem. adv. com. Heckerling Estate Planning Inst., U. Miami, Fla., 1974-87, 92—, mem. faculty, 1974, 91-2000; past dir. Myrtle V. Fitchen Charitable Trust. Mem. ABA, Am. Coll. Trust and Estate Counsel, Bar Assn. San Francisco, State Bar Calif. (cert. in estate planning, probate and trust law Bd. Legal Specialization 1991). Estate planning, Probate (including wills, trusts), Estate taxation. Office: Bancroft & McAlister LLP Ste 120 300 Drake's Landing Rd Greenbrae CA 94904-3123 E-mail: abonapart@bamlaw.com.

BOND, RICHARD LEE, lawyer, state senator; b. Kansas City, Kans., Sept. 18, 1935; s. Clarence Ivy and Florine (Hardison) B.; m. Sue S. Sedgwick, Aug. 23, 1958; children: Mark, Amy. BA, U. Kans., 1957, JD, 1960. City atty., Overland Park, Kans., 1960-62; adminstrv. asst. to Congressman Robert Ellsworth, Washington, 1961-66, Congressman Larry Winn, Washington, 1967-85, Congressman Jan Meyers, Washington, 1986; chmn. bd. dirs. Home State Bank, Kansas City, 1983-94; ptnr. Bennett, Lytle, Wetzler et al, Prairie Village, Kans., 1986-89; senator State of Kans., Topeka, 1985-2001, senate pres., 1997-2001. Vice chmn. Guaranty Bank and Bancshares, Kansas City, Kans., 1995-2002. Mem. Kans. Bd. Regents, 2002—. Named State Legislator of Yr. Governing Mag., 2002. Republican. Presbyterian. Avocations: gardening, tennis, hunting, fishing. Home: 9823 Nall Ave Shawnee Mission KS 66207-2915

BONDOC, ROMMEL, lawyer; b. June 23, 1938; s. Nicholas Rommel and Gladys Sue (Buckner) Bondoc; m. Ariel Guiberson, Aug. 20, 1960 (div. 1963); m. Alberta Linnea Young, Dec. 13, 1967; children: Daphne, Patience, Margaret, Nicholas. AB, Stanford U., 1959, JD, 1963. Bar: Calif. 1964, U.S. Ct. Appeals (9th cir.) 1965, U.S. Supreme Ct. 1969. Assoc. Melvin Belli, San Francisco, 1964—66, Vincent Hallinan, San Francisco, 1966—69; sole practice San Francisco, 1969—. Mem.: Calif. Attys. for Criminal Justice (bd. dir. 1975—80), No. Calif. Criminal Trial Lawyers Assn. (bd. dir. 1972—, pres. 1978—79), San Francisco Bar Assn. (judiciary com. 1982—85). Democrat. Methodist. Criminal. Home: 509 Canyon Rd Novato CA 94947-4330 Office: 819 Eddy St San Francisco CA 94109-7701

BONDS, JOHN WILFRED, JR., lawyer; b. Jackson, Tenn., May 6, 1943; s. John Wilfred Sr. and Louise (Robinson) B.; m. Mary Anne Hatchett, July 18, 1969; children: Kathleen Lucile, Mary Julia. BS, U.S. Air Force Acad., 1965; JD, Vanderbilt U., 1973. Bar: Ga. 1973. Commd. 2nd lt. USAF, 1965, advanced through grades to capt., 1965-70, resigned, 1970; assoc. Sutherland, Asbill & Brennan, Atlanta, 1973-79, ptnr., 1979—. Editor in chief Vanderbilt Law Rev., 1973. Mem. ABA, Ga. Bar Assn., Atlanta Bar Assn., Lawyers Club Atlanta, Order of Coif. Presbyterian. General civil litigation, Insurance. Office: Sutherland Asbill & Brennan 999 Peachtree St NE Atlanta GA 30309-3996

BONDURANT, EMMET JOPLING, II, lawyer; b. Athens, Ga., Mar. 16, 1937; s. John Parnell and Mary Claire (Brannon) B.; m. Jane E. Fahey, Aug. 12, 1990; children by previous marriage: Emmet Jopling III, Katherine Elizabeth, Melissa Eileen, Christopher Scott, Miles Stephen. AB cum laude, U. Ga., 1958, LL.B. magna cum laude, 1960; LL.M., Harvard U., 1962. Bar: Ga. 1959. Law clk. to Judge Clement Haynsworth, Jr. U.S. Ct. Appeals, 4th Circuit, 1960-61; assoc. Kilpatrick, Cody, Rogers, McClatchey & Regenstein, Atlanta, 1962-68, ptnr., 1968-77; ptnr. firm Bondurant, Mixson & Elmore and predecessor, Atlanta, 1977—. Vis. lectr. in antitrust law U. Ga., spring 1971; pres. Atlanta Legal Aid Soc., 1972-73; vice chmn. Ga. Gov.'s Commn. on Criminal Justice Standards and Goals, 1974 Contbr. articles on antitrust and reapportionment, right to counsel, bankruptcy, and local govt. issues to profl. jours.; co-editor: Antitrust Law Developments, 1974. Mem. Joint Atlanta-Fulton County Citizens Adv. Com. on Consolidation, 1969; chmn. Atlanta Charter Commn., 1971-72; co-chmn. Com. for Sensible Rapid Transit, Atlanta, 1971-72; trustee Am. Inns of Ct., 2002--; pres. Common Cause of Ga., 2002--; chmn. bd. Ga. Appellate Resource Ctr. Named 1 of 5 Outstanding Young Men, Atlanta Jaycees, 1970; recipient Ga. Trial Lawyer of Yr., Am. Bd. Trial Advocates (Ga. chpt.), Good Govt. award, LWV Atlanta-Fultin County, 1980, Dufree award, Calif. Western Sch. Law, 1984, Elbert P. Tuttle Jurisprudence award, 2001, Harold G. Clarke award, Ga. Indigent Def. Coun., 2001. Fellow Am. Bar Found.; mem. ABA (exec. com. Atlanta lawyers com. for civil rights), Ga. Bar Assn., Atlanta Bar Assn. (exec. com. 1975-81, Leadership award 1992), State Bar Ga. (chmn. sect. antitrust law 1972-73, chmn. jud. sys. comm. 1991—), Am. Law Inst., Am. Coll. Trial Lawyers, Am. Acad. Appellate Lawyers, Am. Judicature Soc., Ga. Law Sch. Alumni Assn. (pres. 1996-97), Lawyers Club Atlanta (sec. 1971-72), Phi Beta Kappa, Phi Delta Phi, Phi Kappa Phi, Kappa Alpha. Methodist. Home: 2930 Habersham Rd NW Atlanta GA 30305-2846 Office: Bondurant Mixson & Elmore Ste 3900 1201 W Peachtree St NW Atlanta GA 30309-3417

BONEE, JOHN LEON, III, lawyer; b. Hartford, Conn., Dec. 16, 1947; s. John Leon, Jr. and M. Elaine (Sheridan) B. BA, Trinity Coll., Hartford, 1970; JD, Suffolk U., Boston, 1974; postgrad., Hague Acad. Internat. Law, The Netherlands, 1975. Bar: Conn. 1974, U.S. Dist. Ct. Conn. 1974; U.S. Ct. Appeals (2d cir.) 1975, U.S. Supreme Ct. 1979. Assoc. McCook, Kenyon and Bonee, Hartford, 1974-78; ptnr. Bonee Law Offices, LLP, Hartford, Conn., 1979—. Contbr. articles to profl. jours. Mem. bd. edn. Town West Hartford, 1981-83, corp. counsel, 1983, mem. community planning adv. com., 1984, mem. town coun., 1985-89; bd. dirs. World Affairs Coun., Hartford, 1980-91. Mem. ABA (litig. gen. practice and internat. law sects., mem. ho. dels. 1996—), Conn. Bar Assn. (editor-at-large jour. 1978-84, probate, litigation and family law sects., mem. ho. of dels. 1995—, com. on professionalism 2000—), Hartford County Bar Assn. (bd. dirs. 1991-97, treas. 1992-93, sec. 1993-94, pres. elect 1994-95, pres. 1995-96, past pres. 1996-97, co-chair bench/bar leadership conf. com. 1992-93). General civil litigation, General practice, Probate (including wills, trusts). Office: 1 State St Hartford CT 06103-3100 E-mail: boneelaw@aol.com.

BONER, ELEANOR KATZ, lawyer; b. N.Y.C., Jan. 20, 1922; d. Louis and Della (Cherry) Katz; m. Mitchell Boner, June 14, 1942; children: Ethel, Alexander, Lawrence. BA cum laude, Hunter Coll., 1941; LLB, St. Lawrence U., 1943; D in Jud. Sci. cum laude, Bklyn. Law Sch., 1945, JD, 1967; PhD, Columbia U., 1967. Bar: N.Y. 1943, U.S. Dist. Ct. D.C. 1972, U.S. Ct. Appeals D.C. 1972, U.S. Supreme Ct. 1971, U.S. Customs Ct. 1978, U.S. Ct. Internat. Trade 1981. Pvt. practice, N.Y.C., 1943-71; ptnr. Boner & Glod, Washington, 1972-75, Boner, Gold & Oesch, St. Gallen, Switzerland; gen. counsel to Mark Berger, N.Y.C., 1975-80; pvt. practice New Rochelle, N.Y., 1981—. Author: The Hypothetical Question in the Law of Evidence, 1945, Alexander, Child of Love, 1990. Mem. ABA, N.Y. Bar Assn., Assn. Bar of City of N.Y., Westchester County Bar Assn., Phi Beta Kappa. Avocation: art. General practice, Private international, Public international.

BONESIO, WOODROW MICHAEL, lawyer; b. Hereford, Tex., Dec. 27, 1943; s. Harold Andre and Elizabeth (Ireland) B.; m. Michaele Ann Dougherty; children: Elizabeth Eaton, Jo Kristin, William Michael. BA, Austin Coll., 1966; JD, U. Houston, 1971. Bar: Tex. 1971, U.S. Dist. Ct. (we., no., so., and ea. dists.) Tex. 1973, U.S. Ct. Appeals (5th cir.) 1973, U.S. Ct. Appeals (11th cir.) 1981. Law clk. to U.S. dist. Judge Western Dist. Tex., San Antonio, 1971-73; ptnr. Akin, Gump, Strauss, Hauer & Feld, Dallas, 1973-92, Kuntz & Bonesio LLP, Dallas, 1992—2002, Shackelford, Melton & McKinley L.L.P., Dallas, 2003—. Speaker profl. confs. Precinct chmn. Dallas County Dems.; bd. dirs. Grace Presbytery Devel. Bd., 1986—89; ruling elder First Presbyterian Ch., Dallas, 1999—2001. Fellow: Dallas Bar Found., Tex. Bar Found.; mem.: FBA, ABA, Nat. Assn. Rec. Artists, Vocal Majority (bd. dirs., 1990—, pres. 2002—03), U. Houston Law Alumni Assn. (chpt. pres. 1982), Austin Coll. Alumni Assn. (bd. dirs. 1983, Disting. Alumni award 2001), Common Cause Tex. (bd. dirs. 1999—), Dallas Assn. Def. Counsel, Tex. Bar Coll., Dallas Bar Assn., Am. Judicature Soc., Assn. Atty. Mediators, Am. Arbitration Assn., Lake Highlands Exch. Club, Soc. for Preservation and Encouragement Barber Shop Quartet Singing in Am. (internat. chorus champions 1975, 1979, 1982, 1985, 1988, 1991, 1994, 1997, 2000), Order of Barons, Phi Alpha Delta. General civil litigation, Commercial, consumer (including collections, credit), State and local taxation. Office: Shackelford, Melton & McKinley LLP 10100 N Central Expressway Ste 600 Dallas TX 75231 E-mail: mbonesio@shacklaw.net.

BONHAM, JOHN DWIGHT, retired lawyer; b. Tuscaloosa, Ala., Sept. 13, 1928; s. Harry Dwight and Mamie Marie (Griffith) B.; m. Bobbye Claire Maxwell, Sept. 13, 1952; 1 child, Mary Bonham Ward. BS in Commerce, U. Ala., 1950, JD, 1952. Bar: Ala. 1952, U.S. Dist. Ct. (so. dist.) Ala. 1960. Staff atty. Legis. Ref. Svc., Montgomery, Ala., 1952-55; ptnr. Hare & Bonham Attys., Monroe County, Ala., 1955-60; asst chief, trial atty. Ala. Conservation Dept., Montgomery, 1960-70; asst. dir., chief atty. Ala. Legis. Ref. Svc., Montgomery, 1970-95. 1st lt. USAR, 1953-60. Presbyterian. Avocations: hunting, fishing.

BONIELLO, RALPH ANTHONY, III, judge; b. Niagara Falls, N.Y., June 18, 1944; s. Ralph Anthony Boniello and Dorothea Lagomaggiore Boniello; m. Kathleen J. Boniello; children: Ralph A. IV, Michael D., Kristen Kathleen. BA, Ohio U., 1966; JD, SUNY, Buffalo, 1969. Ptnr. Boniello, Anton, Conti & Boniello, Niagara Falls, 1970—95; agy. counsel Niagara County Indsl. Devel. Agy., Niagara Falls, 1990—94, 1998—2000; pvt. practice Niagara Falls, 1995—2000; atty. Niagara County, Lockport, NY, 1999—2000; judge N.Y. State Supreme Ct., Niagara Falls, 2000—; gen. counsel Niagara Falls C. of C., 1990—2000. Trustee Niagara Falls Family YMCA, 1995—2000; mem. adv. bd. Niagara U., Lewiston, NY, 1988—98. Recipient Pres.'s award, Niagara Falls C. of C., 1995. Mem.: N.Y. State Supreme Ct. Justices Assn., N.Y. State Bar Assn. Avocations: hiking, running. Office: NY State Supreme Ct 775 3d St Niagara Falls NY 14301 Office Fax: 716-278-1827. Business E-Mail: rboniell@courts.state.ny.us.

BONNER, ROBERT WILLIAM, lawyer, director; b. Vancouver, B.C., Can., Sept. 10, 1920; s. Benjamin York and Emma Louise (Weir) B.; m. Barbara Newman, June 16, 1942; children: Barbara Carolyn (Mrs. Massie), Robert York, Elizabeth Louise (Mrs. McPhee). BA in Econs. and Polit. Sci, U. B.C., 1942, LL.B., 1948. Bar: B.C. 1948, created Queen's counsel 1952. With firm Clark Wilson White Clark & Maguire, Vancouver, 1948-52; atty. gen. Province of B.C., 1952-68; sr. v.p. adminstrn. MacMillan Bloedel Ltd., 1968-70, exec. v.p. adminstrn., 1970-71, vice chmn., 1971-72, pres., chief exec. officer, 1972-73, chmn. bd., 1973-74, ret., 1974; chmn. B.C. Hydro & Power Authority, 1976-85; ptnr. Bonner & Fouks, 1974-84, Robertson, Ward, Suderman, Vancouver, 1985-89. Mem. B.C. Legislature, 1952-69; mem. Energy Supplies Allocation Bd., bd. dirs. Served to maj. Royal Canadian Army, 1942-45; lt. col. Res. (ret.). Mem. Canadian Bar Assn., Law Soc. B.C. (life bencher), Delta Upsilon. Mem. Social Credit Party. Clubs: Mason, Vancouver; Union (Victoria). Home: 5679 Newton Wynd Vancouver BC Canada V6T 1H6 Office: Box 18162 2225 W 41st Ave Vancouver BC Canada V6M 2A3 Fax: 604-264-6142. E-mail: rwbonner@attcanada.ca.

BONNESON, PAUL GARLAND, lawyer; b. Milw., May 12, 1959; s. Garland Waldemar and Marilyn Adah (Giese) B. BA cum laude, Marquette U., 1981; JD, Drake U., Des Moines, 1984. Bar: Wis. 1984, U.S. Dist. Ct. (ea. dist.) Wis. 1984, U.S. Ct. Appeals (7th cir.) 1991, U.S. Supreme Ct. 1992. Assoc. Riemer Law Offices, Delavan, Wis., 1984-87, Tikalsky, Raasch & Tikalsky, Waukesha, Wis., 1987-90, Rudolph Law Offices, Elm Grove, Wis., 1990-91; pvt. practice Wauwatosa, Wis., 1991—. Mem. Badger State Vettes, Ltd., 1990—. Mem. Rep. Party of Waukesha County, 1996—; active Elmbrook Ch., Brookfield, Wis. Mem. State Bar of Wis. (pres. young lawyers divsn. 1994-95, exec. com. 1995-96, bd. govs. 1995-96, continuing legal edn. com. 1996-2000, chair mentor coun. com. 2000-02), Waukesha County Bar Assn. (bd. dirs. 1998-2001, sec.-treas. 2001-02, pres.-elect 2002-03, pres. 2003—), Corvette Club. Republican. Criminal, Family and matrimonial, Personal injury (including property damage). Home: 20185 A Independence Dr Brookfield WI 53045-5385 Office: 631 N Mayfair Rd Wauwatosa WI 53226-4249 E-mail: vettlaw@execpc.com.

BONNET ESCULIER, SERVANE MICHÈLE, lawyer; b. Greenwich, Conn., May 31, 1962; d. Michel and Thais (Guillemet) Bonnet; m. Jacques Esculier, May 28, 1993. M in European and Internat. Law, U. Paris II, 1985; diploma, Paris Inst. Polit. Scis., 1986; LLM, Columbia U., 1988. Bar: N.Y. 1990, Paris 1992. Tchg. asst. U. Paris II, 1982-86; assoc. Briard & Delaporte, Paris, 1986-87, Rogers & Wells, N.Y.C., 1988-91, Paris, 1991-95, mng. counsel Singapore, 1996-99; ptnr. in charge of European clientele Coudert Bros., Singapore, 1999—2002; ptnr. with Coudert Bros. focusing on cross-border and regional work Brussels. Co-author: Dalloz, 1994; contbr. articles to profl. jours. Scholar Rotary Found., 1987. Mem. ABA. Avocations: tennis, golf, jogging. Office: Coudert Bros LLP Ave Louise 81 Brussels 1050 Belgium E-mail: bonnets@coudert.com.

BONNEY, HAL JAMES, JR., federal judge; b. Norfolk, Va., Aug. 27, 1929; s. Hal J. and Mary (Shackelford) B.; m. Marie McBee, July 4, 1963 (div. 1979); children: David James, John Wesley. BA, U. Richmond, 1951, MA, 1953; JD, Coll. William and Mary, 1969. Bar: Va. 1969. Instr. Norfolk public schs., 1951-61; supt. Douglas MacArthur Acad., 1961-67; practiced law, 1969-71; law clk. U.S. Dist. Ct., 1969; prof. U. Va., 1964-71, Coll. William and Mary, 1969-71; U.S. bankruptcy judge Norfolk, 1971-95; ret., 1995. Adj. prof. law Regent U. Law Sch., 1987—97; prodr. Hal Bonney Prodns. Author: Overturning Applecarts, 2002. Tchr. Wesleymen Bible Class Sta. WTAR-AM, 1962-98, tchr. emeritus, 1998; tchr. Good News TV Network, 1989—; treas. Wesleymen Found., Inc., Billy Graham Crusades, 1974-76; pres. adv. coun. CBN U., 1986-95; vice-chmn. Va. Meth. Bd. Edn., Inc., 1991-99; bd. visitors Duke Div. Sch., 1991—; bd. dirs. Norfolk Union Mission, 1994—, 1st v.p.; v.p. The Tidewater Winds; mem. City of Norfolk Task Force on Pub. Housing, 1995-96; advisor Film Sch., Regent U., 1996-2000, assoc. prodr. 2000—; mem. City of Norfolk Parks and Recreation Commn.; vice chair rules com. Va. United Meth. conf., 1996—; bd. ordained ministry United Meth. Ch., Va; commr. City of Norfolk Parks and Recreation, 2003—; active World Affairs Coun. Recipient S.A.R. Good Citizenship medal, Woodmen of the World History medal, U. Richmond Gold medal, George Washington honor medal Freedoms Found., Alli award Cultural Alliance Greater Hampton Rds., 1998; Judge Hal Bonney Day named in honor by City of Norfolk, Jan. 27, 1998. Mem. Nat. Conf. Bankruptcy Judges (pres. 1983, chmn. editl. bd. The Am. Bankruptcy Law Jour.), Va. State Bar, Norfolk and Portsmouth Bar Assn., Nat. Film Soc., Am. Film Inst. (Second Decade coun.), Brit. Film Inst., Am. Cinematheque (moving picture ball benefit com.), James Kent Inn of Ct. (hon., pres. 1994-96), Phi Alpha Theta, Pi Sigma Alpha, Phi Alpha Delta, Masons, Shriners, Elks, Kiwanis (dir.). Methodist. Home: 1357 Windsor Point Rd Norfolk VA 23509-1311 Office: The Wesleymen 408 Boush St Norfolk VA 23510-1215 E-mail: bonney@erols.com.

BONNIE, RICHARD JEFFREY, law educator, lawyer; b. Richmond, Va., Aug. 22, 1945; s. Herbert Herman and Helene Selma (Berz) B.; m. Kathleen Ford, June 15, 1967; children: Joshua Ford, Zachary Andrew, Jessica Katherine. BA, Johns Hopkins U., 1966; LLB, U. Va., 1969. Var: Va. 1969, U.S. Dist. Ct. (ea. dist.) Va. 1969; U.S. Ct. Appeals (4th cir.) 1969, U.S. Supreme Ct. 1986. Asst. prof. law U. Va., Charlottesville, 1969-70, assoc. prof., 1973-77, prof., 1977-87, John S. Battle prof., 1987—; dir. Inst. Law, psychiatry, and Pub. Policy, 1979—. Vis. prof. Cornell Law Sch., 1993-94; assoc. dir. nat. Commn. Marijuana and Drug Abuse, 1971-73; reporter Nat. Conf. Commrs. on Uniform State Laws, 1972-74; cons. Spl. Action Office for Drug Abuse Prevention Exec. Office of the Pres., 1973-75; spl. asst. to U.S. Atty. Gen., 1975; mem. and sec. Nat. Adv. Coun. on Drug Abuse, 1975-80; mem. Com. on Problem of Drug Dependence, Inc., 1979-84; charter fellow Coll. Problems of Drug Dependence, 1992—; cons. Am. Psychiat. Assn., Coun. Psychiatry and Law, 1979—; mem. U.S. State Dept. Del. to investigate psychiat. practices in the Soviet Union, 1989; mem. World Psychiat. Assn. rev. team to investigate Soviet psychiatry, 1991; mem. adv. bd. permanent coordination office Reforms in psychiatry in Ctrl. and Ea. Europe, former Soviet Union, 1993—; bd. dirs. Geneva Initiative on Psychiatry, 1996—; pres. Am. Friends of Geneva Initiatives on Psychiatry, 1997—, mem. MacArthur Found. Network on Mental Health and the Law, 1988-96; bd. dirs. Va. Capital Representation Resource Ctr., 1994-97, 2002—; mem. MacArthur Found. Network on Mandated Treatment, 2000—. Author: The Marijuana Conviction: The History of Marijuana Prohibition in the United States, 1974, 2d edit. 1999, Legal Aspects of Drug Dependence, 1975, Psychiatrists and the Legal Process: Diagnosis and Debate, 1977, Marijuana Use and Criminal Sanctions: Essays in the Theory and Practice of Decriminalization, 1980, Criminal Law: Cases and Materials, 1982, 2d edit., 1986, The Trial of John W. Hinckley, Jr.: A Case Study in the Insanity Defense, 1986, rev. edit. 2000, Criminal Law, 1997, Growing Up Tobacco Free, 1994, Mental Disorder, Work Disability and the Law, 1997, Reducing the Burden of Injury, 1999, The Evolution of Mental Health Law, 2001, Elder Mistreatment, 2002, Adjudicative Competence, 2002. Chmn. Va. Human Rights Com., Dept. mental Health and Mental Retardation, 1979-85; bd. dirs. Coll. on Problem of Drug Dependence, 1996-2000. Served to capt. USAF, 1970-73. Inst. Criminology fellow Cambridge U., 1977. Fellow Va. Law Found.; mem. Inst. Medicine of NAS (mem. bd. neurosci. and behavioral health, 1992-2001, mem. com. on preventing nicotine dependence in children and youths, 1993-94, mem. membership com. 1995-98, chair com. on opportunities in drug abuse rsch. 1995-96, chair com. injury prevention control 1997-98, mem. com. to assess sci. base for tobacco harm reduction 1999-2001, mem. com. to assess the sys. for the protection of human rsch. subjects 2000-2002, chair com. to propose strategy to prevent and reduce underage drinking 2002-03), Nat. Rsch. Coun. (mem. comm. on data and rsch. for policy on illicit drugs 1998-2000, chair com. elder abuse and neglect 2001-2002, mem. common law and justice com. 2002—. chair com. underage drinking, 2002—, mem. div. com. behavioral and social scis. and edn. 2003—), ABA (mem. criminal justice-mental health stds. project adv. bd. 1981-87), NAS, Am. Psychiat. Assn. (Isaac Ray award 1998, Spl. Presdl. Commendation 2003), Va. Bar Assn. (chmn. com. mentally disabled 1981-90, mem. criminal law sect. coun. 1992-96), World Psychiat. Assn. (rev. team to investigate Soviet Psychiatry 1991), Am. Acad. Psychiat. Law (Amicus award 1994), Inst. Medicine (Yarmolinsky medal 2002), Va. Law Found. (fellow), Nat. Acad. Sci. (nat. assoc.). Office: U Va Sch Law 580 Massie Rd Charlottesville VA 22903

BONO, RANDALL AIAN, lawyer; b. Granite City, Ill., Oct. 23, 1951; s. Ben Charles and Alice Marie Terrell B.; m. Jo Ann Meisenheimer, June 30, 1973; children: Olivia Nicole, Christopher Terrell, Stacie Elizabeth. BA, Millikin U., 1973; JD, U. Louisville, 1976. Bar: Ill. 1976. Atty. Smith Allen, East Alton, Ill., 1976-77, Bono & Haine, Wood River, Ill., 1977-95; cir. judge 3d cir., Edwardsville, Ill., 1995-96; assoc. judge U.S. Ct. Appeals (3d cir.), Edwardsville, 1997-2000; pvt. practice Wood River, 2000—. Mcpl. atty., Madison County, 1976-95; cons., lawyer Simmons Firm, LLC, Wood River, 2000—. Mem. exec. com. Madison County (Ill.) Dem., 2000—. Roman Catholic. Avocations: golfing, fishing. Home: 610 E Bethalto Blvd Bethalto IL 62010 Office: 301 Evans Ave PO Box 559 Wood River IL 62095

BONVILLIAN, WILLIAM BOONE, lawyer; b. Honolulu, Mar. 7, 1947; s. William Doughty and Florence Elizabeth (Boone) B.; m. Janis Ann Sposato, Apr. 12, 1980; children: Raphael William Boone, Marcus Doughty. AB, Columbia U., 1969; MA in Religion, Yale U., 1972; JD, Columbia U., 1974. Bar: Conn. 1975, D.C. 1976, U.S. Supreme Ct. 1983. Law clk. to Hon. Jack B. Weinstein U.S. Dist. Ct. (ea. dist.) N.Y., 1974-75; assoc. Steptoe & Johnson, Washington, 1975-77; dep. asst. sec., dir. congl. affairs, liaison officer U.S. Dept. Transp., Washington, 1977-81; ptnr. Brown, Roady, Bonvillian & Gold, Washington, 1981-85, Jenner & Block, Washington, 1985-89; chief counsel, legis. dir. to Sen. Joseph Lieberman U.S. Senate, Washington, 1989—. Bd. editors Columbia Law Rev. 1973-74; contbr. articles to law and sci. jours. Recipient 2 outstanding Performance awards U.S. Sec. Transp., Washington, 1979, 80. Mem. Conn. Bar Assn., D.C. Bar Assn. Democrat. Episcopalian. Administrative and regulatory, Legislative, Property, real (including real estate development, water). Home: 930 Hickory Run Ln Great Falls VA 22066-1903 Office: Office Sen Lieberman 706 Hart Senate Office Bldg Washington DC 20510-0001

BOOCHEVER, ROBERT, judge; b. N.Y.C., Oct. 2, 1917; s. Louis C and Miriam (Cohen) Boochever; m. Lois Colleen Maddox, Apr. 22, 1943 (dec.); children: Barbara K, Linda Lou, Ann Paula, Miriam Deon; m. Rose Marie Borden, Aug. 31, 2001. AB, Cornell U., 1939, JD, 1941; HD (hon.) , U. Alaska, 1981. Bar: N.Y. 1944, Alaska 1947. Law clk. Nordlinger, Riegel & Cooper, 1941; asst. U.S. atty. Juneau, 1946—47; partner firm Faulkner, Banfield, Boochever & Doogan, Juneau, 1947—72; assoc. justice Alaska Supreme Ct., 1972—75, 1978—80, chief justice, 1975—78; judge U.S. Ct. Appeals (9th cir.), Pasadena, Calif., 1980—86; sr. judge U.S. Ct. Appeals, Pasadena, Calif., 1986—. Mem. 9th cir. rules com. U.S. Ct. Appeals, 1983—85, chmn. 9th cir. libr. com., 1995—2001; chmn. Ala. Jud. Coun., 1975—78; mem. appellate judges seminar NYU Sch. Law, 1975; mem. Conf. Chief Justices, 1975—79, vice chmn., 1978—79; mem. adv. bd. Nat. Bank of Ala., 1968—72; guest spkr. Southwestern Law Sch. Disting. Lecture Series, 1992. Contbr. articles to profl. jours. Chmn. Juneau chpt. ARC, 1949—51, Juneau Planning Commn., 1956—61; mem. Alaska Devel. Bd., 1949—52, Alaska Jud. Qualification Commn., 1972—75; mem. adv. bd. Juneau-Douglas C.C. Capt. U.S. Army, 1941—45. Named Juneau Man of Yr., Rotary, 1974, The Boochever & Bird Chair for Study and Tchg. of Freedom and Equality, U. Calif. Sch. Law, Davis, 2000; recipient Disting. Alumnus award, Cornell U., 1989. Fellow: Am. Coll. Trial Attys.; mem.: ABA, Am. Law Inst., Am. Judicature Soc. (dir. 1970—74), Juneau Bar Assn. (pres. 1971—72), Alaska Bar Assn. (pres. 1961—62), Alaskans United (chmn. 1972), Juneau C. of C. (pres. 1952, 1955), Altadena Town and County Club, Cornell Club L.A. Office: US Ct Appeals PO Box 91510 125 S Grand Ave Pasadena CA 91105-1652 E-mail: boochever@ca9.uscourts.gov.

BOOCOCK, STEPHEN WILLIAM, lawyer; b. Wilkinsburg, Pa., Sept. 25, 1948; s. William Samuel and Zelda Elizabeth (Heginbotham) B.; m. Carol Ann Bennett, July 11, 1970; children: Eric Alan, Allison Anne, Megan Leigh. BS in Acctg., Pa. State U., 1970; JD, U. Pitts., 1973. Bar: Pa. 1974, U.S. Dist. Ct. (we. dist.) Pa. 1973. Supervising tax specialist Coopers & Lybrand (now part of PricewaterhouseCoopers), Pitts., 1973-76; tax counsel Incom Internat., Inc., Pitts., 1977-81; asst. treas., dir. tax Allegheny Ludlum Corp., Pitts., 1981—94, asst. v.p. taxes, 1994-96; asst. v.p. taxes, chief tax officer Allegheny Technologies, Inc., Pitts., 1996—2002; dir. tax controversy svcs. Deloitte & Touche LLP, Chgo., 2003—. Treas. Meadow Wood Homeowner's Assn., 1990-2001. Served to capt. U.S. Army, 1970-79; with USAR. Mem.: ABA, AICPA, Tax Execs. Inst. (treas. Pitts. chpt. 1985—86, sec. 1986—87, sr. v.p. 1987—88, pres. 1988—89, nat. inst. dir. 1989—91, v.p. region VI 1992—93, 50th ann. task force 1993—95, membership com. 1993—97, mem. IRS adminstrv. affairs com. 1993—2003, nominating com. 1994—95, vice chmn. 1995—97, chmn. 1997—99, tax info. sys. com. 1995—97, mem. alternative tax sys. com. 1995—97, nominating com. 1997—98, nat. inst. dir. 1999—2001, mem. nat. exec. com. 1999—2003, nat. treas. 2001—02, nat. sec. 2002—03), Pa. Inst. CPAs, Allegheny County Bar Assn., Pa. Bar Assn. Republican. Avocation: golf. Corporate taxation, Taxation, general, Personal income taxation. Home: 1350 N Lake Shore Dr # 1904 Chicago IL 60610-5149 Office: Deloitte & Touche LLP Tax Svcs 200 E Randolph St Chicago IL 60601-7002

BOOHER, ALICE ANN, lawyer; b. Indpls., Oct. 6, 1941; d. Norman Rogers and Olga (Bonke) B. BA in Polit. Sci., Butler U., 1963; LLB, Ind. U., 1966, JD, 1967. Bar: Ind. 1966, U.S. Dist. Ct. (so. dist.) Ind. 1966, U.S. Tax Ct. 1970, U.S. Ct. Customs and Patent Appeals 1969, U.S. Ct. Mil. Appeals 1969, U.S. Ct. Appeals (D.C. cir.) 1969, U.S. Supreme Ct. 1969; cert. tchr., Ind. Rsch. asst., law clk. Supreme and Appellate Cts. Ind., Indpls., 1966; legal intern, atty., staff legal advisor Dept. State, Washington, 1966-69; staff legal adviser Bd. Vets. Appeals, Washington, 1969-78, sr. atty., 1978—, counsel, 1991—. Former counselor D.C. Penal Facilities and Shelters. Author: The Nuclear Test Ban Treaty and the Third Party Non-Nuclear States, also children's books; contbr. articles to various publs., chpts. to Whiteman Digest of International Law; exhibited crafts, needlepoint in juried artisan fairs; originator U.S. postage stamps Women in Mil. Svc., 1980-97, POWs/MIAs, 1986-96. Bd. dirs. community groups including D.C. Women's Commn. for Crime Prevention, 1980-81, Friends of Nat. Vets Mus.; pres., legal adviser VA employees Assn. Recipient various awards; named Ky. Col., 1988. Mem. DAV (life), VFW Aux. (life), LWV, Women's Bar Assn. D.C., D.C. Sexual Assault Coalition (chmn. legal com.), Life Mem. Judge Advocates Assn., Butler U. Alumni Assn., Nat. Mus. Women in Arts, Kennedy Ctr. Stars, Sackler/Freer Galleries (patron), Women in Mil. Svcs. to Am. Found., Bus. and Profl. Women (pres. D.C. 1980-81, nat. UN fellow 1974, nat. bd. dirs. 1980-82, 87-94, Woman of Yr. award D.C. 1975, Marguerite Rawalt award D.C. 1986), USO, Navy League U.S.A. (life), Am. Legion Aux. (life), Women Officers Profl. Assns., Nat. Vets. Mus. Task Force, Nat. Task Force on Women of the Mil. and Women Mil. POWS (chair Esther Peterson Tribute 1995, panel, paper moderator conf. 1997, book reviewer, contbr. to Stars & Stripes, Ex POWs Bull., others), Assn. Former Intelligence Officers (assoc.), Army Women Officers Profl. Assn., Am. News Womens Club, Cons., Saigon Tourist, Inc., Alliance Nat. Defense.

BOOKER, JAMES DOUGLAS, retired lawyer, government official; b. Columbus, Ohio, June 27, 1933; s. Homer Newton and Grace Bernice (Hermann) Booker; m. Onda Lee Minshall, Aug. 31, 1958; children: Christine E. Booker Garrett, Linda K. Booker Stanek, Molly A. Booker Lary, Andrew W. JD, Ohio State U., 1961. Bar: Ohio 1961, U.S. Dist. Ct. (so. dist.) Ohio 1962, U.S. Ct. Appeals (6th cir.) 1972, U.S. Supreme Ct. 1971. Asst. atty. gen. State of Ohio, Columbus, 1961-62; ptnr. Williams, Deeg, Ketcham, Booker & Obetz, Columbus, 1962-75; adminstrv. law judge SSA, Columbus, 1975-98. Former PTA officer, ch. deacon and Sunday Sch. tchr. Served with U.S. Army, 1953-55. Mem. Ohio State Bar Assn. Republican. Avocations: chess, music, history. Administrative and regulatory. Home: 1290 Smallwood Dr Columbus OH 43235-2503 E-mail: jamesdbooker@prodigy.net.

BOOKER, LEWIS THOMAS, lawyer; b. Richmond, Va., Sept. 22, 1929; s. Russell Eubank and Leslie Quarles (Sessoms) B.; m. Nancy Electa Brogden, Sept. 29, 1956; children: Lewis Thomas Jr., Virginia Frances, Claiborne Brogden, John Quarles. BA, U. Richmond, 1950, LLD, 1977; JD, Harvard U., 1953. Bar: Va. 1953, U.S. Ct. Mil. Appeals 1954, U.S. Supreme Ct. 1958, D.C. 1980, N.Y. 1985. Assoc. Hunton & Williams, Richmond, Va., 1956-63, ptnr., 1963-95, sr. coun., 1995—; substitute Judge 13th Dist., Va., 1996—. Lectr. in law Seinan Gakuin U., Fukuoka, Japan, 1985; vis. lectr. in law St. Thomas U., Miami, Fla., 1993; maj. gen., sr. mil. aide to Gov. of Va., 1997-2001. Mem. Va. Coun. on Human Rights, 1987; commr. chmn. Richmond Redevel. and Housing Authority, 1961-70; mem., v. chmn. Richmond Sch. Bd., 1971-80; trustee U. Richmond, 1972-2002, emeritus, 2002—, rector, 1973-77, 81-85, 91-94, vice rector, 1985-87, chmn. exec. commn., 1977-81; trustee Va. Inst. Sci. Rsch., 1981-94, Richmond Symphony, 1987-92, Rouse-Bottom Found., 1989—; mem. Coun. Richmond Symphony, 1995, Westminster-Canterbury Found. Richmond, 1995-2001, chmn., 1998-2001; mem. Robins Found., 1996—, Richmond Symphony Orch. Found., 1999—, Christian Children's Fund, 2000—, Christian Children's Fund Internat., 2002-, CCF Internat., 2002—, Richmond Eye and Ear Hosp., 2000—, Homeward, 2001—; chmn. Richmond Eye and Ear Fedn., 2001—. Fellow Am. Coll. Trial Lawyers, Am. Bar Found.; mem. ABA, Va. Bar Assn., Va. Law Found. (chmn. fellows coun. 1996-2001), Richmond Bar Assn., Westwood Racquet Club. Democrat. Baptist. General civil litigation. Office: Hunton & Williams East Tower Riverfront Pla PO Box 1535 Richmond VA 23218-1535 E-mail: lbooker@hunton.com.

BOOKER, RUSSELL STUART, lawyer; b. Maidstone, Kent, Eng., Aug. 21, 1957; s. Wilfred Bryan and Irene (Netherton) B.; m. Beverley Morel; children: Luke, Dominique. LLB with honors, Birmingham U., Eng., 1978. Assoc. Booth & Blackwell, London, 1981—84, ptnr., 1984—86; assoc. Masons, London, 1986-88; ptnr., 1988—. Bd. dirs. Masons Ltd., London. Author: Buying and Selling a Business, 1990. Avocations: golf, sailing. Corporate, general, Mergers and acquisitions, Securities. Office: Masons 30 Aylesbury St EC1R 0ER London England Home Fax: 020 8295 4603; Office Fax: 020 7490 2545. E-mail: russell.booker@masons.com.

BOONE, CELIA TRIMBLE, lawyer; b. Clovis, N.Mex., Apr. 3, 1953; d. George Harold and Barbara Ruth (Foster) T.; m. Billy W. Boone, Apr. 21, 1990. BS, Ea. N.Mex. U., 1976, MA, 1977; JD, St. Mary's U., San Antonio, 1982. Bar: Tex. 1982, U.S. Ct. Appeals (5th cir.) 1985, U.S. Supreme Ct. 1986; cer. family law Tex. Bd. Legal Specialization, 1987, family law examination commn., 2002. Instr. English Ea. N.Mex. U., Portales, 1977-78; editor Curry County Times, Clovis, 1978-79; assoc. Schultz & Robertson, Abilene, Tex., 1982-85, Scarborough, Black, Tarpley & Scarborough, Abilene, Tex., 1985-87; ptnr. Scarborough, Black, Tarpley & Trimble, Abilene, Tex., 1988-90, Scarborough, Black, Tarpley & Boone, Abilene, Tex., 1990-94; of counsel Scarborough, Tarpley, Boone & Fouts, Abilene, Tex., 1994-96; prin. Law Office of Celia Trimble Boone, Abilene, Tex., 1996—. Instr. legal rsch. and writing St. Mary's Sch. Law, 1981-82; mem. family law exam. com. Tex. Bd. Legal Specialization, 2002--. Legal adv. bd. to bd. dirs. Abilene Kennel Club, 1983-85; landmarks commn. City of Abilene, 1989-90. Recipient Outstanding Young Lawyer of Abilene, 1988. Mem. ABA, State Bar Tex. (disciplinary rev. com. 1989-93), Am. Trial Lawyers Assn., Tex. Trial Lawyers Assn., Tex. Criminal Def. Lawyers Assn., Tex. Acad. Family Law Specialists, Abilene Bar Assn. (bd. dirs. 1985-88, sec.-treas. 1985-86), Abilene Young Lawyers Assn. (bd. dirs. 1985-89, treas. 1985-86, pres.-elect 1987-88, pres. 1988-89). Avocations: needlework, gardening. Bankruptcy, General civil litigation, Family and matrimonial. Office: 104 Pine St Ste 316 Abilene TX 79601-5930

BOONE, RICHARD WINSTON, SR., lawyer; b. Washington, July 19, 1941; s. Henry Shaffer and Anne Catherine (Huehne) B.; m. Jean Knox Logan, Dec. 17, 1966; children: Elizabeth Anne, Richard Winston, Jr., Katheryn Jeanne. BA with honors, U. Ala., 1963; JD, Georgetown U., 1970. Bar: Va. 1970, D.C. 1970, Md. 1984, U.S. Ct. Appeals (D.C. cir.) 1970, U.S. Ct. Appeals (2nd cir.) 1973, U.S. Ct. Appeals (4th cir.) 1972, U.S. Supreme Ct. 1974, U.S. Ct. Claims 1975. Ptnr. Carr, Jordan, Coyne & Savits, Washington, 1977-81; shareholder, dir. Wilkes, Artis, Hedrick & Boone, P.C., McLean, Va., 1984-95; pres. Richard W. Boone, P.C., McLean, 1984-95, The Law Offices of Richard W. Boone, 1995-97, Boone & Assocs., P.C., 1998—. Capt. USAR, 1964-67. Mem. D.C. Def. Lawyers Assn., Va. Trial Lawyers Assn., Va. Assn. Def. Attys., Barristers Assn. Avocations: model railroading, photography. General civil litigation, Health, Personal injury (including property damage). E-mail: rwboone@aol.com.

BOONE, THOMAS CALEB, lawyer; b. Hays, Kans., May 31, 1957; s. Thomas Clayton and Sarah Lillian (Floyd) B. BA in Econs., Washburn U., 1979, JD, 1982. Bar: Kans. 1982, U.S. Dist. Ct. Kans. 1982, U.S. Ct. Appeals (10th cir.) 1983. Aide A. B. Dickman, Econ. Cons., Anglo Am. Corp. of South Africa, Ltd., Johannesburg, Transvaal, 1980; legal intern Jerry R. Palmer, P.A., Topeka, 1981-82; pvt. practice Hays, Kans., 1982—. Chmn. Students for Stephan for Kans. Atty. Gen., Topeka, 1978. Mem. Ellis County Bar Assn., Sagamore Men's Hon. Soc. (Topeka) (pres. 1978-79). Republican. Avocation: vocal music. General civil litigation, Personal injury (including property damage). Home: 332 W 24th St Hays KS 67601-3008 Office: 1200 Main St Ste 304 Hays KS 67601-3649

BOOS, ROBERT WALTER, II, lawyer; b. Lawton, Okla., Sept. 18, 1954; s. Robert W. and Martha Boos. BA with honors, U. Notre Dame, 1976; JD, UCLA, 1979. Bar: Ill. 1979, Fla. 1986. Ptnr. Arnstein, Gluck, Weitzenfeld & Minow, Chgo., 1979-85; atty. Taub & Williams, P.A., Tampa, Fla., 1986-88; ptnr. Honigman, Miller, Schwartz & Cohn, Tampa, 1988-97, Ruden McClosky Smith Schuster & Russell, P.A., Tampa, 1997—. Federal civil litigation, General civil litigation, State civil litigation. Office: Ruden McClosky Smith et al 401 E Jackson St Ste 2700 Tampa FL 33602-5230

BOOTH, EDGAR HIRSCH, lawyer; b. Bklyn., June 8, 1926; s. Benjamin H. and Lee (Benzman) B.; m. Joan E. Blumberg, Oct. 7, 1956; children— Charles, Janet. Student, U. Va., 1944, 46-47; BA, Stanford, 1949; JD, Harvard, 1953. Bar: N.Y. State bar 1954. Since practiced in, N.Y.C.; assoc. Booth, Lipton & Lipton, N.Y.C., 1954-65, ptnr., 1965-84, Booth, Marcus & Pierce, N.Y.C., 1984-87, Myerson & Kuhn, N.Y.C., 1988-89, Warshaw Burstein Cohen Schlesinger & Kuh, N.Y.C., 1989-2000, of counsel, 2000—02; ret. Mem. mediators panel U.S. Bankrupty Ct. So. Dist. N.Y. Mem. Glen Rock Bd. Edn., 1971-77, pres., 1973-74; bd. dirs. S.M. Louis Fund, Inc., N.Y.C. Served with AUS, 1944-46. Mem. Am. Bankruptcy Inst., N.Y. State Bar Assn., Assn. Bar City N.Y. Bankruptcy, Federal civil litigation, Commercial, contracts (including sales of goods; commercial financing). Home: 25 Belmont Rd Glen Rock NJ 07452-2305 Office: 555 5th Ave New York NY 10017-2416 E-mail: ebooth@wbcsk.com.

BOOTH, EDMUND A., JR., prosecutor; BA, U. Georgia; LLD, UGA Sch. Law. First asst. U.S. Atty., 1986—; interim U.S. Atty. Southern Dist., Savannah, Ga., 2001. Office: One 10th St Augusta GA 30901*

BOOTH, HAROLD WAVERLY, lawyer, finance and investment company executive; b. Rochester, N.Y., Aug. 8, 1934; s. Herbert Nixon and Mildred B. (Anderson) B.; m. Flo Rae Spelts, July 4, 1957; children: Rebecca, William, Eva, Harold, Richard. BS, Cornell U., 1955; JD, Duke U., 1961. Bar: Nebr. 1961, Ill. 1967, Iowa 1974; CLU; chartered fin. counselor; cert. fin. planner. Staff atty. Bankers Life Nebr., Lincoln, 1961-67; pres. First Nat. Bank, Council Bluffs, Iowa, 1970-74; exec. v.p., treas. Blue Cross-Blue Shield Ill., Chgo., 1974-77; pres., chief exec. officer, chmn. Bankers Life Nebr., Lincoln, 1977-84; exec. v.p. Colonial Penn Group, Phila., 1985-87; chmn., chief exec. officer VGVR Cos., 1985—. Served to 1st lt. USAF, 1955-58. Fellow Life Mgmt. Inst. (pres. 1981-84); mem. Ins. Fedn. Nebr. (past pres.) Finance, Insurance. Home: 1000 Stony Ln Gladwyne PA 19035-1128

BOOYSEN, WILLEM HENDRIK, lawyer; b. Durban, South Africa, Feb. 15, 1968; arrived in The Netherlands, 1994; LLB in South African Law, U. South Africa, 1992; LLM in European Law, U. Leiden, 1995; LLM in Dutch Law, U. Amsterdam, 1998. Bar: Rotterdam 1998. Lawyer Du Toit, Haveman & Krog, Durban, South Africa, 1992—94, Loyens & Loeff, Rotterdam, Netherlands, 1995—2001, ptnr., 2002—. Mergers and acquisitions, Corporate, general, Securities. Office: Loyens & Loeff Weena 690 3012 CN Rotterdam Netherlands Fax: +31 10 4047590. E-mail: willem.booysen@loyensloeff.com.

BOPP, JAMES, JR., lawyer; b. Terre Haute, Ind., Feb. 8, 1948; s. James and Helen Marguerite (Hope) B.; m. Cheryl Hahn, Aug. 8, 1970 (div.); m. Christine Marie Stanton, July 3, 1982; children: Kathleen Grace, Lydia Grace, Marguerite Grace. BA, Ind. U., 1970; JD, U. Fla., 1973. Bar: Ind. 1973, U.S. Supreme Ct. 1977. Dep. atty. gen. State of Ind., Indpls., 1973-75; ptnr. Bopp & Fife, Indpls., 1975-79, Brames, Bopp, Abel & Oldham, Terre Haute, Ind., 1979-92, Bopp, Coleson & Bostrom, Terre Haute, 1992—; of counsel Webster, Chamberlain and Bean, Washington, 1997—. Dep. prosecutor Vigo County, Terre Haute, 1979-86; gen. counsel Nat. Right to Life Com., Washington, 1978—; pres. Nat. Legal Ctr. for Medically Dependent and Disabled, 1984—; gen. counsel James Madison Ctr. Free Speech, 1997—; instr. law Ind. U., 1977-78. Editor: Human Life and Health Care Ethics, 1985, Restoring the Right to Life: The Human Life Amendment, 1984; editor-in-chief Issues in Law and Medicine, 1985—. Mem. Pres.'s Com. on Mental Retardation, 1984-87, mem. congl. biomed. ethics adv. com., 1987-89; Vigo County Election Bd., 1991-93; vice chmn. Early for Gov., 1995-96; del. Rep. State Conv., Indpls., 1980, 82, 84, 86, 90, 92, 94, 96, 98, 2000, 2002; alt. del. Rep. Nat. Conv., 1992, 96, del., 2000; chmn. Vigo County Rep. Ctrl. Com., 1993-97, White House Conf. on Families, Washington, 1980, White House Conf. on Aging, Mpls., 1981; bd. dirs. Leadership Terre Haute, 1986-89, Nat. Rep. Pro-Life Com., Washington, 1983-91, Alliance for Growth and Progress, Terre Haute, 1993-97; chmn. bd. dirs. Hospice of Wabash Valley, Terre Haute, 1982-88; mem. The Federalist Soc., Free Speech & Election Law Practice Group, co-chmn. election law subcom., 1996—. Mem. Ind. State Bar Assn., Terre Haute Bar Assn., Terre Haute Rotary (bd. dirs. 1984-86). Roman Catholic. General civil litigation, Constitutional, Non-profit and tax-exempt organizations. Home: 1124 S Center St Terre Haute IN 47802-1116 Office: Bopp Coleson & Bostrom 1 S 6th St Terre Haute IN 47807-3510 E-mail: jboppjr@bopplaw.com.

BORCHARD, WILLIAM MARSHALL, lawyer; b. N.Y.C., Nov. 19, 1938; s. Bernard Philip and Helen (Marshall) B.; m. Myra Cohen, Dec. 13, 1969; children: Jillian, Thomas. BA, Princeton U., 1960; JD, Columbia U., 1964. Bar: N.Y. 1964, U.S. Dist. Ct. (so. and ea. dists.), U.S. Ct. Appeals (2d, 3d, fed. cirs.), U.S. Supreme Ct. Assoc. Kaye, Scholer, Fierman, Hays and Handler, N.Y.C., 1964-74, ptnr., 1974-83, Cowan, Liebowitz and Latman, N.Y.C., 1983—. Mem. editl. bds. Art and the Law, 1982—, The Trademark Reporter, 1983-99 Author: Trademarks and the Arts, 1999, A Trademark is Not a Copyright or a Patent, 2003. Staff sgt. USAFR, 1961-67. Stone scholar Columbia Law Sch. N.Y.C., 1962. Mem. ABA (coun. 1987-90), Am. Law Inst. (adv. com. 1986-92), Internat. Trademark Assn. (legal counsel 1988-91). Democrat. Jewish. Avocations: tennis, boating, biking. Trademark and copyright. Office: Cowan Liebowitz & Latman 1133 Ave of Americas New York NY 10036-6799 E-mail: wmb@cll.com.

BORDEN, DAVID M. state supreme court justice; b. Hartford, Conn., Aug. 4, 1937; BA magna cum laude, Amherst Coll., 1959; LLB cum laude, Harvard U., 1962. Bar: Conn. 1962, U.S. Dist. Ct. Conn. 1962, U.S. Ct. Appeals (2d cir.) 1965, U.S. Supreme Ct. 1969. Pvt. practice, Hartford, Conn., 1962-77; judge Conn. Ct. Common Pleas, 1977-78, Conn. Superior Ct., 1978-83, Conn. Appellate Ct., 1983—90; assoc. justice Conn. Supreme Ct., 1990—. Chief counsel joint com. on judiciary Conn. Gen. Assembly, 1975-76; lectr. Law U. Conn. Sch. Law, 1968-70, 85-92, 94—; exec. dir. Conn. Commn. to Revise Criminal Statutes, 1963-71. Mem. Conn. Bar Assn., Hartford County Bar Assn., Phi Beta Kappa. Democrat. Jewish. Avocations: hiking, reading. Office: PO Drawer N Sta A Hartford CT 06106

BORDEN, DIANA KIMBALL, lawyer; BA magna cum laude, Harvard and Radcliffe Colls., 1979; JD with honors, U. Tex., 1983. Bar: Tex. 1983, U.S. Dist. Ct. (we. dist.) Tex. 1986. Assoc. McGinnis, Lochridge & Kilgore, Austin, 1983-89, ptnr., 1989-91; assoc. prof. law St. Mary's U., San Antonio, 1991-93; v.p., gen. counsel Evolutionary Technologies Internat. Inc., Austin, 1993-97; shareholder Graves, Dougherty, Hearon & Moody, Austin, 1998—. Commercial, contracts (including sales of goods; commercial financing), Computer, Corporate, general. Office: Graves Dougherty Hearon & Moody 515 Congress Ave Ste 2300 Austin TX 78701-3508

BORDER, JAMES ROBERT, lawyer, accountant; b. Oakland, Calif., Nov. 28, 1956; s. George Robert and Nancy Arden (Brown) B.; m. Rebecca J. Hanson, Nov. 10, 1990; children: Kaitlin Janet, Alexander Robert, Christian Berends. AA, AS, Miami-Dade Community Coll., 1976; BBA, Fla. Atlantic U., 1978; MS in Mgmt., Fla. Internat. U., 1981; JD, U. Miami, 1985. Bar: Fla. 1985, D.C. 1998, U.S. Dist. Ct. (so. dist.) Fla. 1992, U.S. Tax Ct. 1985, U.S. Ct. Appeals (11th cir.) 1986, U.S. Ct. Appeals (D.C. cir.) 1995; CPA, Fla. Funeral dir. various orgns., cities, 1971-78; tax cons. Arthur Young & Co., Miami, 1979-81; corp. tax mgr. Cordis Corp., Miami, 1981-87; internat. tax mgr. Hasbro Inc., Pawtucket, R.I., 1987-88; sr. tax mgr. Price Waterhouse, Miami, 1988-89; corp. dir. taxation, tax counsel Carnival Cruise Lines, Miami, 1989-92, v.p. taxation, tax counsel, 1992—. Mem., exec. bd. dirs., v.p. program So. Fla. coun. Boy Scouts Am.; bd. dirs. Cruise Industry PAC, chmn. charitable found; coach girls youth softball and boys youth baseball, West Pembroke Pines Optimist. Mem. ABA, AICPA, Fla. Inst. CPAs, Nat. Eagle Scout Assn., Phi Kappa Phi, Beta Gamma Sigma. Avocations: scuba diving, tennis. Corporate taxation, Taxation, general. Office: Carnival Corp 3655 NW 87th Ave Miami FL 33178-2428 E-mail: jborder@carnival.com.

BORDY, MICHAEL JEFFREY, lawyer; b. Kansas City, Mo., July 24, 1952; s. Marvin Dean and Alice Mae (Rostov) B.; m. Marjorie Enid Kanof, Dec. 27, 1973 (div. Dec. 1983); m. Melissa Anne Held, May 24, 1987; children: Shayna Robyn, Jenna Alexis, Samantha Falyn. Bar: Calif., 1986, U.S. Dist. Ct. (cen. dist.) Calif., 1986, (so. dist.) Calif., 1987, U.S. Ct. Appeals (9th cir.), 1986. Tchg. asst. biology U. Kans., Lawrence, 1975-76, rsch. asst. biology, 1976-80; post-doctoral fellow Johns Hopkins U., Balt., 1980-83; tchg. asst. U. So. Calif., L.A., 1984-86; assoc. Thelen, Marrin, Johnson & Bridges, L.A., 1986-87, Wood, Lucksinger & Epstein, L.A., 1987-89, Cooper, Epstein & Hurewitz, Beverly Hills, Calif., 1989-93; ptnr. Jacobson, Runes & Bordy, Beverly Hills, 1994-96, Jacobson, Sanders & Bordy, LLP, Beverly Hills, 1996-97, Jacobson White Diamond & Bordy, LLP, Beverly Hills, 1997—2001, White, Bordy & Levey, LLP, 2002—. Bd. govs. Beverly Hills (Calif.) Bar Barristers, 1988-90, chair real estate law sect. 1998-2000, exec. com. 2000—; bd. govs. Cedars-Sinai Med. Ctr., L.A., 1994—; bd. dirs. Sinai Temple, 1998—; cabinet United Jewish Fund/Real Estate, L.A., 1995—; mem. exec. com. Moriah Soc. for U. Judaism, 2002--; mem. planning com. Am. Cancer Soc., 1996—; mem. Guardians of the Jewish Home for the Aging, 1995—, Fraternity of Friends, 1997-99; active Lawyers Against Hunger, 1995—. Pre-Doctoral fellow NIH, Lawrence, 1977-80; post-doctoral fellow Mellon Found., Balt., 1980-83. Mem. ABA, State Bar Calif., L.A. County Bar Assn., Beverly Hills Bar Assn. (gov., barrister 1988-92, chair real estate sect. 1998-00), Profl. Network Group. Democrat. Jewish. Avocations: running, triathlons, reading. Corporate, general, Environmental, Property, real (including real estate development, water). Office: White Bordy & Levey 9777 Wilshire Blvd Ste 918 Beverly Hills CA 90212-1902 E-mail: mjbordy@jwbl.com.

BOREL, STEVEN JAMES, lawyer; b. Kansas City, Mo., Nov. 12, 1947; s. Mark and Margaret (Gibson) B.; m. Nancy Jean Dunaway, Aug. 31, 1967; children: Lindsay Kay, Emily Jean, Amy Lynn. BSBA, Pitts. State U., 1969; JD with distinction, U. Mo., Kansas City, 1972. Bar: Mo. 1972, Kans. 1989. Assoc. Stubbs, Epstein & Mann, Kansas City, 1972-79; pvt. practice Kansas City, 1979—. Rsch. editor U. Mo.-Kansas City Law Rev., 1971-72. Capt. U.S. Army, 1969-74. Mem. ATLA, Mo. Assn. Trial Attys., Kans. Trial Lawyers Assn., Kansas City Met. Bar Assn. (chmn. workers' compensation com. 1991-93). Personal injury (including property damage). Office: 1580 Mahaffie Cir Olathe KS 66062- E-mail: sborel@borelfirm.com.

BOREN, JAMES EDGAR, lawyer; b. New Orleans, Nov. 16, 1949; s. John E. and Katherine (Savage) B.; m. Teresa Anne Berlin, Mar. 7, 1971; children: Anna Blynn, Katherine Lenore, Rebecca Camille. BA, La. Tech U., 1971; JD, La. State U., 1975. Bar: La. 1975, U.S. Dist. Ct. (mid. dist.) La. 1975, U.S. Ct. Appeals (5th cir.)1975, U.S. Dist. Ct. (we. dist.) La. 1976, U.S. Dist. Ct. (ea. dist.) La. 1977, U.S. Supreme Ct. 1979, U.S. Ct. Appeals (11th cir.) 1981. Asst. dist. atty. Parish of East Baton Rouge, 1975-76; ptnr. Boren, Holthaus & Perez, Baton Rouge, 1976-88; pvt. practice Baton Rouge, La., 1988—. Chair La. Atty. Discipline Bd. Hearing Com., 1994-2000. Contbr. articles to profl. publs. Mem. ACLU (bd. dirs. 1988-92), La. State Bar Assn. (ho. of dels. 1998—), La. Assn. Criminal Def. Lawyers (bd. dirs. 1985—, pres. commendation 1986, pres. 1990-91, chair edn. com. 1997—, Tate award 2000), Nat. Assn. Criminal Def. Lawyers (bd. dirs. 1992-95, chmn. death penalty com. 1994-98, indigent def. co-chair 1998-2002). Democrat. Criminal. Home: 2035 E Lakeshore Dr Baton Rouge LA 70808-1464 Address: 830 Main St Baton Rouge LA 70802-5597 E-mail: jimboren@bellsouth.net.

BORGER, JOHN EMORY, lawyer; b. Warren, Pa., Apr. 26, 1952; s. Lee James and Patricia Marie (Ulam) B. BA, Dickinson Coll., 1974; JD, Fordham U., 1982. Bar: Conn. 1982, N.Y. 1983. Assoc. Walter, Conston, N.Y.C., 1982-83, Law Offices of J. Russell Clune, Harrison, N.Y., 1983-87; atty. PHH Real Estate Svcs., 1987-95; sr. v.p., gen. counsel Cedant Mobility Svcs. Corp., Danbury, Conn., 1995—2001; exec. v.p., gen. counsel Resort Condominiums Internat., LLC, Parsippany, NJ, 2001—. Avocations: coin collecting, classic cars, sports, reading. Commercial, contracts (including sales of goods; commercial financing), Corporate, general, Property, real (including real estate development, water). Home: 64 Old Washington Rd Ridgefield CT 06877-5917 Office: Resort Condominiums Internat LLC 7 Sylvan Way Parsippany NJ 07054

BORGER, JOHN PHILIP, lawyer; b. Wilmington, Del., Apr. 19, 1951; s. Philip E. and Jane (Smyth) B.; m. Judith Marie Yates, May 24, 1974; children: Jennifer, Christopher, Nicholas. BA in Journalism with high honors, Mich. State U., 1973; JD, Yale U., 1976. Bar: Minn. 1976, U.S. Dist. Ct. Minn. 1976, U.S. Ct. Appeals (8th cir.) 1979, U.S. Supreme Ct. 1983, N.D. 1988, U.S. Dist. Ct. N.D. 1988, Wis. 1993. Editor-in-chief Mich. State News, East Lansing, 1972-73; assoc. Faegre & Benson, LLP, Mpls., 1976-83, ptnr., 1984—. Bd. dirs. Milkweed Edits., 1995-01; adj. prof. U. Minn. Sch. Journalism and Mass Comm., 1999. Contbr. articles to profl. jours. Recipient Freedom of Info. award, Minn. Soc. Profl. Journalists, 2002, First Amendment Award, St. Cloud State U. Dept. Mass. Comms., 2001. Mem. ABA (chmn. media law and defamation torts com. torts and ins. practice sect. 1996-97), Minn. Bar Assn., State Bar Assn. N.D., Wis. Bar Assn., Hennepin County Bar Assn. Appellate, General civil litigation, Libel. Office: Faegre & Benson LLP 2200 Wells Fargo Ctr 90 S 7th St Ste 2200 Minneapolis MN 55402-3901 E-mail: jborger@faegre.com.

BORGERDING, FRANCIS XAVIER, JR., lawyer; b. Balt. s. Francis Xavier Sr. and Betty Bernice (Wilson) B.; m. Amy Kristina Gorena, Apr. 24, 1993. BS, Towson U., 1985; JD, U. Balt., 1988. Bar: Md. 1988, D.C. 1990, U.S. Dsit. Ct. md. 1990, U.S. Tax Ct. 19945 U.S. Supreme Ct. 1998. Law clk. to Hon. A. Owen Hennegan Cir. Ct. Balt. County, 1987-88; assoc. Dinenna & Breschi, Towson, Md., 1989-95; atty. Law Offices of Francis X. Borgerding, Jr., Towson, 1996—. Chmn. Lawyers Have a Heart 5K Run Am. Heart Assn., Towson, 1998. Mem. D.C. Bar Assn., Md. State Bar Assn., Balt. County Bar Assn. (guest editor monthly Advocate 1993-2003, chair young lawyers com. 1996-97, young lawyers rep. to exec. coun. 1996-97, chmn. state, local and zoning laws com. 2000-2001). General civil litigation, General practice, Land use and zoning (including planning). Office: 409 Washington Ave Ste 600 Towson MD 21204-4907

BORGESON, EARL CHARLES, law librarian, educator; b. Boyd, Minn., Dec. 2, 1922; s. Hjalmer Nicarner and Doris (Danielson) B.; m. Barbara Ann Jones, Sept. 21, 1944; children— Barbara Gale, Geoffrey Charles, Steven Earl. BS in Law, U. Minn., 1947, LLB, 1949; BA in Law Librarianship, U. Wash., 1950. Libr. Harvard U. Law Sch. Libr., 1952-70; assoc. dir. Stanford U. Librs., 1970-75; assoc. law libr. Los Angeles County (Calif.) Law Libr., 1975-78; prof. and law libr. So. Meth. U., Dallas, 1978-88, prof. emeritus of law, 1988; lectr. UCLA Grad. Sch. Libr. Sci., 1975-78; adj. prof. Tex. Women's U., 1979-80; adj. prof. U. North Tex., Denton, 1988-90; librarian AccuFile, Inc., 1992-2001; cons. in field. With USNR, 1943-46. Mem. Am. Assn. Law Librs. Home: 867 Tangle Oaks Ct Bellville TX 77418-2861

BORISOFF, RICHARD STUART, lawyer; b. Rochester, N.Y., May 4, 1945; s. Samuel M. and Ida. B.; m. Risa W. Polgar, Aug. 17, 1967; children: Mindy, Dara. AB, U. Pa., 1967; JD, Columbia U., 1970. Bar: N.Y. 1971, D.C. 1981, U.S. Dist. Ct. (so. dist.) N.Y. 1973, U.S. Ct. Appeals (2nd cir.) 1973. Assoc. Paul, Weiss, Rifkind, Wharton & Garrison, N.Y.C., 1970-78, ptnr., 1978—. Mem.: ABA. Corporate, general, Mergers and acquisitions, Securities. Office: Paul Weiss Rifkind Wharton & Garrison Ste 2320 1285 Avenue Of The Americas New York NY 10019-6064 E-mail: rborisoff@paulweiss.com.

BORISON, SCOTT CRAIG, lawyer; b. N.Y.C., Feb. 8, 1961; s. E.B. and Joan B. Borison; m. Janet S. Legg, May 22, 1988; children: Ian, Madison. BA in Russian Studies, Fairleigh Dickinson U., 1982; JD, U. Okla., 1987. Bar: Okla. 1987, D.C. 1994, Md. 1995, U.S. Dist. Ct. Md., U.S. Dist. Ct. D.C., U.S. Ct. Appeals (4th and 10th cirs.), U.S. Tax Ct., U.S. Ct. Vets. Appeals. Law clk. Okla. Ct. Appeals, Oklahoma City, 1987-89; counsel Centurion Oil, Inc., Oklahoma City, 1989-93; atty., mem. Legg Law Firm, LLC, Frederick, Md., 1994—. Bd. dirs. Religious Coalition for Emergency Human Needs. Mem. Nat. Assn. Consumer Bankruptcy Attys., Trial Lawyers for Pub. Justice, Frederick County Bar Assn., Bankruptcy Bar Dist. Md. Bankruptcy. Office: Legg Law Firm LLC 5500 Buckeystown Pike Frederick MD 21703-8331

BORJA, MARY ELLEN MURPHY, lawyer; b. Buffalo, May 14, 1942; d. Walter Timothy and Mary Elizabeth (Strauss) Murphy; m. William Arthur Borja, Aug. 16, 1966 (div. 1986); children: William W., Mary Elizabeth, Jennifer Stacey, Mark Edward, Catherine Anne, Susan Eileen; m. Raymond Philip Mack Jr., Dec. 27, 1997 (div. 2001). BA, Trinity Coll., Washington, 1963; JD, SUNY, Buffalo, 1966. Bar: N.Y. 1967, Fla. 1985, U.S. Dist. Ct. (middle dist.) Fla. 1989, U.S. Supreme Ct. 1990; cert. family ct. mediator, Fla. With trust dept. First Nat. Bank of Chgo., 1966-67; assoc. Peacock & Cope, P.A., Clearwater, Fla., 1985-87, William L. Lyman, P.A., Clearwater, Fla., 1987-88; pvt. practice Palm Harbor, Fla., 1988-90; ptnr. Carrion & Borja, Palm Harbor, Fla., 1990-92; pvt. practice Clearwater, Fla., 1992—. Master Canakaris Inns of Ct. Pres. Parish Coun., Espiritu Santo Ch., Safety Harbor, Fla., 1982-85; co-chmn. sch. bd. St. Cecelia Sch., Clearwater, 1984-85. Mem. N.Y. State Bar Assn., Fla. Bar Assn. (cert. marital and family law, mem. family law sect.), Clearwater Bar Assn. (chmn. mentor com.). Family and matrimonial. Office: 1st Flr East 2536 Countryside Blvd Clearwater FL 33763-1633

BORK, ROBERT HERON, lawyer, author, educator, former federal judge; b. Pitts., Mar. 1, 1927; s. Harry Philip and Elizabeth (Kunkle) B.; m. Claire Davidson, June 15, 1952 (dec. 1980); children: Robert Heron, Charles E., Ellen E.; m. Mary Ellen Pohl, Oct. 30, 1982. BA, U. Chgo., 1948, JD, 1953; LLD (hon.), Creighton U., 1975, Notre Dame Law Sch., 1982; LHD, Wilkes-Barre Coll., 1976; JD (hon.), Bklyn. Law Sch., 1984; ThD, DeSales Sch. Theology, 1990; LLD honoris causa, Adelphi U., 1990. Bar: Ill. 1953, D.C. 1977. Assoc., then ptnr. Kirkland, Ellis, Hodson, Chaffetz & Masters, Chgo., 1955-62; assoc. prof. Yale Law Sch., 1962-65, prof. law, 1965-75, on leave, 1973-75; solicitor gen. U.S. Dept. Justice, Washington, 1973-77, acting atty. gen., 1973-74; Chancellor Kent prof. law Yale Law Sch., 1977-79, Alexander M. Bickel prof. pub. law, 1979-81; ptnr. Kirkland & Ellis, Washington, 1981-82; judge U.S. Ct. Appeals for D.C. Cir., 1982-88, resigned, 1988; resident scholar Am. Enterprise Inst. for Pub. Policy Rsch., Washington, 1977, adj. scholar, 1977-82, John M. Olin scholar in legal studies, 1988-99, sr. fellow, 2000—; prof. law Ave Maria Sch. Law, 2000—03. Mem., trustee Woodrow Wilson Internat. Ctr. for Scholars, 1973-78; nominated for position assoc. justice U.S. Supreme Ct., 1987, confirmation denied by U.S. Senate; Tad and Dianne Taube Disting. vis. fellow Hoover Instn., 2003. Author: The Antitrust Paradox: A Policy at War with Itself, 1978, 2d edit., 1993, The Tempting of America: The Political Seduction of the Law, 1990, Slouching Towards Gomorrah: Modern Liberalism and American Decline, 1996, Coercing Virtue: The Worldwide Rule of Judges, 2002. With USMCR, 1945-46, 50-52. Recipient Francis Boyer award Am. Enterprise Inst., 1984, Henry Salvatori prize Intercollegiate Svcs. Inst., 1998. Fellow AAAS; mem. Federalist Soc. (co-chmn., bd. trustees). E-mail: rbork@aei.org.

BORMAN, JOHN, trial lawyer, arbitrator, mediator; b. Little Falls, Minn., Mar. 21, 1946; s. Myron Francis and Bernadette Mary (Burggraff) B.; 1 child, Mac A. Nelson II. BA in Political Sci., U. Minn., 1973; JD, Notre Dame, 1979. Bar: Minn. 1979, Wis. 1987, U.S. Dist. Ct. Minn. 1980, U.S. Dist. Ct. (we. dist.) Wis. 1990, U.S. Dist. Ct. (we. dist.) Mich. 1996, U.S. Ct. Appeals (8th cir.) 1986, U.S. Ct. Appeals (6th cir.) 1996, U.S. Supreme Ct. 1986; cert. civil trial specialist Minn. State Bar Assn. Law clk. to Hon. Glenn E. Kelley Minn. Dist. Ct., Winona, 1979-80; ptnr. Robins, Kaplan, Miller & Ciresi LLP, Mpls., 1981-97, Streater & Murphy PA, Winona, Minn., 1997-99. Researcher, organizer Minn. Pub. Interest Research Group, Mpls., 1973-76; bd. govs. Minn. Trial Lawyers Assn., 1990—; pres. Minn. Consumer Alliance, Mpls., 1995-97; bd. dirs. Minn. Advocates for Human Rights, Mpls., 1991—, Diversity Found., 2000—. Contbr. to profl. jours. Troop com. chair Boy Scouts of Am., Golden Valley, Minn., 1990-95; Served sgt. USMC, 1964-68. Named Super Lawyer Minn. Jour. Law & Politics, 1998, Leading Am. Atty. Am. Rsch. Corp., 1999, 2000. Mem. atla, ABA, Minn. Bar Assn., Wis. State Bar, Ramsey County Bar Assn., Winona County Bar Assn., Hennepin County Bar Assn., Minn. Trial Lawyers Assn. (bd. govs. 1981—, Excellence award 1997), Acad. Cert. Trial Lawyers. Personal injury (including property damage), Product liability, Professional liability. Office: Trial Lawyer 502 West Broadway Winona MN 55987 Fax: 507-454-8862. E-mail: johnborman@mymailstation.com.

BORMES, JAMES X. lawyer; b. Aberdeen, S.D., Sept. 1, 1962; s. Robert E. and Patricia A. Bormes; m. Anne C. Hussey; children: Margaret, James, Mary, Grace. BA, St. Louis U., 1984, JD, 1988. Bar: Ill. 1988, U.S. Dist. Ct. (no. dist.) Ill. 1990, U.S. Dist. Ct. (we. dist.) Tex. 1996, U.S. Dist. Ct. (so. dist.) Ill. 2000, U.S. Ct. Appeals (7th cir.) 1991. Law clk., Judge William L. Beatty U.S. Dist. Ct. (so. dist.) Ill., Chgo., 1988—89; assoc. Joyce Kubusiak, Chgo., 1989—94, O'Brien, O'Rourke & Hogan, Chgo., 1994—98; ptnr. Law Office James X. Bormes, PC, Chgo., 1998—. Tutor Mercy Home for Boys, Chgo., 2000—. Mem.: Chgo. Athletic Assn. Roman Catholic. Commercial litigation, Construction. Office: Law Office James X Bormes PC 8 S Michigan Ste 2600 Chicago IL 60603

BORN, BROOKSLEY ELIZABETH, lawyer; b. San Francisco, Aug. 27, 1940; d. Ronald Henry and Mary Ellen (Bortner) Born; m. Alexander Elliot Bennett, Oct. 9, 1982; children: Nicholas Jacob Landau, Ariel Elizabeth Landau, Andrew E. Bennett, Laura F. Bennett, Peter J. Bennett. AB, Stanford U., 1961, JD, 1964. Bar: DC 1966. Law clk. U.S. Ct. Appeals, Washington, 1964—65; legal rschr. Harvard Law Sch., 1967—68; assoc. Arnold and Porter, Washington, 1965—67, 1968—73, ptnr., 1974—96, 1999—2002; chair U.S. Commodity Futures Trading Commn., Washington, 1996—99. Lectr. law Columbus Sch. Law, Cath. U. Am., 1972—74; adj. prof. Georgetown U. Law Ctr., Washington, 1972—73. Pres.: Stanford Law Rev., 1963—64. Chair bd. visitors Stanford Law Sch., 1987; trustee Ctr. for Law and Social Policy, Washington, 1977—96, Women's Bar Found., 1981—86; bd. dirs. Nat. Legal Aid and Defenders Assn., 1972—79, Washington Legal Clinic for Homeless, 1993—96, Lawyers Com. for Civil Rights Under Law, 1993—96, Am. Bar Found., 1989—99, Washington Lawyers Com. for Civil Rights and Urban Affairs, 1992—96, Nat. Women's Law Ctr., 1981—. Mem.: ABA (chair sect. ind. rights and responsibilities 1977—78, chair fed. judiciary com. 1980—83, chair consortium on legal svcs. and the pub. 1987—90, bd. govs. 1990—93, chair resource devel. coun. 1993—95, chair coun. Fund for Justice and Edn. 1995—96, state del. from DC 1994—), Southwestern Legal Found. (trustee 1993—96), Am. Law Inst., DC Bar (sec. 1975—76, mem. bd. govs. 1976—79), Order of Coif. Administrative and regulatory, Federal civil litigation, Finance. Office: Arnold & Porter 555 12th St NW Washington DC 20004-1206 E-mail: brooksley_born@aporter.com.

BORN, DAVID PEARSON, lawyer; b. Elkins, W.Va., Feb. 28, 1954; s. Donald D. and Sara B. (Pratt) B.; m. Beverly Rush, Aug. 14, 1976; children:

Hannah, Elliott, Meredith. BA, W.Va. U., 1976, JD, 1979. Bar: W.Va. 1979, U.S. Dist. Ct. (so. dist.) W.Va. 1979, U.S. Dist. Ct. (no. dist.) W.Va. 1983. Pvt. practice, Fairmont, W.Va., 1979-84; asst. pros. atty. Marion County, Fairmont, 1984-86, Family Law Master Supreme Ct. Appeals, Fairmont, 1986—2001; family court judge, 2002. Mem. Marion County Bar Assn. (pres. 1985-86). Methodist. Office: 306 Courthouse 219 Adams St Fairmont WV 26554

BORN, SAMUEL ROYDON , II, lawyer; b. Atwood, Ill., Apr. 19, 1945; s. Samuel Roydon and Mary Elizabeth (Derr) B.; m. Brenda Alice Anderson, June 18, 1988; children: Samuel R. III, Holly Jean; 1 stepchild, Julie Chamberlain Sipe. Student, Northwestern U., 1963-64, Am. U., fall 1966; BA, Simpson Coll., 1967; JD, Ind. U., 1970. Bar: Ind. 1970, U.S. Dist. Ct. (so. dist.) Ind. 1970, U.S. Ct. Appeals (7th crct.) 1975, U.S. Dist. Ct. (no. dist.) Ind. 1990, U.S. Supreme Ct. 2003. Ptnr. Ice Miller, Indpls., 1970—. Mem. safety com. Associated Gen. Contractors Ind., 1988—. Co-author: Safety and Health Guide for Indiana Business, 1999, 4th edit., 2002; mem. bd. editors: Ind. Law Jour., 1969—70; contbr. articles to profl. jours. Mem. bd. visitors Ind. U. Sch. Law, 1988-89, 95-98; chmn. ch. cmty. athletics First Bapt. Ch., Indpls., 1975-78, trustee, 1978-80. Mem. ABA (mem. nat. conf. bar pres. 1987-99, ho. of dels. 1988-98, labor and employment law sect.), Am. Bar Found., Ind. State Bar Assn. (bd. govs. 1990-99, pres. 1997-98, labor law sect.), Ind. Bar Found., Indpls. Bar Assn. (bd. mgrs. 1987-95, pres. 1988), U.S. C. of C. (occupl. safety and health adminstrv. coun. 1981-86, 2000—), Ind. C. of C. (past chmn. occupl. safety health com.), Ind. Mfrs. Assn. (pers. labor rels. com. 1982-99), Highland Golf and Country Club, Crooked Stick Golf Club, Univ. Club, Indpls. Lawyers Club, Masons, Shriners, Kiwanis, Phi Eta Sigma, Sigma Alpha Epsilon. Presbyterian. Avocations: downhill skiing, golf, fly fishing, public speaking. Administrative and regulatory, Civil rights, Labor (including EEOC, Fair Labor Standards Act, labor-management relations, NLRB, OSHA). Home: 5202 Grandview Dr Indianapolis IN 46228-1938 Office: Ice Miller 1 American Sq Indianapolis IN 46282-0020 E-mail: born@icemiller.com.

BORNHEIMER, ALLEN MILLARD, lawyer; b. Brewer, Maine, June 10, 1942; s. Millard Genthner and Gertrude Evelyn (Kinney) B.; m. Deborah Russell Hill, June 17, 1967; children: Anneliese, Charles, Elizabeth. Student, Phillips Exeter Acad., 1961; AB, Harvard U., 1965, LLB, 1968. Bar: Mich. 1968, Mass. 1971. Assoc. Dickinson, Wright, McKean & Cudlip, Detroit, 1968-70, Choate, Hall & Stewart, Boston, 1970-76, ptnr., 1976-99, mng. ptnr., 1988-95; principal, gen. counsel Cargex Properties, Inc., Boston, 2000—. Bd. dirs. Cargex Properties, Inc. and affiliated cos., Portland, Maine. Town moderator, Duxbury, Mass., 1982—, chmn. fin. com., 1974-76, mem. capital budget com., 1977; bd. dirs. Jordan Hosp., Plymouth, Mass., 1974-81; trustee North Yarmouth (Maine) Acad., 1976-79. Mem. ABA, Mass. Bar Assn., Boston Bar Assn., Am. Coll. Investment Counsel, Mass. Moderators Assn., Duxbury Yacht Club (bd. dirs. 1982-84), Harvard Club (Boston). Republican. Avocations: golf, piano, sailing. Corporate, general, Finance, Property, real (including real estate development, water). Home: 15 Summerhouse Lane Duxbury MA 02332-3930 Office: 20th Fl 50 Milk St Boston MA 02109-5003 E-mail: allen.bornheimer@cargex.com.

BOROFSKY, STEPHEN ERIC, lawyer; b. Concord, N.H., Nov. 17, 1946; s. Martin and Marion (Criden) B.; m. Linda Carol Dyke, Aug. 27, 1972; children — Deborah Nicole. B.A., Dartmouth Coll., 1968; J.D., Columbia U., 1973. Bar: N.H. 1973, U.S. Dist. Ct. N.H. 1974. Law clk. U.S. Dist. Ct. N.H., Concord, 1973-74; assoc. McLane, Graf et al., Manchester, N.H., 1974-78; atty., ptnr. The Legal Clinics, Manchester, Nashua, Portsmouth, N.H., 1978-97; shareholder Borofsky, Amodeo-Vickery & Bandazian, PA, Manchester, 1997—; mem. N.H. Supreme Ct. Specialization Com., 1980—; bd. dirs., v.p. N.H. Legal Aid, 1977-83. Mem. ABA, N.H. Bar Assn. (mem. coms. prepaid legal services, code of profl. responsibility revision, ethics, econs. of law, delivery of legal services, publicity and pub. relations), Manchester Bar Assn. (pres. 1978-79), Nashua Bar Assn. Democrat. Jewish. Family and matrimonial, General practice, Personal injury (including property damage). Home: 404 Wallace Rd Bedford NH 03110-4831 Office: Borofsky Amodeo-Vickery & Bandazian PA 708 Pine St Manchester NH 03104-3103

BOROS, JEROME S. lawyer; b. N.Y.C., Apr. 28, 1926; s. Edwin N. Boros and Margaret G. Guttman; m. Elayne N. Nossiter, Nov. 23, 1969; stepchildren: Richard, Ronald, Jill LeVine. AB, Syracuse U., 1947, MA, LLB, Syracuse U., 1950; LLM, Yale U., 1951. Bar: N.Y. 1950, D.C. Bar 1966, U.S. Dist. Ct. (so. dist.) N.Y. 1950, U.S. Ct. Appeals (D.C. cir.) 1966. Atty. CAB, Washington, 1950-53, FCC, Washington, 1953-55; assoc. Fly, Shuebruk, Gaguine, Boros & Braun, N.Y.C., Washington, 1955-62, ptnr., 1962-88, Rosenman & Colin, N.Y.C., 1988—96; of counsel Robinson, Silverman, Pearce, Aaronsohn & Berman, N.Y.C., 1996—2002; chmn. telecomm. group Conn. Bryan Cave, 2002—; of counsel Bryan Cave, 2002—. Faculty sch. speech Syracuse U., 1947; adj. prof. law NYU Sch. Law, 1971-95; chmn. Workshop on Broadcasting Practising Law Inst., 1969, lectr., 1969-76; gen. counsel Internat. Radio and TV Soc., N.Y.C., 1973-93, sec., 1973-93, gov., 1973-93; co-trustee radio sta. WYRM, New Britain, Conn., 1987-96. Acting village justice Village of Sands Point, N.Y., 1988-2000, village justice 2000—; chmn. Sands Point Cable Com., 1993—. With U.S. Army, 1944-45. Mem. City Athletic Club (gov., chmn. legal legis. com. 1999-02), Harmonie Club Republican. Jewish. Office: Bryan Cave 1290 Ave of Americas New York NY 10104-0199

BOROWITZ, ALBERT IRA, lawyer, author; b. Chgo., June 27, 1930; s. David and Anne (Wolkenstein) B.; m. Helen Blanche Osterman, July 29, 1950; children: Peter Leonard, Joan, Andrew Seth. BA in Classics summa cum laude, Harvard U., 1951, MA in Chinese Regional Studies, 1953, JD magna cum laude, 1956. Bar: Ohio 1957. Assoc. firm Hahn, Loeser, Freedheim, Dean & Wellman, Cleve., 1956-62, ptnr., 1962-83, Jones, Day, Reavis & Pogue, Cleve., 1983-90, of counsel, 1991-94; cons., 1994—99. Author: Fiction in Communist China, 1954, Innocence and Arsenic: Studies in Crime and Literature, 1977, The Woman who Murdered Black Satin: The Bermondsey Horror, 1981, A Gallery of Sinister Perspectives: Ten Crimes and a Scandal, 1982, The Jack the Ripper Walking Tour Murder, 1986, The Thurtell-Hunt Murder Case: Dark Mirror to Regency England, 1987, This Club Frowns on Murder, 1990, Jones, Day, Reavis & Pogue: The First Century, 1993, Unhappy Endings, 2001, Blood and Ink: An International Guide to Fact-Based Crime Literature, 2002; author: (with H.O. Borowitz) Pawnshop and Palaces: The Fall and Rise of the Campana Art Museum, 1991; series editor: True Crime. Hon. consul of France in Cleve., 1990-95; v.p. French-Am. C. of C. of No. Ohio, 1993-99; co-founder Borowitz True Crime Collection at Kent State U. Librs. Recipient Cleve. arts prize for lit., 1981 Mem. Am. Law Inst., Rowfant Club (Cleve.), Union Club (Cleve.), Harvard Club (N.Y.C.), Vidocq Soc. Phila. (hon.). E-mail: alborowitz@aol.com.

BOROWSKY, PHILIP, lawyer; b. Phila., Oct. 9, 1946; s. Joshua and Gertrude (Nicholson) B.; m. Judith Lee Goldwasser, Sept. 5, 1970 (div. 1996); children: Miriam Isadora, Manuel, Nora Jo. BA, UCLA, 1967; JD, U. San Francisco, 1973. Bar: Calif. Pres. and mng. ptnr. Cartwright, Slobodin, Bokelman, Borowsky, Wartnick, Moore & Harris, San Francisco, 1987-95; pres. Law Offices Philip Borowsky, Inc., San Francisco, 1996—2002; mng. ptnr. Borowsky & Hayes LLP, San Francisco, 2002—. Mem. faculty Practicing Law Inst., N.Y.C., 1983-84; mem. adj. faculty Hastings Coll. Law, San Francisco, 1982-83; arbitrator Superior Ct., San Francisco, 1982—, Am. Arbitration Assn., 1982—, Nat. Assn. Securities Dealers, 1994—. Co-author: Unjust Dismissal and At-Will Employment, 1985; mem. bd. editl. cons. Bad Faith Law Update, 1986—. With U.S. Army, 1968-70, Vietnam. Mem. Consumer Attys. Calif. Democrat. Federal civil litigation, State civil litigation, General practice. Office: 1 Market Plz San Francisco CA 94105-1420 E-mail: borowsky@borowsky.com.

BORSARI, GEORGE ROBERT, JR., lawyer, broadcaster; b. Washington, July 30, 1940; s. George Robert and Sara Totton (Dunning) B.; m. Regis Ann Herron, Oct. 23, 1964 (div. Jan. 1985); children: George Robert, III, William Grant. BS, Va. Poly. Inst., 1962; LL.B., George Washington U., 1965. Bar: D.C. 1966. Since practiced in, Washington; ptnr. Borsari & Paxson, 1969—. Pres. Local TV Systems, Inc., 1981-89, Outdoor Inst., Inc., 1978—; chmn. Core Group Inc., 1991—. Councilman Town of Glen Echo, Md., 1969-74, mayor, 1977-81, 89-91; mem. Montgomery County (Md.) Muncipality Advisory Bd., 1972-74, Montgomery County CATV Task Force, 1973-74, 80-85, Cable TV Adv. Com., 1979-85; pres. Montgomery County chpt. Md. Mcpl. League. Served to lt. col. JAG USAR. Decorated Army Meritorious Service medal with oak leaf cluster, Army Commendation medal with 2 oak leaf clusters; recipient Presdl. commendation, 1970; St. George award Roman Catholic Archdiocese Washington, 1970; Silver Beaver award Nat. Capital Area council Boy Scouts Am., 1974 Mem. ABA (chmn. cable TV com. sect. sci. and tech. 1982-86, chmn. Broadcast Com. 1986-90, chmn. Mass Media Com. 1990-92, mem. coun. sect. sci. and tech.), D.C. Bar Assn., Fed. Comms. Bar Assn., Isaac Walton League, Kenwood Golf and Country Club, Phi Delta Phi. Democrat. Home: 6107 Princeton Ave Glen Echo MD 20812-1125 Office: Borsari & Paxson 4000 Albemarle St NW Ste 100 Washington DC 20016

BORSODY, ROBERT PETER, lawyer; b. N.Y.C., Oct. 6, 1937; s. Benjamin F. and Edith Nora (Corcoran) B.; m. Paula Jane Bercutt, Oct. 14, 1973; children: Lisa M., Daniel B., Sarah E., Alexander S. B.E.E., U. Va., 1961, LL.B., 1964; diploma, U. Teheran, Iran, 1959. Bar: N.Y. 1965, D.C. 1978. Assoc. firm Sullivan & Cromwell, N.Y.C., 1964-69; founder, dir. Legal Services for Elderly Poor, 1969-71, Community Health Law Project, 1971-73; pvt. practice law N.Y.C., 1973-78; ptnr., founder Epstein Becker Borsody & Green, N.Y.C., 1978-87; of counsel Epstein, Becker & Green, N.Y.C., 1987-99, Fischbein, Badillo, Wagner & Harding, N.Y.C., 1999—. Adj. prof. Manhattan Coll., 1978-82, Pace U. Sch. Law, 1986-90; mem. N.Y. State Coun. Health Care Financing, 1978—; sec. N.Y. Statewide Health Coordinating Coun., 1978-87; chmn. bd. dirs. N.Y. Bus. Group on Health, 1984-87. Bd. dirs. N.Y.C. Mental Health Assn. Mem. ABA, N.Y. State Bar Assn. Health Law Section (chmn. pub. health com. 1974-78), Assn. of Bar of City of N.Y. Health Law Com., Am. Assn. Hosp. Attys., Nat. Health Lawyers Assn., Hosp. Fin. Mgmt. Assn. (advanced), Yale Club. Home: 23 Winged Foot Dr Larchmont NY 10538-1124 Office: 17th Fl 909 3rd Ave New York NY 10022-5508

BORSOS, ROBERT BRUCE, lawyer; b. Kalamazoo, Mich., Aug. 19, 1951; s. Robert Louis and Shirley (Isabelle) B.; m. Sandra Sue Asquini, Aug. 3, 1974; children: Mark, Eric. BS, Western Mich. U., 1973; JD, Notre Dame U., 1976. Bar: Mich. 1985, U.S. Dist. Ct. (we. dist.) Mich. 1985, U.S. Ct. Appeals (6th cir.). Ptnr. Kreis, Enderle, Callander & Hudgins, Kalamazoo, 1976—. Mem. Ambucs Club, Rotary, County C. of C. (chmn.). Bankruptcy, Corporate, general, Estate planning. Office: Kreis Enderle Callander & Hudgins One Moors Bridge Kalamazoo MI 49002

BORTMAN, DAVID, lawyer; b. Detroit, Sept. 17, 1938; s. Erwin Arne and Miriam Elaine (Shapiro) B. BA, U. Mich., 1962, JD, 1965. Bar: Mich. 1965, Ill. 1971. Asst. prosecutor Wayne County, Detroit, 1965-71; staff atty. Fed. Defender, Chgo., 1971-73; trial atty. SEC, Chgo., 1974-77; sole practice Chgo., 1977-79; ptnr. Bortman, Meyer & Barasa, Chgo., 1980-90; pvt. practice L.A., 1990—. Mem. Fed. Ct. Jury Instrns. Com., Chgo., 1984—85; mem. adv. bd. Air Force Office of Pub. Affairs. Chmn. telethon com. Muscular Dystrophy Assn., Chgo., 1984; pres. Met. Chgo. Air Force Comty. Coun., 1985-88; mem. World Affairs Coun. Mem. ABA, ATLA, Acad. of TV Arts and Scis., State Bar Calif., Los Angeles County Bar Assn. (mem. lawyer referral com.), Fed. Bar Assn. (bd. dirs. Chgo. chpt. 1985-90), Rotary, U. Mich. Club of L.A., U. Mich. Club of Chgo. (bd. govs. 1987-89), Union League of Chgo. (bd. dirs. 1986-89), Variety Club Children's Charities, Jonathan Club, Thalians Charity, West L.A. C. of C. (bd. dirs.), Century City C. of C. (bd. dirs., co-chmn. Entertainment Industry Coun.). Jewish. Federal civil litigation, Criminal, Securities. Home: 11908 Dorothy St Apt 102 Los Angeles CA 90049-5330

BOSKEY, BENNETT, lawyer; b. N.Y.C., Aug. 14, 1916; s. Meyer and Janet (Lauterstein) B.; m. Shirley Ecker, July 3, 1940 (dec. 1998). AB, Williams Coll., 1935; LL.B., Harvard U., 1939. Bar: N.Y. 1940, U.S. Supreme Ct. 1943, D.C. 1949. Spl. asst. to Atty. Gen. U.S. Dept. Justice, Washington, 1943; advisor on enemy property U.S. Dept. State, Washington, 1946-47; atty. U.S. Atomic Energy Commn., Washington, 1947-49, dep. gen. counsel, 1949-51; ptnr. firm Volpe, Boskey & Lyons (and predecessors), Washington, 1951-96. Law clk. Judge Learned Hand, 1939-40, Justice Stanley Reed, 1940-41, Chief Justice Harlan F. Stone, 1941-43; trustee Analytic Svcs. Inc., Arlington, Va., 1962-91; adv. bd. internat. legal studies program Am. U., 1987-99. Chmn. bd. trustees Primary Day Sch., Bethesda, Md., 1969— . Served with U.S. Army, 1943-46. Mem. ABA, Am. Law Inst. (treas. 1975—, mem. coun., Am. Law Inst.-ABA com. on continuing profl. edn. 1985—), Am. Soc. Internat. Law (bd. rev. and devel. 1973-88). Non-profit and tax-exempt organizations, Probate (including wills, trusts), Alternative dispute resolution. Office: Ste 600 1800 Massachusetts Ave NW Washington DC 20036-1222

BOSL, PHILLIP L. lawyer; b. Feb. 27, 1945; BA, U. Calif., Santa Barbara, 1968; JD, U. So. Calif., 1975. Bar: Calif. 1975. Ptnr. Gibson, Dunn & Crutcher LLP, L.A., 1983—. Mem. U. So. Calif. Law Rev., 1973-75. Officer USCG, 1969-72. Mem. ABA, Los Angeles County Bar Assn., Fed. Bar Assn., Assn. Bus. Trial Lawyers Am., Securities Industry Assn. (compliance and legal divsn.), Inst. Corp. Counsel (gov.), Nat. Assn. Securities Dealers (arbitrator), Order of Coif. General civil litigation, Securities, Alternative dispute resolution. Home: 6226 Napoli Ct Long Beach CA 90803-4800 Office: Gibson Dunn & Crutcher LLP 333 S Grand Ave Ste 5300 Los Angeles CA 90071-3197 E-mail: pbosl@gibsondunn.com.

BOSLY, THIERRY H. lawyer; b. Brussels, Nov. 22, 1968; s. Henri Bosly and Ghislaine Vanhalewyn; m. Maïte Rapaille; children: Harien, Victoria, Madeleine. JD, U. Cath. Louvain, 1992; LLM, Georgetown U., 1995. Bar: Brussels. Atty. Vander Borght, Brussels, 1992—97; sr. assoc. Linklaters, Brussels, 1997—2003; ptnr. White & Case, Brussels, 2003—. Cons. House of Reps. Belgium, Brussels. Author: Insolvency Law, 2002. Recipient prize, Am. Bankruptcy Law Jour., 1995. Mergers and acquisitions, Bankruptcy. Home: Brederode 13 1000 Brussels Belgium Office: White & Case Rue de la Loi 52 1040 Brussels Belgium Fax: 23-2 213.16.26. E-mail: tbosly@whitecase.com.

BOSS, AMELIA HELEN, law educator, lawyer; b. Balt., Apr. 3, 1949; d. Myron Theodore and Loretta (Oakjones) B.; m. Roger S. Clark, Mar. 3, 1979; children: Melissa, Seymour, Edward, Ashley. Student, Oxford (Eng.) U., 1968; BA in Sociology, Bryn Mawr, 1970; JD, Rutgers U., 1975. Bar: N.J. Pa., U.S. Dist. Ct. (ea. dist.) N.J., U.S. Dist. Ct. (ea. dist.) Pa., U.S. Supreme Ct., U.S. Ct. Appeals (3d cir.). Law clk. Hon. Milton B. Cranford N.J. Supreme Ct., 1975-76; assoc. Pepper, Hamilton & Scheetz, Phila., 1976-78; assoc. prof. law Rutgers U. Sch. Law, Camden, N.J., 1983-87, Temple U., Phila., 1989-91; prof. law Temple U. Sch. Law, Phila., 1991—, Charles Klein prof. law, 1999—. Vis. prof. law U. Miami Sch. Law, Coral Gables, Fla., 1985-86; Leo Goodwin disting. vis. prof. law Nova U., Sch. Law, 1998; mem. coms. Nat. Conf. Commrs. on Uniform State Laws; U.S. rep. to UN Commn. on Internat. Trade Law. Author: (books) Electronic Data Interchange Agreements: A Guide and Sourcebook, 1993, ABCs of the UCC: Article 2A, ABCs of the UCC: Article 5; editor-in-chief The Data Law Report, 1993-97, The Business Lawyer, 1998-99, ABCs of the UCC; mem. permanent editl. bd. Uniform Comml. Code; contbr. articles to profl. jours. Named among top 50 women lawyers in U.S. Nat. Law Jour., 1998. Fellow Am. Bar Found.; mem. ABA (chmn. bus. law sect. 2000-01, chmn. sect. officers conf. 2001—), Internat. Bar Assn., Am. Law Inst. (coun. 2000—), Am. Bankruptcy Inst., Am. Coll. Comml. Fin. Lawyers, Nat. Assn. Women Lawyers. Home: 309 Westmont Ave Haddonfield NJ 08033-1714 Office: Temple U Sch Law 1719 N Broad St Philadelphia PA 19122-6002

BOSS, LENARD BARRETT, lawyer; b. Passaic, N.J., Mar. 6, 1960; s. Lawrence Steven and Laura (Ziegler) Boss. BA in Rhetoric, Bates Coll., 1982; JD with high honors, George Washington U., 1985. Bar: Pa. 1985, DC 1986, Md. 1995, US Ct Appeals (4th and 11th cirs) 1986, US Dist Ct DC 1987, US Ct Appeals (DC cir) 1987, US Ct Appeals (3d cir) 1988, US Supreme Ct 1989. Assoc. Asbill, Junkin, Myers & Buffone, Washington, 1986-91; ptnr. Asbill, Junkin & Myers, Washington, 1991-95; asst. fed. pub. defender Fed. Pub. Defender's Office, Washington, 1995-2000; ptnr. Asbill, Junkin, Moffitt & Boss, Washington, 2000—02, Asbill, Moffitt & Boss, Washington, 2002—. Adj. prof. George Washington U. Law Sch., 1999—; co-chair practitioners adv. group U.S. Sentencing Commn., 2000—. Avocations: films, music, sports. General civil litigation, Criminal. Office: Ste 200 1615 New Hampshire Ave NW Washington DC 20009-2520 E-mail: boss@ambdc.com.

BOSSES, STEVAN J. lawyer; b. Bronx, N.Y., July 29, 1937; s. Fred and Frieda (Picard) B.; m. Abbye Z. Bosses, May 24, 1964; children: Donna Lynne, David Keith, Gary Philip. BME, Cornell U., 1960; LLB, Columbia U., 1963. Bar: N.Y. 1963, U.S. Dist. Ct. (so. dist.) N.Y. 1964, U.S. Dist. Ct. (ea. dist.) N.Y. 1964, U.S. Patent Office 1964, U.S. Ct. Appeals (2d cir.) 1970, U.S. Ct. Appeals (3rd cir.) 1979, U.S. Ct. Appeals (fed. cir.) 1982, U.S. Supreme Ct. 1989. Assoc. Watson Leavenworth Kelton & Taggart, N.Y.C., 1963-71, ptnr., 1972-81, Fitzpatrick, Cella, Harper & Scinto, N.Y.C., 1981—. Mem. ABA, ASME, N.Y. State Bar Assn., Am. Intellectual Property Law Assn., Fed. Bar Coun. (trustee 1989-94), Fed. Cir. Bar Assn. N.Y. Intellectual Property Law Assn. Federal civil litigation, Patent, Trademark and copyright. Home: 19 Springdale Rd Scarsdale NY 10583-7330 Office: 30 Rockefeller Plz New York NY 10112-0002 E-mail: sbosses@fchs.com.

BOSSON, RICHARD CAMPBELL, judge; b. Balt., Mar. 19, 1944; s. Albert D. and Elizabeth S. (Schoeffer) B.; m. Gloria Candelaria, Jan. 9, 1971; children: Christopher, Monica. BA, Wesleyan U., Middletown, Conn., 1966; JD, Georgetown U., 1969. Bar: Conn. 1969, N. Mex. 1970, U.S. Dist. Ct. N. Mex. 1970. Atty Legal Aid Soc. of Albuquerque, 1970-73; staff atty. Mexican Am. Legal Def. Fund, 1974, Latin Am. Tchg. Fellow, Tufts U., Bogota, Colombia, 1975; chief of civil div. Atty. Gen. Office, Santa Fe, 1976-78; sr. ptnr. Bosson & Campa P.A., Santa Fe, 1980—94; judge Ct. of Appeals, 1994—2002, State Supreme Ct., 2002—. Candidate Dem. nomination for Atty. Gen of N. Mex., 1978; active in Dem. Orgn. of N. Mex., 1978—; trustee Orchestra, Santa Fe. Reginald Heber Smith fellow. Mem. N.Mex. Bar Assn., N.Mex. Trial Lawyers Assn. (bd. dirs. 1980—), Nat. Assn. Bond Lawyers, Am. Trial Lawyers Assn. Avocations: running athletics, music, reading, politics. Home: 1470 Miracerros Loop N Santa Fe NM 87505-4022*

BOST, THOMAS GLEN, lawyer, educator; b. Oklahoma City, July 13, 1942; s. Burl John and Lorene Bell (Croka) B.; m. Sheila K. Pettigrew, Aug. 27, 1966; children: Amy Elizabeth, Stephen Luke, Emily Anne, Paul Alexander. BS in Acctg. summa cum laude, Abilene Christian U., 1964; JD, Vanderbilt U., 1967. Bar: Tenn. 1967, Calif. 1969. Instr. David Lipscomb Coll., Nashville, 1967; asst. prof. law Vanderbilt U., Nashville, 1967-68; ptnr. Latham & Watkins, Los Angeles, 1968-99; prof. law Pepperdine U., 2000—. Lectr. on taxation subjects. Chmn. bd. regents, law sch. bd. visitors Pepperdine U., Malibu, Calif., 1980-2000; chmn. bd. trustees Pacific Legal Found., 2000-02. Mem. ABA (chmn. standards of tax practice com., sec. taxation 1988-90), State Bar of Calif., Los Angeles County Bar Assn. (chmn. taxation sect. 1981-82), Calif. Club (L.A.), Beach Club (Santa Monica). Republican. Mem. Ch. of Christ. Corporate taxation, Personal income taxation, State and local taxation.

BOSTICK, GEORGE HALE, lawyer; b. Birmingham, Ala., Dec. 9, 1944; s. Raymond Ellis and Elizabeth (George) Bostick; m. Rebecca Ann Vernon, Dec. 28, 1968; children: Matthew Ellis, Katherine Martin. BA in Econs., Emory U., 1967; JD, U. Va., 1973. Bar: Va. 73, DC 74, U.S. Tax Ct. 77, U.S., Ct. Claims 78, U.S. Supreme Ct. 79. Law clk. to judge U.S. Ct. Appeals (5th cir.), Montgomery, Ala., 1973—74; assoc. Sutherland, Asbill & Brennan, Washington, 1974—79, ptnr., 1979—. Adj. prof. law Georgetown U. Law Sch., Washington, 1978—80; spkr. in field. Mem., notes editor: U. Va. Law Rev., 1971—73; contbr. articles to profl. jours. Mem. Barkley Forum Found., Atlanta, 1968—; alumni rep. Emory U. Admissions Office, Atlanta, 1978—88; trustee Old Presbyn. Meeting House, Alexandria, Va., 2003—. Stipe scholar, 1963—64, Lockheed Leadership scholar, 1963—67. Fellow: Am. Coll. Employee Benefits Counsel; mem.: ABA (bus. law sect. rep. ABA joint com. on employee benefits 1983—88, bus. law sect. employee benefits and exec. compensation com. 1986—88, chmn. 1987—88, chmn. tax sect. subcom on unfunded deferred compensation 1988—91, chmn. 1988—92, exec. compensation task force mem. 1991—94, vice chmn.), Nat. Inst. on Compensation for Execs. and Dirs. (co-chmn. 1987—93). Pension, profit-sharing, and employee benefits, Corporate taxation. Home: 920 Vicar Ln Alexandria VA 22302-3421 Office: Sutherland Asbill & Brennan LLP 1275 Pennsylvania Ave NW Washington DC 20004-2415 E-mail: gbostick@sablaw.com.

BOSTWICK, JAMES STEPHEN, lawyer; b. Pasadena, Calif., Jan. 15, 1943; s. Jack Raymond and Rhoda Loraine (Fox) B.; children from a previous marriage: Brenton Reid, Grant Evan, Blake Powell; m. Marti Philips; children: Taylor, Carter. MS, U. Wash., 1965; JD, Hastings Coll. Law, 1968. Bar: Calif. 1968, Hawaii 1981. Pvt. practice, San Francisco, 1968; assoc. Walkup, Downing, Sterns & Poore, 1968-73; ptnr. Walkup, Downing & Sterns, 1973-77, Sterns, Bostwick & Tehin, 1977-79; sr. ptnr. Bostwick & Tehin, 1979-96, Bostwick & Assocs., 1996—. Faculty Coll. Advocacy, 1976—, Hastings seminar on trial practice; lectr. in field. Recipient Trial Achievement award San Francisco Trial Lawyers Assn., 1979, Presidential Award of Merit, CAOC. Fellow Internat. Acad. Trial Lawyers (sec. internat. rels. 1997-99, bd. dirs. 1993—, dean 2000—, v.p. 2001, pres. elect 2002); mem. Consumer Attys. Calif. (Presdl. Merit award), Inner Circle Advocates (chmn. profl. liability legis. com. 1975-77, bd. dirs. 1978-85), Am. Bd. Profl. Liability Attys. (diplomate, founding mem.), Hawaii Acad. Plaintiff's Attys., San Francisco Trial Lawyers Assn. (bd. dirs., chmn. patients litigation fund com., chmn. jud. liaison com., nat. cert. com., Best Lawyer Am. personal injury litgation sect. 1987—). Democrat. General civil litigation, Personal injury (including property damage), Professional liability. Office: 4 Embarcadero Ctr Ste 750 San Francisco CA 94111-4171 E-mail: james@bostwickfirm.com.

BOSTWICK, RICHARD RAYMOND, retired lawyer; b. Billings, Mont., Mar. 17, 1918; s. Leslie H. and Maude (Worthington) B.; m. Margaret Florence Brooks, Jan. 17, 1944; children: Michael, Patricia, Ed, Dick. Student, U. Colo., 1937-38; AB, U. Wyo., 1943, JD, 1947. Bar: Wyo. 1947. Claim atty. Hawkeye Casualty Co., Casper, Wyo., 1948-49; ptnr. Murane & Bostwick, Casper, 1949-91; ret., 1991. Lectr. U. Wyo. Coll. Law. Contbr. articles profl. jours. Past trustee Casper YMCA; dep. dir. Civil Def., 1954-58; chmn. local SSS, 1952-70; mem. curriculum coordinating com. Natrona Co. Sch. Dist. 2, High Sch. Dist.; Wyom. rep. adv. com. U.S. Tenth Circuit Ct. Appeals, 1985-87; mem. U. Wyo. Coll. Law Adv. Com.,

1987-91. Capt. AUS, 1943-46. Decorated Bronze Star medal; recipient Silver Merit awards Am. Legion. Mem. ABA (Harrison Tweed award 1968), Am. Coll. Trial Lawyers, Wyo. Bar Assn. (pres. 1964-65, 1st Pro Bono award 1987), Natrona County Bar Assn. (pres. 1956), Am. Judicature Soc. (exec. com. 1973-75, sec. 1975-77 Herbert Harley award), Internat. Assn. Def. Counsel, Fedn. Ins. and Corp. Counsel, Nat. Conf. Bar Pres. (exec. council 1970-72), Internat. Soc. of Barristers (dir. 1971-76, pres. 1975), Am. Legion (dir. 1951-58, post comdr. 1953-54), Wyo. Alumni Assn. (trustee 1955-57), Casper C. of C. (chmn. legis. com. 1955-57, dir. 1959-62, v.p.). Lodges: Masons, Shriners, KT. Presbyterian. Home: 1137 Granada Ave Casper WY 82601-5932

BOSWELL, WILLIAM PARET, lawyer; b. Washington, Oct. 24, 1946; s. Yates Paret and Mary Frances (Hyland) B.; m. Barbara Stelle Schroeder, Sept. 6, 1969; children: Susan Anne, Sarah Mary, Christina Catherine. BA cum laude, Cath. U., 1968; JD, U. Va., 1971. Bar: Va. 1971, D.C. 1972, U.S. Ct. Mil. Appeals 1972, U.S. Supreme Ct. 1975, Pa. 1978. Atty. Peoples Natural Gas Co., Pitts., 1978-82, asst. sec., gen. atty., 1982-85, sec., gen. counsel, 1985-88, v.p., gen. counsel, sec., 1989-99; gen. counsel Hope Gas, Inc., Pitts., 1998—99; dep. gen. counsel Consol. Natural Gas Co., Pitts., 1999-2000, Dominion Resources, Inc., Pitts., 2000; ptnr. McGuireWoods LLP, Pitts., 2000—. Mem. exec. com. Gas Industry Stds. Bd., 1994—97, bd. dirs., 1998—2001, chmn., 2001; bd. dirs. N.Am. Energy Stds. Bd., 2002—, chmn., 2002—03; named founding chmn. 2003N.Am. Energy Stds. Bd. Pres. Borough Coun., Osborne, Pa., 1984-97, mayor, 1998—; bd. dirs. Mendelssohn Choir Pitts., 1986-2001, pres. 1997-98; trustee Laughlin Found., 1995—. Capt. JAGC, USAF, 1971-78, col. USAFR, 1978-98, ret. Decorated Legion of Merit; knight Order of Malta, knight Equestrian Order of Holy Sepulchre (Vatican). Mem. ABA (chair gas com. 1995-2000, chair infrastructure security com. 2003—), Pa. Bar Assn., D.C. Bar Assn., Va. Bar Assn., Am. Gas Assn. (chair regulatory com. 1996-98), Pa. Gas Assn. (chmn. 1989-90), Am. Corp. Counsel Assn. (pres. Pa. chpt. 1991-92, Excellence in Corporate Practice award 1998), Am. Soc. Corp. Secs., City Club Pitts., Army and Navy Club D.C. Republican. Roman Catholic. Avocations: reading, walking. Corporate, general, Oil, gas, and mineral, Utilities, public. Home: 405 Hare Ln Sewickley PA 15143-2050 Office: Dominion Tower 23 Fl 625 Liberty Ave Pittsburgh PA 15222-3142

BOTELHO, BRUCE MANUEL, former state attorney general, mayor; b. Juneau, Alaska, Oct. 6, 1948; s. Emmett Manuel and Harriet Iowa (Tieszen) Botelho; m. Guadalupe Alvarez Breton, Sept. 23, 1988; children: Alejandro Manuel, Adriana Regina. Student, U. Heidelberg, Federal Republic of Germany, 1970; BA, Willamette U., 1971, JD, 1976. Bar: Alaska 1976, U.S. Ct. Appeals (9th cir.) 1976, U.S. Supreme Ct. 1979. Asst. atty. gen. State of Alaska, Juneau, 1976—83, 1987—89, dep. commr., acting commr. Dept. of Revenue, 1983-86; mayor City, Borough of Juneau, 1988—91, dep. atty. gen., 1991—94; atty. gen. State of Alaska, 1994—2002. Chmn. Alaska Resources Corp., 1984—86; exec. com. Conf. of Western Attys. Gen., 1997—2002. Editor: Willamette Law Jour., 1975—76; contbr. articles to profl. jours. Pres. Juneau Human Rights Commn., 1978—80, Alaska Coun. Am. Youth Hostels, 1979—81, Juneau Arts and Humanities Coun., 1981—83; pres. S.E. Alaska Area Coun. Boy Scouts Am., 1991—93, 2001—, commr. S.E. Alaska Area Coun., 1993—2000; pres. Juneau World Affairs Coun., 2000—; chmn. Gov.'s Conf. on Youth and Justice, 1995—96, Gov. Task Force on Confidentiality of Childrens Procs., 1998—2002; trustee Alaska Children's Trust, 1996—2000, Alaska Permanent Fund, 2000—02; co-chmn. Alaska Justice Assessment Commn., 1997—2002; active Commn. for Justice Across the Atlantic, 1999—; chmn. Alaska Criminal Justice Coun., 2000—02; Assembly mem. Borough of Juneau, 1983—86; bd. dirs. Found. for Social Innovations, Alaska, 1990—93, Alaska Econ. Devel. Coun., 1985—87; chmn. adminstrv. law sect. Alaska Bar Assn., 1981—82. Recipient Silver Beaver award, Boy Scouts Am., 2000. Mem.: Nat. Assn. Attys. Gen. (exec. com. 1998—). Democrat. Methodist. Avocation: dancing.

BOTHWELL, ANTHONY PEIRSON XAVIER, SR., lawyer, educator; b. Washington, Aug. 12, 1944; s. Frederick Charles Jr. and Catherine Hannon Bothwell; m. Chung Thi Nguyen, Dec. 22, 1973 (div. Nov. 1999); children: Anthony Peirson Xavier Jr., Thomas Theodore Nguyen. BS in Fgn. Svc., Georgetown U., 1966; MS, Boston U., 1968; JD, John F. Kennedy Sch. Law, 1998; LLM with highest honors, Golden Gate U., 2000. Bar: Calif. 2000, U.S. Dist. Ct. (no. dist.) Calif., U.S. Ct. Appeals D.C. Editor AP, Miami, Fla., 1970-73; comms. coord. Fla. Power and Light Co., Miami, 1973-78; cmty. rels. mgr. Wis. Power and Light Co., Madison, 1978-83; dir. pub. affairs Lawrence Livermore Nat. Lab., Livermore, Calif., 1983-85; cons. Livermore, 1985-88; tax specialist IRS, Oakland, Calif., 1988—2001; pvt. practice San Francisco, 1999—; law prof. John F. Kennedy U. Sch. Law, Walnut Creek, Calif., 2000—. Newsroom clk. The Washington Post, 1969-70; acting news dir. Radio Sta. WBRK-AM, Pittsfield, Mass., 1967; cons. Atomic Indsl. Forum, Washington, 1981-83. Contbr. studies to profl. publs.; asst. editor: Computer World, 1967-68. City campaign chmn. Jesse Jackson for Pres., Livermore, 1988; cons. policy ethics Ams. for Energy Independence, Washington, 1980-82; cons. energy ethics com. Nat. Conf. of Cath. Bishops, Washington, 1981-83; chmn. City Coun. Adv. Com. on Energy and Environment, Livermore, 1985-87; asst. to chmn. Mass. Rep. Fin. Com., 1967-68. Recipient 1st pl. award on Commemoration of 50th Anniversary of Universal Declaration of Human Rights, San Francisco chpt. UN Assn. of USA, 1999. Mem. Internat. Bar Assn., State Bar Calif., Hist. Soc. of U.S. Dist. Ct. for No. Calif., San Francisco Bay Area chpt. Nat. Lawyers Guild (exec. bd. 1995-98), Chinese for Affirmative Action, U.S. Holocaust Mus., Rotary Internat. Democrat. Avocation: philately. Office: Law Offices of Anthony P X Bothwell Ste 100 PMB 314 350 Bay St San Francisco CA 94133 E-mail: esquire001@msn.com.

BOTTITTA, JOSEPH ANTHONY, lawyer; b. Mar. 9, 1949; s. Anthony S. and Elizabeth (Bellisano) B.; m. Lynda Joan Kloss, Apr. 14, 1979;children: Michelle Emma, Gregory Joseph. BSBA, Seton Hall U., 1971, JD, 1974. Bar: U.S. Dist. Ct. N.J. 1974, U.S. Supreme Ct. 1981. Ptnr. Rusignola & Pugliese, Newark, 1974-78; sr. ptnr. Joseph A. Bottitta, West Orange, N.J., 1979-88, Gilbert, Gilbert, Schlossberg and Bottitta, 1988-89; pvt. practice, 1989-95; with Bottitta and Bascelli, 1995-99. Chmn. Supreme Ct. Fee Arbitration Com. Dist. V-B., 1984-85; mem. N.J. Uniform Law Commn., 1987-91; mem. N.J. Commn. on Professionalism in Law, 1997—; pres. N.J. Lawyers Svc., 2000—; pres., E-Law.com, 2000—. Fellow: Am. Bar Found.; mem.: ABA, Essex County Bar Assn. (sec. 1983—84, treas. 1984—85, pres.-elect 1985—86, pres. 1986—87), NJ State Bar Assn. (trustee 1988, treas. 1994—95, v.p. 1995—97, pres.-elect 1997—98, pres. 1998—99). Republican. Roman Catholic. Communications, Computer, Corporate, general. Office: c/o NJ Lawyers Svc 2333 Route 22 W Union NJ 07083-8517 E-mail: joeb@njls.com.

BOUCHER, JOSEPH W(ILLIAM), lawyer, accountant, educator, writer; b. Menominee, Mich., Oct. 28, 1951; s. Joseph W. and Patricia (Coon) B.; m. Susan M. De Groot, June 4, 1977; children: Elizabeth, Bridget, Joseph William III. BA, St. Norbert Coll., 1973; JD, U. Wis., 1977, MBA in Fin., 1978. Bar: Wis. 1978, U.S. Dist. Ct. (we. dist.) Wis. 1978; CPA, Wis. Adminstrv. aide to Senator Wis. Senate, Madison, 1977; from assoc. to ptnr. Murphy, Stolper et al., Madison, 1977-84; ptnr. Stolper, Koritzinsky, Brewster & Neider, Madison, 1985-94; mng. ptnr. Stolper, Koritzinsky, Brewster, Neider, Madison, 1989-92, Neider & Boucher, S.C., 1995—. Lectr. bus. U. Wis., Madison, 1980—. Co-author: Organizing a Wisconsin Business Corporation, 1995, 3d edit., 2003, Wisconsin LLCs and LLPs Handbook, 1996, 3d edit., 2003; contbr. articles to Wis. Bar Assn. Bd. dirs. Jackson Found., 1994—99, West Met. Bus. Assn., 1990—95, Dane County United Way., 1986—89, Wis. Chamber Orch., 1990—94, pres., 1993—94; bd. dirs. St. Coletta's, 1997—2001, Edgewood H.S., 1997—2003, chair, 2001—03; mem. bd. advisors St. Mary's Med. Ctr., Madison, 1989—91. Named one of Outstanding Young Men of Am., 1979; named Wis. Lawyer Advocate of Yr., SBA, 1983. Mem. ABA, AICPA (mem. bd. examiners, mem. bus. law subcom. 1987-90), Wis. Bar Assn., Wis. State Bar Assn. (mem. corp. com. 1991—, co-chairperson interprofl. com. 1992-95, chair ltd. liability co. subcom.), Dane County Bar Assn., Wis. Inst. CPAs, U. Wis. Bus. Alumni Assn. (bd. dirs. 1980-87). Roman Catholic. Avocations: sports, reading. Commercial, contracts (including sales of goods; commercial financing), Corporate, general, Corporate taxation. Office: Neider & Boucher SC 440 Science Dr Madison WI 53711-1064

BOUDIN, MICHAEL, federal judge; b. N.Y.C., Nov. 29, 1939; s. Leonard and Jean Boudin; m. Martha Field, Sept. 18, 1984. BA, Harvard Coll., 1961, LLB, 1964. Bar: N.Y. 1964, D.C. 1967. Law clk. U.S. Ct. Appeals (2d cir.), 1964—65, U.S. Supreme Ct., 1965—66; assoc. firm Covington & Burling, Washington, 1966—72, ptnr., 1972—87; dep. asst. atty. gen. anti-trust divsn. Dept. Justice, Washington, 1987—90; judge U.S. Dist. Ct. (D.C. dist.), Washington, 1990—92, U.S. Ct. Appeals, Boston, 1992—98. Vis. prof. Harvard Law Sch., 1982—83, lectr., 1983—98, U. Pa. Law Sch., 1984—85. Contbr. articles to profl. jours. Mem.: ABA, Am. Law Inst. Office: US Ct Appeals 1st Cir 1 Courthouse Way Ste 7710 Boston MA 02210-3009

BOUDREAU, DANIEL J. state supreme court justice; b. Natick, Mass., 1947; m. Faith Boudreau, 1972. BA, Boston Coll., 1969; MA, Rutgers U., 1972; JD, U. Tulsa, 1976. Pvt. practice, Broken Arrow, Okla., 1976—80; trial judge Tulsa County, Okla., 1980—92; judge, then vice-chief judge Okla. Ct. Civil Appeals, 1992-99; justice Okla. Supreme Ct., Oklahoma City, 1999—, Appellate Ct. on the Judiciary, 2001. E-mail: daniel.boudreau@oscn.net.

BOUKIS, KENNETH, lawyer; b. Cleve., Aug. 28, 1940; s. John and Georgia Boukis; m. Pascalia Mageros, Sept. 8, 1968; children: John Paul, Peter M., Elayna G., Andrew C. BBA, Fenn Coll., Cleve., 1963; JD, Case Western Res. U., 1966; LLM, Cleve. State U., 1976. BAr: Ohio 1966. Ptnr. Strangward, Marshman, Lloyd & Malaga, Cleve., 1966-69, Schaaf, Chalko & Boukis, Cleve., 1970-71, Hohmann, Boukis & Boukis, Cleve., 1971-98, Hohmann, Boukis & Curtis, Cleve., 1998—. Mem. adv. com. Fed. Ct. Chmn. Cleve. Metro. Com., Internat. Orthodox Christian Charities. Mem. Nat. Lawyers Assn., Ohio Bar Assn., Cleve. Bar Assn., Am. Hellenic Edn. and Progressive Assn. (pres.), Cleveland Met. Area Intl. Orthodox Christian Charities (chmn.). Republican. Greek Orthodox. Avocations: bible study, church work, fishing, health foods, exercise. General civil litigation, Commercial, contracts (including sales of goods; commercial financing), General practice. Home: 8230 W Ridge Dr Broadview Heights OH 44147-1033 Office: Hohmann Boukis Curtis Co LPA 520 Standard Bldg 1370 Ontario St Cleveland OH 44113-1701 E-mail: kboukis@clevelandlawyers.cc.

BOULANGER, CAROL SEABROOK, lawyer; b. N.Y.C., Sept. 14, 1942; d. John M. and Anne (Schlaudecker) Seabrook; m. Jacques P. Boulanger, June 1, 1974; children: Rodolphe, Adriana. BA, Swarthmore Coll., 1964; LLB, U. Pa., 1969. Bar: N.Y. 1970, U.S. Tax Ct. 1970. Assoc. Baker & McKenzie, N.Y.C., 1969-71, Wender, Murase & White, N.Y.C., 1971-75, ptnr., 1975-82, Boulanger, Finley & Hicks, N.Y.C., 1982-84, Drinker, Biddle & Reath, N.Y.C., 1984-89, Boulanger, Finley & Hicks, P.C., N.Y.C., 1989—96, Winthrop Stimson Putnam & Roberts, N.Y.C., 1996—2000, Pillsbury Winthrop, LLP, N.Y.C., 2001—. Founding mem. ARCS Found. Inc., N.Y.C., sec. 1973-75, v.p. 1975-80; bd. dirs. Swarthmore Coll., 1977-81; trustee, treas. Am. Friends of the Victoria and Albert Mus., Inc., 1999—. Mem. ABA (tax sect., internat. law sect.), Assn. Bar City of N.Y. (internat. law com. 1980-84, fgn. and comparative law com., 1984-85, chmn. 1985-88). Private international, Taxation, general.

BOUMA, JOHN JACOB, lawyer; b. Ft. Dodge, Iowa, Jan. 13, 1937; s. Jacob and Gladys Glennie (Cooper) B.; m. Bonnie Jeanne Lane, Aug. 15, 1959; children: John Jeffrey, Wendy Sue, Laura Lynne, Jennifer Ann. BA, U. Iowa, 1958, JD, 1960. Bar: Iowa 1960, Wis. 1960, Ariz. 1962, U.S. Ct. Appeals (9th cir.) 1971, U.S. Ct. Appeals (D.C. cir.) 1971, U.S. Ct. Appeals (10th cir.) 1982, U.S. Tax Ct., 1983, U.S. Supreme Ct. 1975. Assoc. Foley, Sammond & Lardner, Milw., 1960, Snell & Wilmer, Phoenix, 1962-66, ptnr., 1967—, chmn., 1983—. Contbr. articles to profl. jours. Chmn. Phoenix Human Rels. Commn., 1972-75; mem. Phoenix Commn. on LEAP, 1971-72, Phoenix Cmty. Alliance, 1991—; bd. dirs. Phoenix Legal Aid Soc., 1970-76, Ariz. Econ. Coun., 1989-93, Mountain States Legal Found., 1977-95; trustee Ariz. Opera Co., 1984-2002, pres., 1989-91; trustee Phoenix Art Mus., 1994-2000, 2002-, pres., 1996-98. Capt. JAGC, U.S. Army, 1960-62. Recipient Walter E. Craig Disting. Svc. award, 1998, Cmty. Legal Svcs. Decade of Dedication award, 1998, Disting. Achievement medal Ariz. State U. Coll. Law, 1998, Dist. Alumni Award U. Iowa, 2003. Fellow Am. Coll. Trial Lawyers; mem. ABA (Ho. of Dels. 1989—, bd. govs. 1998-2001, editl. bd. 1996-98), Maricopa County Bar Assn. (pres. 1977-78), Nat. Conf. Bar Pres. (exec. coun. 1984-91, pres. 1989-90), Western States Bar Conf. (pres. 1988-89), Ariz. Bar Assn. (pres. 1983-84), Ariz. Bar Found. (pres. 1987-88), Iowa Bar Assn., Wis. Bar Assn., Phoenix Assn. Def. Counsel (pres. 1972), Attys. Liability Assurance Soc. Ltd. (bd. dirs. 1987—, chair 2002-), Iowa Law Sch. Found. (bd. dirs. 1986-2003), Phoenix C. of C. (bd. dirs. 1988-94), Ariz. State Coll. Law Soc. (bd. dirs., pres. 1997-2000), Ariz. Suprme Ct. Spl. Com. on Lawyer Discipline and Profl. Conduct, Order of Coif, Phi Beta Kappa, Phi Eta Sigma, Omicron Delta Kappa. Avocations: fishing, hunting, skiing, travel, golf. Antitrust, Alternative dispute resolution, Federal civil litigation, General civil litigation, State civil litigation, Professional liability, Securities. Home: 800 E Circle Rd Phoenix AZ 85020-4144 Office: Snell & Wilmer One Arizona Ctr Phoenix AZ 85004-2202

BOUMANN, ROBERT LYLE, lawyer; b. Holdrege, Nebr., June 9, 1946; s. John G. (dec.) and Loretta M. (Eckhardt) B. BS, U. Nebr., 1968, JD, 1974. Bar: Nebr. 1974, Colo. 1987; CPA, Nebr. Sr. acct. Peat, Marwick, Main and Co., Denver, 1968-71; atty., asst. sec. K N Energy, Inc., Lakewood, Colo., 1974-96; pvt. practice Golden, Colo., 1996—; nat. claims mgr. Aon Risk Svcs., Inc., Golden, Colo., 1998—. Bd. dirs. Srs. Independence Agy. West Jefferson County, Inc., 1999-2001. Treas. YMCA, Hastings, 1979-80. Mem. Nebr. Soc. CPAs, Nebr. State Bar Assn., Colo. State Bar Assn., ABA, Jaycees (treas. Hastings chpt. 1977-78), Phi Eta Sigma, Beta Gamma Sigma, Pi Kappa Alpha. Republican. Roman Catholic. Avocations: racquetball, golf. Corporate, general, Pension, profit-sharing, and employee benefits, Taxation, general. Office: 14118 W 1st Ave Golden CO 80401-5353 E-mail: rboumann@aol.com.

BOUNDS, CURTIS PRESTON, lawyer; b. Salisbury, Md., July 29, 1961; s. Boyd Ira Warren and Shirley Ann Bounds; m. Pamela Frances Farinella, May 31, 1987; children: Thomas, Elizabeth, Raymond, Mary, John, Margaret. BA, U. Dallas, 1983; JD, U. Va., 1990. Bar: Del. 1990, U.S. Dist. Ct. Del. 1991. Mgmt. analyst U.S. Dept. Edn., Washington, 1985—87; atty., dir. The Bayard Firm, Wilmington, Del., 1990—. Mem.: Del. State Bar Assn. (vice chair family law sect. 2001—). Republican. Roman Catholic. Family and matrimonial, Labor (including EEOC, Fair Labor Standards Act, labor-management relations, NLRB, OSHA). Office: The Bayard Firm 9th Fl 222 Delaware Ave Wilmington DE 19801

BOURGOIN, DAVID L. lawyer, real estate broker, trade broker, educator, video/television producer; b. Jersey City, Mar. 5, 1946; s. Louis Joseph and Irene Mary Bourgoin. BS, St. Peter's Coll., Jersey City, 1968; MBA, UCLA, 1970; JD, U. San Diego, 1987. Bar: Hawaii 1988, Pa. 1989, U.S. Ct. Appeals (fed. cir.) Hawaii 1988, U.S. Internat. Ct. Appeals. Fin. mgr. Mattel Toys, Hawthorne, Calif., 1969-71; music prodr. Topanga Canyon Records, Redondo Beach, Calif., 1971-76; stock broker Dean Witter, LA, 1976-78; prof. U. Hawaii, Honolulu, 1978-80; trade broker Hawaii chi Trading Co., Honolulu, 1978—; pvt. practice Honolulu, 1988—; real estate broker Realty Offices of D.L.B., Honolulu, 1991—. Prof. U. Md., Heidelburg, Germany, 1983-95; vis. prof. mgmt. & internat. studies U. Hawaii, 2003; prodr. TCR Prodns. Capt. USAR, 1973-85. Mem. Hawaii State Bar, Japanese C. of C., K. of C. Avocations: culture, music, sports. Entertainment, Property, real (including real estate development, water), Private international. Office: 1188 Bishop St Ste 2010 Honolulu HI 96813-3308 E-mail: theofficesnet@yahoo.com.

BOURNE, JAMES E. lawyer; b. Charleston, W.Va., Jan. 13, 1940; BA, Ind. U., 1962, JD, 1965. Bar: Ind. 1965. Law clk. to Hon. William E. Steckler, U.S. Dist. Ct. (so. dist.) Ind., 1965—67; atty. Wyatt, Tarrant & Combs, LLP, New Albany, Ind. Mem. faculty Nat. Inst. for Trial Advocacy. Fellow: Am. Coll. Trial Lawyers; mem.: ABA, Ind. State Bar Assn. (pres.-elect 2001—02), Leadership So. Ind., Def. Trial Counsel Ind., Def. Rsch. Inst. Commercial, consumer (including collections, credit), Insurance, General civil litigation. Office: Wyatt Tarrant Combs LLP Cmty Bank Bldg 101 W Spring St New Albany IN 47150-3440*

BOUTIN, PETER RUCKER, lawyer; b. San Francisco, Oct. 6, 1950; s. Frank J. and Charlotte (Downey) B.; m. Suzanne Jones, Aug. 31, 1974; children: Jennifer, Lisa, Kevin. AB, Stanford U., 1972; JD magna cum laude, Santa Clara U., 1975. Bar: Calif. 1975, U.S. Dist. Ct. (no., ea., so. and ctrl. dists.) Calif. 1976, U.S. Ct. Appeals (9th cir.) 1977, U.S. Supreme Ct. 1982. Assoc. Keesal, Young & Logan, Long Beach, Calif., 1975-78, ptnr., 1978-84, mng. ptnr. San Francisco office San Francisco, 1984—. Arbitrator San Francisco Superior Ct., 1989—, Nat. Assn. Securities Dealers, San Francisco, 1980—; mediator San Francisco Superior Ct., 1989—; early neutral evaluation panel U.S. Dist. Ct., 1993—. Co-author: Am. Arbitration Assn. Arbitrator Tng. Materials, 1992; bd. editors: Securities Arbitration Commentator. Mem. Bar Assn. San Francisco, Securities Industry Assn. Compliance and Legal Divsn., Stanford Buck/Cardinal Club. General civil litigation, Labor (including EEOC, Fair Labor Standards Act, labor-management relations, NLRB, OSHA), Securities. Office: Keesal Young & Logan 4 Embarcadero Ctr Ste 1500 San Francisco CA 94111-4122 E-mail: peter.boutin@kyl.com.

BOVA, VINCENT ARTHUR, JR., lawyer, consultant, photographer; b. Pitts., Apr. 25, 1946; s. Vincent A. and Janie (Pope) B.; m. Breda Murphy, Mar. 20, 1971; 1 child, Kate Murphy Bova. BA in Bus. Adminstrn., Alma (Mich.) Coll., 1968; MPA, Ohio State U., 1972; JD, Oklahoma City U., 1975. Bar: Okla. 1975, N.Mex. 1976, U.S. Dist. Ct. 1976, U.S. Tax Ct., 1976, U.S. Ct. Appeals (10th cir.) 1976, U.S. Supreme Ct. 1979. Mktg. and systems rep., computer systems div. RCA, 1968-70; research analyst Research Atlanta, 1972-73; assoc. Threet, Threet, Glass, King & Maxwell, 1976-78; ptnr. Lill & Bova, P.A., 1978-81; sole practice Albuquerque, 1981—. Past pres. Bare Bulls Investment, 1982, Fumilan Investment, 1983, Toastmasters; rsch. analyst urban affairs Ohio Dept. Urban Affairs, Columbus, 1971; panel mem. N.Mex. Med. Rev. Commn., 1981—, N.Mex. Legal/Dental/Osteopathic Podiatry Com., 1981—; v.p. Albuquerque Com. on Fgn. Rels., 2001—; co-owner Albuquerque Photography Gallery. Contbr. articles on organizational behavior and mgmt. to profl. jours. Bd. dirs. Rio Grande Nature Ctr.; pres., v.p. spl. projects S.W. Arts and Crafts Festival, Albuquerque, 1986-89; pol. cons. Nov. Group; mem. N.Mex. Estate Planning Coun., 1978—; sec.-treas., vice-chmn., pres. adv. bd. Salvation Army, 1987—; contbr. Ctr. for Home for Prevention of Domestic Violence, 1984-85, Ronald McDonald House, 1984; past chmn. N.Mex. Workers' Compensation Monthly; mem. advt. com. Supreme Ct. Panel; pres. Salvation Army Adv. Bd., Albuquerque; mem. Edn. Forum; pres., bd. mem. Albuquerque com. on fgn. rels.; moot ct. judge, Albuquerque. With Air N.G., 1969-75. Recipient Pacesetters award Ohio State U., 1972; named one of Outstanding Young Men of Am., 1975, 76. Mem. ATLA (advanced grad. Nat. Coll. Advocacy), Ct. Practice Inst. (advanced diplomate), ABA, N.Mex. Bar Assn. (pres. small firm and solo sect.), State Bar N.Mex. (mem. med. legal panel, med.-dental podiatry legal panel, rep. probate, wills and trusts ann. report), Nat. Def. Lawyers, Assn. (staff chmn. 1986), N.Mex. Trial Lawyers Assn., Internat. Assn. Fin. Planners, Nat. Assn. Social Security Claimants Reps. (past state chmn.), Business Round Table, Albuquerque Bar Assn., N.Mex. Fin. Planning Assn., Sole Practitioners Assn., Image Profls. of the Southwest (pres., bd. mem.), Internat. Credit Assn. (lectr.), Ohio State U. Alumni Assn. of N.Mex. (pres.), Image Profls. of the S.W. (bd. dirs., print chmn. 1996—, pres.), Image Profls. S.W. (photography award 1996, Best of Show 2000, 10 others, 14 awards 1999), Profl. Photography Assn., Photog. Soc. Am. (pres. chpt.), Toastmasters (past pres., v.p., edn. chmn., Able Toastmaster award), Millionaires Tip Club, Enchanted Lens Camera Club (pres.), Profl. Photographers Am. (assoc. mem.; 8 awards 1999), Albuquerque Knife and Fork (pres., v.p., sec.-treas., bd. dirs.), Inn of the Ct., Zia Scuba Club, Phi Alpha Delta, Sigma Tau Gamma (pres. Albuquerque com. on fgn. rels.), co-owner of Albuq. Photographors Gallery. Democrat. Presbyterian. Avocations: flower gardening, photography - video and still, computers, investing, reading. General civil litigation, Commercial, consumer (including collections, credit), Probate (including wills, trusts). Office: 5716 Osuna Rd NE Albuquerque NM 87109-2527

BOVAIRD, BRENDAN PETER, lawyer; b. N.Y.C., Mar. 9, 1948; s. John Francis and Margaret Mary (Endrizzi) B.; m. Carolyn Warren Boyle, Dec. 18, 1971; children: Anne Warren, Sarah Grant. BA, Fordham U., 1970; JD, U. Va., 1973. Bar: N.Y. 1974, D.C. 1980, Pa. 1983, U.S. Dist. Ct. (so. and ea. dists.) N.Y. 1974, U.S. Ct. Appeals (2d cir.) 1974. Atty., Dewey, Ballantine, Bushby, Palmer & Wood, N.Y.C., 1973-82; asst. gen. counsel Campbell Soup Co., Camden, N.J., 1982-90; sr. v.p., gen. counsel, sec. Orion Pictures Corp., N.Y.C., 1990-91; counsel, mem. exec. com. Wyeth-Ayerst Internat. Inc., St. Davids, Pa., 1992-95; pres. KDH Inc., 1994—; v.p., gen. counsel UGI Corp., Valley Forge, Pa., 1995—; v.p., gen. counsel AmeriGas Propane, Inc., Valley Forge, 1995—; bd. dirs. Motion Picture Export Assn. Am., Inc., 1990-91, United Valley Ins. Co. Mem. MPAA (legal com. 1990-91), ABA (corp., bus. law sect., internat. law sect.), Aircraft Owners and Pilots Assn., Phila. Country Club, Phi Delta Phi. Corporate, general, Private international, Mergers and acquisitions. Office: UGI Corp PO Box 858 Valley Forge PA 19482-0858

BOVARNICK, PAUL SIMON, lawyer; b. N.Y.C., Sept. 15, 1952; s. Murray Elliott and Esther (Waters) B.; m. Nan Garner Waller, Aug. 31, 1980; children: Polly Ames, Kate Garner, Samuel Patton. BA, Claremont Men's Coll., 1974; JD, U. Oreg., 1979. Bar: Oreg. 1979, Mont. 1980, Wash. 2002, U.S. Dist. Ct. Mont. 1980, U.S. Ct. Appeals (9th cir.) 1981, U.S. Dist. Ct. Oreg. 1983, U.S. Dist. Ct. Colo. 1997. Staff atty. Mont. Legal Services, Billings, 1979-80, mng. atty., 1980-82, Oreg. Legal Services, Hillsboro, 1982-83; assoc. Bricker, Zakovics, Portland, Oreg., 1983-85; sole practice Portland, 1985-92; ptnr. Rose, Senders & Bovarnick, Portland, 1993-98, of counsel, 1998—. Designated legal counsel Brotherhood of Locomotive Engrs., Transp. Comms. Union. Chmn., bd. dirs. Forest Park Children's Ctr., Portland, 1986-88, mem., 1985-89; treas. Yellowstone Valley Dem. Club, Billings, 1982; bd. dirs. Oregonians for Individual Rights, Portland, 1984, ACLU, Billings, 1981-82, Rita's Place, 1991-94; sec., bd. dirs. Bridlewide Found. Mem. ATLA, ABA, Mont. Bar Assn., Multnomah County Bar Assn., Oreg. Trial Lawyers Assn., Wash. State Trial Lawyers Assn., Acad. Rail Labor Attys. Avocation: skiing. Labor (including EEOC, Fair Labor Standards Act, labor-management relations, NLRB, OSHA), Personal injury (including property damage), Workers' compensation. Home: 2323 SW 64th Ave Portland OR 97221-1338 Office: 1205 NW 25th Ave Portland OR 97210 E-mail: pbovarnick@rsblaw.net.

BOWDEN, GEORGE NEWTON, judge; b. East Orange, N.J., Nov. 21, 1946; s. W. Paul and Catherine A. (Porter) B. BA, Bowdoin Coll., 1971; JD, U. Maine, 1974. Bar: Wash. 1974, Maine 1975, U.S. Dist. Ct. (we. dist.) Wash. 1978, U.S. Ct. Appeals (9th cir.) 1980, U.S. Supreme Ct. 1982. Asst. county atty. Lincoln County, Wiscasset, Maine, 1974; dep. pros. atty. Grays Harbor County, Montesano, Wash., 1974-76, King County, Seattle, 1976, Snohomish County, Everett, Wash., 1976-79; ptnr. Senter & Bowden, Everett, Wash., 1979-97; judge Snohomish County Superior Ct., Everett, Wash., 1997—. Bd. dirs. Snohomish County Legal Svcs., 2003—. Bd. dirs. Everett Symphony Orch. 1993—, pres. 1996-98; v.p. Driftwood Players, Edmonds, Wash., 1978. Sgt. USMC, 1966-68. Mem. ATLA, NADCL, Wash. State Bar Assn. (CLE com., fee arbitration bd., legal aid and pro bono com.), Wash. Assn. Criminal Def. Lawyers (bd. govs., sec. 1993), Wash. State Trial Lawyers Assn., Snohomish County Bar Assn. (pres. 1995), Rotary. Avocations: scuba diving, skiing, bicycling. Office: Snohomish County Courthouse Superior Ct 3000 Rockefeller Ave M/S502 Everett WA 98201-4046

BOWEN, DUDLEY HOLLINGSWORTH, JR., federal judge; b. Augusta, Ga., June 25, 1941; AB in Fgn. Lang., U. Ga., 1964, LLB, 1965; profesor invitado (hon.), Universidad Externada de Bogotá, 1987. Bar: Ga. 1965, U.S. Dist. Ct. (so. dist.) Ga. 1997-. Pvt. practice law, Augusta, 1968-72; bankruptcy judge U.S. Dist. Ct. (so. dist.) Ga., Augusta, 1972-75, judge, 1979-97, chief judge, 1997—; ptnr. firm Dye, Miller, Bowen & Tucker, Augusta, 1975-79. Bd. dirs. Southeastern Bankruptcy Law Inst., 1976-87; mem. Ct. Security Com. Jud. Conf. U.S., 1987-92. Mem. bd. visitors U. Ga. Sch. Law, 1987-90. Served to 1st lt. inf., U.S. Army, 1966-68. Decorated Commendation medal. Mem. State Bar Ga. (chmn. bankruptcy law sect. 1977), Fed. Judges Assn. (bd. dirs. 1985-90), 11th Cir. Dist. Judges Assn. (sec.-treas. 1988-89, pres. 1991-92). Presbyterian. Office: US Dist Ct PO Box 2106 Augusta GA 30903-2106

BOWEN, LOWELL REED, lawyer; b. Prince Frederick, Md., Jan. 29, 1931; s. Perry Gray and Melba (Hutchins) B.; m. Marilyn Sack, June 14, 1958; children: Mark Holdsworth, David Stockbridge. BA, U. Md., 1952; LLB, U. Md., Balt., 1957. Bar: Md. 1957, U.S. Dist. Ct. Md. 1958, U.S. Ct. Appeals (4th cir.) 1959, U.S. Supreme Ct. 1964. Law clk. to chief judge U.S. Dist. Ct. Md., Balt., 1957—58; assoc. Miles & Stockbridge, Balt., 1958—65, ptnr., 1966—, mng. ptnr., 1974—91, chmn., 2001—02. Lectr. U. Md. Law Sch., 1958-63, U. Balt. Law Sch., 1965-70. Mem., chmn. various coms. Md. Commn. to Revise Annotated Code Md., Annapolis, 1973—; mem. Standing Com. on Rules of Practice and Procedure, Md. Ct. Appeals, Annapolis, 1980—; trustee, chmn. Balt. Opera Co., Inc., 1977-92; mem. Md. Humanities Coun., 1992-97; trustee, pres. Lyric Found., Inc., 1997—. 1st lt. USAF, 1952-54. Mem. ABA, Md. State Bar Assn., Maryland Club, Ctr. Club (bd. govs. 1984-93, sec. 1985-93). Corporate, general. Office: Miles & Stockbridge 36 Iron Mill Garth Cockeysville MD 21030 E-mail: lbowen@milesstockbridge.com.

BOWEN, PATRICK HARVEY, lawyer, consultant; b. Cin., July 7, 1939; s. Albert Vernon and Elsie Matilda (Harvey) B.; m. Karen A. Hunter; 1 child, Harvey Shaw. BA, Marietta Coll., 1961; JD, Duke U., 1964; MBA, Columbia U., 1975. Bar: N.Y. 1965, Conn. 1990. Assoc. Mudge, Rose, Guthrie & Alexander, N.Y.C., 1964-66; atty. Kennecott Copper Corp., N.Y.C., 1966-71, asst. counsel, 1971-79, asst. gen. counsel, 1979-83, asst. sec., 1980-83; sr. assoc. atty. Allied Stores Corp., N.Y.C., 1983-87, v.p., gen. counsel, sec., 1987-88, v.p., 1988-89; pvt. practice Stamford, Conn., 1990—. Mem. ABA, Conn. Bar Assn., N.Y. State Bar Assn., Assn. of Bar of City of N.Y., Am. Soc. Corp. Secs. Avocation: traditional jazz musician. Office: 2001 W Main St Ste 140 Stamford CT 06902-4562 E-mail: phbowen@aol.com.

BOWEN, PETER GEOFFREY, arbitrator, business educator; b. Iowa City, Iowa, July 10, 1939; s. Howard Rothmann and Lois Berntine (Schilling) B.; m. Shirley Johns Carlson, Sept. 14, 1968; children: Douglas Howard, Leslie Johns. BA in Govt. and Econs., Lawrence Coll., 1960; postgrad., U. Wis., 1960-61, U. Denver, 1963-64, U. Colo., 1994. Cert.: expert witness, Denver. V.p. Perry & Butler, Denver, 1972-73; exec. v.p., dir. Little & Co., Denver, 1973; pres. Builders Agy. Ltd., Denver, 1974-75; CEO, gen. ptnr. The Investment Mgmt. Group Ltd., Denver, 1975—. Arbitrator NASD Regulation, Inc., 1996—, Am. Arbitration Assn., 1996—; adj. prof. bus. Colo. Mt. Coll., 1992-2000; arbitrator Eagle County Colo. Atty.'s Office, 1997; asst. prof. bus. adminstrn. and law Regis U., 2000—; continuing legal edn. lectr. on real estate syndications, 1983. Author: A Small Business Primer for Displaced Corporate Executives, 2000; contbr. articles to profl. publs. Vice-chmn. Greenwood Village (Colo.) Planning and Zoning Commn., 1983-85; mem. Vail Planning and Environ. Commn., 1992-96; chmn. emeritus Vail Partnership Environ. Edn. Programs, Inc., 1993-2000; elected mem. City Council Greenwood Village, 1985-86, also mayor pro tem, 1985-86; trustee Vail Mountain Sch. Found., 1987-88. Mem. Colo. Bar Assn. (legal fee arbitration com.), Denver Bar Assn. (legal fee arbitration com. 1997—), Rotary Club (bd. dirs. Vail chpt., named Rotarian of Yr. 1992), Lawrence U. Alumni Assn. (bd. dirs. 1966-72, 82-86). Home: 16006 Double Eagle Dr Morrison CO 80465-9617 E-mail: jsbowen@pcisys.com.

BOWEN, STEPHEN STEWART, lawyer; b. Peoria, Ill., Aug. 23, 1946; s. Gerald Raymond and Frances Arlene (Stewart) B.; m. Ellen Claire Newcomer, Sept. 23, 1972; children: David, Claire. BA cum laude, Wabash Coll., 1968; JD cum laude, U. Chgo., 1972. Bar: Ill. 1972, U.S. Dist. Ct. (no. dist.) Ill. 1972, U.S. Tax Ct. 1977. Assoc. Kirkland & Ellis, Chgo., 1972-78, ptnr., 1978-84, Latham & Watkins, Chgo., 1985—. Adj. prof. DePaul U. Masters in Taxation Program, Chgo., 1976-80; lectr. Practicing Law Inst., N.Y.C., Chgo., L.A., 1978-84, N.Y.C., 1986—. Mem. vis. com. U. Chgo. Div. Sch., 1984—, mem. vis. com. Sch. Law, 1991-93; mem. planning com. U. Chgo. Tax Conf., 1985—, chair, 1995-98; trustee Wabash Coll., 1996—. Fellow Am. Coll. Tax Counsel; mem. ABA, Ill. State Bar Assn., Order of Coif, Met. Club (Chgo.), Econ. Club Chgo., Phi Beta Kappa. Corporate taxation. Office: Latham & Watkins Sears Tower Ste 5800 Chicago IL 60606-6306

BOWEN-MORRIS, NIGEL VAUGHAN, solicitor; b. Barmouth, Wales, Aug. 17, 1961; s. Bernard and Maureen (Towers) Bowen-M. BA with honors, St. Catherine's Coll., Oxford, 1980. Solicitor, Supreme Ct. of Eng. and Wales. Solicitor Watson, Farley & Williams, Greece, 1988-96; mng. ptnr., solicitor Stephenson Harwood, Greece, 1996—. Fellow Royal Geog. Soc. Admiralty, Banking, Finance. Office: Stephenson Harwood Cons Ant Abatielou 1 (Pal Trapezis) 185 36 Piraeus Greece

BOWER, ALLAN MAXWELL, lawyer; b. Oak Park, Ill., May 21, 1936; s. David Robert and Frances Emily Bower; m. Deborah Ann Rottmayer, Dec. 28, 1959. BS, U. Iowa, 1962; JD, U. Miami, Fla., 1968. Bar: Calif. 1969, U.S. Supreme Ct. 1979. Internat. aviation law practice, L.A., 1969—; ptnr. Kern & Wooley, L.A., 1980-85, Bronson, Bronson & McKinnon, L.A., 1985-90, Lane Powell Spears Lubersky, L.A., 1990-99, Bailey & Ptnrs., Santa Monica, Calif., 1999—. Contbr. articles to profl. publs. Mem. Lawyer-Pilots Bar Assn. Republican. Presbyterian. Aviation, General civil litigation, Product liability. Office: Bailey & Ptnrs 2nd Fl 2828 Donald Douglas Loop N Santa Monica CA 90405-2959 Fax: 310-392-8091.

BOWER, GLEN LANDIS, lawyer; b. Highland, Ill., Jan. 16, 1949; s. Ray Landis and Evelyn Ferne Bower. BA, So. Ill. U., 1971; JD (hon.) , Ill. Inst. Tech., 1974. Bar: Ill. 1974, US Ct. Mil. Appeals 1975, US Ct. Appeals (7th cir.) 1976, US Dist Ct. (so. dist.) Ill. 1977, US Dist. Ct. (cen. dist.) Ill. 1992, US Supreme Ct. 1978, US Tax Ct. 1984, US Ct. Claims 1986, US Dist. Ct. (no. dist.) Ill. 1994, US Ct. Veterans Appeals 1995. Sole practice, Effingham, Ill., 1974-83; prosecutor Effingham County, Ill., 1976-79; mem. Ill. House of Reps., Springfield, 1979-83; asst. dir., gen. counsel Ill. Dept. Revenue, Springfield, Ill., 1983-90; Presdl. apptd. chmn. US R.R. Retirement Bd., Chgo., 1990-97; asst. to Ill. Sec. of State, Chgo., 1998-99; apptd. dir. revenue State of Ill., 1999—2003. Mil. aide to Gov. of Ill., 1999-2003; liaison mem. Adminstrv. Conf. of US, 1991-95; mem. Nat. Adv. Com. for Juvenile Justice and Delinquency Prevention, Washington, 1976-80, US Econ. Adv. Bd. of US Dept. Commerce, Washington, 1981-85, Ill. Gen. Assembly State Adv. Com. on Cir. Ct. Fin., Springfield, 1984; mem. Revenue Bd. Appeals, Chgo., 1985-87, chmn., 1986-87; mem. Com. of 50 on Ill. Constn., 1987-88; adv. com. on electronic tax adminstrn. IRS, 2000-2003, So. Ill. U. Pub. Policy Inst., 2000. Co-editor: Handbook on State Taxation, 1991; contbr. articles to profl. jour. Alt. del. Rep. Nat. Conv., Miami Beach, Fla., 1972, Rep. Nat. Conv., New Orleans, 1988, Rep. Nat. Conv. Houston, 1992, Phila., 2000; vice chmn. Effingham County Rep. Ctrl. Com., Ill., 1976-90; bd. dir. Dana-Thomas House Found., Springfield, Ill., 1989-90, So. Ill. U. at Carbondale Found., 1993-2002, pres.'s coun.; trustee McKendree Coll., Lebanon, Ill., 1978-81; chmn. State of Ill. Organ and Tissue Donors Adv. Bd., 1993-98. Lt. col. USAFR, 1974-99, ret. Recipient The Univ. Disting. Svc. award, 1971, Recognition citation Am. Legion, 1980, Outstanding Svc. cert. to tchg. profession Ill. Edn. Assn., 1981, Disting. Svc. award Am. Vets., 1980, 82, Presdl. citation Navy League US, 1981, Constitution award Mus. of Our Nat. Heritage, 1988, Silver Good Citizenship medal Ill. Soc. SAR, 1990, Profl. Achievement award Ill. Inst. Tech., 1993, Friend of History award Ill. State Hist. Soc., 1994, Alumni Achievement award So. Ill. U., 1994, Disting. Alumnus award So. Ill. U. Coll. Liberal Arts, 2000, Outstanding Civilian Svc. Medal, Dept. Army, 2003; named Outstanding Freshman Legislator, Ill. Edn. Assn., 1980, Legislator of Yr., Ill. Assn. Rehab. Socs., 1981, 82, One of 10 Dels. to China, Am. Coun. Young Polit. Leaders, 1988. Fellow: Am. Bar Found. (life), Ill. Bar Found. (life); mem.: ABA (employment taxes com. 1990, adminstrv. practice com. of taxation sect., ct. procedure com., mem. exec. com. nat. assn. state tax bar sects.), Judge Advs. Assn., Am. Coun. Young Political Leaders, US Capitol Hist. Soc. (charter), Effingham County Mental Health Assn. (pub. affairs com. 1977—78), SBA Adv. Coun., Effingham Regional Hist. Soc. (bd. dir. 1973—77), Ill. State Hist. Soc. (v,o, 1979—81, Ralph C. Francis award 1967), Nat. Assn. Tax Adminstrs. (vice chmn. attys. sect. 1985—86, chmn. 1986—88, vice chmn. attys. sect. 1988—89), Effingham County Bar Assn. (sec. 1976—77, pres. 1983—84), Ill. State Bar Assn. (labor law sect. coun. 1976—77, sec. state taxation sect. coun. 1987—88, vice-chair 1988—89, 1988—89, chair 1989—90, sect. coun. on employee benefits 1991—98, 1991—98, sect. coun. on adminstrv. law 2000, Bd. Gov.'s award 1999), Rep. Nat. Lawyers Assn., Fed. Tax Adminstrs. (bd. trustees 2001—03), Fed. Bar Assn., Sons of Am. Revolution, Art Inst. of Chgo., So. Ill. Univ. Alumni Assn. (life), Res. Officers Assn. (life), Effingham County Old Settlers Assn. (pres., bd. dir. 1983—86), Abraham Lincoln Assn., U.S. Supreme Ct. Hist. Soc., The Nat. Sojourners, Smithsonian Assocs., Am. Legion, So. Ill. U. Carbondale Found. (bd. dir. 1993—2002), Field Mus. of Natural History, Army and Navy Club Washington D.C., Kiwanis (pres. 1977—78), Phi Alpha Delta. Republican. Methodist. Home: PO Box 1106 Effingham IL 62401-1106

BOWER, JEAN RAMSAY, lawyer, writer; b. N.Y.C., Nov. 25, 1935; d. Claude Barnett and Myrtle Marie (Scott) Ramsay; m. Ward Swift Just, Jan. 31, 1957 (div. 1966); children: Jennifer Ramsay, Julia Barnett; m. Robert Turrell Bower, June 12, 1971 (dec. June 1990). AB, Vassar Coll., 1957; JD, Georgetown U., 1970. Bar: D.C. 1970. Exec. dir. D.C. Dem. Ctrl. Com., Washington, 1969-71; pvt. practice Washington, 1971-78, 94—; dir. Counsel of Child Abuse and Neglect Office D.C. Superior Ct., 1978-94. Mem. Mayor's Com. on Child Abuse and Neglect, 1973-94, vice chmn., 1975-79; mem. Family Div. Rules Adv. Com., 1977-94; pres., bd. dirs. C.B. Ramsay Found., 1984—; cons. child welfare issues, writer. Contbr. poetry to In a Certain Place. Active D.C. Child Fatality Rev. Com., 1992-; bd. dirs. Friends D.C. Superior Ct., 1994—, pres. bd. dirs., 2002-; Family & Child Svcs., D.C., 1995-2003; Folger poetry bd. (chair 2002-), Folger Shakespeare Libr., 1998-. Named Washingtonian of the Yr. Washington Mag., 1978. Mem. Women's Bar Assn. (bd. dirs. 1993-96, found. 1986-91, Woman Lawyer of Yr. 1986), D.C. Bar Assn. (election bd. 1994-96, Beatrice Rosenberg award sect. com. 1994—), Women's Bar Assn. Found. (bd. dirs. 1986-91).

BOWER, WARD ALAN, management consultant, lawyer; b. Carlisle, Pa., Feb. 10, 1947; s. Dale Luther and Margaret Louise (Chapman) B.; m. Linda Elliott; children: Miles Robert, Chase Batchelor, Reid Alan, Seth Elliott. BA in Econs., Bucknell U., 1969; JD, Dickinson Sch. Law, 1975. Bar: Pa. 1975. Group pension adminstr. Prudential ins. Co., Newark, 1969-70; methods analyst Liberty Mut. Ins. Co., Boston, 1972; prin. Altman Weil, Inc., Newtown Square, Pa., 1977—, pres., 1989—, also bd. dirs. Author: (with Frank Arentowicz, Jr.) Law Office Automation and Technology, 1980. Bd. govs. Dickinson Sch. Law of Pa. State U., 1994—. With U.S. Army, 1970-71. Recipient Outstanding Alumni award Dickinson Sch. Law, 1997. Fellow Am. Bar Found., Coll. of Law Practice Mgmt.; mem. ABA (law practice mgmt. sect. divsn. chair 1986-92, coun. 1990-94), Internat. Bar Assn. (chair com. practice mgmt. and tech. 1992-96, working group on multidisciplinary practices 1996—, coun. sect. on legal practice 1996-2002), Pa. Bar Assn. Corporate, general. Office: Altman Weil Inc PO Box 625 Two Campus Blvd Newtown Square PA 19073 E-mail: wbower@altmanweil.com.

BOWERS, CHRISTI C. mediator, law educator, lawyer; b. Hagerstown, Md., Nov. 4, 1970; BA in Psychology, BS in Bus., Shepherd Coll., 1993; JD, MS, U. Balt., 1998, MBA, 2000. Bar: Md. 2000, cert.: Md. Inst. Continuing Profl. Edn. Lawyers (mediator), Md. Inst. Continuing Profl. Edn. Lawyers (domestic/custody and visitation mediator), Md. Inst. Continuing Profl. Edn. Lawyers (domestic property/fin. issues mediator) 2000, Md. Inst. Continuing Profl. Edn. Lawyers (advanced transformative mediator) 2002, Md. Inst. Continuing Profl. Edn. Lawyers (worker's compensation mediator) 2002, Dist. Ct. of Md. (advanced mediator) 2002. Freelance mediator- custody/visitation, civil disputes, landlord/tenant/neighbors, marriage/relationships, tng. programs for businesses, Hagerstown, 2000—; tchr.,presenter co-parenting workshop for adults and children Children of Separation and Divorce (now Nat. Family Resiliency Program), Balt., 2000—. Vol. mediator civil large and small claims cases Dist. Ct. Md., Annapolis, 2000—; vol. faculty critiquer Md. Inst. Continuing Profl. Edn. Lawyers Mediation Tng., Balt., 2001—; substitute tchr. Bd. Edn. Washington County, Hagerstown, 1999—. Author: Mediation In Maryland; editor: Resolving Issues newsletter. Exec. bd.- mem. at large Md. Coun. Dispute Resolution, Balt., 2002; bd. dirs., sec. Washington County Cmty. Mediation Ctr., Hagerstown, 2002—03. Recipient cert. appreciation for vol. mediation, Dist. Ct. of Md., 2002. Mem.: ABA, Assn. Conflict Resolution, Washington County Bar Assn., Md. State Bar Assn., Sigma Iota Epsilon (hon.). Avocations: writing, singing, travel, writing- poems, songs, guidebooks, fiction, creating things. Office: Mediation Svcs in Md PO Box 642 Hagerstown MD 21740 E-mail: christicbo@aol.com.

BOWERSOX, THOMAS H. lawyer; b. Beatrice, Nebr., May 1, 1941; s. William H. Bowersox and Fairy (Casey) Huff; m. Barbara Mathieson, Aug. 23, 1963; children: William T., Christopher T., Elizabeth A. BBA, U. Houston, 1965, JD, 1969. Bar: U.S. Dist. Ct. (so. and ea. dists.) Tex., U.S. Ct. Appeals (5th and 11th cirs.). Instr. South Tex. Jr. Coll., Houston, 1967-72; assoc. prof. Sam Houston State U., Huntsville, 1972-74; assoc. Baker & Botts, Houston, 1975-76; from assoc. gen counsel to pres. subs. co. Zapata Corp., Houston, 1976-93, exec. v.p., 1993-94; ptnr. Bowersox, Herron & Williamson, Houston, 1996-98; of counsel Hope & Causey, Conroe, Tex., 1998—. Adv. com. energy trade policy, U.S. trade rep. industry sector Dept. of Commerce, 1989-93. Bd. dirs. Offhore Energy Ctr., Houston, 1988-92, mem. adv. bd. 1992-98; mem. adv. com. Sam Houston State U. Coll. Bus., 1985—. Mem. Internat. Assn. Drilling Contractors (vice chmn. contracts and risk mgmt. com. 1984-85, chmn. govt. affairs com. 1986-87, v.p. Tex. gulf coast 1989, v.p. offshore 1990-91, chmn., bd. dirs., 1992), Am. Bureau of Shipping. Avocations: golf, camping, reading. Office: Hope & Causey PO Box 3188 Conroe TX 77305-3188 Fax: 936-441-4674. E-mail: thbowersox@earthlink.net.

BOWIE, PETER WENTWORTH, judge, educator; b. Alexandria, Va., Sept. 27, 1942; s. Beverley Munford and Louise Wentworth (Boynton) B.; m. Sarah Virginia Haught, Mar. 25, 1967; children: Heather, Gavin. BA, Wake Forest Coll., 1964; JD magna cum laude, U. San Diego, 1971. Bar: Calif. 1972, D.C. 1972, U.S. Dist. Ct. D.C. 1972, U.S. Dist. Ct. Md. 1973, U.S. Dist. Ct. (so. dist.) Calif. 1974, U.S. Ct. Appeals (D.C. cir.) 1972, U.S. Ct. Appeals (9th cir.) 1974, U.S. Supreme Ct. 1980. Trial atty. honors program Dept. of Justice, Washington, 1971-74; asst. U.S. Atty. U.S. Atty.'s Office, San Diego, 1974, asst. chief civil div., 1974-82, chief asst. U.S. atty., 1982-88; lawyer rep. U.S. Ct. Appeals (9th cir.) Jud. Conf., 1977-78, 84-87; judge U.S. Bankruptcy Ct., San Diego, 1988—. Lectr. at law Calif. Western Sch. Law, 1979-83; exec. com. mem. 9th Cir. Judicial Conf., 1991-94; mem. com. on codes of conduct Jud. Conf. of U.S., 1995—. Bd. dirs. Presidio Little League, San Diego, 1984, coach, 1983-84; mem. alumni adv. bd. Sch. Law U. San Diego, 1998-2002. Lt. USN, 1964-68, Vietnam. Mem. State Bar Calif. (hearing referee ct. 1982-86, mem. rev. dept. 1986-90), Fed. Bar Assn. (pres. San diego chpt. 1981-83), San Diego County Bar Assn. (chmn. fed. ct. com. 1978-80, 83-85), Assn. Bus. Trial Lawyers (bd. govs.), San Diego Bankruptcy Forum (bd. dirs.), Phi Delta Phi. Republican. Mem. Unitarian Ch. Office: US Bankruptcy Court 325 W F St San Diego CA 92101-6017

BOWLER, MARIANNE BIANCA, judge; b. Boston, Feb. 15, 1947; d. Richard A. and Ann C. (Daly) B. BA, Regis Coll., 1967; JD cum laude, Suffolk U., 1976, LLD (hon.) , 1994, Regis Coll., 2003. Bar: Mass. 1978. Rsch. asst. Harvard Med. Sch., Boston, 1967-69; med. editor Mass. Dept. of Pub. Health, Boston, 1969-76; law clk. Mass. Superior Ct., Boston, 1976-77, dep. chief law clk., 1977-78; asst. dist. atty. Middlesex Dist. Atty.'s Office, Cambridge, Mass., 1978; asst. U.S. atty. U.S. Dept. of Justice, Boston, 1978-90, exec. asst. U.S. atty., 1988-89, sr. litigation counsel, 1989-90; magistrate judge U.S. Dist. Ct. Mass., Boston, 1990—2002, chief U.S. magistrate judge, 2002—. Chmn. bd. trustees New England Bapt. Hosp., Boston, 1990-95. Trustee Suffolk U., Boston, 1994—, Discovering Justice, 2003—; bd. dirs. The Boston Found., 1995—; dir. South Cove Nursing Facilities Found., Inc., 1995—; co-pres. Boston Coll. Inn of Ct., 1998—; bd. dirs. Discovering Justice, 2003-. Mem. Jr. League Boston, Suffolk Law Sch. Alumni Assn. (pres. 1979-80), Vincent Club, Isabel O'Neil Found., Save Venice. Democrat. Roman Catholic. Avocations: faux finishing, trompe l'oeil painting. Office: 1 Courthouse Way Ste 8420 Boston MA 02210-3010

BOWLES, MARGO LA JOY, lawyer; b. Stillwater, Okla., Jan. 26, 1949; d. Joseph Worth and Vivian Alice (Sears) B.; m. Francis E. Jones Jr., Dec. 22, 1987. BS, Okla. State U., 1971; JD, U. Tulsa, 1983. Bar: Okla. 1985, U.S. Dist. Ct. (no. dist.) Okla. Sole practice, Tulsa, 1985—. Instr. U. Ctr. Tulsa, Langston U., 1988-90, Northeastern State U., 1992—. Precinct officer Tulsa Dem. Party, 1987. Mem. ABA, Okla. Bar Assn., Tulsa County Bar Assn. (pres. solo practice/small firm sect. 1993-94). Methodist. Avocation: travel. Estate planning, Probate (including wills, trusts). Office: 1821 E 71st St Ste 200 Tulsa OK 74136 Fax: 918-491-2055. E-mail: mbowlesattorney@aol.com.

BOWMAN, CAROL ANN, lawyer; b. Marion, Ind., Jan. 20, 1952; d. James Russell and Carol Joan (Horner) B. BA with honors, Georgetown Coll., 1974; JD, Valparaiso U., 1977; postdoctoral, John Marshall Law Sch., 1980-81. Bar: Ind. 1977, U.S. Dist. Ct. (so. dist.) Ind. 1977, U.S. Dist. Ct. (no. dist.) Ind. 1978, U.S. Ct. Appeals (7th cir.) 1979; U.S. Supreme Ct., 1997. Dep. atty. gen. State of Ind., Indpls., 1977-79; gen. counsel, corp. sec. Whiteco Industries, Inc., Merrillville, Ind., 1979—, gen. counsel, 1995—, corp. sec., 1994—. Mem. adv. com. Atty. Gen. Ind., 1980-87; mem. nat. coun. to dean Valparaiso U. Sch. Law, 2000-; bd. dirs. The Caring Place, Inc., 1992-94, pres., 1994. Trustee Unity in the Dunes, 2000-2002. Fellow Ind. Bar Found.; mem. ABA, Ind. Bar Assn., Women Lawyers Assn. Lake and Porter Counties (pres. 1982), Lake County Bar Assn., South Lake County Bar Assn., Valparaiso U. Law Sch. Alumni Assn. (bd. dirs. 1980-85, 94-97). Avocations: reading, golf, tennis, sailing, theater. Commercial, contracts (including sales of goods; commercial financing), Corporate, general, Property, real (including real estate development, water). Home: 516 Glade Pl Valparaiso IN 46383-3162 Office: Whiteco Industries Inc 1000 E 80th Pl Ste 700 Merrillville IN 46410-5608 E-mail: abowman@whiteco.com.

BOWMAN, CATHERINE MCKENZIE, lawyer; b. Tampa, Fla., Nov. 10, 1962; d. Herbert Alonza and Joan Bates (Baggs) McKenzie; m. Donald Campbell Bowman, Jr., May 21, 1988; children: Hunter Hall, Sarah McKenzie. BA in Psychology and Sociology, Vanderbilt U., 1984; JD, U. Ga., 1987. Bar: Ga. 1987, U.S. Dist. Ct. (so. dist.) Ga. 1987. Assoc. Ranitz, Mahoney, Forbes & Coolidge, P.C., Savannah, Ga., 1987-91; ptnr. Forbes and Bowman, 1991—. Bd. dirs. Greenbriar Children's Ctr., 1994-98, exec. com. 1995, pres. 1996-98; sustainer Jr. League Savannah; with Leadership Savannah, 1994-96, Savannah Found. Distbn. Com., 1994-2002; ball com. Telfair Arts Acad., 2001-02, ball com. Historic Savannah Found., 2002. Mem. Am. Employment Law Coun., Ga. Def. Lawyers Assn., Savannah Young Lawyers Assn. (pres. 1996-97), 2000 Club (membership chair 1990-91, pres. 1992), South Atlantic Found. (bd. dirs. 1992). Insurance, Labor (including EEOC, Fair Labor Standards Act, labor-management relations, NLRB, OSHA), Workers' compensation. Home: 17 Franklin Creek S Savannah GA 31411 Office: Forbes and Bowman PO Box 13929 7505 Waters Ave Ste D-14 Savannah GA 31406-3824

BOWMAN, DENISE MARIE, lawyer; b. Cheverly, Md., July 6, 1965; d. Arthur Belden and Joyce Elaine Smithwick; m. Daniel Walton Bowman, Sept. 12, 1992; children: Danielle Marie, Caitlin Paige. BS, U. Md., 1987; JD, U. Balt., 1990. Bar: U.S. Ct. Appeals 1990, U.S. Dist. Ct. Appeals (D.C. cir.) 1993, U.S. Dist. Ct. Md. 1992, U.S. Dist. Ct. D.C. 1998, U.S. Supreme Ct. 1997. Atty. Alexander & Cleaver, P.A., Ft. Washington, Md., 1990—. Author: (guide) Ethics Guide, A Summary of Maryland State Ethics Laws, 2002. Mem.: ABA, Prince George's County Bd. Trade, Prince George's County Bar Assn., Md. State Bar Assn., Charles County C. of C., Prince George's County C. of C., So. Prince George's County Bus. and Profl. Women. Corporate, general, Government ethics compliance, Campaign finance compliance. Office: Alexander & Cleaver PA 11414 Livinston Rd Fort Washington MD 20744 Office Fax: 301-292-3264. E-mail: dbowman@alexander-cleaver.com.

BOWMAN, GEORGE ARTHUR, JR., b. Milw., Dec. 1, 1917; s. George Arthur and Edna Oral (Hunter) B.; m. Rose Mary Thorpe, Aug. 8, 1947 (dec. 1980); children: George A. III, Daniel Andrew. Student, U. Wis., 1936-39; JD, Marquette U., 1943. Bar: Wis. 1943, U.S. Supreme Ct. 1943. Asst. dist. atty. Milw. County, 1947-48, children's ct. judge, 1967-72; asst. city atty. City of Milw., 1948-67; adminstrv. law judge Office of Hearing and Appeals Social Security Adminstrn. Dept. HHS, Chgo., 1973-97, adminstrv. law judge emeritus, 1997; pvt. practice, 1997—. Appointed Pres.'s Task Force, Law Enforcement Assistance Adminstrn., 1972; former counsel Milw. Police Dept.; advisor Nat. Council of Juvenile Ct. Judges, Nat. Conv., Atlanta; chmn. conv. com. Nat. Council of Juvenile Ct. Judges, Milw., 1972; chmn. State Task Force on Juvenile Delinquency, 1970-71; legis. com. Wis. Bd. Juvenile Ct. Judges, 1970-71; former mem. numerous legis. coms., Milw.; pioneered Legal Defender System in Children's Ct.; lecturer, Marquette U. Co-author: LEAA Uniform Standards for Police

Departments, 1973 (Pres.'s citation). Bd. dirs. Am. Indian Info. and Action Group, Inc. "Project Phoenix", Juneau Acad.; chmn. Milw. County Rep. Party, 1961-62; active supporter numerous community juvenile programs, including Milw. Boys' Club, St. Joseph's Home for Children, Mt. Mary Coll. Proglram for Truant and Delinquent Girls, Operation Outreach, others; Social Security judge. With USN, 1943-46. Recipient Continious Svc. award Office of Hearings and Appeals Soc. Security Adminstr., 1991. Mem. Fed. Assn. Adminstrv. Law Judges, Assn. Office of Hearing and Appeals Adminstrv. Law Judges, Wis. State Bar Assn., Milw. Bar. Assn., Nat. Council Juvenile Ct. Judges, Am. Judicature Soc., Nat. Council of Sr. Citizens, Inc., Internat. Juvenile Officers Assn., Am. Legion (former post comdr.), Nat. Probate Judges Assn., New Trier Rep. Orgn., Committee-man's Club, Hawthorne Turf Club, Sigma Alpha Epsilon. Roman Catholic. Home: 2824 Orchard Ln Wilmette IL 60091-2144

BOWMAN, PASCO MIDDLETON, II, judge; b. Timberville, Va., Dec. 20, 1933; s. Pasco Middleton and Katherine (Lohr) Bowman; m. Ruth Elaine Bowman, July 12, 1958; children: Ann Katherine, Helen Middleton, Benjamin Garber. BA, Bridgewater Coll., 1955; JD, NYU, 1958; LLM, U. Va., 1986; LLD (hon.), Bridgewater Coll., 1988. Bar: N.Y. 1958, Ga. 1965, Mo. 1980. Assoc. firm Cravath, Swaine & Moore, N.Y.C., 1958—61, 1962—64; asst. prof. law U. Ga., 1964—65, assoc. prof., 1965—69, prof., 1969—70, Wake Forest U., 1970—78, dean, 1970—78; vis. prof. U. Va., 1978—79; prof., dean U. Mo., Kansas City, 1979—83; judge U.S. Ct. Appeals (8th cir.), Kansas City, Mo., 1983—98, 1999—, chief judge, 1998—99. Mng. editor: NYU Law Rev., 1957—58, reporter, chief drafts-man: Georgia Corporation Code, 1965—68. Col. USAR, 1959—84. Scholar Root-Tilden scholar, 1955—58; Fulbright scholar, London Sch. Econs. and Polit. Sci., 1961—62. Mem.: Mo. Bar, N.Y. Bar. Office: US Ct Appeals 8th Circuit 10-50 US Courthouse 400 E 9th St Kansas City MO 64106-2607

BOWMAN, REID C. lawyer; b. Buffalo, Sept. 16, 1960; s. Walter D. and Judith W. Bowman; m. Kimberly H. Holben, Aug. 9, 1986; children: Christopher G., William D. BS, Cornell U., 1982; JD with honors, U. Md., 1987. Bar: Md. 1987, U.S. Dist. Ct. Md. 1988. Assoc. Piper & Marbury, Balt., 1984—87; sr. counsel USF&G, 1994—98; asst. gen. counsel Allied Signal, Inc., Morristown, NJ, 1998—99; asst. gen. counsel and acting head, human resources Ameritrade Holding Co., Balt., 1999—2000; asst. gen. counsel Allegis Group, Inc., Hanover, 2000—. Mem. Human Resources Com. of Bd. of Governors, Nat. Aquarium of Balt., Balt., 2001; adj. prof. U. Md. Sch. of Law, 1993—95. Chmn., adminstrv. coun. Bethany Unite Meth. Ch., Ellicott City, Md., 2002. Recipient Order of the Coif, Md. chpt., Order of the Coif, 1987. Mem.: ABA, ACCA. Labor (including EEOC, Fair Labor Standards Act, labor-management relations, NLRB, OSHA), Alternative dispute resolution. Personal E-mail: rbowman@allegisgroup.com. E-mail: rbowman@allegisgroup.com.

BOWMAN, SCOTT MCMAHAN, lawyer; b. Shaker Heights, Ohio, Mar. 16, 1962; s. George Henry and Patricia (McMahan) B.; children: Chad Marshall, David Chandler, Elizabeth Brooks; stepchildren: Garrett Richard Sevek, Grant Allen Sevek. AA in Bus., Fullerton Coll., 1987; BBA, Calif. State U., Fullerton, 1989; JD, U. Cin., 1992. Pvt. practice, Salem, Ohio, 1992—. Asst. city solicitor Salem, 1992-94; advisor YWCA Salem, 1994—; advisor Butler Inst. Art, Salem, 1994—; intermediary, counsel Unorganized Militia, 1996—. Author: The Turning Point, A Personal Account of the Montana Freemen Standoff, 1997. Mem. Design Review Bd. City of Salem (Ohio), 1993-95, v.p., 1995; mem. Salem Planning and Zoning Commn., 1993-95, v.p., 1995; co-founder, trustee Salem Preservation Soc., 1993-95. Mem. Columbiana County Bar Assn. Episcopal. Avocations: camping, hunting, surfing, coaching football, politics. Estate planning, Probate (including wills, trusts), Property, real (including real estate development, water). Office: PO Box 558 Salem OH 44460-0558 E-mail: SBowmanEsq@aol.com.

BOWNES, HUGH HENRY, judge; b. N.Y.C., Mar. 10, 1920; s. Hugh Gray and Margaret (Henry) Bownes; m. Irja C. Martikainen, Dec. 30, 1944 (dec. Jan. 1991); m. Mary Davis, July 12, 1992. BA, Columbia U., 1941, LLB, 1948. Bar: N.H. 1948. Since practiced in, Laconia; ptnr. firm Nighswander, Lord & Bownes, 1951—66; assoc. justice N.H. Superior Ct., 1966—68; judge U.S. Dist. Ct. N.H., Concord, 1968—77, U.S. Ct. Appeals (1st cir.), 1977—90, sr. judge, 1990—. Chmn. Laconia chpt. ARC, 1951—52; pres. bd. Laconia Hosp. Assn., 1963—64; mem. Laconia City Coun., 1953—57; chmn. Laconia Dem. Com., 1954—57; mayor Laconia, 1963—65; mem. Dem. Nat. Com. for N.H., 1963—66. Maj. USMC, 1941—46. Decorated Silver Star, Purple Heart. Mem.: ABA, Belknap County Bar Assn. (pres. 1965—67), N.H. Bar Assn., Am. Law Inst., Laconia C. of C. (past pres.), Lions Club (past pres. Laconia). Office: US Ct Appeals 1st Cir US Courthouse 1 Courthouse Way Ste 6730 Boston MA 02210-3008

BOXER, ANDREW CAREY, lawyer; b. Yonkers, N.Y., May 28, 1969; s. Jeffrey Victor and Joyce Elaine Boxer. AB, Harvard U., 1991; JD, Cornell U., 1994. Bar: Vt. 1995, U.S. Dist. Ct. Vt. 1995, U.S. Ct. Appeals (2d cir.) 2000. Assoc. Kiel & Ellis, Springfield, Vt., 1994-2000; ptnr. Kiel Ellis & Boxer, Springfield, 2000—. Mem. Vt. Bar Assn., Def. Rsch. Inst., Luclloro Devel. Rev. Bd. (chmn. 1999-2002). Avocations: snowboarding, hiking, camping, mountain biking, bike racing. Administrative and regulatory, General civil litigation, Insurance. Office: Kiel Ellis & Boxer 20 Park St # 948 Springfield VT 05156-3023 E-mail: acboxer@keblaw.com.

BOXER, LEONARD, lawyer; b. N.Y.C., Feb. 11, 1939; s. Max Boxer and Sally (Grill) Koffler; m. Enid Feuer, Nov. 24, 1965; children: Michael, Jason, Douglas. BS, NYU, 1960, LLB, 1963. Bar: N.Y. 1963, U.S. Dist. Ct. (so. and ea. dists.) N.Y. 1985, U.S. Supreme Ct. Assoc. Eisenberg & Weiss, Bklyn., 1964-65; ptnr. Olnick, Boxer, Blumberg, Lane & Troy, N.Y.C., 1965-86, Stroock & Stroock & Lavan, N.Y.C., 1987—. Mem. adv. bd. Chgo. Title Ins. Co., N.Y.C., 1980—; mem. exec. com., gov. NY Real Estate Bd. Trustee NYU Law Sch., 1994—, Nat. Jewish Ctr. Immunology and Respiratory Medicine, Jewish Assn. Svcs. for the Aged, Children's Hearing Inst.; bd. of trustees Lenox Hill Hosp.; trustee NYU, 2000—, Cancer Rsch. Inst., 2001. Mem. N.Y. State Bar Assn., Bklyn. Bar Assn., Tax Certiorari Bar Assn. (bd. dirs. 1983-97), Beta Alpha Psi. Property, real (including real estate development, water). Home: 875 Park Ave New York NY 10021 Office: Stroock & Stroock & Lavan 180 Maiden Ln Fl 17 New York NY 10038-4937

BOXER, LESTER, lawyer; b. N.Y.C., Oct. 19, 1935; s. Samuel and Anna Lena (Samovar) B.; m. Frances Barenfeld, Sept. 17, 1961; children: Kimberly Brett, Allison Joy. AA, UCLA, 1955, BS, 1957; JD, U. So. Calif., 1961. Bar: Calif. 1962; U.S. Dist. Ct. (cen. dist.) Calif. 1962. Assoc. Bautzer & Grant, Beverly Hills, Calif., 1961-63; pvt. practice Beverly Hills, 1963-65, 69—; ptnr. Boxer & Stoll, Beverly Hills, 1965-69. Mem. Calif. Bar Assn., L.A. County Bar Assn., Beverly Hills Bar Assn. Corporate, general, Entertainment, Property, real (including real estate development, water). Office: 1801 Century Park E Ste 2513 Los Angeles CA 90067-4703

BOXX, KAREN ELIZABETH, lawyer, educator; Of counsel Keller Rohrback LLP, Seattle; asst. prof. U. Wash., Seattle. Contbr. articles to profl. jours. Mem. adv. com. NCCUSL. Fellow: Am. Coll. Trust and Estate Counsel. Probate (including wills, trusts), Taxation, general, Family and matrimonial. Office: Keller Rohrback LLP 1201 3d Ave Ste 3200 Seattle WA 98101-3052 Office Fax: 206-623-3384. Business E-Mail: kboxx@kellerrohrback.com.*

BOYD, JOSEPH ARTHUR, JR., lawyer; b. Hoschton, Ga., Nov. 16, 1916; s. Joseph Arthur and Esther Estelle (Puckett) B.; m. Ann Stripling, June 6, 1938; children: Joanne Louise Boyd Goldman, Betty Jean Boyd Jala, Joseph Robert, James Daniel, Jane N. Ohlin. Student, Piedmont Coll., Demorest, Ga., 1936-38, LLD, 1963; student, Mercer U., Macon, Ga., 1938-39; JD, U. Miami, Coral Gables, Fla., 1948; LLD, Western State U. Coll. Law, San Diego, 1981. Bar: Fla. 1948, U.S. Supreme Ct. 1959, D.C. 1973, N.Y. 1982. Practice law, Hialeah, 1948-68; city atty., 1951-58; mem. Dade County Commn., Miami, Fla., 1958-68, chmn., 1963; vice mayor Dade County, 1967; justice Fla. Supreme Ct., Tallahassee, 1969-87, chief justice, 1984-86; assoc. Boyd Lindsey & Sliger P.A., Tallahassee, 1987—99. Mem. Hialeah Zoning Bd., 1946-48; juror Freedoms Found., Valley Forge, Pa., 1971, 73 Bd. dirs. Bapt. Hosp., Miami, 1962-66, Miami Coun. Chs., 1960-64; emeritus trustee Piedmont Coll. Recipient Nat. Top Hat award Bus. and Profl. Women in U.S. for advancing status of employed women, 1967 Mem. ABA, Fla. Bar Assn., Hialeah-Miami Springs Bar Assn. (pres. 1955), Tallahassee Bar Assn., Hialeah-Miami Springs C. of C. (pres. 1956), Am. Legion (comdr. Fla. 1953-54), VFW, Shriners, Masons (33 deg.), Lions, Elks, Wig and Robe, Iron Arrow, Phi Alpha Delta. Democrat. Baptist (deacon). Federal civil litigation, Probate (including wills, trusts). Office: 1407 Piedmont Dr E Tallahassee FL 32308-7943

BOYD, LAWRENCE GREGORY, lawyer; b. Dallas, Nov. 1, 1953; s. Taylor and Ethelda Faye (Meason) B.; m. Vicki Lynn Torbert; children: Benjamin, Rebecca. BA, Trinity U., 1975; JD, Southern Meth. U., 1978. Bar: Tex. 1978, U.S. Dist. Ct. (no. dist.) Tex. 1980, U.S. Supreme Ct. 1992. Assoc. Johnston & Feather, Dallas, 1979-81; pvt. practice law Dallas, 1981—. Spkr. in field. Fellow Coll. State Bar Tex.; mem. Dallas Bar Assn., Dallas Criminal Def. Lawyers Assn., Tex. Criminal Def. Lawyers Assn. Home: 3601 Legendary Ln Plano TX 75023-1008 Office: 5630 Yale Blvd Dallas TX 75206-5035

BOYD, THOMAS MARSHALL, lawyer; b. Yorktown, Va., Sept. 10, 1946; s. Laurel Barnett and Mildred Warner Wellford (Marshall) B.; m. Torri Carol Tyler, Oct. 2, 1976; children: Brooke Warner, Tyler Randolph. BA in History, Va. Military Inst., 1968; JD, U. Va., 1971. Bar: Calif. 1973, D.C. 1974. Law clk. to fed. judge U.S. Dist. Ct. (cen. dist.) Calif., Los Angeles, 1973-74; trial atty., atty. advisor U.S. Dept. Justice, Washington, 1974-76; assoc. counsel com. on judiciary U.S. Ho. of Reps., Washington, 1976-86; dep. asst. atty. gen. Dept. Justice Office Legis. Affairs, Washington, 1986-88, asst. atty. gen., 1988-89, dir. office policy devel., 1989-91; dep. gen. counsel Kemper Corp., Washington, 1991-93, v.p. and legis. counsel, 1993-96; v.p. for legis. affairs Investment Co. Inst., Washington, 1996-98; ptnr. Ramsey, Cook, Looper & Kurlander LLP, Washington, 1998-99, Alston & Bird, LLP, Washington, 1999—. House counsel Presdl. Transition Com. on Criminal Justice, Washington, 1980-81; pub. mem. Adminstrv. Conf. U.S., 1992-95. Co-editor U.S. Atty.'s Criminal Trial Manual, 1971; contbr. articles to profl. jours. and pub. interest articles to newspapers. Served to capt. USAF, 1968-73. Recipient Nat. Media award Delta Soc., 1985, Edmund J. Randolph award, 1988. Mem. U.S. Supreme Ct. Bar Assn., Calif. Bar Assn., D.C. Bar Assn., Army-Navy Country Club, Leland Country Club, Golf Club of Va. Republican. Episcopalian. Avocations: golf, jogging, writing. Constitutional, Legislative.

BOYER, DENNIS LEE, lawyer, lobbyist, writer; b. Allentown, Pa., July 13, 1949; s. Erwin A. and Grace Benner (Choyce) Boyer. BA, Kutztown State Coll., 1975; JD, W.Va. U., 1978. Bar: W.Va. 1978, Wis. 1981. Legal counsel W.Va. Dept. Labor, Charleston, 1978—79; govt. rels. counsel Am. Fedn. State, County and Mcpl. Employees, Madison, Wis., 1980—. Author: Public Employee Bargaining, 1978, Prevailing Wages, 1979, Driftless Spirits, 1997, Giants in the Land, 1998, Great Wisconsin Taverns, 2000, Prairie Whistles, 2001, Gone Missing, 2002. Del. Dem. Nat. Conv., Miami, 1972, Rainbow Coalition, 1986, 1st Nat. Green Politics Conf., 1987; candidate for Pa. State Assembly, 1974. Served to sgt. USAF, 1967—71. Grantee, Dept. Labor, 1977. Mem.: VFW, Scottish Rite, Masonic Lodge. Mem. Wis. Green Party. Home: 3302 Bethlehem Rd Dodgeville WI 53533-8526 Office: AFSCME 8033 Excelsior Dr Madison WI 53717-1903

BOYER, PETER JAY, lawyer; b. Lebanon, Pa., May 5, 1950; s. Peter P. and Ruth (Kleinfelter) B.; m. Debra B. Salins, Oct. 18, 1981; children: Sarah M., Philip H. BA, U. Pa., 1972; JD, Georgetown U., 1977. Law clk. Lancaster County Common Pleas Ct., Pa., 1977-78; assoc. Blank, Rome, Comisky & McCauley, Phila., 1978-86, ptnr., 1986—98; spl. counsel Spector Gaden & Rosen, P.C., 1998—2001, McCarter & English, LLP, Phila., 2002—. Chmn. attys. divsn. United Way Camden County, N.J., 1992-94. Mem. Camden County Bar Assn., N.J. State Bar Assn., U. Pa. Coll. Alumni Soc. (bd. mgrs. 1985—), N.J. Supreme Ct. (dis. IV ethics com., chair 1995-96). Democrat. Avocations: skiing, tennis, choral music. Home: 916 Francine Dr Cherry Hill NJ 08003-2810 Office: McCarter & English LLP Mellon Bank Ctr 1735 Market St Ste 700 Philadelphia PA 19103-

BOYER, TYRIE ALVIS, lawyer; b. Williston, Fla., Sept. 10, 1924; s. Alton Gordon and Mary Ethel (Strickland) B.; m. Elizabeth Everett Gale, June 9, 1945; children: Carol, Tyrie, Kennedy, Lee. BA, U. Fla., 1953, LLB, JD, 1954. Bar: Fla. Atty. Crawford, May & Boyer, Jacksonville, Fla., 1954-58, Boyer Law Offices, Jacksonville, 1958-60; judge Civil Ct. of Record, Jacksonville, 1960-63; cir. judge 4th Jud. Cir. of Fla., Jacksonville, 1963-67; atty. Dawson, Galant, Maddox, Boyer, Sulik & Nichols, Jacksonville, 1967-73; appellate judge 1st Dist. Ct. Appeal, Tallahassee, 1973-79; chief judge 1st Dist. Ct. Appeals, Tallahassee, 1975-76; atty. Boyer, Tanzler, Blackburn & Boyer, Jacksonville, 1979-84, Boyer, Tanzler & Sussman, Jacksonville, 1984—. Adj. prof. Fla. Coastal Sch. Law, Jacksonville, 1996—, U. North Fla., 1998—; chmn. Supreme Ct. Com. on Standard Conduct Governing Judges, Tallahassee, 1976-79. Contbr. articles to profl. jours. Chmn. Duval County Hosp. Authority, Jacksonville, 1970-73, Jacksonville Bldg. Fin. Authority, 1980-81; pres. Jacksonville Legal Aid Assn., 1954-61; bd. dirs. Jones Coll., Jacksonville, 1978-85; bd. advs. Fla. Coastal Sch. Law, 1996—; adj. prof. U. North Fla., 1998—. With USN, 1942-45, PTO. Mem. ABA, Am. Judicature Soc., Fla. Bar, Amer. Bar Assn., Jacksonville Bar Assn., Fla. Acad. Trial Lawyers, Am. Bd. Trial Advs., SCV (comdr.), Mil. Order Stars and Bars (comdr.), Masons, dir., Safari Club Internat., Fla. Blue Key, Order of Coif, Phi Beta Kappa, Phi Kappa Phi. Methodist. Avocation: big game hunting. Appellate, General civil litigation, Condemnation (eminent domain). Home: 3966 Cordova Ave Jacksonville FL 32207-6019 Office: Boyer Tanzler & Sussman 210 E Forsyth St Jacksonville FL 32202-3320

BOYES, PATRICE FLINCHBAUGH, lawyer; b. York, Pa., Aug. 1, 1957; d. Glenn Dale Flinchbaugh and Patricia Ann (Frey) Shultz. BA, Dickinson Coll., 1978; MA, U. Mich., 1980; JD, U. Fla., 1991. Bar: Fla. 1991, Fed. 1994. Law clk. Rakusin & Ivey, Gainesville, Fla., 1989; summer assoc. Hopping, Boyd, Green & Sams, Tallahassee, 1990; gen. counsel GeoSolutions, Inc., Gainesville/Tallahassee, Fla., 1986—2002; pres. Boyes & Assocs., PA, Gainesville, Fla., 1991—, Wildcat Tech. Svc., Inc., 1995-99. Pres. Wildcat Tech. Svcs., Inc., Gainesville, 1995-99. Pres. Hist. Gainesville, Inc.; chair City's Hist. Preservation Adv. Bd.; vol. Kanapha Bot. Gardens; counsel Duckpond Neighborhood Assn., Inc. Recipient Keystone Press award Pa. Soc. Newspaper Editors and Pubs., 1981, City Beautification award, 1994, Hist. Preservation award, 1994, Fla. Trust for Hist. Preservation award, 1996; grad. fellow Modern Media Inst., St. Petersburg, Fla. Mem. Fed. Bar Assn., Fla. Bar Assn. (pub. interest com. for environ. and land use sect.), 8th Jud. Cir. Bar Assn., Fla. Assn. Women Lawyers, Gainesville C. of C., Pi Delta Epsilon, Haile Plantation Golf & Country Club. Avocations: golf, historical preservation, photography, gardening, reading. Corporate, general, Environmental, Land use and zoning (including planning). Office: 4719 NW 53rd Ave Ste C Gainesville FL 32606-4356

BOYKO, CHRISTOPHER ALLAN, lawyer, judge; b. Cleve., Oct. 10, 1954; s. Andrew and Eva Dorothy (Zepko) B.; m. Roberta Ann Gentile, May 29, 1981; children: Philip, Ashley. B in Polit. Sci. cum laude, Mt. Union Coll., 1976; JD, Cleve. Marshall Coll. Law, 1979. Bar: Ohio 1979, Fla. 1985, U.S. Dist. Ct. (no. dist.) Ohio 1979, H.S. Ct. Appeals (6th cir.) 1990, U.S. Tax Ct. 1986, U.S. Supreme Ct., 1988. Prin. Boyko & Boyko, Parma, Ohio, 1979—95; asst. prosecutor City of Parma, 1981-87, dir. of law, 1987-93; exec. v.p., gen. counsel copy Am., Inc., 1993-94; judge Parma Mcpl. Court, 1993, Ct. Common Pleas, Cuyahoga County, Ohio, 1996—, Judicial Corrections Bd., 1999—; chair Ct. Vet. Svc. Com., 2000—. Guardian ad litem Juvenile Ct., 1979-93; legal advisor spl. weapons and tactics divsn. City of Parma Police Dept., 1984-93; chief counsel S.W. Enforcement Bur., 1991-93; mem. faculty Ohio Jud. Coll., Nat. Jud. Coll., lectr. FBI Nat. Acad. jud. editor Law and Fact Com., 1999—. Active Citizens League of Greater Cleve., 1985—; trustee Cops & Kids, Inc., Cleve. Bar Assn., 2000—, County Bar Assn.; mem. Parma Drug Task Force, 1987—; mem. adv. com. Parmadale Children's Svcs., 1991—; mem. St. Anthony's Sch. Commn. Mem.: Nat. Inst. Trial Advocacy (steering com. 2003—), Mt. Union Coll. Alumni Assn., Cleve. Am. Mid. Eastern Orgn., Am. Inns of Ct. Found. (master of bench 2001—, William K. Thomas Inn of Ct.), Narcotics Law Officers Assn., Ukrainian Bar Assn., Parma Bar Assn. (pres., trustee), Cleve. Bar Assn. (bd. trustees, lectr. in law), Cuyahoga County Bar Assn., Ohio Bar Assn., Fla. Bar Assn., ABA, Cuyahoga County Police Chiefs Assn. (assoc.), Elks. Byzantine Catholic. Avocations: martial arts, phys. fitness. General practice, Municipal (including bonds), Probate (including wills, trusts). Office: Justice Ctr 1200 Ontario St Cleveland OH 44113-1604

BOYLE, JANE J. lawyer; b. Sharon, Pa., Dec. 15, 1954; BS, U. of Tex., Austin, 1977; JD, So Meth. U., Dallas, 1981. Asst. dist. atty. Dist. Atty.'s Office, 1981-87; asst. U.S. atty. U.S. Dist. Ct. (no. dist.) Tex., 1987-90, magistrate judge U.S., 1990—2002, U.S. atty., 2003—. Office: 1100 Commerce St 3d Fl Dallas TX 75242-1027

BOYLE, KEVIN RICHARD, lawyer; b. Belleville, Ill., June 24, 1972; s. Richard E. and Janet E. Boyle. BA, Vanderbilt U., 1994; JD, U. Ariz., 1997. Bar: Calif. 1997, U.S. Ct. Appeals (9th cir.) 1998, DC 1999, U.S. Dist. Ct. (ctrl. and no. dists.) Calif. 2001. Law clk. to Hon. Melvin Brunetti U.S. Ct. Appeals (9th cir.), Reno, 1997—98; assoc. Kirkland & Ellis, Washington, 1998—99; law clk. to Hon. William H. Rehnquist U.S. Supreme Ct., Washington, 1999—2000; assoc. Greene, Broillet, Panish & Wheeler, Santa Monica, Calif., 2001—. Product liability, Aviation, Personal injury (including property damage). Office: Greene Broillet Panish and Wheeler 100 Wilshire Blvd Ste 2100 Santa Monica CA 90407 Office Fax: 310-576-1220. Business E-Mail: kboyle@gbpwlaw.com.

BOYLE, LYNNETTE ZELLNER, lawyer, nurse, mediator; b. Sandusky, Ohio, July 9, 1952; d. Berlin C. Zellner and Betty May Grube; m. James Edward Boyle Sr., Oct. 7, 1972; children: James E. Jr., Matthew C. AA, Palm Beach Jr. Coll., 1972; BS in Nursing, Vanderbilt U., 1974; MS, Kans. State U., 1977; JD, U. Nebr., 1985; M in Strategic Studies, U.S. Army War Coll., 2001. Bar: Nebr. 1985, U.S. Dist. Ct. Nebr. 1985, U.S. Ct. Mil. Appeals 1989; comml. pilot, SEL-Instrument. Nurse VA Med. Ctr., Omaha, 1978-85; flight instr. Werner Aviation, Omaha, 1982-84; assoc. Tate and Alden, Lincoln, Nebr., 1985-86; ptnr. Tietjen, Simon & Boyle, Omaha, 1986—; nurse ICU, Midlands Cmty. Hosp., 1986—87, 1997—2001, 2003—. Bd. dirs. Millard Atheltic Assn., 1991—92; mem. bd. edn. Daniel J. Gross H.S., 1994—; bd. dirs.. Utah Youth Symphony, Utah Fulton Assn. Capt. Army Nurse Corps USAR, 1974—82, col. JA USAR, 1987—. Mem. Nebr. State Bar Assn. Republican. Methodist. Avocations: aviation, reading. Family and matrimonial, Juvenile, Labor (including EEOC, Fair Labor Standards Act, labor-management relations, NLRB, OSHA). Office: Tietjen Simon & Boyle Blackstone Ctr No 212 302 S 36th St Omaha NE 68131

BOYLE, PATRICK OTTO, lawyer; b. St. Louis, Nov. 15, 1935; s. Otto William and Wilma Louise (Bowers) B.; m. Jane Adeline Roberts, Nov. 22, 1966; children— Laura Jane, Daniel Patrick. B.S.B.A., Washington U., 1957, J.D., 1960. Bar: Mo. 1960, Ill., 1970. Assoc. firm Lucas & Murphy, St. Louis, 1963-67; assoc. counsel Interco Inc., St. Louis, 1967-69; counsel Energy Systems divsn. Olin Corp., East Alton, Ill., 1969-74; assoc. Winchester Group Counsel, 1974-77; asst. sec., 1970-77; ptnr. Boyle & Stillwell, East Alton, 1977-80; sole practice, St. Louis and E. Alton, 1980—2001; mgr. The Boyle Law Firm, LLC, 2002--. Bd. dirs. Ferguson-Florissant Sch. Bd., 1981-96. Served to comdr. USCGR, 1960-82. Mem. Mo. Bar Assn., Ill. Bar Assn., Madison County Bar Assn., Metro. Bar St. Louis, Beta Gamma Sigma. Club: Mo. Athletic. Education and schools, Estate planning, General practice. Office: 755 Rue Saint Francois Florissant MO 63031-4921 Home: 3715 Greengrass Dr Florissant MO 63033-6634

BOYLE, RICHARD EDWARD, lawyer; b. Westville, Ill., Mar. 27, 1937; s. Kelley George and Florence (Weisert) B.; m. Janet E. Peskar, Nov. 22, 1968; children: Kevin, Douglas, Leslie. BA, U. Ill., 1959, LLB, 1961. Bar: Ill. 1962, Mo. 1985, U.S. Dist. Ct. (so. dist.) Ill. 1962, U.S. Dist. Ct. (cen. dist.) Ill. 1962, U.S. Dist. Ct. (ea. dist.) Mo. 1991, U.S. Ct. Appeals (7th cir.) 1975, U.S. Supreme Ct. 1985. Assoc. Costello, Wiechert, Roberts & Gundlach, 1962-68; ptnr. Gundlach, Lee, Eggmann, Boyle & Roessler, Belleville, Ill., 1968—. With USAFR. Fellow Am. Coll. Trial Lawyers, Am. Bar Found. (mem. Adv. Group Civil Justice Reform Act 1990—); mem. Nat. Assn. R.R. Trial Counsel (pres. 1991-92), St. Clair County Bar Assn. (pres. 1979-80). General civil litigation, Personal injury (including property damage), Product liability. Home: 13 Oak Knoll Pl Belleville IL 62223-1817 Office: Gundlach Lee Eggmann Boyle & Roessler Box 23560 5000 W Main St Belleville IL 62226-4727

BOYLES, WILLIAM ARCHER, lawyer; b. Lakeland, Fla., Aug. 16, 1951; s. Jesse V. and Louise B.; m. Laura M. Rose, June 12, 1977; children: William Archer Jr., John H. BSBA, U. Fla., 1973, JD, 1976, LLM in Taxation, 1978. CPA Fla.; bar: Fla. 1977, U.S. Tax Ct. 1978, U.S. Dist. Ct. (mid. dist.) Fla. 1979. Assoc. Gray, Harris & Robinson, P.A., Orlando, Fla., 1978-82, shareholder, 1982—. Mem. Cen. Fla. Estate Planning Coun. Bd. dirs. Christian Family Svcs., Inc., Gainesville, Fla., 1977-86, Ctrl. Fla. YMCA, Orlando, 1979-81; treas. Univ. Blvd. Ch. of Christ, Orlando, 1979-88; bd. dirs., treas. Orlando Shakespeare Festival, Inc., 1989-97, bd. dirs., 1992, 2d v.p., 1992-95; bd. dirs. Better Bus. Bur. Ctrl. Fla., 1994-02, chair-elect, exec. com. 1994, 95, chmn., 1996-97; chmn. Leadership Orlando, Leadership Fla.; mem. Planned Giving Coun. Ctrl. Fla. Mem. ABA, Fla. Bar (exec. coun. tax sect.), Orange County Bar Assn., AICPA, Fla. Inst. CPA's, Am. Assn. Atty.-CPA's, Small Bus. Coun. Am. (polit. action com.), Citrus Club. Republican. Estate planning, Corporate taxation, Taxation, general. Office: Gray Harris & Robinson PA 301 E Pine St Ste 1400 Orlando FL 32801-2798

BOYNTON, FREDERICK GEORGE, lawyer; b. Yokohama, Japan, May 9, 1948; s. Fred Wenderoth and Buelah Eleanor (Nygaard) B.; m. Nancy Jeanne McLendon, Aug. 3, 1985; children: Emily Margaret, Charlotte Clayton, Susan Jeanne. BA, The Citadel, 1970; JD, Tulane U., 1973. Bar: S.C. 1973, Ga. 1976, U.S. Dist. Ct. Ga. 1976, U.S. Ct. Appeals (5th and 11th cirs.). Assoc. Smith, Gambrell & Russell, and predecessors, Atlanta, 1976-82, ptnr., 1982-88; sole practice law Atlanta, 1988—2002; of counsel Jackson and Hardwick, 2002—. Author: Criminal Defense Techniques, 1976; editor articles Tulane Sch. Law Rev. Exec. com. Southside Progress Assn., Atlanta, 1983-84, Leadership Sandy Springs, 1989-90; bd. dirs. Atlanta Union Mission, 1990-97, exec. com., 1991, sec., 1992, adv. bd., 1998—; mem. Local Advisory Coun., Ridgeview Middle Sch. 2001-03. Served to capt. JAGC, U.S. Army, 1973-76. Fellow Lawyers Found. Ga.; mem. ABA, Fed. Bar Assn. (pres. Atlanta chpt. 1981-82, mem. exec. com. 1982—, dep. chmn. adminstrv. law sect. 1986-87, bd. dirs. younger lawyers divsn. 1981-84, v.p. 11th cir. 1985-87), State Bar Ga. (chmn. adminstrv. law sect. 1987-88), Order of Coif. Property, real (including real estate development, water), Federal civil litigation, State civil litigation. Home: 4860 Northway Dr NE Atlanta GA 30342-2424 Office: 2325 Lakeview Parkway Ste 275 Alpharetta GA 30004 E-mail: fboynton@jhlaw.net.

BOZEMAN, FRANK CARMACK, lawyer; b. Greenwood, Miss., Oct. 16, 1933; s. Frank Carmack and Mamie Hyatt (Pyle) B.; m. Mary Ireland Callcott, Dec. 29, 1961; children: Frank C. III, William Pyle, Thomas Anderson. BA, U. of South, 1955; MA, U. Va., 1956; JD, Washington and Lee U., 1960. Bar: Fla. 1960, Va. 1960. Assoc. Beggs and Lane, Pensacola, Fla., 1960-65; ptnr. Harrell, Wiltshire, Bozeman, Clark & Stone, Pensacola, 1965-75, Carlton, Fields, Ward, Emmanuel, Smith & Cutler, P.A., Pensacola, 1975-93, Bozeman, Jenkins & Matthews, Pensacola, 1993—. Editor Washington and Lee Law Rev., 1960. Chmn. Eagle Scout rev. com., Boy Scouts Am., Pensacola, 1961-63; trustee U. Of South, 1990-96. Capt. USAF, 1956-57. Mem. Am. Bd. Trial Advs. (pres. Pensacola chpt. 1989-90), Fla. Def. Lawyers Assn., Fedn. Ins. and Corp. Counsel, Register of Pre-Eminent Lawyers, Def. Rsch. Inst., Phi Delta Phi (Grad. of Yr. award 1960). Republican. Episcopalian. Avocations: sailing, gardening, civil war history and research. General civil litigation, Health, Insurance. Home: 122 W Lloyd St Pensacola FL 32501-2637 Office: Bozeman Jenkins & Matthews PO Box 13105 Pensacola FL 32591-3105

BRACEY, WILLIE EARL, lawyer, university program director; b. Jackson, Miss., Dec. 21, 1950; s. Dudley and Alvaretta (King) B. AA, Wright Jr. Coll., 1971; BS, Mt. Senario Coll., 1974; MS, Eastern Ill. U., 1976; JD, So. Ill. U., 1979. Bar: Ill. 1979. Dir. student legal services Western Ill. U., Macomb, 1979-86, adj. prof., 1981-84, asst. v.p. student affairs, spl. services, 1986-99, assoc. v.p., 1999—. Asst. pub. defender McDonough County, Macomb, 1983-84. Mem. Ill. Com. on Concern of Blacks in Higher Edn., 1984—, Chgo. Com. on Fgn. Realtions, 1986—, McDonough/Fulton County Youth Service Bd., Macomb, 1985-86. Mem. ABA, Ill. Bar Assn., McDonough County Bar Assn., Assn. Trial Lawyers Am., Nat. Legal Aid and Defender Assn., Ill. Student Atty. Assn., (v.p. 1984—), Nat. Assn. Student Personnel Adminstrs., NAACP. Avocations: chess, cooking. Home: 2012 W Adams St Macomb IL 61455-1210 Office: Western Ill U Univ Union 1 University Cir Macomb IL 61455-1367

BRACKETT, COLQUITT PRATER, JR., judge, lawyer; b. Norfolk, Va., Feb. 24, 1946; s. Colquitt Prater Sr. and Antoinette Gladys (Cacace) B.; m. Carol Ann Roberts, Dec. 29, 2000; 1 child, Susan Elizabeth Brackett Brooks. BS, U. Ga., 1966, MA, 1968, JD, 1973, LLM, 1976; travel mktg. profl. diploma, S.E. Tourism Soc. Mktg. Coll., 1999. Bar: Ga. 1973, U.S. Dist. Ct. (so. dist.) Ga. 1974, U.S. Dist. Ct. (mid. dist.) Ga. 1977, U.S. Supreme Ct. 1980, Tenn. 1987. Assoc. Surrett & CoCroft, Augusta, Ga., 1972-74; ptnr. Surrett & Brackett, Augusta, 1974-76; faculty Sch. Law, U. Ga., Athens, 1977-82; mng. ptnr. Brackett, Prince & Neufeld, Athens, 1982-90; adminstrv. law judge Ga. Dept. Med. Assistance, Athens, 1990-98. Hearing officer Ga. State Bd. Edn., 1979-91; v.p. Mus. Dolls & Gifts, Inc., Watkinsville, Ga., 1983—; pres. Bear Country Lodge and Conf. Ctr., Pigeon Forge, Tenn., 1996—, chmn. bd. Adventures in Toy Land, 1999-2000; CEO Toy Mus. at Natural Bridge Va., 2002-; exec. dir. Soc. Preservation of Am. Childhood Effects, 2002-; curator Toy Mus., Natural Bridge, Va., 2002-. Author: Court Administration, 1972; (monograph) The Security Inventors Protection Corporation and the Operations of SIPC, 1976; (musical play) Americanization of Mary Poppins, 1995. Pres. Athens/Clarke Mental Health Assn., 1985; chmn. bd. dirs. N.E. Ga. Mental Health Assn., 1989-90; bd. dirs. Coalition for The Blue Ridge Pkwy., 1994-2000, Oconee Cultural Arts Found., 1995-97, Blue Ridge Pkwy. Assn., 1997-2001. Mem. ABA, Ga. State Bar Assn., Ga. Assn. Adminstrv. Law Judges (bd. dirs. 1990-91), Ga. Trial Lawyers Assn., Shenandoah Valley Travel Assn. (bd. dirs.), Internat. Platform Assn., S.E. Tourism Soc., Rotary Internat., Ea. Nat. Parks Assn., Sevier County Bar Assn., Soc. Am. Poets, Soc. Magna Carta Barons, Phi Alpha Delta. Episcopalian. Avocations: reading, music, golf, cross-country skiing. E-mail: smokymts@ntelos.net.

BRACKETT, MARTIN LUTHER, JR., lawyer; b. Charlotte, N.C., Feb. 23, 1947; s. Martin Luther and Helen Virginia (Smith) B.; m. Lisa Nichol; children— Martin Hunter, Alexander Jones, Amelia Kathleen, Lauren Hart. B.A., Davidson Coll., 1969; J.D., U. N.C., 1972. Bar: N.C. 1972, U.S. Dist. Ct. (we. dist.) N.C. 1973, U.S. Ct. Appeals (4th cir.) 1975. Ptnr. Bailey, Brackett & Brackett, P.A., Charlotte, N.C., 1973-83, Brackett & Sitton, Charlotte, 1983-85, Robinson, Bradshaw & Hinson, P.A., 1985—. Mem. Auditorium-Coliseum-Conv. Ctr. Authority, Charlotte, 1981-87, chmn., 1985-87. Served to capt. U.S. Army, 1972-73. Recipient Van Hecke-Wettach award U. N.C., 1972. Fellow Am. Coll. Trial Lawyers; mem. N.C. Acad. Trial Lawyers (bd. govs. 1980-86, 88-95, v.p. 1984-86). Democrat. Presbyterian. Criminal, Personal injury (including property damage). Office: 1900 Independence Ctr 101 N Tryon St Charlotte NC 28246-0100

BRADDOCK, DONALD LAYTON, lawyer, accountant, real estate broker, investor; b. Jacksonville, Fla., Dec. 14, 1941; s. John Reddon and Harriet Braddock; children: Stella Helene Knowlton, Leslie Ann Meshad, Donald Layton Jr. BS in Bus. Adminstrn., U. Fla., 1963; JD, 1967. Bar: Fla. 1968, U.S. Dist. Ct. (mid. and no. dists.) Fla. 1968, U.S. Ct. Appeals (5th cir.) 1968, U.S. Ct. Appeals (4th and 11th cirs.) 1968, U.S. Supreme Ct. 1976, U.S. Tax Ct. 1970; CPA; registered real estate broker. Staff acct. Coopers and Lybrand, CPAs, 1964-65, Keith C. Austin, CPA, 1965-67; assoc. Kent, Durden & Kent, attys. at law, 1967-71; sole practice, 1971-73; ptnr. Howell, Kirby, Montgomery, D'Aiuto & Dean, attys. at law, 1974-76; pres., dir. Howell, Liles, Braddock & Milton, attys. at law, Jacksonville, Fla., 1976-88; ret., 1988. Bd. dirs., mem. exec. com. Fla. Lawyers Mutual Ins. Co.; pres., dir. Donald L. Braddock Chartered dba Mandarin Realty, 1970—; mgr. Wildcat Venture, LLC, 2000—; mgr. Bryant Hill, LLC, 2000—. Bd. dirs. Jacksonville Vocat. Edn. Authority, 1971-75; mem. Jacksonville Bicentennial Commn., 1976; bd. govs. Fla. Bar Found., 1984-86, sec.-treas., 1986-88; sec., dir. Laurel Grove Plantation, Inc., 1988—. Served with Air N.G., 1963-69. Mem. Fla. Bar (bd. govs. young lawyers sec. 1972-77), Fla. Inst. CPAs, Jacksonville C. of C. (com. of 100), Jacksonville Bar Assn. (pres. 1983-84, bd. govs. 1978-84), U. Fla. Alumni Assn. (pres. 1975, bd. dirs. 1968-75), Fla. Blue Key, Friars Club, Phi Delta Phi, Alpha Tau Omega. Republican. Corporate, general, Property, real (including real estate development, water), Estate taxation. Office: PO Box 57385 Jacksonville FL 32241-7385

BRADEN, BERWYN BARTOW, lawyer; b. Pana, Ill., Jan. 10, 1928; s. George Clark and Florence Lucille (Bartow) B.; m. Betty J.; children— Scott, Mark, Mathew, Sue, Ralph, Ladd, Brad Student, Carthage Coll., 1946-48, U. Wis., 1948-49, JD, 1959. Bar: Wis. 1959, U.S. Supreme Ct. 1965. Ptnr. Genoar & Braden, Lake Geneva, Wis., 1959-63; individual practice law Lake Geneva, Wis., 1963-68, 72-74; ptnr. Braden & English, Lake Geneva, Wis., 1968-72, Braden & Olson, Lake Geneva, Wis., 1974—2002, Gagliardi O'Brien Braden Olson and Kapelli, Lake Geneva, 2002—. City atty. City of Lake Geneva, 1962-64; tchr. Law Sch., U. Wis., 1977 Bd. dirs. Lake Geneva YMCA. Mem. ABA, Walworth County Bar Assn. (pres. 1962-63), State Bar Wis. (chmn. conv. and entertainment com. 1979-81, chmn. adminstrn. Justice and Judiciary com., 1986-87, bench bar rels. com., 1987-90, mem. exec. com. Wis. Bicentennial Com. on Constn.), Wis. Acad. Trial Lawyers (sec. 1975, treas. 1976, dir. 1977-79), Assn. Trial Lawyers Am. Home: 1031 W Main St Lake Geneva WI 53147-1700 Office: 716 Wisconsin St Lake Geneva WI 53147-1826 also: PO Box 940 Lake Geneva WI 53147-0940 E-mail: bando@genevaonline.com.

BRADFORD, CARL O. judge; b. Dallas, Nov. 16, 1932; s. Montie Leroy and Vivian Ila (Milan) B.; m. Claire Solange Chaloux, Jan. 15, 1955 (dec. 1972); children: Timothy, Kathleen, Elizabeth; m. Mary Ellen Sanborn, July 7, 1973; children: Bethany, Michael. Student, U. Detroit, 1956-59; JD, U. Maine, Portland, 1962. Bar: Maine 1963, U.S. Dist. Ct. Maine 1963, U.S. Ct. Appeals (1st cir.) 1963, U.S. Supreme Ct. 1978. Asst. atty. gen. State of Maine, Augusta, 1963-64, justice Superior Ct., 1981-98, active-ret. justice Superior Ct., 1998—. Ptnr. Powers & Bradford, Freeport, Maine, 1964-81; commr. Uniform State Laws, 1972-76; mem. drafting com. Uniform Exemptions Act, 1974-76. Bd. dirs. Nat. Ctr. State Cts., Williamsburg, Va., 1997—2000; trustee Nat. Jud. Coll., Reno, 2001—. With USN, 1951—55. Fellow Am. Bar Found., Maine Bar Found.; mem. Maine Bar Assn. (bd. govs. 1970-78, pres. 1977-78), Maine Trial Lawyers Assn. (bd. govs., sec. 1970-81), ABA (ho. of dels. 1978-81, 90-95, state bar del. 1978-81, bd. govs. 1st dist. 1990-93, bd. lisiaon to Nat. Conf. Spl. Ct. Judges 1990-91, liaison to Criminal Justice Sect. 1990-93, liaison to Nat. Conf. State Trial Judges 1991-93, chair subcom. nominations and awards com. 1991-93, bd. govs. program com. 1990-91, mem. oper. com. 1991-93, project 2000 subcom. 1991-93, bd. govs. chair compensation com. 1993, bd. govs. exec. com. 1993, bd. govs. exec. dir. search com. 1990, mem. comm. on multi-disciplinary practice 1998-2000), Nat. Conf. State Trial Judges (del. 1982-97, jud. immunity com. 1984-97, chair 1991-96, conf. vice chair 1993, chair-elect 1994-95, chair 1995-96), Am. Judicature Soc. Home: 225 Sea Meadows Ln Yarmouth ME 04096-5523 Office: Superior Ct PO Box 287 Portland ME 04112-0287

BRADFORD, DANA GIBSON, II, lawyer; b. Coral Gables, Fla., Sept. 29, 1948; s. Dana Gibson and Jeanette (Ellis) B.; m. Mary E. Bradford, June 20, 1970 (div. Jan. 1982); 1 child, Jeffrey Dana; m. Donna P. Bradford, Apr. 14, 1984; 1 child, Shannon Claire. BA, U. Fla., 1970; JD, Duke U., 1973. Bar: Fla. 1973, U.S. Dist. Ct. (mid. dist.) Fla. 1974, U.S. Dist. Ct. (so. and no. dists.) Fla. 1979, U.S. Ct. Appeals (5th cir.) 1974, U.S. Ct. Appeals (11th cir.) 1982, U.S. Supreme Ct. 1977. Lawyer, ptnr. Mahoney, Hadlow & Adams, Jacksonville, Fla., 1973-82, Baumer, Bradford & Walters, Jacksonville, 1982—2000, Smith, Gambrell & Russell, LLP, Jacksonville, 2000—. Mem. Fla. Bd. Bar Examiners, 1989-94, chmn. bd., 1992-93; mem. Fla. Supreme Ct. Commn. on Professionalism, 1996-98; seminar lectr. Contbr. chpt. to book, articles to profl. jours. Mem. Leadership Jacksonville, 1982; spl. counsel Jacksonville Sports Authority. Capt. U.S. Army Res., 1972-80. Mem. ABA, ATLA, Jacksonville Bar Assn. (bd. govs. young lawyers sect. 1976-78, chmn. trial sects. 1989-90), Jacksonville Assn. Def. Counsel (pres. 1978-79). Republican. Methodist. Federal civil litigation, General civil litigation, State civil litigation. Office: Smith Gambrell & Russell LLP 50 N Laura St Ste 2200 Jacksonville FL 32202-3625 E-mail: dgbradford@sgrlaw.com.

BRADIE, PETER RICHARD, lawyer, engineer; b. Bklyn., Feb. 19, 1937; s. Alexander Robert and Blanche Isabelle Bradie; m. Anna Barbara Corcoran, Jan. 22, 1960; children: Suzanne J., Barbara L., Michell S. BSME, Fairleigh Dickinson U., 1960; JD, South Tex. Coll. Law, 1978. Bar: Tex. 1978, U.S. Dist. Ct. (so. dist.) Tex. 1981; registered profl. engr., Ala. Performance engr. Pratt & Whitney Aircraft, West Palm Beach, Fla., 1961-63; sr. engr. Hayes Internat. Corp., Huntsville, Ala., 1963—68, Lockheed Missiles and Space, Huntsville, 1964—68; fluidics engr. Double A Products Co., Manchester, Mich., 1968-69; cons. Spectrum Controls, Montvale, N.J., 1969-72; sr. project mgr. Materials Research Corp., Orangebury, N.Y., 1972-74; sr. contracts adminstr. Brown & Root Inc., Houston, 1974-85; sole practice Houston, 1985-91; ptnr. Bradie, Bradie & Bradie, Houston, 1991—. Counsel Inverness Forest C.A., Houston., 1978-80; sr. counsel Raymond-Brown & Root-Molem, J.V., Houston, 1982-84. Contbr. articles on fluidic controls to mags.; patentee. Dem. committeeman Bergen County, Haworth, N.J., 1959; del. Harris County Reps., Houston, 1984; officer, bd. dirs. Inverness Forest Civic Assn., Houston, 1975-78. Served to 2d lt. USMCR, 1958-61. Mem.: ATLA, Comml. Law League Am., Houston N.W. Bar Assn. (treas. 1986, bd. dirs. 1988, pres.-elect 1988—89, pres. 1990—91), Tex. Bar Assn., N.W. Houston Sunrise Rotary Club, Montvale Rotary Club (bd. dirs. 1973—74), Rotary Internat., Am. Inn of Ct. Republican. Jewish. Avocations: classical music, history, computers. General civil litigation, Commercial, contracts (including sales of goods; commercial financing), General practice. Home: 22007 Kenchester Dr Houston TX 77073-1315 Office: Bradie Bradie & Bradie 3845 Fm 1960 Rd W Ste 330 Houston TX 77068-3519 E-mail: bradiex3@bradie-law.com.

BRADLEY, AMELIA JANE, lawyer; b. Columbia, S.C., Apr. 18, 1947; d. Hugh Wilson and Amelia Jane (Wylie) B.; m. Richard Bancroft Hovey, Apr. 1, 1977. BA, U. Va., 1968; MA, George Washington U., 1971. Bar: Va. 1976, D.C. 1985. Budget and mgmt. analyst NLRB, Washington, 1968-71, 72; clk. Cohen and Vitt, PC, Alexandria, Va., 1972-76; assoc. Cohen, Vitt & Annand, PC, Alexandria, 1976-80; White House fellow USDA, Washington, 1980-81, Office U.S. Trade Rep., Exec. Office of Pres., Washington, 1981, asst. gen. counsel, 1981-82, assoc. gen. counsel, 1982-84, legal advisor to U.S. GATT del. Geneva, 1984-87; prin. dep. gen. counsel Office U.S. Trade Rep., Exec Office of Pres., Washington, 1989-92; asst. U.S. trade rep. for dispute resolution Office U.S. Trade Rep., Exec. Office of Pres., Washington, 1994; assoc. dir. for global environment White House Office on Environ. Policy, Washington, 1994-95; assoc. dir. internat. trade and devel. Coun. on Environ. Quality, Washington, 1994—95; asst. U.S. trade rep. for monitoring, enforcement Exec. Office of Pres., Washington, 1996—2002. Chief negotiator U.S. GATT Uruguay Round Dispute Settlement Negotiating Group, 1986-87, 89-93; chmn. interagy. Sect. 301 Com., Washington, 1988-92; vis. rsch. assoc. Fletcher Sch. Law and Diplomacy, Tufts U., Medford, Mass., 1987-88; vis. rschr. Harvard U. Law Sch., Cambridge, Mass., 1988. Mem., chmn. Alexandria Human Rights Commn., 1975-80; pres., trustee Alexandria Law Libr., 1978-80; founding mem. Lawyer Referral Svc., Alexandria, 1978. NEH fellow, 1978. Mem. ABA, Va. State Bar (mem., chmn. com. on legal edn. and admission to bar 1977-84), D.C. Bar (chmn. internat. trade com. 1989-90). Episcopalian.

BRADLEY, ANN WALSH, state supreme court justice; married; 4 children. BA, Webster Coll., 1972; JD, U. Wis., 1976. Tchr. HS; pvt. law practice; former judge Marathon County Circuit Ct., Wausau, Wis.; justice Wis. Supreme Ct., Madison, Wis., 1995—. Office: Wis Ct Sys PO Box 1688 Madison WI 53701-1688

BRADLEY, CHARLES HARVEY, lawyer; b. Indpls., July 17, 1923; s. Charles Harvey and Carolyn (Coffin) Bradley; m. Mary Jo Albright, Aug. 26, 1944; children: Sally A., Jane C. AB, Yale U., 1945, LLB, 1949. Bar: Ind. 1949. Ptnr. Thomson, O'Neal & Smith, Indpls., 1950—60; mgr. legal dept. Eli Lilly and Co., Indpls., 1960—63, asst. sec., dir. legal div., 1963, sec., gen. counsel, 1964—84, v.p., gen. counsel, 1984—86, sr. v.p., gen. counsel, 1986—87. Mem. com. on character and fitness Ind. Supreme Ct., 1965—87; Supreme Ct. Com. on Continuing Legal Edn., 1984—87. Trustee Hussey-Mayfield Meml. Pub. Libr., Zionsville, Ind., 1990—96. Served to 2d lt. USMC, 1943—45, to capt. USMC, 1952—53. Decorated Air medal with 8 oak leaf clusters, D.F.C. with 3 oak leaf clusters. Fellow: Ind. Bar Found.; mem.: Yale Law Sch. Assn. (pres. 1977—79, pres.'s commn. mgmt. agy. for internat. devel. 1991—92, mem. exec. com.), Indpls. C. of C. (dir. emeritus), Assn. Gen. Counsel, Indpls. Bar Assn., Ind. Bar Assn., Yale of Ind. Club (past pres.), Indpls. Lawyers Club. Corporate, general. Home: 1310 S Us Highway 421 Zionsville IN 46077-9762

BRADLEY, DONALD EDWARD, lawyer; b. Santa Rosa, Calif., Sept. 26, 1943; s. Edward Aloysius and Mildred Louise (Kelley) B.; m. Marianne Stark, Apr. 22, 1990; children: Evan Patrick, Matthew Jordan, Andrea Phelps. AB, Dartmouth Coll., 1965; JD, U. Calif., San Francisco, 1968; LLM, N.Y.U., 1972. Bar: Calif. 1968, U.S. Dist. Ct. (no. dist.) Calif. 1968, U.S. Ct. Appeals (9 cir.) 1968, U.S. Tax Ct. 1972, U.S. Ct. Claims 1973, U.S. Supreme Ct. 1981. Assoc. Pillsbury, Madison & Sutro, San Francisco, 1972-77, ptnr., 1978-84; mem. Wilson Sonsini Goodrich & Rosati, Palo Alto, Calif., 1984—. Mng. dir. Wilson Sonsini Goodrich & Rosati, Palo Alto, 1995—; adj. prof. Golden State U., San Francisco, 1973-82; pres., chmn. bd. dirs. Atty.'s Ins. Mut. Risk Retention Group, Honolulu, 1986—. Capt. U.S. Army, 1969-70. Recipient Charles M. Ruddick award N.Y.U., 1972, award Bureau of Nat. Affairs, Washington, 1968. Mem. ABA, Internat. Bar Assn., Santa Clara Bar Assn., San Francisco Bar Assn., Internat. Tax Club, Peninsula Tax Club. Finance, Private international, Corporate taxation. Office: Wilson Sonsini Goodrich & Rosati 650 Page Mill Rd Palo Alto CA 94304-1050 E-mail: dbradley@wsgr.com.

BRADLEY, JEAN MARIE, lawyer; b. Bluffton, Ind., Sept. 16, 1961; d. Louis Francis and Ruth Edna Bradley. BA in Psychology cum laude, St. Mary's of Notre Dame, 1984; JD, U. Houston, 1992. Bar: Tex. 1992, U.S. Dist. Ct. (no., so. and ea. dists.) Tex. 1993, U.S. Ct. Appeals (5th cir.) 1993, U.S. Ct. Appeals (6th cir.) 1997. Dep. bail bond commr. Allen County Superior Ct., Ft. Wayne, Ind., 1985-87; probation officer Dallas County Adult Probation Dept., Dallas, 1987-89; atty. McLeod, Alexander, Powel & Apffel, Galveston and Houston, 1992-94, Liddell, Sapp, Zively, Hill & LaBoon, L.L.P., Dallas, 1995-98, Paul VanNess & Assocs., Dallas, 1999—. Mem. Evergreen Gala, Dallas, 1996-97; mem. Habitat for Humanity, Dallas, 1998-2002; mem. Make-A-Wish Found., Dallas, 1998; vol. Housing Crisis Ctr., Dallas, 1996—, Lawyers Mentoring Kids Program, Dallas, 1996, 2001=02; mem. Attys. Serving the Cmty., Dallas, 1996—. Recipient Citizen's Citation award Ft. Wayne Police Dept., 1985, Vol. Atty. award Housing Crisis Ctr., 1997; named to Outstanding Young Women of Am., 1998. Mem. ABA, State Bar Tex., Tex. Young Lawyers Assn. Avocations: aerobics, skiing, cooking, reading. General civil litigation, Insurance. Office: Paul VanNess & Assocs Founders Sq 900 Jackson Ste 700 Dallas TX 75202

BRADLEY, LAWRENCE D., JR., lawyer; b. Santa Monica, Calif., Feb. 19, 1920; s. Lawrence D. Bradley and Virginia L. Edwards; m. Joan Worthington, Feb. 1, 1945; children— Gary W., Brooks, Eric Scott BS, U.S. Coast Guard Acad., 1942; LL.B., Stanford U., 1950. Bar: Calif. 1950, U.S. Dist. Ct. (cen. dist.) Calif. 1950, U.S. Dist. Ct. (so. dist.) Calif. 1967. Assoc. Pillsbury, Madison & Sutro, L.A., 1950-59, ptnr., 1959—; of counsel Pillsbury Winthrop LLP. Lectr. admiralty and ins. law U. So. Calif., 1952-80 Pres. Stanford Law Rev., 1949-50; assoc. editor Am. Maritime Cases, 1990-2000. Mem. adv. bd. Tulane Admiralty Law Inst., 1990—. With USN, 1942-48; to lt. comdr. Res. Mem. ABA, Calif. Bar Assn., Maritime Law Assn. U.S. (mem. exec. com. 1974-78, chmn. cruise line com. 1991-94), Inst. Navigation, Order of Coif, Calif. Club, Chancery Club, Calif. Yacht Club, San Diego Yacht Club, Propeller Club, Transpacific Yacht Club, Tutukaka South Pacific Yacht Club. Admiralty, Insurance, Private international. Office: Pillsbury Winthrop LLP 725 S Figueroa St Ste 2800 Los Angeles CA 90017-5443

BRADSHAW, CONRAD ALLAN, lawyer; b. Campbell, Mo., Dec. 22, 1922; s. Clarence Andrew and Stella (Cashdollar) B.; m. Margaret Crassous Sanderson, Dec. 31, 1959; children— Dorothy A., Lucy E., Charlotte L. AB, U. Mich., 1943, JD, 1948. Bar: Mich. bar 1948. Since practiced in Grand Rapids with firm Warner, Norcross & Judd. Served to lt. USNR, 1943-46. Mem. Am. Bar Assn., State Bar Mich. (chmn. corp., fin. and bus. law sect. 1976), Grand Rapids Bar Assn. (pres. 1970) Home: 3261 Lake Dr SE Grand Rapids MI 49506-4320 Office: 900 Fifth Third Ctr 111 Lyon St NW Grand Rapids MI 49503

BRADSHAW, JEAN PAUL, II, lawyer; b. May 12, 1956; married; children: Andrew, Stephanie. BJ, JD, U. Mo., 1981. Bar: Mo. 1981, U.S. Dist. Ct. (we. dist.) Mo. 1982, U.S. Dist. Ct. (so. dist.) Ill. 1988, U.S. Ct. Appeals (8th cir.) 1986, U.S. Supreme Ct. 1987. Assoc. Neale, Newman, Bradshaw & Freeman, Springfield, Mo., 1981-87, ptnr., 1987-89; U.S. atty. we. dist. Mo. U.S. Dept. Justice, Kansas City, 1989-93; of counsel Lathrop & Gage, Kansas City, 1993-99, mem., 2000—, chair dept. health law, 2000—. Named Spl. Asst. Atty. Gen. State of Mo., 1985-89; mem., chmn. elect U.S. Atty. Gen.'s adv. com., office mgmt. and budget subcom., sentencing guidelines subcom. Chmn. Greene County Rep. cen. com., 1988-89; pres. Mo. Assn. Reps., 1986-87; bd. dirs. Greene County TARGET, 1984-89; mem. com. on resolutions, family and community issues and del. 1988 Rep. Nat. Conv.; mem. platform com. Mo. Reps., 1988; chmn. Greene County campaign McNary for Gov., 1984, co-chmn. congl. dist. Dole for Pres., 1988, regional chmn. Danforth for Senate, 1988, co-chmn. 7th congl. dist. Webster for Atty. Gen., 1988; county chmn. U. Mo.-Columbia Alumni Assn., 1985-87; bd. dirs. Springfield Profl. Baseball Assn., Inc.; past mem. Mo. Adv. Coun. for Comprehensive Psychiat. Svcs., former bd. dirs. Ozarks Coun. Boy Scouts Am.; pres. bd. trustees St. Paul's Episcopal Day Sch., 1997-2002. Named Outstanding Recent Grad. U. Mo.-Columbia Sch. Law, 1991. Mem. ABA, Mo. Bar Assn., Kansas City Met. Bar Assn., U. Mo.-Columbia Law Sch. Alumni Assn. (v.p. 1988-89, pres. 1990-91), Law Soc. U. Mo.-Columbia Law Sch. Office: 2345 Grand Blvd Ste 2800 Kansas City MO 64108-2612 E-mail: jpbradshaw@rathropgage.com.

BRADY, EDMUND MATTHEW, JR., lawyer; b. Apr. 24, 1941; s. Edmund Matthew and Thelma (McDonald) B.; m. Marie Pierre Wayne, May 14, 1966; children: Edmund Matthew III, Meghan, Timothy BSS, John Carroll U., 1963; JD, U. Detroit, 1966; postgrad., Sch. Law, Wayne State U., 1966—69; DHL (hon.) , U. Detroit, 1998. Bar: Mich. 1966, U.S. Dist. Ct. (ea. dist.) Mich. 1966, U.S. Ct. Appeals (6th cir.) 1973, U.S. Supreme Ct. 1974. Sr. ptnr. Vandeveer & Garzia, 1973-90, Plunkett & Cooney, P.C., 1990—. Village clk. Grosse Pointe Shores, Mich., 1975-80; trustee St. John Hosp. and Med. Ctr., Detroit, 1992-2000, chmn., 1994-2000, Grosse Pointe Acad., Mich., 1977-83, adv. trustee, 1983-89; vice chmn. St. John Physicians Hosp. Orgn., 1994-95; supr. Grosse Pointe Twp., 1994-2000, trustee, 1989-2000; pres., dir. Grosse Pointe Hockey Assn., 1969-70; bd. dirs., chmn. maj. gifts divsn. 1st Fund, St. John Hosp. Guild; bd. dirs., pres. Friends of Bon Secours Hosp.; trustee, mem. exec. com., mem. fin. com. St. John Health Sys., 1998-2000. Recipient award of distinction U. Detroit Law Alumni, 1981, Michael Franck award State Bar of Mich. Rep. Assembly, 1998, Respected Advocate award Mich. Trial Lawyers Assn., 1998. Fellow Am. Bar Found, Mich. State Bar Found. (life); mem. ABA, Am. Coll. Trial Lawyers, Inter. Soc. Barristers, Am. Bd. Trial Advocates, Internat. Assn. Def. Counsel, Assn. Def. Trial Counsel (dir. 1975-80, pres. 1980-81), Mich. Def. Trial Counsel (dir. 1980-81), Def. Rsch. Inst. (Exceptional Performance citation 1981), Cath. Lawyers Soc., Soc. Irish-Am. Lawyers (founding dir. 1979-81), Mediation Tribunal Assn. (mem. panel Wayne County, Macomb County mediator 1989-98), Detroit Bar Assn. (dir. 1986-91, sec.-treas. 1988, pres.-elect 1989-90, pres. 1990-91), State Bar Mich. (commr. 1991-98, treas. 1994, v.p. 1995, pres.-elect 1996, pres. 1997-98), Country Club of Detroit, Detroit Athletic Club, Delta Theta Phi. Republican. Roman Catholic. Federal civil litigation, General civil litigation, State civil litigation. Office: Plunkett & Cooney 535 Griswold St Ste 2400 Detroit MI 48226 E-mail: ebrady@plunkettcooney.com.

BRADY, EDWARD THOMAS, judge; b. Bklyn., N.Y., Nov. 1, 1943; s. Thomas and Virginia (Briggs) Brady; m. Dianne Downing; children: Thomas Robert, Ryan Ashley. Grad., Officer Candidate Sch., 1966; BA in Criminal Justice, U. Nebr., 1972; MA in Criminal Justice, CUNY, 1977; JD, U. Calif., San Diego, 1978. Bar: N.C., Ga., D.C., (U.S. Supreme Ct.), (U.S. Ct. Appeals (4th cir.)), (U.S. Ct. Appeals (5th cir.)), (U.S. Ct. Appeals (D.C. cir.)), (U.S. Army Ct. Mil. Rev.), (U.S. Ct. Mil. Appeals). Enlisted pvt. U.S. Army, 1965; ret. as col. USAR, 1995; pvt. practice in law Fayetteville, NC, 1978—; spl. agt., criminal investigator Dept. Treas., Bur. Alcohol, Tobacco and Firearms; assoc. justice N.C. State Supreme Ct., Raleigh, 2002—. Decorated DFC, Bronze Star medal, Air Medal with Valor Device for heroism and 2d-18th oak leaf cluster, Vietnam Cross of Gallantry with Bronze Star. Office: Justice Bldg PO Box 1841 Raleigh NC 27602

BRADY, GEORGE EOGHAN, lawyer; b. Dublin, May 4, 1971; s. George and Margaret (Lysaght) B. Student, DePaul U., 1993; B of Civil Law, U. Coll. Dublin, 1994. Atty. Baker & McKenzie, Dublin, 1994-98, assoc., 2000—, Matheson Ormsey Prentice Dudin, London, 1998—2003, ptnr., 2003—. Mem. Law Soc. Ireland, Law Soc. Eng. and Wales, Dublin Bar Assn. Corporate, general, Mergers and acquisitions. Office: Matheson Ormsby Prentice 30 Herbert St Dublin 2 Ireland E-mail: george.brady@mop.ie.

BRADY, JACK EDGAR, lawyer; b. Dallas, Aug. 13, 1925; s. V.E. and Thelma (Hill) B.; m. Kathryn Ann Barngrover, Jan. 14, 1951; children: Douglas W., Julia Ann, Susan Lynn. BBA, U. Tex., 1947, LLB, 1949. Bar: Tex. 1949, U.S. Dist. Ct. (no. dist.) Tex. 1951, U.S. Ct. Appeals (5th cir.). Sr. ptnr. Brady & Drake, Dallas, 1951-54, Brady, Drake & Yates, Dallas, 1954-61, Brady, Drake & Wilson, Dallas, 1961-80; pres. Law Offices of Jack E. Brady, P.C., Dallas, 1980—. Pres. Dallas Jr. Bar, 1954-55; speaker Various Tex. State Bar courses. Chmn. deacons First Bapt. Ch., Dallas, 1984; chmn. trustees Criswell Coll., Dallas, 1992-98; chmn. bd. dirs. BankDallas, 2001. Served with USN, 1947-49. Republican. Club: Lakewood Country. Banking, Corporate, general, Probate (including wills, trusts). Office: Law Offices of Jack E Brady PC 2000 Republic Ctr 325 N St Paul Dallas TX 75201

BRADY, LAWRENCE PETER, lawyer; b. Jersey City, July 26, 1940; s. Lawrence Peter and Evelyn (Mauro) B.; div; children: Deegan, Tara, Kerry, Melissa, James; m. Mary Helen Reynolds, Mar. 28, 1984. BS in Acctg., St. Peters Coll., 1961; JD, Seton Hall U., 1964; LLM, Bklyn. Law Sch., 1966. Bar: N.J. 1964, U.S. Dist. Ct. N.J. 1964, U.S. Supreme Ct. 1969, U.S. Ct. Appeals (3rd cir.) 1972, N.Y. 1991; cert. civil trial atty. State of N.J. 1982; cert. Nat. Bd. Trial Advocacy 1989. Asst. prosecutor Hudson County, Jersey City, 1964-70; prosecutor Town of Kearny, N.J., 1971-74; sr. ptnr. Doyle & Brady, Kearny, 1974—. Dir. and founding incorporator Growth Bank, New Vernon, N.J. Mem. ATLA, Nat. Bd. Trial Advocacy, N.J. State Bar Assn., Hudson County Bar Assn., West Hudson Bar Assn. (sec. 1980, treas. 1981, v.p. 1982, pres. 1983), Am. Trial Lawyers N.J. (bd. govs.), Roxiticus Golf Club (Mendham, N.J.), Sandalfoot Country Club (Boca Raton, Fla.), Ocean Reef Club (Key Largo, Fla.), Ocean Reef Yacht Club. Roman Catholic. Avocations: golf, tennis, travel, fishing, boating. General civil litigation, State civil litigation, Personal injury (including property damage). Office: Doyle & Brady 377 Kearny Ave Kearny NJ 07032-2600

BRADY, M. JANE, state attorney general; b. Wilmington, Del., Jan. 11, 1951; m. Michael Neal. BA, U. Del., 1973; JD, Villanova U., 1976. Dep. atty. gen. Wilmington and Kent County, 1977—90; chief prosecutor Sussex County, 1987—90; solo law practice, 1990—94; atty. gen. State of Del., Wilmington, 1994—. Republican. Office: Office of Atty Gen Carvel State Office Bldg 820 N French St Wilmington DE 19801-3509 E-mail: jbrady@state.de.us.

BRADY, PHILLIP DONLEY, lawyer; b. Pasadena, Calif., May 20, 1951; s. Donley L. and Evelyn M. (Dorweiler) B.; m. Kathleen Ryan; children: Ryan Donley, Conor Phillip, Sean Patrick. BA cum laude, U. Notre Dame, 1973; JD cum laude, Loyola U., Los Angeles, 1976. Bar: Calif. 1976, U.S. Ct. Appeals (D.C. cir.) 1978, U.S. Supreme Ct. 1980, U.S. Ct. Mil. Appeals 1990. Assoc. atty. Spray, Gould & Bowers, L.A., 1976-78; dep. atty gen. State of Calif., L.A., 1978-79; legis. counsel U.S. Rep. Daniel E. Lungren, Washington, 1979-81; regional dir. ACTION Agy., San Francisco, 1981-82; dir., Congl. Affairs, Immigration and Naturalization Svc. Dept. of Justice, Washington, 1982-83, assoc. dep. atty. gen., 1983-84, acting asst. atty. gen., 1984-85; dep. asst. to V.P. The White House, Washington, 1985-88, dep. counsel to Pres., 1988-89; gen. counsel Dept. Transp., Washington, 1989-91; asst. to Pres. and staff sec. The White House, Washington, 1991-93; v.p, gen. counsel Am. Automobile Mfrs. Assn., Washington, 1993—99; COO ind. rels. Nat. Automobile Dealers Assn., McLean, Va., 1999—2001, pres., 2001—. Mem. Coun. of the Administrv. Conv. of the U.S., 1988-93. Mem. ABA, Calif. State Bar Assn., FBA (chair gen. counsels sect. 1989-91, nat. coun. 1989—). Home: 5916 Colfax Ave Alexandria VA 22311-1024 Office: Nat Automobile Dealers Assn 8400 Westpark Dr Mc Lean VA 22102-3522

BRADY, RICHARD ALAN, lawyer; b. Newark, Sept. 17, 1934; s. Andrew Joseph and Katherine (Bogan) B.; m. Kathleen R. Sweeney, June 12, 1965; children: Cecilia, Kathleen, Andrew, Joshua. BS, Yale U., 1956, LLB, 1959. Bar: D.C. 1960. Ptnr. Covington & Burling, Washington, 1959—. Corporate taxation. Office: Covington & Burling 1201 Pennsylvania Ave NW PO Box 7566 Washington DC 20044-7566

BRADY, RUPERT JOSEPH, lawyer; b. Washington, Jan. 24, 1932; s. John Bernard and Mary Catherine (Rupert) B.; m. Maureen Mary MacIntosh, Apr. 20, 1954; children: Rupert Joseph Jr., Laureen Zegowitz, Kevin, Warren, Jeanine Hartnett, Jacqueline Rada, Brian, Barton. BEE, Cath. U. Am., 1953; JD, Georgetown U., 1959. Bar: Md. 1961, U.S. Ct. Appeals (D.C. cir.) 1964, U.S. Patent Trademark Office 1961, D.C. 1962, U.S. Supreme Ct. 1969, U.S. Ct. Appeals (fed. cir.) 1961. Elec. engr. Sperry Gyroscope Co., L.I., 1953-56; patent specifications writer John B. Brady, patent atty., 1956-59; patent agt. B.P. Fishburne, Jr., Washington, 1959-61; pvt. practice patent agt. Washington and Md., 1961; practice Washington, Md. and Va., 1961—; sr. ptnr. Brady, O'Boyle & Gates, Washington & Chevy Chase, Md., 1963-95; of counsel Birch, Stewart, Kolasch & Birch, LLP, Va., 1996—. V.p. Minstr-O-Media Inc. Patentee crane booms, moldboard support assembly. Mem. ABA, Am. Intellectual Property Law Assn., Md. Patent Law Assn., Senator's Club Alumni. Republican. Roman Catholic. Intellectual property, Patent, Trademark and copyright. Home: 7201 Pyle Rd Bethesda MD 20817-5623 Office: 8110 Gatehouse Rd Ste 500E Falls Church VA 22042-1210

BRADY, TERRENCE JOSEPH, judge; b. Chgo., Dec. 24, 1940; s. Harry J. and Othele R. Brady; m. Debra René, Dec. 6, 1969; children: Tara René, Dana Rose. BA cum laude, Coll. St. Thomas, 1963; JD, U. Ill., 1968. Bar: Ill. 1969, U.S. Dist. Ct. (no. dist.) Ill. 1970, U.S. Ct. Appeals (7th cir.) 1971. Pvt. practice, Crystal Lake, Ill., 1969-70, Waukegan, Ill., 1970-77; assoc. judge 19th Jud. Cir., Ill. Cir. Ct., Waukegan, 1977—. Lectr. Ann. Ill. Assoc. Judge Seminars, Statewide Ill. Traffic Conf., 1982, Lake County Bar Assn. Seminar, 1983, 88, others; invited participant Law and Econs. Seminar, U. Kans., 2000, Judicial Faculty Development, Ill. Judicial Conf., 2000; vis. jud. faculty Nat. Jud. Coll., U. Nev. Reno, 1997, condr. seminar civil mediation, 1999; materials author and lectr. in field, 1997; author, presenter, lectr. in field, 1998-; long range planning com. 19th Jud. Circuit, Lake County, Ill., 1999; alt. faculty mem., Chancery and Miscellaneous Remedies, 2000, Settlement Techniques, 2002; mem. delegation of Am. judges, Mexican Govt. Jud. Visitation Program, Mex.,2001. Author: Settle It, The Docket, 1998, The Six Steps of a Jury Trial, 1999, Civil Discovery-Rule 213-Keys to Compliance, 1999; author and lectr., SCR 213-2000 Update, The Docket, 2000; mem. editl. bd. The Docket; contbr. articles to profl. jours. Served with U.S. Army, 1963-64, 68-69. Mem. ISBA (bench and bar sect. coun., adv. polls com.), LCBA (civil trial, med., legal coms.), Ill. Bar Assn. (com. on jud. adv. polls 1994—, vice-chair adv. polls 1998, task force on domestic violence 1998—, chair jud. adv. polls, 1999, sec. com. on jud. adv. polls 1997-99, bench and bar coms., judicial polls), Ill. Judges Assn. (bd. govs.), Ill. Bar Found., Lake County Bar Assn., Libertyville Racquet Club, Am. Inns of Ct. Avocations: tennis, golf, writing, reading. Office: Lake County Courthouse 18 N County St Waukegan IL 60085-4304 E-mail: tbrady@co.lake.il.us.

BRADY, THOMAS CARL, lawyer; b. Malone, N.Y., Sept. 5, 1947; s. Francis Robert and Rosamond Ethel (South) B.; m. Joan Marie Murray, Dec. 4, 1971; children: Erin Marie, Ryan Thomas, Trevor Michael. BA, Niagara U., 1969; JD, SUNY, Buffalo, 1972. Bar: N.Y. 1973, U.S. Dist. Ct. (we. dist.) N.Y. 1973, Fla. 1981. City ct. judge City of Salamanca, N.Y., 1973; atty. County of Cattaraugus, Little Valley, N.Y., 1973-76; ptnr. Eldredge, Brady, Peters & Brooks, Salamanca and Ellicottville, NY, 1976-82; sr. ptnr. Brady, Brooks & Smith, Salamanca, 1982—96, Brady, Brooks & O'Connell, L.L.P., Salamanca, 1996—2001, Brady & O'Connell, L.L.P., Salamanca, 2001—02, Brady & Swenson, Salamanca, 2002—. Trustee St. Patrick's Roman Cath. Ch., Salamanca, 1991—; mem. N.Y. State Office Parks, Recreation and Hist. Preservation Allegany Region Commn., 1998—, vice chair, 1999—; mem. 8th Dist. Atty. Grievance Com., 1994-2000. Capt. USAR, 1969-76. Mem.: ATLA, N.Y. State Trial Lawyers Assn., Cattaraugus County Bar Assn. (pres. 1984), N.Y. State Bar Assn. (mem. ho. of dels. 2003), Fla. Bar Assn., Kiwanis (pres. Salamanca club 1983—84). Republican. Roman Catholic. Avocations: skiing, golf, swimming, boating. General civil litigation, Personal injury (including property damage), Product liability. Home: 6894 Woodland Dr Great Valley NY 14741-9752 Office: Brady & Swenson 41 Main St Salamanca NY 14779-0227 Fax: 716-945-3566. E-mail: tbrady@bradyandswenson.com.

BRAFFORD, WILLIAM CHARLES, lawyer; b. Pike County, Ky., Aug. 7, 1932; s. William Charles and Minnie (Tacket) B.; m. Katherine Jane Prather, Nov. 13, 1954; children— William Charles III, David A. JD, U. Ky., 1957; LLM (fellow), U. Ill., 1958. Bar: Ky. 1957, Ga. 1965, Tax Ct. U.S 1965, Ct. Claims 1965, Ohio 1966, U.S. Ct. Appeals 1966, U.S. Supreme Ct. 1970, Pa. 1973. Trial atty. NLRB, Washington and Cin., 1958-60; atty. Louisville & Nashville R.R. Co., Louisville, 1960-63, So. Bell Telephone Co., Atlanta, 1963-65; asst. gen. counsel NCR Corp., Dayton, Ohio, 1965-72; v.p., sec., gen. counsel Betz Dearborn, inc., Trevose, Pa., 1972-97, ret., 1997. Former dir. Betz Process Chems., Inc., Betz, Ltd. U.K., Betz Paper Chem. Inc., Betz Energy Chems., Inc., Betz S.A. France, B.L. Chems., Inc., Betz GmbH, Germany, Betz Entec, Inc., Betz Ges. GmbH, Austria, Betz NV Belgium, Betz Sud S.p.A., Italy, Betz Internat. Inc., Betz Europe Inc., Primex Ltd., Barbados. Served as 1st lt. C.I.C. AUS, 1954-56. Mem. Am. Soc. Corp. Secs., Nat. Assn. Corp. Dirs., Atlantic Legal Found. Republican. Presbyterian.

BRAGG, ELLIS MEREDITH, JR., lawyer; b. Washington, Jan. 30, 1947; s. Ellis Meredith Sr. and Lucille (Tingstrum) B.; m. Judith Owens, Aug. 18, 1968; children: Michael Andrew, Jennifer Meredith. BA, King Coll., 1969; JD, Wake Forest U., 1973. Bar: N.C. 1973, U.S. Dist. Ct. (we. and mid. dists.) N.C. 1974, U.S. Ct. Appeals (4th cir.) 1980, Admission Supreme Ct. of the U.S.A. May 2002. Assoc. Bailey, Brackett & Brackett, P.A., Charlotte, N.C., 1973-76; ptnr. Howard & Bragg, Charlotte, 1976-77, McConnell, Howard, Johnson, Pruitt, Jenkins & Bragg, Charlotte, 1977-79; pvt. practice, , Charlotte, 2002—. Dist. chmn. Mecklenburg County Dems., Charlotte, 1978; coach youth soccer program YMCA, Charlotte, 1982-83; mem. Headstart Policy Council, Charlotte, 1985. Mem. ABA, N.C. Bar Assn., N.C. Acad. Trial Lawyers. Presbyterian. Avocations: reading, jogging, gardening. State civil litigation, Family and matrimonial, General practice. Home: 6407 Honegger Dr Charlotte NC 28211-4718 Office: 500 E Morehead St Ste 210 Charlotte NC 28202-2694 E-mail: Bragglaw@aol.com.

BRAGG, MICHAEL ELLIS, lawyer, insurance company executive; b. Holdrege, Nebr., Oct. 6, 1947; s. Lionel C and Frances E (Klinginsmith) Bragg; m. Nancy Jo Aabel, Jan. 19, 1980; children: Brian Michael, Kyle Christopher, Jeffrey Douglas. BA, U. Nebr., 1971, JD, 1975. CLU; bar: Alaska 1976, Nebr 1976; cert. ChFC, CPCU. Assoc. White & Jones, Anchorage, 1976-77; field rep. State Farm Ins., Anchorage, 1977-79, atty. corp. law dept. Bloomington, Ill., 1979-81, sr. atty., 1981-84, asst. counsel, 1984-86, counsel, 1986-88; asst. v.p., counsel gen. claims dept. State Farm Fire and Casualty Co., Bloomington, 1988-94; v.p., counsel, gen. claims dept. State Farm Ins. Cos., Bloomington, Ill., 1994-97, assoc. gen. counsel corp. law dept., 1997—. Lectr, contbr legal seminars. Contbr, ed: articles to legal and ins jours. Pres. McLean County Crime Detection Network, 1988—95. With USNG, 1970—76. Recipient Disting. Legal Svc. Award, Corp. Legal Times, 1998, 2003. Fellow: Am. Bar Found.; mem.: ABA (vice chmn property ins law comt 1986—91, chmn. ins. coverage litigation com. 1991—92, various offices tort and ins practices sect. 1986—2003, chair task force on ins staff counsel 2000—02, coun. 2000—03, mem standing comt on ethics and profl responsibility 2001—), Internat. Assn. Def. Counsel, Fedn. Def. and Corp. Counsel (chair industry coop sect 1995—97), Def. Rsch. Inst., Am. Corp. Counsel Assn. Republican. Avocations: golf, tennis. General civil litigation, Insurance, Personal injury (including property damage). Office: State Farm Ins Cos Assoc Gen Counsel One State Farm Plz E-3 Bloomington IL 61710 E-mail: buck.bragg.achk@statefarm.com.

BRAGGION, ANTONIO, lawyer; b. Milan, Oct. 31, 1953; JD, Cath. U., Milan, 1984; LLM, McGeorge Sch. Law, Sacramento, 1991. Bar: Italy 1986. Pvt. practice, Milan, 1986—92; ptnr. Corciulo Braggion & Ptnrs., Milan, Udine, 1992—. Contbr. Commercial, contracts (including sales of goods; commercial financing), Intellectual property, Private international. Office: Corciulo Braggion & Ptnrs Via Roma 43 33100 Udine Italy

BRAID, FREDERICK DONALD, lawyer; b. N.Y.C., Aug. 10, 1946; s. Donald Michael and Margaret Anna (Fluty) B.; m. Eleanor Mae Friedman, Oct. 23, 1980; children: Andrew Harris, Roy Leal, Josh Perry, David Barnett, Steven Gabriel. BS in Econs., St. John's U., Jamaica, N.Y., 1968; JD, St. John's U., Bklyn., 1971; LLM, NYU, 1979. Bar: N.Y. 1972, U.S. Dist. Ct. (so. and ea. dists.) N.Y. 1973, U.S. Ct. Appeals (2d cir.) 1973, (D.C. and 4th cirs.) 1997, U.S. Supreme Ct. 1975. Assoc. Rains & Pogrebin, Mineola and N.Y.C., N.Y., 1971-77, ptnr., 1978-99; bd. dirs. Rains & Pogrebin, P.C., Mineola and N.Y.C., N.Y.; ptnr. Holland and Knight LLP, 2000—. Mem. adv. bd. NYU Sch. Law Ctr. for Labor and Employment Law, 1997—. Mng. editor St. John's Law Rev., 1970-71; contbr. articles to profl. jours. Served to capt. USAR, 1972-80. St. Thomas More scholar, St. John's U. Sch. Law, 1968-71. Mem. ABA, N.Y. Bar Assn., Omicron Delta Epsilon, Delta Mu Delta. Federal civil litigation, State civil litigation, Labor (including EEOC, Fair Labor Standards Act, labor-management relations, NLRB, OSHA). Home: 17 E 96th St New York NY 10128-0783 Office: Holland & Knight LLP 195 Broadway New York NY 10007-3100

BRAITHWAITE, KUNBI, lawyer, researcher; b. Benin City, Edo, Nigeria, Jan. 29, 1969; s. Bankole Akinwumi Braithwaite and Grace Evelyn Osifo; m. Funmi Ronke Adegbite, May 19, 2001; 1 child, Oreoluwatomi. LLB, Lagos (Nigeria) State U., 1995. Bar: Nigeria 1998, cert.: Supreme Ct. (barrister). Co. sec., legal advisor Nigen Co. Ltd., Lagos, 1998—99; assoc. Strachan Ptnrs., Lagos, 1999—2000, F.O. Akinrele & Co., Lagos, 2000—. Exec. dir. Granni Orgn., Lagos, 2001—; trustee, dir. Eklessia Internat., Lagos, 2002. Mem.: Internat. Bar Assn., Nigerian Spanish Assn. Avocations: music, reading, watching television, writing, basketball. Admiralty, Alternative dispute resolution, General practice. Home: 6 Chilaka Close Surulere Lagos Nigeria Office: FO Akinrele & Co 188 Awolowo Rd SW Ikoyi Lagos Nigeria

BRAKE, TIMOTHY L. lawyer; b. St. Joseph, Mo., Apr. 8, 1948; s. Douglas E. and Ruth E. (Fahling) B.; m. Julia Marie Gerkin, Sept. 3, 1977; children: Jennifer L., Douglas M. BA in English, Regis Coll., 1970; JD, U. Mo., 1973. Bar: Mo. 1973, U.S. Dist. Ct. (we. dist.) Mo. 1973. Assoc. Margolin & Kirwan, Kansas City, 1973-79, ptnr., 1979-80; sole practice Kansas City, 1980-2001; of counsel Davis, Bethune & Jones, L.L.C., 2001—. Bd. dirs. Ozanam Home for Boys, 1990—2001, Lantz Welch Charitable Found., 1991—96. Fellow U. Mo. Law Found.; mem. Def. Lawyers Assn. (dir. western sect. 1979-80), Assn. Trial Lawyers Am., Mo. Assn. Trial Attys., Mo. Bar Assn., Kansas City Met. Bar Assn., Friends Art, Friends Zoo, Kansas City Athletic Club (dir. 1986-87), Hallbrook Country Club, Homestead Country Club. General civil litigation, Personal injury (including property damage). Home: 3620 Wyncote Ln Shawnee Mission KS 66205-2739 Office: 1100 Main St Kansas City MO 64105-2105 E-mail: tbrake@dbjlaw.net.

BRAMBLE, RONALD LEE, business and legal consultant; b. Pauls Valley, Okla., Sept. 9, 1937; s. Homer Lee and Ethyle Juanita (Stephens) B.; m. Kathryn Louise Seiler, July 2, 1960; children: Julia Dawn, Kristin Lee. AA, San Antonio Coll., 1957; BS, Trinity U., 1959, MS, 1964; JD, St. Mary's U., 1975; DBA, Ind. No. U., 1973; cert. lay spkr. Meth. Ch. Mgr., buyer Fed-Mart, Inc., San Antonio, 1959-61; tchr. bus. San Antonio Ind. Sch. Dist., 1961-65, edn. coordinator, bus. tng. specialist, 1965-67; assoc. prof., chmn. dept. mgmt. San Antonio Coll., 1967-73; prin. Ron Bramble Assocs., San Antonio, 1967-77; pres. Adminstrv. Research Assocs., Inc., 1977-82; v.p. PIA, Inc., 1982-83; v.p. fin. Solar 21 Corp., 1983-84, sr. staff Ausburn, Astoria & Seale (formerly Ausburn, O'Neill & Assocs.), San Antonio, 1984-89; pvt. practice, 1990—; cons., comptr. TEL-STAR Systems, Inc., 1993-95; v.p. MegaTronics Internat. Corp., 1995—; lectr. bus., edn. and ch. groups, 1965—. Cons. editor: Prentice-Hall, Inc., Englewood Cliffs, N.J., 1969-71; contbr. articles to profl. jours. Mem. Am. Soc. Trial Cons., World Affairs Coun. of San Antonio, diplomat. Served with AUS, 1959. Recipient Wall Street Jour. award Trinity U., 1959, U.S. Law Week award St. Mary's Sch. of Law, 1975. Mem. ABA, Am. Soc. Trial Cons., San Antonio C. of C., Adminstrv. Mgmt. Soc. (pres. 1966-68, Merit award 1968), Bus. Edn. Tchrs. Assn. (pres. 1964), Sales and Mktg. Execs. San Antonio (bd. dirs. 1967-68, Disting. Salesman award 1967), Internat. Platform Assn., Internat. Assn. Cons. to Bus., Nat. Assn. Bus. Economists, Acad. Mgmt., Christian Legal Soc., Comml. Law League Am., Toastmasters, Phi Delta Phi, Lions. Republican. Corporate, general, Private international. Home: 127 Palo Duro St San Antonio TX 78232-3026

BRAME, JOSEPH ROBERT, III, lawyer; b. Hopkinsville, Ky., Apr. 18, 1942; s. Joseph Robert and Atwood Ruth (Davenport) B.; m. Mary Jane Blake, June 11, 1966; children: Rob, Blake, Virginia, John, Thomas. BA with high honors, Vanderbilt U., 1964; LLB, Yale U., 1967. Bar: Va. 1968, D.C. 2001. Assoc. McGuire, Woods, Battle & Boothe, Richmond, Va., 1967-72, ptnr., 1972-97; mem. NLRB, 1997-2000; shareholder Ogletree, Deakins, Nash, Smoak & Stewart, P.C., Washington, 2000—02, McGuire Woods, LLP, 2002—. Lectr. in field. Contbr. articles to profl. jours. Mem. adv. bd. Salvation Army, Richmond, 1980-97, chmn., 1989-91; troop com. chmn. Robert E. Lee coun. Boy Scouts Am., 1980-91; chair 10th Amendment Litig. com., Gov.'s Adv. Coun. on Federalism and Self Determination, 1994-97; gen. counsel Rep. Party Va., 1993-96. Mem. Am. Bar Found., Am. Coll. Labor and Employment Lawyers, Va. State Bar, Phi Beta Kappa. Presbyterian. Constitutional, Labor (including EEOC, Fair Labor Standards Act, labor-management relations, NLRB, OSHA). Office: McGuire Woods LLP Washington Sq 1050 Connecticut Ave NW Ste 1200 Washington DC 20036-5317 E-mail: rbrame@mcguirewoods.com.

BRAMLETT, JEFFREY OWEN, lawyer; b. Detroit, Nov. 13, 1953; s. Melvin C. and Edith H. Bramlett; m. Nancy E. Frakes, May 30, 1981; children: Cynthia, Melissa, Robert, Susanna. BA, U. Md., 1975; JD, U. Tex., 1980. Bar: Tex. 1980, U.S. Ct. Appeals (5th and 11th cirs.) 1980, Ga. 1981, U.S. Dist. Ct. (all dists.) Ga. 1981, U.S. Dist. Ct. (we. dist.) Mich. 1995, U.S. Supreme Ct. 1985. Legis. aide Hon. Robert Eckhardt, U.S. Congress, Washington, 1974-77; law clk. to judge Jerre S. Williams U.S. Ct. Appeals (5th cir.), Austin, Tex., 1980-81; assoc., then ptnr. Bondurant, Mixson & Elmore, Atlanta, 1981—. Bd. trustees State Bar Ga. Client Security Fund, Atlanta, 1992—97. Mem. Bar Assn. of Ga. (bd. govs. 1994—), Atlanta Bar Assn. (pres., 2000-01, bd. dirs. 1993—, chmn. litigation sect. 1994-95), ACLU, (bd. dirs. 1993-97, pres. Ga. affiliate 1987-89, bd. dirs. 1983-97). Civil rights, General civil litigation, Constitutional. Office: Bondurant Mixson & Elmore 1201 W Peachtree St NW Ste 3900 Atlanta GA 30309-3417 E-mail: bramlett@bmelaw.com.

BRAMLETT, PAUL KENT, lawyer; b. Tupelo, Miss., May 31, 1944; s. Virgil Preston and McDuff (Goggans) B.; m. Shirley Marie Wilhelm, June 14, 1966; children: Paul Kent II (dec.), Robert Preston. AA with honors, Itawamba Jr. Coll., Fulton, Miss., 1962-64; BA, David Lipscomb Coll., 1966; postgrad., George Peabody Coll., 1966; JD, U. Miss., 1969. Bar: Miss. 1969, U.S. Dist. Ct. (no. dist.) Miss. 1969, U.S. Ct. Appeals (5th cir.) 1974, U.S. Supreme Ct. 1974, U.S. Dist. Ct. (we. dist.) Tenn. 1976, Tenn. 1980, U.S. Dist. Ct. (mid. dist.) Tenn. 1980, U.S. Ct. Appeals (6th cir.) 1980, U.S. Ct. Appeals (11th cir.) 1981, U.S. Dist. Ct. (so. dist.) Miss. 1983, U.S. Dist. Ct. (ea. dist.) Tenn. 2003. Pvt. practice, Tupelo, Miss., 1969-80, Nashville, 1980—. Mem. Million Dollar Advs. Forum, 1998. Mem. ABA, Miss. Trial Lawyers Assn. (bd. govs. 1976-79), Tenn. Bar Assn., Miss. Bar Assn. (pub. info. com. 1979-81), Nashville Bar Assn. (fed. ct. com. 1980-81), Million Dollar Advocates Forum, Am. Arbitration Assn. (comml. panel), Civitan Club (past gov. and legal counsel no. dist. Miss.). Mem. Ch. of Christ. Avocation: music. Product liability, Entertainment, Personal injury (including property damage), Securities. Office: PO Box 150734 2828 Renaissance Tower Nashville TN 37215-0734

BRAMLETTE, DAVID C., III, federal judge; b. New Orleans, Nov. 27, 1939; BA, Princeton U., 1962; JD, U. Miss., 1965. Assoc., then ptnr. Adams, Forman, Truly, Ward & Bramlette, Natchez, Miss., 1975-91; spl. cir. judge Dist. Ct. (6th dist.) Miss., 1977, 79; fed. judge Dist. Ct. (so. dist.) Miss., 1991—. Trustee Miss. Nature Conservancy, 1990—; pres. BBCHA, 1989-90; active Arcole Hunting Camp, Ducks Unlimited, Nat. Wild Turkey Fedn.; mem. adv. bd. Natchez Lit. Celebration. Office: PO Box 928 Natchez MS 39121-0928 E-mail: connie_davis@mssd.uscourts.gov.

BRAMMELL, WILLIAM HARTMAN, lawyer; b. Shelbyville, Ky., Dec. 11, 1955; s. Billy Duard and Helen Combs (Hartman) B.; m. Eleanor Agnes Pesek, Apr. 3, 1982; children: William Hartman Jr., Katherine Elizabeth, Emily Marie. BA, Transylvania U., 1977; JD, U. Louisville, 1980. Bar: Ky. 1980. Atty. pvt. practice, New Castle, Ky., 1980—. City atty. Eminence and Pleasureville, Ky., 1982—; Henry County Planning and Zoning Atty., 1988—; pub. defender Henry and Trimble Counties, Ky., 1983; asst. atty. commr. 12th Jud. Dist., LaGrange, Ky., 1984; trial commr. 12th Jud. Dist., Henry County, 1985—; atty. Farmers Deposit Bank, Simpsonville Sewer Bd., City of Smithfield. Sec. Protect Our Children, Inc., Henry County, 1981-82; bd. dirs. Eminence Christian Ch., 1986; pres. Henry County Heart Assn., 1985-86, Henry County Hist. Soc., 1987-89. Mem. Ky. Bar Assn., Carroll County Bar Assn., Ky. Assn. for Gifted Edn. (treas. 1992-95). Avocations: civil war history, fishing, travel. Commercial, consumer (including collections, credit), General practice, Property, real (including real estate development, water). Home: 118 Tolle Ct Eminence KY 40019-2009 Office: PO Box 629 New Castle KY 40050-0629 E-mail: whbrammell@aol.com.

BRAMNIK, ROBERT PAUL, lawyer; b. N.Y.C., Nov. 17, 1949; s. Abe and Ruth (Richman) B.; m. Sheryl Ann Kalus, Aug. 12, 1973; children: Michael Lawrence, Andrew Martin. BA, CCNY, 1970; JD, Bklyn. Law Sch., 1973. Bar: N.Y. 1974, Ill. 1980, U.S. Dist. Ct. (so. and ea. dists.) N.Y. 1974, U.S. Dist. Ct. (no. dist.) Ill. 1980, U.S. Dist. Ct. (ctrl. dist.) Ill. 1982, U.S. Ct. Appeals (2d cir.) 1974, U.S. Ct. Appeals (4th cir.) 1987, U.S. Ct. Appeals (3d and 7th cirs.) 1992, U.S. Ct. Fed. Claims 1994, U.S. Supreme Ct. 1977. Sr. trial atty. NYSE, Inc., N.Y.C., 1973-75; asst. gen. counsel E.F. Hutton & Co., Inc., N.Y.C., 1975-77, Nat. Securities Clearing Corp., N.Y.C., 1977-79; with Arvey, Hodes, Costello and Burman, Chgo., 1979-86, ptnr., 1982-86, Wood, Lucksinger & Epstein, Chgo., 1987-88, Altheimer & Gray, Chgo., 1988-97, Wildman, Harrold, Allen & Dixon, Chgo., 1997—2003, Duane Morris LLC, Chgo., N.Y.C., 2003—. Lectr. Securities Industry Assn. Compliance and Legal div., N.Y.C., 1980-91, 95-2001. Vice chmn. Ill. Adv. Com. on Commodity Regulation, Chgo., 1985-89, chmn., 1989-95. Fellow: Ill. Bar Found.; mem.: ABA (coms. on futures and derivatives regulation, co-chmn. subcom. on futures commn. merchants), Nat. Futures Assn. (hearing com. 2001—), Nat. Assn. Sec. Dealers, Assn. of Bar of City of N.Y. Jewish. Federal civil litigation, Finance, Securities. Office: Duane Morris LLC 227 W Monroe St Ste 3400 Chicago IL 60606 E-mail: rpbramnik@duanemorris.com.

BRAMS, JEFFREY BRENT, lawyer; b. Ft. Worth, Jan. 24, 1966; s. Samuel David and Barbara Parness B. BS in Fin., Oral Roberts U., 1988; JD, U. Fla., 1992. Bar: Fla. 1993. Assoc. Perry Shapiro Miller & Sarkesy, West Palm Beach, Fla., 1992-94; v.p., gen. counsel Khaki Kamel Exotic Imports, Palm Beach Gardens, Fla., 1993-95; gen. counsel Speedy Sign-A-Rama, West Palm Beach, 1995—2000; v.p., assoc. gen. counsel Arby's Inc., 2000—. Vice-chmn., founder S. Fla. Franchise Bus. Network, Ft. Lauderdale, 1997—. Mem. Big Brother/Big Sister program Covenant Cmty. Ch., 1997—. Mem. Internat. Franchise Assn. (mem. corp. counsel com., mem. legal/legis. com., spkr. legal forum). Avocations: travel, golf, tennis, weightlifting. Corporate, general, Franchising, Private international. Home: 10201 Siena Oaks Cir S West Palm Beach FL 33410-5127

BRAMSON, ROBERT SHERMAN, lawyer; b. NYC, Nov. 11, 1938; s. Oscar David and Gertrude (May) B.; m. Ruth Schaffer, June 27, 1942; children: Jonathan, Jennifer, James, Julia. B.M.E., Rensselaer Poly. Inst., 1959; JD, Georgetown U., 1963; postgrad., U. Chgo. Sch. Bus., 1963-64. Bar: Ill. 1963, Pa. 1968, N.Y. 1984. Patent examiner US Patent Office, Washington, 1959-60; patent agt. Stevens, Davis, Miller & Mosher, Washington, 1960-63; atty. Abbott Labs., North Chgo., Ill., 1963-66, Scott Paper Co., Phila., 1966-68; ptnr., head computer and tech. law group Schnader, Harrison, Segal & Lewis, Phila., 1968-89; v.p., gen. patent and tech. counsel Unisys Corp., Blue Bell, Pa., 1989-90; founder Bramson and Pressman, Conshohocken, Pa., 1991, 95—; pres., CEO InterDigital Tech. Corp., King of Prussia, Pa., 1992-95; pres. VAI Patent Mgmt. Corp., Conshohocken, Pa., 1995—. Adj. prof. Temple U. Law Sch., Phila. Mem. ABA, Internat. Bar Assn., Am. Law Inst., Am. Patent Law Assn., Phila. Patent Law Assn., Phila. Bar Assn. Computer, Intellectual property, Patent. Home: 112 Booth Ln Haverford PA 19041-1752 Office: VAI Patent Mgmt Corp 1100 E Hector St Ste 410 Conshohocken PA 19428-2378 E-mail: rbramson@b-p.com.

BRANAGAN, JAMES JOSEPH, lawyer; b. Johnstown, Pa., Mar. 5, 1943; s. James Francis and Caroline Bertha (Schreier) B.; m. Barbara Jeanne Miller, June 19, 1965; children: Sean Patrick, Erin MacKay, David Michael. BA in English Lit. with honors magna cum laude (Woodrow Wilson fellow), Kenyon Coll., Gambier, Ohio, 1965; LL.B. cum laude, Columbia U., 1968. Bar: Ohio 1968. Assoc. Jones, Day, Reavis & Pogue, Cleve., 1968-72; with Leaseway Transp. Corp., Cleve., 1972-81, gen. counsel, 1975-80, sec., 1979-81, v.p. corp. affairs, 1980-81; also officer, dir. Leaseway Transp. Corp. (subsidiaries); v.p. Premier Indsl. Corp., Cleve., 1981-82; sr. counsel TRW Inc., 1982-88; pvt. practice Cleve., 1988—; treas., gen. counsel, sec. Biomec Inc., 1998—. Mem. ABA, Ohio Bar Assn., Cleve. Bar Assn., Phi Beta Kappa. Corporate, general, Private international, Property, real (including real estate development, water). E-mail: bizlaw@stratos.net.

BRAND, GEORGE EDWARD, JR., lawyer; b. Detroit, Oct. 25, 1918; s. George Edward and Elsie Bertie (Jones) B.; m. Patricia Jean Gould, June 7, 1947; children— Martha Christine, Carol Elsie, George Edward. BA, Dartmouth Coll., 1941; postgrad., U. Minn., Harvard U., 1941; JD, U. Mich., 1948. Bar: Mich. 1948, U.S. Supreme Ct. 1958. Mem. firm George E. Brand, Detroit, 1948-63, Butzel, Long, Gust, Klein & Van Zile, P.C., Detroit, 1963—; ptnr., dir., pres. Butzel, Long, Gust, Klein & Van Zile, 1974-89. Served with USNR, 1942-46. Fellow Am. Bar Found., Am. Coll. Trial Lawyers; mem. ABA, Am. Judicature Soc., Detroit Bar Assn., VFW. Clubs: N.S.S.C. Home: 1233 Kensington Ave Grosse Pointe Park MI 48230-1101 Office: 150 W Jefferson Ave Ste 900 Detroit MI 48226-4416

BRAND, RONALD ALVAH, lawyer; b. McCook, Nebr., Sept. 19, 1952; s. Marvin Ray and LaVaughn R. (Nelson) B.; m. Mary M. Schmitz, June 5, 1976; children: Joshua, Megan. Lindsey. BA, U. Nebr., 1974; JD, Cornell U., 1977. Bar: Wis. 1977, Pa., 1997, U.S. Dist. Ct. (ea. and we. dists.) Wis. 1980, U.S. Ct. Appeals (3d cir.) 1985, U.S. Ct. Appeals (fed. cir.) 1988, Ct. of Internat. Trade 1988. Assoc. Godfrey & Kahn S.C., Milw., 1977-79, Godfrey, Pfeil & Neshek, Elkhorn, Wis., 1979-82; asst. prof. law U. Pitts., 1982-87, assoc. prof., 1987-91, prof., 1991—. Vis. prof. U. Augsburg, spring 1989, U. Brussels, fall 1989, 92; dir. Ctr. for Internat. Legal Edn., 1995—. Author: Basic Documents of International Economic Law, 1990, Disclaimers in Estate Planning: A Guide to Their Effective Use, 1990, Enforcing Foreign Judgments in the United States and United States Judgments Abroad, 1992, Fundamentals Internat. Bus. Transactions, 2000; contbr. articles to profl. jours. Mem. U.S. Del. Hague Conf. on Pvt. Internat. Law, 1994—. Recipient Excellence-in-Teaching award SBA, 1988, Chancellor's Disting. Teaching award, 1989, Chancellor's Disting. Pub. Svc. award, 2003; Fulbright rsch. scholar Belgium, 1989-90; sr. rsch. fellow U. Ctr. Internat. Studies, 1990 Mem. Pa. Bar Assn., Am. Soc. Internat. Law (vice chmn. internat. econ. law group 1985-87, chmn. 1987-89). Democrat. Avocations: family, music. Home: 217 Falconhurst Dr N Pittsburgh PA 15238-2627 Office: U Pitts Sch Law 3900 Forbes Ave Pittsburgh PA 15213

BRANDES, JOEL R. consultant, publisher, writer; b. Bklyn., Dec. 15, 1943; s. Murray and Evelyn (Levine) B.; children: Bari, Evan. Student, U. Tampa, 1961-62; BA, Queens Coll., 1965; JD, Bklyn. Law Sch., 1968; LLM in Corp. Law, NYU, 1974; postgrad., U. Tampa, 1961-62. Assoc. Wallman & Kramer, N.Y.C., 1972-77; pvt. practice Garden City, N.Y., 1977-87; ptnr. Brandes & Stamler, Garden City, 1987-90, Brandes Weidman & Spatz P.C., N.Y.C. and Garden City, 1991-93; prin. The Law Firm of Joel R. Brandes P.C., N.Y.C., Garden City, 1993—2002. Instr. matrimonial law Adelphi U., Garden City, 1976-88; vis. lctr. Sch. Law Hofstra U., Advanced Practice Inst., 1981. Co-author: Digest of Equitable Distribution Cases, 1981, A Practical Guide to the New York Equitable Distribution Law, 1980, Contemporary Matrimonial Law Issues, 1986, Encyclopedia of Matrimonial Practice, 1992, A Comprehensive Analysis of All Reported Equitable Distribution Cases to Date, 1982, Equitable Distribution Case Law, 1983, Law and the Family, New York, 2d edit. (9 vols.), 1986-98, Law and the Family, New York Forms (4 vols.), 1995; contbr. articles to profl. jours; editor: N.Y. Family Law Reporter; internet pub. New York Divorce and Family Law. Pres. Old Lindenmere Civic Assn., Merrick, N.Y., 1975-80, Community Council Merricks, 1977-80; arbitrator Civil Ct. of City of N.Y. Mem. ABA (family law sect., assoc. editor Family Law Newsletter 1971-78, litigation sect., trial evidence com. 1975-77, exec. mem. child custody com. 1982-83, panel mem. Law in the Fifty States 1986-87), Am. Soc. Writers on Legal Subjects, N.Y. State Bar Assn. (family law sect. 1975-2002, Family Law Rev. Edil. Bd. 1975-2002, sec. com. on legis. 1975-77, com. continuing legal edn. 1980-92, chmn. com. continuing legal edn. 1982-92, fin. officer 1990-92, sec. 1992, mem. com. profl. discipline 1992-93, mem. com. on children and the law 1997-2000, mem. com. on Cts. of Appellate Jurisdiction 1998-2000), Nassau County Bar Assn. (com. matrimonial and family law 1975-2002, mem. newsletter subcom. 1976, chmn. legis. subcom. 1978-80, chmn. continuing legal edn. subcom. 1980-82, chmn. matrimonial and family law 1982-84), Am. Arbitration Assn. (panel mem 1974-82). Internat. Acad. Matrimonial Lawyers, Am. Acad. Matrimonial Lawyers (legal edn. com. 1978, bd. mgrs. 1979-83, bd. examiners 1979-80, chmn. legis. com. 1979-80, com. legal fees in matrimonial matters 1980-81, ad hoc com. on revisions of equitable distbn. law 1980-81). Jewish. Office: 155 Washington St Jersey City NJ 07302 E-mail: divorce@brandeslaw.com.

BRANDRUP, DOUGLAS WARREN, lawyer; b. Mitchel, S.D., July 11, 1940; s. Clair L. and Ruth M. (Wolverton) B.; m. Patricia R. Tuck, Dec. 20, 1986; children: Kendra, Monika, Peter. AB in Econs., Middlebury Coll., 1963; JD, Boston U., 1966. Bar: N.Y. 1969, U.S. Dist. Ct. (so. dist.) N.Y. 1970, U.S. Ct. Appeals (2d cir.) 1970. Assoc. Donovan, Leisure, Newton & Irvine, N.Y.C., 1968-72; ptnr. Griggs, Baldwin & Baldwin, N.Y.C., 1972-80, sr. ptnr., 1980—. Chmn. Equity Oil Co.; mem. disciplinary com. first dept. appellate divsn. Supreme Ct. State of N.Y., 2003. Mem. Govs. Security Adv. Com., State of N.J., 1975-90. Capt. U.S. Army, 1966-68. Recipient Ellis Island medal of Honor, 1999, Order of St. John, 2002. Mem. ABA, N.Y. County Bar Assn., N.Y. State Bar Assn., Met. Club (N.Y.C., pres.), Mashomack Preserve Club. Republican. Episcopalian. Commercial, contracts (including sales of goods; commercial financing), Estate planning, Probate (including wills, trusts). Office: 57 Old Post Rd No 2 Greenwich CT 06830 Fax: 203-629-7983.

BRANDT, FOLKE, lawyer; b. Göteborg, Sweden, Jan. 25, 1932; s. Hugo and Margit (Rosell) B.; m. Elisabeth Nordqvist, Dec. 30, 1982; children: Tomas, Olof, Monica, Richard, Arthur. Student, Hvitfeldtska h.a.l., Göteborg, 1951; grad., Merchant Sch., Göteborg, 1953; postgrad., City of London Coll., 1956; LLB (Jur.Kand.), Lund U., Göteborg, 1961. Bar: Sweden, 1966. Notary Ct. of Ljungby, Sweden, 1961-63, Advokaterna Sjögren & Hedén, Göteborg, 1963-69; pvt. practice Göteborg, 1970—. Counsel to Italian, British, German Gen. Counsulate. Mem. Swedish Bar Assn., European Consultants Unit, Verein Europäischen Rechtsanwäite, Euro-Link for Lawyers, Gothenburg Maritime Law Assn. Office: F Brandt Advokatbyrå F Brandt Advokatbyra Box 7086 S-402 32 Göteborg 7 Sweden Fax: 31 135373. E-mail: brandtlaw@swipnet.se.

BRANDT, JÜRGEN FRANZ PAUL, legal counsel, management consultant; b. Duesseldorf, Germany, May 8, 1940; s. Richard Ernst and Marianne (George) B.; m. Alexa Kunze, Feb. 23, 1973; children: Inga, Nadja. M in Econs., U. Dortmund, 1982; MBA, U. Utrecht, 1969; Diploma in Engring., Tech. Fachhochschule Berlin, 1971; Diploma, IMEDE, Lausanne, Switzerland, 1971; Diploma Kaufmann, Diploma Ökonom, Diploma in Engring., Diploma in Pedagogue, LLM. With Euro Engring. (FEANI), Sofia, Bulgaria, 1984—. Guest prof. Staatliche U., Miskolc, Hungary, 1991. Author 5 books; contbr. articles to profl. jours. Col. German Army Res. Recipient Verdienstmedaille der Bundesrepublik Deutschland, 1974, Verdienstkreuz am Bande der Bundesrepublik Deutschland, 1991, others. Mem. Düsseldorf Bar Assn., NRW, Rotary. Address: 32 Nelkenstrasse D-40668 Meerbusch Germany

BRANFMAN, ERIC JAY, lawyer; b. N.Y.C., Sept. 18, 1947; s. Theodore George Branfman and Gloria (Shapiro) Stern; m. Beverly Joyce Tash, Jan. 6, 1979; children: Melissa, Joshua. BA magna cum laude, Columbia U., 1969; JD, Yale U., 1972. Bar: D.C. 1973, U.S. Dist. Ct. D.C. 1976, U.S. Ct. Appeals (8th cir.) 1977, U.S. Ct. Appeals (D.C. cir.) 1984. Trial atty. FTC, Washington, 1972-74; atty. advisor to Elizabeth Dole FTC Commr. Elizabeth Dole, Washington, 1974-75; assoc. Bergson, Borkland, Margolis & Adler, Washington, 1975-78, ptnr., 1978-83; of counsel Deso, Greenberg & Thomas, Washington, 1983-86, Swidler Berlin Shereff Friedman, LLP, Washington, 1986-95, tenured counsel, 1995-99, ptnr., 1999—. Mem. ABA, D.C. Bar Assn., Phi Beta Kappa. Avocation: bridge. Home: 3640 Appleton St NW Washington DC 20008-2959 Office: Swidler Berlin Shereff Friedman LLP 3000 K St NW Fl 3 Washington DC 20007-5109 E-mail: ejbranfman@swidlaw.com.

BRANHAM, C. MICHAEL, lawyer; b. Columbia, S.C., Nov. 6, 1957; s. Mack C. and Jennie Louise (Jones) B.; m. Teresa Barrett; children: Anthony, Mark. BS, Auburn U., Montgomery, Ala., 1979; JD, U. S.C., 1983. Bar: S.C.; cert. tax law specialist; CPA. Acct. Wilson, Price, Barranco & Billingsley, CPAs, Montgomery, 1979-80; law clk. Atty. Gen.'s Office, State of S.C., Columbia, 1981-82; acct. Price, Waterhouse, Columbia, 1983-86; tax lawyer Young, Clement, Rivers & Tisdale, LLP, Charleston, SC, 1986—, chmn. tax, estate planning and probate group, 1999—, firm mgmt. com., 1999—, asst. mng. ptnr., 1999—2001, mng. ptnr., 2002—. Chmn. taxation law specialization adv. bd. S.C. Supreme Ct., 1995-97; pres. Charleston Tax. Coun., 1993-94; dean's adv. bd. Med. U. S.C. Nursing Sch., Charleston, 1994-97; chmn. MUSC Planned Giving adv. coun., 1993-97; S.C. case reporter ABA sect. real property, probate and trust law, 1997-2002; mem. Bishop Gadsden Estate Planning Adv. Coun., Charleston, 1998—. Coach Hungryneck Internat. Soccer Assn., Mt. Pleasant, S.C., 1989-99, James Island/Trident United Soccer Assn., Charleston, 1999-2000; sec., bd. dirs. S.C. Youth Soccer Assn., 2000-02; active Charleston Estate Planning Coun. Mem. ABA, AICPA, S.C. Assn. CPAs, S.C. Bar Assn., Charleston Breakfast Rotary. Avocations: soccer coaching, weight lifting. Estate planning, Probate (including wills, trusts), Estate taxation. Home: 829 Detyens Rd Mount Pleasant SC 29464-5181 Office: Young Clement Rivers & Tisdale LLP 28 Broad St Charleston SC 29401-3070

BRANNEN, JEFFREY RICHARD, lawyer; b. Tampa, Fla., Aug. 27, 1945; s. Jackson Edward and Tobiah M. (Lovitz) B.; m. Mary Elizabeth Strand, Nov. 24, 1972; 1 child, Samuel Jackson. BA in English, U. N.Mex., 1967, JD, 1970. Bar: N.Mex. 1970, U.S. Dist. Ct. N.Mex. 1970, U.S. Ct. Appeals (10th cir.) 1976, U.S. Supreme Ct. 1978. Law clk. N.Mex. State Supreme Ct., Santa Fe, 1970-71; from assoc. to pres., shareholder Montgomery & Andrews, pa, Santa Fe, 1972-93; pres. Jeffrey R. Brannen, P.A., Santa Fe, 1993—; of counsel Comeau, Maldegan, Templeman & Indall (formerly known as Carpenter, Maldegan, Templeman & Indall), Santa Fe, 1995—. Faculty Nat. Inst. Trial Advocacy, Hastings Ctr. for Trial & Appellate Advocacy, 1980-93; co-chmn. Pers. Injury Inst., Hastings, 1992. Mem. ABA, Am. Bd. Trial Advocates (N.Mex. pres. 1998), Assn. Def. Trial Attys. (state chmn. 1992—), Def. Rsch. Inst. (Exceptional Performance Citation 1989), N.Mex. Def. Lawyers Assn. (pres. 1989). Democrat. Avocations: skiing, soccer, fly fishing, travel. General civil litigation, Personal injury (including property damage), Product liability. Office: Comeau Maldegan Templeman & Indall 141 E Palace Ave Santa Fe NM 87501-2041 Fax: (505) 982-4611. E-mail: jbrannen@cmtisantafe.

BRANSCOMB, HARVIE, JR., lawyer; b. Dallas, Mar. 24, 1922; s. Bennett Harvie and Margaret (Vaughan) B.; m. Mary Josephine Goodearle, Dec. 28, 1951; children: Mary Margaret, Bennett Hill, Richard Lee. AB, Duke U., 1943; LL.B., Yale U., 1948. Bar: Tex. 1948, D.C. 1980, CPA, Tex. Shareholder Matthews & Branscomb, Attys.-at-Law, Corpus Christi, Tex., 1948—. Contbr. articles to profl. jours. Trustee Found. Scis. and Arts, Corpus Christi, Tex. A&M U. Corpus Christi Found.; trustee emeritus Southwestern Legal Found.; trustee, pres. Una Chapman Cox Found.; bd. dirs. Corpus Christi Indsl. Found. Served with USNR, 1943-46. Fellow Am. Coll. Tax Counsel; mem. ABA, (chmn. tax sect. 1979-80), State Bar Tex. (chmn. sect. taxation 1961-62), Am. Law Inst., Am. Inst. CPA's, Phi Beta Kappa, Phi Delta Phi. Episcopalian. Home: 4500 Ocean Dr Apt 8B Corpus Christi TX 78412-2500 Office: 802 N Carancahua St Ste 1900 Corpus Christi TX 78470-0102

BRANSDORFER, STEPHEN CHRISTIE, lawyer; b. Lansing, Mich., Sept. 18, 1929; s. Henry and Sadie (Kohane) B.; m. Peggy Ruth Deisig, May 24, 1952; children: Mark, David, Amy, Jill. AB with honors, Mich. State U., 1951; JD with distinction, U. Mich., 1956; LLM, Georgetown U., 1958. Bar: Mich. 1956, U.S. Supreme Ct. 1959, U.S. Dist. Ct. (we. dist.) Mich. 1959; cert. mediator U.S. Dist. Ct. (we. dist.) Mich. 1995. Trial atty. Dept. Justice, Washington, 1956—58; atty., editor Office of Public Info., Office of Atty. Gen., 1958—59; spl. asst. U.S. Atty. for D.C., 1958—59; assoc. Miller, Johnson, Snell & Cummiskey, Grand Rapids, Mich., 1959—63, ptnr., 1963—89; dep. asst. atty. gen. civil div. U.S. Dept. Justice, Washington, 1989—92; pres. Bransdorfer & Bransdorfer, P.C., Grand Rapids, 1993—2000; ptnr. Bransdorfer & Russell, LLP, Grand Rapids, 2000—. Pres. State Bar of Mich., 1974-75, commr., 1968-75, chmn. sr. lawyers sect., 1994-95; pres. Grand Rapids chpt. Am. Inns of Ct., 1995-96; trustee Am. Inns of Ct. Found., 1997-2001; chmn. Mich. Civil Svc. Commn., 1977-78, mem., 1975-78; adv. com. 6th Cir. Jud. Conf., 1984-89; co-chair Mich. polit. leadership program Mich. State U., 1992-94; mem. comml. panel Am. Arbitration Assn., 1998-2001. Asst. editor: U. Mich. Law Rev, 1956. Pres. Grand Rapids Child Guidance Clinic, 1969-71; chmn. Kent County Coms., Griffin for Senator, 1972, Lenore Romney for Senator, 1966; mem. council legal advisers Rep. Nat. Com., 1981-89; Rep. candidate for atty. gen., Mich., 1978; trustee, v.p., Mich. State Bar Found., 1985-87, chmn., fellows, 1987-89; chmn. Mich. State Bd. Canvassers, 1985-87, Commn. on Future Directions in Health Care, West Mich., 1987-89; trustee Hist. Soc. for U.S. Dist. Ct. (we. dist.) Mich., 2002—. With U.S. Army, 1951-53. Recipient Spl. award for Superior Performance Civil Divsn. U.S. Dept. Justice, 1990. Fellow Am. Bar Found.; mem. ABA, 6th Cir. Jud. Conf. (life, mem. mems. com., sr. counsel to 6th cir. ct., 1999—), Grand Rapids Bar Assn., FBA (pres. West Mich. chpt. 1984, Disting. Life Svc. award 1989), Rep. Nat. Lawyers Assn. (bd. govs. 1985-89), Mich. Rep. Party (Svc. award 1989), Rotary, Cascade Hills Country Club, Phi Kappa Phi. Presbyterian. Alternative dispute resolution, General civil litigation, Personal injury (including property damage). Home: 7250 Bradfield Ave SE Ada MI 49301-9130 Office: Bransdorfer & Russell LLP Ste 411-S Waters Bldg 161 Ottawa Ave NW Grand Rapids MI 49503-2705 Fax: 616-774-0326. E-mail: sbrans@iserv.net.

BRANSON, ALBERT HAROLD (HARRY BRANSON), judge, educator; b. Chgo., May 20, 1935; s. Fred Brooks and Marie (Vowell) B.; m. Siri-Anne Gudrun Lindberg, Nov. 2, 1963; children: Gunnar John, Gulliver Dean, Hannah Marie, Siri Elizabeth. BA, Northwestern U., 1957; JD, U. Chgo., 1963. Bar: Pa. 1965, Alaska 1972. Atty. Richard McVeigh law offices, Anchorage, 1972-73; ptnr. Jacobs, Branson & Guetschow, Anchorage, 1973-76, Branson & Guetschow, Anchorage, 1976-82; pvt. practice Law Offices of Harry Branson, Anchorage, 1982-84, 85-89; atty. Branson, Bazeley & Chisolm, Anchorage, 1984-85; U.S. magistrate judge U.S. Dist. Ct., Anchorage, 1989—. Instr., adj. prof. U. Alaska Justice Ctr., 1980—93; U.S. magistrate, Anchorage, 1975—76; mem. 9th Cir. Magistrate Judges Exec. Bd., 2001. Mem. steering com. Access to Civil Justice Task Force, 1997-98. With U.S. Army, 1957-59. Mem. Alaska Bar Assn. (bd. dirs., v.p. bd. govs. 1977-80, 83-86, pres. bd. govs. 1986, Disting. Svc. award 1992, Spl. Svc. award 1988, editor-in-chief Alaska Bar Rag 1978-86), Anchorage Bar Assn. (bd. dirs., bd. govs. 1982-86), Anchorage Inn of Ct. (pres. 1995). Democrat. Avocations: book collecting, cooking, poetry. Office: US Dist Ct 222 W 7th Ave Unit 33 Anchorage AK 99513-7504

BRANSTAD, CHRISTINE ELLEN, lawyer; b. Forest City, Iowa, Nov. 23, 1968; d. Monroe David and Elizabeth Ellen B.; m. David Lee Phillips, June 14, 1997. BS, U. Iowa, 1991; JD, Drake U., 1994. Bar: Iowa 1995, D.C. 1995, U.S. Dist. Ct. (so. dist.) Iowa 1997. Rsch. asst. Drake Law Sch., Des Moines, 1993-94; prosecuting intern Polk County Attys., Des Moines, 1993; law clk. Verne Lawyer & Assocs., Des Moines, 1992-94; asst. county atty. Jasper County, Newton, 1995-97; atty. Hopkins & Huebner, Des Moines, 1997—. Spkr. in field. Co-editor: Trial Handbook Supplement, 1993. Mem. ABA, Assn. Trial Lawyers Am. (asst. editor 1992-93, Iowa Bar Assn., Iowa Trial Lawyers Assn., Iowa Sex Crimes Investigators Assn., Jasper County Bar Assn., Blackstone Inn Ct. Avocations: sports, skiing, reading, swimming, scuba diving. Criminal, Personal injury (including property damage), Workers' compensation. Office: Wandro Lyons & Baer PC 2501 Grand Ave Ste 8 Des Moines IA 50312 Home: 3818 Wolcott Ave Des Moines IA 50321-1866

BRANSTETTER, CECIL DEWEY, SR., lawyer; b. Deer Lodge, Tenn., Dec. 15, 1920; s. Miller Henry and Lillie Mae (Adams) B.; m. Charlotte Virginia Coleman, Aug. 5, 1944; children: Kay Frances Johnson, Linda Charlotte Mauk, Kathy Jane Stranch , Cecil Dewey Jr. BA, George Washington U., 1947; JD, Vanderbilt U., 1949. Bar: U.S. Supreme Ct. 1957, U.S. Ct. Appeals (6th cir.) 1963. Ptnr. Branstetter, Kilgore, Stranch & Jennings, Nashville, 1990—. Chmn. Bd. Profl. Responsibility Supreme Ct. Tenn. Contbr. articles to profl. jours. Mem. Gen. Assembly Tenn., Nashville, 1950-53; chmn. Charter Commn. and Charter Revision Commn., Nashville, 1957-62, 78-90; mem. Met. Action Commn., Nashville, 1964-68; pres. Coun. Community Agys. and Tenn. Environ. Coun., Nashville, 1970, 71-73. Sgt. U.S. Army, 1943-46, lt. Res., 1946-52, ETO. Mem. ACLU (bd. dirs.), ABA, Met. Human Rels. Commn., Am. Judicature Soc., Tenn. Conservation League (Carter Patten award), Am. Trial Lawyers Assn., Tenn. Bar Assn., Tenn. Trial Lawyers Assn., Nashville Bar Assn., Davidson County Sportsman Club, Order of Coif. Democrat. Baptist. Avocations: farming, fishing, hunting, raising angus cattle. Labor (including EEOC, Fair Labor Standards Act, labor-management relations, NLRB, OSHA), Utilities, public, Workers' compensation.

BRANT, JOHN GETTY, lawyer; b. Apr. 13, 1946; BBA, U. Okla., 1968; JD, U. Tex., 1972. Bar: US Dist. Ct. Colo. 1974, US Tax Ct. 1974. Atty. IRS, Houston, 1972—74; ptnr. Bradley, Campbell & Carney, Golden, Colo., 1975—83, Doussard, Brant, Hodel & Markman, Lakewood, Colo., 1983—86; pvt. practice Lakewood, Colo., 1986—2000; ptnr. Brant, Stevens & Graf, Lakewood, 2000—02. Arbitrator Nat. Assn. Securities Dealers. Bd. dirs. U. Tex. Law Sch. Assn., Austin, 1983-86, Nat. Multiple Sclerosis Soc., Denver, 1975-91. Mem.: Centennial Estate Planning Coun. (pres. 1976). Estate planning, Probate (including wills, trusts), Estate taxation. Office: 710 Kipling St Ste 305 Lakewood CO 80215-8006

BRANTON, JAMES LAVOY, lawyer; b. Albany, Tex., Apr. 19, 1938; s. George Lyndon Branton and Oletha Imogene (Westerman) Johnson; m. Molly Branton, May 18, 1968; children: Christina, Victoria, Claudia. BA, U. Tex., 1961, LLB, 1962. Bar: Tex., U.S. Dist. Ct. (we., so, ea. and no. dists.) Tex., U.S. Ct. Appeals (5th cir.). Ptnr. Hardberger, Branton & Herrera, Inc., San Antonio, 1974-78, Branton & Mendelsohn, Inc., San Antonio, 1978-83, Branton, Warncke, Hall & Gonzales, P.C., San Antonio, 1983-88, Branton & Hall, P.C., San Antonio, 1988—. Bd. dirs. Tex. Lawyers' Ins. Exch. Co-author: Trial Lawyer's Series, 1981-91. Capt. USAF, 1962-65. Fellow Am. Coll. Trial Lawyers (state com. 1993-95, chair 1996-98), Internat. Soc. Barristers, Internat. Acad. Trial Lawyers, Tex. Bar Found. (chair 1989-90); mem. Tex. Trial Lawyers Assn. (pres. 1975-76), State Bar Tex. (pres. 1994-95), Am. Bd. Trial Advocates (pres. San Antonio chpt. 1990-91, Tex. Trial Lawyer of Yr. 1994). Avocations: flying, scuba diving. Personal injury (including property damage), Product liability, Professional liability. Home: 403 Evans Ave San Antonio TX 78209-3725 Office: Branton & Hall PC One Riverwalk Pl Ste 1700 700 N St Mary's St San Antonio TX 78205 E-mail: jimbranton@branton-hall.com.

BRANTZ, GEORGE MURRAY, retired lawyer; b. Phila., Oct. 19, 1930; s. Louis Paul and Jeannette (Vinitz) B.; m. Joan Nadler, Mar. 29, 1953; children: Nancy Brantz Ginsberg, Amy L. Brantz Bedrick. AB, Princeton U., 1952; LLB magna cum laude, Harvard U., 1957. Bar: Pa. 1957, U.S. Dist. Ct. (ea. dist.) Pa., U.S. Ct. Appeals (3rd cir.). Ptnr. Wolf, Block, Schorr and Solis-Cohen, Phila., 1966-93; ret., 1993. Pres. Council Migration Service, Phila., 1971-73; bd. dirs. Phila. Port Corp., 1982-84. With U.S. Army, 1952-54. Mem. Am. Law Inst., Jane Austen Soc. (treas. 1993-98), Locust Club. Jewish. Avocation: sailing. Corporate, general.

BRASFIELD, EVANS BOOKER, lawyer; b. Richmond, Va., Sept. 21, 1932; s. George Frederick and Minna (Booker) B.; children: Evans Booker, John McDonald, Elizabeth Lee; m. Anne Dobbins Heilig, June 28, 1980; stepchildren: J. Randall Heilig, Mollie P. Heilig. BA, U. Va., 1954, LLB, 1959. Bar: Va. 1959. Pvt. practice, Richmond; ptnr. Hunton & Williams, Richmond, 1965-99; gen. counsel Va. Electric & Power Co., Richmond, 1976-94, Dominion Resources, 1983-91. Pres. Children's Home Soc. Va., 1972-73, bd. dirs., 1965-91; chmn. Cen. Va. Ednl. TV Corp., 1978-84, bd. dirs., 1965—; bd. dirs. Richmond Cmty. Action Program, 1974-76, Richmond Area Cmty. Coun., 1973-75, Big Bros. Richmond, 1970-75, Sheltering Arms Hosp., 2001--. With USNR, 1954-56. Fellow Am. Bar Found., Va. Law Found.; mem. ABA (chmn. sect. pub. utility law 1996-97), Va. Bar Assn. (exec. com. 1981-86, pres. 1985), Richmond Bar Assn., , Va. State Bar, Phi Beta Kappa (pres. Richmond chpt. 1982-83). Clubs: Country of Va., Commonwealth, (Richmond). Presbyterian. Administrative and regulatory, Utilities, public. Home: 2 Ampthill Rd Richmond VA 23226-2233

BRASWELL, LOUIS ERSKINE, lawyer; b. Selma, Ala., Mar. 11, 1937; s. Erskine McKinley and Leota (Grubb) B.; m. Anne, June 1, 1985 (dec. Feb. 20, 1996); children by previous marriage: Margaret, Anne, Helen; m. Hollis, Apr. 29, 2002. AB, Birmingham So. Coll., 1959; JD, Harvard U., 1962. Bar: Ala. bar 1962. Assoc. firm Hand, Arendall, Bedsole, Greaves & Johnston, Mobile, Ala., 1963-68; ptnr. Hand Arendall LLC, Mobile, 1968—. Participant Nat. Conf. on Discovery Reform, U. Tex. Law Sch., 1982; program participant 11th Cir. Jud. Conf., 1984, others Bd. dirs. Children's Dental Clinic, Mobile, 1965-75; past pres. Friends of Mobile Public Library; bd. dirs. Jr. Achievement of Mobile; past pres. YMCA Rockies Alumni Assn.; bd. dirs. Kidney Found. South Ala., 1978-85, Ecumenical Ministries, Inc., 2001--. With U.S. Army, 1962-63. Mem. ABA, Am. Law Inst., Ala. Law Inst., Ala. Bar Assn., Ala. Def. Lawyers Assn., Athelstan Club, Rotary Internat., Point Clear Rotary Club (bd. dirs. 1997-2000, pres. 1998-99). Presbyterian. General civil litigation, Commercial, contracts (including sales of goods; commercial financing), Property, real (including real estate development, water). Home: 459 Satsuma St Fairhope AL 36532- Office: PO Box 123 Mobile AL 36601-0123

BRATT, HERBERT SIDNEY, lawyer; b. Milw., Sept. 8, 1931; s. Ishmael and Freda (Nelson) B.; m. Rosalee Bender, Dec. 22, 1957; children: Jay, Annie, Jennifer. BS, U. Wis., 1953; JD, Yale U., 1956. Bar: Wis. 1956, N.Y. 1981. Assoc. M.J. Levin, Milw., 1956-61; ptnr. Bratt & Shapiro, Milw., 1961-64, Zubrensky, Padden, Graf & Bratt, Milw., 1964-80, Laikin, Bratt & Laikin, Milw., 1980-81; pvt. practice Milw., 1981-91; ptnr. Churchill, Duback & Smith, Milw., 1991-94; pvt. practice Milw., 1994—. Chpt. 7 panel trustee U.S. Trustee's Office for Ea. Dist. Wis., Milw., 1984-90. Trustee, Congregation Sinai, Milw., 1972-86, pres., 1979-81. Recipient William Gorham Rice Civil Liberties award Wis. Civil Liberties Union, 1968. Mem. ABA, Am. Judicature Soc., State Bar Wis., N.Y. Bar Assn., Milw. Bar Assn. Avocation: running. Corporate, general, Probate (including wills, trusts), Property, real (including real estate development, water). Home: 1610 N Prospect Ave Apt 201 Milwaukee WI 53202-2402 Office: 735 N Water St Ste 704 Milwaukee WI 53202-4104

BRATTER, JOSHUA PEPPERCORN, lawyer; b. N.Y.C., Apr. 2, 1972; s. Warren Michael and Ena Peppercorn Bratter; m. Samantha Remy Reder. BA, Hamilton Coll., 1995; JD, U. Mmiami, 1998. Bar: Fla. 1999, U.S. Dist. Ct. (so. dist.) Fla. 1999. Assoc. Bander, Fox-Iscicoff & Assocs., PA, Miami, 1998—2000; ptnr. Bratter & Krieger, Miami, 2000—. Rsch. assoc., Hon. Judge Caminos U. Miami; lectr. on immigration matters. Contbr. articles to newspapers. Mem. beautification com., Miami Beach, Fla., 2002—03; bd. dirs. Am. Jewish Com., Miami, 2000—. Mem.: Inter-Am. Bar Assn., Am. Immigration Lawyers Assn., Fla. Bar. Immigration, naturalization, and customs, Public international. Office: Bratter & Krieger 777 17th St Penthouse Ste Miami Beach FL 33139 Fax: 305-695-4398. E-mail: joshua@bkvisa.com.

BRATTON, JAMES HENRY, JR., lawyer; b. Pulaski, Tenn., Oct. 9, 1931; s. James Henry and Mabel (Shelley) B.; m. Alleen Sharp Davis, Oct. 15, 1960; children: Susan Shelley McGonigle, James Henry III, Margaret Alleen Schilling. BA optime merens, U. South, 1952; BA, Oxford (Eng.) U., 1954, MA, 1978; LL.B., Yale U., 1956. Bar: Tenn. 1956, Ga. 1957. With antitrust div. Dept. Justice, summer 1955; since practiced in Atlanta; sr. ptnr. firm Smith, Gambrell & Russell. Vis. lectr. U. Ga. Law Sch., 1967; adj. prof. law Emory U., 1984— Editor Yale Law Jour.; contbr. articles to profl. jours. Mem. Gov.'s Citizens Adv. Council on Environ. Affairs, 1970-74; trustee Trust Fund for Sibley Park, Ga. chpt. Multiple Sclerosis Soc., U. of the South, 1984-87, 95-98, Pembroke Coll. Found., Peachtree Rd. United Meth. Ch., chmn. bd. trustees; bd. dirs. Soccer in the Streets, Buckhead Christian Ministry, pres., 1996; pres. Peachtree Heights West Civic Assn., 1984-99; co-chmn. Sewanee Parents Council, 1987-88; v.p. Pembroke Coll. Soc. of N.Am.; mem. Williams Parents' Fund, 1984-86; mem. parents adv. coun. Hamilton Coll., 1988-91. Named Alumnus of Yr., Sewanee Club Atlanta, 1990. Fellow Lawyers Found. Ga., Am. Law Inst.; mem. ABA (standing com. on aero. law 1962-84, chmn. 1977-80), Ga. Bar Assn. (founding chmn. environ. law sect. 1970-73), Fed. Bar Assn., Atlanta Bar Assn., Lawyers Club Atlanta, Old Warhorse Lawyers Club, Am. Acad. Polit. and Social Scis., Am. Judicature Soc., Associated Alumni U. of South (v.p. admissions 1993-95, pres. 1995-97), Yale Law Alumni Assn. (exec. com. 1976-79), Phi Beta Kappa, Phi Delta Phi, Pi Gamma Mu, Gridiron. Democrat. Methodist. Antitrust, Federal civil litigation, Commercial, contracts (including sales of goods; commercial financing). Home: 63 N Muscogee Ave NW Atlanta GA 30305-3542 Office: 1230 Peachtree St NE Atlanta GA 30309-3592 E-mail: jbratton@sgrlaw.com.

BRAUDRICK, ARTHUR C., JR., lawyer; b. Honolulu, Sept. 22, 1941; s. Arthur Carl and Evelyne (Van Horn) B.; m. Marilyn Grace Webb, Dec. 8, 1979; children: Christian, Aaron, Colin, Melody. AB, U. Calif., Berkeley, 1968; JD, U. Calif., Davis, 1971. Bar: Calif. 1971. Dep. dist. atty. Monterey County, Salinas, Calif., 1972-78, dep. pub. defender, 1979-86, asst. dist. atty., 1986-87; dep. pub. defender Los Angeles County, L.A., 1988—. Vol. fireman Carmel (Calif.) Fire Dept., 1972-83. Mem. Calif. State Bar Assn. Democrat. Roman Catholic. Avocations: climbing, fishing, dog training. Office: Los Angeles County Pub Defenders Office 210 W Temple St Fl 19 Los Angeles CA 90012-3210 E-mail: abraudri@co.la.caus.

BRAULT, LISA J. prosecutor; b. L.A., Apr. 2, 1961; BA in Theatre Arts, Calif. State U., Northridge, 1984; JD, Southwestern U., 1991. Bar: Calif. Supreme Ct. 1991, U.S. Dist. Ct. (ctrl. dist.) Calif. 1991, U.S. Ct. Appeals (9th cir.) 1991. Dep. atty. gen. III Calif. Atty. Gen.'s Office, L.A., 1992—. Mem. League Women Prosecutors (v.p., events and spkrs. chairperson 1997—). Democrat. Office: Office Calif Atty Gen 300 S Spring St Fl 5 Los Angeles CA 90013-1230 E-mail: Lisa.brault@doj.ca.gov.

BRAUN, JEFFREY LOUIS, lawyer; b. N.Y.C., Oct. 2, 1946; s. Arthur and Berta (Freimark) B.; m. Beth Essig, June 6, 1982; children: Arthur Paul, Emily Claire. BA, Rutgers U., 1968; JD, Yale U., 1971. Bar: N.Y. 1974, U.S. Dist. Ct. (so. and ea. dists.) N.Y., U.S. Tax Ct., U.S. Ct. Appeals (2d cir.), U.S. Ct. Appeals (9th cir.), U.S. Supreme Ct. Law clk. to Judge Harry Pregerson U.S. Dist. Ct. (cen. dist.) Calif., L.A., 1971—72; assoc. Paul, Weiss, Rifkind, Wharton & Garrison, N.Y.C., 1972—74, Rosenman & Colin LLP, N.Y.C., 1974—80, ptnr., 1980—2002; of counsel Kramer Levin Naftalis & Frankel LLP, N.Y.C., 2002—. Mem. Assn. of the Bar of the City of N.Y. (com. on internat. human rights 1985-88, com. on mcpl. affairs 1988-91, com. on recruitment and retention of lawyers 1992-94, long-range planning com. 1994-97), Fed. Bar Coun. (com. on cts. of the second cir. 1995—). General civil litigation, Land use and zoning (including planning). Home: 15 Park Rd Irvington NY 10533-2008 Office: Kramer Levin Naftalis & Frankel LLP 919 Third Ave New York NY 10022-3852 E-mail: jbraun@kramerlevin.com.

BRAUN, JEROME IRWIN, lawyer; b. St. Joseph, Mo., Dec. 16, 1929; s. Martin H. and Bess (Donsker) B.; children: Aaron, Susan, Daniel; m. Dolores Ferriter, Aug. 16, 1987. AB with distinction, Stanford U., 1951, LLB, 1953. Bar: Mo. 1953, Calif. 1953, U.S. Dist. Ct. (no. dist.) Calif., U.S. Tax Ct., U.S. Ct. Mil. Appeals, U.S. Supreme Ct., U.S. Ct. Appeals (9th cir.). Assoc. Long & Levit, San Francisco, 1957-58, Law Offices of Jefferson Peyser, San Francisco, 1958-62; founding ptnr. Farella, Braun & Martel (formerly Elke, Farella & Braun), San Francisco, 1962—. Instr. San Francisco Law Sch., 1958-69; mem. U.S. Dist. Ct. Civil Justice Reform Act Adv. Com., 1991—; spkr. various state bar convs. in Calif., Ill., Nev., Mont.; requent moderator/participant continuing edn. of bar programs; past chmn. 9th Cir. Sr. Adv. Bd., past chmn. lawyer reps. to 9th Cir. Jud. Conf.; mem. appellate lawyers liaison com. Calif. Ct. Appeals 1st dist.; jud.conf. U.S. Com. Long Range Planning; founder Jon Samuel Abramson Scholarship Endowment Stanford U. Law. Revising editor: Stanford U. Law Rev.; contbr. articles to profl. jours. Mem. Jewish Community Fedn. San Francisco, The Peninsula, Marin and Sonoma Counties, pres., 1979-80; past pres. United Jewish Community Ctrs. 1st lt. JAGC, U.S. Army, 1954-57, U.S. Army Res., 1957-64. Recipient Lloyd W. Dinkelspiel Outstanding Young Leader award Jewish Welfare Fedn., 1967, Professionalism award 9th cir. Am. Inns of Ct., 1999. Fellow Am. Acad. Appellate Lawyers, Am. Coll. Trial Lawyers (teaching trial and appellate advocacy com.), Am. Bar Found.; mem. ABA, Calif. Bar Assn. (chmn. adminstrn. justice com. 1977), Bar Assn. San Francisco (spl. com. on lawyers malpractice and malpractice ins.), San Francisco Bar Found. (past trustee), Calif. Acad. Appellate Lawyers (past pres., mem. U.S. Dist. Ct. Civil Justice Reform Act adv. com., Calif. Ct. of Appeals 1st Dist. Appellate Lawyers liaison com., jud. conf. of the U.S., com. on long-range planning, panelist 1994), Am. Judicature Soc. (past dir.), Stanford Law Sch. Bd. of Visitors, U.S. Dist. Ct. of No. Dist. Calif. Hist. Soc. (past pres., bd. dirs.), 9th Cir. Ct. of Appeals Hist. Soc. (past. pres.), Mex.-Am. Legal Def. Fund (honoree), Order of Coif. Antitrust, Federal civil litigation, General civil litigation. E-mail: jbraun@fbm.com.

BRAUNER, DAVID A. lawyer; b. N.Y.C., Mar. 4, 1942; s. Herman M. and Mary (Trachtenberg) B.; m. Amy Jo Kaplan, May 3, 1981; children: Sara Lynne, Jesse Howard. AB, Dickinson Coll., Carlisle, Pa., 1963; JD, Columbia U., 1966. Bar: N.Y. 1968. Vol. VISTA, Denver, 1966-67; staff atty. Mobilization for Youth, N.Y.C., 1967-68; ptnr. Brauner Baron et al, N.Y.C., 1968—. Bd. dirs. Helen M. DeMario Found. Bd. dirs. Herman Goldman Found., N.Y.C., 1981—; dir. The Bridge, Inc., N.Y.C., 1980—. Mem. N.Y. State Bar Assn. Democrat. Jewish. Avocations: travel, squash, carpentry. Corporate, general, Estate planning, Property, real (including real estate development, water). Home: 315 W 106th St New York NY 10025-3445 Office: Brauner Baron et al 61 Broadway New York NY 10006-2701 E-mail: dbrauner@braunerbaron.com.

BRAUNSDORF, PAUL RAYMOND, lawyer; b. South Bend, Ind., June 18, 1943; s. Robert Louis and Marjorie (Breitenstein) Braunsdorf; m. Margaret Buckley, June 18, 1966; children: Christopher, Mark, Douglas, Amy. BA magna cum laude, U. Notre Dame, 1965; LLB, U. Va., 1968. Bar: NY 1968, US Dist Ct (western dist) NY 1969, US Dist Ct (northern dist) NY 1980, US Ct Appeals (2d cir) 1975, US Supreme Ct 1980. Assoc. Harris Beach LLP, Rochester, 1968-75; ptnr., 1976—. Instr Nat Inst Trial Advocacy, Rochester, 1988; lectr in field. Author (contbg auth): (book) Antitrust Health Care Handbook II, 1993, Antitrust Law in New York, 1995, 2d edit., 2002. Bd dirs McQuaid Parent's Club, 1984—90, pres, 1986—87; bd dirs Mercy Parent's Club, 1989—90, Brighton Baseball, 1987—90. Republican. Roman Catholic. Avocations: tennis, photography, music. Antitrust, Federal civil litigation, State civil litigation. Office: Harris Beach LLP 99 Garnsey Rd Pittsford NY 14534

BRAUTIGAM, DAVID CLYDE, lawyer, judge; b. Westfield, N.Y., Nov. 11, 1950; s. Frank C. and Edna M. Brautigam; m. Amy S. Konz, Apr. 30, 1988; children: Sarah, Susanna, Sharon. BA, Houghton Coll., 1972; JD, U. Pitts., 1979. Bar: N.Y. 1980, U.S. Dist. Ct. (we. dist.) N.Y. 1983. Assoc. Shane & Franz, Olean, N.Y., 1979-84; ptnr. Richardson, Pullen & Brautigam, Fillmore, N.Y., 1984-93; town justice Town of Rushford, N.Y., 1997—; pvt. practice Houghton, N.Y., 1993—. Bd. dirs. So. Tier Legal Svcs., Bath, N.Y., 1981-85, Odosagih Bible Conf., Inc., Mchias, N.Y., 1990-93; chmn., bd. dirs. 1st Bapt. Ch., Rushford, N.Y., 1996-2000, deacon, 1988-2000, 2002--. Mem. Nat. Lawyers Assn., Allegany County Bar Assn. (sec.), Christian Legal Soc. Republican. Baptist. Avocations: hunting, gardening, farming, reading. General practice, Probate (including wills, trusts), Property, real (including real estate development, water). Office: 9888 County Road 23 Houghton NY 14744-8742

BRAUTIGAM, PETER BRYAN, lawyer; b. Anchorage, Mar. 3, 1959; s. E. P. and E. R. Brautigam; m. Marian M. Brautigam. BA in Econs., PAcific Luth. U., 1981; JD, U. Pacific, 1984, LLM in Taxation, 1985. Bar: Alaska, U.S. Dist. Ct. Alaska, U.S. Tax Ct., U.S. Ct. Claims. With Hartig Rhodes, Anchorage, 1985—. Mem. Alaska Planned Giving Coun., Nat. Com. Planned Giving; com. mem. Providence Alaska Found. Planned Giving. Fellow: Am. Coll. Trust & Estate Counsel (state chair, bd. dirs. 1990—); mem.: Alaska Soc. CPA's, Alaska Bar Assn. (probate & planning law sect., past chmn., tax law sect.), Anchorage Estate Planning Coun. Avocation: skiing. Estate planning, Estate taxation. Office: Hartig Rhodes 717 K St Anchorage AK 99501-3330

BRAVERMAN, ALAN N. lawyer; b. Mass. BA, Brandeis U., 1969; JD, Duquesne U., 1975. Bar: D.C. 1976. Assoc. Wilmer, Cutler & Pickering, 1976-82, ptnr., 1983-93; exec. v.p., gen. counsel ABC, Inc., NYC, 1993-2000; deputy, gen. counsel The Walt Disney Co., Burbank, Calif., 2000—03; exec. v.p. & gen. coun. Disney, 2003—. Office: ABC Inc 500 S Buena Vista St Burbank CA 91521-0922*

BRAVERMAN, HERBERT LESLIE, lawyer; b. Buffalo, Apr. 24, 1947; s. David and Miriam P. (Cohen) B.; m. Janet Marx, June 11, 1972; children: Becca Danielle, Benjamin Howard. BS in Econs., U. Pa., 1969; JD, Harvard U., 1972. Bar: Ohio 1972, U.S. Dist. Ct. Ohio 1972, U.S. Supreme Ct. 1975, U.S. Ct. Appeals (6th cir.) 1980, U.S. Ct. Claims 1980. Assoc. Hahn, Loeser, Freedheim, Dean & Wellman, Cleve., 1972-75; sole practice Cleve., 1975-87; ptnr. Porter, Wright, Morris & Arthur, Cleve., 1987-95, Walter & Haverfield LLP, Cleve., 1996—. Councilman Orange Village, Ohio, 1988—, pres., 1998-2001. Capt. USAR, 1970-82. Fellow Am. Coll. Trust and Estate Counsel; mem. ABA, Ohio Bar Assn., Bar Assn. Greater Cleve. (former chmn. estate planning trust and probate sect.), Suburban East Bar Assn. (pres. 1978-80), Rotary (Cleveland Heights pres. 1980), B'nai Brith (local pres. 1978-84), Wharton Club Cleve. (pres. 1991—), Am. Jewish Congress (Ohio pres. 1992—). Avocations: golf, symphony, reading. Corporate, general, Estate planning, Probate (including wills, trusts). Home: 3950 Orangewood Dr Cleveland OH 44122-7406 Office: Walter & Haverfield LLP 1300 Terminal Tower 50 Public Sq Ste 1300 Cleveland OH 44113-2253 also: 2000 Auburn Dr Ste 200 Beachwood OH 44122 E-mail: hbraverman@walterhav.com., hbraverman@ameritech.com.

BRAVERMAN, JANIS ANN BREGGIN, lawyer; b. Rochester, N.Y., Mar. 5, 1955; d. Arnold H. and Eleanor (Wingo) Breggin; m. Joseph T. Braverman; children: Rachel Tyler, Cadiz Safira, Theo Socrates, Arielle. BA, U. Denver, 1976, JD, 1980. Bar: Colo. 1980, U.S. Ct. Appeals (10th cir.) 1980. Assoc. Sherman & Howard, Denver, 1980-82, Jeffrey M. Nobel & Assocs., Denver, 1982-84; assoc. in house counsel Bill L. Walters Cos., Englewood, Colo., 1984-85; assoc. Deutsch & Sheldon, Englewood, 1985-87; ptnr. Breggin & Assocs. P.C., Denver, 1987-95, The Breggin Law Firm, P.C., Denver, 1995—. Mem. Denver Women's Commn., 1990-93, chmn. 1991-92. Mem. Colo. Bar Assn., Denver Bar Assn., Colo. Women's Bar Assn. Property, real (including real estate development, water). Office: The Breggin Law Firm PC 1546 Williams St # 101 Denver CO 80218-1635

BRAWER, MARC HARRIS, lawyer; b. N.Y.C., June 11, 1946; s. Leonard and Diana R. Brawer; m. Susan L. Brunswick, Nov. 23, 1975; 3 children. BA, Queens Coll., 1967; JD, Bklyn. Law Sch., 1969. Bar: N.Y. 1970, Fla. 1978, U.S. Dist. Ct. (ea. and so. dists.) N.Y. 1974, U.S. Ct. Appeals (2nd cir.) 1974, U.S. Supreme Ct. 1975, U.S. Dist. Ct. (so. dist.) Fla. 1981, U.S. Ct. Appeals (5th cir.) 1980; cert. marital and family lawyer, family mediator. Staff atty. Legal Aid Soc., N.Y.C., 1972-78; ptnr. Meyerson Resnicoff & Brawer, N.Y.C., 1978-83, Meyerson & Brawer, Tamarac, Fla., 1983-84; head firm Marc H. Brawer, Sunrise, Fla., 1984—2001; of counsel Resnicoff, Samanowitz & Brawer, Great Neck, N.Y., 1985-91; sr. ptnr. Brawer, Klein & Mandell, LLP, Sunrise, 2001—. Adj. prof. family law St. Thomas Law Sch., 1992; spkr. various orgns. and colls., 1980-96. Contbr. articles to profl. jours., 1970-84. Fellow Am. Acad. Matrimonial Lawyers; mem. Broward County Bar Assn., Queens County Bar Assn. (cert. of svc. 1982-83), Fla. Bar (sec. Family Law Commentator). Avocations: scuba diving, photography, ornamental horticulture. Family and matrimonial. Office: 7771 W Oakland Park Blvd Fort Lauderdale FL 33351-6749

BRAY, AUSTIN COLEMAN, JR., lawyer, investor; b. Dallas, Oct. 25, 1941; s. Austin Coleman and Mary Thelma (Pettigrew) B.; m. Sherrill Ann Farr, Nov. 28, 1964 (div. 1970). Diploma, U. Vienna, Austria, 1962; BA cum laude, Washington and Lee U., 1963; LLB, Columbia U., 1967. Bar: Tex. 1967, U.S. Dist. Ct. (no. dist.) Tex. 1967, U.S. Ct. Appeals (5th cir.) Tex. 1967, U.S. Supreme Ct. 1970, U.S. Dist. Ct. (we. dist.) Tex. 1978, U.S. Ct. Appeals (11th cir.) Tex. 1981. Assoc. Gardere, Wynne & Sewell, Dallas, 1967-69; asst. atty. gen. State of Tex., Austin, 1969-73; subcom. counsel U.S. Rep. Richard White, Washington, 1973-74; exec. asst. to State Senator Mike McKinnon, Austin, 1974-76; atty. Tex. R.R. Commn., Austin, 1977-78; exec. asst. to State Rep. Bob Close, Austin, 1978-79; sr. staff atty. Tex. Sec. State, Austin, 1979-82, sole practice, 1982-87; asst. gen. counsel Tex. Sec. of State, Austin, 1987-98; pvt. practice Austin, 1998—. Editor-in-chief Columbia Law Sch. News, 1966-67. Mem. ABA, State Bar Tex., English-Speaking Union, Kent Ct., Kappa Alpha Order. Episcopalian. Constitutional, Legislative, Election. Office: Ste 106 1218 Baylor St Austin TX 78703-4140

BRAY, JOHN MARTIN, lawyer; b. St. Louis, Feb. 7, 1939; s. Edward Joseph and Rosemary Margaret Bray; m. Joan Maguire, Nov. 24, 1971; children: Kathleen, John P. BS, St. Louis U., 1960, LLB, 1962. Bar: Mo. 1962, D.C. 1968. Atty. U.S. Dept. Justice, Washington, 1962-66, Monsanto Co., St. Louis, 1966-68; assoc. Arent Fox Kintner, Plotkin & Kahn, Washington, 1968-73; ptnr. Arent Fox Kintner Plotkin & Kahn, Washington, 1973-78, Schwalb, Donnenfeld, Bray & Silbert, Washington, 1978-97, King & Spalding, Washington, 1997—. Trustee St. Louis U., 1980-93, 95—. Lt. JAGC, USNR, 1965-70. Fellow Am. Coll. Trial Lawyers (state chmn. Dist. Columbia); mem. J. Edgar Murdock Am. Inn of Ct. (master of bench). Avocation: irish history. Antitrust, Federal civil litigation, Criminal. Home: 3202 Cleveland Ave NW Washington DC 20008-3451 Office: King & Spalding Ste 1200 1730 Pennsylvania Ave NW Washington DC 20006-4706

BRAY, LAURACK DOYLE, lawyer; b. New Orleans, Nov. 13, 1949; s. Laudrack Doyle Bray and Helen Davis. AA, L.A. City Coll., 1969; BA, Long Beach State U., 1972, MS, 1977, MPA, 1981; JD, Howard U., 1984. Bar: Pa. 1986, D.C. 1986, U.S. Ct. Appeals (D.C. and fed. cirs.) 1987, U.S. Dist. Ct. D.C. 1987, U.S. Ct. Appeals (4th cir.) 1991, Md. 1991, U.S. Supreme Ct. 1992. Cmty. rsch. worker Crenshaw Consortium, L.A., 1977-79; adminstrv. intern City of Lawndale, Calif., 1981; legis. intern U.S. Congress, Washington, 1982; law clk. FDIC, Washington, 1983-84; pvt. practice Washington, 1987—. Mem. moot ct. team Howard U., Washington. Contbr. articles to law jours. Recipient Am. Jurisprudence award, 1982, Best Brief award ABA, 1984. Mem. D.C. Bar Assn., Pi Alpha Alpha, Phi Kappa Phi. Democrat. Avocations: sports, dancing, travel. Appellate, Federal civil litigation, Criminal. Home and Office: 1019 E Santa Clara St Ventura CA 93001-3034

BRAZIER, JOHN RICHARD, lawyer, physician; b. Olean, N.Y., Mar. 11, 1940; s. John R. and Edith (Martin) B.; children: Mark, Jennifer. AAS, SUNY, Alfred, 1960; BS in Engring. Physics, U. Colo., 1963, MD, 1969; JD, Santa Clara U., 1989. Bar: Calif., 1989. Intern in surgery Downstate Med. Ctr., Bklyn., 1969-70; resident in surgery U. Colo., Denver, 1970-75; fellowship thoracic and cardiovascular surgery NYU, 1975-77; asst. prof. surgery UCLA, 1977-78; pvt. practice Northridge, 1978-84, Newport News, Va., 1984-86, Sacramento, 1989—. Fellowship NIH, UCLA, 1972-74. Mem. AMA, ACS, Calif. Bar. Avocation: law. General civil litigation, Commercial, contracts (including sales of goods; commercial financing), Corporate, general. Home: 1401 36th St Sacramento CA 95816-6606 Office: 915 21st St Sacramento CA 95814-3117

BREARTON, JAMES JOSEPH, lawyer; b. Troy, N.Y., Aug. 12, 1950; s. James Edward and Lois Marie (Mesnig) B.; m. Margaret Anne Cassidy, Aug. 27, 1977. BA, Coll. Holy Cross, 1972; JD, Albany Law Sch., 1975. Bar: N.Y. 1976, U.S. Dist. Ct. (no. dist.) N.Y. 1976. Assoc. Wager, Taylor, Howd, Brearton & Kessler, Troy, N.Y., 1975-87; ptnr. Wager, Taylor, Howd & Brearton, Latham, NY, 2001—; pvt. practice, Latham, NY, 1987—2001. Mem. bd. arbitrators Nat. Assn. Securities Dealers, Inc., 1992—; mem. Am. Prepaid Legal Svcs. Inst.; mem. examining counsel Monroe Title Ins. Corp.; examining counsel Fidelity Nat. Title Ins. Co.; instr. Am. Inst. Banking, 1994; mem. law guardian liaison com. 3d Jud. Dist., N.Y., 1987-2002. Co-author: Alternate Dispute Resolution, American Jurisprudence, 2nd rev. edit., 1995. Pres. Alumni Assn. LaSalle Inst., Troy, N.Y., 1997-98, mem., ex-officio, Bd.Trustees, 1998. Mem. ABA, N.Y. State Bar Assn., Rensselaer County Bar Assn., Albany County Bar Assn., Capital Dist. Trial Lawyers Assn., Mensa, Uncle Sam Toastmasters, K.C. Democrat. Roman Catholic. Personal injury (including property damage), Probate (including wills, trusts), Personal income taxation. Office: PO Box 889 950 New Loudon Rd Latham NY 12110-2116 E-mail: JJBREARTON@aol.com.

BREATHITT, EDWARD THOMPSON, JR., lawyer, railroad executive, former governor; b. Hopkinsville, Ky., Nov. 26, 1924; s. Edward Thompson Sr. and Mary Josephine (Wallace) B.; m. Lucy Alexander Breathitt; children: Mary Frances, Linda Key, Susan Holleman, Edward Thompson III. BS in Commerce, U. Ky., 1947, LLB, 1950, JD, 1970, LLD (hon.), 1965, U. Marshall, 1966, U. Ky., 1967. Bar: Ky. 1950, U.S. Supreme Ct. 1974. Ptnr. Trimble, Soyars & Breathitt, Hopkinsville, 1960-62; gov. State of Ky., Frankfort, 1963-67; ptnr. Trimble, Soyars & Breathitt, Hopkinsville, 1968-72; v.p. Southern Ry. Co., Washington, 1972-82, Norfolk Southern Corp., Washington, 1982-86, sr. v.p., 1986-92; with Wyatt Tarrent & Combs Law firm, Lexington, Ky., 1992—. Mem. adv. bd. Am. Security Bank, Washington, 1987-90; mem. Ky. Econ. Devel. Corp., 1979—; chmn. bd. trustees U. Ky., 1992-99. Mem. legis. State of Ky., Frankfort, 1952-56; chmn. and pres. Commn. on Rural Property, Washington, 1965-67; pres. Commn. to Fulfill These Rights, Washington, 1965-67. With USAAF, 1942-45. Named Conservationist of Yr. Nat. Wildlife Fedn. and Outdoor Life Mag., 1966; recipient Conservationist award U.S. Dept. of Interior, 1967, Lincoln Key award for Civil Rights, 1966. Fellow U. Ky.; mem. Ky. Bar Assn., D.C. Bar Assn., Chevy Chase Club, Pendenis Club. Democrat. Methodist. Avocations: fishing, hunting, golf, tennis, hiking. Home: 1703 Fairway Dr Lexington KY 40502-1648 Office: Wyatt Tarrant and Combs Lexington Fin Ctr 250 W Main St Ste 1700 Lexington KY 40507-1746

BREAULT, THEODORE EDWARD, lawyer; b. N.Y.C., Mar. 7, 1938; m. Gretchen S. Clements, Dec. 10, 1966; children: Victoria Ann, Theodore Edmund, Heidi Sherwin, Edmund Clements. BS, Manhattan Coll., 1960; JD, Cath. U. Am., 1963. Bar: D.C. 1964, Va. 1964, Pa. 1970, U.S. Ct. Appeals (D.C. cir.) 1964, (4th cir.) 1969, U.S. Supreme Ct. 1967. Assoc. Seltzer & Suskind, Washington, 1964-69, Egler & Reinstadtler, Pitts., 1969-77; pvt. practice Fairfax, Va., 1967-69, Pitts., 1977—. Lectr. Cath. U. Am. Sch. Nursing, 1968, Robert Morris Coll., 1973-74; mem. Pa. Workmen's Compensation Sect.; spl. master Allegheny County Ct. of Common

Pleas; arbitrator U.S. Dist. Ct. Pres. Sewickley (Pa.) Symphony Orch., 1974-75. Fellow: Pa. Bar Found. (life); mem.: Am. Coll. Legal Medicine (assoc. in law), Am. Arbitration Assn. (arbitrator accident and comml. claims), Pa. Def. Inst., Am. Soc. Law and Medicine, Allegheny County Bar Assn. (health law sect., chmn. workmen's compensation sect. 2001—02), D.C. Bar Assn., Va. State Bar Assn., Pa. Bar Assn. (civil litigation sect.), Matrimonial Inns of Ct. (master). General civil litigation, Personal injury (including property damage), Workers' compensation. Home: 108 Claridge Dr Moon Township PA 15108-3204 Office: Breault & Assocs PC 428 Forbes Ave 1509 Lawyers Bldg Pittsburgh PA 15219

BREAUX, PAUL JOSEPH, lawyer, pharmacist; b. Franklin, La., Mar. 11, 1942; s. Sidney J. and Irene (Bodin) B.; m. Marilyn Anne Jones, Aug. 21, 1965; children: Jason E., James P. BS in Pharmacy, Northeast La. U., 1965; JD, La. State U., 1972. Bar: La. 1972, U.S. Supreme Ct. 1975. Pharmacist Belanger's Pharmacy, Morgan City, La., 1965-66, Clinic Pharmacy, Morgan City, La., 1966-69; pvt. practice of law Lafayette, La., 1972-73, 93—; assoc. Allen, Gooch, Bourgeois, Breaux, Robison, Theunissen Attys., Lafayette, 1973-75; ptnr. Allen, Gooch, Bourgeois, Breaux, Robison & Theunissen, Lafayette, 1975-93. Sec., bd. dirs. Bank of Lafayette. Bd. dirs. Lafayette Community Health Care Clinic, Inc., 1992-, vice chmn., 1996-2002, pres. 2003-; bd. dirs. Hospice of Acadiana, Inc., 1996-, v.p., 1999-2003, pres. 2003-; bd. dirs. The Hospice Found., pres. 1998-; mem. Gov.'s Universal Health Care Law Reform Commn., 1992-; active Boy Scouts Am., 1984-92. Named Vol. of Yr., Lafayette Cmty. Health Care Clinic, Inc., 2000. Mem.: ABA, Soc. Hosp. Attys. of La. Hosp. Assn., Acad. Hosp. Attys. of Am. Hosp. Assn., Am. Health Lawyers Assn., Am. Soc. Pharmacy Law, Am. Soc. Law & Medicine, Nat. Assn. Retail Druggists, Am. Compliance Inst., La. Pharmacists Assn. (bd. dir. 1991—99, 2001—, Pharmacist of Year award 1992), Am. Pharm. Assn., La. Bankers Assn. (mem. bank counsel com. 1983—85, 1988—90, La. banking code legis. revision com. 1983), Lafayette Parish Bar Assn., La. Bar Assn., Lafayette C. of C., Phi Eta Sigma, Kappa Psi. Republican. Roman Catholic. Corporate, general, Health, Property, real (including real estate development, water). Office: 600 Jefferson St Ste 503 Lafayette LA 70501-6998

BRECZINSKI, MICHAEL JOSEPH, lawyer; b. El Paso, Tex., Mar. 16, 1953; s. Julius W. and Rosemarie (Kelly) B.; m. Arlene Ann Szafranski, Apr. 20, 1979 (div. Jul. 1999); children: Emily, Nathan, Jacob. AA, Oakland Community Coll., 1973; BA, Mich. State U., 1976; JD, Thomas M. Cooley Law Sch., Lansing, Mich., 1981. Bar: Mich. 1982, Minn. 1983. Sole practice, Lansing, 1982-83, Flint, Mich., 1983-85, Mt. Morris, Mich., 1985-87, Burton, Mich., 1987—. Mem. Mich. Bar Assn., Minn. Bar Assn., Genesee County Bar Assn, Assn. Trial Lawyers Am., Cath. Attys. Guild. Clubs: Flint Rogues Rugby. Republican. Construction, Criminal, General practice. Home and Office: 5005 Lapeer Rd Burton MI 48509-2017 E-mail: Breczinski@yahoo.com.

BREDEHOFT, ELAINE CHARLSON, lawyer; b. Fergus Falls, Minn., Nov. 22, 1958; d. Curtis Lyle and Marilyn Anne (Nesbitt) Charlson; m. Keenan P. Frank; children: Alexandra Charlson, Michelle Charlson. BA, U. Ariz., 1981; JD, Cath. U. Am., 1984. Bar: Va. 1984, U.S. Ct. Appeals (4th cir.) 1984, U.S. Bankruptcy Ct. (ea. dist.) Va. 1987, D.C. 1994, U.S. Ct. Appeals (D.C. cir.) 1994. Assoc. Walton and Adams, McLean, Va., 1984-88, ptnr., 1988-91, Charlson Bredehoft, P.C., Reston, Va., 1991—. Spkr. Fairfax Bar Assn., CLE, 1992—, VB Assn., CLE, 1993—, 12th Ann. Multistate Labor and Employment Law Update, 1993—, Va. Women's Trial Lawyers Assn. Ann. Conf., 1998, Va. Bar. Assn. Labor and Employment Conf., 1994-97, 99—, Va. Trial Lawyers Assn., 1995, 97, Va. Law Found., 1995—, Va. Assn. Def. Attys., 1996, 2001; mem. faculty Va. State Bar Professionalism Com., 1997-2000, Va. State Bar Law Student Professionalism Com., 2001—; invitee 4th Circuit Judicial Conf., 1997-99, permanent mem., 1999—; invitee Boyd Graves Conf., 1999—; substitute judge 19th Judicial Dist., 1998—; chair Fairfax Bar Assn. Diversity Taskforce, 1998-99 (Pres. Vol. award 1998). Bd. dirs. Va. Commn. on Women and Minorities in the Legal System, 1987-90, sec., 1988-90. Mem. Va. Bar Assn. (mem. exec. com. young lawyers sect., mem. litigation com., mem. nominating com., chmn. model jud. com.), Am. Coll. Trial Lawyers, Va. Trial Lawyers Assn. (vice chmn. ann. conv. 1996-98, mem. com. on long-range planning 1996-97, spkr. 1995, 97), Minn. State Soc., Fairfax Bar Assn. (co-chair subcom. on minorities, Pres.'s Vol. award 1998, 99), George Mason Inns of Ct. (master 1996—). Civil rights, General civil litigation, Personal injury (including property damage). Office: Charlson Bredehoft PC 11260 Roger Bacon Dr Ste 201 Reston VA 20190-5252

BREDEHOFT, JOHN MICHAEL, lawyer; b. N.Y.C., Feb. 22, 1958; s. John William and Viola (Struhar) B.; m. Ivana Terango; children: Alexandra Charlson, Michelle Charlson , John Paris. AB magna cum laude, Harvard Coll., 1980, JD cum laude, 1983. Bar: D.C. 1983, U.S. Dist. Ct. D.C. 1985, U.S. Ct. Appeals (D.C. cir.) 1985, U.S. Ct. Appeals (1st cir.) 1986, U.S. Supreme Ct. 1987, U.S. Ct. Appeals (9th cir.) 1988, U.S. Ct. Appeals (3d and 5th cir.) 1989, U.S. Tax Ct. 1989, U.S. Ct. Appeals (4th Cir.) 1990, U.S. Dist. Ct. Mont. 1991, Va. 1992, U.S. Dist. Ct. (ea. dist.) Va. 1992. Assoc. Cleary, Gottlieb, Steen & Hamilton, Washington, 1983-91; prin. Charlson & Bredehoft, Fairfax, Va., 1991-98; ptnr. Venable, Baetjer & Howard L.L.P., McLean, Va., 1998—. Contbg. editor Employment Law in Virginia, 1997. Bd. dirs. Falls Brook Assn., Herndon, Va., 1988-91; nat. class 1983 reunion gift chmn. Harvard Law Sch. Fund, Cambridge, 1988, class agt., 1994—; mem. Harvard Debate Centennial Com., 1992. Named Lawyer of Yr., Met. Washington Employment Lawyers Assn., 1996, Va. Legal Elite, Va. Bus., 2000. Mem. ABA (sect. on litigation), Va. Bar Assn. (sect. on labor and employment law, governing coun. mem.), Va. Trial Lawyers Assn. (founding officer, employment law sect.), Fairfax Bar Assn. (sect. on employment law, vice chmn. 1997-98, chmn. 1998-99), Def. Rsch. and Trial Inst. (appellate advocacy com.), Va. Law Found./Va. CLE (employment law com.), Va. Women Attys. Assn. Civil rights, Federal civil litigation, Labor (including EEOC, Fair Labor Standards Act, labor-management relations, NLRB, OSHA). Office: 8010 Towers Cres Vienna VA 22182-

BREECE, ROBERT WILLIAM, JR., lawyer; b. Blackwell, Okla., Feb. 5, 1942; s. Robert William Breece Sr. and Helen Elaine (Maddox) Breece Robinson; m. Elaine Marie Keller, Sept. 7, 1968; children: Bryan, Justin, Lauren BSBA, Northwestern U., 1964; JD, U. Okla., 1967; LLM, Washington U., St. Louis, 1970. Bar: Oklahoma 1967, Mo. 1970. Pvt. practice, St. Louis, 1968—. Pres., chmn. bd. dirs. Crown Capital Corp., St. Louis. Mem. ABA, Internat. Bar Assn., Mo. Bar Assn., Okla. Bar Assn., Phi Alpha Delta, Beta Theta Pi, Melrose Club, Univ. Club, Forest Hills Country Club (pres. 1978). Home: 35 Crown Manor Dr Chesterfield MO 63005-6805 Office: 540 Maryville Centre Dr Ste 12 Saint Louis MO 63141-5828

BREECHER-BREEN, SHEILA RAE, lawyer; b. Nephi, Utah, Aug. 14, 1953; d. Leo Neil and Jeannine (Cole) Van Ausdal; children: Michael Erin, Anthony Edward, Kelsey Nichole. BS, MS, Utah State U., 1974; JD, Brigham Young U., 1984. Bar: Ariz. 1985, U.S. Dist. Ct. Ariz. 1985, U.S. Ct. Appeals (9th cir.) 1985. Speech pathologist Maricopa Spl. Svcs. Consortium, Buckeye, Ariz., 1974-75; speech pathologist Phoenix Union High Sch. Dist. (Ariz.), 1975-81; assoc. Charles, Smith & Bellah, Glendale, Ariz., 1986; speech pathologist Phoenix Union High Sch. Dist., 1986-88; judge pro tem City of Peoria (Ariz.) Mcpl. Ct., 1987—; of counsel Smith & Breecher, Scottsdale, Ariz., 1987-97; tchr. Legal Magnet High Sch. Program Phoenix Union High Sch. Dist., 1988-89; coord. policy and legal assistance, spl. edn. sect. Ariz. Dept. Edn., Phoenix, 1989-94, dir. adult edn., 1995-96; CEO SolED, PLLC, Phoenix, 1996—; cons. Ednl. Mgmt. Group, Scottsdale, 1997; fin. advisor Prudential Securities, Pasadena, Calif., 1998-99; dir. exceptional student programs Phoenix Union H.S. Dist., 1999—2003; supt. Grand Canyon Unified Sch. Dist., 2003—. Legal cons. Flagstaff (Ariz.) Pub. Schs., 1987-89, Phoenix Union High Sch. Dist., 1986-89; mem. legis. team Ariz. Dept. Edn., Phoenix, 1991-95. Editor: Criminal Procedure, 1983. Precinct committeeperson Dem. Party, Glendale, Ariz., 1979-81; adv. Ariz. Dept. Edn., Phoenix, 1988-90; dep. registrar Maricopa County Elections Dept., Phoenix, 1987-92; authorized pub. lobbyist, 1989-95; mem. Edn. Policy Fellowship Program, 1991-92; bd. dirs. Phoenix Day, 1992-96; bd. dirs. Cmty. Info. and Referral, 1992-96; mem. hon. bd. Tempe Ctr. Habilitation, 1994-97; mem. adv. bd. Inst. Cultural Affairs, 1995-97. Mem. Ariz. Bar Assn., Valley Leadership Class XII (Phoenix). Avocations: reading, writing, traveling, foreign languages. Home: 16005 S 42d St Phoenix AZ 85048-7484 E-mail: srbreen@aol.com.

BREEN, DAVID HART, lawyer; b. Ottawa, Ont., Can., Mar. 27, 1960; came to U.S., Aug. 19, 1978; naturalized, 1993; s. Harold John and Margaret Rae (Hart) B.; m. Pamela Annette Mitchell, Sept. 17, 1988; 1 child, Matthew Mitchell. BA cum laude, U. S.C., Columbia, 1982, JD, 1986. Bar: S.C., U.S. Dist. Ct. S.C., U.S. Ct. Appeals (4th cir.), U.S. Bankruptcy Ct. S.C. 1987. Law clk. to Hon. Don S. Rushing Cir. Ct. (6th cir.), S.C., 1986-87; English instr. humanities U. Coastal Carolina Coll., Conway, 1987-88; criminal law instr. Horry-Georgetown Tech. Coll., Conway, 1987-88; sr. ptnr. David H. Breen, P.A., Myrtle Beach, 1988—. C.J.A. panel atty. U.S. Dist. Ct. S.C., 1991-97; mem. family ct. adv. com. 15th Jud. Ct., 1998—. Campaign asst. Joe Clark for Prime Minister, Ottawa, 1975-76. Recipient Province of Ontario Achievement Award, 1976, Nat. Dean's List Award of Merit, 1981—82, Gold Medal - Rifle Shooting, Canada Summer Games, 1977, Provincial Champion Rifle Shooting, Ontario, 1977. Mem. ABA, ATLA, S.C. Trial Lawyers Assn., S.C. Bar Assn., Horry County Bar Assn., Am. Bankruptcy Inst., Oshawa Gun Club, Phi Delta Phi. Methodist. Avocations: swimming, computers. Bankruptcy, Family and matrimonial, Personal injury (including property damage). Home: Prestwick Country Club 2187 N Berwick Dr Myrtle Beach SC 29575-5835 Office: 4603 Oleander Dr Ste 6 Myrtle Beach SC 29577-5738

BREEN, RICHARD F., JR., law librarian, lawyer, educator; b. Providence, Aug. 1, 1940; s. Richard F. and Elizabeth (Hurlin) B.; children: Stephanie, Jonathan. AB in Econs., Dartmouth Coll., 1962; LLB, U. Maine, Portland, 1967; MLS, U. Oreg., 1973. Bar: Maine, N.H. Asst dean U. Maine Sch. Law, Portland, ., 1967-70; with firm Tesreau and Gardner, Lebanon, N.H., 1970-72; assoc. law libr., assoc. prof. law U. Maine Sch. Law, Portland, 1974-76; law libr., assoc. prof. law Willamette U. Coll. Law, Salem, Oreg., 1976-80, law libr., prof. law, 1980—, interim adminstrv. dean., law libr., 1986-87. Mem. U.S. Olympic Biathlon Tng. Team, 1963. Capt. USAR, 1962-64. Mem. Am. Assn. Law Librs., Oreg. Libr. Assn., Casque and Gauntlet Honor Soc. Democrat. Congregationalist. Avocations: cross-country skiing, hiking. Office: Willamette U Law Libr 245 Winter St SE Salem OR 97301-3916

BREESKIN, MICHAEL WAYNE, lawyer; b. Washington, Dec. 25, 1947; s. Nathan and Sylvia (Raine) B.; m. Frances Cox Lively, May 29, 1982; children: Molly Louise, Laura Rose. BA cum laude, U. Pitts., 1969; JD, Georgetown U., 1975. Bar: D.C. 1975, Colo. 1983, U.S. Dist. Ct. D.C. 1977, U.S. Dist. Ct. Colo. 1983, U.S. Ct. Appeals (D.C. cir.) 1978, U.S. Ct. Appeals (10th cir.) 1984, U.S. Supreme Ct. 1995. Mng. atty. Tobin & Covey, Washington, 1977-79; assoc. Donald M. Murtha & Assocs., Washington, 1979-80; counsel NLRB Office Rep. Appeals, Washington, 1980-83; trial atty. NLRB Denver Regional Office, 1983-88; assoc. Wherry & Wherry, Denver, 1989-91; sr. atty. The Legal Ctr. for People with Disabilities and Older People (formerly The Legal Ctr. Serving Persons with Disabilities), Denver, 1991—98; gen. counsel Assn. Cmty. Living Boulder County, Inc. (formerly the Assn. for Retarded Citizens in Boulder County, Inc.), 1998—2000; counsel Fox & Robertson, PC, Denver, 2000—02, Arc of Denver, Inc., 2002—. Presenter, lectr. in field. Adv. com. Domestic Violence Initiative for Women with Disabilities, 1997—. Recipient Outstanding Work for People with Disabilities acknowledgement Very Spl. Arts Colo., 1996; named Profl. of Yr., The Arc of Adams County, 1997; recipient Adv. of the Year award Assn. Cmty. Living in Boulder County Inc., 1996, Schenkein award Arc of Denver, Inc., 1997, award Disability Ctr. Ind. Living and Colo. Cross-Disability Coalition, 1999, Colo. Cross Disability Coalition Meml. award for Civil Rights Legal Advocacy, 2000. Mem. ABA, Colo. Bar Assn. (disability law forum com.), Arapahoe County Bar Assn., Disability Rights Roundtable. Avocations: bicycling, skiing, reading. Civil rights, Education and schools, Labor (including EEOC, Fair Labor Standards Act, labor-management relations, NLRB, OSHA). Office: Arc of Denver 1905 Sherman St Ste 300 Denver CO 80203

BREGA, CHARLES FRANKLIN, lawyer; b. Callaway, Nebr., Feb. 5, 1933; s. Richard E. and Bessie (King) B.; m. Betty Jean Witherspoon, Sept. 17, 1960; children: Kerry E., Charles D., Angie G. BA, The Citadel, 1954; LLB, U. Colo., 1960. Bar: Colo. 1960. Assoc. firm Hindry & Meyer, Denver, 1960-62, partner, 1962-75, dir., 1975; dir. firm Roath & Brega, Denver, 1975-89, Brega & Winters, Denver, 1989—. Lectr. in field; guest prof. U. Colo., U. Denver, U. Nev. (numerous states and), Can. Trustee Pres.'s Leadership Class, U. Colo., 1977— . Served with USAF, 1954-57. Mem. Colo. Trial Lawyers Assn. (pres. 1972-73), Assn. Trial Lawyers Am. (gov. 1972-79), ABA, Am. Law Inst., Am. Bd. Trial Advs., Internat. Acad. Trial Lawyers, Internat. Soc. Barristers, Cherry Hills Country Club, Denver Athletic Club. Episcopalian. Criminal, Family and matrimonial, Personal injury (including property damage). Home: 4501 S Vine Way Englewood CO 80110-6027 Office: Brega & Winters PC 1700 Lincoln St Ste 1300 Denver CO 80203-4522

BREGLIO, JOHN F. lawyer; b. N.Y.C., June 5, 1946; s. John N. and Sylvia V. (Calucci) B.; m. Nan K. Proctor, May 22, 1976; children: Eliza Mason, Nola Keene. BA, Yale U., 1968; JD, Harvard U., 1971. Bar: N.Y. 1972, U.S. Dist. Ct. (ea. and so. dists.) 1974, U.S. Ct. Appeals (2d cir.) 1975, U.S. Ct. Appeals (D.C. cir.) 1982. Ptnr. Paul, Weiss, Rifkind, Wharton & Garrison, N.Y.C., 1971—. Adj. prof. Sch. of Arts, Columbia U.; chmn., lectr. on entertainment industry N.Y. Law Jour. Seminars, N.Y.C., 1984—88, Practising Law Inst. Bd. dirs. The Acting Co., N.Y.C., 1982-92, The Golden Fund, N.Y.C., 1989—, The Alliance for the Arts, Inc., 1989—, Am. Found. for AIDS Rsch., N.Y.C., 1994—, Young Playwrights Inc., 1995—; chmn. bd. Theater Devel. Fund, N.Y.C., 1982—; mem. adv. com. Theatre Collection Coun., Mus. of City of N.Y. Mem. ABA, N.Y. State Bar Assn., Assn. of Bar of City of N.Y., Am. Arbitration Assn. (panel arbitrators), The Century Assn. (N.Y.C.), Yale Club (N.Y.C.), Waccabuc Country Club (Westchester, N.Y), Phelps Assn. (New Haven). Entertainment, Trademark and copyright. Home: 1120 5th Ave New York NY 10128-0144 also: 41 School House Rd Waccabuc NY 10597 also: 52 W Miacomet Rd Nantucket MA 02554-4369 Office: Paul Weiss Rifkind Wharton & Garrison Rm 200 1285 Avenue Of The Americas New York NY 10019-6065 E-mail: jbreglio@paulweiss.com.

BREGMAN, ARTHUR RANDOLPH, lawyer, educator; b. Phila., Dec. 9, 1946; s. Nathan and Stella (Husock) B.; m. Patrice Rosalie Gancie, May 30, 1980. BA, Columbia U., 1968; MA, Yale U., 1969; JD, Georgetown U., 1985. Bar: D.C. 1985, U.S. Ct. Appeals (D.C. cir.) 1985, U.S. Dist. Ct. D.C. 1985, U.S. Claims Ct. 1985. Treas. Nat. Coun. for Soviet and E. European Rsch., Washington, 1981-83; law clk. Washington Lawyers' Com. for Civil Rights, 1983-84; assoc. Klores, Feldesman and Tucker, Washington, 1985-86; dir. Soviet and E. European Svcs. APCO, Washington, 1988-91; of counsel Steptoe & Johnson, Washington, Moscow, USSR, 1991-92, ptnr. Washington D.C. and Moscow, 1992-99, Squire, Sanders & Dempsey, Washington, 1999—2003, Salans, Washington, N.Y., 2003—. Adj. prof. Georgetown U. Law Ctr., Washington, 1986-89; program dir. Internat. Law Inst., Washington, 1986-91; chmn. bd. adv. U.S.-Russia Bus. Law Report, 1990—. Editor: U.S.-Soviet Contract Law, 1987. Recipient Civil Procedure prize Lawyers Coop. Pub. Co., Balt., 1982. Mem. ABA (internat. bar sect.), D.C. Bar. Private international, Public international. Home: 3059 Porter St NW Washington DC 20008-3272 Office: 1330 Connecticut Ave NW Washington DC 20036 also: 620 Fifth Ave New York NY 10020 E-mail: rbregman@salans.com.

BREHL, JAMES WILLIAM, lawyer; BS engring., U. Notre Dame, 1956; JD, U. Mich., 1959. Bar: Wis. 1989; Minn. and various fed. cts. Lawyer Maun & Simon, St. Paul, 1963-2000; law practice and mediation/arbitration Nuetral Svcs., 2000—. Contbr. articles to law jours. Mem. Minn. Bar Assn. (exec. com. 1996-97), Ramsey County Bar Assn. (exec. coun. 1977-80, 87-90, pres. 1993-94). Labor (including EEOC, Fair Labor Standards Act, labor-management relations, NLRB, OSHA), Property, real (including real estate development, water). Fax: 651-436-5679.

BREITENBACH, ROY W. lawyer; b. Queens Village, N.Y., Nov. 3, 1966; s. Alfred G. Breitenbach and Alicia T. Jancovic; m. Jacqueline M. Kucich, Sept. 4, 1994; children: Julia Alicia, Stephen John. BA, St. John's U., Jamaica, N.Y., 1988, JD, 1991. Bar: N.Y. 1992, U.S. Dist. Ct. (so. and ea. dists.) N.Y. 1992, U.S. Dist. Ct. (no. and we. dists.) N.Y. 1995, U.S. Ct. Appeals (2d cir.) 1997. Assoc. atty. Kelley, Drye & Warren, N.Y.C., 1991—94, Garfunkel, Wild & Travis, P.C., Great Neck, NY, 1994—2000, ptnr., 2000—. Mem.: KC. Republican. Roman Catholic. General civil litigation, Health. Home: 5 Blue Grass Ct Huntington NY 11743 Office: Garfunkel Wild and Travis PC 111 Great Neck Rd Great Neck NY 11021 Office Fax: 516-466-5964. Business E-Mail: rbreitenbach@gwtlaw.com.

BREMER, HOWARD WALTER, consulting patenting and licensing lawyer; b. Milw., July 18, 1923; s. Walter Hugo and Lydia Martha (Schmidt) B.; m. Caryl Marie Faust, May 28, 1948; children: Katharine, William (dec.), Thomas, Timothy, Margaret. BSChemE, U. Wis., 1944, LLB, 1949. Bar: Wis. 1949, U.S. Patent and Trademark Office 1954, U.S. Supreme Ct. 1957, U.S. Ct. Appeals (fed. cir.) 1959, U.S. Dist. Ct. (so. dist.) Ohio 1960. Patent atty. Procter & Gamble Co., Cin., 1949-60; patent counsel Wis. Alumni Rsch. Found., Madison, 1960-88; cons., Madison, 1988—. Mem. adv. com. Coun. on Govtl. Rels., Washington, 1975-93; panel mem. Office Tech. Assessment, Washington, 1981-83; mem. Adv. Commn. on Patent Law Reform, Washington, 1991-92. Mem. internat. adv. bd. Industry and Higher Edn. Jour., 1996—; contbr. articles to profl. jours. Pres. Edgewood Campus Sch. PTA, Madison, 1967-69; mem. adv. bd. Edgewood H.S., 1971-80, chmn. adv. bd., 1973-74. With USN, 1944-46. Recipient alumni appreciation award Edgewood H.S., 1990, Hon. Recognition award, U. Wis. Coll. Agrl. and Life Scis., 2000. Mem. ABA (chmn. com. 1993-2001), Am. Intellectual Property Law Assn. (chmn. com. 1996-99), State Bar Wis. (chmn. intellectual property sect. 1967-68, 79-80), Wis. Intellectual Property Law Assn. (pres. 1989-90), Assn. Univ. Tech. Mgrs. (trustee 1977-78, 80-82, pres. 1978-80, com. chmn. 1985-93, mem. editl. bd. jour. 1990—, Birch award 1980). Avocations: building furniture, home maintenance, model railroading, travel, reading. Intellectual property, Legislative, Patent. Home: 1106 Brookwood Rd Madison WI 53711-3116 E-mail: hwbremer@warf.org.

BREMER, JOHN M. lawyer; b. 1947; BA, Fordham U., 1969; JD, Duke U., 1974. Bar: Wis. 1974. From atty. law dept. to sr. exec. v.p., COO Northwestern Mutual Life Ins., Milw., 1974—2002, COO, 2002—. Corporate, general, Insurance, Property, real (including real estate development, water). Office: Northwestern Mutual Life Ins Co 720 E Wisconsin Ave Milwaukee WI 53202-4703

BREMER, WILLIAM RICHARD, lawyer; b. San Francisco, Jan. 5, 1930; m. Margaret Herrington; children: Mark Richard (dec.), Karen Elizabeth, William Richard Jr. BS in Bus. Adminstrn., Menlo Coll., 1952; JD, U. San Francisco, 1958. Bar: Calif. 1959, U.S. Dist. Ct. (no. dist.) Calif. 1959, U.S. Ct. Appeals (9th cir.) 1959, U.S. Supreme Ct. 1965, U.S. Ct. Mil. Appeals 1973. Pvt. practice San Francisco Bay area, 1959—. Officer, dir. Marshall Hale Meml. Hosp., 1986-88, Childrens Hosp. San Francisco, 1988-91; bd. dirs. Bridgeway Plan for Health, 1988-92. Bd. dirs. Bay Area USO, 1980-89; arbitrator Marin County and San Francisco County Cts., 1977—; animal control hearing officer Marin County, 1998—; city councilman Town of Tiburon (Calif.), 1966-70, mayor, 1968-69; v.p., bd. dirs. Tiburon Peninsula Found.; regional v.p. No. Calif. Naval War Coll. Found., 1997-2000. Lt. USMC, 1952-54, Korea; col. USMC Res. (ret.), 1954-82. Mem. Am. Arbitration Assn. (panel arbitrator 1965—), ATLA, San Francisco Trial Lawyers Assn., Marin County Bar Assn., Calif. Trial Lawyers Assn., Navy League U.S. (life mem. San Francisco Coun., pres. 1978-80, nat. bd. dirs. 1978-88, no. Calif. state pres. 1981-82, nat. dep. JAG 1997-2001, nat. dir. emeritus 2000), Marine Corps Res. Officers Assn. (life), Res. Officers Assn. (life), Naval Order of U.S. (life, San Francisco commandery, comdr. 1982, 83, comdr. gen., nat. pres. 1993-95), Corinthian Yacht (commodore 1986-87), Montgomery St. Motorcycle (pres. 1974-75), Marines Meml. San Francisco (pres. 1985-86), Kiwanis (bd. dirs. San Francisco chpt. 1981-83), Tiburon-Belvedere Rotary (bd. dirs. 1997—, chair cmty. svc., pres. 2001-02). General civil litigation, Criminal, Personal injury (including property damage). Office: 120 Taylor Rd Belvedere Tiburon CA 94920-1061 E-mail: BillBrem@aol.com.

BRENMAN, ALBERT, lawyer; b. Batavia, N.Y., Mar. 28, 1926; s. Joseph M. and Helen (Shapiro) B.; m. Rosalie Rhea Feldman, Oct. 23, 1952; children— Jeffrey M., Cynthia Sue, David W. B.S., B.A., Denver U., 1950, J.D., 1953. Bar: Colo., 1953. Pres., dir., stockholder Brenman, Raskin , Friedlob & Tenenbaum P.C., Denver, 1961— . Fmr. pres., trustee Temple Micah, Denver; pres. Denver chpt. Am. Soc. for Handicapped Children in Israel, 2002-03. Served as 1st lt. U.S. Army, 1945-48. Mem. Denver U. Law Sch. Alumni Council (chmn. 1981-83, chmn. Alumni Fund Drive 1978-81). Beta Alpha Psi (pres. 1950), Beta Gamma Sigma, Phi Delta Phi. Democrat. Jewish. Home: 4400 E Oxford Pl Englewood CO 80110-5044

BRENNAN, DANIEL CHRISTOPHER, lawyer; b. N.Y.C., Oct. 7, 1954; s. Robert H. and Winifred M. (Gerdes) B.; m. Maryann C. Riviello, May 24, 1987. BA cum laude, Fordham U., 1976; JD cum laude, Cornell U., 1980. Bar: N.Y. 1981, D.C. 1982, U.S. Dist. Ct. (no. dist.) N.Y. 1983. Fellow crime and correction com. N.Y. State Senate, Albany, 1978-79; law asst. appellate div., 3d dept., Albany, 1980-81, staff atty., with, 1983—; assoc. Haight, Gardner, Poor & Havens, Washington, 1981-82. Co-editor Law Guardian Reporter, 1985-90; assoc. editor Cornell U. Internat. Law Jour., 1979-80. Mem. Town of Guilderland Conservation Adv. Coun., 1989-94. Mem. N.Y. State Bar Assn. (legal edn., admission coms.), Fordham Club (Bronx, N.Y.), Schuyler Meadows Club (Loudonville). Office: Appellate Div 3d Dept Capitol Sta PO Box 7288 Albany NY 12224-0288

BRENNAN, DANIEL EDWARD, JR., state judge; b. Houston, Oct. 2, 1942; s. Daniel E. and Emily (Tabor) B.; m. Ruth Miriam Gonchar, Nov. 16, 1973; children: Danna Julie, Benjamin Tabor. AA, U. State N.Y., 1974, BS, 1976; JD, U. Bridgeport, 1981; IEM, Harvard U., 1974. Bar: Conn. 1981, U.S. Dist. Ct. Conn. 1981, U.S. Supreme Ct. Exec. asst. to pres. Hunter Coll., N.Y.C., 1970-77; pres. S&B Mgmt. Systems, N.Y.C., 1977-80; ptnr. Brennan, McNamara & Baldwin, P.C., Bridgeport, Conn., 1981-96; judge Superior Ct. Conn., 1999—. Chief legal advisor Bridgeport Police Dept., 1983—85; chief labor counsel City of Bridgeport, 1981—85. Mem.: Conn. Bar Assn. (former chair Litigation sect.), Am. Judges Assn. (bd. govs. 2001—). State civil litigation, General practice, Labor (including EEOC, Fair Labor Standards Act, labor-management relations, NLRB, OSHA). Home: 57 Gray Rock Rd Trumbull CT 06611-3307 Fax: 203-268-8498. E-mail: BDJudgeCT@aol.com., Daniel.Brennan@Jud.State.CT.us.

BRENNAN, JAMES JOSEPH, lawyer, banking and financial services executive; b. Chgo., July 14, 1950; s. John Michael and Rosemary (Rickard) B.; m. Donna Jean Blessing, June 2, 1973; children: Michael James, Laura Jessica. BS, Purdue U., 1972; JD, Indiana U., 1975. Bar: Ind. 1975, U.S. Dist. Ct. (so. dist.) Ind. 1975, U.S. Tax Ct. 1975, U.S. Ct. Appeals (6th cir.) 1976 U. S. Ct. Appeals (4th cir.) 1977, Ill., 1978, U.S. Dist. Ct. (no. dist.) Ill. 1978, U.S. Ct. Appeals (7th cir.) 1978, U.S. Supreme Ct. 1981. Law clk. to judge U.S. Dist. Ct. (ea. dist.), Tenn., 1975-77; ptnr. Pope, Ballard, Shepard & Fowle, Ltd., Chgo., 1977-87, Hopkins & Sutter, Chgo., 1987-91; ptnr., co-chmn. fin. svcs. group Barack, Ferrazzano, Kirschbaum & Perlman, Chgo., 1991-99; exec. v.p. corp. affairs, gen. counsel BankFinancial Corp., 2000—. Chmn. legal affairs com. Ill. Bankers Assn., Chgo., 1986, chmn. bank counsel sect., 1987; lectr. programs for bankers, bank examiners, accts. and bank counsel; participant drafting of various Ill. banking laws; adj. prof. grad. sch. bank law Ill. Inst. Tech. Kent Coll. Law, 1992-2000. Articles editor Ind. Law Rev., 1974-75; editor: Ill. Bankers Assn. Law Watch, 1988-94; contbr. articles to profl. jours. 1st recipient Disting. Bank Counsel award Ill. Bankers Assn., 1989. Mem. Riverside Golf Club (bd. dirs. 1992-2000, sec.-treas. 1995-98), Western Golf Assn. (bd. dirs. 1998—, Evans Scholars (Purdue chpt. 1968-72, pres. 1970-71). Banking. Office: 15 WO60 N Frontage Rd Burr Ridge IL 60527 Business E-Mail: jbrennan@bankfinancial.com.

BRENNAN, JOHN JOSEPH, lawyer, legal administrator; b. Troy, N.Y., Nov. 1, 1958; s. James Patrick and Grace Marie (Bartolomeo) B. AAS, Schenectady (N.Y) Community Coll., 1978; BA cum laude, Siena Coll., 1981; JD cum laude, Union U., 1985. Bar: N.Y. 1986, U.S. Dist. Ct. (no. dist.) N.Y. 1986, U.S. Supreme Ct. 1999. Law clk. to Appellate Divsn. Justice 4th Dept., Herkimer, N.Y., 1985-86; assoc. law ck. to justice State Supreme Ct., Herkimer, 1986-90; law clk. to U.S. Magistrate-Judge, Utica, N.Y., 1991-92; assoc. law clk. to justice N.Y. Supreme Ct., Utica, 1992—2001, 2002—. Adj. prof. Herkimer County CC, 2003—; mem. panel Surrogate Decision Making Program, 2002—. Bd. dirs. Mohawk Valley Red Cross, Utica Zoo. Mem. ABA, N.Y. State Bar Assn., Oneida County Bar Assn. (bd. dirs.), Herkimer County Bar Assn. (treas. 1990), KC, Pi Gamma Mu. Roman Catholic. Avocations: running, skiing. General practice. Home: 119 Court St Herkimer NY 13350-1923 Office: Herkimer County Ct House Utica NY 13350

BRENNAN, JOHN WILLIAM, lawyer, real estate broker; b. Norfolk, Va., May 26, 1940; s. John Leo and Ann Virginia B.; m. Sarah Charlotte Albrecht, July 2, 1966; children: John William, Jr., Anne Alexander, James Rayfield. BA, Duke U., 1963; JD, U. Va., 1966. Staff atty. Fed. Trade Commn., Washington, 1966-70; asst. Washington counsel U.S. Savings and Loan League, Washington, 1970-77; pres., CEO, dir. Mt. Vernon Savings Assn., Alexandria, 1977-80; dir. Va., Md. and D.C. Foremost Guaranty Corp., Madison, Wis., 1980-82; pvt. practice Fairfax, Va., 1982-92; assoc. Scanlon & Assocs., Manassas, Va., 1992-93; pvt. practice Portsmouth, Va., 1993-95; commercial realtor, legal counsel Barrick Tri-City Real Estate, Portsmouth, 1995—. Bd. dirs. Fairfax County United Way, Annandale, Va., 1985-86; pres., dir. Hampton Roads Affordable Housing, Inc., Portsmouth, 1997-2000. Placed 1st Ann. Golf Tournament , Fed. Home Loan Bank Bd., Washington, 1971,75, 79, State Savings and Loan Suprs., Colorado Springs, Colo., 1973, Va. Savings and Loan League, Hilton Head, S.C., 1980; recipient Grand Prize Vince Lombardi Golf Tournament Vince Lombardi Meml. Fund., 1975. Mem. Am. Philatelic Soc., U. Va. Alumni Assn. (life), Va. State Bar Assn., SAR, Olde Towne Civic Assn. Episcopalian. Avocations: antique collecting, golf, stamp collecting, swimming, hiking. Commercial, contracts (including sales of goods; commercial financing), Landlord-tenant, Property, real (including real estate development, water). Home: 416 North St Portsmouth VA 23704-2522 Office: Barrick Tri-City Real Estate 3403 County St # C Portsmouth VA 23707-3233

BRENNECKE, ALLEN EUGENE, lawyer; b. Marshalltown, Iowa, Jan. 8, 1937; s. Arthur Lynn and Julia Alice (Allen) B; m. Billie Jean Johnstone, June 12, 1958; children: Scott, Stephen, Beth, Gregory, Kristen BBA, U. Iowa, 1959, JD, 1961. Bar: Iowa 1961. Law clk. U.S. Dist. Judge, Des Moines, 1961-62; assoc. Mote, Wilson & Welp, Marshalltown, Iowa, 1962-66; ptnr. Harrison, Brennecke, Moore, Smaha & McKibben, Marshalltown, 1966—. Contr. articles to profl. jours. Bd. dirs. Marshalltown YMCA, 1966-71; mem. bd. trustees Iowa Law Sch. Found., 1973-86, United Meth. Ch., Marshalltown, 1978-81, 87-89; fin. chmn. Rep. party 4th Congl. Dist., Iowa, 1970-73, Marshall County Rep. Party, Iowa, 1967-70. Fellow ABA (chmn. ho. of dels. 1984-86, bd. govs. 1982-86), Nat. Jud. Coll. (bd. dirs. 1982-88), Am. Coll. Trusts and Estates Counsel, Am. Coll. Tax Counsel, Am. Bar Found., Iowa Bar Assn. (pres. 1990-91, award of merit 1987); mem. Masons, Shriners, Promise Keepers. Republican. Methodist. Avocations: golf, travel, sports. Home: 703 Circle Dr Marshalltown IA 50158-3809 Office: Harrison Brennecke Moore Smaha & McKibben 302 Masonic Temple Marshalltown IA 50158

BRENNEMAN, DELBERT JAY, lawyer; b. Albany, Oreg., Feb. 4, 1950; s. Calvin M. and Velma Barbara (Whitaker) B.; m. Caroline Yorke Allen, May 29, 1976; children: Mark Stuart, Thomas Allen. BS magna cum laude, Oreg. State U., 1972; JD, U. Oreg., 1976. Bar: Oreg. 1976, U.S. Dist. Ct. Oreg. 1977, U.S. Ct. Appeals (9th cir.) 1977. Assoc. Schwabe, Williamson, and Wyatt, Portland, Oreg., 1976-83, ptnr., 1984-92, Hoffman, Hart & Wagner, Portland, Oreg., 1993—. Spkr. Oreg. Self-Ins., 1978, 90; seminar instr. U. Oreg. Law Sch., Eugene, 1980. Mem. ABA, Oreg. State Bar Assn., Multnomah County Bar Assn. (spkr. 1983-84), Order of Coif, Multnomah Athletic Club, Propeller Club of U.S. (bd. dirs. 1983-85), Phi Kappa Phi, Beta Gamma Sigma. Administrative and regulatory, Insurance, Workers' compensation. Office: Hoffman Hart & Wagner 1000 SW Broadway Fl 20 Portland OR 97205-3035 E-mail: djb@hhw.com.

BRENNEMAN, HUGH WARREN, JR., judge; b. Lansing, Mich., July 4, 1945; s. Hugh Warren and Irma June Brenneman; m. Catherine Brenneman; 2 children. BA, Alma Coll., 1967; JD, U. Mich., 1970. Bar: Mich. 1970, D.C. 1975, U.S. Dist. Ct. (we. dist.) Mich. 1974, U.S. Dist. Ct. Md. 1973, U.S. Ct. Mil. Appeals 1971, U.S. Ct. Appeals (6th cir.) 1976, U.S. Ct. Appeals (D.C. cir.) 1981, U.S. Supreme Ct. 1980. Law clk. Mich. 30th Jud. Cir., Lansing, 1970-71; asst. U.S. atty. Dept. Justice, Grand Rapids, Mich., 1974-77; assoc. Bergstrom, Slykhouse & Shaw PC, Grand Rapids, 1977—80; magistrate judge US Dist. Ct. (we. dist.) Mich., Grand Rapids, 1980—. Instr. Western Mich. U., Grand Valley State U., 1989-92. Mem. exec. bd. and adv. coun. Gerald R Ford coun. Boy Scouts Am., 1984—, v.p., 1988-92; mem. Grand Rapids Hist. Commn., 1991-97, pres., 1995-97; dir. Cmty. Reconciliation Ctr., 1991. Capt. JAGC, U.S. Army, 1971-74. Recipient Disting. Alumnus award Alma Coll., 1998. Fellow Mich. State Bar Found.; mem. FBA (pres. Western Mich. chpt. 1979-80, nat. del. 1980-84), U.S. Dist. Ct. Hist. Soc. (pres. 2002--), State Bar Mich. (rep. assembly 1984-90), D.C. Bar Assn., Grand Rapids Bar Assn. (chmn. U.S. Constn. Bicentennial com., co-chmn. Law Day 1991), Fed. Magistrate Judges Assn., Am. Inns of Ct. (master of bench Grand Rapids chpt., pres.), Phi Delta Phi, Omicron Delta Kappa, Peninsular Club, Rotary (past pres., Charities Found. of Grand Rapids v.p., Paul Harris fellow), Econ. Club of Grand Rapids (past bd. dirs.). Congregationalist. Office: US Dist Ct West Mich 110 Michigan St NW Rm 580 Grand Rapids MI 49503-2313

BRENNEMAN HARRAH, SANDRA, lawyer; b. Charleston, W.Va., Nov. 3, 1970; d. Samuel Lee and Patricia Ruth B. BS in Bus. Adminstrn., BA in Polit. Sci., Alderson-Broaddus Coll., 1993; JD, W.Va. U., 1996. Bar: W.Va. 1996, U.S. Dist. Ct. (so. dist.) W.Va. 1996, (no. dist.) 2000. Assoc. Calwell & McCormick, Charleston, W.Va., 1996-97, Hill, Peterson, Carper, Bee & Deitzler, PLLC, Charleston, W.Va., 1997—. Mem. Assn. Trial Lawyers Am., W.Va. Trial Lawyers Assn. Avocations: skiing, scuba diving. Insurance, Personal injury (including property damage), Product liability. Office: Hill Peterson Carper Bee & Deitzler 500 Tracy Way Charleston WV 25311-1261 E-mail: sandra@hpcbd.com.

BRENNER, ANITA SUSAN, lawyer; b. LA, Aug. 18, 1949; d. Morris I. and Lillian F. Brenner; m. Leonard E. Torres, Aug. 19, 1973; children: Andrew, Rachel. BA, UCLA, 1970, JD, 1973. Bar: Calif. 1974, U.S. Dist. Ct. (ctrl. dist.) Calif. 1974. Atty. Grtr. Watts Justice Ctr., L.A., 1974-75; pvt. practice L.A., 1975; dep. pub. defender L.A. County, 1975-84; assoc. Tyre and Kamins, L.A., 1979; ptnr. Torres-Brenner, Pasadena, Calif., 1984—. Lectr. criminal law. Mem. editl. bd., assoc. editor UCLA Law Rev., 1971-73; editor FORUM mag., 1980-83; contbr. articles to profl. jours. Bd. dirs. One Stop Immigration, 1979-81, Lanterman Ho. Mus., 2003—; vol. LA Area Coun. on Child Passenger Safety, 1981; joint com. on med.-legal issues LA County Med. Assn., 1983. Mable Wilson Richards scholar, 1971-72. Mem. Calif. Attys. for Criminal Justice (bd. govs. 1980-86). State civil litigation, Computer, Criminal. Office: Torres-Brenner 301 E Colorado Blvd Ste 614 Pasadena CA 91101-1918

BRENNER, EDGAR H. law administrator; b. N.Y.C., Jan. 4, 1930; s. Louis and Bertha B. (Guttman) B.; m. Janet Maybin, Aug. 4, 1979; children from previous marriage— Charles S., David M., Paul R. BA, Carleton Coll., 1951; JD, Yale U., 1954. Bar: D.C. 1954, U.S. Ct. Claims 1957, U.S. Supreme Ct. 1957. Mem. 2d Hoover Commn. Legal Task Force Staff, Washington, 1954; trial atty. U.S. Dept. Justice, Washington, 1954-57; assoc. Arnold & Porter, Washington, 1957-62, ptnr., 1962-89. Co-dir. Inter Univ. Ctr. for Legal Studies, 1999—. Co-editor: Legal Aspects of Terrorism in the United States, Terrorism and the Law, U.S. Federal Legal Responses to Terrorism, The United Kingdom's Legal Responses to Terrorism; contbr. articles to profl. jours. Commr. Fairfax County Econ. Devel. Corp., Va., 1963—78; v.p., bd. dirs. Stella and Charles Guttman Found., N.Y.C.; bd. dirs. Ams. for Med. Progress, Arlington, Va. Recipient Disting. Achievement award Carleton Coll., 2001; fellow Coll. Problems of Drug Dependency. Mem.D.C. Bar Assn., Yale Club, Explorers Club (N.Y.C.). Democrat. Home: 340 Persimmon Ln Washington VA 22747-1845 Office: 4620 Lee Hwy Ste 216 Arlington VA 22207-3400 E-mail: edgarhbrenner@email.com.

BRENNER, JOHN FINN, lawyer; b. Eglin AFB, Fla., Aug. 18, 1956; s. Theodore Engelbert and Maria Theresa (Finn) B.; m. Lydia Snel, Dec. 29, 1979; children: Meredith R., Corinne J., Elise H. BA, Dartmouth Coll., 1977; JD, U. Va., 1980. Bar: N.J. 1980, U.S. Dist. Ct. N.J. 1980, U.S. Ct. Appeals (3d cir.) 1984, N.Y. 1988. Assoc. McCarter & English, LLP, Newark, N.J., 1980-88, ptnr., 1988—. Contbr.: New Jersey Product Liability Law, 1994. Chmn. planning bd. Borough of Fair Haven, N.J., 1998—. Mem. ABA, Def. Rsch. Inst., N.J. State Bar Assn., Phi Beta Kappa. Appellate, General civil litigation, Product liability. Office: McCarter & English LLP 100 Mulberry St Newark NJ 07102-4096 E-mail: jbrenner@mccarter.com.

BRESNAHAN, ARTHUR STEPHEN, lawyer; b. Chgo., Dec. 26, 1944; s. Arthur Patrick and Margaret Genevieve (Gleason) B.; m. Patricia Margaret Wetz, June 29, 1968; children: Arthur Patrick, Maureen Justina, Brian Michael, Brendan Robert, Sean Matthew. BA in Psychology, Loras Coll., 1967; JD, Ill. Inst. Tech., 1975. Bar: Ill. 1975, U.S. Dist. Ct. (no. dist.) Ill. 1975, U.S. Ct. Appeals (7th cir.) 1978, U.S. Supreme Ct. 1986, U.S Ct. Claims 1986. Assoc. Garbutt, Jacobson & Lee, Chgo., 1975-77; sr. assoc. atty. Purcell & Wardrope, Chgo., 1977-83; ptnr. Bresnahan & Garvey, Chgo., 1983-88, 1988-98; pvt. practice Arthur S. Bresnahan & Assocs., Chgo., 1998—. Speaker in field. Asst. scoutmaster Boy Scouts Am., Chgo., 1980—, Webelos Den leader. Capt. USMC, 1967-72. Mem. ABA, VFW, Fed. Bar Assn., Ill. Bar Assn., Fed. Trial Bar, Chgo. Bar Assn., Trial Lawyers Club, Vietnam Vets. Am., Lawyer Pilots Bar Assn., Am. Legion. Lodges: KC, Moose. Democrat. Roman Catholic. Avocations: golf, girl/boy scouts. Federal civil litigation, State civil litigation, Insurance. Home and Office: 4715 N Kenneth Ave Chicago IL 60630-4004

BRESS, MICHAEL E. retired lawyer; b. Mpls., Aug. 23, 1933; s. Michael J. and Anna (Tema) B.; m. Grace Billings, June 3, 1966; 1 child, Anne Ruth. BA, U. Minn., 1954, LLB, 1957. Bar: N.Y. 1958, Minn. 1959. Assoc. Donovan Leisure Newton & Irvine, N.Y.C., 1957-59, Dorsey & Whitney LLP, Mpls., 1959-64; ptnr. Dorsey & Whitney LLP, Mpls., 1964-91, of counsel, 1992-97, ret., 1998. Trustee St. Vladimir's Orthodox Theol. Sem., Crestwood, N.Y. Mem. Minn. Bar Assn., Hennepin County Bar Assn., Phi Beta Kappa. Antitrust, Health. Home: 2007 W Franklin Ave Minneapolis MN 55405-2422 E-mail: mbress@mn.rr.com.

BRESSAN, PAUL LOUIS, lawyer; b. Rockville Centre, N.Y., June 15, 1947; s. Louis Charles Bressan and Nance Elizabeth Batteley. BA cum laude, Fordham Coll., 1969; JD, Columbia U., 1975. Bar: N.Y. 1976, Calif. 1987, U.S. Dist. Ct. (so., ea. and no. dists.) N.Y. 1976, U.S. Dist. Ct. (no. and ctrl. dists.) Calif. 1987, U.S. Ct. Appeals (2d cir.) 1980, U.S. Supreme Ct. 1980, U.S. Ct. Appeals (1st and 4th cirs.) 1981, U.S. Ct. Appeals (11th cir.) 1982, U.S. Ct. Appeals (9th cir.) 1987, U.S Ct. Appeals (7th cir.) 1991, U.S. Dist. Ct. (ea. dist.) Calif. 1995; U.S. Dist. Ct. (so. dist.) Calif. 1997. Assoc. Kelley, Drye & Warren, N.Y.C., 1975-84, ptnr. N.Y.C. and Los Angeles, 1984—2003; shareholder Buchalter, Nemer & Fields, 2003—. Served to lt. USNR, 1971-72. Named One of Outstanding Coll. Athletes of Am., 1969; Harlan Fiske Stone scholar Columbia Law Sch. Mem. ABA, Calif. Bar Assn., Phi Beta Kappa. Republican. Roman Catholic. Federal civil litigation, State civil litigation, Labor (including EEOC, Fair Labor Standards Act, labor-management relations, NLRB, OSHA). Office: Buchalter Nemer Fields & Younger 601 S Figueroa St Ste 2400 Los Angeles CA 90017 E-mail: pbressan@buchalter.com.

BRESSLER, BARRY E. lawyer; b. Phila., Apr. 7, 1947; s. Joseph and Shirley M. (Eiseman) B.; m. Risé Sharon Cohen, June 14, 1970 (dec.); children: Allison Ivy, Michelle Amy. AB, Franklin and Marshall Coll., Lancaster, Pa., 1968; JD, U. Pa., 1971. Bar: Pa. 1971, U.S. Dist. Ct. (ea. dist.) Pa. 1973, U.S. Ct. Appeals (3d cir.) 1977, U.S. Supreme Ct. 1988, U.S. Dist. Ct. (mid. dist.) Pa. 1990. Law clk. to judge Superior Ct. Pa., Phila., 1971-73; assoc. Meltzer & Schiffrin, Phila., 1973-79, ptnr., 1979-86, Fox, Rothschild, O'Brien & Frankel, Phila., 1987-88; mem., sr. lawyer real estate litigation & creditors' rights Pelino & Lentz, P.C., Phila., 1988-2000; ptnr. Schnader, Harrison, Segal & Lewis, LLP, Phila., 2000—. Adj. instr. landlord-tenant law Delaware County C.C., Media, Pa., 1985—, Montgomery County C.C., Blue Bell, Pa., 1987—. V.p. English Ceramic Study Group, Phila.; v.p., sec. Temple Sinai, Dresher, Pa., 1991-97, 2003-; grad. Leadership, Inc., Phila. Mem. ABA (litigation sect.), Pa. Bar Assn. (corp. banking and bus. sect.), Phila. Bar Assn. (real property sect.), Bankruptcy Conf. Ea. Dist. Pa. (treas. 1995-2000), Am. Arbitration Assn. Republican. Jewish. Avocations: tennis, ceramics, bridge. Bankruptcy, General civil litigation, Landlord-tenant. Office: Schnader Harrison Segal and Lewis LLP 1600 Market St Ste 3600 Philadelphia PA 19103-7286 E-mail: bbressler@schnader.com.

BRESSLER, GARY DAVID, lawyer; b. Phila., July 27, 1956; s. Joseph and Shirley Maxine (Eiseman) B.; m. Daryl Jacobs, Oct. 29, 1983; children: Paul Jacob, Alexis Leigh, Dana Lynne. BA cum laude, U. Pa., 1978; JD cum laude, Villanova U., 1981. Bar: Pa. 1981, U.S. Dist. Ct. (ea. dist.) Pa. 1982, U.S. Ct. Appeals (3d cir.) 1984. Law clk. Ct. Commons Pleas. of Phila., 1981-82; assoc. Adelman, Lavine, Gold & Levin, Phila., 1982-87, ptnr., 1988-91, stockholder, 1992—. Author: case note Villanova Law Rev., 1981. Mem. ABA, Pa. Bar Assn., Phila. Bar Assn. (corp., banking, bus. law bankruptcy com. sect.), Order of Coif, Pi Sigma Alpha. Avocation: sports. Bankruptcy, Federal civil litigation. Office: Adelman Lavine Gold & Levin 1900 Two Penn Center Plz Philadelphia PA 19102

BREST, PAUL A. law educator; b. Jacksonville, Fla., Aug. 9, 1940; s. Alexander and Mia (Deutsch) B.; m. Iris Lang, June 17, 1962; children: Hilary, Jeremy. AB, Swarthmore Coll., 1962; JD, Harvard U., 1965; LLD (hon.), Northeastern U., 1980, Swarthmore Coll., 1991. Bar: N.Y. 1966. Law clk. to Hon. Bailey Aldrich U.S. Ct. Appeals (1st cir.), Boston, 1965-66; atty. NAACP Legal Def. Fund, Jackson, Miss., 1966-68; law clk. Justice John Harlan, U.S. Supreme Ct., 1968-69; prof. law Stanford U., 1969—, Kenneth and Harle Montgomery Prof. pub. interest law, Richard E. Lang prof. and dean, 1987-99; pres. William and Flora Hewlett Found., Menlo Park, Calif., 1999—. Author: Processes of Constitutional Decision-making, 1992. Mem. Am. Acad. Arts and Scis. Home: 814 Tolman Dr Palo Alto CA 94305-1026 Office: William and Flora Hewlett Found 2121 Sand Hill Rd Menlo Park CA 94025 E-mail: pbrest@hewlett.org.

BRETT, THOMAS RUTHERFORD, federal judge; b. Oklahoma City, Oct. 2, 1931; s. John A. and Norma (Dougherty) B.; m. Mary Jean James, Aug. 26, 1952; children: Laura Elizabeth Brett Tribble, James Ford, Susan Marie Brett Crump, Maricarolyn Swab. BBA, U. Okla., 1953, LL.B., 1957, JD, 1971. Bar: Okla. 1957. Asst. county atty., Tulsa, 1957; mem. firm Hudson, Hudson, Wheaton, Kyle & Brett, Tulsa, 1958-69, Jones, Givens, Brett, Gotcher, Doyle & Bogan, 1969-79; judge U.S. Dist. Ct. (no. dist.) Okla., Tulsa, 1979—. Bd. regents U. Okla., 1971-78; mem. adv. bd. Salvation Army; trustee Okla. Bar Found. Col. JAG, USAR, 1953-83. Named to Okla. Heritage Assn. Hall of Fame, 2000. Fellow Am. Coll. Trial Lawyers, Am. Bar Found.; mem. Okla. Bar Assn. (pres. 1970), Tulsa County Bar Assn. (pres. 1965), Am. Judicature Soc., U. Okla. Coll. Law Alumni Assn. (bd. dirs.), Order of Coif (hon.), Phi Alpha Delta. Democrat. Office: Crown & Dunley Kennedy Bldg 4th & Boston Ste 500 Tulsa OK 74103

BRETTSCHNEIDER, RITA ROBERTA FISCHMAN, lawyer; b. Bklyn., Nov. 12, 1931; d. Isidore M. and Augusta T. (Singer) Fischman; m. Bertram D. Brettschneider, June 25, 1950 (dec. Nov. 17, 1986); children: Jane Brettschneider, Joseph Brettschneider; m. Bertram D. Cohn, June 30, 1991 (dec. July 2002). BA, CUNY, 1953; JD, Bklyn. Law Sch., 1956; postgrad., NYU, 1968-69, Nat. Inst. Trial Advocacy, 1976. Bar: N.Y. 1961, U.S. Dist. Ct. N.Y. 1971. Pvt. practice, Huntington, NY, 1961. Instr. women and the law C.W. Post Coll., Brookville, N.Y., 1969-70; arbitrator med. malpractice arbitration com. Suffolk County (N.Y.), 1974-76; spl. assoc. prof. philosophy and law New Coll. Hofstra U., Hempstead, N.Y., 1974-76; faculty N.Y. Law Jour. Conf. Changing Concepts in Matrimonial Law, 1976; legal advisor Am. Arbitration Assn., 1977-84; arbitrator night small claims ct. Nassau County, 1978-83; of counsel Nassau County Psychol. Assn., 1987—, Suffolk County Psychol. Assn., 1990-95. Contbr. numerous articles to profl. jours. Pres., bd. dirs. For Our Children and Us, 1992—2001. Mem. Nassau-Suffolk Women's Bar Assn. (chair judiciary com. 1974-80), Nassau County Bar Assn. (demonstrating atty. mock trial contested matrimonial action 1975), Suffolk County Bar Assn. (demonstrating atty. mock trial contested matrimonial action 1976), Am. Arbitration Assn. (legal advisor 1977-84), Nassau-Suffolk Women's Bar Assn. (pres. 1980-81). Family and matrimonial. Home: 2 Crosby Pl Cold Spring Harbor NY 11724-2403 Office: Brettschneider & Brettschneider 83 Prospect St Huntington NY 11743-3306 E-mail: vember@aol.com.

BREWER, CHARLES MOULTON, lawyer; b. Washington, June 9, 1931; BS, U. Md., 1953; JD, George Washington U., 1957. Bar: Ariz. 1959. Since practiced in, Phoenix; law clk. to Chief Justice Ariz. Supreme Ct. Levi S. Udall, 1958-59; pvt. practice, 1959—; pres. Charles M. Brewer Ltd.; airline transport pilot, 1977—. Guest lectr. Stanford U. Law Sch., Ariz. State U. Law Sch. (Charles M. Brewer professorship of trial advocacy established 1985); mem. plaintiffs steering com. Northwest Crash Case, 1987. Contbr. articles to profl. jours. Bd. visitors Ariz. State U. Law Sch. Named one of Best Lawyers in Am. Mem.: ATLA, ABA, Atty.'s Info. Exch. Group, Fed. Bar Assn., Nat. Bar Assn., Trial Lawyers for Pub. Justice, Lawyers-Pilots Bar Assn., Assn. Trial Lawyers Am., Lawyers-Pilots Bar Assn., Assn. Trial Lawyers, Internat. Acad. Trial Lawyers, Am. Bd. Trial Advs., Ariz. Trial Lawyers Assn., Am. Judicature Soc., Maricopa County Bar Assn., Ariz. Bar Assn. Personal injury (including property damage). Mailing: 5500 N 24th st Phoenix AZ 85016

BREWER, DAVID MADISON, lawyer; b. Bordeaux, Gironde, France, July 8, 1953; s. Herbert L and Paulyne B (Ver Benec) Brewer; m. Andrea M Bordiga, May 20, 1978; children: James David Madison, Caroline Elizabeth, Geoffrey Andrew. AB summa cum laude, Yale U., 1975, JD, 1978. Bar: NY 1979. Assoc. atty. Cravath Swaine & Moore, N.Y.C., 1978-84; assoc. gen. tax counsel Union Pacific Corp., N.Y.C. and Bethlehem, Pa., 1984-89; pres. Madison Co., Inc., N.Y.C., 1990—; pres., CEO Madison Oil Co., Dallas, 1993-2000, vice chmn., 2000—01, chmn., 2001—. Bd. dirs. Toreador Resources Corp., Dallas, 2002—. Editor: Yale Law Rev., 1977—78. Spec gifts chmn Yale Univ Class 1975 and Law Sch Class 1978, 1985—; mem Yale Develop Bd, 2000—; nat vice-chmn Smithsonian Friends First Ladies, 1989—92; mem. world bd. USO, 1995—2002; vice chmn Bush/Quayle '92 Fin Comt; policy asst Office Campaign Mgr, Bush-Quayle campaign, 1988; bd. govs. Am. Friends of the Anglican Ctr. in Rome, 2002—; bd dirs Yale Univ Law Sch Fund, 1989—93, Yale Alumni Fund, 1989—95; trustee Pine Ridge Sch, Vt., 1998—. Assoc. fellow, Saybrook Coll., Yale U., 2000—. Mem.: NY Bar Assn., Mory's (New Haven), Cercle de L'Union Interalliee (Paris), Yale Club (N.Y.C.), Phi Beta Kappa. Republican. Episcopalian. Taxation, general. Office: Toreador Resources Corp 4809 Cole Ave Ste 108 Dallas TX 75205

BREWER, EDWARD CAGE, III, law educator; b. Clarksdale, Miss., Jan. 20, 1953; s. Edward Cage Brewer Jr. and Elizabeth Blair (Alford) Little; m. Nancy Corr Martin, Dec. 27, 1975 (div. Sept. 1985); children: Katherine Martin, Julia Blair; m. Laurie Carol Alley, June 27, 1993 (div. Dec. 1999); 1 child, Caroline Elizabeth McCarty; m. Karlyn Ann Schnapp; children: Matthew Karl Schnapp, Andrew Cage Schnapp. BA, U. of the South, 1975; JD, Vanderbilt U., 1979. Bar: Ala. 1980, U.S. Ct. Appeals (5th and 11th cirs.) 1981, U.S. Dist. Ct. (so. dist.) Ala. 1981, Ga. 1982, U.S. Dist. Ct. (no. dist.) Ga. 1982, U.S. Dist. Ct. (so. dist.) Ga. 1988, U.S. Ct. Appeals (3d and 8th cirs.) 1983, U.S. Dist. Ct. (mid. dist.) Ga. 1992, U.S. Supreme Ct. 1996. Law clk. to Hon. Virgil Pittman U.S. Dist. Ct. (so. dist.) Ala., Mobile, 1979-81; law clk. to Hon. Albert J. Henderson U.S. Ct. Appeals (5th and 11th cirs.), Atlanta, 1981-82; pvt. practice Atlanta, 1982-96; instr. Coll. of Law Ga. State U., Atlanta, 1992, 94; adj. prof. legal writing Emory U., Atlanta, 1994-96; asst. prof. law No. Ky. U., Highland Heights, 1996-2000, assoc. prof. law, 2000—02, prof. law, 2002—. Co-author: Railway Labor Act of 1926: Legislative History, 1988, Georgia Appellate Practice, 1996, 2d edit., 2002; author: Powerpoint Materials for Morgan and Rotunda, Professional Responsibility, 1997, 2003; contbr. articles to profl. jours. Mem.: Omicron Delta Kappa, Phi Beta Kappa. Episcopalian. Avocations: choral music, guitar, bicycling, hiking, canoeing. E-mail: brewerec@nku.edu.

BREWER, LEWIS GORDON, judge, lawyer, educator; b. New Martinsville, W.Va., Sept. 6, 1946; s. Harvey Lee and Ruth Carolyn (Zimmerman) B.; m. Kathryn Anne Yunker, May 25, 1985. BA, W.Va. U., 1968, JD, 1971; LLM, George Washington U., 1979. Bar: W.Va. 1971, Calif. 1978. Commd. 2d lt. USAF, 1968, advanced through grades to col., 1988, dep. staff judge adv., 1976-78, chief civil law San Antonio Air Logistics Ctr. Kelly AFB, Tex., 1979-83, staff judge adv. MacDill AFB, Fla., 1983-86, chief Air Force Cen. Labor Law Office Randolph AFB, Tex., 1987-88, dep. staff judge adv.

Air Tng. Command, 1988-89, staff judge adv. 7th Air Force Osan AFB, Korea, 1989-91, 45 Space Wing Patrick AFB, 1991-93; adminstrv. law judge W.Va. Edn. and State Employee Grievance Bd., Charleston, 1993-2000, mediator, 1994—; legal counsel W.Va. Ethics Commn., Charleston, 2000—. Instr. bus. law No. Mich. U., Marquette, 1972, Solano Coll., Suisun City, Calif., 1978; instr. labor law Webster U., Ft. Sam Houston, 1983. Decorated Air Force Commendation medal, Meritorious Service medal, Legion of Merit. Mem. ABA, Assn. for Conflict Resolution, W.Va. Bar Assn., State Bar Calif., W.Va. U. Alumni Assn., George Washington U. Alumni Assn. Roman Catholic. Home: 528 Sheridan Cir Charleston WV 25314-1063 Office: 1207 Quarrier St Charleston WV 25301-1826 E-mail: Mede8wv@abanet.org., LBrewer@GWMail.state.wv.us.

BREWER, ROY EDWARD, lawyer; b. Atlanta, Dec. 22, 1949; s. Roy Mullins and Martha Joan (Still) Brewer; m. Catherine Elizabeth Schindler, May 5, 1979; children: Garrett Edward, Alex Winston. BA in Polit. Sci., U. Fla., 1971, MA in Polit. Sci., 1973; JD, U. Pacific, 1982. Bar: Calif. 1984, U.S. Dist. Ct. (ea. dist.) Calif. 1984, U.S. Supreme Ct. 1990. Regional planner North Cen. Fla. Regional Planning Council, Gainesville, Fla., 1975-78; dir. met. affairs Sacramento Met. C. of C., 1978-79; dir. land planning Raymond Vail and Assocs., Sacramento, 1979-84; pvt. practice Sacramento, 1984-89; ptnr. Hunter McCray Richey & Brewer, Sacramento, 1989-95, Hunter, Richey, DiBenedetto & Brewer, Sacramento, 1995—2000, mng. ptnr., 1993—2000; ptnr. The Brewer Law Firm, 2000—. Bd. dirs. Am. River Natural History Assn., 1986—90, pres., 1988—89; bd. dirs. No. Calif. Rugby Football Union, 1985—88, pres., 1985—88; chmn. Sacramento Ad-hoc Charter Comm., 1988—90; bd. dirs. Healthcare, 1987—90, chmn., 1988—89; bd. dirs. Sacramento Met. C. of C., 1985—91, pres., 1990; trustee ARC, 1989—90; chmn. Local Govt. Reorgn. Com., 1988; chair Leadership Sacramento, 2000, co-chair, 2001—03; bd. dirs. Sacramento Symphony Assn., 1987—95, Am. Lung Assn., 1988—92, Sacramento Downtown Partnership, 1997—99. Named among Best and Brightest, Sacramento Mag., 1985; recipient Sacramento Regional Pride award for cmty. devel., 1991, Exceptional Performers award, Air Force Assn., 1991, Sacramentan of the Yr. award, 1991. Mem.: Am. Inst. Cert. Planners. Avocations: rugby , scuba diving, snowboarding. Environmental, Land use and zoning (including planning), Property, real (including real estate development, water). Office: The Brewer Law Firm 980 Ninth St Ste 2050 Sacramento CA 95814

BREWSTER, CLARK OTTO, lawyer; b. Marlette, Mich., Nov. 5, 1956; s. Charles W. and June V. (Hoff) B.; m. Deborah K. Trowhill, Aug. 3, 1974; children: Cassie Mae, Corbin Clark, Cade Otto. BA cum laude, Cen. Mich. U., 1977; JD with honor, Tulsa U., 1980. Bar: Okla. 1981, U.S. Dist. Ct. (ND,WD,ED) Okla. 1982, Tex. 1993. Assoc. Riddle and Assocs., Tulsa, 1981, Braly and McEachin, Tulsa, 1981-82; ptnr. Brewster & DeAngelis, Tulsa, 1982—. Bd. dirs. Redy Corp., Tulsa, Cottontail Oil Corp., Tulsa. Mem. ABA, ATLA, Okla. Bar Assn., Okla. Trial Lawyers Assn. (pres. 1998), Tulsa County Bar Assn., Order of Curule chair, Order of Barristers. Avocations: golf, hunting, horseback riding. Criminal, Personal injury (including property damage). Home: 2109 E 30th Pl Tulsa OK 74114-5429 Office: Brewster & DeAngelis 2617 E 21st St Tulsa OK 74114

BREWSTER, FRANCIS ANTHONY, lawyer; b. Foochow, China, Jan. 28, 1929; s. Francis Thoburn and Eva (Melby) B.; m. Susan Brewster, Apr. 6, 1974; 1 dau., Melissa Leigh; children by previous marriage— Sara, Julia, Anne, Ellen, Rebecca. BS, U. Wis., 1950, LL.B., 1955. Bar: Wis. 1955, U.S. Dist. Ct. (ea. and we. dists.) Wis. Corporate counsel Scott Paper Co., Phila., 1955-56, labor counsel, 1957; div. personnel mgr. Scott Paper Co. (Detroit div.), 1958-60; corp. counsel RCA, Camden, N.J., 1961; pvt. practice law Madison, Wis., 1961—. Dir. Nat. Guardian Life Ins. Co., Stephan & Brady, Inc.; lectr. law U. Wis., 1961— . Contbr. articles to profl. jours. Gen. counsel Four Lakes coun. Boy Scouts Am., 1980—94; mem. gen. counsel Wis. Privacy Coun., 1991—95; chair Gov.'s Task Force on Privacy, 1999—2001; pres. Hill Farms Assn., 1999—; counsel John Knox Presbytery, 2001—; Chmn. personnel bd. City of Madison, 1970—75; bd. dirs. Capitol div. A.R.C., 1965—74, chmn. div., 1973; bd. dirs. Madison Symphony, Inc., 1968—75, gen. counsel, 1961—91; bd. visitors U. Wis. System, 1972—85, pres. bd. visitors, 1978—80. Served to capt. USMC, 1950—53, Korea. Recipient Certificate of Merit U. Mich.-Wayne State U., 1959; named Outstanding Madisonian, 1969, Wis. Man of Distinction, 1972, State Atty. of Yr. for Pro Bono Svc., 1998. Mem. ABA, Dane County Bar Assn. (past sec. and program chmn.), State Bar of Wis. (chmn. dist. 2 fee arbitration panel 1978—; mem. lawyer dispute resolution panel 1998—), Wis. Bar Found. (bd. dirs. 1981-87, chmn. investment com.), Interfraternity Alumni Council U. Wis. (pres. 1968-74), Delta Upsilon (pres. Wis. 1965-72, Outstanding Alumnus 1984). Republican. Presbyn. (elder). Club: Kiwanian (Madison) (pres. 1969). Corporate, general, Labor (including EEOC, Fair Labor Standards Act, labor-management relations, NLRB, OSHA), Non-profit and tax-exempt organizations. Office: PO Box 55418 Madison WI 53705-9218 Fax: 608-231-1163. E-mail: fabrewst@facstaff.wisc.edu.

BREWSTER, RUDI MILTON, judge; b. Sioux Falls, S.D., May 18, 1932; s. Charles Edwin and Wilhemina Therese (Rud) B.; m. Gloria Jane Nanson, June 27, 1954; children: Scot Alan, Lauri Diane (Alan Lee), Julie Lynn Yahnke. AB in Pub. Affairs, Princeton U., 1954; JD, Stanford U., 1960. Bar: Calif. 1960. From assoc. to ptnr. Gray, Cary, Ames & Frye, San Diego, 1960-84; judge U.S. Dist. Ct. (so. dist.) Calif., San Diego, 1984—98, sr. judge, 1998—. Capt. USNR, 1954-82 Ret. Fellow Am. Coll. Trial Lawyers; mem. Am. Bd. Trial Advs., Internat. Assn. Ins. Counsel, Am. Inns of Ct. Republican. Lutheran. Avocations: skiing, hunting, gardening. Office: US Dist Ct Ste 4165 940 Front St San Diego CA 92101-8902 Fax: 619-702-9927. E-mail: Rudi_Brewster@casd.uscourts.gov.

BREYER, STEPHEN GERALD, United States supreme court justice; b. San Francisco, Aug. 15, 1938; s. Irving G. and Anne R. Breyer; m. Joanna Hare, Sept. 4, 1967; children: Chloe, Nell, Michael. AB, Stanford U., 1959; BA (Marshall scholar), Oxford U., 1961; LLB, Harvard U., 1964; LLD (hon.) , U. Rochester, 1983. Bar: Calif. 1966, D.C. 1966, Mass. 1971. Law clk. Justice Goldberg, U.S. Supreme Ct., 1964—65; spl. asst. to asst. atty. gen. U.S. Dept. Justice, 1965—67; asst. prof. law Harvard U., 1967—70, prof., 1970—81, lectr., 1981—, prof. govt. J.F. Kennedy Sch., 1978—81; asst. spl. prosecutor Watergate Spl. Prosecution Force, 1973; spl. counsel U.S. Senate Judiciary Com., 1974—75, chief counsel, 1979—81; judge U.S. Ct. Appeals (1st cir.), Boston, 1981—90, chief judge, 1990—94; Oliver Wendell Holmes lectr. Harvard Law Sch., 1992; assoc. justice U.S. Supreme Ct., Washington, 1994—. Mem. U.S. Sentencing Commn., 1985—89, Jud. Conf. of U.S., 1990—94; vis. lectr. Coll. Law, Sydney, Australia, 1975, Salzburg (Austria) Seminar, 1978, 93; Jud. Conf. rep. to Adminstrv. Conf. U.S., 1981—94; vis. prof. U. Rome, 1993. Author (with Paul MacAvoy): The Federal Power Commission and the Regulation of Energy, 1974; author: (with Richard Stewart) Administrative Law and Regulatory Policy, 1979, Administrative Law and Regulatory Policy, 3rd edit., 1992; author: Regulation and its Reform, 1982, Breaking the Vicious Circle, 1993; contbr. articles to profl. jours. Trustee U. Mass., 1974—81; bd. overseers Dana Farber Cancer Inst., Boston, 1977—. Mem.: ABA, Coun. Fgn. Rels., Am. Acad. Arts and Scis., Am. Law Inst., Am. Bar Found. Office: US Supreme Ct Supreme Ct Bldg 1 1st St NE Washington DC 20543-0001*

BREYFOGLE, EDWIN HOWARD, lawyer; b. Ann Arbor, Mich., May 16, 1949; s. Ernest Edwin and Dorothy Winefred (Frye) Breyfogle; children: James Edwin, Thomas David. BA, Ohio State U., 1971, JD, 1976; postgrad., Va. Theol. Sem, 1972—74. Bar: Ohio 1976, U.S. Dist. Ct. (no. dist.) Ohio 1976. Pvt. practice, Massillon, Ohio, 1976—. Sec. Interfaith Campus Ministries, Inc., North Canton, Ohio, 1979—80. Mem.: Stark County Bar Assn., Am. Bankruptcy Inst., Ohio State Bar Assn. (exec. com. 1993—95, chmn. bankruptcy com. 1996—97, 2001—02, exec. com. 2002—), Massillon Lawyers Club (pres. 1980—81). Republican. Bankruptcy, Commercial, consumer (including collections, credit). Home: 7785 Hills & Dules NW Massillon OH 44646 Office: 921 Lincoln Way E Massillon OH 44646-6833

BRIACH, GEORGE GARY, lawyer, consultant; b. Youngstown, Ohio, Apr. 11, 1954; s. George William and Donna Jean (Phillips) B.; m. Loretta Ann Lepore, May 17, 1985; 1 child, Rachel Renee. BS magna cum laude, Youngstown State U., 1976; JD, U. Akron, Ohio, 1982. Bar: Ohio 1983, Mahoning County, 1983. Assoc. Flask & Policy, Youngstown, 1983-91; asst. atty. gen. State Atty. Gen.'s Office, Youngstown, 1984-90; solicitor Poland (Ohio) Village, 1988-89; cons., dir. Mahoning County (Ohio) Auditor, 1990—; ptnr. White & Briach, Youngstown, 1991—. Fundraiser United Way, Youngstown, 1989-92; bd. dirs., treas., pres. D&E Counseling Ctr., Youngstown, 1992-98, 2000—; trustee, treas. Children' Challenge Found., Inc., 1998-2000, 2002—; bd. dirs. Interfaith Home Maintenance, 1999—. Mem. Ohio Bar Assn., Mahoning County Bar Assn., Youngstown State U. Alumni Assn., Tippecanoe Country Club. Avocations: aerobic and weight training, golf, reading, travel. Family and matrimonial, General practice, Probate (including wills, trusts). Home: 45 Russo Dr Canfield OH 44406-9666 Office: White & Briach 755 Boardman Canfield Rd Youngstown OH 44512-4300

BRICE, ROGER THOMAS, lawyer; b. Chgo., May 7, 1948; s. William H. and Mary Loretta (Ryan) B.; m. Carol Coleman, Aug. 15, 1970; children: Caitlin, Coleman, Emily. AB, DePaul U., 1970; JD, U. Chgo., 1973. Bar: Ill. 1973, Iowa 1973, U.S. Ct. Appeals (10th, 4th, 6th and 7th cirs.) 1975, U.S. Dist. Ct. (no. and ctrl. dists.) Ill. 1977, 1995, U.S. Trial Bar (no. dist.) 1982, U.S. Supreme Ct. 1978. Staff atty. Office of Gen. Counsel NLRB, Washington, 1974-76; assoc. Kirkland & Ellis, Chgo., 1976-79, Reuben & Proctor, Chgo., 1979-80, ptnr., 1980-86, Isham, Lincoln & Beale, Chgo., 1986-88, Sonnenschein, Nath & Rosenthal, Chgo., 1988—. Legal counsel, bd. dirs. Boys and Girls Clubs Chgo., 1991—. Fellow Coll. Labor and Employment Lawyers. Roman Catholic. Civil rights, General civil litigation, Labor (including EEOC, Fair Labor Standards Act, labor-management relations, NLRB, OSHA). Home: 3727 N Harding Ave Chicago IL 60618-4026 Office: Sonnenschein Nath & Rosenthal 233 S Wacker Dr Ste 8000 Chicago IL 60606-6491 E-mail: rbrice@sonnenschein.com.

BRICKLER, JOHN WEISE, lawyer; b. Dayton, Ohio, Dec. 29, 1944; s. John Benjamin and Shirley Hilda (Weise) B.; m. Marilyn Louise Kuhlmann, July 2, 1966; children: John, James, Peter, Andrew, Matthew. AB, Washington U., St. Louis, 1966; JD, Washington U., 1968. Bar: Mo. 1968, U.S. Supreme Ct. 1972, U.S. Dist. Ct. (ea. dist.) Mo. 1974, U.S. Ct. Appeals (8th cir.) 1974. Assoc. Peper, Martin, Jensen, Maichel and Hetlage, St. Louis, 1973-77, ptnr., 1978-98, Blackwell Sanders Peper Martin LLP, St. Louis, 1998—2003, Spencer Fane Britt & Browne LLP, 2003—. Bd. dirs. Concordia Pub. House, St. Louis, 1993-, chmn. 1998-2001. Bd. dirs. Luth. Family and Children's Svcs. Mo., St. Louis, 1988-93, vice chmn., 1988-89. Capt. JAGC, U.S. Army, 1969-73. Mem. ABA, Nat. Assn. Bond Lawyers, Bar Assn. Met. St. Louis. Corporate, general, Securities, Municipal Finance. Office: Blackwell Sanders Peper Martin LLP 720 Olive St Fl 24 Saint Louis MO 63101-2338 E-mail: jbrickler@blackwellsanders.com.

BRICKWEDDE, RICHARD JAMES, lawyer; b. Bklyn., Dec. 12, 1944; s. George L. and Rose M. (McCarthy) B.; m. June Minsch Gamber, Sept. 2, 1978; stepchildren: Stephanie, Karen, Frances. AB, Syracuse U., 1966; JD, Fordham U., 1969. Bar: N.Y. 1970, D.C. 1971, U.S. Tax Ct. 1972, U.S. Supreme Ct. 1991. Staff asst. Syracuse (N.Y.) office Senator Robert F. Kennedy, 1965-66; adminstrv. asst. U.S. P.O. and OEO/VISTA, Washington, 1966; mgmt. cons. Washington, 1969-71; gen. counsel The Student Vote, Washington, 1971; pvt. practice law Syracuse, 1971-80; regional counsel N.Y. State Dept. Environ. Conservation, Syracuse, 1980-91, acting regional dir., 1984; with Green, Seifter Attys. PLLC, 1992—. Head environ. law practice; assoc. counsel to majority leader N.Y. State Assembly, 1975, asst. counsel to spkr. N.Y. State Assembly, 1976-77. Author: The Student's Right to Vote, 1971, Duke's Tale, 1991, Interstate Garbage: The Carbone Case and the Commerce Clause, 1994, The Superfund Recycling Equity Act of 1999, 2000; contbg. editor Network, 1975-76; contbr. articles to profl. jours. and trade publs. Treas. Legal Svcs. of Ctrl. N.Y., Inc., 1980—81, pres., 1981—82; Goodwill amb. Internat. Ctr. of Syracuse, 2000; chmn. voting rights task force Dem. Nat. Com., 1970—71; bd. dirs. Legal Svcs. of Ctrl. N.Y., Inc., 1978—83, Internat. Ctr. of Syracuse, 1992—2000, bd. dirs., pres., 1998—99; bd. dirs. N.Y. Alpha Tau Omega Student Aid Fund, Inc., Syracuse, 1972—2000, Huntington Family Ctrs., Inc., Syracuse, 1971—89, v.p., 1980; bd. dirs. Onondaga County (N.Y) Child Care Coun., Inc., 1978—80, Appleseed Trust, 2000—, The Nature Conservancy of Ctrl. and Western N.Y., 2001—. Named Hon. Citizen State of Tex., 1976; recipient Pub. Citizenship award N.Y. Pub. Interest Rsch. Group 1980. Mem. ABA (vice chair spl. com. on solid waste 1998-2002, state and local govt. vice-chair environ. com. 1998—), N.Y. Bar Assn., Onondaga County Bar Assn. (co-chair CLE com. 1999-2000, bd. dirs., 2002—), Nat. Solid Waste Mgmt. Assn. (mem. steering com. N.Y. chpt. 1992—) Democrat. Office: Green & Seifter Attys PLLC 1 Lincoln Ctr Ste 900 Syracuse NY 13202-1387 E-mail: rbrickwedde@greenseifter.com.

BRICKWOOD, SUSAN CALLAGHAN, lawyer; b. Sydney, NSW, Australia, Dec. 6, 1946; d. Graham Callaghan Brickwood and Nan (Cahaley) Nichols). BA, Swarthmore Coll., 1969; postgrad., Harvard U., 1969-71; JD, U. So. Calif., 1980. Bar: Calif. 1980, U.S. Tax Ct. 1981. Controller Howard Smith, Ltd., Sydney, 1972-74; assoc. Rifkind & Sterling, Beverly Hills, Calif., 1980-81, Armstrong, Hendler & Hirsch, Century City, Calif., 1981-82; pvt. practice L.A., 1982—. Author: Start Over!, 1990. Bankruptcy. Office: 9107 Wilshire Blvd #500 Beverly Hills CA 90210

BRIDENSTINE, LOUIS HENRY, JR., lawyer; b. Detroit, Nov. 13, 1940; s. Louis and Mary Ellen (O'Keefe) B.; m. Lucia Elizabeth Pucci, June 18, 1966; 1 child, Lucia McMullin. BS, John Carroll U., 1962; MA, U. Detroit, 1966, JD, 1965. Bar: Mich. 1966, U.S. Dist. Ct. (ea. dist.) Mich. 1966. Trial atty., atty.-advisor FTC, Washington, 1966-72; sr. legal counsel, v.p. dir. comms. Motor Vehicle Mfrs. Assn. U.S., Inc., Detroit, 1972-81; sr. v.p., gen. counsel, sec. Campbell-Ewald Co., Warren, Mich., 1981—. Exec. dir. Motorists Info., Inc., Detroit, 1977; legal affairs com. Am. Assn. Advt. Agys., N.Y.C., 1990—, chair, 2000—. Youth allocations panelist United Way Cmty Svcs., Detroit, 1991-98, chair, 1993-98, fund distbn. panelist, 1994-98, admissions compliance com. panelist, 2001-02; trustee, bd. dirs. Catholic Youth Orgn., Detroit, 1981-97, 99-2000, chair bd. dirs., 1990-92. Fellow Mich. State Bar Found. (life); mem. Mich. Bar Assn., Am. Corp. Counsel Assn., Alpha Sigma Nu, Blue Key, Detroit Athletic Club. Avocations: travel, reading. Administrative and regulatory, Corporate, general, Labor (including EEOC, Fair Labor Standards Act, labor-management relations, NLRB, OSHA). Office: Campbell Ewald Co 30400 Van Dyke Ave Warren MI 48093-2368 E-mail: libridens@campbell-ewald.com.

BRIDESTOWE, Lord See MOORE, THOMAS

BRIDGE, BOBBE J. state supreme court justice; m. Jonathan J. Bridge; children: Rebecca, Don. BA magna cum laude, U. Wash; MA, PhD in Polit. Sci., U. Mich.; JD, U. Wash., 1976. Superior Ct. judge King County, Wash., 1990-1999; chief judge King County Juvenile Ct., Wash., 1994-97, asst. presiding judge, 1997-98, presiding judge, 1998-99; judge Wash. State Supreme Ct., 1999—; mem. faculty Wash. State Jud. Coll. Chmn. King County Criminal Justice Coun., King County Truancy Steerin Com., Juvenile Justice Operational Master Plan Oversight Com., Pub. Trust and Confidence Com. Bd. Jud. Adminstrn.; co-chmn. Unified Family Ct. Bench-Bar Task Force. Bd. dirs. YWCA, Seattle Children's Home, Families for Kids Permanency Oversight Com., Tech. Adv. Com. Female Juvenile Offenders, Adv. Com. Adolescent Life Skills Program, Street Youth Law Program, Northwest Mediation Svc., Woodland Pk. Zoological Soc., Wash. Coun. Crime and Delinquency, Women's Funding Alliance, Alki Found., Privacy Fund, Seattle Arts Commn., U. Wash. Arts and Sci. Devel., Greater Seattle C. of C., Metrocenter YMCA, Juvenile Ct. Conf. Com.; mem. King County Task Force on Children and Families, Wash. State's Dept. Social and Health Svcs. Children., Youth, Family Svcs. Adv. Com., Child Protection Roundtable, Govs. Juvenile Justice Adv. Com.; chmn. State Task Force on Juvenile Issues, Coun. Youth Crisis Work Group, Families-at-Risk sub-com., Bd. Dirs. Ctr. Career Alternatives, Candidate Evaluation Com. Seattle-King Mcpl. League, Law and justice Com. League Women Voters; co-chmn. Govs. Coun. on Families, Youth, and Justice; pres. Seattle Women's Commn., Seattle Chpt. Am. Jewish Com.,bd. dirs., asst. sec.-treas. Jewish Fedn. Greater Seattle, chmn., vice chmn. Cmty. Rels. Coun. Named Judge of Yr. Wash. Women Lawyers, 1996; recipient Hannah G. Solomon award Nat. Coun. Jewish Women, 1996, Cmty. Catalyst award Mother's Against Violence in Am., 1997, Women Making a Difference award Youthcare, 1998; honored "woman helping women" Soroptimist Internat. of Kent, 1999. Mem. Phi Beta Kappa. Office: Wash Supreme Ct PO Box 40929 Olympia WA 98504-0929

BRIDGES, B. RIED, lawyer; b. Kansas City, Mo., Oct. 20, 1927; s. Brady R. and Mary H. (Nieuwenhuis) B.; 1 son, Ried George. BA, U. So. Calif., 1951, LLB, 1954. Bar: Calif. 1954. Assoc. Overton, Lyman & Prince, L.A., 1956-58, ptnr., 1958-63, Bonne, Jones & Bridges, L.A., 1963-74, Bonne, Bridges, Mueller & O'Keefe, L.A., Santa Ana, San Luis Obispo, Riverside, San Francisco, 1974—. Served with U.S. Army, 1954-56. Fellow Am. Coll. Trial Lawyers, Internat. Acad. Trial Lawyers; mem.Calif. Bar Assn., Assn. So. Calif. Def. Counsel, L.A. County Bar Assn., Santa Barbara County Bar Assn., Am. Bd. Trial Advs. (diplomate), Pacific Corinthian Yacht Club, Balboa of Mazatlan (Sinaloa, Mex.). Republican. Avocation: sportfishing. Federal civil litigation, State civil litigation, Personal injury (including property damage). Home: 2551 Victoria Ave Oxnard CA 93035-2931 Office: Bonne Bridges Mueller O'Keefe & Nichols 3699 Wilshire Blvd 10th Flr Los Angeles CA 90010 E-mail: rbridges@bbmon.com.

BRIDGES, DAVID MANNING, lawyer; b. Berkeley, Calif., May 22, 1936; s. Robert Lysle and Alice Marion (Rodenberger) B.; m. Carmen Galante de Bridges, Aug. 16, 1973; children: David, Stuart. AB, U. Calif., Berkeley, 1957, JD, 1962. Assoc. Thelen, Marrin, Johnson & Bridges, San Francisco, 1962-70, ptnr., 1970-94, mng. ptnr. Houston, 1981-91. Served as lt. (j.g.) USN, 1957-59. Mem. ABA, State Bar of Tex., Tex. Bar Assn., Houston Bar Assn., Internat. Bar Assn., Houston Club, Coronado Club, Pacific-Union Club. Banking, Commercial, contracts (including sales of goods; commercial financing), Construction. Office: 700 Louisiana St Ste 4600 Houston TX 77002-2732 E-mail: dbridhou@aol.com.

BRIDGES, ROBERT LYSLE, retired lawyer; b. Altus, Ark., May 12, 1909; s. Joseph Manning and Jeffa Alice (Morrison) B.; m. Alice Marian Rodenberger, June 10, 1930; children: David Manning, James Robert, Linda Lee. AB, U. Calif., 1930, JD, 1933. Bar: Calif. 1933, U.S. Supreme Ct 1938. Pvt. practice, San Francisco, 1933-92; assoc. firm Thelen Marrin Johnson & Bridges, 1933-39, ptnr., 1938-92. Trustee, former chmn. U. Calif. Berkeley Found.; trustee, hon. dir. John Muir Found., 1992—. Mem. ABA, Calif. Bar Assn., San Francisco Bar Assn., Commonwealth Club of Calif., Pacific Union Club, Claremont Country Club (Oakland). Republican. Home: 3972 Happy Valley Rd Lafayette CA 94549-2426 Office: 101 Second St Ste 1800 San Francisco CA 94105-3601

BRIDGMAN, G(EORGE) ROSS, lawyer; b. New Haven, Dec. 27, 1947; s. George Ross Bridgman and Betty Jean (Soderquist) Burrows; m. Patricia Hess; children: Taylor Wilson, Katharine June, Elizabeth Honey. BA cum laude, Yale U., 1970; JD, Northwestern U., 1973. Bar: Ohio 1973, U.S. Dist. Ct. (so. dist.) Ohio 1974, U.S. Dist. Ct. (no. dist.) Ohio 1976, U.S. Ct. Appeals (6th cir.) 1984, U.S. Supreme Ct. 1990. Assoc. Vorys, Sater, Seymour & Paese, Columbus, Ohio, 1973-80, ptnr., 1980—. Mem. editorial bd. Northwestern U. Law Rev., Chgo., 1972-73. Trustee Columbus Jr. Theatre of the Arts, 1976-80, pres., 1978-80; trustee, v.p. London (Ohio) Pub. Libr., 1979-84; bd. dirs. Ctrl. Ohio Regional Coun. on Alcoholism, Columbus, 1987-89; trustee Kidscope, Columbus, 1988-89, Recovery Alliance, Columbus, 1989-97, Ohio Parents for Drug-Free Youth, 1991-99; mem. exec. bd. Simon Kenton coun. Boy Scouts Am., 1996—; mem. Columbus Symphony Chorus, 1999—. Mem. ABA, Columbus Bar Assn., Ohio Bar Assn., Nat. Assn. Coll. and Univ. Attys., Capital Club, Columbus Country Club. Republican. Episcopalian. Civil rights, Education and schools, Labor (including EEOC, Fair Labor Standards Act, labor-management relations, NLRB, OSHA). Office: Vorys Sater Seymour & Pease PO Box 1008 52 E Gay St Columbus OH 43215-3161 E-mail: grbridgman@vssp.com.

BRIDGMAN, THOMAS FRANCIS, retired lawyer; b. Chgo., Dec. 30, 1933; s. Thomas Joseph and Angeline (Gorman) B.; m. Patricia A. McCormick, May 16, 1959; children: Thomas, Kathleen Ann, Ann Marie, Jane T., Molly. BS cum laude, John Carroll U., 1955; JD cum laude, Loyola U., Chgo., 1958. Bar: Ill. 1958, U.S. Dist. Ct. 1959. Assoc. McCarthy & Levin, Chgo., 1958, Baker & McKenzie, Chgo., 1958—96, ptnr., 1962—96. Trustee John Carroll U., 1982-88. Fellow Am. Coll. Trial Lawyers, Am. Bd. Trial Advs. (adv.), Internat. Acad. Trial Lawyers (past pres.), Union Club, Beverly Country Club (Chgo., pres. 1983). Democrat. Roman Catholic. Federal civil litigation, State civil litigation. Home: 9400 S Pleasant Ave Chicago IL 60620-5646 Office: Baker & McKenzie 1 Prudential Plaza 130 E Randolph St Ste 3700 Chicago IL 60601-6342

BRIEANT, CHARLES LA MONTE, federal judge; b. Ossining, N.Y., Mar. 13, 1923; s. Charles La Monte and Marjorie (Hall) B.; m. Virginia Elizabeth Warfield, Sept. 10, 1948. BA, Columbia U., 1947, LL.B., 1949. Bar: N.Y. 1949. Mem. firm Bleakley, Platt, Schmidt & Fritz, White Plains, 1949-71; water commr. Village of Ossining, 1948-51; town justice, 1952-58; town supr., 1960-63; village atty.; also spl. asst. dist. atty. Westchester County, 1958-59; asst. counsel N.Y. State Joint Legis. Com. Fire Ins., 1968; judge U.S. Dist. Ct. (so. dist.) N.Y., N.Y.C., 1971-86, chief judge, 1986-93; judge U.S. Dist Ct. So. Dist. N.Y., White Plains, 1993—. Adj. prof. Bklyn. Law Sch.; mem. Jud. Conf. U.S., 1989-95, mem. exec. com., 1991-95. Mem. Westchester County Republican Com., 1957-71; mem. Westchester County Legislature from 2d Dist., 1970-71. Served with AUS, World War II. Mem. ABA, N.Y. State Bar Assn., Westchester County Bar Assn., Ossining Bar Assn. Episcopalian (vestryman). Club: SAR. Office: US Dist Ct US Courthouse 300 Quarropas St White Plains NY 10601-4140

BRIEGER, GEORGE, lawyer; b. Hungary, Apr. 30, 1966; came to the U.S., 1977; s. Jenö and Miriam Brieger. BS in Computer Sci. cum laude(hon.) , Bklyn. Coll., 1988; postgrad., Yeshiva U., 1988-90; JD, Cardozo Sch. Law, 1993; postgrad., George Washington U. Bar: N.Y. 1994, D.C. 2002, U.S. Dist. Ct. (so. and ea. dists.) N.Y. 1995, U.S. Ct. Internat. Trade, 1999, registered patent atty. Internat. counsel Bacher & Ptnrs. Atty. at Law, Budapest, Hungary, 1996-98; atty. Internat. Trade Litigation U.S. Customs Svc., N.Y.C., 1998-2000; atty. Sughrue Mion, Washington, 2001—. Cons. Fin. Svcs. Vol. Corps, NYC, 1996. Editor New Europe Law Rev. Cardozo Sch. Law, N.Y.C., 1992-93, Sughrue Rev., 2001-03; contbr. chpt. to book. Adv. bd. Budapest-N.Y. Sister City Com., N.Y.C., 1996—. Revel Grad. Sch. fellow in Medieval European history, N.Y.C., 1988-90. Mem. Am. Intellectual Property Law Assn. Avocations: linguistics, philosophy, computer technology, tai chi, swimming. Business E-Mail: gbrieger@sughrue.com.

BRIER, BONNIE SUSAN, lawyer; b. Oct. 19, 1950; d. Jerome W. and Barbara (Srenco) B.; m. Bruce A. Rosenfield, Aug. 15, 1976; children: Rebecca, Elizabeth, Benjamin. AB in Econs. magna cum laude, Cornell U., 1972; JD, Stanford U., 1976. Bar: Pa. 1976, U.S. Dist. Ct. (ea. dist.) Pa., U.S. Tax Ct., U.S. Ct. Appeals (3d cir.), U.S. Supreme Ct. Law clk. to chief judge U.S. Dist. Ct. Pa. (ea. dist.), Phila., 1976-77, asst. U.S. atty. criminal prosecutor, 1977-79; from assoc. to ptnr. Ballard, Spahr, Andrews & Ingersoll, Phila., 1979-90; gen. counsel Children's Hosp. of Phila., Phila., 1990—. Legal counsel Womens Way, 1979—2001; lectr. U. Pa., 1988-95; lectr., speaker various orgns. and seminars. Editor Stanford Law Rev., 1974-76; contbr. articles to profl. jours. Bd. dirs. U.S. Com. for UNICEF, 1994—2000, vice chmn., 1998-2000. Fellow Am. Coll. Tax Counsel; mem. ABA (exempt orgn. com. on tax sect., chair 1991-93, mem. health law sect.), Pa. Bar Assn. (tax sect., health law sect., mem. com. charitable orgn., children's rights), Phila. Bar Assn. (tax sect., health law sect., bd. dir. 1998—, chmn. 2002—), Am. Health Lawyers Assn. Education and schools, Health, Taxation, general. Home: 132 Fairview Rd Narberth PA 19072-1331 Office: Children's Hosp of Pa 34th St and Civic Ctr Blvd Philadelphia PA 19104

BRIGGS, JOHN MANCEL, III, lawyer; b. Muskegon, Mich., May 24, 1942; s. John M. Jr. and Margaret Jane (Wren) B.; m. Janice R. Dykema, May 20, 1967; children: Jennifer Anne, Jill Margaret. BS, U. Mich., 1964, JD, 1967. Bar: Mich. 1968, U.S. Dist. Ct. (we. dist.) Mich. 1968, U.S. Ct. Appeals (6th cir.) 1974, U.S. Supreme Ct. 2000. Assoc. Parmenter, Forsythe, Rude, Van Epps, Briggs & Fauri and predecessors, Muskegon, 1967-70, ptnr., 1970-92; shareholder Parmenter O'Toole, Muskegon, Mich., 1992—. Active Muskegon United Appeal, 1968-73; bd. dirs. Big Bros., Muskegon, 1969-74; bd. dirs. Y Family Christian Assn., 1970-80, 81-83, 1st v.p., 1973-76, pres., 1977-78; bd. dirs. Muskegon-Oceana Legal Aid Soc., 1970-73, pres., 1972-73; bd. dirs. Berean Ch., 1985-86, 88-90, 93-94, 99-2001, sec., 1988-90, v.p., 1993, pres., 1994, 99, 2000. With USAR, 1967-73. Recipient Disting. Svc. award Muskegon Jaycees, 1977. Fellow Mich. State Bar Assn.; mem. ABA, Muskegon County Bar Assn. (sec. 1970-71, v.p. 1974-75, pres. 1975-76), Rotary (bd. dirs. 1981-85, pres.-elect 1982-83, pres. 1983-84, Presdl. Citation). Republican. Condemnation (eminent domain), Estate planning, Property, real (including real estate development, water). Office: Parmenter O'Toole PO Box 786 175 W Apple Ave Muskegon MI 49443-0786

BRIGHAM, HENRY DAY, JR., retired lawyer; b. Pittsfield, Mass., Dec. 12, 1926; s. Henry Day and Gladys M. (Allen) B.; m. Catherine T. Van't Hul, Dec. 16, 1961; children: Henry Day, Johan Van't Hul, Alexander Frederick. BA, Yale U., 1947, JD, 1950. Bar: N.Y. 1951, Mass. 1966. Assoc. Milbank, Tweed, Hope & Hadley, N.Y.C., 1951-52, 54-56, Simpson Thacher & Bartlett, N.Y.C., 1956-66; v.p., gen. counsel, dir. Eaton & Howard, Inc., Boston, 1966-73, pres., 1973-79; v.p., chmn. exec. com. Eaton & Howard, Vance Sanders, Inc., Boston, 1979-81, Eaton Vance Corp., Boston, 1981—96; ret., 1996. Former trustee Eaton Vance Cash Mgmt. Fund, Boston; former v.p., trustee Eaton Vance Tax Free Reserves, Boston; former sec., clk., dir. Investors Bank & Trust Co., Boston; v.p., sec., trustee Wright Managed Income Trust, Boston, Wright Managed Equity Trust, Boston. Pres. Trustees of Donations of Episc. Diocese Mass., 1984-89; sr. warden Ch. of the Redeemer, Chestnut Hill, 1975-79; sec., bd. dirs. Chestnut Hill Assn. (Mass.), 1969—. Lt. USNR, 1952-54. Mem.: Assn. Yale Alumni (bd. govs.) Investment Co. Inst. (bd. govs.), Investment Counsel Assn. Am. (bd. govs.), Tarratine Club (Islesboro, Maine), Longwood Cricket Club (Chestnut Hill, Mass.), Downtown Club (Boston), The Country Club (Brookline, Mass.), Soc. Colonial Wars (Mass.), Somerset Club (Boston)., Tennis & Racquet Club (Boston), Harvard Club (Boston), Phi Delta Phi, Phi Beta Kappa. Episcopalian. Corporate, general.

BRIGHT, MYRON H. federal judge; b. Eveleth, Minn., Mar. 5, 1919; s. Morris and Lena A. Bright; m. Frances Louise Reisler, Dec. 26, 1947; children: Dinah Ann, Joshua Robert. AA, Eveleth Junior Coll, 1939; BSL, U. Minn., 1941, JD, 1947. Bar: N.D. 1947, Minn. 1947. Assoc. Wattam, Vogel, Vogel & Bright, Fargo, ND, 1947, ptnr., 1949—68; judge 8th U.S. Cir. Ct. Appeals, Fargo, 1968—85, sr. judge, 1985—; disting. prof. law St. Louis U., 1985—88, emeritus prof. of law, 1989—95. Capt. USAF, 1942—46. Recipient Francis Rawle award, ALI-ABA, 1996, Lifetime Achievement award, U. N.D. Law Sch., 1998, Herbert Harley award, AJS, 2000. Mem.: ABA, U.S. Jud. Conf. (com. on adminstrn. of probation sys. 1977—83, adv. com. on appellate rules 1987—90, com. on internat. jud. rels. 1996—2003), N.D. Bar Assn. Office: US Ct Appeals 8th Cir 655 1st Ave N Ste 340 Fargo ND 58102-4952 also: Thomas F Eagleton US Cthse 111 S 10th St Rm 26 325 Saint Louis MO 63102 E-mail: judge_myron_bright@ca8.uscourts.gov.

BRIGHT, THOMAS LYNN, lawyer; b. Omaha, June 3, 1948; B in Bus., Emporia State U., 1970; JD, Kans. U., 1974; MBA, Tulsa U., 1989. Bar: Okla. 1975, U.S. Ct. Appeals (10th cir.) 1989, U.S. Supreme Ct. 1989. Tax atty. Phillips Petroleum Co., Bartlesville, Okla., 1974-79; assoc. tax counsel Phillips Petroleum Europe/Africa, London, 1979-83, Phillips Petroleum Co., Bartlesville, 1984-87; pvt. practice Tulsa, 1987—. Adj. prof. Tulsa U., 1989-92. Mem.: ABA, Nat. Employment Lawyers Assn., Okla. Bar Assn. General civil litigation, Labor (including EEOC, Fair Labor Standards Act, labor-management relations, NLRB, OSHA), Pension, profit-sharing, and employee benefits. Office: 2303 Ragland Rd Mansfield TX 76063 E-mail: tlbright@webzone.net.

BRIGNONE, MARCO SALVATORE, lawyer, consultant; b. Milan, Apr. 17, 1971; s. Ubaldo Lucio Maria Brignone and Maria Antonietta Modica; m. Elena Maria Ferraresi, Oct. 23, 1999; 1 child, Matteo. LLD, Cath. U., 1994. Bar: Italy 1999. Apprenticeship Studio Macri Difino & Assocs., Milan, 1994—95, Studio Marco De Luca, 1996; atty. Studio Rossini, 1996; cons. Studio De Berti Jacchia, 2000—. Lt. Italian Mil., 1995—96. Grantee, Telecom Italia S.P.A., 1994, Pirelli S.P.A., 1999. Avocations: gardening, swimming, jogging. Office: Studio Brignone-Ferraresi Viale Monte Nero 33 20135 Milan Italy Fax: +39 02 55191738. E-mail: studioelma@tin.it.

BRIHAMMAR, B. NIKLAS, lawyer; b. Stockholm, Apr. 12, 1964; s. Bengt Axel and Solbritt Linnea Elisabeth (Pettersson) B.; m. Marta Kristina Sjoevall, Dec. 21, 1995. BS in Econs., U. South Ala., Mobile, 1989; JD, U. Miami, 1993. Bar: Fla. 1993, U.S. Dist. Ct. (so. dist.) Fla. 1995. Asst. mgr. Daiwa Securities, Ltd., Stockholm, 1990; assoc. atty. John E. Bigler, P.A., Key West, Fla., 1994, John R. Fiore, P.A., Miami, Fla., 1995, Sheri Smallwood, Chartered, Key West, 1995-99; pvt. practice Key West, Fla., 1999—. Mem. Gala Task Force, Key West, 1997-99. Mem. Fla. Bar (family law sect.), Monroe County Bar Assn., Swedish-Am. Bar Assn. Avocations: computers, reading, chess, tennis, film. General civil litigation, Family and matrimonial, Personal injury (including property damage). Office: 417 Eaton St Key West FL 33040-6548 E-mail: brihammar@yahoo.com.

BRILL, STEVEN CHARLES, financial advisor, lawyer; b. Miami, Fla., Aug. 21, 1953; s. Arthur W. and Joan K. (Caveretta) B. AB, Boston U., 1975; JD, Western New Eng. Coll., 1978; LLM, NYU, 1986. Advanced underwriting cons. Equitable Life Assurance Soc., N.Y.C., 1978-79; sr. advanced underwriting cons. Met. Life Ins. Co., N.Y.C., 1979-85; asst. v.p. personal fin. planning group Dean Witter Reynolds, N.Y.C., 1985-87; v.p., dir. asset allocation group Chase Pvt. Bank, N.Y.C., 1987-98; prin. Spielberger, Dampf, Brill & Levine, LLC, 1998—. Chmn. Cmty. Housing Innovations, Inc.; past pres., dir. Wychwood Owner's Corp., Great Neck, N.Y., Realty of Bay Terr. Inc., Bayside, N.Y. Contbr. articles to Mature Outlook Mag. Avocations: skiing, tennis, golf. Home: 16625 12th Ave Whitestone NY 11357-2261 E-mail: brilladvis@aol.com.

BRIM, JEFFERSON KEARNEY, III, (JAY), lawyer; b. Sulphur Springs, Tex., July 15, 1945; s. J. Kearney and June Marie (Wester) B.; m. Jeanine Eloise Clymer, July 3, 1971; children: Cari Christen, Brandon Taylor, Jessica Merrill. BA, U. Tex., 1971, JD, 1975. Bar: Tex. 1974, U.S. Dist. Ct. (no. and ea. dists.) Tex. 1976, U.S. Dist. Ct. (we. dist.) Tex. 1978, U.S. Dist. Ct. (so. dist.) Tex. 1981, U.S. Ct. Appeals (5th cir.) 1981. Ptnr. Carter & Brim, Commerce, Tex., 1974-77; staff atty. Tex. Edn. Agy., Austin, 1977-79; state pres. Tex. Jaycees, Austin, 1979-80; assoc. Davis & Davis, Austin, 1981-83; ptnr. Brim, Tingley & Arnett, Austin, 1983-86, Brim & Arnett, Austin, 1986-94, 96-97, Brim, Arnett and Judge, P.C., 1994-96, Brim, Arnett, Robinett, Hanner & Conners P.C., 1997—. Mcpl. judge City of Rollingwood, Tex., 1988-96; alderman City of Rollingwood, 1996-2000; counsel Assn. Tex. Profl. Educators, 1980—. Chmn. Travis County Dem. Party, 1998-2000; founding bd. dirs. JustPeace Ctr. For Mediation and Conflict Transformation, 2000—. Staff sgt. USAF, 1967-70. Decorated Air medal; recipient Clayton Frost Meml. award U.S. Jaycees, 1979-80. Mem. State Bar Tex. (com. chmn. 1982-84), U.S. Jaycees (nat. v.p. 1980-81), Kappa Delta Pi. Methodist. Administrative and regulatory, Civil rights, Education and schools. Home: 1506 W 13th St Apt 15 Austin TX 78703-4064 Office: 2525 Wallingwood Dr Bldg 14 Austin TX 78746-6900 E-mail: jbrim@barpc.net.

BRIMMER, CLARENCE ADDISON, federal judge; b. Rawlins, Wyo., July 11, 1922; s. Clarence Addison and Geraldine (Zingsheim) B.; m. Emily O. Docken, Aug. 2, 1953; children: Geraldine Ann, Philip Andrew, Andrew Howard, Elizabeth Ann. BA, U. Mich., 1944, JD, 1947. Bar: Wyo. 1948. Pvt. practice law, Rawlins, 1948-71; mcpl. judge, 1948-54; U.S. commr., magistrate, 1963-71; atty. gen. Wyo., 1971-74; U.S. atty., 1975; chief judge U.S. Dist. Ct. Wyo., Cheyenne, 1975-92, dist. judge, 1975—. Mem. panel multi-dist. litigation, 1992-2000; mem. Jud. Conf. U.S., 1994-97, exec., 1995-97. Sec. Rawlins Bd. Pub. Utilities, 1954-66; Rep. gubernatorial candidate, 1974; trustee Rocky Mountain Mineral Law Found., 1963-75. With USAAF, 1945-46. Mem. ABA, Wyo. Bar Assn., Laramie County Bar Assn., Carbon County Bar Assn., Am. Judicature Soc., Masons, Shriners, Rotary. Episcopalian. Office: US Dist Ct 2120 Capitol Ave Rm 2603 Cheyenne WY 82001

BRIN, ROYAL HENRY, JR., lawyer; b. Dallas, Oct. 9, 1919; BA, JD, U. Tex., 1941; postgrad. fellow, Harvard U., 1941-42. Bar: Tex. 1941. Atty. OPA, Washington, 1942; asso. firm Strasburger & Price, Dallas, 1946-56, ptnr., 1956—. Editor-in-chief Tex. Law Rev., 1940-41; contbr. articles to profl. jours. Fellow Am. Bar Found. (life); mem. ABA, Am. Acad. of Appellate Attorneys, State Bar Tex., Tex. Assn. Def. Counsel (pres. 1981-82), Dallas Bar Assn., Dallas Assn. Def. Counsel, Def. Rsch. Inst., Am. Acad. Appellate Lawyers, Internat. Brotherhood Magicians (pres. 1969-70), The Chancellors (grand chancellor), Order of Coif, Phi Beta Kappa, Phi Eta Sigma. Federal civil litigation, State civil litigation, Insurance. Home: 6506 Lupton Dr Dallas TX 75225-2323 Office: 4300 Bank of Am Plz 901 Main St Dallas TX 75202-3714

BRIND, DAVID HUTCHISON, lawyer, judge; b. Albany, N.Y., Feb. 4, 1930; s. Charles Albert and Laura Stuart (Hutchison) B.; m. Shirley Jean Hodgins, Mar. 6, 1954; children: Susan Brind Morrow, Charles. AB, Union Coll., 1951; LLB, Albany Law Sch., 1954, JD, 1968; LHD, N.Y. Inst. Technology, 1971. Bar: N.Y. 1954, U.S. Supreme Ct. 1970. Atty. law divsn. N.Y. State Dept. Edn., Albany, 1954-55; ptnr. Chacchia & Brind, Geneva, N.Y., 1957-64; sole practice Geneva, 1964-95; presiding judge Geneva City Ct., 1974-95; ret., 1995; apptd. jud. hearing officer N.Y. State Supreme Ct., 1995—. Hearing officer N.Y. State and Local Ret. Sys., 1997—; counsel real estate N.Y. State Dormitory Auth., 1970-86; gen. counsel Geneva Gen. Hosp., 1966-85; local counsel Conrail. Bd. dirs. Geneva United Way, 1965-89; campaign chmn. United Way Greater Rochester (N.Y.), 1966-69, pres., 1969-71; trustee Geneva Gen. Hosp., 1962-73; pres., 1969-71; trustee Geneva Hist. Soc., 1963-90, pres., 1968-70; chmn. Geneva Hist. Commn., 1969-89; mem. exec. bd. Finger Lakes coun. Boy Scouts Am., 1965—; bd. dirs. 7 Lakes Coun. Girl Scouts U.S.A., 1966-73; bd. dirs. Geneva Gen. Hosp. Nursing Home, pres., 1969-71; v.p. Geneva Bd. Edn., 1962-67; mem. pres.'s coun. Eisenhower Coll., 1972-79, Hobart & William Smith Colls., 1967—. Recipient Geneva Cmty. Chest/Red Cross Svc. citation, 1969, named Man of Yr., Geneva C. of C., 1971. Mem. Am. Assn. Homes for Aging, N.Y. State Sch. Bds. Assn. (law revisions com. and constnl. conv. com. 1964-68), Monroe County Jud. Com., 1976-80, Ontario County Bar Assn., N.Y. State Bar Assn. (jud. coun.), Fedn. N.Y. State Judges (pres. 1989-91), N.Y. State Assn. Jud. Hearing Officers (treas. 1995—), St. Andrews Soc. Albany, Rotary (pres. 1967-68), Finger Lakes Forum (pres. 1991—). Republican. Presbyterian. Probate (including wills, trusts), Property, real (including real estate development, water). Home: 43 Delancey Dr Geneva NY 14456-2809 Office: 37 Seneca St Geneva NY 14456-0409 E-mail: dbrind@rochester.rr.com.

BRING, MURRAY H. retired lawyer; b. Denver, Jan. 19, 1935; s. Alfred Alexander and Ida (Molinsky) B.; m. Constance Brooks Evert, Dec. 30, 1963 (div. June 1989); children: Beth, Catherine, Peter; m. Kathleen Delaney, May 19, 1990. BA, U. So. Calif., 1956; LLB, NYU, 1959. Bar: N.Y. 1960, D.C. 1963, U.S. Supreme Ct. 1966. Law clk. to Chief Justice Earl Warren U.S. Supreme Ct., Washington, 1959-61; spl. asst. to asst. atty. gen. civil div. Dept. Justice, Washington, 1961-62; spl. asst to dep. undersec. state Dept. State, Washington, 1962-63; dir. policy planning anti-trust divsn., 1963-65; ptnr. Arnold & Porter, Washington, 1965-87; sr. v.p., gen. counsel Philip Morris Cos., Inc., N.Y.C., 1988-94, exec. v.p. external affairs and gen. counsel, 1994-97, vice chmn., gen. counsel, 1997-2000; ret., 2000. Editor-in-chief N.Y. Law Rev., 1958-59. Bd. dirs. Guild Hall East Hampton, NYU Law Sch. Found. Mem. ABA, Assn. Bar City N.Y., D.C. Bar Assn., Order of Coif, Phi Beta Kappa, Phi Kappa Phi. Avocations: fishing, photography, art. Corporate, general. Office: Philip Morris Cos Inc 120 Park Ave New York NY 10017-5592

BRINGMAN, JOSEPH EDWARD, lawyer; b. Elmhurst, N.Y., Jan. 31, 1958; s. Joseph Herman and Eileen Marie (Sheehy) B.; m. Laurie Lynn Cunningham, July 11, 1992; children: Joseph Edward Jr., Elizabeth Grace. BA, Yale U., 1980; JD, Stanford U., 1983. Bar: N.Y. 1984, Wash. 1985, U.S. Dist. Ct. (we. dist.) Wash. 1986, U.S. Ct. Appeals (9th cir.) 1986, U.S. Ct. Appeals (fed. cir.) 1988, U.S. Dist. Ct. (ea. dist.) Wash. 2000. Acting asst. prof. U. Wash. Law Sch., Seattle, 1983-85; assoc. Perkins Coie, Seattle, 1985-91, of counsel, 1992—. Dir. Perkins Coie Cmty. Fellowship, Seattle, 1990-96, chair assoc. tng. com., 1997-2000. Editor: Stanford Jour. Internat. Law, 1980-83; author Fed. Trial Practice chpt. Washington Lawyers' Practice Manual, 2002-03. Mem. Yale Alumni Schs. Com., Seattle, 1980—. Nat. Merit scholar, 1976; recipient Pro Bono Publico award Trumbull Coll. (Yale U.), 1980. Mem. ABA, Wash. State Bar Assn., King County Bar Assn. (jud. screening com. 1993-96, chair fair campaign practices com. 1997-99, judiciary and cts. com. 1999—, sec. 2003-, trustee 2003-). Democrat. Roman Catholic. Federal civil litigation, State civil litigation, Professional liability. Office: Perkins Coie LLP 1201 3rd Ave Fl 48 Seattle WA 98101-3099 E-mail: brinj@perkinscoie.com.

BRINK, DAVID RYRIE, lawyer; b. Mpls., July 28, 1919; s. Raymond Woodard and Carol Sybil (Ryrie) B.; m. Irma Lorentz Brink; children: Anne Carol, Mary Claire, David Owen, Sarah Jane. BA with honors, U. Minn., 1940, BSL with honors, 1941, JD with honors, 1947; LLD, Capital U., 1981, Suffolk U., 1981, Mitchell Coll. Law, 1982. Bar: Minn. 1947, U.S. Dist. Ct. Minn. 1947, U.S. Tax Ct. 1967, U.S. Supreme Ct. 1980, U.S. Ct. Appeals (D.C. Cir.) 1982. Assoc. firm Dorsey & Whitney, Mpls., 1947-53, ptnr., 1953-89, head Washington office, 1982-84, ret. ptnr. Trustee Lawyers Com. Civil Rights Under Law, 1978—; bd. dirs. Nat. Legal Aid and Defender Assn., 1978-80; U.S. panelist for Dispute Resolution under Free Trade Agreement with Can.; bd. visitors U. Minn. Law Sch., 1978-81; chmn. trust and estates dept. Dorsey & Whitney, 1956-82 Bd. editors: U. Minn. Law Rev, 1941-42; contbr. numerous articles to law jours. Bd. govs. Am. Coll. Trust and Estate Counsel Found., 1987-95. Served to lt. comdr. USNR, 1943-46. Recipient Outstanding Achievement award U. Minn., 1982 Fellow Coll. Law Practice Mgmt. (hon.), Am. Coll. Trust and Estate Counsel (regent, exec. com.); mem. ABA (gov. 1974-77, 80-83, pres. 1981-82), Ctrl. and Ea. European Legal Initiative, Com. on Law and Nat. Security, Com. on Substance Abuse, 2002—, Adv. Com. to Commn. on Lawyers Assisstance Programs, 2000— Com. on Specialization, Fund for Pub. Edn. of ABA (pres. 1981-82), Am. Bar Found. (state chmn. 1977-80, gov. 1980-83), Am. Bar Retirement Assn. (pres. 1976-77), Am. Judicature Soc. (bd. dirs. 1988—), Nat. Conf. Bar Pres., Inst. Jud. Adminstrn., Am. Arbitration Assn. (trustee 1981—), Can.-U.S. Law Inst. (adv. bd. 1987—), Minn. Bar Assn. (pres. 1978-79), Internat. Mgmt. and Devel. Inst., Hennepin County Bar Assn. (pres. 1967-68), Nat. Inst. Citizen Edn. in Law (nat. adv. bd. 1982-85, chmn. 1983-84), N.W. Athletic Club, Sr. Tennis Players Club, Inc. Public international, Probate (including wills, trusts). Office: Dorsey & Whitney # 50 S 6th St Minneapolis MN 55402

BRINKLEY, JACK THOMAS, lawyer, former congressman; b. Faceville, Ga., Dec. 22, 1930; s. Lonnie Elester and Pauline (Spearman) B.; m. Alma Lois Kite, May 29, 1955; children: Jack Thomas Jr., Fred Alen II. Student, Young Harris Coll., 1947-49, Okla. A. and M. Coll., 1952; LL.B. cum laude, U. Ga., 1959. Bar: Ga. 1958, D.C. 1973. Sch. tchr., Ga., 1949-51; assoc. firm Young, Hollis & Moseley, Columbus, Ga., 1959-61; ptnr. firm Coffin & Brinkley, Columbus, 1961-66; mem. Ga. Ho. Reps., 1965-66; sr. ptnr. Brinkley and Brinkley, 1983-95, of counsel, 1996-2000, of counsel emeritus, 2001—; mem. 90th-97th Congresses from 3d Ga. dist.; chmn. mil. facilities and installations subcom. 97th Congress. Mem. Ga. Ho. Rep., 1965-66. Trustee Young Harris Coll. Mem. Ga. Bar Assn., Columbus Bar Assn., Young Lawyers Club of Columbus (pres. 1963-64), Blue Key, Civitan Club, Masons. Democrat. Baptist. Legislative, Personal injury (including property damage), Probate (including wills, trusts). Office: Corporate Ctr Ste 901 Columbus GA 31902

BRINKMAN, DALE THOMAS, lawyer; b. Columbus, Ohio, Dec. 10, 1952; s. Harry H. and Jean May (Sandel) B.; m. Martha Louise Johnson, Aug. 3, 1974; children: Marin Veronica, Lauren Elizabeth, Kelsey Renee. BA, U. Notre Dame, 1974; JD, Ohio State U., 1977. Bar: Ohio 1977, U.S. Dist. Ct. (so. dist.) Ohio 1979. Assoc. Schwartz, Shapiro, Kelm & Warren, Columbus, 1977-82; asst. tax counsel Am. Elect. Power, Columbus, 1982; gen. counsel Worthington Industries, Inc., Columbus, 1982-99, v.p. adminstrn., gen. counsel, sec., 1999—. Author: Ohio State U. Law Jour.,1975-76, editor, 1976-77. Trustee, officer Friends of Dahlberg Ctr., Columbus, 1980-86; dir., officer Assn. for Developmentally Disabled, Columbus, 1986-94. Mem. ABA, Ohio Bar Assn., Columbus Bar Assn. Republican. Roman Catholic. Corporate, general, Mergers and acquisitions, Securities. Office: Worthington Industries Inc 1205 Dearborn Dr Columbus OH 43085-4769 E-mail: dtbrinkm@worthingtonindustries.com.

BRINKMANN, ROBERT JOSEPH, lawyer; b. Cin., Dec. 25, 1950; s. Robert Harry and Helen R. (Streuwing) B.; children: Christopher, Julia. BA, U. Notre Dame, 1972; postgrad., Alliance Française, 1974-75; AM, Brown U., 1977; JD, Loyola U., Los Angeles, 1980. Bar: Calif. 1980, D.C. 1981, U.S. Ct. Appeals (D.C. and 9th cirs.) 1981, U.S. Supreme Ct. 1984, U.S. Ct. Appeals (6th cir.) 1987. Tchr. secondary schs., Los Angeles and Paris, 1974-77; assoc. Hedrick & Lane, Washington, 1980-82; gen. counsel Nat. Newspaper Assn., Washington, 1982-92; exec. dir. Red Tag News Publs. Assn., 1990-92; v.p., counsel postal and regulatory affairs Newspaper Assn. Am., Reston, Va., 1992—2002. Mem. faculty Am. Press. Inst., Reston, 1982-92; adj. faculty U. Md., 1996—. Mem. ABA, Fed. Communications Bar Assn. (former vice chmn. postal affairs com.). Roman Catholic. Administrative and regulatory, Communications, Legislative. Home: 204 Lynn Manor Dr Rockville MD 20850-4431 Office: Newspaper Assn Am National Press Bldg 529 14th St NW Ste 440 Washington DC 20045-1407 E-mail: brinb@naa.org.

BRINKMEYER, SCOTT S. lawyer; b. Chgo., Sept. 27, 1949; BA, DePauw U., 1971; JD, St. Louis U., 1975. Bar: Mich. 1975. Atty. Mika, Meyers, Beckett & Jones, PLC, Grand Rapids, Mich. Fellow: Mich. State Bar Found., Am. Bar Found.; mem.: ABA, Am. Inns of Ct., Grand Rapids Bar Assn., Def. Rsch. Inst., Mich. Def. Trial Counsel, State Bar Mich. (bd. commrs. 1995—, exec. com. 1996—98, 1999—, v.p., rep. assembly 1992—, chair 1997—98, sects. on environ. law, litigation, negligence law). Product liability, Commercial, consumer (including collections, credit), Environmental. Office: Mika Meyers Beckett and Jones 900 Monroe Ave NW Grand Rapids MI 49503-1423*

BRINSMADE, LYON LOUIS, retired lawyer; b. Mexico City, Feb. 24, 1924; s. Robert Bruce and Helen (Steenbock) B. (Am. citizens); m. Susannah Tucker, June 9, 1956 (div. 1978); children: Christine Fairchild, Louisa Calvert; m. Carolyn Hartman Lister, Sept. 22, 1979. Student, U. Wis., 1940-43; BS, Mich. Technol. U., 1944; JD, Harvard U., 1950. Bar: Tex. 1951. Assoc. Butler, Binion, Rice, Cook & Knapp, Houston, 1950-58, ptnr. in charge internat. dept., 1958-83, Porter & Clements, Houston, 1983-91; sr. counsel Porter & Hedges (formerly Porter & Clements), Houston, 1991-99. Bd. dirs. Houston br. English-Speaking Union of U.S., 1972-75. Served with AUS, 1946-47. Mem. ABA (chmn. com. internat. investment and devel. of sect. internat. law and practice 1970-76, council 1972-76, 81-82, vice chmn. 1976-79, chmn.-elect 1979-80, chmn. 1980-81, co-founder and co-chmn. com. Mex. 1982-85), Internat. Bar Assn., Inter-Am. Bar Assn. (co-chmn. sect. oil and gas laws, com. natural resources 1973-76, council 1984-87), Houston Bar Assn., State Bar Tex. (chmn. internat. law com. 1970-74, mem. council sect. internat. law 1975-78), Am. Soc. Internat. Law (exec. council 1984-86), Houston World Trade Assn. (sec., dir. 1967-70), Houston World Trade Assn. (chmn. legis. com. 1967-72), Houston C. of C. (chmn. legis. subcom. internat. bus. com. 1970-72), SAR, Allegro of Houston, Harvard Club (Houston), Sigma Alpha Epsilon Episcopalian. Home: PO Box 1149 Wimberley TX 78676-1149

BRINSON, GAY CRESWELL, JR., retired lawyer; b. Kingsville, Tex., June 13, 1925; s. Gay Creswell and Lelia (Wendelkin) B.; m. Bette Lee Butter, June 17, 1979; children from former marriage: Thomas Wade, Mary Kaye. Student, U. Ill., Chgo., 1947-48; BS, U. Houston, 1953, JD, 1957. Bar: Tex. 1957, U.S. Dist. Ct. (so. dist.) Tex. 1959, U.S. ct. Appeals (5th cir.) 1962 U.S. Dist. Ct. (ea. dist.) Tex. 1965, U.S. Supreme Ct. 1974; U.S. Dist. Ct. (no. dist.) Tex. 1990; diplomate Am. Bd. Trial Advocates, Am. Bd. Profl. Liability Attys. Spl. agt. FBI, Washington and Salt Lake City, 1957-59; trial atty. Liberty Mut. Ins. Co., Houston, 1959-62; assoc. Horace Brown, Houston, 1962-64, Vinson & Elkins, Houston, 1964-67, ptnr., 1967-91; of counsel McFall, Sherwood & Sheehy, Houston, 1992-2000. Lectr. U. Houston Coll. Law, 1964-65; mem. staff Tex. Coll. Trial Advocacy, Houston, 1978-86; prosecutor Harris County Grievance Com.-State Bar Tex., Houston, 1965-70 Served with AUS, 1943-46, ETO. Fellow Tex. Bar Found. (life); mem. Tex. Acad. Family Law Specialists (cert.), Tex. Assn. Def. Counsel, Tex. Bd. Legal Specialization (cert.), Fedn. Ins. Counsel, Nat. Bd. Trial Advocacy (cert.), Houston Ctr. Club, Phi Delta Phi. Federal civil litigation, State civil litigation, Personal injury (including property damage). Home: 3740 Del Monte Dr Houston TX 77019-3018 E-mail: gbrinson@houston.rr.com.

BRIONES, DAVID, judge; b. El Paso, Tex., Feb. 26, 1943; m. Delia Garcia; four children. BA, U. Tex., El Paso, 1969; JD, U. Tex., Austin, 1971. Ptnr. Moreno & Briones, 1971-91; judge El Paso County Ct. No. 1, El Paso, 1991-94; dist. judge U.S. DIst. Ct. (we. dist.) Tex., El Paso,

1994—. With U.S. Army, 1964-66. Fellow Tex. Bar Found.; mem. State Bar of Tex., El Paso Bar Assn., Mexican-Am. Bar Assn. Office: US Courthouse Courtroom 1 511 E San Antonio Ave El Paso TX 79901-2401 E-mail: David_Briones@txwd.uscourts.gov.

BRISCOE, JOHN, lawyer; b. Stockton, Calif., July 1, 1948; s. John Lloyd and Doris (Olsen) B.; divorced; children: John Paul, Katherine. JD, U. San Francisco, 1972. Bar: Calif. 1972, U.S. Dist. Ct. (no., ea. and ctrl. dists.) Calif. 1972, U.S. Supreme Ct. 1978, U.S. Ct. Appeals (9th cir.) 1981. Dep. atty. gen. State of Calif., San Francisco, 1972-80; ptnr. Washburn and Kemp, San Francisco, 1980-88, Washburn, Briscoe & McCarthy, San Francisco, 1988—2001, Stoel Rives LLP, San Francisco, 2001—. Author: Surveying the Courtroom, 1984, rev. edit., 1999, Falsework, 1997, Tadich Grill, 2002; editor: Reports of Special Masters, 1991; contbr. articles to profl. and lit. jours. Mem.: ABA, Am. Soc. Internat. Law, San Francisco Bar Asn. Roman Catholic. General civil litigation, Land use and zoning (including planning), Property, real (including real estate development, water). Office: Stoel Rives LLP 111 Sutter St #700 San Francisco CA 94104 E-mail: jbriscoe@stoel.com.

BRISTER, BILL H. lawyer, former bankruptcy judge; b. Sieper, La., Mar. 5, 1930; s. Clayton Houston and Era (Price) B.; m. Carolyn Lee McDowell, June 11, 1955; children— Jeff, Julie. B.S. in Chemistry, Northwestern State U. Natchitoches, La., 1948; J.D., U. Tex., 1958. Bar: Tex. 1957, U.S. Dist. Ct. (no. dist.) Tex. 1959, U.S. Ct. Appeals (5th cir.) 1971, U.S. Supreme Ct. 1971. Pvt. practice, Lubbock, Tex., 1958-79; bankruptcy judge U.S. Dist. Ct. (no. dist.) Tex., 1979-85; of counsel Winstead, Sechrest & Minick and predecessor firm, 1986—. Served to col. USMCR, 1951-52. E-mail: billbrist@aol.com. Bankruptcy. Office: Winstead Sechrest & Minick 5400 Renaissance Tower 1201 Elm St Ste 5400 Dallas TX 75270-2199

BRISTOL, NORMAN, lawyer, arbitrator, former food company executive; b. Bronx, N.Y., June 14, 1924; s. Lawrence and Bell (Allchin) B.; m. Doreen Kingan, Mar. 28, 1952; children: Charles L., Norman, Alexander, Barnaby. Grad., Phillips Exeter Acad., 1941; AB, Yale, 1944; LLB, Columbia Law Sch., 1949. Bar: N.Y. bar 1950, Mich. bar 1954. Atty. Root, Ballantine, Harlan, Bushby & Palmer, N.Y.C., 1949-53; with Kellogg Co., Battle Creek, Mich., 1954-78, asst. gen. counsel, 1958-64, sec., 1960-78, gen. counsel, 1964-78, sr. v.p., 1968-75, dir., 1972-78, exec. v.p., 1975-78; atty. Howard & Howard, Kalamazoo, 1979-93. Mem. Gull Lake Comty. Schs. Bd. Edn., 1963-70, pres., 1965-67; trustee Kalamazoo Symphony Soc., Inc., 1983-94, pres., 1990-91; bd. dirs. Southwest Mich. Land Conservancy, Inc., 1996-2001. Lt. (j.g.) USNR, 1943-46. Mem. State Bar Mich., Kalamazoo Bar Assn., Am. Soc. Corp. Secs., SCORE (counsellor). Home and Office: 2962 Sylvan Dr Hickory Corners MI 49060-9319

BRISTOW, WALTER JAMES, JR., retired judge; b. Columbia, S.C., Oct. 14, 1924; s. Walter James and Caroline Belser (Melton) B.; m. Katherine Stewart Mullins, Sept. 12, 1952; children: Walter James III, Katherine Mullins (dec.). Student, Va. Mil. Inst., 1941-43; AB, U. N.C., 1947; LLB cum laude, U. S.C., 1949; LLM, Harvard U., 1950. Mem. Marchant, Bristow & Bates, 1953-76, S.C. Ho. of Reps., 1956-58, S.C. Senate, 1958-76; resident judge 5th Cir. Ct. S.C., 1976-88; ret., 1988. Nat. pres. Conf. Ins. Legislators, 1974-75. Trustee Elvira Wright Fund for Crippled Children, 1963-76; mem. bd. visitors ex officio The Citadel, Charleston, S.C., 1967-76. Served with AUS, 1943-45; ETO, brig. gen. S.C. Army N.G. Decorated Meritorious Svc. medal; recipient Order of Palmetto, 1999, Order of Cypress, 1999. Mem. ABA, Wig and Robe, S.C. Law Inst., S.C. Coun. on Holocaust, Capital City Club, Cotillion Club, Forest Lake Club, Palmetto Club, Columbia Ball Club, Sertoma, Alpha Tau Omega. Democrat. Office: PO Box 1147 Columbia SC 29202-1147

BRITT, EARL THOMAS, lawyer; b. Phila., July 14, 1940; s. Earl Francis and Marie Rita (Lawless) B.; m. Maureen Wong, Dec. 26, 1964; children: Denise, Karen, Eileen, Mary, Kevin, Stephen. AB, St. Joseph's U., Phila., 1961; JD, U. Pa., 1964. Bar: Pa. 1964, U.S. Dist. Ct. (ea. dist.) Pa. 1964, U.S. Ct. Appeals (3rd cir.) 1964, U.S. Dist. Ct. Appeals (D.C. cir.) 1981, U.S. Supreme Ct. 1982. Atty. Pa. Mfrs. Assn. Ins. Co., Phila., 1964-67; assoc. Swartz Campbell & Detweiler, Phila., 1967-68; assoc., then ptnr. Duane Morris & Heckscher, Phila., 1968-92; founder, ptnr., chmn. Britt, Hankins, Schaible & Moughan, Phila., 1992—; judge pro tem Ct. Common Pleas, Phila., 1991—. Lectr. Comey Inst. Indsl. Rels. St. Joseph's U., 1961-92; adj. faculty Temple U. Sch. Law-Acad. Advocacy, 1994—. Mem. adv. bd. Norwood-Fontbonne Acad., 1997-2002. Mem. ABA, Pa. Bar Assn., Phila. Bar Assn. (trustee campaign for qualified judges 1989, hon. trustee 1990-91), Phila. Assn. Def. Counsel (bd. dirs. 1983-89, 93-94, pres. 1988-89), Pa. Def. Inst. (lectr. Trial Acad. 1990—), Internat. Assn. Def. Counsel, Def. Rsch. Inst., Lawyer's Club Phila. (bd. dirs. 1988-90). Republican. Roman Catholic. Home: 106 Sparango Ln Plymouth Meeting PA 19462-1115 Office: Britt Hankins Schaible & Moughan 11 E Airy St Norristown PA 19401 E-mail: ebritt@bhsm-pm.com.

BRITT, W. EARL, federal judge; b. McDonald, N.C., Dec. 7, 1932; s. Dudley H. and Martha Mae (Hall) B.; m. Judith Moore, Apr. 17, 1976. Student, Campbell Jr. Coll., 1952; BS, Wake Forest U., 1956, JD, 1958. Bar: N.C. 1958. Pvt. practice law, Fairmont, N.C., 1959-72, Lumberton, N.C., 1972-80; judge U.S. Dist. Ct. (ea. dist.) N.C., from 1980, chief judge, 1983-90, sr. judge, 1997—. Mem. Jud. Conf. Com. on Automation and Tech., 1990-95; 4th cir. dist. judge rep. to Jud. Conf. U.S., 1991-97. Trustee Southeastern Community Coll., 1965-70, Southeastern Gen. Hosp., Lumberton, 1965-69, Pembroke State U., 1967-72; bd. govs. U. N.C. Served with U.S. Army, 1953-55. Mem. N.C. Bar Assn., Fed. Judges Assn. (bd. dirs., v.p., 1993-95, pres. 1995-97). Baptist. Office: US Dist Ct PO Box 27504 Raleigh NC 27611-7504*

BRITTIGAN, ROBERT LEE, lawyer; b. Columbus, Ohio, Aug. 24, 1942; s. Virgil Devan and Ruth (Clark) B.; m. Sharon Lynn Amore, Aug. 22, 1964; children: Eric Clark, Robert Lee II. BSBA cum laude, Ohio State U., 1964, JD summa cum laude, 1967. Bar: Ohio 1967, U.S. Ct. Mil. Appeals 1974, U.S. Ct. Claims 1977, U.S. Ct. Appeals (5th cir.) 1978, U.S. Ct. Appeals (6th cir.) 1992, U.S. Supreme Ct. 1974. Commd. 2d lt. U.S. Army, 1968, advanced through grades to maj., 1977, chief mil. justice, 1972-73, dep. staff judge adv. 5th Inf. Divsn. (Mech.) Ft. Polk, La., 1974-76, action atty. litig. divsn. Office of JAG Washington, 1976-80, resigned, 1980; gen. counsel Def. Threat Reduction Agy., Washington, 1980—. Col. Res. ret. Decorated Bronze Star medal, Meritorious Svc. medal with oak leaf cluster; recipient Exceptional Civilian Svc. medal Def. Nuc. Agy., Meritorious Civilian Svc. medal, Sec. Defense, Presdl. Rank award, Meritorious Exec. Office: General Counsel Def Threat Reduction Agy 8725 John J Kingman Rd Fort Belvoir VA 22060-6201

BRITTON, ANDREW JAMES, lawyer; b. Conneaut, Ohio, Sept. 15, 1945; s. Charles A. and Geraldine A. (Sill) B.; children: James E., Richard K. BA in Econs. with honors, Wittenberg U., 1967; BA with honors, Duke Univ.; JD with honors, Ariz. State U., 1972. Bar: Fla. 1976, Calif. 1972, Ga. 1974, U.S. Dist. Ct. (mid. dist.) Fla. 1979, U.S. Ct. Appeals (11th cir.) 1981. Clerk U.S. Ct. Appeals, San Francisco, 1972-73; assoc. Hansell, Post et al, Atlanta, 1973-76, Isphording, Payne et al, Venice, Fla., 1978—83; pvt. practice Venice, Fla., 1983—. Adj. prof. Manatee C.C., 1988—. Pres., dir. Venice (Fla.) H.S. Found., 1989—; dir. Venice Endowment, Inc., 1998—; pres. Venice Estate Planning Coun., 2001-02; adv. bd. Venice Econ. Devel. Bd., Boys and Girls Club of Sarasota County, Inc., 2000—; dir. Venice Symphony, pres., 1997-98; United Way South Sarasota County (pres., 1986-87); mem., chmn. Venice Area Chamber Commerce Econ. Devel. Com.; adv. bd. Sarasota County Cmty. Found., bd. dir. Consortium Children and Youth of Sarasota, Inc., bd. dir. Venice Little League, Inc. (pres., 1980-82); bd. dir. Major League Baseball Old-Timers, Inc.; mgr. Babe Ruth and Sr. League Baseball, 1980-88. Mem. Fla. Bar Assn., Sarasota County Bar Assn., Venice (Fla.) Golf & Country Club (bd. govs.), Sertoma Club Venice (pres., 1989-90), Sarasota County Com. of 100. Avocations: golf, skiing, softball. Corporate, general, Estate planning, Probate (including wills, trusts). Home: 430 Palmetto Cres Nokomis FL 34275-3030 Office: 151 Center Rd Venice FL 34292 E-mail: ajbpa@hotmail.com.

BRITTON, CLAROLD LAWRENCE, lawyer, consultant; b. Soldier, Iowa, Nov. 1, 1932; s. Arnold Olaf and Florence Ruth (Gardner) B.; m. Joyce Helene Hamlett, Feb. 1, 1958; children: Laura, Eric, Val, Martha. BS in Engring., U. Mich., Ann Arbor, 1958, JD, 1961, postgrad. Bar: Ill. 1961, U.S. Dist. Ct. (no. dist.) Ill. 1962, U.S. Ct. Appeals (7th cir.) 1963, U.S. Supreme Ct. 1970, Mich. 1989. Assoc. Jenner & Block, Chgo., 1961-70, ptnr., 1970-88; pres. Britton Info. Systems, Inc., 1991—. Lectr. DePaul U., 1988. Author: Computerized Trial Notebook, 1991, Trial By Notebook, 2002; asst. editor Mich. Law Rev., 1960. Comdr. USNR, 1952-57. Fellow Am. Coll. Trial Lawyers; mem. ABA (litigation sect., antitrust com., past regional chmn. discovery com. 1961), Ill. State Bar Assn. (chmn. Allerton House Conf. 1984, 86, 88, chmn. rule 23 com. 1985-87, chmn. civil practice and procedure coun. 1987-88, antitrust com.), Chgo. Bar Assn. (past chmn. fed. civil procedure com., mem. judiciary and computer law coms., civil practice com.), 7th Cir. Bar Assn., Def. Rsch. Inst. (com. on aerospace 1984), Mich. Bar Assn., Ill. Assn. Trial Lawyers, Order of Coif, Law Club (Chgo.), Racine Yacht Club (Wis.), Macatawa Yacht Club (Mich.), Masons, Alpha Phi Mu, Tau Beta Pi. Republican. Lutheran. Antitrust, Federal civil litigation, State civil litigation. Office: 411 E Washington St Ann Arbor MI 48104-2015 E-mail: britton@ic.net.

BRITTON, LOUIS FRANKLIN, lawyer; b. Terre Haute, Ind., Mar. 5, 1953; s. Charles J. and Deneta (Reichert) B.; m. Debra Lynne Brown, May 15, 1977; children: Louis J., Laura Elizabeth. BA cum laude, Ind. U., 1974, JD magna cum laude, 1977. Bar: Ind. 1977, U.S. Dist. Ct. (so. dist.) Ind. 1977, U.S. Ct. Appeals (7th cir.) 1997. Assoc. Cox, Zwerner, Gambill & Sullivan, Terre Haute, 1977-81, ptnr., 1981—. Bd. dirs. Regional Mfrs. Coop., 1995-. Mem. parish coun. Sacred Heart Ch., 1978-81, St. Benedicts Ch., 1998-2002; treas. Vigo County Taxpayers Assn., 1995—; v.p. agy. rels., bd. rels., bd. dirs. United Way, 1981-84; v.p., bd. dirs. Terre Haute Humane Soc., 1982-84; pres., bd. dirs. Leadership Terre Haute Alumni Assn., 1984-85, Vigo Preservation Alliance, 1985-95, pres. 1993; youth chmn., bd. dirs. local YMCA, 1987-88; bd. dirs. Terre Haute YMCA, 1985-88, Leadership Terre Haute, 1987-90, pres., 1989-90; active Friends of The Woods, St. Mary of the Woods Coll., 1998—; bd. dirs. Woods Day Care, 1993-98, Greater Terre Haute C.C., 1998-, treas., 2000-03, v.p., 1999. Ira C. Batman fellow, 1976-77; named one of Outstanding Young Men Am., 1982; recipient Outstanding Svc. award Leadership Terre Haute, 1987. Mem. ABA, Ind. Bar Assn., Terre Haute Bar Assn., Terre Haute Area C. of C. (treas. 1999—), Order of Coif, Phi Beta Kappa. Commercial, contracts (including sales of goods; commercial financing), General practice, Property, real (including real estate development, water). Home: 2206 N 7th St Terre Haute IN 47804-1802 Office: Cox Zwerner Gambill & Sullivan PO Box 1625 Terre Haute IN 47808-1625

BRIZZI, CARL, prosecutor; m. Melanie Brizzi; 4 children. Grad., Ind. U., Valparaiso U. Sr. investigative counsel U.S. Ho. Reps.; dep. pros., chief pros. Metro Gang Task Force Marion County, Ind., 1995—99, pros., 2003—; co-founder Brizzi, Collignon & Dietrick. Precinct committeeman Rep. Party, ward chmn., asst. twp. chmn., GOP club pres. Office: 200 E Washington Indianapolis IN 46204*

BRIZZOLARA, CHARLES ANTHONY, lawyer, director; b. Chgo., Nov. 20, 1929; s. Ralph D. and Florence H. (Hurley) B.; m. Audree Doyle, Aug. 24, 1968. BA, Lake Forest (Ill.) Coll., 1951; JD, Ill. Inst. Tech., 1957. Bar: Ill. 1959. Practiced law, Chgo., 1959-67; with Walter E. Heller & Co., also Walter E. Heller Internat. Corp. (later Amerifin Corp.), Chgo., 1967-85; v.p., sec., gen. counsel Walter E. Heller & Co., also Walter E. Heller Internat. Corp., 1974-85, sr. v.p., 1980-85; v.p. Chgo. Bears Football Club, Inc., 1975-88; mem. firm Chadwell & Kayser Ltd., 1985-90; ptnr. Michael Best & Friedrich, LLC, Chgo., 1990—2002; of counsel Berger, Newmark and Fenchel P.C., Chgo., 2003—. Bd. dirs. Abacus Real Estate Fin. Co., Walter E. Heller & Co. S.E., Heller Factoring (Hong Kong) Ltd., Factoring Serfin, S.A., Chandler Leasing Corp., 1975-80; lectr. seminars Am. Mgmt. Assn. Editor: Chgo.-Kent Law Rev, 1956. Bd. dirs. Cath. Charities Archdiocese of Chgo., 1978-99, sec., 1991-94; bd. dirs. Ill. Inst. Tech. Chgo. Kent Alumni Assn., 1980-89. Served with AUS, 1952-54. Mem. Internat. Bar Assn., ABA, Ill. Bar Assn. Roman Catholic. Corporate, general. Home: Apt 20G 253 E Delaware Pl Chicago IL 60611-1758 Office: 222 N LaSalle St Chicago IL 60601

BROADHURST, JEROME ANTHONY, lawyer; b. Cleve., Feb. 4, 1945; s. William and Estelle M. (Bozak) B.; m. Annette Lou Wilt, Sept. 3, 1966; children: Stephanie Ann, Jerome A., Elizabeth Marie. BS in Bus., U. Akron, 1967, JD, 1971. Bar: Ohio 1973, Tenn. 1987. Acctg. supr., fin. analyst B.F. Goodrich Co., Akron, Ohio, 1971-73, corp. counsel, 1973-76; counsel, asst. sec. The Weatherhead Co., Cleve., 1976-77; asst. counsel Gen. Tire and Rubber Co., Akron, 1977-80; sr. corp. atty. Holiday Inns, Inc. (subs. Holiday Corp.), Memphis, 1980-81, sec., sr. corp. atty., 1981-84; sec., assoc. gen. counsel Holiday Corp., Memphis, 1984-87, v.p., sec., assoc. gen. counsel, 1987-88; v.p., gen. counsel, sec. Perkins Family Restaurants, L.P., Memphis, 1989-91; pvt. practice law, 1991—; ptnr. Armstrong Allen, PLLC, 2000—. Mediator Tenn. Mediation/Arbitration Svc., 1994-95; adj. prof. MBA program Christian Brothers U. Sch. Bus., Memphis, 1997-99. Bd. dirs. Memphis Urban League, 1987-94; trustee Memphis Urban League Endowment Fund, 1987—. Mem. ABA (mem. bus. law sect. subcoms. on corp. litigation and environ. control 1995—, intellectual property law sect. com. on unfair comp.-trade identity 1996—), Tenn. Bar Assn., Ohio Bar Assn., Memphis Bar Assn., Shelby County Bar Assn., Am. Soc. Corp. Secs. (corp. practices com. 1981-97, 99-2001, public company affairs com. 2003-). Republican. Roman Catholic. Avocations: photography, jogging, fishing, racquetball. Corporate, general, Environmental, Trademark and copyright. Office: Brinkley Plaza Ste 700 80 Monroe Ave Memphis TN 38103-2467 E-mail: jbroadhurst@armstrongallen.com.

BROADWATER, DOUGLAS DWIGHT, lawyer; b. Preston, Minn., May 31, 1944; s. George and Marion Elaine (Gleason) B.; m. Beatrice (Kinney), July 8, 1978; children: Ian Dwight, George Francis, Mark Fowler. BA, U. Mass., 1966; JD, U. Mo., 1969. Bar: NY., 1969. Staff atty. employment project Ctr. Social Welfare Policy and Law, N.Y.C., 1969—71; assoc. Cravath, Swaine & Moore LLP, N.Y.C., 1971—78, ptnr., 1978—. General civil litigation. Office: Cravath Swaine & Moore LLP. Worldwide Plz 825 8th Ave 41st Fl New York NY 10019-7475

BROCHIN, MURRY DAVID, lawyer; b. Hackensack, N.J., June 11, 1930; m. Leona Nelkin, Sept. 20, 1959; children: Esther Elizabeth children: James Lewis, Nathaniel Edward. BA, Yale U., New Haven, 1952; LLB, Yale U., 1955. Bar: N.J. 1956. Ptnr. Lowenstein Sandler Brochin Kohl & Fisher, Roselan, NJ, 1961—86; judge law divsn. Superior Ct. of N.J., Newark, 1987—89, judge appellate divsn., 1989—2000; counsel Orloff, Lowenbach, Stifelman & Siegel PA, Roseland, NJ, 2000—; judge, appellate divsn. NJ Superior Ct., NJ, 1989—2000. Appellate. Home: 605 Mountain Dr South Orange NJ 07079 Office: Orloff Lowenbach Stifelman & Siegel PA 101 Eisenhower Pkwy Roseland NJ 07068 Office Fax: 973-622-3073. E-mail: mdb@olss.com.

BROCK, DAVID ALLEN, state supreme court chief justice; b. Stoneham, Mass., July 6, 1936; s. Herbert and Margaret B.; m. Sandra Ford, 1960; 6 children. AB, Dartmouth Coll., 1958; LLB, U. Mich., 1963; postgrad., Nat. Jud. Coll., 1977. Bar: N.H. 1963. Assoc. Devine, Millimet, McDonough, Stahl & Branch, Manchester, N.H., 1963-69; U.S. atty. State of N.H., 1969-72; ptnr. Perkins, Douglas & Brock, Concord, N.H., 1972-74, Perkins & Brock, 1974-76; spl. counsel to gov. and exec. coun. N.H., 1974-76; legal counsel to gov. N.H., 1976; assoc. justice N.H. Superior Ct., 1976-78, N.H. Supreme Ct., 1978-86, chief justice, 1986—. Chmn. State of N.H. Legal Svcs. Adv. Commn., 1977-79; chmn. dist. ct. reform subcom. Gov.'s Commn. for Ct. System Improvement, 1974-75; chmn. N.H. Commn. Ct. Accreditation, 1986—; mem. Select Commn. on Unified Ct. System, 1980-84, chmn. N.H. Supreme Ct. Com. on Jud. Conduct, 1981-89, rules adv. com., 1985-97; mem. State N.H. Jud. Coun., 1979-87; mem. nat. adv. bd. Leadership Inst. for Jud. Edn., 1989-96, Nat. Jud. Coll. long range planning com., 1990-91; mem. Jud. Edn. and Tech. Assistance Consortium, 1989-97; chmn. Interbranch Coun. on Substance Abuse and the Criminal Justice System, 1991-95; bd. dirs. State Justice Inst., 1992-98, vice-chmn., 1994-95, co-chmn., 1995-98; bd. dirs. Conf. Chief Justices, 1993-94, v.p., 1996-97, pres-elect 1997-98, pres., 1998-99; bd. dirs. Nat. Ctr. for State Cts., 1996-2000, chmn.-elect, 1997-98, chmn., 1998-99; mem. Nat. Criminal Justice Info. Svcs. Adv. Policy Bd., 1999—. Bd. dirs. Manchester Cmty. Guidance Ctr., 1966-72, pres., 1969-72; chmn. Manchester Rep. Com., 1967-69; vice chmn. N.H. Rep. State Com., 1968-69; Rep. candidate U.S. Senate, 1972; del. N.H. Constl. Conv., 1974: mem. Gov.'s Commn. for Handicapped, 1978-79. Fellow ABA (mem. edn. com. of appellate judges conf. 1981-97, appellate advocacy com. 1982-84, faculty appellate judges' seminar program 1984-89, del. ho. of dels. 1994-96), N.H. Bar Assn. (chmn. constl. revision com. 1976-77), N.H. Bar Found. (hon.). Office: NH Supreme Ct Noble Dr Concord NH 03301

BROCK, GLEN PORTER, JR., lawyer; b. Mobile, Ala., Nov. 13, 1937; s. Glen Porter Sr. and Esther Alitha (Goodwin) B.; m. Shirley Ann Forbes, Jan. 7, 1961; children: Glen Porter III, Susan Forbes. BS, Auburn U., 1959; JD, U. Ala., 1963; LLM in Taxation, NYU, 1964. Bar: Ala. 1963. Assoc. Hand, Arendall, Bedsole, Greaves & Johnston, Mobile, 1964-69, ptnr., 1970-94; mem. Hand Arendall, LLC, 1995—. Capt. USAR, 1959-67. Mem. ABA, Ala. Bar Assn. (chmn. tax sect. 1974-75), Mobile Bar Assn., Lions (pres. 1982-83). Baptist. Avocations: travel, computers, photography. Estate planning, Probate (including wills, trusts), Taxation, general. Home: 737 Westmoreland Dr W Mobile AL 36609-6132 Office: Hand Arendall LLC 3000 AmSouth Bank Bldg 107 Saint Francis St Mobile AL 36602-3334 E-mail: porterb@handarendall.com.

BROCK, MITCHELL, lawyer; b. Wyncote, Pa., Nov. 10, 1927; s. John W. and Mildred A. (Mitchell) B.; m. Gioia Connell, June 21, 1952; children: Felicity, Marina, Mitchell Hovey, Laura. AB, Princeton U., 1950; LLB, U. Pa., 1953. Bar: N.Y. 1954. Assoc. firm Sullivan & Cromwell, N.Y.C., 1953-59, ptnr., 1960-92, Paris, 1965-68, ptnr. in charge Tokyo, 1987-90. Bd. dirs. Frost Valley YMCA, Oliverea, N.Y., 1980-87, 1990-2000, Am. Found. Blind, 1967-87; pres., trustee Helen Keller Internat., N.Y.C., 1970-87, 90-94, chmn., trustee, 1994-96, sec., 1996—. Served with USN, 1945-46. Mem. Anglers Club, Princeton Club, Ivy Club, Boca Grande Pass Club. Republican. Episcopalian. Corporate, general, Private international. Home: PO Box 452 Boca Grande FL 33921-0452 E-mail: gimibrock@ewol.com.

BROCK, RALPH HANEY, lawyer; b. Amarillo, Tex., Aug. 6, 1948; s. Charles and Waurika (Haney) B.; m. Carolyn Frances Moore, Nov. 14, 1981. BA, Tex. Tech U., 1971, JD, 1975. Bar: Tex. 1975, U.S. Dist. Ct. (no. dist.) Tex. 1976, U.S. Ct. Appeals (5th cir.), 1978, U.S. Supreme Ct. 1979. Briefing atty. 7th Ct. Civil Appeals Tex., 1975—76; assoc. Brown & Harding, Lubbock, Tex., 1976—79; legal counsel 7th Ct. Appeals Tex., 1981—82; faculty Tex. Tech U. Sch. Law, Lubbock, 1996—97; sole practice law Lubbock, 1979—81, 1982—. Contbr. articles to profl. jours. Fellow Tex. Bar Found. (sustaining life fellow, Dan Rugeley Price Meml. award 1999); mem. State Bar Tex. (sect. rep. to bd. dirs. 2000-02, bd. dirs. 2002—, chair jour. com. 1994-95, chair appellate practice advocacy sect. 1987-88, women and the law sect. 1999-2002, sec. computer sect. 1998-2000, opportunities for minorities in the profession com. 1998-2001, Women in the Profession Com. 1998-2001, Pres. award 2002, Ma'at Justice award 1997), ABA, ACLU, Tex. Women Lawyers, Bar Assn. 5th Fed. Cir., Lubbock County Bar Assn. (Pro Bono Atty. of Yr. award 1986), Lubbock County Women Lawyers Assn., Lubbock Criminal Def. Lawyers Assn., Amateur Radio Relay League, Nat. Eagle Scout Assn., Lubbock Amateur Radio Club, Phi Alpha Theta, Pi Sigma Alpha. Democrat. Unitarian Universalist. Avocations: amateur radio, collecting soda pop bottles. Appellate, Criminal, General practice. Office: PO Box 959 Lubbock TX 79408-0959 E-mail: Brock@abanet.org.

BRODER, AARON J. lawyer; b. N.Y.C., May 21, 1924; BS cum laude, CCNY, 1945; LLB, NYU, 1949. Bar: N.Y. 1949. Pvt. practice, N.Y.C., 1949—; ptnr. F. Lee Bailey & Aaron J. Broder, 1970—; mem. legal adv. com. N.Y.C. Community Coll., 1973. Lectr. in field; mem. legal adv. com. N.Y.C. Community Coll., 1973. Author: Trial Handbook for New York Lawyers, 1973, 2d edit., 1986, 3rd edit. 1996, Dealing with Damages in Personal Injury and Wrongful Death Trials; columnist: N.Y. Law Jour, 1971-95, also numerous articles, chpts. in books. Mem. ABA, Am. Trial Lawyers Assn. (gov. 1974, mem. faculty, aviation law com., editor-in-chief quar., 6 vols. 1964-67), Internat. Acad. Law and Sci., N.Y. State Trial Lawyers Assn. (pres. 1965-67), N.Y. State Trial Lawyers Assn., Assn. Bar City N.Y., Bronx County Bar Assn., Nassau County Bar Assn. Home: 11 Beech Ln Great Neck NY 11024-1230 Office: 350 5th Ave New York NY 10118-0110

BRODER, DOUGLAS FISHER, lawyer; b. Cleve., Sept. 30, 1948; s. Harry M. and Peggy (Fisher) B.; m. Rebecca Northey, Jan. 24, 1976; 1 child, Julia N. BA, Vassar Coll., 1970; JD cum laude, Boston U., 1977. Bar: N.Y. 1978, U.S. Dist. Ct. (so. and ea. dists.) N.Y. 1978, U.S. Ct. Appeals (2d cir.) 1983, U.S. Ct. Appeals (6th cir.) 1986, U.S. Ct. Appeals (4th cir.) 1987, U.S. Dist. Ct. (ea. dist.) Mich. 1987, U.S. Supreme Ct. 1993, U.S. Ct. Appeals (9th cir.) 1997. Assoc. Lord, Day & Lord, N.Y.C., 1977-86; ptnr. Coudert Bros. LLP, N.Y.C., 1986—2002, Nixon Peabody LLP, 2002—. Spkr. and lectr. on continuing legal edn. Author: Antitrust Law Desk Book, 2001; lead editor: "International Joint Ventures" Professional Information Publishing Ltd., 1996; mem. editl. bd. European Competition Law Rev.; contbr. articles to profl. publs. Mem. ABA, Assn. of Bar of City of N.Y. Antitrust, General civil litigation, Securities. Home: 300 Central Park W New York NY 10024-1513 Office: Nixon Peabody LLP 437 Madison Ave New York NY 10022 Business E-mail: dbroder@nixonpeabody.com.

BRODER, GAIL STEINMETZ, lawyer; b. Bklyn., Oct. 18, 1944; m. Samuel Broder, 1966. BA, CUNY, 1966; MA, U. Mich., 1971; JD with honors, George Washington U., 1979; MS in Clin. Counseling, Jpohns Hopkins U., 2002. Bar: Md., 1980. Pvt. practice, Rockville, Md., 1980-84; staff atty. Vet. Adminstrn., Washington, 1984-89; sr. atty. U.S. Dept. HHS, Washington, 1989-95; pres., founder, exec. dir. Cancer Survivorship Alliance of South Fla., Ft. Lauderdale, 1995—98. Office: 9309 Sprinklewood Ln Potomac MD 20854-2258

BRODER, JOSEPH ARNOLD, lawyer; b. Hartford, Conn., Jan. 19, 1939; s. Morris H. and Dora (Levine) B.; m. Andrea L. Goldstein, Feb. 23, 1967; 1 child, Michael. AB, Trinity Coll., 1960; JD, Harvard U., 1963. Bar: Conn. 1963, N.Y. 1964, U.S. Dist. Ct. Conn. 1965, U.S. Military Ct. 1968, U.S. Supreme Ct. 1976. Assoc. Dammann, Blank, Hirsh & Heming, N.Y.C., 1964-65, Broder & Broder, Colchester, Conn., 1965; pvt. practice Colchester, 1966-80; sr. ptnr. Broder & Butts, Colchester, 1981—. Dir. Yankee Inst. for Pub. Policy Studies, 1993—; corporator Norwich (Conn.) Savs. Soc.,

1982-87; bd. dirs., v.p. Colchester Publs., 1982-88. Mem. Conn. Ho. of Reps., 1981-82; mem. Rep. State Ctrl.Com., 1980-81, 87-93; mem. Glastonbury (Conn.) City Coun., 1993-97. Comdr. USNR ret. Mem. ABA, ATLA, Conn. Bar Assn., Nat. Acad. Elder Law Attys., Am. Legion, Rotary Internat. Avocations: tennis, skiing, hunting, fishing, flying. Estate planning, General practice, Personal injury (including property damage). Home: PO Box 208 East Glastonbury CT 06025-0208 Office: Broder & Butts PO Box 270 188 Norwich Ave Colchester CT 06415-1256

BRODERICK, JOHN T., JR., state supreme court justice; BA magna cum laude, Coll. Holy Cross, 1969; JD, U. Va., 1972. Atty. Devine, Millimet, Stahl & Branch, Manchester, N.H., 1972-89; shareholder Broderick & Dean (formerly Merrill & Broderick), Manchester, 1989-95; assoc. justice N.H. Supreme Ct., Concord, N.H., 1995—. Bd. dirs. Legal Svcs. Corp. Fellow Am. Coll. Trial Lawyers, N.H. Bar Found. (bd. dirs. 1985-91); mem. ABA, Mass. Bar Assn., N.H. Bar Assn. (bd. govs. 1985-91, pres. 1990-91), N.H. Trial Lawyers Assn. (bd. govs. 1977-82, pres. 1982-83). Office: NH Supreme Ct One Noble Dr Concord NH 03301

BRODHEAD, DAVID CRAWMER, lawyer; b. Madison, Wis., Sept. 16, 1934; s. Richard Jacob and Irma (Crawmer) B.; m. Nancie Christensen, Aug. 17, 1963; children: Compton, Peter, Christoffer. BS, U. Wis., 1956, LLB, 1959. Bar: N.Y. 1960, Wis. 1959, D.C. 1979. Assoc. firm Paul, Weiss, Rifkind, Wharton & Garrison, N.Y.C., 1959-68, ptnr., 1969—. Dir. Centennial Industries, Inc., N.Y.C. Editor-in-chief: Wis. Law Rev, 1958-59. Trustee Collegiate Sch., N.Y.C., 1978-85; vestryman Christ and St. Stephen's Episcopal Ch., 1972-82. Mem. N.Y. State Bar, Assn. of Bar of City of N.Y., Wis. Bar. Assn., D.C. Bar Assn., ABA, Westside C. of C. of City of N.Y. (dir. 1970-83), Order of Coif, Delta Theta Phi Clubs: Washington (Conn.); Holland Soc. of N.Y. Commercial, contracts (including sales of goods; commercial financing), Corporate, general, Finance.

BRODIE, RONALD, lawyer, author; b. N.Y.C., Sept. 22, 1941; s. S. Robert and Ann Brodie. BA in Econs., U. Pa., 1963; SM in Mgmt., MIT, 1965; JD, U. Miami, Fla., 1967, LLM in Taxation, 1968. Bar: Fla. 1967, U.S. Tax Ct. 1976, U.S. Ct. Appeals (11th cir.) 1981. Sole practice, Miami and Miami Beach, Fla., 1967—; pres. Taxplan, Inc., Miami Beach, 1979—. Lectr. Fla. Bar continuing legal edn. seminars, guest lectr. U Miami Law Sch. Author Real Estate Tax Planning Newsletter, 1981-86; author, editor tax column Jour. Property Mgmt., 1981-99; contbr. numerous articles on taxation to profl. jours. Mem. counsel Conservative Caucus of Dade, Inc., Miami, 1980-86; mem. U. Miami Endowment Com., 1969—. Mem. Miami Beach Bar Assn., Real Estate Assn. of Profls. (founder, pres., counsel 1979-80), Fla. Bar (chmn. tax aspects of real property law com. 1979-90, exec. coun. real property, probate and trust law sect. 1979-90), U. Miami Law Alumni Assn., U. Pa. Dade Alumni Club, MIT Club of Miami, U. Miami Alumni Ass., Wharton Sch. Club, Delta Theta Phi, Mensa, Intertel. Republican. Probate (including wills, trusts), Corporate taxation, Personal income taxation. Home: 951 W 47th Ct Miami Beach FL 33140-2906 Office: 134 Mirasol Internat Ctr 2699 Collins Ave Miami Beach FL 33140-4716 E-mail: ronaldbrodie@webtv.net.

BRODKA, MARK A. lawyer; b. Montebello, Calif., Dec. 8, 1956; s. George and Jesse (Koziel) B. BA, Loyola U., L.A., 1979, JD, 1982. Bar: Calif. 1982. Assoc. Arthur J. Crowley Profl. Corp., L.A., 1982-89; sole practice L.A., 1990--. Mem. L.A. County Bar Assn., L.A. Trial Lawyers Assn., Alpha Sigma Nu. General civil litigation. Office: 12100 Wilshire Blvd Ste 700 Los Angeles CA 90025-7125

BRODL, RAYMOND FRANK, lawyer, former lumber company executive; b. Cicero, Ill., June 1, 1924; s. Edward C. and Lillian (Cerny) B.; m. Ethel Jean Johnson, Aug. 15, 1953; children: Mark Raymond, Pamela Jean, Susan Marie. Student, Norwich U., Northfield, Vt., 1943, Ill. Coll., 1946-48; JD, Loyola U., Chgo., 1951. Bar: Ill. 1951. Atty. law office Joseph A. Ricker, Chgo., 1951-58, Brunswick Corp., Chgo., 1958-62; sec., gen. atty. Edward Hines Lumber Co., Chgo., 1962-84, atty., cons., 1985—, sr. counselor, 2001. Democratic candidate for local jud. office, 1953, 57. Served with AUS, 1943-46. Mem. Ill. Bar Assn. Home and Office: 366 Lance Dr Des Plaines IL 60016-2628

BRODSKY, DAVID MICHAEL, lawyer; b. Providence, Oct. 16, 1943; s. Irving and Naomi (Richman) B.; m. Stacey J. Moritz; children: Peter, Isabel, Nell. AB cum laude, Brown U., 1964; LLB, Harvard U., 1967. Bar: N.Y. 1968, U.S. Dist. Ct. (so. dist.) N.Y. 1969, U.S. Ct. Appeals (2d cir.) 1974, U.S. Dist. Ct. (ea. dist.) N.Y. 1977, U.S. Supreme Ct. 1977, U.S. Ct. Appeals (D.C. cir.) 1981, U.S. Ct. Appeals (3d cir.) 1984, U.S. Tax Ct. 1984, U.S. Dist. Ct. (no. dist.) Tex. 1986. Law clk. to U.S. Dist. judge U.S. Dist. Ct. (so. dist.) N.Y., 1967-69; asst. U.S. atty. So. Dist. N.Y., 1969-73; assoc. Guggenheimer & Untermyer, N.Y.C., 1973-75, ptnr., 1976-80; ptnr., chmn. litig. dept. Schulte Roth & Zabel, N.Y.C., 1980-99; mng. dir., gen. counsel-Ams., Credit Suisse First Boston, 1999—2002; ptnr., co-chair securities and profl. liability litigation group Latham & Watkins LLP, 2002—. Lectr. in field. Co-author: Federal Securities Litigation: A Deskbook for the Practitioner, 1997. Chmn., bd. dirs. N.Y. Lawyers for Pub. Interest, Inc., 1991-94, vice-chmn., 1994-96; bd. dirs. Equal Justice Works, N.Y. Lawyers for the Pub. Interest, Assn. of the Bar Fund. Recipient Pathways to Justice award. Fellow Am. Coll. Trial Lawyers (mem. access to justice com., mem. downstate N.Y. com.); mem. ABA, (litig. sect., co-chmn. ann. meeting 1998, co-chmn. trial practice com. 1990-94, task force on jury sys. 1995-2001), Assn. of Bar of City of N.Y., Anti-Defamation League (exec. com., legal com. 1994—), Am. Law Inst., N.Y. County Lawyers Assn., Fed. Bar Coun., Harvard Club, Scarsdale Golf Club. Jewish. General civil litigation, Criminal, Securities. Office: Latham & Watkins LLP 885 Third Ave New York NY 10022 E-mail: david.brodsky@lw.com.

BRODSKY, FELICE ADRIENNE, lawyer; b. Utica, N.Y., July 21, 1952; d. Emile Borden and Harriet Maxine (Berman) Skraly; m. Keith E. Brinkley, Nov. 4, 2002. BA, U. Rochester, 1973; MBA, SUNY, Buffalo, 1984, JD, 1993. Bar: N.Y. 1994, Fed. 1994. Claims rep. U.S. Govt./Social Security Adminstrn., Batavia, N.Y., 1976-90; pvt. practice Lockport, N.Y., 1994—. Instr. Nat. Coll., Rapid City, S.D., 1973-75, Niagara U., Niagara Falls, N.Y., 1989. Treas. Temple Beth El, Niagara Falls, 1987-93; adv. bd. Salvation Army, Lockport, 1995—; bd. dirs. Niagara County Legal Aid Soc., 1996—, v.p. 1999-2000, pres. 2000—; mem. adv. bd. Planned Parenthood, 2002—. Mem. ABA, N.Y. State Bar Assn., Erie County Bar Assn., Lockport Bar Assn., Women Lawyers of Western N.Y., Nat. Orgn. Social Security Claimants Reps. (sustaining mem.), Phi Delta Phi. Democrat. Jewish. Avocations: travel, reading, civic activities. General practice, Pension, profit-sharing, and employee benefits. Home: 71 Bridlewood Dr PO Box 557 Lockport NY 14095-0557 Office: 556 S Transit St Lockport NY 14094-5933 E-mail: Feliceesq@aol.com.

BRODSKY, SAMUEL, lawyer; b. Kansas City, Mo., June 12, 1912; s. Abraham and Anne (Brodsky) B.; m. Margery J. Bach, Oct. 17, 1944; children: Joan E., Alice E. BA, U. Tulsa, 1933; LL.B., Harvard U., 1936. Bar: N.Y. 1937. Since practiced in, N.Y.C.; law clk. to Fed. Circuit Ct. Judge Julian W. Mack, 1936-37; asst. U.S. atty. So. Dist. N.Y., 1937-43, 46, charge civil div., 1942-43, 46; partner firm Aranow, Brodsky, Bohlinger, Einhorn & Alter, 1947-79, Botein, Hays & Sklar, 1979-89; counsel Robinson, Brog, Leinwand, Greene, Genovese & Gluck, N.Y.C., 1989-97. Lectr. taxation NYU Law Sch., 1953, 56-64, also; Inst. on Fed. Taxation, NYU, Practicing Law Inst. Contbr. articles to profl. jours. Served to lt. USNR, 1943-46. Mem. ABA, N.Y. State Bar Assn. (past chmn. tax sect.), Harvard Law Sch. Assn. N.Y. Jewish (past pres., trustee synagogue). Home: 55 Grasslands Rd Apt B224 Valhalla NY 10595 Office: care Robinson Brog Leinwand Greene Genovese & Gluck 1345 Avenue Of The Americas New York NY 10105-0302

BRODY, JAY HOWARD, lawyer; b. Detroit, Jan. 4, 1953; s. Robert David and Rhea Antoinnette (Orley) B.; m. Helene Cheryl Brodsky, Aug. 11, 1974 (div. Nov. 1998); children: Stuart, Rachel; m. Susan Logar, Oct. 15, 1999. BA in Anthropology, U. Mich., 1974; JD, Wayne State U., 1976. Bar: Mich. 1977, U.S. Dist. Ct. (ea. dist.) Mich. 1977, U.S. Ct. Appeals (6th cir.) 1977, U.S. Tax Ct. 1979. Acct. Arther Andersen, Detroit, 1977-79; assoc. Raymond & Dillon, Detroit, 1979-80, Rubenstein & Isaacs, Southfield, Mich., 1980-81; pvt. practice Farmington Hills, Mich., 1981-01; with Kemp, Klein, Umphrey, Endelman & May PC, Troy, Mich., 2001—. Dir. Thomas Found., Farmington Hills, 1984—. Exec. producer (film) KillZone, 1997. Mem. ABA, AICPAs, State Bar Mich., Mich. Assn. CPAs. Pension, profit-sharing, and employee benefits, Probate (including wills, trusts), Taxation, general. Office: Kemp Klein Umphrey Endelman & May PC 201 W Big Beaver Rd Ste 600 Troy MI 48084

BRODY, RICHARD ERIC, lawyer; b. N.Y.C., Sept. 9, 1947; s. Harold I. and Lillian C. (Albert) B.; m. V. Jane Cohen, May 25, 1974; children: Lauren, Erica. BA, Washington and Jefferson Coll., 1969; JD, Boston U., 1975. Bar: Mass. 1975, U.S. Dist. Ct. Mass. 1975, U.S. Ct. Appeals (1st cir.) 1975, U.S. Supreme Ct. 1987. Law clk. Mass. Superior Ct., Boston, 1975-76, chief law clk., 1976-77; assoc. Sisson, Lee & Bloomenthal, Boston, 1977-78; asst. dist. atty. Atty.'s Office Middlesex County Dist., Cambridge, Mass., 1978-82; assoc. Morrison, Mahoney & Miller, Boston, 1982-85, ptnr., 1985-95, Brody, Hardoon, Perkins & Kesten, Boston, 1995—. Lectr. Nat. Inst. Trial Advocacy, trial practice series Harvard U., Mass. Continuing Legal Edn., Def. Rsch. Inst.; evaluator Middlesex Multi-Door Courthouse, Cambridge, 1989—; mediator Arbitration Forums, Inc., Tarrytown, N.Y., 1989—, cons. Liability Cons., Inc., Sudbury, 1988—; mem. nat. adv. bd. Govtl. Liability Ins., Richmond, 1985—. Trustee Mass. Civil Liability Ins., Boston, 1983-89. Mem. Mass. Bar Assn. (civil litigation sect. coun.), Mass. Assn. Trial Lawyers, Boston Bar Assn., Def. Rsch. Inst., City Solicitors and Town Counsel Assn. Civil rights, General civil litigation, Personal injury (including property damage). Office: Brody Hardoon Perkins & Kesten 1 Exeter Plz Fl 12 Boston MA 02116-2848

BROEKER, JOHN MILTON, lawyer; b. Berwyn, Ill., May 27, 1940; s. Milton Monroe and Marjorie Grace (Wilson) B.; m. Linda J. Broeker, Dec. 9, 1983; children: Sara Elizabeth, Ross Goddard; stepchildren: Terrance Mercil Jr., Johnny Mercil, Veronica Mercil. BA, Grinnell Coll., 1962; JD cum laude, U. Minn., 1965. Bar: Minn. 1965, Wis. 1982, U.S. Ct. Appeals (8th cir.) 1966, U.S. Dist. Ct. Minn. 1967,. U.S. Tax Ct. 1969, U.S. Ct. Appeals (5th cir.) 1971, U.S. Dist. Ct. (we. dist.) Wis. 1982, U.S. Supreme Ct. 1984. Law clk. to presiding judge U.S. Ct. Appeals (8th cir.), 1965-66; ptnr. Gray, Plant, Mooty, Mooty & Bennett, Mpls., 1966-71, Broeker, Geer, Fletcher & LaFond and predecessor firms, Mpls., 1971-91; v.p., gen. counsel NordicTrack, Inc., Mpls., 1991-94; founder Broeker Enterprises, 1992—; pres. Legal Mgmt. Strategies, Inc., Mpls., 1994—; of counsel Popham, Haik, Schnobrich & Kaufman, Ltd., Mpls., 1995-96, Halleland, Lewis, Nilan, Sipkins & Johnson, Mpls., 1996-97; pvt. practice, 1997—. Instr. U Minn. Law Sch., 1967-72; lectr. convs. and seminars, 1969—; lectr. U. Minn. Ctr. for Long Term Care Edn., 1972-77, Gt. Lakes Health Congress, 1972, Sister Kenney Inst., 1972. Contbr. articles to legal jours. Bd. dirs. Minn. Environ. Scis. Found., Inc., 1971-73; bd. dirs. Project Environ. Found., 1977-83, chmn., 1980-82; mem. alumni bd. Grinnell Coll., 1968-71; chmn. MInnetonka Environ. Quality and Natural Resources Commn., 1971-72; trustee The Writers Project, Inc., 1999-2001. Recipient Outstanding Alumni award Grinnell Coll., 1973. Mem. ABA (forum com. on health law 1978-91), Minn. Bar Assn. (chmn. environ. law com. 1970-72), State Bar Wis., Hennepin County Bar Assn. (chmn. environ. law com. 1976-77, legis. com. 1972-76, health law com. 1977-79), Am. Soc. Hosp. Attys., Minn. Soc. Hosp. Attys., Am. Health Care Assn. (legal coordinating com. 1970-75, labor com. 1973-74), Nat. Health Lawyers Assn., Minn. Thoroughbred Assn. (bd. dirs. 1991-92), Minn. Quarterhorse Racing Assn. (bd. dirs. 1994—, pres. 1997-99), Sierra Club (nat. dir. 1974-76, chmn. chpt. 1971-72, regional v.p. 1973-74). Corporate, general, Health, Labor (including EEOC, Fair Labor Standards Act, labor-management relations, NLRB, OSHA). Home: 11402 Burr Ridge Ln Eden Prairie MN 55347-4717 Office: 8120 Penn Ave S Ste 151Q Bloomington MN 55431-1326 E-mail: jbroeker@msn.com.

BROGDON, W.M. "ROWE", lawyer; b. Columbia, S.C., Oct. 14, 1953; s. Wallace M. and Helen (Deloach) B.; m. Cynthia S. Brogdon, Feb. 28, 1987; 1 child, Emily Elizabeth. BS in Biology magna cum laude, Ga. So. U., 1976; JD cum laude, Mercer U., 1982. Bar: Ga. 1982. Law clk. to Hon. B. Avant Edenfield U.S. Dist. Ct. (so. dist.) Ga.; ptnr. Smith & Brogdon Attys., Savannah, Ga., 1983-87, Brannan & Brogdon Attys., Claxton, Ga., 1987-93, Franklin, Taulbee, Rushing & Brogdon, P.C., Statesboro, Ga., 1994-2000; sole practitioner, 2000—. Contbr. articles to profl. jours. Vice chmn. bd. trustees Bulloch Acad. Sch., Statesboro, 1998—; bd. govs. Mercer U. Law Sch., 1979-81. State of Ga. law scholar, 1980. Mem. ATLA, Am. Bd. Trial Advocates, Ga. Trial Lawyers Assn. (chmn. Amicus com. 1996-98, v.p. mid. cir. 1996-97), Atlantic Cir. Bar Assn. (pres. 1991-92), Ogeechee Cir. Bar Assn. (pres. 1996-97), Nat. Bd. Trial Advocacy (cert.), Am. Bd. Trial Advocates, Rotary (treas. 1992-93), Phi Delta Phi. Methodist. Avocation: fishing. General civil litigation, Personal injury (including property damage), Product liability. Home: 4599 Country Club Rd Statesboro GA 30458-9007 Office: PO Box 189 Statesboro GA 30459-1002 E-mail: rowebrog@frontiernet.net.

BROHMAN, MARK ALLEN, lawyer, biologist; b. McCook, Nebr., Oct. 12, 1963; s. Harold Horatio and Judy Louise (Neben) B.; m. Anessa Jo Schreiner, Aug. 1, 1987. BA in Biology and Chemistry, Chadron (Nebr.) State Coll., 1985; JD, U. Nebr., 1990, MS in Forestry, Fisheries and Wildlife, 1991. Bar: Nebr. 1990, U.S. Dist. Ct. Nebr. 1990. Rsch. biologist Chadron State Coll., 1981-85, Nebr. Game and Parks Commn., Lincoln, Nebr., 1988-91, U. Nebr., Lincoln, Nebr., 1985-87, legal rschr., 1987-88; legis. asst. Nebr. Legislature, Lincoln, Nebr., 1991; wetlands biologist Nebr. Dept. Roads, Lincoln, Nebr., 1991-93; environ. analyst supr. Nebr. Game and Parks Commn., Lincoln, Nebr., 1993-98, divsn. adminstr., legis. liaison, 1998—. Mem.: Lincoln Engrs. Club, Nebr. Bar Assn., Elks. Democrat. Home: 2637 Washington St Lincoln NE 68502-2955

BROILES, DAVID, lawyer; b. Ft. Worth, Feb. 23, 1938; s. Rowland and Hazel Broiles; m. Linda Broiles, Sept. 19, 1959 (div. Feb. 1, 1988); children: Jim, Lisa, Kathy; m. Patty Broiles, Nov. 10, 2000. BA, So. Meth. U., 1959, MA, 1960; PhD, Ohio State U., 1963; LLB cum laude, Yale U., 1968; LLM with distinction, Georgetown U., 1994; MLA, Tex. Christian U., 1997. Bar: Conn. 1968, Tex. 1972, U.S. Supreme Ct. 1972, U.S. Ct. Appeals (5th cir.), U.S. Ct. Appeals (D.C. cir.), U.S. Ct. Claims. Assoc. Jacobs Jacobs Grudberg & Clifford, New Haven, 1967—71; ptnr. Hooper Kerry Chappell & Broiles, Ft. Worth, 1971—78, Brown Herman Scott Dean & Miles, Ft. Worth, 1978—91, Kirkley Schmidt & Cotten, Ft. Worth, 1992—99; pvt. practice Ft. Worth, 1999—. Author: Moral Philosophy of David Hame, 1965; contbr. articles to profl. jours. Fellow: Am. Coll. Trial Lawyers. Democrat. Avocation: travel. Personal injury (including property damage), Appellate, Alternative dispute resolution. Home: 2400 Indian Cove Fort Worth TX 76108 Office: 1619 Pennsylvania Ave Fort Worth TX 76104

BROMBERG, JOHN E. lawyer; b. Dallas, May 9, 1946; s. Edward S. and Mildred J. (Rosenberg) B.; children from previous marriage: Spencer Harkness, Whitney Payne, Kemp Howitt, Campbell Wynne; m. Beth Jenkins; children: Susan Elizabeth, Melissa Anne. BA, Columbia U., 1968; JD, U. Tex., 1972. Bar: Tex. 1972. Chmn. Stutzman, Bromberg Esserman & Plifka PC, Dallas, 1984—. Past pres. Preston Hollow Park Assn., pre-sch. playground, Dallas. Mem. Am. Contract Bridge League (past pres. Dallas unit) Commercial, contracts (including sales of goods; commercial financing), Property, real (including real estate development, water). Home: 9 Hallshire Ct Dallas TX 75225-1824 Office: 2323 Bryan St Ste 2200 Dallas TX 75201-2655 E-mail: bromberg@sbep-law.com.

BROMBERG, MYRON JAMES, lawyer; b. Paterson, N.J., Nov. 5, 1934; s. Abraham and Elsie (Baker) B.; m. Lisa Murtha, Nov. 28, 1987; children— Kenneth Karl, Eric Edward, Bruce Abraham. BA, Yale U., 1956; LLB, Columbia U., 1959. Bar: N.J. bar 1960, N.Y. bar 1981. Law asst. to dist. atty., N.Y. County, 1958; law asst. U.S. atty. So. Dist. N.Y., 1958-59; asso. mem. firm Ralph Porzio, Morristown, N.J., 1960-61; ptnr. Porzio, Bromberg & Newman, Morristown, 1962-77, mng. prin., 1980-96. Atty. Morris County Bd. Elections, 1963-64; town atty., Town of Morristown, 1965-67; lectr. trial practice Rutgers Inst. CLE, 1965-94; mem. faculty Kraft-Eidson trial techniques seminar Emory U., 1997—. Chmn. fund and membership Morristown chpt. ARC, 1965; chmn. retail div. Community Chest Morris County, 1963; chmn. Keep Morristown Beautiful Com., 1963; mem. Morris Twp. Com., 1970-72; committeeman Morris County Democratic Com., 1962-63, 72-77; lay trustee Delbarton Sch., Morristown, 1972-75; trustee Morris Mus., 1973-79. Fellow Am. Coll. Trial Lawyers (chmn. com. on admission to fellowship 1986-91, com. on complex litigation 1992-98, com. on tchg. of trial and appellate advocacy 1998—), Am. Law Inst. (cons. group product libility), Am. Bar Found. (life); mem. ABA, Internat. Acad. Trial Lawyers (chair N.J. 1997-99, regional chair 3d jud. cir. 1997-2000, dir. 2002—), N.J. Bar Assn. (named outstanding young lawyer 1970, chmn. joint conf. com. with N.J. Med. Soc. 1970-72), Morris County Bar Assn., Am. Judicature Soc., Trial Attys. N.J. (pres. 1976-77, Trial Bar award 1989), Internat. Soc. Barristers (N.J. State chmn., bd. govs., sec.-treas. 1996-97, v.p. 1998-00, pres. 2000-01), Found. Internat. Soc. Barristers (pres. 2002—), Internat. Assn. Def. Counsel (chair com. on toxic and hazardous substances 1994-96, dir. Def. Counsel Trial Acad. 1996), Andover Alumni Assn. N.Y.C., Columbia U. Law Sch. Assn. of N.J. (bd. dirs. 1986-95, 2001—), Yale Club (N.Y.C. and ctrl. N.J.), Park Ave. (N.J.) Club, Chi Phi, Phi Delta Phi. Environmental, Product liability, Professional liability. Home: 9 Thompson Ct Morristown NJ 07960-6326 Office: PO Box 1997 100 Southgate Pkwy Morristown NJ 07962-1997 E-mail: mjbromberg@pbnlaw.com.

BROMBERG, ROBERT SHELDON, lawyer; b. Bklyn., May 3, 1935; s. Jack and Bertha (Toskey) B.; m. Barbara W. Schwartz, Apr. 1, 1978; children: Jason, David. AB, Columbia U., 1956, LLB, 1959; LLM in Taxation, NYU, 1966. Bar: N.Y. 1960, D.C. 1972, Ohio 1972, U.S. Ct. Claims 1976, U.S. Supreme Ct 1975. Practiced law, N.Y.C., 1960-66; atty. exempt orgns. br. IRS, Washington, 1966-70, Office Chief Counsel, 1970-72; partner firm Baker, Hostetler & Patterson, Cleve., 1972-79; prin. Robert S. Bromberg, L.P.A., Cleve., 1979-81, Paxton & Seasongood, Cin., 1981-85; sole practice Cin., 1985—. Lectr. tax and health law confs. Author: Tax Planning for Hospitals and Health Care Organizations, 2 vols., 1979; cons. editor: Prentice Hall Tax Exempt Organizations Service, 1973-84; nat. adv. bd. Integrated Healthcare Report; adv. bd. The Exempt Organization Tax Review; contbr. articles to profl. jours. Recipient award (5) Dept. Treasury, 1966-72, citation Am. Assn. Homes for Aged, 1973 Mem. Am. Health Lawyers Assn. (pres. 1986-87, program chmn. Ann. Tax Inst. 1975-95). Home and Office: 1144 E Rookwood Dr Cincinnati OH 45208-3334

BROME, THOMAS REED, lawyer; b. NYC, Aug. 24, 1942; s. Robert Harrison and Mary Elizabeth (Reed) B.; m. Marie Olszewski, June 5, 1971; children: Clinton Reed, Bethan, Heather. AB, Harvard Coll., 1964; LLB, NYU, 1967. Bar: DC 1967, NY 1968. Law clk. to hon. Warren E. Burger U.S. Ct. Appeals, Washington, 1967-68; assoc. Cravath, Swaine & Moore, NYC, 1968-75, ptnr., 1975—. Dir. Legal Aid Soc., NYC, 1989-98, pres., 1994-96. V.p. sch. bd., Ridgewood, NJ, 1989—90, pres., 1991—92; trustee NYU Law Ctr. Found., NY, 1992—2003, vice chair, 2001—; pres. Ridgewood Pub. Edn. Found., NJ, 1993—96. Mem. ABA, NY State Bar Assn., Assn. Bar of City of NY Republican. Episcopalian. Corporate, general, Finance, Securities. Home: 500 Knollwood Rd Ridgewood NJ 07450-4700 Office: Cravath Swaine & Moore 825 8th Ave New York NY 10019-7475

BROMLEY, MARILYN MODLIN, librarian; b. Cleve., Mar. 14, 1951; d. Robert A. and Helen F. (Hicks) Modlin; m. Haworth P. Bromley, Nov. 7, 1987. BA magna cum laude, Randolph-Macon Woman's Coll., 1973; MSLS, Cath. U. Am., 1978. Librarian ICF Inc., Washington, 1978-83, Bur. Nat. Affairs Inc., Washington, 1983—94, libr. dir., 1994—. Editor: Direct-Line Distances: U.S. Edition, 1986, Direct-Line Distances: International Edition, 1986, BNA's Directory of State Courts, Judges and Clerks, 1986. Recipient Dialog Corp. Infostar award, 2002. Mem. Spl. Librs. Assn. (treas. Washington chpt. 1984-87, 96-99, bd. dirs. 1988-90, v.p., pres.-elect 1991-92, pres. 1992-93, bylaws com. 2001-03), Phi Beta Kappa, Beta Phi Mu. Episcopalian. Office: Bur Nat Affairs Inc 1231 25th St NW Washington DC 20037-1197 E-mail: mbromley@bna.com.

BRONFIN, FRED, lawyer; b. New Orleans, Nov. 30, 1918; m. Carolyn Pick; children by previous marriage: Daniel R., Kenneth A. BA, Tulane U., 1938, JD, 1941. Bar: La. 1941, U.S. Dist. Ct. (ea. dist.) La. 1941, U.S. Ct. Appeals (5th cir.) 1951, U.S. Supreme Ct. 1973. Assoc. Rittenberg & Rittenberg, New Orleans, 1946-50; ptnr. Rittenberg, Weinstein & Bronfin, New Orleans, 1950-60, Weinstein & Bronfin, New Orleans, 1960-63, Bronfin, Heller, Steinberg & Berins and precessor firms, New Orleans, 1963-91; of counsel Bronfin & Heller, 1991-98, Heller, Draper, Hayden, Patrick & Horn, 1998—. With USN, 1942-46. Mem. ABA, La. Bar Assn., New Orleans Bar Assn., Order of Coif, Phi Beta Kappa. Office: Heller Draper Hayden Et Al 650 Poydras St Ste 2500 New Orleans LA 70130-6175 E-mail: fbronfin@hellerdraper.com.

BRONIS, STEPHEN JAY, lawyer; b. Miami, Fla., Feb. 23, 1947; s. Larry and Thelma (Berger) B.; children: Jason Michael, Tyler Adam, Kenneth Lawrence. BSBA, U. Fla., 1969; JD, Duke U., 1972. Bar: Fla. 1972, D.C. 1973, U.S. Dist. Ct. (so. dist.) Fla. 1973, U.S. Ct. Appeals (5th cir.) 1977, U.S. Supreme Ct. 1978, U.S. Ct. Appeals (11th cir.) 1981, U.S. Dist. Ct. (mid. dist.) Fla. 1989, Colo. 1994, U.S. Dist. Ct. Colo. 1996, U.S. Ct. Appeals (10th cir.) 1996, U.S. Tax Ct. 1998. Asst. pub. defender 11th Jud. Cir. Fla., Miami, 1972-75; ptnr. Rosen & Bronis, P.A., Miami, 1975-77, Rosen, Portela, Bronis, et al, Miami, 1977-82, Bronis & Potela, P.A., Miami, 1982-90; pvt. practice Miami, 1990-93; ptnr. Davis, Scott, Weber & Edwards, Miami, 1993-95, Zuckerman, Spaeder, LLP, Miami, 1996—. Mem. faculty Nat. Inst. of Trial Adv., U. N.C., Yeshiva U, Nova Sch. Law; appointed to Fla. Supreme Ct. Commn. on Professionalism, 2000—; Fla. Bar rep. to 11th Cir. Jur. Conf., 2001—. Contbr. articles to profl. jours. Recipient Am. Jurisprudence award Bancroft-Whitney Co., 1972. Mem. ABA (ho. of dels. 1999—, Fla. rep. 2000—, chmn. def. function com. of criminal justice sect. 2001--), ATLA, Nat. Criminal Def. Attys. Assn., Am. Bd. Criminal Lawyers (v.p. 1981-82), Fla. Criminal Def. Attys. Assn. (Outstanding Svc. award 1981), Calif. Attys. Criminal Justice, Acad. Fla. Trial Lawyers (criminal law sect. dir.). Democrat. General civil litigation, Corporate, general, Criminal. Home: 3 Grove Isle Dr Apt 1506 Miami FL 33133-4103 Office: 201 S Biscayne Blvd Ste 900 Miami FL 33131-4326 E-mail: sbronis@zuckerman.com.

BRONNER, JAMES RUSSELL, retired lawyer; b. Chgo., Nov. 14, 1943; s. Maurice Henry and Elaine R. (Rosenberg) B.; m. Barbara Henley, July 3, 1968; children: Michael, Jamie. BA, U. Mich., 1965; JD, Northwestern U.,

1968, LLM, 1970. Bar: Ill. 1968, U.S. Dist. Ct. (no. dist.) Ill. 1968, U.S. Ct. Appeals (7th cir.) 1969. Asst. prof. law sch. Northwestern U., Chgo., 1970-72; ptnr. Davis, Miner, Barnhill & Bronner, Chgo., 1972-75; prin. Ct. Club Cir., Chgo., 1975-82; ptnr. Speakers Sport, Inc., Northbrook, Ill., 1976-2000; exec. v.p. SFX Sports, Northbrook, 2000-01, ret., 2001. Lectr. law sch. Northwestern U., 1972-79; vice chmn. Gov.'s Com. on State Salaries, Chgo., 1978. Exec. v.p. Chgo. Shakespeare Repertory Co., 1988-91; masters chmn. U.S. Team for 1993, open sports chmn., 1997 World Maccabiah Games. Named Northwestern Law Sch. Disting Alumni Sports, 2002; fellow, Ford Found., 1968—70. Mem. ABA, Am. Arbitration Assn. (panel mem. 2001—), Chgo. Bar Assn., Nat. Ct. Club Assn. (pres. 1980). Sports.

BRONSON, MERIDITH J. lawyer; b. N.Y.C., Dec. 4, 1958; d. Ira D. and Carolyn Bronson; children: Logan Alexa, Jordan Alanna. BA, Drew U., 1980; JD, Seton Hall U., 1984. Cert. matrimonial atty. Jud. law clk., Newark, N.J., 1984-85; ptnr. Stern Steiger Croland, Paramus, 1985-95, Shapiro & Croland, Hackensack, N.J., 1995—. Master Family Law Inns of Ct., N.J., 1996—. Mem. Phi Beta Kappa. Family and matrimonial. Office: Shapiro & Croland 411 Hackensack Ave Fl 6 Hackensack NJ 07601-6365

BRONSTEIN, ALVIN J. lawyer; b. Bklyn., June 8, 1928; LLD, N.Y. Law Sch., 1951, LLD (hon.), 1990. Bar: N.Y. 1952, Miss. 1967, La. 1971, U.S. Ct. Appeals (D.C., 1st, 2d, 3d, 4th, 5th, 9th, 10th and 11th cirs.), U.S. Supreme Ct. 1961. Ptnr. Bronstein & Bronstein, Bklyn., 1952-63; pvt. practice Elizabethtown, N.Y., 1963-64; chief staff counsel Lawyers Constl. Def. Com., Jackson, Miss., 1964-68; fellow Inst. Politics, Kennedy Sch. Govt. Harvard U., Cambridge, Mass., 1968-69, assoc. dir. Inst. Politics, Kennedy Sch. Govt., 1969-71; ptnr. Elie, Bronstein, Strickler & Dennis, New Orleans, 1971-72; exec. dir. Nat. Prison Project, Nat. Jail Project ACLU Found., Washington, 1972-96, cons. nat. legal dept., 1996—. Cons., trial counsel CORE, NAACP, NAACP Legal Def. Fund, SCLC, SNCC, Miss. Freedom Dem. Party, Black Panther Party, Nat. Inst. for Edn. in Law and Poverty, and others; guest lectr. various law schs., 1964—; cons. various state corrections depts., 1972—; adj. prof. Am. U. Law Sch., 1973; expert witness in various prison litigations, 1978—; appointed mem. Fed. Jud. Ctr. Adv. Com. on Experimentation in the Law, 1978-81. Contbg. author: The Evolution of Criminal Justice, 1978, Prisoners' Rights Sourcebook, Vol. II, 1980, Confinement in Maximum Custody, 1980, Sage Criminal Justice Annual, Vol. 14, 1980, Readings in the Justice Model, 1980, Our Endangered Rights, 1984, Prisoners and the Courts: The American Experience, 1985; author: (with Rudovsky and Koren) The Rights of Prisoners, 1988; author, editor: Representing Prisoners, 1981; editor: Prisoners' Self-Help Litigation Manual, 1977; contbr. articles to profl. jours. MacArthur Found. fellow, 1989; named one of the 100 most influential lawyers in Am., Nat. Law Jour., 1985, 88, 91, 94; recipient Roscoe Pound award Nat. Coun. on Crime and Delinquency, 1981, Karl Menninger award Fortune Soc., 1982, Pa. Prison Soc. award, 1991. Office: Penai Eform Internat 1120 19th St NW Washington DC 20036

BRONSTEIN, RICHARD M. lawyer; b. N.Y.C., Feb. 20, 1945; s. Benjamin and Betty Bronstein; m. Ethel Leder; children: Rachel, Susan. BS, Queens Coll., 1965; JD, NYU, 1968. Bar: N.Y. 1969, U.S. Dist. Ct. (so. and ea. dists.) N.Y. 1971. Assoc. N.Y. State Divsn. Human Rights, N.Y.C., 1969-71; asst. dist. atty. Suffolk County Dist. Atty.'s Office, Riverhead, N.Y., 1972-79; assoc. Lustig & Bronstein, Deer Park, N.Y., 1979-94; pvt. practice Central Islia, N.Y., 1994—. Fin. v.p. North Shore Jewish Ctr., Port Jefferson Station, N.Y., 1994-95. Mem. ATLA, N.Y. State Trial Lawyers Assn., Suffolk County Bar Assn. Avocations: golf, tennis, skiing. General civil litigation, Criminal. Office: 115 Carleton Ave # 100 Central Islip NY 11722-3619

BRONSTEIN, ROBERT, retired lawyer; b. East Chicago, Ind., Dec. 8, 1919; s. Phillip and Sarah (Gross) B.; m. Sonia Zeidman, July 4, 1922; children: Eric, Scott. MA in Sociology, U. Chgo., 1948, JD, 1951. Bar: Ill. 1951, Colo. 1961. Dir. mgmt. analysis State of Colo., 1961-64, dir. budget, 1964-70, coordinator environ. problems, 1970-72; sec. Colo. Environ. Commn., 1970-72; project dir. Boulder (Colo.) Area Growth Study, 1972, mgmt. cons., 1973-75; asst. dept. dir. Colo. Dept. Labor and Employment, 1975-76; assoc. dir. Colo. Div. Employment and Tng., 1976-80; pvt. practice Denver, 1981-2000; ret., 2000. Faculty U. Denver Grad Sch. Pub. Adminstrn., 1973, U. Colo. Grad. Sch. Pub. Affairs, 1973. Writer screenplays, books. Bd. dirs. Colo. Citizens Com. on Govt., 1975-79, Citizens Inquiry into Colo. Constitution, 1977; mem. arbitration panel Am. Arbitration Assn., Better Bus. Bur., Denver County Assessment Appeals, Nat. Assn. Securities Dealers, 1985-95; mediator Ctr. Dispute Resolution, 1984-87. Lt. USAF, 1941—45, lt. col. USAF, 1960, ret. USAF, 1960. Mem. ACLU, Common Cause. Alternative dispute resolution, Criminal, Family and matrimonial. Home: 2457 S Dahlia Ln Denver CO 80222-6119

BROOKE, EDWARD WILLIAM, lawyer, former senator; b. Washington, Oct. 26, 1919; s. Edward W. and Helen (Seldon) B. BS, Howard U., 1940, LL.D., 1967; LL.B. (editor Law Rev.), Boston U., 1948, LL.M., 1949, LL.D., 1968, George Washington U., 1967, Skidmore Coll., 1969, U. Mass., 1971, Amherst Coll., 1972; D.Sc., Lowell Tech. Inst., 1967; D.Sc. numerous other hon. degrees. Bar: Mass. 1948, D.C. Ct. Appeals 1979, D.C. Dist. Ct. 1982, U.S. Supreme Ct. 1962. Chmn. Boston Fin. Com., 1961-62; atty. gen. State of Mass., Boston, 1963-66; mem. U.S. Senate from Mass., 1967-79; chmn. Nat. Low-Income Housing Coalition; former ptnr. O'Connor & Hannan, Washington; formrly of counsel Csaplar & Bok, Boston. Former pub. mem. Adminstrv. Conf. U.S.; chmn. bd. dirs. Boston Bank Commerce; bd. dirs. Meditrust, Inc., Wellesley, Mass., Grumman Corp., Bethpage, N.Y. Chmn. Boston Opera Co.; former commr. Pres.'s Commns. on Housing and of Wartime Relocation and Internment of Civilians; bd. dirs. Washington Performing Arts Soc. Served as capt. inf. AUS, World War II, ETO. Decorated Bronze Star; recipient Disting. Svc. award Amvets, 1952, Charles Evans Hughes award NCCJ, 1967, Springarn medal, NAACP, 1967 Fellow Am. Bar Assn., Am. Acad. Arts and Scis. Office: 6437 Blantyre Rd Warrenton VA 20187-7147

BROOKE, WILLIAM WADE, business executive, lawyer; b. Baton Rouge, Apr. 5, 1956; s. Frederick Dixon and Sybil Stringer (Vogtle) B.; m. Margaret Lee Williamson, June 2, 1979; children: William W. Jr., Robert A., Sarah M. BA in Gen. Bus. Mgmt., U. Ala., 1978, JD, 1981. Bar: Ala. 1981. Assoc. Burr & Forman, Birmingham, Ala., 1981-87; mng. ptnr. Wallace, Brooke & Byers, Birmingham, 1987-91; gen. counsel Harbert Corp., Birmingham, 1991-94, COO, 1995—2001; exec. v.p. and mng. dir. Venture Capital, 2001—; chmn. Harbert Realty Svcs., Inc., 1998—. Trustee Bus. Coun. Alabama, 1998—. Trustee Discovery 2000 Mus., Birmingham, 1987-2000; trustee Mountain Brook City Schs. Found., 1993—, pres., 1995-97, chmn., 1997—; trustee Ctrl. Alabama United Way, 1998—, Cornerstone Schs. Ala., 1996—; bd. visitors U. Ala. CSBA Sch., 2001—. Mem. ABA, Ala. Bar Assn., Birmingham Bar Assn., Rotary. Republican. Presbyterian. Avocations: sport fishing, golf, reading. Banking, Commercial, contracts (including sales of goods; commercial financing), Corporate, general. Office: Harbert Mgmt Corp 1 Riverchase Pkwy S Birmingham AL 35244-2008 E-mail: wbrooke@harbert.net., will@wbrooke.com.

BROOKMAN, ANTHONY RAYMOND, lawyer; b. Chgo., Mar. 23, 1922; s. Raymond Charles and Marie Clara (Alberg) B.; m. Marilyn Joyce Brookman, June 5, 1982; children: Meribeth Brookman Farmer, Anthony Raymond, Lindsay Logan Christensen. Student, Ripon Coll., 1940-41; BS, Northwestern U., 1947; JD, U. Calif., San Francisco, 1953. Bar: Calif. 1954. Law clk. to presiding justice Calif. Supreme Ct., 1953-54; ptnr. Nichols, Williams, Morgan, Digardi & Brookman, 1954-68; sr. ptnr. Brookman & Talbot, Inc. (formerly Brookman & Hoffman, Inc.), Walnut Creek, Calif., 1969-92, Brookman & Talbot Inc., Sacramento, 1992—. Pres. Young Reps. Calif., San Mateo County, 1953-54. 1st lt. USAF. Mem. ABA, Alameda County Bar Assn., State Bar Calif., Lawyers Club Alameda County, Alameda-Contra Costa County Trial Lawyers Assn., Assn. Trial Lawyers Am., Calif. Trial Lawyers Assn., Athenian Nile Club, Masons, Shriners. Republican. General civil litigation, State civil litigation, Personal injury (including property damage). Office: 901 H St Ste 200 Sacramento CA 95814-1808 also: Ste B-201 675 Ygnacio Valley Rd Walnut Creek CA 94596 also: 1746 Grand Canal Blvd Ste 11 Stockton CA 95207-8111

BROOKS, DAVID EUGENE, lawyer; b. Chickasha, Okla., Apr. 14, 1953; s. Shirey Sherman and Joyce Faye Brooks; m. Victoria Lynn Ward, Aug. 11, 1973; children: Kristina Kaye, Leah Kathene, Stephen Sherman. BA, Southwestern Okla. State U., 1975; JD, U. Tulsa, 1978. Bar: Okla. 1978, U.S. Dist. Ct. (we. dist.) Okla. 1979. Pvt. practice, Chickasha, 1978-81; assoc. dist. judge State of Okla., Mangum, 1981-91, asst. dist. atty. Sayre, 1991-92; pvt. practice Sayre, 1992—. Pres. bd. Beckham County Law Libr., Sayre, 1996—. Mem. Beckham County Bar Assn. (pres. 1993), Kiwanis of Mangum (pres. 1984), Masons (master, 33 degree). Methodist. Criminal, Family and matrimonial, General practice. Office: Brooks and Israel 119 E Main St Sayre OK 73662-2913 Fax: 580-928-2648. E-mail: davidbrooks@cableone.net.

BROOKS, JOHN WHITE, lawyer; b. Long Beach, Calif., Sept. 3, 1936; s. John White and Florence Belle (O'Grady) B.; m. Elizabeth Ann Bellmore, June 21, 1958; children: Stephen Sanford, John Tinley. AB, Stanford U., 1958, LLB, 1966. Assoc. Luce, Forward, Hamilton and Scripps, San Diego, 1966-71, ptnr., 1971-81, sr. ptnr., 1981—; chmn. Internat. Svcs. Group, 1989—. Mem. Internat. Coun. Inst. Ams., Pacific Coun. Internat. Policy. 1996-98; panelist Ctr. for Internat. Comml. Arbitration, 1987—; bd. dirs. Union of Pan-Asian Communities, , 1989-98, Ctr. for Dispute Resolution, 1986—; chmn. Pacific Rim Adv. Coun., 1984-91. Author: Passport Pal, The Pacific Rim, 1996—, The Heads Up Report; contbr. articles to profl. jours. Mem. Commn. of the Californias, 1977—79; chmn. San Diego Regional Yr. 2000 Working Group, 1998—2000; dir. Corp. Fin. Coun. of San Diego, 1977—82, chmn., 1980—81; bd. visitors Stanford Law Sch., 1978—80. With USN, 1958—63. Named Alfred P. Sloan scholar Stanford U., 1958, Rocky Mountain Mineral Law Found. Research scholar, 1966. Mem. ABA (bus. law sect., com. on internat. commercial transactions, subcom. on Asia-Pacific law and internat. bus. structures and agreements, com. on negotiated transactions, internat. law sect., subcom. on multinat. corps., com. on internat. comml. transactions), Calif. Bar Assn. (bus. law sect. com. on corps. 1977, vice chmn. com. on internat. practice 1986-87, exec. com. internat. law sect. 1987), San Diego County Bar Assn., Internat. Bar Assn. (com. on issues and trading in securities 1980-89, com. on procedures for settling disputes 1980—, com. on bus. orgns. 1989—), Inter-Pacific Bar Assn. (com. on internat. trade), Am. Arbitration Assn. (panel of arbitrators 1975-96), State Bar Calif. Avocations: greenhouse gardening, horse competitions, helicopters, wine, food. Private international, Mergers and acquisitions, Securities. Office: Luce Forward Hamilton & Scripps 600 W Broadway Ste 2600 San Diego CA 92101-3372 E-mail: jwbrooks@luce.com.

BROOKS, LARRY ROGER, judge; b. Oklahoma City, Mar. 8, 1949; s. Stanley James and Dorothy Marguerite (Miller) B.; m. Rebecca Jean Nix, June 5, 1971. BS in Agronomy, Okla. State U., 1971, MS in Agronomy, 1973; JD, U. Okla., 1976. Bar: Okla. 1976. Pvt. practice law, Idabel, Okla., 1977; asst. dist. atty. Craig County Dist. Attys. Office, Vinita, Okla., 1978, Logan County Dist. Attys. Office, Guthrie, Okla., 1979-94; assoc. judge Dist. Ct., Logan County, Okla., 1995—. Ch. bd. mem. Guthrie (Okla.) Ch. of the Nazarene. Mem. Okla. Bar Assn., Guthrie Lions Club (pres. 1991-92), Train Collectors Assn., Nat. Ry. Hist. Soc. Avocations: toy train and railroad memorabilia, railroad history, riding trains. Home: 324 N Capitol St Guthrie OK 73044-3640 Office: Assoc Dist Judge Logan County Courthouse Guthrie OK 73044

BROOKS, LORIMER PAGE, patent lawyer; b. Swampscott, Mass., May 11, 1917; s. William Lorimer and Maude (Page) B.; m. Arlene M. Cook, Nov. 9, 1941; children: Lorraine E. Brooks Phillips, Jr., Rosalind P. Brooks O'Malley. BS in elec. engring. with honors, Northeastern U., 1939; JD, Fordham U., 1948; postgrad., NYU Law Sch., 1951. Bar: N.Y. 1948, U.S. Dist. Ct. (so. dist.) N.Y. 1952, U.S. Dist. Ct. (ea. dist.) N.Y. 1957, U.S. Ct. Appeals (2d cir.) 1964, U.S. Dist. Ct. (we. dist.) N.Y. 1971, U.S. Supreme Ct. 1971, U.S. Ct. Appeals (fed. cir.) 1982. Patent agt. ITT, 1939-41, patent atty., 1945-50, Ward, Crosby, & Neal, N.Y.C., 1950-54; ptnr. firm Ward, McElhannon, Brooks & Fitzpartrick, N.Y.C., 1954-71, Brooks, Haidt, Haffner & Delahunty, N.Y.C., 1971-98; ptnr. Norris McLaughlin & Marcus, PA, N.Y.C., 1998—. Rep. Nat. Council Patent Law Assns., 1976-77. Patentee in field. Sec. Westchester Park Citizens Assn., 1950-52, pres., 1952-54; dir. Westchester County Cerebral Palsy Assn., 1962-64; mem. Young Men's Republican Club Eastchester, N.Y., 1952-56. Served with AUS, 1941-45. Mem. Westchester County Bar Assn. (ethics com. 1978-86), N.Y. Patent Law Assn. (bd. govs. 1961-64, 74-78, chmn. subcom. practice and procedure in cts. 1961-62, chmn. com. ethics and grievances 1973-74, 1st v.p. 1974-75, pres. 1975-76, past pres. com. 1976—), IEEE, Aircraft Owners and Pilots Assn., Tau Beta Pi. Patent, Trademark and copyright. Home: 6 Hyatt Rd Briarcliff Manor NY 10510-2610 Office: Norris McLaughlin and Marcus 220 East 42nd St New York NY 10017

BROOKS, NORMA NEWTON, legal assistant; b. Granite, Okla., Oct. 30, 1936; d. Ralph David and Bessie M. (Elkins) Newton; m. Rex Dwain Brooks, May 16, 1964; children: Jonathan Douglas, Elizabeth Ann. Student, U. Okla., 1979, BS in Edn., 1970; MEd, Ctrl. State U., 1972. Cert. secondary sch. tchr., Okla. Legal asst. Rex D. Brooks Atty.-At-Law, Oklahoma City, 1974—. Mem. Am. Home Econs. Assn., Women in the Arts, Kappa Delta Pi. Baptist. Avocations: art, education. Home: 2323 N Indiana Ave Oklahoma City OK 73106-1632 Office: Rex D Brooks Atty-At-Law 1900 NW 23rd St Oklahoma City OK 73106-1202

BROOKS, PATRICK WILLIAM, lawyer; b. May 11, 1943; s. Mark Dana and Madge Ellen (Walker) B.; m. Mary Jane Davey, Dec. 17, 1966; children: Carolyn Walker, Mark William. BA, State Coll. Iowa, 1966; JD, U. Iowa, 1971. Bar: Iowa 1971, U.S. dist. Ct. (so. dist.) Iowa 1972, U.S. Sup. Ct. 1974, U.S. Ct. apls. (8th cir.) 1979. Tchr. Waterloo (Iowa) Cmty. Schs., 1966-68; mem. staff Donahue & Brooks, West Union, Iowa, 1971-72; ptnr. Mowry, Irvine, Brooks & Ward, Marshalltown, Iowa, 1972-84, 92—, Brooks, Ward & Trout, Marshalltown, Iowa, 1984-92. Mem. Fayette County (Iowa) Republican Ctrl. com., chmn. platform resolutions com., 1971-72; pres. Marshall County Young Reps., 1974; trustee Iowa Law Sch. Found., 1970-71; bd. dirs. Iowa Hist. Found., 1991-96. Mem. Am. Judicature Soc., Iowa Bar Assn., Marshall County Bar Assn. (pres. 1985-86), Iowa Trial Lawyers Assn., Iowa Def. Counsel Assn., Buick Am. Club (bd. dir. 2001—). Lutheran. Avocation: international road rally driver and mechanic. Federal civil litigation, Insurance, Personal injury (including property damage). Office: Box 908 6 W Main St Marshalltown IA 50158-4941

BROOKS, SONDRA, lawyer; b. Bklyn., Mar. 29, 1957; d. Frank Harry and Roslyn Louise Brooks; m. Lance Hillel Edwards, May 29, 1982; children: Devon Wesley, Alexandra Nell. BS, SUNY, Stony Brook, 1978; JD, Syracuse U., 1981. Bar: N.Y. 1982, U.S. Dist. Ct. (so. dist.) N.Y. 1982, U.S. Supreme Ct. 1985. Asst. dist. atty. Nassau County Dist. Attys. Office, Mineola, N.Y., 1981-87; asst. county atty. Suffolk County Attys. Office, Hauppauge, N.Y., 1987-88; ptnr. Boland & Brooks, Smithtown, N.Y., 1988—. Legal cons. Plaza Employment Agy., Lynbrook, N.Y., 1981—, Suffolk Ob-gyn. Assn., Pt. Jefferson, N.Y., 1981—. Editor Deviance and Delinquency, 1978, Syracuse Law Rev., 1980-81. Named Hon. Asst. Atty. Gen., State Ark., 1983, Outstanding Young Women of Am., 1986. Mem. NOW, Nassau County Bar Assn., Suffolk County Womens Bar Assn. (award 1995). Jewish. Avocations: skiing, tennis, reading, flying, travel. Criminal, Family and matrimonial, Personal injury (including property damage). Home: 12 Crane Neck Rd East Setauket NY 11733-1628 Office: 222 E Main St Ste 212 Smithtown NY 11787-2814

BROOKS, SUSAN W. prosecutor; Grad., Miami U.; JD, Ind. U. Ptnr. McClure, McClure & Kammen, 1985—88, Kammen & Brooks, 1989—97; dep. mayor Indpls., 1998—99; of counsel Ice Miller Law Firm , Indpls., 2000—01; U.S. atty. so. dist. Ind., 2001—. Office: 10 W Market St Ste 2100 Indianapolis IN 46204 Office Fax: 317-226-6125.

BROOMFIELD, ROBERT CAMERON, federal judge; b. Detroit, June 18, 1933; s. David Campbell and Mabel Margaret (Van Deventer) B.; m. Cuma Lorena Cecil, Aug. 3, 1958; children: Robert Cameron Jr., Alyson Paige, Scott McKinley. BS, Pa. State U., 1955; LLB, U. Ariz., 1961. Bar: Ariz. 1961, U.S. Dist. Ct. Ariz. 1961. Assoc. Carson, Messinger, Elliot, Laughlin & Ragan, Phoenix, 1962-65, ptnr., 1966-71; judge Ariz. Superior Ct., Phoenix, 1971-85, presiding judge, 1974-85; judge U.S. Dist. Ct. Ariz., Phoenix, 1985—, chief judge, 1994-99; judge Fgn. Intelligence Surveillance Ct., 2003—. Faculty Nat. Jud. Coll., Reno, 1975-82. Contbr. articles to profl. jours. Adv. bd. Boy Scouts Am., Phoenix, 1968-75; tng. com. Ariz. Acad., Phoenix, 1980—; pres. Paradise Valley Sch. Bd., Phoenix, 1969-70; bd. dirs. Phoenix Together, 1982—, Crisis Nursery, Phoenix, 1976-81; chmn. 9th Cir. Task Force on Ct. Reporting, 1988—; space and facilities com. U.S. Jud. Conf., 1987-93, chmn., 1989-93, chmn. security, space and facilities com., 1993-95, budget com., 1997—; founding mem. Sandra Day O'Connor Inn of Ct., 1988-94. Recipient Faculty award Nat. Jud. Coll., 1979, Disting. Jurist award Miss. State U., 1986. Mem. ABA (chmn. Nat. Conf. State Trial Judges 1983-84, pres. Nat. Conf. Met. Cts. 1978-79, chmn. bd. dirs. 1980-82, Justice Tom Clark award 1980, bd. dirs. Nat. Ctr. for State Cts. 1980-85, Disting. Svc. award 1986), Ariz. Bar Assn., Maricopa County Bar Assn. (Disting. Pub. Svc. award 1980), Ariz. Judges Assn. (pres. 1981-82), Am. Judicature Soc. (spl. citation 1985), Maricopa County Med. Soc. (Disting. Svc. medal 1979). Lodges: Rotary. Office: US Dist Ct Sandra Day O'Connor Cthse 401 West Washington St #626 SPC 61 Phoenix AZ 85003-2158

BROOTEN, KENNETH EDWARD, JR., retired lawyer, rancher, author, chief counsel United States Congress; b. Kirkland, Wash., Oct. 17, 1942; s. Kenneth Edward Sr. and Sadie Josephine (Assad) B.; m. Patricia Anne Folsom, Aug. 29, 1965 (div. Apr. 1986); children: Michelle Catherine, Justin Kenneth; m. Judy Diane Robinette, July 14, 2001. Diploma, Lewis Sch. Hotel, Restaurant and Club Mgmt., Washington, 1963; student, U. Md., 1964-66; AA with honors, Santa Fe C.C., Gainesville, Fla., 1969; BS in Journalism with highest honors, U. Fla., 1971, MA in Journalism and Communications with highest honors, 1972, JD with honors, 1975; law student, U. Idaho, 1972-73; diploma in internat. law, Polish Acad. Scis., Warsaw, 1974; postgrad. in Internat. Law, Trinity Coll.,Cambridge (Eng.) U., 1974. Bar: Fla., D.C., U.S. Dist. Ct. (no., mid. and so. dists.) Fla., U.S. Dist. Ct. D.C., U.S. Tax Ct., U.S. Ct. Appeals (5th, 9th, 11th and D.C. circs.), U.S. Supreme Ct., Trial Counsel Her Majesty's Govt. of United Kingdom. Asst. to several congressmen U.S. Ho. of Reps., Washington, 1962-67; adminstrv. asst. VA Cen. Office, Washington, 1967; adminstrv. officer VA Hosp., Gainesville, Fla., 1967-72; ptnr. Carter & Brooten, P.A., Gainesville, Fla., 1975-78, Brooten & Fleisher, Chartered, Washington and Gainesville, Fla., 1978-80; pvt. practice, Washington and Gainesville, 1980-86, Washington, 1987-88, Washington and Orlando, Fla., 1988-91, Washington and Winter Park, Fla., 1991-98; ret., 1998. Permanent spl. counsel, acting chief counsel, dir. Select Com. Assassinations U.S. Ho. of Reps., 1976-77; counsel Her Majesty's Govt. of U.K. (in U.S.). Author: Malpractice Guide to Avoidance and Treatment, 1987; episode writer TV series Simon and Simon; nat. columnist Pvt. Practice, 1988-90, Physicians Mgmt., 1991-93; commentator Med. News Network, 1993-94; contbr. more than 250 articles to profl. jours.; composer. Served with USCGR, 1960-68. Named one of Outstanding Young Men Am., U.S. Jaycees, 1977. Mem. Fla. Bar Assn., D.C. Bar Assn., Sigma Delta Chi. Roman Catholic. Avocations: writing, marksmanship, dangerous game hunting. Federal civil litigation, Family and matrimonial, Public international. Address: The Oxbow Ranch Bascom FL 32423-9361

BROPHY, GILBERT THOMAS, lawyer; b. Southampton, N.Y., July 15, 1926; s. Joseph Lester and Helen Veronica (Scholtz) B.; m. Canora Woodham Brophy, Sept. 3, 1957; m. Isabel Blair Porter; children: Laure Porter Thompson, Erin Brophy Caraballo. BS in Acctg. with high honors, U. Fla., 1949; LLB, George Washington U., 1960; postgrad., U. Miami, 1970-73. Bar: Fla. 1960, U.S. Supreme Ct. 1965, U.S. Dist. Ct. D.C. 1970, D.C. 1974. Title examiner Jesse Phillips Klinge & Kendrick, Arlington, Va., 1959-60; ptnr. Beall, Beall & Brophy, Palm Beach, Fla., 1962-65; asst. city atty. West Palm Beach, Fla., 1965-67; ptnr. Brophy & Skrandel, Palm Beach, 1968-70, Brophy & Aksomitas, Tequesta, Fla., 1974-75, Brophy, Genovese & Sayler, Jupiter, Fla., 1977-78, Brophy & Genovese, 1978-83; town atty. Lantana, Fla., 1967-70; judge ad litem Village of Tequesta, 1970-72; town atty. Jupiter, 1974-75. Bd. dirs., disaster chmn. ARC, Palm Beach; past corr. sec. Palm Beach County Hist. Soc.; del. Fla. Caucus for Presidency, 1979, 87; mem. Rep. Com. Martin County, 1984-87. With AUS, 1944-46, ETO, USA, 1951-54, FECOM, Japan and Korea. Recipient Dedicated Svc. plaque Town of Jupiter, 1975. Mem. NRA (endowment), Nat. CIC Assn., Assn. Former Intelligence Officers (life), Attys. Title Ins. Fund, Fla. Bar, Palm Beach County Bar Assn., Attys. Bar Assn. Palm Beach County, Rotary Club (pres. 1977-78, dist. 6930 ethics chair-4 way test, Paul Harris fellow), Univ. Club (Washington), Elks, Everglades Rifle and Pistol Club (hon. life), Kappa Sigma Alumni. Family and matrimonial, General practice, Probate (including wills, trusts). Home: 717 S US Highway 1-504 Jupiter FL 33477-5905 Office: 810 Saturn St Ste 16 Jupiter FL 33477-4398

BROSSEIT, A. KIMBERLY ROCKWELL, lawyer; b. Atlanta, Mar. 22, 1968; d. Ramon Richard and Alice (Scott) Rockwell; m. Brett Anthony Brosseit, Aug. 17, 1996. BA, Bryn Mawr Coll., 1990; JD with high honors, Fla. State U., 1996. Bar: Fla. 1996, D.C. 1998, Del. 1998. Atty. Treiser Koboza & Volpe, Chartered, Naples, Fla., 1996-97, Duane Morris & Hecksher LLP, Wilmington, Del., 1998-99, Klehr Harrison Harvey Branzburg & Ellers. LLP, Wilmington, Del., 1999-2000, Blank Rome Comisky & McCauley, LLP, Wilmington, Del., 2000—. Grad. Leadership Del. 1998; pro-bono counsel Ctrl. Del. Habitat for Humanity, 1999—. Land use and zoning (including planning), Property, real (including real estate development, water). Office: Blank Rome Comisky & McCauley LLP 1201 Market St Ste 1200 Wilmington DE 19801-1163

BROTHERTON, KATHRYN PIELE, lawyer; b. Springfield, Oreg., Oct. 16, 1972; d. Philip Kern and Sandra Jean Piele. BA magna cum laude, U. Ariz., 1993; JD, U. Oreg., 1997. Bar: Oreg. 1998, U.S. Dist. Ct. Oreg. 1999, U.S. Ct. Appeals (9th cir.) 2000. Jud. clk. Alaska Supreme Ct., Anchorage, 1997—98; litigation assoc. atty. Law Office of Robert Franz, Springfield, Oreg., 1998—2000; assoc. atty. Harrang Long Gary Rudnick P.C., 2001—. Contbr. articles; assoc. editor: Oreg. Law Rev. Mem.: Order of the Coif. Land use and zoning (including planning), Municipal (including bonds). Office: Harrang Long Gary Rudnick PC 360 East 10th Ave Eugene OR 97401

BROTMAN, STANLEY SEYMOUR, federal judge; b. Vineland, N.J., July 27, 1924; s. Herman Nathaniel and Fanny (Melletz) B.; m. Suzanne M. Simon, Sept. 9, 1951; children: Richard A., Alison B. BA, Yale U., 1947; LLB, Harvard U., 1950. Bar: N.J. 1950, D.C. 1951. Pvt. practice, Vineland, 1952-57; ptnr. Shapiro, Brotman, Eisenstat & Capizola, Vineland, 1957-75; judge U.S. Dist. Ct. N.J., Camden, 1975—; acting chief judge Dist. Ct. of V.I., 1989-92; judge U.S. Fgn. Intelligence Surveillance Ct., 1997—. Mem.

N.J. Bd. Bar Examiners, 1970-74. Chmn. editl. bd. N.J. State Bar Jour, 1969-74; contbr. articles to profl. jours. Trustee Newcomb Hosp., Vineland, 1953-68. With U.S. Army, 1943-45, 51-52. Fellow Am. Bar Found., Jud. Conf. U.S. (space and facilities com. 1987-93); mem. ABA (ho. of dels. 1975-80, state del. 1982-93, mem. judicial immigration edn. project, chmn. adv. com. 1996—), Nat. Conf. Fed. Trial Judges (exec. com. 1984-87, chmn.-elect 1986-87, chmn. 1987-88, chmn. standing com. jud. selection, tenure and compensation 1988-92, chmn. steering com. of nominating com. 1992-93, standing com. Fed. Jud. Improvements 1992-2003), Am. Judicature Soc. (dir. 1995-2000), N.J. State Bar Assn. (pres. 1974-75), Cumberland County Bar Assn. (pres. 1969-70), Assn. of Fed. Bar of State of N.J., Harvard U. Law Sch. Assn. N.J. (pres. 1974-75), Fed. Judges Assn. (v.p. 1993-97), Yale U. Alumni Assn., Am. Legion, Jewish War Vets., Yale Club, B'nai B'rith, Masons, Shriners. Office: MH Cohen US Courthouse 6030 MH Cohen US Courthouse 4th and Cooper St Camden NJ 08102

BROTT, IRVING DEERIN, JR., lawyer, judge; b. Buffalo, June 28, 1930; s. Irving Deerin and Lillian May (Cooke) B.; m. Suzanne Hunt, July 11, 1959 (dec. Sept. 1979); children: Megan Cooke, Meryl Hunt, Gordon Alexander MacDonald; m. Donna Rey Kohl, Apr. 19, 1986. BS, Bowling Green State U., 1952; JD, U. Buffalo, 1955. Bar: N.Y. 1955. Assoc. Phillips, Lytle, Hitchcock, Blaine & Huber, Buffalo, 1957-68, ptnr., 1968-94; retired, 1995. Town justice Town of Aurora Ct., East Aurora, N.Y., 1966-94; asst. treas., treas., chmn. fin. com. Camp Fire Girls Buffalo and Erie County, 1966-79; bd. dirs. N.Y. Employee Benefits Conf., 1979-94, v.p., 1993-94. Mem. Erie County Bar Assn., N.Y. State Magistrates Assn., East Aurora Country Club, Myakka Pines Golf Club. Avocations: golf, tennis. Pension, profit-sharing, and employee benefits. Home: 950 Inlet Circle Rd Venice FL 34285

BROUDE, RICHARD FREDERICK, lawyer, educator; b. L.A., June 6, 1936; s. Leo Martin and Frances (Goldman) B.; m. Paula Louise Galnick, June 8, 1958; children: Julie Sue, James Matthew, Mark Allen. BS, Washington U., St Louis, 1957; JD, U. Chgo., 1961. Bar: Ill. 1961, Calif. 1971, N.Y. 1989. Prof. law U. Nebr., Lincoln, 1966-69, Georgetown U., Washington, 1969-71; ptnr. Commons & Broude, L.A., 1974-77, Irell & Manella, L.A., 1977-80, Sidley & Austin, L.A., 1980-87, White & Case, L.A., 1987-90, Mayer, Brown & Platt, N.Y.C., 1990-99. Adj. prof. law U. So. Calif., L.A., 1978-90, St. Johns U., 2000—; adv. panel World Bank Insolvency Initiative; cons. OECD Forum for Asian Insolvency Reform. Author: Reorganizations Under Chapter 11, 1986—2003, Cases and Materials on Land Financing, 3rd, 1985; editor: Insolvency and Finance in the Transportation Industry, 1993, Collier Internat. Bus. Guide; mem. editl. bd.: Collier on Bankruptcy, contbg. editor: Collier Bankruptcy Practice Guide. Fellow Am. Bar Found., Am. Coll. Bankruptcy; mem. ABA (com. on bus. bankruptcy), Am. Law Inst. (advisor Transnat. Insolvency Project), Internat. Bar Assn. (chair insolvency and credit rights com. 1996-2000), Bar Assn. of City of N.Y., Calif. Bar Assn., Nat. Bankruptcy Conf. (conferee, chair com. on internat. aspects, vice chair legis. com.). Bankruptcy, Commercial, contracts (including sales of goods; commercial financing). Office: Law Offices of Richard Broude 400 E 84th St # 22A New York NY 10028-5611 E-mail: rfbroude@cs.com.

BROUGHEL, ANDREW JOSEPH, lawyer; b. Bridgeport, Conn., Sept. 8, 1938; s. Edward Robbins and Florence (Lavery) B.; m. Josephine Ann Maugeri, July 13, 1968; 1 child, Kevin Paul. B in Social Scis., Fairfield U., 1960; JD, Georgetown U., 1963. Bar: Conn. 1964, U.S. Supreme Ct. 1967, U.S. Ct. Appeals (2d cir.) 1969, U.S. Dist. Ct. Conn. 1972. Legal counsel Milford (Conn.) Housing Authority, 1972-76; adjudicator Conn. Dept. Motor Vehicles, Wethersfeld, Conn., 1973-75; trial counsel City of Milford, Conn., 1977-82; pvt. practice Milford, 1970—. Panelist Am. Arbitration Assn., Hartford, Conn., 1976; fact finder Judicial Dist. Ansonia/Milford, 1983-89, trial referee, 1990-96. Sec. Milford Charter Revision Commn., 1972-73; mem. Milford Pension and Retirement Bd., 1973-76, chmn. 75-76. Mem. KC (bd. dirs. Milford 1978-83, Spl. Svc. award 1994), Milford Bar Assn. (pres. 1984-88, other offices. 1972-84), Milford C. of C. (bd. dirs. 1984-87, Outstanding Achievement award 1986, 87). Republican. Roman Catholic. General practice, Probate (including wills, trusts), Property, real (including real estate development, water). Home: 18 Berner Ter Milford CT 06460-6756 Office: 243 Broad St Milford CT 06460-3235

BROUGHTON, PHILLIP CHARLES, lawyer, director; b. Findlay, Ohio, Sept. 21, 1930; s. Harold C. and Marian (Pierson) B.; children: Margaret Crockett, Phillip Charles, Anne Duvall, Elizabeth Cox. BA, Bowling Green U., 1953; JD, U. Mich., 1957; LLM, NYU, 1962. Bar: N.Y. 1957. Practiced in, N.Y.C., 1957—; mem. firm Thacher, Proffitt and Wood, 1957-93, of counsel, 1993—. Pres., bd. dirs. Midgard Found., N.Y.C.; pres., bd. trustees Asheville (N.C.) Art Mus.; trustee United Way Asheville, N.C. Mus. Art. Mem. ABA.

BROUN, KENNETH STANLEY, lawyer, educator; b. Chgo., July 26, 1939; s. Fred G. and Helene (Smith) B.; m. Marjorie Enid Shagam, Jan. 29, 1961; children: Jonathan, Daniel. BS, U. Ill., 1960, JD, 1963. Bar: Ill. 1963, N.C. 1976. From assoc. prof. to prof. U. N.C. Law Sch., Chapel Hill, 1969—, hon. Brandis prof. law, 1990—; dir. Nat. Inst. Trial Advocacy, Chapel Hill, 1976-79; dean Sch. Law U.N.C., Chapel Hill, 1979-87; of counsel Petree & Stockton, Raleigh, N.C., 1988-94; mayor Town Chapel Hill, N.C., 1991-95. Co-dir. program in trial advocacy Black Lawyers Assn. South Africa; mem. Adv. Com. on Fed. Rules of Evidence, 1993-99, cons., 1999—. Author: Black Lawyers, White Courts, 2000; co-author (with R. Mosteller): Problems in Evidence, 4th edit., 2001; co-author: (with J. Strong et al) Handbook of Evidence, 5th edit., 1999; author: Brandis and Broun, North Carolina Evidence, 1998; co-author (with R. Mosteller et al): Cases and Materials in Evidence, 6th edit., 2002. Recipient award for teaching excellence U. N.C., 1978; fellow Internat. Soc. Barristers, 1978 Fellow Am. Bar Found., Internat. Soc. Barristers; mem. ABA, Nat. Inst. Trial Advocacy (chmn. 1993-94), N.C. Bar Assn. (v.p. 1991-92), Order of Coif. Home: 414 Whitehead Cir Chapel Hill NC 27514-4833 Office: U NC Sch Law Cb # 3380 Chapel Hill NC 27599-0001

BROUNTAS, PAUL PETER, lawyer; b. Bangor, Maine, Mar. 19, 1932; s. Peter Nicholas and Penelope (Spiropoulos) B.; m. Lynn Barrett Thurston, Sept. 7, 1963; children— Paul Peter, Jennifer VanWoert, Barrett Penelope AB summa cum laude, Bowdoin Coll., 1954; BA, Oxford (Eng.) U., 1956, MA, 1960; LLB, Harvard U., 1960. Bar: Mass. 1960. Assoc. Hale and Dorr LLP, Boston, 1960-64, jr. ptnr., 1964-68, sr. ptnr., 1968—2002, sr. counsel, 2003—. Guest presenter Harvard U. Bus. Sch., Cambridge, Mass., 1981-87; corp. sec. various corps.; panelist, lectr. corp., venture capital and securities law. Overseer Bowdoin Coll., Brunswick, Maine, 1974-82, pres. bd. overseers, 1979-82, trustee, 1983-96, chmn. bd. trustees, 1993-96; chmn. com. for Michael S. Dukakis Gov. of Mass., 1976-88; chmn. Dukakis for Pres. Com., 1987-88; mem. corp. Children's Hosp. Med. Ctr., Boston, 1965-87, Boston Mus. Sci., 1966-91, Mass. Gen. Hosp., Boston, 1983-94; mem. bd. overseers Newton Wellesley Hosp., 1990-96; mem. Marshall Scholar Selection Com. N.E. Region, 1973-75, 88-92; mem. Weston Planning Bd., Mass., 1967-72, chmn., 1970-72; chmn. Met. Boston Citizen's Coalition for Cleaner Air, 1969-71; bd. dirs. Mass. Ctrs. of Excellence Corp., 1985-87. Served with U.S. Army, 1956-58. Marshall scholar, 1954 Mem. ABA, Mass. Bar Assn., Boston Bar Assn., Assn. Marshall Scholars and Alumni (treas. 1965-71, bd. dirs. 1988-90). Avocations: skiing, golf. Corporate, general, Mergers and acquisitions, Securities. Office: Hale and Dorr LLP 60 State St Boston MA 02109-1816 E-mail: paul.brounta@haledorr.com.

BROUPHY, GRETA MANNING, lawyer; b. New Orleans, Nov. 4, 1968; d. Meryl Joseph and Patricia Enright Manning; m. Kevin Patrick Brouphy, Dec. 12, 1992; children: Emma Bailey, Kelsey Marie. BS in Acctg., U. New Orleans, 1990; JD, Loyola U., New Orleans, 1999. Cert.: (paralegal). Assoc. Harvey Jacobson, New Orleans, 1999—2000, Heller, Draper, Hayden, Patrick & Horn, LLC, New Orleans, 2000—. Mem. Rep. Vitter Women's Orgn., New Orleans, 2002—. Mem.: La. Bar Assn., Fed. Bar Assn. (bd. dirs. 2002—). Republican. Bankruptcy, Commercial, contracts (including sales of goods; commercial financing). Office: Heller Draper Hayden Patrick & Horn 650 Poydras St Ste 2500 New Orleans LA 70130 Office Fax: 504-592-0949. Business E-Mail: gbrouphy@hellerdraper.com.

BROUS, THOMAS RICHARD, lawyer; b. Fulton, Mo., Jan. 7, 1943; s. Richard Pendleton and Augusta (Gilpin) B.; m. Patricia Catlin, Sept. 12, 1964; (dec. Sept. 1999); children: Anna Catlin Brous, Joel Pendleton Brous; m. Mary Lou McClelland Kroh, Sept. 8, 2001. BSBA, Northwestern U., 1965; JD cum laude, U. Mich., 1968. Bar: Mo. 1968, U.S. Dist. Ct. (we. dist.) Mo. 1968, U.S. Ct. Mil. Appeals 1968, U.S. Supreme Ct. 1971. Assoc. Watson & Marshall L.C., Kans. City, Mo., 1968-78, ptnr., 1978-96, mng. ptrn., 1992-94; shareholder Stinson, Mag & Fizzell, P.C., Kans. City, Mo., 1996—2002; ptnr. Stinson Morrison Hecker LLP, Kans. City, 2002—. Mem. steering com. U. Mo. Kansas City Law Sch. Employee Benefits Inst., 1990—2001, chmn. 1992-93; with Ctrl. Mtn. TE/GE Coun. IRS, 1997—. Author: Chapter 26, III Missouri Business Organizations, 1998; asst. editor Mich. Law Rev., 1966-68. Mem. vestry St. Andrews Episcopal Ch., Kansas City, 1974-77, Grace & Holy Trinity Cathedral, 1994—, chancellor, 1998—; trustee Mo. Repertory Theatre, Inc., Kansas City, 1990—, pres., 1995-98; v.p., treas. Barstow Sch., Kansas City, 1982-86; dir. Met. Orgn. to Counter Sexual Abuse, Kansas City, 1992-95. Capt. U.S. Army, 1968-72. Mem. ABA, Univ. Club (pres. 1988-89), Greater Kansas City Soc. Hosp. Attys., Kansas City Met. Bar Assn., Heart of Am. Employee Benefit Conf., The Mo. Bar Assn. (vice-chair employee benefits com. 1997-2000), Mo. Soc. Hosp. Attys., Delta Upsilon, Beta Gamma Sigma. Episcopalian. Avocations: reading, hiking, gardening. Corporate, general, Health, Pension, profit-sharing, and employee benefits. Office: Stinson Morrison Hecker LLP 1201 Walnut Ste 2800 Kansas City MO 64106 E-mail: tbrous@stinsonmoheck.com.

BROUSSARD, THOMAS ROLLINS, lawyer; b. Houston, May 30, 1943; s. Charles Hugh and Ethel (Rollins) B.; m. Mollie Brewster, Jan. 13, 1968. BS cum laude in Econs., U. Pa., 1964; JD cum laude, Harvard U., 1967. Bar: N.Y. 1968, Calif. 1973. Tax atty. Esso Standard Eastern, Inc., N.Y.C., 1967-70; gen. tax counsel Atlantic Richfield Co., N.Y.C., Los Angeles, 1970-74; v.p. corp. affairs, sec., gen. counsel Technicolor, Inc., Los Angeles, 1974-80; mem. firm Nelson & Broussard, Los Angeles, 1980-81; pres. Thomas R. Broussard, Ltd., P.C., Los Angeles, 1981—; of counsel Law Offices of Joseph E. Bachelder, N.Y.C., 2002—. Mem. ABA, Calif., Los Angeles County bar assns., Assn. of the Bar of the City of N.Y. Office: 172 N Las Palmas Ave Los Angeles CA 90004

BROWDY, JOSEPH EUGENE, lawyer; b. Bklyn., July 23, 1937; s. Philip and Fannie (Asherowitz) B.; m. Anita Sue Rubenstein, June 18, 1958; childrenF: Jennifer, Daniel. BA, Oberlin Coll., 1958; LLB, NYU, 1961. Bar: N.Y. 1962, D.C. 1982. Assoc. Paul, Weiss, Rifkind, Wharton & Garrison, N.Y.C., 1962-71, ptnr., 1972-97, of counsel, 1998—. Adj. asst. prof. real estate NYU, 1976-86; lectr. in field. With U.S. Army Res., 1961-62. Mem. Assn. of Bar of City of N.Y. (com. real property law, chmn. subcom. on leasing 1989-92), Am. Coll. Real Estate Lawyers, Order of Coif, Phi Beta Kappa. Property, real (including real estate development, water). Office: Paul Weiss Rifkind Wharton & Garrison 1285 Avenue of the Americas New York NY 10019-6065 E-mail: jbrowdy@paulweiss.com.

BROWER, CHARLES NELSON, lawyer, judge; b. Plainfield, N.J., June 5, 1935; s. Charles Hendrickson and Mary Elizabeth (Nelson) B.; children: Michael Claudio Joseph Hutchings, Carmen Dèsirèe Ponti, Frederica Anne Amity, Jasmin Maria Plekavich, Charles Hendrickson II. BA cum laude, Harvard U., 1957, JD, 1961; cert. Parker Sch. Comp. & Internat. Law, Columbia U., 1962. Bar: N.Y. 1962, D.C. 1970, U.S. Supreme Ct. 1967, U.S. Ct. Appeals (D.C. cir., 2d, 5th, 6th, 7th, 8th, 9th, 11th and fed. cirs.), U.S. Ct. Internat. Trade, U.S. Dist. Ct. (so. and ea. dists.) N.Y., U.S. Dist. Ct. D.C. Assoc., then ptnr. White & Case LLP, N.Y.C., 1961-69; asst. legal adviser European affairs Dept. State, Washington, 1969-71, dep. legal adviser, 1971-73, acting legal adviser, 1973; ptnr. White & Case LLP, Washington, 1973-84, 88-00, spl. counsel, 2001—; mem. 20 Essex St. Chambers, London, 2001—. Judge Iran-U.S. Claims Tribunal, The Hague, 1984—88, 2001—, substitute judge, 1983—84, 1988—2000; dep. spl. counselor to the Pres., Washington, 1987; counsel and advocate for U.S., 92, Costa Rica, 98, Internat. Ct. Justice, The Hague; mem. Register of Experts UN Compensation Commn., 1991—; mem. sec. of state adv. com. on internat. law, 1996—; mem. panels of arbitrators and conciliators Internat. Ctr. for Settlement of Investment Disputes, 1998—; judge ad hoc Inter-Am. Ct. of Human Rights, 1999—. Fulbright scholar Rheinische Friedrich-Wilhelms-Universitaet, Bonn, and Hochschule fuer Politik, Berlin, 1957-78. Mem. ABA (chmn. sect. internat. law 1981-82, mem. ho. of dels. 1982, 84-98, bd. govs. 1985-88, mem. nominating com. 1992-94), Internat. Law Assn. (hon. v.p. Am. br.), Internat. Bar Assn., Am. Soc. Internat. Law (v.p. 1994-96, pres. 1996-98, hon. v.p. 1998—), Am. Law Inst., Assn. of Bar of City of N.Y., Coun. Fgn. Rels., Inst. Transnat. Arbitration (chmn. adv. bd. 1994-2000), Ctr. for Am. and Internat. Law (trustee 1996—), Met. Club, Chevy Chase Club. Episcopalian. Federal civil litigation, Private international, Public international. Home and Office: Parkweg 13 2585 JH The Hague Netherlands E-mail: cbrower@20essexst.com., cbrower@whitecase.com.

BROWER, DAVID JOHN, lawyer, urban planner, educator; b. Holland, Mich., Sept. 11, 1930; s. John J. and Helen (Olson) B.; m. Lou Ann Brown, Nov. 26, 1960; children: Timothy Seth, David John, II, Ann Lacey. BA, U. Mich., 1956, JD, 1960. Bar: Ill. 1960, Mich. 1961, Ind. 1961, U.S. Supreme Ct. 1971. Asst. dir. div. community planning Ind. U., Bloomington, 1960-70; rsch. prof. dept. city and regional planning U. N.C., Chapel Hill, 1970—, assoc. dir. Ctr. for Urban and Regional Studies, 1970-94; pres. Coastal Resources Collaborative, Ltd., Chapel Hill and Manteo, N.C., 1980—; counsel Robinson & Cole, Hartford, Conn., 1986—. Vis. prof., Vt. Law Sch., South Royalton, summers, 1994—. Author: (with others) Constitutional Issues of Growth Management, 1978; Growth Management, 1984, Managing Development in Small Towns, 1984, Special Area Management, 1985, Catastrophic Coastal Storms, 1989, Understanding Growth Management, 1989, Coastal Zone Management: An Evaluation, 1991, An Introduction to Coastal Zone Management, 1994, rev. edit. 2002, Natural Hazard Mitigation, 1999. Fellow Am. Inst. Cert. Planners (Coll. of Fellows); mem.Am. Planning Assn. (bd. dirs. 1982-85, chmn.-founder planning and law div. 1978, co-chmn. sbstainable devel. group 1995—). Democrat. Episcopalian. Home: 612 Shady Lawn Rd Chapel Hill NC 27514-2009 Office: U NC CB # 3140 Chapel Hill NC 27599-0001 E-mail: brower@email.unc.edu.

BROWER, JOSHUA CHRISTOPHER ALLEN, lawyer; b. Boston, Oct. 2, 1965; s. Robert Samuel and Donna (Romero) B.; m. Erin Elizabeth Allen, Aug. 1, 1993; children: Owen Samuel, Eliza Avery. BA, Hampshire Coll., 1988; JD, Seattle U., 1995. Bar: Wash. 1995, U.S. Dist. Ct. (we. dist.) Wash. 1995. Assoc. Law Office of James C. Middlebrooks, Seattle, 1995-96, Preg, O'Donnell, Sargeant & Gillett, Seattle, 1996-99, Stoel Rives, LLP, Seattle, 1999—. Contbr. articles to profl. jours. Appellate, Land use and zoning (including planning), Property, real (including real estate development, water). Office: Stoel Rives LLP 600 University St Ste 3600 Seattle WA 98101-4109 E-mail: jcabrower@stoel.com.

BROWN, ALAN CRAWFORD, lawyer; b. Rockford, Ill., May 12, 1956; s. Gerald Crawford and Jane Ella (Herzberger) B.; m. Dawn Lestrud, Apr. 16, 1998; children: Parker Crawford, Sydney Danielle, Sarah Kate, Drew Kristen, Connor Austin. BA magna cum laude, Miami U., Oxford, Ohio, 1978; JD with honors, U. Chgo., 1981. Bar: Ill. 1981, U.S. Dist. Ct. (no. dist.) Ill. 1981, U.S. Tax Ct. 1986. Assoc. Kirkland & Ellis, Chgo., 1981-87; sr. assoc. Coffield Ungaretti Harris & Slavin, Chgo., 1987-89; ptnr. McDermott, Will & Emery, Chgo., 1989—2001, Neal, Gerber & Eisenberg, Chgo., 2001—. Deacon Northminster Presbyn. Ch., Evanston, Ill., 1989-92; apiarist Chgo. Botanic Garden, Glencoe, Ill., 1988-97; active Kenilworth (Ill.) Union Ch. Mem. Order of Coif, Phi Beta Kappa. Estate planning, Probate (including wills, trusts), Estate taxation. Office: Neal Gerber & Eisenberg Ste 2200 Two North LaSalle St Chicago IL 60602-3801 E-mail: acbrownesq@aol.com ., abrown@ngelaw.com.

BROWN, BARBARA A. lawyer; b. Yonkers, N.Y., Feb. 14, 1950; d. Morton Herbert and Pauline (Willis) Kleinman; m. Bruce G. Brown, June 14, 1981 (div. Aug. 1988); children: Sara Elise, Joshua Charles. BA, U. Mass., 1974; JD magna cum laude, New England Sch. of Law, Boston, 1978. Atty. student legal svcs. U. Maine, Orono, 1979-80; atty. Law Offices of Marshall Stern, Bangor, Maine, 1985-93, Leen & Emery, Bangor, 1993-94; prin. Barbara A. Brown, Bangor, 1994—95, Sharon, Mass., 1995—; of counsel Bayer Corp., Medfield, Mass., 1996—2000; contract specialist Siebec Systems, Inc., 2000—02. Estate planning, Family and matrimonial. Office: PO Box 179 Sharon MA 02067-0179

BROWN, BOBBY WAYNE, lawyer, educator, accountant; b. Columbia, Tenn., Mar. 26, 1955; s. William R. and Sara (Cummins) R.; m. Joy Gill, May 18, 1985. BS, David Lipscomb Coll., 1977; MBA, U. Tenn., 1978, JD, 1982. Bar: Tenn. 1983; CPA, Tenn.; cert. valuation analyst. Staff auditor Coopers an Lybrand, Memphis, 1979-80; tax specialist Pugh and Co., Knoxville, 1981-82, Peat, Marwick, Mitchell and Co., Nashville, 1983-84; fin. analyst Taylor Fin. Corp., Nashville, 1984-85; asst. prof. bus. law David Lipscomb Coll., Nashville, 1985-90; pvt. cons. Brentwood, Tenn., 1993; corp. sec. Pratt & Co., Inc., Nashville, 1991-93, consulting analyst, 1993—. Mem. AICPA, Tenn. Bar Assn., Tenn. Soc. CPAs, Nat. Assn. Cert. Valuation Analysts. Republican. Mem. Ch. Christ. Avocations: tennis, auto repair. Home: 5114 Dorchester Cir Brentwood TN 37027-6815 Office: Bobby W Brown CPA,CVA 207 Brentwood Pointe Brentwood TN 37027 E-mail: bwbrowncpa@juno.com.

BROWN, BONNIE MARYETTA, lawyer; b. North Plainfield, N.J., Oct. 31, 1953; d. Robert Jeffrey and Diana (Parket) B. AB, Washington U., St. Louis, 1975; JD, U. Louisville, 1978. Bar: Ky. 1978, U.S. Dist. Ct. (we. dist.) Ky. 1979, U.S. Dist. Ct. (ea. dist.) Ky. 1993. Pvt. practice, Louisville, 1978—; of counsel Morris, Garlove, Waterman and Johnson PLLC, 1998—. Lectr., seminar leader various profl., ednl., govtl. and civic groups; cons. marital rape; registered lobbyist 1994 Ky. Gen. Assembly for Ky. Assn. Marriage and Family Therapy. Editor Ky. Appellate Handbook, 1985; contbr. articles to profl. jours. Vol. legal panel Ky. Civil Liberties Union, Louisville, 1984—; author, chief lobbyist Marital Rape Bill, Ky. Coalition Against Rape and Sexual Assault, 1984-90, Sexual Harassment bill, 1996; vol. advocate Louisville RAPE Relief Ctr., 1975—; treas. Family Support Group/Family Readiness Program. of USAR, 1994-96, 3d Bat., 2nd. bge, 87th divsn., 1996-2000, acting coord. 10th bat., 6th bge, 100th divsn. Recipient Cert. Spl. Recognition RAPE Relief Ctr., 1980, Cert. Outstanding Contbn., Louisville YWCA, 1983, Cert. of Appreciation, James Graham Brown Cancer Ctr., 1984, Decade of Svc. award YWCA/Rape Relief Ctr., Outstanding Victim Adv. award Fayette County Govt., 1990, cert. of Recognition Jefferson County Family Ct., 1995, other awards. Mem. ABA (family law sect.), Am. Acad. Matrimonial Lawyers (interdisciplinary com., treas. Ky. chpt. 1999-2001), Ky. Collaborative Family Law Network (treas. 2002—), Ky. Bar Assn. (family law sect., chair 1996-97, seminar spkr., task force solo practitioners and small law firms 1992, chair subcom. on law office automation and networking, solo practitioner and small Law Firm sect., chmn. 1999-2000, CLE award 1981, 97-2002, Louisville Bar Assn. (liaison to mental health sect., organizer marital rape seminar, chmn. family law sect., mediation com. property divsn., seminar spkr., organizer joint custody child abuse seminars, solo practitioner and small law firm sect., chair 1995, pro bono consortium), Ky. Acad. Trial Attys. (spkr. seminar, editor The Advocate family law sect. 1995-2001), Bus. and Profl. Women (pres. River City chpt. 1983-84), Ky. Fedn. (legis. chair 1986-87, 90-92, legal counsel 1992, 96-2001, lobby corps chair 1993-95), Louisville Internat. Cultural Ctr. Republican. Avocations: basketball fan, classic cars. Family and matrimonial, Appellate. Office: Ste 1000 One Riverfront Plz Louisville KY 40202

BROWN, C. HAROLD, lawyer; b. Mendenhall, Miss., July 28, 1931; m. Alicia Brown; children: Tracey Gwen, Terry Lynne, Allison Anne, Harold Allen. BA, Vanderbilt U., 1957; LLB, U. Tex., 1960. Bar: Tex. 1960. Sr. ptnr. Brown Pruitt Peterson & Wambsganss , P.C., Ft. Worth, 1960—. Pres. A.J. and Jessie Duncan Found. Past chmn. Ft. Worth Civil Svc. Commn.; past chmn. bd. dirs., past pres. Tarrant County Conv. Ctr., 1980; active Com. for Greater Tarrant County; past bd. dirs. Ft. Worth Camp Fire Girls; past bd. dirs. Nat. Com. for Adoption, Gladney Ctr., Adopt a Spl. Kid/Tex.; past bd. dirs. Tex. Assn. Licensed Children's Svcs.; mgr. campaign R.M. Stovall for Mayor of Ft. Worth, 1969, 71, 73, Richard T. Andersen for Tarrant County Commr., 1972, 76, 80, 84, Senator Al Gore for Pres., Tarrant County, Tex., 1988; past deacon U. Christian Ch., Ft. Worth. Sgt. U.S. Army, 1953-55. Recipient cert. Carnegie Hero Fund Commn., 1972; named Outstanding Young Texan, 1976; named to Gladney Ctr. Hall of Fame. Fellow Tex. Bar Found. (life), Southwestern Legal Found., Tarrant County Bar Found. (life), Ft. Worth-Tarrant County Bar Assn. (charter, life, bd. dirs. family law sect. 1978-80); mem. ABA, Tex. Bar Assn., Tarrant County Probate Bar, Ft. Worth Jr. Bar Assn. (pres. 1963), Am. Acad. Adoption Attys., Am. Acad. Hosp. Attys., Nat. Health Lawyers Assn., Pro Bono Coll. of State Bar of Tex., Badge and Shield, Vanderbilt U. Alumni Assn. (pres. 1966-67), Am. Brittany Club (Hall of Fame), Ridotto Club (pres. 1974), Petroleum Club, River Crest Country Club, Steeplechase Club, Nat. Commodore Club (adm.), Rotary, Masons, Shriners, Jesters, Alpha Tau Omega, Phi Delta Phi. Corporate, general, General practice, Probate (including wills, trusts). Office: Brown Pruitt Peterson & Wambsganss PC 201 Main St Ste 801 Fort Worth TX 76102-3817 E-mail: brownpruittlaw@ad.com.

BROWN, CHARLES DODGSON, lawyer; b. N.Y.C., Dec. 31, 1928; s. James Dodgson and Leonora Rose (Nichols) B.; m. Martha Lockhart Spindler, Apr. 5, 1963; children: Gregory Spindler, William Howard. BA, NYU, 1949, JD, 1952. Bar: N.Y. 1952, U.S. Dist. Ct. (so. and ea. dists.) N.Y. 1955, U.S. Supreme Ct. 1958, U.S. Ct. Appeals (2d cir.) 1988. Counsel, former ptnr. Thacher Proffitt & Wood, N.Y.C., 1954—. Co-author: Equipment Leasing, 1995—. Chmn. zoning bd. Asharoken, N.Y., 1965, alt. chmn. environ. bd., 1967, trustee, 1967, village justice, 1980—; chmn. Boy Scout Am., Northport, N.Y., 1989—; elder 1st Presbyn. Ch., Northport; mem. admiralty law inst. faculty Tulane U. Sch. Law, 1999. With U.S. Army, 1952-54. Mem. ABA, N.Y. Bar Assn., Maritime Law Assn. U.S. (proctor in Admiralty 1956, former chair to marine fin. com. 1996-2000), N.Y. State Magistrate Assn., Suffolk County Magistrate Assn., Northport Tennis Club. Republican. Avocations: scuba diving, wind surfing, tennis. Admiralty, Banking, Commercial, contracts (including sales of goods; commercial financing). E-mail: cbrown@tpwlaw.com., cbrown2@optonline.net.

BROWN, CHARLES FREEMAN, II, lawyer; b. Boston, Mar. 7, 1914; s. Arthur Harrison and Nellie Abigail (Kenney) B.; m. Caroline Gotzian Tighe, Nov. 12, 1949 (dec. Jan. 1951); m. Pamela Judith Wedd, Nov. 29, 1952; children— Penelope Susan, Nicholas Wedd. AB, Harvard U., 1936, LL.B., 1941. Bar: Mass. 1941. Assoc. atty. Sherburne, Powers & Needham, Boston, 1941-43; asst. gen. counsel, gen. counsel OSRD, Washington, 1943-47; counsel rsch. and devel. bd. and mil. liaison com. Office of Sec.

of Def., patent advisor, mem. govt. patents bd., counsel Def. Prodn. Bd.; dep. asst. sec. gen. for prodn. and logistics NATO detailed from Office Sec. Def., Washington, London, Paris, 1947-53; asst. to pres. Hydrofoil Corp., Annapolis, Md., 1953-54; asso. gen. counsel CIA, Washington, 1954-60; v.p., treas. Sci. Engring. Inst., Waltham, Mass., 1960-66; dep. gen. counsel NSF, Washington, 1966-73, gen. counsel, 1973-76, chmn. interim compliance panel, 1970-71. Cons., 1976— Trustee Belmont (Mass.) Day Sch., 1963-66; bd. dirs. Hillcrest Children's Ctr., Washington, 1978-87, pres., 1980-83; pres. Cleveland Park Book Club, 1980-83, 91-94; bd. dirs. Cleveland Park Hist. Soc. Recipient Disting. Service award NSF. Mem. Fed. Bar Assn., Cosmos Club. Home and Office: 3500 Macomb St NW Washington DC 20016-3162

BROWN, CHRISTOPHER ROBERT, lawyer; b. Teaneck, NJ, Sept. 3, 1959; s. Robert L. and Martha E. Brown; m. Diane M. Steely, Mar. 28, 1987; children: Katharine, Adam. BA, Rutgers U., 1981; JD, NY Law Sch., 1985. Bar: NJ 1985. Assoc. Law Office of Ernest J. Gikas, Farmingdale, NJ, 1985—87, Pincus, Gordon & Zuckerman, New Brunswick, NJ, 1987—88; sr. assoc. Drazin and Warshaw, Hazlet, NJ, 1988—. Vol. Trial Lawyers Care, N.Y.C., 2002. Mem.: ATLA, Monmouth County Bar Assn., Sigma Pi Internat. (bd. dirs. 2000—). Personal injury (including property damage), Criminal, Juvenile. Office: Drazin & Warshaw PC 3315 Hwy 35 Hazlet NJ 07730

BROWN, DAVID NELSON, lawyer; b. Harrodsburg, Ky., May 29, 1940; s. Irmel Nelson and Pauline (Harmon) B.; m. Lois Aileen Everett, June 20, 1964; 1 child, Ian Richard. A.B., Cornell U., 1963; J.D., U. Chgo., 1966; Bar: D.C. 1967. Assoc., Covington & Burling, Washington, 1966-74, ptnr., 1974—. mgmt. com. Covington & Burling, 1989-93. Comment editor U. Chgo. Law Rev. Mem. ABA, Order of Coif, Cosmos Club. Episcopalian. Mergers and acquisitions, Private international, Securities. Office: Covington & Burling 1201 Pennsylvania Ave NW Washington DC 20004-2401 E-mail: dbrown@cov.com.

BROWN, DAVID RONALD, lawyer; b. Turtle Creek, Pa., Jan. 25, 1939; s. James R. and Mary A. (Barnes) Brown; m. Debra W. Brown; children: Michelle, Adrienne, Aaron, Eden, Jeremy. Student, Brown U., 1956-57; BS, U. Pitts., 1960; JD, Duquesne U., 1967. Bar: Penn. 1968, U.S. Dist. Ct. (we. dist.) Penn. 1967, U.S. Ct. Appeals (3d cir.) 1972, U.S. Tax Ct. 1986. Rschr. phys. chemistry Mellon Inst., Pitts., 1960-66; real estate lawyer Redevel. Authority of Allegheny County, Pitts., 1966-69; ptnr. Litman, Litman, Harris & Brown, Pitts., 1969-2000, Sherrard, German & Kelly, Pitts., 2000—. Lectr. Robert Morris Coll., 1978-84. Councilman Borough of Turtle Creek, Penn., 1963-67. Mem. ABA (real property and probate sect., bus. law sect.), Pa. Bar Assn., Allegheny County Bar Assn. (com. legal svcs. 1973-74, real property sect., probate and trust law sect.). Commercial, contracts (including sales of goods; commercial financing), Probate (including wills, trusts), Property, real (including real estate development, water). Home: 1411 Grandview Ave Apt 202 Pittsburgh PA 15211-1157 Office: Sherrard German & Kelly 35th Fl Free Markets Ctr Pittsburgh PA 15222

BROWN, DONALD ARTHUR, lawyer; b. Washington, Feb. 1, 1929; s. Louis S. and Rose (Kliban) B.; m. Ann Winkelman, July 13, 1959; children: Cathy, Laura. BA in Econs., George Washington U., 1949, LL.B. (Case Club oral argument competition winner), 1952, LL.M., 1958. Bar: D.C. 1952. Sr. partner Brown, Gildenhorn & Jacobs (and predecessor), Washington, 1955—. Mem. faculty Practising Law Inst.; faculty Harvard U. Sch. Bus., Cambridge, Mass., 1984-93, Yale U. Sch. Mgmt., New Haven, 1986, George Washington U. Sch. Bus., Washington, 1994—; guest lectr. Am. U., Nat. Assn. Real Estate Counselors, Nat. Assn. Real Estate Investors; pres., sec. JBG Constrn., Inc.; partner JBG Assocs.; v.p., treas. JBG Properties, Inc.; trustee, gen. counsel Nat. Bank Rosslyn, Arlington, Va.; mem. minority enterprises com. SBA; finance com. Housing Devel. Corp.; mem. Model Cities Com. D.C.; apptd. by Pres. of U.S. commr. Internat. Cultural and Trade Ctr., 1988. Co-author: Understanding Real Estate Investments, 1967; contbr. articles to profl. jours. Exec. bd. Forest Hills Citizens Assn.; bd. dirs. D.C. Jr. C. of C.; mem. Friends Kennedy Center, Friends Corcoran Gallery, Big Bros. Orgn. D.C.; bd. dirs. Washington Area Tennis Patrons Found., 1964—, pres., 1973-75, Fed. city council; trustee Woodley House, psychiat. half-way house, Washington, 1973—, pres. bd. dirs., 1975—; trustee U. D.C., Sidwell Friends Sch., The Phillips Collection, 1984—; mem. art adv. council Washington Conv. Ctr. com. D.C. Conv. Ctr. Served as officer USNR, 1952-55. Named Washingtonian of Yr., Washingtonian mag., 1989. Mem. ABA, Fed. Bar Assn., D.C. Bar Assn., Washington Bd. Realtors (chmn. lawyer-realtor liaison com. 1972, chmn. investment property com. 1970), Economics Club of Washington, Burning Tree Club. Jewish (bd. mgrs. congregation 1962, treas. 1965). Club: Georgetown (Washington). Property, real (including real estate development, water). Home: 2734 Rhone Dr Palm Beach Gardens FL 33410-1280 Office: Brown Gildenhorn & Jacobs 5301 Wise Ave NW Washington DC 20015

BROWN, DONALD JAMES, JR., lawyer; b. Chgo., Apr. 21, 1948; s. Donald James Sr. and Marian Constance (Scimeca) B.; m. Donna Bowen, Jan. 15, 1972; children: Megan, Maura. AB, John Carroll U., 1970; JD, Loyola U., Chgo., 1973. Bar: Ill. 1973, U.S. Dist. Ct. (no. dist.) Ill. 1973, U.S. Tax Ct. 1982. Asst. to state's atty. Cook County, Ill., 1973-75; assoc. Baker & McKenzie, Chgo., 1975-82, ptnr., 1982-95, Donohue, Brown, Mathewson & Smyth, Chgo., 1995—. State civil litigation, Personal injury (including property damage). Office: Donohue Brown et al 140 S Dearborn St Chicago IL 60603-5202

BROWN, DONALD WESLEY, lawyer; b. Cleve., Jan. 2, 1953; s. Lloyd Elton Brown and Nancy Jeanne Hudson. AB summa cum laude, Ohio U., 1975; JD, Yale U., 1978. Bar: Calif. 1978, U.S. Dist. Ct. (no. dist.) Calif. 1978, U.S. Dist. Ct. (cen. dist.) Calif. 1990. Assoc. Brobeck, Phleger & Harrison, San Francisco, 1978-85, ptnr., 1985—2003, Covington & Burling, San Francisco, 2003—. Democrat. Federal civil litigation, State civil litigation. Home: 2419 Vallejo St San Francisco CA 94123-4638 Office: Covington & Burling One Front St San Francisco CA 94111

BROWN, ENOLA T. lawyer; b. Tampa, Fla., Nov. 30, 1953; d. Fred G. and Enola C. Tobi; m. Edward C. Brown, Oct. 6, 1984. BS, Fla. State U., 1975, MS, 1977; JD, U. Fla., 1984. Bar: Fla. 1984, U.S. Dist. Ct. (mid. dist.) Fla. 1984, , U.S. Dist. Ct. (no. dist.), 2002, U.S. Ct. Appeals (11th cir.) 2000. Environ. scientist Hillsborough County, Tampa, 1978-81; atty. Lawson McWhirter Grandoff & Reeves, Tampa, 1984-89, ptnr., 1989-93, Annis Mitchell Cockey Edwards & Roehn, Tampa, 1993-2001, Enola Brown, PA, Tampa, 2001—; spl. counsel environ. matters Tampa Port Auth., 2001—. Atty. Jr. League Tampa, Inc., 1990-92; lectr. Fredrick Levin Coll. of Law, 2002-; mem. exec. coun. environ. and land use sect. Fla. Bar Assn., 2002-. Environmental. Office: Enola Brown PA 442 W Kennedy Blvd Ste 340 Tampa FL 33606 E-mail: enola@enolabrown.com.

BROWN, GEORGE E. judge, educator; b. Hammond, Ind., July 27, 1947; s. George E. and Violet M. (Matlon) B.; m. Patricia A. Schneider, June 6, 1970; children: Janet M., Elizabeth A. BS, Ball State U., 1969; JD, DePaul U., 1974; grad., Ind. Jud. Coll., 1996. Bar: Ind. 1974, Ill. 1974, U.S. Dist. Ct. (no. dist.) Ind. 1979, U.S. Supreme Ct. 1977, U.S. Tax Ct. 1977. Pvt. practice, LaGrange & Lake Counties, Ind., 1974-84; judge LaGrange County Ct., 1984-87, LaGrange Superior Ct., 1988—. Part-time chief dep. prosecutor LaGrange County, 1975—77; adj. faculty Tri-State U., Angola, Ind., 1991—. Vol. Jr. Achievement, 1997-2000, 01—. Mem.: Nat. Conf. State Trial Judges (criminal justice com.), Ind. Judges Assn. (com. protective orders), LaGrange County Bar Assn. (pres. 1978), Ind. State Bar Assn. (ho. of dels., written publs. com., com. on improvements in the jud. sys., written pub. com.), ABA, LaGrange Rotary (past dir., v.p. 1999—2000, pres. 2000—01, dir. 2002—). Office: Lagrange Superior Ct Courthouse Lagrange IN 46761

BROWN, GREGORY K. lawyer; b. Warren, Ohio, Dec. 9, 1951; s. George K. and Dorothy H. (Gaynor) B.; m. Joy M. Feinberg, Apr. 10, 1976. BS in Bus. & Econs., U. Ky., 1973; JD, U. Ill., 1976. Bar: Ill. 1976. Assoc. atty. McDermott, Will & Emery, Chgo., 1976-80, Mayer, Brown & Platt, Chgo., 1980-84; ptnr. Keck, Mahin & Cate, Chgo., 1984-93, Oppenheimer Wolff & Donnelly, Chgo., 1994-97, Seyfarth, Shaw, Fairweather & Geraldson, Chgo., 1997-2000, Gardner, Carton & Douglas, Chgo., 2000—. Contbg. author: The Handbook of Employee Ownership Plans, 1989, Employee Stock Ownership Plans, 1989 Active Chgo. Coun. Fgn. Rels. Named One of the Top Benefits Lawyers Nat. Law Jour., 1998. Mem.: ABA (chair employee stock ownership plan com., tax law sect. Nat. Ctr. Employee Ownership, Employee Stock Ownership Plan Assn. chair legis. and regulatory adv. c 1997—99), Chgo. Bar Assn. (chmn. employee benefits com. 1988—89). Avocations: basketball, bicycling, golf, opera, theatre. Mergers and acquisitions, Pension, profit-sharing, and employee benefits. Office: Gardner Carton & Douglas 191 N Wacker Dr Ste 3700 Chicago IL 60606-1698 E-mail: gkbrown@gcd.com.

BROWN, HAROLD EUGENE, retired magistrate; b. Damascus, Ark., Jan. 6, 1935; s. Amos Eugene and Hazel Gladys (Thomas) B.; m. Carolyn Marie Sanders, Aug. 26, 1972; children: James Daryl, Deena Leigh, Cynthia Marie. Student, U. Md. Overseas Divsn., Verdun, France, 1962-64, Germanna C.C., 1978-84. Enlisted U.S. Army, 1954, advanced through grades to sgt. maj., 1977; White House liaison Chief of Staff Army, Washington, 1969—73; dep. dir. Def. Coop. Agy., New Delhi, 1973—77; post sgt. maj., co. comdr Fort A.P. Hill, Bowling Green, Va., 1977—81; magistrate 15th dist. Supreme Ct. Va., Fredericksburg, 1982—2002, apptd. chief magistrate, 1987—2000, apptd. magistrate VI, 2000—02; ret., 2002. Marriage commr. Commonwealth Va., 1984. Bd. dirs., former dir. Rappahannock Coun. Domestic Violence; bd. dirs. Rappahannock United Way. Decorated Cross of Gallantry (Republic of Vietnam). Mem. Am. Judges Assn., Va. Magistrates Assn., Va. Cmty. Criminal Justice Assn., Ret. Sgts. Maj. Assn. Avocations: golf, photography, computer programming. Home: 21 Rosewood Dr Fredericksburg VA 22408-1521 E-mail: hebrown5@aol.com.

BROWN, HARRY M. lawyer, consultant; b. Oradia-Mare, Romania, Oct. 9, 1947; came to U.S., 1951; s. Bernard and Lydia Brown; m. Perl Keller, Aug. 10, 1969; children: Michael, Elissa, Rochel, Bentzion, Shmuel. BA, Yeshiva Coll., 1969; JD, NYU, 1972. Bar: Ohio 1972. Atty., ptnr. Benesch, Friedlander, Coplan & Aronoff, Cleve., 1972—. Finance, Health. Office: Benesch Friedlander Coplan 200 Public Sq Cleveland OH 44114-2301 E-mail: hbrown@bfca.com.

BROWN, HERBERT RUSSELL, lawyer, writer; b. Columbus, Ohio, Sept. 27, 1931; s. Thomas Newton and Irene (Hankinson) B.; m. Beverly Ann Jenkins, Dec. 2, 1967; children: David Herbert, Andrew Jenkins. BA, Denison U., 1953; JD, U. Mich., 1956. Assoc. Vorys, Sater, Seymour and Pease, Columbus, Ohio, 1956, 60-64, ptnr., 1965-82; treas. Sunday Creek Coal Co., Columbus, 1970-86; assoc. justice Ohio Supreme Ct., Columbus, 1987-93. Commr. Ohio Ethics Commn., 2002—, examiner Ohio Bar, 1967-72, Multi-State Bar, 1971-76, Dist. Ct. Bar, 1968-71; commr. Fed. Lands, Columbus, 1967-68, Lake Lands, Columbus, 1981; bd. dirs. Thurber House, 1992-94, Sunday Creek Coal Co.; adj. prof. Ohio State U. Coll. Law, 1997-2000; panelist Am. Arbitration Assn., 1993—. Author: (novels) Presumption of Guilt, 1991, Shadows of Doubt, 1994, (plays) You're My Boy, 1999, Peace with Honor, 2000, Mano A Mano, 2000, Power of God, 2002; mem. editl. bd. U. Mich. Law Rev., 1955-56. Trustee Columbus Bar Found., 1993—, pres., 2001—; candidate Ohio State Legis.; deacon, mem. governing bd. 1st Cmty. Ch., 1966—80; bd. dirs. Ctrl. Cmty. House Columbus, 1967—75. Capt. JAGC U.S. Army, 1956—57. Fellow Am. Coll. Trial Lawyers; mem. Ohio Bar Assn., Columbus Bar Assn. Democrat. Office: 5 E Long St Columbus OH 43215

BROWN, HERMIONE KOPP, lawyer; b. Syracuse, N.Y., Sept. 29, 1915; d. Harold H. and Frances (Burger) Kopp; m. Louis M. Brown, May 30, 1937 (dec. Sept. 1996); children— Lawrence D., Marshall J., Harold A. BA, Wellesley Coll., 1934; LLB, U. So. Calif., 1947. Bar: Calif. 1947. Story analyst 20th Century-Fox Film Corp., 1935-42; assoc. Gang, Kopp & Tyre, Los Angeles, 1947-52; ptnr. to sr. ptnr. Gang, Tyre, Ramer & Brown, Inc., Los Angeles, 1952—. Lectr. copyright and entertainment law U. So. Calif. Law Sch., 1974-77. Contbr. to profl. publs. Fellow Am. Coll. Trust and Estate Coun.; mem. Calif. Bar Assn. (chair probate law cons. group nd. legal specialization 1977-82, trust and probate law sect., exec. com. 1983-86, advisor 1986-89), L.A. Copyright Soc. (pres. 1979-80), Order of Coif, Phi Beta Kappa. Avocations: literature, theatre, music. Entertainment, Probate (including wills, trusts), Trademark and copyright. Office: Gang Tyre Ramer & Brown Inc 132 S Rodeo Dr Beverly Hills CA 90212-2415

BROWN, IFIGENIA THEODORE, lawyer; b. Syracuse, N.Y., Mar. 14, 1930; d. Gus and Christine Theodore; m. Paul Frederick Brown, Sept. 16, 1956; 1 child, Paul Darrow. BA, Syracuse U., 1951, LLB, JD, 1954. Bar: N.Y. 1956. Acting police justice Village of Ballston Spa, NY, 1960—62; sr. ptnr. Brown & Brown, Ballston Spa, 1958—95; ptnr. Brown Brown & Peterson Esqs, Ballston Spa, 1995—2000; of counsel Brown, Peterson and Craig, Ballston Spa, 2000—. Chmn. N.Y. State Bd. Real Property Svcs., Albany, 1996—. Mem. Charlton Sch. Bd., 1989-93, Ballston Spa Libr. Bd., 1991-94; founder, pres. Saratoga County Women's Rep. Club; vice-chmn. Saratoga County Rep. Com., 1958-72. Mem. N.Y. State Bar Assn., Saratoga County Bar Assn. (treas. 1983-84, pres. 1984-85), Zonta (pres. Saratoga County 1962, 90), Order Ea. Star. Republican. Greek Orthodox. Avocations: church choir, piano. Family and matrimonial, Probate (including wills, trusts), Property, real (including real estate development, water). Home: 42 Hyde Blvd Ballston Spa NY 12020-1608 Office: Brown Peterson and Craig One E High St Ballston Spa NY 12020

BROWN, JAMES BENTON, lawyer; b. Pitts., Jan. 18, 1945; s. Sidney J. and Marian R. (Bailiss) B.; m. Susan M. Brenner, Aug. 6, 1967; children: Jessica Lynn, Joshua David. BA, U. Louisville, 1967; JD, Duquesne U., 1971. Bar: Pa. 1971, U.S. Dist. Ct. (we. dist.) Pa. 1971, U.S. Ct. Appeals (3d cir.) 1974, U.S. Supreme Ct. 1982. Dir., ptnr. Cohen & Grigsby, P.C., head labor and employment group. Lectr. Pa. Bar Inst.; mediator Justus ADR; arbitrator Am. Arbitration Assn. Mem. ABA, Fed. Bar Assn., Am. Acad. Hosp. Attys., Pa. Bar Assn. (past vice chmn. labor and employment law sect.), Allegheny County Bar Assn., Internat. Assn. Def. Counsel, Akmont Yacht Club. Democrat. Federal civil litigation, Labor (including EEOC, Fair Labor Standards Act, labor-management relations, NLRB, OSHA). Home: 6739 Wilkins Ave Pittsburgh PA 15217-1318 Office: 15th fl 11 Stanwix St Ste 15 Pittsburgh PA 15222-1312 E-mail: jbrown@cohenlaw.com.

BROWN, JAMES JOSEPH, judge; b. Mineola, N.Y., Mar. 1, 1944; s. Thomas Patrick and Sally (Casey) B.; m. Alice May Manningham, Aug. 3, 1965; children: Thomas P., Scott L., Christine M., Daniel J. BA in History, U. Tex., 1968; JD, Boston Coll., 1971. Bar: Mass. 1971, U.S. Dist. Ct. Mass. 1971, U.S. Dist. Ct. Vt. 1972, U.S. Supreme Ct. 1973, U.S. Ct. Appeals (4th cir.) 1980, U.S. Ct. Appeals (5th cir.) 1983, U.S. Ct Appeals (10th cir.) 1984, Md. 1985, U.S. Dist. Ct. Md. 1985, U.S. Dist. Ct. D.C. 1986. Assoc. Levy & Winer PC, Greenfield, Mass., 1971-75; trial atty., dep. chief commercial litigation U.S. Dept. Justice, Washington, 1976-85, supervisory trial atty. environ. enforcement sec., 1987-90; supervisory trial atty. Asset Forfeiture Office Criminal div. U.S. Dept. Justice, 1990-95; U.S. adminstrv. law judge Office of Hearings and Appeals, Raleigh, N.C., 1995—. Sr. assoc. Saul, Ewing, Weinberg & Green, Balt., 1985-87; lectr., tchr. U.S. Dept. Justice, Washington, 1978-85, Russian Law Acad., Moscow and Samara, Russia, 1999. Author: Judgment Enforcement, 1994, pocket supplements, 1995-2003, 2d edit., 1999; editor: Scientific Evidence and Experts Handbook, 1999, pocket supplements, 2000-03. Sch. com. Town of Greenfield, 1973-75; bd. elders Forcey Meml. Ch., Silver Spring, Md., 1981-82, missions com. 1980-83, 88-90; bd. dirs. New Life Christian Camp, Raleigh, N.C., 2001—. With USNR, 1962-64. Recipient Outstanding Performance awards U.S. Dept. Justice, 1980-85, Spl. Achievement award, 1983, Disting. Svc. award, 1985. Mem. Mass. Bar Assn., Md. Bar Assn. Republican. Avocations: golf, poetry, writing. Office: US Administrative Law Judge Office of Hearings & Appeals 1305 Navaho Dr Raleigh NC 27609-7454 E-mail: james.j.brown@ssa.gov., jbrown358@nc.rr.com.

BROWN, JAN HOWARD, lawyer; b. Bklyn., Nov. 13, 1948; s. Monroe and Ruth B.; m. Deborah Lugo, Sept. 28, 1981 (dec. Feb. 26, 1992); children: Richard, Andrew; m. Elizabeth Jo Spaeth, Mar. 3, 1996. BA, Antioch Coll., 1973; JD, Western New Eng. Coll., 1976. Bar: N.Y. 1978, U.S. Dist. Ct. (so. dist. and ea. dist.) N.Y. 1978. Internat. lectr. U.S. immigration. Contbg. author: Visa Processing Guide, 1998—. Mem. Am. Immigration Lawyers Assn., N.Y. State Bar Assn. (chmn. immigration law com.). Immigration, naturalization, and customs. Office: Jan H Brown PC 225 W 57th St Ste 400 New York NY 10019 E-mail: jhb@janhbrown.com.

BROWN, JANICE ROGERS, state supreme court justice; b. Laverne, AL, May 11, 1949; BA , Ca. St. U., Sacramento, 1974; JD, UCLA, 1977. Assoc. justice Calif. Supreme Ct., San Francisco, 1996—. Office: Calif Supreme Ct 350 Mcallister St Rm 1295 San Francisco CA 94102-4783

BROWN, JEAN WILLIAMS, state supreme court justice; b. Birmingham, Ala. m. E. Terry Brown; 2 children. Grad. with honors, Samford U., 1974; JD, U. Ala., 1977. Bar: Ala. 1977, U.S. Ct. Appeals (11th cir.), U.S. Supreme Ct. Law clerk Tucker, Gray & Thigpen; asst. atty. gen. criminal appeals divsn., chief extradition officer Ala. Atty. Gen.'s Office; judge Ala. Ct. Criminal Appeals, 1997-99; justice Supreme Ct. Ala., 1999—. Tchr. kindergarten Sunday sch. 1st Bapt. Ch. Mem. Montgomery Jr. League. Office: Ala Supreme Ct 300 Dexter Ave Montgomery AL 36104-3741

BROWN, JERROLD STANLEY, lawyer; b. Little Falls, N.Y., Nov. 8, 1953; s. Stanley Clayton and Ruth Jane Brown; m. Catherine M. Agnello, Aug. 2, 1980. BA, SUNY, Albany, 1975; JD, Union U., 1979. Bar: N.Y. 1980, U.S. Dist. Ct. (no. dist.) N.Y. 1980, U.S. Dist. Ct. (we. dist.) N.Y. 1982, U.S. Ct. Appeals (2nd cir.) 1983, U.S. Supreme Ct. 1989. Law clk. to judge N.Y. Ct. Appeals, Albany, 1979-81; assoc. Hodgson Russ LLP, Buffalo, 1981-85; ptnr. Hodgson, Russ, Andrews, Woods & Goodyear, Buffalo, 1986—. Mem. adv. panel N.Y. Clean Air Act, 1996—. Note and comment editor Albany Law Rev., 1978-79. Mem. adv. bd. Salvation Army, Buffalo Area, 1999—; dir. Studio Arena Theatre, 1999—, v.p. bd. dirs., 2001—; ward leader Del. Dist. Rep. Party, 1992; Trustee Westminster Presbyn. Ch., Buffalo, 1986, pres., 1988, elder, 1992—93, 1997—2000. Mem. N.Y. State Bar Assn. (task force on commerce and industry 1998—). Federal civil litigation, State civil litigation, Environmental. Office: Hodgson Russ LLP Ste 2000 One M & T Plz Buffalo NY 14203

BROWN, JOE BLACKBURN, judge; b. Louisville, Dec. 9, 1940; s. Knox and Miriam (Blackburn) B.; m. Marilyn McGowen, Aug. 10, 1963; children: Jennifer Knox, Michael McGowen. BA cum laude, Vanderbilt U., 1962, JD, 1965. Bar: Ky. 1965, Tenn. 1972, U.S. Supreme Ct. 1979. Asst. U.S. atty. Dept. Justice, Nashville, 1971-73, 1st asst. U.S. atty., 1974-81, U.S. atty., 1981-91, spl. asst. U.S. trustee, 1991-98; U.S. magistrate judge, U.S. Dist. Ct. (mid. dist.) Tenn., Nashville, 1998—. Lectr. law Atty. Gen.'s Advocacy Inst., 1982—; vice chmn. Atty. Gen.'s Adv. Com., 1986-87, chmn. subcom. on sentencing guidelines, mem. subcom. on budget and office mgmt., 1982-91; instr. math. and bus. law Augusta (Ga.) Coll., 1966-69; instr. law Nashville Sch. Law, 1999—. Contbr. articles to legal jours. Bd. dirs. Mid-Cumberland Drug Abuse Coun., Nashville, 1977-86; asst. scoutmastr Boy Scouts Am.; vestryman St. David's Episcopal Ch., sr. warden, 1982, 90; ch. atty. Episcopal Diocese of Tenn., 1995-98; lt. col. CAP, 1996—. Maj. U.S. Army, 1965-71; col. JAGC, USAR ret. Decorated Legion of Merit, Meritorious Svc. medal with 3 oak leaf clusters; recipient Disting. Svc. award Atty. Gen.'s Adv. Com., 1988. Fellow Tenn. Bar Assn., Nashville Bar Found.; mem. FBA (treas. 1978), Nashville Bar Assn. (bd. dirs. 1995-97, exec. com. 1996-97, v.p. 1997), Radio Amateur Transmitting Soc. (pres. 1997-98), Nat. Assn. Flight Instrs., Profl. Assn. Div Instrs., Ky. Bar Assn., NRA (life, Disting. Rifleman award), Harry Phillip Inn of Ct. (master of bench and bar 1994—), Order of Coif, Phi Beta Kappa. Republican. Home: 3427 Woodmont Blvd Nashville TN 37215-1421 Office: US Courthouse Rm 797 801 Broadway Nashville TN 37203-3816 E-mail: joe_b_brown@tnmd.uscourts.gov.

BROWN, JOHN ROBERT, lawyer; b. Muskogee, Okla., Apr. 22, 1948; s. John Robert and Betty Jane (Singleterry) B. BA, MA, Cambridge U., 1972; STB, Gen. Theol. Sem., 1973; STM, Union Theol. Sem., 1978, Harvard U., 1982; MA, STL, U. Louvain, Belgium, 1979; JD, Howard U., 1991. Bar: Ga. 1991, D.C. 1991, U.S. Supreme Ct. 1997; admitted Middle Temple, London, 2000; ordained priest Episcopal Ch., 1972, received into Roman Cath. Ch., 2001. Tchr., headmaster St. John's Sch., Oklahoma City, 1973-77; novice Soc. St. John the Evangelist, Cambridge, Mass., 1979-81; minor canon Pro-Cathedral of Holy Trinity, Brussels, 1981-83; assoc. rector St. James Ch., L.A., 1983-87; hon. assisting priest Ch. of the Ascension and St. Agnes, Washington, 1987-91; legis. aide U.S. Ho. of Reps., Washington, 1987-91; hon. asst. priest Ch. of Our Savior, Atlanta, 1991—2001; staff atty. Ga. Legal Svcs., Atlanta, 1991-1995; asst. gen. counsel State Bar Ga., Atlanta, 1996—. Reader Ecumenical Inst. World Coun. Ch., Geneva, 1978, Huntington Libr., San Marino, Calif., 1985-86, Coll. of Preachers, Nat. Cathedral, Washington, 1987, fellow, Center for Ethics in Public Policy and the Professions, Emory U., 1996-98. Contbr. articles to profl. jours. Vol. NIH, 1987—88, Fed. Charitable Campaign, Washington, 1988—89, Atlanta Project, 1991—96; spiritual adv. com. AIDS Project, L.A., 1984—86; mem. Mayor's Task Force on Family Diversity, 1984—86, Mcpl. Elections Com. L.A., 1984—86; governing bd. Robert Wood Johnson Homeless Health Care Project, L.A., 1985—87; trustees com. Opera Am., 1994—2001; co-trustee Freeman Found., 1994—97; adv. bd. Caring Hands Programs, 1983—87; mem. adv. bd. United Way of Metro Atlanta, 1993—97; adv. bd. Metro Atlanta Cmty. Found., 1994—97; chmn. social justice grants com. Threshold Found., 1994—96; capt. The Old Guard of The Gate City Guard, Atlanta, 1998—; bd. dirs. S.W. Assn. Episcopal Schs., 1974—77, Anglican Roman Cath. Commn. of Belgium, 1981—83; chaplain Most Venerable Order of St. John of Jerusalem, 1996—; bd. dirs. Cmty. Counseling Svc., L.A., 1983—86, Acad. Performing Arts, L.A., 1984—85, Right to Life League So. Calif., 1984—86, Cape Coast Outreach Found., 1984—86, Coun. Battered Women, Atlanta, 1991—94, AID Atlanta, 1993—2002, Atlanta Opera, 1993—, ACLU of Ga., 1994—2002, Fund for So. Cmtys., 1995—98, Funding Exch., 1997—99, Cathedral of St. Philip Bookstore, 1998—2003. Named one of Outstanding Young Men of Am., 1974; Yale U. rsch. fellow, 1983; recipient Mayor's Phoenix award, Atlanta, 1997. Fellow: Ga. Bar Found. (life); mem.: ABA (vice-chmn. fed. legis. com. gen. practice sect. 1989—91), Soc. Colonial Wars, Patrons of the Vatican Mus., Commerce Club (Atlanta), City Tavern Club, Harvard Club (Washington), United Oxford and Cambridge U. Club (London). Administrative and regulatory, General civil litigation, Health. Office: State Bar of Ga 104 Marietta St # 100 Atlanta GA 30303

BROWN, JOSEPH WENTLING, lawyer; b. Norfolk, Va., July 31, 1941; s. Edwin Wallace and Nancy Jack (Wentling) B.; m. Pamela Jones, Aug. 18, 1966; children: Tyree, Palmer, Jeffrey, Hunter. BA, U. Va., 1965; LLB,

Washington and Lee U., 1968. Bar: Nev. 1969, D.C. 1976, U.S. Dist. Ct. Nev. 1969. Pres. Jones Vargas Law Firm, Las Vegas, 1997—. Commr. Nev. Dept. of Wildlife, 1979-85; mem. U.S. Fgn. Claims Settlement Commn., 1981-87; bd. dirs. State Justice Inst., 1988-89, Wells Fargo Bank (Nev.); mem. Bd. of Litigation, Mountain States Legal Found., 1978-82. Editor: Washington and Lee Lawyer, 1967-68. Bd. dirs. Nev. Devel. Authority, Las Vegas C. of C., Nev. Cath. Cmty. Svcs.; dep. counsel Rep. Nat. Conv., 1984; mem. Rep. Nat. Com., 2002—. Served with USMCR, 1963-69. Mem. ABA, ATLA, Nev. Bar Assn., Clark County Bar Assn., Spanish Trail Country Club, Rotary. Republican. Roman Catholic. Administrative and regulatory, Corporate, general, General practice. Home: 17 Sawgrass Ct Las Vegas NV 89113-1326 Office: Jones Vargas 3773 Howard Hughes Pkwy Suite 300 S Las Vegas NV 89109

BROWN, JOSEPH WILLIAM, retired patent agent; b. Evanston, Wyo., Sept. 19, 1919; s. James Jr. and Mary (Duncombe) Brown. BS, U. Wyo., 1943, JD, 1947. Bar: (Patent) 1947. Patent agt. Shell Devel., Calif., 1946-54, mgr. polymer divsn., 1954-72, mgr. patents, 1972-80, ret., 1980. Capt. U.S. Army, 1944—46. Patent, Trademark and copyright. Home: 698 E 2320 N Provo UT 84604-1749

BROWN, KENNETH LLOYD, lawyer; b. N.Y.C., Sept. 28, 1927; s. Edythe Schneider; m. Freya Dorothy Finkelstein, July 10, 1954; children: Ivy Hope Brown Hill, Patrice Shari Botting. BS, NYU, 1951; LLB, St. John's U., Bklyn., 1954. Bar: N.Y. 1955. Pvt. practice, Forest Hills, N.Y., 1955-61; asst. corp. counsel City of N.Y., 1962-78; ptnr. Rivkin, Radler & Kremer and predecessor firms, Uniondale, N.Y., 1977-98; pvt. practice Jamaica, N.Y., 1998—. Dem. dist. leader Queens County Dem. Orgn., Forest Hills, until 1982; mem. Forest Hills Jewish Ctr. With U.S. Army, 1945-47. Mem. Queens County Bar Assn. (various coms.), Am. Legion, Jewish War Vet. Post, Continental Regular Dem. Club (founder), Robert F. Kennedy, Jr. Dem. Club, B'nai B'rith, Masons, Knights of Pythias. Avocation: politics. Home: PO Box 457 Flushing NY 11375-0457 Office: 15049 Hillside Ave Jamaica NY 11432-3319 Fax: 718-297-5588.

BROWN, LAWRENCE CHARLES, lawyer; b. Johnson City, N.Y., Apr. 5, 1951; s. Charles Hugh and Cora Rose (O'Connor) B.; m. Constance Angela Grimes, July 28, 1973; children: Jason P., Christina M. BS, Cornell U., 1973; MA, SUNY, Albany, 1974; JD, Syracuse U., 1977. Bar: N.Y. 1978, U.S. Dist. Ct. (we. dist.) N.Y. 1978, U.S. Dist. Ct. (so. dist.) N.Y. 1986, U.S. Tax Ct. 1987, U.S. Court Appeals (2nd Circuit) 1998, U.S. Supreme Court 1998. Assoc. Phillips, Lytle, Hitchcock, Blaine & Huber, Buffalo, N.Y., 1977-78, Hodgson, Russ, Andrews, Woods & Goodyear, Buffalo, 1978-82; ptnr. Lipsitz, Green, Fahringer, Roll, Salisbury & Cambria, Buffalo, 1982-94, Kavinoky & Cook, LLP, 1994-96; prin. Law Offices of Lawrence C. Brown, Buffalo, 1996—. Treas. Fund for Pub. Edn./Comml. Law Found., 2002-; advisor high sch. moot ct. teams for state bar program; presenter in field. Rsch. editor Syracuse U. Law Rev., 1976-77; mem. editl. bd. Comml. Law Jour., 1998—, Comml. Law Bull., 1998-, bd. editors, DePaul Business & Commercial Law Journal, 2002-; contbr. articles to profl. jours. Mem. ABA, N.Y. State Bar Assn., Erie County Bar Assn., Comml. Law League Am. (nat. vice chmn. practice and procedure com. 1989-91, nat. vice chmn. uniform laws com. 1990—, nat. chmn. uniform laws com. 1992-95, advisor 1995-2002), Pi Kappa Alpha. Methodist. Avocation: public speaking. Bankruptcy, General civil litigation, Commercial, contracts (including sales of goods; commercial financing). Office: 360 Dingens St Buffalo NY 14206-2353 E-mail: lcbrown36000@cs.com., brownl724@aol.com.

BROWN, MARY RAWSON, retired lawyer; b. Pitts., May 7, 1945; d. Daniel P. and Mary P. (Wilson) B. AB with honors, Middlebury (Vt.) Coll., 1966; MA, Northwestern U., 1969; EdD, Cath. U. Am., 1980; JD cum laude, Harvard U., 1985. Bar: Mass. 1985. House dir. Northwestern U., 1968; dist. mgr., other positions New Eng. Telephone, AT&T, Boston, other locations, 1969-84; assoc. Bingham, Dana & Gould, Boston, 1985-86; pvt. practice Mashpee, Mass., 1986—95, Vineyard Haven, Mass., 1995—2002; ret., 2002. Mem. Conservation Commn., Mashpee, 1985-89; bd. dirs. Hospice of Martha's Vineyard, Martha's Vineyard Hosp., Shellfish Adv. Coun. Mem. Mass. Conveyancers Assn. (exec. com. 1992-94), Mortar Board. Avocations: sailing, cooking, nordic track skiing, tennis. Address: PO Box 1356 Vineyard Haven MA 02568-1356

BROWN, MEREDITH M. lawyer; b. N.Y.C., Oct. 18, 1940; s. John Mason Brown and Catherine (Screven) Meredith; m. Sylvia Lawrence Barnard, July 17, 1965; 1 child, Mason Barnard. AB, Harvard U., 1961, JD, 1965. Bar: N.Y. 1965, U.S. Ct. Appeals (2d cir.) 1966, U.S. Dist. Ct. (so. dist.) N.Y. 1976. Law clk. to Hon. Leonard P. Moore U.S. Ct. Appeals (2d cir.), N.Y.C., 1965-66; assoc. Debevoise & Plimpton, N.Y.C., 1966-72, ptnr., 1973—, co-chair corp. dept., 1993—2001, chair or co-chair mergers and acquisitions group, 1985—. Author: (with others) Takeovers: A Strategic Guide to Mergers & Acquisitions, 2001, Global Offerings, 1994, Privatisations, 1994, Mechanics of Global Equity Offerings, 1995, International Mergers and Acquisitions: An Introduction, 1999; contbr. articles to profl. publs. Mem. ABA (fed. regulation of securities com., bus. law sect.), Assn. of Bar of City of N.Y. (chmn. profl. responsibility com. 1987-90), Internat. Bar Assn. (co-chmn. com. on issues and trading of securities, sect. on bus. law 1994-98, co-chmn. capital markets forum, sec. bus. law 1998-2002). Corporate, general, Mergers and acquisitions, Securities. Home: 1021 Park Ave New York NY 10028-0959 E-mail: mmbrown@debevoise.com.

BROWN, MICHAEL DEWAYNE, federal agency administrator, lawyer; b. Guymon, Okla., Nov. 11, 1954; s. Wayne E. and R. Eloise B.; m. Tamara Ann Oxley, July 19, 1973; children: Jared Michael, Amy Aryann. Student, Southeastern State Coll., 1973-75; BA in Polit. Sci. and English, Cen. State U., Edmond, Okla., 1978; JD, Oklahoma City U., 1981. Bar: Okla. 1982, Colo. 1992, U.S. Dist. Ct. (no. and we. dists.) Okla. 1982, U.S. Ct. Appeals (10th cir.) 1982, U.S. Ct. Appeals (D.C. cir.) 1987. Assoc. Long, Ford, Lester & Brown, Enid, Okla., 1982-87; pvt. practice Enid, 1987—; gen. counsel & deputy dir. Fed. Emergency Mgmt. Agy., 2001—02; under secy. Preparedness & Response U.S. Dept. Homeland Security, Wash., DC, 2003—. Adj. prof. state and local govt. law legis. Oklahoma City U.; cons. No. Okla. Devel. Assn., Enid, 1983-91; gen. counsel Alpha Oil Co., Duncan, Okla., 1985—, Physicians Mgmt. Svc. Corps., 1985-90, Physicians of Okla., Inc., Physicians Med. Plan Okla., Inc., City Nat. Bank & Trust Co., 1987-88, Stanfield Printing Co., 1987—, Hammell Newspapers, Inc., 1987-90, Dillingham Ins., 1989-91, Suits Rig Corp., Suits Drilling Co., 1989-91; chmn. bd. dirs. Okla. Mcpl. Power Authority, Edmond, 1982-88, judges & stewards commr. Internat. Arabian Horse Assn., 1991—. Councilman City of Edmond, 1981; cons. Okla. Reps., Oklahoma City, 1983; bd. dirs. Okla. Christian Home, Edmond, 1985; Rep. nominee 6th Dist. U.S. Congress, 1988; co-chmn. Nat. Challengers Polit. Coalition, 1989-91; trustee, co-chair fin. com. Theodore Roosevelt Assn., 1994—. Michael D. Brown Hydroelectric Power Plant and Dam named in his honor, Kaw Reservoir, Okla., 1987. Mem. Okla. Bar Assn. (assoc. bar examiner 1984—), MD Physicians Okla., Ariz. and La., MD Physicians of Tulsa. Mem. Christian Ch. (Disciples Of Christ). Avocations: travel, photography, reading, wilderness adventures, swimming. Office: Dept Homeland Security Washington DC 20528*

BROWN, NORMAN JACK, lawyer; b. Liberal, Kans., Apr. 21, 1934; s. Oliver Scott and Doris Evelyn (Thompson) B.; m. Sharon Kay Crawford, Aug. 19, 1956; children: Deborah Kay, Dale Scott, Deanna Patricia. AB, U. Kans., 1956, JD, 1958. Bar: Kans. 1959, U.S. Dist. Ct. Kans. 1959, U.S. Ct. Appeals (4th cir.) 1966. Claims adjuster Am. Family Mut. Ins. Co., Kansas City, Mo., 1958-59, subrogation atty. St. Joseph, Mo., 1959, regional claims counsel, 1959-60; assoc. Boddington & Boddington, Kansas City, Kans., 1960—65; ptnr. Boddington, Boddington & Brown, Kansas City, 1965-67, Boddington & Brown, Kansas City, 1967-70, 78-87, Boddington, Brown & Unverferth, Kansas City, 1970-78; shareholder, bd. dirs., pres. Boddington & Brown, Chartered, Kansas City, 1987—. City atty. City of Fairway, Kans., 1974—; mcpl. judge City of Westwood, Kans., 1966-67; mediator U.S. Dist. Ct. Kans., Kansas City, 1992—. Pres. Roeland Park (Kans.) City Coun., 1964-66; pres. Kansas City (Kans.) Jaycees, 1966, Johnson County Boys Clubs, Fairway, Kans., 1968, Terrace Club, Kansas City, 1986, Toastmasters Internat., St. Joseph, 1960; chmn. Mayor's Adv. Coun. of Johnson County, Kans., 1967-69; mem. future direction com. Kans. Jaycees, 1967-68. Named one of Three Outstanding Young Men of Kans. 1966, Young Man of Yr., Shawnee Mission Jaycees, 1966, Sen., Jaycees Internat., 1968; recipient Spl. Svc. award Boys Club Am., 1969, State Speak-Up award Kans. Jaycees, 1968. Mem. ABA, Am. Bd. Trial Advocates (advocate), Kans. Bar Assn., Wyandotte County Bar Assn. (bd. govs. 1986-87). Republican. Avocations: fishing, hunting, cooking, reading. General civil litigation, Insurance, Personal injury (including property damage). Office: Boddington & Brown Chartered 100 Security Bank Bldg 7th And Ann Kansas City KS 66101-3077

BROWN, OMER FORREST, II, lawyer; b. Somerville, N.J., Mar. 4, 1947; s. George Alvin and Frances (Schnitzler) B.; m. Sandra J. Cannon, Apr. 3, 1982. AB, Rutgers U., 1969; JD, Cornell U., 1972. Bar: N.J. 1972, D.C. 1974, U.S. Supreme Ct. 1976. Dept. atty. gen. dept. law and pub. safety State of N.J., Trenton, 1972-75; sr. trial atty. U.S. Dept. Energy, Washington, 1979-83; ptnr. Davis Wright Tremaine, Washington, 1987-96, Harmon, Wilmot & Brown, LLP, Washington, 1997—. Bd. dirs., sec. VideoTakes, Inc., Arlington, Va., 1986—; vis. lectr. Cornell U., 1993-95, 2002; guest lectr. Cornell U. Law Sch., 1993-95, 2002—; mem. OECD Contact Group on Nuclear Safety Assistance for Eastern Europe, 1994—; mem. G-7 Joint Task Force on Ukrainian Nuclear Legislation, 1996—. Contbr. numerous articles on energy, enviro. and ins. law to legal jours. Capt. USAR, 1969-75. Recipient Class of 1931 award Rutgers U. Alumni Assn., 1979, Loyal Son of Rutgers award, 1980. Mem. ABA (various offices tort and ins. practice sect. 1981-96, coord. group on energy law 1995-99), Internat. Bar Assn., Fed. Bar Assn., Univ. Club (Washington). Democrat. Roman Catholic. Nuclear power, Environmental, Public international. Address: PO Box 419 Saint Michaels MD 21663-0419 E-mail: omerb@aol.com.

BROWN, PATRICIA IRENE, retired law librarian, lawyer; b. Boston; d. Joseph Raymond and Harriet A. (Taylor) B. BA, Suffolk U., 1955, JD, 1965, MBA, 1970; MST, Gordon Conwell Theol. Sem., 1977. Bar: Mass. 1965. Libr. asst. Suffolk U., Boston, 1951-60, asst. libr., 1960-65, asst. law libr., 1965-85, assoc. law libr., 1985-92; ret.; human resources counselor Winthrop (Mass.) Sr. Ctr., 1993—. Dir. Referral/Resource Ctr., Union Congl. Ch., Winthrop, Mass.; vol. health benefits counselor Mass. Dept. Elder Affairs, 1994—. First Woman inducted into Nat. Baseball Hall of Fame, Cooperstown, N.Y., 1988, All- Am. Girls Profl. Baseball League, 1950-51. Mem. Assn. Am. Law Librs., Am. Congl. Assn. (bd. dirs. 1992—), Mass. Bar Assn. Avocations: television and movie history, walking, computers. Home: 1100 Governors Dr Apt 26 Winthrop MA 02152-3254 E-mail: pbrown@acad.suffolk.edu.

BROWN, PAUL EDMONDSON, lawyer; b. Van Buren County, Iowa, Dec. 24, 1915; s. William Allen and Margaret (Edmondson) B.; m. Lorraine Hill, Jan. 9, 1944; 1 child, Scott. BA, U. Iowa, 1938, JD with distinction, 1941. Bar: Iowa 1941, U.S. Supreme Ct. 1966. Ptnr. Mahoney, Brown, Mahoney, Boone, Iowa, 1946-52; v.p., counsel Bankers Life Co. (now Prin. Fin. Group), Des Moines, 1952-80; of counsel Grefe & Sidney, Des Moines, 1980-84, Davis, Hockensberg, Wine, Brown, Koehn, Shors, Des Moines, 1984-91; pvt. practice Des Moines, 1991—. Atty. County of Boone, Iowa, 1948-52; pres. Iowa Life Ins. Assn., Des Moines, 1980-85. With U.S. Army, 1942-46, col. USAR, 1946-70. Named Outstanding Young Man of Iowa, Iowa State Jr. C. of C., 1948; named to Iowa Ins. Hall of Fame, 2001. Mem. ABA, Iowa Bar Assn., Polk County Bar Assn., Assn. Life Ins. Counsel, U. Iowa Alumni Assn. (mem. Pres.' Club and various coms.), Civil War Roundtable, World War II State Monument Com., Downtown Des Moines Kiwanis Club (pres. 1961, Hixson fellow 1999). Republican. Congregationalist. Corporate, general, Insurance, Legislative. Home and Office: 5804 Harwood Dr Des Moines IA 50312-1206 Fax: 515-255-7900. E-mail: peb200@aol.com.

BROWN, PAUL M. lawyer; b. Jan. 10, 1938; s. I. Harry and Rose L. (Kresge) B.; m. Helga J. Fischer, Aug. 4, 1962 (div. 1977); children: Stephanie J., William A.; m. Ruth Reiter, June 28, 1986. Student, Williams Coll., 1955-57; BS in Econs., U. Pa., 1959; LLB, Columbia U., 1962. Bar: N.Y. 1963, U.S. Ct. Appeals (2d cir.) 1963, U.S. Dist. Ct. (so. and ea. dists.) N.Y. 1964, U.S. Dist. Ct. Mass. 1981, U.S. Ct. Appeals (3d cir.), U.S. Ct. Appeals (1st cir.) 1982, U.S. Dist. Ct. (we. dist.) N.Y. 1983, U.S. Ct. Appeals (6th cir.) 1983, U.S. Dist. Ct. R.I. 1985, U.S. Dist. Ct. (ea. dist.) Mich. 1986. Assoc. Berman & Frost, N.Y.C., 1963-66; ptnr. Havens, Wandless, Slitt and Tighe, N.Y.C., 1966-74, Whitman and Ransom, N.Y.C., 1975-94, Parson & Brown, N.Y.C., 1994-99, Satterlee Stephens Burke & Burke, N.Y.C., 1999—. Councilman Closter, N.J., 1970-74; police commr. Closter, 1970-73; trustee No. Valley Regional H.S., Demarest, N.J., 1972. With USAR, 1962-68. Mem. Assn. of Bar of City of N.Y., N.Y. State Bar Assn., Fed. Bar Coun., Am. Arbitration Assn. (panel of arbitrators), Univ. Club, Columbia Golf & Country Club, Las Campanas (N.Mex.) Club. Democrat. Federal civil litigation, State civil litigation, Construction. Office: Satterlee Stephens Burke & Burke 230 Park Ave New York NY 10169-0079 E-mail: pbrown@ssbb.com.

BROWN, PAUL NEELEY, federal judge; b. Denison, Tex., Oct. 4, 1926; s. Arthur Chester and Nora Frances (Hunter) B.; m. Frances Morehead, May 8, 1955; children: Paul Gregory, David H. II. JD, U. Tex., 1950. Assoc. Keith & Brown, Sherman, Tex., 1951-53, Brown & Brown, Sherman, 1953; asst. U.S. atty. for Ea. Dist. Tex. Texarkana and Tyler, Tex., 1953-59; U.S. atty. Ea. Dist. Tex., Tyler, 1959-61; ptnr. Brown & Brown and Brown Brothers & Perkins, Sherman, 1961-65, Brown and Perkins, Sherman, 1965; sole practice, Sherman, 1965-67; ptnr. Brown & Hill, Sherman, 1967, Brown Kennedy Hill & Minshew, Sherman, 1967-71, Brown & Hill, Sherman, 1971-76, Brown Hill Ellis & Brown, Sherman, 1976-85; U.S. dist. judge U.S. Dist. Ct. (ea. dist.) Tex., Sherman, 1985—. Served with USN, 1944-46, 50-51. Fellow Tex. Bar Found.; mem. Rotary. Presbyterian. Office: US Dist Ct Fed Bldg 101 E Pecan St Sherman TX 75090-5989

BROWN, PAUL SHERMAN, lawyer; b. June 26, 1921; s. Paul Michael and Norma (Sherman) Brown; m. Ann Wilson, Feb. 7, 1959; 1 child, Paul S. BS in Commerce, St. Louis U., 1943, JD cum laude, 1951. Bar: Mo. 51, U.S. Dist. Ct. (ea. dist.) Mo. 51, U.S. Ct. Appeals (8th cir.) 51, U.S. Supreme Ct. 66. Shareholder Brown & James, P.C., St. Louis, 1980—. Instr. St. Louis U. Night Law Sch., 1978—; lectr. in field; mem. com. on civil pattern jury instructions Mo. Supreme Ct. Contbr. articles to profl. jours. Fellow: Internat. Soc. Barristers, Internat. Acad. Trial Lawyers, Am. Coll. Trial Lawyers; mem.: ABA (vice-chmn. com. consumer products liability 1977—78), Am. Judicature Soc., Bar Assn. Met. St. Louis (pres. 1970—71), Lawyers Assn. St. Louis, Am. Bd. Trial Advocates, Mo. Bar Assn. (bd. govs. 1963—67), Order of Woolsack, St. Louis Amateur Athletic Assn. (bd. dirs. 1974—76, pres. 1976—78), Alpha Sigma Nu. Roman Catholic. Federal civil litigation, State civil litigation, Insurance. Home: 7331 Kingsbury Blvd Saint Louis MO 63130-4143 Office: Brown & James 1010 Market St Ste 18 Saint Louis MO 63101-2270

BROWN, PETER MEGARGEE, lawyer, writer, lecturer; b. Cleve., Mar. 15, 1922; s. George Estabrook and Miriam (Megargee) B.; m. Alexandra Johns Stoddard, May 18, 1974; children: Peter, Blair Tillyer, Andree de Rapalyee, Nathaniel Holmes; stepchildren: Alexandra, Brooke Stoddard, Wallace Davis. Student, U. Calif., Berkeley, 1943-44; BA, Yale U., 1945, JD, 1948. Bar: N.Y. 1949. Spl. asst. atty. gen. State N.Y. and asst. counsel N.Y. State Crime Commn., 1951-53; asst. U.S. atty. So. Dist. N.Y., 1953-55, spl. asst., 1956; ptnr. firm Cadwalader, Wickersham & Taft, N.Y.C., 1959-82, head litigation and ethics coms.; ptnr. Brown & Seymour, N.Y.C., 1983-96; counsellor-at-law Peter Megargee Brown, N.Y.C., 1996—. Mem. Mayor's Com. on Judiciary, 1965-72, vice chmn., 1972-74 Author: The Art of Questioning: Thirty Maxims of Cross-Examination, 1987, Flights of Memory-Days Before Yesterday, 1989, Rascals: The Selling of the Legal Profession, 1989, One World at a Time: Tales of Murder, Joy and Love, 1991, Village: Where to Live and How to Live, 1997, Riot of the Century (Civil War Draft Riot 1863), 1999; author essays, articles on law profession, life and humor, pub. nationally. Mem. N.Y. County Rep. Com., 1958—; counsel on crime to Nelson Rockefeller, Campaign for Gov. N.Y.S., 1968; bd. dirs. Yale Alumni Fund, 1979-84; bd. dirs., pres. Episcopal Ch. Found., 1989-93; master of ceremonies Yale Class of 1944 50th Reunion, 1994, 55th reunion, 1999; chmn., co-founder Design and Art Soc., Ltd., N.Y.C.; pres. Trustees Riot Relief Fund; bd. regent Cath. St. John Divine; founding mem. Henry Morrison Flagler Mus., Palm Beach, Fla.; mediator, East Side N.Y. gang warfare, 1956-57; counsel Grand Jury Assn. N.Y. County, 1956-79; orientation specialist U.S. Army WWII, 1943-46; editor in ch. Camp Bowie Blade (commendation). Decorated knight Order St. John of Hosp. of Jerusalem, Soc. of Anchor Cross; recipient award for svc. to profession Fed. Bar Assn., N.Y., N.J. and Conn., 1962; recipient Trustees Gold medal for disting. svc., Fed. Bar Coun., 1971; Chmn.'s award Yale Alumni Fund, 1979, Disting. Svc. award Class of 1944, Yale U., 1983, Henry Knox Sherrill medal for outstanding svc. Episcopal Ch. Found., 1993, Speakers prize Browning Sch., Headmaster's medal for pub. svc. St. Andrew's Sch.; Named record scorer U.S. Army Phys. Efficiency Test 1943 (697 out of possible 700 a score still unbroken). Fellow Am. Bar Found., Am. Coll. Trial Lawyers, N.Y. State Bar Found.; mem. ABA, World Assn. Lawyers (founding), Soc. Colonial Wars, New England Soc., Sons of the Revolution, N.Y. State Bar Assn., Assn. of Bar of City of N.Y., Fed. Bar Coun. Found. (trustee, pres. 1961-62, chmn. bd. 1962-64, chmn. judiciary com. 1960-85), chmn. planning and program com. 2d cir. judicial conf. 1976-80), St. Nicholas Soc. (past pres.), Delta Kappa Epsilon (Phi chpt. Yale), Phi Delta Phi (magister Waite Inn 1947, pres. province I 1950-55). Episcopalian (vestryman, sr. warden 1961-77). Clubs: Union (N.Y.C.); Coral Beach (Bermuda). Federal civil litigation, General civil litigation, State civil litigation. Office: 1125 Park Ave Ste 6A New York NY 10128-1243

BROWN, RALPH SAWYER, JR., retired lawyer, business executive; b. Cohasset, Mass., July 21, 1931; s. Ralph Sawyer and Rosemary (Wyman) B.; m. Elizabeth Atkinson Rash, June 12, 1953; children— Lucy Victoria Phillips, Alexander Sawyer Batson. BA, Swarthmore Coll., 1954; LLB, Harvard U., 1957. Bar: Mass. bar 1957, N.Y. State bar 1963. Assoc. Hutchins & Wheeler, Boston, 1957-62, Carter, Ledyard & Milburn, N.Y.C., 1962-68; ptnr. Janklow & Traum, N.Y.C., 1968-71; sec., asst. gen. counsel Indian Head, Inc., N.Y.C., 1971-76, v.p., treas., 1976-79; v.p., gen. counsel, sec. Esquire, Inc., N.Y.C., 1979-83, sr. v.p., gen. counsel, sec., 1983-84; assoc. counsel Paramount Communications Inc., N.Y.C., 1984-93, sr. counsel, 1993-94. Mem. Phi Beta Kappa. Home: 160 W 86th St Ph 4 New York NY 10024-4074

BROWN, RHONDA ROCHELLE, chemist, health facility administrator, lawyer; b. Shelbyville, Ky., July 13, 1956; d. Clifton Theophilus and Fannie Mae (Lawson) B. BA in Chemistry, U. Md., 1978; MA, Central Mich. U., 1983; JD, No. Va. Law Sch., 1992. Bar: Wash. 1998, D.C. 1994, U.S. Dist. Ct. D.C., U.S. Dist. Ct. Md. Analytical chemist Dept. Health and Mental Hygiene, Annapolis, Md., 1978-83, epidemiologist Balt., 1983-88; patent examiner U.S. Patent and Trademark Office, Xtal City, Va., 1989-90; freelance researcher New Carrollton, Md., 1990—; lawyer, pvt. practice Washington, 1998—. Mem. Am. Chem. Soc., Washington, 1978-82; mem., exec. bd. Nat. Lawyers Guild, Washington, 1987—; pres. Voucher Express, 1993—; mediator Superior Ct., Washington, 1993—; legal advt. mgr. Sentinel Newspaper. Subcommittee chmn. Anne Arundel County Task Force for Drug and Alcohol Abuse, 1979-80; pres., bd. mem. Md. Ornithological Soc., 1979-82; mem., exec. bd. Md. Condominium and Homeowners Assn., Rockville, Md., 1988-91. Named Outstanding Young Women of Am., 1983. Mem. ABA, ATLA (family divsn. 1999—), Nat. Assn. Criminal Def. Lawyers, Superior Ct. Trial Lawyers Assn. (criminal and family divsn.), Nat. Intellectual Propery Law Assn., Anne Arundel County Tennis Assn., Sigma Iota Epsilon.

BROWN, RICHARD L. lawyer; b. N.Y.C., Nov. 9, 1944; s. S. Robert and Frances S. B.; children: Jesselyn Alicia, Justin Alexander, Jeremy Brandon, Matthew Tyler, Garrett William. BA, Emory U., 1966; JD, NYU, 1969. Bar: N.Y. 1969, D.C. 1973, U.S. Ct. Appeals (D.C. cir.) 1974, U.S. Ct. of Claims 1980, U.S. Supreme Ct. 1980. Atty., advisor FCC, Washington, 1969-72; assoc. firm Farrow, Cahill, Kaswell & Schildhause, Washington, 1972-75; sr. ptnr. Brown Nietert & Kaufman, Chartered, Washington, 1975—. Gen. counsel Community Antenna TV Assn., 1972-75; pres. Alaskan Cable Network, Inc., Fairbanks, 1980-85; v.p., gen. counsel Soc. for Pvt. and Comml. Earth Stas., 1980-86; chmn. bd. trustees Rock Creek Internat. Sch., Washington, 2999-2002. Author: Low Power TV Handbook, 1981, licensing manual for land mobile radio-TV, 1980; co-author: The Satellite Earth Station Zoning Book, Questions & Answers About Satellite Earth Stations, The Business of Private Cable Television, The Low-Power TV Manual; contbr. articles to profl. jours. Mem. ABA, Fed. Communications Bar Assn. Communications. Office: Brown Nietert & Kaufman Chartered 2000 L St NW Ste 817 Washington DC 20036

BROWN, RICHARD LAWRENCE, lawyer; b. Evansville, Ind., Dec. 8, 1932; s. William S. and Mildred (Tenbarge) B.; m. Alice Rae Costello, June 14, 1957; children: Richard, Catherine, Vanessa, Mary, James. AA, Vincennes U., 1953; BA, Ind. State U., 1957; JD, Ind. U., 1960. Bar: Ind., 1960, U.S. dist. ct. (so. dist.) Ind., 1961, U.S. Ct. Apls. (7th cir.), 1972, U.S. Sup. Ct., 1972. Mng. ptnr. Butler, Brown, Hahn and Little, and predecessor firms, Indpls., 1961-85, Butler, Brown and Blythe, Indpls., 1985-92; city atty. City of Beech Grove, Ind., 1967—; pvt. practice, Beech Grove, 1992-2001; of counsel Blythe & Ost, Indpls., 1994-96, Holwager, Byers & Caughy, Beech Grove, 1996-2001. Sec., treas. Internat. Bus. Inst., Dayton, Ohio, 1987—, Internat. Pub. Inst., Dayton, 1987-96; bd. dirs. Vincennes U. Found. Editor: Indiana Municipal Lawyers Assn. Newsletter, 1985—. Chmn. bd. zoning appeals small cities and towns Marion County, Ind., 1965-66; gen. counsel Habitat for Humanity Greater Indpls., 1985-95; parish chmn. St. Jude's Ch. With U.S. Army, 1953-55. Fellow Indpls. Bar Assn.; mem. ABA, Ind. Bar Assn., Ind. Mcpls. Lawyers Assn. (co-editor newsletter, bd. dirs., pres. 1987-88), Vincennes U. Alumni Assn. (pres., bd. dirs. 1990-92), KC, Delta Theta Phi. Roman Catholic. Avocation: golf. Federal civil litigation, State civil litigation. Office: 1818 Main St Beech Grove IN 46107-1418 E-mail: rbrown080@comcast.net.

BROWN, RICHARD LEE, lawyer, director; b. Ft. Worth, Dec. 7, 1925; s. Marvin H. and Janie (McIntosh) B.; m. Elizabeth McPherson, Nov. 19, 1949; children: Beverly Elizabeth, Leigh Ann (dec.). Student, Rice U., 1942-43; LLB, U. Tex., 1949; LLM, George Washington U., 1954. Bar: Tex. 1949. Asst. dist. atty., Tarrant County, 1949- 50; spl. atty. Chief Counsel's Office, IRS, Washington, 1953-56; partner Friedman & Brown, 1956-60, Stone, Parker, Snakard & Brown, 1961-66, Law, Snakard, Brown & Gambill, 1967-81, 83-84; of counsel Bishop Payne Harvard & Kaitler, Ft. Worth, 1984-89, 91—; judge Ct. Appeals Tex. 2d Dist., 1981-83; chief civil div. Tarrant County Dist. Atty's Office, 1989-91. Former mem. bd. commrs. Pub. Housing Authority Ft. Worth, chmn., 1976-77; Chmn. bd., chmn. competition Van Cliburn Internat. Piano Competition, 1966-69. Served with

AUS, 1944-46; Served with U.S. Army, 1950-53. Decorated Bronze Star medal, Combat Infantry badge and 3 battle stars. Fellow Tex. Bar Found. (life); mem. Tex. Bar Assn., Tarrant County Bar Assn. (pres. 1977-78) Office: 1800 Bank of Am Bldg 500 W 7th St Fort Worth TX 76102-4700

BROWN, ROBERT CARROLL, lawyer; b. Ridley Park, Pa., June 24, 1948; s. Robert Carroll Sr. and Marjorie Elizabeth (Nowell) B.; m. Charlene M. Lipp, Oct. 4, 1986; children: Robert Charles, Gregory Scott, Michael Joseph. AB in Polit. Sci., Pa. State U., 1970; JD, Temple U., 1973. Bar: Pa.; U.S. Dist. Ct. (ea. dist.) Pa. 1977, Pa. Supreme Ct. 1973, U.S. Ct. Appeals (3d cir.) 1980. Judicial law clk. Ct. Common Pleas/Northampton County, Easton, Pa., 1973-74; assoc. Fox & Oldt, Easton, 1974-82; ptnr. Fox, Oldt & Brown, Easton, 1982—. Sec. Greater Easton Corp., 1977-82, Two Rivers Area Commerce Coun., Easton, 1983-85; officer Lehigh Valley Flying Club, Allentown, Pa., 1979-99. Mem. Northampton County Bar Assn. (sec. 1983-84), Pa. Bar Assn., Pa. Trial Lawyers Assn., Pa. Def. Inst. Republican. Presbyterian. Avocations: private pilot, sports cars, golf, spectator sports. Probate (including wills, trusts), Personal injury (including property damage), Product liability. Home: 420 Wedgewood Dr Easton PA 18045-5753 Office: Fox Oldt & Brown 6 S 3rd St Ste 508 Easton PA 18042-4591 E-mail: rcbjr2001@cs.com.

BROWN, ROBERT CHARLES, lawyer; b. Southington, Conn., Oct. 26, 1954; s. Herbert L. and Agnes Reba (Lewis) B.; children: Matthew Justin, Allyn Michelle. BA, Wofford Coll., 1976; JD, U. S.C., 1979. Bar: S.C. 1979, U.S. Dist. Ct. S.C. 1978, U.S. Ct. Appeals (4th cir.) 1980, U.S. Supreme Ct. 1991. Assoc. Alford & Johnson, Columbia, SC, 1979—82; ptnr. Alford, Johnson & Salane, Columbia, SC, 1982—84, Brown & Brehmer (formerly Brown & Woods), Columbia, 1984—. Mem. S.C. Def. Trial Attys. Assn., Def. Rsch. Inst., Am. Bd. Trial Advocates, Phi Beta Kappa, Omicron Delta Kappa. Republican. Episcopalian. Avocations: snow skiing, sailing, scuba diving. General civil litigation, Insurance, Personal injury (including property damage). Office: Brown & Brehmer 1720 Main St Ste 201 Columbia SC 29201-2850

BROWN, ROBERT LAIDLAW, state supreme court justice; b. Houston, June 30, 1941; s. Robert Raymond and Warwick (Rust) B.; m. Charlotte Banks, June 18, 1966; 1 child, Stuart Laidlaw. BA, U. of the South, 1963; MA in English and Comparative Lit., Columbia U., 1965; JD, U. Va., 1968. Bar: Ark. 1968, U.S. Dist. Ct. (ea. and we. divs.) Ark. 1968. Assoc. Chowning, Mitchell, Hamilton & Burrow, Little Rock, 1968-71; dep. prosecuting atty. 6th Jud. Dist., Prosecuting Atty. Office, Little Rock, 1971-72; legal aide Office Gov. Dale Bumpers, Little Rock, 1972-74; legis. asst. U.S. Senator Dale Bumpers, Washington, 1975-76; adminstrv. asst. Congressman Jim Guy Tucker, Washington, 1977-78; ptnr. Harrison & Brown, P.A., Little Rock, 1978-85; pvt. practice law, 1985-90; assoc. justice Ark. Supreme Ct., Little Rock, 1991—. Contbr. articles to profl. jours. Trustee U. of the South, Sewanee, Tenn., 1983-89, bd. regents, 1989-95. Fellow ABA, Ark. Bar Found (cert. of recognition 1981); mem. Ark. Bar Assn. Episcopalian. Fax: 501-683-4003. E-mail: Robert.Brown@mail.state.ar.us.

BROWN, ROBERT WAYNE, lawyer; b. Allentown, Pa., July 6, 1942; s. P.P. and Rose (Ferrara) B.; m. Rochelle Kaplan, Oct. 23, 1977; m. Shelley Sherman, Mar. 3, 1973; children: Courtney Sherman, Robin Thea, Ryan Palmer; m. Lupe Pearce, Nov. 22, 1996. AB, Franklin and Marshall Coll., 1964; JD, Cornell U., 1967. Bar: Ill. 1969, Pa. 1971. VISTA atty. Cmty. Legal Svcs., Detroit, 1967-68; asst. prof. law U. Ill., 1968-70; ct. adminstr., law clk. Lehigh County Ct. Common Pleas, 1971-72; ptnr. Gross & Brown, Allentown, 1972-76; pvt. practice law Allentown, 1976-77; sr. ptnr. Brown & Brown, Allentown, 1977-82, Brown, Brown & Solt, Allentown, 1982-85, Brown, Brown, Solt & Krouse, Allentown, 1985-89, Brown, Brown, Solt & Ferretti, Allentown, 1989—; city solicitor Allentown, 2002—. Instr. bus. law Muhlenburg Coll., 1973-76; pub. defender Lehigh County, 1973-74; mem. adv. bd. PNC Bank. Mem. Rape Crisis Coun. Lehigh Valley, 1978-84, Lehigh County Pre-trial Svcs., 1975-82; bd. dirs. Hispanic Am. Orgn., 1982-90, treas., 1983-86; bd. dirs. Lehigh County Sr. Citizens, 1980-88, pres., 1984-86; bd. dirs. Lehigh County Legal Svcs., 1973-77, Boys and Girls Club Allentown, 1994—, pres., 1998-2000; founding trustee Robert Clemente Charter Sch., 1998—. Recipient Cmty. Svc. award Hispanic Am. Orgn., 1985, Human Rels. Commn. award, Allentown, 1986; Lindback scholar Franklin and Marshall Coll., 1963-64. Mem. ABA, Pa. Bar Assn., Lehigh County Bar Assn., Order of Coif, Rotary (bd. dirs. Allentown 1998—). Democrat. State civil litigation, Commercial, contracts (including sales of goods; commercial financing), Property, real (including real estate development, water). Home: 225 Parkview Ave Allentown PA 18104-5323 Office: 1425 W Hamilton St Allentown PA 18102-4224 E-mail: rwbrown@onemain.com.

BROWN, ROGER GORDON, lawyer; b. Sedalia, Mo., Mar. 19, 1952; s. Virgil Brown and Kathryn Virginia Brown; m. Corrine Marion White, May 26, 1979 (div. Nov. 1994). BA, U. Mo., 1974, MA, 1976; JD, Gonzaga U., 1979. Assoc. Bushman, Nett & Gallaher, Jefferson City, Mo., 1980—82; ptnr. Bushman, Nett, Gallaher & Brown, Jefferson City, 1982—87; owner, sr. atty. Roger Brown & Assocs., Jefferson City, 1987—. Pres. Mo. Assn. Trial Attys., Jefferson City, 1996—97, Cole County Bar, 1995. Democrat. Avocations: gardening, coaching baseball. Home: 4601 Tanner Bridge Rd Jefferson City MO 65101 Office: Roger Brown & Assocs 216 E McCarty Jefferson City MO 65101 Office Fax: 573-634-7679. E-mail: rgblaw@socket.net.

BROWN, RONALD WELLINGTON, lawyer, educator, consultant, business executive, entrepreneur; b. Oct. 17, 1945; s. Leroy Harry and Mollie (Fitch) Brown; m. Geraldine Reed, Aug. 20, 1972; children: Kimberly Diana, Michael David. BA, Rutgers U., 1967; JD, Harvard U., 1971, MBA, 1973; postgrad., Columbia U., 1975. Bar: N.Y. 1975, U.S. Dist. Ct. (so. and ea. dists.) N.Y. 1975, U.S. Ct. Appeals (2d cir.) 1975, U.S. Supreme Ct. 1978. From atty. legal dept. to staff counsel litigation ITT, N.Y.C., NY, 1973—84, staff counsel litigation, 1984—85; dir. N. Am. commonwealth antipiracy ops. Motion Picture Assn. Am., N.Y.C., 1986—87; real estate devel. and property mgmt. N.J. Transit Corp., Newark, 1988; exec. v.p. Reed, Brown Consulting Group, Montclair, NJ, 1991—; dir. bus. affairs Norjean Entertainment Mgmt., N.Y.C., 1997—2002; mng. dir. legis. regulatory and legal affairs Office Info. Tech., State of N.J., Trenton, 2003—. Vis. prof. Huston-tillotson Coll., Austin, Tex., 1978; of counsel Spooner & Burnett, N.Y.C., 1997—97; pres., CEO BRS & W Prodns., Inc., N.Y.C., 1992—94; adj. prof. law sch. Rutgers U., 1995; sec., dir., mem. exec. com. Studio Mus. in Harlem, N.Y.C., 1979—81. Author: (non-fiction) Economic and Trade Related Aspects of Transborder Flow: Elements of A Code for Transnational Commerce, 1986, Legal Aspects of Doing Business in the Middle East, 1975, Joint Ventures: A Tool for Small, Women, and Minority Owned Businesses, 2000; contbr. articles to profl. jours.; editor (mem. bd. editors): (law rev.) Harvard Civil Rights-Civil Liberties Law Rev., 1969—71; exec. prodr.(articles editor): (law rev.) Harvard Civil Rights-Civil Liberties Law Rev., 1970. Dir. Operation Crossroads Africa, Inc., N.Y.C., 1976—, v.p., 1981—86; pres., exec. dir., COO Sammy Davis Jr. Nat. Liver Inst., 1988—91; moderator White House Conf. Small Bus., 1995; mem. small bus. com. Prosperity N.J., 1996—; mem. N.J. Bd. Pub. Utilities Supplier Diversity Coun., 1997—; chmn. N.J. United Minority Bus. Brain Trust, 1997—2000, U.S. Small Bus. Adminstrn., 1999; CEO W.F. Golf Enterprises, Inc., 2000—; mem. environ. commn. Twp. of Monclair, 2002—03; chmn. staff parish rels. com. St. Marks United Meth. Ch., 1998—2000, vice chmn. Ch. coun., 2001—; mem. Bd. Edn., Montclair, NJ, 1986—, v.p., 1987, pres., 1988—; bd. dirs. One Hundred Black Men, N.Y.C., 1982—88, 1st v.p., 1985—87; bd. dir. Friends of the Davis Ctr. for the Performing Arts, 1987—88, Leonard Davis Ctr. for the Performing Arts, N.Y.C., 1984—89; mem. Planning bd. Twp. of Montclair, 1997—. Named Black Achiever in Industry, Harlem YMCA, 1984. Mem.: ABA (mem. coun., chmn. Euripean law com., sect. internat. law and practice 1984—86, assoc. editor Internat. Law News 1983—86), Union Internat. des Avocats, Am. Soc. Internat. Law, Internat. Law Assn., N.Y. State Bar Assn., Assn. Bar City N.Y. (chmn. subcom. on fed. legis. of com. on art law 1983—86), Am. Arbitration Assn., Omega Psi Phi. Methodist. Entertainment, Private international, Property, real (including real estate development, water). Home: 180 Union St Montclair NJ 07042-2125 Office: PO Box 407 Montclair NJ 07042-0407 also: PO Box 212 300 Riverview Plaza Trenton NJ 08625

BROWN, SANFORD DONALD, lawyer; b. Neptune, N.J., May 16, 1952; s. Richard B. and Janet (Flint) B.; m. Joan Miller, Sept. 5, 1978; children: Jennifer, Sanford Flint, Edward. BA, Brown U., 1974; JD, Seton Hall U., Newark, 1978. Bar: N.J. 1978, U.S. Dist. Ct. N.J. 1978, U.S. Ct. Appeals (3d cir.) 1998, U.S. Supreme Ct. 1999. Law clk. to Hon. Patrick J. McGann, Freehold, N.J., 1978-79; assoc. Dawes & Youssouf, Freehold, 1979-81; ptnr. Dawes & Brown, Freehold, 1981-86, Cerrato, O'Connor, Dawes, Collins et al, Freehold, 1986-89, Cerrato, Dawes, Collins et al, Freehold, 1989—2002; mem. Brown & Connelly, LLC, 2002—. Gen. counsel Manalapan-Englishtown Regional Bd. Edn., N.J., 1979-85, 87—, Monmouth Vocat. Bd. Edn., Colts Neck, N.J., 1979—, Allenhurst Bd. Edn., 1990-98, Interlaken (N.J.) Bd. Adjustment/Planning Bd., 1990—, Manasquan River Regional Sewer Authority, Howell, 1979-91, Pioneer Farm Credit, 1990—, United Meth. Homes N.J., 1992—, Ocean Twp. Bd. Adjustment Spl. Counsel, 1995—; fee arbitrator N.J. Supreme Ct., 1995-99, panel chair, 1998-99. Chancellor, So. N.J. Ann. Conf., United Meth. Ch., 1995-2000, co-chancellor Greater N.J. Ann. Conf., 2000—; coach Ocean Twp. (N.J.) Recreation League, 1986-97, Ocean Twp. Little League, 1992-95; chmn. bd. trustees United Meth. Ch., 1986-91; mem., chmn. county advancement com. Boy Scouts Am., 1989-92, atty., county exec. bd., 1992—, gen. counsel, 1995—, dist. chmn., 1996-9, at. rep., 1997-99, 2001—, v.p. 2000—. Recipient Monmouth Legal Sec. assn. Employer of the Year award, 1993, Monmouth Coun. Boy Scouts Disting. Adult Eagle Scout award, 1997, Silver Beaver award, 1998, Dist. Award of Merit, 1999. Mem.: NJ Sch. Bd. Attys. Assn. (regional v.p. 1991), NJ Bar Assn., Monmouth Bar Assn., Rotary, Wemrock Profl. Condo Assn. (pres. 1988—96, v.p. 1996—2001), Brown U. Alumni Assn. (chpt. pres. 1986—89, 1995—), United Meth. Scouters Assn. (life), Nat. Eagle Scout Assn. (life). Methodist. Avocation: swimming. General civil litigation, Education and schools, Land use and zoning (including planning). Office: Brown & Connelly LLC 1127 Hwy 35 Ocean Twp Freehold NJ 07728-5302 E-mail: Sdbrown509@aol.com.

BROWN, SEYMOUR R. lawyer, director; b. Cleve., Oct. 24, 1924; s. Leonard and Ella (Rubinstein) B.; m. Madeline Kusevich, July 8, 1956; children: Frederic M., Thomas R., Barbara L. N. Rybicki. BA, Case-Western Res. U., 1948; JD, Cleve. State U., 1953. Bar: Ohio 1953. Prin. Seymour R. Brown & Assocs., Cleve.; ptnr. Brown-McCallister Real Estate, Residential & Comml. Constrn., Melbourne, Fla., 1973-81. Spl. counsel to atty. gen. State of Ohio, 1963-70. Editor, pub.: Gt. Lakes Architecture, 1955-59. Chmn. CSC, University Heights, Ohio, 1978-82, 84-86, mem., 1976—; mem. exec. com. Cuyahoga County Rep. Orgn., 1966—; pres. Nat. Permanent Endowment Fund, Inc., 1988-92. With AUS, 1943-45. Decorated Purple Heart, Bronze Star; named to Ohio Mil. Hall of Fame, 2003. Mem. ABA, Ohio Bar Assn., Cleve. Bar Assn., Am. Arbitration Assn. (comml. arbitration panel), Zeta Beta Tau (nat. dir., nat. pres. 1978-80), Masons. State civil litigation, Commercial, contracts (including sales of goods; commercial financing), Property, real (including real estate development, water). Home: 3718 Meadowbrook Blvd Cleveland OH 44118-4422

BROWN, STEPHEN THOMAS, judge; b. N.Y.C., Feb. 1, 1947; s. Albert and Ruth Hope (Kaff) B.; m. Yvonne Tobias Brown, Aug. 10, 1968. BS, Fla. State U., 1968; JD, U. Miami, Fla., 1972. Bar: Fla. 1972, U.S. Dist. Ct. (so. dist.) Fla. 1973, U.S. Dist. Ct. (mid. dist.) Fla. 1989, U.S. Ct. Appeals (11th cir.) 1973, U.S. Supreme Ct. 1976. Atty. Preddy, Kutner & Hardy, Miami, Fla., 1972-77, ptnr., 1977-86, Preddy, Kutner, Hardy, Rubinoff, Brown & Thompson, Miami, 1986-91; U.S. magistrate judge U.S. Dist. Ct. (so. dist.) Fla., Miami, 1991—. Adj. prof. U. Miami Sch. Law, 1983-84; vice chmn. auto ins. com. Fla. Bar, 1979-80, chmn. grievance com., 1981-84; mem. adv. com. on rules and procedures So. Dist. Fla., 1995--; mem. leadership coun. Fla. State U. Sch. of Arts & Scis. Mem. ABA, Acad. Fla. Trial Lawyers, Dade County Bar Assn., Fla. State U. Alumni Assn. (dist. v.p. 1993-99), Seminole Boosters Inc. (bd. dirs. 1988-93), Seminole Club Dade County (pres. 1984-87), U. Miami Law Sch. Alumni Assn. (bd. dirs. 1994—, v.p. 2000—). Avocations: snow skiing, golf. Office: US Dist Ct 300 NE 1st Ave Miami FL 33132-2126

BROWN, STEVEN SPENCER, lawyer; b. Manhattan, Kans., Feb. 26, 1948; s. Gerald James and Buelah Marie (Spencer) B. BBA, U. Mo., 1970, JD, 1973. Bar: Mo. 1973, U.S. Tax Ct. 1974, Ill. 1977, U.S. Dist. (no. dist.) Ill. 1979, U.S. Ct. Appeals (7th cir.) 1980, U.S. Ct. Claims 1986, Calif. 1989, U.S. Ct. Appeals (11th cir.) 1989, U.S. Ct. Appeals (5th cir.) 2000. Trial atty. IRS Regional Counsel, Chgo., 1973-78; sr. trial atty. IRS Dist. Counsel, Chgo., 1978-79; assoc. Silets & Martin Ltd., Chgo., 1979-85, ptnr., 1985-92, Martin, Brown & Sullivan Ltd., Chgo., 1992—. Adj. prof. John Marshall, Chgo., 1985—. Republican. Presbyterian. Avocations: golf, tennis. Administrative and regulatory, Federal civil litigation, Personal income taxation. Home: 1340 N Astor St Apt 2903 Chicago IL 60610-8438 Office: Martin Brown & Sullivan Ltd 10th Fl 321 S Plymouth Ct Chicago IL 60604-3912 E-mail: brown@mbslaw.com.

BROWN, T. MICHAEL, lawyer; b. New Orleans, Aug. 17, 1964; s. William Alton and Gayle Timphony Brown; m. Allison Leigh McKee; children: Katherine Alton, Margaret Alice, Michael Louis, Frank McKee. BA in History, Auburn U., 1986; JD, Vanderbilt U., 1989. Assoc. Bradley Arant Rose & White LLP, Birmingham, Ala., 1989—97, ptnr., 1997—. Environmental, Toxic tort, Product liability. Office: Bradley Arant Rose & White LLP 1819 5th Ave N Birmingham AL 35203 Office Fax: 205-488-6462. E-mail: mbrown@bradleyarant.com.

BROWN, THOMAS CARTMEL, JR., lawyer; b. Marion, Va., June 20, 1945; m. Sally Guy Lynch; children: Sarah Preston, Taylor Cardwell. AB, Davidson Coll., 1967; JD, U. Va., 1970. Bar: Va 1971. Assoc. Boothe, Prichard & Dudley, Alexandria, Va., 1971-76, ptnr., 1976-86, McGuire-Woods LLP and predecessors, McLean, Va., 1986—. Mem. lawyers com. Nat. Ctr. State Cts., 1993—2003; sec., gen counsel Potomac Knowledge-Way, 1995—99. Mem. Va. Child-Day Coun., Richmond, 1987—91, No. Va. Roundtable, 1995—2001; pres. Alexandria Libr. Co., 2002—03; bd. dirs. Alexandria chpt. ARC, 1982—88; bd. dirs. Nat. Capital Area coun. Boy Scouts Am., 2002—. Fellow: Va. Law Found. (bd. dirs. 1997—, pres. 2003), Am. Bar Found.; mem.: Warren E. Burger Soc., Va. State Bar (chmn bus law sect 1987—88, bd govs health law sect 1998—, chair 2002—03), Va. Bar Assn. (pres. 1992), Omicron Delta Kappa. Corporate, general, Health, Mergers and acquisitions. Office: McGuireWoods LLP 1750 Tysons Blvd Ste 1800 Mc Lean VA 22102-4231

BROWN, WESLEY ERNEST, federal judge; b. Hutchinson, Kans., June 22, 1907; s. Morrison H. H. and Julia (Wesley) B.; m. Mary A. Miller, Nov. 30, 1934 (dec.); children: Wesley Miller, Loy B. Wiley; m. Thadene N. Moore. Student, Kans. U., 1925-28; LLB, Kansas City Law Sch., 1933. Bar: Kans. 1933, Mo. 1933. Pvt. practice, Hutchinson, 1933-58; county atty. Reno County, Kans., 1935-39; referee in bankruptcy U.S. Dist. Ct. Kans., 1958-62, judge, 1962-79, sr. judge, 1979—. Apptd. Temporary Emergency Ct. of Appeals of U.S., 1980-93; dir. Nat. Assn. Referees in Bankruptcy, 1959-62; mem. bankruptcy divsn. Jud. Conf., 1963-70; mem. Jud. Conf., U.S., 1976-79. With USN, 1944-46. Mem. ABA, Kans. Bar Assn. (exec. council 1950-62, pres. 1964-65), Reno County Bar Assn. (pres. 1947), Wichita Bar Assn., S.W. Bar Kan., Delta Theta Phi. Office: US Dist Ct 414 US Courthouse 401 N Market St Wichita KS 67202-2089

BROWN, WILLIAM A. lawyer, mediator, arbitrator; b. Memphis, Nov. 6, 1957; s. Winn D. Sr. and Annie Ruth (Hurt) B.; m. Mary Lee Walker, Dec. 27, 1980. BBA, U. Miss., 1978, JD, 1981. Bar: Miss. 1981, U.S. Dist. Ct. (no. and so. dists.) Miss. 1981, U.S. Dist. Ct. (we. dist.) Tenn. 1987. Ptnr., pres. Walker, Brown & Brown, P.A., Hernando, Miss., 1981—. Pres. DeSoto Literacy Coun., Hernando, 1988, Am. Cancer Soc., Hernando, 1988, DeSoto County Econ. Devel. Coun., 1995—96; mem. Leadership 2000, 1990—91; chmn. Ch. Coun. Hernando United Meth. Ch.; vice-chmn. Hernando Preservation Commn., 1997—2000, chmn., 2001—; chmn. design com. Main St. Project, 1997—2000; allocations chmn. United Way of Mid-South DeSoto County. James O. Eastland scholar, 1978-81; Paul Harris fellow Rotary Internat., 1997. Mem. Miss. Bar Assn. (bd. dirs. young lawyers sect. 1988-89, Bd. Bar Commrs. 2002—), DeSoto County Bar Assn. (v.p. 1988-89, pres. 1996-98, bar commr. 2002—), Rotary (pres. Hernando chpt. 1989-90), Boy Scouts Am., N.W. Miss. (membership chmn. 1990, activities chmn. 1991). Methodist. Avocations: gardening, design and construction projects. Alternative dispute resolution, Personal injury (including property damage), Property, real (including real estate development, water). Home and Office: Walker Brown & Brown PA PO Box 276 Hernando MS 38632-0276

BROWN, WILLIAM HILL, III, lawyer; b. Phila., Jan. 19, 1928; s. William H. Jr. and Ethel L. (Washington) B.; m. Sonya Morgan Brown, Aug. 29, 1952 (div. 1975); 1 child, Michele D.; m. D. June Hairston, July 29, 1975; 1 child, Jeanne-Marie. BS, Temple U., 1952; JD, U. Pa., 1955. Bar: Pa. 1956, D.C. 1972, U.S. Ct. Appeals (3d cir.) 1959, U.S. Ct. Appeals (4th cir.) 1978, U.S. Dist. Ct. (ea. dist.) Pa. 1957, U.S. Ct. Appeals (10th cir.) 1986, U.S. Ct. Appeals (5th cir.) 1988, U.S. Dist. Ct. D.C. 1994, U.S. Ct. Appeals (D.C. cir.) 1994, U.S. Ct. Appeals (fed. cir.) 1997, U.S. Ct. Appeals (8th cir.) 2002. Assoc. Norris, Schmidt, Phila., 1955-62; ptnr. Norris, Brown, Hall, Phila., 1962-68, Schnader, Harrison, Segal & Lewis, Phila., 1974—, mem. exec. com., 1983-87; chief of frauds Dist. Atty.'s Office, 1968, dep. dist. atty., 1968; commr. EEOC, Washington, 1968-69, chmn., 1969-73. Lectr. S.W. Legal Found., Practising Law Inst., Nat. Inst. Trial Advocacy; bd. dirs. United Parcel Svc., Inc., 1983—, Lawyers Com. Civil Rights Under Law; chmn. Phila. Spl. Investigation Commn. MOVE; pres. Nat. Black Child Devel., Inc., 1986-90; bd. dirs. Cmty. Legal Svcs., 1986—; mem. exec. com. Schnader, Harrison, Segal & Lewis, 1983-87; bd. dirs., mem. exec. com. Lawyers Com. Civil Rights Under law, 1977—, co-chair, 1991-93; mem. Commn. on Comml. Operation of U.S. Customs Svc., 1994-98. Contbr. articles to profl. jours. Bd. dirs. Mid. States Colls. and Secondary Schs., 1983-89, Main Line Acad., 1982—, Nat. Sr. Citizens Law Ctr., 1988-94; mem. nat. bd. govs. Am. Heart Assn., 1994-96, mem. audit com., mem. pub. affairs policy com., bd. dirs., 1986-94, mem. audit com., mem. pub. affairs policy com.; mem. adv. com. on appellate ct. rules Supreme Ct. Pa., 1989-95. With USAF, 1946-48. Recipient award of merit Fed. Bar Assn., Columbus, 1971, NAACP award, 1971, Dr. Edward S. Cooper award Am. Heart Assn., 1995, Whitney M. Young Jr. Leadership award Urban League, 1996, Whitney North Seymor award Lawyers Com. for Civil Rights Under Law, 1996, Champions for Social Justice and Equality award Black Law Students Assn. Rutgers-Camden, 1997, Earl G. Harrison Pro Bono award, 1998, law alumni award U. Pa., 2000. Fellow Internat. Acad. Trial Lawyers, Am. Law Inst.; mem. ABA, Phila. Bar Assn. (Fidelity award 1990), D.C. Bar Assn., Pa. Bar Assn., Fed. Bar Assn., Nat. Bar Assn., Inter-Am. Bar Assn., World Assn. Lawyers (founding mem.), Am. Arbitration Assn. (past bd. dirs.), Barrister's Assn. Phila., Inc. (J. Austin Norris award 1987), Citizens Commn. on Civil Rights, NAACP (bd. dirs. legal def. and edn. fund), Alpha Phi Alpha (Recognition award 1969). Republican. Episcopalian. Federal civil litigation, State civil litigation, Labor (including EEOC, Fair Labor Standards Act, labor-management relations, NLRB, OSHA). Office: Schnader Harrison Segal & Lewis 1600 Market St Suite 3600 Philadelphia PA 19103-7213

BROWN, ZENELL BRIDGETTE, lawyer, mediator; b. Detroit, Aug. 22, 1964; d. John D. and Gendoly Onita Beard; m. James Arthur Brown, Jr., Feb. 15, 1995; children: Rashondra, Asha. BA, U. Detroit, 1985; JD, Wayne State U., 1993. Bar: Mich. 1994. Regulations officer Dept. of State, Detroit, 1993—97; sr. staff atty. 3d Cir. Ct., Detroit, 1997—, mediation team leader, 2002—. Congl. precinct del. Mich. Dems., Detroit, 2000—02. Mem.: Met. Future Lawyers Club (program dir. 2001—), Wayne County Family Bar (sec., officer 2002—), Mich. State Bar (mem. day com. 2001), Toastmasters (v.p. edn. 2001). Office: 3d Cir Ct 645 Griswold 3d Fl Detroit MI 48226 Personal E-mail: zenellbrown@aol.com.

BROWNE, JEFFREY FRANCIS, lawyer; b. Clare, South Australia, Australia, Mar. 1, 1944; came to U.S., 1975; s. Patrick Joseph and Irene Kathleen (Cormack) B.; m. Deborah Mary Christine West, Aug. 28, 1971; children: Veronique Namur Irene, Jeffrey James, Nicholas Patrick, Sophie Christina, Amy Elizabeth. LLB, Adelaide U., South Australia, 1966; LLM, Sydney U., Australia, 1968, Harvard U., 1976. Bar: South Australia 1969, Australian Capital Territory 1973, N.Y. 1978, Victoria 1982, New South Wales 1983, Western Australia 1983. Assoc. High Ct. Australia, Canberra, Australian Capital Territory, 1967-68; diplomat Dept. Fgn. Affairs, Canberra, 1969; 2d sec. Australian High Commn., London and Malaysia, 1970-71, acting high commr. Ghana, 1972; counsel nuclear tests case Internat. Ct. Justice, 1973-74; assoc. Sullivan & Cromwell, N.Y.C., 1976-81, ptnr., 1983—; gen. counsel Alcoa of Australia, Melbourne, 1981-82. Bd. dirs. Compinvest Pty. Ltd. Mem. Law Inst. Victoria, Australian Mining and Petroleum Law Assn., Law Coun. Australia (chmn. fin. and securities subcom., internat. trade and bus. law com.), Inst. Dirs. of Australia, Internat. Bar Assn. (sect. on energy and natural resources), Am. C. of C. in Australia (bd. dirs.), Am. Soc. Internat. Law, N.Y. Yacht Club, Melbourne Club. Commercial, contracts (including sales of goods; commercial financing), Corporate, general, Securities. Office: Sullivan & Cromwell 125 Broad St Fl 28 New York NY 10004-2489 also: 101 Collins St Melbourne Victoria 3000 Australia E-mail: brownej@sullcrom.com.

BROWNE, RICHARD CULLEN, lawyer; b. Akron, Nov. 21, 1938; s. Francis Cedric and Elizabeth Ann (Cullen) Browne; m. Patricia Anne Winkler, Apr. 23, 1962; children: Richard Cullen, Catherine Anne, Paulette Elizabeth, Maureen Frances, Colleen Marie. BS in Econs., Holy Cross Coll., 1960; JD, Cath. U. Am., 1963. Bar: Va. 1963, U.S. Ct. Claims 1963, U.S. Ct. Customs and Patent Appeals 1963, D.C. 1964, U.S. Ct. Mil. Appeals 1963, U.S. Ct. Appeals (D.C. cir.) 1964, U.S. Supreme Ct. 1966, U.S. Ct. Appeals (fed. cir.) 1982, U.S. Ct. Appeals (9th cir.) 1983, U.S. Ct. Appeals (6th cir.) 1991, U.S. Ct. Appeals (7th cir.) 1998. Assoc. Browne, Beveridge, DeGrandi & Kline, Washington, 1963-68, ptnr., 1968-72, Schaffert, Miller & Browne, Washington, 1972-74; sr. counsel Office of Enforcement EPA, Washington, 1974-76; asst. chief hearing counsel U.S. Nuclear Regulatory Commn., Washington, 1976-78; sole practice Washington, 1978-79; ptnr. Winston & Strawn, Washington, 1980-2001, of counsel, 2001—. Lectr. U. R.I., 1975, Washburn U., 1978, Legal Ins., CSC, 1975—78, Hofstra U., 1987—, Nat. Inst. for Trial Advocacy, 1986—. Del. Montgomery County Civic Fedn., 1970—74; chmn. Citizens Adv. Com. on Rockville Corridor, 1972—77; mem. Montgomery County Potomac River Basin Adv. Com., 1972—74; chmn. Cath. U. Am. Fund, 1996—2001. Capt. JAGC USAF, 1963—66, capt. USAFR, 1966—69. Named Disting. Mil. Grad., Holy Cross Coll., 1960. Mem.: Cath. U. Gen. Alumni Assn. (bd. govs. 1992—, chair Gibbons medal com. 1995—2001, exec. com. 1995—2001), Cath. U. Law Sch. Alumni Soc. (bd. dirs. 1991—, pres. 1992—93, bd. visitors 1998—), Coll. Holy Cross General Alumni Assn. (bd. dirs. 1971—78, alumni senate 1978—97, nominations and elections com. 1995—, pres. 2002—03, bd. dirs. 1996—). Republican. Corporate, general, Intellectual property, Non-profit and tax-exempt organizations. Home: 7203 Old Stage Rd Rockville MD 20852-4438 Office: Winston & Strawn 1400 L St NW Ste 1000 Washington DC 20005-3508 E-mail: Enworb@earthlink.net.

BROWNE, STANHOPE STRYKER, lawyer; b. Colorado Springs, Colo., July 22, 1931; s. Samuel Stanhope Stryker and Florence Jeanette (Reynolds) B.; m. Elizabeth Whitney Sturges, Sept. 12, 1964; children: Katrina C., Whitney R. AB, Princeton U., 1953; LL.B., Harvard U., 1956. Bar: Pa. 1957. Assoc. Dechert LLP, Phila., 1956-65, ptnr., 1965-97, of counsel, 1998—, resident ptnr. Brussels, 1972—76. Lectr. internat. law. Contbr. articles to profl. jours. Chmn. Penn's Landing Corp., Phila., 1981-97, Com. to Preserve Am.'s Birthplace, 1965-72; vice chmn. World Affairs Council, 1978-90; bd. dirs. Phila. 1976 Bicentennial Corp., 1971-72, Greater Phila. Movement, 1970-71, Phila. Port Corp., 1984-90, Ecole Française Internationale de Philadelphie, 1991-99, The Ch. Found., 1998-2001, French Heritage Soc., Inc., 1999—; mem. exec. com. Cen. Phila. Devel. Corp., 1968-72, 77-99; mem. Phila. Dist. Export Council U.S. Dept. Commerce, 1983-96; vice pres. Pa. Prison Soc., 1962-69; pres. Greater Phila. Council of Chs., 1966-67; mem. Diocesan Coun. Episcopal Diocese of Pa., 1967-71; rector's warden St. Peter's Ch., 1983-90; chmn. Democrats Abroad, Belgium, 1975-76, Pa. Internat. Trade Conf., 1977-79; mem. adv. commn. Independence Nat. Hist. Park, Phila., 1969-72; hon. consul of France in Phila., 1986-96; mem. vestry Am. Cathedral in Paris, 2001-02. Recipient Pub. Service and Polit. Courage award Southeastern Pa. chpt. Ams. for Democratic Action, 1965; decorated Nat. Order of Merit, France, 1998. Mem. Phila. Bar Assn., French-Am. C. of C. (bd. dirs. Phila. chpt. 1989-2001), Independence Hall Assn. (bd. dirs. 1978-90, adv. com. 1990-99), Phila. Com. on Fgn. Rels., Brook Club (N.Y.C.), Phila. Club (bd. dirs. 1988-92), Phi Beta Kappa Democrat. Episcopalian. Estate planning, Private international, Probate (including wills, trusts). Office: Dechert LLP 4000 Bell Atlantic Tower 1717 Arch St Philadelphia PA 19103-2793 E-mail: stanhopesb@aol.com.

BROWNE, WILLIAM BITNER, lawyer; b. Springfield, Ohio, Nov. 23, 1914; s. John Franklin and Etta Blanche (Bitner) B.; m. Dorothy Ruth Gilbert, Aug. 31, 1939; children: Franklin G., Dale Ann Browne Compton. AB, Wittenberg U., 1935, LLD (hon.), 1970; postgrad., U. Bordeaux, 1935-36; JD cum laude, Harvard U., 1939. Bar: Ohio 1939, U.S. Dist. Ct. (so. dist.) Ohio 1941, U.S. Ct. Appeals (6th cir.) 1950, U.S. Supreme Ct. 1970. Assoc. Donovan, Leisure, Newton & Lumbard, N.Y.C., 1939-40; assoc. Corry, Durfey & Martin, Springfield, Ohio, 1940-48; ptnr. Corry, Durfey, Martin & Browne and successors, Springfield, Ohio, 1948-88; of counsel Martin, Browne, Hull & Harper, Springfield, 1988-94. Contbr. (articles to legal jours.). Bd. dirs. Wittenberg U., 1955-89; pres. Greater Springfield & Clark County Assn., 1948-49; vice chmn. Clark County Republican Central and Exec. coms., 1948-52; mem. Springfield City Bd. Edn., 1950-53; mem. exec. com. United Appeals Clark County, 1956-62. Capt. OSS Signal Corps, U.S. Army, 1942-46. Decorated Bronze Star; decorated Croix de Guerre with palm, Medaille de Reconnaissance Francaise; laureate Springfield Area Bus. Hall of Fame, 1993. Fellow Am. Coll. Trial Lawyers (ret.), Am. Bar Found., Am. Coll. Trust and Estate Counsel (ret.), Ohio Bar Found. (pres. 1979, Fellows rsch. and svc. award 1976); mem. ABA (del. 1971-76), Ohio Bar Assn. (pres. 1969-70, medal of honor 1973), Springfield Bar Assn. (pres. 1967), Springfield C. of C. (pres. 1961-62), Zanesfield Rod and Gun Club, Springfield Country Club, Rotary, Masons. Episcopalian. General practice, Probate (including wills, trusts). Office: Martin Browne Hull & Harper 1 S Limestone St PO Box 1488 Springfield OH 45501-1488

BROWNER, CAROL M. former federal agency administrator; d. Michael Browner and Isabella Harty Hugues; m. Michael Podhorzer; 1 child, Zachary. Grad., U. Fla., 1977, JD, 1979. Gen. counsel govt. ops. com. Fla. Ho. of Reps., 1980; with Citizen Action, Washington; chief legis. aide environ. issues to Sen. Lawton Chiles, 1986—88; legis. dir. to Sen. Al Gore, Jr., 1988-91; sec. Dept. Environ. Regulation, Fla., 1991-93; administr. EPA, Washington, 1993—2000; principal The Albright Group L.L.C., 2001—. Mem. adv. coun. Harvard Med. Sch., Ctr. for Health and the Global Environment. Democrat. Office: The Albright Group 901 15th St NW Ste 1000 Washington DC 20005*

BROWNING, JAMES ROBERT, federal judge; b. Great Falls, Mont., Oct. 1, 1918; s. Nicholas Henry and Minnie Sally (Foley) Browning; m. Marie Rose Chapell. BA, Mont. State U., Missoula, 1938; LLB with honors, U. Mont., 1941, LLD (hon.) , 1978, Santa Clara U., 1989. Bar: Mont. 1941, D.C. 1953, U.S. Supreme Ct. 1952. Spl. atty. antitrust div. Dept. Justice, 1941—43, spl. atty. gen. litigation sect. antitrust div., 1946—48, chief antitrust dept. N.W. regional office, 1948—49; asst. chief gen. litigation sect. antitrust div. Dept. Justice (N.W. regional office), 1949—51, 1st asst. civil div., 1951—52; exec. asst. to atty. gen. U.S., 1952—53; chief U.S. (Exec. Office for U.S. Attys.), 1953; pvt. practice Washington, 1953—58; lectr. N.Y.U. Sch. Law, 1953, Georgetown U. Law Center, 1957—58; clk. Supreme Ct. U.S., 1958—61; judge U.S. Ct. Appeals 9th Circuit, 1961—76, chief judge, 1976—88, judge, 1988—. Reed justice com. on continuing edn., tng. and adminstrn. Jud. Conf. of U.S., 1967—68, com. on ct. adminstrn., 1969—71, chmn. subcom. on jud. stats., 1969—71, com. to study the illustrative rules of jud. misconduct, 1969, com. on the budget, 1971—77, adminstrn. office, subcom. on budget, 1974—76, mem., 1976—88, exec. com. of conf., 1978—87, com. to study the illustrative rules of jud. misconduct, 1985—87, com. to study U.S. jud. conf., 1986—88, com. on internat. conf. of appellate judges, 1987—90; David T. Lewis disting. judge-in-residence U. Utah, 1987; Blankenbaker lectr. U. Mont., 1987; Sibley lectr. U. Ga., 1987; lectr. Human Rights Inst., Santa Clara U. Sch. Law, Strasbourg. Editor-in-chief: Mont. Law Rev. Dir. Western Justice Found.; chmn. 9th Cir. Hist. Soc. 1st lt. U.S. Army, 1943—46. Decorated Bronze Star; named to, Order of the Grizzly, U. Mont., 1973; recipient Devitt Disting. Svc. to Justice award, 1990; scholar in residence, Santa Clara U., 1989, U. Mont., 1991. Mem.: FBA (bd. dirs. 1945—61, nat. coun. 1958—62), ABA (judge adv. com. to standing com. on Ethics and Profl. Responsibility 1973—75), Am. Soc. Legal History (adv. bd. jour.), Am. Judicature Soc. (chmn. com. on fed. judiciary 1973—74, bd. dirs. 1972—75, Herbert Harley award 1984), Inst. Jud. Adminstrn., Am. Law Inst., Mont. Bar Assn., D.C. Bar Assn., Nat. Lawyers Club (bd. govs. 1959—63). Office: US Ct Appeals 9th Cir PO Box 193939 San Francisco CA 94119-3939

BROWNING, WILLIAM DOCKER, federal judge; b. Tucson, May 19, 1931; s. Horace Benjamin and Mary Louise (Docker) B.; children: Christopher, Logan, Courtenay; m. Zerilda Sinclair, Dec. 17, 1974; 1 child, Benjamin. BBA, U. Ariz., 1954, LLB, 1960. Bar: Ariz. 1960, U.S. Dist. Ct. Ariz. 1960, U.S. Ct. Appeals (9th cir.) 1965, U.S. Supreme Ct. 1967. Pvt. practice, Tucson, 1960-84; judge U.S. Dist. Ct., Tucson, 1984—. Mem. jud. nominating com. appellate ct. appointments, 1975-79; mem. Commn. on Structural Alternatives, Fed. Ct. Appeals, 1997-99. Del. 9th Cir. Jud. Conf., 1968-77, 79-82; trustee Inst. for Ct. Mgmt., 1978-84; mem. Ctr. for Pub. Resources Legal Program. 1st lt. USAF, 1954-57, capt. USNG, 1958-61. Recipient Disting. Citizen award U. Ariz., 1995. Fellow Am. Coll. Trial Lawyers, Am. Bar Found.; mem. ABA (spl. com. housing and urban devel. law 1973-76, com. urban problems and human affairs 1978-80), Ariz. Bar Assn. (chmn. merit selection of judges com. 1973-76, bd. gove. 1968-74, pres. 1972-73, Outstanding Mem. 1980), Pima County Bar Assn. (exec. com. 1964-68, med. legal screening panel 1965-75, pres. 1967-68), Am. Bd. Trial Advocates, Am. Judicature Soc. (bd. dirs. 1975-77), Fed. Judges Assn. (bd. dirs.). Office: US Courthouse 405 W Congress St Ste 6160 Tucson AZ 85701-5061

BROWNLEE, JOHN L. prosecutor; BA, Washington and Lee U.; MBA, Golden Gate U.; JD, Coll. William and Mary. Law clk. U.S. Dist. Ct. (we. dist.) Va., 1994—96; asst. U.S. atty. D.C., 1997—2001; assoc. Woods, Rogers and Hazlegrove, Richmond, Va., 2001; U.S. atty. we. dist. U.S. Dept. Justice, Va., 2001—. With U.S. Army, 1987—91, Capt. JAG USAR. Office: 180 W Main St Abingdon VA 24210*

BROWNRIGG, JOHN CLINTON, lawyer; b. Detroit, Aug. 7, 1948; s. John Arthur and Sheila Pauline (Taffe) B.; children: Brian M., Jennifer A., Katharine T. BA, Rockhurst Coll., 1970; JD cum laude, Creighton U., 1974. Bar: Nebr. 1974, U.S. Dist. Ct. Nebr. 1974, U.S. Tax Ct. 1977, U.S. Ct. Appeals (8th cir.) 1990. Ptnr. Eisenstatt, Higgins, Kinnamon, Okun & Brownrigg, P.C., Omaha, 1974-80, Erickson & Sederstrom, P.C., Omaha, 1980—. Lectr. law trial practice Creighton U. Sch. Law, Omaha, 1978-83; dir. Legal Aid Soc., Inc., Omaha, 1982-88, pres., 1987-88, devel. coun., 1989—; dir. Nebr. Continuing Legal Edn., Inc., 1991-93. Chmn. law sect. Archbishop's Capital Campaign, Omaha, 1991; dir. Combined Health Agys. Drive, 2001—. Sgt. USAR, 1970-76. Fellow ABA (commn. on lawyer assistance programs 1996-2000), Nebr. State Bar Found. (dir. 1991-93); mem. Nebr. State Bar Assn. (pres. 1992-93), Nebr. Assn. Trial Attys., Omaha Bar Assn. (pres. 1990-91). Avocations: golf, bicycling, hiking. Alternative dispute resolution, General civil litigation. Office: Erickson & Sederstrom PC Ste 100 10330 Regency Parkway Dr Omaha NE 68114-3761

BROWNWOOD, DAVID OWEN, lawyer; b. L.A., May 24, 1935; s. Robert Scott Osgood and Ruth Elizabeth (Bellamy) B.; m. Sigrid Carlson, Mar. 3, 1956 (div. 1972); children: Jeffrey Owen, Kirsten, Scott David, Daniel Stuart; m. Susan Sloane Jannicky, July 4, 1975; 1 child, Mary Ruth Bellamy; stepchildren: Bradbury, Stephanie Ellington. AB with distinction, Stanford U., 1956; LLB magna cum laude, Harvard U., 1964. Bar: Calif. 1965, N.Y. 1969. Law clk. Ropes & Gray, Boston, 1963; assoc. McCutchen, Doyle, Brown & Enersen, San Francisco, 1964-66; lectr. law U. Khartoum, Sudan, 1966-67, Kenya Inst. Adminstrn., Lower Kabete, 1967-68; assoc. Cravath, Swaine & Moore, N.Y.C., 1968-72, ptnr., 1973—, recruiting ptnr., 1978-82, mng. ptnr. for legal staff, 1983-86; ptnr. in charge London office, 1995—2001. Treas. N.Y. Law Inst., 1978-83, chmn. exec. com., 1983-88, pres., 1988-93. Mem. editorial bd. Harvard U. Law Rev., 1963-64. Nat. chair Harvard U. Law Sch. Fund, 1991—93; dir. Royal Oak Found., 2003—; pres. Benjamin Franklin House, 2002—; dir. Literacy Assistance Ctr., N.Y.C., 1983—94, co-chmn. bd. dirs., 1987—94; trustee Greenwich (Conn.) Country Day Sch., 1985—92, v.p., 1986—88, pres., chmn. bd. trustees, 1988—92; co-chmn. Harvard U. Law Sch. 25th Reunion Gift, 1988—89; N.Y. regional com. campaign Harvard Law Sch., 1991—95; com. on univ. resources Harvard U., 1991—, mem. Harvard law sch. vis. com., 1995—2001; keystone regional vice chair centennial campaign Stanford U., 1986—92; exec. com. Stanford U. N.Y. Coun., 1992—95; vice chmn. Stanford U. N.Y. Major Gifts Com., 1993—95; co-chair Stanford U. Ea. Coun., 1993; bd. govs. Stanford Assocs., 1993—95, pres., chmn. bd. govs., 1994—95; bd. advisors Stanford Trust (U.K.), 1995—2002; mem. Stanford U. UK/Western Europe Regional Adv. Bd., 2003—; mem. nat. bd. Outward Bound USA, 1993—96. 1st lt. USAF, 1956—61, fighter pilot Air Def. Command, capt. USAFR, Mass. Air N.G., 1961—66. Recipient Centennial medallion Stanford U., Stanford Assocs. award. Fellow Am. Bar Found., N.Y. State Bar Found.; mem. ABA, Internat. Bar Assn., N.Y. State Bar Assn., Assn. Bar City N.Y., The Pilgrims, Round Hill Club (Greenwich), Field Club (Greenwich), Sankaty Head Club (Nantucket), Siasconset Casino Assn. (Nantucket), Harvard Club (N.Y.C.). Banking, Corporate, general, Securities. Home: 602 St Johns 79 Marsham St London SW1P 4SB England also: 39 Baxter Rd Siasconset MA 02564 Office: Cravath Swaine & Moore CityPoint One Ropemaker St London EC2Y 9HR England also: Cravath Swaine & Moore 825 8th Ave Fl 46 New York NY 10019-7416 E-mail: dbrownwood@cravath.com.

BRUCE, E(STEL) EDWARD, lawyer; b. Hutchinson, Kans., Nov. 23, 1938; s. Kenneth Dean and Josephine (Vigna) B.; m. Marnell Elaine Higley, Aug. 9, 1960; children: Anthony Dean, Caroline Bruce Macaulay. BA summa cum laude, Yale U., 1960, LLB magna cum laude, 1966. Bar: D.C. 1967, U.S. Ct. Appeals (1st, 2d, 3d, 4th, 5th, 6th, 8th, 9th, 10th, 11th, D.C. and Fed. cirs.), U.S. Supreme Ct. Law clk. U.S. Supreme Ct., Washington, 1966-67; assoc. Covington & Burling, Washington, 1967-73, ptnr., 1973—; adj. prof. constitutional law Georgetown U. Law Center, 1970-75. Mem. Appellate Judges Conf., Com. on Appellate Practice, 1993-2000; mem. faculty ABA Appellate Inst., 1992-2000. Mem. adminstrv. bd. Cornell Lab. Ornithology, 1998—; bd. dirs. Young Concert Artists, 2003—, Washington Area Lawyers for the Arts, 1993-99, Yale Law Sch. Fund, 1992-98, Audubon Nat. Soc., 1986-92. Lt. jg. USN, 1960—63. Mem.: ABA, Edward Coke Appellate Inn of Ct. (v.p. 2000—02, pres. 2002—), D.C. Bar Assn., Am. Acad. Appellate, Am. Law Inst., Chevy Chase Club, Met. Club, Phi Beta Kappa, Order of Coif. Administrative and regulatory, Federal civil litigation, Environmental. Home: 2701 Foxhall Rd NW Washington DC 20007-1128 Office: Covington & Burling 1201 Pennsylvania Ave NW Washington DC 20004-2401

BRUCE, ROBERT DENTON, lawyer; b. Houston, Tex., Jan. 29, 1943; s. Simeon Kelley and Lucy Jane B.; m. Norma Gene Durant, June 5, 1965; children: Denton, Jennifer, Stuart. BBA, U. Tex., 1966; JD, St. Mary's U., San Antonio, 1972. Bar: Tex. 1972. Pvt. practice, Mineola, Tex., 1972—. City atty., Mineola, 1976—77, Alba, Tex., 1981—, Yantis, Tex., 2002—. Trustee sch. bd. Mineola Ind. Sch. Dist., 1976-82; pres. Mineola Indsl. Found., 1980-2000, adminstrv. bd. Meth. Ch., Mineola, 1978-80. With USNR, 1960-70. Avocations: tennis, reading, hunting. Office: PO Box 266 Mineola TX 75773-0266 E-mail: wctc@lcii.net.

BRUCHS, AMY O'BRIEN, lawyer; b. Portage, Wis., Jan. 19, 1968; d. John Gregory O'Brien and Maxine O'Brien Hibner; m. Michael L. Bruchs, Jan. 1, 1994; children: Tanner, Elizabeth, Garrett. BA magna cum laude, U. Wis., Green Bay, 1990; JD cum laude, U. Wis., Madison, 1993. Bar: Wis. 1993, U.S. Dist. Ct. (we. and ea. dists.) Wis. 1993, U.S. Ct. Appeals (7th cir.) 1993. Ptnr. Michael, Best & Friedrich LLP, Madison, 1993—. Bd. dirs., vol. Badger chpt. ARC, Madison, 1998-2002, Family Svc., Madison, 2001—, Wis. Ctr. Mfg. and Productivity, 2001—. Avocations: fishing, watching sports, basketball, reading, dog training. Federal civil litigation, Labor (including EEOC, Fair Labor Standards Act, labor-management relations, NLRB, OSHA), Workers' compensation. Office: Michael Best & Friedrich 1 S Pinckney St Madison WI 53703-2892

BRUCKEN, ROBERT MATTHEW, lawyer; b. Akron, Ohio, Sept. 15, 1934; s. Harold M. and Eunice B. (Boesel) B.; m. Lois R. Gilbert, June 30, 1960; children: Nancy, Elizabeth, Rowland, Gilbert. AB, Marietta Coll., 1956; JD, U. Mich., 1959. Bar: Ohio 1960. Assoc. Baker & Hostetler, Cleve., 1960-69; ptnr., 1970—. Trustee Lakeside Assn., 1979-97, Marietta Coll., 1983—; sec., treas. Leader Shape, Inc., 1990—. Served with AUS, 1959-60. Mem. ABA, Ohio State Bar Assn. (chmn. probate and trust law sect. 1981-83), Cleve. Bar Assn. (chmn. probate ct. com. 1973-75), Am. Coll. Trust and Estate Counsel, Phi Beta Kappa. Congregationalist. Estate planning, Probate (including wills, trusts), Estate taxation. Office: Baker & Hostetler 3200 Nat City Ctr 1900 E 9th St Ste 3200 Cleveland OH 44114-3475 E-mail: rbrucken@bakerlaw.com.

BRUCKER, WILBER MARION, retired lawyer; b. Saginaw, Mich., Apr. 13, 1926; s. Wilber Marion and Clara (Hantel) B.; m. Doris Ann Shover, June 23, 1951; children: Barbara Ann, Wilber Marion, Paul Bradford. Student, Wayne State U., 1943; AB, Princeton U., 1949; JD, U. Mich., 1952. Bar: Mich. 1953. Assoc. Clark, Klein, Brucker & Waples, Detroit, 1952-58; pvt. practice Detroit, 1958-61; ptnr. Brucker & Brucker, Detroit, 1961-67, McInally, Rockwell & Brucker, Detroit, 1968-78, McInally, Brucker, Newcombe, Wilke and DeBona, Detroit, 1978-86; pres. Alliance Fin. Corp., 1986-89; sr. legal counsel Riley and Roumell, Detroit, 1990-96; dir. Bank of Dearborn, Mich., 1970-89, Alliance Fin. Corp., 1982-89; ret. Legal counsel Econ. Club Detroit, 1968-86; arbitrator Am. Arbitration Assn., 1965-79; bd. dirs. Cmty. Bank Dearborn. Bd. govs. Wayne State U., Detroit, 1967-78, chmn. bd. govs., 1972; pres. bd. trustees Arnold Home, 1968-96; mem. Witanagamote, 1956—, Centurions, 1977-96, Woodworkers, 1991—; mem. bd. canvassers City of Grosse Pointe Farms, Mich., 1972-74; pres. Grosse Pointe Sr. Mens Club, 1998-99. Mem. ABA, Mich. Bar Assn., Country Club of Detroit, Masons. Banking, Commercial, consumer (including collections, credit), Probate (including wills, trusts). Home: 253 Touraine Rd Grosse Pointe Farms MI 48236-3308

BRUEN, JAMES A. lawyer; b. South Hampton, N.Y., Nov. 29, 1943; s. John Francis and Kathryn Jewell (Arthur) B.; m. Carol Lynn Heller, June 13, 1968; children: Jennifer Lynn, Garrett John. BA cum laude, Claremont Men's Coll., 1965; JD, Stanford U., 1968. Bar: Calif. 1968, U.S. Dist. Ct. (no., ea., so. and cen. dists.) Calif. 1970, U.S. Ct. Claims 1972, U.S. Tax Ct. 1972, U.S. Ct. Appeals (9th cir.) 1972, U.S. Supreme Ct. 1973, Ariz. 1993. Atty. FCC, Washington, 1968-70; asst. U.S. atty. criminal div. Office of US. Atty., San Francisco, 1970-73, asst. U.S. atty. civil div., 1973-75, chief of civil div., 1975-77; ptnr. Landels, Ripley & Diamond, San Francisco, 1977-2000, Farella Braun & Martel LLP, San Francisco, 2000—. Mem. faculty Nat. Jud. Coll. ABA; lectr. Am. Law Inst. Am. Bd. Trial Advocates, Practising Law Inst. Def. Rsch. Inst., others. Co-author: Pharmaceutical Products Liability, 1989; contbg. editor: Hazardous Waste and Toxic Torts Law and Strategy, 1987-92; contbr. numerous articles to profl. jours. Mem. ABA (vice chmn. environ. quality com. nat. resources sect. 1989-93, co-chmn. enforment litigation subcom. environ. litigation com. litigation sect. 1990-92), Am. Inn of Ct. (master-at-large), Internat. Soc. for Environ. Epidemiology. Avocations: scuba diving, travel. Criminal, Environmental, Product liability. Office: Farella Braun & Martel Russ Bldg 30th Fl 235 Montgomery St San Francisco CA 94104 Fax: (415) 954-4480. E-mail: jbruen@fbm.com.

BRUESEKE, HAROLD EDWARD, magistrate; b. Sandusky, Ohio, Mar. 19, 1943; s. Edward W. and Jolanda (Sommer) B.; m. Bonnie A. Beaver, Aug. 12, 1967; children: Matthew E., Michael A. BA with honors, Elmhurst Coll., 1965; JD, Ind. U., 1968; grad., Ind. Judicial Coll., 2000. Bar: Ind., 1968, U.S. Dist. Ct. (no. and so. dists.) 1968, U.S. Supreme Ct. 1978; lic. real estate broker, Ind. Staff atty. Legal Svcs./Legal Edn., South Bend, Ind., 1968-70; pvt. practice South Bend, 1971-92; dep. pros. atty. St. Joseph County, South Bend, 1971-73; juvenile referee St. Joseph Probate Ct., South Bend, 1973-92, judge pro tem, 1993, magistrate, 1993—. Instr. Ivy Tech. State Coll., South Bend, Ind., 2003—. Contbg. author: Juvenile Benchbook, 1980-92. Bd. dirs. Eden Theol. Sem., St. Louis, 1989-2001, various other civic orgns., South Bend, 1968—; bd. dirs., elder Zion United Ch. of Christ, South Bend, 1994-96. Mem. ABA, Ind. State Bar Assn., St. Joseph County Bar Assn., Nat. Coun. Juvenile and Family Ct. Judges, Ind. Coun. Juvenile and Family Ct. Judges (bd. dirs., sec., v.p. pres. 1980-2000), Jud. Conf. Ind. (dir. 1998-2000). Avocations: amateur radio, recreational vehicles, computers. Home: 52741 Arbor Dr South Bend IN 46635-1205 Office: Juvenile Justice Ctr 1000 S Michigan St South Bend IN 46601-3426 E-mail: bhbruese@attbi.com., hbrueseke@jjconline.org.

BRUESS, CHARLES EDWARD, lawyer; b. St. Paul, Oct. 15, 1938; s. Edward Charles and Eleanor Mabel (Hammerstein) B.; m. Jean Ellen Gustafson, Aug. 26, 1962; children: Steven Charles, Karen Jean. BA, U. Minn., 1959; student, Ohio U., 1959-60; JD, Ind. U., 1963. Bar: Ind. 1963, U.S. Dist. Ct. (so. dist.) Ind. 1968, U.S. Supreme Ct. 1966. Assoc. Barnes, Hickam, Pantzer & Boyd, Indpls., 1967-71; ptnr. Barnes & Thornburg (formerly Barnes, Hickam, Pantzer & Boyd), Indpls., 1972-94, of counsel, 1995-96, ret., 1996; dep. clk. U.S. Dist. Ct. (so. dist.) Ind., 1999—. Trustee Eagle-Union Community Sch. Corp., Zionsville, Ind., 1978-90; dir. Tri-County Ctr. Inc., 1991-94, dir., sec. Zionsville Pub. Libr., Leasing Corp., 1992—; bd. dirs. Hussey-Mayfield Meml. Pub. Libr. Found., 1999—. Fellow Ind. Bar Found.; mem. Ind. Bar Assn., Lawyers Club (Indpls.). Republican. Methodist. Home: 3517 Inverness Blvd Carmel IN 46032

BRUFF, HAROLD HASTINGS, dean; b. 1944; BA in Am. History and Lit., Williams Coll.; JD magna cum laude, Harvard U. Law faculty Ariz. State U., Tempe, 1971-79; sr. atty.-advisor Office of Legal Counsel, U.S. Dept. Justice, 1979-81; cons. to chmn. Pres.'s Commn. on the Accident at Three Mile Island, 1981; law faculty U. Tex., Austin, 1983-85, John S. Redditt prof. law, 1985-92; Donald Rothschild rsch. prof. George Washington U. Law Sch., Washington, 1992-96; dean U. Colo. Sch. Law, Boulder, 1996—. Contbr. articles to profl. jours. Mem. ABA, Phi Beta Kappa. Office: U Colo Boulder Sch Law Campus Box 401 Boulder CO 80309-0001

BRUGGER, GEORGE ALBERT, lawyer; b. Erie, Pa., Jan. 19, 1941; s. Albert F. and Georgia V. (Bach) B.; children from previous marriage: Laura, Linda, Mark; m. Ann Rosenberg. BA, Gannon Coll., 1963; JD, Georgetown U., 1967. Bar: Md. 1968, D.C. 2002, U.S. Dist. Ct. Md. 1972, U.S. Supreme Ct. 1972. Law clk. to U.S. asst. atty. gen. U.S. Dept. of Justice, Washington, 1963-66; mgr. pub. affairs Air Transport Assn. of Am., Washington, 1966-68; ptnr. Beatty & McNamee, Hyattsville, Md., 1968-75; sr. ptnr., pres. Fossett & Brugger, Chartered, Greenbelt, Md., 1975—. Bd. dirs. Prince George's County Fin. Svcs. Corp. Chmn. bd. dirs. Prince George's Econ. Devel. Corp.; pres. Laurel Regional Hosp. Found. Recipient Disting. Alumni award Gannon Coll. Fellow Md. Bar Found.; mem. ABA (chmn. land use regulation com.), Md. Bar Assn. (bd. dirs.), Prince George's County Bar Assn. (pres. 1982), Prince George's Law Found., (bd. dirs.), Prince George's County C. of C. (Disting. Svc. award 1980, 83, 85), Fed. Bar Assn. (dir.). Roman Catholic. Avocations: collecting classic sports cars, marine tropical fish. Administrative and regulatory, Condemnation (eminent domain), Property, real (including real estate development, water). Home: The Colonnade 2801 New Mexico Ave NW Washington DC 20007 also: 5546 N Harbor Village Dr Vero Beach FL 32967 Office: Fossett & Brugger Chartered 6404 Ivy Ln Ste 720 Greenbelt MD 20770-1425

BRUMBAUGH, GEORGE EDWIN, JR., lawyer; b. Abington, Pa., Jan. 20, 1950; s. George E. and Mary C. (Wabecz); m. Kathleen A. Magreta, June 23, 1973; children: Geoffrey, Timothy, Stacey. BS, U. Detroit, 1971, JD, 1974. Bar: Mich. 1974, U.S. Dist. Ct. (ea. dist.) Mich. 1975, U.S. Supreme Ct. 1981, U.S. Ct. Appeals (6th cir.) 1990. Assoc. LaBarge, Zatkoff & Dinning, Roseville, Mich., 1974-83; asst. corp. counsel Macomb County, Mt. Clemens, Mich., 1983-90, corp. counsel, dir., 1990—. Mem. Macomb County Bar Assn. Roman Catholic. Avocation: golf. Office: Macomb County 1 S Main St Fl 8 Mount Clemens MI 48043-2306

BRUMBAUGH, JOHN MOORE, lawyer; b. Lima, Peru, Aug. 3, 1945; s. John Granville and Annie Lee (Moore) B.; m. Caroline Patterson, Aug. 12, 1967; children: John Patterson, David Elliott, Katherine Anne, Caroline Moore. BA, Wabash Coll., 1967; JD, U. Fla., 1970. Bar: Fla. 1970, U.S. Ct. Appeals (5th and 11th cirs.), U.S. Dist. Ct. (so. dist.) Fla., U.S. Supreme Ct. Law clk. to judge U.S. Dist. Ct. (so. dist.) Fla., Miami, Fla., 1970-72; assoc. Frates, Floyd, Pearson, Miami, 1972-76; ptnr. Richman, Greer, Weil Brumbaugh Mirabito & Christensen, PA, Miami, Fla., 1976—, mng. ptnr., 1990—. Trustee Trinity Episcopal Sch., Miami, 1985-89, chmn. bd. trustees, 1987-90; trustee St. Thomas Episc. Day Sch., 1988-90, Palmer Trinity Sch., 1996—, vice-chmn., 1999-2001, chair, 2001—; bd. dirs. Miami City Club, 1998-2002. Fellow Am. Coll. Trial Lawyers, Internat. Soc. Barristers; mem. ABA (standing com. on specialization 1997—, chair

2000—), Am. Bar Found., Fla. Bar (mem. bd. legal specialization and edn. 1984-85, 87-2001, chmn. 1993-94, cert. civil trial lawyer), Blue Key, Phi Delta Phi. Federal civil litigation, General civil litigation, State civil litigation.

BRUMM, JAMES EARL, lawyer, trading company executive; b. San Antonio, Dec. 19, 1942; s. John Edward and Marie Oletha (Gault) B.; m. Alicia Joan Pine, Aug. 17, 1968 (div. Mar. 1991); children: Christopher Kenji, Jennifer Kimiko, Laurie Kiyoko; m. Yuko Tsuchida, Apr. 17, 1991. AB, Calif. State U., Fresno, 1965; LLB, Columbia U., 1968. Bar: N.Y. 1969. Assoc. Reid & Priest, N.Y.C., 1968-72, Logan, Takashima & Nemoto, Tokyo, 1973-76; exec. v.p., gen. counsel, dir. Mitsubishi Internat. Corp., N.Y.C., 1977—; pres. Mitsubishi Internat. Corp. Found., N.Y.C., 1992—. Bd. dirs. Brunei LNG, Tembec, Inc., Mitsubishi Corp., Japan, 1995—2002. Trustee Spuyten Duyvil Nursery Sch., Bronx, NY, 1991—95; bd. dirs. Sanctuary for Families, 2000—, Forest Trails, 2003—; bd. visitors Columbia Law Sch., 1998—; mem. corp. adv. coun. Earthwatch; mem. adv. bd. Global Forest Trade Network; bd. dirs. Jr. Achievement Internat., 1997—2000, Internat. Sch. Svcs., 1997—99, Forest Trends, 2003—, Am. Bird Conservancy, 2003—. Mem. ABA, bd. dirs. Forest Trends, 2003-, Internat. Bar Assn., Assn. Bar City N.Y. (chmn. com. on internat. trade 1990-93, chmn. task force on internat. legal svcs. 1998-2001, rep. to Internat. Bar Assn. 2001--), Univ. Club, Nippon Club. Corporate, general, Private international. Home: 255 W 84th St Apt 6C New York NY 10024-4327 Office: Mitsubishi Internat Corp 520 Madison Ave New York NY 10022-4213

BRUNDIGE, ROBERT WILLIAM, JR., lawyer; b. Dayton, Ohio, Feb. 4, 1944; s. Robert W. and Elizabeth (Marquardt) B.; m. Katherine D. Muller, Dec. 18, 1971; children: Elizabeth, Allyson. BA, Yale U., 1966; JD, Vanderbilt U., 1969. Bar: N.Y. 1970, U.S. Dist. Ct. (so. and ea. dists.) N.Y. 1972, U.S. Tax Ct. 1973, U.S. Ct. Appeals (2d cir.) 1975, U.S. Ct. Appeals (11th cir.) 1983, U.S. Ct. Appeals (5th cir.) 1985, U.S. Supreme Ct. 1996, N.J. 1997, U.S. Dist. Ct. N.J. 1997, U.S. Ct. Appeals (3rd cir.) 2000. Assoc. Sage, Gray, Todd & Sims, N.Y.C., 1969-75, ptnr., 1976-86, Hughes, Hubbard & Reed, LLP, N.Y.C., 1987—. Mem. Vanderbilt Law Sch. Nat. Alumni Bd., Nashville, 1993-98; del. Yale U. Assn. of Yale Alumni, 1994-98; mem. Yale Alumni Fund, 1971—; mem. Yale Club of Bergen County and Vicinity, 1977—; presenter in field. Author: (with others) The McGraw-Hill Construction Business Handbook, 2d edit., 1985; mem. adv. bd. Vanderbilt Jour. Transnational Law, 2000—; contbr. article to profl. jours. Trustee Ridgewood Pub. Edn. Found., 1990-97, pres., 1990-93; pres. dean's coun. Vanderbilt U. Law Sch., Nashville, 1996—. Recipient Disting. Svc. award Vanderbilt Law Sch., 1995. Mem. ABA (sect. litigation, chmn. subcom. on commodities 1984-86). Episcopalian. Avocations: tennis, fly fishing, gardening. Banking, General civil litigation, Private international. Home: 251 Palmer Ct Ridgewood NJ 07450-2316 Office: Hughes Hubbard & Reed 1 Battery Park Plz Fl 17 New York NY 10004-1405

BRUNER, PHILIP LANE, lawyer; b. Chgo., Sept. 26, 1939; s. Henry Pfeiffer and Mary Marjorie (Williamson) B.; m. Ellen Carole Germann, Mar. 21, 1964; children: Philip Richard, Stephen Reed, Carolyn Anne. AB, Princeton U., 1961; JD, U. Mich., 1964; MBA, Syracuse U., 1967. Bar: Wis. 1964, Minn. 1968. Mem. Briggs and Morgan P.A., Mpls., St. Paul, 1967-83; founding shareholder Hart and Bruner P.A., Mpls., 1983-90; ptnr. Faegre & Benson, Mpls., 1991—, head constrn. law group, 1991—2001. Adj. prof. William Mitchell Coll. Law, St. Paul, 1970-76, U. Minn. Law Sch., 2003-; lectr. law seminars, univs., bar assns. and industry; chmn. Supreme Ct. Minn. Bd. Continuing Legal Edn., 1994-98. Co-author: Bruner and O'Conner on Construction Law, 7 vols., 2002; contbr. articles to profl. jours. Mem. Bd. Edn., Mahtomedi Ind. Sch. Dist. 832, 1978-86; bd. dirs. Mahtomedi Area Ednl. Found., 1988-94, 2002—, pres., 1988-91, 2002—; bd. dirs. Minn. Ch. Found., 1975—, pres., 1989-97; chmn. constrn. industry adv. bd. West Group, 1991—. Served to capt. USAF, 1964-67. Decorated Air Force Commendation Medal; recipient Disting. Service award St. Paul Jaycees, 1974; named One of Ten Outstanding Young Minnesotans, Minn. Jaycees, 1975. Fellow Am. Coll. Constrn. Lawyers (founding mem., bd. govs. 1999-2002, sec. 2003—), Nat. Contract Mgmt. Assn., Am. Bar Found.; mem. ABA (chmn. internat. constrn. divsn. forum com. on constrn. industry 1989-91, chmn. fidelity and surety law com. 1994-95, regional chmn. pub. contract law sect. 1990-96), Internat. Bar Assn., Inter-Pacific Bar Assn. (vice chmn. internat. constrn. com. 1995-97), Fed. Bar Assn., Minn. Bar Assn. (vice chmn. litigation sect. 1979-81), Wis. Bar Assn., Hennepin Bar Assn., Am. Arbitration Assn. (nat. panel arbitrators), Mpls. Club. Presbyterian. General civil litigation, Construction, Government contracts and claims. Home: 8432 80th St N Stillwater MN 55082-9331 Office: Faegre & Benson 2200 Wells Fargo Ctr 90 S 7th St Minneapolis MN 55402-3901 E-mail: pbruner@faegre.com., Philipbruner@hotmail.com.

BRUNER, WILLIAM GWATHMEY, III, lawyer; b. Gadsden, Ala., Nov. 29, 1951; s. William G. and Nicolette A. (Diprima) B.; m. Eloisa Fernandez, Aug. 7, 1976; children: Nicolette, Virginia, William, Weston. BSE, U. Mich., 1973; JD, U. Va., 1976. Bar: Ind., Pa. Assoc. Bingham, Summers, Indpls., 1976-78; corp. counsel Scott Paper Co., Phila., 1978-86; group counsel Emhart Corp., Farmington, Conn., 1986-89; corp. counsel Black & Decker, Towson, Md., 1989-93, sr. corp. counsel, 1994—. Mem. ABA (EEO com. labor and employment law sect., taxation sect.). Republican. Roman Catholic. Corporate, general, Labor (including EEOC, Fair Labor Standards Act, labor-management relations, NLRB, OSHA), Pension, profit-sharing, and employee benefits. Office: Black & Decker Corp 701 E Joppa Rd Baltimore MD 21286-5502

BRUNETTI, MAURIZIO, international lawyer; b. Milan, Sept. 10, 1957; s. Franco and Afra Margherita (Agnetti) B. Licentiatus iuris magna cum laude, U. Zurich, Switzerland, 1982. Bar: Canton of Ticino, Switzerland, atty.-at-law, 1987, civil law notary, 1987. Acad. asst. ETH, Zurich, 1983-84; law clerk Pretura di Lugano, Switzerland, 1985; articles atty. Bolla & Bonzanigo, Lugano, 1985-87, assoc., 1987-88; legal adviser Iran-U.S. Claims Tribunal, The Hague, The Netherlands, 1989-95, dep. sec.-gen., 1995—. Instr. LL.M. program Leiden U., The Netherlands, 1997; arbitrator in field. Contbr. articles to law jours. Mem.: Internat. Law Assn., Nederlandse Vereniging voor Internationaal Recht, Swiss Arbitration Assn., Am. Soc. Internat. Law, ABA (assoc.). Avocations: running, fitness, skiing, cooking. Office: Iran-US Claims Tribunal Parkweg 13 2585 JH The Hague Netherlands E-mail: mbrunetti@compuserve.com.

BRUNETTI, MELVIN T. federal judge; b. Reno, 1933; m. Gail Dian Buchanan; children: Nancy, Bradley, Melvin Jr. Attended, U. Nev., 1951-53, 1956-57, 1960; JD, U. Calif., San Francisco, 1964. Mem. firm Vargas, Bartlett & Dixon, 1964-69, Laxalt, Bell, Allison & Lebaron, 1970-78, Allison, Brunetti, MacKenzie, Hartman, Soumbeniotis & Russell, 1978-85; judge U.S. Ct. Appeals (9th cir.), Reno, 1985-99, sr. judge, 1999—. Mem. Council of Legal Advisors, Rep. Nat. Com., 1982-85. Served with U.S. Army N.G., 1954-56. Mem. ABA, State Bar of Nev. (pres. 1984-85, bd. govs. 1975-84). Office: US Ct Appeals US Courthouse 400 S Virginia St Ste 506 Reno NV 89501-2194*

BRUNIG, ROBERT ARTHUR, lawyer; b. New Orleans, Feb. 15, 1946; s. Arthur John and Marie Louise (Engelhardt) B.; m. Donna Jean Bahn, Aug. 2, 1968 (div. Dec. 1980); children: Jennifer Lynn, Adam Robert, Scott Arthur. AA, Concordia Luth. Coll., Austin, Tex., 1963-65; BA with high distinction, Concordia Sr. Coll., 1967; M. in Div., Concordia Sem., St. Louis, 1971; JD magna cum laude, Washburn U., 1976. Bar: Kans. 1976, Minn. 1976, D.C. 1987, U.S. Dist. Ct. Kans. 1976, U.S. Dist. Ct. Minn. 1977, U.S. Ct. Appeals (8th cir.) 1979, U.S. Dist. Ct. D.C. 1987, U.S. Tax. Ct. 1984, U.S. Supreme Ct. 1985, U.S. Ct. Appeals (D.C. cir.) 1990. Pastor Zion Lutheran Ch., Vassar, Kans., 1971-76; law clk. to judge U.S. Dist. Ct., St. Paul, 1976-78; assoc. O'Connor & Hannan, Mpls., 1978-83, ptnr., 1983-94; shareholder Moss & Barnett, P.A., Mpls., 1994—. Chmn. merit selection panel magistrates/bankruptcy judges U.S. Dist. Ct., Minn., 1984, mem. merit selection panel, magistrate, 1989; bd. dirs. Coffey County Hosp. Assn., Burlington, Kans., 1971-76; bd. advisors Hilltop Nursing Home, Lyndon, Kans., 1971-76. Bd. dirs. Coffey County Hosp. Assn., Burlington, Kans., 1971-76; bd. advisors Hilltop Nursing Home, Lyndon, Kans., 1971-76. Mem. ABA, Minn. State Bar Assn., Hennepin County Bar Assn. Lutheran. Federal civil litigation, State civil litigation, Criminal. Home: 918 Strafford Dr Southlake TX 76092-7110 Office: SEC Ft Worth Dist Office 801 Cherry St Ste 1900 Fort Worth TX 76102-6815

BRUNING, JON CUMBERLAND, state attorney general; b. Lincoln, Nebr., Apr. 30, 1969; s. Roger Howard and Mary Genevieve (Cumberland) B.; m. Deonne Leigh Niemack, July 8, 1995, two children, Lauren Caroline, Jon Cumberland Jr. BA with high distinction, U. Nebr., 1990, JD with distinction, 1994. Bar: Nebr. 1994, U.S. Dist. Ct. Nebr. 1994, U.S. Ct. Appeals (8th cir.) 1994. Pvt. practice, Papillion, Nebr., 1993-97; mem. Nebr. Legislature from 3rd dist., Lincoln, 1997—2002; atty. gen. State of Nebr., 2003—. Mem., Gretna United Methodist Church, Nebr. State Bar Assoc., Phi Beta Kappa. Republican. Methodist. Home: 17501 Riviera Dr Omaha NE 68136-1951 Office: State Capitol PO Box 98920 Lincoln NE 68509

BRUNNER, KIM M. insurance company executive; Chief counsel Ill. Ins. Dept.; atty. Nationwide Ins. Co.; with State Farm Ins. Cos., Bloomington, Ill., 1987—, assoc. gen. counsel, 1991-93, v.p.-counsel, 1993-97, sr. v.p., gen. counsel, 1997—. Office: State Farm Ins Cos 1 State Farm Plz Bloomington IL 61710-0001*

BRUNO, ANTHONY D. lawyer; b. Newark, N.J., May 3, 1956; s. Frank and Delores (Fleming) B.; m. Gina Mabey, Aug. 1982; children: Chris, Dan, Will. BA in Polit. Sci., Syracuse U., 1978; JD, George Washington U., 1981. Bar: N.Y. 1981, N.J. 1981. Atty. Shearman & Sterling, N.Y.C., 1981-84; assoc. gen. counsel Warner-Lambert, Morris Plains, NJ, 1984-2000; exec. v.p., gen. counsel Galen Holdings Plc, Rockaway, NJ, 2001—. Office: 100 Enterprise Dr Ste 280 Rockaway NJ 07866 E-mail: tbruno@wclabs.com.

BRUNO, LISA, law librarian; b. N.Y.C., Apr. 1, 1951; d. Dominic A. and Earline H. (Reed) B. BA, U. South Fla., 1973; MLS, Fla. State U., 1976. Cert. libr., N.Y. Law libr. Carlton, Fields, Ward, Emmanuel, Tampa, Fla., 1986-88; info. specialist Consumers Union, Yonkers, N.Y., 1991; law libr. Libr. of U.S. Cts., 11th Cir., Atlanta, 1992; sales rep. Lawyers Coop. Pub., Rochester, N.Y., 1994-95; cons. Info. Brokers, Atlantic Beach, Fla., 1995—; sr. account exec. Questel Orbit Telecom grp., France, 1999—. Lectr./guest spkr. in field. Contbr. articles to profl. jours. Avocations: ballet, art appreciation, travel. Office: Information Brokers 377 Plaza St Atlantic Beach FL 32233-5441 also: 377 Plaza St Atlantic Beach FL 32233-5441

BRUNS, BEVERLY A. lawyer; b. Pensacola, Fla., June 18, 1957; d. Kenneth Alvin and Nina Arnold Bruns. Cert. legal asst., U. Calif., Irvine, 1984; B in Polit. Sci. and Philosophy, Ind. U., 1996; JD, Ind. U., Bloomington, 1999. Bar: Ind., U.S. Dist. Ct. (no. and so. dists.) Ind. Paralegal, Ind.; legal editor Lexis-Nexis, 1999—2000; pvt. practice Indpls., 2000—02; atty. O'Koon Hindtermeister, Indpls., 2002—. Usher 2d Presbyn. Ch., Indpls. Named Miss Jr. Achievement, Ft. Wayne, Ind. Mem.: ATLA, ABA, Christian Legal Soc., Ind. Trial Lawyers Assn. (young lawyers divsn.), Ind. State Bar Assn. Personal injury (including property damage), Family and matrimonial, Bankruptcy. Home: 6102 Rosslen Ave Indianapolis IN 46220 Office: O'Koon Hindtermeister 101 W Ohio Ste 1401 Indianapolis IN 46204 Fax: 317-951-8470. E-mail: babruns.jd@juno.com., bbruns@okoon.com.

BRUNSON, DENISE M. lawyer; b. Madison, Wis., Dec. 12, 1965; d. Thomas J. and Virginia L. Schuh; children: Joshua, Anna. BA, U. Wis., 1989; JD, No. Ill. U., 1994. Bar: Tex. 94, Minn. 96, U.S. Dist. Ct. Minn. 97, Pa. 02. Assoc. McKenna & Cuneo LLP, Dallas, 1994—96, Gray, Plant, Mooty, Mooty & Bennett, Mpls., 1997—98, Best & Flanagan LLP, Mpls., 1998—2001; v.p. Fulton Fin. Advisors, N.A., Lancaster, Pa., 2001—. Contbr. to law rev. articles. Chmn. profl. advisors com. Leave-A-Legacy, Lancaster, 2002—; alt. mem. employee rev. bd. City of Crystal, Minn., 1997—2001; mem. estate planning coun. Lancaster County, Pa., 2001—. Fellow: ABA (mem. estate planning for bus. owners com. 2002—, sect. real property, probate and trust); mem.: Lancaster Bar Assn., Pa. Bar Assn. Office: Fulton Fin Advisors NA 1 Penn Sq Lancaster PA 17602 Fax: 717-392-1324. E-mail: dbrunson@fultonfinancialadvisors.com.

BRUSTAD, ORIN DANIEL, lawyer; b. Chgo., Nov. 11, 1941; s. Marvin D. and Sylvia Evelyn (Peterson) B.; m. Ilona M. Fox, July 16, 1966; children: Caroline E., Katherine L., Mark D. BA in History, Yale U., 1963, MA, 1964; JD, Harvard U., 1968. Bar: Mich. 1968, U.S. Dist. Ct. (so. dist.) Mich. 1968. Assoc. Miller, Canfield, Paddock and Stone, Detroit, 1968-74, sr. ptnr., 1975—, chmn. employee benefits practice group, 1989-96, dep. chmn. tax dept., 1989-93. Bd. dirs. Electrocon Internat., Inc., Ann Arbor, Mich. Mem. editl. adv. bd. Benefits Law Jour.; contbr. articles to profl. jours. Fellow Am. Coun. Employee Benefits Counsel (charter); mem. ABA, Mich. Bar Assn., Detroit Bar Assn., Mich. Employee Benefits Conf. Avocations: sailing, skiing, reading, piano. Corporate, general, Pension, profit-sharing, and employee benefits. Home: 1422 Macgregor Ln Ann Arbor MI 48105-2836 Office: Miller Canfield Paddock & Stone 150 W Jefferson Ave Fl 25th Detroit MI 48226-4432 E-mail: odbrusta@aol.com., brustad@millercanfield.com.

BRUVOLD, KATHLEEN PARKER, lawyer; BS in Math., U. Denver, 1965; MS in Math., Purdue U., 1967; JD, U. Cin., 1978. Bar: Ohio 1978, U.S. Dist. Ct. (so. dist.) Ohio 1978, U.S. Dist. Ct. (ea. dist.) Ky. 1979. Mathematician bur. rsch. and engrng. U.S. Post Office, 1967; instr. math. Purdue U., West Lafayette, Ind., 1967-68, asst. to dir., tng. coord., programmer Administrv. Data Processing Ctr., 1968-71; instr. math. Ind. U., Kokomo, 1969-70; pvt. practice Cin., 1978-80; asst. dir. Legal Adv. Svcs. U. Cin., 1980-89, assoc. gen. counsel, 1989—2002; asst. atty. gen. State of Ohio, 1983—. Chair Ohio pub. records com. Inter-univ. Coun. Legal Advisors, 1980-84; presenter various confs. and symposiums. Active com. group svcs. allocation United Way and Community Chest; v.p. Clifton Recreation Ctr. Adv. Coun., 1983-84; vice chair Cin. Bilingual Acad. PTA, 1989-90. U. Denver scholar, Jewel Tea Co. scholar. Mem. ABA, Nat. Assn. Coll. and Univ. Attys. (bd. dirs., co-chair taxation sect., com. ann. meeting arrangements, program com., publs. com., bd. ops. com., JCUL editl. bd. nominations com., honors and award com., intellectual property sect., com. continuing legal edn. 1992—), Cin. Bar Assn. (com. taxation, program chmn. 1985-86, sec. 1986-87, com. computer law). Home: 536 Evanswood Pl Cincinnati OH 45220-1527

BRYAN, BARRY RICHARD, lawyer; b. Orange, N.J., Sept. 5, 1930; s. Lloyd Thomas and Amy Rufe (Swank) B.; m. Margaret Susannah Elliot, July 24, 1953; children— Elliot Christopher, Peter George (dec.), Susannah Margaret, Sallie Catharine. BA, Yale U., 1952, JD cum laude, 1955; diploma in comparative legal studies, Cambridge U., Eng., 1956. Bar: N.Y. 1959. Legal advisor to gen. counsel Sec. of U.S. Air Force, Washington, 1956-58; assoc. Debevoise & Plimpton, N.Y.C., 1958-62, ptnr., 1963-93, presiding ptnr., 1993-98, of counsel, 1999—. Served to 1st lt. USAF, 1956-58. Fulbright scholar Trinity Coll., Cambridge U., 1956. Mem. ABA, Assn. of Bar of City of N.Y., Union Internationale des Avocats, Country Club of New Canaan, Fishers Island Club, Order of Coif, Phi Beta Kappa. Episcopalian. Corporate, general, Private international, Securities. Home: PO Box 197 Isabella Beach Rd Fishers Island NY 06390 Office: Debevoise & Plimpton 919 3rd Ave Fl 43 New York NY 10022

BRYAN, HENRY C(LARK), JR., retired lawyer; b. St. Louis, Dec. 8, 1930; s. Henry Clark and Faith (Young) B.; m. Sarah Ann McCarthy, July 28, 1956; children— Mark Pendleton, Thomas Clark, Sarah Christy Nussbaum. AB, Washington U., St. Louis, 1952, LL.B., 1956. Bar: Mo. 1956. Law clk. to fed. judge, 1956; assoc. McDonald & Wright, St. Louis, 1956-60; ptnr. McDonald, Bernard, Wright & Timm, St. Louis, 1961-64, McDonald, Wright & Bryan, St. Louis, 1964-81, Wright, Bryan & Walsh, St. Louis, 1981-84; pvt. practice law, 1984-96; ret., 1996. V.p., dir. Harbor Point Boat & Dock Co., St. Charles, Mo., 1966-80, Merrell Ins. Agy., 1966-80. Served to 1st lt. AUS, 1952-54 Mem. ABA, Mo. Bar Assn., St. Louis Bar Assn. (past chmn. probate and trust sect., marriage and div. law com.), Kappa Sigma, Phi Delta Phi Lodges: Elks. Republican. Episcopalian. Corporate, general, Family and matrimonial, Probate (including wills, trusts). Home: 41 Ladue Ter Saint Louis MO 63124-2047

BRYAN, RICHARD H. lawyer, educator, former senator; b. Washington, July 16, 1937; m. Bonnie Fairchild; 3 children. BA, U. Nev., 1959; LLB, U. Calif., San Francisco, 1963. Bar: Nev. 1963, DC 2002. Dep. dist. atty., Clark County, Nev., 1964—66; pub. defender, 1966—68; counsel Clark County Juvenile Ct., 1968—69; mem. Nev. Assembly, 1969—73, Nev. Senate, 1973—79; atty. gen. State Nev., 1979—83, gov., 1983—89; senator from Nev. U.S. Senate, 1989—2001; ptnr., mem. exec. com. Lionel, Sawyer & Collins, 2001—. Former mem. U.S. Senate coms. on commerce, sci. and transp., Dem. Policy Com., Fin. Com., Banking, Housing and Urban Affairs Com., Senate Nominating Steering and Coord. Com., Select Com. on Intelligence; adj. prof. polit. sci. U. Nev., Las Vegas, 2001—. Former pres. Clark County Legal Aid Soc.; bd. dirs. Las Vegas C. of C.; bd. trustees Nev. Devel. Authority, 2001—. 2d lt. U.S. Army, 1959—60. Recipient Disting. Svc. award, Vegas Valley Jaycees. Mem.: ABA, Coun. of State Govts. (past pres.), Am. Judicature Soc., Clark County Bar Assn., Elks, Masons, Lions, Phi Alpha Theta, Phi Alpha Delta. Democrat. Office: Lionel Sawyer & Collins 1700 Bank Am Plaza 300 S 4th St Las Vegas NV 89101

BRYAN, ROBERT J. federal judge; b. Bremerton, Wash., Oct. 29, 1934; s. James W. and Vena Gladys (Jensen) B.; m. Cathy Ann Welander, June 14, 1958; children: Robert James, Ted Lorin, Ronald Terence. BA, U. Wash., 1956, JD, 1958. Bar: Wash. 1959, U.S. Dist. Ct. (we. dist.) Wash. 1959, U.S. Tax Ct. 1965, U.S. Ct. Appeals (9th cir.) 1985. Assoc., then ptnr. Bryan & Bryan, Bremerton, 1959-67; judge Superior Ct., Port Orchard, Wash., 1967-84; ptnr. Riddell, Williams, Bullitt & Walkinshaw, Seattle, 1984-86; judge U.S. Dist. Ct. (we. dist.) Wash., Tacoma, 1986—. Mem. State Jail Comm., Olympia, Wash., 1974-76, Criminal Justice Tng. Com., Olympia, 1978-81, State Bd. on Continuing Legal Edn., Seattle, 1984-86; mem., sec. Jud. Qualifications Commn., Olympia, 1982-83; chair Wash. Fed.-State Jud. Coun., 1997-98. Author: (with others) Washington Pattern Jury Instructions (civil and criminal vols. and supplements), 1970-85, Manual of Model Criminal Jury Instructions for the Ninth Circuit, 1992, Manual of Model Civil Jury Instruction for the Ninth Circuit, 1993. Chmn. 9th Ct. Jury Com., 1991-92; bd. dirs. Fed. Jud. Ctr., 2000—. Served to maj. USAR. Mem.: 9th Cir. Dist. Judges Assn. (sec.-treas. 1997—99, v.p. 1999—2001, pres. 2001—). Office: US Dist Ct 1717 Pacific Ave Rm 4427 Tacoma WA 98402-3234

BRYAN, THOMAS LYNN, lawyer, educator; b. Wichita, Kans., June 10, 1935; s. Herbert Thomas and Ruth Marjorie (Williams) B.; m. Virginia Alice Cooper, June 13, 1981; children from previous marriage— Victoria Lynne Hague, Douglas Edward BA, U. Kans., 1957; LLB, Columbia U., 1960. Bar: N.Y. Assoc. Willkie Farr & Gallagher, N.Y.C., 1960-66, ptnr., 1967-92; adj. prof. Stetson U. Coll. Law, 1993-97. Co-author: Business Acquisitions, 1971, 2d edit. 1981 Mem. Longboat Key Club, Upper Ridgewood Tennis Club, Phi Beta Kappa Republican. Avocations: tennis, sports, golf, theatre. Home: 77 Lakewood Ave Ho Ho Kus NJ 07423-1507 also: 3448 Mistletoe Ln Longboat Key FL 34228-4146

BRYANT, ARTHUR H. lawyer; b. Harrisburg, Pa., Aug. 11, 1954; s. Albert Irwin and Marjorie (Weinrib) B.; m. Nancy Kaye Johnson, Aug. 17, 1991; 1 stepchild, Vinnie Johnson; 1 child, Wallace Johnson Bryant. AB with hons., Swarthmore Coll., 1976; JD, Harvard U., 1979; D (hon.), Ripon Coll., 1998. Bar: Pa. 1981, U.S. Dist. Ct. (ea. dist.) Pa. 1981, U.S. Ct. Appeals (3d cir.) Pa. 1981, U.S. Ct. Appeals (11th cir.) Ga. 1985, U.S. Ct. Appeals (6th cir.) Ohio 1986, U.S. Ct. Appeals (D.C. cir.) 1986, U.S. Ct. Appeals (9th cir.) Calif. 1987, U.S. Ct. Appeals (7th cir.) Ill. 1988, U.S. Ct. Appeals (5th cir.) Tex. 1988, D.C., 1989, U.S. Supreme Ct. 1989, U.S. Ct. Appeals (1st cir.) 1996. Intern Rosenman, Colin & Freund, N.Y.C., 1978, N.Y. Civil Liberties Union, N.Y.C., 1978, Cambridge & Somerville Legal Svcs., Cambridge, Pa., 1979; law clk. U.S. Dist. Ct. (so. dist.), Tex., 1979-80; atty. Kohn, Savett, Marion & Graf., Phila., 1980-84; staff atty. Trial Lawyers for Pub. Justice, Washington, 1984-87, exec. dir., 1987—. Recipient George Moscone Meml. award Consumer Atty. Assn. L.A., 2003; named one of 20 young lawyers making a difference in the world ABA Barrister mag., 1991, one of 50 most influential people in coll. sports Coll. Sports Mag., 1994, one of 45 lawyers whose vision and commitment are changing lives The Am. Lawyer, 1997, one of 100 most influential lawyers in Am. Nat. Law Jour., 2000; recipient Wasserstein Pub. Interest law fellowship, 1996. Mem. ABA (Pursuit of Justice award 2003), ATLA. General civil litigation, Constitutional, Public interest. Office: Trial Lawyers Pub Justice Ste 275 One Kaiser Plaza Oakland CA 94612

BRYANT, HUBERT HALE, lawyer; b. Tulsa, Jan. 4, 1931; s. Roscoe Conkling and Curlie Beatrice (Marshall) B.; m. Elnora Geraldine Roberson, Oct. 25, 1952; children— Cheryl Denise, Tara Kay. BA, Fisk U., 1952, LL.B., Howard U., 1956. Bar: Okla. bar 1956, U.S. Dist. Ct. bar for No. Dist. Okla 1956, U.S. Ct. Appeals (10th cir.) 1967, U.S. Supreme Ct. bar 1980. Individual practice law, Tulsa, 1956-67, 81-84, 86—. Asst. city prosecutor, City of Tulsa, 1961-63, chief city prosecutor, 1963-67, asst. U.S. atty., No. Dist. Okla., 1967-77, U.S. atty., 1977-81; mcpl. ct. judge City of Tulsa, 1984-86. Trustee 1st Bapt. Ch., Tulsa, 1970-75, 96-2002; bd. dirs. Tulsa Urban League, 1962-64. Recipient Outstanding Alumni award Howard U. Sch. Law, 1981, 30 Yr. Outstanding African Am. Lawyer award Met. Tulsa Urban League, 1997 Mem. NAACP, Nat. Bar Assn. (Named to Hall of Fame), Okla. Bar Assn., Tulsa County Bar Assn., Okla. Trial Lawyers Assn., Nat. Set, Masons (named Mason of Yr. local chpt. 1963, Outstanding Citizen award 1978), Sigma Pi Phi, Alpha Theta Boule, Alpha Phi Alpha. Democrat. General practice, Personal injury (including property damage), Workers' compensation. Home: 1818 N Boston St Tulsa OK 74106 Office: 2623 N Peoria Ave Tulsa OK 74106-2512

BRYANT, J(AMES) BRUCE, lawyer; b. Dettlebach, Fed. Republic Germany, Jan. 23, 1961; came to U.S., 1964; s. John Thomas and Doris Jean (Hazenbuahler) B.; 1 child, James Bruce II. BA, Northwestern State U., Natchitoches, La., 1984; MJ, La. State, 1986; JD, Miss. Coll., 1989. Bar: Miss., Tex. 1995, U.S. Dist. Ct. (no. and so. dists.) Miss., U.S. Ct. Appeals (5th cir.) La. 1991, U.S. Dist. Ct. (we. dist.) La. 1994. With residential life La. State U., Baton Rouge, 1985-86; law libr. worker Miss. Coll. Sch. Law, Jackson, 1986-87; clk. Brunini Law Firm, Jackson, 1987-88; ptnr. Cook & Bryant, Bay St. Louis, Miss., 1989-90; assoc. Cook, Yancey, King & Galloway, Shreveport, La., 1990-93; prof. bus. law La. State U., 1991-92, prof. paralegal sci., 1994-96; staff atty. State of La. Office of Support Enforcement, Shreveport, 1993-95; atty. Storm Operating Co. Inc. of La., 1994-98; sr. regional atty. State of La. Dept. Health and Hosps., Shreveport-Bossier City, La., 1995—; prof. comms. law, pub. rels and advt. Northwestern State U., 1996—; spl. asst. dist. atty. 1st Jud. Dist., Caddo Parish, La., 1998—. Bd. dirs. Extra Mile; cons. Wyman Fed. Credit Union,

Geismar, La., 1989-90, Comml. Nat. Bank, Shreveport, 1990-93; owner, pres. SHOWBIZZ Entertainment Agys., Shreveport, 1992—; v.p. Godfather Prodns., Inc., Shreveport-Bossier City, La., 1994—; owner La. Ctr. for Law and Justice, 1995—; spl. asst. dist. atty. Caddo Parish, 1998—; owner, pres. Dreamworks Internat., 1999—. Editor, author (with others): Art & Bylaws for Moot Court, 1989; contbr. to The Silence Within, 2000. Del. Republican Dist. IV, 1994—; bd. dirs. Shreveport Little Theatre, 1995-2000, Extra Mile, 1996—; vol. N.W. La. Coalition for Mentally Ill, 1995—, pres., 2002-; vol. Shreveport/Bossier Svc. Connection, 2001—; mem. L.A. Pro Bono Project, Tex. Bar Assn. Pro Bono Project (Outstanding Svc. Award 2002). Recipient Outstanding Svc. award, Tex. State Bar Pro Bono Project, 2002. Mem. ABA, La. Bar Assn. (mem. health law sect.), Miss. Pro Bono Project, Miss. Bar Assn., Assn. Trial Lawyers Am., La. Trial Lawyers Assn., Hancock County Bar Assn. (social chmn.), Shreveport Bar Assn. (comml. litigation sect., editor newsletter), TKE Alumni Assn. (pres.), Univ. Club (mem. com. 1994—). Roman Catholic. Avocations: martial arts, weightlifting, skiing, shooting. Commercial, contracts (including sales of goods; commercial financing), Communications, Entertainment. Home: PO Box 444 Shreveport LA 71162-0444 Office: La Ctr for Law and Justice 711 Texas Advocates Bldg Shreveport LA 71120

BRYANT, RICHARD TODD, lawyer; b. Kansas City, Mo., Sept. 3, 1952; s. Francis Todd and Marion Audrey (Weum) B.; m. Carol H. Olsen, Mar. 24, 1979. AA, AAS., Longview Community Coll., 1972; BBA, U. Mo.-Kansas City, 1974, M.P.A., 1975, JD, 1978. Bar: Mo. 1978, D.C. 1995, U.S. Dist. Ct. (we. dist.) Mo. 1978, D.C. 1995, U.S. Dist. Ct. (ea. dist.) Mo. 1995, Kans. 1996, Territorial Ct. of the Virgin Islands 1999. Assoc. Harding & Copilevitz P.C., Kansas City, Mo., 1978-85; ptnr. Copilevitz, Bryant, Gray & Jennings, P.C., Kansas City, 1985-95; bailiff ct. Overland Park, Kans., 1974-84; ptnr. Richard T. Bryant & Assocs. PC, Kansas City, 1995-98, mng. shareholder, 1998—. Contbr. articles to legal jours. Cons. Westwood & Lenexa (Kans.) Police Dept., 1977-78; adminstrv. hearing officer Housing Authority of Kansas City, 1988—; chmn. ad hoc com. Kansas City (Mo.) City Coun., 1992. Mem. ABA (liaison standing com. assn. standards criminal justice 1978, com. adminstrn. criminal justice 1977-78), Am. Arbitration Assn. (bd. of arbitrators, bd. of mediators), Kansas City (Mo.) Bar Assn. (mcpl. ct. com., vice chmn. 1991-94, chmn. 1994-95), First Amendment Lawyers Assn., Phi Delta Phi, Omicron Delta Kappa, Phi Theta Kappa. Family and matrimonial, Insurance, Land use and zoning (including planning). Office: 804 Bryant Bldg 1102 Grand Blvd Kansas City MO 64106-2316 E-mail: dick2479@aol.com.

BRYANT, ROBERT W., JR., lawyer; b. Raleigh, N.C., Mar. 8, 1953; s. Robert W. Bryant and Patricia Joan Johnson; m. Elizabeth Gale Lucas, May 10, 1975; children: Katherine, Sarah, Robert. BS in Bus. Adminstrn., U. N.C., 1975, JD, 1982. Bar: N.C. 1982, U.S. Dist. Ct. N.C. 1984, U.S. Ct. Appeals (4th cir.) 1985. Law clk. N.C. Ct. Appeals, Raleigh, 1982—83; lawyer Hornthal, Riley, Ellis & Maland, Elizabeth City, NC, 1983—87, Lucas, Bryant, Denning & Ellerbe, P.A., Selma, NC, 1987—. Chmn., mem. Johnston-Harnett County chpt. ARC, Selma, 1989—91; mem. N.C. State Health Coordinating Coun., Raleigh, 1995—; vice chair bd. trustees Johnston C.C., Smithfield, NC, 1999—; sec. Johnston County Dem. Party, 1987—2003. Recipient Pro Bono Atty. of the Yr. award, East Ctrl. Cmty. Legal Svcs. N.C., 1999. Mem.: N.C. Bar Assn. (mem. family law sect. coun. 1986—, chmn. family law sect. 1991, mem. small firm and solo practitioners com. 1994, mem. curriculum CLE com. 1997—2001). Methodist. Avocations: sports, scuba diving, fishing. Family and matrimonial, Personal injury (including property damage). Office: Lucas Bryant Denning & Ellerbe PA PO Box 309 208 N Webb St Selma NC 27576

BRYCE, ROBERT W. lawyer; b. Defiance, Ohio, Jan. 10, 1954; s. F. William and Jeanette A. Bryce; m. Francelia A. Yagelski, Aug. 16, 1975; children: Bobbi Ann, Christa Jean, Teresa Marie. BS, Mich. State U., 1976; JD, U. Toledo, 1980. Bar: Ohio 1981, U.S. Dist. Ct. (no. dist., we. divsn.) Ohio 1983, U.S. Ct. Appeals (6th cir.) 1993, cert.: Nat. Bd. Trial Advocacy (bd. cert. civil trial adv.). Jr. high sci. tchr. Toledo Pub. Schs., 1976—80; biology tchr. Montpelier (Ohio) H.S., 1980—81; asst. county prosecutor Defiance County, 1981—83; civil trial atty. Frank W. Cubbon, Jr. & Assocs., Toledo, 1983—88, Huffman, Gallagher, Schlageter & Breier, Oregon, Ohio, 1988—92, Schlageter, Breier & Bryce, Oregon, 1992—2003, Schlageter & Bryce Co., L.P.A., Oregon, 2003—. Trustee Anthony Wayne Sch. Edn. Found., Whitehouse, Ohio, 1997—2000. Mem.: Toledo Bar Assn. (mem. fee grievance com. 1986—88, mem. common pleas ct. com. 1988—90, mem. grievance com. 1998—2000), Ohio State Bar Assn., Ohio Acad. Trial Lawyers (trustee 1996—98), Am. Acad. Trial Lawyers, Sons Am. Legion (adj. 2003—), Mich. State Alumni Assn., Fraternal Order Eagles, Sigma Chi. Avocations: skiing, golf, entomology, landscaping. Home: PO Box 2666 11015 Stiles Rd Whitehouse OH 43571 Office: Schlageter & Bryce Co LPA 715 S Coy Rd Oregon OH 43616

BRYCE, WILLIAM DELF, lawyer; b. Georgetown, Tex., Aug. 7, 1932; s. D.A. Bryce and Frances Maxine (Wilson) Bryce Bakke; m. Sarah Alice Riley, Dec. 20, 1954; children: Douglas Delf, David Dickson. BA, U. Tex., 1955; LLB, Yale U., 1960. Bar: Tex. 1960, U.S. Dist. Ct. (we. dist.) Tex. 1963, U.S. Ct. Claims 1964, U.S. Supreme Ct. 1971. Briefing atty. Tex. Supreme Ct., Austin, 1960-61; sole practice, 1961—. Lectr. U. Tex., 1965-66. Editor, Tex. Supreme Ct. Jour. Served to 1st lt. USAF, 1955-57. Fellow Tex. Bar Found. (sustaining; life); mem. ABA, State Bar Tex., Travis County Bar Assn., Williamson County Bar Assn., Rotary Internat. (dist. 5870 gov. 1999-2000). Corporate, general, General practice, Probate (including wills, trusts). Home: 308 E University Ave Georgetown TX 78626-6813 also: 511 S Main St Georgetown TX 78626-5609

BRYDGER, GORDON CHARLES, lawyer; b. Miami, Fla., May 30, 1952; s. Lee and Sylvia (Balaban) B.; m. Marjorie Anne Gelber, Aug. 6, 1977; 1 child, Melanie. BS, U. Fla., 1974; JD cum laude, Emory U., 1977. Bar: Fla. 1977, Ga. 1977, Fla. Supreme Ct. 1977, U.S. Dist. Ct. (so. dist.) Fla. 1977, U.S. Ct. Appeals (5th cir.) 1977; bd. cert. marital and family law Fla. Bar. Assoc. Bradford, Williams, McKay, Kimbrell, Hamman & Jennings, PA, Miami, 1977-79, Kaplan, Jaffe & Gates, PA, Hollywood, Fla., 1979-81; ptnr. Brydger & Levitt, PA, Ft. Lauderdale, Fla., 1981-89; pvt. practice Ft. Lauderdale, 1989—. Mem. jud. nominating commn. State Fla., 1999—; lectr. in field. Contbr. chpt. to book. Fellow Am. Acad. Matrimonial Lawyers (bd. mgrs. 1997—); mem. Fla. Bar Asn. (mem. exec. com. family law sect. 1991-98, family law rules com. 1996—), Broward Bar Assn. (chmn. family law sect. 1992-93), Anti-Defamation League, Phi Beta Kappa. Avocation: wine. Family and matrimonial. Office: Ste 601 600 S Andrews Ave Fort Lauderdale FL 33301-2851

BRYDGES, THOMAS EUGENE, lawyer; b. Niagara Falls, N.Y., June 1, 1942; s. Earl W. and Eleanor M. (Mahoney) B.; m. Melissa May, May 26, 1990; children: Andrew MacLeod, Elizabeth Hendricks. BA in History, Syracuse U., 1971, JD, 1973. Bar: N.Y. 1974, U.S. Dist. (we. dist.) N.Y. 1974, U.S. Ct. Appeals (2d cir.) 1978. Assoc. Jaeckle, Fleischmann & Mugel, Buffalo, 1973-78, ptnr., 1979—. Bd. dirs., sec. Theodore Roosevelt Inagural site, 1999—. Author: (with others) Employment Discrimination Law, 1980—. Trustee Daemen Coll., Amherst, N.Y., 1988—; bd. dirs., v.p. Art Park & Co., Lewiston, N.Y., 1976—. Capt. U.S. Army, 1962-68, Vietnam. Decorated Bronze Star, Air medal, Army Commendation (2). Mem. ABA (labor sect.), Erie County Bar Assn. (bd. dirs. 2002--), N.Y. Bar Assn. (labor law com.). Labor (including EEOC, Fair Labor Standards Act, labor-management relations, NLRB, OSHA). Office: Jaeckle Fleischmann & Mugel 700 Fleet Bldg Buffalo NY 14202 E-mail: tbrydges@jaeckle.com.

BRYK, WILLIAM MICHAEL, lawyer, writer; b. Troy, N.Y., Mar. 12, 1955; s. William Zygmundt and Joy Kathleen (Hart) B.; m. Catherine Leitch Black, 1990 (div. 2002); m. Mimi Kramer, Jan. 12, 2003. BS, Manhattan Coll., 1977; JD, Fordham U., 1989. Bar: N.Y. 1990, U.S. Supreme Ct. 1993. Adminstrv. asst. N.Y. City Comptroller's Office, N.Y.C., 1977-82; asst. to pres. Manhattan Borough Pres.'s Office, N.Y.C., 1982-85; chief of staff N.Y. City Coun. Mem. W. L. McCaffrey, N.Y.C., 1986-87; spl. asst. to pres. N.Y. City Coun. Pres.'s Office, N.Y.C., 1987-89, 91-93; assoc. Bondy & Schloss, N.Y.C., 1989-90; ct. atty. N.Y. City Civil Ct., N.Y.C., 1990-91; atty. N.Y. City Dept. Social Svcs., N.Y.C., 1994, 95-97; spl. asst., mem. N.Y. City Bd. Edn., Bklyn., 1994-95; pvt. practice, 1997—99, 2002—03; assoc. Spinelli & Assocs., 1999—2000, Levy Boonshoft & Spinelli, 2000—02; staff counsel N.Y.C. Dept. Correction, 2002—. Columnist, N.Y. Press, 1998—. Mem. Manhattan Cmty. Bd. #6, N.Y.C., 1981-82, 89-90. Recipient N.Y. State Meritorious Svc. medal, 1998. Mem. Equestrian Order of the Holy Sepulchre of Jerusalem (knight). Roman Catholic. Avocations: reading, writing, railways, Portugal and the Portuguese. Home: 467 Central Park W Apt 5C New York NY 10025-3885

BRYNER, ALEXANDER O. state supreme court justice; b. Tientsin, China; m. Carol Crump; children: Paul, Mara. BA, Stanford U., 1966, JD, 1969. Law clk. to Chief Justice George Boney, Alaska Supreme Ct., 1969-71; legal editor Bancroft Whitney Co., San Francisco, 1971; with Pub. Defender Agy., Anchorage, 1972-74; ptnr. Bookman, Bryner & Shortell, 1974; Alaska dist. ct. judge Anchorage, 1975-77; U.S. atty. Alaska, 1977-80; chief judge Alaska Ct. Appeals, 1980-97; state supreme ct. justice Alaska Supreme Ct., Anchorage, 1997—. Office: Alaska Supreme Ct 303 K St Anchorage AK 99501-2013

BRYSON, WILLIAM HAMILTON, law educator; b. Richmond, Va., July 29, 1941; s. William Alexander and Lillian Sutton (Wilkinson) B. BA, Hampden_Sydney Coll., 1963; LLB, Harvard U., 1967; LLM, U. Va., 1968; PhD, Cambridge (Eng.) U., 1972. Bar: Va. 1967. Asst. prof. U. Richmond Sch. Law, 1973-76, assoc. prof., 1976-80, prof., 1980—; Blackstone prof. law U. Richmond Sch. Law, 2001. Adv. com. on rules of ct. Jud. Council Va. Author: Equity Side of the Exchequer, 1975, Legal Education in Virginia 1779-1979: A Biographical Approach, 1982, Virginia Civil Procedure, 1997, Virginia Circuit Court Opinions, 1985—, Virginia Law Books, 2000, Samuel Dodd's Reports, 2000, Cases Concerning Equity, 2001; mem. editl. bd. Am. Jour. Legal History, 1976—. William Senior scholar, 1970-72; Max Planck Inst. fellow, Frankfurt, Germany, 1972-73; Fulbright grant, 1963, Am. Coun. Learned Socs. grant, 1980; recipient Yorke prize Cambridge U., 1973 Fellow Royal Hist. Soc.; mem. Selden Soc. (Va. corr.), Va. Hist. Soc., Va. Bar Assn., Am. Soc. Legal History (bd. dirs. 1981-84), Phi Beta Kappa. Episcopalian. Office: U Richmond Sch Law Richmond VA 23173

BRZUSTOWICZ, JOHN CINQ-MARS, lawyer; b. Rochester, N.Y., Feb. 1, 1957; s. Richard J. and Alice (Cinq-Mars) B.; m. Diane Day, Aug. 22, 1981; children: Richard Reed, Megan Day, Emily Day-Hanson. BA, Coll. Wooster, 1979; JD, Case Western Res. U., 1985; cert., Cornell Inst. Labor Rels., 1982. Bar: Pa. 1985, U.S. Dist. Ct. (we. dist.) Pa. 1985, U.S. Ct. Appeals (3d cir.) 1986, U.S. Supreme Ct. 1990. Asst. to dir. Inst. Am. Music U. Rochester, Rochester, 1979-82; assoc. Peacock, Keller, Yohe, Day & Ecker, Washington, Pa., 1985-88, Sable, Makoroff & Libenson, Pitts., 1988-90; pvt. practice Brzustowicz Law Offices, McMurray, Washington, Pa., 1990-94; shareholder Day, Brzustowicz & Malkin, P.C., McMurray, Pa., 1995—. Chmn. bd. dirs. Inst. for Am. Music of Eastman Sch. Music, 1997—; chmn. law libr. Washington County (Pa.) Bar, 1992; mem. com. Jud. Inquiry Bd., Pa., 1991-94; dir. Hanson Inst. of Am. Music of the Eastman Sch. of Music, U. Rochester, 1995. Co-author: Pennsylvania School Law, 1992, Pennsylvania Adminstrative Law, 1987; editor: So You Want to Be A Lawyer, 1990; advisor on PBC documentary: Life of Howard Hanson, An American Masterpiece, 1987. Pres. Newman Club, Coll. Wooster, 1976-79; v.p. Young Reps., Wooster, Ohio, 1977-79; co-founder, officer Wooster Polo and Hunt Club, 1976-79; bd. dirs. Hanson Inst. Am. Music of Eastman Sch. Music, 1996, Washington County Fund, 1998-2000, Pyramid Gallery, Rochester, N.Y., 1997—; mem. fin. com. JFK Sch., 1998—. Recipient Merit award Inst. Am. Music, 1981, Outstanding Scholar award Rotary, Albert H. Robbins award for Meritorious Svc. in Advancement of Am. Art, 2000. Mem.: KC, ATLA, ABA, Pa. Young Lawyers for Washington County (state rep. 1988), Washington County Bar Assn. (legis. com. 2001—), Allegheny County Bar Assn., Pa. Bar Assn. (del. 1992), Wash. C. of C., Peters Twp. C. of C. Roman Catholic. Avocations: reading, woodworking, biology. General civil litigation, Commercial, contracts (including sales of goods; commercial financing), Banking. Home: 56 Mckennan Ave Washington PA 15301-3531 Office: 3821 Washington Rd Mc Murray PA 15317-2964 E-mail: dexterdawg@aol.com.

BUBALO, GREGORY JOE, lawyer; b. Evansville, Ind., June 3, 1955; s. Joe Jr. and Mayme Lee (Villines) B.; m. Linda Rose Lamping (div.); m. Pamela L. Klinner. BA in History, Philosophy and Religion, Ill. Coll., 1977; JD, Ind. U., 1980. Bar: Ind. 1980, Ky. 1980, U.S. Dist. Ct. (so. dist.) Ind. 1980, U.S. Dist. Ct. (we. and ea. dists.) Ky. 1980, U.S. Ct. Appeals (6th and 7th cirs.) 1980. Assoc. Greenebaum, Doll & McDonald, Louisville, 1980-81; ptnr. Ogden, Newell & Welch, Louisville, 1981—95; v.p., gen. counsel Paradigm Insurance Co., 1995—99; of counsel Ogden, Newell & Welch, Louisville; ptnr. Becker Law Office, 1999—. Assoc. editor Ind. U. Law Rev., 1979, notes and devel. editor, 1980. Mem. ABA, Ky. Bar Assn., Ind. Bar Assn. Bankruptcy, General civil litigation, Insurance. Office: Becker Law Office 800 Brown & Williamson Tower Louisville KY 40202

BUC, NANCY LILLIAN, lawyer; b. Orange, N.J., July 27, 1944; d. George L. and Ethel Buc. AB, Brown U., 1965, LLD (hon.), 1994; LLB, U. Va., 1969. Bar: Va. 1969, N.Y. 1977, D.C. 1978. Atty. Fed. Trade Commn., Washington, 1969-72; assoc. Weil, Gotshal & Manges, N.Y., 1972-77, ptnr., 1977-78, Washington, 1978-80, 81-94, Buc & Beardsley, Washington, 1994—; chief counsel FDA, Rockville, Md., 1980-81. Mem. recombinant DNA adv. com. NIH, 1990-94; consensus panelist NIH Consensus Devel. Conf. on Effective Med. Treatment of Heroin Addiction, 1997; adj. prof. law Georgetown U. Law Ctr., 2000-2002. Mem. editl. bd. Food Drug and Cosmetic Law Jour., 1981-87, 94-97, Jour. of Products Liability, 1981-92, Health Span: The Jour. of Health, Bus. & Law, 1984-95. Mem. adv. com. on new devels. in biotech. 1986-89, mem. adv. com. on govt. policies and pharm. R & D, 1989-93, Office of Tech. Assessment, Washington, mem. com. to study drug abuse medications devel. and rsch., 1993-95; mem. com. on contraceptive R & D, Inst. Medicine, Washington, 1994-96; trustee Brown U., 1973-78, 1998—; fellow, 1980-92. Recipient Disting. Svc. award Fed. Trade Commn., Washington, 1972, Award of Merit FDA, Rockville, 1981, Sec.'s Spl. citation HHS, Washington, 1981, Ind. award Associated. Alumni of Brown U., 1991. Mem. ABA (mem. spl. com. to study FTC 1988-89), Com. of 200, Nat. Partnership for Women and Families (bd. dirs.). Administrative and regulatory. Office: Buc & Beardsley 919 18th St NW Ste 600 Washington DC 20006-5507

BUCCINO, ERNEST JOHN, JR., lawyer; b. Oct. 29, 1945; s. Ernest J. and Rachel (Talarico) B.; m. Martha Mollinedo, Dec. 27, 1968; 1 child, Tasha. BS, Temple U., 1967, MEd, 1969, JD, 1973. Bar: Pa. 1973, N.J. 1974, U.S. Dist. Ct. (ea. dist.) Pa. 1973, U.S. Ct. Appeals (3d cir.) 1973, U.S. Supreme Ct. 1978. Officer, counsel Blue Cross Greater Phila., 1973-74; law clk. Supreme Ct. Pa., Phila., 1974; mem. Gross & Buccino, P.A., Phila., 1975-96; pvt. practice Phila., 1996-97; prin. Buccino Law Office, Phila., 1997—. Lectr. Roscoe Pound, 1986, Trial Advocacy Found. Pa., Phila., 1984; mem. civil procedure rules com. Supreme Ct. Pa., 1994—. Author: The Barrister Vol. XVI, #3, 1985. Chmn. eastern dist. LAWPAC, Harrisburg, Pa., 1983—. Mem. ABA, ATLA, Pa. Bar Assn., Pa. Trial Lawyers Assn. (bd. dirs. 1982—), Phila. Trial Lawyers Assn. (bd. dirs. 1982—, lectr. luncheon series 1986), Justinian Soc. (bd. dirs. 1982—), Phila. Bar Assn. (chmn. econs. of law practice 1983, nominating com. 1982-83), Sons of Italy. Personal injury (including property damage). Office: 2112 Walnut St Philadelphia PA 19103-4808 E-mail: EJB@buccino.com.

BUCHANAN, JOHN MACLENNAN, Canadian provincial official; b. Sydney, N.S., Can., Apr. 22, 1931; s. Murdoch William and Flora Isabel (Campbell) B.; m. Mavis Forsyth, Sept. 1, 1954; children: Murdoch, Travis, Nichola, Natalie, Natasha. BSc, Mt. Allison U., cert. engring., 1954; LLB, Dalhousie U., Halifax, N.S., 1958; DEng (hon.), N.S. Tech. Coll., 1979; LLD (hon.), St. Mary's U., 1982; DCL, Mt. Allison U., 1981; LLD (hon.), St. Francis Xavier U., 1986; D Polit. Sci. (hon.), U. de St. Anne, 1989. Bar: Called to bar, created queen's counsel 1972. Pvt. practice, Halifax, 1958-71; mem. N.S. Legislative Assembly, Halifax, from 1967; min. public works, then fisheries; premier of N.S., 1978-90. Created Queen's Counsel, 1972; leader Progressive Conservative Party in N.S., from 1971; elected mem. legis. assembly for Halifax-Atlantic provinces gen. election, 1967, 70, 74, 78, 81, 84, 88, apptd. Privy Coun., 1972; apptd. to Senate of Can., 1990, bd. dirs. Legal Aid for N.S. Barristers Assn. Active Boy Scouts Am., pres. exec. oun., chmn. policy bd., 1978-90. Mem. Can. Bar Assn., N.S. Barristers Assn., Can.-U.S. Parliamentary Assn. (bd. dirs.), Royal Can. Legion, Buchanan Soc. of Glasgow, Scotland (bd. dirs.), Halifax Club, City Club, Lions, Masons, Shriners, Odd Fellows. Progressive Conservative. Mem. Progressive Ch. Can. Office: The Senate Ottawa ON K1A OA4 Canada

BUCHANAN, MARY BETH, prosecutor; BA, U. Pa.; JD, U. Pittsburgh Sch. Law. Assoc. Strassburger, McKenne, Gutnick and Potter, Pittsburgh, 1987—88; asst. US Atty. Western Dist. of Pa., 1988—2001, US Atty., 2001—. Office: US Attorney 633 US Post Office & Courthouse Pittsburgh PA 15219*

BUCHANAN, PHILLIP HOGE, lawyer, foundation executive, educator, academic administrator; b. Pearisburg, Va., Dec. 17, 1960; s. Wiley Blake Jr. and Mary Ella (Hedrick) B.; m. Katharine Berkeley Bernard, Aug. 23, 1997. BS in Mgmt., Va. Tech., 1983; JD, Washington and Lee U., 1988. Bar: Va. 1988, U.S. Dist. Ct. (ea. dist.) Va. 1988, U.S. Ct. Appeals (4th cir.) 1988, U.S. Supreme Ct. 1992. Territory mgr., dir. health products info., dist. mgr. Mid-Atlantic div. Ralston-Purina Co., Charlotte, N.C., 1983-85; atty. Willcox & Savage, P.C., Norfolk, Va., 1988-92; officer, in-house counsel FCFT, Inc., Bluefield, W.Va., 1992; dir. will and trust programs, dir. planned giving, sr. dir. devel. Va Tech., Blacksburg, 1992—2001; pvt. practice Charlottesville, Va., 1992—; dir., atty. Duke U., Durham, NC, 2002—. Judge Va. Acad. Decathlon, U. Va., 1999, 2000. Mem. fin. com. United Way of the Va., Montgomery County Christmas Store, Nat. Com. Planned Giving, N.C. Planned Giving Coun.; bd. dirs. United Methodist Fedn. Recipient Am. Electric Power Co. Scholarship. Mem. ABA (mem. forum on constrn. industry, environ. sect., sports and entertainment law, young lawyers sect., litigation sect.), Fed. Bar Assn. (mem. transp. law sect.), Va. Bar Assn., Va. State Bar (young lawyers sec. 1988, vice-chair for S.E. regional trial competition), Norfolk-Portsmouth Bar Assn. (young lawyers sect., pub. rels. com.), Montgomery County/Radford Bar Assn., Masons, Scottish Right, Shriners, Ducks Unltd. Methodist. Avocations: fishing, skiing, scuba diving, Karate, travel. Estate planning, Non-profit and tax-exempt organizations, Taxation, general. Office: Duke Univ 2127 Campus Dr Durham NC 27708

BUCHANAN, ROBERT MCLEOD, lawyer; b. N.Y.C., Oct. 4, 1932; s. Albert William and Elizabeth (McLeod) B.; m. Jane Vidaud Britton, July 6, 1957; children: Robert M. Jr., Jamy B., Stephen S., Genevra V. Buchanan Casais. BA, Dartmouth Coll., 1954; JD, Harvard U., 1959. Bar: N.Y. 1960, Mass. 1969, U.S. Supreme Ct. 1973. Assoc. Debevoise & Plimpton, N.Y.C., 1959-68; ptnr. Sullivan & Worcester LLP, Boston, 1968-2000, of counsel, 2000—. Contbr. articles on antitrust law to profl. jours. Moderator Town of Weston, Mass., 1980—, mem., chmn. fin. com., 1975-80; chmn. weston Hist. Dist. Study Com., 1973. With U.S. Army, 1954-56. Mem. Mass. Bar Assn. (ethics com. 1986—), Boston Bar Assn. (chmn. antitrust com. 1980-86), Harvard Faculty Club. Unitarian Universalist. Avocations: reading, guitar playing, sailing. Antitrust, General civil litigation, Legal Ethics. Office: Sullivan & Worcester LLP 1 Post Office Sq Ste 2300 Boston MA 02109-2129 E-mail: RMB@SANDW.COM.

BUCHANAN, WILLIAM H., JR., retired lawyer, venture capitalist; b. Summit, N.J., July 2, 1937; s. William Hobart and Margaret R. B.; m. Eleanor A. Lincoln, June 18, 1966; children: Diana A., Jessica R. AB, Princeton U., 1959; LL.B., Harvard U., 1963. Bar: N.Y. 1964. Assoc. firm Shearman & Sterling, N.Y.C., 1963-70; v.p., sec., gen. counsel Reuben H. Donnelley Corp., N.Y.C., 1970-91, sr. v.p., chief legal counsel, 1991-97; asst. sec., assoc. gen. counsel Dun & Bradstreet Corp., N.Y.C., 1976-79, v.p., sec., assoc. gen. counsel, 1979-91, v.p. law, 1991-96, v.p. law, sec., 1996-97; pres. Spencer Trask Spin-Off Group LLC, 1998—2001; exec. v.p. Spencer Trask Intellectual Capital Co. LLC, 1999—2001; ret., 2001. Served with USMCR, 1959-60. Mem. Am. Soc. Corp. Secs. (pres. N.Y. regional group 1979-80, nat. treas. 1979-83, bd. dirs. 1983-86). Clubs: Princeton (N.Y.C.); New Canaan Field, Port Royal Club, Naples, Fl., Grey Oaks County Club, Naples, Fl. Republican. Presbyterian.

BUCHBINDER, DARRELL BRUCE, lawyer; b. N.Y.C., Oct. 17, 1946; s. Julian and Bernice (Levy) Buchbinder; m. Janet Grey McLean, Jan. 22, 1977; children: Julian Bradford, Andrew Grey, Ian Jeffress. BA in Politics with honors, NYU, 1968, JD, 1971. Bar: N.Y. 1972, U.S. Dist. Ct. (so. and ea. dists.) N.Y. 1973. Sole practice, N.Y.C., 1972-79; atty. Port Authority of N.Y. and N.J., N.Y.C., 1979-83, prin. atty., 1983-86, dep. chief fin. divsn. Law Dept., 1986-92, chief pub. securities law divsn. law dept., 1992-2001, asst. gen. counsel, 2001—02, dep. gen. counsel, 2002—03, 1st dep. gen. counsel, 2003—. With USNR, 1968—70. Mem.: Nat. Assn. Bond Lawyers, Pi Sigma Alpha. Republican. Business E-Mail: dbuchbin@panynj.gov.

BUCHENROTH, STEPHEN RICHARD, lawyer; b. Bellefontaine, Ohio, Feb. 8, 1948; s. Richard G. and Patricia (Muller) B.; m. Vicki Anderson, June 6, 1974; children: Matthew Brian, Sarah Elizabeth. BA, Wittenburg U., Springfield, Ohio, 1970; JD, U. Chgo., 1974. Bar: Ohio 1974, U.S. Dist. Ct. (so. and no. dists.) Ohio 1974, U.S. Ct. Appeals (6th cir.) 1974. Ptnr. Vorys, Sater, Seymour & Pease, Columbus, Ohio, 1974—. Author: Ohio Mortgage Foreclosures, 1986, Ohio Franchising Law, 1990, also chpts. in books. Trustee, v.p. Godman Guild Assn., Columbus, 1977-83; trustee, sec. Neighborhood Homes, Inc., Columbus, 1977-85; mem. bd. rev. Worthington Pers., 1981—; pres. Worthington Alliance for Quality Edn., 1989-91; chmn. bd. advisors paralegal program Capitol U. Law Sch., 1991; pres. bd. trustees Worthington Edn. Found., 1997-98; mem. Ohio Supreme Ct. Commn. on CLE, 1994-2000, chmn., 1999; bd. advisors C.H.A.D.D. of Ctrl. Ohio, 1993-97; bd. trustees Wittenberg U., 2000—. Recipient Cmty. Svc. award Legal Assts. Ctrl. Ohio, 1987. Mem.: ABA (forum com. franchising), Am. Coll. Real Estate Lawyers, Columbus Bar Assn. (pres. 1992—93, bd. govs., Bar Svc. medal 2000), Ohio State Bar Assn. (coun. dels., chmn. legal assts. com., bd.govs. real property sect., chmn. 2003). Republican. Lutheran. Commercial, contracts (including sales of goods; commercial financing), Franchising, Property, real (including real estate development, water). Home: 2342 Collins Dr Columbus OH 43085-2810 Office: Vorys Sater Seymore & Pease 52 E Gay St PO Box 1008 Columbus OH 43215-3161 E-mail: SRBuchenroth@vssp.com.

BUCHMAN, KENNETH WILLIAM, lawyer; b. Plant City, Fla., Nov. 20, 1956; s. Paul Sidney and Beryle (Solomon) B.; m. MarDee H. Buchman, May 9, 1985; 1 child, Katherine Elizabeth. AA, U. Fla., 1976, BBA, 1978, JD, 1981. Bar: Fla. 1981; U.S. Dist. Ct. (Mid. dist.) Fla. 1981; U.S. Ct. Appeals (11th cir.) 1986; U.S. Supreme Ct. 1988; bd. cert. city, county, local govt. law. Ptnr. Buchman and Buchman, Plant City, 1981-85, Buchman and Buchman, PA, Plant City, 1985-91; pvt. practice Plant City, 1991-2000; asst. city atty. City of Plant City, 1982-91, city atty., 1991—. City atty. San Antonio, Fla., 1995-2000; mem. exec. coun. city, county and local govt. law sect. Fla. Bar., 1997—. Mem.: Plant City Bar Assn., Fla. Mcpl. Attys. Assn. (steering com. 1999—2002, exec. bd. 2002—), Masons. Jewish. Municipal (including bonds), Property, real (including real estate development, water). Office: 302 W Reynolds St Plant City FL 33566-3314

BUCHMAN, LAWRENCE JAY, lawyer; b. Bklyn., Aug. 20, 1965; s. Abraham and Janet Buchman; m. Tavora Ann Leitman, Dec. 1, 1998; children: Leah, Rebecca. BS Magna cum laude, Springfield Coll., 1987. Bar: NJ 92, NY 93, DC 95. Assoc. Hurley & Vasios, Short Hills, NJ, 1992—94, Marvin Bergman, Esquire, Forest Hills, NY, 1994—95, Friedman, Levy & Goldfarb, N.Y.C., 1995—97, McCabe, Colins, McGeough & Fowler, Mineola, NY, 1997—2000; mng. atty. MacKay & Wrynn, Douglaston, NY, 2000—01; pvt. practice Law Office of Lawrence J. Buchman, Rockville Centre, NY, 2001—. Coach, mgr. RVC Little League, Rockville Centre, 2002—; asst. coach South Hempstead PAL Baseball, Rockville Centre, 2001—. Mem.: ATLA, ABA, Queens County Bar Assn., Nassau County Bar Assn., NY State Bar Assn., NY State Trial Lawyer Assn. Avocations: baseball, basketball, Civil War history. Property, real (including real estate development, water), Personal injury (including property damage), General civil litigation. Home: 392 Westminster Rd Rockville Centre NY 11570 Office: Law Office of Lawrence J Buchman 7-11 Front St Rockville Centre NY 11570 Office Fax: 516-255-9380. E-mail: L.J.Buchman@hotmail.com.

BUCHWALD, DON DAVID, lawyer; b. Bklyn., May 10, 1944; BA, Cornell U., 1965, JD, 1968. Assoc. Marshall, Bratter, Greene, Allison & Tucker, N.Y.C., 1970-73; asst. U.S. atty. So. Dist. of N.Y., N.Y.C., 1973-80, dep. chief criminal, 1977-80; ptnr. Buchwald & Kaufman, N.Y.C., 1980-99; pvt. practice Don Buchwald, LLP, N.Y.C., 1999—. Served to sgt. U.S. Army, 1968-70. Mem. ABA, Fed. Bar Council, Assn. of the Bar of the City of N.Y., N.Y. State Bar Assn. Federal civil litigation, State civil litigation, Criminal. Office: 100 Park Ave New York NY 10017-5516

BUCHWALD, NAOMI REICE, judge; b. Kingston, N.Y., Feb. 14, 1944; BA cum laude, Brandeis U., 1965; LLB cum laude, Columbia U., 1968. Bar: N.Y. 1968, U.S. Ct. Appeals (2d cir.) 1969, U.S. Dist. Ct. (so. and ea. dists.) N.Y. 1970, U.S. Supreme Ct. 1978. Litigation assoc. Marshall, Bratter, Greene, Allison & Tucker, N.Y.C., 1968-73; asst. U.S. atty. So. Dist. N.Y., N.Y.C., 1973-80, dep. chief civil divsn., 1976-79, chief civil divsn., 1979-80; U.S. magistrate judge U.S. Dist. Ct. (so. dist.) N.Y., N.Y.C., 1980-99, chief magistrate judge, 1994-96, U.S. dist. judge, 1999—. Editor Columbia Jour. Law and Social Problems, 1967-68. Recipient spl. citation FDA Commrs., 1978, Robert B. Fiske Jr. Assn. William B. Tendy award, Outstanding Pub. Svc. award Seymour Assn., Columbia Law Sch. Class of 1968 Excellence in Pub. Svc. award, 1998. Mem. Fed. Bar Coun. (trustee 1976-82, 97-2000, v.p. 1982-84), N.Y. State Bar Assn., Assn. of the Bar of the City of N.Y. (trademarks and unfair competition com. 1988-89, mem. long range planning com. 1993-95, litigation com. 1994-96, ad hoc com. on jud. conduct 1996-99; prof., jud. ethics com. 2002-2003), Phi Beta Kappa, Omicron Delta Epsilon. Office: US Ct House Foley Square New York NY 10007-1316

BUCK, GURDON HALL, lawyer, urban planner; b. Hartford, Conn., Apr. 10, 1936; s. Richard Saltonstall and Aloha Frances (Hall) B.; children: Keith Saltonstall, Frances Josephine, Daniel Winthrop; m. Martha Finder, 1996. BA in English, Lehigh U., 1958; JD, U. Pa., 1965. Bar: Conn. 1965, U.S. Dist. Ct. 1966, U.S. Ct. Appeals (2d cir.) 1966. Assoc. Shipman & Goodwin, Hartford, 1965-67; v.p., counsel R. F. Broderick & Assocs., Hartford, 1968-69; ptnr. Pelgrift, Byrne, Buck & Connolly, Hartford and Farmington, Conn., 1969-75, Byrne, Buck & Steiner and predecessor Byrne & Buck, Farmington, 1975-78; sr. ptnr. real estate and land use sects., chmn. common interest group Robinson & Cole, Farmington and Hartford, 1979—. Author: Condominium Development, Forms with Commentary, 1990, 2d edit., 1992; prin. co-author: The Connecticut Condominium Manual, 1972, 2d edit., 2003, Real Estate Brokers Community Associations Handbook, rev. edit., 1982, Connecticut Common Interest Ownership Manual, 1984, 2d edit., 2003, The Alaska Common Interest Ownership Manual, 1985, Attorney's and Lenders Guide to Common Interest Communities, 1989, 2nd edit., 1999; contbr. articles on zoning, condominiums, planned unit devels. to profl. jours.; columnist various newspapers. Lt. USCGR, 1958-62. Recipient Disting. Svc. award Glastonbury (Conn.) Jaycees, 1968. Mem. ABA (common interest com. law com., real property and probate, joint editl. bd. real property laws, adv. Uniform Planned Cmty. Act, Model Real Estate Coop. Act, Uniform Common Interest Ownership Act), Am. Law Inst. (advisor, Restatement on Property 3d Servitudes), Am. Coll. Real Estate Lawyers (bd. dirs. 1986-92, common ownership com.), Anglo-Am. Real Property Inst. (bd. govs. 1994—), Cmty. Assns. Inst. (nat. trustee 1982-88, pres. Conn. chpt. 1980-83, sec. 1986-89, bd. dirs. 1992-98, pres. rsch. found. 1980-83, Century Club, Byron Hanke Disting. Svc. award, Acad. of Authors), Am. Planning Assn., Am. Inst. Cert. Planners, Internat. Bar Assn. (panelist common ownership consumer protection 1987), Conn. Bar Assn. (chmn. com. opinions, vice chair real estate sect., pro bono com., chair comty. svc. com., ed. Conn. Bar Jour.), Statewide Legal Svcs. (bd. dirs., pres.), Hartford County Bar Assn., Conn. Assn. Homebuilders Orgn. (developer's coun., pres. statewide legal svcs. 1998—). Environmental, Land use and zoning (including planning), Property, real (including real estate development, water). Office: 1 Commercial Plz Hartford CT 06103-3509

BUCK, THOMAS RANDOLPH, retired lawyer, financial services executive; b. Washington, Feb. 5, 1930; s. James Charles Francis and Mary Elizabeth (Marshall) B.; m. Alice Armistead James, June 20, 1953; children: Kathryn James, Thomas Randolph, Douglas Marshall, David Andrew; m. Sunny Clark, Sept. 15, 1971; 1 child, Carey Virginia; m. Yvonne Brackett, Nov. 27, 1981. BA summa cum laude, Am. U., 1951; JD, U. Va., 1954. Bar: Va. 1954, Ky. 1964, Fla. 1974. Asst. gen. atty. Seaboard Air Line R.R. Co., 1958-63; sec., gen. counsel Am. Comml. Lines. Inc., Houston, 1963-68; asst. gen. counsel Tex. Gas Transmission Corp., 1968-72; sec., gen. counsel Leadership Housing Inc., 1972-77; pres. law firm Buck and Golden, P.A., 1975-92; exec. v.p., gen. counsel Buck Fin. Svcs., Inc., Ft. Lauderdale, Fla., 1992-99. Chmn. Hanover Bank Fla.; adj. prof. bus. law Broward C.C., Fla. Bd. dirs. Sheridan House for Youth; trustee Fla. Bapt. Found. Served to capt. USMCR, 1954-58. Mem. Assn. ICC Practitioners (nat. v.p., mem. exec. com.), Maritime Law Assn. U.S., Am. Judicature Soc., Omicron Delta Kappa, Alpha Sigma Phi, Delta Theta Phi. Clubs: Kiwanian, Propeller of U.S. Banking, Corporate, general, Education and schools. Home: 2873 SW 13th Dr Deerfield Beach FL 33442

BUCKAWAY, WILLIAM ALLEN, JR., lawyer; b. Bowling Green, Ky., Dec. 3, 1934; s. William Allen and Kathryn Anne (Scoggin) B.; m. Bette Joan Cross, July 27, 1963; 1 child, William Allen III. AB, Centre Coll. of Ky., 1956; JD, U. Louisville, 1961. Bar: Ky. 1961, U.S. Dist Ct. (we. dist.) Ky. 1961, U.S. Dist. Ct. (ea. dist.) Ky. 1986, U.S. Supreme Ct. 1975. Assoc. Tilford, Dobbins, Caye & Alexander, Louisville, 1961-78; ptnr. Tilford, Dobbins, Alexander, Buckaway & Black, Louisville, 1978—. Atty. Masonic Homes of Ky., Louisville, 1985—; gen. counsel Kosair Charities. Elder 2d Presbyn. Ch., Louisville, 1975; emeritus mem. bd. govs. Lexington (Ky.) unit Shriners Hosp. for Crippled Children, 1986, sec., 1989-94; mem. children's oper. bd. Kosair Children's Hosp., 1986-99; mem. bd. govs. Norton Health Care, Louisville, 1999—. With USNR, 1956-58. Named Disting. Alumnus U. Louisville Sch. Law, 1986, Centre Coll., 1986. Mem. SAR (pres. Ky. soc. 1999-2000, pres. Louisville-Thrusion chpt., 2002-03), Nat. Eagle Scout Assn., Soc. of the Cin. in State of Va., Sons Confederate Vets. (adj. John Hunt Morgan Camp 1993-96), Masons (33 deg., past master Crescent Hill lodge 1967, chmn. jurisprudence and law com. imperial coun. Shrine of N.Am. 1989-91), Kosair Shrine Temple (potentate 1986), Rotary, Soc. Colonial Wars (Ky. coun.), Soc. War of 1812 (pres. Ky. soc. 1998-2000, judge adv. gen., gen. sec.), Sigma Chi, Phi Alpha Delta. Corporate, general, Non-profit and tax-exempt organizations, Probate (including wills, trusts). Home: 1761 Sulgrave Rd Louisville KY 40205-1643 Personal E-mail: bbuckaway@aol.com. E-mail: wbuckaway@tilfordlaw.com.

BUCKLEY, CHARLES ROBINSON, III, lawyer; b. Richmond, Va., Oct. 9, 1942; s. Charles Robinson and Eleanor (Small) B.; m. Virginia Lee, Apr. 17, 1971; children: Richard, Rebecca. BS, U. N.C., 1965, JD, 1969. Bar: N.C. 1969, U.S. Supreme Ct. 1979. Asst. city atty. City of Charlotte, N.C., 1969-78; ptnr. Constagny, Goines, Buckley & Boyd, 1978-81, Taylor & Buckley, Charlotte, 1981-85, Buckley McMullen & Buie, P.A., Charlotte, 1994—. Town atty. Town of Matthew (N.C.), 1978—; faculty Ctrl. Piedmont C.C., 1970. Bd. dirs. Charlotte City Employees Credit Union, 1974-78; pre. PTA, 1980-82; bd. visitors Luth. Theol. So. Sem., 1989-93. Recipient Cert. of Merit, City of charlotte, 1982. Mem.: N.C. Assn. Mcpl. Lawyers (bd. dirs. 1979—81, v.p. 1995—96, 1st v.p. 1996—97, pres. 1997—98), N.C. Bar Assn., Optimist Club (pres. 1982—83), Rotary Club (pres. Charlotte South Rotary Found. 2003—), Phi Alpha Delta. Democrat. Lutheran. Commercial, consumer (including collections, credit), General practice, Municipal (including bonds). Home: 6813 Linda Lake Dr Charlotte NC 28215-4019 E-mail: CRB3@bellsouth.net.

BUCKLEY, FREDERICK JEAN, lawyer; b. Wilmington, Ohio, Nov. 5, 1923; s. William Millard and Martha (Bright) B.; m. Josephine K. Buckley, Dec. 4, 1945; children: Daniel J., Fredrica Buckley Elder, Matthew J. Student, Wilmington Coll., 1941-42, Ohio State U., 1942-43; AB, U. Mich., 1948, LLB, 1949. Bar: Ohio 1950, U.S. Dist. Ct. (so. dist.) Ohio 1952, U.S. Supreme Ct. 1978, U.S. Ct. Appeals (6th cir.) 1981, Fla. 1982, U.S. Dist. Ct. (mid. dist.) Fla. 1991; cert. cir. ct. mediator, Fla.; cert. arbitrator Fla. state and fed. cts. Assoc. G.L. Schilling, Sr., Wilmington, 1951-52; ptnr. Schilling & Buckley, Wilmington, 1953-56; sole practice Wilmington, 1956-62; sr. ptnr. Buckley, Miller & Wright, Wilmington, 1962—2002. Chmn., counsel The Wilmington Savs. Bank, 1971— , also dir.; solicitor City of Wilmington, 1954-63. Contbr. articles in field. With AUS, 1943-46, ETO. Joint program Mich. Inst. Pub. Adminstrn. fellow, 1948. Fellow Am. Coll. Trial Lawyers; mem. ABA, Am. Arbitration Assn. (comml. panel), Ohio State Bar Assn., Clinton County Bar Assn., Fla. Bar, Fla. Acad. Profl. Mediators, Assn. for Conflict Resolution, Collier County Bar Assn., Ohio State Bar Found. Republican. Methodist. Alternative dispute resolution, General civil litigation, Probate (including wills, trusts). Home and Office: # 95 4031 Gulf Shore Blvd N Naples FL 34103

BUCKLEY, JEREMIAH STEPHEN, lawyer; b. San Francisco, Oct. 12, 1944; s. Jeremiah Stephen and Flora (Saur) Buckley; m. Deborah Stanley, Nov. 5, 1983. AB, Fairfield U., 1966; JD, U. Va., 1969. Bar: Conn. 1969, D.C. 1972, U.S. Supreme Ct 1980. VISTA vol. Wayne County Legal Svcs., Detroit, 1969-70; asst. counsel govt. ops. com. U.S. Ho. of Reps., Washington, 1971-73; minority counsel housing subcom. U.S. Senate, Washington, 1973-77, minority staff dir. banking com., 1977-79; ptnr. Leighton, Lemov, Jacobs & Buckley, Washington, 1979-84, Thacher Proffitt & Wood, Washington, 1984-93, Goodwin Procter LLP, 1994—. Mem.: ABA, Fed. Bar Assn., Electronic Fin. Svcs. Coun., Millwood Golf Club, Kenwood Golf Club. Banking, Legislative, Property, real (including real estate development, water). Office: 1717 Pennsylvania Ave NW Washington DC 20006-4614 E-mail: jbuckley@goodwinprocter.com.

BUCKLEY, JOHN JOSEPH, JR., lawyer; b. N.Y.C., May 18, 1947; m. Jane Emily Genster, Jan. 12, 1980; children: Emily, Darcy, Claire, Connor. AB, Georgetown U., 1969; JD, U. Chgo., 1972. Bar: N.Y. 1973, D.C. 1977. Law clk. to judge John Minor Wisdom U.S. Ct. Appeals, New Orleans, 1972-73; law clk. to justice Lewis F. Powell Jr. U.S. Supreme Ct., Washington, 1973-74; spl. asst. to atty. gen. Edward H. Levi U.S. Dept. Justice, Washington, 1975-77; assoc. Williams & Connolly, Washington, 1977-80, ptnr., 1981—. Fellow: Am. Coll. Trial Lawyers; mem.: ABA, Phi Beta Kappa, Order of Coif. General civil litigation, Criminal. Home: 2955 Newark St NW Washington DC 20008-3339 Office: Williams & Connolly 725 12th St NW Washington DC 20005-5901 E-mail: JBuckley@wc.com.

BUCKLEY, MICHAEL EDWARD, lawyer; b. L.A., June 13, 1950; s. Robert and Barbara Ann (Johansing) B.; m. Catherine Delores Busch, Oct. 14, 1978; children: Robert Timothy, Mara Busch, Jeffrey Johansing, Thomas Elliot. BA, UCLA, 1972; JD, Santa Clara U., 1975. Bar: Nev. 1975, Calif. 1976, D.C. 1982, U.S. Dist. Ct. Nev. 1975. Shareholder Jones Vargas, Las Vegas, Nev., 1975—. Instr. dept. fin. U. Nev. Las Vegas, spring 1987, fall 1989; mem. Block Grant Com., State of Nev. Dept. Human Resources, 1996—, chair, 1998-99. Author: (with others) Nevada Real Estate Transactions, 1988. Bd. trustees HELP of So. Nev., Las Vegas, 1985-91, adv. bd., 1991—, pres. 1987-89; mem. City of Las Vegas Planning Commn., 1994-2002, chmn., 1999-2000. Mem. ABA, Cmty. Assn. Inst. (legis. action com.), State Bar Nev. (chair real estate com., bus. law com.), Am. Coll. Real Estate Lawyers, State Bar Calif., D.C. Bar. Democrat. Roman Catholic. Avocations: reading, writing, travel. Commercial, contracts (including sales of goods; commercial financing), Property, real (including real estate development, water). Office: Jones Vargas 3rd Fl S 3773 Howard Hughes Pkwy Las Vegas NV 89109-0949 E-mail: meb@jonesvargas.com.

BUCKLEY, MICHAEL FRANCIS, lawyer; b. Saranac Lake, N.Y., Nov. 1, 1943; s. Francis Edward and Marjorie (Mooney) B.; m. Mary Thornton, June 26, 1965; children: Sean, Kathleen. BA, Dartmouth Coll., 1965; JD, Cornell U., 1968. Bar: N.Y. 1969, Fla. 1982, U.S. Dist. Ct. (we. dist.) N.Y. 1970. Assoc. Harter, Secrest & Emery, Rochester, N.Y., 1968-75, ptnr., 1976—. Contbg. author: Estate Planning and Probate in New York, 1985; co-editor: Administration of New York Estates, 1990. Bd. dirs. Highland Hosp. Found., Rochester, 1981-95, pres., 1984-87; bd. dirs. Highland Hosp., 1987—, pres., 1992-94; bd. dirs. Highland Health Sys., Inc., 1995-97, Strong Ptnrs. Health System, Inc., 1997—, YMCA of Greater Rochester, 1997—, Highland Cmty. Devel. Corp., 1998-2002, Highland Living Ctr., Inc., 1998-2002, Rochester Area Cmty. Found., 1999—, James B. Wilmot Found., Inc., 2000—, U. Rochester Med. Ctr., 2000—. Fellow Am. Coll. Trusts and Estates Counsel; mem. N.Y. State Bar Assn. (exec. com. trusts and estates law sect. 1988-92), Monroe County Bar Assn. (chmn. trusts and estates sect. 1984-85, banking liaison com. 1985-86), Fla. Bar Assn., Estate Planing Coun. Rochester, Internat. Assn. Fin. Planners. Roman Catholic. Avocations: basketball, platform tennis. Estate planning, Probate (including wills, trusts), Estate taxation. Home: 571 Thomas Ave Rochester NY 14617-1432 Office: Harter Secrest & Emery 1600 Bausch & Lomb Pl Rochester NY 14604-2711 E-mail: mbuckley@hselaw.com.

BUCKLEY, MIKE CLIFFORD, lawyer; b. Atlanta, Sept. 1, 1944; s. Clifford Robert Buckley and Winifred Davis (Clayton) Coleman; m. Elizabeth Trimble, June 17, 1967. AB, U. Calif., Berkeley, 1966; JD, U. Calif., 1969. Bar: Calif. 1969. Assoc. Lawler, Felix & Hall, L.A., 1969-72; asst. West Coast counsel ITT, L.A., 1972-74; ptnr. Crosby, Heafey, Roach & May, Oakland, Calif., 1974—. Pres. TeleNetwork, Inc., Oakland, 1984-92; treas. Salem Luth. Home of the East Bay Inc., 1992-98; lectr. Calif. Continuing Edn. of Bar, Berkeley, 1978—; workshop leader Hastings Coll. Advocacy, San Francisco, 1981-85; adv. com. U.S. Bankruptcy Ct., San Francisco, 1984-89. Mem. ABA, Calif. Bar Assn., Alameda Bar Assn., San Francisco Bar Assn. Democrat. Bankruptcy, Commercial, contracts (including sales of goods; commercial financing). Home: 246 Pershing Dr Oakland CA 94611-3235 Office: Reed Smith Crosby Heafey LLP PO Box 2084 Oakland CA 94604-2084 E-mail: mbuckley@chrm.com.

BUCKLEY, SUSAN, lawyer; b. Rockville Center, N.Y., Dec. 24, 1951; BA, Mt. Holyoke Coll., 1973; JD, Fordham U., 1977. Bar: N.Y. 1978, D.C. 1980. Ptnr. Cahill Gordon & Reindel, N.Y.C., 1985—. Mem. ABA, N.Y. State Bar Assn. (com. on media law 1992-95), Bar Assn. N.Y.C. (com. comm. law 1986-89). Communications, Constitutional, Libel. Office: Cahill Gordon & Reindel 80 Pine St Fl 17 New York NY 10005-1790

BUCKLEY, TERRENCE PATRICK, lawyer; b. N.Y.C., May 7, 1945; s. Cornelius and Catherine (Sheehan) B.; m. Patricia Ann McComb, Oct. 7, 1976; children: Shannondoah, Heather. BA, Iona Coll., 1967; JD, Bklyn. Law Sch., 1972. Bar: N.Y. 1972, U.S. Dist. Ct. (so. and ea. dists.) N.Y. 1977, U.S. Supreme Ct. 1993. Asst. dist. atty. Dist. Atty.'s Office, N.Y.C., 1972-74; law instr. Western State U., Fullerton, Calif., 1975; assoc. McDonald, Pulaski & Harlan, San Diego, 1975-77; atty.-in-charge Nassau-Suffolk Law Svcs., Riverhead, N.Y., 1977-78; spl. asst. atty. gen. N.Y. State Atty. Gen. Office, N.Y.C., 1978-86; trial counsel Pelletreau & Pelletreau, Patchogue, N.Y., 1986-87; pvt. practice Islandia, N.Y., 1988—. Instr. health law SUNY, Stony Brook, 1988, 90; adminstrv. law judge Divsn. Parole, L.I. City, N.Y., 1987-88. With U.S. Army, 1969-71. Recipient Excellence award Am. Jurisprudence, 1972. Mem. ATLA, NACDL, Suffolk County Bar Assn., Am. Inns of Ct. (Alexander Hamilton Inn), Brehon Law Soc., Frank Hogan Assocs. Roman Catholic. Avocations: skiing, running, sailing, hiking, kayaking. Criminal, Personal injury (including property damage), Professional liability. Office: 1 Suffolk Sq Ste 520 Islandia NY 11749-1528

BUCKLIN, DONALD THOMAS, lawyer; b. Providence, July 11, 1938; s. Elmer F. and Anne (Scott) B.; m. Kathryn L. Alfera, Nov. 30, 1963; children: Donald R., Heather Anne. BS in Acctg., Providence Coll., 1960; JD cum laude, Am. U., 1967. Bar: Va. 1968, D.C. 1968. Supervisory acct. GAO, 1960-67; law clk. to judge U.S. Dist. Ct. D.C., 1967-68; asst. U.S. atty. for D.C. Dept. Justice, Washington, 1968-71; ptnr. Rowley & Scott, Washington, 1971-74, Truitt, Fabrikant, Bucklin & Lenzner, Washington, 1974-76, Wald, Harkrader & Ross, Washington, 1977-85, Squire, Sanders & Dempsy, 1986—. Contbg. author: Antitrust Counseling and Litigation Techniques, 1984. Served to 1st lt. USAR, 1960-68. Fellow Am. Coll. Trial Lawyers; mem. ABA (criminal law sect. white collar crimes and offenders 1976-77, litigation sect. com. on liaison with state and local bar assns.), D.C. Bar Assn. (treas. Criminal Practice Inst. 1972-73, exec. coun. young lawyers sect. 1973-75, Young Lawyer of Yr.), D.C. Bar (litigation sect. steering com., treas. 1985, bd. govs. 1986-89, bd. dirs., exec. com. 1989—, pres. 1995-96). Federal civil litigation, State civil litigation, Criminal. Office: Squire Sanders & Dempsey 1201 Pennsylvania Ave NW PO Box 407 Washington DC 20044-0407

BUCKLIN, MARK RICHARD, lawyer; b. Seattle, May 9, 1950; s. Harold L. and Catherine A. (Sater) B.; m. Colleen M. Black, Oct. 19, 1969; children: Heather A., Bryan W. BA in Polit. Sci., Wash. State U., 1972; JD, U. Puget Sound, 1975. Bar: Wash. 1975, U.S. Dist. Ct. Wash. 1977, U.S. Ct. Appeals (9th cir.) 1982. Dep. prosecutor Snohomish County Prosecutor, Everett, Wash., 1975-79; atty., shareholder Keating, Bucklin, McCormack, Seattle, 1979—, pres., mng. shareholder, 1983—; gen. coun. Washington Cities Ins. Authority, Seattle, 1981—. Pres. Stevens Meml. Hosp. Bd., Edmonds, Wash., 1989. Bd. dirs. Stevens Meml. Hosp. Found., Edmonds, 1983-93. Named Super Lawyer, Law and Politics Mag., 1999—2001. Mem. Wash. Def. Trial Lawyers, Def. Rsch. Inst., Fedn. Def. and Corp. Counsel, Phi Beta Kappa. General civil litigation, Government contracts and claims, Insurance. Office: Keating Bucklin & McCormack 800 5th Ave Ste 4141 Seattle WA 98104-3175

BUCKMAN, JAMES EDWARD, lawyer; b. N.Y.C., Oct. 2, 1944; s. John Burr and Mary Dolores (Ullery) B.; m. Nancy Lee McLaughlin, Aug. 23, 1969; children: Elizabeth Ahern, Anne Tracy, Julia Walsh. AB, Fordham U., 1966; JD, Yale U., 1969. Bar: N.Y. 1969, Ga. 1974, U.S. Dist. Ct. (no. dist.) Ga. 1974. Assoc. Dewey, Ballantine, Bushby, Palmer & Wood, N.Y.C., 1969-72; asst. gen. counsel Gable Industries, Inc., Atlanta, 1972-74; assoc. then ptnr. Troutman, Sanders, Lockerman & Ashmore, Atlanta, 1974-85, ptnr., 1990-92; exec. v.p., gen. counsel Days Inns of Am., Inc., Atlanta, 1985-89, HFS Inc., Parsippany, N.J., 1992-96; now vice chmn., gen. counsel Cendant Corp, Parsippany, 1996—. 1st lt. USAFR, 1969-75. Mem. ABA, Atlanta Bar Assn., State Bar Ga. Roman Catholic. Avocation: running. Corporate, general, Finance, Securities. Office: Cendant Corp 9 W 57th St 37th Fl New York NY 10019

BUCKSTEIN, MARK AARON, lawyer, mediator, educator; b. N.Y.C., July 1, 1939; s. Henry Al and Minnie Sarah (Russ) B.; children: Robin Beth, Michael Alan. BS in Math., CCNY, 1960; JD, NYU, 1963. Bar: N.Y. 1963, U.S. Dist. Ct. (so. and ea. dists.) N.Y. 1965, U.S. Supreme Ct. 1981. Assoc. Russ & Weyl, Massapequa, N.Y., 1963-64; assoc. counsel Mut. Life Ins. Co. N.Y., N.Y.C., 1964-65; assoc. Moses & Singer, N.Y.C., 1965-67, Leinwand, Maron & Hendler, N.Y.C., 1967-68; sr. ptnr. Baer Marks & Upham, N.Y.C., 1968-86; sr. v.p. external affairs, gen. counsel TWA, Inc., N.Y.C., 1986-92; exec. v.p. Am. Arbitration Assn., N.Y.C., N.J., 1992-93; exec. v.p., gen. counsel GAF Corp. and Internat. Specialty Products, Wayne, NJ, 1993-96; counsel Greenberg Traurig, Ft. Lauderdale, Fla., 1996-99, Profl. Dispute Resolution, Inc., Boca Raton, Fla., 1999—. Spl. prof. law Hofstra U. Law Sch., Hempstead, N.Y., 1981-93; adj. prof. law Rutgers U. Law Sch., Newark, 1994-96; bd. dirs. Bayswater Realty & Capital Corp., N.Y.C., Travel Channel Inc., N.Y.C., TWA, GAF Corp., Internat. Specialty Products, Consultis; mem. exec. com. Herzfeld & Stern, N.Y.C., 1981-84; mem. nat. arbitration and mediation com. NASD, 1998-2001. Trustee Bronx H.S. Found., 1984-96. Mem. ABA, N.Y. Bar Assn., Assn. of Bar of City of N.Y., KP (past dep. grand chancellor 1978). Jewish. Avocations: tennis, music, theater, puzzles. Commercial, contracts (including sales of goods; commercial financing), Corporate, general, Securities. Office: Profl Dispute Resolution 2424 N Federal Hwy Boca Raton FL 33431 E-mail: mabresolve@aol.com.

BUCKWALTER, RONALD LAWRENCE, federal judge; b. Lancaster, Pa., Dec. 11, 1936; s. Noah Denlinger and Carolyn Marie (Lawrence) B.; m. Dollie May Fitting, May 9, 1963; children: Stephen Matthew, Wendy Susan. AB, Franklin and Marshall Coll., 1958; JD, Coll. William and Mary, 1962. Prin. Ronald L. Buckwalter, Esquire, Lancaster, 1963-71; ptnr. Shirk, Reist and Buckwalter, Lancaster, 1971-80; dist. atty. Lancaster County, Lancaster, 1978-80; judge 2nd Jud. Dist. Commonwealth Pa., 1980-90, U.S. Dist. Ct., Phila., 1990—. Sec. City Lancaster Authority, 1970; bd. dirs. Am. Cancer Soc., Lancaster, 1982, Boy Scouts Am., Lancaster, 1984, YMCA, Lancaster, 1990. 1st lt. U.S. Army NG, 1962-68. Recipient Pub. Life and Letter award Phi Sigma Alpha, 1990. Mem. Am. Judicature Soc., Fed. Bar Assn., Fed. Judges Assn., Pa. Bar Assn., Lancaster Bar Assn. (pres. 1988). Office: US Dist Ct 14614 US Courthouse 601 Market St Philadelphia PA 19106-1713*

BUCKWALTER, WAYNE CLARK, lawyer; b. Upland, Pa., May 20, 1955; s. Robert Clark and Mae Margaret (Sweeten) B.; m. Nancy Jeanne Sagurton, Jan. 26, 1985; children: Brian Clark, Elise Marie, Corinne Ann. BA cum laude, Villanova U., 1977, JD cum laude, 1980. Bar: Pa. 1980, U.S. Supreme Ct. 1986. Shareholder Buckwalter Law, PC, Exton, Pa. Solicitor Domestic Rels. sect. of Ct. of Common Pleas, Chester County, 1986—; mem. adv. bd. First Fin. Bank; solicitor Habitat for Humanity of Chester County, Inc., Pa. Home of the Sparrow, Inc. Mem. Pa. Bar Assn., Chester County Bar Assn., Ocean City Surf Boating Assn. Republican. Episcopalian. Avocations: sailing, tennis. Probate (including wills, trusts), Estate planning, Estate taxation. Office: 347 N Pottstown Pike Exton PA 19341-2222 also: 108 W Evergreen St West Grove PA 19390-1006 E-mail: wayne@buckwalterlaw.com.

BUDA, JAMES B. lawyer, manufacturing executive; b. South Bend, Ind., Mar. 9, 1947; BA, Ball State U., 1969; JD, U. Notre Dame, 1973. Bar: Ind. 1973, Ill. 1987, U.S. Ct. Appeals (7th cir.) 1987, U.S. Supreme Ct. 1987. V.p., gen. counsel, sec. Caterpillar, Inc., Peoria, Ill., 1996—2001. Mem. Prevent Child Abuse, Ill., Civil Justice Reform Group. Mem.: ATLA, ABA, Gen. Counsel Roundtable, Corp. Exec. Bd., CLO Roundtable, Assn. Gen. Counsels, Am. Soc. Corp. Secs., Internat. Assn. Def. Counsel, Fedn. Corp. and Ins. Counsel, Def. Rsch. Inst., Am. Corp. Counsel Assn., Ind. State Bar Assn., Ill. State Bar Assn. Office: Caterpillar Inc Legal Dept 100 NE Adams St Peoria IL 61629-7310*

BUDD, DAVID GLENN, lawyer; b. Dayton, Ohio, May 19, 1934; s. Glenn E. and Anna Elizabeth (Purdy) B.; m. Barbarann Dumbaugh, Apr. 4, 1964; children: Anne Elizabeth, David Glenn II. AB with honors, Ohio U., 1959; JD with honors, U. Cin., 1962. Bar: Ohio 1962, U.S. Dist. Ct. (so. dist.) Ohio 1963, U.S. Dist. Ct. (no. dist.) Ohio 1967, U.S. Supreme Ct. 1967, Fla. 1980, U.S. Dist. Ct. (mid. dist.) Fla. 1981, U.S. Tax Ct. 1989. Assoc. Young, Pryor, Lynn, Strickland & Falke, Dayton, 1962-65; trial atty. U.S. Dept. Justice, Cleve., 1965-67; chief antitrust sect. Atty. Gen. Ohio, Columbus, Ohio, 1967-69; ptnr., sr. corp. atty. Cox & Brandabur Attys., Xenia, Ohio, 1969-74; asst. v.p., asst. sec. law Jim Walter Corp., Tampa, Fla., 1974-76; sec., gen. counsel, asst. treas. Gardinier Big River, Inc., Gardinier, Inc., Tampa, 1976-80; assoc. Young, Van Assenderp, Varnadoe & Benton, P.A., Naples, Fla., 1981-84; ptnr. Van Koughnet & Budd, Naples, 1984-85; sr. ptnr. Budd, Hines & Thompson, Naples, 1985-88, Budd & Thompson, Naples, 1989-92, Budd, Thompson & Zuccaro, Naples, 1993-95, Budd & Zuccaro, Naples, 1996-97, Budd and Bennett, Naples, 1998—. Legal counsel to bd. dirs. of numerous corps. Vol. Legal Aid Soc., Xenia, 1972; active Newcomen Soc. N.Am. With USN, 1952-54. Mem. ABA (bus. law sect.), Fla. Bar Assn., Collier County Bar Assn., Blue Key Club, Omicron Delta Kappa, Pi Gamma Mu, Phi Kappa Tau. Republican. Presbyterian. Avocations: health fitness club, tennis, golf, boating. Corporate, general, Probate (including wills, trusts), Property, real (including real estate development, water). Home: 3757 Fountainhead Ln Naples FL 34103-2734 Office: Budd and Bennett 3033 Riviera Dr Ste 201 Naples FL 34103-2750 E-mail: buddbennett@aol.com.

BUDD, THOMAS MATTHEW, solicitor; b. Murwillumbah, NSW, Australia, Sept. 12, 1958; arrived in U.K., 1984; s. Derek Knight and Gwenda Molly (Gregor) B.; m. Gillian Susan Grendale, June 27, 1992; children: Matthew Charles Hamilton, Rory Edward Andrew, Lachlan Thomas Harry. B Comm., U. Queensland, Brisbane, Australia, 1980, LLB, 1982; LLM, U. Cambridge, Eng., 1985. Cert. solicitor, Queensland, New South Wales, Eng., Wales. Articled clk. Morris, Fletcher & Cross, Brisbane, 1982-84, solicitor, 1984, Slaughter and May, London, 1985-92; ptnr. Jones Day Gouldens, London, 1992—. Mem. Internat. Bar Assn. Office: Jones Day Gouldens 10 Old Bailey London EC4M 7NG England

BUDD, THOMAS WITBECK, lawyer; b. Phila., Nov. 1, 1939; s. Reginald Masten and Elizabeth (Charlton) B.; divorced; children: Kelly Budd Tinsley, Paige Budd Glickman; m. Bernadette Smith Budd, July 4, 1988; stepchildren: Amanda Kronin, Karen Kronin Campisi. BA, Washington and Lee U., 1961, LLB, 1964. Bar: Va. 1964, N.Y. 1965, U.S. Supreme Ct. 1982. Assoc. Buell Clifton & Turner, N.Y.C., 1964-69, ptnr., 1969-70, Clifton Budd & Burke, N.Y.C., 1970-76, Clifton Budd Burke & Demaria, N.Y.C., 1976-88, Clifton, Budd & Demaria, N.Y.C., 1988—. Contbr. ; editor (newsletter): Labor and Employment Law; co-author: (Labor and Employment Aspects of Bankruptcy Re-organization) Jour. of Bankruptcy Law and Practice, 2002. Mem. law coun. Washington and Lee U., 1978-81, 84-85. Mem. ABA (labor law sect.), N.Y. Bar Assn. (labor law sect.), N.Y.C. Bar Assn. (labor law sect.), Washington Soc. Washington and Lee U., Princeton Club (N.Y.C.), St. George's Golf and Country Club (Stony Brook, N.Y.). Labor (including EEOC, Fair Labor Standards Act, labor-management relations, NLRB, OSHA), Pension, profit-sharing, and employee benefits. Home: 3 Colgate Ct Shoreham NY 11786-1221 Office: Clifton Budd & Demaria 420 Lexington Ave New York NY 10170-0002 E-mail: twbudd@cbdm.com.

BUDIGAN, WILLIAM CLAY, lawyer, educator; b. Seattle, Mar. 25, 1957; s. Kenneth Leo and Beverly Jean (Cate) B. BA in European History, U. Chgo., 1977, MA in Internat. Rels., 1978; JD, U. Ill., 1983. Bar: Wash. 1983, Alaska 1984, U.S. Dist. Ct. (we. dist.) Wash. 1983, U.S. Dist. Ct. Alaska 1986, U.S. Ct. Appeals (9th cir.) 1984. Legal asst. Keck, Mahin & Cate, Chgo., 1979-80; assoc. Cable, Barrett, Langebach & McInerney, Seattle, 1983-84; prin. Budigan Law Firm, Seattle, 1985—. Instr. U. Wash. Extension Legal Asst. Progran, Seattle, 1985-94. Mem. Pioneer Sq. Preservation Bd., Seattle, 1986-91. Mem. ABA, Wash. State Bar Assn., Alaska State Bar Assn., Wash. State Trial Lawyers Assn., Seattle-King County Bar Assn., Am. Trial Lawyers Assn., Wash. Assn. Criminal Def. Lawyers, U. Chgo. Alumni Assn. Avocation: sailing. General civil litigation, General practice, Personal injury (including property damage). Home and Office: 2601 42d Ave W Seattle WA 98199-2522 E-mail: info@budiganlaw.com.

BUDMAN, ALAN DAVID, lawyer, law educator; b. Phila., Feb. 18, 1953; s. Harry and Ida G. B.; m. Susan Arlene Schwartz, Apr. 4, 1981; children: Heather Jana Budman, Traci A. Budman. BS, Penn State U., 1974; JD, Del. Law Sch., 1977. Bar: Pa. 1977, U.S. Dist. Ct. (ea. dist.) Pa. 1977, U.S. Supreme Ct. 1997. Corp. tax atty. Penn Ctrl. Corp., Phila., 1977-79; grad. sch. instr. Villanova U., Phila., 1980; law instr. Penn State U., Abington, 1979—; pvt. practice Phila., Abington, 1979—. Co-author: Comparative Negligence, 1984. Vol. Big Brother, Phila., 1978-84; committeeman Dem. City Com., Phila., 1983-87; v.p. Melrose B'Nai Israel, Cheltenham, Pa., 1985-88; pres. Ctrl. H.S. Alumni Assn., Phila., 1988-91: chmn. Devel. Com. Am. Heart Assn., Phila., 1990-92; bd. dirs. Temple Sinai, Dresher, Pa., 1997—. Mem. Comml. Law League, Pa. Bar Assn., Phila. Bar Assn., Montgomery Bar Assn. Democrat. Jewish. Avocations: skiing, golf, the internet. Bankruptcy, Commercial, consumer (including collections, credit), General practice. Office: 1150 Old York Rd Ste 2 Abington PA 19001-3712

BUECHEL, WILLIAM BENJAMIN, lawyer; b. Wichita, Kans., July 27, 1926; s. Donald William and Bonnie S. (Priddy) B.; m. Theresa Marie Girard, Nov. 3, 1955; children: Sarah Ann, Julia Elaine. Student, U. Wichita, 1947-49; BS, U. Kans., 1951; LLB, 1954. Sole practice, Concordia, Kans., 1954-56; stockholder Paulsen, Buechel, Swenson, Uri & Brewer Chartered, Concordia, 1971-75; sec.-treas., 1975-77; pres., 1977-92; of counsel, 1993-95; ret. Bd. dirs. County Bank & Trust, Concordia, 1971-92, mem. trust and adminstrn. com. Citizens Nat. Bank, 1992—. Bd. dirs. Cloud County C.C. Found., 1983-89. Mem. ABA, Kans. Bar Assn. (mem. exec. coun. 1966-68, chmn. adv. sect. profl. ethics com. 1974-76), Cloud County Bar Assn. (pres. 1984-86), Elks, Moose, Rotary. Republican. Methodist. Estate planning, Probate (including wills, trusts), Estate taxation.

BUECHNER, JACK W(ILLIAM), lawyer, government affairs consultant, educational association administrator; b. St. Louis, June 4, 1940; s. John Edward and Gertrude Emily (Richardson) B.; children from previous marriage: Patrick John, Terrence J.; m. Nancy Chanitz; 1 child, Charles Chanitz. BA, Benedictine Coll., 1962; JD, St. Louis U., 1965. Bar: Mo. 1965, U.S. Dist. Ct. (ea. dist.) Mo. 1965, D.C., 1998, U.S. Ct. Appeals (8th cir.) 1965, U.S. Ct. Appeals (D.C. cir.) 1998. Ptnr. Buechner, McCarthy, Leonard, Kaemmerer, Owen & Laderman, Chesterfield, Mo., 1965-93; mem. 100th-102d U.S. Congresses from 2d Mo. dist., 1987-91; dep. minority whip, 1989-90; vice-chmn. Rep. study group, pres. Internat. Rep. Inst., Washington, 1991-93; prin., dir. internat. svcs. The Hawthorn Group, Arlington, Va., 1993-95; ptnr. Manatt Phelps & Phillips, Washington, 1995—2001; pres., CEO, A Presdl. Classroom for Young Americans, 2002—; of counsel Schmeltzer, Aptaker and Shepard. State rep. 94th dist. Mo. Gen. Assembly, 1972-82, minority leader, 1974-78; mem. state adv. com. U.S. Commn. on Civil Rights, 1975-82; bd. dirs. Coun. Cmty. Democracies. Lay advisor St. Louis Med. Soc., 1989-92; Mo. Tourism Commn., 1976, 82-85; prin. Coun. for Excellence in Govt.; bd. dirs. Presdl. Classroom. Recipient Meritorious Svc. award St. Louis Globe-Democrat, 1973, Legis. Achievement award St. Louis Police Officers, 1982, Pub. Svc. award Women's Polit. Caucus, Mo., Disting. Svc. award Cardinal Glennon Hosp., Mo., 1982, Nat. Security Leadership award Am. Security Coun. Found., 1988, 89, Family and Freedom award, Golden Bulldog award, 1987, 88, Guardian of Small Bus. award Nat. Fedn. Ind. Bus., 1987, 88, 90, 91, Enterprise award U.S. C. of C., 1988, 89, 90, Sound Dollar award, 1988, Eagle of Freedom award Am. Security Coun. Foun., 1990. Mem. Mo. Bar Assn., D.C. Bar Assn., Met. Bar Assn., Mo. Soc. Washington (pres.), Nat. Conf. State Socs. (1st v.p.), Ctr. Nat. Policy (bd. dirs. 1997—, bd. dirs. Alliance for responsible Cuba policy), Assn. Former Mems. of Congress (bd. dirs., v.p.), The Pericles Inst. (pres. 2001-), The Zorig Found., John Marshall Club (Outstanding Atty. award 1986), Lions, Phi Delta Phi. Republican. Episcopalian. Avocations: golf, reading, travel. Private international, Public international, Legislative. Home: 1303 Altamira Ct Mc Lean VA 22102-2201 Office: Presdl Classroom 119 Oronoco Alexandria VA 22314-2015 also: Schmeltzer Aptaker and Shepard 2600 Virginia Ave NW Washington DC 20037 E-mail: jackb@presidentialclassroom.org.

BUECHNER, ROBERT WILLIAM, lawyer, educator; b. Syracuse, N.Y., Oct. 29, 1947; s. Donald F. and Barbara (Northrup) B.; m. Angela Marian Hoetker, May 28, 1978; children: Julie Marie, Robert William Jr., Leslie Ann, James Bradley. BSE, Princeton U., 1969; JD, U. Mich., 1974. Bar: Ohio, 1974, Fla. 1974, U.S. Dist. Ct. (so. dist.) Ohio 1974, U.S. Tax Ct. 1974. Assoc. Frost & Jacobs, Cin., 1974-79; pres. Buechner, Haffer, O'Connell, Meyers & Healey Co., L.P.A., Cin., 1979—. Adj. prof. Salmon P. Chase Coll. Law, No. Ky., 1975-82; instr. Cin. chpt. Chartered Life Underwiters, 1976-96; lectr. Million Dollar Roundtable, Atlanta, 1981; prodr., host TV show Greater Cin. Bus. Rev., 1993—. Author: (with others) Why Universal Life, 1982, Prosper Through Tax Planning, 1982, Living Gangbusters, 1986, The 8 Pathways to Financial Success, 1987, 93, 98. Mem. planning divsn. Cin. Cmty. Chest, 1978-84; trustee Cin. Venture Assn., 1994-99, pres., 1997-98; trustee Cin. Country Day Sch., 1979-93, pres., 1990-93. Recipient Alumnus of Yr. award Cin. Country Day Sch., 1985, First winner of John Warrington Cmty. Svc. award, 1997. Mem. Cin. Bar Assn. (chmn. taxation sect. 1984-85), S.W. Ohio Tax Inst. (chmn. 1981-82), Cin. Assn. (trustee 1999—, pres. 2002—), Gyro Club (sec. 1982-83, v.p. 1999-2000), Princeton Club (pres. 1982-84). Republican. Methodist. Avocations: golf, tennis, bridge. Estate planning, Probate (including wills, trusts), Corporate, general. Office: Buechner Haffer O'Connell Meyers Healey Co LPA 105 E 4th St Ste 300 Cincinnati OH 45202-4023 E-mail: rhuechner@bhomh.com.

BUELL, BRUCE TEMPLE, lawyer; b. Pueblo, Colo., Mar. 18, 1932; s. Jewett C. and Eva Lorraine (Allen) B.; m. Joan Carol Souders, June 20, 1953; children: Alan D., Susan L. Buell, Bonnie L. Iten. AB, Princeton U., 1953; postgrad., Harvard Law Sch., 1953-54, George Washington U. Law Sch., 1955-57; LLB, U. Denver, 1958. Bar: Colo. Asst. trust dept. Cen. Bank & Trust Co., Denver, 1957-58; assoc. Holland & Hart, Denver, 1958-64, ptnr. Colorado Springs and Denver, Colo., 1964-96; atty. pvt. practice, Colorado Springs, Colo., 1996—. Bd. dirs., counsel Jefferson Bank & Trust, Lakewood, Colo., 1971-76; counsel, sec. Colo. Bus. Devel. Corp., Denver, 1965-83; gen. counsel Colo. Bankers Assn., Denver, 1961-85. Pres. Colo. Lawyer Trust Account Found., Denver, 1982-85, 88-89, Arvada (Colo.) Hist. Soc., 1974-75; chmn. adv. coun. Arvada Ctr. for Arts, 1978-79; dir. North Jeffco Recreation and Pk. Dist., Arvada, 1976-80; trustee, chmn. Presbytery of Denver Trust Fund, 1983-85; trustee, sec.-treas. Viola Vestal Coulter Found., 1964—, pres., 1998—; trustee Edmondson Found., 1996—, v.p., 2000—; trustee Pikes Peak Cmty. Found., 1998—; bd. dirs., v.p. Samaritan Counseling Ctr., Colorado Springs, 1991-96; mem. Colo. Forum, Denver, 1989-93. Served to capt. USNR, 1954-76. Recipient Vol. of Yr. award Denver Bar Assn., 1982, Man of Yr. award Arvada C. of C., 1983, Bruce T. Buell award Colo. Lawyer Trust Acct. Found., 1991, U. Denver Law Sch. Professionalism award, 1995. Fellow Colo. Bar Found.; mem. ABA, Colo. Bar Assn., El Paso County Bar Assn. (treas. 2000-2002), Colorado Springs Estate Planning Coun., Winter Night Club (pres. 1996-97). Presbyterian. Avocations: tennis, music, prison ministry, church work. Banking, Estate planning. Home: 2512 Rigel Dr Colorado Springs CO 80906-1031 Office: Buell & Ezell LLP 118 S Wahsatch Ave Ste 210 Colorado Springs CO 80903-3679 E-mail: buell-law@msm.com.

BUELL, MARK PAUL, lawyer; b. St. Petersburg, Fla., Mar. 9, 1951; s. Harold E. and Jeane Charlotte (Russell) B.; m. Ellen Courtney Rendall, Apr. 28, 1984; children: Mary Ellen, Johnston Rodd, Rendall Jeane. BS, U. Fla., 1973, JD, 1976. Bar: Fla. 1976, U.S. Ct. Appeals (5th and 11th cirs.), U.S. Dist. Ct. (mid., so. and no. dists.) Fla. Assoc. Shackleford, Farrior, Stallings & Evans, P.A., Tampa, Fla., 1976-82, shareholder, 1982-90, Schropp, Buell & Elligett, P.A., Tampa, 1990—. Mem. Hillsborough County Bar Assn. (pres. young lawyers sect. 1981-82, pres. 1992-93, chmn. eminent domain com. 1993-94), Fla. Bar (young lawyers bd. govs. 1981-87, vice chmn. eminent domain com. 1995-97, bd. govs. 1997-2001, bd. cert. civil trial lawyer and bus. litigation law), Am. Bd. Trail Advocates (pres. 2003 Tampa Bay chpt.) Federal civil litigation, Condemnation (eminent domain), Personal injury (including property damage). Office: Schropp Buell & Elligett PA 3003 Azeele St Ste 100 Tampa FL 33609

BUELL, RODD RUSSELL, lawyer; b. Pitts., Mar. 31, 1946; s. Harold Ellsworth and Jeanne Charlotte (Russell) Buell. BS, Fla. State U., 1968; JD, U. Fla., 1970; LLM, U. Miami, 1978. Bar: Fla. 1971, U.S. Dist. Ct. (so., mid. and no. dists.) Fla. 1971, U.S. Ct. Appeals (5th and 11th cirs.) 1971. Gen. ptnr. Blackwell & Walker, P.A., Miami, 1970-95; shareholder Fleming, O'Bryan & Fleming, Ft. Lauderdale, Fla., 1995-97; pvt. practice, Coral Gables, Fla., 1997—. Mem. Dade County Def. Bar Assn. (pres. 1985-86), Def. Trial Attys. Assn. (exec. counsel 1986-88), Maritime Law Assn., Am. Bd. Trial Advs., Internat. Assn. Def. Counsel, Bath Club, Riviera Country Club, Miami Club, Univ. Club. Republican. Methodist. Admiralty, General civil litigation, Personal injury (including property damage). Home: 11883 Maidstone Dr Wellington FL 33414 Office: 288 Aragon Ave Ste C Coral Gables FL 33134

BUETENS, ERIC D. lawyer; b. Rochester, N.Y., Jan. 30, 1953; s. Melvin and Shirley Doris (Gerber) B.; m. Carol Rebecca Osborn, Feb. 7, 1986; children: Rachel Catherine, Sarah Louise. BFA, U. N.Mex., 1976; JD magna cum laude, Syracuse U., 1986. Bar: Fla. 1986. Ptnr. Buetens & Buetens, Hobe Sound, Fla., 1986—. Chmn. Martin County Law Libr. Com., 2001—; mem. strategic planning com. Martin County Sch. Dist., 2000—; chmn. com. Martin County Law Libr., 2001—; pres. Friends of the Mid-County Libr., Inc., 1995—2001; chmn. Sch. Improvement Plan, 1995—96. Mem. Fla. Bar Assn. (vice-chmn. individual rights com. 1988, legis. com. pub. interest sect. 1990-91). Democrat. Personal injury (including property damage), Probate (including wills, trusts), Property, real (including real estate development, water). Home: 381 SW Timber Trl Stuart FL 34997-6289 Office: 8965 SE Bridge Rd Hobe Sound FL 33455-5327

BUFFORD, SAMUEL LAWRENCE, federal judge; b. Phoenix, Ariz., Nov. 19, 1943; s. John Samuel and Evelyn Amelia (Rude) B.; m. Julia Marie Metzger, May 13, 1978. BA in Philosophy, Wheaton Coll., 1964; PhD, U. Tex., 1969; JD magna cum laude, U. Mich., 1973. Bar: Calif., N.Y., Ohio. Instr. philosophy La. State U., Baton Rouge, 1967-68; asst. prof. Ea. Mich. U., Ypsilanti, 1968-74; asst. prof. law Ohio State U., Columbus, 1975-77; assoc. Gendel, Raskoff, Shapiro & Quittner, L.A., 1982-85; atty. Paul, Weiss, Rifkind, Wharton & Garrison, N.Y.C., 1974-75, Sullivan Jones & Archer, San Francisco, 1977-79, Musick, Peeler & Garrett, L.A., 1979-81, Rifkind & Sterling, Beverly Hills, Calif., 1981-82, Gendel, Raskoff, Shapiro & Quittner, L.A., 1982-85; U.S. bankruptcy judge Ctrl. Dist. Calif., 1985—. Bd. dirs. Fin. Lawyers Conf., L.A., 1987-90, Bankruptcy Forum, L.A., 1986-88; lectr. U.S.-Romanian Jud. Delegation, 1991, Internat. Tng. Ctr. for Bankers, Budapest, 1993, Bankruptcy Technical Legal Assistance Workshop, Romania, 1994, Comml. Law Project for Ukraine, 1995-96, 99, Ea. Europe Enterprise Restructuring and Privitization Project, U.S. AID, 1995-96, World Bank Global Judges Forum, 2003, Morocco Jud. Tng.Program; cons. World Bank Project, 2002; cons. Calif. State Bar Bd. Examiners, 1989-90; bd. trustees Endowment for Edn.; bd. dirs. Nat. Conf. Bankruptcy Judges, 1994-2000; bd. dirs. San Pedro Enterprise Community, 1997—. Sr. author: International Insolvency, 2001, editor-in-chief: Am. Bankruptcy Law Jour., 1990—94; contbr. articles to profl. jours. Younger Humanist fellowship NEH. Mem. ABA, L.A. County Bar Assn. (mem. profl. responsibility and ethics com. 1979—, chair profl. responsibility and ethics com. 1985-86, chair ethics 2000 liaison com. 1997—), Order of Coif. Office: US Bankruptcy Ct 255 E Temple St Ste 1582 Los Angeles CA 90012-3332

BUFORD, FLOYD MOYE, JR., lawyer; b. Macon, Ga., Dec. 9, 1957; s. Floyd Moye and Mary Frances (Watson) B. AB, U. Ga., 1981; JD, Mercer U., 1984. Bar: Ga. 1985, U.S. Ct. Appeals (11th cir.) 1985. Ptnr. Buford & Buford, Macon, 1985—. Mem. Ga. Ho. Reps., 1986—. Mem. Ga. Ho. of Reps., 1986-90. Mem. State Bar Ga., Macon Bar Assn., Ga. Trial Lawyers Assn., Assn. Trial Lawyers Am., Ga. Assn. Criminal Def. Lawyers. Democrat. Baptist. Avocation: golf. Criminal, Personal injury (including property damage).

BUFORD, ROBERT PEGRAM, lawyer; b. Roanoke Rapids, N.C., Sept. 7, 1925; s. Robert Pegram and Edith (Rawlings) B.; m. Anne Bliss Whitehead, June 26, 1948; children: Robert, Bliss, Peyton. LLB, U. Va., 1950. Bar: Va. 1949. sr. counsel Hunton & Williams, Richmond, Va. Bd. visitors U. Va., Charlottesville, 1972-80; chmn. Met. Richmond C. of C., 1973; vice chmn., bd. trustees St. Paul's Coll., Lawrenceville, Va., 1977-85. Lt. (j.g.) USNR, 1943-46. Recipient Disting. Service award Jr. C. of C., 1961, Va. Profl. Assn., 1965, Good Govt. award Richmond First Club, 1967. Fellow Am. Bar Found., Va. Law Found.; mem. ABA, Va. Bar (assoc.), Country Club of Va., Commonwealth Club. Banking, Corporate, general, Securities. Home: 506 Kilmarnock Dr Richmond VA 23229-8102 Office: Hunton & Williams Riverfront Pla E Tower PO Box 1535 Richmond VA 23218-1535

BUILDER, J. LINDSAY, JR., lawyer; b. Miami, Fla., Feb. 6, 1943; s. John Lindsay and Majorie (Merrell) L.; m. Jean Fern, Aug. 3, 1968; children Margaret Merrell, John Lindsay III. BE, Vanderbilt U., 1965, JD, 1970. Bar: Fla. 1970, U.S. Dist Ct. (mid. dist.) Fla. 1971, U.S. Supreme Ct. 1976. Assoc., ptnr. Maguire, Voorhis & Wells P.A, Orlando, Fla., 1970-84; ptnr. Godbold, Allen, Brown & Builder P.A., Winter Park, Fla., 1984-88, Allen, Brown & Builder P.A., Winter Park, 1988-90, Honigman, Detroit, Orlando, 1991-96, Graham, Builder, Jones, Pratt and Marks, Winter Park, Fla., 1996—. Mem. bd. trust Vanderbilt U., Nashville, 1990-92, Winter Park Mem. Hosp., chmn. 1994-96. Lt. (j.g) USN, 1965-67. Mem. Orange County Bar Assn. (pres. 1983-84), Vanderbilt U. Law Sch. Alumni (bd. dirs. 1985, pres.), Vanderbilt U. Alumni (pres. bd. dirs. 1989-90). Republican. Episcopalian. Avocations: golf, running. Office: Graham Builder Jones Pratt & Marks 369 N New York Ave Winter Park FL 32789-3124 E-mail: lbuilder@grahambuilder.com.

BULL, HOWARD LIVINGSTON, lawyer; b. Binghamton, N.Y., Oct. 7, 1942; s. Glen Chapel Bull and Martha Gertrade (Mott) Skinner; m. Sheila Kay Settle, Apr. 22, 1977; children: John Keese, Jason Howard, Justin Thomas. AB, DePauw U., 1964; JD, U. Va., 1967. Bar: Calif. 1973, U.S. Dist. Ct. (no. dist.) Calif. 1973, U.S. Ct. Appeals (9th cir.) 1973. Assoc. Owen, Melbye & Rohlff, Redwood City, Calif., 1973-74; corp. atty. Varian Assocs., Inc., Palo Alto, Calif., 1974-99; pvt. practice Mountain View, Calif., 1999—. Pres. Midpeninsula chpt. UN Assn.-USA, 1985, Northern Calif. div., Palo Alto, 1987; trustee Ben Lomond (Calif.) Quaker Ctr., 1975-80. Served to capt. USAF, 1968-72. Mem. ABA, Am. Corp. Counsel Assn., Santa Clara County Bar Assn. (steering com. corp. counsel sect. 1984-86), Palo Alto Area Bar Assn., DePauw Alumni Club (pres. 1975). Republican. Mem. Soc. of Friends. Avocations: sports, camping, bicycling, woodworking. Commercial, contracts (including sales of goods; commercial financing), Computer. Home: 1457 Isabelle Ave Mountain View CA 94040-3039 Office: Counsel to Bus in Comml Law 1457 Isabelle Ave Mountain View CA 94040 E-mail: howardbull@earthlink.net.

BULLOCK, BRUCE STANLEY, lawyer; b. Kissimmee, Fla., Oct. 29, 1933; s. Arthur Stanley and Athalia (Griffin) B.; m. Lydia Austill, July 8, 1960; children: Bruce Stanley Jr., Margaret Bullock Martin. BA, U. Fla., 1955, JB, 1967. Bar: Fla. 1962, U.S. Dist. Ct. (mid. and no. dists.), U.S. Supreme Ct., U.S. Ct. Appeals (11th crct.); diplomate Am. Bd. Trial Advocates; cert. crct. ct. mediator. Atty. assoc. Marks Gray Conroy & Gibbs, Jacksonville, Fla., 1962-66, atty., ptnr., 1966-73; atty., pres. Bullock & Alexander, Jacksonville, 1973-74, Bullock, Childs, Pendley & Reed, Jacksonville, 1974-95; ptnr. Bullock, Childs, Pendley & Reed, PA, Jacksonville, 1995—. Pres. N.E. Fla. Med. Malpractice Claims Coun. Dir., committeeman, gen. counsel Duval County (Fla.) Rep. Party. Lt. USAF, 1955-59. Mem. Jacksonville Bar Assn., Jacksonville Assn. Def. Counsel (pres.), Fla. Def. Lawyers Assn., Def. Trial Lawyers Assn., Def. Rsch. Inst., U. Fla. Alumni Club (pres.), Rotary Club (v.p. S. Jacksonville chpt.), Am. Bd. Trial Advocates (pres. local chpt. 1999). Republican. Episcopalian. Avocations: fishing, boating, nature. General civil litigation, Personal injury (including property damage), Product liability. Home: 2510 Hickory Bluff Ln Jacksonville FL 32223-6503 Office: Bullock Childs Pendley Reed 1551 Atlantic Blvd 2d Fl Jacksonville FL 32207 E-mail: bbullock@bcprlaw.com.

BULLOCK, FRANK WILLIAM, JR., federal judge; b. Oxford, N.C., Nov. 3, 1938; s. Frank William and Wilma Jackson (Long) B.; m. Frances Dockery Haywood, May 5, 1984; 1 child, Frank William III BSBA, U. N.C., 1961, LLB, 1963. Bar: N.C. 1963. Assoc. Maupin, Taylor & Ellis, Raleigh, N.C., 1964-68; asst. dir. Adminstrv. Office of Cts. of N.C., Raleigh, 1968-73; ptnr. Douglas, Ravenel, Hardy, Crihfield & Bullock, Greensboro, N.C., 1973-82; judge U.S. Dist. Ct. N.C., Greensboro, 1982—, chief judge, 1992-99. Mem. bd. editors N.C. Law Rev., 1962-63; contbr. articles to profl. jours. Mem. N.C. Bar Assn., Greensboro Bar Assn., N.C. Soc. of Cin., Fla. Soc. Colonial Wars, Greensboro Country Club. Republican. Presbyterian. Avocations: golf, tennis, running, history. Office: US Dist Ct PO Box 3223 Greensboro NC 27402-3223*

BULLOCK, STEPHEN C. lawyer; b. Miami, Fla., May 9, 1949; BS, NYU, 1973; JD cum laude, Harvard U., 1989. Bar: Conn. 1989, Pa. 1989. Asst. counsel Pratt & Whitney; staff atty. United Tech. Corp.; asst. gen. counsel Carrier Corp., Syracuse, NY; v.p., counsel Carrier Sales and Distbn., LLC, Syracuse, NY. Mem. ABA (mem. business law and antitrust sects.). Antitrust, Corporate, general, Mergers and acquisitions. Office: Carrier Corp Carrier Pkwy PO Box 4800 Syracuse NY 13221-4800

BULLOCK, STEVEN CARL, lawyer; b. Anderson, Ind., Jan. 19, 1949; s. Carl Pearson and Dorothy Mae (Colle) B.; m. Debra Bullock; children: Bradford, Christine, Justin, Evan. BA, Purdue U., 1971; JD, Detroit Coll., 1985. Bar: Mich. 1985, U.S. Dist. Ct. (ea. dist.) 1985, Ct. of Appeals (6th cir.) 1993, U.S. Supreme Ct. 1993. Pvt. pracitce, Inkster, Mich., 1985—. With USAF, 1971-75. Mem. Mich. Bar Assn. (criminal law sect.), Detroit

Bar Assn., Detroit Funder's Soc., Recorder's Ct. Bar Assn., Suburban Bar Assn., Criminal Def. Lawyers of Mich. Avocations: golf, travel. Criminal, Family and matrimonial. Office: 2228 Inkster Rd Inkster MI 48141-1811 E-mail: lawone123@aol.com.

BULMAN, JOHN, lawyer; b. Washington, July 13, 1958; s. John Shea and Louise Bronson Bulman; m. Kathryn Marlow, June 7, 1980; children: Kimberly, Alison, Evan. BA, Hobart Coll., 1980; JD cum laude, Georgetown U., 1984. Bar: RI 84, U.S. Dist. Ct. RI 85, U.S. Ct. Appeals (1st cir.) 87, Mass. 90, U.S. Dist. Ct. Mass. 90, U.S. Ct. Appeals (11th cir.) 96. Assoc. Tillinghast, Collins & Graham, Providence, 1984—90, ptnr., 1990—95; prin. Little, Bulman & Reardon, Providence, 1995—99, Little, Bulman Medeiros and Whitney, Providence, 1999—. Bd. dirs., sec. Barrington (RI) Land Trust, 1987—; mem. adv. bd. Providence Cmty. Mediation Ctr., 2000—. Mem.: ABA (chmn. subcom. litigation sect. 1998—), Am. Arbitration Assn. (bd. dirs. 2002—, panel mem. comml., mediation and complex case panels 1991—). Avocations: woodworking, golf, fishing. Construction, Alternative dispute resolution. Office: Little Bulman Medeiros & Whitney PC 72 Pine St Providence RI 02903 Fax: 401-521-3555. E-mail: jbulman@LBMWLAW.com.

BUMBLEBURG, JOSEPH THEODORE, lawyer; b. Lafayette, Ind., Jan. 5, 1937; s. Theodore Joseph and Elizabeth Mary (Delaney) B.; m. Constance J. Peterson, Dec. 26, 1966; children: Theodore William, Amy Ann. BA, U. Notre Dame, 1958; JD, Ind. U., 1961. Bar: Ind. 1961, U.S. Ct. Mil. Appeals 1962, U.S. Dist. Ct. (no. dist.) Ind. 1964, U.S. Ct. Appeals (7th cir.) 1970, U.S. Supreme Ct. 1970, U.S. Ct. Appeals (fed. cir.) 1985. Capt., judge adv. U.S. Army, Ft. Gordon, Ga., 1961-64; ptnr. Ball, Eggleston, Bumbleburg, McBride, Walkey & Stapleton PC, Lafayette, 1964—. Commr. City of Lafayette Police Civil Svc. Commn., 1971-75, v.p., 1971-72, pres., 1972-75; sec. Tippecanoe County Sheriff's Merit Bd., 1968—; mem. Lafayette Bd. Zoning Appeals, 1970-71; advisor to registrants SSS, 1967-69, 72-75; mem. pastoral coun. St. Mary's Cathedral, 1968-70, 74-78; mem. nat. bd. govs. ARC, 1975-81; bd. dirs. United Way, Lafayette, 1972-75; mem. cmty. adv. coun. Sch. Nursing, Purdue U., 1979-85; state trustee Ivy Tech. State Coll., vice-chmn., 1998-00, chmn., 2000-02; elected Acad. of Law Sch. Alumni Fellows, Ind. U. Law Sch., Bloomington, 2002. Recipient Cert. appreciation Chief Naval Edn., 1978, Gold award United Way, 1978, Pres. U.S. Citation for Community Achievement, 1979, Cert. appreciation ARC, 1972, 81, Harriman award ARC, 1992. Fellow Ind. Bar Found. (master); mem. Ind. Bar Assn., Greater Lafayette C. of C. (bd. dirs. 1986-91, chmn. 1988-89), Am. Legion (nat. security coun. 1970-83, Ind. judge advocate, 1999—, Post II Legionnaire of Yr. 1982-83, Dept. Ind. Disting. Svc. award 2001), K.C., Phi Theta Kappa (hon.). Land use and zoning (including planning), Property, real (including real estate development, water). Home: 726 Owen St Lafayette IN 47905-1878 Office: Ball Eggleston Bumbleburg McBride Walkey & Stapleton PC PO Box 1535 Lafayette IN 47902-1535 E-mail: jbumbleburg@ball-law.com.

BUMGARNER, JAMES MCNABB, judge; b. Peru, Ill., Sept. 13, 1919; s. Joshua Mills and Ethel (McNabb) Bumgarner; m. Helen D Welker, Feb. 7, 1942 (dec. May 1981); children: Barbara Malany, Sally Guth; m. Elizabeth L Miller, Feb. 12, 1983; stepchildren: Tad Miller, Brian Miller, Mathew Miller. BS in Psychology with honors, U. Ill., 1941, JD, 1946. Commd. 2nd lt. USAAF, 1942; advanced through grades to col. USAF, 1967, ret., 1974; pvt. practice Rantoul, Ill., 1947, Hannah, Mattoon, Ill.; cir. judge 10th Jud. Cir. of Ill., 1979—. Mem. pres. coun. U. Ill. Named Disting. Grad. of, U. Ill. Coll. Law; named to, Sr. Illinoisians Hall of Fame. Mem.: VFW, Air War Col Alumni Asn, Judge Advs Asn, Timber Growers Asn, Putnam County Hist Soc, Putnam County Bar Asn, Univ Ill Alumni Asn, Ill Bar Asn, Vietnam Vets Bar Asn, Ret Judge Advs Asn, Ret Officers Asn, Vietnam Vets Ill, Am Legion, Ill Col Law Deans Club, Rotary, Phi Alpha Delta. Home: 1010 Market St PO Box 225 Hennepin IL 61327-0225 E-mail: jimbum@bumgarner.org.

BUMPAS, STUART MARYMAN, lawyer; b. Little Rock, Oct. 7, 1944; s. Hubert Wayne Bumpas and Martha Conway (Maryman) Gaylord; m. Diane Ellen DeWare, Oct. 1, 1977. BA, Brown U., 1966; JD, U. Tex., 1969; LLM, George Washington U., 1973. Bar: Tex. 1969, D.C. 1972. Atty.-advisor Office of Chief Counsel, Washington, 1969-72; asst. to commr. IRS, Washington, 1973-74; ptnr. Locke, Purnell, Rain, Harrell, Dallas, 1974-98, Locke, Liddell & Sapp, Dallas, 1999—. Adj. prof. employee benefits So. Meth. U., Dallas, 1975; lectr. Washington Non-Profit Tax Conf., Am. Law Inst., Ann. Non-Profit Orgns. Inst. Contbr. articles to profl. jours. Exec. com. Meadows Sch. of Arts, So. Meth. U., Dallas; bd. dirs. Callier Ctr. for Comm. Disorders, Dallas, 1984—, Friends of Alzheimer's Dis. Ctr., Southwestern Med. Sch., Goodwill Industries, Dallas; bd. dirs., v.p. Dallas Grand Opera Assn., 1984; mem. Mayor's Commn. on Internat. Devel. Task Force on Arts and Culture, Dallas, 1988; nat. counsel Am. Heart Assn., Dallas, 1979—; trustee The Lamplighter Sch.; gen. counsel The Hockaday Sch.; gen. counsel, bd. trustees, exec. com. Dallas Mus. Art; bd. trustees Southwestern Med. Found. Mem. ABA (mem. exempt orgns. com.), Tex. Bar Assn. (former chmn. legal aspects of arts com.), Dallas Bar Assn., Bus. Adv. Com., Am. Coun. on Germany, Coun. on Fgn. Rels. Clubs: Dallas Petroleum, Brook Hollow Golf, Idlewild (Dallas); Soc. Cin. (Washington), Coral Beach and Tennis (Bermuda). Episcopalian. Non-profit and tax-exempt organizations, Pension, profit-sharing, and employee benefits, Corporate taxation. Home: 5306 Surrey Cir Dallas TX 75209-2427 Office: Locke Liddell & Sapp 2200 Ross Ave Ste 2200 Dallas TX 75201-6776 E-mail: sbumpas@lockeliddell.com.

BUNCH, W(ALTER) EDWARD, lawyer; b. Asheboro, N.C., July 5, 1955; s. John C. and Claudine (Cox) B.; m. Nancy E. Hord, Mar. 8, 1980; children: Mary Eoline, Rebekah Hord, Julia Lowe. Student, Wake Forest U., 1973-74, N.C. State U., 1974-75; BA in English, U. N.C., 1976; JD, Wake Forest U., 1980. Assoc. Bell & Browne, P.A., Asheboro, 1980-82; sole practice Asheboro, 1982-85; ptnr. Beck, O'Briant, O'Briant & Bunch, Asheboro, 1985-89, O'Briant, O'Briant & Bunch, Asheboro, 1990, O'Briant, O'Briant, Bunch, Whatley & Robins, Asheboro, 1991-97, O'Briant, Bunch & Robins, Asheboro, 1997—. Chmn. Randolph County Dems., Asheboro, 1983-85. Mem. N.C. Bar Assn., Randolph County Bar Assn., N.C. Acad. Trial Lawyers, Assoc. Trial Lawyers of Am., Phi Alpha Delta. Democrat. United Meth. Criminal, General practice, Personal injury (including property damage). Home: 1833 Lake Country Drive Ext Asheboro NC 27205-0539 Office: O'Briant Bunch and Robins 117 Sunset Ave Asheboro NC 27203-5607

BUNDA, STEPHEN MYRON, political advisor, counselor, lawyer, classical philosopher; b. Jersey City, N.J., Oct. 5, 1949; s. Stephen and Anna (Yaschak) B. BA summa cum laude, St. Peter's Coll., Jersey City, 1971; MA with honors, New Sch. Grad. Faculty, N.Y.C., 1976; JD, Rutgers Law Sch., Newark, N.J., 1987. Bar: N.J. Pol. cons. Democratic Party, N.J., 1977-92; pol. adv. Govt. of Ukraine, 1991—; counsellor-at-law Bunda & Co., Lyndhurst, N.J., 1994—. Advisor on Ukraine to U.S. Congress, Office of the Pres., Nat. Security Coun., Washington, 1991—. Mem. Nat. Honor Soc., Am. Hist. Assn., Am. Philos. Assn., Ukrainian-Am. Bar Assn., N.J. Bar Assn., Soc. for Ukrainian-Jewish Rels., Ukrainian Nat. Assn., Lawyers Com. for Human Rights. Democrat. Mem. Ukrainian Catholic Ch. Avocations: reading philosophy and history, educational travel and sight-seeing, music, art, literature, theatre. Home: 691 Union Ave Lyndhurst NJ 07071-2815 Office: Stephen Myron Bunda Esquire PO Box 461 Lyndhurst NJ 07071

BUNDERSON, JON J. lawyer; b. Brigham City, Utah, Sept. 14, 1947; s. Dean L. and Velma L. (Straub) B.; m. Peggy L. Howlett, Dec. 14, 1971; children: Eric, Lisa, Adam. BS, Utah State U., 1971; JD, U. Utah, 1974. Bar: Utah 1974, U.S. Dist Ct. Utah. 1974. Assoc. Brandt, Miller & Nelson, Salt Lake City, 1974-75; sole practice Brigham City, 1975-80; ptnr. Bunderson & Baron, Brigham City, 1980—2002; pros. atty. Box Elder County, Brigham City, 1975—2002. Pres., bd. dirs. Greater Brigham City C. of C., 1980-84; precinct chmn. cen. com. Box Elder County Reps., 1978-83. Served with USN, 1967-69. Mem. ABA, Utah State Bar Assn. Clubs: Brigham City Golf and Country. Mem. Lds Ch. Avocations: fly fishing, scouting. General practice. Home: 257 Sycamore Dr Brigham City UT 84302-2371 Office: Jon Bunderson Atty at Law 45 N 1st E Brigham City UT 84302-2121

BUNDY, DAVID HOLLISTER, lawyer; b. Boston, Feb. 21, 1947; s. Frederick McGeorge and Anita (Hollister) B.; m. Jean Wellington Nelson, Mar. 13, 1969; children: Jennifer, Nicholas, Elliott, Oliver, Madeleine. BA, Yale Coll., 1969; JD, Harvard U., 1972. Bar: Alaska 1972, U.S. Dist. Ct. Alaska 1972, U.S. Ct. Appeals (9th cir.) 1973; cert. bus. bankruptcy Am. Bd. Cert., 1995. Assoc. Ely, Guess & Rudd (named changed to Guess & Rudd 1984), Anchorage, 1972-76, ptnr., 1976-91; mng. ptnr. Ely, Guess & Rudd (name changed to Guess & Rudd 1984), Anchorage, 1991-92; ptnr. Bundy & Christianson, Anchorage, 1992—2002. Mem. Alaska Bar Assn. (bd. govs. 1994—2000, pres. 1997-98). Episcopalian. Bankruptcy, Commercial, contracts (including sales of goods; commercial financing), Probate (including wills, trusts). Office: David H Bundy PC 3201 C St Ste 301 Anchorage AK 99503 E-mail: dhb@alaska.net.

BUNGE, JONATHAN GUNN, lawyer; b. La Crosse, Wis., Oct. 20, 1936; s. Jonathan Clement and Anne Liddell (Gunn) B.; m. Gertrude Shoemaker Bunge, June 18, 1961; children— Jonathan C., William H., Katherine E. A.B. cum laude, Princeton U., 1958; J.D., Harvard U., 1961. Bar: Ill. 1961, U.S. Supreme Ct. 1968. Assoc. Lees & Bunge, Chgo., 1961-62; assoc. Keck, Mahin & Cate, Chgo., 1964-71, ptnr., 1971-95; ptnr. Ross & Hardies, Chgo., 1995-2000; atty. Law Offices of Jonathan G. Bunge, P.C., Chgo., 2000—; pres. De Paul Mgmt. Co., 1985—; instr. John Marshall Law Sch., 1968-73; mem. adv. panel East-West Trade, U.S. Dept. Commerce, 1977-78. Bd. dirs. Mid-Am. chpt. ARC 1975-87, vice chmn. 1982-85, Chgo. region, 1981-95, vice chmn., 1981-82, chmn., 1983-86; vestryman Holy Comforter Ch., Kenilworth, Ill. 1979-84, 98-2001; bd. dir. Chgo. Work Ethic Corp., 1988-94, St. Gregory's Episcopal Sch., 1990—. Served with U.S. Army 1962-64. Mem. ABA, Chgo. Bar Assn., Internat. Bar Assn., Ill. State Bar Assn., Bar Assn. 7th Cir., Maritime Law Assn., Econ. Club, Sheridan Shores Yacht Club, Lawyers Club, Chgo. Yacht Club, Michigan Shores Club (Chgo). Episcopalian. Antitrust, Federal civil litigation, Corporate, general. Home: 821 Sheridan Rd Wilmette IL 60091 Office: 3014 N Racine Ste 1 Chicago IL 60657 E-mail: jbunge@bungelaw.com.

BUNN, ROBERT BURGESS, lawyer; b. Boise, Idaho, May 31, 1933; s. Marion Roy and Lois Lucile (Burgess) B.; m. Frances Patten Bull, Sept. 12, 1959; children: Carolyn B., F. Robin, Andrew R., Kathryn B. AB cum laude, Harvard U., 1955, LLB, 1961. Bar: Hawaii 1961, U.S. Dist. Ct. Hawaii 1961, U.S. Ct. Appeals (9th cir.) 1963, U.S. Supreme Ct. 1973. Ptnr. Cades, Schutte, Fleming & Wright, Honolulu, 1961—. Counsel Honolulu Symphony Soc., 1974-80, Hawaii Opera Theatre, Honolulu, 1980-82, 86—, pres., 1982-86, bd. dirs., 1980—. Lt. USN, 1958-61. Mem. ABA, Am. Coll. Real Estate Lawyers, Hawaii Bar Assn., Pacific Club. Avocations: tennis, wine, investments. Condemnation (eminent domain), Estate planning, Property, real (including real estate development, water). Home: 2493 Makiki Heights Dr Honolulu HI 96822-2547 Office: Cades Schutte Fleming & Wright PO Box 939 Honolulu HI 96808-0939 E-mail: rbunn@cades.com.

BUNNELL, GEORGE ELI, lawyer; b. Miami, Fla., Apr. 28, 1938; s. George A. and Lillian E. (Hurley) B.; Dianne Railton, Dec. 1, 1990; children: Kelley, Courtney. BA, U. Fla., 1960, LLB, 1962. Bar: Fla. 1963, U.S. Dist. Ct. (so. dist.) Fla. 1963, U.S. Supreme Ct. 1970, U.S. Ct. Appeals (11th cir.) 1982. Assoc. Nicholson, Howard & Brawner, Miami, 1963-64, Dean, Adams, George & Wood, Miami, 1964-67, ptnr., 1968-71; officer, dir. Huebner, Shaw & Bunnell, P.A., Ft. Lauderdale, Fla., 1972-77; pres., dir. Bunnell, Woulfe, Kirschbeum, Keller, McIntyre & Gregoire, Ft. Lauderdale, 1977—. Mem. advance staff White House, 1974-76; mem. City of Ft. Lauderdale Marine Adv. Bd., 1974-76, City of Ft. Lauderdale Civil Svc. Bd., 1977-79; bd. dirs., sec. Ft. Lauderdale Mus. Art, 1990—. Fellow Am. Coll. Trial Lawyers; mem. Internat. Assn. of Def. Counsel, Am. Bd. Trial Advs. (pres. Ft. Lauderdale chpt. 1992), Def. Rsch. inst., Fla. Def. Lawyers Assn., Broward County Bar Assn., Fla. Acad. of Hosp. Attys., Am. Health Lawyers Assn., Lauderdale Yacht Club. Republican. State civil litigation, Insurance, Personal injury (including property damage). Office: Bunnell Woulfe Kirschbaum Keller McIntyre Gregoire 888 E Las Olas Blvd Fl 4 Fort Lauderdale FL 33301-2272 E-mail: geb@bunnellwoulfe.com.

BUNNER, WILLIAM KECK, lawyer; b. Fairmont, W.Va., Sept. 2, 1949; s. Scott Randolph and Virginia Lenore (Keck) B. BS in Secondary Edn. magna cum laude, W.Va. U., 1970, MA in History, 1973, ABD in History, 1975, JD, 1978, postgrad., 1998—. Bar: W.Va. 1978, U.S. Dist. Ct. (so. dist.) W.Va. 1978, U.S. Dist. Ct. (no. dist.) W.Va. 1985. Tchr. Monongalia County Bd. Edn., Morgantown, W.Va., 1970-78; contract lawyer dept. fin. and adminstrn. State of W.Va., Charleston, 1978-79; pvt. practice law Fairview, W.Va., 1979-84; pres. Farm Home Svc., Inc., 1983—; ptnr. Bunner & Bunner, Morgantown and Fairview, 1984-92. Pres. Climates, 1988—; presenter History of Barn Dance in U.S.A., Rush D. Holt History Conf., W. Va. U., 1999. Author: Planting Churches: A Case Study of Western Monongalia County, West Virginia, 2000, Anxiety, Alienation and Adjustment: Filmnoir and the Returning Warriorfrom WWII, 2000. Pres. Monongalia County Young Dems., 1974; parliamentarian Monongalia County Dem. Exec. Com., 1982-94; counsel, parliamentarian Young Dem. Clubs W.Va., 1974-77; bd. dirs., supr. Monongahela Soil Conservation Dist., 1982—; advisor West Run Watershed Improvement Dist., 1983—; mem. W.Va. Commn. on Rural Abandoned Mines, Rural Alliance, Monongalia County Solid Waste Auth., 1989—, also chmn., 1990-92. Mem. ABA, Monongalia County Bar Assn., Assn. Rural Conservation, Soil Conservation Soc. Am., United Taxpayers' Assn. (counsel), Monongalia County Hist. Soc., Marion County Hist. Soc., Marion County Bar Assn., W.Va. Trial Lawyers Assn, Phi Alpha Delta, Phi Alpha Theta. Democrat. Avocations: music, politics, farming, videos, regional history and genealogy. Environmental, General practice, Property, real (including real estate development, water). Home and Office: 15 Devine Rd Fairview WV 26570-8711

BUNT SMITH, HELEN MARGUERITE, lawyer; b. LA, Oct. 8, 1942; d. Alan Verbanks and Nettie Virginia (Crandall) Bunt; m. Charles Robert Smith, Jan. 12, 1974; children: John, Sharon. BS, U. Calif., L.A., 1964; JD, Southwestern U., 1972. Bar: Calif. 1972; cert. secondary tchr., Calif. Tchr. L.A. City Schs., 1965-72; pvt. practice Pasadena, Calif., 1973—. Law Day chmn. Pasadena Bar Assn., 1980, sec., 1981. Editor (newsletter) Lawyer's Club, 1984-85. Sunday sch. tchr. Lake Ave. Congrl. Ch., Pasadena, 1978-1999, church choir 1999-2003; mem. Pasadena Sister Cities Com., 1994-96. Mem. San Gabriel Bar Assn. (bd. dirs., sec. 1999—, pres.). Avocations: jogging, singing, stained glass. Office: 465 E Union St Ste 102 Pasadena CA 91101-1783

BUQUICCHIO, STEVEN T. lawyer; b. N.Y.C., Nov. 9, 1969; s. Frank and Carmela Buquicchio; m. Kelly Anne Maskell, Aug. 28, 1999; 1 child, Spencer. BA, CUNY, 1994; JD, Thomas M. Cooley Law Sch., 1997. Bar: Mich. 2000, U.S. Dist. Ct. (ea. and we. dists.) Mich., U.S. Dist. Ct. (no. dist.) Ill. 00. Litigation cons. Compulit-Litigation Cons., Grand Rapids, Mich., 1997—99; assoc. Stenger & Stenger, P.C., Grand Rapids, 1999—. Substitute tchr. Kent Intermediate Sch. Dist., Grand Rapids, 1997; lectr. Lorman Edn. Svcs., Wis., 2001—. Contbg. author Avoiding Gad Debt in Michigan, 2001. Mem.: ATLA, ABA (litigation sect.), Nat. Bus. Inst. (mem. 2003—), State Bar Mich. (litigation sect.), Mich. Trial Lawyers Assn., Fed. Bar Assn. Avocations: golf, travel, woodworking, baseball, reading. Commercial, consumer (including collections, credit), receiverships, General civil litigation. Office: Stenger & Stenger PC 4095 Embassy Dr SE Grand Rapids MI 49546 E-mail: Steven@stengerlaw.com.

BURACK, MICHAEL LEONARD, lawyer; b. Willimantic, Conn., Oct. 10, 1942; s. Meyer and Rose Ann (Kravitz) B.; m. Maria Gallego, Oct. 20, 1978; children: Victoria Luisa, Cristina Maria. BA summa cum laude, Wesleyan U., Middletown, Conn., 1964; postgrad. in physics, Calif. Inst. Tech., 1965; MS in Applied Physics, Stanford U., 1967, JD, 1970. Bar: Calif. 1971, D.C. 1972. Law clk. to judge U.S. Ct. Appeals for 9th Cir., San Francisco, 1970-71; assoc. Wilmer, Cutler & Pickering, Washington, 1971-77, ptnr., 1978-2000, of counsel, 2001—. Mem. staff D.C. Jud. conf. Com. on Adminstrn. of Justice under Emergency Condition, 1972-73; mem. adv. com. govt. applications of ADR of Ctr. for Pub. Resources, 1988; mem. jud. evaluation com. D.C. Bar, 1991-94. Assoc. editor Jour. Pub. Contract Law, 1988-94. Mem. ABA, Order of the Coif, Phi Beta Kappa, Sigma Xi. Office: Wilmer Cutler & Pickering 2445 M St NW Washington DC 20037-1487 E-mail: mburack@wilmer.com.

BURAK, H(OWARD) PAUL, lawyer; b. N.Y.C., July 9, 1934; s. Harry and Bette (Hauer) B.; m. Edna K. Goodman, Oct. 18, 1970; children: Hally Ann., Jason Lewis. BS, Cornell U., 1954; LLB, Columbia U., 1957. Bar: N.Y. 1958, D.C. 1967, U.S. Dist. Ct. (so. and ea. dists.) N.Y. 1967, U.S. Ct. Appeals (2d cir.) 1960, U.S. Supreme Ct. 1964. Assoc. Cadwalader, Wickersham & Taft, N.Y.C., 1957-63; dep. asst., asst. gen. counsel Agy. for Internat. Devel. U.S. State Dept., Washington, 1963-67; assoc. Rosenman Colin Kay Petschek & Freund, N.Y.C., 1967-69; ptnr. Rosenman & Colin, N.Y.C., 1969—2002, Katten Muchin Zavis Rosenman, N.Y.C., 2002—. Bd. dirs. Sony Corp. Am., N.Y.C., Sony Music Entertainment, Inc., N.Y.C., Sony Pictures Entertainment, Inc., Culver City, Calif., Sony USA Found., N.Y.C. Rev. editor Columbia Law Rev., 1956-57; author pamphlets. Mem. adv. bd. N.Y.C. Ballet. Mem. ABA, Assn. of Bar of City of N.Y., Fed. Bar Coun., N.Y. Bar Assn., Internat. Bar Assn., Univ. Club. Corporate, general, Private international, Mergers and acquisitions. Office: Katten Muchin Zavis Rosenman 575 Madison Ave New York NY 10022-2585 Business E-Mail: hpburak@kmzr.com.

BURBANK, STEPHEN BRADNER, law educator; b. NYC, Jan. 8, 1947; s. John Howard and Jean (Gedney) B.; m. Ellen Randolph Coolidge, June 13, 1970; 1 child, Peter Jefferson. AB, Harvard U., 1968, JD, 1973. Bar: Mass. 1973, Pa. 1976, U.S. Supreme Ct. 1977. Law clk. Supreme Jud. Ct. of Mass., Boston, 1973-74, Chief Justice Warren Burger, Washington, 1974-75; gen. counsel U. Pa., Phila., 1975-80, asst. prof. law, 1979-83, assoc. prof. law, 1983-86, prof. law, 1986—, Fuller prof. law, 1991-95; Berger prof. law, 1995—. Reporter 3rd Cir. Jud. Discipline Rules, Phila., 1981-82, 84, 3rd Cir. Task Force on Rule 11, Phila., 1987-89; mem. Nat. Commn. on Jud. Discipline and Removal, 1991-93; mediator, arbitrator Ctr. for Pub. Resources, NY, 1986—; cons. Dechert, Price & Rhoads, Phila., 1986—; mem. CPR Arbitration Commn., 1997-2000; spl. master NFL, 2002—. Mem. Com. to Visit Harvard and Radcliffe Coll., Cambridge, Mass., 1979-85; mem. adv. bd. Inst. Contemporary Art, Phila., 1982-99; charter trustee Phillips Acad., Andover, Mass., 1980-97. Mem. Am. Law Inst. (life, adviser transnational rules of civil procedure 1997—, adviser internat. jurisdiction and judgments 1999—), Am. Arbitration Assn. (mem. panel of arbitrators 1985—), Century Assn., Am. Jud. Soc. (mem. exec. com. 1997-2002, v.p. 1997-99), Phi Beta Kappa. Avocations: swimming, travel, tennis. Office: U Pa Sch Law 3400 Chestnut St Philadelphia PA 19104-6204 E-mail: sburbank@law.upenn.edu.

BURCAT, JOEL ROBIN, lawyer; b. Phila., Oct. 28, 1954; s. David Sidney and Jessie (Goldberg) B.; m. Gail Rene Hartman, May 30, 1982; children: Dina Michelle, Shira Elizabeth. Student, Temple U., 1972-73; BS, Pa. State U., 1976; JD, Vt. Law Sch., 1980. Bar: Pa. 1980, U.S. Dist. Ct. (mid. dist.) Pa. 1980, U.S. Dist. Ct. (we. dist.) Pa. 1988, U.S. Dist. Ct. (ea. dist.) Pa. 1993, U.S. Ct. Appeals (3d cir.) 1981, U.S. Ct. Appeals (fed. cir.) 2001, U.S. Supreme Ct. 1984, U.S. Ct. Fed. Claims 2001. Asst. atty. gen. Pa. Dept. Environ. Resources, Harrisburg, 1980—83; assoc. Rhoads & Sinon, Harrisburg, 1983—88, Kirkpatrick & Lockhart, Harrisburg, 1988—91, ptnr., 1992—2002, Saul Ewing LLP, Harrisburg, 2002—, vice chair environ. dept., 2003—. Spl. counsel Pa. Senate Com. on Environ. Resources and Energy, Harrisburg, 1986—87; gen. counsel Nat. Wilderness Inst., Washington, 1991—93; mem. rules com. Pa. Environ. Hearing Bd., 1984—88. Author, editor: Pennsylvania Environmental Law and Practice, 1994, 2002. Trustee United Jewish Cmty., Harrisburg, 1991—94, v.p., 1996—97, Yeshiva Acad., Harrisburg, 1986—, pres., 1996—97; dir. Friends of State of Pa. Mus., 1999—2002. Recipient Best Publ. award Assn. Continuing Legal Edn., 1999. Mem. ABA (standing com. environ. law 1979-80, law student liaison), Pa. Bar Assn. (sec. environ. mineral and natural resource law sect. 1990-91, vice-chmn. 1991-92, chmn. 1992-93, ethics com. 1984-97, chmn. pro bono com. 1999—, Spl. Achievement award 1993, cert. of recognition 1994). Republican. Jewish. Avocations: guitar playing, classical music, jogging, hiking, gardening. Administrative and regulatory, General civil litigation, Environmental, Natural Resources. Office: Saul Ewing LLP Two N Second St 7th Flr Harrisburg PA 17101 E-mail: jburcat@saul.com.

BURCH, FRANCIS BOUCHER, JR., lawyer; b. Balt., Feb. 27, 1948; s. Francis Boucher and Mary Patricia (Howe) B.; children: Sara E., Francis B. III, Michael F.; m. Elisabeth J. Harper, Sept. 29, 2002. Student, U. Fribourg, Switzerland, 1968-69; BA, Georgetown U., 1970; JD with honors, U. Md., 1974. Bar: Md. 1974, U.S. Ct. Appeals (4th cir.) 1975, U.S. Supreme Ct. 1994. Assoc. litigation dept. Piper & Marbury LLP, Balt., 1974-81, ptnr. litigation dept., 1981—, chmn. litigation dept., 1991-94, chmn., 1994-99; co-chmn. Piper Rudnick LLP, Balt., 1999—. Contbr. articles to profl. jours. Bd. dirs. Greater Balt. Com., 1996—, vice-chmn., 1998—2001, chmn., 2001—; mem. Leadership Program, 1990—, bd. dirs., 1993—98, vice-chmn., 1994—96, chmn., 1996—98, chmn. selection com., 1994—95; trustee Calvert Sch., 1989—2000, exec. com., 1991—2000, chmn., 1991—95, sec., 1991—95; trustee Western Md. Coll., 1996—2001, Johns Hopkins Health Sys. Corp., 1994—96, Johns Hopkins Hosp., 1994—96, Johns Hopkins Medicine, 1996—, Balt. Mus. Art., 1990—96, 1998—2000, mem. exec. com., 1991—96, chmn. ann. giving com., 1991—93, treas., 1992—94, v.p., 1994—96, co-chmn. devel., 1994—96; bd. visitors U. Md. Sch. Law, Balt., 1993—, U. Md., 1995—; campaign cabinet, chmn. emerging markets United Way Ctrl., Md., 1994; chmn. Leadership Giving, 1999. With U.S. Army N.G., 1970—76. Fellow Am. Bar Found., Am. Coll. Trial Lawyers, Md. Bar Found.; mem. ABA, Am. Law Inst., Md. Bar Assn. (Disting. Svc. award litigation sect. 1981), Balt. City Bar Assn. (chmn. jud. appts. com. 1990-91, exec. coun. 1990-91), 4th Cir. Jud. Conf., Rule Day Club, Lawyers' Round Table Balt., Center Club, River Bend Club. Democrat. Roman Catholic. Avocations: skiing, surfing. General civil litigation, Product liability, Securities. Office: Piper Rudnick LLP 6225 Smith Ave Baltimore MD 21209-3600

BURCH, JOHN THOMAS, JR., lawyer; b. Balt., Feb. 22, 1942; s. John T and Katheryn Estella (Peregoy) Burch; m. Linda Anne Shearer, Nov. 1, 1969; children: John Thomas, Richard James. BA, U. Richmond, 1964, JD, 1966; LLM, George Washington U., 1971. Bar: Va 1966, US Supreme Ct 1969, DC 1974, Mich 1983, Md 1993. Pvt. practice, Richmond, 1966, Washington, 1974-77; pres. Burch, Kerns and Klimek, 1977-82, Burch & Assocs., Washington, 1982-95, Burch & Bennett, P.C., Washington, 1983-85; ptnr. Alagia, Day, Marshall, Mintmire & Chauvin, Washington, 1985-90, Maloney & Burch, Washington, 1990-96; pres. Burch & Cronauer, P.C., Washington, 1995—2001, Burch & Assocs., Washington, 1982-95; with office of gen. counsel Dept. of Vets Affiars, 2001—. Rep committeeman

City of Alexandria, Va., 1975—92; aide-de-camp brigadier gen to gov State of Va, 1976—; alt del Rep Nat Conv, 1988, 1994. Decorated Bronze Star, Meritorious Serv Medal. Mem.: VFW (dep comdr 1986—87), ABA (secy pub contract law sect 1976—77), Va War Meml Found (trustee), Nat Vietnam and Gulf War Vets Coalition (nat chmn 1983—2001), Spec Forces Asn, Fed Bar Asn (nat coun, dep secy 1982—83), Scabbard and Blade, Soc of War 1812, Va Soc SAR (pres 1975—76, Patriots Medal 1978, Good Citizenship Award 1970), Am Legion, Sons of Confederate Vets, Cheveliar, Order St Constantine Magna, Phi Sigma Alpha, Phi Alpha Delta. Republican. Episcopalian. State civil litigation, General practice, Government contracts and claims. Home and Office: Burch & Cronauer PC 1015 N Pelham St Alexandria VA 22304

BURCH, MARY SEELYE QUINN, law librarian, consultant; b. Worcester, Mass., Oct. 16, 1925; d. James Henry and Mary Seelye (O'Donnell) Quinn; m. Walter Douglas Burch, Aug. 18, 1972; children: Cathi, Andrew, David, John, Joan. BS, Suny, 1976; MLS, Pratt Inst., 1979. Law libr. N.Y. Supreme Ct., Troy, 1969-82; chief law libr. Office Ct. Adminstrn., Albany, N.Y., 1982-86; libr. N.Y. State Libr., 1986-89, ret., 1989; owner Mary S. Burch Law Libr. Svc., 1983—2003. Instr. legal rsch. SUNY, 1981; selected to meet with deans of law schs. in China for improvement of legal reference materials in China. Mem. N.Y. State Bar Assn. (lectr. 1980), Ulster County Bar Assn. (cons. 1980), Am. Assn. Law Librs., Assn. Law Librs. Upstate N.Y. (pres. 1971, v.p. 1981). Roman Catholic. Avocations: pilot, swimming, sewing. Home: 312 Diamond Rock Cir Troy NY 12182

BURCH, VORIS REAGAN, retired lawyer, mediator, arbitrator; b. Liberty, Tex., Feb. 10, 1930; s. Voris Reagan and Jessamae (Coffey) B.; m. Claudia Ramsland, Dec. 30, 1978; children: Melissa Burch Lively, Voris Reagan III. BBA, Tex. A&M U., 1952; JD, U. Tex., 1957. Bar: Tex. 1957. Assoc. Baker & Botts, Houston, 1957-69, ptnr., 1969-95, ret., 1995. Served to 1st lt. USAF, 1952-54. Mem. State Bar Tex. (chmn. labor law sect. 1970-71), Houston Bar Assn., Phi Delta Phi. Federal civil litigation, State civil litigation, Oil, gas, and mineral. Home and Office: 5761 Indian Cir Houston TX 77057-1302 E-mail: reaganburch@houston.rr.com.

BURCH, WILLIAM MARK, II, retired lawyer; b. Peabody, Mass., Oct. 28, 1917; s. Charles Bell and Jane Montgomery (Bell) B.; m. Irene Ethel Miller, June 5, 1954; children: Barbara, Elizabeth. JD, Detroit Coll. of Law, 1949; LLM, George Washington U., 1967. Bar: Mich. 1949, U.S. Ct. Mil. Appeals 1955, U.S. Supreme Ct. 1955. Commd. 2d. lt. USAF, 1942, advanced through grades to col., 1966; navigator instr. various assignments, 1943-45, staff judge, 1950-72, the dir. USAF Judiciary, 1972-77; claims adjustor Mich. Unemployment Commn., Detroit, 1945-49; chmn. pers. coun. Brevard County, Melbourne, Fla., 1972-99; ret., 1999. Bd. dirs. Snug Harbor Homeowners Assn. Mem. ABA, FBA, Mich. Bar Assn. Home: 2 W Point Dr Cocoa Beach FL 32931-5304 E-mail: wburch2@earthlink.net.

BURCHFIELD, BOBBY ROY, lawyer; b. Middlesboro, Ky., Oct. 23, 1954; s. Roy and Anna Lee (McCreary) B.; m. Teresa J. Miller, Apr. 6, 1996; 1 child, Taylor Nicole. BA, Wake Forest U., 1976; JD, George Washington U., 1979. Bar: D.C. 1980, U.S. Ct. Appeals (3rd cir.) 1981, U.S. Dist. Ct. D.C. 1982, U.S. Dist. Ct. Md. 1982, U.S. Ct. Appeals (D.C. cir.) 1982, U.S. Ct. Appeals (9th cir.) 1985, U.S. Supreme Ct. 1986, U.S. Ct. Appeals (5th cir.) 1989, U.S. Ct. Appeals (6th cir.) 1993. Law clk. to Judge Ruggero J. Aldisert U.S. Ct. Appeals (3rd cir.), Pitts., 1979-81; assoc. Covington & Burling, Washington, 1981-87, ptnr., 1987—. Gen. counsel Bush-Quayle '92, 1992. Editor-in-chief George Washington U. Law Rev., 1978-79. Gen. counsel Rep. Nat. Lawyers Assn., 1991—; nat. chmn. George Washington U. Nat. Law Ctr. Ann. Fund, 1990—91, Wake Forest U. Coll. Fund, 1999—2000; pres. Wake Forest U. Alumni Coun., 2000—01, mem., 1990—91, 1997—2001; vol. George Bush for Pres., Washington, 1986—88. Mem.: ABA. Republican. Antitrust, Constitutional, Federal civil litigation. Office: Covington & Burling 1201 Pennsylvania Ave NW PO Box 7566 Washington DC 20044-7566 E-mail: BBurchfield@cov.com.

BURCHFIELD, JAMES RALPH, lawyer; b. Vincennes, Ind., Feb. 6, 1924; s. James R. and Doris (Marchal) B.; m. Dorothey Alice Underwood, July 31, 1949; children— Susan Burchfield Holliday, J. Randolph, Stephanie D. B.A., Ohio State U., 1947, J.D., 1949. Bar: Ohio 1949, U.S. Supreme Ct. 1960. Sole practice, Columbus, Ohio, 1949-77; ptnr. Burchfield & Burchfield, Columbus, 1978— ; pres. Ohio Bar Liability Ins. Co., 1978-92, chmn. bd. dirs. Exec. dir. Franklin County Eisenhower Orgn., Ohio, 1952; mem. Mayor's Spl. Com. on Transit, Columbus, 1955-58; trustee Columbus Goodwill, 1970; mem. Ohio Soc. Colonial Wars, 1972. Served with USAF, 1943-45. Recipient Outstanding Young Man award Columbus Jaycees, 1956, Mil. Hon. award, Scabbard & Blade, 1948. Fellow Ohio State Bar Found. (life); mem. Bexley Am. Legion (post comdr. 1954), Columbus Bar Assn., Am. Arbitrator's Assn., ABA, Ohio State Bar Assn., Am. Jud. Assn., Eastside Bus. Assn. (pres. 1955), Phi Alpha Theta. Republican. Clubs: Sertoma Internat. (pres. 1967), Sertoma Found. (pres. 1977-79). Lodges: Masons (treas. 1952-86), Shriners. Avocations: world travel, hiking, fishing, reading. Personal injury (including property damage), Probate (including wills, trusts), Property, real (including real estate development, water). Home: 9330 White Oak Ln Westerville OH 43082-9606 Office: Burchfield & Burchfield 1313 E Broad St Columbus OH 43205-3500

BURD, MICHAEL, lawyer; b. N.Y.C., Feb. 7, 1958; arrived in Eng., 1978; s. Donald and Shane (Gale) B.; m. Jacqueline Margaret Thomas; children: Hannah Rebecca, Molly Rose, Sarah May. BA, Columbia U., 1980; MPhil, Cambridge (Eng.) U., 1982; law finals, Coll. Law, London, 1984. Solicitor Lewis Silkin, London, 1984-88, ptnr., 1988—. Editor: Employment Law Section-Practical Tax Planning and Precedents; adv. editor Managing Termination of Employment, 1996; contbr.: Employment Law Cases: Practical Implications for HR Managers. Kellett fellow Columbia U., Clare Coll., Cambridge, 1980-82. Mem. London Solicitors Litigation Assn. (com. mem. 1994—), City Westminster Law Soc. (pres. 1995-96). Labor (including EEOC, Fair Labor Standards Act, labor-management relations, NLRB, OSHA). Office: Lewis Silkin 12 Gough Sq London EC4A 3DW England Office Fax: 44 0 20 7832 1722. E-mail: michael.burd@lewissilkin.com.

BURDEN, JAMES EWERS, lawyer; b. Sacramento, Oct. 24, 1939; s. Herbert Spencer and Ida Elizabeth (Brosemer) B.; m. Kathryn Lee Gardner, Aug. 21, 1965; children: Kara Elizabeth Crabtree, Justin Gardner. BS, U. Calif., Berkeley, 1961; JD, U. Calif., Hastings, 1964; postgrad., U. So. Calif., 1964-65. Bar: Calif. 1965, Tax Ct. U.S. 1969, U.S. Supreme Ct. 1970. Assoc. Elliott and Aune, Santa Ana, Calif., 1965, White, Harbor, Fort & Schei, Sacramento, 1965-67, Miller, Starr & Regalia, Oakland, Calif., 1967-69, ptnr., 1969-73, Burden, Aiken, Mansuy & Stein, San Francisco, 1973-82, James E. Burden, Inc., San Francisco, 1982—; founder, dir., COO KineMed, Inc., Emeryville, Calif., 2001—, sec., 2001—, bd. dirs., 2001—. Of counsel Aiken, Kramer & Cummings, Oakland and San Francisco, 1999-2002; bd. dirs. IP Floor Products, Inc., San Leandro, Calif., Denver; founder Gloucestershire Innovation Centre, Gloucester, Eng., EuroGen Pharmas. Ltd., Gloucester; underwriting mem. Lloyds of London, 1986-93; instr. U. Calif., Berkeley, Merritt Coll. 1968-74; pres., prin. Dorset Capital LLC; founder Info4cars.com., Inc., Asheville, N.C. Contbr. articles to profl. jours. Mem.: ABA, Inst. of Dirs. (London), St. Andrews Golf Club (Fife, Scotland), Faculty Club U. Calif. Berkeley, The Univ. Club, Commonwealth Club of Calif., Claremont Country Club. Corporate, general, Finance, Property, real (including real estate development, water). Office: One Maritime Plz 4th Fl San Francisco CA 94111-3407 E-mail: jeburden@compuserve.com.

BURDETTE, ROBERT BRUCE, retired lawyer; b. Cin., Oct. 8, 1945; s. Lumas Carter and Myrtle Margaret (Diesel) B. AB, Columbia Coll., 1967; JD, U. Cin., 1973. Bar: Ohio 1973, U.S. Supreme Ct. 1978. Legis. atty. Libr. Congress, Washington, 1973—2003. Author: A Step Beyond The Graetz Prepayment Analysis, 1992. Mem. Mensa, St. Andrew Club, W.A.R. Goodwin Soc. Colonial Williamsburg. Methodist. Avocation: gilding and rum collecting. Home: 323 Dogleg Dr Williamsburg VA 23188

BURFORD, ANNE MCGILL, lawyer; b. Casper, Wyo., Apr. 21, 1942; d. Joseph John and Dorothy Jean (O'Grady) McGill; m. David Gorsuch, June 4, 1964 (div. 1982); children: Neil, Stephanie, J.J.; m. Robert Fitzpatrick Burford, Feb. 20, 1983 (dec. 1993). Student, Nat. U. Mex., 1955-56, 58, Regis Coll., Denver, 1959; BA, U. Colo., 1961, LLB, 1964. Bar: Colo. 1964, D.C. 1985. Asst. trust adminstr. 1st Nat. Bank of Denver, 1966-67; instr. Metro State Coll., 1966-67; asst. dist. atty. Jefferson County, 1968-71; dep. dist. atty. City and County of Denver, 1971—73; hearing officer Real Estate Commn., State Bds. Cosmetology, State Bd. Vet. Medicine, State Bd. Optemetric Examiners and Profl. Nursing, 1974-75; corp. counsel Mountain Bell Telephone Co., Denver, 1975-81; mem. Colo. Ho. of Reps., 1977-81, chmn. state affairs com., 1979-80, chmn. legal svcs. com., 1980; adminstr. EPA, Washington, 1981—83; lectr., author Washington, 1983—89; pvt. practice Denver, 1993—. Author: Are You Tough Enough, 1986. Del. Nat. Conf. State Legislators; mem. Nat. Conf. Commrs. on Uniform State Law, 1979, 80; presdl. del. to Kenya's Independence, 1983; loaned exec. mgmt. and efficiency task force Colo. Dept. Regulatory Agys., 1976; adminstr. EPA, Washington, 1981-83; former bd. dirs. YMCA. Fulbright scholar, Jaipur, India, 1964-65. Mem. Mortar Bd., Phi Alpha Delta, Delta Delta Delta. Republican. Roman Catholic. Home and Office: 3853 S Hudson St Denver CO 80237-1050

BURG, BRENT LAWRENCE, lawyer; b. Houston, Mar. 2, 1940; s. Abner Danford and Bess (Levin) B.; m. Patricia S. Petitt, 1980; 1 child, Brook Lawrence. BA, U. Tex., 1962; JD, 1966. Bar: Tex. 1966, U.S. Dist. Ct. (so. dist.) Tex. 1966, U.S. Ct. Appeals (5th cir.) 1966, U.S. Supreme Ct. 1970, U.S. Ct. Appeals (4th cir.) 1976, U.S. Dist. Ct. Md. 1976, U.S. Ct. Appeals (11th cir.) 1981. Dist. judge 309th Dist. Ct., Harris County, Tex., 1981-82; assoc. mcpl. judge City of Piney Point Village, 1990-98, City of Bunker Hill Village, 1991-98; ptnr. Rentz, Burg and Assocs., Houston, 1983-95; pvt. practice Brent Burg, Houston, 1995-98; assoc. judge 312th Dist. Ct., Houston, 1999—; of counsel Fouts & Moore, L.L.P., 1996-98. Chairperson Houston Vol. Lawyers Program, Inc., 1988-89, 89-90. Fellow Tex. Bar Found.; mem. Houston Bar Found., State Bar Tex. (grievance com.), Houston Bar Assn. (family law sect. treas. 1978-79, chairperson elect 1980-81, dir. 1982-83, chairperson 1984-85; mem. Supreme Ct. of Tex. child support and visitation guidelines adv. com. 1986-87, 96-97), Phi Alpha Delta. Family and matrimonial. Office: 312th District Ct 1115 Congress St Houston TX 77002-1927

BURGDOERFER, JERRY, lawyer; b. Jeffersonville, Ind., May 3, 1958; s. Jerry Jack and Barbara Jean Burgdoerfer. BS, Ind. U., 1980, MBA, JD cum laude, Ind. U., 1983. Bar: Ill. 1984, U.S. Dist. Ct. (no. dist.) Ill. 1984, U.S. Tax Ct. 1984. Assoc. Adams, Fox, Adelstein, Rosen & Bell, Chgo., 1983-88, ptnr., 1988-89; assoc. Jenner & Block, Chgo., 1989-90, ptnr., 1991—, mem. mgmt. com., 2002—, co-chair securities practice group, 2000—, co-chair corp. dept., 1999—2002; with Mori Hamada Matsumoto, Tokyo, 1991—93. Author: (book) Director and Officers Liability: Prevention, Insurance and Indemnification, 2000; contbr. articles to profl. jours. Vol. United Cerebral Palsy Assn., 1995—, dir., 1999—; mem. exec. com. Northwestern U. Sch. Law Ann. Garrett Corp. and Securities Law Inst. Named 2d Benton, Nat. Moot Ct. Competition, 1982. Mem.: ABA, Chgo. Coun. Fgn. Rels., Chgo. Bar Assn. (chairperson '34 Act Com. 1996—98, reporter securities com. 1997—98, vice chair 1998—99, chair 1999—2000), Ill. Bar Assn., Inter Pacific Bar Assn., Internat. Bar Assn., Japan Am. Soc. Chgo., Exec. Club Chgo., Ind. U. Alumni Club Chgo. (vol. 1988—89), Econ. Club Chgo., Phi Delta Theta (sec. chpt. 1977—78, co-founder, mem. steering com. Chgo. alumni club 1988—89), Phi Delta Phi, Phi Eta Sigma. Avocations: bicycling, water-skiing, Japanese language. Corporate, general, Private international, Securities. Office: Jenner & Block 1 E Ibm Plz Fl 4000 Chicago IL 60611-7603

BURGE, DAVID ALAN, patent lawyer, writer; b. Anderson, Ind., July 22, 1943; s. James Swisher and Esther M. (Sheppard) B.; m. Carolyn J. Alter, Nov. 24, 1966; children: Benjamin, Thomas. BS in Gen. Engring. with highest honors, U. Ill., 1966; JD, U. Louisville, 1970. Registered patent atty. Pres. David A. Burge Co LPA, Cleve., 1975—. Author: Patent and Trademark Tactics and Practice, 1980, 3rd edition, 1999; contbr. chpts. in books. Pres. Gen. Engring. Constituent Alumni Assn., 1984, 85. Mem.: ABA, Sigma Delta Kappa, Gamma Epsilon, Associated Locksmiths of Am., Am. Intellectual Property Law Assn., Cleve. Bar Assn., Phi Eta Sigma, Sigma Tau, Phi Kappa Phi. Avocations: antique tools, woodworking. Intellectual property, Patent, Trademark and copyright. Office: David A Burge Co LPA 2901 S Park Blvd Cleveland OH 44120-1842

BURGESS, DAVID, lawyer; b. Detroit, Nov. 30, 1948; s. Roger Edward and Claire Theresa (Sullivan) B.; m. Rebecca Culbertson Stuart, 1985 (dec. 1988); m. Catherine Mounteer, 1993; children: Jalil Riahi, Leila Riahi, Bryan Valentine, Grace Catherine. BS in Fgn. Svc., Georgetown U., 1970, MS in Fgn. Svc., JD, Georgetown U., 1978. Bar: D.C. 1978, U.S. Dist. Ct. D.C. 1979, U.S. Ct. Appeals (D.C. cir.) 1979, U.S. Ct. Appeals (fed. cir.) 1988, U.S. Ct. Internat. Trade 1988. Rsch. asst. Georgetown U. Sch. Bus. Adminstrn., Washington, 1975, asst. to dean, 1975-76; rsch. assoc., prof. Acad. in the Pub. Svc., Washington, 1976-79; asst. editor Securities Regulation Law Report, Washington; legal editor Internat. Trade Reporter Bur. Nat. Affairs, Washington, 1978-79; atty. Cadwalader, Wickersham & Taft, Washington, 1979-81; mng. editor Bur. Nat. Affairs, Washington, 1981-82; dir. U.S. Peace Corps, Niamey, Niger, 1982-84, Rabat, Morocco, 1984-85; dir. policy planning, mgmt. Peace Corps, Washington, 1985-87; dir. Bur. Human Rights and Humanitarian Affairs U.S. Dept. State, Washington, 1987-92; regional dir. Lawyers for Bush-Quayle Re-Election Campaign, 1992; chief party Rwanda Dem. and Governance Project, 1994, Russia NGO Sector Project, Moscow, 1994. Dir. democracy and civil soc. program, sr. advisor World Learning, Washington, 1995, dir. U.S. Democracy Fellows program, Washington, 1995-2002, dir. bus. devel., 2002-03; exec. v.p. Am.'s Devel. Found., Alexandria, Va., 2003—; spkr. workshops Minority Legis. Edn. Program, Ind. Assn. Cities and Towns, Georgetown U. Continuing Edn. Program, Comms. Workers Am., Colo. State U., U. Wis. Alumni rep. Internat. Sch. Bangkok, 1972-74; adj. prof. Inst. of World Politics, Washington, 2002—. Author: Financing Local Government, 1977, 2d edit., 1978, Preparation of the Local Budget, 2 vols., 1976, 2d edit., 1978, Local Government Accounting Fundamentals, 2d edit., 1977, Understanding Federal Assistance Programs, 2d edit., 1978, The POW/MIA Issue: Perspectives on the National League of Families, 1978; contbr. articles to publs. Mem. adv. com. Arlington County Fiscal Affairs, 1993-94; mem. pres. coun. Mary Washington Coll.; mem. Rep. Nat. Com.; vol. G.W. Bush Campaign, 1999-2000; bd. mem. U.S. Selective Svc. Sys., Va., 2002-. Mem. D.C. Bar Assn., Washington Fgn. Law Soc., Hoyas Unltd. (pres. 1992-94), Federalist Soc., Georgetown U. Alumni Assn. (bd. govs. 1975-00, class rep. 1971-91, mem. alumni senate 2000—), Rep. Nat. Lawyers Assn., Pachyderm Club No. Va. (pres. 1992-93), Pres.'s Club. Republican. Roman Catholic. Home: 3115 1st Pl N Arlington VA 22201-1037 Office: 101 N Union St Ste 200 Alexandria VA 22314 E-mail: dburgess@adfusa.org.

BURGESS, HAYDEN FERN, lawyer; b. Honolulu, May 5, 1946; s. Ned E. and Nora (Lee) B.; m. Puanani Sonoda, Aug. 28, 1968. B in Polit. Sci., U. Hawaii, JD, 1976. Bar: Hawaii 1976, U.S. Tax Ct., U.S. Ct. Appeals (9th cir.). Pvt. practice, Waianae, Hawaii, 1976—; pres. Hawaii Coun. for 1993 and Beyond, Honolulu, 1991—; exec. dir. Waianae Coast Cmty. Mental Health Ctr., 1997—. V.p. World Coun. Indigenous Peoples before UN, 1984-90; human rights adv., writer, speaker in field; pres. Pacific and Asia Coun. Indigenous Peoples; cons. on indigenous affairs, 1984; indigenous expert to ILO Conv.; expert UN seminar on effects of racism and racial discriminations on social and econ. rels. between indigenous peoples and states, 1989—; del. Native Hawaiian Convention, chmn. Trustee Office Hawaiian Affairs, Honolulu, 1982-86; mem. Swedish Nat. Commn. on Mus., 1986; leader Hawaiian Independence Movement; mem. Hawaiian Sovereignty Elections Coun. Mem. Law Assn. Asia and Western Pacific (steering com. on human rights 1988), Union of 3d World Journalists. General practice, Health, Public international. E-mail: plaenui@pixi.com.

BURGESS, TIMOTHY M. prosecutor; BA, MBA, U. of Alaska; JD, Northeastern U. Assoc. Gilmore and Feldman, Anchorage, 1987—89; Asst. U.S. Atty. Dist. of Alaska, 1989—2001, U.S. Atty., 2001—. Office: Fed Bldg & US Courthouse 222 W 7th Ave #9 Rm 253 Anchorage AK 99513-7567

BURGET, MARK EDWARD, lawyer; b. Wiesbaden, Fed. Republic Germany, Feb. 11, 1954; came to U.S., 1955; s. Carl Edward and Mary Sue (McMinimy) B.; m. Elaine Pasque, May 17, 1975; children: Bradley, Brian, Blake, David, Matthew. BBA, U. Okla., 1976, JD, 1979; LLM in Taxation, NYU, 1982. Bar: Okla. 1979, U.S. Dist. Ct. (we. dist.) Okla., U.S. Tax Ct., U.S. Ct. Appeals (10th cir.). Assoc. McAfee & Taft, Oklahoma City, 1979—85, ptnr., 1985—2001, of counsel, 2001—. Mem. ABA, Okla. Bar Assn., Okla. County Bar Assn., Am. Inst. CPA's, Okla. Soc. CPA's. Republican. Avocation: young life leader. Corporate taxation, Personal income taxation. Office: McAfee & Taft 2 Leadership Sq Fl 10 Oklahoma City OK 73102

BURGIN, CHARLES EDWARD, lawyer; b. Marion, N.C., Dec. 16, 1938; m. Ellen Salsbury Burgin; children: Ellen, Lucy. BA, U. N.C., 1961; LLB, Duke U., 1964. Bar: N.C.; U.S. Supreme Ct. Law clk. to Hon. J. Braxton Craven Jr. U.S. Dist. Ct., U.S. Ct. Appeals, 1964-66; prosecuting atty. McDowell County Criminal Ct., 1966-68; sr. ptnr. Dameron, Burgin & Parker, P.A., Marion, N.C., 1968—. Bd. dirs. Shadowline, Inc.; lectr. in field. Contbr. articles to profl. jours. Bd. dirs. McDowell County Recreation Commn. 1977-87, First Union Nat. Bank 1975—; McDowell County Mountain Rescue Team 1980—; McDowell Arts and Crafts Assn. 1980—. Fellow Am. Coll. Trial Lawyers (state chmn. 1996-98, named Best Lawyers in Am. 1993—), Internat. Soc. Barristers, Am. Bar Found.; mem. ABA, N.C. Bar Assn. (pres. 1993-94), Defense Rsch. Inst., Am. Soc. Hosp. Attys., N.C. Assn. Defense Lawyers, U.S. Supreme Ct. Bar Assn. Insurance, Libel, Personal injury (including property damage). Office: Dameron Burgin & Parker PA PO Drawer 1049 26 W Court St Marion NC 28752-3906 E-mail: cburgin@dameronburginlaw.com.

BURGMAN, DIERDRE ANN, lawyer; b. Logansport, Ind., Mar. 25, 1948; d. Ferdinand William Jr. and Doreen Walsh Burgman. BA, Valparaiso U., 1970, JD, 1979; LLM, Yale U., 1985. Bar: Ind. 1979, U.S. Dist. Ct. (so. dist.) Ind. 1979, N.Y. 1982, U.S. Dist. Ct. (so. dist.) N.Y. 1982, U.S. Ct. Appeals (7th cir.) 1982, U.S. Ct. Appeals (D.C. and 2d cirs.) 1984, U.S. Supreme Ct. 1985, D.C. 1988, U.S. Dist. Ct. (ea. dist.) N.Y. 1992. Law clk. to chief judge Ind. Ct. Appeals, Indpls., 1979-80; prof. law Valparaiso (Ind.) U., 1980-81; assoc. Dewey, Ballantine, Bushby, Palmer & Wood, N.Y.C., 1981-84, Cahill Gordon & Reindel, N.Y.C., 1985-92; v.p., gen. counsel N.Y. State Urban Devel. Corp., N.Y.C., 1992-95; dep. insp. gen. State N.Y., 1992-95; of counsel Vandenberg & Felieu, N.Y.C., 1995-99; counsel Salans, N.Y.C., 1999—. Note editor Valparaiso U. law rev., 1978-79; contbr. articles to law jours. Mem. bd. visitors Valparaiso U. Sch. Law, 1986—95, chmn., 1989—92, mem. nat. coun., 2001—. Ind. Bar Found. scholar, 1978. Mem. ABA (trial evidence com. 1983-86, profl. liability com. 1986-89, ins. coverage litigation com. 1990-92), Assn. Bar City N.Y. (com. profl. responsibility 1988-91, com. profl. and jud. ethics 1991-95, mem. coun. jud. adminstrn. 1997-99), New York County Lawyers Assn. (com. Supreme Ct. 1987-94, chmn. 1990-93, bd. dirs. 1991-97, 2002—, exec. com. bd. dirs. 1992-95, fin. and pers. com. 1994-95), N.Y. State Bar Assn. (mem. Ho. Dels. 1994-98, mem. com. on profl. stds. for atty. conduct 2002—). Home: 345 E 56th St Apt 5C New York NY 10022-3744

BURGUM, BRADLEY JOSEPH, lawyer; BS, N.D. State U., 1974; JD, U. N.D., 1977. Bar: N.D. 1977, U.S. Dist. Ct. N.D. 1977; CPA, N.D. Assoc. Woell & Woell, Casselton, ND, 1977; ptnr. Woell, Woell & Burgum, Casselton, 1977—81; pvt. practice Casselton, 1981—85; ptnr. Burgum & Irby P.C., Casselton, 1986—2002; owner Burgum Law Firm, P.C., Casselton, 2002—. Mng. ptnr. Burgum Farms, Arthur, N.D., 1970—; atty. City of Casselton 1981—; pres. Millennium Devel. Co., Casselton; bd. dirs. Arthur Cos., Inc., Cass County Mut. Ins. Co., Casselton. Mem. Casselton Econ. Devel. Commn., 1985—; pres. Casselton Community Club, 1985-87; sec. Casselton Vol. Ambulance, 1978—; bd. dirs. Casselton Community Med. Ctr. Inc., 1983—. Mem. ABA, N.D. Bar Assn., Cass County Bar Assn., N.D. Soc. CPAs, Nat. Registry Emergency Med. Techs., Sigma Alpha Epsilon Alumni Assn. (treas. 1982—), Cass County Twp. Officers Assn. (sec.-treas. 1978—). Clubs: Pelican Lake (Minn.) Yacht (treas. 1985—). Probate (including wills, trusts), Property, real (including real estate development, water), Personal income taxation. Home: PO Box 886 Casselton ND 58012-0886 Office: Burgum Law Firm PC PO Box 308 Casselton ND 58012-0308

BURGWEGER, FRANCIS JOSEPH DEWES, JR., lawyer; b. Evanston, Ill., July 5, 1942; s. Francis Dewes and Helen Theodosia (Chancellor) B.; m. Kathleen Marie Wessel, Sept. 3, 1978; children: Lauren Elizabeth, Francis Joseph Dewes III, Sherman Ward Chancellor. BA, Yale U., 1964; JD, U. Pa., 1970. Bar: Calif. 1971, N.Y. 1988, U.S. Ct. Appeals (9th cir.) 1971, U.S. Dist. Ct. (cen. dist.) Calif. 1971. Law clk. to Hon. Shirley M. Hufstedler U.S. Ct. Appeals 9th Cir., L.A., 1970-71; assoc. O'Melveny & Myers, L.A., 1971-78, ptnr., 1978-85, O'Melveny & Myers LLP, N.Y.C., 1985-97, sr. counsel, 1997—2003. Contbr. articles on environ. law. Capt. U.S. Army, 1964-67, Vietnam. Mem. Assn. of Bar of City of N.Y., N.Y. State Bar Assn., L.A. County Bar Assn. (exec. com. R.P. sect.). Avocations: books, wine, agriculture. Environmental, Finance, Property, real (including real estate development, water). Office: O'Melveny & Myers LLP 153 E 53rd St Fl 54 New York NY 10022-4611

BURIAN, LAWRENCE J. lawyer; b. Bklyn., Nov. 17, 1969; s. Andrew and Ruth Yellen Burian; m. Adina Miriam Schainker, Sept. 3, 1998; children: Jonah Alec, Ethan Marc. BA in Econs., Yeshiva U., 1991; JD, Yale U., 1994. Bar: N.Y., N.J. Law clk. Justice Aharon Barak Supreme Ct. Israel, Jerusalem, 1995; assoc. Davis Polk & Wardwell, N.Y.C., 1994—2000, London, 1995; asst. gen. counsel Cablevision Sys. Corp., Bethpage, NY, 2000—02, v.p., assoc. gen. counsel, 2002—. Bd. dirs. Camp Morasha, 2000—, Princeton Video Image, Inc., Lawrenceville, NJ, 2001—03, PVI Virtual Media Svcs. LLC, N.Y.C., 2003—, Safe3W, Inc., Garden City, NY, 2003—. Dir. Young Leadership Am. Soc. for Yad Vshem, 1997. Recipient Intern award, Inst. for Pub. Affairs, 1998. Corporate, general, General civil litigation. Office: Cablevision Sys Corp 1111 Stewart Ave Bethpage NY 11714

BURICK, LAWRENCE T. lawyer; b. Dayton, Ohio, May 15, 1943; s. Lee and Ida (Brenner) B.; m. Cynthia Joy Rosen, Aug. 31, 1969; children: Carrie R., Samuel J. BA, Miami U., 1965; JD, Northwestern U., 1968. Bar: Ohio 1968. Assoc. Smith & Schnacke, Dayton, 1969-78, ptnr., 1978-89, Thompson Hine LLP, Dayton, 1989—. Chmn. Dayton Jewish Ctr., Ohio, 1982—83, Jewish Cmty. Rels. Coun., 1980—81; pres. Jewish Fedn. Greater Dayton, Ohio, 1989—93, bd. dir., 1977—; chmn. United Jewish Campaign, 1997—99, Nat. Conf. Cmty. and Justice, 2002—; bd. dir. Jewish Edn. in

Svc. to N.Am., 1994—99, v.p., 1997—99; chmn. Dayton region Nat. Conf. Cmty. and Justice, 1997—, v.p., 1999—2002, chair, 2002—; bd. dir. Beth Abraham Synagogue, 1997—. Recipient Wasserman Leadership award, Jewish Fedn. Greater Dayton, 1978. Mem. Ohio State Bar Assn., Dayton Bar Assn., Am. Bankruptcy Law Forum, Am. Bankruptcy Inst. Office: Thompson Hine LLP PO Box 8801 200 Courthouse Plz NE Dayton OH 45401-8801 E-mail: larry.burick@thompsonhine.com.

BURK, ROBERT S. lawyer; b. Mpls., Jan. 13, 1937; s. Harvey and Mayme (Cottle) B.; m. Eunice L. Silverman, Mar. 22, 1959; children: Bryan, Pam, Matt. BBA in Indsl. Rels., U. Minn., 1959; LLB, William Mitchell Coll. Law, 1965. Bar: Minn. 1966; qualified neutral under Rule 114 of the Minn. Gen. Rules of Practice, 1995—. Labor rels. cons. St. Paul Employers Assn., 1959-66; labor rels. mgr. Koch Refining Co., St. Paul, 1966-72, mgr. indsl. rels., 1972-75, mgr. indsl. rels., environ. affairs, 1975-77; sr. atty. Popham, Haik, Schnobrich & Kaufman, Ltd., Mpls., 1977-95, pres., CEO, 1986-90; ptnr. Burk & Seaton, P.A., Edina, Minn., 1995-2001, Burk & Landrum, P.A., Edina, 2001—. Chair bd. trustees William Mitchell Coll. Law, St. Paul, 1994-96, sec. 1991. Recipient Hon. Ronald E. Hachey Outstanding Alumnus award William Mitchell Coll. Law Alumni Assn., 1993. Mem. ABA (labor sect.), Minn. Bar Assn. (labor sect.). Administrative and regulatory, Labor (including EEOC, Fair Labor Standards Act, labor-management relations, NLRB, OSHA). Office: Burk & Landrum PA 7400 Metro Blvd Ste 100 Edina MN 55439 Office Fax: 952-835-1867. E-mail: rburk@burklandrum.com.

BURKE, EDMUND JAMES, III, lawyer; b. N.Y.C., May 10, 1949; s. Edmund James Burke Jr. and Mary Virginia Hahn. BA, Bates Coll., 1971; postgrad., U. Glasgow, Scotland, 1970; JD, Western New Eng. Coll., 1976. Bar: Maine 1976, U.S. Dist. Ct. Maine 1977, U.S. Ct. Appeals (1st cir.) 1990. Ptnr. Burke, Meyer & Bates, Lewiston, Maine, 1977-82, Burke & Gauvreau, Lewiston, 1982-84; pres. Longley, Whalen & Burke, Lewiston, 1984-86, Whalen & Burke, Lewiston, 1986-87; sole practice Lewiston, 1987-88; pres. Bell & Burke P.A., Lewiston, 1988-96; pvt. prac., 1996—. Complaint justice 8th Jud. Dist., Lewiston, 1982-85, fee arbitration commn. 1997-2001, chair, 2001—; vis. prof. law U. Maine, 2002, 2003. Bd. dirs. Maine Civil Liberties Union, Portland, 1986—, v.p., 1988, pres., 1989-91, Pathways, Inc., 1996— (pres. 1997-99); bd. dirs. Lewiston-Auburn Children's Home, 1982-88; trustee, clk. Androscoggin County Law Libr., Auburn, 1978—. Fellow Maine Bar Found. (grants com. 1987-91); mem. ABA, Maine Bar Assn., Maine Trial Lwyers Assn., Androscoggin County Bar Assn. (treas. 1978-97, pres. 1998-99). State civil litigation, Constitutional, Personal injury (including property damage). Office: E James Burke PA 621 Main St Lewiston ME 04240-5938 E-mail: burke@megalink.net.

BURKE, GAY ANN WOLESENSKY, lawyer; b. Crete, Nebr., Apr. 16, 1954; d. Robert Melvin and Camille Mary (Fountain) Wolesensky; m. Richard Donald Crosier, May 12, 1973 (div. 1981); 1 child, Joshua Jay; m. Kenneth John Burke, June 4, 1983; 1 child, John Tynan. BS, Nebr. Wesleyan U., 1975; JD with high distinction, U. Nebr., 1981. Bar: Colo. 1982, Nebr. 1987, U.S. Dist. Ct. Colo. 1983, U.S. Tax Ct. 1987, U.S. Ct. Appeals (10th cir.) 1987. Assoc. Holme Roberts & Owen, Denver, 1982-86, Otten, Johnson, Robinson, Neff & Ragonette, Denver, 1986; ptnr. Burke & Burke, Denver, 1986-88, Massey Burke & Showalter, Denver, 1988-90; sole practice Denver, 1990—; gen. counsel, exec. v.p. E.J. Renner & Assocs. Inc. (dba Malott Peterson Renner Inc.), 1991-93. Lectr. U. Denver Coll. Law, 1988-97. Pres., CEO, bd. dirs. Pumpkin Ltd. dba Pumpkin Masters, Inc. 1993—; bd. dirs. Mackintosh Acad. Mem. ABA, Colo. Bar Assn., Nebr. Bar Assn., Order of Coif. Democrat. Presbyterian. Avocation: fly fishing. Corporate, general, Insurance, Taxation, general. Office: 1905 Sherman #1000 Denver CO 80203 E-mail: gburke@pumpkinmasters.com.

BURKE, JOHN MICHAEL, lawyer; b. Chgo., Oct. 9, 1941; s. John and Catherine Mary (Barrett) B.; m. Maureen Kay Fox, Oct. 5, 1968; children: Brian, Timothy, Michael. BBA, Loyola U., 1964, JD, 1965. Bar: Ill. 1965, U.S. Dist. Ct. (no. dist.) Ill. 1965, U.S. Ct. Appeals (7th cir.) 1968, U.S. Dist. Ct. (no.dist.) Ind. 1986. Assoc. Pretzel & Stouffer, Chgo., 1965-69, Shaheen, Lundberg & Callahan, Chgo., 1969-70; ptnr. Burke & Burke, Ltd., Chgo., 1970—. Sgt. U.S. Army, 1965-68. Mem. AATLA, BA, Ill. State Bar Assn. (chmn. tort coun., svc. award 1984, mem. civil practice com. 1997—, mem. jud. evaluation com. 2002—), Ill. Trial Lawyers (bd. mgrs. 1988—), Appellate Lawyers Ill., Westmoreland Country Club (Wilmette, Ill.). Federal civil litigation, State civil litigation, Personal injury (including property damage). Home: 2241 Kenilworth Ave Wilmette IL 60091-1523 Office: Burke & Burke Ltd 30 N LaSalle St Ste 2800 Chicago IL 60602 E-mail: jburke@burke-burke.com.

BURKE, KATHLEEN B. lawyer; b. Bklyn., Sept. 2, 1948; BA, St. John's U., 1969, JD, 1973. Bar: Ohio 1973. Ptnr. Jones, Day, Reavis & Pogue, Cleve. Chair Notre Dame Coll. of Ohio, 2002—. Pres. Cleve. Skating Club, 2000-2002. Fellow Ohio State Bar Found. (pres. 2000); mem. Ohio State Bar Assn. (pres. 1993-94). Office: Jones Day Reavis & Pogue North Point 901 Lakeside Ave E Cleveland OH 44114-1190

BURKE, MICHAEL HENRY, lawyer; b. Washington, Oct. 28, 1952; s. John Joseph and Mary Catherine (Gaul) B.; m. Ann McFarland, Jan. 31, 1981; children: Allison M., Andrew M. BA magna cum laude, Tufts U., 1974; JD, Georgetown U., 1977. Bar: Mass. 1977, U.S. Dist. Ct. Mass. 1979. Assoc. Bulkley, Richardson and Gelinas L.L.P., Springfield, Mass., 1977-83, ptnr., 1983—. Pub. adminstr. Commonwealth of Mass., 1980-90. Mem. ABA, Mass. Bar Assn., Hampden County Bar Assn. Roman Catholic. Administrative and regulatory, General civil litigation, Professional liability. Home: 50 Meadowbrook Rd Longmeadow MA 01106-1341 Office: Bulkley Richardson and Gelinas LLP 1500 Main St Springfield MA 01115-0001 E-mail: mburke@bulkley.com.

BURKE, RICHARD WILLIAM, lawyer; b. Chgo., Oct. 3, 1933; s. James William and Helen (Creed) B.; m. Maryjeanne Ryan, Feb. 11, 1961; children: Mary, Richard, Sarah, Will. BA cum laude, U. Notre Dame, 1955; JD, U. Chgo., 1958. Bar: Ill. 1959, U.S. Dist. Ct. Ill. 1959, U.S. Ct. Appeals (7th cir.) 1965, U.S. Supreme Ct. 1977. Assoc. William T. Kirby & Assocs., Chgo., 1958-65, Hubachek, Kelly, Rauch & Kirby, Chgo., 1965-67, ptnr., 1967-80, Burke, Griffin, Chomicz & Wienke, Chgo., 1980-88, Burke, Wilson & McIlvaine, Chgo., 1989-92, Burke, Warren & MacKay, P.C., Chgo., 1992-97, Burke, Warren, MacKay & Serritella, PC, Chgo., 1997—. Bd. dirs. various charities. Mem. Ill. Bar Assn., Chgo. Bar Assn. Roman Catholic. Avocations: skiing, reading, travel. Banking, Mergers and acquisitions, Property, real (including real estate development, water). Office: Burke Warren MacKay & Serritella 330 N Wabash Ave Chicago IL 60611-3603

BURKE, ROBERT BERTRAM, lawyer, political consultant, lobbyist; b. Cleve., July 9, 1942; s. Max and Eve (Miller) B.; m. Helen Choate Hall, May 5, 1979 (div. Oct. 1983). BA, UCLA, 1963, JD, 1966; LLM, London Sch. Econs., 1967. Bar: D.C. 1972, U.S. Supreme Ct. 1977, Calif. 1978. Exec. dir. Lawyer's Com. Civil Rights Under Law, Washington, 1968-69; ptnr. Fisk, Wolfe & Burke, Paris, 1969-71; assoc. O'Connor & Hannan, Washington, 1972-74; pvt. practice Washington, 1974-79, L.A., 1978-93; contract lobbyist Rose & Kindel, L.A., Sacramento, Washington, 1993—. Cons. Commonwealth Pa., Harrisburg, 1973. Chmn. So. Calif. Hollings for Pres., 1984; pres. Bldg. and Appeals Bd. City of L.A.; bd. dirs. Vols. of Am.; mem. exec. com. State Bar of Calif. pub. law sect. Mem. ABA UCLA Law Alumni Assn. (pres.). Jewish. Administrative and regulatory, Private international. Home: 277 S Irving Blvd Los Angeles CA 90004-3809 E-mail: bburke@rosekindel.com.

BURKE, THOMAS JOSEPH, JR., lawyer; b. Oct. 23, 1941; s. Thomas Joseph and Violet (Green) B.; m. Sharon Lynne Forke, Aug. 29, 1964; children: Lisa Lynne, Heather Ann. BA, Elmhurst Coll., 1963; JD, Chgo.-Kent Coll. Law, 1966. Bar: Ill. 1966, U.S. Dist. Ct. (no. dist.) Ill. 1967, U.S. Ct. Appeals (7th cir.) 1972, U.S. Supreme Ct. 1972, U.S. Ct. Appeals (11th cir.) 1994, U.S. Ct. Appeals (6th cir.) 1995. Assoc. Lord, Bissell & Brook, Chgo., 1966-74, ptnr., 1974—. Fellow: Am. Coll. Trial Lawyers; mem.: Assn. Advancement Automotive Medicine, Soc. Automotive Engrs., Product Liability Adv. Coun., Ill. Assn. Def. Trial Counsel, Def. Rsch. Inst., Soc. Trial Lawyers, Chgo. Bar Assn., Mid-Day Club, Phi Delta Phi, Pi Kappa Delta. Republican. Roman Catholic. Federal civil litigation, State civil litigation, Product liability. Office: Lord Bissell & Brook 115 S La Salle St Ste 3300 Chicago IL 60603-3801 E-mail: tburke@lordbissell.com.

BURKE, THOMAS MICHAEL, lawyer; b. Summit, N.J., Feb. 10, 1956; s. Robert William and Eleanor Mary (Kelley) B.; m. Nancy Robin Mogab, Sept. 24, 1983; children: Colleen Margaret, Michael Thomas, Brendan Robert. BA, Notre Dame U., 1978; JD, St. Louis U., 1981. Bar: Mo. 1981, Ill. 1982, U.S. Dist. Ct. (ea. dist.) 1981. Assoc. Moser, Marsalek, Carpenter, Cleary & Jaeckel, St. Louis, 1981-86; ptnr. Noonan & Burke, St. Louis, 1986-92; prin. Thomas M. Burke, PC, St. Louis, 1992—. Bd. dirs. Legal Svcs. Ea. Mo., 1995-97. Active Vol. Lawyers program, St. Louis, St. Louis Hills Homeowner's Assn., 1984-94. Mem. Mo. Bar Assn. (bd. govs., 1998—, chair fin. com. 2002--), Ill. Bar Assn., Interest On Lawyers' Trust Accounts (bd. dirs. 1997-2002, pres. 2000-01), Bar Assn. Met. St. Louis (treas. 1992-93, sec. 1993-94, v.p. 1994-95, pres.-elect 1995-96, pres. 1996-97), St. Louis Bar Found. (sec. 1993-94, treas. 1995-96), Lawyers Assn. St. Louis (exec. com. 1987-92, sec. 1992-93, treas. 1992-93, v.p. 1993-94). General civil litigation, Personal injury (including property damage), Workers' compensation. Office: 701 Market St Ste 1075 Saint Louis MO 63101-1886 E-mail: tburke@burkelawfirm.com.

BURKE, THOMAS RAYMOND, lawyer; b. Lincoln, Nebr., Apr. 15, 1928; s. Raymond C. and Florine (Kost) B.; children from previous marriage: Thomas R., Timothy J. (dec. 1998), Melanie A., Pamela (dec. 1963), Laura M., Lisa M., Daniel C.; m. Barbara Schafer, Apr. 17, 1993; stepchildren: Robyn, Stephen, Holly, Jamie. JD, Creighton U., 1951. Bar: Nebr. 1951. Assoc. Kennedy, Holland, DeLacy & Svoboda, Omaha, 1956-62, ptnr., 1963—, sr. ptnr., 1970-98; of counsel Lamson Dugan & Murray LLP, 1998—. Lectr. Coll. St. Mary, 1960-80. Past pres. adv. bd. Archbishop Bergan Mercy Hosp., past chmn. fin. com.; co-chmn. NCCJ, 1969-77, nat. trustee, 1972-78, bd. dirs., 1969-95, bd. govs., 1995—; mem. Archbishop's Com. for Ednl. Devel., 1975-98, chmn., 1975-78, 87-95; founding trustee, pres., gen. counsel Omaha Archdiocesan Ednl. Found.; co-chair Archbishop's $25 Million Campaign for Ednl. Excellence, 1991; adv. bd. Mercy HS; mem. pres.'s coun. U. Nebr., 1979-85, Coll. St. Mary, 1979-85; bd. dirs. Duchesne Acad., 1979-82, trustee, 1982-87, pres., trustee, 1985-87; bd. dirs. Christian Urban Edn. Svc., 1982-97, United Arts Omaha, 1983-98; trustee Nat. Jewish Hosp. (humanitarian award 1983), Denver, 1983; bd. dirs., exec. com., fin. com. United Way of Midlands, 1984-90, ann. campaign chmn., 1986; mem. st. Joseph High Devel. Bd., 1983-88; diocesan rep., trustee Nat. Cath. Ednl. Assn., 1984-87; chmn. bd. dirs. Bergan Mercy Found., 1992-98, bd. dirs. 1992—; founding chmn. bd. dirs. New Cassel Found., 2000-01, bd. dirs., 2001-; mem. com. Stephen Ctr. Devel., 2000-, hon. chair ann. campaign, 2002. Named Citizen of Yr., United Way of Midlands, 1992; named to Aksarben Ct. of Honor, 1998, Face on Barroom Floor Press Club, 2001; recipient Brotherhood award, 1991, Humanitarian award, 1991, Spirit of Francis award, Hew Passel Fedn., 2002. Fellow Am. Bar Found.; mem. Omaha Bar Assn. (pres. 1971), Am. Coll. of Trust and Estate Counsel, Nebr. Bar Assn. (pres. 1978-79, exec. coun. 1966-72, 78-87, pres.'s adv. coun. 2000—), Omaha Bus. Men's Assn. (pres. 1962, Man of Yr. 1970), Rotary Found. (trustee), Omaha Rotary Club (pres. 1992-93), Nat. Lawyers Assn., Omaha Press Club. Corporate, general, Estate planning, Probate (including wills, trusts). Office: 10306 Regency Parkway Dr Omaha NE 68114-3708 E-mail: Tburke@ldmlaw.com.

BURKE, TIMOTHY MICHAEL, lawyer, educator; b. Cleve., Feb. 10, 1948; s. Ralph and Frances (Dilley) B.; m. Patricia Kathleen LaGrange, June 6, 1970; children: Nora Frances, Tara Kathleen, Michael Ralph. AB, Xavier U., Cin., 1970; JD, U. Cin., 1973. Bar: Ohio 1973, U.S. Dist. Ct. (so. dist.) Ohio 1979, U.S. Ct. Appeals (6th cir.) 1978, U.S. Supreme Ct. 1979. Legis. asst. to coun. mem. Cin. City Coun., 1971-74; spl. asst. to Congressman Tom Luken Cin., 1974, 76-77; exec. dir. Little Miami, Inc., Cin., 1975-76; prin. Manley Burke and predecessor firm, Cin., 1977—; spl. counsel to atty. gen. State of Ohio, 1978-95; law dir. Village of Lockland, Ohio, 1982—2003, Village of Evendale, Ohio, 2003—. Lectr. Xavier U., 1975-78, 81, 82-83, adj. asst. prof., 1983-85; adj. assoc. prof. U. Cin., 1977-78, 79, dir. law enforcement tech. program, 1977-78. Bd. dirs. Tri State Air Com., 1972-80, chmn., 1976-78; chmn. land use subcom. water quality adv. com. Ohio-Ky.-Ind. Regional Coun. Govts., 1975-76; bd. dirs. Lower Coun. Little Miami, Inc., 1976-82; mem. alumni bd. govs. Xavier U., 1970-76, 78-79, v.p., 1980-81, pres., 1981-82; candidate for U.S. Ho. of Reps. from 1st dist. Ohio, 1978; chmn. legal com. Cin. Zoo, bd. dirs., 1980-91; co-chmn. Zoo Tax Levy Campaign, 1982, 86; commr. Cin. Park Bd., 1991-94; participant Fgn. Policy Conf. for Young Am. Polit. Leaders, U.S. Dept. State, 1980; chmn. Hamilton County Bd. Elections, 1993—; exec. co-chmn. Hamilton County Dem. Party, 1982-86, 88-89, chmn., 1993-99, co-chmn., 1999-; co-chmn. Cin. Dem. Com., 1983-89, chmn., 1989-97; 1st v.p. Ohio Dem. County Chairs Assn., 1995-99; internat. supr. Bosnia Mcpl. Elections, 1997, Elections Tng. Slovakia, 2002; team leader Law Enforcement and Justice Team, Cinti, Can. Served to 1st lt. U.S. Army, 1974. Recipient svc. award Ohio River Valley Com. for Occupational Safety and Health, 1983, Leadership award Xavier U., 1984; named Ohio Dem. of Yr. Ohio Dem. Party, 1995. Mem. ABA, Am. Planning Assn. (legal sect.). Roman Catholic. General civil litigation, Land use and zoning (including planning), Municipal (including bonds). Home: 3560 Mcguffey Ave Cincinnati OH 45226-1919

BURKE, WILLIAM JOSEPH, lawyer; b. Chgo., Aug. 9, 1949; BS in Acctg., U. Ill., Chgo., 1974; JD, Ill. Inst. Tech., 1978. Bar: Ill. 1978, U.S. Dist. Ct. (no. dist.) Ill. 1978, U.S. Ct. Appeals (7th cir.) 1978, U.S. Supreme Ct. 1993. Ptnr. Demos & Burke, Chgo., 1980—2002, Costello McMahon & Burke, Chgo., 2002—. General civil litigation, Personal injury (including property damage), Product liability. Office: Costello McMahon & Burke 150 N Wacker Dr Ste 3050 Chicago IL 60606

BURKE, WILLIAM TEMPLE, JR., lawyer; b. San Antonio, Oct. 30, 1935; s. William Temple and Adelaide H. (Raba) B.; m. Mary Sue Johnson, June 8, 1957; children: William Patrick, Michael Edmond, Karen Elizabeth. BBA, St. Mary's U., San Antonio, JD, 1961. Bar: Tex. 1961. Practice law, Dallas; founder, pres. Burke Wright & Keiffer, PC, 1985-98; of counsel Hance/Scarborough/Wright, Dallas, 1998-2000, Hance, Scarborough, Wright Ginsberg and Brusilow, Dallas, 2000—. Co-founder, v.p., dir. Tex. Cath. Cmty. Credit Union, 1966-69, vice chmn. bd. dirs., 1990-91; pres., dir. Dallas County Small Bus. Devel. Ctr., 1966-67; v.p. Dallas County Hist. Survey Com., 1966; pres. Dallas Mil. Govt. Assn., 1962-63; pres. men's club St. Patrick's Parish Roman Cath. Ch., 1963, prin. jr. H.S. Christian devel. program, 1970, chmn. scout troop com., 1976-78, chmn. fin. com., 1984-87, mem. bldg. com., 1978-87, chmn. bd. consultors, 1978-81; bd. dirs. Dallas County War on Poverty, 1965-66, pres. Dallas Cnty. Small Bus. Devel. Ctr., 1966-67; trustee Montserrat Jesuit Retreat House, 1995-2000, treas., 1996-97; bd. dirs. The Montserrat Found., 1999-2000; vice-chmn. Cath. Commn. Appeal Diocese of Dallas, 1993-97. 1st lt. U.S. Army, 1958-60; capt. USAR ret. Fellow Tex. Bar Found. (life), Coll. of State Bar Tex., Dallas Bar Found. (sr. life); mem. ABA, Tex. Bar Assn., Dallas Bar Assn. (chmn. bankruptcy and comml. law sect. 1976-77, 86-87, courthouse liaison com. 1985—, lectr. 1985—, chmn. spkrs. com. 2001—02), Am. Bankruptcy Inst., John C. Ford Am. Inn Ct. (co-founder, pres. 2000—, Serjeant of the Inn (Hon.), 2003), Dallas C. of C., Dallas Safari Club, Serra Internat. Met. Club (pres. Met. Dallas 1997-98, Outstanding Mem. award 1995), Internat. Order Alhambra (exemplar 1978-95), KC (co-founder Greater Dallas chpt., council 799 grand knight, trustee 1964-69, dist. examplar 4th degree 1968-69, Man of Yr. award 1970), Sgt. of the Inn (hon.), Optimists (v.p., bd. dirs. Dallas 1965-66, Man of Yr. award 1966, Pres.'s award 1968), Phi Delta Phi (life), Tau Delta Sigma (pres., 1957). Home: 9751 Larchcrest Dr Dallas TX 75238-2112 Office: 1401 Elm St Ste 4750 Dallas TX 75202 E-mail: wburke@hswgb.com.

BURKETT, GERALD ARTHUR, lawyer, musician; b. Oklahoma City, Apr. 23, 1939; s. Francis Gerald and Leta Carey (Weaver) B.; m. Carolyn Ruth Hicks, Aug. 7, 1960; 1 child, Debora Lynne Burkett Nutt. BA, David Lipscomb U., 1962; MA, Peabody Coll., 1967; JD, Nashville Sch. of Law, 1974. Bar: Tenn. 1975, U.S. Dist. Ct. (mid. dist.) Tenn., 1976, U.S. Ct. Appeals (6th cir.), 1977, U.S. Tax Ct., 1981, U.S. Supreme Ct. 1993. Leader Fritz's German Band, Nashville, 1972-97; pvt. practice law office Nashville, 1975—; jud. commr. Met. Nashville/Davidson County, Tenn., 1999—. Adj. prof. Vol. State C.C., Gallatin, Tenn., 1979-93, 2001—, Nashville State Tech. Inst., 1984-89; band leader Strohaus, 1982 World's Fair, Knoxville, 1982; appears on Metro Night Ct., Channel 50, Nashville. Condr.German band for commls. and concerts including Monday Night Football, 1994-2000, Super Bowl, 1995, Oktoberfest Concert, Soldier Field, Chgo., 1995; appeared on weekly TV show Metro Night Ct., Channel 50, Nashville, 2000. Accordionist Charlie Rich's Bi-Centennial Album, 1976, film soundtrack Sweet Dreams, 1983. Mem. Nashville Assn. Musicians, Alliance Francaise (treas. 1985-86), Nashville Bar Assn., Tenn. Assn. of Spanish Spkg. Attys., Phi Delta Kappa (treas. 1967-68). Mem. Ch. of Christ. Avocations: travel, foreign languages. Commercial, contracts (including sales of goods; commercial financing), Probate (including wills, trusts), General practice. Office: PO Box 8566 Hermitage TN 37076-8566 E-mail: geraldburkett@hotmail.com.

BURKEY, LEE MELVILLE, lawyer; b. Beach, N.D., Mar. 21, 1914; s. Levi Melville and Mina Lou (Horner) B.; m. Lorraine Lillian Burghardt, June 11, 1938; 1 child, Lee Melville, III BA, U. Ill., 1936, MA, 1938; JD with honor, John Marshall Law Sch., 1943. Bar: Ill., 1944, U.S. Dist. Ct., 1947, U.S. Ct. Appeals, 1954, U.S. Supreme Ct.; 1983; cert. secondary tchr., Ill. Tchr. Princeton Twp. High Sch., Princeton, Ill., 1937-38, Thornton Twp. High Sch., Harvey, Ill., 1938-43; atty. Office of Solicitor, U.S. Dept. Labor, Chgo., 1944-51; ptnr. Asher, Gubbins & Segall and successor firms, Chgo., 1951-94; of counsel, 1995—. Lectr. bus. law Roosvelt Coll., Chgo., 1949—52. Contbr. numerous articles on lie detector evidence. Trustee, Village of La Grange, Ill., 1962-68, mayor, 1968-73, village atty., 1973-87; commr., pres. Northeastern Ill. Planning Commn., Chgo., 1969-73; mem. bd. dirs. United Ch. Christ, Bd. of Homeland Ministries, 1981-87; mem. exec. com. Cook County Coun. Govts., 1968-70; life mem. La Grange Area Hist. Soc.; bd. dirs. Better Bus. Bur. Met. Chgo., Inc., 1975-82, Plymouth Place, Inc., 1973-82; mem. exec. bd., v.p. S.W. Suburban Ctr. on Aging, 1993—. Brevet 2nd Lt. Ill. Nat. Guard, 1932. Recipient Disting. Alumnus award John Marshall Law Sch., 1973, Meritorious Svc. award Am. Legion Post 1941, 1974, Honor award LaGrange Area Hist. Soc., 1987, Cmty. Svc. award S.W. Suburban Ctr. on Aging, 2000; named to Order of Ky. Cols. Fellow: Coll. Labor and Employment Lawyers. (charter); mem.: S.R., SAR (state pres. 1977, Good citizenshp medal 1973, Patriot medal 1977), ABA (coun. sect. labor and employment law 1982—86, governance officer 1986—96), Chgo. Bar Assn., Ill. Bar Assn., United Empire Loyalists Assn. Can., La Grange Country Club, Masons, Theta Delta Chi, Order John Marshall. Mem. First Congl. Ch. Labor (including EEOC, Fair Labor Standards Act, labor-management relations, NLRB, OSHA).

BURKHARDT, DONALD MALCOLM, lawyer; b. N.Y.C., Jan. 21, 1936; s. Seymour and Ruby Victoria (Brownrigg) B.; m. Gail Lee Burkhardt; children: Susan Lynn McIlhenny, Steven Lee. BA, Dartmouth Coll., 1957; LLB, U. Mich., 1961. Bar: Colo. 1961, U.S. Dist. Ct. Colo. 1961, U.S. Ct. Appeals (10th cir.) 1962, U.S. Supreme Ct. 1988. Assoc. Grant, Shafroth, Toll & McHendrie, Denver, 1961-66; ptnr. Grant McHendrie, P.C., Denver, 1967-93; spl. counsel Inman Flynn & Biesterfeld, P.C., Denver, 1993-2001. Scoutmaster Boy Scouts Am., Denver, 1962-64; pres. Rangers Club, Young Am. League, Denver, 1972-76; ski patroller Nat. Ski Patrol System, Winter Park, Colo., 1967—. Republican. Presbyterian. Avocations: sports, outdoors. Home: 2833 E 8th Ave Denver CO 80206-3827

BURNETT, ARTHUR LOUIS, SR., judge; b. Spotsylvania County, Va., Mar. 15, 1935; s. Robert Louis and Lena Victoria (Bumbry) B.; m. Ann Lloyd, May 14, 1960; children: Darnellena, Arthur Louis II, Darryl, Darlisa, Dionne. BA summa cum laude, Howard U., 1957; LLB, NYU, 1958; grad., Fed. Exec. Inst., 1978. Bar: D.C. 1958, U.S. Dist. Ct. Md. 1963, U.S. Supreme Ct. 1964. Atty. Gen.'s Honor Program atty. fraud sect. criminal divsn. U.S. Dept. Justice, Washington, 1958, atty. to acting dep. chief gen. crimes sect., 1960-65; spl. asst. U.S. atty., Balt. and East St. Louis, Ill., 1961-63; asst. U.S. atty. D.C., 1965-68; legal adviser, gen. counsel D.C. Dept. Met. Police, 1968-69; U.S. magistrate U.S. Dist. Ct., Washington, 1969-75; asst. gen. counsel legal adv. divsn. U.S. CSC, 1975-78; assoc. gen. counsel Office of Personnel Mgmt., 1979-80; U.S. magistrate U.S. Dist. Ct. D.C., 1980-87; judge Superior Ct. D.C., 1987-98, sr. judge, 1998—; faculty Fed. Jud. Center, 1970—, Nat. Jud. Coll., 1974—. Judge-in-residence Children's Def. Fund, 1998—; program chmn. ann. meeting Nat. Conf. Spl. Ct. Judges, Washington, 1973, chmn. elect, acting chmn., 1974-75, chmn., 1975; program chmn. ann. meeting Nat. Council U.S. Magistrates, Williamsburg, Va., 1974, pres., 1983-84; program participant D.C. Circuit Jud. Conf., 1974, U.S. Ct. Claims Jud. Conf., 1979; adj. prof. Columbus Sch. Law, Cath. U. Am., 1997—, Cath. U., 1997—, Sch. Law Howard U., 1998—. Mem. NYU Law Rev., 1957-58 Bd. dirs. Fellowship of Christian Athletes, Washington, Nat. Assn. for Children of Alcoholics, 2000—. Recipient Founders Day award NYU, 1958, Sustained Superior Performance award U.S. Atty. Gen., 1963, Disting. Service award CSC, 1978, Meritorious Service award U.S. Office of Personnel Mgmt., 1980, Jud. award of excellence Washington Met. Trial Lawyers Assn., 1999, award of excellence Nat. Conf. State Trial Judges, 1999, Outstanding Disting. Service award Fed. Bar Assn., 1983. Mem. ABA (Franklin N. Flashner jud. award as outstanding judge on ct. of spl. jurisdiction 1985, coun. adminstrv. law and regulatory practice sect. 1987-90, liaison rep. of adminstrv. law and regulatory practice sect. to adminstrv. conf. of U.S. 1990-94, mem. JAD task force on improving opportunities for minorities 1988-97, 98—, judge Edward R. Finch Law Day USA speech award 1991, asst. sec. 1991-93, chair civil right and employment discrimination com. 1992-95, sec. adminstrv. law and regulatory practice 1993-95, chmn. CJS com. on criminal rules and evidence 1993-97, standing com. on substance abuse 1995-99, co-chmn. editl. bd. Criminal Justice Mag. 1997-2000, adv. com. and standing com. on pro bono and pub. svc. 2001-, State Justice Initiatives award, 2002), FBA (sect. coord. 1987-88, chmn. fed. litigation sect. 1984-85, chmn. standing com. on U.S. magistrates, dep. chmn. sect. adminstrn. of justice 1983-84, chmn. standing com. on U.S. magistrate, chmn. sect. adminstrn. of justice 1983-84, 95-97, pres. D.C. chpt. 1984-85, chmn. profl. ethics com. 1991-93, chmn. audit com. 1999—, Disting. Svc. award 1978, The Pres.'s award 1994, Earl Kintner award, 2002), Washington Bar Assn. (chmn. jud. coun. 2000-01, Ollie Mae Cooper award 1997), Nat. Bar Assn. (chmn. cmty. and youth action com. jud. coun. 1995—, chmn. profl. ethics com., jud. coun. asst. sec., The Pres.'s award 1996), Bar Assn. D.C., D.C. Unified Bar, Am. Judicature Soc., Am. Judges Assn. (sec-treas. Prettyman-Leventhal Inn of Ct. Washington 1991-94, pres.

1994-95), Phi Beta Kappa, Omega Psi Phi. Office: Superior Ct DC Chambers JM-680 500 Indiana Ave NW Washington DC 20001-2131 E-mail: albsr2alb@aol.com., burnetta@dcsc.gov.

BURNETT, E. C., III, state supreme court justice; b. Spartanburg, S.C., Jan. 26, 1942; s. E.C. Jr. and Lucy (Byars) B.; m. Jami Grant, 1963; children: Curry, Sharon, Jeffrey. AB, Wofford Coll., 1964; JD, U. S.C., 1969. Bar: S.C. 1969. Mem. S.C. Ho. of Reps., 1973-74; probate judge Spartanburg County, 1976-80; judge family ct., 1980-81, Seventh Jud. Cir., 1981-95; assoc. justice S.C. Supreme Ct., 1995—. Elder Mt. Calvary Presbyn. Ch. Mem. ABA, S.C. Bar Assn. Home: 200 Burnett Rd Pauline SC 29374-2610 Office: State Supreme Court PO Box 11330 Columbia SC 29211

BURNETT, HENRY, lawyer; b. N.Y.C., Feb. 24, 1927; s. Lucien Dallam and Ruth (Hinkle) B.; m. Florence Stewart, July 19, 1952; children: Marian Starr, Betsy Callaway, Henry Stewart. BA, U. Va., 1947, LLB, 1950. Bar: Va. bar 1950, Fla. bar 1951. Ptnr. Fowler, White, Burnett, Hurley, Banick & Strickroot, Miami, Fla., 1957-93, pres., 1957-93; ptnr. Fowler, White, Burnett and predecessor firm, Miami, Fla., 1993—. Bd. dirs. Dade County Citizens Safety Council, Travelers Aid, United Family and Children's Services. Served with USNR, 1945-46. Fellow Am. Coll. Trial Lawyers; mem. Am., Fla., Dade County bar assns., Fla. Def. Lawyers Assn. (pres. 1967-68), Dade County Def. Bar Assn. (pres. 1966-67), Internat. Assn. Def. Counsel (exec. com. 1972-74, pres. 1976-77). Clubs: Riviera Country. Episcopalian. Federal civil litigation, State civil litigation, Personal injury (including property damage). Home: 8871 SW 68th Ave Miami FL 33156 Office: Nations Bank Tower 100 SE 2nd St Fl 18 Miami FL 33131-2195

BURNETT, RALPH GEORGE, lawyer; b. Milw., Apr. 13, 1956; s. Ralph G. and Joan T. Burnett; m. Eileen M. Gallagher, May 31, 1980; children: Christopher, Jessica, Thomas, Sarah, Andrew. BA, Marquette U., 1978; JD, U. Wis., 1981. Bar: Wis. 1981, U.S. Dist. Ct. (ea. and we. dists.) Wis. 1981, U.S. Ct. Appeals (7th cir.) 1981, U.S. Dist. Ct. (we. dist.) Mich. 1997, U.S. Ct. Appeals (6th cir.) 1997. Law clk. to Hon. Judge Harlington Wood U.S. Ct. Appeals 7th Cir., Chgo., 1981-82; lawyer Smith & O'Neil, Milw., 1983-84, Trowbridge, Planert & Schaefer, Green Bay, Wis., 1985-86, Liebmann, Conway, Olejniczak & Jerry, S.C., Green Bay, 1986—. Officer Robert J. Parins Inn of Ct., Green Bay, 1997—. Co-author: Wisconsin Trial Practice, 1999. Mem. allocations com. United Way N.E. Wis., Green Bay, 1988-91; bd. mem. paralegal program N.E. Wis. Tech. Coll., Green Bay, 1993—; bd. mem. parish coun. St. Mary's Ch., De Pere, 1997—; bd. mem. Cerebral Palsy, Green Bay, 1989-92; bd. mem. steering com. Notre Dame Sch., De Pere, 1998—. Mem. ABA, State Bar Wis. (bd. dirs., chmn. litigation sect. 1996—), Wis. Acad. Trial Lawyers (bd. dirs. 1995—; amicus commuter, constitutional challenge com., exec. com., regional dir. N.E. Wis. chpt., pres.-elect 2002-03). Avocations: woodworking, athletics. General civil litigation, Personal injury (including property damage), Product liability. Home: 806 Lawton Pl De Pere WI 54115-2623 Office: PO Box 23200 Green Bay WI 54305 E-mail: RGB@lcojlaw.law.*

BURNETTE, MARY MALISSA, lawyer; b. Morven, N.C., May 23, 1950; d. Harvey Lorraine and Mary Malissa (Ratliff) B. BA, U. S.C., 1971, JD, 1977. Bar: S.C. 1977, U.S. Dist. Ct. S.C. 1978, U.S. Ct. Appeals (4th cir.) 1978, U.S. Supreme Ct. 1998; cert. specialist in employment and labor law. Dir. Richland/Lexington Sr. Citizens Ctr., Columbia, S.C., 1973-74; atty. S.C. Gov.'s Office, Columbia, 1977-78; dep. lt. gov. State of S.C., Columbia, 1979-82; ptnr. Gergel, Burnette, Nickles, Grant & Leclair, Columbia, 1982-96, Burnette & Leclair, Columbia, 1996—. Disting. alumni spkr. U. S.C., 1995—. Campaign mgr. Medlock for Atty. Gen., Columbia, 1982; bd. dirs. Family Svc. Ctr., 1985-89, Men's Resource Ctr., 1987-89, The Nurturing Ctr., 2002—; chmn. adv. bd. S.C. Crime Victims, 1984-89; chmn. bd. visitors Columbia Coll., 1989-90; coun. on ministries Washington St., United Meth. Ch., 1988-89, chmn. adminstrv. bd., 1990-93, chmn. staff-parish rels. com., 1997-98; pres. Greater Columbia Cmty. Rels. Coun., 1995—; chair Gov.'s Task Force on Domestic Violence, 2000. Recipient Ten for the Future award Columbia Record, 1978, Career Woman award Columbia YWCA, 1980. Mem. ATLA, S.C. Bar (various coms. 1977—, chair quality of life com. 1994, chair jud. qualifications com. 1999-2001), S.C. Trial Lawyers (chair employment law sect. 1990-95, 2001—), S.C. Bus. and Profl. Women (Career Woman award 1987, S.C. Young Career Woman 1979), S.C. Women Lawyers Assn. (pres. 2001). Democrat. Avocations: travel with family, baseball. General civil litigation, Family and matrimonial, Labor (including EEOC, Fair Labor Standards Act, labor-management relations, NLRB, OSHA). Office: Burnette & Leclair PA 2322 Devine St Columbia SC 29205-2404 E-mail: mmburnette@mindspring.com.

BURNETTE, RALPH EDWIN, JR., judge; b. Lynchburg, Va., Sept. 25, 1953; s. Ralph Edwin and Carlease (Samuels) B. BA, Coll. William & Mary, 1975, JD, 1978. Bar: Va. 1978. Assoc. Edmunds & Williams, Lynchburg, 1978-83, ptnr., 1983-2001; gen. dist. ct. judge 24th Jud. Dist. Ct. Va., 2001—. Adj. prof. law Coll. William and Mary, 1996-2002, Washington & Lee U. Deacon Peakland Bapt. Ch., Lynchburg, 1983-86; pres. Kaleidoscope Festival, Lynchburg, 1985, Lynchburg Symphony Orch., 1989-91; bd. dirs. Centra Health, Inc., 1987-97, United Way Cen. Va., 1989-90, Amazement Sq. Children's Mus. Mem. Va. Bar Assn., Va. State Bar (pres. 1993-94, pres. young lawyers conf. 1985, chmn. com. on alternative dispute resolution 1985-89, mem. bar coun., 1986-95, vice chmn. standing com. on legal ethics 1986-88, chmn. com. on long range planning 1988-91, mem. exec. com. 1990-95), Lynchburg Bar Assn. (pres. 1991-92), Avocations: golf, music, boating. Office: Lynchburg Gen Dist Ct 905 Court St Lynchburg VA 24504

BURNETTE, SUSAN LYNN, lawyer; b. Sylva, N.C., Nov. 20, 1955; d. William M. and Mary (McGrady) B.; m. Mark Howard Morey, June 2, 1984; children: Barbara Elizabeth Morey, Marianne McGrady Morey. Student, Institut d'Etudes Politiques, Paris, 1974-75; BA, U. S.C., 1975, BS, 1976; JD, U. Va., 1979. Bar: Va. 1979, S.C. 1979, Tex. 1980, U.S. Dist. Ct. (no. dist.) Tex. 1980, U.S. Ct. Appeals (5th cir.) 1984, U.S. Tax Ct. 1985; bd. cert. estate planning and probate law Tex. Bd. of Legal Specialization. Ptnr. Whittenburg, Whittenburg & Schachter, Amarillo, Tex., 1983-90; shareholder Conant Whittenburg Whittenburg & Schachter, P.C., Amarillo, 1991-95, Conant Whittenburg French & Schachter, P.S.C., Amarillo, 1995-99, Whittenburg, Whittenburg & Schachter, P.C., Amarillo, 1999—2002, Susan L. Burnette, P.C., 2002—. Lectr. in field. Fellow: Tex. Bar Found. (life); mem.: Amarillo Area Estate Planning Coun., Amarillo Bar Assn. (pres. 2003—), Tex. Acad. Probate and Trust Counsel, Va. Bar Assn., S.C. Bar Assn., Tex. Bar Assn. (dist. 13A grievance com. pres. 1994—95, course dir. Advanced Tax Law Course 1999, coun. tax sect. 1999—2002), ATLA, ABA. General civil litigation, Estate planning, Probate (including wills, trusts). Home: 2709 Sunlite St Amarillo TX 79106-6113 Office: Susan L Burnette, PC Lobby Box 206 500 S Taylor Ste 504 Amarillo TX 79101-2445 E-mail: susan@burnettelawfirm.com.

BURNEY, RHETT D. lawyer; b. Charlotte, NC, Mar. 13, 1970; s. D.F. and Joy Burney. BA, Presbyn. Coll., Clinton, SC, 1992; JD, U. SC, 1995. Bar: SC 1995, U.S. Dist. Ct. SC 1996, cert.: (domestic mediator). Ptnr. Turner and Burney, PC, Laurens, SC, 1995—. Atty. to assist disciplinary counsel SC Bar, Columbia, 1999—. Elder 1st Presbyn. Ch. Laurens, 2000—; bd. dirs. YMCA, Laurens, 1998—2001, Hospice, Laurens, 2002—. Mem.: Laurens County Bar (pres. 1997—). Family and matrimonial, Property, real (including real estate development, water), Personal injury (including property damage). Office: Turner & Burney PC 105 W Public Sq Laurens SC 29360 Office Fax: 864-984-5451. E-mail: rdburney@backroads.net.

BURNHAM, BRYSON PAINE, retired lawyer; b. Chgo., Oct. 11, 1917; s. Raymond and Patti (Paine) B.; m. Frances Katherine Burns, Feb. 8, 1941; children: Janice Young, Stephanie Paine. BA, U. Chgo., 1938, JD, 1940. Bar: Ill. 1940, Colo. 1983. Assoc., then ptnr. Mayer, Brown & Platt, Chgo., 1940-83; of counsel Shand, McLachlan and Newbold, Durango, Colo., 1985-93. Bd. dirs. Fort Lewis Coll. Found., 1986-2002. Antitrust, General civil litigation. Home: 315 Highland Hill Dr Timberline View Estates Durango CO 81301

BURNISON, BOYD EDWARD, lawyer; b. Arnolds Park, Iowa, Dec. 12, 1934; s. Boyd WIlliam and Lucile (Harnden) B.; m. Mari Amaral; children: Erica Lafore, Alison Katherine. BS, Iowa State U., 1957; JD, U. Calif., Berkeley, 1961. Bar: Calif. 1962, U.S. Supreme Ct. 1971, U.S. Dist. Ct. (no. dist.) Calif. 1962, U.S. Ct. Appeals (9th cir.) 1962, U.S. Dist. Ct. (ea. dist.) Calif. 1970, U.S. Dist. Ct. (ctrl. dist.) Calif. 1992. Dep. counsel Yolo County, Calif., 1962-65; assoc. Steel & Arostegui, Marysville, Calif., 1965-66, St. Sure, Moore & Hoyt, Oakland, Calif., 1966-70; ptnr. St. Sure, Moore, Hoyt & Sizoo, Oakland and San Francisco, 1970-75; v.p. Crosby, Heafey, Roach & May, P.C., Oakland, 1975-2000, also bd. dirs.; pres. Boyd E Burnison A Profl. Law Corp., Walnut Creek, Calif., 2001—. Advisor Berkeley YMCA, 1971—, Yolo County YMCA, 1962—65, bd. dirs., 1965; trustee, sec., legal counsel Easter Seal Found., Alameda County, 1974—79, hon. trustee, 1979—; trustee Alameda County Law Libr., 2001—; bd. dirs. Easter Seal Soc. Crippled Children and Adults of Alameda County Calif., 1972—75, Moot Ct. Bd., U. Calif., 1960—61, East Bay Conservation Corps, 1997—2000, treas., 2000. Named Vol. of Yr., Berkeley YMCA, 1999. Fellow: ABA Found. (life); mem.: ABA (labor rels. and employment law sect., equal employment law com. 1972—), Sproul Assoc. Boalt Hall Law Sch. U. Calif. Berkeley, Indsl. Rels. Rsch. Assn., Contra Costa County Bar Assn. (labor law sect.), Bar Assn. San Francisco (labor law sect.), Yuba Sutter Bar Assn., Yolo County Bar Assn. (sec. 1965), Alameda County Bar Found. (bd. dirs. 1993—95), Alameda County Bar Assn. (chmn. memberships and directory com. 1973—74, 1980, chmn. law office econs. com. 1975—77, assn. dir. 1981—85, pres. 1984, vice chmn. bench bar liaison com. 1983, chmn. 1984, Disting. Svc. award 1987), State Bar Calif. (spl. labor counsel 1981—84, labor and employment law sect. 1982—), Nat. Conf. Bar Pres.'s, Rotary (Paul Harris fellow), Round Hill Country Club, Iowa State Alumni Assn., Order Knoll, Phi Delta Phi, Pi Kappa Alpha. Democrat. Labor (including EEOC, Fair Labor Standards Act, labor-management relations, NLRB, OSHA). Home: PO Box 743 2500 Caballo Ranchero Dr Diablo CA 94528 Office: Boyd E Burnison A Profl Law Corp 1600 South Main Plz Ste 130 Walnut Creek CA 94596 Fax: (925) 817-2411. E-mail: boyd@bburnison.com.

BURNS, ARNOLD IRWIN, lawyer; b. N.Y.C., Apr. 14, 1930; s. Herman Leon and Rose (Lauterstein) B.; m. Felice Bernstein, June 17, 1951; children: Linda Susan, Douglas Todd. AB, Union Coll., Schenectady, 1950; LL.B., Cornell U., 1953; postgrad., Parker Sch. Internat. Law, 1960; JD, Hofstra U., 1986. Bar: N.Y. 1953, D.C. 1977. Ptnr. Burns Summit Rovins & Feldesman (and predecessors), N.Y.C., 1960-86; assoc. atty. gen. U.S. Govt., Washington, 1986; dep. atty. gen. U.S. Dept. Justice, Washington, 1986-88; mem. Proskauer Rose LLP, N.Y.C., 1988-99; mng. dir. Natexis Bleichroeder Inc., N.Y.C., 1999—. Bd. dirs., mem. exec. com. New Valley Corp. Note editor: Cornell Law Quar, 1952-53. Former chmn., life trustee Union Coll., Schenectady; former chmn., now chmn. emeritusbd. dirs. Freedom Found., Valley Forge, Pa.; emeritus chmn. nat. bd. govs. Boys and Girls Clubs Am.; mem. adv. com., co-chmn. nat. capital campaign Cornell Law Sch., Ithaca, N.Y.; former chmn. N.Y.C. Commn. on Youth Empowerment Svcs.; former mem. N.Y.C. Commn. to Monitor Police Corruption; former chmn. Nat. Ctr. for Victims of Crime, Internat. Ctr. for Missing and Exploited Children; vice chmn. Nat. Ctr. for Missing and Exploited Children; bd. dirs. Vis. Nurse Svc., N.Y., YES Newtork; chmn. emeritus Coun. for Unity; active Nat. Prison Indsl. Task Force. Capt. U.S. Army, 1953-57. Mem. Am. Israeli Polit. Action Com. (nat. exec. bd.), Anti-Defamation League (life; nat. com.), Fed. Bar Coun., Cornell Law Inst., Army Navy Club, N.Y. Athletic Club, Friars Club, Order of Coif, Phi Kappa Phi, Kappa Nu, Alpha Phi Omega. Republican. Jewish. Corporate, general, General practice, Public international. Home: 25 Sutton Pl S Apt 11F New York NY 10022-2462 Office: Natexis Bleichroeder Inc 1345 Avenue Of The Americas Fl 43 New York NY 10105-4300

BURNS, BERNARD JOHN, III, public defender; b. Alexandria, Va., Apr. 28, 1956; s. Bernard John and Mary Theresa (O'Malley) B.; m. Pamela Sue Endres, June 9, 1990; 1 child, Kristie Keener. BA in Journalism, U. Iowa, 1982, JD with distinction, 1984. Bar: Iowa 1985, U.S. Dist. Ct. (so. dist.) Iowa 1987, U.S. Supreme Ct. 1989, U.S. Ct. Appeals (8th cir.) 1992. Asst. appellate defender Iowa Appellate Defender, Des Moines, 1985-94; asst. pub. defender Des Moines Adult Pub. Defender, 1994-99; asst. fed. defender Office of Fed. Defender, Des Moines, 1999—. Author: 4A Iowa Practice: Criminal Procedure Bd. dirs. Met. Arts Alliance Greater Des Moines, 1996—, pres., 2000; mem. Iowa Criminal and Juvenile Justice Planning Commn., 1993-99; chmn. Jazz in July Planning Com., Des Moines, 1997—; keyboard player Goodnight Dallas. Named Outstanding Sr., Iowa Sch. Journalism, 1982. Mem. Nat. Assn. Fed. Defenders, Iowa Pub. Defenders Assn. (pres. 1991-99), Chopin Soc. (v.p. 1982), Blackstone Inn of Ct., Am. Mock Trial Assn., Judges Hall of Fame, Friends of Iowa Civil Rights, Inc. 1998. Phi Beta Kappa. Avocations: composer, actor, writer, tae kwon do instructor, musician. Office: Fed Defender 300 Walnut St Ste 295 Des Moines IA 50309-2258

BURNS, EDWARD MORRIS, protective services official; b. Somerville, Mass., Oct. 3, 1946; s. Edward Joseph and Ruth Irene (Mayer) Burns. A in Aeronautics, Daniel Webster Coll., 1967; BSBA, Suffolk U., 1970, JD, 1978; MPA, Harvard U., 1980. Bar: Mass. 1979, U.S. Dist. Ct. Mass. 1979, U.S. Ct. Appeals (1st cir.) 1979, U.S. Supreme Ct. 1983, cert.: Commonwealth Caribbean, Nassau, Bahamas (legal edn.) 1999. Asst. dist. atty., dir. grand jury Suffolk Dist. Atty.'s Office, Boston, 1979—94; chief legal counsel Mass. Aeronautics Commn., Boston, 1994—97; spl. sheriff Middlesex Sheriff's Office, Cambridge, Mass., 1997—. 1st mate Gt. Congress St. and Atlantic Steam Navigation Co., Boston, 1979—81; capt. Skyline Cruises, Inc., Boston, 1983—85; leading U.S. commentator on Class A tall ships, 1976—. Named Ofcl. Boston Harbor Historian, Mayor and City Coun., Boston, 1983. Mem.: Clover Club Boston (actor, singer), Harvard Club Boston, Ancient and Hon. Arty. Co. Avocations: travel, nautical historian. Home: 208 Grandview Ave Winthrop MA 02152-1456 Office: Middlesex Sheriff's Office 17th Fl 40 Thorndike St Cambridge MA 02141 Office Fax: 617-577-8373. E-mail: edburns@socialaw.com.

BURNS, ELLEN BREE, federal judge; b. New Haven, Conn., Dec. 13, 1923; d. Vincent Thomas and Mildred Bridget (Bannon) Bree; m. Joseph Patrick Burns, Oct. 8, 1955 (dec.); children: Mary Ellen, Joseph Bree, Kevin James. BA, Albertus Magnus Coll., 1944, LLD (hon.), 1974; LLB, Yale U., 1947; LLD (hon.), U. New Haven, 1981, Sacred Heart U., 1986, Fairfield U., 1991. Bar: Conn. 1947. Dir. legis. legal svcs. State of Conn., 1949-73; judge Conn. Cir. Ct., 1973-74, Conn. Ct. of Common Pleas, 1974-76, Conn. Superior Ct., 1976-78, U.S. Dist. Ct. Conn., New Haven, 1978—, chief judge, 1988-92, sr. judge, 1992—. Trustee Fairfield U., 1978-85, Albertus Magnus Coll., 1985—. Recipient John Carroll of Carrollton award John Barry Council K.C., 1973, Judiciary award Conn. Trial Lawyers Assn., 1978, Cross Pro Ecclesia et Pontifice, 1981, Law Rev. award U. Conn. Law Rev., 1987, Judiciary award Conn. Bar Assn., 1987, Raymond E. Baldwin Pub. Svc. award Bridgeport Law Sch., 1992. Mem.: ABA, Conn. Bar Found., Conn. Bar Assn., New Haven County Bar Assn., Am. Bar Found. Roman Catholic. Office: US Dist Ct 141 Church St New Haven CT 06510-2030

BURNS, GEORGE F. lawyer; b. Boston, Oct. 4, 1947; s. George and Bridget Burns O'Keefe; m. Elizabeth A. Burns; children: Michael, Abigail. BS in Internat. Affairs, Georgetown U., 1969; JD, NYU, 1972. Bar: Maine, NY. Assoc. Nixon Hargrave Devans & Doyle, Rochester, N.Y., 1973-78; ptnr. Jensen Baird Gardner & Henry, Portland, Maine, 1978-80, Burns Ray DeLano & MacDonald, P.A., 1980-2000; shareholder Bernstein Shur Sawyer & Nelson, Portland, 2001—. Mem. Maine Securities Law Revision Com., 1978-81. Contbr. articles to profl. jours. Mem., chmn. Town Coun., Falmouth, Maine, 1981-83; mem. Falmouth Charter Rev. Commn., 1987, 97; bd. dirs. LARK Soc. for Chamber Music, 1980-97, pres., 1993-97; trustee Salt Mag., 1991-93; bd. dirs. Spurwink Inst. and the Spurwink Sch., 1997-2000; pres. Spurwink Sch., 1997-2000. Fellow Maine Bar Found.; mem. ABA (sects. on litigation and bus.), Maine State Bar Assn., Cumberland County Bar Assn., Am. Arbitration Assn. (arbitrator, comml. panel), listed, Best Lawyers in Am. Office: 100 Middle St Portland ME 04101-4100 E-mail: gburns@bssn.com.

BURNS, JENNIFER D. advocate, lawyer; b. Camden, N.J., Jan. 25, 1968; d. Roger Johnson Burns and Patricia Pearson Ross; m. Matthew Langdon Cost, July 20, 1991 (div. Oct. 2000); children: Brittany S. Cost, Pearson G. Cost. BA, Trinity Coll., 1990; JD, U. Maine, 1996. Bar: Maine 1996. Legal vol. Maine Audubon Soc., Falmouth, 1993; student atty. Maine Sch. Law, Environ. Law Clinic, Portland, 1994; legal asst. Maine Health Care Fin. Com., Augusta, 1994; legal intern Maine Atty. Gen.'s Office, Augusta, 1995; legal vol. Maine Atty. Gen., Augusta, 1996; staff atty., advocate Maine Audubon Soc., Falmouth, 1997—. Mem. Citizens Adv. Com. to Secure the Future of Maine's Wildlife and Fish, Augusta, 1999—2001, Mercury-Added Products Adv. Com., Augusta, 2001—. Mem. Christian Edn. Com., 1st Parish Ch., Brunswick, Maine, 1989—, co-chair, 2001—03; mem. long range planning com. 1st Parish Church, Brunswick, Maine, 2003—; Bd. dirs. Friends of Merry Meeting Bay, Bowdoin, Maine, 1999—2002. Mem.: Maine State Bar Assn. Home: 6 Aspen Dr Brunswick ME 04011 Office: Maine Audubon Soc 20 Gilsland Farm Rd Falmouth ME 04105

BURNS, JOHN MACDOUGAL, III, lawyer; b. Ft. Worth, Aug. 23, 1933; s. John MacDougal and Mary Tabitha (Kenney) B.; m. Lorraine Lovell, Aug. 31, 1957; 1 son (dec.). A.B., Columbia U., 1955, M.A., 1960, LL.B., 1961. Bar: N.Y. 1961, U.S. Dist. Ct. (so., ea. and no. dists.) N.Y. 1962, U.S. Ct. Appeals (2d cir.) 1963, U.S. Ct. Appeals (3d cir.) 1980, U.S. Ct. Appeals (6th cir.) 1989. Assoc. Hughes, Hubbard, Blair & Reed, N.Y.C., 1961-68; legis. counsel to State Senator Whitney North Seymour, Jr., N.Y.C., 1965-68; ptnr. Spear & Hill, N.Y.C., 1969-70, 71-74; exec. asst. U.S. atty. So. Dist. N.Y., 1970-71; ptnr. Alexander, Katz & Rosenberg, N.Y.C., 1974-76; sole practice, N.Y.C., 1976-81; ptnr. Burns & Fox, N.Y.C., 1981-86; sole practice, 1986-87, 94—; ptnr. Burns, Beck & Stumpp, 1988, Burns & Beck, 1989-93. Mem. ABA, Assn. of Bar of City of N.Y., Gipsy Tr. Club (Carmel, N.Y.) Democrat. Federal civil litigation, State civil litigation, Corporate, general. Home: 33 Greenwich Ave Apt 7H New York NY 10014-2788

BURNS, MARVIN GERALD, lawyer; b. Los Angeles, July 3, 1930; s. Milton and Belle (Cytron) B.; m. Barbara Irene Fisher, Aug. 23, 1953; children: Scott Douglas, Jody Lynn, Bradley Frederick. BA, U. Ariz., 1951; JD, Harvard U., 1954. Bar: Calif. 1955. Bd. dirs. Inner City Arts for Inner City Children. With AUS, 1955-56. Mem.: Beverly Hills Tennis, Sycamore Park Tennis. General civil litigation, Land use and zoning (including planning), Property, real (including real estate development, water), Commercial, contracts (including sales of goods; commercial financing). Home: 10350 Wilshire Blvd Ph 4 Los Angeles CA 90024-4734 Office: 9107 Wilshire Blvd Ste 800 Beverly Hills CA 90210-5533 E-mail: mburns@lurie-zepeda.com.

BURNS, MICHAEL WILLIAM, lawyer former state legislator; b. Balt., Feb. 16, 1958; s. William Charles and Helen Kearns Burns. BS magna cum laude, U. Md., Towson, 1980; JD with honors, U. Md., 1983. Clk. Circuit Ct. Judge, 1983-84; atty. Balt., 1984—; Rep. state del. State of Md., 1995-99. Mem., ranking Rep. house jud. com. 1997-99, mem. subcom. on civil law and procedure, 1995-99; devel. and comm. cons. Mem. Md. State Rep. Ctrl. Com., 1978-81, 86-90, 94-97, 98-2001; legal counsel Md. State Rep. Party, 1987-88; exec. dir. Dole for Pres. Com., Md., 1987-88, Md. State Rep. Party, 1988-89; bd. dirs. Md. Underage Drinking Prevention Coalition, 1995-2002, Chesapeake Ctr. for Creative Arts, 1996-2002; del. Rep. Nat. Conv., 1988, 96; past pres. adv. bd. Salvation Army of Glen Burnie, Md., 1999; mem. Mothers Against Drunk Drivers. Mem.: KC. Home: 201 Homewood Rd Linthicum MD 21090-2605

BURNS, RICHARD GORDON, retired lawyer, writer, consultant; b. Stockton, Calif., May 15, 1925; s. Earl Gordon and Alberta Viola (Whale) B.; m. Eloise Estelle Beil, June 23, 1951 (div. May 25, 1985); children: Kenneth Charles, Donald Gordon. AA with honors, U. Calif., Berkeley, 1948; AB, Stanford U., 1949, JD, 1951. Atty. Clausen & Burns, San Francisco, 1951—61; cons. Wyo. Pacific Oil Co., L.A., 1956—; pvt. practice Corte Madera, Calif., 1961—86; pub. Good Book Pub., Kihei, Hawaii, 1991—; cons. Universal Network Identification Tech., Inc., Hawaii, 2001—. Bd. dirs. Clean Fuels Hawaii. Co-author (with Bill Pittman): Courage To Change, 1998; author (as Dick B.): New Light on Alcoholism: God, Sam Shoemaker and A.A., 1999; author: The Akron Genesis of Alcoholics Anonymous, 1998, Anne Smith's Journal, 1998, Dr. Bob and His Library, 1998, The Good Book and The Big Book: AA's Roots in the Bible, 1998, The Oxford Group and Alcoholics Anonymous, 1998, That Amazing Grace, 1996, The Books Early AAs Read for Spiritual Growth, 1999, Good Morning!Quiet Time, Morning Watch, Meditation, and Early A.A., 1998, Turning Point: A History of Early A.A.'s Spiritual Roots and Successes, 1997, Utilizing A.A.'s Spiritual Roots for Recovery Today, 1999, The Golden Text of A.A., 1999, By the Power of God, 2000, Why Early A.A. Succeeded: The Good Book in Alcoholics Anonymous Yesterday and today, 2001, An 11 Year Project, 2001, Making Known the Biblical Roots of A.A., 2002, God and Alcoholism: A Growing Opportunity in the 21st Century, 2002, Hope!: The Story of Geraldine Owen Delaney, Alina Lodge and Recovery, 2002, Cured! A Proven Solution for Alcoholics and Addicts, 2003, Twelve Steps for You, 2003, Comments at First Nationwide AA History Conference, 2003; editor: Stanford Law Rev., 1950. Dir. Almonte Sanitary Bd., Marin County, Calif., 1962-64; v.p./sec. Lions Club, Corte Madera, 1961-64; pres. Almonte Improvement Club, Mill Valley, Calif., 1960, Cmty. Ch., Mill Valley, 1971, C. of C., Corte Madera, 1972, Corte Madera Ctr. Merchant Co., 1975, Redwoods Retirement Ctr., Mill Valley, 1980. Sgt. U.S. Army, 1943-46. Mem. Am. Hist. Assn., Alcohol and Temperance History Group, Authors Guild, Maui Writers Guild, Christian Assn. for Psychol. Studies, Assn. Med. Edn. and Rsch. in Substance Abuse, Stanford Alumni Assn., Phi Beta Kappa, Delta Tau Delta, Phi Delta Phi. Avocations: travel, bible study, swimming, walking. Estate planning, General practice, Non-profit and tax-exempt organizations. Office: PO Box 837 Kihei HI 96753-0837 E-mail: dickb@dickb.com.

BURNS, RICHARD OWEN, lawyer; b. Bklyn., Nov. 16, 1942; s. James I. and Ida (Shore) B.; m. Lynda Gail Birnbaum, Dec. 24, 1967; children: Marc Adam, Lisa Ann, Susan Danielle. BS, Wilkes Coll., 1964; JD, Bklyn. Law Sch., 1967. Bar: N.Y. 1967, U.S. Dist. Ct. (so. dist.) N.Y. 1969, U.S. Dist. Ct. (ea. dist.) N.Y. 1979. Assoc. Clune & O'Brien, Mineola, N.Y., 1967-73, Clune, Burns, White & Nelson, Harrison, N.Y., 1973-78; ptnr. Schurr & Burns, P.C., Spring Valley, N.Y., 1978-98; pvt. practice, Chestnut Ridge, N.Y., 1998—. Bd. dirs. Rockland County unit Am. Cancer Soc., West Nyack, N.Y., 1979-85, 86-92, pres., 1981-83; bd. dirs. Hudson Valley Health System Agy., Sterling Park, N.Y., 1979, Vets. Meml. Assn., Congers, N.Y., 1980-86; mem. Wilkes U. Coun., Wilkes-Barre, Pa., 1995—. Recipient Reese D. Jones award Wilkes Coll. Jr. C. of C., 1964. Mem. Rockland

County Bar Assn., N.Y. State Bar Assn., N.Y. State Trial Lawyers Assn. Democrat. Jewish. State civil litigation, Labor (including EEOC, Fair Labor Standards Act, labor-management relations, NLRB, OSHA), Personal injury (including property damage). Home: 140 Waters Edge Congers NY 10920-2622 Office: 500 Chestnut Ridge Rd Chestnut Ridge NY 10977-5646

BURNS, RICHARD RAMSEY, lawyer; b. Duluth, Minn., May 3, 1946; s. Herbert Morgan and Janet (Strobel) B.; Jennifer, Brian; m. Elizabeth Murphy, June 15, 1984. BA with distinction, U. Mich., 1968, JD magna cum laude, 1971. Bar: Calif. 1972, U.S. Dist. Ct. (no. dist.) Calif. 1972, U.S. Ct. Appeals (9th cir.) 1972, Minn. 1976, U.S. Dist. Ct. Minn. 1976, Wis. 1983, U.S. Tax. Ct. 1983. Assoc. Orrick, Herrington, Rowley & Sutcliffe, San Francisco, 1971-76; ptnr. Hanft, Fride, P.A., Duluth, 1976—. Gen. counsel Murphy, McGinnis Media, Duluth, Minn., 1982—, Murphy TV Stas., Madison, Wis., 1982—. Chmn. Duluth-Superior Area Comty. Found., 1988-90; chair United Way of Greater Duluth, Inc., 1998-99; bd. dirs. Miller Dwan Found., Northland Coll., Ashland, Wis. Fellow Am. Coll. Trust and Estate Counsel; mem. Calif. Bar Assn., Wis. Bar Assn., Minn. Bar Assn. (past. exec. com., past chmn. probate and trust coun.), 11th Dist. Bar Assn. (past pres., past chmn. ethics com.), Arrowhead Estate Planning Coun. (pres. 1980), Northland Country Club (pres. 1982), Boulders Club, Kitchi Gammi Club (bd. dirs.). Republican. Avocations: travel, golf, tennis, fishing. Communications, Estate planning, Pension, profit-sharing, and employee benefits. Home: 180 Paine Farm Rd Duluth MN 55804-2609 Office: Hanft Fride PA 1000 First Bank Pl 130 W Superior St Ste 1000 Duluth MN 55802-2056 E-mail: rrb@hanftlaw.com.

BURNS, SANDRA, lawyer, educator; b. Bryan, Tex., Aug. 9, 1949; d. Clyde W. and Bert (Rychlik) B.; 1 son, Scott. BS, U. Houston, 1970; MA, U. Tex., 1972, PhD, 1975; JD, St. Mary's U., 1978. Bar: Tex. 1978; cert. tchr., adminstr., supr. instrn., Tex. Tchr. Austin (Tex.) Ind. Sch. Dist., 1970-71; prof. child devel./family life and home econs. edn. Coll. Nutrition, Textiles and Human Devel. Tex. Women's U., Denton, 1974-75; instrnl. devel. asst. Office of Ednl. Resources divsn. instr U. Tex. Health Sci., San Antonio, 1976-77; legis. aide William T. Moore Tex. Senate, Austin, fall 1978, com. clk.-counsel, spring 1979; legal cons. Colombotti & Assocs., Aberdeen, Scotland, 1980; corp. counsel 1st Internat. Oil and Gas, Inc., 1983; contracted atty. Humble Exploration Co., Inc., Dallas, 1984; assoc. Smith, Underwood, Dallas, 1986-88; pvt. practice Dallas, 1988—. Atty. contracted to Republic Energy Inc., Bryan, Tex., 1981-82, ARCO, Dallas, 1985; vis. lectr. Tex. A&M U., fall 1981, summer, 1981; lectr. home econ. Our Lady of the Lake Coll., San Antonio, fall, 1975. Contbr. articles on law and edn. to profl. jours. Mem. Coll. of the State Bar of Tex., Phi Delta Kappa. Office: Preston Commons West 300 8117 Preston Rd Dallas TX 75225 E-mail: burns@attorney-mediator.com.

BURNS, STEVEN DWIGHT, judge; b. Marshalltown, Iowa, Mar. 20, 1948; s. Dwight Harry and Cleo Maxine (England) B.; 1 child, Natalie Stone. BArch, U. Nebr., 1971, JD, 1973. Bar: Nebr. 1973, U.S. Dist. Ct. Nebr. 1973, U.S. Ct. Appeals (8th cir.) 1980, U.S. Supreme Ct. 1985. Sole practice, Lincoln, Nebr., 1973-74; assoc. Luedtke, Radcliffe, Burns, Lincoln, Nebr., 1974-77; ptnr. Noren & Burns, Lincoln, 1978-82, Burns & Grenier, P.C., Lincoln, 1982-88, Burns & Assocs., P.C., 1988-97; judge Nebr. Dist. Ct., Lincoln, 1997—. Dem. candidate for Congress from 1st Dist., Nebr., 1986; chmn. Gov.'s Coun., 1991-97. Recipient Outstanding Service award Nebr. Assn. Pub. Employees, 1983. Office: Nebr State Dist Ct PO Box 30333 575 S 10th St Lincoln NE 68508-2810

BURNS, TERRENCE MICHAEL, lawyer; b. Evergreen Park, Ill., Mar. 2, 1954; s. Jerome Joseph Burns and Eileen Beatrice (Collins) Neary; m. Therese Porucznik, Mar. 24, 1979; children: David, Steven, Theresa, Daniel. BA, Loyola U., Chgo., 1975; JD, DePaul U., 1978. Bar: Ill. 1978, U.S. Dist. Ct. (no. dist.) Ill. 1978, U.S. Ct. Appeals (7th cir.) 1979, U.S. Supreme Ct. 1985, U.S. Dist. Ct. (no. dist.) Ind. 1989. Asst. state's atty. Cook County, Chgo., 1979-85; ptnr. Rooks, Pitts & Poust, Chgo., 1985—. Mem. inquiry bd. Ill. Supreme Ct. Atty. Registration and Disciplinary Commn., Chgo., 1986-90, chair hearing bd., 1990—. Mem. ABA (ann. meeting adv. com.), Chgo. Bar Assn. (treas. 1997-99, 2d v.p. 1999-2000, 1st v.p. 2000-01, pres. 2001—, bd. mgrs. 1995-97, chair fin. com. 1997-99, criminal law com. 1979-83, jud. candidate evaluation com. 1981-86, 87-95, chmn. investigation divsn. evaluation com. 1991-92, chmn. hearing divsn. evaluation com. 1992-93, gen. chmn. 1993-95, ct. liaison com. 1993-95, tort reform subcom. 1997), Chgo. Bar Found. (bd. dirs. 1999-2000). Roman Catholic. General civil litigation, Personal injury (including property damage). Office: Rooks Pitts & Poust 10 S Wacker Dr Ste 2300 Chicago IL 60606-7407

BURNSTEIN, DANIEL, lawyer; b. Hartford, Conn., Oct. 12, 1946; s. Lawrence J. and Margaret (Le Vien) B. AB, U. Calif., Berkeley, 1968; JD cum laude, New Eng. Sch. Law, 1975. Bar: Mass. 1975, U.S. Dist. Ct. Mass. 1976, U.S. Ct. Appeals (1st cir.) 1976. Pres. Beacon Expert Systems, Inc., 1989-99. Dir. Interactive Video Project Harvard Law Sch., Cambridge, 1985-89, clin. instr.; pres. Ctr. for Atomic Radiation Studies, Acton, Mass., 1982—; advisor Am. Mgmt. Assn. for Negotiation Curriculum to Mgrs., 1993; pres.-COO BuzzIT.com, 1999—. Editor: The Digital MBA, 1995. Mem. Mass. Adv. Coun. on Radiation Protection, 1990—2002. Mem.: ABA. Communications, Computer, Private international. Office: 35 Gardner Rd Brookline MA 02445-4512

BURR, FRANCIS HARDON, lawyer; b. Nahant, Mass., July 21, 1914; AB cum laude, Harvard U., 1935, LL.B, 1938, LL.D., 1982. Bar: Mass. 1938. Assoc. Ropes & Gray, Boston, 1938-47, ptnr., 1947-87, of counsel, 1988—. Dir. emeritus AMR Corp., Corning, Inc., Raytheon Co. Hon. trustee Mass. Gen. Hosp., McLean Hosp.; pres. Humane Soc., Commonweath of Mass.; dir emeritus Cotting Sch. Fellow Harvard Coll., 1954-82; sr. fellow Harvard Coll., 1971-82 Fellow AAAS, Am. Bar Found; mem. ABA, Boston Bar Assn., Am. Law Inst. Corporate, general. Office: Ropes & Gray One International Pl Boston MA 02110 E-mail: fhburr@ropesgray.com.

BURR, SCOTT ALLEN, lawyer; b. Reading, Pa., May 2, 1964; s. Walter B. III and Patricia (Lord) Rothenberger. BA, Albright Coll., 1985; JD, The Dickinson Sch. Law, 1988; LLM in Internat. Law, Georgetown U., 1994; LLM in Trial Advocacy, Temple U. Law Sch., 1999. Bar: Pa. 1988, U.S. Dist. Ct. (ea. dist.) Pa. 1988, N.J. 1988, U.S. Dist. Ct. N.J. 1988. Sr. assoc. Spector, Gadon & Rosen, Phila., 1994—2000; sr. counsel Astigarraga Davis, Miami, 2002—. V.p. Nite & Day Mag., Ltd., Phila., 1990—. Author: (published law review article) 15 U. Pa. J. Int'l. Bus. L. 221 (1994), 6 Dick. J. Int.'l L. Active 237, 1987, ACLU, Phila., 1989—. Scholar, Albright Coll., 1985. Mem. ABA (internat. law sect., litigation and ins. and torts sect.), Fla. Bar Assn., Dade County Bar Assn. Democrat. Lutheran. Avocations: sailing, equestrian riding, body building, water-skiing. General civil litigation, Private international, Labor (including EEOC, Fair Labor Standards Act, labor-management relations, NLRB, OSHA). Office: Astigarraga Davis 701 Brickell Ave Ste 1650 Miami FL 33131 Fax: 305-372-8202. E-mail: sburr@astidavis.com.

BURR, TIMOTHY FULLER, lawyer; b. New Bedford, Mass., Oct. 18, 1952; s. John Thayer and Joan (Ames) B.; m. Marguerite Conti, Feb. 28, 1981; children: Emily Ames, Lisa Conti, David Thayer. AB, Harvard U., 1975; JD, U. Miami, 1979. Bar: La. 1979, Tex. 1993, Fla. 1996, U.S. Supreme Ct., U.S. Cir. Ct., U.S. Dist. Ct. Admiralty and litigation atty. Galloway, Johnson, Tompkins, Burr & Smith, New Orleans, Houston, Lafayette, Gulf Breeze, 1979—, mng. dir. firm New Orleans, Gulf Breeze, 1987—. Past chmn. St. Tammary Parish Zoning Bd.; mem. Gulf Breeze Devel. Rev. Bd.; pres. Optimist Club Gulf Breeze, Fla., 2001-02. Mem. La. Bar Assn., Tex. Bar Assn., Fla. Bar Assn., Maritime Law Assn. U.S., Tammany Yacht Club, Pensacola Yacht Club. Republican. Admiralty, General civil litigation, Personal injury (including property damage). Home: 281 Plantation Hill Rd Gulf Breeze FL 32561-4050 Office: 1101 Gulf Breeze Pky Ste 2 Gulf Breeze FL 32561-4468

BURROW, ALISTAIR STEWART, solicitor; b. Glasgow, Scotland, Oct. 14, 1951; s. James Edward and Helen Dickson (White) B.; m. Mary Anne Lockhart Crombie, Sept. 15, 1978; children: Sheona, Kirsty, Mairi. MA with hons., U. Glasgow, 1973, LLB, 1976. Notary public, 1978. Apprentice Boyds, Glasgow, 1976—78, asst. solicitor, 1978-81, Neill Clerk & Murray, Greenock, Scotland, 1981-82, ptnr. Glasgow, 1982-90, McClure Naismith, Glasgow, 1990—2001, Tods Murray WS, Glasgow, 2001—. Tutor law faculty U. Strathclyde, Scotland, 1980-83, U. Glasgow, 1988-91. Co-author: International Banking Law and Regulation, Offshore Financing: Security and Insolvency. Clerk Inc. Hammermen of Glasgow, 1988—; hon. treasurer Global Fellowship of Christian Youth, Eng., 1994-. Mem. Law Soc. Scotland, Internat. Bar Assn., Assn. Bus. Recovery Profls. Presbyterian. Avocations: youth leadership, hill walking, reading. Bankruptcy, Corporate, general, Mergers and acquisitions. Office: Tods Murray WS 33 Bothwell St Glasgow G2 6NL Scotland Fax: 0141 275 4781. E-mail: alistair.burrow@todsmurray.com.

BURROWS, JAY EDWARD, lawyer; b. Council Bluffs, Iowa, Aug. 2, 1949; s. David E. and R. Nerine (Harris) B.; m. Valrie J. Wheaton, Oct. 14, 1972; children: Clifford D., John H. BA, Mich. State U., 1973; JD, U. Mich., 1976. Bar: Mich. 1976. Ptnr. Prince, Nicholas & Burrows, LLP, Shelby, Mich., 1976—. Pres. Muskegon-Oceana chpt. ARC, 1985-86; bd. dirs. West Mich. Shores coun. Boy Scouts Am., 1977--2001. Mem. State Bar Assn. Mich., Rotary, Shelby Optimist Club (pres. 1990-91, 2002-03). General practice, Probate (including wills, trusts), Property, real (including real estate development, water). Office: Prince Nicholas & Burrows LLP Nicholas & Burrows 191 N Michigan Ave Shelby MI 49455-1024

BURROWS, MICHAEL DONALD, lawyer; b. Oak Park, Ill., May 23, 1944; s. Milford Denton and Helen Jean (Spitali) B.; m. Sandi Miller, Feb. 6, 1982; 1 child, Matthew Denton. BA, Williams Coll., 1967; JD, N.Y. Law Sch., 1973. Bar: N.Y. 1974, U.S. Dist. Ct. (ea. and so. dists.) N.Y. 1974, U.S. Ct. Appeals (2d cir.) 1978, U.S. Supreme Ct. 1981. Assoc. Baker & McKenzie, N.Y.C., 1973-80, ptnr., 1980-95, of counsel, 1995-99, mem. internat. exec. com., 1986-88; ptnr. Winston & Strawn, N.Y.C., 1999—, exec. com., chmn. N.Y. Litigation dept., 2000—. Co-author: The Practice of International Litigation, 1992. With USMC, 1968-70. Mem. ABA, Assn.of Bar of City of N.Y. Federal civil litigation, General civil litigation, State civil litigation. Office: Winston & Strawn 200 Park Ave New York NY 10166-0005

BURSKY, HERMAN AARON, lawyer; b. Bklyn., Jan. 16, 1938; s. Abraham S. and Anna R. (Polstein) B.; m. Dolores Kelner, Sept. 3, 1961; children: Daniel Jay, Jennifer Dina. BA, B in Hebrew Lit., Yeshiva U., 1959; LLB, Cornell U., 1962. Bar: N.Y. 1963. Assoc. Levin & Weintraub, N.Y.C., 1963-69; atty. CIT Fin. Corp., N.Y.C., 1969-70; assoc. Otterbourg, Steindler, Houston & Rosen, P.C., N.Y.C., 1970-71; ptnr. Shea & Gould, N.Y.C., 1971-91, Rosenman & Colin, N.Y.C., 1991-98; counsel Fischbein, Badillo, Wagner and Harding, 2000—. Contbg. author: Practical Guide to Bankruptcy and Debtor Relief, 1964. Served as pvt. U.S. Army, 1962-63. Mem. ABA, N.Y. State Bar Assn., Fed. Bar Council, Assn. Comml. Fin. Attys., N.Y. County Lawyers Assn. (bankruptcy com. 1973-80). Clubs: Inwood Country (N.Y.). Jewish. Bankruptcy, Commercial, contracts (including sales of goods; commercial financing). Home: 25 Muriel Ave Lawrence NY 11559-1810 Office: Fischbein Badillo Wagner Harding 909 3rd Ave Fl 18 New York NY 10022-4731 E-mail: hbursky@fbwhlaw.com.

BURSTEIN, RICHARD JOEL, lawyer; b. Detroit, Feb. 9, 1945; s. Harry Seymour and Florence (Rosen) B.; m. Gayle Lee Handmaker, Dec. 21, 1969; children: Stephanie Faith, Melissa Amy. Grad., U. Mich., 1966; JD, Wayne State U., 1969. Bar: Mich. 1969, U.S. Ct. Appeals (ea. dist.) Mich. 1969. Ptnr. Smith Miro Hirsch & Brody, Detroit, 1969-81, Honigman Miller Schwartz & Cohn, Detroit, 1981-96. Bd. dirs. Sandy Corp., Troy, Mich.; bd. dirs. Met. Affairs Corp., Detroit; co-chmn. Artrain. Mem. Am. Coll. Real Estate Lawyers. Property, real (including real estate development, water). Office: Honigman Miller Schwartz & Cohn 32270 Telegraph Rd Ste 225 Bingham Farms MI 48025

BURT, JEFFREY AMSTERDAM, lawyer; b. Phila., Apr. 27, 1944; s. Samuel Matthew and Esther (Amsterdam) B.; m. Sandra Cas, Dec. 17, 1967; children: Stephen, Daniel, Jonathan, Andrew. BA, Princeton, 1966; LLB, Yale U., 1970; MA in Econs., 1970. Bar: Md. 1971, DC 1971. Law clk. to judge U.S. Ct. Appeals (4th cir.), Balt., 1970-71; assoc. Arnold & Porter, Washington, 1971-77; ptnr., 1978—. Adj. prof. law Georgetown U., 1987-95; frequent lectr. Pres., Green Acres, Inc. Ind. Sch., Rockville, Md., 1984-86. Author: (with others) International Joint Ventures, 1986, 2nd edit., 1992; co-editor: Joint Ventures with Internat. Ptnrs., 1997. Mem. ABA (co-chairperson NIS Law Com. Sect. Internat. Law and Practice 1992-98), Russian Am. C. of C. (dir., sec.). Administrative and regulatory, Federal civil litigation, Private international. Office: Arnold & Porter 555 12th St NW Washington DC 20004-1206

BURTON, CHARLES HENNING, lawyer; b. Washington, Nov. 25, 1915; s. Charles Henry and Bessie R. (Harrell) B.; m. Mary Sheppard, Sept. 6, 1941; children: Nancy Leigh Burton Wysling, Susan C. Burton Roberts, Mary Ellen Burton Graves, Charles S. Attended, George Washington U., 1937-41; LLB, Am. U., 1936, LLM, 1937. Bar: D.C. 1936, Md. 1957. Gen. counsel D.C. Unemployment Compensation Bd., 1938-42; mem. firm MacCracken & O'Rourke, Washington, 1946-50; mem. Law Offices Robert Ash, Washington, 1950-56; gen. partner Bauersfeld, Burton, Hendricks and Vanderhoff, Bethesda, Md., 1956—. Ltd. ptnr. A.W.S. Assocs., S & H Assocs.; pres., dir. North Shore Corp., Links, Inc., Charles H. Burton, P.A.; dir. Mattos, Inc., Sisk Mailing Svc. Inc., Sisk Fulfillment, Inc.; gen. counsel Bapt. World Alliance, McLean, Va., 1958, Calvary Bapt. Ch., 1950. Bd. dirs. Jovius Found., Mustard Seed Found., F.W. Harris Found. for Personal Evangelism; trustee Kendall Mission Fund; v.p. Cen. Union Mission; nat. chmn. World Peace Through Law of World Jurist Assn. Comdr. USNR, 1942-46. Fellow Am. Bar Found.; mem. Am. Bar Assn. (editor Young Lawyer 1946-48, nat. sec. Jr. Bar 1949, nat. vice-chmn. 1950, nat. chmn. 1951, ho. of dels. 1952-59), Sigma Chi, Sigma Nu Phi. Clubs: Montgomery County Country. Estate planning, Probate (including wills, trusts), Corporate taxation. Home: 21600 Davis Mill Rd Germantown MD 20876-4418 Office: Bauersfeld Burton Hendricks & Vanderhoff 7101 Wisconsin Ave Ste 1011 Bethesda MD 20814-4805

BURTON, DAVID K. lawyer; b. Phila., July 11, 1970; s. Kenneth Burton and Georgia May Peters; m. Tyler Katherine Bradford, Dec. 28, 1993; children: Joshua David, Alexander Bradford. BA, Ithaca Coll., 1993; JD, Georgetown U., 1996. Bar: Pa. 1996, N.J. 1996, U.S. Tax Ct. 1997. Atty. Morgan, Lewis & Bolkius LLP, Phila., 1996—2000; tax counsel GE Capital Corp., Stamford, Conn., 2000—. Contbr. articles to profl. jours. Dailey scholar, Georgetown U. Law Ctr., 1994. Mem.: ABA (tax sect.), Phi Kappa Phi. Personal income taxation, Finance, Aviation. Office: GE Capital Corp 777 Long Ridge Rd Stamford CT 06927

BURTON, JOHN PAUL (JACK BURTON), lawyer; b. New Orleans, Feb. 26, 1943; s. John Paul and Nancy (Key) Burton; m. Anne Ward; children: Jennifer, Michele Kfouri, Marcos Maiken, Susanna, Derek, Catherine. BBA magna cum laude, La. Tech. U., 1965; LLB, Harvard U., 1968. Bar: N.Mex. 1968, U.S. Dist. Ct. N.Mex. 1968, U.S. Ct. Appeals (10th cir.) 1973, U.S. Supreme Ct. 1979. Assoc. Rodey, Dickason, Sloan, Akin & Robb, Albuquerque, 1968-74, dir., 1974—, chmn. comml. dept., 1980-81, mng. dir. Santa Fe, 1986-90. Settlement facilitator N.Mex. Second Jud. Dist., 1997—. Co-author: Boundary Disputes in New Mexico, 1992, Unofficial Update on the Uniform Ltd. Liability Co. Act, 1994. Pres. Brunn Sch., 1987—89; active Nat. Coun. Commrs. on Uniform State Laws, 1989—, drafting com. UCC Article 5, 1990—95, UCC Article 9, 1993—95, UCC Articles 2 and 2A, 1999—2001; active Power-of Sale Foreclosure Act, 1999—2002, Uniform Ltd. Liability Co. Act, 1993—95, Legis. Coun., 1991—99, divsn. chmn., 1993—95, 1999—2001, 1995—99; chmn. drafting com. on uniform durable powers of atty. Nat. Coun. Commrs. on Uniform State Laws, 2003—; joint editl. bds. Uninc. Bus. Orgns., 1994—95, Trust and Estates Acts, 1999—2001. Fellow Am. Coll. Real Estate Lawyers; mem. ABA, Am. Law Inst. (rep. to UCC Article 5 drafting com. 1992-95), Am. Coll. Mortgage Attys., Am. Arbitration Assn. (mem. comml. panel arbitrators), N.Mex. State Bar Assn. (chmn. comml. litig. and antitrust sect. 1985-86). Federal civil litigation, Commercial, contracts (including sales of goods; commercial financing), Property, real (including real estate development, water). Office: Rodey Dickason Sloan Akin & Robb PA PO Box 1357 Santa Fe NM 87504-1357 E-mail: jpburton@rodey.com.

BURTON, JOSEPH RANDOLPH, lawyer; b. Houston, Sept. 10, 1951; s. Joseph Milburn and Lee (Hillegeist) B.; m. Regina Helen O'Brien, Mar. 13, 1982; children: Cara Eileen, Ross Andrew. BS, Yale U., 1974; JD, South Tex. Coll., Houston, 1982. Bar: Tex. 1983, U.S. Dist. Ct. (so. and ea. dists.)Tex. 1983, U.S. Supreme Ct. 1996. Asst. dist. atty. Harris County Dist. Atty's Office, Houston, 1984-87; litigation assoc. Kennedy, Sanford, Kuhl & Hackney, Houston, 1987-90; ptnr. Moerer & Burton, Houston, 1990—. Contbr. articles to profl. jours.; featured on TV shows, including ABC News Prime Time Live, 20/20, HBO, Discovery Channel, Donahue, Good Morning Am. Founder, spokesperson Justice for Children, Houston, 1987—, Citizens Response Group; bd. dirs. Houston Area Women's Ctr., 1987-89, Aid to Victims of Domestic Abuse, 1987, Children's Trust Fund of Tex. Coun., 1994-98; child advocate mem. Tex. Child Fatality Rev. Com. Recipient AIA Pres.'s award, 1998, Victims' Resource Inst. with U. Houston Kim Houston award, 1999; named Outstanding Young Lawyer of Houston, Houston Young Lawyers' Assn., 1987-88, Mayor's award Outstanding Vol. Svc., 1998; finalist 5 Outstnding Young Houstonians, Houston Jr. C. of C., 1988. Fellow Tex. Bar Found.; mem. ABA, Houston Bar Assn., South Tex. Coll. of Law Alumni Assn., Garland Walker Inns of Ct. Democrat. Avocation: golf. General civil litigation, General practice, Juvenile. Home: 18418 Snowwood Dr Spring TX 77388-5100 Office: Moerer and Burton 440 Louisiana St Ste 1150 Houston TX 77002-1634

BURTON, RANDALL JAMES, lawyer; b. Sacramento, Feb. 4, 1950; s. Edward J. and Bernice Mae (Overton) B.; m. Kimberly D. Rogers, Apr. 29, 1989; children: Kelly Jacqueline, Andrew Jameson. BA, Rutgers U., 1972; JD, Southwestern U., 1975. Bar: Calif. 1976, U.S. Dist. Ct. (ea. dist.) Calif. 1976, U.S. Dist. Ct. (no. dist.) Calif. 1990, Supreme Ct. 1991. Assoc. Brekke & Mathews, Citrus Heights, Calif., 1976; pvt. practice Sacramento, 1976—93; ptnr. Burton & White, Sacramento, 1993—; judge pro tem Sacramento Samll Claims Ct., 1982—. Bd. dirs. North Highlands Recreation and Park Dist., 1978—86, Family Svc. Agy. Sacramento, 1991—96; active local bd. 22 Selective Svc., 1982—2001; active 20-30 Club Sacramento, 1979—90, pres., 1987. Recipient Disting. Citizen award Golden Empire Coun., Boy Scouts Am. Mem.: Sacramento Young Lawyers Assn., Sacramento Bar Assn., Rotary (pres. Foothill-Highlands club 1980—81). Presbyterian. Family and matrimonial, Personal injury (including property damage), Probate (including wills, trusts). Office: 1540 River Park Dr Ste 224 Sacramento CA 95815-4609

BUS, ROGER JAY, lawyer; b. Kalamazoo, Mich., Oct. 15, 1953; s. Charles J. and Sena (Wolthuis) B.; m. Lida Margaret Sell, Aug. 27, 1977; children: Emily Lynn, Stephen Charles. Student, Calvin Coll., 1971-73; BA, U. Mich., 1975; JD, U. Toledo, 1979. Bar: Mich. 1979, U.S. Dist. Ct. (we. dist.) Mich. 1979. Law clk. to presiding justice Kalamazoo Cir. Ct., 1978; intern Toledo Legal Aid, 1979; staff atty. Legal Aid Bur. SW Mich., Kalamazoo, 1979-81; assoc. Stanley, Davidoff & Gray, Kalamazoo, 1981-83; owner, atty. Debt Relief Law Ctr., Kalamazoo, 1983—. Deacon Ref. Bapt. Ch., Kalamazoo, 1983-85; precinct del. Kalamazoo County Reps., 1986-88; bd. dirs., atty. Kalamazoo Gospel Mission, 1983-86, v.p., 1997—, bd. dirs., 1996—, chmn. bd., 2000-02; adult Sunday sch. tchr. Calvary Bible Ch., elder, 1988-91, 92-98, elder clk., 1989-91, 97, 98, missions coun., 1999—; mem. missions team Richland Bible Ch., 2000—, adult Sunday Sch. tchr., 2001--, elder, 2002--; team mem. Operation Mobilization, Grenada, 2002. Mem. Fed. Bar Assn. (lectr. western dist. Mich. bankruptcy div. 1990-92, 97, 2001, spkr. we. dist. Mich. 2001), Am. Bankruptcy Inst., Mich. Bar Assn., Kalamazoo County Bar Assn., Nat. Assn. Chpt. 13 Trustees. Avocations: global missions, reading, religious book collecting, gospel music, evangelism. Bankruptcy. Home: 5330 Stoney Brook Rd Kalamazoo MI 49009-3850 Office: Debt Relief Law Ctr 903 E Cork St Kalamazoo MI 49001-4875

BUSBEE, KLINE DANIEL, JR., law educator, lawyer; b. Macon, Ga., Mar. 14, 1933; s. Kline Daniel and Bernice (Anderson) B.; children: Rodgers Christopher, Jon Edward. BBA, So. Meth. U., 1961, JD, 1962. Ptnr. Worsham, Forsythe, Sampels & Busbee, Dallas, 1962-70, Locke, Purnell, Rain & Harrell, P.C., Dallas, 1970-98, Gibson, Dunn & Crutcher, Dallas, 1998-99. Adj. prof. law So. Meth. U. Sch. Law, 1974—83, 1992; adj. prof. pub. internat. law U. Tex. Grad. Sch. Mgmt., Dallas; bd. dirs. Atmos Energy Corp.; vis. sr. fellow Ctr. for Comml. Law Studies, Queen Mary U. London, 2001—, Brit. Inst. Internat. and Comparative Law, Russell Sq., 2001—; sr. fellow So. Meth. U. Sch. Law Inst. Internat. Banking and Fin., 2001—. Mem.: ABA, Dallas Com. on Fgn. Rels., Tex. Bar Assn., Dallas Petroleum Club, Snowmass Club, Dallas Country Club. Home: 4360 San Carlos St Dallas TX 75205-2052 E-mail: danbusbeelaw@msn.com.

BUSBY, DAVID, lawyer; b. Ada, Okla., Jan. 29, 1926; s. Orel and Hope B.; m. Mary Beth Baker, June 9, 1962; children: Helen Hope Busby Burleigh, Alison Sears Busby Vareika, Robert David, John Orel. BA, 1948; LL.B., Okla. U., 1951. Bar: Okla. 1950, D.C. 1959, N.Y. 1959, U.S. Supreme Ct. 1959. Assoc. Busby, Harrell & Trice, Ada, 1951-55; counsel Subcom. on Automobile Mktg. Practices, Com. on Interstate and Fgn. Commerce, U.S. Senate, Washington, 1955-58, Subcom. Fgn. Commerce, 1958; ptnr. Hays, Busby & Rivkin, N.Y.C., 1958-77, Busby, Rehm & Leonard, 1977-87; of counsel Dorsey & Whitney, Washington, 1988—. Trade advisor Ministry of Fin., Republic of Latvia, 1996; lectr., Moscow, Kiev, Chisinev, Kampala, 1995-98; mem. accountability rev. bd. terrorist attack on U.S. Embassy, Dar Es Salaam, 1998-99. Mem. Nat. Motor Vehicle Safety Adv. Coun., 1966-68; pres. League Young Dems. of Okla., 1951; city judge, Ada, 1952-53; bd. dirs. Legal Aid Soc. D.C.; mem. Washington Nat. Cathedral chpt., 1984-91. Served with USNR, 1944-46. Mem. ABA (chmn. standing com. on customs law 1973-76), Fed. Cir. Bar Assn. (bd. dirs.), Customs and Internat. Trade Bar Assn. (bd. dirs.), Nat. Cathedral Assn. (bd. trustees 1992-96), Met. Club. Episcopalian. Private international. Office: Dorsey & Whitney 1001 Pennsylvania Ave NW Washington DC 20004-2505 E-mail: busby.david@dorseylaw.com.

BUSCEMI, PETER, lawyer; b. Bklyn., Sept. 25, 1950; s. Vincent and Ilse (Griesser) Buscemi; m. Judith Ann Miller, June 27, 1981. BA, Columbia U., 1969, JD, 1976; MA, Princeton U., 1971. Bar: N.Y. 1977, D.C. 1979, U.S. Supreme Ct. 1980, U.S. Dist. Ct. (D.C. dist.) 1981, U.S. Ct. Appeals (D.C. cir.) 1981, U.S. Dist. Ct. (so. dist.) N.Y. 1982, U.S. Ct. Appeals (5th and 11th cirs.) 1982, U.S. Ct. Appeals (2d cir.) 1985, U.S. Ct. Appeals (fed. cir.)

1986, U.S. Ct. Appeals (3d and 4th cirs.) 1990, U.S. Ct. Appeals (6th cir.) 1993, U.S. Ct. Appeals (1st cir.) 1994, U.S. Ct. Appeals (7th cir.) 1995, U.S. Ct. Appeals (10th cir.) 1998. Law clk. to Hon. Carl McGowan U.S. Ct. Appeals (D.C. cir.), Washington, 1976-77; asst. to solicitor gen. U.S. Dept. Justice, Washington, 1977-81; spl. asst. U.S. atty. U.S. Atty.'s Office, Alexandria, Va., 1980; assoc. Paul, Weiss, Rifkind, Wharton & Garrison, Washington, 1981-86, Morgan, Lewis & Bockius, LLP, Washington, 1986-87, ptnr., 1987—. Federal civil litigation, General civil litigation, Criminal. Home: 5215 Chamberlin Ave Chevy Chase MD 20815-6646 Office: Morgan Lewis & Bockius LLP 1111 Pennsylvania Ave NW Washington DC 20004 E-mail: pbuscemi@morganlewis.com.

BUSCH, JOHN ARTHUR, lawyer; b. Indpls., Mar. 23, 1951; s. John L. and Betty (Thomas) B.; m. Barbara Ann Holt, June 23, 1973; children: Abigail, Elizabeth, Amanda, Rachel. BA, Wabash Coll., 1973; JD, Duke U., 1976. Bar: Wis. 1976, U.S. Dist. Ct. (ea. we. dists.) Wis., U.S. Ct. Appeals (5th and 7th cirs.) 1976. Assoc. Michael, Best & Friedrich, Milw., 1976-83, ptnr., 1983—; chmn. litigation dept. Michael Best & Friedrich, Milw., 1990-95, mgmt. com., 1995-2001, mng. ptnr. Milw. office, 2003—. Mem. ad hoc com. on alternative dispute resolution Milw. Cir. Ct., ad hoc com. on multidisciplinary practices State Bar, mem. bd. govs., 2001—. Treas. North Shore Rep. Club, Milw., 1984-85, vice chmn., 1985-86, chmn., 1987-89; del. Rep. State Conv., Milw., 1986; mem. local rules adv. com. Ea. dist., Wis.; mem. com. Fed. Bench Bar. Master Am. Inns of Ct.; mem. ABA, Wis. Bar Assn. (v.p. ednl. devel. 2002—), Milw. Bar Assn. Federal civil litigation, State civil litigation, Health. Home: 1025 E Lyon St Milwaukee WI 53202 Office: Michael Best & Friedrich 100 E Wisconsin Ave Ste 3300 Milwaukee WI 53202-4108 E-mail: jabusch@mbf-law.com.

BUSDICKER, GORDON G. retired lawyer; b. Winona, Minn., Oct. 12, 1933; s. Harry John and Edna Mae (Rogers) B.; m. Noreen Decker; children— Karla E., Pamela J., Alison G., Neal A. BA, Hamline U., St. Paul, 1955; JD, Harvard U., 1958. Bar: Minn. Atty. Aluminum Co. of Am., Pitts., 1958-61; assoc. Faegre & Benson, Mpls., 1961-67, ptnr., 1967-99, ret., 1999. Trustee Hamline U., St. Paul, 1973— Mem. ABA, Minn. Bar Assn., Interlachen Golf Club. Republican. Congregationalist. Avocations: boating, geanealogy. Home: 3833 Abbott Ave S Minneapolis MN 55410-1036 E-mail: busdick1@mn.rr.com.

BUSEY, PHIL GORDON, lawyer; b. Oklahoma City, Okla., Jan. 22, 1952; s. C.L. and Hazel (Brown) B.; m. Catherine Jean Callaway, Sept. 17, 1977; children: Phil G. Jr., Brian Marshall, Emily C. BA in Polit. Sci. and History, Oklahoma City U., 1974; JD, Okla. U., 1977. Bar: Okla. 1978, U.S. Dist. Ct. (we. dist.) Okla., U.S. Ct. Appeals (10th cir.) 1987. Aircraft and ins. examiner Insured Aircraft Title Service, Inc., Oklahoma City, 1975-77; asst. v.p., trust officer Am.-First Title and Trust Co., Oklahoma City, 1977-79; asst. gen. counsel First Nat. Bank and Trust Co. and First Oklahoma Bancorp., Inc., Oklahoma City, 1979-81; atty. Linn, Helms, Kirk & Burkett, Oklahoma City, 1981-82; v.p., atty. Penn Sq. Bank, Oklahoma City, 1982; atty. Kornfeld Franklin & Phillips, Oklahoma City, 1982-84, Robinson, Boese & Davidson, Tulsa, 1984-85; of counsel Kirk & Chaney, Tulsa, 1985-91; shareholder Pats & Payne, P.C., 1987-91, Hall, Estill, Attys. at Law, 1991-95; of counsel Phillips McFadden, 1995-97; sr. v.p., global counsel Advanica Corp., 1997-99; pres., CEO ProForma Group Inc., 1999-2000; pres., founder Busey Resource Group Inc., 2000—; pvt. practice, 2000—; founder, chmn, CEO Del. Resource Gap, Inc., 2002—. Adj. prof. South Oklahoma City Jr. Coll. and Inst. of Banking, 1979-82, Oklahoma City U., 1983-95; mem. Okla. Regents Coun. for Career and Tech., 1999—. Contbr. articles to profl. jours. Baseball coach YMCA Youth Baseball team, Oklahoma City, 1977-93; bd. dirs. Ch. of the Servant, Oklahoma City, 1983; pres. Classen Awards Alumni Assn., Oklahoma City, 1983-95; mem. adminstrv. bd. St. Lukes United Meth. Ch., 1998—; mem. alumni bd. Oklahoma City U., 1997-99. Mem. ABA, Okla. Bar Assn., Oklahoma County Bar Assn., Nat. Assn. Bond Lawyers, Del. Chamber Indian Nations, Okla. State C. of C., So. Oklahoma City C. of C. (bd. dirs. 2000—), Phi Alpha Delta, Oklahoma City Young Men's Dinner Club. Democrat. Home: 6401 Winchester Dr Oklahoma City OK 73162-1722 Office: 2800 NW 36 Ste 202 Oklahoma City OK 73112 E-mail: pbuseylaw@aol.com.

BUSH, FRED MARSHALL, JR., lawyer; b. Newhebron, Miss., Jan. 25, 1917; s. Frederick Marshall Sr. and Elizabeth Stewart (Buck) B.; m. Katie Ruth Field, May 8, 1942; children: Frederick Marshall III, Carl J., Richard S. AA, Hinds Jr. Coll., 1935; BS, U.S. Naval Acad., 1939; LLB, U. Miss., 1950. Bar: Miss. 1948, U.S. Dist. Ct. Miss. 1948, U.S. Ct. Appeals (5th and 11th cirs.) 1948, U.S. Supreme Ct. 1965. Commd. ensign USN, 1939, advanced through grades to capt., resigned, 1948, with Res., 1948-60; ptnr. Fant & Bush, Holly Springs, Miss., 1950-60, Mitchell, McNutt, Bush, Lagrone & Sams, Tupelo, Miss., 1962-89, Phelps Dunbar, Tupelo, Miss., 1989—. Bd. dirs. Miss. Bd. Econ. Devel., Jackson, Miss., 1960-68, exec. dir., 1960-62; bd. dirs. Tenn.-Tombigbee Waterway Devel. Authority, Columbus, Miss., 1980-84. Fellow Miss. Bar Found. (chmn. 1978); mem. ABA (ho. of dels. 1986-87, 89-90), Miss. Bar Assn. (pres. 1986-87, various coms. and offices), Miss. Def. Lawyers Assn. (pres. 1973-74). Lodges: Rotary (pres. local club 1954-55). Episcopalian. Corporate, general, Insurance, Municipal (including bonds). Office: Phelps Dunbar PO Box 1220 Tupelo MS 38802-1220 E-mail: bushf@phelps.com.

BUSH, MICHAEL KEVIN, lawyer; b. Davenport, Iowa, May 23, 1952; s. Roy Alvin and A. Carmelita (Gilroy) B.; m. Kathleen M. Grace, Nov. 26, 1977; children: Kelly Anne, Daniel Stephen, Brendan Michael. BA, U. Notre Dame, South Bend, Ind., 1974; JD, Valparaiso (Ind.) U., 1977. Bar: Iowa 1977, U.S. Dist. Ct. (no. dist.) Iowa 1980, U.S. Ct. Appeals (7th cir.) 1980, U.S. Dist. Ct. (ctrl. dist.) Ill. 1983, U.S. Ct. Appeals (8th cir.) 1996, U.S. Supreme Ct. 1990, Ill. 1999. Mem. Wells, McNally & Bowman, Davenport, 1977-80; prosecutor Scott County Atty.'s Office, Davenport, 1980-82; mem. Henninger & Henninger, Davenport, 1979-82; founding ptnr. Walton, Creen & Bush, Davenport, 1982-86; ptnr. Carlin, Hellstrom & Bittner, Davenport, 1987—; sr. ptnr. Bush, Motto, Creen, Hoffman and Koury, Davenport, 2000—. Recipient Iowa Trial Lawyer's Public Justice award, 2001. Mem. ATLA (sustaining mem.), Am. Bd. Trial Advocates (assoc.), Iowa Assn. Trial Lawyers (Pub. Justice award 2000), Million Dollar Advocates Forum, Iowa Bar Assn., Scott County Bar Assn., Am. Coll. Barristers (sr. counsel). Roman Catholic. Avocation: tennis. Personal injury (including property damage). Home: 2806 E 42nd Ct Davenport IA 52807-1576 Office: Carlin Hellstrom & Bittner 5505 Victoria Ave Ste 100 Davenport IA 52807

BUSHNELL, GEORGE EDWARD, III, lawyer; b. Detroit, Feb. 18, 1952; s. George Edward Jr. and Elizabeth (Whelden) B.; m. Eileen Mary Maguire, Sept. 16, 1989; children: Ann-Elizabeth, Emily Spears, George Edward. BA, Bucknell U., 1974; JD, Emory U., 1981. Bar: Ga. 1981, D.C. 1983, N.Y. 1986. Vol. U.S. Peace Corps, Burkina Faso, 1974-76, tng. dir., 1976-77; staff asst. to hon. Lucien Nedzi U.S. Ho. of Reps., Washington, 1977-78; assoc. Duncan, Allen and Mitchell, Washington, Ivory Coast, Congo, 1981-85, Shearman & Sterling, N.Y.C., 1985-91; corp. counsel Joseph E. Seagram & Sons, Inc., N.Y.C., 1991-2001; v.p., corp. counsel Vivendi Universal S.A., N.Y.C., 2001—. Mem. ABA, N.Y. State Bar Assn. Corporate, general, Finance, Mergers and acquisitions. Home: 1075 Park Ave Apt 2A New York NY 10128-1003 Office: Vivendi Universal 800 3rd Ave New York NY 10022-7604

BUSHNELL, RODERICK PAUL, lawyer; b. Buffalo, N.Y., Mar. 6, 1944; s. Paul Hazen and Martha Atlee Bushnell; m. Suzann Yvonne Kaiser, Aug. 27, 1966; 1 child, Arlo Phillip. BA, Rutgers U., 1966; JD, Georgetown U., 1969. Bar: Calif. 1970, U.S. Supreme Ct. 1980.; cert. Civil Trial Advocate, Nat. Bd. Trial Advocates. Atty. dept. water resources, Sacramento, 1969-71; ptnr. Bushnell, Caplan & Fielding, San Francisco, 1971—. Adv. bd. dirs. Bread & Roses, Inc., Mill Valley, Calif. Mem. ATLA, ABA (labor and employment sects.), San Francisco Bar Assn. (labor and employment sects.; arbitrator), San Francisco Superior Ct. (arbitrator), Fed. Ct. Early Neutral Evaluator, Calif. Bar Assn. (labor and employement sects.), Consumer Attys. Calif., San Francisco Trial Lawyers Assn., Nat. Employment Lawyers Assn., Calif. Employment Lawyers Assn. Federal civil litigation, State civil litigation, Labor (including EEOC, Fair Labor Standards Act, labor-management relations, NLRB, OSHA). Office: Bushnell Caplan & Fielding 221 Pine St Ste 600 San Francisco CA 94104-2705

BUSNER, PHILIP H. retired lawyer; b. Bklyn., Mar. 26, 1927; s. Joseph and Ray (Grajewer) B.; m. Naomi Marcia Greenfield, June 24, 1951; children: Joan Alexandra, Carey Elizabeth. BA cum laude, NYU, 1949; LLB, Harvard U., 1952. Bar: N.Y. 1953, U.S. Dist. Ct. (so. dist.) N.Y. 1956, U.S. Dist. Ct. (ea. dist.) N.Y. 1958, U.S. Ct. Appeals (2d cir.) 1956, U.S. Supreme Ct. 1974. Assoc. Rein, Mound & Cotton, N.Y.C., 1953, Hess, Mela, Segall, Popkin & Guterman, N.Y.C., 1954-55, Carroad & Carroad, N.Y.C., 1955-72; ptnr. Young, Sonnenfeld & Busner, N.Y.C., 1972-75, Sonnenfeld & Busner, N.Y.C., 1976-78, Sonnenfeld, Busner & Weinstein, N.Y.C., 1978-85, Sonnenfeld, Busner & Richman, N.Y.C., 1986-88; pvt. practice Great Neck, N.Y., 1989-97; ret., 1998. Trustee Asthmatic Children's Found. N.Y., 1978-87; adminstrv. judge N.Y.C. Dept. Transp., 1989-93; arbitrator N.Y.C. Civil Ct., 1990-92, Nassau County Dist. Ct., 1990-95, Suffolk County Dist. Ct., 1990-93. With USAAF, 1945-47. Mem. Am. Arbitration Assn. (arbitrator 1990-92), Phi Beta Kappa. Home: One Todd Dr Sands Point NY 11050

BUSSEWITZ, ROY JON, lawyer, pharmacist; b. Hartford, Wis., Mar. 19, 1944; s. Reginald Max and Bernice (Kadolph) B.; m. Joyce Ann O'Donnell, Aug. 24, 1980; children: Kathleen Ann, Christine Marie. BS in Pharmacy, U. Wis., 1967; JD, Valparaiso U., 1973. Bar: Wis. 1973. Prof. health law U. Wis., Milw., 1973-78; legal cons. State of Wis., Madison, 1978; legis. asst., health U.S. Senator Gaylord Nelson, Washington, 1979—80; legis. counsel Am. Health Care Assn., Washington, 1981; exec. dir. Nat. Assn. Med. Equipment Suppliers, Alexandria, Va., 1982—83; dir. govt. rels. Nat. Assn. Pvt. Psychiat. Hosps., Washington, 1984; dir. fed. govt. affairs Glaxo Inc., Alexandria, 1984-88; cons., 1988-91; v.p. managed care/telecomms. Nat. Assn. Chain Drug Stores, Alexandria, 1991—. Bd. dirs., mem. working group Electronic Data Exch., Nat. Coun. Prescription Programs. Mem. Wis. Bar Assn. Avocations: tennis, golf, gardening, photography. Home: 1103 Potomac Ln Alexandria VA 22308-2534 Office: 413 N Lee St Alexandria VA 22314-2301 E-mail: rbussewitz@nacds.org.

BUSSMAN, DONALD HERBERT, lawyer; b. Lakewood, Ohio, July 15, 1925; s. Herbert L. and Hilda L. (Henrichs) B. PhB, U. of Chgo., 1947, JD, 1951. Bar: Ill. 1951. Atty. Swift & Co., Chgo., 1950-84; pvt. practice Chgo., 1985—. With U.S. Army, 1944-46. Mem. ABA, Chgo. Bar Assn., Am. Assn. of Individual Investors, Club Internat. (Chgo.). General practice. Office: Ste 2102 860 N Dewitt Pl Chicago IL 60611-5780

BUSTAMANTE, NESTOR, lawyer; b. Havana, Cuba, Apr. 20, 1960; came to the U.S., 1961; s. Nestor and Clara Rosa (Sanchez) B.; m. Marilyn Gonzalez, Sept. 20, 1986; children: Tiffany Alexandra, Nestor C. AA, U. Fla., 1980, BS in Journalism, 1982, JD, 1985. Bar: Fla. 1986, U.S. Dist. Ct. (so. dist.) Fla. 1989, U.S. Supreme Ct. 1991. Asst. state atty. State Atty.'s Office 11th Cir., Miami, 1986-88; juvenile serious offender prosecutor State Atty.'s Office, Miami, 1987-88, spl. prosecutor, gang prosecutor, 1987-88; asst. divsn. chief State Atty.'s Office-11th Jud. Cir., Miami, 1987-88; of counsel Fernandez-Caubi, Fernandez & Aguilar et al., Miami, 1988-89; atty. Ferencik, Libanoff, Brandt and Bustamante PA, Ft. Lauderdale, Fla., 1989—, ptnr., 1996—. Mem. code and rules of evidence com. The Fla. Bar, 1989—90, jud. evaluation com., 2000; mem. Dade County Constrn. Trades Qualifying Bd.; adj. faculty dept. constrn. mgmt. Fla. Internat. U. Contbr. articles to newsletters. Mem. Miami-Dade Constrn. Trades Qualifying Bd. Named Hon. mem. Quien es Quien Publs., Inc., N.Y.C., 1990. Mem. ATLA (scoring judge nat. finals student trial advocacy competition 1994, 95), Fed. Bar Assn., Dade County Bar Assn. (mem. juvenile divsn. com. 1988-92, mem. media and pub. rels. com. 1989-91, mem. constrn. law com. 1990-91), Phi Delta Phi, U. Fla. Alumni Assn. Commercial, contracts (including sales of goods; commercial financing), Construction, State civil litigation. Office: Ferencik Libanoff Brandt & Bustamante PA 150 S Pine Island Rd Ste 400 Fort Lauderdale FL 33324-2667 E-mail: flbbnb@mindspring.com.

BUSTIN, GEORGE LEO, lawyer; b. Perth Amboy, N.J., Feb. 10, 1948; s. George and Agnes W. (Bulvanoski) B.; m. Halina Orestovna Kaniuka, July 9, 1979; children: Michael G., Alexander G. AB summa cum laude, Princeton U., 1970; JD magna cum laude, Harvard U., 1973. Bar: N.Y. 1973, U.S. Dist. Ct. (so. dist.), U.S. Ct. Appeals ((2nd cir.), 1974. Assoc. Cleary, Gottlieb, Steen & Hamilton, N.Y.C., 1973-81, ptnr., 1982-84; vis. prof. Princeton (N.J.) U., 1991; ptnr. Cleary, Gottlieb, Steen & Hamilton, Brussels, 1984-90, 1992—; chair Brussels chpt. Internat. divsn. N.Y. State Bar Assn., 1996—. Chair Princeton Alumni Schs. Com., Belgium, 1998—; dir. Sabre Found. (Europe) S.p.r.l.; co-chair Fall 2003 meeting ABA section Internat. Law and Practice. Author: Business Transactions with the USSR, 1975, International Business Transactions, 1980, International Financial Law Review, 1990, Insights, 1990. Mem. Cercle Gaulois Artistique et Litteraire, Harvard Law Sch. Assn. (sec. Brussels 1989-92), Am. European Union Assn. (pres.'s group), N.Y. State Bar Assn., Assn. Bar City N.Y. (co-chair coms. on rels. with European bars 2001—), Ordre Francais du barreau de Bruxelles, Brussels Sports Assn. (bd. dirs. 1996-98), Commn. des membres associés du barreau de Bruxelles (ABA liaison rep. 2001—). Corporate, general, Private international, Product liability. Home: 39 Rue de La Gendarmerie 1380 Lasne Belgium Office: Cleary Gottlieb Steen & Hamilton 57 Rue de La Loi 1040 Brussels Belgium

BUTCHER, BRUCE CAMERON, lawyer; b. N.Y.C., Feb. 17, 1947; s. John Richard and Dorothy Helen (Wehner) B.; m. Kathryn Ann Fiddler, Oct. 12, 1979; 1 child, Kristen Ann. BS, Belknap Coll., 1969; JD, St. John's U., N.Y.C., 1972. Bar: N.Y. 1973, U.S. Dist. Ct. (so. dist.) N.Y. 1974, La. 1980, U.S. Dist. Ct. (ea. dist.) La. 1980, U.S. Ct. Appeals (5th and 11th cirs.) 1981, Tex. 1993. Assoc. Laporte and Meyers, N.Y.C., 1972-73; asst. chief contract and comml. litigation divsn. Corp. Counsel's Office City of N.Y., 1973-79; ptnr. Chaffe, McCall, Phillips, Toler & Sarpy, New Orleans, 1980-84; prin. Bruce C. Butcher, P.C., Metairie, La., 1985-93; of counsel Smith Martin & Schneider, New Orleans, 1993-94; gen. coun. The Vulcan Group, Birmingham, Ala., 1994-95, Favalora Constructors, Inc., 1995—2002; gen. counsel Tailgators Restaurant, LLC, New Orleans, 1994-99; pvt. practice Law Offices of Bruce Cameron Butcher & Assocs., New Orleans, 1999—. Mem. ABA (regional chmn. pub. report 1975, state chmn. pub. contracts sect. 1984-95, cert. of performance 1975), La. Bar Assn., Am. Arbitration Assn. (mem. arbitration panel U.S. Coun. on Internat. Bus. Arbitration 2001—), New Orleans Country Club, New Orleans Athletic Club, Crescent Club. Home: 402 Julia St Ste 307 New Orleans LA 70130-3689 Office: 402 Julia St Ste 307 New Orleans LA 70130-3689 E-mail: bbutch@bellsouth.net.

BUTLER, CHARLES RANDOLPH, JR., federal judge; b. N.Y.C., Mar. 28, 1940; BA, Washington and Lee U., 1962; LLB, U. Ala., 1966. Assoc. Hamilton Butler Riddick and LaTour, Mobile, Ala., 1966-69; asst. pub. defender Mobile County, 1969-70, dist. atty., 1971-75; ptnr. Butler and Sullivan, Mobile, 1975-84, Hamilton Butler Riddick Tarlton and Sullivan P.C., Mobile, 1984-88; dist. judge U.S. Dist. Ct. (so. dist.) Ala., Mobile, 1988-94, chief dist. judge, 1994—2002, dist. judge, 2002—. Adj. prof. criminal justice program U. So. Ala., 1972-76; mem. jud. coun. 11th cir., 1994-2003, jud. conf. com. on criminal law, 1993-99, jud. conf. com., 1999-2002; past liaison mem. to long-range planning com. of the AO; past mem. program and adminstrn. subcom., planning for the future and automation subcom., probaton and pretrial umbrella group; mem. exec. com. Jud. Conf. of U.S., 1999-2002. Lst lt. USAR, 1962-64. Named One of Outstanding Young Men of Am., Mobile County Jaycees, 1971. Office: US Dist Ct 113 Saint Joseph St Mobile AL 36602-3683

BUTLER, DAVID, lawyer; b. St. Paul, June 11, 1930; s. Francis David and Alida (Bigelow) B.; m. Diana Dodge Duffy, Aug. 29, 1952 (div. 1957); children: Anne, Lawrence David; m. Barbara Williams Clark, July 12, 1958; children: Molly Elizabeth, Peter, Katherine BA, Princeton U., 1952; LLB, Harvard U., 1957. Bar. Colo. 1958, U.S. Dist. Ct. Colo. 1958. Assoc. Holland & Hart, Denver, 1957-63, ptnr., 1963-95, chmn. mgmt. com., 1990-95; of counsel, 1996—. Gen. counsel 1st Interstate Bank Denver, 1984-86; bd. dirs. UMB Bank Colo., Denver. Mem. bd. editors Harvard Law Rev., 1955-57. Chmn. lawyers adv. com. United Way, Denver, 1989—94; trustee Graland Country Day Sch., Denver, 1971—79, Legal Aid Found., Colo., 1991—97, chmn., 1993—97, Colo. Planning Group for Legal Svcs. to the Poor, 1995—2002; bd. dirs. Met. Denver Legal Aid Soc., 1971—74, Colo. Lawyers Trust Account Fund, 2000—; chmn. Colo. Lawyers Trust Account Found., 2003—, Colo. Access to Justice Commn., 2003—. 1st lt. U.S. Army, 1952—54. Mem. ABA, Colo. Bar Assn. (chmn. tax sect. 1970, Jacob V. Schaetzel pro bono award 2002), Denver Bar Assn. Office: Holland & Hart 555 17th St Ste 2900 Denver CO 80202-3979

BUTLER, GEORGE MORTON, lawyer; b. Worthington, Minn., Mar. 10, 1949; s. James Milton and Mary Irene (Morton) Butler; m. Carol Ann Telford, Sept. 26, 1981; children: Christopher, Alison, Charles. BA, Antioch Coll., Yellow Springs, Ohio, 1973; JD, Tulane U., 1978. Bar: La., Guam, U.S. Dist. Ct. (ea. dist.) La., DC, U.S. Ct. Appeals (5th and 9th cirs.), Federated States Micronesia. Pvt. practice, New Orleans, 1978—79, Hagatna, 1997—98; staff atty. Micronesian Legal Svcs., Moen Truk, 1979—81; asst. legis. counsel FSM Congress, Moen Truk, 1981—83; ptnr. Keog and Butler, Hagatna, 1983—96, Butler & Telford Butler, Hagatna, 1998—. Pres. Cantate - Cmty. Choir, 1002. Mem.: Am. Bankruptcy Inst., Rotary (pres. Guam chpt. 1989). Bankruptcy, Commercial, consumer (including collections, credit), Probate (including wills, trusts). Home and Office: 137 Murray Blvd Hagatna GU 96910 Office Fax: 671-475-0203. Business E-Mail: butlergu@guam.net.

BUTLER, JOHN EDWARD, lawyer; b. Teaneck N.J., Dec. 8, 1946; s. John Edward and Alice Mary (Knorr) B.;children: Jennifer, Kathryn, John Michael; m. Elizabeth M. Fair, Mar. 12, 1994. General practice, Personal injury (including property damage), Probate (including wills, trusts). Home: 120 E Washington St Ste 825 Syracuse NY 13202-4014

BUTLER, MANLEY CALDWELL, retired lawyer; b. Roanoke, Va., June 2, 1925; s. W.W.S. Butler Jr.; m. June Nolde, June 26, 1950; children: Manley, Henry, James, Marshall. AB, U. Richmond, 1948; JD, U. Va., 1950; LLD (hon.), Washington & Lee U., 1978. Bar: Va. 1950. Mem. Va. Ho. Dels., 1962-72, minority leader; mem. 92d-97th Congresses from 6th Va. dist., Judiciary Com., Com. on Govt. Ops., Woods, Rogers & Hazlegrove, P.L.C., 1983—99; ret., 1999. Mem. Nat. Bankruptcy Rev. Commn., 1995-97. Lt. USNR, 1943-46. Fellow Am. Bar Found., Am. Coll. Bankruptcy, Va. Law Found.; mem. ABA, Va. Bar Assn., Va. State Bar Assn., Roanoke Bar Assn., Am. Bankruptcy Inst., Raven Soc. Order of Coif, Phi Beta Kappa, Tau Kappa Alpha, Omicron Delta Kappa, Phi Gamma Delta. Episcopalian. Bankruptcy, Corporate, general. Home: Unit 202 4434 Pheasant Ridge Rd Roanoke VA 24014-5279 E-mail: nuniepapa@cox.net.

BUTLER, MICHAEL FRANCIS, lawyer; b. Pitts., Aug. 17, 1935; s. Frank J. and Mary M. (Montgomery) B. BA magna cum laude, Harvard U., 1957; LLB, Yale U., 1960. Bar: Pa., D.C. Mem. Kirkpatrick & Lockhart, Pitts., 1960-69; asst. gen. counsel for domestic and internat. bus., then dep. gen. counsel U.S. Dept. Commerce, Washington, 1969-73; v.p., gen. counsel Overseas Pvt. Investment Corp., Washington, 1973-75; gen. counsel Fed. Energy Adminstrn., Washington, 1975-77; ptnr. Andrews & Kurth, Washington, 1977-92. Bd. dirs., chmn. audit com. Three Rivers Bancorp, Inc., Three Rivers Bank & Trust Co.; mem. adv. com. Fagan & Co.; mem. panel of arbitrators Dispute Settlement Ctr., Internat. Energy Agy., Paris; past mem. or chmn. U.S. dels. to OECD coms., Berne Union, Adminstrv. Conf. of U.S. Contbr. articles to profl. publs. Past vice chmn. class spl. gifts com. Harvard Coll. and Yale Law Sch.; past bd. dirs., sec. Three Rivers Arts Festival, Pitts.; past bd. dirs. Bryce Harlow Found. Fellow Am. Bar Found. (life); mem. ABA (past chmn. com. on fgn. investment in U.S. internat. law sect.), Am. Arbitration Assn. (mem. comml. panel of arbitrators), Pa. Bar Assn., D.C. Bar Assn., Allegheny County Bar Assn., Am. Law Inst., Am. Judicature Soc., Am. Soc. Internat. Law, Internat. Bar Assn., Washington Fgn. Law Soc., Inter-Am. Bar Assn., Harvard Club West Pa. (past. sec.), Harvard Club of D.C. (past bd. dirs.), Met. Club, Rolling Rock Club (Ligonier, Pa.), Harvard-Yale-Princeton Club (Pitts.). Republican. Presbyterian. Administrative and regulatory, Corporate, general, Private international. Home and Office: 2214 Massachusetts Ave NW Washington DC 20008-2812

BUTLER, PAUL BASCOMB, JR., lawyer; b. Charleston, S.C., Nov. 27, 1947; s. Paul B. and Mary Anna (Tisdale) B.; m. Virginia Eldridge, June 14, 1969; children: Jeffrey Bryan, Robert Paul. BA, Emory U., 1969, MDiv cum laude, 1972, JD with distinction, 1976. Bar: Ga. 1976, Fla. 1977; ordained to ministry United Meth. Ch., 1970. United Meth. Ch., 1970—; assoc. min. First United Meth. Ch., Phoenix, 1972-73; assoc. Swift, Currie, McGhee and Hiers, Atlanta, 1976-79; ptnr. Butler Pappas, Tampa, Fla., 1979-97, of counsel, 1998—. Chancellor Fla. Ann. Conf. United Meth. Ch., 1997—. Contbr. articles to profl. jours. Chair com. on new church devel. Fla. annual conf. United Meth. Ch., 1996-2000, chair bd. missions and ch. ext. Tampa dist. United Meth. Ch., Inc., 1992-96; pastor Temple Terrace United Meth., Tampa, 1998-2000, sr. pastor, 2000-2002; vision facilitator Tampa Dist. United Meth. Ch., 2002-; bd. dirs. United Meth. Ch. Found., 1999-2000. Mem. ABA (chmn. Nat. Inst. sect. of trial tort and ins. practice 1987-89, ho. of dels. 1993-95, coun. mem. sect. of trial tort and ins. practice 1990-93, chmn. task force on civil justice reform, chmn. property ins. law com. 1985-86, editor So. Region Annotated Homeowner's Policy), Fedn. of Def. and Corp. Counsel (dean Litigation Mgmt. Coll. 1996-98, chair litigation mgmt. coll. adv. coun. 1998-2000, bd. deans 2000—), Def. Rsch. Inst. (chmn. ins. law com. 1989-92, chmn. Amcus com. 1994-97, bd. dirs. 1995-98, vice chair law inst. 1998-99, chair law inst. 1999-2001, immediate past chair 2001-), Fla. Def. Lawyers Assn., Hillsborough County Bar Assn., Internat. Assn. Def. Counsel (vice chair property ins. com. 1993-96), Assn. Def. Trial Attys. Clubs: Temple Terr. (Fla.) Golf and Country. Democrat. Avocations: golf, tennis. Federal civil litigation, State civil litigation, Insurance. Office: Butler Pappas Ste 1100 6200 W Courtney Campbell Cswy 1100 Tampa FL 33607-5946 E-mail: pbutler@butlerpappas.com.

BUTLER, ROBERT CARLYLE, III, lawyer; b. Tulsa, Okla., Mar. 1, 1973; s. Robert Carlyle and Mary Virginia Butler; m. Erin Sutherland, May 30, 2000. BA, U. Tulsa, 1996, JD, 2000. Bar: Okla. 2000, U.S. Dist. Ct. (no. dist.) Okla. 2000, U.S. Ct. Appeals (10th cir.) 2000. Counsel Wagner & Grandy LLP, Tulsa, Okla., 2000—02; counsel, owner Butler Law Office PLLC, Tulsa, 2002—. Bd. dirs. Comml. Bank, Tulsa. Author: Pre and Post Nuptial Agreements, 2001. Mem.: ABA, Tulsa County Bar Assn., Okla. Bar Assn. Republican. Avocations: tennis, coaching Pop Warner, German language, Big Brothers and Big Sisters. Estate planning, Family and matrimonial, Commercial, contracts (including sales of goods; commercial financing). Office: 5508 S Lewis Tulsa OK 74105

BUTLER, SAMUEL COLES, lawyer, director; b. Logansport, Ind., Mar. 10, 1930; s. Melvin Linwood and Jane Lavina (Flynn) B.; m. Sally Eugenia Thackston, June 28, 1952; children: Samuel Coles, Leigh F., Elizabeth J. AB magna cum laude, Harvard U., 1951, LLB magna cum laude, 1954. Bar: D.C. 1954, Ind. 1954, N.Y. 1957. Law clk. to Justice Minton U.S. Supreme Ct., 1954; assoc. Cravath, Swaine & Moore, N.Y.C., 1956-60, ptnr., 1961—. Trustee Vassar Coll., 1969-77, N.Y. Pub. Libr., 1979—, chmn. bd., 1999—; trustee Am. Mus. Natural History, 1989-93, The September 11 Fund, 2001—; chmn. Harvard Coll. Fund, 1977-85; bd. overseers Harvard U., 1982-88, pres. bd., 1986-88; bd. dirs. Culver Ednl. Found., 1981-2001. With U.S. Army, 1954-56. Mem. Coun. Fgn. Rels. Corporate, general, Mergers and acquisitions, Securities. Home: 1220 Park Ave New York NY 10128-1733 Office: Cravath Swaine & Moore 825 8th Ave New York NY 10019-7475

BUTLER, WILLIAM ELLIOTT, comparative law educator, lawyer; b. Mpls., Oct. 20, 1939; came to Eng., 1970; s. William Elliott and Maxine Swan (Elmberg) B.; m. Darlene Mae Johnson, Sept. 2, 1961 (dec. Nov. 23, 1989); children: William III, Bradley; m. Maryann Elizabeth Gashi, Dec. 6, 1991. AA, Hibbing Jr. Coll., 1959; BA, Am. Univ., Washington, 1961; MA, Johns Hopkins U., 1963; JD, Harvard U., 1966; PhD, Johns Hopkins U., 1970; LLD, London U., 1979; LLM, Russian Acad. Scis., 1997. Bar: D.C. 1967, U.S. Supreme Ct. 1970, Uzbekistan 1996, Russia 1997. Rsch. asst. Johns Hopkins U., Washington, 1966-68; rsch. assoc. Harvard Law Sch., Cambridge, Mass., 1968-70; reader in comparative law U. London, 1970-76, prof. comparative law, 1976—; ptnr. White & Case, London, 1994-96; resident ptnr. PricewaterhouseCoopers CIS Law Firm, Moscow, 1997—2001; sr. ptnr. Phoenix Law Assocs. CIS, Moscow, 2002—, Jurisphoenix, Moscow, 2003—. Dir. The Vinogradoff Inst., Univ. Coll. London; dean and M.M. Speranskii prof. internat. and comparative law, Moscow Sch. Social and Econ. Scis., 1995—; prof., chair civil law Moscow State Legal Acad., 2002. Editor Bookplate Internat., 1994—, Sudebnik, 1996—; contbr. numerous articles to profl. jours.; author more than 150 books including Russian Law, 2d edit., 2003, Civil Code of Russian Federation, 2003, Russian Company and Commerical Legislation, 2003. Rsch. fellow Leverhulme Trust, London, 1991, FSA. Mem. Internat. Fedn. Ex-Libris Socs. (exec. sec.), Russian Acad. Natural Sci. (academician 1992—), Nat. Acad. Scis. Ukraine (academician 1992—), Russian Acad. Legal Scis. Avocations: book collecting, bookplate collecting. Home: Stratton Audley Park Bicester Oxon OX27 9AB England Office: Univ Coll London 4/8 Endsleigh Gardens London WC1H OEG England E-mail: webakademik@aol.com.

BUTT, EDWARD THOMAS, JR., lawyer; b. Chgo., Oct. 27, 1947; s. Edward T. and Helen Kathryn (Guy) B.; m. Leslie Laidlaw Hilton, Oct. 20, 1972; children: Julie Guy, Andrew McNaughton. BA, Lawrence U., 1968; JD, U. Mich., 1971. Bar: Ill. 1971, U.S. Dist. Ct. (no. dist.) Ill. 1971, Wis. 1975, U.S. Dist. Ct. (ea. dist.) Wis. 1978, U.S. Ct. Appeals (7th cir.) 1978, U.S. Ct. Claims 1982, U.S. Ct. Appeals (6th cir.) 1986, U.S. Ct. Appeals (6th cir.) 1987, Mich. 1997. Assoc. Wildman, Harrold, Allen & Dixon, Chgo., 1971-75, 76-78, ptnr., 1979-94, Lund & Butt, S.C., Minocqua, Wis., 1975-76; of counsel Swanson, Martin & Bell, Chgo. and Wheaton, Ill., 1994—. Bd. dirs. Constl. Rights Found., Chgo. Mem. ABA, State Bar Wis., State Bar Mich., 7th Cir. Bar Assn., Def. Rsch. Inst., Crystal Lake Yacht Club, Crystal Downs Country Club. Avocations: distance running, sailing, golf. General civil litigation, Insurance, Product liability. Home: Michabou Shores 1006 Tiba Rd Frankfort MI 49635-9216 also: 3903 Forest Ave Western Springs IL 60558-1049 Office: Swanson Martin & Bell 2100 Manchester Rd Ste 1420 Wheaton IL 60187-4534

BUTTENWIESER, LAWRENCE BENJAMIN, lawyer; b. N.Y.C., Jan. 11, 1932; s. Benjamin Joseph and Helen (Lehman) B.; m. Ann Harriet Lubin, July 13, 1956; children— William Lawrence, Carol Helen Sharp, Jill Ann Schloss, Peter Lubin BA, U. Chgo., 1951, MA, 1955; JD, Yale U., 1956; DHL (hon.), Yeshiva U., 1974. Bar: N.Y. 1956. Assoc. Rosenman & Colin, N.Y.C., 1956-66, ptnr., 1966—2002; counsel KMZ Rosenman, 2002—. Chmn., bd. dirs. Gen. Am. Investors Co., Inc., N.Y.C. Past pres., trustee Associated YM-YWHAs of Greater N.Y.; past v.p., dir. Citizens Housing and Planning Coun. of N.Y.; past treas., dir. City Ctr. of Music and Drama, Inc.; past dir. Coun. on Social Work. Edn.; past trustee Dalton Sch. ; past. hon. chmn. bd., trustee, past pres. Fedn. Jewish Philanthropies N.Y.; past chmn. bd., trustee Montefiore Med. Ctr.; past gen. campaign chmn. United Neighborhood Houses N.Y.; past trustee UJA/Fed. Joint Campaign; past chmn., past trustee Am. Jewish World Svc.; past chmn., trustee Citizens Budget Commn.; dir. Playwrights Horizons Inc., N.Y. Acad. Sci.; trustee U. Chgo. Mem. Assn. Bar City of N.Y. Probate (including wills, trusts). Office: KMZ Rosenman Fl 21 575 Madison Ave Fl 21 New York NY 10022-2511 E-mail: lawrence.buttenwieser@kmzr.com.

BUTTERFIELD, G. K., JR., state supreme court justice; b. Wilson, N.C., Apr. 27, 1947; s. G. K. and Addie (Davis) Butterfield; children: Valeisha Monique, Jenetta Lenai. BS, NC Central U., 1971, JD, 1974. Sr. ptnr. law firm, 1974—88; resident judge NC Superior Ct Dist 7B, 1988—2001; assoc. justice Supreme Ct. N.C., 2001. Office: PO Box 2170 Raleigh NC 27602

BUTTERMAN, JAY RONALD, lawyer; b. N.Y.C., June 15, 1958; s. Louis and Ellen (Schmeltzer) B. BA, Vassar Coll., 1983; JD, Yeshiva U., 1988. Bar: N.J. 1988, N.Y. 1989, U.S. Dist. Ct. (so. dist.) N.Y. 1991, U.S. Dist. Ct. (ea. dist.) N.Y. 1996, U.S. Dist. Ct. N.J. 1988, U.S. Supreme Ct. 2002. Assoc. Hoffinger Friedland Dobrish Bernfeld & Hasen, N.Y.C., 1988-91; sole practitioner N.Y.C., 1991-95; mng. ptnr. Law firm of Jay R. Butterman, N.Y.C., 1995-99; sr. ptnr. Butterman, Kahn & Gardner, LLP, 1999—. Recipient Outstanding Acad. Achievement award Acad. Am. Matrimonial Lawyers, 1988. Mem. ABA, ATLA, N.Y. State Bar Assn., Assn. Bar City N.Y. Democrat. Avocations: oriental art, antiquarian books. General civil litigation, Entertainment, Family and matrimonial. Office: 425 Park Ave Fl 26 New York NY 10022-3506

BUTTERWORTH, ROBERT A. dean, former state attorney general; b. Passaic, N.J., Aug. 20, 1942; m. Marta Prado. BA, BS, U. Fla., 1965; JD, U. Miami, 1969. Prosecutor, Fla., 1970—74; circuit and county judge, 1974—78; adj. prof. Nova Univ. Grad. Sch. Criminal Law, 1976—78; sheriff Broward County Sheriff's Office, 1978—82; head Fla. Dept. Hwy. Safety and Motor Vehicles, Tallahassee, 1982—84; mayor City of Sunrise, 1984—87; atty. gen. State of Fla., Tallahassee, 1987—2002; sr. judge Broward County, Fla., 2002—; dean St. Thomas Univ. Law Sch., Fla., 2003—. Democrat. Office: St Thomas U Law Sch 16400 NW 32nd Ave Miami FL 33054*

BUTTREY, DONALD WAYNE, lawyer; b. Terre Haute, Ind., Feb. 6, 1935; s. William Edgar and Nellie (Vaughn) B.; children: Greg, Alan, Jason; m. Karen Lake, Mar. 23, 1985. BS, Ind. State U., 1956; JD, Ind. U., 1961. Bar: Ind. 1961, U.S. Dist. Ct. 1961, U.S. Ct. Appeals (7th cir.) 1972, U.S. Tax Ct. 1972, U.S. Supreme Ct. 1972. Law clk. to chief judge Steckler, U.S. Dist. Ct. So. Dist. Ind., 1961-63; mem. McHale, Cook & Welch, P.C., Indpls., 1963—2001, pres., 1986-93, chmn., 1993—2001; of counsel Wooden & McLaughlin, LLP, 2001—. Chmn. Ctrl. Region IRS-Bar Liaison Com., 1984; mem. jud. nominating com. Marion County Mcpl. Ct., 1993-96; mem. Estate Planning Coun. Indpls., 1990—. Note editor Ind. Law Jour., 1960-61. Trustee Ind. State U., 1992-2000, v.p. bd., 1997-2000; bd. dirs. Ind. State U. Found., 1991—. With AUS, 1956-58, Korea. Fellow Am. Coll. Tax Counsel, Am. Bar Found., Ind. State Bar Found., Indpls. Bar Found. (pres. 1993-96, Buchanan award 1999); mem. ABA (taxation, real property, probate and trust sect., liaison IRS-Bar Liaison com., taxation sect. 1995-96), Ind. State Bar Assn. (bd. govs. 1994-96, taxation, real property, probate and trust sect., chmn. taxation sect. 1982-83), Indpls. Bar Assn. (pres. 1990, mem. probate, taxation sects.), Highland Golf and Country Club, Indpls. Athletic Club (bd. dirs. 1982-88), Skyline Club, Univ. Club (bd. dirs. 1997-2000). Presbyterian. Corporate, general, Estate planning, Corporate taxation. E-mail: dbuttrey@woodmaclaw.com.

BUTTS, J. DAVID, lawyer, pharmacist; b. Glace Bay, N.S., Can., Feb. 22, 1962; arrived in Hungary, 2001; s. Charles William Butts and Rita Monica Yorke; m. Irena Kralova, Aug. 22, 1998; 1 child, Tatiana Marie. BSc (Pharm._), Dalhousie, Halifax, 1983; LLB, BCL, McGill, Montreal, 1990. Bar: Quebec, Budapest (foreign legal advisor). Dir. hosp. pharmacy Glace Bay Cmty. Hosp., Glace Bay, 1983—86; lawyer Stikeman Elliott, Montreal, 1991—94; dir. legal affairs Burroughs Wellcome Inc., Montreal, 1994—95; sole proprietor J. David Butts Avocat, Montreal, 1995—97; ptnr. O'Connor Greenspoon, Senc, Montreal, 1997—2000, Greenspoonnn Butts, Senc, Montreal, 2000—01; prin. Hayhurst Berlad Robinson, Budapest, Hungary, 2002—, Bucharest, Romania, 2002—, Sofia, Bulgaria, 2002—. Dir. Lupus Quebec, 1996—99, Bioniche Life Sci. Inc., Toronto, 1998—, Bioniche Pharma Group Ltd, Galway, Ireland, 2000—. Contbr. articles to prof. jour.; co-author: (manual) Lupus Patient Advocacy Handbook , 1997. Recipient First Pl. Common Law, McGill Faculty of Law, 1990. Mem.: Barreau de Quebec, Can. Pharmacists Assn., Kanawaki Golf Club, Delta Theta Phi (Disting. Scholarship Key 1990). Roman Cath. Avocations: golf, scuba diving, theater , travel. Home: 46 Bem RKP 1024 Budapest Hungary Office: Hayhurst Berlad Robinson 46 Terez Krt 1066 Budapest Hungary

BUTZNER, JOHN DECKER, JR., retired federal judge; b. Scranton, Pa., Oct. 2, 1917; BA, U. Scranton, 1939; LLB, U. Va., 1941. Bar: Va. 1941. Pvt. practice law, Fredericksburg, 1941—58; judge 15th and 39th Jud. Cir. of Va., 1958—62; U.S. judge Ea. Dist. Va., 1962—67; cir. judge U.S. Ct. Appeals (4th cir.), Richmond, Va., 1967—98; judge for appointment of ind. counsel U.S. Ct. Appeals for D.C. Cir., 1988—98. With USAAF, 1942—45. Office: 10th And Main St 443 Courthouse Rd Richmond VA 23219-

BUX, WILLIAM JOHN, lawyer; b. Wadsworth, Ohio, Nov. 10, 1946; s. William J. and Helen M. (Sybelnik) B.; m. Linda Alice Zenar, Feb. 13, 1971. BSME, Ohio State U., 1969, MS, 1970; JD, So. Meth. U., 1977. Bar: Tex. 1977, U.S. Dist. Ct. (so. dist.) Tex. 1978, U.S. Ct. Appeals (5th cir.) 1978, U.S. Dist. Ct. (no. dist.) Tex. 1980, U.S. Dist. Ct. (ea. and we. dists.) Tex. 1981, U.S. Ct. Appeals (11th cir.) 1981, U.S. Supreme Ct. 1982; cert. Labor & Employment Law Tex. Bd. Legal Specialization. Assoc. Vinson & Elkins, Houston, 1977-85; ptnr. Hughes & Luce, Dallas, 1985-93; shareholder Locke Purnell Rain Harrell, Dallas, 1994-97; ptnr. Liddell, Sapp, Zivley, Hill & La Boon, Houston, 1997-98, Locke, Liddell & Sapp, Houston, 1999—. Author: Developing and Enforcing Drug and Alcohol Abuse Work Rules: A Primer for Texas Employers, 1984. Sec. So. Meth. U. Law Sch. Alumni Council, Dallas, 1986-88. Capt. USAF, 1971-74. Mem. ABA, Tex. Bar Assn. (chmn. labor and employment law sect. 1992-93), Houston Bar Assn., 5th Cir. Bar Assn. Republican. Roman Catholic. Labor (including EEOC, Fair Labor Standards Act, labor-management relations, NLRB, OSHA). Home: 2511 Westgate St Houston TX 77019-6609 Office: Locke Liddell & Sapp 600 Travis St 3400 JP Morgan Chase Twr Houston TX 77002-3095

BUXBAUM, RICHARD M. law educator, lawyer; b. 1930; AB, Cornell U., 1950, LLB, 1952; LLM, U. Calif., Berkeley, 1953; Dr. (hon.), U. Osnabrück, 1992, Eötvös Lorand U., Budapest, Hungary, 1993. Bar: Calif. 1953, N.Y. 1953. Practice law pvt. firm, Rochester, N.Y., 1957-61; prof. U. Calif., Berkeley, 1961—, dean internat. and area studies, 1993-99. Hon. prof. U. Peking, 1998. Editor-in-chief Am. Jour. Comparative Law. Property commn. mem. Found. for Responsibility, Remembrance, and the Future, Germany, 2001—. Recipient Humboldt prize, 1991, German Order of Merit, 1992, Officier Arts et Lettres, France, 1997, Order of Rio Branco, Brazil, 1998. Mem. AAAS, German Soc. Comparative Law (corr.), Coun. on Fgn. Rels. Office: U Calif Sch Law 888 Simon Hall Berkeley CA 94720-0001 E-mail: bux@uclink.berkeley.edu.

BUZAK, EDWARD JOSEPH, lawyer; b. Jersey City, Apr. 20, 1948; s. Edward and Nellie (Scalone) B.; m. Gail Marie Capizzi, July 24, 1971; children: Craig E., Lindsay T. BA, Union Coll., 1970; JD, Georgetown U., 1973. Bar: N.J. 1973, D.C. 1974. Assoc. Villoresi & Flanagan, Boonton, N.J., 1973-75; ptnr. Villoresi & Buzak, Boonton, 1976-82; pvt. practice, Montville, N.J., 1983—. Trustee Housing Partnership of Morris County, Morristown, N.J., 1992—. Contbr. articles to profl. jours. Chmn. affordable housing com., asst. counsel N.J. State League of Municipalities, Trenton, N.J., 1986—; asst. counsel N.J. Planning Ofcls., 1998-2000. Mem. Assn. Environ. Authorities (chmn. legis. com. 1986-2000), N.J. Inst. Local Govt. Attys.(pres.), N.J. Bar Assn. (chmn. local gov. com. 1985-87). Roman Catholic. Avocations: running, skiing, music, reading. Environmental, Land use and zoning (including planning), Municipal (including bonds). Office: 150 River Rd Ste N4 Montville NJ 07045-8920

BUZARD, DAVID ANDREW, lawyer; b. Evanston, Ill., Dec. 8, 1961; s. Clifford Howard and Mary Louise (Dole) B.; children: Clémentine, Victor. Student, Carleton Coll., 1980-82; BA in Linguistics, Northwestern U., 1984; JD, Tulane U., 1990. Bar: Ill. 1991, Va. 1997, U.S. Ct. Mil. Appeals 1991, U.S. Ct. Appeals (4th cir.) 1991, U.S. Dist. Ct. (ea. dist.) Va. 1997, U.S. Dist. Ct. (no. dist.) Ill. 1998, U.S. Supreme Ct. 1998; cert. qualified guardian ad litem for incapacitated adults, Va. Law clk. U.S. Atty.'s Office, New Orleans, 1988-90; judge advocate U.S. Navy, 1990-97; assoc. Glasser & Glasser, PLC, Norfolk, Va., 1997-98, Bennett & Zydron, P.C., Virginia Beach, Va., 1998—. Adj. asst. prof. Old Dominion U., 2002; lectr. law and ethics U.S. Joint Forces Staff Coll., 2002-03; counsel Alliance Française Chapitre de Grasse, Norfolk, Va., 1996—; judge Jessup Internat. Law Moot Ct. Competition, 1998. Contbr. articles to profl. jours. Lt. USN, 1990-97; lt. comdr. USNR, 1998—. Nat. Merit scholar. Mem. ATLA (fed. tort liability and mil advocacy sect., nursing homes litigation group), Va. State Bar (bd. govs. mil. law sect.), Virginia Beach Bar Assn., Va. Trial Lawyers Assn. (del. 2003—), Norfolk and Portsmouth Bar Assn. (founder, chair mil. law and lawyers com. 1997-2002, Walter E. Hoffman award 2001), Judge Advocates Assn., DAV, Naval Res. Assn., Pan European Orgn. Personal Injury Lawyers Avocations: civic activities, travel. Military, Personal injury (including property damage), Professional liability. Office: Bennett & Zydron PC 120 S Lynnhaven Rd Virginia Beach VA 23452 E-mail: dbuzard@bandzlaw.com.

BUZZARD, STEVEN RAY, lawyer; b. Centralia, Wash., May 22, 1946; s. Richard James and Phylis Margaret (Bevington) B.; m. Joan Elizabeth Merrow, Nov. 11, 1967; children: Elizabeth Jane, Richard Wolcott, James Merrow. BA, Cen. Wash. State Coll., 1972; postgrad., U. Wash., 1973; JD, U. Puget Sound, 1975. Bar: Wash. 1975, U.S. Dist. Ct. (we. dist.) Wash. 1976, U.S. Supreme Ct. 1979, U.S. Tax Ct. 1983. Assoc. Shires, Kruse, Wallace, Roper & Kamps, Port Orchard, Wash., 1975-77; ptnr. Buzzard & O'Connell, Centralia, 1978-80, Buzzard & Tripp, Centralia, 1980-94, Buzzard & Assoc., Centralia, 1994—. City atty. Mossyrock, Wash., 1979-94, Vader, Wash., 1989-96, Bucoda, Wash., 1989-99; judge Centralia, 1980-84, Winlock, Wash., 1983—; sec. Consol. Enterprizes Inc., Centralia, 1986-88; judge Chehalis (Wash.) Mcpl. Ct., 1998—, Winlock Mcpl. Ct., 1983—, Napavine Mcpl. Ct., 2001—, Vader Mcpl. Ct., 2001—; past pres. Reliable Enterprises, Inc. Chmn. bd. dirs. Lewis County Cmty. Svcs., Chehalis, Wash., 1981-84; bd. dirs. Lewis County United Way, 1993-95; mem. adv. bd. Centralia Sch. Dist., 1995—; founding mem., trustee, treas. Dollars for Scholars, Scholarship Found., 1997-2002. Mem. ABA (rural judges com. 1986), Wash. State Bar Assn. (ct. rules com. 1992-), Lewis County Bar Assn. (past pres.), Assn. Trial Lawyers Am., Wash. State Trial Lawyers Assn., Wash. State Govt. Lawyers Bar Assn. (former trustee), Wash. State Dist. and Mcpl. Ct. Judges Assn. (dist. and mcpl. rural judges com.), Wash. Bd. Jud. Adminstrn. (best practices com. 2001—, ct. improvement com., 2001-), Dist. and Mcpl. Judges Assn. (dist. and mcpl. rural judges com., ct. improvement com., long range planning com.), Kiwanis (pres.-elect 1991, pres. 1992-93, Disting. Past Pres. award 1994), Elks (trustee Centralia 1981—). Avocations: running, boating, hiking, biking, fishing. State civil litigation, General practice, Personal injury (including property damage). Office: Buzzard & Assoc 314 Harrison Ave Centralia WA 98531-1326 Fax: (360) 330-2078.

BYARS, WALTER RYLAND, JR., lawyer; b. Birmingham, Ala., Oct. 5, 1928; s. Walter Ryland and Essie (Hopper) B.; m. Mildred Lucile Rhodes, Dec. 22, 1950; children: Debra Leigh Byars Patterson, Walter Ryland III, Rebecca Lynn Byars Pradat, John Baxter. BS, U. Ala., 1948, LLB, 1952, JD, 1969. Bar: Ala. 1952, U.S. Ct. Appeals (5th and 11th cirs.), U.S. Dist. Ct. (no., mid. and so. dists.) Ala., U.S. Supreme Ct. Pvt. practice, Troy, Ala., 1953-57; atty. legal dept. So. Bell. Tel. & Tel. Co., Atlanta, 1957-59, gen. atty. Birmingham, 1959-68; ptnr. Steiner, Crum & Baker, 1968—; city atty. Montgomery, Ala., 2002—; ptnr. Steiner, Crum & Byars, PC, Montgomery, 2003—. Bd. editors Ala. Law Rev., 1951-52. Lt. (j.g.) USNR, 1952-53. Fellow Am. Bar Found., Internat. Soc. Barristers (gov. 1977-83, sec.-treas. 1979-80, 2d v.p. 1980-81, 1st v.p. 1981-82, pres. 1982-83), Am. Coll. Trial Lawyers; mem. ABA (Young Lawyers past mem. exec. council, com. chmn.), Ala. Bar Assn. (pres.-elect 1983-84, pres. 1984-85, past pres. Young Lawyers, past sect. chmn., past com. chmn.), Pike County Bar Assn. (past pres.), Birmingham Bar Assn. (past com. chmn.), Montgomery County Bar Assn. (past com. chmn., bd. dirs. 1976-79, v.p. 1978, pres. 1979), Ala. Law Inst. (council), Montgomery Area Com. of 100, Masons, Sigma Chi, Phi Alpha Delta. Methodist. General practice. Home: 1744 Fairforest Dr Montgomery AL 36106-2602 Office: Regions Bank Bldg PO Box 668 Montgomery AL 36101-0668 E-mail: wbyars@steinercrum.com.

BYBEE, JAY SCOTT, judge, federal agency administrator; b. Oakland, Calif., Oct. 27, 1953; s. Rowan Scott and Joan (Hickman) B.; m. Dianna Jean Greer, Feb. 15, 1986; children: Scott, David, Alyssa, Ryan. BA, Brigham Young U., 1977, JD, 1980. Bar: D.C. 1981, U.S. Ct. Appeals (4th cir.) 1983, U.S. Supreme Ct. 1985, U.S. Ct. Appeals (5th cir.) 1986, U.S. Ct. Appeals (2d, 9th, 10th and D.C. cirs.) 1987. Law clk. to judge U.S. Ct. Appeals (4th cir.), 1980-81; assoc. Sidley & Austin, Washington, 1981-84; atty., advisor U.S. Dept. Justice, Washington, 1984-89; assoc. counsel to Pres. of U.S. The White House, 1989-91; prof. law La. State U., Baton Rouge, 1991-98, U. Nev., Las Vegas, 1999—2000; asst. atty. gen. off. legal counsel U.S. Dept. Justice, Washington, 2001—02; judge U.S. Ct. Appeals (9th cir.), San Francisco, 2003—. Contbr. articles to profl. jours. Missionary Mormon Ch., Santiago, Chile, 1973-75. Edwin S. Hinckley scholar, Brigham Young U., 1976-77. Mem. Phi Kappa Phi. Avocations: piano, all sports, reading. Office: US Ct of Appeals PO Box 193939 San Francisco CA 94119-3939*

BYCZYNSKI, EDWARD FRANK, lawyer, financial executive; b. Chgo., Mar. 17, 1946; s. Edward James and Ann (Ruskey) B.; children: Stefan, Suzanne. BA, U. Wis., 1968; JD, U. Ill., 1972; Cert. de Droit, U. Caen (France), 1971. Bar: Ill. 1972, U.S.Dist. Ct. (no. dist.) Ill. 1972, U.S. Supreme Ct. 1976. Title officer Chgo. Title Inst. Co., 1972-73; ptnr. Haley, Pirok, Byczynski, Chgo., 1973-76; pres. Alderstreet Investments, Portland, Oreg., 1976-82, Nat. Tenant Network, Portland, 1981—. Asst. regional counsel SBA, Chgo., 1973-76; pres. Bay Venture Corp., Portland, 1984—. Contbr. articles to profl. jours. Mem. ABA, Ill. Bar Assn. Independent. Banking, Franchising, Property, real (including real estate development, water). Home: PO Box 2377 Lake Oswego OR 97035-0614 Office: 525 1st St Ste 105 Lake Oswego OR 97034-3100 E-mail: efb@ntnnet.com.

BYE, KERMIT EDWARD, federal judge, lawyer; b. Hatton, N.D., Jan. 13, 1937; s. Kermit Berthrand and Margaret B. (Brekke) Bye; m. Carol Beth Soliah, Aug. 23, 1958; children: Laura Lee, William Edward, Bethany Ann. BS, U. N.D., 1959, JD, 1962. Bar: N.D. 1962, U.S. Dist. Ct. N.D. 1962, U.S. Ct. Appeals (8th cir.) 1969, U.S. Supreme Ct. 1974, Minn. 1981. Dep. securities commr. State of N.D., 1962—64, spl. asst. atty. gen., 1964—66; asst. U.S. atty. U.S. Atty.'s Office, Dist. N.D., 1966—68; ptnr. Vogel Brantner Kelly Knutson Weir & Bye, Fargo, ND, 1968—2000; judge U.S. Ct. Appeals (8th cir.), Fargo, 2000—. Contbr. articles. Chmn. Red River Human Svcs. Found., 1980—83; S.E. Mental Health and Retardation Ctr., Inc. Fellow: Am. Bar Found.; mem.: ABA (state del. 1986—95, bd. govs. 1999—2001, state del. 2002—), Minn. Bar Assn., Cass County Bar Assn., N.D. State Bar Assn. (pres. 1983—84). Lutheran. Office: 655 1st Ave N Ste 330 Fargo ND 58102

BYERS, DAVID W. human resources specialist; b. Lodi, Ohio, Oct. 6, 1941; s. Waldo E. Byers and Elsie C. Bennett; m. Christine Haberkorn, June 20, 1970 (div.); children: Brian, Jennifer; m. Nancy H. Hornbuckle, Mar. 21, 1992. BA, Miami U., 1963; JD, U. Cin., 1966. Bar: Ohio. Office: Employment Law Consulting Group LLC 3425 Swanson Ste 101 Plano TX 75025 Office Fax: 972-618-1731. Business E-Mail: dbyers@elcg.com.

BYERS, FRANKLIN HAYS, II, lawyer; b. Rantoul, Ill., June 1, 1952; s. Franklin Hays and Florence Aileen (Nichols) B.; children: Franklin Hays, III, Barrett Jameson. BS, U. Ill., 1974, JD, 1977. Bar: Ill. 1977, U.S. Ct. Appeals (7th cir.) 1985, U.S. Supreme Ct., 1986. Pvt. practice, Decatur, Ill., 1977—. Mem. Ill. State Bar Assn. (assembly mem., 1988-90). General practice. Office: 3795 N Woodford St Ste 100 Decatur IL 62526-2717

BYERS, MATTHEW T(ODD), lawyer, educator; b. Ridley Park, Pa., May 30, 1963; s. Richard Lynn and Joyce Ann (Ralston) B.; m. Lori Byers; children: Amanda Michelle, Amber, Helen, David, Saren, Loren. BA, U. N. Mex., 1985, JD, 1990. Bar: N.Mex. 1990, U.S. Dist. Ct. N.Mex. 1991, U.S. Ct. Appeals (10th cir.) 1991, U.S. Tax Ct. 1991, Pa. 1997. Staff Los Alamos (N.Mex.) Nat. Lab., 1989—90; assoc. Marek, Francis & Byers, P.A., Carlsbad, N.Mex., 1990—2001, ptnr., 1998—2001; assoc. Forry, Ullman, Ullman & Forry, Reading, Pa., 1997; pvt. practice Matthew T. Byers, Carlsbad, N.Mex., 2001—. Assoc. editor N. Mex. U. Law Review, 1990. Bd. dirs. United Way of Carlsbad, 1990-93. Recipient Cert. of Achievement Renaissance Program, Carlsbad, 1991. Mem. ABA, State Bar Assn. N.Mex., Eddy Cty. Bar Assn. (pres. 1993), George L. Reese Jr. Inn of Court, Pa. Bar Assn. Democrat. Baptist. Avocations: softball, music, reading. Bankruptcy, General practice, Probate (including wills, trusts). Office: 211 W Mermod Carlsbad NM 88220

BYRAM, JAMES ASBERRY, JR., lawyer; b. Gadsden, Ala., July 27, 1954; s. James Asberry Sr. and Barbara Anne (Ryals) B.; m. Virginia Elisabeth Nicholas, Apr. 17, 1982; 1 child, Nicholas Byram. BS, U. Ala., 1976, JD, 1979. Bar: Ala. 1979, U.S. Dist. Ct. (mid. and no. dists.) Ala. 1980, U.S. Ct. Appeals (11th cir.) 1981, U.S. Supreme Ct. 1985, U.S. Dist. Ct. (so. dist.) Ala. 1992. Assoc. Steiner, Crum & Baker, Montgomery, Ala., 1979-83, ptnr., 1984-89, Balch & Bingham, Montgomery, Ala., 1989—. Bd. dirs. Trinity Presbyn. Sch., Inc., pres., chmn. 1998-99. Chmn. Young Life Montgomery, 1990-92; deacon Local Presbyn. ch., chmn. 1999. Hugo Black scholar U. Ala., 1978. Mem. Ala. Bar Assn. (bd. bar examiners 1992-96), Montgomery County Bar Assn. (grievance com. 1984-88, panel chmn. 1988-94), Bench and Bar Soc., Montgomery Country Club, Kiwanis. Federal civil litigation, State civil litigation, General practice. Home: 1749 Pineneedle Rd Montgomery AL 36106-2615 Office: Balch & Bingham 2 Dexter Ave Montgomery AL 36104-3574 E-mail: jbyram@balch.com.

BYRD, CHRISTINE WATERMAN SWENT, lawyer; b. Oakland, Calif., Apr. 11, 1951; d. Langan Waterman and Eleanor (Herz) Swent; m. Gary Lee Byrd, June 20, 1981; children: Amy, George. BA, Stanford U., 1972; JD, U. Va., 1975. Bar: Calif. 1976, U.S. Dist. Ct. (ctrl., so. no., ea. dists.) Calif., U.S. Ct. Appeals (9th cir.). Law clk. to Hon. William P. Gray, U.S. Dist. Ct.,

L.A., 1975-76; assoc. Jones, Day, Reavis & Pogue, L.A., 1976-82, ptnr., 1987-96; asst. U.S. atty. criminal divsn. U.S. Atty.'s Office-Cen. Dist. Calif., L.A., 1982-87; ptnr. Irell & Manella, L.A., 1996—. Mem. Calif. Law Revision Commn., 1992-97. Author: The Future of the U.S. Multinational Corporation, 1975; contbr. articles to profl. jours. Mem.: Assn. Bus. Trial Lawyers (bd. govs. 1996—99), 9th Jud. Cir. Hist. Soc. (bd. dirs. 1986—, pres. 1997—2002), Century City Bar Assn. (bd. govs. 2001—), Stanford Profl. Women Los Angeles County, Am. Arbitration Assn. (large and complex case panel 1992—, nat. energy panel 1998—, bd. dirs. 1999—), Women Lawyers Assn. Los Angeles County, Los Angeles County Bar Assn., Calif. State Bar (com. fed. cts. 1985—88), ABA (assoc.; Vice Chmn, com. on ADR Advocacy in Lit.), Stanford U. Alumni Assn. Republican. General civil litigation, Alternative dispute resolution. Office: Irell & Manella LLP 1800 Ave Of Stars Ste 900 Los Angeles CA 90067-4276

BYRD, GARY ELLIS, lawyer; b. Dothan, Ala., Mar. 8, 1957; m. Emily Marie Reid; children: Elizabeth, Virginia and Victoria (twins). BS in Pre-Law and Am. History summa cum laude, Troy State U., 1979; JD, U. Ala., 1982. Bar: Ga. (no. and middle dists.) 1983, U.S. Dist. Ct. (no. and so. dists), Ga., U.S. Ct. Appeals. Pntr. Bishoff & Byrd, Talbotton, Ga., 1982-86; assoc. Bunn & Kirby, Hamilton, Ga., 1993—, 1993-96; ptnr. Bunn & Byrd, Hamilton, Ga., 1996—2000; city atty. Woodland, Ga., 1986—, Geneva, Ga., 1988—, Shiloh, Ga., 1994—; ptnr. Bunn, Byrd, Newsom & Hix, 2001—. Chmn. bd. dirs. Talbot County Law Libr., Talbotton, 1992-2003; bd. dirs. Harris County Law Libr., Hamilton, 1998-2003. Contbr. numerous articles to newspapers and profl. jours., chpt. to book; author City of Woodland city code, 1986, City of Geneva charter, 2000, City of Shiloh charter, 2001. Bd. dirs. Chattahoochie-Flint RESA, Americus, Ga., 1986-87, Pine Mountain Regional Arts Coun., Manchester, Ga., 1986-88; pres., chmn. exec. com. Talbot County 2000 Group, Talbotton, 1987-88; coach debate team dept. social studies Manchester (Ga.) H.S., 1982; chmn. appropriations com. Harris County YMCA, Hamilton, 1994-2000, 2002-03, bd. dirs. 1994-2000, 2002-03; mem. budget com. City of Talbotton, 1989-92, councilman, 1985-92, mem. policy adv. com., 1986-92, vol. fireman, 1982-93; ct. apptd. adminstr. City of Geneva, Ga., 1992; mem. adv. com. Am. Security Coun., Washington, 1976-82; dir. Harris County Indigent Def. Program, 1999-2003. Recipient Outstanding Svc. award Talbot County Jaycees, 1983, Mem. Ga. Bar Assn., Ga. Mcpl. Assn. (atty.'s sect.), Talbot County C. of C. (chmn. membership com. 1992-93, bd. dirs. 1993), Harris County C. of C. (bd. dirs. 2000-02), Troy State U. Alumni Assn. (membership com. East Ala./West Ctrl. Ga. chpt. 1993-99, Rotary (chmn. internat. svc. com. 2002-03), Phi Kappa Phi, Phi Alpha Theta (State Hist. Rsch. award 1979). Author, City of Geneva, GA Charter, 2000; Author, City of Shiloh, GA Charter, 2001. Avocations: model trains, stock car racing. General practice, Probate (including wills, trusts), Property, real (including real estate development, water). Home: PO Box 119 Hamilton GA 31811-0119 Office: 103 N College St PO Box 489 Hamilton GA 31811-0489

BYRD, L(AWRENCE) DEREK, lawyer; b. Bradenton, Fla., Feb. 5, 1968; s. H. Lawrence and Peggi Jean Byrd; m. Heather Solnoki, Oct. 15, 1996. BS in Criminology, Fla. State U., 1990; JD cum laude, Quinnipiac Coll., 1995. Bar: Fla. 1996, U.S. Dist. Ct. (mid. dist.) Fla. 1997; bd. cert. Criminal Trial Practice. Assoc. Mark Lipinski, PA, Bradenton, 1996; atty. Pub. Defender's Office, Sarasota, Fla., 1996-98; ptnr. Byrd Law Firm, Sarasota, 1998—. Bd. dirs. YMCA, Sarasota, 1997—. Mem.: ACLU, Sarasota County Bar Assn., Fla. Assn. Criminal Defense Lawyers (Cert. in Criminal Trial Law, pres.), Am. Inn of Ct. Avocations: tennis, golf, softball. Criminal, Family and matrimonial, Personal injury (including property damage). Office: Byrd Law Firm Ste 201 2151 Main St Sarasota FL 34237 E-mail: byrdlaw@thebyrdlawfirm.com.

BYRD MISCHE, RICHARD J. lawyer; b. Washington, July 28, 1937; B in Electonics Engring., George Washington U., 1960, JD magna cum laude, 1972; postgrad., U. Calif., San Diego. Bar: VA. 1972, U.S. Dist. Ct. (ea. and we. dists.) Va. 1973, DC 1976, U.S. Ct. Appeals (4th cir.) 1976. Founder, sr. prin. Byrd Mische, P.C., Fairfax, Va., 1972—. Co-author: (software) VADER. Commr. Chancerty Fairfax Cir. Ct.; mem. Fairfax Electronic Filing Taskforce; bd. dirs. No. Va. Mediation Svc., 1993—97, Va. Info. Providers Network. Named one of 50 Best Divorce Lawyers in Met. Washington Area, Washingtonian Mag., 2000; recipient Lifetime Achievement award. Mem.: Fairfax Bar Assn. (chmn. family law sect., mem. cir. ct. com., mem. tech. com., editor Fairfax Bar Support Guidelines 1988—2002, lectr.), Va. State Bar (bd. govs. family law sect., mem. tech. task force, lectr.). Family and matrimonial, Property, real (including real estate development, water). Office: 10521 Judicial Dr Ste 120 Fairfax VA 22030 Office Fax: 703-591-4226.*

BYRNE, DONNA J. law librarian; AS in Bus. Adminstrn., Onondaga C.C., 1992; BS in Info. Mgmt. and Tech., Syracuse U., 1994, MLS, 1996. Analyst jr. ct. N.Y. State Supreme Ct. Libr., Syracuse, 1996—99; law libr. Hancock & Estabrook, LLP, Syracuse, 1999—. Mem.: Am. Assn. Law Librs. (assoc.). Office: Hancock & Estabrook LLP 1500 MONY Tower 1 Syracuse NY 13221 E-mail: dbyrne@hancocklaw.com.

BYRNE, GRANVILLE BLAND, III, lawyer; b. San Antonio, Jan. 26, 1952; s. Granville Bland and Mary (Dowling) B.; divorced; children: Peyton Smith, Fulton Buckner; m. Monique Renée Wise, 1999. AB, U. N.C., Chapel Hill, 1974; JD, Harvard U., 1978. Bar: Ga. 1978, U.S. Dist. Ct. (no. dist.) Ga. 1978, U.S. Ct. Appeals (5th cir.) 1978, U.S. Ct. Appeals (11th cir.) 1981. Assoc. Swift, Currie, McGhee & Hiers, Atlanta, 1978-84, ptnr., 1984-94; prin. Byrne & Davis, P.C., Atlanta, 1994-99, Byrne, Moore & Davis, PC, Atlanta, 1999—2002, Byrne, Eldridge, Moore & Davis PC, Atlanta, 2003—. Bd. dirs. Compeer Atlanta, Inc., chmn., 1993-, 1996-2002; bd. dirs. Cagle's, Inc. Elder, mem. session 1st Presbyn. Ch. Atlanta, 1993-96, 99-2002. Mem. ABA, Ga. Bar Assn., Atlanta Bar Assn. Democrat. Presbyterian. Commercial, contracts (including sales of goods; commercial financing), Corporate, general, Securities. Home: 3555 Castlegate Dr NW Atlanta GA 30327-2601 Office: Byrne Davis PC 3340 Peachtree Rd NE Atlanta GA 30326-1000 E-mail: gbb@bmdlaw.net.

BYRNE, GREGORY WILLIAM, lawyer; b. Chgo., Aug. 18, 1939; s. William Daniel and Theresa (Gregory) B.; m. Debra Demert, Oct. 12, 1984; children: Kathleen Minde, Gregory W. Jr., Julianna Rowe, Elizabeth Hering. AB, U. S.C., 1968; JD, Harvard U., 1971. Bar: Oreg. 1971, U.S. Dist. Ct. Oreg. 1971, U.S. Ct. Appeals (9th cir.) 1973, U.S. Supreme Ct. 1990, U.S. Ct. Fed. Claims 1993. Enlisted USMC, 1959, advanced through grades to capt., 1965, resigned, 1967; sole practice Portland, Oreg., 1971—. Judge pro tem Multnomah County Cts., Portland, 1983-90; dir. Harvard Legis. Rsch. Bur., 1970-71; adj. scholar Cascade Policy Inst., 2002. Mem. Multnomah Bar Assn. Republican. General civil litigation, Constitutional, Property, real (including real estate development, water). Office: 5550 SW Macadam Ave Portland OR 97201 E-mail: gbyrne@att.net.

BYRNE, ROBERT WILLIAM, lawyer; b. Frankfurt, Germany, Dec. 12, 1958; s. Robert Patrick and Anne Lise (Brondelsbo) B. BA, Rutgers U., 1981; JD, Seton Hall U., 1984; LLM, Golden Gate U., 2002. Bar: N.J. 1984, U.S. Dist. Ct. N.J. 1984, D.C. 1986, U.S. Ct. Appeals (3d cir.) 1987, U.S. Ct. Appeals (D.C. and fed. cirs.) 1988, (11th cir.), 1993, U.S. Dist. Ct. D.C. 1989, U.S. Supreme Ct. 1989, N.Y. 1991, U.S. Dist. Ct. (so. and ea. dists.) N.Y. 1991, Fla. 1992, U.S. Dist. Ct. (no. and mid. dists.) Fla. 1992, Calif. 2001., U.S. Dist. Ct. (no. dist.) Calif. 2001, U.S. Ct. Appeals (9th cir.) 2001. Law clk. to Judge Sylvan G. Rothenberg, Superior Ct. Passaic County N.J., 1984-85; asst. prosecutor Bergen County, N.J., 1985-88; assoc. Harwood Lloyd, Hackensack, NJ, 1988-90, Mudge Rose Guthrie Alexander & Ferdon, N.Y.C., 1990-91; sr. assoc. O'Connor, Reddy & Jensen, N.Y.C., 1991-92; pvt. practice Panama City, Fla., 1992-94; v.p., gen. counsel Bay Bank & Trust Co., Panama City, Fla., 1994-2000; dep. atty. gen. Calif. Dept. Justice, San Francisco, 2002—. Contbr. Seton Hall Legislative Jour., 1983-84. Mem. Phi Alpha Delta, Pi Sigma Alpha. Democrat. Lutheran. Environmental, FERC practice, Antitrust. Home: 267 Roosevelt Way San Francisco CA 94114-1431 Office: 455 Golden Gate Ave Ste 11000 San Francisco CA 94102-7004 Fax: 415-703-5480. E-mail: robert.byrne@doj.ca.gov.

BYRNE, THOMAS J. lawyer; b. Rochester, N.Y., June 17, 1944; m. Brenda C. Byrne, June 4, 1994; children: Thomas, David, Heather. AB, U. Rochester, 1967; JD, U. Denver, 1976. Bar: Colo. 1977, Calif. 1977, U.S. Ct. Appeals (10th cir.) 1977, U.S. Dist. Ct. Colo. 1977, U.S. Dist. Ct. (so. dist.) Tex. 1990, N.Y. 1990, U.S. Ct. Appeals (3d cir.) 1992, U.S. Dist. Ct. (ea. dist.) Pa. 1992, U.S. Dist. Ct. (ea. dist.) Va. 1992, U.S. Ct. Appeals (4th cir.) 1993, U.S. Dist. Ct. (no. dist.) Ill. 1993, U.S. Dist. Ct. Ariz. 1993, U.S. Dist. Ct. Utah 1996, U.S. Dist. Ct. (so. dist.) N.Y. 1997. Law clk. Dist. Ct. Colo., Denver, 1976-77; assoc. Ullstrom Law Offices, Denver, 1978-83; ptnr., Denver mgr. Conklin & Adler, Ltd., Denver and Chgo., 1983-86; mng. ptnr. Byrne, Kiely & White LLP, Denver, 1986—. Mem. fin. com. Citizens for Romer, Denver, 1990—. Capt. USAF, 1967-73. Mem. ABA (tort and ins. practice sect., vice chair aviation and space law com., litigation sect., forum on air and space law), Internat. Bar Assn., Colo. Bar Assn., Denver Bar Assn., State Bar Calif., N.Y. State Bar Assn., Def. Rsch. Inst., Colo. Def. Lawyers Assn., Nat. Bus. Aircraft Assn., Lawyer-Pilot Bar Assn., Aviation Ins. Assn. Avocations: flying, travel, sports. Aviation, Insurance, Product liability. Office: Byrne Kiely & White LLP 1120 Lincoln St Ste 1300 Denver CO 80203-2140

BYRNE, WALTER ROBBINS, JR., lawyer; b. Clarksville, Tenn., May 30, 1947; s. Walter Robbins and Elisabeth (Cross) B.; children: Walter Robbins III, William Hardwick. BA in English, U. Ky., 1969, MBA, 1974; JD, U. Louisville, 1980. Bar: Ky. 1980. Vice pres. First Nat. Bank of Louisville, 1974-80; ptnr. Stites & Harbison, Lexington, 1980—. Bd. dirs. People's Exch. Bank, Beattyville, Ky. 1st lt. U.S. Army, 1969-72. Mem. ABA, Ky. Bar Assn., Fayette Bar Assn. Republican. Banking, Corporate, general. Home: 239 Queensway Dr Lexington KY 40502-1625 Office: Stites and Harbison 250 W Main St Ste 2300 Lexington KY 40507-1758

BYRNES, WILLIAM JOSEPH, lawyer; b. Bklyn., Apr. 11, 1940; s. William James and Margaret Mary (English) B.; m. Catherine Belle Rollings, Aug. 15, 1970 (dec. 2002); children: Jennifer, Suzanne. BS, Fordham U., 1961; JD, Yale U., 1964. Bar: N.Y. 1965, D.C. 1970, Va. 1992. Atty. AEC, Washington, 1964-68; internat. mgr. Comm. Satellite Corp., Washington, 1968-70; ptnr. Haley, Bader & Potts, Arlington, Va., 1970-95; of counsel Irwin Campbell & Tannenwald, Washington, 1995-96; pvt. practice, McLean, Va., 1997—; v.p. Shared Spectrum Co. Author: Telecommunications Regulation: Something Old and Something New in the Communications Act: A Legislative History of the Major Amendments, 1934-1996, 1999; co-author: The Common Carrier Provisions--A Product of Evolutionary Development in A Legislative History of the Communications Act, 1989, Decency Redux: The Curious History of the New FCC Broadcast Indecency Policy, 1989, A New Telecommunications Paradigm, 1993; bd. dirs. Great Falls Players; mem. Elden Street Players, Rockville Little Theatre, Am. Music Stage, Sterling Playmakers, Vienna Theater Co. Candidate Fairfax County Bd. Suprs., 1995; bd. dirs. McLean Citizens Assn (ex. pres.) Recipient cert. U.S. Atomic Energy Commn., 1967. Mem. Fed. Comms. Bar Assn., Va. State Bar, D.C. Bar Assn. Avocations: acting, videography. Administrative and regulatory, Appellate, Communications. Office: 7921 Old Falls Rd Mc Lean VA 22102-2414

CABLE, JOHN FRANKLIN, lawyer; b. Hannibal, Mo., Dec. 22, 1941; s. John William and Dorothy (Stanley) C.; m. Leslie Gibbs, Apr. 5, 1965; children: Coventry, Tory, John. AB, Stanford U., 1964; LLB, Harvard U., 1967. Bar: Oreg. 1967. Assoc. Miller, Nash, Wiener, Hager & Carlsen, Portland, Oreg., 1967-73, ptnr., 1973—. Corporate, general, Finance, Intellectual property. Office: Miller Nash LLP 111 SW 5th Ave Fl 35 Portland OR 97204-3604 E-mail: cable@millernash.com.

CABRANES, JOSÉ ALBERTO, judge; b. Mayaguez, P.R., Dec. 22, 1940; s. Manuel and Carmen López Cabranes; m. Kate Stith, Sept. 15, 1984; children: Alejo, Benjamin José;children from previous marriage: Jennifer Ann, Amy Alexandra. AB, Columbia U., 1961; JD, Yale U., 1965; MLitt in Internat. Law, Cambridge (Eng.) U., 1967; LLD (hon.) , Colgate U., 1988, other instns., 1989—2000. Bar: N.Y. 1968, D.C. 1975, U.S. Dist. Ct. Conn. 1976. Assoc. Casey, Lane & Mittendorf, N.Y.C., 1967—71; assoc. prof. law sch. Rutgers U., Newark, 1971—73; spl. counsel to gov. P.R., head Office Commonwealth P.R., Washington, 1973—75; gen. counsel Yale U., New Haven, 1975—79; judge U.S. Dist. Ct. Conn., New Haven, 1979—94, chief judge, 1992—94; judge U.S. Ct. Appeals (2nd cir.), 1994—. Mem. Pres.'s Commn. White House Fellowships, 1993—96, Pres.'s Commn. Mental Health, 1977—78; U.S. del. Conf. Security and Coop. in Europe, Belgrade, 1977—78; bd. dirs. James Madison Meml. Fellowship Found., 1995—; founding mem. P.R. Legal Def. and Edn. Fund, 1972, chmn. bd., 1977—80; cons. to sec. Dept. State, 1978; mem. Fed. Cts. Study Com., 1988—90; instr. history P.R. Colegio San Ignacio de Loyola, Rio Piedras, PR, 1962; supr. in internat. law Queens' Coll., Cambridge U., 1966—67. Author: Citizenship and the American Empire, 1979; co-author (with Kate Stith): Fear of Judging: Sentencing Guidelines in the Federal Courts, 1998 (Cert. of Merit, ABA); author: articles on law and internat. affairs. Trustee Yale U., 1987—99, Yale-New Haven Hosp., 1978—80, 1984—87, Colgate U., 1981—90, Century Found., N.Y.C., 1983—2000, Columbia U., 2000—. Fed. Jud. Ctr., 1986—90; mem. Coun. on Fgn. Rels.; bd. dirs. Aspira of N.Y. (Puerto Rican edn. agy.), chmn., 1971—73. Recipient Life Achievement award, Nat. P.R. Coalition, 1987, John Jay award, Columbia Coll., 1991, Life Achievement award student divsn., Nat. Hispanic Bar Assn., 1991, Learned Hand medal for excellence in fed. jurisprudence, Fed. Bar Coun., 2000; Kellett rsch. fellow, Columbia Coll. at Cambridge U., 1965—67. Fellow: ABA, Mex.-Am. Lawyers Assn. (Spl. Recognition award 1994); mem.: Nat. Hispanic Bar Assn., Am. Law Inst., Conn. Bar Assn. (Naruk Jud. award 1993). Roman Catholic. Office: US Ct of Appeals US Courthouse 141 Church St New Haven CT 06510-2030

CACACE, MICHAEL JOSEPH, lawyer; b. Apr. 20, 1952; s. Jerry F. and Margaret F. (Pesditsch) Cacace; m. Maureen R. Brown, May 24, 1975; children: Joseph M., Christine M. BA, Fordham U., 1974; JD, N.Y. Law Sch., 1978. Bar: Conn. 1978, N.Y. 1979, U.S. Dist. Ct. Conn. 1979, U.S. Ct. Appeals (2d cir.) 1981, U.S. Dist,. Ct. (so. dist.) N.Y. 1982. Atty. Saxe, Bacon & Bolan, N.Y.C., 1978—79, Abate, Fox & Farrell, Stamford, Conn., 1979—82; pvt. practice law Stamford, Conn., 1982—87; ptnr. D'Andrea & Cacace, Stamford, Conn., 1988—94, Cacace Tusch & Santagata, Stamford, Conn., 1994—. Co-chmn. 13th Charter Revision Com., Stamford, 1982—83; bd. dirs. The Vol. Ctr., Stamford, 1980—86, pres., 1984—86; v.p. Gateway Cmtys., Inc., Stamford, 1981—89; bd. dirs. Stamford Commn. on Aging, 1975—80, chmn., 1978—80; bd. dirs. Vis. Nurses Assn., Stamford, 1982—87, Shippan Point Assn., Stamford, 1980—83, Stamford Ctr. for the Arts, 1986—, v.p., 1989—2000, pres., 2000—; bd. dirs. Stamford Sr. Svcs., 1998—. Named one of Best Lawyers in Am.; recipient Cmty. Leader of Yr. award, The Stamford Adv., 1986, Good Scout award, Conn. Yankee coun. Boy Scouts Am., 2001, Dr. Max Reich award, N.Y. Law Sch., Humanitarian award, Southwestern Conn. Assn. Life Underwriters, 1987—88, Lawyers Co-op Book award, Lawyers Co-op Book Co., 1977, Thomas F. Richardson Pres.'s award, United Way Stamford, 1995, Citizen of Yr. award, The Fred Robbins Post #142 Jewish Vets. of U.S., 1995. Mem.: ATLA, Conn. Trial Lawyers Assn., N.Y. Bar Assn., Conn. Bar Assn. (chair planning and zoning sect. 1994—97), Stamford/Darien Bar Assn. (mem. exec. com. 1980—92, treas. 1986—87, sec. 1987—88, 2d v.p. 1988—89, 1st v.p. 1989—90, pres. 1990—91), Urban Inst., Am. Planning Assn. (Conn. chpt.), State St. Debating Soc., Stamford C. of C. (bd. dirs. 1999—), Landmark Club (bd. govs. 1995—2001), Roasters Club (Stamford). Democrat. Roman Catholic. State civil litigation, General practice, Property, real (including real estate development, water). Home: 316 Scofieldtown Rd Stamford CT 06903-4012 Office: Cacace Tusch & Santagata PO Box 15859 777 Summer St Stamford CT 06901-1022

CACCAVALE, STEPHEN JOSEPH, lawyer; b. Belleville, N.J., May 9, 1961; s. Joseph Michael and Eileen (Tully) C. BA, Bethany Coll., 1983; MBA, Rutgers U., Newark, 1985; JD, Seton Hall U., 1989. Bar: N.J. 1990, U.S. Dist. Ct. N.J. 1990. Ptnr., shareholder LaPenna, Teitelbaum & Caccavale, P.C., Clifton, N.J., 1991-95, Teitelbaum, Caccavale, & Wiseberg, LLC, Bloomfield, 1995—2001. Cons. Rutgers U. Small Bus. Devel. Ctr. Mem. N.J. State Bar Assn. (mem. elder law sect. 1997—), Passaic County Bar Assn. (chmn. environ. law sect. 1996-97), Ocean County Bar Assn. Avocations: running, golf, tennis, coin collecting. Bankruptcy, Federal civil litigation, Commercial, contracts (including sales of goods; commercial financing). Office: 300 Broadacres Dr Bloomfield NJ 07003 E-mail: tcitcaccscaccavale@comcast.net.

CACCESE, MICHAEL STEPHEN, lawyer; b. Penn Valley, Pa., Nov. 21, 1954; s. Frederick D. and Mary J. Caccese; m. Barbara Mitchel, Jan. 7, 1978; chldren: Stephen M., Michelle L. BA, Pa. State U., 1977; JD, Temple U., 1980. Bar: Pa. 1980, Va. 1993, U.S. Dist. Ct. (we. dist.) Va. 1997, Mass. 2001. Corp. counsel Federated Ivestors, Inc., 1980-83; sr. v.p., assoc. counsel Frank Russell Co., Tacoma, 1983-93; sr. v.p., gen. counsel, sec. Assn. for Investment Mgmt. and Rsch., Charlottesville, Va., 1993-2000; ptnr. Kirkpatrick & Lockhart, Boston, 2001—. Mem. editl. bd. Villanova Jour. Law and Investment Mgmt., 1997—, Jour. for Performance Measurement, 1997—. Mem. ABA, Boston Soc. Security Analysts, Assn. for Investment Mgmt. and Rsch. Corporate, general, Non-profit and tax-exempt organizations, Securities. Home: 34 Choate Ln Ipswich MA 01938 Office: Kirkpatrick & Lockhart 75 State St Boston MA 02109 E-mail: mcaccese@kl.com.

CACCIATORE, S. SAMMY, lawyer; b. Tampa, Fla., Aug. 2, 1942; s. Sam and Margarita C.; m. Carolyn Michels, Aug. 10, 1963; children: Elaine Michel, Sammy Michel. BA, JD, Stetson U., DeLand, Fla., 1966. Bar: Fla. 1966, U.S. Ct. Appeals (5th cir.) 1967, U.S. Supreme Ct. 1971, U.S. Ct. Appeals (11th cir.) 1981, U.S. Dist. Ct. (mid. dist. 1966) Fla. Asst. public defender 9th jud. cir. State of Fla., State of Fla., 1966; assoc. firm Orlando, Fla., 1966-67; pvt. practice Melbourne, Fla., 1967—; ptnr. Nance, Cacciatore & Hamilton, Melbourne, Fla., 1970—. Mem. 5th Dist. Appellate Nomination Commn., 1979-83; mem. Fla. Med. Malpractice Adv. Com., 1982; mem. jud. nominating commn. Fla. Supreme Ct. 1986-90, mem. jury instrn. com., 2001—; bd. overseers Stetson U. Coll. Law, 1995—, trustee, 2000—; lectr. in field. Contbr. articles to profl. jours., chpts. to books. Trustee A. Max Brewer Meml. Law Libr., Brevard County, Fla., 1972-76, chmn., 1972-75. Mem. ABA, ATLA, Am. Law Inst., Internat. Acad. Trial Lawyers, Am. Bd. Profl. Liability Lawyers, Am. Bd. Trial Advocates, Nat. Bd. Trial Advocacy, Acad. Fla. Trial Lawyers (bd. dirs. 1970—, pres. 1984-85, Pres.'s award 1983), Internat. Acad. Trial Lawyers Assn. (adminstrn. of justice com. 1989), Fla. Bar (bd. govs. 1994-99, exec. com. 1995-99, vice chmn. advt. task force 1995-97, budget com. 1994-97, chmn. 1996, mem. exec. com. trial lawyer sect. 1975, chmn. constl. revision com. 1997—, mem. legis. com. 1995-99, chmn. 1998-99, mem. jury instrn. com. Fla. Supreme Ct., 2001—), So. Trial Lawyers Assn., Stetson Lawyers Assn. (1st v.p. 1992-93, pres.-elect 1994-95, pres. 1995-96), Brevard County Bar Assn. (bd. dirs., Pres.'s award 1975), Vassar Carlton Inn of Ct. (emeritus), Eau Gallie Yacht Club (gov., vice commodore 1981-82, commodore 1983-84). Democrat. Roman Catholic. General civil litigation, Personal injury (including property damage), Product liability. Office: 525 N Harbor City Blvd Melbourne FL 32935-6837

CADDELL, JOHN A. lawyer; b. Tuscumbia, Ala., Apr. 23, 1910; s. Thomas Arthur and Florence Lee (Huff) C.; m. Lucy Bowen Harris, Sept. 1, 1935; children— Thomas A., Lucinda Lee, Henry Harris and John A. (twins). AB, U. Ala., 1931, LLB, 1933, LLD (hon.), 1982. Bar: Ala. bar 1933. Since practiced in, Decatur. Sec., dir. Southeastern Metals Co., Inc., Birmingham, 1946-68; chmn. bd. First Nat. Bank Decatur, 1976-81; City atty., Decatur, 1936-59; counsel com. investigating campaign expenditures U.S. Ho. of Reps., 1944; bd. commrs. Ala. State Bar, 1939-54, Jud. Council Ala., 1946-58; mem. bd. Bar Examiners Ala., 1949, 50 Mem. Ala. Democratic Exec. Com., 1938-50; Trustee U. Ala., 1954-79, also pres. pro tem, 1974-78. Fellow Am. Coll. Trust and Estate Counsel, Am. Coll. Trial Lawyers, Am. Bar Found.; mem. ABA, Ala. Bar Assn. (pres. 1951-52), Morgan County Bar Assn., U. Ala. Alumni Assn. (pres. 1953), Decatur C. of C. (pres. 1943-44), Ala. Acad. Honor, Pi Kappa Alpha, Omicron Delta Kappa, Phi Delta Phi. Democrat (mem. Ala. exec. com. 1938-50). Presbyn. (elder). Clubs: Athletic, U. Alabama, Decatur Kiwanis (pres. 1939). Home: PO Box 2688 Decatur AL 35602-2688 Office: 214 Johnston St SE Decatur AL 35601-2516 E-mail: jcaddell2200@aol.com.

CADDY, MICHAEL DOUGLAS, lawyer; b. Long Beach, Calif., Mar. 23, 1938; s. Frank Edward and Tabitha (Miles) C. BS in Fgn. Svc., Georgetown U., 1960; JD, NYU, 1966. Bar: DC 1970, Tex. 1979. Practiced in, Washington and, Tex.; exec. dir. com. on pub. affairs McGraw-Edison Co., N.Y.C., 1960-61; asst. to lt. gov. State of N.Y., 1962-65; asst. to exec. v.p. NAM, N.Y.C., 1966-67; Washington liaison Gen. Foods Corp., 1968-70; assoc. Gall, Lane, Powell & Kilcullen, 1970-74; legis. counsel Nat. Assn. Realtors, Washington, 1975-76; atty. Office Tex. Sec. of State, Austin, 1980-81. Author: The Hundred Million Dollar Payoff, 1974, How They Rig Our Elections, 1975, Understanding Insurance, 1984, Legislative Trends in Insurance Regulation, 1985, Exploring America's Future, 1987. Mem. Rep. County Com., N.Y.C., 1965-66; nat. dir. Young Ams. for Freedom, 1960-62. Scholar Intercollegiate Studies Inst., 1957-59. Mem.: FBA, ACLU, ABA, ATLA, Nat. Lesbian and Gay Law Assn., Nat. Trust Hist. Preservation, People for Am. Way, Supreme Ct. Hist. Soc., Nat. Coun. Crime and Delinquency, Internat. Platform Assn., Am. Acad. Polit. and Social Sci., Am. Econ. Assn., Assn. Former Intelligence Officers, Am. Judicature Soc., Stonewall Lawyers Assn. Houston, Houston Bar Assn. Office: 7941 Katy Fwy Ste 296 Houston TX 77024-1924 E-mail: douglascaddy@justice.com.

CADENHEAD, ALFRED PAUL, lawyer; b. LaGrange, Ga., Oct. 14, 1926; s. Roy E. and Omie (Bishop) C.; m. Sara Davenport, Oct. 14, 1945; children: Steven Paul, David James. Jr. coll. certificate, W. Ga. Coll., 1944; LL.B., Emory U., 1949. Bar: Ga. 1949. Sr. counsel, ptnr. Hurt, Richardson, Garner, Todd & Cadenhead, Atlanta; with Hurt, Richardson, 1977-92; now of counsel Fellows, Johnson & La Briola, Atlanta, 1993—. Pres. Atlanta Legal Aid Soc., 1958 Pres. Met. Atlanta Mental Health Assn., 1964-65, Ga. Assn. Mental Health, 1968; past trustee Queens Coll., Charlotte, N.C.; lifetime trustee West Ga. Found. Served with paratroops U.S. Army, 1944-46. Recipient West Ga. Coll. Disting. Svc.award, 1993, Emory U. Law Sch. Disting. Alumnus award, 1996, Ben F. Johnson Pub. Svc. award Ga. State U., 1999, Founders award State U. West Ga., 2001. Fellow ABA, Am. Acad. Matrimonial Lawyers, Am. Coll. Trial Lawyers, Internat Soc. Barristers; mem. State Bar Ga. (past bd. govs.), Atlanta Bar Assn. (pres. 1970-71, Charles E. Watkins award for disting. and sustained svc. 1992, Leadership award 2000), Atlanta Estate Planning Coun. (pres. 1976). Presbyterian. General practice. Home: 6305 Riverside Dr NW Atlanta GA 30328-3646 Office: South Tower Peachtre Ctr Ste 2300 225 Peachtree St NE Atlanta GA 30303-1731

CADENILLAS, ADOLFO ALBERTO, lawyer; b. Lima, Peru, Apr. 10, 1941; s. Francisco Cadenillas and Clotilde Galvez; m. Nedda Astrid Reymer; children: Adolfo, Nedda. Bachellor, San Marcos U., Lima, Peru,

1964, JD, 1968. With Galvez Tafur Law Office, Peru, 1958-69, ptnr., 1970-84, mgr., 1985-89; pres. bd. Cadenillas & Galvez Tafur Law Office, Peru, 1989; ptnr. G&R Consellors, Lima, Peru, 1980-99; pres. bd. ONG, Lima, 1990-98. Mem.: Latin Am.-German Jurist Assn., Peruvian Bar Lawyers, Japanese-Peruvian Chamber Industry and Commerce, World Jurist Assn., Inter-Am. Assn. Indsl. Property, Inter-Pacific Bar Assn., Internat. Assn. Protection Indsl. Property, Bar of Lawyers, World Assn. Lawyers (chmn. 2003), Club Social Miraflores, Jockey Club, Club of Union, Lions Club, Grand Lodge of Peru (grand warden 2002). Office: Av Los Libertadores 533 Ste 201 Lima 27 Peru Fax: 51-1-4426687. E-mail: galveztafur@galveztafur.com.

CADLE, JERRY NEAL, lawyer; b. Swainsboro, Ga., June 3, 1951; s. F.H. and Eugenia (Baker) Cadle; m. Paula Kay Ferre, Dec. 27, 1971; children: Ivy Neal, Donald Jacob, Jean Marie. Student, Mid. Ga. Coll., 1969—70, Ga. So. Coll., 1970—71; BBA, U. Ga., 1972, JD, 1975. Bar: Ga. 1975, U.S. Dist. Ct. (so. dist.) Ga. 1975, U.S. Tax Ct. 1976, U.S. Ct. Appeals (11th cir.) 1981. Assoc. Rountree & Rountree, Swainsboro, 1975—76; ptnr. Rountree & Cadle, Swainsboro, 1977—87, Rountree Cadle & McNeely, Swainsboro, 1987—. Commr. Emanuel County, 1997—2000; chmn. Emanuel County Commn., 2000—. Chmn. East Georgia Coll. Found., 1990—2000; pres. Swainsboro Devel. Corp., 1977—; deacon First Bapt. Ch., Swainsboro, 1983—85, 1987—, chmn. deacons, 1988—89, chmn. bd. trustees, 1984—85; bd. dirs. Emanuel County 4-H Found., 1975—2003, v.p., 1979—2003. Mem.: Mid. Jud. Cir. Bar Assn. (sec.-treas. 1978, 1983, pres. 1988), Ga. Sch. Bd. Attys. Assn., Swainsboro Country Club (dir. 1981—85, pres. 1984). Commercial, contracts (including sales of goods; commercial financing), Probate (including wills, trusts), Property, real (including real estate development, water). Home: 957 W Main St Swainsboro GA 30401 Office: Rountree Cadle & McNeely 130 S Main St Swainsboro GA 30401-3618

CADY, ELWYN LOOMIS, JR., medico legal consultant, educator; b. Ames, Iowa, Feb. 21, 1926; s. Elwyn Loomis Sr. and Annabel (Lacey) C.; m. Jane Carolyn Elliott, Jan. 27, 1964 (dec. Dec. 1989); children: James Anson, Kathryn Anne; stepchildren: Martin Norman Jensen III, Paul Elliott Jensen. BS in Medicine, U. Mo., 1955; JD, Tulane U., 1951. Bar: Mo. 1951, U.S. Supreme Ct. 1965. Sci. comml. tchr., athletic dir. and coach Vermillion (Kans.) Rural High Sch., 1948-49; pvt. practice Kansas City, St. Louis, Independence, Mo., 1951—; dir. law-medicine program U. Kansas City, 1951-56; asst. dir. Law-Sci. Inst. U. Tex., Austin, 1956-57, sec. Law-Sci. Acad. Am., 1956-57; of counsel Koenig & Dietz, St. Louis, 1959-74; gen. counsel Elliott Oil, Inc., Independence, 1966—, Overland Park Dry Cleaners, Inc. Mem. com. on mgmt. Ea. Jackson County Planned Parenthood Clinics, Independence, 1970-75. Author: (book) Law and Contemporary Nursing, 1961, 1st. rev. edit., 1963; Author: (with others) Immediate Care of the Acutely Ill and Injured, 1974, Cardiac Arrest and Resuscitation, 1958, 4th rev. edit., 1974, West's Federal Practice Manual, 1960, rev. 2nd edit., 1989, Gradwohl's Legal Medicine, 1954; book reviewer: sci. books and films. Legal Counsel Friends of the Truman Campus, U. Mo.-Kansas City, Independence, 19 87-97, Cmty. Assn. for the Arts, Independence, 1991—; charter mem. Friends of Nat. Frontier Trails Ctr., Independence, 1990—, Independence Hist. Trails City Com., 1991—. With U.S. Army, 1944-45, ETO. Fellow Harry S. Truman Libr. Inst. for Nat. and Internat. Affairs (hon.), Am. Acad. Forensic Sci. (ret.); mem. AAAS (life), Nat. Geog. Soc. (life), Am. Legion (past comdr., judge adv., chaplain, chmn. state blood donor program, chmn. dist. oratorical contest), Mo. Writers' Guild (past pres., historian), Soc. Mayflower Descs. (gov. Heart of Am. colony), Phi Alpha Delta (life), Phi Beta Pi, Tau Kappa Epsilon. Health. Home and Office: 1919 Drumm Ave Independence MO 64055-1836

CADY, MARK S. judge; b. Rapid City, SD, July 12, 1953; married; 2 children. Undergrad. degree, Drake U., JD, 1978. Law clk. 2d Jud. Dist. Ct., 1978-79; asst. Webster County atty.; with law firm; dist. assoc. judge, 1983—86; dist. ct. judge, 1986—94; judge Iowa Ct. Appeals, 1994—98, chief judge, 1997—98; justice Iowa Supreme Ct., 1998—. Author: (book) "Curbing Litig. Abuse and Misuse: A Jud. Response". Chmn. Supreme Ct. Task Force on Ct.'s and Cmty.'s Response to Domestic Abuse. Mem.: Webster County Bar Assn., Iowa State Bar Assn. Office: Iowa Supreme Ct State House Des Moines IA 50319-0001 E-mail: MarkS.Cady@jb.state.ia.us.*

CAFFEE, LORREN DALE, lawyer; b. Decatur, Ind., Oct. 22, 1947; s. Howard Dale and Maxine Faye (Smith) C.; m. Mary Katherine Hostetler, May 25, 1968 (div. Apr. 1982); children: Liesl Katherine, Evan Dale, Colin Dale (dec.); m. Mary Jannice Dyer, June 14, 1986. BA, Bluffton Coll., 1969; JD, Georgetown U., 1972. Bar: Ind. 1972, U.S. V.I. 1994, U.S. Dist. Ct. (no. dist.) Ind. 1974. Pvt. practice, Decatur, 1972-73, 74-76; assoc. DeVoss & DeVoss Law Offices, Decatur, 1973-74; judge Adams County Ct., Decatur, 1976-84, Adams Superior Ct., Decatur, 1985-90, Adams Cir. Ct., Decatur, 1991-99; assoc. A.J. Weiss & Assoc. Law Office, 1999—. Mem. county ct. com. Ind. Jud. Ctr., 1978-88, chmn., 1983-86; mem. juvenile benchbook com. Jud. Conf. of Ind., 1991-99, bd. dirs., 1995-99. Bd. dirs. Ind. Right to Life, 1974-76; mem. constn. and by-laws com. Ind. Young Reps. Fedn., 1974, of counsel, 1975-76; chmn. Adams County Young Reps., 1973-76. Mem. Ind. State Bar Assn., Adams County Bar Assn. (pres. 1975-76), Ind. Judges' Assn., Am. Judges Assn., Nat. Coun. Juvenile and Family Ct. Judges, Federalist Soc. Lutheran. Avocations: jazz music, aviation, sports cars, art, reading. Criminal. Home: PO Box 11479 St Thomas VI 00801-4479 Office: Law Offices of Norman Jones 4002 Raphune Hill Ste 407 St Thomas VI 00802

CAHN, JAMES, lawyer, martial arts educator; b. Cleve., Apr. 16, 1946; s. Sherman D. and Barbara Cahn; m. Jean A. Johnson, May 20, 1978; children: Rachel, Lucy. BA, U. Pa., 1968; JD, Ohio State U., 1973; 7th Degree Black Belt, Oriental Martial Arts Coll., 2001. Bar: Ohio 1973. Assoc. Calfee, Halter & Griswold, Cleve., 1973-75; pvt. practice Cleve., 1975-77; ptnr. Hermann, Cahn & Schneider, Cleve., 1977—. Instr., Master Oriental Martial Arts Coll., Cleve. and Columbus, Ohio, 1975—; legal counsel U.S. Taekwondo Union, Colorado Springs, Colo., 1977-81, 85-86; lectr. Ohio Jud. Coll., others. Founding mem. Ctr. for Principled Family Advocacy, pres., 2002. Fellow Am. Acad. Matrimonial Lawyers (pres. Ohio chpt. 1997-98); mem. ABA, Ohio State Bar Assn., Cuyahoga County Bar Assn. (chair family law sect. 1990-91), Cleve. Bar Assn. (family law sect.), Oakwood Club. Family and matrimonial. Office: Hermann Cahn & Schneider 1301 E 9th St Ste 500 Cleveland OH 44114-1876

CAHN, JEFFREY BARTON, lawyer; b. N.Y.C., Jan. 1, 1943; s. Harold Leon and Vivian (Loewy) C.; m. Miriam Epstein, Jan. 22, 1965; children: Lauren Samantha, Vanessa Shari. BA, Ind. U., 1964; JD, Rutgers U., 1967. Bar: N.J. 1967, U.S. Dist. Ct. N.J. 1967, U.S. Ct. Appeals (3d cir.) 1971, U.S. Supreme Ct. 1971, U.S. Tax Ct. 1973, U.S. Ct. Appeals (D.C. cir.), 1979, N.Y. 1980, U.S. Ct. Appeals (9th cir.) 1981, U.S. Claims Ct. 1981, U.S. Dist. Ct. (so. dist.) N.Y. 1992, U.S. Dist. Ct. (ea. dist.) N.Y. 1994, U.S. Ct. Appeals (2nd cir.) 1998. Law clk. to sr. presiding judge Appellate Div. N.J. Superior Ct., Trenton, N.J., 1967-68; assoc. Schapira, Steiner & Walder, Newark, 1968-72; ptnr. Sills, Cummis, Radin, Tischman, Epstein & Gross, Newark, 1972—. Author: (with others) New Jersey Transaction Guide, Vol. 12, 1993, The Use of Another's Trademark: A Review of the Law in The United States, Canada, and Western Europe, 1997; co-author, editor: Trademark Law Basics Coursebook, 2001; rsch. editor: Rutgers Law Rev., 1966-67; cons. editor Trademark Administration, 1999; contbr. articles to profl. jours. Mem. ATLA, ABA, N.J. State Bar Assn., Essex County Bar Assn., Internat. Trademark Assn. (publs. bd., 2002, projects editl. bd. 2001-), N.Y. State Bar Assn. (sect. intellectual property, chair copyright law com.), Am. Intellectual Property Law Assn., N.J. Intellectual Property Law Assn., Phi Delta Phi (Outstanding Grad. 1967). Jewish. Federal civil litigation, General civil litigation, Trademark and copyright. Home: 72 Winged Foot Dr Livingston NJ 07039-8229 Office: Sills Cummis Radin Tischman Epstein & Gross Legal Ctr 1 Riverfront Plz Fl 13 Newark NJ 07102-5401

CAHN, RICHARD CALEB, lawyer; b. Bklyn., June 11, 1932; s. Irving and Pearl (Abel) C.; m. Vivian Isabel Meksin, Dec. 24, 1961; children: Michael, Lisa, Daniel, Sara. AB, Dartmouth Coll., 1953; LLB, Yale U., 1956; U. London, 1959. Bar: NY 1956, Fla. 1966, US Supreme Ct. 1960. Student asst. US atty. So. Dist. NY, NYC, 1955; atty. U.S. Dept. Justice, Washington 1956-57; ptnr. Cahn & Cahn, LLP, Melville, NY; prin. asst. dist. atty. Suffolk County (NY), 1965-66; dep. atty. Town of Huntington (NY), 1966-68; spl. counsel towns of Smithtown, Islip, Brookhaven, Babylon, Southhampton (NY), 1967-68, Islip, NY, 1976-83, Huntington, NY, 1981-92; counsel Brentwood Sch. Dist., 1977-82, 86-90; spl. counsel Amityville Sch. Dist., 1978-79, Village of North Hills, 1978-79, Merrick Pub. Library; adj. prof. Touro Coll., 1987-90, 93—; hearing officer NY State Edn. Dept., Nassau and Suffolk Counties, 1971-77; spl. dist. atty. Suffolk County, 1972; participant World Peace Through Law Conf., 1967, Malpractice Mediation Panel, 2d dept., 1974-84, Gov.'s Jud. Nominating Com. 2d dept., 1975-81; screening com. bankruptcy judges U.S. Dist. Ct. Dist. NY, 1976-81, screening com. US magistrates, 1977-81; regional counsel SUNY, Stony Brook, 1972-90. Bd. dirs. Stony Brook Found., 1974-86, Ea. Dist. Civil Litigation Fund, 1982-86; del. Moscow Conf. on Law & Jurisprudence, 1990; trustee Adelphi U., 1997—. Fellow Soc. Values in Higher Edn., 1984-96; mem. ABA, NY Bar Assn. (ho. of dels. 1981-83, chmn. condemnation, zoning and property use com. 1989—), Suffolk County Bar Assn. (pres. 1981-82), Fed. Bar Assn., Am. Judicature Soc., Fed. Bar Council (v.p. 1982-84, trustee 1984-89), Huntington Lawyers Club. Contbr. articles to profl. jours.; mem. editl. bd. Yale Law Jour., 1954. Federal civil litigation, State civil litigation. Office: 445 Broadhollow Rd Ste 332 Melville NY 11747 Personal E-mail: rcahn@aol.com. Business E-Mail: rcahn@cahnlaw.com.

CAHOON, PETER THOMAS, lawyer; b. Nyack, N.Y., July 22, 1953; s. Thomas Arthur Cahoon and Carol (Wohlgemuth) Reynolds; m. Heidi Marlene Eve, Mar. 19, 1977; children: Laura Elizabeth, Elizabeth Allison, Faith Ann. BA, NYU, 1974; JD, U. Akron, 1977. Bar: Ohio 1977, U.S. Dist. Ct. (no. dist.) Ohio 1978; cert. criminal trial advocate Nat. Bd. Trial Advocacy. Assoc. Oestreicher, Sternberg & Manes, Akron, Ohio, 1978-79, Metz & Cahoon, Akron, 1979-81, Hershey & Browne, Akron, 1981-86, Baker, Chapman & Diefenbach, Akron, 1986-93, Baker, Chapman & Cahoon, Akron, 1993—98, Buckingham, Doolittle & Burroughs, LLP, Akron, 1998—, co-chair litigation practice group, 2003—. With USMC, 1976. Mem. Ohio State Bar Assn., Akron Bar Assn. (treas. 1992-93). Avocations: reading, sports, family activities. General civil litigation, Criminal, Family and matrimonial. Office: Buckingham Doolittle & Burroughs LLP PO Box 1500 Akron OH 44309-1500

CAHOON, ROBERT STRANGE, lawyer; b. Plymouth, N.C., Dec. 25, 1915; s. Louis Clyde and Minnie Harrison Cahoon; m. Ermah Yelverton Cahoon, July 5, 1941; children: Marilyn, Robert S. Cahoon, Jr.(dec.). LLB, Waike Forest U., 1941. Bar: N.C., U.S. Dist. Ct. (mid. dist.) N.C., U.S. Ct. Appeals (4th cir.), U.S. Supreme Ct. Pvt. practice, Wilmington, NC, 1941—44, Greensboro, NC, 1944—; ptnr. Cahoon, Edgerton, Alspaugh, Greensboro, 1954—61, Cahoon & Swisher, Greensboro, 1961—. Cpl. U.S. Army, 1944—46. Mem.: Greensboro Criminal Def. Attys. (1st pres. 1972—), Greensboro Bar Assn., N.C. Bar Assn., N.C. State Bar. Democrat. Methodist. Avocations: horses, gardening. Condemnation (eminent domain), Criminal, General practice. Home: 213 W Avondale Dr Greensboro NC 27403

CAIN, DOUGLAS MYLCHREEST, lawyer; b. Chgo., Sept. 8, 1938; s. Douglas M. Jr. and Louise C. (Coleman) C.; m. Constance Alexis Adams Moffit, Apr. 18, 1970; children: Victoria Elizabeth Moffit, Alexandra Catherine Moffit. AB, Harvard U., 1960; JD with distinction, U. Mich., 1966; LL.M., N.Y. U., 1970. Bar: Colo. 1966, U.S. Ct. Appeals (10th cir.) 1972, U.S. Supreme Ct. 1972. Assoc. Sherman & Howard, L.L.C., Denver, 1966-72, ptnr., 1972-93; equity mem., 1993—; chmn. policy council Sherman & Howard, Denver, 1984-87; adj. prof. law U. Denver, 1972-78. Mem. Rocky Mountain Estate Planning Council, pres., 1976-77 Assoc. editor: Mich. Law Rev, 1964-66; contbr. articles to profl. jours. Bd. dirs. Craig Hosp. Found., 1980-86, v.p., 1984-85, pres., 1986-87, 88-89; bd. dirs. Colo. Jud. Inst., 1990-96, chmn., 1992-93; bd. dirs. Colo. chpt. Am. Diabetes Assn., 1993, Breathe Better Found., 1993—, Colo. Coun. Econ. Edn., 1996-98, Fortune Found., 1998—; mem. Estate Planning Seminar Group. With USN, 1960-63. Fellow Am. Coll. Tax Coun., Am. Coll. Trust and Estate Counsel; mem. ABA, Colo. Bar Assn. (gov. 1980-82), Greater Denver Tax Coun. Assn. (v.p. 1987, pres. 1988), Assn. Harvard Alumni (regional dir. 1978-81), Rocky Mountain Harvard Club (pres. 1977-78, 92-93), Denver Country Club, Mile High Club, Rotary. Estate planning, Corporate taxation, Taxation, general. Home: 1960 Hudson St Denver CO 80220-1459 Office: Sherman & Howard LLC 633 17th St Ste 3000 Denver CO 80202-3665

CAIN, GEORGE HARVEY, lawyer, business executive; b. Washington, Aug. 3, 1920; s. J. Harvey and Madeleine (McGettigan) C.; m. Patricia J. Campbell, Apr. 23, 1946 (div.); children: George Harvey, James C., John P., Paul J.; m. Constance S. Collins, Aug. 10, 1985 BS, Georgetown U., 1942; JD, Harvard U., 1948. Bar: N.Y. 1949, Ohio 1972, Conn. 1977, U.S. Supreme Ct. 1995. Practiced law, N.Y. State, 1949-71, 73-76; pvt. practice, 1972-73; sec., gen. counsel Nat. Carloading Corp., 1949-54; mem. firm Spence & Hotchkiss, 1954-55; gen. atty., asst. sec. Cerro Corp., 1955-68, sec., gen. atty., 1968-72; v.p., gen. counsel Pickands Mather Co., Cleve., 1971-73; v.p., sec., gen. counsel Flintkote Co., White Plains, N.Y., 1973-76, Stamford, Conn., 1976-80; spl. counsel Day, Berry & Howard, Hartford and Stamford, Conn., 1980-82, ptnr. Stamford, 1983-90, of counsel, 1991—. Sec. Cerro Sales Corp., 1955-71; bd. dirs., sec. Leadership Housing Sys., Inc., 1970-71; bd. dirs., gen. counsel Atlantic Cement Co., Inc., 1962-71; bd. dirs. Hajoca Corp., 1975-79, Polymer Bldg. Sys., Inc.; adj. prof. U. Bridgeport Law Sch., 1983-86. Author: Turning Points: New Paths and Second Careers for Lawyers, 1994, Law Firm Partnership: Its Rights and Responsibilities, 1995, 2nd edit., 1999, Law Partnership Revisited, 2002. Served to 1st lt. USAAF, 1942-46; to capt. USAF, 1951-52. Fellow Am. Bar Found.; mem. ABA (chair sr. lawyers divsn. 2002—), N.Y. State Bar Assn., N.Y.C. Bar Assn., Ohio Bar Assn., Conn. Bar Assn., Am. Law Inst., Am. Soc. Corp. Secs., Georgetown U. Alumni Assn. (mem. Alumni senate), Harvard Club N.Y., Dutch Treat Club. Home: 14 Burnt Hill Rd Farmington CT 06032-2039 Office: Day Berry & Howard City Place I Hartford CT 06103-3499 E-mail: cainghsr@worldnet.att.net.

CAIN, HOWARD GUESS, JR., lawyer; b. Fullerton, Calif., Nov. 15, 1943; s. Howard Guess and Dixie Marie Cain; m. Sharron Sue Jennings, Sept. 22, 1962; children: Destari, Trey, Blakeney. JD, U. Ark., 1972. Bar: Ark., U.S. Dist. Ct. (we. dist.) Ark. Dep. pros. atty. State of Ark., Huntsville, 1972-94; atty. City of Huntsville, 1972—. Bd. dirs. Madison Bank and Trust, Huntsville, 1981—; counsel Meadowview Rehab. Ctrs., Huntsville, 1988—. Atty. County of Madison, Ark., 1972-94. Mem. ABA, Ark. Bar Assn., Carroll/Madison Bar Assn., City Attys. Assn. (Appreciation award 1998), Masons. Baptist. Office: Cain Law Office 104 E Main St Box 539 Huntsville AR 72740

CAIN, ROBERT GAYNOR, lawyer; b. Natick, Mass., July 21, 1951; s. Robert Nolan and Mary Elizabeth (Gaynor) C.; m. Jill Sikora, Apr. 7, 1989; children: Sarah C., R. Nolan, Sikora E. BA cum laude, U. Vt., 1973; JD with distinction, John Marshall Law Sch., 1977. Bar: Vt. 1978, U.S. Dist. Ct. Vt. 1978, U.S. Ct. Appeals (2nd cir.) 1986, N.Y. 1989, U.S. Supreme Ct., 1999. Law clk., chief law clk. to presiding justice Vt. Supreme Ct., Montpelier, 1977-79; assoc. Paul, Frank & Collins, Inc., Burlington, Vt., 1979-83, ptnr., 1983—. Instr. law Champlain Coll., Burlington, 1982-85; assoc. mem. Vt. Bd. Bar Examiners, 1982-87, mem., 1987-96. Exec. rsch. editor John Marshall Jour. Practice and Procedure, 1976-77. Mem. Burlington Zoning Bd. Adjustment, 1983-86; trustee Ruggles Found., Burlington, 1986-2002; clk. ward 4 City of Burlington, 1986-87. Mem. ABA, Vt. Bar Assn., Chittenden County Bar Assn., Vt. Handball Assn. (treas. 1981-2000). Republican. Roman Catholic. Avocations: handball, skiing, running, water skiing. General civil litigation, Insurance, Workers' compensation. Home: 29 John Stark Rd South Hero VT 05486-4909 Office: Paul Frank & Collins Inc 1 Church St Burlington VT 05401-4451 E-mail: rcain@pfclaw.com.

CAIN, TIM J. lawyer; b. Angola, Ind., July 12, 1958; s. Nancy J. (Nichols) C.; m. Debra J. VanWagner, Feb. 28, 1976; children: Christine M., Stephanie L., Katherine S., Jennifer A. BA in Polit. Sci. with honors, Ind. U., 1980; JD, Valparaiso U., 1984; MBA, Ind. Wesleyan U., 1991; LLM in Internat. Bus. and Trade with honors, John Marshall Law Sch., 2001. Bar: Ind. 1984, U.S. Dist. Ct. (no. and so. dists.) Ind. 1984, U.S. Supreme Ct., 2002. Assoc. Hartz & Eberhard, LaGrange, Ind., 1984-85; pub. defender LaGrange Cir. Ct., 1985-86; sr. assoc. Eberhard & Assocs., LaGrange, 1985-86; chief dep. to Pros. Atty.'s Office, LaGrange, 1986-87; ptnr. Eberhard & Cain, LaGrange, 1986-89; pvt. practice LaGrange, 1989-95; pros. atty. La Grange (Ind.) County, 1991—2002; ptnr. Williams and Cain, Ft. Wayne, Ind., 2002—. Asst. atty. La Grange County, La Grange; atty. Town of Shipshewana, Ind., 1984-93. Coach Orland (Ind.) Little League, 1977-79, Prairie Hts. Baseball, LaGrange, 1986-90; pres. Prairie Hts. H.S. Dollars for Scholars, LaGrange, 1989; active LaGrange County Coun. on Aging, 1989-91, Prairie Hts. At-Risk Students Com., 1989—, LaGrange County 4-H Fair Assn., 1993-97. Mem.Ind. Bar Assn., LaGrange County Bar Assn. (sec.-treas. 1986-87, v.p. 1987-89, pres. 1990-93). Clubs: Exchange (pres. 1988-89). Republican. Corporate, general, Private international, Labor (including EEOC, Fair Labor Standards Act, labor-management relations, NLRB, OSHA). Home: 360 S 900 E Lagrange IN 46761-9529 Office: 110 W Berry Ste 1910 Fort Wayne IN 46802 E-mail: tim@williams-cain.com.

CAIRNS, JAMES DONALD, lawyer; b. Chelsea, Mass., Aug. 7, 1931; s. Stewart Scott and Kathleen (Hand) C.; m. Alice Crout Cairns, June 18, 1988; children from previous marriage: Douglas S., Timothy H., Pamela S., Heather M. AB, Harvard U., 1952; JD, Ohio State U., 1958. Bar: Fla. 1974, Ohio 1958, U.S. Dist. Ct. (no. dist.) Ohio 1975, U.S. Tax Ct. 1963. Ptnr. Squire, Sanders & Dempsey, Cleve., 1958-95, Spieth, Bell, McCurdy & Newell, Cleve., 1995—. Served to lt. (j.g.) USNR, 1952-55. Mem. ABA, Am. Coll. Trust and Estate Counsel, Fla. Bar Assn., Ohio State Bar Assn., Bar Assn. Greater Cleve., Union Club, Edgewater Yacht Club, Shoreby Club. Democrat. Episcopalian. Estate planning, Probate (including wills, trusts). Office: Spieth Bell McCurdy Newell 2000 Huntington Bldg 925 Euclid Ave Cleveland OH 44115-1408 E-mail: dcairns@spiethbell.com.

CAJIAO, XIMENA T. lawyer; b. Oakland, Calif., Oct. 20, 1966; Law Degree, U. Los Andes, Bogotá, Colombia, 1990, Georgetown U., 1992. Bar: Colombia 1990, N.Y. 1997. Lawyer for internat. dept. Banco de Bogota, Bogota, 1990—91; assoc. Gomez Pinzón y Asociados, Bogota, 1993—94; legal cons. IIC-Interamerican Devel. Bank, Washington, 1995; fgn. assoc. Morrison & Foerster, Washington, 1996—97; assoc. Kaye, Scholer, Fierman, Hays & Haendler, Washington, 1997—98; sr. assoc. Prieto, Carrizosa, Bogota, 1998—2000, Lewin & Wills, Bogota, 2000—. Commercial, contracts (including sales of goods; commercial financing), Corporate, general, Mergers and acquisitions. Office: Lewin & Wills Abogados Calle 72 #4-03 Bogotá Colombia

CALABRESE, ARNOLD J. lawyer; b. Summit, N.J., Nov. 18, 1960; s. Jack and Valentine (Pannullo) C.; m. Kathryn DeRosa, Aug. 16, 1986. BS in Econs. and Fin., Fairleigh Dickinson U., 1983; JD, U. Bridgeport, 1986. Bar: N.J. 1986, U.S. Dist. Ct. N.J. 1986. Law clk. intern to judge U.S. Dist. Ct. Conn., Hartford, 1985; assoc. Robert J. Hueston (merged with E. Richard Kennedy 1987), Florham Park, Montville, N.J., 1986-88, Rosenberg & Rosenberg, Florham Park, 1988-89; ptnr. Rosenberg, Rosenberg & Calabrese, Florham Park, 1990-96; atty. Law Offices Arnold J. Calabrese PC, 1996—. Lectr. N.J. chpt. Community Assn. Inst., Pennington, 1987—. Mem. ABA, N.J. Bar Assn., Morris County Bar Assn., Phi Delta Phi. Construction, Personal injury (including property damage), Property, real (including real estate development, water). Home: 4 Jolen Ct Florham Park NJ 07932-2519 Office: 171 Ridgedale Ave Ste A Florham Park NJ 07932-1764 E-mail: loajcpc@aol.com.

CALABRESI, GUIDO, judge, law educator; b. Milan, Oct. 18, 1932; s. Massimo and Bianca Maria (Finzi Contini) C.; m. Anne Gordon Audubon Tyler, May 20, 1961; children: Bianca Finzi Contini, Anne Gordon Audubon, Massimo Franklin Tyler BS in Analytical Econs., Yale U., 1953, LLB, 1958, MA (hon.), 1962; BA in Politics, Philosophy and Econs., Oxford U., 1955, MA in Politics, Philosophy and Econs., 1959; LLD (hon.), Notre Dame U., 1979, Villanova U., 1984, U. Toronto, 1985, Boston Coll., 1986, Cath. U. Am., 1986, U. Chgo., 1988, Conn. Coll., 1988, Chgo.-Kent-I.T.T., 1989, William Mitchell Coll. Law, 1992, Princeton U., 1992, Detroit Mercy Sch. Law, 1994, Seton Hall U., 1995, Albertus Magnus Coll., 1995, Lewis and Clark Coll., 1996, St. John's U., 1997, Pace U., 1998, Iona Coll., 1998, Roger Williams U., 1999, Hofstra U., 1999, N.Y. Law Sch., 1999, Skidmore Coll., 2000, Colby Coll., 2001, U. San Diego, 2001; Dott. Ius SD (hon.), U. Turin, Italy, 1982; JD (hon.), U. Pavia, Italy, 1987, U. Stockholm, 1993; PhD (hon.), U. Haifa, Israel, 1988; DPhil, U. Tel Aviv, 1998; LHD (hon.), U. New Haven, 1989, Williams Coll., 1991, Quinnipiac Coll., 1993; DSc in Politics (hon.), U. Padua, Italy, 1990; Dott. Jur. (hon.), U. Bologna, Italy, 1991, U. Milan, 1998. Bar: Conn. 1958. Asst. instr. dept. econs. Yale U., New Haven, Conn., 1955-56; law clk. to Hon. Hugo Black U.S. Supreme Ct., Washington, 1958-59; asst. prof. Yale U. Law Sch., 1959-61, assoc. prof., 1961-62, prof., 1962-70, John Thomas Smith prof. law, 1970-78, Sterling prof. law, 1978-95; prof. emeritus, lectr. Yale U., 1995—; dean Yale U. Law Sch., 1985-94, Sterling prof. law emeritus, lectr., 1995—; judge U.S. Ct. Appeals 2d cir., New Haven, 1994—. Fellow Timothy Dwight Coll., 1960—; vis. prof. Harvard U. Law Sch., 1969-70, Japan Am. Studies Seminar, Kyoto-Doshisha Univs., summer 1972, European U. Inst., Florence, Italy, 1979; Arthur L. Goodhart prof. legal sci. Cambridge U., also fellow St. John's Coll., 1980-81. Author: The Costs of Accidents: A Legal and Economic Analysis, 1970; (with P. Bobbitt) Tragic Choices, 1978; A Common Law for the Age of Statutes, 1983 (ABA citation of merit, Order of Coif Triennial Book award); Ideals, Beliefs, Attitudes and the Law: Private Law Perspectives on a Public Law Problem (Silver Gavel award ABA), 1985; contbr. articles to profl. jours. Hon. trustee Hopkins Grammar Sch., pres. 1976-80; trustee St. Thomas More Chapel, Yale U.; vice-chmn. bd. trustees Carolyn Found., Minn. Rhodes scholar, 1953; named one of Ten Outstanding Young Men Am., U.S. Jaycees, 1962; recipient Laetare Medal, U. Notre Dame, 1985, Marshall-Wythe medal Coll. William and Mary, 1985, award for outstanding rsch. in law and govt. Fellows of Am. Bar Found., 1998, Thomas Jefferson medal in law Jefferson Found./U. Va. Law Sch., 2000. Fellow Am. Acad. Arts & Scis., Associazione Italiana di Diritto Comparato, Brit. Acad. (corr.), Royal Swedish Acad. Scis. (fgn.), Nat. Acad. dei Lincei (fgn.), Acad. delle Sci. di Torino (fgn.); mem. Conn. Bar Assn., Assn. Am. Law Schs. (exec. com. 1986-89), Am. Philos. Soc. Home: 639 Amity Rd Woodbridge CT 06525-1206 Office: US Ct Appeals 2d Cir 157 Church St New Haven CT 06510-2100

CALAMARI, JOSEPH AUGUST, legal educator; b. N.Y.C., Feb. 20, 1919; s. August Alexander and Margaret Elizabeth (Casella) C.; m. Marie Jean Sileo, June 30, 1951; children— Betty Jo, Ann-Marie, Maryellen, James. B.A., Fordham U., 1939, LL.B., 1942; M.Law, NYU, 1949. Bar:

N.Y. 1942, U.S. Dist. Ct. (so. dist.) N.Y. 1946, (ea. dist.) N.Y. 1947, U.S. Ct. Apls. (2d cir.) 1947, Va. 1952, U.S. Supreme Ct. 1951, U.S. Ct. Mil. Apls. 1951. Assoc. counsel Alexander Ash & Schwartz, N.Y.C., 1946-50; post judge adv. Post Headquarters, Ft. Myer, Va., 1950-52; dep. gen. counsel/gen. counsel Mil. Sealift Command Atlantic, Bklyn., 1952-73; prof. law St. John's U. Sch. Law, Jamaica, N.Y., 1973— ; hearing officer U.S. EEO, Washington, 1979— . Contbr. articles to profl. jours. Mem. Western Property Owners of Garden City, N.Y., 1956— ; sponsor Nat. Republican. Congl. Com., 1984; mem. Republican Nat. Com., 1983. Served to col., USAR, 1972-77. Decorated Bronze Star, Army Commendation medal. Mem. Fed. Bar Assn., ABA, Martime Law Assn. U.S., Bar Assn. Nassau County (arbitrator), Res. Officers Assn., Am. Judicature Soc. Roman Catholic. Clubs: Garden City Country, Mast Hope Lodge. Home: 14 Glen Rd Garden City NY 11530-1012

CALAMARO, RAYMOND STUART, lawyer; b. Cairo, May 28, 1944; came to U.S., 1947, naturalized, 1960; s. Albert and Charlotte (Golub) C.; m. Jaana Pirinen; 1 child, Alexander M. AB, Cornell U., 1966; JD, NYU, 1969. Bar: N.Y. State 1970, U.S. Supreme Ct. 1975, D.C. 1976. Legis. dir. Sen.Gaylord Nelson, Washington, 1973-75; exec. dir. Com. for Pub. Justice, N.Y.C., 1975-76; adj. faculty New Sch. Social Rsch., N.Y.C., 1976; staff profl. Carter/Mondale Transition Team, Washington, 1976-77; dep. asst. atty. gen. Office Legis. Affairs, Dept. Justice, Washington, 1977-79; pvt. practice Washington and Brussels, 1979-95; team leader Clinton-Gore Transition Team, 1992-93; ptnr. Hogan & Hartson, Washington, 1995—. U.S. vice-chmn. U.S.-Korea Com. on Bus. Coop., 1997-99. Recipient Royal Order of Polar Star King Carl XVI Gustav, Sweden, 1989. Mem. Met. Club (Washington), St. Albans Tennis Club (Washington). Home: 5073 Lowell St NW Washington DC 20016-2616 Office: Hogan & Hartson 555 13th St NW Ste 800E Washington DC 20004-1161 also: rue de l'Industrie 26 1040 Brussels Belgium E-mail: RSCalamaro@HHLaw.com.

CALCAMUGGIO, LARRY GLENN, lawyer; b. Toledo, Feb. 9, 1951; s. Glenn L. and Darlene M. (Brown) C.; m. Diane L. Seagert, June 30, 1973; children: Jeffrey, Todd, Scott. BBA, U. Toledo, 1973, JD, 1977. Bar: Ohio 1977, U.S. Dist. Ct. Ohio 1979, U.S. Tax Ct. 1984. Auditor Blue Cross N.W. Ohio, Toledo, 1973-75; trust officer Ohio Citizens Bank, Toledo, 1975-78; assoc. Brown, Baker, Schlageter & Craig, Toledo, 1979-80; ptnr. Rohrs, Rimelspach & Calcamuggio, Toledo, 1980-82; trust officer new bus. BancOhio Nat. Bank, Toledo, 1982-84; pvt. practice Toledo, 1984-94; ptnr. Sprenger, Douglas and Calcamuggio Attys., Toledo, 1994-95; pvt. practice Toledo, 1996—. Mem. adv. com. legal assisting tech. U. Toledo, 1980-92, instr., 1987-89. Coach Little League Baseball, 1986-92; trustee Luth. Social Svcs., Toledo, 1989-92, sec. 1992; trustee Luth. Homes Soc. Found., 1997—, Interfaith Hospitality Network of Metro Toledo, 2000-2001. Mem. NRA, Ohio Bar Assn., Toledo Bar Assn., Toledo Estate Planning Coun., Nat. Fedn. Ind. Bus., Toledo Planned Giving Coun. Lutheran. Avocations: shooting, hunting, gun collecting, choir singing. Estate planning, Probate (including wills, trusts), Estate taxation. Office: Ste 4 4149 Holland-Sylvania Rd Toledo OH 43623-2590 E-mail: Larrycal@mynra.com.

CALDAS DE SA, RODRIGO CESAR, lawyer; b. Jaboatão, Brazil, Apr. 1, 1975; s. Bartolomeu Leal De Sá and Diva Maria Caldas de Sá. BA in Law, Cath. U., Recife, 1998; postgrad., U. Fed. Ruralde Pernambuco, Recife, 1999—2000; LLM in Tax Law, U. London, 2002. Bar: Brazil, 1999. With Trigueiro Fontes Advogados, Brazil, 1997—, ptnr., 2001—. Contbr. articles to profl. jours. Chevening scholar, Brit. Coun., London, 2001—02, postgrad, Fund Getulio Vargas, Recife, 2003—. Mem.: Am. C. of C., Ctr. for Internat. Legal Studies of Salzburg Austria (Portuguese, English, & French spkr.). Taxation, general. Home: R Dom Bosco 632/701 50070-070 Boa Vista Recife Brazil Office: Trigueiro Fontes Advogados Av Domingos Ferreira 801 51011 050 Recife Brazil E-mail: rod.recife@trigueirofontes.com.br.

CALDERON, ERNEST, lawyer; b. Morenci, Ariz., Oct. 24, 1957; BS, No. Ariz. U., 1979; JD, U. Ariz., 1982. Bar: Ariz. 1983, U.S. Dist. Ct. Ariz. 1983, U.S. Ct. Appeals (9th cir.) 1984, U.S. Ct. Appeals (D.C. cir.) 1984, U.S. Supreme Ct. 1986. Law clk. to Judge Walter E. Craig, U.S. Dist. Ct., 1982—84; atty. Jennings, Strouss & Salmon, PLC, Phoenix. Fellow: Ariz. Bar Found.; mem.: Am. Bar Found., Am. Law Inst., State Bar Ariz. (pres. 2002—03). Construction, General civil litigation. Office: Jennins Strouss and Salmon 201 E Washington St Phoenix AZ 85004-2385*

CALDWELL, COURTNEY LYNN, lawyer, real estate consultant; b. Washington, Mar. 5, 1948; d. Joseph Morton and Moselle (Smith) C. Student, Duke U., 1966-68, U. Calif., Berkeley, 1967, 1968-69; BA, U. Calif., Santa Barbara, 1970, MA, 1975; JD with highest honors, George Washington U., 1982. Bar: D.C. 1984, Wash. 1986, Calif. 1989. Jud. clk. U.S. Ct. Appeals for 9th Cir., Seattle, 1982-83; assoc. Arnold & Porter, Washington, 1983-85, Perkins Coie, Seattle, 1985-88; dir. western ops. Edn. Real Estate Svcs., Inc., Irvine, Calif., 1988-91, sr. v.p., 1991-98; ind. cons., Orange County, Calif., 1998—. Bd. dirs. Univ. Town Ctr. Assn., 1994; bd. dirs. Habitat for Humanity, Orange County, 1993-94, chair legal com., 1994. Named Nat. Law Ctr. Law Rev. Scholar, 1981-82. Mem. Calif. Bar Assn. Avocation: foreign languages. Home and Office: 140 Cabrillo St #15 Costa Mesa CA 92627 E-mail: clcaldwell@earthlink.net.

CALDWELL, GARNETT ERNEST, lawyer; b. Houston, July 2, 1934; s. William Ernest and Ethel Leona (Jones) C. BA, U. Houston, 1957, JD, 1959. Bar: Tex. 1958. Pvt. practice law, Houston, 1959-64; ptnr. Ginther, Erwin, Dillard & Caldwell, Houston, 1964-65, Prappas, Caldwell & Moncure, Houston, 1965-77, Caldwell & Baggott, Houston, 1977-82, Caldwell, Wallis, Pruitt & Baggott, Houston, 1982; pvt. practice Houston, 1982-85, 87-90, Houston and Galveston, 1990—; ptnr. Caldwell & Lareau, 1985-87. Lectr. govt. U. Houston, 1961-62 2d lt. U.S. Army, 1957, lt. col. Res., 1977—. Decorated knight and knight comdr. Royal Yugoslavian Order St. John of Jerusalem. Mem. Galveston County Bar Assn., Houston Bar Assn., Houston Bankruptcy Conf., Res. Officers Assn., Houston Early Music Soc., Delta Theta Phi. Roman Catholic. Bankruptcy, Probate (including wills, trusts), Property, real (including real estate development, water). Home and Office: 1619 Post Office St Galveston TX 77550-4813

CALDWELL, RODNEY KENT, lawyer; b. Washington, Feb. 19, 1937; s. Rodney Huntington and Marion Elisabeth Caldwell; m. Marjorie Lee Zink, Apr. 15, 1965 (div. 1975); children: Dana Kent, Susan Ashley; m. Yolanda Silva, June 22, 1979; 1 child, David Huntington. BChemE, U. Va., 1959; JD, U. Houston, 1969. Bar: Tex. 1969, U.S. Supreme Ct. 1975. With Howrey Simon Arnold & White, LLP (formerly Arnold, White & Durkee), Houston, 1970—. Author: Patent Litigation: Procedure & Tactics, 1978-84. Lt. USAF, 1959-62. Fellow Tex. Bar Found., Houston Bar Found.; mem. ABA, Am. Intellectual Property Law Assn., Internat. Bar Assn., Internat. Intellectual Property Assn., Univ. Club, Army and Navy Club. Methodist. Federal civil litigation, Patent, Trademark and copyright. Home: 4021 Ella Lee Ln Houston TX 77027-3910 Office: Howrey Simon Arnold & White LLP 750 Bering Dr Houston TX 77057-2198 E-mail: caldwellr@howrey.com.

CALE, CHARLES GRIFFIN, lawyer, private investor; b. St. Louis, Aug. 19, 1940; s. Julian Dutro and Judith Hadley (Griffin) C.; m. Jessie Leete Rawn, Dec. 30, 1978; children: Whitney Rawn, Walter Griffin, Elizabeth Judith. BA, Principia Coll., Elsah, Ill., 1961; LLB, Stanford U., 1964; LLM, U. So. Calif., 1966. Bar: Calif. 1965. Pvt. practice, L.A., 1965—90; ptnr. Adams, Duque & Hazeltine, L.A., 1970—81, Morgan, Lewis & Bockius, L.A., 1981—91. Bd. dirs., co-chmn., CEO World Cup USA 1994, Inc., L.A., 1991. Group v.p. sports L.A. Olympic Organizing Com., 1982-84; assoc. counselor U.S. Olympic Com., 1985, spl. asst. to pres., 1985-89, asst. to pres, dir. olympic del., 1989-92; bd. dirs. Century 21 Real Estate-Can. Ltd., 1995-97, Rapattoni Corp., 2001—, Foresters Equity Services Corp., 2001—. Trustee St. John's Hosp. and Med. Ctr., Santa Monica, Marymount H.S.; asst. chief de mission U.S. Olylmpic Team, 1988; bd. dirs. Hallum Prevention of Child Abuse Fund, 1976-96. Recipient Gold medal of Youth and Sports, France, 1984. Mem. State Bar Calif., Calif. Club, L.A. Country Club, The Beach Club, Ind. Order Foresters (bd. dirs. 1993-2001), Eagle Springs Golf Club, Country Club of the Rockies. Office: PO Box 688 Pacific Palisades CA 90272-0688

CALHOUN, DONALD EUGENE, JR., federal judge; b. Columbus, Ohio, May 15, 1926; s. Donald Eugene and Esther C.; m. Shirley Claggett, Aug. 28, 1948; children: Catherine C., Donald Eugene III, Elizabeth C. BA in Polit. Sci., Ohio State U., 1949, JD, 1951. Bar: Ohio 1951. Pvt. practice, 1951-68; ptnr. Folkerth, Calhoun, Webster, Maurer & O'Brien, 1968-82, Guren, Merritt, Feibel, Sogg & Cohen, 1982-84; of counsel Lane, Alton, Horst, 1984-85; judge U. S. Bankruptcy Ct., Columbus, 1985-99, ret., 1999, recalled, 2000—. Gen. counsel Ohio Conf. United Ch. of Christ, 1964-85 Chmn. City-wide Citizens Com. for Neighborhood Seminars on Sch. Program and Fin., 1963; mem. Columbus Bd. Edn., 1963-71, pres., 1966, 70. With USNR, 1944-46. Mem. Columbus Bar Assn. (pres. 1967-68, Community Svc. award 1972), Nat. Conf. Bar Pres., Am. Arbitration Assn., Columbus Jaycees (life), Athletic Club, Masons. Congregationalist. Office: US Bankruptcy Ct 170 N High St Columbus OH 43215-2403

CALHOUN, JOHN R. lawyer; b. Fairfield, Iowa, Nov. 22, 1933; m. Elizabeth Calhoun; four children. BA in Polit. Sci., U. Iowa, 1956, JD, 1958. Bar: Iowa, 1958, Calif. 1960, U.S. Ct. Appeals (9th cir.) 1987, U.S. Ct. Appeals (fed. cir.) 1997, U.S. Dist. Ct. (cen. dist.) Calif. 1960, U.S. Supreme Ct. 1963, U.S. Ct. Mil. Appeals 1963. Commd. 2d lt. U.S. Army Res., 1958, advanced through grades to col., JAG Corp., ret., 1988; atty. U.S. Securities and Exch. Commn., 1960, Automobile Club of So. Calif., 1960-61; dep. dist. atty. L.A. Dist. Atty.'s Office, 1961-62; dep. city prosecutor Long Beach (Calif.) City Prosecutor's Office, 1962-67; dep. city atty. Long Beach City Atty.'s Office, 1967-78, asst. city atty., 1978-85, city atty., 1985-98; commr., v.p. Long Beach Harbor Commn., 1999—. Decorated Legion of Merit, Meritorious Svc. medal. Mem. Calif. Bar Assn., Long Beach Bar Assn. (bd. govs. 1974-75, 87-88), Rotary, Res. Officers Assn., Long Beach Area C. of C., Phi Delta Phi, Phi Delta Theta. Home: 4011 Chestnut Ave Long Beach CA 90807-3207

CALHOUN, SCOTT DOUGLAS, lawyer; b. Aurora, Ill., May 1, 1959; s. Ellsworth L. Calhoun and Mary Louise (Mummert) Wire; m. Gloria Jean Fulvi, Aug. 1, 1987; 1 child, John Daniel. BA cum laude, Knox Coll., 1981; JD, Coll. of William and Mary, 1984. Bar: Ga. 1984, U.S. Dist. Ct. (no. dist.) Ga. 1984, U.S. Ct. Appeals (11th cir.) 1984. Assoc. Swift, Currie, McGhee & Hiers, Atlanta, 1984-90, ptnr., 1990-92; pvt. practice Atlanta, 1992-94; prin. Byrne, Eldridge, Moore & Davis, PC, Atlanta, 1994-95; ptnr. Mozley, Finlayson & Loggins, Atlanta, 1996—. Spkr. in field. Bd. dirs. Atlanta Symphony Assocs., 1991-97, Wildwood Civic Assn., Atlanta, 1991-98; elder Trinity Presbyn. Ch., Atlanta, 1994-97, 2001—. Mem. Mortar Bd. Avocations: golf, music. Commercial, contracts (including sales of goods; commercial financing), Corporate, general, Estate planning. Office: Mozley Finlayson & Loggins 5605 Glenridge Dr NE Ste 900 Atlanta GA 30342-1380 E-mail: scalhoun@mfllaw.com.

CALHOUN-SENGHOR, KEITH, lawyer; b. Richmond, Va., June 14, 1955; s. Clarence Calhoun Jr. and Senegal Senghor; m. Sharon White. AB with honors, Stanford U., 1977; JD, Harvard U., 1981. Bar: D.C. 1981, U.S. Ct. Appeals (4th cir.) 1982. Law clk. to judge U.S. Ct. Appeals for 4th Cir., Richmond, 1981-82; assoc. Gibson, Dunn & Crutcher, L.A. and Washington, 1983-85; fgn. legal fellow Kreuz, Niebler & Mittl, Munich, 1986; v.p., gen. counsel Tech. Applications, Inc., Alexandria, Va., 1986-90; pres. Noma Internat. Enterprises, Inc., Washington, 1990-93; of counsel Wood, Williams, Rafalsky & Harris, Washington, 1991-93; dir. Office of Space Commercialization U.S. Dept. Commerce, Washington, 1993-99; v.p. internat. and legal affairs, gen. counsel Edenspace Systems Corp., Reston, Va., 1999—2000; legal and fin. cons., 2000—. Fulbright scholar U. Bonn., 1977-78; German Acad. Exch. Svc. Fgn. fellow, 1985-86. Mem. ABA, D.C. Bar Assn.

CALISE, WILLIAM JOSEPH, JR., lawyer; b. N.Y.C., May 22, 1938; s. William Joseph and Adeline (Rota) C.; m. Elizabeth Mae Gagne, Apr. 16, 1966; children: Kimberly Elizabeth, Andrea Elizabeth. BA, Bucknell U., 1960; MBA, JD, Columbia U., 1963. Bar: N.Y. 1963, D.C. 1981. Assoc., then ptnr. Chadbourne & Parke, NYC, 1967—94; sr. v.p., gen. counsel, sec. Rockwell Automation, Inc., Milw., 1994—. Dir. Henry St. Settlement, N.Y.C., 1977-94; mem. Allendale (N.J.) Sch. Bd., 1977-80. Capt. U.S. Army, 1964-66. Mem. Assn. Bar N.Y.C., Milw. Club. Roman Catholic. Corporate, general, Securities, Mergers and acquisitions. Office: Rockwell Automation Inc 777 E Wisconsin Ave Milwaukee WI 53202-5300 E-mail: wjcalise@corp.rockwell.com.

CALISSENDORFF, AXEL, lawyer; b. Stockholm, May 25, 1953; s. Gotthard and Karin Calissendorff; m. Kerstin Calissendorff, Sept. 1, 1984; children: Karin, Kaj. LLM, Stockholm U., 1978. Law clk. Nacka Dist. Ct., Stockholm, 1978—80; jr. judge Adminstrv. Ct. Appeals, Stockholm, 1980—81; asst. Mannheimer & Zetterlof, Gothenburg/Stockholm, 1981—86, ptnr. Stockholm, 1986—90, Mannheimer Swartling, Stockholm, 1990—, mng. ptnr., 1993—94. Councillor Stockholm Ctr. for Commendation, 2001—. Mem.: Swedish Bar Assn. (pres. 2001—). Office: Mannheimer Swartling Norrmalmstorg 4 PO Box 1711 SE 111 87 Stockholm Sweden

CALKINS, STEPHEN, law educator, lawyer; b. Balt., Mar. 20, 1950; s. Evan and Virginia (Brady) C.; m. Joan Wadsworth, Oct. 18, 1981; children: Timothy, Geoffrey, Virginia. BA, Yale U., 1972; JD, Harvard U., 1975. Bar: N.Y. 1976, D.C. 1977, U.S. Dist. Ct. D.C. 1979. Law clk. to FTC commr. S. Nye, Washington, 1975-76; assoc. Covington & Burling, Washington, 1976-83; assoc. law prof. Wayne State U., Detroit, 1983-88, prof., 1988—; gen. counsel FTC, Washington, 1995-97; of counsel Covington & Burling, Washington, 1997—, program dir. conf. bd. antitrust conf., 2001—. Vis. assoc. prof. law U. Mich., Ann Arbor, 1985, U. Pa., Phila., 1987; vis. prof. law U. Utrecht, Netherlands, 1989; chair career devel. Wayne State U., 1990-91. Editor: Antitrust Law Developments, 1984, 86, 88; (legal book revs.) The Antitrust Bulletin, 1986—; (articles) Antitrust, 1991-95. Counsel Ind. Commn. on Admissions Practices in Cranbrook Sch., Detroit, 1984-85; mem. Northville Zoning Bd. Appeals, 1987-95; rep.-at-large Assn. Yale Alumni Assembly, 1989-92; bd. dirs. yale Alumni Assn. of Mich., 2002—; elder First Presbyn. Ch. of Northville, 1989-92. Research fellow Wayne State U., 1984; USAID grantee, 1999-2000; recipient FTC award disting. svc., 1997. Mem.: ABA (counsel to com. on FTC 1988—89, coun. antitrust sect. 1988—91, 1997—2000, coun. adminstrv. law sect. 1999—2002, co-chair 50th Anniversary com., Antitrust sect. 50th anniversary pub. award 2002), Am. Assn. Law Schs. (sec. antitrust sect. 1987—91, chair-elect 1991—93, chair 1993—95), Am. Law Inst., Northville Swim Club, Yale Club (Detroit), Harvard Club. Avocations: reading, skiing, rollerblading. Administrative and regulatory, Antitrust, Corporate, general. Home: 317 W Dunlap St Northville MI 48167-1404 Office: Wayne State U Law Sch 471 W Palmer Detroit MI 48202 E-mail: calkins@wayne.edu.

CALKINS, SUSAN W. judge; Grad., U. Colo.; JD, U. Maine. Staff atty., exec. dir. Pine Tree Legal Assistance; judge Maine Dist. Ct., 1980-90, chief judge, 1990; judge Maine Superior Ct., 1995; justice Maine Supreme Jud. Ct., 1998—. Office: Cumberland County Courthouse PO Box 368 142 Federal St Portland ME 04112-0368

CALLAGHAN, GEORGANN MARY, lawyer; b. Bklyn., June 25, 1944; d. George Louis and Jean (Russo) Carpenito; m. Matthew John Callaghan, June 7, 1969; children: Matthew, Michael, Christian. BS in Hist. Studies, SUNY Empire State Coll., 1994; JD, Pace U., 1999. Bar: Conn. 1999, N.Y. 2000, D.C. 2000. Adminstr. Wood & Scher, Scarsdale, 1986—99, atty., 1999—2001; assoc. Colucci & Umans, 2001—. Exec. com. Boy Scouts Am. Mem. ABA, N.Y. State Bar Assn., Westchester County Bar Assn., Conn. Bar Assn., D.C. Bar Assn., Westchester Women's Bar Assn., Scarsdale Town and Village Club. Home: 49 Carman Rd Scarsdale NY 10583-6328 Office: Colucci & Umans 670 White Plains Rd Scarsdale NY 10583

CALLAHAN, CONSUELO MARIA, judge; b. Palo Alto, Calif., June 9, 1950; married; 2 children. BA, Leland Stanford Jr. Univ., 1968—72; JD, McGeorge Sch. of Law, Univ. of the Pacific, 1972—75; grad LLM, Univ. of Va. Sch. of Law, 2002—. Bar: Calif. 1975. Dep. city atty. City of Stockton, Stockton, Calif., 1975—76; dep. dist. atty. Dist. Atty. Office, San Joaquin County, Calif., 1976—82, sup. dist. atty., 1982—86; ct. comm. Mcpl. Ct. of Stockton, Stockton, Calif., 1986—92; judge San Joaquin County Superior Ct., San Joaquin, Calif., 1992—96; Assoc. judge Ct. of Appeal , State of Calif., Calif., 1996—2003. Recipient Award for Criminal Justice Programs, Gov., Susan B. Anthony Award for Women of Achievement, Stockton Peacemaker of the Yr., 1997, Mexican-Am. Hall of Fame, San Joaquin County, 1999. Office: US Ct Appeals 95 Seventh St San Francisco CA 94103*

CALLAHAN, MICHAEL THOMAS, lawyer, writer; b. Kansas City, Mo., Oct. 7, 1948; s. Harry Leslie and Venita June (Yohn) C.; m. Stella Sue Paffenbach, Mar. 21, 1970; children: Molly Leigh, Michael Kroh. BA, U. Kans., 1970; JD, U. Mo., 1973, LLM, 1979; postgrad., Temple U., 1976-77. Bar: Kans. 1973, N.J. 1975, Mo. 1977. V.p. T.J. Constrn., Inc., Lenexa, Kans., 1973-74; sr. cons. Wagner-Hohns-Inglis, Inc., Mt. Holly, N.J., 1974-77, v.p. Kansas City, Mo., 1977-86; exec. v.p. CCL Constrn. Cons., Overland Park, Kans., 1986-88, pres., 1988—. Adj. prof. U. Kans., Iowa State U.; arbitrator, lectr. in field, author; chmn. CCL Pacific Corp.; pres. Handcrafted Wines Kans., Inc. Home: 9011 Delmar St Shawnee Mission KS 66207-2343 Office: CCL Constrn Cons 4600 College Blvd Ste 104 Overland Park KS 66211-1606

CALLAHAN, ROBERT JEREMIAH, retired judge, mediator; b. Norwalk, Conn., June 3, 1930; s. Jeremiah J. and Elizabeth A. (Connolly) C.; m. Dorothy B. Trudel, Jan. 24, 1959; children: Sheila, Kerry, Denise, Janine, Patrick, Megan, Jane, Robert Jr. BS in History and Govt., Boston Coll., 1952; JD, Fordham U., 1955. Judge Cir. Ct. Conn., 1970-75, Ct. Common Pleas, Conn., 1975-76, Conn. Superior Ct., 1976-85; assoc. justice Conn. Supreme Ct., 1985-96, chief justice, 1996-99; ret., 1999. Judge trial referee Superior Ct., Stamford, Conn.; mem. Bd. Pardons, Conn., 1985-87. Served with U.S. Army, 1956-58. Recipient Fordham U. Sch. Law Dean's medal of recognition, 1986, Fordham Law Alumni Assn. medal of excellence, 1997, Fordham Disting. Alumnus award, 1998, U. Conn. Alumni Assn. Disting. Svc. award, 1998. Roman Catholic. Office: Superior Ct 123 Hoyt St Stamford CT 06905

CALLAHAN, ROBERT JOHN, JR., lawyer, arbitrator; b. St. Louis, July 3, 1923; s. Robert John and Elizabeth Mae Deck (Gentner) C.; m. Dorothy Foley, Apr. 18, 1958 (dec. Nov. 1980); m. Barbara Kelsall Couture, May 22, 1982. Grad., Chaminade Coll., 1941; BS in Bus. Adminstrn., Washington U., 1944; JD cum laude, Notre Dame U., 1948. Bar: Mo. 1948, U.S. Ct. Appeals (fed. cir.) 1951, U.S. Supreme Ct. 1955, U.S. Ct. Mil. Appeals. Ptnr. Callahan and Callahan, St. Louis, 1948-56; sole practice St. Louis, 1956—. Contbr. articles to legal jours. Candidate for judge St. Louis County Cir. Ct., 1960. Served with FBI and USCGR, 1944-45; former liaison officer USAF Acad. Served to capt. JAGC, USAFR. Coro fellow. Mem. ABA, Lawyers Assn. of St. Louis, St. Louis Bar Assn., Am. Assn. Trial Lawyers, Notre Dame U. Law Assn., U. Notre Dame Alumni Assn., Nat. Panel Consumer Arbitrators, Ret. Air Force Officers Assn., Phi Delta Theta. Republican. Roman Catholic. Civil rights, Personal injury (including property damage), Probate (including wills, trusts). Office: 32 Normandy Dr Lake Saint Louis MO 63367-1502

CALLAHAN, TIMOTHY J. lawyer, investment advisor; b. Yokohama, Japan, Jan. 6, 1948; parents Am. citizens; s. Frank T. and Jane A. Callahan; m. Margan Raphael, Aug. 15, 1970; children: Katie E., Zachary P., Carmen C., Elizabeth G. BS in Commerce, U. Va., 1970; JD, Cath. U., 1974. Bar: Va. 1974. Atty./assoc. Simmonds, Coleburn, Towner and Carman, Arlington, Va., 1974-76, Farley, Harrington & Sickels, Fairfax, Va., 1977-79; atty., ptnr. Merrell & Callahan, McLean, Va., 1980-87, Clary, Lawrence, Lickstein and Moore, Falls Church, Va., 1987-91, Tener & Callahan, Vienna, Va., 1992-2000, McCandlish & Lillard PC, Vienna, Va., 2000—. Bd. dirs. Joe Gibbs' Youth for Tomorrow, Manassas, Va., 1997, Fresta Valley Christian Sch., Marshall, Va., 1987—; adminstr. I Found It campaign, Washington, 1976. Mem. Christian Legal Soc., Fin. Planning Assn., No. Va. Estate Planning Coun. Republican. Evangelical Christian. Estate planning, Probate (including wills, trusts), Estate taxation. Office: McCandlish & Lillard PC 11350 Random Hills Rd Ste 500 Fairfax VA 22030

CALLEGARI, WILLIAM A., JR., lawyer, mediator; b. Baton Rouge, La., Sept. 3, 1961; s. William A. and Ann T. (Roy) C.; m. Denise Bordelon, Dec. 17, 1993; children: Will, Michael, John, Elizabeth. BA, La. State U., 1982; MBA, Emory U., 1985; JD, South Tex. Coll. Law, Houston, 1993. Bar: Tex. 1994. Comml. loan rep. Tex. Commerce Bank, Houston, 1985-86; project mgr. AM-TEX Corp., Houston, 1986-90, project devel. mgr., 1990-94; seconded atty. Vinson & Elkins, LLP, Houston, 1995-96; v.p., sec., gen. counsel S T Environ. Svcs., Houston, 1994-97; sole practitioner Houston, 1997—; fee atty. Stewart Title Co., 2001—. Mem. Alpha Tau Omega. Corporate, general, General practice, Labor (including EEOC, Fair Labor Standards Act, labor-management relations, NLRB, OSHA). Office: 15040 Fairfield Village Dr Ste 200 Cypress TX 77433 E-mail: wcj1304@msn.com.

CALLETON, THEODORE EDWARD, lawyer, educator; b. Newark, Dec. 13, 1934; s. Edward James and Dorothy (Dewey) C.; m. Elizabeth Bennett Brown, Feb. 4, 1961; children: Susan Bennett, Pamela Barritt, Christopher Dewey.; m. Kathy E'Beth Conkle, Feb. 22, 1983; 1 child, James Frederick. BA, Yale U., 1956; LLB, Columbia U., 1962. Bar: Calif. 1963, U.S. Dist. Ct. (so. dist.) Calif. 1963, U.S. Tax Ct. 1977. Assoc. O'Melveny & Myers, L.A., 1962-69, Agnew, Miller & Carlson, L.A., 1969, ptnr., 1970-79; pvt. practice L.A., 1979-83; ptnr. Kindel & Anderson, L.A., 1983-92, Calleton & Merritt, Pasadena, Calif., 1992-99, Calleton & Trytten, Pasadena, 1999—2002; pvt. practice Pasadena, 2002—. Academician Internat. Acad. Estate and Trust Law, 1974—; lectr. Calif. Continuing Edn. Bar, 1970—96, U. So. Calif. Tax Inst., 1972, 76, 91, Calif. State U., L.A., 1974—93, Practicing Law Inst., 1976—86, Am. Law Inst., 1985; bd. dirs. UCLA/Continuing Edn. of Bar Estate Planning Inst., 1979—; adj. prof. Golden Gate U. Law Sch., 1997—2000, Loyola U. Sch. Law, 2002—. Author: The Short Term Trust, 1977, A Life Insurance Primer, 1978, Calleton's Wills and Trusts, 1992—2003; co-author: California Will Drafting Practice, 1982, Tax Planning for Professionals, 1985, California Estate Planning, 2002; contbr. articles to profl. jours. Chmn. Arroyo Seco Master Planning Commn., Pasadena, Calif., 1970-71; bd. dirs. Montessori Sch., Inc., 1964-68, chmn., 1966-68, Am. Montessori Soc., N.Y.C., 1967-72, chmn., 1969-72; trustee Walden Sch. of Calif., 1970-86, 90-94, chmn., 1980-86; trustee Episc. Children's Home of L.A., 1971-75; bd. dirs. L.A. Master Chorale Assn., 1989-94, San Gabriel Valley Coun., Boy Scouts of Am., 2002—. Lt. USMC, 1956-59. Fellow Am. Coll. Trust and Estate Counsel; mem. L.A. County Bar Assn. (chmn. taxation sect. 1980-81, chmn. probate and trust law sect. 1981-82, Dana Latham Meml. award

1996), Aurelian Honor Soc., Elihu, Beta Theta Pi, Phi Delta Phi. Estate planning, Probate (including wills, trusts), Estate taxation. Home: 301 Churchill Rd Sierra Madre CA 91024-1354 Office: 200 S Los Robles Ave Ste 678 Pasadena CA 91101-4600 E-mail: ted@calletonlaw.com.

CALLIES, DAVID LEE, lawyer, educator; b. Chgo., Apr. 21, 1943; s. Gustav E. and Ann D. Callies; m. Laurie Breeden, Dec. 28, 1996; 1 child, Sarah Wayne. AB, DePauw U., 1965; JD, U. Mich., 1968; LLM, U. Nottingham, England, 1969. Bar: Ill. 1969, Hawaii 1978, U.S. Supreme Ct. 1974. Spl. asst. states atty., McHenry County, Ill., 1969; assoc. firm Ross, Hardies, O'Keefe, Babcock & Parsons, Chgo., 1969-75, ptnr., 1975-78; prof. law Richardson Sch. Law, U. Hawaii, Honolulu, 1978—; Benjamin A. Kudo prof. law U. Hawaii, Honolulu, 1995—. Mem. adv. com. on planning and growth mgmt. City and County of Honolulu Coun., 1978-88, mem. citizens adv. com. on State Functional Plan for Conservation Lands, 1979-93. Author: (with Fred P. Bosselman) the Quiet Revolution in Land Use Control, 1971 (with Fred P. Bosselman and John S. Banta) The Taking Issue, 1973, Regulating Paradise: Land Use Controls in Hawaii, 1984, (with Robert Freilich and Tom Roberts) Cases and Materials on Land Use, 1986, 3d edit., 1999, Preserving Paradise: Why Regulation Won't Work, 1994 (in Japanese 1994, in Chinese 1999), Land Use Law in the United States, 1994; editor: After Lucas: Land Use Regulation and the Taking of Property Without Compensation, 1993, Takings! Land Development Conditions and Regulatory Takings: After Dolan and Lucas, 1995, (with Hylton, Mandelker and Franzese) Property Law and the Public Interest, 1998, 2nd edit., 2003 (with Kotaka) Taking Land, 2002, (with Curtin & Tappendorf) Bargaining For Development: A Handbook, 2003; co-editor Environ. and Land Use Law Rev., 2000—. Named Best Prof., U. Hawaii Law Sch., 1990-91, 91-92; Mich. Ford Found. fellow U. Nottingham (Eng.), 1969, life mem. Clare Hall, Cambridge U., 1999. Fellow Am. Inst. Cert. Planners, Am. Planning Assn.; mem. ABA (chmn. com. on land use, planning and zoning 1980-82, coun. sect. on state and local govt. 1981-85, 95—, exec. com. 1986-90, sec. 1986-87, chmn. 1989-90), Am. Law Inst., Am. Planning Assn., Hawaii State Bar Assn. (chair, real property and fin. svc. sect., 1997), Am. Bar Found., Ill. Bar Assn., Internat. Bar Assn. (coun. Asia Pacific Forum 1993-96, co-chair Acads. Forum 1994-96, chair 1996-98), Nat. Trust for Hist. Preservation, Royal Oak Soc., Lambda Alpha Internat. (pres. Aloha chpt. 1989-90, internat. v.p. Asia-Pacific region 2001—, Internat. Mem. of Yr. 1994). Home: 1532 Kamole St Honolulu HI 96821-1424 Office: U Hawaii Richardson Sch Law 2515 Dole St Honolulu HI 96822-2328 E-mail: dcallies@hawaii.edu.

CALLISON, JAMES W. former lawyer, consultant, airline executive; b. Jamestown, N.Y., Sept. 8, 1928; s. J. Waldo and Gladys A. C.; m. Gladys I. Robinson, Oct. 3, 1959; children: Sharon Elizabeth, Maria Judith, Christopher James. AB with honors, U. Mich., 1950, JD with honors (Overbeck award 1952, Jerome S. Freud Meml. award 1953), 1953. Bar: D.C. 1954, Ga. 1960. Atty. Pogue & Neal, Washington, 1953-57; with Delta Air Lines, Inc., Atlanta, 1957-93, v.p. law and regulatory affairs, 1974-78, sr. v.p., gen. counsel, 1978-81, sr. v.p., gen. counsel, corp. sec., 1981-88; sr. v.p. legal and corp. affairs, sec. Delta Air Lines Inc., 1988-90; sr. v.p. corp. and external affairs Delta Air Lines, Inc., 1990-91, sr. v.p. corp. affairs, 1991-93; ret., 1993; cons. Inman Deming Internat., Washington. Contbr. articles to legal jours.; asst. editor: Mich. Law Rev, 1952-53. Bd. dirs. St. Joseph's Mercy Found. (chmn. planned giving com.); mem. adv. bd. Atlanta Union Mission. Recipient Papal Pro Ecclesia Et Pontifice award, 1966. Mem. State Bar Ga. (chmn. corp. counsel sect. 1989-90, mem. emeritus), Atlanta Bar Assn. (life), Atlanta Athletic Club, Order of Coif. Corporate, general, Legislative, Transportation. Home: 2034 Dunwoody Club Way Dunwoody GA 30338-3024

CALLISON, JAMES WILLIAM, lawyer; b. Albemarle County, Va., Dec. 24, 1955; s. James Crofts and Jan (Richelsen) C. AB, Oberlin Coll., 1977; JD, U. Colo., 1982; LLM, Yale U., 2000. Law clk. to judge Dist. Ct. Colo., Boulder, 1982; ptnr. Moye, Giles, O'Keefe, Vermeire & Gorrell, Denver, 1982-96, Faegre & Benson L.L.P., 1997—. Lectr. law U. Denver, 1988-90; adj. prof. U. Colo. Law Sch., 1997—. Author: Partnership Law and Practice, 1992, Limited Liability Companies, 1994; contbr. articles to profl. jours. Mem. Leadership Denver, 1989-90, Denver Community Leadership Forum, 1991. Mem. ABA (bus. law sect., tax sect.), Colo. Bar Assn. (tax sect., exec. council 1986—, chmn. 1988-89), Denver Bar Assn., Order of Coif. Democrat. Corporate, general, Corporate taxation, Taxation, general. Home: 4622 S Vine Way Cherry Hills Village CO 80110-6045 Office: Faegre & Benson LLP 370 17th St Ste 2500 Denver CO 80202-5665 E-mail: wcallison@faegre.com.

CALLISON, RUSSELL JAMES, lawyer; b. Redding, Calif., Sept. 4, 1954; s. Walter M. and Norma A. (Bruce) C. BA in Polit. Sci., U. of Pacific, 1977, JD cum laude, 1980. Bar: Calif. 1980, U.S. Dist. Ct. (ea. dist.) Calif. 1981, U.S. Dist. Ct. (no. dist.) Calif. 1986, U.S. Ct. Appeals (9th cir.) 1989. Assoc. Memering & DeMers, Sacramento, 1980-85; pres. DeMers, Callison & Donovan, P.C., Sacramento, 1985-95; ptnr. Lewis Brisbois Bisgaard & Smith, San Francisco, 1995—. Spl. master Calif. State Bar, 1991—; arbitrator, judge pro tem Calif. Superior Cts., 1986—. Co-author: Premises Liability in California, 1996. Mem. ABA (litig. sect.), SAR (chpt. pres. 1992-93), Am. Arbitration Assn. (panel of arbitrators), Assn. Def. Counsel No. Calif., Commonwealth Club, Natomas Racquet Club, Order of Coif, Phi Alpha Delta. Republican. Episcopalian. Avocations: golf, hunting, fishing, antique restoration. General civil litigation, Insurance, Professional liability. Home: 3889 20th St San Francisco CA 94114-3018 Office: Lewis Brisbois Bisgaard & Smith LLP One Sansome St Ste 1400 San Francisco CA 94104-4431 E-mail: callison@lbbslaw.com.

CALLISTER, LOUIS HENRY, JR., lawyer; b. Aug. 11, 1935; s. Louis Henry and Isabel (Barton) C.; m. Ellen Gunnell, Nov. 27, 1957; children: Mark, Isabel, Jane, Edward, David, John Andrew, Ann. BS, U. Utah, 1958, JD, 1961. Bar: Utah 1961. Asst. atty. gen., Utah, 1961; sr. ptnr. Callister Nebeker & McCullough, Salt Lake City, 1961—2002, of counsel, 2002—. Bd. dirs. Am. Stores Co., 1985-97, Quailbluff Devel. Co., 1971-2000; Vice-chmn. Salt Lake City Zoning Bd. Adjustment, 1979-84; bd. govs. Salt Lake Valley Hosps., 1983-91; treas. exec. com. Utah Rep. Com., 1965-69; chmn. Utah chpt. Rockefeller for Pres. Com., 1964-68; sec., trustee Salt Lake Police/Sheriff Hon. Cols., 1982-97; trustee, mem. exec. com. Utah Econ. Devel. Corp., 1992—, chmn., 1998-2000; trustee U. Utah, 1987-99, vice-chmn., 1989-99, bd. dirs. U. Utah Hosp., 1993-99; trustee Grand Canyon Trust, 2001—. Mem. Lds Ch. Banking, Corporate, general, Mergers and acquisitions. Home: 3860 Highland Ct Bountiful UT 84010-3365 Office: Callister Nebeker & McCullough Gateway Tower E Ste 900 Salt Lake City UT 84133-1102 E-mail: Lhcallister@cnmlaw.com.

CALLOW, THOMAS EDWARD, lawyer; b. Menominee, Mich., Mar. 12, 1954; s. James Kewley and Janet Marie (Drury) C.; m. Kathy Ann Cain, Oct. 26, 1985. BGS, U. Mich., 1976, JD, 1979. Bar: Mich. 1979. Prin. Vestevich, Mallender, DuBois & Dritsas, P.C., Bloomfield Hills, Mich., 1986—. Pres. Beverly Hills (Mich.) Homeowners Assn., 1986. Mem. Mich. Bar Assn., Southeastern Mich. Computer Orgn. (dir. 1988—). Corporate, general, Pension, profit-sharing, and employee benefits, Taxation, general. Home: 53034 Whitby Way Shelby Township MI 48316-2747 Office: Vestevich Mallender Et Al 800 W Long Lake Rd Ste 200 Bloomfield Hills MI 48302-2058 E-mail: tcallow@vmddlaw.com.

CALLOW, WILLIAM GRANT, retired judge; b. Waukesha, Wis., Apr. 9, 1921; s. Curtis Grant and Mildred G. C.; m. Jean A. Zilavy, Apr. 15, 1950; children: William G., Christine S., Katherine H. PhB in Econs, U. Wis., 1943, JD, 1948. Bar: Wis.; cert. for Fla. mediation. Asst. city atty., Waukesha, 1948-52; city atty., 1952-60; county judge, 1961-77; justice Supreme Ct. Wis., Madison, 1978-92. Asst. prof. U. Minn., 1951-52; mem. faculty Wis. Jud. Coll., 1968-75; Wis. commr. Nat. Conf. Commrs. on Uniform State Laws, 1967—; arbitrator Wis. Employment Rel. Commn.; arbitrator-mediator bus. disputes; arbitration and mediation nat. and internat. res. judge, 1992—. With USMC, 1943-45; with USAF, 1951-52, Korea. Recipient Outstanding Alumnus award U. Wis., 1973 Fellow Am. Bar Found.; mem. ABA, Dane County Bar Assn., Waukesha County Bar Assn. Episcopalian. Fax: 608-241-9923, 715-588-3452, 941-642-8889. E-mail: wgc@mymailstation.com., justice4@newnorth.net.

CALOGERO, PASCAL FRANK, JR., judge; b. New Orleans, Nov. 9, 1931; s. Pascal Frank and Louise (Moore) C.; children— Deborah Ann Calogero Applebaum, David, Pascal III, Elizabeth, Thomas, Michael, Stephen, Gerald, Katie, Chrissy. Student, Loyola U., New Orleans, 1949-51, JD, 1954; ML in the Jud. Process, U. Va., 1992; LLD (hon.) , Loyola U., New Orleans, 1991. Bar: La. Ptnr. Landrieu, Calogero & Kronlage, 1958-69, Calogero & Kronlage, 1969-73; gen. counsel La. Stadium and Expn. Dist., 1970-73; assoc. justice Supreme Ct. La., New Orleans, 1973-90, chief justice, 1990—. Mem. La. Democratic State Central Com., 1963-71; mem. subcom. on del. selection La. Dem. Party, 1971; del. Dem. Nat. Conv., 1968. Served to capt. JAGC U.S. Army, 1954-57. Recipient Disting. Jurist award La. Bar Founds., 1991; Judge Bob Jones Meml. award, Am. Judges Assn., 1995. Mem. ABA, La. Bar Assn., New Orleans Bar Assn., Greater New Orleans Trial Lawyers Assn. (v.p. 1967-69), Order of the Coif. Office: Supreme Ct La 301 Loyola Ave New Orleans LA 70112-1814 E-mail: icaloger@lasc.org.

CALVANI, TERRY, lawyer; b. Carlsbad, N.Mex., Jan. 29, 1947; s. Torello Howard and Mary Virginia (Hawkins) C.; m. Mary Virginia Anderson, May 3, 1969; m. 2d, Judith Thompson, Aug. 28, 1980; children: Dominic Mario, Torello Howard. BA, U. N.Mex., 1969; JD with distinction, Cornell U., 1972. Bar: N.Mex. 1972, Calif. 1972, Tenn. 1978, D.C. 1992, U.S. Dist. Ct. N.Mex. 1972, U.S. Dist. Ct. (no. dist.) Calif. 1972, U.S. Dist. Ct. (mid. dist.) Tenn. 1978, U.S. Dist. Ct. D.C. 1994, U.S. Ct. Appeals (9th cir.) 1972, U.S. Ct. Appeals (6th cir.) 1977, U.S. Ct. Appeals (5th cir.) 1981, U.S. Ct. Appeals (11th cir.) 1981, U.S. Ct. Appeals (D.C. cir.) 1994, U.S. Supreme Ct. 1985. Tchg. fellow Stanford U. Law Sch., 1972-73; asst. prof. law Vanderbilt U. Sch. Law, Nashville, 1974—77, assoc. prof., 1977—80, prof., 1980—83; assoc. Pillsbury, Madison & Sutro (now Pillsbury Winthrop LLP), San Francisco, 1973-74, ptnr., 1990—2002; mem. The Competition Authority Republic of Ireland , 2002. Vis. prof. law U. Va., Charlottesville, 1981—82; of counsel Haksell Slaughter & Young, Birmingham, 1980—83; commr. U.S. F.T.C., 1983—90; acting chmn., 1985—86; lectr. Harvard U. Sch. Law, 1998—2002; sr. lectrg. fellow Duke U. Sch. Law, 2000. Author: (with John Siegfried) Economic Analysis and Antitrust Law, 1979, 2d edit., 1988; bd. editors Antitrust Bull., 1982—, Bur. Nat. Affairs RICO Report, 1986-96. Mem.: ABA (chmn. spl. com. to study antitrust penalties and damages antitrust sec 1979—82, chmn. Robinson-Patman com. antitrust sect. 1981—83, coun. mem. 1985—86), Order of the Coif, Adminstrv. Conf. U.S. 1985-90, Am. Law Inst. (coun. mem. 1990—93), 6th Jud. Conf. (life), Malahide Tennis & Croquet Club, The Stephen's Green Club (Dublin), Olympic Club (San Francisco), Richland Country Club, Colonnade Club (Charlottesville), Riverside Country Club (Carlsbad), Pacific Union Club (San Francisco), The G.C. Club Tenn. (Nashville), The Club (Birmingham). Roman Catholic. Antitrust. Office: Competition Authority Parnell Ho 14 Parnell Sq Dublin Ireland Fax: +353 1 804 5401. E-mail: tc@tca.ie.

CALVANICO, THOMAS PAUL, lawyer; b. Jersey City, Oct. 18, 1955; s. Emanuel Paul and Helen A. (Miller) C. AB in Polit. Sci., St. Peter's Coll., 1976; JD, N.Y. Law Sch., 1979. Bar: N.J. 1979, N.Y. 1986, U.S. Dist. Ct. N.J. 1979, U.S. Dist. Ct. (ea. and so. dists.) N.Y. 1985. Asst. prosecutor Hudson County, Jersey City, 1979-81; sole practice Jersey City, 1981-87; asst. corp. counsel Jersey City Law Dept., 1981-87; gen. counsel The Ryan Group, Middletown, N.J., 1987-90; ins. mgr. County of Hudson, Jersey City, 1990-95, chief of staff to county exec., 1995-98; exec. dir. Hudson County Improvement Authority, Jersey City, 1998—2002; gen. counsel Stamato Waste Svcs., North Bergen, NJ, 2003—. Pres. bd. edn., Hudson County Schs. of Tech., 1997-2001; mem. Hudson County Ins. Fund Commn., 1995-2001. Mem. Hudson County Bar Assn., 200 Club of Hudson County (trustee 1999—). Democrat. Home: 11 Gail Pl Secaucus NJ 07094-3808 Office: 4711 Dell Ave North Bergen NJ 07047 E-mail: tcalvanico@comcasdt.net.

CALVARUSO, JOSEPH ANTHONY, lawyer; b. N.Y.C., Oct. 9, 1949; BEE, Manhattan Coll., 1971; JD, Fordham U., 1974. Bar: N.Y., U.S. Dist. Ct. (so. and ea. dists.) N.Y. 1975, U.S. Ct. Appeals (2d and 3d cirs.), U.S. Ct. Appeals (2nd and 3d cirs.) 1984, U.S. Supreme Ct. Atty. N.Y. City Corp. Counsel, N.Y.C., 1974-76; assoc. Law Office of Anthony J. Casella, N.Y.C., 1976-78; ptnr. Morgan & Finnegan, N.Y.C., 1978—. Lectr. in Elect. & Computer Law Seminar, 1990. Mem. ABA (litigation sect.), Am. Intellectual Property Law Assn., N.Y. Intellectual Property Law Assn., Internat. Trademark Assn. General civil litigation, Patent, Trademark and copyright. Office: Morgan & Finnegan 345 Park Ave New York NY 10154-0053

CALVERT, JAY H., JR., lawyer; b. Charleston, S.C., Mar. 19, 1945; m. Ann E., June 14, 1969; children: Amanda, Emily, Sarah. BA, Amherst (Mass.) Coll., 1967; JD, U. Va., 1970. Bar: Pa. 1970, U.S. Dist. Ct. (ea. dist.) Pa. 1970, U.S. Ct. Appeals (3d cir.) 1971, U.S. Dist. Ct. (mid. dist.) Pa. 1973, U.S. Ct. Appeals (2d cir.) 1980, U.S. Ct. Appeals (8th cir.) 1987, U.S. Supreme Ct. 1989, U.S. Dist. Ct. Ariz. 1994, U.S. Dist. Ct. (we. dist.) Pa. 2000. Assoc. Morgan, Lewis & Bockius LLP, Phila., 1970—78, ptnr., 1987—89, exec. ptnr., 1987—90; mgr. litigation sect., firm governing bd. Morgan Lewis & Bockius LLP, Phila., 1989—94; mng. ptnr. Morgan, Lewis & Bockius LLP, Phila., 1990—94; mem. exec. com. Morgan Lewis & Bockius LLP, Phila., 1997—98, sr. ptnr. litigation sect., 1990—. Trustee Agnes Irwin Sch., Rosemont, Pa., 1988-94, Leukemia and Lymphoma Soc. Am., Phila., 1982—; bd. dirs. St. David's Nursery Sch., Wayne, Pa., 1980-94; chmn. devel. com. Phila. Zool. Soc., 1993-96, chmn. facilities, exhibits and safety com., 1997-2001, bd. dirs., 1992—, vice-chmn. bd. dirs., 1994-96.; mem. ann. fund campaign com. Inglis House, 1998—. Mem. ABA, Pa. Bar Assn., Phila. Bar Assn., Lawyers Club of Phila. Avocations: biking, gardening, hiking, horseback riding, animal husbandry. Antitrust, Federal civil litigation, General civil litigation. Office: Morgan Lewis & Bockius LLP 1701 Market St Philadelphia PA 19103-2903 Office Fax: 215-963-5299. E-mail: jcalvert@morganlewis.com.

CALVERT, MATTHEW JAMES, lawyer; b. Lynchburg, Va., Apr. 24, 1953; s. George Edward and Helen Owen Calvert; m. Helen Baldwin Saer, Oct. 3, 1981; children: McQueen Saer, Anne Russell, Helen Hardie. BA, Washington & Lee U., 1975, JD, 1979. Bar: Va. 1980, Ga. 1995. Law clk. to hon. John Minor Wisdom 5th Cir. Ct. Appeals, La., 1979-80; assoc. Hunton & Williams, Richmond, Va., 1980-87, ptnr. Richmond and Atlanta, 1987—, chmn. pro bono com. Atlanta, 1995—. Chmn. young lawyers sect. Richmond Bar Assn., 1987-88; 6th dist. disciplinary com. Va. State Bar, Richmond, 1993-94. Editor-in-chief Washington & Lee Law Rev., 1978-79. Chmn. workplace com. Metro Coalition on Drugs, Richmond, 1990-93; major gifts com. Woodruff Arts Ctr., Atlanta, 1995—. Recipient Dir.'s award FBI, Richmond, 1993, Charles R. Yates award for fundraising leadership Woodruff Arts Ctr., Atlanta, 1998. Avocations: camping, hunting, golfing. Federal civil litigation, General civil litigation, Product liability. Office: Hunton & Williams 600 Peachtree St NE Ste 4100 Atlanta GA 30308-2217

CALVERT, MELANIE A. lawyer; b. Nashville, Nov. 11, 1954; d. Allen Dalton and Edna (Jones) Shoffner; m. David Roll Calvert, May 1977 (div. 1980); children: Sarah Randolph, Elizabeth Megan. BS cum laude in Gen. Biology, Vanderbilt U., 1977; JD, George Washington U., 1984. Bar: Calif. 1984, U.S. Patent and Trademark Office, 1984, U.S. Dist. Ct. (cen. dist.) Calif. 1985, U.S. Ct. Appeals (9th cir.) 1987, U.S. Supreme Ct. 1996. Rsch. technician Emory U. Sch. Medicine, Atlanta, 1978-81; assoc. Lyon & Lyon, L.A., 1984-85; pvt. practice, Pasadena, Calif., 1985—. Spkr. in field. Active Women's Legal Clinic, L.A., 1987-89. Recipient Commendation award Calif. Bd. of Govs., 1987-88. Democrat. Avocations: reading, yoga. Appellate, State civil litigation, Labor (including EEOC, Fair Labor Standards Act, labor-management relations, NLRB, OSHA). Office: Ste 950 150 S Los Robles Ave Pasadena CA 91101-2486 E-mail: calvertlaborlaw@aol.com.

CAMBRICE, ROBERT LOUIS, lawyer; b. Nov. 23, 1947; s. Eugene and Edna Bertha (Jackson) C.; m. Christine Jackson, Jan. 7, 1972; children: Bryan, Graham. BA cum laude, Tex. So. U., 1969; JD, U. Tex., 1972. Bar: Tex. 1973, U.S. Dist. Ct. (so. dist.) Tex. 1975, U.S. Ct. Appeals (5th cir.) 1975, U.S. Ct. Appeals (11th cir.) 1981, U.S. Supreme Ct. 1981. Asst. atty. City of Houston, 1974-76; pvt. practice, Houston, 1976-81; asst. atty. Harris County, Tex., 1981-85, City of Houston, 1986—, sr. trial atty. legal dept., 1990-92, chief def. litigation dept., 1992—. Earl Warren fellow, 1969-72. Mem. ABA, NAACP, Nat. Bar Assn., Alpha Kappa Mu. Roman Catholic. E-mail: Robert.Cambrice@cityofhouston.net.

CAMERON, DUNCAN HUME, lawyer; b. Brandon, Man., Can., May 26, 1934; s. Donald Ewen and Jean Carruthers (Rankine) Cameron; m. Caroline I. Gilbert, 1975; children: Sarah, Anne. BA cum laude, Harvard U., 1956; LLB, Columbia U., 1959, PhD, 1965. Bar: N.Y. 1959, D.C. 1967, U.S. Supreme Ct. 1970. Assoc. Paul, Weiss, Rifkind, Wharton & Garrison, 1959-62; atty. office gen. counsel AID U.S. Dept. State, Washington, 1963-67, legal advisor mission to Dominican Republic, 1966; ptnr. Appleton, Rice & Perrin, 1967-71; mng. ptnr. Cameron & Hornbostel, Washington, 1972—2001, ptnr., 1972—. Adj. prof. Law Ctr., Georgetown U., Washington, 1970—80, Washington, 1989—2001, adj. prof. Sch. Fgn. Svc., 1973—88; vis. prof. Victoria U., New Zealand, 1986; vis. lectr. INCAE, Costa Rica, 2001—. Contbr. articles to profl. jours. Bd. dirs. Pan Am. Sch. Agr., 1986—2002, chmn. bd. dirs., 1991—97, trustee emeritus, 2002—; bd. dirs. Washington Tennis Found., 1995—99. Mem.: ABA, Washington Fgn. Law Soc. (bd. govs. 1988—90), Hist. Soc. Washington (bd. dirs. 1999—), Chilean-Am. C. of C. Washington (pres. 1992—96, bd. dirs. 1992—), Cosmos Club. Private international, Public international. Home: 3532 Chesapeake St NW Washington DC 20008-2957 Office: Cameron & Hornbostel 818 Connecticut Ave NW Washington DC 20006-2702 E-mail: dcameron@cameron-hornbostel.com.

CAMERON, JOHN CLIFFORD, lawyer, health science facility administrator; b. Phila., Sept. 17, 1946; m. Eileen Duffy, July 12, 1975; children: Christopher, Meghan. BA, U. Pitts., 1969; MBA, Temple U., 1972; JD, Widener U., 1976; LLM, NYU, 1980. Bar: Pa. 1977, N.J. 1977, Md. 1995. Asst. adminstr. Phila. Psychiatric Ctr., 1972-76; jud. clk. to presiding justice N.J. Superior Ct., Newark, 1976-77; asst. adminstr. St. Elizabeth Hosp., Elizabeth, N.J., 1977; v.p. corp. legal affairs Methodist Hosp., Phila., 1978-94; solicitor, 1988-94; legal cons. North Penn Hosp, Lansdale, Pa., 1994-95; counsel, legal adminstr. Hodes, Ulman, Pessin & Katz, P.A., Towson, Md., 1995-96; asst. to pres. Temple U. Health Sys., Phila., 1996—; asst. sec. Neumann Med. Ctr., Phila., 1997—2002, Jeanes Hosp., Phila., 1997—, Northwood Nursing Home, Phila., 1997—2002, Temple Physicians, Inc., Phila., 1997—, Temple Univ. Hosp., Phila., 1997—, Lower Bucks Hosp., Bristol, Pa., 1997—2002, Episcopal Hosp., Phila., 1997—, Temple U. Children's Med. Ctr., Phila., 1997—, Northeastern Hosp., Phila., 1997—, Temple Continuing Care Ctr., Phila., 1997—2002. Sec. Suthbrelt Properties, Ltd., Phila., 1981-94, Asbury Corp., Wilmington, Del., 1982-94, Healthmark, Inc., Moorestown, N.J., 1982-94, Meth. Hosp. Nursing Ctr., Phila., 1983-94; asst. sec. various hosps. and nursing homes, 1997—, instr. Grad. Sch. Mgmt., Pa. State U., 1991—; instr. mgmt. dept. Neumann Coll., 1991-96; instr. bus. divsn. Rosemont Coll., 1995-96. Contbr. articles to profl. jours. Mem. campaign United Way, Phila., 1979-94; mem. health and welfare com. United Meth. Eastern Pa. Conf., 1978-94; advisor Explorer Post, Boy Scouts Am., 1988-94; mem. steering com. Golden Cross, Phila., 1984-94; sec. Tredyffrin Twp. Park and Recreation Bd., 1987-95; alumni rep. Widener U.; mem. environ. adv. com. and open space task force Tredyffrin Twp., 1991-95. Fellow Am. Coll. Healthcare Execs. (chmn. bylaws com. 1995-96); mem. ABA, N.J. Bar Assn., Pa. Bar Assn., Phila. Bar Assn., Am. Hosp. Assn., Hosp. Assn. Pa., Swedish Colonial Soc. (bd dirs. 1992—, gov. 1993-95), Sons of Union Vets. of Civil War, SAR. Avocations: swimming, music. Corporate, general, Health. Home: 1410 Church Rd Malvern PA 19355-9714

CAMERON, MARK ALAN, lawyer; b. Boston, Aug. 20, 1954; s. Alan Bruce and Marilyn Ruth (Waldron) C.; m. Sandra Karen Bakko, June 18, 1983; children: Matthew Bruce, Gregory Cronquist. Student, Calif. State, Chico, 1972-74; BA in Econ., U. Calif., Davis, 1976, MA in Econ., 1978; JD, U. Calif., Hastings, 1981. Bar: Calif. 1981, U.S. Dist. Ct. (no. and ctrl. dists.) Calif. 1982, U.S. Dist. Ct. (ea. dist.) Calif. 2002, U.S. Ct. Appeals (9th cir.) 1983, U.S. Supreme Ct. 1985. Atty. Kindel & Anderson, Los Angeles, 1981-83, Miller, Starr & Regalia, Walnut Creek, Calif., 1983—. Co-author: chpt. 29, Defective Construction, Miller & Starr California Real Estate 3d edit., 2001. Mem. Calif. State Bar, Contra Costa County Bar Assn. Republican. Avocations: tennis, skiing, volleyball. General civil litigation, Construction, Property, real (including real estate development, water). Office: Miller Starr & Regalia 5th Fl 1331 N California Blvd Fl 5 Walnut Creek CA 94596-4537 E-mail: mac@msandr.com.

CAMERON, NINA RAO, lawyer, government official; b. N.Y.C., Apr. 28, 1925; d. Paul and Grace (Malatino) Rao; m. John D. Cameron, Jan. 9, 1950 (div.); 1 child, Scott; m. Robert M. Gewald. BA, Manhattanville, 1945; LLB, Bklyn. Law Sch., 1950; JD, U. Mex., 1968. Bar: N.Y. 1951, U.S. Ct. Appeals (2nd cir.) 1962, U.S. Supreme Ct. 1966. Pvt. practice, N.Y.C., 1951, 55, 90—; atty. adviser U.S. Immigration and Naturalization Svc., N.Y.C., 1952-54, dist. counsel, 1968-84, spl. counsel, 1985-90; asst. dir. commerce City of N.Y., 1956-58; asst. commr. dept. pub. events, dir. UN Consular Corps Coms. N.Y.C., 1958-65; law sec. Supreme Ct. State of N.Y., 1967; dep. asst. sec. Dept. of Interior, 2002—. Chmn. govt. officials com. Internat. Debutante Ball, 1980—. Decorated Orden de Ruben Dario (Nicaragua), Order Nacional al Merito (Ecuador), Order of Merit (Italy), Officers Cross of Merit (Germany), Order of the Brilliant Star (China), Officer of the Natural Order of the Cedar (Lebanon); recipient Amita award to Women of Outstanding Achievement of Italian Ancestry, 1956, Vespu CCI award to Outstanding Ams. of Italian Ancestry, 1957, award Soc. Fgn. Consuls in N.Y., 1961, 63, award for community svc. JFK Libr. for Minorities of Am. Heritage, 1972. Mem. Am. Soc. Italian Legions of Merit (bd. dirs., officer), Am. Immigration Lawyers' Assn. Republican. Roman Catholic. Avocations: gardening, theatre. Immigration, naturalization, and customs, Probate (including wills, trusts). Office: 58 W 58th St New York NY 10019-2502

CAMIC, DAVID EDWARD, lawyer; b. Indpls., June 11, 1954; s. Edward Franklin Camic and Carolyn (Hooker) Camic-Longland. BA, Aurora U., 1982; postgrad., DePaul U., 1982-83; JD cum laude, John Marshall Law Sch., 1987. Bar: Ill. 1987, U.S. Dist. Ct. (no. dist.) Ill. 1990, N.Y. 1996. Ptnr. Camic, Johnson, Wilson & McCulloch P.C., Aurora, Ill., 1987—. Mem. faculty, lectr. Aurora U.; lectr. in criminal law Regional Police Tng., Aurora, 1987—. Contbr. articles to profl. jours. Chmn. Rape Def. Seminar, Aurora, 1986. Named Man of Yr. Todays Orgn. Youth, 1987. Mem. ATLA, ABA, Ill. Bar Assn. (past-chair criminal justice sect.), Kane County Bar Assn. (past chair criminal law com., bd. dirs. 2000-01), Nat. Assn. Criminal Lawyers, Phi Delta Phi. Criminal. Office: Camic Johnson Wilson & McCulloch PC 546 W Galena Blvd Aurora IL 60506-3855

CAMMARANO, DENNIS A. lawyer; b. N.Y.C., Jan. 9, 1957; s. Joseph Cammarano and Josephine Saez; m. Terri Lee Wagner, Mar. 25, 1994; children: Ellen, Marlon. BA, SUNY, Stonybrook, 1979; JD, Fordham U., 1982. Bar: N.Y. 1983, Calif. 1986. Assoc. Vincent, Berg, Russo, N.Y.C., 1982—85, Fisher & Porter, Long Beach, Calif., 1985—87; ptnr. Grayson & Cammarano, L.A., 1987—89, Law Offices Dennis A. Cammarano, Long Beach, 1989—. Admiralty, Transportation. Office: Law Offices Dennis A Cammarano 555 E Ocean Blvd # 501 Long Beach CA 90802 Office Fax: 562-495-3674. Business E-Mail: dac@cargolawyers.com.

CAMP, JACK TARPLEY, JR., judge; b. Newnan, Ga., Oct. 30, 1943; s. Jack Tarpley and Sophia (Stephens) C.; m. Elizabeth Thomas, Apr. 24, 1976; children: Thomas Henry, Sophia Rose. BA, The Citadel, Charleston, S.C., 1965; MA, U. Va., 1967, JD, 1973. Bar: Ala. 1973, Ga. 1975. Atty. Cabaniss, Johnston, Dumas & O'Neal, Birmingham, Ala., 1973-75, Glover & Davis, P.A., Newnan, 1975-88; U.S. dist. judge Atlanta, 1988—. Mgr. family timber land holdings. Mem. Newnan Hist. Soc., 1975—, Ga. Trust for Hist. Preservation, Atlanta, 1975—. Capt. U.S. Army, 1967-70, Vietnam. Decorated Bronze Star; Ford Found. fellow U. Va., 1965-66. Mem. Ga. State Bar (bd. govs. 1987-89), Newnan-Coweta Bar Assn. (pres. 1978), Fed. Judges Assn., Kiwanis. Presbyterian. Office: US Dist Ct 2142 US Courthouse 75 Spring St SW Atlanta GA 30303-3309

CAMP, JAMES CARROLL, lawyer; b. Greenville, S.C., Jan. 7, 1951; s. Willard Alford and Joy (Mills) C. BA, Duke U., 1973; JD, Emory U., 1976. Bar: Ga. 1976, Calif. 1977, U.S. Dist. Ct. (cen. dist.) Calif. 1977, U.S. Tax Ct. 1981. Assoc. Strother, Weiner & Dwyer, Atlanta, 1976; atty. Pacific Lighting Corp., L.A., 1977-78; ptnr. Greenberg, Bernhard, Weiss & Rosin, L.A., 1978-84, Brown, Winfield & Canzoneri, L.A., 1984—. Coun. mem. Emory U. Law Sch., 1998-2000, Duke U. Regional Coun., 1999—; Adj. prof. of law real estate sales transactions Southwestern Univ. Sch. of Law, 2002—. Mem. editl. bd. Los Angeles Lawyer, 1984-88, chmn. 1986-87. Mem. ABA (real estate fin. subcom.), Los Angeles County Bar Assn. (chmn. lawyer and arts com. 1982-83), Century City Bar Assn. (chmn. real property com. 1983-84). Commercial, contracts (including sales of goods; commercial financing), Corporate, general, Property, real (including real estate development, water). Office: Brown Winfield & Canzoneri 300 S Grand Ave Ste 1500 Los Angeles CA 90071-3125 E-mail: jcamp@bwclaw.com.

CAMP, JOHN CLAYTON, lawyer; b. Arab, Ala., Sept. 23, 1923; s. Roy Hubert and Alice Mellie (Cox) C.; m. Frances Elizabeth Spencer, Nov. 3, 1944; children: John, Elizabeth Camp Bower, Martha Camp Cox, Charles. Student, Birmingham-So. Coll., 1940-42, U. Ala., 1943, Auburn U., 1944; JD, La. State U., 1948. Bar: La. 1948, U.S. Supreme Ct. 1958, D.C. 1974. Assoc. Thompson, Lawes and Cavanaugh, Lake Charles, La., 1948-55; ptnr. Camp, Carmouche, Barsh, Gray, Hoffman & Gill, Lake Charles, 1955-84, Camp, Barsh & Tate, Washington, 1984-94, Patton Boggs LLP, Washington, 1994—. Active Internat. Top Mgmt. Roundtable Confs., London, Milan, Amsterdam, Brussels, Frankfurt, Rome, Dusseldorf, Ditchley Park, Stockholm and Toronto, 1982-87. Mem. Presdl. Trade Commn. to People's Republic of China, 1979; trustee Athens (Greece) Coll., 1985-91; mem. exec. com., vice chmn. Meridian House Internat., 1986-96; past mem. med. ctr. adv. coun. George Washington U. With USAF, 1943-46; bd. advs. Internat. Mgmt. and Devel. Inst., Fowler McCracker Commn. (chmn. policy planning group, 1982-87); pres., mem. exec. com. Metro USO, 1989-92; bd. exec. com. Wolf Trap Found., 1984-91. Mem. ABA, D.C. Bar Assn., La. State Bar Assn., Southwestern La. Bar Assn., Congl. Country Club. Democrat. Presbyterian. Avocations: golf, photography, reading. Administrative and regulatory, Corporate, general, Legislative. Office: Patton Boggs LLP 2550 M St NW Ste 800 Washington DC 20037-1301 Home: Apt CT 411 3122 Gracefield Rd Silver Spring MD 20904-5804

CAMP, RANDY COLEMAN, lawyer; b. Alamo, Tenn., Nov. 15, 1952; s. W.L. and Ara (Coleman) C.; m. Lisa Roland, Oct. 27, 1984; children: Catherine Nicole, Leigh Elizabeth. AA, Jackson State Coll., 1972; BS, U. Tenn., 1975; JD, Memphis State U., 1980. Bar: Tenn. 1980, U.S. Dist. Ct. (ea., mid., we. dists) Tenn. 1982. Pvt. practice, Alamo, 1980-99; exec. asst. to lt. gov. State of Tenn., Nashville, 1984-87, asst. dist. atty. gen. 28th jud. dist., 1988-90; gen. session and juvenile judge Crockett County, 1990-98. County atty. Crockett County, Alamo, 1981-91, election commr., 1981-90; bank atty. People's Bank, Alamo, 1981-96; commr. Tenn. Claims Commn., 1999-2003, Tenn. Dept. Pers., 2003—. Chmn. Crockett County Dem. Party, Alamo, 1980-87. Mem. Crockett County C. of C. (pres. 1988-89). Democrat. Baptist. Banking, General practice, Property, real (including real estate development, water). Office: James K Polk Bldg Dept Persone 2nd Fl Nashville TN

CAMPAGNA, MARK V. lawyer; b. Pittsfield, Mass., Apr. 23, 1970; s. Alfred J. and Eileen K. Campagna; m. Robyn Campagna, Aug. 27, 2000. BSEE, Fla. State U., 1994; JD, John Marshall Law Sch., 1997. Bar: Ill. 1997, U.S. Patent and Trademark Office 1997, D.C. 1998. Assoc. Arnold White & Durkee, Chgo., 1997—2000, Jones Day, Chgo., 2000—. Mem.: ABA (co-chair intellectual property law sect. young lawyers com. 2001, chair intellectual property law sect. pro bono com. 2002). Intellectual property, Patent, Trademark and copyright.

CAMPANIE, SAMUEL JOHN, lawyer; b. Oneida, N.Y., May 30, 1952; s. Samuel G. Campanie and Kathryn A. McCarthy Warner, stepson George A. Warner; m. Susan Noyes Garner, June 14, 1975; children: Joseph Warner, Abigail Noyes. AB cum laude, Colgate U., 1974; JD, Albany Law Sch., 1978; postgrad., Syracuse U., 1982—. Bar: N.Y. 1979, U.S. Dist. Ct. (no. and we. dists.) N.Y. 1994. Assoc. Kiley, Feldman, Whalen, Devine & Patane, Oneida, 1977-81; mgr. Mid-east and African divs. Oneida (N.Y.) Ltd. Silversmiths, 1981-83, mgr. export div., 1982-85, mgr. export and mil. divs., 1985; ptnr. Kohn, Moseman, Campanie, Oneida and Remsen, 1986-88; county atty. Madison County, N.Y., 1987—; dir. Kiley, Feldmann, Whalen, Devine & Patane P.C., Oneida, 1988-2000; mem., pres. Campanie & Wayland-Smith PLLC, Sherrill, N.Y., 2000—. Dir., counsel, Madison-Oneida County Indian Land Claim Litigation Task Force, 1999—; accredited rep. Svc. Core of Retired Execs./Active Core Execs., Utica, N.Y., 1979-90; cons. to various firms, 1985-89; pvt. cons. practice Kenwood Assocs. Internat., Oneida, 1986-89. Mem. City of Oneida Planning Commn., 1979-91, chmn. 1990-91; legislator Madison County Bd. Suprs., Wampsville, N.Y., 1986-87; bd. dirs. Madison County Indsl. Devel. Agy., 1986-90, Oneida-Madison Red Cross, 1979-87, Mansion House Svc. Corp., 1988-98, pres. 1997-98; mem. platform com. N.Y. State Rep. Com., Albany, 1986; mem. exec. com. Madison County Rep. Com., 1979-87; chmn. City of Oneida Rep. Com., 1979-87; mem. N.Y. State Oneida Lake Adv. Com., 1986—, chmn., 1988—. Named one of Outstanding Young Men in Am., 1985. Mem. ABA, N.Y. State Bar Assn., Madison County Bar Assn., N.Y. State County Attys. Assn. (dir. 1988—, pres. 1989-90, treas. 1997—), Oneida Jaycees. Republican. Roman Catholic. Avocations: sailing, biking, skiing, reading, computers. Commercial, contracts (including sales of goods; commercial financing), Corporate, general, General practice. Home: 209 Kenwood Ave Oneida NY 13421-2809 Office: Campanie & Wayland-Smith PLLC PO Box 70 60 E State St Sherrill NY 13461 Fax: (315) 363-1952. E-mail: nybizlawyer@yahoo.com., sjclaw@twcny.rr.com., sjc@mad.co.ny.us.

CAMPBELL, BERNARD ALEXANDER, JR., lawyer; b. Trenton, N.J., Jan. 22, 1940; s. Bernard Alexander and Laura (Hill) C.; m. Barbara Russell, Oct. 6, 1990; children: Bernard A. III, Sarah K. BA, Yale U., 1962; LLB, U. Pa., 1965. Bar: N.J., U.S. Dist. Ct. N.J., U.S. Ct. Appeals (3d cir.). Assoc. Pitney, Hardin & Kipp, Newark, 1965-67, McLaughlin, Dawes & Abbots, Trenton, 1967-70, Pelletieti & Rabstein, Trenton, 1970-79; ptnr. Mason, Griffin & Pierson, Princeton, N.J., 1979-86, Destribats Campbell DeSantis & Magee, Trenton, 1986—. Counsel Am. Boy Choir Sch., Princeton, 1980—. Mem. ABA, N.J. State Bar Assn. Clubs: Nassau Gun (Princeton) (bd. dirs. 1983—). Avocations: fly fishing, shooting, hunting. Federal civil litigation, State civil litigation, Personal injury (including property damage). Office: 247 White Horse Ave Trenton NJ 08610-2625

CAMPBELL, BERT LOUIS, lawyer, mediator, arbitrator; b. Tyler, Tex., Aug. 11, 1939; s. Bert M. and Jocelyn M. (Day) C.; m. Mary Ann Suatoni, July 17, 1965; children: Stephen, Brian, Rebecca. BA, U. Tex., 1961, B in Journalism, JD, U. Tex., 1970. Ptnr. Vinson & Elkins, Houston, 1970—2001. Writer, lectr. in field. Trustee Cullen Found. Lt. (j.g.) USN, 1963-66. Mem. ABA, Tex. Bar Assn., Houston Bar Assn., Am. Health Lawyers Assn. (ADR panel), Am. Arbitration Assn., Atty.-Mediators Assn. Corporate, general, Health, Mergers and acquisitions. Office: 3017 Nottingham Blvd Houston TX 77005

CAMPBELL, BRUCE IRVING, lawyer; b. Mason City, Iowa, July 7, 1947; s. E. Riley Jr. and Donna May (Andresen) C.; children: Anne, John; m. Beverly J. Evans. BA, Upper Iowa U., 1969; JD, Harvard U., 1973. Bar: Iowa 1973, U.S. Dist. Ct. (so. dist.) Iowa 1973, U.S. Dist. Ct. (no. dist.) Iowa 1974, U.S. Tax Ct. 1976, U.S. Ct. Appeals (8th cir.) 1977, U.S. Ct. Claims 1982. Shareholder Davis, Brown, Koehn, Shors & Roberts, P.C., Des Moines, 1973—. Adj. prof. law Drake U., Des Moines, 1974-90. Trustee Upper Iowa U., Fayette, 1978—, chair bd. trustees, 1992—2002; sec., dir. Iowa Natural Heritage Found., 2001—. Mem. ABA, Iowa State Bar Assn., Polk County Bar Assn. Republican. Estate planning, Estate taxation, Taxation, general. Home: 62 Meadowbrook Cir Cumming IA 50061-1014 Office: Davis Brown Koehn Shors & Roberts PC 666 Walnut St Ste 2500 Des Moines IA 50309-3904 E-mail: bruce.campbell@lawiowa.com.

CAMPBELL, CHARLES EDWARD, lawyer; b. Atlanta, Jan. 12, 1942; s. Borden Burr and Bonnie (McPherson) C.; m. Ann Grovenstein, Apr. 12, 1976; 1 child, Garrett McPherson. Student, Emory U., 1960-61; BA, MA, U. Ga., 1964; JD, Georgetown U., 1971. Bar: Ga. 1972. Legis. asst. to U.S. Sen. Richard B. Russell, Washington, 1965-67; exec. sec., 1967-69; adminstrv. asst., 1969-71; assoc. Heyman & Sizemore, Atlanta, 1971-73, ptnr., 1974-77, Hicks, Maloof & Campbell, Atlanta, 1977-98, McKenna Long & Aldridge LLP (formerly Long, Alridge & Norman, LLP), 1998—. Trustee Richard B. Russell Found., 1978—, mem. exec. com., 1980—, chmn., 1990—. Fellow Am. Coll. Trial Lawyers, Am. Coll. Bankruptcy; mem. Ga. Bar Assn. (mem. legis. com. 1978-79), Southeastern Bankruptcy Law Inst., Inc. (bd. dirs., pres. 1993-94). Administrative and regulatory, Bankruptcy, General civil litigation. Home: 2485 Dellwood Dr NW Atlanta GA 30305-4075 Office: McKenna Long & Alridge LLP 303 Peachtree St NE Ste 5300 Atlanta GA 30308-3264

CAMPBELL, CLAIR GILLILAND, lawyer; b. Aberdeen, Md., Nov. 27, 1961; d. Bobby Eugene and Sara Frances (Matkins) G. BA, U. Ala., 1982; JD, Cumberland U., 1985. Bar: N.C. 1985, U.S. Dist. Ct. (we. and mid. dists.) N.C. 1985, S.C. 1986. Ptnr. Karney, Campbell & Karney, Charlotte, N.C., 1985-91, Campbell & Taylor, Charlotte, 1991—, 1996—. Instr. Paralegal Inst., Queens, Coll., 1990; participant Wild Dolphin Project. Author: Twas the Night Before the Orange Bowl, 1988. Mem. ABA, ATLA, Mecklenburg County Bar Assn. (program coord. edn. com. 1986-88, panel televised lawyers discussion 1991, mem. speakers forum com. 1992, silent ptnr., law day com. 1996), N.C. Acad. Trial Lawyers, Ducks Unltd., Cumberland Alumni Assn. (reunion com. 1989-90), DAR (vice-regent 1993-94), Nat. Soc. Colonial Dames (sec. 1995—), Nat. Soc. Magna Charta Dames, Alpha Omicron Pi (sec. 1994—). Avocations: private pilot, equestrian, water- and snow-skiing, films, reading. Personal injury (including property damage). Office: Campbell & Taylor 717 East Blvd Charlotte NC 28203-5113

CAMPBELL, DIANA BUTT, lawyer; b. Ayer, Mass., Nov. 14, 1943; d. Lester A. and Genevieve P. (Ash) Butt; m. James W. Campbell, Feb. 3, 1961; children: James R., Lisa J., Alan D. BS magna cum laude, Suffolk U., 1980; JD, New Eng. Sch. Law, 1984. Bar: Mass. 1984, U.S. Dist. Ct. Mass. 1986, U.S. Supreme Ct. 1988. Editor Danvers (Mass.) State Hosp. Newsletter, 1977, Mass. Press Assn. Bull., 1978-79; mediator, case coord. Salem (Mass.) Mediation Program, 1979-83; legal adv. Help for Abused Women and Their Children, Salem, 1980-82; pvt. practice, Hamilton, Mass., 1984—. Mem., chair Hamilton Housing Authority, 1975-80; vol. Danvers State Hosp., 1978-92; mem. Cape Ann Area bd. Dept. Social Svc., Beverly, Mass., 1982-84; merit badge counselor Boy Scouts Am., Hamilton, 1984-93; assoc. mem. Hamilton Cable Adv. Bd., 1987-91; bd. dirs. United Way of North Shore, Beverly, 1988-94; adv. bd. of money mgmt. program North Shore Elder Svcs., 1993—; mem. adv. coun. SeniorCare, Inc. 2001—. Mem. Nat. Acad. Elder Law Attys., Assn. Trial Lawyers Am., Mass. Acad. Trial Lawyers, Mass. Bar Assn., Soc. Profl. Journalists, Essex County Bar Assn., Salem Bar Assn., North Shore Women Lawyers' Assn., Kiwanis (pres. 1990-91). Avocations: volkssporting, photography, travel. Family and matrimonial, Estate planning, Probate (including wills, trusts). Home: 30 East St Topsfield MA 01983 Office: 65 Railroad Ave South Hamilton MA 01982-2218

CAMPBELL, EDWARD ADOLPH, judge, electrical engineer; b. Boonville, Ind., Jan. 16, 1936; s.Revis Allen and Sarah Gertrude (Hunsaker) C.; m. Nancy Colleen Keys, July 26, 1957; children: Susan Elizabeth Campbell Frisse, Stephen Edward, Sara Lynne. BEE, U. Evansville, 1959; JD, Ind. U., 1965; grad. Nat. Coll. Dist. Attys., U. Houston, 1972; grad. Nat. Jud. Coll., U. Nev., 1978; grad. Am. Acad. Jud. Edn., U. Va., 1979; grad., Ind. Jud. Coll., 1981; grad. Ind. Grad. Program for Judges, Ind. Jud. Ctr., 1999. Bar: Ind. 1965, U.S. Dist. Ct. (so. dist.) Ind. 1965, U.S. Ct. of Customs and Patent Appeals 1967, U.S. Supreme Ct. 1973, U.S. Ct. Appeals (fed. cir.) 1982. Patent examiner U.S. Patent Office Digital Computer Divsn., Washington, 1959-60; patent adv. U.S. Naval Avionics, Indpls., 1960-65; patent atty. Gen. Elec. Co., Ft. Wayne, Ind., 1965-66; ptnr. Weyerbacher & Campbell, attys., Boonville, Ind., 1966-71; pros. atty. 2nd Jud. Cir., Warrick County, Ind., 1971-77; judge Warrick Superior Ct. No. 1, 1977-2001; sr. judge Ind. State Trial Cts., 2001—. Fellow Ind. Bar Found.; mem. IEEE, Ind.State Bar Assn., Evansville Bar Assn., Warrick County Bar Assn., Ind. Judges Assn., Nat. Coun. Juvenile and Family Ct. Judges, Ind. Coun. Juvenile and Family Ct. Judges, Warrick County C. of C. (bd. dirs. 1978-84, 97—), Lions Club, Sigma Pi Sigma, Phi Delta Phi. Democrat. Methodist. Home: 911 Julian Dr Boonville IN 47601-9556

CAMPBELL, FRANK ANDREW SCOTT, lawyer; b. Paterson, N.J., July 19, 1955; s. Donald and Frances C. BA, Lafayette Coll., 1977; JD, George Washington U., 1980. Bar: D.C. 1980, U.S. Dist. Ct. D.C. 1981, U.S. Ct. Appeals (D.C. cir.) 1981, U.S. Supreme Ct. 1984, U.S. Ct. Claims 1990. Ptnr. Hemsley & Campbell, Washington, 1980-83; sole practice Washington, 1984-94; asst. gen. counsel FBI, Washington, 1995—99; dep. asst. atty. gen., office of legal policy U.S. Dept. Justice, Washington, 1999—. Recipient Benjamin N. Cardoza citation of merit Anti-Defamation League B'nai Brith, 1987. Administrative and regulatory, Federal civil litigation, General practice.

CAMPBELL, FREDERICK HOLLISTER, retired lawyer, historian; b. Somerville, Mass., June 14, 1923; s. George Murray and Irene Ivers (Smith) C.; m. Amy Holding Strohm, Apr. 14, 1951; 1 child, Susan Hollister. AB, Dartmouth Coll., 1944; JD, Northwestern U., 1949; postgrad., Indsl. Coll. Armed Forces, 1961-62; MA in History, U. Colo., 1984, PhD in History, 1993. Bar: Ill. 1950, U.S. Supreme Ct. 1967, Colo. 1968. Joined USMC, 1953, advanced through grades to lt. col., 1962; assoc. editor Callaghan and Co., Chgo., 1949-50; pvt. practice Colorado Springs, Colo., 1968-88; ptnr. Gibson, Gerdes and Campbell, 1969-79; pvt. practice, 1980-88; gen. counsel 1st Fin. Mortgaage Corp., 1988-96; vice-chmn., corp. sec. 1st Fin. Mortgage Corp., 1993-96; hon. instr. history U. Colo., Colorado Springs, 1986—. Judge adv. USMC, Camp Lejeune, N.C., Korea, Parris Island, S.C., 1950-67, El Toro, Calif., Vietnam, Washington, 1950-67; vis. instr. Colo. Coll., 1993-95, asst. prof., 1996—. Author: John's American Notary and Commissioner of Deeds Manual, 1950; contbr. articles to profl. jours. Mem. Estate Planning Coun., Colorado Springs, 1971—81, v.p., 1977—78; trustee Frontier Village Found., 1971—77; precinct committeeman Rep. Party, 1971—86; del. Colo. State Conv., 1972, 1974, 1976, 1980; bd. dirs. Rocky Mountain Nature Assn., 1975—2001, pres., 1979—92; bd. dirs. Rocky Mountain Nat. Park Assocs., 1986—2001, v.p., 1986—92, sec., 1992—95; bd. dirs. Colorado Springs Symphony Assn., 2002—. Mem. Colo. Bar Assn., El Paso County Bar Assn. Am. Arbitration Assn., Marines Meml. Club, Phi Alpha Theta. Congregationalist. Corporate, general, Finance.

CAMPBELL, GEORGE EMERSON, lawyer; b. Piggott, Ark., Sept. 23, 1932; s. Sid and Mae (Harris) C.; m. Anna Claire Janes, June 22, 1960 (dec. Mar. 1971); children: Dianne, Carole; m. Joan Stafford Rule, Apr. 7, 1973. JD, U. Ark., Fayetteville, 1955. Bar: Ark. 1955, U.S. Supreme Ct. 1971. Law clk. to judge Ark. Supreme Ct., 1959-60; mem. Rose Law Firm, P.A., Little Rock, 1960—; Del. 7th Ark. Constl. Conv., 1969-70; regional v.p. Nat. Mcpl. League, 1974-86. Mem. Ark. Ednl. TV Commn., 1976-92, chmn., 1980-82, 88-91; bd. dirs. Ark. Ednl. TV Found., 1984-92, chmn., 1988-91. Chmn. bd. Pulaski County Law Libr., 1980—; bd. dirs. Ark. Arts Ctr., 1991-95, sec. 1992-93), Ark. Symphony Orch. Soc., 1982-87, Ark. Capital Corp., pres. 2001-; bd. dirs. Ark. Cert. Devel. Corp., Downtown Partnership, 1978-2002; bd. dirs. Youth Home Inc., 1986-92, pres., 1991-92. With USNR, 1955-77, comdr. ret. Fellow Am. Bar Found.; mem. ABA, Ark. Bar Assn., Pulaski County Bar Assn., Am. Law Inst. (life mem.), Am. Judicature Soc., Nat. Assn. Bond Lawyers. Corporate, general, Finance, Property, real (including real estate development, water). Office: Rose Law Firm PA 120 E 4th St Little Rock AR 72201-2893 Office Fax: 501-375-1309. E-mail: gcampbell@roselawfirm.com.

CAMPBELL, HUGH BROWN, JR., judge; b. Charlotte, N.C., Feb. 19, 1937; s. Hugh Brown and Thelma Louise (Welles) C.; m. Mary Irving Carlyle, Nov. 3, 1962; children: Hugh B. III, Irving Carlyle, Thomas Lenoir. AB, Davidson Coll., 1959; JD, Harvard U., 1962. Atty. Craighill, Rendleman, Charlotte, 1964-77, Weinstein & Sturges, Charlotte, NC, 1977-94, Cansler Lockhart Charlotte, 1995-2000; judge N.C. Ct. Appeals, Raleigh, 2001—02, 26th Jud. Dist. Ct., Charlotte, 2003—. Chmn. Jury Commn., Mecklenburg County, N.C., 1985-97; exec. com. County Bar Assn., Mecklenburg County, 1989-92, civil cts. com. chair, 1990-92. Rep. N.C. House Reps., Raleigh, 1969-71; legis. liaison Charlotte/Mecklenburg County, Raleigh, 1971-72; state chmn. N.C. Zoo Bond Campaign, 1972; chmn. Carolinas Med. Ctr. Bond Campaign, 1976. Col. JAG U.S. Army, 1962-64, Res., 1964-92. Decorated Legion of Merit, Meritorious Svc. medal (2); Honored Order of Hornet, Mecklenburg County, 1976. Mem. N.C. Bar Coun. (exec. com., chair ethics 1981-90), Planned Parenthood Charlotte (bd. dirs., chmn. 1980-81), YMCA Charlotte (adv. bd. 1992—), Rotary Club E. Charlotte (pres. 1976-77). Democrat. Episcopalian. Avocations: tennis, swimming, hiking, reading, politics. Home: 1428 Scotland Ave Charlotte NC 28207-2561 Office: 26th Jud Dist 700 E 4th St Charlotte NC 28202

CAMPBELL, JAMES SARGENT, lawyer; b. Chgo., Sept. 19, 1938; m. Mary Tydings Eager, Sept. 3, 1960; children: Catherine, Julia, John. BA summa cum laude, Yale U., 1960; LLB, Stanford U., 1964. Bar: D.C. 1966. Carnegie teaching fellow Yale U., 1960-61; law clk. Justice William O. Douglas, U.S. Supreme Ct., 1964-65; spl. asst. antitrust div. Dept. Justice, 1967-68; gen. counsel Nat. Commn. Causes and Prevention Violence, 1968-69; assoc. Wilmer, Cutler & Pickering, Washington, 1965-67, 70-71, ptnr., 1972-2000, of counsel, 2001—. Cons. Office Sec. HUD, 1977-78, HHS, 1979. Author, editor: Law and Order Reconsidered, 1970, Doctor Faustus: Archetypal Subtext at the Millenium, 1999. Trustee Eastern Shore Chamber Music Festival, 2000—, pres., 2002—; vestry Wye Parish, 2003—; co-chair Eastern Shoreway Alliance, 2003—. Mem.: MLA, ABA, Save Our County, Cosmos Club, Elizabethan Club, Phi Beta Kappa, Order of Coif. Antitrust, Transportation. Office: Wilmer Cutler & Pickering 2445 M St NW Washington DC 20037-1420

CAMPBELL, JENNIFER LOUISE, lawyer; b. Encino, Calif., Sept. 9, 1962; d. Robert Joseph and Margaret Helen Campbell; m. Juan Carlos Cruz, Mar. 20, 1993. BA, Whittier Coll., 1985; JD, U. Calif. Hastings Coll. Law, 1991. Bar: Calif. 1991, U.S. Tax Ct. 1996. Assoc. Pillsbury, Madison & Sutro, San Francisco, 1991-94; assoc. Fenwick & West, Palo Alto, Calif., 1994-96, Rosenfeld, Meyer & Susman, Beverly Hills, Calif., 1996-98, Hoffman, Sabban & Watenmaker, L.A., 1998—. Mem. Jr. League of L.A. (asst. chair rummage sale com. 1997-98), Order of the Coif. Estate planning, Probate (including wills, trusts), Estate taxation. Office: Hoffman Sabban & Watenmaker 10880 Wilshire Blvd Ste 2200 Los Angeles CA 90024-4123

CAMPBELL, JOEL RODERICK, lawyer; b. Cleve., Dec. 10, 1946; s. Ralph L. and Jean M. (Roderick) C.; children: Kristie A., Scott R.; m. Robin Ann Rentfrow, Jan. 22, 1982. BA in Bus. Adminstrn., Ohio State U., 1968; JD, U. Akron, 1972. Bar: Ohio 1972. Asst. pros. atty. Franklin County, Columbus, Ohio, 1972-73; ptnr. Britt, Campbell & Nagel, Columbus, 1973— . Mem. Dublin City Coun., 1990-98, mayor, 1994-95. Recipient Merit award Ohio Legal Ctr. Inst., Columbus, 1978. Mem. ABA, Ohio State Bar Assn., Columbus Bar Assn., Ohio State U. Pres.'s Club. State civil litigation, Family and matrimonial, Personal injury (including property damage). Office: 490 City Park Ave Columbus OH 43215-5780

CAMPBELL, JOHN WILLIAM, prosecutor; b. Honolulu, Jan. 6, 1955; s. George Willis and Leona Ruth Campbell; m. Lisa Jo Hale, Dec. 31, 1984. BA in Polit. Sci. and History, Washburn U., 1977; JD, U. Kans., 1979, MPA, 1980. Bar: Kans. 1979, U.S. Dist. Ct. Kans. 1979, U.S. Ct. Appeals (10th cir.) 1986, U.S. Supreme Ct. 1986, U.S. Ct. Appeals (D.C. cir.) 1992. Asst. county atty. Ford County Atty.'s Office, Dodge City, Kans., 1979-80; asst. atty. gen. Kans. Atty. Gen.'s Office, Topeka, 1981-86, dep. atty. gen., 1986-95, sr. dep. atty. gen., 1995—2003, gen. counsel Kans. Dept. Ins., 2003—. Chmn. Gov.'s Indian Gaming Group, Topeka, 1995; trustee Western Hills Bapt. Ch., Topeka, 1997-2000. Recipient Gen. Pres.'s award Nat. Assn. Attys., 2000, Marvin award Nat. Assn. Attys., 2001. Mem. Kans. Bar Assn., Topeka Bar Assn. Republican. Avocations: motorcycles, reading.

CAMPBELL, LEONARD M. lawyer; b. Denver, Apr. 12, 1918; s. Bernard Francis and May (Moran) C.; m. Dot J. Baker, Sept. 23, 1944; children: Brian T., Teri Pat, Thomas P. AB, U. Colo., 1941, LLB, 1943. Bar: Colo. 1943. Of counsel Gorsuch, Kirgis, Campbell, Walker and Grover, 1948-88, sr. ptnr., 1951-88; city atty. Denver, 1951-53; of cousel Gorsuch, Kirgis LLC, 1989—. Cons. pub. utility matters Colo. Mcpl. League. Mem. Denver Charter Com., 1947; mgr. Safety and Excise for Denver, 1947-48; chmn. Denver Com. Human Relations, 1954; mem. Denver Planning Bd., 1950-51; mem. Bd. Water Commrs., Denver, 1965-70, pres., 1968-69; mem. Gov.'s Com. on Jud. Compensation, 1972; chmn. U. Colo. Law Alumni Devel. Fund, 1962. Served with USAAF, 1943-46. Mem. ABA, Colo. Bar Assn. (pres. 1978-79, Award of Merit 1967), Denver Bar Assn. (pres. 1969), Am. Coll. Trial Lawyers, Cath. Lawyers Guild Denver (pres. 1962, St. Thomas More award 1978), Nat. Inst. Mcpl. Law Officers (v.p. 1952), Colo. Judicial Inst. (Chancellor Chester Alter award 1987). Clubs: Denver Athletic (Denver) (sec. 1960-61, pres. 1962), Cherry Hills Country (Denver). Democrat. Roman Catholic. State civil litigation, Utilities, public. Home: 3447 S Birch St Denver CO 80222-7212 Office: Gorsuch Kirgis LLC LLP 1515 Arapahoe St Ste 1000 Denver CO 80202-2120

CAMPBELL, LEVIN HICKS, judge; b. Summit, N.J., Jan. 2, 1927; s. Worthington and Louise (Hooper) Campbell; m. Eleanor Saltonstall Lewis, June 1, 1957; children: Eleanor S., Levin H., Sarah H. AB cum laude, Harvard U., 1948, LLB, 1951; postgrad., Nat. Coll. State Judiciary, 1970; LLD (hon.) , Suffolk U., 1975; LLD (hon.) , Colby Coll., 1982. Bar: D.C. 1951, Mass. 1954. Assoc. firm Ropes & Gray, Boston, 1954—64; mem. Mass. Ho. of Reps., 1963—64; asst. atty. gen. State of Mass., 1965—66, spl. asst. atty. gen., 1966—67, 1st asst. atty. gen., 1967—68; assoc. justice Superior Ct. of Mass., 1969—72; judge U.S. Dist. Ct. Mass., Boston, 1972, U.S. Ct. Appeals (1st cir.), Boston, 1972—, chief judge, 1983—90, sr. judge, 1992—. Fellow Inst. of Politics J.F. Kennedy Sch. Govt. Harvard U., 1968—69, study group leader, 1980; faculty chmn. law sessions Salzburg Seminar in Am. Studies, 1981. Pres. Cambridge 9 Neighborhood Assn., 1960—62; treas. Cambridge Ctr. for Adult Edn., 1961—64; campaign chmn. Cambridge United Fund, 1965; mem. bd. overseers Boston Symphony Orch., 1969—75, 1977—80; pres. bd. overseers Shady Hill Sch., 1969—70; mem. vis. com. Harvard U. Press, 1958—64; v.p. Cambridge Cmty. Svcs.; corp. mem. SEA Ednl. Assn., 1982—; trustee Colby Coll., Waterville, Maine, 1981—90, 1991—99, Asheville (N.C.) Sch., 1987—98; overseer U.S. Constn. Mus. 1st lt. (j.g.) U.S. Army, 1951—54, Korea. Mem.: ABA, Mass. Hist. Soc. (coun. 1993—96, v.p. 1996—99, pres. 2000—02, coun. 2003—), U.S. Jud. Conf. (ct. adminstrn. com. 1975—83, chmn. subcom. on supporting pers. 1980—83, exec. com. 1985—90, ad hoc com. study jud. conf. 1987, fed. ct. study com. 1988—90, chmn. com. to rev. cir. coun. conduct and disability orders 1989—94, nat. commn. on jud. discipline and removal 1991—93), Boston Bar Assn., Mass. Bar Found. (long range planning com. 1999—2000), Am. Bar Found., Am. Law Inst. Office: US Ct of Appeals US Courthouse 1 Courthouse Way Ste 6720 Boston MA 02210-3008

CAMPBELL, PAUL, III, lawyer; b. Chattanooga, Feb. 1, 1946; children: Paul IV, Kolter M. BA, Vanderbilt U., 1968; MA, Middlebury Coll., 1972; postgrad., So. Meth. U., 1971-72, Emory U., 1972-73; JD, U. Tenn., 1975. Bar: Tenn. 1976, Ga. 1977. Tchr. English St. Mark's Sch., Dallas, 1968-72; ptnr. Campbell & Campbell, Chattanooga, 1976-98; mem. Witt, Gaither & Whitaker, Chattanooga, 1998—2002, Shumacker Witt Gaither & Whitaker, Chattanooga, 2002—. Adj. prof. English, U. Tenn., Chattanooga, 1976, adj. prof. law, 1979-81, adj. prof. pre-trial litigation, Knoxville, 1996, adj. prof. pol. sch., 2002-; mem. Tenn. Ct. of Judiciary, 1995-2003; mem. Tenn. Jud. Evaluation Guidelines Commn., 1994-95. Author: Tennessee Admissibility of Evidence in Civil Cases, 1987; co-author: Tennessee Automobile Liability Insurance, 1986, 95, 96, 99, 2002; editor-in-chief Tenn. Law Rev., 1975; contbr. articles to profl. jours. Bd. mgrs. YMCA Youth Residential Ctr., 1977-80; mem. McCallie Sch. Alumni Coun., 1987-93, U. Tenn. Dean's Alumni adv. coun. law coll., 1979—; trustee, Harbison Found., 1994-96; bd. Cmty. Found. Greater Chattanooga, 2002-. Recipient Am. Jurisprudence award U. Tenn., 1974, U. Ten. Coll. Law Pub. Svc. award, 1995; Alumni Achievement award McCallie Sch., 1994. Mem. ABA, Am. Bar Found., Tenn. Bar Assn. (bd. govs. 1985-94, pres. 1992-93, ho. del., 2002-), Tenn. Bar Found., Chattanooga Bar Found., Chattanooga Bar Assn. (bd. govs. 1983-85), State Bar Ga., Fed. Bar Assn. (dir. chpt. 1983-88), Fed. Defense and Corp. Counsel, Def. Rsch. Inst., Internat. Assn. Def. Counsel, Order of Coif, Phi Kappa Phi. Federal civil litigation, State civil litigation, Insurance. Office: Shumacker Witt Gaither & Whitaker 736 Market St Ste 1100 Chattanooga TN 37402-4856

CAMPBELL, RICHARD BRUCE, lawyer; b. Phila., Jan. 5, 1947; s. George B. and Edith (Neithammer) C.; m. Patricia Ann James, Mar. 7, 1981; children: Ron Martin, Rebecca Joi. BA, U. S.C., 1968, JD, 1974. Bar: U.S. Dist. Ct. S.C. 1975, U.S. Ct. Appeals (4th cir.) 1976, U.S. Ct. Appeals (5th cir.) 1983, Colo. 1985, U.S. Dist. Ct. Colo. 1986, U.S. Ct. Appeals (fed. cir.) 1989, Fla. 1989, U.S. Dist. Ct. (mid. dist.) Fla., U.S. Ct. Appeals (11th cir.) 1992. Law clk. to presiding justice U.S. Dist. Ct., Columbia, S.C., 1975; ptnr. Henderson & Salley, Aiken, S.C., 1975-80; atty. TVA, Knoxville, 1980-85; ptnr. Wells, Love & Scoby, Boulder, Colo., 1986-89; shareholder Carlton, Fields, Ward, Emmanuel, Smith & Cutler, P.A., Tampa, Fla., 1989—. Lectr. in field. Contbr. articles to profl. jours. Served to capt. USAF, 1968-72. Mem. ABA, Am. Arbitration Assn. (panelist), Fla. Bar Assn., Colo. Bar Assn., Hillsborough County Bar Assn. Avocations: travel, skiing, photography. General civil litigation, Construction, Government contracts and claims. Office: Carlton Fields Ward Emmanuel Smith & Cutler PC PO Box 3239 Tampa FL 33601-3239 E-mail: rcamp@carltonfields.com.

CAMPBELL, ROBERT HEDGCOCK, investment banker, lawyer; b. Ann Arbor, Mich., Jan. 16, 1948; s. Robert Miller and Ruth Adele (Hedgcock) C.; m. Katherine Kettering, June 17, 1972; children: Mollie DuPlan, Katherine Elizabeth, Anne Kettering. BA, U. Wash., 1970, JD, 1973. Bar. Wash. 1973, Wash. State Supreme Ct. 1973, Fed. 1973, U.S. Dist. Ct. (we. dist.) Wash. 1973, Ct. Appeals (9th cir.) 1981. Assoc. Roberts & Shefelman, Seattle, 1973-78, ptnr., 1978-85; sr. v.p. Lehman Bros., Inc., Seattle, 1985-87, mng. dir., 1987—. Bd. dirs. Pogo Producing Co., 1999—; dir., treas. Nat. Assn. Bd. Lawyers, Hinsdale, Ill., 1982-85; pres., trustee Wash. State Soc. Hosp. Attys., Seattle, 1982-85; mem. econs. dept. vis. com. U. Wash., 1995-97; mem. Law Sch. dean's adv. bd. U. Wash., 1999—. Contbr. articles to profl. jours. Trustee Bellevue (Wash.) Schs. Found., 1988-91, pres., 1989-90; nation chief Bellevue Eastside YMCA Indian Princess Program, 1983-88; trustee Wash. Phikeia Found., 1983-91, Sandy Hook Yacht Club Estates, Inc., 1993-98; mem. Wash. Gov.'s Food Processing Coun., 1990-91. Mem. U. Wash. Varsity Swimming Alumni Bd. Republican. Avocations: skiing, wind surfing, bike riding, physical fitness, golf. Home: 8604 NE 10th St Medina WA 98039-3915 Office: Lehman Bros Bank of America Tower 701 5th Ave Ste 7101 Seattle WA 98104-7016 E-mail: ibe2ski@msn.com., rhcampbe@lehman.com.

CAMPBELL, ROBERT ROE, lawyer; b. Knoxville, Tenn., Nov. 7, 1930; s. Lacy Roe and Anita Tromp (Wilson) C.; m. Ruth Eleanor VerMeulen, July 7, 1956; children: Robert Roe Jr., Willard B., Cady Ruth. BS, U. Tenn., 1953, JD, 1956. Bar: Tenn. 1956, U.S. Dist. Ct. (ea. dist.) Tenn. 1956, U.S. Ct. Appeals (6th cir.) 1965, U.S. Supreme Ct. 1971. Sole practice Knoxville, 1956-58; assoc. Poore, Cox, Baker & McAuley, 1958-62, Hodges, Doughty & Carson, 1962-63, ptnr., 1963—. Bd. dirs., vice chmn. Maryville Coll., 1976-82; bd. dirs. Ft. Sanders Hosp., 1969-86; elder 2d Presbyn. Ch., Knoxville, 1960—; active Republican Party. Served with U.S. Army, 1953-55. Mem. ABA, Tenn. Bar Assn., Knoxville Bar Assn., Am. Coll. Trial Lawyers, Tenn. Bar Found., Am. Bar Found., Internat. Assn. Def. Counsel, Am. Bd. Trial Advs., LeConte Club, Cherokee Country Club (Knoxville). Alternative dispute resolution, General civil litigation, Corporate, general. Office: PO Box 869 Knoxville TN 37901-0869 E-mail: rcampbell@hdclaw.com.

CAMPBELL, SCOTT ROBERT, lawyer, former food company executive; b. Burbank, Calif., June 7, 1946; s. Robert Clyde and Jenevieve Anne (Olsen) C.; m. Teresa Melanie Mack, Oct. 23, 1965; 1 son, Donald Steven. BA, Claremont Men's Coll., 1970; JD, Cornell U., 1973. Bar: Ohio 1973, U.S. Dist. Ct. (so. dist.) Ohio 1974, Minn. 1976, Calif. 1989, U.S. Dist. Ct. (no. dist.) Calif. 1989, U.S. Ct. Appeals (9th cir.) 1989, U.S. Dist. Ct. (cen. and so. dists.) Calif. 1990, U.S. Ct. Appeals (5th cir.) 1991, U.S. Tax Ct. 1991, U.S. Ct. Appeals (fed. cir.) 2001. Assoc. Taft, Stettinius & Hollister, Cin., 1973-76; atty. Mpls. Star & Tribune, 1976-77; sr. v.p., gen. counsel, sec. Kellogg Co., Battle Creek, Mich., 1977-89; ptnr. Furth Fahrner Mason, San Francisco, 1989-2000, Zelle, Hofmann, Voelbel, Mason & Gette, LLP, San Francisco, 2000—. U.S. del. ILO Food and Beverage Conf., Geneva, 1984; participant, presenter first U.S.-USSR Legal Seminar, Moscow, 1988; speaker other legal seminars. Mem. ABA, Ohio Bar Assn., Minn. Bar Assn., Calif. Bar. Assn. Antitrust, Corporate, general, Securities. Office: Zelle Hofmann Voelbel Mason& Gette LLP 44 Montgomery St Ste 3400 San Francisco CA 94104- E-mail: srclaw@ix.netcom.com., scampbel@zelle.com.

CAMPBELL, SELAURA JOY, lawyer; b. Oklahoma City, Mar. 25, 1944; d. John Moore III and Gyda (Hallum) C. AA, Stephens Coll., 1963; BA, U. Okla., 1965; MEd, Chapel Hill U., 1974; JD, N.C. Cen. U., 1978; postgrad. atty. mediation courses, South Tex. Sch. of Law, Houston, 1991, Atty. Mediators Inst./Dallas, Dallas, 1992. Bar: Ariz 1983; lic. real estate broker, N.C.; cert. tchr. N.C. With flight svc. dept. Pan Am. World Airways, N.Y.C., 1966-91; lawyer Am. Women's Legal Clinic, Phoenix, 1987. Charter mem. Sony Corp. Indsl. Mgmt. Seminar, 1981; guest del. Rep. Nat. Conv., Houston, 1992; judge all-law sch. mediation competition for Tex., South Tex. Sch. Law, Houston, 1994. Mem. N.C. Cen. U. Law Rev., 1977-78. People-to-People del. People's Republic of China, 1987; guest del. Rep. Nat. Conv., Houston, 1992. Mem. Ariz. Bar Assn., Humane Soc. U.S., Nat. Wildlife Fedn., People for the Ethical Treatment of Animals, Amnesty Internat., Phi Alpha Delta. Republican. Episcopalian. Avocations: climbed Mt. Kilimanjaro, 1983, also Machu Pichu, Peru, Mt Kenya, Africa, horseback riding, photography. General civil litigation, Family and matrimonial, General practice. Home: 206 Taft Ave Cleveland TX 77327-4539

CAMPBELL, THOMAS DOUGLAS, lawyer, consultant; b. N.Y.C., Jan. 5, 1951; s. Edward Thomas and Dorothy Alice (Moore) C.; m. Mary Anne Makin, Dec. 22, 1978; 1 child, Kristen Anne. BA, U. Del., 1972; JD, U. Pa., 1976. Bar: Del. 1977. Law clk. Law Offices Bayard Brill & Handleman, Wilmington, Del., 1974-77; govt. affairs rep. Northeastern U.S. Std. Oil Co. Ind., 1977-78; Washington rep. Std. Oil Co., Ind., 1978-85; pres. Thomas D. Campbell and Assocs., Inc., Alexandria, Va., 1985—; chmn. bd. dirs. Compressus, inc., 2001—. Govt. affairs rep. Northeastern U.S., Std. Oil Co. Ind., 1977-78. With U.S. Army, 1968-69, Del. Air N.G., 1969-77. Elected to Wall of Fame, U. Del., 2000. Mem. ABA, Del. Bar Assn., Congl. Awards Found. (chmn. bd. dirs.), Duke of Edinburgh's Internat. Award Assn. (internat. trustee), Phi Beta Kappa, Phi Kappa Phi, Omicron Delta Epsilon, Omicron Delta Kappa. Republican. Episcopalian. Legislative. Home: 6215 Ventnor Ave C2 Ventnor City NJ 08406 also: PO Box 37 Cruz Bay St John VI 00831

CAMPBELL, VINCENT BERNARD, judge, lawyer; b. Rochester, N.Y., Nov. 1, 1943; s. Paul and Lucy C.; m. Geraldine Miceli, July 4, 1970; children: Dina, Tracy. BS, Syracuse U., 1965, LLD, 1968. Bar: N.Y. 1969. Lawyer Goldman and Shinder, Rochester, N.Y., 1970-74, Vincent B. Campbell Law Firm, Rochester, N.Y., 1974—; businessman Flower City Builders Supply Corp., Rochester, N.Y., 1974—; real estate developer V.R.J.D. Devel. Inc., 40 West Ave. Properties, Rochester, N.Y., 1970—; judge Town of Greece, N.Y., 1994—. V.p. Monroe County Legislature, Rochester, 1976-88; N.Y. state committeeman Rep. Party, Rochester, 1988-93; town councilman Town of Greece, 1990-94; bd. trustees N.Y. Chiropractic Coll., Seneca Falls, N.Y., 1992; econ. devel. com. Nazareth Coll., Rochester, 1991-93. Recipient Robert Roantree award Syracuse Credit Mfrs. Assn., 1965, Am. Jurisprudence award Lawyers Coop., 1969; named Legislator of the Yr., Monroe County Conservative Party, 1983-84. Mem. ABA, N.Y. State BarAssn., Monroe County Bar Assn., N.Y. State Magistrate's Assn., Rochester Yacht Club. Avocations: sailing, golfing, hunting, winemaking.

CAMPBELL, WILLIAM F., III, lawyer; b. Nyack, NY, Jan. 14, 1949; s. William F. and Marie J. Campbell; m. Ellen Fisher Campbell, July 29, 1972; children: Katherine, Marie, Ryan. BA, Lehigh U., 1970; MBA, JD, Rutgers U., 1974; LLM in Corp. Law, NYU, 1980. Bar: NJ 74, U.S. Dist. Ct. NJ 74, U.S. Supreme Ct. 00. Law clk. to Justice Mountain NJ Supreme Ct., Morristown, 1974—75; assoc. Dillon Bitar & Luther, Morristown, 1975—90, ptnr., 1980—. Adj. prof. Seton Hall Law Sch., Newark, 1983—2000; cons. NJ Corp. Law Pension Commn., 1976—80; mem. adm. com. NJ Bd. Securities, 1995. Corporate, general, Securities, Commercial, contracts (including sales of goods; commercial financing). Office: Dillon Bitar & Luther 53 Maple Ave Morristown NJ 07960 Fax: 973-292-2970. E-mail: wcampbell@DBL-Law.com.

CAMPBELL, WILLIAM GANT, lawyer, consultant; b. Atlantic City, Aug. 31, 1941; s. Edward T. and Dorothy (Moore) C.; m. Roberta A. Taylor, Nov. 20, 1964; children: Beth, Heather. BA, U. Del., 1963; JD, Temple U., 1966. Bar: Del. 1967, D.C. 1990. With Bayard, Handelman & Murdoch, P.A. and predecessor, Wilmington, Del., 1966—, ptnr., 1971—, mng. dir., 1976-82; counsel Del. Workmen's Compensation Study Commn., 1980; mem. Gov.'s Med. Malpractice Commn., 1975-76; chmn. Del. Ann. Bench and Bar Conf., 1981; counsel Workers' Compensation Coalition, 1980-82. Mem. Rep. State Exec. Com., 1976-77; media chmn. counsel Del. Nixon-Agnew Com., 1968; mem. bus. and govt. adv. coun. State Legis. Leaders Found., 1982-86; bd. dirs. Am. Tort Reform Assn., 1986—, vice-chair, 1986-88. Mem. ABA (chmn. membership com. Del. 1972-80, chair ins. com. sect. of adminstrv. law and regulatory practice 1997—), Del. Bar Assn., Capital Hill Club (Washington), Rodney Square Club (Wilmington), Masons. Administrative and regulatory, Corporate, general, Legislative. also: 1212 New York Ave NW Ste 510 Washington DC 20005-3987

CAMPBELL, WILLIAM J. lawyer; b. Grand Junction, Colo., Feb. 10, 1945; s. Timothy Samuel and Narcissa Cooke C.; m. Marsha Logan Campbell, June 16, 1979; children: John Bradford Geiger, Elizabeth Weir Geiger, Anne Wentworth Campbell, Amy Logan Campbell. BA cum laude, Colo. Coll., 1967; JD, U. Colo., 1971. Bar: Colo. 1971, U.S. Dist. Ct. Colo. 1971. Shareholder Bradley, Campbell, Carney & Madsen, P.C., Golden, Colo., 1971-95; ptnr. Faegre & Benson LLP, Denver, 1995—. Mem. U. Colo. Law Rev., 1970-71. Bd. trustees Colo. Colo.; mem. St. Andrews Vestry; bd. dirs. World Trade Ctr. , Denver. Named Outstanding Young Lawyer, First Jud. Dist. Bar Assn., 1982; Boettcher scholar Boettcher Found., 1963-67; Grad. fellow Rotary Found., 1969. Mem. ABA, Colo. Bar Assn., Colo. Assn. Corp. Counsel, Phi Beta Kappa. Republican. Episcopalian. Avocation: golf. Corporate, general, Private international, Securities. Home: 6781 Lupine Cir Arvada CO 80007 Office: Faegre & Benson LLP 3200 Wells Fargo Ctr 1700 Lincoln St Denver CO 80203

CAMPION, RENÉE, lawyer; b. Balt. BS, U. Md., 1980; JD, U. Balt., 1987. Bar: Md. 1987; cert. mediator. Atty. Legal Aid Bur., Inc., Balt., 1988-96; pvt. practice Balt., 1996—. Mem.: ABA, Bar Assn. Balt. City, Women's Law Ctr., Balt. County Bar Assn., Md. State Bar Assn., Women's Bar Assn. Family and matrimonial, Juvenile. Office: 401 Washington Ave Ste 803 Towson MD 21204-4905 E-mail: rlcesq8080@aol.com.

CAMPION, THOMAS FRANCIS, lawyer; b. Bklyn., Aug. 15, 1935; s. Thomas Francis and Genevieve Agnes (Schantz) C.; m. Virginia Grosscup, Aug. 21, 1965; children: Caroline, Michael. AB, Fordham U., 1957; LLB, Cornell U., 1961. Bar: N.J. 1961, U.S. Dist. Ct. N.J. 1961, U.S. Ct. Appeals (3d cir.) 1965, U.S. Supreme Ct. 1966, U.S. Dist. Ct. D.C. 1970, N.Y. 1988. Law clk. to judge Appellate Div.-Superior Ct. N.J., 1961-62; assoc. Shanley & Fisher, Newark and Morristown, NJ, 1962-67, ptnr. Morristown, 1968-99, Drinker, Biddle & Shanley, LLP, Florham Park, NJ, 1999—2002, Drinker, Biddle & Reath, LLP, Florham Park, NJ, 2003—. Bd. on trial atty. cert. N.J. Supreme Ct., 1982—89, chmn., 1987—89, chmn. disciplinary oversight com., 1994—2001, vice chmn. commn. on rules of profl. conduct, 2001—. Contbr. articles to profl. jours. Mem. N.J. Gov.'s Mgmt. Commn., 1970. 1st lt. USAR, 1957-61. Fellow Am. Bar Found., Am. Coll. Trial Lawyers; mem. ABA, N.J. Bar Assn. (past chmn. jud. and county prosecutor appointments com., civil cts. task force), Essex County Bar Assn., Morris County Bar Assn., Assn. Fed. Bar N.J. (pres. 1980-82), Univ. Club (N.Y.C.). Federal civil litigation, State civil litigation, Insurance. E-mail: thomas.campion@dbr.com.

CAMPOS, ALFRED, lawyer; b. Bklyn., Oct. 28, 1968; s. Adelfo and Mildred Campos; m. Lorraine Mullings, Nov. 10, 2001. BA in Polit. Sci., SUNY, Albany, 1990; JD, Western New Eng. Coll., 1998. Bar: Conn. 98, DC 99, U.S. Tax Ct. 00, U.S. Supreme Ct. 02. Underwriter Chubb & Son, Inc., N.Y.C. and New Providence, NJ, 1990—94, sr. underwriter Boston, 1994—95; assoc. Porter, Wright, Morris & Arthur LLP, Washington, 1998—99; legis. asst. U.S. Senator Charles S. Robb, Washington, 1999—2002; counsel, asst. dir. govt. rels. Fin. Planning Assn., Washington, 2000—. Recipient Arthur Osman Acad. scholarship, Union of Dist. 65, 1986—90, Howard I. Kalooner Acad. scholarship, Western New Eng. Coll. Sch. of Law, 1995. Mem.: ABA, DC Bar Assn., Western New Eng. Coll. Sch. of Law Alumni Assn. (bd. dirs. 2001—), Phi Alpha Delta. Roman Catholic. Avocations: Renaissance art and history, cooking, political biographies, jogging. Taxation, general, Personal income taxation. Home: 1600 S Joyce St Apt 407 Arlington VA 22202 Office: Fin Planning Assn 1615 L St NW Ste 650 Washington DC 20036 Fax: 202-626-8233. E-mail: alfred.compos@fpanet.org.

CAMPOS, DENNIS M. lawyer, mediator; b. Sacramento, Calif., Oct. 6, 1946; m. Nancy Younger; children: Paul, Jake, Jessica. BA, U. Calif., Davis, 1968, JD, 1971. Assoc. Diepenbrock, Wulff, Plant & Hannigan, Sacramento, 1971—76, ptnr., 1977—98; founding ptnr. Riegels Campos & Kenyon, Sacramento, 1998—. Dir., pres. U. Calif. Davis Law Sch. Alumni Assn., 1976—79, Sutter Club, Sacramento, 1998—2001. Mem.: Assn. Def. Counsel No. Calif. (past dir.), Am. Bd. Trial Advs. (assoc.). Insurance, Alternative dispute resolution, Product liability. Home: 37 Parkside Dr Davis CA 95616 Office: Riegels Campos & Kenyon LLP #220 2500 Venture Oaks Way Sacramento CA 95833

CAMPOS-ORREGO, NORA PATRICIA, lawyer, consultant; b. Lima, Peru, Sept. 3, 1959; came to U.S., 1984; d. Victor M. and Ofelia A. Campos. BA, Cath. U. Peru, 1979, LLB, 1983, Lawyer, 1984; JD magna cum laude, InterAm. U. P.R., San Juan, 1989. Bar: P.R. 1989, Peru, 1984. Legal asst. women's affairs commn. P.R. Gov.'s Office, San Juan, 1988-89, lawyer women's affairs commn., 1989-93, P.R. Gov.'s Office/Immigration Law Practice, Miami, Fla., 1993-94; women's discrimination cons. San Juan, P.R., 1994-95; pvt. practice Miami Beach, 1995—. Co-author: How to Write Public Police and Internal Process to Sexual Harassment Claims, 1989; editor Law Sch. Mag., 1988-89. All Am. scholar U. P.R., 1988-89. Mem. ABA, InterAm. Bar Assn., P.R. Bar Assn., Peru Bar Assn. Roman Catholic. Avocations: sightseeing, reading, dancing, walking. Civil rights, Labor (including EEOC, Fair Labor Standards Act, labor-management relations, NLRB, OSHA). Address: Apostolic Mission Christ 261 NE 23 St Miami FL 33137 Home: 15864 W Wind Cir Fort Lauderdale FL 33326

CANAN, THOMAS MICHAEL, lawyer; b. Appleton, Wis., Mar. 22, 1964; s. Michael Edward and Jean Ellen (McLaughlin) C.; m. Elizabeth Jane Levy, Aug. 5, 1989; children: Katherine, William. BA, U. Wis., Eau Claire, 1986; JD, U. Minn., 1989. Bar: Minn. 1989, U.S. Dist. Ct. Minn. 1990. M.J. Murdock fellow Washington Legal Found., 1987; student atty. Civil Practice Clinic, Mpls., 1987-88; summer assoc. Davis & Kuelthau, Milw., 1988; rsch. asst. Minn. Ho. of Rep. Rsch. Dept., Mpls., 1988-89; jud. clk. Olmsted County Dist. Ct., Rochester, Minn., 1989-90; assoc. Streater, Murphy, Gernander, Winona, Minn., 1990-91; asst. city atty. City of Rochester, Minn., 1991-99; pvt. practice Rochester, 1999—. Presenter in field. Presenter of various programs including Domestic Abuse Prosecution, Abating Gang Graffiti, Criminal Law Update. Tour guide Olmsted County Hist. Soc., Rochester, 1991-96; vol. Rochester Pk. and Recreation, 1989-93, Woodside Nursing Home, Rochester, 1993-97. Mem. Minn. State Bar Assn., Olmsted County Bar Assn. (bd. dirs.), Kiwanis, Lions (1st v.p.). Avocations: bicycling, swimming, sea kayaking. Home: 3117 Tremont Ln SW Rochester MN 55902-6316 Office: Merchants Exchange Bldg 18 3rd St SW Ste 200 Rochester MN 55902-3022 E-mail: tomcanan@worldnet.att.net.

CANARY, LEURA, prosecutor; Grad., Huntington Coll.; JD, U. Ala. Asst. Atty. Gen. Ala. Atty. Gen. Office, 1981—90; trial atty. Dept. of Justice Civil Dist., Ala., 1990—94; asst. U.S. Atty. Middle Dist., Ala., 1994—2001, U.S. Atty., 2001—. Office: US Atty'sOffice One Ct Sq Ste 201 Montgomery AL 36104 Fax: 334-223-7560.

CANARY, NANCY HALLIDAY, lawyer; b. Cleve., Apr. 21, 1941; d. Robert Fraser and Nanna (Hall) Halliday; m. Sumner Canary, Dec. 1975 (dec. Jan. 1979). BA, Case Western Res. U., 1963; JD, Cleve. State U., 1968. Bar: Ohio 1968, Fla. 1972, U.S. Dist. Ct. (no. dist.) Ohio 1975, U.S. Supreme Ct. 1974, U.S. Dist. Ct. (so. dist.) Fla. 1994. Law clk. to presiding judge Ohio Ct. Appeals, Cleve., 1968—69; ptnr. McDonald, Hopkins & Hardy, Cleve., 1969—83, Thompson, Hine, LLP, Cleve., 1984—2002. Trustee Beck Ctr. for Cultural Arts, Lakewood, Ohio, 1980—90, Ohio Motorists Assn., 1989—95, Ohio Chamber Orch.; trustee, mem. devel. adv. com. Fairview Gen. Hosp., Cleve., 1980—96; chairperson Sumner Canary Lectureship com. Case Western Res. U. Law Sch.; sec. bd. govs. Churchill Ctr., Washington, 2000—02; bd. dirs. Comerica Bank & Trust Co., F.S.B., 1993—2000. Mem. Ohio State Bar Assn., Cleve. Bar Assn., Palm Beach County Bar Assn., Estate Planning Coun. Cleve., Estate Planning Coun. Palm Beach County, Gulf Stream (Fla.) Golf Club, Westwood Country Club (Cleve.). Republican. Avocations: music, horseback riding, collecting Churchill books. Home: Unit 1806 12500 Edgewater Dr Cleveland OH 44107-1677 also: 200 N Ocean Blvd Delray Beach FL 33483-7126 Office: 125 Worth Ave # 117 Palm Beach FL 33480

CANAS, EDUARDO, lawyer; b. San Benito, Tex., Dec. 27, 1941; BGS, U. Nebr., Omaha, 1970; JD, Tex. Tech U., 1985. Commd. pvt. U.S. Army, 1959, advanced through grades to maj., 1975, ret., 1979; retail sales exec., 1979-82; pvt. practice, 1985—. Decorated Bronze Star. Mem. KC. Roman Catholic. Office: 600 N Main St Ste A Fort Worth TX 76106-9416

CANBY, WILLIAM CAMERON, JR., judge; b. St. Paul, May 22, 1931; s. William Cameron and Margaret Leah (Lewis) Canby; m. Jane Adams, June 18, 1954; children: William Nathan, John Adams, Margaret Lewis. AB, Yale U., 1953; LLB, U. Minn., 1956. Bar: Minn. 1956, Ariz. 1972. Law clk. U.S. Supreme Ct. Justice Charles E. Whittaker, 1958—59; asso. firm Oppenheimer, Hodgson, Brown, Baer & Wolff, St. Paul, 1959—62; asso., then dep. dir. Peace Corps, Ethiopia, 1962—64, dir., 1964—66; asst. to U.S. Senator Walter Mondale, 1966; asst. to pres. SUNY, 1967; prof. law Ariz. State U., 1967—80; judge U.S. Ct. Appeals (9th cir.), Phoenix, 1980—96, sr. judge, 1996—; chief justice High Ct. of the Trust Ter. of the Pacific Islands, 1993—94. Bd. dirs. Ariz. Ctr. Law in Pub. Interest, 1974—80, Maricopa County Legal Aid Soc., 1972—78, D.N.A.-People's Legal Svcs., 1978—80; Fulbright prof. Makerere U. Faculty Law, Kampala, Uganda, 1970—71. Author: American Indian Law, 1998; note editor: Minn. Law Rev., 1955—56; contbr. articles to profl. jours. Precinct and state committeeman Dem. Party Ariz., 1972—80; bd. dirs. Ctrl. Ariz. Coalition for Right to Choose, 1976—80. With USAF, 1956—58. Mem.: Maricopa County Bar Assn., State Bar Ariz., Order of Coif, Phi Beta Kappa. Office: Sandra Day O'Connor US Courthouse 401 W Washington St SPC 55 Phoenix AZ 85003-2156

CANDITO, JOSEPH, lawyer; b. Santa Eufemia, Reggio, Italy, Mar. 23, 1954; came to the U.S., 1956; s. Joseph (dec.) and Claudia (Sabina) C.; m. Doris Ann Beutner, Oct. 1, 1983; children: Claudia Christine, Joseph

Michael, Jonathan Matthew. AB, Ohio U., 1976, MEd, 1979; JD, U. Dayton, 1986. Bar: Ohio 1986, U.S. Dist. Ct. (so. and we. dist.) Ohio 1986. Staff assoc. Citizens Fed. Savs. and Loan, Dayton, Ohio, 1984-86; mng. atty. Hyatt Legal Svcs., Blue Ash, Ohio, 1986-94; owner Joseph Candito & Assocs., Blue Ash, 1994—. Mem. Ohio State Bar Assn., Cin. Bar Assn. Roman Catholic. Avocations: christian apologetics, weight lifting, reading, dancing, writing. Bankruptcy, Family and matrimonial, Probate (including wills, trusts). Address: 9403 Kenwood Rd Ste A-106 Cincinnati OH 45242-6811 E-mail: jcandito@candito.com.

CANDLAND, D. STUART, lawyer; b. Madison, Wis., Sept. 6, 1942; s. Don Charles and Dorothy Jane (Nelson) C.; m. Evelyn McComber, Dec. 3, 1982; children: Ashley, Tara Lynn, Brett. BA with honors, Brigham Young U., 1967; JD, U. Calif., Berkeley, 1970. Bar: Calif. 1971, U.S. Dist. Ct. (no. dist.) Calif. 1971, U.S. Ct. Appeals (9th cir.) 1971. Dep. atty. gen. State of Calif., San Francisco, 1970-73; dep. dist. atty. Solano County Dist. Atty.'s Office, Fairfield, Calif., 1973-75; assoc. Law Offices of M. Craddick, Walnut Creek, Calif., 1976-78; ptnr. Craddick, Candland & Conti, Danville, Calif., 1979—. Asst. prof. law Armstrong Sch. Law, Berkeley, 1971-77. Mem. ABA, Assn. Def. Counsel, Contra Costa County Bar Assn. Federal civil litigation, Insurance, Professional liability. Office: Craddick Candland & Conti Ste 260 915 San Ramon Valley Blvd Danville CA 94526-4021

CANDLER, JAMES NALL, JR., lawyer; b. Detroit, Jan. 25, 1943; s. James Nall and Lorna Augusta (Blood) C.; m. Jean Ward McKinnon, Mar. 8, 1974; children: Christine, Elizabeth, Anne. AB, Princeton U., 1965; JD, U. Mich., 1970. Bar: Mich. 1970. Assoc. Dickinson Wright PLLC, Detroit, 1970-77, ptnr., 1977—. Adj. prof. real estate planning U. Detroit Sch. of Law, 1975-80. Bd. dirs. Detroit Inst. Ophthalmology Grosse Pointe Park, Mich., 1983—, chmn., 1994—. Lt. USNR, 1965-67. Mem. Internat. Assn. Attys. and Execs. in Corp. Real Estate, State Bar Mich. (chmn. real property law sect. 1998-99), Am. Coll. of Real Estate Lawyers, Grosse Pointe Club (chmn. 1987-89), Country Club of Detroit. Republican. Avocations: sailing, golf, platform tennis. Construction, Landlord-tenant, Property, real (including real estate development, water). Home: 211 Country Club Dr Grosse Pointe Farms MI 48236-2901 Office: 500 Woodward Ave Ste 4000 Detroit MI 48226-3416 E-mail: jcandler@dickinson-wright.com.

CANDRIS, LAURA A. lawyer; b. Frankfort, Ky., Apr. 5, 1955; d. Charles M. and Dorothy (King) Sutton; m. Aris S. Candris, Dec. 22, 1974. AB with distinction in polit. sci., Transylvania Coll., 1975; postgrad., U. Pitts., 1975-77, U. Fla., 1977-78; JD, U. Pitts., 1978. Bar: Fla. 1978, U.S. Dist. Ct. (mid. dist.) Fla. 1978, U.S. Ct. Appeals (4th cir.) 1980, Pa. 1981, U.S. Dist. Ct. (we. dist.) Pa. 1982, U.S. Ct. Appeals (3d cir.) 1983. Assoc. Coffman, Coleman, Andrews & Grogan, Jacksonville, Fla., 1978-80, Manion, Alder & Cohen, Pitts., 1981-85, Eckert, Seamans, Cherin & Mellott, Pitts., 1985-86, ptnr., 1987-96, vice chmn. labor and employment law dept, mem. practice mgmt. com., mem. strategic planning com.; ptnr. Meyer Unkovic & Scott, LLP, Pitts., 1996—, chair labor, employment law and employee benefits sect., mem. litigation and transactions depts. Contbr. over 30 articles to profl. jours. including Compensation and Benefits Rev., Forum Reporter, Employment Law Inst. manuals, Ref. Manual for the 34th Ann. Mid-West Labor Law Conf. Dynamic Bus. Mem. O'Hara Twp., 1986—90, O'Hara Twp. Planning Commn., 1990; bd. dirs. Tri-State Employers Assn., 1991—93, Parent and Child Guidance Ctr., 1991—2001, v.p., 1998—99, mem. exec. com., 1998—2001, pres., 1999—2000, sec., 2000—01; treas., mem. exec. com. SMC Bus. Couns., 1993—94, bd. dirs., 1993—96, Big Bros. & Big Sisters Greater Pitts., 1998—, v.p. planning, 2001—02, mem. exec. com., 2001—, v.p. adminstrn., 2003—; bd. dirs. The Whale's Tale, 2000—01; bd. dirs., mem. exec. com. The FamilyLinks, 2000—01. Nat. Merit Found. scholar 1972-75; named Ky. Col., 1974. Mem.: ABA (EEO com. labor sect., labor and employment law com. litigation sect.), Pitts. Human Resources Assn., Allegheny County Bar Assn. (coun. on professionalism 1990—2000, employment and fed. cts. sect., women in the law div., hqrs. com. and pers. subcom.), Pa. Bar Assn. (elected mem. employment sect.), Fla. Bar Assn. Republican. Avocations: skiing, traveling, bicycling, reading. Federal civil litigation, Labor (including EEOC, Fair Labor Standards Act, labor-management relations, NLRB, OSHA), Pension, profit-sharing, and employee benefits. Office: Meyer Unkovic & Scott LLP 1300 Oliver Bldg Pittsburgh PA 15222

CANE, MARILYN BLUMBERG, lawyer, educator; b. Rockville Center, N.Y., Feb. 26, 1949; d. Howard Godfrey and Lilly Ruth (Goldberg); m. Edward M. Cane, Dec. 24, 1970 (div.); children: Daniel Eric, Jonathan Marc Howard; life ptnr. Karen E. Michaels, June 18, 2001. BA magna cum laude, Cornell U., 1971; JD cum laude, Boston Coll., 1974. Bar: N.Y. 1975, U.S. Dist. Ct. (so. dist.) N.Y. 1975, U.S. Ct. Appeals (2d cir.) 1976, Conn. 1977, Fla. 1981. With Reavis & McGrath, N.Y.C., 1974-76, Badger, Fisher & Assocs., Greenwich, Conn., 1977-80; counsel Corp Components divsn. GE, Fairfield, Conn., 1980-81; with Gunster, Yoakley & Assocs., Palm Beach, Fla., 1981-83; asst. prof. law Nova Southeastern U., Fort Lauderdale, Fla., 1983-85, assoc. prof. law, 1985-88, prof. law, 1988—. Author: Securities Arbitration: Law and Procedure, 1991; contbr. articles to profl. jours. Dir. Jewish Cmty. Day Sch. Palm Beach County, West Palm Beach, Fla., 1983-88; mem. adv. com. Conn. Banking Commn., Hartford, 1979-81; trustee Temple Beth Torah, Wellington, Fla., 1985-87, 92-98, Sta. WXEL, 1992—. Fellow Am. Bar Found.; mem. ABA (bus. law sect., bank holding cos. subcom.), Fla. Bar Assn., (advisor exec. coun. bus. law sect. 1988—, chair corp./securities com. bus. law sect. 1992-93, vice chair 1999-2000), Am. Law Inst., Order of Coif, Human Rights Campaign. Home: 1580 NW 100th Terr Plantation FL 33322 Office: Nova Southeastern U Law Ctr 3305 College Ave Fort Lauderdale FL 33314-7721 E-mail: canem@nsu.law.nova.edu.

CANER, EMIN DAVID, lawyer; b. N.Y.C., June 27, 1960; s. Ali Riza and Anjela Josephine Caner; m. Eva Chovancakova, May 19, 2002; stepchildren: Michaela Chovancakova, Pavlina Chovancakova. AS, McHenry County Coll., Crystal Lake, Ill., 1983; AAS, Ind. Vocat. Tech. Coll., Evansville, 1988; BA, Calif. State U., LA, 1992; JD, Thomas M. Cooley Law Sch., 1998. Bar: Ill. 1999, U.S. Dist. Ct. (no. dist.) Ill. 1999. Data entry clk. Can. Nat./Ill. Ctrl. R.R., Chgo., 1999—2000; pvt. practice Chgo., 2000—. Metros scholar, Sixty Plus Elderlaw Clinic, Lansing, Mich., 1997. Mem.: ABA, Ill. State Bar Assn., Chgo. Bar Assn. Avocations: walking, bicycle riding. Family and matrimonial, Personal injury (including property damage). Office: 1300 W Belmont Ave Ste 210 Chicago IL 60657 Business E-Mail: david_caner@attymail.com.

CANFIELD, ANDREW TROTTER, lawyer, writer; b. NYC, Apr. 30, 1953; s. Edward Francis and Janet Powell (Trotter) C.; m. Marguerite Southworth Dove, May 30, 1987; children: Augusta Phillips, Lilian Sinclair. BA in History, U. Va., 1976; JD, Am. U., 1991. Bar: Pa. 1991, D.C. 1993. Rsch. assoc. Planning Rsch. Corp., McLean, Va., 1977-79; legal asst. Casey, Scott and Canfield P.C., Washington, 1979-88, law clk., 1988-91, assoc., 1991-93, Canfield and Smith, Washington, 1993-94, of counsel, 1994—. Technical and legal writer on solar energy, environ. law, manufactured housing, computer products liability and govt. timber contracts, 1976—. Republican. Episcopalian. Avocations: history, audio, photography, poetry, skiing. Home: PO Box 758 Shelburne VT 05482-6357

CANFIELD, EDWARD FRANCIS, lawyer, business executive; b. Phila., Apr. 7, 1922; s. Frank James and Eunice C. (Sullivan) C.; m. Janet Powell Trotter, 1952 (div. 1991); children: Andrew Trotter, Janet Powell; m. Margaret Harvey O'Brien, 1993. BA, St. Joseph's U., 1943; JD, U. Pa., 1949. Bar: Pa. 1949, D.C. 1972. Practice in, Phila., 1949-51; with RCA, 1953-60, Philco-Ford Corp., 1960-69, corp. dir. govt. planning and mktg., 1961-69; pres. Leisure Time Industries, Inc., 1969; mng. ptnr. Casey, Scott & Canfield, 1971-93; ptnr. Canfield & Smith, Washington, 1993—. Lt. comdr. USNR, ret. Mem. Fed. Bar Assn., D.C. Bar Assn., Phila. Bar Assn., Congl. Country Club (Bethesda, Md.), Overbrook Golf Club (Bryn Mawr, Pa., Atlantic City (N.J.) Country Club. General civil litigation, Commercial, contracts (including sales of goods; commercial financing), Corporate, general. Home: 1 Andover Rd Haverford PA 19041-1002 Office: Canfield & Smith 910 17th St NW Ste 800 Washington DC 20006-3604 also: 117 S 17th St Philadelphia PA 19103-5025

CANNELL, JOHN REDFERNE, lawyer; b. Cambridge, Mass., Apr. 3, 1937; s. John and Thyra (Larson) C.; m. Elizabeth Ann May, May 28, 1960; children: John R. Jr. (dec.), James C., William H. AB, Princeton U., 1958; LLB, Columbia U., 1961. Bar: NY 1961. Assoc. Simpson Thacher & Bartlett, NYC, 1961-70, ptnr., 1970-95, of counsel, 1996—. Gov. Am. Bus. Council, Singapore, 1982-85, vice chmn., 1984-85. Trustee Kessler Inst. for Rehab., West Orange, NJ, 1986-97, vice chmn., 1989-92, chmn., 1992-95; trustee Henry H. Kessler Found., 1992—, chmn., 1996-99; trustee Marcus Ward Home, Maplewood, NJ, 1996—; dir. Kessler Rehab. Corp., 1992—, Kessler Med. Rehab. Rsch. and Edn. Corp., 1997—; bd. dir. New Alternatives for Children, Inc., 1996—. Mem. Montclair Golf Club (trustee 2001—), Univ. Club, Singapore Cricket Club, Tanglin Club. Episcopalian. Avocations: squash, golf. Bankruptcy, Corporate, general, Finance. Office: Simpson Thacher & Bartlett 425 Lexington Ave Fl 17 New York NY 10017-3903

CANNON, HUGH, lawyer; b. Albemarle, N.C., Oct. 11, 1931; s. Hubert Napoleon and Nettie (Harris) C.; m. Jo Anne Weisner, Mar. 21, 1988. AB, Davidson Coll., 1953; BA, Oxford U., 1955, MA, 1960; LLB, Harvard U., 1958. Bar: N.C. 1958, D.C. 1978, S.C. 1979. Mem. staff U. N.C. Inst. Govt., Chapel Hill, 1959; mem. firm Sanford, Phillips, McCoy & Weaver, Fayetteville, N.C., 1960; asst to Gov. of N.C., Raleigh, 1961; dir. adminstrn. State of N.C., 1962-65, state budget officer, 1963; mem., mng. ptnr. Sanford, Cannon, Adams & McCullough, Raleigh, 1965-79; pvt. practice Charleston, S.C., 1979—; mem. Everett, Gaskins, Hancock and Stevens attys., Raleigh, 1990—; v.p. gen. counsel Palmetto Ford, Inc., Charleston, 1979—. Author: Cannon's Concise Guide to Rules of Order, 1992. Parliamentarian NEA, 1965—; mem. nat. adv. coun. Am. Inst. Parliamentarians; pres. Friends of Coll., Raleigh, 1963; alt. de. Dem. Nat. Conv., 1964, chief parliamentarian, 1976, 80, 84, 88, 92, 96; bd. govs. U. N.C., 1972-81; trustee Davidson Coll., 1966-74, N.C. Sch. Arts, 1963-72; mem. sch. bd. Charleston County, 2000—. Rhodes scholar, 1955. Mem. Phi Beta Kappa, Omicron Delta Kappa, Phi Gamma Delta. Episcopalian. Administrative and regulatory, Corporate, general. Home: PO Box 31820 Charleston SC 29417-1820 Office: 1625 Savannah Hwy Charleston SC 29407-2236

CANNON, JOHN, III, lawyer; b. Phila., Mar. 19, 1954; s. John and Edythe (Grebe) C. BA, Denison U., 1976; JD, Dickinson Sch. Law, 1983. Bar: Pa. 1983, Hawaii 1986, U.S. Dist. Ct. (ea. dist.) Pa. 1983, U.S. Ct. Appeals (3d cir.) 1985. Account exec. PRO Services, Inc., Flourtown, Pa., 1976-79, br. officer mgr. Pitts., 1979-80; law clk. Montgomery County Ct. of Common Pleas, Norristown, Pa., 1983-84; assoc. Rawle & Henderson, Phila., 1984-88; comml. litigation counsel CIGNA Corp., Phila., 1988-90; counsel CIGNA Internat. Fin. Svcs. Divsn., Phila., 1990-93; sr. counsel CIGNA Internat., Phila., 1993-95, v.p., sr. counsel, 1995-97, sr. v.p., chief counsel, 1997-2000, CIGNA Healthcare, Bloomfield, Conn., 1999—2003, Conn. Gen. Life Ins. Co., Bloomfield, Conn., 1999—2003; sr. v.p. pub. affairs, assoc. gen. counsel CIGNA Corp., Phila., 2003—. V.p. Life Ins. Co. N.Am.; trustee U.S.-China Legal Coop. Fund, Washington, 1998—. Comments editor Dickinson Internat. Law Ann., 1983. Mem. ABA, Pa. Bar Assn., Hawaii State Bar Assn., Kappa Sigma (pres. 1975-76), Gamma Xi (v.p., trustee 1982-86). Republican. Episcopalian. General civil litigation, Private international, Pension, profit-sharing, and employee benefits. Office: Cigna Cos PO Box 7716 2 Liberty Pl Philadelphia PA 19192

CANNON, KIM DECKER, lawyer; b. Salt Lake City, Oct. 15, 1948; s. Morris Nibley Cannon and Bette Jeanne (Decker) Sage; m. Jane B. Howard, June 10, 1972 (div. Sept. 1985); children: Sage, Meredith; m. Susan Margaret Clinch, Sept. 6, 1986; 1 child, Grace. AB, Dartmouth Coll., 1970; JD, U. Colo., 1974. Bar: Wyo. 1974, U.S. Dist. Ct. Wyo. 1974, U.S. Ct. Appeals (10th cir.) 1974. Ptnr. Burgess & Davis, Sheridan, Wyo., 1974-90, Burgess, Davis, Carmichael & Cannon, Sheridan and Cheyenne, Wyo., 1990-94, Davis & Cannon, Sheridan and Cheyenne, 1994—. Pres. Sheridan County Fulmer Pub. Librs., 1980-85, Wyo. Theater, Inc., Sheridan, 1986-91, Wyo. Outdoor Coun., Lander, 1987-91; chmn. Wyo. Environ. Quality Coun., 1992-96; active Commn. on Jud. Conduct and Ethics, 1997-2001, chair, 2001-03; chmn. Rhodes Scholarship Selection Com., Wyo., 1998—. Mem. Sheridan Bar Assn. (pres. 1982). Avocations: polo, training horses, fly fishing, skiing. General civil litigation, Environmental, Product liability. Home: PO Box 401 Big Horn WY 82833-0401 Office: Davis & Cannon 40 S Main St Sheridan WY 82801-4222 E-mail: cannon@davisandcannon.com.

CANNON, THOMAS ROBERTS, lawyer; b. Durham, N.C., May 22, 1940; s. Edward Lee and Elizabeth Hendren (Roberts) C.; m. Martha Craig White, Feb. 19, 1966; children: Caroline Craig, Thomas Roberts Jr. AB, U. N.C., 1962, JD, 1965; postgrad., U. Va., 1962-63. Bar: N.C. 1965, U.S. Dist. Ct. (we. dist.) N.C. 1969, U.S. Ct. Appeals (4th cir.) 2000; cert. specialist in family law. Ptnr. Helms, Cannon, Henderson & Porter, P.A. , Charlotte, NC, 1985—2000, Horack, Talley, Pharr & Lowndes, Charlotte, 2000—. Served with USNR, 1968-89. Recipient John Motley Morehead scholarship, 1958-62. Fellow Am. Acad. Matrimonal Lawyers; mem. ABA, N.C. Bar Assn. (chmn. family law sect. 1982-83), N.C. State Bar (bd. legal specialization, family law certification com. 1988-94), Charlotte Country Club, Charlotte City Club, Soc. of the Lees of Va.. Presbyterian. State civil litigation, Family and matrimonial. Home: 2611 Beretania Cir Charlotte NC 28211-3635 Office: 301 S College St Ste 2600 Charlotte NC 28202-6044 E-mail: tcannon@horacktalley.com.

CANO, KRISTIN MARIA, lawyer; b. McKeesport, Pa., Oct. 27, 1951; d. John S. and Sally (Kavic) C. BS in Biochemistry, Pa. State U., 1973; MS in Forensic Sci., George Washington U., 1975; JD, Southwestern U., 1978; LLM in Securities Regulation, Georgetown U., 1984. Bar: Calif. 1978, U.S. Dist. Ct. (cen., no. and so. dists.) Calif. 1984, U.S. Dist. Ct. Ariz., 1988, U.S. Supreme Ct. 1988, U.S. Ct. Appeals (9th cir.) 1992. Assoc. Yusim, Cassidy, Stein & Hanger, Beverly Hills, Calif., 1979-81, Walker and Hartley, Newport Beach, Calif., 1981-82, Milberg, Weiss, Bershad, Spethrie & Lerach, San Diego, 1984; pvt. practice Newport Beach, 1984—. Bd. dirs., v.p. Sandcastle Community Assn., Corona del Mar, Calif., 1987-97; active Leadership Tomorrow Class of 1994. Mem. Orange County Bar Assn., Balboa Bay Club. Democrat. Roman Catholic. Avocations: ballet, ice skating, bicycling, photography, golf. Corporate, general, Mergers and acquisitions, Securities. Office: 1 Corporate Plaza Dr Ste 110 Newport Beach CA 92660-7924 E-mail: cano@securities-law.com.

CANO, MARIO STEPHEN, lawyer; b. Miami, Fla., Sept. 2, 1953; s. Mario Arturo Cano and Irene H. Moreno; m. Johanna Marie Van Rossum, Oct. 13, 1979. AA, Miami Dade Jr. Coll., 1973; BA, Fla. Internat. U., 1975; JD, U. Santa Clara, 1978. Bar: Fla. 1979, U.S. Dist. Ct. (so. dist.) Fla. 1979, U.S. Ct. Claims 1979, U.S. Tax Ct. 1979, U.S. Ct. Mil. Appeals 1979, U.S. Ct. Appeals (9th cir.) 1979, U.S. Dist. Ct. (no. and mid. dists.) Fla. 1980, U.S. Dist. Ct. (no. dist.) Calif. 1980, U.S. Ct. Appeals (3d cir.) 1980, U.S. Ct. Internat. Trade 1981, U.S. Ct. Appeals (11th cir.) 1981, U.S. Ct. Appeals (6th and 10th cirs.) 1983, U.S. Supreme Ct. 1983, Nebr. 1984, U.S. Dist. Ct. Nebr. 1984, U.S. Dist. Ct. (no. dist.) Okla. 1984, U.S. Dist. Ct. Hawaii 1984, U.S. Ct. Appeals (2d, 4th, 5th, 7th 8th and D.C. cirs.) 1984, N.Y. 1985, U.S. Dist. Ct. (no., we., ea. and so. dists.) N.Y. 1985, U.S. Ct. Appeals (1st cir.) 1987, U.S. Dist. Ct. (no. and so. dist.) Tex. 1988, U.S. Dist. Ct. (ea. dist.) Wis. 1988, U.S. Dist. Ct. (we. dist.) Pa. 1988, U.S. Dist. Ct. (no. dist.) Ill. 1991, Mass., 1998, U.S. Dist. Ct. Mass. 1999. Assoc. Orta and Assocs., Miami, 1979-80, Law Office of J. Ramirez, Coral Gables, Fla., 1980, Law Office of I.G. Lichter, Miami, 1980-82, Gelb & Spatz, Miami, 1982; pvt. practice Coral Gables, 1982—. Mem. Am. Immigration Lawyers Assn., Cuban Am. Bar Assn., Nat. Assn. Criminal Def. Lawyers. Democrat. Criminal, Family and matrimonial, Immigration, naturalization, and customs. Office: Ste 600 2121 Ponce De Leon Blvd Coral Gables FL 33134-5222 Fax: 305-567-0423.. E-mail: canolawmiami@msn.com.

CANONI, JOHN DAVID, lawyer; b. Newton, Mass., May 11, 1939; s. John Joseph and Olga Elizabeth (Mangini) C.; m. Katherine Ariadna Bryant, Aug. 18, 1962; children: Lisa Ann, Peter Christopher, John Charles, Scott Francis. BA, Amherst Coll., 1960; LLB, Yale U., 1963. Bar: N.Y. 1964, U.S. Ct. Appeals (2d cir.) 1966, U.S. Ct. Appeals (3d cir.) 1967, U.S. Ct. Appeals (4th cir.) 1968, U.S. Ct. Appeals (1st cir.) 1969, U.S. Supreme Ct. 1971, U.S. Ct. Appeals (7th cir.) 1972. Assoc. Townley & Updike, N.Y.C., 1963-71, ptnr., 1971-95, Nixon Peabody LLP, N.Y.C., 1995—. Mem. Lt. Gov.'s Task Force on Plant Closings, N.Y., 1984-85. Mem. N.Y. State Bar Assn. (chmn. labor & employment law sect. 1983-84), Yale Club. Republican. Roman Catholic. Alternative dispute resolution, Labor (including EEOC, Fair Labor Standards Act, labor-management relations, NLRB, OSHA), Pension, profit-sharing, and employee benefits. Home: 20 High Meadows Mount Kisco NY 10549-3847 Office: Nixon Peabody LLP 437 Madison Ave New York NY 10022-7001 E-mail: jcanoni@aol.com., jcanoni@nixonpeabody.com.

CANTERO, RAOUL G., III, judge; b. Madrid, Aug. 1, 1960; m. Ana Maria Cantero; children: Christian, Michael, Elisa. BA in English and Bus. summa cum laude, Fla. State U.; JD cum laude, Harvard U. Bd. cert. in appellate practice:. Law clk. to Hon. Edward B. Davis U.S. Dist. Ct. (so. dist.) Fla.; shareholder, head appellate divsn. Adorno & Yoss, Miami; justice Supreme Ct. Fla., Tallahassee, 2002—. Lectr. in field. Contbr. articles to legal jours., short stories to anthologies. Mem. planning and zoning bd. City of Coral Gables, 1993—2001; mem. pastoral coun. St. Augustine Ch., 1990—97, chmn., 1997—2001, head Men's Retreat Ministry, 1994—2000; bd. dirs. Legal Svcs. of Greater Miami, Inc., 1991—95. Mem.: Dade County Bar Assn. (mem. appellate ct. com. 1998—99), Fla. Bar Assn. (mem. appellate rules com. 1993, sec. 1997—99, treas. appellate practice sect. 1999—2000, vice-chair 2001—02, sec. appellate practice sect. 2000—01, mem. 11th jud. cir. jud. nominating commn. 2001—02). Office: Supreme Ct Fla 500 S Duval St Tallahassee FL 32399

CANTOR, BERNARD JACK, patent lawyer; b. N.Y.C., Aug. 18, 1927; s. Alexander J. and Tillie (Henzeloff) C.; m. Judith L. Levin, Mar. 25, 1951; children, Glenn H., Cliff A., James E., Ellen B., Mark E. B. Mech. Engring., Cornell, 1949; JD, George Washington U., Washington, 1952. Bar: D.C. 1952, U.S. Patent Office 1952, Mich. 1953; registered patent atty. U.S., Can. Examiner U.S. Patent Office, Washington, 1949-52; pvt. practice Detroit, 1952-88; ptnr. firm Harness, Dickey & Pierce, Troy, Mich., 1988—. Lectr. in field. Contbr. articles on patent law to profl. jours. Mem. exec. coun. Detroit Area Boy Scouts Am., 1972—. Served with U.S. Army, 1944-46. Recipient Ellsworth award patent law George Washington U., 1952, Shofar award Boy Scouts Am., 1975, Silver Beaver award, 1975, Disting. Eagle award, 1985. Fellow Mich. State Bar Found.; mem. ABA, Mich. Bar Assn. (dir. econs. sect., arbitrator State of Mich. grievance com.), Detroit Bar Assn., Oakland Bar Assn., Mich. Patent Law Assn., Am. Intellectual Property Law Assn., Am. Arbitration Assn. (arbitrator), Cornell Engring. Soc., Am. Technion Soc. (bd. dirs. Detroit 1970—), Pi Tau Sigma, Phi Delta Phi, Beta Sigma Rho. Intellectual property, Patent, Trademark and copyright. Home: 5685 Forman Dr Bloomfield Hills MI 48301-1154 Office: Harness Dickey & Pierce 5445 Corporate Dr Troy MI 48098-2683

CANTOR, HERBERT I. lawyer; b. N.Y.C., Dec. 10, 1935; s. David and Ethel C.; m. Lynn Hardie, July 8, 1972; children: David, Susan. BA in Chemistry, NYU, 1965; JD, Cath. U. Am., 1970. Bar: Md. 1970, U.S. Dist. Ct. Md. 1970, D.C. 1971, U.S. Dist. Ct. D.C. 1971, U.S. Ct. Appeals (5th, D.C. and fed. cirs.) 1971, U.S. Supreme Ct. 1974, U.S. Ct. Appeals (4th cir.) 1981, U.S. Ct. Claims 1987. Patent examiner U.S. Patent Office, Washington, 1965-67; agt. Jacobi, Davidson & Jacobi, Washington, 1967-68; pvt. practice Washington, 1968-70; with Kraft, Cantor & Singer, Cantor & Lessler, Washington, 1971-85; ptnr. Cantor & Lessler, Washington, 1982-85, Wegner, Cantor, Mueller & Player, Washington, 1985-94; Evenson, McKeown, Edwards & Lenahan, Washington, 1994-2001; Crowell & Moring, 2001—. Adj. prof. Law Ctr. Georgetown Univ., Washington, 1988-89. Assoc. editor Cath. U. Law Rev., 1969-70. Mem. Am. Chem. Soc., Fedn. Internat. des Conseils Propriete Industrielle, Am. Intellectual Property Assn. Intellectual property, Patent, Trademark and copyright. Office: Crowell & Moring 1001 Pennsylvania Ave NW Washington DC 20004 E-mail: hcantor@crowell.com.

CANTOR, IRVIN VICTOR, lawyer; b. Richmond, Va., June 9, 1953; s. Leo Joseph and Mary Frances (Cohen) C. BS, U. Va., 1975, JD, 1978. Bar: Va. 1978. Law clk. Va. Supreme Ct., Richmond, Va., 1978-79; ptnr. Rilee Cantor Arkema Edmonds (now Cantor, Arkema, P.C.), Richmond, Va., 1979—, World Class, Inc., Richmond, 1983—. Bd. dirs. Richmond Tennis Patrons, Tennis Found. Richmond, Hist. Richmond Found. Zeta Beta Tau Nat. Found. scholar, 1973. Mem. Am. Bd. Trial Advocates, Nat. Head Injury Found., Brain Injury Assn. Va. (bd. dirs. 2002—), Va. Bar Assn., Richmond Bar Assn., Va. Trial Lawyers Assn. (bd. govs. 1992—, legis. chmn. 1993—, v.p. 1997-99, pres.-elect 2001, pres. 2002—), Richmond Trial Lawyers, U. S. Tennis Assn., U. Va. Alumni Assn., Westwood Racquet Club. Personal injury (including property damage), Product liability. Office: Cantor Arkema & Edmonds PO Box 561 Richmond VA 23218-0561 E-mail: icantor@cantorarkema.com.

CANTOR, JAMES ELLIOT, lawyer; b. Detroit, Mar. 14, 1958; s. Bernard J. and Judith (Levin) C.; m. Susan Elaine Finger, Dec. 26, 1983; children: Tilly Samantha, Brian Alexander. BS in Natural Resources, U. Mich., 1980; JD, Cornell U., 1986. Bar: Alaska 1986. Assoc. Perkins Coie, Anchorage, 1986-91; asst. atty. gen. environ. sect. Alaska, Atty. Gen.'s Office, Anchorage, 1991-98, supervising atty. transp. sect., 1998—. Mem. Eagle River (Alaska) Pk. and Recreation Bd. of Suprs., 1989-95, chmn., 1991-92; dir. Anchorage (Alaska) Trails and Greenways Coalition, 1994-97; commr. Municipality of Anchorage, The Municipality of Anchorage Heritage Land Bank Adv. Commn., 1999—, chmn., 2002—. Mem. Anchorage Inn of Ct. Avocation: dog sled racing. Office: Atty Gen Office 1031 W 4th Ave Ste 200 Anchorage AK 99501-5903

CANTOR, MELVYN LEON, retired lawyer; b. Boston, Aug. 13, 1942; s. Manuel and Adeline (Raffel) C.; m. Susan Gershen, June 7, 1964 (div. Jan. 1981); children: Matthew, Douglas; m. Kathryn Gabler, Jan. 3, 1982; 1 child, Joanna. BA, U. Vt., 1964; LLB magna cum laude, U. Pa., 1967. Bar: N.Y. 1969, U.S. Dist. Ct. (so. and ea. dists.) N.Y. 1971, U.S. Ct. Appeals (2nd cir.) 1971, U.S. Ct. Appeals (3d cir.) 1974, U.S. Ct. Appeals (5th cir.) 1986, U.S. Supreme Ct. 1987. Law clk. to Hon. Stanley A. Weigel U.S. Dist. Ct., San Francisco, 1967-68; assoc. Simpson, Thacher & Bartlett, N.Y.C., 1968-74, ptnr., 1974-97; of counsel, 1998—. Adj. prof. Yeshiva U. Benjamin Cardozo Sch. Law, N.Y.C., 1977-81, lectr. in law, Columbia U. Contbr. numerous articles to profl. jours. Fellow Am. Coll. Trial Lawyers; mem. ABA, Am. Law Inst., Bar Assn. of City of N.Y., Fed. Bar Coun. General civil litigation, State civil litigation. Office: Simpson Thacher & Bartlett 425 Lexington Ave Fl 14 New York NY 10017-3903

CANTOR, SAMUEL C. lawyer, company executive; b. Phila., Mar. 11, 1919; s. Joseph and Miryl (Ginzberg) C.; m. Dorothy Van Brink, Apr. 9, 1943; children: Judith Ann Stone, Barbara Ann Palm. BSS, CCNY, 1940;

JD, Columbia, 1943. Bar: N.Y. 1943, U.S. Dist. Ct. (so. and ea. dists.) N.Y. 1951, U.S. Supreme Ct 1969, D.C. 1971. Asst. dist. atty., N.Y.C., 1943-48; legislative counsel N.Y. State Senate; counsel N.Y.C. Affairs Com. N.Y. State Senate, 1949-59; mem. firm Newcomb, Woolsey & Cantor, Newcomb & Cantor, N.Y.C., 1951-59; 1st dep. supt. ins. State of N.Y., 1959-64, acting supt. ins., 1963-64; 2d v.p., gen. solicitor Mut. Life Ins. Co. N.Y., 1964-66, v.p., gen. counsel, 1967-72, sr. v.p., gen. counsel, 1973-74, sr. v.p. law and external affairs, 1974-75, sr. v.p. law and corp. affairs, 1975-78, exec. v.p. law and corp. affairs, 1978-84; counsel Rogers & Wells, 1984-89. Bd. dir. Mut. Life Ins. Co N.Y., Mony Reins. Corp., Monyco, Inc., Key Resources, Inc., Mony Advisors, Inc.; chmn. exec. com. N.Y. Life Ins. Guaranty Corp., 1974-84; mem. spl. com. on ins. holding holding cos. N.Y. Supt. Ins., 1967, N.Y. State select com. pub. employee pensions, 1973 Contbr. articles to Golf and other mags., legal and ins. jours. Fellow Am. Bar Found.; mem. Ins. Fedn. N.Y. (pres. 1967-68), Am. Bar Assn., N.Y. State Bar Assn., Am. Life Conv. (v.p. N.Y. State 1965-70), Am. Coun. Life Ins. (chmn. legal sect. 1977, chmn. legis. com. 1977-78, N.Y. State v.p. 1977-84), Health Ins. Assn. Am. (chmn. govt. rels. com. 1975, chmn. health care com. N.Y. State 1974-80), Assn. Life Ins. Counsel (dir.), Am. Judicature Soc., Bar Assn. City N.Y., N.Y. Law Inst., Nat. Attys. Assn., N.Y. State Dist. Attys. Assn., Union Internationale des Avocats, Columbia U. Law Sch. Alumni Assn. (dir.) Clubs: Mason. (N.Y.C.), University (N.Y.C.); Met., Univ. (Washington); Fort Orange (Albany, N.Y.); Sawgrass Country, Marsh Landing, Ponte Vedra (Fla.); La Costa Country (Carlsbad, Calif.); Confrérie des Chevaliers du Tastevin; Fairview Country (Greenwich, Conn.); Royal Dornoch Golf (Scotland), Am. Seniors Golf Assn., U.S. Golf Assn. (committeeman). Home: 10 Audubon Ln Greenwich CT 06831-2501 also: 34 Little Bay Harbor Dr Ponte Vedra Beach FL 32082-3707

CANTRELL, CHARLES L. lawyer, educator; b. Waco, Tex., Aug. 24, 1948; m. Ann Marie Howard, Dec. 29, 1970; children: Jennifer Lee, Jeffrey Davis. JD, Baylor U., 1972; LLM, U. Tex., 1976. Bar: Tex. 1972, Wis. 1978, U.S. Supreme Ct. 1980. Pvt. practice, Waco, 1972-76; asst. prof. law Marquette U. Law Sch., Milw., 1976-81; prof. law Oklahoma City U. Law Sch., 1981—. Author: Oklahoma Criminal Defense Manual, 1987, Okla. Criminal Rules and Statutes Annotated, 1996, Oklahoma Uniform Jury Instructions, 2000, Missouri Criminal Rules and Statutes Annotated, 2002; contbr. articles to profl. jours. Coord. Friends of Met. Library, 1988. Mem. Assn. Internat. de Droit Penal, Internat. League for Human Rights, Internat. Antitrust Assn., Am. Assn. Law Schs. (sects. of constl. and criminal law), Masons. Episcopalian. Avocations: handball, record collecting, guitar. Constitutional, Criminal, Public international. Home: 5609 NW 110th St Oklahoma City OK 73162-5826 Office: Oklahoma City U Sch Law 2501 N Blackwelder Ave Oklahoma City OK 73106-1493

CANTWELL, ROBERT, lawyer; b. Buffalo, Sept. 12, 1931; s. Thomas and Helen (Robinson) C.; m. Barbara Hurlbert, Oct. 19, 1963; children: Robert, Helen Virginia, Sara Elizabeth. AB, Cornell U., 1953, JD, 1956; LLM, NYU, 1959. Bar: N.Y. State bar 1956. Assoc. firm Jaeckle, Fleischmann & Mugel (and predecessor firm), Buffalo, 1956-62; mem. legal dept. Colgate-Palmolive Co., N.Y.C., 1962-68, London dep. gen. counsel, 1972-73, v.p., gen. counsel, 1973-86, sec., 1974-86; v.p., sec., gen. counsel Roblin Industries, Inc., Buffalo, 1968-72; ptnr. Serchuk, Wolfe and Zelermyer, White Plains, N.Y., 1986-87, Cantwell and Chen, N.Y.C., 1988-89; pvt. practice Greenwich, Conn., 1989—. Mem. ABA, N.Y. State Bar Assn., Assn. of Bar of City of N.Y., Am. Soc. Corp. Secs., Saturn Club (Buffalo), Belle Haven, Greenwich Horseneck Club. Corporate, general, Private international, Securities. Home and Office: 5 Meadow Dr Greenwich CT 06831-4504

CANTWELL, WILLIAM PATTERSON, lawyer; b. Saranac Lake, N.Y., Dec. 2, 1921; s. Francis Barry and Genevieve (Godfrey) C.; m. Hendrika Antonia Bestebreurtje, June 19, 1947; children: Peter F., Rebecca D., Christopher A. BA with highest honors, Williams Coll., 1942; JD, Yale U., 1948. Bar: N.Y. 1948, Colo. 1953. Assoc. Moot, Sprague, Marcy & Gulick, Buffalo, 1948-52, Holland & Hart, 1953-64; ptnr. Sherman & Howard, 1964-87, of counsel, 1988-95. Vis. lectr. law U. Denver, 1956-60, 64-65, U. Colo., 1962, 87, U. Miami, 1976; lectr. various continuing legal edn. insts. and legal meetings; reporter on Uniform Marital Property Act Nat. Conf. Commrs. on Uniform State Laws, 1980-83. Contbr. articles to profl. jours. Recipient Treat award Nat. Coll. Probate Judges for Probate Excellence, 1983 Mem. ABA (ho. of dels. 1964-66, 73-78, chmn. real property probate and trust law sect. 1971-72), Am. Coll. Trust and Estate Counsel (pres. 1975-76, Trachtman lectr. 1980), Colo. Bar Assn. (pres. 1970-71, gov. 1959-65, chmn. taxation law sect. 1959-60, probate and trust law sect. 1960-61), Denver Bar Assn. (pres. 1962-63, award of merit 1969), Order of Coif (hon.). Home: 700 West 140 North Driggs ID 83422

CANUP, JAMES W.C. lawyer; b. Washington; s. William C. and Mireille R. Canup; m. Winnie Perilla, May 30, 1987; children: Elise, William, Ann Charlotte. BA, U. Va., 1980; JD, Washington & Lee U., 1984; LLM, Georgetown U., 1992. Bar: Va. 1984, Md. 1987, D.C. 1987. Sr. atty.-advisor Chief Counsel, IRS, Washington, 1987-93; assoc. Brown & Wood, LLP, Washington, 1993-95; ptnr. McGuire Woods LLP, Richmond, Va., 1996—. Mem. Nat. Assn. of Real Estate Investment Trusts (govt. rels. com. 1994—), Mortgage-Backed Securities Industry Group, Jr. Achievement of Ctrl. Va. Inc. (bd. dirs. 1999—). Securities, Corporate taxation, Taxation, general. Office: McGuire Woods LLP One James Ctr 901 E Cary St Richmond VA 23219-4057

CAPECELATRO, MARK JOHN, lawyer; b. New Haven, June 2, 1948; s. Ralph Ettore and Elaine (Scialla) C.; m. Jane Beals, June 19, 1971; children: Christopher Beals, Kate Rowley, Jonathan Mark. BA, Colgate U., 1970; JD, U. Conn., 1973. Bar: Conn. 1973. Assoc. Ells, Quinlan, Eddy & Robinson, Canaan, Conn., 1973-77; ptnr. Ells, Quinlan & Robinson, Canaan, 1977-90, Capecelatro & Nelligan LLP, Canaan, 1991—2001; pvt. practice, 2002—. Bd. advisors Canaan Nat. Bank, 1982—; mortgage counsel People's Bank, Canaan and Hartford, Conn., 1983—; trustee Sharon (Conn.) Hosp., 1984-91, vice chmn., 1990-91, chmn. exec. com., 1990-91; trustee Salisbury Congl. Ch., 1990-98, 2000—, vice chmn., 1990-93, chmn., 1993-2000, 2002—, fin. com., 1998—. Bd. dirs. Housatonic Homemaker Health Aide, West Cornwall, Conn., 1977-80, Housatonic Day Care Ctr., Inc., Lakeville, Conn., 1981-90, Salisbury Pub. Health Nursing, Lakeville, 1983-85, Salisbury Vol. Ambulance Svcs., Inc., 1997-2003, Salisbury Winter Sports Assn., 1983-87, Salisbury (Conn.) Congl. Ch.; mem. adv. com. Parkside Med. Svcs. Corp., 1988-93. Mem. ABA, Conn. Bar Assn., Litchfield County Bar Assn., Model A Ford Club Am. Republican. Avocations: guitar, fishing, canoeing. General practice, Probate (including wills, trusts), Property, real (including real estate development, water). Home: 196 Belgo Rd Lakeville CT 06039-1003 Office: 117 Main St Canaan CT 06018-1045 Address: PO Box 1045 Canaan CT 06018 Office Fax: 860-824-9869. E-mail: mjc@mohawk.net.

CAPEHART, CRAIG EARL, lawyer; b. Indpls., Oct. 13, 1951; s. H. Earl, Jr. and Harriet Jane (Holmes) C.; m. Lynn Dee Barker, Dec. 29, 1988 (div. Dec. 3, 1997); 1 child, Kelly Anne. BA, George Washington U., 1974, MA, 1976; MBA, Ind. U., 1978, JD, 1988. Bar: Ind. 1989, N.Y. 1989, U.S. Dist. Ct. (no. and so. dists.) Ind. 1989, D.C. 1991, Minn. 1991, U.S. Dist. Ct. Minn. 1992, U.S. Supreme Ct. 1992. Internat. analyst Abbott Lab., N. Chgo., 1978-80; mgr. consulting Arthur Andersen & Co., Chgo., 1980-81; v.p., gen. mgr. MPMS, Inc., Northfield, Ill., 1981-84; prin. MMC, Inc., Lake Bluff, Ill., 1984-87; atty. IBM, Armonk, N.Y., 1989-94, Capehart Law Office, Indpls., 1994—; pres. Capehart Farms, Inc., 1996-99. Dir. Capehart Farms, Inc., Washington, Ind., 1986-2000; faculty sch. bus. Univ. Indpls., 1999—, Coll. Bus. Adminstrn., Butler U., 2000-01. Trustee Epsilon Edn. Found., Washington, 1980-2002; v.p. Chgo. Alumni Sigma Chi, 1981-84, bd. dirs., Indpls., 2001—. Mem. Am. Intellectual Property Law Assn., Am. Bankruptcy Inst., Computer Law Assn., Ind. Software Assn., Venture Club of Ind., Columbia Club (fin. com. 1996-2002), Sigma Chi (dir. Indpls. Alumni). Republican. Avocation: pvt. pilot. Contract Law, Business Law, Bankruptcy. Home: 11526 Creek Side Ln Carmel IN 46033-3715 Office: Capehart Law Office Ste 220 8200 Haverstick Rd Indianapolis IN 46240 E-mail: down2biz@aol.com.

CAPIZZI, MICHAEL ROBERT, prosecutor; b. Detroit, Oct. 19, 1939; s. I.A. and Adelaide E. (Jennelle) C.; m. Sandra Jo Jones, June 22, 1963; children: Cori Anne, Pamela Jo. BS in Bus. Adminstrn., Ea. Mich. U., 1961; JD, U. Mich., 1964. Bar: Calif. 1965, U.S. Dist. Ct. (so. dist.) Calif. 1965, U.S. Ct. Appeals (9th cir.) 1970, U.S. Supreme Ct. 1971. Dep. dist. atty., Orange County, Calif., 1965-68; head writs, appeals and spl. assignments sect., 1968-71; asst. dist. atty., dir. spl. ops., 1971-86; legal counsel, mem. exec. bd. Interstate Organized Crime Index, 1971-79, Law Enforcement Intelligence Unit, 1971-95, chief asst. dist. atty., 1986-90, dist. atty., 1990-99. Instr. criminal justice Santa Ana Coll., 1967-76, Calif. State U., 1976-87. Commr. City Planning Commn., Fountain Valley, Calif., 1971-80, vice chmn. 1972-73, chmn. 1973-75, 79-80; candidate for Rep. nomination Calif. Atty. Gen., 1998. Fellow Am. Coll. Trial Lawyers; mem. Nat. Dist. Attys. Assn. (bd. dirs. 1995-96, v.p. 1996-99), Calif. Dist. Attys. Assn. (outstanding prosecutor award 1980, v.p. 1995, pres. 1996), Calif. Bar Assn., Orange County Bar Assn. (chmn. cts. com. 1977, chmn. coll. of trial advocacy com. 1978-81, bd. dirs. 1977-81, sec.-treas. 1982, pres. 1984). Office: PO Box 1938 Santa Ana CA 92702-1938 E-mail: mrclaw@socal.rr.com.

CAPLIN, MORTIMER MAXWELL, lawyer, educator; b. N.Y.C., July 11, 1916; s. Daniel and Lillian (Epstein) C.; m. Ruth Sacks, Oct. 18, 1942; children: Lee Evan, Michael Andrew, Jeremy Owen, Catherine Jean. BS, U. Va., 1937, LLB, 1940; JSD, NYU, 1953; LLD (hon.), St. Michael's Coll., 1964. Bar: Va. 1941, N.Y. 1942, D.C. 1964. Law clk. to Hon. Armistead M. Dobie U.S. Ct. Appeals (4th cir.), Richmond, 1940-41; assoc. Paul, Weiss, Rifkind, Wharton & Garrison, N.Y.C., 1941-42, 45-50; prof. law U. Va., Charlottesville, 1950-61, vis. prof. law, 1965-87, prof. emeritus, 1988—; ptnr. Perkins, Battle & Minor, Charlottesville, 1952-61; U.S. commr. IRS, Washington, 1961-64; sr. ptnr. Caplin & Drysdale, Washington, 1964—. Mem. Pres.'s Task Force on Taxation, 1960; bd. dirs. Danaher Corp., Washington, Fairchild Corp., Dulles, Va., Presdl. Realty Corp., White Plains, N.Y., Environ. and Energy Study Inst.; mem. pub. rev. bd. Arthur Andersen & Co., Chgo., 1980-88; reorgn. trustee Webb & Knapp, Inc., 1965-72. Author: Proxies, Annual Meetings and Corporate Democracy, 1953, Doing Business in Other States, 1959; editor-in-chief Va. Law Rev., 1939-40; contbr. numerous articles on tax and corp. matters to profl. jours. Past chmn. bd. dirs. Nat. Civic Svc. League, Am. Coun. on Internat. Sports; past chmn. nat citizens adv. com. Assn. Am. Med. Colls.; trustee Arena Stage, U. Va. Law Sch. Found., Wolf Trap Found. Performing Arts, Shakespeare Theatre, Washington, Arena Stage, Washington, Peace Through Law Found., Washington; bd. overseers U. V.I.; chmn. adv. bd. Hospitality and Info. Svc., Washington; chmn. Coun. for Arts, U. Va.; past pres. Atlantic Coast Conf.; emeritus trustee George Washington U.; mem. bd. visitors U. Va., 1992-97; pres., bd. dirs. Indigent Civil Litigation Fund. Decorated mem. initial landing force Normandy Invasion USN; recipient, Va. State Bar and Va. Soc. CPAs award, 1960, Achievement award, Tax Soc. of NYU, 1962, Judge Learned Hand Human Rels. award, Am. Jewish Com., 1963, 1993, Alexander Hamilton award, U.S. Treasury Dept., 1964, Disting. Svc. award, Tax Execs. Inst., 1964, medal in law, U. Va. Thomas Jefferson Found., 2001. Fellow Am. Bar Found., Am. Tax Policy Inst., Am. Coll. Tax Counsel; mem. ABA (ho. of dels. 1980-92, mem. fed. jud. com. 1993-96, ALI-ABA com. continuing profl. edn., chair DC Fellows), Nat. Conf. of Lawyers and CPAs, Am. Law Inst. (life), N.Y. State Bar Assn., Va. Bar Assn., D.C. Bar Assn., D.C. Bar Found. (adv. com.), Univ. Club (Washington), Fed. City Club (bd. govs.), Colonnade Club (Charlottesville), Order of Coif, Phi Beta Kappa, Phi Beta Kappa Assocs., Omicron Delta Kappa. Democrat. Jewish. Avocations: swimming, tennis, hiking. Corporate, general, Corporate taxation, Taxation, general. Home: 5610 Wisconsin Ave Apt 18E Chevy Chase MD 20815-4415 Office: One Thomas Circle NW Washington DC 20005-5802 E-mail: mmc@capdale.com.

CAPORALE, D. NICK, lawyer; b. Omaha, Sept. 13, 1928; s. Michele and Lucia Caporale; m. Margaret Nilson, Aug. 5, 1950; children: Laura Diane Stevenson, Leland Alan. BA, U. Nebr.-Omaha, 1949, M.Sc., 1954; JD with distinction, U. Nebr.-Lincoln, 1957. Bar: Nebr. 1957, U.S. Dist. Ct. Nebr. 1957, U.S. Ct. Appeals 8th cir. 1958, U.S. Supreme Ct. 1970. Judge Nebr. Dist. Ct., Omaha, 1979-81, Nebr. Supreme Ct., Lincoln, 1982-98; of counsel Baird Holm Law Firm, 1998—. Lectr. U. Nebr., Lincoln, 1982-84, 2000—. Pres. Omaha Community Playhouse, 1976. Served to 1st lt. U.S. Army, 1952-54, Korea. Decorated Bronze Star; recipient Alumni Achievement U. Nebr.-Omaha, 1972 Fellow Am. Coll. Trial Lawyers, Internat. Soc. Barristers; mem. Order of Coif. Office: Baird Holm Law Firm 1500 Woodmen Tower Omaha NE 68102 E-mail: ncaporale@bairdholm.com.

CAPOUANO, ALBERT D. lawyer; b. Montgomery, Ala., 1945; BS, U. Ala., 1967, JD, 1970; LLM in Taxation, NYU, 1971. Bar: Ala. 1970, Fla. 1973. Mem. Dean, Mead, Egerton, Bloodworth, Capouano & Bozarth P.A., Orlando, Fla. Mem. Fla. Bar, Ala. State Bar. Corporate, general, Mergers and acquisitions, Taxation, general. Office: Dean Mead Egerton Bloodworth Capouano & Bozarth 800 N Magnolia Ave # 1500 PO Box 2346 Orlando FL 32802-2346 E-mail: acapouano@deanmead.com.

CAPPELLA, ELENA A. lawyer, legal association administrator; b. Bklyn., June 17, 1947; m. Joseph N. Cappella. AB in Math. magna cum laude, LeMoyne Coll., 1969; MA in Comm., Mich. State U., 1974; JD magna cum laude, U. Wis., 1979. Bar: Wis. 1979, Pa. 1992. Law clk. to Hon. Alfred T. Goodwin U.S. Ct. Appeals (9th cir.), 1979-80; lectr. Law Sch. and Women Studies Program U. Wis., Madison, 1980-81; asst. state pub. defender State of Wis., 1981-84; exec. dir. Wis. Jud. Commn., 1984-90; dep. to exec. v.p. Am. Law Inst., Phila., 1990-92, dep. dir., 1993—. Program chair Legal Assn. Women, Madison, 1983-90; mem. comm. com. State Bar Wis., 1987-89. Mem. task force on women and criminal justice sys. Wis. Women's Network, 1982-86, chair, 1983-84; mem. adv. com. Ctr. for Jud. Conduct Orgns., Am. Judicature Soc., 1985-86, chair, 1986, Madison chpt. NOW, 1974, chpt. coord., 1975-76. Mem. Am. Law Inst., Order of Coif. Office: Am Law Inst 4025 Chestnut St Philadelphia PA 19104-3054

CAPPELLETTI, FRANCO ALBERTO, law educator; b. Cecina, Livorno, Italy, Mar. 20, 1948; s. Gianfranco and Wanda (Stoppa) C. Law degree, U. Pisa, Italy, 1972; doctorate, The Sorbonne, Paris, 1984. Prof. philosophy of law U. Sannio, Benevento, Italy, 1987—. Author: Una Teoria per la Politica, 1980, Differenza e Potere, 1984, Legge Coustume Alteritá lo Scetticismo Moderno e il Diritto, 1989. Office: U Sannio Dept Econs via Calandra 82100 Benevento Italy

CAPPELLO, A. BARRY, lawyer; b. Bklyn., Feb. 21, 1942; s. Gus and Ann (Klukoff) C.; children: Eric Rheinschild, Blythe, Brent, Dominic, Vincent. AB, UCLA, 1962, JD, 1965. Bar: Calif. 1966, U.S. Dist. Ct. (cen. dist.) Calif. 1966, U.S. Ct. Appeals (9th cir.) 1974, U.S. Dist. Ct. (no. dist.) Calif. 1981, U.S. Ct. Appeals (7th cir.) 1985, U.S. Supreme Ct. 1985, U.S. Dist. Ct. (ea. dist.) Calif. 1986, U.S. Ct. Appeals (10th cir.) 1986. Dep. atty. gen. State of Calif., L.A., 1965-68; chief trial dep., asst. dist. atty. Santa Barbara County, 1968-70, asst. dist. atty., 1970-71, city atty., 1971-77; pvt. practice, mng. ptnr. Cappello & McCann, Santa Barbara, 1977—. Lectr. complex bus. litigation, lender liability, adv. trial techniques. Author: Lender Liability, 3d edit., 1994, Lender Liability: A Practical Guide, 1987, AmJur Model Trials and Proofs of Facts; contbr. more than 150 articles to profl. legal and bus. jours. Mem. ABA, ATLA, Consumer Attys. Calif. Avocation: triathalons. Banking, General civil litigation, Commercial, consumer (including collections, credit). Office: Cappello & McCann 831 State St Santa Barbara CA 93101-3227

CAPPS, JAMES LEIGH, II, lawyer, reserve military career officer; b. Brunswick, Ga., 1956; s. Thomas Edwin Sr. and Betty Marie C.; m. Nancy Ann Fisher, 1978; children: Bonnie Lynn, James Leigh III. AA, Seminole C.C., Sanford, Fla., 1976; BA in History, U. Cen. Fla., 1981; JD, U. Fla., 1987. Bar: Fla. 1987, U.S. Ct. Mil. Appeals 1988, Colo. 1990, U.S. Ct. Appeals (4th cir.) 1997. Enlisted USAF, 1976, advanced through grades to maj., 1995, med. svc. specialist, 1977-79, air weapons dir., 1982-84, claims officer, 1987-88, area def. counsel, 1988-90, dep. staff judge adv. Onizuka AFB, Calif., 1990-93; atty. office of state atty. 18th Jud. Ct., Sanford, Fla., 1994; assoc. Dominick Salfi Law Offices, Maitland, Fla., 1993-94; res. judge adv. Moody AFB, Ga., 1993-99; of counsel Dominick Salfi Law Offices, Maitland, Fla., 1994—; pvt. practice, 1996—; res. judge adv. Patrick AFB, Fla., 2000—; civilian contract specialist for Naval Air Warfare Ctr. USN, Orlando, Fla., 1999—. Assigned to 16th Air Force Hdqs., Aviano AFB, Italy, Operation Joint Endeavor, 1996; atty. Vietnam Vets. Ctrl. Fla., 1998-99; implementation force Dayton Peace Accords UN. Maj. USAFR, 1993—. Recipient McCarthy award for legal svc. Air Combat Command, 1995. Mem. DAV, VFW. Democrat.

CAPPUCCIO, PAUL T. lawyer, communications executive; b. West Peabody, Mass., June 5, 1961; AB, Georgetown U., 1983; JD, Harvard U., 1986. Bar: Ohio 1989, DC 1990. Law clk. to Hon. Alex Kozinski U.S. Ct. Appeals (9th cir.), 1986—87; law clk. to Hon. Antonin Scalia U.S. Supreme Ct., 1987—88, law clk. to Hon. Anthony M. Kennedy, 1989; assoc. Jones, Day Reavis & Pogue, 1989—91; assoc. dep. atty. gen. U.S. Dept. Justice, 1991—93; ptnr. Kirkland & Ellis, 1993—99; sr. v.p., gen. counsel Am. Online, Inc., 1999—2001; exec. v.p., gen. counsel, sec. AOL Time Warner Inc., N.Y.C., 2001—. Adj. prof. U. Calif., Berkeley, 1990, Berkeley, 91, Georgetown U. Law Ctr., Washington, 1991, Washington, 93, Columbia U. Sch. Law, N.Y.C., 1996, N.Y.C., 97. Bd. dirs. Washington Scholarship Fund, 1997—. Office: AOL Time Warner Inc Law Dept 75 Rockefeller Plz New York NY 10019*

CAPPY, RALPH JOSEPH, judge; b. Pitts., Aug. 25, 1943; s. Joseph R. and Catherine (Miljus) C.; m. Janet Fry, Apr. 19, 1985; 1 child, Erik. BS in Psychology, U. Pitts., 1965, JD, 1968. Bar: Pa. 1968, U.S. Dist. Ct. (we. dist.) Pa. 1968, U.S. Supreme Ct. 1975. Law clk. to pres. judge Ct. Common Pleas of Allegheny County, Pitts., 1968-70, apptd. judge, 1978-79, assigned family div., 1978-79, elected judge, 1979-85; judge criminal div. Ct. Common Pleas of Allegheny County, Pitts., 1980-85; judge civil div. Allegheny County Ct. Common Pleas of Allegheny County, Pitts., 1985-86, former presiding adminstrv. judge, from 1986; pvt. practice Pitts., 1968-78; now chief justice Supreme Ct. Pa. Lectr. constl. law U. Pitts., 1970-72; instr. criminal law and trial tactics City of Pitts. Police Acad., Allegheny County Police Acad., 1970-74; trial defender, 1st asst. homicide atty. Office Pub. Defender Allegheny County, Pa., 1970-75; pub. defender Allegheny County, Pa., 1975-78. Mem. Pitts. Health and Welfare Planning Agy., 1984—; mem. jud. ethics com. Pa. Law Jour., 1980-82; trustee U. Pitts., 1992—, bd. visitors, 1992—. Fellow Am. Bar Found.; mem. ABA, Pa. Bar Assn., Allegheny Bar Assn., Pa. Conf. State Trial Judges (legis. and planning com. 1978-83, legis. com., zone rep. 1984—, chmn. edn. com. 1985-88), Pa. Coll. Judiciary (lectr. 1983—, treas. 1987—, sec. 1988—), NACCP (life), Pitts. Athletic Assn. Office: Pa Supreme Ct 1 Oxford Ct Ste 3130 Pittsburgh PA 15219-1407

CAPRON, ALEXANDER MORGAN, lawyer, educator, philosopher; b. Hartford, Conn., Aug. 16, 1944; s. Willaim Mosher and Margaret (Morgan) Capron; m. Barbara A. Brown, Nov. 9, 1969 (div. Dec. 1985); 1 child, Jared Capron-Brown; m. Kathleen West, Mar. 4, 1989; children: Charles Spencer West Capron, Christopher Gordon West Capron, Andrew Morgan West Capron. BA, Swarthmore Coll., 1966; LLB, Yale U., 1969; MA (hon.) , U. Pa., 1975. Bar: D.C. 1970, Pa. 1978. Law clk. to presiding judge U.S. Ct. Appeals, Washington, 1969—70; lectr., rsch. assoc. Yale U., 1970—72; asst. prof. law U. Pa., 1972—75, vice dean, 1976, assoc. prof., 1975—78, prof. law and human genetics, 1978—82; exec. dir. Pres.'s Commn. for Study of Ethical Problems in Med. and Biomedical and Behavioral Rsch., Washington, 1980—83; prof. law, ethics and pub. policy Law Ctr. Georgetown U., Washington, 1983—84, inst. fellow Kennedy Inst. Ethics, 1983—84; Topping prof. law, medicine and pub. policy U. So. Calif., LA, 1985—89, Univ. prof., 1989—, prof. medicine and law, 1991—, Henry W. Bruce prof. equity, 1991—; co-dir. Pacific Ctr. for Health Policy and Ethics, LA, 1990—; dir. ethics and health WHO, 2002—. Mem. bd. advisors Am. Bd. Internal Medicine, 1985—95, chmn., 1991—95; cons. NIH, mem. subcom. on human gene therapy, 1984—92, mem. recominent DNA com., 1990—95; chmn. Congrl. Biomedical Ethics Adv. Commn., 1987—91; mem. Joint Commn. on Accreditation of Healthcare Orgns., 1994—, mem. ethics adv. com., 1984—85; mem. Nat. Bioethics Adv. Commn., 1996—2001. Author (with Katz): Catastrophic Diseases: Who Decides What?, 1976; author: (with others) Genetic Counseling: Facts, Values and Norms, 1979, Law, Science and Medicine, 1984, supplements, 1987, 1989, 2d edit., Treatise on Health Care Law, 1991; contbr. articles to profl. jours. Bd. mgrs. Swarthmore Coll., 1982—85; bd. trustees The Century Found. Fellow: AAAS, Hastings Ctr. (Inst. Soc., Ethics and Life Scis., bd. dirs. 1975—98), Am. Coll. Legal Medicine (hon.); mem.: AAUP (exec. com. Pa. chpt.), Am. Soc. Law, Medicine and Ethics (pres. 1988—89), Inst. Medicine of NAS (bd. dirs. 1985—90), Swarthmore Coll. Alumni Soc. (v.p. 1974—77). Office: DGO/ETH WHO Avenue Appia 20 1211 Geneva 27 Switzerland E-mail: capronа@who.int.

CAPSHAW, TOMMIE DEAN, judge; b. Oklahoma City, Sept. 20, 1936; m. Dian Shipp; 1 child, Charles W. BS in Bus., Oklahoma City U., 1958; postrad., U. Ark., 1958-59; JD, U. Okla., 1961. Bar: Okla. 1961, Wyo. 1971, Ind. 1975. Assoc. Looney, Watts, Looney, Nichols and Johnson, Oklahoma City, 1961-63, Pierce, Duncan, Couch and Hendrickson, Oklahoma City, 1963-70; trial atty., v.p. Capshaw Well Service Co., Liberty Pipe and Supply Co., Casper, Wyo.; adminstrv. law judge Evansville, Ind., 1973-75, 96-99; hearing office chief adminstrv. law judge Chgo., 1975-96; acting regional chief adminstrv. law judge, 1977-78; sr. adminstrv. law judge, 1999—. Acting appeals coun. mem., Arlington, Va., 1980, acting chief adminstrv. law judge, 1984; mem. faculty U. Evansville, 1977, So. Ill. U. Sch. Law, 1988—, So. Ind. U., 1990; lectr. in field. Author: A Manual for Continuing Judicial Education, 1981, Practical Aspects of Handling Social Security Disability Claims, 1982, Judicial Practice Handbook, 1990, A Quest for Quality, Speedy Justice, 1991; contbr. numerous articles to profl. jours., chpt. to textbook. Mem. adv. coun. Boy Scouts Am., scoutmaster, den leader, 1969—, Nat. Jud. Coll. U. Nev.; bd. dirs. Casper Symphony, 1972-73, Casper United Fund, 1972-73, Midget Football Assn., Casper, 1972-73, German Twp. Water Dist., 1984-85; pres. Evansville Unitarian Universalist Ch., 1984-86; performer Evansville Philharmonic Orch., 1986-98; bd. dirs. German Twp. Vol. Fire Dept., 1998—. Recipient Kappa Alpha Order Ct. of Honor award, 1962, Silver Beaver award Boy Scouts Am., 1980, presentation for vol. svc. contbg. betterment of cmty. Office Hearings and Appeals, 1992, presentation outstanding jud. mentor tng. Supreme Ct. Iowa, 1992, presentation disting. mentor tng. Fla. Jud. Coll., 1992, Robert V. Payant award Nat. Jud. Coll., 2002. Mem. Okla. Bar Assn., Okla. County Bar Assn. (v.p. 1967), Wyo. Bar Assn., Evansville Bar Assn. (jud. rep. 1986-87, James Bethel Gresham Freedom award 1988), Young Lawyers Assn., Assn. Adminstrv. Law Judges HHS (bd. dirs. 1979-82, Tic Vickery award 1998), Oklahoma City U. Alumni Assn. (bd. dirs. 1965). Home: 6105 School Rd # 6 Evansville IN 47720

CAPUTO, KATHRYN MARY, paralegal; b. Bklyn., June 29, 1948; d. Fortunato and Agnes (Iovino) Villacci; m. Joseph John Caputo, Apr. 4, 1976. AS in Bus. Adminstrn., Nassau C.C., Garden City, N.Y., 1989. Legal asst. Jacob Jacobson, Oceanside, N.Y., 1973-77; legal asst., office mgr. Joseph Kaldor, P.C., Franklin Square, N.Y., 1978-82, William H. George, Valley Stream, N.Y., 1983-89; exec. legal asst., office adminstr. Katz & Bernstein, Westbury, N.Y., 1990-93; sr. paralegal and office adminstr. Blaustein & Weinick, Garden City, N.Y., 1993—. Instr. adult continuing edn. legal sec. procedures Lawrence (N.Y.) H.S., 1992—. Spl. events coord. Bklyn.-Queens Marriage Encounter, 1981, 82, 83, 85, 86; mem. Lynbrook Civic Assn., St. Raymond's R.C. Ch. Pastoral Coun., 1999-2002, sec. 2000-02, Renew 2000, mem. rev. bd.; mem. St. Vincent DePaul Soc., sec., 2001—. Mem. L.I. Paralegal Assn. Avocations: traveling, reading, theatre, gardening. Office: Blaustein & Weinick 1205 Franklin Ave Garden City NY 11530-1629 E-mail: kacapbwparalgl@hotmail.com.

CARAVASOS, NIALENA, lawyer; b. Ridley Park, Pa., Oct. 20, 1966; BS in Econs. with honors, U. Pa., 1988; JD, Boston U., 1993. Bar: Mass. 1993, Pa. 1994, U.S. Dist. Ct. (ea. dist.) Pa. 1997, U.S. Ct. Appeals (3rd cir.) 1997, U.S. Supreme Ct. 1997. Law clk. to presiding judge Lisa Aversa Richette Ct. Common Pleas, Phila., 1995-97; assoc. F. Emmett Fitzpatrick, P.C., Phila., 1997—. CLE speaker at 2000 Criminal Law Symposium, Pa. Bar Inst. Edward F. Hennessey scholar; recipient Commencement award, Am. Jurisprudence award in Criminal Trial Practice. Mem. Pa. Bar Assn., Hellenic Lawyers Assn. Phila., Phila. Bar Assn. (criminal justice sect.), Fed. Bar Assn. (criminal law com.). Criminal. Office: 926 Public Ledger Bldg 610 Chestnut St Philadelphia PA 19106 E-mail: nialena@toplaw.com.

CARBARY, JONATHAN LEIGH, lawyer; b. Elgin, Ill., Nov. 6, 1949; s. Warren Edward and Barbara Jean (Leigh) C.; m. Janice Kay Weingartner, Dec. 29, 1973; children: Nicole, Dana, Jonathan. BA, Knox Coll., 1972; JD, Hamline U., 1978. Bar: Ill. 1978, U.S. Dist. Ct. (no. dist.) Ill. 1979. Assoc. Robert A. Chapski, Ltd., Elgin, 1978-83; ptnr. Roeser, Vucha & Carbary, Elgin, 1984-96; pvt. practice Elgin, 1996—. 1st lt. U.S. Army, 1972-73. Recipient Am. Jurisprudence award Lawyer Co-op Pub. Co., 1978. Mem. Ill. State Bar Assn., Kane County Bar Assn. Republican. State civil litigation, Personal injury (including property damage), Workers' compensation. Home: 11 N 205 Johnstown Rd Elgin IL 60123 Office: 1814 Grandstand Pl Elgin IL 60123-4981 E-mail: jcarbary@msn.com.

CARBINE, JAMES EDMOND, lawyer; b. Scotts Bluff, Nebr., June 3, 1945; s. Edmond Horace Carbine and Mabel (Porterfield) Hukle; m. Marianne Lemly, Aug. 5, 1972; 1 child, Matthew. BA, Mich. State U., 1967; JD, U. Md., 1972. Bar: Md. 1972. Assoc. Weinberg and Green, Balt., 1972-79, ptnr., 1980-96, chmn. litigation dept., 1985-95; pvt. practice Balt., 1996—. Panel mem. Nat. Press Club Symposium, 1974. Reporter Govs. Landlord Tenant Commn., Md., 1973-76; mem. Mayor's Bus. Roundtable, Balt., 1983-85; bd. dirs. Greater Homewood Community Corp., Balt., 1980-82; trustee Roland Park Found., 1986-87; bd. dirs. Md. Vol. Lawyers Svc., 1991-2002. With U.S. Army, 1968-70. Named one of Outstanding Young Men Am., Jaycees, 1977. Mem. ABA (computer litigation com., corp. coun. com., co-chair trial practice com. 1994-97), Md. Bar Assn., Balt. City Bar Assn., Nat. Press Club (panelist 1974). Avocation: outdoor sports. Federal civil litigation, State civil litigation. Office: 111 S Calvert St Ste 2700 Baltimore MD 21202-6143

CARBULLIDO, F. PHILIP, judge; b. Tamuning, Guam, Feb. 5, 1953; s. Francisco Chaco and Maria Salas (Castro) Carbullido; m. Fay Diana Lizama Garrido; children: Brandon Philip, Kristina Joy, Adam Philip, Steven Philip. BS in Polit. Sci., U. Oreg., 1975; JD, U. Calif., Davis, 1978. Intern to asst. atty. gen. Office Atty. Gen.; assoc. Arriola and Lamorena, Arriola & Cowan, ptnr., Carbullido & Pipes, P.C., 1983—97, Carbullido Bordallo & Brooks, LLP, 1997, Carbullido & Brooks LLP; judge Supreme Ct. Guam, Hagåtña, 2000—. Recipient award of Merit, Pacific Jaycees, 1983; Profl. Tech. scholar, Govt. of Guam. Office: Supreme Ct Guam Jud Ctr Ste 300 120 W O'Brien Dr Hagatna GU 96910 Office Fax: 671-475-3140. Business E-Mail: justice@guamsupremecourt.com.*

CARDAMONE, RICHARD J. judge; b. Utica, N.Y., Oct. 10, 1925; s. Joseph J. and Josephine (Scala) Cardamone; m. Catherine Baker Clarke, Aug. 28, 1946. BA, Harvard U., 1948; LLB, Syracuse U., 1952. Bar: N.Y. 1952. Pvt. practice, Utica, 1952—62; judge N.Y. State Supreme Ct., 1963—71, judge appelate divsn. 4th dept., 1971—81; judge U.S. Ct. Appeals (2d cir.), Utica, 1981—. Lt. (j.g.) USNR, 1943—46. Mem.: Oneida County Bar Assn., N.Y. State Bar Assn., Am. Law Inst. Roman Catholic. Office: US Ct Appeals 10 Broad St Utica NY 13501-1233

CARDEA, JAMES DONALD, lawyer; b. Englewood, NJ, May 1, 1967; s. Donald John and Barbara Flade Cardea; m. Frances Fato Cardea, Aug. 8, 1992; children: Jaimie Frances, Katherine Anne. BA, McDaniel Coll., Westminster, Md., 1989; JD cum laude, U. of Balt., 1995. Bar: U.S. Ct. Appeals of Md. 1995, DC Ct. of Appeals 1996, U.S. Dist. Ct. Md. 1996, U.S. Dist. Ct. DC 1996. Atty. DeCaro, Doran, Siciliano, Gallagher, Sonntag & DeBlasis, Lanham, Md., 1995—97, Horowitz, Foran & Sonntag, Greenbelt, Md., 1997—2000, Schochor, Federico and Staton, P.A., Balt., 2000—. Staff editor U. Balt. Law Rev., 1994—95. Co-founder Dr. Don Cardea Meml. Charity Golf Tournament, Cherry Hill, NJ, 1998—2002. Named to Heuisler Honor Soc., U. of Balt. Sch. of Law, 1995; recipient Am. Jurisprudence Award in Legal Analysis, Rsch. and Writing, 1992, Am. Jurisprudence Award in Domestic Rels., 1995. Mem.: ATLA, Md. State Bar Assoc., Md. Trial Lawyers Assn., Balt. City Bar Assn., Prince George's County Bar Assn., Million Dollar Advocates Forum. Personal injury (including property damage), Product liability. Office: Schochor Federico and Staton, PA 1211 St Paul S Baltimore MD 21202 Office Fax: 410-234-1010. E-mail: jcardea@sfspa.com.

CARDEN, CONSTANCE, law educator, lawyer; b. D.C., July 15, 1944; d. George Alexander and Constance (Sullivan) C.; m. John Dinsmore Adams, Jun. 7, 1975 (div. Jun. 1988); 1 child, Elizabeth; m. Bernard Lawrence Goldstein, Aug. 7, 1998. BA, Radcliffe Coll., 1966; MA in Teaching, Harvard Grad. Sch. Edn., 1967; JD, N.Y. Univ., 1972. Bar: N.Y. 1973. Assoc. Webster & Sheffield, N.Y.C., 1972-73; law clerk U.S. Dist. Judge Kevin Thomas Duffy, N.Y.C., 1973-74; staff atty. Legal Aid Soc., N.Y.C., 1974-81; sr. staff atty. Legal Svcs. for the Elderly, N.Y.C., 1981-90; dir. litig. Bklyn. Neighborhood Office Legal Aid Soc., N.Y.C., 1990-96; supervising atty. gen. legal svcs. N.Y. Legal Assistance Group, N.Y.C., 1997-98, dir. spl. litig., 1998—. Revson fellow, City Coll. N.Y. Law Sch., N.Y.C., 1981-82; adj. asst. prof., Bkln. Law Sch., N.Y.C., 1985-86; adj. prof., Pace Law Sch., White Plains, NY, 1993—. Author, editor: Medical Assistance in New York State, 1988, revised annually. Pres., Project Greenhope Svcs. for Women, N.Y.C., 1986-97; bd. dirs. Medicare Rights Ctr., 1988-95, Correctional Assn., Osborne Assn., N.Y.C., Project Greenhope Svcs., 1986—. Recipient Legal Svcs. award, Bar Assn. City of N.Y., 1990. Mem. Century Assn., Canterbury Choral Soc., Essex Hunt Club. Avocations: running, singing, foxhunting, playing piano, reading. Home: 115 E 90th St New York NY 10128-1509 Office: New York Legal Asst Group 130 E 59th St New York NY 10022-1302 E-mail: ccarden@nylag.org.

CARDENAS, ALEJANDRO, lawyer; b. Mexico City, Mex., Oct. 27, 1970; s. Raul Fernando Cardenas and Dolores Eychenne. Law degree, U. Anahuac, Mexico City, 1996, M of Corp. Law, 1998; M of Intellectual Property, U. Alicante, Spain, 2001. Assoc. Basham, Ringe & Correa, Mexico City, 1996—2002; trademark dir. Clarke, Modet & Co., Mexico City, 2003; prof. post grad. intellectual property U. Latina de America, Morelia, Mich., 2002—03, U. Anáhuac, Toluca, Mexico. Intellectual property, Patent, Trademark and copyright. Office: Clarke Modet & Co San Francisco 310 03100 Mexico City Mexico Office Fax: 5255 53236418. E-mail: acardenas@clarkemodet.com.mx.

CARDINALE, PHILIP JOHN, lawyer, educator; b. Bklyn., Dec. 14, 1948; s. Alerio A. and Louise D. Cardinale; m. Susan Marie Porreco, Aug. 19, 1972; children: Philip Jr., Cristina, Joseph. AB, Georgetown U., 1970, MA, 1971, JD, 1973. Bar: N.Y., U.S. Dist. Ct. (ea. dist.) N.Y. 1974. Asst. dist. atty. Suffolk County (N.Y.) Dist. Atty.'s Office, Riverhead, 1973-80; ptnr. Cardinale & Cardinale, Jamesport, NY, 1980—; assoc. adj. prof. Suffolk County C.C., Selden, NY, 1978—. Councilman Town of Riverhead, 1997-2001; trustee Riverhead Lib., 1996-2002. Mem. Rotary. Roman Catholic. Municipal (including bonds), Probate (including wills, trusts), Property, real (including real estate development, water). Home: 785 Peconic Bay Blvd Riverhead NY 11901-5906 Office: Cardinale & Cardinale 1451 Main Rd Jamesport NY 11947

CARDON, LAWRENCE MARC, lawyer; b. Bklyn., Apr. 3, 1943; s. Leon and Selma (Bennett) C.; m. Lucy Ann Proto, June 27, 1970; children: David Aaron, Rebecca Lynn. BS in Commerce, U. Va., 1965; JD, U. Richmond, 1973. Ptnr. Decker, Cardon, Thomas, Norfolk, Va. Mem. Norfolk Portsmouth Bar Assn., Virginia Beach Bar Assn. Home: 446 Discovery Rd Virginia Beach VA 23451-2158 Office: Decker Cardon Thomas 201 E Plume St Norfolk VA 23510-1706

CARELLA, CHARLES CARMINE, lawyer; b. Newark, Nov. 21, 1933; s. Peter A. and Rose P. (Rizzo) C.; m. Joan Loprete Carella, June 16, 1956; children— Charles M., Robert P., Mary Catherine, JoAnne. B.S., Fordham U., 1955; LL.B., Rutgers U., 1958. Bar: N.J. 1959, N.Y. 1983, U.S. Ct. Apls. (3d cir.) 1968, U.S. Supreme Ct. 1968. Sr. mng. ptnr. Carella, Byrne, Bain, Gilfillan, Cecchi, Stewart & Olstein, Roseland, 1976— ; asst. prosecutor County of Essex (N.J.), 1961-63, spl. prosecutor 1965; commr. Ethical Standards Commn. N.J., 1974-75; dir. N.J. State Lottery Commn. 1974-75; mem. exec. sec. to Gov. N.J. 1975-76; chmn. N.J. State Racing Commn., 1976-82; formerly chief counsel Passaic Valley Sewerage Commrs.; bd. dirs. DiGiorgio Corp. Mem. fin. coun. Archdiocese of Newark; former chmn. Found. for Ednl. Alternatives. Mem. ABA, N.J. Bar Assn., Essex County Bar Assn., Rock Spring Club (West Orange, N.J.), Rifle Club (N.Y.C.), W.M.O. Assn. Inc. (Windham, N.Y.), Sailfish Point Golf Club (Stuart, Fla.). Democrat. Roman Catholic. Administrative and regulatory, Banking, Corporate, general. Home: 411 Ridgewood Ave Glen Ridge NJ 07028-1617 Office: 6 Becker Farm Rd Roseland NJ 07068-1735

CAREY, ANTHONY MORRIS, lawyer; b. Balt., May 31, 1935; s. Anthony Morris and Louise (Waterman) C.; m. Eleanor MacKey, Oct. 7, 1967. AB, Princeton U., 1957; LLB, Harvard U., 1963; MLA, Johns Hopkins U., 1970. Bar: Md. 1963, U.S. Dist. Ct. (fed. dist.) Md. 1965, U.S. Supreme Ct. 1968. Assoc. Venable, Baetjer & Howard, Balt., 1963-67, ptnr., 1972-79, 87—; former chmn. environ. dept., asst. atty. gen. State of Md., Balt., 1967-69; spl. asst. for energy affairs HUD, Washington, 1979-81; pres. Carey-Tidewater, Inc., Balt., 1981-86; regional dir., gen. counsel HEC Energy Corp., Balt., 1986-87. Former bd. dirs. Carey Machinery Supply Co., Inc., Balt.; former bd. dirs. Eberhard Faber, Inc; former exec. sec. Md. Bd. Ethics. Former trustee Citizen's Planning and Housing Assn.; former dir. Nat. Civic League, Denver, 1979-90; chmn. bd. trustees Balt. Sch. for the Arts Found., current chmn. emeritus bd. overseers; vice chmn. Lillie Carroll Jackson Mus.; trustee, sec. Robert Garrett Fund for Surg. Treatment of Children; mem. Balt. City Commn. on Resource Conservation and Recycling. With USAF, 1957-60. Mem. ABA, Md. State Bar Assn., Balt.City Bar Assn., Ivy Club, Hamilton St. Club. Democrat. Episcopalian. Avocations: skiing, hiking, reading. Office: Venable Baetjer & Howard 1800 Merc Bank & Trust Bldg 2 Hopkins Plz Ste 2100 Baltimore MD 21201-2982

CAREY, JANA HOWARD, lawyer; b. Huntsville, Ala., Apr. 20, 1945; d. Ernest Randall and Mary Regna (Baites) Howard; m. James Johnston Hale Carey, Jan. 15, 1983. BS in Home Econs., Auburn U., 1967; MS in Audiovisual Communications, Towson State U., 1973; JD, U. Balt., 1976. Bar: (U.S. Ct. Appeals (4th cir.)) 1977, (U.S. Dist. Ct. (Md. dist.)) 1978, (U.S. Ct. Appeals (3d cir.)) 1994, (U.S. Supreme Ct.) 1995, (U.S. Ct. Appeals (Md. cir.)) 1996. Tchr. Hampton High Sch., Melbourne, Australia, 1967; home economist U. Ga., Athens, 1967-70, devel. specialist state youth program, 1970-72, U. Md., College Park, 1972-73; clk. appellate div. Pub. Defender's Office, Balt., 1974; assoc. Venable, Baetjer & Howard, Balt., 1975, 76-84, ptnr., 1984—, past chair labor and employment group, 1995-97. Spkr in field. Co-author: (book) Legal Aspects of the Employment Relationship: An Introduction for the General Practitioner, 1978; mem ed bd: Employment Testing Law and Policy Reporter, Nat Employment Law Inst Adv Bd, Am Employment Law Coun Adv Bd; contbr. articles to profl jours. Chair dean's adv coun Univ Baltimore Law Sch; mem Univ Baltimore Educ Found, Univ Baltimore Bd Visitors; past mem pres adv coun St Mary's Col, Pension Oversight Comn Anne Arundel County. Named Top 100 Women for Oustanding Achievement, Daily Record, 1997, 2000, Circle of Excellence, 2002; recipient Top 100 Women for Outstanding Achievement, 2002. Mem.: ABA (chair sect coun labor and employment law sect, past mgt co-chair insts and meetings comt, EEOC liaison comt sects comt equal employment opportunity law, mem standing comt CLE, dep chair labor & employment law comt sect pub utility, comm, transp, health law forum), Nat Asn Women Lawyers (mem gender bias comt), Am Col Labor and Employment Lawyers, Nat Labor Lawyers Adv Comt CUE. Labor (including EEOC, Fair Labor Standards Act, labor-management relations, NLRB, OSHA). Office: Venable Baetjer & Howard 1800 Mercantile Bank & Trust Bldg Two Hopkins Plaza Baltimore MD 21201 E-mail: jhcarey@venable.com.

CAREY, JOHN, lawyer, judge; b. Phila., June 11, 1924; s. Henry Reginald and Margaret Howell (Bacon) C.; m. Patricia F. Frank, Feb. 24, 1951; children: Henry Frank, John, Douglas, Jennifer Patricia. Grad., Milton Acad., 1942; BA, Yale U., 1947; LL.B., Harvard U., 1949; LL.M. in Internat. Law, N.Y.U., 1965; LL.D., U. W.I., 1985. Bar: Pa. 1950, N.Y. 1957. Practiced in, Phila., 1949-55; asst. dist. atty., 1952-54; cons. spl. com. fed. loyalty-security program Assn. Bar City N.Y., 1955-56; ptnr. Coudert Bros., 1961-87; justice N.Y. Supreme Ct., 1987; judge Westchester County Ct., White Plains, N.Y., 1988-94; mem. faculty NYU Law Sch., 1966-73; jud. hearing officer N.Y. State, 1995—. Author: UN Protection of Civil and Political Rights, 1970; editor: United Nations Law Reports, 1966—. Mem. Rye (N.Y.) City Coun., 1964-68, 72-74, mayor, 1974-82; alt. mem. UN Subcommn. on Prevention Discrimination and Protection of Minorities, 1966-82, 84-91, mem. 1983; alt. U.S. rep. UN Human Rights Commn., 1968; trustee Little Harbor Chapel, Portsmouth, N.H. Mem. ABA, N.Y. State Bar Assn., Assn. Bar City N.Y., Am. Soc. Internat. Law (v.p. 1987-88), Coun. on Fgn. Rels., Phi Beta Kappa. Home and Office: 860 Forest Ave Rye NY 10580-3145 Office: County Ct House White Plains NY 10601 E-mail: jncarey@westnet.com.

CAREY, JOHN LEO, lawyer; b. Morris, Ill., Oct. 1, 1920; s. John Leo and Loretta (Conley) C.; m. Rhea M. White, July 15, 1950; children: John Leo III, Daniel Hobart, Deborah M. BS, St. Ambrose Coll., Davenport, Ia., 1941; JD, Georgetown U., 1947, LLM, 1949. Bar: Ind. DC 1947, Ill. 1947. Legislative asst. Sen. Scott W. Lucas, 1945-47; spl. atty. IRS, Washington, 1947-54; since practiced in South Bend; ptnr. Barnes & Thornburg, 1954—, now of counsel; law prof. taxation Notre Dame Law Sch., 1968-90. Trustee LaLumire Prep. Sch., Laporte, Ind. Served with USAAF, World War II; to lt. col. USAF, Korean War. Decorated D.F.C., Air medal. Mem. ABA (bd. govs. 1986-89, treas. 1990-93), Ind. Bar Assn. (pres. 1976-77), St. Joseph County Bar Assn., Signal Point Country Club, Quail Walley City Club. Corporate, general, Corporate taxation. Home: # 114 1250 W Southwinds Blvd Vero Beach FL 32963 Office: 600 1st Source Bank Ctr 100 N Michigan St South Bend IN 46601-1630

CAREY, SARAH COLLINS, lawyer; b. N.Y.C., Aug. 12, 1938; d. Jerome Joseph and Susan (Atlee) Collins; m. James J. Carey, Aug. 28, 1962 (div. 1977); 1 child, Sasha; m. John D. Reilly, Jan. 27, 1979; children: Sarah Reilly, Katherine Reilly. BA, Radcliffe Coll., 1960; LLB, Georgetown U., 1965. Bar: D.C. 1966, U.S. Supreme Ct. 1977. Soviet specialist USIA/U.S. Dept. State, 1961-65; assoc. Arnold & Porter, Washington, 1965-68; asst. dir. Lawyers Com. for Civil Rights, Washington, 1968-73; ptnr. Heron, Burchette, Ruckert & Rothwell/predecessor firms, Washington, 1973-90; chair CIS Practice Steptoe and Johnson, Washington, 1990-99; chair CIS Practice, sr. ptnr. internat. Squire, Sanders & Dempsey, Washington, 1999—. Cons. Ford Found., 1975—83; bd. dirs. Yukos Oil Co., 2001—. Chair bd. dirs. Eurasia Found., 1994—; bd. dirs. Russia-Am. Enterprise Fund, 1993—95, Def. Enterprise Fund, 1994—2001, Georgetown U. Sch. Law Inst. Pub. Representation, 1971—85, Am. Arbitration Assn., 1975—82, Women's Fgn. Policy Group. Mem.: Atlantic Coun., Coun. Fgn. Rels. Democrat. General practice, Private international, Legislative. Office: 1201 Pennsylvania Ave NW Washington DC 20004-2401 E-mail: scarey@ssd.com.

CARGILL, ROBERT MASON, lawyer; b. Atlanta, Nov. 15, 1948; s. George Slade Jr., and Emma Elizabeth (Matthews) C.; m. Sharon McEver, June 12, 1971; children: Ansley Lauren, Kristin Lucille. BS summa cum laude, Ga. Inst. Tech., 1970; JD magna cum laude, Harvard U., 1973. Bar: Ga. 1973, D.C. 1975. Assoc. atty. Hansell & Post, Atlanta, 1976-81, ptnr., 1981-89, Jones & Day, Atlanta, 1989—. Lt. USNR 1973-76. Mem. Swedish Am. C. of C. Atlanta (bd. dirs.), Swiss Am. C. of C. (bd. dirs. Atlanta chpt.), World Trade Ctr. Atlanta (bd. dirs.), Cherokee Town Country Club. Methodist. Avocations: tennis, travel. Commercial, contracts (including sales of goods; commercial financing), Corporate, general, Private international. Home: 230 Colewood Way NW Atlanta GA 30328-2923 Office: Jones & Day 303 Peachtree St NE Ste 3500 Atlanta GA 30308-3263 E-mail: rcargill@jonesday.com.

CARGO, DAVID FRANCIS, lawyer; b. Dowagiac, Mich., Jan. 13, 1929; s. Francis Clair and Mary E. (Harton) C.; children: Veronica Ann, David Joseph, Patrick Michael, Maria Elena Christina, Eamon Francis. AB, U. Mich., 1951, M of Pub. Adminstrn., 1953, JD, 1957. Bar: Mich. 1957, N.Mex. 1957, Oreg. 1974. Practice in, Albuquerque, 1957; asst. dist. atty., 1958-59; mem. N.Mex. Ho. of Reps., 1962; gov. N.Mex., 1967-71; practice law, 1970-73, Portland, Oreg., 1973-83. Chmn. Four Corners Regional Commn., 1967-71, Oil and Gas Conservation Commn.; chmn. N.Mex. Young Reps., 1959-61, Clackamas County Rep. Ctrl. Com.; mem. Israel Bond Com.; former mem. bd. govs. St. John Coll.; bd. dirs. Albuquerque Tech. Vocat. Sch.; chmn. governing bd. Albuquerque Tv.I. C.C.; mem. Albuquerque City Pers. Bd.; adv. bd. mem. N.Mex. State Fair; exec. bd. Found. for Open Govt. With AUS, 1953-55; bd. dirs. N.M. State Libr. Found.; elected state chair libr. bond chmn., 2002; pres. Calvin Coolidge Found. and Libr. Named Man of Yr. Albuquerque Jr. C. of C., 1964, Congregation Albert Brotherhood Man of Yr., 2001, 2002; recipient Outstanding Conservationist award N.Mex. Wildlife Assn., 1969, 70. Mem. Mich. Bar Assn., Oreg. Bar Assn., N.Mex. Bar Assn., Albuquerque Bar Assn., Isaac Walton League (past v.p. N.Mex.), World Affairs Coun. Oreg. (pres.), Interstate Oil and Gas Compact, Isaak Walton League Oreg., Hispano C. of C., Am. Leadership Conf. (bd. dirs.), Nat. Fedn. Blind, Calvin Coolidge Presidential Found. (nat. bd. mem.), Oegon State Film Commn. Family and matrimonial, Personal injury (including property damage), Workers' compensation. Home: 6422 Concordia Rd NE Albuquerque NM 87111-1228

CARITOUX, VALÉRIE FRANCOISE CECILE, lawyer; b. Feb. 4, 1970; d. James Caritoux and Mireille Gregoire; 1 child, Matis Bobet. M in Comml. Law, Lyon III, Tex. Tech. U., 1993; DESS in Internat. Trade Law, Paris X, Nanterre, 1994, DEA in Econ. Internat. Rels., 1995. Bar: Paris 1996. Lawyer Thomas & Assocs., Paris, 1997—98, NOMOS, Paris, 1998—. Contbr. articles to profl. jours. Commercial, consumer (including collections, credit), Antitrust, Advertising, Internet, Distbn. Office: NOMOS 13 Rue Alphonse de Neuville 75017 Paris France Fax: 33 1 43 18 55 55. Business E-Mail: vcaritoux@nomosparis.com.

CARLBERG, JAMES EDWIN, lawyer; b. Jeffersonville, Ind., May 3, 1950; s. Dale Levan and Nanette (Prendergast) C.; m. Donna S. Funk, Oct. 28, 1950; children: Jason, Lindsay, Kelly. BS highest distinction, Ind U., 1972, JD cum laude, 1974. Bar: Ind. 1974, U.S. Dist. Ct. (no. and so. dists.) Ind. 1974. Ptnr. Klineman, Rose, Wolf & Wallack, Indpls., 1974-94, Bose, McKinner & Evans, Indpls., 1994—. Author: (with others) Indiana Continuing Legal Education Forum. Mem. ABA (secured creditors' sub com. of bankruptcy com., bus. and banking sect.), Ind. State Bar Assn., Indpls. Bar Assn. Bankruptcy, Commercial, contracts (including sales of goods; commercial financing), Corporate, general. Office: Bose McKinney & Evans 2700 1st Indiana Pla Indianapolis IN 46204

CARLENO, HARRY EUGENE, lawyer; b. Denver, Mar. 3, 1928; s. Benjamin Edward and Elizabeth Bess (De Rose) C.; m. Ann Marie Kraft, Sept. 14, 1957; children: Gregory S., Paul C., Jennifer A., Machelle L. BBA, U. Denver, 1951, LLB, 1955, JD, 1970. Bar: Colo. 1955, U.S. Dist. Ct. Colo. 1955, U.S. Ct. Appeals (10th cir.) 1959, U.S. Supreme Ct. 1959. Pres., atty. H.E. Carleno & Assoc., P.C., Englewood, Colo., 1955—80; atty. H.E. Carlino & Assocs. P.C., Littleton, Colo., 1980—. Mcpl. judge City of Wheat Ridge, Colo., 1970-77; dep. dist. atty. Arapahoe County, Littleton, 1968-78; owner, broker Eagle Real Esate Co, Denver, Colo., 1998—. Chmn. Dem. Com., Arapahoe County, 1958-60; chmn. Career Service Commn., Englewood, 1961-64; pres. Inter Faith Task Force Found., Englewood, 1986-88. Col. USAF, 1947-53. Recipient St. George award Denver Area council Boy Scouts Am., 1980. Mem. ABA (life), Res. Officers Assn. of U.S. (life), Ret. Officers Assn. (life), Fraternal Order of Eagles (life). Lodges: Kiwanis (local pres. 1966-67). Roman Catholic. Estate planning, General practice. Home and Office: 5471 S Sherman St Littleton CO 80121-1253 E-mail: hecarleno@msn.com.

CARLETON, JOSEPH GEORGE, JR., lawyer, state legislator; b. Bklyn., July 21, 1945; s. Joseph G. and Ellen (Gabriel) C. AB, Dartmouth Coll., 1969; JD, Boston U., 1972. Atty. Calderwood & Ouellette, Dover, N.H., 1972-79; pvt. practice Wells, Maine, 1979-83, 88—; atty., ptnr. Patterson Carleton & Mongue, Wells, 1983-88; mem. Maine Ho. of Reps., Augusta, 1990-98, asst. Rep. leader, 1994-96; commr. Gov.'s Blue Ribbon Commn. on Health, 2000, Maine Health Performance Coun., 2001—02. Chmn. Wells Site Rev. Bd., 1985-86; town meeting moderator Town of Wells; 1983—; mem. adv. bd. York County Tech. Coll., 1996—. Sgt. N.H. Air N.G., 1966-74. Mem. Wells C. of C. (pres. 1984), Elks, Masons. Republican. Avocations: golf, history, politics. Home and Office: PO Box 369 Wells ME 04090-0369 E-mail: atty@maine.rr.com.

CARLEY, DONALD MARTIN, lawyer; b. Mpls., Feb. 28, 1968; s. Harold Edwin and Mary Elizabeth Carley. BS, Coll. William and Mary, 1990; JD, Temple U., 1995. CPCU, Coll., 2001; bar: Calif. 1995, U.S. Dist. Ct. (no. dist.) Calif. 1995, U.S. Ct. Appeals (9th cir.) 1995, U.S. Dist. Ct. (ea. dist.) Calif. 1996, U.S. Dist. Ct. (so. dist.) Calif. 1997, U.S. Dist. Ct. (ctrl. dist.) Calif. 1999, U.S. Patent and Trademark Office 2001, U.S. Supreme Ct. 2002. Environ. claims rep. The PMA Group, Phila., 1990-92, CIGNA Property and Casualty, Phila., 1992-95; assoc. Gordon & Rees, LLP, San Francisco, 1995-97, Luce Forward Hamilton & Scripps LLP, San Francisco, 1997-98; ptnr. Sonnenschein Nath & Rosenthal, San Francisco, 1998—. Contbr. articles to profl. jours. Mem. ABA, CPCU Soc. (mem.

Golden Gate chpt. 1995—, exec. com. mem. Golden Gate chpt. 1998—, bd. dirs. 2000—), Calif. Bar Assn., San Francisco Bar Assn., Barristers Club San Francisco (vice chair bridging the gap com. 1996, chair bridging the gap com. 1997, 98, bd. dirs. 1999—, pres. 2000—), Alpha Lambda Delta, Phi Eta Sigma. Avocations: cycling, travel, fly fishing, photography. Office: Sonnenschein Nath & Rosenthal 685 Market St Ste 6 San Francisco CA 94105-4202 Fax: 415-543-5472. E-mail: d3c@sonnenschein.com.

CARLEY, GEORGE H. judge; b. Jackson, Miss., Sept. 24, 1938; s. George L. Jr. and Dorothy (Holmes) C.; m. Sandra M. Lineberger, 1960; 1 child, George H. Jr. AB, U. Ga., 1960, LLB, 1962. Bar: Ga. 1961. Pvt. practice, Atlanta and Decatur, Ga., 1961-71; ptnr. McCurdy & Candler, Decatur, Ga., 1971-79; also spl. asst. atty. gen. Office. Atty. Gen.; judge Ct. Appeals Ga., 1979-89, chief judge, 1989-91, presiding judge, 1991-93; justice Supreme Ct. Ga., Atlanta, 1993—. Chmn. bd. visitors U. Ga. Law Sch., 1995-96. Bd. Visitors U. Ga. Law Sch.; past pres. U. Ga. Law Sch. Assn. Coun., 1989-90, active, 1986-91; trustee Ga. Legal History Found., Inc.; active Holy Trinity Episc. Ch., Decatur. Mem. ABA, State Bar Ga., Ga. Bar Found., Lawyers Club Atlanta, Old Warhorse Lawyers Club (pres. 1997-98), Joseph Henry Lumpkin Am. Inn of Ct. (pres. 1994-95), Pythagoras Lodge, Scottish Rite. Office: Supreme Court 244 Washington Street Atlanta GA 30334-9007

CARLEY, JOHN HALLIDAY, lawyer; b. N.Y.C. s. John T. and Edna May (Halliday) C.; m. Pia Lingström, 2000; children: Melinda S., Caroline H. BA, Rutgers Coll., 1962; LLB, Yale U., 1968. Bar: N.Y. 1969. Assoc. Mudge Rose Guthrie & Alexander, N.Y.C., 1968-72; assoc., ptnr. Rogers & Wells, N.Y.C., 1972-81; gen. counsel FTC, Washington, 1981-85, Office Mgmt. & Budget, The White House, Washington, 1985-87; ptnr. Donovan Leisure Newton & Irvine, N.Y.C., 1987-94; spl. coun. to deputy mayor N.Y.C., 1994-95; deputy atty. gen. Pub. Advocacy N.Y. State, 1995-96; exec. v.p., gen. counsel Avis, Inc., Garden City, N.Y., 1997-98; sr. v.p. law & regulatory affairs Cendant Corp., N.Y.C., N.J., 1998—. 1st lt. U.S. Army, 1963-65. Mem. Assn. Bar of City of N.Y. General civil litigation. Office: Cendant Corp 9 W 57th St New York NY 10019-2701 E-mail: john.carley@cendant.com.

CARLIN, CLAIR MYRON, lawyer; b. Sharon, Pa., Apr. 20, 1947; s. Charles William and Carolyn L. (Vukasich) C.; children: Eric Richard, Elizabeth Marie, Alexander Myron. BS in Econs., Ohio State U., 1969, JD, 1972. Bar: Ohio 1973, Pa. 1973, U.S. Dist. Ct. (so. dist.) Ohio 1973, U.S. Dist. Ct. (no. dist.) Ohio 1975, U.S. Supreme Ct. 1976, U.S. Ct. Claims, 1983, U.S. Tax Ct. 1985. Staff atty. Ohio Dept. Taxation, Columbus, 1972-73; asst. atty. City of Warren, Ohio, 1973-75; assoc. McLaughlin, DiBlasio & Harshman, Youngstown, Ohio, 1975-80; ptnr. McLaughlin, McNally & Carlin, Youngstown, 1980-98, Carlin & Vasvari, LLC, Poland, Ohio, 1998-2000, Clair M. Carlin, LLC, 2000—. Mem. editl. bd. Ohio Trial mag. Mem. Trumbull County Bicentennial Commn., Ohio, 1976; v.p. Svcs. for the Aging, Trumbull County, 1976-77; mem. Pres.' Club Ohio State U., Polit. Action Com. Maj. Ohio NG, 1972-82. Fellow Ohio State Bar Found.; mem. ATLA (bd. govs. 1996-2002, trustee PAC 1996-98), ABA, Ohio State Bar Assn. (negligence law com. 1991—), Ohio State Bar Coll., Mahoning County Bar Assn. (chmn. legal edn. com. 1985-86, counsel 1986-87, trustee 2000—), Ohio Acad. Trial Lawyers (trustee 1988-92, polit. action com. chmn. 1991, exec. com. 1991-97, treas. 1992-93, sec. 1993-94, pres.-elect 1994-95, pres. 1995-96), Mahoning-Trumbull Acad. Trial Lawyers (pres. 1991), Ohio State U. Alumni Assn. (pres. Trumbull County chpt. 1985—), Cath. War Vets. (Ohio state commdr., Vet. of Yr. 1988), Rotary, Million Dollar Advocate Forum. Democrat. Roman Catholic. Personal injury (including property damage), Product liability, Professional liability. Home: 3524 Hunters Hl Poland OH 44514-5303 Office: Clair M Carlin LLC PO Box 5369 Youngstown OH 44514-0369 E-mail: cmc@carlin-law.com.

CARLIN, DENNIS J. lawyer; b. Chgo., Aug. 23, 1941; s. Herbert E. and Lillian (Schnelder) C.; m. Fern Carlin, Nov. 25, 1964; children: Gregory A., H. David, Stuart B. BBA, U. Wis., 1963; JD, DePaul U., 1967; LLM in Taxation, Georgetown U., 1971. Bar: Ill. 1967; CPA. Auditor Checkers, Simon & Rosner, Chgo., 1963-67; assoc. tax ct. litigation divsn. IRS, Washington, 1967-71; ptnr. Frankel, McKay, Orlikoff, Denten & Kostner, Chgo., 1971-77, Horwood & Carlin, Chgo., 1977-82, Gardner, Carton & Douglas, Chgo., 1982—, vice-chmn., 1998—2003. Contbr. articles to profl. jours. Mem. atty. div. Jewish United Fund; bd. dirs., exec. com. Coun. for Jewish Elderly. Mem. ABA, Am. Coll. Tax Counsel, Chgo. Bar Assn. (former chmn. fed. tax com.), Nat. Strategy Forum, NYU Inst. Fed. Taxation, DePaul U. Alumni Coun., Am. Israeli C. of C., Twin Orchard Country Club. Avocations: golf, skiing, reading, music, theatre. Office: Gardner Carton & Douglas LLC 191 N Wacker Dr Ste 3400 Chicago IL 60606-1698

CARLIN, PAUL VICTOR, legal association executive; b. McKeesport, Pa., Nov. 11, 1945; BA, Grove City Coll., 1967; JD, Dickinson Law Sch., 1970. Bar: Pa. 1971, D.C. 1978, U.S. Dist. Ct. (we. dist.) Pa. 1971, U.S. Dist. Ct. D.C. 1978, U.S. Supreme Ct. 1979. Exec. dir. Balt. City Bar Assn., 1981-84, Conn. Bar Assn., Rocky Hill, 1984-85, Md. State Bar Assn., Balt., 1985—. Exec. v.p. Pro Bono Resource Ctr., 1990—; asst. sec. treas. Md. Bar Found. Mem. Am. Soc. Assn. Execs. (mem. devel. com. 1995-97, legal sect. coun. 1997—), Legal Mut. Liability Soc. Md. (charter, bd. dirs. 1986—), Phila. Bar Assn. (dir. legal svcs. 1975-77), ABA (standing com. lawyer referral 1977-80, standing com. delivery of legal svcs. com. 1987-89, standing com. assn. com. 1992-96, standing com. on legal assts. 1996-99), DC Bar (dir. pub. svc. activities 1977-81), Nat. Assn. Bar Execs. (state del. 1987-89, treas. 1989-91, v.p. 1991, pres. elect 1992, pres. 1993, Bolton award for profl. excellence), Internat. Inst. Law Assn. Chief Execs. Office: Md State Bar Assn Inc 520 W Fayette St Baltimore MD 21201-1781

CARLING, FRANCIS, lawyer, mediator; b. N.Y.C., Nov. 2, 1945; s. James Andrew and Mary Amelia (Lorenzo) C.; m. Elisabeth Morse Kelley, Aug. 30, 1969 (div. Apr. 1979); 1 child, Duncan Campbell; m. Christina Ellen Black, Sept. 28, 1991 (div. Sept. 2000); children: Graham Black, Gillian Kirova. AB, Fordham U., 1967; JD, Yale U., 1970. Bar: Conn. 1970, U.S. Dist. Ct. Conn. 1971, N.Y. 1972, U.S. Dist. Ct. (so. and ea. dists.) N.Y. 1972, U.S. Ct. Appeals (2nd cir.) 1972, U.S. Supreme Ct. 1973, U.S. Dist. Ct. (no. dist.) Ohio 1978, U.S. Ct. Appeals (3d cir.) 1980, U.S. Dist. Ct. (we. dist.) N.Y. 1981, U.S. Ct. Appeals (6th cir.) 1986, U.S. Ct. Appeals (4th cir.) 1990. Staff atty. New Haven Legal Assistance Assn., 1970-72; assoc. Sullivan & Cromwell, N.Y.C., 1972-80, Winthrop, Stimson, Putnam & Roberts, N.Y.C., 1980-82, ptnr., 1982-97, Collazo Carling & Mish LLP, N.Y.C., 1997—. Author: Move Over: Students, Politics, Religion, 1969. Bd. dirs. Big Bros., Inc. N.Y., N.Y.C., 1974—, pres., 1993-95; v.p. Friends of Afghanistan, Inc., N.Y.C., 1985-90; bd. dirs. Vol. Cons. Group, Inc., N.Y.C., 1988-97. Mem. ABA, N.Y. State Bar Assn., Assn. Bar City N.Y., Union Club. Episcopalian. Avocation: music. General civil litigation, Labor (including EEOC, Fair Labor Standards Act, labor-management relations, NLRB, OSHA), Pension, profit-sharing, and employee benefits. Home: 205 E 69th St New York NY 10021-5431 Office: Collazo Carling & Mish LLP 747 3rd Ave New York NY 10017-2803 E-mail: fcarling@ccmlaw.com.

CARLISLE, DALE L. lawyer; b. Walla Walla, Wash., Apr. 24, 1935; BA, U. Idaho, 1957; JD, George Washington U. School of Law, 1960. Judge advocate USAF, 1960—63; asst. U.S. atty. Wash. State (western dist.), 1964—66; with Gordon, Thomas, Honeywell, Malanca, Peterson & Daheim PLLC, Tacoma, 1966—; gen. counsel Levitt West, Inc., 1970—73; mng. ptnr. Gordon, Thomas, Honeywell, Malanca, Peterson & Daheim PLLC, Tacoma, 1990—2000, of counsel. Mem.: Wash. State Bar Assn. (pres.-elect 2000—01, pres. 2001—02, bd. govs. 1999—2002). Securities. Address: 1201 Pacific Ave Ste 2200 Tacoma WA 98402-4314 Mailing: PO Box 1157 Tacoma WA 98402*

CARLOTTI, STEPHEN JON, lawyer; b. Providence, Apr. 28, 1942; s. Albert Edward and Rose C.; m. Nancy Ann Arnold, Sept. 16, 1961; children: Stephen J., Cristina C. AB, Dartmouth Coll., 1963; LLB, Yale U., 1966. Bar: R.I. 1966, U.S. Ct. Mil. Appeals 1967, U.S. Ct. Appeals (9th cir.) 1969, U.S. Dist. Ct. R.I. 1970, U.S. Supreme Ct. 1972. Assoc. Hinckley, Allen, Salisbury & Parsons, Providence, 1966, 70-72; ptnr. Hinckley, Allen, & Snyder, Providence, 1972-89, 91, mng. ptnr., 1986-89, 92-96; with The Mut. Benefit Life Ins. Co., Newark, 1989-91. Chmn. Town Com., 1975-76; trustee Roger Williams U., 1978-93; chmn. Health Provider Svcs., R.I. Pub. Expenditures Coun. Capt. JAGC, U.S. Army, 1967-70. Mem. ABA, R.I. Bar Assn., R.I. Country Club, Univ. Club. Republican. Roman Catholic. Avocations: golf, sailing. Corporate, general, Property, real (including real estate development, water), Securities. Office: Hinckley Allen & Snyder 1500 Fleet Ctr Providence RI 02903-2319 E-mail: scarlotti@haslaw.com.

CARLSEN, HELLE, lawyer; b. Odense, Fyn, Denmark, Oct. 17, 1966; d. Erik and Rosa Marie Carlsen; m. Tonny Andersen (div. Mar. 2000); children: Karen Marie, Jens Peter, Valdemar. LLM, U. Aarhus, Denmark, 1991. Advocate Bech-Bruun Dragsted Advokatfirma, Aarhus, Denmark, 1992—. Contbr. articles to profl. jours. Mem. Assn. Lawyers and Asst. Lawyers (pres. 1997-98, bd. dirs. 1993-98), Danish Bar and Law Soc. (environ. law com. gen. coun. 1999—), Danish Assn. Environ. Law, Internat. Assn. Young Lawyers. Office: Bech-Bruun Dragsted Adv Frue Kirkeplads 4 8000 Aarhus C Jylland Denmark E-mail: helle.carlsen@bechbruundragsted.com.

CARLSON, ALAN DOUGLAS, lawyer; b. Omaha, May 24, 1951; s. John Peter and Elizabeth Jean (Pflasterer) C.; m. Sarah Louise Ware, June 28, 1975 (div. Mar., 1995); children: Elizabeth, Anne, Sally. AB, Augustana Coll., Rock Island, Ill., 1973; postgrad., Luth. Sch. Theology, 1974-75; JD, Creighton U., 1978. Bar: Nebr. 1978, U.S. Dist. Ct. Nebr. 1978, Colo. 1981, U.S. Dist. Ct. Colo. 1981, U.S. Ct. Appeals (10th cir.) 1989. Staff asst. govt. rels. Luth. Coun. USA, Washington, 1973-74; assoc. Holtorf, Kovarik & Nuttleman, Gering, Nebr., 1978-80; ptnr. Hopp, Carlson & Beckmann, Longmont, Colo., 1981-89, Ozer, Kiel, Trueax, Pribila & Kullman, P.C., Denver, Colorado Springs, Colo., 1989-91; Ozer and Carlson, Ft. Collins, Colo., 1990-91; pvt. practice Ft. Collins, Colo., 1991—99; ptnr. Carlson & Swanson, P.C., 1999—. Guest lectr. Trial Advocacy Program U. Colo. Sch. Law; adj. faculty Regis U., 1999--, Colo. Christian U., 2000--. Del. County Rep. Conv., Nebr. Rep. Conv., 1976, Colo. Rep. Conv., 1988; mem. subcom. social ministry Rocky Mountain Synod, Denver, 1984-88, adv. bd. Luth. Office Govt. Ministry, Denver, 1984-92; intern for U.S. Sen. Mark Hatfield, 1971; mem. Long Range Planning Bd. St. Vrain Sch. Dist. Mem. ATLA, Colo. Bar Assn., Colo. Trial Lawyers Assn. (speakers bur.), Alliance Def. Fund, Nat. Litigation Acad., Christian Legal Soc., Longmont C. of C. (vice chmn. govt. affairs com. 1988-89). Republican. Avocations: showing horses, tournament tennis. State civil litigation, Personal injury (including property damage), Workers' compensation.

CARLSON, DAVID BRET, lawyer; b. Jamestown, N.Y., Aug. 16, 1918; s. David Albert and Gertrude (Johnson) C.; m. Jane Tapley, Apr. 12, 1947; children: Christopher Tapley, David Kurt, Nancy Berners-Lee. AB, Brown U., 1940; LL.B., Harvard U., 1947. Bar: N.Y. 1947, U.S. Supreme Ct. 1972. Assoc. Debevoise & Plimpton, N.Y.C., 1947-53, ptnr., 1953-87. Contbr. articles to profl. publs. Mem. ABA, N.Y. State Bar Assn., Bar Assn. City of N.Y. Pension, profit-sharing, and employee benefits, Corporate taxation, Personal income taxation. Home: PO Box 32 275 W Falmouth Hwy West Falmouth MA 02574

CARLSON, GEORGE CLARENCE, JR., judge; b. Greenwood, Miss., May 23, 1946; s. George Clarence and Gusta Christine (Wooley) C.; m. Jane Ivy Russel, July 25, 1970; children George Russel, Meredith Christine. BS in History, Miss. State U., 1969; JD, U. Miss., 1972; grad., Nat. Judicial Coll. U. Nev., Reno, 1982. Bar: Miss. 1972, U.S. Dist. Ct. (no. dist.) Miss. 1972. Practiced law, Panola County, Miss., 1972-82; cir. ct. judge 17th Judicial Dist. Miss., Batesville, Miss., 1982—2001; justice magistrate Miss. Supreme Ct., 2001—. Sch. bd. atty. S. Panola Sch. Dist., 1972-82; state chmn. Miss. Sch. Bds. Assn. Coun. of Sch. Bd. Attys., 1980-81; mcpl. judge pro tem City of Batesville, 1979-82; atty. 2d ct. dist. Indsl. Devel. Authority, Panola County, 1980-82; mem. Govs'. Criminal Justice Task Force, 1991, Commn. on the Cts. in the 21st Century, 1992-93. Elected del. precinct, county, congressional dist. caucuses and to state Dem. conv., 1976; elected judge cir. ct. 1982, re-elected 1989, 90, 94, 98. Named Boss of Yr. Panola County Legal Secs. Assn., 1981; elected King Batesville Jr. Aux. Charity Ball, 1985. Fellow Miss. Bar Found.; mem. ABA, Miss. Bar Assn. (bd. dirs. young lawyers divsn. 1975-78), Panola County Bar Assn. (pres. 1975-76), Am. Judges Assn., William C. Keady Am. Inns of Ct. (past pres.). Presbyterian. Avocations: golf, skiing. Office: Miss Supreme Ct PO Box 779 Batesville MS 38606-0779

CARLSON, JON GORDON, lawyer; b. Wakefield, Mich., June 25, 1943; s. John Edwin and Irene Anne (Erickson) C.; m. Jane McCann, June 17, 1965; children: Christine, Eric, Susan. BA, U. Ill., 1965, JD, 1967. Bar: Ill. 1967, Mo. 1990. Assoc. Edward F. O'Malley, East St. Louis, Ill., 1967-68, Kassly, Weihl & Bone, Belleville, Ill., 1968-70; ptnr. Kassly, Weihl, Bone, Becker & Carlson, Belleville, 1970-78, Chapman & Carlson, Ill., 1978-84, Talbert, Carlson & Mallon, Ill., 1985-86, Carlson & Alfeld, Edwardsville, Ill., 1986-87; prin. Jon G. Carlson & Assocs., P.C., Edwardsville, Ill., 1987-94, Carlson, Wendler & Assocs., P.C., Edwardsville, Ill., 1994-99, St. Louis, 1996-99, Carlson & Carlson, P.C., 1999—. Fellow Am. Bar Found.; mem. Ill. Trial Lawyers Assn. (pres. 1987-88), Mo. Trial Lawyers Assn. Trial Lawyers Am., Ill. Bar Assn., Mo. Bar Assn. Democrat. Avocations: flying (multi-engine instrument rated pilot), walking, hiking. Labor (including EEOC, Fair Labor Standards Act, labor-management relations, NLRB, OSHA), Personal injury (including property damage), Product liability. Office: 90 Edwardsville Profl Park PO Box 527 Edwardsville IL 62025-0527

CARLSON, KATHLEEN BUSSART, law librarian; b. Charlotte, N.C., June 25, 1956; d. Dean Allyn and Joan (Parlette) Bussart; m. Gerald Mark Carlson, Aug. 15, 1987. BA in Polit. Sci., Ohio State U., 1977; JD, Capital U., 1980; MA in Libr. and Info. Sci., U. Iowa, 1986. Bar: Ohio 1980 (inactive). Editor Lawyers Coop. Pub. Co., Rochester, N.Y., 1980-83; asst. state law libr. State of Wyo., Cheyenne, 1987-88, state law libr., 1988—. Mem. Bd. Adjustment, City of Cheyenne, 2001--; 2d v.p., bd. dirs. Wyo. coun. Girl Scouts U.S., Casper, 1990-92, 1st v.p., bd. dirs., 1993-96. Mem. Am. Assn. Law Librs. (sec.-treas., State Ct. and County Law Librs. nat. exec. bd. 2003-2006 spl. interest sect.1992-95, edn. com. 1991-92, chair grants com. 1997-98 spl interest sect., nominating com. 1998-99 spl. interest sect., indexing legal periodical lit. adv. com. 1993-96, chair 1994-96, scholarship com. 1996-98, citation format com. 1998-2000, 2002--, co-chair State, Court and Co. Librs. membership com. 2000-01, chair edn. com. 2000-01, mem. fair bus. practices com. 2000-02), Western Pacific Assn. Law Librs. (pres. 1996-97, 2003-04), Wyo. Libr. Assn. (sec. acad. and spl. librs. sect. 1990-92, pres. 1994-95), Bibliog. Ctr. for Rsch. (trustee 1991-95), Zonta (pres. local club 2002--), Kappa Delta, Beta Phi Mu. Avocations: arts and crafts, baking, travel. Home: 911 E 18th St Cheyenne WY 82001-4722 Office: State Law Libr 2301 Capitol Ave Cheyenne WY 82002-0001 E-mail: kcarls@state.wy.us.

CARLSON, RAYMOND HOWARD, retired naval officer, prosecutor; b. Evergreen Park, Ill., June 19, 1951; s. Howard E. and Elizabeth J. (Lee) C. BSChE, Purdue U., 1973; JD summa cum laude, Ind. U., 1981; LLM, U. Va., 1988; MA in Nat. Security and Strategy, USN War Coll., 1997. Bar: Ind. 1981, Fla. 1993. Commd. ensign USN, 1973, advanced through grades to comdr., 1990; with Navy Legal Office, Seattle, 1981-84; Naval Sta., Rota, Spain, 1984-88; Navy Legal Office, Subic Bay, Philippines, 1988-91; prin. legal advisor to comdr. Naval Base, Jacksonville, Fla., 1991-95; prof. jt. mil. ops., internat. law Naval War Coll., Newport, R.I., 1995-97, Navy Legal Office, Mayport, Fla., 1997-2000; asst. state atty. Duval County Courthouse, Jacksonville, Fla., 2000—. Mem. Fed. Bar Assn., Judge Advocates' Assn., Jacksonville Bar Assn. Office: State Attys Office Duval County Courthouse Jacksonville FL 32202-2484

CARLSON, ROBERT M. lawyer; b. Billings, Mont., May 8, 1954; BA with honors, U. Mont., 1976, JD, 1979. Bar: Mont. 1979. Assoc. Corette, Pohlman & Kebe, Butte, Mont. Mem.: ABA (bd. govs. 13th dist. 2001—, state bar del. 1999—2001), Mont. Def. Trial Lawyers, Silver Bow County Bar Assn., State Bar Mont. (pres. 1993—94). Product liability, Environmental, Insurance. Office: Corette Pohlman & Kebe PO Box 509 129 W Park St Butte MT 59703-0509*

CARLSON, RONALD LEE, lawyer, educator; b. Davenport, Iowa, Dec. 10, 1934; s. Arthur A. and Louise (Sehmann) C.; m. Mary Murphy, Apr. 10, 1965; children: Michael, Andrew. BA, Augustana Coll., 1956; JD (Clarion DeWitt Hardy law scholar), Northwestern U., 1959; LL.M. (E. Barrett Prettyman law scholar), Georgetown U., 1961. Bar: Ill. 1959, Iowa 1959, D.C. 1960, U.S. Supreme Ct. 1966. Mem. firm Betty, Neuman, McMahon, Hellstrom & Bittner, Davenport, Iowa, 1961-65; U.S. commr. So. Dist. Iowa, 1964-64; prof. law U. Iowa, Iowa City, 1965-73, Washington U., St. Louis, 1973-84; John Byrd Martin prof. law U. Ga., 1984-95, Fuller E. Callaway prof. law, 1995—. Vis. prof. Wayne State U., Detroit, 1974, Detroit, 1976—77, Detroit, 1979, U. Tex., 1978, St. Louis U., 1982—86, 1988, U. Iowa, 1986—87, 1996; cons. Legis. Com. Criminal Code Revision Iowa, 1969—73; lectr. Nat. Coll. State Judiciary, Reno, 1974, Nat. Coll. Dist. Attys., West Palm Beach, Fla., 1980, Chgo., 83, Inst. Cont. Legal Edn., Atlanta, 1990, 2000—02, Amelia Island, 2001, Nat. Pract. Inst., Kansas City, 1991, 93, 98, Omaha, 91, 96, 2001, Davenport, 00, Des Moines, 1991, Chgo., 91, San Francisco, 91, San Francisco, 96, St. Louis, 1992—93, St. Louis, 1997—98, St. Louis, 2000, Honolulu, 1992, 94, 96, 2001, New Orleans, 1992, 2001, 03, Seattle, 1992, Minn., 1992—97, 2001, 03, Boston, 1992, Houston, 92, Houston, 97, Cleve., 92, 97, 2001, Tampa, 1992, Miami, 92, San Diego, 93, L.A., 93, Phoenix, 93, 96, Detroit, 93, Portland, 93, Denver, 93, 95, Washington, 93, 97, Little Rock, 93, 97, 98, Newark, 94, Richmond, 94, Atlanta, 94, 95, 97, N.Y.C., 94, Birmingham, 95, Oklahoma City, 95, Nashville, 95, 2001, Salt Lake City, 1995, Charlotte, 98, Phila., 98, 2002, Las Vegas, 1998, Hartford, 2000, Columbus, 2000—02, Raleigh, 2001, Providence, 02; moderator Robert Vance Forum on The Bill of Rights, 1990—96, 2002—03; lectr. in field. Author (with M. Ladd): Cases on Evidence, 1972; author: (with J. Yeager) Criminal Law and Procedure, 1979; author: Criminal Law Advocacy, 1982, Successful Techniques for Civil Trials, 1983, rev. edit., 1992, Adjudication of Criminal Justice, 1986; author: (with M. Bright) Maine Objections at Trial, 1991, New Hampshire Objections at Trial, 1992, Oregon Objections at Trial, 1992; author: (with A. Montgomery and M. Bright) Minnesota Objections at Trial, 1992; author: (with R. Aronson and M. Bright) Washington Objections at Trial, 1992; author: Pocket Proof of Facts, 1993, Trial Handbook for Georgia Lawyers, 1993; author: (with J. Young, K. Curtis, and M. Bright) Virginia Objections at Trial, 1998; author: Criminal Justice Procedure, 1999; author: (with E. Imwinkelried, E. Kionka and K. Strachan) Evidence Teaching Materials for an Age of Science and Statues, 2002; author: (with M. Bright and E. Imwinkelried) Objections at Trial: A Concise Guide, 2002; author: (with E. Imwinkelried) Dynamics of Trial Practice: Problems and Materials, 2002. V.p. alumni bd. Augustana Coll., Rock Island, Ill., 1968. Recipient Roscoe Pound Found. Jacobson award, ATLA, 1987, Harrison Tweed award, Ali-Baba, 2000. Mem.: ABA, Fed. Ins. and Corp. Counsel, Am. Inns. of Ct., Fed. Practice Inst. (dir. 1980—83, dean 1985—89), Iowa Bar Assn., Fed. Bar Assn. (chmn. law sch. divsn. 1978—79, nat. coun. 1994—95, Earl W. Kintner award for disting. svc. 1992), Am. Assn. Law Schs. Republican. Home: 283 Skyline Pkwy Athens GA 30606-3842 Office: U Ga School of Law Sch of Law Athens GA 30602 E-mail: mlfield@arches.uga.edu.

CARLSON, THOMAS JOSEPH, real estate developer, lawyer, mayor; b. St. Paul, Jan. 12, 1953; s. Delbert George and Shirley Lorraine (Willardson) C.; m. Chandler Elizabeth Campbell, July 15, 1973; 1 child, Thomas Chandler. BA, George Washington U., 1975; JD, U. Mo., Kansas City, 1979. Reporter Springfield (Mo.) News-Leader, 1975-76; editor Buffalo (Mo.) Reflex, 1976-77; assoc. Woolsey Fisher, Springfield, 1980-83; pvt. practice law Springfield, 1983-86; ptnr. Carlson & Clark, 1986-93, Carmichael, Carlson, Gardner & Clark, Springfield, 1993-94; mayor City of Springfield, 1987-93, 2001—; U.S. Bankruptcy trustee Springfield, 1982-98; pvt. practice, 1994-98. CEO, Resorts Mgmt., Inc., 1995—; bd. dirs. ITEC Attractions, Inc., Great So. Bancorp; lectr. in field. Contbr. articles to profl. jours. Mem. Springfield City Coun., 1983-87, 97—, Airport Bd. Springfield, 1994-97; chmn. Springfield-Branson Leadership Com., 1993—; bd. dirs. Mo. Cmty. Devel. Corp. Iniative, Mo. Commn. on Intergovernmental Cooperation; mem. bd. govs. S.W. Mo. State U., 2003—. Mem. Mo. Bar Assn. (Disting. Young Lawyer award 1989). Presbyterian. Bankruptcy, Commercial, contracts (including sales of goods; commercial financing). Office: 205 W Walnut Ste 200 Springfield MO 65806-2115

CARLTON, ALFRED PERSHING, JR., lawyer; b. Raleigh, N.C., Aug. 27, 1947; s. Alfred P. and Katherine (Singleton) C.; m. Blair Creech Carlton, Apr. 21, 2001; children: Mary Elizabeth, Troy Eugene. BSBA, U. N.C., 1969, JD, 1975; MPA, U. Dayton, 1973. Bar: N.C. 1975, U.S. Dist. Ct. (ea. dist.) N.C. 1975, U.S. Ct. Appeals (4th cir.) 1976, U.S. Supreme Ct. 1993. Pvt. practice, Raleigh, 1975-77; counsel N.C. Bankers Assn., Raleigh, 1977-79; sec., gen. counsel Bancshares N.C., Inc., Raleigh, 1979-82; adj. prof. law Campbell U., Buies Creek, N.C., 1979-82; ptnr. Sanford, Adams, McCullough & Beard, Raleigh, 1983-89; shareholder McNair & Sanford, Raleigh, 1990-95; ptnr. The Sanford Holshouser Law Firm, Raleigh, 1995—2001, Kilpatrick Stockton LLP, 2002—. Founding chmn. State Law Resources Inc., 1999—. Active City of Raleigh Hist. Properties and Hist. Dists. Commn., 1978-82; exec. bd. Occoneechee coun. Boy Scouts Am., 1983-94; trustee U. N.C. at Wilmington, 1997—; mem. Chief Justice's Commn. on Professionalism, 1998-2001. 1st lt. Med. Svc. Corps, USAF, 1970-73. Fellow Am. Bar Found.; mem. ABA (ho. of dels. 1987—, chmn. of the house 1996-98, bd. govs. 1996-98, chmn. standing com. on jud. independence 1998-2001, pres.-elect 2001—02, pres. 2002—), N.C. Bar Assn. (bd. govs. 1981-82, 92-95), Am. Law Inst., N.C. Legis. Rsch. Commn. (study com. on pub. financing 1985-88). Democrat. Episcopalian. Avocations: tennis, gardening. Banking, Municipal (including bonds), Securities. Office: Kilpatrick Stockton LLP 3737 Glenwood Ave Ste 400 Raleigh NC 27612 E-mail: acarlton@kilpatrick.com.

CARLTON, DIANE MICHELE, lawyer; b. L.A., Sept. 26, 1950; d. Thomas Neal and Fanny Jean (Crawford) Moon; m. Gregory Carlton, Sept. 12, 1969; children: Brendan, Dylan. BA in Spanish and Criminal Justice, U. Calif., Irvine, 1972; JD, U. Denver, 1976. Bar: Colo. 1977, U.S. Dist. Ct. Colo. 1977, U.S. Ct. Appeals (10th cir.) 1977. Pub. defender State of Colo., Denver, 1978—82; ptnr. Carlton & Jacobi, Denver, 1983—89; pvt. practice law Englewood, Colo., 1989—97; ptnr. Gutterman, Carlton & Heckenbach, 1997—2002, Heckenbach Carlton LLP, Lone Tree, Colo., 2002—. Judge City of Aurora, Colo., 1983-90. Fellow Am. Acad. Matrimonial Lawyers (Colo. pres. 2001); mem. ABA, Colo. Bar Assn., Arapahoe Bar Assn. (pres. 1997-98), Douglas/Elbert Bar Assn., Colo. Criminal Def. Bar Assn. Democrat. Avocations: reading, hiking, gardening, skiing. Criminal, Family and matrimonial, Personal injury (including property damage). Home: 14063 E Fair Ave Centennial CO 80111-6008 E-mail: dcarlton@familylawcolorado.com.

CARLUCCI, JOSEPH P. lawyer; b. Port Chester, N.Y., Aug. 21, 1942; m. Elizabeth Smith; children: Susan Elizabeth, Kathleen Ann. B.S, in Econs., Georgetown U., 1964; JD, Fordham U., 1967. Bar: N.Y. 1969. Ptnr. Pierro

& Carlucci, Port Chester, N.Y., 1969-76; pvt. practice, Rye, N.Y., 1977-78; mng. ptnr. Cuddy & Feder & Worby LLP, White Plains, N.Y., 1979-99. Chief legis. counsel to N.Y. senator from Westchester County, 1971-73; chief counsel N.Y. State Select Com. on State's Economy, 1973-74. Co-founder, v.p. Rye Town-Port Chester Rep. Club, 1972; trustee Village of Port Chester, 1974-77; chmn. Port Chester Indsl. Devel. Agy., 1974-76; mem. Westchester County Econ. Devel. Coun., 1976-80, Narcotics Guidance Coun. Port Chester, 1970-74; chmn. Met. N.Y. YMCA Key Leaders Conf., 1984; mem. Parent's Coun., Wheaton Coll., 1986-87; bd. dirs. Port Chester YMCA, 1970-79, sec., 1972-77, v.p., 1978; mem. Port Chester Govt. Study Commn., 1971-73; commr. appraisal White Plains and Greenburgh Urban Renewal; counsel to South Shore Hotline, 1973-74; mem. Port Chester Pub. Employees Rels. Bd., 1973-77; mem. adv. bd. bd. dirs. Salvation Army, 1973-77; mem. adv. bd. Security Title and Guaranty Co., 1986-90; bd. dirs. Rye YMCA, 1979-87, pres., 1982-85, trustee, 1989—; trustee Rye Hist. Soc., 1979-83, 90-96, sec., 1980-81, v.p., 1982-83, 92-94, pres., 1994-96; interviewer alumni admissions program Georgetown U., 1988-96; bd. visitors Pace U. Sch. Law, 1990—; bd. dirs. Vol. Ctr. United Way Westchester County, 1991-97; mem. Westchester divsn. Cardinal's Com. for Laity, 1991-2001, vice chmn., 1992, chmn., 1993-95; mem. paralegal curriculum adv. com. SUNY-Westchester C.C., 1994; bd. dirs. March of Dimes Birth Defects Found., 1994-96, Westchester Bus. Partnership, 1995-98, Westchester Partnership for Econ. Devel., 1996-97, Jacob Burns Film Ctr., Ind., 2000—; trustee Westchester Arts Coun., 2000—, Mercy Coll., 2002—. Recipient Golden R award Rennaissance Project, Inc., Gold Man award YMCA, 1985, Cmty. Svc. award Rotary Internat. Club, 1995. Mem. ABA (vice chmn. econs. of law practice com. on lawyering skills 1984-85), N.Y. State Bar Assn., Westchester County Bar Assn. (real property com. 1978-82), Port Chester-Rye Bar Assn. (sec. 1970-75, pres. 1976-77, bd. dirs. student assistance svcs. alcohol and drug abuse prevention program 1989-95, adv. bd. 1995—), Westchester C.C. Found. (bd. dirs. 1997—), Real Estate Fin. Assn. (bd. dirs. 2000—), Coveleigh Club (bd. govs. 1978-86, sec. 1979, v.p. 1980, pres. 1981-84), Georgetown U. Met. Club (bd. dirs. 1980-82), Hundred Club Westchester (bd. dirs.). Corporate, general, Probate (including wills, trusts), Property, real (including real estate development, water). Office: Cuddy & Feder LLP 90 Maple Ave White Plains NY 10601

CARLUCCI, PAUL PASQUALE, lawyer; b. N.Y.C., Sept. 26, 1949; s. Nicholas Carlucci and Anastasia Di Vincenzo; m. Marie A. McNamee, Aug. 18, 1973; children: Christine Marie Anastasia, Patricia Ann Rebecca. BS, Fordham U., 1971, JD, 1974. Bar: N.Y. 1975, Fla. 1999, U.S. Dist. Ct. (so. and ea. dists.) N.Y. 1975, U.S. Supreme Ct. 1982. Staff atty. Legal Aid Soc., N.Y.C., 1975; atty. of record Liberty Mutual Ins., Scarsdale, N.Y., 1975-88; atty. Belkin, Natale & Oxman, Hawthorne, N.Y., 1988-90; prin. law sec. Hon. Harold L. Wood N.Y. State Supreme Ct., White Plains, 1990-95; mng. atty. Nat. Grange Mutual Ins. Co., N.Y.C., 1995-99; sr. atty. Ct. Appeals for 2d Dist. Fla., Tampa, 2001; atty. Santos, Dutton, Lynott & Henry, PA, Tampa, 2001—02; program atty. Guardian ad Litem Program, 2003—. Contbr. articles to profl. jours. Chmn. Cons. Bd., New Castle, N.Y., 1987-88, Environ. Rev. Bd., New Castle, 1988-90; councilman Town Bd., New Castle, 1990-95. Regents scholar, Nat. Merit scholar. Mem. N.Y. State Bar Assn. (civil practice com., surrogate decision making com.). Avocations: legal writing, camping, reading, volunteer work. Home: 3916 Appletree Dr Valrico FL 33594-4315 Office: 801 E Kennedy Blvd Tampa FL 33602

CARMACK, MILDRED JEAN, retired lawyer; b. Folsom, Calif., Sept. 3, 1938; d. Kermit Leroy Brown and Elsie Imogene (Johnston) Walker; m. Allan W. Carmack, 1957 (div. 1979); 1 child, Kerry Jean Carmack Garrett. Student, Linfield Coll., 1955-58; BA, U. Oreg., 1967, JD, 1969. Bar: Oreg. 1969, U.S. Dist. Ct. Oreg. 1980, U.S. Ct. Appeals (9th and fed. cirs.) 1980, U.S. Claims Ct. 1987. Law clk. to Hon. William McAllister Oreg. Supreme Ct., Salem, 1969-73, asst. to ct., 1976-80; asst. prof. U. Oreg. Law Sch., Eugene, 1973-76; assoc. Schwabe, Williamson & Wyatt, Portland, Oreg., 1980-83, ptnr., 1984-96, ret., 1996. Writer, lectr., legal educator, Oreg., 1969—; mem. exec. bd. Appellate sect. Oreg. State Bar, 1993-95. Contbr. articles to Oreg. Law Rev., 1967-70. Mem. citizen adv. com. State Coastal Planning Commn., Oreg., 1974-76, State Senate Judiciary Com., Oreg., 1984; mem. bd. visitors Law Sch. U. Oreg., 1992-95; mem. Oreg. Law Commn. Working Group on Conflict of Laws, 2000. Mem. Oreg. State Bar Assn., Order of Coif. General civil litigation, Personal injury (including property damage), Product liability.

CARMAN, ERNEST DAY, lawyer; b. Mpls. s. Ernest Clarke and Juanita Howland (Day) C.; children Eric, Brooke (dec.), Christiane, Dayna. BA, U. So. Calif.; MA, Stanford U.; Dr. ès Sci. Pol., U. Geneva, Switzerland; JD, U. San Franicsco. Bar: Calif. 1957, U.S. Supreme Ct. 1973. Ptnr. Adams, Carman, Mansfield, Ball and Wenzel, 1959-65, Carman and Mansfield, 1965-70. Judge protem Santa Clara County Superior Ct., Orange County Superior Ct.; dir. various corps. Contbr. articles to profl. jours. Past chmn. Santa Clara County Dem. Cen. Com. Maj. USMCR. Mem. ABA, Calif. Employment Lawyers Assn. Civil rights, General civil litigation, General practice. Office: 1 Corporate Plaza Dr Ste 110 Newport Beach CA 92660-7924 E-mail: eday99@earthlink.net.

CARMICHAEL, CARSON, III, lawyer; b. Abingdon, Va., Sept. 29, 1954; s. Carson Jr. and Frances Rosemary (Clarkston) C.; m. Deborah Nell Murray, May 19, 1984; children: Neil McCall, Davis Alexander. BSChemE, BS in Pulp, Paper Sci. and Tech., N.C. State U., 1976; JD, Wake Forest U., 1980. Bar: N.C. 1981, U.S. Dist. Ct. (ea. dist.) N.C. 1981, U.S. Ct. Appeals (4th cir.) 1981, U.S. Dist. Ct. (mid. dist.) N.C. 1989. Project engr. Fed. Paper Bd., Riegelwood, N.C., 1977; assoc. Bailey & Dixon, Raleigh, N.C., 1981-85, ptnr., 1985—. Mem. legal com. Gov.'s Waste Mgmt. Bd., Raleigh, 1986-88 Mem. ABA, N.C. Bar Assn. (environ. law sect. 1984—, constrn. law sect. 1988—, chair 1999-2000, adminstrv. law sect. 1990—), Wake County Bar Assn., N.C. Soc. Healthcare Attys., Am. Soc. Pharmacy Law. Democrat. Methodist. Administrative and regulatory, Environmental, Utilities, public. Office: Bailey & Dixon 2 Hannover Square PO Box 1351 Raleigh NC 27602-1351

CARMO, LIE UEMA DO, lawyer; d. Leao Neto do Carmo and Kei Uema. LLB, Pontificia Universidade Catolica de Sao Paulo, Sao Paulo, SP Brazil, 1994—98; LLM, U. of Chgo., 2002—03, Pontificia Universidade Catolica de Sao Paulo, 2001—. Bar: Brazil 1999. Ptnr. Lilla, Huck, Malheiros, Otranto, Ribeiro, Camargo e Messina Advogados, Sao Paulo, 1999—. Bd. of directors mem. Lilla, Huck, Malheiros, Otranto, Ribeiro, Camargo e Messina Advogados, 2001—02. Constitution. Mergers and acquisitions, Securities, Corporate, general. Office: Lilla Huck Malheiros Otranto Ribeiro Av Brig Faria Lima 1744 - 6th floor Sao Paulo São Paulo 01451-010 Brazil Office Fax: 55 11 3038-1103. E-mail: lie@lhm.com.br.

CARMODY, JAMES ALBERT, lawyer; b. St. Louis, Nov. 21, 1945; m. Helen Tippy Valin, mar. 22, 1969; children: Paul Valin, Leigh Christin. BA, Vanderbilt U., 1967; JD, U. Ark., 1973. Bar: Tex. 1974, U.S. Dist. Ct. (so. dist.) Tex. 1974, U.S. Ct. Appeals (5th and 10th cirs.) 1975, U.S. Supreme Ct., 1996. Assoc. Mabry & Gunn, Texas City, Tex., 1974-75; mcpl. ct. judge Texas City, Tex., 1975; assoc. Chamberlain & Hrdlicka, Houston, 1975-78, ptnr., 1978-89, Keck Mahin & Cate, Houston, 1989-94, Carmody & Yokubaitis, L.L.P., Houston, 1995-2000. Assoc. editor U. Ark. Law Rev., 1973. Incorporator, Gulf Coast Big Bros. and Sisters, Inc., Galveston County, Tex., 1975; mem. St. Maximillian Cath. Community Bldg. Com., Houston, 1985-88; mem. I CANN Uniform Dispute Resolution Policy Task Force, 2001—. Lt. USN, 1967-71. Mem. Nat. Arbitration Forum, Galveston County Jr. Bar Assn. (pres. 1975, Outstanding Young Lawyer award 1975), Houston Bar Assn. (arbitrator fee dispute com. 1997-99), Entrepreneurship Inst. Houston (chmn. 1991-94), Delta Theta Phi (master insp. 1983-85, dean Houston alumni senate 1988, bd. dirs. Found.). Republican. Roman Catholic. Avocations: ham radio, international travel. General civil litigation, Commercial, contracts (including sales of goods; commercial financing), Private international. Office: 6363 Woodway Ste 910 Houston TX 77057 E-mail: carmody@lawyer.com.

CARMODY, RICHARD PATRICK, lawyer; b. Chgo., June 2, 1942; s. Thomas Francis and Margaret (Tully) C.; m. Alison Pierce Cutter, Dec. 27, 1968; children: Elizabeth Carmody Gonzalez, Emily Pierce Carmody. BA, U. Ill., 1964; JD, Vanderbilt U., 1975. Bar: Ala. 1975, U.S. Dist. Ct. (no., mid. and so. dists.) Ala. 1975, U.S. Ct. Appeals (11th cir.) 1985, U.S. Supreme Ct. 1988. Assoc. Lange, Simpson, Robinson & Somerville, Birmingham, Ala., 1975-81, ptnr., 1981—2002; chmn. exec. com. Lange, Simpson Robinson & Somerville, Birmingham, Ala., 1987-93; ptnr. Adams and Reese/Lange Simpson LLP, Birmingham, 2003—. Mem. Am. Bankruptcy Inst., Washington, 1985—, co-chair ethics com. 1999—; bd. dirs. Am. Bd. Cert., 2000—, mem. exec. com., 2001—; bd. cert. Bus. Bankruptcy Am. Bd. of Cert. Bd. dirs. Birmingham coun. Campfire Boys and Girls Inc., 1978-90, pres., 1983-85; bd. dirs. Ala. region NCCJ, 1995—, state chair, 2000-02; bd. dirs. St. Vincent's Hosp. Foudn., 2002—; active Leadership Birmingham, 1998—. Fellow Am. Coll. Bankruptcy, 1999—. Mem. Ala. Bar Assn. (chmn. bankruptcy and comml. law sect. 1985, exec. com. 1986-93), Greystone Golf & Country Club, Kiwanis. Roman Catholic. Avocations: golf, sports. Banking, Bankruptcy, Commercial, contracts (including sales of goods; commercial financing). Office: Adams & Reese LLP 2100 3d Ave N Ste 1100 Birmingham AL 35203 Business E-Mail: richard.carmody@arlaw.com.

CARNAHAN, JOHN ANDERSON, lawyer; b. Cleve., May 8, 1930; s. Samuel Edwin and Penelope (Moulton) C.; m. Katherine A. Halter, June 14, 1958; children: Peter M., Allison E., Kristin A. BA, Duke U., 1953, JD, 1955. Bar: Ohio 1955. Pvt. practice, Columbus, Ohio, 1955-78; ptnr. Arter & Hadden, Columbus, 1978-99; in-house counsel The Excello Spity. Co., Cleve., 2000—. Lectr. Ohio Legal Ctr. Inst., 1969, 73-74. Editor Duke Law Jour., 1954-55; chmn. bd. editors Ohio Lawyer, 1986-91; contbr. articles to profl. jours. Chmn. UN Day, Columbus, 1960; pres. Capital City Young Republican Club, 1960; bd. dirs. Columbus Cancer Clinic, pres., 1978-81; bd. dirs. Columbus chpt. ARC, 1979-87; mem. governing bd. Hannah Neil Mission, Inc., 1974-78; chmn. Duke Alumni Admissions Adv. Com., 1965-79. Named one of Outstanding Young Men of Columbus, 1965. Fellow Am. Bar Found. (life, chmn. Ohio fellows 1988-95), Columbus Bar Found. (life); mem ABA (ho. of dels. 1984-95), Ohio State Bar Found. (trustee 1986-90), Nat. Conf. Bar Pres., Ohio State Bar Assn. (coun. of dels. 1965-67, exec. com. 1977-81, 82-85, pres.-elect 1982-83, pres. 1983-84, Ritter award for outstanding contbns. adminstrn. justice 1987), Columbus Bar Assn. (bd. govs. 1970-72, sec.-treas. 1974-75, pres. 1976-77, Professionalism award 1996), Kit Kat Club (past pres.). Presbyterian. Corporate, general, General practice, Probate (including wills, trusts). Home and Office: 767 S 5th St Columbus OH 43206-2145 E-mail: jac5830@aol.com.

CARNALL, GEORGE HURSEY, II, lawyer, business executive; b. Ft. Smith, Ark., Feb. 19, 1947; s. George and Kathleen (Browne) C.; m. Janet Spaulding, Aug. 28, 1971; children: Clayton Wilson, Abigail Browne, Kevin Joseph. BS in Econs. and Bus. Adminstrn., Millikin U., Decatur, Ill., 1969; JD, Vanderbilt U., 1974. Bar: Tenn. 1974, U.S. Dist. Ct. (we. dist.) Tenn. 1974. Assoc. Arnoult & May, Memphis, 1974-76, Watson Cox & Arnoult, Memphis, 1976-79; gen. counsel S.M.R. Enterprises, Memphis, 1980-82, pres., 1982-87; pres. internat. divsn. Fantastic Sam's Internat., Inc., Memphis, 1987-91; pres. LP Svcs., Inc., Memphis, 1992-97, Mid South FS, Inc., Olive Branch, Miss., 1997—, Carnall Franchise Group, Memphis, 1991—. Contbr. articles to legal jours., mags., newspapers. Bd. dirs. Teen Challenge, Memphis, 1982-87. Served with U.S. Army, 1969-71. Mem. ABA, Tenn. Bar Assn., Memphis Bar Assn., Shelby Bar Assn. Mem. Assembly of God Ch. Franchising. Home: 6155 Timber Oaks Dr Olive Branch MS 38654-6935 Office: Carnall Franchise Group 6155 Timber Oaks Olive Branch MS 38654

CARNEAL, GEORGE UPSHUR, lawyer; b. N.Y.C., May 31, 1935; AB, Princeton U., 1957; LLB, U. Va., 1961. Bar: Va. 1961, D.C. 1962. Law clk. to judge U.S. Ct. Appeals, D.C. Circuit, 1961-62; asso. firm Hogan & Hartson, Washington, 1962-68, partner, 1973—. Spl. asst. to sec. Dept. Transp., Washington, 1969-70; gen. counsel FAA, Washington, 1970-73; lectr. Georgetown U. Law Ctr., 1965-68; chmn. bd. trustees D.C. Bar Clients Security Trust Fund, 1973-78; gen. counsel Nat. Aeronautic Assn., 1984—. Decisions editor: Va. Law Rev, 1960-61; contbr. articles to legal jours. Bd. govs. Flight Safety Found., 1982-95; mem. exec. com. Princeton U. Alumni Coun., 1984-87; bd. dirs. Nat. Aviation Rsch. Inst., 2001—. Mem. ABA, Fed. Bar Assn., Raven Soc., Order of Coif. Clubs: Princeton (pres. 1984-86), Aero (pres. 1982) (Washington), Metropolitan, Chevy Chase. Aviation, Public international, Transportation. Office: Hogan & Hartson 555 13th St NW Washington DC 20004-1161 E-mail: gucarneal@hhlaw.com.

CARNES, JULIE ELIZABETH, judge; b. Atlanta, Oct. 31, 1950; m. Stephen S. Cowen. AB summa cum laude, U. Ga., 1972, JD magna cum laude, 1975. Bar: Ga. 1975. Law clk. to Hon. Lewis R. Morgan U.S. Ct. Appeals (5th cir.), 1975-77; spl. counsel U.S. Sentencing Commn., 1989, commr., 1990-96; asst. U.S. Atty. U.S. Dist. Ct. (no. dist.) Ga., Atlanta, 1978-90, judge, 1992—. Office: US Courthouse 75 Spring St SW Ste 2167 Atlanta GA 30303-3309

CARNEY, DEBORAH LEAH TURNER, lawyer; b. Great Bend, Kans., Aug. 19, 1952; d. Harold Lee and Elizabeth Lura Turner; m. Thomas J.T. Carney, Mar. 20, 1976; children: Amber Blythe, Sonia Briana, Ross Dillon. BA in Human Biology, Stanford U., 1974; JD, U. Denver, 1976. Bar: Kans. 1977, U.S. Dist. Ct. Kans. 1977, U.S. Ct. Appeals (10th cir.) 1982, Colo. 1984, U.S. Dist. Ct. Colo. 1984, U.S. Supreme Ct. 1989, U.S. Claims Ct. 1990. With Turner & Boisseau, Great Bend, 1976-84, of counsel, 1984-93; assoc. Lutz & Oliver, Arvada, Colo., 1984-85; prin. Deborah Turner Carney, P.C., Golden and Lakewood, Colo., 1985-92; shareholder Carney Law Office, Golden, Colo., 1992-95, owner, 1995—. Author (newsletter) Profl. Solutions, 1984, (chpt.) Courtroom Handbook, 1998; editor Apple Law newsletter, 1984-86; contbr. articles to profl. jours. Pres. Canyon Area Residents for the Environment (C.A.R.E.), 1998. Mem. Colo. Trial Lawyers Assn., 1st Jud. Dist. Bar Assn. (Colo.), Genesee Daytime Bookclub (co-chair 1997-98), Kiwanis (bd. dirs. Denver club 1988-90, trustee 1990-92, sec. 1992-93). Republican. Avocations: horses, dancing, computers. Federal civil litigation, State civil litigation, Personal injury (including property damage). Office: 21789 Cabrini Blvd Golden CO 80401-9488 E-mail: deb@carneylaw.net.

CARNEY, GERARD BARRY, lawyer; b. Brockton, Mass., Aug. 9, 1949; s. John T. and Helen G. (Butler) C.; m. Cynthia A. Jones, June 25, 1976; children: Brendan Gerard, Meredith Patricia. BS, Boston Coll., 1971; JD, Suffolk U., 1980. Bar: Mass. 1980, U.S. Ct. Appeals (1st cir.) 1980, U.S. Dist. Ct. R.I. 1981, U.S. Supreme Ct. 1984. Asst. dist. atty. Bristol County, Mass., 1980; ptnr. Ashcraft & Gerel, Boston and Washington, 1980-86, Wynn & Wynn P.C., Raynham, Mass., 1986-90, Hislop, Carney & Troupe, Boston, 1990-98, Carney & Troupe, Boston, 1999—. Fides patron Boston Coll. Alumni Assn., Chestnut Hill, Mass., 1991—. Mem. ATLA, ABA, Mass. Acad. Trial Attys. (co-chair worker's compensation sect. 1998—), Mass. Bar Assn., Sports Lawyers Assn. Avocations: outdoor sports, jogging, student pilot. Personal injury (including property damage), Sports, Workers' compensation. Office: Carney & Troupe 5th Fl 10 High St Ste 5 Boston MA 02110-1605 E-mail: carnlaw8949@aol.com.

CARNEY, T.J, lawyer; b. Denver, July 18, 1952; s. Thomas Joseph Carney and Patricia (Amack) Carney Calkins; m. Deborah Leah Turner, Mar. 20, 1976; children: Amber Blythe, Sonia Briana, Ross Dillon. BA in Econs., U. Notre Dame, Ind., 1974; JD, U. Denver, 1976. Bar: Colo. 1977, Kans. 1977, U.S. Dist. Ct. Colo. 1977, U.S. Dist. Ct. Kans. 1977, U.S. Dist. Ct. Ariz. 1995, U.S. Ct. Appeals (10th cir.) 1983. Legal asst. Turner & Hensley, Chartered, Great Bend, Kans., 1977; atty.-shareholder Turner and Boisseau, Chartered, Great Bend, 1977-84; atty., shareholder Bradley, Campbell, Carney & Madsen, Golden, Colo., 1984-92, 95-97; atty.-shareholder Deborah TJ Carney, P.C., Lakewood and Golden, 1992-95; atty. officer Carney Law Office, Golden, Colo., 1997-99; spl. counsel Oliver & Kirven, P.C., Arvada, Colo., 1999; atty., shareholder Oliver and Carney, P.C., Arvada, 1999—. CLE instr. Nat. Inst. Trial Advocacy, 1st Jud. Bar Assn., Colo. Inc., Rocky Mountain Child Advocacy Tng. Inst.; cons. Vocat. Econs., Inc., 1998, others. Precinct com. Rep. Party, Jefferson County, Colo., 1988-94, 2000—, area capt., 1994-96, 2002—; bd. dirs. Jefferson County Libr. Found., 1999—, pres., 2002-03; area vice-chmn. West Area sch. accountability com. Jefferson R-1 Pub. Schs., 1985-89, mem. fin. oversight com., 1987-88, textbook com., 1988-89; bd. dirs. Table Mountain Soccer Assn., 1985-92, treas., 1990-92. Mem. Colo. Bar Assn., Colo. Trial Lawyers Assn., Kansas Bar Assn., Kans. Trial Lawyers Assn., 1st Jud. Dist. Bar Assn. (trustee 1990-94), Phi Delta Phi (Province Grad. of Yr. 1977). Avocations: flying, martial arts, skiing, lacrosse, ballroom dancing. General civil litigation, Commercial, contracts (including sales of goods; commercial financing), Property, real (including real estate development, water). Office: Oliver and Carney PC 7903 Ralston Rd Arvada CO 80002-2435 Fax: 303-424-3629., 720-294-0480. E-mail: tjc@jeffcolawyers.net.

CAROME, PATRICK JOSEPH, lawyer; b. Cleve., Nov. 20, 1957; s. Edward Francis and Jeanne Marie (Carrabine) C.; m. Elsie Elizabeth Orr, Oct. 7, 1989. BA, Boston Coll., Chestnut Hill, Mass., 1980; JD, Harvard U., 1983. Bar: Mass. 1984, D.C. 1985, U.S. Dist. Ct. D.C. 1985, U.S. Ct. Appeals (D.C. cir.) 1987, U.S. Supreme Ct. 1988, U.S. Ct. Appeals (4th cir.) 1989, U.S. Ct. Appeals (9th cir.) 1993, U.S. Ct. Appeals (10th cir.) 1999. Law clk. to Judge Milton Pollack, U.S. Dist. Ct. for So. Dist. N.Y., N.Y.C., 1983-84; staff atty. Washington Post, 1984-86; staff counsel select com. to investigate covert arms trans. U.S. Ho. of Reps., Washington, 1987; assoc. Wilmer, Cutler & Pickering, Washington, 1986-87, 88-90, ptnr., 1991—. Mem. ABA (vice chmn. com. on govt. info. and right to privacy com. adminstrv. law sect. 1988-90, chmn. 1990-94). General civil litigation, Communications, Libel. Office: Wilmer Cutler & Pickering 2445 M St NW Ste 500 Washington DC 20037-1487

CARON, WILFRED RENE, retired lawyer; b. N.Y.C., July 23, 1931; s. Joseph Wilfred and Eva Caron; m. Anne Theresa Flanagan, AUg. 2, 1958. JD, St. John's U., 1956. Bar: N.Y. 1956, D.C. 1977, U.S. Dist. Ct. D.C. 1977, U.S. Dist. Ct. (no. dist.) N.Y. 1957, U.S. Dist. Ct. (so. and ea. dists.) N.Y. 1961, U.S. Ct. Appeals (2d cir.) 1965, U.S. Ct. Appeals (3d cir.) 1973, U.S. Ct. Appeals (5th cir.) 1977, U.S. Ct. Appeals (6th cir.) 1973, U.S. Ct. Appeals (8th cir.) 1975, U.S. Ct. Appeals (9th cir.) 1976, U.S. Ct. Appeals (D.C. cir.) 1975, U.S. Supreme Ct. 1961. Law clk. to chief judge N.Y. State Ct. Appeals, 1956-59; spl. asst. atty. gen. N.Y., 1959-60; assoc. Goldman & Drazen, 1960-64, Corner, Finn, Cuomo & Charles, N.Y.C., 1964-69; asst. gen. counsel Ronson Corp., Woodbridge, N.J., 1969-71; assoc. gen. counsel Securities Investor Protection Corp., Washington, 1972-80; gen. counsel U.S. Cath. Conf., Inc., Washington, 1980-87, Nat. Conf. Cath. Bishops, 1980-87, Cath. Telecom. Network Am., Inc., N.Y.C., 1981-88; ptnr. O'Connor & Hannan, Washington, 1987-88; sr. advisor Office of Policy Devel., U.S. Dept. of Justice, Washington, 1988-90; appellate counsel Travelers Ins. Co., 1990-92; ret., 1992. Contbr. articles to profl. jours. Adv. bd. St. Thomas More Inst. Legal Rsch., St. John's U. Sch. Law, N.Y.C., 1981-92; exec. bd. Ctr. for Ch.-State Studies, DePaul U. Law Coll., Chgo., 1982—. Served to 1st lt. U.S. Army, 1952-54, Korea. Mem.: ABA, D.C. Bar Assn., Am. Legion, VFW. Roman Catholic. Home: 44 Old Main Rd Little Compton RI 02837-1321

CARP, LARRY, lawyer; b. St. Louis, Jan. 26, 1926; s. Avery and Ruth C. Student, U. Mo., Columbia, 1944; cert., Sorbonne U., Paris, 1946; BA, Washington U., St. Louis, 1947; postgrad., Grad. Inst. Internat. Studies, Geneva, 1949; JD, Washington U., St. Louis, 1951. Bar: Mo. 1951, U.S. Dist. Ct. (ea. dist.) Mo. 1951. Mem. U.S. Dept. of State, Washington, 1951-53; mem. staff Senator Paul H. Douglas (Dem. Ill.), Washington, 1953-54; assoc. Fordyce, Mayne, Hartman, Renard, and Stribling, St. Louis, 1954-63; sole practice St. Louis, 1963-68; ptnr. Carp & Morris, St. Louis, 1968-90, Carp, Sexauer and Carr, St. Louis, 1990-94, Carp and Sexauer, St. Louis, 1994—. Assoc. counsel, acting chief counsel U.S. Senate Subcom. on Constitutional Rights, Washington, 1956; mem. St. Louis Regional U.S. Export Expansion Coun., 1964-74; mem. Mo. Commn. on Human Rights, 1966-78, vice chmn., 1977-78; vice chmn., bd. dirs. Pastoral Counselling Inst. for Greater St. Louis, 1964-91; mem. bd. trustees The Acad. Sci., St. Louis, 1984—, asst. treas., 1992-2003; mem. adv. bd. George Engelmann Math. and Science Inst., 1992-96; bd. dirs. St. Louis Ctr. for Internat. Rels., 1998—; legal advisor Image, Inc., St. Louis, 1998—; mem. cmty. adv. panel Double Helix (TV and Radio) Corp., 1999—. Co-author: (musicals) Pocahontas, The Pied Piper, Androcles; author: (musicals) For the Love of Adam, The Red Ribbon, Famous Last Words, GOD KNOWS!; contbr. articles to newspapers and mags. on subjects relating to immigration and nationality law. Mem. Common Cause, 1966-78, chmn. Mo. chpt., 1973-75; bd. dirs. Internat. Inst. of Metro St. Louis, 1980-86, English Speaking Union, St. Louis, 1985—, Mo. Prison Arts Program, 1999—; U.S. presdl. appointee as sr. adviser and U.S. pub. del. to UN 55th Gen. Assembly, 2000-2001. With U.S. Army, 1944-46, ETO. Decorated (2) Battle Stars; Rotary Internat. fellow Grad. Inst. Internat. Studies, Geneva, 1948-49; award for Outstanding Service in Recognition of Spl. Needs of Hispanic Community IMAGE, St. Louis, 1984; selected in immigration and naturalization law by his peers as one in Best Lawyers in Am., 1992— Fellow Am. Acad. Matrimonial Lawyers (cert.); mem. ABA (immigration law coord. com., chmn. immigration law com. gen. practice sect. 1981-86), Mo. Bar Assn., Bar Assn. Met. St. Louis (chmn. internat. law and trade com. 1973-79, chmn. immigration law com. 1989-92), Am. Immigration Lawyers Assn., St. Louis Ctr. for Internat. Rels. (bd. dirs. 1998—), UNA-USA Assn. (bd. dirs. St. Louis chpt. 1999—), Phi Delta Phi. Family and matrimonial, General practice, Immigration, naturalization, and customs. Office: Carp and Sexauer Notary Pub 225 S Meramec Ave Ste 325 Saint Louis MO 63105-3511 Fax: 314-727-0308. E-mail: candslaw@earthlink.net.

CARPENETI, WALTER L. judge; b. San Francisco, 1945; m. Anne Dose, 1969; children: Christian, Marianna, Lia, Bianca. AB in History with distinction, Stanford U., 1967; JD, U. Calif., Berkeley, 1970. Law clk. Justice John H. Dimond Alaska Supreme Ct., 1970-71; pvt. practice San Francisco, 1972-74; pub. defender Juneau, Alaska, 1974-78; pvt. practice, 1978-81; judge Alaska Superior Ct., Juneau, 1981-98, state supreme ct. justice, 1998—. Office: Alaska Supreme Ct PO Box 114100 Juneau AK 99811-4100

CARPENTER, CHARLES ELFORD, JR., lawyer; b. Greenville, S.C., Nov. 3, 1944; s. Charles Elford and Mary Charlotte (Campbell) C.; m. Nancy Townsend, June 8, 1968; children: Charlotte Elizabeth, John Morrison. BA, Furman U., 1966; JD, U. Va., 1969; MPA, U. S.C., 1976. Bar: Va. 1969, S.C. 1972, U.S. Dist. Ct. S.C. 1974, U.S. Ct. Appeals (4th cir.) 1978, U.S. Ct. Appeals (11th cir.) 1984, U.S. Supreme Ct. 1983. Assoc. Leatherwood, Walker, Todd & Mann, Greenville, 1969, Richardson, Plowden, Grier & Howser, Columbia, S.C., 1974-78; ptnr. Richardson, Plowden, Carpenter & Robinson, P.A., Columbia, S.C., 1978—. Mem. com. on grievances and discipline S.C. Supreme Ct., 1986-89, 1996; spkr. Law Seminars, Inc., Columbia, 1987, Outline for Post-Trial Practice, 1988, 89, 90; mem. S.C. Supreme Ct. Bd. Law Examiners, 1995-2001. Editor Appeal and Error, S.C. Jurisprudence; contbr. articles to legal jours. Mem. bd. visitors Presbyn. Coll., Clinton, S.C., 1983-87; trustee James H. Hammond Sch., Columbia, 1986-89, Trinity Presbytery; pres. A.C. Flora PTO; elder Eastminster Presbyn. Ch. Capt. U.S. Army, 1969-72. Fellow Am. Acad. Appellate Lawyers (bd. dirs.); mem. ABA (speaker appellate process program 1990, editor Appellate Practice Jour. 1989-2000, co-chair oral argument subcom. litigation sect., mem. task force on unreported opinions 1996—), S.C. Bar Assn. (mem. Richland County fee dispute com. 1984-88, speaker 1987, appellate practice, panel mem. proposed rules of appellate practicefor S.C. Bar ann. meeting 1989, mem. practice and procedure com., health and hosp. law subcom., appellate rules subcom., chmn. merit selection of judges subcom., alternative dispute resolution com. 1993—), Richland County Bar Assn., S.C. Def. Trial Attys. (chmn. amicus curiae com. 1981-85), Forest Lake Club, St. Andrews Soc., Tarantella Club, Columbia Ball Club, Torch Club (pres. 2000-01). Avocations: reading, hunting, tennis, fishing. Administrative and regulatory, General civil litigation, Insurance. Office: Richardson Plowden Carpenter & Robinson PA 1600 Marion St # 7788 Columbia SC 29201-2913

CARPENTER, CHARLES FRANCIS, lawyer; b. Raleigh, N.C., Apr. 3, 1957; s. William Lester and Mattie Frances (Wallace) C.; m. Heidi Ann Athanas, June 14, 1980. BA with honors, U. N.C., 1979, JD, 1982. Bar: N.C. 1982, U.S. Dist. Ct. (mid. dist.) N.C. 1982, U.S. Dist. Ct. (ea. dist.) N.C. 1986, U.S. Ct. Appeals (4th cir.) 1986, U.S. Dist. Ct. (we. dist.) N.C. 1988. Assoc. Newsom, Graham, Hedrick, Murray, Bryson & Kennon, Durham, N.C., 1982-87; ptnr. Newsom, Graham, Hedrick, Bryson & Kennon, Durham, 1988-93; pvt. practice Charles F. Carpenter, P.A., Durham, 1993-98; ptnr. Pulley, Watson, King & Lischer, PA, Durham, 1998—. Trustee N.C. Conf. United Meth. Ch., 1993-2002; mem. exec. bd. Occoneechee Coun. Boy Scouts Am., 1988—. Mem. ABA, N.C. State Bar, N.C. Bar Assn., Durham County Bar Assn. (medico-legal com. 1994-2002, bd. dirs. 1998—), Order of the Old Well, Honorable Order of Ky. Colonels, Phi Beta Kappa. Democrat. Avocations: Karate, golf, softball, jogging, skiing. Bankruptcy, General civil litigation, Commercial, consumer (including collections, credit). Home: 1325 Arnette Ave Durham NC 27707-1601 Office: 905 W Main St Ste 21 F Durham NC 27701-2076 E-mail: cfc@pwkl.com.

CARPENTER, CRAIG M. lawyer; b. Plymouth, Ind., Dec. 12, 1968; BS in Bus., Ind. U., 1991; JD, MBA, Ind. U., Indpls., 1995. Bar: Ind. 1995, U.S. Dist. Ct. (so. and no. dists.) Ind. 1995. Assoc. Kroger, Gardis & Regas, Indpls., 1995—96, Sommes & Barnard, PC, Indpls., 1996—2000; v.p. ops. and assoc. gen. counsel ProValent, Inc., Indpls., 2000; assoc. gen. counsel Brightpoint, Inc., Indpls., 2000—. Commercial, contracts (including sales of goods; commercial financing), Corporate, general, Mergers and acquisitions. Office: Brightpoint Inc 501 Airtech Pkwy Plainfield IN 46168

CARPENTER, EDMUND NELSON, II, retired lawyer; b. Phila., Jan. 27, 1921; s. Walter S. and Mary (Wootten) C.; m. Carroll Morgan, July 18, 1970; children: Mary W., Edmund Nelson III, Katherine R.R., Elizabeth Lea; stepchildren: John D. Gates, Ashley du Pont Gates. AB, Princeton U., 1943; LLB, Harvard U., 1948; LLD (hon.), Widener U., 1985, U. Del., 1999. Bar: Del. 1949, U.S. Supreme Ct. 1957. Assoc. Richards, Layton & Finger, Wilmington, Del., 1949-53, ptnr., 1953-78, dir., 1978-91, pres., 1982-85; retired, 1991. Dep. atty. gen. State of Del., 1953-54, spl. dep. atty., 1960-62; chmn. Del. Superior Ct. Jury Study Com., 1963-66, Del. Supreme Ct. Cts. Consol. Com., 1985-87; mem. Del. Gov.'s Commn. Law Enforcement and Adminstrn. Justice, 1969; chmn. Del. Supreme Ct. Adv. Com. on Profl. Fin. Accountability, 1974-75, Del. Jud. Nominating Commn., 1977-83, Del. Superior Ct. Study Com., 1991-92; mem. Long Range Cts. Planning Com., 1976-89, Del. Ct. Common Pleas Study Com., 1992, Del. Supreme Ct. Com. on Judicial Code of Conduct, 1991-93; co-chmn. Del. Justice Ctr. Com., 1994-97; mem. lawyers adv. com. U.S. Ct. Appeals (3d cir.) 1975-80, chmn., 1975-77; chmn. local rules com. U.S. Dist. Ct. Del., 1978-83, Del. Ct. on the Judiciary Rules Com., 1996-98; bd. dirs. Bank of Del., Barclay's Bank. Trustee Wilmington Med. Ctr., 1965—, U. Del., 1971-77, Princeton U., 1974-85, 86-91, Winterthur Mus., 1991-99, World Affairs Coun. Wilmington, 1968-80, Woodrow Wilson Found., 1985—, Lawrenceville Sch., 1953-74, trustee emeritus, 1974—; trustee Nat. Humanities Ctr., 1995-98; bd. dirs. Good Samaritan Inc., 1973—, pres., 1998—; mem. Del. Health Care Injury Ins. Study Commn., 1976-80. With U.S. Army, 1942-46, 50-52. Decorated Bronze Star, Soldier's medal, Chinese Order of the Flying Cloud with four battle stars; recipient 1st State Disting. Svc. award, Del. State Bar Assn., 1984, Josiah Marvel Cup award Del. State C. of C., 1990, Benjamin Franklin Disting. Pub. Svc. award Am. Philos. Soc., 1996. Fellow Am. Coll. Trial Lawyers, Am. Bar Found.; mem. ABA (ho. of dels. 1979-86), Del. State Bar Assn. (pres. 1971-72, Presdl. citation 1987), ATLA, Am. Judicature Soc. (bd. dirs. 1974-83, exec. com. 1978-80, v.p. 1980-81, pres. 1981-83, Justice award 1991). Federal civil litigation, State civil litigation, Corporate, general. Home and Office: 600 Center Mill Rd Wilmington DE 19807-1502 E-mail: Nedcarp@aol.com.

CARPENTER, KEVIN STARR, lawyer; b. Moorhead, Minn., Nov. 3, 1954; s. Roger Frank and Delores Fae (Starr) C.; m. Julianna Marshall Schupp, July 17, 1976; children: Clinton John Marshall, Anysia Starr, Ian Albert, Myrna Elizabeth, Raissa Riley, George Roger. BA, St. John's U., Collegeville, Minn., 1975; JD, St. Louis U., 1979. Bar: Minn. 1979, N.D. 1993, U.S. Dist. Ct. Minn. 1980, U.S. Ct. Appeals (8th cir.) 1999, Nat. Bd. Trial Advocacy 1995; cert. civil trial specialist Minn. State Bar Assn., 1994. Law clk. Minn. Dist. Ct., St. Cloud, 1979-80; assoc. Quinlivan, Sherwood, Spellacy & Tarvestad, P.A., St. Cloud, 1980-87, mem., 1987-97, Holmen & Carpenter, 1997-99; atty. pvt. practice, St. Cloud, Minn., 1999—. Panel mem. Am. Arbitration Assn., Mpls., 1987—. Trustee Stearns Benton County Law Libr., St. Cloud, 1980-84, Sts. Peter, Paul & Michael Sch., St. Cloud, 1986-92; mem. St. Peter Parish Coun., 1992-98. Mem. ABA, Am. Bd. of Trial Advocates, Minn. Bar Assn., Minn. Trial Lawyers Assn., Assn. Trial Lawyers of Am., Stearns-Benton County Bar Assn. Roman Catholic. Alternative dispute resolution, Personal injury (including property damage), Product liability. Office: 204 Midsota Ctr 3701 12th St N Saint Cloud MN 56303-2255

CARPENTER, NORMAN ROBLEE, retired lawyer; b. Cambridge, Mass., Aug. 26, 1932; s. Norman Roblee and Mary P. (Hannigan) C.; m. Janet (Gerhauser); children: Kevin D., Cynthia L., Kathryn Carpenter Nelson, Kim G. Powers, Jill Griffiths, Guy Griffiths. BA, Dartmouth Coll., 1953; JD, U. Mich., 1960. Bar: Minn. 1960. Assoc. Faegre & Benson, Mpls., 1960-67, ptnr., 1969-98; dep. atty. gen. State of Minn., St. Paul, 1967-69. Dir. Walter Judd Found., Mpls., 1963-70 Contbr. articles to profl. jours., short stories and poetry to lit. mags. Bd. regents Augsburg Coll., Mpls., 1970-82; chmn. bd. YMCA Camp Warren, Mpls., 1978-80, Charter Commn., City of St. Louis Park, Minn., 1965-67; trustee Plymouth Congl. Ch., Mpls., 1978-82; bd. dirs. Citizens League, Mpls., 1970-74, The Loft, 1994-2000; mem. Hennepin County Adv. Commn. on Chem. Dependency, 1977-79; vol. United Way, 1983-92. Capt. USMC, 1953-55. Mem. ABA, Minn. Bar Assn., Hennepin County Bar Assn., Dartmouth Coll. Alumni Coun., Minikahda Club. Republican. Antitrust, Federal civil litigation, Insurance. Home: 2223 Sherwood Ct Minnetonka MN 55305

CARPENTER, RANDLE BURT, lawyer; b. Raleigh, N.C., Oct. 19, 1939; s. Randle Burt and Adonis (Watson) C.; m. Suzanne Gronemeyer, Aug. 21, 1965; children: Randle III, Christine. BA in Internat. Rels., Duke U., 1962, LLB, 1965; LLM in Fgn. Law, NYU, 1969. Bar: N.Y. 1967, N.C. 1965, U.S. Supreme Ct., U.S. Ct. Appeals (2d cir.), U.S. Dist. Ct., U.S. Ct. Internat. Trade. Official asst. First Nat. City Bank, N.Y.C., 1965-67; with Exxon Internat. Inc., N.Y.C., 1967-68; gen. counsel Occidental Crude Sales Inc., N.Y.C., 1968-75; v.p. law Wesco Internat. Inc., N.Y.C., 1975-76; gen. counsel A. Johnson & Co., Inc., N.Y.C., 1976-81; ptnr. Davidson Dawson & Clark, N.Y.C., 1981-84, Schoeman, Marsh & Updike, N.Y.C., 1984-97, Jackson & Nash, N.Y.C., 1997—. Adj. prof. law Pace U., White Plains, N.Y., 1984—. Contbr. articles to profl. jours. Angier B. Duke scholar Duke U., 1958. Mem. Am. Arbitration Assn., Assn. of Bar of City of N.Y. (inter-Am. affairs com.), Maritime Law Assn., Church Club N.Y., Colonial Order of the Acorn (companion). Private international, Commercial, contracts (including sales of goods; commercial financing), Corporate, general. Home: 29 Hazel Ln Larchmont NY 10538-4007 Office: Jackson & Nash 330 Madison Ave Rm 1800 New York NY 10017-5001

CARPENTER, RICHARD NORRIS, lawyer; b. Cortland, N.Y., Feb. 14, 1937; s. Robert P. and Sylvia (Norris) C.; m. Elizabeth Bigbee, Aug. 1961 (div. June 1975); 1 child, Andrew Norris; m. Leslie Nordby, July, 1991. BA magna cum laude, Syracuse U., 1958; LLB, Yale U., 1962. Bar: N.Y. 1962, N.Mex. 1963, U.S. Dist. Ct. (no. dist.) N.Y., U.S. Dist. Ct. N.Mex., U.S. Ct. Appeals (D.C. and 10th cirs.), U.S. Supreme Ct. Assoc. Breed, Abbott & Morgan, N.Y.C., 1962-63, Bigbee Law Firm, Santa Fe, 1963-78; ptnr. Carpenter Law Firm, Santa Fe, 1978-2000, owner, 2000—02; bd. regents N.Mex. Inst. Mining and Tech., 2003—. Spl. asst. atty. gen., State of N.Mex., 1963-74, 90-96; sec. Bokum Corp., Miami, Fla., 1969-70; bd. dirs. N.Mex. Ednl. Assistance Found. Mem. adv. bd. Interstate Mining Compact, N.Mex., 1981-88; elder 1st Presbyn. Ch., Santa Fe, 1978-80, 86-89, trustee, 1975-77, pres., 1977; bd. dirs. Santa Fe Community Coun., 1965-67, St. Vincent Hosp. Found., Santa Fe, 1980-84; trustee Santa Fe Prep. Sch., 1981-84, pres., 1982-84; trustee St. Vincent Hosp., 1980-86, 87-2001, chmn. 1985-86, 90-93, 98-2000; bd. dirs. Santa Fe YMCA, 1964-69, pres., 1969; trustee Santa Fe Prep. Permanent Endowment Fund., 1987-90; bd. dirs., treas. Con Alma Health Found., 2002—; bd. regents N.Mex. Inst. Mining and Tech., 2003—; bd. dirs. N.Mex. Edn. Assistance Found., 2003—. Rotary Found. fellow, Panjab U., Pakistan, 1959-60. Mem. N.Mex. Bar Assn., N.Y. State Bar Assn., The Best Lawyers of Am., Phi Beta Kappa, Pi Sigma Alpha, Phi Beta Phi. Legislative, Natural resources, Utilities, public. Home and Office: 1048 Bishops Lodge Rd Santa Fe NM 87501-1009 E-mail: rncarpenter@aol.com.

CARPENTER, ROBERT BRENT, lawyer; b. Newton, Mass., Feb. 9, 1949; s. Edward N. and Charlotte F. (Grant) C.; m. L. Deborah Gorchov, Mar. 25, 1978; children: Stephen Michael, Matthew Jeremy, Meredith Anne. AB, Bowdoin Coll., 1971; JD, Boston Coll., 1975; LLM, Temple U., 1977. Bar: Mass. 1975, U.S. Dist. Ct. Mass. 1977, U.S. Ct. Appeals (1st cir.) 1977, U.S. Supreme Ct. 1980, U.S. Ct. Appeals (fed. cir.) 2000. Teaching fellow, lectr. Temple U., Phila., 1975-77; shareholder, dir. Goldstein & Manello, P.C., Boston, 1977-99; ptnr. Schnader, Harrison, Goldstein & Manello, 2000—03, Seyfarth Shaw, 2003—. Contbr. articles to profl. jours. Mem. ABA, Mass. Bar Assn., Boston Bar Assn. Federal civil litigation, General civil litigation, State civil litigation. Home: 1 Commonwealth Park Wellesley MA 02481-3213 Office: Seyfarth Shaw World Trade Ctr Two Seaport Lane ste 300 Boston MA 02210 E-mail: rcarpenter@seyfarth.com.

CARPENTER, RUSSELL H., JR., lawyer; b. Providence, May 17, 1941; AB, Princeton U., 1963; BPhil in Politics, Oxford U., Eng., 1965; LLB, Yale U., 1968. Bar: D.C. 1968. Law clk. to Hon. David Bazelon U.S. Ct. Appeals (D.C. cir.), 1968-69; mem. Covington & Burling, Washington. Contbr. articles to profl. jours. Mem. Order Coif. Federal civil litigation, Insurance, Private international. Office: Covington & Burling PO Box 7566 1201 Pennsylvania Ave NW Washington DC 20004-2401 E-mail: rcarpenter@cov.com.

CARPENTER, SUSAN KAREN, defender; b. New Orleans, May 6, 1951; d. Donald Jack and Elise Ann (Diehl) C. BA magna cum laude with honors in English, Smith Coll., 1973; JD, Ind. U., 1976. Bar: Ind. 1976. Dep. pub. defender of Ind. State of Ind., Indpls., 1976-81, pub. defender of Ind., 1981—; chief pub. defender Wayne County, Richmond, Ind., 1981. Bd. dirs. Ind. Pub. Defender Coun., Indpls., 1981—; Ind. Lawyers Comm., Indpls., 1984-89; trustee Ind. Criminal Justice Inst., INdpls., 1983—. Mem. Criminal Code Study Commn., Indpls., 1981—, Supreme Ct. Records Mgmt. Com., Indpls., 1983—, Ind. Pub. Defender Commn., 1989—, Ind. Supreme Ct. Commn. on Race and Gender Fairness, 2000—. Mem. Ind. State Bar Assn. (criminal justice sect.), Nat. Legal Aid and Defender Assn., Nat. Assn. Defense Lawyers, Phi Beta Kappa. E-mail: scarpenter@iquest.net.

CARPENTER, VICTORIA J. lawyer; b. Evanston, Ill., Mar. 08; d. Robert Duane and Jaqueline Joan Carpenter. BA, U. Ill., 1979; MA, U. Mo., 1983; JD, Ill. Inst. Tech., 1996. Bar: Ill. 2001, U.S. Ct. Appeals (4th cir.) 2001, U.S. Dist. (no. dist.) Ill. 2001. Ind. contractor, Chgo., 1996—2001; pvt. practice, 2001; bankruptcy assoc. Legal Rescues, Chgo., 2003—. Bd. dirs. Kindred Hearts Inc., Evanston, Ill., 1990—. Mem.: ABA, Chgo. Bar Assn., Ill. State Bar Assn., Pi Delta Phi. Bankruptcy, Trademark and copyright, Property, real (including real estate development, water).

CARPIO, MIGUEL ANGEL, lawyer; s. Guillermo Carpio and María del Pilar Pertierra; m. Dinorah Del Mazo, Dec. 16, 2000. LLB, Anahuac U., Mex. City, 1999. Bar: Mex. Bar Assn. 1999. Assoc. Ogarrio Daguerre, S.C., Mexico City, 1996—. Intellectual property, Patent, Trademark and copyright, Corporate, general. Home: Juan de Dios Batiz 96 Col Vistabella Tlalnepantla 54050 Mexico Office: Ogarrio Daguerre SC Av Constituyentes 345 7 floor Mexico City 11830 Mexico Office Fax: 5255 52713665. E-mail: macarpio@ogarrio.com.mx.

CARR, CYNTHIA, lawyer; b. San Antonio, Nov. 4, 1953; d. Robert Claude Carr and Alta Mae (Bletsch) Holmes; m. Marc Allan Wallman; children: Lydia Michael, Aidan Holmes. BA, Austin Coll., 1975; JD, Harvard U., 1984; LLM, NYU, 1990. Bar: N.Y. 1985, Conn. 1988. Coord. Cambodian sect. Internat. Rescue Com., Bangkok, Thailand, 1980-81; legal intern Mental Health Legal Advisers Com., Boston, 1982-83; assoc. White & Case, N.Y.C., 1984-87; assoc. gen. counsel, exec. dir. planned giving Yale U., New Haven, 1988-2000; gen. counsel Save the Children, Westport, Conn., 2000—. Vis. lectr. Yale U. Law Sch., New Haven, 1988-90. Vol. Peace Corps, West Africa, 1975-77, 79-80; bd. dirs. Yale Law Sch. Early Learning Ctr., 1990-95; trustee Yale U. Hong Kong Charitable Trust, 1997-2000, Oak Leaf Endowment Trust for Yale, 1997-2000. Mem. ABA (vice chair lifetime and charitable gift planning com. 2000—, probate and trust divsn. 2000-01), Conn. Bar Assn. (mem. charitable giving exempt orgns. subcom.), Trusts and Estates Mag. (charitable giving mini bd. mem. 1996-99), Jewish Found. New Haven (tax and legal com. 1999—), Conn. Planned Giving Group (bd. dirs. 2000-01). Estate planning, Taxation, general. Home: 30 Hawley Rd Hamden CT 06517-2128 Office: Save the Children 54 Wilton Rd Westport CT 06880-3131 E-mail: ccarr@savechildren.org.

CARR, DAVID J. lawyer; m. Sandra S. Carr; children: Jacob, Angela, Alex. BA summa cum laude, DePauw U., 1981; JD, Georgetown U., 1984. Bar: Ind., U.S. Dist. Ct. (so. dist.) Ind. 1984, U.S. Ct. Appeals (7th cir.) 1987, U.S. Supreme Ct. 1989. Assoc. Bingham Summers Welsh & Spilman, Indpls., 1984-90, Johnson Smith LLP, Indpls., 1990-92, ptnr., 1992—2001, Ice Miller, Indpls., 2001—. Contbr. articles to profl. publs. Coun. mem. Zionsville Town Coun., 1998—; bd. dirs. Zionsville Parks and Recreation Bd., 1996-98. Mem. ABA, Ind. State Bar Assn., Indpls. Bar Assn., Christian Legal Soc., Federalist Soc., Ct. Practice Inst. (diplomate), Delta Chi, Phi Beta Kappa. General civil litigation, Entertainment, Labor (including EEOC, Fair Labor Standards Act, labor-management relations, NLRB, OSHA). Office: Box 82001 One American Sq Indianapolis IN 46282-0002 E-mail: carr@icemiller.com.

CARR, DAVIS HADEN, lawyer; b. Richmond, Va., July 21, 1940; s. Frederick and Bernice (Haden) Clifton; m. Judith A. Guerry, Aug. 1959 (div. Apr. 1979); children: Wendy, Judith Carr Stewart; m. Martha Cash, Feb. 12, 1983. BEE, U. Va., 1961; JD, Vanderbilt U., 1970. Bar: Tenn. 1970, Ky. 1989. Assoc. Boult, Cummings, Conners & Berry PLC, Nashville, 1970-74, ptnr., 1974—; mng. ptnr. Boult, Cummings, Conners & Berry, 1984-94, chmn., 1995-99. Active Leadership Nashville, 1977-78, chmn. alumni assn., 1978-79, bd. trustees 1997—, finance chair 2000-01; pres. Cumberland Museums, Nashville, 1978-80; bd. dirs. Greater Nashville Arts Found., 1991-97; bd. dirs. Jr. Achievement Mid. Tenn., 1991-99, chmn., 1995-97; trustee Vol. State Horsemen's Found., 1988-, Houghland Found., 1988—, The Bright Hour Trust, 2000— ; mem. bd. trustees, exec. com. Fisk U., 1996—, vice-chmn., 2000—; bd. dirs. Nashville Downtown Partnership, 1994-99, chmn., 1994-95, exec. com., 1997-99. Mem. ABA, Tenn. Bar Found., Tenn. Bar Assn., Nashville Bar Found., Nashville Bar Assn., Vanderbilt U. Law Alumni Assn. (bd. dirs.), Cumberland Club (pres. 1986-87), Belle Meade Country Club, Nashville Area C. of C. (gen. counsel, mem. exec. com. 1992-96, bd. govs.). Corporate, general, Finance, Mergers and acquisitions. Home: Martlesham Heath 1344 Carnton Ln Franklin TN 37064-3258 Office: Boult Cummings Conners & Berry PO Box 198062 Nashville TN 37219-8062 E-mail: dcarr@bccb.com.

CARR, EDWARD A. lawyer; b. Borger, Tex., July 31, 1962; AB with honors and distinction, Stanford U., 1984; JD, UCLA, 1987. Bar: Tex. 1988, D.C. 1989, U.S. Dist. Ct. (so. dist.) Tex. 1989, U.S. Ct. Appeals (5th cir.) 1989, U.S. Ct. Appeals (fed. cir.) 1989. Assoc. Vinson & Elkins, Houston, 1988-97, ptnr., 1997—. Lectr. in field. Contbr. articles to profl. jours., contbg. author: Business and Commercial Litigation in Federal Courts, 1998, Texas Legal Ethics in the American Legal Ethics Library, Cornell Law School, 1998; mem. UCLA Law Rev., 1985-87, mem. editl. bd., 1986-87. Fellow Tex. Bar Found. (life), Coll. State Bar Tex.; mem. ABA (sects. antitrust law, litigation), Am. Judicature Soc. (life), D.C. Bar, Fed. Bar Assn., State Bar Tex.(panel chair, dist. 4B5 grievance com. 2001-), Houston Bar Assn. Federal civil litigation, State civil litigation. Address: Vinson & Elkins LLP First City Tower 1001 Fannin St Ste 2300 Houston TX 77002-6760

CARR, GARY THOMAS, lawyer; b. El Reno, Okla., July 25, 1946; s. Thomas Clay and Bobbye Jean (Page) C.; m. Ann Elizabeth Smith, Jan. 5, 1985. AB, Washington U., St. Louis, 1968, BSCE, 1972, JD, 1975. Bar: Mo. 1975, U.S. Dist. Ct. (ea. and we. dists.) Mo. 1975, U.S. Ct. Appeals (8th cir.) 1977, U.S. Ct. Appeals (fed. cir.) 1980, U.S. Ct. Appeals (5th cir.) 1991. Jr. ptnr. Bryan, Cave, McPheeters & McRoberts, St. Louis, 1975-83, ptnr., 1984-99. Lectr. law Washington U., 1978-82, adj. prof., 1982-85; sec., dir. Bruton-Stroube Studios, Inc., 1978—, bd. dirs. Trustee Parkview Subdiv. Assn., St. Louis, 1982-90. 1st lt. U.S. Army, 1968-71, Vietnam. Mem. ABA, Mo. Bar Assn., St. Louis Bar Assn., Order of Coif. Avocations: woodworking, hunting, fishing, automobiles. General civil litigation, Commercial, contracts (including sales of goods; commercial financing), Government contracts and claims. Office: PO Box 3030 Saint Louis MO 63130-0430 E-mail: gtc10485@aol.com.

CARR, GEORGE FRANCIS, JR., lawyer; b. Bklyn., Feb. 11, 1939; s. George Francis and Edith Frances (Schaible) C.; m. Patricia Louise Shiels, Jan. 30, 1965; children: Frances Virginia, Anne McKenzie, Margaret Edith. BA, Georgetown U., 1961; LLB, Harvard U., 1964. Bar: Ohio 1964, U.S. Dist. Ct. Ohio 1964. Assoc. Kyte, Conlan, Wulsin & Vogeler, Cin., 1964-70, ptnr., 1970-78, Frost & Jacobs, Cin., 1978-82; sec., counsel Baldwin-United Corp., Cin., 1982-84, v.p., spl. counsel, 1984-85; sole practice Cin., 1985-86; ptnr. Douglas, Carr and Pettit, Milford, Ohio, 1987-88; staff v.p., assoc. gen. counsel Penn Cen. Corp., Cin., 1988-92, Gen. Cable Corp., Highland Heights, Ky., 1992-95, ret., 1995. Bd. dirs. Ctr. for Comprehensive Alcoholism Treatment, Cin., 1975-87, pres., 1980-83; bd. dirs. NCCJ, Cin., 1975-82. Served with U.S. Army, 1965—67. Avocations: farming, geology, hiking, physical fitness. Corporate, general. Home: 7150 Ragland Rd # 4 Cincinnati OH 45244-3148

CARR, JAMES FRANCIS, lawyer; b. Buffalo, May 7, 1946; s. Maurice Kilner and Cecelia Francis (Harmon) C.; children: James Robert, Marguerite Louise. BS, USAF Acad., 1968; JD, George Washington U., 1971. Bar: D.C. 1972, Mich. 1972, Pa. 1972, U.S. Dist. Ct. D.C. 1972, U.S. Ct. Appeals (D.C. cir.) 1972, U.S. Supreme Ct. 1975, Colo. 1979, U.S. Dist. Ct. Colo. 1979, U.S. Ct. Appeals (10th cir.) 1979. Atty. Unity Ctr., Meadville, Pa., 1971-73; asst. pros. atty. Genesee County, Flint, Mich., 1973-79; sr. asst. atty. gen. State of Colo., Denver, 1979-82, 85—; assoc. Sumners, Miller & Clark, Denver, 1982-83, Miles & McManus, Denver, 1983-85. Mem. Colo. Bd. Law Examiners, 1992-02; spkr. in field. Contbr. articles to profl. jours. Mem. Mich. Pub. Consultation Panel of Internat. Joint Commn., 1976-78; treas. Denver South High Sch. PTSA, 1988-91, pres., 1991-93; athletic dir. Most Precious Blood Sch., 1988-90; bd. dirs. Pioneer Jr. Hockey Assn., 1988-90. Mem. ABA (house of dels. 1997-2002, chmn. commn. on mental & physical disability law, 1998-2001, commn. on mental and phys. disability law 1995-2001, standing com. pub. edn., 2001-, tort and ins. practice sect., chmn. environ. law com. 1978-81, liaison jud. adminstrn. divsn. 1987-90, chmn. govt. liability com. 1988-89, 92-93, chmn. emerging issues com. 1996-97, sect. sec. 1997-99, TIPS coun. 1999-2002, mem. coun. govt. and pub. sector lawyers divsn. 1991-97, editor-in-chief The Brief 1981-87), ATLA, Denver Bar Assn. (chmn. pub. legal ednl. com. 1989-91, 99—, ABA del. 1997-2002, bd. trustees 2002—), Colo. Bar Assn. (chmn. health law sect. 1993-94, chmn. law edn. com. 1993-96, coun. licensure, enforcement and regulation, chmn. profl. discipline com. 1992-93, 98-99, program chmn. ann. meeting 1993-94, chair publs. com. 1995-97, chair elect 2003—. Democrat. Roman Catholic. Home: 10406 W Glasgow Ave Littleton CO 80127-3468 Office: Atty Gen Office 1525 Sherman St Fl 5 Denver CO 80203-1760 E-mail: jim.carr@state.co.us.

CARR, JAMES GRAY, judge; b. Boston, Nov. 14, 1940; s. Edmund Albert and Anna Frances C.; m. Eileen Margaret Glynn, Dec. 17, 1966; children: Maureen M., Megan A., Darrah E., Caitlin E. AB, Kenyon Coll., 1962; LLB, Harvard U., 1966. Bar: Ill. 1966, Ohio 1972, U.S. Dist. Ct. (no. dist.) Ill. 1966, U.S. Dist. Ct. (no. dist.) Ohio 1970, U.S. Supreme Ct. 1980. Assoc. Gardner & Carton, et al., Chgo., 1966-68; staff atty. Cook County Legal Asst. Found., Evanston, Ill., 1968-70; prof. U. Toledo Law Sch., 1970-79; U.S. magistrate judge U.S. Dist. Ct., Toledo, 1979-94, U.S. dist. judge, 1994—. Adj. prof. law Chgo. Kent Law Sch., 1969, Loyola U., Chgo., 1970; reporter, juvenile rules com. Ohio Supreme Ct., Columbus, 1971-72; reporter, mem. nat. wiretap com. U.S. Congress, Washington, 1976-77. Contbr. articles to profl. law jours. Founder, bd. dirs. Child Abuse Ctr., Toledo, 1970-84; active Lucas County Mental Health Bd., Toledo, 1984-89, Lucas County Children Svcs. Bd., Toledo, 1989-94. Fulbright fellow, 1977-78. Mem. ABA (reporter, elec. survey stds. 1979-80, mem. task force on tech. and law enforcement 1995-99, mem. task force on jury initiatives 1995-98), Toledo Bar Assn. (bd. dirs.), Phi Beta Kappa. Roman Catholic. Office: US Dist Ct 203 US Courthouse 1716 Spielbusch Ave Toledo OH 43624-1363 E-mail: james_g_carr@ohnd.uscourts.gov.

CARR, KATHLEEN M. lawyer; b. Whittier, Calif., May 3, 1960; d. Jim and Lori Carr; 1 child, Mariah Kate. BA, Marylhurst U.; JD, Williamette U. Law. Bar: Oreg. Pvt. practice, Portland; trial atty. Mem.: Oreg. Trial Lawyers Assn., Assn. Trial Lawyers Am. Family and matrimonial, Personal injury (including property damage). Office: 5550 SW Macadam #215 Portland OR 97239 Fax: 503-226-3232. E-mail: kathleencarr002@aol.com.

CARR, LAWRENCE EDWARD, JR., lawyer; b. Colorado Springs, Colo., Aug. 10, 1923; s. Lawrence Edward and Lelah R. (Rubert) C.; m. Agnes Isabel Dyer, Dec. 26, 1946; children— Mary Lee, James Patrick, Lawrence Edward III, Eileen Louise, Thomas Vincent. BS, U. Notre Dame,

1948, LL.B., 1949; LL.M., George Washington U., 1954. Bar: Colo. 1949, D.C. 1952, Md. 1961. With Travelers Ins. Co., 1949-51; practiced in Washington, 1952—; sr. ptnr. Carr Goodson, PC, Washington, 1984—2001, Carr Maloney, PC, 2001—. Mem. adv. coun. U. Notre Dame Coll. Law, 1985—. With USMCR, 1943-46, 51-52; col. Res.; ret. Fellow Am. Bar Found.; mem. ABA (ho. of dels. 1973-75), Bar Assn. D.C. (dir. 1969-71, pres. 1974-75), D.C. Def. Lawyers Assn. (pres. 1978-79), Bar Assn. D.C. Rsch. Found. (pres. 1985-86). Federal civil litigation, Environmental, Insurance. Home: 111 Storm Haven Ct Stevensville MD 21666-3707 Office: Carr Maloney PC 1667 K St NW 11th Fl Washington DC 20006-1605 E-mail: lec@carmaloney.com.

CARR, OSCAR CLARK, III, lawyer; b. Apr. 9, 1951; s. Oscar Clark Carr Jr. and Billie (Fisher) Carr Houghton; m. Mary Leatherman, Aug. 4, 1973; children: Camilla Fisher, Oscar Clark V. BA in English with distinction, U. Va., 1973; JD with distinction, Emory U., 1976. Bar: Tenn. 1976, U.S. Dist. Ct. (we. dist.) Tenn. 1977, (no. dist.) Miss. 1977, U.S. Ct. Appeals (6th cir.) 1985, (5th cir.) 1995, U.S. Dist. Ct. (so. dist.) Miss. 2000; cert. mediator Tenn. Assoc. Glankler Brown, PLLC (formerly Glankler, Brown, et al, Memphis, 1976-82, ptnr., 1982—, chief mgr., 1998-00. Treas., vestryman St. John's Episcopal Ch., Memphis, 1988—91, sr. warden, 1991; mem. Commn. on Ministry Diocese of West Tenn., 1987—90; King of Carnival Memphis, 1994; bd. dirs. West Tenn. chpt. Juvenile Diabetes Found., 1998—, dir., 1998—2002; bd. dirs. Memphis Ballet Soc., 1980, Memphis-Shelby County Unit Am. Cancer Soc., Memphis Oral Sch. Deaf, 1988—91, Carnival Memphis. Recipient Living and Giving award, West Tenn. chpt. Juvenile Diabetes Rsch. Found., 2002. Mem. ABA, Tenn. Bar Assn. (we. dist. coun. environ. law 1992—), Memphis-Shelby County Bar Assn. (bd. dirs. 1985-87), Memphis Country Club (atty. 1997—). Federal civil litigation, State civil litigation, Environmental, Appellate. Office: Glankler Brown PLLC 1700 One Commerce Sq Memphis TN 38103 E-mail: ocarr@glankler.com.

CARR, STEPHEN KERRY, lawyer; b. L.A., Apr. 30, 1930; s. Richard Bruce and Katherine Ward C.; m. Vivian Manno. BA, U. Toronto, Can., 1951; JD, Georgetown U., 1954. Bar: N.Y. 1957, U.S. Dist. Ct. (so. and ea. dists.) N.Y. 1958, U.S. Supreme Ct. 1966, U.S. Dist. Ct. Ga. 1975, U.S. Dist. Ct. (no. dist.) N.Y. 1984, Pa. 1995, U.S. Dist. Ct. (ea. dist.) Pa. 1997, U.S. Dist. Ct. Conn. 1998, U.S. Ct. Appeals (2nd, 3d, 4th and 11th cirs.). Assoc. Haight, Gardner, Poor & Havens, N.Y.C., 1957-68, ptnr., 1969-95; pvt. practice Pipersville, Pa., 1996—. With Counter Intelligence Corps U.S. Army, 1954—56. Fellow Am. Coll. Trial Lawyers; mem. Maritime Law Assn., Bucks County Bar Assn. Democrat. Roman Catholic. Avocations: sailing, rowing, tennis, mentoring. Admiralty, Federal civil litigation, Personal injury (including property damage). Home and Office: 6057 Schlentz Hill Rd Pipersville PA 18947-1318 E-mail: unpluged@comcat.com.

CARR, WALTER STANLEY, lawyer; b. Chgo., May 5, 1945; s. Robert Adams and Margaret (Wiley) C.; m. Mary Baine, Sept. 20, 1969. BS, U. Pa., 1967; JD, U. Chgo., 1970. Bar: Ill. 1970. From assoc. to ptnr. McDermott, Will & Emery, Chgo., 1970-86; v.p. Miami Corp., Chgo., 1987—. Pres. Hull House Assn., Chgo., 1989; bd. dirs. Planned Parenthood Assn. Chgo. Area, 1980—. Mem. ABA, Ill. Bar Assn., Chgo. Bar Assn., Chgo. Estate Planning Council. Clubs: Univ. (Chgo.). Estate planning, Probate (including wills, trusts), Estate taxation. Home: 507 W Briar Pl Chicago IL 60657-4633 Office: Miami Corp 410 N Michigan Ave Ste 590 Chicago IL 60611-4252

CARR, WILLARD ZELLER, JR., lawyer; b. Richmond, Ind., Dec. 18, 1927; s. Willard Zeller and Susan (Brownell) C.; m. Margaret Paterson, Feb. 15, 1952; children: Clayton Paterson, Jeffrey Westcott. BS, Purdue U., 1948; JD, Ind. U., 1951. Bar: Calif. 1951, U.S. Supreme Ct. 1963. Ptnr. Gibson, Dunn & Crutcher, Los Angeles, 1952—. Mem. nat. panel arbitrators Am. Arbitration Assn.; former labor relations cons. State of Alaska; lectr. bd. visitors Southwestern U. Law Sch.; mem. adv. council Southwestern Legal Found., Internat. and Comparative Law Ctr. Trustee Calif. Adminstrv. Law Coll.; bd. dirs. Employers' Group, Calif. State Pks. Found., Los Angeles coun. Boy Scouts Am.; mem. Mayor's Econ. Devel. Policies Com.; past chmn. Pacific Legal Found.; past chmn. men's adv. com. Los Angeles County-USC Med. Ctr. Aux. for Recruitment, Edn. and Service; past chmn. bd. Wilshire Republican Club; past mem. Rep. State Central Com.; past mem. pres.'s coun. Calif. Mus. Sci. and Industry; mem. Nat. Def. Exec. Res., Los Angeles World Affairs Coun.; bd. dirs., sec. Los Angeles Police Meml. Found.; past chmn. Los Angeles sect. United Way; mem. adv. com. Los Angeles County Human Rels. Commn., past commr., Calif. State World Trade Commn.; Los Angeles chpt. ARC. Fellow Am. Bar Found.; mem. Internat. Bar. Assn. (past chmn. labor law com. of bus. law sect., past chmn. labor employment practice group), The Federalist Soc., Calif. Bar Assn., L.A. County Bar Assn., L.A. C. of C. (past chmn. 1991), Calif. C. of C. Administrative and regulatory, Labor (including EEOC, Fair Labor Standards Act, labor-management relations, NLRB, OSHA). Home: 2185 Century Hl Los Angeles CA 90067-3516 Office: Gibson Dunn & Crutcher 333 S Grand Ave Ste 4400 Los Angeles CA 90071-3197 E-mail: wcarr@gibsondunn.com.

CARRERA, VICTOR MANUEL, lawyer; b. Rio Grande City, Tex., Nov. 20, 1954; s. Eladio and Ines Olivia (Guerra) C. BS, U. Tex., 1975, BA with honors, 1976, JD, 1979. Bar: Tex. 1979, U.S. Dist. Ct. (so. dist.) Tex. 1980, U.S. Dist. Ct. (we. dist.) Tex. 1996, U.S. Dist. Ct. (no. dist.) Tex. 2001, U.S. Ct. Appeals (5th cir.) 1986; cert. civil trial law, personal injury trial law, civil appellate law, Tex. Assoc. Cardenas & Whitis, McAllen, Tex., 1979-80; briefing atty. U.S. Dist. Ct. (so. dist.) Tex., Brownsville, 1980-81; assoc. Keys, Russell & Seaman, Corpus Christi, Tex., 1981-84, Wood, Boykin, Wolter & Keys, Corpus Christi, 1984-86, ptnr., 1987-88; participating mem. Law Offices of Ramon Garcia, P.C., Edinburg, Tex., 1988-90; ptnr. Munoz, Hockema & Reed, McAllen, Tex., 1990-96, Reed & Carrera, Edinburg, Tex., 1997, Reed, Carrera & McLain, 1997. Lectr. South Tex. Coll. Law, Houston, 1987, U. Houston, 1989-90, 96-99, State Bar Tex., 1992. Mng. editor Tex. Internat. Law Jour., 1978-79. Recipient Outstanding Individual Contbn. Award Vol. Lawyers of Coastal Bend, 1985. Mem.: Hidalgo County Bar Assn. (lector - 2000, 2002), Tex. Trial Lawyers Assn. (dir. 1991—96, lectr. 1993—94), Tex. Bar Assn. Democrat. Avocations: history, archaeology. General civil litigation, Private international, Personal injury (including property damage). Home: 5400 N 1st St Mcallen TX 78504-2211 Office: Reed Carrera & McLain PO Box 9702 Mcallen TX 78502-9702 also: Reed Carrera & McLain Bldg 101 1 Paseo del Prado Edinburg TX 78539 E-mail: vmcarrera@rcmlaw.com.

CARRERE, CHARLES SCOTT, law educator, judge; b. Dublin, Ga., Sept. 26, 1937; 1 son, Daniel Austin. BA, U. Ga., 1959; LLB, Stetson U., 1961. Bar: Ga. 1960, Fla. 1961. Law clk. U.S. Dist. Judge, Orlando, Fla., 1962-63; asst. U.S. Atty. Middle Dist. Fla., 1963-66, 68-69, chief trial atty., 1965-66, 68-69; ptnr. Harrison, Greene, Mann, Rowe & Stanton, 1970-80; judge Pinellas County, Fla., 1980-96; vis. prof. law Stetson Coll. Law, 1997-98, Cumberland Law Sch., 1998-99. Recipient Jud. Appreciation award St. Petersburg Bar Assn., 1996, Alumnus of Yr. award Stetson Student Bar Assn., 1998. Mem. State Bar Ga., Fla. Bar, Phi Beta Kappa. Presbyterian. Address: PO Box 22034 Gateway Mall Sta Saint Petersburg FL 33742 Fax: 727-395-0444.

CARREY, NEIL, lawyer, educator; b. Bronx, N.Y., Nov. 19, 1942; s. David L. and Betty (Kurtzburg) C.; m. Karen Krysher, Apr. 9, 1980; children: Jana, Christopher; children by previous marriage: Scott, Douglas, Dana. BS in Econs., U. Pa., 1964; JD, Stanford U., 1967. Bar: Calif. 1968. Mem. firm, v.p. corp. DeCastro, West, Chodorow, Inc., L.A., 1967-97; of counsel Jenkens & Gilchrist, L.A., 1998—. Instr. program legal paraprofls., U. So. Calif., 1977-89; lectr. U. So. Calif. Dental Sch., 1987—, Employee Benefits Inst., Kansas City, Mo., 1996; legal cons. 33rd Dist. Calif. PTA, 1997—. Author: Nonqualified Defered Compensation Plans-The Wave of the Future, 1985. Treas. Nat. Little League, Santa Monica, Calif., 1984—85, pres., 1985—86, coach, 1990—95; referee, coach Am. Soccer Youth Orgn., 1989—95; officer Vista Del Mar Child Care Ctr., L.A., 1968—84; coach Bobby Sox Softball Team, Santa Monica, 1986—88, bd. dirs., 1988, umpire in chief, 1988; curriculum com. Santa Monica-Malibu Sch. Dist., 1983—84, comm. health adv. com., 1988—95, chmn., 1989—95, sports and phys. edn. adv. com., 1991—2000, chmn., 1991—99, dist. com. for sch. based health ctr., 1991—94, title IX/gender equity com. chmn., 1992—, athletic study com. chmn., 1989—91, fin. adv. com., 1994, ad hoc com. dist. facilities chmn., 1998, fin. task force, 1999—2000, parcel tax com., 2000; dir. The Santa Monica Youth Athletic Found., 1995—, exec. comm., 1997—98, v.p., 1998—, mem. parcel tax com., 1999; dir. The Small Bus. Coun. of Am., 1995—, Santa Monica H.S. Booster Club, 1995—97, Santa Monica Police Activities League, 1995—97, v.p. fin., 1997—98, pres.-elect, 1998—99, pres., 1999—2001, past pres., 2001—; pres. Gail Dorin Music Found., 1994—; v.p. Sneaker Sisters, 1996—2001; pres. Santa Monica Jr. Rowing, 1997—2002; legal cons. 33d Dist. Calif. PTA, 1997—99; recreation and parks commr. City of Santa Monica, 1999—; sec. Santa Monica Leaders Club, 1999—2000; mem. U. Pa. Women's Sports Adv. Bd., 1998—; mem. resource bd. Santa Monica-Malibu Edn. Found., 2000—; pres. Chris Carrey Charitable Found., 2000—; chmn. parcel tax com. Santa Monica-Malibu Sch. Dist., 2002; v.p. bd. Ivan and Sam Found., 2002—; chmn. Save Our Sch. com. Santa Monica Malibu Sch. Dist., 2002—03; bd. dirs. Padres Contra el Cancer, 2001—03, v.p., 2002—. Mem.: LWV (dir. 1997—), Children's Hosp. L.A. (adv. coun. 2001—), Children's Ctr. for Cancer and Blood Diseases, U. Pa. Alumni Soc. (pres. 1971—79, dir. 1979—87), Mountaingate Tennis Club, Alpha Kappa Psi (life). Jewish. Corporate, general, Health, Pension, profit-sharing, and employee benefits. Home: 616 23d St Santa Monica CA 90402-3130 Office: 12100 Wilshire Blvd Fl 15 Los Angeles CA 90025-7120 E-mail: ncarrey@aol.com., ncarrey@jenkens.com.

CARRICO, HARRY LEE, retired judge; b. Washington, Sept. 4, 1916; s. William Temple and Nellie Nadalia (Willett) C.; m. Betty Lou Peck, May 18, 1940 (dec. 1987); 1 child, Lucretia Ann; m. Lynn Brackenridge, July 1, 1994. Jr. cert., George Washington U., 1938, JD, 1942, LLD, 1987, U. Richmond, 1973, Coll. William & Mary, 1993. Bar: Va. 1941. With Rust & Rust, Fairfax, Va., 1941-43; trial justice Fairfax, Va., 1943-51; pvt. practice, 1951-56; judge 16th Jud. Cir., Va., 1956-61; justice Va. Supreme Ct., Richmond, 1961-81, chief justice, 1981—2003, sr. justice, 2003—. Chmn. bd dirs. Nat. Ctr. for State Cts., 1989-90. With USNR, 1945-46. Recipient Alumni Profl. Achievement award George Washington U., 1981. Mem. McNeill Law Soc., Conf. Chief Justices (bd. dirs. 1985-91, 1st v.p. 1987, pres.-elect. 1988, pres. 1989-90, co-chmn. nat. jud. coun. 1991-97), Order of Coif, Phi Delta Phi, Omicron Delta Kappa. Episcopalian. Office: Supreme Court of Va 100 N 9th St 4th Fl Richmond VA 23229-7610

CARRICO, LUCRETIA A. lawyer; b. Alexandria, Va., May 17, 1942; d. Harry L. and Betty Lou C.; m. Robert Langston Irby, Nov. 28, 1961 (div. 1975); children: Ann Temple Irby Roberts, Robert Lee Irby; m. Wallace Lafayette Cliborne, Dec. 11, 1990. BA, U. Richmond, 1976, JD, 1978. Bar: Va. 1978. Asst. gen. counsel The Life Ins. Co. Va., Richmond, 1978-83; asst. corp. sec. Blue Cross Blue Shield Va., Richmond, 1983-84; pvt. practice Cumberland, Va., 1985-87; lawyer Hayes & Carrico, P.C., Powhatan, Va., 1987—2000, Blandford, Carrico & Newlon, P.C., 2000—; sub. judge 11th Jud. Dist. Comments editor U. Richmond Law Rev., 1977-78. Pres., dir. Neighbor to Neighbor Literacy Counsel, Powhatan, 1990-96, Goochland Powhatan Cmty. Svcs. Bd., 1991-95; dir. Children at Risk Today, Chesterfield, Va., 1996—. Mem. Powhatan Bar Assn. (pres. 2001-), Powhatan C. of C. (pres., dir.), McNeil Law Soc. Episcopalian. Avocations: restoring old houses and decorating, gardening, reading, antiques. General practice, Family and matrimonial, Criminal. Home: PO Box 222 Powhatan VA 03139-5203 Office: PO Box 809 3864 Old Buckingham Rd Ste B Powhatan VA 23139-0809 Fax: 804-598-0280. E-mail: LACarrico@aol.com.

CARRIGAN, JIM R. arbitrator, mediator, retired judge; b. Mobridge, S.D., Aug. 24, 1929; s. Leo Michael and Mildred Ione (Jaycox) C.; m. Beverly Jean Halpin, June 2, 1956. Ph.B., JD, U. N.D., 1953; LL.M. in Taxation, NYU, 1956; LLD (hon.), U. Colo., 1989, Suffolk U., 1991, U. N.D., 1997. Bar: N.D. 1953, Colo. 1956. Asst. prof. law U. Denver, 1956-59; vis. assoc. prof. NYU Law Sch., 1958, U. Wash. Law Sch., 1959-60; Colo. jud. adminstr., 1960-61; prof. law U. Colo., 1961-67; partner firm Carrigan & Bragg (and predecessors), 1967-76; bd. regents U. Colo., 1975-76; justice Colo. Supreme Ct., 1976-79; judge U.S. Dist. Ct. Colo., 1979-95. Mem. Colo. Bd. Bar Examiners, 1969-71; lectr. Nat. Coll. State Judiciary, 1964-77, 95; bd. dirs. Nat. Inst. Trial Advocacy, 1971-73, 78—, chmn. bd. 1986-88, also mem. faculty, 1972—; adj. prof. law U. Colo, 1984, 1991—; bd. dirs. Denver Broncos Stadium Dist., 1996—. Editor-in-chief: N.D. Law Rev., 1952-53, Internat. Soc. Barristers Quar., 1972-79; editor: DICTA, 1957-59; contbr. articles to profl. jours. Bd. visitors U. N.D. Coll. Law, 1983-85. Recipient Disting. Svc. award Nat. Coll. State Judiciary, 1969, Outstanding Alumnus award U. N.D., 1973, Regent Emeritus award U. Colo., 1977, B'nai Brith Civil Rights award, 1986, Thomas More Outstanding Lawyer award Cath. Lawyers Guild, 1988, Oliphant Disting. Svc. award Nat. Inst. Trial Advocacy, 1993, Constl. Rights award Nat. Assn. Blacks in Criminal Justice (Colo. chpt.), 1992, Disting. Svc. award Colo. Bar Assn., 1994, Amicus Curiae award ATLA, 1994, Colo. Trial Lawyers Assn. Lifetime Achievement award, 2000. Fellow Colo. Bar Found., Boulder County Bar Found.; mem. ABA (action com. on tort system improvement 1985-87, TIPS sect. long range planning com., 1986-97; coun. 1987-91, task force on initiatives and referenda 1990-92, size of civil juries task force 1988-90, class actions task force 1995-97), Colo. Bar Assn., Boulder County Bar Assn., Denver Bar Assn., Cath. Lawyers Guild, Inns. of Ct., Internat. Soc. Barristers, Internat. Acad. Trial Lawyers (bd. dirs. 1995—), Fed. Judges Assn. (bd. dirs. 1985-89), Am. Judicature Soc. (bd. dirs. 1985-89), Tenth Circuit Dist. Judges Assn. (sec. 1991-92, v.p. 1992-93, pres. 1994-95), Order of Coif, Phi Beta Kappa. Roman Catholic. Office: Judicial Arbiter Group 1601 Blake St Ste 400 Denver CO 80202-1328 E-mail: carrigan2350@earthlink.net.

CARRINGTON, PAUL DEWITT, lawyer, educator; b. Dallas, June 12, 1931; s. Paul and Frances Ellen (DeWitt) C.; m. Bessie Meek, Aug., 1952; children: Clark DeWitt, Mary Carrington Coults, William James, Emily Carrington. BA, U. Tex., 1952; LLB, Harvard U., 1955. Bar: Tex. 1955, Ohio 1962, Mich. 1967. Practice, Dallas, 1955; teaching fellow Harvard U., 1957-58; asst. prof. law U. Wyo., 1958-60, Ind. U., 1960-62; assoc. prof. Ohio State U., 1962-65; prof. U. Mich., 1965-78; dean Duke U. Sch. Law, Durham, N.C., 1978-88, prof., 1978—. Reporter civil rules adv. com. Jud. Conf. of U.S., 1985-92. Author: (with Meador and Rosenberg) Justice on Appeal, 1977, (with Meador and Rosenberg) Appeals, 1994, (with Babcock) Civil Procedure, 1977, 3d edit., 1983, Stewards of Democracy, 1999. Mem. Ann Arbor (Mich.) Bd. Edn., 1970-73; pres. Pvt. Adjudication Ctr., Inc., 1988-94, chmn., 1995-2002. With U.S. Army, 1955-57. Guggenheim fellow, 1988-89. Fellow Am. Bar Found., Am. Acad. Arts & Scis.; mem. ABA, Am. Law Inst. Episcopalian. Office: Duke U Sch Law Durham NC 27708-0362 E-mail: pdc@law.duke.edu.

CARRIO, ALEJANDRO DANIEL, lawyer, educator; b. Buenos Aires, Oct. 15, 1953; s. Genaro Ruben Carrió and Margarita Martha Baistrocchi; m. Alicia Angelica Maqueda de Carrió; children: Juan Francisco, Tomas. LLB, Buenos Aires U., 1976; LLM, La. State U., 1982. Ptnr. Law Firm Landaburu & Carrió, Buenos Aires, 1977—. Adj. prof. law Buenos Aires U., 1984-88, prof. law, 1989-99, Palermo U., 1996-; rsch. assoc. La. State U., 1985; vis. prof. law Syracuse U., 1990, 91, 92, 94, 2001; vis. scholar Columbia U. Law Sch., N.Y., 1989. Author: Garantías Constitucionales en el Proceso Penal, 1984, 4th edit., 2000, The Criminal Justice System of Argentina, 1986, El Enjuiciamiento Penal en Argentina y Estados Unidos, 1989, Presidential Systems in Stress: Emergency Powers in Argentina and The United States (together with William C. Banks), 1993, La Corte Suprema y Su Independencia, 1996, (together with Alejandro M. Garro) Criminal Procedure: A Worldwide Study, Chapter 1: Argentina, 2000. Mem. Internat. Acad. Trial Lawyers, Assn. por Los Derechos Civiles (pres. 1996—). Home: Av Libertador 4710 1426 Buenos Aires Argentina Office: Landaburu & Carrió Cerrito 1294 Piso 10 1010 Buenos Aires Argentina

CARROLL, DIANE C. lawyer; b. Mineola, N.Y., Apr. 16, 1960; d. Manuel Niceto and Irene Louisa (Mandra) Lopez; m. Paul J. Antico, May 10, 1992; children: Bryan Paul, Jared Joseph. BA, Hofstra U., 1982; JD, Bklyn. Law Sch., 1985. Bar: N.Y. 1986, U.S. Dist. Ct. (ea. dist.) N.Y. 1986, U.S. Ct. Mil. Appeals 1991, U.S. Ct. Claims 1991, U.S. Ct. Appeals (fed. cir.) 1991, U.S. Supreme Ct. 1991. Assoc. Ansell & Weiss, Huntington, N.Y., 1986-90; litigating atty. Alan Paul Ansell, Huntington, 1990-91; pvt. practice Melville, N.Y., 1991—. Mem. Suffolk County Matrimonial Com., Commack, N.Y., 1988—, chair fee dispute com., 1993—; arbitrator Suffolk County Small Claims Ct., Hauppauge, N.Y., 1989—; matrimonial arbitrator, 1996—; co-chmn. Suffolk County Free Dispute Com., Dispute Resolution Panel, Bench Bar Com. Mem. Suffolk Womens Bar Assn., N.Y. State Bar Assn., Suffolk County Bar Assn., Queens County Bar Assn. Avocations: reading, gardening. Bankruptcy, Family and matrimonial, General practice.

CARROLL, EARL HAMBLIN, federal judge; b. Tucson, Mar. 26, 1925; s. John Vernon and Ruby (Wood) C.; m. Louise Rowlands, Nov. 1, 1952; children— Katherine Carroll Pearson, Margaret Anne BSBA, U. Ariz., 1948, LLB, 1951. Bar: Ariz., U.S. Ct. Appeals (9th and 10th cirs.), U.S. Ct. of Claims, U.S. Supreme Ct. Law clk. Ariz. Supreme Ct., Phoenix, 1951-52; assoc. Evans, Kitchel & Jenckes, Phoenix, 1952-56, ptnr., 1956-80; judge U.S. Dist. Ct. Ariz., Phoenix, 1980—, sr. judge, 1994—. Spl. counsel City of Tombstone, Ariz., 1962-65, Maricopa County, Phoenix, 1968-75, City of Tucson, 1974, City of Phoenix, 1979; designated mem. U.S. Fgn. Intelligence Surveillance Court by Chief Justice U.S. Supreme Ct., 1993-99; chief judge Alien Terrorist Removal Ct., 1996-01, 2001—. Mem. City of Phoenix Bd. of Adjustment, 1955-58; trustee Phoenix Elem. Sch. Bd., 1961-72; mem. Gov.'s Council on Intergovtl. Relations, Phoenix, 1970-73; mem. Ariz. Bd. Regents, 1978-80. Served with USNR, 1943-46; PTO Recipient Nat. Service awards Campfire, 1973, 75, Alumni Service award U. Ariz., 1980, Disting. Citizen award No. Ariz. U., Flagstaff, 1983, Bicentenial award Georgetown U., 1988, Disting. Citizen award U. Ariz., 1990, Sidney S. Woods Alumni Svc. award, 2000. Fellow Am. Coll. Trial Lawyers, Am. Bar Found.; mem. ABA, Ariz. Bar Assn., U. Ariz. Law Coll. Assn. (pres. 1975), Sigma Chi (Significant Sig award 1991), Phi Delta Phi. Democrat. Office: US Dist Ct US Courthouse Ste 521 401 W Washington SPC 48 Phoenix AZ 85003-2151

CARROLL, FRANK JAMES, lawyer, educator; b. Albuquerque, Feb. 10, 1947; s. Francis J. and Dorothy (Bloom) C.; m. Marilyn Blume, Aug. 9, 1969; children: Christine, Kathleen, Emily. BS in Acctg., St. Louis U., 1969; JD, U. Ill., 1973. Bar: Iowa 1973, U.S. Dist. Ct. Iowa, U.S. Tax Ct., U.S. Ct. Appeals (8th cir.); CPA, Mo., Iowa. Acct. Arthur Young & Co., St. Louis, 1969-70; shareholder Davis, Brown, Koehn, Shors & Roberts, P.C., Des Moines, 1973—. Lectr. law Drake U. Law Sch., Des Moines, 1976-86, lectr. Sch. of Bus., 1988-92; bd. dirs. Iowa Agr. Devel. Authority, Iowa State Bar Assn., Variety Club. Mem. commr.'s adv. group IRS, Washington, 1989; mem. grad. tax adv. bd. U. Mo. Kansas City Sch. Law, 1995. Mem. ABA, Iowa Bar Assn. (chair bus. law sect. 1995-98, chair corp. counsel sect. 2001-2003), Polk County Bar Assn., Des Moines C. of C., Wakonda Club, Des Moines Variety Club (bd. dirs. 1998), Beta Gamma Sigma. Corporate, general, Corporate taxation. Home: 5725 Harwood Dr Des Moines IA 50312-1203 Office: Davis Brown Koehn Shors Roberts PC 666 Walnut St Ste 2500 Des Moines IA 50309-3904

CARROLL, J. SPEED, lawyer, financial executive; b. Sherman, Tex., Apr. 23, 1936; s. Horace Bailey and Mary Joe (Durning) C.; m. Martha Coleman Huff, Apr. 12, 1957; 1 child, Charles Durning. BA, U. Tex., 1957; LLB cum laude, Harvard U., 1962. Bar: N.Y. 1964, U.S. Supreme Ct. 1971, Japan (fgn. legal cons.) 1993-95. Assoc. Cleary, Gottlieb, Steen & Hamilton, N.Y.C. and Paris, 1963-70, ptnr. N.Y.C., London, Tokyo, 1971-97, counsel, 1997—2002; mng. dir. Emerging Markets Partnership, Washington, 1997—. Cons. fgn. law Nagashima & Ohno, Tokyo, 1964-65; instr. Internat. Law Inst., Washington, 1973-83; bd. dirs. Mitsubishi Trust and Banking Corp., U.S.A., N.Y.C. Contbr. chapters to books and articles to profl. jours. Mem. Coun. on Fgn. Rels., N.Y.C., 1973—; trustee Parker Sch. Internat. and Comparative Law Columbia U., 1992—. Lt. USNR, 1957-59. Knox fellow Harvard U., 1962-63. Mem. Phi Beta Kappa. Finance, Private international, Mergers and acquisitions. Office: Emerging Markets Partnership 2001 Pennsylvania Ave NW Washington DC 20006-1850

CARROLL, JOSEPH J(OHN), lawyer; b. N.Y.C., Sept. 18, 1936; s. James J. and M. Catherine (Molloy) C.; m. Barbara Ann Lediger, May 16, 1959; 1 child, Barbara Ann (dec.). BS, Manhattan Coll., 1958; LLB, St. John's U., 1963; LLM, NYU, 1968. Bar: N.Y. 1964, U.S. Supreme Ct. 1967. Ins. underwriter Atlantic Mut. Ins. Co., N.Y.C., 1959-63; pub. adminstrn. intern N.Y. State Housing Fin. Agy., N.Y.C., 1963-64, adminstrv. asst., 1964-67; assoc. Mudge, Rose, Guthrie, Alexander & Ferdon, N.Y.C., 1967-77, ptnr., 1977-95; of counsel Sullivan Donovan & Gentile, P.C., N.Y.C., 1995—. Mem. nat. coun. trustees Nat. Jewish Med. and Rsch. Ctr., Denver; trustee Manhattan Coll., N.Y.C., Queen of the Most Holy Rosary Parish, Roosevelt, N.Y. Mem.: ABA (health law sect.), Nat. Assn. Coll. and Univ. Attys., Am. Health Lawyers Assn., N.Y. State Bar Assn. (mcpl. health law sects.). E-mail: jjbacarroll@juno.com.

CARROLL, JULIAN MORTON, lawyer, former governor; b. Paducah, Ky., Apr. 16, 1931; s. Elvie B. and Eva (Heady) C.; m. Charlann Harting, July 22, 1951; children: Kenneth Morton, Iva Patrice, Bradley Harting, Ellyn Kriston. AA, Paducah Jr. Coll., 1952; AB, U. Ky., 1954, LLB, 1956. Bar: Ky. 1956. Ptnr. Emery & Carroll, Paducah, 1960-68; mem. Ky. Ho. of Reps., 1962-71, speaker, 1968-71; lt. gov. State of Ky., 1971-74, gov., 1974-79; of counsel Reed, Scent & Walton, Paducah, 1968-71; ptnr. Carroll & Assocs., Frankfort, Ky., 1980—. Chmn. Nat. Conf. Lt. Govs., 1974, Nat. Govs. Assn., 1978-79. Trustee Paducah Jr. Coll., Regency U. Lt. USAF, 1956-59. Recipient Minerva award U. Louisville, 1977, Man of Yr. award Advt. Club Louisville, 1978. Mem. ABA, Ky. Bar Assn., Franklin County Bar Assn., Optimist Club, Phi Delta. Democrat. Avocation: golf. Office: Carroll & Assocs 25 Fountain Pl Frankfort KY 40601-1942

CARROLL, MARK THOMAS, lawyer; b. Queens, N.Y., May 12, 1956; s. Bernard James and Thalia (Antypas) C.; m. Joanne Mary Grinnell, Aug. 4, 1979; children: Stephen, Thomas. BA, Columbia U., 1977; JD, Harvard U., 1980. Bar: Pa. 1980, U.S. Ct. Appeals (3d cir.) 1980, U.S. Dist. Ct. (ea. dist.) Pa. 1980. Assoc. Duane, Morris & Heckscher, Phila., 1980-82; asst. dir. ALI-ABA, Phila., 1982-85, dir. office of publs., 1985—. Bd. dirs. Bradford Glen Homeowners Assn., 1988-90; founding mem. Joseph's People Com. Mem. ABA, Assn. for Continuing Legal Edn. (pres. 2003—). Republican. Roman Catholic. Home: 1402 Ashcom Dr Downingtown PA 19335-3566 Office: ALI-ABA 4025 Chestnut St Ste 500 Philadelphia PA 19104-3099 E-mail: mcarroll@ali-aba.org.

CARROLL, RAOUL LORD, lawyer, investment banker; b. Washington, Mar. 16, 1950; s. John Thomas and Gertrude Barbara (Jenkins) C.; m. Elizabeth Jane Coleman, Mar. 22, 1980; children: Alexandria Nicole,

Christina Elizabeth. BS, Morgan State U., 1972; JD, St. Johns U., Jamaica, N.Y., 1975; postgrad., Georgetown U., 1980-81. Bar: N.Y. 1976, D.C. 1979, U.S. Dist. Ct. D.C. 1979, U.S. Supreme Ct. 1979, U.S. Dist. Ct. (so. and ea. dist.) N.Y. 1982. Asst. U.S. atty. Office U.S. Atty., Dept. Justice, Washington, 1979-80. Assoc. mem. U.S. Bd. Vets. Appeals, Washington, 1980-81; ptnr. Hart, Carroll & Chavers, Washington, 1981-86, Bishop, Cook, Purcell & Reynolds, Washington, 1986-89; gen. counsel U.S. Dept. Vets. Affairs, 1989-91; pres. Govt. Nat. Mortgage Assn., HUD, 1991-92; COO, M.R. Beal & Co., 1993-95; chmn. Christalex Ptnrs., Inc., 1995-2002, Am. Ctr. for Internat. Leadership, Balt.; trustee Christian Bros. Investment Svcs., Inc., N.Y.C., WINCOM, Inc., Century City, Calif., chmn. 1997—, pres. Pro-Banker Securities LLC, 2002—. Trustee The Enterprise Found., Columbia, Md. Capt. U.S. Army, 1975-79. Decorated Joint Service Commendation medal, Army Commendation medal; named Outstanding Young Man Am., U.S. Jaycees, 1979. Em. N.Y. State Bar Assn., D.C. Bar Assn., Washington Bar Assn., Asst. U.S. Attys. Assn., Omega Psi Phi. Republican. Baptist. Finance, Municipal (including bonds). Home: 7821 Morningside Dr NW Washington DC 20012-1448 Office: 1900 Ave of the Stars 5th Flr Los Angeles CA 90067

CARROLL, W. DONALD, JR., lawyer, consultant; b. N.Y.C., Aug. 12, 1945; children: Nora Sawrie Crosby Carroll, William Wise Crosby Carroll. AB, Davidson Coll., 1967; MPhil, U. Dundee, Scotland, 1970; JD, U. Va., 1971. Bar: Va. 1971, N.C. 1973, U.S. Dist. Ct. N.C. 1974, U.S. Supreme Ct. 1979. Law clk. to judge U.S. Dist. Ct. N.C., Charlotte, 1972-74; assoc. Helms, Mulliss and Johnston, Charlotte, 1975-80; ptnr. Smith, Helms Mulliss and Moore and predecessor, Charlotte, 1980-90; of counsel Conrad Trosch Kenny, Charlotte, 1991-93; dir. N.C. State Bar Lawyer Assistance Program, Raleigh, 1993—. Mem. Charlotte City Coun., 1977-81; commr. Charlotte Housing Authority, 1981-91, mem. bd. dirs. Charlotte Chemical Dependency Ctr. Mem.: ABA (commn. on lawyer assistance programs). Home: 607 Pinecrest St Davidson NC 28036-8072 Office: 907 Barra Row Ste 205 Davidson NC 28036

CARROLL, WAYNE JACKSON, lawyer; b. Earlington, Ky., Mar. 1, 1933; s. Herbert E. and Van (Josey) C.; m. Lorraine Y. Yancey, Feb. 8, 1958; children: Cynthia, Scott. BS in Commerce, U. Ky., 1955, JD, 1957. Bar: Ky. Asst. atty. gen. Commonwealth of Ky., Frankfort, 1960-61; asst. U.S. atty. U.S. Dep. Justice, Louisville, 1961-65; atty., shareholder Mackenzie & Peden, Attys., Louisville, 1965—. Lectr. U. Louisville Law Sch., 1968-71; ct. com. U.S. Ct. Mil. Appeals, Washington, 1987-89; pres. Louisville chpt. Fed. Bar Assn., 1963-65. 1st lt. USAF, 1957-60. Mem. ABA, Def. Rsch. Inst., Ky. Bar Assn., Louisville Bar Assn., Ky. Def. Counsel (bd. dirs. 1985). General civil litigation, Insurance. Home: 2205 Glenview Ave Louisville KY 40222-6343 Office: Mackenzie & Peden PSC 7508 New La Grange Rd No 3 Louisville KY 40222

CARROLL, WILLIAM RICHARD, lawyer; b. Charleroi, Pa., Nov. 26, 1946; s. J. Regis and Virginia (Steen) C.; m. Amy R. Woy, Feb. 14, 1981; children: Benjamin A., Nicholas A., Greta A., Joseph A. BA, St. Vincent Coll., 1968; MA, U. Notre Dame, 1969; JD, Duquesne U., 1976. Bar: Pa. 1976, U.S. Dist. Ct. (we. dist.) Pa. 1976. Law clk. Ct. Common Pleas, Somerset, Pa., 1976-78; pvt. practice, 1978—; pub. defender Somerset County, 1990—. Served to 1st lt. U.S. Army, 1969-73. Mem. Pa. Bar Assn., Somerset County Bar Assn. Democrat. Lutheran. Criminal, Family and matrimonial, Property, real (including real estate development, water). Office: PO Box 604 Somerset PA 15501-0604

CARROW, ROBERT DUANE, lawyer, barrister; b. Marshall, Minn., Feb. 5, 1934; s. Meddie Joseph and Estelle Marie (Kough) C.; m. Jacqueline Mary Givens, Sept. 3, 1960; children: Leslie, Tamara, Amelia, Vanessa, Creighton, Jessica, Ramsey. Student, U. Colo., 1952; BA, U. Minn., 1956; JD, Stanford U., 1958. Bar: Calif. 1959, U.S. Supreme Ct. 1978, N.Y. 1983; barrister: Eng. 1981. Sole practice, Calif., 1959—; barrister London, 1981—. Judge pro tem Superior Ct. of Calif., San Francisco, 1992—. Bd. editors Minn. Law Rev., 1956-57. Mayor City of Novato, Calif., 1962-64. Fellow Ctr. Internat. Legal Studies, Soc. Advanced Legal Studies (assoc.); mem. ABA, N.Y. Bar Assn., L.A. Bar Assn. (litigation sect. 1988—), San Francisco Bar Assn., Internat. Bar Assn., Chartered Inst. Arbitrators, Assn. Conflict Resolution, Honourable Soc. Middle Temple. General civil litigation, Criminal. Office: Chambers 33 Bedford Row London WC1 England also: Goldstein & Musto 1 Embarcadero Ctr Ste 880 San Francisco CA 94111-3607 also: 7 Mounthassen Dr Ste C134 San Rafael CA 94903-1170

CARRUTHERS, PHILIP CHARLES, lawyer, public official; b. London, Dec. 8, 1953; s. J. Alex and Marie Carruthers. BA, U. Minn., 1975, JD, 1979. Bar: Minn. 1979, U.S. Dist. Ct. Minn. 1979, U.S. Ct. Appeals (8th cir.) 1979. Assoc. Nichols & Kruger, and predecessor firm, 1979-81; ptnr. Nichols, Starks, Carruthers and Kister, Mpls., 1982-84, Luther, Ballenthin & Carruthers, Mpls., 1985—92, Carruthers & Tallen, Mpls., 1992—93; pvt. practice Mpls., 1994—2000; pros. atty. City of Deephaven, Minn., 1979-2000, City of Woodland, Minn., 1980-2000; mem. Minn. Ho. of Reps., St. Paul, 1987-2000, majority leader, 1993-96, spkr. of house, 1997-98; dir. prosecution divsn. Ramsey County Attys. Office, St. Paul, 2000—. Co-author: The Drinking Driver in Minnesota: Criminal and Civil Issues, 1982; note and comment editor Minn. Law Rev., 1978-79. Mem. Met. Coun. of Twin Cities Area, St. Paul, 1983-87. Mem. Minn. Trial Lawyers Assn. (bd. govs. 1982-86), Minn. State Bar Assn., Ramsey County Bar Assn. Democratic Farmer-Labor Party. Roman Catholic. Criminal, Personal injury (including property damage), Alternative dispute resolution. Home: 6018 Halifax Pl Brooklyn Center MN 55429-2440 Office: 315 Government Ctr W 50 W Kellogg Blvd Saint Paul MN 55102-1657 E-mail: Phil.Carruthers@Co.Ramsey.mn.us.

CARSON, CHRISTOPHER LEONARD, lawyer; b. Washington, Dec. 28, 1940; s. Leonard O. and Evelyn (Watters) C.; m. Cynthia Caffey, Dec. 27, 1963; 1 dau., Melissa Ann. AB, Duke U., 1962; JD, U. Mich., 1965. Bar: N.Y. 1965, Fla. 1968, Ga. 1970. Assoc. Olwine, Chase, O'Donnell & Weyher, N.Y.C., 1965-66; ptnr. Hansell & Post, Atlanta, 1969-89, Jones Day, Atlanta, 1989—. Contbg. author: Modern Real Estate Transactions; contbr. articles to legal publs. and mags. Bd. dirs., adv. coun. Atlanta Area Boy Scouts Am., 1974-80; bd. dirs. Young Life Urban Atlanta, 1983—. Lt. sr. grade USNR, 1960-69. Fellow Am. Coll. Coml. Fin. Lawyers; mem. ABA (Uniform Comml. Code Com., Subcoms. on Secured Transactions and Letter of Credit 1982—), Southeastern Bankruptcy Law Inst. (dir. 1973—, pres. 1980-81, chmn. 1981-82), Atlanta Bar Bankruptcy Sect. (chmn. 1981-82), Ga. Bar Uniform Code Com. (chmn. 1984-87), Cherokee Club. Republican. Baptist. Avocations: running, reading, traveling. Banking, Bankruptcy, Finance. Office: Jones Day SunTrust Plz 303 Peachtree St NE Ste 3500 Atlanta GA 30308-3263 E-mail: clcarson@jonesday.com.

CARSON, TIMOTHY JOSEPH, lawyer; b. Darby, Pa., Feb. 17, 1949; s. Joseph Timothy and Marian (Maloney) C.; m. Janet Louise Duffy, May 30, 1975; children: Lindsey, Anne, Timothy J. BS in Econs., U. Pa., 1970; JD, Villanova Sch. Law, 1975. Bar: Pa. 1975, U.S. Ct. Claims 1976, U.S. Tax Ct. 1976. Assoc. Lentz, Riley, Cantor, Kilgore & Massey, Paoli, Pa., 1975-77, Townsend, Elliott & Munson, Phila., 1977; assoc. Saul, Ewing, Remick & Saul, Phila., 1977-81, ptnr. 1981—, chmn. dept. pub. fin., mem. policy com., 1994—; Mng. editor Villanova Law Rev., 1974-75; contbr. articles to profl. jours. and newsletters. Chmn. Tri-State Rep. Alliance, 1984—; mem. SBA Adv. Coun., Phila., 1982-85., Del. Valley Regional Planning Commn., 1996—; spl. advisor Pa. Ho. Local Govt. Com., 1985-88, Pa. Senate Intergovt. Affairs Com., 1989-93; chmn. fin. com. Rep. State Com. Pa., 1986-90, mem. leadership com. 1986-93; del. 1988, alt. del. 1992, Rep. Nat. Conv. Recipient Spl. awards and commendations U. Pa. Bd. Trustees, U.S. Navy and NASA, 1971, Rep. State Com. Pa., 1989, March of Dimes Birth Defects Found., 1990, commnr. Pa. Turnpike Commn., 2000; Fellow Am. Bar Found. (life), Pa. Bar Found., Phila. Bar Found. (trustee 1989-93, pres. 1992, Spl. award 1993, commnr. 1996-2001), Del. Valley Planning Commn. (chmn. 2000-01), Am. Coll. Bond Lawyers; mem. ABA, Phila. Bar Assn. (exec. com. young lawyers sect. 1981-84, bd. govs. 1997-99), Pa. Bar Assn. (bd. govs. 1979-82, 96—, chmn. young lawyers sect. 1980-81, ho. of dels. 1979—, del. 3d cir. jud. conf. 1979, chmn. commn. mcpl. fin. mcpl. law sect. 1984-87, chmn.'s award young lawyers sect. 1981, exec. officer, mem. bd. govs. 1997—, v.p. 2000-01, pres.-elect 2001-02, pres. 2002-03), , Nat. Assn. Bond Lawyers, Pa. Assn. of Bond Lawyers (bd. dirs. 1988-90), Mcpl. Bond Club Phila. Republican. Roman Catholic. Clubs: Racquet (Phila.), U. Pa. Faculty, Merion Golf (Ardmore, Pa.). Municipal (including bonds). Office: Saul Ewing LLP Centre Sq W 1500 Market St 38th Fl Philadelphia PA 19102-2186*

CARSON, WALLACE PRESTON, JR., judge; b. Salem, Oreg., June 10, 1934; s. Wallace Preston and Edith (Bragg) C.; m. Gloria Stolk, June 24, 1956; children: Scott, Carol, Steven (dec. 1981). BA in Politics, Stanford U., 1956; JD, Willamette U., 1962. Bar: Oreg. 1962, U.S. Dist. Ct. Oreg. 1963, U.S. Ct. Appeals (9th cir.) 1968, U.S. Supreme Ct. 1971, U.S. Ct. Mil. Appeals 1977; lic. comml. pilot FAA. Pvt. practice law, Salem, Oreg., 1962-77; judge Marion County Cir. Ct., Salem, 1977-82; assoc. justice Oreg. Supreme Ct., Salem, 1982-92, state supreme ct. chief justice, 1992—. Mem. Oreg. Ho. of Reps., 1967-71, maj. leader, 1969-71; mem. Oreg. State Senate, 1971-77, minority floor leader, 1971-77; dir. Salem Area Community Council, 1967-70, pres., 1969-70; mem. Salem Planning Commn., 1966-72, pres., 1970-71; co-chmn. Marion County Mental Health Planning Com., 1965-69; mem. Salem Community Goals Com., 1965; Republican precinct commiteeman, 1963-66; mem. Marion County Rep. Central Exec. Com., 1963-66; com. predinct edn. Oreg. Rep. Central Com., 1965; vestryman, acolyte, Sunday Sch. tchr., youth coach St. Paul's Episcopal Ch., 1935— ; task force on cts. Oreg. Council Crime and Delinquency, 1968-69; trustee Willamette U., 1970— ; adv. bd. Cath. Ctr. Community Services, 1976-77; mem. comporehensive planning com. Mid-Willamette Valley Council of Govts., 1970-71; adv. com. Oreg. Coll. Edn. Tchr. Edn., 1971-75; pres. Willamette regional Oreg. Lung Assn., 1974-75, state dir., exec. com., 1975-77; pub. relations com. Williamette council Campfire Girls, 1976-77; criminal justice adv. bd. Chemeketa Community Coll., 1977-79; mem. Oreg. Mental Health Com., 1979-80; mem. subcom. Gov's Task Force Mental Health, 1980; you and govt. adv. com. Oreg. YMCA, 1981— . Served to col. USAFR, 1956-59. Recipient Salem Disting. Svc. award, 1968; recipient Good Fellow award Marion County Fire Svc., 1974, Minuteman award Oreg. N.G. Assn., 1980; fellow Eagleton Inst. Politics, Rutgers U., 1971 Mem. Marion County Bar Assn. (sec.-treas. 1965-67, dir. 1968-70), Oreg. Bar Assn., ABA, Willamette U. Coll. Law Alumni Assn. (v.p. 1968-70), Salem Art Assn., Oreg. Hist. Soc., Marion County Hist. Soc., Stanford U. Club (pres. Salem chpt. 1963-64), Delta Theta Phi. Office: Oregon Supreme Ct Supreme Ct Bldg 1163 State St Salem OR 97310-1331

CARTEN, FRANCIS NOEL, lawyer; b. Bryn Mawr, Pa., Dec. 25, 1935; s. Francis Patrick and Louise Cathleen (Leach) C. BS, U. Notre Dame, 1960; JD, Villanova U., 1964. Bar: Pa. 1967, N.Y. 1967, Conn. 1976. Assoc. Eyre, Mann & Lucas, N.Y.C., 1966-74; pvt. practice Danbury and Stamford, Conn., 1975-78, Stamford, 1985-88; patent counsel TIE/Comm., Inc., Shelton, Conn., 1978-79, Automation Industries, Inc., Greenwich, Conn., 1979-85; ptnr. Wyatt, Gerber & O'Rourke), LLP, Stamford, 1988—. With U.S. Army, 1954-56. Mem. N.Y. Intellectual Property Law Assn., Seawanhaka Corinthian Yacht Club (Oyster Bay, N.Y.). Republican. Intellectual property, Patent, Trademark and copyright. E-mail: fncarten@att.net.

CARTER, BARRY EDWARD, lawyer, educator, administrator; b. L.A., Oct. 14, 1942; s. Byron Edward and Ethel Catherine (Turner) C.; m. Kathleen Anne Ambrose, May 17, 1987; children: Gregory Ambrose, Meghan Elisabeth. AB with great distinction, Stanford U., 1964; M.P.A., Princeton U., 1966; JD, Yale U., 1969. Bar: Calif. 1970, D.C. 1972. Program analyst Office of Sec. Def., Washington, 1969-70; mem. staff NSC, Washington, 1970-72; rsch. fellow Kennedy Sch., Harvard U., Cambridge, Mass., 1972; internat. affairs fellow Coun. on Fgn. Rels., 1972; assoc. Wilmer, Cutler & Pickering, Washington, 1973-75; sr. counsel Select Com. on Intelligence Activities, U.S. Senate, Washington, 1975; assoc. Morrison & Foerster, San Francisco, 1976-79; assoc. prof. law Georgetown U. Law Ctr., Washington, 1979-89, prof., 1989-93, 96—; exec. dir. Am. Soc. Internat. Law, Washington, 1992-93; acting undersec. for export adminstrn. U.S. Dept. Commerce, Washington, 1993-94, deputy undersec., 1994-96. Vis. prof. law Stanford U. Law Sch., 1990; bd. dirs. RWE Nukem, Inc., 1998—; chmn. adv. bd. Def. Budget Project, 1990—93; mem. UN Assn. Soviet-Am. Parallel Studies Project, 1976—87; adv. coun. Zurich Emerging Markets Solutions, 2001—. Author: International Economic Sanctions: Improving the Haphazard U.S. Legal Regime, 1988 (Am. Soc. Internat. Law Cert. of Merit 1989); co-author: International Law, 4th edit., 2003; co-editor: Internat. Law: Selected Documents, 2003—; contbr. articles to profl. jours. With U.S. Army, 1969-71. Mem.: ABA, Am. Soc. Internat. Law (hon. v.p. 1993—99, counselor 1999—2000), Coun. on Fgn. Rels., DC Bar Assn., Calif. Bar Assn., Am. Law Inst., Am. Bar Found., Phi Beta Kappa. Democrat. Roman Catholic. Home: 2922 45th St NW Washington DC 20016-3559 Office: Georgetown U Law Ctr 600 New Jersey Ave NW Washington DC 20001-2075 E-mail: carter@law.georgetown.edu.

CARTER, BRET ROBERT, lawyer; b. Muscatine, Iowa, Oct. 8, 1959; s. Burt Eugene and Mary Esther Carter; m. Hazel Mary Williams, Oct. 5, 1991. BS, Iowa State U., 1982; JD, Pepperdine U., 1987. Bar: Calif. 1987, U.S. Dist. Ct. (so. dist.) Calif., 1987, U.S. Dist. Ct. (cen., no. dists.) Calif., 1988, U.S. Dist. Ct. (ea. dist.) Calif., 1990, U.S. Ct. Appeals (9th cir.), 1993. Atty. Booth Mitchell & Strange, L.A., 1986-88, John T. Heaney, A Law Corp., L.A., 1988-93, Hart & Watters, L.A., 1993—. Contbr. articles to profl. jours. Mem. ARC, Santa Monica, Calif., City Hope-Bus. L.A. Recipient Young Lawyer award Achievement ABA, 1990. Mem. L.A. Venture Assn., Beverly Hills Bar Assn. (v.p. bd. govs. 1990-92), L.A. Bus. Property Coun. Avocations: hiking, biking. Corporate, general, Estate planning, Property, real (including real estate development, water). Office: Hart & Watters 12400 Wilshire Blvd Ste 500 Los Angeles CA 90025-1055

CARTER, GENE, judge; b. Milbridge, Maine, Nov. 1, 1935; s. K.W. and S. Loreta (Beal) C.; m. Judith Ann Kittredge, June 24, 1961; children: Matthew G., Mark G. BA, U. Maine, 1958, LLD (hon.), 1985; LLB, NYU, 1961. Bar: Maine 1962. Ptnr. Rudman, Winchell, Carter & Buckley (and predecessors), Bangor, Maine, 1965-80; assoc. justice Maine Supreme Jud. Ct., 1980-83; judge U.S. Dist. Ct. Maine, 1983-89, 1996—2003, chief judge, 1989-96, sr. dist. judge, 2003—. Chmn. adv. com. on rules of civil procedure Maine Supreme Jud. Ct., 1976-80. Chmn. Bangor Housing Authority, 1970-77. Mem. Am. Trial Lawyers Assn., Internat. Soc. Barristers, Am. Coll. Trial Lawyers. Office: US Dist Ct 156 Federal St Portland ME 04101-4152

CARTER, J. DENISE, lawyer; b. Kansas City, Mo., Mar. 21, 1963; d. Ronald Ira and Sharon Kay (Williams) C. AA, Longview C.C., 1986; BA, U. Mo., Kansas City, 1989, JD, 1992. Bar: Mo. 1992. Pvt. practice, Kansas City, 1993—. Republican. Avocations: golf, tennis, scuba diving. Bankruptcy, Criminal, General practice. Office: 4218 Roanoke Rd Ste 300 Kansas City MO 64111-4735

CARTER, JAMES H. judge; b. Waverly, Iowa, Jan. 18, 1935; s. Harvey J. and Althea (Dominick) C.; m. Jeanne E. Carter, Aug. 1965; children: Carol, James. BA, U. Iowa, 1956, JD, 1960. Law clk. to judge U.S. Dist. Ct, 1960-62; assoc. Shuttleworth & Ingersoll, Cedar Rapids, Iowa, 1962-73; judge 6th Jud. Dist., 1973-76, Iowa Ct. Appeals, 1976-82; justice Iowa Supreme Ct., Des Moines, 1982—. Office: Iowa Supreme Ct State House Des Moines IA 50319-0001 E-mail: James.carter@jb.state.us.

CARTER, JAMES HAL, JR., lawyer; b. Ames, Iowa, Sept. 25, 1943; s. James H. Sr. and Louise (Benge) Carter; m. Theresa Carter; children: Janet, Faith, Katherine. BA, Yale U., 1965, LLB, 1969. Bar: N.Y. 1971, U.S. Ct. Appeals (2d cir.) 1971, U.S. Dist. Ct. (so. dist.) N.Y. 1972, U.S. Dist. Ct. (ea. dist.) N.Y. 1975, U.S. Supreme Ct. 1976, U.S. Ct. Internat. Trade 1980, U.S. Dist. Ct. Conn. 1981, U.S. Ct. Appeals (1st and 5th cirs.) 1984, U.S. Ct. Appeals (fed. cir.) 1988, U.S. Ct. Appeals (3d cir.) 1990, U.S. Dist. Ct. (no. dist.) N.Y. 1992, U.S. Dist. Ct. (we. dist.) Mich. 1992. Law clk. U.S. Ct. Appeals (2d cir.), 1969-70; with Sullivan & Cromwell, N.Y.C., 1970—77, ptnr., 1977—. Lectr. internat. comml. arbitration Practicing Law Inst. Corr. editor: Internat. Legal Materials; contbr. articles to profl. jours. Mem. adv. bd. Southwestern Legal Found. Internat.; bd. dirs. Am. Bar Found. Fulbright scholar, Cambridge (Eng.) U., 1965—66. Mem.: ABA (past chair internat. law and practice sect., former co-chmn. internat. comml. arbitration com.), Coun. Fgn. Rels., Assn. Bar City N.Y. (former chmn. internat. affairs coun.), N.Y. State Bar Assn. (former chmn. internat. dispute resolution com.), Am. Law Inst., Am. Soc. Internat. Law (pres.-elect), U.S. Coun. Internat. Bus. (mem. com. arbitration). Federal civil litigation, Private international. Office: Sullivan and Cromwell 125 Broad St 32d Fl New York NY 10004-2498 E-mail: carterj@sullcrom.com.

CARTER, JAMES M. lawyer; b. Ridley Park, Pa., Jan. 17, 1972; s. Michael J. and Georgette M. Carter; m. Kristine Prieto, June 8, 1996; 1 child, Ian Andrew. BA, Rowan U., 1995; JD, Rutgers U., 1998. Bar: N.Mex. 1998, N.J. 2000, U.S. Dist. Ct. N.J. 2000. Assoc. Lamb, Metgar, Lines & Dahl, Albuquerque, 1998—99; jud. law clk. State of N.J., Flemington, 1999—2000; assoc. Angelini, Vinio & Freedman, Woodbury, 2000—. Mem.: ABA, Gloucester County Bar Assn., N.J. State Bar Assn. Labor (including EEOC, Fair Labor Standards Act, labor-management relations, NLRB, OSHA), Trademark and copyright, Corporate, general. Office: Angelini Vinior & Freedman 70 Euclid St Woodbury NJ 08096 Fax: 856-384-1230. E-mail: jkicarter@earthlink.net.

CARTER, JEANNE WILMOT, lawyer, publisher; b. Iowa City, Iowa, Oct. 25, 1950; d. John Robert and Adelaide Wilmot (Briggs) Carter; m. Daniel Halpern, Dec. 31, 1982; 1 child, Lily Wilmot. BA cum laude, Barnard Coll., N.Y.C., 1973; MFA, Columbia U., 1977; JD, Yeshiva U., N.Y.C., 1986. Bar: N.Y. 1987. Assoc. Raoul Lionel Felder, P.C., N.Y.C., 1986—; pres., co-owner, dir. Ecco Press, Hopewell, N.J., 1992—. Author: Dirt Angel, 1997, Tales from the Rain Forest, 1997; editor: On Music, 1994; contbr. articles to profl. jours. and books including Reading the Fights, N.Am. Rev., O'Henry Prize Stories 1986, Antaeus, Antioch Rev., Arts and Entertainment Law Jour., Ont. Rev., Denver Quar., Jour. Blacks in Higher Edn., others. Bd. dirs. Nat. Poetry Series, 1981—, AIDS Helping Hand, N.Y.C., 1987-95, Planned Parenthood of Mercer County, 1998—; vol. litigator Womanspace, Princeton, N.J., 1994; mem. Jr. League of N.Y.C., 1980-91. N.Y. Found. of the Arts fellow, 1989. Mem. ABA, N.Y. State Bar Assn. Family and matrimonial.

CARTER, JOHN LOYD, lawyer; b. Clayton, N.Mex., Oct. 2, 1948; s. John Allen and Ruth (Laughlin) C.; m. Dorel Susan Payne, Sept. 20, 1975; children: Matthew, Caroline, Susan. BA, So. Meth. U., 1970, JD cum laude, 1973. Bar: Tex. 1973, U.S. Ct. Appeals (5th and 11th cirs.) 1975, U.S. Supreme Ct. 1976, U.S. Dist. Ct. (so. dist.) Tex. 1974, U.S. Dist. Ct. (no. dist.) Tex. 1978, U.S. Dist. Ct. (ea. dist.) Tex. 1985, U.S.Dist. Ct. (we. dist.) Tex. 1999. Assoc. Vinson & Elkins, Houston, 1973-80, ptnr., 1980—. Fellow Am. Coll. Trial Lawyers, Am. Bar Found., Tex. Bar Found., Houston Bar Found. Antitrust, General civil litigation, Securities. Office: Vinson & Elkins 2300 First City Tower Houston TX 77002-6760 E-mail: jcarter@velaw.com.

CARTER, JOSEPH CARLYLE, JR., lawyer; b. Mayfield, Ky., June 3, 1927; s. Joseph Carlyle and Cynthia Elizabeth (Stokes) Carter; m. Dianne C. Dinwiddie, July 14, 1949; children: Joseph Carlyle, Hugh D., William H., Henry S., Dianne C. BA, U. Va., 1948, LLB, 1951. Bar: Va. 1951. Assoc. firm Hunton & Williams, Richmond, Va., 1951-58, ptnr., 1958-93, mng. ptnr., 1972-82, sr. counsel, 1993—. Chmn. Richmond Pub. Libr. Bd., 1967—77, mem., 1980—85; vice-chmn. Richard City Sch. Bd., 1990—94; trustee Colonial Williamsburg Found., 1977—93, Assn. Preservation Va. Antiquities, Med. Coll. Va. Found., 1976—99, pres., 1984—87; trustee U. Va. Law Sch. Found., 1985—99, pres., 1988—98; elder, trustee 2d Presbyn. Ch., Richmond. Recipient Algernon Sidney Sullivan award, 1948, Good Govt. award, Richmond First Club, 1994. Mem.: ABA, Am. Judicature Soc., Am. Law Inst., Richmond Bar Assn., Va. Bar Assn., Newcomen Soc., Country Club Va. (Richmond), Commonwealth Club (Richmond). Presbyterian. Commercial, contracts (including sales of goods; commercial financing), Corporate, general, Securities. Home: 5102 Harlan Cir Richmond VA 23226-1637 Office: Hunton & Williams 951 E Byrd St Richmond VA 23219-4074

CARTER, MARY ANDREWS, paralegal; b. Greenville, S.C., Sept. 27, 1958; d. Harold M. Andrews and Mary Nancy Dollar; m. Donald P. Carter, Aug. 1, 1982 (div. Sept. 27, 1986); children: Christina Marie, Jason Paul. Diploma in paralegal, Greenville Tech., 1988. Paralegal Alan. O Campbell, P.E., Inc., Sullivan's Island, SC, 1995—99; pvt. practice, 1999—2001; paralegal Campbell, Schneider & Assocs., John's Island, SC, 2001—. Mem. adv. coun. Clark Acad., Charleston, 1998—2000; guardian, litem State of S.C., Charleston, 1999—2001. Office: Campbell Schneider and Assocs 3690 Bohicket Rd Ste 1D Johns Island SC 29455

CARTER, RICHARD DENNIS, lawyer, educator; b. Newburgh, N.Y., Feb. 17, 1949; s. Edward Francis and Catherine Florence (Harding) C. BA, Pace U., 1977; JD, George Washington U., 1980. Bar: D.C. 1980, Va. 1991, Md. 1991, U.S. Dist. Ct. D.C. 1981, U.S. Dist. Ct. Md. 1990, U.S. Dist. Ct. (ea. dist.) Wis. 1994, U.S. Dist. Ct. Ariz. 1994, U.S. Ct. Appeals (4th cir.) 1991, U.S. Supreme Ct. 1987. Supervising atty., adj. prof. law D.C. Law Students in Ct., Washington, 1980-90, dep. dir., 1981-85, exec. dir., 1985-90; adj. prof. trial advocacy Georgetown U., Washington, 1982-2000; ptnr. Cunningham and Hudgins, Alexandria, Va., 1990, Hudgins, Carter & Coleman, Alexandria, 1990-98, Carter & Coleman, Alexandria, 1998—. Contbr. articles to profl. jours. Mem. ABA, D.C. Bar Assn., Washington Bar Assn., Alexandria Bar Assn., Am. Inns of Ct. Episcopalian. Avocation: motor sports. Federal civil litigation, State civil litigation, Health. Home: 1802 Jamieson Ave Alexandria VA 22314 Office: Carter & Coleman 602 Cameron St Alexandria VA 22314-2506

CARTER, RICHARD MURRELL, lawyer, director; b. Dandridge, Tenn., May 11, 1950; s. Willard Susong and Edna S. (Swann) C.; children: Leslie Marie, Melanie Cruse. BS, U.S. Mil. Acad., 1973; JD, Memphis State U., 1980. Bar: Tenn. 1980, U.S. Dist. Ct. Md. 1981, U.S. Army Ct. Mil. Rev. 1982, Ct. Mil. Appeals 1984, U.S. Supreme Ct. 1984, U.S. Dist. Ct. (ea. and we. dists.) Tenn. 1985, U.S. Dist. Ct. (ea. dist.) Ark. 1986, U.S. Ct. Appeals (11th cir.) 1986, D.C. Ct. Appeals 1986, U.S. Ct. Appeals (6th cir.) 1989, U.S. Ct. Appeals (8th cir.) 1989, U.S. Dist. Ct. (no. dist.) Miss. 1990. Commd. 2d lt. U.S. Army, 1973, advanced through grades to maj., infantry platoon leader, co. exec. officer, 1974-76, asst. brigade adjutant Bad Windsheim, Federal Republic of Germany, 1976-77, funded legal edn. program (law sch.) Memphis, 1977-80, prosecutor, chief prosecutor Ft. Meade, Md., 1980-82, sr. def. counsel, asst. regional def. counsel, 1982-84; assoc. Martin, Tate, Morrow & Marston, Memphis, 1984-89, shareholder, 1989—, chief litigation sect., 1996—; also bd. dirs. Co-author: (NBI booklets) Wrongful Death Law in Tennessee, 1996, Insurance Coverage Law in Tennessee, 1995; author articles and legal edn. materials. Deacon Ind. Presbyn. Ch., Memphis, 1997. Mem. ABA, ATLA, Tenn. State Bar Assn., Memphis Bar Assn., West Point Soc. of Mid-South (sec. 1985-87, pres. 1987-89, chair West Point bicentennial 1996-2002), Omicron Delta Kappa. Democrat. Avocations: running, racquetball, woodworking, studying and teaching various books of the bible. General civil litigation, Construction, Intellectual property. Office: Martin Tate Morrow & Marston PC 22 N Front St Fl 11 Memphis TN 38103-1182 Home: 2173 Massey Rd Memphis TN 38119-6526 E-mail: rcarter@martintate.com.

CARTER, STEVE, state attorney general; b. Lafayette, Ind. BA in Econs., Harvard U., 1976; JD, MBA, Ind. U. Chief city-county atty. Indpls.-Marion County; atty. gen. State of Ind., 2001—. Republican. Office: Ind Govt Ctr S 5th Fl 402 W Washington St Indianapolis IN 46204*

CARTER, T(HOMAS) BARTON, law educator; b. Dallas, Aug. 6, 1949; s. Sydney Hobart and Josephine (Wren) C.; m. Eleonore Dorothy Alexander, June 3, 1978 (div. 1988); 1 child, Richard Alexander. BA in Psychology, Yale U., 1971; JD, U. Pa., 1974; MS in Mass Communication, Boston U., 1978. Bar: Mass. 1974, U.S. Dist. Ct. Mass. 1975, U.S. Ct. Appeals (1st cir.) 1975. Asst. prof. law Boston U., 1979-85, assoc. prof., 1985-96, prof., 1996—; pvt. practice Boston, 1974—. Pres. Tanist Broadcasting Corp., Boston, 1981—2001. Co-author: The First Amendment and the Fourth Estate, 1985, 8th edit., 2000, The First Amendment and the Fifth Estate, 1986, 6th edit., 2003, Mass Communications Law in a Nutshell, 1988, 5th edit., 2000. Mem. ABA, Assn. for Edn. in Journalism and Mass Comm. (clk. 1981-82, asst. head 1982-83, head 1983-84), Broadcast Edn. Assn. (chair law and policy divsn. 1989-90), Fed. Comm. Bar Assn., Univ. Club. Avocation: bridge. Home: 109 Commonwealth Ave Apt 6 Boston MA 02116-2345 Office: Boston U 640 Commonwealth Ave Boston MA 02215-2422 E-mail: comlaw@bu.edu.

CARTER, WILLIAM G. lawyer, legal association administrator; b. Oct. 1940; BS, LLB, U. Oreg. Bar: Oreg. 1965. Pres.-elect Oreg. State Bar, 2003—. Office: 900 W Eighth St Medford OR 97501*

CARTER, WILLIAM JOSEPH, lawyer; b. Balt., Sept. 1, 1949; s. Henry Merle and Florence (Rogan) C.; m. Monica Anne Urlock, July 17, 1976. BS in Psychology, Va. Poly. Inst., 1971; JD, Coll. William and Mary, 1974. Bar: Va. 1974, Pa. 1974, Md. 1980, D.C. 1980, U.S. Dist. Ct. D.C. 1981, U.S. Dist. Ct. Md. 1983, U.S. Dist. Ct. (ea. dist.) Va. 1985, U.S. Ct. Claims 1977, U.S. Tax Ct. 1977, U.S. Ct. Mil. Appeals 1975, U.S. Ct. Appeals (D.C. and 4th cirs.) 1979, U.S. Ct. Appeals (fed. cir.) 1982, U.S. Ct. Appeals (6th cir.) 1988, U.S. Ct. Appeals (3d and 5th cirs.) 1992, U.S. Ct. Appeals (11th cir.) 2002, U.S. Supreme Ct. 1977. Commd. 2d lt. U.S. Army, 1971, advanced through grades to capt., 1974, served with JAGC, 1971-79, resigned, 1979; assoc. Carr, Jordan, Coyne & Savits, Washington, 1979-84; shareholder Carr, Goodson & Lee, P.C., 1984-95, Carr Goodson Lee & Warner Profl. Corp., Washington, 1996-98, Carr Goodson Warner Profl. Corp., Washington, 1999-2000, Carr Goodson, P.C., Washington, 2000—01, Carr Maloney, P.C., Washington, 2001—. Mem. Deans adv. roundtable Coll. Arts and Scis., Va. Poly. Inst. Author: Appellate Practice Handbook for Maryland, Virginia and District of Columbia, 1996; editor: Appellate Practice Manual for the District of Columbia Court of Appeals, 1992. Mem.: ABA, D.C. Bar Assn. (cts. and adminstrn. of justice sect., ct. rules com., chair 1998—2001), Counselors, Bar Assn. D.C., Rotary (pres. Olney, Md. chpt. 1999—2000). Episcopalian. Avocations: ice hockey, tennis, music, scuba diving, skiing. Appellate, General civil litigation, Insurance. Office: Carr Maloney PC Ste 1100 1667 K St NW Washington DC 20006

CARTER, ZACHARY W. lawyer; BA, Cornell U., 1972; JD, NYU, 1975. Bar: N.Y., U.S. Dist Ct. (ea. dist.) N.Y., U.S. Dist. Ct. (so. dist.) N.Y., U.S. Ct. Appeals (2d cir.), U.S. Supreme Ct. Asst. U.S. atty. U.S. Dist. Ct. (ea. dist.) N.Y., 1975-80; mem. Patterson, Belknap, Webb & Tyler, 1980-81; exec. asst. dist. atty. King County Dist. Atty's. Office, Bklyn., 1982-87; exec. asst. to dep. chief adminstrv. judge N.Y. City Cts., 1987; judge criminal ct. City of N.Y., 1987-91; U.S. magistrate judge E.D.N.Y., 1991-93; U.S. atty. ea. dist. N.Y. U.S. Dept. Justice, Bklyn., 1993-99; ptnr. Dorsey & Whitney, N.Y.C., 1999—. Mem. N.Y. Bar Assn. (chmn. Mayor's adv. com. on jud. selection). Office: Dorsey & Whitney LLP 250 Park Ave New York NY 10177-0001 E-mail: carter.zachary@dorseylaw.com.

CARTY, AMOS W. lawyer; b. V.I., 1966; m. Verna Carty. Chief legal counsel Legis.; counsel to Gov., 1997. Mem.: V.I. Bar Assn. (pres.-elect, ABA del. 2003). Office: Roy Lester Schneider Hosp St Thomas VI 00802*

CARTY, JOHN WESLEY, lawyer; b. Lansing, N.C., Oct. 29, 1923; s. John Arthur and Bertha (Eller) C.; m. Doris Frances Barnes, June 27, 1948; children: Dixie Lynne, John Jeffrey. BA, Buena Vista Coll., 1950; JD, Drake U., 1952. Bar: Iowa 1952, U.S. Dist. Ct. (so. dist.) Iowa 1952, U.S. Ct. Appeals (8th cir.) 1965. Assoc. Pryor, Hale, Plock, Riley & Jones, Burlington, Iowa, 1952-54; ptnr. Carty & Jones, Des Moines, 1960-75; pvt. practice Winfield, Iowa, 1955—. Bd. dirs. Farmers Nat. Bank, Winfield, Iowa, pres., chmn. 1984—; pres. Oxidex, Inc., Winfield, 1971—; broker, dir. Winfield Realty Co., 1956-98; pres., chmn. Winfield Health Care & Retirement Ctr., 1972-77; dir., sec., treas. Satellite Mill, Inc., 1961-63. Co-author: Business Law & The Cooperative, 1962; assoc. editor Drake U. Law Rev., 1951-52. City atty. City of Winfield, Iowa, 1954-89, City of Wayland, Iowa, 1962-70; mem. Henry County Conservation Bd., Mt. Pleasant, Iowa, 1972-74; chmn. Henry County Compensation Commn., 1987-92; sec. S.E. Iowa Planning Coun., 1973-74; mem. Gov.'s Heartland Leadership Coun., Iowa, 2003; dir. S.E. Iowa Health Care Coun., Ft. Madison, 1974-76; mem. Iowa Archaeol. Soc., 1991—; mem. commn. eminent domain Henry County, 1993-98. With combat infantry U.S. Army, 1944-46, ETO. Decorated Combat Infantryman's badge, Bronze star; recipient Spl. award Bur. Nat. Affairs, 1952, Annual award Greene County Conservation Bd., 1987. Mem. Henry County Bar Assn. (pres. 1961-62), S.E. Iowa Bar Assn. (pres. 1962), Iowa State Bar Assn., Hawkeye Archeol. Soc., Am. Legion, VFW, Masons, Phi Alpha Delta. Presbyterian. Home: 1586 Oasis Ave Mount Union IA 52644-9506 Office: Carty Law Office Farmers Nat Bank Bldg Winfield IA 52659

CARTY, PAUL VERNON, lawyer; b. Uchitomari, Okinawa, Aug. 2, 1954; s. Leo Sylvester and Dolores Iola (Inniss) C.; m. Kimberly Ann Fickett, Jan. 23, 1982; children: Rachel Lee, Paul Jr., Trevor Dudley. BA, Wesleyan U., Middletown, Conn., 1977; JD, U. Conn., 1985. Bar: Conn. 1985, U.S. Dist. Ct. (Conn.) 1992, Mashantucket Pequot Tribal Ct. 1995. Claims adjustor Liberty Mut. Ins. Co., Bklyn., 1977-80; sr. claims rep. Cigna Corp., Farmington, Conn., 1980-85; assoc. Farren & King, New Haven, 1985-97; solo practitioner New Haven, 1997—. Chmn. West Haven (Conn.) Bd. Ethics, 1987-90. Mem. ABA, Nat. Bar Assn., Conn. Bar Assn., Conn. Trial Lawyers Assn., Conn. Criminal Def. Lawyers Assn., New Haven County Bar Assn., West Haven Bar Assn., George Crawford Law Assn. Episcopalian. Avocations: Karate, photography. General civil litigation, Criminal, Personal injury (including property damage). Home: 20 Swampscott St West Haven CT 06516-1424 Office: 506 Whalley Ave PO Box 3192 New Haven CT 06515-0292 E-mail: PVCartyEsq@aol.com.

CARUSO, DANIEL F. lawyer, judge, former state legislator; b. Greenwich, Conn., Dec. 12, 1957; s. Frederick A. Caruso and Ruth Collins. BA, U. Conn., 1980; JD, U. Vt., 1983. Bar: Conn. 1983, U.S. Dist. Ct. Conn. 1984. Atty. Paul M. Tymniak & Assocs., Fairfield, Conn., 1984-88; sole practice Fairfield, 1988-97; mem. Conn. Gen. Assembly, Hartford, 1989-94, asst. house minority leader, 1992-94, ranking mem. gen. law com., 1991; judge of probate Probate Dist. of Fairfield, 1995—; adminstrv. judge Probate Dist. of New Cannan, 2001, Probate Dist. of Greenwich, 2002; atty. Owen, Schine & Nicola, P.C., Fairfield, Conn., 1997—. Co-chmn. House Rep. Policy Group on Drug Control Strategy; mem. gen. law com. Conn. Gen. Assembly, 1991-94, mem. judiciary com., 1989-94, mem. regulation rev. com., 1989-94. Mem., advisor Nat. Heritage Trust Adv. Bd., 1990-91; treas. Town of Fairfield, 1993-95, mem. bd. fin., 1985-89; del. Rep. Nat. conv., Houston, 1992. Mem. Kiwanis, Eagle Scouts Am., Pi Sigma Alpha, Phi Alpha Theta, Alpha Phi Omega. Roman Catholic. Home: 160 Fairfield Woods Rd Apt 61 Fairfield CT 06432-3348 Office: 53 Sherman St Fairfield CT 06430-5821

CARUSO, MARK JOHN, lawyer; b. L.A., Apr. 27, 1957; s. John Mondella and Joyce Dorothy C.; m. Judy F. Velarde, Aug. 15, 1987. BS cum laude, Pepperdine U., 1979, JD cum laude, 1982. Bar: Calif. 1982, N.Mex. 1987, U.S. Dist. Ct. (ctrl. dist.) Calif. 1982, U.S. Dist. Ct. N.Mex. 1987, U.S. Dist. Ct. (no. and so. dists.) Calif. 1995, U.S. Ct. Appeals (9th cir.) 1983, U.S. Ct. Appeals (10th cir.) 1987. Law clk. Fed. Trade Commn., L.A., 1981-82; pvt. practice, Burbank, Calif., 1982—, Albuquerque, 1987—. Mem. N.Mex. Ho. of Reps., 1990-94, mem. labor com., consumer and pub. affairs com., workers compensation oversight interim com., ct. correction and justice interim com., jud. com., labor com., workers compensation oversight com.; lobbyist Nat. Right to Work Com., 1984-86. Col., aide de camp to gov. State of N. Mex., 1987; chmn. N. Mex. Mcpl. Boundary Commn., 1988—; del. Rep. Nat. Conv., 1988, 92; lectr. breast implant litigation, Fen Phen diet drug litigation; Sandoval county chmn. George Bush for Pres., 1988; campaign mgr. Boulter for U.S. Congress, Tex., 1983-84. Recipient platinum award N.Mex. Free Enterprise Adv., 1986. Mem. ATLA, Breast Implant Litigation Group, Consumer Attys. of Calif., Albuquerque Hispano C. of C., Greater Albuquerque C. of C. General civil litigation, Personal injury (including property damage), Product liability. Office: 4302 Carlisle Blvd NE Albuquerque NM 87107-4811 Fax: 505-883-5012. E-mail: mark@carusolaw.com.

CARVAJAL, ARTHUR GONZALEZ, editor, lawyer; b. San Antonio, Dec. 14, 1962; s. Arthur Carrillo Carvajal and Maria Antonia Gonzalez Berumen. BA, St. Mary's U., San Antonio, 1985; JD, U. Notre Dame, 1988. Bar: Ill. 1989, Tex. 1998. Assoc. Kralovec, Marquard, Doyle & Gibbons, Chartered, Chgo., 1989-93, Robert S. Fritzshall & Assocs., Chgo., 1995-96; sr. legal editor Dearborn Fin. Pub., Inc., Chgo., 1997—. Pro bono counsel Chgo. Vol. Legal Svcs., 1990. Mem. Tex. Bar Assn., Chgo. Bar Assn., Lambda Chi Alpha. Roman Catholic. Office: Dearborn Fin Pub Inc 30 S Wacker Dr Ste 2500 Chicago IL 60606-7481 Fax: 312-577-2458. E-mail: carvajal@dearborn.com.

CARVER, GEORGE ALLEN, JR., retired lawyer; b. Washington, Nov. 8, 1940; s. George Allen and Barbara Ellen (Bristol) C.; m. Joan Page, Dec. 13, 1964; children: George Allen III, Robert William. BS, U.S. Mil. Acad., 1964; JD, U. Va., 1972. Bar: Va. 1972, D.C. 1978, U.S. Ct. Appeals (D.C. cir.) 1979, U.S. Ct. Appeals (9th cir.) 1986, U.S. Ct. Appeals (4th cir.) 1988. Trial atty. gen. crimes sect. Criminal divsn. U.S. Dept. Justice, Washington, 1972-76, trial atty. pub. integrity sect., 1976-81, dir. conflicts of interest crimes br., pub. integrity sect., 1981-88, dep. chief fraud sect., 1988-92, prin. dep. chief fraud sect., 1992-95, sr. counsel to chief asset forfeiture/money laundering sect., 1995-96, dep. chief, sr. counsel to the chief, 1996-2000; ret., 2000. Capt. inf. U.S. Army, 1964-69. Decorated Silver Star, Bronze Star, Purple Heart. Avocations: photography, fishing, boating, walking, reading. Home: 6049 Makely Dr Fairfax Station VA 22039-1324

CARVER, TERESA ANN, lawyer; b. La Grange, Tex., Oct. 21, 1966; d. Clarence G. and Dorris V. Chovanec; m. William Matthew Carver, Mar. 6, 1993; children: Keleigh Ann, Kyle Matthew. BBA, S.W. Tex. State U., 1988; JD, South Tex. Coll. Law, 1992. Bar: Tex. 1992, U.S. Dist. Ct. (so. and ea. dists.) Tex. 1995. Mem. Lorance & Thompson, P.C., Houston, 1992—. Mem. Am. Law Firm Assn. (ins. practice group), Def. Rsch. Inst., Tex. Assn. Def. Counsel, Houston Bar Assn. Avocations: hunting, fishing, travel, family activities. Appellate, Insurance, Personal injury (including property damage). Office: Lorance & Thompson PC 2900 North Loop W Ste 500 Houston TX 77092-8826 E-mail: tac@lorancethompson.com.

CARY, CHARLES MUSE, lawyer; b. Salina, Kans., May 23, 1948; s. Charles Muse and Carolyn Elizabeth (Blalock) C. BS, U. Tenn., 1969, JD, 1972; postgrad., Command and Gen. Staff Coll., 1986; M in Strategic Studies, U.S. Army War Coll., 2002. Bar: Tenn. 1972, U.S. Dist. Ct. (mid. dist.) Tenn. 1972, U.S. Dist. Ct. (we. dist.) Tenn. 1974, U.S. Ct. Mil. Appeals 1980, U.S. Supreme Ct. 1984. Staff atty. Div. Water Quality Control, Nashville, 1972-74; assoc. H. Morris Denton, Bolivar, Tenn., 1974-75; ptnr. Denton and Cary, Bolivar, 1975—. Atty. Hardeman County, Bolivar, 1976—; atty. City of Middleton, Tenn., 1976—, City of Grand Junction, Tenn., 1981—. Mayor Town of Whiteville, Tenn., 1976-79. Served to col. Tenn. Army Nat. Guard, 1979—. Fellow Tenn. Bar Assn. (ho. dels. 1982-87); mem. ABA, Hardeman County Bar Assn. Presbyterian. Avocations: piloting, tennis, traveling. State civil litigation, General practice, Property, real (including real estate development, water). Home: 701 Pebble Springs Dr Bolivar TN 38008 Office: Denton and Cary PO Box 306 Bolivar TN 38008-0306

CASANUEVA, FERNANDO, lawyer; b. Oviedo, Spain, Aug. 27, 1958; m. Victoria Feliu. Degree in Econs., MBA, Escuela Superior de Administración y Dirección de Empresas, Barcelona, Spain, 1980; Law Degree, U. Barcelona, 1995. Bar: 1996. Ptnr. Garrigues (Andersen), Barcelona, 1984—. Author: Insurance and Pension Scheme, 2000. Corporate taxation, Mergers and acquisitions. Office: Garrigues Abogados Asesores Tributarios Avenida Diagonal 654 08034 Barcelona Spain

CASE, DAVID LEON, lawyer; b. Lansing, Mich., Sept. 22, 1948; s. Harlow Hoyt and Barbara Jean (Denman) C.; m. Cynthia Lou Rhinehart, Jan. 28, 1968; children: Beau, Ryan, Kimberly, Darren, Stephanie. BS with distinction, Ariz. State U., 1970, JD cum laude, 1973. Bar: Calif. 1973, U.S. Dist. Ct. (cen. dist.) Calif. 1973, U.S. Tax Ct. 1974, Ariz. 1976, U.S. Supreme Ct. 1997. Assoc. Willis, Butler & Scheifly, Los Angeles, 1973-75; from assoc. to mem. Ryley, Carlock & Applewhite, Phoenix, 1975—. Fellow Ariz. Bar Found., Am. Coll. Trust and Estate Counsel; mem. ABA (tax sect., corp. sect., probate and trust sect.), Ariz. Bar Assn., Ctrl. Ariz. Estate Planning Coun. (bd. dirs., pres. 1988-89), Beta Gamma Sigma. Republican. Presbyterian. Avocations: guitar, sports. Corporate, general, Estate planning, Taxation, general. Office: Ryley Carlock & Applewhite PO Box 634 Phoenix AZ 85001-0634 E-mail: dcase@rcalaw.com.

CASE, DOUGLAS MANNING, lawyer; b. Cleve., Jan. 3, 1947; s. Manning Eugene and Ernestine (Bryan) Case; m. Marilyn Cooper, Aug. 23, 1969. BA, U. Pa., 1969; JD, MBA, Columbia U., 1973. Bar: N.Y. 1974, N.J. 1975, Calif. 1980, Ohio 1991, Fla. 2000. Assoc. Brown & Wood, N.Y.C., 1973-77; corp. counsel PepsiCo Inc., Purchase, NY, Irvine, Calif., 1977—83, Nabisco Brands Inc., N.Y.C., East Hanover, N.J. and London, 1983-89; asst. gen. counsel Chiquita Brands Internat., Inc., Cin., 1989-92; prin. Douglas M. Case Law Offices, Cin., Vero Beach, Fla., 1993—. Lectr. numerous seminars. Contbr. articles to profl. jours. Chmn. Olde Colonial Dist.; active Morris-Sussex area coun. Boy Scouts Am., 1986—88; sec., trustee Marble Scholarship Com., N.Y.C., 1983—88; trustee Cin. Opera Guild, 1994—99, pres., 1997—98, chmn., 1998—99, hon. trustee, 1999—; bd. dirs., mem. exec. com. Cin. Opera Assn., 1997—98. Mem.: ABA, Quality in Law (chmn. 1996—98), Cin. Bar Assn. (continuing legal edn. chair internat. law com. 1994—96, chair solo and small firm practitioners com. 1995—97, sec. 1996—97, vice chair 1997—98, chair 1998—2000), Fla. Bar Assn., Internat. Bar Assn., Munich Sister City Assn. Greater Cin. (chmn. econ. devel. com. 1995—96), Kenwood Country Club, Columbia Bus. Sch. Club (N.Y.C.) (pres., bd. dirs. 1974—79), Morris County Golf Club, Met. Club (N.Y.C.), Lawyers Club Cin. (mem. exec. com. 1995—2000, treas. 1996, sec. 1997, 2d v.p. 1998, 1st v.p. 1999, pres. 2000). Avocation: golf. Commercial, contracts (including sales of goods; commercial financing), Corporate, general, Private international. Office: 501 Bay Dr Vero Beach FL 32963-2163 E-mail: dcaselaw@bellsouth.net.

CASE, JAMES HEBARD, lawyer; b. Lihue, Hawaii, Apr. 10, 1920; s. Adrial Hebard and Elizabeth (McConnell) C.; m. Suzanne Catherine Espenett, Sept. 18, 1948; children: Edward E., John H., Suzanne D., Russell L., Elisabeth C. Marguleas, Bradford Case. AB, Williams Coll., 1941; JD, Harvard U., 1949. Bar: Hawaii 1949, U.S. Supreme Ct. 1985. Assoc. Pratt, Tavares & Cassidy, Honolulu, 1949-51, Carlsmith & Carlsmith, Hilo, Hawaii, 1951-59; ptnr. Carlsmith Ball, Honolulu, 1959—2002, of counsel, 2002—. Bd. dirs. ML Resources, Honolulu. Trustee Hanahauoli Sch., Honolulu, 1970-82, Cen. Union Ch., Honolulu, 1984-88, Arcadia Retirement Residence, Honolulu, 1985-91. Lt. comdr. USNR, 1943-46, PTO. Mem. ABA, Hawaii Bar Assn., Hawaii Yacht Racing Assn. (bd. dirs. 1994-2000). Clubs: Pacific (bd. dirs. 1978-82); Kaneohe Yacht (Honolulu). Republican. Congregationalist. Avocations: sailing, tennis. Corporate, general, Utilities, public, Securities. Home: 3757 Round Top Dr Honolulu HI 96822-5043 Office: Carlsmith Ball PO Box 656 Honolulu HI 96809-0656 E-mail: jhc@carlsmith.com.

CASE, JEFF DEAN, lawyer; b. Harlingen, Tex., Jan. 7, 1955; s. Gene Carl and Lois Faye Case; children: Robert Gene, Caitlin Anne, Julia Faye. BJ with highest honors, U. Tex., 1978, JD, 1990. Bar: Tex. 1990. Atty. pvt. practice, San Antonio, 1990—. Editor, publisher: The Belton Journal, 1982-86. Trustee Liberty Hill Sch. Bd., 1992-98, v.p., 1995-96, pres., 1996-97; vice-chmn. Liberty Hill Econ. Devel. Found., 1992-93. Mem. ABA, State Bar Coll., Williamson County Bar Assn., Assn. Trial Lawyers Am., Nat. Wildlife Fedn., Liberty Hill C. of C. (pres. 1993). Avocations: family, music, travel, ranching. General civil litigation, Corporate, general, General practice. Office: PO Box 701952 San Antonio TX 78270 E-mail: jeffdeancase@go.com.

CASE, KAREN ANN, lawyer; b. Milw., Apr. 7, 1944; d. Alfred F. and Hilda M. (Tomich) Case. BS, Marquette U., 1963, JD, 1966; LLM, NYU, 1973. Bar: Wis. 1966, U.S. Ct. Claims 1973, U.S. Tax Ct. 1973. Ptnr. Meldman, Case & Weine, Milw., 1973-85, Meldman, Case & Weine divsn. Mulcahy & Wherry, S.C., 1985-87; Sec. of Revenue State of Wis., 1987-88; ptnr. Case & Drinka, S.C., Milw., 1989-91, Case, Drinka & Diel, S.C., Milw., 1991-97, CoVac, 1997—. Lectr. U. Wis., Milw., 1974-78; guest lectr. Marquette U. Law Sch., 1975-78; dir. WBBC, 1998—. Contbr. articles to legal jours. Mem. gov.'s Commn. on Taliesin, 1988, gov.'s Econ. Adv. Commn., 1989-91, pres.'s coun. Alverno Coll., 1988-94, nat. coun., 1998-2000; bd. dirs. WBCC, 1998—. Fellow Wis. Bar Found. (dir. 1977-90, treas. 1980-90); mem. ABA, Milw. Assn. Women Lawyers (founding mem., bd. dirs. 1975-78, 81-82), Milw. Bar Assn. (bd. dirs. 1985-87, law office mgmt. chair 1992-93), State Bar Wis. (bd. govs. 1981-85, 87-90, dir. taxation sect. 1981-87, vice chmn. 1986-87, 90-91, chmn. 1991-92), Am. Acad. Matrimonial Lawyers (bd. dirs. 1988-90), Nat. Assn. Women Lawyers (Wis. del. 1982-83), Milw. Rose Soc. (pres. 1981, dir. 1981-83), Friends of Boerner Bot. Gardens (founding mem., pres. 1984-90), Profl. Dimensions Club (dir. 1985-87), Tempo Club (sec. 1984-85). Probate (including wills, trusts), Corporate taxation, Personal income taxation. Home: 2212 Harbour Ct Longboat Key FL 34228-4174 Office: CoVac 9803 W Meadow Park Dr Hales Corners WI 53130-2261

CASE, THOMAS LOUIS, lawyer; b. Dallas, June 14, 1947; s. Donald L. and Ellen (Hanson) C.; m. Bonnie Nally, July 8, 1972. BA, Vanderbilt U., 1969, JD, 1972; cert. civil trial law, Tex. Bd. Legal Specialization. Bar: Tex. 1972, U.S. Dist. Ct. (no. dist.) Tex. 1973, U.S. Dist. Ct. (we. and ea. dists.) Tex. 1978, U.S. Dist. Ct. (so. dist.) Tex. 1979, U.S. Dist. Ct. (ea. dist.) Ark. 1981, U.S. Ct. Appeals (5th cir.) 1977, U.S. Supreme Ct. 1978, U.S. Ct. Appeals (8th cir.) 1984, U.S. Ct. Appeals (11th cir.) 1981. Assoc. Johnson, Bromberg, Leeds & Riggs, Dallas, 1972-77; ptnr. Bickel & Case, Dallas, 1977-84, St. Claire & Case, Dallas, 1984-93, Thomas L. Case & Assocs., P.C., Dallas, 1993-2000; shareholder Case Carter Salyers & Henry, Dallas, 2000—01; ptnr. Bell, Nunnally & Martin, Dallas, 2002—. Mem. ABA, Tex. Bar Assn., Tex. Assn. Def. Coun., Dallas Assn. of Def. Counsel, Dallas Bar Assn. Federal civil litigation, General civil litigation, Labor (including EEOC, Fair Labor Standards Act, labor-management relations, NLRB, OSHA). Office: Bell Nunnally & Martin 3232 McKinney Ave Ste 1400 Dallas TX 75204 E-mail: tomc@bellnunnally.com.

CASELLA, PETER F(IORE), patent and licensing executive; b. June 5, 1922; s. Fiore Peter and Lucy (Grimaldi) C.; m. Marjorie Eloise Enos, March 9, 1946 (dec. Aug. 1989); children: William Peter, Susan Elaine, Richard Mark. BChE, Poly. U., Bklyn., 1943; student in chemistry, St. John's U., N.Y.C., 1940. Registered to practice by the U.S. Patent and Trademark Office, Can. Patent and Trademark Offices. Head patent sect. Hooker Electrochem. Co., Niagara Falls, N.Y., 1943-54; mgr. patent dept. Occidental Chem. Corp. (formerly Hooker Chem. Corp.), Niagara Falls, N.Y., 1954-64, dir. patents and licensing, 1964-81, asst. sec., 1966-81, ret., 1981. Pres. TFA Products, Inc., Houston, Intra Gene Internat., Inc., Lewiston, N.Y., 1981-92; chmn. bd. In Vitro Internat., Inc., Linthicum, Md., 1983-86; cons. patents and licensing, Lewiston, N.Y., 1981—; Dept. Commerce del. on patents and licensing exchange, USSR, 1973, 90, Poland and German Dem. Rep., 1976. Editor: Drafting the Patent Application, 1957. Mem. Lewiston Bd. Edn., 1968-70. With AUS, 1944-46, Mediterranean Theater of Operation. Recipient Centennial citation Poly. U., Bklyn., 1955, Golden Jubilee Soc., 1993. Mem. ACS, AIChE, Assn. Corp. Patent Counsel (emeritus, exec. com. 1974-77, charter mem.), N.Y. Intellectual Property Law Assn. (Niagara Frontier chpt. pres. 1973-74, founder award 1974), Licensing Execs. Soc. (v.p. 1976-77, Trustees award 1977), Chartered Inst. Patent Agts. Gt. Britain (emeritus), Patent and Trademark Inst. Can., Internat. Patent and Trademark Assn. (emeritus), U.S. Trademark Assn., Nat. Assn. Mfrs. (patent com.), Mfg. Chemists Assn., Pacific Indsl. Property Assn., U.S. Patent Office Soc. (assoc.), U.S. Trademark Office Soc. (assoc.), Chemists Club (emeritus N.Y.C. chpt.), Niagara Club (Niagara Falls pres. 1973-74).

CASELLAS, SALVADOR E. judge; b. 1935; BS in Fgn. Svc. cum laude, Georgetown U., 1957; LLB magna cum laude, U. P.R., 1960; LLM, Harvard U., 1961. Ptnr. Fiddler, Gonzalez & Rodriguez, 1962-72, 77-94; judge U.S. Dist. Ct. P.R., San Juan, 1994—. Mem. P.R. Acad. Jurisprudence, P.R. Commn. on Bicentennial of U.S. Constn., 1987-89; aide to Sec. of U.S. Army, 1985-89, emeritus, 1990—. Dir. Alliance for Drug Free P.R., 1993-94. 1st lt. U.S. Army, 1961-62, Res., JAGC, 1963-67. Recipient Comdrs. medal Second U.S. Army, 1990, P.R. Nat. Guard medal, 1990. Mem. ABA, Am. Bar Found., P.R. Bar Assn., P.R. Bar Assn. Found., Caparra Country Club, Banker's Club. Office: US Dist Ct PR US Courthouse 150 Ave Carlos Chardon # 111 San Juan PR 00918-1703

CASEY, BERNARD J. lawyer; b. June 4, 1942; s. Andrew J. and Theresa (Lennon) C.; m. Kathleen A. Wall; children: Brendan, B. John. AB, Providence Coll., 1964; JD, Catholic U., 1967. Bar: R.I. 1967, D.C. 1971, U.S. Supreme Ct. 1972, U.S. Cir. Ct. (D.C. cir., 4th cir., 6th cir.). Assoc. Gall, Lane & Powell, Washington, 1971-76, ptnr., 1976, Reed Smith LLP, Washington, 1976—. Bd. dirs. Cath. Charities, 1994-99, chmn., 1997-98. Served to capt. AUS, 1967-71. Decorated Bronze Star medal. Mem. ABA (litigation com.), Barristers, Lawyers Club, Univ. Club (bd. govs. 1989-97, pres. 1990-92), Chevy Chase Country Club. Roman Catholic. General civil litigation, Labor (including EEOC, Fair Labor Standards Act, labor-management relations, NLRB, OSHA), Product liability. Home: 4700 Connecticut Ave NW Apt 607 Washington DC 20008-5613 Office: Reed Smith LLP East Tower 1301 K St NW Ste 1100 Washington DC 20005-3317

CASEY, JOHN FREDERICK, lawyer; b. Martinsville, Ohio, May 19, 1939; s. Raymond J. and Esther E. (Read) C.; m. Karen S. Bollenbacher, Sept. 2, 1978. BS, Ohio State U., 1961, JD, 1965. Bar: Ohio, 1965, U.S. Dist. Ct. (so. dist.) Ohio 1967, D.C. 1981, U.S. Tax Ct. 1967. Ptnr. Means, Bichimer & Burkholder, Columbus, Ohio, 1965-70, Chamblin, Snyder & Casey, Columbus, 1971-75; pvt. practice Columbus, 1976-83, 91-93; ptnr., shareholder Wiles, Doucher, Van Buren, Boyle & Casey, Columbus, 1984-85; ptnr. Thompson, Hine & Flory, Columbus, 1986-88, Casey & Christensen, Columbus, 1989, Casey, McFadden & Winner, Columbus, 1990, Harris, McClellan, Binau & Cox, Columbus, 1994; prin. John F. Casey, A Legal Profl. Assn., 1994—. Adv. coun. mem. U.S. Small Bus. Adminstrn., Columbus, 1985-93. Mem. gov.'s Ohio Farmland Preservation Task Force, 1996-97. Mem. Ohio State Bar Assn. (bd. govs. 1990-99, emeritus 2000, estate planning, trust, and probate law sect.), Fin. Planning Assn. Ctrl. Ohio (founding trustee 2000), Columbus Bar Found., Ohio State U. Coll. Law (nat. coun.), Greater Columbus C. of C. Avocations: gardening, golf. Corporate, general, Estate planning, General practice. Home: 207 E Whittier St Columbus OH 43206-2638 Office: Lucas Predergast Albright Gibson & Newman 600 S High St Columbus OH 43215-5656

CASEY, PATRICK ANTHONY, lawyer; b. Apr. 20, 1944; s. Ivanhoe and Eutimia (Casados) C.; m. Gail Marie Johns, Aug. 1, 1970; children: Christopher Gaelen, Matthew Colin. BA, N.Mex. State U., 1970; JD, U. Ariz., 1973. Bar: N.Mex. 1973, Ariz. 1973, U.S. Dist. Ct. N.Mex. 1973, U.S. Ct. Appeals (10th cir.) 1979, U.S. Supreme Ct. 1980, U.S. Dist. Ct. Ariz. 1999. Assoc. Bachicha & Casey, Santa Fe, 1973-76; Patrick A. Casey, P.A. Santa Fe, 1976—. Bd. dirs. Santa Fe Sch. Arts and Crafts, 1974, Santa Fe Animal Shelter, 1975-81, Cath. Charities of Santa Fe, 1979-82, Old Santa Fe Assn., 1979-88, Santa Fe Fiesta Coun., 1982—; bd. dirs. United Way, 1986-89, N.Mex. State U. Found., 1985-93. Served with USN, 1961—67. Mem.: VFW, Vietnam Vets. of Am., Am. Legion, Hispanic Bar Assn., Bar Assn. 1st Jud. Dist. (pres. 1980), N.Mex. Trial Lawyers Assn. (dir. 1977—79, treas. 1979—83, pres. 1983—84, dir. 1985—, treas. 2000—01), Western Trial Lawyers Assn. (gov. 1987—90, bd. dirs. 1988—91, parliamentarian 1990—91, sec. 1991—92, treas. 1991—95, pres. 1996—97, treas. 2000—), ABA, ATLA (state del. 1988—89, bd. govs. 1990—91, 1993—95), B.P.O. Elks. General civil litigation, Personal injury (including property damage), Product liability. Office: 1421 Luisa St Ste P Santa Fe NM 87505-4073

CASEY, PAULA JEAN, former prosecutor; b. Charleston, Ark., Feb. 16, 1951; d. Arthur Clinton and Mildred Aleene (Underwood) C.; m. Gilbert Louis Glover II, Mar. 13, 1981. BA, Ea. Cen. (Okla.) U., 1973; JD, U. Ark., 1977. Staff atty. Ctrl. Ark. Legal Services, Hot Springs, Ark., 1977-79; dep. pub. defender 6th Jud. Dist. Pub. Defender, Little Rock, 1979; clinic supr. U. Ark. at Little Rock Law Sch., 1979-81, asst. prof., 1981-84, assoc. prof., 1984-92, prof., 1992-93, assoc. dean, 1986-90; legis. dir., chief counsel U.S. Senator Dale Bumpers, 1990-92; lobbyist Ark. Bar Assn., 1993; U.S. atty. Ea. Dist. Ark., 1993—2001; prof. law U. Ark. at Little Rock Law Sch., 2001—. Cons. for juvenile affairs 6th Jud. Dist. Judges, Ark., 1987. Author, editor: Poverty Law Practice Manual, 1985. Sec. Pulaski County Dem. Com., Little Rock, 1984-89; mem. Ark. Dem. Com., 1984-89; mem. Juvenile Adv. Group, Little Rock, 1985-89; mem. Gov.'s Task Force on Juvenile Cts., Ark., 1987; chmn. Ark. Dem. Jud. Com., 1987; bd. dirs. Ctrl. Ark. Legal Svcs., Little Rock, 1986-89. Named One of Top 100 Women in Ark., Ark. Bus. Pubs., 1996, 98, 99; recipient Gale Pettus Pontz award U. Ark.-Fayetteville Law Sch. Women Students Assn., 1994, award of merit Organized Crime Drug Enforcement Task Force, 1997. Fellow Ark. Bar Found. (bd. dirs.); mem. Ark. Bar Assn. (del. 1986-90), Am. Inns Ct., Overton Am. Inns of Ct., 8th Cir. Ct. Appeals (fed. adv. comm. 2001-05). Democrat. Office: U Ark at Little Rock Sch Law 1201 McMath Blvd Little Rock AR 72202 E-mail: pjcasey@ualr.edu.

CASHMAN, GIDEON, lawyer; b. N.Y.C., Sept. 10, 1929; s. Abba Morris and Rachel (Cashman) Cashman; m. Kathryn Batchelder, 1985; children: Adam Parker, Lindsey Avril, Emily Parker Hyle. AB, NYU, 1951; JD, Columbia U., 1954. Bar: D.C. 1954, N.Y. 1954. Asst. counsel Waterfront Commn. N.Y., 1954-55; asst. U.S. atty. criminal divsn. So. Dist. Ct. N.Y., 1958-61, chief criminal aplls., 1959-61; assoc. Christy Perkins & Christy, N.Y.C., 1961-63; sr. ptnr. Pryor, Cashman, Sherman & Flynn LLP, N.Y.C., 1963—. Lectr. trial tactics Practicing Law Inst.; bd. dirs. Irvington Inst. for Med. Rsch. Trustee Friars Found., Heart Rsch. Found., Eugene O'Neill Teatre Ctr. 1st lt. U.S. Army, judge advocate Gen.'s Corps, 1955-58. Mem. ABA, N.Y. State Bar Assn., Assn. Bar City N.Y., N.Y. County Lawyers Assn., Friars Club (N.Y.C.). Jewish. Federal civil litigation, State civil litigation, Corporate, general. Home: 812 Park Ave New York NY 10021-2759 Office: 410 Park Ave New York NY 10022-4441

CASILLAS, MARK, lawyer; b. Santa Monica, Calif., July 8, 1953; s. Rudolph and Elvia C.; m. Natalia Settembrini, June 2, 1984. BA in History, Loyola U., L.A., 1976; JD, Harvard U., 1979. Bar: N.Y. 1982, Calif. 1983. Clk. to chief judge U.S. Ct. Appeals (10th cir.), Santa Fe, 1979-80; assoc. Breed, Abbott & Morgan, N.Y.C., 1980-82; counsel Bank of Am. Nat. Trust and Savs. Assn., San Francisco, 1982-84; assoc. Lillick & Charles, San Francisco, 1984-87, ptnr., 1988-95, Russin & Vecchi LLP, San Francisco, 1995-96; of counsel LeBoeuf, Lamb, Greene & MacRae, LLP, San Francisco, 1997-2000; atty. Wilson Sonsini Goodrich & Rosati, Palo Alto, Calif., 2000—. Counsel Internat. Bankers Assn. in Calif., L.A., 1984-89, 94-97. Co-author: California Limited Liability Company: Forms and Practice Manual, 1994; mng. editor Harvard Civil Rights-Civil Liberties Law Rev., 1978-79. Mem. ABA (apptd. mem. airfin. subcom. 1991—), N.Y. Bar Assn., Calif. Bar Assn. (vice-chmn. fin. instn. com. 1987-88), Internat. Bar Assn., The Japan Soc., Bankers Club (bd. dirs. 1996—, pres. 2003-). Avocations: skiing, travel. Office: Wilson Sonsini Goodrich & Rosati 650 Page Mill Rd Palo Alto CA 94304 E-mail: mcasillas@wsgr.com.

CASO, DAWN MARIE, lawyer, consultant, law educator; b. Boynton Beach, Fla., Sept. 4, 1967; AA in Psychology, Palm Beach (Fla.) C.C., 1992; BA, Barry U., 1994; JD, Nova Southeastern U., 2000. Cert.: (notary pub.) 1998. Novelist, Rome and other cities, Italy, 1992—93; asst. editor The National Enquirer, Lantana, Fla., 1993—96; editor self employed, Boca Raton, Fla., 1996—98; jud. asst. to judges Palm Beach County, West Palm Beach, Fla., 1998—99; law clk., legal rschr. Legal Help, West Palm Beach, Fla., 1999—2000; legal instr., asst. prof. law Kaplan Coll.-Kaplan, Inc. , Boca Raton, Fla., 2000—01. Legal cons., provider free legal aid, educator Caso, Inc., Deerfield Beach, Fla., 2001—. Author: (Numerous Books and Study Guides) Every Major Legal Subject- Torts, Contracts, Mediation, etc., 2001 (Specialty Publication acknowlegement, 2001), numerous books and study guides, 2001—. Supporter Families Against Mandatory Minimum Sentences, 1998—; contbr., supporter Broward Outreach Ctr., Hollywood, Fla., 2000—; pro choice advocate NOW, Washington, 1993—; active polit. advocate for women's rights West Palm Beach, 1985—. Mem.: ABA, Broward County Bar Assn., Nat. Assn. Pub. Interest Law, Fla. Assn. Women Lawyers (assoc.), Broward County Bar Association (Featured in Journal), National Association of Public Interest Law, Florida Association of Women Lawyers, American Bar Association (Permitted to Remain a member). Liberal. Home and Office: 441 NE 20th Ave # 205 Deerfield Beach FL 33441 Personal E-mail: DMC98SAW@aol.com.

CASPER, DENISE JEFFERSON, lawyer; b. East Patchogue, N.Y., Jan. 9, 1968; d. Eugene and Marcia Jefferson; m. Marc N. Casper, Aug. 20, 1994. BA, Wesleyan U., 1990; JD, Harvard, 1994. Bar: Mass. 1994, N.Y. 1995; U.S. Dist. Ct. Mass. 1995, U.S. Ct. Appeals (1st. cir.) 1996. Law clk. to Hon. Justice Edith Fine and Hon. Justice J. Harold Flannery Mass. Appeals Ct., Boston, 1994-95; assoc. Bingham Dana L.L.P., Boston, 1995-98; asst. U.S. atty. U.S. Atty's Office, Boston, 1999—. Bd. dirs. Vol. Lawyer's Project Boston, 1998—. Chair, bd. dirs. People Making a Difference Through Community Svc. Inc. Boston 1995-99. Mem. Mass. Black Women's Atty's Assn. (exec. bd. mem. 1998-2000), Boston Bar Assn. (coun., 2002-) Women's Bar Assn. (bd. trustees, sec.), Delta Sigma Theta. Office: US Atty's Office US Courthouse 1 Courthouse Way Ste 9200 Boston MA 02210-3011

CASPER, ERIC MICHAEL, lawyer; b. Long Branch, N.J., Feb. 27, 1959; s. Walter Jr. and Lois Ann (Countryman) C. BS in Polit. Sci. with high honors, U. Iowa, 1980, MBA, JD with high honors, 1984. Bar: Ariz. 1985, U.S. Dist. Ct. Ariz. 1985, U.S. Tax Ct. 1986, U.S. Ct. Appeals (9th cir.) 1997. Assoc. Snell & Wilmer, Phoenix, 1984-91; trial atty. civil tax litigation Dept. Justice, Washington, 1991-95; pvt. practice Phoenix, 1995—; ptnr. Walker Silver, PLC, Phoenix. Contbr. articles to profl. publs. Tchr. Jr. Achievement, various Phoenix area jr. high and high schs., 1986-91; tutor Dept. Labor TEAM Project; vol. Phoenix chpt. Am. Cancer Soc., 1987-91. Mem. Ariz. Bar Assn. (tax and bankruptcy sects.), Mensa, Kiwanis (dir. Camelback), Am. Bankruptcy Inst. Methodist. Avocations: basketball, volleyball, science fiction. Home: 5778 W Corrine Dr Glendale AZ 85304-1890 Office: Walker Silver PLC 4800 N Scottsdale Rd 6th Flr Scottsdale AZ 85251

CASPER, RICHARD HENRY, lawyer; b. Chgo., Nov. 4, 1950; s. Edson Lee and Dorothy Ellen (Klemp) C.; m. Betty Gene Ward, Aug. 26, 1972; children: Terrance, Laura, Russell, Jeremy. AB, Bowdoin Coll., 1972; JD, Northwestern U., 1975. Bar: Wis. 1975, U.S. Dist. Ct. (ea. dist.) Wis. 1975. Assoc. Foley & Lardner, Milw., 1975-82, ptnr., 1982—. James Bowdoin scholar Bowdoin Coll, 1972. Mem. Wis. Bar Assn., Milw. Bar Assn., Order of the Coif. Bankruptcy, Commercial, contracts (including sales of goods; commercial financing), Franchising. Office: Foley & Lardner Firstar 777 E Wisconsin Ave Milwaukee WI 53202-5367 E-mail: rcasper@foleylaw.com.

CASS, ROBERT MICHAEL, lawyer, consultant; b. Carlisle, Pa., July 5, 1945; s. Robert Lau and Norma Jean (McCaleb) C.; m. Patricia Ann Garber, Aug. 12, 1967 (dec. Jan. 1999); children: Charles McCaleb, David Lau. BA, Pa. State U., 1967; JD, Temple U., 1971. Bar: N.Y. 1974; cert. arbitrator AIDA Reins. and Ins. Arbitration Soc. Benefit examiner Social Security Adminstrn., Phila., 1967-68; mktg. rep. Employers Comml. Union Ins. Co., Phila., 1968-70; asst. sec. Nat. Reins. Corp., N.Y.C., 1970-77; asst. v.p. Skandia Am. Reins. Corp., N.Y.C., 1977-80; mgr. Allstate Reins. divsn., South Barrington, Ill., 1980-86, R.K. Carvill, Inc., Chgo., 1986-87; pres. R. M. Cass Assocs., Chgo., 1987—. V.p. Assurance Alliance, Inc., Crystal Lake, Ill., 1989; lectr. Ins. Sch. Chgo., Coll. of Ins. N.Y., U. Wis., Am. Inst. for Chartered Property Casualty Underwriters. Author: (with others) Reinsurance Contract Wording, Reinsurance Practices, 2d edit.; editor, reviewer: (with others) The Legal Environment of Insurance, 4th edit. Mem. ABA (tort and ins. practice sect., past chair com. on excess, surplus lines and reins. law, standing com. on professionalism, standing com. on emerging issues, com. on long range planning, past chmn. internat. com., liaison to ABA Ctrl. & East European Law Initiative, chair 3rd Chinese-Am. law seminar, Guangzhou, China, 1999, chair 4th Chinese-Am. law seminar Beijing and Shanghai 2001, dispute resolution sect., past chair com. large complex case arbitration), Soc. CPCUs (past chair risk mgmt. sect. com., mem. excess, surplus and splty. lines sect. com., reinsurance sect. com., past officer Chgo. N.W. suburban chpt.), Am. Arbitration Assn. (panel neutrals), Assn. Ind. Reins. Cons. (pres.), Internat. Assn. Ins. Receivers (publs. com., past chair membership com.), Fellows of Am. Bar Found., N.Y. State Bar Assn., Assn. Internat. de Droit des Assurances, Ill. Captive and Alternative Risk Funding Ins. Assn. (pres. bd. dirs.), Coalition Alternative Risk Funding Mechanisms (bd. dirs.). Alternative dispute resolution, Insurance, Private international. Home: 330 N Jefferson Ct #1705 Chicago IL 60661-1212 Office: PO Box 543460 Chicago IL 60654-3460 E-mail: mikecassre@aol.com.

CASS, RONALD ANDREW, dean; b. Washington, Aug. 12, 1949; s. Millard and Ruth Claire (Marx) C.; m. Valerie Christina Swanson, Aug. 24, 1969; children: Laura Rebecca, Alexander Stephan. BA with high distinction, U. Va., 1970; JD with honors, U. Chgo., 1973. Bar: Md. 1973, D.C. 1974, U.S. Dist. Ct. D.C. 1974, U.S. Ct. Appeals (D.C. cir.) 1974, U.S. Supreme Ct. 1977, Va. 1979. Law clk. to chief judge U.S. Ct. Appeals (3d cir.), Wilmington, Del., 1973-74; assoc. Arent, Fox, Kintner, Plotkin & Kahn, Washington, 1974-76; asst. prof. law U. Va. Sch. Law, Charlottesville, 1976-81; assoc. prof. law Boston U., 1981-83, prof., 1983-95; dean Boston U. Law Sch., 1990—; Melville Madison Bigelow prof. Boston U., 1995—; legal advisor Office Plans and Policy, FCC, Washington, 1987-88; mem. U.S. Internat. Trade Commn., Washington, 1988-90, vice chmn., 1989-90. Cons. comm. program Aspen (Colo.) Inst., 1977-78, Adminstrv. Conf. U.S. Washington, 1980-87, Helsell, Fetterman, Martin, Todd & Hokanson, Seattle, 1984-85, Assn. Trial Lawyers Am., Phila., 1985-87, UN Conf. Trade and Devel., Geneva, 1991, U.S. Dept. Justice, 1998, Microsoft Corp., 1998-; spl. cons. Nat. Econ. Rsch. Assn., Cambridge, Mass., 1990-94; arbitrator Biogen v. Schering-Plough, 1999-2000, Telesia Sistemas v. Lucent Tech., 2000-2002, UPS v. Canada, 2001-; adj. scholar Am. Enterprise Inst., Washington, 1993-; sr. fellow Internat. Ctr. Econ. Rsch., Turin, 1996-97, 99-02; sesquicentennial assoc. Ctr. Advanced Studies U. Va. Law Sch., 1980-81; mem. nat. adv. bd. Case Western Res. U. Sch. Law, 1996-97; disting. lectr. U. Francisco Marroquin, Guatemala City, 1996, IMADEC Internat. Bus. Sch., Vienna, 2000, U. Aix en Provence, 2002, Boston U. London Program, 2002. Author: Revolution in the Wasteland: Value and Diversity in Television, 1981, (with Colin S. Diver) Administrative Law: Cases and Materials, 1987, (with Colin S. Diver and Jack M. Beermann) Administrative Law: Cases and Materials, 2nd edit., 1994, 3d edit., 1998, 4th edit., 2002, (with John R. Haring) International Trade in Telecommunications, 1998, The Rule of Law in America, 2001; contbr. articles and essays to profl. jours., also chpts. to books. Bd. dirs. Northwestern Va. Health Systems Agy., Culpeper, 1980; bd. govs. Sightsavers Internat., Washington, 1989-91; bd. dirs. Telecomm. Policy Rsch. Conf., Washington, 1989-91, sec.-treas. 1989-90, vice chmn., 1991-92; bd. dirs. New Eng. Legal Found., 1994-2002, New England Coun., 1995-; bd. overseers Boston Bar Found., 1992-94, Supreme Jud. Ct. Hist. Soc., 1997-2000; sr. Europe Discussion Group, Ctr. for Strategic and Internat. Studies, 1989-96; bd. advisors George Mason U. Law Sch. Law & Econs. Ctr., 1996-99, Inst. Dem. Comm., Boston, 1991-92, Fundación de la Commn. Social, Madrid, 1995-, IMADEC Internat. Bus. Sch., Vienna, 1999-2001, Legal Issues in Econ. Integration, Amsterdam, 2000-. Fellow Am. Bar Found.; mem. ABA (adminstrv. law and regulatory practice sect., coun. 1993-95, chair 1998-99, legal edn. and admission bar sect., review commn. 1994-95, ho. of dels. 2000-02), Am. Law Inst., Am. Law Deans Assn. (bd. dirs. 1995—, pres. 1995-97), Mont Pelerin Soc., Boston Bar Assn. (coun. 1992-95), Adminstrv. Conf. U.S. (pub. mem. 1990-95, govt. mem. 1988-90), Transatlantic Policy Network (U.S. Working Group), Spring Valley C. C., Order of Coif, Phi Beta Kappa, Bay Club, Federalist Soc., Internat. Law (exec. com. 2001-). Republican. Jewish. Home: 36 Forest St Wellesley Hills MA 02481-6818 Office: Boston U Sch Law 765 Commonwealth Ave Boston MA 02215-1401

CASSAR, GEORGE V., JR., lawyer; b. Detroit, Aug. 24, 1971; s. Margaret Cassar; m. Carolyn M. Boakes, July 18, 1998. BA in Psychology, U. of Mich., 1993; JD with honors, Drake U., Des Moines, 1996; LLM in Tax, Wayne State U., Detroit, 1997. Bar: Mich. 1996, Iowa 1996, U.S. Dist. Ct. (ea. dist.) Mich. 1996, U.S. Tax Ct. 1997. Law clk. Fisher, Fisher & Fisher, P.C., Adair, Iowa, 1994—96, Law Offices of Jacques D. Schira, Des Moines, 1994—96; jud. clk. U.S. Dist. Ct. for Ea. Dist. of Mich., Detroit, 1994—95; tchg. asst. Drake U. Law Sch., Des Moines, 1994—96; atty. Downey & Sosin, P.C., Southfield, Mich., 1996—98, Maddin, Hauser, Wartell, Roth & Heller, P.C., Southfield, Mich., 1998—. Vol. Big Bros./Big Sisters of Mich. Mem.: ABA, Bldg. Industry Assn. of Southeastern Mich., Fed. Bar Assn., State Bar of Mich. Avocations: motorcycle riding, classic muscle cars, hockey, football. Environmental, Probate (including wills, trusts), Estate taxation. Office: Maddin Hauser Wartell Roth & Heller 28400 Northwestern Hwy 3rd floor Southfield MI 48034 Office Fax: 248-359-6144. E-mail: gvc@maddinhauser.com.

CASSELL, RICHARD EMMETT, lawyer; b. N.Y.C., Jan. 3, 1949; s. Max and Sylvia (Cohen) Cassell; m. Madeline Gail Erdman, June 13, 1970; children: Lori Faith, Marc Joshua. BA cum laude, SUNY, Buffalo, 1971; JD, Georgetown U., 1974. Bar: D.C. 1974, Va. 1974, Md. 1985. Assoc. Ira Lechner, Washington, 1974-75, Benson, Stien & Braunstien, Washington, 1975-85; sole practice Alexandria, Va., 1986—. Mem. Landlord-Tenant Commn., Arlington, 1974-76. Committeeperson Arlington Dems., 1973-76, Arlingtonians for Better County, 1973-76. Mem. ABA, Va. Bar Assn., D.C. Bar Assn., Md. Bar Assn. Family and matrimonial, Personal injury (including property damage), Workers' compensation. Home: 7497 Covent Wood Ct Annandale VA 22003-5731 Office: 1513 King St Alexandria VA 22314-2716

CASSELMAN, WILLIAM E., II, lawyer; b. Washington, Pa., July 8, 1941; s. William E. and Lucy (Bobbs) C.; m. Mia Kang, June 15, 1993; children: Katharine Carr, Lee Wilson. BA, Claremont-McKenna Coll., 1963; postgrad., U. Madrid, 1963-64; JD, George Washington U., 1968. Bar: Va. 1968, D.C. 1972, U.S. Supreme Ct. 1975. Legis. asst. to Robert McClory U.S. Ho. of Reps., 1965-68; staff asst. Office of Pres., 1969, dep. spl. asst. to Pres., 1969-71, counsel to Pres., 1974-75; gen. counsel Gen. Svcs. Adminstrn., 1971-73; legal counsel to Vice Pres. U.S., 1973-74; ptnr. Ambrose & Casselman, P.C., 1975-79; pvt. practice Washington, 1979-82; ptnr. Dorsey & Whitney, 1982-84, Popham, Haik, Schnobrich & Kaufman, Ltd., Washington, 1985-93; of counsel Stairs Dillenbeck Finley & Rendon, N.Y.C., 1993—; pvt. practice Washington, Va., 1993—. Mem. adminstrv. conf. U.S., 1971-73; adv. mem. Nat. Conf. Commrs. on Uniform State Laws, 1975; mem. Gerald R. Ford Commemorative Com., 1977-82; bd. dirs. gen. counsel, mem. fin. com., fellow Georgetown U. Ctr. for Internat. Bus. and Trade (formerly Nat. Ctr. Export-Import Studies), 1983-93. Recipient Disting. Alumni Achievement award George Washington U., 1975. Mem. ABA, Fed. Bar Assn. (chmn. gen. counsels com. 1973-74, nat. coun. 1974-79, Disting. Svc. commendation 1974), George Washington Law Assn. (bd. dirs. 1976-81), Nat. Trust for Hist. Preservation (mem. com. on legal svcs. 1978-80), Delta Theta Phi, Theta Chi. Republican. Corporate, general, Government contracts and claims, Private international.

CASSERLY, JAMES LUND, lawyer; b. Norfolk, Va., Dec. 26, 1951; s. James Robert and Patricia (Lund) C.; m. Kathleen Ann Flynn, Apr. 25, 1981; 1 child Laura Flynn. AB magna cum laude, Tufts Coll., 1973; JD, Columbia U., 1976. Bar: D.C. 1976, U.S. Dist. Ct. D.C. 1980, U.S. Ct. Appeals (D.C. cir.) 1981. Law clk. to trial judges U.S. Ct. Fed. Claims, Washington, 1976-77; law clk. to judge Marion Bennett U.S. Ct. Appeals Fed. Cir., Washington, 1977-78; assoc. Wilkinson, Cragun & Barker, Washington, 1978-82, Squire Sanders & Dempsey, Washington, 1982-85, ptnr., 1985-94; sr. legal advisor to Commr. Susan Ness FCC, Washington, 1994-99; ptnr. Mintz Levin Cohn Ferris Glovsky & Popeo PC, Washington, 1999—2002, Willkie Farr & Gallagher, Washington, 2003—. Communications, Legislative. Home: 2839 Allendale Pl NW Washington DC 20008 Office: Willkie Farr & Gallagher 1875 K St NW Washington DC 20006-1238 E-mail: jcasserly@willkie.com.

CASSIDY, BRETT, lawyer; b. Jersey City, N.J., Mar. 28, 1972; s. Harold J. and Randee S. Cassidy. BS, U. So. Calif., 1994; JD, Vanderbilt U., 1998. Bar: Calif. Atty. Latham & Watkins, L.A., 1998—2000, London, 2000—. Mem.: Order of Coif. Securities, Mergers and acquisitions. Office: Latham & Watkins 99 Bishopsgate London EC2M 3XF England Fax: +44 207 3744460. E-mail: brett.cassidy@lw.com.

CASSIDY, DAVID MICHAEL, lawyer; b. Amityville, N.Y., May 31, 1954; s. Paul Francis and Theresa Alice (Britts) C.; children: Daniel B., Caitlin E. BA, SUNY, Stony Brook, 1981; JD, St. John's U., Jamaica, N.Y., 1985. Bar: N.Y. 1986. Assoc. Rivkin Radler LLP, Uniondale, NY, 1985-92, ptnr., 1992—. Mem. Suffolk County Bar Assn., L.I. Assn. General civil litigation, Insurance. Office: Rivkin Radler LLP Eab Plz Uniondale NY 11556-0001

CASSIDY, EDWARD Q. lawyer; b. Pekin, Ill., July 15, 1951; s. Clement James and Patricia Quinn Cassidy; m. Michele A. Cohn, Oct. 30, 1982. JD, Hamline U., 1981. Ptnr. Felhaber, Larson, Fenlon & Vogt, St. Paul, 1994—. General civil litigation, Labor (including EEOC, Fair Labor Standards Act, labor-management relations, NLRB, OSHA), Workers' compensation. Office: Felhaber Larson Fenlon & Vogt 2100 World Trade Ctr Saint Paul MN 55105

CASSIDY, ROBERT CHARLES, JR., lawyer; b. Beaumont, Tex., May 16, 1946; s. Robert Charles and Peggy (Timken) C.; m. Leslie Fleming Iben, Sept. 2, 1949; children: Robert Charles III, Thomas Reinhard, Leslie Anne Vallandingham. BA, Johns Hopkins U., 1968; JD, U. Pa., 1973; LLM, Georgetown U., 1977. Bar: Pa. 1973, U.S. Dist. Ct. D.C. 1975, U.S. Ct. Appeals (D.C. cir.) 1975, U.S. Ct. Internat. Trade 1982, U.S. Ct. Appeals (fed. cir.) 1982. Asst. counsel Office of Legis. Counsel U.S. Senate, 1973-75, internat. trade counsel Com. on Fin., 1975-79; gen. counsel Office of U.S. Trade Rep., Exec. Office of Pres., Washington, 1979-81; ptnr. Kaye, Scholer, Fierman, Hays & Handler, Washington, 1982-83, Wilmer, Cutler & Pickering, Washington, 1983—, internat. practice group leader, 1995-2000, trade group leader, 1985—2001. Bd. dirs. Cordell Hull Inst., 1999—. With U.S. Army, 1968—70. Mem.: ABA (chmn. internat. trade law com. 1986—89), Am. Soc. Internat. Law., D.C. Bar Assn. Administrative and regulatory, Private international, Legislative. Office: Wilmer Cutler & Pickering 2445 M St NW Washington DC 20037-1487 E-mail: Robert.Cassidy@wilmer.com.

CASSIDY, SAMUEL H. lawyer, lieutenant governor, state legislator, humanities educator; children: Rachael, Sarah, Samuel H. IV. BA, U. Okla., 1972; JD, U. Tulsa, 1975; postgrad., Harvard U., 1991. Bar: Okla., 1975, U.S. Supreme Ct. 1977, U.S. Ct. Appeals (10th cir.), 1977, Colo. 1982. Pvt. practice law, 1975—; mem. Colo. State Senate, 1991-94; lt. gov. State of Colo., 1994-95; pres. Jefferson Econ. Coun., 1995-97; pres., CEO Colo. Assn. Commerce and Industry, 1997-2000; chair dept. bus. ethics and legal studies U. Denver, 2001—. Bd. dirs. Capital Reporter; instr. U. Tulsa, 1978-81, Tulsa Jr. Coll., 1979; owner High Country Title Co.; developer of residential and commercial real estate, pres. Sam Cassidy, Inc. oil and gas exploration and production co., mem. agriculture and natural resources com., 1991-92, state, mil. and vet. affairs com., 1991-92, local govt. com. 1991, legal svcs. com. 1991-92, hwy. legis. review com. 1991-93, nat. hazards mitigation coun., 1992-93, appropriations com., 1993, judiciary com., 1993; pres. Econ. Devel. Coun. of Colo., 1997-98; exec. com. legis coun., 1993-94, senate svcs. com. 1993; elected Senate Minority Leader, 1993-94, exec. com. Colo. Gen. Assembly; sr. fellow U. Denver, 1997—. Bd. dirs. Colo. DLC, 1993-95, Leadership Jefferson County, Rocky Flats Local Impacts Initiative, dir.; chmn. bd. Arts Comm., Inc. Named Outstanding Legislator for 1991 Colo. Bankers Assn., ACLU Outstanding Legis. 1994; recipient Outsatnding Legis. Efforts award Colo. Counties, Guardian of Small Bus. award, NFIB, 1992, 94; fellow Gates Found., 1991, U. Denver sr. fellow. Mem. Colo. Bar Assn. (bd. gov. 1993-94), S.W. Colo. Bar Assn., Nat. Conf. State Legis. (Colo. rep., task force on state-tribe rels.), Rotary (hon. mem., sustaining Paul Harris fellow), Club 20 (bd. dirs.), San Juan Forum (chmn., bd. dirs.). Avocations: fine art photography, skiing, fishing. Home: # 128 2800 S University Blvd Denver CO 80210 E-mail: scassidy@du.edu.

CASSON, RICHARD FREDERICK, lawyer, travel bureau executive; b. Boston, Apr. 11, 1939; s. Louis H. and Beatrix S. C. AB, Colby Coll., 1960; JD, U. Chgo., 1963. Bar: Ill. 1963, Mass. 1964. Ptnr. Casson & Casson, Boston, 1967-68; assoc. counsel, corp. sec. Bankers Leasing Corp., 1968-75; asst. gen. counsel, corp. sec. Commonwealth Planning Corp., 1975-76; assoc. gen. counsel, asst. sec. Prudential Capital Corp., 1976-92; pres. Autumn Crest Corp., 1991-98; v.p. Casseden Corp. Asst. innkeeper Jackson House Inn, Woodstock, Vt. Capt. JAGC U.S. Army, 1964-67. Decorated Bronze Star. Jewish. Home and Office: 6648 John Smith Ln Hayes VA 23072 E-mail: rfc0439@3bubbas.com.

CASTAGNA, CHARLES NELSON, mediator; b. Clearwater, Fla., June 8, 1955; BA in Pub. Affairs, George Washington U., 1975—77; JD, Fla. State U., Tallahassee, 1977—80. Law clk. to James C. Adkins Fla. Supreme Ct., Tallahassee, 1980—82, Carr, Jordan, Coyne & Savits, Washington, 1982—83; assoc. Alcalde, Henderson, & O'Bannon, Arlington, Va., 1983—85, Battaglia Ross, St. Petersburg, Fla., 1985—87, McMullen, Everett, Clearwater, Fla., 1987—90; pvt. practice Charles N. Castagna, PA, Clearwater, Fla., 1990—94; pres. Mediation Ctr. of Tampa Bay, Inc., Clearwater, Fla., 1994—. Contbr. articles to profl. jours. Vol. Pinellas County Pub. Schs., 1990—. Recipient Outstanding Family Mediator, 13th Jud. Cir., Hillsborough County, Fla., 1998. Mem.: Fla. Assn. Profl. Family Mediators (pres. 2000—02), Fla. Acad. Profl. Mediators (pres. 2002—, Pres.'s Award 2001). Avocations: boating, hiking, reading, cooking, tennis. Office: Mediation Ctr of Tampa Bay Inc 611 Druid Rd E Ste 512 Clearwater FL 33756 Fax: 727-462-0196. E-mail: mediators.mediate@verizon.net.

CASTAGNA, WILLIAM JOHN, federal judge; Student, U. Pa., 1941-43; LLB, JD, U. Fla., 1949. Bar: Fla. 1949. Ptnr. MacKenzie, Castagna, Bennison & Gardner, 1970-79; judge U.S. Dist. Judge (mid. dist.) Fla., 1979—, now sr. judge. Democrat.

CASTAGNOLA, GEORGE JOSEPH, JR., lawyer, mediator, secondary education educator; b. Scotia, Calif., July 6, 1950; s. George Joseph and Olga Esther Castagnola; m. Sandra Annette Castagnola, June 7, 1975; children: George Joseph III, Laura, Joseph. Grad., U. San Francisco, 1974; JD, N.W. Calif. U., Sacramento, 1990, D Juridical Sci., 1992. BAr: Calif. 1990. Tchr. El Molino H.S., Forestville, Calif., 1977—; charter boat capt. Castagnola Fishing, Petaluma, Calif., 1971—; prof. law N.W. Calif. U., 1990—; atty., mediator Law and Mediation Office of George Castagnola, Petaluma, Calif., 1990—. Cpl. USMCR, 1968-74. Mem. Calif. Bar Assn., Sonoma County Bar Assn., Calif. Tchrs. Assn., Golden Gate Sport Fishing Assn. Roman Catholic. Avocations: weightlifting, fishing. Home and Office: 802 Wine Ct Petaluma CA 94954-7420

CASTANO, GREGORY JOSEPH, lawyer; b. Kearny, NJ, Feb. 17, 1929; s. Nicholas and Marianna (Prestinaci) C.; m. June Dwyer, Oct. 15, 1966; children: Gregory, Christopher, John, Timothy. BS, Seton Hall U., 1950; JD, Fordham U., 1953; LLM, NYU, 1956. Bar: NJ 1956, US Ct. Appeals (3d cir.) 1957, US Supreme Ct. 1959, US Tax Ct. 1974, NY 1985. Sports writer Newark Star-Ledger, 1946—53; pvt. practice Harrison, NJ, 1959—78; atty. Bd. Adjustment, Harrison, 1978; judge Superior Ct. N.J., Jersey City, 1978—85; ptnr. Tompkins, McGuire & Wachenfeld, Newark, 1985—88, Waters, McPherson & McNeill, Secaucus, NJ, 1988—2002, Castano Quigley LLC, West Caldwell, NJ, 2002—. Asst. atty. Town of Harrison, 1959-64; asst. prosecutor County of Hudson, NJ, 1963-71; atty. Town of West New York, NJ, 1977-78, Town of Kearny, NJ, 1999—, Harrison Redevel. Agy., 1997—; adj. prof. Seton Hall U. Sch. Law, Newark, 1988—; master com. to computerize criminal cts. Essex County; mediator US Dist. Ct., Superior Ct. Tax assessor Town of Harrison, 1964-78; del. NJ Constl. Conv., 1964; mem. juvenile conf. com. Twp. West Caldwell, NJ, 1977-78; trustee Caldwell (NJ) Coll., 1985-91, chmn. acad. affairs com. bd. trustees, 1987-91; chmn. County Govt. Transition Com., Hudson County, 1987-88; mem. Hudson County Community Coll. Blue Ribbon Task Force, 1992-93. With US Army, 1953-55. Named Man of Yr., Kearny Jaycees, 1963, Alumnus of Yr., Dorf Feature Service, 1987, Caldwell Coll., 2003, Pres. Award. Fellow Am. Bar Found.; mem. ABA, NJ Bar Assn., Hudson County Bar Assn. (Justice medallion 1985), Essex County Bar Assn., West Hudson Bar Assn. (pres. 1977-78), Assn. Fed. Bar NJ, Essex Fells Country Club. General practice, Municipal (including bonds), Property, real (including real estate development, water). Home: 19 Sunset Rd West Caldwell NJ 07006-6540 Office: Castano Quigley LLC 1120 Bloomfield Ave W Caldwell NJ 07007

CASTEEL, STEVEN W. federal agency administrator; b. Ill. Degree in Zoology, Degree in Chemistry, So. Ill. U. Dep. sheriff Ill. Sheriffs Dept., 1971—72; spl. agt. U.S. Dept. Justice-Bur. Narcotics and Dangerous Drugs (now Drug Enforcement Adminstrn.), 1972; exec. asst. to the career bd. Drug Enforcement Adminstrn., Washington, exec. asst. to dep. adminstr., sr. exec. svc., head Office Inspections, 1994—96, assoc. spl. agt. in charge Houston field divsn., 1996—98, spl. agt. in charge Seattle field divsn., 1998—99, asst. adminstr. for intelligence Alexandria, Va., 1999—. Office: Drug Enforcement Adminstrn Washington DC 20537

CASTEL, P. KEVIN, lawyer; b. N.Y.C., Aug. 5, 1950; s. Peter A. and Mildred (Cronin) C.; m. Patricia A.; 2 children. BS, St. John's U., Jamaica, N.Y., 1972, JD, 1975. Bar: N.Y. 1976, U.S. Dist. Ct. (so. and ea. dists.) N.Y. 1976, U.S. Ct. Appeals (2nd cir.) 1979, U.S. Supreme Ct. 1983, U.S. Ct. Appeals (fed. cir.), 1986, U.S. Ct. Appeals (10th cir.), 1988, U.S. Ct. Appeals (3rd cir.) 1989, U.S. Ct. Appeals (4th cir.) 1991, U.S. Ct. Appeals (7th cir.) 1995, U.S. Ct. Appeals (11th cir.) 1997. Law clk. to judge U.S. Dist. Ct. (so. dist.) N.Y., 1975-77; assoc. Cahill Gordon & Reindel, N.Y.C., 1977-83, ptnr., 1983—; nominated by Pres. George W. Bush for U.S. Dist. Judge (so dist.) N.Y., 2003. Mem. departmental disciplinary com. appellate divsn. 1st dept., 1987—93, hearing panel chair, 1991—93, mem. policy com., 1997—2002. Articles editor St. John's Law Rev., 1974-75. Mem. mayor's panel Martin Luther King Jr. Inst. for Law and Social Justice, 1987—89; nat. chmn. ann. giving campaign St. John's U., 1994—95; bd. dirs. The Legal Aid Soc., 2000—. Recipient Pres.'s medal St. John's U., 2000. Fellow: N.Y. Bar Found., Am. Bar Found.; mem.: N.Y. County Lawyers Assn., Fed. Bar Coun. (pres. 2000—02, sec. 1983—85, trustee 1985—93, 1997—, chmn. publs. com. 1984—95, chmn. program com. 1995—98, v.p. 1988—90), Assn. Bar City of N.Y. (com. profl. and jud. ethics 1994—97, coun. on jud. adminstrn. 1997—), N.Y. State Bar Assn. (com. on cts. of appellate jurisdiction 1979—86, com. fed. cts. of appellate jurisdiction 1979—86, com. fed. cts. 1986—89, chmn. com. fed practice 1989—91, exec. vice chmn. comml. and fed. litig. sect. 1991—92, chmn. 1993—94, ho. of dels. 1994—95), St. John's U. Law Sch. Alumni Assn. (bd. dirs. 1991—, v.p. 1998—), Supreme Ct. Hist. Soc. Federal civil litigation, General civil litigation, State civil litigation. Office: Cahill Gordon & Reindel 80 Pine St Fl 17 New York NY 10005-1790

CASTELLANO, CHRISTINE MARIE, lawyer; b. Jacksonville, Fla., Jan. 10, 1966; d. James Todd and Constance Marie (Wallis) Drylie; m. Ralph Castellano, Sept. 15, 1997. BA summa cum laude, U. Colo., 1987; JD cum laude, U. Mich., 1990. Bar: Colo. 1990, Ill. 1991, U.S. Dist. Ct. Colo. 1991, U.S. Dist. Ct. (no. dist.) Ill. 1991, U.S. Dist. Ct. (ctrl. dist.) Ill. 1994, U.S. Ct. Appeals (10th cir.) 1991, U.S. Ct. Appeals (7th cir.) 1993, U.S. Supreme Ct. 1995. Clk. to chief judge Sherman G. Finesilver U.S. Dist. Ct. Colo., Denver, 1990-91; income ptnr. McDermott, Will & Emery, Chgo., 1991-96; ops. atty. Corn Products divsn. of CPC Internat. Inc., Summit-Argo, Ill., 1996-97; atty. Corn Products Internat., Inc., 1998—2002, counsel, U.S. and Can., 2002—. Adminstr. Family Law Project, Ann Arbor, Mich., 1988-91; judge Julius H. Miner Moot Ct., Northwestern U. Sch. Law, 1993-95, Northwestern U. Sch. Law Negotiation Competition, 1992-94. Writer newspaper The Res Gestae, 1987-90; editor yearbook The Quadrangle, 1988-90; contbg. editor Jour. of Law Reform, 1988-90. Vol. Lincoln Park Homeless Shelter, Chgo., 1991-92, Chgo. Cares, 1993-96; co. coord. Youth Motivation Program, 1991-96. Recipient Negligence Sect. award Mich. Bar Assn., 1990; Carl B. Gussin Meml. prize U. Mich., 1991; scholar Elk's, 1983-84, faculty U. Colo., 1983-84; U. Colo. grantee, 1987. Mem. ABA, Colo. Bar Assn., Ill. Bar Assn., Denver Bar Assn. (vol. teen ct. 1991), Chgo. Bar Assn., Chgo. Coun. Laywers, Women Law Students Assn., U. Colo. Alumni Assn., U. Mich. Alumni Assn., Moot Ct., Mortar Bd., Phi Beta Kappa, Pi Sigma Alpha. Avocations: photography, ice skating, camping, hiking. General civil litigation, Commercial, contracts (including sales of goods; commercial financing), Corporate, general. Office: Corn Products Internat 5 Westbrook Corporate Ctr Westchester IL 60154

CASTELLO, RAYMOND VINCENT, lawyer; b. San Jose, Calif., Apr. 25, 1939; s. Joseph V. and Josephine M. (Gallina) C.; m. W. Karla Grusonik, July 29, 1963; children: Joseph W., Julie A. BS, Calif. State U., San Jose, 1961; JD, Stanford U., 1964. Bar: Calif. 1965, U.S. Dist. Ct. (no. dist.) Calif. 1965, U.S. Ct. Appeals (9th cir.) 1965, U.S. Supreme Ct. 1976. Sole practice, Campbell, Calif., 1965-68; ptnr. Finch, Castello & Tennant, Campbell, 1968-78, Castello, Daily & Gerbino, Campbell, 1978—. Gen. ptnr. Castello, Marino & Orr, Tracy, Calif., 1963—, Castello Farms, Tracy, 1963—, Castello Properties, San Jose, 1975—, Southgate Shopping Ctr., Modesto, Calif., 1995—, Modesta Plz. Shopping Ctr., 2000. Coach Police Athletic League, San Jose, 1973-83; pres. Dry Creek Community Assn., San Jose, 1975—. Mem. Calif. Bar Assn., Santa Clara County Bar Assn. (trustee 1973-80), West Valley Bar Assn. (pres. 1973), Am. Arbitrary Assn., Phi Alpha Delta. Clubs: Civic of Santa Clara County (San Jose) (pres. 1982-84). Lodges: Rotary (bd. dirs. Campbell club 1966-74). State civil litigation, Personal injury (including property damage), Probate (including wills, trusts). Office: Law Office of Raymond V Castello 1790 Winchester Blvd Ste 1 Campbell CA 95008-1150

CASTILLE, RONALD D. judge; b. Miami, Mar. 16, 1944; s. Henry and Marie Nash Castille. BS in Econs., Auburn U., 1966; JD, U. Va., 1971. Asst. dist. atty., 1971-81; chief asst. dist. atty. Career Criminal Unit, 1982-84; dep. dist. atty. Pre-Trial Unit, 1984-85; dist. atty. Phila., 1986-91; with litigation dept. Reed Smith Shaw & McClay, Phila., 1991-93; justice Supreme Ct. Pa., 1993—. Co-chmn. Pa. Anti-Crime Coalition for George Bush for Pres., 1988, 92; commr. Pres.'s Commn. on Model State Drug Laws, 1992. Lt. USMC, 1966-68. Decorated Bronze Star with Combat V, Purple Heart (2); recipient Disting. Pub. Svc. award Pa. County and State Detectives Assn., 1987, Layman award Pa. Chiefs of Police Assn., 1987, Spirit of Am. award Inst. for Study of Am. Wars, 1988, Pres.'s award for Outstanding Svc., Nat. Dist. Attys. Assn., 1991; named Man of Yr., Fraternal Order of Police Lodge #5, 1988, Outstanding Disabled Vet. of Yr., Nat. Disabled Am. Vets., 1988. Mem. Nat. Dist. Attys. Assn. (v.p. 1986-91), Pa. Dist. Attys. Assn. (legis. chmn. 1986-91). Office: 1818 Market St Ste 3730 Philadelphia PA 19103-3639

CASTILLO, ANGEL, JR., lawyer; b. Havana, Cuba, Nov. 29, 1946; came to U.S., 1960; s. Angel and Graciela (Blanco) C. m. Stormie G. Stafford, Dec. 16, 1977; children: Arielle Caridad, Angel Marti. BA, Stetson U., 1968; JD with high honors, U. Fla., 1978; LLM, Yale U., 1980. Bar: Fla. 1979, U.S. Supreme Ct. 1982. Various positions in pub. and journalism, 1968-80; legal affairs reporter The N.Y. Times, N.Y.C., 1980-81; assoc. Shutts & Bowen, Miami, Fla., 1981-83; sr. assoc. Morgan, Lewis & Bockius, Miami, 1983-86; ptnr. Soto & Castillo, Miami, 1987-89, Castillo, Stafford & Wald, Miami, 1989-99; of counsel Morgan, Lewis & Bockius LLP, Miami, 1999—. Exec. asst. to chmn. Ways and Means Com., Fla. Senate, Tallahassee, 1978-79; mem. jud. nominating com. Fla.Dist. Ct. Appeal (3d dist.), 1992-95. Exec. editor U. Fla. Law Rev., 1978. Del. Creative Crime Control Conf., Fla., 1982. Mem. ABA, Dade County Bar Assn. (chmn. internat. law com.), Cuban-Am. Bar Assn., Hispanic Nat. Bar Assn., Inter-Am. Bar Assn., Order of Coif, Phi Kappa Phi. General civil litigation, Private international, Trademark and copyright. Office: Morgan Lewis & Bockius LLP 200 S Biscayne Blvd Ste 5300 Miami FL 33131-2339 Fax: 305-415-3001. E-mail: casstawal@aol.com.

CASTLE, JAY FRANK, lawyer; b. Sarasota, Fla., July 24, 1963; s. Frank Douglas and Nan Hunter Castle; m. Jennifer Annette Levi, Feb. 14, 1993; children: Jaager, Maddux, Lillian. BA with high honors, U. Fla., 1985; JD with distinction, Emory U., 1988. Bar: Ga. 1988, U.S. Dist. Ct. (no., mid. and so. dists.) Ga., U.S. Ct. Appeals (11th cir.). Assoc. King & Spalding, Atlanta, 1988—92, Lord Bissell & Brook, 1992—93; ptnr. Holt Ney Zatcoff & Wasserman, 1993—2003; group leader, litigator Winn-Dixie Stores, Inc., 2003—. Mem.: Am. Trial Lawyers Assn., State Bar Ga. (eminent domain sect.). Appellate, General practice. Office: 5050 Edgewood Ct Jacksonville FL 32203

CASTLE, PERCY, lawyer, law educator; b. Lima, Peru, Dec. 19, 1963; s. Charles E. and Nelly Castle; m. Sandra Indacochea Conetta, Sept. 8, 1990; children: Derek Castle Indacochea, Anneliese Castle Indacochea. Law Degree, U. Lima, 1987, M in Corp. Law, 1997. Bar: Lima 1989. Lawyer Estudio Llona & Bustamante Abogados, Lima, 1987—93, ptnr., 1993—96; mgr. PricewaterhouseCoopers, Lima, 1996—99, acting ptnr., 2000—01; ptnr. Estudio Navarro Abogados, Lima, 2001—. Prof. corp. law U. Lima, 1989—, prof. comml. contracts, 1994—99. Contbr. articles to profl. jours. Mem.: Centro de Mercados y Capitales, Instituto Peruano de Derecho Mercantil, Instituto Peruano de Derecho Tributario. Avocations: sailing, tennis, soccer. Corporate, general, Bankruptcy, Taxation, general. Home: Alameda de Las Palmas #237 Lima 9 Peru Office: Estudio Navarro Abogados Avenida del Parque 195 Lima 27 Peru

CASTLEBERRY, JAMES NEWTON, JR., retired law educator, dean; b. Chatom, Ala., Dec. 28, 1921; s. James Newton and Nellie (Robbins) C.; m. Mary Ann Blocker, Feb. 12, 1944 (dec.); children: Jean, Nancy, James III (dec.), Elizabeth, Cynthia, Robert, Mary Ann. JD magna cum laude, St. Mary's U., 1952; diploma in comparative law, Nat. U. Mex., 1960; diploma in tchg. of comparative law, Strasburg, 1963. Bar: Tex. 1952. Asst. atty. gen. State of Tex., 1953-55; prof. law St. Mary's U., San Antonio, 1955-92, dean, 1978-89, dean emeritus, 1989—, ret., 1992. Dir. St. Mary's U. Summer Program in Internat. and Comparative Law, Innsbruck, Austria, 1986-89; exec. dir. Tex. Ctr. for Legal Ethics and Professionalism, 1990-92; lectr. comparative law fgn. legal study tours Corp. for Profl. Confs., 1990—. Co-author: Water & Water Rights, 1970; contbr. articles to law jours. Bd. dirs. Preservation Tex., San Antonio Conservation Soc.; trustee Tex. Supreme Ct. Hist. Soc. Mem. ABA, Am. Bar Found., San Antonio Bar Assn., Tex. Bar Found., San Antonio Bar Found., Tex. State Bar, Phi Delta Phi (internat. pres. 1977-79). Home: 7727 Woodridge Dr San Antonio TX 78209-2223

CASTLETON, DAVID J. lawyer; b. Cedar City, Utah, May 24, 1954; s. David B. and Maurine (Jordan) C.; m. Cynthia Sue Anderson, June 4, 1976; children: Natalie, Cameron, Heather, Melissa, Ryan, Lindsay, Cody, Jordan. BS, U. Utah, 1978; JD, Cornell U., 1981. Bar: Utah 1981. Internal auditor Castletons, Inc., Salt Lake City, 1975-77; asst. dir. U. Utah Alumni Assn., 1977-78; assoc. Snow, Christensen & Martineau, Salt Lake City, 1981-85, ptnr., 1986-93, Blackburn & Stoll, Salt Lake City, 1993—. Lectr. Utah Assn. CPA, 1987-88. Coord. Boy Scouts Am., Murray, Sandy, Utah, 1982-88; coach Utah Soccer Assn., 1985—; active Utah Vol. Lawyers Project, Salt Lake City; charitable giving com. Primary Children's Hosp. Fellow Am. Coll. of Trust and Estate Coun.; mem. ABA, Utah State Bar Assn. (exec. com. probate and estate planning sect. 1989—, chmn. estate planning sect. 1992-93). Mem. Lds Ch. Avocations: snow skiing, water skiing, soccer, tennis, running. Commercial, contracts (including sales of goods; commercial financing), Estate planning, Property, real (including real estate development, water). Office: Blackburn & Stoll 77 W 200 S Ste 400 Salt Lake City UT 84101-1613

CASTRATARO, BARBARA ANN, lawyer; b. Bethpage, N.Y., Apr. 25, 1958; d. Vincent James and Theresa (Chiarini) C. BA in Music, L.I. U., 1984; JD, N.Y. Law Sch., 1989. Bar. N.Y. 1990, U.S. Dist. Ct. (so. dist.) N.Y. 1990. Music dir. CBS Network, N.Y.C., 1979-81, exec. ops., 1985-88; music dir. NBC Network/Score Prodns., N.Y.C. and L.A., 1983-84, Score Prodns./ABC Network, N.Y.C. and L.A., 1980-84; assoc. Donald Frank Esq., N.Y.C., 1989-93, Law Offices of Joel C. Bender, White Plains, N.Y., 1993-99, Bender, Jenson, Silverstein & Castrataro, LLP, White Plains, 1999-2000; pvt. practice Law Offices of Barbara A. Castrataro, Chappaqua, N.Y., 2000—. Lectr. on divorce and separation parenting; founder Castrataro Artist Mgmt., 1997-99; adj. faculty mem. Berkeley Coll., White Plains, N.Y. Recipient 3 Emmy nominations N.Y. Acad. TV Arts and Sci., 1979, 82-83. Mem. N.Y. State Bar Assn., Womens Bar Assn. Avocations: sailing, gourmet cooking, gardening. Entertainment, Family and matrimonial. Office: PO Box 132 Chappaqua NY 10514 E-mail: cambac233@aol.com.

CASTRO, ALEXANDRO C. judge; b. Tinian, Northern Marianas, Apr. 23, 1952; m. Carmen Moses; children: Patrick, Eric, Yvonne, Alex Jr., Rodney, Ariel. BL, U. Papua New Guinea, 1979. Bar: U.S. Ct. Appeals (9th cir.), U.S. Dist. Ct. No. Mariana Islands. Mem. Rota Mcpl. Coun., 1972; asst. prosecutor Atty. Gen.'s Office, 1979—86, atty. gen., 1986—89; assoc. judge CNMI Superior Ct., 1989—93, presiding judge, 1993—98; assoc. judge CNMI Supreme Ct., 1998—. Office: Ho Justice Guma Hustisia, Imwaal Aweewe PO Box 502179 Saipan MP 96950-2179 Office Fax: 670-236-9897. Business E-Mail: cnmilaw@itecnmi.com.*

CASTRO, LEONARD EDWARD, lawyer; b. L.A., Mar. 18, 1934; s. Emil Galvez and Lily (Meyerholtz) C.; 1 son, Stephen Paul. A.B., UCLA, 1959, J.D., 1962. Bar: Calif. 1963, U.S. Supreme Ct. 1970. Assoc. Musick, Peeler & Garrett, Los Angeles, 1962-68, ptnr., 1968— . Mem. ABA, Los Angeles County Bar Assn.Bd. editors, note and comment editor: UCLA Law Review, 1961-62. Contbd. chpts. to books. Panelist, spkr., various legal edn. programs. Corporate, general, Private international, Securities. Office: Musick Peeler & Garrett 1 Wilshire Blvd Ste 2000 Los Angeles CA 90017-3876

CASTRO, RAUL HECTOR, lawyer, former ambassador, former governor; b. Cananea, Mexico, June 12, 1916; came to U.S., 1926, naturalized, 1939; s. Francisco D. and Rosario (Acosta) C.; m. Patricia M. Norris, Nov. 13, 1954; children— Mary Pat, Beth. BA, Ariz. State Coll., 1939; JD, U. Ariz., 1949; LL.D. (hon.), No. Ariz. U., 1966, Ariz. State U., 1972, U. Autonoma de Guadalajara, Mex. Bar: Ariz. bar 1949. Fgn. service clk. Dept. State, Agua Prieta, Mexico, 1941-46; instr. Spanish U. Ariz., 1946-49; practiced in Tucson, 1949-51; dep. county atty. Pima County, Ariz., 1951-54; county atty., 1954-58; judge Superior Ct., Tucson, 1958-64, Juvenile Ct., Tucson, 1961-64; U.S. ambassador to El Salvador, 1964-68, to Bolivia, La Paz, 1968-69; practice internat. law Tucson, 1969-74, Phoenix, 1980—; gov., 1975-77; U.S. ambassador to, 1977-80; operator Castro Pony Farm, 1954-64. Pres. Pima County Tb and Health Assn., Tucson Youth Bd., Ariz. Horseman's Assn.; Bd. dirs. Tucson chpt. A.R.C., Tucson council Boy Scouts Am., Tucson YMCA, Nat. Council Christians and Jews, YWCA Camp; Bd. Mem. Ariz. N.G., 1935-39. Recipient Outstanding Naturalized Citizen award Pima County Bar Assn., 1964, Outstanding Am. Citizen award D.A.R., 1964; Pub. Service award U. Ariz., 1966; John F. Kennedy medal Kennedy U., Buenos Aires. Mem. Am. Fgn. Service Assn., Am. Judicature Soc., Inter-Am. Bar Assn., Ariz. Bar Assn., Pima County Bar Assn., Nat. Council Crime and Deliquency (bd. dirs.), Assn. Trial Lawyers Am., Council Am. Ambassadors, Nat. Assn. Trial Judges, Nat. Council Juvenile Ct. Judges, Fed. Bar Assn., Nat. Lawyers Club, Phi Alpha Delta. Clubs: Rotarian. Democrat. Roman Catholic. Immigration, naturalization, and customs, Private international, Public international.

CASTRO-BLANCO, JAMES, professional society administrator; b. Bronx, N.Y., 1959; Bachelor, SUNY, Albany, 1988; JD, Bklyn. Law Sch., 1991. Litigation assoc. Winthrop Stimson Putnam & Roberts; asst. U.S. atty. Ea. Dist. N.Y.; asst. dean, adj. prof. law St. John's U. Sch. Law; mgr. assoc. devel. Shearman & Sterling. Mem. faculty N.Y.C. Corp. Counsel Trial Program, 1999—; coach mock trial teams Bklyn. Law Sch. and St. Johns U. Sch. Law. Mem. Mayor's adv. com. on judiciary, N.Y.C.; exec. coun. Network of Bar Leaders. Mem.: N.Y. State Bar Assn. (com. on legal edn. and admission to bar), Assn. of Bar of City of N.Y. (com. on recruitment and retention of lawyers), Puerto Rican Bar Assn. (pres., former v.p., treas., co-chair 45th Ann. Scholarship Banquet). Office: Puerto Rico Bar Assn Colegio de Abogados de Puerto Rico PO Box 9021900 San Juan PR 00902-1900*

CASTRO DIAZ, ALFONSO, lawyer, educator; b. Mexico City, Fed. Dist., Mexico, Jan. 21, 1977; s. Alfonso Castro Urueta and Rosa María Díaz Bujons. JD, U. Anáhuac, Mex. City, 2000. Bar: Fed. and local cts. United Mexican States (Lic.) 2001. Assoc. Santamarina y Steta, S.C., Mex. City, 1999—. Instr. U. Iberoamericana, Mex. City, Mexico, 2002—. Avocations: running, reading. Finance, Securities, Mergers and acquisitions. Office: Santamarina y Steta SC Campos Elíseos 345 - 1 floor Mexico Mexico City 11560 Mexico Office Fax: (5255) 52795458. E-mail: acastro@s-s.com.mx.

CASTRO Y CASTRO, JUVENTINO VICTOR, judge; b. Mexico, July 16, 1918; Law Degree, Nat. Autonomous U. Mexico, 1940, LLD, 1951. Chair dept. constnl. law Escuela Libre de Derecho, 1969—95; chair postgrad. studies dept. law Nat. Autonomous U. Mexico, 1992—; min. Supreme Ct. Justice, Mexico City, 1995—, pres. House of Civil and Criminal Affairs, 1995—97. Office: Suprema Corte de Justicia de la Nacion Pino Suarez No 2 Col Centro 06065 Mexico City Mexico*

CATALFO, ALFRED, JR., (ALFIO CATALFO), lawyer; b. Lawrence, Mass., Jan. 31, 1920; s. Alfio and Vincenza (Amato) C.; m. Caroline Joanne Mosca (dec. Apr. 1968); children: Alfred Thomas, Carol Joanne, Gina Marie; m. Gail Varney, 1988. BA, U. N.H., 1945, MA in History, 1952; LLB, Boston U., 1947, JD (hon.), 1969; postgrad., Suffolk U. Sch. Law, 1955-56, Am. Law Inst., N.Y.C., 1959. Bar: N.H. 1947, U.S. Dist. Ct. 1948, U.S. Ct. Appeals 1978, U.S. Supreme Ct. 1979. Pvt. practice, Dover, N.H., 1948—; ptnr. Catalfo Law Firm, Dover, 1980—; county atty. Strafford County, Dover, N.H., 1949-50, 55-56; bd. immigration appeals U.S. Dept. Justice, 1953—; football coach Berwick Acad., South Berwick, Maine, 1944, Mission Catholic H.S., Roxbury, Mass., 1945-46. Author: Laws of Divorces, Marriages, and Separations in New Hampshire, 1962, History of the Town of Rollinsford, 1623-1973, 1973. Pres. Young Dems. of Dover, 1953-55; 1st vice-chmn. Young Dems., N.H., 1954-56; mem. Strafford County Dem. Com., 1948-75; vice-chmn. N.H. Dem. Com., 1954-56, 1st chmn., 1956-58, chmn. spl. activities, 1958-60; del. Dem. Nat. Conv., 1956-60, 76; chmn. N.H. Dem. Conv., 1958, conv. dir., 1960; mem. Dem. state exec. com., 1960-70; Dem. nominee for U.S. Senate, 1962; vice-chmn. Dover Cath. Sch. Com., 1969-71; mem. Dover Bd. Adjustment, 1960-65; apptd. lt. commdr. N.H. Govs. Mil. Staff. Pilot U.S. Naval Air Corp., lt. commdr. USNR, 1942-44. Recipient keys to cities of Dover, Somersworth, Concord, Berlin, Manchester and Rochester N.H., 6 nat. plaques DAV, 3 disting. svc. awards Am. Legion, Am. Legion Life Membership award, spl. recognition award Berwick Acad., 1985. Mem. ABA, N.H. Bar Assn., Strafford County Bar Assn. (v.p. 1966-67, pres. 1968-69), Assn. Trial Lawyers Am., N.Y. State Trial Lawyers Assn., Mass. Trial Lawyers Assn., N.H. Trial Lawyers Assn., Tex. Trial Lawyers Assn., Nat. Assn. Criminal Def. Lawyers, N.H. Assn. Criminal Def. Lawyers, Am. Judicature Soc., Phi Delta Phi, DAV (judge adv. N.H. dept. 1950-68, 72— ; comdr. chpt. 1953-54, comdr. N.H. 1956-57), Am. Legion (life, chmn. state conv. 1967, 77, 84), Navy League, N.H. Hist. Soc., Dover Hist. Soc., Rollinsford Hist. Soc., Eagles Club, Sons of Italy, Lions, Elks, K.C. (grand knight 1975-77), Moose, Lebanese Club. Clubs: Eagles (Somersworth, N.H.), Sons of Italy (Portsmouth, N.H.). Lodges: Lions, Elks, K.C. (grand knight 1975-77),

Moose, Lebanese (Dover). General civil litigation, Criminal, Family and matrimonial. Home: 20 Arch St Dover NH 03820-3602 Office: 450 Central Ave Dover NH 03820-3451

CATANANTE, ALESSANDRA, lawyer; b. Rio De Janeiro, Brazil, June 10, 1972; LLB, JD, Sch. Of Law - U. Candido Mendes, Rio De Janeiro, 1989—93; M in Bus. Law, Cath. U., Rio De Janeiro, 1997—98. Bar: Brazil 1994. Legal mgr. Navegação Vale do Rio Doce S/A, Docenave, 1992—2000; head, maritime law dept. Castro, Barros, Sobral, G.gomes Advogados, 2000—02; specialist, internat. and maritime law Stroeter, Royster & Ohno Advogados, Rio de Janeiro, 2002—. Contbr. articles; spkr.: Brazilian delegation IBA an. meeting, Brazilian delegation, internat. maritime com. CMI biannual meeting. Grantee Representing Brazilian Del. In The 24Th Ann. Symposium - Ctr. For The Study Of The Presidency, Wash., D.c., Americas Found., N.Y., 1993. Mem.: Internat. Bar Assn. (Maritime Com. 2000—03), Am. C. of C., Brazilian Maritime Law Assn. Office: Stroeter Royster & Ohno Advogados Av Rio Branco 108/ 30th Floor Rio De Janeiro Rio De Janeiro 20040-001 Brazil Office Fax: 55 21 2509 5783.

CATHCART, DAVID ARTHUR, lawyer; b. Pasadena, Calif., June 1, 1940; s. Arthur James and Martelle C.; m. Janet Eileen Farley, June 19, 1973; children: Sarah Emily, Rebecca Eileen. BA with gt. distinction, Stanford U., 1961; MA, Harvard U., 1966, LLB cum laude, 1967. Bar: Calif. 1968, U.S. Dist. Ct. (cen. dist.) Calif. 1969, U.S. Dist. Ct. (so., no. dists.) 1975, U.S. Dist. Ct. (ea. dist.) 1979, U.S. Ct. Appeals (9th cir.) 1975, U.S. Supreme Ct. 1979. Assoc. Gibson, Dunn & Crutcher LLP, L.A., 1968-70, 72-75, ptnr., 1975—. Legis. asst. U.S. Senate, Washington, 1971-72; mem. NLRB Adv. Com., 1994-98. Editor-in-chief: Employment Discrimination Law Five-Year Cumulative Supplement, 1989, Employment-At-Will: A 1989 State-By-State Survey, 1990; co-author: California Employment Litigation Practice Guide, 2002; contbr. chpts. to legal texts, articles to profl. jours. Bd. dirs. Western Ctr. on Law and Poverty, LA, 1985-88, US-South Africa Leadership Devel. Program, 1992—, Employers Group, 2000-03. Woodrow Wilson fellow, 1961-62, Danforth fellow, 1961-64. Fellow Coll. of Labor and Employment Lawyers; mem. ABA (mem. coun. 1997—, mgmt. co-chmn. equal employment opportunity law com., 1994-96, sect. labor and employment law, co-chmn. employment and labor rels. law com., 1985-88, litigation sect., class action task force 2002-03), LA County Bar Assn. (chmn. labor & employment law sect. 1991-92), Am. Employment Law Coun. (chmn. 1993—), Chancery Club, City Club on Bunker Hill, Harvard Club NYC, Phi Beta Kappa. General civil litigation, Labor (including EEOC, Fair Labor Standards Act, labor-management relations, NLRB, OSHA), Pension, profit-sharing, and employee benefits. Office: Gibson Dunn & Crutcher LLP 333 S Grand Ave Los Angeles CA 90071-3197

CATHCART, ROBERT JAMES, lawyer; b. Palo Alto, Calif., Sept. 28, 1945; s. Arthur James and Martelle Leeper Cathcart; m. Joan Anglin Kirkland, Mar. 29, 1969; children: Benjamin Patrick, Barbara Wynne, Kara Anglin. AB, Stanford U., 1968; JD, U. Wash., 1972. Bar: Calif. 1972, Wash. 1973, U.S. Dist. Ct. Calif. 1973, U.S. Ct. Appeals (9th cir.) 1973. Law clk. to Judge David Soukup, Superior Ct., Seattle, 1972-73; assoc. McCutchen, Doyle, Brown & Enersen, San Francisco, 1973-75; assoc., ptnr. Severson, Werson, Berke & Melchior, San Francisco, 1975-82; ptnr. Allen, Matkins, Leck, Gamble & Mallory, L.A., 1982—. Mem. adv. bd. Inst. Corp. Counsel, L.A., 1996—; panelist EDUC panels CEB, 1990—; mem. State Bar Com. on AD Justice, L.A. and San Francisco, 1979-83; temp. judge L.A. Superior and Mcpl. Cts., 1982—. Mem. Assn. Bus. Trial Lawyers. Avocations: golf, swimming, hiking, sailing, reading. General civil litigation, Construction, Property, real (including real estate development, water). Office: Allen Matkins Leck Et Al 515 S Figueroa St Fl 8 Los Angeles CA 90071-3301

CATHELL, DALE ROBERTS, judge; b. Berlin, Md., July 30, 1937; s. Dale Parsons Cathell and Charlotte Robert (Hocker) Terrell; m. Charlotte M. Kerbin; children: Kelly Ann, Dale Kerbin, William Howard. Student, U. Md., 1962-64; LLB, U. Balt., 1967; cert., Nat. Jud. Coll., 1983. Bar: Md. 1967. Atty. City of Ocean City, Md., 1970-76; assoc. judge Md. Dist. Ct., Worcester County, 1980-81; judge Md. Cir. Ct., Worcester County, 1981-89, Ct. Spl. Appeals, 1st Appellate Cir., 1989-97, Ct. Appeals, 1997—. Adj. prof. law U. Balt., 1997—; mem. family and domestic rels. law com. Md. Jud. Conf., 1995-97, past mem. exec. com.; instr. WOR-WIC C.C., 1973, Salisbury State U., 1978. Mem. Pub. Service Commn. Adv. Panel, Md., 1970, charity revision com. Mayor City Council, Ocean City, 1970; mem. Worcester County Shoreline Com., Md., 1971; mem. charter revision com. City of Ocean City, 1973, mem. utility consumer adv. panel, 1978; creator Alt. Com. Service Program, Md., 1980—; organizer Legal Intern Program Pub. Schs., Worcester County, 1981—. Served with USAF, 1955-59. Mem. Md. Bar Assn. (jud. appointment com. 1970), Worcester County Bar Assn. (pres. 1970), Balt. City Bar Assn. Democrat. Episcopalian. Office: Ct Appeals Md Robert C Murphy Cts Apl Bld 361 Rowe Blvd Annapolis MD 21401-1672 also: PO Box 4306 Salisbury MD 21803-4306

CATINA, JANET K. lawyer; b. East Stroudsburg, Pa., Apr. 7, 1962; d. James R. and Helen J. Marsh; BA in Polit. Sci. and Acctg., Muhlenberg Coll., 1984; JD, Dickinson U., 1987. Bar: Pa. 1987, U.S. Dist. Ct. (mid. dist.) Pa. 1989, U.S. Ct. Appeals (3rd cir.) 1989, U.S. Dist. Ct. (ea. dist.) Pa. 1994, U.S. Supreme Ct. 1998. Assoc. James F. Marsh Law Offices, Stroudsburg, 1987-88; asst. dist. atty. Monroe County, Stroudsburg, 1988-90; assoc. Hanna, Young, Upright & Pazuhanich, Stroudsburg, 1988-94; ptnr. Hanna, Young, Upright & Catina, Stroudsburg, 1995—. Solicitor Paradise Twp. Planning Commn., Cresco, Pa., 1991-93. V.p. Am. Heart Assn., 1992-94, bd. dirs. Monroe County div.; chmn. daffodil days Am. Cancer Soc., 1993-94, bd. dirs. Monroe unit, 1994-95, chmn. spkrs. bur., 1996—; chmn. profl. divsn. United Way Monroe County, 1998—; tchr. Sunday sch. Christ Hamilton United Luth. Ch.; youth sports coach YMCA; bd. dirs. United Way of Monroe County, campaign chair, 2003. Mem. ATLA (mem. PAC task force), NACDL, Pa. Bar Assn. (quality of life task force, professionalism com.), Pa. Trial Lawyers Assn., Monroe County Bar Assn., Pocono Mountains C. of C. (chair legis. com. 1997-99, chair employment com. 1999-2001, bd. dirs.), Pi Sigma Alpha, Omicron Delta Epsilon. Federal civil litigation, State civil litigation, Criminal. Office: Young Upright Catina & Parker LLP 300 Stroud Bldg Stroudsburg PA 18360-1602 E-mail: jcatina@pennlawyers.com.

CATLETT, RICHARD H., JR., retired lawyer; b. Boston, May 1, 1921; s. Richard Henry and Martha Barton (Taylor) Catlett; m. Marion Frances Buckey, Apr. 3, 1948 (dec. Sept. 1967); children: Ross C. Rose, Richard H. III, Thomas Y., Maria C. Eldredge; m. Barbara Ann L'Orange, May 1, 1969. BSEE, Va. Mil. Inst., 1943; LLB, U. Richmond, 1952. Engr. C&P Tel. Co., Richmond, Va., 1946-47, Catlett-Johnson Corp., Richmond, Va., 1947-50; assoc., ptnr. Christian & Barton, Richmond, Va., 1952-76; ptnr. McGuire Woods LLP, Richmond, Va., 1976-91; ret., 1991. Bd. dirs. Ga. Pacific Corp., gen. counsel, sec., 1969—90; gen. counsel Signet Banking Corp. (now First Union Corp.), Richmond, 1985—89; adj. asst. prof. law U. Richmond, 1990—93. Chmn. City of Richmond Personnel Bd., 1971—80; dir. Westminster-Canterbury Ho., Richmond, 1985—89, chmn., 1987—89; mem. vestry St. James Episc. Ch., Richmond, 1954—75. 1st lt. U.S. Army, 1943—46, ETO. Mem.: ABA, Va. State Bar Assn. (chmn. bus. law sect. 1972—73), Va. State Bar (chmn. bus. law sect. 1971—72), Commonwealth Club (Richmond), Country Club Va. (dir. 1966—69, 1971—74). Home: 11 Robin Rd Richmond VA 23226-3205 E-mail: rcatlett@mcguirewoods.com.

CATRON, STEPHEN BARNARD, lawyer; b. Bowling Green, Ky., Feb. 4, 1949; s. Eugene and Gladys (Bell) C.; m. Deborah Faye Grigsby, Nov. 28, 1981. BA, Western Ky. U., Bowling Green, 1971; JD, U. Miss., 1974. Bar: Ky. 1974, Miss. 1974, Tenn. 1988, U.S. Dist. Ct. (we. dist.) Ky, 1974, U.S. Dist. Ct. (no. dist.) Miss. 1974, U.S. Supreme Ct. 1982, U.S. Ct. Appeals (6th cir.) 1983. Atty. Ky. Dept. Human Resources, Bowling Green, Ky., 1974-75; atty., ptnr. Reynolds, Catron, Johnson & Hinton, Bowling Green, Ky., 1975-95, Lewis, King, Krieg, Waldrop and Catron, P.C., Bowling Green, Ky., 1995-2001; ptnr. Wyatt, Tarrant & Combs, LLP, Bowling Green, Ky., 2001—. Pres. Bowling Green-Warren County Bar, 1989-90; chair., bd. trustees Ky. IOLTA Fund, Frankfort, Ky., 1990-94; bd. dirs. Nat. Assn. IOLTA Programs, Chgo., 1991-92. Author: Kentucky Corporations Law, 1989. Bd. dirs. Bowling Green (Ky.) Human Rights Commn., 1976-78; vice chair Ky. Ednl. TV Auth., Lexington, Ky., 1988-92; bd. regents Western Ky. U., Bowling Green., 1991-92; chairperson Bowling Green-Warren County Indsl. Authority; trustee Western Ky. U. Found. Fellow Am. Bar Found.; mem. Ky. Bar Assn. (bd. govs. 1992-2000, v.p. 2000-01, pres.-elect 2001-02, pres. 2002-03), Bowling Green C. of C. Democrat. Episcopalian. Avocations: reading, jogging, golf, computers. Banking, Finance, Corporate, general. Home: 231 Greenview Way Bowling Green KY 42103 Office: Wyatt Tarrant & Combs LLP PO Box 1220 918 Main St Bowling Green KY 42102-1220 E-mail: stephenc@wyattfirm.com.

CATUZZI, J(EROME) P(RIMO), JR., lawyer; b. N.Y.C., Aug. 23, 1938; s. J.P. Sr. and Ida (Ghezzi) C.; m. Chantal Mauricette Marais, Nov. 10, 1979; children: Daniella Firenze, Vanessa Carmen, Lee. BA, Columbia U., 1958; JD, Georgetown U., 1961; LLM in Internat. Law, NYU, 1963; PhD in Internat. Bus., La Salle U., 1998. Bar: N.Y., D.C., Asesor Legal, Spain 1973. Assoc. Baker & McKenzie, N.Y.C. and Chgo., 1963-65; gen. counsel, exec. v.p. Royal Bus. Fund Corp. (Amex), N.Y.C., 1965-72; exec. v.p., gen. counsel Holmes Protection, Inc. (Amex); internat. counsel, mng. dir. Occidental S.A., Madrid and Geneva, 1972-84; counsel U.S. Consulate, Costa del Sol, Spain, Sotogrande, S.A.; U.S. gen. counsel Soparind S.A., N.Y.C. and Paris, 1984-86; resident U.S. ptnr. Berlioz, Ferry, David, Lutz & Rochefort, N.Y.C., 1986-88; resident prin. J.P. Catuzzi, Jr. & Assocs., N.Y.C., 1989—; internat. counsel Colina la Ropa, S.A.; Mexico, 1987. Adj. prof. law and fin. C.W. Post campus Long Island U., N.Y.C., 1985—; nat. lectr. Internat. Bus. Network, N.Y.C. and Santa Monica, Calif., 1980-84; internat. cons. Eums Pharma, S.A., Geneva, Switzerland, Magellan, GmbH, MNG Industries, GmbH, Fed. Republic Germany, GEFI Holdings, Ltd., Gibraltar, ChartHouse Holdings, Ltd., Ireland, Galia, Ltd., Lausanne, Switzerland,, Centro Geotecnico, S.R.L., Rome, Geosaf, Inc., Montreal, Can., Hanover Trust House, Ltd., Ireland; internat. coun. Chropi, S.A., Greece, Igos Comm., S.A., Paris, Ireland, Lenzburg Capital Corp, Calgary, Alta., Can.; gen. internat. counsel Centrum European Securities, Ltd., Geneva, Switzerland; int. counsel golden Hat Resources, Inc., Vancouver, B.C., Canada; gen. counsel Orbis Capital Investment, Ltd., Dublin, Irelandm South Winds, LLC, Isle of Man; cons. Fond D'aide au Devel. NGO Econ. and Social Coun. UN, Geneva, N.Y.C., 1999—; pres. Pyramids Unltd., Inc., Nevada, Ingenicard Trust, Zug, Switzerland, KI-Int. Mgmt. Group, London. Legis. cons. to Gov. Rockefeller div. human rights State of N.Y., Albany, 1968-70; mem. legal com. N.Y. County Rep. Party, 1967-72. Mem. Confrerie des Chevalier du Tastevin (N.Y.C.) (chevalier 1985—), Knights of Malta. Roman Catholic. Corporate, general, Private international, Mergers and acquisitions. E-mail: ilmaestro7@hotmail.com.

CAUDILL, WILLIAM HOWARD, lawyer; b. Memphis, Mar. 18, 1951; s. John W. Caudill and Elizabeth (Rivers) Stayton; m. Chris Looney, Sept. 2, 1978; children: Lucy L., W. Christopher. BSBA, U. Ark., 1973; M in Pub. Acctg., U. Tex., 1977, JD, 1978. Bar: Tex. 1978, U.S. Dist. Ct. (so. dist.) Tex. 1978, U.S. Tax Ct. 1978, U.S. Claims Ct. 1978, U.S. Ct. Appeals (5th cir.) 1978; CPA. Ptnr. Fulbright & Jaworski, LLP, Houston, 1986—; pres. Meml. Endowment Fund, 1995—. Mem. Tex. Quarter Dollar Coin Design Com., 2002-03; mem. vestry St. John the Divine Episc. Ch., Houston, 1982-86, 89-93; coun. del. Episcopal Diocese of Tex., 2003. Mem. ABA (chair spl. projects subcom., vice chair partnership com. 2000-03, tax sect. 1994-98, chair CLE subcom., 1998-2000), State Bar Tex. (bd. dirs. taxation sect. 1987-92, chair-elect 1990, chair 1991-92, dir. tax course 1986-87). Avocations: fishing, music, golf. Taxation, general. Office: Fulbright & Jaworski LLP 1301 Mckinney St Ste 5100 Houston TX 77010-3031

CAULEY, MICHAEL A. prosecutor; b. 1948; B.A., Bethany Coll.; J.D., U. of Pittsburgh. Former U.S. atty. mid. dist., Fla. Office Fax: 813-274-6246.*

CAUTHRON, ROBIN J. federal judge; b. Edmond, Okla., July 14, 1950; d. Austin W. and Mary Louise (Adamson) Johnson. BA, U. Okla., 1970, JD, 1977; MEd, Cen. State U., Edmond, Okla., 1974. Bar: Okla. 1977. Law clk to Hon. Ralph G. Thompson U.S. Dist. Ct. (we. dist.) Okla., 1977-81; staff atty. Legal Svcs. Ea. Okla., 1981-82; pvt. practice law, 1982-83; spl. judge 17th Jud. Dist. State Okla., 1983-86; magistrate U.S. Dist. Ct. (we. dist.) Okla., Oklahoma City, 1986-91, judge, 1991—. Editor Okla. Law Rev. Bd. dirs. Juvenile Diabetes Found. Internat., 1989-92; mem. nominating com. Frontier Coun. Boy Scouts Am., 1987, Edmond Ednl. Endowment; trustee, sec. First United Meth. Ch., 1988-90. Mem. ABA, Okla. Bar Assn., Okla. County Bar Assn. (bd. dirs. 1990— bench and bar com.), McCurtain County Bar Assn. (pres. 1986), Am. Judicature Soc., Nat. Assn. Women Judges, Fed. Bar Assn., Nat. Coun. Women Magistrates (bd. dirs. 1990-91), Okla. Jud. Conf. (v.p. 1985), Am. Inns of Ct. (pres. 1991-92), Order of Coif, Phi Delta Phi. Office: US Courthouse 200 NW 4th St Ste 3108 Oklahoma City OK 73102-3029*

CAVALLINI, DONNA FRANCESCA, law librarian; b. St. Louis, Nov. 3, 1962; d. Giovanni Iader and Yolanda Marie (Boveri) Cavallini; m. Jeffrey Alan Mills, Jan. 13, 1986 (div. Nov. 1991); m. Gregory Joseph Kern, Aug. 31, 2000. BA, Washington U., St. Louis, 1983; JD, St. Louis U., 1990. Ref. libr. Huey, Guilday, Kuersteiner & Tucker, P.A., Tallahassee, 1988-91; libr. program adminstr. Office of the Atty. Gen., Tallahassee, 1991-96; ref. libr. Kilpatrick Stockton, LLP, Atlanta, 1996-99, mgr. competitive knowledge, 1999—. Fla. State Ct. and County Law Librs. scholar, 1992; recipient Davis Productivity award Fla. Taxwatch Inc., 1994. Mem. Am. Assn. Law Librs., Soc. Competitive Intelligence Profls. Home: 1961 Dorset Dr Fort Collins CO 80526 Office: 1100 W Peachtree St NW Ste 2800 Atlanta GA 30309-3609

CAVANAGH, MICHAEL FRANCIS, state supreme court justice; b. Detroit, Oct. 21, 1940; s. Sylvester J. and Mary Irene (Timmins) C.; m. Patricia E. Ferriss, Apr. 30, 1966; children: Jane Elizabeth, Michael F., Megan Kathleen BA, U. Detroit, 1962, JD, 1966. Bar: Mich. 1966. Law clk. to judge Ct. Appeals, Detroit, 1966-67; atty. City of Lansing, Mich., 1967-69; ptnr. Farhat, Story, et al., Lansing, Mich., 1969-73; judge 54-A Dist. Ct., Lansing, 1973-75, Mich. Ct. Appeals, Lansing, 1975-82; justice Supreme Ct., Lansing, 1983—, chief justice, 1991-94; Supreme Ct. liaison Mich. Indian Tribal Cts./Mich. State Cts. Supervising justice Sentencing Guidelines Com., Lansing, 1983-94, Mich. Jud. Inst., Lansing, 1986-94, 2001-03; bd. dirs. Thomas M. Cooley Law Sch., 1979-88; chair Mich. Justice Project, 1994-95, Nat. Interbranch Conf., Mpls., 1994-95. Bd. dirs. Am. Heart Assn. Mich., 1982—, chmn. bd. Am. Heart Assn. Mich., Lathrup Village, 1984-85; bd. dirs. YMCA, Lansing, 1978. Mem. ABA, Fed. Bar Assn., Ingham County Bar Assn., Inst. Jud. Adminstrn. (hon.), Inc. Soc. of Irish/Am. Lawyers (pres. 1987-88). Democrat. Roman Catholic. Avocations: jogging, racquetball, fishing. Office: Mich Supreme Ct PO Box 30052 925 W Ottawa St Lansing MI 48933-1067

CAVANAUGH, JOHN JOSEPH, JR., lawyer; b. Albany, N.Y., June 14, 1936; s. John J. Sr. and Jane A. (McKeon) C.; m. Judith A. Myers, Sept. 5, 1964. BA cum laude, Siena Coll., 1958; JD, Albany Law Sch., 1961. Bar: N.Y. 1961, U.S. Dist. Ct. (no. dist.) N.Y. 1961, U.S. Supreme Ct. 1967. Assoc. Donohue & Bohl, Albany, 1961-64, Arthur J. Harvey, Albany, 1964-67; pvt. practice Albany, 1967—. Ind. counsel Rosenblum & Sarachan, Albany, 1978-87. Assoc. editor Albany Law Rev., 1961. Cpl. U.S. Army, 1956-63. Mem. N.Y. State Bar Assn., Albany County Bar Assn., Capital Dist. Trial Lawyers Assn., Am. Arbitration Assn. (arbitrator), Am. Legion, K.C. Avocations: reading, tennis, travel, coin collector. Family and matrimonial, General practice, Personal injury (including property damage). Home: 28 Bancroft St Albany NY 12208-1615 Office: 210 Delaware Ave Delmar NY 12054-1221

CAVAZOS-GARZA, BELINDA, lawyer; b. San Antonio, Sept. 17, 1962; d. Roger Cavazos and Corina Cortez; m. Roger E. Garza; 1 child, Miranda C. Garza. BA, U. Tex., 1985; JD, U. Houston, 1992. Bar: Tex. 1993. Tchr. Edgewood Ind. Sch. Dist., San Antonio, 1985—90; pvt. practice San Antonio, 1993—2001; atty. Tex. Dept. Human Svcs., San Antonio, 2002—. Troop leader Girls Scouts U.S., 2002. Democrat. Roman Catholic. Home: 11310 Candle Park San Antonio TX 78249 Office: Tex Dept Human Svcs 11307 Roszell San Antonio TX 78223 Office Fax: 210-619-8159.

CAVEDA, DAVID MARTIN, lawyer; b. Miami, Fla., Nov. 27, 1965; s. Manuel Ramon and Irma Molina Caveda; m. Maritza Villavicencio, Aug. 14, 1999; children: Katherine, Christopher Manuel. BA, U. South Fla., 1987; JD, U. Fla., 1991. Bar: Fla. 1992, U.S. Dist. Ct. (so. and mid. dists.) Fla. 1993. Assoc. Law Office of Jerry Green, PA, Miami, Fla., 1992—93, Mensh and MacIntosh, PA, New Port Richey, Fla., 1994; pvt. practice Miami, 1995—98, Tampa, Fla., 1998—2000; assoc. Knox and Givens, PA, Tampa, 2000—. Co-author: Florida Family Law Practice for Paralegals, 2002. Lt. USAR, 1991—99. Mem.: Tampa Family Law Inn of Ct. Family and matrimonial. Office: Knox & Givens PA 607 W Horatio St Tampa FL 33606 Fax: 813-254-5698. E-mail: caveda@tampafamilylaw.com.

CAVIN, CLARK, lawyer; b. Bunch, Okla., Aug. 17, 1939; s. Champ Clark and Ruby Madeline (Mitchell) c. BA, U. Wash., 1961; postgrad., U. Calif., Irvine, 1972-73; JD, U. Calif., San Francisco, 1976. Bar: Calif. 1976, Wash. 1977, U.S. Dist. Ct. (no. dist.) Calif. 1976, U.S. Dist. Ct. (we. dist.) Wash. 1977. Pvt. practice, Seattle, 1977—. Magistrate pro tem. Mpcl. Ct., Seattle, 1981, judge pro tem., 1987-91. With USMC, 1961-72. Mem. Tchrs. Assn. Can., Royal Scottish Country Dance Soc. (Seattle br., cert. tchr.). Avocations: fiddling, geneology. Estate planning, General practice, Probate (including wills, trusts). Office: 6003 Phinney Ave N Seattle WA 98103-5511

CAVIN, KRISTINE SMITH, lawyer; b. Decatur, Ga., Mar. 26, 1969; d. Richard Theodore and Sherri (Nash) Smith; m. James Michael Cavin, May 13, 1995. BA, Furman U., 1991; JD, Calif. Western Sch. Law, 1995. Bar: Ga. 1995. Legal asst. Smith & Jenkins, P.C., Atlanta, 1991-92; intern child abuse and domestic violence unit San Diego City Atty.'s Office, 1995; assoc. Smith, Ronick & Corbin, L.L.C., Atlanta, 1995—. Mem. ABA, Nat. Assn. Women Lawyers, Nat. Assn. Profl. Mortgage Women, Mortgage Bankers Assn. (assoc.), Ga. Bar Assn., Ga. Assn. for Women Lawyers, Ga. Real Estate Closing Attys. Assn. (sec. 1997—), Atlanta Bar Assn. Avocations: gourmet cooking, wine, gardening. General practice, Property, real (including real estate development, water). Office: Smith Ronick & Corbin LLC 750 Hammond Dr NE Bldg 11 Atlanta GA 30328-5532 E-mail: kristinecavin@closingattorney.com.

CAYTAS, IVO GEORGE, lawyer; b. Plovdiv, Bulgaria, Feb. 3, 1958; s. George I. and Hilda (Plankl) Kaitasow. MA in Diplomacy, U. St Gallen, Switzerland, 1982, PhD in Law, 1984, PhD in Fin., 1986; LLM, Yale U., 1986. Bar: D.C. 1997, U.S. Ct. Internat. Trade, U.S. Claims Ct., U.S. Tax Ct., U.S. Dist. Ct. (so. and ea. dists.) N.Y. 1992, (no. and ctrl. dists.) Calif. 1992, U.S. Ct. Appeals (1st-11th cirs., fed. and D.C. cir.), U.S. Supreme Ct. 1996. Asst. to chmn. IMAG Corp., Vienna, Austria, 1979-80; ptnr. Caytas & Cie, St. Gallen, 1984-89, CCCC, St. Gallen, 1989-91; mng. dir. Swissconsult Corp., N.Y.C., 1990-91; pres., gen. counsel Swiss Am. Group Inc., N.Y.C., 1991-95; ptnr. Caytas & Assocs., 1996—. Bd. dirs. The London Ct. of Internat. Abritration. Author: Investment Banking, 1988, Global Political Risk, Modern Financial Instruments, 1992, Transnational Legal Practice, 1992; contbr. articles to profl. publs. Fellow Swiss Nat. Sci. Found., 1985, 88, Max Planck Inst., 1987; recipient Walther-Hug Found. award, 1984. Mem. ABA (sect. of internat. law and practice, internat. investment com., internat. taxation com.), Assn. of Bar of City of N.Y. (com. on govt. ethics), Calif. Bar Assn. (internat. law com., task force on internat. legal svcs.), Yale Club. Roman Catholic. Banking, Finance, Securities. Office: 146 W 57th St New York NY 10019-3301

CAZALAS, MARY REBECCA WILLIAMS, lawyer, nurse; b. Atlanta, Nov. 11, 1927; d. George Edgar and Mary Annie (Slappey) Williams; m. Albert Joseph Cazalas (dec.). BS in Pre-medicine, Oglethorpe U., Atlanta, 1954; MS in Anatomy, Emory U., 1960; JD, Loyola U., 1967, Loyola U., New Orleans, 1967. RN, Ga.; Bar: La. 1967, U.S. Dist. Ct. (ea. dist.) La. 1967, U.S. Ct. Appeals (5th cir.) 1972, U.S. Supreme Ct. 1975, U.S. Ct. Appeals (fed. cir.) 1999. Gen. duty nurse, 1948-68; instr. maternity nursing St. Josephs Infirmary Sch. Nursing, Atlanta, 1954-59; med. rschr. in urology Tulane U. Sch. Medicine, New Orleans, 1961-65; legal rschr. for presiding judge La. Ct. Appeals (4th cir.), New Orleans, 1965-71; pvt. practice New Orleans, 1967-71; asst. U.S. atty., 1971-79; sr. trial atty. Equal Employment Opportunity Commn., New Orleans, 1979-84; owner Cazalas Apts., New Orleans, 1962—. Lectr. in field. Contbr. articles to profl. jours. Bd. advisors Loyola U. Sch. Law, New Orleans, 1974, v.p. adv. bd., 1975; active New Orleans Drug Abuse Adv. Com., 1976-80; task force Area Agy. on Aging, 1976-80, pres. coun. Loyola U., 1978—; adv. bd. Odyssey House, Inc., New Orleans, 1973; chmn. womens com. Fed. Exec. Bd., 1974; bd. dirs. Bethlehem House of Bread, 1975-79. Named Hon. La. State Senator, 1974; recipient Superior Performance award U.S. Dept. Justice, 1974, Cert. Appreciation Fed. Exec. Bd., 1975-78, Rev. E.A. Doyle award, 1976, Commendation for tchg. Guam Legislature, 1977, Career Achievement award Mt. de Sales Acad., 1995. Mem. Am. Judicature Soc., La. Sate Bar Assn., Fed. Bus. Assn. (v.p. 1976—, pres. 1976-78, bd. dirs. 1972-75), Fed. Bar Assn. (1st v.p. 1973, pres. New Orleans chpt. 1974-75, nat. coun. 1974-79), Assn. Women Lawyers, Nat. Health Lawyers Assn., DAR, Bus. and Profl. Womens Club, Am. Heart Assn., Emory Alumni Assn., Oglethorpe U. Alumni Assn., Loyola U. Alumni Assn. (bd. dirs. 1974-75, 77, v.p. 1976), Jefferson Parish Hist. Soc., Sierra Club, Zonta, Leconte Hon. Sci. Soc., Phi Delta Delta (merged with Phi Alpha Delta pres. 1970-72, bd. dirs., vice justice 1974-75), Alpha Epsilon Delta, Phi Sigma. Democrat. Health, Property, real (including real estate development, water).

CECI, LOUIS J. former state supreme court justice; b. N.Y.C., Sept. 10, 1927; s. Louis and Filomena C.; m. Shirley; children— Joseph, Geraldine, David; children by previous marriage: Kristin (dec.), Remy, Louis. Ph.B., Marquette U., 1951, JD, 1954. Bar: Wis. 1954, U.S. Dist. Ct. (ea. dist.) Wis. 1954, U.S. Dist. Ct. (we. dist.) Wis. 1987; cert. mediator-arbitrator. Sole practice, Milw., 1954-58, 63-68; asst. city atty. City of Milw., 1958-63; mem. Wis. Assembly, Madison, 1965-66; judge Milw. County Ct., 1968-73, Milw. Circuit Ct., 1973-82; justice Wis. Supreme Ct., Madison, 1982-93, retired, 1993; res. judge State of Wis., 1993—. Lectr. Wis. Jud. Confs., 1970-79 Lectr. Badger Boys State, Ripon, Wis., 1961, 1982-84; asst. dist. commr. Boy Scouts Am., 1962. Recipient Wis. Civic Recognition PLAV, Milw., 1970; recipient Community Improvement Pompeii Men's Club, Milw., 1971, Good Govt. Milw Jaycees, 1973, Community-Judiciary Pompeii Men's Club, 1982 Mem. ABA, Wis. Bar Assn., Dane County Bar Assn., Milw. County Bar Assn., Waukesha County Bar Assn., Am. Legion (comdr. 1962-63). E-mail: appeal301@aol.com.

CEDARBAUM, MIRIAM GOLDMAN, federal judge; b. N.Y.C., 1929; d. Louis Albert and Sarah (Shapiro) Goldman; married; 2 children. BA, Barnard Coll., 1950; LLB, Columbia U., 1953. Bar: N.Y. 1954, U.S. Dist. Ct. (so. dist.) N.Y. 1956, U.S. Ct. Appeals (2d cir.) 1956, U.S. Ct. Claims 1958, U.S. Supreme Ct. 1958, U.S. Dist. Ct. (ea. dist.) N.Y. 1980, U.S. Ct.

Appeals (5th and 11th cirs.) 1981. Law clk. to judge Edward Jordan Dimock U.S. Dist. Ct. (so. dist.) N.Y., 1953-54, asst. U.S. atty., 1954-57; atty. Dept. Justice, Washington, 1958-59; part-time cons. to law firms in litig. matters, 1959-62; 1st asst. counsel N.Y. State Moreland Act Commn., 1963-64; assoc. counsel Mus. Modern Art, N.Y.C., 1965-79; assoc. litig. dept. Davis, Polk & Wardwell, N.Y.C., 1979-83, sr. atty., 1983-86; acting village justice Village of Scarsdale, NY, 1978—82, village justice, 1982-86; judge U.S. Dist. Ct. (so. dist.) N.Y., 1986-98, sr. judge, 1998—. Mem. com. defender svcs. Jud. Conf. U.S., 1993—99; bd. vis. Columbia Law Sch.; trustee Barnard Coll. Contbr. articles to profl. jours. Recipient Medal of Distinction Barnard Coll., 1991; James Kent scholar. Mem. ABA (chmn. com. on pictorial graphic sculptural and choreographic works 1979-81, copyright com. fed. practice and procedure 1983-84), Am. Law Inst., N.Y. State Bar Assn. (chmn. com. on fed. legis. 1978-80, com. on dist., city, village, and town cts. 1983-84), Assn. of Bar of City of N.Y. (com. on copyright and lit. property 1982-84, com. on the Bicentennial 1988-92), Fed. Bar Coun., Copyright Soc. U.S.A. (trustee, exec. com. 1979-82), Supreme Ct. Hist. Soc. Jewish. Office: US Dist Ct US Courthouse 500 Pearl St Rm 1330 New York NY 10007-1312

CEMBER, M. NATHAN, lawyer, speaker; b. N.Y.C., July 18, 1928; s. Arthur and Lilly (Schuster) C.; m. Esther Weissman, June 29, 1952; children: Richard, Mark, William. LLB, Bklyn. Law Sch., 1950, LLM, 1955. Bar: N.Y. 1951, U.S. Dist. Ct. (so. dist.) N.Y. 1960, U.S. Supreme Ct. 1967. House counsel Tenax, Inc., N.Y.C., 1953-66, Cember & Cember PC, Nyack, N.Y., 1966—. Chmn. Rockland County Com. for Soviet Jewry, N.Y., 1975; pres. Congregation Sons of Israel, Nyack, 1964-65. With U.S. Army, 1950-52, Korea. Mem. N.Y. State Bar Assn., Rockland County Bar Assn., Comml. Law League, B'nai B'rith (v.p. dist. 1 1982-85, pres. 1985-86, internat. v.p. 1990-92). Democrat. Commercial, contracts (including sales of goods; commercial financing), Property, real (including real estate development, water). Office: Cember & Cember PC 10 S Broadway Nyack NY 10960-3119 E-mail: bignat28@aol.com.

CENTNER, CHARLES WILLIAM, lawyer, educator; b. Battle Creek, Mich., July 4, 1915; s. Charles William and Lucy Irene (Patterson) C.; m. Evi Rohr, Dec. 22, 1956; children: Charles Patterson, David William, Geoffrey Christopher. AB, U. Chgo., 1936, AM, 1938, 39, PhD, 1941; JD, Detroit Coll. Law, 1970; LLB, LaSalle Extension U., 1965. Bar: Mich. 1970. Asst. prof. U. N.D., 1940-41, Tulane U., New Orleans, 1941-42; liaison officer for Latin Am., Dept. State at Lend-Lease Adminstrn., 1942; assoc. dir. Western Hemisphere divsn. Nat. Fgn. Trade Coun., N.Y., 1946-52; exec. Ford Motor Co., Detroit, 1952-57, Chrysler Corp. and Chrysler Internat. S.A., Detroit and Geneva, Switzerland, 1957-70. Adj. prof. Pace U., N.Y.C., 1950-52, Wayne State U., Detroit, 1971-78, U. Detroit, 1970-72, Wayne County C.C., 1970-2001. Author: Great Britian and Chile, 1810-1914, 1941. Lt. comdr. USNR, 1942-45, Res., 1945-75. Mem. ABA, State Bar Mich., Oakland County Bar Assn., Masons. Republican. Episcopalian. Home: 936 Harcourt Rd Grosse Pointe Park MI 48230-1874

CERIANI, GARY JAMES, lawyer; b. Kremmling, Colo., Oct. 1, 1947; s. Ernest G. and Bernetha M. C.; m. Marianne L. Wormley, June 29, 1974; children: Kelly, Barbara. BA, Colo. Coll., 1968; postgrad., U. Edinborough, 1968-69; JD, U. Colo., 1972. Bar: Colo. 1972, U.S. Dist. Ct. Colo. 1972, U.S. Ct. Appeals (10th cir.) 1972, U.S. Ct. Claims 1989. Assoc. Helmick, Conover & Burkhardt, Denver, 1972-76; pvt. practice Denver, 1976-78; ptnr. Davis & Ceriani P.C., Denver, 1979--. Editor: U. Colo. Law Review, 1970-72. Mem. ATLA, ABA, Colo. Bar Assn., Denver Bar Assn., Colo. Trial Lawyers Assn. Avocations: hunting, fishing, golf, skiing. Alternative dispute resolution, General civil litigation, State civil litigation. Office: Davis & Ceriani 1350 17th St Ste 400 Denver CO 80202-1575

CERJAN, MARTIN, dean, law educator; Grad., U. Mich., U. N.C. Dep. law libr. U. Maine Sch. Law; assoc. dir. Alyne Queener Massey Law Libr., 1999—2003; asst. dean for libr. and info. tech., asst. prof. law Vanderbilt U. Law Sch., Nashville, 2003—. Office: 131 21st Ave South Nashville TN 37203-2615*

CERMAK, KAREL, lawyer; b. Prague, Sept. 13, 1934; s. Karel and Marie (Sudova) C.; m. Vera Kuchynkova, 1963; 1 child, Karel. Degree in Law, Charles U., Prague, 1959, JD, 1966. Bar: Czech Republic, 1961. Legal asst., Pelhrimov, Czech Republic, 1959-61; lawyer Prague, 1961-90; sr. ptnr. Cermak, Horejs, Myslil, Law and Patent Offices, Prague, 1990—. Arbitrator Arbitration Ct. in Vienna, 1992—, Arbitration Ctr. of WIPO, Geneva, 1996—. Recipient Grosses Ehrenzeichen fur Verdienste um die Republik Osterreich, Pres. Austrian Rep., Vienna, 1993, award of Antonin Randa, Assn. of Czech Lawyers, 1996. Mem. Bar Assn. of Prague (pres. 1968-70), Czech Bar Assn. (pres. 1990-93, 96-2002). Roman Catholic. Avocations: classical music, playing piano and organ. Intellectual property, Commercial, contracts (including sales of goods; commercial financing), Mergers and acquisitions. Office: Cermak/Horejs Myslil Law Of Národní 32 110 00 Prague 1 Czech Republic E-mail: intelprop@apk.cz.

CERNIGLIARO, MICHAEL JOSEPH, lawyer; b. Englewood, N.J., Mar. 31, 1938; s. Sebastian and Cernigliaro; m. Patricia Goy, June 8, 1963; children: Allison, Nicole. BA, Rutgers U., 1960, JD, 1963. Bar: N.J. 1963, D.C. 1963, U.S. Dist. Ct. N.J. 1963, U.S. Supreme Ct. 1969. Assoc., ptnr. Campbell, Foley, Lee, Murphy & Cernigliaro, Asbury Park, N.J., 1963—; mcpl. ct. judge Twp. of Ocean, N.J., 1972-80; atty. Bd. of Adjustment, Eatontown, N.J., 1966—, mcpl. ct. judge Interlaken, N.J., 1989—. Vice chmn. ethics com. Monmouth County, NJ, 1981—82. Bd. govs. Jersey Shore Med. Ctr., Neptune, N.J., 1974-85; founder, pres. Ocean Twp. Italian-Am. Assn., 1977-80. Served as cpl. USMC, 1956-62. Mem. ABA, N.J. Bar Assn., Trial Lawyers of N.J., N.J. Def. Assn. (pres. 1976), Monmouth Mcpl. Judges Assn. (pres. 1975). Republican. Roman Catholic. Insurance, Personal injury (including property damage), Probate (including wills, trusts). Home: 412 Windermere Ave Asbury Park NJ 07712-4321 Office: 601 Bangs Ave Asbury Park NJ 07712-6936

CERNY, JIRI, lawyer; b. Kladno, Czech Republic, Feb. 14, 1971; s. Jiri Cerny and Stanislava Cerna; 1 child, Jan. ML, Charles U. of Prague, 1995. Bar: Czech Republic 1998, Slovak Bar of Comml. Lawyers, Slovakia 2001. Jr. atty. at law JUdr. Karol Hradela, Prague, 1995—98; atty. associated with Andrej Peterka, Prague, 1998—99; assoc. Peterka & Leuchterova v.o.s., 2000—01; ptnr. Peterka, Leuchterova & Ptnrs. v.o.s., 2001—. Avocation: sports. Alternative dispute resolution, Antitrust, General civil litigation. Office: Peterka Leuchterova & Partners vos Na Prikope 15 Prague 110 00 Czech Republic

CERULLO, JULIUS FACSON, lawyer, consultant; b. Sao Luis, Brazil, June 16, 1969; s. Handel Armstrong and Janet Phil Cerullo; m. Uche Salome Cerullo, Feb. 1, 2002. LLB, U. Lagos, Nigeria, 1988; advanced diploma in comml. law and practice, U. Lagos, 1998; BL, Nigerian Law Sch., Lagos, 1990; M in Internat. Law and Econs., U. Berne, Switzerland, 1999. Bar: Nigeria 1990. Mgr. credit Continental Mcht. Bank, Lagos, 1992—96; head external rels. Sheriea Oil and Gas, Lagos, 1996—98; mng. ptnr. Armstrong Handel & Cerullo, Lagos, 1998—. Office: Armstrong Handel and Cerullo 1 Aerodrome Rd Apapa GRA Lagos Nigeria

CHABAN, LAWRENCE RICHARD, lawyer; b. Pitts., Apr. 8, 1955; s. Donald W. and June H. (Klee) Chaban; children: Matthew A., Micah R. BA, U. Pitts., 1977, JD, 1980. Bar: Pa. 1980, U.S. Dist. Ct. (we. dist.) Pa. 1980, U.S. Ct. Appeals (3rd cir.) 1981, U.S. Ct. Appeals (4th cir.) 1984, U.S. Ct. Appeals (6th cir.) 1993. Compensation atty. Dist. 5 United Mine Workers Am., Pitts., 1980-81; with Yablonski, Costello & Leckie, P.C., Washington, Pa., 1980—2003; sole practitioner Pitts., 2003—. Mem. ABA, Nat. Employment Lawyers Assn., Pa. Bar Assn., Allegheny County Bar Assn., Order of Coif, Pa. Trial Lawyers Assn., Nat. Orgn. Social Security Claimant's Reps. Democrat. Jewish. Avocations: miniature gaming, golf. Labor (including EEOC, Fair Labor Standards Act, labor-management relations, NLRB, OSHA), Pension, profit-sharing, and employee benefits, Workers' compensation. Home: 111 Overlook Dr Pittsburgh PA 15216-1434 Office: 825 Grant Bldg 310 Grant St Pittsburgh PA 15216 Office Fax: 412-434-7795. E-mail: lchaban@lydonschubert.com.

CHABANEIX, JEAN PAUL, lawyer; b. Cusco, Peru, July 1964; s. Ferdinand and Luz Marina Chabaneix; m. Giselle Chabaneix; children: Benoit, François, Philippe. Degree in law, Cath. U., Lima, Peru, 1990; LLM, NYU, 1995. Assoc. Rodrigo, Elias & Medrano Abogados, Lima, 1987-93, ptnr., 1994—. Fellow Org. Am. States, 1994. Commercial, contracts (including sales of goods; commercial financing), Corporate, general, Finance. Office: Rodrigo Elias & Medrano Abogados Ave San Felipe 758 Lima 11 Peru Office Fax: 511 6191919. E-mail: jpchabaneix@estudiorodrigo.com.

CHABOT, ELLIOT CHARLES, lawyer; b. Anniston, Ala., Mar. 29, 1955; s. Herbert L. and Aleen (Kerwin) C.; m. Christine H. Swan, July 3, 1998. BA with honors, U. Md., 1977; JD, George Washington U., 1980. Bar: D.C. 1980, U.S. Dist. Ct. D.C. 1981, U.S. Ct. Fed. Claims 1981, U.S. Ct. Internat. Trade 1981, U.S. Tax Ct. 1981, U.S. Ct. Appeals Armed Forces 1981, U.S. Temporary Emergency Ct. Appeals 1981, U.S. Ct. Appeals (D.C. cir.) 1981, U.S. Ct. Appeals (4th, 5th, 8th, 9th, 10th, 11th, fed. cirs.) 1982, U.S. Ct. Appeals (7th cir.) 1983. Applications analyst, atty., House Info. Systems U.S. Ho. of Reps., Washington, 1980-81, project leader integrated law revision and retrieval project, 1981-89, legal support project leader House Info. Sys., 1989-95, webmaster internet law libr., 1994-99, legal sys. team leader House Info. Resources, 1995—. Bd. dirs. Am. Revenue Assn., Rockford, Iowa, 1983-87, Threshold Services, Inc., Silver Spring, Md., 1984-89; v.p. Banor Housing Inc., Kensington, Md., 1987-88, 90—, dir., 1987—. Columnist Aspen Hill Gazette, 1987-96. Pres. Aspen Hill (Md.) Civic Assn., 1985—95, dir., 1995—2000; adv. com. Aspen Hill Libr., 1972, 1986—2001; sec. Friends Aspen Hill Libr., 1994—96, dir., 1996—; mem. exec. com. Allied Civic Group, Silver Spring, 1987—89, corr. sec., 1992—94; mem. Sta. 21 com. Kensington Vol. Fire Dept., 1989; mem. Greater Layhill Community Night Com., 1989, Aspen Hill Master Plan Citizens Adv. com., 1990—94, Wheaton Action Group, 1990—95; chmn. Wheaton Woods Recreation Ctr. Adv. Com., 1990; mem. Bauer Drive Community Ctr. Adv. Com., 1992—; rec. sec. Dist. 19 Dem. Club, Montgomery County, 1983—86, 2d v.p., 1986—89, 1st v.p., 1989—92; sec. Montgomery County Dem. Party, 1994—, chmn. rules com., 1994—, chmn. Internet Svcs. com., 1995—2002, mem. ballot questions adv. com., 1988—90, 1998—2002; vice chmn. precint orgn. com. of the party opers. task force, 1991—92; area coord. Dist. 19, 1992—94, chmn. Precinct 13-43, 1987—92, treas. Precinct 13-45, 1978—85; campaign chmn. Dist. 19 Democratic Team, 1989—90; dir. dist. 3 Montgomery Citizens Polit. Action Com., 1991—92; sec. Montgomery County United Democrats, 1997—2002; mem. Md. State Dem. Ctrl. Com., 1994—, alt. mem. exec. com., 2002—, mem. rules com., 2003—; vice chmn. homeless com. Temple Shalom, Chevy Chase, Md., 1992—93; pres. Parkland Community Sch. Coun., Aspen Hill, 1983—87, 1994—96, v.p., 1971—73, mem. coun., 1970—74, 1982—96; chmn. community svcs. com. Greater Wheaton (Md.) Citizens Adv. Bd., 1986—92; chmn. Ga. Ave. Men's Shelter Adv. Bd., Aspen Hill, 1989—96, Community Edn. Devel. subcom. of Citizens Adv. com. to the Interagency Coordinating Bd. for Community Use of Ednl. Facilities and Svcs., 1985—88; dist. 3 v.p. Montgomery County Civic Fedn., 1990—91; exec. com. Robert E. Peary High Sch. PTA, Aspen Hill, 1972—73, Montgomery County Coun. com. on re-use of Peary High Sch., 1986, task force to examine the regional dist. act, 1991; corr. sec. Area 2 adv. coun. Montgomery County Pub. Schs., 1972—74, adv. com. spl. edn. programs, 1974; commr. Gov.'s Commn. on Student Affairs, Md., 1976—77; legal and acctg. div. steering com. Washington Israel Bonds, 1984—86; chmn. Kensington/Wheaton Human Svcs. Area Plan Adv. Group, 1988; sec. Robert E. Peary H.S. Alumni Assn., Aspen Hill, Md., 2001—. Recipient George Washington award, George Washington U., 1980, Donald R. Spivak award Montgomery County Interagency Coordinating Bd. Community Use of Edn. Facilities and Services, 1987, Total Quality Team award Chief Adminstrv. Officer of U.S. Ho. of Reps., 1996; named One of Outstanding Young Men, U.S. C. of C., 1982, Ky. Col. Hon. Order Ky. Cols., 1967, Citizen of Yr. Greater Wheaton Citizen's Adv. Bd., 1990, One of the Federal 100 Federal Computer Week, 1994. Mem. ABA, FBA, Internat. Law Inst. (mem. faculty legis. drafting 2000—), George Washington U. Law Alumni Assn. (pres. Capitol Hill chpt. 1987-89, sec. 1985-87), Phi Alpha Delta (clk. Jay chpt. 1979-80), Omicron Delta Kappa. Home: 3501 Beret Ln Aspen Hill MD 20906 Office: US Congress House Info Resources H2-641 Ford Ho Office Bldg Washington DC 20515-6165 E-mail: elliotchabot@abanet.org.

CHABOT, HERBERT L. judge; b. N.Y.C., July 17, 1931; s. Meyer and Esther (Mogilansky) C.; m. Aleen Carol Kerwin, June 16, 1951; children: Elliot C., Donald J., Lewis A., Nancy Jo. BA, CCNY, 1952; LLB, Columbia U., 1957; LLM, Georgetown U., 1964. Bar: N.Y. 1958. Staff counsel Am. Jewish Congress, 1957-60; law clk. U.S. Tax Ct., Washington, 1961-65, judge, 1978—, judge sr. status, 2001—. Atty. Joint Congl. Com. Taxation, 1965—78. Del. Md. Constl. Conv., 1967-68. With U.S. Army, 1953-55. Mem. ABA, Fed. Bar Assn. Office: US Tax Ct 400 2nd St NW Washington DC 20217-0002

CHABROW, PENN BENJAMIN, lawyer; b. Phila., Feb. 16, 1939; s. Benjamin Penn and Annette (Shapiro) Chabrow; m. Sheila Sue Steinberg, June 18, 1961; children: Michael Penn, Carolyn Debra, Frederick Penn. BS, Muhlenberg Coll., 1959; JD, George Washington U., 1962, LLM in Taxation, 1968; postgrad. in econs., Harvard U. Bar: Va. 1963, D.C. 1964, U.S. Ct. Appeals (D.C. cir.) 1964, U.S. Tax Ct. 1964, U.S. Supreme Ct. 1966, Fla. 1972, U.S. Ct. Claims 1974, U.S. Ct. Appeals (5th and 11th cirs.) 1981, bd. cert. tax atty. Fla. tax law specialist IRS, Washington, 1961—67; tax counsel C. of C. U.S., Washington, 1967—74; pvt. practice Miami, 1974—; shareholder Wampler, Buchanan, Walker, Chabrow & Banciella, PA, Miami, 1993—. Pres. Forum Realty Co., Phila., Pure Poultry Enterprises, Inc., Miami, Heartland Farms of Fla., Inc.; lectr. fed. taxation Barry U. Grad. Schl. of Bus., 1977—81. Contbr. articles to profl. jours. Founding dir. The Dan Marino Found., Inc., The Melissa Inst. for Violence Prevention and Treatment, Inc. Fellow: Am. Coll. Tax Counsel; mem.: ABA, D.C. Bar Assn., Va. Bar Assn., Fed. Bar Assn., Fla Bar Assn., Muhlenberg Coll. Internat. Vis. Com., Phi Sigma Tau, Phi Alpha Delta. Corporate, general, Estate planning, Taxation, general. Office: SunTrust Internat Ctr 1 SE Third Ave Ste 1700 Miami FL 33131

CHACON, GERALD GILBERT, lawyer; b. San Jose, Calif., Oct. 28, 1966; s. Gerald Gilbert and Barbara Kaye C. BS, Stanford U., 1988; JD, U. Calif., Davis, 1991; LLM, Boston U., 1995. Lawyer Hopkins & Carley, San Jose, 1991-94, Rosenblum Parish & Isaacs, San Jose, 1995—99, Wilson, Sonsini, Goodrich, & Rosati, Palo Alto, 1999—. Adj. lectr. Golden Gate U. Sch. Taxation, San Francisco, 1998—. Sr. campaign staff Tom Campbell for Congress, San Jose, 1995. Republican. Roman Catholic. Commercial, contracts (including sales of goods; commercial financing), Mergers and acquisitions, Taxation, general. Office: Wilson Sonsini Goodrich & Rosati 650 Page Rd Palo Alto CA 94304

CHADWICK, ROBERT, lawyer, judge; b. Jackson, Miss., Apr. 5, 1924; s. Hudson and Annie (Eley) C.; m. Helen Faye Josey, Apr. 5, 1953; children: Robert Hudson, Celia, Dan, Lea Ann, Robin. BA, Auburn U., 1950; JD, Miss. Coll., 1957; postgrad., U. So. Calif., 1973, 75-76. Bar: Miss. 1963, U.S. Supreme Ct. 1970, U.S. Ct. Mil. Appeals 1975, Ky. 1980, U.S. Dist Ct. (ea. dist.) Ky. 1987. Chief regulation staff div. pesticide regulation USDA, Washington, 1965-70; atty., ecologist div. enforcement EPA, Washington, 1970-75, chmn. com. pesticide misuse rev., 1975-79; asst. gen. counsel Presdl. Clemency Bd. White House Dept. Justice, Washington, 1975; pvt. practice law Frankfort, Ky., 1980-82, 83—; law judge parole bd. Corrections Cabinet, Frankfort, 1982-83; asst. dir. div. hazardous materials Ky. Dept. Natural Resources and Environ. Protection, Frankfort, 1983—. Chmn. bd. Exis, Inc.; staff atty., gen. counsel Ky. Cabinet for Human Resources, 1989-90. Pres. PTA Oxon Hill (Md.) Jr. High Sch., 1974, Frankfort Audubon Soc., 1981-83. Cpl. U.S. Army, 1943-45. Mem. ABA, Nat. Assn. Adminstrv. Law Judges, Miss. State Bar Assn., Ky. State Bar Assn., Franklin County Bar Assn., VFW, Masons. Criminal, Environmental, General practice. Home and Office: 16 Ryswick Ln Frankfort KY 40601-3848

CHAFFIN, VERNER FRANKLIN, lawyer, educator; b. Martin, Ga., Sept. 26, 1918; s. Emory Franklin and Mabel Lea (Verner) C.; m. Corinne Ethel Tison, July 17, 1943; children— Ethel, Verner Franklin, Mary Davis, John Edwards. AB, U. Ga., LL.B., 1942; J.S.D., Yale, 1961. Bar: Ga. bar 1942, Ala. bar 1953, U.S. Supreme Ct. bar 1965. Atty. Dept. Justice, 1946-47; mem. faculty U. Ala., 1947—57, U. Ga., Athens, 1957—, prof. law, 1954-69, Fuller E. Callaway prof., 1969—89, Fuller E. Callaway prof. emeritus, 1989—; mem. nat. labor panel Am. Arbitration Assn., 1957—89, mem. pub. employment disputes settlement panel, 1969—89; mem. panel arbitrators Fed. Mediation and Conciliation Service, 1973—89. Trustee Inst. Continuing Legal Edn. Ga., 1969-76 Author: Georgia Annotations to the Restatement (Second) Trusts, 1970, Studies in the Georgia Law of Decedents' Estates and Future Interests, 1979, The Rule Against Perpetuities in Georgia, 1984; Contbr. numerous articles to legal jours. Mem. permanent jud. commn. Gen. Assembly, Presbyn. Ch. U.S.A., 1972-75; elder 1st Presbyn. Ch., Athens, 1966-71, 74-79, 96-98; pres. Athens chpt. Am. Cancer Soc., 1968-69, Athens Community Concert Assn., 1966-67; with USN; Lt. Cmdr. USNR. Sterling fellow Yale, 1950-51 Fellow Am. Coll. Trust & Estate Council (life), Lawyers Found. GA (life); mem. Am. Law Inst., ABA, Internat. Acad. Law and Sci.,Pres. Athens Historical Soc., Western Circuit, Ga., Am. bar assns., Ga. Hist. Soc., Athens-Clarke Heritage Found., Blue Key, Sphinx, Order of Coif, Phi Beta Kappa, Phi Kappa Phi, Phi Delta Phi, Omicron Delta Kappa, Sigma Nu. Clubs: Athens City, Yale club Ga. Home: 510 Riverview Rd Athens GA 30606-4830 Office: University of Georgia Law School Athens GA 30602

CHAIT, GREGORY MARSHALL, lawyer; b. Atlanta, Oct. 4, 1960; s. Donald Carl and Jean Tillman Chait; m. Dorinda Dee Healy, Jan. 7, 1993; children: Healy Leah Tillman, Sarah Wilkes Davis. BA, George Washington U., 1982; JD, NYU, 1985. Bar: N.Y. 1987, Ga. 1994. Staff asst. W. Wyche Fowler, Jr., M.C., Atlanta and Washington, 1981—82; assoc. Mudge Rose Guthrie Alexander & Fender, N.Y.C., 1985—89, Shea & Gould, N.Y.C., 1989—93; gen. counsel Insignia Fin. Group, Inc., Greenville, SC, 1993—94; capital ptnr. Powell Goldstein Frazer & Murph LLP, Atlanta, 1994—. Sr. articles editor: NYU Jour. Internat. Law and Politics, 1984—85. Mem.: ABA, Assn. of Bar of City of N.Y., Ga. Bar Assn., Phi Beta Kappa. Securities, Mergers and acquisitions, Corporate taxation. Office: Powell Goldstein Frazer & Murph LLP 191 Peachtree St NE Atlanta GA 30303 Office Fax: 404-572-6999. E-mail: gchait@pgfm.com.

CHAITMAN, HELEN DAVIS, lawyer; b. N.Y.C., July 5, 1941; d. Philip and Miriam (Pfeffer) D.; m. Edmund Chaitman, Feb. 29, 1964 (div. 1978); children: Jennifer, Alison; m. George B. Gelman, Oct. 21, 1979. AB cum laude, Bryn Mawr Coll., 1963; JD, Rutgers U., 1976. Bar: N.Y. 1978, N.J., 1976, SDNY, 1978, EDNY, 1978, US Supreme Ct., 1981, Ct. Fed. Chairs, 2001, 8th Cir, 2002, U.S. Dist. Ct. N.Y., U.S. Dist. Ct. N.J., U.S. Ct. Appeals (3d cir.), U.S. Supreme Ct. Assoc. Paul, Weiss, Rifkind, Wharton & Garrison, N.Y.C., 1977-82; ptnr. Wilentz, Goldman & Spitzer, Woodbridge, N.J., 1983-87, Ross & Hardies, Somerset, N.J., 1987-99, Wolf Haldenstein Adler Freeman & Herz LLP, N.Y.C., 1999—2002. Author: The Law of Lender Liability, 1990; contbg. author: Commercial Damages, 1985; editor Emerging Theories of Lender Liability, 1985-87. Mem.: ABA (chmn. comml. fin. svcs. com. 1994—97, sect. bus. law), Pub. Law Inst., Am. Law Inst. (sustaining mem. 1992—2003). Bankruptcy, Commercial, contracts (including sales of goods; commercial financing). Home: The Farm 115 Fairview Rd Frenchtown NJ 08825-3013 Office: Phillips Niza LLP 666 Fifth Ave New York NY 10103-0084 also: 45 Essex St Hackensack NJ 07601 E-mail: hchaitman@phillipsnizer.com.

CHAJEC, ANDRZEJ BOGDAN, lawyer; b. Kamienica Polska, Poland, May 27, 1966; s. Stanisław and Irena Chajec; m. Marzena Chajec. MA in Law, U. Warsaw, Poland, 1991; Atty. at Law, Legal Advisor's Apprenticeship Chamber Legal Advisors, Warsaw, 1995. Asst. to dept. dir. Nat. Bank Poland, Warsaw, 1990—91; lawyer KPMG Reviconsult Sp. z O.O., Warsaw, 1991—93, Vinson & Elkins Sp. z O.O., Warsaw, 1993; ptnr. Beata Gessel, Andrzej Chajec & Ptnrs., Warsaw, 1993—. Mem.: Internat. Bd. Assn., Internat. Assn. Bus. Leaders (life). Corporate, general, Mergers and acquisitions. Office: Beata Gessel Andrzej Chajec and Ptnrs Ul Widok 8 00-023 Warsaw Poland

CHALFANT, WILLIAM YOUNG, lawyer, author, historian; b. Hutchinson, Kans., Oct. 3, 1928; s. Claude Edward and Junia Maurine (Young) C.; m. Martha Ann Wallbillich, June 30, 1956; children: William David, Kristin. AB, U. Kans., 1950; JD, U. Mich., 1956. Bar: Kans. 1956, U.S. Ct. Appeals (10th cir.), U.S. Supreme Ct. Ptnr. Branine, Chalfant & Hill, Hutchinson, 1956—. Bd. dirs. First Nat. Bank, Hutchinson; mem. Kans. State Bd. of Law Examiners, 1966—92, chmn., 1986—92; mem. constnl. law drafting com. Nat. Conf. of Bar Examiners, 1974—85. Author: Cheyennes and Horse Soldiers, 1989, Dangerous Passage, 1993, Without Quarter, 1991, Cheyennes at Dark Water Creek, 1997. Drive chmn. Reno County Cmty. Chest, Hutchinson, 1957-581 bd. dirs. Reno County Red Cross, Hutchinson, 1960-64; dist. commr. Boy Scouts Am., 1965-75. Capt. USMC, 1950-53. Recipient Gold award Santa Fe Nat. Hist. Trail/Nat. Park Svc., 1995. Mem. ABA, Kans. Bar Assn., Santa Fe Trail Assn. (bd. dirs., award of merit 1995), Western History Assn. (chmn. fin. com.). Avocations: history, writing. Commercial, contracts (including sales of goods; commercial financing), Constitutional, General practice. Home: 1007 W 95th Ave Hutchinson KS 67502-8325 Office: Branine Chalfant & Hill 418 First Nat Ctr Hutchinson KS 67501

CHALK, JOHN ALLEN, SR., lawyer; b. Lexington, Tenn., Jan. 16, 1937; AA, Freed-Hardeman Coll., 1956; BS, Tenn. Tech. U., 1962, MA, 1967; JD, U. Tex., 1973. Bar: Tex. 1973, D.C. 1977; ordained to ministry Ch. of Christ, 1956. Pastor chs., Dayton, Ohio, 1956-60, Cookeville, Tenn., 1960-66, Abilene, Tex., 1966-71; assoc. Rhodes and Seamster, Abilene, 1973-74, Rhodes and Doscher, Abilene, 1974; ptnr. Rhodes, Doscher, Chalk and Heatherly, Abilene, 1975-78; gen. counsel La Jet, Inc., Abilene, 1978-84, also v.p., sec; exec. v.p. Dabney Corp., Dallas, 1984-86; pres. Dabney Capital, Dallas, 1984-86; assoc. Gandy, Michener, Swindle, Whitaker & Pratt, Ft. Worth, 1986, ptnr., 1987-93, Michener Larimore Swindle Whitaker Flowers Sawyer Reynolds & Chalk, Ft. Worth, 1993-2000, Whitaker Chalk Swindle & Sawyer LLP, Ft. Worth, 2000—. Pres. Equity, Inc., 1982-90; bd. dirs. Osteo. Health Sys. Tex., Inc.; mem. strategic alliances com. for edn. Nat. Ct. Reporters Assn., 1994-95; cert. master mediator Dispute Resolution Svcs. Tarrant County, Tex.; Tex. court-approved mediator; mem. panel of comml. and employment neutrals Am. Arbitration Assn.; contract mediator EEOC, Dallas, 1999-2001. Author: The Praying Christ, 1964, Three American Revolutions, 1970, Jesus' Church, 1970, The Christian Family, 1973, Great Biblical Doctrines, 1973, The Devil, You Say!, 1974; author numerous articles on U.S. Dept. Edn. fed. student fin. assistance, domestic and internat. arbitration and mediation, also articles on religion; presenter in fields. Trustee Abilene Regional Mental Health Retardation Ctr., 1978—80, Christian Scholarship Found., Inc., Atlanta, 1980, chmn. bd., 1992—93; chmn. Ailene Bicentennial Com., 1975—76; mem. nat. adv. coun. Am. United for Separation of Ch. and State, 1979—82, pres. bd. trustees, 1981—82; mem. nat. devel. coun. Abilene Christian U.; featured spkr. radio and TV programs Herald of Truth, 1966—69; trustee Osteo. Health Care Found., Inc., Ft. Worth, 1987—96, sec.-treas., 1990—91, sr. v.p., pres.-elect, 1991—92, pres., 1992—93; mem. Strategy for 2000, City of Ft. Worth, 1995—2000; bd. dirs. Health Care of Tex., Inc., 1987—2003. Fellow Tex. Bar Found. (life), Chartered Inst. Arbitrators London (chartered arbitrator), Tarrant County Bar Found. (founding, life); mem. ABA (acting assoc. editor, mem. editl. bd. Family Adv. 1977-78), FBA, Coll. State Bar Tex. (maintaining), Am. Health Lawyers Assn. (disput resolution svc. panel of neutrals), Am. Arbitration Assn. (panel arbitrators and mediators), Internat. Ctrs. for Arbitration (panel arbitrators and mediators), Tex. Assn. Mediators, Tarrant County Assn. Mediators, Tex. Ct.-Approved Mediators, State Bar Tex., Ft. Worth Bar Assn., Nat. Arbitration Forum (panel of neutrals), London Ct. Internat. Arbitration. Administrative and regulatory, Corporate, general, Finance. Home: 3601 Verde Vista Ct W Aledo TX 76008-3679 Office: Whitaker Chalk Swindle & Sawyer 3500 City Ctr II Fort Worth TX 76102-4186 E-mail: jchalk@whitakerchalk.com.

CHAMBERLAIN, DAVID ALANSON, writer; b. Warren, Pa., Oct. 20, 1937; s. Alanson Wilder and Rachel (Hazeltine) C.; m. Mary Dell Lentz, July 2, 1979; children: Lynn, Verna Reynolds, David Jr., Scott D. BS summa cum laude, Ariz. State U., 1971, JD, 1974. Bar: Ariz. 1974, U.S. Dist. Ct. Ariz. 1974, U.S. Supreme Ct. 1978, U.S. Ct. Appeals (9th cir.) 1986, U.S. Dist. Ct. (no. dist.) Calif. 1990, U.S. Dist. Ct. (ea. dist.) Wis. 1992, U.S. Dist. Ct. (no. dist.) Ill. 1993, U.S. Dist. Ct. Nebr. 1993, U.S. Dist. Ct. (no. dist.) Tex. 1993, U.S. Dist. Ct. (we. dist.) Tex. 1995, White Mountain Apache Tribal Ct. 1977. Pvt. practice, Pinetop, Ariz., 1975—76, Prescott, Ariz., 1976—. Fellow Ariz. Bar Found.; mem. State Bar Ariz. (cert. specialist bankruptcy bd. legal specialization), Ariz. State U. Coll. Law Alumni Assn. (bd. dirs. 1993-95). Avocations: writing, photography. Bankruptcy, Commercial, consumer (including collections, credit), Public international. Office: PO Box 10668 Prescott AZ 86304-0668

CHAMBERLAIN, DOUGLAS REGINALD, lawyer; b. Burlington, Vt., Sept. 8, 1951; s. Reginald B. and Ethelda B. (Towle) C.; m. Linda J. Canfield, Sept. 11, 1982; children: Samuel Douglas, Sarah Riley. AB, Harvard U., 1973; JD, Columbia U., 1976. Bar: N.H. 1976, U.S. Dist. Ct. N.H. 1976. Assoc. Wiggin & Nourie, Manchester, N.H., 1976-81, ptnr., 1982-91, chmn. corp. dept., 1987-93; shareholder Wiggin & Nourie, P.A., Manchester, 1992—2002; mem. Sulloway & Hollis, P.L.L.C., Concord, NH, 2002—. N.H. Minimum CLE (bd. mem. 1992—, chmn. 1997—). Bd. dirs. N.H. Performing Arts Ctr., Manchester, 1981-89; mem. Mayor's Child Care Comn., 1988-92; mem. vestry Grace Episcopal Ch., 1995-98, jr. warden, 1999-2002, sr. warden, 2002—; mem. Constn. and Canons Com., Episcopal Diocese of N.H., 1999—, chair, 2002--. Mem. ABA (employee benefits com. 1982—, taxation sect.), N.H. Employee Benefits Coun. (pres. 1983-84, bd. dirs., sec. 1997-2000, v.p. 2000-01, pres. 2001-03), N.H. Med. Group Mgmt. Assn., Human Resources Assn. Greater Concord (bd. dirs., sec. 2003—), N.H. Bar Assn. (com. on ethics 1981-86, chmn. 1986-88, chmn. group ins. pension plan com. 1984-85, continuing legal edn. com. 1988-98, legis. com. 1996—, lawyer dispute resolution com. 1988-90, tax sect., vice chair, 2001-03, chair 2003--, bus. law sect.). Republican. Corporate, general, Pension, profit-sharing, and employee benefits, Health. Office: Sulloway & Hollis PLLC PO Box 1256 Concord NH 03302-1256 E-mail: dchamberlain@sulloway.com.

CHAMBERLIN, MICHAEL MEADE, lawyer; b. Omaha; s. Cecil Meade and Helen Gail (Russell) C. AB in Econs., Princeton U., 1972; JD, George Washington U., 1975. Bar: N.Y. 1976. Assoc. Shearman & Sterling, N.Y.C., 1975-83, ptnr., 1984-93; CEO, exec. dir. EMTA, 1994—. Avocations: conservation, running, choral music, skiing, flying. Private international, Securities. E-mail: mchamb@emta.org.

CHAMBERS, GUY WAYNE, lawyer; b. Harvey, Ill., Feb. 18, 1956; s. Robert Rood and Martha (Wayne) C. BS in Chem. Engring. with highest honors, U. Calif., Santa Barbara, 1978; JD, Columbia U., 1981. Bar: Calif. 1981, U.S. Ct. Appeals (fed. cir.) 1982, U.S. Patent and Trademark Office 1982, U.S. Ct. Appeals (9th cir.) 1992, U.S. Supreme Ct. 1995. Trial atty. civil div. U.S. Dept. Justice, Washington, 1981-84; assoc. Townsend and Townsend and Crew, San Fransisco, 1984-91, ptnr., 1991—. Project mgr. NIH Patent Svcs. Contract; spkr. PLI high tech. licensing, 2001-02. Contbr. articles to profl. publs. Mem. San Francisco Intellectual Property Law Assn. Intellectual property, Trademark and copyright, Patent. Office: Townsend & Townsend & Crew 8th flr 2 Embarcadero Ctr San Francisco CA 94111 Office Fax: (415) 576-0300. E-mail: gwchambers@townsend.com.

CHAMBERS, JULIUS LEVONNE, lawyer; b. Montgomery County, N.C., Oct. 6, 1936; BA, N.C. Cen. U., 1958; MA, U. Mich., 1959; LLB, U. N.C., 1962; LLM, Columbia U., 1963. Bar: N.C. 1962, N.Y. 1986. Ptnr. Chambers, Ferguson, Stein, Chambers, Adkins, Gresham & Sumter, Charlotte, NC, 1964-84; dir., counsel NAACP Legal Def. and Ednl. Fund, N.Y.C., 1984-92; chancellor N.C. Ctrl. U., Durham, 1993-2000; with Ferguson, Stein, Wallas, Adkins, Gresham & Sumter, Charlotte, 2000—. Former trustee N.J. State Bd. Higher Edn.; former bd. visitors Harvard U., Columbia U. Law Sch.; former trustee U. Pa., mem. bd. overseers Law Sch.; former bd. dirs. Children's Def. Fund, Legal Aid Soc. N.Y. Mem. ABA (bd. editors ABA jour.), N.C. Bar Assn., Mecklenburg County Bar Assn., N.Y. State Bar Assn., Assn. of Bar of City of N.Y., Nat. Bar Assn., Assn. Black Lawyers N.C., Order of Coif, Order of Golden Fleece, Phi Alpha Theta. Office: Ferguson Stein Wallas Adkins Gresham & Sumter 741 Kenilworth Ave Ste 300 Charlotte NC 28204

CHAMBERS, THOMAS JEFFERSON, lawyer, state supreme court justice; b. Yakima, Wash., Oct. 11, 1943; s. Thomas J. and Doris May (Ellyson) C.; m. Judy Larene Cable, June 11, 1967; children: Jolie, Jana, Tommy. BA in Polit. Sci., Wash. State U., 1966; JD, U. Wash., 1969. Bar: Wash., U.S. Dist. Ct. (we. and ea. dists.) Wash. 1969. Assoc. Lycette, Diamond & Sylvester, Seattle, 1969-71, Barokas & Martin, Seattle, 1972; sole practice Seattle, 1972—2001; justice Wash. State Supreme Ct., 2001—. Mem. congestion com. Wash. State Cts., 1984, King County Mandatory Arbitration Council, 1981-86, Damages Atty. Roundtable, 1983-86. Editorial adv. bd. Everday Law mag.; contbr. articles to profl. jours. Mem. jud. evaluation com. Mcpl. League, 1982. Mem. Wash. State Trial Lawyers Assn. (pres. 1985-86, pres.-elect 1984-85, bd. govs. 1976—, various coms.), Am. Bd. Trial Advs. (past pres. Wash. chpt.), Am. Trial Lawyers Assn. (past mem. bd. govs.), Wash. State Bar Assn. (pres. 1996-97). Avocation: flying airplanes. Personal injury (including property damage). Home: 4514 193rd Pl SE Issaquah WA 98027-9308 Office: PO Box 40929 Olympia WA 98504-0929

CHAMPION, SARA STEWART, lawyer; b. Boston, Apr. 1, 1942; d. William Julius Champion and Mary Stewart Cunningham; m. Wayne L. Kinsey, Dec. 12, 1964 (div. Feb. 1971); m. John Q. Adams, Apr. 25, 1998 (div. Oct. 2000). BA, Duke U., 1963; MA, U. Calif., Davis, 1974; JD cum laude, N.Y. Law Sch., 1992. Bar: N.Y. 1992, Conn. 1992. Rsch. analyst Nat. Security Agy., Ft. Meade, Md., 1963-65; instr. Russian Def. Lang. Inst., Monterey, Calif., 1970-72; claims rep. Social Security Adminstrn., San Francisco, 1974-78, claims rep., ops. supr. N.Y.C., 1978-87; office adminstr. Bachelder Law Offices, N.Y.C., 1987-97, assoc., 1992-97, ptnr., 1997—2002, Vedder, Price, Kaufman and Kammholz, N.Y.C., 2002—. Head N.Y. Exec. Comp Group, 2002—. Mem.: DAR, New England Soc., Soc. Mayflower Descs., Silver Spring Country Club (Ridgefield, Conn.), Univ. Club, Wianno Yacht Club (Osterville, Mass.). Avocation: genealogy. Office: Vedder Price Kaufman & Kammholz 805 3d Ave New York NY 10022 E-mail: schampion@vedderprice.com.

CHAN, DANIEL CHUNG-YIN, lawyer; b. Kowloon, Hong Kong, June 5, 1948; came to U.S., 1969; s. David Chi-Kwong and Betty Wai-Lan (Kwok) C.; m. Mary Ching-Fay Wong, June 11, 1977; children: Pamila Wai-Sum (dec.), Derrick Ming-Deh. BA cum laude, Azusa Pacific U., 1972; post-grad., Calif. State U., L.A., 1973-75; JD, U. West L.A., 1983. Bar: Calif. 1984, U.S. Dist. Ct. (cen. dist.) Calif. 1984, U.S. Ct. Appeals (9th cir.) 1984, U.S. Dist. Ct. (so. dist.) Calif. 1985, U.S. Dist. Ct. (no. dist.) Calif. 1986. Mgr. Elegant Sewing Co., L.A., 1977; legal asst. Otto Frank Swanson Law Office, Marina Del Ray, Calif., 1978-84, assoc., 1984-87; pvt. practice, Pasadena, Calif., 1987—. Legal counsel Chinese Grace Missions Internat., Inc., Duarte, Calif., 1984—, Diao Jiou Chinese Christian Ch. L.A., Highland Park, Calif., 1988—, Ruth Hitchcock Found. Mem. ABA, Assn. Trial Lawyers Am., So. Calif. Chinese Lawyers Assn., Am. Immigration Lawyers Assn., Delta Epsilon Chi, Alpha Chi. Family and matrimonial, Immigration, naturalization, and customs, Private international. Office: 283 S Lake Ave Ste 219 Pasadena CA 91101-4818

CHAN, DAVID RONALD, tax specialist, lawyer; b. L.A., Aug. 3, 1948; s. David Yew and Anna May (Wong) Chan; m. Mary Anne Chan, June 21, 1980; children: Eric, Christina. AB in Econs., UCLA, 1969, MS in Bus. Adminstrn., 1970, JD, 1973. Bar: Calif. 1973, U.S. Tax Ct. 1974, U.S. Ct. Appeals (9th cir.) 1974, U.S. Dist. Ct. (ctrl. dist.) Calif. 1980. Acct. Oxnard Celery Distbrs., L.A., 1968-73, Touche Ross & Co., L.A., 1970; tax prin. Kenneth Leventhal & Co. (name now E&Y Kenneth Leventhal Real Estate Group), L.A., 1973—. Contbr. chpts. to books and articles to profl. jours. Founder, dir. Chinese Hist. Soc. So. Calif., L.A., 1975—; mem. spkrs. bur. L.A. 200 Bicentennial, L.A., 1981; spkr. Project Follow Through, L.A., 1981, EY Tax Forum, UCLA Real Estate Forecast, Merril Lynch Symposium, Calif. CPA Soc. Recipient Forbes Gold medal Calif. Soc. CPAs, L.A., 1970, Elijah Watt Sells cert. AICPA, L.A., 1970, cert. recognition Chinese Hist. Soc. So. Calif., L.A., 1985. Mem. So. Calif. Chinese Lawyers Assn., L.A. County Bar Assn., Chinese Am. CPAs So. Calif., Asian Bus. League, Chinese For Affirmative Action. Republican. Avocations: chinese cuisine, sports memorabilia, philately. Office: E&Y Kenneth Leventhal Real Estate Group Ste 1800 2049 Century Park E Los Angeles CA 90067-3119 E-mail: david.chan02@ey.com.

CHAN, LAI LEE, lawyer; b. Jan. 18, 1969; BA, NYU, 1991, JD, 1994. Bar: N.Y. 1997, U.S. Dist. Ct. (so. and ea. dists.) N.Y. 1997. Assoc. Law Offices Richard S. Missan, N.Y.C., 1994-97; pvt. practice N.Y.C., 1997—. Civil rights, Federal civil litigation, Labor (including EEOC, Fair Labor Standards Act, labor-management relations, NLRB, OSHA). Office: Ste 15D 404 E 76th St New York NY 10021

CHAN, THOMAS TAK-WAH, lawyer; b. Kowloon, Hong Kong, 1950; BA magna cum laude, U. Wis., Whitewater, 1973; JD, U. Wis., 1979. Bar: Wis. 1979, Minn. 1983, Calif. 1987. Judicial intern Wis. Supreme Ct., 1978; atty. Wausau (Wis.) Ins., 1979-82; staff atty. CPT Corp., Eden Prairie, Minn., 1982-84; gen. counsel Lee Data Corp., Eden Prairie, 1984-85; dep. gen. counsel Ashton-Tate Corp., Torrance, Calif., 1985-87; pres. Chan Law Group LC, L.A., 1987—. Mem. adv. bd. SBA Export Devel. Ctr., 1992-2000; founder Bus. Software Alliance, Washington, 1987; mem. industry sector adv. com. and U.S. trade rep., U.S. Dept. Commerce, 1988-91; founder Asian Pacific Am. Coord. Com., 1996; bd. dirs. Asian Pacific Am. Legal Ctr., 2002—. Bd. dirs. Torrance Meml. Med. Ctr. Found., 2000—. Mem. Asian Pacific Am. Bar Assn. (founder, dir. 1998-00), Wis. Bar Assn., Calif. Bar Assn. (lectr. 1988) Computer Law Assn., So. Calif. Chinese Lawyers Assn. (gov. 1990-92) Export Mgrs. Assn. So. Calif. (dir. 1990-92), S.Bay Chinese Am. C. of C. (founder, dir. 1997—), S.Bay Chinese Culture Ctr. (dir. 1998-01), Cause (dir. 1994-97, chmn. 1995-96), Phi Kappa Phi. Avocations: skiing, hiking, tai chi. Computer, Intellectual property, Private international. Office: Chan Law Group LC Ste 1880 1055 W Seventh St Los Angeles CA 90017 E-mail: thelaw@chanlaw.com.

CHANDER, ANUPAM, lawyer; b. Punjab, India, Apr. 15, 1967; s. Harish and Yash (Garg) C. AB, Harvard U., 1989; JD, Yale U., 1992. Bar: N.Y. 1993. Clk. to Judge W. Norris U.S. Ct. Appeals (9th cir.), L.A., 1992-93; clk. to Chief Judge Newman U.S. Ct. Appeals (2d cir.), Hartford, Conn., 1993-94; assoc. Cleary, Gottlieb, Steen & Hamilton, N.Y.C., 1994-99; assoc. prof. law Ariz. State U., Tempe, 1999-00; prof. U. Calif., Davis, 2000—. Contbg. author: UNHCR Human Rights Manual, 1998. Co-dir. South Asian Youth Action, N.Y.C., 1998-99. Mem. Assn. Bar City N.Y. (human rights com. 1997-99). Avocation: reading. Finance, Intellectual property, Private international. Office: U Calif Sch Law 400 Mrak Hall Dr Davis CA 95616-5201 E-mail: anupam@post.harvard.edu.

CHANDLER, ALBERT BENJAMIN, III, state attorney general; m. Jennifer Chandler; children: Lucie Brasher, Albert Benjamin IV, Russell Branham. BA in History with distinction, U. Ky., JD, 1986. Bar: Ky. 1986. Assoc. Brown, Todd & Heyburn, Lexington, Ky., Reeves & Graddy, Versailles, Ky.; auditor State of Ky., 1991—94, atty. gen., 1995—. Recipient Achievement of Yr. award, Assn. Govt. Accts., 1993—94. Mem.: ABA, Woodford County Bar Assn., Ky. Bar Assn. (named Outstanding Young Lawyer 1993). Democrat. Office: Office of Atty Gen Ste 118 Capitol Bldg Frankfort KY 40601-2831*

CHANDLER, KENT, JR., lawyer; b. Chgo., Jan. 10, 1920; s. Kent and Grace Emeret (Tuttle) C.; m. Frances Robertson, June 19, 1948; children: Gail, Robertson Kent. BA, Yale U., 1942; JD, U. Mich., 1949. Bar: Ill. 1949, U.S. Dist. Ct. (no. dist.) Ill. 1949, U.S. Ct. Appeals (7th cir.) 1955, U.S. Ct. Claims 1958. Assoc. Wilson & McIlvaine, Chgo., 1949-56, ptnr., 1957-94, spl. counsel to firm, 1994-98; of counsel Bell Jones & Quinlisk, Chgo., 1998—. Bd. dirs. No. Trust Bank, Lake Forest, Ill., 1969-90, A.B. Dick Co., 1971-79, Internat. Crane Found., 1988—. Mem. zoning bd. appeals City of Lake Forest, Ill., 1953-63, chmn., 1963-67, mem. plan commn., 1955-69, chmn., 1969-70, pres. bd. local improvements, 1970-73, mayor, 1970-73, mem. bd. fire and police commn., 1975-82, chmn., 1982-84. Served to maj. USMCR, 1941-46. Mem. ABA, Ill. State Bar Assn., Chgo. Bar Assn., Lake County Bar Assn., Lawyers Club Chgo. (pres. 1985-86), Univ. Club, Onwentsia Club (Lake Forest), Old Elm Club (Highland Park, Ill.). Republican. Presbyterian. Estate planning, Probate (including wills, trusts), Personal income taxation. Office: 200 W Adams St Ste 2600 Chicago IL 60606-5233

CHANDLER, LAWRENCE BRADFORD, JR., lawyer; b. New Bedford, Mass., June 20, 1942; s. Lawrence Bradford and Anne (Crane) C.; m. Madeleine Bibeau, Sept. 7, 1963 (div. June 1984); children: Dawn, Colleen, Brad. BS in Bus. Adminstrn., Boston Coll., 1963; LLB, U. Va., 1966, JD, 1970. Bar: Mass. 1966, U.S. Supreme Ct. 1967, Va. 1970, W.Va. 1993; diplomate Nat. Bd. Trial Advocacy; advocate Am. Bd. Trial Advocates. Ptnr. Chandler, Franklin & O'Bryan, Charlottesville, Va., 1971—. Pres. Western Va. Chpt., 1992-93. Capt. U.S. Army, 1967-71. Mem.: ATLA (chair state dels. 1993—94, exec. com. 1993—94, bd. govs. 1995—2001), ABA, Am. Assn. Profl. Liability Attys., Am. Soc. on Law, Medicine and Ethics, Am. Coll. Legal Medicine, Charlottesville Bar Assn., Nat. Bd. Trial Advocacy (bd. examiners), Am. Bd. Trial Advs. (pres. Va. chpt.), Va. Trial Lawyers Assn. (pres. 1985—86), Assn. U.S. Army (pres. 1971—73). Roman Catholic. Personal injury (including property damage), Professional liability, Transportation. Home: 1445 Old Ballard Rd Charlottesville VA 22901-9469 Office: Chandler Franklin & O'Bryan PO Box 6747 Charlottesville VA 22906-6747 E-mail: goofyc@mindspring.com.

CHANDLER, MARK, telecommunications industry executive; b. 1956; AB, Harvard U.; JD, Stanford U. Gen. counsel Cisco Systems, Inc., San Jose, Calif., 2001—. Office: Cisco Sys Inc 255 W Tasman Dr San Jose CA 95134-1705

CHANDLER, RONALD JAY, lawyer; b. Springfield, Mo., Jan. 15, 1949; s. Jack Dempsey and Esta Lee (Cravens) C.; m. Patricia Ann Meyer, June 17, 1973; 1 child, Mary Coday. BA, Mo. So. State Coll., 1975; JD, U. Tulsa, 1979. Bar: Okla. 1979, U.S. Dist. Ct. (no. dist.) Okla. 1980, U.S. Ct. Appeals (10th cir.) 1981. Asst. dist. atty. Office of Dist. Atty., Tulsa, 1979-80; ptnr. Chandler & Cantrell, Tulsa, 1980; atty. Cities Svc. Co., Tulsa, 1980-82; assoc. Prichard, Norman & Wohlgemuth, Tulsa, 1982-84; ptnr. Norman, Wohlgemuth & Thompson, Tulsa, 1984-89, Norman Wohlgemuth Chandler & Dowdell, Tulsa, 1989—. Instr. Tulsa Jr. Coll., 1980-83, 86; vis. asst. prof. Univ. Ctr., U. Okla., Tulsa, 1990-97. With U.S. Army, 1968-70. Mem. ABA, Okla. Bar Assn., Tulsa County Bar Assn., Summit Club, Tulsa So. Tennis Club, Phi Alpha Delta. Republican. Episcopalian. Avocations: sailing, tennis, reading. Commercial, contracts (including sales of goods; commercial financing), Corporate, general, Property, real (including real estate development, water). Office: Norman Wohlgemuth Chandler & Dowdell 2900 Mid-Continent Tower Tulsa OK 74103

CHANDONNET, SHEILA WOHL, lawyer; d. Alan and Gail Wohl; m. Raymond E. Chandonnet, Jan. 16, 1999. BS, Pa. State U., 1987; MBA, U. of Del., Newark, 1992; JD, Rutgers U., 1996. Bar: N.J. 1996, Pa. 1996, N.C. 2000. Treasury mgr., ops. mgr. Verizon, Various, Del., 1987—93; assoc. Morgan, Lewis and Bockius, Phila., 1996—99, Kennedy Covington Lobdell and Hickman, Charlotte, NC, 1999—2001; sr. atty. Aventis Pharms. Inc., Bridgewater, NJ, 2001—. Recipient Grad. 2nd in class, Rutgers Sch. of Law, 1996. Corporate, general, Mergers and acquisitions, Securities. Office: Aventis Pharmaceuticals Inc 300 Somerset Corporate Blvd Bridgewater NJ 07901 Personal E-mail: s_chandonnet@yahoo.com.

CHANEY, KIM J. judge; b. Ariz., Apr. 12, 1957; s. James Nevada Chaney and Jean Ann Owens; m. Maureen Cecilia Murphy, June 12, 1982; children: Alex J., Emily Ann. BA in Criminal Justice, U. Ala., 1979, MA in Criminal Justice, 1985, JD, 1986. Bar: Ala. 1986, U.S. Dist. Ct. (no. dist.) Ala. 1986. Dep. sheriff Cullman County Sheriff's Dept., Ala., 1979—80; pvt. practice Carbon Hill, Ala., 1986—87; asst. dist. atty. Office of Dist. Atty., Cullman, Ala., 1987—92; presiding dist. judge Cullman County, 1992—. Bd. dirs. DayStar Homeless Shelter, Cullman, 1995—2002, Cullman Caring for Kids, 1992—2002; mem. adv. bd. Cullman County Ext. Office, 1995—2002; chmn. bd. Cullman Children's Policy Coun., Mitnick Juvenile Boot Camp, Jasper, Ala. Named Cullman County Disting. Citizen, Cullman Times newspaper, 2001. Mem.: Ala. Juvenile and Family Court Judges (v.p. 2001—02, mem. exec. bd.), Ala. Bar Assn. Office: Cullman Dist Ct County Courthouse Rm 213 Cullman AL 35055

CHANEY, MICHAEL THOMAS, lawyer; b. Charleston, W.Va., Feb. 4, 1948; s. Vincent V. and Caroline (O'Neale) C.; m. Nancy Jane Bierly, May 25, 1974; children: Matthew Thomas, Megan O'Neale, Christopher Michael. BA, Duke U., 1970; JD magna cum laude, U. Mich., 1973. Bar: W.Va. 1973, U.S. Dist. Ct. (so. dist.) W.Va. 1973, U.S. Dist. Ct. (no. dist.) W.Va. 1974, U.S. Ct. Appeals (4th cir.) 1982. Assoc. Kay, Casto & Chaney PLLC, Charleston, 1973—76, mem., 1977—. Bd. dirs. Marmet Hosp. Found. for Crippled Children, Inc., 1992—, pres., 2000—; bd. dirs. W.Va State Bar Found., Inc., 1992-2000, pres. 1999-2000; disciplinary bd. W. Va. State Bar, 1998—; United Way of Kanawha Valley, Inc., 1997-2002. Mem. ABA, W.Va. State Bar (exec. com. young law sect. 1981-84, bd. govs. 1987-90), Kanawha County Bar Assn., Order of Coif. Bankruptcy, Commercial, contracts (including sales of goods; commercial financing), Corporate, general. Office: 1600 Bank One Ctr Charleston WV 25301-2723 E-mail: m.chaney@kaycasto.com.

CHANEY, VINCENT VERLANDO, lawyer; b. Elkins, W.Va., June 12, 1913; s. Thomas H. and Anna Gertrude (Merge) C.; m. Caroline O'Neale, Feb. 5, 1939; children— Michael Thomas, Malcolm L. A.B., W.Va. U., 1936, J.D., 1938. Bar: W.Va. 1938, U.S. Dist. Ct. (so. dist.) W.Va. 1938, U.S. Dist. Ct. (no. dist.) W.Va. 1938, U.S. Ct. Apls. (4th cir.) 1939. Assoc., Kay, Casto & Amos, 1938-50, ptnr. Kay Casto & Chaney, Charleston, W.Va., 1950— ; sec., gen. counsel, dir. Ray Resources Corp., Charleston, 1969-75, Mountaineer Gas Co., Charleston, 1984— ; dir. Allegheny & Western Energy Corp., Charleston, 1981— ; mem. inspection teams USIA, Venezuela, 1971, Thailand, 1974, Poland, Czechoslovakia, 1976, U.S. Internat. Communication Agy., Hong Kong, 1978. Trustee Charleston Area Med. Ctr., 1972— , chmn. bd., 1975-78; bd. dirs. Sunrise Ctr. and Mus., 1972-74, Kanawha Valley Dental Health Found., 1965-70; vis. com. W.Va. U. Coll. Law, 1980-84. Served from 1st lt. to lt. col. AUS, 1941-46. Fellow Am. Bar Found.; mem. ABA, W.Va. Bar Assn., W.Va. State Bar (bd. govs. 1956-62, pres. 1962-63), Kanawha County Bar Assn., Am. Judicature Soc., Am. Law Inst., Am. Arbitration Assn. (panel 1972—), W.Va. U. Alumni Assn. (exec. council 1965-72, pres. 1971-72), Order of Coif, Phi Beta Kappa. Democrat. Club: Edgewood Country. Bd. editors W.Va. Law Rev., 1936-38. Corporate, general, Oil, gas, and mineral, Utilities, public. Home: Charleston, W.Va. Died 1997.

CHANG, DEANNA J. lawyer; b. Winston-Salem, N.C., Aug. 2, 1970; BA, Mt. Holyoke Coll., South Hadley, Mass., 1992; JD, Boston U., 1995. Bar: Md. 1996, DC 1998, U.S. Dist. Ct. DC 1998. Trial atty. U.S. Dept. Justice, Washington, 1995—99; assoc. Resolution Law Group, P.C., Washington, 2000—. Gen. counsel Jet Set Pets, LLC, Washington, 1999—. Mem.: ABA, DC Bar Assn. Environmental, General civil litigation. Office: Resolution Law Group PC 5335 Wisconsin Ave NW Ste 305 Washington DC 20015 Office Fax: 202-686-4843. Business E-Mail: deanna.chang@resolutionlawgroup.com.

CHANG, JANICE MAY, lawyer, naturopathic doctor, psychologist; b. Loma Linda, Calif., May 24, 1970; d. Belden Shiu-Wah (dec.) and Sylvia (Tan) C. BA, cert. paralegal studies, Calif. State U., San Bernardino, 1990, cert. creative writing, 1991; JD, LaSalle U., 1993; D in Naturopathy, Clayton Sch. Natural Healing, 1993; DFA in Creative Writing: Poetry, Am. Internat. U., 1999; MD in Alternative Medicines, Open Internat. U., 2001; DPsychology, Calif. Coast U., 2002; LLM in Taxation, Wash. Sch. of Law, 2003. Cert. bd. cert. alternative med. practitioner Am. Alternative Med. Assn.; Notary Pub. Calif. Victim/witness contact clk.-paralegal Dist. Atty.'s Office Victim/Witness Assistance Program, San Bernardino, Calif., 1990; gen. counsel JMC Enterprises, Inc., Riverside, Calif., 1993—; law prof. LaSalle U., Mandeville, La., 1994-97; corp. counsel, CFO, JDS Assocs., Inc., Loma Linda, 1998-99; corp. counsel, CFO DJS, L.P., Loma Linda, 1998-99; trust officer/trust svcs. Southeastern Calif. Conf. Seventh-Day Adventists, Riverside, 1998—; CFO/mgr. Stanberden Properties, 2001—. Spkr. graduation ceremony/conv. Internat. U., Las Vegas, 1998. Contbr. poetry to anthologies, including Am. Poetry Anthology, 1987-90, The Pacific Rev., 1991, The Piquant, 1991, River of Dreams, 1994, Reflections of Light, 1994, Musings, 1994 (Honorable Mention award 1994), Treasured Poems of America, 1994, Windows of the Soul, 1995, Best Poems of 1995 (Celebrating Excellence award 1995, Inspirations award 1995), Am. Poetry Annual, 1996, 99, Best New Poems of 1996, Interludes, 1996, Meditations, 1996, Perspectives, 1996 (Honorable Mention award 1996), Keepsakes, 1997 (Honorable Mention award 1997), Best Poems of 1997, Poetic Voices of America, 1997, The Isle of View, 1997, The Other Side of Midnight, 1997, Treasures, 1998, Best Poems of 1998, Writingscapes: Insights & Approaches to Creative Writing, 1998, Mirrors, 1999 (Pres.'s Lit. Excellence award), Pieces of the Heart, 2000, The Silence Within, 2001, Nature's Echoes, 2001, The Best Poems and Poets of 2001, The Best Poems and Poets of 2002; Theatre of the Mind, Noble House, 2003, contbr. to Internat. Libr. Photography: Tapestry of Dreams, 1999, Mystical Seasons, 1999,

Candid Captures, 2001, The Mirror's Reflection, 2003. Vol. Health Fair Expo La Sierra U., 1988, 1989, Path of the Just Tree Project, 1998; vol. first aid, CPR, other classes ARC, 1994—; sponsor Student Employement Recognition Banquet La Sierra U., Riverside, Calif., 1999, 2000, 2001, sponsor Student Employment Recognition Banquet, 2002—, 2003. Recipient Poet of Merit award, Am. Poetry Assn., San Francisco, 1989, Golden Poet award, World of Poetry, Washington, 1989, Publisher's Choice award, Watermark Press, 1990, Editor's Choice award, The Nat. Libr. Poetry, 1990—97, Pres.'s award for lit. excellence, Iliad Press, 1995—99, Editor's Choice award, Poetry.com, 2002. Fellow Am. Coll. Internat. Physicians; mem. ACA, APA, ATLA, Nat. Bar Assn., Nat. Notary Assn., Brit. Guild Drugless Practitioners (life). Republican. Seventh-Day Adventist. Avocations: poetry writing, photography, music, drama, literature, numismatics. Home: 1025 Crestbrook Dr Riverside CA 92506-5662 Office: Southeastern Calif Conf 7th-Day Adventists PO Box 8050 11330 Pierce St Riverside CA 92515-8050 E-mail: changjm@secc-sda.org.

CHANIN, LEAH FARB, law library administrator, lawyer, consultant, law educator; b. Glaveston, Tex., Nov. 29, 1929; d. A.C. and Celia (Rubenstein) Farb; m. Louis Chanin, Feb. 4, 1951 (dec. 1991); children: Scott, Leonard, Johanna, Rebecca. BA, So. Meth. U., 1950; LLB, Mercer U., 1954. Bar: Ga. 1954, U.S. Dist. Ct. (mid. dist.) Ga. 1954. Practice, Macon, Ga., 1959-63; mem. Kenmore & Culpepper, 1959-63; mem. faculty Walter F. George Sch. Law, Mercer U., 1964-92, ast. prof. law, 1969-72, assoc. prof., 1972-77, prof., 1977-92, dir. law libr., 1964-92, dean pro tem, 1986-87; disting. prof., dir. libr. U. D.C. Sch. Law, 1992-96; head pub. svcs. Howard U. Law Libr., Washington, 1997—2001. Mem. Fed. Merit Rev. Com., 1979-81; bd. visitors Mercer Law Sch., 1992-98. Author: Specialized Legal Research, 1987, Georgie Legal Research, 1990, Legal Research in D.C., Maryland and Virginia, 1995, 2d edit., 1999; contbr. articles to profl. jours. Mem. State Bar Ga. (adv. ethics opinions bd., pres. author's ct. 1985-86). Democrat. Jewish. Home: 3001 Veazey Ter NW Apt 1027 Washington DC 20008-5416 E-mail: leahfchanin@aol.com.

CHANIN, MICHAEL HENRY, lawyer; b. Atlanta, Nov. 11, 1943; s. Henry and Herma Irene (Blumenthal) C.; m. Margaret L. Jennings, June 15, 1968; children: Herma Louise, Richard Henry, Patrick Jennings. AB, U. N.C., 1965; JD, Emory U., 1968. Bar: Ga. 1968, D.C. 1981. Dir. So. Ctr. for Studies in Pub. Policy, Atlanta, 1968-69; asst. and acting legal officer 1st Coast Guard Dist., Boston, 1969-72; atty. Powell, Goldstein Frazer & Murphy, Atlanta, 1972-77; spl. asst. to sec. U.S. Dept. Commerce, Washington, 1977-78; dep. asst. to pres. The White House, Washington, 1978-81; ptnr. Powell, Goldstein, Frazer & Murphy, Washington, 1981—. Served to lt. USCGR, 1969-72. Mem. ABA, D.C. Bar Assn., State Bar Ga. Democrat. Corporate, general, Finance, Private international. Office: Powell Goldstein Frazer & Murphy 1001 Pennsylvania Ave NW Fl 6 Washington DC 20004-2505

CHANSAY WILMOTTE, PHILIPPE, lawyer; b. Liège, Belgium, Aug. 12, 1957; s. Robert Chansay Wilmotte and Frédérique De Bruyn; m. Soraya Benmestoura, May 14, 1994; children: Elisabeth, Benedicte. LLB, Cath. U. Louvain, 1984. Bar: Brussels. Pvt. practice, Brussels, 1985—. Author: (study) The Lockerbie Case, 1995, Guide about Congolese Dialogue, 2002. Former chmn. internat. com. Social Christian Party's Youth, 1989; former rep. in Vienna UN Econ. and Social Com. North South XXI, Geneva, 1995. Mem. Kiwanis Internat. (club officer 1989). Avocation: horseback riding. Home: 37 Chée de Liège B 4500 Huy Belgium Office: 1 rue de la Pepiniere B-1000 Brussels Belgium

CHAPLIN, ANSEL BURT, lawyer; b. Deerfield, Ill., June 12, 1931; s. Robert Tappan and Ruth (Burt) C.; m. Maud Denise Hazeltine, 1959 (div. 1993); children: Rawson, Margaret, Jane; m. Anne Carol Kenney, 1995. BA magna cum laude, Princeton U., 1953; postgrad., Inst. Polit. Sci., Paris, U. Algiers; JD, Harvard U., 1959. Boston Bar Found: Mass. 1959. Law clk. to chief justice Mass. Supreme Ct., 1959-60; ptnr. Chaplin & Chaplin, Boston; practice Boston, 1960-99, Cape Cod, Mass., 1981—. Owner Cape Cod Fishnet Industries, North Truro, Mass., 1980-96; chmn. com. legal edn. Mass. Supreme Ct., 1979-90, mem. com. lawyer advt., 1979-82; vice chmn. commn. on legal profession and the economy of New Eng., New Eng. Bd. Higher Edn., 1991; mem. U.S. Dist. Ct. Ad. Practice Com., 1981-85; chmn. vis. com. So. New England Sch. Law, 1992-93; bd. dir. Housing Land Trust for Cape Cod, 2002—. Author papers in field. Pres. Truro Neighborhood Assn., 1979-83; mem. corp. Perkins Sch. for Blind, Watertown, Mass., 1973—, Winsor Sch., Boston, 1980-83; sec., adminstrv. trustee Truro Conservation Trust, 1981—; trustee Payomet Performing Arts Charitable Trust, 1998-2000, Dexter Keezer Cmty. Fund, 1998—, Truro Parks Preservation Trust, 2003—; pres. Compact of Cape Cod Conservation Trusts, 1986-2001; pres. Friends of the Pamet, Inc., 1994-96; mem. bd. dirs. Mass. Appleseed Ctr. for Law and Justice, 1994-96; mem. Truro Planning Bd., 2001—. Recipient Thoreau award Cape Cod Mus. Natural History, 1987, Environmental Merit award EPA, 2000; Fulbright fellow, 1953-54 Fellow Am. Bar Found., Mass. Bar Found.; Mem. ABA, Am. Law Inst., Mass. Bar Assn. (chmn. law practice sect. 1978-80), Boston Bar Assn. (co-chair peer support com. 1997—), Harvard Law Sch. Assn. Mass. (pub. interest coord. 1994—), Harvard Law Sch. Assn. (mem. coun. 1997-2000), Wellesley Boat Club, Harvard Club (Boston). Democrat. Unitarian Universalist. General civil litigation, Environmental, General practice. Office: 165 Cranberry Hwy PO Box 340 Orleans MA 02653-0340 E-mail: abchaplin@cs.com.

CHAPMAN, CONRAD DANIEL, lawyer; b. Detroit, July 31, 1933; s. Conrad F. and Alexandrine C. (Baranski) C.; m. Carol Lynn DeBash, Sept. 1, 1956; children: Stephen Daniel, Richard Thomas, Suzanne Marie. BA, U. Detroit, 1954, JD summa cum laude, 1957; LLM in Taxation, Wayne State U., 1964. Bar: Mich. 1957, U.S. Dist. Ct. (so. dist.) Mich. 1957. Pres., chmn. bd. dirs. Powers, Chapman, DeAgostino, Meyers & Milia and predecessor firms, Troy, Mich., 1964—. Mem. ABA, Detroit Bar Assn., Oakland Bar Assn., Am. Arbitration Assn., Met. Detroit Estate Planning Coun., Nat. Assn. Estate Planning Coun., Detroit Athletic Club, Detroit Golf Club, Elks. Corporate, general, Estate planning, Corporate taxation. Office: Powers Chapman DeAgostino Meyers & Milia 3001 W Big Beaver Rd Ste 704 Troy MI 48084-3108

CHAPMAN, RALPH E. lawyer; b. Memphis, Dec. 30, 1950; s. Edwin Volney and Mary Ruth Chapman; m. Lisa Harlow, Sept. 10, 1977; children: William Brennan, Elizabeth Camille. BA, Miss. State U., 1972; JD, U. Miss., 1974. Bar: Miss. 1974, U.S. Dist. Ct. (no. and so. dists.) Miss. 1974, U.S. Dist. Ct. (no. dist.) N.Y. 1974, U.S. Dist. Ct. (we. dist.) Tenn. 1974, U.S. Dist. Ct. (ea. dist.) Ark. 1974, U.S. Ct. Appeals (5th and 6th cir.) 1977, U.S. Supreme Ct. 1977. Pres. U. Miss. Sch. Law, 1974; mem. Miss. Jud. Nominating Com., 1984. Capt. USAR. Mem. ATLA, ABA, Miss. State Bar (mem. by-laws study com. 1979-80), Coahoma County Bar Assn., Miss. Trial Lawyers Assn. (bd. govs.), Civil Justice Found., Nat. Assn. Criminal Def. Attys., Million Dollar Advs. Forum, Am. Bd. Trial Advs., Omicron Delta Kappa, Phi Delta Phi, Lamar Order, Scabbard and Blade. Episcopalian. Avocations: outdoor recreation, hunting, fishing. Personal injury (including property damage), Product liability. Office: Chapman Lewis & Swan PO Box 428 501 1st St Clarksdale MS 38614-4409 Fax: 662-627-4171.

CHAPMAN, ROBERT FOSTER, judge; b. Inman, S.C., Apr. 24, 1926; s. James Alfred and Martha (Marshall) Chapman; m. Mary Winston Gwathmey, Dec. 21, 1951 (dec. Sept. 1998); children: Edward, Foster, Winston; m. Mary Vail St. Georges, Sept. 30, 2000. BS, U. S.C., 1945, LLB, 1949, LLD (hon.) , 1986, Coll. Charleston, 1999. Bar: S.C. 1949. Assoc. firm Butler & Moore, Spartanburg, 1949—51; partner firm Butler, Chapman & Morgan, Spartanburg, 1953—71; U.S. dist. judge for S.C., 1971—81; U.S. cir. judge, 1981—. Chmn. S.C. Rep. Party, 1961—63. Lt. USNR, 1943—46, lt. USNR, 1951—53. Recipient Nat. Patriot's award, Congl. Medal of Honor Soc., 1985. Fellow: Am. Coll. Trial Lawyers. Presbyterian. Home: PO Box 1043 Camden SC 29020-1043

CHAPMAN, ROBERT T. lawyer; b. Sioux City, Iowa, Aug. 30, 1956; s. William J. and Edith K. Chapman; m. Vicki Lynn McLemore, Jan. 21, 1984; 1 child, Lauren Christina. BSBA, U. So. Calif., 1978; JD, So. Meth. U., 1981, LLM, 1986. CPA; bar: Tex. 1981. Nat. ptnr. in charge tax cosourcing Deloitte & Touche, Dallas. Mem. adv. bd. Tex. Stampede, Dallas, 2002; exec. bd. mem. March of Dimes, chmn., 2001—02. Mem.: U. So. Calif. Alumni CLub North Tex. (v.p. membership, pres. 2001—02). Republican. Episcopalian. Taxation, general. Office: Deloitte & Touche 2200 Ross Ave Ste 1600 Dallas TX 75201 E-mail: bchapman@deoitte.com.

CHAPMAN, WILLIAM LANSING, lawyer; b. Hackensack, N.J., May 4, 1942; s. William L. Jr. and Suzanne P. (Becton) C.; children: Jeffrey L., Michael B. BA in History, Williams Coll., 1964; JD, U. Colo., 1972. Bar: N.H. 1972, U.S. Dist. Ct. N.H. 1972, U.S. Ct. Appeals (1st cir.) 1972. Assoc. Orr and Reno, Concord, NH, 1972-77, shareholder, dir., 1977—. Pres., 2001-; chmn. bd. trustees N.H. Pub. Radio; chmn. Williams Coll. Planned Giving Exec. Com. Mem. ABA, N.H. Bar Assn. (Pres.'s award 1982, professionalism award 1999). General civil litigation, Communications, Libel. Office: Orr and Reno PO Box 3550 Concord NH 03302-3550

CHAPPANO, PERRY MICHAEL, lawyer, consultant; b. Mingo Junction, Ohio, Sept. 9, 1961; s. Ralph Anthony and Rose Marie (Fiora) C. BA, Ohio State U., 1983, JD, 1986; diploma advanced internat. legal studies, Faculty of Law, Salzburg, Austria, 1986; LLM, U. Pacific, 1987. Bar: Ohio 1986, Ind. 1987, U.S. Dist. Ct. (no. and so. dists.) Ind. 1987, U.S. Tax Ct. 1987, D.C. 1988, U.S. Dist. Ct. (so. dist.) Ohio 1989. Fgn. assoc. Rubino-Sammartano & Assocs., Milan, Italy, 1986; staff atty. United Student Aid Funds Inc., Indpls., 1987; corp. atty. USA Funds Inc./ELSC Inc., Indpls., 1987-88; assoc. Fontana & Shuman, P.C., Washington, 1988-89, Carlile Patchen & Murphy, Columbus, Ohio, 1989-92, Buckingham, Doolittle & Burroughs, L.P.A., Columbus, 1992-94; shareholder, pres. Overly Spiker Chappano & Wood, L.P.A., Dublin, Ohio, 1994-98; ptnr. Chappano Wood PLL, Columbus, 1999—. Cons. Chappano Legal Internat., Mingo Junction, Ohio, Indpls., Washington, 1986-88; pres. Polestar Inc., Columbus, 1989—; mem. ad hoc adv. com. Quest Health Enterprises, Inc.; mediator Franklin County Common Pleas and Mcpl. Cts., Columbus; adj. faculty Franklin U., Columbus. Active Big Bros./Big Sisters of Columbus. Mem. ABA (internat. sect. publs. com. adv. bd.), Ohio State Bar Assn., Ind. Bar Assn., Internat. Bar Assn., Columbus Bar Assn. (mediator pre-suit claims mediation program, chmn. internat. law com. 1992-94, chmn. lawyer referral svc. com. 1994-96, mem. editorial adv. bd. 1994—), Columbus Bar Found., Nat. Assn. Bond Lawyers, Ordine Degli Avocati E Procuratori, Nat. Lawyers Club, Am. Inns of Ct., Columbus C. of C. (internationalization com.), KC, Delta Theta Phi, Alpha Phi Delta. Democrat. Roman Catholic. Avocations: philately, aviation, sports, travel, languages. Corporate, general, Intellectual property, Private international. Home: 1625 Goodale Blvd Columbus OH 43212-3358 Office: Chappano Wood PLL 145 N High St # 12th-fl Columbus OH 43215-3006

CHAPPARS, TIMOTHY STEPHEN, lawyer; b. Cin., July 23, 1952; s. Gregory S. and Helen (Maragos) C.; m. Laurie A. Kress, Dec. 24, 1986 (div. Sept. 1987); m. Laurie A. Kress, Apr. 18, 1990; children: Alexander T., Jake A. BS, Duke U., 1974; JD, U. Cin., 1978. Assoc. Cox & Chappars, Xenia, Ohio, 1978-94, Bryant Law Office, Wilmington, Ohio, 1981—. Trial atty. Pub. Defender's Office, Clinton County, Wilmington, 1978-88; lectr. So. State Jr. Coll., Wilmington, 1982. Mem. Ohio Bar Assn., Am. Trial Lawyers Acad., Ohio Acad. Trial Lawyers. Methodist. Avocations: tennis, piano, hiking, cycling, skiing. Criminal, Personal injury (including property damage). Home: 2025 Winding Brook Way Xenia OH 45385-9382 Office: PO Box 280 Xenia OH 45385-0280

CHAPPELEAR, STEPHEN ERIC, lawyer; b. Columbus, Ohio, Dec. 25, 1952; s. Thornton White and Phyllis Evelyn (Williams) C.; m. Sharon Sue Starr, June 8, 1974; children: Katherine Sue, Christopher Charles. BA, Ohio State U., 1974, JD, 1977. Bar: Ohio 1977, U.S. Dist. Ct. (so. dist.) Ohio, U.S. Dist. Ct. (no. dist.) Ohio, U.S. Dist. Ct. (ea. dist.) Wis., U.S. Tax Ct., U.S. Ct. Appeals (6th cir.). Assoc. Emens, Hurd, Kegler & Ritter, Columbus, 1977-82, prin., 1983—2001, Kegler Brown Hill & Ritter, Columbus; ptnr. Hahn, Loeser & Parks, Columbus, 2001—. Mem. exec. coun. Nat. Conf. Bar Pres., 1997-2000; pres. Met. Bar Caucus, 2001-02. Author: The Complete Book of Jury Verdicts II, Franklin County, Ohio, 1985-91, The Complete Book of Franklin County Jury Verdicts, 1990, So What's Your Case Reaaly Worth?: A Decade of Jury Trial Verdicts, 1995; editor jour. Bar Briefs, 1986-88; contbr. articles to profl. jour. Fellow Ohio State Bar Found. (trustee), Columbus Bar Found.; mem. ABA (litig. sect., trial practice com., trial and ins. practice sects. com. on, trial techniques and comml. torts) Ohio State Bar Assn. (bd. gov., coun. dels., former chair fed. cts. and practice com., litigation sect., bd. gov., pres. 2002-03), Columbus Bar Assn. (bd. govs., pres. 1995-96), Am. Inns of Ct. (Franklin chpt. pres. 1994-95), Million Dollar Adv. Forum, Lawyers Club of Columbus, New Albany Country Club. Avocations: sports, movies, theater, writing. Appellate, General civil litigation, Personal injury (including property damage). Office: Hahn Loeser & Parks 21 E State St Ste 1050 Columbus OH 43215-4213 E-mail: sechappelear@hahnlaw.com.

CHAPPELL, DAVID FRANKLIN, lawyer; b. St. Louis, Apr. 18, 1943; married; children: Libbey Paige, Wade Garrett. BA in Polit. Sci., U. Tex., 1964, JD with honors, 1968. Bar: Tex., U.S. Ct. Appeals (5th, 9th, and 11th cirs.); cert. civil trial law, Tex. Bd. Legal Specialization, 1978. Ptnr. Chappell, Hill & Lowrance, LLP, Ft. Worth. Mem. task force on delay Supreme Ct. Tex., 1985, spl. master U.S. Dist. Ct. (no. dist.) Tex., Ft. Worth; mem. Ft. Worth City Coun., 1989-93; chair nat. adv. coun. U.S. SBA, 1998-2000. Editorial bd. The Texas Lawyer, 1985-86. V.p., gen. counsel Tarrant County Arts Coun., 1980-86; vice chmn. City of Ft. Worth Human Rels. Com.; chair Area Ambulance Authority, 1994-98; chair adv. bd. U. Tex. at Arlington-Ft. Worth, 2001. Fellow Tex. Bar Found. (chmn. bd. trustees 1987-88); mem. Am. Bar Found., Tex. Bar Assn. (bd. dirs. 1982-86, chmn. bd. 1984-85, chmn. health law sect. 1985-86, spl. com. to revise grievance process), ABA (editor Practice TIPS 1980, sec., exec. council of tort and ins. practice sect. 1983-87, chmn. young lawyers div. 1978), Am. Judicature Soc. (exec. com, bd. dirs. 1979), Tex. Young Lawyers Assn. (pres. 1976), Ft. Worth and Tarrant County Young Lawyers Assn. (pres. 1974, Outstanding Young Lawyer award 1979). Federal civil litigation, State civil litigation, Personal injury (including property damage). Office: Chappell Hill & Lowrance LLP 400 City Center Tower I 201 Main St Fort Worth TX 76102-4140 E-mail: chappell@cmlaw.com.

CHAPPELL, JOHN CHARLES, lawyer; b. Minden, Nebr., Jan. 28, 1935; s. Charles Arthur and Eletta Hope (Pattison) C.; m. Joyce Joan Dawson, Sept. 1, 1957; children: Laura, Pamela, James, Allegra. BS in Edn., U. Nebr., 1956; JD, NYU, 1960. Bar: N.Y. 1960. Summer assoc. firm Dewey Ballantine, N.Y.C., 1959, assoc., 1960-68; ptnr. Dewey Ballantine LLP, N.Y.C., 1968-00, of counsel, 2000—. Served to 1st lt. U.S. Army, 1957. Root-Tilden scholar NYU, 1956 Mem.: Assn. Bar City N.Y. Corporate, general, Mergers and acquisitions, Securities. Home: 2 Galloping Hill Cir Holmdel NJ 07733-1848 Office: Dewey Ballantine LLP 1301 Ave Of The Americas New York NY 10019-6022

CHAPPELL, MILTON LEROY, lawyer; b. Accra, Ghana, Mar. 25, 1951; (parents Am. citizens); s. Derwood Lee and Helen Jean (Freeman) C.; m. Margot Cecelia Shields, Dec. 18, 1972; children: Marton Gerald, Monet Louise. BA summa cum laude, Columbia Union Coll., 1973; JD, Cath. U., 1976; diploma, Nat. Inst. Trial Advocacy, Boulder, Colo., 1978; cert., U. Miami, 1982. Bar: Md. 1976, D.C. 1977, U.S. Ct. Appeals (4th, 5th, 9th and D.C. cirs.) 1977, U.S. Dist. Ct. D.C. 1978, U.S. Ct. Appeals (6th cir.) 1979, U.S. Supreme Ct. 1980, U.S. Ct. Appeals (11th cir.) 1981, U.S. Dist. Ct. Md. 1982, U.S. Ct. Appeals (7th cir.) 1988, U.S. Dist. Ct. (no. dist.) Calif., 1990, U.S. Ct. Appeals (3rd cir.) 2000. Sole practice, Silver Spring, Md., 1976—; staff atty. Nat. Right to Work Legal Def. Found., Springfield, Va., 1976—. Lectr. Columbia Union Coll., Takoma Park, Md., 1976-77; legal cons. JNA Elem. Sch., Takoma Park, 1980-83; gen. counsel Playgrounds Unltd., Inc., 1988-2000, Internat. Play Equipment Mfrs. Assn., Inc., 1995—, Park Dreams Internat., Ltd., 2000—; participant play settings subcom. recreation access adv. com. U.S. Archtl. and Transp. Barriers Compliance Bd., 1993-94. Contbr. to Ohio No. U. Law Rev., Govt. Union Rev., Calif. Pub. Employee Rels. Mem. Hillandale Civic Assn., Silver Spring, 1980—; legal cons., bd. dirs. Silver Spring Seventh-day Adventist Ch., 1976-84, Takoma Park.; participant U.S. Arch. and Trans. Barriers Compliance Bd., Recreation Access Adv. Com., Play Settings subcom., 1993-94. Mem. ABA, Md. Bar Assn. D.C. Bar Assn. Federal civil litigation, General practice, Labor (including EEOC, Fair Labor Standards Act, labor-management relations, NLRB, OSHA). Home: 10321 Royal Rd Silver Spring MD 20903-1616 Office: Nat Right to Work Legal Def Found 8001 Braddock Rd # 600 Springfield VA 22151-2110 E-mail: mlc@nrtw.org.

CHAR, VERNON FOOK LEONG, lawyer; b. Honolulu, Dec. 15, 1934; s. Charles A. and Annie (Ching) C.; m. Evelyn Lau, June 14, 1958; children: Richard, Daniel, Douglas, Charles, Elizabeth. BA, U. Hawaii, 1956; LLB, Harvard U., 1959. Bar: Hawaii 1959. Dep. atty. gen. Office of Atty. Gen., Honolulu, 1959-60, 62-65; ptnr. Damon Key Char & Bocken, Honolulu, 1965-89, Char, Sakamoto, Ishii, Lum & Ching, Honolulu, 1989—. Chmn. Hawaii Ethics Commn., Honolulu, 1968-75, Hawaii Bicentennial Com., 1986-91. Mem. ABA (bd. govs. 1991-94), Hawaii Bar Assn. (pres. 1985), U. Hawaii Alumni Assn. (pres. 1989-90). Antitrust, Aviation, Corporate, general. Home: 351 Anonia St Honolulu HI 96821-2052 Office: Char Sakamoto Ishii Lum & Ching Davies Pacific Ctr 841 Bishop St Ste 850 Honolulu HI 96813-3957 E-mail: vflchar@lawcsilc.com.

CHARFOOS, LAWRENCE SELIG, lawyer; b. Detroit, Dec. 7, 1935; s. Samuel and Charlotte (Salkin) C.; m. Jane Emerson. Student, U. Mich., 1953-56; LLB, Wayne State U., 1959. Bar: Mich. 1959, Ill. 1965. Pvt. practice, Detroit, 1960-63; pres., ptnr. Charfoos & Christensen PC, Detroit, 1967—; theatrical producer, legitimate theater mgr. Chgo., 1963-67. Cons. med.-legal problems Mich. Med. Soc., Mich. Hosp. Coun., State Bar Mich., ATLA; lead counsel N.W. Airlines, 1999. Author: The Medical Malpractice Case: A Complete Handbook, 1974, Daughters at Risk, 1981, Personal Injury Practice, Technique and Technology, 1986; contbr. articles to profl. jours. Trustee Lawrence S. Charfoos Found. Elected to Inner Circle of Advocates, 1973 Mem. ABA, Mich. Bar Assn., Detroit Bar Assn. (past dir.), Am. Bd. Profl. Liability Attys. (founder, past pres.), Internat. Acad. Trial Lawyers, Plaintiff's Steering Com./Breast Implant Cases. Office: 5510 Woodward Ave Detroit MI 48202-3804

CHARLA, LEONARD FRANCIS, lawyer; b. New Rochelle, NY, May 4, 1940; s. Leonard A. and Mary L. Charla; m. Kathleen Gerace, Feb. 3, 1968 (div. Dec. 1988); children: Larisa, Christopher; m. Elizabeth A. Du Mouchelle, Aug. 27, 1993. BA, Iona Coll., 1962; JD, Cath. U., 1965; LLM, George Washington U., 1971. Bar: D.C. 1967, N.J. 1970, Mich. 1971. Tech. writer IRS, Washington, 1966-67; atty. adv. ICC, 1967, atty., 1968-69; mgmt. intern HEW, 1967-68; atty. Bowes & Millner, Transp. Cons., Newark, 1969-71; atty. legal staff GM, Detroit, 1971-85, sr. counsel, 1985-87, asst. gen. counsel, 1987-89; sr. v.p. Clean Sites Inc., Alexandria, Va., 1989-90; shareholder Butzel Long, Detroit, 1990—. Mem. faculty Coll. Creative Studies, Detroit, 1978-89, adj. asst. prof., 1982-89; faculty art U. Mich., 1980, 84-89, adj. asst. prof. 1988-89. Author: Never Cooked Before/Gotta Cook Now!, 1999. Bd. dirs. Gt. Lakes Performing Artists Assocs., 1983-85; bd. dirs. Mich. Assn. Cmty. Arts Agys., 1983-89, 92-93, vice-chair, 1986-88, chair, 1988-89; bd. govs. Cath. U. Am. Alumni, 1982-2002, v.p., 1993-99; active Info. Network Superfund Settlements, 1988—; bd. regents Cath. U. Am., 1992-2002, Birmingham Bloomfield Art Assn., 1987-88, 94-95; bd. dirs. Friends Modern Art, Detroit Inst. Arts, 1996—, v.p., 1998—; bd. dirs. Art Ctr. Mt. Clemens, Mich., 1997—, chair facilities com., 2001-, v.p. 2001-. Fellow N.Y. State Regents, 1962; scholar Cath. U. Law Sch., 1962-65. Mem. ABA, Nat. Spkrs. Assn., Mich. State Bar Assn. (arts com. entertainment and sports sect. 1979-87, chmn., 1980-81, 92—). Environmental, Art. Office: Butzel Long 100 Bloomfield Pkwy Ste 200 Bloomfield Hills MI 48304 E-mail: charla@butzel.com.

CHARLES, ROBERT BRUCE, lawyer; b. Portsmouth, Va., Aug. 23, 1960; s. Roland Wilbur Charles Jr. and Doris Anne (Hassell) Babineau; m. Marina Timasheff, Oct. 16, 1988; children: Nicholas Westcote, Sophia Anne. AB, Dartmouth Coll., 1982; MA, Oxford U., 1984; JD, Columbia U., 1987. Bar: N.Y. 1989, Conn. 1989, Maine 1990. Law clk. to judge U.S. Ct. Appeals (9th cir.), Seattle, 1987-88; assoc. Kramer, Levin et al, N.Y.C., 1988-91, Weil, Gotshal & Manges, N.Y.C., 1991-92, Washington, 1993-95; dep. assoc. dir. office of policy devel The White House, Washington, 1992-93; chief staff, chief counsel nat. security, internat. affairs and criminal justice subcommittee U.S. Ho. of Reps., Washington, 1995-99; chief staffer Speaker's Task Force on Drug Free Am., 1997-99; prof. govt. and cyberlaw Harvard U. Extension Sch., 1998—2001; pres. The Charles Group, 1999—. Summer assoc. The White House, Washington, 1982-84, Supreme Ct. India, 1985. Contbr. articles to profl. jours., chpts. to books. Active Coun. on Fgn. Rels. Theodore Roosevelt Assn. Officer USNR, 1998—. Keasbey scholar, Phila. 1982, Tony Patino fellow Columbia U., 1984; recipient Petra T. Shattuck Disting. Tchg. award Harvard U., 2000. Republican. Avocations: distance running, hiking, writing. E-mail: RCharlesZZ@aol.com.

CHARLTON, PAUL, lawyer; BA in Spanish, U. Ariz.; grad. in Law, Ariz. State U., 1988. Law clk. to Atty. Gen. Bob Corbin; prosecutor Atty. Gen. Office; asst. U.S. atty. U.S. Atty.'s Office, 1991—2001; U.S. atty., 2001—. Recipient Nat. Pros. award, Fed. law Enforcement Officer's Assn., 1997. Office: Dist Ariz Ste 1200 2 Renaissance S, 40 N Central Ave Phoenix AZ 85004-4408*

CHARVAT, ANN MARIE, mediator; b. Peoria, Ill., Apr. 25, 1953; s. Harold Alois Charvat and Patricia Ann Hagel; m. John Charles Dedert, Mar. 10, 1990; children: Gabriel, Abigail, Colleen Dedert, Rebecca Dedert. BS, Western Ill. U., 1974; EdM, Oreg. State U., 1978; PhD, So. Ill. U., 1989. Cert. sociol. practitioner, family mediator. Grad. asst. sociology dept. So. Ill. U., Carbondale, 1984—88; instr. Western Ky. U., Bowling Green, Ky., 1988—89; regional family liaison Eckerd Family Youth Alternatives, Deerlodge, Tenn., 1989—92; adj. instr. Tenn. State U., Nashville, 1993—98; mitigation specialist Capital Case Resource Ctr., Nashville, 1994—95, Capital Case Cons., Nashville, 1989—; pres. In Svc., Inc., Nashville, 2000—. Mem. adv. coun. Tenn. Protection and Advocacy, Nashville, 2000—. Vol. Tying Nashville Together, 2000—; mediator juvenile ct. CASA, 1996—. Mem.: Sociol. Practice Assn. (cert. chmn., bd. dirs.). Democrat. Unitarian Universalist. Office: InSvc Inc 2112 Acklen Ave Nashville TN 37212 Fax: 615-383-7609. E-mail: ann@inserviceinc.net.

CHASANOW, DEBORAH K. federal judge; b. 1948; BA, Rutgers U., 1970; JD, Stanford U., 1973. Pvt. practice atty. COle & Groner, Washington, 1975; asst. atty. gen. State of Md., 1975-79; chief criminal appeals divsn. Md. Atty. Gen.'s Office, 1979-87; U.S. magistrate judge U.S. Dist. Ct. Md., 1987-93, dist. judge, 1993—. Instr. law schs. U. Balt., U. Md., 1978-84. Mem. Fed. Magistrate Judges Assn., Md. Bar Assn., Prince George's County Bar Assn., Women's Bar Assn., Marlborough Am. Inn. Ct. (pres. 1988-90), Phi Beta Kappa. Office: US Courthouse 6500 Cherrywood Ln Rm 465A Greenbelt MD 20770-1249*

CHASANOW, HOWARD STUART, retired judge, lecturer, mediator; b. Washington, Apr. 3, 1937; 1 child from previous marriage, Andrea; m. Deborah Hovis Koss, May 15, 11983. BA, U. Md., 1959, JD, 1961; LLM, Harvard U., 1962. Bar: Md. 1961, U.S. Supreme Ct. 1965. Asst. states atty. Prince George County, Upper Marlboro, Md., 1963-64, dep. states atty., 1964-67; judge Dist. Ct., Upper Marlboro, 1971-77, 7th Jud. Cir., 1977-90, Ct. Appeals of Md., 1990-99, ret., 1999. Lectr. Sch. Law U. Md., Balt., 1973—, Nat. Jud. Coll., Reno, 1980—, Am. Acad. Jud. Edn., 1984—; founder Prince George's County Drinking Driving Sch.; chmn. adv. bd. Sentencing Guidelines, Md., 1982-90, chmn. jud. adminstrn. sect., 1982-84; mem. Md. Commn. on Criminal Sentencing Policy, 1996—; mem. standing com. on rules of practice and procedure Ct. Appeals, 1985-90; mem. govs. task force to Revise Criminal Code, 1992—. Contbr. law rev. articles. Served with USAF, 1968-69. Office: Ct Appeals Md Prince George County Courthouse PO Box 399 Upper Marlboro MD 20773-0399

CHASE, CURT J. lawyer; b. Oskaloosa, Iowa, Sept. 10, 1968; s. Carlos J. Chase and Carolyn J. Tschetter; m. Lisa A. Tweedy, Aug. 12, 1995; 1 child, Greta A. BA, Yale U., 1991; MA, JD, U. Iowa, 1995. Bar: Mo. 1995, Kans. 1996, Iowa 2002. Assoc. Blackwell, Sanders, Peper, Martin, Kansas City, Mo., 1995—2001, ptnr., 2002—. Bd. dirs. Cabot Westside Clinic. Health. Home: 4650 Millbrook Shawnee KS 66218 Office: Blackwell Sanders Peper Martin 2300 Main Ste 1000 Kansas City MO 64108-2415

CHASE, ERIC LEWIS, lawyer; b. Princeton, N.J., Sept. 21, 1946; s. Harold William and Bernice Mae (Fadden) C.; m. Jamie Campbell, Dec. 29, 1979; children: Eric Campbell, Kathryn Dianne, John Harold. BA, Princeton U., 1968; JD cum laude, U. Minn., 1974. Bar: N.J. 1974, D.C. 1975, U.S. Ct. Appeals (3d cir.) 1979, U.S. Supreme Ct. 1981, U.S. Claims Ct. 1982, U.S. Tax Ct. 1982, N.Y. 1983, U.S. Ct. Appeals (2d cir.) 1988, U.S. Ct. Appeals (6th cir.) 2003. Trial atty. FCC, 1974-78; asst. U.S. atty. Dist. N.J., Newark, 1978-80; ptnr. Margolis Chase, Verona, N.J., 1980-90, Hannoch Weisman, Roseland, N.J., 1990-93, Bressler, Amery & Ross, Florham Park, N.J., 1993—. Prof. law of war Marine Corps Command and Staff Coll., Quantico, Va., 1990-99. Author: Automobile Dealers and the Law, 1994, 7th edit., 2000; contbr. articles on law and mil. to profl. publs., including N.Y. Times, Washington Post, Newsweek mag. With USMC, 1968-71; col. Res., ret. Mem. ABA (mem. task force on internat. criminal ct.), N.J. State Bar Assn. (franchise com 1997—, co-chair franchise com. 1999-2001). General civil litigation, Communications, Franchising. Office: Bressler Amery & Ross 325 Columbia Tpke Ste 8 Florham Park NJ 07932-1212 E-mail: echase@bressler.com.

CHASE, NORMA, lawyer; b. Evergreen Park, Ill., Dec. 30, 1952; d. Harry and Joan (Sirutis) C. AB, U. Pitts., 1972; JD, Duquesne U., 1978. Bar: Pa. 1978, U.S. Dist. Ct. (fed. dist.) 1978, U.S. Ct. Appeals (3rd cir.) 1983, U.S. Supreme Ct. 1984. Pvt. practice, Pitts., 1978—. Contbr. articles to Word Perfect for the Law Office, 1995. Mem. Pa. Bar Assn. (atty. discipline study com. 1991-97, client security fund study com. 1991-94, vice chair latter com. 1991-93, chmn. 1993-94, vice-chair plain English com. 1998—, mem. coun. of solo and small firm practice sect. 1998—; editor coun. newsletter 2000—). Democrat. Avocations: reading, writing, computing, hiking. Family and matrimonial. Office: 220 Grant St Pittsburgh PA 15219-2123 E-mail: normac@angstrom.net.

CHASE, OSCAR G(OTTFRIED), law educator, consultant, author; s. Sidney and Helen G. Chase; m. Jane Monell, June 12, 1969; children: Arlo M., Oliver G. BA (hon.), NYU, 1960; JD, Yale U., 1963. Bar: N.Y. 1963, U.S. Dist. Ct. (so. and ea. dists.) N.Y. 1968, U.S. Ct. Appeals (2nd cir.) 1970, U.S. Supreme Ct. 1972, U.S. Ct. Appeals (D.C. cir.) 1975. Staff mem voter edn. project SNCC, Jackson, Miss., 1963-64; counsel Lower West Side Cmty. Corp., N.Y.C., 1966-67; lawyer M.F.Y. Legal Svcs., Inc., 1967-68; asst. gen. counsel, dir. law reform, 1968-72; prof. law Bklyn. Law Sch., 1972-78; vis. prof. law NYU, 1978-79; prof. law, 1979—. Assoc. dean law sch., 1990-94, vice dean law sch., 1994-99. Author: CPLR Manmual, rev. edit., 1980, Civil Litigation in New York, 1983, end. edit., 1990, 4th edit., 2002, New York Practice Guide: Negligence, 4 vols., 1989; co-author: Cases and Materials on Civil Procedure, 1987; contbr. New York Practice, bi-monthly column for N.Y. Law Jour., 1982-84; contbr. articles to profl. jours. Bd. dirs. Untapped Resources, Inc., 1970—81; mem. adv. com. ACLU Reproductive Freedom Project, 1977—82; mem. civil litigation com. Ea. Dist. N.Y.; mem. joint AALS, ABA, Law Sch. Admission Coun. on Fin. Aid, 1991—94; bd. dirs. Inst. Judicial Adminstrn., 1992, co-exec. dir., 2000—. Office: NYU Sch Law 40 Washington Sq S New York NY 10012-1099

CHASEY, JACQUELINE, lawyer; Bar: N.J. 1983, N.Y. 1984. Formerly counsel Bertelsmann, Inc.; sr. counsel Bertelsmann, Inc., 1990-93, v.p. legal affairs, 1994—2002, sr. v.p. legal affairs, 2002—. Corporate, general. Office: Bertelsmann Inc 1540 Broadway New York NY 10036-4039

CHASNOFF, JULES, retired lawyer; b. St. Louis, July 15, 1927; s. Jacob and Julia Linenthal C.; m. Martha Slay, Aug. 21, 1949; children: David M., Paul E., Richard A. AB, Washington U., St. Louis, 1949; LLB, Harvard U., 1952. Bar: Mo. 1952, U.S. Dist. Ct. (ea. dist.) Mo. 1953, U.S. Ct. Claims 1960. Assoc. Tucker & Chasnoff, St. Louis, 1952-54, Grand, Peper, Martin & Roudebush and predecessors, St. Louis, 1954-59, Lowenhaupt & Chasnoff, St. Louis, 1959-63, ptnr., 1963-2001, ret., 2001. Mem. ABA, Mo. Bar Assn., Met. St. Louis Bar Assn., Am. Judicature Soc. Jewish. Corporate, general, Probate (including wills, trusts), Property, real (including real estate development, water). E-mail: julescha@swbell.net.

CHATIGNY, ROBERT NEIL, judge; b. 1951; AB, Brown U., 1973; JD, Georgetown U., 1978. Atty. Williams & Connolly, Washington, 1981-83; ptnr. Chatigny and Palmer, Hartford, Conn., 1984-86, Chatigny & Cowdery, Hartford, 1991-94; pvt. practice Hartford, 1986-90; dist. judge U.S. Dist. Ct., Hartford, Conn., 1994—. Office: 450 Main St Hartford CT 06103-3022

CHATOFF, MICHAEL ALAN, lawyer; b. N.Y.C., Aug. 18, 1946; s. Alexander Zelig and Leona Rhoda (Weiss) C. BA, CUNY, 1967; JD, Bklyn. Law Sch., 1971; LLM, NYU, 1978. Bar: N.Y. 1971, U.S. Dist. Ct. (so. and ea. dists.) N.Y. 1978, U.S. Ct. Appeals (2d cir.) 1980, U.S. Supreme Ct. 1980. Reader Chgo. Title Ins. Co., N.Y.C., 1972; chief U.S. Code Congl. and Adminstrv. News West Pub. Co., Westbury, N.Y., 1972-97. Cons. N.Y. Sch. for Deaf, N.Y.C. Mayor's Office for Disabled, Westchester County Legis.; lectr. N.Y. State Dept. of Edn. Vocat. Ednl. Svcs. for Individuals with Disabilities, N.Y. Sch. Deaf, Lexington Sch. for Deaf, Parents for Deaf Awareness, Am. Profl. Soc. for Deaf, N.Y. Ctr. for Law and the Deaf, Coun. on Jewish Deaf Edn. and Rehab., Nat. Coun. on Deaf People and Deafness, NYU. Assoc. law editor Ency. on Deaf People and Deafness; contbr. articles to Nat. Law Jour., N.Y. Law Jour., Able Adv., Communication Outlook, Deaf Spectrum. Bd. dirs. Westchester Cmty. Svcs. for Hearing Impaired; counsel Conn. African-Am. Deaf Advocate; mem. Supreme Ct. Hist. Soc.; del. nominee Dem. Nat. Conv., 1992. Mem. ABA, Queens County Bar Assn., Assn. of Bar of City of N.Y., Nat. Assn. Deaf, Am. Contract Bridge League, Nassau Bar Assn. Avocations: bridge, jogging, weight-lifting. Civil rights, Education and schools, Legislative. Home: 26909T Grand Central Pkwy Floral Park NY 11005-1010

CHATROO, ARTHUR JAY, lawyer; b. N.Y.C., July 1, 1946; s. George and Lillian (Leibowitz) C.; m. Christina Daly, Aug. 6, 1994; 1 child, Alexander. BChemE, CCNY, 1968; JD cum laude, New York Law Sch., 1979; MBA with distinction, NYU, 1982. Bar: N.Y. 1980, Ohio 1992, Calif. 1993, U.S. Patent Office 1998. Process engr. Std. Oil Co. of Ohio, various locations, 1968-73; process specialist BP Oil, Inc., Marcus Hook, Pa., 1974-75; sr. process engr. Sci. Design Co., Inc., N.Y.C., 1975-78; mgr. spl. projects The Halcon SD Group, N.Y.C., 1978-82; corp. counsel, tax and fin. The Lubrizol Corp., Wickliffe, Ohio, 1982-85, sr. counsel spl. investment projects, 1989-90; gen. counsel Lubrizol Enterprises, Inc., Wickliffe, 1985-89; chmn. Correlation Genetics Corp., San Jose, Calif., 1990-91; gen. counsel Agrigenetics Co., Eastlake, Ohio, 1990-92; gen. counsel, dir. comml. contracting Agrigenetics, L.P., San Diego, 1992-93; counsel Agrigenetics, Inc. dba Mycogen Seeds, Mycogen Corp., San Diego, 1994-97; dir. legal affairs Mycogen Corp., San Diego, 1997-98; exec. v.p. bus. devel., legal and regulatory affairs Global Agro, Inc., Encinitas, Calif., 1998-99; exec. v.p., gen. counsel Akkadix Corp., San Diego, 1999—2001; legal and bus. cons. San Diego, 2001—. Mem. Met. Parks Adv. com., Allen County, Ohio, 1973. Mem. ABA, AIChE, Am. Chem. Soc., N.Y. State Bar Assn., San Diego County Bar Assn., Am. Corp. Counsel Assn., Jaycees (pers. dir. Lima, Ohio chpt. 1972-73), Licensing Execs. Soc., Toastmasters, Omega Chi Epsilon, Beta Gamma Sigma. Clubs: Toastmasters. Avocations: sailing, photography, skiing. Corporate, general, Intellectual property, Private international. Home and Office: 3525 Del Mar Hts Rd # 285 San Diego CA 92130-2122 E-mail: achatroo@earthlink.net.

CHAUVIN, LEONARD STANLEY, JR., lawyer; b. Franklin, Ky., Feb. 13, 1935; s. Leonard Stanley Sr. C.; m. Cecilia McKay; children: Leonard Stanley III, Jacqueline, McKay. Grad., Castle Heights Mil. Acad., 1953; AB in Polit. Sci., U. Ky., 1957; JD, U. Louisville, 1961, LLD (hon.), 1990, Ohio No. U., 1990. Bar: Ky. 1961, U.S. Dist. Ct. (we. dist.) Ky. 1962, U.S. Ct. Appeals (6th cir.) 1964, U.S. Ct. Mil. Appeals 1966, U.S. Ct. Claims 1966, U.S. Supreme Ct. 1966, N.Y. 1983, Ind. 1983, Tenn. 1983, D.C. 1983, U.S. Dist. Ct. (so. and na. dists.) Ind. 1983, U.S. Dist. Ct. D.C. 1983, U.S. Ct. Appeals (7th, D.C. and Fed. cirs.) 1983, U.S. Tax Ct. 1983, U.S. Ct. Internat. Trade 1983, Wis. 1984, U.S. Dist. Ct. (so.and ea. dist.) 1984, U.S. Ct. Appeals (2d cir.) 1984, Fla. 1985, Nebr. 1985, Minn. 1985, Mass. 1986, W.Va. 1986. Assoc. Daniel B. Boone, Louisville, 1962-63, Laurence E. Higgins, Louisville, 1963-68; ptnr. Brown & Chauvin, Louisville, 1968-78, Carroll, Chauvin, Miller & Conliffe, Louisville, 1978-82; sole practice Louisville, 1982-83; ptnr. Barnett & Alagia, Louisville, 1983-92, Chauvin & White, Louisville, 1992-93, Chauvin & Chauvin, 1993—. Asst. Commonwealth atty. Jefferson County Commonwealth Attys. Office, Louisville, 1962-63; asst. gen. counsel dept. hwys. Commonwealth of Ky., Louisville; judge pro tem Louisville Police Ct.; master commr. Jefferson Cir. Ct., Louisville, 1992—; asst. county atty. of Jefferson County, 1978-87. Chmn. Registry of Election Fin.; mem. Ky. jud. retirement form system, Frankfort, Ky. Fellow Am. Bar Found. (chmn.); mem. ABA (chmn. ho. of dels. 1982-84, pres. 1989-90), Am. Coll. Tax Counsel, Ky. Bar Assn. (Lawyer of Yr. award), Nat. Jud. Coll., Am. Judicature Soc. (pres. 1986-88, Harley award), Am. Coll. Trust and Estate Counsel. Federal civil litigation, State civil litigation, Probate (including wills, trusts). Office: 235 S 5th St Ste 300 Louisville KY 40202 Home: 1028 Cherokee Rd Louisville KY 40204-1226

CHAVERS, DANE CARROLL, lawyer; b. Cleve., Mar. 20, 1956; s. Clarence Louis and Lee Myrtle (Simpson) C.; m. Christine Kumer, Sept. 21, 1991; stepchildren: Mary Elizabeth Curtin, Laura Louise Curtin. BA, Hiram Coll., 1978; JD, Ohio State U., 1981. Bar: U.S. Dist. Ct. (so. dist.) Ohio 1981. Staff atty. common pleas unit Franklin County Pub. Defender, Columbus, Ohio, 1980—. Lectr. Ohio Assn. Criminal Def. Attys., Columbus, 1997—. Bd. dirs. Friends of Homeless, Columbus, Summit United Meth. Ch., Columbus, West Ohio Conf. United Meth. Ch. Bd. Ministry. Democrat. Avocations: reading, tennis, church choir. Bus. Office: Franklin County Pub Defender 373 S High St Columbus OH 43215-4591 E-mail: dcchaver@co.franklin.oh.us., dchavers@allvantage.com.

CHAVEZ, CARMELA BERNADETTE, lawyer, consultant; b. Estancia, N.Mex., Feb. 2, 1950; d. Alfred Salomon and Frances Refugio (Lucero) C. B Univ. Studies, U. N.Mex., 1974; JD, Harvard U., 1979. Bar: N.Mex. 1982. Pvt. practice, Albuquerque, 1983-97. Instr. bus. law U. Albuquerque, 1983-84. Author: (newsletter) Paper View; contbr. articles to law jours. Mem. N.Mex. State Bar (hist. com., 1996). Democrat. Unitarian Universalist. Home: PO Box 3868 Albuquerque NM 87190-3868 E-mail: bcchavez@hotmail.com.

CHAVEZ, EDWARD L. judge; b. Santa Fe, Oct. 15, 1957; BA in Pers. Mgmt. with honors, Eastern N.Mex U., 1978; JD, N.Mex Sch Law, 1981. Bar: N.Mex 1981. Ptnr. Carpenter & Chavez, Ltd.; assoc. judge Ariz. Supreme Ct., Santa Fe, 2003—. Spl. counsel N.Mex Disciplinary Bd., 1987—95; lectr. Nat. Inst. Trial Advocacy, 1998—99; adj. prof. U. N.Mex; chmn. disciplinary bd. Supreme Ct. N.Mex. Mem. Ctr. Civic Values; trustee U. N.Mex Mental Health Ctr., 1989; mem. Task Force Regulation Lawyer Advt., 1990. Fellow: Internat. Acad. Trial Lawyers, Am. Coll. Trial Lawyers; mem.: ATLA (minority del.), Hispanic Nat. Bar Assn., N.Mex. Hispanic Bar Assn., Am. Inns Ct., Trial Lawyers Pub. Justice, State Bar N.Mex, N.Mex Trial Lawyers Assn. (feature editor newsletter 1987—90, bd. dirs. 1990—, pres. 1997—98), Nat. Spinal Cord Injury Assn. Office: NMex Supreme Ct Box 848 Santa Fe NM 87504*

CHAVEZ, JOHN ANTHONY, lawyer; b. Auburn, Calif., Oct. 5, 1955; s. Marco Antonio and Barbara Ann (Lawrence) Chavez-Rivas. BA, U. Calif., Santa Barbara, 1977; JD, Stanford U., 1981. Bar: Calif. 1981, Tex. 1982, U.S. Dist. Ct. (so. and no. dists.) Calif. 1982, (cen. dist.) Calif. 1983, U.S. Dist. Ct. (so. dist.) Tex. 1982, (we. dist.) Tex. 1983, (no. dist.) Tex. 1991, N.Y. 1986, U.S. Dist. Ct. (ea. and so. dists.) N.Y. 1986, U.S. Supreme Ct. 1986. With legal dept. Exxon Co. U.S.A., Houston, 1981-85, N.Y.C., 1985-86; assoc. gen. counsel Sybron Corp., Saddlebrook, N.J., 1986-88, Crown Equipment Corp., New Bremen, Ohio, 1989-90; trial atty. Exxon Co. U.S.A., Houston, 1990-92; counsel complex litigation Exxon Chem. Co., Houston, 1992-95; counsel internat. oil and gas exploration Exxon Exploration Co., Houston, 1995-96; counsel antitrust, mergers and acquisitions Exxon Chem. Co., Houston, 1996-2000; counsel intellectual property licensing ExxonMobil Chem. Co., Baytown, Tex., 2000—. Presenter numerous legal edn. seminars and programs. Contbr. articles to profl. jours. Mentor Ft. Bend Ind. Sch. Dist., 1998, Houston Bar Assn., 1998. Chancellor's scholar U. Calif., 1976; Univ. Svc. award for dist. svc. to campus cmty. U. Calif., Santa Barbara, 1977. Fellow Houston Bar Found.; mem. ABA (antitrust sect., vice chair corp. counseling com. 1998-2000, vice chair intellectual property com. 2000-03, vice chair Sherman Act sect. 2003—), Houston Bar Assn. (chair antitrust and trade regulation sect., 1997-98, vice-chair 1996-97, sec.-treas. 1995-96, coun. 1993-95), Wong Sun Soc. Republican. Avocations: hiking, theatre, travel. Antitrust, Federal civil litigation, Trade. Home: 4908 Cedar St Bellaire TX 77401 Office: Exxon Chem Co 5200 Bayway Dr Baytown TX 77520-2100 Fax: 281-834-2911. E-mail: J.Anthony.Chavez@exxonmobil.com.

CHAVEZ, MARTIN JOSEPH, lawyer, mayor; b. Albuquerque, Mar. 2, 1952; s. Lorenzo Armijo and Sara (Baca) C.; m. Margaret Aragon de Chavez, July 29, 1988; children: Martinique, Ezequiel Lorenzo. BS, U. N.Mex., 1975; JD, Georgetown U., 1978. Staff asst. U.S. Senate, Washington, 1976-77; dep. dir. LULAC Nat. Scholarship Fund, Washington, 1977-78; law clk. N.Mex. Atty. Gen., 1978-79; pvt. practice, 1979-86, 87-93, 98—; first and founding dir. N.Mex. Workers Compensation Adminstrn., 1986-87; mem. N.Mex. Senate, 1988-93; mayor City of Albuquerque, 1993-97, 2001—. Mem. Med. Rev. Commn., 1990—; bd. dirs. Senior Arts Project, 1987—, Tree New Mex., 1991-92. Mem. Citizens Rev. Bd., 1988—; bd. dirs. N.Mex. First, Sr. Arts; founding mem., bd. dirs. Tree N.Mex.; mem. Citizens Adv. Bd., N.Mex. Med. Rev. Commn.; Dem. candidate for Gov., 1998. Recipient Outstanding Young Men of Am. award, 1984, Appreciation award Friends of Albuquerque Petroglyphs, 1989, Cert. Appreciation, Am. Merchant Marines, 1989, Disting. Svc. award N.Mex. Dietetic Assn., 1989, Appreciation award West Mesa Little League, 1989, Excellence in Edn. award Friend of Edn., 1990, Appreciation award FHP N.Mex., Inc., 1990, Devoted and Invaluable Svc. award Indian Pueblo Cultural Ctr., 1990, Recognition award Ind. Ins. Agts. N.Mex., 1991, Accomplishment, Dedication and Performance award West Mesa High Sch., 1991, N.Mex. State Meml. award, 1991, Exemplary Dedication and Svc. award Sec. of State, 1991, Cert. Spl. Appreciation, MADD, 1991, Disting. Svc. award Hispanic Bar Assn., 1992, Legis. Recognition award Dem. Party N.Mex., 1992, Commitment to Edn. award Alamosa Elem. Sch., 1992, Recognition and Appreciation award N.Mex. First, 1992, Dedication award Albuquerque Hispano C. of C., 1993, Pride of N.Mex. award Hispanic Round Table, 1993; named Outstanding Youth Advocate, Youth Devel., Inc., 1993. Mem. N.Mex. State Bar Assn. (Pub. Svc. Recognition award 1989). Avocation: fly fishing. Office: Office of the Mayor PO Box 1293 Albuquerque NM 87103

CHAYKIN, ROBERT LEROY, manufacturing and marketing executive; b. Miami, Fla., May 2, 1944; s. Allan Leroy and Ruth (Levine) C.; m. Patty Jean Patton, Feb. 1971 (div. May 1975); m. Evalyn Marcy Slodzina, Sept. 3, 1989; children: Stephanie Lee, Michele Alee, Catrina Celia, Ally Sue. BA in Polit. Sci., U. Miami, Fla., 1965, LLB, 1969. Owner, operator Serrating Svcs. Miami, 1969-71, Serrating Svcs. Las Vegas, Nev., 1971-84; pres. Ser-Sharp Mfg., Inc., Las Vegas, 1984—; nat. mktg. dir. Coserco Corp., Las Vegas, 1987—. Patentee in mfg. field. With U.S. Army, 1962. Recipient 2d degree black belt Tae Kwon Do, Profl. Karate Assn., 1954-61. Avocations: travel, camping.

CHAZEN, HARTLEY JAMES, lawyer; b. N.Y.C., Feb. 14, 1932; s. Joseph and Helen (Jacobson) C.; m. Lois Audrey, Dec. 12, 1967; 1 child, Nicole Joanna. AB, CCNY, 1953; LLB, Harvard U., 1958; LLM, NYU, 1959. Bar: N.Y. 1959. Assoc. Hays, St. John, Abramson & Heilbron, N.Y.C., 1959-65, Shea & Gould, N.Y.C., 1965-68, Rosenman & Colin, N.Y.C., 1968-70; ptnr. Monasch Chazen & Stream, N.Y.C., 1970-82; pvt. practice N.Y.C., 1982-88; ptnr. Chazen & Fox, N.Y.C., 1988—; of counsel McLaughlin & Stern, N.Y.C., 1992-2000. Lectr. in field. Capt. USAR, 1958-68. Mem. Assn. Bar City N.Y., ABA (subcom. corp. taxation 1987—), Harvard Club. Corporate, general, Health, Securities. Home: 75 Perkins Rd Greenwich CT 06830-3510 Office: Chazen & Fox 767 Third Ave Fl 35 New York NY 10017 E-mail: hchazen@chazenfox.com.

CHECK, MELVIN ANTHONY, lawyer; b. Milw., Nov. 12, 1951; s. Mathew N. and Lorraine L. (Michels) C.; m. LuAnn E. Mueller, July 10, 1976. BBA, U. Wis., Milw., 1976; JD, Marquette U., 1979. Assoc. atty. Miller Law Office, Jefferson, Wis., 1979-81; atty. Check Law Office, Port Washington, Wis., 1981-82, 85—; corp. counsel Mutual Savs. and Loan Assn., Milw., 1982-85; owner Coldwell Banker N. Suburban Realty, Port Washington, Wis., 1994—. Instr. Wis. Realtors Assn., Madison, 1991—, Milw. Area Tech. Coll., 1985-91. Bd. dirs. Econ. Devel. for Grafton Enhancement, Inc., Grafton, 1990-93. With U.S. Army, 1971-73. Recipient Outstanding Svc. by an Individual Atty. Milw. Young Lawyers Assn. Vol. Lawyers Project, 1987. Mem. Ozaukee Realtors Assn. (Affiliate of Yr. 1990, Realtor of Yr. 1995), Wis. Realtors Assn. (Instr. of Yr. 1995, 2001), Nat. Assn. of Realtors, Ozaukee County Bar Assn., State Bar of Wis., Beta Gamma Sigma. Avocations: softball, bowling, woodworking. Probate (including wills, trusts), Property, real (including real estate development, water). Office: 429 W Grand Ave Port Washington WI 53074-2143 E-mail: melcheck@coldwellbanker.com.

CHECKMAN, NEIL BRUCE, lawyer; b. N.Y.C., Mar. 26, 1947; s. Joseph and Berenice Dorothy (Price) C.; children: Alexandra Josephine, Joseph Jacob. AB, Herbert Lehman Coll., 1968; JD, Bklyn. Law Sch., 1971. Bar: N.Y. 1971, U.S. Ct. Appeals (2d cir.) 1973, U.S. Dist. Ct. (so. and ea. dists.) N.Y. 1975, U.S. Dist. Ct. (no. dist.) N.Y. 2002. Assoc. atty. criminal def. divsn. Legal Aid Soc., N.Y.C., 1971-83; spl. asst. atty. gen. Office of Spl. Prosecutor for Medicaid Fraud Control, N.Y.C., 1983-90; pvt. practice N.Y.C., 1990—. Mem. Assn. of Bar of City of N.Y., N.Y. County Lawyers Assn., N.Y.C. Criminal Bar Assn. (bd. dirs.), N.Y. State Assn. Criminal Def. Lawyers, Nat. Assn. Criminal Def. Lawyers. Criminal. Office: 319 Broadway 5th Fl New York NY 10007-1187 E-mail: neilchec@optononline.net., neilchec@rcn.com.

CHEEK, JAMES HOWE, III, lawyer, educator; b. Nashville, Nov. 28, 1942; s. James H. and Anne H. C.; m. Sigourney Woods, June 1, 1968; children— James Howe, IV, Daniel W., Matthew H. AB, Duke U., 1964; JD, Vanderbilt U., 1967; LL.M., Harvard U., 1968. Bar: Tenn. 1967. Assoc. firm Shearman & Sterling, N.Y.C., 1967; asst. dean, asst. prof. law Vanderbilt U. Law Sch., 1968-70, adj. prof. law, 1970—; ptnr. Bass, Berry & Sims, PLC, Nashville, 1970—; chmn. legal adv. com. N.Y. Stock Exch., 1989-92. Vis. fellow Jesus Coll., Cambridge U., 1985—86; cons. Securities and Investments Bd. U.K., 1985—86; cons. comml. crime unit Commonwealth Secretariat, 1985—85; trustee Elliott E. Cheatham Fund; pres. dean's coun. Vanderbilt U. Law Sch., 1986—89, pres. law alumni bd., 1997—99; chair San Diego Securities Regulation Inst., 2000—; chmn. legal adv. bd. NASD Inc., 1996—98; lectr. CLE at seminars and insts. Contbr. articles to law jours. Trustee SEC Hist. Soc., 2000—02, Montgomery Bell Acad., Nashville, 2000—; chmn. Met. Nashville Airport Authority, 2000—. Recipient Disting. Alumnus award Vanderbilt Univ., 1994. Fellow Tenn. Bar Found. (trustee 1993-97); mem. ABA (chmn. subcom. on 1933 Act 1978-85, sec. com. on corp. law 1980-85, chmn. fed. regulation of securities com. 1987-91, chmn. sect. bus. law 1998-99, chmn. nat. task force on corp. responsibility 2002--), Nashville Bar Assn., Am. law Inst., Order of Coif, Belle Meade Country Club, Queen's Club. Corporate, general, Mergers and acquisitions, Securities. Home: 4404 Honeywood Ave Nashville TN 37205-3404 Office: Bass Berry & Sims PLC AmSouth Ctr Nashville TN 37238

CHEEK, MICHAEL CARROLL, lawyer; b. Fostoria, Ohio, Aug. 28, 1948; s. Carroll Wright and Mabel A. (Smith) C. BA, Hanover Coll., 1970; JD, U. Cin., 1974. Bar: Ohio 1974, Fla. 1974, U.S. Dist. Ct. (mid. dist.) Fla. 1975. Pub. defender, Clearwater, Fla., 1974-77; lawyer sole practice, 1977—. Vice chmn. bar grievance Clearwater, 1990-94; trustee Pinellas County Law Libr., Clearwater, 1977-92; chmn. Ct. Law Libr., 1982-89. Pres. 1st Step Corp., Clearwater, 1986-93; vice chmn. Long Ctr. Found., Clearwater, 1994-95; founder Head Start Learn-to-Swim Program, 1994. With Ohio NG, 1970—74, with Fla. NG, 1974—76. Mem. Nat. Assn. Criminal Def. Lawyers, Pinellas Criminal Def. Assn. (v.p. 1987). Criminal.

CHEMERS, ROBERT MARC, lawyer; b. Chgo., July 24, 1951; s. Donald and Florence (Weinberg) C.; m. Lenore Ziemann, Aug. 16, 1975; children: Brandon J., Derek M. BA, U. So. Calif., 1973; JD, Ind. U.-Indpls., 1976. Bar: Ind. 1976, Ill. 1976, U.S. Dist. Ct. (so. dist.) Ind. 1976, U.S. Dist. Ct. (no. and so. dists.) Ill. 1977, U.S. Ct. Appeals 7th cir.) 1977, U.S. Ct. Appeals (5th cir.) 1985. Assoc. Pretzel & Stouffer, Chgo., 1976-79, officer, 1979-81, dir., 1981—. Author: IICLE - Civil Practice, 1978, rev. edit. 1982, 87; IICLE Settlements, 1984. Mem. ABA, Ill. State Bar Assn., Chgo. Bar Assn., Def. Rsch. Inst., Ill. Def. Counsel, Appellate Lawyers Assn. Federal civil litigation, State civil litigation, Insurance. Office: Pretzel & Stouffer One S Wacker Dr Chicago IL 60606

CHEN, EDWARD M. judge; b. 1953; AB, JD, U. Calif., Berkeley. Law clk. to Hon. Charles Renfrew U.S. Dist. Ct.; law clk. to Hon. James Browning U.S. Ct. Appeals (9th cir.); with Coblentz, Patch, Duffy & Bass; atty. ACLU, San Francisco, 1985—2001; judge U.S. Dist. Ct., San Francisco, 2001—. Office: US Dist Ct San Francisco divsn 450 Golden Gate Ave 16th Rm 1111 Panorama City CA 91402*

CHEN, WESLEY, lawyer; b. N.Y.C., Nov. 29, 1954; s. Tom Y.M. and Mary (Don) C.; m. Vivien Wong, Dec. 10, 1983; 2 children: Marissa, Jocelyn. BA, N.Y. U., 1976, JD, 1980. Bar: N.Y. 1981, U.S. Dist. Ct. (so. and ea. dists.) N.Y. 1981. Lawyer Meissner, Tisch & Kleinberg, N.Y.C.,

1980-81; pvt. practice N.Y.C., 1982—85, 2003—, 1989—90; of counsel Serchuk, Wolfe & Zelermyer, White Plains, N.Y., 1985-88; ptnr. Cantwell & Chen, N.Y.C., 1988, Kimmelman, Sexter, Warmflash & Leitner, N.Y.C., 1990-91, Krasner & Chen, N.Y.C., 1992-94, Serchuk & Zelermyer, N.Y.C., 1995—2003. Bd. dirs. United Orient Bank, N.Y.C., 1982-92, MFY Legal Svcs., Inc., 1993-96; mem. N.Y. State Banking Bd., 1992—. Pres. bd. trustees Union Ch. of Pocantico Hills, 2000—. Mem. ABA, N.Y. State Bar Assn. (mem. banking law com.), N.Y.County Lawyers Assn. (mem. banking law com.), Asian-Am. Bar Assn. of N.Y., Chinese C. of C. (legal adviser 1982—). Banking, Commercial, contracts (including sales of goods; commercial financing), Property, real (including real estate development, water). Office: 641 Lexington Ave Fl 20 New York NY 10022-4503

CHENAULT, JAMES STOUFFER, judge; b. Richmond, Ky., May 1, 1923; s. Joe Prewitt and Russell (Stouffer) C.; m. Dorothy Neff, Apr. 21, 1960; children: Jean Russell. AB, Ea. Ky. U., 1949, LLD (hon.), 1975; LLB, U. Ky., 1949. Bar: Ky. 1949, U.S. Ct. Mil. Appeals 1956, U.S. Supreme Ct. 1960. Prosecuting atty. City of Richmond, Ky., 1950-57; commonwealth's atty. 25th Jud. Ct. of Ky., Clark, Jessamine and Madison Counties, 1964-66, cir. judge, 1966-80, chief cir. judge Clark and Madison Counties, 1980-93; chief regional judge Bluegrass Region of Ky., 1978-93; spl. judge Ky. Ct. of Appeals, 1973, Ky. Supreme Ct., 1984. Ky. rep. Nat. Ctr. State Cts., 1972-78; mem. Ky. Commn. on Corrections and Community Svc., 1973-77, Ky. Crime Commn. Cts. Sect., 1972-80, chmn., 1976-80, Task Force on Office for Pub. Advocacy, 1981-82, Gov.'s Jud. Adv. Coun., 1972-75, Ky. Jud. Coun., 1977-81, State and Fed. Jud. Coun., 1979-84; vol. faculty intensive trial seminar U. Ky., 1983, 85, 87, 90; lectr. So. Police Inst., 1970-80, Nat. Conf. Appellate Ctr. Clks., 1985, Nat. Conf. U.S. Dist. Ct. Clks., 1988, Nat. Conf. on Tech. and the Cts., Chgo., 1984, Denver, 1988, 3rd Fed. Jud. Cone, 1987, Ala. Appellate Judges Conf., 1990; adj. faculty Sch. Law Enforcement Ea. Ky. U., 1967-73; lectr. numerous state jud. confs.; presenter 1st Nat. Jud. State of the Art Conf., Phoenix, 1987. Councilman City of Richmond, 1949-50. Lt. (j.g.) USN, 1943-46, PTO. Recipient Outstanding Contbn. award Ky. Coun. Crime and Delinquency, 1974, Outstanding Contbn. award City of Richmond, 1977, Disting. Svc. award Dept. Mass Comm. Ea. Ky. U., 1993, Outstanding Trial Judge award Ky. Acad. Trial Attys., 1993, Ky. Chief Justice Spl. award, 1994; named Outstanding Alumnus Ea. Ky. U., Richmond, 1982; inducted into U. Ky. Law Sch. Hall of Fame, 2000. Mem. ABA (lectr., presenter ann. meeting San Francisco chpt. 1987), Am. Judicature Soc., Internat. Acad. Trial Judges, Ky. Bar Assn. (pres. younger lawyers conf. 1956-57), Ky. Assn. Cir. Judges (pres. 1970-75, editor newsletter 1976-93, Outstanding Contbn. award 1978), Ky. Commonwealth's Attys. Assn. (pres. 1965-66), Richmond C. of C. (Outstanding Svc. award 1983, Outstanding Achievement award 1989), Exch. Club (pres. Richmond chpt. 1955), Elks. Avocations: Ky. history, home gardening. Home and Office: 302 High St Richmond KY 40475-1344

CHENEY, KIMBERLY BUNCE, lawyer; b. Manchester, Conn., Nov. 25, 1935; s. Kimberly and Margreta (Swenson) C.; m. Dorthy Tod, Feb. 7, 1977; children: Alison, Margreta, Benjamin. BA, Yale U., 1957, LLB, 1964. Bar: Conn. 1964, U.S. Ct. Appeals (2d cir.) 1965, Vt. 1968. Assoc. Gumbart, Corbin, New Haven, 1964-67; asst. atty. gen. State of Vt., Montpelier, 1967-68, atty. gen., 1972-75; state's atty. Washington County, Montpelier, 1968-72; ptnr. Cheney, Brock and Saudek, Montpelier, 1975—. Chmn. Vt. Labor Relations Bd., Montpelier, 1978—; mem. Vt. adv. com. US Civil Rights Commn., 1982—. Bd. dirs. ARC, Montpelier, 1976, Vt. State Employees Credit Union; mem. Montpelier Sch. Bd., 1978-81. Served to lt. USNR, 1959-61. Mem. Assn. Trial Lawyers Am., Vt. Bar Assn. (del. family proceedings com., Montpelier, 1985), Am. Arbitration Assn. (arbitrator). Democrat. Administrative and regulatory, State civil litigation, Family and matrimonial. Office: Cheney Brock & Saudek PO Box 489 Montpelier VT 05601-0489

CHENG, ANDREW YUAN-SUNG, lawyer; b. Ann Arbor, Mich., Mar. 20, 1967; s. Chu-yuan and Alice (Hua) C.; m. Yvonne Chan, Jan. 5, 1967; children: Samuel, Joshua, Anne. BA, Columbia U., 1989; JD, Yale U., 1992. Bar: Calif. 1993, U.S. Dist. Ct. (no. dist.) Calif. 1993, U.S. Ct. Appeals (9th cir.) 1993, U.S. Dist. Ct. (ea. dist.) Calif. 1995. Assoc. atty. Pillsbury Madison Sutro, San Francisco, 1992-93; jud. law clk. Hon. Sarah Evans Barker, Indpls., 1993-95; assoc. atty. Steinhart & Falconer, San Francisco, 1995-97; dep. city atty. San Francisco City Atty.'s Office, 1997—2003; asst. U.S. Atty., U.S. Atty.'s Office, San Francisco, 2003—. Lectr. Boalt Hall Law Sch., U. Calif., 1996-97. Contbr. articles to profl. jours. Commr. Civil Svc., Piedmont, Calif., 2002—; elder Old First Presbyn. Ch., San Francisco, 1997—99, chair pastoral nominating com., 2000—01. Mem. Asian Am. Bar Assn., Bar Assn. of San Francisco (commr.), Piedmont Civil Svc. Commn. Avocations: piano, literature, Scrabble, tennis, theology. Home: 1045 Harvard Rd Piedmont CA 94610-1128 Office: US Attys Office 450 Golden Gate Ave 10th Fl San Francisco CA 94102-5342 E-mail: andrew.cheng@usdoj.gov.

CHERCHIGLIA, DEAN KENNETH, lawyer; b. Cold Springs, N.Y., Apr. 11, 1956; s. Patrick Joseph and Bella (Feld) C.; m. Susan Elaine Sonkin, July 5, 1980; children: Brian Alden, Evan James. BBA cum laude, Ohio U., 1977; JD, Case Western Res. U., 1984. Bar: Ohio 1984. Contract specialist NASA Lewis Rsch. Ctr., Cleve., 1980; atty. Hermann, Cahn & Schneider, Cleve., 1984-85; assoc. Schwarzwald, Robiner, Wolf & Rock, Cleve., 1985; asst. counsel HealthAm. Corp., Cleve., 1986-87; atty. TransOhio Savs. Bank, Cleve., 1987-91; asst. v.p., counsel Chase Fin. Corp., Cleve., 1991-97; of counsel Benesch, Friedlander, Coplan & Aronoff, Cleve., 1997-99; counsel CompliSource, LLC, 1999-2000; assoc. counsel, asst. sec. Ohio Savs. Bank, 2000—. Mem. Case Western Res. U. Law. Rev., 1982-84. Mem. Ohio State Bar Assn., Cleve. Bar Assn., Amnesty Internat. Avocations: photography, scuba diving, weightlifting. Commercial, consumer (including collections, credit), Commercial, contracts (including sales of goods; commercial financing), Corporate, general. Home: 3620 Stoer Rd Shaker Heights OH 44122-5116 E-mail: dcherchiglia@ohiosavings.com.

CHEREWKA, MICHAEL, lawyer; b. Taylor, Pa., July 3, 1955; s. Michael Jr. and Anne (Regan) C.; m. Michele Mary Robinson, Aug. 2, 1980; children: Michael Colin, Matthew Bryan, Meaghan Kelly. Student, U. Bristol, Eng., 1976-77; BSBA cum laude, Bucknell U., 1978; JD cum laude, Dickinson Sch. Law, 1981. Bar: Pa. 1981, U.S. Dist. Ct. (mid. dist.) Pa. 1983, U.S. Tax Ct. 1983, U.S. Ct. Appeals (3d cir.) 1983, U.S. Supreme Ct. 1985. Sr. mem. tax staff Ernst & Whinney, Harrisburg, Pa., 1981-83; assoc. Ball, Skelly, Murren & Connell (formerly Ball & Skelly), Harrisburg, 1983-89; pvt. practice Harrisburg, 1989—96, Wormleysburg, Pa., 2002—; mng. ptnr. Cherewka & Radcliff, LLP, 1996—2002; pvt. practice, 2002—. Mem. Keystone Family Bus. Ctr., LLC, 2000—. Co-author: Pennsylvania Tax Service, 1987; contbg. editor (legal column) Cen. Penn Bus. Jour., 1985-88, Strictly Business, 2002; adviser Dauphin County Law Explorers Post, 1982-88. Mem. Country Club Park Civic Assn., 1983-98, pres., 1987-88; mem. Hist. Harrisburg Assn., 1982-84; active Tri-County United Way, 1985-90, cons. planning giving, mem. adv. com., 1988-90; bd. dirs. Capital divsn. Am. Heart Assn., chmn. 1989-91, bd. dirs. Pa. affiliate, 1989-98 , exec. com., 1989-90, 93, treas., 1994-95, incoming chmn. bd., 1995-96, chmn. 1996-97; chrm., bd. dirs. Concertante Chamber Ensemble, 1996-97; bd. dirs. Pa. Assn. Nonprofit Orgns., 1996-; mem. planned giving com. Keystone Svc. Sys. Found., 1995-2000; mem. adv. bd. Found. Caths. United in Svc., Cath. Diocese of Harrisburg, 1991-97. Named Outstanding Young Man Am., U.S. Jaycees, 1983. Mem. Nat. Network Estate Planning Attys., Pa. Bar Assn. (tax sect. 1981—, real estate, probate and trust law sect. 1981—, com. state taxation 1984-99, chmn. subcom. on compromise tax 1986-97), Dauphin County Bar Assn. (interprofl. rels. com. 1984-89, estate planning sect. 1992—), Estate Planning Coun. Cen. Pa. (chmn. CPA subcom. 1982-83, bd. dirs. 1988-96, treas. 1989-90, v.p. 1990-91, pres. 1991-92), Polit. Info. Com. CPAs Pa. (treas. 1982-83), Greater Harrisburg C. of C. (bus. liaison com. 1984-87, econ. devel. com. 1988-89, 92-93, reaccreditation task force 1996), Nat. Assn. Estate Planners (charter 1988—), Pa. Chamber Bus. and Industry (bus. subcom. 1989), Greater West Shore Area C. of C. (comml.-indsl. devel. com. 1987-89), Alzheimer's Assn. of So. Ctrl. Pa. (bd. dirs. 1998-2001), Pa. Assn. Nonprofit Orgns. (bd. dirs. 2000—), Delta Mu Delta, Omicron Delta Kappa. Republican. Roman Catholic. Avocations: coin collecting, golf, basketball. Corporate, general, Estate planning, Taxation, general. Home: 125 Pelham Rd Camp Hill PA 17011-1353 Office: 624 N Front St Wormleysburg PA 17043-1022

CHERKEN, HARRY SARKIS, JR., lawyer; b. Phila., Dec. 8, 1949; s. Harry Sarkis and Lorna G. (Demurjian) Cherken. BA, Lafayette Coll., 1971; JD, Villanova U., 1976. Bar: Pa. 1976, U.S. Dist. Ct. (ea. dist.) Pa. 1976, U.S. Supreme Ct. 1983. Assoc. counsel Albert M. Greenfield & Co., Inc., Phila., 1976-79; assoc. Drinker, Biddle & Reath, Phila., 1979-84, ptnr., 1984—, co-chmn. real estate group, 1991—, mng. ptnr., 1996-2000. Mem. Phila. adv. bd. Chgo. Tile Ins. Co., 1986—; assoc. mem. Wharton Real Estate Rsch. Ctr., U. Pa., 1996—; mem. adv. bd. Advanced Comml. Leasing Inst., Georgetown U. Law Ctr.; bd. dirs. Urban Outfitters, inc., Mikronite Techs. Group, Inc., Law Dept. Am. U. Armenia. Trustee Kulicke Fund, Phila., 1985—, Balch Inst., 1992—2000, Woodmere Art Mus., 2002—; fellow trustee Armenian Assembly Am., 1986—, bd. dirs., 1988—2000, vice-chmn. bd. dirs., 1988—91, 1994—95; bd. dirs. Howard Karagheusian Commemorative Corp., 2003—; sec., bd. dirs. Reading Terminal Market Preservation Fund, 1991—. Mem.: ABA, Am. Coll. Real Estate Lawyers, Pa. Land Title Assn. (affiliate), Phila. Bar Assn., Pa. Bar Assn., Internat. Coun. Shopping Ctrs. (assoc.). Armenian Apostolic. Property, real (including real estate development, water). Home: 630 St Andrews Rd Philadelphia PA 19118 Office: Drinker Biddle & Reath LLP One Logan Sq 18th & Cherry Sts Philadelphia PA 19103-6996

CHERNETT, ROBERT IRWIN, lawyer, banker; b. Cleve., Aug. 13, 1946; s. Joseph and Bessie C.; m. Barbara Jean Kesler, Sept. 5, 1970 (dec. Mar. 1980); Jorey, Lee, Brian; m. Sande Gerth Jablow, Oct. 6, 2001. B.S., Ohio State U., 1968; J.D., Cleve. State U., 1972. Bar: Ohio 1972, U.S. Dist. Ct. (no. dist.) Ohio 1973. Ptnr. Gottsegen Tucker Chernett, Cleve., 1972-79; assoc. Burke Haber Berick, Cleve., 1979-83; ptnr. Honohan Harwood Chernett & Wasserman, Cleve., 1983-92, Kohrman, Jackson & Krantz, LLP, 1993-; mem. Cuyahoga Co. Bar Assn. (ethics com.), Beachwood Bd. of Recreation (pres.); Served to capt. U.S. Army, 1969-70. Jewish. Corporate, general, Family and matrimonial, Property, real (including real estate development, water). E-mail: ric@aol.com.

CHERNEY, JAMES ALAN, lawyer; b. Boston, Mar. 19, 1948; s. Alvin George and Janice (Elaine) Cherney; m. Linda Bienenfeld. BA, Tufts U., 1969; JD, Columbia U., 1973. Bar: Ill. 1973, U.S. Supreme Ct. 1977, U.S. Ct. Appeals (7th cir.) 1979, U.S. Ct. Appeals (3d cir.) 1982, U.S. Ct. Appeals (10th cir.) 1984, U.S. Ct. Appeals (8th and 9th cirs.) 1987. Assoc. Kirkland & Ellis, Chgo., 1973-76, Hedlund, Hunter & Lynch, Chgo., 1976-79, ptnr., 1979-82, Latham & Watkins, Chgo., 1982—. Mem. ABA, Chgo. Bar Assn. Federal civil litigation, State civil litigation, Health. Office: Latham & Watkins Sears Tower Ste 5800 Chicago IL 60606-6306

CHERNOW, JEFFREY SCOTT, lawyer, educator, author; b. Phila., Mar. 8, 1951; s. William and Sylvia Ann (Rosenberg) C.; m. Debra Sharon Shapiro, Dec. 29, 1974; children: William Ross, Stephanie Lynne. BS, Pa. State U., 1972; JD, U. Balt., 1976. Bar: Md. 1976, U.S. Dist. Ct. Md. 1977, U.S. Supreme Ct. 1980, U.S. Ct. Claims 1991. Assoc. Goodman, Meagher & Enoch, Balt., 1977-79; asst. atty. gen. State of Md., Balt., 1980-85; assoc. Cardin & Cardin, P.A., Balt., 1985-86; pvt. practice law Balt., 1986-89; ptnr. Kandel, Klitenic, Kotz, Betten & Chernow LLP, Owings Mills, Md., 1990—2002; pvt. practice law, 2002—. Asst. prof. Towson (Md.) State U., 1978-83, assoc. prof., 1983-86; panel chmn. Md. Health Claims Arbitration Office, 1983-84; lectr. Md. Inst. for Continuing Profl. Edn. of Lawyers, Inc., 1986; dir. Altex Industries, Inc., 1989. Contbr. chpt. to book. Sec., trustee Basic Cancer Rsch. Found., Inc., 1986—; chmn. bldg. com. Congregation Adat Chaim, 1985-86, trustee, 1986-90. Mem. ABA, Md. Bar Assn., Bar Assn. Balt. City, N.Am. Securities Adminstrs. Assn. (mem. various coms. 1980-85, chmn. franchise and bus. opportunities com. 1984-85), Md. State Bar Assn. (sec. bus. law, franchise law com. 1991). Corporate, general, Franchising, Securities. Home: 214 Berry Vine Dr Owings Mills MD 21117-4500 Office: Jeffrey S Chernow PA 1838 Greene Tree Rd Ste 360 Baltimore MD 21208-7102

CHEROUTES, MICHAEL LOUIS, lawyer; b. Chgo., Apr. 27, 1940; s. Louis Samuel Cheroutes and Maria Jane (Zimmerman) Dodd; m. Trisha Flynn, Oct. 30, 1965; children: Michael Louis Jr., Trisha Francesca, Matthew Dodd. BA, Harvard U., 1962; LLB, Stanford U., 1965. Bar: Colo. 1965. Assoc., then ptnr. Sherman & Howard, Denver, 1965-85; chief of staff to Rep. Patricia A. Shroeder U.S. Ho. of Reps., Washington, 1972-74; ptnr. Davis, Graham & Stubbs, Denver, 1985-93, Hogan & Hartson LLP, various, Colo., 1993—. Contbr. articles to profl. jours. Mem. Colo. Commn. on Higher Edn., 1988-91, chmn., 1989-91; mem. state bd. Gt. Outdoors Colo. Trust Fund, 1996-97. Mem. ABA, Colo. Bar Assn., Nat. Assn. Bond Lawyers. Avocation: sailing. Home: 2625 E Cedar Ave Denver CO 80209-3205 Office: Hogan & Hartson 1200 17th St Ste 1500 Denver CO 80202-5840

CHEROVSKY, ERWIN LOUIS, lawyer, writer; b. Dover, N.J., Dec. 31, 1933; s. Sam and Ida (Bluestein) C.; m. Edith Mayer, June 26, 1966; children: Kim, Karen; children by previous marriage: Debra, Jill. AB, U. Rochester, 1955; LLB, Harvard U., 1958. Bar: N.Y. 1958, U.S. Dist. Ct. (so. dist.) N.Y. 1964, U.S. Ct. Appeals (2d cir.) 1964. Assoc. Stamer & Haft, N.Y.C., 1958-63, Summit Rovins & Feldesman, N.Y.C., 1963-68, ptnr., 1968-88, Proskauer Rose LLC, 1988-89; chmn., legal cost containment cons. WIK Cons. Inc., N.Y.C., 1992-97; pres. Old Quarry Devel., Englewood, N.J., 1996—. Sec. Space & Leisure Time, Ltd., N.Y.C., 1972-80, Ghiordian Knot, Ltd., N.Y.C., 1978-88, ORS Automation, Inc., Princeton, N.J., 1983-86, Cook United, Inc., Cleve., 1986; lit. agt. for Random House Russian-English Dictionary of Idioms, Sophia Lubensky, 1995, From Central Park to Sinai, Roy S. Neuberger, 2000. Author: The Guide to New York Law Firms, 1991, Competent Counsel: The Business Guide to Selecting, Hiring Lawyers and Monitoring Their Work, 1992; contbr. articles to profl. jours. Fellow Phi Beta Kappa Soc.; mem. N.Y.State Bar Assn., Assn. Bar City of N.Y., Fed. Bar Coun. (chmn. winter meeting 1980, mem. alternative dispute resolution com. 1984), Can. Club (N.Y.C.) (bd. govs. 1988-89, editor Maple Leaf 1984-89), Met. Club (N.Y.C.). Corporate, general, Securities, Corporate finance.

CHERRY, PAUL STEPHEN, lawyer; b. Phila., Oct. 6, 1943; s. Herbert Isdor and Toby (Ring) C.; m. Hilary Kirwan, Apr. 8, 1972. BA, Temple U., 1966; JD, Widener U., 1982. Pa. 1983, U.S. Dist. Ct. (ea. dist.) Pa. 1983, U.S. Ct. Appeals (3d and fed. cirs.) 1983, U.S. Ct. Internat. Trade 1983, U.S. Ct. Claims 1983, U.S. Tax Ct. 1983, U.S. Supreme Ct. 1986, U.S. Ct. Vets. Appeals 1995, U.S. Ct. Appeals (11th cir.) 1996, Fla. 1997; registered sanitarian. Sci. tchr. Cen. High Sch., Phila., 1966-67; instr. physiology Regional Sch. Nursing, Owen Sound, Ont., Can., 1967-68; tchr. natural sci. Sir Sanford Fleming Coll., Peterborough, Ont., 1968-69; sanitarian Dept. Pub. Health, Phila., 1972-73, Chester County Health Dept., West Chester, Pa., 1974-79; pvt. practice law Wayne, Pa., 1983-95; asst. pub. defender 20th Jud. Cir., Fla., 1998—2001; sr. atty. child welfare svcs. Fla. DCF, 2001—. Operating engr. Sound and Light Show at Independence Hall, Phila., 1961-82; bd. dirs. Hist. Soc. of U.S., Dist. Ct. (ea. dist.) Pa., Phila., 1985-95; mem. traffic com. Tredyffrin Twp., Berwyn, Pa., 1991. Recipient Annual recognition Women Against Abuse, Phila., 1986. Fellow Lawyers in Mensa (main line coord. 1985-95); mem. Pa. Bar Assn., B'nai B'rith (pres. Freedom Valley Lodge, Valley Forge, Pa. 1992-95). Democrat. Jewish. Avocations: classical music, acoustics, computers, pipe organ constrn. Commercial, contracts (including sales of goods; commercial financing), Criminal, General practice. Home: 6625 Taeda Dr Sarasota FL 34241-9149 Office: 805 N Mills ave Arcadia FL 34266 E-mail: paul_s_cherry_esquire@msn.com.

CHERRY, SANDRA WILSON, lawyer; b. Dec. 31, 1941; d. Berlin Alexander and Renna Glen (Barnes) Wilson; m. John Sandefur Cherry, Sept. 24, 1976; 1 child, Jane Wilson. BA, U. Ark., 1962, JD, 1975. Bar: Ark. 75, U.S. Dist. Ct. (ea. dist.) Ark. 79, U.S. Supreme Ct. 79, U.S. Ct. Appeals (8th cir.) 79. Tchr. social studies Little Rock Sch. Dist., 1966—70; chmn. social studies dept. Horace Mann Jr. H.S., Little Rock, 1970—72; asst. U.S. atty. Dept. Justice, Little Rock, 1975—81, 1983—, 1st asst. U.S. atty., 2002—; commr. Ark. Pub. Svc. Commn., Little Rock, 1981—83. Adj. instr. U. Ark. Sch. Law, Little Rock, 1980; mem. 8th cir. gender fairness task force, Ark. dist. ct. magistrate selection panel, 2001. Contbr. Pres. bd. dirs. Gaines House, Inc.; pres. U. Ark. at Little Rock Law Sch. Assn., 1980—81, bd. dirs., 1982, Jr. League Little Rock, 1974, Ark. Cmty. Found., 1997—, Gov.'s Mansion Assn., 1998—. Recipient Gayle Pettus Pontz award, U. Ark. Law Sch. Women Lawyers Assn., 1990. Mem.: ABA, Little Rock C. of C., Ark. Bus. Assn. (com. on the status of women and minorities), Ark. Women Lawyers Assn., Pulaski County Bar Assn. (bd. dirs. 1989—90, 1991—92, pres.-elect 1993—94, pres. 1994—), Ark. Bar Assn. (Ho. of Del. 1984—86, sec.-treas. 1986—89, Ho. of Del. 1989—, tenured del. 1994, exec. coun. chair 1995—, pres. 2001—02, 8th cir. gender fairness task force, Golden Gavel award 1992), Phi Beta Phi. Republican. Presbyterian. Home: 4100 S Lookout St Little Rock AR 72205-2030 Office: US Atty's Office PO Box 1229 Little Rock AR 72203-1229

CHERTOFF, MICHAEL, judge; b. Elizabeth, NJ, Nov. 28, 1953; BA, Harvard U., 1975, JD, 1978. Bar: D.C. 1980, N.Y. 1987, N.J. 1990. Summer assoc. Miller, Cassidy, Larroca & Lewin, 1978; law clk. to Hon. Murray Gurfein U.S. Ct. Appeals (2d cir.), N.Y.C., 1978-79; law clk. to Hon. William J. Brennan Jr. U.S. Supreme Ct., Washington, 1979-80; assoc. Latham & Watkins, Washington, 1980-83, ptnr., 1994—2001; asst. U.S. atty. U.S. Atty.'s Office, N.Y.C., 1983-87, 1st asst. U.S. atty. Newark, 1987-90, U.S. atty., 1990—94; spl. counsel for Whitewater com. U.S. Senate, 1994—96; asst. atty. gen. criminal div. U.S. Dept. Justice, Washington, 2001—03; circuit judge U.S. Ct. Appeals, 3rd cir., 2003—. Mem. lawyer's adv. com. U.S. Dist. Ct. N.J., Newark, 1990—, U.S. Atty. Gen.'s Adv. com. of U.S. Atty.'s, Washington, 1991—. Recipient John Marshall award U.S. Dept. Justice, Washington, 1987. Office: James A Byrne Cthse 601 Market St Philadelphia PA 19106*

CHESLEY, STANLEY MORRIS, lawyer; b. Cin., Mar. 26, 1936; s. Frankl and Rachel (Kinsburg) C.; children: Richard A., Lauren B. BA, U. Cin., 1958, LLB, 1960. Bar: Ohio 1960, Ky. 1978, W.Va. 1981, Tex. 1981, Nev. 1981. Ptnr. Waite, Schneider, Bayless & Chesley Co., Cin., 1960—. Contbr. articles to profl. jours. Bd. dirs., past chmn. bd. commrs. on grievances and discipline Supreme Ct. Ohio; past pres. Jewish Fedn. Cin.; nat. vice chair, bd. govs., trustee, joint distbn. com. United Jewish Coms.; exec. bd., nat. bd. govs. Am. Jewish Com.; nat. bd. govs. Hebrew Union Coll.; exec. com. U.S. Holocaust Meml. Mus. Mem. ABA, ATLA, FBA, Am. Judicature Soc., Melvin M. Belli Soc., Ohio Bar Assn., Ky. Bar Assn., W.Va. Bar Assn., Tex. Bar Assn., Nev. Bar Assn., Cin. Bar Assn. General civil litigation, Personal injury (including property damage), Product liability. Office: Waite Schneider Bayless & Chesley 1513 Central Trust Towers Cincinnati OH 45202 E-mail: wsbclaw@aol.com.

CHESSON, CALVIN WHITE, lawyer, educator; b. Williamston, N.C., July 23, 1936; s. Bruce Cecil Chesson and Debby Beatrice White; m. Ann Cooke; children: Courtney Ann Haas, Stephanie Lynn. BA in Bus. Adminstrn., East Carolina U., 1958; JD, U. N.C., 1962. Bar: N.C. 1962, U.S. Dist. Ct. (ea., we. and mid. dists.) N.C. 1995, U.S. Ct. Appeals (4th cir.) 1998. Assoc. Lassiter, Moore & Van Allen, Charlotte, N.C., 1962-65; dist. atty. for Mecklenburg County N.C. Superior Ct., Charlotte, 1965-68; sr. ptnr. Cole & Chesson, Charlotte, 1968-80, Curtis, Millsaps & Chesson, Charlotte, 1980-85; pvt. practice law Charlotte, 1985—. Dir., chmn. Voluntary Action Ctr.-United Way, Charlotte, 1983-86; pres. Lions Club, Charlotte, 1984-85, 92-93; commr. Mecklenburg County Pk. and Recreation Commn., Charlotte, 1986-88; dir. Family Support Ctr., Charlotte, 1989-90, Hope Springs, Charlotte, 1991-93. Pvt. USAR, 1959-65. Mem. N.C. Bar Assn., N.C. State Bar, Mecklenburg County Bar Assn. Democrat. Methodist. Avocation: tennis. General civil litigation, Commercial, contracts (including sales of goods; commercial financing), Corporate, general. Office: 7804 Fairview Rd PMB 287 Charlotte NC 28226 E-mail: cchesson@mindspring.com.

CHESTER, JOHN JONAS, lawyer, educator; b. Columbus, Ohio, July 13, 1920; s. John J. and Harriet Bonnadine (Rice) C.; m. Cynthia Johnson, Apr. 18, 1959; children: John, James, Joel, Cecily. AB cum laude, Amherst Coll., 1942; JD, Yale U., 1948. Bar: Ohio 1948. Ptnr. Chester & Chester, Columbus, 1948-57, Chester & Rose, Columbus, 1958-70, Chester Willcox and Saxbe and predecessor firm, Columbus, 1971—. Spl. counsel Pres. of U.S.., 1974. adj. prof. Ohio State U. Coll. Law. Past bd. dirs. Grant Riverside Meth. Hosps.; past chmn. Doctor's Hosp.; chmn. bd. dirs. Ohio Health, 2001—; past trustee Doctor's Hosp., Columbus Sch. for Girls, Columbus Acad., Shepherd Hill Hosp., Ohio Hist. Found., Ohio Hist. Soc.; active Ohio Gen. Assembly, 1953-58. Lt. USNR, 1942-46. Mem. ABA, Ohio State Bar Assn., Columbus Bar Assn., Am. Coll. Trial Lawyers, Columbus Club (bd. dirs.), Columbus Athletic Club, Rocky Fork Hunt and Country Club. Republican. Episcopalian. General civil litigation, Property, real (including real estate development, water), General practice. Home: 4906 Riverside Dr Columbus OH 43220-2876 Office: Chester Willcox & Saxbe 65 E State St Ste 1000 Columbus OH 43215-3442

CHESTER, ROBERT SIMON GEORGE, lawyer; b. Chelmsford, Essex, England, Feb. 11, 1949; arrived in Can., 1971. s. Robert John and Elizabeth Poyitt (Forteath) C.; m. Anna Tharyan, Sept. 18, 1975; 1 child, Rahael Elizabeth Anna. BA, Oxford U., England, 1971, MA, 1979; postgrad., Osgoode Hall Law Sch., Toronto, 1971-72. Bar: Ontario 1982, England and Wales 1988. Vis. lectr. Osgoode Hall Law Sch., Toronto, 1972-74; rsch. staff Ontario Law Reform Commn., Toronto, 1974-77; exec. counsel Dep. Atty. Gen. Ontario, Toronto, 1977-82; counsel policy devel. Ministry Atty. Gen., Ontario, 1982-85; dir. rsch. McMillan Binch, Toronto, 1985—; ptnr. KNOWlaw Group, Toronto, 1988—. Counsel Study on Access to Legal Svcs. by Disabled, Ontario, 1982-83; cons. Royal Commn. on Employment Equity, 1983-84, Royal Commn. on Electoral Reform, 1990-91, Royal Commn. on Aboriginal Peoples, 1992. Author: (with others) Environmental Rights in Canada, 1981, The Quality Pursuit, 1988, ABA Guide to Legal Marketing, 1995, Barristers and Solicitors in Practice, 1998; co-editor: Winning with Computers, 1991, 2d vol., 1993; contbr. articles to profl. jours. Can. Rhodes Found. scholar, 1972; sec., trustee and fellow Coll. Law Practice Mgmt. Mem. ABA (chmn. New Media and Internet bd., chmn. edn. bd. law practice mgmt. sect. 1994-96, chmn. Techshow 1992-93), Can. Bar Assn. (com. legal opinions 1992—, Pres. tech. impact adv. group). Anglican. Intellectual property, Private international, Libel. Home: 41 Walmsley Blvd Toronto ON Canada M4V 1X7 Office: McMillan Binch LLP Royal Bank Plz PO Box 38 Toronto ON Canada M5J 2J7 E-mail: simon.chester@mcmillanbinch.com.

CHESTON, GEORGE MORRIS, lawyer; b. Phila., Aug. 18, 1917; s. Radcliffe and Sydney (Ellis) C.; m. Winifred Dodge Seyburn, May 5, 1955; 1 dau., Sydney. AB, Harvard U., 1939, LL.B., 1947. Bar: Pa. 1947. Since practiced in, Phila.; atty. firm Ballard, Spahr. Andrews & Ingersoll, Phila., 1947-52; farmer Georgetown, S.C., 1968-94. Treas. Nat. Citizens for Eisenhower, 1955-56 Pres. Phila. Soc. for Svcs. to Children, 1959-69;

trustee United Fund, Phila., 1958-69; bd. dirs. Phila. Zool. Soc., 1977-86, Saratoga Performing Arts, Am. Fedn. Arts; trustee Phila. Mus. Art, 1962—, pres., 1968-76, Nat. Mus. of Racing. Served to comdr. USNR, 1941-46, PTO. Mem. S.C. Plantation Soc. Home: 229 Spruce St Philadelphia PA 19106-3906

CHESTON, SHEILA CAROL, lawyer; b. Washington, Nov. 5, 1958; d. Theodore C. and Gabrielle Joan (Hellings) C. BA, Dartmouth Coll., 1980; JD, Columbia U., 1984. Bar: N.Y. 1986, D.C. 1986, U.S. Dist. Ct. D.C. 1987, U.S. Ct. Appeals (D.C. cir.) 1987, U.S. Dist. Ct. (so. and ea. dists.) N.Y. 1989, U.S. Ct. Appeals (2d cir.), U.S. Supreme Ct. 1989. Law clk. to judge U.S. Ct. Appeals for 9th Cir., L.A., 1984-85; assoc. Wilmer, Cutler & Pickering, Washington, 1985-92, ptnr., 1992-93; gen. counsel Def. Base Closure and Realignment Commn., 1993; spl. assoc. counsel to Pres. of U.S., 1994; dep. gen. counsel Dept. Air Force, 1993-95, gen. counsel, 1995-98; ptnr. Wilmer, Cutler & Pickering, Washington, 1998—2002; sr. v.p., gen. counsel BAE Systems N.A., Rockville, Md., 2002—. Adj. prof. in internat. litigation Georgetown Law Sch., 1991—. Mem. ABA, D.C. Bar Assn., Women's Bar Assn., Am. Soc. Internat. Law. Democrat. Episcopalian. Administrative and regulatory, Antitrust, Aviation. Office: BAE Systems NA 1601 Research Blvd Rockville MD 20850-3173 E-mail: sheila.cheston@baesystems.com.

CHEWNING, MARTHA FRANCES MACMILLAN, lawyer; b. Orlando, Fla., Oct. 11, 1951; d. James Francis and Frances Sybil (Es'Dorn) MacMillan; m. John Quinton Chewning, June 3, 1978. BA in Social Work magna cum laude, LaGrange Coll., 1972; JD, Mercer U., 1979. Bar: Ga. 1979. Pvt. practice, Pine Mountain, Ga., 1979—85; judge probate ct., traffic ct., supt. of elections Harris County, Hamilton, Ga., 1985—98; pvt. practice Hamilton, Ga., 1985—. Bd. dirs. First Union Nat. Bank, Pine Mountain. Mem. State Bar Assn. Ga., Pine Mountain C. of C. (pres. 1985), Harris County C. of C. (pres. 1998). Methodist. Avocations: scuba diving, motorcycles. Office: PO Box 354 Hamilton GA 31811-0354

CHIARA, MARGARET MARY, United States attorney; BA, Fordham U.; MA Pace U.; JD, Rutgers U. Assoc. French and Lawrence, Cassopolis, Mich., 1979—82; prosecuting atty. Cass County Prosecutor's Office, 1982—96; adminstr. Trial Ct. Assessment Commn., 1997—98; policy and planning dir. Office of Chief Justice of Mich. Supreme Ct., 1999—2001; U.S. atty. We. Dist. Mich. U.S. Dept. Justice, 2001—. Office: PO Box 208 Grand Rapids MI 49501

CHIATE, KENNETH REED, lawyer; b. Phoenix, June 24, 1941; s. Mac Arthur and Lillian (Lavin) C.; m. Jeannette Jensen, Aug. 21, 1965; children: Gregory Jensen, Carley MkKay. BA with honors, Claremont Men's Coll., 1963; JD, Columbia U., 1966; postgrad., U. So. Calif. Law Sch., 1967. Bar: Calif. 1967, U.S. Dist. Ct. (cen. dist.) Calif. 1967, Ariz. 1971, U.S. Dist. Ct. Ariz. 1971, U.S. Dist. Ct. (no. Dist.) Calif. 1982. Law clk. presiding justice U.S. Dist. Ariz., 1971; ptnr. Lillick McHose & Charles, L.A., 1971-91, Pillsbury Winthrop, LLP (formerly Pillsbury Madison), L.A., 1991—. Arbitrator Los Angeles Superior Ct. Arbitration Panel, 1979-82; mcpl. ct. judge protem Los Angeles, 1979-81; vice chmn. Los Angeles Open Com., 1969-71. Named among Calif. Lawyers of Yr. 2000, Calif. Mag. Mem. ABA, L.A. County Bar Assn., Calif. State Bar Assn., Ariz. State Bar Assn., Maricopa County Bar Assn., Am. Trial Lawyers Assn., L.A. Bus. Trial Lawyers Assn. Federal civil litigation, State civil litigation, Personal injury (including property damage). Office: Quinn Emanuel Urquhart Oliver & Hedges LLP 865 Figueroa St 10th Fl Los Angeles CA 90017 E-mail: kennethchiate@quinnemanuel.com.

CHIAVASSA, TERCIO, lawyer, researcher; b. São Paulo, Brazil, Aug. 11, 1972; s. Francisco Antonio and Helena Maria (Filardi) Chiavassa; m. Carolinne Degen, May 22, 1999. Civil Procedure Cert., U. Degli Studi Milan, Italy, 1997; LLM, U. of Sao Paulo, Sao Paulo - Brazil, 2003. Bar: Sao Paulo, Brazil 1995. Sr. assoc. Pinheiro Neto Advogados, Sao Paulo, Brazil, 1993—; prof. Carlos Chagas Found., Sao Paulo, 2001—. Mem.: Tax Rsch. Inst. (founding mem.), Brazulian Inst. Tax Law, Sao Paulo. Taxation, general, General civil litigation. Office: Pinheiro Neto Advogados Boa Vista 254 90 Andar São Paulo 01014-907 Brazil Office Fax: 55 11 3247.8600. E-mail: tercio@pinheironeto.com.br.

CHIDNESE, PATRICK N. retired lawyer; b. Neptune, N.J., May 26, 1940; s. Louis and Helen Chidnese; 1 child, Krista; m. Kathy J. Chidnese, Feb. 16, 1985; children: Patrick, Nicole. BA, U. Miami, 1964, JD, 1968. Assoc. Sinclair, Louis & Huttoe, Miami, 1968-69, Stephens, Demos, Magil & Thornton, Miami, 1969-70, Howell, Kirby, Montgomery, D'Aiuto, Dean & Hallowes, Ft. Lauderdale, Fla., 1970-71; sole practice Ft. Lauderdale, 1971-88; ret., 1988. County atty. Broward County Juvenile Ct., 1971—72. Mem. Fla. Bar Assn. (chmn. auto ins. com. 1977-78, chmn. 17th jud. circuit legis. com. 1977-80), Broward County Bar Assn., Acad. Fla. Trial Lawyers, Broward County Trial Lawyers Assn. (bd. dirs. 1974-80). Insurance, Personal injury (including property damage), Workers' compensation. Home: PO Box 18419 Asheville NC 28814-0419

CHIECHI, CAROLYN PHYLLIS, federal judge; b. Newark, Dec. 6, 1943; BS magna cum laude, Georgetown U., 1965, JD, 1969, LLM in Taxation, 1971, LLD honoris causa, 2000. Bar: DC 1969, U.S. Dist. Ct. DC, U.S. Ct. Fed. Claims, U.S. Tax Ct., U.S. Ct. Appeals (5th, 6th, 9th, DC, and fed. cirs.), U.S. Supreme Ct. Atty. advisor to Hon. Leo H. Irwin U.S. Tax Ct., Washington, 1969-71; assoc. Sutherland, Asbill & Brennan, Washington, 1971—76, ptnr., 1976—92; judge U.S. Tax Ct., 1992—. Mem. bd. regents Georgetown U., 1988—94, Washington, 1995—2001, mem. nat. law alumni bd., 1986—93; mem. bd. govs. Georgetown U. Alumni Assn., 1994—2000; bd. dirs. Stuart Stiller Meml. Found., 1986—99; prin. Coun. for Excellence in Govt., 1990—92. Dept. editor: Jour. Taxation, 1986—92; contbr. articles to profl. jours. Fellow: Am. Coll. Tax Counsel, Am. Bar Found.; mem.: FBA, ABA, Am. Judicature Soc., Women's Bar Assn., DC Bar Assn., Georgetown U. Law Alumni Assn. (Law Ctr. Alumnae Achievement award 1998). Office: US Tax Ct 400 2nd St NW Washington DC 20217-0002

CHILDRESS, STEVEN ALAN, law educator; b. Mobile, Ala., Feb. 9, 1959; s. Roy and Mary Helen (Gillion) C.;children: Ani, Steven; m. Victoria Holstein, Oct. 19, 2002. BA, U. Ala., 1979; JD, Harvard U., 1982; PhD in Jurisprudence and Social Policy, U. Calif., Berkeley, 1995. Bar: Calif. 1983, U.S. Ct. Appeals (5th cir.) 1984, D.C. 1986, U.S. Ct. Appeals (9th cir.) 1986, U.S. Supreme Ct. 1987. Law clk. to judge U.S. Ct. Appeals (5th cir.), Shreveport, La., 1982-83; assoc. Morrison & Foerster, San Francisco, 1983-84; adj. lectr. law Golden Gate U. Sch. Law, San Francisco, 1984-86; grad. instr. U. Calif., Berkeley, 1985-86; assoc. Brobeck, Phleger & Harrison, San Francisco, 1987-88; assoc. prof. law Tulane U. Law Sch., New Orleans, 1988-96, prof. law, 1996—. Co-author: Federal Standards of Review, 1986, 3d edit., 1999; contbr. articles to profl. jours. Regents fellow U. Calif. at Berkeley, 1985. Mem. Law and Soc. Assn., Phi Beta Kappa. Office: Tulane U Sch Law School of Law New Orleans LA 70118 E-mail: achildress@law.tulane.edu.

CHILDS, DAVID ROBERT, lawyer; b. Woking, Surrey, England, June 28, 1951; m. Julie Childs. LLB, Sheffield Univ., Eng., 1972; LLM, Univ. Coll. London, Eng., 1973. Bar: Eng. and Wales. Ptnr. Clifford Chance, 1981—; global heaad of corp. practice Clifford Chance LLP, 2000—. Corporate, general, Mergers and acquisitions. Office: Clifford Chance LLP 200 Aldersgate St London ECIA 4JJ England

CHILDS, LARRY BRITTAIN, lawyer; b. Feb. 26, 1952; s. Don and Mattie Frances (Brittain) C.; m. Julie Truss; children: Lucy, Elizabeth, George. BA, U. Ala., 1974; JD, U. Va., 1977. Bar: Ala. 1977. Law clk. to sr. judge U.S. Dist. Ct. (no. dist.) Ala., Birmingham, 1977-78; assoc. Cabaniss, Johnston, Gardner, Dumas & O'Neal, Birmingham, 1978-83, ptnr., 1984-91, Walston, Wells, Anderson & Bains, LLP, Birmingham, 1991—. Mem. ABA, Ala. Bar Assn., Birmingham Bar Assn. Presbyterian. Banking, Federal civil litigation, General civil litigation. Home: 2676 Alta Glen Dr Birmingham AL 35243-4508 Office: Walston Wells Anderson & Bains LLP 505 N 20th St Ste 500 Birmingham AL 35203-4628

CHILES, STEPHEN MICHAEL, lawyer; b. July 15, 1942; s. Daniel Duncan and Helen Virginia (Hayes) C.; m. Deborah E. Nash, June 13, 1964; children: Stephen, Abigail. BA, Davidson Coll., 1964; JD, Duke U., 1967. Bar: N.Y. 1970, Pa. 1978, Wis. 1981, Ill. 1986, U.S. Dist. Ct. (ea. dist.) Pa. 1978, U.S. Tax Ct. 1978, U.S. Supreme Ct. 1978. Officer trust dept. Irving Trust Co., N.Y.C., 1970-75, v.p., 1975-77; assoc. atty. Stassen Kostos & Mason, Phila., 1978-79, mem., shareholder, 1979-85; ptnr. McDermott, Will & Emery, Chgo., 1986—. Contbr. articles to profl. jours. Served to capt. U.S. Army, 1967-69. Decorated Bronze Star, Army Commendation medal. Mem. ABA, State Bar Wis., Exmoor Country Club (Highland Park, Ill.). Republican. Episcopalian. Estate planning, Estate taxation. Office: McDermott Will & Emery 227 W Monroe St Ste 3100 Chicago IL 60606-5096 E-mail: schiles@mwe.com.

CHILIVIS, NICKOLAS PETER, lawyer; b. Athens, Ga., Jan. 12, 1931; s. Peter Nickolas and Wessie Mae (Tanner) C.; m. Patricia Kay Tumlin, June 3, 1967; children— Taryn Tumlin, Nicole Tumlin, Nickolas Peter Tumlin. LL.B., U. Ga., Athens, 1953; LL.M., Atlanta Law Sch., Ga., 1955. Bar: Ga. 1952, U.S. Supreme Ct. 1965. Ptnr. Lester & Chilivis, Athens, Ga., 1953-58; ptnr. Erwin, Epting, Gibson & Chilivis, Athens, Ga., 1958-75; commr. of revenue State of Ga., Atlanta, 1975-77; ptnr. Powell, Goldstein, Frazer & Murphy, Atlanta, 1977-84, Chilivis & Grindler, Atlanta, 1984-95, Chilivis, Cochran, Larkins & Bever, Atlanta, 1995—. Adj. prof. U. Ga. Sch. Law, Athens, 1965-75. Author: Termination Settlement, 1955. Contbr. chpts. to books, articles to profl. jours. Bd. visitors U. Ga., Athens, 1983-85; trustee Skandalakis Found., Atlanta, 1984, Found. of the Holy Apostles; former trustee U. Ga. Found.; former mem. U. Ga. Rsch. Found. Bd.; pres. and sr. warden Ch. of Apostles. With USAFR, 1953-55. Recipient Archdiocesan medal Archbishop of North and South Am., 1980. Fellow Internat. Soc. Barristers, Am. Coll. Trial Lawyers, Am. Acad. Appellate Lawyers; mem. Am. Inns. of Ct. (emeritus, master), Old War Horse Lawyers Club, Lawyers Club Atlanta, Commerce Club, Heritage Club, (Atlanta), Pres.'s Club (U. Ga.), Elks. Avocations: handball, tennis, writing, lecturing. General civil litigation, Criminal. Home: 855 W Paces Ferry Rd NW Atlanta GA 30327-2655 Office: Chilivis Cochran Larkins & Bever Chilivis Bldg 3127 Maple Dr NE Atlanta GA 30305-2503

CHILSTROM, ROBERT MEADE, lawyer; b. San Diego, July 1, 1945; s. Arne Oswald and Margaret Myra (Kippax) C.; m. Buena Lelia Hamlin, Aug. 24, 1968; children: Per Benjamin, Mikaela Lynn. BA, Princeton U., 1967; MA, Columbia U., 1969; JD, Yale U., 1973. Bar: N.Y. State 1975, U.S. Dist. Ct. (so. dist., ea. dist.) N.Y. 1975, U.S. Ct. Appeals (2d cir.) 1975. Assoc. Cravath, Swaine & Moore, N.Y.C., Paris, London, 1973-85, Skadden, Arps, Slate, Meagher & Flom LLP, N.Y.C., 1985-87, ptnr., 1987—. Corporate, general, Finance, Private international. Office: Skadden Arps Slate Meagher & Flom LLP Rm 31-100 4 Times Sq New York NY 10036-6595 E-mail: rchilstr@skadden.com.

CHILTON, BRADLEY STEWART, law educator, educator; b. Rockford, Ill., Oct. 28, 1955; s. Ermal Rural and Maybelle Rose (McNair) C.; m. Lisa Marie Hartmann, May 21, 1977. BA, Milton Coll., 1977; JD, U. Toledo, Ohio, 1980, MA, 1981, U. Wis., 1982; PhD, U. Ga., 1988; MLS, U. So. Miss., 1989. Instr. S.E. Mo. State U., Cape Girardeau, 1985-86; asst. prof. U. So. Miss., Hattiesburg, 1986-89, Wash. State U., Pullman, 1989-93; assoc. prof. U. Toledo, 1993-2000, U. North Tex., 2000—. Pre-law advisor U. Toledo, 1993—99; fellow Tex. Ctr. for Digital Knowledge, U. North Tex. Author: Prisons Under the Gavel, 1991. Recipient Ann. Dissertation award NASPAA, 1988. Mem. Acad. Criminal Justice Scis., Am. Polit. Sci. Assn., Am. Soc. Criminology, Am. Soc. Pub. Adminstrn. Avocations: music, home design and building, religion. Office: Criminal Justice Univ North Texas PO Box 305130 Denton TX 76203-5130

CHILVERS, ROBERT MERRITT, lawyer; b. Long Beach, Calif., Oct. 23, 1942; s. James Merritt and Elizabeth Louise (Blackburn) C.; m. Sandra Lee Rigg, Sept. 5, 1969; children: Jeremy Merritt, Jessica Rigg. AB, U. Calif., Berkeley, 1972; JD, Harvard U., 1975. Bar: Calif. 1975, U.S. Dist. Ct. (no. dist.) Calif. 1975, U.S. Ct. Appeals (9th cir.) 1980, U.S. Supreme Ct. 1980, U.S. Dist. Ct. (ctrl. dist.) Calif. 1981, U.S. Ct. Fed. Claims, 1984, U.S. Dist. Ct. (ea. dist.) Calif. 1987, U.S. Ct. Appeals (fed. cir.) 1987, U.S. Dist. Ct. (no dist.) Calif. 2002. Assoc. Brobeck, Phleger & Harrison, San Francisco, 1975-82, ptnr., 1982-93; spl. master U.S. Dist. Ct. (no. dist.) Calif., 1994-99; pres. Chilvers & Taylor, PC, San Rafael, Calif., 1996—; neutral evaluator and mediator, 2001—. Faculty U. Calif., Hastings Sch. Law, San Francisco, 1983-89, Emory U., Atlanta, 1984-90, fed. practice program U.S. Dist. Ct. (no. dist.) Calif., 1984-86, Nat. Inst. for Trial Advocacy, 1986—, Cardozo Law Sch., Yeshiva U., N.Y.C., 1993-99, Stanford U. Law Sch., 1994—, Widener U. Sch. Law, Wilmington, 1994-96, U. San Francisco Sch. Law, 1994—. Mem. Calif. Sch. Bds. Assn., 1985—89; trustee Mill Valley Sch. Dist., Calif., 1985—89, chmn., 1987—89; bd. dirs. Marin County Sch. Bds. Assn., Calif., 1985—86, Artisans, Mill Valley, Calif., 1999—2001. With USMC, 1964—71. Mem. Calif. Bar Assn. (commendation for Outstanding Contbns. to the delivery of vol. legal svcs. 1984), Marin County Bar Assn., Tau Beta Pi, Sigma Tau. Alternative dispute resolution, Federal civil litigation, State civil litigation. Office: Chilvers & Taylor PC 83 Vista Marin Dr San Rafael CA 94903-5228

CHIMPLES, GEORGE, lawyer; b. Canton, Ohio, Oct. 8, 1924; s. Mark and Katherine (Hines) C.; m. Margaret Joanna Cavalaris, July 31, 1949; children: Alicia Candace, Mark II, John Hines, Katherine Hines. AB, Princeton U., 1951; LLB, Harvard Coll., 1954. Bar: Pa. 1955, U.S. Dist. Ct. (ea. dist.) Pa. 1955, U.S. Ct. Appeals (3d cir.) 1955, U.S. Ct. Claims, 1965, U.S. Tax Ct., 1965. Assoc. Stradley, Ronon, Stevens & Young, Phila., 1954-61, gen. ptnr., 1961-92; pvt. practice Wayne, Pa., 1993—. Adj. prof. law U. Pa., Drexel U. Grad. Sch. Bus.; co-authored establishment of overseas infrastructure for securities mktg. in Europe and the Antilles. Trustee Christ Ch. Preservation Trust; permament assoc. Phila. Mus. Art. Capt. USAAF, 1942-46, ETO. Decorated D.F.C., Air medal with four oak leaf clusters, Air Force Commendation medal, Victory medal, four Battle Stars; recipient Royal Air Force plaque, 1994. Mem. ABA (chmn. subcom. regulated investment cos.), Phila. Bar Assn. (tax sect.), Internat. Bar Assn., Internat. Fiscal Assn. (tax treaty sect.), Mid-Atlantic Coun., Commanderie de Bordeaux aux Etats-Unis d'Amerique (archivist), Newcomen Soc. U.S. (com. chmn., nat. trustee, life mem.) Army and Navy Club (Washington chpt.), Penn Club (life, bd. dirs., historian) Athenaeum of Phila. (life), Libr. Co. of Phila. (life), Phila. Mus. Art (permanent assoc.), Phila. Club, Princeton Club N.Y., Cannon Club (Princeton chpt.), Merion Cricket Club. Corporate, general, Estate planning, Taxation, general. Home: 1179 Lafayette Rd Wayne PA 19087-2110 Office: 1522 Overington St Philadelphia PA 19124-5808

CHIN, DAVIS, lawyer; b. Evansville, Ind., Dec. 13, 1947; s. Frank S. M. and Mamie (Shu) C.; m. Pauline C., Aug. 3, 1974; 1 child, Davis M. BS, Rose-Hulman Inst. Tech., Terre Haute, Ind., 1969; JD, U. Balt., 1974; LLM in Taxation, John Marshall Law Sch., 1981. Bar: Ill. 1974, U.S. Dist. Ct. (no. dist.) 1974, U.S. Ct. Appeals (7th cir.) 1974, U.S. Patent and Trademark Office 1974, U.S. Claims Ct. 1977, U. S. Tax Ct. 1977, U.S. Supreme Ct. 1977, U.S. Ct. Appeals (fed. cir.) 1982. Staff atty. CTS Corp., Elkhart, Ind., 1974; assoc. Petherbridge, Lindgren & Gilhooly, Chtd., Chgo., 1974-78; staff atty. Borg-Warner Corp., Chgo., 1978-80, Container Corp. Am., Chgo., 1980-84; pvt. practice Chgo., 1984—. Instr. Prairie State Coll., Chgo. Heights, 1987-90, 94, South Suburban Coll., South Holland, Ill., 1989-91, Roosevelt U., Olympia Fields, Ill., 1990-93. Elder United Presbyn. Ch., South Holland, 1986—; panel program atty. Chgo. Vol. Legal Svcs., 1988—. Mem. Am. Intellectual Property Law Assn., Chgo. Bar Assn., Intellectual Property Law Assn. Chgo., Patent Law Assn. Chgo. (bd. mgrs. 1985-87, 94-96). Avocations: tennis, golf, travel. General practice, Intellectual property, Taxation, general. Home: 11428 Plattner Dr Mokena IL 60448-9228 Office: 16061 S 94th Ave Tinley Park IL 60477-4623 E-mail: davischin@juno.com.

CHIN, KELVIN HENRY, university ombudsperson; b. Boston, Jan. 7, 1951; s. Henry W.F. and King (Lee) C.; m. Peggy Abbott, July 26, 1987; children: Jesse, Samantha. Student, U. Strasbourg, France, 1971; AB cum laude, high distinction in French, Dartmouth Coll., 1973; MA, Yale U., 1974; JD, Boston Coll., 1983. Dir. in East Asia, Found. for Creative Intelligence, Hong Kong, 1974-78; co-founder Microtex Corp., Cambridge, Mass., 1978-83; life ins. agent Sun Life of Canada, Wellesley, Mass., 1979-81; law clerk Bingham, Dana & Gould, Boston, 1980-83; summer assoc. to assoc. Choate, Hall & Stewart, Boston, 1982-84; employee benefits cons. Hicks Pension Svcs., Lexington, Mass., 1984-86; pres. Bus. Consulting Assocs., Boston, San Diego, 1986-92; dir. mediation Ctr. for Mediation, Am. Arbitration Assn., San Diego, 1992-93, regional v.p. Las Vegas, Nev., 1993-96, L.A., 1996-2000; co-founder The Health Accord LLC, N.Y.C., 2000; pres. AgreeOnline, Inc., L.A., 2000; bus. cons., 2000—02; ombudsperson Office of the Pres., MIT, Cambridge, 2002—. Mem. nat. adv. bd. Ctr. for Med. Ethics and Mediation, San Diego, 1992—. Editor: International Law Dictionary, 1983. Ombudsman Calif. Dept. on Aging, San Diego, 1991-93; com. mem. Waldorf Sch. of San Diego PTA, 1992-93; mediator Ctr. for Mcpl. Dispute Resolution City Atty.'s Office, San Diego, 1990-93; bd. advs. U. West L.A., 1996-2000. Rufus Choate scholar Dartmouth Coll., 1971-73; Nat. Def. Fgn. Language fellow U.S. Dept. Edn., 1973-74. Mem. ABA (dispute resolution sect.), Am. Arbitration Assn. (blue ribbon mediator panel 1992—), San Diego County Bar Assn. (treas. alternative dispute resolution sect. 1991-93), Assn. for Conflict Resolution, So. Calif. Mediation Assn., The Ombudsman Assn., Univ. and Coll. Ombudsman Assn. Avocations: basketball, philosophy. E-mail: kelchin@attbi.com.

CHIN, MING, state supreme court justice; b. Klamath Falls, Oreg., Aug. 31, 1942; m. Carol Lynn Joe, Dec. 19, 1971; children: Jennifer, Jason. BA in Polit. Sci., U. San Francisco, 1964, JD, 1967. Bar: Calif. 1970, U.S. Fed. Ct., U.S. Tax Ct. Assoc., head trial dept. Aiken, Kramer & Cummings, Oakland, Calif., 1973—76, prin., 1976—88; dep. dist. atty. Alameda County, Calif., 1970—72; judge Alameda County Superior Ct., 1988—90; assoc. justice divsn. 3 Ct. Appeal 1st Dist., 1990—94; presiding justice 1st Dist. Ct. Appeal Divsn. 3, San Francisco, 1994—96; state supreme ct. assoc. justice Calif. Supreme Ct., San Francisco, 1996—. Capt. U.S. Army, 1967—69, Vietnam, Capt. USAR, 1969—71. Mem.: ABA, Asian Am. Bar Assn., San Francisco Dist. Atty.'s Commn. Hate Crimes, Alameda County Bar Assn., State Bar Calif., Calif. Judges Assn., Commonwealth Club of Calif. (pres. 1998), Alpha Sigma Nu. Office: Supreme Court Calif 350 Mcallister St Fl 1 San Francisco CA 94102-4783

CHIN, SYLVIA FUNG, lawyer; b. N.Y.C., June 27, 1949; d. Thomas and Constance (Yao) Fung; m. Edward G.H. Chin, July 10, 1971; children: Arthur F., Benjamin F. BA, NYU, 1971; JD, Fordham U., 1977. Bar: N.Y. 1978, U.S. Dist. Ct. (so. and ea. dists.) N.Y. 1979, U.S. Supreme Ct. 1990. Law clk. to dist. judge U.S. Dist. Ct. (so. dist.), N.Y.C., 1977-79; assoc. White & Case, N.Y.C., 1979-86, ptnr., 1986—. Adj. assoc. prof. law Fordham U., N.Y.C., 1979-81. Mem. editl. bd.: Bus. Law Today, 1996—2002; contbr. articles to profl. jours. Mem.: ABA, Am. Coll. Comml. Fin. Lawyers, Am. Coll. Investment Counsel (bd. dirs. 1999—, pres. 2002—03), Nat. Asian Pacific ABA (treas. 1997—98), Women's World Banking (bd. dirs.), Asian Am. Bar Assn. N.Y. (bd. dirs. 1991—97, pres. 1994—96), N.Y. County Lawyers Assn., Assn. Bar City N.Y., AABANY Found. (treas.), Fordham Law Alumni Assn. (bd. dirs.). Commercial, contracts (including sales of goods; commercial financing), Corporate, general, Finance. Office: White & Case LLP 1155 Ave of Americas New York NY 10036-2711

CHING, GALE LIN FONG, lawyer; b. Honolulu, Nov. 27, 1954; s. Richard L. and Helen Y.C. (Wong) C. BA in Psychology with Distinction, U. Hawaii, 1976; JD, Gonzaga U., 1980. Bar: Hawaii 1980, U.S. Dist. Ct. Hawaii 1980, U.S. Ct. Appeals (9th cir.) 1981, U.S. Supreme Ct. 2001. Law clerk Hawaii 3rd Cir. Ct., 1980-81; dep. pros. atty. County of Hawaii Ct., Hilo, 1981-86; dep. atty. gen. State of Hawaii, Honolulu, 1986-90; ptnr. Moon, O'Connor, Tam & Yuen, Honolulu, 1990-95, Hisaka, Stone & Goto, Honolulu, 1995-98, Hisaka Stone Goto Yoshida Cosgrove & Ching, 1998—; per diem judge Dist. Ct. First Cir., Honolulu, 1997—. Mem. ABA, Am. Judicature Soc., Hawaii Bar Assn., Def. Rsch. Inst. General civil litigation, Commercial, contracts (including sales of goods; commercial financing), Insurance. Home: 2315 Auhuhu St Pearl City HI 96782-1142 Office: Hisaka Stone Goto Yoshida Cosgrove & Ching Pacific Guardian Ctr 737 Bishop St Ste 3000 Honolulu HI 96813-3214 E-mail: gching@objectionsustained.com.

CHING, LOUIS MICHAEL, lawyer; b. New Orleans, June 26, 1956; BS, Tulane U., 1979; JD, Willamette U., 1985. Bar: Oreg. 1986, Hawaii, 1986, U.S. Dist. Ct. Hawaii 1986, U.S. Ct. Appeals (9th cir.) 1989, U.S. Supreme Ct. 1990. Pvt. practice law, Honolulu, 1986-87, 90—; arbitrator, 1999. Mem. Hawaii Assn. Crimimal Def. Lawyers, Phi Beta Kappa. Avocations: tennis, diving. Criminal. E-mail: Louismichaelching@hotmail.com.

CHING, WESLEY H. H. lawyer; b. Honolulu, Sept. 10, 1949; s. Donald H. H. and Beatrice (Liu) C.; m. June W. J. Yim, Aug. 14, 1976; children: David, Krystal. BA, Claremont Men's Coll., 1971; JD, Boston U., 1975. Bar: Ill. 1976, U.S. Dist. Ct. (no. dist.) Ill. 1976, U.S. Ct. Appeals (7th cir.) 1977, U.S. Supreme Ct. 1980, Hawaii 1981, U.S. Dist. Ct. Hawaii 1981, U.S. Ct. Appeals (9th cir.) 1982; arbitrator and mediator, Am. Arbitration Assn., Dispute Prevention and Resolution, 1st cir. ct. State of Hawaii, Honolulu. Rsch. counsel, dir. law student div. Office of Pres. ABA, Chgo., 1976-78; asst. state's atty. spl. prosecutions Office of State's Atty. of Cook County, Chgo., 1978-81; ptnr. Reinwald, O'Connor, Marrack, Hoskins & Playdon, Honolulu, 1981-93, Fukunaga, Matayoshi, Hershey & Ching, Honolulu, 1993—. Mem. ABA, Hawaii State Bar Assn., Defense Rsch. Inst. Avocations: jogging, tennis. General civil litigation, Insurance, Personal injury (including property damage). Office: Fukunaga Matayoshi Hershey & Ching 841 Bishop St Ste 1200 Honolulu HI 96813-3920

CHINN, MARK ALLAN, lawyer; b. Jackson, Miss., June 9, 1953; s. Rollin J. and Ann M. (Heiberg) C.; m. Cathy Hawkinson, Aug. 6, 1978; children: Courtney, Casey, Carly, Conley. BA in Polit. Sci., Iowa State U., 1975; JD, U. Miss., 1978. Bar: U.S. Dist. Ct. (no. dist.) Miss. 1978, U.S. Dist. Ct. (so. dist.) Miss. 1980; U.S. Ct. Appeals (5th and 11th cirs.) 1981; U.S. Supreme Ct. 1980; cert. civil trial expert Nat. Bd. Trial Advocacy. Staff atty. Miss. Senate, Jackson, 1978-79; spl. asst. Atty. Gen. Office, Jackson, 1979-80; assoc. Louis Baine, Jackson, 1980-82, Law Office William Latham, Jackson, 1982-88; atty. pvt. practice, Jackson, 1988—. Adj. prof. law Miss. Coll. Sch. Law; vice chair Supreme Ct. Gender Fairness Task Force; v.p. Gov. Children's Justice Task Force, 2001—. Bd. dirs. Arts Alliance, Jackson, 1990-97, Miss. Children's Home, Jackson, 1990-95; pres. Jackson Urban League Bd., 1995-2000; bd. dirs. Jubilee Jam Found., 1995-97, chmn. Jubilee! Jam '96; chair Lamar Order U. Miss. Law Alumni,

2001-02. Mem. ABA (v.p., mem. family law sect. governing coun.), Miss. Bar Assn. (chmn. family law sect. 1995-96, 2000-01, chmn. small firm practice com. 1995-96, Award of Merit 1996), Hinds County Bar Assn. (dir. 1994-95, pres. 1998—), Am. Inn of Ct. (master Charles Clark), Rotary, Jackson C. of C., Miss. Bar Found., Miss. Law Alumni Assn. (chmn. 2001-02). Avocations: golf, physical fitness, Karate, tae kwan do (black belt), flying. Administrative and regulatory, Family and matrimonial, Personal injury (including property damage). Office: Chinn & Assocs 4316 Old Canton Rd Ste 200 Jackson MS 39211-5920 E-mail: mark@chinnandassociates.com.

CHIORAZZI, MICHAEL GERARD, law librarian, educator; b. Jersey City, Dec. 3, 1954; s. John Dominic and Dolores (Bonn) C.; m. Vickie Bletso, May 30, 1982. BA, U. Miami, 1976; JD, Gonzaga U., 1980; MLL, U. Wash., 1981. Editor Legal Reference Svcs. Quaterly. Democrat. Office: U Arizona Coll Law 1201 E Speedway Blvd Tucson AZ 85721 Home: 3854 E Marble Peak Pl Tucson AZ 85718

CHIPMAN, DEBRA DECKER, paralegal; b. Oneonta, N.Y., Sept. 21, 1959; d. Leon Hannibal and Patricia Elizabeth (Ainsworth) Decker; m. Michael A. Chipman, May 24, 1980 (div. Sept. 1990); 1 child, Amanda Michelle. Student, Robert Morris Coll., 1988-94. Sec., receptionist Power Engring. Corp., Binghamton, N.Y., 1977-78; accts. payable clk. Old Dominion U. Rsch. Found., Norfolk, Va., 1978-80; adminstrv. asst. U. Pitts., 1980-81; paralegal Papernick & Gefsky, Attys. at Law, Pitts., 1981-93; mgr. Preferred Settlement Svcs., Inc., Pitts., 1993-97; asst. v.p., agy. rep. First Am. Title Ins. Co., Pitts., 1997-2000, Fidelity Nat. Title Ins. Co. of N.Y., 2000—. Recipient award Otsego County Bankers Assn., 1977. Mem.: Pa. Land Title Assn. (western Pa. chpt. sec., chair 2002), Pa. Assn. Notaries, Pitts. Paralegal Assn. (co-chair fundraising com. 1990). Methodist. Avocations: golf, skiing. Home: 2593 Hunters Point Ct S Wexford PA 15090-7986 Office: Fidelity Nat Title Ins Co Grant Building Ste 1412 Pittsburgh PA 15219-2203 E-mail: dchipman@fnf.com.

CHIPMAN, MARION WALTER, retired judge; b. Penokee, Kans., May 5, 1920; s. James Edwin and May Maude (Hatcher) C.; m. Thelma Nadine Clark, Nov. 1, 1941 (div. 1965); m. Nancy Jo Payne, May 28, 1983; children: Clark D., Jill Ellen. AB in Social Sci., Ft. Hays (Kans.) State U., 1942; JD, Washburn U., 1948. Bar: Kans. 1948, U.S. Dist. Ct. Kans. 1948, U.S. Ct. Appeals 1970, U.S. Supreme Ct. 1970. Supt. Prairieview (Kans.) Sch., 1942; dir. edn. Bous Indsl. Sch., Topeka, 1945—46; atty. County of Graham, Hill City, Kans., 1949-53; counselor County of Johnson, Olathe, Kans., 1967-68; judge 10th Jud. Dist. Kans. Dist. Ct., Olathe, 1980-91, sr. judge, 1996-2001. Sgt. USAAF, 1942-45. Mem. ABA (life), Johnson County Bar Assn. (life), Kans. Bar Assn. (life), Am. Judicature, Am. Judge's Assn., Am. Arbitration Assn., Am. Legion (life), Masons (life), Shriners (life), Elks (life). Methodist. Home: 6398 17th Pl N Saint Petersburg FL 33710-5520

CHIREZ, ALAIN, lawyer; b. Orchies, Nord, France, Sept. 28, 1947; s. Gaston and Paule (de Marecaux) C.; m. Christine Danielle Dallard, Sept. 15, 1979; children: Maelle, Matthieu, Frederic, Pierre. M in Law, Social Scis. U., Grenoble, France, 1970; Specialized Diploma in Fundamental Law, Law and Econ. Scis. U., Nice, France, 1971, Specialized Diploma in Law/Social Facts, 1973, Law State Doctorate, 1977. Lawyer profl. aptitude cert. Lawyer Chirez-Tourneur-Zalma-D'Aste Lawyers, Valbonne Sophia Antipolis, France, 1971—; law prof. Professionalized U. Inst., Valbonne/Sophia Antipolis, France, 1993—; asst. law prof. Law and Econ. Scis. U., Nice, 1971-77, assoc. law prof., 1978-86, law prof., 1986—. Law prof. various schs., Nice, Valbonne, Toulon, France, 1996—; rschr. Ctr. for Econ. Law Rsch. and Studies, Valbonne, Sophia-Antipolis, 1991—; mentor for student theses, Law and Econ. Scis. U., 1978—; seminary tutor and rschr. in field, 1993—. Author: (book) The Notion of Trust in Contractual Law, 1977; co-author: Legal Problems in Sports, The Sports Person and Sports Associations, 1981, Companies Takeovers and Similar Situations, 1985, Labour Law Reference Manual, 1993; contbr. articles to profl. jours. Mem. Social Law Practicing Lawyers Assn. of Maritime ALPS (pres. 1996—), Assn. for Aids and Comms. (v.p. 1996—), Assn. for Assisting Handicapped Students. Avocations: literature, art, cinema, writing, travel. Office: 45 alleé des Ormes Batiment B 06526 Sophie Antipolis Rougirs France

CHISHOLM, DEAN D. lawyer; b. Missoula, Mont., Feb. 15, 1967; s. Richard L. and Marilyn R.W. Chisholm; m. Penni L. Chisholm, Sept. 4, 1993; children: Henry R., Ava P. BA, Colo. State U., 1989; JD, U. Mont., 1992. Bar: Mont. 1992, U.S. Dist. Ct. Mont. 1992, U.S. Ct. Appeals (9th cir.) 1992, Colo. 2001. Dep. county atty. Cascade County, Great Falls, Mont., 1992—94, acting county atty., 1994; ptnr. Lynch & Chisholm, P.C., Great Falls, Mont., 1995—96, Kaplan & Chisholm, P.L.L.P., Columbia Falls, Mont., 1996—; dep. city atty. Columbia Falls, 1998—; apptd. spl. prosecutor Mont. Supreme Ct. Commn. on Practice, 2001—02. Bd. mem. Fed. Law Enforcement Grant Bd., Great Falls, 1994—96. Named one of Best Lawyers in Am., 2001—; recipient cert. of recognition for Nat. Mid. East Studies Symposium, Pa. State U., 1989, Am. Jurisprudence award for outstanding achievement in constl. law, 1991. Mem.: Colo. Bar Assn., N.W. Mont. Bar Assn., Mont. Trial Lawyers Assn., Mensa. Avocations: literature, golf. Office: Kaplan & Chisholm PLLP PO Box 2071 Columbia Falls MT 59912

CHISHOLM, TOMMY, lawyer, utility company executive; b. Baldwyn, Miss., Apr. 14, 1941; s. Thomas Vaniver and Rubel (Duncan) C.; m. Janice McClanahan, June 20, 1964; children: Mark Alan (dec.), Andrea, Stephen Thomas, Patrick Ervin. BSCE, Tenn. Tech. U., 1963; JD, Samford U., 1969; MBA, Ga. State U., 1984. Registered profl. engr., Ala., Del., Ga., Fla., Ky., La., N.H., Miss., N., Pa., Tenn., S.C., Va., W.Va. Civil engr. TVA, Knoxville, Tenn., 1963-64; design engr. So. Co. Svcs., Birmingham, Ala., 1964-69, coord. spl. projects Atlanta, 1969-73, sec., house counsel, 1977-82, v.p., sec., house counsel, 1982-98; v.p., assoc. gen. counsel, sec. So. Co., Atlanta, 1998—, asst. to pres., 1973-75, sec., asst. treas., 1977—; mgr. adminstrv. svcs. Gulf Power Co., Pensacola, Fla., 1975-77; sec. So. Energy, Inc., Atlanta, 1981-82; v.p., sec. So. Energy Resources Inc., Atlanta, 1982-2000. Mem. ABA, State Bar Ala., Am. Soc. Corp. Secs., Am. Corp. Counsel Assn., Nat. Assn. Corp. Dirs., Phi Alpha Delta, Beta Gamma Sigma. Corporate, general. Office: The Southern Co 270 Peachtree St NW Ste 2200 Atlanta GA 30303-1247

CHISM, TIMOTHY KIRKPATRICK, JR., lawyer; b. Tompkinsville, Ky., Mar. 24, 1954; s. Timothy Kirkpatrick and Jean Major (Swift) C.; m. Lynn Eve France, Aug. 1, 1984 (div. Nov. 1992); 1 child, Timothy Major; m. Dorothea Anne Highland, Feb. 2, 1996. BA, Western Ky. U., 1976; JD, U. Louisville Sch. Law, 1980. Bar: Ky. 1980, Fla. 1982, Hawaii 1984, U.S. Dist. Ct. Hawaii 1984, U.S. Ct. Appeals (6th cir.) 1991, Navy-Marine Corps Ct. Mil. Rev. 1994. Officer USN, R.I., Fla., Hawaii, 1980-84; assoc. Steven Songstad, Maui, Hawaii, 1984, Richard L. Rost, Maui, 1985-88; asst. atty. Warren County, Bowling Green, Ky., 1988-90, 92—; assoc. Hughes & Coleman, Bowling Green, 1990-92. Assoc. editor Bar Tabloid, Bowling Green, 1992-99. Served to comdr. USNR, 1980-84, Res. 1984—. Mem. ABA, Ky. Trial Lawyers Assn., Bowling Green-Warren County Bar Assn. (pres. 1999-2000), Lions (pres. 2001-02), Naval Res. Lawyers Assn., Naval Res. Assn. Methodist. Office: Warren County Atty 1001 Center St Ste 206 Bowling Green KY 42101-2191

CHIULLI, E. ANTOINETTE, lawyer; b. Pescara, Italy, Oct. 30, 1950; arrived in U.S., 1955; d. Nino and Maria (Mezzanotte) C.; children: Christopher J., Jason A. BA, Marymount Coll., 1972; JD, Rutgers-Camden Sch. Law., 1976. Legal asst. Judge Manuel Greenberg, Atlantic City, N.J., 1976-77; pvt. practice Somerdale, N.J., 1978-86. Econ. analyst Nat. Econ. Research Assocs., N.Y.C., 1972-73; panelist Matrimonial Settlement Program, 1985—. Cons., Alternatives for Women Now, Camden, 1978-80, Women's Counseling Ctr., 1981-83, Glassboro (N.J.) Coll. Together Program, Jaycettes of Camden County; trustee, Haddonfield Child Care, 1989—. Mem. N.J. State Bar Assn., Camden County Bar Assn. (family law com., scholarship com.), Burlington Co. Bar. Assn. Family and matrimonial. Office: 100 Grove St Haddonfield NJ 08033 E-mail: eachiulli1@aol.com.

CHIVERS, JAMES LEEDS, lawyer; b. Pitts., Jan. 8, 1939; s. Joseph Hobart and Lorraine Anna (Silhol) C.; m. Patricia Ann Dolan, Sept. 3, 1960; children: Catherine Ann, Christopher John, Matthew Leeds. AB, Colgate U., 1960; LLB cum laude, Union U., Albany, N.Y., 1967. Bar: N.Y. 1967, U.S. Dist. Ct. (no. dist.) N.Y. 1967, U.S. Ct. Appeals (2d cir.) 1982, Fla. 1987, U.S. Dist. Ct. (so. and ea. dists.) N.Y. 1988, U.S. Supreme Ct. 1989, U.S. Dist. Ct. (we. dist.) N.Y. 1993. Assoc. Hinman, Howard & Kattell, Binghamton, N.Y., 1967-75, ptnr., 1975—, ptnr.-in-charge dept. litigation, 1981—. Bd. govs. N.Y. State Atty.-Client Fee Dispute Resplution Program, 2003—. Past pres. Vol. Am. Binghamton, bd. dirs., 1969-93; bd. govs. N.Y. State Atty.-Client Fee Dispute Resolution Program, 2003-. Lt. USNR, 1960-64, Vietnam. Mem. ABA (tort and ins. practice sect.), N.Y. State Trial Lawyers Assn., Internat. Def. Counsel, Am. Arbitration Assn. (arbitrator), Def. Rsch. Assn. (bd. govs. N.Y. State Disput Resolution Program, 2003—), N.Y. State Bar Assn. (torts, ins. and compensation, trial lawyers exec. com. 1996—, environ., comml. and fed. litigation sects., com. on profl. ethics 1994-98, spl. com. on unlawful practice of law 1998-2002), Broome County Bar Assn., Broome County C. of C., Broome County YMCA Found., Justinian Soc., Binghamton Club (pres. 1987-89), Harpur Forum, Am. Legion. Republican. Roman Catholic. Avocations: fishing, winemaking, gardening. Federal civil litigation, General civil litigation, State civil litigation. Office: Hinman Howard & Kattell 700 Security Mutual Bldg Binghamton NY 13901 E-mail: chivers@HHK.com.

CHO, TAI YONG, lawyer; b. Seoul, Republic of Korea, May 27, 1943; came to U.S., 1966; s. Nam Suck and Sun Yeo (Yoon) C; m. Hea Sun Cho, July 14, 1973; children: Robert, Richard, Susan. BS, Seoul U., 1965; MS, Cooper Union, 1971; CE, Columbia U., 1971; JD, Fordham U., 1981. Bar: N.Y., 1982; registered profl. engr., N.Y., 1973. Engr. Ministry of Constrn., Seoul, 1965-66, Andrews & Clark, N.Y.C., 1967-68, Parsons, Brinckerhoff, Quade & Douglas, N.Y.C., 1969-71; v.p. John R. McCarthy Corp., N.Y.C., 1972-80. Mem. ASCE, ABA, N.Y. State Bar Assn., Am. Arbitration Assn. (panel of arbitrators), Am.-Korean Lawyers Assn. of N.Y. (pres. 1988), Korean TV Broadcasters Assn., Am. (pres. 1990), Internat. Korean Lawyers Assn. (v.p. 1991). Commercial, contracts (including sales of goods; commercial financing), Corporate, general, Private international. Home: 56 Tuttle Rd Briarcliff Manor NY 10510-2233 Office: 445 5th Ave New York NY 10016-6509 E-mail: taicho7@aol.com.

CHOBOT, JOHN CHARLES, lawyer; b. N.Y.C., Feb. 14, 1948; s. Arthur E. and Eleanore L. (Lotito) Chobot; m. Catherine Anne Moran, Aug. 24, 1974; children: Christine, Keith. BA, Cornell U., 1969; MS in Edn., CCNY, 1971; JD, Fordham U., 1975. Bar: N.Y. 1976, U.S. Dist. Ct. (we. dist.) N.Y. 1976, N.J. 1985, U.S. Dist. Ct. N.J. 1985. Assoc. Phillips, Lytle, Hitchcock, Blaine & Huber, Buffalo, 1975-85; with The CIT Group/Sales Financing, Inc., Livingston, N.J., 1985-90; sr. v.p., chief counsel bus. fin. divsn. AT&T Capital Corp., 1990-98; v.p. law, asst. gen. counsel Newcourt Credit Group Inc., Parsippany, N.J., 1998-99, The CIT Group, Inc., 1999-2000; counsel Am. Express Co., 2000-01; corp. counsel Lucent Techs. Inc., Murray Hill, NJ, 2001—. Adj. prof. law Seton Hall Law Sch., 2000—. Contbr. articles to legal jours. Mem.: ABA, Comml. Law League, Am. Bankruptcy Inst., N.Y. State Bar Assn., Kappa Alpha Soc. Bankruptcy, Commercial, contracts (including sales of goods; commercial financing), Corporate, general. Home: 23 Laurel Hill Dr Randolph NJ 07869-4632 Office: Lucent Techs Inc 600 Mountain Ave New Providence NJ 07974 Fax: 908-582-8048. Business E-Mail: chobot@lucent.com.

CHOI, JAE HOON, retired university administrator, legal educator; b. San Cheong, Korea, Apr. 8, 1929; s. Ki Seop and Bok Cho (Jeong) C.; m. So Hee Kim, Apr. 15, 1952; children: Shi Hyun, Jang Hyun, Jee Hee. LLB, Seoul Nat. U., 1953, LLM, 1955; PhD, Pusan Nat. U., 1971; researcher The Hague (Netherlands) Acad. Internat. Law, 1971; LL.D. (hon.), Nat. Chengchi U., Republic of China, 1984; LL.D. (hon.), U. S.C., 1987. Prof. law Pusan Nat. U., 1956-83, dean Coll. Law and Polit. Sci., 1971-73, dir. Inst. Problem of Korean Unification, 1974-77, dean Grad. Sch. Public Adminstrn., 1981-83, pres., 1983-87, prof. emeritus, 1990—; prof. law Kyushu Nat. U., Japan, 1988-89; chmn., pres. Hyunbum Rsch. Inst. for Internat. Affairs, 1990—; prof. law Seinangakuin U., Fukuoka, Japan, 1992-2000. Mem. Korean Assn. Internat. Law (v.p. 1974-77, pres. 1983-84), Am. Soc. Internat. Law, Japanese Assn. Internat. Law. Author: International Law, 1996; contbr. articles to profl. jours. Office: # 1407 Samhwan B/D 830-295 Bumil-Dong Tong-ku Pusan 601-709 Republic of Korea

CHOI, JAY JUNEKUN, lawyer; b. Seoul, Korea, Oct. 19, 1956; came to U.S., 1972; s. Lim and Ok Lim Choi; m. Grace Hyesook Kim, Dec. 21, 1982; children: Aretha, Jessica. BA, U. No. Colo., 1976; MBA, Regis U., 1982; JD, U. Denver, 1988. Bar: Colo. 1989, D.C. 1990; CPA. Ptnr. Law Office Jay Choi, Englewood, Colo., 1989-97; dir. Cohen Brame & Smith, Denver, 1997-98, Burns Figa and Will P.C., 1999—. Commr. Jud. Performance Commn., Aurora, Colo., 1994-98; mem. Multicultural Commn. Colo. Supreme Ct., 1995-97, U.S.-- Korea Com. Bus. Coop., 1996-99. Staff editor: Asia Pacific Lawyers Assn. Jour., 1988. Mem. Colo. delegation Colo./Kangwon-Do 10th Anniversary Sister Statehood, 2001. With USN. Recipient World Friendship award Martin Luther King Commn., 1996, Cmty. Activist award Asian Pacific Devel. Ctr., 1996. Mem. ABA (amb. bus. law sect. 2003—), Colo. Bar Assn. (vice chair internat. law sect. 2002-03). Corporate, general, Private international, Securities. Office: Burns Figa & Will PC Ste 1030 6400 S Fiddlers Green Cir Englewood CO 80111-4957 E-mail: jayjkchoi@aol.com.

CHONG, CLAYTON ELLIOTT, lawyer; b. Hilo, Hawaii, July 6, 1950; s. Wing Kong and Ethel (Ishii) C. BS in Bus., Miami U., Oxford, Ohio, 1972, MBA, 1973; JD, Ohio No. U., 1977. Bar: U.S. Dist. Ct. Hawaii 1978, U.S. Ct. Appeals (9th cir.) 1978. Sole practice, Hilo, 1978-79; ptnr. Chong & Chong, Hilo, 1979—; pres. Island Designs Hawaii, LLC, 2000—. Named Outstanding Young Man of Am. U.S. Jaycees, 1989, YWCA Vol. of the Year, 1988-89, Hawaii Businessman of Yr., 2003. Mem. Hawaii State Bar Assn., Hawaii County Bar Assn., Miami U. Alumni Assn., Ohio No. U. Law Alumni Assn., U. Hawaii Founders Alumni Assn., Lehua Jaycees, Kuilima Jaycees (pres. 1989-90), Lions (pres. Hilo club 1986-87, Lion of Yr.), Delta Theta Phi (dist. chancellor 1983-2001, Hawaii State chancellor 2001—, Clarence W. Pierce award 1983), Delta Sigma Pi (pres. Hawaii Alumni chpt. 1987-89, dist. dir. 1989-92, Hawaii Hall of Fame 1999). Avocation: rock collecting. General practice. Home and Office: PO Box 1483 Hilo HI 96721-1483 E-mail: cechong@aol.com.

CHONG, STEPHEN CHU LING, lawyer; b. Lakewood, Ohio, Aug. 1, 1957; s. Richard Seng Hoon C. and Betty J. (Chong) Wamego; m. Sheryl Kay Horton, Nov. 23, 1984; children: Evan M. G., Erin M.L., Elena M.L., Eric M.K., Ethan M.L. BA, Calvin Coll., 1979; JD, Ohio State U., 1982. Bar: Fla. 1982, U.S. Dist. Ct. (mid. dist.) Fla. 1983, U.S. Ct. Appeals (11th cir.) 1982, U.S. Tax Ct. 1985; bd. cert. real estate lawyer Fla. Bar Bd. Legal Specialization and Edn. Assoc. Caudill, Drage, de Beaubien, Orlando, Fla., 1982-83; shareholder Caudill, Chong & Migliaccio, Winter Garden, Fla., 1983-84; assoc. Thomas R. Rogers & Assocs., Longwood, Fla., 1984-90; of counsel Litchford, Christopher, Orlando, 1990-92; pres., shareholder Marks & Chong, Orlando, 1992-2001; ptnr. Arnold Matheny & Eagan PA, Orlando, 2001—. Mem. nominating bd. City of Orlando, 1993-98, chmn. 1996-97; mem. area bus. com. Naval Tng. Ctr. Reuse Com., Orlando, 1994-95; bd. trustees Minority/Women Bus. Enterprise Alliance, Orlando, 1994-99; chair Realtor Rels. Com., Orlando, 1992-93; presenter in field. Contbr. articles to profl. jours. Mem. cultural diversity com. Orlando Sci. Ctr., 1993-2000; mem. cmty. adv. bd. WMFE-TV/FM, Orlando, 1994-95; mem. adv. bd. Ctrl. Fla. Family, Orlando, 1994-2000; mem. 9th Jud. Cir. Grievance Com., 2002—; pres. Asian Am. C. of C., Orlando, 1993-94; vol. Income Tax Assistance, 1996—; trustee Calvin Coll., Grand Rapids, Mich., 1999—; bd. dirs. Econ. Devel. Commn. of Mid-Fla., Inc., 2001—. Recipient Vision award-Small Bus. Downtown Orlando Partnership, 1994. Mem. ABA, Fla. Bar Assn., Orange County Bar Assn., Christian Legal Soc. Ctr. Fla. (pres. 1999-2000). Presbyterian. Corporate, general, Franchising, Property, real (including real estate development, water). Office: Arnold Matheny & Eagan PA 801 N Magnolia Ave Ste 201 Orlando FL 32803

CHOPIN, L. FRANK, lawyer; b. New Orleans, Apr. 29, 1942; s. Alton Francis and Floretta (Thensted) C.; children: Philip, Alexandra, Christopher. BBA, Loyola U., New Orleans, 1964, JD, 1966; diploma in mil. law, Judge Adv. Gen.'s Sch., U. Va. Sch. Law, 1966; postgrad., Nat. Law Ctr., George Wash. U., 1967-68; LLM in Taxation, U. Miami, Fla., 1976; PhD in Law, Cambridge U., Eng., 1986. Bar: La. 1966, Fla. 1968, Iowa 1980, U.S. Dist. Ct. (so. dist.) Fla. 1968, U.S. Ct. Appeals (5th cir.) 1968. Ptnr. Chopin & Chopin, Miami, 1969-77; assoc. prof. law Drake U., Des Moines, 1979-80; ptnr. Cadwalader, Wickersham & Taft, Palm Beach, Fla., 1980-94, Chopin, Miller & Yudenfreund, Palm Beach, Fla., 1994-98, Chopin & Miller, Palm Beach, Fla., 1999—. Adj. prof. law U. Miami, 1982-96, U. Sherbrooke, Can., 1982-94. Author: The New Residency Rules for Canadian Tax Considerations, 1985; also numerous articles in legal jours. Mem. Housing Fin. Authority; trustee Preservation Found., Palm Beach Community Chest, Inc. Served to capt. U.S. Army, 1966-68. Mem. ABA, Internat. Bar Assn., Fed. Bar Assn., Fla. Bar (tax sect.), Loyola U. Alumni Assn., U. Miami Alumni Assn., St. Thomas More Law Soc., Phi Alpha Delta (charter). Republican. Roman Catholic. Estate taxation, Taxation, general, Personal income taxation. Office: Chopin & Miller 505 S Flagler Dr Ste 300 West Palm Beach FL 33401-5942

CHOPIN, SUSAN GARDINER, lawyer; b. Miami, Fla., Feb. 23, 1947; d. Maurice and Judith (Warden) Gardiner; children: Philip, Alexandra, Christopher. BBA, Loyola U., New Orleans, 1966; JD cum laude, U. Miami, 1972; MLitt (Law), Oxford U., Eng., 1983. Bar: Fla. 1972, Iowa 1979. Sr. law clk. to judge U.S. Dist. Ct. (so. dist.) Fla., Miami, 1972-73; ptnr. Chopin & Chopin, Miami, 1973-77; assoc. prof. law sch. Drake U., Des Moines, 1979-80; pvt. practice law Palm Beach, Fla., 1981—; ptnr. Chopin & Chopin, 1999—2003, Chopin, Chopin & Chopin, 2003—. Lectr. in family law. Editor (mem. editl. bd.): (jour.) Fla. Bar Jour., 1975; editor: (co-chair editl. bd.) Fla. Bar Family Law Commentator, 2000—01. Trustee Preservation Found. of Palm Beach, 1986-89. Mem.: Palm Beach County Bar Assn., Soc. Wig and Robe, Fla. Assn. Women Lawyers, Fed. Bar Assn., Iowa Bar Assn., Fla. Bar Assn., ABA, Phi Alpha Delta, Phi Kappa Phi. State civil litigation, Family and matrimonial, General practice. Office: Esperante Bldg 222 Lakeview Ave Ste 220 West Palm Beach FL 33401-6149

CHOPLIN, JOHN M., II, lawyer; b. Cedar Rapids, Iowa, Nov. 10, 1945; s. John M. and Joyce G. (Mickelson) C.; m. Linda H. Kutchen, Feb. 14, 1969; children: Julie, John, James. BA, Drake U., 1967; JD, U. Mich., 1974. Bar: Ind. 1974, U.S. Dist. Ct. (so. dist.) Ind. 1974, U.S. Ct. Appeals (7th cir.) 1976, U.S. Supreme Ct. 1977, U.S. Ct. Appeals (6th cir.) 1983, U.S. Dist. Ct. (no. dist.) Ind. 1991. Assoc. Wilson, Tabor & Holland, Indpls., 1974-80; ptnr. Norris, Choplin & Schroeder, Indpls., 1980—. Committeeman precinct Carmel Reps., Ind., 1982-84. Served to capt. USAF, 1969-73. Mem. ABA, Ind. Bar Assn., Indpls. Bar Assn., 7th Fed. Cir. Bar Assn., Lawyers-Pilots Bar Assn., Ind. Trial Lawyers Assn., Assn. Trial Lawyers Am., Christian Legal Soc., Phi Beta Kappa, Omicron Delta Kappa. Baptist. Avocations: water sports, tennis, flying. General civil litigation, Insurance, Personal injury (including property damage). Home: 8553 Twin Pointe Cir Indianapolis IN 46236-8903 Office: Norris Choplin & Schroeder 101 W Ohio St Ste 900 Indianapolis IN 46204-4213

CHOSY, JAMES LOUIS, lawyer, brokerage house executive; b. Madison, Wis., Dec. 17, 1963; s. Louis W. and Shirley A. Chosy; m. Julie Knox, Sept. 16, 1995; children: Emma Joy, Annabel. BA, U. Wis., 1986; JD magna cum laude, U. Minn., 1989. Assoc. atty. Dorsey & Whitney, Mpls., 1989—95; corp. atty. Deluxe Corp., Shoreview, Minn., 1995; assoc. gen. counsel, asst. sec. U.S. Bancorp Piper Jaffray, Mpls., 1995—2000, assoc. gen. counsel, corp. sec., 2000—01, mng. dir., gen. counsel, 2001—. Mem.: ACCA, SIA, ABA. Securities, Corporate, general. Office: US Bancorp Piper Jaffray 800 Nicollet Mall J1012057 Minneapolis MN 55402 Office Fax: 612-303-1772. Business E-Mail: jchosy@pjc.com.

CHOUKAS-BRADLEY, JAMES RICHARD, lawyer; b. Hartford, Conn., Sept. 11, 1950; s. William Lee and Paula Ann (Elliott) Bradley; m. Melanie Rose Choukas, June 21, 1975; children: Sophia Crane, Jesse Elliott. BA cum laude, U. Vt., 1974; JD cum laude, Georgetown U., 1980. Bar: D.C. 1980, U.S. Ct. Appeals (D.C. cir.) 1981, U.S. Ct. Appeals (11th cir.) 1984, U.S. Ct. Appeals (10th cir.) 1985, U.S. Ct. Appeals (4th cir.) 1990, U.S. Ct. Appeals (6th cir.) 1993. Reporter, editor The Berlin (N.H.) Reporter, The Groveton (N.H.) News, The Northland News, 1973—74; editor, pub., creative dir. Ad Lib, Gorham, NH, 1974—75; asst. to city mgr. City of Berlin, 1975—77; contbg. reporter The Lewiston (Maine) Sun, 1976; legal intern Congl. Budget Office, Washington, 1978; rsch. assoc. Schlossberg-Cassidy & Assocs., Washington, 1978—80; assoc. Miller, Balis & O'Neil, P.C., Washington, 1980—84, mem., v.p., 1985—, exec. com., 1993—97. Legal advisor, first v.p. Sugarloaf Citizens Assn., Barnesville, Md., 1987-2000; counsel Mcpl. Gas Authority of Ga., Natural Gas Acquisition Corp. of City of Clarksville, Tenn., S.E. Ala. Gas Dist., Mcpl. Gas Authority of Miss.; gen. counsel Tenn. Energy Acquisition Corp., Lower Ala. Gas Dist.; spkr. in field; pioneer in joint action and pub. financing in deregulated natural gas industry. Author: The Early Days, 1975. Pres. D.C. Dukes Athletic Club, Washington, 1978-81, Montgomery Dukes, 1987-92; com. chmn. Berlin Bicentennial Commn., Berlin, 1975-76; youth soccer and flag football coach Seneca Sports Assn., 1999-. Regents scholar State of N.Y., 1968. Mem.: Hist. Medley Dist., Energy Bar Assn., For A Rural Montgomery, Nat. Youth Sports Coaches Assn., Sugarloaf Citizens Assn., Randolph Mountain Club, Phi Beta Kappa. Avocations: softball, guitar, songwriting, hiking, travel. Administrative and regulatory, FERC practice, Oil, gas, and mineral. E-mail: jchoukasbradley@mbolaw.com.

CHOVANES, EUGENE, lawyer; b. Hazleton, Penn., Jan. 1, 1926; s. Michael and Anna (Watro) C.; m. Claire Amelia Puhak, Mar. 27, 1952; children: Michael, George, Nicholas, Joseph, John. BS in Engring., Lehigh U., 1950; JD, Villanova U., 1960. Bar: Pa. 1961. Assoc. William Steell Jackson & Sons, Phila., 1957-63; ptnr. Jackson & Chovanes, Phila. and Bala-Cynwyd, Pa., 1963—. Lectr. patent law Villanova U., 1957-80. Sgt. U.S. Army, 1943-46, to 1st lt. Ordnance Corps, 1951-52. Mem. ABA, Phila. Intellectual Property Law Assn., Phila. Bar Assn., Soc. Registered Profl. Engrs., Am. Intellectual Property Law Assn. Patent, Trademark and copyright. Office: 1 Bala Plz Ste 319 Bala Cynwyd PA 19004-1405

CHOW, AMY HAU KUEN, lawyer, contract negotiator, consultant; b. Hong Kong, May 31, 1963; d. Yun-Yin and Lin-Wan (Wong) C. B in Social Scis., U. Hong Kong, 1985; M in Japanese Bus. Studies, Chaminade U., Honolulu, Hawaii, 1987; B in Law, Beijing (China) U., 1996. Bar: solicitor Hong Kong, solicitor Eng. and Wales. Tchg. asst. Chinese U. of Hong Kong, 1985-86; officer Fuji Bank Ltd., Hong Kong, 1987-88; asst. to gen. mgr. Internat. Broadway Devel. Co., Ltd., Hong Kong, 1988-90; trainee solicitor Peter C. Hong, Chow & Chow Solicitors, Hong Kong, 1992-94; solictor and

China gen. counsel Counselors at Large Ltd., Hong Kong, 1994-95; sr. contract consultant Hewlett Packard Asia Pacific Ltd., Hong Kong, 1995-98; asst. solicitor Johnston Stokes & Master, Hong Kong, 1998, Jewkes Chan & Ptnrs., Hong Kong, 1999; legal mgr. Beijing Oriental Plaza Co., Beijing, 1999-2001; asst. v.p. contract mgmt. PCCW, Ltd., Hong Kong, 2001—. Bd. dirs. Chediston Co., Ltd., Hong Kong, 1993—; cons. Cal Internat. Ltd., Hong Kong, 1996-97. Sec. The Incorporated Owners of Happy Ct., Hong Kong, 1995-97; chairlady The Inc. Owners of Happy Ct., Hong Kong, 1997-98; mem. St. Andrew's Ch. Choir. Named Model Teenager of Hong Kong, Island Jaycees, Hong Kong, 1978; recipient Fujitsu scholarship, Fujitsu Ltd., Honolulu, Tokyo, 1986-87. Mem. Law Soc. of Hong Kong, Hong Kong China Lawyers Tng. Course Alumni Ltd. (bd. dirs. 1994—), Rotary Club of Happy Valley Hong Kong (v.p. 1998-99, dir. cmty. svcs. 1996-98, dir. club svcs. 2002-03). Mem. Anglican Ch. Avocations: squash, badminton, swimming, scuba diving. Home: Flat A 6th Fl Happy Ct 39E Sing Woo Rd H Valley Hong Kong Hong Kong

CHOW, STANLEY, lawyer; B in Commerce with honors, Queen's U., Kingston, Ont., Can., 1986; LLB with honors, U. Toronto, Ont., 1989. Bar: B.C. (barrister and solicitor) 1994, Ont. 1991, Eng. and Wales (solicitor) 1994, Hong Kong 1995. Assoc. Aird & Berlis, Toronto, 1991—93, Boughton Peterson Yang Anderson, Hong Kong, 1994—95; sr. mgr. listing divsn. The Stock Exch. Hong Kong Ltd., 1995—96; assoc. Allen & Overy, Hong Kong, 1996, cons., 1999, ptnr., 2000. Mem.: Law Soc. Eng. and Wales, Law Soc. Hong Kong. Securities, Mergers and acquisitions, Corporate, general. Office: Allen & Overy Three Exch Sq 9th Fl Hong Kong Hong Kong

CHOW, STEPHEN Y(EE), lawyer; b. Cleve., Miss., Sept. 8, 1952; s. Chester H. and June (Eng) C.; children: Astrid Crockett, Augustus Stephen. AB cum laude, SM in Applied Physics, Harvard U., 1975; JD, Columbia U., 1979. Bar: N.Y. 1980, Mass. 1983, U.S. Supreme Ct. 1983, U.S. Patent Office 1984. Assoc. Donovan Leisure Newton & Irvine, N.Y.C., 1979-82, Gaston Snow & Ely Bartlett, Boston, 1982-85, Cesari and McKenna, Boston, 1985-88; ptnr. Nutter, McClennen & Fish, Boston, 1988-90, Cesari and McKenna, Boston, 1990-93, Perkins, Smith & Cohen, Boston, 1993—. Adj. faculty Suffolk U. Law Sch., 1995—; mem. Nat. Conf. Commrs. on Uniform State Laws, 1994—; Nat. Conf. Drafting Com. Uniform Comml. Code, 1995—, Drafting Com. Uniform Electronic Transactions Act, 1996—; mem. study com. on taxation of electronic commerce; mem. Mass. Jud. Nom. Commn., 2003—. Author: E-Commerce and Communications, 2002; bd. editors Mass. Law Rev., 1991-98. Trustee Hawthorne Pl. Condominium Trust, Boston, 1985-92; spl. asst. dist. atty. N.Y. County, 1980-82. Mem. ABA, IEEE, Am. Intellectual Property Law Assn. (chmn. uniform comml. code com. 1997-99), Am. Law Inst. (elected), Mass. Bar Assn. (chmn. uniform comml. code project 1990-98, chmn. banking and comml. law com. 1998—), Licensing Execs. Soc. (chmn. uniform comml. code com. 1991-93), Boston Bar Assn. (chmn. intellectual property com. 1991-95, mem. governing coun. 1994-96), N.Y.C. Bar Assn., Boston Patent Law Assn. (chmn. trade secrets law com. 1996—), Assn. Computing Machinery (chmn. ad hoc com. on software patenting 1991-93), Asian Am. Law Assn. Mass. (dir.), Boston Racquet Club. Republican. Avocations: painting, squash, sculling. Computer, Private international, Patent. Home: 9 Hawthorne Pl Boston MA 02114-2344 Office: Perkins Smith & Cohen LLP One Beacon St Boston MA 02108

CHOY, HERBERT YOUNG CHO, federal judge; b. Makaweli, Hawaii, Jan. 6, 1916; s. Doo Wook and Helen (Nahm) Choy; m. Dorothy Helen Shular, June 16, 1945. BA, U. Hawaii, 1938; JD, Harvard U., 1941. Bar: Hawaii 1941. Law clk. City and County of Honolulu, 1941; assoc. Fong & Miho, 1947—48; ptnr. Fong, Miho and Choy, 1948—57; atty. gen. Territory of Hawaii, 1957—58; ptnr. Fong, Miho, Choy & Robinson, Honolulu, 1958—71; sr. judge U.S. Ct. Appeals (9th cir.), Honolulu, 1971—. Adv. com. on constrn. judiciary bldgs. Chief Justice Hawaii, 1970—71; compilation commn. to compile Revised Laws of Hawaii, 1955, 1953—57; com. to draft Hawaii rules of criminal procedure Supreme Ct., 1958—59; com. on pacific ocean territories Jud. Conf. of U.S., 1976—79. Dir. Legal Aid Soc. Hawaii, 1959—61; trustee Hawaii Loa Coll., 1963—79. Capt. U.S. Army, 1941—46, lt. col. USAR. Recipient Order of Merit award, Republic of Korea, 1973. Fellow: Am. Bar Found.; mem.: ABA, Hawaii Bar Assn. (exec. com. 1953, 1957, 1961, legal ethics and unauthorized practices com. 1953, com. on legis. 1959). Office: US Ct Appeals 300 Ala Moana Blvd Rm C305 Honolulu HI 96850-0305

CHRISS, TIMOTHY D.A. lawyer; b. Balt., Oct. 26, 1950; s. Evan Alevizatos and Ceres (Rogokos) C.; m. Karin Elizabeth Jones, Feb. 25, 1978; children: Alexander Wilhelm Alevizatos, Caroline Elizabeth. BA, Washington and Lee U., 1972; JD, Cath. U. Am., 1976. Bar: Md. 1976, U.S. Dist. Ct. Md. 1976. Assoc. Gordon, Feinblatt, Rothman, Hoffberger & Hollander, Balt., 1976-83, ptnr., 1983—. Com. on character Ct. Appeals Md., 1991—. Fellow: Md. Bar Found.; mem.: ABA, Bar Assn. Balt. City (exec. coun. 1988—90), Md. Bar Assn. (coun. real property sect. 1988—2000, sec. 1992—94, chmn.-elect 1994—96, chmn. 1996—98, chmn. real property code revision com. 1988—92), Am. Coll. Real Estate Lawyers, Balt. City C. of C. (bd. dirs. 1993—2002), Md. Club, Ctr. Club, Balt. Country Club (bd. govs. 2001—). Republican. Greek Orthodox. Corporate, general, Landlord-tenant, Property, real (including real estate development, water). Office: Gordon Feinblatt Rothman Hoffberger & Hollander 233 E Redwood St Baltimore MD 21202-3332 E-mail: tchriss@gfrlaw.com.

CHRISTALDI, BRIAN, lawyer; b. Passaic, N.J., June 8, 1940; s. Peter Samuel and Helen (O'Brien) C.; m. Amy Edmonds, May 4, 1968; children: Kevin, Justin. BA, Amherst Coll., 1962; LLB, Harvard U., 1965. Bar: D.C. 1966, N.Y. 1967, Calif. 1988. Maxwell Pub. Svc. fellow, Papua, Guinea, 1965—66; with legal dept. Allied Chem. Corp., N.Y.C., 1967-69; assoc. then ptnr. Kelley Drye & Warren, N.Y.C., 1969-1995; counsel Kaye, Scholer, Fierman, Hays & Handler, LLP, N.Y.C., 1995-97; sr. comml. counsel, later asst. gen. counsel, then assoc. gen. counsel project fin. Overseas Pvt. Investment Corp., Washington, 1997—. Finance, Private international, Public international. Home: 4031 Oliver St Chevy Chase MD 20815-3432 Office: Overseas Pvt Investment Corp 1100 New York Ave NW Washington DC 20527-0001 E-mail: bchri@opic.gov.

CHRISTENFELD, ALAN M. lawyer; b. N.Y.C., Apr. 19, 1951; s. Paul and Renee Christenfeld. BA, Bowdoin Coll., 1974; JD, Cornell U., 1976; LLM in Taxation, NYU, 1978. Bar: N.Y. 1977, U.S. Dist. Ct. (ea. and so. dists.) 1978, U.S. Dist. Ct. Ariz. 1994, U.S. Dist. Ct. D.C. 1998, U.S. Ct. Appeals (2d cir.) 1978). Assoc. Rathheim, Hoffman, Kassel & Silverman, N.Y.C., 1978-83, ptnr., 1984-86, Sidley & Austin, N.Y.C., 1987-90, Rosenman & Colin, N.Y.C., 1991-93, Clifford Chance US, N.Y.C., 1994—. Co-author bi-monthly column N.Y. Law Jour., 1996—; contbr. chpt. to book, articles to profl. jours. Mem. gov.'s bd. Comml. Fin. Assn. Edn. Found., N.Y.C., 1992—; mem. exec. bd. Assn. Comml. fin. Attys., N.Y.C., 1992—. Fellow Am. Coll. Comml. Fin. Lawyers. Avocations: american history, classical music, ice hockey. Banking, Bankruptcy, Commercial, contracts (including sales of goods; commercial financing). Office: Clifford Chance US 200 Park Ave New York NY 10166-0800 E-mail: alan.christenfeld@cliffordchance.com.

CHRISTENSEN, CHARLES BROPHY, lawyer; b. Altadena, Calif., July 3, 1948; s. Charles Warren and Barbara Louise (Kruger) C.; m. Susan Marie Stricklin, Aug. 22, 1970; children: Charles Brophy, Michelle K., Courtney Marie, Timothy Patrick. BA in Biology, Claremont Men's Coll., Calif., 1970; JD, U. San Diego, 1973. Bar: Calif. 1973, U.S. Dist. Ct. (so. dist.) Calif. 1973, U.S. Dist. Ct. (cen. dist.) Calif. 1994, U.S. Ct. Appeals (9th cir.) 1995, U.S. Supreme Ct. 1997. Assoc. Biafora & Weiner, Reseda, Calif., 1974-76; ptnr. Biafora, Weiner & Christensen, Reseda, 1977-78; gen. counsel Charles W. Christensen & Assocs., San Diego, 1978-90; ptnr. Detisch, Christensen & Wood, San Diego, 1983-95, Detisch & Christensen, San Diego, 1995—2002; mng. ptnr. Christensen Schwerdtfeger & Spath LLP, San Diego, 2002—. Mem. ABA, San Diego County Bar Assn. Republican. Roman Catholic. Avocations: golf, tennis. State civil litigation, Insurance. Home: 2684 Jonquil Dr San Diego CA 92106-1135 Office: Christensen Schwerdtfeger & Spath LLP 444 W C St Ste 200 San Diego CA 92101-3582 E-mail: cbc@csslawllp.com.

CHRISTENSEN, HENRY, III, lawyer; b. Jersey City, Nov. 8, 1944; s. Henry Jr. and M. Louise (Brooke) C.; m. Constance L. Cumpton, July 1, 1967; children: Alexander, Gustavus, Elizabeth, Katherine. BA, Yale U., 1966; JD, Harvard U., 1969. Bar: N.Y. 1970, U.S. Tax Ct. 1973, U.S. Ct. Appeals (2d. cir.) 1973, U.S. Supreme Ct. 1975. Assoc. Sullivan & Cromwell, N.Y.C., 1969-77, ptnr., 1977—. Adj. assoc. prof. NYU, N.Y.C., 1985-88, U. of Miami Law Sch., 1997—. Author: International Estate Planning, 1999, ann. supplements, 1999—; contbr. articles to profl. jours. Chmn. Prospect Park Alliance, Bklyn., 1985—; trustee, 1st vice chmn. Peddie Sch., Hightstown, N.J., 1986—; trustee Am. Fund for the Tate Gallery, 1987—, Bklyn. Acad. Music, 1992—, Vincent Astor Found., 1993—, Alex Hillman Family Found., 2000—, Friends of the Prince's Trust, 2001—; dir., sec. Freedom Inst., N.Y.C., 1980—; dir., v.p. Am. Friends of Whitechapel Art Gallery Found., 1991—; trustee, mem. exec. com. Am. Ctr. Oriental Rsch. in Amman, 1993—. Fellow Am. Coll. Trust and Estate Counsel (chmn. internat. estate planning com. 2003—; mem. N.Y. State Bar Assn. (chmn. estate and gift tax com. 1983-84, chmn. exempt orgn. com. 1986, chmn. income taxation of trusts com. 1984-85, 87-89, exec. com. tax sect. 1983-89), Internat. Acad. Estate and Trust Law (academician). Probate (including wills, trusts), Estate taxation, Personal income taxation. Home: 35 Prospect Park W Apt 8/9B Brooklyn NY 11215-2370 Office: Sullivan & Cromwell 125 Broad St Fl 29 New York NY 10004-2498

CHRISTENSEN, KAREN KAY, lawyer; b. Ann Arbor, Mich., Mar. 9, 1947; d. Jack Edward and Evangeline (Pitsch) C.; m. Kenneth Robert Kay, Sept. 2, 1977; children: Jeffrey Smithson, Braden, Bergen. BS, U. Mich., 1969; JD, U. Denver, 1975. Bar: Colo. 1975, D.C. 1976, U.S. Supreme Ct. 1979. Atty., advisor office of dep. atty. gen. U.S. Dept. of Justice, Washington, 1975-76, trial atty. civil rights div., 1976-79; legis. counsel ACLU, Washington, 1979-80; staff atty. D.C. Pub. Defender Service, Washington, 1980-85; asst. gen. counsel Nat. Pub. Radio, Washington, 1985-93; gen. counsel Nat. Endowment Arts, Washington, 1993-98, acting dep. chmn. for grants and partnership, 1997-98, dep. chmn. grants and awards, 1998—2001; arts cons., 2002—. Mem. D.C. Bd. Profl. Responsibility, 1990-98, chair, 1996-98; arts cons. Bd. dirs. Corcoran Art Mus., 2001—, Liz Lerman Dance Exchange, 2002—. Mem. D.C. Bar Assn., NCA/ACLU (exec. bd. 1986-93, chair 1993), Phi Beta Kappa. Civil rights, Communications, Criminal.

CHRISTENSEN, PATRICIA ANNE WATKINS, lawyer; b. Corpus Christi, Tex., June 24, 1947; d. Owen Milton Jr. and Margaret (McFarland) Watkins; m. Steven Ray Christensen, May 28, 1977 (dec. 1985); children: Geoffrey Holland, Jeremy Ladd. BS, U. North Tex., 1971; JD, U. Houston, 1977. Bar: Utah 1977, Tex. 1977, U.S. Dist. Ct. Utah 1977, U.S. Ct. Appeals (10th cir.) 1977, U.S. Supreme Ct. 1990. Assoc. Berman & Giauque, Salt Lake City, 1977-80; ptnr. Parr, Waddoups, Brown, Gee & Loveless, Salt Lake City, 1980—, pres., 1991-93, 2002—. Adj. prof. law U. Utah Law Sch., Salt Lake City, 1979-81; judge pro tem Third Dist. Ct., 1995—. Legis. asst. U.S. Senate, 1970-74; bd. dirs. Comml. Law Affiliate, 1997-2001, co-chair litigation sect.; trustee Rowland Hall St. Mark's Sch., chair devel. com., 1987-90; mem. steering com., comprehensive capital campaign U. Utah Sch. Nursing; mem. steering com. Utah Electronic Law Project. Named Utah Woman Lawyer of Yr., 1992. Mem. ABA, Utah State Bar (Dorothy Merrill Brothers award 1996), State Bar of Tex., Salt Lake County Bar Assn. (exec. com. 1979-87, author editor Utah Lawyers Practice Manual 1986), Women Lawyers Utah (pres. 1988-89, bd. dirs. 1987-90), Phi Delta Phi, Delta Gamma, Alpha Lambda Delta. Avocations: hiking, mountain biking, writing, travel, languages. Federal civil litigation, State civil litigation. Office: Parr Waddoups Brown Gee & Loveless 185 S State St Ste 1300 Salt Lake City UT 84111-1537 E-mail: pwc@pwlaw.com.

CHRISTENSEN, RAY RICHARDS, lawyer; b. Salt Lake City, July 7, 1922; s. E.R. and Carrie (Richards) C.; m. Carolyn Crawford, July 9, 1954 (dec. 1986); children: Carlie, Paul Ray, Joan, Eric.; m. Jeanne F. Pyke, June 24, 1989. LL.B., U. Utah, 1944. Bar: Utah 1944. Enforcement atty. OPA, 1946; law clk. to Utah Supreme Ct. Justice Wolfe, 1947-48; practice in Salt Lake City, 1949—; ptnr. Christensen & Jensen, P.C. (and predecessors), 1949—. Mem. Utah Bar Commn., 1963-66. Bd. dirs. Salt Lake City Jr. C. of C., 1949-53, v.p., 1950-52. Served with AUS, 1943-46. Fellow Internat. Acad. Trial Lawyers (bd. dirs. 1982-88), Am. Coll. Trial Lawyers (state chmn. 1984-85); mem. ABA (mem. council jr. bar conf. 1952-56, ho. of dels. 1966-68, 73-79, mem. council bar activities sect. 1967-70), Utah State Bar (pres. 1965-66, Utah Lawyer of Yr. 1981, Utah Trial Lawyer of Yr. 1993), Salt Lake County Bar Assn., Western States Bar Conf. (pres. 1969-70), Internat. Assn. Def. Counsel, Fedn. Defense and Corp. Counsel, Phi Eta Sigma, Phi Kappa Phi. Federal civil litigation, State civil litigation, Product liability. Home: 992 Oak Hills Way Salt Lake City UT 84108-2022 Office: Christensen & Jensen PC 50 S Main St Ste 1500 Salt Lake City UT 84144-2044 E-mail: ray.christensen@chrisjen.com.

CHRISTENSEN, ROBERT PAUL, lawyer; b. Mpls., June 26, 1949; s. Otto and Cora Alice C.; m. Cindy G. Christensen, July 15, 1972; children: Nicholas, Lindsey, Callie. BA, U. Minn., 1971, JD cum laude, 1974. Ptnr. Carlsen, Greiner & Law, Mpls., 1974-86, Dunkley, Bennett Christensen & Madigan, Mpls., 1986—. Mem. Minn. Trial Lawyers Assn. (bd. dirs. 1986-96), Creative Dispute Resolution Assn. (bd. dirs. 1995-97, pres. 1998—), Coll. of Master Advocates & Barristers, NBTA 1993-, Million Dollar Advocates Forum, 1997-. General civil litigation, Personal injury (including property damage), Product liability. Office: Dunkley Bennett Christensen& Madigan PA 701 4th Ave S Ste 700 Minneapolis MN 55415-1812 E-mail: rpchristensen@visi.com.

CHRISTENSON, GORDON A. law educator; b. Salt Lake City, June 22, 1932; s. Gordon B. and Ruth Arzella (Anderson) C.; m. Katherine Joy deMik, Nov. 2, 1951 (div. 1977); children: Gordon Scott, Marjorie Lynne, Ruth Ann, Nanette; m. Fabienne Fadeley, Sept. 16, 1979. BS in Law, U. Utah, 1955, JD, 1956; SJD, George Washington U., 1961. Bar: Utah 1956, U.S. Supreme Ct. 1971, D.C. 1978. Law clk. to chief justice Utah Supreme Ct., 1956-57; assoc. firm Christenson & Callister, Salt Lake City, 1956-58; atty. Dept. of Army, Nat. Guard Bur., Washington, 1957-58; atty., acting asst. legal adviser Office of Legal Adviser, U.S. Dept. State, Washington, 1958-62; asst. gen. counsel for sci. and tech. U.S. Dept. Commerce, 1962-67, spl. asst. to undersec. of commerce, 1967, counsel to commerce tech. adv. bd., 1962-67, chmn. task force on telecommunications missions and orgn., 1967, counsel to panel on engring. and commodity standards, tech. adv. bd., 1963-65; assoc. prof. law U. Okla., Norman, 1967-70, exec. asst. to pres., 1967-70; univ. dean for ednl. devel., central adminstrn. State U. N.Y., Albany, 1970-71; prof. law Am. U. Law Sch., Washington, 1971-79, dean, 1971-77; on leave, 1977-79; Charles H. Stockton prof. internat. law U.S. Naval War Coll., Newport, R.I., 1977-79; dean, Nippert prof. law U. Cin. Coll. Law, 1979-85, univ. prof. law, 1985-99, prof. emeritus, dean emeritus, 1999—. Assoc. professorial lectr. in internat. affairs George Washington U., 1961-67; vis. scholar Harvard U. Law Sch., 1977-78, Yale Law Sch., 1985-86, Law Sch. U. Maine, Portland, 1997; Wallace S. Fujiyama vis. disting. prof. law Univ. Hawaii Law Sch., 1997; participant summer confs. on internat. law Cornell Law Sch., Ithaca, N.Y., 1962, 64; cons. in internat. law U.S. Naval War Coll., Newport, R.I., 1969; faculty mem., reporter seminars for experienced fed. dist. judges Fed. Jud. Center, Washington, 1972-77. Author: (with Richard B. Lillich) International Claims: Their Preparation and Presentation, 1962, The Future of the University, 1969; Contbr. articles to legal jours. Cons. to Center for Policy Alternatives Mass. Inst. Tech., Cambridge, 1970-81; mem. intergovtl. com. on Internat. Policy on Weather Modification, 1967; Vice pres. Procedural Aspects of Internat. Law Inst., N.Y.C., 1962-2001, trustee, 1962—. Served with intelligence sect. USAF, 1951-52, Japan. Recipient Silver Medal award Dept. Commerce, 1967; fellow Grad. Sch. U. Cin. Mem. Am. Soc. Internat. Law (mem. panel on state responsibility), Utah Bar Assn., Cin. Bar Assn., Order of Coif, Phi Delta Phi, Kappa Sigma. Clubs: Literary (Cin.); Cosmos (Washington). Home and Office: 3465 Principio Ave Cincinnati OH 45208-4242 E-mail: christga@msn.com.

CHRISTIAN, BETTY JO, lawyer; b. Temple, Tex., July 27, 1936; d. Joe and Mattie Manor (Brown) Wiest; m. Ernest S. Christian, Jr., Dec. 24, 1960. BA summa cum laude, U. Tex., 1957, LL.B. summa cum laude, 1960. Bar: Tex. 1961, U.S. Supreme Ct. 1964, D.C. 1980. Law clk. Supreme Ct. Tex., 1960-61; atty. ICC, 1961-68, asst. gen. counsel, 1970-72, assoc. gen. counsel, 1972-76, commr., 1976-79; ptnr. Steptoe & Johnson, Washington, 1980—. Atty. Labor Dept., Dallas, 1968-70 Fellow Am. Bar Found., Tex. Bar Found.; mem. ABA, FBA (Younger Fed. Lawyer award 1964), Tex. Bar Assn., Am. Law Inst., Am. Acad Appellate Lawyers, Adminstrv. Conf. U.S., City Tavern Club. Administrative and regulatory, Federal civil litigation, Transportation. Office: 1330 Connecticut Ave NW Washington DC 20036-1704 E-mail: bchristi@steptoe.com.

CHRISTIAN, ERNEST SILSBEE, JR., lawyer; b. Gonzales, Tex., Jan. 15, 1937; s. Ernest Silsbee and Ruby Ruth (Hamon) Christian; m. Betty Jo Wiest, Dec. 24, 1960. LLB cum laude, U. Tex., 1961. Bar: Tex. 1961, D.C. 1961, U.S. Supreme Ct. 1978. Atty. Treasury Dept., Washington, 1970-72, tax legis. counsel, 1973-74, dep. asst. sec. treasury (tax policy), 1974-75; ptnr. Patton, Boggs & Blow, Washington, 1975-94, E.S. Christian, 1995—. Mem.: ABA, Am. Law Inst. Republican. Home: Willows Farm PO Box 1140 Union Bridge MD 21791-0582 Office: 800 Connecticut Ave NW Washington DC 20006-2709

CHRISTIAN, GARY IRVIN, lawyer; b. Albany, Ga., July 7, 1951; s. Rupert Irvin and Alice Amelia (Smith) C.; 1 child, Amy Margaret. BA in History, Polit. Sci., David Lipscomb Coll., 1973; MPA, U. Tenn., 1974; JD, Vanderbilt U., 1979. Bar: Fla. 1979, U.S. Dist. Ct. (no. and mid. dists.) Fla 1979. Rsch. dir. Ala. League of Mcpls., Montgomery, 1974-76; instr. in pub. adminstrn. David Lipscomb Coll., Nashville, 1977-79; assoc. Rogers, Towers, Bailey, Jones & Gay, Jacksonville, Fla., 1979-83, Foley & Lardner, Jacksonville, 1983-86; ptnr. Christian, Prom, Korn & Zehmer, Jacksonville, 1986-92, Rumph, Stoddard & Christian, Jacksonville, 1992—. Editor-in-chief Vanderbilt Jour. of Transnational Law, 1978-79. Bd. dirs. PACE Ctr. for Girls, Inc., Jacksonville, 1984-92, pres., 1984-86; mem. Leadership Jacksonville, 1986-87; chmn. site selection com. St. Johns County Sch. Bd., 1993-95; mem. site selection com., St. Johns County Sch. Bd., 1989-91. Mem. ABA (condominiums and planned devels. com.), Jacksonville Bar Assn. (coord. continuing edn. 1984-85, vice chmn. real property sect. 1986-87, chmn. 1987-88, chmn. corps., banking & bus. sect. 1991-92), Wavemasters Soc. (pres. 1986-87), Jacksonville C. of C. (com. 100 1986-94), Southpoint Bus. Assn. (bd. dirs. 1990-2001, pres. 1991-93), Oak Bridge Country Club, Seminole Club, Salt Creek Homeowners Assn. (bd. dirs. 1993-97, pres. 1994-96), Univ. Club, Deer Creek Country Club. Republican. Mem. Ch. of Christ. Avocations: golf, fishing, racquetball, hunting, stamp collecting. Banking, Commercial, contracts (including sales of goods; commercial financing), Property, real (including real estate development, water). Home: 1719 Girvin Rd Jacksonville FL 32225-2620 Office: Rumph Stoddard & Christian 3100 University Blvd S Ste 101 Jacksonville FL 32216-2777

CHRISTIAN, JOHN CATLETT, JR., lawyer; b. Springfield, Mo., Sept. 12, 1929; s. John Catlett and Alice Odelle (Milling) C.; m. Peggy Jeanne Cain, Apr. 12, 1953; children: Cathleen Marie, John Catlett, Alice Cain. AB, Drury Coll., 1951; LLB, Tulane U., 1956. Bar: La. 1956, Mo. 1956, U.S. Supreme Ct. 1975. Assoc. Porter & Stewart, Lake Charles, La., 1956-58, Wilkinson, Lewis, Wilkinson & Madison, Shreveport, La., 1958-62, ptnr., 1962-64, Milling, Benson, Woodward, Hillyer, Pierson & Miller, New Orleans, 1964-92, of counsel, 1993-94. Pres. Sherburne Land Co., 1974-83, Pointe-Martin Mgmt., Inc., 1990-2000; dir. Emerald Land Corp. Pres. Kathleen Elizabeth O'Brien Found., 1963—. Served with USMCR, 1951-53. Fellow Am. Coll. Trial Lawyers; mem. ABA, Fed. Bar Assn., Mo. Bar Assn., La. Bar Assn., La. Landowners Assn. (bd. dirs. 1983-2001), Boston Club, Beau Chene Country Club, Kappa Alpha Order, Omicron Delta Kappa, Phi Delta Phi. Home: 807 Tete Lours Dr Mandeville LA 70471-1774 Office: PO Box 1317 Mandeville LA 70470-1317 E-mail: jcchristiansr@aol.com.

CHRISTIAN, WARREN HAROLD, JR., lawyer; b. Greenville, S.C., June 11, 1949; s. Warren Harold Sr. and Doris Marie (Hopkins) C.; m. Connie Sue Collett, June 19, 1971; children: Matthew, Joshua, Jill. BA, Carson Newman Coll., 1971; JD, U. S.C., 1975. Bar: S.C. 1975, U.S. Dist. Ct. S.C. 1977, U.S. Ct. Appeals (4th cir.) 1982. Assoc. Law Offices of John Bolt Culbertson, Greenville, 1975-80; ptnr. Christian & Davis, Greenville, 1980—. Vis. instr. paralegal program Greenville Tech. Edn. Ctr. Coach youth soccer teams YMCA; v.p. Dem. precinct, 1978; mem. sch. bd. Shannon Forest Christian Sch., 1990-97, chmn., 1995-97. Named one of Outstanding Young Men of Am., U.S. Jaycees, 1978. Mem. S.C. Trial Lawyers Assn. (sustaining mem.), ATLA (sustaining mem.), S.C. Bar Assn. (spkr. S.C. Workers Compensation Seminar 1984, 87), Greenville County Bar Assn. Baptist. Avocations: basketball, tennis. Personal injury (including property damage), Workers' compensation. Home: 33 Bateswood Dr Greer SC 29651-7681 Office: Christian & Davis PO Box 332 1007 E Washington St Greenville SC 29601-3128

CHRISTIANSEN, KEITH ALLAN, lawyer; b. Madison, Wis., Dec. 14, 1943; s. Herman Louis and Faith Louise (Haase) C.; m. Sheila Irene Stangel, Apr. 11, 1966; children: Douglas, Jeffrey. BS, U. Wis., 1965, JD, 1968. Bar: Wis. 1968, Fla. 1973, U.S. Dist. Ct. (ea. dist.) Wis. 1968. Assoc. Foley & Lardner, Milw., 1968-74, ptnr., 1975—. Co-author: Marital Property Law in Wisconsin, 1984, supplements. Active Potawatomi Coun. Boy Scouts Am. (past pres.), 1975—; v.p. Ctrl. Region Boy Scouts. Am., 1992—. Fellow Am. Coll. Trust & Estate Counselors; mem. Mid-winter Estate Planning Clinic, Estate Counselors Forum. Republican. Estate planning, Probate (including wills, trusts), Estate taxation. Office: Foley & Lardner 777 E Wisconsin Ave Ste 3800 Milwaukee WI 53202-5367 E-mail: kchristiansen@foleylaw.com.

CHRISTIANSEN, MARK D. lawyer; b. Olney, Tex., June 10, 1955; s. Leon H. and Doris J. (Jennings) C. BA, U. Okla., 1977, JD, 1980. Bar: U.S. Dist. Ct. (we. dist.) Okla. 1984, U.S. Dist. Ct. (ea. dist.) Okla. 1993, U.S. Ct. Appeals (10th cir.) 1987. Assoc. Crowe & Dunlevy, Oklahoma City, 1980-85, mem., 1986—. Editor: The Oil and Gas Reporter. Mem.: ABA (chmn. energy and natural resources litigation 2001—, chmn. oil and natural gas exploration and prodn. com. 1999—2001), Okla. Bar Assn., Oklahoma City Mineral Lawyers Soc. (pres. 1989—90). General civil litigation, Oil, gas, and mineral. Home: 20 N Broadway Ave Ste 1800 Oklahoma City OK 73102-8296 Office: Crowe & Dunlevy Mid America Tower 20 N Broadway Ave Ste 1800 Oklahoma City OK 73102-8273

CHRISTIANSEN, PATRICK T. lawyer; b. Mpls., 1947; BSEE summa cum laude, U. Notre Dame, 1969; JD, Harvard U., 1972. Bar: Fla. 1972, Minn. 1974, U.S. Tax Ct. 1977, U.S. Supreme Ct. 1980. Mem. Akerman, Senterfitt & Eidson P.A., Orlando, Fla. Chmn. bd. Orlando Mus. Art; mem., bd. dirs. The Greater Orlando C. of C., Jobs and Edn. Partnership; chmn. Orange County Transp. Roundtable, BusinessForce, 2002--; mem. Orange County Blue Ribbon Commn., steering com., chmn. transp. com.; bd. dirs. United Arts Cen. Fla., Orlando Downtown Devel. Bd.; trustee, chmn. Orlando Repertory Theatre, 2002--, U. Ctrl. Fla. Found., 2001--; bd. trustees U. Ctrl. Fla.; mem. Orange County Arts & Cultural Affairs Adv. Com., chmn. advancement com., 2001--. Mem. ABA (sects. on bus. law, taxation, real property), Fla. Bar (trial lawyers sect., co-chmn. land trust com. real property, probate and trust law sect. 1978-82, dir. real property divsn. 1982-84, vice chmn. 1984-85, chmn. 1985-86, vice-chmn. UCC subcom. corp., banking and bus. law sect. 1979-84, bd. govs. young lawyers sect. 1981-83), Am. Coll. Real Estate Lawyers, Minn. State Bar Assn., Orange County Bar Assn. Banking, Commercial, consumer (including collections, credit), Property, real (including real estate development, water). Office: Akerman Senterfitt & Eidson PA Citrus Ctr 17th Fl PO Box 231 255 S Orange Ave Orlando FL 32801-3445

CHRISTIE, CHRISTOPHER JAMES, lawyer; b. Mendham, N.J., 1963; m. Mary Pat Foster; children: Andrew, Sarah Anne, Patrick. BA, U. Del.; JD, Seton Hall U., 1987. Bar: N.J. 1987, U.S. Dist. Ct. N.J. 1987. Atty. Dughi & Hewit, Cranford, NJ, 1987—93, ptnr., 1993—; U.S. atty. U.S. Dist. Ct. N.J., 2001—. Bd. trustees Daytop Village-N.J., Mendham, 1998—2002; officer Christie Family Found., 2001—; chmn. Morris County Ins. Commn.; bd. dirs. United way Morris County, Family Svcs. Morris County, Morris County Bd. Social Svcs.; dir. bd. Morris County Bd. Chosen Freeholders, 1997—. Office: Peter Rodino Fed Bldg 970 Broad St Ste 700 Newark NJ 07102*

CHRISTMAN, BRUCE LEE, lawyer; b. Bethlehem, Pa., Apr. 1, 1955; s. Raymond J. Jr. and Irene May (Bowman) C.; m. Lynn Eloise Brodt, Oct. 11, 1980; children: Jennifer Lynn, Amy Nicole. BA, Coll. William and Mary, 1977; JD, U. Pa., 1980. Bar: Va. 1980, U.S. Ct. Appeals (4th cir.) 1980, U.S. Dist. Ct. (ea. dist.) Va. 1980. Assoc. Hunton & Williams, Richmond, Va., 1980-84; prin., ptnr. Reed Smith LLP, Fairfax, Va., 1984—. Adj. prof. George Mason Sch. Law. Mem. Leadership Fairfax Class of 1993, bd. dirs. 1997, 2000-02—. Mem. Va. State Bar Assn., Phi Beta Kappa, Omicron Delta Kappa, Kappa Sigma. Democrat. Avocations: tennis, basketball, swimming, bicycling, camping. Banking, Finance, Property, real (including real estate development, water). Home: 13610 Flintwood Pl Herndon VA 20171-3331 Office: Reed Smith LLP 3110 Fairview Park Dr Falls Church VA 22042-4503

CHRISTOL, CARL Q(UIMBY), lawyer, political science educator; b. Gallup, S.D., June 28, 1913; s. Carl and Winifred (Quimby) C.; m. Jeannette Stearns, Dec. 18, 1949 (dec.); children: Susan Quimby Christol-Deacon, Richard Stearns (dec.). AB, U. S.D., 1934, LLD (hon.), 1977; AM, Fletcher Sch. Law and Diplomacy, 1936; postgrad., Institut Universitaire des Hautes Etudes Internationales, Geneva, 1937-38, U. Geneva, 1937-38; PhD, U. Chgo., 1941; LLB, Yale U., 1947; postgrad., Acad. Internat. Law, The Hague, 1950. Bar: Calif. 1949, S.D. 1948. Assoc. firm Guthrie, Darling and Shattuck, Los Angeles, 1948-49; of counsel Fizzolio, Fizzolio & McLeod, Sherman Oaks, Calif., 1949-94; assoc. prof. polit. sci. U. So. Calif., 1949-59, prof., 1959-87, prof. emeritus, 1987—, chmn. dept. polit. sci., 1960-64, 75-77. Stockton chair internat. law U.S. Naval War Coll., 1962-63, cons., 1963-70 ; cons. World Law Fund; mem. L.A. Mayor's Adv. Com. Human Rels., Commn. to Study Orgn. of Peace; mem. adv. panel on internat. law Dept. State, 1970-76; v.p. Ct. of Man Found., 1971-77; scholar-in-residence Rockefeller Found. Bellagio Conf. and Study Ctr., Italy, 1980. Author: Transit by Air in International Law, 1941, Introduction to Political Science, 1957, 4th edit., 1982, Readings in International Law, 1959, The International Law of Outer Space, 1966, The International Legal and Institutional Aspects of the Stratosphere Ozone Problem, 1975, The Modern International Law of Outer Space, 1982, Space Law: Past, Present and Future, 1991; bd. editors: Western Polit. Quar, 1970-75, Internat. Lawyer, 1975-84, Space Policy, 1985— , Internat. Legal Materials, 1985—, Australian Internat. Law Jour., 1998—; contbr. articles on legal, polit. and mil. subjects to profl. jours. Bd. dirs. Los Angeles County Heart Assn., 1956-61. Served to lt. col. AUS, 1941-46; col. Res. ret. Decorated Bronze Star medal; recipient Dart award U. So. Calif., 1970, Assos. award for excellence in teaching, 1977, Raubenheimer award, 1982, Disting. Emeritus award, 1990, Rockefeller Found. fellow, 1958-59; Borchard Found. lectr., 2002. Mem. Am., Los Angeles bar assns., Am. Soc. Internat. Law (exec. council 1973-76), Internat. Studies Assn. (chmn. internat. law sect. 1977-78), Internat. Acad. Astronautics, State Bar Calif., UN Assn. Los Angeles (pres. 1961-63), Am. Polit. Sci. Assn., Internat. Inst. Space Law (pres. Am. br. 1973-75, Lifetime Achievement award 1998), Town Hall, AIAA, Internat. Law Assn., UN Assn. U.S. (dir. 1967-69), Masons, Blue Key, Skull and Dagger, Rotary, Phi Beta Kappa, Phi Kappa Phi (award 1987), Alpha Tau Omega. Republican. Presbyterian. Home: 1041 Anoka Pl Pacific Palisades CA 90272-2414 Office: U So Calif Polit Sci Dept Los Angeles CA 90089-0044

CHRISTOPHER, WILLIAM GARTH, lawyer; b. Beaumont, Tex., Oct. 14, 1940; s. Garth Daugherty and Ollye Mittie (Harkness) C.; m. Kathleen S. Christopher; children: John William, David Noah, Michael O'Hara. BS in Engring., U.S. Mil. Acad., 1962; JD, U. Va., 1970. Bar: Va. 1970, D.C. 1970, U.S. Supreme Ct. 1975, Mich. 1977, Fla. 1988, Tex. 1989. Atty. Steptoe & Johnson, Washington, 1970-77; ptnr. Honigman MIller Schwartz & Cohn, Detroit, 1977-94, Holland & Knight, Tampa, Fla., 1994-95, Brown Clark Christopher & DeMay, P.A., Sarasota, Fla., 1995—. Contbr. articles to legal publ. Pres. Birmingham (Mich.) Hockey Assn., 1982-84; mem. Epsc. Diocese of Mich. Commn. on Ministry, 1983-88, co-chmn., 1987-88, standing com., 1988. Capt. C.E. U.S. Army, 1962-67. Mem.: Tex. Bar Assn., The Fla. Bar, Nat. Bd. Trial Advocacy, Sarasota County Bar Assn., Va. Bar, Order of Coif, Phi Delta Phi. Episcopalian. General civil litigation, Commercial, contracts (including sales of goods; commercial financing), Construction. Office: Brown Clark Christopher & DeMay PA 1819 Main St Ste 1100 Sarasota FL 34236-5975 E-mail: wchristopher@sarasotafirm.com .

CHRISTOPHERSON, DAVID VICTOR, lawyer; b. Edina, Minn., June 2, 1974; s. David Lee and Diane Kay Christopherson; m. Lindsay Brown. AB, Davidson Coll., 1996; JD, Harvard U., 1999. Bar: N.Y. 2000. Assoc. Sullivan & Cromwell LLP, N.Y.C., 1999—. Mem.: ABA, Assn. Bar City of N.Y. Republican. Episcopalian. Mergers and acquisitions, Corporate, general, Banking. Office: Sullivan & Cromwell LLP 125 Broad St New York NY 10004-2400

CHRISTOPHILLIS, CONSTANTINE S. lawyer; b. Greenville, S.C., Nov. 27, 1953; s. Gus and Fofo (Stamati) C.; m. Catherine Lynn Carr, May 14, 1978; children: Tina, Cory, Anna Kate. BA, Wofford Coll., 1975; JD, U. S.C., 1977. Bar: S.C. 1978, U.S. Dist. Ct. S.C. 1978, U.S. Ct. Appeals (4th cir.) 1981. Ptnr. Christophillis Law Offices, Greenville, 1978-88; shareholder Culbertson & Christophillis, Greenville, 1988—. Mem. ABA, S.C. Bar Assn., Greenville County Bar Assn., S.C. Trial Lawyers Assn., Nat. Orgn. Social Security Claimants Reps., Assn. S.C. Claimant Attys. for Workers Compensation, Rotary (bd. dirs. Greenville, Paul Harris fellow 1996). General civil litigation, Personal injury (including property damage), Workers' compensation. Office: Culbertson & Christophillis 707 E North St Greenville SC 29601-3010

CHRISTY, ARTHUR HILL, lawyer; b. Bklyn., July 25, 1923; s. Francis Taggart and Catherine Virginia (Damon) C.; m. Gloria Garvin Osborne, Feb. 14, 1980; children by previous marriage: Duncan Hill, Alexandra. AB, Yale U., 1945; LL.B., Columbia U., 1949. Bar: N.Y. 1950. Assoc. firm Baldwin, Todd & Lefferts, N.Y.C., 1950-52; spl. asst. atty. gen. Saratoga Investigation, N.Y., 1952-53; asst. U.S. atty. So. Dist. N.Y., 1953-54; chief prosecutor spl. asst. atty. gen. Saratoga and Columbia County Investigations, 1954-55; asst. atty. gen. N.Y., 1955; chief criminal div. U.S. atty.'s Office, So. Dist. N.Y., 1955-57; chief asst. U.S. atty., 1957-58; U.S. atty., 1958-59; partner firm Christy & Viener (and predecessors), N.Y.C., 1959—. Spl. asst. to Gov. Rockefeller, 1959-61; apptd. 1st spl. prosecutor Under Ethics in Govt. Act of 1978 to investigate charges against White House Chief of Staff, 1979-80. Artist in scrimshaw. Trustee, vice chmn. Bklyn. Hosp., Cmty. Svc. Soc.; v.p., gen. counsel, mem. coun. N.Y. Heart Assn. Lt. USNR, 1944-46. Mem. ABA, N.Y. State Bar Assn., Fed. Bar Assn., Assn. Bar City N.Y. (chmn. exec. com. 1966-67, v.p. 1968-69), Am. Coll. Trial Lawyers, Century Assn., Rockefeller Luncheon Club, Univ. Club (N.Y.C.), Mastigouche Fish and Game Club (Que., Can.). Republican. Episcopalian. Home: 430 E 57th St New York NY 10022-3061 Office: 620 5th Ave New York NY 10020-2402 E-mail: achristy@salans.com.

CHROMOW, SHERI P. lawyer; b. N.Y.C., Aug. 27, 1946; d. Abe and Sara L. Pinsky. BA, Barnard Coll., N.Y.C., 1968; JD, NYU, 1971. Ptnr. Shearman & Sterling, N.Y.C., 1979—2001, Katten, Muchin, Zavis Rosenman, N.Y.C., 2001—. Lectr. Practising Law Inst., N.Y. County Bar Assn., Urban Land Inst.; mem. exec. com. N.Y. dist. coun. U. L.I.; mem. adv. bd. N.Y.U. Law Sch. Real Estate Inst.; mem. adv. bd. Ticor Title Ins. Co. Mem. Urban Land Inst., Assn. Fgn. Investors in Real Estate (gen. counsel). Commercial, contracts (including sales of goods; commercial financing), Finance, Property, real (including real estate development, water). Office: Katten Muchin Zavis Rosenman 575 Madison Ave New York NY 10022 E-mail: sheri.chromow@kmzr.com.

CHU, MORGAN, lawyer; b. N.Y.C., Dec. 27, 1950; m. Helen M. Wong, Dec. 29, 1970. BA, UCLA, 1971, MA, 1972, PhD, 1973; MSL, Yale U., 1974; JD magna cum laude, Harvard U., 1976. Bar: Calif. 1976, U.S. Dist. Ct. (ctrl. dist.) Calif. 1977, U.S. Dist. Ct. (no. dist.) Calif. 1980, U.S. Ct. Appeals (9th cir.) 1980, U.S. Dist. Ct. (so. dist.) Calif. 1984, U.S. Dist. Ct. (ea. dist.) Calif. 1986, U.S. Ct. Appeals (fed. cir.) 1989, U.S. Supreme Ct. 1991. Law clk. to judge U.S. Ct. Appeals (9th cir.), San Francisco, 1976-77; assoc. Irell & Manella, LLP, L.A., 1977-82; ptnr. Irell & Manella, L.A., 1982—, co-mng. ptnr., 1997—, exec. com., 1984—. Adj. prof. UCLA Sch. Law, 1979-82; judge pro tem L.A. Mcpl. Ct., 1980—. Mem. editl. bd. Litigation News, 1981-84. Named Best Intellectual Property Lawyer in Nation, 2001 Survey of Co. Dirs., Law Sch. Deans and Lawyers by Corp. Bd. Mem., one of 12 Superstars in all practice areas, one of 10 New Superstars of 1st ammendment law, Legal Times of Washington, 1986, one of 100 Most Influential Lawyers in Am., Nat. Law Jour., 1994, 1997, 2000, one of Top Ten Trial Lawyers in U.S., 1995, one of top 45 Lawyers in U.S. Under 45 Years Old, Am. Lawyer, 1995, Exec. of Yr. in Law, L.A. Bus. Jour., 1994, one of top 20 lawyers in L.A., Calif. Law and Bus., one of top 100 Most Influential Lawyers in Calif., Calif. Law Bus., 1998, 1999, 2000, 2001, one of top 100 Most Inluential Lawyers in Calif., 2002; recipient Significant Achievement award for excellence and innovation in alternative dispute resolution, Ctr. for Pub. Resources, 1987; fellow postdoctoral fellow, Yale U., 1974. Mem.: ABA (chmn. high tech. intellectual property and patent trials subcom. 1986—90, trial practice com., litigation sect.), L.A. Intellectual Property Law Assn. (bd. dirs. 1991—93, bd. dirs. pub. counsel 1993—, exec. com. bd. dirs. pub. counsel 1995—), L.A. County Bar Assn. (judiciary com. 1983—2001), Calif. Bar Assn. General civil litigation, Patent, Trademark and copyright. Office: Irell & Manella LLP Ste 900 1800 Avenue Of The Stars Los Angeles CA 90067-4276 E-mail: mchu@irell.com.

CHUBIN, ELLEN LISA, lawyer; b. Phila., Pa., Apr. 12, 1968; d. Herbert Maurice and Selma (Parris) C. AB, Harvard-Radcliffe, 1990; JD, Harvard U., 1993. Bar: D.C. 1994, N.Y. 1994. Assoc. Covington and Burling, Washington, 1993-97; sr. trial atty. office of spl. investigations, criminal divsn. U.S. Dept. Justice, Washington, 1997—2001; asst. US Atty. US Dept. of Justice, Washington, 2001. Mem. ABA, Internat. Assn. Jewish Lawyers and Jurists (bd. dirs., v.p. Washington chpt. 1994-2001), Bar Assn. DC (bd. dirs., sec. young lawyers sect. 1999-2002), Women's Bar Assn., Harvard Club Washington (bd. dirs., v.p. 1998-2002). Democrat. Jewish. Avocation: member of a cappella singing group. Administrative and regulatory, Federal civil litigation, Immigration, naturalization, and customs. Home: 3003 Van Ness St NW Apt S-1103 Washington DC 20008-4708 Office: US Attorney's Office for DC 555 4th St NW Washington DC 20530

CHUN-HOON, LOWELL KOON YING, lawyer; b. Honolulu, Aug. 23, 1949; s. Kenneth Chew Ming and Alice Mee Chan (Yee) C.-H.; m. Catherine A. Chun-Hoon, July 1, 1989. BA, Yale U., 1971; MA, UCLA, 1974; JD, U. Calif., Berkeley, 1977. Bar: Hawaii 1977, U.S. Dist. Ct. Hawaii 1977, U.S. Ct. Appeals (9th cir.) 1980, U.S. Ct. Appeals (fed. cir.) 1985. Assoc. Bouslog & Symonds, Honolulu, 1977-79; ptnr. King, Nakamura & Chun-Hoon, Honolulu, 1979—. Bd. dirs. Na Loio No Na Kanaka, Honolulu, Hawaii Justice Found., 1993-99; mem. com. on jud. evaluation Hawaii Supreme Ct., 1991-95. Named one of Outstanding Young Men of Am., U.S. Jaycees, 1984. Mem. ABA, Hawaii Bar Assn. Labor (including EEOC, Fair Labor Standards Act, labor-management relations, NLRB, OSHA), Workers' compensation. Home: 254 Hao St Honolulu HI 96821-1846 Office: King Nakamura & Chun-Hoon 220 S King St Ste 980 Honolulu HI 96813-4539

CHURCH, DALE WALKER, lawyer; b. Portland, Oreg., Dec. 17, 1939; s. Floyd Walker and Lydia Belle (Barnette) C.; m. Mollie Ann Harper, Apr. 11, 1964; 1 child, Forrest Gregory. BS, Oreg. State U., 1961; JD, George Washington U., 1967. Bar: D.C. 1968, Calif. 1971. Contracting officer, exec. sec. contract rev. bd. CIA, Langley, Va., 1963-69; corp. gen. counsel, asst. sec. directory of contracts ESL, Inc., Sunnyvale, Calif., 1969-77; dep. under sec. research and engring. U.S. Dept. Def., Washington, 1977-80; ptnr. Surrey and Morse, Washington, 1980-84, Seyfarth, Shaw, Fairweather & Geraldson, Washington, 1984-88, Pillsbury, Madison & Sutro, Washington, 1988-93, McDermott, Will & Emery, Washington, 1993-97; chmn., CEO, Ventures & Solutions, LLC, Williamsburg, Va., 1998—, Intelligent Inspection Corp., 1999—, Mechanical Tech., Inc., 2002—. Counsel def. mgmt. to pres.'s Blue Ribbon Commn.; cons. Def. Sci. Bd., Washington, 1980—; lectr. profl. orgns. and colls. Mem. task force on Industry-to-Industry Coop.; active Ctr. Strategic and Internat. Studies Def. Orgn. Project; trustee Oratorio Soc. Washington; co-founder, counsel, treas. Youth Engaged in Svc. Am. Mem. ABA, Am. Electronics Assn. (former gen. counsel, chmn. def. conversion com.), Nat. Security Indsl. Assn. (trustee, chmn. acquisition reform task force), Nat. Contracts Mgmt. Assn., Def. Sci. Bd. Acquisition Reform Task Force, Calif. Bar Assn., D.C. Bar Assn., Fed. Bar Assn., Soc. Logistics Engrs. (hon.), Delta Theta Phi, Sigma Phi Epsilon. Corporate, general, Private international, Mergers and acquisitions. Home: 9 Franklin St Alexandria VA 22314-3828 Office: Ventures & Solutions LLC 704 Fairfax Way Williamsburg VA 23185-8202

CHURCH, GLENN J. lawyer; b. Grand Island, Nebr., Aug. 20, 1932; s. Glenn Jennings and Rachel Frances (Cochran) C.; m. Mary L. Church; children: Susan Jo, Zackary William. AB, U. Ill., 1954, JD, 1959. Bar: Ill. 1959, U.S. Dist. Ct. (cen. dist.) Ill. 1960, U.S. Ct Appeals (7th cir.) 1967, U.S. Supreme Ct. 1971, Ohio 1983. Assoc. Kavanaugh, Bond, Scully, Sudow & White, Peoria, Ill., 1959-62; ptnr. Smith & Church, Peoria, 1962-64, Smith, Whitney & Church, Peoria, 1964-65; pvt. practice Peoria, 1965-88, Columbus, Ohio, 1988—. Spl. asst. atty. gen. water pollution div. State of Ill., 1960-61; hearing officer Am. Arbitration Assn., Chgo., 1966—; mem. Ill. Fair Employment Practice Commn., 1974-79. Liasion officer Air Force Acad., Colorado Springs, Colo., 1968-82; bd. dirs. W.D. Boyce council Boy Scouts Am., 1970-86, Heart of Ill. Fair and Exposition Gardens, Peoria, 1978-84; exec. bd. chmn. eagle rev. com. Boy Scouts Am. , Peoria, 1977-86. Served to lt. col. USAF, 1954-82. Mem. Ill. Bar Assn., Ohio Bar Assn., Peoria Bar Assn., Assn. Trial Lawyers Am., Phi Alpha Delta. Lodges: Sertoma. Republican. Methodist. Non-profit and tax-exempt organizations, Personal injury (including property damage). Home and Office: Apt 502 3740 Ocean Beach Blvd Cocoa Beach FL 32931-5405 Fax: 321-868-4343. E-mail: churchbells@bellsouth.net.

CHURCH, RANDOLPH WARNER, JR., lawyer; b. Richmond, Va., Nov. 6, 1934; s. Randolph Warner and Elizabeth Lewis (Gochnauer) C.; m. Lucy Ann Canary, July 4, 1970; children: Leslie R. Pennell, L. Weeks Kerr. BA with honors, U. Va., 1957, LLB, 1960. Bar: Va. 1960, U.S. Dist. Ct. (ea. dist.) Va. 1962, U.S. Ct. Appeals (4th cir.) 1981, U.S. Supreme Ct. 1999. Assoc. McCandlish, Lillard & Marsh, Fairfax, Va., 1960-63; ptnr. McCandlish, Lillard, Rust & Church, Fairfax, 1963-84; city atty. Fairfax, 1968-72; mng. ptnr. McCandlish, Lillard, Rust & Church, Fairfax, 1975-83, Hunton & Williams, Fairfax, 1984-99, mem. exec. com., 1988-94, sr. counsel, 2000—. Bd. dirs. George Mason Bank, George Mason Bankshares, Inc., George Mason Mortgage Co., 1991-98, Va. Found. for Rsch. and Econ. Edn., Inc., 1994-2000. Author: Appellate Civil Litigation, 1984; panelist: Lawyer Professionalism: Is Change in Order? 1988, Marketing Legal Services: What's Hot and What's Not, 1990, (with others) Equity Practice and Tips on Brief Writing. Active Fairfax Com. of 100, 1988—, bd. dirs., 1989-92; bd. visitors George Mason U., Fairfax, 1982-90, rector, 1983-86, chmn. adv. bd. Coll. Arts and Scis., 1999—; bd. dirs. Fairfax Symphony, 1991-2002, gen. counsel, exec. com., 1996-2002; bd. dirs. Fairfax Symphony Orch. Found., Inc., 1999-, Va. Found. for Humanities and Pub. Policy, 1993-99, vice chmn., 1997-99; active Va. Mus. of Fine Arts Found., 2000—; pres. Fall for the Book, Inc., 2001—. Fellow Va. Law Found., Am. Bar Found.; mem. Va. Bar Assn. (v.p. 1975), Country Club Fairfax County, U. Va. Club, Phi Beta Kappa. State civil litigation, Corporate, general. Home: 5114 Forsgate Pl Fairfax VA 22030-4507 Office: Hunton & Williams 1751 Pinnacle Dr Ste 1700 Mc Lean VA 22102-3836

CHURCHILL, DAVID A. lawyer; b. Ft. Collins, Colo., May 13, 1952; s. A. Paul and Anna Marie Churchill; m. Barbara Jean Schultz, Sept. 15, 1972; children: Julia Marie, Heather E. BA, U. Colo., 1974; JD, Cornell U., 1979. Bar: D.C. 1979. Law clk. U.S. Ct. of Claims, Washington, 1979—80; ptnr. McKenna & Cuneo, Washington, 1980—2000, Jenner & Block, Washington, 2000—. Mem.: ABA (chair contract law sect. 1998—99), Ct. Fed. Claims Bar Assn. (pres.-elect 2002). Avocations: flying (airplane single engine and glider), hiking. Government contracts and claims. Office: Jenner & Block LLC 601 13th St NW 1200 S Washington DC 20005 Office Fax: 202-637-6370. E-mail: dchurchill@jenner.com.

CHYNOWETH, W. EDWARD, retired lawyer, farmer; b. Washington, Sept. 1, 1923; s. Bradford Grethen and Grace (Woodruff) C. BS in Mil. Sci. and Engring., U.S. Mil. Acad., 1946; MS in Mech. Engring., U. Calif., Berkeley, 1959; LLB, Stanford U., 1963. Bar: Calif. Pvt. practice law, Fresno, Calif., 1963—69; dep. dist. atty. Tulare County, Visalia, Calif., 1969—78; farmer Sanger, Calif., 1968—. Contbr. articles on social-constl. issues to cultural jours. of opinion and politics. With U.S. Army, 1946-57, maj. Res. Civil rights, Criminal, Other. Home: 403 S Indianola Ave Sanger CA 93657-9436

CIACCIO, KARIN MCLAUGHLIN, lawyer; b. Galesburg, Ill., Feb. 9, 1947; d. Cleo Edward and Kathryn Louise (Payton) McLaughlin; m. Frederick Steven Ciaccio, May 4, 1968; children: John, Jennifer. BS, So. Ill. U., 1969; postgrad., Temple U. Law Sch., 1971-72; JD, DePaul U., 1975. Bar: Ill. 1975, U.S. Dist. Ct. (7th cir.) Ill. 1975. Tchr. French Sherrard (Ill.) High Sch., 1969-70; prof. law U. Wis., Racine, 1975, Coll. DuPage, Glen Ellyn, Ill., 1976, Am. Paralegal Inst., Chgo., 1997—98; sole practice Chgo. and Lombard, Ill., 1975-80, Galesburg and Woodhull, Ill., 1980-90, 96-98; internat. rels. Woodhull, Japan, 1990-93; deputy city attorney City of Moline, Ill., 1993-96; real estate attorney U.S. Army Corps. of Engrs., Rock Island, Ill., 1998—2001; lawyer U.S. Army Ops. Support Command, Rock Island, Ill., 2001—. Lectr. on consumer law, various orgns., 1976-90; city atty. Woodhull, 1983-90. Ofcl. Lombard Zoning Bd., 1978-80; mem. Alpha (Ill.) Cemetary Bd., 1980-, St. John's Cemetary Bd., Woodhull, 1983-90; legis. chmn. Rep. Women Henry County, 1981-83; bd. dirs. Alwood Bus. Assn., 1984-86, People to People and Japanese Internat. bd. rels., Japan, 1990-92; v.p. AlWood Music Boosters, 1987-89; adv. rights of the mentally ill. Mem. ABA, Ill. Bar Assn., Henry County Bar Assn., Ninth Jud. Circuit Women's Bar Assn., Phi Alpha Delta. Lodges: Altrusa. General practice, Probate (including wills, trusts), Property, real (including real estate development, water). Office: AMSOS-GC 1 Rock Island Arsenal Rock Island IL 61299-6000 Mailing: PO Box 488 Woodhull IL 61490-0488

CIANI, JUDITH ELAINE, retired lawyer; b. Medford, Mass., July 24, 1943; d. A. Walter and Ruth Alice (Bowman) C.; m. Marion M. Smith, Sept. 29, 1982. Grad., Thayer Acad., Braintree, Mass., 1961; MA, Mt. Holyoke Coll., 1965; JD, Boston Coll., 1970. Bar: Calif. 1971, U.S. Dist. Ct. (no. dist.) Calif. 1971, U.S. Ct. Appeals (9th cir.) 1971. Aide/press sec. Rep. James A. Burke, Washington, 1965-67; atty. Pillsbury, Madison & Sutro, San Francisco, 1970-78, ptnr., 1978-90; ret., 1990. Del. Calif. Bar Conv., San Francisco, 1973-78, 83-85. Mem. San Francisco Police Commn., 1976-80, Juvenile Justice Task Force, San Francisco, 1981-83; bd. dirs. Bernard Osher Found., San Francisco, 1977—; pres. Common Fund for Legal Svcs., San Francisco, 1985—, Sinfonia San Francisco, 1985-86. Fellow Am. Bar Found.; mem. Bar Assn. San Francisco (bd. dirs., pres. Found. 1978—, bd. dirs. 1981-83, treas. 1987). Home: PO Box 960 Inverness CA 94937-0960 E-mail: jeciani@svn.net.

CICERO, FRANK, JR., lawyer; b. Nov. 30, 1935; s. Frnk and Mary (Balma) Cicero; m. Janice Pickett, July 11, 1959; children: Erica, Caroline. AB with hons., Wheaton Coll., 1957; M in Pub. Affairs, Woodrow Wilson Sch. of Pub. & Internat. Affairs, 1962; JD, U. Chgo., 1965. Bar: Ill., U.S. Supreme Ct. 1965, various U.S. Ct. of Appeals and Dist. Cts. Polit. sci. instr. Wheaton Coll., Ill., 1957—58; assoc. Kirkland & Ellis, Chgo., 1965—70, ptnr., 1970—. Mem. vis. com. U. Chgo. Law Sch., 1971—74, 1996—99, lectr., 1989—90, 1991—92; del. 6th Ill. Constl. Conv., 1969—70. Bd. editors: law rev. U. Chgo. Law Rev.; contbr. articles to profl. jours. Recipient Joseph Henry Beale prize, U. Chgo., 1963, Outstanding Young Man award, Evanston Jaycees, 1970. Fellow: Am. Coll. Trial Lawyers; mem.: ABA, Bar Assn. 7th Fed. Cir., Ill. State Bar Assn., Internat. Bar Assn., Saddle and Cycle Club (bd. govs. 1984), Mid-Am. Club (gov. 1981—84), Ventana Canyon Golf Club, Glen View Club, Chgo. Club. Federal civil litigation, State civil litigation, Private international. Office: Kirkland & Ellis 200 E Randolph Dr Ste 6000 Chicago IL 60601-6636

CICET, DONALD JAMES, lawyer; b. New Orleans, May 24, 1940; s. Arthur Alphonse and Myrtle (Ress) C.; m. Iona Perry. BA, Nicholls State U., 1963; JD, Loyola U., New Orleans, 1969. Bar: La. 1969, U.S. Dist. Ct. (ea. dist.) La. 1972, U.S. Dist. Ct. (mid. dist.) La. 1978, U.S. Dist. Ct. (we. dist.) La. 1979, U.S. Ct. Appeals (5th cir.) 1972, U.S. Supreme Ct. 1972. Pvt. practice, Reserve, La., 1969—88, LaPlace, La., 1988—; staff atty. La. Legis. Coun., 1972-73; legal counsel Nicholls State U. Alumni Fedn., 1974-76, 78-80; spl. counsel Pontchartrain Levee Dist., 1976—2001. Adminstrv. law judge La. Dept. Civil Svc., 1981—. Pres. Boys' State of La. Inc., 1990-92, bd. dirs., 1988—. With AUS, 1964, USNG, 1964-70. Recipient Am. Jurisprudence award Loyola U., 1968. Fellow La. Bar Found.; mem. ABA, La. Bar Assn. (ho. dels. 1973-77, 79-85), 40th Jud. Dist. Bar Assn. (pres. 1985-87). ATLA, La. Trial Lawyers Assn., Nicholls State U. Alumni Fedn. (exec. coun. 1972-76, 77-85, pres. 1982, James Lynn Powell award 1980), Am. Legion (post cmdr. 1976-77, dist. judge adv. 1975-95, judge adv. La. dept. 1990-92, 93-96, mem. La. dept. commn. on nat. security and govtl. affairs 1974-89, chmn. 1977-78, 79-81, 85-89, M.C. Gehr blue cap award 1983). Roman Catholic. Administrative and regulatory, Juvenile. Home: 263 Central Ave Reserve LA 70084-6003 Office: 197 Belle Terre Blvd La Place LA 70069-0461

CICIO, ANTHONY LEE, lawyer; b. Birmingham, Ala., July 8, 1926; s. Joseph and Rosa (Tombrello) C.; m. Yvonne Antonio, Nov. 4, 1959; children: Valerie, Anthony Jr., Mark. BS, Samford U., 1951; LLB, Birmingham Sch. Law, 1955. Bar: Ala. 1956, U.S. Dist. Ct. Ala. 1956, U.S. Supreme Ct. 1961, U.S. Ct. Appeals (11th cir.) 1968. Ptnr. Cicio & Cicio, Birmingham, 1976—, sr. ptnr., 1994—. Served as Spl. asst. Atty. Gen. State of Ala., 1980; served Brimingham-Jefferson County Transit Authority, 1962; appt. Birmingham-Jefferson County regional planning com., 1999—. Served with USAF, 1944-46, PTO. Mem. ABA, Ala. Bar Assn. (chmn. pub. relations com.), Birmingham Bar Assn. (ethics com., ch. com. on media and pub. relations), Trial Lawyers Assn. Am., Ala. Trial Lawyers Assn. (exec. com. 1983—), State Indsl. Revenue Bond (adv. coun.), The Club, Vestavia Country Club (Birmingham). Democrat. Roman Catholic. General practice, Personal injury (including property damage), Probate (including wills, trusts). Home: 3128 N Woodridge Rd Birmingham AL 35223-2750 Office: Cicio & Cicio PC Cicio Profl Bldg 2153 14th Ave S Birmingham AL 35205-3921

CIFELLI, JOHN LOUIS, lawyer; b. Chicago Heights, Ill., Aug. 19, 1923; s. Antonio and Domenica (Liberatore) C.; m. Irene Romandine, Jan. 4, 1948; children— Carla, David, John L., Bruce, Thomas, Carol. Student, Bowdoin Coll., 1943, Norwich Mil. Acad., 1943, Mt. Piliar Acad., 1943, U. Ill. Extension Ctr., 1946-47; LLB, DePaul U., 1950, JD (hon.), 1975. Bar: Ill. 1950, U.S. Supreme Ct. 1960. Ptnr. Piacenti, Cifelli & Sims, Chicago Heights, 1950-78; pres. John L. Cifelli & Assocs., Chicago Heights, 1978-85; sr. ptnr. Cifelli Baczynski & Scrementi Ltd. (now Cifelli & Scrementi), Chicago Heights, 1985—; spl. counsel City of Chicago Heights, 1961-72; village atty. Village of Richton Park, Ill., 1962-77, Village of Ford Heights, Ill., 1984-89. Counsel Maj. League Umpires Assn., 1973-78, Ill. High Sch. Baseball Coaches Assn., 1975-89. Sec. Bd. Fire and Police, Chicago Heights, 1959-65; co-founder Small Fry Internat. Basketball, 1969, pres., 1969— ; coach, baseball coordinator Chicago Heights Park Dist., 1970-75; coach Babe Ruth League Baseball, 1972, 74, 75, asst. Ill. dir., 1973; dir. Ill. tournament, 1973. Served to 2d lt. USAAF, 1942-45, ETO. Mem. ABA, Ill. Bar Assn., Ill. Trial Lawyers Assn., Asns. Trial Lawyers Am., Justinian Soc. Lawyers, Isaac Walton League, Italo Am. Vets. Group, VFW (judge adv. 1951-72), Cath. War Vets. (judge adv. 1951-70), Am. Legion. Clubs: Chicago Heights Country (bd. dirs. 1972-76), Mt. Carmel; Pike Lake Fishing (Wis.). Lodges: Moose, Amaseno. Republican. Avocations: hunting, fishing, golf. Criminal, General practice, Personal injury (including property damage). Home: 879 Amico Dr Chicago Heights IL 60411 Office: Cifelli & Scrementi 1700 S Halsted St Ste 201 Chicago Heights IL 60411-3555 E-mail: cifellilawfirm@msn.com.

CILZ, DOUGLAS ARTHUR, lawyer; b. Rugby, N.D., Feb. 22, 1949; s. Fred W. and Arliene (Nelson) C.; m. Kathy Ann Walker, June 10, 1972; children: Jennifer, Nicholas. BS, Dickinson State U., 1976; JD, U. N.D., Grand Forks, 1980. Bar: N.D. 1980, U.S. Dist. Ct. N.D. 1980, Minn. 1981, U.S. Tax Ct. 1981, U.S. Claims Ct. 1981. Atty. Qualley Larson & Jones, Fargo, N.D., 1980-81, Pearson & Christensen, Grand Forks, N.D., 1981-87; ptnr. Juntunen, Cilz & Hager, Grand Forks, 1987—98; atty. N.D. Dept. Transp., Grand Forks, 1998—. Instr. East Grand Forks (Minn.) Tech. Coll., 1989-92; apptd. spl. asst. atty. gen. Bank N.D., 1993—; apptd. temporary adminstrv. law judge N.D. Office Adminstrv. Hearings, 1995-2003. Sgt. USAF, 1968-71. Mem. ABA, Minn. Bar Assn., N.D. Bar Assn., Grand Forks C. of C. Lutheran. Avocations: golf, sailing, fishing. General civil litigation, Estate planning, Taxation, general. Office: ND Dept Transportation 1951 N Washington St Grand Forks ND 58203-1420

CIMINI, JOSEPH FEDELE, law educator, lawyer, former magistrate; b. Scranton, Pa., Sept. 8, 1948; s. Frank Anthony and Dorothy Theresa (Musso) C. AB in German and Polit. Sci., U. Scranton, 1970; JD Columbus Sch. Law, Cath. U. Am., 1973. Bar: Pa. 1973, U.S. Dist. Ct. (mid. dist.) Pa. 1973, D.C. 1976, U.S. Ct. Appeals (3d cir.) 1978, U.S. Supreme Ct. 1978. Law clk. to judge Ct. Common Pleas Lackawanna County (Pa.), 1973-75; asst. U.S. atty. Middle Dist. Pa., Pa. Dept. Justice, 1975-80; spl. asst. to U.S. Atty. Middle Dist. Pa., 1980-81; asst. prof. sociology/criminal justice U. Scranton, 1980-94, assoc. prof., 1994—, chmn. dept., 2001—. U.S. magistrate judge U.S. Dist. Ct. (mid. dist.) Pa., 1981-92; spl. trial master Lackawanna County Ct. Common Pleas, 1995—. Past pres., trustee Lackawanna Hist. Soc.; v.p. adv. bd. Holy Family Residence, Scranton, Pa., 1997-2001, pres., 2002—; v.p. pastoral coun. St. Francis Ch., 1994-96; mem. cmty. adv. bd. MINSEC-Scranton, 2003. Recipient Meritorious award Dept. Justice; German Acad. Exchange Service fgn. study travel grantee, W.Ger., 1981. Mem. ABA, Fed. Bar Assn. (past v.p. mid. dist. Pa. chpt.), Am. Judges Assn., Fed. Magistrate Judges Assn., Am. Justinian Soc. of Jurists, Acad. Criminal Justice Scis., Pa. Bar Assn., Northeastern Assn. Criminal Justice Scis. (pres. 1987-88), Lackawanna Bar Assn., Pa. Sociol. Soc. (treas.), U. Scranton Alumni (nat. sec. 1997-99), Cath. U. Law Alumni, Purple Club, Victor Alfieri Lit. Soc., UNICO Nat., Dante Lit. Soc. Republican. Roman Catholic. Address: Univ Scranton Dept Sociology/Criminal Justice Scranton PA 18510-4605 E-mail: ciminij1@scranton.edu.

CIMINO, RICHARD DENNIS, lawyer; b. Omaha, June 6, 1947; s. Lewis Raymond and Louise (Monaco) C.; m. Mary Scott Reins, Feb. 12, 1977; children: John Damon, Mary Drusilla, Robert Andrew, Ann Marie. BBA, U. Notre Dame, 1969; JD, St. Louis U., 1974. Bar: Nebr. 1975, Kans. 1989, Fla. 1994, U.S. Dist. Ct. Nebr. 1975, U.S. Dist. Ct. Kans. 1989, U.S. Dist. Ct. Fla. 1995. Assoc. Kutak, Rock & Campbell, Omaha, 1975-78, ptnr., 1979; v.p., gen. counsel Silvey Refrigerated Carriers, Omaha, 1980-86, pres., 1987; ptnr. Dwyer, Pohren, Wood, Heavey & Grimm, Omaha, 1988-89; pvt. practice St. Marys, Kans., 1989-93; ptnr. Treadwell, Cimino & McElrath, Naples, Fla., 1993—. Editor St. Louis U. Law Jour., 1972-74. Bd. dirs. Bergan Mercy Hosp. Found., Omaha, 1986-87. With U.S. Army, 1969-71, Vietnam. Mem. Fla. Bar Assn., Kans. Bar Assn., Nebr. Bar Assn., Collier County Bar Assn., Notre Dame Alumni Club (pres. Omaha chpt. 1980), Alpha Sigma Nu. Republican. Roman Catholic. Avocations: golf, family activities. State civil litigation, Estate planning, General practice. Office: 3838 Tamiami Trl N Naples FL 34103-3590 E-mail: dome96@aol.com.

CINABRO, ROBERT HENRY, lawyer; b. Kalamazoo, June 10, 1948; s. Louis and Maria (Breviglieri) C.; m. Pamela Mae Eschenburg, Aug. 19, 1972; children: Jennifer Elise, Michael Thomas. BA cum laude, Kalamazoo Coll., 1970; JD, Cornell U., 1973. Bar: Mich. 1973, U.S. Dist. Ct. (we. dist.) Mich., 1975, U.S. Supreme Ct. 1979, U.S. Ct. Appeals (6th cir.) 1983, Fla. 1987. Law clk. to presiding judge 9th Judicial Ct., Kalamazoo, 1973-74; asst. city atty. City of Kalamazoo, 1974-77, dep. city atty., 1977-88, city atty., 1988—. Civil mediator 9th Jud. Cir. Ct., Kalamazoo, 1985—; civil arbitrator U.S. Dist. Ct. for We. Dist. Mich., Grand Rapids, 1986—; legal counsel Kalamazoo Met. Transit Authority, 1985-88. Mem. Kalamazoo Criminal Justice Commn., 1982-83, Kalamazoo Safety Coun., Drunk Driving Task Force, 1983—85 commr. Kalamazoo Hosp. Fin. Authority, 1988—; bd. dirs. Kalamazoo County Humane Soc., 1983-85. Mem. ABA, Kalamazoo County Bar Assn., Fed. Bar Assn., Fla. Bar Assn., Phi Beta Kappa. Roman Catholic. Avocations: civil war history, travel, animal welfare. Home: 2525 Frederick Ave Kalamazoo MI 49008-2149 Office: Office of City Atty 234 W Cedar St Kalamazoo MI 49007-5151 E-mail: cinabror@kalamazoocity.org.

CIOFFI, MICHAEL LAWRENCE, lawyer; b. Cin., Feb. 2, 1953; s. Patrick Anthony and Patricia (Schroeder) C.; children: Michael A., David P., Gina M. BA magna cum laude, U. Notre Dame, 1975; JD, U. Cin., 1979. Bar: Ohio 1979, U.S. Dist. Ct. (so. dist.) Ohio 1980, U.S. Dist. Ct. (no. dist.) Ohio 1983, U.S. Ct. Appeals (6th cir.) 1985. Asst. atty. gen. Ohio Atty. Gen., Columbus, 1979-81; from assoc. to ptnr. Frost & Jacobs, Cin., 1981-87; staff v.p., asst. gen. counsel Penn Cen. Corp., Cin., 1988-93; v.p., asst. gen. counsel Am. Fin. Group, Cin., 1993-2000; ptnr. Blank Rome Comisky & McCauley, Cin., 2001—. Adj. prof. law U. Cin. Coll. Law, 1983—. Author: Ohio Pretrial Litigation, 1991; co-author: Sixth Circuit Federal Practice Manual, 1993. Bd. dirs. Charter Com. of Greater Cin., 1985—88. Recipient Goldman Prize for Tchg. Excellence U. Cin. Coll. Law, 1995, Nicholas Longworth Disting. Alumni award, 1996. Mem. ABA, Fed. Bar Assn. (mem. exec. com., pres.1994), Ohio Bar Assn., Cin. Bar Assn. Avocations: tennis, travel. Federal civil litigation, General civil litigation, Environmental. Office: Blank Rome LLP 201 E 5th St Cincinnati OH 45202

CIOLINO, DANE STEPHEN, law educator; b. New Orleans, Jan. 28, 1964; s. John Charles Ciolino and Edith (Hummell) Fedoroff; m. Wendy Dehan, May 14, 1988; children, Dane Hale, Henry Prince, Camille Elise. BA cum laude, Rhodes Coll., 1985; JD magna cum laude, Tulane U., 1988. Bar: N.Y. 1989, La. 1989. Law clk. U.S. Dist. Ct., New Orleans, 1988-89; assoc. Cravath, Swaine & Moore, N.Y.C., 1989-91, Stone, Pigman, Walther, Wittmann & Hutchinson, New Orleans, 1991—95. Mem. Criminal Justice Act Panel, New Orleans, 1991—. Mem. Order of Coif. Home: 127 Hector Ave Metairie LA 70005-4018 Office: Loyola Law Sch New Orleans 526 Pine St New Orleans LA 70118

CIPARICK, CARMEN BEAUCHAMP, judge; b. N.Y.C., 1942; Grad., Hunter Coll., 1963; JD, St. John's U., 1967. Staff atty. Legal Aid Soc., N.Y.C.; asst. counsel Office of Jud. Conf., 1969—72; chief law asst. N.Y.C. Criminal Ct., 1972—74, judge, 1978—82; counsel Office of N.Y.C. Adminstrv. Judge, 1974—78; judge N.Y. Supreme Ct, 1982—94; assoc. judge N.Y. State Ct. Appeals, N.Y.C., 1994—. Former mem. N.Y. State Commn. Jud. Conduct. Trustee Boricua Coll.; bd. dirs. St. John's U. Sch. of Law Alumni Assn. Named to Hunter Coll. Hall of Fame, 1991. Office: NY State Ct Appeals 122 E 42nd St New York NY 10168-0002

CIPOLLONE, ANTHONY DOMINIC, judge, educator; b. N.Y.C., Mar. 15, 1939; s. Domenico and Caterina (Brancazio) C.; m. Eileen Mary Patricia Kelly, Sept. 14, 1963; children: Catherine Mary, Kelly Ann, Mary Rose. BA, CCNY, 1961, MA, 1968; JD, Seton Hall U., 1978. Bar: N.J. 1978, Pa. 1978, U.S. Patent Office 1978, Fla. 1980, N.Y. 1984, D.C. 1985, Mass. 1988; cert. civil trial atty. N.J., 1987. Chemist Am. Chicle Co., Long Island City, N.Y., 1961-65; research chemist Denver Chem. Mfg. Co., Stamford, Conn., 1965-66; chem. sales engr. GAF Corp., N.Y.C., 1966-68; nat. acct. rep. Stauffer Chem., N.Y.C., 1968-72; sales mgr. Rhone-Poulenc Inc., South Brunswick, N.J., 1972-78; prosecutor Town of Elmwood Park, N.J., 1981-85, Town of Paramus, N.J., 1982-85; mcpl. ct. judge Town of Paramus (N.J.), 1985-90, Town of Little Ferry (N.J.), 1986-89; atty. planning bd. Twp. Saddle Brook, 1986-87; mcpl. ct. judge Town of Elmwood Park (N.J.), 1991, Town of Saddle Brook (N.J.), 1991-94; atty. Twp. Saddle Brook, 1987-90. Adj. faculty MBA program for chmn. and pharm. mgrs. Fairleigh Dickinson U.; atty. Zoning Bd., City of Hackensack, N.J., 1989-90, atty. Planning Bd., 1991—. Served to sgt. USMC, 1961-66. Mem. ABA, Bergen Bar Assn., N.J. Bar Assn., Pa. Bar Assn., N.Y. Bar Assn., D.C. Bar Assn., Fla. Bar Assn., Mass. Bar Assn., Am. Chem. Soc., Am. Mensa. Roman Catholic. Home: 130 Overlook Ave Hackensack NJ 07601 Office: 15 Main St Ste 215 Hackensack NJ 07601 E-mail: cipollone@aol.com.

CIRANDO, JOHN ANTHONY, lawyer; b. Syracuse, N.Y., June 25, 1942; s. Daniel John and Anne Marie (Farone) C.; m. Carolyn Joyce Lace, Sept. 17, 1966; children: Lisa Marie, Julie Lynn, Jennifer Mary. BA in History, St. Bonaventure (N.Y.) U., 1963; JD, SUNY, Buffalo, 1966. Bar: N.Y. 1966, U.S. Dist. Ct. (no. dist.) N.Y. 1966, U.S. Dist. Ct. (we. dist.) N.Y. 1994, U.S. Claims Ct. 1991, U.S. Ct. Mil. Appeals 1967, U.S. Ct. Appeals (2d cir.) 1985, U.S. Supreme Ct. 1974. Chief asst. dist. atty. Onondaga County Dist. Atty.'s Office, Syracuse, N.Y., 1971-87; atty. D.J. & J.A. Cirando, Syracuse, 1966—. Treas. N.Y. State Dist. Atty.'s Assn., 1977-87; chair Govs. Jud. Screening Com. 4th Jud. Dept., 1997—. Pres. bd. dirs. Vera House, Shelter for Women and Children in Crisis, Syracuse, 1988-90, gen. counsel, 1991—; bd. trustees Leukemia Soc. Am., 1995—, asst. sec., 1995-96, sec., 1996-2000, adv. bd., 2000—. Capt. JAG, U.S. Army, 1967-71. Mem. N.Y. State Bar Assn. (chair com. on county cts. 1975-78, chair com. on pub. rels. 1979-83), Onondaga County Bar Assn. (bd. dirs. 1974-77, sec. 1979). Appellate, Probate (including wills, trusts), Property, real (including real estate development, water). Office: DJ & JA Cirando 101 S Salina St Ste 1010 Syracuse NY 13202-4303

CIRESI, MICHAEL VINCENT, lawyer; b. St. Paul, Apr. 18, 1946; s. Samuel Vincent and Selena Marie (Bloom) Ciresi; m. Ann Ciresi; children: Dominic, Adam. BBA, U. St. Thomas; JD, U. Minn.; LLD, Southwestern U., 2001. Bar: Minn. 1971, U.S. Dist. Ct. Minn. 1974, U.S. Ct. Appeals (8th cir.) 1971, U.S. Supreme Ct. 1981, U.S. Ct. Appeals (2d cir.) 1986, U.S. Ct. Appeals (9th cir.) 1987, U.S. Ct. Appeals (10th cir.) 1990, NY 1995, Fed. Cir. 1998, U.S. Ct. Appeals (5th cir.) 1999. Assoc. Robins, Kaplan, Miller & Ciresi, Mpls., 1971—78, ptnr., 1978—, exec. bd., 1983—, chmn. exec. bd., 1995—. Adv. bd. Ctr. Advanced Litig. Nottingham (Eng.) Law Sch. Trustee U. St. Thomas; candidate U.S. Senate, 2000. Named Product Liability Lawyer of Yr., Australian Nat. Consumer Law Assn., 1989, Trial Lawyer of Yr., Trial Lawyers for Pub. Justice Found., 1998. Mem.: ABA, Am. Acad. Trial Lawyers, Internat. Acad. Trial Lawyers, Trial Lawyers for Pub. Justice (bd. dirs.), Inner Cir. of Advocates, Internat. Bar Assn., Am. Bd. Trial Advocates, Assn. Trial Lawyers Am., Ramsey County Bar Assn., Hennepin County Bar Assn., Minn. State Bar Assn. Roman Catholic. Avocations: sports, U.S. history. Federal civil litigation, State civil litigation. Home: 1247 Culligan Ln Saint Paul MN 55118-4151 Office: Robins Kaplan Miller & Ciresi 2800 Lasalle Plz Minneapolis MN 55402

CIRILLO, RICHARD ALLAN, lawyer; b. N.Y.C., Feb. 7, 1951; s. Paul F. and Edith A. (Flanagan) C.; m. Kathleen V. Rossi, Aug. 23, 1975; children: Benjamin F., Theodore T., Amanda K. BA, Yale U., 1972; JD cum laude, Fordham U., 1975. Bar: N.Y. 1976, U.S. Dist. Ct. (so. dist.) N.Y. 1977, U.S. Dist. Ct. (no. dist.) N.Y. 1990, U.S. Ct. Appeals (5th and 10th cirs.) 1978, U.S. Ct. Appeals (2d cir.) 1982, U.S. Ct. Appeals (9th cir.) 1984, U.S. Ct. Appeals (11th cir.) 1994, U.S. Tax Ct. 1984, U.S. Supreme Ct. 1983. Assoc. Rogers & Wells, N.Y.C., 1975-83, ptnr., 1983—99, King & Spalding, N.Y.C., 1999—. Bd. dirs. MIM Corp. Editor: Fordham Law Rev.; contbr. articles to profl. jours. Trustee Colony Found., New Haven, 1982-84. Republican. Presbyterian. Antitrust, Federal civil litigation, Securities. Home: 246 E 33d St New York NY 10016 Office: King & Spalding LLP 1185 Ave of the Americas Ste 3400 New York NY 10036

CIRKVENI, NEVEN, lawyer, consultant; b. Slavonski Brod, Croatia, Mar. 20, 1957; s. Ivica Cirkveni and Anka Djurić-Cirkveni; m. Irena Nakić, May 3, 1969; 1 child, Neva. JD, U. Zagreb, Croatia, 1981; LLM, U. Belgrade, Yugoslavia, 1985; PhD, U. Conn., 1989. Bar: Croatian Bar Assn. 1998. Instr. U. Zagreb, 1981—83, U. Conn., Storrs, 1986—88; pvt. practice bus. cons. Zagreb, 1989—; sr. advisor Ministry Fgn. Affairs, Zagreb, 1992—92; atty. at law Odvjetniki ured Cirkveni, Zagreb, 1998—. Advisor Coun. Econ. Advisors to the Govt. Croatia, Zagreb, 2000—. Contbr. articles to profl. jours. Advisor Coun. of the Social Dem. Party, Zagreb, 1998—2003; founding mem. Zaklada 2020, Zagreb, 2000—03; dir. Leadership Forum Croatia, Zagreb, 2003—03. Decorated Meml. of the Homeland War 1991 - 1992 Pres. Republic Croatia; named Hon. Citizen Kansas City, Mayor Kansas City, 1975; Secondary Sch. scholar, Am. Field Svc., 1974, Lang. Study fellow, Tech. U., Dresden, Germany, 1984, pre-doctoral fellow, U. Conn., 1985—89, doctoral fellow, 1990. Mem.: German-Croatian Lawyers' Assn., Am. C. of C. in Croatia (v.p. 2002—). Roman Catholic. Avocations: photography, skiing, private flying, sailing, shooting. Corporate, general, Mergers and acquisitions, Finance. Office: Law Offices Cirkveni Radiceva 27 10000 Zagreb Croatia Office Fax: 0113854813221. Personal E-mail: neven.cirkveni@zg.tel.hr. E-mail: neven.cirkveni@cirkveni.hr.

CISSELL, JAMES CHARLES, lawyer; b. Cleve., May 29, 1940; s. Robert Francis and Helen Cecelia (Freeman) C; children: Denise, Helene-Marie, Suzanne, James. Student, Sophia U., Tokyo, 1961; AB, Xavier U., 1962; JD, U. Cin., 1966; postgrad., Ohio State U., 1973-74; D. Tech. Letters, Cin. Tech. Coll., 1979. Bar: Ohio 1966, U.S. Dist. Ct. (so. dist.) Ohio 1967, U.S. Ct. Appeals (6th cir.) 1978, U.S. Supreme Ct. 1980, U.S. Dist. Ct. (ea. dist.) Ky. 1981. Pvt. practice law, 1966-78, 82—; asst. atty. gen. State of Ohio, 1971-74; first v.p. Cin. Bd. Park Commrs., 1973-74; vice mayor City of Cin., 1976-77; U.S. atty. So. Dist. Ohio, Cin., 1978-82. Adj. instr. law No. Ky. U., 1982-86; pres. Nat. Assn. Former U.S. attys., 2001—02. Author: Oil and Gas Law in Ohio, 1964, Federal Criminal Trials, 5th edit., 1999; editor; Proving Federal Crimes. Gen. chmn. amateur pub. links championship U.S. Golf Assn., 1987; mem. coun. City of Cin., 1974-78, 85-87, 89-92; clk of cts., Hamilton County, 1992-2003; judge Hamilton County Probate Ct., 2003-; commr. Recreation Bd. Cin., 1974, Planning Bd. Cin., 1977; pres. Ohio Clk. of Cts. Assn., 1998; mem. Ohio Bicentennial Commn., 1998-2003; mem. Ohio Cts. Futures Commn., 1998-2000; mem. Ohio Supreme Ct. Adv. Com. on Tech. and the Cts., 2000—, privacy of access subcom. of Supreme Ct. adv. com. on tech. of the Cts. Recipient Econ. Opportunity award, Dr. Martin Luther King Jr. Holiday Commn., 2002; fellow, Ford Found., 1973—74. Mem. Ohio Bar Assn., Cin. Bar Assn., Fed. Bar Assn. (pres. 2002-03), Former U.S. Attys. Assn. Avocations: golf, jogging. Federal civil litigation, Criminal, Probate (including wills, trusts). Home: 201B Belvedere 3900 Rose Hl Cincinnati OH 45229 Office: William Howard Taft Law Ctr 230 E 9th St 10th Fl Cincinnati OH 45202 E-mail: jcissell@cms.hamilton-co.org.

CITRO, VINCENT A. prosecutor, educator; b. Daytona Beach, Fla., Oct. 19, 1976; s. Albert E. and Dorothy P. Citro. BBA, Stetson U., 1998, MBA, JD, Stetson U., 2000. Bar: Fla. 2001, U.S. Dist. Ct. (no., mid. and so. dists.) Fla. 2001, U.S. Ct. Appeals (11th cir.) 2001. Atty. Lowndes, Drosdick, et. al., Orlando, Fla., 2001—02; asst. U.S. atty. U.S. Atty.'s Office, Orlando, 2002—. Editor: (book) ABA Family Law Guide, 2002. Mem.: ABA (vice chair criminal and juvenile justice com. 2000—01, chair 2001—, vice chair litig. com. 2001—). Office: US Attys Office 80 N Hughey Ave Ste 201 Orlando FL 32801 Office Fax: 407-648-7643. Business E-Mail: Vincent.Citro@usdoj.gov.

CITRON, BEATRICE SALLY, law librarian, lawyer, educator; b. Phila., May 19, 1929; d. Morris Meyer and Frances (Teplitsky) Levinson; m. Joel P. Citron, Aug. 7, 1955 (dec. Sept. 1977); children: Deborah Ann, Victor Ephraim. BA in Econs. with honors, U. Pa., 1950; MLS, Our Lady of the Lake U., 1978; JD, U. Tex., 1984. Bar: Tex. 1985; cert. all-level sch. libr., secondary level tchr. Tex. Claims examiner Social Security Adminstrn., Pa., Fla. and N.C., 1951-59; head libr. St. Mary's Hall, San Antonio, 1979-80; media, reference and rare book libr., asst. and assoc. prof. St. Mary's U. Law Libr., San Antonio, 1984-89; asst. dir. St. Thomas U. Law Libr., Miami, Fla., 1989-96, assoc. dir./head pub. svc., 1996-99, acting dir., 1997-98. Law libr. cons., 2000—. Mem.: ABA, South Fla. Assn. Law Librs. (treas. 1992—94, v.p. 1994—95, pres. 1995—96), S.E. Assn. Law Librs. (newsletter, program and edn. coms. 1991—98), S.W. Assn. Law LIbrs. (continuing edn. com. 1986—88, chmn. local arrangements 1987—88), Am. Assn. Law Librs. (publs. com. 1987—88, com. on rels. with info. vendors 1991—93, bylaws com. 1994—96).

CLABAUGH, ELMER EUGENE, JR., retired lawyer; b. Anaheim, Calif., Sept. 18, 1927; s. Elmer Eugene and Eleanor Margaret (Heitshusen) C.; m. Donna Marie Organ, Dec. 19, 1960 (div.); children: Christopher C., Matthew M. BBA cum laude, Woodbury U.; BA summa cum laude, Claremont McKenna Coll., 1958; JD, Stanford U., 1961. Bar: Calif. 1961, U.S. Dist. Ct. (cen. dist.) Calif., U.S. Ct. Appeals (9th cir.) 1961, U.S. Supreme Ct. 1971. With fgn. svc. U.S. Dept. State, Jerusalem, Tel Aviv, 1951-53, Pub. Adminstrn. Svcs., El Salvador, Ethiopia, U.S., 1953-57; dep. dist. atty. Ventura County, Calif., 1961-62; pvt. practice, 1962-97; mem. Hathaway, Clabaugh, Perrett and Webster and predecessors, 1962-79, Clabaugh & Perfloff, Ventura, 1979-97; state inheritance tax referee, 1968-78; ret. Bd. dirs. San Antonio Water Conservation Dist., Ventura Cmty. Meml. Hosp., 1964-80; trustee Ojai Unified Sch. Dist., 1974-79; bd. dirs. Ventura County Found. for Parks and Harbors, 1982-96, Ventura County Maritime Mus., 1982-94. With USCGR, 1944-46, USMCR, 1946-48. Mem. NRA, Calif. Bar Assn., Safari Club Internat., Mason, Shriners, Phi Alpha Delta. Republican. Commercial, contracts (including sales of goods; commercial financing), Probate (including wills, trusts), Property, real (including real estate development, water).

CLAGETT, BRICE MCADOO, lawyer, writer; b. Washington, July 6, 1933; s. Brice and Sarah Fleming (McAdoo) Clagett; m. Virginia Lawrence Parker, Sept. 18, 1965 (div.); children: John Brice, Ann Calvert Brooke; m. Diana Wharton Sinkler, July 26, 1987. AB summa cum laude, Princeton U., 1954; postgrad., U. Allanabad, India, 1954-55; JD magna cum laude, Harvard U., 1958. Bar: D.C. 1958, U.S. Supreme Ct. 1962. Assoc. Covington & Burling, Washington, 1958-67, ptnr., 1967-2000, sr. counsel, 2000—02. Jud. counsellor Cambodian del. Internat. Ct. Justice, 1960—62; legal advisor Transition Team U.S. Dept. State, 1980—81; mem. nat. steering com. U.S. Iran Claimants Com., 1982—99; adv. bd. Inst. Transt. Arbitration, 1989—2000; mem. lawyers com. Ctr. Individual Rights, 1992—. Co-author: (book) The Valuation of Property in International Law, vol. 4, 1987, An Illustrated History of St. Albans School, 1981; bd. editors: Harvard Law Rev., 1956—58; contbr. articles to legal, geneal. and hist. jours. Trustee Md. Hist. Trust, 1971—78, chmn., 1972—78; trustee Md. State Ho. Trust, 1972—76, Md. Environ. Trust, 1978—, vice chmn., 1981—85, chmn., 1985—89; bd. dirs. Chester-Sassafras Found., 1985—89; trustee New Eng. Hist. Geneal. Soc., 1989—92, 1995—98, Tudor Place Found., 1992—96, Found. Preservation hist. Georgetown, 2000—; bd. advisors Nat. Trust Hist. Preservation, 1978—81; Clagett family com. Chesapeake Bay Found., 1982—; mem. Human Rights Law Group del. to Romania, 1990; counselor to the Pres. Gen. Soc. Cin., 1988—89, solicitor, 1998—; mem. adv. coun. Accokeek Found., 1989—91, trustee, 1991—94; comdr. Royal Order Cambodia, 1962. Recipient Cert. Disting. Citizens, State of Md., 1978. Mem.: So. Md. Soc., Federalist Soc., Washington Inst. Fgn. Affairs, Internat. Law Assn., Am. Arbitration Assn., Am. Law Inst., Am. Soc. Internat. Law, Mil. Order Stars and Bars, City Tavern Club (D.C.), Radnor Hunt Club (Pa.), Soc. Cin. Md., Met. Club (D.C.), Marlborough Hunt Club (Upper Marlboro, Md.), Sons Confederate Vets., Phi Beta Kappa. Republican. Episcopalian. Federal civil litigation, Private international, Public international. Home: Holly Hill PO Box 86 Friendship MD 20758-0086 also: 3331 O St NW Washington DC 20007-2814 Office: Covington & Burling PO Box 7566 1201 Pennsylvania Ave NW Washington DC 20044 E-mail: bclagett@cov.com.

CLAPMAN, PETER CARLYLE, lawyer, insurance company executive; b. N.Y.C., Mar. 11, 1936; s. Jack and Evelyn (Clapman); m. Barbara Posen, May 8, 1966; children: Leah, Alice. AB, Princeton U., 1957; JD, Harvard U., 1960. Bar: N.Y. 1961, Conn. 1972. Assoc. Sage, Gray, Todd & Sims, N.Y.C., 1961-63; asst. counsel Stichman Commn., N.Y.C., 1964; legal cons. OEO, Washington, 1965; assoc. counsel Equitable Life, N.Y.C., 1965-72; sr. v.p., chief counsel investments Tchrs. Ins. and Annuity of Am., Coll. Ret. Equities Fund, N.Y.C., 1972—. Chmn. Internat. Corp. Govt. Network; bd. dirs. Nat. Com. for Quality Assurance, Investor Responsibility Rsch. Ctr.

Author: Fiduciary Responsibilities of Institutional Managers on Proxy Issues, Iowa Law Jour., 1994, SEC Market 2000 Report; co-author: Notre Dame U. Law Rev., 1981. Mem. ABA, Assn. Bar City N.Y. (com. on securities regulation spl. com. on mergers), Am. Law Inst. Administrative and regulatory, Commercial, contracts (including sales of goods; commercial financing), Private international. Home: 3 Valley Rd Scarsdale NY 10583-1123 Office: Tchrs Ins & Annuity Assn Am 730 3rd Ave New York NY 10017-3206

CLARK, BRUCE ARLINGTON, JR., lawyer; b. Hopewell, Va., Nov. 17, 1951; s. Bruce Arlington Sr. and Thelma (Givens) C.; m. Catherine Mary Lambert, Aug. 11, 1973; children: Andrew, David, Caryn. BA, Coll. William and Mary, 1973; JD, U. Richmond, 1979. Bar: Va. 1979, U.S. Dist. Ct. (ea. dist.) Va. 1979, U.S. Ct. Appeals (4th cir.) 1979. Law clk. to presiding justice U.S. Bankruptcy Ct., Richmond, Va., 1979-80; assoc. Marks, Stokes & Harrison, Hopewell, 1980-82; sole practice Hopewell, 1982—. Asst. commonwealth atty. City of Hopewell, 1986—. Pres. PTO, Hopewell, 1985; chmn. Hopewell chpt. Am. Heart Soc., 1986—; mem. Hopewell chpt. Am. Cancer Soc., 1985—; bd. dirs. Hopewell Youth Soccer League, 1984. Served with U.S. Army, 1973-77. Mem. ABA, Va. Bar Assn., Hopewell Bar Assn. (pres. 1986—), Va. Trial Lawyers Assn., Hopewell-Prince George C. of C. (vice chmn. 1986—, chmn. bd. dirs. 1987—, pres. 1987), Ducks Unltd. (chmn. 1986—). Methodist. Avocations: golf, fishing, youth soccer. Bankruptcy, General practice. Home: 2703 Princess Anne Ave Hopewell VA 23860-1929 Office: 105 N 2nd Ave Hopewell VA 23860-2701

CLARK, BRUCE F. lawyer; b. Jacksonville, Fla., May 17, 1946; s. Charles H. and Martha Jean Clark; m. Monika Weidner, May 30, 1970; children: Thomas, Stephen, Benjamin. BSBA, Western Ky. U., 1968; JD, U. Of Ky., 1976. Bar: Ky. 1976. Atty. Stites & Harbison, Pllc, Frankfort, Ky., 1976—. Chmn. Frankfort C. of C., 1992—93. Capt. U.S. Army, 1968—71, Germany/Vietnam. Avocation: golf. State and local taxation. Office: Stites & Harbison Pllc 421 West Main St Frankfort KY 40602-0634 Office Fax: 502-223-4124. E-mail: bclark@stites.com.

CLARK, CELIA RUE, lawyer; b. N.Y.C., Aug. 16, 1951; d. Edward Frank and Rosemary (Reddick) Clark, Jr.; m. Edgar Crawford Gentry, Jr., Aug. 11, 1979; children: Diana Marron, Carl Edgar. BA with distinction, U. Wis., 1974; JD, U. Chgo., 1979; LLM, NYU, 1988. Bar: N.Y. 1980. Mng. editor Heldref Publs., Washington, 1974-78; assoc. Rogers & Wells, N.Y.C., 1979-84; adj. asst. prof. law Yeshiva U., 1985; assoc. Weitzner, Levine & Hamburg, N.Y.C., 1988-92; counsel Pirro, Collier, Cohen, Crystal & Block, White Plains, NY, 1992—96; ptnr. Smith, Buss & Jacobs, L.L.P., N.Y.C., 1996—2002; pvt. practice N.Y.C., 2002—. Contbg. author: Asset-Based Financing, 1984; contbr. articles to profl. jours. Mem. planned giving coun. Am. Cancer Soc.; bd. govs. N.Y. chpt. Arthritis Found.; bd. dirs. Louis R. Cappelli Found. Mem. ABA, Westchester County Bar Assn. Democrat. Corporate, general, Estate planning, Taxation, general. Office: Law Offices of Celia R Clark 100 Park Ave 33d Fl New York NY 10017 E-mail: cclark@cclarklaw.com.

CLARK, CHARLES EDWARD, arbitrator; b. Cleve., Feb. 27, 1921; s. Douglas James and Mae (Egermayer) C.; m. Nancy Jane Hilt, Mar. 11, 1942; children: Annette S. (Mrs. Paul Gernhardt), Charles Edward, John A., Nancy P. Gonzalez, Paul R., Stephen C., David G. Student, Berea Coll., 1939-40, King Coll., 1945; JD, U. Tex., 1948. Bar: Tex. 1948, Mass. 1956, U.S. Supreme Ct. 1959. Sole practice, San Antonio, 1948-55; writer legal articles, editor NACCA Law Jour., Boston, 1955-58; legal asst. to vice chmn., chief voting sect. U.S. Commn. on Civil Rights, Washington, 1958-61; spl. counsel Pres.'s Com. on Equal Employment Opportunity, Washington, 1961-65; sr. compliance officer Office Fed. Contract Compliance, Washington, 1965-66; regional dir. Equal Employment Opportunity Commn., Kansas City, Mo., 1966-79, arbitrator, 1979—. Prof. law, asst. dean St. Mary's U. Sch. Law, 1948-55; lectr. Rockhurst Coll., 1980-91, Longview Coll., 1988—. Contbr. articles to legal jours. Active Boy Scouts Am. Served with AUS, 1943-44. Mem. VFW, Assn. Conflict Resolution, State Bar Tex., Tex. Law Rev. Assn., Am. GI Forum (D.C. vice chmn. 1962-63), Soc. Fed. Labor Rels. Profls., Indsl. Rels. Rsch. Assn. (exec. bd. Kansas City 1976-91, pres. chpt. 1986), Profl. Men's Club K.C. (treas. 2002—), Phi Delta Phi (province pres. 1951-55). Home and Office: 6418 Washington St Kansas City MO 64113-1732

CLARK, CORNELIA, lawyer; b. Johannesburg, South Africa, Feb. 2, 1966; arrived in U.S., 96; d. Carel Johannes and Maria Magaretha Jarrard; m. William Robert Clark, Oct. 7, 1995; 1 child, Carlene. BA in Law, U. Stellenbosch, Cape Town, South Africa, 1986, LLB, 1988. Article clk. Mazahams Attys., Johannesburg, 1989—91; pvt. practice, Johannesburg, 1991—95; assoc. Roger Knowles Attys., Durban, South Africa, 1995; pvt. practice Law Offices of Cornelia Clark, Seattle, 1998—. Family and matrimonial. Office: 7200 S 180th St Ste 101 Seattle WA 98188 E-mail: corneliaclark@seanet.com.

CLARK, DAVID EDWARD, lawyer; b. N.Y.C., Apr. 19, 1960; s. Edward White Clark and Croll Margaret; m. Jessica Ruth Towne, Sept. 3, 1988; children: Phoebe Merrill, Gordon Allistair. BA, SUNY, Fredonia, 1981; JD, U. Ga., 1989. Bar: Ga. 89. Assoc. Boyce, Thompson & O'Brien, Norcross, Ga., 1989—91; ptnr. Clark & Towne P.C., Lawrenceville, Ga., 1991—. Contbr. column to Atlanta Jour.-Constitution. Mem. Dems. of Gwinnett County, Lawrenceville, 2001—. Mem.: Ga. DODD DUI Group (Lawyer of Yr. 1999), Ga. Assn. Criminal Def. Lawyers. Criminal. Office: Clark & Towne PC 600 Perry St Lawrenceville GA 30045 Fax: 770-338-2341. E-mail: dclark@clarktowne.com.

CLARK, DAVID LEWIS, lawyer; b. Forest Grove, Oreg., Mar. 11, 1946; s. Virgil James and Lovina (Culbertson) C.; divorced; children: Emily Janis, Bradley David. BS in Sociology, U. Oreg., 1968, JD, 1975. Bar: Oreg. 1975, U.S. Dist. Ct. Oreg. 1976. Ptnr. Nicholson & Clark, Florence, 1978-86; sole practice Florence, 1986—. Atty. City of Florence, 1975-81, Port of Siuslaw, Florence, 1975-92. Bd. dirs. Western Ln. County Found., Florence, 1982-89; justice of peace, Florence, 1983-90. Served with USAF, 1968-72. Mem. U. Oreg. Law Sch. Alumni Assn. (bd. dirs. 1982-83). Lodges: Rotary (pres., bd. dirs. 1982-89), Elks (justice 1976—). Roman Catholic. Avocations: family activities, reading. Estate planning, Family and matrimonial, Probate (including wills, trusts). Office: PO Box 146 Florence OR 97439-0005 E-mail: davec616@hotmail.com.

CLARK, DAVID MCKENZIE, lawyer; b. Greenville, N.C., Sept. 1, 1929; s. David McKenzie and Myrtle Estelle (Brogdon) C.; m. Martha McKellar Early; children: David, Martha Dockery, Marietta Brogdon, Carolyn Elizabeth; m. Susan Summers Mullally; 1 child, McKenzie Lawrence. BA, Wake Forest Coll., 1951; LLD, NYU, 1957. Law clerk Chambers of Justice Black U.S. Supreme Court, Washington, D.C., 1957-59; assoc. Smith, Moore, Smith, Schell & Hunter, Greensboro, N.C., 1959-63; ptnr. Stern Rendleman & Clark, Greensboro, N.C., 1964-68, Clark & Wharton, Greensboro, N.C., 1968-98, Clark Bloss & Wall, Greensboro, 1999—. Mem. bd. dirs. Legal Svcs. of N.C., Raleigh, 1976-82; pres. Summit Rotary Club, Greensboro, 1967; mem. bd. trustees W. Market Street Methodist Ch., Greensboro; chmn., co-founder Greensboro Legal Aid Found., 1965-68. Mem. ABA, Am. Trial Lawyers Assn., Am. Bd. Trial Advocates, N.C. Bar Assn. (bd. govs. 1982-85), N.C. Acad. Trial Lawyers, Greensboro Bar Assn. (bd. dirs.). Avocations: golf, tennis. General civil litigation, Personal injury (including property damage), Securities. Home: 21-C Fountain Manor Dr Greensboro NC 27405 Office: Clark Bloss & Wall 125 S Elm St Ste 600 Greensboro NC 27401-2644

CLARK, DAVID ROBERT, lawyer; b. Streator, Ill., May 28, 1953; s. Robert Allen and Marcia Grace (Hile) C.; m. Patricia Kathleen Bostock, Sept. 26, 1982; 1 child, Ryan Michael. BA, Purdue U., 1975; JD, U. So. Calif., 1978. Bar: Calif. 1978, U.S. Dist. Ct. (all dists.) Calif., U.S. Tax Ct. 1979, U.S. Ct. Appeals (9th cir.) 1979, U.S. Supreme Ct. 1982. Assoc. Higgs, Fletcher & Mack, San Diego, 1978-81; ptnr. Aylward, Kintz & Stiska, San Diego, 1981-87, Jenkins & Perry, San Diego, 1987-90, Musick, Peeler & Garrett, San Diego, 1990-91, Higgs, Fletcher & Mack, San Diego, 1991—. Bd. dirs. Defenders Program of San Diego, 1984-87. Mem. ABA, Calif. Bar Assn., San Diego County Bar Assn., San Diego Country Club, Phi Beta Kappa, Phi Kappa Phi. Avocation: golf. Federal civil litigation, General civil litigation, Property, real (including real estate development, water). Office: Higgs Fletcher & Mack 401 W A St Ste 2600 San Diego CA 92101-7913 E-mail: drclark@higgslaw.com.

CLARK, DAVID SCOTT, law educator, consultant; b. San Diego, Nov. 24, 1944; s. Homer Granville and Edna Susan (Maunus) C.; m. Marilee Oakes Wilson, Mar. 29, 1970; children: Richard, Susanna, Eliina, Liisa, David Scott II. AB, Stanford U., 1966, JD, 1969, JSM, 1972. Bar: Calif. 1972. Vis. prof. law U. Costa Rica, San Jose, 1969-71; asst. dir. studies in law and devel. Stanford (Calif.) Law Sch., 1973-75; asst. prof. law La. State U., Baton Rouge, 1976-78; assoc. prof. law U. Tulsa, 1978-81, prof., 1981—2002, dir. comparative and internat. law ctr., 1993—2001; Wilson prof. law Willamette U., Salem, Oreg., 2002—. Vis. scholar Max Planck Inst., Hamburg, Germany, 1984-85, 92; disting. vis. prof. So. Ill. U., Carbondale, 1987; vis. prof. law U. Colo., 1989; disting. vis. prof. Loyola U., Chgo., 1996; Fulbright sr. chair in comparative law, U. Trento, Italy, 1999; vis. prof. law U. Houston, 1999. Author: Comparative Law, 1978, Law and Social Change, 1979, The Civil Law Tradition, 1994, Oklahoma Civil Pretrial Procedure, 1995; editor: Comparative and Pvt. Internat. Law, 1990, Introduction to the Law of the United States, 1992, 2d edit., 2002, Oxford Companion to American Law, 2002, (jours.) Am. Jour. Comparative Law; contbr. articles to profl. jours. NEH grantee, 1981; von Humboldt Stiftung sr. research fellow, 1984-87. Mem. ABA (internat. law and practice sect.), Am. Soc. Comparative Law (exec. com. 1986-88, treas. 1989-95, v.p. 1998-2002, pres. 2002—), Internat. Acad. Comparative Law, Am. Soc. Legal History, Am. Coun. Learned Socs. (exec. com. 1996-99, chair 1997-99, bd. dirs. 1997-99). Democrat. Unitarian Universalist. Avocations: running, bicycling. Office: Willamette U Coll Law 245 Winter St Salem OR 97301

CLARK, DAVID WILLIAM, lawyer, councilman; b. Manchester, Eng., Jan. 27, 1954; s. Chandler Kinney and May Clark; m. Sally Catherine Clark, June 27, 1987; children: Hilary Alexandra, Gillian Noelle. AB in History, Princeton U., 1975; JD, Duke U., 1978. Bar: Calif. 1978, Colo. 1990, Fla. 1992. Assoc. Thelen, Marrin, Johnson & Bridges, L.A., 1978-84; counsel Ultrasys. Inc. (later Hadson Corp.), Irvine, Calif., 1984-89, Oxbow Corp., West Palm Beach, Fla., 1989—2003, FPL Energy, LLC, Juno Beach, Fla., 2003—. Councilman City of Palm Beach Gardens, Fla., 1993—, mayor, 1994-95; bd. dirs. Palm Beach County chpt. ARC, West Palm Beach, 1998-2001. Mem. State Bar Calif., Colo. Bar Assn., Fla. Bar Assn. Republican. Avocations: reading, history, ships and the sea. Home: 24 Thurston Dr Palm Beach Gardens FL 33418-7097 Office: FPL Energy LLC 700 Universe Blvd Juno Beach FL 33408 E-mail: David_W_Clark@fpl.com.

CLARK, DAVID WRIGHT, lawyer; b. West Point, Miss., May 19, 1948; s. Douglas Earl and Sarah Evelyn (Wright) C.; m. Victoria Baugher, Oct. 16, 1976; children: Alexander, Nicholas, Peter. BA with high honors, Millsaps Coll., 1970; MA, Harvard U., 1971; JD, U. Mich., 1974. Bar: Ill. 1974, Miss. 1978, U.S. Dist. Ct. (no. dist.) Ill. 1974, U.S. Ct. Appeals (7th cir.) 1974, U.S. Dist. Ct. (so. and no. dists.) Miss. 1978, U.S. Ct. Appeals (5th cir.) 1978. Adj. prof. Miss. Coll. Sch. Law, Jackson, 1978-82; assoc. Wildman, Harrold, Allen & Dixon, Chgo., Friedman & Koven, Chgo., 1974-78; shareholder Wise Carter Child & Caraway, P.A., Jackson, 1978-96; ptnr. Lake Tindall, LLP, Jackson, 1996-2001, Bradley Arant Rose & White LLP, Jackson, 2001—. Pres. Miss. Bar Rev., 1979—. Mem. Miss. Constitution Study Commn., Jackson, 1985-87; bd. dirs. Miss. First, Inc., Jackson, 1983-87; pres. U.S.A. Internat. Ballet Competition, Jackson, 1990-98; mem. Leadership Jackson, 1989-90. Mem. ABA (sect. litigation, dir. divsn., com. chmn. and task force chmn. 1987-2000, chmn. gun violence coord. com. 1998-2002), Miss. Bar Assn. (chmn. litigation sect. 1994-95), Am. Law Inst., Charles Clark Am. Inn of Ct. Avocations: musicals, opera. Federal civil litigation, State civil litigation, Corporate, general. Home: 110 Olympia Fields Jackson MS 39211-2509 Office: Bradley Arant Rose & White LLP One Jackson Pl Ste 450 Jackson MS 39201 E-mail: dclark@barw.com.

CLARK, DIDDO, lawyer; b. Oakland, Calif., Jan. 20, 1950; d. Johnson and Louise Clark. AA, Diablo Valley Coll., 1968; BA, U. Calif., San Diego, 1973; JD, Georgetown U., 1976. Bar: Calif. 1978, U.S. Ct. Appeals (9th cir.) 1978, D.C. 1979. Internat. law atty. U.S. Dept. Labor, 1979-83; pvt. practice Lafayette, Calif. Named nat. champion Jessup Internat. Moot Ct. Competition of Am. Soc. of Internat. Law, 1975. Mem. Alameda County Bar Assn. (co-chair Alameda delegation to state bar conf. of dels.). Alternative dispute resolution. Office: 3530 Deer Hill Rd Lafayette CA 94549-3108

CLARK, DONALD H. lawyer; b. Washington, Jan. 29, 1937; BS, U.S. Naval Acad., 1959; JD, George Washington U., 1968. Bar: Va. 1968, U.S. Dist. Ct. (ea. dist.) Va. 1969, U.S. Ct. Appeals (4th cir.) 1974, U.S. Supreme Ct. 1974, U.S. Ct. Fed. Claims 1998. Engr. Naval Elec. Sys., Washington, 1965—68; assoc. Kellam & Kellam, Norfolk, 1968—72; ptnr. Clark & Stant, Virginia Beach, Va., 1972—99; pres., COO Williams, Mullen, Virginia Beach, 1999—. Appointed to Va. State Bar disciplinary bd., 1982-86, med. malpractice rev. panel, 1978-85, 2d dist. ethics com. 1975-77, vice chmn. 1976, chmn. 1977; lectr. continuing legal edn. Co-author: Virginia Construction Law. Vice chmn., chmn. bd. dirs. Sentara Health Care, 1998—; chmn. bd. dirs., mem. exec. com. Tidewater Health Care Inc., 1993-98; chmn. bd. dirs. Virginia Beach Gen. Hosp., 1988-91; chmn. mayor's com. for reapportionment; mem. vestry Eastern Shore Chapel, 1971-74, sr. warden, 1974. Lt. USN, 1959-65. Fellow ACTL; mem. ABA (litigation and law practice mgmt. sects.), Va. State Bar Assn. (litigation and constrn. law sects., bd. govs. constrn. law sect. 1983-86), Virginia Beach Bar Assn. (pres. 1982), Am. Inns of Ct. James Kent Inn (master 1995—). Federal civil litigation, General civil litigation, State civil litigation. Office: Williams Mullen 222 Central Park Ave Ste 1700 Virginia Beach VA 23462-6762 E-mail: dclark@williamsmullen.com.

CLARK, DONALD OTIS, lawyer; b. Charlotte, N.C., May 30, 1934; s. Otis and Ruby Lee (Church) C.; m. Jo Ann Hager, June 15, 1957 (div. 1980); children: Deborah Elise, Stephen Merritt; m. Anja Maria Smith, Nov. 5, 1983. AB, U. S.C., 1956, JD cum laude, 1963; MA, U. Ill., 1957. Bar: S.C. 1963, Ga. 1964, D.C., 1999. Practice law, Atlanta, 1963-83; mem. Candler, Cox, McClain & Andrews, 1968-70, McClain, Mellen, Bowling & Hickman, 1970-75; ptnr. King & Spalding, 1975-78; sr. ptnr. Hurt, Richardson, Garner, Todd & Cadenhead, 1978-83; ptnr. Bishop, Liberman, Cook, Purcell & Reynolds, Washington, 1983-86, Kaplan Russin & Vecchi, Washington, 1986-92, Whitman & Ranson (merged with Breed Abbot & Morgan 1993), Washington, 1992-93; sr. ptnr. Whitman Breed Abbott & Morgan, Washington, 1993-95; ptnr. Keck, Mahin & Cate, Washington, 1995-97, Reed Smith LLP, Washington, 1997—. Mem. dist. export council U.S. Dept Commerce, 1974—; adj. prof. law Emory U., 1970—, U.S.C., 1974; lectr. Ga. State U., 1972; lectr. numerous internat. trade seminars and workshops Author: German govt. study on doing bus. in Southeastern U.S., 1974; editor-in-chief: S.C. Law Rev., 1963; contbr. articles to profl. jours. Served to capt. USAF, 1957-60. Decorated knight Order St. John of Jerusalem, Knights of Malta, knight Order St. Stanislas, knight and minister of justice Order of New Aragon, Sungrye medal Korea; recipient Nat. Leadership medal Air Force Assn., 1956, Coll. award Am. Legion, Outstanding Sr. award U. S.C., 1956, hon. consul Republic of Korea, 1972—. Mem. Atlanta Bar Assn., ABA, S.C. Bar Assn., Ga. Bar Assn., D.C. Bar Assn., Lawyers Club Atlanta, Am. Judicature Soc., Am. Soc. Internat. Law, Atlanta C. of C., Ga. C. of C. (exec. com. Internat. Councils), Inst. Internat. Edn. (chmn. Southeastern regional adv. bd. 1974— , nat. trustee), So. Consortium Internat. Edn. Inc. (dir.), Wig & Robe, Sigma Chi (pres. 1956 Province Balfour award), Omicron Delta Kappa, Kappa Sigma Kappa, Phi Delta Phi (pres. 1963 Province Grad. of Yr. award) Private international, Public international, Taxation, general.

CLARK, DOUGLAS H., JR., lawyer; b. Phoenix, July 17, 1941; s. Douglas H. Clark and Virginia Lee Russel; m. Kathryn Lewis (div. 1973); children: Gregory R., Devon A. Glasco. BS, JD, LLB, U. Ariz., 1966. Bar: Ariz. 1966, U.S. Dist. Ct. Ariz. 1966. Atty. Mesch, Marquez & Rothschild, Tuscon, 1967—73; ptnr. Mesch, Marquez, Clark & Rothschild, PC, Tuscon, 1973—83, Mesch, Clark & Rothschild, PC, Tuscon, 1983—. Mem.: ATLA, ABA, Ariz. State Bar, Ariz. Trial Lawyers Assn. Republican. Avocations: water-skiing, handball. Personal injury (including property damage), Product liability. Office: Mesch Clark and Rothschild 259 N Meyer Tucson AZ 85701 Office Fax: 520-798-1037. Business E-Mail: dclark@mcrazlaw.com.

CLARK, GARY CARL, lawyer; b. Flippin, Ark., Mar. 4, 1947; m. Jane W. Clark; children: Ross, Lauren. BS in Agrl. Edn., Okla. State U., 1969, MS, 1972; JD with honors, U. Tex., 1975. Bar: Okla. 1975, U.S. Dist. Ct. (no. dist.) Okla. 1975, U.S. Ct. Appeals (10th cir.) 1979. Tchr. Laverne H.S., Okla., 1969—70; assoc. Conner, Winters, Ballaine, Barry & McGowen, 1975—81, ptnr., 1981, Baker & Hoster, Tulsa, 1981—97; dir. Crowe & Dunlevy, PC, Tulsa, 1997—. Lawyer-staffed Panel of Ct. Appeals, 1991; speaker in field. Vol. Legal Svcs. Ea. Okla., 1993—; trustee Okla. State Univ., Tulsa, 1999-2001; mem. bd. regents Okla. State Univ. and A&M Colls., 1993-2001, chmn., 1997-98; past v.p. Jane Addams Elem. Sch. PTA, sch. vol.; chair site adv.; mem. Okla. Jud. Evaluation Com., 1999—. Recipient Silver Beaver award Boy Scouts Am., 1996. Fellow Am. Coll. Trust and Estate Coun., Am. Bar Found., Okla. Bar Found. (trustee); mem. Okla. Bar Assn. (pres. 2002, bd. govs. 1997-99, 2001-2003, John Shipp Ethics award 1999, chair estate planning and probate sect. 1988-89, vice chair probate code com. 1991, bd. dirs. young lawyers divsn., mem. real property sect.), Tulsa County Bar Assn. (pres. 1993-94, Golden Rule award 1993, Outstanding Sr. Lawyer 1996), Tulsa County Bar Found. (pres. 1994-95, treas. 1995-99, charter fellow), Tulsa Title and Probate Lawyers Assn. (pres. 1989-90), Okla. State U. Alumni Assn. (life), FFA Alumni Assn. (life), Order of Coif, Alpha Gamma Rho Alumni Assn. (Okla. chpt. dir., past pres.), Phi Delta Phi. Bankruptcy, Estate planning, Probate (including wills, trusts). Home: 5505 S 97th West Ave Sand Springs OK 74063-4726 Office: Crowe & Dunlevy 500 Kennedy Bldg Tulsa OK 74103 E-mail: clarkg@crowedunlevy.com.

CLARK, GLEN EDWARD, judge; b. Cedar Rapids, Iowa, Nov. 23, 1943; s. Robert M. and Georgia L. (Welch) C.; m. Deanna D. Thomas, July 16, 1966; children: Andrew Curtis, Carissa Jane. BA, U. Iowa, 1966; JD, U. Utah, 1971. Bar: Utah 1971, U.S. Dist. Ct. Utah 1971, U.S. Ct. Appeals (10th cir.) 1972. Assoc. Fabian & Clendenin, 1971-74, ptnr., 1975-81, dir., chmn. banking and comml. law sect., 1981-82; judge U.S. Bankruptcy Ct. Dist. Utah, Salt Lake City, 1982-86, chief judge, 1986—. Bd. govs. nat. Conf. Bankruptcy Judges, 1988-94; mem. com. on bankruptcy edn. Fed. Jud. Ctr., 1989-92; vis. prof. U. Utah, Salt Lake City, 1977-79, 83; pres. Nat. Conf. Bankruptcy Judges, 1992-93; chair bd. trustees Nat. Conf. Bankruptcy Judges Endowment for Edn., 1990-92; vis. assoc. prof. law Univ. Utah; instr. adv. bus. law Univ. Utah. Articles editor: Utah Law Review. With U.S. Army, 1966-68. Finkbine fellow U. Iowa. Fellow Am. Coll. Bankruptcy (charter, mem. bd. regents 1995-2000, dir. found. 2002—); mem. Jud. Conf. U.S. (mem. com. jud. br. 1992-99, 10th cir. bankruptcy appellate panel 1996—), Utah Bar Assn., Order of Coif. Presbyterian. Office: 365 US Courthouse 350 S Main St Salt Lake City UT 84101-2106

CLARK, GRANT LAWRENCE, corporate lawyer; b. Syracuse, NY, Apr. 15, 1954; s. Robert William and Linda (Grant) C.; m. Diana Christine Baker, Aug. 5, 1983. BA, Framingham State Coll., 1979; JD, Suffolk U., 1983. Bar: Mass. 1983, Calif. 1992, U.S. Dist. Ct. Mass. 1983, U.S. Dist. Ct. (so. dist.) Calif. 1992, U.S. Ct. Appeals (D.C. cir.) 1995, U.S. Ct. Claims 1995, U.S. Ct. Mil. Appeals 1984. Judge advocate USAF, Washington, 1983-87; asst. gen. counsel GSA, Washington, 1987-88; assoc. Rivkin, Radler, Dunne & Bayh, Washington, 1988-91; assoc./ptnr. McKenna & Cuneo, Washington, 1991-94; asst. gen. counsel Sci. Applications Internat. Corp., San Diego, 1994-99; sr. v.p., gen. counsel Telcordia Tech., Inc., Morristown, NJ, 1999—. Instr. Fed. Publ., Inc., Washington, 1991—99. Capt., USAF, 1983-87. Mem.: ABA. Avocations: mountain biking, latin dance, medieval history. General civil litigation, Commercial, contracts (including sales of goods; commercial financing), Government contracts and claims. Home: 229 Mount Kemble Ave Morristown NJ 07960-6209 Office: Telcordia Tech Inc 445 South St Morristown NJ 07960-6454 E-mail: gclark@telcordia.com.

CLARK, JAMES E. lawyer; b. Strong, Ark., Feb. 10, 1929; s. Carey Eugene Clark and Mary (Braswell) Matthews; m. Susie Erskine (dec.); children: Christopher G., David D., Jeffrey F.; m. Linda Savoy. BBA, La. Tech U., 1952; JD, La. State U., 1957. Bar: La. 1957, U.S. Dist. Ct. (we. dist.) La. 1957, U.S. Ct. Appeals (5th cir.) 1957, U.S. Supreme Ct. 2001. Sr. ptnr. Cook, Clark, Egan, Yancey and King, Shreveport, La., 1957-72; dist. judge State of La. 1st Jud. Dist., Shreveport, La., 1972-90; pvt. practice arbitration and mediation Shreveport, La., 1991—. Pres. La. Dist. Judges Assn., 1982-83; mem. State-Fed. Jud. Coun., 1983-90. Active Caddo Parish Dem. Exec. Com., Shreveport, 1964-72, La. State Dem. Exec. Com., 1964-72; del. Dem. Nat. Conv., 1964, 68; chmn. bd. Live Oak Retirement Cmty., Shreveport. Capt. USAFR, 1952-64; corp. USMC, 1946-48. Recipient Communication award Shreveport Toastmaster Internat., 1987. Mem. ABA, La. State Bar Assn. (del. 1968-72), Shreveport Bar Assn., Mason, Scottish Rite, Shriner, Elks, Rotary (pres. 1990-91). Democrat. Episcopalian. Avocation: reading. Alternative dispute resolution, General civil litigation. Office: 400 Travis St Ste 211 Shreveport LA 71101

CLARK, JAMES RICHARD, lawyer; b. Madison, Wis., Mar. 30, 1946; s. James F. and Gloria J. Clark; m. Martha C. Conrad, Mar. 18, 1950; children: Lindsey Kelley, Chad. BA, Ripon Coll., 1968; JD, U. Wis., 1971. Bar: Wis. 1971, U.S. Dist. Ct. (we. and ea. dists.) Wis. 1972, U.S. Ct. Appeals (7th cir.) 1973, U.S. Dist. Ct. (no. dist.) Ill. 1974, U.S. Supreme Ct. 1976. Assoc. Foley & Lardner, Milw., 1971-78, ptnr., 1978—. Editor-in-chief Wis. Law Rev., 1971. Trustee Ripon Coll., 1985—. 1st lt. U.S. Army, 1971. Mem. ABA, Am. Coll. Trial Lawyers, Am. Bd. Trial Advs., Def. Rsch. Inst., 7th Cir. Bar Assn., Wis. Bar Assn., Ripon Coll. Alumni Assn. (past pres.), Milw. Athletic Club, Tripoli Country Club, Order of Coif, Phi Beta Kappa. General civil litigation, Construction, Product liability. Home: 9719 N Dalewood Ln Mequon WI 53092-6210 Office: Foley & Lardner Firstar Ctr 777 E Wisc Ave Milwaukee WI 53202

CLARK, JENNIE L. lawyer, webmaster; b. Spokane, Apr. 17, 1966; BS, Portland State U.; JD, U. Calif., San Francisco, 1997. Bar: Oreg. 2000. Pvt. practice, Portland, Oreg., 2000—. Personal injury (including property damage). Office: PO Box 42622 Portland OR 97202 E-mail: counselclark@justice.com.

CLARK, JOHN H., JR., lawyer; b. Chester, Pa., June 6, 1928; s. John H. and Emma E. (Higler) C.; m. Esther F. Giaccio, June 12, 1954 (dec. Feb. 2002); 1 child, Jacqueline Ann. BA with honors, U. Pa., 1948, JD cum laude, 1951. Bar: Pa. 1951. Pvt. practice, Ridley Park, Pa., 1973—. Chmn. hearing com. Pa. Supreme Ct. Disciplinary Bd., 1980-86. Pres. Historic Delaware County, Inc., 1972; del. Democratic Nat. Conv., 1960; solicitor Tinicum Twp., 1960-64, Folcroft Borough Sch. Dist., 1959-63, Norwood Borough, 1972-76, Folcroft Borough, 1973-74. Served with USAF, 1952-53; to maj. Res. Mem. ABA, Pa. Bar Assn. (ho. of dels. 1972-82), Delaware County Bar Assn., Delaware County Hist. Soc. (pres. 1989-92), Rotary (pres. Chester Pike club 1973-74). Roman Catholic. Office: PO Box 152 204 E Chester Pike Ridley Park PA 19078-0152 Home: 207 Knoll Rd Wallingford PA 19086

CLARK, JONATHAN MONTGOMERY, lawyer; b. Bklyn., Oct. 20, 1937; s. Russell Inslee and Lillian (Longmore) C.; m. Priscilla M. Jorgensen, Sept. 24, 1960; children: Jonathan M. Jr., Christopher D. BA, Yale U., 1959; LLB, U. Va., 1964. Bar: N.Y. 1965. Assoc. Davis Polk & Wardwell, N.Y.C., 1964-71, ptnr., 1971-93; gen. counsel, mng. dir. Morgan Stanley & Co., Inc., N.Y.C., 1993—98; sr. counsel Davis, Polk & Wardell, N.Y.C., 1999—. Advisor mission to Poland, Fin. Svcs. Vol. Corps, 1990, 92; cons. Warren Commn., Washington, 1965; bd. dirs. Greenwich Hosp. Assn., 1990-98, Prentice Cup Com. bd. dirs. Caramoor Ctr. Music & the Arts. 1st lt. USMC, 1959-61. Mem. ABA, N.Y. State Bar Assn., Assn. Bar City N.Y., Securities Industry Assn. (bd. dirs., 1995-96), N.Y. Stock Exchange Legal Adv. Com. Republican. Episcopalian. Avocations: golf, fly fishing, birding. Office: Davis, Polk & Wardell 450 Lexington Ave New York NY 10017 E-mail: jonathan.clark@dpw.com.*

CLARK, JOSEPH FRANCIS, JR., lawyer; b. Tulsa, Okla., Jan. 20, 1949; s. Joseph F. and Betty Sue C.; m. Carol J. Coleman, Nov. 2, 1974 (div. 1981); m. Cathy A. Baker, Jan. 6, 1989; children: Joseph F. Clark III, Thomas S. Clark, Joshua B. Baker. BA, Villanova U., 1971; JD, Tulsa U., 1973. Bar: Okla. 1974. Atty. Gibbon, Gladd, Clark et al, Tulsa, 1974-78; pvt. practice Tulsa, 1979-80; atty. Williams, Clark et al, Tulsa, 1980-90; ptnr. Clark & Stainer, Tulsa, 1990-94, Layon, Cronin, Clark & Kaiser, P.L.L.C., Tulsa, 1994-99; pvt. practice Tulsa, 1999—. Mem.: Tulsa County Bar Assn. (fee dispute com. 1998—99, profl. responsibility com. 2001—), Am. Inns of Ct. (Council Oak chpt., term master 1996—98, master 1999—). Democrat. Roman Catholic. Appellate, General civil litigation, Insurance. Home: 2922 E 39th St Tulsa OK 74105-3704 Office: 1622 S Denver Ave Tulsa OK 74119-4232 E-mail: jclarkatt@sbcglobal.net.

CLARK, KAREN HEATH, lawyer; b. Pasadena, Calif., Dec. 17, 1944; d. Wesley Pelton and Lois (Ellenberger) Heath; m. Bruce Robert Clark,Dec. 30, 1967; children: Adam Heath, Andrea Pelton. Student, Pomona Coll., Claremont, Calif., 1962-64; BA, Stanford U., 1964-66; MA in History, U. Wash., 1968; JD, U. Mich., 1977. Bar: Calif. 1978. Instr. Henry Ford Community Coll., Dearborn, Mich., 1968-72; assoc. Gibson, Dunn & Crutcher LLP, Irvine, Calif., 1977-86, ptnr., 1986—. Bd. dirs. Dem. Found. Orange County, 1989-91, 94—, Planned Parenthood Orange County, Santa Ana, Calif., 1979-82, New Directions for Women, Newport Beach, 1986-91, Human Options, 2001—, Erin Greenwell Edn. Project, 2003—; bd. dirs. Women in Leadership, chair, 1995-99; trustee Newport Beach Pub. Libr., 2001—; mem. deans adv. coun. Sch. Humanities, U. Calif., Irvine. Recipient 1996 Choice award Planned Parenthood of Orange & San Bernardino Counties. Mem. Women in Leadership (founder 1993), Comml. Real Estate Women, Bldg. Industries Assn. So. Calif., Internat. Coun. Shopping Ctrs., Calif. Mortgage Bankers Assn. Property, real (including real estate development, water). Office: Gibson Dunn & Crutcher LLP 4 Park Plz Ste 1400 Irvine CA 92614-8557 E-mail: kclark@gibsondunn.com.

CLARK, KEVIN P. protective services official; b. N.Y.C., May 20, 1956; B in Polit. Sci., John Jay Coll. Criminal Justice, 1992. Police officer N.Y.C. Police Dept., N.Y.C., 1981—2003, narcotics lt., 1995—97, comdg. officer, 1997—2002, exec. officer narcotics divsn., 2002—03; police commr. Balt. Police Dept., 2003—. Office: Police Dept 601 E Fayette St Baltimore MD 21202*

CLARK, KIM ROGERS, lawyer, real estate developer; b. Ottawa, Ill., Dec. 2, 1936; s. Ted Rogers and Helen (Clare) C.; children: Anna, John, Damon, Joshua, Lynsey; m. Deborah Stinsman, July 15, 1996. AB, Princeton (N.J.) U., 1958; JD, U. Calif., Berkeley, 1964. Bar: Calif. 1965, US Supreme Ct. Commd. ensign USN, 1958, advanced through grades to lt. comdr., 1966, resigned, 1968; assoc. to ptnr. Chickering & Gregory, San Francisco, 1964-76; ptnr. Capron, Hodge & Clark, San Francisco, 1976-80, Clark & Sheppard, San Francisco, 1980-85; pvt. practice San Francisco, 1986—. Personal injury (including property damage). Office: 561 Silva Ave Santa Rosa CA 95404-2407

CLARK, LEROY D. legal educator, lawyer; b. 1934; BA, CCNY, 1956; LLB, Columbia U., 1961. Bar: N.Y. 1961. Staff atty. Office of N.Y. Atty. Gen., 1961-62; asst. cousnel NAACP Legal Def. and Edn. Fund, Inc., N.Y.C., 1962-68; prof. law NYU Law Sch., N.Y.C., 1969-79, Cath. U., 1981—. Gen. counsel EEOC, 1979-81; arbitrator Am. Arbitration Assn., Fed. Mediation and Conciliation Svc.; mem. Pub. Employee Rels. Bd. Author: The Grand Jury: The Use and Abuse of Political Power, 1975, Employment Discrimination Law--Cases and Materials, 5th edit., 2000. Office: Law School Catholic Univ Am 3600 John Mccormack Rd NE Washington DC 20064-0001 E-mail: clarkl@law.cua.edu.

CLARK, MARCIA RACHEL, former prosecutor; b. Berkeley, Calif., 1954; d. Abraham I. Kleks; m. Gabriel Horowitz, 1976 (div. 1980); m. Gordon Clark (div. 1994); 2 children. BA in Polit. Sci., UCLA, 1974; JD, Southwestern U., 1979. Atty. Brodey and Price, LA, 1979-81, LA County Dist. Atty. Office, LA, 1981-97; legal analyst/commentator NBC, CNBC, MSNBC, 1998; host "Lie Detector", for FOX, 1998. Ms. Clark toured the US and Canada giving lectures on a variety of women's issues, including domestic violence, inspirational/motivational speeches, as well as lectures on pub. svc. careers, and , of course, the Trial of the Century. Author (with Teresa Carpenter) Without a Doubt, 1997. Ms. Clark hosted "Rivera Live" on Friday nights and during all of Geraldo Rivera's vacations. Mailing: William Morris Agency One William Morris Pl Beverly Hills CA 90212*

CLARK, MARK JEFFREY, paralegal, researcher; b. Alton, Ill., Nov. 2, 1953; s. William Alfred and Winifred May (Young) C.; m. Patricia Ann Newell, July 29, 1989; children: Jason William, Brandi Leigh. AS in Bus. Adminstrn., Lewis & Clark Coll., 1978; cert. paralegal, diploma in civil lit. and bus. law, Paralegal Inst., Atlanta, 1994. Commd. spl. officer Lake Ozark (Mo.) Police Dept., 1975-78; ind. paralegal J & B Enterprises, Woodriver, Ill., 1994—; criminal rschr. Pinkerton Svcs. Group, Charlotte, N.C., 1998—, MPC Legal Rsch. Consulting Svcs., Battle Creek, Mich., 1999—. Cons., rschr. Nationwide Corps., 1994—. With USN, 1972-75, Vietnam. Mem. Nat. Paralegal Assn., KC (4th degree), Am. Legion. Democrat. Roman Catholic. Avocations: scuba diving, golf, bowling. Home: 318 S Pence East Alton IL 62024 Personal E-mail: MJC3562002@yahoo.com. Business E-Mail: MJC356@netscape.net.

CLARK, MARK LEE, lawyer; b. Muskegon, Mich., July 13, 1953; s. Alva Lee and Esther Luella (Bellinger) C.; m. Jane Ellen Lyons, Sept. 3, 1983; children: Zachary, Caitlin. BA with high honors, Mich. State U., 1975; JD with honors, Wayne State U., 1978. Bar: Mich. 1978, U.S. Dist. Ct. (ea. dist.) Mich. 1982. Assoc. McLean & Mijak, Romeo, Mich., 1978-82; ptnr. McLean, Mijak & Clark, P.C., Romeo, 1982—; mcpl. atty. City of Richmond, Mich., 1993—. Mcpl. atty. Village of Romeo, 1985—. Pres. bd. trustees, bd. dirs. Romeo Dist. Library, 1981-85. Mem. ATLA, Mich. Bar Assn., Macomb County Bar Assn. Avocations: running, golf. State civil litigation, General practice, Municipal (including bonds). Home: 268 W Saint Clair St Romeo MI 48065-4662 Office: McLean Mijak & Clark P C 137 W Saint Clair St Romeo MI 48065-4657 E-mail: mmc@ees.eesc.com.

CLARK, MARTIN F(ILLMORE), JR., judge; b. Winston-Salem, N.C., June 23, 1959; s. Martin Fillmore Sr. and Hazel Victoria (Young) C. BA cum laude, Davidson Coll., 1981; JD, U. Va., 1984. Bar: Va. 1984, U.S. Dist. Ct. (we. and ea. dists) Va. 1985. Judge 21st Jud. Cir., Stuart, Va., 1992—. Patrick County escheator, Stuart, 1984; commr. of accounts, 21st Jud. Cir., Patrick County, 1986. Author: The Many Aspects of Mobile Home Living, 2000 (N.Y. Times Notable Book, Book-of-the-Month Club selection, Stephen Crane Fiction award finalist). Bd. dirs. Patrick County Spl. Edn. Adv. Bd.; trustee Stuart Presbyn. Ch. Recipient Vereen Bell Creative Writing award Author's Panel, Davidson Coll., 1979, 81. Mem. ATLA, Patrick County C. of C. (bd. dirs.), Phi Beta Kappa. Avocations: writing fiction, horses, fishing. Office: PO Box 762 Stuart VA 24171-0762 E-mail: maclark@neocom.net.

CLARK, MERLYN WESLEY, lawyer; b. Grand Forks, British Columbia, Can., Oct. 27, 1937; came to U.S., 1938; s. Robert Wesley and Lilia Ann (Frechette) C.; m. Sandra Sue Bolan, Mar. 15, 1969. JD, U. Idaho, 1964. Bar: Idaho 1964, U.S. Dist. Ct. Idaho 1964, U.S. Supreme Ct. 1987, U.S. Ct. Appeals (9th cir.) 1989, U.S. Ct. of Fed. Claims 1994; approved mediator Idaho Fed. Cts., Idaho State Cts. Assoc. Blake, Givens & Feeney, Lewiston, Idaho, 1964-66; ptnr. Blake, Givens, Feeney & Clark, Lewiston, 1966-68; pvt. practice law, 1968-74, 78-79; ptnr. Clark, Curtin & Creason, Lewiston, 1974-78, Hawley, Troxell, Ennis & Hawley, Boise, Idaho, 1979—; mng. mem. Clark Dispute Resolution LLC, 2001—. Pros. atty. Nez Perce County, Lewiston, 1974-77; mem. Idaho Supreme Ct. Civil Rules Adv. com., Boise, 1975-86; mem. Idaho Supreme Ct. Evidence Rules com., Boise, 1986-92. Fellow Am. Coll. of Trial Lawyers; mem. ABA, Idaho Bar Assn. (commr. 1977-79, cert. appreciation 1984, Distinguished Lawyer Award, 2001), Boise Bar Assn., Assn. Trial Lawyers Am., Idaho Assn. Def. Counsel, Idaho Law Found. (pres. 1984-86), Idaho Trial Lawyers Assn., Idaho Mediation Assn. (cert.), Am. Inns of Ct. Found. (master lawyer), Boise CXXX. Alternative dispute resolution, Federal civil litigation, State civil litigation. Home: 3983 W Quail Ridge Dr Boise ID 83707-3855 Office: Hawley Troxell Ennis & Hawley PO Box 1617 Boise ID 83701-1617

CLARK, MERRELL EDWARD, JR., lawyer; b. Bklyn., Apr. 30, 1922; s. Merrell Edward and Eleanor Everest (Wild) C.; m. Hollis Logan, May 22, 1943; children: Julie Clark Goodyear, Kenyon Wild. BA, Yale U., 1943, LLB, 1948. Bar: N.Y. 1948, U.S. Dist. Ct. (so. dist.) 1949, U.S. Ct. Appeals (2d cir.) 1949, U.S. Tax Ct. 1951, Conn. 1952, U.S. Dist. Ct. (ea. dist.) N.Y. 1952, U.S. Dist. Ct. (ea. dist.) N.Y. 1952, U.S. Supreme Ct. 1956, U.S. Ct. Appeals (6th cir.) 1965, U.S. Ct. Appeals (8th cir.) 1973, U.S. Ct. Appeals (4th cir.) 1974, U.S. Dist. Ct. (no. dist.) N.Y. 1982, U.S. Dist. Ct. (we. dist.) N.Y. 1982. Assoc. Winthrop, Stimson, Putnam & Roberts, N.Y.C., 1948-55, ptnr., 1956-91. Editor Yale Law Sch. Jour., 1947-48. Mem. Town Meeting, Greenwich, Conn., 1953-56, com. on jud. appointments (Appelate Div. 1st Dept.), 1978-82, 2d cir. jud. conf. evaluation com., 1980-87; dir.; trustee Perrot Meml. Library, Old Greenwich, Conn., 1956-63, Pomfret (Conn.) Sch., 1966-74, Richard Found., N.Y.C., 1965-2002, William Nelson Cromwell Found., N.Y.C., 1979—, Steep Rock Assn., Washinton, Conn., 1993—, Internat. Coll. Hospitality Mgmt., 1994-2002; adviser women's rights project ACLU, 1976-90; mem. N.Y.C. Bd. Ethics, 1987-89; chair N.Y.C. Conflicts of Interest Bd., 1989-90, N.Y.C. Hardship Appeals Bd., 1993-2001; bd. dirs. N.Y. Legal Aid Soc., 1985-88. Served to capt. AUS, 1943-46. Decorated Bronze Star with two battle stars. Mem. ABA (ho. of dels. 1985-89), Assn. of Bar of City of N.Y. (pres. 1978-80), Am. Law Inst., Am. Coll. Trial Lawyers, River Club (N.Y.C.), India House Club (N.Y.C.), Washington Club (Conn.). Antitrust, Federal civil litigation. Office: Pillsbury Winthrop LLP 1 Battery Park Plz New York NY 10004-1490 Personal E-mail: htgclark@aol.com. Business E-Mail: mclerk@pillsbury-winthrop.com.

CLARK, MORTON HUTCHINSON, lawyer; b. Norfolk, Va., Apr. 21, 1933; s. David Henderson and Catharine Angelica (Hutchinson) C.; m. Lynn Harrison Adams, Aug. 12, 1961; children: Allison Adams, David Henderson, Susan West, Julia Dixon. BA in English, U. Va., 1954, LLB, 1960. Bar: Va. 1960, U.S. Dist. Ct. (ea. dist.) Va. 1960, U.S. Ct. Appeals (4th cir.) 1976, U.S. Ct. Appeals (1st cir.) 1993, U.S. Supreme Ct. 1993. Assoc. Vandeventer Black LLP, Norfolk, 1960-65, ptnr., 1965—. Co-editor: The Virginia Lawyer, 1991-93. Chmn. Va. Commn. for Children and Youth, Richmond. Fellow Am. Coll. Trial Lawyers, Va. Law Found.; mem. Maritime Law Assn. (exec. com. 1984-87), Hoffman I'Anson Am. Inns of Ct. (exec. com. 1993-95), The Harbor Club (pres.), Town Point Club, Princess Anne Country Club, Farmington Country Club. Episcopalian. Avocations: off shore racing, cruising. Admiralty, Federal civil litigation. Home: 103 Rivers Edge Kingsmill Williamsburg VA 23185-8930 Office: Vandeventer Black LLP 500 World Trade Ctr Norfolk VA 23510-1679

CLARK, PAT ENGLISH, lawyer; b. Austin, Tex., Feb. 26, 1940; s. Pat Wheeler and Jennie Bell (Lagrone) C.; m. Peggy Arnold Gray, March 16, 2002; 1 child, Susan Louise Beisert. BA, JD, U. Tex. Bar: Tex. 1963, U.S. Ct. Mil. Appeals 1964, U.S. Dist. Ct. (so. and no. dists.) Tex. Staff atty. Phillips Petroleum Co., Houston, 1967-69; atty. Amoco Production Co., Houston, 1969-75; ptnr. Vinson & Elkins, Houston, 1975-95, Borrego & Clark, 1996-99. Capt. JAGC, U.S. Army, 1964-67. Presbyterian. Oil, gas, and mineral, Property, real (including real estate development, water). Office: 9809 Villa Maria Cove Austin TX 78759

CLARK, PAUL JAY, lawyer, police detective; b. Oceanside, N.Y., Dec. 5, 1963; s. Paul Francis and Mary Ann (Genoese) C. BA, Hofstra U., Hempstead, N.Y., 1984, JD, 1988; grad., Fed. Bur. Investigation Nat. Acad., 2000. Bar: N.Y. 1988. Police officer Precinct 4, Nassau Co. Police Dept., Mineola, NY, 1985-87, detective legal bur., 1987-92; pvt. practice lawyer Mineola, 1988—; detective 6th squad Nassau Co. Police Dept., Mineola, NY, 1992-98; sgt. legal bur. Nassau County (N.Y.) Police Dept., 1998—2000, sgt. Fifth Precinct, 2000—01, lt. Fourth Precinct, 2001—02, comdg. officer Legal Bur., 2002—. Instr. Nassau County Police Acad., 1987—. Mem. Mensa. Avocations: reading, weight training, computers, golf. General practice. Office: 190 Mineola Blvd Ste 2L Mineola NY 11501-2535

CLARK, PAUL THOMAS, lawyer; b. Long Beach, Calif., Oct. 10, 1954; s. Thomas Joseph and Lois (Olney) C.; m. Deborah Elaine Myers, May 18, 1991 (div. 2000). AB in History, U. Calif., 1976, JD, 1980. Bar: D.C. 1980. Legis. asst. Congressman Mark W. Hannaford, Washington, 1976-77; assoc. Williams & Jensen, P.C., Washington, 1980-84, Seward & Kissel, Washington, 1984-87, legis. counsel, 1987-88, ptnr., 1989—. Bd. dirs. Bank 2000, N.A., 1985-91. Pres. Calif. State Soc., Washington, 1986; bd. dirs. Washington Chamber Symphony, 1996-2000. Mem. ABA, D.C. Bar Assn., Internat. Bar Assn., Berkeley Alumni Club (pres.). Avocations: tennis, golf, bicycling. Banking, Legislative, Securities. Office: Seward & Kissel 1200 G St NW Ste 350 Washington DC 20005-3881

CLARK, RICHARD EDWARD, lawyer; b. Geneva, N.Y., Jan. 4, 1947; s. Henry F. and Leona (Naughton) C.; m. Sherilyn Johns, Dec. 30, 1972 (div. 1995); children: Robert F., Jennifer P. AB summa cum laude, Syracuse U., 1972; JD, Albany Law Sch. of Union U., 1976. Bar: N.Y. 1977, U.S. Dist. Ct. (no. dist.) N.Y. 1977, Ariz. 1983, U.S. Dist. Ct. Ariz. 1983. Assoc. Carey, LaRocque & Piasecki, Malone, N.Y., 1977-78, ptnr., 1978-83; pvt. practice Scottsdale, Ariz., 1983-2000; mng. atty. Salt River Pima-Maricopa Indian Cmty. Legal Svcs. Office, 2000—. Mem. council Our Lady Perpetual Help Ch., Scottsdale, 1985-87. Served with USAF, 1967-71, Vietnam. Mem. ABA, N.Y. State Bar Assn., Ariz. Bar Assn., Scottsdale Bar Assn., Am. Arbitration Assn. (assocs. comml. panel), Scottsdale C. of C., KC (chancellor 1985-86), Phi Kappa Phi. Democrat. Roman Catholic. Native American, Personal injury (including property damage), Probate (including wills, trusts).

CLARK, ROBERT CHARLES, dean, law educator; b. New Orleans, Feb. 26, 1944; s. William Vernon and Edwina Ellen (Nuessly) C.; m. Kathleen Margaret Tighe, June 1, 1968; children— Alexander Ian, Matthew Tighe. BA, Maryknoll Sem., 1966; PhD, Columbia U., 1971; JD, Harvard U., 1972. Bar: Mass. 1972. Assoc. firm Ropes & Gray, Boston, 1972-74; asst. prof. Yale U. Law Sch., New Haven, 1974-76, assoc. prof., 1976-77, prof., 1977-78; prof. law Harvard U., Cambridge, Mass., 1978—, dean of Law Sch., 1989—. Contbr. articles to profl. jours. Mem. Am. Bar Assn.

CLARK, ROBERT MUREL, JR., lawyer; b. Dallas, Mar. 7, 1948; s. Robert M. Sr. and Dorrace Helen (Schaerdel) C.; m. Kimberly Ann Kerss, Oct. 25, 1986; 1 child, Ashley Pendleton. BBA, U. Tex., 1972; MBA, So. Meth. U., 1978; JD, Oklahoma City U., 1982. Bar: Tex. 1982, U.S. Dist. Ct. (no. dist.) Tex. 1982, U.S. Ct. Appeals (5th cir.) 1982, U.S. Supreme Ct. 1988; cert. in civil trial law Tex. Bd. Legal Specialization; cert. trial specialist Nat. Bd. Trial Advocacy. Ptnr. Eddleman & Clark, Dallas, 1989—. Author: The Evangelical Knights of Saint John, 2003; contbr. articles to profl. jours. Del. state conv. Tex. Rep. Party, 1970, 72, 74, 82, 90; bd. dirs. Haile Selassie Fund for Ethiopian Children in Need; sec., bd. dirs. Dallas Goethe Ctr.; bd. dirs. Tex. Conf. of Chs. Decorated grand officer Order of Ethiopian Lion, 1998, hon. knight Order of Vitez (Hungary), 1997, knight Order of St. John (Brandenburg), 1996; recipient Grand Cross, Rwanden Order of the Lion, 2000. Fellow Tex. Bar Found. (life), Soc. Antiquaries (Scotland); mem. State Bar Tex., Am. Bd. Trial Advs. (Dallas chpt.), Oak Cliff Bar Assn. (pres. 1990), Am. Soc. Legal History, Soc. of the Cin., Aztec Club, Sons Republic of Tex., Founders and Patriots Am. (dep. atty. gen.), Nat. Huguenot Soc. (former coun. gen. and 3d v.p. gen.), St. Nicholas Soc., Johanniterorden-Bailiwick of Brandenburg, Johanniter Hilfsgemeinschaften (bd. dirs., Washington), Army and Navy Club (Washington), City Tavern Club (Washington), Phi Delta Phi, Phi Delta Theta. Episcopalian. General civil litigation, Commercial, contracts (including sales of goods; commercial financing). Office: 4627 N Central Expy Dallas TX 75205-4022

CLARK, ROSS BERT, II, lawyer; b. Lafayette, Ind., Dec. 23, 1932; s. Ross Bert and Pauline Frances (Wilkinson) C.; m. Madge Logan, Dec. 27, 1959; 1 stepchild, George W. Johnson III. BA in History, U. of the South, 1954; JD, U. Tenn., 1960. Bar: Tenn. 1961, U.S. Dist. Ct. (we. dist.) Tenn. 1961, U.S. Dist. Ct. (no. dist.) Miss. 1981, U.S. Dist. Ct. (ea. dist.) Ark. 1996, U.S. Ct. Appeals (6th cir.) 1962. Law clk. to presiding judge U.S. Dist. Ct. (we. dist.) Tenn., Memphis, 1961-62; assoc. Rupert & Ewing, Memphis, 1962-64, Laughlin, Watson, Garthright & Halle, Memphis, 1964-68; ptnr. Laughlin, Halle, Clark, Gibson, McBride, Memphis, 1968-84, McKnight, Hudson, Lewis, Henderson & Clark, Memphis, 1985-91, Apperson, Crump, Duzane & Maxwell, Memphis, 1991-96, Armstrong Allen PLLC, Memphis, 1996—. Instr. med. and dental jurisprudence U. Tenn., Memphis, 1963-72; asst. city atty. City of Memphis, 1972-78. Tenn. commr. Nat. Conf. Commrs. on Uniform Laws, 1998—; chmn. bd. dirs. Memphis Heart Assn., 1971—72; mem. adv. coun. U. Tenn. Law Sch., 1983—90, chmn. adv. coun., 1986—88; trustee U. of the South, 1992—95, 1998—. Fellow: Tenn. Bar Found. (trustee 1989—98, chmn. 1996—97), Am. Bar Found.; mem.: Memphis Bar Assn. (treas. 1981, sec. 1982, v.p. 1983, pres. 1984), Tenn. Bar Assn. (ho. of dels. 1986—88, bd. govs. 1988—94), Tenn. Supreme Ct. Hist. Soc. (bd. dirs. 2002—), Rotary (sec. 1988, bd. dirs. 1988—90, 2002—, Paul Harris fellow 2002). Republican. Episcopalian. Federal civil litigation, Labor (including EEOC, Fair Labor Standards Act, labor-management relations, NLRB, OSHA). Office: Armstrong Allen PLLC Brinkley Plz Ste 700 80 Monroe Ave Memphis TN 38103-2481

CLARK, R(UFUS) BRADBURY, lawyer, director; b. Des Moines, May 11, 1924; s. Rufus Bradbury and Gertrude Martha (Burns) C.; m. Polly Ann King, Sept. 6, 1949; children: Cynthia Clark Maxwell, Rufus Bradbury, John Atherton. BA, Harvard U., 1948, JD, 1951; diploma in law, Oxford U., Eng., 1952; D.H.L., Ch. Div. Sch. Pacific, San Francisco, 1983. Bar: Calif. 1952. Assoc. O'Melveny & Myers, L.A., 1952-62, sr. ptnr., 1961-93; mem. mgmt. com., 1983-90; of counsel O'Melveny & Myers LLP, L.A., 1993—. Bd. dirs. Econ. Resources Corp., Brown Internat. Corp., Brown Citrus Sys., Inc., Avoco Internat. Corp., John Tracy Clinic, also pres. 1982-88, Tracy Family Hearing Ctrs., Ch. Charitable Found. Episcopal Diocese L.A., 2000—. Editor: California Corporation Laws, 7 vols, 1976—. Chancellor Prot. Episcopal Ch. in the Diocese of L.A., 1967—, hon. canon, 1983—. Capt. U.S. Army, 1943-46. Decorated Bronze Star with oak leaf cluster, Purple Heart with oak leaf cluster; Fulbright grantee, 1952. Mem. ABA (com. law and acctg., task force on audit letters 1976-93, com. on opinions 1988-92), State Bar Calif. (chmn. drafting com. on gen. corp. law 1973-81, drafting com. on nonprofit corp. law 1980-84, mem. exec. com. bus. law sect. 1977-78, 84-87, sec. 1986-87, mem. com. nonprofit orgns. 1991—, mem. task force on opinions 1999—), L.A. County Bar Assn., Harvard Club, Chancery Club, Alamitos Bay Yacht Club (Long Beach, Calif.). Republican. Banking, Corporate, general, Non-profit and tax-exempt organizations. Office: O'Melveny & Myers LLP 400 S Hope St Los Angeles CA 90071-2899

CLARK, WILLIAM H., JR., lawyer; b. Phila., Apr. 10, 1951; s. William H. and Alice Kimes (Metts) C.; m. Cristine D. Merkel, Aug. 18, 1973; children: Matthew, Alison, Daniel. BA summa cum laude, Amherst Coll., 1973; MA in Religion, Westminster Sem., 1979; JD magna cum laude, Temple U., 1983. Bar: Pa. 1983. Assoc. Morgan, Lewis & Bockius, Phila., 1983-89; ptnr. Klett Lieber Rooney & Schorling, Pitts., 1989-98, Phila., 1998-99, Drinker Biddle & Reath LLP, Phila., 1999—. Chmn. corp. bur. advisory com. Pa. Dept of State, 1991—; cons. rules disciplinary bd. Supreme Ct. Pa., Harrisburg, 1983—. Fellow Am. Bar Found.; mem. ABA (com. on corp. laws, com. on bus. courts), Pa. Bar Assn. (draftsman, lobbyist, corp. law com. 1984—, coun. sect. corp. banking and bus. law 1989-93, officer 1993-2001), Allegheny County Bar Assn. (coun. sect. corp. banking and bus. law 1991-97, officer 1997-98), Phila. Bar Assn. (coun. bus. law sect. 1998—), Am. Law Inst., Phi Beta Kappa. Republican. Presbyterian. Corporate, general, Mergers and acquisitions, Securities. Office: Drinker Biddle & Reath LLP One Logan Sq Philadelphia PA 19103 E-mail: clarkwh@dbr.com.

CLARK, WILLIAM NORTHINGTON, lawyer, former army reserve officer; b. Meridian, Miss., Jan. 16, 1941; s. Oliver Watson and Mildred Catherine (Northington) C.; m. Faye Virginia Baker, Feb. 1, 1964; children: Helen Catherine Smith, William Northington Jr. BS, U.S. Mil. Acad., 1963; JD, U. Ala., 1971. Bar: Ala. 1971 (pres.-elect 2002-03, chmn. com. on indigent defense 1975-81, chmn. Fed. judiciary liason com. 1983-85), U.S. Ct. Appeals (5th and 11th cirs.), U.S. Supreme Ct., Ala. Law Inst. (chmn. Children's Code Com. 1986-93), Nat. Assn. Criminal Def. Lawyers. Law clk. to Judge Walter P. Gewin U.S. Ct. Appeals (5th cir.), 1971—72; assoc. Rogers Howard Redden & Mills, Birmingham, Ala., 1972-74, ptnr., 1974-79, Redden Mills & Clark, Birmingham, 1979—. Adj. prof. evidence U. Ala. Sch. Law, 1979, adj. prof. criminal procedure, 2000, adj. prof. bus. fraud, 01; mem. Ala. Supreme Ct. Advisory Com. on Criminal Procedure, 1979—94. Bd. dirs. Metro YMCA of Birmingham, 1989—, chmn., 1992-94; bd. dirs. Boys and Girls Club of Cen. Ala., Birmingham, 1987—. Capt. U.S. Army, 1963-68, Vietnam; maj. gen. USAR. Mem. Birmingham Bar Assn. (sec., treas. 1987-88, pres.-elect 1992, pres. 1993). Methodist.

General civil litigation, Criminal, Family and matrimonial. Home: 2915 Canterbury Rd Birmingham AL 35223-1203 Office: Redden Mills & Clark 940 Financial Ctr 50520th St N Birmingham AL 35203-3288*

CLARKE, ALAN WILLIAM, lawyer; b. Arlington, Va., Aug. 19, 1949; s. William Garland and Josephine Sessions (Cornell) C.; 1 child, Benjamin Alan; m. Laurie Anne Whitt, Oct. 22, 1994. BA, William and Mary Coll., 1972, JD, 1975; LLM, Queen's U., Kingston, Ont., Can., 1994; postgrad., Western Mich. U., 1998—. Bar: Va. 1975, Mich. 1994, U.S. Dist. Ct. (ea. dist.) Va., U.S. Dist. Ct. (we. dist.) Mich., U.S. Ct. Appeals (4th and 6th cirs.), U.S. Bankruptcy Ct. (ea. dist.) Va., U.S. Supreme Ct. Assoc. Clarke & Johnston, P.C., Lively, Va., 1975-81; ptnr. Clarke & Clarke, Kilmarnock, Va., 1981-93; sole practitioner Chassell, Mich., 1994-97; asst. prof. criminal justice Ferris State U., 1997-2001, U. Wis.-Parkside, 2001—. Cons. in field; dir. Rappahanock Legal Svcs. Corp., Fredericksburg, Va.; adj. prof. bus. Rappahanock C.C., 1987-88; adj. prof. criminal justice Gogebic C.C., 1995-96; vis. scholar humanities dept. Mich. Technol. U., summers 1998, 2000; lectr. in field. Contbr. articles to legal jours. Fireman, Upper Lancaster Fire Dept.; bd. dirs. York chpt. Chesapeake Bay Found., 1974, No. Neck Audubon Soc., Kilmarnock, Va., 1982. Recipient Spl. Recognition award Lancaster County br. NAACP, 1993, Cert. of Recognition for pub. svc.. Coll. William and Mary, 1993, Cert. of Appreciation, Va. State Bar, 1993. Mem. ACLU, Am. Soc. Criminology, Can. Law and Soc. Assn., Nat. Assn. Criminal Def. Lawyers, Va. Bar Assn., Nat. Lawyers Guild, Upper Lancaster Ruritan (pres. 1982-83). Democrat. Episcopalian. Club: Upper Lancaster Ruritan (pres. 1982-83). Federal civil litigation, State civil litigation, Criminal. Office: U Wis-Parkside Molinaw 380 900 Kenosha Rd Kenosha WI 53141-2000

CLARKE, CHARLES FENTON, lawyer; b. Hillsboro, Ohio, July 25, 1916; s. Charles F. and Margaret (Patton) C.; m. Virginia Schoppenhorst, Apr. 3, 1945 (dec. July 1989); children: Elizabeth, Margaret, Jane, Charles Fenton, IV; m. Lesley Wells, Nov. 13, 1998. AB summa cum laude, Washington and Lee U., Lexington, Va., 1938; LLB, U. Mich., 1940; LLD (hon.), Cleve. State U., 1971. Bar: Mich. 1940, Ohio 1946. Pvt. practice, Detroit, 1942, Cleve., 1946—; ptnr. firm Squire, Sanders & Dempsey, 1957—, adminstr. litigation dept., 1979-85. Trustee Cleve. Legal Aid Soc., 1959-67; pres. Nat. Assn. R.R. Trial Counsel, 1966-68; life mem. 6th Circuit Jud. Conf.; chmn. legis. com. Cleve. Welfare Fedn., 1961-68; master bencher Celebrezze Inn of Ct., 1991—; bd. dirs. Wheeling and Lake Erie R.R. Co. Pres. alumni bd. dirs. Washington and Lee U., 1970-72; pres. bd. dirs. Free Med. Clinic Greater Cleve., 1970-86; trustee Cleve. Citizens League, 1956-62, Cleve. chpt. ACLU, 1986-93, Cleve. Works Inc., 1995—; bd. dirs. citizens adv. bd. Cuyahoga County (Ohio) Juvenile Ct., 1970-73; bd. dirs. George Jr. Republic, Greenville, Pa., 1970-73, Bowman Tech. Sch., Cleve., 1970-91; vice chmn. Cleve. Crime Commn., 1973-75; exec. com. Cuyahoga County Rep. Orgn., 1950—; councilman Bay Village, Ohio, 1948-53; pres., trustee Cleve. Hearing and Speech Ctr., 1957-62, Laurel Sch., 1962-72, Fedn. Cmty. Progress, 1984-90; mem. planning commn. Cleveland Heights, 1994-2003. Fellow Am. Coll. Trial Lawyers; mem. Greater Cleve. Bar Assn. (trustee 1983-86), Cleve. Civil War Round Table (pres. 1968), Cleve. Zool. Soc. (dir. 1970), Phi Beta Kappa. Clubs: Skating, Union (Cleve.); Tavern, Rowfant. Presbyterian. Home: 2262 Tudor Dr Cleveland Heights OH 44106-3210 Office: Squire Sanders & Dempsey 4900 Key Tower 127 Public Sq Cleveland OH 44114-1304 E-mail: cclarke@ssd.com.

CLARKE, DAVID ALAN, lawyer; b. Hillsboro, Ohio, Apr. 15, 1950; s. Thomas C. and Dorothea S. Clarke; m. Marilee Ann Miller, Dec. 27, 1980; children: Douglas, Kevin. BA, Claremont McKenna Coll., 1972; JD, Stanford U., 1975. Bar: Ariz. 1975, U.S. Dist. Ct. Ariz. 1976. Assoc. Rawlins, Ellis, Burrus & Kiewit, Phoenix, 1975-81; asst. corp. counsel Greyhound Capital Corp., Phoenix, 1981-86; assoc. corp. counsel Bell Atlantic Sys. Leasing Internat., Inc., Phoenix, 1986-93; corp. counsel BHFC Fin. Svcs., Inc., Phoenix, 1994—. Mem. Maricopa County Bar Assn. Democrat. Methodist. Avocations: golf, biography. Commercial, consumer (including collections, credit), Commercial, contracts (including sales of goods; commercial financing), Corporate, general. Office: BHFC Financial Svcs Inc 3320 W Cheryl Dr Ste 120B Phoenix AZ 85051-9560

CLARKE, EDWARD OWEN, JR., lawyer; b. Balt., Dec. 19, 1929; s. Edward Owen and Agnes Oakford C.; m. P. Rhea Parker, Dec. 18, 1954; children: Deborah Jeanne, Catherine Ann, Carolyn Agnes, Edward Owen III. AB magna cum laude, Loyola Coll., Balt., 1950; JD with honors, U. Md., 1956. Bar: Md. 1956, U.S. Dist. Ct. Md. 1956. Law clk. U.S. Dist. Ct. Md., 1956-57; assoc. Smith, Somerville & Case, Balt., 1957-62, ptnr., 1962-71, Piper & Marbury, Balt., 1971-94, mem. policy and mgmt. com., 1981-94, mng. ptnr., 1987-90, co-chmn. bus. div., 1991-94. Mem. Gov.'s Com. to Study Blue Sky Law, 1961; mem. Md. Commn. on Revision Corp. Law, 1965-66. Bd. dirs. Bon Secours Hosp., 1964-73, sec., 1968-73; bd. dirs. Hosp. Cost Analysis Svc., 1966-81; bd. pres. mem. exec. coun. Md. Hosp. Assn., 1968-74, chmn. com. on legislation, 1971-73, treas., 1973; trustee St. Mary's Coll. Md., 1983-94, chmn. bd., 1988-94; trustee St. Mary's Sem., U. Balt., 1986-89, Loyola H.S., Balt., 1984-90, Hannah More Ctr., 1980-83; bd. dirs. Helix Health Sys., Inc., 1995-98, Med Star Health, 1998—; mem. Md. Higher Edn. Commn., 1994—, chmn. 1995-2000. Lt. USNR, 1952-55. Recipient Alumni Laureate award Loyola Coll. in Md., 2001. Mem. ABA, Md. State Bar Assn. (mem. sect. coun. corp., banking and bus. law sect. 1968-71, chmn. 1970-71), Wednesday Law Club (sec., treas. 1984-88, v.p. 1988-89, pres. 1990), Center Club (Balt., bd. govs. 1988-94), Order of Coif, Order of the Ark and the Dove, Phi Beta Kappa, Alpha Sigma Nu, Tau Kappa Alpha. Corporate, general, Health, Securities.

CLARKE, HUGH B., JR., lawyer; b. Detroit, July 14, 1954; s. Hugh B. Sr. and Gwendolyn Clarke; 1 child, Hugh B. IV. BS, Wayne State U., 1975; JD, Thomas M. Cooley U., 1975. Bar: Mich. 1979, U.S. Dist. Ct. (ea. and we. dists.) 1980, U.S. Ct. Appeals (6th cir.) 1982. Assoc. gen. counsel State of Mich./State Senate, Lansing, 1979-81; pvt. practice Lansing, 1981—. Legal counsel NAACP, Lansing, 1984-87; dir. Capital Area Substance Abuse Com., Lansing, 1994-96; pres. Lansing Black Lawyers, 1994-96. Recipient BLSA Alumni of the Year, Thomas M. Cooley Law School, 1992. Mem.: St. Bar Mich. Com. Standard Criminal Jury Inst., 2000-. General civil litigation, Criminal, Family and matrimonial. Office: 109 W Michigan Ave Ste 1025 Lansing MI 48933

CLARKE, J. CALVITT, JR., federal judge; b. Harrisburg, Pa., Aug. 9, 1920; s. Joseph Calvitt and Helen Caroline (Mattson) C.; m. Mary Jane Cromer, Feb. 1, 1943 (dec.1985); children: Joseph Calvitt III, Martha Tiffany; m. Betty Ann Holladay, May 29, 1986. BS in Commerce, JD, U. Va., 1945. Bar: Va. 1944. Practiced in, Richmond, Va., 1944-74; partner firm Bowles, Anderson, Boyd, Clarke & Herod, 1944-60; firm Sands Anderson, Marks and Clarke, 1960-74; judge U.S. Dist. Ct. (ea. dist.) Va., 1975-91, sr. judge, 1991—. Mem. 4th Circuit Judicial Conf., 1963; hon. consul for Republic of Bolivia, 1959-75 Chmn. Citizen's Advisory Com. on Joint Water System for Henrico and Hanover counties, Va., 1968-69; mem. Mayor's Freedom Train Com., 1948-50; del. Young Republican Nat. Conv., Salt Lake City, 1949, Boston, 1951; chmn. Richmond (Va.) Republican Com., 1952-54; candidate for Congress, 1954; chmn. Va. 3d Dist. Rep. Com., 1955-58, 74-75, Va. State Rep. Conv., 1958— ; co-founder Young Rep. Fedn. of Va., 1950, nat. committeeman, 1950-54, chmn., 1955; chmn. 3d dist. Speakers Bur., Nixon-Lodge campaign, 1960, mem. fin. com., 1960-74; chmn. Henrico County Republican Com., 1956-58; fin. chmn. 1956; pres. Couples Sunday Sch. class Second Presbyn. Ch., Richmond, Va., 1948-50, mem. bd. deacons, 1948-61, elder, 1964-99, 1st Presbyn. Ch., Virginia Beach, 1999— ; bd. dirs. Family Service Children's Aid Soc., 1948-61, Gambles Hill Community Center, 1950-60, Christian Children's Fund, Inc., 1960-67, Children, Inc., 1967-75, Norfolk Forum, 1978-83; mem. bd. of chancellors Internat. Consular Acad., 1965-75; trustee Henrico County Pub. Library, chmn., 1971-73. Fellow Va. Law Found.; mem. Va. State Bar (mem. 3rd dist. com. 1967-70, chmn. 1969-70), Richmond Bar Assn., Norfolk-Portsmouth Bar Assn., Va. Bar Assn., Thomas Jefferson Soc. of Alumni U. Va. Lile Law Soc., McGuires U. Sch. Alumni (pres. 1995-96), Am. Judicature Soc., ABA, Va. Bar Assn. (vice chmn. com. on cooperation with fgn. bars 1960-61), Richmond Jr. C. of C. (dir. 1946-50), Windmill Point Yacht Club, Westwood Racquet Club (pres. 1961-62), Commonwealth Club, Delta Theta Phi. Office: US Dist Ct 600 Granby St Norfolk VA 23510-1915

CLARKE, MILTON CHARLES, lawyer; b. Chgo., Jan. 31, 1929; s. Gordon Robert and Senoria Josephine (Carlisa) C.; m. Dorothy Jane Brodie, Feb. 19, 1955; children: Laura, Virginia, Senoria K. BS, Northwestern U., 1950, JD, 1953. Bar: Ill. 1953, Mo. 1956, U.S. Dist. Ct. (we. dist.) Mo. 1961, U.S. Ct. Appeals (8th cir.) 1961. Assoc. Swanson, Midgley, Gangwere, Clarke & Kitchin, Kansas City, Mo., 1955-61, ptnr., 1961-91; of counsel Olsen & Talpers, P.C., Kansas City, 1994—. Served with U.S. Army, 1953-55. Mem. Rotary. State civil litigation, Probate (including wills, trusts). Office: Olsen and Talpers PC 2100 City Center Square 1100 Main St Kansas City MO 64105-2125 E-mail: miltonclarke@hotmail.com.

CLARKE, THOMAS HAL, lawyer; b. Atlanta, Aug. 10, 1914; s. James Caleb and Mary Cox (DeSaussure) C.; m. Mary Louise Hastings, July 12, 1951; children: Thomas Hal Jr., Katie Clarke Hamilton, Rebecca DeSaussure Morrison. LLB, Washington and Lee U., 1938. Bar: Ga. 1939, U.S. Dist. Ct. (no. dist.) Ga., U.S. Ct. Appeals (5th cir.), U.S. Supreme Ct., 1973. Ptnr. Clarke & Anderson, Atlanta, 1948-60, Mitchell, Clarke, Pate & Anderson, Atlanta, 1960-69, 73-85; of counsel Gambrell, Clarke, Anderson & Stolz, Atlanta, 1985-92. Copyright trustee Gone With the Wind and sequels, 1983—. Mem. Fed. Home Loan Bank Bd., Washington, 1969-73; past pres., bd. dirs. Atlanta Hist. Soc.; past bd. visitors Emory U.; trustee emeritus Washington and Lee U.; mem. Hibernian United Service Club, Dublin, Ireland. Served with USNR, 1942-46, ETO, PTO. Mem. Internat. Bar Assn. (past chmn. savs. and bldg. socs. com.), ABA (chmn. savs. and loan com. 1970-73, chmn. corp. banking and bus. law sect. 1973-74, mem. ho. of dels. 1974-80, editor The Business Lawyer 1972), Ga. Bar Assn., Atlanta Bar Assn., Am. Law Inst., Atlanta Lawyers Club (past pres.), Selden Soc., English Speaking Union (past pres., chmn. bd.), Metropolitan Club (Washington D.C.), Commerce Club, Piedmont Driving Club (Atlanta). Presbyterian. Home: 186 15th St NE Atlanta GA 30309-3511 Office: 600 W Peachtree St NW Ste 1580 Atlanta GA 30308-3631

CLARKE, WM. A. LEE, III, lawyer; b. Balt., May 7, 1949; s. William Anthony Jr. and Eileen Sheila (Walsh) C.; m. Dara Ford, May 8, 1994. Student, John Carroll U., 1969-72; JD magna cum laude, U. Balt., 1975. Bar: Md. 1975, U.S. Dist. Ct. Md. 1975, U.S. Supreme Ct. 1979, U.S. Ct. Appeals (4th cir.) 1981. Trial atty. Tenn. Valley Authority, Knoxville, 1975-76; pvt. practice Salisbury, Md., 1977—. Vis. lectr. criminal law U. Md. Eastern Shore, Princess Anne, 1989. Pres. Wicomico County Dems., Salisbury, 1981-83; commr. Md. Human Rels. Commn., Balt., 1983-85. Served to cpl. USMC, 1967-69, Vietnam. Mem.: Nat. Bd. Trial Adv. (cert. criminal trial advocate 1987—2002), Md. Criminal Def. Attys. Assn. (bd. dirs. 1984—93), Salisbury Jaycees (legal counsel 1977—79). Federal civil litigation, State civil litigation, Criminal. Office: 30644 Brandywine Ct Salisbury MD 21804-2558 E-mail: walc@clarkelaw.com.

CLARY, BRADLEY G. lawyer, educator; b. Richmond, Va., Sept. 7, 1950; s. Sidney G. and Jean B. Clary; m. Mary-Louise Hunt, July 31, 1982; children: Benjamin, Samuel. BA magna cum laude, Carleton Coll., 1972; JD cum laude, U. Minn., 1975. Bar: Minn. 1975, U.S. Dist. Ct. Minn. 1975, U.S. Ct. Appeals (10th cir.) 1977, U.S. Ct. Appeals (8th cir.) 1979, U.S. Ct. Appeals (6th cir.) 1980, U.S. Ct. Appeals (7th cir.) 1981, U.S. Supreme Ct. 1986, U.S. Ct. Appeals (4th cir.) 1989, U.S. Ct. Appeals (9th cir.) 1991. Assoc. Oppenheimer Wolff & Donnelly, St. Paul, 1975-81, ptnr., 1982-2000; legal writing dir. Law Sch. U. Minn., 1999—, clin. prof. Law Sch., 2000—. Adj. prof. Law Sch. U. Minn., Mpls., 1985-99; adj. instr. William Mitchell Coll. Law, St. Paul, 1995-96, 98, adj. prof., 1997, 99. Author: Primer on the Analysis and Presentation of Legal Argument, 1992; co-author: Advocacy on Appeal, 2001, Successful First Depositions, 2001, Successful Legal Analysis and Writing: The Fundamentals, 2003. Vestryman St. John Evangelist Ch., St. Paul, 1978-81, 98-00, pledge drive co-chmn., 1989-90, sr. warden, 2000-2002; mem. alumni bd. Breck Sch., Mpls., 1981-85, 89-96, exec. com., 1991-96, dir. emeritus, 1996—; mem. adv. bd. Glass Theatre Co., West St. Paul, Minn., 1982-87; mem. antitrust adv. panel dept. health State of Minn., 1992-93. Mem. ABA (adv. group antitrust sect. 1987-89, corp. counseling com.), Minn. Bar Assn. (program chmn. antitrust sect. 1986-87, treas. 1987-88, vice-chmn. 1989-90, co-chmn. 1990-92, governing coun. appellate practice sect. 2001--), Phi Beta Kappa. Avocations: tennis, sailing. Antitrust, General civil litigation. Office: U Minn Law Sch 229 19th Ave S Rm 444 Minneapolis MN 55455-0400

CLARY, RICHARD WAYLAND, lawyer; b. Tarboro, N.C., Oct. 10, 1953; s. S. Grayson and Jean (Beazley) C.; m. Suzanne Clerkin, July 21, 1991; children: Grayson Edward, Taryn Fenner. BA magna cum laude, Amherst Coll., 1975; JD magna cum laude, Harvard U., 1978. Bar: N.Y. 1981, U.S. Dist. Ct. (so. and ea. dists.) N.Y. 1981, U.S. Dist. Ct. (no. dist.) N.Y. 1998, U.S. Dist. Ct. (no. dist.) Calif., 1982, U.S. Ct. Appeals (9th cir.) 1983, U.S. Supreme Ct. 1989, U.S. Ct. Appeals (3d cir.) 1990, U.S. Ct. Appeals (2d cir.) 1994, U.S. Ct. Appeals (fed. cir.) 1995, U.S. Ct. Appeals (11th cir.) 1999, U.S. Ct. Appeals (6th cir.) 2000, U.S. Ct. Appeals (5th cir.) 2003. Law clk. to judge U.S. Ct. Appeals (2d cir.), N.Y.C., 1978-79; law clk. to Justice Thurgood Marshall U.S. Supreme Ct., Washington, 1979-80; assoc. Cravath, Swaine & Moore LLP, N.Y.C., 1980-85; ptnr. Cravath, Swaine & Moore, N.Y.C., 1985—, mng. ptnr. litigation, 1997—. Bd. dirs. Legal Aid Soc., 1998—.(vice chair, 2003-) John Woodruff Simpson fellow Amherst Coll., 1975-76. Mem. ABA, Fed. Bar Found. (bd. dirs. 1998-2001), N.Y. State Bar Assn., Assn. Bar City N.Y., Fed. Bar Coun., Phi Beta Kappa. Roman Catholic. Antitrust, Securities, Intellectual property. Office: Cravath Swaine & Moore LLP Worldwide Pla 825 8th Ave New York NY 10019-7475 E-mail: rclary@cravath.com.

CLASSENS, MICHAEL JOHN, lawyer; b. Jacksonville, Fla., Mar. 2, 1955; s. Raymond E. and Melanie J. (Warwick) C.; m. Laura Anne Pollock, Jan. 9, 1982; children: Jessica Ruth, Carolina Michelle. BS in Psychology, Ga. So. Coll., 1978; JD, U. Tenn., 1984. Bar: Ga. 1985, U.S. Dist. Ct. (no. and so. dists.) Ga. 1985, U.S. Ct. Appeals (11th cir.) 1996. Assoc. Allen, Brown & Edenfield, Statesboro, Ga., 1985-88; pvt. practice Statesboro, 1989-93; pub. defender Ogeechee Jud. Cir., 1989-91; asst. prof. criminal justice Ga. So. U., Statesboro, Ga., 1991-97; ptnr. Allen & Classens, Statesboro, 1993-96, Edenfield, Cox & Classens, Statesboro, 1997-98, Edenfield, Cox, Bruce, and Classens, Statesboro, 1998—. Mem. ABA, ATLA, Nat. Assn. Criminal Def. Lawyers, Ga. Assn. Criminal Def. Lawyers, Ga. Bar Assn., Ogeechee Cir. Bar Assn., Statesboro Jaycees (Keyman Award 1981), Statesboro-Bulloch County C. of C., chmn. Bulloch County Democratic com., Cumberland Island Athletic Club (charter), Optimist Club, Masons. Democrat. Roman Catholic. Avocations: racquetball, golf. General civil litigation, Criminal, Family and matrimonial. Office: PO Box 1700 Statesboro GA 30459-1700

CLAUSS, C. DAVID, lawyer; b. Louisville, Sept. 22, 1948; BS, Ohio State U., 1970; JD, U. Louisville, 1973. Bar: Ky. 1973, U.S. Supreme Ct. 1978, Wyo. 1981, U.S. Dist. Ct. (ea. and we. dists.) Ky., U.S. Dist. Ct. Wyo. 1982, U.S. Ct. Appeals (6th cir.). Law clk. to assoc. justice Ky. Supreme Ct., Frankfort, 1973-74; asst. atty. gen. Commonwealth of Ky., Frankfort, 1977-80; sole practice Jackson, Wyo., 1982—, Lander, Wyo., 1981; Louisville, 1974-77. Served to capt. USAR. Mem. ABA, Wyo. Bar Assn., Ky. Bar Assn., Teton County Bar Assn., Wyo. State Soccer Assn. (pres. 1985), Rotary (bd. dirs. Jackson Hole club 1985-92, v.p. 1987-88, pres. 1988-89). State civil litigation, Family and matrimonial, Personal injury (including property damage). Office: PO Box 1172 Jackson WY 83001-1172

CLAWSON, ALICIA KATHERINE, lawyer, educator; b. Fairbanks, Alaska, Mar. 20, 1965; d. James Daniel and Sara Roberta Clawson; children: Sara Katherine, Caroline Elizabeth. Student, U. N.Mex., 1983—86; BA in Sociology, U. S.C., 1987, JD, 1990. Bar: S.C. 1990. Judicial law clk. Honorable Richard E. Fields, Charleston, SC, 1990—92; asst. solicitor 14th Cir. Solicitor, Hampton, SC, 1992—94; from atty. to dep. dir. S.C. Dept. Ins., Columbia, SC, 1994—97, dep. dir., 1997—99; exec. dir. S.C. Workers Compensation Commn., Columbia, 1999—. Adj. prof. Saint Leo U., Shaw AFB, SC, 1995—. Mem.: So. Assn. Workers Compensation Adminstrs. (bd. dirs. 1999—), S.C. Occupl. Safety Coun. (bd. dirs. 1999—2003), S.C. Workers Compensation Ednl. Assn. (bd. dirs. 1999—). Roman Catholic. Avocations: golf, reading, family. Office: SCWCC 211 Village Walk Ln Columbia SC 29209

CLAYCOMB, HUGH MURRAY, lawyer, author; b. Joplin, Mo., May 19, 1931; s. Hugh and Fern (Murray) C.; m. Jeanne Cavin, May 6, 1956; children: Stephen H., Scott C. BS in Bus., U. Mo., 1953, JD, 1955; LLM, U. Miss., 1969. Bar: Mo. 1955, Ark. 1957, U.S. Tax Ct. 1956, U.S. Dist. Ct. (ea. dist.) Ark. 1957, U.S. Supreme Ct. 1979. Asst. staff judge advocate USAF, 1955-57; law clerk Ark. Supreme Ct., Little Rock, 1957-58; ptnr. Gregory & Claycomb, Pine Bluff, Ark., 1958-69; partner Haley, Claycomb, Roper & Anderson, Warren, Ark., 1969—. Dir. The Strong Co., Inc., Pine Bluff, Ark. Author: Arkansas Corporations, 1967, 82, 92. Pres. Jefferson County Bar Assn., Pine Bluff, 1969, Warren YMCA, 1973-75, S.E. Ark. Legal Inst., 1980-81, Ctrl. Ark. Estate Planning Coun., 1963-64; trustee Bradley County YMCA Found.; spl. assoc. justice Ark. Supreme Ct., 1978, 87. Lt. USAF, 1955-57. Recipient Pres.'s award Ark. Trial Lawyers Assn., 1985. Mem. Ark. Bar Found. (pres. 1990), Ark. Bar Assn. (sec.-treas. 1998-2000, C.E. Ransick award 1996, pres. 2002-03), Warren Rotary (pres. 1972, Paul Harris fellow). Episcopalian. Corporate, general, Estate planning, Probate (including wills, trusts). Home: 619 E Cedar St Warren AR 71671-3001

CLAYTON, CLAUDE F., JR., lawyer; b. Tupelo, Miss., June 15, 1948; s. Claude F. and Bronson (Munday) C.; children from a previous marriage: Frances, Claude III; m. Tacey Clark, July 25, 1997. Student, Stanton Mil. Acad., 1966; BA, Tulane U., 1971; JD, U. Miss., 1973. Bar: Miss. 1973. Mem. judiciary com. U.S. Senate, Washington, 1968; ptnr. Mitchell, Voge, Clayton and Beasley, Tupelo, 1973-85, Mitchell, McNutt & Sams, Tupelo, 1985—2001; pres. Mitchell, NcNutt & Sams, Tupelo, 1995—97; ptnr. Clayton Law Firm, PLLC, 2001—03, Clayton O'Donnell Walsh, PLLC, 2003—. Mem. complaints tribunal Supreme Ct. Miss., 1990-93; speaker Miss. Jud. Coll., also various trial practice and ethics seminars; special justice Miss. Supreme Ct., 2000. Mem. ABA (young lawyers div., chmn. justice dept. liaison com. 1978-79), Miss. State Bar (pres. fellows of young lawyers 1990-91, vice chmn. specialization com. 1990-92, chmn., 1980-82, lawyer econs. com. 1988-89, ethics com. 1982-85, vice chmn. continuing legal edn. com. 1980-81, law jour.-law sch. liaison com. 1974-76, various coms. young lawyers sect. 1985-90, bd. dirs. 1975-80), Miss. Def. Lawyers Assn. (bd. dirs. 1992-95), Def. Rsch. Inst., Internat. Assn. Def. Counsel. General civil litigation, Personal injury (including property damage), Product liability. Office: Clayton O'Donnell Walsh PLLC 115 N Broadway PO Box 755 Tupelo MS 38802-4869 E-mail: cclayton@northmslaw.com.

CLAYTON, DAVID WILLIAM, lawyer; b. N.Y.C., July 23, 1940; s. Kenneth Gordon and Charlotte (Coomber) C.; married; children—Jonathan, Christopher, Kenneth. B.A., Cornell U., 1963; J.D., Bklyn. Law Sch., 1969. Bar: N.Y. 1969, U.S. Dist. Ct. (ea. and so. dist.) N.Y. 1969. Asst. dist. atty. Suffolk County, N.Y., 1969-76; ptnr. Clayton, Miller & Mayer, Hauppauge, N.Y., 1981— . Served to capt. U.S. Army, 1963-66. Mem. Nat. Assn. Criminal Def. Attys., Suffolk County Bar Assn. State civil litigation, Criminal. Office: 38 Kings Hwy Hauppauge NY 11788-4205

CLEAR, JOHN MICHAEL, lawyer; b. St. Louis, Dec. 16, 1948; s. Raymond H. and Marian (Clark) Clear; m. Isabel Marie Bone, May 10, 1980; 1 child, Thomas Henry. BA summa cum laude, Washington U., St. Louis, 1971; JD with honors, U. Chgo., 1974. Bar: Mo. 1974, D.C. 1975, U.S. Ct. Appeals (5th and D.C. cirs.) 1975, U.S. Supreme Ct. 1977, U.S. Ct. Appeals (3d cir.) 1978, U.S. Ct. Appeals (8th cir.) 1980, U.S. Ct. Appeals (9th cir.) 1990, U.S. Dist. Ct. (so. dist.) Ill. 1995, U.S. Ct. Appeals (7th cir.) 1997. Law clk. to judge U.S. Ct. Appeals (5th cir.), Atlanta, 1974-75; assoc. Covington & Burling, Washington, 1975-80; jr. ptnr. Bryan, Cave, McPheeters & McRoberts, St. Louis, 1980-81, ptnr., 1982—. Mem. ABA, Mo. Bar Assn., D.C. Bar Assn., St. Louis Met. Bar Assn., Am. Law Inst., Order of Coif., Racquet Club, Noonday Club, Fox Run Golf Club, Phi Beta Kappa. Antitrust, Federal civil litigation, Securities. Office: Bryan Cave LLP One Metropolitan Sq Saint Louis MO 63102-2750 E-mail: jmclear@bryancave.com.

CLEARY, WILLIAM JOSEPH, JR., lawyer; b. Wilmington, N.C., Aug. 14, 1942; s. William Joseph and Eileen Ada (Gannon) C. AB in History, St. Joseph's U., 1964; JD, Villanova U., 1967. Bar: N.J., 1967, Calif. 1982, U.S. Ct. Appeals (3d cir.) 1969, U.S. Ct. Appeals (9th cir.) 1983, U.S. Dist. Ct. (ctrl. dist.) Calif. 1983, U.S. Supreme Ct. 1992. Law sec. to judge N.J. Superior Ct., Jersey City, 1967-68; assoc. Lamb, Blake, H&D, Jersey City, 1968-72; dep. pub. defender State of N.J., Newark, 1972-73; 1st asst. city corp. counsel Jersey City, N.J., 1973-76; assoc. Robert Wasserwald, Inc., Hollywood, Calif., 1984-86, Gould & Burke, Century City, Calif., 1986-87; pvt. practice Hollywood, 1989—. Mem. ABA, FBA, N.J. State Bar Assn., Calif. Bar Assn., L.A. County Bar Assn. (appellate cts. com.), Nat. Jesuit Hon. Soc., Alpha Sigma Nu. Democrat. Roman Catholic. Appellate, Constitutional, General practice. Office: 1853 1/2 Canyon Dr Los Angeles CA 90028-5607 E-mail: wjclaw42@aol.com.

CLEAVER, WILLIAM LEHN, lawyer; b. Harrisburg, Pa., Dec. 7, 1949; s. Gene Franklin and Goldie Jean (Haldeman) C.; children: Benjamin Neville, Valerie Anne. BA, Augustana Coll., 1971; JD, U. Iowa, 1974. Bar: Iowa 1974, Ill. 1975, U.S. Dist. Ct. (so. dist.) Iowa 1975, U.S. Dist. Ct. (so. dist.) Ill. 1975. Ptnr. Bozeman, Neighbour, Patton & Noe, Moline, Ill., 1991—. Chmn. bd. govs. BBB Ctrl. Ea. Iowa. Mem. adv. coun. Luth. Social Svcs. of Ill. Adult Day Care Ctr., Rock Island; v.p., bd. dirs. United Way of Quad Cities, Rock Island; pres. adv. coun. Ret. Sr. Vol. Program, Moline; bd. govs. Rock Island Cmty. Found.; commr., chmn. Rock Island Preservation Commn.; mem. Citizen's Adv. Com.; bd. dirs. Quad Cities chpt. ARC; mem. Rock Island/Milan Dist. 41 Sch. Bd. Col. USAR. Mem. ABA, Ill. State Bar Assn. (mem. assembly), Iowa State Bar Assn., Rock Island County Bar Assn., Scott County Bar Assn. Lodges: Kiwanis (pres. 1983-84, bd. dirs. 1984-85). Lutheran. Avocations: fine arts, racquet sports. Commercial, consumer (including collections, credit), Commercial, contracts (including sales of goods; commercial financing), Property, real (including real estate development, water). Home: 8806 Ridgewood Rd Rock Island IL 61201-7655 Office: Bozeman Neighbour Patton & Noe 1630 5th Ave Moline IL 61265-7910 E-mail: wcleaver@bnpn.com.

CLELAND, EDWARD GORDON, lawyer; b. Montreal, Que., Can., Aug. 16, 1949; came to U.S. 1979; s. Edward Samuel and Diana Elizabeth (McLennan) C.; m. Thelma Alicia Chen, Jan. 2, 1992. BCommerce, McGill U., 1970; LLB, York U., 1974; LLM in Taxation, NYU, 1980. Bar: Ont. 1976, Conn. 1987, N.Y. 1987, U.S. Tax Ct. 1990. Adv. counsel Dept. Justice, Ottawa, Ont., Can., 1976-79; mgr. Coopers & Lybrand, N.Y.C.,

1979-86; pvt. practice N.Y.C., 1987—. Treas. Alden Owners, Inc., N.Y.C., 1987-88. Mem. ABA, N.Y. State Bar Assn., Law Soc. Upper Can. Clubs: Can Soc. N.Y., St. Andrews Soc. (N.Y.C.). Lodges: Loyal Orange. Republican. Episcopalian. Corporate, general, Corporate taxation, Personal income taxation. Home: 65 Beech Tree Ln Monroe CT 06468-4214 Office: 500 Purdy Hill Rd #7 Monroe CT 06468-1661

CLEMEN, JOHN DOUGLAS, lawyer; b. Mineola, N.Y., Dec. 18, 1944; s. John Douglas and Amy Gertrude (Ackerson) C.; m. Judith Anne Davis, June 3, 1967; children: Elizabeth, Jennifer. BA, Hobart Coll., 1966; JD cum laude, Seton Hall U., 1974. Bar: N.J. 1974, U.S. Dist. Ct. N.J. 1974, U.S. Ct. Appeals (3d cir.) 1980, U.S. Supreme Ct. 1982, N.Y. 1984, U.S. Dist. Ct. (so. dist.) N.Y. 1985, U.S. Dist. Ct. (ea. dist.) N.Y. 1989, U.S. Ct. Appeals (2d cir.) 1989. Law sec. to assoc. justice N.J. Supreme Ct., Trenton, 1974-75; assoc. Shanley & Fisher, P.C., Newark, 1975-83, ptnr., 1983-99; founding ptnr. Hooker, Pucciarelli, Clemen & Tibbs (and predecessor firm), Woodcliff Lake, NJ, 1999—. Arbitrator U.S. Dist. Ct. N.J., 1985—, N.J. Superior Ct., Morristown, 1986—; guest lectr. Acad. Medicine N.J., 1980-82. Contbg. editor Seton Hall Law Rev., 1973-74. Bd. dirs. Acad. Decathalon of N.J., 1997—; mem. Mass Disaster Response Team, ARC, 1997—. Capt. USAF, 1966-71, Vietnam. Decorated Air medal. Mem. ABA, N.J. Bar Assn. (chmn. aviation sect. 1992-94), N.Y. State Bar Assn., Assn. Bar City N.Y. (mem. aeronautics com. 1992—), Trial Attys. N.J., Bergen County Bar Assn., Commerce and Industry Assn. N.J. (bd. dirs. 1986—, counsel 1988-92). Aviation, General civil litigation, Insurance. Home: 574 Colonial Rd River Vale NJ 07675-6107 Office: Hooker Pucciarelli Clemen & Tibbs 172 Broadway Woodcliff Lake NJ 07677-8077 E-mail: jdclemen@aol.com.

CLEMENS, RICHARD GLENN, lawyer; b. Chgo., Oct. 8, 1940; s. James Ralston and Jeanette Louise (Moellering) C.; m. Judith B. Clemens, Aug. 19, 1967; 1 child, Kathleen. BA, U. Va., 1962, JD, 1965. Bar: Ill. 1965. Assoc. Sidley Austin Brown & Wood, Chgo., 1965—66, Washington, 1968—71, Brussels, 1972—73, ptnr. Chgo., 1973—. Served to capt. U.S. Army, 1966-68. Mem. ABA, Chgo. Bar Assn., Lawyers Club, Mid-Day Club. Corporate, general, Mergers and acquisitions, Securities. Office: Sidley Austin Brown & Wood 10 S Dearborn St Chicago IL 60603 E-mail: rclemens@sidley.com.

CLEMENT, EDITH BROWN, federal judge; b. Birmingham, Ala., Apr. 29, 1948; d. Erskine John and Edith (Burrus) Brown; m. Rutledge Carter Clement Jr., Sept. 3, 1972; children: Rutledge Carter III, Catherine Lanier. BA, U. Ala., 1969; JD, Tulane U., 1972. Bar: La. 1973. Law clk. to Hon. Herbert W. Christenberry U.S. Dist. Ct., New Orleans, 1973-75; ptnr. Jones, Walker, Waechter, Poitevent, Carrere & Denegre, New Orleans, 1975-91; judge U.S. Dist. Ct. (ea. dist.) La., New Orleans, 1991—2001, U.S. Ct. Appeals (5th cir.), New Orleans, 2001—. Fellow La. Bar Found. (life); mem. Am. Law Inst., La. Bar Assn., Federalist Soc. Advisory Bd. Louisiana Chpt., Maritime Law Assn. U.S., Fed. Bar Assn., Am Inn Ct., Com. Admin. Office of the Judicial Conference of the U.S., 5th Cir. Judicial Coun. Office: US Ct Appeals 5th Cir 600 Camp Street Rm 200 New Orleans LA 70130-3313

CLEMENT, FRANCES ROBERTS, lawyer, mediator, nurse, consultant; b. Columbia, S.C., Oct. 1, 1945; d. Ralph Winfred and Frances Lucille (Harter) Roberts; m. Tom F. Clement; children: Everett Hudson Smith, Armenta Harter Smith. BS in Biology, U. Ala., 1967; MS in Counseling, Fla. State U., 1970; AA in Nursing, Victoria Coll., Tex., 1978; JD with honors, Jones Sch. Law, Montgomery, Ala., 1986. Bar: Ala. 1987, U.S. Supreme Ct. 1997. Staff nurse Citizen's Meml. Hosp., Victoria, Tex., 1978-81, DeTar Hosp., Victoria, Tex., 1981, Bapt. Med. Ctr., Montgomery, 1982-84; adminstr sch. nurse Bloomington (Tex.) Sch. Dist., 1981-82; supr. Humana Hosp., Montgomery, 1985; legal asst. Kaufman, Rothfeder & Blitz, Montgomery, 1985-87; assoc. Powers & Willis, Montgomery, 1987-88; pvt. practice Montgomery, 1988-90; with Office of Atty. Gen., 1990-2001; mediator, 1999—. Adj. prof. U. Houston, Victoria, 1980, Auburn U., Montgomery, 1988-90. Mem. Montgomery County Bar Assn. Methodist. Avocation: computers. Home: 3502 Bankhead Ave Montgomery AL 36111-2018 Office: 312 Scott St Montgomery AL 36104 E-mail: FrClement@aol.com.

CLEMENTE, MARK ANDREW, lawyer; b. Newark, Nov. 12, 1951; s. Celestino and Marie (Strangio) C. BS, Cornell U., 1974, MPS in Hotel Adminstrn., 1977; JD cum laude, Seton Hall U., 1981. Bar: N.J. 1981, U.S. Dist. Ct. N.J. 1981, U.S. Ct. Appeals (3d cir.) 1991. Law sec. to Hon. Paul B. Thompson Judge Superior Ct., Newark, 1981-82; assoc. Lum, Biunno & Tompkins (Tompkins, McGuire & Wachenfeld), Newark, 1982-84; trial atty. Law Offices of Robert W. McAndrew, Roseland, N.J., 1984-85; mng. trial atty. CNA Ins. Cos., Roseland, Fairfield, N.J., 1986-89; pvt. practice Catania and Harrington, 1989-90; mng. atty. Clemente & Gesicki (Royal Ins.), 1990-2000; pvt. practice Montclair, NJ, 2000—; of counsel Clemente, Mueller & Tobia, P.A., Morristown, NJ. Mem. Cornell Soc. Hotelmen, Delta Upsilon. Republican. Roman Catholic. General civil litigation, Insurance, Personal injury (including property damage). Home: 366 Ridgewood Ave Glen Ridge NJ 07028-1513 Office: Clemente Mueller & Tobia PA PO Box 1296 Morristown NJ 07962 also: PO Box 1570 Montclair NJ 07042 E-mail: mac@cmt-law.com.

CLENDENEN, WILLIAM HERBERT, JR., lawyer; s. William H. and Ethel L. (Clifford) C.; children: William, Patrick, Allison, Derek, Luke; m. Corinna P. Smith. BA, Providence Coll., 1964; JD, Cath. U. Am., 1967. Bar: Conn. 1967, U.S. Dist. Ct. Conn. 1971, U.S. Dist. Ct. (so. dist.) N.Y. 1977, U.S. Dist. Ct. R.I. 1977, U.S. Ct. Clms. 1977, U.S. Ct. Appeals. (2d cir.) 1971, U.S. Sup. Ct. 1976. Reginald Heber Smith Cmty. Lawyer fellow U. Pa. 1967-68; staff atty. New Haven Legal Assistance Assn., Inc., 1968-73; prin. William H. Clendenen Jr., PC, New Haven, 1973-2002; mng. mem. Clendenen & Shea LLC, New Haven, 2002—; supervising atty. Yale Law Sch., 1981; alt. pub. mem. Conn. State Bd. Mediation and Arbitration, 1976-78; co-chmn. U.S. Dist. Ct. Conn. Spcl. Masters Com., New Haven, 1985-89. Fellow Am. Coll. Trial Lawyers, Conn. Bar Found. (life, dir. 1991—, treas. 1992—); mem. ABA, ATLA, Conn. Bar Assn. (chmn. consumer law sect. 1974-78, chmn. lawyer referral com. 1987-89, jud. independence task force 1998—), New Haven County Bar Assn. (sec. 1986-87, treas. 1987-88, v.p. 1988-89, pres. 1989-90), Conn. Trial Lawyers Assn., New Haven County Bar Found. (dir. 1993—). Federal civil litigation, State civil litigation, Commercial, consumer (including collections, credit). Home: 102 River Edge Farms Rd Madison CT 06443-2756

CLENDINEN, CRAIG P. lawyer; b. Savannah, Fla., Mar. 11, 1961; s. Norman W. and Virginia L. Clendinen; m. Cynthia Creel (div. Aug. 1998); 1 child, Anissa Nicole; m. Carolyne Anne Clendinen, July 17, 1999. BA in Econs. and Polit. Sci., Fla. So. Coll., 1983; JD with honors, Fla. State U., 1986. Bar: U.S. Dist. Ct. (mid. and so. dists.) Fla. 88, U.S. Ct. Appeals (11th cir.) 89, Fla. 96. Assoc. Trenam, Simmons, Kemker et al, Tampa, Fla., 1986—91, Stearns Weaver Miller, Tampa, 1992—94, Bales Weinstein, Tampa, 2001—; gen. counsel, v.p. Fla. Employers Safety Assn., Lakeland, 1991—92; asst. states atty. Hillsborough County States Atty., Tampa, Fla., 1994—2001. Bd. dirs. Bay Area Legal Svcs., Tampa, Samaritan Counseling Ctrs., Tampa; mem. adv. bd. tememarketing fraud Am. Prosecutors Rsch. Inst., Washington, 1998—2000; lectr. in field. Author: Commercial Arbitration, 1990, Creditors Right in Florida, 1993. Pres., dist. gov. Sertoma, Tampa, 1993; chmn. Tampa Drug Nuicance Bd., 1989—91; pres. Human Devel. Ctr., Tampa. Named Sertoman of Yr., Sertoma, 1993; grantee, Dept. Justice. Master: Tampa Bay Inn of Ct. (sec. 1991—99); mem.: Hubert Goldbert Criminal Inn of Ct. (barrister). Avocations: tennis, sailing, hiking, canoeing. Personal injury (including property damage), Criminal. Home: 10605 Coquita Ln Tampa FL 33618 Office: Bales Weinstein 625 E Twiggs Tampa FL 33602

CLERMONT, KEVIN MICHAEL, law educator; b. N.Y.C., Oct. 25, 1945; s. William Theodore and Rita Ruth (Healy) C.; m. Emily Sherwin; 1 child, Adrienne Shaine. AB summa cum laude, Princeton U., 1967; postgrad., U. Nancy, France, 1967-68; JD magna cum laude, Harvard U., 1971. Bar: Mass. 1971, N.Y. 1974, U.S. Dist. Ct. (so. and ea. dists.) N.Y. 1974, U.S. Ct. Appeals (2d cir.) 1974. Law clk. to judge U.S. Dist. Ct. (so. dist.) N.Y., 1971-72; assoc. Cleary, Gottlieb, Steen & Hamilton, N.Y.C., 1972-74; asst. prof. Sch. Law Cornell U., Ithaca, N.Y., 1974-77, assoc. prof., 1977-80, prof., 1980-89, Flanagan prof. law, 1989—. Vis. prof. Sch. Law Harvard U., Cambridge, 1991. Author: (with another) Res Judicata: A Handbook on Its Theory, Doctrine, and Practice, 2001, Civil Procedure: Territorial Jurisdiction and Venue, 1999, (with others) Materials for a Basic Course in Civil Procedure, 8th edit., 2003, Civil Procedure, 6th edit., 2001, (with others) Law: Its Nature, Functions, and Limits, 3d edit., 1986; editor Harvard Law Rev., 1969-71. Fulbright scholar, 1967-68. Mem. ABA, Assn. Am. Law Schs., Order of Coif, Phi Beta Kappa, Sigma Xi. Home: 100 Iroquois Rd Ithaca NY 14850-2223 Office: Cornell U Sch Law Myron Taylor Hall Ithaca NY 14853 E-mail: kmc12@cornell.edu.

CLEVELAND, EDWARD D. lawyer; b. Lafayette, Ind., Dec. 11, 1921; s. Clarence Rugg and Helen Mary Cleveland; m. Shirley B. Housam, Aug. 29, 1943; children: Michael, Anne, John, Geoffrey. AB, Western Mich. Coll., 1942; PhD, Johns Hopkins U., 1950; LLB, U. Wis., 1955. Bar: Wis. 1955, Colo. 1969. Instr. English U. Wis., Madison, Wis., 1950—55; assoc., ptnr. Whyte, Hirschbeck, Minahan, Milw., 1955—69; ptnr. Geddes, Weir, Sparks & O-Brien, Colorado Springs, 1969—70; pres. Edward D. Cleveland P.C. (formerly Cleveland, Wengler & Robbins), Colorado Springs, 1970—. Capt. U.S. Army Air Corps, 1942—45, ETO. Mem.: Colo. Bar Assn., Order of Coif. General practice. Office: Ste 8 2985 Broadmoor Valley Rd Colorado Springs CO 80906-4484

CLEVELAND, LILA VIRGINIA, lawyer; b. Mobile, Ala., Nov. 15, 1968; d. Henry Brooks and Marjorie Virginia Cleveland; m. Gregory Wayne Boyington, Aug. 24, 1999. BA in Polit. Sci. and History, Auburn U., 1991; JD, Auburn U. Birmingham Sch. Law, 1995. Bar: Ala., U.S. Dist. Ct. (mid. and so. dists.) Ala. 1996, U.S. Ct. Appeals (11th cir.) 1996. Pvt. practice, Mobile, Ala., 1996—. Instr. U. South Ala., Mobile, 1998—. Mem.: ABA, Ala. Criminal Def. Lawyers Assn., Nat. Assn. Criminal Def. Lawyers. Avocation: reading. Criminal, Family and matrimonial, Appellate. Office: 312 N Joachim St Mobile AL 36603

CLEVENGER, RAYMOND CHARLES, III, federal judge; b. Topeka, Kans., Aug. 27, 1937; s. Raymond and Mary Margaret (Ramsey) Clevenger; m. Celia Faulkner, Sept. 6, 1961 (div. Mar. 1987); children: Winthrop, Peter. BA, Yale U., 1959, LLB, 1966. Law clerk to Justice Byron S. White U.S. Supreme Court, Washington, 1966—67; ptnr. Wilmer Cutler & Pickering, Washington, 1967—71, 1972—90; special assist. to gen. counsel John W. Barnum US Dept. of Transp., Washington, 1971—72; judge U.S. Ct. Appeals (Fed. Cir.), Washington, 1990—. Mem.: ABA, D.C. Bar Assn. Office: Howard T Markey Nat Ct Bldg 717 Madison Pl NW Washington DC 20439-0002*

CLICK, DAVID FORREST, lawyer, investment advisor; b. Miami Beach, Fla., Dec. 17, 1947; s. David Gorman and Helen Margaret (McPhail) C.; m. Helaine London, June 2, 1974; children: Kenneth Randall, Adam Elliott. BA, Yale U., 1969, JD, 1973, MA, 1974. Bar: Conn. 1973, Md. 1983, U.S. Supreme Ct. 1983, Fla. 1984, Maine 1984. Asst. prof. Western New England Sch. Law, Springfield, Mass., 1974-77; assoc. prof. Ind. U., 1977-78, U. Md., Balt., 1978-84; assoc. Nixon, Hargrave, Devans and Doyle, Jupiter, Fla., 1984-86; pvt. practice, Jupiter, 1986—. Pres., dir. Click Farms, Inc., Clewiston, Fla.; pres. Click Capital Mgmt., LLC. Contbr. articles to profl. jours. Mem. Christmas Cove (Maine) Improvement Assn., Palm Beach County Estate Planning Coun., pres. 1988-89; participant Leadership Palm Beach County, 1991-92. Mem. ABA, Fla. Bar Assn., Palm Beach County Bar Assn. (cultural activities award 1992), Nat. Soc. Arts and Letters, Yale Club of the Palm Beaches (pres.), Kiwanis. Presbyterian. Estate planning, Probate (including wills, trusts), Property, real (including real estate development, water). Home: 19216 Pinetree Dr Jupiter FL 33469-2002 Office: 810 Saturn St Ste 15 Jupiter FL 33477-4456

CLIFF, JOHN WILLIAM, JR., lawyer; b. Bonham, Tex., Mar. 25, 1949; s. John William and Betty Lou (Wheeler) C.; m. Rebecca Munos; children: Jacob, Heidi, Jordan, Hillary, Holli, Harrison. BS, U. Houston, 1971, JD, 1974. Bar: Tex. 1974, U.S. Dist. Ct. (we. dist.) Tex. 1975, U.S. Ct. Appeals (5th cir.) 1977, U.S. Dist. Ct. (no. dist.) Tex. 1982. Ptnr. Kenworthy & Cliff, Odessa, Tex., 1974-76; assoc. Childs & Bishop, Odessa, 1976-77, Ater & Hirsch, Odessa, 1977-79; ptnr. Moore & Cliff, Odessa, 1979-81, Smith & Cliff, P.C., Odessa, 1981-88; pvt. practice Odessa, 1988—. Instr. legal rsch. Odessa Coll., 1985, 88, 89, 95—, instr. rules of evidence, 1988, instr. legal writing and family law, 1994—. Mem. Order of Barristers, Order of Barons Criminal, Family and matrimonial, General practice. Home: 1407 Spur Ave Odessa TX 79761-3327 Office: Ste 722 700 N Grant Ave Odessa TX 79761-4555

CLIFFORD, EUGENE THOMAS, lawyer; b. Utica, N.Y., July 15, 1941; s. James Anthony and Mary Margaret (Ellard) C.; m. Joyce Victoria Siwinski, Sept. 4, 1965; children: Michael Sean, Elizabeth Joyce, Thomas More. BA, Boston Coll., 1963, LLB, 1966. Bar: N.Y. 1967, U.S. Dist. Ct. (we. dist.) N.Y. 1967. Assoc. Chamberlain, D'Amanda, Bauman, Chatman & Oppenheimer, Rochester, N.Y., 1967-72, Lamb, Webster, Walz, Telesca & Donovan, Rochester, 1972-76; ptnr. Webster, Sullivan, Santoro & Clifford, Rochester, 1976-86, Fulreader, Rosenthal, Sullivan, Clifford, Santoro & Kaul, Rochester, 1986-2001, Davidson, Fink, Cook, Kelly & Galbraith, 2001—. Bd. dirs. N.Y. state divsn. Am. Cancer Soc., Syracuse, 1972-78, 82-88, 90-97, chmn. bd. dirs., 1982-83, nat. bd. dirs., 1991-97; bd. dirs. Urban League of Rochester, 1988-91. Recipient Nat. Bronze award N.Y. state divsn. Am. Cancer Soc., 1984, Hope award Monroe County unit, 1983. Mem.: Monroe County Bar Assn. (pres. 2002—03). Estate planning, Probate (including wills, trusts), Property, real (including real estate development, water). Office: 28 Main St E Ste 1700 Rochester NY 14614 E-mail: eclifford@dfckg.com.

CLIFFORD, JOHN A. lawyer; b. Detroit, Dec. 22, 1956; BS in Physics, Creighton U., 1978, JD, 1981. Bar: Minn. 1981, U.S. Patent and Trademark Office 1981. Ptnr. Merchant & Gould P.C., Mpls., 1981—. Filing cntr. over 1,900 U.S. trademark applications. Intellectual property. Office: Merchant & Gould PC 3200 IDS Ctr 80 S 8th St Minneapolis MN 55402-2215 E-mail: jclifford@merchant-gould.com.

CLIFFORD, PETER, lawyer; b. Danbury, Conn., July 30, 1964; s. Paul J. and Ann (Malloy) C.; m. Stephanie Perkins, Sept. 12, 1992; children: Meghan, Olivia. BS, Boston Coll., 1986; JD cum laude, U. Maine, 1991. Bar: Maine 1991, Mass. 1991, U.S. Dist. Ct. Maine 1991, U.S. Ct. Appeals (1st cir.) 1992, U.S. Dist. Ct. Mass. 1992, U.S. Supreme Ct. 1994. Fin. analyst Raytheon Co., Lexington, Mass., 1986-88; assoc. Monaghan Leahy Hochadel & Libby, Portland, Maine, 1991-92; pvt. practice Kennebunk, Maine, 1992—. Lectr. in field. Bd. dirs. KIDS, Inc., Kennebunk, 1994-95. Mem. Maine State Bar Assn., Maine Trial Lawyers Assn., York County Bar Assn., Kennebunk C. of C. (bd. dirs. 1994-95), Kennebunk Rotary. Avocations: sailing, tennis. General civil litigation, Criminal. Office: Hodsdon & Clifford LLC 56 Portland Rd Kennebunk ME 04043-6658

CLIFFORD, ROBERT WILLIAM, state supreme court justice; b. Lewiston, Maine, May 2, 1937; s. William H. and Alice (Sughrue) C.; m. Clementina Radillo, Jan. 18, 1964; children: Laurence M., Matthew P. BA, Bowdoin Coll., 1959; LLB, Boston Coll., 1962; LLM, U. Va., 1998. Bar: Maine 1962, U.S. Dist. Ct. Maine 1965. Ptnr. Clifford & Clifford, Lewiston, 1964-79; justice Maine Superior Ct., Auburn, 1979-83, chief justice, 1984-86; assoc. justice Maine Supreme Jud. Ct., Auburn, 1986—. Mem. Lewiston City Coun., 1968-70, mayor, 1971-72; mem. Maine State Senate, 1973-76; chmn. Lewiston Charter Commn., 1978-79; mem. Maine Probate Law Revision Commn., 1973-79; bd. overseers St. Joseph's Coll. Maine, 2000—. Mem. Maine Bar Assn., Androscoggin County Bar Assn., Am. Judicature Soc. Roman Catholic. Home: 14 Nelke Pl Lewiston ME 04240-5318 Office: Maine Supreme Jud Ct PO Box 3488 Auburn ME 04212-3488

CLIFTON, RICHARD RANDALL, judge; b. Framingham, Mass., Nov. 13, 1950; s. Arthur Calvin and Vivian Juanita (Himes) C.; m. Teresa Morano Aleshire, Oct. 15, 1988; children: David Madison, Katherine Kaleilani. AB, Princeton U., 1972; JD, Yale U., 1975. Bar: Ill. 1975, Hawaii 1976, U.S. Dist. Ct. Hawaii 1976, U.S. Ct. Appeals (9th cir.) 1976, U.S. Ct. Appeals (2d cir.) 1979, U.S. Supreme Ct. 1982. Law clk. to judge U.S. Ct. Appeals (9th cir.), Honolulu, 1975-76; from assoc. to ptnr. Cades, Schutte, Fleming & Wright, Honolulu, 1977—2002; judge U.S. Ct. of Appeals (9th cir.), 2002—. Adj. prof. law U. Hawaii, Honolulu, 1979-89. Co-author: The Shreveport Plan: An Experiment in the Delivery of Legal Services, 1974. Mem. dist. com. Nancy J. Stivers Meml. Fund, Honolulu, 1984—; bd. dirs. Hawaii Pub. Radio, Honolulu, 1991—, chmn., 1995-2000; mem. Hawaii State Jud. Conf., 1987-90; 1st vice chmn. Hawaii Rep. Party, 1989-93, chmn. rules com., 1987-90, gen. counsel, 1993-2001; bd. dirs. Hawaii Women's Legal Found., 1987—, Ninth Jud. Cir. Hist. Soc., 1996—; mem. Hawaii State Reapportionment Com., 1991-92. Mem. ABA, Hawaii Bar Assn. Office: US Ct of Appeals 1132 Bishop St Ste 601 Honolulu HI 96813

CLINARD, ROBERT NOEL, lawyer; b. Welch, W.Va., Nov. 1, 1946; s. Vernon Carlos and Mary Elizabeth (Noel) C.; m. Margaret Hawthorne Higgins, May 21, 1977; children: Elizabeth Kercheval, Edward Noel, Margaret Graham Robinson, Kathryn Moir. BA, Washington & Lee U., 1968, JD, 1976. Bar: N.Y. 1977, Va. 1978, U.S. Dist. Ct. (so. dist.) N.Y. 1977, U.S. Dist. Ct. (ea. dist.) Va. 1978, U.S. Ct. Appeals (4th cir.) 1986, U.S. Supreme Ct. 1990. Assoc. Winthrop, Stimson, Putnam & Roberts, N.Y.C., 1976-78, Hunton & Williams, Richmond, Va., 1978-86, ptnr., 1986—. Sec. Va. Cultural Laureate Soc., Richmond, 1981-86, bd. dirs., 1981-90. Served to lt. USNR, 1969-72. Mem. ABA (antitrust sect., franchising and healthcare coms.), Va. State Bar (vice chmn. antitrust com. health law sect. 1985-86, chmn. 1986-87, bd. govs. antitrust sect. 1989-95, vice chmn. antitrust sect. 1992, chmn. 1993), Nat. Health Lawyers Assn., Coun. of Franchise Suppliers, Internat. Franchise Assn., Order of Coif, Phi Beta Kappa, Omicron Delta Kappa. Republican. Episcopalian. Avocations: boating, saltwater fishing, house renovation. Antitrust, Federal civil litigation, Franchising. Home: 6010 York Rd Richmond VA 23226-2737 Office: Hunton & Williams Riverfront Plaza East Tower 951 E Byrd St Richmond VA 23219-4074

CLINE, LANCE DOUGLAS, lawyer; b. Columbus, Ind., Oct. 8, 1951; s. Leon Dale and Jo Ann Alice (Fauser) C.; children: Rachel Ann, Natalie Brooke, Kathleen Nagle. BA, Ind. U., 1973, JD, 1980. Bar; Ind. 1980, U.S. Dist. Ct. (so. dist.) Ind. 1980. Ptnr. Cline, Farrell, Christie, Lee & Caress, Indpls., 1980—. Contbr. articles to profl. jours. Mem. ABA, ATLA, Am. Coll. Trial Lawyers, Am. Coll. Legal Medicine, Ind. Trial Lawyers Assn. (bd. dirs. 1984—), Ind. State Bar Assn., Indpls. Bar Assn., Trial Lawyers Pub. Justice, Phi Beta Kappa. Personal injury (including property damage). Home: 8645 Bay Colony Dr Indianapolis IN 46234-2912 Office: Cline Farrell Christie Lee & Caress 951 N Delaware St Indianapolis IN 46202 E-mail: lance@cfclc-law.com.

CLINE, MICHAEL ROBERT, lawyer; b. Parkersburg, W.Va., Oct. 13, 1949; s. Robert Rader and Hazel Mae (Boice) C.; m. Carole R. Davis, Aug. 28, 1972. A.B., Morris Harvey Coll., 1972; J.D., Wake Forest U., 1975. Project coordinator Gov.'s Office Fed.-State Relations, Charleston, W.Va., 1970-72; spl. asst. W.Va. Office Econ. Opportunity, 1973; spl. asst. W.Va.-Dept. Labor, Charleston, 1974; staff asst., hearing officer, 1975-77; sole practice, Charleston, 1977— . Mem. ABA, Assn. Trial Lawyers Am., Comml. Law League Am., So. Mems. Assn. (bd. dirs.), Nat. Assn. Criminal Defense Lawyers, W.Va. Trial Lawyers Assn. (bd. dirs. 1982—, treas. 1984, v.p. 1985-86, Outstanding Mem. 1983), W.Va. State Bar (chmn. com. on econs. of law practice 1986, 91-92), Pi Kappa Delta, Phi Alpha Delta. Republican. Methodist. Lodge: Elks, Rotary. E-mail: mcline@clinelaw.com. Commercial, consumer (including collections, credit), Criminal, Personal injury (including property damage). Home: 1531 Dixie St Charleston WV 25311-1903 Office: 323 Morrison Bldg Charleston WV 25301

CLINE, RICHARD ALLEN, lawyer; b. Columbus, Ohio, Oct. 1, 1955; s. Ralph S. and Myrtle O. (Harrison) C.; m. Nora Jean Arth, Oct. 2. 1982; children: Caitlin, Patrick. BA in Polit. Sci., BS in Criminal Justice, Kent State U., 1977; JD, Ohio State U., 1981. Bar: Ohio 1981, U.S. Dist. Ct. (so. dist.) Ohio 1981, U.S. Ct. Appeals (6th cir.) 1983, U.S. Supreme Ct. 1985. Assoc. David Riebel, Columbus, 1981-84; ptnr. Riebel & Cline, Columbus, 1984-85; ptnr., pres. Durkin, Cline and Co. L.P.A., Columbus, 1985-88; pres. Richard Cline & Co. L.P.A., Columbus, 1988-92; mem. Mitchell Allen Catalano & Boda Co. LPA, Columbus, 1992—, ptnr., 1996—. Prosecutor City of Whitehall, Ohio, 1980-81, Village of Powell, Ohio, 1983-85, Powell Village Coun., 1996—; instr. Ohio Peace Officers Tng. Counsel, Columbus, 1985. Bd. dirs. Woodbridge Village Assn., Columbus, 1983-86. Served with JAGC, Ohio Nat. Guard, 1983-2003. Mem. Ohio Bar Assn., Jaycees (named one of Outstanding Young Men of Am., 1979), Phi Alpha Delta, Omicron Delta Kappa. Republican. Baptist. Avocations: martial arts, military history. State civil litigation, Criminal, General practice. Home: 290 Weatherburn Ct Powell OH 43065-9103 Office: Mitchell Allen Catalano & Boda 490 S High St Columbus OH 43215-5603

CLINE, VIVIAN MELINDA, lawyer; b. Seneca, S.C., Oct. 6, 1953; d. Kenneth H. and Wanda F. (Simmons) Fuller; m. Terry S. Cline, June 15, 1974 (div. Oct. 1986); 1 child, Alicia C. BSBA, Calif. State U., Northridge, 1974; JD, Southwestern U., L.A., 1983. Bar: Calif. 1983, Tex., 1990. Paralegal Internat. House Pancakes, North Hollywood, Calif., 1976-78; assoc. Tuohey & Prasse, Santa Ana, Calif., 1983-85; paralegal Smith Internat., inc., Newport Beach, Calif., 1978-83, sr. corp. counsel Houston, 1985—. Bus. cons. Jr. Achievement, Houston, 1992—94, 1997—99. Mem. Exec. Women's Network (sec. 1993, pres. 1994, dir. programs 1995, sec. 1996, 2000, treas. 1998-2001), Am. Soc. Corp. Secs. Inc. (sec. Houston chpt. 1995-96, treas. 1996-97, v.p., program dir. 1997-98, pres. 1998-99). Republican. Presbyterian. Commercial, contracts (including sales of goods; commercial financing), Corporate, general, Securities. Office: Smith Internat Inc 16740 Hardy Rd Houston TX 77032-1125 E-mail: vcline@smith.com.

CLINTON, EDWARD XAVIER, lawyer; b. Chgo., July 13, 1930; s. Michael Xavier and Mary Agnes (Joyce) C.; m. Margaret Mary Clinton, May 1, 1965 (div. Oct. 1978); 1 child, Edward Xavier Jr. Student, DePaul U., 1949-50; JD, John Marshall U., 1953. Bar: Ill. 1953, U.S. Dist. Ct. (no. dist.) Ill. 1955, U.S. Ct. Appeals (7th cir.) 1955, U.S. Supreme Ct. 1995. Assoc. Schultz & Biro, Chgo., 1955-56; with securities dept. Ill. State Dept., Springfield, 1956-57; assoc. Hough, Young & Coale, Chgo., 1957-65, Keck, Mahin & Cate, Chgo., 1965-92; pvt. practice Chgo., 1992—; spl. counsel Bullwinkel Ptnrs., Ltd. Instr. John Marshall Law Sch., Chgo., 1965-74; arbitrator N.Y. Stock Exch. Contbr. articles to profl. jours.;

speaker in field. Mem. adv. bd. Steppenwolf Theatre, Chgo., 1988—89; pastoral coun. Holy Name Cathedral, 1989—94; Chgo. Opera Theatre, 1983—88, Children's Care Found., v.p.; bd. dirs. Records Mgmt. Svcs., 1966—97. With U.S. Army, 1953—55. Postgrad. scholar John Marshall Law Sch., 1953, John Jewell scholar, 1953. Mem. ABA, Ill. Bar Assn., Chgo. Bar Assn., Bar. Assn. of 7th Cir., Lawyers Club of chgo., Rotary, Law Club, Union League Club, Execs. Club of Chgo. (bd. dirs. 1985-95), Evanston Golf Club, Am. Legion, KC. Roman Catholic. Avocations: golf, prisoner appeals (pro bono). Corporate, general, Property, real (including real estate development, water), Securities. Home: 990 N Lake Shore Dr Chicago IL 60611-1366 Office: 19 S La Salle St Ste 1300 Chicago IL 60603-1406 E-mail: EClinton@mac.com.

CLINTON, RICHARD M. lawyer; b. Milw., June 25, 1941; s. William J. and Idella (Loftis) C.; m. Barbara Lynch, June 14, 1969; children: Amanda, Camille, Rebecca. BS, U. Wis., 1963, JD, 1967; LLM, George Washington U., 1971. Bar: Wis. 1967, Wash. 1971, U.S. Dist. Ct. (ea. dist.) Wash. 1975, U.S. Ct. Appeals (9th cir.) 1972. Instr. legal writing U. Wis. Law Sch., Madison, 1966-67; trial atty. antitrust div. U.S. Dept. Justice, Washington, 1967-71; assoc. Bogle & Gates, Seattle, 1971-75, mem., 1975-99; ptnr. Dorsey & Whitney LLP, 1999—. Fellow Am. Coll. Trial Lawyers; mem. ABA, Wash. Bar Assn. (pres. antitrust sect. 1982-83), Fed. Bar Assn. (pres. 1986-87), Wash. Athletic Club, Columbia Tower Club. Roman Catholic. Avocations: sailing, skiing, fishing, hiking, travel. Antitrust, General civil litigation. Home: 3863 50th Ave NE Seattle WA 98105-5235 Office: Dorsey & Whitney LLP US Bank Centre 1420 5th Ave Seattle WA 98101-4087

CLIPPARD, RICHARD F. prosecutor; Graduate, U. Miss., 1976; JD, U. Miss. Law Sch., 1980. Private practice Butler, Lackey, Holt and Snedeker, 1980—83; special asst. US atty. US Small Bus. Adminstrn., 1983—88; asst. US atty. US Atty. Office, Nashville, 1988—2000, chief of Civil Division, 2000—01; interim U.S. atty. Middle Dist., Tenn., 2001—02; U.S. trustee for Tenn. & Ky. Exec. Off. for U.S. Trustees, 2003—. Office: 200 Jefferson Ave Ste 400 Memphis TN 38103*

CLIPPERT, CHARLES FREDERICK, lawyer; b. Detroit, May 21, 1931; s. Harrison Frank and Ethelyn (Reuss) C.; m. Lynne Davison, June 6, 1959; children: Martha G. Shannon, Charles Frederick III, Thomas Harrison. BA, U. Mich., 1953, LLB, 1959. Bar: Mich. 1959. Assoc. Dickinson, Wright, Moon, Van Dusen & Freeman, Bloomfield Hills, Mich., 1959-67, ptnr., 1967-97, mem. exec. com., 1986-89; mem. Dickinson Wright PLLC, Bloomfield Hills, Mich., 1998-2000, cons. mem., 2001—. Commr. City of Birmingham, Mich., 1964-70, mayor, 1969-70; gov. Cranbrook Schs., Bloomfield Hills, 1978-99; trustee Cranbrook Ednl. Community, Bloomfield Hills, 1980-98, sec., 1989-93. Lt. (j.g.) USNR, 1953-56; mem. endowment com. The Consortium of Endowed Episcopal Parishes, 1998—. Fellow Am. Bar Found., Mich. Bar Found.; mem. ABA, State Bar Mich. (real property law coun. 1980-85, mem. select com. on professionalism 1992-99, mem. alternate dispute resolution coun. 1999—), Oakland County Bar Assn. (bd. dirs. 1985-91, pres. 1990-91), Orchard Lake Country Club (gov. 1986-92, pres. 1991-92), Am. Arbitration Assn. (panel of neutral arbitrators 1997—), Pi Sigma Alpha. General civil litigation, Commercial, contracts (including sales of goods; commercial financing), Property, real (including real estate development, water). Office: Dickinson Wright PLLC Ste 2000 38525 N Woodward Ave Bloomfield Hills MI 48304-2971 Mailing: PO Box 509 Bloomfield Hills MI 48303-0509 E-mail: cclippert@dickinson-wright.com.

CLODFELTER, DANIEL GRAY, state legislator, lawyer; b. Thomasville, N.C., June 2, 1950; s. Billy G. and Marie Lorene (Wells) C.; m. Elizabeth Kay Bevan, Aug. 20, 1974; children: Julia Elizabeth, Catherine Gray. BA, Davidson Coll., 1972; AB, Oxford U., Eng., 1974; JD, Yale U., 1977. Bar: N.C. 1977, U.S. Dist. Ct. (we. dist.) N.C. 1977, U.S. Dist. Ct. (ea. dist.) N.C. 1979, U.S. Ct. Appeals (4th cir.) 1984, U.S. Dist. Ct. (mid. dist.) N.C. 1985. Law clk. to presiding judge U.S. Dist. Ct., Charlotte, N.C., 1977-78; assoc. Moore & Van Allen, Charlotte, 1978-82, ptnr., 1983—. Mem. N.C. Senate, 1999—. Mem. Charlotte City Coun., 1987-93, Charlotte-Mecklenburg Planning Commn., 1984-87, chmn., 1986-87; state sec. Rhodes Scholarship Trust, N.C., 1986-97; trustee Z. Smith Reynolds Found., Inc., Winston-Salem, N.C., 1983—; bd. dirs. N.C. Ctr. for Pub. Policy Rsch., 1994-96. Rhodes scholar, 1972. Mem. N.C. Bar Assn. (antitrust law com., bankruptcy sect. coun.). Office: Moore & Van Allen 100 N Tryon St 4700 Charlotte NC 28202-4003

CLONEY, TERENCE J. lawyer; b. Chgo., Oct. 29, 1953; s. John Edward and Helen (Junginger) C.; m. Katherine Giam, 1985; children: Sean Christopher, Michael Brendan. AB, Columbia U., 1975; JD, NYU, 1979. Bar: N.Y. 1980, Ill. 1989. Assoc. Milbank, Tweed, Hadley & McCloy, N.Y.C., 1979-83, Hong Kong, 1983-86, Singapore, 1986-89; ptnr. Gardner, Carton & Douglas, Chgo., 1989-97, Altheim & Gray, Chgo., 1997—. Bd. dirs. Juvenile Diabetes Found., Chgo., 1993-2001, mem. exec. com., 1994-96. Mem. ABA. Banking, Securities, Private international. Home: 421 Concord Ln N Barrington IL 60010-2207

CLORE, LAWRENCE HUBERT, lawyer; b. Tulsa, July 31, 1944; s. Hubert Charles and Jessie Louada (Fowler) C.; m. Carol Jean Roegelein, June 3, 1967 (div. 1981); children: Robert William, James Lawrence; m. Martha Jo Lawyer; children: Kathryn Denise, Michael Hubert. BBA, Tex. Christian U., 1966; JD, U. Tex., 1969. Bar: Tex. 1969. Assoc. Fulbright & Jaworski, Houston, 1971-77, ptnr., 1977—. Capt. U.S. Army, 1969-71, Vietnam. Mem. ABA, Tex. Bar Assn. (labor and employment sect., coun. 1990-93, vice chair 1993-94, chair 1994-95), Indsl. Rels. Rsch. Assn., Houston Mgmt. Lawyers Forum (chmn. 1976-77). Republican. Methodist. Avocations: hunting, fishing, golf. Civil rights, Labor (including EEOC, Fair Labor Standards Act, labor-management relations, NLRB, OSHA). Office: Fulbright & Jaworski 1301 Mckinney St Ste 5100 Houston TX 77010-3031 E-mail: lclore@fulbright.com.

CLOSE, DAVID PALMER, lawyer; b. N.Y.C., Mar. 16, 1915; s. Walter Harvey and Louise De Arango (Palmer) C.; m. Margaret Howell Gordon, June 26, 1954 (dec. July 1992); children: Louise, Peter, Katharine, Barbara. BA, Williams Coll., 1938; JD, Columbia U., 1942; LHD, Mount Vernon Coll., 1998. Bar: N.Y. State bar 1942. Practice law, Washington, 1946—; ptnr. Dahlgren & Close. Mem. adv. council Nat. Capital area Boy Scouts Am., 1961— ; bd. dirs. Nat. Soc. Prevention Blindness, 1961-63, Internat. Eye Found., 1965—, chmn., 1985-89; bd. dirs. D.C. Soc. Prevention of Blindness, 1957-63, pres., 1961-63; bd. dirs. Internat. Humanities, Inc., 1960—, pres., 1989—; bd. dirs. Marjorie Merriweather Post Found., 1974—, sec.-treas., 1974-76, sec., 1991—; trustee Williams Coll., 1963-68; trustee Hill Sch., 1965-85, chmn., 1973-85 ; trustee Mount Vernon Coll., 1963-75 , bd. pres., 1971-74; mem. Am. coun. UN U., 1980—. Served with O.N.I., USN, 1942-46. Mem. ABA, Inter-Am. Bar Assn., D.C. Bar Assn., Assn. Bar City of N.Y., Pilgrims, Order of St. John, Chevy Chase (Md.) Club, Fauquier Springs Country Club (Warrenton, Va.), Univ. Club (Washington). Administrative and regulatory, General practice, Probate (including wills, trusts). Home: 40 Hungry Run Farm Ln Amissville VA 20106-4017 Office: Dahlgren & Close 1000 Connecticut Ave NW Ste 204 Washington DC 20036-5337 E-mail: dahlgrenclose@cs.com.

CLOSE, MICHAEL JOHN, lawyer; b. Sandusky, Ohio, Jan. 24, 1943; s. Robert J. and Mary Lee (Graefe) C.; m. Nancy L. Schelp, June 18, 1995; children: Christina C., Karen L. AB in History, Lafayette Coll., Easton, Pa., 1965; JD cum laude, U. Mich., 1968. Assoc. Dewey, Ballantine, Bushby, Palmer & Wood, N.Y.C., 1968-76; ptnr. Dewey Ballantine, N.Y.C., 1976-96. Chmn. Tax Rev., N.Y.C. Author: Tax Aspects of Oil and Gas Drilling Funds, 1972, Drilling Funds: The 1977 Perspective, 1977, Special Allocations in Oil and Gas Ventures, 1982, The Final Section 704 (b) Regulations: Special Allocations Reach New Heights of Complexity, 1986, Fringe Benefit Regulation and the New York Law Firm Culture: A New Era, 1989, Off Balance Sheet Financings, 1994; contbr. articles to profl. jours. Bd. dirs., adminstrv. vice-chmn. Conn. Swimming, Inc., 1992-99, ad-hoc com. on by-laws, 1995-96; bd. dirs. Sharks Swim Team, Inc., 1991-94, pres., 1992-94. Mem. ABA (mem. tax sect. com. on partnerships), Assn. of Bar of City of N.Y., N.Y. Law Inst. (life mem.), N.Y. State Bar Assn. (mem. tax sect. com. partnerships), Ohio State Bar Assn., India House (N.Y.C.), Burning Tree Country Club (Greenwich), Meadows Country Club (Sarasota, Fla.), Phi Delta Phi, Theta Chi. Republican. Home: 4951 Windsor Pk Sarasota FL 34235-2610 E-mail: thecloses@comcast.net.

CLOSSON, WALTER FRANKLIN, child support prosecutor; b. Phila., Dec. 24, 1944; s. David Mayard Jr. and Florence Louise (Anderson) C.; m. Irene Veronica Jones, Aug. 10, 1968; children: Forrest Troy, Carey-Walter Franklin. BS in Music Edn., West Chester U., 1967; JD, Potomac Sch. Law, Washington, 1981. Bar: Ga. 1983, Md. 1985. Tchr. music D.C. Pub. Schs., Washington, 1967-77; tchr. woodwinds D.C. Youth Orch. Program, Washington, 1969-71; dist. ct. commr. Dist. Ct. of Md., Ellicott City, 1978-89; supervising dist. ct. commr. Dist. Ct. of Howard County, Ellicott City, 1984-89; asst. state's atty. State's Atty.'s Office, Ellicott City, 1989-99, chief child support divsn., 1999-2000; supervising atty. Bur. of Supoort Enforcement, Howard County Dept. Social Svcs., Columbia, Md., 2000—. Mem.. Howard County Bar Assn., Waring-Mitchell Law Soc. (pres. 1992-94, Man of Yr. 1990), Masons (sr. deacon 1996-97, sr. warden 1997-98, worshipful master, 1998-99, Lodz treas. 2002-), Delta Theta Phi (v.p. 1979-80). Office: Howard County Dept Social Svcs 7121 Columbia Gateway Dr Columbia MD 21046 E-mail: walt024@earthlink.net.

CLOUES, EDWARD BLANCHARD, II, lawyer; b. Concord, N.H., Dec. 28, 1947; s. Alfred Samuel and H. Jeannette (Callas) C.; m. Mary Anne Matthews, Aug. 21, 1971; children: E. Matthew, M. Elizabeth. BA, Harvard U., 1969; JD, NYU, 1972. Bar: Pa. 1972, U.S. Dist. Ct. (ea. dist.) Pa. 1973. Law clk. to hon. judge James Hunter III U.S. Ct. Appeals (3d cir.), Phila. and Camden, N.J., 1972-73; assoc. Morgan, Lewis & Bockius LLP, Phila., 1973-79, ptnr., 1979-98; chmn., CEO K-Tron Internat., Inc., Pitman, N.J., 1998—. Bd. dirs. K-Tron Internat., Pitman, N.J., vice chmn. bd., 1987-94; bd. dirs. Amrep Corp., chmn., 1995—; bd. dirs. Penn Va. Corp., Penn Va. Resource Ptnrs., L.P.. Republican. Lutheran. Avocations: travel, reading. Bankruptcy, Corporate, general, Mergers and acquisitions. Office: K-Tron Internat Inc PO Box 888 Rtes 55 & 553 Pitman NJ 08071

CLOUSE, JOHN DANIEL, lawyer; b. Evansville, Ind., Sept. 4, 1925; s. Frank Paul and Anna Lucille (Frank) C.; m. Georgia L. Ross, Dec. 7, 1978; 1 child, George Chauncey. AB, U. Evansville, 1950; JD, Ind. U., 1952. Bar: Ind. 1952, U.S. Supreme Ct. 1962, U.S. Ct. Appeals (7th cir.) 1965. Assoc. Firm of James D. Lopp, Evansville, 1952-56; pvt. practice law James D. Lopp, Evansville, 1956—. Guest editorialist Viewpoint, Evansville Courier, 1978—86, Evansville Press, 1986—98, Focus, Radio Sta. WGBF, 1978—84; 2d asst. city atty. Evansville, 1954—55; mem. Com. for Implementation of Criminal Justice Act of 1964, 1965; mem. appellate rules sub-com. Ind. Supreme Ct. Com. on Rules of Practice and Procedure, 1980. Pres. Civil Svc. Commn. Evansville Police Dept., 1961-62, v.p., 1988; pres. Ind. War Memls. Com., 1963-69; mem. jud. nominating com. Vanderburgh County, Ind., 1976-80; dir. Ind. Fed. Cmty. Defender Project, Inc., 1993-98. With inf. U.S. Army, 1943-46. Decorated Bronze Star; named one of World's Most travelled Man Guinness Book of Records, 1993, Most Travelled Man, 1995-2001. Fellow Ind. Bar Found.; mem. Internat. Wood Collector's Soc., Evansville Bar Assn. (v.p. 1972, James Bethel Gresham Freedom award 1997), Ind. Bar Assn. (chmn. com. on civil rights 1991-92), 87th Inf. Divsn. Assn., Internat. Wood Collectors Soc., Club Internat. Des Grand Voyageurs, Travelers Century Club (L.A.), Pi Gamma Mu. Republican. Methodist. State civil litigation, Criminal, Family and matrimonial. Office: 123 NW 4th St Ste 317 Evansville IN 47708-1712 E-mail: JDCMJS@aol.com.

CLUBB, BRUCE EDWIN, retired lawyer; b. Blackduck, Minn., Feb. 6, 1931; s. Ernest and Abigail (Gordy) Clubb; m. Martha Lucia Trapp, Dec. 19, 1954 (dec. Nov. 2001); children: Bruce Allen, Christopher Wade. BBA, U. Minn., 1955, LL.B. cum laude, 1958. Bar: DC 1959. Atty. Covington & Burling, 1958-61, Devel. Loan Fund, 1961-62, Chapman, DiSalle and Friedman, 1962-67; commr. U.S. Tariff Commn., 1967-71; ptnr. firm Baker & McKenzie, Washington, 1971-96; disting. lawyer in residence U. Minn. Law Sch., 1981-82. Chmn. bd. dirs. Sunrise Properties, Inc., 1989—99. Author: (treatise) United States Foreign Trade Law (2 vols.), 1991; contbr. law revs. Served with U.S. Army, 1952—54. Mem. D.C. Bar Assn., Am. Arbitration Assn. (arbitrator 1994-2000), Order of Coif, Cosmos Club (pres. 1986), Met. Club, Army Navy Club. Republican. Commercial, contracts (including sales of goods; commercial financing), Private international, Public international. Home: 630 Tennis Club Dr Fort Lauderdale FL 33311-4055 E-mail: bclubb2@aol.com.

CLULO, PAUL JACQUES, judge; b. Marquette, Mich., Dec. 19, 1939; s. William R. and Corinne (Jacques) C.; m. Carolyn L. Frepan, June 15, 1963; children: Timothy, David, Jacquelynn. BS in Chemistry, Notre Dame U., 1962; LLB, Marquette U., 1965. Bar: Wis. 1965, Mich. 1965, U.S. Dist. Ct. (ea. dist.) Mich. 1966, U.S. Ct. Appeals (6th cir.) 1966. Staff atty. Dow Chem. Co., Midland, Mich., 1965-66; ptnr. Sinclair & Clulo, Midland, 1966-84; cir. judge State of Mich., Midland, 1985—. Mem. faculty Mich. Jud. Inst., Lansing, 1985—, Inst. for Ct. Mgmt., Denver, 1987-91. Named Judge of Yr., Nat. Child Support Enforcement Assn., 1990. Mem. ABA, Mich. Bar Assn., Mich. Judges Assn. (exec. com. 1989—, chmn. domestic rels. com. 1989-93, chmn. ct. reorgn. com. 1994-95, pres. 1999). Home: 405 Cherryview Dr Midland MI 48640-5914 Office: 42d Cir Ct 301 W Main St Midland MI 48640-5162

CLUNAN, AMY MARIE, lawyer; b. Memphis, June 8, 1969; d. Paul W. Clunan II and Charlotte M. Clunan. BS in Computer Sci., Econs. and Math., Vanderbilt U., 1991, JD, 1994; MBA in Fin. and Real Estate, U. Memphis, 1997. Bar: Tenn. 1994, U.S. Dist. Ct. (we. dist.) Tenn. 1997, U.S. Supreme Ct. 2001. Atty. Streibich & Seale, Memphis, 1994—95, Law Office Charles Pope, Memphis, 1995—97; real estate mgr. AutoZone, Inc., Memphis, 1997—98, corp. atty., 1998—2002, sr. corp. atty., 2002—. Vol. Habitat for Humanity, Memphis, 2001—; coach Youth Soccer, Memphis, 1999—2001. Mem.: Memphis Bar Assn. (corp. counsel, pres. and treas.), Jr. League of Memphis. Avocations: scuba diving, soccer, tennis, reading. Corporate, general, Commercial, contracts (including sales of goods; commercial financing), Securities. Office: AutoZone 123 S Front St Memphis TN 38103 E-mail: amy.clunan@autozone.com.

CLYMER, JOHN HOWARD, lawyer; b. Boston, Nov. 19, 1939; s. Russell Sturgis and Eileen Newell (Williams) C.; m. Diana Payne Walker, Aug. 22, 1964; children: Sarah Payne, Amy Newell. BA, Princeton U., 1962; JD, Harvard U., 1965. Bar: Mass. 1965. Assoc. Hutchins & Wheeler, Boston, 1965-71; ptnr. Hutchins Wheeler & Dittmar, Boston, 1972—2003, Nixon Peabody LLP, Boston, 2003—. Trustee Hyams Found. Contbr. articles to profl. jours. Mem. Concord Planning Bd., Mass., 1972-77, Concord Bd. Selectmen, 1988-94; trustee, treas. Walter E. Fernald State Sch., Waltham, Mass., 1975-82; bd. dirs., clk. Anatolia Coll., Boston, 1984—; trustee clk. Sofia Am. Schs., Boston, 1985—. Mem. Am. Bar Assn. (bus. law section, com. chmn. health law 1987, real propr., probate and trust law sect., com. chmn. exempt orgn. 1996-2000), Mass. Bar Assn., Boston Bar Assn., Am. Coll. Trust and Estate Coun., Union Club (Boston), Concord Country Club. Unitarian Universalist. Avocations: photography, travel. Estate planning, Non-profit and tax-exempt organizations, Probate (including wills, trusts). Office: Nixon Peabody LLP 100 Summer St Boston MA 02110

COATES, FREDERICK ROSS, lawyer; b. Madison, Va., June 27, 1933; s. Fred Icer and Sarah (Hale) C.; m. Rebecca White, Nov. 25, 1959; children: Stephanie Renee Piper, Susan C. McCoy. BA, U. Richmond, 1954, JD, 1959. Bar: Va., U.S. Dist. Ct. (we. dist.) Va. 1959. Vice chmn. Madison County Rep. Party, 1968-88; mem. Rescue Squad Madison County, Madison County Planning com.; commr. accounts Madison County; asst. commn. accounts Greene County, Va.; mem. Madison COunty Sch. Bd.; mem., chmn. bd. Germanna C.C.; chmn. bd. dirs. Jefferson Nat. Bank br. office. Served with U.S. Army, 1954-57. Recipent Key Man award Madison Jaycees, 1962-64. Mem. ABA, Va. State Bar. Assn., Madison-Greene Bar Assn., Red Land Club, Greene Hills Club, Masons, Boosters Club, Lions, Shriners. Baptist. Avocation: golf. Estate planning, Probate (including wills, trusts), Property, real (including real estate development, water). Home and Office: PO Box 328 Madison VA 22727-0328

COATES, GLENN RICHARD, lawyer; b. Thorp, Wis., June 8, 1923; s. Richard and Alma (Borck) C.; m. Dolores Milburn, June 24, 1944; children— Richard Ward, Cristie Joan Student, Milw. State Tchrs. Coll., 1940-42, NMA and MA, 1943-44; LLB, U. Wis., 1949, SJD, 1953. Bar: Wis. 1949. Atty. Mil. Sea Transp. Service, Dept. Navy, 1951-52; pvt. practice law Racine, Wis., 1952—; of counsel Dye, Foley, Krohn, Shannon, S.E. Sec., gen. counsel Racine Federated Inc.; lectr. U. Wis. Law Sch., 1955-56. Author: Chattel Secured Farm Credit, 1953; contbr. articles to profl. publs. Chmn. bd. St. Luke's Meml. Hosp., 1973-76, bd. dirs., 1990-91; pres. Racine Area United Way, 1979-81; bd. curators State Hist. Soc. Wis., 1986-2001, pres., 1995-97; bd. dirs. Racine County Area Found., 1983-89; bd. dirs. Wis. History Found., Inc., 1983-99, Hist. Sites Found., Inc., 1987-89, St. Luke's Hosp./St. Mary's Med. Ctr. Healthcare Found., 1992-96. With U.S. Army, 1943-46. Fellow Am. Bar Found. (life); mem. ABA, State Bar Wis. (bd. govs. 1969-74, chmn. bd. 1973-74), Wis. Jud. Coun. (chmn. 1969-72), Am. Law Inst. (life), Racine Country Club, Masons, Order of Coif. Methodist (chmn. fin. com. 1961-67). Corporate, general, Estate planning, Mergers and acquisitions. Home: 2830 Michigan Blvd Racine WI 53402-4254 Office: 1300 S Green Bay Rd Racine WI 53406-4469

COATS, ANDREW MONTGOMERY, lawyer, former mayor, dean; b. Oklahoma City, Okla., Jan. 19, 1935; s. Sanford Clarence and Mary Ola (Young) C.; m. Linda M. Zimmerman; children— Andrew, Michael, Jennifer, Sanford BA, U. Okla., 1957, JD, 1963. Assoc. Crowe and Dunlevy, Oklahoma City, Okla., 1963-67, ptnr., 1967-76, sr. trial ptnr., 1980—; dist. atty. Oklahoma County, Oklahoma City, Okla., 1976-80; mayor City of Oklahoma City, 1983-87; dean U. Okla. Coll. Law. Pres. Okla. Young Lawyers Conf., 1968-69; dir. Local Okla. Bank, Oklahoma City. Democratic nominee U.S. Senate, 1980; pres. Oklahoma County Legal Aid Soc., 1972-73. Served to lt. USN, 1960-63 Named Outstanding Lawyer in Okla., Oklahoma City U., 1977 Fellow Am. Coll. Trial Lawyers (pres. 1996-97, 10th Cir. regent 1992-96), Am. Bd. Trial Advocates (charter pres. Okla. 1986); mem. ABA, U.S. Supreme Ct. Hist. Soc. (trustee), Okla. Bar Assn. (pres. 1992-93), Oklahoma County Bar Assn. (pres. 1976-77), Order of Coif, Oklahoma City Golf and Country Club (bd. dirs. 1977-80, 93-96), Petroleum Club (pres. 1995), Phi Beta Kappa (pres. 1975), Pi Kappa Alpha (pres. 1956), Phi Delta Phi (pres. 1962). Clubs: Oklahoma City Golf and Country, Petroleum. Democrat. Episcopalian. Avocations: music, golf. General civil litigation, Product liability. Office: Crowe and Dunlevy Mid-Am Tower 20 N Broadway Ave Ste 1800 Oklahoma City OK 73102-8273 also: U Okla Coll Law 300 Timber Dell Rd Norman OK 73019-5081 E-mail: acoats@ou.edu.

COATS, NATHAN B. state supreme court justice; m. Mary Ricketson; 1 child, Johanna. BA in Econs., U. Colo., 1971, JD, 1975. Assoc. Hough, Grant, McCarren and Bernard, 1977-78; asst. atty. gen. Appellate Sect., Colo., 1978-83, dep. atty. gen., 1983-86; adj. prof. U. Colo., Colo., 1990; chief appellate dep. dist. atty. 2d Jud. Dist., Denver, 1986-2000; justice Colo. Supreme Ct., 2000—. Chief reporter Erickson Commn. on Officer-Involved Shootings, 1996-97; lectr. Denver Police Acad., 1986-97; reporter Govs. Columbine Commn., 1999-2000; mem. Colo. Supreme Ct. Criminal Rules Com., 1983-2000, chmn., 1997-2000, Colo. Bd. Law Examiners, 1984-94, Colo. Supreme Ct. Appellate Rules Com., 1985-2000, Colo. Supreme Ct. Civil Rules Com., Colo. Supreme Ct. Criminal Pattern Jury Instructions Com., 1987-2000, Colo. Supreme Ct. Jury Reform Pilot Project Com., 1998-2000, Colo. Dist. Attys. Coun. Legis. Com., 1990-2000. Office: Colo State Supreme Ct Judicial Bldg 2 E 14th Ave Denver CO 80203-2115

COBAU, JOHN REED, lawyer; b. New Castle, Pa., Aug. 28, 1934; s. William D. and Sarah M. (Weinschenk) C.; m. Arlene L. Gilbert, June 22, 1960; children: William, Joseph, Thomas, John. BA, Princeton U., 1956; LLB, Harvard U., 1960. Bar: D.C. 1960, Ohio 1961, Mich. 1966. Assoc. Kyte, Conlan, Wulsin & Vogeler, Cin., 1960-66, Freud, Markus, Slavin & Mountain, Detroit, 1966-73; pvt. practice Grosse Pointe Woods, Mich., 1974—. Mem. ABA, Mich. Bar Assn., Macomb County Bar Assn., Grosse Pointe Hunt Club (bd. dirs. 1976-78), Rotary (pres., bd. dirs. Grosse Pointe). Corporate, general, Probate (including wills, trusts), Property, real (including real estate development, water). Office: 20233 Mack Ave Grosse Pointe MI 48236-1769 E-mail: jrcobaulawyer@ameritech.net.

COBB, CALVIN HAYES, JR., lawyer; b. San Diego, Aug. 2, 1924; s. Calvin Hayes and Frances King (Halm) C.; m. Olive Latimer Watson, Mar. 19, 1955; children: Alice Cobb Parte, Joan Cobb Pettit, Calvin Hayes III, Robert Watson, Olive Latimer Waxter. BS with distinction, U.S. Naval Acad., 1944; LLB, Georgetown U., 1950. Bar: D.C. 1950, Md. 1950, U.S. Supreme Ct. 1953. Assoc. Law Offices of Elisha Hanson, Washington, 1950-55; ptnr. Hanson, Cobb & O'Brien, Washington, 1955-69; sr. ptnr. Steptoe & Johnson, Washington, 1969—. Leading article editor Georgetown Law Jour., 1949; contbr. articles to law revs. and profl. jours. Trustee Naval Hist. Found., 1983—, Found. Mid. East Peace, 1969—. Lt. (j.g.) USN, 1944-47. Recipient Disting. Pub. Svc. award Sec. of Navy, 1979, 91, Pub. Svc. award USCG, 1991. Mem. Navy League of US (nat. judge adv. 1975-89, bd. dirs. 1975—, sr. v.p. 1988-89, pres. 1989-91, Nat. Pres.'s award 1976, 83, 86), US Naval Acad. Alumni Assn. (trustee 1955-58), Soc. of Cin., Lawyers Club, Chevy Chase Club (pres. 1974-75), Gibson Island Club, Royal Poinciana Golf Club (Fla., pres. 2003—), Naples Bath and Tennis Club, Barristers Club (pres. 1974), The Forum Club (bd. dirs. 2000—), Naples Athletic Club. Republican. Roman Catholic. Avocations: tennis, golf, bridge. Corporate, general, Securities. Home: 3571 Hamlet Pl Chevy Chase MD 20815-4822 Office: 1330 Connecticut Ave NW Washington DC 20036-1704 E-mail: chcobbjr@aol.com, ccobb@steptoe.com.

COBB, G. ELLIOTT, JR., lawyer; b. Franklin, Va., July 11, 1939; s. Gardner E. and Thelma L. (Whitley) C.; m. Betty Minor, July 15, 1961; children: Polly, Susan, Gardner. BS, U. Va., 1960, LL.B., 1966. Bar: Va. 1966, Supreme Ct. U.S 1974. Asso. counsel Union Camp Corp., Wayne, N.J., 1967-74, counsel, mgr. adminstrn., 1974-76, gen. counsel, asst. sec., 1976, v.p., gen. counsel, sec., 1976-78; ptnr. Moyler, Rainey & Cobb, Franklin, 1978—. Mem. adv. bd. SunTrust Bank, Franklin. Mem. Franklin City Coun., 1980-88; vice mayor of Franklin, 1982-84, mayor, 1984-88; bd. dirs. SFranklin Southampton Charieies. Served with USMC, 1960-61. Mem. Va. Bar Assn., Southampton-Franklin Bar Assn. Clubs: Cypress Cove Country, Rotary. Episcopalian. Home: 913 Clay St Franklin VA 23851-1306 Office: Moyler Rainey & Cobb 506 N Main St Franklin VA 23851-1438

COBB, HOWELL, federal judge; b. Atlanta, Dec. 7, 1922; s. Howell and Dorothy (Hart) C.; m. Torrance Chalmers (dec. 1963); children: Catherine Cobb Cook, Howell III, Mary Ann Cobb Walton; m. Amelie Suberbielle, July 3, 1965; children: Caroline Cobb Ervin, Thomas H., John L. Student, St. John's Coll., Annapolis, Md., 1940-42; LLB, U. Va., 1948. Assoc. Kelley & Ryan, Houston, 1949-51, Fountain, Cox & Gaines, Houston, 1951-54, Orgain, Bell & Tucker, Beaumont, 1954-57, ptnr., 1957-85; judge U.S. Dist. Ct. (ea. dist.) Tex., Beaumont, 1985—. Mem. jud. coun. U.S. Ct. Appeals (5th cir.), 1994-97; mem. adv. com. East Tex. Legal Svcs., Beaumont. Pres. Beaumont Art Mus., 1969, bd. dirs., 1967-68; mem. vestry St. Stephens Episcopal Ch., Beaumont, 1973; mem. bd. adjustment City of Beaumont, 1972-82; trustee All Saints Episcopal Sch., Beaumont, 1972-76. 1st lt. USMC, 1942-45, PTO. Mem.: ABA, Maritime Law Assn. U.S., Am. Bd. Trial Advs., Am. Judicature Soc., Jefferson County Bar Assn. (sec. 1960, bd. dirs. 1960—61, 1967—68), State Bar Tex. (grievance com. 1970—72, chmn. 1972, admissions com. 1974—, bd. dirs. 1993—94, adv. mem.). Office: US Dist Ct 118 US Courthouse PO Box 632 Beaumont TX 77704-0632 Business E-Mail: druann_wiley@txed.uscourts.gov.

COBB, KAY BEEVERS, state supreme court justice, former state senator; m. Larry Cobb; children: Barbara Cobb Murphy, Elizabeth Cobb DeBusk. BS, Miss. U. Women; JD, U. Miss. Former spl. asst. atty. gen. North Miss.; assoc. justice Miss. Supreme Ct. Mem. Nat. Alliance/Model State Drug Laws, Vets. Aux., C. of C. Baptist. Office: Miss Supreme Ct PO Box 117 450 High St Jackson MS 39205 Home: PO Box 604 Oxford MS 38655-0604

COBB, PETER Z. lawyer; b. Northfield, Minn., Oct. 10, 1943; Grad., Pomona Coll., 1965; PhD in Math., CUNY, 1972; JD, Columbia U., 1979. Bar: N.Y., (U.S. Tax Ct.). With Fried, Frank, Harris, Shriver & Jacobson, N.Y.C., 1979—84, ptnr., 1984—91; bus. tax counsel Congress's Joint Com. on Taxation, dep. chief of staff, 1993, acting chief of staff, 1994; co-mng. ptnr., tax ptnr. Fried, Frank, Harris, Shriver & Jacobson, N.Y.C., 1994—. Mem.: ABA, N.Y. State Bar Assn. (mem. exec. com. sect. taxation 1995—2001). Office: Fried Frank Harris Shriver & Jacobson 1 New York Plz New York NY 10004

COBB, STEPHEN A. lawyer; b. Moline, Ill., Jan. 27, 1944; s. Archibald William and Lucile Bates C.; m. Nancy L. Hendrix, Dec. 18, 1972. AB cum laude, Harvard U., 1966; MA in Sociology, Vanderbilt U., 1968, PhD in Sociology, 1971, JD, 1977. Bar: Tenn. 1978, U.S. Dist. Ct. (mid. dist.) Tenn. 1978. Asst. prof. Tenn. State U., Nashville, 1970-74, dept. head, 1972-74; mem., chair edn. oversight com. Tenn. Ho. Reps., Nashville, 1974-86; pvt. practice law Nashville, 1978-86; with Waller Lansden Dortch & Davis, Nashville, 1986-90, ptnr., 1990—. Fullbright Jr. lectr. U. Caen, France, 1977-78; lectr. dept. sociology Fisk U., 1981-86. Former pres. Sister Cities of Nashville, Inc.; former vice chmn. commn. ednl. quality So. Regional Edn. Bd. Decorated officer Ordre des Palmes Academiques (France); recipient Paul Simon Internat. award, 1990, Edwin Cudeki Internat. Bus. award, 1992; NDEA fellow, NIMH fellow, 1966-70. Mem. ABA, Am. Immigration Lawyers Assn., So. Sociol. Soc., Tenn. Bar Assn., Tenn Fgn. Lang. Inst., Nashville Bar Assn., Fedn. Alliances Francaises (former pres.), Order of Coif. Government contracts and claims, Immigration, naturalization, and customs. Home: 1929 Castleman Dr Nashville TN 37215-3901 Office: 511 Union St Ste 2100 Nashville TN 37219-1760

COBBETT, STUART HANSON, lawyer; b. Montreal, June 3, 1948; s. Stuart Ashton and Adrienne Cobbett; m. Jill Rankin, Sept. 7, 1973; children: Alexander, William, Anne. BA, McGill U., 1969, BCL, 1972. Bar: Que. Ptnr. Heenan Blaikie, Montreal, 1974-85; sr. v.p., dir. Astral Comms., Montreal, 1985-92; sr. ptnr. Stikeman Elliott, Montreal, 1992, mng. prin. London, 1996-99, mng. ptnr. Montreal, 2000—. Bd. dirs. Aldeavision Inc., Montreal, Formula Growth Ltd., Montreal, McCord St. Sites, Montreal. Bd. dirs. Bishop's Coll. Sch., Lennoxville, Que., Can., 1982-95; chmn., bd. dirs. McGill News, Montreal, 1991-96; chmn. bd. visitors in arts McGill U., 1991-96. Mem. Can. Bar Assn., Internat. Bar Assn., N.Y. State Bar Assn., McGill Alumni Assn. U.K. (pres. 1996, 2002—). Anglican. Avocations: skiing, tennis, golf, hiking. Office: Stikeman Elliott 1155 Rene Levesque Blvd Montreal QC Canada H3B 3V2 E-mail: scobbett@stikeman.com.

COBBS, LOUISE BERTRAM, lawyer; b. Miami, Fla., Dec. 7, 1947; d. Sidney and Annette (Gottlieb) Stolman; m. Andrew R. Doctor, Aug. 16, 1970 (div. Sept. 1982); m. Nicholas H. Cobbs, Mar. 26, 1983 (div. Sept. 2002); children: Robert, Rebecca. AB, Smith Coll., 1969. Bar: N.Y. 1978, U.S. Ct. Appeals (D.C. cir.) 1984, U.S. Ct. Appeals (9th cir.) 1985, U.S. Dist. Ct. D.C. 1985, U.S. Supreme Ct., 1985, U.S. Ct. Appeals (5th cir.) 1986, U.S. Ct. Appeals (4th cir.) 1996, U.S. Ct. Appeals (3d cir.) 1997. Assoc. Haight, Gardner Poor and Havens, Washington, 1980-83, counsel, 1989-93, ptnr., 1994-97; assoc. Finley, Kumble, Underberg, Manley, Myerson & Casey, Washington, 1983—89; ptnr. Holland & Knight, Washington, 1997—. Mem. ABA, FBA (chair transp. sect.), Aero Club of Washington, Internat. Aviation Club. Office: 2099 Pennsylvania Ave NW Washington DC 20006 Fax: 202-955-5564. E-mail: lcobbs@hklaw.com.

COCALIS, DIMITRI N. lawyer; b. Athens, Attica, Greece, Feb. 1, 1951; s. Nicholas D. and Clio Cocalis; m. Naya K. Raxi; children: Nicholas, Ilia. Law Degree, U. Thessaloniki, Greece, 1973; postgrad., Panteion U. Econ. Scis., Athens, 1976. Bar: Athens. Trainee Katis Law Offices, Athens, 1973—76; assoc. Tsecouras & Athanassakos, Athens, 1977—79, ptnr., 1979—81, Tsecouras & Cocalis, Athens, 1981—83, mng. ptnr., 1985—; ptnr. Tsecouras, Cocalis & Grafanakis, Athens, 1983—85. Bd. dirs. Sara Lee HBC, Athens, Sara Lee C&T Hellas, Athens, NetMed Group of Cos., Athens. Author: Unfair Trading Practices, 1996. Fellow: Ctr. Internat. Legal Studies. Avocations: computers, music, hiking, sailing. Commercial, contracts (including sales of goods; commercial financing), Communications, Mergers and acquisitions. Office: Tsecouras & Cocalis 14 Solonos 106 73 Athens Greece

COCCIA, MICHEL ANDRE, retired lawyer; b. Sept. 17, 1922; BS in Indsl. Engring., Ill. Inst. Tech., 1944; JD, John Marshall Law Sch., 1951; docteur, l'Universite de Paris, 1965. Bar: Ill. 1951, U.S. Supreme Ct. 1951. Ptnr. litigation Baker & McKenzie, Chgo., 1951-88; justice Ill. Appellate Ct., Chgo., 1988-91. Lectr. in fields. Contbr. articles to profl. jours. With USNR. Fellow: Internat. Soc. Barristers, Internat. Acad. Trial Lawyers, Am. Coll. Trial Lawyers, Am. Bar Found.; mem.: ABA (various coms., past ho. of dels.), Justinian Soc. (Man of Yr. 1981), Def. Rsch. Inst. (chmn. products liabiltiy com. 1971—77, bd. dirs. 1977—80), Internat. Assn. Ins. Counsel (sec., treas. 1975—78, products liability com., fed. ruls com.), Soc. Trial Lawyers (past pres.), Am. Judicature Soc., Chgo. Bar Assn. (various coms.), Ill. Bar Assn. (pres. 1981—82, past bd. govs., various coms.), John Marshall Law Sch. Alumni Assn. (past pres., Citation of Merit 1971), Ill. Inst. Tech. Alumni Assn. (past. pres., past trustee, various awards), Mid Am. Club, Union League Club, Trial Lawyers Club Chgo. Avocations: french, barbershop chorus, amateur radio, boating. Home and Office: 203 Smoky Lake Dr Phelps WI 54554-9311

COCHRAN, GEORGE MOFFETT, retired judge; b. Staunton, Va., Apr. 20, 1912; s. Peyton and Susie (Robertson) C.; m. Marion Lee Stuart, May 1, 1948; children— George Moffett, Harry Carter Stuart. BA, U. Va., 1934, LLB, 1936; LLD (hon.), James Madison U., 1991. Bar: Va. 1935, Md. 1936. Asso. law firm, Balt., 1936-38; partner firm Peyton Cochran and George M. Cochran, Staunton, 1938-64, Cochran, Lotz & Black, Staunton, 1964-69; justice Supreme Ct., Richmond, Va., 1969-87. Pres. Planters Bank & Trust Co., Staunton, 1963-69 Chmn. Woodrow Wilson Centennial Commn. Va., 1952-58, Va. Cultural Devel. Study Commn., 1966-68, Frontier Culture Mus. Va., 1986-98; mem. Va. Commn. Constl. Revisi on, 1968-69, Jud. Coun. Va., 1963-69, Va. Ho. Dels., 1948-66, Va. Senate, 1966-68; chmn. bd. dirs. Stuart Hall, 1971-86; mem. bd. visitors Va. Poly. Inst., 1960-68; trustee Mary Baldwin Coll., 1967-81, U. Va. Law Sch. Found., 1975-89, Woodrow Wilson Birthplace Found., 1955-93. Lt. comdr. USNR, 1942-46. Recipient Algernon Sydney Sullivan award Mary Baldwin Coll., 1981. Mem. ABA, Va. Bar Assn. (pres. 1965-66), Raven Soc., Soc. of Cin., Phi Beta Kappa, Phi Delta Phi, Beta Theta Pi. Episcopalian.

COCHRAN, JOHN M., III, lawyer; b. N.Y.C., June 26, 1941; s. John M. Jr. and Mildred Lee (Ford) C.; m. Véronique Bouchet du Val Jolie de Bonneau. AB, Coll. William and Mary, 1963; JD, George Washington U., 1967; Doctorat de l'Université, U. Paris, 1971. Bar: N.Y. 1967, Calif. 1974, France 1973; avocat à la Cour d'Appel de Paris 1992-98. Barrister Chambers of Lord Rippon of Hexham, London, 1974-98; ptnr. Willkie, Farr & Gallagher, Paris, 1984-93, Curtis, Mallet-Prevost, Colt & Mosle, Paris, 1993-98. Editor Butterworth's Jour. of Internat. Banking and Finance Law, 1986. Mem. Soc. Sportive du Jeu de Paume et des Raquettes (Paris). Alternative dispute resolution, Mergers and acquisitions. Home: Chateau Falfas 33710 Bayon France also: 16 rue Montevideo 75116 Paris France

COCHRAN, JOHNNIE L., JR., lawyer; b. Shreveport, La., Oct. 2, 1937; BS, UCLA, 1959; JD, Loyola U., 1962; postgrad., U. So. Calif. Bar: Calif. 1963, U.S. Dist. Ct. (we. dist.) Tex. 1966, U.S. Supreme Ct. 1968. Dep. city atty. criminal divsn. City of L.A., 1963-65; asst. dist. atty. L.A. County, 1978-82; now pvt. practice atty. L.A. Former adj. prof. law UCLA Sch. Law, Loyola U. Sch. Law; lawyer rep. U.S. Dist .Ct. (ctrl. dist.) Calif., 1990, U.S. Ct. Appeals (9th cir.) Judicial Conf., 1990; bd. dirs. L.A. Family Housing Corp., Lawyers Mut. Ins. Co. Spl. counsel, chmn. rules com. Dem. Nat. Convention, 1984; spl. counsel com. on standard ofcl. conduct, ethics com. 99th congress U.S. Ho. Reps.; bd. dirs. L.A. Urban League, Oscar Joel Bryant Found., 28th St. YMCA, ACLU Found. So. Calif. Fellow Am. Bar Found.; mem. Am. Coll. Trial Lawyers, State Bar Calif. (co-chair bd. legal svc. corps 1993), L.A. African Am. C. of C. (bd. dirs.), Airport Commrs. City of L.A., Black Bus. Assn. L.A. (pres. 1989). Office: 4929 Wilshire Blvd Ste 1010 Los Angeles CA 90010-3825

COCHRAN, SHIRLEY ANN, assistant attorney general; b. Akron, Ohio, Apr. 18, 1953; d. Harry Blaine and Ruth Shirley (Keifer) Cool; m. Mitchell Stephen Cochran, Dec. 4, 1982. BA, U. Akron, 1974, postgrad., 1974-75, JD, 1979. Bar: Ohio 1979, U.S. Dist. Ct. (so. dist.) Ohio 1980, U.S. Dist. Ct. (no. dist.) Ohio 1981. Rep. Avon Products, Akron, 1972-73; clk. bookstores U. Akron, 1973-74; teaching asst. U. Akron, 1974-75; student dir. Appellate Rev. Office, Akron, 1976-78, legal intern, 1978-79; asst. atty. gen. State of Ohio, Columbus, 1979-90; pvt. practice, 1990-2002; Magistrate Clermont County Common Pleas Ct., 2002-. Mem. Ohio State Bar Assn. (chairperson young lawyers sect. 1984-86), ABA, Columbus Bar Assn. (com. chairperson 1982-83, 90), Assn. Women Lawyers of Franklin County, Independence Village Civic Assn., Clermont County Bar Assn., Ohio Women's Bar Assn., Delta Theta Phi (bailiff local chpt. 1985). Democrat. Club: Aux. United Fellowship (Barberton, Ohio). Home: 2897 Liberty Bell Ln Reynoldsburg OH 43068-3930 E-mail: scochran@co.clermont.oh.us.

COCHRAN, STEPHEN GREY, lawyer; b. N.Y.C., Aug. 7, 1947; s. John M. and Madeline (Grey) C.; m. Irene Gomberg, Oct. 10, 1975 (div.); m. Ruth Swart, Jan. 8, 1982; children: Stephanie Alice, Michael Edward. BA, William and Mary Coll., 1969; JD, Am. U., Washington, 1972. Bar: Va., U.S. Supreme Ct. 1972, U.S. Ct. Appeals (4th cir.) 1978, U.S. Tax Ct. 1980. Assoc. Furniss, Davis & Sachs, Norfolk, Va., 1972-74; ptnr. Bennett, Goram & Cochran, Vienna, Va., 1974-79, Gattsek, McConnel & Cochran, Annandale, Va., 1979-80, Clary & Pijor, Springfield, Va., 1980-85, Cochran & Pijor, McLean, Va., Peterson, Pesner, Cochran & Basha, P.C., Vienna, Va., 1991-92, Cochran & Rathbun, P.C., McLean, 1992-97, The Jefferson Law Firm PLC, Vienna, 1997—. Mem. faculty Nat. Inst. Trial Advocacy, Georgetown U. Law Ctr. Mem. Assn. Trial Lawyers Am., Va. Trial Lawyers Assn. (chmn. comml. litigation sect.), Fairfax Bar Assn. (chmn. civil litigation sect. 1984—, law day com. 1982-84). General civil litigation, Family and matrimonial, Personal injury (including property damage). Home: 6155 Farver Rd Mc Lean VA 22101-3239 Office: Womble Carlyle Sandridge & Rice PLLC 4th Fl 8065 Leesburg Pike Vienna VA 22182-2738 E-mail: scochran@wcsr.com.

COCKE, JOHN HARTWELL, lawyer; b. Clarksdale, Miss., Oct. 9, 1947; s. Cary H. Cocke and Mary Edmonds Peacock; m. Robin Page, Nov. 20, 1971; 1 child, David B. BA in Econs., U. Va., 1969, JD, 1975. Bar: Miss. 1975, Tenn. 1992. Ptnr. Hollomb Dunbar, Clarksdale, Miss., 1975-82; founding ptnr. Merkel & Cocke, Clarksdale, 1982—. With U.S. Army, 1969-72. Mem. ABA (co-chair med. malpractice sub com. 1997-98), Miss. Trial Lawyers Assn. (bd. govs. 1992-98), Rotary Club. Episcopalian. Avocations: flying, fishing, skiing, scuba, tennis. Federal civil litigation, Personal injury (including property damage), Professional liability. Office: Merkel & Cocke PA PO Box 1388 Clarksdale MS 38614-1388

COCKRIEL, STEPHEN EUGENE, lawyer; b. Long Beach, Calif., June 9, 1948; s. John Robert and Patricia D. (Carroll) C.; m. Helen K. Mulford, Dec. 19, 1968 (div. Feb. 1988); children: Jonathan Ryan, Timothy; m. Dee Ann Kahler, Apr. 17, 1987; stepchildren: John Brandon Kahler, Zachary Robert Kahler, Sara Courtney Kahler. BS, U. So. Calif., 1970; JD, Loyola U., L.A., 1973. Bar: Calif. 1973. Assoc. Munns, Kofford, Hoffman, Hunt & Throckmorton, Pasadena, Calif., 1973-74; atty. Thrifty Drug Stores Co., Inc., L.A., 1974-75; pvt. practice Long Beach, 1975-81, 87—; ptnr. Bergmann, Cockriel & Forrester, Long Beach, 1975-87. Assoc. legal counsel U.S. Jaycees, Tulsa, 1978-79, legal counsel, 1979-80. Pres. Grand Prix Charities Found., Long Beach, 1979-80, Local Devel. Corp., Long Beach, 1987-89; chmn. bd. Community Svcs. Devel. Corp., Long Beach, 1986-90. Mem. Long Beach Jaycees (pres. 1978-79). Republican. Methodist. Avocations: golf, stamp collecting. Corporate, general, Probate (including wills, trusts), Estate taxation. Office: 333 W Broadway Ste 306 Long Beach CA 90802-4440

COCO, MARK STEVEN, lawyer; b. Alliance, Ohio, Nov. 1, 1952; s. John Robert and Mabel Ann (Paletti) C.; children: Steven, Matthew. BA cum laude, Ohio State U., 1974, JD summa cum laude, 1977. Bar: Ohio 1977, U.S. Dist. Ct. (no. and so. dists.) Ohio 1977. Assoc. Schwartz, Kelm, Warren & Rubenstein, Columbus, Ohio, 1977-80, Jones, Day, Reavis & Pogue, Columbus, Ohio, 1980-87; ptnr. Minton, Leslie & Coco, Columbus, Ohio, 1987-89, Jones, Troyan, Coco, Pappas & Perkins, Columbus, 1989-94, Harris, McClellan, Binau & Cox, Columbus, 1994—. Mem. ABA (litigation sect.), Ohio Bar Assn. (labor and litigation sect.), Columbus Bar Assn., Ohio State U. Alumni Assn., Order of Coif. Federal civil litigation, State civil litigation, Labor (including EEOC, Fair Labor Standards Act, labor-management relations, NLRB, OSHA). Home: 8622 Gairloch Ct Dublin OH 43017-9754 E-mail: mcoco@hmbc.com.

CODDING, FREDERICK HAYDEN, lawyer; b. Hopewell, Va., Dec. 13, 1938; s. Francis Chadwick and Ruthcille Sharon (Craven) C.; m. Judith Willis Hawkins, Apr. 30, 1966; children: Forrest Hayden, Judith Chadwick, Cally Willis, Clare Catharine. AB, Coll. William and Mary, 1962; JD, Georgetown U., 1966. Bar: Va. 1966, D.C. 1968, U.S. Supreme Ct. 1979. Legal asst. VA, Washington, 1963-65; Capitol Hill reporter, editor Congressional Monitor, Washington, 1966; law clk. to chief judge D.C. Ct. Appeals, 1966-68; individual practice law Va. and Washington; v.p., counsel Nat. Assn. Miscellaneous, Ornamental and Archtl. Products Contractors, Fairfax, Va., 1970—; counsel, dir. Nat. Assn. Reinforcing Steel Contractors, Fairfax, 1970—. Editor pub. legis., adminstrv., bldg. and constrn. industry newsletters, reports. Mem. federally established rev. bds. for constrn., OSHA and industry; counsel, pres. Fairfax Police Youth Club; appointee Fairfax City Sch. Bd., 1983-88. Mem. ABA, D.C. Bar Assn., Va. Bar Assn., Fairfax Bar Assn., Nat. Council Erectors, Fabricators and Riggers, Sigma Nu. Office: 10382 Main St Fairfax VA 22030-2412

CODDINGTON, CLINTON HAYS, lawyer; b. Honolulu, July 8, 1939; s. L. Clinton and Patricia Carolyn (Richer) C.; m. Martha Ann Stevens, June 20, 1970; children: Clinton Stevens, Catherine Hadley. BSCE, U.S. Mil. Acad., 1961; JD, U. Calif., Berkeley, 1968. Bar: Calif. 1969, U.S. Ct. Appeals (2nd, 5th, 7th, 8th and 9th cirs.), U.S. Supreme Ct. 1974. Assoc. Bronson, Bronson & McKinnon, San Francisco, 1969-70, Rogers Majeski Kohn Bentley Wagner & Kane, Redwood City, Calif., 1970-77, Tucker & Coddington, Palo Alto, Calif., 1977-78; ptnr., pres. Coddington, Hicks & Danforth, Redwood City, 1978—. Contbr. articles to profl. jours. Chmn. Easter Seals; vestryman, sr. warden, chancellor various Episcopal chs.; pres. Chinquapin Homeowners Assn., Lake Tahoe, Calif., 1991-92, Stanford Hills Homeowners Assn., Palo Alto, Calif. Capt. U.S. Army, 1961-64. Mem. ABA, Assn. Def. Counsel of No. Calif., Lawyer/Pilot Bar Assn., Internat. Assn. Def. Counsel, San Mateo County Bar Assn., Calif. Bar Assn., Def. Rsch. Inst., Am. Bd. Trial Advocates. Republican. Avocations: guitar, classical music, aviation, boating, reading. Aviation, Federal civil litigation, State civil litigation. Office: Coddington Hicks & Danforth 555 Twin Dolphin Dr Ste 300 Redwood City CA 94065-2133 E-mail: codsqd@attbi.com., ccoddington@chdlawyers.com.

CODURRI, MAURIZIO, lawyer, international business law specialist; b. Brescia, Italy, Mar. 7, 1961; s. Gabriele Andrea and Jole Maria (Tanghetti) C.; m. Piera Daru, May 6, 1989; 1 child, Alexandre Michel. D in Civil Law, State U. Pavia, Italy, 1986. Assoc. Valseristi Law Firm, Brescia, 1982-90; jr. ptnr. Monti & Ptnrs., Milan, 1990-91, ptnr., 1991-93; mng. ptnr. Frau & Ptnrs., Milan, 1993—. Dir. for Italy, formal rep. Internat. Found. of Airline Passengers Assn., Geneva, 1984—; guest spkr., chmn. in field. Contbr. articles to profl. jours. Mem. ABA, Internat. Bar Assn., N.Y. State Bar Assn. (chair Italian chpt. internat. law and practice sect. Milan 1994—), The Offshore Inst., Internat. Tax Planning Assn., European Air Law Assn., Union Internat. des Avocats (sec. commn. 1992-96, chmn. commn. 1996—, dep. sec. gen. 1998—), Assn. Bar City of N.Y., Soc. Trust and Estate Practitioners. Avocations: music, theater, golf. Banking, Commercial, contracts (including sales of goods; commercial financing), Private international. Office: Frau & Ptnrs Via C Poerio 15 20129 Milan Italy Fax: 39-0276003311. E-mail: codurri@itpa.org.

CODY, DANIEL SCHAFFNER, lawyer; b. Columbus, Ohio, Nov. 21, 1948; s. Ralph Eugene and Grace (Schaffner) C.; m. Susan Ragsdale, Mar. 27, 1992 (div.); 1 child, Sean. Student, Kent State U., 1977; BA, Ohio State U., 1970, BSEd, 1973; JD, U. Akron, 1990. Bar: Ohio 1990, U.S. Dist. Ct. (no. dist.) Ohio 1990, U.S. Ct. Appeals (6th cir.) 1990, U.S. Ct. Appeals (4th cir.) 1992. Tchg. Archbishop Hoban H.S., Akron, Ohio, 1973-88, athletic dir., 1980-84; rsch. asst. Hon. Arthur Goldberg (ret.) U.S. Supreme Ct., U. Akron, 1989, staff intern Appellate Rev. Office, 1990-91; jud. clk. Ohio Ct. Appeals (9th dist.), Akron, 1990-91; assoc. Jacobson, Maynard, Tuschman & Kalur, Cleve., 1991-93; pvt. practice Akron, 1993—. Trustee U. Akron Law Alumni Assn., 1992—, pres., 2000-01; trustee Archbishop Hoban H.S., 1995-2001. Mem.: Akron Bar Assn., Ohio State Bar Assn. Democrat. Roman Catholic. Criminal, Personal injury (including property damage). Office: 17 S Main St Ste 201 Akron OH 44308-1803

COELHO DA ROCHA, PAULO FRANK, lawyer; b. Rio de Janeiro, Mar. 9, 1971; s. Luiz Henrique Rocha and Karin Frank. JD, U. São Paulo, Brazil, 1993; LLM in Corp. Law, NYU, 1997. Bar: Brazil 1994. Assoc. Demarest e Almeida, São Paulo, 1993—97; fgn. assoc. Cravath, Swaine & Moore, N.Y.C., 1997—99; sr. assoc. Demarest e Almeida, São Paulo, 1999—2003, ptnr., 2003—. Avocations: tennis, wine tasting, history. Mergers and acquisitions, Corporate, general, Commercial, contracts (including sales of goods; commercial financing). Office: Demarest e Almeida Advogados Av Pedroso de Moraes 1201 05419-001 São Paulo Brazil

COERPER, MILO GEORGE, lawyer, priest; b. Milw., May 8, 1925; s. Milo Wilson and Rose (Schubert) C.; m. Lois Hicks, Apr. 11, 1953; children: Milo Wilson, Allison Lee, Lois Paddock. BS, U.S. Naval Acad., 1946; LLB, U. Mich., 1954; MA, Georgetown U., 1957, PhD, 1960. Bar: D.C. 1954, Md. 1960, N.Y. 1980. Since practiced in, Washington; asso. firm Wilmer & Broun, 1954-60; firm Coudert Bros., 1961-63, mem. firm, 1964-96, retired ptnr., 1996—; ordained deacon Episcopal Ch., 1978, priest, 1979. Cathedral chaplain Washington Nat. Cathedral, 1986—. Contbr. articles to profl. jours. Trustee, vice chmn. for U.S., Canterbury Cathedral Trust in Am., 1982-97, acting chmn., 1991, 97; mem. coun. The Friends of Canterbury Cathedral in U.S., 1999—. Ensign USN, 1946-49; to lt. 1951-53. Mem.: ABA, Internat. Assn. for Protection of Indsl. Property, Am. Soc. Internat. Law, Am. Law Inst., Md. State Bar Assn., Bar Assn. DC, Chevy Chase Club, Met. Club (pres. 1986), Army and Navy Club. Corporate, general, Probate (including wills, trusts), Trademark and copyright. Home: 7315 Brookville Rd Chevy Chase MD 20815-4057 Office: Coudert Bros 1627 I St NW Washington DC 20006-4007

COEY, DAVID CONRAD, lawyer; b. Chgo., Oct. 20, 1930; s. David R. and Marion E. (Sullivan) C.; divorced; children: David R., Kurt T.; m. Barbara Stephenson, Aug. 24, 1972; 1 child, Deborah. BS, Mich. State U., 1956; JD, U. Mich., 1959. Bar: Mich. 1959, U.S. Dist. Ct. (ea. and we. dists.) M ich. 1960, U.S. Ct. Appeals (6th cir.) 1965. Ptnr. Foster, Swift, Collins & Coey, P.C., Lansing, Mich., 1966-89, Howard & Howard P.C., Lansing, 1990-97, Dickinson, Wright, Lansing, 1997—. Lectr. Mich. State U. Med. Sch., U. Mich. Inst. Continuing Legal Edn.; past chmn. workers' disability compensation sect. State Bar Mich.; lectr., adv. Am. Bd. of Trial Advocates. With USN, 1950-54. Recipient Outstanding Lawyer of the Yr. award Ingham County Bar, 1995, Excellence in Def. award Mich. Def. Trial Counsel, 1995. Fellow Am. Coll. Trial Lawyers; mem. ABA, Am. Bd. Trial Advs., Mich. Trial Lawyers Assn., Mich. Def. Trial Counsel Assn., Univ. Club (East Lansing, Mich.), Mich. Bar Found., Am. Bar Found. Federal civil litigation, State civil litigation, Personal injury (including property damage). Home: 988 Lantern Hill Dr East Lansing MI 48823-2832 Office: 215 S Washington Sq Ste 200 Lansing MI 48933-1888 E-mail: dcoey@dickinson-wright.com.

COFFEE, MELVIN ARNOLD, retired lawyer; b. Chgo., July 8, 1934; s. Charles Hyman and Ida (Berson) C.; m. Beverly N. Segal, Aug. 26, 1956; children: Ronald M., Babette S. BS in Law, LLB, U. Denver, 1957; LLM, NYU, 1959. Bar: Colo. 1958. Ptnr. Drexler, Wald, Sobol & Coffee, Denver, 1959-63, Inman, Flynn & Coffee, Denver, 1963-78; sr. ptnr. Melvin Coffee & Assocs., Denver, 1978-2000; ret., 2000. Adj. prof. tax law U. Denver, 1974-83; chmn. IRS liaison com. Southwest Bar, 1989. Author: Taxation for Accountants, 1970, Protecting Client in Tax Fraud Investigation, 1972, New Directions in Guarding Client Records, 1973, Criminal Tax Investigations, 1983, The Colorado Lawyer, 1983. Prin. draftsman statute Colo. Income Tax Act 1964; pres. Denver and Tri-County Respiratory Disease Assn., 1962; active Citizen Budget Rev., 1963; Dem. rep. Colo. Ho. of Reps., 1967-69. With U.S. Army, 1958-64. Mem. Colo. State Bd. Accountancy (bd. dirs., pres. 1981), Colo. Soc. CPAs (hon.), Colo. Bar Assn. (bd. govs. 1980-82, chmn. taxation sect. 1970, chmn. continuing legal edn. 1981), Arapahoe County Bar Assn. (trustee 1980-82), Nat. Assn. State Bds. Accountancy (v.p. 1981-84), Greater Denver Tax Counsel (pres., sec. 1963-65), Masons, Columbine. Criminal, Taxation, general, State and local taxation. Office: Melvin Coffee PC 4296 S Dahlia St Englewood CO 80110-5004

COFFEE, RICHARD JEROME, II, lawyer; b. Chgo., Nov. 12, 1954; s. James F. and Jean Marie (Hackman) C.; children: David Patrick Coffee, Brent William Coffee; m. Sue Heberlie, Dec. 12, 1997. BS, So. Ill. U., 1975; JD, U. Ill., 1978. Bar: Ill. 1978, U.S. Dist. Ct. (no. dist.) Ill. 1978, U.S. Dist. Ct. (ctrl. dist.) Ill. 1980, U.S. Dist. Ct. (so. dist.) Ill. 1998. Staff atty. Ill. Dept. Ins., Springfield, 1979-80; counsel Ill. State Employees Assn., Springfield, 1980-84; staff counsel Ill. Bd. Regents, Springfield, 1984-87, legal counsel Chancellor's Office, 1987-89; univ. legal counsel Sangamon State U., Springfield, 1989-90; chief legal advisor Ill. State Bd. Edn., Springfield, 1990-96; assoc. Rau & Rau Attys., Waterloo, Ill., 1997—. Mem.: Monroe County Bar Assn. (sec. 1998—99, treas. 1999—2000, v.p. 2000—01, pres. 2001—02), Chgo. Bar Assn. Avocations: licensed pilot, licensed amateur radio operator. Office: 119 E Mill St Waterloo IL 62298-1518 E-mail: coffee@ljextra.com., raulaw@htc.net.

COFFEY, JOHN LOUIS, judge; b. Milw., Apr. 15, 1922; s. William Leo and Elizabeth Ann (Walsh) Coffey; m. Marion Kunzelmann, Feb. 3, 1951; children: Peter Coffey-Robbins, Elizabeth Mary Coffey-Robbins. BA, Marquette U., 1943, JD, 1948; MBA (hon.) , Spencerian Coll., 1964. Bar: Wis. 1948, U.S. Dist. Ct. 1948, U.S. Supreme Ct. 1980. Asst. city atty. City of Milw., 1949—54; judge Civil Ct., Milw. County, 1954—60, Milw. County Mcpl. Ct., 1960—62; judge criminal divsn. Cir. Ct., Milw. County, 1962—72, sr. judge criminal divsn., 1972—75, chief presiding judge criminal divsn., 1976, judge civil divsn., 1976—78; justice Wis. Supreme Ct., Madison, 1978—82; cir. judge U.S. Ct. Appeals (7th cir.), Chgo., 1982—; mem. Wis. Bd. Criminal Ct. Judges, 1960—78, Wis. Bd. Circuit Ct. Judges, 1962—78. Mem. adv. bd. St. Mary's Hosp., 1964—70; bd. dirs., mem. exec. bd. Milw.-Waukesha chpt. ARC; mem. Milw. County coun. Boy Scouts Am., 1970—78; chmn. vol. svcs. adv. com. Milw. County Dept. Pub. Welfare, 1970—72; chmn. St. Eugene's Sch. Bd., 1967—70; pres. St. Eugene's Ch. Coun., 1974; chmn. adv. bd. St. Joseph's Home for Children, 1958—65. With USNR, 1943—46. Named Outstanding Young Man of Yr., Milw. Jr. C. of C., 1951; recipient Marquette Univ. H.S. Alumni Merit award, 2001. Fellow: Am. Bar Found.; mem.: State Bar Assn. Wis., Ill. State Bar Assn., 7th Cir. Bar Assn., Marquette U. Law Alumni Assn. (Disting. Profl. Achievement Merit award 1985), Marquette U. M Club (former dir.), Nat. Lawyers Club, Am. Legion (Disting. Svc. award 1973), Alpha Sigma Nu, Phi Alpha Delta (hon.). Roman Catholic.

COFFEY, THOMAS WILLIAM, lawyer; b. Cin., Jan. 19, 1959; s. Joseph Paul and Doris June (Adams) C.; m. Shirley Ann Strode, July 24, 1982. MusB, U. Cin., 1981, JD, 1987. Bar: Pa. 1987, U.S. Dist. Ct. (we. dist.) Pa. 1987, U.S. Ct. Appeals (3d cir.) 1988, Ohio 1990, U.S. Dist. Ct. (so. dist.) Ohio 1990, U.S. Ct. Appeals (6th cir.) 1990. Dir. band Ea. Local Sch., Brown County, Ohio, 1981-83, Goshen (Ohio) High Sch., 1983-84; assoc. Buchanan Ingersoll, P.C., Pitts., 1987-90; chmn. bankruptcy group Cors & Bassett, Cin., 1990—. Mem. ABA, Ohio Bar Assn., Cin. Bar Assn., Am. Fedn. Musicians, Masons, Shriners. Avocation: symphonic and dixieland jazz. Banking, Bankruptcy, Commercial, contracts (including sales of goods; commercial financing). Home: 933 Monastery St Cincinnati OH 45202-1510 Office: Cors & Bassett 537 E Pete Rose Way Ste 400 Cincinnati OH 45202-3578 E-mail: twc@eors.bassett.com.

COFFIN, FRANK MOREY, judge; b. Lewiston, Maine, July 11, 1919; s. Herbert Rice and Ruth (Morey) Coffin; m. Ruth Ulrich, Dec. 19, 1942; children: Nancy, Douglas, Meredith, Susan. AB, Bates Coll., 1940, LLD, 1959; postgrad. indsl. adminstrn., Harvard U., 1943, LLB, 1947; LLD, Bates Coll., 1959, U. Maine, 1967, Bowdoin Coll., 1969; degree (hon.) , Colby Coll., 1975. Bar: Maine 1947. Law clk. to fed. judge Dist. of Maine, 1947—49; engaged in practice, 1947—52; with Verrill, Dana, Walker, Philbrick & Whitehouse, Portland, Maine, 1952—56; mem. 85th-86th Congresses from 2d Dist. Maine, House Com. Fgn. Affairs; mng. dir. joint econ. com. Devel. Loan Fund, Dept. State, Washington, 1961; dep. adminstr. AID, 1961—64; U.S. rep. devel. assistance com. Orgn. Econ. Coop. and Devel., 1964—65; judge 1st circuit U.S. Ct. Appeals, 1965—, chief judge, 1972—83, sr. judge, 1989—; chmn. com. jud. br. U.S. Jud. Conf., 1984—90. Adj. prof. U. Maine Sch. Law, 1986—89. Author: Witness for Aid, 1964, The Ways of a Judge-Reflections from the Federal Appellate Bench, 1980, A Lexicon or Oral Advocacy, 1984, On Appeal, 1994. Emeritus Bates Coll.; dir. The Governance Inst., 1987—; mem. emeritus The Examiner; chair Maine Justice Action Group, 1996—2001. Lt. USNR, 1943—46. Recipient Edward J. Devitt Disting. Svc. to Justice award, 2001. Mem.: ABA, ABA (co-chmn. com. on loan forgiveness and repayment 2001—02), Am. Acad. Arts and Sci., Am. Acad. Arts and Sci. Office: US Ct Appeals 156 Federal St Portland ME 04101-4152

COFFIN, MARY MCCARTHY, lawyer; b. Syracuse, NY, Oct. 15, 1920; m. Louis F. Coffin, Apr. 24, 1943; children: John, Sally, Laurie, Robert, Patricia, Deborah, Louis, Margaret. AB, Radcliffe Coll., 1942; postgrad., MIT, 1942-43; LLB, Albany Law Sch., 1967. Bar: N.,Y. 1968, U.S. Supreme Ct. 1974. Rsch. tech. Children's Hosp., Boston, 1941-43; law clk. County Ct., Schenectady, N.Y., 1968-70; counsel Schenectady Urban Renewal Agy., 1970-72; pvt. practice Schenectady, 1972-79; ptnr. Antokol & Coffin, Schenectady, 1979-97, of counsel, 1990; ret., 1996. Legal counsel Sch. Urban Renewal Agy, Schenectady, 1970-73; past pres., incorporator Schenectady County Legal Aid; trustee, YWCA, 1975-90; mem. Schenectady Housing Code Commn., 1973-76, Hospice of Schenectady, 1982-88, Law, Order and Justice, 1975-82, Schenectady Family and Child Service, 1977-82; bd. dirs. Schenectady County Legal Aid, 1968-81, pres., 1970; bd. dirs. N.E. Legal Aid Soc., 1979-82. Recipient Susan B. Anthony award Schenectady County LWV, 1982; named Schenectady Jr. League Vol. of Yr., 1957; recipient Schenectady Law, Order and Justice award for Svc., 1982; Cmty. Svc. award YWCA, 1982. Mem. ABA, Schenectady Bar Assn., N.Y. Bar Assn. (Root/Stimson award), Torch Club. Democrat. Criminal, Family and matrimonial, Property, real (including real estate development, water). Home: 235 Walker St Apt 172 Lenox MA 01240-2747 E-mail: marylouco@webtv.net.

COFFMAN, JENNIFER BURCHAM, federal judge; b. 1948; BA, U. Ky., 1969, MA, 1971, JD, 1978. Ref. libr. Newport News (Va.) Pub. Libr., 1972-74, U. Ky. Libr., 1974-76; atty. Law Offices Arthur L. Brooks., Lexington, Ky., 1978-82; ptnr. Brooks, Coffman and Fitzpatrick, Lexington, 1982-92, Newberry, Hargrove & Rambicure, Lexington, 1992-93; judge U.S. Dist. Ct. (ea. dist. and we. dist.) Ky., 1993—. Adj. prof. Coll. Law, U. Ky., 1979-81. Elder Second Presbyn. Ch., 1993—96; bd. dirs. YWCA Lexington, 1986—92, Shepherd Ctr., 2000—. Mem. Ky. Bar Assn., Fayette County Bar Assn., U. Ky. Law Sch. Alumni Assn. Office: 306 US Courthouse 101 Barr St Lexington KY 40507-1313

COFFMAN, PENELOPE DALTON, judge; b. Pulaski, Va., Apr. 16, 1938; d. Gomez and Hazel (Davis) Dalton; m. Aldine J. Coffman, Mar. 27, 1965; children: D'Maris, Derek. AB, Randolph-Macon Women's Coll., 1958; JD, Coll. William and Mary, 1965. Bar: Va. 1966, Utah 1977, Colo. 1984. Law clk. Va. Supreme Ct., Richmond, 1966-68; asst. commonwealth atty. Commonwealth Atty.'s Office, Virginia Beach, va., 1970-73; ptnr. Coffman & Coffman, Virginia Beach, 1968-75, Moab, Utah, 1975-88, Dodd, Scott, Stockton & Coffman, Lakewood, Colo., 1990-94; substitute judge Cherry Hills Village and Greenwood Village, Colo., 1992—. Articles editor William and Mary Law Rev., 1964-66; book reviewer. Bd. dirs. Four County Travel Coun., Grand County, Utah, 1978-82, Health Coun., Grand County, 1978-82, Mental Health, Grand County, 1978-82, Va. Coun. Ednl. TV, 1970-72. Mem. Denver Women's Press Club (bd. dirs., treas.). Republican. Episcopalian. Avocation: competitive bridge. Home: 6 Cherry Lane Dr Englewood CO 80110-4210

COGAN, JOHN FRANCIS, JR., lawyer; b. Boston, June 13, 1926; s. John Francis and Mary (Galligan) C.; m. Mary T. Hart, May 1, 1951 (div.); m. Mary L. Cornille, June 24, 1989; children: Peter G., Pamela E., Jonathan C., Gregory M. AB cum laude, Harvard U., 1949, JD, 1952. Bar: Mass. 1953. Ptnr. Hale and Dorr, Boston, 1957—2000, mng. ptnr., 1976—84, chmn., 1984—96, of counsel, 2000—; dep. chmn. Pioneer Global Asset Mgmt., SpA, Milan, 2000—; chmn. Pioneer Investment Mgmt., USA, Inc., Boston, 2000—. Trustee various Pioneer Funds, Inc., Boston, 1963—; bd. dirs. ICI Mutual Inst. Co.; chmn. exec. com. Western Res. Life Assurance Co., Ohio, 1968—79. Trustee Boston Symphony Orch., 1989—, overseer, 1984—92, chmn., 1989—92; overseer Mus. Fine Arts, 1989—90, trustee, 1990—, chmn., 1994—98; trustee Boston Ballet, 1986—89; mem. Mass. Dem. State Com.; trustee Univ. Hosp., Boston, 1965—95, chmn. bd., 1972—89; trustee Boston Med. Ctr., 1995—; bd. dirs. Wendell P. Clark Meml. Assn., Walker Home for Children, 1972—2000, Brigham Surg. Group, Inc., 1981—95, The Med. Found., 1986—90; trustee Boston U. Med. Ctr., 1973—90; bd. govs. Investment Co. Inst., 1971—74, 1975, 1981, 1982, chmn. bd. govs., 1978—80, 1982—85, 1986—89, 1991—. Served with USNR, 1944—46. Mem. ABA, Internat. Bar Assn., Mass. Bar Assn. (chmn. corp. banking and bus. law com. 1973-76), Boston Bar Assn. (past chmn. profl. svcs. sect., mem. bench-bar com.), Boston Estate and Bus. Planning Coun. (past pres.), Boston Probate and Estate Planning Forum (sec. 1958-73), Nat. Assn. Security Dealers (bd. dirs. 1983-86, legal adv. bd. 1988-94). Home: 975 Memorial Dr Apt 802 Cambridge MA 02138-5755 Office: Pioneer Investment Mgmt USA Inc 60 State St Boston MA 02109-1820

COGAN, MARY JO GLEBER, lawyer; b. Wilmington, Del., Aug. 13, 1954; d. Jacob Adam and Marilyn Roberta (Fox) Gleber; m. Julian N. Cogan; children: Caitlin, Amanda. BA in Polit. Sci., U. Del., 1978; JD, U. San Diego, 1981. Bar: Calif. 1982. Assoc. Stebleton, Waters & May, El Cajon, Calif., 1982-83; ptnr. George & Allred, El Cajon, 1983-84; assoc. O'Dorisio, Wedell & Wade, San Diego, 1984-85; sole practice San Diego, 1985—. Lillian Kratter Women's scholar U. San Diego, Law Sch., 1980-81. Mem. Calif. State Bar Assn., San Diego County Bar Assn., U. San Diego Law Sch. Alumni Assn. Democrat. Home: 11145 Calle Dario San Diego CA 92126-1714

COGAN, STEW, arbitrator; b. L.A., Calif., Apr. 1, 1952; s. Benjamin H. and Edna L. Cogan; children: Bradley Benjamin, David Daniel. BA, U. Calif. Berkeley, 1973; JD, Harvard U., 1976. Bar: Wash. 1976, U.S. Dist. Ct. (we. dist.) Wash. 1980, U.S. Ct. Appeals (9th cir.) 1981, U.S. Tax Ct. 1981, U.S. Supreme Ct. 1982. Counsel Davis Wright Tremaine, Seattle, 1976—81; prin. Mills Cogan Meyers Swartling, Seattle, 1981—96; arbitrator, mediator Stew Cogan Arbitrator-Mediator, Seattle, 1996—. Bd. dirs. Physician's Ins., Seattle, Alpha One Found., Miami, Fla.; trustee Instn. for Family Devel., Federal Way, Va., 1996—. Recipient Helen M. Geisness Meml. award, King County Bar Assn., 1992, Founders Spirit award, Alpha One Found., 2000. Home: 2600 2d Ave #2202 Seattle WA 98121-1221 Office: 1301 5th Ave Ste 2600 Seattle WA 98101-2618

COGGINS, PAUL EDWARD, JR., lawyer; b. Hugo, Okla., May 21, 1951; s. Paul E. and Rebecca (Cates) C.; m. Regina T. Montoya, June 12, 1976; 1 child, Jessica Chandler. BA in Polit. Sci. summa cum laude, Yale U., 1973; BA with honors, Oxford U., 1975; JD cum laude, Harvard U., 1978. Bar: Tex. 1978. Tchr. Project New Gate N.Mex. State Penitentiary, 1973; law clk. Mass. Ct. Appeals, 1978-79; fed. prosecutor U.S. Attys. Office, Dallas, 1980-83; assoc. Johnson & Swanson, Dallas, 1979-80, ptnr., 1983-86, Meadows, Owens, Collier, Reed & Coggins, Dallas, 1986-93; U.S. atty. U.S. Dept. of Justice, Dallas, 1993-2001. Mem. adv. com. Magnet Sch. in Dallas, 1984—. Author: The Lady is the Tiger, 1987; co-author: Out of Bounds, 1992. Pres. bd. dirs. Dem. Forum, Dallas, 1985—. Rhodes scholar, 1973-76. Mem. ABA, Dallas Bar Assn. (mem. pro bono panel), Harvard Club (v.p. 1987—), Yale Club. Criminal, Entertainment, Intellectual property. Office: Fish & Richardson PC 5000 Bank One Ctr 1717 Main St Dallas TX 75201 Fax: (214) 747-2091. Business E-Mail: coggins@fr.com. E-mail: Coggins@fr.com.

COGGIO, BRIAN D. lawyer, educator; b. Yonkers, N.Y., Apr. 25, 1949; s. Joseph G. and Catherine T. Coggio; m. Nancy L. Sourbeck, Aug. 17, 1974; children: Jennifer, Brian Jr. BChemE, Manhattan Coll., 1971; JD, Fordham U. cum laude, 1974; LLM in Trade Regulations, NYU, 1980. Bar: N.Y., U.S. Ct. Appeals (2d cir.), U.S. Ct. Appeals (fed. cir.), U.S. Patent and Trademarks. Assoc. Pennie & Edmonds LLP, N.Y.C., 1974-82, ptrn., 1982-93, sr. ptnr., 1994—. Adj. prof. law N.Y. Law Sch., 1996-98, Fordham U. Sch. of Law, 1999—; mem. bd. editors Intellectual Property Litigator, 1995—. Contbr. articles to profl. jours. Avocation: piano. Patent. Home: 34 Moore Rd Bronxville NY 10708-5410 Office: Orrick Herrington & Sutcliffe LLP 666 Fifth Ave New York NY

COGHILL, WILLIAM THOMAS, JR., retired lawyer; b. St. Louis, July 20, 1927; s. William Thomas and Mildred Mary (Crenshaw) C.; m. Patricia Lee Hughes, Aug. 7, 1948; children: James Prentiss, Victoria Lynn, Cathryn Anne. JD, U. Mo., 1950, undergrad., 1944-45, 46-47. Bar: Mo. 1950, Ill. 1958. Pvt. practice, Farmington, Mo., 1950-51; spl. agt. FBI, 1951-52; ptnr. Smith, Smith & Coghill, Farmington, 1952-57; assoc. Coburn & Croft, St. Louis, 1957-58; ptnr. Thompson Coburn (formerly Thompson & Mitchell and predecessor firm), Belleville, Ill., 1958—2001, ret., 2001. Co-author: Illinois Products Liability, 1991, Cavaliers, 1999. With USN, 1945-46. Fellow Am. Coll. Trial Lawyers; mem. ABA, Ill. State Bar Assn., Mo. State Bar Assn. Federal civil litigation, State civil litigation, Insurance. Home: 715 W Moon Valley Dr Phoenix AZ 85023-6234 E-mail: tcoghill@rni.net.

COGHLAN, KELLY JACK, lawyer; b. Longview, Tex., Sept. 3, 1952; s. Howard and Peggy Coghlan. BBA with honors, So. Meth. U., 1975, JD cum laude, 1978. Bar: Tex. 1978, U.S. Dist. Ct. (so. dist.) Tex. 1979, U.S. Tax Ct. 1981, U.S. Ct. Appeals (5th cir.) 1981, U.S. Supreme Ct. 1984. Law clk. to presiding judge Finis E. Cowan U.S. Dist. Ct. (so. dist.) Tex., 1978-79; assoc. Vinson & Elkins, Houston, 1979-84; equity ptnr. Dotson, Babcock & Scofield, Houston, 1984-88, chmn. risk mgmt. com., head gen. litigation group, 1987-88; pvt. practice, Houston, 1988—. Bd. dirs. Sta. KSBJ, Houston, sec., 1990-93, chmn. long range planning com., 1989-93, mem. exec. com., 1990-97, v.p., 1994-97. Mem. So. Meth. U. Law Sch. Southwestern Law Jour. Mem. steering com. Palmer Drug Abuse Program, Houston, 1980-82; vol. jr. high and H.S. youth programs, 1990—, 2d Bapt. Ch., Houston, 1990—; mem. 1st Meth. Ch., Longview, Tex., 1962—; youth min., Wesley United Meth. Ch., Longview, 1972-77. Recipient So. Meth. U. M award, 1975, Russell Baker Moot Ct. 1st pl. award So. Meth. U. Law Sch., 1976; named Players of 1999, Tex. Lawyer. Fellow Houston Bar Found., Pro Bono Coll. State Bar Tex.; mem. ABA, Tex. Bar Assn., Houston Bar Assn., Houston Young Lawyers Assn. (chmn. com. on consumer rights 1981-82), Nat. Eagle Scout Assn. (life), So. Meth. U. Student Found. (hon.), Order of Coif (hon.), Am. Mensa, Gulf Coast Mensa, Blue Key Soc. (hon., pres. 1974-75), Beta Gamma Sigma (hon.), Phi Delta Phi (hon.), Lambda Chi Alpha. Avocations: drumming, singing, youth work. General civil litigation, Personal injury (including property damage). Office: 505 Lanecrest Ln Ste 1 Houston TX 77024-6716

COGSWELL, PAUL REID, barrister, solicitor; m. Sandra Gay Pallmer. LLB, Auckland Univ., Auckland, New Zealand, 1992. Bar: New Zealand (soliciter high ct.) 1992. Ptnr. Hesketh Henry, Auckland, New Zealand, 1992—. Mem.: New Zealand Ins. Law Assn., INSOL. Office: Hesketh Henry 41 Shortland St Auckland New Zealand E-mail: paul.cogswell@heskethhenry.co.nz.

COHAN, LEON SUMNER, lawyer, retired electric company executive; b. Detroit, June 24, 1929; s. Maurice and Lillian (Rosenfeld) C.; m. Heidi Ruth Seelmann, Jan. 22, 1956; children: Nicole, Timothy David, Jonathan Daniel. BA, Wayne State U., 1949, JD, 1952. Bar: Mich. 1953. Pvt. practice, Detroit, 1954-58; asst. atty. gen. State of Mich., Lansing, 1958-61, dep. atty. gen., 1961-72; v.p. legal affairs Detroit Edison Co., 1973-75, v.p., 1975-79, sr. v.p., gen. counsel, 1979-93; counsel Barris, Sott, Denn & Driker, Detroit, 1993—. Bd. dirs. Oakland Commerce Bank. Trustee Mich. Cancer Found.; bd. dirs. Concerned Citizens for Arts in Mich., U. Mich. Musical Soc.; mem. arts commn. Detroit Inst. Arts; mem. Race Rels. Coun. Met. Detroit. With U.S. Army, 1952-54. Recipient Disting. Alumni award Wayne State U. Law Sch., 1972, Disting. Svc. award Bd. Govs., Wayne State U., 1973, Judge Ira W. Jayne award NAACP, 1987, Israel Histadrut Menorah award, 1987, Knights of Charity award Pontifical Inst. for Fgn. Missions, 1989, Fellowship award Am. Arabic and Jewish Friends of Met. Detroit, Judge Learned Hand Human Rels. award, 1991, Gov.'s Arts award for Civic Leadership in the Arts, Michiganian of Yr. award Detroit News, 1993. Mem. ABA, Detroit Bar Assn., State Bar Mich. (Champion of Justice award 1993), Mich. Gen. Counsel Assn., Detroit Club. Democrat. Jewish. Home: 17 Eastbury Ct Ann Arbor MI 48105-1402 Office: Barris Sott Denn & Driker 15th Fl 211 W Fort St Lbby 15 Detroit MI 48226-3244 E-mail: icohan@aol.com.

COHEN, ANITA MARILYN, retired lawyer; b. Pitts., Dec. 4, 1945; d. Rosalie (Agger) C. BA, U. Pitts., 1967; JD, Duquesne U., 1970. Bar: Pa. 1970, U.S. Dist. Ct. (ea. dist.) Pa. 1978, U.S. Dist. Ct. (we. dist.) Pa. 1970. Law clk., asst. pub. defender Appellate divsn. Office Pub. Defender of Allegheny County, 1968-71; asst. dist. atty. trial divsn. Office of Dist. Atty. of Philadelphia County, 1971-78; pvt. practice Phila., 1978-99; ret., 1999. Lectr. in field; counsel Phila. Boosters Assn., 1982-86. Contbr. articles to profl. jours. Bd. dirs. Girls Coalition of Southeastern Pa., 1981-85, cousel, 1983-86; bd. dirs. Planned Parenthood Southeastern Pa., 1981-85. Mem. ABA, Pa. Bar Assn. (legal ethics and profl. responsibility com. 1985-95), Am. Judicature Soc., Nat. Dist. Atty. Assn., Shomrim Club, F.O.P. State civil litigation, Criminal, Family and matrimonial.

COHEN, CYNTHIA MARYLYN, lawyer; b. Bklyn., Sept. 5, 1945; AB, Cornell U., 1967; JD cum laude, NYU, 1970. Bar: N.Y. 1971, U.S. Ct. Appeals (2nd cir.) 1972, U.S. Dist. Ct. (so. and ea. dists.) N.Y. 1972, U.S. Supreme Ct. 1975, U.S. Dist. Ct. (ctrl. and no. dists.) Calif. 1980, U.S. Ct. Appeals (9th cir.) 1980, U.S. Dist. Ct. (so. dist.) Calif. 1981, U.S. Dist. Ct. (ea. dist.) Calif. 1986. With Paul, Hastings, Janofsky & Walker, LLP, L.A., N.Y.C. Lawyer del. 9th Cir. Jud. Conf. Bd. dirs. N.Y. chpt. Am. Cancer Soc., 1977-80; active Pres.'s Coun. Cornell Women; lawyer del. Ninth Cir. Jud. Conf. Recipient Am. Jurisprudence award for evidence, torts and legal instns., 1968-69; John Norton Pomeroy scholar NYU, 1968-70, Founders Day Cert., 1969. Mem. ABA, Assn. Bar City N.Y. (trade regulation com. 1976-79), Assn. Bus. Trial Lawyers, Fin. Lawyers Conf., N.Y. State Bar Assn. (chmn. class-action com. 1979), State Bar Calif., Los Angeles County Bar Assn., Order of Coif, Delta Gamma. Avocations: tennis, bridge, rare books, wines. Antitrust, Bankruptcy, General civil litigation. Home: 4531 Dundee Dr Los Angeles CA 90027-1213 Office: Paul Hastings Janofsky & Walker LLP 515 S Flower St 25th Fl Los Angeles CA 90071 E-mail: cynthiacohen@paulhastings.com.

COHEN, EDMUND STEPHEN, lawyer; b. Newark, June 25, 1946; s. Louis William and Edna (Medresch) C.; m. Lisa Beth Sonenthal, June 30, 1968; children: Ellen Paige, Paul Lawrence. BA cum laude, Dartmouth Coll., 1968; JD cum laude, Harvard U., 1971; LLM in Taxation, NYU, 1975. Bar: N.Y. 1972, U.S. Ct. Appeals (2d cir.) 1972, U.S. Ct. Claims, 1973, U.S. Tax Ct. 1973, U.S. Dist. Ct. (so. dist.) N.Y. 1975. Assoc. Davis Polk & Wardwell, N.Y.C., 1971-78; ptnr. Cole & Deitz, N.Y.C., 1978-81, Coudert Bros., 1981—. Adj. prof. law grad. tax program NYU Law Sch., 1977-86; chmn. seminars World Trade Inst., N.Y.C., 1977—, Practicing Law Inst., N.Y.C., 1977—, NYU Fed. Tax Inst. Mem. ABA, N.Y. State Bar Assn., Assn. Bar City N.Y., Internat. Fiscal Assn. Private international, Corporate taxation, Taxation, general. Office: Coudert Bros LLP Fl 43 1114 Avenue Of The Americas New York NY 10036-7710

COHEN, EDWARD, lawyer; b. Hamilton, Ohio, Dec. 20, 1954; s. Alfred Sylvan and Marilyn (Melnikoff) C.; m. Dee Anne Bryll; children: Daniel, Briana L. BA, U. Cin., 1976; MA, Ind. U., 1982; JD, U. Cin., 1982. Bar: Ohio 1982, U.S. Dist. Ct. (so. dist.) Ohio 1982, U.S. Ct. Appeals (6th cir.) 1982. Doctoral fellow U. Cin., 1978-79, instr. coll. law, 1982-83; assoc. Goodman & Goodman Co., Cin., 1982-84, Kondritzer, Gold & Frank Co., Cin., 1984-88; ptnr. Clements, Mahin & Cohen, LLP, Cin., 1988—. Mem. ABA, ASCAP, Ohio Acad. Trial Lawyers, Ohio Bar Assn., Cin. Bar Assn. (sec. workers compensation com. 1990-91, chmn. 1992—), Order of Barristers, Ohio Cmty. Theatre Assn. (bd. dirs. 1995-98). General civil litigation, Personal injury (including property damage), Workers' compensation. Office: Clements Mahin & Cohen LLP 708 Walnut St Ste 600 Cincinnati OH 45202-2022 Fax: 513-763-6415. E-mail: ecohen@cmclawyers.com.

COHEN, EDWARD HERSCHEL, lawyer; b. Lewistown, Pa., Sept. 30, 1938; s. Saul Allen and Barbara (Getz) C.; m. Arlene Greenbaum, Aug. 12, 1962; children: Fredrick, James, Paul. AB, U. Mich., 1960; JD, Harvard U., 1963. Bar: N.Y. 1964. Assoc. Katten Muchin Zavis Rosenman, N.Y.C., 1963-72, ptnr., 1972—86, 1988—2002, counsel, 1987, 2003—; v.p., gen. counsel, sec. Phillips-Van Heusen Corp., N.Y.C., 1987. Mem. Fenway Golf Club (Scarsdale, N.Y.), Ventana Golf and Racquet Club (Tucson). Republican. Jewish. Avocations: golf, travel. Corporate, general, Securities. Office: Katten Muchin Zavis Rosenman 575 Madison Ave New York NY 10022-2585 Home: 45 Club Pointe Dr White Plains NY 10605

COHEN, EDWARD BARTH, lawyer; b. Washington, Oct. 13, 1949; s. Stanley Edward and Marjorie Cohen; m. Charlene Barshefsky, Jan. 25, 1976; two children. BA with acad. honors, U. Wis., 1971; JD, Georgetown U., 1974. Bar: D.C. 1975, U.S. Ct. Appeals (D.C. and 9th cirs.) 1981, U.S. Supreme Ct. 1981, U.S. Ct. Internat. Trade 1982, U.S. Tax Ct. 1983. Mem. profl. staff, counsel commerce com. U.S. Senate, Washington, 1971-77; gen. counsel U.S. Office Consumer Affairs, Washington, 1977-79; dep. spl. asst. Pres. Jimmy Carter, Washington, 1979-81; assoc. Davis, Wright & Jones, Washington, 1981—93; ptnr. Davis Wright Tremaine (and predecessor firm Davis, Wright & Jones), Washington, 1983-94; counselor to Sec. of Interior U.S. Dept. Interior, Washington, 1994-95, dep. solicitor, 1995-2000; v.p. govt. & industry rels. Honda North Am. Inc., Washington, 2000—. Mem. Bar of D.C. Administrative and regulatory, Communications, Legislative. Office: Honda N Am Inc Ste 950 1001 G St NW Washington DC 20001

COHEN, EDWIN LOUIS, lawyer; b. Louisville, May 7, 1930; s. Abe and Belle (Bass) C.; m. Helen Lois Kasdan, July 23, 1967; children: Deborah, Jennifer, Joseph. AB, U. Louisville, 1955, LLB, 1958. Bar: Ky. 1958, U.S. Dist. Ct. (we. dist.) Ky. 1960, U.S. Ct. Appeals (6th cir.) 1980, U.S. Supreme Ct. 1981. Ptnr. Cohen & Cohen, Louisville, 1958—. Served to staff sgt. USAF, 1951-55, Korea. Mem. Ky. Bar Assn. Democrat. Jewish. Federal civil litigation, Condemnation (eminent domain), Construction. Office: Cohen & Cohen 3415 Bardstown Rd Ste 306 Louisville KY 40218-4605 E-mail: cohenattorneys@aol.com.

COHEN, EDWIN SAMUEL, lawyer, educator; b. Richmond, Va., Sept. 27, 1914; s. LeRoy S. and Miriam (Rosenheim) C.; m. Carlyn Labenberg, June 27, 1936 (dec. 1942); m. Helen Herz, Aug. 31, 1944; children: Edwin C., Roger, Wendy. BA, U. Richmond, 1933; JD, U. Va., 1936. Bar: Va. 1935, N.Y. 1937, D.C. 1973. Assoc. Sullivan & Cromwell, N.Y.C., 1936-49; ptnr. Root, Barrett, Cohen, Knapp & Smith (and predecessor firm), N.Y.C., 1949-65; counsel Root, Barrett, Cohen, Knapp & Smith, 1965-69; prof. law U. Va., Charlottesville, 1965-68, Joseph M. Hartfield prof., 1968-69, 73-85, prof. emeritus, 1985—, professorial lectr. law, 1994—; asst. sec. treasury for tax policy, 1969-72; under sec. treasury, 1972-73; of counsel Covington & Burling, Washington, 1973-77, ptnr., 1977-86, sr. counsel, 1986—. Vis. prof. Benjamin N. Cardozo Sch. Law, Yeshiva U., 1987-92, U. Miami Law Sch., 1993, 95-99, chmn. grad. program in taxation and estate planning, 1995-98; mem., counsel adv. group on corp. taxes ways and means com. U.S. Ho. of Reps., 1956-58; spl. cons. on corps. fed. income tax project Am. Law Inst., 1949-54; mem. adv. group Fed. Estate and Gift Tax Project, 1964-68; mem. Va. Income Tax Conformity Study Commn., 1970-71; cons. Va. Income Tax Conformity Study Commn., 1966-68; mem. adv. group to commr. IRS, 1967-68. Author: A Lawyer's Life Deep in the Heart of Taxes, 1994. Recipient Alexander Hamilton award Treasury Dept. Mem. Am. Judicature Soc., ABA (chmn. com. on corporate stockholder relationships 1956-58, mem. council 1958-61, chmn. spl. com. on substantive tax reform 1962-63, chmn. spl. com. on formation tax policy 1977-80, Disting. Svc. award taxation sect. 1997), Va. Bar Assn., D.C. Bar Assn., N.Y. State Bar Assn., Va. Tax Conf. (planning com. 1965-68, 85-95, trustee emeritus 1995—), C. of C. of U.S. (bd. dirs., chmn. taxation com. 1979-84), Assn. Bar City N.Y., N.Y. County Lawyers Assn., Am. Law Inst., Am. Coll. Tax Counsel, Order Coif, Raven Soc., Colonnade Club, Boar's Head Club, Farmington Club, City Club, Phi Beta Kappa, Omicron Delta Kappa, Pi Delta Epsilon, Phi Epsilon Pi (Nat. Achievement award) Home: 104 Stuart Pl Ednam Forest Charlottesville VA 22903 E-mail: ecohen@virginia.edu.

COHEN, EZRA HARRY, lawyer; b. Macon, Ga., Mar. 13, 1942; s. Harry M. and Rena C. Cohen; m. Bonnie E. Cohen, Feb. 1, 1969 (div. Mar. 1988); children: Aaron M., Eileen R.; m. Katherine C. Meyers, June 18, 1989. BA, Columbia U., 1964; JD, Emory U., 1969. Bar: Ga. 1969. Ptnr. Troutman, Sanders, Lockerman & Ashmore, Atlanta, 1969-76, 79—; judge U.S. Bankruptcy Ct., U.S. Dist. Ct. (no. dist.) Ga., Atlanta, 1976-79. Dir. S.E. Bankruptcy Law Inst., Atlanta. Contbg. author: Cowan's Bankruptcy Laws & Practices, 1979. Mem. Emory U. Law Sch. Coun., Atlanta, 1988—. With U.S. Army, 1964-66, ETO. Fellow Am. Coll. Bankruptcy; mem. Ga. Bar Assn. (chmn. bankruptcy law sect.), Assn. Former Bankruptcy Judges (bd. dirs.), Nat. Assn. Bank Judges (assoc.), Atlanta Bar Assn. (bd. dirs. 1988-90), Lawyers Club of Atlanta. Bankruptcy. Home: 546 W Wesley Rd Atlanta GA 30305-3534 Office: Troutman Sanders 600 Peachtree St NE Ste 5200 Atlanta GA 30308-2216 E-mail: ezra.cohen@troutmansanders.com.

COHEN, GEORGE LEON, lawyer; b. Covington, Ga., June 20, 1930; s. Leon and Callie (Harrison) C.; m. Jacqueline Lanier Edwards, Nov. 17, 1951 (dec. May 2001); children— George Leon, Gardner Edwards. AB, Va. Mil. Inst., 1951; LLB, U. Va., 1956. Bar: Ga. 1957, U.S. Ct. Appeals (11th cir.). Assoc. Sutherland, Asbill & Brennan, Atlanta, 1956-62, ptnr., 1962—. Editorial bd. Va. Law Rev., 1954-56 Mem.: ABA (various coms.), Am. Law Inst. (advisor to corp. governance project), Lawyers Club Atlanta, Atlanta Bar Assn., Ga. State Bar (chmn. corp. and banking law sect. 1968—69, chmn. Ga. bus. corp. code revision com. 1986—89, various coms.), Peachtree Club, Omicron Delta Kappa, Order of Coif. Corporate, general, Mergers and acquisitions, Securities. Office: Sutherland Asbill & Brennan 999 Peachtree St NE Ste 2300 Atlanta GA 30309-3996

COHEN, HENRY RODGIN, lawyer; b. Charleston, W.Va, May 7, 1944; s. Louis W. and Bertie (Rodgin) C.; m. Barbara Latz, Aug. 31, 1969; children: Sarah Abigail, Jonathan David. BA, Harvard U., 1965, LLB, 1968; LLB (hon.), U. Charleston, 1998. Bar: W.Va. 1968, N.Y. 1970. Assoc. Sullivan & Cromwell, N.Y.C., 1970-77, ptnr., 1977—, vice chmn., 1999-2000, chmn., 2000—. Contbg. editor Fin. Svcs. Regulation Newsletter, 1985; bd. advisors Banking Law Rev.; mem. editorial adv. bd. Banking Expansion Reporter; mem. nat. bd. contbrs. Am. Lawyers Newspaper Group. Trustee N.Y. Presbyn. Hosp.; trustee Hampton Coll., Hackley Sch. With U.S. Army, 1968—70. Banking, Mergers and acquisitions, Corporate, general. Office: Sullivan & Cromwell 125 Broad St Fl 28 New York NY 10004-2489

COHEN, HOWARD MARVIN, lawyer; b. Bklyn., Mar. 22, 1926; s. A. Louis and Claire (Bisgier) C.; m. Judith Rothstein, July 6, 1952 (div. Apr. 1967); children: Jonathan David, Tamara Beth; m. Marjory Hexter, Oct. 12, 1969; children: Theresa Abrams, John Abrams. Student, Yale U., 1945; AB cum laude, Columbia U., 1947; JD magna cum laude, Harvard U., 1949. Bar: N.Y. 1949. Ptnr. Kaye Scholar Fierman, Hays & Handler, N.Y.C., 1963-65; v.p., gen. counsel Revlon Inc., N.Y.C., 1966-71; ptnr. Finley, Kumble, Underberg, Persky & Roth, N.Y.C., 1971—72, Poletti, Freidin, Prashker, Feldman & Gartner, N.Y.C., 1973-78, Warshaw, Burstein, Cohen, Schlesinger & Kuh, N.Y.C., 1978-2000, of counsel, 2001—. Past editor Harvard Law Rev. Trustee Assoc. YM-YWHA, N.Y.C., 1972-90. With U.S. Army, 1943-45. Mem. ABA, Bar of Assn. of City of N.Y., Phi Beta Kappa, Harvard Club, Euro-Am. Lawyers Group (mem. mgmt. com. 1997-2001), Internat. Inst. of Space Law. Jewish. Avocations: skiing, tennis, computers, reading, travel. Corporate, general, Private international, Mergers and acquisitions. Home: 16 Sutton Pl Apt 16A New York NY 10022-3057 Office: Warshaw Burstein Cohen 555 5th Ave Fl 12 New York NY 10017-2456 E-mail: hcohen@wbcsk.com.

COHEN, HYMAN K. lawyer; b. Balt., July 26, 1925; s. Jacob and Tillie Cohen; m. Eileen Ruth Manko, Nov. 7, 1954; children: Jill Leslie, Brent Paul (dec.). AB, U. N.C., 1948; JD, U. Balt., 1954. Bar: Md. 1954, U.S. Dist. Ct. Md. 1955, U. S. Supreme Ct. 1959, D.C. 1979. Pvt. practice, Balt., 1954—. Adj. asst. prof. U. Md., Baltimore County, 1983—; bd. dirs. Fgn. Motors Ltd., Koren Furniture House, Inc.; bd. dirs. 7800, Ltd. Pres. Liberty Rd. Recreation and Parks Coun., Randallstown, Md., 1977-81; pres. Res. Officers Assn. Balt. Naval Chpt., 1963-67, treas. 1967—; bd. dirs. Cockpit in Ct., Essex Cmty. Coll., Balt. 1983—; vol. Jewish Big Brother League. Named Big Brother of Yr. Jewish Big Brother League, 1983, Vol. of Yr. Liberty Rd. Recreation and Parks Council, 1984. Mem. Md. State Bar Assn. Democrat. Jewish. Avocations: theater, reading, community activities. Family and matrimonial, General practice, Personal injury (including property damage). Office: 514 Saint Paul St Baltimore MD 21202-2282 Home: Apt 2 3 Stonehenge Cir Pikesville MD 21208-3222 E-mail: hycohen.law@juno.com.

COHEN, JASON JAY, lawyer; b. Boston, Dec. 1, 1931; s. Philip W. and Doris (Winetsky) C.; m. Barbara Ann Levin, Aug. 28, 1955; children— Susan Lori Cohen Gower, Ellen Terry. B.S. in Bus. Adminstrn., Boston U., 1953, J.D., 1957. Bar: Mass. 1957, U.S. Dist. Ct. Mass. 1958, U.S. Supreme Ct. 1965. Assoc., Wassermen & Salter, Boston, 1 1957-58, Winetsky & Zuker, 1958-59; ptnr. Cohen & Gaffin, Framingham, Mass., 1959—97, ret. 1997; lectr. Mass. Continuing Legal Edn. New England Law Inst., 1982— . Pres. Temple Beth Sholem, Framingham, 1965-67. Served with USAR, 1954-58. Fellow Mass. Bar Found., Am. Acad. Matrimonial Lawyers (pres. chpt.); mem. Mass. Bar Assn. (delegate 1978, 81), S. Middlesex Bar Assn. (pres. 1977-78), ABA, Am. Trial Lawyers Assn., Mass. Acad. Trial Lawyers. Clubs: 21st Century, Mt. Pleasant Country. (pres.). Family and matrimonial.

COHEN, JAY ALLEN, lawyer, accountant; b. Bklyn., Oct. 7, 1951; s. Nathan and Sheila (Ginsberg) C.; m. Judith Sue Rosenthal, June 29, 1986. BS in Acctg., Bklyn. Coll., 1973; MBA in Taxation, St. John's U., 1976; JD, Pace U., 1983. Bar: N.Y. 1983; CPA, N.Y.; notary pub., N.Y. Acct. Miller & Perry, CPA's, N.Y.C., 1973-75; assoc. acct. N.Y.C. Dept. Fin., 1976-77; sr. acct. Price Waterhouse & Co., 1978-79; legal asst. Bronx (N.Y.) Dist. Atty.'s Office, 1980-83; pvt. practice Bklyn., 1984-85; v.p., chief fin. officer Big Apple Credit Corp., Lynbrook, N.Y., 1986-90; CFO, Orthopaedic & Sports Medicine Assocs., Emerson, N.J., 1990-95; pvt. practice L.I., 1996—. Mem. AICPA, Masons (dist. dep. grand master 1985-86), K.P. (chancellor comdr. 1982-83). Avocations: ham radio, stamps, bowling, softball. Fax: 516-569-5622. E-mail: jayallenc@hotmail.com.

COHEN, JEFFREY, lawyer; b. Bklyn., Jan. 31, 1956; s. Fred and Ann (Piel) Cohen. AB in Politics and Philosophy with depart mental honors magna cum laude, Brandeis U., 1977; JD, Bklyn. Law Sch., 1980. Bar: N.Y. 1981, Colo. 1981. Assoc. Freedman & May, N.Y.C., 1980—81, Alter, Zall & Haligman, Denver, 1981—82; ptnr. Quiat & Dice, Denver, 1982—84, Koransky, Friedman & Cohen, P.C., Denver, 1984—89, Cohen & Kenney, 1989—. Recipient Am. Jurisprudence Award, 1977, Rose Meml. scholar, 1977. Mem.: ABA (bus. bankruptcy com.), Denver Bar Assn., Colo. Bar Assn., Colo. Mountain Club. Republican. Jewish. Bankruptcy, State civil litigation, Corporate, general. Office: 600 17th St Ste Denver CO 80202-

COHEN, JON STEPHAN, lawyer; b. Omaha, Nov. 9, 1943; s. Louis H. and Bertha N. (Goldstein) C.; children: Carolyn, Sherri, Barbara, Shayna, Jordan; m. Cheryl A. Jiroux, Oct. 7, 1994. Student, London Sch. Econs., 1963-64; BA, Claremont Men's Coll. (now Claremont McKenna Coll.), 1965; JD, Harvard U., 1968. Bar: Ariz. 1968. Assoc. Snell & Wilmer, Phoenix, 1968-73, ptnr., 1973—. Bd. dirs. Vika Corp., Phoenix, Enterprise Network, Phoenix, Ariz. Tech. Coun., Phoenix, Ariz. Sci. Ctr., Phoenix. Bd. dirs. Kronos Found., Phoenix, Aurora Found., Phoenix. Fellow Ariz. Bar Found.; mem. ABA, Ariz. Bar Assn., Maricopa County Bar Assn., Village Athletic Club, City Sq. Athletic Club. Avocations: record collecting, skiing, racquetball. Finance, Mergers and acquisitions, Securities. Home: 6528 N 27th St Phoenix AZ 85016 Office: Snell & Wilmer One Arizona Ctr Phoenix AZ 85004-0001 E-mail: jcohen@swlaw.com.

COHEN, LAURA, lawyer; b. Pitts., Feb. 26, 1958; d. Alfred and Rita K. Cohen; (div.); children: Sarah Hackney, Beth Hackney. BA in Polit. Sci. with honors, Chatham Coll., 1993; JD, U. Pitts., 1996. Bar: Pa. 1996, U.S. Dist. Ct. (we. dist.) Pa. 1996, U.S. Supreme Ct., 2000. Lawyer, owner Family Legal Ctr., Monroeville, Pa., 1996—. Mem.: ABA, Greater Pitts. Bus. Connection (v.p. 1997—99, pres. 2000—), Matrimonial Inns of Ct., Allegheny County Bar Assn., Pa. Bar Assn. Family and matrimonial, Juvenile, Probate (including wills, trusts). Office: Family Legal Ctr 2526 Monroeville Blvd Monroeville PA 15146-2133 E-mail: lauracohen@adelphia.net.

COHEN, LEWIS ISAAC, lawyer; b. N.Y.C., July 27, 1932; s. Benjamin and Jeannette (Klotzko) C.; m. Sheila Lipman, Sept. 8, 1957; children— Leslie, Bruce, Wendy. BA, U. Calif. at Los Angeles, 1953; LL.B., Columbia, 1958. Bar: N.Y. State bar 1959, D.C. bar 1964, U.S. Supreme Ct. bar 1966. Atty. FCC, Washington, 1959-64; 1995practiced in Washington, 1964—95; ptnr. Cohen & Berfield, 1964-95. Served with AUS, 1954-56. Mem. Fed., D.C. bar assns., FCC Bar Assn. Home: 45 Sunset Ct Edinburg VA 22824 E-mail: lihcohen@shentel.net.

COHEN, LOUIS RICHARD, lawyer; b. Washington, Nov. 28, 1940; s. Milton Howard and Rowna (Chaffetz) C.; m. Bonnie Rubenstein, Aug. 29, 1965; children: Amanda Carroll, Eli Augustus. AB, Harvard U., 1962, LLB, 1966; student, Wadham Coll., Oxford, Eng., 1962-63. Bar: DC. Law clk. to Hon. John M. Harlan U.S. Supreme Ct., Washington, 1967-68; assoc. Wilmer, Cutler & Pickering, Washington, 1968-74, ptnr., 1974-86, 88—; dep. solicitor gen. U.S. Dept. Justice, Washington, 1986-88; ptnr. Wilmer, Cutler & Pickering, Wash., DC, 1988—. Vis. prof. Stanford (Calif.) Law Sch., 1981; lectr. law Harvard Law Sch., Cambridge, Mass., 1986. Author: Book Review Michigan Law Review, 1993. Chair Harvard Law Sch. Fund, 1993-96; mem. overseers com. to Visit Harvard Law Sch., 1986-92; bd. dirs. Woolly Mammoth Theatre Co., Washington, 1988-91, 96—; bd. of dir.; Ptnrs. for Sacred Places, 2002--. Mem.: Bd. of Dir., Telluride Soc. for Jazz (bd. dirs. 2001—), Am. Law Inst., Am. Acad. Appellate Lawyers, Supreme Ct. Hist. Soc. Jewish. Avocation: hiking. Federal civil litigation, Corporate, general, Securities. Office: Wilmer Cutler & Pickering 2445 M St NW Ste 500 Washington DC 20037-1420 E-mail: louis.cohen@wilmer.com.

COHEN, MARK L. lawyer; b. Springfield, Mass. s. Irving Maurice Cohen and Sylvia Hess; m. Clottilde A. Santi; children: Alexander, Edward, Katia. BA, Syracuse U., 1963; JD, Boston Coll., 1966. Bar: Mass., Paris, US Ct. of Appeals (1st circuit). Law clk. Chief Justice Superior Ct., Boston, 1966—67; asst. atty. gen. Mass., 1967—71; sr. program analyst Ford Found., Washington, 1971—75; dir., UNESO overseas UNESCO, Paris, 1973—74; internat. lawyer Pechiney, Paris, 1975—83, sr. legal cons., 1983—2000; counsel White & Case, 2000—. Cons. NET/PBS, The Advocates, Boston, 1968—70. Avocations: sailing, skiing, tennis. Office: White & Case Madeleine 11 Blfd De La 75001 Paris France

COHEN, MARY ANN, judge; b. Albuquerque, July 16, 1943; d. Gus R. and Mary Carolyn (Avriette) C. BS, UCLA, 1964; JD, U. So. Calif., 1967. Bar: Calif. 1967. Ptnr. Abbott & Cohen, P.C. and predecessors, L.A., 1967-82; judge U.S. Tax Ct., Washington, 1982—, chief judge, 1996-2000. Mem. ABA (sect. taxation), Legion Lex. Republican. Office: US Tax Ct 400 2nd St NW Washington DC 20217-0002

COHEN, MELANIE ROVNER, lawyer; b. Chgo., Aug. 9, 1944; d. Millard Jack and Sheila (Fox) Rovner; m. Arthur Wieber Cohen, Feb. 17, 1968; children: Mitchell Jay, Jennifer Sue. AB, Brandeis U., 1965; JD, DePaul U., 1977. Bar: Ill. 1977, U.S. Dist. Ct. (no. dist.) Ill., U.S. Ct. Appeals (7th cir.). Law clk. to Justice F.J. Hertz U.S. Bankruptcy Ct., 1976-77; ptnr. Antonow & Fink, Chgo., 1977-89, Altheimer & Gray, Chgo., 1989—. Mem. Supreme Ct. of Ill. Atty. Registration and Disciplinary Commn. Inquiry Bd., 1982-86, hearing bd., 1986-94; instr. secured and consumer transactions creditor-debtor law DePaul U., Chgo., 1980-90; bd. dirs. Bankruptcy Arbitration and Mediation Svcs., 1994-96; instr. real estate and bankruptcy law John Marshall Law Sch., Chgo., 1996-98. Contbr. articles to profl. jours. Panelist, spkr., bd. dirs., v.p. Brandeis U. Nat. Alumni Assn., 1981—; life mem. Brandeis Nat. Women's Com., 1975—, pres. Chgo. chpt., 1975-82; mem. Glencoe (Ill.) Caucus, 1977-80; chair lawyers com. Ravinia Festival, 1990-91, chmn. sustaining com., 1991, mem. annual fund, 1991—. Brandeis U. fellow. Fellow: Am. Coll. Bankruptcy; mem.: ABA (co-chair com. on enforcement of creditors' rights and bankruptcy), Internat. Women's Insolvency and Restructuring Confederation, Internat. Fedn. Insolvency Profls., Internat. Insolvency Inst., Turnaround Mgmt. Assn. (pres. Chgo./midwest chpt. 1990—92, internat. bd. dirs. 1990—, mem. mgmt. com. 1995—, pres. internat. bd. dirs. 1999—2000, chmn. internat. bd. dirs. 2000—01), Comml. Fin. Assn. Edn. Found. (bd. govs.), Ill. Trial Lawyers Assn., Comml. Law League, Chgo. Bar Assn. (chmn. bankruptcy reorgn. com. 1983—85), Ill. State Bar Assn. Banking, Bankruptcy, Commercial, contracts (including sales of goods; commercial financing). Home: 167 Park Ave Glencoe IL 60022-1351 Office: Altheimer & Gray 10 S Wacker Dr Ste 4000 Chicago IL 60606-7407 E-mail: cohenm@altheimer.com.

COHEN, MORRIS LEO, retired law librarian and educator; b. N.Y.C., Nov. 2, 1927; s. Emanuel and Anna (Frank) C.; m. Gloria Weitzner, Feb. 1, 1953; children— Havi, Daniel Asher. BA, U. Chgo., 1947; LLB, Columbia U., 1951; MLS, Pratt Inst., 1959. Bar: N.Y. bar 1951. Pvt. practice, N.Y.C., 1951-58; asst. law librarian Rutgers U. Law Sch., 1958-59, Columbia Law Sch., 1959-61; law librarian, assoc. prof. law State U. N.Y. at, Buffalo, 1961-63; Biddle law librarian, prof. law U. Pa. Law Sch., Phila., 1963-71; law librarian, prof. law Harvard U. Law Sch., 1971-81, Yale U. Law Sch., New Haven, 1981-91; prof. emeritus, 1991—. Lectr. Drexel Inst. Sch. Libr. Sci., 1964-70, Columbia Sch. Libr. Svc., 1965-70; vis. prof. Simmons Coll. Libr. Sch., 1977-80; mem. exec. bd. Phila. chpt. ACLU; bd. visitors Columbia U. Law Sch., 1977-95. Author: Legal Research in a Nutshell, 1968, 8th edit., 2003, How to Find the Law, 9th edit., 1989, Law and Science: A Selected Bibliography, 1980, Finding the Law, 2d edit., 1989, Law: The Art of Justice, 1992, A Guide to the Early Reports of the Supreme Court of the United States, 1995, The Bench and Bar: Great Legal Caricatures from Vanity Fair, 1997, Bibliography of Early American Law, 1998. Mem. Am. Antiquarian Soc. NEH grantee. Mem. ABA, ALA (chmn. law and polit. sci. sect. 1967-69), AAUP (pres. U. Pa. chpt. 1966-67), Am. Assn. Law Librs. (pres. 1970-71), Am. Soc. Legal History (hon. fellow), Jewish Publs. Soc. (v.p. 1975-80), Bibliog. Soc. Am., Internat. Assn. Law Librs., Grolier Club, Yale Club of N.Y.C. Jewish. Office: Yale U Sch Law PO Box 208215 New Haven CT 06520-8215 E-mail: morris.cohen@yale.edu.

COHEN, NELSON CRAIG, lawyer; b. Harrisburg, Pa., Nov. 8, 1947; s. Raymond and Rhea (Jaschik) C. BS in Acctg., Pa. State U., 1969; JD, George Washington U., 1973. Bar: Md. 1973, D.C. 1974. Assoc., ptnr. Levitan Ezrin West & Kerxton, Bethesda, Md., 1973-84; ptnr. Kerxton & Cohen Chartered, Bethesda, 1984-87, Zuckerman & Spaeder LLP, Washington, 1987—. Speaker on bankruptcy matters. Mem. ABA (bus. banking sec.), Bankruptcy Bar Assn. Md., Montgomery County Bar Assn., Md. State Bar Assn. Republican. Jewish. Avocation: golf. Bankruptcy, Commercial, consumer (including collections, credit). Office: Zuckerman Spaeder LLP 1201 Connecticut Ave NW Washington DC 20036-2605

COHEN, NORTON JACOB, lawyer; b. Detroit, Nov. 5, 1935; s. Norman and Molly Rose (Natinsky) C.; m. Lorelei Freda Schuman, June 16, 1957 (dec. Jan. 1998); children: Debrah Anne, Sander Ivan. Student, U. Mich., 1953-55, U. Detroit, 1955-56; JD, Wayne State U., 1959. Bar: Mich. 1959, Tex. 1962, U.S. Dist. Ct. (ea. dist.) Mich. 1963, U.S. Ct. Appeals (6th cir.) 1966, U.S. Supreme Ct. 1970. Law clk. to presiding justice Mich. Supreme Ct., Lansing, 1959; assoc. Zwerdling, Miller, Klimist & Maurer, Detroit, 1963—68; legal dir. ACLU of Mich., Detroit, 1968—69; sr. dir. Miller, Cohen, Martens, Ice & Geary, P.C., Southfield, Mich., 1971—97, Miller Cohen, P.L.C., Detroit, 1997—. Chmn. Southfield (Mich.) Dem. Party, 1965-67; co-chair Robert F. Kennedy for Pres., Oakland County, Mich., 1968; mem. exec. bd. Met. Detroit ACLU, 1969-93, chmn., 1972-74; vice chair Equal Justice Coun., Detroit, 1970-74; spl. counsel workers compensation Mich. AFL-CIO, 1983-86; mem. dir.'s adv. coun. Workers Compensation Bur., Mich. Dept. Labor, 1986-1999. Served to capt. U.S. Army, 1960-63. Recipient Spirit of Detroit award Detroit Common Coun., 1982; elected to Mich. Workers' Compensation Hall of Fame, 2000. Mem. ABA (labor co-chair workers compensation com. sect. labor and employment law 1989-96), Fed. Bar Assn., B'nai B'rith, Am. Jewish Com. Jewish. Labor (including EEOC, Fair Labor Standards Act, labor-management relations, NLRB, OSHA), Workers' compensation. Office: Miller Cohen PLC 600 W Lafayette Blvd Fl 4 Detroit MI 48226-3125

COHEN, PHILIP GARY, lawyer; b. N.Y.C., Aug. 15, 1950; s. Herbert and Anna (Kohn) C.; m. Linda Ann Silverberg, July 20, 1975; children: Laurie Debra, Ellen Melissa. BA in Polit. Sci., NYU, 1971, LLM in Labor Law, 1975, LLM in Taxation, 1982; JD, Duke U., 1974; MBA in Acctg., George Washington U., 1979. Bar: N.Y. 1975. Tax cons. Touche Ross & Co., N.Y.C., 1978-80; tax atty. SCM Corp., N.Y.C., 1980-83; sr. tax atty. Colt Industries, Inc., N.Y.C., 1983-85; gen. tax counsel, head rsch., planning and audit Unilever U.S., Inc., Englewood Cliffs, N.J., 1985-2000, v.p. tax, gen. tax counsel, 2000—. Adj. asst. prof. tax Lubin Grad. Sch. Bus., Pace U., 1989—. Contbr. articles to profl. jours. Lt. JAGC USNR, 1975-78. Mem. ABA, N.Y. State Bar Assn. (tax sect. com. on corps. 1989—, com. on fin. instruments), Tax Execs. Inst. (publs. com. 1988, chmn. 1994-96, editl. rev. bd. 1988-96, fed. tax com. 1990—, vice chmn. 1996-98, chmn. 1998-2000). Democrat. Jewish. Corporate taxation. Office: Unilever US Inc 700 Sylvan Ave Englewood Cliffs NJ 07632-3201 E-mail: Philip.Cohen@unilever.com.

COHEN, RICHARD GERARD, lawyer; b. N.Y.C., June 11, 1931; m. Evelyn Streit, June 22, 1952; Children: Frances, Andrew Steven, Emilie, Sarah Jane Grossbard. BS in Econs, U. Pa., 1952; LL.B., Columbia U., 1955. Bar: N.Y. 1956. With Office Chief Counsel, IRS, Treasury Dept., 1957-64, tech. asst. to chief counsel, 1961-64; with Lord, Day & Lord, N.Y.C., 1964-86, ptnr., 1966-86, Pillsbury Winthrop LLP, N.Y.C., 1986—. Chmn. adv. bd. NYU Inst. Fed. Taxation, 1991; lectr. in field. Contbr. articles to profl. jours. Served with Audit Agy. U.S. Army, 1955-57. Mem. ABA, N.Y. State Bar Assn. (chmn. tax sect. 1986-87), Assn. Bar City N.Y. (chmn. coun. on taxation 1989-93), Am. Law Inst. (cons. fed. income tax project 1974-95, reporter ptnrship tax issues 1976-84). Jewish. Corporate taxation, Estate taxation, Personal income taxation. Office: Pillsbury Winthrop LLP One Battery Park Plaza New York NY 10004 E-mail: rcohen@pillsburywinthrop.com.

COHEN, RICHARD PAUL, lawyer; b. Bklyn., Nov. 18, 1945; s. Morris T. and Ida (Tepletsky) C.; m. Laura Diane Keller, July 4, 1968; 1 child, Adam Morris. BME, CCNY, 1968; JD, Fordham U., 1973. Bar: N.Y. 1974, W.Va. 1979, U.S. Ct. Appeals (2d cir.) 1974, U.S. Dist. Ct. (so. dist.) N.Y. 1974, U.S. Dist. Ct. (so. and no. dists.) W.Va. 1979, U.S. Ct. Appeals (fed. cir.) 1994, U.S. Supreme Ct. 1977, U.S. Ct. Vets Appeals 1993. Asst. counsel Waterfront Commn. N.Y. Harbor, N.Y.C., 1973-78; asst. atty. Westchester County Atty's. Office, White Plains, N.Y., 1977-78; asst. prosecutor Wetzel County Atty's. Office, New Martinsville, W.Va., 1980-82; pvt. practice law Hundred and Fairmont, W.Va., 1979-83; ptnr. Cohen, Abate & Cohen, L.C., Fairmont, W.Va., 1984—. Named One of Oustanding Young Men of Am., Outstanding Young Men of Am., 1981; recipient Meritorious Svc. award Am. Assn. Mental Dificiency, 1987. Mem. ABA, Nat. Assn. Soc. Sect. Claimants Rep, Nat. Assn. Vets. Advocates, W.Va. State Bar Assn. Commercial, consumer (including collections, credit), Pension, profit-sharing, and employee benefits, Military. Home: 116 Lincoln Ave Morgantown WV 26501-6512 Office: PO Box 846 Morgantown WV 26507-0846

COHEN, ROBERT, medical device manufacturing and marketing executive; b. Glen Cove, N.Y., Sept. 23, 1957; s. Alan and Selma (Grossman) C.; m. Nancy A. Arey, Jan. 17, 1981. BA, Bates Coll., 1979; JD, U. Maine, 1982. Bar: N.Y. 1983, U.S. Dist. Ct. (so. and ea.) N.Y. 1983. Atty. Pfizer Inc., N.Y.C., 1982-86; asst. corp. counsel, asst. sec. Pfizer Hosp. Products Group, Inc., N.Y.C., 1986-88; v.p. bus. devel., dir. for med. device mfr. and marketer Deknatel Inc., Fall River, Mass., 1988-92; pres., CEO GCI Med., Braintree, Mass., 1992-93; v.p. bus. devel. Sulzermedica USA, Inc., Angleton, Tex., 1993-94, group v.p., 1994-98; v.p. bus. & tech. devel. St. Jude Med., Inc., St. Paul, 1998—2002; CEO, dir. of Advanced Circulatory Sys., Inc. Eden Prairie, Minn., 2003—; dir. Horizon Med. Products, Inc., Atlanta, 1998-2001, CardioFocus, Inc., Boston, 1999-2000; CEO Advanced Circulating Sys., Inc., Eden Prairie, Minn., 2003—. Author: 19th Century Maine Authors, 1978. Mem. ABA, Am. Corp. Counsel Assn. Republican. Home: 18683 Bearpath Trl Eden Prairie MN 55347-3476 Office: Advanced Circulatory Systems Inc 7615 Golden Triangle Dr Ste A Eden Prairie MN 55344 E-mail: rcohenmeddev@aol.com.

COHEN, ROBERT STEPHAN, lawyer; b. N.Y.C., Jan. 14, 1939; s. Abraham and Florence C.; children: Christopher, Ian, Nicholas; m. Stephanie J. Stiefel, Jan. 29, 1998. BA, Alfred U., 1959; LLB, Fordham U., 1962. Bar: N.Y. 1963, U.S. Dist. Ct. (so. and ea. dists.) N.Y. 1964, U.S. Ct. Appeals (2d cir.) 1965. Assoc. Saxe, Bacon & O'Shea, N.Y.C., 1963-68; mng. ptnr., chmn. Morrison, Cohen Singer and Weinstein and predecessor firms, N.Y.C., 1968—. Lectr. in field; mem. faculty Am Acad. Psychiatry and the Law, 1984—. Author: Reconcilable Differences, 2002; contbr. articles to legal jours. Bd. dirs. N.Y. Pops, 1983-02. 1st lt. JAG, USAR, 1965-67. Fellow Am. Coll. Family Trial Lawyers; mem. ABA, FBA, ATLA, N.Y. State Bar Assn., N.Y.C. Bar Assn., N.Y. Acad. Matrimonial Lawyers, Univ. Club (N.Y.C.). Federal civil litigation, State civil litigation, Family and matrimonial. Office: 750 Lexington Ave New York NY 10022-1200

COHEN, RONALD J. lawyer; b. Englewood, N.J., Dec. 16, 1950; s. Irwin and Shirley (Kushel) C.; m. Jeanne K. Houser, June 22, 1981; children: Shay, Emily. BA, U. Fla., 1973; JD, U. Miami, 1976. Asst. city atty. City of Miami, 1979-83; assoc. Paul, Landy, Beiley & Harper, Miami, 1983-87; ptnr. Klausner & Cohen, PA, Hollywood, Fla., 1987-97; pvt. practice Ronald J. Cohen, PA, Miami, 1997—. Civil rights, Labor (including EEOC, Fair Labor Standards Act, labor-management relations, NLRB, OSHA), Pension, profit-sharing, and employee benefits. Office: 8100 Oak Ln Ste 403 Miami Lakes FL 33016-7051

COHEN, SAUL, lawyer; b. Los Angeles, June 19, 1927; s. Jack and Sarah (Ostrofsky) C.; m. Anne-Lise Engel, June 12, 1954; children: Adam D., Mikala L., Elizabeth R. AB, UCLA, 1950; JD, Stanford U., 1953. Bar: Calif. 1954, N.Mex. 1971. Sole practice, Beverly Hills, Calif., 1954-55; assoc. MCA, Beverly Hills, 1955-56; sole practice Los Angeles, 1957-70, Santa Fe, N.Mex., 1971—. Author: (with John Hogan) An Author's Guide to Scholarly Publishing and the Law, 1965, (with Harvey Fergusson) Southwest Writer, 2001; contbr. book reviews, articles and essays to profl. jours. and mags. Trustee emeritus Mus. N.Mex. Found.; pres. bd. regents NM Sch. for the Deaf; trustee Georgia O'Keeffe Mus., Internat. Folk Art Found.; former trustee Santa Fe Inst. Fine Arts, Friends of Bandelier, Rio Grande Hist. Collections, Santa Fe Hist. Found., Santa Fe Animal Shelter, Santa Fe Pub. Libr., Santa Fe Prep. Sch., Guadalupe hist. Found., Santa Fe Concert Assn., St. John's Coll. Libr. Assocs.; former chairperson City Hist. Design Rev. Bd.; mem. Supreme Ct. Bldg. Commn. With U.S. Army, 1945-46. Mem. ABA, 10th Jud. Cir. Conf., N.Mex. State Bar (Outstanding Contbn. award 1975, 85, 87), Zamorano Club (hon.), Baker St. Irregulars Club. Democrat. Jewish. Avocations: book collecting, running, writing. Property, real (including real estate development, water), Trademark and copyright. Home: 54 Bauer Rd Santa Fe NM 87506-0053 Office: Sutin Thayer & Browne PO Box 2187 Santa Fe NM 87504-2187

COHEN, SHELDON IRWIN, lawyer; b. Newark, July 25, 1937; BS in Ceramic Engring., AB in Humanities, Rutgers U., 1959; LLB, Georgetown U., 1964. Bar: Va. 1964, D.C. 1964, U.S. Ct. Appeals (D.C. and 4th cirs.) 1964, U.S. Supreme Ct. 1967. Assoc. Chapman, Disalle & Friedman, Washington, 1964-70; pvt. practice law Washington, Arlington, Va., 1970—. Author: Security Clearances and the Protection of National Security Information, Law and Procedure, 2000. Vice chmn. Arlington Dem. Com., 1968-70; mem. Va. Dem. Cen. Com., 1969-70. Capt. USAR, 1959-67. Mem. ABA (chmn. govt. pers. com. 1986-89, chmn. nat. security interests com. 1990-95), D.C. Bar Assn. (chmn. civil svc. law com. 1984-86). Democrat. Administrative and regulatory, Labor (including EEOC, Fair Labor Standards Act, labor-management relations, NLRB, OSHA), Military. Office: 2009 14th St N Ste 708 Arlington VA 22201-2514 E-mail: sicohen@sheldoncohen.com.

COHEN, SHELDON STANLEY, lawyer; b. Washington, June 28, 1927; s. Herman and Pearl (Jaffe) C.; m. Faye Fram, Feb. 21, 1951; children: Melinda Ann Cohen Goetzl, Laura Eve Cohen Apelbaum, Jonathan Adam, Sharon Ruevena Cohen Liebman. AB with spl. honors, George Washington U., 1950, JD with highest honors (Charles W. Dorsey scholar), 1952; DLit (hon.) , Lincoln Coll.; LLD (hon.) , George Washington U., 2003. Bar: D.C. 1952, U.S. Dist. Ct. D.C. 1952, U.S. Ct. Appeals (D.C. cir.) 1952, U.S. Claims Ct. 1956, U.S. Tax Ct., 1956, U.S. Supreme Ct. 1956, U.S. Ct. Appeals (fed. cir.) 1986; CPA, Md. Acct., 1950-52; legis. atty. Office Chief Counsel, IRS, Dept. Treasury, 1952-56, chief counsel, 1963-65, commr. internal revenue, 1965-69; assoc. Paul, Weiss, Rifkind, Wharton & Garrison, 1956-60; ptnr. Arnold, Fortas & Porter, Washington, 1960-63, Cohen & Uretz, Washington, 1969-85, Morgan, Lewis & Bockius, Washington, 1985—. Lectr. Howard U. Law sch., 1957-58; professorial lectr. George Washington U. Law Sch., 1958-81; adj. prof. U. Miami Law Sch., Fla., 1974-85; mem. adv. com. Inst. Estate Planning, U. Miami Law Ctr., 1969-86; chmn. exec. compensation com. U.S. Pay Bd., 1971-72; cons. Commn. for Revision of Tax Laws, 1969-71; cons. Filer Commn. on Pvt. Philanthropy and Pub. Needs, 1975-76; mem. Commn. on Founds. and Pvt. Philanthropy, 1969-70; mem. adv. group to commr. IRS, 1969-70; chmn. steering com. Adminstrv. Conf. U.S., 1974-84; mem. exec. com. Washington Lawyer's Com. for Civil Rights Under Law, 1975-, co-chmn., 1988-90; mem. Jimmy Carter Tax Task Force, 1976; advisor on tax and econs. Walter F. Mondale Campaign, 1984; mem. cons. panel to controller gen. U.S. Gen. Acctg. Office, 1982-2000, chmn. Audit Adv. Com, 1995-; pres. Am.-Israel Tax Found., 1969-80; mem. coun. Sch. Govt. and Bus. Adminstrn. George Washington U., 1969-79, mem. commn. on governance, 1970, trustee, 1980-2002, chmn. bd. of trustees, 2000-02, chmn. emeritus, 2003; pres. Law Assn., 1978-79; rapporteur CIAT Conf. in Can., 1987; adv. bd. The Lincoln Legals, 1988-; v.p. presdl. Inaugural Found., 1992-93; bd. dirs. Supreme Ct. Hist. Soc., treas. 1995-. Editorial and bus. sec.: George Washington U. Law Rev, 1952; case notes editor, 1951-52; bd. editors Nat. Law Jour., 1978—85; editorial bd. advisors Corporate Taxation. Mem. adv. com. to D.C. Ct. Appeals Admission Com.; past pres. Jewish Social Service Agy., Washington; bd. dirs. Adas Israel Congregation, Jewish Welfare Bd., United Synagogues Am., Common Cause, Nat. Council for a Responsible Firearms Policy, Inc., Nat. Found. for Jewish Culture, 1968-72, Am. Jewish Joint Distbn. Com., United Jewish Appeal Found. of D.C., 1969-2002, Supreme Ct. Hist. Soc., 1993-, treas. 1997-; past v.p. Jewish Community Ctr. Greater Washington; bd. dirs., past v.p. Jewish Community Found.; bd. regents Omar N. Bradley Found., U.S. Army Hist. Collection, 1970-73; bd. dirs., chmn. devel. com. Community Found. Greater Washington, 1982—; trustee B'nai B'rith Found. of U.S.; spl. tax counsel Democratic Nat. Com., 1969-72, gen. counsel, 1972-77; bd. overseers Jewish Theol. Sem. Am., 1972-; trustee United Jewish Endowment Fund, 1980-2002, trustee emeritus, 2003-; counsel Project Judaica Found., Inc., 1980—; v.p. Am. Jewish Hist. Soc., 1980-92, chmn., 1993-2000, honorary chair, 2001—; bd. dirs. Am. Assocs. Ben-Gurion U. of the Negev, Israel, v.p., 1988-90; sec., tax counsel Ctr. for Nat. Policy, 1981-2000; bd. dirs. Gomez Found. for Mill House, 1982-95, Ulysses S. Grant Assn., 1976-, v.p. 1994—, B'nai B'rith, 1979-85; treas. Nat. Jewish Dem. Coun., 1991-; chmn. endowment steering com. Coun. Jewish Fedns., 1991-2000, Am. Jewish Hist. Soc., 1993-; v.p. Presdl. Inaugural Found., 1992-93. With USNR, 1945-46, adv. com. Abraham Lincoln Bicentennial Commn., 2002-. Recipient Alumni Achievement award George Washington U., 1965, Arthur Flemming award, 1966, Alexander Hamilton award U.S. Treasury Dept., 1969, Joseph Ottenstein community service award Jewish Social Agy., 1976. Ourisman award for comm. svc. 1999. Mem. Nat. Acad. Pub. Adminstrn. (chmn. com. on energy 1978-79, trustee, sec. 1983-90, com. on ethics), ABA (chmn. spl. com. on retirement benefits legis. tax csect. 1972-73), Fed. Bar Assn. (coun. tax sect.), D.C. Bar Assn. (bd. dirs. 1969-72), D.C. Bar (Unified) (bd. govs. 1972-75, tax counsel 1972-, chair Iolta Study), Am. Coll. Tax Counsel, Am. Law Inst., J. Edgar Murdock Am. Inn of Ct. (counselor 1988—), D.C. Inst. CPAs (hon.), Inter-Am. Ctr. for Tax Adminstrs. (pres. 1967-68), Am.-Israel C. of C. (chmn. tax com.), Cosmos Club, Tournament Players Assn., Golf Avenel Club, Masons. Corporate taxation, Estate taxation, Personal income taxation. Home: 5518 Trent St Bethesda MD 20815-5512 Office: Morgan Lewis & Bockius 1111 Penna Ave NW Washington DC 02004-5802

COHEN, STEPHEN IRA, lawyer, state legislator; b. Memphis, May 24, 1949; s. Morris David and Genevieve (Goldsand) C. BA, Vanderbilt U., 1971; JD, U. Memphis, 1973. Bar: Tenn. 1974. Sole practice, 1974-75; legal advisor Memphis Police Dept., 1975-78; mem. Shelby County Commn., 1978-80; sole practice Memphis, 1978—; mem. Tenn. Senate, 1982—, deputy spkr., 2000—, chair, Senate State & Local Govt. Comm., 1991, mem., Senate Judiciary, Transp. & Fiscal Review Comm. Interim judge Gen. Sessions Ct., 1980; v.p. Tenn. Constnl. Conv., 1977; del. Democratic Nat. Conv., 1980, 92; chair lottery info. and recommendation com.; mem. coun. state govts. exec. com., 2002, exec. com. Nat. Conf. State Legislators. Trustee Memphis Coll. Art, 2000, bd. trustees, 1988-2002; mem. Redbirds Found., Memphis Shelby County Center City Commn, Memphis Zoological Soc., 1998-, (bd. dirs. 1988-). Recipient Public Leadership award, Tenn. Human Rights Campaign, 2002, Legislator of the Year, Boys & Girls Clubs of Tenn., 2003, Leadership Award, Gov.'s Awards in the Arts. Mem. Memphis Bar Assn., Shelby County Charter Commn. Democrat. Home: 349 Kenilworth Pl Memphis TN 38112-5405 Office: Legislative Plz Ste 8 Nashville TN 37243-0030*

COHEN, SUSAN J. lawyer; b. Hackensack, NJ, Sept. 8, 1957; m. Michael Walter Klein, Apr. 4, 1982; children: Gabriel Klein, Noah Klein. BA, Brandeis U., 1980; JD, Yeshiva U., 1985. Bar: Mass. 1985, U.S. Ct. Appeals (1st cir.) 1986, U.S. Dist. Ct. Mass. 1986. Assoc. Mintz Levin Cohen Ferris Glousky & Popeo, P.C., Boston, 1998—98, mem., chair immigration sect., 1998—. Mem.: ABA (sect. internat. law, vice chair immigration and nationality com. 1997—, editor newsletter 1998—), Am. Immigration Lawyers Assn. (bus. immigration com. 2002—). Immigration, naturalization, and customs. Office: Mintz Levin Cohn Ferris Glovsky & Popeo PC One Financial Ctr Boston MA 02111 Office Fax: 617-542-2241. Business E-Mail: scohen@mintz.com.

COHEN, WILLIAM MARK, lawyer; b. N.Y.C., May 22, 1951; s. Martin and Annabelle (Turner) C.; m. Melinda Pauline Salomon, Aug. 3, 1975; children: Jessica, Adam. AB, Rutgers U., 1973; JD, Georgetown U., 1976. Bar: Tenn. 1976, U.S. Dist. Ct. (mid. dist.) Tenn. 1976, U.S. Ct. Appeals (6th cir.) 1977, U.S. Supreme Ct. 1980. Law clk. to chief judge U.S. Dist. Ct. (mid. dist.) Tenn., Nashville, 1976-78; asst. U.S. atty. U.S. Atty.'s Office, 1978—93, 1st asst. U.S. atty., 1983—92, chief criminal divsn., 1992—98, asst. U.S. atty., 1998—2002, 2003—, sr. litigation counsel, 2002—03; adj. prof. law Vanderbilt U. Law Sch., 2003—. Home: 6021 Foxland Dr Brentwood TN 37027-5733 Office: US Attys Office 110 9th Ave S Ste A961 Nashville TN 37203-3870

COHILL, MAURICE BLANCHARD, JR., federal judge; b. Pitts., Pa., Nov. 26, 1929; s. Maurice Blanchard and Florence (Clarke) C.; m. Suzanne Miller, June 27, 1952 (dec. May 1986); children: Cynthia Cohill Plattner, Jonathan, Jennifer Cohill O'Connor, Victoria. AB, Princeton U., 1951; LLB, U. Pitts., 1956. Bar: Pa. 1957. Judge family div. Common Pleas Ct., Allegheny County, Pitts., 1965-76; judge U.S. Dist. Ct. Pa. (we. dist.), 1976-94, chief judge, 1985-92, sr. judge, 1994—. Bd. dirs. Pa. George Jr. Republic, Grove City; chmn. bd. fellows Nat. Ctr. for Juvenile Justice. Served to capt. USMCR, 1951-53. Mem. ABA, Pa. Bar Assn. Allegheny County Bar Assns., Nat. Coun. Juvenile Ct. Judges (past v.p.), Pa. Coun. Juvenile Ct. Judges (past pres.), Phi Delta Phi. Republican. Presbyterian. Office: US Dist Ct US Courthouse 8th Fl Rm 803 7th and Grant Sts Pittsburgh PA 15219

COHN, ALBERT LINN, lawyer; b. Paterson, NJ, June 18, 1928; s. David and Rose (Yolken) C.; m. Sylvia J. Jacoby, June 14, 1959; children: Melissa Lynn, Joshua Peter, Priscilla Betsy, Liza-Faith Michaelis, Thaddeus Augustus David. BS, Georgetown U., 1948; JD, Harvard U., 1951. Bar: D.C. 1951, N.J. 1954, cert.: Supreme Ct. N.J. Bd. Trial Atty. Cert. (civil trial atty.). Assoc. David L. Cohn, Paterson, 1954—59; ptnr. David & Albert L. Cohn, 1959—66; sr. ptnr. Cohn & Lifland, Saddle Brook, NJ, 1967—. Adj. prof. law Rutgers U., Newark, 1979—, Inst. Cont. Legal Edn., 1980, 1982—, chmn. curriculum adv. com., 1984—85; vis. instr. Mass. Cont. Legal Edn., Nat. Inst. Trial Attys., Harvard U. Law Sch., 1981; trustee N.J. Inst. Cont. Legal Edn., chair, 1993—; master Arthur T. Vanderbilt Inn. Ct., 1988—90, Morris Pashman Inn of Ct., 1990—98, mem. coord. com., 1992—98. Mem. editl. bd. Divorce Litigation, 1996—; contbr. articles. Pres. Temple Shomrei Emunah, 1968—70. 1st lt. USAF, 1951—53. Fellow, Am. Bar Found., 2000—. Mem.: ABA, Harvard Law Sch. Assn. N.J., Saddle Brook C. of C. (past pres., trustee), Million Dollar Advs. Forum, Trial Attys. N.J., Soc. Med. Jurisprudence, N.J. State Bar Assn., Bergen County Bar Assn., Passaic County Bar Assn. (trustee 1978—86), Hamilton (Paterson), Harvard (N.Y.C.). General civil litigation, Family and matrimonial, Probate (including wills, trusts). Home: Llewellyn Park 14 Mountain Ave West Orange NJ 07052 Office: Cohn & Lifland 1 Park 80 Plz W Saddle Brook NJ 07663-5830

COHN, ANDREW HOWARD, lawyer; b. N.Y.C., Jan. 17, 1945; s. Maurice John and Margaret Ethel (Gordon) C.; m. Marcia Bliss Leavitt, July 10, 1977; children: Marisa Leavitt, David Herman. BA, U. Pa., 1966; AM, Harvard U., 1970, PhD, 1972; JD, Yale U., 1975. Bar: Mass. 1975, U.S. Dist. Ct. Mass. 1976, U.S. Ct. Appeals (1st cir.) 1976. Law clk. to presiding justice U.S. Ct. Appeals (1st cir.), Providence and Boston, 1975-76; assoc. Hill & Barlow, Boston, 1976-80; sr. ptnr. Hale and Dorr, Boston, 1980—. Chmn. exec. com. Hale and Dorr, 1990-91, real estate dept., 1991-97, energy group, 1992—; cons. for juvenile justice standards project ABA and Inst. for Judicial Adminstrn., N.Y.C., 1973-74; rsch. fellow MIT-Harvard U. Joint Ctr. for Urban Studies, Cambridge, Mass., 1969-71, Univ. Coll., Nairobi, Kenya, 1968. Contbr. articles to profl. jours.; note and project editor Yale Law Jour., New Haven, 1974-75. Advisor Newton (Mass.) Community SChs. Found., 1987-88. Named Law and Social Sci. fellow Russell Sage Found., 1972-74. Mem. ABA (environ.controls com., bus. law sect.), Am. Coll. Real Estate Lawyers, Boston Bar Assn. (chmn. real estate sect. 95-97), Yale Law Sch. Assn. Mass. (treas. 1985-87). Democrat. Jewish. Environmental, Finance, Property, real (including real estate development, water). Office: Hale and Dorr 60 State St Ste 25 Boston MA 02109-1816

COHN, AVERN LEVIN, district judge; b. Detroit, July 23, 1924; s. Irwin I. and Sadie (Levin) C.; m. Joyce Hochman, Dec. 30, 1954 (dec. Dec. 1989); m. Lois Pincus Cohn, June 1992; children: Sheldon, Leslie Cohn Magy, Thomas. Student, John Tarleton Agrl. Coll., 1943, Stanford U., 1944; JD, U. Mich., 1949. Bar: Mich. 1949. Practiced in, Detroit, 1949-79; mem. firm Honigman Miller Schwartz & Cohn, Detroit, 1961-79; sr. judge U.S. Dist. Ct., 1979—. Mem. Mich. Civil Rights Commn., 1972-75, chmn., 1974-75; Mem. Detroit Bd. Police Commrs., 1975-79, chmn., 1979; bd. govs. Jewish Welfare Fedn., Detroit, 1972—. Served with AUS, 1943-46. Mem. ABA, Mich. Bar Assn., Am. Law Inst. E-mail: avern_cohn@mied.uscourts.gov.

COHN, DAVID STEPHEN, lawyer; b. Richmond, Va., June 19, 1945; s. Alfred Jerome and Jane Shaffer Cohn; m. Jane Boyle, Nov. 22, 1970; children: Elizabeth, Sarah. AB, U. Pa., 1967; JD, Harvard U., 1971. Bar: Pa. 1971, U.S. Dist. Ct. (ea. dist.) Pa. 1971, U.S. Ct. Appeals (3d cir.) 1971, Va. 1973. Assoc. Schnader, Harrison, Segal & Lewis, Phila., 1971-73; asst. prof. law T.C. Williams Sch. Law, U. Richmond, 1973-75; counsel Hunton & Williams, Richmond, 1975-84; mem., chmn., real estate dept. Browder, Russell, Morris & Butcher, P.C., Richmond, 1984-89; ptnr. Troutman Sanders LLP, Richmond, 1989—. Arbitrator Am. Arbitration Assn., 1972—; lectr. Marshall Wythe Sch. Law, Coll. William and Mary, Williamsburg, Va., 1977—81; mem. Va. Gov.'s Regulatory Reform Adv. Bd., 1983—85, Va. Gov.'s Com. on Efficiency in Govt., Richmond, 1985—87; chmn. Va. com. Harvard Law Sch. Fund, Cambridge, Mass., 1986—88, Cambridge, 2002—. Editor: (book) The Residential Real Estate Transaction, 1975. Bd. dirs., pres. Sci. Mus. Va. Found., 1987—2002; mem. Va. Hist. Landmarks Bd., 1988—89; chmn., pres. Richmond Goodwill Industries, Inc., 1988—2002; mem. Va. Vol. Formulary Bd., 1989—; mem. adv. coun. Va. Gov.'s Sch. Govt. and Internat. Studies for Gifted, 1991—93; mem. regulatory climate subcom. Va. Gov.'s Econ. Recovery Coun., 1991—92; mem. orgnl. structure team Gov.'s Commn. on Efficiency and Effectiveness, 2002; mem. state ctrl. com. Va. Dem. Party, Richmond, 1985—93; assoc. trustee U. Pa., Phila., 1984—94; bd. dirs. Better Housing Coalition, 1988—99; trustee, vice chair Sci. Mus. Va., 2002—. Mem.: ABA (chmn. govtl. assistance for real estate programs com. 1989—93), Va. State Bar (mem. bd. govs. real estate sect. 1984—87), Va. Bar Assn. (chmn. real estate com. 1985—87), Am. Coll. Real Estate Lawyers (chmn. affordable housing com. 1991—97). Jewish. Land use and zoning (including planning), Landlord-tenant, Property, real (including real estate development, water). Office: Troutman Sanders LLP Bank of Am Ctr PO Box 1122 Richmond VA 23218-1122 E-mail: david.cohn@troutmansanders.com.

COHN, DON STEPHEN, lawyer; b. Manchester, Conn., Mar. 3, 1950; s. Harold and Elaine Lois (Ackerman) C.; m. Beth Ann Abramson, Sept. 16, 1995; 1 child, Kimberly. BA, U. Conn., 1972; JD, U. Miami, 1975. Bar: Fla. 1975; U.S. Dist. Ct. (so. dis.) Fla. 1983, U.S. Ct. Appeals (5th cir.) 1976, (11th cir.) 1981, (10th cir.) 1980, (4th cir.) 1981. Assoc. Law Office of Max Engel, Miami, 1975-77, Engel, Aronson, Fried & Cohn, Miami, 1977-80; ptnr. Aronson, Ansel & Cohn, Miami, 1980-82, Ansel & Cohn, Miami, 1982-83; pvt. practice Miami, 1983-96. Bd. dirs. Informed Families, Miami, 1988—, Nat. Soc. to Prevent Blindness, Miami, 1987—, Lions Conklin Ctr. for the Multi-Handicapped Blind; sec. B'nai B'rith, Miami, 1987—, pres. Mem. Nat. Assn. Criminal Def. Attys., Fla. Assn. Criminal Def. Lawyers, Fla. Bar Assn. (mem. criminal law rules com.), B'nai B'rith (pres. 1989-92), Lions Club (pres. Miami 1987-88). Republican. Jewish. Avocations: golf, sports. Criminal, General practice. Office: 1504 NW 14th St Miami FL 33125-2612 E-mail: dons.cohnpc@bellsouth.net.

COHN, JULIUS W. lawyer; b. N.Y.C., Apr. 6, 1937; m. Ona Cohn, July 30, 1986. BBA, Western Res. U., 1959; JD, NYU, 1964. Bar: N.Y., Fla. 1981, U.S. Dist. Ct. (so., ea., we. and no. dists.) N.Y., U.S. Supreme Ct., U.S. Ct. Appeals (2d, 5th and 11th cirs.). Asst. dist. atty. Bronx County Dist., 1967—68; 1st asst. corp. counsel City of Yonkers, 1968—69; sr. assty. county atty. County of Westchester, 1969—71; ptnr. Sweeney Cohn Stahl Spector & Frank, White Plains, 1971—. With U.S. Army, 1960—66. Personal injury (including property damage), General practice, Family and matrimonial. Office: Sweeney Cohn Stahl Spector & Frank 200 E Post Rd White Plains NY 10601 Fax: 914-428-0519. E-mail: sweeney.cohn@gte.net.

COHN, MARK BARRY, lawyer; b. Cleve., Dec. 28, 1947; s. David J. and Dorothy (Camin) C.; m. Marlene Sherman, Dec. 27, 1969; children: Mindy D., Laurie A., Jill R. BS, Ohio State U., 1969, JD, 1973. Bar: Ohio 1974, Fla. 1976. Assoc. Jones, Day, Reavis & Pogue, Cleve., 1973-76, Trenam, Simmons, Kemkar et al, Tampa, Fla., 1976-79, Kadish & Krantz, Cleve., 1979-82; pvt. practice Cleve., 1982-87; prin. McCarthy, Lebit, Crystal & Haiman Co., L.P.A., Cleve., 1987—. Author: Smith's Review of Civil Procedure, 1985. Mem. ABA, Cleve. Bar Assn., Ohio Bar Assn., Fla. Bar Assn., Am. Trial Lawyers Assn., Am. Bd. Trial Advocates, Order of Coif. Democrat. Jewish. General civil litigation, Personal injury (including property damage), Taxation, general. Home: 31349 Gates Mills Blvd Cleveland OH 44124-4352 Office: McCarthy Lebit Crystal & Haiman 101 W Prospect Ave Ste 1800 Cleveland OH 44115-1027 E-mail: mbc@mccarthylebit.com.

COHN, NATHAN, lawyer; b. Charleston, S.C., Jan. 20, 1918; s. Samuel and Rose (Baron) C.; 1 child, Norman; m. Carolyn Venturini, May 18, 1970. JD, San Francisco Law Sch., 1947. BAr: Calif. 1947, U.S. Supreme Ct. 1957. Pvt. practice law, San Francisco, 1947—. Judge pro tem Mcpl. Ct., Superior Ct. Columnist, San Francisco Progress, 1982-86; contr. and author seminars in field. Mem. Calif. State Recreation Commn., 1965-68; former mem. Dem. State Ctrl. Com. Served to 1st lt. USAF, 1950-55. Named to San Francisco Law Sch. Hall of Fame, 2000. Fellow Am. Bd. Criminal Lawyers (founder, past pres.), Am. Bd. Trial Advs. (diplomate; chpt. pres. 1984), Internat. Acad. Law and Sci., San Francisco Trial Lawyers (past pres., Lifetime Achievement award 2000), Criminal Trial Lawyers Assn. No. Calif., Irish-Israeli-Italian Soc. (co-founder, co-pres.), Internat. Footprinters Assn., Regular Vets. Assn. (national judge advocate), Calamari Club, Godfathers Club (past pres.), St. Vincent Sch. for Boys, Press Club (life), Masons (32 deg.), Shriners, South of Market Boys (past pres.), Ancient Order Hibernians Am. (hon. life). Jewish. Criminal, General practice, Personal injury (including property damage). Office: 2107 Van Ness Ave Ste 200 San Francisco CA 94109-2596

COHRSSEN, JOHN JOSEPH, lawyer, consultant; b. N.Y.C., Nov. 4, 1939; s. Hans and Alice (Natt) C.; m. Roberta Gross, Aug. 27, 1965; children: James, Noah. BS with honors, CCNY, 1961; MSc, McGill U., Montreal, Que., Can., 1963; JD, George Washington U., 1967. Bar: Va. 1968, D.C. 1972, U.S. Dist. Ct. D.C., U.S. Ct. Appeals (D.C. cir.), U.S. Supreme Ct. Sr. asso. Pres.'s Adv. Council Exec. Orgn., 1970; exec. dir. White House Conf. Youth, Drug Task Force, 1971; counsel U.S. Nat. Commn. Diabetes, 1976, White House Conf. Librs. and Info. Svcs., 1979, U.S. Regulatory Council, 1979-81, office of sci. and tech. policy Exec. office Pres., 1985-86, atty. advisor Council on Environ. Quality, Exec. Office of the Pres., 1986-89, sr. advisor to the chmn. 1989-1990, policy adv. to v.p., assoc. dir., Pres. Coun. on Competitiveness 1990-92; U.S. Senate Labor and Human Resources Com.; staff dir., Aging Subcom., Labor Subcom., Chief Minority coun. 1993-94; counsel, U.S. House of Reps. Com. on Commerce 1995-1997; staff dir., Congressional Biotechnology caucus 1995-97; cons. John J. Cohrssen 1998-2000; mem. adv. bd.Pub. Health Policy 2000-, exec. dir., 2003--; exec. office pres., sr. advisor Nat. Sci. Found., 1986-89; mem. drug abuse adv. com. FDA, 1978-80; of counsel Boasberg, Klores, Feldsman & Tucker, Washington, 1977-85; pres. John J. Cohrssen, P.C., Washington and Arlington, Va., 1972-86; cons. to various White House and govt. agencies on adminstrv. regulatory and health law, info. systems, 1972-86; sr. policy advisor NSF, 1986-89; cons. Bur. Justice Statistics, Bur. Narcotics and Dangerous Drugs, Can. Commn. Inquiry into Non-Med. Use of Drugs, Drug Abuse Council, EPA, FDA, Nat. Ctr. Health Statistics, Nat. Commn. Marihuana and Drug Abuse, NIMH, Nat. Inst. Alcohol Abuse and Alcoholism, Nat. Inst. Drug Abuse, Office Mgmt. and Budget, Exec. Office of Pres., White House Office of Planning and Eval., White House Spl. Action Office for Drug Abuse Prevention; mem. drug abuse adv. com. FDA, Org. on Economic Cooperation and Devel. Served to maj. USPHS, 1967-70. Mem. Va. Bar Assn., D.C. Bar Assn., Arlington County Bar Assn. Contbr. articles to profl. jours. Office: 2175 K St NW Washington DC 20037

COKER, HOWARD COLEMAN, lawyer; b. Jacksonville, Fla., Apr. 30, 1947; B in Journalism, U. Fla., 1969, JD, 1971. Bar: Fla. 1972. Asst. state atty. Fourth Jud. Cir., 1972; assoc. Howell, Kirby, Montgomery, D'Aiuto & Dean, P.A., 1973-76; pres., dir. Coker, Myers, Schickel, Sorenson & Green, Jacksonville, Fla., 1976—. Guest lectr. more than 40 CLE seminars on litig. and trial matters throughout Fla., for Fla. Bar Assn., Acad. Fla. Trial Lawyers; advisor mock trial team U. Fla. Law Sch., 1991-98; adj. prof. U. North Fla. Chair edn. adv. coun. U. North Fla., 1992-94, chair adv. bd. for paralegals, 1990-92. Fellow Am. Bar Found., Internat. Soc. Barristers; mem. ABA (ho. of dels., jud. qualifications commn.), ATLA, Am. Arbitration Assn. (panel arbitrators 1983—), Fla. Bar Assn. (pres. 1998-99, bd. govs. 1994-99, exec. com. 1995-97, all bar fconf. del. 1990-92, 94, 96, 97, budget com. 1995-97, bd. rev. coml. on profl. ethics chair 1995-96, disciplinary rev. com. 1994-95, jud. qualification screen com. 1994-95, legis. com. 1994-95, profl. retreat chair 1996, program evaluation com. chair 1996-97, 4th jud. cir. grievance com. reviewer 1994-97, com. sects. 1991-94, chair 1993-94, sect. leadership conf. chair 1995, trial lawyers sect. exec. coun. 1987-94, bd. govs. liaison 1996, chair 1992-93, exec. co. 1989-93, legis. com. 1988-93), Am. Bd. Trial Advocates (pres. Jacksonville chpt. 1988—, media rep. 1988, exec. com. 1988—, diplomate), Am. Judicature Soc., Chester Bedell Meml. Found. (trustee 1996-2001), First Coast Trial Lawyers Assn., Acad. Fla. Trial Lawyers (bd. dirs. 1995—, pres. 2002-2003, Eagle sponsor 1990—), Fla. Lawyers Assn. for Maintenance of Excellence (bd. dirs. 1995-97), So. Trial Lawyers, Nat. Conf. Bar Presidents, Fla. Supreme Ct. Hist. Soc., Jacksonville Bar Assn., Roscoe Pound Found., U.S. Supreme Ct. Hist. Soc., Internat. Acad. Trial Lawyers, Fla.

Conservation Assn. (pres. 1993-94), Fla. Ducks Unltd. (Sportsman of Yr. 1994), Fla. Wildlife Fedn., Seminole Club (bd. dirs. 1988, pres., 1989), U. Fla. Nat. Alumni Assn. (pres.'s coun. 1992-2001), Sigma Alpha Epsilon, Phi Delta Phi. General civil litigation, Commercial, consumer (including collections, credit), Personal injury (including property damage). Office: PO Box 1860 136 E Bay St Jacksonville FL 32201 Home: 4931 River Point Rd Jacksonville FL 32207 E-mail: hcoker@cokerlaw.com.

COLAGIOVANNI, JOSEPH ALFRED, JR., lawyer; b. Providence, Dec. 26, 1956; s. Joseph Alfred Sr. and Rosemarie (Giordano) C.; m. Mary Jo Gagliardo, Aug. 9, 1980. AB in Polit. Sci. and Philosophy, Brown U., 1979; JD, Boston U., 1982. Bar: Mo. 1982, U.S. Dist. Ct. (ea. and we. dists.) Mo. 1982, U.S. Ct. Appeals (7th cir.) 1992. Asst. atty. gen. State of Mo., Jefferson City, 1982-84; ptnr., co-leader constrn. group Bryan, Cave, St. Louis, 1984—. Adj. prof. of law Wash. U. Sch. of Law, 1997—; hon. vice consul of Italy, 1997—. Mem. ABA, Mo. Bar Assn., Noonday Club. Avocations: tennis, music, collecting matchbooks. Construction. Office: Bryan Cave 211 N Broadway Ste 3600 Saint Louis MO 63102-2733 E-mail: jcolagiovanni@bryancave.com.

COLANTUONO, THOMAS PAUL, state legislator; b. Newton, Mass., Oct. 4, 1951; m. Pamela E. Chaloge. BA, Duke U., 1973; JD, Boston Coll., 1976. Bar: N.H. 1976. Assoc. Hamblett & Kerrigan, Nashua, N.H., 1976-78; asst. atty gen. N.H. Atty. Gen.'s Office, 1978-81; pvt. practice Derry, N.H., 1981—; state sen. State of New Hampshire, 1990-96; vice chmn. exec. dept., adminstrn. coms.; exec. councilor State of N.H., 1999—2001; U.S. atty. U.S. Dept. of Justice, NH, 2002—. Former chmn ways and means com., N.H. Senate, mem. capitol budget, fin., judiciary, ins. coms., vice chmn. exec. dept., adminstrn. coms. Mem. ABA, N.H. Bar Assn., Derry Rotary, Londonderry and Hudson C. of C. Office: 55 Pleasant St Rm 352 Concord NH 03301*

COLASURD, RICHARD MICHAEL, lawyer; b. Navarre, Ohio, Apr. 1, 1928; s. Michael and Adeline (Manack) C.; m. Jane Cooley, Dec. 20, 1986; children: Steven Michael, David Gerard, Cathie Marie. AB, U. Notre Dame, 1950; JD, Harvard U., 1953. Bar: Ohio 1953. Practice in, Toledo, 1960-99; spl. agt. FBI, 1953-56; asst. U.S. atty. charge Northwestern Ohio, 1956-60; mem. firm Shumaker, Loop & Kendrick, 1960-64; asst. city law dir. Toledo, 1964; mem. firm Mulholland, Hickey & Lyman, 1964-73; U.S. commr., 1963-67. Mem. Ohio Bar Assn., Toledo Bar Assn., Soc. Former Spl. Agts. FBI, Lexington C.C., Rotary. Roman Catholic. Home: 16133 Edgemont Dr Fort Myers FL 33908-3651

COLAW, THIERRY PATRICK, judge; b. Kansas City, Mo., Jan. 9, 1947; s. Albert E. and Josette Colaw; m. Jeri Williams, Oct. 11, 1980; children: Case, Clayton. BA cum laude, UCLA, 1974; JD, U. Santa Clara, Calif., 1977. Bar: Calif. Assoc. Smith & Brissenden, Santa Ana, Calif., 1978-79, Vernon W. Hunt, Inc., Santa Ana, 1979-84; ptnr. Hunt, Colaw & Roe, Inc., Santa Ana, 1984-89, Hunt, Colaw & Adams, Inc., Santa Ana, 1989-97; judge Calif. Superior Ct., Santa Ana, 1997—. With USN, 1968-72. Named Judge of Yr., Am. Bd. Trial Advs. Mem. Orange County Bar Assn. (bd. dirs. 1983-96), Orange County Trial Lawyers Assn. (pres. 1989), Orange County Barristers (pres. 1983). Roman Catholic. Avocations: photography, classical music. Office: Orange County Superior Ct 700 Civic Center Dr W Santa Ana CA 92701-4045

COLBERT, DOUGLAS MARC, lawyer; b. N.Y.C., Feb. 8, 1948; s. Leonard M. and Estelle (Ginsberg) C.; m. Amy Jo Guryan, May 1, 1976 (div. 1977); m. Angel Mendez, Dec. 28, 1986. Student, Hunter Coll., N.Y.C., 1964-67; BBA cum laude, Bernard Baruch Coll., N.Y.C., 1969; JD, Bklyn. Law Sch., 1972. Bar: N.Y. 1974. Honor law intern N.Y. County Dist. Atty., N.Y.C., 1971; law asst. N.Y.C. Corp. Counsel, 1972-74; campaign staff writer, media coord. Gov. Hugh. L. Carey, 1974; arbitrator N.Y.C. Civil Ct., 1979—; atty. Hauser & Rosenbaum Esq., N.Y.C., 1974-76; pvt. practice law N.Y.C., 1974—. Vol. atty. Vol. Lawyers for the Arts, N.Y.C., 1979-85; spl. investigator N.Y. State Bd. Elections, N.Y.C., 1981-84. Mem. N.Y. State Trial Lawyers Assn., N.Y. County Lawyers Assn., USCG Aux., Moot Ct., Sigma Alpha Mu (founder). Avocations: scuba, health & fitness, travel, boating. Family and matrimonial, Personal injury (including property damage), Property, real (including real estate development, water). Office: 350 5th Ave Ste 7220 New York NY 10118-7299

COLBERT, JAMES W., III, lawyer; b. N.Y.C., Sept. 1, 1945; AB magna cum laude, Yale U., 1967; JD magna cum laude, Harvard U., 1970. Bar: Calif. 1971. Law clk. to Hon. Shirley M. Hufstedler U.S. Ct. Appeals (9th cir.), 1970-71; mem. O'Melveny & Myers, L.A. Mem. L.A. County Bar Assn. Office: O'Melveny & Myers 400 S Hope St Los Angeles CA 90071-2899

COLBY, KAREN LYNN See WEINER, KAREN COLBY

COLBY, WILLIAM MICHAEL, lawyer; b. Pontiac, Mich., Jan. 24, 1942; s. Orville Edgar and Jeannette (Nadon) C.; m. Brenda Schneckenburger, Nov. 28, 1964; children: Kathleen C. Scott, Thomas Brownell. AB, U. Mich., 1963, JD, 1966. Bar: N.Y. 1966, U.S. Tax Ct. 1969, U.S. Supreme Ct. 1972, Fla. 1982. Assoc. Harter, Secrest & Emery, Rochester, N.Y., 1966-74, ptnr., 1975-99, counsel, 2000—. Cons. various tax pubs. Contbr. articles to profl. jours.; editor various tax publs. Bd. dirs., hon. mem. Rochester Mus. and Sci. Ctr.; chmn. bd. dirs. Genesee Cmty. Charter Sch. Fellow Am. Bar Found.; mem. Monroe County Bar Found. (pres. 1980-81), Oak Hill Country Club. Avocations: golf, wine tasting, collecting ancient greek coins, travel. Estate planning, Pension, profit-sharing, and employee benefits, Taxation, general. Home: 39 Granite Dr Penfield NY 14526-2851 Office: Harter Secrest & Emery LLP 1600 Bausch & Lomb Pl Rochester NY 14604-2711 E-mail: colbyw@hselaw.com.

COLDREN, IRA BURDETTE, JR., lawyer; b. Uniontown, Pa., June 15, 1924; s. Ira Burdette and Eleanor Clarke (Lincoln) C.; m. Phyllis Miles, Sept. 7 (div. Oct. 1970); children: Kathy, Lee Ellen, Janice, David; m. Frances Thomas, Aug. 27, 1971. BS, U.S. Mil. Acad., 1945; LLB, U. Pa., 1952; LLM in Estate Planning, U. Miami, 1982. Bar: Pa. 1952, U.S. Dist. Ct. (we. dist.) Pa. 1953, U.S. Ct. Appeals (3d cir.) 1983. Commd. 2d lt. U.S. Army, 1945, advanced through grades to lt. col., 1952, ret., 1956; assoc. Ray, Coldren & Buck, Uniontown, Pa., 1956-59; ptnr. Coldren & Coldren, Uniontown, 1959-62, Coldren & Adams, Uniontown, 1962-75, Coldren, DeHaas & Radcliffe, Uniontown, 1983-92, Coldren Adams, Uniontown, 1992—. Pres. Greater Uniontown United Fund, 1962, Fayette County Devel. Council, 1971-75. Fellow Am. Bar Found., Am. Coll. Trust and Estate Counsel; mem. Pa. Bar Assn. (ho. of dels. 1976-79, bd. govs. 1979-82, v.p. 1985-86, pres. 1986-87), Pa. Bar Inst. (pres. 1982-83), Fayette County Bar Assn. (pres. 1983), Am. Law Inst., Am. Judicature Soc., Internat. Assn. Ins. Counsel, Pa. Jaycees (pres. 1959), Club: Uniontown Country (pres. 1969-71). Lodges: Rotary (pres. Uniontown club 1964), Masons (master 1964, 69, mem. Scottish Rite Supreme Coun. 1991—). Democrat. Presbyterian. Estate planning, Probate (including wills, trusts), Estate taxation. Home: 117 Belmont Cir Uniontown PA 15401-4759 Office: Coldren Adams 2 W Main St Ste 700 Uniontown PA 15401 E-mail: CALawFirm@aol.com.

COLE, CHARLES DEWEY, JR., lawyer; b. Lower Merion Twp., Pa., Aug. 12, 1952; s. Charles Dewey and Margaret Ann (Leach) C. AB, Columbia U., 1974; JD, St. John's U., Jamaica, N.Y., 1979; ML Info. Sci., U. Tex., 1982; LLM, NYU, 1988; LLM in Environ. Law, Pace U., 1993; LLM in Trial Advocacy, Temple U., 1999; LLM in Advanced Litigation, Nottingham Trent U., 2003. Bar: N.Y. 1980, Tex. 1980, N.J. 1986, D.C. 1988, U.S. Dist. Ct. (we. and ea. dists.) Tex. 1980, U.S. Dist. Ct. (so. and ea. dists.) N.Y. 1980, U.S. Dist. Ct. (no. dist.) Tex. 1982, U.S. Dist. Ct. (no. dist.) N.Y. 1983, U.S. Dist. Ct. (we. dist.) N.Y. 1984, U.S. Dist. Ct. N.J. 1986, U.S. Dist. Ct. D.C. 1994, U.S. Ct. Internat. Trade 1980, U.S. Tax Ct. 1984, U.S. Ct. Appeals (5th and 11th cirs.) 1981, U.S. Ct. Appeals (Fed. cir.) 1982, U.S. Ct. Appeals (2d cir.) 1984, U.S. Ct. Appeals (D.C. cir.) 1987, U.S. Ct. Appeals (3d cir.) 1993, U.S. Supreme Ct. 1984; solicitor, Eng. and Wales, 1995; Higher Rights of Audience (civil procs.) Qualification, 2002. Law clk. to chief judge U.S. Dist. Ct. (ea. dist.), Beaumont, Tex., 1979-80, U.S. Ct. Appeals (5th cir.), Austin, Tex., 1981-82; assoc. Moore, Berson, Lifflander & Mewhinney, Garden City and N.Y.C., N.Y., 1982-85; assoc. and ptnr. Newman Schlau Fitch & Burns P.C., N.Y.C. and Mineola, N.Y., 1985-88; assoc. Meyer, Suozzi, English & Klein, P.C., Mineola and N.Y.C., 1988-95; of counsel Newman Fitch Altheim Myers, P.C., N.Y.C. and Newark, 1995—. Instr. trial techniques program Hofstra Law Sch., 1994-2000; instr. intensive trial advocacy program Widener Law Sch., 1999—. Author: Law Books as a Charitable Contribution, 1975, The EPA Lender Liability Regulations: EPA's Questionable Authority to Promulgate the Regulations as Part of the National Contingency Plan, 1993; contbr. book revs. to profl. publs. Mem.: Solicitors Assn. of Higher Ct. Advs., The Coll. of State Bar Tex., State Bar Tex., Selden Soc., Supreme Ct. Hist. Soc., Soc. Advanced Legal Studies, Am. Soc. for Legal History, Osgoode Soc., Brit. and Irish Assn. Law Librs., Law Libr. Assn. Greater N.Y., Am. Assn. Law Librs., Fed. Bar Coun., Bar Assn. 5th Fed. Cir., Maritime Law Assn. U.S. (proctor), N.Y. County Lawyers Assn. (com. on fed. cts.), D.C. Bar, N.Y. State Bar Assn. (exec. and appellate practice coms., comml. and fed. litigation sect.), The Law Soc. (reference group on multi-party actions), Clarity, Scribes (dir., chair brief-writing competition com.). Republican. Appellate, Federal civil litigation, State civil litigation. Home: 16 94th St Apt 3B Brooklyn NY 11209-6643 Office: Newman Fitch Altheim Myers PC 14 Wall St New York NY 10005-2101 E-mail: dcole@nfam.com., cdc27@columbia.edu.

COLE, CHARLES DUBOSE, II, law educator; b. Monroeville, Ala., May 14, 1938; BSBA, Auburn U., 1960; JD cum laude, Samford U., 1966; LLM, NYU, 1971; D (hon.), Faculdade Marcelo Tupinamba, Sao Paulo, Brazil, 1991. Bar: Ala. 1966, U.S. Supreme Ct., 1971, U.S. Ct. Appeals (fed. cir.) 1997, U.S. Ct. Internat. Trade, 1997. Law clk., assoc. atty. Porterfield & Sch., Birmingham, Ala., 1965-66; prof. law Cumberland Sch. Law Samford U., Birmingham, 1966-75, 81—; Lucille S. Beeson prof. law and dir. internat. programs, master comparative law degree program Cumberland Sch. Law, Birmingham, Ala., 1993—; dir. permanent study commn. Ala. Jud. System, 1972-74; dir. Ala. Jud. Conf. Criminal Justice Survey, 1973; dir. adv. com. Ala. jud. article implementation Ala. Dept. Ct. Mgmt., 1974-75; dir. so. regional office Nat. Ctr. for State Cts., Atlanta, 1975-79; adminstrv. dir. cts. Commonwealth of Ky., Frankfort, 1979-81. Lectr. Cumberland Inst. for Continuing Legal Edn., Ala. Continuing Legal Edn., Josephson/Kluwer Bar Rev. Ctr. Am., Inc., 1967-87; law and social sci. adv. coun. Coll. Liberal Arts/Auburn U., 1991-96, dean's coun., 1996—; chmn. profl. adv. com. Office Advancement Auburn U., 1992-93; reporter civil justice adv. group Middle Dist. Ala., 1991-93; del. Moscow Conf. on Law and Econ. Coop., The Kremlin Palace, 1990; legal specialist (pro bono) Parliament of Ukriane, 1993; v.p. faculty Samford U., 1989-90; policy com. mem. Cumberland Sch. Law, 1989-92, 2000-02; mem. faculty exec. com. Samford U., 1988-89; del. U.S./Japan Bilateral Session, 1988; presenter USIA, Internat. Meeting Brazil/U.S., 1988; participant seminar Claremont McKenna Coll./NEH, 1986; presenter in field. Author: (with Brewer) Alabama Constitutional Law, 1992, 2d edit., 1997; contbr. articles to profl. jours.; mem. editl. bd. Ala. Lawyer, 2000—. Bd. dirs. Auburn U. Bar Assn., 1991—. Named Outstanding Prof. Student Bar Assn./Cumberland Sch. Law, 1972-73, 83-84, Outstanding Alumnus, Phi Alpha Delta, 1973, Samford U. Cumberland Sch. Law, 1998. Mem. ABA (lectr. appellate judges seminar 1977-78), Am. Judicature Soc. (bd. dirs. 2000—, exec. com. 2000—), Supreme Ct. Hist. Soc., Am. Trial Lawyers Assn. (faculty mem.), Ala. Bar Assn. (action group mem. 1984-85, chmn. 1985-88, reporter task force on jud. selection 1988-89, com. on the future of the profession 1990-91, task force on legal edn. 1992-93, com. on judicial and legal reform 1994-95, chmn. 1995-96), Ukrainian Legal Found. (bd. fgn. advisors 1993-98), Birmingham Bar Assn. (mem. civil ct. rules com. 1998-99), Auburn U. Bar Assn. (adv. bd. 1992—), Phi Alpha Delta. Home: 2419 Dove Pl Birmingham AL 35216 E-mail: cdcole@samford.edu., colecdII@aol.com.

COLE, CURTIS ALLEN, lawyer; b. Niles, Mich., Aug. 17, 1946; s. Keith Arnold and Persis Elizabeth (Kelley) C.; m. Sharon Gail Lozoya, July 25, 1981; children: Richard, Cassidy, Kirsten, Cameron. BA, UCLA, 1968, JD, 1972. Bar: Calif. 1972, U.S. Dist. Ct. (cen., so., no. and ea. dists.) Calif. 1972, U.S. Supreme Ct. 1976, U.S. Ct. Appeals (6th and 9th cir.s) 1972, Cert. Appellate Specialist, State Bar of Calif., Bd. of Legal Specialization, 1997. Dep. city atty. City of L.A., 1972-73; assoc. Thelen, Marrin, Johnson & Bridges, L.A., 1973-80, ptnr., 1980—98, Thelen, Reid and Priest, 1998—. Chmn. ins. law com. Calif. State Bar, 1991-92; rep. decisions include Madden v. Kaiser Found. Hosps., 1976, Fein v. Permanente Med. Group, 1985, Adams v. Murakami, 1991, Guz v. Bechtel Nat. Inc., 2000. Mem. ABA, L.A. County Bar Assn., Am. Health Lawyers' Assn. Appellate, General civil litigation. Office: Thelen Reid and Priest 333 S Hope St Ste 2900 Los Angeles CA 90071-3048

COLE, EMRIED DARGAN, JR., lawyer; b. Hattiesburg, Miss., Nov. 6, 1945; m. Wandaleen Poynter. BA in History with high honors, Emory U., 1967; JD, Harvard U., 1970. Bar: Md. 1990, US Ct. Appeals (5th, 6th, 7th, 11th and DC cir.) 1974, US Supreme Ct. 1974. Assoc. Powell, Goldstein, Frazer and Murphy, Atlanta, 1970—73; asst. gen. atty., asst. gen. solicitor Louisville and Nashville R.R. Co., Louisville, 1973—77; gen. atty. Seaboard System R.R., Jacksonville, 1977—83, gen. solicitor, 1983—86; v.p. law and risk mgmt. CSX Transp.-Equipment Group, Balt., 1986—90; of counsel, ptnr. Venable, Baetjer & Howard LLP, Balt., 1990—. Adj. faculty Johns Hopkins Univ. Sch. of Profl. Studies in Bus. and Ed., 2002. Mem.: ABA, Assn. Transp. Practitioners (chmn. com. profl. ethics 1982—84), State Bar Ga., Nat. Assn. R.R. Trial Counsel, Fla. Bar Assn. Administrative and regulatory, Antitrust, Utilities, public. Office: Venable Baetjer & Howard LLP 2 Hopkins Plz Ste 1800 Baltimore MD 21201-3805 Business E-Mail: edcole@venable.com.

COLE, GEORGE THOMAS, lawyer; b. Orlando, Fla., Mar. 14, 1946; s. Robert Bates and Frances (Arnold) C.; m. Peggy Ellen Stimson, May 23, 1981; children: Leslie Elizabeth, Ashley Ellen, Robert Warren. AB, Yale U., 1968; JD, U. Mich., 1975. Bar: Ariz. 1975, U.S. Dist. Ct. Ariz. 1975, U.S. Ct. Appeals (9th cir.) 1978; cert. real estate specialist Ariz. Bar. With Fennemore, Craig, von Ammon, Udall & Powers, Phoenix, 1975-81; ptnr. Fennemore Craig, P.C., Phoenix, 1981—. Mem. Ariz. State U. Coun. for Design Excellence. Served to lt. (j.g.) USN, 1968-71. Fellow: Ariz. Bar Found. (founding); mem.: Maricopa Bar Assn., Ariz. Bar Assn. (coun.real property sect. 1985—88, chmn. 1987—88), Cmty. Assns. Inst., Nat. Golf Found. (assoc.), ULI (cmty. devel. coun. 1995—2001), Ariz. Assn. Home Bldrs., Nat. Assn. Home Bldrs., White Mountain Country Club (Pinetop, Ariz.), Paradise Valley Country Club (Phoenix), Yale Club (pres. 1984). Republican. Methodist. Property, real (including real estate development, water). Home: 5102 E Desert Park Ln Paradise Valley AZ 85253-3054 Office: Fennemore Craig 3003 N Central Ave Ste 2600 Phoenix AZ 85012-2913 E-mail: gcole@fclaw.com.

COLE, JAMES OTIS, lawyer; b. Florence, Ala., Feb. 6, 1941; s. Calloway and Eula (Reynolds) C.; m. Ada Dolores Cole, Dec. 16, 1961; children: James Otis Jr., Lerone Barrington. BA, Talladega Coll., 1963; JD, Harvard U., 1971. Bar: Ill. 1971, U.S. Dist. Ct. (no. dist.) Ill. 1971, Calif. 1977, U.S. Supreme Ct. 1981. Assoc. Kirkland & Ellis, Chgo., 1971-73; div. counsel The Clorox Co., Oakland, Calif.; sr. v.p., gen. counsel, sec. AutoNation, Inc., Ft. Lauderdale; of counsel Ruden, McClosky, Smith, Schuster & Russell, 2002—. Arbitrator Contra Costa County Superior Ct., Martinez, Calif., 1980—. Counsel East Oakland Youth Devel. Ctr.; bd. dirs. Oakland Ballet, Bay Area Urban League, Oakland; bd. dirs. Black Filmmakers Hall of Fame, Oakland, pres. 1980-83. Mem. ABA, Nat. Bar Assn. (bd. govs. 1981—), Calif. Assn. Black Lawyers (pres.-elect 1986—), Charles Houston Bar Assn. (pres. 1985—), Calif. Bar Jud. Nominees Evaluation Commn. (commr. 1985—). Clubs: Oakland Athletic, Lakeview (Oakland). Corporate, general. Home: 10 Nurmi Dr Fort Lauderdale FL 33301-1403 Office: Ruden McClosky Smith Schuster & Russell 200 E Broward Blvd Fort Lauderdale FL 33302*

COLE, JAMES YEAGER, foundation executive; b. Cleve., Sept. 20, 1957; s. Charles and Nancy C. JD, Blackstone Sch. Law, Dallas, 1980, U. N.C., 1989; MA, M.C.I., London, 1981; PhD, N.W. London U., 1981. CEO Cole Corp., Tallahassee, 1979-81; judge Inst. Advanced Law Study, Las Vegas, 1981-84; cons., sentencing advocate Cullowhee, N.C., 1984-2001. Recipient Presdl. medal of Merit Pres. Ronald Reagan, Washington, 1980; Knight Comdr. Royal Knights of Justice, London, 1981; Venerable Order of the Knights of Michael the Archangel Knight Chevalier, Disting. Leadership award ABA Jud. Divsn., 1997; lifetime dep. gov. Am. Biog. Rsch. Inst. Mem. Am. Judges Assn., World Judges Assn., Nat. Judges Assn., Internat. Bar Assn., Human Rights Inst., Island Found., Am. Fedn. of Police, Heirs, Inc., Nat. Sheriff's Assn., N.C. Sheriff's Assn., Haywood County C. of C., Maggic Valley C. of C., N.C. Fraternal Order of Police. Avocations: swimming, snow/water skiing, volleyball, tennis, cinema. Home and Office: 389 Chestnut Walk Dr Waynesville NC 28786 E-mail: jim@maggievalley.com.

COLE, JANICE MCKENZIE, former prosecutor; b. Feb. 16, 1947; m. James Carlton Cole. BA summa cum laude, John Jay Coll Criminal Justice, 1975, MPA, 1978; JD, Fordham U., 1979. Bar: N.Y. 1980, N.C. 1983. Asst. U.S. atty. Eastern Dist. N.Y., 1979-83; sole practitioner, 1983-89; with firm Cole & Cole, 1989-90; dist. ct. judge First Jud. Dist. N.C., 1990-94; U.S. atty. N.C. Eastern Dist., 1994—2001; sole practitioner, 2001—. Office: Ste 106 1072 Harvey Point Rd Hertford NC 27944-1461

COLE, JOHN PRINCE, lawyer, university official; b. Carrollton, Ga., Mar. 18, 1963; m. Mary Stewart Donovan. AB, Harvard U., 1985; JD magna cum laude, Mercer Law Sch., 1991. Bar: Ga. 1991, U.S. Dist. Ct. (no., mid. dist.) Ga. 1991, U.S. Ct. Appeals (11th cir.) 1991. Law clerk Mitchell, Coppedge, Wester, Bisson & Miller, Dalton, Ga., 1989, Ga. Atty. Gen., Atlanta, 1990; assoc. Anderson, Walker & Reichert, Macon, Ga., 1991-94; gen. asst. to pres. Mercer U., Macon, Ga., 1994—2000, v.p. univ. admissions, 2001—. Trustee First Bapt. Ch., Macon, 1993-97, Ga. Children's Home, 1996-2000, bd. chair, 1999-2000; funds allocation com. United Way Ctrl. Ga., 1992-94. Maj. USAR, Bosnia, 2001. Mem. ABA, Nat. Assn. Coll. and Univ. Attys., Macon Bar Assn. (treas. 1997-98, sec. 1998-99, pres. elect 1999-2001, pres. 2001-02), Lawyers Found. Ga., Leadership GA, Phi Kappa Phi. Democrat. Avocations: hiking, music, golf. Office: Mercer U 1400 Coleman Ave Macon GA 31207-0003

COLE, LEWIS GEORGE, lawyer; b. N.Y.C., Mar. 9, 1931; s. Ralph David and Emma (Balterman) C.; m. Sara Livingston, June 22, 1952; children: Elizabeth, Peter. BS in Econ., U. Pa., 1951; LLB, Yale U., 1954. Bar: N.Y. 1954. Ptnr. Stroock & Stroock & Lavan, LLP, N.Y.C., 1958—. Bd. dirs. Ametek, Inc. Served as 1st lt. U.S. Army, 1954-57. Mem. ABA, Assn. Bar City N.Y., N.Y. State Bar Assn. Corporate, general, Securities. Office: Stroock & Stroock & Lavan LLP 180 Maiden Ln New York NY 10038-4925

COLE, PHILLIP ALLEN, lawyer; b. Washington, Mar. 3, 1940; s. Gordon Harding and Dorothy Barbara (Jugel) C.; m. Mary Jo Ruff, July 2, 1994; children: Jennifer Leigh, Christopher Harding, Catherine Anne. BA, U. Md., 1961; JD, Georgetown U., 1964. Bar: Md. 1964, Minn. 1968, U.S. Supreme Ct. 1967, U.S. Ct. Appeals (8th cir.) 1968, U.S. Dist. Ct. Minn. 1965, U.S. Ct. Mil. Appeals 1965; cert. civil trial specialist. Assoc. Beatty & McNamee, Hyattville, Md., 1968; founder, sr. mem. Lommen, Nelson, Cole & Stageberg, Mpls., 1969—. Spl. counsel Md. Ho. of Dels., 1968. Contbr. articles to profl. jours. Capt. USMC, 1965-67. Mem. ATLA, Am. Bd. Profl. Liability Attys., Internat. Assn. Def. Counsel. Avocations: golf, reading. General civil litigation, Professional liability, Securities. Office: Lommen Nelson Cole & Stageberg 1800 IDS Ctr Minneapolis MN 55402 E-mail: phil@lommen.com.

COLE, R. DENO, lawyer; b. St. Louis, Mo., Aug. 7, 1971; s. Robert Reland Cole and Cynthia Lamperson Azari; m. Sara Christine Head, Aug. 17, 2002. BA in English, The Citadel, 1993; JD, Touro Law Ctr., 1997. Bar: 1997. Atty. Law Offices of Felicia Pasculli, Bayshore, NY, 1996—97, Yancey, Cooper, Simpson and Cole, Knoxville, 1997—2001, McGehee, Newton, Stewart, Dupree and Boswell, 2001—. ALTA moot ct. judge ATLA, Knoxville, 2001; judge, H.S. moot ct. competition Knoxville Bar Assn., 2000—02, coach, H.S. moot ct. competition, 2002. V.p. Optimist Club, Knoxville, 2002—03; bd. mem. Boy Scouts of Am., Knoxville, 2000—03; active mem. atty. Knoxville Pro Bono Project. Mem.: Assn. of Trial Lawyers of Am., Knoxville Bar Assn., ABA. Republican. Episcopal. Avocation: hiking in the Smoky Mtns. and enjoying mtn. home.. Office: McGehee, Newton, Stewart, Cole, Dupree and Boswell 709 Market St Suite 2 Knoxville TN 37902

COLE, RANSEY GUY, JR., federal judge; b. Birmingham, Ala., May 23, 1951; s. Ransey Guy and Sarah Nell (Coker) Cole; m. Kathleine Kelley, Nov. 26, 1983; children: Justin Robert Jefferson, Jordan Paul, Alexandra Sarah. BA, Tufts U., 1972; JD, Yale U., 1975. Bar: Ohio 1975, D.C. 1982. Assoc. Vorys, Sater, Seymour and Pease, Columbus, Ohio, 1975—78, ptnr., 1980—86, 1993—95; trial atty. U.S. Dept. Justice, Washington, 1978—80; judge U.S. Bankruptcy Ct., Columbus, 1987—93; circuit judge U.S. Ct. Appeals (6th cir.), Cinn., 1995—. Mem.: ABA, Columbus Bar Assn., Nat. Bar Assn. Office: US Courthouse 85 Marconi Blvd Rm 127 Columbus OH 43215-2823 also: US Court of Appeals 6th Circuit 532 Potter Stewart US Courthouse 100 E Fifth St Cincinnati OH 45202*

COLE, RICHARD A. retired lawyer; b. Syracuse, N.Y., Feb. 21, 1951; s. Victor and Marie (Pogacar) C.; m. Lois Hallonquist, Sept. 27, 1975. AB, Brown U., 1973; JD, Cornell U., 1976. Bar: Ill. 1976, U.S. Dist. Ct. (no. dist.) Ill. 1976. Assoc. Mayer, Brown, Rowe & Maw, Chgo., 1976—82, ptnr., 1983—2002. Trustee U. Notre Dame, London, 1981-2002. Avocation: travel. Banking, Corporate, general, Private international. Home: 29 Beverley Rd London SW 13 England E-mail: randlcole@dial.pipex.com.

COLE, RICHARD CHARLES, lawyer; b. Albany, N.Y., Apr. 23, 1950; s. Charles Stanley and Doris Jean (Hatch) C.; m. Margaret O'Leary; children: Jack Patrick, Charles Michael. BA magna cum laude, Cornell U., 1972; JD, Harvard U., 1975. Bar: N.Y. 1976, U.S. Dist. Ct. (so. and ea. dits.) N.Y. 1977, U.S. Ct. Apeals (D.C. cir.) 1980, U.S. Ct. Appeals (2d and 5th cirs.) 1981, U.S. Dist. Ct. (no, ea., so. and ctrl. dists.) 1989, U.S. Supreme Ct. 1995. Assoc. LeBoeuf, Lamb, Leiby & MacRae, N.Y.C., 1975-83, ptnr., 1984-89, LeBoeuf, Lamb, Greene & MacRae, San Francisco, 1989-95; pvt. practice Mill Valley, 1996—. Mem. ABA. Avocations: woodwind instruments, sch. vol. Federal civil litigation, Insurance, Mergers and acquisitions. Office: 41 Buena Vista Ave Mill Valley CA 94941-1231

COLE, ROBERT THEODORE, lawyer; b. Bklyn., Mar. 16, 1932; s. Harold I. and Bella (Weissman) C.; m. C. Margaret Hall, Oct. 25, 1959; children: Elizabeth, Tanya, Judith Amy. BS, U. Pa., 1953; LLB magna cum laude, Harvard U. Law Sch., 1956; diploma in law, London Sch. Econs.,

1958. Bar: N.Y. 1956, D.C. 1972. Assoc. Law Office Frank Boas, Brussels, 1960-62, Nixon Mudge Rose et al, N.Y.C., 1962-67; atty. U.S. Treasury Dept., Washington, 1967-73, internat. tax counsel, 1971-73; ptnr. Cole Corette & Abrutyn, Washington, 1973-96; ptnr., sr. counsel Alston & Bird LLP, Washington, 1997—; co-owner The Little Gym, Va. Lectr. on internat. tax. Editor, prin. author Practical Guide U.S. Transfer Princing; contbr. articles on internat. taxes to legal jours. Capt. USAF, 1957-59. Recipient exceptional svc. award U.S. Treasury Dept., 1973. Fellow Am. Coll. Tax Counsel; mem. Assn. Bar City N.Y., Nat. Fgn. Trade Coun. (vice-chair tax com. 1989-95), Harvard Club (N.Y.C.). Avocations: hiking, theatre. Private international, Corporate taxation. Home: 4000 Chancery Ct NW Washington DC 20007-2140 Office: Alston & Bird LLP 601 Pennsylvania Ave NW No Bldg 10th Fl Washington DC 20004-2601

COLE, ROLAND JAY, lawyer; b. Seattle, Dec. 15, 1948; s. Robert J. and Josephine F. C.; m. Elsa Kircher, Aug. 16, 1975; children: Isabel Ashley, Madeline Aldis. AB in Econs. magna cum laude, Harvard U., 1970, M in Pub. Policy, 1972, PhD in Pub. Policy, JD, 1975. Bar: Wash. 1975, U.S. Supreme Ct. 1980, U.S. Dist. Ct. (we. dist.) Wash. 1984, Mich. 1989. Rsch. scientist Battelle Human Affairs Rsch. Ctrs., Seattle, 1975-83; assoc. Appel and Glueck, P.C., Seattle, 1984-89; gen. counsel Indsl. Tech. Inst., Ann Arbor, Mich., 1990-94; founder, exec. dir. Software Patent Inst., Indpls., 1994—; of counsel Shughart Thomson & Kilroy PC, Overland Park, Kans., 1997-2000, Barnes & Thornburg, Indpls., 2000—. Co-author: Government Requirements of Small Business, 1980, The Containment of Organized Crime, 1984; co-programmer Quadrant I software program, 1983. HUD fellow, 1970-71. Mem. Assn. Personal Computer User Groups (dir., founding pres. 1986), Wash. Athletic Club, Indpls. Athletic Club. Congregationalist. Avocations: squash, racquetball, volleyball, music. Computer, Intellectual property, Trademark and copyright. Office: Barnes & Thornburg 11 S Meridian St Indianapolis IN 46204-3535 E-mail: rcole@btlaw.com.

COLE, SARAH, law enforcement librarian; b. Ill., Nov. 8, 1963; BA, North Cen. Coll., Naperville, Ill., 1985; MA in Libr. Studies, No. Ill. U., 1988. Law enforcement libr. North East Multi-Regional Tng., North Aurora, Ill., 1988—. Editor Precious Nonsense newsletter, 1984—. Active Midwestern Gilbert and Sullivan Soc., North Aurora. Mem. Spl. Librs. Assn., Ill. Librs. Assn., Nat. Sheriffs Assn. Office: NE Multi-Regional Tng 355 Smoke Tree Plz North Aurora IL 60542 E-mail: sarah@nemrt.com.

COLE, THOMAS AMOR, lawyer; b. Phila., Nov. 2, 1948; s. George Lough and Elizabeth (Bush) C.; m. Carol L. Owen, Dec. 27, 1969 (div. 1979); children: Kirsten E., Lauren E.; m. Constance J. Ward, Nov. 17, 1979; children: Lindsay W., Emily C. BA, Johns Hopkins U., 1970, JD, U. Chgo., 1975. Bar: Ill. 1975, U.S. Dist. Ct. (no. dist.) Ill. 1975. Assoc. Sidley & Austin, Chgo., 1975-81; v.p. law Northwest Industries, Chgo., 1982-85; ptnr. Sidley & Austin, Chgo., 1981—, mgmt. com., 1988—, chair exec. com., 1998—. Adj. prof., U. Chgo. Law Sch.; chmn. exec. com. Northwestern U. Sch. Law, Garrett Corp., Securities Law Inst.; co-chair Tulane Corp. Law Inst., Practising Law Inst., Northwestern U. Kellogg Grad. Sch. Mgmt.; bd. dirs. U. Chgo., Northwestern Meml. Hosp., Chgo. Coun. Fgn. Rels. U. Chgo. Bd. dirs. Ravinia Festival; Joffrey Ballet. Mem. ABA, Chgo. Bar Assn., Am. Law Inst., Chgo. Club, Econ. Club, Comml. Club, Law Club of Chgo., Order of Coif, Phi Beta Kappa. Democrat. Mem. Soc. Friends. Finance, Mergers and acquisitions, Securities. Office: Sidley Austin Brown & Wood 1 S First National Plz Chicago IL 60603-2000

COLEMAN, FRANCIS J., JR., lawyer; b. McCook, Nebr., Jan. 28, 1945; BA, Rice U., 1966; JD (with hons.), U. Tex., 1972. Bar: Tex. 1972. City atty. City of Houston, Tex., 1982-84; ptnr. Vinson & Elkins L.L.P., Houston. Finance. Office: Vinson & Elkins 2300 1st City Tower 1001 Fannin St Houston TX 77002-6760

COLEMAN, JAMES H., JR., former state supreme court justice; b. Lawrenceville, VA, May 4, 1933; s. James H. Sr. and Neda Coleman; m. Sophia Coleman, May 12, 1962; 2 children. BA cum laude, Va. State U., 1956, LLD (hon.) , 1995; JD, Howard U., 1959. Bar: N.J. 1960, U.S. Dist. Ct. N.J. 1960, U.S. Supreme Ct. 1963. Asst. and/or cons. various N.J. commns. and divs., 1960-64; pvt. practice law Elizabeth and Roselle, N.J., 1960-70; judge N.J. Workers' Compensation Ct., 1964-73, Union County Ct., 1973-78, Law div. N.J. Superior Ct., 1978-81; mem. spl. three-judge resentencing panel N.J. Superior Ct., 1979-81; judge Appellate div. N.J. Superior Ct., 1981-87, presiding judge, 1987-94; assoc. justice Supreme Ct. of N.J., Springfield, 1994—. Mem. various Supreme Ct. coms.; lectr. in field. Chmn. Elizabeth Good Neighbor Coun.; mem. Elizabeth Adv. Bd. on Urban Renewal; incorporator, bd. dirs. Union County Legal Svcs., Elizabeth Anti-Poverty Program; v.p., bd. dirs., counsel to Urban League of Union County; counsel to Elizabeth NAACP; v.p. Scotch Plains-Fanwood Human Rights Coun.; Mem. N.J. Com. on Hiring the Handicapped; mem. Union County Coordinating and Adv. Com. on Higher Edn.;mem. Essex County Coll. Equal Edn. Opportunity Fund Bd., others. Fellow ABA; mem. Nat. Bar Assn. (judicial coun.), N.J. Bar Assn., Union County Bar Assn., Am. Law Inst., Am. Judicature Soc., Garden State Bar Assn., Omega Psi Phi. Baptist. Avocations: tennis, gardening. Office: Supreme Ct of NJ 99 Mount Bethel Rd Warren NJ 07059-5126*

COLEMAN, JAMES JULIAN, JR., lawyer, industrialist, real estate executive; b. New Orleans, May 7, 1941; s. James Julian Sr. and Dorothy Louise (Jurisich) C.; m. Carol Campbell Owen, Dec. 19, 1970 (dec. Sept. 1979); 1 child, James Owen; m. Mary Olivia Cochrane Cushing, Oct. 12, 1985. BA, Princeton U., 1963; postgrad. in law, Oxford (Eng.) U., 1963-65; JD, Tulane U., 1968. Bar: La. 1969, U.S. Supreme Ct. 1969. Chmn. Internat.-Matex Tank Terminals, New Orleans, 1969—; pres. Coleman Devel. Co., New Orleans, 1969—, IMTT, Quebec, 1993—, Nfld. Transhipment Terminal Inc.; ptnr. Coleman, Johnson & Artigues, New Orleans, 1972—; chmn. DownTown Parking Service, New Orleans, 1978—; pres. City Ctr. Properties, New Orleans, 1980—. Mng. ptnr. Windsor Court Hotel, New Orleans Hilton Hotel, Exxon Bldg., Chevron Bldg., Freeport Cooper Gold Bldg., Internat. River Ctr.; chmn. East Jersey R.R. and Terminal Co., 1993; trustee Loving Found., New Orleans, R.L. Blaffer Found., Houston; dir., v.p. U.S. Coast Guard Found., pres. Natl. Coast Guard Museum Assn. 2001—. Author: Gilbert Antoine de St. Maxent: The Spanish Frenchman of New Orleans, 1975. Mem. history coun. Princeton U., 1982—; mem. N.J. Commn. on Sci. and Tech., 1992—; bd. dirs. Hampden Sydney Coll., 1982-92, Liberty Sci. Ctr., Liberty State Park, N.J., 1999—; bd. overseers N.J. Inst. Tech., 1999—; mem. N.J. Commn. on Jobs and Econ. Growth, 2003—. Named H.M. Hon. Brit. Consul for La., Brit. Consulate, New Orleans, 1975—, to Order of Brit. Empire, Queen Elizabeth II, London, 1986. Mem. ABA, La. Bar Assn., N.Y. Yacht Club, N.Y. Racquet Club, Newport Reading Room, So. Yacht Club, New Orleans Lawn Tennis Club, USN League (bd. dirs. New Orleans), Union League Club. Corporate, general, Environmental, Property, real (including real estate development, water). Office: Coleman Johnson & Artigues 321 St Charles Ave 10th Fl New Orleans LA 70130-3145 E-mail: jimmyjr504@aol.com.

COLEMAN, JEROME P. lawyer; b. Washington, July 3, 1948; s. Francis Thomas and Helen Theresa (Hile) C. AB, Princeton U., 1970; JD, Georgetown U., 1973. Bar: D.C. 1973, N.Y. 1976, U.S. Dist. Ct. (so. and ea. dists.) N.Y. 1976, U.S. Ct. Appeals (2d cir.) 1976, U.S. Ct. Appeals (3d cir.) 1978, U.S. Supreme Ct. 1988. Atty., advisor Nat. Labor Rels. Bd., Washington, 1973-74; assoc. Townley & Updike, N.Y.C., 1974-81, ptnr., 1982-95, Nixon Peabody LLP, N.Y.C., 1995—. Co-chair Inner-City Schs. Lawyers Com., N.Y.C., 1998—; pres., Princeton Class of 1970, 2000, 2005. Mem. ABA, Federal Bar Assn. (chmn. labor law com. 1978-82), N.Y. State Bar Assn.(chmn. labor arbitration com. 1983-86), Univ. Club (governing coun. 1991-95, sec. 1996-99, v.p. 1999-2000, pres. 2000—). Federal civil litigation, Labor (including EEOC, Fair Labor Standards Act, labor-management relations, NLRB, OSHA). Home: 124 E 84th St Apt 8B New York NY 10028-0917 Office: Nixon Peabody LLP 437 Madison Ave New York NY 10022-7001

COLEMAN, JOHN MICHAEL, lawyer, consumer products executive; b. Boston, Dec. 28, 1949; s. John Royston Coleman and Mary Norrington Irwin; m. Susan Lee Lavine, Oct. 29, 1978; children: William L., Anne H. L. BA, Haverford (Pa.) Coll., 1975; JD, U. Chgo., 1978. Bar: N.Y. 1978, Pa. 1979, U.S. Ct. Appeals (3rd and 4th cirs.) 1979, U.S. Dist. Ct. (ea. dist.) Pa. 1979, U.S. Dist. Ct. (so. dist.) N.Y. 1981, U.S. Supreme Ct., 1982, N.J. 1988. Law clk. to judge U.S. Ct. Appeals, Richmond, Va., 1978-79; law clk. to chief justice Warren Burger U.S. Supreme Ct., Washington, 1980-81; assoc. Dechert Price & Rhoads, Phila., 1981-86, ptnr., 1986-89; v.p., gen. counsel Campbell Soup Co., Camden, N.J., 1989-90, sr. v.p. law and pub. affairs, 1990-97; sr. v.p., gen. counsel The Gillette Co., Boston, 1997-99; mng. dir., CEO, Cambridge (Mass.) Capital Ptnrs. LLP, 1999-2000, chmn., CEO, 2000—. Adj. prof. law U. Pa., Phila., 1985-88; bd. dirs. CDI Corp. Contbr. articles to profl. jours. Chmn. bd. trustees Campbell Soup Found., 1990-97; trustee N.J. State Aquarium, 1991-94, Food and Drug Law Inst., 1991-98, Inst. for Law and Econs., 1993-97, Am. Judicature Soc., 1995—; mem. vis. com. U. Chgo. Law Sch., 1993-95; mem. corp. Haverford Coll., 1994—; bd. dirs. The Guidance Ctr., treas., 2000—. Mem. Am. Law Inst., Order of the Coif, Phi Beta Kappa. Mem. Religious Soc. of Friends. Corporate, general.

COLEMAN, RICHARD WILLIAM, retired lawyer; b. Brookline, Mass., Dec. 9, 1935; s. Michael John and Mary Ellen (Motherway) C.; m. Mary M. Kilcommins, June 3, 1961; children: Lauren, Christopher. BS, Boston Coll., Newton, Mass., 1957; JD, Boston Coll., Brighton, Mass., 1960. Bar: Mass. 1960, U.S. Dist. Ct. Mass. 1961, U.S. Ct. Appeals (1st cir.) 1981. Field atty. NLRB, Newark, 1960-61; assoc. Segal & Flamm, Boston, 1961-69; labor rels. advisor Scott Paper Co., Phila., 1969-70; labor rels. mgr. Harvard U., Cambridge, Mass., 1970-72; ptnr. Segal, Roitman & Coleman, Boston, 1972-93; pres. Richard W. Coleman, P.C., Needham, 1994—2002; ret. Contbg. editor Development of Law Under National Labor Relations Act, 1988. Bd. dirs. Little Bros. of St. Francis, 1998-2001. Recipient Cushing award Cath. Labor Guild Boston, 1976. Mem. ABA, Am. Prepaid Legal Svcs. Inst. (bd. dirs. 1997—), Indsl. Rels. Rsch. Assn., Mass. Bar Assn., Boston Bar Assn., AFL-CIO Lawyers Coord. Com. Democrat. Roman Catholic. Avocations: golf, reading, choir singing. Labor (including EEOC, Fair Labor Standards Act, labor-management relations, NLRB, OSHA), Pension, profit-sharing, and employee benefits. E-mail: rcolegolf@aol.com.

COLEMAN, ROBERT J. lawyer; b. Phila., Dec. 24, 1936; s. Francis Eugene and Mary Veronica (McCullough) C.; m. Mary Patricia Coleman, June 26, 1955; children: Debra, Robert P., Linda, Martin S. AB, Villanova U., 1959; JD, Temple U., 1964. Bar: Pa., U.S. Dist. Ct. (ea. dist.) Pa., U.S. Ct. Appeals (3d cir.), U.S. Supreme Ct. With First Pa. Bank, Phila., 1955-57; underwriter Employer's Mut. Co., Phila., 1957-59; claim adjuster Safeco Ins. Co., Phila., 1959-62; claim supr. Gen. Accident Ins., Phila., 1962-64; assoc. Rappaport & Lagakos, Phila., 1964; trial atty. Allstate Ins. Co., Phila., 1964-67; chmn., CEO Marshall, Dennehey, Warner, Coleman & Goggin, Phila., 1967—. Chmn. hearing com. Pa. Disciplinary Bd., Phila., 1986-94; mem. Pa. Bd. Law Examiners, 1997-2003; bd. dirs. Republic First Bancorp., 2003-. Assoc. editor Phila. County Reporter, 1984-96; contbr. articles to legal publs. Bd. dirs. Ins. Soc. Phila., HERO Scholarship Fund Delaware County; bd. vis. Temple U. Law Sch. With USAR, 1954-62. Mem. ABA, Pa. Bar Assn., Phila. Bar Assn., Phila. Bar Found. (trustee), Pa. Def. Inst., Internat. Assn. Def. Lawyers, Def. Rsch. Inst. Republican. Roman Catholic. Avocations: tennis, boating, travel. Personal injury (including property damage), Product liability. Home: 908 Penn Valley Rd Media PA 19063-1652 Office: Marshall Dennehey Warner Coleman & Goggin 1845 Walnut St Philadelphia PA 19103-4797

COLEMAN, ROBERT LEE, retired lawyer; b. Kansas City, June 14, 1929; s. William Houston and Edna Fay (Smith) C. BMus Edn., Drake U., 1951; LLB, U. Mo., 1959. Bar: Mo. 1959, Fla. 1973. Law clk. to judge U.S. Dist. Ct. (we. dist.) Mo., Kansas City, 1959-60; assoc. Watson, Ess, Marshall & Engas, Kansas City, 1960-66; asst. gen. counsel Gas Svc. Co., Kansas City, 1966-74; v.p., corp. counsel H & R Block, Inc., Kansas City, 1974-94; retired, 1994. With U.S. Army, 1955-57. Mem. ABA. Corporate, general.

COLEMAN, ROBERT WINSTON, lawyer; b. Oklahoma City, Mar. 1, 1942; s. Clint Sheridan and Genevieve (Ross) C.; m. Judith Moore, Sept. 7, 1963; children: Robert Winston, Jr., Claire Elizabeth. BA, Abilene Christian Coll., 1964; JD with hons., U. Tex., 1968. Bar: Tex. 1968, Ga. 1970. Law clk. to presiding justice U.S. Ct. Appeals (5th cir.), Montgomery, Ala., 1968-69; assoc. Kilpatrick, Cody, Rogers, McClatchey & Regenstein, Atlanta, 1969-75; ptnr. Meyers, Miller, Middleton, Weiner & Warren and predecessor, Dallas, 1975-80, Jones, Day, Reavis & Pogue, Dallas, 1981-85; dir. Baker, Glast and Middleton, P.C., Dallas, 1985-92; ptnr. Vial, Hamilton, Koch & Knox, LLP, Dallas, 1992-2000, Brown McCarroll LLP, Dallas, 2000—. Mem. exec. com. Dallas County Dem. Com., 1980-87. Mem. ABA, Dallas Bar Found., Dallas Bar Assn., Tex. Bar Assn., Ga. Bar Assn., Am. Judicature Soc. Federal civil litigation, State civil litigation, Professional liability. Office: Brown McCarroll LLP 2000 Trammell Crow Ctr 2001 Ross Ave Dallas TX 75201 E-mail: RColeman@mailbmc.com.

COLEMAN, THOMAS, federal lawyer; b. Rochester, N.Y., May 12, 1950; s. Thomas James and Amy Desmond Coleman. BA, U. Kans., 1972, JD, 1976; MS, Johns Hopkins U., 1999. Dir. energy project Kans. Legal Svcs., Topeka, 1977-82; asst. atty. gen. State of Kans., Topeka, 1982-84; atty. advisor U.S. Dept. of Housing and Urban Devel., Kansas City, Mo., 1984-86, regional counsel, 1996—, assoc. field counsel Denver, 1986-89, chief counsel, 1989-96. Avocations: music, flyfishing, canoeing, marital arts. Home: 1217 W 71st Ter Kansas City MO 64114-1237 Office: US Dept of Housing and Urban Devel 400 State Ave Fl 5 Kansas City KS 66101-2425 Fax: 913-551-5857. E-mail: Thomas_J._Coleman@hud.gov.

COLEMAN, THOMAS YOUNG, lawyer; b. Richmond, Va., Jan. 6, 1949; s. Emmett Macadium and Mary Katherine (Gay) C.; m. Janet Clare Norris, Aug. 30, 1980; children: Dana Alicia (dec.), Amanda Gay, Blair Norris. BA, U. Va., 1971, JD, 1975. Bar: Va. 1975, U.S. Dist. Ct. (we. dist.) Va. 1975, U.S. Ct. Appeals (4th cir.) 1976, Calif. 1977, U.S Dist Ct. (no. dist.) Calif. 1977. Law clk. chief judge U.S. Dist. Ct. (we. dist.) Va., Charlottesville, 1975-76; assoc. Morrison & Foerster, San Francisco, 1976-79; v.p., counsel Calif. 1st Bank (now Union Bank of Calif.), San Francisco, 1979-85; of counsel Orrick, Herrington & Sutcliffe, San Francisco, 1985-86, ptnr., 1987—. Speaker in field; vis. atty. Clifford-Turner Solicitors (now Clifford Chance), London, 1984. Mem. bus. gifts com. San Francisco Symphony. Mem. Internat. Bankers Assn. in Calif. (co-counsel). Office: Orrick Herrington & Sutcliffe 400 Sansome St San Francisco CA 94111-3143

COLEMAN, WILLIAM THADDEUS, JR., lawyer; b. Germantown, Pa., July 7, 1920; s. William Thaddeus and Laura Beatrice (Mason) Coleman; m. Lovida Hardin, Feb. 10, 1945; children: William Thaddeus III, Lovida Hardin Jr., Hardin L. AB summa cum laude, U. Pa., 1941; LLB magna cum laude, Harvard U., 1943. Bar: Pa. 1947, DC 1977. Law sec. Judge Herbert F. Goodrich, U.S. Ct. of Appeals, 3d Cir., 1947—48, Justice Felix Frankfurter (assoc. justice Supreme Ct. U.S.), 1948—49; assoc. Paul, Weiss, Rifkind, Wharton & Garrison, N.Y.C., 1949—52, Dilworth, Paxson, Kalish, Levy & Green, Phila., 1952—56; ptnr. Dilworth, Paxson, Kalish, Levy & Coleman, 1956—75; sec. Dept. Transp., Washington, 1975—77; sr. counsellor, sr. ptnr. O'Melveny & Myers, Washington, L.A., San Francisco, N.Y.C., Tokyo, London, Hong Kong, Shanghai, Beijing, China, 1977—. Spl. counsel for transit matters City of Phila., 1952—63; rep. atty. gen. Pa. and Commonwealth of Pa. in litig. to remove racial restrictions at Girard Coll., 1965; mem. Pres.'s Com. on Govt. Employment Policy, 1959—61; cons. ACDA, 1963—74; sr. cons., asst. counsel Pres.'s Commn. on Assassination of Pres. Kennedy, 1964; co-chmn. planning sessions White House Conf. to Fulfill These Rights, 1965—66; mem. U.S. del. 24th Session UN Gen. Assembly, 1969; mem. legal adv. com. Coun. on Environ. Quality, 1970; pub. mem. Pres.'s Nat. Commn. on Productivity, 1970; commr. Price Commn., 1971—72, Phila. Fairmount Pk. Commn., 1967—75, White House Commn. Aviations Safety and Security, 1996—97; mem. Gov.'s Commn. on Constl. Revision, 1963—65. Contbr. articles to profl. jours. Former chmn. bd. NAACP Legal Def. and Ednl. Fund; v.p., trustee, mem. exec. com. Phila. Art Mus.; trustee Brookings Instn., Nat. Gallery Art, 1999; mem. Trilateral Commn.; mem. exec. com. Lawyers Com. for Civil Rights Under Law; bd. overseers Harvard U., 1975—81; bd. dirs., adv. dir. NY City Ballet. Decorated officer French Legion of Honor; recipient Joseph E. Beale prize, 1946, Presdl. Freedom medal, Pres. Clinton, 1995, NAACP Legal Def. Fund Thurgood Marshall Lifetime Achievement award, 1997, Marshall Wythe medallion, 2003; fellow Langdell, 1946—47. Fellow: Am. Coll. Trial Lawyers; mem.: Coun. Fgn. Rels., Am. Arbitration Assn. (gov.), Am. Acad. Arts and Scis., Am. Philos. Soc., Phila. Bar Assn. (past chmn. jud. com.), Am. Law Inst. (coun., Henry J. Friendly medal 2000), Am. Acad. Appellate Lawyers, Met. Club (Washington), Jr. Legal Club (Phila.), Alfalfa Club, Cosmos Club, Order of Coif, Harvard Law Sch. Club, Pi Gamma Nu (Wickersham award 1997, The Fordham-Stein prize 2000), Phi Beta Kappa. Administrative and regulatory, Federal civil litigation, Corporate, general. Office: O'Melveny & Myers 555 13th St NW Ste 500W Washington DC 20004-1159

COLEN, FREDERICK HAAS, lawyer; b. Pitts., May 16, 1947; married, 1972. BSChemE, Tufts U., 1969; JD, Emory U., 1975. Bar: Pa. 1975, Ga. 1975, U.S. Patent Office 1976, U.S. Dist. Ct. (we. dist.) Pa. 1975, U.S. Dist. Ct. (no. dist.) Ga. 1975, U.S. Ct. Appeals (fed. and 3d cirs.) 1975, U.S. Supreme Ct. 1980. Chem. engr. Shell Oil Co., New Orleans, 1969-71; san. engr. USPHS, Morgantown, W.Va., 1971-73; patent atty. Mobay Chem. Corp., Pitts., 1975-79; assoc. Reed Smith, LLP, Pitts., 1979-86, ptnr., 1986—. Contbr. articles to profl. jours. Mem. ABA, Allegheny County Bar Assn., Pa. Bar Assn., Ga. Bar Assn., Am. Intellectual Property Law Assn. Intellectual property, Patent, Trademark and copyright. Home: 4940 Ellsworth Ave Pittsburgh PA 15213-2807 Office: Reed Smith LLP 435 6th Ave Ste 2 Pittsburgh PA 15219-1886 E-mail: fcolen@reedsmith.com.

COLESON, RICHARD EUGENE, lawyer, minister; b. Bulsar, India, Feb. 6, 1951; came to U.S., 1952; s. Ralph James and Olive Leone Coleson; m. Linda Sue McCrory, Aug. 19, 1972; children: Nathan Edward, Heather Anne, Jason Andrew. BA, Ind. Wesleyan U., 1973; MA in Religion, Asbury Theol. Sem., Wilmore, Ky., 1975; JD, Ind. U., 1987. Bar: Ind. 1987, U.S. Dist. Ct. (so. and no. dists.) Ind. 1987, U.S. Ct. Appeals (7th cir.) 1994, U.S. Ct. Appeals (5th cir.), 1991, U.S. Ct. Appeals (4th cir.) 1995, U.S. Supreme Ct. 1990. Pastor Wyoming (Mich.) Wesleyan Ch., 1975-78; prof. Bartlesville (Okla.) Wesleyan Coll., 1978-82; pastor Blue River Wesleyan Ch., Arlington, Ind., 1983-87, Oak Hill & Riley (Ind.) United Meth. Chs., 1990—; assoc. Brames, Bopp, Abel & Oldham, Terre Haute, Ind., 1987-92; staff counsel Nat. Legal Ctr. for the Medically Dependent and Disabled, Terre Haute, Ind., 1992-99; sr. assoc. Bopp, Coleson & Bostrom, Terre Haute, Ind., 1992—. Contbr. articles to profl. jours. Mem. Vigo County Election Bd., Terre Haute, 1993-97. Recipient Outstanding Achievement award Ind. Wesleyan U. Alumni Assn., 1997. Appellate, Federal civil litigation, Constitutional. Office: Bopp Coleson & Bostrom 1 South 6th St Terre Haute IN 47807-3510

COLESSIDES, NICK JOHN, lawyer; b. Kavala, Greece, Jan. 14, 1938; came to U.S., 1958; s. John T. and Maroula C.; m. Sophia Simons Symeonidis, Oct. 5, 1970. BS in Polit. Sci., U. Utah, 1963, MS Polit. Sci., 1967, JD, 1970. Bar: Utah 1970, U.S. Dist. Ct. Utah 1970, U.S. Ct. Appeals (10th cir.) 1970, U.S. Dist. Ct. (so. dist.) Ohio 1975, U.S. Ct. Appeals (9th cir.) 1976. Chief deputy county atty. Salt Lake County (Utah) Atty.'s Office, 1970-74; city atty. West Jordan (Utah) City Atty.'s Office, 1971-78, Park City (Utah) Atty.'s Office, 1976-80; atty. pvt. practice, Salt Lake City, 1970—. Bd. dirs. Merrill Lynch Bank, U.S.A., Salt Lake City City. Trustee Greek Orthodox Ch., SaltLake City, 1976, 77, 87, 88, 98, 99, Utah Cmty. Reinvestment Corp. Mem. Assn. Trial Lawyers Am., Utah Trial Lawyers Assn., U. Utah Coll. of Law Alumni Assn. (trustee 1995-98), Utah State Bar Assn., Salt Lake County Bar Assn., Am. Inn of Ct. VII (master of the bench, pres. 1997, 98). Greek Orthodox. Avocations: gardening, cooking, reading. Federal civil litigation, State civil litigation, Property, real (including real estate development, water). Office: 466 S 400 E Ste 100 Salt Lake City UT 84111-3301 Home: Apt 410 150 S 300 E Salt Lake City UT 84111-2087

COLETTA, RALPH JOHN, retired lawyer; b. Chillicothe, Ill., Dec. 13, 1921; s. Joseph and Assunta Maria (Aromatario) C.; m. Ethel Mary Meyers, Nov. 19, 1949; children: Jean, Marianne, Suzanne, Joseph, Robert, Michele, Renee. BS, Bradley U., 1943; JD, U. Chgo., 1949. Bar: Ill. 1949. Practice law, Peoria, Ill., 1949-99; gen. ptnr. Ralet Ltd. Partnership, Peoria, Ill.; ret., 1999. Pres. White Star Corp., Mark Tidd, Inc.; asst. state's atty. Peoria County. Chmn. United Fund. Served to 1st lt. AUS, 1943-46. Mem. ABA, Ill. State Bar Assn., Peoria County Bar Assn., Chgo. Bar Assn., Creve Coeur Club, Mt. Hawley Country Club, K.C., Union League Club. Republican. Roman Catholic. Estate planning, Probate (including wills, trusts), Property, real (including real estate development, water). Home: 301 W Crestwood Dr Peoria IL 61614-7328

COLETTI, JOHN ANTHONY, lawyer, furniture and realty company executive; b. Cherry Point, N.C., Sept. 22, 1952; s. Joseph Nicholas and Gloria Lucy (Fusco) C.; m. Barbara Nancy Carlotti, July 20, 1975; children: Lisa M., Kristen B. Student, Biscayne Coll., 1970-72; BA summa cum laude, Boston Coll., 1974, JD, 1977. Bar; R.I. 1977, U.S. Dist. Ct. R.I. 1977. Assoc. Resmini, Fornaro, Colagiovanni & Angell, Providence, 1979-81; ptnr. Coletti & Tente, Cranston, R.I., 1981—. Pres. Coletti's Furniture, Inc., Johnston R.I., 1983-95, Coletti's Realty, Inc., Johnston, 1983-96. Legal counsel Cranston Housing Authority, 1988—; interviewer alumni admissions coun. Boston Coll., 1980—. Mem. ABA, R.I. Bar Assn., R.I. Conveyancers Assn., Nat. Assn. Retail Collection Attys., Phi Beta Kappa. Roman Catholic. Avocations: horseback riding, golf, figure skating. Commercial, consumer (including collections, credit), General practice, Property, real (including real estate development, water). Office: Coletti & Tente 311 Doric Ave Cranston RI 02910-2903

COLFIN, BRUCE ELLIOTT, lawyer, video producer; b. Bklyn., June 9, 1951; s. Abraham and Sylvia (Laykin) C.; m. Virginia Mary Faszczewski, Sept. 27, 1981. BA, CUNY, 1977; JD, N.Y. Law Sch., 1980. Bar: N.Y. 1982, U.S. Dist. Ct. (so., ea. dists.) N.Y., 1987, U.S. Ct. Internat. Trade, 1990. Audio engr. Snowball Sound Systems, N. Bergen, N.J., 1974-77; producer, dir. cable TV program What's On, N.Y.C., 1976-84; stage mgr. Peter Tosh U.S. tour Rolling Stones Records, 1978; v.p., producer Upswing Artists Mgmt., N.Y.C., 1979-86; pres., producer, dir. LegalVision, Inc., N.Y.C., 1982-87; ptnr. Jacobson & Colfin, N.Y.C. and Washington, 1985-90; mem. Jacobson & Colfin, P.C., N.Y.C. and Washington, 1990—; pres. Fifth Ave. Media, Ltd., N.Y.C., 1996—. Assoc. prof. music bus. and tech. Five Towns Coll., 1999—; spkr. Discovery Ctr., N.Y., 1st Ann. Musicians Seminar, L.I., N.Y. Law Sch. Media Law Soc., 1986; vis. lectr. SUNY, Oneonta, 1988—; panelist New Eng. Music Orgn. Conf., 1998, Emerging Artists and Talent in Music, 1999, 2002. Assoc. producer music video Blues Alive, 1982; exec. prodr., dir. video series Entertainment Law Video Primer, 1984; exec. prodr. (CD) Zen Tricksters, 1999; monthly columnist Ind. Music Producers Soc. Jour., NARAS N.Y. chpt. newsletter; contbr. articles to profl. jours.;

columnist: Replication News, 1998, Medialine, 2000. Mem. ABA (com. on entertainment sports law, subcom. chmn. patent, trademark and copyright com. 1989, subcom. chmn. internat. law and practice, internat. intellectual property rights com., spl. subcom. on multimedia 1994—, editl. advisor pubs. com. internat. law sect. 1990-92, exec. com. entertainment law cir. 1989-91, com. on authors of intellectual property law sect. 2001--), NATAS (N.Y. chpt., mem. new media com., internet sub-com.), N.Y. State Bar Assn. (entertainment, arts and sports law sect., com. on talent agys. and talent mgmt., com. on rights of publicity 1994—), Nassau County Bar Assn. (vice chmn. entertainment, sports and media law com.), Spkrs. Bur. Entertainment and Sports Law Comm., Copyright Soc. U.S.A. (editl. bd. 1986-88), Nat. Acad. of Recording Arts and Scis. (N.Y. chpt.). Jewish. Avocations: traveling, writing, stamp collecting, hockey. General civil litigation, Entertainment, Trademark and copyright. Office: Jacobson & Colfin PC 19 W 21st St Rm 603A New York NY 10010 E-mail: BRUCE@Thefirm.com.

COLGAN, JEREMY SPENCER, lawyer; b. Belfast, Jan. 14, 1972; s. John Michael and Kathleen C. LLB with honors, Queens U., Belfast, 1995. Bar: Eng., Wales 1996, N.Y. 2001. Barrister Chambers of Michael Ashe Q.C., London, 1996-97, Queen Elizabeth Bldg. Chambers of Lindsey Burn, London, 1997-98; assoc. Gide Loyrette Nouel, Paris, 1998-99; sr. assoc. Beijing, 1999—2001; assoc. Hawkins, Delafield & Wood, NY, 2002—. Contbr. articles to profl. jour. Key note spkr. All-China Fin. and Tax. Mgmt. Summit, Beijing, 2000. Accomodation scholar Honorable Soc. Inner Temple, 1996; named bursary Honorable Soc. Inner Temple, 1995. Mem. Honorable Soc. Knights Round Table (esquire, Sunley prize 1996). Municipal (including bonds). Office: Hawkins Delafield & Wood 67 Wall St New York NY 10005 Office Fax: 212-820-9615. E-mail: jeremycolgan@hotmail.com., jscolgan@hdw.com.

COLISTRA, BRIAN WILLIAM, lawyer; b. Islip, NY, Sept. 25, 1969; s. Joseph Anthony and Monica Kathleen Colistra; m. Nancimarie Rose Pullo, Sept. 22, 2002. BS, Canisius Coll., 1991; JD, NY Law Sch., 1995. Bar: NY, U.S. Dist. Ct. (so. dist.) NY. Asst. dist. atty. Orange County Dist. Atty.'s Office, Goshen, NY, 1995—2000; trial assoc. Pino and Assocs., White Plains, NY, 2000—. Republican. Roman Catholic. Avocations: running, rugby , reading, politics. Construction, Product liability, Toxic tort. Office: Pino & Assocs 50 Main St White Plains NY 10606 E-mail: bcolistra@pinolaw.com.

COLL, JOHN PETER, JR., lawyer; b. Pitts., Oct. 5, 1943; s. John Peter and Lelia (Nicolussi) C.; m. Nancy Kaye Swan; children: John Peter, Alexis S. AB in Polit. Sci., Duke U., 1965; JD, Georgetown U., 1968. Bar: N.Y. 1969, U.S. Dist. Ct. (so. dist.) N.Y. 1970, U.S. Dist. Ct. (ea. dist.) N.Y. 1974, U.S. Ct. Appeals (2d cir.) 1972, U.S. Supreme Ct. 1974, U.S. Ct. Appeals (5th cir.) 1981, U.S. Ct. Appeals (11th cir.) 1981, U.S. Ct. Appeals (8th cir.) 1980, U.S. Ct. Appeals (6th cir.) 1991, U.S. Ct. Appeals (1st cir.) 1993, U.S. Ct. Appeals (3d cir.) 1994, U.S. Ct. Appeals (9th cir.) 1994, U.S. Dist. Ct. (no. dist.) Calif. 1983, U.S. Dist. Ct. (no. dist.) N.Y. 1984, U.S. Dist. Ct. (we. dist.) N.Y. 1988, U.S. Tax Ct. 1990, U.S. Ct. Appeals (fed. cir.) 1999. Assoc. Donovan Leisure Newton & Irvine LLP, N.Y.C., 1968-76, ptnr., 1976-98, chmn. exec. com., 1989-98; ptnr. Orrick, Herington & Sutcliffe, LLP, N.Y.C., 1998—, mem. exec. com., 2000—. Bd. advisors product safety and liability rep. BNA, 1991—; mem. litigation steering com. Def. Rsch. Inst., 1991—97. Contbg. author: Preparing for and Trying the Civil Law Suit, 1987, Supplement, 2003, Commercial Litigation in New York State Courts, 1995, Supplement, 2003, Products Liability in New York, Strategy and Practice, 1997. Mem. ABA (litigation sect. 1983—), Fed. Bar Coun., N.Y. State Bar Assn., Assn. of Bar of City of N.Y., N.Y. Coun. Law Assocs. (mem. steering com. 1971-72), Lawrence Beach Club (bd. govs. 1991-2000), Cherry Valley Club, Univ. Club. Democrat. Roman Catholic. Federal civil litigation, General civil litigation, State civil litigation. Home: 385 Stewart Ave Garden City NY 11530-4615 Office: Orrick Herrington and Sutcliffe LLP 666 5th Ave New York NY 10103-1798

COLLEN, JOHN, lawyer; b. Chgo., Dec. 26, 1954; s. Sheldon and Ann Collen; m. Lauren Kay Smulyan, Sept. 20, 1986; children: Joshua, Benjamin, Sarah, Joel. AB summa cum laude, Dartmouth Coll., 1977; JD, Georgetown U., 1980. Bar: Ill. 1980, U.S. Dist. Ct. (no. dist.) Ill. 1980, Trial 1982, U.S. Ct. Appeals (7th cir.) 1984, U.S. Supreme Ct. 1990. Ptnr. Duane Morris, LLC, Chgo. Mem. editl. adv. bd. Journal of Bankruptcy Law & Practice. Author: Buying and Selling Real Estate in Bankruptcy, 1997; contbr. articles to profl. jours.; lectr. in field. Mem. ABA, Chgo. Bar Assn., Am. Bankruptcy Inst. (co-chmn. com. real estate bankruptcy), Phi Beta Kappa. Avocations: water sports, magic, biographies. Bankruptcy, Property, real (including real estate development, water). Office: Duane Morris LLC 227 W Monroe St Chicago IL 60606-5016 Fax: 312-499-6701. E-mail: jcollen@duanemorris.com.

COLLERAN, KEVIN, lawyer; b. Spalding, Nebr., July 16, 1941; s. James Edward and Helen Marcella (Vybiral) C.; m. Karen Ann Rooney, Aug. 1, 1964; children: Mary Jane, Patrick. BS, U. Nebr., 1964, JD with distinction, 1968. Bar: Nebr. 1968, U.S. Dist. Ct. Nebr. 1968, U.S. Dist. Ct. (we. dist.) La. 1975, U.S. Dist. Ct. (no. dist.) Tex. 1978, U.S. Supreme Ct. 1980, U.S. Ct. Appeals (8th cir.) 1981. Law. clk. U.S. Dist. Ct. Nebr., 1968-69; assoc. Cline, Williams, Wright, Johnson & Oldfather, LLP, Lincoln, Nebr., 1969-74, ptnr., 1975—, mng. ptnr., 1985-89, 96—. Bd. dirs. Lancaster County unit Am. Cancer Soc., 1972-83, pres., 1979. Fellow Am. Coll. Trial Lawyers; mem. ABA, Am. Bd. Trial Advocates, Nebr. Bar Assn. (chmn. worker's compensation com. 1980-82, chmn. civil practice and procedure com. 2001-02), Internat. Assn. Def. Counsel, Nat. Assn. Trial Attys., Order of Coif. Democrat. Federal civil litigation, State civil litigation, Environmental. Office: Cline Williams Wright Johnson & Oldfather LLP US Bank Bldg Ste 1900 233 S 13th St Lincoln NE 68508 E-mail: kcolleran@cline-law.com.

COLLIER, CHARLES ARTHUR, JR., lawyer; b. Columbus, Ohio, Apr. 18, 1930; s. Charles Arthur and Gertrude Clara (Roe) C.; m. Linda Louise Biggs, Aug. 5, 1961; children: Sheila Collier Rogers, Laura Collier Prescott. AB magna cum laude, Harvard U., 1952, LLB, 1955. Law clk. U.S. Dist. Ct. (cen. dist.) Calif., L.A., 1959-60; assoc. Freston & Files, L.A., 1960-66; assoc., ptnr. Mitchell, Silberberg & Knupp, L.A., 1967-82; ptnr. Irell & Manella, L.A., 1982-95, of counsel, 1995—. Lectr. Calif. Continuing Edn. of Bar, 1976-89; advisor Restatement of Property, Donative Transfers, 1990—; speaker numerous local bar assns. Contbr. articles to profl. jours. Recipient Arthur K. Marshall award Probate and Trust sect. L.A. County Bar Assn. Fellow Am. Coll. Trust and Estate Counsel (chmn. state laws com. 1986-89, regent 1989-98, joint editl. bd. uniform trust and estate acts, 1988—, chmn. expanded practice com. 1989-92, chmn. nominating com. 1998-99, spkr. 1988, exec. com. 1989-98, treas. 1992-93, sec. 1993-94, v.p. 1994-95, pres.-elect 1995-96, pres. 1996-97, immediate past pres. 1997-98), ABA Found.; mem. ABA (mem. real property, trust and probate law sect. spkr. 1985, 89, moderator teleconf. 1998, coun. 1989-93, chmn. com. trust adminstrn. 1982-85, chmn. task force on fiduciary litigation 1986-89, sr. lawyers divsn., vice chair wills, probate and trusts com. 1999-2000, chair 2000-2001, vice chair book pub. com. 2000-2002, chair editl. bd. 2001--, others), Estate Planning, Trust and Probate Law Sect. of State Bar Calif. (chmn. 1980-81, vice chmn. 1979-80, mem. exec. com. 1977-82, advisor 1982-85, chmn. probate com. 1977-78, mem. legislation com. 1977-80, sect. liaison to Calif. Law Revision Commn. 1982-88), Internat. Acad. Estate and Trust Law, Harvard Alumni Assn. (dir. 1975-77, v.p. 1979-82), Harvard Club So. Calif. (pres. 1970-72). Republican. Methodist. Office: Irell & Manella LLP 1800 Ave Of Stars Ste 900 Los Angeles CA 90067-4276 E-mail: ccollier@irell.com.

COLLIER, JAMES BRUCE, lawyer; b. Ironton, Ohio, Sept. 25, 1920; s. James W. and Faye L. (Clark) C.; m. Bette E. Fawcett, Mar. 24, 1943; children: James B. Jr., Gretchen J. Randall. Student, Miami U., Oxford, Ohio, 1938-41; LLB, State U. Iowa, 1949. Bar: Iowa 1949, Ohio 1949, U.S. Dist. Ct. (so. dist.) Ohio 1950, U.S. Ct. Appeals (6th cir.) 1961, U.S. Supreme Ct. 1960. Pvt. practice, Ironton, 1949—. Chmn. Lawrence County Rep. Ctrl. Com., Ironton, 1955-85; mem., pres. Ironton City Sch. Bd., 1962-66. Capt. USAAF, 1941-46. Mem. Ohio Bar Assn., Lawrence County Bar Assn. Episcopalian. Avocations: fishing, boating, competitive pistol shooting. General civil litigation, Probate (including wills, trusts). Home: 1111 Mastin Ave Ironton OH 45638-2223 Office: Collier & Collier 411 Center St Ironton OH 45638-1506

COLLIER, JAMES WARREN, lawyer; b. Dallas, July 31, 1940; s. J.W. and Mary Gertrude (Roberts) C.; m. Judith Lane, Dec. 27, 1964; children: Anne Elizabeth, Jennifer Susan. BA, U. Mich., 1962, JD, 1965. Bar: N.Y. 1966, Mich. 1968. Assoc. Simpson Thacher & Bartlett, N.Y.C., 1965-66; tax atty. office gen. counsel Ford Motor Co., 1966-67; assoc. Dykema Gossett, Detroit, 1967-73, ptnr., 1973—. Mem. Dykema Gossett. Mem. ABA, Mich. Bar Assn., Econ. Club Detroit, Lochmoor Club. Commercial, contracts (including sales of goods; commercial financing), Corporate, general, Environmental. Office: Dykema Gossett 400 Renaissance Ctr # 3500 Detroit MI 48243-1603 E-mail: jcollier@dykema.com.

COLLIN, THOMAS JAMES, lawyer; b. Windom, Minn., Jan. 6, 1949; s. Everett Earl and Genevieve May (Wilson) C.; m. Victoria Gatov, Oct. 11, 1985; children: Arielle, Elise, Sarah. BA, U. Minn., 1970; AM, Harvard U., 1972; JD, Georgetown U., 1974. Bar: Ohio 1975, U.S. Dist. Ct. (no. dist.) Ohio 1975, U.S. Ct. Appeals (10th cir.) 1977, U.S. Supreme Ct. 1980, U.S. Ct. Appeals (6th cir.) 1981, U.S. Ct. Appeals (8th cir.) 1982, U.S. Ct. Appeals (7th cir.) 1997, U.S. Ct. Appeals (11th cir.) 1999. Law clk. to Judge Myron Bright U.S. Ct. Appeals, 8th Cir., St. Louis, Mo., 1974-75; assoc. Thompson, Hine & Flory, LLP, Cleve., 1975-82, ptnr., 1982--. Author: Ohio Business Competition Law, 1994, (with others) Criminal Antitrust Litigation Manual, 1983; editor: Punitive Damages and Business Torts: A Practitioner's Handbook, 1998; contbr. articles to profl. jours. Active Citizens League, Cleve., bd. trustees, 1994-99, v.p., 1995-97, pres. 1997-99; bd. trustees Citizens League Rsch. Inst., Cleve., 1999-2002. Mem. ABA (chair bus. torts and unfair competition com. antitrust sect. 1995-98, chair annual mtg. com. 2001-02, chmn. franchise and dealership com. 2002-), Ohio State Bar Assn. (bd. govs. antitrust sect. 1988-98). Republican. Avocations: book collecting, music. Antitrust, Federal civil litigation, Intellectual property. Home: 7879 Oakhurst Dr Cleveland OH 44141-1123 Office: Thompson Hine LLP 127 Public Sq Cleveland OH 44114-1216

COLLINGS, ROBERT L. lawyer; b. May 22, 1950; AB, Harvard U., 1972; JD, Boston Coll., 1977. Bar: Pa. 1977, U.S. Ct. Appeals (D.C. cir.) 1981, U.S. Dist. Ct. (ea. dist.) Pa. 1985, U.S. Ct. Appeals (3d cir.) 1984, U.S. Dist. Ct. (mid. dist.) 1992. Atty. U.S. EPA, 1977-84, sect. chief, 1979-81, br. chief, 1981-84; ptnr., chair litigation dept., mem. exec. com. Schnader, Harrison, Segal & Lewis LLP, Phila., 1984—. Editor: Environmental Spill Reporting Handbook; contbr. Municipal Solicitors Handbook, 1994, 1999, 2003, Brownfields: A Comprehensive Guide, 1997, 2d edit., 2002. Mem. Phila. Bar Assn. (chair environ. law com. 1986), Water Resources Assn. (sec. exec. com. 1990—). Administrative and regulatory, Environmental, Personal injury (including property damage). Office: Schnader Harrison Segal & Lewis LLP 1600 Market St Ste 3600 Philadelphia PA 19103-7287

COLLINS, AUDREY B. judge; b. 1945; BA, Howard U., 1967; MA, Am. U., 1969; JD, UCLA, 1977. Asst. atty. Legal Aid Found. L.A., 1977-78; with Office L.A. County Dist. Atty., 1978-94, dept. dist. atty., 1978-94, asst. dir. burs. ctrl. ops. and spl. ops., 1988-92, asst. dir. atty., 1992-94; judge. U.S. Dist. Ct. (Ctrl. Dist.) Calif., 1994—. Dep. gen. counsel Office Spl. Acad. scholar Howard U.; named Lawyer of Yr., Langston Bar Assn., 1988; honoree Howard U. Alumni Club So. Calif., 1989; recipient Profl. Achievement award UCLA Alumni Assn., 1997, Ernestine Stahlhut award, Women Lawyers Assn., 1999. Mem. FBA, Nat. Assn. Women Judges, Nat. Bar Assn. (life), State Bar Calif. (com. bar examiners, chmn. subcom. on moral character 1992-93, co-chmn. 1993-94), Los Angeles County Bar Assn. (task force on criminal justice sys. 2002-03), Assn. Los Angeles County Dist. Attys. (pres. 1983), Black Women Lawyers Los Angeles County, Women Lawyers L.A. (life, Ernestine Stahlhut award 1999), Calif. Women Lawyers (life), Order of Coif, Phi Beta Kappa. Office: US Dist Ct Edward R Roybal Fed Bldg 255 E Temple St Ste 670 Los Angeles CA 90012-3334

COLLINS, DANIEL FRANCIS, lawyer; b. N.Y.C., Mar. 5, 1942; s. Daniel Joseph and Madeline Elizabeth (Berger) C.; m. Margaret Mary Heyden, Jan. 15, 1966; children: Matthew C., Elizabeth C. BA in History and Polit. Sci., Hofstra U., 1964; JD, Am. U., 1967. Bar: D.C. 1968. Law clk. to E. Barrett Prettyman U.S. Ct. Appeals, Washington, 1967-68; assoc. Ross, Marsh & Foster, Washington, 1970-74, mem., 1974-78; ptnr. Brackett & Collins, P.C., Washington, 1978-87; v.p. regulatory law The Coastal Corp., Washington, 1987-2001; sr. v.p., dep. gen. counsel El Paso Corp., Washington, 2001—. Administrative and regulatory, FERC practice, General civil litigation. Office: El Paso Corp Ste 750 555 11th St NW Washington DC 20004 E-mail: daniel.collins@elpaso.com.

COLLINS, J. BARCLAY, II, lawyer, oil company executive; b. Gettysburg, Pa., Oct. 21, 1944; s. Jennings Barclay and Golda Olevia (Hook) C.; m. Janna Claire Fall, June 25, 1966; children: J. Barclay III, L. Christian. AB magna cum laude, Harvard U., 1966; JD magna cum laude, Columbia U., 1969. Bar: N.Y. 1969. Law clk. to presiding judge U.S. Ct. Appeals (2d cir.), N.Y.C., 1969-70; assoc. Cravath, Swaine and Moore, N.Y.C., 1970-78; v.p., asst. gen. counsel City Investing Co., N.Y.C., 1978-84; exec. v.p., gen. counsel Amerada Hess Corp., N.Y.C., 1984—, also bd. dirs. Bd. dirs. Premier Oil plc, Nuvera Fuel Oils Inc. Trustee Bklyn. Hosp., Bklyn.; bd. dirs. United Hosp. Fund N.Y., past gov. Bklyn. Heights Assn. Mem. ABA, N.Y. Bar Assn., N.Y.C. Yacht Club. Clubs: Heights Casino (Bklyn.); Harvard N.Y.C. Office: Amerada Hess Corp Ste 810 1185 Avenue Of The Americas Fl 800 New York NY 10036-2601

COLLINS, JAMES SLADE, II, lawyer; b. St. Louis, June 9, 1937; s. James Slade and Dolma Ruby (Neilsen) C.; m. Neva Frances Guinn, June 27, 1959; children: Shari, Camala Ann. BSBA, Washington U., 1958, JD, 1961. Bar: Mo. 1961, U.S. Supreme Ct. 1969, U.S. Dist. Ct. (ea. dist.) Mo. 1972, U.S. Ct. Appeals (8th cir.) 1972. Assoc. Whalen, O'Connor, Grauel & Sarkisian, St. Louis, 1961-70, ptnr., 1970-72, Whalen, O'Connor, Collins & Danis, St. Louis, 1972-75; assoc. Hullverson, Hullverson & Frank, Inc., St. Louis, 1975-78; pvt. practice St. Louis, 1979—. Trustee Village of Hanley Hills, Mo., 1966-69, mayor, 1967, mcpl. judge, 1967-68, 69-70. Mem. ABA, ATLA, Mo. Trial Lawyers Assn., Bar Assn. Met. St. Louis, Lawyers Assn. St. Louis, Phi Delta Phi. Republican. Baptist. Federal civil litigation, State civil litigation, Personal injury (including property damage). Home: 916 Parkwatch Dr Ballwin MO 63011-3640 Office: 6654 Chippewa St Saint Louis MO 63109-2527 E-mail: jcollinslaw@aol.com.

COLLINS, JEFFREY G. lawyer; b. Detroit, Mar. 16, 1959; m. Lois Collins; 2 children. BA in Psychology, Northwestern U., 1981; JD, Howard U. Sch. Law, 1984. Pvt. practice, 1984—94; appointed judge Detroit Recorder's Ct., 1994—96; cir. judge Wayne County Cir. Ct., 1997—98; judge Mich. Supreme Ct., 1998—2000; appointed judge Mich. Ct. Appeals, 2000—. Mentor Man to Man program Paul Robeson Acad.; mem. Plymouth United Ch. of Christ, Detroit. Mem.: Mich. Assn. for Leadership Devel. (founder, dir. Wayne County chpt.). Office: Ea Dist Mich 211 W Fort St Ste 2000 Detroit MI 48226-3211*

COLLINS, JOHN F. lawyer; b. N.Y.C., Dec. 15, 1948; AB, Fordham U., 1970; JD, U. Chgo., 1973. Bar: N.Y. 1974. Ptnr. Dewey Ballantine, N.Y.C. Mem. ABA, N.Y. State Bar Assn., Assn. Bar of City of N.Y., Phi Beta Kappa. Antitrust, General civil litigation, Securities. Office: Dewey Ballantine 1301 Avenue Of The Americas New York NY 10019-6022

COLLINS, JOHN PETER, lawyer; b. New Rochelle, N.Y., Mar. 3, 1944; s. William Thomas and Diane G. Collins; m. Martha Ann Gorman; children: Patrick Michael, Matthew Peter, Kathryn Corby, John Peter Jr., Meighan O'Connor. BS, Xavier U., 1966; JD, U. Cin., 1969. Bar: N.Y. 1969, U.S. Ct. Mil. Appeals 1970, U.S. Dist. Ct. (so. dist.) N.Y. 1978, U.S. Supreme Ct. 1988, U.S. Dist. Ct. (ea. dist.) N.Y. 2002. Asst. dist. atty. Westchester County Dist. Atty., White Plains, NY, 1969—70; assoc. King Edwards O'Connor, White Plains, 1977—79; ptnr. O'Connor, McGuinness Conte Doyle Oleson & Collins, White Plains, 1980—99, Burchetta Collins and Hanley, Carmel, NY, 1999—2002, Collins, Hanley & LaFrance, Carmel, NY, 2003—. Justice Town of Kent, NY, 2000—. Maj. U.S. Army, 1970—77. Mem.: ATLA, Strathmore's (life), Putnam County Bar Assn., N.Y. State Bar Assn. Personal injury (including property damage). Office: Collins Hanley & LaFrance LLP 9 Fair St Carmel NY 10512-1301

COLLINS, KEVIN HEATH, lawyer; b. Cedar Rapids, Iowa, May 7, 1955; s. Thomas Martin and Joanne (Heath) C.; m. Sally A. Stephenson, June 11, 1985. BA, Creighton U., 1978; JD, U. Iowa, 1981. Bar: Iowa 1980, Hawaii 1982, U.S. Dist. Ct. (no. and so. dist.) Iowa 1981, U.S. Dist. Ct. Hawaii, 1982, U.S. Ct. Appeals (8th cir.) 1981, U.S. Ct. Appeals (9th cir.) 1982, U.S. Supreme Ct. 1984. Sr. v.p. Shuttleworth & Ingersoll, P.C., Cedar Rapids, 1980-82, 84—; assoc. Dinman & Yokoyama, P.C., Honolulu, 1982-84. Exec. com. United Way of East Cen. Iowa, Cedar Rapids, 1986—, Retired Sr. Vol. Program, Cedar Rapids, 1986—. Mem. ABA, Am. Arbitration Assn. (panel mem.), Iowa State Bar Assn. (co-chair com. on delivery of legal svcs. to the elderly 1989-90, mem. law practice mgmt. sect. 1991-98, bd. govs. 1998-2001, v.p. 2001-02, pres.-elect 2002-), Hawaii State Bar Assn. General civil litigation, Computer, Immigration, naturalization, and customs. Office: Shuttleworth Ingersoll PLC PO Box 2107 Cedar Rapids IA 52406-2107*

COLLINS, SAMUEL W., JR., judge; b. Caribou, Maine, Sept. 17, 1923; s. Samuel Wilson Collins & Elizabeth Black C; m. Dorothy Small, 1952; children: Edward, Elizabeth, Diane. BA, U. Maine; JD, Harvard U. Lawyer, Rockland, Maine, 1947—; justice Supreme Jud. Ct., Portland, Maine. Trustee Rockland Sch. Dist, 1949-61; Maine State Senate Dist. 21, 1975-84, majority leader, 1981-82, minority leader, 1983-84. Recipient Disting. Svc. award Jaycees, 1978. Mem. Maine Bar Assn., Rotary, Phi Beta Kappa, Phi Kappa Phi, Delta Tau Delta. Unitarian Universalist. Republican. Office: Knox County Courthouse 62 Union St Rockland ME 04841-2836

COLLINS, STEVEN M. lawyer; b. Atlanta, Oct. 22, 1952; s. E.B. and Judith (Morse) C.; divorced; 1 child, Erin M.; m. Anne Frances Garland, Oct. 31, 1987; 1 child, Timothy G. AB, Harvard U., 1974, JD, 1977. Bar: Ga. 1977, U.S. Dist. Ct. (no. dist.) Ga. 1977, U.S. Ct. Appeals (11th cir.) 1981, U.S. Dist. Ct. (mid. dist.) Ga. 1982, U.S. Tax Ct. 1984, U.S. Ct. Appeals (4th cir.) 1986, U.S. Ct. Appeals (6th cir.) 2001, U.S. Supreme Ct. 1994. Assoc. Alston & Bird, Atlanta, 1977-83, ptnr., 1983—. Editor-in-chief Ga. State Bar Journal, Atlanta, 1982-84. Mem. ABA, State Bar Ga., Atlanta Bar Assn. Banking, General civil litigation, Securities. Office: Alston & Bird One Atlantic Ctr 1201 W Peachtree St NW Atlanta GA 30309-3424 E-mail: scollins@alston.com.

COLLINS, THEODORE JOHN, lawyer; b. Walla Walla, Wash., Oct. 2, 1936; s. Robert Bonfield and Catherine Roselle (Snyder) C.; m. Patricia Spengler Pasieka, May 11, 1968; children: Jonathan, Caitlin, Matthew, Patrick, Flannary. BA, U. Notre Dame, 1958; postgrad., U. Bonn, Fed. Republic Germany, 1959; LLB, Harvard U., 1962. Bar: Wash. 1962, U.S. Supreme Ct. 1982, U.S. Ct. Appeals (fed. cir.) 1982, U.S. Dist. Ct. (ea. dist.) Wash. 1965, U.S. Dist. Ct. (we. dist.) Wash. 1962. Ptnr. Perkins Coie Law Firm, Seattle, 1962-86; v.p., gen. counsel The Boeing Co., Seattle, 1986-98, sr. v.p., gen. counsel, 1998-2000; of counsel Perkins Coie Law Firm, 2001—. Adj. prof. Seattle U. Law Sch. Mem. ABA, Wash. State Bar Assn., King County Bar Assn., Wash. Athletic Club. General civil litigation, Corporate, general, Government contracts and claims. E-mail: tcoll10236@aol.com., collt@perkinscoie.com.

COLLINS, THOMAS HANSEN, federal agency administrator, coast guard officer; b. Quincy, Mass., June 25, 1946; s. Harley Hartford and Inger Dagmar (Hansen) C.; m. Constance Ann Monahan, June 7, 1968; children: Christine Ann, Kathryn. BS, USCG Acad., New London, Conn., 1968; MA in Liberal Studies, Wesleyan U., 1972; MBA, U. New Haven, 1976. Commd. 1st lt. USCG, 1968, advanced through grades to rear adm., 1994; comdg. officer USCG Cutter, Cape Morgan, Charleston, S.C., 1969-71; instr., prof. USCG Acad., 1972-76; mem. planning program, budget staff Office of R&D USCG Hdqs., Washington, 1976-80; dep. group comdr. USCG Group, St. Petersburg, Fla., 1980-83; mem. program rev. staff USCG Hdqs., Washington, 1983-87; group comdr. USCG Group L.I. Sound, New Haven, 1987-90; chief adminstrn. divsn. USCG Dist. 14, Honolulu, 1990-92; chief program divsn. USCG Hdqs., Washington, 1992-94, dep. chief of staff, 1994—98, chief office of acquisition, 1994—; comdr, Pac. area and 11th Coast Guard dist. U.S. Coast Guard, 1998—2000, vice-commandant, 2000—02, commandant, 2002—. Decorated Legion of Merit, Meritorious Svc. medal (2), Coast Guard Commendation medal (3). Mem. Am. Soc. Naval Engrs. (hon.). Avocations: golf, gardening, reading. Office: Comdt US Coast Guard 2100 2nd St SW Washington DC 20593*

COLLINS, TODD STOWE, lawyer; b. Chgo., Oct. 18, 1952; s. Thomas Hightower and Beulah Stowe Collins; m. Susan Faith Burt, June 19, 1982; children: Rachel, Katherine, Leila. BA, U. Pa., 1973, JD, 1978. Bar: Pa. 1979, Del. 1979, U.S. Dist. Ct. (ea. dist.) Pa. 1979, U.S. Dist. Ct. Del. 1979, U.S. Ct. Appeals (llth cir.) 1989, U.S. Ct. Appeals (9th cir.) 1996. Assoc. Potter Anderson & Carroon, Wilmington, Del., 1978-80, Braemer & Kessler, Phila., 1980-82, Berger & Montague, PC, Phila., 1982-85, shareholder, 1986—. Bd. dirs. Phila. Sr. Ctr., 1994—. Mem. Phila. Bar Assn. Episcopalian. Avocations: tennis, biking, gardening, military history. Federal civil litigation, Securities. Office: Berger & Montague PC 1622 Locust St Philadelphia PA 19103-6305 E-mail: tcollins@bm.net.

COLLINS, WAYNE DALE, lawyer; b. Portsmouth, Va., Dec. 23, 1951; s. Wayne D. Sr. and Mary. L. (Higdon) C.; m. Mary Ann Bradshaw, Aug. 9, 1981; children: Laura, Melissa, Christopher. BS with honors, Calif. Inst. Tech., 1973, MS, 1974; JD, U. Chgo., 1978; postgrad., U. Minn., 1979. Bar: N.Y. 1979, U.S. Supreme Ct. 1983, D.C., 1991. Assoc. Shearman & Sterling, N.Y.C., 1978-81, 83-86, ptnr., 1987—; spl. asst. to V.P. George Bush, Washington, 1981-82; dep. asst. atty. gen. antitrust div. U.S. Dept. Justice, Washington, 1983. Vis. lectr. Yale Law Sch., 1991-95. Co-author: Horizontal Mergers: Law and Policy, 1986, Non-Horizontal Mergers: Law and Policy, 1988, State Antitrust Practice and Statutes, 1991. White House fellow, 1981-82. Fellow Am. Bar Found.; mem. ABA (chmn. antitrust sect. subcom. on fin. markets and instns. 1983-87, chmn. pub. com. 1987-91, coun. mem. antitrust sect. 1991-94, officer antitrust sect. 1994-1999), Am. Law Inst., Assn. of Bar of City of N.Y., Am. Econ. Assn., Econometric Soc., Soc. for Advancement of Econ. Theory, Am. Coun. Nationalities Svc. (bd. dirs. 1988-1999). Republican. Roman Catholic. Antitrust, Constitutional. Office: 599 Lexington Ave New York NY 10022-6030 also: 801 Pennsylvania Ave NW Washington DC 20004-2615

COLLINSON, BRENT PATRICK, lawyer; b. Merced, Calif., Jan. 9, 1952; s. Roger Whitfield and Aileen June C.; m. Dianne Louise West, June 22, 1974. BA, U. Calif., Davis, 1974; JD, U. Pacific, 1979. Bar: Calif. 1979, U.S. Dist. Ct. (ea. dist.) Calif. 1979. Assoc. Law Offices of George L. Pifer, Truckee, Calif., 1979-80, Richard J. Schneider P.C., Truckee, 1981-82; ptnr. Schneider, Collinson & Lange, Truckee, 1983-84; pvt. practice law Truckee, 1985-90; ptnr. Collinson & Clancy, Truckee, 1991-93; pvt. practice Truckee, 1993—. Bd. dirs., Truckee Group Individual & Family Counseling; instr. Sierra Jr. Coll., Truckee, 1981; judge pro tem Nevada and Placer County cts., 1982—; arbitrator Nevada, Lassen & Placer County Cts., 1989; fee arbitrator Nevada County Bar Assn. County chairperson McCloskey for Pres., 1971; mem. Truckee-Tahoe Airport Noise Adv. Com., 2001-02. Recipient Outstanding Community Participation recognition Sacramento Blood Found., 1987. Mem. Truckee Donner C. of C., Tahoe Truckee Bar Assn. (bd. dirs. 1981-83, pres. 1982), Truckee Rotary (bd. dirs. 1984—, v.p. found. 1988-91, pres. found. 1994-96, pres. 1996-97, Paul Harris fellow). Avocations: sports, woodworking, music, flying. Office: 9709 Highway 267 Truckee CA 96161-0348

COLLUM, RICK DANIEL, lawyer; b. Atlanta, Sept. 25, 1969; s. Wesley Daniel and Mary Elizabeth Collum; m. Donna Lee Rogers, Sept. 12, 1992; children: Danielle Elizabeth, Jared Lee. BS in Criminal Justice, BA in Sociology, Valdosta State U., 1992; JD, Cleve. State U., 1999. Bar: Ga. 2000, U.S. Dist. Ct. (no., mid. and so. dists.) Ga. 2001, U.S. Tax Ct. 2001, U.S. Ct. Appeals (11th cir.) 2001. Dep. U.S. marshal U.S. Marshals Svc., Cleve., 1992—99; legal instr. Fed. Law Enforcement Tng. Ctr., Brunswick, Ga., 1999—2000; jud. law clk. Hon. W. Louis Sands, Mid. Dist. Ga., Albany, 2000—02; lawyer Hall, Booth, Smith & Slover, Albany, 2002—. Tchr. Sunday Sch. Autryville (Ga.) Bapt. Ch., 2001—. Baptist. Avocations: golf, fishing, hunting, weightlifting. Labor (including EEOC, Fair Labor Standards Act, labor-management relations, NLRB, OSHA), Personal injury (including property damage), Criminal. Office: Hall Booth Smith & Slover 2417 Westgate Dr Albany GA 31708 Office Fax: 229-888-2156.

COLLYER, MICHAEL, lawyer; b. N.Y.C., Feb. 5, 1942; s. Clayton Johnson and Heloise (Green) Collyer; m. Sandra Karen Schaum, July 28, 1979 (div. Aug. 1999); m. Susan Catherine Bruyn, Nov. 13, 1999; children: Sophie Marie, Matthew Michael Severyn;1 stepchild, Shelley Malia. BA, Williams Coll., 1963; LLB, Columbia U., 1966. Bar: N.Y. 1966. Assoc. Becker & London, N.Y.C., 1966—70; ptnr. Kay Collyer & Boose and predecessors, N.Y.C., 1970—2001, Cascone Cole & Collyer, N.Y.C., 2001—, Collyer & Schutte, 2001—; legal adviser NATAS, N.Y.C., 1978—, trustee, 1982—, nat. officer, 1982—, chmn., 1990—. Instr. bus. law Columbia U., N.Y.C., 1966—69; spkr. conv. Practicing Law Inst., 1977; mem. chpt. motion pictures and TV under new copyright statute, 78. Trustee George Heller Meml. Scholarship Fund; active N.Y.C. Mayor's Adv. Coun. Film and Broadcasting, 1993. With U.S. Army, 1966—71. Mem.: Internat. Coun. Nat. Acad. Arts and Scis. (bd. dirs.), Internat. Radio and TV Soc., N.Y. Bar Assn. (author TV sect. entertainment law 1995), Assn. of Bar of City of N.Y., N.Y. Yacht Club. Entertainment. Home: 25 Chester Ct Cortlandt Manor NY 10567-6361 Office: Cascone Cole & Collyer 711 3d Ave 15th FlPla New York NY 10017 E-mail: collyerlaw@aol.com.

COLMAN, RICHARD THOMAS, lawyer; b. Boston, Sept. 22, 1935; s. Albert Vincent and Marie Catherine (Henehan) C.; m. Marilyn Flavin, Dec. 1, 1962; children: Elizabeth B., Catherine B., Richard T. Jr., Patrick B. AB magna cum laude, U. Notre Dame, 1957; LLB cum laude, Boston Coll., 1962. Bar: Mass. 1962, D.C. 1966. Trial atty. Antitrust Div. U.S. Dept. Justice, Washington, 1962-66; ptnr. Howrey Simon Arnold & White LLP, Washington, 1970—2001. Trustee Indian Mountain Sch., Lakeville, Conn., 1992-98; regional del. Boston Coll. Law Sch. Alumni Assn., 1992-99; adv. bd. Georgetown U. Law Ctr., Corp. Counsel Inst., 1999—2001; bd. overseers Boston Coll. Law Sch., 2001—. Mem.: ABA, DC Bar Assn., Beach Club, Wianno Club. Republican. Roman Catholic. Administrative and regulatory, Antitrust, Federal civil litigation. E-mail: colmanr@howrey.com.

COLMANT, ANDREW ROBERT, lawyer; b. Bklyn., Oct. 10, 1931; s. Edward J. and Mary Elizabeth (Byrne) C.; children: Elizabeth, Carolyn, David (dec.), Stephen, Robert. BBA, St. Johns U., Jamaica, N.Y., 1957, LLB, 1959. Bar: N.Y. 1959, U.S. Dist Ct. (so. and ea. dists.) N.Y. 1961, U.S. Ct. Appeals (2nd cir.) 1969, U.S. Ct. Appeals (4th cir.) 1977, U.S. Supreme Ct. 1991. Assoc. Hill, Rivkins, Carey, Loesberg O'Brien & Mulroy and predecessor firms, 1959-73, ptnr., 1973-87; of counsel Jerrold E. Hyams, 1988-97, Peter F. Broderick, 1992. Proctor in admiralty; active USMC amphibious reconnaissance Army Gen. Intelligence Sch. Author: Outline of General Average. Interpretive vol. Sandy Hook Lighthouse and History House, Fort Hancock, NJ, Navesink Light Sta., Highland, NJ; active Conservation Coun. for Hawaii, Honolulu, St. Stephans Indian Sch., Am. Indian Mus. Natural History; founder Deep Cut Gardens, Middleton, NJ; vol. Twin Lighthouse, NJ, Highlands Hist. Soc., Highlands, NJ; VIP Nat. Park Svc.; vol. Sandy Hook Lighthouse, History House, Hancock, NJ, 2002—, Cmty. St. Benedict, Holmdel, NJ; rep., leader Bayshore Comty. Hosp., Holmdel, NJ, 1978—; min. of eucharist St. Benedict Parish, Holmdel, NJ; extraordinary min. Holy Eucharist Asssigned; Sunday contingent; mem., track chmn. Parish Coun., Fin. Funding, Constl. Lance cpl. USMC, 1952—54. Recipient Social Min. award, Diocese Trenton Bishop Riess, VIP award, Dept. Interior. Mem.: ACLU, ABA (torts and ins. and admiralty com. , sr. com.), St. John's Sch. Law Admiralty Soc., Social Security Com., Assn. Internationale de Droit des Assurances, Pacific Rim Maritime Law Assn., Asia Pacific Lawyers Assn., NY State Bar Assn. (admiralty), Maritime Law Assn. U.S. (life; proctor in admiralty 1960, carriage goods com.), NY County Lawyers Assn. (life; admiralty com. 1963,), Nat. Trust for Hist. Preservation, Nat. Maritime Hist. Soc., Navy League U.S., Amnesty Internat., Anti-defamation League, Nat. Park Conservation Assn., Twin Light Hist. Soc., Nat. Wildlife Fedn., ATLA (admiralty com. 1995), Sierra Club. Admiralty, Insurance, Private international. Home: Bethany Manor 500 Broad St Apt 11Y Keyport NJ 07735-1640

COLODNY, EDWIN IRVING, lawyer, retired air transportation executive; b. Burlington, Vt., June 7, 1926; s. Myer and Lena (Yett) Colodny; m. Nancy Dessoff, Dec. 11, 0965; children: Elizabeth, Mark, David. AB with distinction, U. Rochester, 1948; LLB, Harvard U., 1951; D in Comml. Sci. (hon.) , Robert Morris Coll., 1985; LLD (hon.) , Middlebury Coll., 1986; HHD (hon.) , Kings Coll., 1988. Bar: N.Y. 1951, DC 1958. With Office Gen. Counsel, GSA, 1951-52, CAB, 1954-57, USAirways Inc. (formerly Allegheny Airlines Inc.), 1957-91; exec. v.p. mktg. and legal affairs USAirways, Inc. (formerly Allegheny Airlines Inc.), 1969-75, pres., 1975-90, CEO, 1975-91, chmn. bd. dirs., 1978-92; also chmn. USAirways Group, Inc., 1978-92; ret., 1992; of counsel Paul, Hastings, Janofsky and Walker, Washington, 1991—2002; chmn. Comsat Corp., 1997-2000. Interim pres. U. Vt., 2001—02; interim pres., CEO Fletcher Allen Health Care, Burlington, 2002—. Lt. U.S. Army, 1952—54. Recipient James D. McGill Meml. award, U. Rochester, Wright Bros. Meml. award, 1990, Tony Jannus award, 1990. Mem.: ABA, U. Vt. (bd. trustees), U. Rochester (bd. trustees). E-mail: eic8225@aol.com.

COLOGNE, GORDON BENNETT, lawyer; b. Long Beach, Calif., Aug. 24, 1924; s. Knox M. Cologne; m. Patricia Cologne; children: Steven J., Ann Maureen Meyer. BS, U. So. Calif., 1948; LLB cum laude, Southwestern U. Sch. of Law, L.A., 1951. Bar: Calif. 1951, U.S. Supreme Ct. 1961. Trial atty. U.S. Dept. of Justice, Jacksonville, Fla., 1951-52; pvt. practice Indio, Calif., 1952-61; mayor Indio City Coun., 1954; mem. state assembly Calif. Legis., Sacramento, 1961-65; mem. senate Calif. State Senate, Sacramento, 1965-72; justice Ct. of Appeal, San Diego, 1972-84; govt. rels. atty. Sacramento, 1984-99. With USN, 1944-46. Named one of Outstanding Young Men of Calif., Calif. Jr. C. of C., 1961; recipient Freedom Found. award, 1965.

COLSON, EARL MORTON, lawyer, educator; b. Bklyn., Mar. 8, 1930; s. Abraham and Rebecca (Hecker) C.; m. Helen Theresa Austern, Apr. 24, 1960; children: Adam Thomas, Amy Esther, Deborah Austern. BS magna cum laude, Syracuse U., 1950; LLB magna cum laude, Harvard U., 1957. Bar: N.Y. 1958, D.C. 1960. Assoc. Chadbourne, Parke, Whiteside & Wolff, N.Y.C., 1957-60, Arent, Fox, Kintner, Plotkin & Kahn, Washington, 1960-68, partner, 1968—. Adj. prof. law Georgetown U., 1970— ; lectr on tax subjects. Author: Capital Gains and Losses, 1975; co-author: Federal Taxation of Estates, Gifts and Trusts, 1975. Bd. dirs. Washington Hebrew Congregation, 1979—, v.p., 1984-90, pres., 1990-92; trustee Kingsbury Ctr., 1978-81; mem. N.Y. bd. overseers Hebrew Union Coll., 1995-97; bd. dirs. D.C. chpt. Am. Jewish Com., 1995-98. Mem. ABA (chmn. estate and gift tax com. sect. taxation 1972-73), D.C. Bar Assn. (chmn. tax com. 1971-72, treas., bd. govs. 1974-76), Am. Law Inst., Assn. of Bar of City of N.Y., Cosmos Club Washington. Estate planning, Property, real (including real estate development, water), Corporate taxation. Office: 1050 Connecticut Ave NW Washington DC 20036-5303

COLTON, STERLING DON, lawyer, business executive, missionary; b. Vernal, Utah, Apr. 28, 1929; s. Hugh Wilkins and Marguerite (Maughan) C.; m. Eleanor Ricks, Aug. 6, 1954; children: Sterling David, Carolyn, Bradley Hugh, Steven Ricks. BS in Banking and Fin., U. Utah, 1951; JD, Stanford U., 1953. Bar: Calif. 1954, Utah 1954, D.C. 1967. Ptnr. Van Cott, Bagley, Cornwall & McCarthy, Salt Lake City, 1957-66; vice chair, sr. v.p., gen. counsel, bd. dirs. Marriott Corp. and Marriott Internat., 1954-95. Pres. Can. Vancouver Mission Ch. of Jesus Christ of Latter Day Saints, 1995-98, Washington DC Temple, Ch. of Jesus Christ of Latter Day Saints, 1999-2002; v.p. Colton Ranch Corp., Vernal, 1987—; former bd. dirs. Megaherz Corp. and Dyncorp; former chmn. bd. dirs. Nat. Chamber Litigation Ctr. Former bd. dirs. Polynesian Cultural Ctr.; former chmn. nat. adv. coun. U. Utah, Ballet West, nat. adv. counsel; mem. adv. coun. The Nat. Conservancy. Maj. JAG, U.S. Army, 1954-57. Mem. ABA, Calif. Bar Assn., Utah Bar Assn., D.C. Bar Assn., Washington Met. Corp. Counsel Assn. (former pres., dir.), Sigma Chi. Republican. Mem. Lds Ch. Corporate, general, Finance, Property, real (including real estate development, water). E-mail: sdercolton@aol.com.

COLVILLE, ROBERT E. judge; b. Pitts., May 23, 1935; s. John and Mary M. (Goldbronn) C.; children: Michael C., Robert J., Molly. B.A. Duquesne U., 1963, J.D., 1969. Bar: Pa. 1969, U.S. Dist. Ct. (we. dist.) Pa. 1969. Tchr., coach North Catholic High Sch., Pitts., 1959-64; patrolman, detective Bur. of Police, Dept. Pub. Safety, Pitts., 1964-68, police legal adviser, 1969-70, asst. dir. Dept. Pub. Safety, 1970-71, supt. Bur. of Police, Pitts., 1971-75; clk., detective Dist. Atty.'s Office of Allegheny County, Pitts., 1968-69, dist. atty., 1976-97; judge Allegheny County Ct. Common Pleas, 1998—; adj. prof. law Duquesne U. Sch. of Law, Pitts., 1976-78; instr. in labor law LaRoche Coll., Pitts., 1983-84. Contbr. articles to profl. jours. Past chmn. Joint Allegheny County Narcotics Task Force; chmn. Allegheny County Drug Initiative; mem. Pa. Democratic Com. Served with USMC, 1953-56; foremr trustee Community Coll. of Allegheny County. Recipient Dapper Dan award Pitts. Post Gazette, 1963, Disting. Service award County Detectives Assn., 1977, Service Recognition award Pitts. Community Crime Prevention Coalition, 1980; Law Enforcement award Dep. Sheriff's Assn. of Pa., 1983; Outstanding Grad., Duquesne U., 1969; Jr. C. of C. Man of Yr. in Law, 1973; Phi Alpha Delta Law Alumni of Yr., 1976; Outstanding Grad., Duquesne U. Century Club, 1978; Outstanding Law Alumnus Duquesne U. Law Alumni Assn., 1985. Office: 436 Grant St Pittsburgh PA 15219-2400

COLVIN, SHERRILL WILLIAM, lawyer; b. Jeffersonville, Ind., Sept. 13, 1938; s. Hewitt L. and Mary (Sutton) C.; m. Sarah Albin, Aug. 12, 1962; children: John, Betsy. AB, Wabash Coll., 1960; LLB, Ind. U., 1965. Bar: Ind. 1965, U.S. Supreme Ct. 1968. Pres. Ind. Trial Lawyers Assn., 1991—; ptnr. Haller & Colvin PC, Fort Wayne, Ind., 1965—. Mem. disciplinary commn. Ind. Supreme Ct.; mem. faculty Nat. Inst. Trial Advocacy Fellow Am. Coll. Trial Lawyers; mem. Ind. State Bar Assn. (pres.-elect 2003), disciplinary commn. Supreme Ct. (chair 1995-96). Methodist. General civil litigation, Personal injury (including property damage), Product liability. Home: 5700 Old Mill Rd Fort Wayne IN 46807-3043 Office: Haller & Colvin 444 E Main St Fort Wayne IN 46802-1910*

COMBE, JOHN CLIFFORD, JR., lawyer; b. New Orleans, Jan. 5, 1939; s. John Clifford and Gladys Ann (Reine) C.; m. Lynne Wendel Watson, July 11, 1964; children: John, Wendy, Holly. BBA, Tulane U., 1960, LLB, 1965. Bar: La. 1965, U.S. Dist. Ct. (ea. and mid. dists.) La. 1965, U.S. Ct. Appeals (5th cir.) 1965, U.S. Supreme Ct. 1971, U.S. Ct. Appeals (11th cir.) 1981, U.S. Dist. Ct. (we. dist.) La. 1986. Assoc. Jones, Walker, Waechter, Poitevent, Carrere & Denegre, New Orleans, 1965—, ptnr., 1970—, sr. ptnr., 1989—. Editor: La. Bar Jour., 1975-77; contbr. articles to legal jours. Organizer, mem. Crestmont Pk. Improvement Assn.; organizer Greater New Orleans Law Explorer program Boy Scouts Am., 1974; mem. St. Catherine of Siena Parish Sch. Bd., 1976-89; trustee Acad. of Sacred Heart, 1993-96. Lt. (j.g.) USN, 1960-62. Fellow: ABA (mem. ho. of dels. 1982—88), La. State Bar Found., Am. Bar Found., Am. Coll. Trial Lawyers (state chair 1999—2000); mem.: La. Bar Assn. (mem. bd. govs. 1973—74, sec.-treas. 1975, mem. bd. govs. 1975—76, 1977—78, 1978—80, pres. 1979—80), So. Regional Conf. Bar Pres., Nat. Conf. Bar Pres., Def. Rsch. Inst., Am. Judicature Soc. (mem. bd. govs. 1982—86), La. Assn. Def. Counsel (bd. dirs. 1969—75, faculty trial acad. 2000—02), Internat. Assn. Def. Counsel (speaker 1989, mem. faculty trial acad. 1991), Stratford Club (pres. 1993—95), Boston Club, Metairie Country Club. Republican. Roman Catholic. Federal civil litigation, Insurance, Product liability. Office: Jones Walker Waechter Poitevent Carrere & Denegre 201 Saint Charles Ave Ste 50 New Orleans LA 70170-5100

COMBS, W(ILLIAM) HENRY, III, lawyer; b. Casper, Wyo., Mar. 18, 1949; s. William Henry and Ruth M. (Wooster) Combs; 1 child from previous marriage, J. Bradley. Student, Northwestern U., 1967-70; BS, U. Wyo., 1972, JD, 1975. Bar: Wyo. 1975, U.S. Dist. Ct. Wyo. 1975, U.S. Ct. Appeals (10th cir.) 1990, U.S. Supreme Ct. 1990. Assoc. Murane & Bostwick, Casper, 1975-77, ptnr., 1978—. Mem. com. resolution fee disputes, 1990—92. Mem.: ABA (tort and ins. practice sect., law office mgmt. sect.), U.S. Handball Assn., Nat. Bd. Trail Advocacy (cert.), Assn. Ski Def. Attys., Def. Lawyers Assn. Wyo., Am. Judicature Soc., Def. Rsch. Inst., Natrona County Bar Assn., Waterski USA, Porsche Club Am. Republican. Episcopalian. Avocations: handball, waterskiing, snow skiing, climbing, driving. Federal civil litigation, State civil litigation, Personal injury (including property damage). Office: Murane & Bostwick 201 N Wolcott St Casper WY 82601-1922

COMBS, WILLIAM L. lawyer; b. Rockford, Ill., Sept. 8, 1947; s. Lester LaRue and Edna Maxcene (Brown) C.; m. Joan Elizabeth Sherry, July 4, 1982 (div. Apr. 1992); children: Kellie Anne, William Lawrence II. BA in English Lit., Knox Coll., 1969; JD, U. Wyo., 1986. Bar: Wyo. 1986, U.S. dist. Ct. Wyo. 1986, U.S. Ct. Appeals (10th cir.) 1989, U.S. Supreme Ct. 1993. Asst. pub. defender Wyo. Office Pub. defender, Gillette, 1986-87; assoc. Holland & Hart, Cheyenne, Wyo., 1987-90, Buck Law Office, Cheyenne, 1990; asst. pub. defender Wyo. Office Pub. defender, Evanston, 1990-95; pvt. practice Evanston, 1995—. Atty. Town of LaBarge, Wyo., 1996—. Bd. dirs. Sexual Assault/Family Violence Task Force, Evanston, 1996—, Wyo. ACLU, 1997—. Recipient Svc. award State of Wyo., 1995. Mem. ABA, Wyo. Bar Assn., Uinta County Bar Assn., C. of C., NOW. Avocations: golf, softball, camping, rafting, skiing. Appellate, Criminal, Family and matrimonial. Office: Combs Law Office 318 7th St Evanston WY 82930-3538

COMEAU, MICHAEL GERARD, lawyer; b. Balt., July 13, 1956; s. Joseph Gerard and Irma (Cullison) C.; m. Penny Lee Derrickson, Apr. 14, 1984; children: Joseph Gerard, Nicole Lee. BA, Randolph-Macon Coll., 1978; JD, U. Balt., 1981; postgrad., George Washington U., 1982-83, U.S. Army Judge Advocate Gen.'s Basic Course, 1992; Advanced Course, 1994, command and gen. staff course, 2002. Bar: Md. 1981, U.S. Dist Ct. Md. 1982, U.S. Ct. Mil. Appeals 1982, U.S. Ct. Appeals (4th and D.C. cirs.) 1982, D.C. 1984, U.S. Dist Ct. D.C. 1984, U.S. Supreme Ct. 1985. Law clk. Balt. County Solicitor's Office, Towson, Md., 1980-81; assoc. county atty. Prince George's County, Upper Marlboro, Md., 1981-84, 86-89; assoc. Knight, Manzi, Brennan & Ostrom, Upper Marlboro, 1984-86; chief dep. clk. Ct. Spl. Appeals, Annapolis, Md., 1986; asst. atty. gen. State of Md., Towson, 1989-94; chief of litigation, asst. county atty. Balt. County Atty.'s Office, Towson, Md., 1994-2000; mng. atty. Law Offices of Michael G. Comeau, Balt., 2000—02; mng. atty Law Offices John E. Kelly, 2002—. Mem. adv. com. Loyola Coll. Bar Rev., Balt., 1982; mem. gen. assembly's task force on gaming laws in Prince George's County, 1987. Mem. ch. coun. All Saints Luth. Ch., Bowie, Md., 1986-88, pres., 1987-88; mem. Dem. State Ctrl. Com. for Harford County, 1995-98, 2002-, chmn. 2003-; mem. procurement adv. coun. State of Md., 1995-98, Gubernatorial Transition Team, 1994-95; mem. judiciary com. Md. Ho. of Dels., Harford County, 1997-99. Maj. Md. Army N.G., 1991—. Recipient Exceptional Svc. award, Md. Atty. Gens.'s Office, 1991. Mem. Md. Bar Assn., Harford County Bar Assn., Prince George's County Bar Assn. (bd. dirs. 1988-90), Kappa Alpha. Democrat. Avocations: baseball card collecting, softball. Home: 3509 Glen Oak Dr Jarrettsville MD 21084-1837 Office: 516 Rock Spring Ave Bel Air MD 21014 E-mail: MGComeau@hotmail.com.

COMEY, JAMES B., JR., lawyer; b. Yonkers, N.Y., Dec. 14, 1960; m. Patrice Comey; 5 children. BS, Coll. William and Mary; JD, U. Chgo. Asst. U.S. atty., Manhattan, 1987—93; pvt. practice McGuire Woods, Richmond, Va., 1993—96; mng. asst. U.S. Atty.'s Office, Ea. Dist. Va., 1996—2001; U.S. atty. So. Dist. N.Y., 2002—. Avocations: squash, bicycling, New York Giants and Knicks, teaching Sunday school. Office: One St Andrews Plz New York NY 10007*

COMISKY, IAN MICHAEL, lawyer; b. Phila., Feb. 5, 1950; s. Marvin and Goldye (Elving) C. BS magna cum laude, U. Pa., 1971, JD, 1974; LLM in Taxation, U. Miami, 1984. Bar: Pa. 1974, Fla. 1976, D.C. 1976, U.S. Ct. Appeals (3rd and 11th cirs.), U.S. Ct. Claims, U.S. Tax Ct., U.S. Supreme Ct., U.S. Dist. Ct. (ea. dist.) Pa., U.S. Dist. Ct. (so. dist.) Fla., U.S. Dist. Ct. (mid. dist.) Fla. Law clk. to Hon. Alfred Luongo Jr. U.S. Dist. Ct. Pa., Phila., 1974-75; asst. dist. atty. Office of Dist. Atty., Philadelphia County, Phila., 1975-78; asst. U.S. atty. So. Dist. Fla., 1978-80; spl. asst. Office of Dist. Atty., So. Dist. Fla., 1980; ptnr., comml. litigation and white collar crime Blank Rome LLP, Phila., 1980—. Presenter various profl. confs. seminars, 1981—; guest TV and radio programs, 1990. Co-author: Tax Fraud and Evasion (2 vols.); contbr. articles to profl. publs. Sec. Mann Music Ctr. Mem. ABA (past chmn. civil and criminal tax penalties com. tax sect., mem. CLE com. tax sect., vice chmn. COGS spl. projects, mem. various coms. criminal justice and litig. sect.), ATLA, Am. Law Inst., Am. Coll. Tax Counsel, Fed. Bar Assn., Pa. Bar Assn., Fla. Bar Assn. (bd. govs. 1998), D.C. Bar Assn., Phila. Bar Assn., Assn. Fellows and Legal Scholars or Ctr. for Internat. Legal Studies (hon.). Avocations: sailing, gardening, Karate, jogging. Federal civil litigation, Criminal, Taxation, general.

COMISKY, MARVIN, retired lawyer; b. Phila., June 5, 1918; m. Goldie Elving; children: Ian M., Hope A., Matthew J. BSC. summa cum laude, Temple U., 1938; LL.B., U. Pa., 1941; LL.D., Dickinson Sch. Law, 1970. Bar: Pa. 1942. Law clk. Pa. Superior Ct., 1941-42; law clk. to presiding justice Pa. Supreme Ct., 1946; assoc. Lemuel B. Schofield, Phila., 1946-54; ptnr. Brumbelow & Comisky, 1954-59, Blank, Rome, Comisky & McCauley LLP, Phila., 1959-68, mng. ptnr., 1968-88; chmn. Blank, Rome, Comisky & McCauley, Phila., 1988-90, chmn. emeritus, 1991-99, ret., 1993. Mem. Pa. Bd. Law Examiners, 1974-75; former dir. Midlantic Bank. Co-author: Judicial Selection, Compensation, Ethics and Discipline, 1986 Gen. counsel Pa. Constl. Conv., 1967. Fellow Am. Bar Found., Am. Coll. Trial Lawyers, Internat. Acad. Trial Lawyers; mem. ABA (del. 1965, 70), Phila. Bar Assn. (chancellor 1965), Pa. Bar Assn. (past pres.), Order of Coif, Beta Gamma Sigma. Office: Blank Rome Comisky & McCauley LLP One Logan Square Philadelphia PA 19103

COMITER, LLOYD ALAN, lawyer; b. Phila., Feb. 19, 1965; 3 children. BA in Polit. Sci., Boston U., 1987; JD, St. Thomas U., Miami, Fla., 1990. Bar: Fla. 1991, D.C. 1991, U.S. Dist. Ct. (so. dist.) Fla. 1991, U.S. Ct. Appeals (11th cir.) 1992, U.S. Supreme Ct. 2000. Clk. Law Offices Philip Berman, Pompano Beach, Fla., 1986-91, assoc., 1991-93, Law Offices Berman & Feldman, Pompano Beach, 1993-95; pres. Law Offices of Comiter, P.A., Boca Raton, Fla., 1995—, Deerfield Beach, Fla., 1995—2002; assoc. Mandel, Weisman, Heimberg, Brodie & Griffin, P.A., Boca Raton, Fla., 2002—. Mem. planning com. Am. Diabetes Assn., Boca Raton, 1996, 97; com. mem. Crohn's and Colitis Found., Boca Raton, 1996, 97; mentor Comtys. in Sch., Take Stock in Children, 2001-. Mem. ABA, Fla. Bar (small claims rules com. 2002-), Bar Assn. D.C. Ct. Appeals, Palm Beach County Bar Assn. (small claims ct. clinics com. 2001—), Greater Deerfield Beach C. of C. (facilitator career expo. forum, edn. com. 1996). Republican. Jewish. Avocations: exercise, running, reading. General civil litigation, Commercial, consumer (including collections, credit), Landlord-tenant. Office: 2101 Corporate Blvd Ste 300 Boca Raton FL 33431-9411

COMPTON, ALLEN T. retired state supreme court justice; b. Kansas City, Mo., Feb. 25, 1938; 3 children. BA, U. Kans., 1960; LL.B., U. Colo. 1963. Pvt. practice, Colorado Springs, 1963-68; staff atty. Legal Svcs. Office, Colorado Springs, 1968-69, dir., 1969-71; supervising atty. Alaska Legal Svcs., Juneau, Alaska, 1971-73; pvt. practice Juneau, 1973-76; judge Superior Ct., Alaska, 1976-80; justice Alaska Supreme Ct., Anchorage, 1980-98, state supreme ct. chief justice, 1995-97, ret., 1998.

COMPTON, ASBURY CHRISTIAN, state supreme court justice; b. Portsmouth, Va., Oct. 24, 1929; BA, Washington and Lee U., 1950, LLB, 1953, LLD, 1975. Bar: Va. 1957. Mem. firm May, Garrett, Miller, Newman & Compton, Richmond, 1957-66; judge Law and Equity Ct., City of Richmond, 1966-74; justice Supreme Ct. Va., Richmond, 1974-2000, sr. justice, 2000—. Trustee Collegiate Schs., Richmond, 1972-89, chmn. bd., 1978-80; former chmn. adminstrv. bd. Ginter Park United Meth. Ch., Richmond; former mem. adminstrv. bd. Trinity United Meth. Ch., Richmond; trustee Washington and Lee U., 1978-90. With USN, 1953-56, USNR, 1956-62. Decorated Letter of Commendation. Mem. Va. Bar Assn., Va. State Bar, Bar Assn. City Richmond, Washington and Lee U. Alumni Assn. (past pres., dir.), Omicron Delta Kappa, Phi Kappa Sigma, Phi Alpha Delta. Clubs: Country of Va. Office: Va Supreme Ct 100 N 9th St Richmond VA 23219-2335

COMPTON, CARNIS EUGENE, lawyer; b. Grundy, Va., June 20, 1948; s. Virginia (Compton) Hughart; m. Dollie McGlothlin, Aug. 24, 1966; children: Wade Trent, Nicholas Brian. BA, U. Va.-Clinch Valley, Wise, 1976; JD, Campbell Coll., 1979. Bar: Va. 1979, Fla. 1982, U.S. Dist. Ct. (we. dist.) Va. 1979, U.S. Supreme Ct. 1982, U.S. Ct. Appeals (4th cir.) 1984. Assoc. John L. Bagwell, P.C., Grundy, 1979; ptnr. Bagwell & Compton, P.C., Grundy, 1980-82, Watts & Compton, Deland, Fla., 1982; pvt. practice Honaker, Va., 1982-86; ptnr. Compton & Jessee, P.C., Abingdon and Honaker, Va., 1985—86; pvt. practice Honaker, 1982—88,

Lebanon, Va., 1988—. Sec. Buchanan County Republican Party, Grundy, 1980; chmn. Reagan/Bush Com.-Buchanan County, Grundy, 1980; Republican candidate 40th State Senatorial Dist., Va., 1983; mem. Young Republicans of CVC, Wise, 1975. With USAF, 1967-73, Vietnam. Mem. ATLA, Va. Bar Assn., Va. Trial Lawyers Assn. (com. mem., dist. gov. 1995-96), Russell County Bar Assn. (pres. 1989), Fla. State Bar, Am. Legion. Avocations: bird dog field trials, reading history, horse back riding. General civil litigation, Criminal, Family and matrimonial. Home: Rte 614 PO Box 1090 Lebanon VA 24266 Office: PO Box 1000 Lebanon VA 24266-1000 E-mail: gene@comptonlaw.net.

COMSTOCK, REBECCA ANN, lawyer; b. Mpls., Mar. 13, 1950; d. Clark Franklin and Ruth Carolyn (Sundt) C. Student, Conn. Coll., 1968-70; BA summa cum laude, U. Minn., 1973; JD Order of St. Ives, U. Denver, 1977; MBA, Northwestern U., 2002. Bar: Minn. 1978, U.S. Dist. Ct. Minn., U.S. Ct. Appeals (8th cir.). Ptnr. Dorsey & Whitney, Mpls., 1982—. Bd. dirs. St. Paul Chamber Orch., 1996-2001. Mem. ABA, Minn. Bar Assn., Hennepin County Bar Assn., Legal Aid Soc. Mpls. (bd. dirs. 1988-93), Nat. Assn. Women Bus. Owners, Licensing Exec. Soc. (USA and Can.), Environ. Law Inst. Avocations: skiing, biking, golf, music, theatre. Administrative and regulatory, Environmental. Office: Dorsey & Whitney LLP 50 S 6th St Minneapolis MN 55402-1498 E-mail: comstock.becky@dorsey.com.

COMSTOCK, ROBERT FRANCIS, lawyer; b. Lincoln, Ill., June 4, 1936; s. William Bryan and Mary Euceba (Durham) C.; m. Jean Joyce Herring, May 9, 1970; children: James, Michael, Kelly, Jennifer, Margaret. AB, Cath. U., 1958, LLB, 1964. Bar: U.S. Dist. Ct. 1965, U.S. Ct. Appeals (D.C. cir.) 1965, U.S. Tax Ct. 1971. Ptnr. Comstock & Reilly LLP, Washington, 1965—. Chmn. bd. dirs. Balt. Bancorp, 1991, Met. Fed. Savs. & Loan, Bethesda, Md., 1986-87, Met Holding Co., Bethesda, 1985-87, First Continental Bank, Silver Spring, Md., 1983-86; dir. Nat. Captial Bank Washington, 1999—. Trustee, vice chmn. bd. trustees Cath. U. Am., Washington, 1987—; bd. dirs. Cath. Cemeteries Washington, 1986—, Cath. Youth Orgn. Capt. USAF, 1958-61. Named Knight of St. Gregory, Knight of Holy Sepulchre, Papal Award of Holy See, to Athletic Hall of Fame, Cath. U., 1985. Mem. ABA, D.C. Bar Assn., Cath. U. Alumni Assn. (bd. govs.). Clubs: Columbia Country (Chevy Chase, Md.); Univ. Md. M. Roman Catholic. Avocation: sports. Banking, Probate (including wills, trusts), Property, real (including real estate development, water). Home: 7707 Brookville Rd Bethesda MD 20815-3933 Office: Comstock & Reilly LLP Ste 300 5225 Wisconsin Ave NW Washington DC 20015-2014

CONABOY, RICHARD PAUL, federal judge; b. Scranton, Pa., June 12, 1925; m. Marion Hartnett; children: Mary Ann, Richard, Judith, Conan, Michele, Kathryn, Patrick, William, Margaret, Janet, John, Nancy. BA, U. Scranton, 1945; LLB, Cath. U. Am., 1950. Bar: Pa. 1951. Ptnr. firm Powell & Conaboy, Scranton, 1951-54; dep. atty. gen., 1953-62; assoc. firm Kennedy O'Brien & O'Brien, 1954-62; judge Pa. Ct. Common Pleas, 1962-79, pres. judge, 1978-79; judge U.S. Dist. Ct. (mid. dist.) Pa., Scranton, 1980—, chief judge, 1989-93, now sr. judge. Pres. Pa. Joint Council on Criminal Justice System, 1971-79; mem. Nat. Conf. Juvenile Justice, Nat. Conf. Corrections. Contbr. articles to legal jours. Bd. dirs. Marywood Coll., U. Scranton; apptd. chmn. U.S. States Sentencing Commn., 1994. Mem. Pa. Conf. State Trial Judges (pres. 1976-77, v.p. 1973-76, sec. 1968-73), ABA, Pa. Bar Assn., Am. Judicature Soc. Office: US Dist Courthouse & Post Office Bldg PO Box 189 Scranton PA 18501-0189

CONBOY, KENNETH, lawyer, former federal judge; b. 1938; AB, Fordham Coll., 1961; JD, U. Va., 1964; MA in History, Columbia U., 1980. Asst. dist. atty., exec. asst. dist. atty. Manhattan Dist. Atty.'s Office, 1966-77; dep. commr., gen. counsel N.Y. Police, 1978-83; criminal justice dir. N.Y.C., 1984-86; N.Y.C. commr. of investigation, 1986-87; judge U.S. Dist. Ct. (so. dist.) N.Y, 1987-93; sr. litigation ptnr. Mudge, Rose, Guthrie, Alexander & Ferdon, N.Y.C., 1994-95; ptnr. Latham & Watkins, N.Y.C., 1995—. Summer faculty Cornell Law Sch.; adj. prof. of law Fordham Law Sch. Author: Grand Jury Examination of the Recalcitrant Witness, 1977; contbr. articles to profl. jours. Mem. N.Y. State Crime Control Planning Bd., N.Y. Sovern Commn. Capt. U.S. Army, 1964-66. Mem. Am. Soc. Legal History, N.Y. State Bar Assn., Assn. of Bar of City of N.Y., Fed. Bar Coun. General civil litigation, Constitutional, Securities. Office: Latham & Watkins 885 3rd Ave Ste 1000 New York NY 10022-4834

CONCANNON, JAMES M. law educator, university dean; b. Columbus, Ga., Oct. 2, 1947; s. James M. Jr. and Mary Jane (Crow) C.; m. Melissa P. Masoner, June 9, 1988. BS, U. Kans., 1968, JD, 1971. Law clk. Kans. Ins. Commn., Topeka, 1971; rsch. atty. Kans. Supreme Ct., Topeka, 1971-73; asst. prof. law Washburn U., Topeka, 1973-75, assoc. prof. law, 1976-81, prof., 1981—, dean, 1988-2001. Vis. prof. law Washington U., St. Louis, 1979; active Kans. Commn. on Pub. Understanding of Law, 1983-89, Task Force on Law Enforcement Consolidation, Topeka, 1991-92; mem. Nat. Conf. Commrs. on Uniform State Laws, 1998—; mem. Pattern Instrns. for Kans.-Civil Com., Kans. Jud. Coun., 2001—. Co-author: Kans. Appellate Practice Manual, 1978, Kansas Statutes of Limitations, 1988; sr. contbr. editor: Evidence in America-Federal Rules in the States, 1987. Coord. Citizens to Keep Politics Out of Our Courts, Topeka, 1984; mem. bd. dirs. Kans. Legal Svcs. for Prisoners, 2003— ; co-reporter Citizens Justice Initiative, 1997-99; chmn. legal com. Concerned Citizens Topeka, 1995-99; bd. dirs. Mut. Funds Waddell and Reed, Inc., 1997—, Legal Svcs. for Prisoners, 2002—. Master: Topeka Am. Inn. of Ct. (pres. 2001—02); fellow: Kans. Bar Found., Am. Bar Found. (state chair 2002—); mem.: Assn. Am. Law Schs. (com. on bar admission, lawyer performance 1994—97), Kans. Bar Assn. (CLE com. 1976—2001, Outstanding Svc. award 1982, 2003), Washburn Law Sch. Alumni Assn. (life), Order of Coif. Office: Washburn U Law Sch 1700 SW College Ave Topeka KS 66621-0001

CONDIE, ROBERT STEVENS, lawyer; b. Palo Alto, Calif., May 28, 1950; s. Robert S. Condie and Ellen Jean (Wylie) Barthold; m. Margaret Anne Lieferman, Mar. 13, 1982; children: Matthew Robert, Nicholas Paul, Megan Elizabeth. BA, U. Calif., Berkeley, 1971, JD, 1974. Bar: Calif. 1974, U.S. Dist. Ct. (no. dist.) Calif. 1975, U.S. Supreme Ct. 1990. Pvt. practice, Oakland, Calif., 1975—. Appellate, General civil litigation. Office: 11 Embarcadero W Ste 140 Oakland CA 94607-4543

CONDO, JAMES ROBERT, lawyer; b. Somerville, N.J., Mar. 2, 1952; s. Ralph Vincent and Betty Louise (MacQuaide) C. BS in Bus. and Econs., Lehigh U., 1974; JD, Boston Coll., 1979. Bar: Ariz. 1979, Colo. 2001, U.S. Dist. Ct. Ariz. 1979, U.S. Ct. Appeals (9th cir.) 1982, U.S. Supreme Ct. 1983, U.S. Ct. Appeals (D.C. cir.) 1989, U.S. Ct. Appeals (10th cir.) 1989, U.S. Ct. Appeals (6th cir.) 1991, U.S. Ct. Appeals (4th cir.) 1994. Assoc. Snell & Wilmer, Phoenix, 1979-84, ptnr., 1985—. Judge pro tem Ariz. Ct. Appeals. Active Ariz. Town Hall, 1985—. Fellow Ariz. Bar Found.; mem. ABA, State Bar Ariz., Maricopa County Bar Found., Defense Rsch. Inst. Federal civil litigation, State civil litigation, Product liability. Office: Snell & Wilmer One Arizona Ctr Phoenix AZ 85004-2202 E-mail: jcondo@swlaw.com.

CONDO, JOSEPH A. lawyer; b. Plattsburgh, N.Y., Oct. 12, 1948; BA, Le Moyne Coll., 1970; JD, Cath. U. Am., 1973. Bar: Va. 1973, U.S. Dist. Ct. (ea. dist.) Va. 1973. Founding ptnr. Condo & Masterman, Vienna, Va., 1993—. Instr. paralegal program George Washington U., 1976—79; neutral case evaluator Fairfax Cir. Ct., 1995—. Fellow: Va. Bar Found. (lectr. com. continuing legal edn. 1984—), Am. Bar Found., Am. Acad. Matrimonal Lawyers, Am. Coll. Trail Lawyers; mem.: ABA (mem. ho. dels. 1999—, mem. exec. com. Nat. Conf. Bar Pres. 2001—), Fairfax County Bar Assn. (chmn. domestic rels. sect. 1981—83), Va. State Bar (bd. govs. family law sect. 1983—88, chmn. 1986—87, mem. coun. 1987—93, mem. com. bench-bar rels. 1988—93, chmn. 1990—93, mem. coun. 1995—2002, mem. com. professionalism 1996—99, mem.budget and fin. com. 1996—2000, mem. exec. com. 1997—2002). Family and matrimonial. Office: Condo and Masterman 1921 Gallows Rd Ste 830 Vienna VA 22182 Office Fax: 703-442-0294. Business E-Mail: jac13@condo-masterman.com.*

CONDOMINES, AURÉLIEN, lawyer; JD, U. Paris, France, 1996; LLM, U.Cologne, Germany, 1996, Coll. of Europe, Belgium, 1998. Bar: Paris 2000. Lawyer de Pardieu Brocas Maffei & Leygonie, Paris, 1999—2003; internat. assoc. Simpson Thacher & Bartlett, N.Y.C., 2001—02. Antitrust. Office: de Pardieu Brocas Maffei & Leygonie 64-66 ave d'Lena Paris 75016 France Office Fax: 33 1 53 57 71 70.

CONDON, CHARLES MOLONY, former state attorney general; b. Charleston, S.C., May 2, 1953; s. James Joseph and Harriet (Molony) Condon; m. Emily Yarbrough, June 21, 1980; children: Charles Molony Jr., Patrick Monaghan, Doreen Yarbrough, Emily Elliot. Student, Saltzburg (Austria) Summer Sch., 1972, U. Innsbruck, Austria, 1972—73; BA, U. Notre Dame, 1975; JD, Duke U., 1978. Bar: S.C. 1978, U.S. Dist. Ct. S.C. 1978, U.S. Ct. Appeals (4th cir.) 1987, U.S. Supreme Ct. 1988. Assoc. Nexsen, Pruet, Jacobs & Pollard, Columbus, SC, 1978—79; asst. solicitor S.C. 9th Jud. Cir., Charleston, 1979—80, solicitor, 1980—92; atty. gen. State of S.C., Columbia, 1995—2002. Lectr. med. U. S.C., 1982—83, Coll. Charleston, 1986, bd. visitors com., 1992—; panel mem. Nat. Inst. for Drug Abuse, Washington; prosecuter City of Isle Palms, SC, 1993—; cons. Nat. Consortium for Justice Info. and Stats.; profl. rep. So. Environ. Network, 1990—91. Sect. chmn. govtl. divsn. United Way; ex-officio mem. Friends of Charleston County Courthouse; com. mem. Charleston County Criminal Justice Task Force; bd. dirs. com. for drug free soc. Charleston County Sch. Dist., 1989, Children's Ctr., Charleston, SC, 1990—91, S.C. Commn. on Presecution Coord., 1991—92. Mem.: ABA, S.C. Law Enforcement Assn., S.C. Cir. Solicitors Assn. (v.p. 1987—88, pres. 1988—89), Richland County Bar Assn., S.C. Bar Assn., Silver Elephant Club, Notre Dame Club, Charleston Lawyers Club. Republican.

CONDON, DAVID BRUCE, lawyer; b. Tacoma, May 20, 1949; s. Lester Milo and Ruby Elizabeth (Elson) C.; m. Constance Lynn Montgomery, Aug. 27, 1971; children: Amy M., Anne E. BA, U. Wash., 1971; JD cum laude, Gonzaga U., 1974. Bar: Wash. 1974, U.S. Dist. Ct. (we. dist.) Wash. 1974, U.S. Ct. Appeals (9th cir.) 1976, U.S. Dist. Ct. (ea. dist.) Wash. 1989. Assoc. Griffin & Enslow, Tacoma, 1974-78; ptnr. Welch & Condon, Tacoma, 1978—. Examiner Wash. State Higher Edn. Pers. Bd., 1979-95. Bd. dirs. Bldg. A. Scholastic Heritage, pres., 1991-92; bd. dirs. Tacoma Art Mus., 1993-94. Law. ABA, Wash. State Bar Assn., Tacoma-Pierce County Bar Assn., Assn. Trial Lawyers Am., Wash. Trial Lawyers Assn., Nat. Assn. Social Security Claimants Reps. Avocations: running, swimming. Labor (including EEOC, Fair Labor Standards Act, labor-management relations, NLRB, OSHA), Personal injury (including property damage), Workers' compensation. Office: Welch & Condon PO Box 1318 Tacoma WA 98401-1318 E-mail: condond@harbornet.com.

CONDRA, ALLEN LEE, lawyer, state official; b. Middlesboro, Ky., Apr. 11, 1950; s. Allen and Dorothy Dell (Douglas) C. BA, Western Ky. U., 1972; JD, No. Ky. U., 1978. Bar: Ky. 1979, U.S. Dist. Ct. (we. dist.) Ky. 1980. Staff atty. West Ky. Legal Services, Madisonville, 1979-81; dist. atty. Dept. Transp. Commonwealth of Ky., Madisonville, 1981—. Mem. Ky. Bar Assn., Hopkins County Bar Assn., Phi Alpha Delta. Lodges: Elks, Masons, K.T. Democrat. Methodist.

CONDRELL, WILLIAM KENNETH, lawyer; b. Buffalo, N.Y., Sept. 19, 1926; s. Paul Kenneth and Celia Olga (Schinas) C.; m. Stacie J. Oliver, June 9, 1991; children: Paul, William, Alexander. BS, Yale U., 1946; S.M., MIT, 1947; JD, Harvard U., 1950. Bar: N.Y. 1951, D.C. 1964, U.S. Ct. Appeals (4th cir.) 1974, U.S. Ct. Appeals (Fed. cir.) 1982, U.S. Ct. Appeals (D.C. cir.) 1984, U.S. Supreme Ct. 1965. Assoc. econ. adv. Exec. Office Pres., Washington, 1951—54; mgmt. cons. McKinsey and Co., Chgo., 1954-55; mgr. budgets Hotpoint div. GE, Chgo., 1955—59; sole practice, 1959-68; ptnr. Steptoe & Johnson, Washington, 1968—90, of counsel, 1990—. Adj. prof. Duke U., Durham, NC, 1975—95, chmn. Ctr. for Forestry Investment, 1980—93; chmn. Ctr. for Continuing Edn., Washington, 1980—. Bd. trustees Hope Housing, 1992—96, Kingsbury Ctr., 1994—98; dir. mediation D.C. Pub. Schs., 1998—99. Lt (j.g.) USNR, 1944—46. Mem.: ABA, Congl. Country Club (Bethesda, Md.). Home: 2510 Virginia Ave NW # 502 Washington DC 20037-1904 Office: 1330 Connecticut Ave NW Washington DC 20036-1704

CONETTA, TAMI FOLEY, lawyer; b. Akron, Ohio, Aug. 29, 1965; d. Charles David and Roxanne (Onyett) Foley; m. Anthony Joseph Conetta, July 29, 1989 (div.); 1 child, Emory Elizabeth Conetta; m. Barry Frank Spivey, June 8, 2002. BA in Polit. Sci., Furman U., 1987; JD with honors, U. Fla., 1990. Bar: Fla. 1991; bd. cert. estates, trusts and wills Fla. Bar Bd. Legal Specialization. Ptnr. Gassman & Conetta, PA, Clearwater, Fla., 1990-98, Ruden, McClosky, Smith, Schuster & Russell, PA, Sarasota, Fla., 1998—. Contbr. articles to profl. jours. Mem. planned giving com. All Children's Hosp. Found. Recipient Am. Jurisprudence awards in Estate Planning and Taxation of Gratuitous Transfers, 1990. Mem. Am. Bus. Womens Assn., Sarasota County Bar Assn. (chair probate and estate planning sect. 2000-01), Clearwater Bar Probate Com. (chair 1996-98), Southwest Fla. Estate Planning Coun., Fla. Bar Assn. (chair probate rules com. 2003—, rules jud. adminstrn. com.). Avocations: golf, reading. Estate planning, Probate (including wills, trusts), Estate taxation. Office: Ruden McClosky Smith Schuster & Russell PA 1549 Ringling Blvd Ste 600 Sarasota FL 34236-6772 also: PO Box 49017 Sarasota FL 34230-6017 E-mail: tami.conetta@ruden.com.

CONGALTON, CHRISTOPHER WILLIAM, lawyer; b. N.Y.C., Apr. 8, 1946; s. William Alexander and Jacqueline Rose (Ryan) C.; m. Susan Tichenor, May 29, 1971. AB, Fairfield (Conn.) U., 1968; JD, Georgetown U., 1971. Bar: N.Y. 1972, U.S. Dist. Ct. (so. dist.) N.Y. 1974, U.S. Ct. Appeals (2d cir.) 1974, U.S. Supreme Ct. 1976, Ill. 1988, Colo. 1990. Assoc. Dunnington, Bartholow & Miller, N.Y.C., 1971-78; asst. gen. counsel Diamond Internat. Corp., N.Y.C., 1978-82; gen. counsel, v.p. Children's TV Workshop, N.Y.C., 1987-88; chmn. and ceo Moffitt Co., Schiller Park, Ill., 1988—. Mem. ABA (corp. banking & bus. sect.), Am. Corp. Counsel Assn., N.Y. State Bar Assn., Assn. of Bar of City of N.Y., Chgo. Bar Assn., Eagle Springs Golf Club. Corporate, general, Securities. Home: 1500 N Lake Shore Dr Chicago IL 60610-6657 Office: Moffitt Co 9347 Seymour Ave Schiller Park IL 60176-2206

CONINO, JOSEPH ALOYSIUS, lawyer; b. Hammond, La., Aug. 17, 1920; s. Dominic and Catherine (Tamborella) C.; m. Mae Evelyn Moragas, Feb. 27, 1943; children: Joseph Aloysius Jr., Robert Carl. BBA, Tulane U., 1950; JD, Loyola U., 1961; MBA, U. Pa., 1951. Bar: La. 1961, U.S. Dist. Ct. (ea. dist.) La. 1961, U.S. Ct. Appeals (5th cir.) 1972, U.S. Supreme Ct. 1989. Pvt. practice, Jefferson, La., 1961—. County judge State of La. Parish, Jefferson, 1970; del. State of La. Constnl. Conv., Baton Rouge, 1973-74; asst. atty. Parish of Jefferson, 1977—. With USN, 1942-45. Mem. La. Bar Assn. (ho. of dels. 1963-92, bd. dirs. 1981-83, 96-99), Jefferson Bar Assn. (pres.), New Orleans C. of C. (bd. dirs. 1974-77), Kiwanis (pres. Metairie, La. chpt.). Avocations: golf, swimming, tennis. General civil litigation, Estate planning, Property, real (including real estate development, water). Office: 1920 Jefferson Hwy Jefferson LA 70121-3816

CONKEL, ROBERT DALE, lawyer, pension consultant; b. Oct. 13, 1936; s. Chester William and Marian Matilda (Ashton) Conkel; m. Elizabeth A. Cargill, June 15, 1958; children: Debra Lynn, Dale William, Douglas Alan; m. Brenda Jo Myers, Aug. 2, 1980; 1 child, Chelsea Ashton. BA, Mt. Union Coll., 1958; JD cum laude, Cleve. Marshall Law Sch., 1965; LLM, Case Western Res. U., 1972. Bar: Ohio 1965, U.S. Ct. Appeals (5th cir.) 1979, U.S. Tax Ct. 1974, U.S. Supreme Ct. 1974. Supr. Social Security Adminstrn., Cleve., 1958—65; trust officer Harter Bank & Trust Co., Canton, Ohio, 1965—70; exec. v.p. Am. Actuaries, Inc., Grand Rapids, Mich., 1970—73; mgr. plans and rsch. A.S. Hansen, Inc., Dallas, 1973—74; pvt. practice Dallas, 1973—; pension cons., southwest regional dir. Am. Actuaries, Inc., Dallas, 1974—88. Sr. cons. Coopers & Lybrand, Dallas, 1989; pres. Robert D. Conkel, Inc., 1989—; mem. devel. bd. Met. Nat. Bank, Richardson, Tex.; instr. Am. Mgmt. Assn., 1975, Am. Coll. Advanced Pension Planning, 1975—76; enrolled actuary Joint Bd. Enrollment U.S. Depts. Labor and Treasury. Contbr. articles to legal publs.; mem. editl. adv. bd.: jour. Jour. Pension Planning and Compliance, 1974—83. Mem. Zoning Bd. of Adjustments, City of Richardson, Tex.; sustaining mem. Rep. Nat. Com., 1980—88. Mem.: ABA (employee benefit com. sect. taxation), Am. Acad. Actuaries, Am. Soc. Pension Actuaries (dir. 1973—81), Dallas Bar Assn., Tex. Bar Assn., Ohio State Bar Assn. Estate planning, Pension, profit-sharing, and employee benefits, Personal income taxation. Office: 100 N Central Expy # 519 Richardson TX 75080-5332

CONKLIN, HOWARD LAWRENCE, lawyer; b. N.Y.C., Apr. 16, 1943; s. Weldon F. and Gladys (Meyer) C.; m. Barbara Ann Janas, Aug. 1, 1982. BS, Fairleigh Dickinson U., 1961; MBA, Syracuse U., 1969; JD, Fordham U., 1974. Bar: Fla. 1974, U.S. Dist. Ct. (so. dist.) 1976, U.S. Supreme Ct. 1978, U.S. Dist. Ct. (mid. dist.) Fla. 1980. Mktg. planning specialist Trans World Airlines, N.Y.C., 1969-71; sr. transp. analyst Paine Webber, N.Y.C., 1971-74; ptnr. Tripp, Scott, Conklin & Smith, Ft. Lauderdale, Fla., 1974-97; v.p. govt. and airport rels. Alamo Rent-a-Car, Inc., Ft. Lauderdale, 1997; v.p. govt. rels. AutoNation, Inc., Ft. Lauderdale, 1997—. Chmn. Ft. Pierce Area Coun. C. of C.; chmn. investment advisory com. St. Lucie County; bd. dirs. ARC. Col. USAF, 1964—68, Vietnam. Decorated Bronze Star, Legion of Merit. Mem. ABA, Am. League of Lobbyists, Air Force Assn., Res. Officers Assn., St. Lucie County Bar Assn., Indian River County Bar Assn., Army Navy Club (Washington), Pelican Yacht Club, Sons of Norway. Avocation: flying. Government contracts and claims, Legislative, Trade. Office: Howard L Conklin Atty 2030 Harbortown Dr Ste A Fort Pierce FL 34946-1438

CONKLIN, THOMAS WILLIAM, lawyer; b. Chgo., Mar. 1, 1938; s. Clarence Robert and Ellen Pauline (Gleason) C.; children: Thomas William, Sarah Adrienne. BA, Yale U., 1960; JD, U. Chgo., 1963. Bar: Ill. 1964, Mich. 1997. Ptnr. Upton, Conklin & Leahy, Chgo., 1969-72, Conklin, Leahy & Eisenberg, Chgo., 1972-79, Conklin & Adler, Ltd., Chgo., 1979-87, Conklin & Roadhouse, Chgo., 1988-95; Rivkin, Radler & Kremer, Chgo., 1995-97; ptnr. Conklin, Murphy, Conklin & Snyder, Chgo., 1997—. Contbr. numerous articles to legal jours. With USAF, 1963-64. Mem. ABA, Fed. Bar Assn., Am. Arbitration Assn., Internat. Assn. Ins. Counsel, Chgo. Bar Assn., Maritime Law Assn., Mich. Bar Assn., Ill. State Bar Assn., Chgo. Bar Assn., Union League Club Chgo. Home: PO Box 189 Bangor MI 49013-0189 Office: Conklin Murphy Conklin & Snyder 53 W Jackson Blvd Ste 1150 Chicago IL 60604-3790 E-mail: tconk@msn.com.

CONLEY, DANIEL F. prosecutor; m. Tricia McGillicuddy; children: Jim, Christine. Asst. dist. atty. Suffolk County, Boston, 1984—93, dist. atty., 2002—; mem. Boston City Coun., 1993, chmn. pub. safety com. Mem. adv. bd. Suffolk U. Law Schs. Honor Program in Law and Pub. Svc.; mem. social justice com. Orders Sons Italy in Am. Mem.: Fraternal Order Police (hon.). Office: One Bullfinch Pl Boston MA 02114*

CONLIN, ROXANNE BARTON, lawyer; b. Huron, S.D., June 30, 1944; d. Marion William and Alyce Muraine (Madden) Barton; m. James Clyde Conlin, Mar. 21, 1964; children: Jacalyn Rae, James Barton, Deborah Ann, Douglas Benton BA, Drake U., 1964, JD, 1966, MPA, 1979; LLD (hon.), U. Dubuque, 1975. Bar: Iowa 1966. Assoc. Davis, Huebner, Johnson & Burt, Des Moines, 1966-67; dep. indsl. commr. State of Iowa, 1967-68, asst. atty. gen., 1969-76; U.S. atty. So. Dist. Iowa, 1977-81; ptnr. Conlin, P.C., Des Moines, 1983—. Adj. prof. law U. Iowa, 1977-79; chmn. Iowa Women's Polit. Caucus, 1973-75, del. nat. steering com., 1973-77; cons. U.S. Commn. on Internat. Women's Year, 1976-77; gen. counsel NOW Legal Def. and Edn. Fund, 1985-88, pres., 1986-88; lectr. in field. Contbr. articles to profl. jours. Nat. committeewoman Iowa Young Dems.; pres. Polk County Young Dems., 1965-66; del. Iowa Presdl. Conv., 1972; Dem. candidate for gov. of Iowa, 1982; bd. dirs. Riverhills Day Care Ctr., YWCA; chmn. Drake U. Law Sch. Endowment Trust, 1985-86; bd. counselors Drake U., 1982-86; pres. Civil Justice Found., 1986-88, Roscoe Pound Found., 1994-97; chair Iowa Dem. Party, 1998-99. Named one of Top Ten Litigators, Nat. Law Jour, 1989, 100 Most Influential Attys., 1991, 50 Most Powerful Women Attys., Nat. Law Jour., 1998, 10 Most Influential Women, 2002; recipient award, Iowa ACLU, 1974, Alumnus of Yr. award, Drake U. Law Sch., 1989, ann. award, Young Women's Resource Ctr., 1989, Verne Lawyer award as Outstanding Mem., Iowa Trial Lawyers Assn., 1994, Rosalie Wahl award, Minn. Women Lawyers, 1998, Marie Lambert award, 2000, Mary Louise Smith award, YWCA, 2001, lifetime achievement award, Des Moines Human Rights Commn.; grantee scholarship established in her honor Kansas City Women Lawyers; scholar Reader's Digest scholar, 1963—64, scholar, Fishcher Found, 1965—66. Mem.: ATLA (chmn. consumer and victims coalition com. 1985—87, chmn. edn. dept 1987—88, parliamentarian 1988—89, sec. 1989—90, v.p. 1990—91, pres.-elect 1991—92, pres. 1992—93), ABA, NOW, Trial Lawyers Care (bd. dirs.), Inner Circle of Advocates, Higher Edn. Commn. Iowa (co-chmn. 1988—90), Iowa Acad. Trial Lawyers, Internat. Acad. Trial Lawyers, Assn. Trial Lawyers Iowa (bd. dirs.), Iowa Bar Assn., Chi Omega, Alpha Lambda Delta, Phi Beta Kappa. Civil rights, General civil litigation, Personal injury (including property damage). Office: Griffin Bldg 319 7th St Ste 600 Des Moines IA 50309-3826

CONLON, MICHAEL WILLIAM, lawyer; b. Wilkes Barre, Pa., Nov. 9, 1946; s. William Peter and Dorothy (Stone) C.; m. Alice Cario, June 14, 1969; children: Michele, Stacia. AB, Cath. U., 1968; JD, Duke U., 1971. Bar: Tex. 1971, D.C. 1993. Ptnr. Fulbright & Jaworski, Houston, 1978-93, 98—, ptnr. in charge Washington, 1993-98, co-head corp., banking and bus. practice dept., 1999—, co-ptnr. in charge Houston Office, 2001—. Mergers and acquisitions, Corporate, general, Securities. Office: Fulbright & Jaworski 1301 Mckinney St Houston TX 77010-3031 E-mail: mconlon@fulbright.com.

CONLON, SUZANNE B. federal judge; b. 1939; AB, Mundelein Coll., 1963; JD, Loyola U., Chgo., 1968; postgrad., U. London, 1971. Law clk. to judge U.S. Dist. Ct. (no. dist.) Ill., 1968-71; assoc. Pattishall, McAuliffe & Hostetter, 1972-73, Schiff Hardin & Waite, 1973-75; asst. U.S. atty. U.S. Dist. Ct. (no. dist.) Ill., 1976-77, 82-86, U.S. Dist. Ct. (cen. dist.) Calif., 1978-82; exec. dir. U.S. Sentencing Commn., 1986-88; spl. counsel to assoc. atty. gen., 1988; judge U.S. Dist. Ct. (no. dist.) Ill., 1988—. Asst. prof. law De Paul U., Chgo., 1972-73, lectr., 1973-75; adj. prof. Northwestern U. Sch. Law, 1991-95; vice chmn. Chgo. Bar Assn. Internat. Inst., 1993—; vis. com. U. Chgo. Harris Grad. Sch. Pub. Policy, 1997—. Mem. ABA, FBA, Am. Judicature Soc., Internat. Bar Assn. Judges Forum, Lawyers Club Chgo. (pres. 1996-97). Office: US Dist Ct No Dist Everett McKinley Dirksen Bldg 219 S Dearborn St Ste 2356 Chicago IL 60604-1878*

CONMY, PATRICK A. federal judge; b. 1934; BA, Harvard U., 1955; JD, Georgetown U., 1959. Bar: Va. 1959, N.D. 1959. Ptnr. Lundberg, Conmy et al, Bismarck, N.D., 1959-85; mem. Bismarck City Commn., 1968-76; state rep. N.D. House Reps., Bismarck, 1976-85; judge U.S. Dist. Ct. N.D., Bismarck, 1985—. Office: US Dist Ct Fed Bldg 220 E Rosser Ave Rm 411 PO Box 1578 Bismarck ND 58502-1578*

CONN, DAVID P. lawyer; Grad., Hunter Coll., Columbia U. Bar: Calif. 1978. Dep. dist. atty., L.A.; ptnr. Jeffer, Mangels, Butler & Marmaro LLP, Century City, Calif.; pvt. practice L.A., 1978—. Office: 12400 Wilshire Blvd #400 Los Angeles CA 90025

CONNELL, JAMES BERNARD, lawyer; b. Milw., June 21, 1948; s. Bernard Joseph and mary Susan C.; m. Teresa Mary Seelman Connell, June 15, 1974; children: Elizabeth, Ann, Matthew, Mary, Thomas, Margaret. BA, Regis Coll., Denver, 1970; JD, Marquette U., Milw., 1974. Atty. Crooks Low Connell , Wausau, Wis., 1974—. Mem. Wis. Bar Assn., Madison, 1974—, Wis. Assn. Criminal Def. Lawyers, Madison, 1985—, Marathon County Bar Assn., Wausau, Wis., 1974—. Dir., officer United Cerebral Palsy of No. Ctrl. Wis., Wausau, 1975-80; mem. Task Force on the Legal Sys. and Refuge Population, Wausau, 1990-92. Recipient Outstanding Achievement award State Pub. Defender, 1998. Mem. Wausau Area Softball Assn., Wausau Curling Club, Alpha Delta Gamma, Phi Alpha Delta. Roman Catholic. General civil litigation, Criminal, General practice. Office: Crooks Low & Connell 531 Washington St Wausau WI 54403-5438

CONNELL, WILLIAM D. lawyer; b. Palo Alto, Calif., Apr. 1, 1955; s. Robert Charles and Audrey Elizabeth (Steele) C.; m. Kathy Lynn Mleko, Aug. 13, 1977; children: Hilary Anne, Andrew James. BA in Polit Sci. with honors, Stanford U., 1976; JD cum laude, Harvard U., 1979. Bar: Calif. 1979, U.S. Dist. Ct. (cen., no. and ea. dists.) Calif. 1979, U.S. Ct. Appeals (9th cir.) 1979. Assoc. Gibson, Dunn & Crutcher, L.A., 1979-80, San Jose, Calif., 1980-87, ptnr., 1988-97, Gen. Counsel Assocs. LLP, 1997—. Mem. Christian Legal Soc. Mem. Stanford Alumni Assn. (life), Commonwealth Club Calif., The Churchill Club, U.S. Golf Assn., The Federalist Soc., Phi Beta Kappa. Republican. Avocations: photography, golf. General civil litigation, Environmental, Product liability.

CONNELL, WILLIAM TERRENCE, lawyer, judge; b. Montclair, N.J., July 29, 1949; s. Raymond Charles and Kathryn (Hanley) C.; m. Honor Marilyn McMahon, July 19, 1975; children: Sean William, Heather Erin, Lauren Blythe. AB, Providence Coll., 1971; JD, Seton Hall U., 1976. Bar: N.J. 1977, D.C. 1979, U.S. Dist. Ct. N.J. 1977, U.S. Ct. Appeals (3d cir.) 1984; cert. trial atty. Investigator Comml. Union Ins. Co., West Orange, N.J., 1971, Essex County Prosecutors Office, Newark, 1971-77; mem. Dwyer, Connell & Lisbona, Montclair, NJ, 1977—, Fairfield, N.J., 1997—. Arbitrator Middlesex County Superior Ct., New Brunswick, N.J., 1984—; judge Mcpl. ct. Borough of Roseland, N.J., 1988—. Mem.: Def. Rsch. Inst., Trucking Ind. Def. Assn., Middlesex County Trial Lawyers Assn., Middlesex County Bar Assn., Essex County Bar Assn., N.J. Bar Assn., Am. Bd. Trial Attys. (adv.), Assn. Trial Lawyers Am., ABA, Bear Lakes Country Club (Fla.), Essex Fells Country Club (N.J.). Roman Catholic. Civil rights, Federal civil litigation, Insurance. Home: 18 Ford Ln Roseland NJ 07068-1456 also: 3360 S Ocean Blvd Palm Beach FL 33480 Office: Dwyer Connell & Lisbona Greenbrook Corp Ctr 100 Passaic Ave Fairfield NJ 07004-3508 E-mail: wconnell@dcllaw.com.

CONNELLY, COLIN CHARLES, lawyer; b. Hopewell, Va., Nov. 1, 1956; s. Charles Bernell and Doris Louise (Beasley) C.; m. Stephanie Paige Lowder, May 9, 1981. AA, Richard Bland Coll., 1977; BA, Va. Commonwealth U., 1979; JD, U. Richmond, 1983. Bar: Va. 1983, U.S. Ct. Appeals (4th cir.) 1983. Assoc. Tuck, Freasier, & Herbig, Richmond, Va., 1984-87; ptnr. Tuck & Connelly Profl. Assocs., Inc., Richmond, Va., 1988-95, Connelly & Assocs., P.C., Chester, Va., 1996—. Bd. dirs., v.p. Cen. Title Ins. Agy., Richmond, 1988—; agt. Chgo. Title Ins. Corp., Richmond, 1988—. Mem., assoc./counsel Home Builders Assn. South Side Va. Mem. ABA, Va. Bar Assn., Richmond Bar Assn., Southside Bd. Realtors (affiliate), Chester Jaycees, Omicron Delta Kappa, Phi Kappa Phi, Phi Alpha Delta (justice 1983-86). Baptist. Avocations: biking, racquetball, basketball. Construction, Property, real (including real estate development, water). Home: 14206 Masada Ct Chesterfield VA 23838-8725 Office: Connelly & Assocs 4830 W Hundred Rd Chester VA 23831-1746

CONNELLY, MARY JO, lawyer; b. Chgo., May 19, 1949; d. Joseph Anthony and Veronica Colette (Casey) C. BSN, Coll. St. Teresa, 1971; JD, DePaul U., 1980. Bar: Ill. 1980, U.S. Dist. Ct. (no. dist.) Ill. 1980, U.S. Dist. Ct. (ctrl. dist., no. dist.) Ill. 1990. Head nurse neurosurgery St. Mary's Hosp., Rochester, Minn., 1971-73; head nurse ambulatory care U. Calif., San Francisco, 1973-77; ptnr. Sweeney & Riman Ltd., Chgo., 1980-98. Mem. ABA, Women's Bar Assn. Ill., Ill. Bar Assn., Chgo. Bar Assn. (investigator hearing, bd. dirs. jud. evaluation com. 1984-89). General civil litigation, Personal injury (including property damage). Home: 340 W Diversey Pky Apt 618 Chicago IL 60657-6242 E-mail: maryjo.21stcentury@rcn.com.

CONNELLY, P. KEVIN, lawyer; b. Chgo., Apr. 29, 1950; s. John J. and Dorothy M. (Day) C.; children: Sheila S., J. Neil, D. Owen, Clare C. BS in Fgn. Service, Georgetown U., 1972; JD, Loyola U., Chgo., 1975. Bar: Ill., U.S. Dist. Ct. (no. dist.) Ill., U.S. Ct. Appeals (2d, 3d, 4th, 5th, 7th, 8th, 9th and 11th cirs.), U.S. Supreme Ct. Assoc. Lederer, Fox & Grove, Chgo., 1975-78; ptnr. Lederer, Reich, Sheldon & Connelly, Chgo., 1978-90, Connelly, Sheehan & Moran, Chgo., 1990—. Lectr. Loyola U. Law Sch., Chgo., 1977-85, adj. prof., 1985-97, 2001—. Contbr. articles to profl. jours. Mem. ABA (labor and employment law sect.), Chgo. Bar Assn. Roman Catholic. Federal civil litigation, Labor (including EEOC, Fair Labor Standards Act, labor-management relations, NLRB, OSHA). Home: 441 N Park Blvd Glen Ellyn IL 60137-4677 Office: Connelly Sheehan & Moran 150 S Wacker Dr Chicago IL 60606-4103

CONNELLY, THOMAS JOSEPH, lawyer; b. Kansas City, Kans., Jan. 31, 1940; s. Edward J. and Mary (McCallum) C.; m. Barbara Helen Marciniak, Aug. 1, 1964; children: Catherine, Jennifer. AB, U. Detroit, 1963, JD, 1968. Bar: Mich. 1969, U.S. Dist. Ct. (so. and ea. dists.) Mich. 1969, U.S. Ct. Appeals (6th cir.) 1969. Sr. ptnr. Connelly, Crowley, Groth & Seglund, Walled Lake, Mich., 1975—. Exec. bd. dirs. Oakland County (Mich.) Reps., 1979-82. Mem. Mich. Bar Assn. (rep. assembly 1978—), Oakland County Bar Assn., Internat. Arabian Horse Assn. (pres.), Mich. Arabian Horse Assn. (pres. 1986—), Am. Horse Shows Assn. (bd. dirs., exec. com. 1996—). Roman Catholic. Personal injury (including property damage), Property, real (including real estate development, water). Home: 1635 S Garner Rd Milford MI 48380-4127 Office: Connelly Crowley Groth & Seglund 2410 S Commerce Rd Walled Lake MI 48390-2129 E-mail: ccgs@ismi.net.

CONNELLY, WARREN E. lawyer; b. Mt. Vernon, N.Y., Nov. 18, 1946; BA cum laude, Dartmouth Coll., 1968; JD, Georgetown U., 1973. Bar: D.C. 1973. Atty. Cost of Living Coun., 1973-74; mem. Akin, Gump, Strauss, Hauer & Feld L.L.P., Washington. Active NAFTA Binat. Panel. 1st lt. U.S. Army, 1968-70. Mem. D.C. Bar. Office: Akin Gump Strauss Hauer & Feld LLP 1333 New Hampshire Ave NW Washington DC 20036-1564

CONNER, LEWIS HOMER, JR., lawyer; b. Chattanooga, Mar. 21, 1938; s. Lewis H. Sr. and Cleo (Johnson) C.; m. Ashley Whitsitt, June 1, 1960; children: Holland Ashley, Lewis Forrest. BA, Vanderbilt U., 1960, JD, 1963. Bar: Tenn. 1963, U.S. Dist. Ct. (all dists.) Tenn. 1963, U.S. Ct. Appeals (6th cir.) 1963, U.S. Ct. Mil. Appeals 1964, U.S. Supreme Ct. 1990; cert. mediator, Tenn. Founding ptnr., atty. Dearborn & Ewing, Nashville, 1972-80; judge Ct. Appeals Middle Dist., Nashville, 1980-84; sr. ptnr., atty. Waller Lansden Dortch & Davis, Nashville, 1985-89, Boult, Cummings, Conners & Berry, Nashville, 1989-96; of counsel Stokes & Bartholomew, Nashville, 1997—. Chmn. Willis Coroon, Tenn., 1996-99; spl. chief justice Supreme Ct. Tenn., 1980-81; lectr. law Vanderbilt U. Sch. Law, Nashville, 1984-93; life del. Sixth Cir. Ct. Appeals Jud. Conf. Mng. editor Vanderbilt Law Rev. Elder Westminster Presbyn. Ch.; bd. dirs. Tenn. Golf Assn., Nashville, 1965—, pres., 1985; chmn. Tenn. Golf Found., 1992-93, 96-97, 2000-01; fin. co-chmn. Alexander for Gov., 1974-78; chmn. Tenn. Rep. Fin. Com., 1975, Tenn. Corrections Overcrowding Commn., 1985-86; bd. dirs. Boys & Girls Club Middle Tenn., 1980—, pres., 1991-92; bd. govs. Tenn. State Mus., 1987-91; chmn. Gaylord Music City Bowl, 2002. Recipient Tennesseean of Yr. award, Tenn. Golf Found., 2001, Nat. Achievement award, Boys & Girls Club Mid. Tenn., 2003. Fellow Am. Acad. Matrimonial Lawyers, Am. Bar Found., Tenn. Bar Found., Nashville Bar Found.; mem. ABA, Am. Arbitration Assn. (bd. dirs. 1990-96, chmn. Tenn. large complex case panel 1992—, panel of arbitrators 1975—, panel of mediators 1995—), Tenn. Bar Assn., Tenn. Jud. Conf., Nashville Bar Assn. (pres. 1986-87, bd. dirs., 1984-87), Commn. on the Future of the Cts. in Tenn., Order of the Coif, PGA of Am. (hon. Tenn. sect.), The Golf Club Tenn. (founder, exec. com. 1991-97), Richland Country Club (bd. dirs. 1976-79, pres. 1978-79), Belle Meade Country Club, The Honors Course, Naples Grande Golf Club, Nashville City Club, Nashville Cumberland Club, Nashville Stadium Club, Tenn. Golf Assn. (amateur player of yr., 1973). Republican. Avocations: golf, basketball, softball, politics. Home: 163 Charleston Park Nashville TN 37205-4703 Office: Stokes & Bartholomew 424 Church St Ste 2800 Nashville TN 37219-2386 E-mail: lewconner@stokesbartholomew.com.

CONNER, STEWART EDMUND, lawyer; b. Louisville, Oct. 7, 1941; s. James Pleasant and Lucille (Winter) C.; m. Joan E. Fish, May 20, 1989; children: Shannon Lynn, Erin Eileen, Margaret Eisele; stepchildren: Hunt Rounsavall, Gibbs Rounsavall, Christine Rounsavall. BS, U. Louisville, 1963, JD cum laude, 1966. Bar: Ky. 1966, U.S. Dist. Ct. (ea. and we. dists.) Ky. 1966, U.S. Tax Ct. 1967. Assoc. Wyatt, Tarrant & Combs, Louisville, 1966-72, ptnr., 1972-90, chmn. gen. corp. sect., 1980-90, mng. ptnr., 1988-2001, chmn. exec. com., 1988—. Author, editor: Kentucky Business Practice Handbook, 1988; editor Kentucky Legal Forms, 1988; contbr. to U. Ky. Law Rev. Bd. dirs. Coun. on Higher Edn., 1992-95, Louisville Water Co., 1990—, Lincoln Heritage coun. Boy Scouts Am., 1989—, dePaul Sch., 1996—. With U.S. Army, 1968-69, Vietnam. Fellow Am. Bar Found., Ky. Bar Found.; mem. ABA (banking com. 1983), Ky. Bar Assn., Louisville Bar Assn. (chmn. ethics com. 1980), Ky. C. of C. (bd. dirs. 1992-96), Greater Louisville Inc. (bd. dirs. 1996-2001), Law Club, Harmony Landing Country Club, Louisville Boat Club. Republican. Banking, Corporate, general, Securities. Office: Wyatt Tarrant & Combs 2800 PNC Plz Louisville KY 40202 E-mail: sconner@wyattfirm.com.

CONNER, WILLIAM CURTIS, judge; b. Wichita Falls, Tex., Mar. 27, 1920; s. D.H. and Mae (Weeks) C.; m. Janice Files, Mar. 22, 1944; children: William Curtis, Stephen, Christopher, Molly. BBA, U. Tex., 1941, LLB, 1942; student, Harvard, 1942-43, MIT, 1943. Bar: Tex. bar 1942, N.Y. State bar 1949. Asso., mem. firm Curtis, Morris & Safford (and predecessor firm), N.Y.C., 1946-73; judge U.S. Dist. Ct. (so. dist.) N.Y., White Plains, 1973—, now sr. judge. Editor Tex. Law Rev. Served to lt. USNR, 1942-45, PTO. Recipient Jefferson medal N.J. Patent Law Assn., Outstanding Pub. Svc. award N.Y Intellectual Property Law Assn. Mem. Am. Judicature Soc., N.Y. Patent Law Assn. (pres. 1972-73), St. Andrews Golf Club. Presbyterian (elder). Office: US Dist Ct US Courthouse 300 Quarropas St White Plains NY 10601-4140

CONNER, WILLIAM HERBERT, lawyer; b. Columbus, Ohio, Jan. 29, 1940; s. Herbert Lee and Beulah Doris C.; m. Julie Ann Katzan, Aug. 13, 1966; children: W. David, Kristen Ann. Student, Purdue U., 1960-61; AB magna cum laude, Miami U., Oxford, Ohio, 1964; JD cum laude, U. Mich. Law Sch., 1967. Bar: Ohio 1967, U.S. Dist. Ct. (no. dist.) Ohio 1967. Assoc. Squire, Sanders & Dempsey L.L.P., Cleve., 1967-77, ptnr., 1977—. Contbr. articles to profl. jours. Mem. ABA (tax exempt financing com. 1981--), Ohio Bar Assn. (chmn. taxation com. 1981-84), Cleve. Bar Assn. (chmn. gen. tax com. 1983-84), Nat. Assn. Bond Lawyers (bd. dirs. 1991, 94-99, treas. 1995-96, pres. elect 1996-97, pres. 1997-98, immediate past pres. 1998-99). Republican. Methodist. Municipal (including bonds), Taxation, general, State and local taxation. Home: 3139 Falmouth Rd Shaker Heights OH 44122-2844 Office: Squire Sanders & Dempsey LLP 4900 Key Tower 127 Public Sq Ste 4900 Cleveland OH 44114-1304

CONNOLLY, COLM F. prosecutor; BA, U. of Notre Dame; MSc, London Sch. Econs.; JD, Duke U. Asst. U.S. Atty. Dist. of Del., 1992—99; ptnr. Morris, Nichols, Arsht and Tunnel, Wilmington, Del., 1999—2001; U.S. Atty. Dist. of Del., 2001—. Recipient Director's award for Superior Performance as Asst. U.S. Atty., U.S. Atty. Gen., 1996. Office: US Attorney Chase Manhattan Ctr PO Box 2046 Wilmington DE 19899-2046 Fax: 302-573-6220.

CONNOLLY, GERALD EDWARD, lawyer; b. Boston, Oct. 13, 1943; s. Thomas E. and Grace J. (Fitzgerald) C.; m. Elizabeth Heidi Eckert, Jan. 6, 1968; children: Matthew F., Dennis F., David D., Edward F. BS, Coll. of Holy Cross, 1965; JD, U. Va., 1972. Bar: Wis. 1972, U.S. Tax Ct. 1973. From assoc. to ptnr. Whyte & Hirschboeck S.C., Milw., 1972-78; ptnr. Minahan & Peterson S.C., Milw., 1978-91, Quarles & Brady, 1991—. V.p., bd. dirs., sec. Reinhart FoodService, Inc.; bd. dirs., sec. Reinhart Real Estate Group, Inc., Reinhart Retail Group; sec. Hometown Inc.; bd. dirs. Viterbo U., LaCrosse, Wis., Hatco Corp., Milw., Adaptive Engring. Lab., Inc., Diversatek, Inc., Medovations, Sunlite Plastics, Inc., Milw.; sec. The Medalcraft Mint, Inc., Radisson LaCrosse Hotel, Water Blasting. Trustee Emory T. Clark Family Charitable Found., D.B. Reinhart Family Found.; chmn. Circle of Care Children's Hosp. Wis.; bd. dirs. Children's Hosp. Wis. Found. Lt. USN, 1966-69. Mem. ABA, Milw. Club, Milw. Athletic Club, North Shore Country Club, Order of Coif. Corporate, general, Mergers and acquisitions, Property, real (including real estate development, water). Home: 10134 N Range Line Rd # 27W Mequon WI 53092-5435 Office: Quarles & Brady 411 E Wisconsin Ave Ste 2550 Milwaukee WI 53202-4497 E-mail: gec@quarles.com.

CONNOLLY, JOSEPH THOMAS, lawyer, judge; b. Montclair, NJ, Mar. 22, 1938; s. Patrick Joseph and Ethelyn Marie (Dilkes) Connolly; m. Phyllis Jane Marturano, June 25, 1966; children: James V., Michael J., Victoria L. BS, St. Peter's Coll., Jersey City, 1959; JD, Fordham U., 1966. Bar: N.J. 1967, U.S. Dist. Ct. N.J. 1967, U.S. Supreme Ct. 1972. Claim adjuster Md. Am. Gen. Group, East Orange, NJ, 1962—66; jud. clk. Superior Ct. N.J., Newark, 1966—67; assoc. Feurerstein & Sachs, Newark, 1967—68, Donohue & Donohue, Nutley, NJ, 1969—71; trial lawyer Office Pub. Defender N.J., Newark, 1968—69; ptnr. Brown, Connolly & Karosen, Bloomfield, NJ, 1971—88; sole practitioner Glen Ridge, 1989—; judge Mcpl. Ct., Glen Ridge, NJ, 1980—; acting judge Irvington Mcpl. Ct., Newark Mcpl. Ct. Instr. William Paterson Coll., Wayne, NJ, 1980; lectr. Inst. for Continuing Legal Edn., Trenton and Newark, 1975—82; moot ct. judge Seton Hall U. Sch. Law, Newark, 1980—94. Pres. Glen Ridge Cmty. Fund, 1978—79; trustee League for Family Svc. , Bloomfield and Glen Ridge; pres. Bloomfield Jaycees, 1971—72. Served U.S. Army, 1959—60. Mem.: ABA, Essex County Bar Assn., N.J. Bar Assn. (consultor 1979—84), Glen Ridge Country Club, Bloomfield Lawyers (pres. 1976—77, Outstanding Service award 1977), Kiwanis (pres. 1979—80, sec., bd. dirs., Disting. Pres. award). Roman Catholic. General practice, Probate (including wills, trusts). Home: 13 Winsor Pl Glen Ridge NJ 07028-2124 Office: Office JT Connolly 13 Windsor Pl Glen Ridge NJ 07028

CONNOLLY, K. THOMAS, lawyer; b. Spokane, Wash., Jan. 23, 1940; s. Lawrence Francis and Kathleen Dorothea (Hallahan) C.; m. Laurie Samuel, June 24, 1967; children: Kevin, Megan, Amy, Matthew. BBA, Gonzaga U., Spokane, Wash., 1962; JD, Gonzaga U., 1966; LLM in Taxation, NYU, 1972. Bar: Wash. 1966, U.S. Ct. Mil. Appeals 1967, U.S. Tax Ct. 1983. Assoc. Witherspoon, Kelley, Davenport & Toole, Spokane, 1972-77, ptnr./prin., 1977—. Assoc. prof. law Gonzaga Sch. Law, 1973-77. Bd. overseers Gonzaga Prep. Sch., Spokane, 1988-89; trustee Spokane Guild Sch. for the Handicapped, 1975-78, Wash. State U. Found. Bd., 1992-97, Whitman Coll. Planned Giving Coun., 1994-2001, Holy Family Adult Day Care Bd., 2001—. Capt. U.S. Army, 1966-70. Recipient Wall St. Jur. award, 1962; decorated Bronze Star medal. Mem. Wash. State Bar Assn. (founder, chmn. health law sect. 1989-92, health law coun. 1989-94, pres. state tax sect. 1987-88, mem. tax coun. 1984—), ABA (chmn. health care subcom. 1990-94). Republican. Avocations: tennis, astronomy. Health, Pension, profit-sharing, and employee benefits, Corporate taxation. Office: Witherspoon Kelley Davenport & Toole 1100 US Bank Bldg Spokane WA 99201 E-mail: ktc@wkdtlaw.com.

CONNOLLY, THOMAS EDWARD, judge; b. Boston, Nov. 7, 1942; s. Thomas Francis and Catherine Elizabeth (Skehill) C. AB, St. John's Coll., Brighton, Mass., 1964; JD, Boston Coll., 1969. Bar: Mass., 1969. Assoc. Schneider & Reilly, Boston, 1969-73; ptnr. Schneider, Reilly, Zabin, Connolly & Costello, P.C., Boston, 1973-85, Connolly Leavis & Rest, Boston, 1986-90; judge Mass. Superior Ct., Boston, 1990—. Instr. law Northeastern Law Sch., Boston, 1975-76. Mem. governing coun. Boston Coll. Law Sch. Alumni Coun., 1980—82, 2001—. Fellow Am. Coll. Trial Lawyers; mem. ABA (vice chmn. products liability sect. 1978-80), Trial Lawyers Assn. Am. (nat. gov. 1977-80), Mass. Acad. Trial Lawyers (gov. 1976-90), Univ. Club (Boston). Democrat. Roman Catholic. Home: 253 Marlborough St # 4 Boston MA 02116-1731 Office: The Superior Ct Boston MA 02109

CONNOLLY, WILLIAM M. state supreme court justice; Undergrad., Creighton U., 1956—59, JD, 1963. Dep. atty. Adams County, 1964—66, atty., 1967—72; pvt. law practice Hastings, 1972—91; former judge Nebr. Ct. of Appeals, Lincoln, 1992—94; assoc. justice Nebr. Supreme Ct. , Lincoln, justice, 1994—. Office: Nebr Supreme Ct PO Box 98910 2413 State Capitol Bldg Lincoln NE 68509 Office Fax: 402-471-3480.

CONNOR, TERENCE GREGORY, lawyer; b. Chelsea, Mass., Dec. 28, 1942; s. Joseph Gerard Sr. and Rosalie Cecilia (Ryan) C.; m. Julie Kaye Berry, Dec. 18, 1971; children: Cormac, Kristin, Etain, Brendan. AB, Georgetown U., 1964; LLB, Seton Hall U., 1967; LLM, Georgetown U., 1975. Bar: D.C. 1968, U.S. Supreme Ct. 1976, Fla. 1980. Trial atty. U.S. Dept. Justice, Washington, 1973-76; labor counsel Nat. Airlines Inc., Miami, Fla., 1976-79; practicing atty. Morgan, Lewis & Bockius, Miami, 1979-96, mng. ptnr., 1996—2002. Mem. firm wide governing bd., 1996-2000. Chmn. Miami: Dade citizen com. for Observance Bicentennial of U.S. Constitution, 1986. Served to capt. JAG, USAF, 1968-73. Mem. Fla. Bar Assn. (chair labor and employment law sect. 1994-95, mem. exec. coun. 1986-93), Miami C. of C. (co-chair pers. and Labor mgmt. com. 1993-94) Civil rights, Federal civil litigation, Labor (including EEOC, Fair Labor Standards Act, labor-management relations, NLRB, OSHA). Home: 1517 San Rafael Ave Miami FL 33134-6241 Office: Morgan Lewis & Bockius Wachovia Fin Ctr 200 S Biscayne Blvd Ste 5300 Miami FL 33131-2333

CONNORS, EUGENE KENNETH, lawyer, educator; b. Dobbs Ferry, N.Y., Oct. 3, 1946; s. Edward Micheal and Eileen (Burke) C.; children: Kevin Patrick, Kathryn Margaret. BA in English, Holy Cross Coll., Worcester, Mass., 1968; JD, Columbia U., 1971. Bar: Pa. 1971. Assoc. Reed Smith Shaw & McClay, Pitts., 1971-76; ptnr. Reed Smith LLP (formerly Reed Smith Shaw & McClay), Pitts., 1977—. Adj. prof. St. Francis Coll. Grad. Sch., Loretto, Pa., 1975—; ski instr. Holiday Valley Ski Area, Ellicottville, N.Y., 1987—; bd. dirs. Green Garden Inc., 1985—. Contbr. articles to profl. jours. Bd. dirs. Sch. Vol. Assn. Pitts., 1973-78, Pitts. Human Resources Assn., 1988-95, TEC/Pa. Smallers Mfrs. Coun., 1993-94, Pitts. Pub. Theater, 1999—, exec. com., 2000—. Persuaded U.S. Supreme Ct. to overturn 9-0 employment discrimination decision adverse to employers 442 U.S. 366 (1979). Mem. ABA, Pa. Bar Assn., Allegheny County Bar Assn., Pitts. Human Resources Assn. (bd. dirs. 1988-95, treas. 1987-95), Tri-State Employers Assn. (bd. dirs. 1992-93), Profl. Ski Instrs. Am. Avocations: alpine (downhill) skiing, scuba diving, golf. Federal civil litigation, State civil litigation, Labor (including EEOC, Fair Labor Standards Act, labor-management relations, NLRB, OSHA). Office: Reed Smith LLP PO Box 2009 435 6th Ave Pittsburgh PA 15219-1886

CONNORS, FRANK JOSEPH, lawyer; b. N.Y.C., Oct. 8, 1944; s. Frank Joseph and Nina Florence (Kirk) C.; m. Evelyn Noreen Mills, Oct. 14, 1983. BA, UCLA, 1965; MA, Columbia U., 1966; JD, Harvard U., 1969. Bar: N.Y. 1970, Fla. 1982, Mass. 1986, U.S. Supreme Ct. 1973. Assoc. Dewey, Ballantine, Bushby, Palmer & Wood, N.Y.C., 1969-75; asst. atty. gen. N.Y. State Spl. Prosecutor, N.Y.C., 1975-77; gen. atty. Am. Broadcasting Cos., Inc., N.Y.C., 1977-85; atty. Harvard U., Cambridge, Mass., 1985—; acting gen. counsel, 1992. Arbitrator N.Y.C. Civil Ct., 1980-85; comml. arbitrator Am. Arbitration Assn., N.Y.C., 1984-85. Bd. dirs. World Teach, Inc., 1992-2002. Mem. Am. Judicature Soc., N.Y. State Bar Assn. (copyright com. 1981-85), Assn. of Bar of City of N.Y. (profl. discipline com. 1983-85). Republican. Methodist. Corporate, general, Taxation, general. Office: Harvard U 1350 Massachusetts Ave Cambridge MA 02138-3846 E-mail: frank_connors@harvard.edu.

CONNORS, JAMES PATRICK, lawyer; b. N.Y.C., May 28, 1952; s. Joseph Patrick Connors and Edna Theresa Fitzgerald; m. Gloria Ann Ciccarelli, Jan. 12, 1974; children: Nicholas, Patrick, Jamie Cathleen. BA, Herbert H. Lehman Coll., 1974; JD, N.Y. Law Sch., 1977; LLM, NYU, 1985. Bar: N.Y. 1978, U.S. Dist. Ct. (so. and ea. dists.) N.Y. 1978. Assoc. Bower & Gardner, N.Y.C., 1978-80, Joseph W. Conklin, N.Y.C., 1980-82; ptnr. Jones, Hirsch, Connors & Bull, N.Y.C., 1982—. Lectr. NYU Sch. Medicine, 1983, N.Y. Law Jour., 1984, Bellevue Hosp., 1984, Hillcrest Gen. Hosp., 1984, Mt. Sinai Hosp., 1985, Am. Coll. Ophthalmologists, 1986—88. Contbr. Recipient Am. Jurisprudence award, Lawyers Pub. Coop., 1977. Mem.: ABA, Lawyer Pilot Bar Assn., Def. Assn. of N.Y., N.Y. County Bar Assn., N.Y. State Bar Assn. State civil litigation, Insurance, Personal injury (including property damage). Home: 85 Mayflower Dr Yonkers NY 10710-3801

CONNORS, JOSEPH ALOYSIUS, III, lawyer; b. Washington, June 24, 1946; s. Joseph Aloysius Jr. and Charlotte Rita (Fox) C.; m. Mary Louise Bucklin, June 14, 1969. BBA, U. Southwestern La., 1970; JD, U. Tex., 1973. Bar: Tex. 1973, U.S. Dist. Ct. (so. dist.) Tex. 1975, U.S. Supreme Ct. 1976, U.S. Ct. Appeals (5th cir.) 1976, U.S. Dist. Ct. (ea., we. and no. dists.) Tex. 1981, U.S. Ct. Appeals (11th cir.) 1981, U.S. Ct. Appeals (3d, 4th, 6th, 7th, 8th, 9th, 10th and D.C. cirs.) 1986. Law clk. to assoc. justice Tex. Ct. Civil Appeals, Amarillo, 1973-74; assoc. Rankin & Kern, McAllen, Tex., 1974-76; asst. criminal dist. atty. Hidalgo County, Tex., 1976-78; pvt. practice, McAllen, 1978—. Faculty Criminal Trial Advocacy Inst., Huntsville, Tex., 1981-84; spkr. seminars State Bar Tex., 1980-81, 84; adj. prof. Reynaldo G. Garza Sch. Law, Edinburg, Tex., 1988-89. Contbg. editor Criminal Trial Manual, Tex., 1984-95; contbr. articles to profl. jours. Bd. dirs. Tex. Rural Legal Aid, 1991—, pres. bd. dirs., 1994-96. With USMCR, 1966-71. Mem. NACDL, State Bar Tex. (grievance com. 12B 1984-91, chmn. com. 1989-90, profl. enhancement program 1997-2000), Tex. Assn. Criminal Def. Lawyers (bd. dirs. 1982-89, Excellence award 1983, medal of honor 1987), Hidalgo County Bar Assn. (bd. dirs. 1981-83), Am. Soc. Writers on Legal Subjects, Hidalgo County Criminal Def. Lawyers Assn. (bd. dirs. 1991-98). Democrat. Roman Catholic. Criminal. Home: 605 E

Violet Ave Ste 3 Mcallen TX 78504-2469 Office: Law Offices Joseph A Connors III 605 E Violet Ave Ste 3 Mcallen TX 78504

CONNORS, PETER J. lawyer; b. Huntington, NY, June 25, 1951; s. John Anthony and Jeanne (Labate) Connors; m. Claudine Minieri, Nov. 13, 1979; children: Priscilla, Grayson. BA, Cath. U., 1973; JD, U. Richmond, 1976; LLM, NYU, 1979. CPA N.Y., 1979, Va., 1979; bar: N.Y. 1977. Mgr. JC Penney & Co., NYC, 1983—87; sr. mgr. KPMG, 1987—90; prin., dir. Ernst & Young LLP, 1990—95; ptnr. Baker & McKenzie, 1995—2001, Orrick, Herrington & Sutcliffe LLP, 2001—. Fellow: Am. Coll. Tax Counsel; mem.: ABA. Avocation: squash. Mergers and acquisitions, Corporate taxation, Estate taxation. Office: Orrick Herrington & Sutcliffe LLP 666 5th Ave New York NY 10103 E-mail: pconnors@orrick.com.

CONNUCK, ERIC S. lawyer; b. Bklyn., Nov. 14, 1965; m. Wendy E. DiMarco, Aug. 23, 1991; children: Marc, David. BS, SUNY, Binghamton, 1986; JD, NYU, 1991. Bar: Conn. 1991, N.Y. 1992, U.S. Dist. Ct. (ea. and so. dists.) N.Y. 1992, U.S. Dist. Ct. (no. dist.) N.Y. 1998, U.S. Dist. Ct. Colo. 1998, U.S. Dist. Ct. (ea. and we. dist.) Ark. 1999, U.S. Ct. Appeals (2d cir.) 2000. Assoc. Rogers & Wells, N.Y.C., 1991-94, McCarrick, Finnerty & Mayer, N.Y.C., 1994-96, Piper Marbury Rudnick & Wolfe L.L.P., N.Y.C., 1996—2002; of counsel Piper Rudnick LLP, N.Y.C., 2002—. General civil litigation, Insurance, Professional liability. Office: Piper Rudnick LLP 1251 Ave of Americas New York NY 10020 E-mail: eric.connuck@piperrudnick.com.

CONOUR, WILLIAM FREDERICK, lawyer; b. Indpls., June 21, 1947; s. William E. and Marian L. (Smith) C.; m. Jennifer Conour; children: Tonja, Andrea, Erin, Rachel, Tyler, Elise. BA History, Ind. U., 1970, JD cum laude, 1974. Bar: Ind. 1974, U.S. Dist. Ct. (so. dist.) Ind. 1974, U.S. Dist. Ct. (no. dist.) Ind. 1996, U.S. Ct. Appeals (7th cir.) 1975, U.S. Supreme Ct., 1982; cert. mediator Ind. Supreme Ct., 1992—. Dir. training Ind. Pros. Attys. Council, Indpls., 1974-82; ptnr. Conour & Devis, Indpls., 1974-86; assoc. prof., adj. faculty Ind. U. , 1975—89; pvt. practice Indpls., 1986-88; spl. dep. prosecutor State of Ind. v. Ford Motor Co. (Ford Pinto Prosecution); ptnr. Conour Doehrman , Indpls., 1988—. Assoc. prof., adj. faculty Ind. U. Purdue U. Indpls., 1976-86; lectr. Ind. Law Enforcement Acad., otehr lectrs. in field; rsch. analyst Ind. Criminal Law Study Commn., 1973-74. Contbg. author Indiana Criminal Procedure Sourcebook, 1974, Indiana Penal Code, 1974, Indiana Prosecuting Attorney's Deskbook, New Indiana Penal Code, 1976, Lawyers Cooperative Publishing, 1996, The Indiana Lawyer, 2000 ; editor profl. bulletins; editor, contbg. author: Indiana Prosecuting Attorney's Deskbook, 1978; contbr. articles to profl. jours.; author: Indiana Penal Code, 1977, Res Gestae Mag., 1977-90, The Prosecutor, 1980, Verdict mag., 1992, The Indiana Lawyer, 1996, 99. Guarantor Butler U. Clowes Hall; patron Ind. Repertory Theatre, Indpls. Symphony Orch.; mem. Gov.'s club Ind. Dems., Conner Prairie Pioneer Settlement, Nat. Safety Coun., Hoosier Safety Coun.; mem., co-chmn. task force cmty. based missions second Presbyn. ch.; mem. bd. dirs. U. HS; chess coach U. HS Chess Team; life mem.U.S. Chess Fedn.; life mem. Ind. U. Alumi Assn.; life mem. Woodburn Guild Ind. U.; life mem., mem. bd dirs. Hoosier Salon, U.S. Centenial Olympic Com., Ind., 1996; mem. Five Seasons Country Club; life mem. Ind. Dressage Soc., U.S. Dressage Fedn., NA/WPN, Am. Horse Show Assn.; mem. gold club U.S. Equistrian Team. Recipient commendation Drug Enforcement Adminstrn. U.S. Dept. Justice, 1977, Commendation award Hoosier Safety Coun., 1989, Commendation award Ind. State Bar Assn. Criminal Justice Sect., 1990. Fellow Roscoe Pound Found. (life), Found. Am. Bd. Trial Advocates (sr. life), Indpls. Bar Found. (life); mem. ABA (litigation sect.), Am. Bd. Trial Advocates (pres. Ind. chpt., honoree, charter sr. life fellow 1996), Am. Soc. Safety, Ind. Bar Assn. (sec. litigation 1981-82, ad hoc com. on legal cert., mem. litigation sect., criminal justice sect., sec. 1977-78, treas. 1981-82), Am. Coll. Legal Medicine (assoc.), Indpls. Bar Assn. (grievance com. 1983-91, litigation sect.), Assn. Trial Lawyers Am. (cert. Nat. Coll. Advocacy 1979, Advanced Coll. Advocacy 1981, cons. site litigation group, M Club, lectr., cert. civil trial advocate), Ind. Bar Assn. (grievance com. 1984-91), Coll. of Legal Medicine, Am. Coll. of Legal Medicine, Ind. Trial Lawyers Assn. (sustaining mem., bd. dirs., lectr., amicus curie com., rule of evidence com.), Ind. Lawyers Commn. (ad hoc com. on criminal justice standards and goals 1976-80), Am. Bd. Trial Advs., Ind. U. Alumni Assn. (life), Ind. State Bar Assn. (litig. sect. 1983-, appellate law sect. 1996-, ad hoc com. legal cert., chmn. lawyers adv. com. 1996-98, commendation criminal justice sect. 1990), Trial Lawyers Pub. Justice (sustaining founder), Indpls. Law Club, Indpls. Athletic Club, US Equestrian Team (contbg. mem.), Nat. and Hoosier Safety Coun. (commendation 1989), US Dressage Fedn. Ind. Dressage Soc. (dir.), Indpls. Mus. Art, Sagamore Am. Inn of Ct. (pres. 1999-2001, pres.-elect 1997-99, counselor 2001-), Nat. Am. Inns Ct. Found. (trustee 2001-), Am. Coll. Barristers (sr.counsel), Phi Delta Phi (hon.). Clubs: Inpls. Athletic; Ind. Soc. Chgo., Atla "M". Democrat. Federal civil litigation, General civil litigation, Personal injury (including property damage). Home: 10858 Sedgemoor Cir Carmel IN 46032-9189 Office: 10333 N Meridian St Ste 100 Indianapolis IN 46290-1074 Office Fax: 317-705-4455. E-mail: wfc@indianalaw.com.

CONOVER, FREDERIC KING, lawyer; b. Portchester, N.Y., June 4, 1933; s. Julian D. and Josephine T. Conover; m. Kathryn B. Conover, Dec. 21, 1955; children: Frederic, Elizabeth, Pamela, Margaret; m. 2d, Jacquelyn Wonder, Aug. 24, 1979. B.A., Amherst Coll., 1955; J.D., U. Mich., 1961. Bar: Colo. 1962, U.S. Dist. Ct. Colo. 1962, U.S. Ct. Appeals (10th cir.) 1962. Ptnr. Conover, McClearn & Heppenstall, P.C., Denver, 1972-88, Faegre & Benson, Devner, 1988—, ptnr. in charge dispute resolution svcs. The Faegre Group, 1993—. Trustee Mt. Airy Psychiat. Ctr.; dir. Legal Aid Soc.; chmn. citizens adv. com. Denver Regional Coun. Govts.; bd. govs., trustee, Nat. Ctr. for Preventive Law; mem. panel of disting. neutrals Ctr. for Pub. Resources; bd. dirs. Lawyers Alliance for World Security, Denver Partnership, Colo. Hist. Soc.; founder, bd. dirs. Generation of Hope Fund, The Denver Found. Served to lt. USN, 1955-59. Fellow Am. Coll. Trial Lawyers, Am. Bar Found., Colo. Bar Found.; mem. ABA, Denver Bar Assn. (pres. 1983-84), Colo. Bar Assn. (pres. 1990-91), Law Club (v.p.), Colo. Hi, Generations of Hope Fundst. Soc. (bd. dirs.), City Club of Denver (dir.), Denver Tennis Club. Democrat. State civil litigation, Corporate, general, General practice. Office: The Faegre Group 2500 Republic Plz 370 17th St Denver CO 80202-1370

CONOVER, RICHARD CORRILL, lawyer; b. Bridgeport, Nebr., Jan. 12, 1942; s. John Cedric and Mildred (Dunn) C.; m. Cathy Harlan, Dec. 19, 1970; children— William Cedric, Theodore Cyril. B.S., U. Nebr., Lincoln, 1965, M.S., 1966; J.D., Cornell U., 1969. Bar: N.Y. 1970, Mont. 1982, U.S. Dist. Ct. (so. and ea. dists.) N.Y. 1971, U.S. Supreme Ct. 1977, U.S. Ct. Customs and Patent Appeals 1979, U.S. Ct. Claims 1980, U.S. Dist. Ct. Mont. 1984, U.S. Tax Ct. 1986. Assoc. Brumbaugh, Graves, Donohue & Raymond, N.Y.C., 1969-73; assoc. Townley, Updike, Carter & Rodgers, N.Y.C., 1974-75; assoc. gen. counsel legal office Automatic Data Processing, Inc., Clifton, N.J., 1975-77; assoc. Nims, Howes, Collison & Isner, N.Y.C., 1977-81; sole practice, Mont., 1981— ; lectr. indsl. and mech. engring. dept. Mont. State U., 1981-97. Mem. Mont. Gov.'s Bd. Sci. and Tech., 1985-87. Mem. ABA, Assn. Bar City N.Y., Mont. Bar Assn., Am. Pat. Law Assn. General civil litigation, Patent, Trademark and copyright. Home: PO Box 1329 Bozeman MT 59771-1329 Office: 104 E Main St Ste 404 Bozeman MT 59715-4787

CONRAD, JOHN REGIS, lawyer, engineering executive, consultant; b. Bloomington, Ind., Feb. 23, 1955; s. John Francis and Patricia Ann (English) C.; m. Paula Jane Vessels, July 4, 1980; children: William Celestine Vessels, John Paul Vessels, M. Alexander Vessels, David Thomas Kelamalamalamanokeakua Vessels, Rachel Elizabeth Ho'ouluolaikealoha Vessels. AB cum laude, Harvard U., 1977; MBA, JD, Ind. U., 1981. Bar: Hawaii 1981, Fla. 1994, Tex. 1994, N.C. 1995, U.S. Dist. Ct. Hawaii 1981, U.S. Ct. Appeals (9th cir.) 1981, U.S. Ct. Claims 1981, U.S. Tax Ct. 1981. Assoc. Cades, Schutte, Fleming & Wright, Honolulu, 1981-85, 89-90, Thompson & Chan, Honolulu, 1985-89; ptnr. Cades Schutte Fleming & Wright, Honolulu, 1991-94; regional bus. mgr. Kimley-Horn and Assocs., Inc., West Palm Beach, Fla., 1994-96, regional prodn. mgr., 1996-98, regional bus. mgr., sr. assoc., sr. v.p. Phoenix, 1999—. Lectr. law Kapiolani C.C., Honolulu, 1984-86; adj. prof. Richardson Sch. Law, U. Hawaii, 1989-90; webmaster Conrad-Vessels Genealogy. Author: A Conrad Genealogy, 1979, Hawaii Probate Sourcebook, 1985, rev. 1986, rev. 1992; co-author: Beyond the Basics: Hawaii Estate Planning & Probate, 1985, Hawaii Wills & Trusts Sourcebook, 1986, Hawaii Guardianship Sourcebook, 1988; editor HICLE Fin. and Estate Planning Manual, vol. II, 1989, vol. I, 1990. Planned giving com. Hawaii Heart Assn., Honolulu, 1983-86; arbitrator Hawaii Ct. Annexed Arbitration Program, 1989-94; sch. bd. Star of the Sea Sch., Honolulu, 1992-94, pres., 1993-94, chair Carnival, 1992; chair Cub Scout Pack Aloha Coun. Boy Scouts Am., den leader Cub Scout Pack, Gulf Stream Coun., Grand Canyon Coun.; lector Good Shepherd of the Hills Ch., Cave Creek, Ariz.; trustee St. Paul's Prep. Acad., Phoenix, 2002--. Fellow Am. Coll. Trust and Estate Coun.; mem. ABA, Am. Arbitration Assn., Hawaii Bar Assn. (chmn. estate and gift tax com. 1984-85, CFO probate and estate planning sect. 1989-90), Hawaii Bar Found. (bd. dirs. 1985-92, v.p. 1989, pres. 1989-91), Ancestral Trails Hist. Soc., Sons of Am. Legion, John T. Reilly Hist. Soc., Hawaii Estate Planning Coun. (bd. dirs. 1991-94, sec. 1993), Filson Club Hist. Soc. Roman Catholic. Avocations: running, genealogy, coin collecting, scouting. Office: Kimley-Horn and Assocs Inc 7600 N 15th St Ste 250 Phoenix AZ 85020-4335 Home: 33214 N 61st St Scottsdale AZ 85262-8206 E-mail: jrconrad@post.harvard.edu., john.conrad@kimley-horn.com.

CONRAD, ROBERT J. prosecutor; BA Clemson U., JD U. Va. Pvt. practice Michie, Hamlett, Donato and Lowry, 1983—86, Horn and Conrad, 1986—87; aole practice, 1987—88; ptnr. Bush, Thurman and Conrad, 1988—89; asst. U.S. atty. We. Dist. N.C. U.S. Dept. Justice, 1989—2001, U.S. atty. western dist., 2001—. Office: Carillon Bldg Ste 1700 227 W Trade St Charlotte NC 28202*

CONRAN, JOSEPH PALMER, lawyer; b. St. Louis, Oct. 4, 1945; s. Palmer and Theresa (Bussmann) C.; m. Daria D. Conran, June 8, 1968; children: Andrew, Lisabeth, Theresa. BA, St. Louis U., 1967, JD with honors, 1970. Bar: Mo. 1970, U.S. Ct. Mil. Appeals 1971, U.S. Ct. Appeals (8th cir.) 1974. Assoc. Husch and Eppenberger, St. Louis, 1974-78, ptnr., 1978—, chmn. litigation dept., 1980-95, chmn. mgmt. com., 1995—. Mem. faculty Trial Practice Inst. Capt., JAGC, USAF, 1970-74. Mem. Bar Assn. Met. St. Louis (Merit award 1976, 77), Mo. Bar Assn. (bd. govs. 1987-92), Mo. Athletic Club (pres. 1986-87), Norwood Hills Country Club, St. Louis Club. Roman Catholic. Federal civil litigation, State civil litigation, Securities. Home: 53 Hawthorne Est Saint Louis MO 63131-3035 Office: Husch & Eppenberger 100 N Broadway Ste 1300 Saint Louis MO 63102-2789 E-mail: joe.conran@husch.com.

CONROY, CHRISTOPHER S. lawyer; b. Omaha, Sept. 6, 1971; BS in Comm., Northwestern U., 1994; JD, Washburn U., 1998; MBA in Finance, Kans. U., 2001. Bar: Kans. 1998, U.S. Dist. Ct. Kans. 1998. Asst. counsel AmerUs Annuity Group Co., Topeka, 1997—. Fundraiser Jr. Achievement, Topeka, 2002, Boy Scouts Am., United Way; bd. dirs. Native Am. Jr. Golf Assn., Mayetta, Kans., 2002. Mem.: ABA, Topeka Bar Assn., Kans. Bar Assn., Am. Corp. Counsel Assn. Insurance, Corporate, general, Administrative and regulatory. Office: AmerUS Annuity Group Co 555 S Kansas Ave Topeka KS 66603 Business E-Mail: chrisco@amerusannuity.com.

CONROY, ROBERT JOHN, lawyer; b. Newark, Feb. 17, 1953; s. Michael John and Frances (Goncalves) C.; m. Mary Catherine McGuire, June 7, 1975; children: Caitlin Michaela, Michael Colin. BS, St. Peter's Coll., 1977; M in Pub. Adminstrn., CUNY, 1981; JD, N.Y. Law Sch., 1981; MPH, Harvard U., 1985. Bar: N.Y. 1981, N.J. 1981, U.S. Dist. N.J. 1981, Calif. 1982, U.S. Dist. Ct. (so. and ea. dists.) N.Y. 1982, U.S. Dist. Ct. (we. dist.) Calif. 1990, U.S. Ct. Appeals (2d, 3d and 11th cirs.) 1982, Fla. 1984, D.C. 1984, U.S. Supreme Ct. 1984, Pa., 2000, U.S. Dist. Ct. (ea. dist.), Pa., 2001. Asst. corp. counsel City of N.Y., 1981-83, dep. chief med. malpractice unit, 1983, chief med. malpractice unit, 1984; assoc. Jones, Hirsch, Connors & Bull, N.Y.C., 1985-88; counsel Kern & Augustine, P.A., Morristown, N.J., 1988-90; prin. Kern Augustine Conroy & Schoppmann, P.C., Bridgewater, N.J., 1990—. Spl. counsel pro bono med. malpractice rsch. project, N.Y.C., 1985-88; gen. counsel Med. Soc. N.J., 2002—. Decorated knight of merit Sacred Mil. Constantinian Order St. George, 2002; Solomon scholar, NY Law Sch., 1979; recipient Bronze Pelican award Roman Cath. Archdiocese, Newark, 2000. Fellow: Coll. Law Practice Mgmt.; mem.: ABA (chmn. govt. mgmt. com. 1984—86, mgr. products media bd. 1985—92, chmn. document retrieval com. 1985—86, vice-chmn. ins. and malpractice com. 1986—88, co-chmn. glass ceiling task force 1992—95, vice-chmn. law practice mgmt. phb. bd. 1992—95, coun. mem. 1989—95, co-chmn. law practice mgmt. pub. bd. 1995—98, Foonberg award 1998), Am. Healthcare Lawyers Assn., N.Y. Bar Assn. (mem. health law sect. 1996—), Assn. of Bar of City of N.Y., Cmty. Health Law Project N.J., Inc. (trustee 1988—91), Westfield Sr. Citizens Housing Corp., Inc. (trustee 1994—, v.p. 1996—98, pres. 1998—), Soc. Health Care Risk Mgmt. N.J. (chmn. legis. com. 1987—96), N.J. Bar Assn. (dir., chmn. health hosp. sect. 1993—95, mem. com. health law litigation, mem. subcom. profl. licensing 1997—, del. gen. coun. adminstrn. sect. 1995—97), Mensa, Harvard Club. Administrative and regulatory, General civil litigation, Health. Home: 905 Pennsylvania Ave Westfield NJ 07090-3433 Office: Kern Augustine Conroy & Schoppmann PC 1120 Rt 22 E Bridgewater NJ 08807 E-mail: CONROY@DRLAW.COM.

CONSILIO, BARBARA ANN, legal administrator, management consultant; b. Cleve., June 22, 1938; d. Joseph B. and Anna E. (Ford) C. BS, Kent State U., 1962; MA, U. Detroit, 1973. Cert. social worker, Mich. Tchr. Chagrin Falls (Ohio) High Sch., 1962-64; probation officer Macomb County Juvenile Ct., Mt. Clemens, Mich., 1965-68, casework supr., 1968-74, dir. children's svcs., 1974-79; mgr. foster care and instns. Oakland County Juvenile Ct., Pontiac, Mich., 1979-83; ct. adminstr. Oakland County Probate Ct., Pontiac, 1983-93, ret., 1993. Bd. dirs. Children's Charter Cts. of Mich., Lansing, Statewide Adv. Bd. on Sexual Abuse, Lansing, Havenwyck Hosp., Auburn Hills, Orchards Children's Svcs., Southfield, Oakland County Coun. Children at Risk, Pontiac; mem. Nat. Women's Polit. Caucus, N.Y.C.; bd. dirs. Care House, Pontiac. Mem. Nat. Coun. Juvenile and Family Ct. Adminstrs. Group, Mich. Probate and Juvenile Register's Assn., Mich. Juvenile Ct. Adminstrs. Assn., Nat. Assn. Ct. Mgrs., Supreme Ct. Task Force on Racial and Ethnic Bias, Office of Children and Youth Svcs. (state foster care system rev. com.), Nat. Coun. Juvenile and Family Ct. Judges (Outstanding Ct. Adminstr. award, 1993). Avocations: music, sports, sports cars. Home: 3000 Carefree Blvd M-4 Fort Myers FL 33917

CONSTANTINE, HEIDI CHRISTINE, lawyer; BS, U. La., Lafayette, 1994; JD, Pepperdine U., 1999. Bar: N.Y. 2000. Assoc. LeBoeuf, Lamb, Greene & MacRae, L.L.P., N.Y.C., 1999—. Intellectual property, Trademark and copyright, General civil litigation. Office: LeBoeuf Lamb Greene & MacRae LLP 125 West 55th St New York NY 10019

CONSTANTINO-BANA, ROSE EVA, nursing educator, researcher, lawyer; b. Labangan Zamboanga delSur, Philippines, Dec. 25, 1940; came to U.S., 1964; naturalized, 1982; d. Norberto C. and Rosalia (Torres) Bana; m. Abraham Antonio Constantino, Jr., Dec. 13, 1964; children: Charles Edward, Kenneth Richard, Abraham Anthony III. BS in Nursing, Philippine Union Coll., Manila, 1962; MNursing, U. Pitts., 1971, PhD, 1979; JD, Duquesne U., Pitts., 1984. Lic. clin. specialist in psychiatric-mental health nursing; RN. Instr. Philippine Union Co., 1963-65, Spring Grove State Hosp., Balt., 1965-67, Montefiore Sch. Nursing, Pitts., 1967-70, U. Pitts., 1971-74, asst. prof., 1974-83, assoc. prof., 1983—, chmn. Senate Athletic Com., 1985-86, 89-90, sec. univ. senate, 1991-92, v.p., 1993-95. Project dir. grant divsn. of nursing HHS, Washington, 1983-85; bd. dirs. Am. Jour. Nursing; prin. investigator NIH NINR, 1991-94; bd. dirs. Internat. Coun. on Women's Health Issues, 1986—. Author: (with others) Principles and Practice of Psychiatric Nursing, 1982; contbr. chpts. to books and articles to profl. jours. Mem. Presdl. Task Force, Washington, 1980, Rep. Senatorial Com., Washington, 1980. Fellow Am. Acad. Nursing, Am. Coll. Forensic Examiners; mem. ABA, ATLA, Allegheny County Bar Assn. (bd. cert. forensic examiner), Pa. Bar Assn., Women's Bar Assn., Am. Assn. Nurse Attys., Am. Nurses Assn., Pa. Nurses Assn. (sec. 1994-98), Nat. League Nursing, Pa. League Nursing (chairperson area 6), Allegheny County Bar Assn., U. Pitts. Sch. Nursing Alumni Assn., U. Duquesne Law Alumni Assn., Sigma Theta Tau, Phi Alpha Delta. Seventh Day Adventist. Avocations: cooking, piano. Home: 6 Carmel Ct Pittsburgh PA 15221-3618 Office: U Pitts Sch Nursing 4500 Victoria St Rm 415 Pittsburgh PA 15261-0001

CONSTON, HENRY SIEGISMUND, lawyer; b. Dresden, Germany, Dec. 18, 1928; arrived in U.S., 1947, naturalized, 1952; BSBA, NYU, 1955, JD, 1958, LLM, 1961. Bar: N.Y. 1959. With Calif. Tex. Oil Corp., N.Y.C., 1947-61; sr. ptnr. Walter, Conston, Alexander & Green PC, N.Y.C., 1961—95; sr. counsel Alston & Bird$D, N.Y.C., 2001—. Contbr. Bd. dirs. Margaret Tietz Ctr. for Nursing Care, N.Y. Found. Nursing Homes, Inc. Office: 90 Park Ave New York NY 10016-1301

CONTI, JOY FLOWERS, judge; b. Kane, Pa., Dec. 7, 1948; d. Bernard A. Flowers and Elizabeth (Tingley) Rodgers; m. Anthony T. Conti, Jan. 16, 1971; children: Andrew, Michael, Gregory. BA, Duquesne U., 1970, JD summa cum laude, 1973. Bar: Pa. 1973, U.S. Dist. Ct. (we. dist.) Pa. 1973, U.S. Ct. Appeals (3rd cir.) 1976, U.S. Supreme Ct. 1993. Law clk. Supreme Ct. Pa., Monessen, 1973-74; assoc. Kirkpatrick & Lockhart, Pitts., 1974-76, 82-83, ptnr., 1983-96; shareholder Buchanan, Ingersoll, P.C., Pitts., 1996—2002; dist. judge U.S. Dist. Ct.(we. dist.) Pa., Pitts., 2002—. Prof. law Duquesne U., Pitts., 1976-82; hearing examiner Pa. Dept. State, Bur. Profl. Occupation and Affairs, 1978-82; chairperson search com. for judge U.S. Bankruptcy Ct. (we. dist.) Pa., 1987, 95; active Pa. Futures Commn. on Justice in 21st Century, 1995-97. Contbr. articles to profl. jours. Mem. disciplinary hearing com. Supreme Ct. Pa., 1982-88; v.p. Com. for Justice Edn., Pitts., 1983-84; mem. Leadership Pitts., 1987-88. Named One of Ten Outstanding Young Women in Am., 1981. Fellow Am. Bar Found. (Pa. state chair 1991-97); mem. ABA (ho. of dels. 1980-86, 91-97), Am. Law Inst., Am. Coll. Bankruptcy, Pa. Bar Assn. (gov. 1993-95, ho. of dels. 1978—, Am. Inns of Ct., Pitts. Chpt. (2002-), corp. banking and bus. law sect. coun. 1983-89, treas. 1991-93, v.p. 1993-95, chair-elect 1995-97, chmn. 1997-99, chmn. commn. comml. law 1990-93, co-chair 1995-2002, chair civil rights and responsibilities com. 1986-89, Achievement award 1982, 87, 99, Anne X. Alpern award 1995), Nat. Conf. Bar Pres. (exec. coun. 1993-96), Allegheny County Bar Assn. (adminstrv. v.p. 1984-86, 90, chairperson corp. banking and bus. law sect. 1987-89, treas. 1988-90, gov. 1991, pres.-elect 1992, pres. 1993), Internat. Women's Insolvency and Restructuring Confedn. (chair Tri-State Network 1996), Pa. Bar Inst. (dir. 1991-97), Duquesne Club, Treesdale Country Club. Roman Catholic. Office: US Dist Judge 936 US Courthouse 7th & Grant Sts Pittsburgh PA 15219

CONTI, LEE ANN, lawyer; b. Astoria, Oreg. BA with honors, So. Ill. U., 1970; JD summa cum laude, De Paul U., 1976. Bar: Ill. 1976, U.S. Dist. Ct. (no. dist.) Ill. 1976. Ptnr. Mayer, Brown & Platt, Chgo., 1983-94; assoc. gen. counsel Citizens Comm. Co., Stamford, 1994—2002. Contbr. articles to profl. jours. Mem. Bd. Edn. Cmty. Consol. Sch. Dist. 89, Du Page County, 1987-93. Recipient Am. Jurisprudence awards in Torts, Remedies. Mem. ABA, Am. Corp. Counsel Assn., Ill. State Bar Assn., Du Page County Bar Assn., Chgo. Bar Assn., Phi Kappa Phi, Pi Sigma Alpha, Phi Lambda Pi. Office: 635 S Park Blvd Glen Ellyn IL 60137-6977

CONTI, LOUIS THOMAS MOORE, lawyer; b. Phila., Aug. 31, 1949; s. Alexander and Yolanda (DiLorenzo) Conti; m. Christina M.S. Moore, May 1, 1982; children: Charles Alexander, Whitney Caroline. BS, LaSalle Coll., 1971; MBA, Drexel U., 1972; JD, Creighton U., 1975; LLM, Temple U., 1981. Bar: Pa. 1975, U.S. Claims Ct. 1975, U.S. Tax Ct. 1975, U.S. Dist. Ct. (ea. dist.) Pa. 1978, U.S. Ct. Appeals (3d cir.) 1979, U.S. Supreme Ct. 1981, Fla. 1982, U.S. Dist. Ct. (mid. dist.) Fla. 1988. Tax atty. Office Chief Counsel IRS, Washington and Phila., 1975-81; tax mgr. Touche Ross & Co., Phila., 1981-84; assoc. Saul, Ewing, Remick & Saul, Phila., 1984-87; shareholder Swann & Haddock, P.A., Orlando, Fla., 1987-89; ptnr., chmn. corp. tax and securities dept. Holland & Knight, Orlando, 1989—. Mem. fin. com. S.E. Pa. chpt. ARC, Phila., 1984—87; advisor Vol. Lawyers for Arts, Phila., 1984—87; bd. dirs. Fla. Hosp. Found., Ctrl. Fla. Planned Giving Coun., 1989—97, Cmty. Found. Ctrl. Fla. Inc., World Trade Ctr., Orlando, 1992—95; mem. internat. bus. adv. bd. Metro Orlando; grad. Leadership Orlando, 1994, Leadership Fla., 1996; chair recruiting com. East Ctrl. Region of Leadership Fla., 1997; bd. dirs. Orlando Performing Arts and Edn. Ctr., Inc., 1998—2001. Mem.: ABA (tax and bus. law sect., chmn. task force on drafting prototype ltd. liability co. operating ag 1998—, chmn. Fla. Bar drafting com. 1999), Orange County Bar Assn. (chmn. tax sect. 1990—91), Fla. Bar Assn. (tax and bus. law sect., chmn. drafting com. ltd. liability co. operating agreements 1998—, chair corps. and securities com., bus. law sect. 1999—2001, chair tax sect. 2001—02), Seminole County C. of C. (bd. dirs. 1994—97). Republican. Avocation: travel, skiing, golf, tennis, theatre. Corporate, general, Mergers and acquisitions, Corporate taxation. Home: 603 Genius Drive Winter Park FL 32779 Office: Holland & Knight PO Box 1526 Orlando FL 32802-1526 E-mail: lconti@hklaw.com.

CONTI, SAMUEL, federal judge; b. L.A., July 16, 1922; s. Fred and Katie C.; m. Dolores Crosby, July 12, 1952; children: Richard, Robert, Cynthia. BS, U. Santa Clara, 1945; LLB, Stanford U., 1948, JD. Bar: Calif. 1948. Pvt. practice, San Francisco and Contra Costa County, 1948-60; city atty. City of Concord, Calif., 1960-69; judge Superior Ct. Contra Costa County, 1968-70, U.S. Dist. Ct. (no. dist.) Calif., San Francisco, 1970-88, sr. judge, 1988—. Mem. Ctrl. Contra Costa Bar Assn. (pres.), Concord C. of C. (pres.), Alpha Sigma Nu. Office: US Dist Ct 450 Golden Gate Ave Ste 36052 San Francisco CA 94102-3482

CONTI, WILLIAM ACHILLE, lawyer; b. Torrington, Conn., Apr. 26, 1948; s. Achille William and Catherine Conti; m. Linda Losacano, Aug. 12, 1972; children: Christian, Marissa. BA, Boston Coll., 1970, JD, 1973. Bar: Conn. 1973, Mass. 1974. Assoc. Rozbicki & Assocs., Torrington, Conn., 1973—90; mng. ptnr. Smith, Keefe, Conti & Moraghan, Torrington, Conn., 1990—97; ptnr. Febbroriello, Conti & Levy, Torrington, 1997—. Lectr. N.W. Conn. C.C., Winsted. Mem. Torrington Dem. Town Com., 1974—2002. Mem.: ABA, ATLA, Conn. Criminal Def. Assn., Litchfield County Bar Assn. (pres. 1996—2002). Democrat-Npl. Roman Catholic. Workers' compensation, Personal injury (including property damage), Criminal. Home: PO Box 421 Torrington CT 06790 Office: Febbroriello Conti & Levy 355 Prospect St Torrington CT 06790 Office Fax: 860-489-6306. E-mail: info@fcandl.com.

CONWAY, BERRY LESLIE, II, lawyer; b. Morganfield, Ky., Apr. 14, 1956; m. Darlene Conway; children: Michael, John, Nicole. BA with high distinction, U. Ky., 1979, JD, 1986. Bar: Va. 1987, U.S. Dist. Ct. (we. dist.) Va. 1987. Sr. assoc. Penn, Stuart, Eskridge, Abingdon, Va., 1987-93; ptnr. Conway Law Firm P.L.L.C., Abingdon, 1993—. Mem. Phi Beta Kappa.

Avocation: breeding standardbred horses. General civil litigation, Criminal, Personal injury (including property damage). Office: Conway Law Firm PLLC 165 W Main St Abingdon VA 24210-2837 E-mail: conwayattorneys@naxs.com.

CONWAY, FRENCH HOGE, lawyer; b. Danville, Va., June 11, 1918; s. Lysander Broadus and Mildred (Hoge) C.; BS, U. Va., 1942, JD, 1946; m. Louise Throckmorton, Feb. 3, 1961; children: French Hoge, William Chenery, Helen (Mrs. Carlton Bedsole), Donna (Mrs. Michael Henderson). Starnes. Bar: Va. 1942. Sole practice, Danville, 1942—; mem. firm Clement, Conway & Winston, 1950-60. Sec., Danville City Bd. Rev., 1985— ; v.p. Va. Election Bd. Assn., 1974. Served with USNR, 1942-46. Mem. ABA, Va. Bar Assn., Danville Bar Assn. (pres. 1985-86), Am. Trial Lawyers Assn., Va. Trial Lawyers Assn., Soc. Cincinnati in State of Va., Ret. Officers Assn., Boat Owners Assn. U.S. Lodges: Kiwanis, Masons. General practice, Personal injury (including property damage), Probate (including wills, trusts). Home: 912 Main St Danville VA 24541-1810 Office: 105 S Union St Danville VA 24541-1113

CONWAY, JOHN E. federal judge; b. 1934; BS, U.S. Naval Acad., 1956; LLB magna cum laude, Washburn U., 1963. Assoc. Matias A Zamora, Santa Fe, 1963-64; ptnr. Wilkinson, Durrett & Conway, Alamogordo, N.Mex., 1964-67, Durrett, Conway & Jordon, Alamogordo, 1967-80, Montgomery & Andrews, P.A., Albuquerque, 1980-86; city atty. Alamogordo, 1966-72; mem. N.Mex. State Senate, 1970-80, minority leader, 1972-80; chief fed. judge U.S. Dist. Ct. N.Mex., Albuquerque, 1994—2000, sr. fed. judge, 2000—. Mem. Jud. Resources Com., 1995—98. 1st lt. USAF, 1956-60. Mem. 10th Cir. Dist. Judges Assn. (pres. 1995-98), Fed. Judges Assn. (bd. dirs. 1996-2001), Nat. Commrs. on Uniform State Laws, N.Mex. Bar Assn., N.Mex. Jud. Coun. (vice chmn. 1973, chmn. 1973-75, disciplinary bd. of Supreme Ct. of N.Mex. vice chmn. 1980, chmn. 1981-84, apptd. to fgn. intelligence surveillance ct. 2002). Office: US Dist Ct Chambers #740 333 Lomas Blvd NW Albuquerque NM 87102-2272 E-mail: jconway@nmcourt.fed.us.

CONWAY, MARK ALLYN, lawyer; b. Dayton, Ohio, Dec. 13, 1957; s. Allyn Walter and Doris Jean (Wright) C.; m. Dawn Elizabeth Manning, July 31, 1982; children: Ashley Wright, Alexandra Mills. BA, Denison U., 1980; JD, Calif. Western Sch. of Law, 1983; LLM in Taxation, Georgetown U., 1984. Bar: D.C. 1983, U.S. Tax Ct. 1983, Calif. 1988, Ohio 1991. Ptnr. Thompson Hine LLP, Dayton, 1990—. Fellow Am. Coll. of Trust and Estate Counsel; mem. ABA (real property, probate and trust law sect.), D.C. Bar Assn., Calif. Bar Assn. (real property, probate and trust law sect. 1988—), Dayton Racquet Club. Republican. Presbyterian. Avocations: tennis, skiing, sailing. Estate planning, Probate (including wills, trusts), Estate taxation. Home: 5712 Price Hill Pl Dayton OH 45459-1428 Office: Thompson Hine LLP 2000 Courthouse Plz NE Dayton OH 45402

CONWAY, REBECCA ANN KOPPES, lawyer; b. Colorado Springs, Colo., May 18, 1952; d. Virgil Lee and Betty J. Koppes; children: Kelley, Kathrine; m. Sean P. Conway, Nov. 26, 1994. BA, U. Colo., 1975, JD, 1978. Bar: Colo. 1978, U.S. Dist. Ct. Colo. 1978. Atty. EEOC, Denver, 1978-79, Dist. Atty.'s Office, Adams County, Brighton, Colo., 1979-80; ptnr. Gutierrez & Koppes, Greeley, Colo., 1980-92; pvt. practice Law Office of Rebecca Koppes Conway, Greeley, 1992—. Mem. Colo. Pub. Defenders Commn., 1985-95, chair, 1990-95; chair Civil Justice Task Force, State of Colo., 1999-2000. Chmn. Placement Alternatives Commn., Weld County, Colo., 1987-89; mem. Our Saviors Luth. Ch., Greeley, 1985, exec. dir., 1987-89; chmn. bd. dirs. Colo. Rural Legal Svcs., Denver, 1983-86, 93-96; mem. 19th Dist. Jud. Nominating Commn., 2000—; vice-chair Weld Child Care Network, 1988; chair transition com. jud. Gov. Owens Adminstrn., State of Colo., 1998; mem. state exec. com. Dem. Party, 1993-98, mem. ctrl. com., 1993-99; mem. Weld County Exec. Com., 1990-99, vice chair, 1991-92; co-chair Univ. Schs., bd. govs. k-12 charter, 2000—. Fellow ABA (ho. of dels. 1994-1997), Colo. Bar Found. (dir. 1998, chair bd. dirs. 1999); mem Colo. Bar Assn. (com. mem., exec. coun. 1986-90, 94-98, bd. govs. 1983-90, 94-99, 2001—, pres.-elect. 1996-97, pres. 1997-98, chair young lawyers divsn. 1988-89, Outstanding Young Lawyer 1988, v.p. 1989-90, litigation sect. coun. 1998, chair 1999-2000), Weld County Bar Assn. (pres. 1992-93), Redeye Rotary (bd. dirs. 2001—). Avocation: reading. Personal injury (including property damage), Workers' compensation. Home: 2595 56th Ave Greeley CO 80634-4503 Office: 912 8th Ave Greeley CO 80631-1112

CONWAY, ROBERT GEORGE, JR., lawyer; b. Albany, N.Y., Apr. 26, 1951; s. Robert George Sr. and Kathryn Ann (Kelly) C.; m. Lynda Rae Christenson, Dec. 15, 1979; 1 child, Phillip Christopher. AB, Dartmouth Coll., 1973; JD, Union U., 1976; diploma, U.S. Army JAGC Sch., 1986. Bar: Pa. 1978, U.S. Ct. Mil. Appeals 1978, N.C. 1983, U.S. Dist. Ct. (ea. dist.) N.C. 1983, U.S. Dist. Ct. (no. dist.) N.Y. 1998, U.S. Army Ct. Mil. Rev. 1986, U.S. Supreme Ct. 1986, U.S. Ct. Appeals (4th and fed. cirs.) 1987, N.Y. 1998; cert. USMC judge advocate. Commd. 2d lt. USMC, 1975, advanced through grades to maj., 1983, gen. staff sec., 1982-83, chief rev. officer, 1983-84, spl. asst. U.S. atty., 1984-85, dir. joint law ctr. air sta. Cherry Point, N.C., 1986-88, chief rsch. officer air sta., 1988, dep. asst. staff judge adv. to comdt. Washington, 1989; mil. justice officer Marine Corps Base, Quantico, Va., 1990-91; assoc. counsel for land use law Ea. Area Counsel Office USMC Dept. of Navy Office of Gen. Counsel, Camp Lejeune, N.C., 1991-96; ret. USMC, 1996; counsel, dep. commr. N.Y. State Divsn. Mil. and Naval Affairs, Latham, 1996—. Adj. faculty mem. Ga. Inst. Tech., 1993, Webster U., 1994-96; spkr. in field. Trustee Cath. student ctr. Aquinas House, Dartmouth Coll., Hanover, N.H., 1973-89, sec. Dartmouth class of 1973, 1994—. Recipient Legion of Merit, 1996. Mem.: ABA, Marine Corps Assn., U.S. Naval Inst., Dartmouth Lawyers Assn., Fed. Bar Assn. (contbg. author assn. news and jour. 1990), N.Y. Bar Assn., N.C. Bar Assn., Pa. Bar Assn., Dartmouth Club Ea. N.Y. (v.p. 1998—2001, pres. 2001—), KC (adv. 1984—85), Am. Legion. Roman Catholic. Home: 27 Manor Dr Glenmont NY 12077-3326 Office: NY State Divsn Mil and Naval Affairs Attn MNLA 330 Old Niskayuna Rd Latham NY 12110-3514

COOK, AUGUST JOSEPH, lawyer, accountant; b. Devine, Tex., Sept. 25, 1926; s. August E. and Mary H. (Schmidt) C.; m. Matie M. Brangan, July 12, 1952; children: Lisa Ann, Mary Beth, John J. BS, Trinity U., 1949; BBA, U. Tex., 1954; JD, St. Mary's U., 1960. Bar: Tex. 1960, Tenn. 1975. Bus. mgr., corp. sec. Life Enterprises, Inc. and affil. cos., San Antonio, 1950-58, also bd. dirs.; mgr. Ernst & Young, San Antonio, 1960-69, ptnr., Memphis, 1970-84; ptnr. McDonnel Boyd, Memphis, 1984-91; of counsel Harris, Shelton, Dunlap and Cobb, Memphis, 1991-97, Pietrangelo Cook, Memphis, 1997—. Author: A.J. $ Tax Court, 1987; author newspaper column A.J.'s Tax Fables, 1983—; contbr. articles to profl. jours. Alderman City of Castle Hills, Tex., 1961-63, mayor, 1963-69; chmn. Bexar County Coun. Mayors, 1967-69; v.p. Tex. Mcpl. League, 1968-69; bd. dirs. San Antonio Met. YMCA. With U.S. Army, 1945-46, PTO. Mem. AICPA, Tex. Soc. CPAs, Tex. Bar Assn., Estate Planning Coun. San Antonio (pres. 1967), Tenn. Soc. CPAs, Tenn. Bar Assn. (chmn. tax, probate and trust sect., 1993-95), Estate Planning Coun. Memphis (pres. 1983-84), Toastmasters (pres. 1963), Delta Theta Phi, Kappa Pi Sigma, University Club (Memphis), Canyon Creek Country Club (San Antonio, bd. dirs.), Chickasaw Country Club, Optimists (bd. dirs.), Rotary (treas. 1978, 99, bd. dirs. 1986-87, 96-97). Estate planning, Corporate taxation, Personal income taxation. Home: 6785 Slash Pine Cv Memphis TN 38119-5617 Office: Pietrangelo Cook PLC 6410 Poplar Ave Ste 190 Memphis TN 38119-4841

COOK, BRYSON LEITCH, lawyer; b. Balt., Apr. 17, 1948; s. A. Samuel Cook. BA magna cum laude, Princeton U., 1970; JD cum laude, MBA, U. Pa., 1973. Bar: Md. 1974, U.S. Dist. Ct. Md. 1976, U.S. Tax Ct. 1977. Assoc. Alex Brown & Sons, Balt., 1973-75, Venable, Baetjer & Howard, Balt., 1975-81, ptnr., 1981—. Adj. prof. U. Md. Law Sch., Balt., 1981, Loyola U. Bus. Sch., Balt., 1980-82. Contbr. articles to legal jours.; author tax mgmt. portfolios. Trustee Balt. Ballet, 1980-83, Keswick Home for the Incurables, Balt., 1983—; bd. dirs. Balt. City Jail, 1980-82; counsel Md. Hist. Soc., Balt., 1981—. Recipient Gordon A. Block award U. Pa. Law Sch., 1973. Mem. ABA, Bar Assn. Balt. City, Md. State Bar Assn., Internat. Fiscal Assn., Order of Coif, Elkridge Club (Balt.). Republican. Methodist. Corporate, general, Corporate taxation, Estate taxation. Home: 201 Woodbrook Ln Baltimore MD 21212-1037 Office: Venable Baetjer & Howard LLP Mercantile Bank Trust Bldg 2 Hopkins Plz Ste 1800 Baltimore MD 21201-2971 E-mail: blcook@venable.com.

COOK, CHARLES RYAN, lawyer; b. Seoul, South Korea, Oct. 24, 1969; s. John Ryan and Barbara Sandy Cook; m. Rakel Su Boler, Sept. 25, 1971. BA in Polit. Sci. and Philosophy, U. of Calif., Santa Barbara, 1991; JD, U. of Ariz., 1996. Bar: Wash. 1997. Ptnr. The Bae Law Group, P.S., Seattle, 1998—. Co-chair, DOL liaison com. Am. Immigration Lawyers Assn., Wash. State, Seattle, 2002—. Mem.: ABA, Am. Immigration Lawyers Assn., Phi Delta Phi (treas. 1994—95). Immigration, naturalization, and customs, Corporate, general. Office: The Bae Law Group PS 2505 2nd Ave Seattle WA 98121 E-mail: ryan@us-immigration.net.

COOK, CHARLOTTE SMALLWOOD, lawyer; b. Union Springs, N.Y., Jan. 24, 1923; d. William H. and Alice (Utter) Licht; m. Edward M. Smallwood, May 22, 1943; children: Edward Christopher, Susan Smallwood Grossman; m. Frederick S. Cook, July 25, 1970. BA, Cornell U., 1944; LLB, Columbia U., 1946. Bar: N.Y. 1947, U.S. Supreme Ct. 1958. Ptnr. Smallwood & Smallwood, 1947-52, Smallwood & Ladd, 1970-74, Smallwood, Cook & Stout, 1975-77, 82—, Smallwood, Cook, Stout & Erickson, 1977-82 (all Warsaw, N.Y.); dist. atty. Wyoming County (N.Y.), 1949-52. Mem. ABA, N.Y. State Bar Assn. N.Y. State Bar Found., Am. Bar Found., Western N.Y. Trial Lawyers Assn. (dir. 1987-88), Am. Coll. Trial Attys. State civil litigation, Personal injury (including property damage), Probate (including wills, trusts). Office: 140 N Main St Warsaw NY 14569-1103

COOK, DAVID LEE, lawyer; b. Indpls., Mar. 22, 1952; s. Paul Moore and Opal (Steele) C.; m. Lisa Geib, May 28, 1994; children: Jennifer Lee, Rachel Darby. BA, U. Central Fla., 1974; JD, U. Fla., 1977. Bar: Fla. 1978, U.S. Dist. Ct. (no. dist.) Fla. 1979, U.S. Dist. Ct. (mid. dist.) Fla. 1990; cert. real estate lawyer. Ptnr. Young, van Asssenderp & Varnadoe, Tallahassee, 1977-89, Naples, Fla., 1989-97, Windels Marx Lane & Mittendorf, Bonita Springs, Fla., 1997—. Author: The Collection Process, Florida State and Local Taxes, 1984. Mem. ABA, Fla. Bar Assn., Collier County Bar Assn. Avocations: golf, fishing. Property, real (including real estate development, water). E-mail: dcook@windelsmarxfl.com.

COOK, DEBORAH L. judge, former state supreme court justice; b. Pittsburgh, Feb. 8, 1952; BA in English, U. Akron, 1974, JD, 1978, LLD (hon.), 1996. Ptnr. Roderick & Linton, Akron, 1976-91; judge 9th dist. Ohio Ct. Appeals, 1991-94; justice Ohio Supreme Ct., 1995—2003. Bd. trustees Summit County United Way, Vol. Ctr., Stan Hywet Hall and Gardens, Akron Sch. Law, Coll. Scholars, Inc.; bd. dirs. Women's Network; vol. Mobile Meals, Safe Landing Shelter. Named Woman of Yr., Women's Network, 1991. Fellow Am. Bar Found.; mem. Omicron Delta Kappa, Delta Gamma (pres., Nat. Shield award). Office: 532 Potter Stewart US Courthouse 100 E Fifth St Cincinnati OH 45202-3988*

COOK, GAYLE FREEMAN, lawyer; b. Oklahoma City, Jan. 13, 1949; d. Howard Stanley and Joan (Counts) F.; m. David Milton Cook, April 17, 1981. BS in Edn., U. Okla., 1971, MEd, 1972; JD, Oklahoma City U. Sch. Law, 1974. Bar: Okla., 1975, U.S. Dist. Ct. (we. dist.) Okla., 1977 (no. dist.) Okla., 1981, U.S. Ct. Appeals (10th cir.) 1980, U.S. Supreme Ct., 1980. Jud. counsel to justice Okla. Supreme Ct., Oklahoma City, 1975-78; counsel to presiding judge Okla. Ct. of Criminal Appeals, Oklahoma City, 1978-81; ptnr. Monnett, Hayes, Bullis, Thompson & Edwards, Oklahoma City, 1981—. Bd. dirs. Lyric Theater of Okla., Inc. (sec. 1985, 87), 1977—. Recipient Bronze Letzeiser award U. Okla., 1971, Am. Jurisprudence award in Adminstrv. Law Oklahoma City U. Law Sch., 1974. Mem. ABA, Okla. Bar Assn. (chmn. pub. info. com. 1990-91, vice chmn. 1992), Okla. County Bar Assn. (Cert. Achievement 1981, bench and bar com. 1983-84, mem. house dels. to conv. 1984, fee grievance and ethnic com. 1986—, social com. 1980-81, law day com. 1980-81, chmn. ann. meeting 1980-81), Mortar Bd., Robert J. Turner Am. Inn of Ct. (adminstr. 1999—), Chi Omega Alumni Assn., Phi Delta Phi, Iota Tau Tau (sec. 1977-79). Methodist. Avocations: figure skating, reading, travel, piano. Oil, gas, and mineral, Estate planning, Probate (including wills, trusts). Office: Monnet Hayes Bullis Thompson & Edwards 120 N Robinson 1719 1st Nat Ctr W Oklahoma City OK 73102

COOK, GEORGE VALENTINE, lawyer, consultant; b. Glendale, N.Y., Feb. 14, 1927; s. Walter Preston and Ida Ruth (Smith) C.; m. Edith Wengler, Sept. 4, 1948 (dec. Dec. 2002); children: George V., James, Robert, Laura, Barbara, Mary, Walter, Elizabeth. BA, Columbia U., 1949, LL.B., 1952. Bar: N.Y. 1953, U.S. Dist. Ct. (so. dist.) N.Y. 1955, U.S. Dist. Ct. (ea. dist.) N.Y. 1955, U.S. Ct. Appeals (2d cir.) 1955, U.S. Ct. Appeals (3d cir.) 1982, US. Dist. Ct. (no. dist.) N.Y. 1987. Assoc. Dewey, Ballantine, Bushby, Palmer & Wood, N.Y.C., 1952-56; mem. legal staff N.Y. Telephone Co., N.Y.C., 1956-59, 60-61; atty. AT&T, N.Y.C., 1959-60, 61-65, v.p., 1973-76; v.p. regulatory matters Western Electric Co., Inc., N.Y.C., 1966-72, v.p. gen. counsel, 1976-83, also dir.; exec. v.p., gen. counsel AT&T Technologies, Inc., N.Y.C., 1984-85; counsel Hunton & Williams, 1985-90; cons., 1990—. Contbr. articles to profl. jours. Active alumni activities Columbia U. Served to 2d lt. U.S. Army, 1945-47. Fellow Am. Bar Found.; mem. ABA, N.Y. State Bar Assn., Assn. Gen. Counsel, Assn. of Bar of City of N.Y. Home: 127 Somerset Ave Garden City NY 11530-1348

COOK, GLEN ANDRÉ, lawyer; b. Oakland, Calif., Dec. 31, 1954; s. Curtis Clifton and Mary Lynn (Bostick) C.; m. Melody Waters, Apr. 19, 1980; children: Glen Jr., Sarah, Benjamin, Mary Katherine. BA, U. Okla., 1978; JD, Brigham Young U., 1982; diploma, Nat. Inst. Trial Advocacy, 1991. Bar: Utah 1982, U.S. Dist. Ct. Utah 1982, U.S. Ct. Claims 1991, Ct. Appeals for the Armed Forces 1998, U.S. Supreme Ct. 2000, Supreme Ct. Eng. and Wales 2001. Staff atty. Social Security Adminstrn., Phoenix, 1985-87; trial counsel Salt Lake Legal Def. Assn., Salt Lake City, 1987-88; asst. city prosecutor Salt Lake City, 1988-90; pvt. practice, 1990—; mem. Cook Skeen & Robinson LLC, Salt Lake City, 1997—. Pro-tem judge 3rd dist. ct. Small Claims Divsn., Salt Lake City, 1988—; mil. judge, 2000—; examiner Utah State Bar, 1992—; mem. bd. editors Utah Bar Jour., 1990-99. Author: (with others) Summary of Utah Corporate Law, 1983; editor Jour. Legal Studies, 1981-82; contbr.: Utah Women and the Law, 1991, Navy Legal Assistance Handbook, 1991. Bd. govs. Intermountain Shriner's Hosp. Children, 1998—; bd. dirs. Salt Lake City chpt. NAACP, 1991-96 (Atty. of Yr. 1996); trustee Clan Urquhart Found., 1999—. With JAGC USN, 1982-85, capt. JAGC USNR; dist. counsel USCG Aux., 1995-96. Cortez Ewing fellow, 1976; Internat. Rotary scholar, 1977, Univ. Aberdeen, Scotland. Fellow Soc. Antiquaries of Scotland, Royal Soc. for Protection of Birds (life); mem. ABA, FBA, ATLA, NACDL, Internat. Bar Assn., Law Soc. Eng. and Wales, Naval Res. Assn. (life), Utah State Bar (chair mil. law sect. 1993), Res. Officers Assn. (life), Navy League (life), U.S. Naval Inst. (life), Masonic Youth Found. Utah (bd. dirs. 1995—), Am. Legion (life), Masons (past master), Ind. Order of Foresters, Philatethes Soc. (life), Venerable Order of St. John of Jerusalem, Mil. Order of World Wars, Order Sons of Indian Wars, Order of First World War, Utah Scottish Assn. (life), St. Andrews Soc. Utah (life), Friends of Rosslyn Chapel (life), Friends of Edinburgh Tattoo (life), Friends of Historic Scotland (life), Heraldry Soc. Scotland, Utah Trial Lawyers Assn., Utah Assn. Criminal Def. Lawyers, Nat. Orgn. Social Security Reps., Nat. Trust Scotland (life). Mem. Lds Ch. Criminal, Military, Personal injury (including property damage). also: 3 Ross St Balintore Scotland

COOK, HARRY CLAYTON, JR., lawyer; b. Washington, Mar. 25, 1935; s. Harry Clayton and Lillian June (A'harrah) Cook; m. Jane Clare Mellius, 1963 (div. 1974); children: Christianne Pier, Nicole, Harry Clayton III; m. Judith Ann Taber, 1994; children: Rebecca Lyeth Kelsey, Parker Burr Kelsey. BSChemE, Princeton U., 1956; LLB, U. Va., 1960. Bar: Colo. 1960, N.Y. 1961, Pa. 1966, D.C. 1973. Assoc. Sullivan & Cromwell, N.Y.C., 1960-63, Holme Roberts & Owen, Denver, 1964, Pepper Hamilton & Scheetz, Phila., 1965-69, ptnr., 1969-70, 73; on assignment as sr. tax counsel Sun Oil Co., Phila., 1970; ptnr. Cadwalader Wickersham & Taft, Washington, 1974-87, Bishop, Cook, Purcell & Reynolds, Washington, 1988-90; pvt. practice Langley, Va., 1991—2002; of counsel Bastianelli, Brown and Kelley, Washington, 1992—2002; ptnr. Mgmt. & Transp. Assoc., Inc., Essex, Conn., 2001—; sr. counsel Fulbright & Jaworski LLP, 2002—. Page to U.S. Sen. E. D. Millikin, Colo., 1950—52; gen. counsel Maritime Adminstrn.; mem. Maritime Subs. Bd., U.S. Dept. Commerce, Washington, 1970—73; U.S. del. to Soviet Union Maritime Agreement between U.S. and USSR, 1971—73; mem. Adminstrv. Conf. U.S., 1980—90, chmn. com. jud. rev., 1982—88, sr. fellow, 1988—90; mem. Nat. Def. Exec. Res., U.S. Mil. Sealift Command, 1983—91, U.S. Office Tech. Assessment; mem. citizens adv. panel U.S. Maritime Ind., 1982—85, cargo policy workshop particpant, 1984—85. Mem. editl. bd.: Va. Law Rev., 1958—60, exec. editor: , 1959—60; contbr. articles to profl. jours. Dir. Com. on the Present Danger, 1978—87; bd. dirs. New World Inst., 2000—, Inst. Fgn. Policy Analysis. Mem.: ABA, Maritime Law Assn. U.S. (marine fin. com., proctor in admiralty), D.C. Bar Assn., Am. Law Inst. (life), Raven Soc., Univ. Club (N.Y.C.), Fishers Island Club (N.Y.), Chevy Chase (Md.) Club, Cosmos Club (Washington), Hay Harbor Club (N.Y.), Met. Club (Washington), Order of Coif, Phi Delta Phi. Administrative and regulatory, Admiralty, Finance. Home: 1011 Langley Hill Dr Mc Lean VA 22101-1709 Office: Ste 500 801 Pennsylvania Ave NW Washington DC 20004-2623 E-mail: plimsolldc@aol.com., ccook@fulbright.com.

COOK, JULIAN ABELE, JR., federal judge; b. Washington, June 22, 1930; s. Julian Abele and Ruth Elizabeth (McNeill) C.; m. Carol Annette Dibble, Dec. 22, 1957; children: Julian Abele III, Peter Dibble, Susan Annette. BA, Pa. State U., 1952; JD, Georgetown U., 1957, LLD (hon.), 1992; LLM, U. Va., 1988; LLD (hon.), U. Detroit, 1996, Wayne State U., 1997. Bar: Mich. 1957. Law clk. to judge, Pontiac, Mich., 1957-58; pvt. practice Detroit, 1958-78; judge U.S. Dist. Ct. (ea. dist.) Mich., Detroit, 1978, chief judge, 1989-96, sr. judge, 1996—. Spl. asst. atty. gen. State of Mich., 1968-78; adj. prof. U. Detroit Sch. Law, 1971-74; gen. counsel pub. TV Sta. WTVS, 1973-78; labor arbitrator Am. Arbitration Assn. and Mich. Employment Rels. Commn., 1975-78; mem. Mich. State Bd. Ethics, 1977-78; instr. trial advocacy workshop Harvard U., 1988—, trial advocacy program U.S. Dept. Justice, 1989-90; com. on fin. disclosure Jud. Conf. U.S., 1988-93, chmn., 1990-93; screening panel NYU Root-Tilden-Snow Scholarship Program, 1991, 96—; mem. U.S. Sentencing Commn. Judicial Adv. Group, 1996-98; mem. nat. bd. trustees Am. Inn Ct., 1996—; mem. adv. com. Nat. Publs., 1994-96, chmn. nat. nominations and election com., 1994-95; pres. chpt. XI, Master of Bench, 1984-95. Contbr. articles to profl. jours. Exec. bd. dirs. Child and Family Svcs. Mich., 1968-89, past pres., 1975-76; bd. dirs. Am. Heart Assn. Mich., 1968-89, Hutzel Hosp., 1984-95; chmn. Mich. Civil Rights Commn., 1968-71; co-chair exec. com. Walter P. Reuther Libr. Labor and Urban Affairs, Wayne State U.; mem. bd. visitors Georgetown U. Law Ctr., 1992—. With Signal Corps, U.S. Army, 1952-54. Recipient Merit citation Pontiac Area Urban League, 1971, Pathfinders award Oakland U., 1977, Svc. award Todd-Phillips Home, Inc., 1978, Disting. Alumnus award Pa. State U., 1987, Georgetown U., 1989, Focus and Impact award Oakland U., 1985; resolution Mich. Ho. of Reps., 1971, Outstanding Community Svc. award Va. Park Community Investment Assocs., 1992, 1st Ann. Trailblazers award D. Augustus Straker Bar Assn., 1993, Renowned Jurist award Friends of African Art, 1993, Brotherhood award Jewish War Vets. U.S., 1994, Paul R. Dean award Georgetown U. Law Sch., 1997; named Boss of Yr., Oakland County Legal Secs. Assn., 1974, one of Mich. Most Respected Judges, Mich. Law Weekly, 1990-91; named one of the Best Judges, Detroit Monthly, 1991; named Disting. Citizen of Yr., NAACP Oakland County, Mich., 1970. Fellow Am. Bar Found., Mich. Bar Found. (vice-chmn. 1992-93, chmn. 1993—); mem. NAACP (mem. state constl. revision and legal redress com. 1963, Disting. Citizen of Yr. 1970, Presdl. award North Oakland County, Mich. chpt. 1987), ABA, Fed. Bar Assn. (fed.-state ct. seminar lectr. Detroit chpt. 1981—), Mich. Bar Assn. (chmn. constl. law com. 1969, vice-chmn. civil liberties com. 1970, co-chmn. profl. devel. task force 1984-87, U.S. cts. com. 1988-95, com. on professionalism 1991—, Champion of Justice 1994), Mich. Tribunal Assn. (bd. dirs. 3rd cir. 1992-98), Detroit Bar Assn. (Bench-Bar award 1987), Oakland County Bar Assn. (chmn. continuing legal edn. com. 1968-69, jud. liaison Dist. Ct. com. 1977, unauthorized practice law com. 1977), Wolverine Bar Assn. (Bench-Bar award 1987, D. Augustus Straker award 1988), Mich. Assn. Black Judges, Am. Inn of Ct. (founder Met. Detroit chpt., pres., master of bench, chmn. 6th cir. com. on standard jury instructions 1986—), Am. Law Inst., Union Black Episcopalians (Detroit chpt., Absalom Jones award 1988), Justice Frank Murphy Honor Soc.

COOK, MICHAEL HARRY, lawyer; b. June 9, 1947; s. Leonard James and Ethel (Shapiro) C.; m. Michele Anne Reday, Apr. 21, 1979; children: Noah Reday, Megan Rose. Student, U. Wis., Madison, 1965-66; BA with honors cum laude, Temple U., 1969; JD, Villanova U., 1973. Bar: Pa. 1973, D.C. 1979, U.S. Dist. Ct. (no. dist.) Ill. 1977, U.S. Dist. Ct. D.C. 1981, U.S. Ct. Claims 1982, U.S. Ct. Appeals (3d cir.) 1982, U.S. Ct. Appeals (5th cir.) 1981, U.S. Ct. Appeals (9th cir.) 1979, U.S. Ct. Appeals (11th cir.) 1981, U.S. Ct. Appeals (7th cir.) 1984, U.S. Ct. Appeals (10th cir.) 1984, U.S. Ct. Appeals (fed. cir.) 1984, U.S. Ct. Appeals (D.C. cir.) 1981, U.S. Supreme Ct. 1976. Atty. Gen. Counsel's Office U.S. Dept. Health and Human Svcs., Washington, 1973-80; assoc. Wood, Lucksinger & Epstein, Washington, 1981-85, ptnr., 1985-90, Katten, Muchin & Zavis, Washington, 1991-97; mem. Mintz, Levin, Cohn, Ferris, Glovsky and Popeo, P.C., Washington, 1997-98; shareholder Jenkens & Gilchrist, P.C., Washington, 1998—. Lectr. Am. Health Lawyers Assn., Aspen Sys., Inc., various state and nat. hosps. and long-term care assns. Lectr.: Am. Health Lawyers Assn., : Aspen Sys., Inc., : various state and nat. hosps. and long-term care assns., contbg. author: book Handbook of Subacute Health Care, 1994, Subacute Care: A Guide to Devel., Implementation and Mgmt., 1995, The Long Term Care Handbook: Regulatory, Operational, and Fin. Guideposts, 2000; contbr. articles to profl. health care jours. V.p. Taylor Run Citizens Assn., Alexandria, Va., 1982-84, pres., 1984-85, bd. dirs., 1985—. Named to 100 Most Influential People in Long Term Care, 1996; Pres.'s scholar Temple U., Phila., 1969. Mem.: Nat. Assn. for Support of Long Term Care, Assisted Living Fedn. Am. (former mem. task force on managed care, former mem. public policy force, leadership coun., mem. pres.'s coun., mem. legal task force), ABA, Sword Soc., Tau Epsilon Phi, Phi Eta Sigma. Democrat. Jewish. Administrative and regulatory, Federal civil litigation, Health. Home: 2724 King St Alexandria VA 22302-4009 Office: Jenkens & Gilchrist a Profl Corp Ste 600 1919 Pennsylvania Ave NW Washington DC 20006-3404 E-mail: mhcook@jenkens.com.

COOK, MICHAEL LEWIS, lawyer; b. Rochester, N.H., Mar. 5, 1944; s. Israel J. and Molly L. Cook; m. Roberta Tross, Feb. 25, 1995; children: Jonathan, Alexander. AB, Columbia U., 1965; JD, NYU, 1968. Bar: N.Y. 1968. Assoc. Weil, Gotshal & Manges, N.Y.C., 1970-75, ptnr., 1975-80, Skadden, Arps, Slate, Meagher & Flom, LLP, N.Y.C., 1980-2000; adj. prof. law NYU Sch. Law, 1975—2001; ptnr. Schulte Roth & Zabel LLP, N.Y.C., 2000—. Co-author: A Practical Guide to the Bankruptcy Reform Act, 1979,

Creditors' Rights, Debtors' Protection and Bankruptcy, 1985, rev. edit., 1997; contbr.: Collier on Bankruptcy, 1979, rev. edit., 1999, Collier Bankruptcy Practice Guide, 2003; editor and contbg. author: Bankruptcy Litigation Manual, rev. edit., 2002. Bd. dirs. Goddard Riverside Cmty. Ctr.; bd. dirs., former chair Lawyers Alliance for N.Y. Fellow ABA, Am. Coll. Bankruptcy, Am. Bar Found.; mem. Assn. of Bar of City of N.Y., Practicing Law Inst. (mem. bankruptcy law adv. com.), Columbia Coll. Alumni Assn. (bd. dirs., v.p.). Bankruptcy, Federal civil litigation, Commercial, contracts (including sales of goods; commercial financing). Home: 45 E 89th St New York NY 10128-1251 Office: Schulte Roth & Zabel LLP 919 3d Ave New York NY 10022

COOK, QUENTIN LAMAR, lawyer, healthcare executive, church leader; b. Sept. 8, 1940; s. J. Vernon and Bernice (Kimball) C.; m. Mary Gaddie, Nov. 30, 1962; children: Kathryn Cook Knight, Quentin Laurance, Joseph Vernon III. BS, Utah State U., 1963; JD, Stanford U., 1966. Bar: Calif. 1966. Assoc. Carr, McClellan, Ingersoll, Thompson & Horn, Burlingame, Calif., 1966-69, ptnr., 1969-93; interim pres., CEO Calif. Healthcare Sys., San Francisco, 1993-94, pres., CEO, 1994-95; vice chmn. Sutter Health/Calif. Healthcare Sys., San Francisco, 1996; gen. authority LDS Ch., 1996—. City atty. Town of Hillsborough, Calif., 1982-93; mem. adv. bd. Utah State U., Logan, 1985-95; mem. bd. visitors Brigham Young U. Law Sch., Provo, 1994-96.

COOK, ROBERT MATTHEW, solicitor, barrister; b. Sydney, Australia, May 16, 1955; s. Clive Leonard and Patricia Ann Cook; m. Jenny Maxine Cook, Apr. 21, 1984; children: Sarah Ann, Benjamin Nickolas, Emma Louise. LLB, Queensland (Australia) U. of Tech., 1992. Commd. Australian Air Force, 1976, advanced through grades to wing comdr., ret., 1996; with air force Australian Dept. Def., 1993—95, legal officer, 1993—95, asst. def. force adv., 1995—96; solicitor Clayton Utz Law Firm, Canberra, Australia, 1997—2000, ptnr., 2000—. Dir. welfare fund RAAF Welfare Recreational Trust, Canberra, 1999—2002; head RAAF Legal Panel, 2000—02. Legal adv. Royal Soc. Prevention Cruelty to Animals, Canberra, 1998—. Mem.: Act Rowing Indsl. Rels. Soc. (v.p. 2000—02, team mgr. 2002—), Royal Canberra (Australia) Golf Club. Avocations: golf, rowing. Labor (including EEOC, Fair Labor Standards Act, labor-management relations, NLRB, OSHA). Office: Clayton Utz 40 Marcus Clark St Canberra 2601 Australia E-mail: vcook@claytonutz.com.

COOK, WILLIAM JOHN, lawyer; s. William John and Suzanne Mary Cook; m. Jacqueline Lee Calliott, Oct. 22, 1994; children: Meredith Lee, Samuel Henry. BA, Va. Poly. Inst. and State U., 1990; JD, Stetson U., St. Petersburg, Fla., 1993. Bar: Fla. 1993, U.S. Ct. Appeals (11th cir.) 1994, U.S. Dist. Ct. (mid. dist.) Fla. 1995, U.S. Dist. Ct. (so dist.) Fla. 2001. Lawyer Alpert, Barker, Rodems, Ferrentino & Cook, P.A., Tampa, Fla., 1993—2000; ptnr. Barker, Rodems & Cook, P.A., Tampa, Fla., 2000—. Mem. Fla. Bar Consumer Protection Com., 2000—; barrister Tampa Bay Inn of Ct., Tampa, Fla., 2000—; spkr. various seminars in field. Author: (book) Florida Practice Handbook - Damages, 1995; contbr. Dir. Montessori House of Hyde Pk. Scholarship Found., Tampa, Fla., 2002. Recipient Book Award Bus. Assns., Am. Jurisprudence, 1992. Mem.: Rotary Club of Tampa Bay (pres. 2003—). General civil litigation, Commercial, consumer (including collections, credit), Insurance. Office: Barker Rodems & Cook PA 300 West Platt St Ste 150 Tampa FL 33606 Office Fax: 813-489-1008. E-mail: wcook@barkerrodemsandcook.com.

COOK, WILLIAM LESLIE, JR., lawyer; b. July 1, 1949; s. William Leslie and Mary Elizabeth (Roberts) C.; m. Mary Jo Dorr, July 17, 1976; children: Leslie Patton, William Roberts, Maribeth Dorr. BA, U. Miss., 1971, JD, 1974. Bar: Miss. 1974, U.S. Dist. Ct. (no. dist.) Miss. 1974, U.S. Dist. Ct. (we. dist.) Tenn. 1986. Assoc. Bailey & Trusty, Batesville, Miss., 1974-79; ptnr. Bailey, Trusty & Cook, Batesville, Miss., 1980-90, Bailey & Cook, Batesville, Miss., 1990-92, Bailey, Cook & Womble, Batesville, Miss., 1992—. Chmn., Miss. Coll. Rep. Clubs, 1973, Panola County March of Dimes, Batesville, 1976-78; miss. chmn. Nat. Orgn. Social Security Claimants Reps., 1981-82; rep. Honor Coun., U. Miss. Sch. Law, 1974 King Batesville Jr. Aux. Charity Ball, 2000. Paul Harris fellow 1998—. Mem. ABA (torts and ins. practice sect. 1979—, vice chmn. com. on delivery of legal svcs. tothe disabled young lawyers divsn. 1983-85, gen. practice sect. 1985-86), ATLA, Miss. State Bar (state bd. bar admissions 1978-79, mem. ethics com. 1980-83, bd. dirs. Young Lawyers sect. 1980-83, chmn. com. on unauthorized practice of law 1983-86, workers compensation sect., mem. com. on Kid's Second Chance 1992), Panola County Bar Assn. (pres. 1979-80), Miss. Trial Lawyers Assn. (membership com. 1983-84), Ct. Practice Inst. (diplomate), Lawyer-Pilots Bar Assn., Lamar Soc. Internat. Law, Lamar Order-U. Miss., Batesville Jaycees (legal counsel 1975-77), Masons, Shriners, Rotary (pres. 1991-92, 96-97, asst. dist. gov. 1997-99, dist. gov. nominee 1999-2000, dist. gov. 2000-01, Paul Harris fellow, Four Aves. of Svc. Citation, Rotary Found. Dist. Svc. award, Dist. Found. chmn.), Omicron Delta Kappa, Pi Sigma Alpha, Delta Theta Pi. Methodist. Personal injury (including property damage), Workers' compensation. Home: 110 Shagbark Dr Batesville MS 38606-8470 Office: Panola Plz 118 Highway 6 W Batesville MS 38606-2507 E-mail: wlcook@panola.com.

COOKSON, KIRK S. lawyer; b. Tucson, Ariz., Jan. 4, 1953; d. William C. Scott and R. Judith Williams; m. James M. Cookson, Mar. 25, 1982 (div. Jan. 1997). BS, U. Ariz., 1974; JD, Whittier Coll., 1982. Bar: Calif. 1982, Ariz. 1983, U.S. Dist. Ct. (ctrl. dist.) Calif. 1983, U.S. Ct. Appeals (9th cir.) 1983, U.S. Dist. Ct. Ariz. 1983. Assoc. Ray Bennett, Woodland Hills, Calif., 1982—83, Scott & Renneckar, Tucson, 1983—86; adminstrv. law judge State of Ariz., Tucson, 1986—90; judge pro tempore City of Tucson, 1989—90, County of Pima, Tucson, 1989—91; town atty. City of Marana, Ariz., 1991—92; city prosecutor City of Lake Havasu City, Ariz., 1992—95; pvt. practice atty., 1995. Mem.: Mohave County Bar Assn. (pres. 1993—), We. Ariz. Humane Soc., London Bridge Rep. Women, Lions Club Internat. (dir. 1994—2000). Avocation: sewing. Juvenile, Probate (including wills, trusts), General practice. Office: 2156 McCulloch Blvd N Ste 3 Lake Havasu City AZ 86403

COOLEY, RICHARD EUGENE, lawyer; b. Flint, Mich., Apr. 28, 1935; s. Eugene J. and Helen Frances (Lumbert) C.; m. Wanda Lee Ford, Feb. 20, 1965; children: Scott Richard, Courtney Cooley Breaugh. AB, Albion Coll., 1957; JD, Duke U., 1960. Bar: Mich. 1960, U.S. Supreme Ct. 1970. Asst. pros. atty. Genesee County, Mich., 1962-64; ptnr. Bellairs, Dean, Cooley, Siler, Moulton & Smith, Flint, 1964—; spl. asst. atty. gen. State of Mich., 1975-81. City atty. City of Linden, Mich., 1964-89; twp. atty. Fenton (Mich.) Twp., 1970—; village atty. Village of Gaines, Mich., 1989-96. Past bd. dirs. Tall Pines coun. Boy Scouts Am., Fairwinds coun. Girl Scouts U.S.A.; past pres. Child and Family Svcs. Mich., Flint. Mem. State Bar Mich., Genesee County Bar Assn. (pres. 1977-78), Flint Estate Planning Coun. (pres. 1999-2000), Rotary. Republican. Presbyterian. Avocations: skiing, sailing, travel. Estate planning, Family and matrimonial, Municipal (including bonds). Office: Bellairs Dean Cooley Siler Moulton & Smith 412 S Saginaw St Ste 300 Flint MI 48502-1810 Home: 906 E Kearsley St Flint MI 48503-6119

COOLEY, STEVE, prosecutor; b. L.A., May 1, 1947; m. Jana Cooley; 2 children. Grad., Calif. State U., L.A., U. So. Calif., 1973. Joined Dist. Attys. Office, 1973; dist. atty. L.A. County, 2000—. Named Pros. of the Yr., Century City Bar Assn., 2001, Alumnus of Yr., Calif. State U., L.A., 1998, Champion of the People, Nat. Black Pros. Assn., Crime Victims Star of the Yr., Justice for Homicide Victims; recipient Leaders in Pub. Svc. award, Encino C. of C., Cmty. Justice award, Calif. NAACP. Mem.: Phi Kappa Phi. Office: County of Los Angeles Ste 18000 210 W Temple St Los Angeles CA 90012-3210*

COOLIDGE, DANIEL SCOTT, lawyer; b. Portland, Maine, Sept. 20, 1948; s. John Walter and Mary Louise (Arnold) C.; m. Carolyn Stiles, Nov. 23, 1984; children: Lillian Mae, Lydia Stiles. BS summa cum laude, U. Bridgeport, 1976; JD, Harvard U., 1980. Bar: Conn. 1980, N.H. 1982, Mass. 2001, U.S. Patent Office 1999, U.S. Ct. Appeals (1st cir.) 1983, U.S. Supreme Ct. 1985. Assoc. Cummings & Lockwood, Stamford, Conn., 1980-82, Sheehan, Phinney, Bass & Green PA, Manchester, N.H., 1982-87, ptnr., 1987—. Chmn. juvenile diversion com. Pittsfield (N.H.) Dist. Ct., 1982-85. Author: Survival Guide for Road Warriors, 1996; mem. editl. bd. Law Tech. News; columnist Law Office Computing, 1997—; patentee tel. test equipment. Chmn. Bradford Constitution Bicentennial Com.; mem. Pittsfield Planning Bd., 1984-85; treas., trustee First Congl. Ch., Pittsfield, 1984-85, First Bapt. Ch. Bradford; pres. Pittsfield Arts Coun., 1985; del. N.H. Constl. Conv., Concord, 1984-94; moderator Town of Bradford, N.H., 1999-, Kearsago Reg. Sch. Dist, 2002-; founding bd. dirs., officer U.S. Found. for Inspiration and Recognition of Sci. and Tech. Mem. ABA (environ. law sect., intellectual property law sect., acting chmn., chmn. computer and tech. divsn., vice-chmn. sys. and tools law practice mgmt. sect. 1994—, governing coun. 1996—, advisor UCC article 2B drafting com. 1995-99), N.H. Bar Assn. (vice-chmn. tech. sect. 1993-96, chmn. lex mundi intellectual property sect. 1992-93), Manchester Bar Assn. Avocations: computers, physics, fly fishing, hiking, machining. Computer, Environmental, Intellectual property. Home: 106 Bible Hill Ln Warner NH 03278-3701 Office: Coolidge and Graves 106 Bible Hill Ln Warner NH 03278 Personal E-mail: dancoolidge@yahoo.com. Business E-Mail: dancoolidge@ipbizlaw.com.

COOMBE, GEORGE WILLIAM, JR., lawyer, retired banker; b. Kearny, N.J., Oct. 1, 1925; s. George William and Laura (Montgomery) C.; A.B., Rutgers U., 1946; LL.B., Harvard, 1949; m. Marilyn V. Ross, June 4, 1949; children— Susan, Donald William, Nancy. Bar: N.Y. 1950, Mich. 1953, Calif. 1976, U.S. Supr. Ct. Practice in N.Y.C., 1949-53, Detroit, 1953-69; atty., mem. legal-staff Gen. Motors Corp., Detroit, 1953-69, asst. gen. counsel, sec., 1969-75; exec. v.p., gen. counsel Bank of Am., San Francisco, 1975-90; ptnr. Graham and James, San Francisco, 1991-95; sr. fellow Stanford Law Sch., 1995—. Served to lt. USNR, 1942-46. Mem. Am., Mich., Calif., San Francisco, Los Angeles, N.Y.C. bar assns., Phi Beta Kappa, Phi Gamma Delta. Presbyterian. Banking, State civil litigation, Corporate, general. Home: 2190 Broadway St Apt 2E San Francisco CA 94115-1312 Fax: 415-923-9266. E-mail: gwcoombe@aol.com.

COONEY, CHARLES HAYES, lawyer; b. Nashville, Apr. 25, 1937; s. Robert G. and Annie Lee (Hayes) C.; m. Patsy M. Cooney, Dec. 25, 1986; children: Susan, Hayes Jr. BA, Vanderbilt U., 1959, JD, 1963. Bar: Tenn. 1963. Pvt. practice Cornelius & Collins, Nashville, 1963-67; chief def. atty. gen. State of Tenn., Nashville, 1967-80; ptnr. Watkins, McGugin, McNeilly & Rowan, 1980—. Staff mem. Vanderbilt U. Law Review, 1961-62. Capt. U.S. Army, 1959. Mem. ABA, Rotary, Tenn. Bar Assn. (pres. young lawyers sect., 1961), Nashville Bar Assn. (bd. dirs. 1985-87), Tenn. Bar Found., Nashville Bar Found. Presbyterian. Avocations: golf, travel. Personal injury (including property damage), Professional liability, State civil litigation. Office: Watkins McGugin McNeilly & Rowan 214 2nd Ave N Ste 300 Nashville TN 37201-1638

COONEY, TERESA M. lawyer; b. Washington, June 9, 1972; d. Robert J. and Constence A. Cooney; m. Steve W. Culfogienis, Aug. 15, 2000. BA, Mt. St. Mary's Coll., Emmitsburg, Md., 1994; JD, U. Balt., 2000, MBA, 2001. Bar: Md. 2001. Law clk. to Hon. Ronald Silkworth, Annapolis, Md., 2001; lawyer Law Office James L. Mayer, Columbia, Mo., 2001—. Mem.: ABA, Md. Bar Assn. Avocation: sailing. General practice, Probate (including wills, trusts), Corporate, general. Office: James L Mayer PA 10805 Hickory Ridge Rd Columbia MD 21044 Office Fax: 410-730-9674. Business E-Mail: tmcooney@jlmayerlaw.com.

COONEY, WILLIAM J. lawyer; b. Augusta, Ga., July 31, 1929; s. John F. and Ellen (Joy) C.; m. Martha L. Whaley, May 1, 1971; children: William J. IV, Sarah C. BS, U. Notre Dame, 1951; JD, Georgetown U., 1954, LLM, 1955. Bar: Ga. 1963, Calif. 1961, D.C. 1954. Law clk. U.S. Ct. Appeals, Washington, 1954, U.S. Claims Ct., Washington, 1955; asst. U.S. atty. Washington, 1958-60, San Francisco, 1960-63; sole practice Augusta, 1963—. Capt. JAGC, U.S. Army, 1955-58. Mem. State Bar Ga., Spl. Master State Bar Ga., Augusta Bar Assn. (mem. exec. com.), Am. Arbitration Assn. (arbitrator). Roman Catholic. Alternative dispute resolution, General civil litigation, Probate (including wills, trusts). Office: 1 Habersham Sq 3602 Wheeler Rd Augusta GA 30909-1826 E-mail: cooney@knology.net.

COOPER, ALAN SAMUEL, lawyer, educator; b. June 13, 1942; s. Rudey and Rosalie (Schwartz) C.; m. Maxine Jacobs, Aug. 13, 1966 (dec.); children: Lauren K., Jennifer D.; m. Linda Morguelan Klein, April 18, 1999. BA, Vanderbilt U., 1964, JD, 1968. Bar: Tenn. 1968, D.C. 1969, U.S. Dist. Ct. D.C. 1969, U.S. Supreme Ct. Appeals (Fed. cir.) 1975, U.S. Supremem Ct. 1980. Law clk. U.S. Dist. Ct. (mid. dist.), Tenn., 1967-68; assoc. Browne, Schuyler & Beveridge and Browne, Beveridge & DeGrandi, Washington, 1968—72, Schyler, Birch, Swindler, McKie & Beckett, Washington, 1972-74; ptnr. Schyler, Banner, Birch, McKie & Beckett, Washington, 1974-94; mem. bd. dirs., shareholder Banner & Witcoff, Ltd., Washington, Chgo., Boston, 1995-97; ptnr. Shaw Pittman Potts & Trowbridge, Washington, N.Y.C., L.A., London, 1997—. Adj. prof. Georgetown U. Law Ctr., 1985—; adviser on trademark law to U.S. del. to Diplomatic Conf. on Revision of Paris Conv. for Protection of Indsl. Property, Nairobi, Kenya, 1981. Mem. ABA (faculty Nat. Insts. on Trademark Litigation 1978-79), Internat. Trademark Assn., D.C. Bar, Bar Assn. D.C., Tenn. Bar Assn., Bethesda Country Club. Jewish. Trademark and copyright. Office: 2300 N St NW Washington DC 20037-1122

COOPER, ALMETA E. lawyer, medical association administrator; Gen. counsel Ohio State Med. Assn., Hilliard, Ohio. Mem.: Am. Health Lawyers Assn. (pres.-elect, chair programs com., chair nominating com.). Office: Ohio State Med Assn 3401 Mill Run Dr Hilliard OH 43026 Office Fax: 614-527-6763. Business E-Mail: aecooper@osma.org.*

COOPER, CLEMENT THEODORE, lawyer; b. Miami, Fla., Oct. 26, 1930; s. Benjamin Leon and Louise (Bethel) C.; m. Nan Coles Cooper; children: Patricia, Karen, Stephanie, Bridgette, Jessica (dec.), Stacy. AB, Lincoln U., 1952; student, Boston U., 1954-55; JD, Howard U., 1958; PhD in Bus. Adminstrn. (hon.), Colo. Christian Coll. Bar: D.C. 1960, Mich. 1960, U.S. Ct. Appeals (3rd, 4th, 6th, 9th and 10th cirs.), U.S. Ct. Mil. Appeals, , U.S. Ct. Claims, U.S. Supreme Ct. 1963. Pvt. practice, Washington, 1960—. Adj. prof. Strayer U., Washington, 1991-98; former legal cons. No. Calif. Mining Assn.; arbitrator NY Stock Exch., NASD. Author: Sealed Verdict, 1964; contbr. articles to profl. jours. Adv. coun. D.C. Dept. Welfare, 1963-66; adv. bd. Com. on Irish Ethnicity, N.Y.C. Mem. ABA, ATLA, NASD, D.C. Bar Assn., Nat. Bar Assn., ACLU, Am. Judicature Soc., Rocky Mountain Mining Law Found., Internat. Platform Assn., Nat. Assn. Securities Dealers (arbitrator), Soc. King Charles Martyr, Am. Legion, Knights Templar (Knights fellow), Alpha Phi Alpha (life). Episcopalian. Appellate, General civil litigation, Property, real (including real estate development, water). Home: 728 Dahlia St NW Washington DC 20012-1844 Office: PO Box 76135 Washington DC 20013-6135

COOPER, CORINNE, communications consultant, lawyer; b. Albuquerque, July 12, 1952; d. David D. and Martha Lucille (Rosenblum) C. BA magna cum laude, U. Ariz., 1975, JD summa cum laude, 1978. Bar: Ariz. 1978, U.S. Dist. Ct. Ariz. 1978, Mo. 1985. Assoc. Streich, Lang, Weeks & Cardon, Phoenix, 1978-82; asst. prof. U. Mo., Kansas City, 1982-86, assoc. prof., 1986-94, prof., 1994-2000, prof. emerita, 2000—; pres. Profl. Presence, Comm. Cons., Tucson and Kansas City, Mo., 2001—. Vis. prof. U. Wis., Madison, 1985, 91, U. Pa., Phila., 1988, U. Ariz., 1993, U. Colo., 1994. Author: (with Bruce Meyerson) A Drafter's Guide to Alternative Dispute Resolution, 1991; editor: The Portable UCC, 1993, 3d edit., 2001, Getting Graphic I and II, 1993, 94, The New Article 9, 1999, 2d edit., 2000; editor in chief Bus. Law Today, 1995-97; mem. editl. bd. ABA Jour., 1999—; contbr. articles to profl. jours., chpts. to books. Legal counsel Mo. for Hart campaign, 1984; dir. issues Goddard for Gov. campaign, 1990; bd. dirs. Com. for County Progress, Kansas City, 1985-95. Mem. ABA (mem. coun. bus. sect. 1992-96, uniform comml. code com., chmn. membership com. 1992-94, editl. bd. Bus. Law Today, 1991-97, sect. of bus. law pubs. 1998-2002, standing com. on strategic comm. 2001—), Am. Law Inst., Am. Assn. Law Schs. (comml. law 1982-2000), Ariz. Bar Assn., Mo. Bar Assn. (comml. law com.), Order of Coif, Phi Beta Kappa, Phi Kappa Phi. Democrat. Jewish. Office: Profl Presence 6412 Morningside Dr Kansas City MO 64113 also: 4558 N 1st Ave Tucson AZ 85718

COOPER, GARY ALLAN, lawyer; b. Bristol, Va., Feb. 3, 1947; s. Earl Clarence and Reba Evelyn (Jenkins) C.; chidlren: Drew Kelsey, Gavin Morgan. BS in Journalism, U. Tenn., 1969, JD, 1972. Bar: Tenn. 1972, U.S. Dist. Ct. (ea. dist.) Tenn. 1972, U.S. Supreme Ct. 1979, Fla. 1981. Assoc. Luther, Anderson & Ruth, Chattanooga, 1972-76; ptnr. Luther, Anderson, Cleary, Luhowiak & Cooper, Chattanooga, 1976-79, Luther, Anderson, Cleary & Cooper, Chattanooga, 1979-80, Anderson, Cleary & Cooper, Chattanooga, 1981, Fleissner & Cooper, Chattanooga, 1982, Fleissner, Cooper & Marcus, Chattanooga, 1983-88, Fleissner Cooper Marcus & Steger, Chattanooga, 1988-89, Fleissner Cooper Marcus & Quinn, Chattanooga, 1990-97, Franklin, Cooper & Marcus, PLLC, Chattanooga, 1998—. Author: Tennessee Forms for Trial Practice, 1977, 5th edit., 1999, Tennessee Law Office Adminstration, 1977, Tenese Forms for Trial Practice-Damages, 1997. With USAR, 1972-79. Recipient Herman Hickman Post-grad. scholarship for Athletes U. Tenn., 1969. Mem. ABA, Chattanooga Bar Assn. (bd. dirs. 1984-86), Fla. Bar Assn. (mem. out-of-state practitioners com. 1983-86), Tenn. Bar Assn., Tenn. Def. Lawyers Assn. (chmn. amicus curiae com. 1987-89), Phi Delta Phi. Republican. Methodist. Avocations: golf, reading, boating. Federal civil litigation, State civil litigation, Insurance. Office: Franklin Cooper & Marcus PLLC 837 Fortwood St Chattanooga TN 37403-2313 E-mail: garyacooper@mindspring.com.

COOPER, JAMES RUSSELL, retired law educator; b. New Kensington, Pa., July 21, 1928; s. John Edward and Isabella Bird (Bowen) C.; m. Carolyn Hocker, Sept. 21, 1953 (div. Dec. 1975); children: L. Rachel, Julia Anderoni, Evan Lloyd, Jennifer Meyer; m. Leigh Ann Brian, Feb. 25, 1995 (div. Nov. 1999). BS Econs., U. Pa., 1952, JD, 1955. Bar: D.C., 1955, U.S. Supreme Ct., 1964; ordained to ministry Order of the Holy Spirit, Meeting House for Aspiring Spirits. Pres., chmn. Radio WKPA-AM, WYDD-FM, New Kensington, 1959-64; urban renewal dir. Redevelopment Authority, New Kensington, 1964-68; assoc. prof. U. Ill., Champaign-Urbana, 1968-74; prof. legal studies Ga. State U., Atlanta, 1974-94, emeritus prof., 1994—. Author: Twilights Last Gleaming, 1992, Real Estate Investments, 3d edit. 1992. Sgt. U.S. Army, 1946-48. Mem. Fed. Bar Assn., D.C. Bar Assn., Am. Real Estate Soc. (founder, dir.). Home: 4072 Lebanon Church Rd Athens GA 30607-2924 E-mail: jrcat@opwr.net.

COOPER, JAY LESLIE, lawyer; b. Chgo., Jan. 15, 1929; s. Julius Jerome and Grayce (Wolkenheim) C.; m. Darice Richman, July 30, 1970; children: Todd, Leslie, Keith. JD, De Paul U., 1951. Bar: Ill. 1951, Calif. 1953, U.S. Supreme Ct. 1965, N.Y. 1987. Ptnr. Cooper, Epstein & Hurewitz (and predecessors), Beverly Hills, Calif., 1955-93; ptnr. Manatt, Phelps & Phillips, L.A., 1993—2001; shareholder Greenberg Traurig, LLP, 2002—. Guest lectr. Advanced Profl. Program Legal Aspects of Music and Rec. Industry, U. So. Calif., 1968, 70, 75, Entertainment Industry Conf., 1971, Harvard Law Sch., 1985; guest lectr. Calif. Copyright Conf., 1967, 71, 73, 75, 77, 97, v.p., 1975, pres., 1976-77; co-chmn. ann. program The Rec. Contract, UCLA, 1977—; lectr. Midem, 1977-95, 96-97; adj. prof. entertainment law Loyola U. Law Sch., Los Angeles, 1978-80; moderator UCLA Seminar, 1994. Profl. musician with, Les Brown, Charlie Barnet, Frank Sinatra, Los Angeles Philharm. others, 1945-55; editor: (with Irwin O. Spiegel) Record and Music Publishing Forms of Agreement in Current Use, 1971, Annual Program on Legal Aspects of Entertainment Industry, Syllabus, 1966-70; co-author: Talent in the New Millennium, 2001, The Work Made For Hire Conundrum, 2001. Named Entertainment Lawyer of Yr. Billboard mag., 1975, Best of the Best, 2000. Mem. ABA (chmn. forum com. on entertainment and sports industries 1983-86), NARAS (chpt. pres. 1973-75, nat. pres. 1975-77), Beverly Hills Bar Assn. (co-chmn. entertainment law com. 1972-75), Calif. Copyright Soc. (pres. 1976), Los Angeles County Bar Assn., Calif. Bar Assn., Ill. Bar Assn., L.A. Copyright Soc., Internat. Assn. Entertainment Lawyers (exec. com.). Entertainment. Office: Greenberg Traurig LLP 2450 Colorado Ave #400 E Santa Monica CA 90404

COOPER, JEFFREY, lawyer; b. Phila., Dec. 30, 1950; s. Joseph and Fannie (Forman) C.; m. Nancy Klaus, May 25, 1975; children: Max, Jacob. BA, Northwestern U., 1972; JD, U. Pa., 1975. Bar: Pa. 1975, N.Y. 1975, U.S. Dist. Ct. (ea. dist.) Pa. 1976, U.S. Dist. Ct. (mid. dist.) Pa. 1977, U.S. Ct. Appeals (3rd cir.) 1977. Dep. atty. gen. Commonwealth of Pa., Phila., 1975-78; assoc. Mesirov, Gelman, Jaffe, Cramer & Jamieson, Phila., 1978-84, ptnr., 1985-2000, Schnader Harrison Segal & Lewis, Phila., 2000—02; chief counsel Pa. State Sys. of Higher Edn., 2003—. Bd. dirs. Pub. Interest Law Ctr., Phila., 1986-90, Print Ctr. Phila., chair 1997—2002; treas. Am. Poetry Ctr., Phila., 1986-90, v.p. 1990-91, pres. 1991-93; mem. Greater Phila. Women's Med. Fund; mem. Mural Arts Ads., 1999—. Mem. ABA, Pa. Bar Assn., Phila. Bar Assn. Democrat. Jewish. Avocation: book collecting. General civil litigation, Personal injury (including property damage), Taxation, general. Office: Dixon U Ctr 2986 N Second St Harrisburg PA 17110 E-mail: jcooper@sshechan.edu.

COOPER, JEROME A. lawyer; b. Brookwood, Ala., Jan. 15, 1913; s. Marks Benjamin and Etta (Temerson) C.; m. Lois Harriet McMillen, Aug. 16, 1938; children: Ellen (Mrs. Benjamin L. Erdreich), Carol. AB cum laude, Harvard, 1933, LLB, 1936. Bar: Ala. 1936. Practice in, Birmingham, 1946—; law clk. U.S. Dist. Judge Davis, 1936-37, U.S. Supreme Ct. Justice Hugo L. Black, 1937-40; regional atty. Solicitors Office, Dept. Labor, 1940-41; ptnr. Cooper, Mitch & Crawford, 1950-98; of counsel Gardner, Middlebrooks, Fleming & Gibbons, PC, Birmingham, 1999—. Mem. Pres. Kennedy's Lawyers' Com. for Civil Rights Under Law, 1963—; pres. adv. coun. Pub. Radio Sta. WBHM, 1980—. Mem. editl. adv. bd. The Ala. Lawyer. Mem. Birmingham area Manpower Resource Devel. Planning Bd., 1969; chmn. cmty. devel. com. Operation New Birmingham; mem. Jefferson County Drug Abuse Coordinating Com., 1970-76; pres. Jefferson County Assn. Mental Health, Birmingham Jewish Cmty. Ctr., United Jewish Fund; mem. Southeastern regional adv. bd. Anti Defamation League, 1981; exec. bd. Birmingham Concentrated Employment Program; pres. Positive Maturity; sec., exec. bd. Jefferson County Com. Econ Opportunity; pres. Crisis Ctr., 1976; mem. Gov.'s Task Force on Unemployment, 1983; Democratic candidate for Ala. Senate, 1966; bd. dirs. Birmingham Symphony Assn., 1979-80, Ruffner Mountain Nature Ctr., 1985—, v.p., 1990, pres. 1991-93; bd. dirs. Friends of U. Ala. in Birmingham Psychiatry, 1987, Birmingham Civil Rights Inst., 1992—, adv. com. (HAER) Birmingham Hist. Soc., 1992—. Served to lt. comdr. USNR, 1942-45. Fellow Internat. Soc. Barristers, Coll. Labor and Employment Lawyers (emeritus); mem. Ala. Law Inst., Adminstrv. Conf. U.S., Birmingham Audubon Soc. (v.p. exec. com. 1989—), Disting. Fellow Birmingham-So. Coll., 1995. Jewish (trustee temple). Home: 42 Fairway Dr Birmingham AL 35213-4211 Office: 2013 1st Ave N Ste 450 Birmingham AL 35203-4116

COOPER, LANGDON MCILROY, lawyer; b. Chgo., Ill., Apr. 27, 1941; s. George Langdon and Lois McIlroy Cooper; m. Mary H. Cooper, June 1964 (div.); children: Marya Ladd, Abigail Harrill. BA, Duke U., 1964; JD, U. N.C., 1969. Bar: U.S. Dist. Ct. (we., mid. and ea. dists.) N.C. 1980, U.S. Ct. Appeals (4th and 3rd cirs.), U.S. Supreme Ct. 1992, cert.: N.C. State Bar (bd. cert. bankruptcy law), Am. Bd. Cert. (bd. cert. bus. and consumer bankruptcy). Mng. dir. Alala Mullen Holland & Cooper P.A., Gastonia, NC, 1985—. Mem. panel of chpt. 7 trustees U.S. Bankruptcy Ct. (we. dist.) N.C., 1978—; lectr. in field. Contbr. articles to profl. jours. Initial dir. Jobquest program City of Gastonia, NC. Mem.: ABA, Nat. Assn. Bankruptcy Trustees, Am. Bankruptcy Inst., Gaston County Bar Assn., N.C. Bar Assn. (bd. govs. 1985—88). Bankruptcy, General civil litigation. Office: Alala Mullen Holland & Cooper PA 301 S York St Gastonia NC 28052

COOPER, MARY LITTLE, federal judge, former banking commissioner; b. Fond du Lac, Wis., Aug. 13, 1946; d. Ashley Jewell and Gertrude (McCoy) Little. AB in Polit. Sci. cum laude, Bryn Mawr Coll., 1968; JD, Villanova U., 1972; LLD (hon.), Georgian Ct. Coll., 1987. Bar. N.J. 1972. Assoc. McCarter & English, Newark, 1972-80, ptnr., 1980-84; commr. N.J. Dept. Banking, Trenton, 1984-90; assoc. gen. counsel Prudential Property & Casualty Ins. Co., Holmdel, N.J., 1991-92; judge U.S. Dist. Ct. N.J., 1992—. Chmn. bd. Pinelands Devel. Credt Bank. Bd. trustees Exec. Commn. Ethical Standards, Trenton, 1984-90, Corp. Bus. Assistance, Trenton, 1984-91, N.J. Housing & Mortgage Fin. Agy., Trenton, 1984-90, N.J. Cemetery Bd. Assn., 1984-90, N.J. Hist. Soc., 1976-79., YMCA of Greater Newark, 1973-76; mem. Supreme Ct. N.J. Civil Practice Com., 1982-84, Supreme Ct. N.J. Dist. Ethics Com., 1982-84. Fellow Am. Bar Found.; mem. ABA, N.J. Bar Assn., Princeton Bar Assn., John J. Gibbons Am. Inn of Ct. Office: US Courthouse 402 E State St Ste 5000 Trenton NJ 08608-1507*

COOPER, MICHAEL ANTHONY, lawyer; b. Passaic, N.J., Mar. 29, 1936; BA, Harvard U., 1957, LL.B., 1960. Bar: N.Y. State 1961, U.S. Supreme Ct. 1969. With firm Sullivan & Cromwell, N.Y.C., 1960—, ptnr., 1968—. Pres. Legal Aid Soc., 1981-83; bd. fellows Inst. Jud. Adminstrn., chair, pro bono net, 2000—. Co-chair Lawyers Com. for Civil Rights Under Law, 1993-95; bd. dirs. Equal Justice Works, Fund for Modern Cts., Vols. of Legal Svcs. Fellow: Am. Coll. Trial Lawyers (bd. regents 2000—, sec. 2002—); mem.: ABA, Am. Judicature Soc., Am. Law Inst., Fed. Bar Coun. (trustee 1994—2000), Assn. Bar City N.Y. (chair exec. com. 1996—97, v.p. 1997—98, pres. 1998—2000), N.Y. State Bar Assn. Antitrust, Federal civil litigation, Securities. Office: Sullivan & Cromwell 125 Broad St Fl 28 New York NY 10004-2489

COOPER, N. LEE, lawyer; m. Joy Clark; children: Clark, Catherine. BS, U. Ala., 1963, LLB, 1964. Pvt. practice, Birmingham, Ala., 1966—; founder Maynard, Cooper & Gale, P.C., Birmingham. Vice chair U.S. Congl. Commn. on Structural Alternatives for the Fed. Cts. of Appeals; dir. Lawyers Com. for Civil Rights. Articles and Notes editor Ala. Law Rev., 1962-64. Nat. bd. dirs. U. Ala.; trustee Ala. Law Sch. Found.; bd. overseers Rand Inst. for Civil Jusice. 1st lt. U.S. Army, 1964-66, capt. USAR. Fellow Am. Bar Found.; mem. ABA (chair, litig. sect. 1985-86, sec. litig. sect. 1976-78, Birmingham bar del. to ho. of deps. 1979-80, Ala. del. to ho. of dels. 1980-89, mem. drafting com. on model rules of profl. conduct 1982-84, mem. commn. on professionalism 1985-87, chair select com. on ho. of dels. 1989-90, chair ho. of dels. 1990-92, pres.-elect 1995-96, pres. 1996-97), Am. Judicature Soc. (dir.), Am. Bar Endowment (dir.), Am. Law Inst. (coun., advisor project on restatement of law governing lawyers), Ala. Bar Assn. (pres. young lawyers sect. 1974-75, Merit award 1976), Birmingham Bar Assn. (sec.-treas. 1972). Office: AmSouth Harbert Plz 1901 6th Ave N Ste 2400 Birmingham AL 35203-4604

COOPER, NANCY M. lawyer; b. Boulder, Colo., July 11, 1958; d. John Douglas and Betty Mae (Locke) McCullen; m. Neal David Cooper, July 29, 1984 (dec. Sept. 1998). BS in Pub. Adminstrn., U. Ariz., 1980; JD, Lewis and Clark Coll., 1995. Bar: Oreg. 1995. Juvenile probation officer Gila County, Globe, Ariz., 1980-82, State of Alaska, Anchorage, 1983-92; founding mem. Steinman, Cooper, Wiscarson, LLC, Portland, 1995—2001; with Bullivant Houser Bailey PC, Portland, 2001—. Contbr. articles to profl. jours. Mem. progress bd. City of Gresham, Oreg., 1999-2002. Mem. ABA, Oreg. State Bar Assn. (chair legal ethics com. 2001, mem. svcs. com. new lawyer divsn. 1995-99, family law sect. 1995-2001, litig. sect. 1995—, employment law sect. 1995—), Multnomah County Bar Assn. (professionalsm com. 2000—), Gus Solomon Inns of Court. Family and matrimonial, Labor (including EEOC, Fair Labor Standards Act, labor-management relations, NLRB, OSHA). Office: 300 Pioneer Tower 888 SW Fifth Ave Portland OR 97204 E-mail: nancy.cooper@bullivant.com.

COOPER, PAUL DOUGLAS, lawyer; b. Kansas City, Mo., July 22, 1941; s. W.W. and Emma Marie (Ringo) C.; m. Elsa B. Shaw, June 15, 1963 (div. 1991); children: Richard, Dean; m. Kay J. Rice, Aug. 30, 1992; 1 child, Natanya. BA in English, U. Mich., 1963; LLB, U. Calif., 1966. Bar: Colo. 1966, U.S. Dist. Ct. Colo. 1966, U.S. Ct. Appeals (10th cir.) 1967, U.S. Supreme Ct. 1979. Dep. dist. atty., Denver, 1969-71; asst. U.S. atty. Dist. of Colo., 1971-73; ptnr. Yegge, Hall & Evans, Denver, 1973-80; pres., dir. Cooper & Kelley PC, Denver, 1980-94, Cooper & Clough PC, Denver, 1994—. Faculty trial practice seminar Denver U. Law Sch., 1982; spl. asst. U.S. atty. Dist. of Colo., 1973-75; spl. prosecutor Mar. 1977 term, Garfield County Grand Jury; pres. Bow Mar Owners, Inc., 1976-77; mem. English adv. bd. U. Mich., 2000—. Recipient Spl. Commendation award for outstanding svc., 1972. Mem. ABA, Am. Bd. Trial Advocates, Colo. Bar Assn. (interprofl. com., bd. govs.), Denver Bar Assn. (trustee, 1st v.p. 1982-83), Colo. Med. Soc. (chmn. interprofl. com., Denver bar liaison com), Internat. Assn. Def. Counsel (exec. com. 1989-92). Republican. Professional liability, Libel, Personal injury (including property damage). Home: 11571 Eliot Ct Westminster CO 80234-1665 Office: 1512 Larimer St Ste 600 Denver CO 80202-1610 E-mail: pcooper@cooper-clough.com.

COOPER, RICHARD MELVYN, lawyer; b. Phila., Nov. 13, 1942; s. Arthur Martin and Sophia Phyllis (Gottlieb) C.; m. Sabina Abbe Karp, June 12, 1965 (div. 1978); children: Alexander, Stephanie; m. Judith Carole Areen, Feb. 17, 1979; children: Benjamin, Jonathan. BA summa cum laude, Haverford Coll., 1964; BA 1st class, Oxford U., 1966, MA, 1970; JD summa cum laude, Harvard U., 1969. Bar: D.C. 1970, U.S. Ct. Appeals (5th, 6th and 9th cirs.) 1988, U.S. Ct. Appeals (10th cir.) 1982, U.S. Ct. Appeals (11th cir.) 1984, U.S. Ct. Appeals (fed. cir.) 1985, U.S. Ct. Appeals (4th cir.) 1997, U.S. Supreme Ct. 1973. Law clk. to Justice William J. Brennan, Jr. U.S. Supreme Ct., Washington, 1969-70; sr. lectr. Law Devel. Ctr., Kampala, Uganda, 1970-71; assoc. Williams, Connolly & Califano, Washington, 1971-77; chief counsel FDA, Rockville, Md., 1977-79; ptnr. Williams & Connolly, LLP, Washington, 1980—; mem. exec. com. Williams & Connolly, Washington, 1983-84, 89-92. Sr. mem. Office Energy Policy and Planning, Exec. Office of Pres., Washington, 1977; adj. prof. Georgetown U. Law Ctr., Washington, 1987-92, 96; mem. Adminstrv. Conf. U.S., 1978-79, Jud. Conf. D.C., Washington, 1979; mem. Adv. Panel on Strategies for Med. Tech. Assessment, Washington, 1980-81; mem. coms. NAS, 1980-83, 87-90. Editor: Food and Drug Law, 1991; co-editor: Fundamentals of Law and Regulation, 1997; contbr. articles to profl. jours. Chief counsel credentials com. Dem. Nat. Conv., Washington and N.Y.C., 1976; bd. mgrs. Haverford Coll., 1997—. Rhodes Trust scholar 1964; recipient FDA Award of Merit, 1979. Jewish. Office: Williams & Connolly 725 12th St NW Washington DC 20005-5901 E-mail: rcooper@wc.com.

COOPER, RICHARD ALAN, lawyer; b. Hattiesburg, Miss., July 19, 1953; s. H. Douglas and Elaine (Reece) C. BA, BS, U. Ark., Little Rock, 1976; JD, Washington U., St. Louis, 1979. Bar: Mo. 1979, Ill. 1980, U.S. Dist. Ct. (ea. dist.) Mo. 1980, U.S. Dist Ct. (so. dist.) Ill. 1988. Law clk. U.S. Dist. Ct., St. Louis, 1979-80; assoc. William R. Gartenberg, St. Louis, 1980-81, Danis, Reid, Murphy, Tobben & Cooper, St. Louis, 1983-87, ptnr., 1987-88, Law Office Terry Sharp, P.C., 1988-89; pvt. practice, 1989-90; ptnr. Danis & Boyce, 1990-93, Danis, Cooper, Cavanagh & Hartweger, L.C., 1994-98; CFO MedCard Am., Inc., 1997-99; pvt. practice, 1999—. Liaison to Washington U. Sch. Law, Mo. Assn. Trial Attys., St. Louis, 1983-85; presenter in field. Bus. mgr. Urban Law Jour., 1978-79; editor Bankruptcy Law Reporter, 1983-88, co-mgr., editor, 1984-88; co-author seminars including Debt Collection from Start to Finish in Mo., Planning for the Newly Married Couple, Collection Practice in Missouri from Start to Finish, Impact of Bankruptcy on Family Law, Advanced Consumer Bankruptcy and Fair Debt Collection Practices, Collecting Judgments and Non UCC Liens, Advanced Consumer Bankruptcy; author: supplement to Missouri Desk Book Civil Procedure, 2000; contbg. author: Missouri CLE Deskbook Civil Procedure on Rule 76, Executions.. Recipient Milton F. Napier trial award Lawyers Assn. St. Louis, 1979, Outstanding Sr. Bus. Major award Wall St. Jour., 1976. Mem. Mo. Bar Assn., Boulder Yacht Club (commodore 1998-99), Commonwealth Yacht Club. Avocation: sailing. Bankruptcy, Federal civil litigation, Commercial, contracts (including sales of goods; commercial financing). Office: Law Offices Richard Alan Cooper 2379 Cedar Dale Ct Maryland Heights MO 63043 E-mail: richard@richardalancooperattorney.com.

COOPER, RICHARD EARL, lawyer; b. Louisville, May 1, 1947; s. David Dowell and Lillian Mary Rose (Magel) C.; m. Ellen Zapp, Dec. 29, 1973 (div. Sept. 1979); m. Pamala Ann Murphy, July 18, 1981; children: John David, Shelley Marsh. BA in Edn., U. Ky., 1970; JD, U. Louisville, 1975. Bar: Ky. 1975, U.S. Dist. Ct. (we. dist.) Ky. 1979, U.S. Supreme Ct. 1979, U.S. Ct. Appeals (6th cir.) 1980. Tchr. Jefferson County Bd. Edn., Louisville, 1971-74; pvt. practice, Louisville, 1975—76; prosecutor Commonwealth Atty., Louisville, 1976-80; assoc. Eli George, P.S.C., Louisville, 1980-82; pvt. prac., 1982—. Spl. asst. Ky. atty. gen., Louisville, 1979-80. Named Prosecutor of Yr., Commonwealth Atty., 1979. Mem. ATLA, Ky. Bar Assn., Louisville Bar Assn. (jud. evaluatin com. 1979-82, profl. responsibility com. 1982-88, co-chmn. criminal practice com. 1980-81, 89—, mem. litigation com. 1990—, family law com. 1990—, probate and estate com. 1991—, comm. com. 1992-2000, mem. Ky. lawyer referral svc. 1993-2001, chmn. 1996-98). Democrat. Roman Catholic. Criminal, Family and matrimonial, Personal injury (including property damage). Home: 510 McCready Ave Louisville KY 40206-3026 Office: 310 Starks Bldg Louisville KY 40202

COOPER, ROBERT ELBERT, state supreme court justice; b. Chattanooga, Oct. 14, 1920; s. John Thurman and Susie Inez (Hollingsworth) C.; m. Catherine Pauline Kelly, Nov. 24, 1949; children: Susan Florence Cooper Hodges, Bobbie Cooper Martin, Kelly Ann Smith, Robert Elbert Jr. BA, U. N.C., 1946; JD, Vanderbilt U., 1949. Bar: Tenn. 1948. Assoc. Kolwyck and Clark, 1949-51; ptnr. Cooper and Barger, 1951-53; asst. atty. gen. 6th Jud. Ct. Tenn., 1951-53; judge 6th Jud. Circuit Tenn., 1953-60, Tenn. Ct. Appeals, 1960-70, presiding judge Eastern divsn., 1970-74; justice Tenn. Supreme Ct., 1974-90, chief justice, 1976-77, 84-85. Chmn. Tenn. Jud. Coun., 1967-90; chmn. Tenn. Code Commn., 1976-77, 84-85; mem. Tenn. Jud. Standards Commn., 1971-77. Mem. exec. bd. Cherokee coun. Boy Scouts Am., 1960-64; bd. dirs. Met. YMCA, 1956-65, St. Barnabas Nursing Home and Apts. for Aged, 1966-69. With USNR, 1941-46. Recipient Nat. Heritage award Downtown Sertoma Club, Chattanooga, 1989. Mem. Am., Tenn., Chattanooga bar assns., Conf. Chief Justices, Phi Beta Kappa, Order of Coif, Kappa Sigma, Phi Alpha Delta. Clubs: Signal Mountain Golf and Country, Masons (33 deg.), Shriners. Democrat. Presbyterian. Home and Office: 196 Woodcliff Cir Signal Mountain TN 37377-3147

COOPER, ROY ASBERRY , III, state attorney general, lawyer; b. Rocky Mount, N.C., June 13, 1957; s. Roy Asberry Jr. and Beverly (Batchelor) C.; m. Kristin Bernhardt, Mar. 28, 1992; children: Hilary Godette, Natalie Rose, Claire Kristin. BA, U. N.C., 1979, JD, 1982. Bar: N.C. 1982. Ptnr. Fields and Cooper, Rocky Mount, 1982—2001; atty. gen. State of N.C., 2001—. Mem. N.C. Ho. of Reps., 1987-91, chmn. jud. com., 1989-91; mem. N.C. Senate, 1991-2001, chmn. jud. com., 1991-2000. Morehead scholar U. N.C., 1975-79. Democrat. Presbyterian. Office: NC Dept Justice PO Box 629 Raleigh NC 27602

COOPER, STEPHEN HERBERT, lawyer; b. N.Y.C., Mar. 29, 1939; s. Walter S. and Selma (Herbert) C.; m. Linda Cohen, Aug. 29, 1965 (dec.); m. Karen Gross, Sept. 6, 1981; 1 child, Zachary Noel. AB, Columbia U., 1960, JD cum laude, 1965. Bar: N.Y. 1965. Assoc. Weil, Gotshal & Manges, N.Y.C., 1966-73, ptnr., 1973—. Lectr. Nat. Inst. Securities Regulation U. Colo., Boulder, 1985, Practicing Law Inst. 25th Annual Nat. Inst. Securities Regulation, N.Y.C., 1993, Law Jours. Seminars, 1997, 98; adj. prof. law, N.Y. Law Sch., N.Y.C., 2002-. Served to lt. USNR, 1960-62. Fellow Am. Bar Found.; mem. ABA (com. fed. regulation securities, subcom. internat. securities matters, co-chmn. 1990—). Corporate, general, Private international, Securities. Home: 1125 Park Ave New York NY 10128-1243 Office: Weil Gotshal & Manges LLP 767 5th Ave New York NY 10153-0119 E-mail: stephen.cooper@weil.com.

COOPER, WILLIAM LEWIS, research librarian, lawyer, consultant; b. Highland Park, Mich., Sept. 11, 1944; s. Frank Edward and Margaret Ellen (Hayes) C.; m. Bonnie McIntyre Devine, June 7, 2002. AB, Dartmouth Coll., 1966; JD, U. Mich., 1972, AM in Library Sci., 1974. Bar: Mich. 1972, D.C. 1976. Assoc. Miller-Canfield, Detroit, 1972-74; reference libr. U. Pa., 1974-75; libr. Hogan & Hartson, Washington, 1975-77; dir. legal rsch. Dykema Gossett, Detroit, 1977-91, Williamsbury Assocs., Birmingham, Mich., 1991-95; rsch. libr. Coll. William and Mary, Williamsburg, Va., 1995-99; legal practice prof. U. Mich., 1999-2002; assoc. prof. John Marshall Law Sch., Atlanta, 2002—. Contbr. articles to profl. jours. With US Army, 1967-69. Mem. Mich. State Bar Assn. (legal econs. sect.), Detroit Bar Found. (treas. 1980-82, trustee 1979-85). Episcopalian. Home: 2764 Cosmos Dr Atlanta GA 30345 Office: 1422 W Peachtree St NW Atlanta GA 30309 Personal E-mail: wlcoop44@hotmail.com.

COOPER, WILLIAM S. state supreme court justice; b. Sept. 15, 1941; BA, U. Ky., 1963, JD with high distinction, 1970. Ptnr. Collier, Arnett, Coleman & Cooper, 1970—79; judge Ky. 9th Judicial Cir., Div. 1, 1979—96; justice Ky. Supreme Ct., Frankfort, 1996—. Capt. USAF, 1963-67. Office: Hardin County Justice Ctr 120 E Dixie Ave Elizabethtown KY 42701-1469

COOPERRIDER, LUANN, judge; b. Newark, Ohio, Dec. 30, 1955; d. Carl Richard Cooperrider and Julia Jean Vickers; m. John W. Gillogly, May 4, 1991; 1 child, Cooper John Gillogly. BSW, Ohio State U., 1978; postgrad., Loyola U., Rome, 1980; JD, Capital U., 1983. Asst. pros. Perry County, 1986—90; judge probate-juvenile divsn. Perry County Common Pleas Ct., 1991—. Active numerous civic orgns. Recipient Nettie Cronian Lutes award, Ohio State Bar Assn., 2001. Mem.: Ohio Assn. Juvenile Family Ct. Judges (pres. 2003—). Lutheran. Avocations: bicycling, swimming, boating. Office: Perry County Probate and Juvenile PO Box 167 New Lexington OH 43764-0167

COOTER, DALE A. lawyer; b. Syracuse, N.Y., Aug. 28, 1948; s. Charles Henry and Mavis Elizabeth (Wagner) C.; m. Mary Kathryn Nolan, Oct. 8, 1977; children: John Andrew, Jessica Averie. BA cum laude, SUNY, Fredonia, 1970; JD, Georgetown U., 1975. Bar: Md. 1975, D.C. 1976, Va. 1984, U.S. Dist. Ct. Md. 1976, U.S. Dist. Ct. D.C. 1976, U.S. Ct. Appeals (4th and D.C. cirs.) 1976, U.S. Supreme Ct. 1979. Ptnr. Cooter, Mangold, Tompert & Wayson, LLP, Washington, 1976—. Adj. prof. law Georgetown U., Washington, 1985—. Editor Georgetown U. Law Jour., 1973-75. Served with N.G. Mem. ABA, Va. Bar Assn., Md. Bar Assn., D.C. Bar Assn. Federal civil litigation, State civil litigation. Home: 4675 Kenmore Dr NW Washington DC 20007-1914 Office: Cooter Mangold Tompert & Wayson LLP 5301 Wisconsin Ave NW Ste 500 Washington DC 20015-2015 E-mail: dcooter@cootermangold.com.

COOVER, ANN E. lawyer; b. Sparta, Wis., Aug. 23, 1948; d. Orlin H. Runde and Kathleen Ann Dwyer; m. David M. Coover, July 22, 1972; 1 child, D. Marshall. BS, U. Wis., 1971; JD magna cum laude, U. Houston, 1975. Bar: Tex. 1975, U.S. Dist. Ct. (fed. dist.) 1975, U.S. Supreme Ct. 1978; bd. cert. family law Tex. Bd. Legal Specialization. Sr. law clk. to dist. judge U.S. Dist. Ct., Corpus Christi, Tex., 1976-78; ptnr. Coover & Coover, Corpus Christi, 1978—. Chair Am. Cancer Soc. Cattlemen's Ball, Corpus Christi, 1998; chair Auction for Art Mus. Gala, Corpus Christi, 1997. Mem.: State Bar Family Law Coun. Avocations: gardening, antiques, bridge. Alternative dispute resolution, Environmental. Office: Coover & Coover 921 N Chaparral St Corpus Christi TX 78401-2008

COPE, JOSEPH ADAMS, lawyer; b. Summit, N.J., Jan. 15, 1945; s. Joseph H. and Eunice (Adams) Cope; m. Michele Zeleny, Sept. 25, 1982 (dec. Dec. 2001). BA, U. Colo., 1967, JD, 1976. Bar: Colo. 1967, U.S. Dist. Ct. Colo. 1976, U.S. Ct. Appeals (10th cir.) 1977, U.S. Claims Ct. 1984, U.S. Supreme Ct. 1984; cert. civil trial advocate NBTA, 2001. Assoc. Vranesh & Musick, Boulder, Colo., 1976—78; ptnr. Musick and Cope, Boulder, 1978—91; of counsel Frascona, Joiner, Goodman & Greenstein, P.C., Boulder, 1991—. Served to lt. USN, 1967-73. Mem. ABA, Colo. Bar Assn., Boulder County Bar Assn., State Bar Calif., Lawyer-Pilots Bar Assn., Order of Coif. Avocation: raising shire draft horses. General civil litigation, Natural resources. Home: 8595 N 95th St Longmont CO 80504-7768 Office: Frascona Joiner Goodman & Greenstein PC 4750 Table Mesa Dr Boulder CO 80305-5500 E-mail: jay@frascona.com.

COPE, THOM K. lawyer; b. Bremen, Fed. Republic Germany, Feb. 26, 1948; came to U.S., 1960; s. Ray and Gabriele E. (Meyer) C.; m. Melba D. Van Hemert, Nov. 8, 1980. BA with honors, Syracuse U., 1969; JD, U. Nebr., 1972. Bar: Nebr. 1972, U.S. Dist. Ct. Nebr. 1972, U.S. Ct. Appeals (8th cir.) 1972, Calif. 1976, U.S. Dist. Ct. (no. dist.) Calif. 1976, U.S. Ct. Appeals (9th cir.) 1976, U.S. Supreme Ct. 1987, U.S. Claims Ct. 1988, U.S. Ct. Appeals (D.C. cir.) 1990. Agy. legal counsel Nebr. Workers' Compensation Ct., Lincoln, 1972-73; assoc. counsel Fireman's Fund Ins. Co., San Francisco, 1973-76; asst. gen. counsel Argonaut Ins. Co., Menlo Park, Calif., 1976-78; assoc. counsel Ins. Svcs. Office, N.Y.C., 1978-82; assoc. atty. Tate & Assocs., Nebr., 1982-83, Bailey, Polsky, Cada & Todd, Nebr., 1983-84; ptnr. Bailey, Polsky, Cope & Knapp, Lincoln, 1984-97, Polsky Cope Shiffermiller Coe and Monzon and predecessors, Lincoln, 1997—2002; v.p. human resources Beaudry Motor Co., 2002—. Judge Nebr. Commn. of Indsl. Rels., 1986-91; mem. Nebr. Supreme Ct. Gender Bias Task Force; mem. Nebr. Motor Vehicle Industry Licensing Bd.; mem. Nebr. Atty. Gen. Odometer Fraud Task Force; mem. Fed. Practice Adv. Com.; lectr. in field. Author: Executive Guide to Employment Practices, 1985, 3d edit., 1999. Bd. dirs. Friends of Elderly Found., Lincoln, 1986-90, Capital Humane Soc., Planned Parenthood Lincoln, 1997—, v.p., 1998, pres. 1999—2001; bd. dirs. Child Advocacy Ctr., 1995-97; bd. trustees Lincoln Bar Assn. Fellow Coll. Employment and Labor Law; mem. Nat. Employment Lawyers Assn., Nebr. Bar Assn. (labor and employment sect., exec. com., sec.), Nebr. Trial Lawyers Assn., NOW (bd. dirs. 1999), Soc. Human Resource Mgmt. Avocation: golf. Civil rights, State civil litigation, Labor (including EEOC, Fair Labor Standards Act, labor-management relations, NLRB, OSHA). Home: 9343 N Sunflower Blossom Pl Tucson AZ 85743- Office: Beaudry Motor Co PO Box 12747 Tucson AZ 85732 E-mail: epocgolf@aol.com.

COPELAND, CHARLENE CAROLE, lawyer; b. Gloversville, N.Y., July 22; d. Joseph Frank and Marion (Dye) Born; children: Christopher, Todd, Tiffani. BS in Polit Sci., Lamar U.; JD, John Marshall U. Bar: Ill. 1991, U.S. Dist. Ct. (no. dist.) Ill. 1991, U.S. Ct. Appeals (7th cir.) 1993, Fed. Trial Bar, 1993. Assoc. Brenner, Mavrias & Alm, New Lenox, Ill., 1992-96; assoc. civil divsn. Will County State's Attys. Office, Joliet, Ill., 1997-1999; with Lehrer, Flaherty & Canavan, Wheaton, Ill., 2000—02; asst. atty. gen. Ill. Atty. Gen.'s office Indsl. Commn. Bur., 2002—. Mem. Will County Pro Bono Project; pres. Jaycettes, Port Authur, Tex., 1970-71; fin. chmn. League of Women Voters, 1971, pres. Joliet Region, 1979-81; area capt. March of Dimes Mothers' March, 1971; day chmn. George Bush for Senate Campaign, 1970; mem. Village of Shorewood Ad Hoc Com. on Ordinances, 1975, Fin. Com., 1976-78; pres. United Meth. Women of Grace Meth. Ch., 1980-81; crusade chmn. Shorewood Residential Cancer Crusade, 1982. Named Outstanding Pro Bono Vol., 1995. Mem. Ill. State Bar Assn., Will County Bar Assn., Will County Arbitration Panel, Will County Women's Bar Assn. (chmn. 1999), John Marshall Law Sch. Reunion Com. Federal civil litigation, State civil litigation, Environmental. Home: 516 Ca Crest Dr Shorewood IL 60431-9729

COPELAND, EDWARD JEROME, lawyer; b. Chgo., Oct. 29, 1933; s. Harvey and Lilyan (Rubin) C.; m. Ruth Caminer, Sept. 2, 1962; children: Ellyn, Bradley. BA, Carleton Coll., 1955; JD, Northwestern U., 1958. Bar: Ill. 1959, N.Y. 1981. Mem. Ill. Ho. of Reps., Springfield, 1967-71; ptnr. Foss, Schuman, Drake & Barnard, Chgo., 1971-86, Wood, Lucksinger & Epstein, Chgo., 1986-88, Shefsky & Froelich, Ltd., Chgo., 1988-89, Schuyler, Roche & Zwirner, Chgo., 1989—. Chmn. Bank of North Shore, Northbrook, Ill., 1976-81. Mem. Ill. Bd. Edn., 1975-83, chmn., 1981-83. Mem. ABA, Ill. Bar Assn., Chgo. Bar Assn. Republican. Education and schools, Landlord-tenant, Property, real (including real estate development, water). Office: One Prudential Plaza Ste 3800 Schuyler Roche & Zwirner 130 E Randolph St Chicago IL 60601-6312 E-mail: ecopeland@srzlaw.com.

COPELAND, ROBERT GLENN, lawyer; b. San Diego, Mar. 15, 1941; s. Glenn Howard and Lualla Louise (Schmid) C.; m. Harriet S. Smith, June 27, 1964 (div. Jan. 1977); children: Katherine Louise, Matthew Robert; m. Marcia Diane Cummings, Jan. 8, 1977 (div. June 1990); m. Lynne Newman, Oct. 10, 1993; 1 child, Zachary Newman. AB, Occidental Coll., 1963; JD, U. So. Calif., 1966. Bar: Calif. 1966, U.S. Dist. Ct. Calif. (so. dist.), 1967. Ptnr. Gray, Cary, Ware & Freidenrich, San Diego, 1966-95, Luce, Forward Hamilton & Scripps LLP, 1995—. Mem. ABA, Calif. Bar Assn. Republican. Avocations: shooting, fly fishing, hiking, racquetball. Corporate, general, Mergers and acquisitions. Office: Luce Forward Hamilton & Scripps LLP 600 W Broadway Ste 2600 San Diego CA 92101-3311 E-mail: rcopeland@luce.com.

COPELAND, ROBERT TAYLOE, lawyer; b. Norfolk, Va., June 13, 1947; s. William Robert and Carolyn Penny (Raynor) C.; m. Charlotte Elizabeth Walker, July 7, 1973 (div. 1980); m. Jo Damron Molinary, Jan. 15, 1981; children: Sarah Virginia, Robert Joseph. BA, U. Va., 1969; JD, Coll. William and Mary, 1975. Bar: Va. 1975, U.S. Dist. Ct. (we. dist.) Va. 1975, U.S. Ct. Appeals (4th cir.) 1976, U.S. Supreme Ct. 1980. Assoc. Smith, Robinson & Vinyard, Abingdon, Va., 1975-78; ptnr. Bradshaw, Morris & Copeland, Abingdon, 1978-79; pvt. practice Abingdon, 1979-81; ptnr. Copeland, Molinary & Bieger, Abingdon, 1981—. Bd. dirs., sec. Miners Exchange Bank, Coeburn, Va., pres. Kelly Energy Co., 1981-2001, Inc., Clintwood, Va. Chmn. Va. Pub. Sch. Authority, 1994-2002; mem. Econ. Devel. Coun. With U.S. Army, 1969-75. Mem. ABA, Va. Bar Assn., Washington County Bar Assn. (pres. 1987-88), Downtown Club of Richmond, Kiwanis (bd. dirs. Abingdon 1980-83), Highlands Soccer Club (chair 1995-97). Republican. Avocations: travel, gardening, golf. Banking, Bankruptcy, Federal civil litigation. Office: Copeland Molinary & Bieger PO Box 1296 Abingdon VA 24212-1296

COPENHAVER, JOHN THOMAS, JR., federal judge; b. Charleston, W.Va., Sept. 29, 1925; s. John Thomas and Ruth Cherrington (Roberts) C.; m. Camille Ruth Smith, Oct. 7, 1950; children: John Thomas III, James Smith, Brent Paul. AB, W.Va. U., 1947, LLB, 1950. Bar: W.Va., 1950. Law clerk to presiding judge U.S. Dist. Ct. (so. dist.) W.Va., 1950-51; mem. firm Copenhaver & Copenhaver, Charleston, 1951-58; U.S. bankruptcy judge So. Dist. W.Va. Charleston, 1958-76; U.S. dist. judge (so. dist.) W.Va., 1976—. Adj. prof. law W.Va. U. Coll. Law, 1970-76; mem. faculty Fed. Jud. Center, 1972-76; Pres. Legal Aid. Soc. Charleston, 1954; Chmn. Mcpl. Planning Commn. City of Charleston, 1964; chmn., pres. W.Va. Housing Devel. Fund, 1969-72; chmn. vis. com. W.Va. U. Coll. Law, 1980-83; mem. adv. com. on bankruptcy rules Jud. Conf. U.S., 1978-84. Contbr.: articles in fields of bankruptcy and comml. law to Bus. Lawyer, Am. Bankruptcy Law Jour., Personal Fin. Law Quar., W. Va. Law Rev., others. Served with U.S. Army, 1944-46. Recipient Gavel award W.Va. U. Coll. Law, 1971, Outstanding Judge award W. Va. Trial Lawyers Assn., 1983 Fellow Am. Bar Found.; mem. ABA, W.Va. Bar Assn., Kanawha County Bar Assn., Nat. Bankruptcy Conf., Nat. Conf. Bankruptcy Judges (past pres.), Phi Delta Phi, Beta Theta Pi. Republican. Presbyterian. Office: US Courthouse PO Box 2546 Charleston WV 25329-2546

COPLAN, GREGORY FORREST, lawyer; b. Morrison, Ill., Oct. 11, 1966; s. Ronald Franklin and Rosemary Lynn (Winters) Coplan; m. Lori D. Thompson, Mar. 12, 1994; children: Hailey C., Noah S., Mason B. BA, U. Ill., 1988; JD, No. Ill. U., 1992. Bar: Ill. 1992, U.S. Dist. Ct. (no. dist.) Ill. 1993. Pvt. practice, Morrison, 1992; lawyer Heyl, Royster, Voelker & Allen, Rockford, Ill., 1993—98, Goldberg, Weisman & Cairo, Ltd., Chgo., 1998—2003; pvt. practice, 2003—. Contbr. chapters to books. Bd. dirs. Storefront Cinema, Rockford, 1995—98. Mem.: ATLA, ABA, Ill. Trial Lawyers Assn. (med. negligence com. 1998—), Ill. State Bar Assn. Personal injury (including property damage). Office: Coplan Law Offices Ste 104 1415 W 55th St La Grange IL 60525 Office Fax: 708-354-3530. E-mail: coplanlawoffice@sbcglobal.net.

COPLEY, EDWARD ALVIN, lawyer; b. Memphis, Jan. 17, 1936; m. Connie James Patterson, Nov. 17, 1990; children: Julie, Ward, Drew, Kelly, Zeke. BA, So. Meth. U., 1957, JD, 1960. Bar: U.S. Dist. Ct. (no. dist.) Tex., U.S. Ct. Claims 1962, U.S. Supreme Ct. 1963, U.S. Tax Ct. 1966, U.S. Ct. Appeals (5th cir.) 1968. Atty. U.S. Dept. Justice, Washington, 1960-64, Ft. Worth, 1964-66; assoc. Akin, Gump, Strauss, Hauer & Feld, Dallas, 1966-67, ptnr., 1968—. Fellow Am. Coll. Probate Counsel; mem. Internat. Acad. Estate Trust Law, Dallas Bar Assn. (tax sect.), Dallas Estate Coun. (pres. 1975-76), So. Meth. U. Law Sch. Alumni Assn. (pres. 1978-79), Salesmanship Club, Order of Woolsac, Barristers, Dallas Petroleum Club, Dallas Country Club, Phi Alpha Delta. Avocations: racquetball, photography, hunting, fishing, reading. Estate planning, Estate taxation, Probate (including wills, trusts). Home: 3711 Shenandoah St Dallas TX 75205-2120 Office: Akin Gump Strauss Hauer & Feld Ste 4100 1700 Pacific Ave Dallas TX 75201-4675 E-mail: ecopley@akingump.com.

COPPEL, LAWRENCE DAVID, lawyer; b. Washington, July 3, 1944; s. Albert and Anne (Gold) C.; m. Arlene Cohen, Aug. 10, 1968; children: Jennifer, Allison. BA, U. Md., 1966, JD, 1969. Bar: Md. 1969, U.S. Dist. Ct. Md. 1971, U.S. Ct. Appeals (4th cir.) 1976, U.S. Ct. Appeals (3d cir.) 1983. Law clk. Md. Ct. Appeals, Annapolis, 1969-70; assoc. Gordon, Feinblatt, Rothman, Hoffberger & Hollander, LLC, Balt., 1970-77, mem., 1977—. Fellow Am. Coll. Bankruptcy; mem. ABA, Md. State Bar Assn., Bankruptcy Bar Assn. Dist. Md. (pres. 1988-89), Balt. City Bar Assn. Jewish. Bankruptcy. Office: Gordon Feinblatt Rothman Hoffberger & Hollander LLC 233 E Redwood St Baltimore MD 21202-3332 E-mail: lcoppel@gfrlaw.com.

COPPERSMITH, SAM, lawyer; b. Johnstown, Pa., May 22, 1955; m. Beth Schermer, Aug. 28, 1983; children: Sarah, Benjamin, Louis. AB in Econs. magna cum laude, Harvard U., 1976; JD, Yale Law Sch., 1982. Bar: Calif. 1982, Ariz. 1983. Fgn. svc. officer U.S. Dept. State, Port of Spain, Trinidad and Tobago, 1977—79; law clk. to Judge William C. Canby Jr. U.S. Ct. Appeals (9th cir.), Phoenix, 1982—83; atty. Sacks, Tierney & Kasen, P.A., Phoenix, 1983—86; asst. to Mayor Terry Goddard City of Phoenix, 1984; atty. Jones, Jury, Short & Mast P.C., Phoenix, 1986—88, Bonnett, Fairbourn & Friedman P.C., Phoenix, 1988—92; mem. 103d Congress from 1st Ariz. Dist., 1993—95; atty. Coppersmith Gordon Schermer Owens & Nelson PLC, 1995—. Former dir., pres. Planned Parenthood Ctrl. and No. Ariz.; former chair City of Phoenix Bd. Adjustment; former dir. Ariz. Cmty. Svc. Legal Assistance Found., 1986—89; trustee Devereux Found., 1997—; chair Ariz. Dem. Party, 1995—97. Mem. ABA, Maricopa County Bar Assn. Democrat. Commercial, contracts (including sales of goods; commercial financing), Corporate, general, Property, real (including real estate development, water). Office: Coppersmith Gordon Schermer Owens & Nelson PLC 2800 N Central Ave Ste 1000 Phoenix AZ 85004-1007 E-mail: sam@cgson.com.

COPSETTA, NORMAN GEORGE, real estate executive; b. Pennsauken, N.J., Mar. 11, 1932; s. Joseph J. and Mary P. (DeMello) C.; m. Patricia Fitzpatrick, Mar. 5, 1971; children: Gregory, Margaret, Andrew, Norman G. Jr.; stepchildren: Samuel Sassano, James Sassano. Cert. real estate, Rutgers U. Extension, Camden, N.J., 1952; AA, Internat. Accts. Soc. Schl. Acctg., Chgo., 1968. Lic. title insurance agent, N.J. Settlement clk. Market Street Title Abstract Co., Camden, 1949-53; settlement administrator West Jersey Title & Guaranty Co., Camden, 1953; title examiner, abstract adminstr. Realty Abstract Co., Cherry Hill, N.J., 1954-64; mcpl. treas., tax collector Borough of Somerdale, N.J., 1961-65; title examiner, legal adminstr. Davis, Reberkenny & Abramowitz, Cherry Hill, 1974-97; pres., title officer Cooper Abstract Co., Cherry Hill, 1974-99, chmn. bd., 1997—. N.J. fgn. commr. of deeds in and for Pa., 1959—2000; mem. faculty Title Acad. N.J., The Title Ins. Sch. Custodian of funds Somerdale Bd. Edn., 1960-64. Mem. N.J. Title Ins. Agts. Assn., Haddonfield (N.J.) Hist. Soc., Camden County Hist. Soc. Avocation: local history. Office: Cooper Abstract Co 401 Cooper Landing Rd Ste C6 Cherry Hill NJ 08002-2598

COQUILLETTE, DANIEL ROBERT, lawyer, educator; b. Boston, May 23, 1944; s. Robert McTavish and Dagmar Alvida (Bistrup) C.; m. Judith Courtney Rogers, July 5, 1969; children: Anna, Sophia, Julia. AB, Williams Coll., 1966; MA Juris., U. Coll., Oxford U., Eng., 1969; JD, Harvard U., 1971. Bar: Mass. 1974, U.S. Dist. Ct. Mass. 1974, U.S. Ct. Appeals (1st cir.) 1974. Law clk. Mass. Supreme Ct., 1971-72; to chief justice Warren E. Burger U.S. Supreme Ct., 1972-73; assoc. Palmer & Dodge, Boston, 1973-75, ptnr., 1980-85; assoc. prof. law Boston U., 1975-78; dean, prof. Boston Coll. Law, 1985-93, prof., 1993-96, J. Donald Monan prof. law, 1996—. Vis. assoc. prof. law Cornell U., Ithaca, N.Y., 1977-78, 84; vis. prof. law Harvard U., 1978-79, 84-85, 94-2001, overseers com., Lester Kissel vis. prof., 2001—; reporter com. rules and procedures Jud. Conf. U.S.; mem. task force on rules of atty. conduct Supreme Jud. Ct. of Mass., 1996-97. Author: The Civilian Writers of Doctors Commons, London, 1988, Francis Bacon, 1993, Lawyers and Fundamental Moral Responsibility, 1995, Working Papers on Rules Governing Attorney Conduct, 1997, (with Basile, Beston, Donahue) Lex Mercatoria and Legal Pluralism, 1999, The Anglo-American Legal Heritage, 1999, (with McMorrow) Federal Law of Attorney Conduct, 2001; editor: Law in Colonial Massachusetts, 1985, Moore's Federal Practice, 3d edit., 1997; bd. dirs. New Eng. Quar., 1986—; contbr. articles to profl. jours. Trustee, sec.-treas. Ames Found; bd. overseers vis. com. Harvard Law Sch.; treas. Byron Meml. Fund; propr., trustee Boston Athenaeum. Recipient Kaufman prize in English Williams Coll., 1966, Sentinel of the Republic prize in polit. sci. Williams Coll., 1965; Hutchins scholar, 1966-67, Fulbright scholar, 1966-68 Mem. ABA (com. on profl. ethics 1990-93), Am. Law Inst., Mass. Bar Assn. (task force on model rules of profl. conduct), Boston Bar Assn., Am. Soc. Legal History (bd. dirs. 1985-89), Mass. Soc. Continuing Legal Edn. (bd. dirs. 1985-89), Selden Soc. (state corr.), Colonial Soc. Mass. (v.p., mem. coun.), Anglo-Am. Cathedral Soc. (bd. dirs.), Mass. Hist. Soc., Am. Antiquarian Soc., Phi Beta Kappa. Democrat. Mem. Soc. Of Friends. Home: 12 Rutland St Cambridge MA 02138-2503 Office: Boston Coll Sch Law 885 Centre St Newton MA 02459-1148 E-mail: coquill@bc.edu.

COQUILLETTE, WILLIAM HOLLIS, lawyer; b. Boston, Oct. 7, 1949; s. Robert McTavish and Dagmar (Bistrup) C.; m. Mary Katherine Templeton, June 19, 1971 (div. Oct. 1984); 1 child, Carolyn Patricia; m. Janet Marie Weiland, Dec. 8, 1984; children: Benjamin Weiland, Madeline Marie, Elizabeth Charlotte. BA, Yale U., 1971, Oxford U., 1973; JD, Harvard U., 1975. Bar: Ohio 1976, Mass. 1976. Law clk. to presiding justice Mass. Supreme Ct., Boston, 1975-76; assoc. Jones Day, Cleve., 1976-83, ptnr., 1984—. Trustee Cleve. Foodbank, Playhouse Sq. Found., Greater Cleve. Com. on Hunger. Mem. Kirtland Club, Yale Club (N.Y.C.), Union Club (Cleve.), Cleve. Skating Club, Rowfant Club, N.Y. Yacht Club. Banking, Corporate, general, Private international. Office: Jones Day 901 Lakeside Ave E Cleveland OH 44114-1190

CORAPI, DIEGO, lawyer, educator; b. Rome, May 21, 1940; s. Salvatore and Olga (Scacchi) C.; m. Maria Elisa Bocca, July 16, 1969 (div. 1977); children: Elisabetta, Tommaso; m. Maria Helena Cunha Pitaguari, July 3, 1998. JD, U. Rome, 1962. Bar: Rome 1964. Asst. prof. U. Rome, 1965-68; vis. prof. U. Macerata, Italy, 1968-70, U. Salerno, Italy, 1970-75, prof., 1975-79, U. Naples, Italy, 1979-84, U. Rome-Tor Vergata, 1984—97, U. Rome-La Sapienza, 1997—. Vis. prof. Luiss U., Rome, 1985—2000; lectr. Temple Law Sch., Phila., U. Paris I-Panthéon; dir. Authority for Control on Ins. Cos., Rome, 1987—98; cons. Authority for Stock Exch. and Corps., Rome, 1984—90; chmn. SanPaoloVita Co., 1999—. Editor: Author's Rights in Front of New Technologies, 1994, Essays in European Commercial Law, 1995; author: Companies By-Laws, 1971, Joint Ventures, 1983. Mem.: IAI, LCIA, Clausen Miller Europe, Internat. Acad. De Droit Compare, Internat. Acad. Trial Lawyers. Avocation: poetry. Office: Studio Legale Corapi Via Flaminia 318 00196 Rome Italy E-mail: diego.corapi@studiolegalecorapi.it.

CORASH, RICHARD, lawyer; b. N.Y.C., Mar. 31, 1938; s. Paul and Mildred (Spanier) C.; m. Carol A. McKevitt, Dec. 11, 1966; children: Richard Jr., Sharon, Peter, Amy. BA, Harpur Coll., SUNY, Bingamton, 1959; MA, Bklyn. Law Sch., 1966; JD, Rutgers U., 1963. Bar: N.Y. 1964, U.S. Dist. Ct. D.C. 1964, U.S. Supreme Ct. 1972. Pvt. practice, N.Y.C., 1964-77; pres. Corash & Hollender, P.C ., N.Y.C., 1977—. Pres. NEFM Trading Co., N.Y.C.; chmn. North Eastern Fiscal Mgmt. Co., N.Y.C.; pres. North Eastern Equities, L.L.C.; counsel Caywood Homeowners Assn. Mem. N.Y. State Bar Assn. (real estate and trust and estates sects.), N.Y. State Bar Assn. (chmn. grievance com.), Richmond County Bar Assn. Corporate, general, Estate planning, Property, real (including real estate development, water). Address: 81 Roxiticus Rd Far Hills NJ 07931-2225 E-mail: E-mailchlawnyc@aol.com.

CORBETT, THOMAS WINGETT, JR., lawyer; b. Phila., June 17, 1949; s. Thomas Wingett and Mary Bernadine (Diskin) C.; m. Susan Jean Manbeck, Dec. 16, 1972; children: Thomas Wingett III, Katherine. BA, Lebanon Valley Coll., 1971; JD, St. Mary's U., 1975. Bar: Pa. 1976, U.S. Dist. Ct. (we. dist.) Pa. 1976, U.S. Ct. Mil. Appeals 1979, U.S. Supreme Ct. 1984. Asst. dist. atty. Allegheny County, Pitts., 1976—80; asst. U.S. atty. Office U.S. Atty. for Western Dist. Pa., Pitts., 1980—83; assoc. Rose, Schmidt, Hasley & DiSalle, Pitts., 1983—86, ptnr., 1986—89; U.S. atty. We. Dist. Pa., Pitts., mem. U.S. atty. gen.'s adv. com., 1991—, chmn., 1993; Atty. Gen. State of Pa., Harrisburg, 1995—97; ptnr. Thorp, Reed & Armstrong, Pitts., 1993—95, 1997—98; asst. gen. counsel for govt. affairs Waste Mgmt. Inc., Pitts., 1998—2002; owner Thomas Corbett & Assocs., 2002—. Pres. St. Mary's Parent-Tchr. Guild, Glenshaw, Pa., 1983-85; mem. Allegheny County Republican Com., 1985-89, 2002—; mem. Shaler Twp. Bd. Commrs., 1988-89; chmn. Pa. Commn. on Crime and Delinquency, 1995—. Mem. ABA, Pa. Bar Assn., Allegheny County Bar Assn. (judiciary com.). Roman Catholic. Avocations: skiing, golf, reading. General civil litigation, Criminal. Office: 1720 Gulf Tower 7th and Grant St Pittsburgh PA 15219

CORBIN, DONALD L. state supreme court justice; b. Hot Springs, Ark., Mar. 29, 1938; BA, U. Ark., 1964, JD, 1966. Bar: Ark. 1966, U.S. Dist. Ct. (we. dist.) Ark. 1966. Lawyer Lewisville and Stamps, 1967-80; judge Ark. Ct. Appeals, 1981-87, chief judge, 1987-90; assoc. justice Ark. Supreme Ct., Little Rock, 1991—. State rep. Ark. Gen. Assembly, 1971-80. Served with USMC, 1955-59. Mem. ABA, Ark. Bar Assn., SW Ark. Bar Assn., Sigma Alpha Epsilon. Democrat. Avocation: duck hunting. Office: Supreme Ct Justice Bldg 625 Marshall St, 120 Justice Builiding Little Rock AR 72201-1054

CORBIN, SOL NEIL, lawyer; b. N.Y.C., Apr. 16, 1927; s. Nathan I. and Sarah (Kaiser) Corbin; m. Tanya Jacobs, Aug. 7, 1963; 1 child, David J. BS, Columbia U., 1948; JD cum laude, Harvard U., 1951. Bar: N.Y. 1952. Pvt. practice, N.Y.C., 1952—; law clk. Judge Charles D. Breitel, 1954-56; counsel Gov. of N.Y., 1962-65; ptnr. Corbin, Silverman & Sanseverino LLP, N.Y.C., 1970-96, sr. counsel, 1997—2001, Taylor, Colicchio & Silverman, LLP, N.Y.C., 2001—. Chmn. N.Y. State Commn. Constl. Conv., 1966—67, N.Y. State Crime Control Planning Bd., 1974—75; mem. N.Y. State Banking Bd., 1969—76, N.Y. State Commn. Local Govt. Powers, 1971—73; mem. chief judge's com. to recruit state ct. adminstr., 1973; trustee bankruptcy Franklin N.Y. Corp., 1974—90; spl. counsel to v.p. U.S., 1975; apptd. counsel to trustee BCCI, 1990—97. Trustee N.Y. Pub. Libr., 1977—; mem. chief judge's com. availability legal svcs., 1988—90. With USNR, 1945—46. Mem.: ABA, Am. Law Inst., New York County Bar Assn., Assn. Br. City of N.Y., Lotus Club. Banking, Corporate, general, Securities. Home: 1100 Park Ave New York NY 10128-1202 Office: 99 Park Ave Ste 1703 New York NY 10016

CORBIN WALKER, KAROL, lawyer; b. Jersey City, Oct. 11, 1958; BA cum laude, N.J. City U., 1980; JD, Seton Hall U., 1986. Bar: N.J. 1986, N.Y. 1991, U.S. Dist. Ct. N.J. 1986, U.S. Dist. Ct. (so. and ea. dists.) N.Y. 1987, U.S. Dist. Ct. (no. dist.) N.Y. 1994, U.S. Ct. Appeals (3d cir.) 1991, U.S. Supreme Ct. 1993. Jud. law clk. to Hon. Davis S. Baime, Superior Ct. N.J., Appellate Divsn., 1986—87; adj. prof. law Seton Hall U. Sch. Law, 1988—90; atty. St. John & Wayne, LLC, Newark. Mem. adv. bd. Salvation Army Morristown Corps; active United Way of Essex and West Hudson. Mem.: ABA, Assn. Fed. Bar of State of N.J., Nat. Bar Assn. (treas. 1994—96, sec. divsn. ptnrs. in majority law firms 1999—2002, sec. 1998—99, 2d vice chair 1999—2002, comml. law sect. 1st vice chair 2002—), Garden State Bar Assn. (trustee 1989—91, pres. 1991—93), Essex County Bar Assn. (Young Lawyers divsn. exec. bd. 1990—92, chair minorities in profession com. 1991—93, chair continuing legal edn. com. 1993—97, trustee 1994—97), Morris County Bar Assn., N.J. State Bar Assn. (Young Lawyers divsn. exec. bd. 1990—93, chair minorities in profession com. 1991—93, trustee 1995—99, chair diversity com. 1997—98, chair jud. and prosecutorial appointments com. 1998—99, sec. 1999—2000, treas. 2000—01, 2d v.p. 2001—02, 1st v.p. 2002, pres.-elect 2002—03), Phi Alpha Delta. Commercial, consumer (including collections, credit), Environmental, Toxic tort. Office: St John and Wayne LLC 2 Penn Plz E Newark NJ 07105-2249*

CORCORAN, CLEMENT TIMOTHY, III, judge; b. Kansas City, Mo., Dec. 18, 1945; s. Clement T. and Bette Lou (Hohl) C. BA, U. N.C., 1967; JD, U. Va., 1973. Bar: Fla. 1973, U.S. Dist. Ct. (mid. dist.) Fla. 1973, D.C. 1974, U.S. Dist. Ct. (no. and so. dists.) Fla. 1975, U.S. Supreme Ct. 1979, U.S. Ct. Appeals (11th cir.) 1981. Law clk. U.S. Dist. Ct., Tampa, Fla., 1973-75; assoc. Carlton, Fields, Ward, Emmanuel, Smith & Cutler, P.A., Tampa, 1975-78, ptnr., 1978-89; judge Bankruptcy Ct. (mid. dist.) Fla., Orlando, 1989-93, Tampa, 1993—. Dir. Bay Area Legal Svcs., Inc., Tampa, 1983-89, v.p., 1987, pres., 1988; bd. dirs. Fla. Coun. Bar Pres., 1982-88, pres., 1986-87; arbitrator Ct. Annexed Arbitration Program, U.S. Dist. Ct. (mid. dist.) Fla., 1984-89; counselor U. Tampa, 1981-86, fellow, 1986-89. Co-author: Conflicts of Interest, 1984; contbr. articles to legal jours. Lt. USNR, 1967-70. Mem. ABA (litigation sect., coun. mem. 1999-2002, co-chair comm. com. 1990-92, chair book pub. bd. 1992-98, assoc. editor Litigation News 1982-87, mng. editor 1987, editor-in-chief 1988-90, 2002—, Nat. Conf. of Lawyers and Reps. of Media 1992-95, mem. adv. com. on nominations 1994-95, chair media-law roundtable 1994, chair sect. officers conf. com. on non-dues revenue 1995-96, mem. working group on ABA bus. plan for pub. 1995-96, standing com. on pub. oversight 1996-2002, ho. of dels. 2002—), Fla. Bar (chmn. voluntary bar liaison com. 1985-86, chmn. grievance com. 13-D 1986-88, chmn. legal edn. com. 1981-82, Most Productive Young Lawyer award 1981), Am. Judicature Soc., Hillsborough County Bar Assn. (Robert W. Patton Outstanding Jurist award 2002, Red McEwen award 1980, pres. 1982-83), Am. Inns of Ct. (Master of the Bench 1990-93, 96—). Roman Catholic. Office: Sam M Gibbons US Courthouse 801 N Florida Ave Tampa FL 33602-3849

CORDES, ALEXANDER CHARLES, lawyer; b. Buffalo, Aug. 14, 1925; s. Alexander J. and Margaret (Markens) C.; m. Jane Wells, Feb. 9, 1976; children by previous marriage: John J., Ann T., Susan A. BA, Yale U., 1947; LLB, U. Buffalo, 1950. Bar: N.Y. 1950. Assoc. Kenefick, Bass, Letchworth, Baldy & Phillips, 1950-54; asst. U.S. atty. Western Dist. N.Y., 1954-56; ptnr. Phillips, Lytle, Hitchcock, Blaine & Huber, Buffalo, 1956-90, of counsel, 1990—. Mem. Erie County Bd. Suprs., 1960-61 Trustee The Park Sch. Buffalo, 1993-96. With USNR, 1943-46. Fellow Am. Coll. Trial Lawyers, Am. Bar Found., N.Y. Bar Found. Presbyterian. Federal civil litigation, State civil litigation. Home: 470 Village Pl Apt 316 Longwood FL 32779-6031

CORDOVA, RON, lawyer; b. L.A., Aug. 18, 1946; s. Reuben and Lya (Gruber) C.; m. Mariann Pehrson, June 2, 1970; children: Danielle, Andrea. AB, Dartmouth Coll., 1967; postgrad., Trinity Coll., Dublin, Ireland, 1966; JD, U. So. Calif., 1972. Bar: U.S. Dist. Ct. (ctrl. dist.) Calif., 1979, U.S. Dist. Ct. (so. dist.) Calif., 1989, U.S. Dist. Ct. (no. dist.) Calif., 1995, U.S. Dist. Ct. (we. dist.) Tex., 1996, Ariz., 1994, U.S. Dist. Ct. (ea. dist.) Mich., 1995, U.S. Dist. Ct. Colo., 1999. Dep. dist. atty. Orange County Dist. Atty., Santa Ana, Calif., 1973-76; legis. Calif. State Assembly, Sacramento, 1976-78; trial lawyer Newport Beach, Calif., 1979—. Adj. prof. U. Calif., Irvine, 1975-77, 81-84. Author: Orange County Bar Journal, 1975. Recipient Outstanding Young Men. Am. Jaycees, 1977, 78. Mem. Lincoln Club. Republican. Jewish. Avocations: travel, languages, photography. State civil litigation, Criminal, Family and matrimonial. Office: 120 Newport Center Dr Newport Beach CA 92660-6922 Business E-Mail: advokaat@aol.com.

CORDY, ROBERT J. judge; b. Manchester, Conn., May 18, 1949; married; 4 children. AB cum laude, Dartmouth Coll., 1971; JD, Harvard U., 1974. Def. atty. Mass. Defenders Com., 1974—78; spl. asst. atty. gen. Mass. Dept. Revenue, 1978—79; assoc. gen. counsel in charge of enforcement Mass. State Ethics Commn., 1979—82; asst. U.S. atty., 1982—87; ptnr. Burns & Levinson, Boston, 1987—91; chief legal counsel to Gov. William F. Weld, Boston, 1991—93; mng. ptnr. McDermott, Will & Emery, Boston, 1993—2001; assoc. justice Mass. Supreme Judicial Ct., 2001—. Lectr. Harvard Law Sch., 1987—96. Office: 1300 New Courthouse Pemberton Sq Boston MA 02108*

COREY, BARRY MARTIN, lawyer; b. Louisville, Apr. 15, 1942; s. Joseph and Ann (Friedman) C.; m. Arlene Corey; children: David, Pamela; stepchildren: Vanessa Aldecoa, Sarah Rivera, Esther Rivera. BA, U. Colo., 1963; JD, Georgetown U., 1966. Bar: Ariz. 1967, US Dist. Ct. DC 1967, US Ct. Appeals (9th cir.) 1973, US Supreme Ct. 1990. Law clk. to chief judge U.S. Dist. Ct. for Ariz., Tucson, 1966-7; assoc. Schorr & Karp, P.C., Tucson, 1967-69; asst. city atty. City of Tucson, 1969-71; ptnr. Schorr, Karp & Corey, Tucson, 1971-73; pvt. practice Tucson, 1974-78; shareholder Corey & Kime, PC, Tucson, 1978—. Pres., co-founder Cmty. Food Bank, Inc., Tucson, 1980, bd. dirs. 1975—; bd. dirs. United Way Tucson, 1982-95, chmn. bd., 1990-91. Fellow Ariz. Bar Found.; mem. ABA, ATLA, Am. Judicature Soc., Ariz. Trial Lawyers Assn., State Bar Ariz. (chmn. pub. rels. com. 1987-89), Pima County Bar Assn. (bd. dirs. 1978-85, pres. 1983-84). Democrat. Jewish. Avocations: reading, hiking, music, golf. Labor (including EEOC, Fair Labor Standards Act, labor-management relations, NLRB, OSHA), Education and schools, Personal injury (including property damage). Office: Corey & Kime PC 711 Transamerica Bldg 177 N Church Ave Tucson AZ 85701-1119

CORK, ROBERT LANDER, lawyer; b. Central, S.C., Oct. 27, 1927; s. James Walter and Lila (Mitchell) C.; m. Anne McNeill Ward, Oct. 11, 1952; children: Leah, Robert Jr. (dec.), Travis, Patrick. AB, U. Ga., 1952, LLB, 1953. Bar: Ga. 1951, Fla. 1958, S.C. 1989, U.S. Dist. Ct. (mid. dist.) Ga. 1951, U.S. Ct. Appeals (11th cir.) 1981, U.S. Dist. Ct. (mid. dist.) Fla. 1983. Ptnr. Cork & Gaines, Athens, Ga., 1951-53; pvt. practice law Valdosta, Ga., 1954-83; ptrn. Cork & Cork, Valdosta, 1983—. Gen. counsel Warrior Cattle Co., Sylvester, Ga., 1964-70; legal draftsman charter and mcpl. code Town of Dasher, Ga., 1967; counsel Truman Arnold Co., Texarkana, Ark., 1995—, Internat. Petroleum, Inc., Jacksonville, Fla., 1990—, Strasburg and Assocs. (Petroleum), Waco, Tex., 1996—. County co-chmn. campaign Goldwater for Pres., Valdosta, 1964, county chmn. campaign Wallace for Pres., Valdosta, 1968; precinct chmn., del. to state Rep. Conv., Valdosta, 1983, 84, 87-88, 89, 91, 92, 94, 96, 98, 99, 2000; alt. del. Nat. Rep. Conv., 2000. With AUS, 1953-54. Mem. Am. Legion, Shriners, Masons, St. John the Baptist, Delta Theta Phi. Republican. Methodist. General practice, Probate (including wills, trusts), Property, real (including real estate development, water). Home: Sunnyside Lake Francis Lake Park GA 31634 Office: Cork & Cork 700 N Patterson St Valdosta GA 31601-4527

CORLE, JAMES THOMAS, lawyer; b. Jay County, Ind., Dec. 28, 1927; s. Herbert R. and Mary M. (Reitenour) C.; m. Jean Polhemus, July 16, 1950; children— James Thomas, Sarah Corle Thomas, Kenneth D. B.S. in Engring. Law, Purdue U., 1955; J.D., Ind. U.-Bloomington, 1955. Bar: Ind. 1955, D.C. 1964. With E. I. duPont de Nemours & Co., Wilmington, Del., 1955— , patent counsel, Washington, 1967-70, sr. supervising patent counsel, legal dept., 1970-85, corp. counsel, legal dept., 1986-92, intellectual property cons., 1993—. Served to lt. col. U.S. Army, 1946-52. Mem. ABA, Am. Patent Law Assn., Phila. Patent Law Assn., Del. Bar Assn. Republican. Methodist. E-mail: jimcorle@comcast.net. Patent.

CORLETT, EDWARD STANLEY, III, retired lawyer; b. Miami, May 28, 1924; s. Edward Stanley Jr. and Marjorie (Cook) C.; m. Jeanne Sherouse, Mar. 27, 1948; children: Karen Marie Corlett McCammon, Edward S. AA, U. Fla., 1946, LLB, 1949. Bar: Fla. 1949, U.S. Dist. Ct. (so. dist.) Fla. 1949, U.S. Ct. Appeals (5th cir.) 1949, U.S. Ct. Appeals (11th cir.) 1981. Sole practice, 1949-58; sr. ptnr. Sherouse and Corlett and successor Corlett, Killian, Hardeman, McIntosh and Levi, P.A., Miami, 1958-96. Chmn. bd. Internat. Oceanographic Found.; pres. Miami Met. Fishing Tournament, 1973-80; mem. Fed. Jud. Nominating Panel. Served with USN, 1942-44. Recipient Henry Hyman trophy, 1974. Fellow Am. Coll. Trial Lawyers; mem. ABA, Fla. Bar Assn., Dade County Bar Assn., Fedn. Ins. Counsel (pres. 1978-79, testimonial award 1979), Fla. Def. Lawyers Assn. (pres. 1970), Def. Rsch. Inst. (dir. 1978-79, testimonial award 1979), Internat. Assn. Ins. Counsel, Miami Rod and Reel Club, Riviera Country Club, Bankers Club. Republican. Presbyterian. State civil litigation, Insurance, Personal injury (including property damage). E-mail: ecorl82673@aol.com.

CORLEW, JOHN GORDON, lawyer; b. Dyersburg, Tenn., July 13, 1943; s. Emmett Atkins and Margaret Elizabeth (Swann) C.; m. Elizabeth Lee Scott, July 8, 1967; children: John Scott, William Heath, Carey Elizabeth. BA, U. Miss., 1965; JD, Vanderbilt U., 1968. Bar: Miss. 1968. Clk. to judge U.S. Dist. Ct. (so. dist.) Miss., 1968-69; assoc., then ptnr. Megehee, Brown, Williams & Corlew, Pascagoula, Miss., 1969-74; sole practice Pascagoula, 1975-78; ptnr. Corlew, Krebs & Hammond, Pascagoula, 1978-84, Watkins & Eager, Jackson, Miss., 1984. Mem. Miss. State Senate, 1974-80, chmn. appropriations com., 1979, chmn. constn. com., 1975-79, chmn. legis. audit com., 1978; chmn. Miss. State Bd. Pub. Welfare, 1980-84. Mem. ABA, Miss. Bar Assn., Hinds County Bar Assn., Miss. Bar Found., Order of Coif, Phi Delta Phi. Democrat. Methodist. General civil litigation, Corporate, general, Product liability. Home: 2124 Eastover Dr Jackson MS 39211-6719 Office: Emporium Bldg 400 E Capitol St Jackson MS 39201-2610

CORN, STEPHEN LESLIE, lawyer; b. Danville, Ill., June 12, 1944; s. Clyde C. and Minnie Kathryn (Collins) C.; m. Judith Rae Petkas, June 11, 1966; children: Stephanie Lynn, Suzanne Michelle. BA, U. Ill., 1966, JD, 1969. Bar: Ill. 1969, U.S. Dist. Ct. (so. and cen. dists.) Ill. 1971, U.S. Ct. Appeals (7th cir.) 1976, U.S. Supreme Ct. 1976. Ptnr. Craig & Craig, Mattoon, Ill., 1969—. Bd. dirs. Mattoon Area YMCA, 1981-88, pres., 1987-88; bd. dirs. Harlan E. Moore Heart Rsch. Found., Champaign, Ill., 1982—, Lawyers Trust Fund of Ill., 1991-97. Mem. Ill. Bar Assn., Coles Cumberland Bar Assn. (pres. 1987-88), Ill. Assn. Def. Trial Counsel (pres. 1991-92), Ill. Bar Found., Am. Coll. Trial Lawyers. Episcopalian. General civil litigation, Personal injury (including property damage), Workers' compensation. Office: Craig & Craig 1807 Broadway Ave Mattoon IL 61938-3800 E-mail: slc@craiglaw.net.

CORNABY, KAY STERLING, lawyer, former state senator; b. Spanish Fork, Utah, Jan. 14, 1936; s. Sterling A. and Hilda G. Cornaby; m. Linda Rasmussen, July 23, 1965; children: Alyse, Derek, Tara, Heather, Brandon. AB, Brigham Young U., 1960; postgrad. law, Heidelberg, Germany, 1961-63; JD, Harvard U., 1966. Bar: NY 1967, Utah 1969, U.S. Patent and Trademark Office 1967. Assoc. Brumbaugh, Graves, Donahue & Raymond, N.Y.C., 1966-69; ptnr. Mallinckrodt & Cornaby, Salt Lake City, 1969-72; sole practice Salt Lake City, 1972-85; mem. Utah State Senate, 1977-91, majority leader, 1983-84; shareholder Jones, Waldo, Holbrook & McDonough, Salt Lake City, 1985—. Mem. Nat. Commn. on Uniform State Laws, 1988-93; mem. adv. bd. U. Mich. Ctr. for Study of Youth Policy,1990-93; mem. Utah State Jud. Conduct Commn., 1983-91, chmn., 1984-85; bd. dirs. KUED-KUER Pub. TV and Radio, 1982-88; bd. dirs. Salt Lake Conv. and Visitors Bur., 1985—. Mem. N.Y. Bar Assn., Utah Bar Assn., Utah Harvard Alumni Assn. (pres. 1977-79), Harvard U. Law Sch. Alumni Assn. (pres. 1995—). Patent, Property, real (including real estate development, water), Trademark and copyright. Office: Jones Waldo Holbrook & McDonough Ste 1500 170 S Main St Salt Lake City UT 84101-1644

CORNELL, JOHN ROBERT, lawyer; b. Boston, Nov. 7, 1943; s. Robert Cole Cornell and Thelma Marjorie (Bassett) Strout; m. Susan Lindsay Jordan, June 11, 1966; children: Jared, Joshua, Alexandra, Margaret. AB, Colby Coll., 1965, MA, 1997; JD, Georgetown U., 1968; LLM in Taxation, NYU, 1972. Bar: N.Y. 1969, Maine 1972, U.S. Dist. Ct. Maine 1972, Ohio 1982, U.S. Tax Ct. 1990. Assoc. Dewey Ballantine, N.Y.C., 1968-72; from assoc. to ptnr. Drummond, Woodsum & MacMahon, Portland, Maine, 1972-81; ptnr. Jones Day, Cleve., 1981-98, Atlanta, 1998-2000, former tax group coord. for S.E., ptnr. N.Y.C., 2001—. Former chmn. tax group's employee benefits sect. Jnes Day; lectr. in field. Overseer Colby Coll., 1992-97, trustee, 1997—; trustee Cleve. San Jose Ballet, 1994-98, treas., 1995-98. Mem. ABA, Maine Bar Assn. (chmn. tax sect. 1980-81), Colby Coll. Alumni Assn. (chmn. 1979-82), Cleve. Yachting Club (Rocky River, Ohio), Anglers Club (N.Y.C.), Megantic Club (Eustis, Maine), DKE Club (N.Y.C.). Republican. Avocations: sailing, bicycling, skiing, fly fishing. Pension, profit-sharing, and employee benefits, Corporate taxation, Personal income taxation. Office: 222 E 41st St New York NY 10017 E-mail: jrcornell@jonesday.com.

CORNELL, KENNETH LEE, lawyer; b. Palo Alto, Calif., Feb. 23, 1945; s. Clinton Burdette and Mildred Lucy (Sheafer) C.; m. Barbara J. Smith, June 26, 1966; children: Melinda Lee Van Hise, Geoffery Mark. BBA, BA in Social Sci., Pacific Union Coll., 1966; JD, U. Wash., 1971. Bar: Wash. 1971, U.S. Dist. Ct. (we. dist.) Wash. 1971, U.S. Supreme Ct. 1974. Ptnr. Keller & Rohrback, Seattle, 1971-75, Richard, Rossano & Cornell, Seattle, 1975-77, Moren, Lageschulte (now Cornell, Hansen, Bugni & McConnell), Seattle, 1978-87, Cornell, Hansen, Bugni & McConnell PS (firm name change), 1995-98; pvt. practice Seattle, 1998—. Cons. atty. Town of Clyde Hill, Wash. 1980-87. Editor Wash. U. Law Rev., 1970-71. Bd. dirs. Kirkland (Wash.) Seventh Day Adventist Sch., 1972-78, Auburn (Wash.) Acad., 1974-80, Western Wash. Corp. Seventh Day Adventists, Bothell, 1974-80. Mem. Wash. State Bar Assn., Wash. State Trial Lawyers Assn., Order of Coif. Democrat. Avocations: skiing, reading, gardening. State civil litigation, Personal injury (including property damage), Property, real (including real estate development, water). Office: 11320 Roosevelt Way NE Seattle WA 98125-6228 E-mail: kbcornell@yahoo.com.

CORNELL, RICHARD FARNHAM, lawyer; b. Pitts., June 9, 1952; s. Paul Watson and Margaret Lucy (Boose) C.; m. Denise Vandevelde, May 24, 1975; children: Jonathan Watson, Julie Elizabeth, Benjamin Dunlap. BA in Polit Sci. and Econs., U. Calif., Irvine, 1974; JD, U. San Francisco, 1977. Bar: Calif. 1977, U.S. Dist. Ct. (no. dist.) Calif. 1977, Nev. 1979, U.S. Dist. Ct. Nev. 1979, U.S. Ct. Appeals (9th cir.) 1981, U.S. Supreme Ct. 1999. Law clk. to chief judge U.S. Dist. Ct. Nev., Las Vegas, 1978-80; dep. dist. atty. Washoe County Dist. Atty., Reno, 1980-81; assoc. Raggio, Wooster & Lindell, Reno, 1981-86; sole practice Reno, 1986—. Pro-tem judge Reno Justice Ct., 1992—. Co-editor Nevada Civil Practice Manual, 1985-86. Bd. dirs. Drunk Drivers Inc. d/b/a Call-a-Ride, Reno, 1984-85, Assn. Excellence in Edn., Reno, 1986. Mem. ABA, ATLA, Nev. Bar Assn. (criminal practice and procedures com. 1986, fee dispute com. 1998—), Nat. Assn. Criminal Def. Lawyers. Appellate, Criminal, Family and matrimonial. Office: 150 Ridge St Reno NV 89501-1938 E-mail: Rcornlaw@150.Reno.Nv.Us.

CORNETT, BRADLEY WILLIAMS, lawyer; b. Maryville, Tenn., Apr. 15, 1970; s. Billy Kenneth and Wilda Cornett; m. Wendy Leigh Love, Apr. 27, 1996. BS, U. Tenn., 1991; JD, U. N.C., 1995. Bar: Ala. 1995, U.S. Dist. Ct. (no. dist.) Ala. 1996, U.S. Ct. of Appeals (11th cir.), 2002. Atty. Ford, Howard & Cornett, P.C., Gadsden, Ala., 1996—. Mem. Ala. Def. Lawyers Assn., Def. Rsch. Inst., Am. Inns of Court. General civil litigation, Insurance, Product liability. Office: Ford Howard & Cornett PC PO Box 388 Gadsden AL 35902-0388 E-mail: cornettb@bellsouth.net.

CORNFELD, DAVE LOUIS, lawyer; b. St. Louis, Dec. 24, 1921; s. Abraham and Rebecca (David) C.; m. Martha Herrmann, May 30, 1943; children: Richard Steven, James Allen, Lawrence Joseph. AB, Washington U., St. Louis, 1942, LLB, 1943. Bar: Mo. 1943. Practice law, St. Louis; ptnr. Husch & Eppenberger, 1954—2001, of counsel, 2001—. Adj. prof. Washington U., 1966-87. Co-author: Missouri Estate Planning, Will Drafting and Estate Administration, 2 vol., 1988, supplement, 2002; editor Law Quar. 1943. Bd. dirs. Jewish Fedn., St. Louis, 1977-80, 83-88, Jewish Ctr. for Aged, 1981-88; mem. adv. com. U. Miami Inst. Estate Planning, 1979—. Served with AUS, 1945-46. Mem. ABA (past chmn. com. taxation income estates and trusts, vice chmn. sect. taxation 1977-80, editor-in-chief Tax Lawyer 1977-80, sr. assoc. editor Probate and Property), St. Louis Bar Assn. (past chmn. taxation com), Am. Law Inst., Am. Coll. Trust and Estate Counsel (regent 1984-90), Am. Coll. Tax Counsel (regent 1980-88), Internat. Acad. Estate and Trust Law, Order of Coif. Jewish (trustee temple 1967-91). Club: Masons. Estate planning, Probate (including wills, trusts), Taxation, general. Home: 834 Oakbrook Ln Saint Louis MO 63132-4812 Office: Husch & Eppenberger LLC 190 Carondelet Plz Ste 600 Saint Louis MO 63105-3441 E-mail: dave@cornfeld.net., dave.cornfeld@husch.com.

CORNFIELD, MELVIN, lawyer, university institute director; b. Chgo., June 5, 1927; s. Harry and Annabelle (Maltz) C.; m. Edith Pauline Haas, June 24, 1951; children: Daniel Benjamin, Deborah S. Cornfield Alexander. AB, U. Chgo., 1948, JD, 1951. Bar: D.C. 1951, N.Y. 1958. Atty. durable goods divsn. Office Price Stblzn., Washington, 1951-53; atty., advisor Chief Counsel's Office IRS, Washington, 1953-58; assoc. Willkie, Farr, Gallagher, Walton & FitzGibbon, N.Y.C., 1958-63; dir. taxes NBC, Inc., 1963-66; staff v.p. tax affairs RCA Corp., N.Y.C., 1966-76, v.p., treas., 1976-82, v.p. tax affairs, 1982-85; dir. NYU Tax Inst., 1985-94. With USAAF, 1946-47. Home: 4703 Iselin Ave Bronx NY 10471-3323

CORNING, NICHOLAS F. lawyer; b. Seattle, Nov. 8, 1945; s. Frank C. and Jessie D. (Weeks) C.; m. Patricia A. Tomlinson, Dec. 14, 1968; children: Kristen Marie, Lauren Margaret. BCS cum laude, Seattle U., 1968; JD, U. Wash., 1972. Bar: Wash. 1972, U.S. Ct. Appeals (9th cir.) 1972, U.S. Dist. Ct. (we. dist.) Wash. 1973, U.S. Supreme Ct. 1976, U.S. Ct. Claims 1981. Assoc. Jennings P. Felix, Seattle, 1972-75; ptnr. Lagerquist, McConnell & Corning, Seattle, 1975-77; pres., ptnr. Treece, Richdale, Malone, Corning & Abbott, Inc., P.S., Seattle, 1977-99; atty. Corning Law Firm, Seattle, 1999—. Pres. Windermere Corp., Seattle, 1988, also bd. dirs. Recipient Am. Jurisprudence award in Criminal Law U. Wash., 1971. Mem.: ATLA, King County Bar Assn. (spkrs. bur. 1983—85, chmn. pub. info. com. 1985—87, chmn. judiciary and cts. com. 2001—), Wash. State Trial Lawyers Assn. (pres. 1994—95, bd. dirs.), Wash. State Bar Assn., Nat. Inst. Trial Advocacy, Ballard C. of C. (bd. dirs., pres. 1989—92), Beta Gamma Sigma (Key award 1968). Insurance, Product liability, Personal injury (including property damage). Home: 5640 NE 55th St Seattle WA 98105-2835 Office: The Corning Law Firm 5301 Ballard Ave NW Seattle WA 98107-4061 E-mail: corninglawfirm@seanet.com.

CORNISH, JEANNETTE CARTER, lawyer; b. Steelton, Pa., Sept. 17, 1946; d. Ellis Pollard and Anna Elizabeth (Stannard) C.; m. Harry L. Cornish; children: Lee Jason, Geoffrey Charles. BA, Howard U., 1968, JD, 1971. Bar: N.J. 1976, U.S. Dist. Ct. N.J. 1976. Atty. Newark-Essex Law Reform, 1971-72; technician EEOC, Newark, 1972-73; atty., asst. sec. Inmont Corp., N.Y.C., 1974-82, sr. atty., asst. sec. Clifton, N.J., 1982-85; sr. atty. BASF Corp., Mt. Olive, N.J., 1986-99. Speaker on diversity in bus. Past mem., bd. dirs. YWCA, Paterson, N.J.; trustee Barnert Hosp., Paterson; bd. dirs. Lenni-Lenape coun. Girl Scouts Am. Mem. ABA (commn. on opportunities for minorities in the profession, minority in-house counsel group, diversity vice chair gen. practice sect. corp. counsel com.), Nat. Bar Assn., Assn. Black Women Lawyers, Am. Corp. Counsel Assn., Internat. Trademark Assn. (past mem. editorial bd. The Trademark Reporter, exec. commn. com., meetings com., program quality and evaluation subcom.). Commercial, contracts (including sales of goods; commercial financing), Corporate, general, Trademark and copyright. Business E-Mail: jeannettecornish@1stcounsel.com.

CORNISH, RICHARD POOL, lawyer; b. Evanston, Ill., Sept. 9, 1942; s. William A. and Rita (Pool) C.; children: William Darby, Richard Gordon. BS, Okla. State U., 1964; LLB, U. Okla., 1966. Bar: Okla. 1966, U.S. Dist. Ct. (ea. dist.) Okla. 1969, U.S. Supreme Ct. 1979. Ptnr. Baumert & Cornish, McAlester, Okla., 1967-71, Cornish & Cornish, Inc., McAlester, 1971-77; magistrate U.S. Dist. Ct. for Ea. Dist. Okla., McAlester, 1976—2000; prin. Richard P. Cornish, Inc., McAlester, 1977—. Bd. dirs. McAlester Boys Club, 1970-80, pres., 1974. Capt. JAGC, USAR, 1966-78. Mem. Okla. Bar Assn. (legal aid to servicemen com., legal specialization com.), Pittsburg County Bar Assn., McAlester C. of C. (bd. dirs. 1973-75). Roman Catholic. General practice, Probate (including wills, trusts). Home: 611 E Creek Ave Mcalester OK 74501-6929 Office: PO Box 1106 Mcalester OK 74502-1106 E-mail: cornish@cwis.net.

CORNYN, JOHN, senator; b. Feb. 2, 1952; married; 2 children. BA, Trinity U., 1973; JD, St. Mary's U., 1977; postgrad., U. Va. Cert.: Tex. Bd. Legal Specialization (personal injury trial law). Assoc., ptnr. Groce, Locke & Hebdon, San Antonio, 1977—84; judge 37th Dist. Ct., Bexer County, 1985—90; presiding judge 4th Adminstrv. Jud. Region, 1989—92; justice Supreme Ct. Tex., Austin, 1991—98; atty. Thompson & Knight; atty. gen. State of Tex., Austin, 1999—2002; U.S. senator from Tex., 2003—. Bd. vis. Trinity U., Pepperdine U. Sch. Law; Tex. Supreme Ct. liaison Bd. Law Examiners, 1991—, Gender Bias Task Force, 1993—95; lectr. CLE programs. Fellow: San Antonio Bar Found., Tex. Bar Found.; mem.: Robert W. Calvent Inn of Ct. (pres. 1994—95), William Sessions Inn of Ct. (master bencher 1988—90, pres. 1989—90), Am. Law Inst. Republican. Office: US Senate Washington DC 20510*

CORONADO, SANTIAGO SYBERT (JIM CORONADO), judge; b. Laredo, Tex., Nov. 12, 1951; s. Bill Gee and Lucía (Coronado) Sybert; m. Dawn Dittman, Apr. 27, 1996. BA cum laude, U. Tex., 1974, JD, 1978. Bar: Tex. 1978. Pvt. practice, Austin, Tex., 1979-89; mcpl. judge City of Austin, 1989-91, City of Kyle, Tex., 1989-91; magistrate judge Travis County Dist. Ct., 1991—. Bd. dirs. Am. Heart Assn., Austin, 1990; state pres. Mex. Am. Bar Assn., Tex., 1988-89; pres. Capital Area Mex. Am. Lawyers, Austin, 1986-87. Recipient Lifetime Achievement award Hispanic Issues Sect. State Bar of Tex., 1995, Presdl. citation for disting. svc., 1999. Mem.: Master Robert Calvin Inn of Ct., Travis County Bar Assn. (dir. 1995—2003, pres. 2001—02), State Bar of Tex. (at-large minority dir.), Hispanic Nat. Bar Assn. (regional pres. 1989—90, nat. v.p. 1991—92). Democrat. Home: 5602 Palisade Ct Austin TX 78731-4508 Office: Travis County Ct House Austin TX 78701

CORRADA DEL RIO, BALTASAR, supreme court justice; b. Morovis, P.R., Apr. 10, 1935; s. Romulo and Ana Maria (del Rio) Corrada del R.; m. Beatrice Betances, Dec. 24, 1959; children: Ana Isabel, Francisco Javier, Juan Carlos, Jose Baltasar BA in Social Scis., U. P.R., 1956, JD, 1959. Bar: P.R., 1959. Ptnr. McConnell Valdes Sifre & Ruiz Suria, San Juan, 1959-75; atty., chmn. Civil Right Commn., P.R., 1970-72; mem., resident commr. from P.R. 95th-98th Congress; mayor City of San Juan, P.R., 1985-89; atty. Baltasar Corrada Law Office, 1989-92; sec. of state Govt. of P.R., 1993-95; assoc. justice P.R. Supreme Ct., 1995—. Pres. New Progressive Party, 1986-89. Pres. editorial bd. P.R. Human Rights Rev., 1971-72. Bd. dirs. P.R. Teleradial Inst. Ethics. Recipient Great Cross of Civil Merit of Spain King Juan Carlos I, 1987. Mem. ABA, Fed. Bar Assn., P.R. Bar Assn. Clubs: Exchange, San Juan Rotary. Roman Catholic. Office: P R Supreme Ct PO Box 9022392 San Juan PR 00902-2392

CORRELL, JOANNA RAE, lawyer; b. Indpls., Apr. 17, 1948; d. Philip Ray Correll and Dorothy Jane (Morris) Aslaner; m. Bruce Harold Sheetz, June 15, 1968 (div. 1978); m. Christopher Miles Althof, June 29, 1985; children: Tanya, Dustin, Kurt, Korine, Kiri, Kara. BS in Edn., Ind. U., 1970; JD, Western State U., San Diego, 1978. Bar: Calif. 1979, U.S. Dist. Ct. (no. dist.) Calif. 1981, U.S. Dist. Ct. (ea. dist.) Calif. 1979. Tchr. Laredo (Tex.) Unified Sch. Dist., 1970; subs. tchr. Napa (Calif.) Unified Sch. Dist., 1970-72; investigator Hughes Atty. Svcs., San Diego, 1976-78; assoc. Wagner, Pistole & Correll, Napa, 1978-82; ptnr. Childers & Correll, Weaverville, Calif., 1982-86; pvt. practice Weaverville, 1987—97. Patient's rights adv. State of Calif., Sacramento, 1984-93. Actress/dancer Trinity Players, Weaverville, 1982-84. Mem. Ca. State Bar Assn., Bus. and Profl. Women (v.p. 1983-84). Democrat. Avocations: running long distance, skiing, backpacking, windsurfing. General civil litigation, Criminal. Office: PO Box 1329 248 Main Weaverville CA 96093-0631

CORRERO, ANTHONY JAMES, III, lawyer; b. Monroe, La., Dec. 15, 1941; s. Anthony James Jr. and Robbie Lee (Pace) C.; m. Margaret Aline O'Meara, May 30, 1966; children: Margaret Hollis, Edward Thomas Eliot, Marshall Alan. BA, N.E. La. U., 1962; LLB, La. State U., 1965. Bar: La. 1965, U.S. Supreme Ct. 1968. Spl. asst. atty. gen. State of La., Baton Rouge, 1965-68; assoc. Jones, Walker, Waechter, Poitevent, Carrere & Denegre, New Orleans, 1968-72, ptnr., 1972-94, Correro, Fishman & Casteix, LLP, New Orleans, 1994-96, Correro Fishman Haygood Phelps Walmsley & Casteix, LLP, New Orleans, 1996—. Adj. prof. law La. State U., Tulane U., Loyola U.; bd. dirs. T.L. James & Co., Inc., Ruston, La., La. Partnership for Tech. 1st lt. USAR, 1965-71. Mem. ABA, La. Bar Assn. (chmn. sect. corp. and bus. law 1978-79), Am. Law Inst. Democrat. Roman Catholic. Other, Mergers and acquisitions, Securities. Office: Correro Fishman et al 201 Saint Charles Ave New Orleans LA 70170-4600 E-mail: acorrero@cfhlaw.com.

CORRIGAN, ANN PHILLIPS, lawyer; b. Des Moines, May 20, 1963; d. Lawrence Marvin and Jo Ann S. Phillips; m. William M. Corrigan Jr., Aug. 20, 1988; children: Kathleen, Maura. BJ, U. Mo., 1985; JD, U. Wis., 1988. Bar: Wis. 1988, Mo. 1988, Ill. 1989, U.S. Dist. Ct. (ea. dist.) Mo. 1988. Assoc. Thompson & Mitchell, St. Louis, 1988-91; staff atty. ITT Comml. Fin., Clayton, Mo., 1991-94; assoc. Descher & Schultz, Clayton, 1995-99, Schultz & Little, LLC, Clayton, 1999—. General civil litigation, Trademark and copyright. Office: Schultz & Little LLC 7700 Bonhomme Ave Ste 325 Saint Louis MO 63105-1924

CORRIGAN, MAURA DENISE, judge; b. Cleve., June 14, 1948; d. Peter James and Mae Ardell (McCrone) Corrigan; m. Joseph Dante Grano, July 11, 1976 (dec.). BA with honors, Marygrove Coll., 1969; JD with honors, U. Detroit, 1973; LLD (hon.) , Mich. State U., 2003; JD (hon.) , Mercy Law Sch., 2002. Bar: Mich. 1974. Jud. clk. Mich. Ct. Appeals, Detroit, 1973-74; asst. prosecutor Wayne County, Detroit, 1974-79, asst. U.S. atty., 1979-89, chief appellate divsn., 1979-86, chief asst. U.S. Atty., 1986-89; ptnr. Plunkett & Cooney PC, Detroit, 1989-92; judge Mich. Ct. Appeals, 1992-98, chief judge, 1997-98; justice Mich. Supreme Ct., Detroit, 1999-2001, chief justice, 2001—. Vice chmn. Mich. Ct. to formulate Rules of Criminal Procedure, Mich. Supreme Ct., 1982-89; mem. Mich. Law Revision Commn., 1991-98; mem. com. on standard jury instrns., State Bar Mich., 1978-82; lectr. Mich. Jud. Inst., Sixth cir. Jud. Workshop, Inst. CLE, ABA-Cin. Bar Litigation Sects., Dept. Justice Advocacy Inst. Contbr. chpt. to book, articles to legal revs. Vice chmn. Project Transition, Detroit, 1976-92; mem. citizens Adv. Coun. Lafayette Clinic, Detroit, 1979-87; bd. dirs. Detroit Wayne County Criminal Advocacy Program, 1983-86; pres., bd. dirs. Rep. Women's Bus. and Profl. Forum, 1991. Recipient award of merit Detroit Commn. on Human Rels., 1974, Dir.'s award Dept. Justice, 1985, Outstanding Practitioner of Criminal Law award Fed. Bar Assn., 1989, award Mich. Women's Commn., 1998, Grano award, 2001, U.S. Dept. HHS award for child support, 2002. Mem. Mich. Bar Assn., Detroit Bar Assn., Fed. Bar Assn. (pres. Detroit chpt. 1990-91), Inc. Soc. Irish Am. Lawyers (pres. 1991-92, Achievment award 2001), Federalist Soc. (Mich. chpt.). Office: Mich Supreme Ct 8-500 3034 W Grand Blvd Detroit MI 48202

CORRIGAN, WILLIAM M. lawyer; b. St. Louis, Dec. 3, 1958; BBA, U. Notre Dame, 1981; JD, U. Mo., Columbia, 1985. Bar: Mo. 1985, Ill. 1986. Contbr. articles to profl. jours. Mem.: ABA, St. Louis County Bar Assn. (Outstanding Young Lawyer award 1992), Bar Assn. Met. St. Louis, Ill. State Bar Assn., Mo. Bar (bd. govs. 1995—, chair Young Lawyers sect. 1992—93, Pres.'s award 1993). Personal injury (including property damage), General civil litigation. Office: Armstrong Teasdale LLP One Metropolitan Sq Ste 2600 Saint Louis MO 63102-2740*

CORRY, ROBERT J., JR., lawyer; b. Boston, Aug. 5, 1967; s. Robert J. Corry, Sr. and Linda S. Corry. BA magna cum laude, U. Colo., 1989; JD, Stanford U., 1994. Bar: Calif. 1994, Colo. 2001, D.C. 2001, U.S. Dist. Ct. (no., so., ea. and cen. dists.) Calif. 1995, U.S. Dist. Ct. Colo. 2001, U.S. Dist. Ct. D.C. 2001, U.S. Ct. Appeals 9th cir. 1995, cert.: U.S. Ct. Appeals 10th cir. 2001, bar: U.S. Supreme Ct. 1998. Staff atty. Pacific Legal Found., Sacramento, 1994—97; com. counsel Calif. State Assembly, Sacramento, 1996; counsel U.S. Ho. Jud. Com., Washington, 1997—98; legal counsel Prison Fellowship Ministries, Washington, 1999—2000; staff atty. Jud. Watch, Inc., Washington, 1999—2000; pvt. practice Denver, 2001—02, Washington, 2000—; atty., owner Law Offices of Corry & Fellows LLP, Denver, 2002—. Registered lobbyist U.S. Senate/U.S. Ho. Reps., Washington, 1999—2000. Mng. editor: Stanford Environ. Law Jour.; contbr. articles to profl. jours. Named Stanford Man of Yr., Stanford Rev., 1995; named one of 40 Under 40 Young Leaders, Nat. Law Jour., 1995; recipient Bill Farr Free Speech award, Calif. Soc. Newspaper Editors, San Francisco, 1995. Mem.: ABA, Denver Bar Assn., Federalist Soc. for Law and Policy (chpt. pres. 1992—93), Nat. Assn. Criminal Def. Lawyers, Alliance Def. Fund (affiliate atty. 1999—), Colo. Bar Assn. (bd. mem. young lawyers divsn. exec. coun. 2001—), Colo. Criminal Def. Bar. Republican. Presbyterian. Avocations: skiing, bicycling, swimming, running. Criminal, Civil rights, Constitutional. Office: Law Office Corry & Fellows Ste 2800 South Tower 600 17th St Denver CO 80202 E-mail: robert@corryandfellows.com.

CORSI, PHILIP DONALD, lawyer; b. N.Y.C., Oct. 11, 1928; s. Edward and Emma Catherine (Gillies) C.; m. Marcia Munro, June 3, 1953 (div. 1976); children: Martina Jane O'Donnell, Charles Edward, Philip Munro, Christopher Matthew; m. Lois Joann Cobb, July 20, 1983. AB, Princeton U., 1950; LLB, Columbia U., 1953. Bar: N.Y. 1955, U.S. Dist. Ct. N.Y. 1970. Assoc. Willkie Farr & Gallagher, N.Y.C., 1955-69, ptnr., 1969-88, ret., 1988. Bd. dirs., pres. emeritus LaGuardia Meml. House, N.Y.C., 1964—. With U.S. Army, 1953—55. Mem. Garden City Golf Club, Black Diamond Club. Republican. Avocations: golfing, reading, history. Antitrust, Corporate, general, Securities. Home: 3210 N Pinelake Village Pt Lecanto FL 34461-8140

CORSO, FRANK MITCHELL, lawyer; b. N.Y.C., July 28, 1928; s. Joseph and Jane (DeBenedetto) C.; m. Dorothy G. McVeety, Apr. 7, 1951; chldren: Frank, Elaine, Patricia, Dorothy. LLB, St. John's U., 1952. Bar: N.Y. 1954, D.C. 1981, U.S. Ct. Mil. Appeals 1954, U.S. Supreme Ct. 1960. Ptnr. Corso & Fertig, 1957-61, Corso & Petito, 1966-69, Corso & Landa, Jericho, N.Y., 1971-73, Corso & Engelberg, 1973-82; sr. ptnr. Frank Mitchell Corso, P.C., Westbury, N.Y., 1982—. Bd. dirs. UN Devel. Corp. by N.Y. Gov., N.Y. Mcpl. Bond Bank Agy.; lectr. St. John's U. Sch. of Law; U.S. congl. candidate, N.Y.; trustee WLIW pub. TV channel. Contbr. articles to legal jours.; TV commentator legal topics. With U.S. Army, 1951-53. Decorated Knight of Holy Sepulchre (Vatican City); named Man of Yr., Am.-Italians of L.I., 1966. Mem. ABA, ATLA, N.Y. State Bar Assn., Nassau Bar Assn., Internat. Bar Assn., World Assn. Lawyers (founding mem.). State civil litigation, Corporate, general, Personal injury (including property damage). Home: 1 Southdown Ct Huntington NY 11743-2548 Office: 350 Jericho Tpke Jericho NY 11753-1317 E-mail: fmc28@aol.com.

CORSON, J. JAY, IV, lawyer; b. Richmond, Va., May 19, 1935; s. John Jay III and Mary Turner (Tilman) C.; children: John Jay V, Catherine Anne, Clare Tilman, Jennifer Page. BA, U. Va., 1957, LLB, 1960. Bar: Va. 1960. Assoc. Davis, Polk, Wardwell, Sunderland & Kiendl, N.Y.C., 1960, Boothe, Dudley, Koontz & Blankingship, Fairfax, Va., 1963-68; ptnr. McGuire, Woods, Battle & Boothe & predecessor firms, McLean, Va., 1968-2000. Capt. USAF, 1960-63. Fellow Am. Coll. Trial Lawyers, Am. Bar Found., Va. Law Found.; mem. Va. Assn. Def. Attys. (pres. 1981-82), Va. State Bar (pres. 1988-89, del. ABA 1989-96). Episcopalian. Avocations: golf, skiing, fishing, gardening. Insurance, Personal injury (including property damage). Home: 3137 Trenholm Dr Oakton VA 22124-1529 Office: McGuire Woods LLP 1750 Tysons Blvd Ste 1800 Mc Lean VA 22102-4231

CORSON, KIMBALL JAY, lawyer; b. Mexico City, Sept. 17, 1941; came to U.S., 1942; s. Harland Jerry and Arleen Elizabeth (Jones) C.; m. Ann Dudley Wood, May 25, 1963 (div. Apr. 1978); 1 child, Claudia Ring; m. Joy Lorann Sligh, June 16, 1979; children: Bryce Manning, Jody Darlene. BA, Wayne State U., 1966; MA, U. Chgo., 1968, JD, 1971. Bar: Ariz. 1972, U.S. Dist. Ct. 1971, U.S. Supreme Ct. 1991. Assoc. Lewis & Roca, Phoenix, 1971-74, ptnr., 1974-90, Horne Kaplan & Bistrow, Phoenix, 1990-99; of counsel Shields and Andersen, P.C., 1999—. Co-author: Document Control: The Organization, Management and Production, 1988; co-author: Litigation Support Using Personal Computers, 1989. Co-founder Desert Hills Improvement Assn., Phoenix, 1988—. With U.S. Army, 1961-64. Fellow Woodrow Wilson Found., 1966-67. Mem. ABA (civil practice and procedures com. antitrust sect. 1988-2000), Ariz. Bar Assn. (spkr. 1991—), Maricopa County Bar Assn., Internat. Trademark Assn. (editl. bd. The Trademark Reporter 1993-94, 99-2000, mem. publs. com. 1995-96), INTA Speaker, Phi Beta Kappa. Avocations: music, computers, sailing, photography, first century history. Appellate, Federal civil litigation, Intellectual property. Home: Summit Ranch 35808 N 15th Ave Phoenix AZ 85086-7228 Office: Shields and Andersen 7830 N 23rd Ave Phoenix AZ 85021-6808

CORTESE, ALFRED WILLIAM, JR., lawyer, consultant; b. Phila., Apr. 2, 1937; s. Alfred William and Marie Ann (Coccio) C.; m. Rosanna S. Zimmerman, Aug. 18, 1962 (div. Aug. 1981); children: Aline Elizabeth, Alfred William III, Christina Nicole. BA cum laude, Temple U., 1959; JD, U. Pa., 1962. Bar: Pa. 1963, U.S. Supreme Ct. 1972, D.C. 1977. Assoc., ptnr. Pepper, Hamilton & Scheetz, Phila., 1962-71; asst. exec. dir. FTC, Washington, 1972-73; assoc. Dechert, Price & Rhoads, Phila., 1974-76; ptnr. Clifford & Warnke, Washington, 1977-81; chmn., CEO Cortese & Loughran Inc., Washington, 1982-84; ptnr. Kirkland & Ellis, Washington, 1985-94, Pepper Hamilton, LLP, Washington, 1994-98; mng. mem. Cortese PLCC, Washington, 1999—. Cons. Gen. Motors Corp., Detroit, 1985—. Lt. U.S. Army, 1959-60. Mem. ABA, Am. Law Inst., Pa. Bar, D.C. Bar Assn., Def. Rsch. Inst., Lawyers for Civil Justice (mem. exec. com., bd. dirs.), Racquet Club (Phila.), Univ. Club, Capitol Hill Club. Avocations: vintage automobile racing and restoration, art & antique collecting, cooking. Administrative and regulatory, Federal civil litigation, Legislative. Home: 113 3rd St NE Washington DC 20002-7313 Fax: 202-637-9797. E-mail: awc@corteseplic.com.

CORTESE, JOSEPH SAMUEL, II, lawyer; b. Des Moines, Aug. 17, 1955; s. Joseph Anthony and Kathryn Mary (Marasco) C.; m. Diane Caniglia, Aug. 5, 1978; children: Joseph III, James David, Kathryn Elizabeth. BA, Ind. U., 1977; JD with honors, Drake U., 1980. Bar: Iowa 1981, U.S. Dist. Ct. (no. and so. dists.) Iowa 1981, U.S. Ct. Appeals (8th cir.) 1984. Assoc. Jones, Hoffman & Huber, Des Moines, 1981-85; ptnr. Huber, Book, Cortese, Happe & Lanz, P.L.C., Des Moines, 1985—. Ordained permanent deacon Diocese Des Moines Roman Cath. Ch., Iowa, 1997. Mem. ABA, ATLA, Iowa State Bar Assn., Polk County Bar Assn., Def. Rsch. Inst., Iowa Trial Lawyers Assn. Roman Catholic. Personal injury (including property damage), Product liability, Workers' compensation. Home: 2915 Sherry Ln Urbandale IA 50322-6813 Office: Huber Book Cortese Happe & Lanz PLC 317 6th Ave Ste 200 Des Moines IA 50309-4127 Fax: 515-243-5481. E-mail: jcortese@desmoineslaw.com.

CORTEZ, HERNAN GLENN, lawyer; b. Harlingen, Tex., Nov. 12, 1934; s. Hernan and Laura (Howell) C.; m. Carole Elaine DuBois, Jan. 29, 1958 (div. Aug. 1976); children: Vicky Foss, Marta Stephens, Jill Hubach, Ingrid Smith, H. Glenn Jr.; m.Carole Jean Simms, Dec. 31, 1976; 1 child, Troy Dillinger. BA, U. Tex., 1956, JD, 1962. Bar: Tex. 1962, U.S. Dist. Ct. (we. dist.) Tex. 1970, U.S. Ct. Appeals (5th cir.) 1981; bd. cert. pers. injury trial law Tex. Bd. Legal Specialization. Asst. atty. City of Austin, Tex., 1962-69, assoc. atty., 1969, atty., 1969-70; sole practice Austin, 1971-97; adminstrv. law judge State of Tex., 1997—. Atty. City of Manor, Tex., 1972-90, City of Rollingwood, Tex., 1972-86, City of Pflugerville, Tex., 1974-93, City of Sunset Valley, Tex., 1980-86, City of Granite Shoals, Tex., 1983-86. Served as capt. U.S. Army, 1957-59, USAR. Mem.: Travis County Bar Assn., Tex. Bar Assn. Administrative and regulatory, General civil litigation, Personal injury (including property damage). Home: 4701 Fieldstone Dr Austin TX 78735-6309 Office: 150 E Riverside Dr Austin TX 78704-1202

CORWIN, GRANT LESTER, II, lawyer; b. Mar. 9, 1949; s. Grant Lester Matthew and Barbara Read (McIntosh) C.; children: Mindy Corwin Sutton, Mitsi, Marshal H. BA, Brigham Young U., 1973; JD, Del. Law Sch., 1976. Bar: Vt. 1992, U.S. Dist. Ct. Vt. 1996. Accounts payable clk. Petco Oil Co., South Royalton, Vt., 1976-77; law clk. Griffin & Griffin, Attys., Rutland, Vt., 1977; bus. mgr. Am. River Animal Hosp., Orangevale, Calif., 1978-79; bookkeeper Corwin Enterprises, Royalton, Vt., 1979-81; law clk. Norman S. Case Jr., Esq., Bethel, Vt., 1981-87; asst. ct. clk. Windsor Dist. Ct., White River Junction, Vt., 1987-93; pvt. practice South Royalton, Vt., 1993—. Tenor chorus Vt. Symphony Orch., 1995-99; sousaphone player Royalton Band, Mad Bavarian Brass Band, 1997—; missionary LDS Ch., France and Belgium, 1969-71; chpt. leader John Birch Soc., Royalton, 1992—; notary pub. Windsor County, Woodstock, Vt., 1981—; justice of the peace Bd. of Civil Authority, Royalton, 1986—; town grand juror Town of Royalton, 1995—, sec., treas. town com.; del. Vt. Rep. Convs.; asst. scoutmaster Troop 243, Boy Scouts Am., South Royalton, 1995-99; mem. Vt. Stake Activities com., 1995—; facilitator Royalton Vital Communities, 2003; candidate for Windsor County Senator, 2003. Mem. Royalton Lodge Ind. Order of Odd Fellows (sec. 2002—), Tunbridge Grange, Phi Alpha Delta. Avocations: family history, genealogy. Home: Riverbow Farm 2219 VT RT 110 South Royalton VT 05068-7703 Office: Vt Rt No 110 South Royalton VT 05068

CORWIN, GREGG MARLOWE, lawyer; b. Mpls., May 4, 1947; s. Gerald Sidney Corwin and Shirley Mae (Nathenson) Nadler; m. Frances Gail Shapiro, mar. 21, 1971; children: Mitchell, David. BA summa cum laude, U. Minn., 1969, JD cum laude, 1972. Bar: Minn. 1972, U.S. Dist. Ct. Minn. 1972, U.S. Ct. Appeals (8th cir.) 1976, U.S. Supreme Ct. 1977. Assoc. Fred Burstein Law Firm, Mpls., 1972-77; ptnr. Cortlen Cloutier, Mpls., 1977-78; pvt. practice, Mpls., 1978—. Capt. USAF. Mem. ABA, Minn. Bar Assn., Hennepin County Bar Assn., Phi Beta Kappa. Democrat. Jewish. Avocations: reading, music, sports. Civil rights, Labor (including EEOC, Fair Labor Standards Act, labor-management relations, NLRB, OSHA). Office: 1660 Hwy 100 Ste 508 E Minneapolis MN 55416-1534 E-mail: GCorwin@GCorwin.com.

CORWIN, MELANIE S. lawyer; b. Cin., July 9, 1962; BA, Ea. Ky. U., 1984; JD, No. Ky. U., 1990. Bar: Ohio 1990, Ky. 1998, U.S. Dist. Ct. (so. dist.) Ohio 1991, U.S. Ct. Appeals (6th cir.) 1992. Assoc. Brown, Cummins & Brown Co., L.P.A., 1990-97, ptnr., 1998—2002; atty. Waite, Schneider, Bayless & Chesley Co. LPA, Cin., 2002—. Mem. ABA, Ohio Bar Assn., Ky. Bar Assn. Commercial, contracts (including sales of goods; commercial financing), Labor (including EEOC, Fair Labor Standards Act, labor-management relations, NLRB, OSHA), Mergers and acquisitions. Office: Waite Schneider Bayless & Chesley Co LPA 1513 4th and Vine Tower One W 4th St Cincinnati OH 45202

CORWIN, SHERMAN PHILLIP, lawyer; b. Chgo., June 29, 1917; s. Louis C. and Becky (Goodman) Cohen; m. Betty C. Corwin (dec. Jan. 1998); children: Susan M. Rothberg, Laurie L. Grad. valedictorian, Wilson Jr. Coll., 1937; BA, U. Chgo., 1939, JD cum laude, 1941. Bar: Ill. 1941, Mich. 1946, Colo. 1946. Assoc. Lederer, Livingston Kahn & Adsit, Chgo., 1941-43; assoc. Sonnenschein Nath & Rosenthal, Chgo., 1946-60, ptnr., 1960—, head estate planning and probate group, 1970-88. Editor: Estate Planning Handbook for Lawyers, 6th edit., 1976, 7th edit., 1980 Bd. dirs., officer North Suburban Synagogue Beth El, Highland Park, Ill., 1959-80; bd. dirs. Congregation Moriah, Deerfield, Ill., 1980-84; chmn. profl. adv. com. (estate planning) Jewish Fedn. Met. Chgo., 1985-87. Served to 1st lt. U.S. Army, 1944-46 Fellow Am. Coll. Trust and Estate Counsel; mem. Chgo. Bar Assn. (chmn. trust law com. 1970, chmn. Am. citizenship com. 1955), Chgo. Estate Planning Coun. (pres. 1983), Nu Sigma Kappa (past pres. local chpt.), Nu Beta Epsilon (past pres. local chpt.). Estate planning, Probate (including wills, trusts). Home: 400 E Ohio St Apt 2104 Chicago IL 60611-4615 Office: Sonnenschein Nath Et Al 8000 Sears Tower 233 S Wacker Dr Ste 8000 Chicago IL 60606-6491

CORY, BARBARA ELLEN, lawyer; b. Oak Park, Ill., July 26, 1951; d. Paul Russell and Mary Clark (Holbrook) C.; m. Spencer Richard Knapp, Aug. 21, 1976; children: Emily Cory Knapp, Alexandra Cory Knapp. Student, Dartmouth Coll., 1971-72; BA, Wellesley Coll., 1973; JD, Cornell U., 1976. Bar: Vt. 1977, U.S. Dist. Ct. Vt. 1978. Law clk. to chief judge U.S. Dist. Ct. Vt., Rutland, 1977-78; assoc. Dinse, Knapp & McAndrew (formerly Dinse, Erdmann & Clapp), Burlington, Vt., 1976—83, ptnr., 1983—. Chairperson Adult Day Care Ctr. Inc., Burlington, 1981-85; bd. dirs., v.p., sec. Child Care Ctr. Inc. Scholar, Wellesley Coll., 1973. Mem. ABA, Vt. Bar Assn. (young lawyers sect.), Vis. Nurse Assn. (bd. dirs. 1983—). Avocations: running, swimming, languages. Federal civil litigation, General civil litigation, Personal injury (including property damage). Home: 90 Heather Ln Shelburne VT 05482-7339 Office: Dinse Knapp & McAndrew 209 Battery St Burlington VT 05401-5261

COSTALES, MARCO DANIEL, lawyer; b. L.A., Dec. 14, 1962; s. Armando Aguilar and Sharon Rose (Cooper) C.; m. Virginia Louise Childs, Aug. 7, 1988; children: Michelle Louise, Kevin Daniel. BA in Internat. Rels., Stanford U., 1984; JD, MBA, U. Calif., Berkeley, 1988. Bar: Calif. 1988. Atty. Loeb & Loeb LLP, L.A., 1989-99, Nossaman, Guthner, Knox & Elliott LLP, 1999—. Active La Canada First Presbyn. Ch., 1997-2001, Glendale Presbyn. Ch., 2002-. Avocations: music, scuba diving. Corporate, general, Mergers and acquisitions, Non-profit and tax-exempt organizations. Office: Nossaman Guthner Knox & Elliott LLP 445 S Figueroa St Fl 31 Los Angeles CA 90071-1602 E-mail: mcostales@nossaman.com.

COSTELLO, DANIEL BRIAN, lawyer, consultant; b. Arlington, Va., Apr. 23, 1950; s. James Russell and Hazel Virginia (Caudle) C.; m. Margaret Ruth Dow, June 13, 1970; children: James Brian, Rebecca Ruth, Kathleen Marie. BA, U. Va., 1972; JD, Coll. of William and Mary, 1975. Bar: Va. 1975, U.S. Dist. Ct. (ea. dist.) Va. 1979, U.S. Ct. Appeals (4th cir.) 1979, U.S. Bankruptcy Ct. (ea. dist.) Va. 1979, D.C. 1984. Reporter Globe Newspapers, Vienna, Va., 1965-68; freelance journalist Williamsburg, Va., 1972-73; news dir. Sta. WMBG, WBCI-FM, Williamsburg, 1973-76; spl. asst. atty. gen. Commonwealth of Va., Suffolk, Va., 1976-78, asst. atty. gen. Richmond, Va., 1978-80; ptnr. Dameron, Costello & Hubacher, Alexandria, Va., 1980-89, Costello & Hubacher, Alexandria, 1989-99; pvt. practice Springfield, 1999—; corp. sec., gen. counsel Olivares U.S.A., Inc., Fairfax, Va., 1999-2000, pres., 2000—. Press rels. cons. Va. Bar Assn.; spl. commr. in chancery Alexandria Cir. Ct. Author: Land Use Planning and Eminent Domain, 1997, 2d edit. 1999, Foreclosure in Virginia, 1991; co-editor, co-author The Layman's Guide to Virginia Law, 1977; editor night news Sta. WINA, 1969-72; contbr. articles to profl. jours. Mem. Va. State Bar, D.C. Bar, Soc. Alumni Coll. of William and Mary, U. Va. Alumni Soc., Rolling Hills Club. Presbyterian. Avocations: hunting, fishing, coin collecting. Condemnation (eminent domain), General practice, Property, real (including real estate development, water). Office: Ste A-210 8136 Old Keene Mill Rd Springfield VA 22152-1843 E-mail: dbriancostello@att.net.

COSTELLO, EDWARD J., JR., arbitrator, mediator, lawyer; b. N.Y.C., Apr. 18, 1939; m. Karin Bergstrom, Aug. 21, 1981; 1 child, Catharine A. AB, Fordham U., 1961; JD, NYU, 1964. Bar: Fla. 1965, N.Y. 1967, Calif. 1969, U.S. Supreme Ct. 1973. Assoc. Donovan, Leisure, Newton & Irvine, N.Y.C., 1962-64; spl. agt. FBI, Washington, 1964-67; assoc. O'Melveny & Myers, Los Angeles, 1963, 68-72; ptnr. Costello & Walcher, Los Angeles, 1972-85, Proskauer, Rose, Los Angeles, 1985-89; professional neutral Santa Monica, Calif., 1989—. Adj. assoc. prof. law, evidence and criminal procedure Southwestern U. Sch. Law, Los Angeles, 1970-73, internat. bus. trans. U. So. Calif. Law Ctr., Los Angeles, 1973-75; judge pro tem Los Angeles Mcpl. Ct., 1971—; chmn. bd. dirs. Year Labs. Inc., Los Angeles; instr. arbitration/mediation Loyola Law Sch.; dispute resolution lectr. Am. Arbitration Assn., ABA, Calif. Continuing Edn. of the Bar, Ctr. for Profl. Edn., U. Calif. Editorial bd. mem. NYU Law Review; author: Controlling Conflict: Alternative Dispute Resolution for Business, 1996; author: (with others) Dispute Resolution Alternatives 1994, Insurance Alternative Dispute Resolution Manual, 1994. Chmn., trustee Brentwood Sch., Los Angeles, 1986-87. Root-Tilden scholar NYU. Mem. ABA (litigation and internat. law construction forum sects.), Calif. Bar Asn. (bar examiners com. 1985-86), N.Y. State Bar Assn., Fla. Bar Assn., Los Angeles County Bar Assn. (past mem. juvenile ct. and judiciary coms., trial lawyer sect.), Am. Arbitration Assn. (mem. large complex case panel, specialty panels in construction, employment, healthcare, intellectual property). Office: 620 E Channel Rd Santa Monica CA 90402-1316 E-mail: info@edcostello.com.

COSTELLO, JAMES PAUL, lawyer; b. Elgin, Ill., Nov. 12, 1953; s. John Desmond and Helena (Brennan) C.; m. Kathryn Charlotte Schafer, June 16, 1979; children: James Albert, Robert Francis, Paul Desmond, Philip Schafer Costello. BA, U. Ill., 1975; JD, DePaul U., 1978. Bar: Ill. 1978, U.S. Dist. Ct. (no. dist.) Ill. 1978. Assoc. J. Thomas Demos & Assocs., Chgo., 1978-83; ptnr. Costello, McMahon & Burke Ltd. (formerly James Paul Costello Ltd.), Chgo., 1983—. Contbg. author: Law Enforcement Legal Defense Manual, 1977-78; editor: Jail Law Bulletin, Police Plaintiff, Law Enforcement Employment Digest, 1977-78. Mem. Ill. Bar Assn., Assn. Trial Lawyers Am., Ill. Trial Lawyers Assn. (amicus curiae com. 1981—), Chgo. Bar Assn. (judicial evaluation com.). Democrat. Roman Catholic. Personal injury (including property damage), Product liability, Professional liability. Home: 1202 E Clarendon St Arlington Heights IL 60004-5050 Office: 150 N Wacker Dr Ste 3050 Chicago IL 60606-1660 E-mail: costelaw@core.com.

COSTELLO, JOHN WILLIAM, lawyer; b. Chgo., Apr. 16, 1947; s. William John and June Ester (O'Neill) C.; m. Maureen Grace Matthews, June 13, 1970; children— Colleen, William, Erin, Owen. BA, John Carroll U., 1969; JD, DePaul U., 1972. Bar: U.S. Dist. Ct. (no. dist.) Ill. 1982. Assoc. Arvey, Hodes, Costello & Burman, Chgo., 1972-76; ptnr., 1976-90, ptnr. Wildman, Harrold Allen & Dixon, 1990—. Co-author: (manual) The Bankrupcy Reform Act of 1978, 1981. Served to capt. U.S. Army, 1972-73. Mem. ABA (bus. bankruptcy com., jurisdiction and venue and secured creditors subcoms.), Ill. State Bar Assn. (former vice chmn., chmn. comml. banking and bankrupcy law sect. 1979-81), Am. Bankruptcy Inst., Turnaround Mgmt. Assn. (former bd. dirs. Midwest sect.). Democrat. Roman Catholic. Office: Wildman Harrold Aller & Dixon 225 W Wacker Dr Chicago IL 60606-1224

COSTENBADER, CHARLES MICHAEL, lawyer; b. Jersey City, Dec. 9, 1935; s. Edward William and Marie Veronica (Danaher) C.; m. Barbara Ann Wilson, Aug. 1, 1959; children: Charles Michael Jr., William E., Mary E. BS in Acctg., Mt. St. Mary's Coll., 1957; JD, Seton Hall U., 1960; LLM in Taxation, NYU, 1968. Bar: N.J 1960; U.S. Tax Ct. 1961, U.S. Ct. Appeals (3d cir.) 1973, U.S. Supreme Ct. 1983. Trial atty. office regional counsel IRS, N.Y.C., 1961-69; tax assoc. Shanley & Fisher, Newark, 1969-76; tax ptnr. Stryker, Tams & Dill, Newark, 1976-98; spl. counsel McCarter & English, Newark, 1998—. Mem. N.J. State and Local Expenditure and Revenue Commn., 1985-88. Mem. ABA, N.J. Bar Assn. (chmn. taxation sect. 1984-85), N.J. State C. of C. (chmn. tax coun. com. 1988—), Am. Coll. Tax Counsel. Republican. Roman Catholic. Avocations: gardening, reading, sports. Taxation, general, State and local taxation. Home: 8 Neptune Pl Colonia NJ 07067-2502 Office: Gateway Four Ctr 100 Mulberry St Newark NJ 07102-4056 E-mail: ccostenbader@mccarter.com.

COSTIKYAN, EDWARD N. lawyer; b. Weehawken, N.J., Sept. 14, 1924; s. Mihran Nazar and Berthe (Muller) C.; m. Frances Holmgren, 1950 (div. 1975); chldren: Gregory, Emilie; m. Barbara Heine, Mar. 6, 1977. AB, Columbia U., 1947, LLB, 1949. Bar: N.Y. 1949, U.S. Dist. Ct. (so. dist.) N.Y. 1950, U.S. Ct. Appeals (2d cir.) 1950, U.S. Supreme Ct. 1964. Law sec. to judge Harold R. Medina U.S. Dist. Ct., N.Y.C., 1949-51; ptnr. Paul, Weiss, Rifkind, Wharton & Garrison, N.Y.C., 1960-93, of counsel, 1994—. Spl. advisor to mayor on sch. and borough governance City of N.Y., 1994-96, chairperson mayor's investigative commn. on sch. safety, 1995-96; mem. Commn. on Integrity in Govt., N.Y.C., 1986, mem. joint com. on jud. adminstrn., 1985-92; adj. fellow Ctr. for Edn. Innovation, 1997—. Author: Behind Closed Doors: Politics in the Public Interest, 1966, How to Win Votes: The Politics of 1980, 1980; co-author: Re-Structuring the Government of New York City, 1972, New Strategies for Regional Cooperation, 1973; rsch. editor Columbia Law Rev.; mem. editl. bd. City Jour., 1992—; mem. bd. editors N.Y. Law Jour., 1976—; contbr. articles on legal and polit. subjects to profl. publs. Chmn. N.Y. State Task Force on N.Y.C. Juristiction and Structure, 1971-72; vice chmn. State Charter Revision for N.Y.C., 1972-77; county leader New York County Dem. Com., 1962-64; Dem. presdl. elector, 1964, 88; trustee, mem. exec. com., chmn. alumni adv. bd. Columbia U., 1981-93, trustee emeritus, 1993—; bd. dirs., mem. coun. Mcpl. Art Soc., 1993-98; chmn. bd. dirs. N.Y. Found. for Sr. Citizens, 1993—. 1st lt. inf. U.S. Army, 1943-46. Recipient William J. Brennan Jr. award for Outstanding Cont. to Pub. Discourse, 1997. Fellow Am. Coll. Trial Lawyers; mem. Assn. of Bar of City of N.Y. (mem. exec. com. 1986-90), Century Club. Unitarian Universalist. Home: 50 Sutton Pl S New York NY 10022-4167 Office: Paul Weiss Rifkind Wharton & Garrison Ste 12J 1285 Avenue Of The Americas Fl 21 New York NY 10019-6028

COTCHETT, JOSEPH WINTERS, lawyer, author; b. Chgo., Jan. 6, 1939; s. Joseph Winters and Jean (Renaud) C.; children— Leslie F., Charles P., Rachael E., Quinn Carlyle, Camilla E. BS in Engring., Calif. Poly. Coll., 1960; LLB, U. Calif. Hastings Coll. Law, 1964. Bar: Calif. 1965, DC 1980. Ptnr. Cotchett, Pitre, Simon & McCarthy, Burlingame, Calif., 1965—. Mem. Calif. Jud. Coun., 1975-77, Calif. Commn. on Jud. Performance, 1985-89, Commn. 2020 Jud. Coun., 1991-94; select com. on jud. retirement, 1992—. Author: (with R. Cartwright) California Products Liability Actions, 1970, (with F. Haight) California Courtroom Evidence, 1972, (with A. Elkind) Federal Courtroom Evidence, 1976, (with Frank Rothman) Persuasive Opening Statements and Closing Arguments, 1988, (with Stephen Pizzo) The Ethics Gap, 1991, (with Gerald Uelmen) California Courtroom Evidence Foundations, 1993; contbr. articles to profl. jours. Chmn. San Mateo County Heart Assn., 1967; pres. San Mateo Boys and Girls Club, 1971; bd. dirs. U. Calif. Hastings Law Sch., 1981-93. With Intelligence Corps, U.S. Army, 1960-61; col. JAGC, USAR, ret. Fellow Am. Bar Found., Am. Bd. Trial Advs., Am. Coll. Trial Lawyers, Internat. Acad. Trial Lawyers, Internat. Soc. of Barristers, Nat. Bd. Trial Advs. (diplomate civil trial adv.), State Bar Calif. (gov. 1972-75). Clubs: Commonwealth, Press (San Francisco). Federal civil litigation, State civil litigation. Office: 840 Malcolm Rd Burlingame CA 94010-1401 also: 9454 Wilshire Blvd Ste 907 Beverly Hills CA 90202

COTE, THOMAS JACQUES, lawyer; b. Ste-Foy, Quebec, Can., Oct. 26, 1951; came to U.S., 1970; s. Andre and Virginia C.; m. Josee L. Bourbeau, Aug. 29, 1987; children: Christine J., Julie M. BA, Suffolk U., 1972, JD, 1975. Bar: N.H. 1975. Pvt. practice, Gorham, N.H., 1976—. Former mem. faculty Sch. for Life Long Learning, Berlin. Past pres. United Way, Berlin. Avocations: skiing, hockey, piano, tennis, hiking. Bankruptcy, Family and matrimonial, Personal injury (including property damage). Office: 74 Main St Gorham NH 03581-1622

COTHORN, JOHN ARTHUR, lawyer; b. Des Moines, Dec. 12, 1939; s. John L. and Marguerite (Esters) C.; m. Connie Cason, Aug. 6, 1996; children: Jeffrey, Judith. BS in Math., BS in Aero. Engring., U. Mich., 1961, JD, 1980. Bar: Mich. 1981, U.S. Dist. Ct. (ea. dist.) Mich. 1981, U.S. Ct. Appeals (6th cir.) 1981, U.S. Dist. Ct. (we. dist.) Mich. 1986, U.S. Supreme Ct. Exec. U.S Govt., 1965-78; asst. prosecutor Washtenaw County, Ann Arbor, Mich., 1981-82; ptnr. Kitch, Saurbier, Drutchas, Wagner & Kenney P.C., Detroit, 1982-94, Meganck & Cothorn P.C., Detroit, 1994-97, Meganck, Cothorn & Stanczyk P.C., Detroit, 1997-98, Cothorn & Stanczyk, P.C., Detroit, 1998-2000, Cothorn & Braceful, Detroit, 2000—02, Cothorn & Assocs., P.C., Detroit, 2002—. Served to capt. U.S. Army, 1961-65. Mem. ABA, Nat. Bar Assn. (numerous fed. and state coms.), Soc. Automotive Engrs., Assn. Def. Trial Counsel, Phi Alpha Delta. Republican. Avocations: bridge, golf. Federal civil litigation, State civil litigation, Insurance. Office: 535 Griswold St Ste 530 Detroit MI 48226-3696

COTTER, PATRICIA O'BRIEN, state supreme court justice; b. South Bend, Ind., 1950; m. Michael W. Cotter, 1979; 2 children. BS in Polit. Sci. and History with honors, We. Mich. U, 1972; JD, Notre Dame, 1977. Pvt. practice, South Bend, 1977—83, Great Falls, Mont., 1984; ptnr. Cotter & Cotter, Great Falls, 1985—2000; justice Mont. Supreme Ct., 2001—. Office: Rm 323 PO Box 203003 Helena MT 59620

COTTONGAME, W. BRICE, lawyer; b. Ft. Worth, June 4, 1958; s. William Robert and Nelda Ree Cottongame; m. Elizabeth Cramer, Jan. 9, 1992; children: Kate, Will. BA in Polit. Sci., U. Tex., 1980; JD, S. Tex. Coll. Law, 1984. Bar: Tex., 1984, U.S. Dist. Ct. (no. and so. dists.) Tex., U.S. Ct. Appeals (5th cir.), U.S. Supreme Ct.; bd. cert. personal injury trial law Tex. Bd. Legal Specialization. Atty. Wallace Craig & Assocs., Ft. Worth, 1980-95, Henderson Haksell & Cottongame, Ft. Worth, 1995-98, Law Office W. Brice Cottongame & Assocs., Ft. Worth, 1998—. Fellow State Bar Tex., Tarrant County Bar Found.; Mem. Tex. Trial Lawyers Assn. (assoc. dir. 1986-90, dir. 1990-95), Tarrant County Trial Lawyers Assn. (dir. 1989-93, pres. 1994), Tarrant County Bar Assn. Democrat. United Methodist. General civil litigation, Insurance, Personal injury (including property damage). Office: W Brice Cottongame & Assoc PC 1701 River Run Fort Worth TX 76107 Office Fax: 817-877-0334.

COTTRELL, JAMES RAY, lawyer; b. Norton, Va., Aug. 9, 1952; BA, Va. Mil. Inst., 1974; JD, U. Richmond, 1976. Bar: Va. 1977, DC 1979. Ptnr. Gannon & Cottrell, P.C., Alexandria, Va. Mem.: ATLA, ABA (mem. family law sect.), Fairfax Bar Assn., Alexandria Bar Assn., DC Bar, Va. Trial Lawyers Assn., Va. State Bar (sec. 1987—88, vice chmn. 1988—89, chmn. 1989—90, bd. govs. family law sect.), Phi Delta Phi. Family and matrimonial, General civil litigation, Appellate. Office: Gannon and Cottrell PC PO Box 1286 Alexandria VA 22313-1286 Office Fax: 703-836-9086.*

COTTY, WILLIAM FRANK (BILL COTTY), lawyer; b. Aug. 9, 1946; s. William O. and Marie (Frank) C.; m. Amelia Dunlap, Dec. 26, 1969; children: William D., Mary K., Anne Marie. BA, Erskine Coll., Due West, S.C., 1969; JD, U. S.C., 1974. Bar: S.C. 1974. Adminstrv. asst. Congressman Tom Gettys, Washington, 1969-71; atty., legis. liaison S.C. Wildlife Dept., Columbia, 1974-77; assoc. atty. Ratchford & Eleazer, Columbia, 1977-81; sole practitioner Columbia, 1981-95; with Cotty & Jonas, 1995—; mem. S.C. Ho. of Reps., 1994—. Trustee Richland County Sch. Dist. Two, Columbia, 1986-94. Lt. col. S.C. Army NG. ret. Recipient Legis. Conservationist of the Yr. award S.C. Wildlife Fedn., 1971. Republican. Presbyterian. Estate planning, Probate (including wills, trusts), Property, real (including real estate development, water). Home: 324 Valley Springs Rd Columbia SC 29223-6934 Office: 1328 Blanding St Columbia SC 29201-2903

COUCH, J. O. TERRELL, lawyer, former oil company executive; b. San Antonio, Mar. 3, 1920; s. Quest C. and Mattie H. (Terrell) C.; m. Willynn Miles Brooks, July 31, 1943 (dec. May 1992); children: J.O. Terrell Jr., Leland Brooks, Nancy Couch Davis; m. Margaret Bachtel Atwood, July 17, 1993. Student, San Antonio Jr. Coll., 1937-38; LL.B., U. Tex., 1942; grad., Advanced Mgmt. Program, Harvard, 1968. Bar: Tex. 1942, Ohio 1967. Partner firm Lattimore & Couch, Ft. Worth, 1946-49, Lattimore, Couch & Lattimore, 1949-51; asso. firm McGown, McGown, Godfrey & Logan, Ft. Worth, 1951-52; atty. Marathon Oil Co., Houston, 1952-61, div. atty., 1961-67, gen. counsel, 1967-74, dir., 1969-74; sole practice Houston, 1975; ptnr. Hutcheson & Grundy, Houston, 1976-89; of counsel Hutcheson & Grundy, Houston, 1990-98; arbitrator, 1998—. Mem. adv. bd. Internat. and Comparative Law Center, 1967-2002; mem. adv. bd. Internat. Oil & Gas Ednl. Ctr., 1967—2002, vice chmn., 1973-77; mem. adv. bd. Inst. Transnational Arbitration of Ctr. for Am. and Internat. Law, 1989—. Served with CIC AUS, 1942-46, ETO, PTO. Mem. ABA (mem. natural resources law sect. council 1972-76, vice chmn. 1976, chmn.-elect 1977-78, chmn. 1978-79), Houston Bar Assn. (chmn. oil, gas, mineral law com. 1966), State Bar Tex. (chmn. oil, gas, mineral law sect. 1961-62, mem. internat. law sect. coun. 1976-79), Houston Country Club, Allegro Club, Alpha Tau Omega. Methodist. Home: 5956 Riverview Way Houston TX 77057-1434

COUCH, MARK WOODWORTH, lawyer; b. Albany, N.Y., Sept. 5, 1956; s. Leslie Franklin and Joan Teresa (Dunham) C.; m. Mary Jane Bendon, Oct. 25, 1985; children: Braden Bendon, Dylan Bendon, Tucker Bendon. BA, Worcester State Coll., 1982; JD, Union U., 1985. Bar: N.Y. 1986, U.S. Dist. Ct. (no. dist.) N.Y. 1986, U.S. Dist. Ct. (we. dist.) N.Y. 1995. Prin. Couch & Howard, Albany, 1986-88; atty. Couch, White, Brenner, Howard & Feigenbaum, Albany, 1988-89; prin. Breakell & Couch, Albany, 1989—2003, Couch Dale PC, 2003—. Bd. dirs. Downtown Day Care Ctr. Inc., Albany, 1991-96. Mem. ABA, N.Y. State Bar Assn., Albany County Bar Assn., Schuyler Meadows Club. General civil litigation, Construction, Labor (including EEOC, Fair Labor Standards Act, labor-management relations, NLRB, OSHA). Home: 27 Bergen Woods Dr Cohoes NY 12047-4951 Office: Couch Dale PC 29 British American Blvd Latham NY 12110

COUGHLAN, PATRICK CAMPBELL, lawyer, mediator; b. Orange, N.J., May 28, 1940; s. Gerald Noel and Carter (Van Schaick) C.; m. Joyce Miskuf; children: Kimberly Campbell,Devon Gerald, Carter Turner. BA, Duke U., 1962, JD, 1965. Bar: Fla. 1965, U.S. Supreme Ct. 1968, Calif. 1974, Maine 1985. Assoc. Alley, Maass, Rogers & Lindsay, Palm Beach, Fla., 1969-72, ptnr., 1972-74; judge Mcpl. Ct., Ocean Ridge, Fla., 1970-72; assoc. firm Richards, Watson & Gershon, Los Angeles, 1974-75, ptnr., 1975-84; city atty. City of Rancho Palos Verdes, Calif., 1975-82, City of San Fernando, Calif., 1977-82, City of Seal Beach, Calif., 1978-84, City of La Habra Heights, Calif., 1979-84, 1981-84, Rolling Hills, Calif., 1981-84, Westlake Village, Calif., 1981-84; chair bd. appeals Raymond, Maine, 1985-98; pres. Kingsley Pines, Inc.; prin. Coughlan Assoc., 1987-88; pres. Resolve Disputes, Inc. N.Am., Portland, Maine, 1989-92, Conflict Solutions, Portland, Oreg., 1992—, Naples, Fla., 1992. Pres. No. Pines, Inc., 1980-86; ptnr. Atlanean Ptnrs.; trustee, sec. Gulf Stream Sch. Found., Inc., 1970-85; bd. dirs. Mountains Restoration Trust, 1981-82; trustee North Yarmouth Acad., 1984-93, pres., 1985-89; treas., trustee Natural Resources Coun. Maine, 1989-93; pres. parish coun. Our Lady of Perpetual Help, 1983-85; pres. World Affairs Coun. of Maine, 1986-89, trustee, 1985-93; trustee Portland Stage Co., 1989-93, sec., 1990-91, v.p., 1991-92; trustee Maine Youth Camps Assn., 1989-96, sec., 1990, v.p., 1990-93, pres., 1993-95; trustee Susan Curtis Found., 1991-96; dir. Pvt. Adjudication Ctr. Duke U., 1994-2002, mediator 1998-2002; dir. The Club at La Peninsula, 1997-98. Capt. USAF, 1965-68. Fellow Internat. Acad. Mediators (bd. dirs. 1999—, v.p. 2001—); mem. ABA, State Bar Calif., Fla. Bar, Maine State Bar, Soc. Profls. in Dispute Resolution, Maine Assn. Dispute Resolution Profls. (pres. 1990-92), Am.Coll. Civil Trial Mediators, Woodlands Country Club,Falmouth, ME, Windstar Country Club (Naples, Fla.). Roman Catholic. Home: 47 Coughlan Cove Rd Raymond ME 04071-6274 Home and Office: 1540 Star Pointe Ln Naples FL 34112 E-mail: coglan@aol.com., pat@conflictsolutionsinc.com.

COUGHLIN, FRANCIS RAYMOND, JR., surgeon, educator, lawyer; b. N.Y.C., Feb. 22, 1927; s. Francis Raymond and Isabel (Archibald) C.; m. Barbara Ann Blunt, June 9, 1951; children: Hilary, Mary, Patricia, Christopher Francis, Geoffrey Blunt, Daniel Taylor, Isabel, David Carleton. BS, Fordham U., 1948; MD, Yale U., 1952; MS, McGill U., Montreal, Que., Can., 1955, diploma in surgery, 1959; JD, U. Bridgeport, 1988. Bar: N.Y., Conn., Dist. Columbia, U.S. Supreme Ct.; diplomate Am. Bd. Surgery, Am. Bd. Thoracic Surgery. Intern N.Y. Hosp., N.Y.C., 1952-53; resident McGill U. Teaching Hosp., Montreal, 1953-57, Overholt Thoracic Clin., Boston, 1958-60; mem. staff Stamford (Conn.) Hosp., 1960—; practice medicine specializing in thoracic surgery Stamford, 1960—88; medico-legal cons., 1988—. Dir. thoracic and vascular surgery St. Josephs Hosp., Stamford, 1970-73, 80-85, assoc. chief surgery, 1971-73, chief surgery, 1973-77; assoc. prof. clin. surgery N.Y. Med. Coll., 1981-2002; mem. staff Norwalk Hosp., 1965-89; vice chair Conn. State Commn. Medicolegal Investigations, 1990-2002. With U.S. Maritime Svc., 1945-46. Recipient Encaenia award Fordham U., N.Y.C., 1958; Teaching fellow Harvard U., 1958. Fellow ACS (sec.-treas. Conn. chpt. 1966-70), Royal Coll. Surgeons (Can.), Am. Coll. Cardiology, Am. Coll. Chest Physicians, Royal Soc. Medicine; mem. Soc. Thoracic Surgeons (founding mem.), N.Y. Acad. Medicine, Conn. Heart Assn. (dir. 1961-64), Conn. Lung Assn. (dir. and exec. com. 1963-69, v.p. 1967-69), Lung Assn. So. Fairfield County (pres. 1963-68, dir. 1960-70), Soc. Med. Jursiprudence (v.p. 1992-93, pres. 1995-97), English-Speaking Union, Scottish-Am. Found., Can. Soc. N.Y., Yale Club N.Y., Army Navy Club (Washington), Yale Med. Sch. Alumni Assn. (v.p. 1999-2001, pres. 2001—). Republican. Office: 20 Mead St New Canaan CT 06840-5701 E-mail: fcoughlinmd@att.net.

COUGHLIN, TERRANCE J. lawyer; b. Sioux Falls, S.D., June 11, 1948; s. John William and Blanche (Stekl) C.; m. Suzanne Houghton, June, 27, 1981; children: Michael, Brian. BChemE, S.D. Sch. Mines, 1970; JD with high honors, Ill. Inst. Tech., 1977. Bar: Ill. 1977, U.S. Dist. Ct. (no. dist.) Ill. 1977, U.S. Patent Office 1977, U.S. Ct. Appeals (7th cir.) 1977, U.S. Supreme Ct. 1980; registered profl. engr., Ind., Ill. Engr. E.I. Dupont, East Chicago, Ind., 1970-74, Container Corp. of Am., Carol Stream, Ill., 1974-77; ptnr. Coughlin and Marutzky, Chgo., 1977-80; sole practice Chgo., 1980—. Hearing officer Ill. Pollution Control Bd., 1979-87. Editor: IIT Law Review, 1974-77. Bd. dirs. Catholic Charities, 1993-2000. Mem. ABA, Ill. State Bar Assn. (gen. assembly), Chgo. Bar Assn., K.C. (officer 1986—). Republican. Roman Catholic. Avocations: golf, boating, sports. State civil litigation, Personal injury (including property damage), Probate (including wills, trusts). Home: 410 Ascot Ln Oak Brook IL 60523-2540 Office: 39 S La Salle St Ste 1400 Chicago IL 60603-1706

COULSON, ROBERT, retired association executive, arbitrator, author; b. New Rochelle, N.Y., July 24, 1924; s. Robert Earl and Abby (Stewart) C.; m. Cynthia Cunningham, Oct. 16, 1961; children: Cotton Richard, Dierdre, Crocker, Robert Cromwell, Christopher. BA, Yale U., 1949; LLB, Harvard U., 1953; DSc in Bus. Adminstrn. (hon.), Bryant U., 1985; LLD (hon.), Hofstra U., 1987. Bar: N.Y. 1954, Mass. 1954. Assoc. Whitman, Ransom & Coulson, N.Y.C., 1954-61; ptnr. Littlefield, Miller & Cleaves, N.Y.C., 1961-63; exec. v.p. Am. Arbitration Assn., N.Y.C., 1963-71, pres., 1971-94; ret., 1994. Cons. N.Y. State Div. Youth, 1961-63; pres. Youth Consultation Service of N.Y., 1970 Author: How to Stay Out of Court, 1968, Labor Arbitration: What You Need to Know, 1973, Business Arbitration: What You Need to Know, 1980, The Termination Handbook, 1981, Fighting Fair, 1983, Arbitration in Schools, 1985, Business Mediation, 1987, Alcohol and Drugs in Arbitration, 1988, Empowered at Forty, 1990, Police Under Pressure, 1993, ADR in America, 1994, Family Mediation, 1996; editor: Racing at Sea, 1958; contbr. articles to profl. jours. Bd. dirs. Fedn. Protestant Welfare Agys., pres., 1982-84, chmn. 1985-87; adv. com. Internat. Coun. for Comml. Arbitration. Mem. N.Y. Yacht Club, Cruising Club Am., Riverside Yacht Club. Avocations: sailing, travel, writing. Home: 9 Reginald St Riverside CT 06878-2522 E-mail: coulfamily@aol.com.

COULSON, WILLIAM ROY, lawyer; b. Waukegan, Ill., Oct. 5, 1949; s. Robert E. and Rose (Stone) C.; m. Elizabeth A. Shafernich, Feb. 14, 1986. AB, Dartmouth Coll., 1969; JD, U. Ill., 1972. Bar: Ill. 1972, U.S. Dist. Ct. (no. dist.) Ill. 1974, U.S. Supreme Ct. 1976. Law clk. to judge U.S. Dist. Ct., East St. Louis, Ill., 1972-74, Chgo., 1975; asst. U.S. atty. U.S. Dept. Justice, Chgo., 1975-88, supr. criminal divsn., 1980-88; mng. ptnr. Cherry & Flynn, Chgo., 1988-99, Gold & Coulson, 1999—. Faculty Atty. Gens. Adv. Inst., Washington, 1980-88, Ill. Inst. for Continuing Legal Edn., Springfield, 1983-88, Fed. Law Enforcement Tng. Ctr., Glynco, Ga., 1983-86; co-chmn. U.S. Magistrate Merit Selection Panel, 1989-91. Author: Federal Juvenile Law, 1980; contbg. author Animation mag., 1993—. Served to 2d lt. Ill. N.G., 1965-66. Finalist U.S. Senate Jud. Selection Panel, 1996. Mem. ABA, Chgo. Bar Assn. (jud. evaluation com. 1987-89, vice chair 1990-91), Fed. Bar Assn. (pres. 1991-92), Dartmouth Club. Federal civil litigation, Criminal. Office: 30 N La Salle St Chicago IL 60602-2590

COULTER, CHARLES ROY, lawyer; b. Webster City, Iowa, June 10, 1940; s. Harold L. Coulter and Eloise (Wheeler) Harrison; m. Elizabeth Bean, Dec. 16, 1961; 1 child, Anne Elizabeth. BA in Journalism, U. Iowa, 1962, JD, 1965. Bar: Iowa 1965. Assoc. Stanley, Bloom, Mealy & Lande, Muscatine, Iowa, 1965-68; v.p. Stanley, Lande & Hunter, Muscatine, 1969—, also bd. dirs. County fin. chmn. Leach for Congress, 1980-96; county coord. George Bush for Pres. , 1980, 88, Reagan-Bush Campaign, 1984. Fellow Coll. of Law Practice Mgmt. (dir. 1994-, pres. 2001-), Am. Bar Found., Iowa State Bar Found., Am. Coll. Trust and Estate Counsel; mem. ABA (mem. coun. law practice mgmt. sect. 1984-88, sec. 1988-89, vice chair 1989-90, chair 1991-92, chair coord. commn. legal tech. 1994-97, mem. standing com. on tech. and info. sys. 1997-98), Iowa Bar Assn., Muscatine County Bar Assn., Thirty-Three Club (pres. 1981), Rotary, Order of Coif. Episcopalian. Avocation: tennis. Corporate, general, Probate (including wills, trusts), Property, real (including real estate development, water). Office: Stanley Lande & Hunter 301 Iowa Ave Ste 400 Muscatine IA 52761-3881 E-mail: chuckcoulter@slhlaw.com.

COUNTRYMAN, DAYTON WENDELL, lawyer; b. Sioux City, Iowa, Mar. 31, 1918; s. Cleve and Susie (Schaeffer) Countryman; m. Ruth Hazen, Feb. 2, 1941 (dec.); children: Karen, Joan, James, Kay. BS, Iowa State Coll., 1940; LLB, State U. Iowa, 1948, JD, 1969. Bar: Iowa 1948. Practiced in, Nevada; ptnr. Hadley & Countryman, Nevada, Iowa, 1949-64; mem. Countryman & Zaffarano P.C., 1984-87, Dayton Countryman Law Offices, P.C., 1987—; county atty. Story County, Iowa, 1950-54; atty. gen. State of Iowa, 1954-56. Candidate for U.S. Senate, 1956, 1960, 68. Air Force Res. pilot USAAF, 1941-46. Mem. ABA, Iowa Bar Assn., Story County Bar Assn., VFW, Am. Legion, Iowa State U. Alumni Assn. (pres. 1970-71), Iowa 2B Jud. Dist. Assn., Masons, Lions (pres. 1975-76). Methodist. Office: PO Box 28 Nevada IA 50201-0028 E-mail: dcountryman@midiowa.net.

COURT, LEONARD, lawyer, educator; b. Ardmore, Okla., Jan. 11, 1947; s. Leonard and Margaret Janet (Harvey) C.; m. JoAnn Dilleshaw, Sept. 2, 1967; children: Chris, Todd, Brooke. BA, Okla. State U., 1969; JD, Harvard U., 1972. Bar: Okla. 1973, U.S. Dist. Ct. (we. dist.) Okla. 1973, U.S. Dist. Ct. (no. dist.) Okla., 1978, U.S. Dist. Ct. (ea. dist.) Okla. 1983, U.S. Ct. Appeals (10th cir.) 1980, U.S. Ct. Mil. Appeals 1973. Assoc. Crowe & Dunlevy, Oklahoma City, Okla., 1977-81, shareholder, dir., 1981—. Adj. prof. Okla. U. Law Sch., Norman, 1984-85, 88-89, 99—, Okla. City U. Law Sch., 1998—; planning com. Ann. Inst. Labor Law, S.W. Legal Found., Dallas, 1984—. Contbg. author: (supplement book) The Developing Labor Law, 1978, Corporate Counsel's Annual, 1974, Labor Law Developments, 1993, Employment Discrimination Law, Supplement, 1998, 2000. Chmn. bd. elders Meml. Christian Ch., Oklahoma City, 1980, 98-2000; cubmaster Last Frontier coun. Boy Scouts Am., 1984, co-chmn. sustaining fund raising drive Oklahoma City Downtown YMCA, 1989, mem. bd. mgmt., 1994-96; participant Leadership Oklahoma City, 1987-88, bd. govs. Okla. State U. Found., 1990-2002; Oklahoma City Ronald McDonald House, 1990-93, mem. exec. com. 1991-93; co-chmn. ann. telepathy fundraising drive Am. Heart Assn., Okla. City, 1996-98, bd. dirs., 1996-98. Capt. USAF, 1973-77. Fellow Am. Coll. Labor and Employment Lawyer; mem. Am. Employment Law Coun., U.S. C. of C. (mem. labor rels. com. 1997—, chmn. fair labor stds. act subcom. 1999—, mem. steering com. 1999—), Oklahoma City C. of C. (mem. sports and recreation com. 1982-85, indsl. devel. com. 1986), Okla. State U. Alumni Assn. (nat. bd. dirs. 1989—, nat. exec. com., 1992-97, pres. 1995-96, chmn. alumni ctr. task force 1998—, Disting. Alumni award 1998), Okla. County Alumni Assn. (bd. sec. 1987-88, treas. 1988-89, v.p. 1989-90, pres. 1990-91), Harvard Law Sch. Assn., ABA (labor and employment law sect. com. on devel. of law under Nat. Labor Rels. Act, com. on EEO law, litigation sect./employment and labor rels. law com.), Okla. Bar Assn. (labor and employment law sect. coun. 1978-83, 85-87, chmn. 1986), Okla. County Bar Assn., Fed. Bar Assn., U.S. Tennis Assn. (life). Civil rights, Labor (including EEOC, Fair Labor Standards Act, labor-management relations, NLRB, OSHA). Office: Crowe & Dunlevy Mid America Tower 20 N Broadway Ave Ste 1800 Oklahoma City OK 73102-8273

COURTEAU, GIRARD ROBERT, retired prosecutor; b. St. Paul, Minn., Aug. 21, 1942; s. Robert William and Laura Gertrude Courteau; m. Mary Linda Lucas, Apr. 3, 1964 (div. May 1997); m. Susan Frances DeBaca, Aug. 8, 1997; children: Steven, Girard, Devin, Heather. AA, Coll. Marin, 1965; BA, U. Calif., Berkeley, 1967; JD, U. Calif., 1970. Bar: Calif. 1971, U.S. Dist. Ct. (ctrl. dist.) Calif. 1971, U.S. Dist. Ct. (no. dist.) Calif. 1983. Dep. dist. atty. Monterey County, Calif., 1971, Marin County, San Rafael, Calif., 1972-2001; ret., 2001. Mem. editl. bd. Hasting's Law Jour., 1970; editor Marin Law Enforcement Newsletter, 1974-89. Named Prosecutor of the Yr., Marin County Dist. Attys. Office, San Rafael, Calif., 1987. Mem. Order of the Coif, Thurston Soc., Corvettes of Sonoma County, Palm Springs Corvettes Team ZR-1. Roman Catholic. Avocations: gardening, reading, corvettes. Home: 1307 Park St Santa Rosa CA 95404-3542 E-mail: courvettes@sbcglobal.net.

COURTNEY, ANN M. lawyer; b. 1951; BA, Bridgewater State Coll.; JD, Western New Eng. Coll. Bar: Maine 1989. Pvt. practice, Portland, Maine; asst. V.P. & Litigation counsel Unumprovident Corp. Mem. ABA, Maine State Bar Assn. (pres. 1999). Office: 517 Summit St Portland ME 04103 also: Unumprovident Corp 2211 Congress St Portland ME 04102*

COUSINS, WILLIAM, JR., retired judge; b. Swiftown, Miss., Oct. 6, 1927; s. William and Drusilla (Harris) C.; m. Hiroko Ogawa, May 12, 1953; children: Cheryl Akiko, Noel William, Yul Vincent, Gail Yoshiko. BA, U. Ill., 1948; LLB, Harvard U., 1951. Bar: Ill. 1953, U.S. Dist. Ct. (no. dist.) Ill. 1961, U.S. Supreme Ct. 1975. Title examiner Chgo. Title & Trust Co., 1953-57; asst. state's atty. Cook County, Ill., 1957-61; sole practice Chgo., 1961-67; judge Circuit Ct. Cook County, Chgo., 1976-92; justice Ill. Appellate Ct., 1992—2002. Chair exec. com. 1st Dist. Appellate Ct., 1997-98; lectr. DePaul Law Sch., Chgo.; bd. dirs. Nat. Ctr. State Cts., 1996-2002; faculty advisor Nat. Jud. Coll., 1987; mem. exec. com. Ill. Jud. Conf., 1983-2002, former chmn. exec. com.; liaison assoc. judge coordinating com.; former chmn. Ill. Jud. Coun. Bd. dirs. Ind. Voters Ill., 1964-67, Ams. for Dem. Action, 1968, Operation PUSH, 1971-76, Nat. Ctr. for State Cts.; mem. Chgo. City Coun., 1967-76; del. Dem. Nat. Conv., 1972; asst. moderator United Ch. of Christ, N.Y.C., 1981. Served with U.S. Army, 1951-53. Decorated Army Commendation medal; named Judge of Yr., John Marshall Law Sch., Chgo., 1980; recipient Thurgood Marshall award Ill. Jud. Coun., 1992, Earl Burris Dickerson award Chgo. Bar Assn., 1998, C. Francis Stradford award, 2001. Mem. ABA, Nat. Bar Assn. (jud. coun., Raymond Pace Alexander award 1999, Hall of Fame 1994), Ill. Bar Assn., Cook County Bar Assn. (former bd. dirs., Edward N. Wright award 1968, William R. Ming award 1974, Hall of Fame 1997), Alpha Kappa Alpha (Monarch award for Statesmanship 1995), Kappa Alpha Psi, Sigma Pi Phi, Delta Sigma Rho. Home: 1745 E 83rd Pl Chicago IL 60617-1714 Fax: 773-374-4316. E-mail: wmcousins1@ameritech.net.

COUVILLION, DAVID IRVIN, federal judge; b. Simmesport, La., Oct. 27, 1934; s. J. Forest Couvillion and Leontine Rabalais. BS, La. State U., 1956, JD, 1959; LLM, Georgetown U., 1973. Bar: La. 1959. Pvt. practice, Marksville, La., 1959-67; adminstrv. asst. U.S. Congressman Speedy O. Long, Washington, 1967-72; assoc. McCollister, McCleary, Fazio and Holliday, Baton Rouge, 1974-85; spl. trial judge U.S. Tax Ct., Washington, 1985—. Mem. ABA, La. State Bar Assn. Office: US Tax Ct 400 2nd St NW Washington DC 20217-0002

COVIELLO, FRANK JOSEPH, lawyer; b. Washington, Dec. 27, 1940; s. Francis George and Mary Louise (Martini) C. BA, Western Car. U., 1966; LLB, U. Balt., 1969. Bar: Md. 1971, U.S. Dist. Ct. (4th cir.) 1971, U.S. Dist. Ct. D.C. 1985, U.S. Ct. Appeals (4th cir.) 1985. Law clk. Circuit Ct. for Montgomery County, Rockville, Md., 1969-71; asst. state's atty. Montgomery County, Rockville, 1971-73; pvt. practice, 1974-84; ptnr. Bivona & Cohen, Rockville, 1984-89, Gilberg & Kurent, Gaithersburg, 1989-90; pvt. practice Gaithersburg, 1990—. With U.S. Army, 1961-64. Mem. Montgomery County Bar Assn., D.C. Bar Assn. Roman Catholic. Avocations: tennis, skiing, scuba diving. General civil litigation, Personal injury (including property damage), Product liability. Fax: 301-208-9063. E-mail: fjcoviello_esq@surfmk.com.

COVINGTON, GEORGE MORSE, lawyer; b. Lake Forest, Ill., Oct. 4, 1942; s. William Slaughter and Elizabeth (Morse) C.; m. Shelagh Tait Hickey, Dec.28, 1966 (div. May 1995); children: Karen Morse, Jean Tait, Sarah Ingersoll Covington; m. Barbara Schilling Trentham, Dec. 19, 1998. AB, Yale U., 1964; JD, U. Chgo., 1967. Assoc. Gardner, Carton & Douglas, Chgo., 1970-75, ptnr., 1976-95; atty. pvt. practice, Lake Forest, Ill., 1995—. Lectr. in field. Contbr. articles to profl. jours. Active Grant Hosp. of Chgo., 1974-95, chmn. of bd. 1990-95; bd. dirs. Grant Healthcare Found., 1995—, chmn. 1999—; trustee Chgo. Acad. Sci., 1974-85, pres., 1980-82; trustee, chmn. Ill. chpt. Nature Conservancy, Chgo., 1974-88; bd. dirs. Latin Sch Chgo., 1979-80, Open Lands Project, Chgo., 1972-86, Chgo. Farmers, 1994-96; bd. dirs., sec. Lake Forest Open Lands Assn., 1984—; bd. dirs., sec., treas. Les Cheneaux Found., 1978—; bd. dirs. Student Conservation Assn., 1996—, Little Traverse Conservancy, 1998—, vice chmn., 1999-2002, chmn., 2002—; mem. Bd. Fire and Police Commrs., Village of Lake Bluff, Ill., 1991—. With U.S. Army, 1967-69. Mem. ABA, Ill. Bar Assn., Lake County Bar Assn., Chgo. Bar Assn., Univ. Club (bd. dirs. 1985-88), Commonwealth Club, Legal Club, Shoreacres (Lake Bluff, Ill.), Les Cheneaux Club (Cedarville, Mich.), Lambda Alpha. Land use and zoning (including planning), Property, real (including real estate development, water). Office: 500 N Western Ave Ste 204 Lake Forest IL 60045-1955

COVINGTON, MARLOW STANLEY, retired lawyer; b. Langhorne, Pa., Apr. 25, 1937; s. Marlow O. and Madalyn L. (Johnson) C.; m. Laura Aline Wallace, Aug. 28, 1965; children: Lisa M., Scott, Eric (dec.). BS, Bloomsburg U., 1959; postgrad., Rutgers U., 1960; JD, Howard U., 1965. Bar: D.C. 1971, U.S. Dist. Ct. D.C. 1971, U.S. Supreme Ct. 1975, U.S. Dist. Ct. Md. 1981, Md. 1985. Tchr. Pub. Schs., Long Branch, N.J., 1959-62; referee N.J. Dept. Labor, Newark, 1965-66; claim examiner Allstate's Ins. Co., Verona, N.J., 1966-71, house counsel Washington, Greenbelt, Md., 1971-97; sr. trial atty. Allstate Ins. Co., Greenbelt, Md., 1989-96; ret., 1996. Mem. adv. bd. Inverness Custom Plastics, Inc., Barrington, Ill., 1990—. Recipient cert. of recognition Balt.-Washington area Fellowship Christian Athletes, 1981. Mem. ABA (com. ins. negligence and compensation sect.), D.C. Bar Assn. (com. ins. and compensation sect.), Nat. Bar Assn., Bloomsburg U. Alumni Assn. (bd. dirs. 1977-80), Sigma Delta Tau, Gamma Theta Upsilon. Avocation: collecting antique pocket knives. Corporate, general, Insurance, Personal injury (including property damage). Home: 16001 Amina Dr Burtonsville MD 20866-1039 Fax: 301-421-4329. E-mail: SCoving104@aol.com.

COVINGTON, VONDA RUSSELL, lawyer; b. Kenosha, Wis., Feb. 7, 1958; d. Kenneth Kirk Marshall and Wanda Ann Belmont; m. Ronald L. Russell, Aug. 18, 1990; 1 child, Samantha. BA in Psychology, U. Calif., San Diego, 1980; MA in Psychology, Rice U., 1984; JD, U. Houston, 1992. Bar: Oreg. 1992, 1993 (Tex.). Law clk. Martin, Herring & Fjeldal, Houston, 1990—91; office mgr. Challenger Drywall, Inc., 1991—92; law clk. Fjeldal & Assocs., Houston, 1993, atty., 1993—95; pvt. practice Houston, 1995—. Mem.: Coll. State Bar Tex., Houston Bar Assn. (mem. family law sect.), Internat. Assn. Collaborative Profls., Alliance Collaborative Family Law Attys. (founder, bd. mem.), Assn. Women Attys. Unitarian-Universalist. Avocations: rock climbing, camping, weightlifting. Family and matrimonial, General practice. Office: Ste 1515 1314 Texas Houston TX 77002 Fax: 713-773-4383. E-mail: vonda@pdq.net.

COWAN, BARTON ZALMAN, lawyer; b. Cleve., Mar. 3, 1934; s. Milton Jerome and Clara (Umans) C.; m. Teri Anne Thomas, June 25, 1961; children: Pamela B., Cynthia R. Stewart, Susan L. Kraft AB with honors, U. Mich., 1955; JD cum laude, Harvard U., 1958. Bar: Ohio 1958, Pa. 1962, U.S. Dist. Ct. (we. dist.) Pa., U.S. Ct. Appeals (3d, 4th and D.C. cirs.), U.S. Supreme Ct. Assoc. Eckert Seamans Cherin & Mellott, Pitts., 1961-67; mem. Eckert Seamans Cherin & Mellott LLC, Pitts., 1968-1999, spl. counsel, 2000—. Chmn. lawyers com., mem. policy com. Atomic Indsl. Forum, Washington, 1981—87; chmn. lawyers com. Nuc. Mgmt. and Resource Coun., Washington, 1988—90; vis. prof. law W.Va. Univ. Coll. Law, 2001—. Life trustee, chair Pitts. chpt. Am. Jewish Com.; mem. bd.overseers Hebrew Union Coll. Jewish Inst. Religion Pitts., 1986-2002; Pitts. Symphony Soc.; bd. dirs. ARZA/World Union N.Am., Union Am. Hebrew Congregations; life trustee, past pres. Rodef Shalom Congregation, Pitts. 1st lt. USAF, 1958-61. Recipient Clyde A. Lilly award Atomic Indsl. Forum, Inc., 1985, Hebrew Inst. Pitts. award for leadership, 1991, Jewish Edn. Inst. award for dedication and commitment to Jewish edn., 1992, State of Israel bonds award, 1993, 2002, Am. Jewish Com. Human Rels. award, 1996. Mem. ABA (chmn. energy resources law com., tort and ins. practice sect. 1986-87), Pa. Bar Assn., Allegheny County Bar Assn., Internat. Nuclear Law Assn., Duquesne Club. Republican. Corporate, general, Nuclear power, Labor (including EEOC, Fair Labor Standards Act, labor-management relations, NLRB, OSHA). Office: Eckert Seamans Cherin & Mellott LLC 600 Grant St Ste 44th Pittsburgh PA 15219-2702 E-mail: bzc@escm.com., teribart61@aol.com.

COWAN, CASPAR FRANK, lawyer; b. Calais, Maine, May 7, 1915; s. Frank Irving and Helen Anna (Caspar) C.; m. Nancy Hopkinson Linnell, Oct. 19, 1946; children; Joanna Cowan Allen, Seth W., June Cowan Roelle. AB, Bowdoin Coll., 1936; JD, Harvard U., 1940. Bar: Maine 1940, U.S. Dist. Ct. Maine 1941, U.S. Ct. Appeals (1st cir.) 1946. Assoc. Cowan and Cowan, Portland, Maine, 1940-48, Perkins, Thompson, Hinckley & Keddy, Portland, Maine, 1948-51, ptnr., 1951-93. Author: Maine Real Estate Law and Practice. Chmn. Portland Renewal Authority, 1952-64; chmn. Portland Housing Authority, 1958-59. Lt. U.S. Army, 1942-46. Decorated Bronze

Star. Mem. ABA, Maine State Bar Assn. (econs. practice law com., life stds. com.), Cumberland County Bar Assn., 10th Mt. Divsn. Alumni Assn., Maine Charitable Mechanics Assn., Woodfords Club, Junto Club. Probate (including wills, trusts), Property, real (including real estate development, water), Personal income taxation. Home and Office: 99 Vannah Ave Portland ME 04103-4510

COWAN, DALE HARVEY, internist, lawyer; b. Cleve., Jan. 25, 1938; s. Milton Jerome and Clara (Umans) jC.; m. Deborah Wolowitz, Jan. 28, 1967; children: Rachel, Morris Benjamin, William Ezra. AB, Harvard U., 1959, MD, 1963; JD, Case Western Res. U., 1981. Diplomate Am. Bd. Internal Medicine with subspecialty cert. in hematology and med. oncology. Bar: Ohio 1981. Intern Cleve. Met. Gen. Hosp., 1963-64, resident, 1964-65, 67-70; practice medicine specializing in internal medicine, hematology and oncology; dir. hematology and oncology Marymount Hosp., Cleve., 1982-2001; asst. prof. medicine Case Western Res. U., Cleve., 1970-75, assoc. prof., 1975-84, clin. prof. environ. health scis., 1985—; assoc. Health Sys. Mgmt. Ctr., 1982-90; of counsel Burke, Haber & Berick, 1984-86; pres. med. staff Parma (Ohio) Cmty. Gen. Hosp., 1997-98; med. dir. Cmty. Oncology Group Cleve. Clinic Found., Cleve., 1999—. Spl. cons. President's Commn. on Bioethics, Washington, 1981-82; mem. nat. adv. coun. Nat. Heart Lung and Blood Inst., Bethesda, Md., 1982-85. Author: Preferred Provider Organizations, 1984; co-editor: Human Organ Transplantation, 1987; contbr. articles to profl. jours. Bd. dirs. Bur. Jewish Edn., 1977-87, Northeast Ohio affiliate Am. Heart Assn., 1982-86; pres. Ohio/W.Va. Oncology Soc., 1990-94; trustee No. Ohio Cancer Resource Ctr., 1998-2001, chmn. 1999-2001. Lt. comdr. USPHS, 1965-67. Fellow ACP, Am. Coll. Legal Medicine (bd. govs. 2001—); mem. AMA, Am. Soc. Hematology, Am. Soc. Clin. Oncology, Am. Assn. for Cancer Rsch., Am. Health Lawyers Assn. (bd. dirs. 1988-94), Am. Soc. Law and Medicine, Acad. Medicine Cleve. (pres. 1997-98), Cleve. Med. Libr. Assn. (pres.-elect 2003—), Ohio State Bar Assn., Greater Cleve. Bar Assn. Home: 19600 Shaker Blvd Cleveland OH 44122-1830 Office: 6100 W Creek Rd Ste 15 Cleveland OH 44131-2133 E-mail: cowand@ccf.org

COWAN, FAIRMAN CHAFFEE, lawyer; b. Wellesley Hills, Mass., Apr. 22, 1915; s. James Franklin and Hortense Victoria (Fairman) C.; m. Martha Logan Allis, Apr. 24, 1943; children: Douglas Fairman, Frederick Allis, Leonard Chaffee. AB magna cum laude, Amherst Coll., 1937; LLB, Harvard U., 1940; AMP, Harvard Bus. Sch., 1963. Bar: Mass. 1940. Assoc. Goodwin, Procter & Hoar, Boston, 1940-41; ptnr. Goodwin, Proctor & Hoar, 1952-54; gen. counsel, clk., sec., v.p., dir. Norton Co., 1955-79; counsel Bowditch & Dewey, Worcester, Mass., 1979-90. Mem. Citizen Plan E Assn. Worcester, 1957-87; vice chmn. Worcester Civic Ctr. Commn., 1977-79; chmn. Pvt. Industry Coun., Worcester Area CETA Consortium, 1979-83; bd. dirs. Legal Assistance Corp. of Ctr. Mass., 1982-86, Social Svc. Planning Corp., 1975-88, Worcester Mcpl. Rsch. Bur., Inc., 1986—, Mass. Job Tng. Inc., 1983-92, Elder Home Care Svcs. of Worcester, Inc., 1987-92, Daybreak, Inc., 1993-96; incorporator Alliance for Edn., 1986—, Worcester Dynamy, Inc., 1992—, Worcester YWCA, 2001—, Worcester Hist. Mus., 1995—, YOU, Inc., 1983—, ARC Ctrl. Mass., 2000—; mem. State Job Tng. Coordinating Coun., 1985-87, Worcester Housing Partnership, 1986-93; trustee Clark U., 1964-76, 79—, Meml. Hosp., Worcester, 1967-86, United Way Ctrl. Mass., 2000—; mem. bd. overseers Planned Parenthood League Mass., 1992-2001, mem. adv. bd. Mass. Coastal Resource Bd., 1992—. Lt. USNR, 1942-45. Recipient Isaiah Thomas award, 1995. Mem. Am. Antiquarian Soc., Mass. Civic League (v.p. 1947), Worcester Club, Worcester Com. on Fgn. Rels., Phi Beta Kappa, Alpha Delta Phi. Home: 48 Berwick St Worcester MA 01602-1443 E-mail: fcowan1059@aol.com.

COWAN, FREDERIC JOSEPH, lawyer; b. N.Y.C., Oct. 11, 1945; s. Frederic Joseph Sr. and Mary Virginia (Wesley) C.; m. Linda Marshall Scholle, Apr. 28, 1974; children: Elizabeth, Caroline, Allison. AB, Dartmouth Coll., 1967; JD, Harvard U., 1978. Bar: Ky. 1978, U.S. Dist. Ct. (we. dist.) Ky. 1979, U.S. Ct. Appeals (6th cir.) 1984, U.S. Supreme Ct. 1989. Vol. Peace Corps, Ethiopia, 1967-69; assoc. Brown, Todd & Heyburn, Louisville, 1979-83; ptnr. Rice, Porter, Seiller & Price, Louisville, 1983-87; atty. gen. Commonwealth of Ky., 1988-92; counsel Lynch, Cox, Gilman & Manan P.S.C., 1992—. Ky. State Rep., 32d legis. dist., 1982-87; chair Ky. Child Support Enforcement Commn., 1988-91, Ky. Sexual Abuse and Exploitation Prevention Bd., 1988-91; bd. dirs. Ky. Job Tng. Coordinating Council, Frankfort, Louisville Bar Found., 1986. Vice chmn. judiciary criminal com. Ky. Ho. of Reps., 1985-87; chmn. budget com. on justice Judiciary and Corrections Ky. Ho. of Reps., 1985-87, Leadership Ky., 1985; U.S. del. election mission to Namibia Nat. Dem. Inst. for Internat. Affairs, 1989; U.S. del. dem. instns. seminar Nat. Dem. Inst. for Internat. Affairs, Slovenia, 1992; electoral supr. Orgn. for Security and Cooperation in Europe, Bosnia and Herzogovina, 1996; adv. com. Samara Oblast, Russia, 2001. Mem. ABA (adv. com. east european law initiative 2001), Ky. Bar Assn., Louisville Bar Assn., Ky. Acad. Trial Attys. Methodist. Administrative and regulatory, General civil litigation, Communications. Home: 1747 Sulgrave Rd Louisville KY 40205-1643 Office: 400 W Market St Ste 2200 Louisville KY 40202-3354

COWAN, JOHN JOSEPH, retired lawyer; b. Chester, Pa., Nov. 14, 1932; s. John Joseph and Helen Marie (Frame) C.; m. Hilary Ann Gregory, Dec. 29, 1960; children: Daniel, Patrick, Meg, Jennifer. AB, LaSalle Coll., 1954; JD cum laude, U. Pa., 1959. Bar: D.C. 1960, Ohio 1964, W.Va. 1968, U.S. Supreme Ct. 1971. Tchg. fellow Stanford U., Palo Alto, Calif., 1959-60; trial atty. civil divsn. U.S. Dept. Justice, Washington, 1960-63; assoc. Taft, Stettinius & Hollister, Cin., 1963-67; gen. atty. Chesapeake & Potomac Tel. Co. of W.Va., Charleston, 1968-79; ptnr. Sullivan & Cowan, Charleston, 1979-82; sole practice Charleston, 1982-98; ret., 1998. Sr. adv. editor U. Pa. Law Rev., 1958-59. Served to 1st lt. AUS, 1954-56. Mem. ABA. Federal civil litigation, State civil litigation, Criminal. Home and Office: 300 Sweetbriar Rd Greenville SC 29615

COWAN, STUART MARSHALL, lawyer; b. Irvington, N.J., Mar. 20, 1932; s. Bernard Howard and Blanche (Hertz) C.; m. Marilyn R.C. Toepfer, Apr., 1961 (div. 1968); m. Eleanor Schmerel, June, 1953 (dec.); m. Jane Alison Averill, Feb. 24, 1974 (div. 1989); children: Fran Lori, Catherine R.L., Erika R.L., Bronwen P.; m. Victoria Yi, Nov. 11, 1989. BS in Econs., U. Pa., 1952; LLB, Rutgers U., 1955. Bar: N.J. 1957, Hawaii 1962, U.S. Supreme Ct. 1966. Atty. Greenstein & Cowan, Honolulu, 1961-70, Cowan & Frey, Honolulu, 1970-89; pvt. practice, 1989—; of counsel Price Okamoto Himeno & Lum, 1993—. Arbitrator Fed. Mediation & Conciliation Svc., Honolulu, 1972—, Am. Arbitration Assn., Honolulu, 1968—, Hawaii Pub. Employee Rels. Bd., 1972—. Pres. Hawaii Epilepsy Soc., 1984-86; acquisition chair Hawaii Family Support Ctr., 1995-97. Lt. USN, 1955-61. Mem. ABA, Hawaii Bar Assn., Am. Judicature Soc., Assn. Trial Lawyers Am. (state committeeman for hawii 1965-69, bd. govs. 1972-75), Consumer Lawyers Hawaii, Hawaii Trial Lawyers Assn. (v.p. 1972-78), Japan-Hawaii Lawyers Assn., Soc. Profls. in Dispute Resolution, Inter Pacific Bar Assn., Honolulu Symphony Soc. (bd. dirs. 1989-99), Hawaii Epilepsy soc. (pres. 1984-86), Royal Order of Kamehameha, Order of St. Stanislas, Sovereign Order of St. John of Jerusalem Knights Hospitallers, Mil. Order of Temple at Jerusalem, Queen's Club, Waikiki Yacht Club, St. Francis Yacht Club, Hawaii Yacht Club, Plaza Club, Hawaii Scottish Assn. (chieftain 1983-88), St. Andrews Soc., Caledonian Soc. (vice chieftain 1983-85), Honolulu Pipes and Drums (sec.-treas. 1985-90), New Zealand Police Pipe Band, Masons (York Rite, Scottish Rite no. and so. jurisdictions, 33 deg., Grand Lodge Hawaii, grand orator 1992, sr. grand steward 1993, jr. grand warden 1994, sr. grand warden 1995, grand master 1997), Red Cross of Constantine, Royal Order Scotland, Pearl Harbor (master 1971, chaplain 1992-96), Masonic Kilties N.J., Masada (#51 N.J.), USS Missouri Meml. Assn., Nat. Sojourners (1st v.p.), Elks, Chinese Acacia Club, Royal Hawaiian Ocean Racing Club. Jewish. Home: 47-339 Mapumapu Rd Kaneohe HI 96744-4922 Office: Ste 728 Ocean View Ctr 707 Richards St Honolulu HI 96813-4616 also: 47-653 Kamehameha Hwy # 202 Kaneohe HI 96744-4965 E-mail: stuartgm@juno.com.

COWAN, WALLACE EDGAR, lawyer; b. Jersey City, Jan. 28, 1924; s. Benjamin and Dorothy (Zunz) C.; m. Ruth Daitzman, June 8, 1947; children: Laurie, Paul, Judith. BS magna cum laude, NYU, 1947; JD cum laude, Harvard U., 1950. Ptnr. Stroock, Stroock & Lavan, N.Y.C., 1950-93, of counsel, 1994—. Dir. Ametek, Inc., Paoli, Pa., 1982-93, sec., 1969-93, sec. H.S. Stuttman, Inc., Westport, Conn., to 1996; adv. bd. Hackensack River Greenway, Teaneck, N.J. Mem. Teaneck (N.J.) Adv. Bd. on Parks, Playgrounds and Recreation, 1966—, chmn., 1974—; pres. No. Valley Commuters Assn.; past pres., life trustee Congregation Beth Sholom, Teaneck; mem. Forum adv. bd. Sch.-Based Youth Svcs. Project, 1998—. 1st lt. USAF, 1942-45, ETO. Decorated Air medal with silver cluster; recipient Vol. in the Parks award Bergen County, N.J., 1993, Disting. Svc. award Bergen County, N.J., 1994, Disting. Achievement award Bergen County, N.J., 2001. Mem. Beta Gamma Sigma. Commercial, contracts (including sales of goods; commercial financing), Corporate, general, Securities. Home: 499 Emerson Ave Teaneck NJ 07666-1927 Office: Stroock Stroock & Lavan 180 Maiden Ln New York NY 10038-4937

COWART, T(HOMAS) DAVID, lawyer; b. San Benito, Tex., June 12, 1953; s. Thomas W. Jr. and Glenda Claire (Miller) C.; children: Thomas Kevin, Lauren Michelle, Megan Leigh; m. Greta E. Gerberding, Aug. 12, 1995. BBA, U. Miss., 1975, JD, 1978; LLM in Taxation, NYU, 1979. CPA Tex., Miss.; bar: Miss. 1978, Tex. 1979. Assoc. Dossett, Magruder & Montgomery, Jackson, Miss., 1978, Strasburger & Price, Dallas, 1979-87; ptnr., assoc., shareholder Johnson & Gibbs, Dallas, 1988-90; shareholder Jenkens & Gilchrist, Dallas, 1991—. Adj. prof. law So. Meth. U. Sch. Law, 1988; mem. key dist. adv. coun. IRS, Dallas, 1989—95, chmn., 1990—93; mem. Coll. State Bar Tex.; lectr. in field. Mem. editl. bd.: Flexible Benefits, 1993—, 401k Advisor, 1994—, COBRA, 1996—. Mem. adv. com. Goals for Dallas, 1984-85; vol. Children's Med. Ctr., 1992-96. Recipient Best Lawyer in Am. award, 2001—02, 2003—, Best Lawyer in Dallas award, 2003. Mem.: ABA (sect. taxation, employee benefit com., vice-chmn. 1995—97, chmn. elect 1997—98, chmn. 1998—99, sect. 83 issues task force, chmn. health plan designs issues subcom. 1992—95, health care task force 1991—98, chmn.-designate joint com. on employee benefits 1997—99, chmn. joint com. employee benefits 1999—2000), Dallas Bar Found., Am. Law Inst., Phi Alpha Phi, Dallas Benefits Soc. (co-moderator 1991—92, bd. dirs. 1991—93), S.W. Benefits Assn. (bd. dirs. 1994—97), Dallas Bar Assn. (lectr. 1985—, coun. mem. employee benefits sect. 1989—92, treas. 1992, sec. 1993, v.p. 1994, pres. 1995), State Bar Tex. (sect. taxation, com. compensation and employee benefits, fed. legislation, regulations and revenue rulings subcom. 1986—87, chmn. fiduciary stds. for trustees subcom. 1987—88), Am. Coll. Employee Benefits Counsel (1st chair, charter mem.), Beta Alpha Psi, Omicron Delta Kappa. Pension, profit-sharing, and employee benefits. Office: Jenkens & Gilchrist 1445 Ross Ave Ste 3200 Dallas TX 75202-2785 E-mail: dcowart@jenkens.com.

COWDEN, JOHN WILLIAM, lawyer; b. Springfield, Mo., June 3, 1945; s. John Marshall and Laura Alice (Lemmon) C.; m. Carol Jean Avery, Jan. 27, 1968; children: Jennifer, John. BA, Southwest Mo. State U., 1967; JD, U. Mo., 1970. Bar: Mo. 1970, U.S. Dist. Ct. (we. dist.) Mo. 1971, U.S. Ct. Appeals (8th cir.) 1980, U.S. Supreme Ct. 1982. Asst. atty. gen. State of Mo., Jefferson City, 1970-71; assoc. Morrison, Hecker, Curtis, Kuder & Parrish, Kansas City, Mo., 1971-76, ptnr., 1976-89, Baker, Sterchi & Cowden, Kansas City, 1989—. Co-author: Missouri Evidence Restated. Chmn. human devel. bd. YMCA, Kansas City; bd. dirs. Gt. Am. Basketball League, Johnson City, Kans., 1986-88. Mem. ABA, Mo. Bar Assn., Kansas City Bar Assn., Lawyers Assn. Kansas City, Am. Bd. Trial Advs., Am. Coll. Trial Lawyers, Internat. Assn. Def. Counsel, Def. Rsch. Inst., U. Mo. Law Soc., Indian Hills Country Club, Univ. Club. Avocations: golf, travel. Federal civil litigation, General civil litigation, State civil litigation. Home: 6827 Linden St Prairie Village KS 66208-1427 Office: 2400 Pershing Rd Kansas City MO 64108-2504

COWDERY, ALLEN CRAIG, lawyer; b. Bartlesville, Okla., July 1, 1943; s. Herman Charles and Jane (Sparr) C.; m. Jane Reed, May 31, 1969; children: Elizabeth, Owen. B.A., Okla. U., 1965, J.D., 1968. Bar: Okla. 1968, Kans. 1973, Tex. 1976. Staff atty. Koch Industries, Inc., Wichita, Kans., 1968-74; sr. assoc. counsel Mitchell Energy & Devel. Corp., Houston, 1974-81; v.p., gen. counsel, sec. Tex. Internat. Petroleum Corp., Oklahoma City, 1981-83; gen. counsel, v.p. Samson Resources Co., Tulsa, 1983-86; sole practice, 1986—. Mem. ABA, Okla. Bar Assn., Kans. Bar Assn., Tex. Bar Assn., Tulsa Bar Assn., Oklahoma City Bar Assn. Republican. Episcopalian. Fax: 918-495-0653. Criminal, Family and matrimonial, General practice. Home: 6816 E 105th St Tulsa OK 74133-6757 Office: PO Box 701583 Tulsa OK 74170-1583

COWDERY, CHARLES KENDRICK, lawyer, writer, consultant; b. Mansfield, Ohio, Sept. 5, 1951; s. Joseph Kendrick and Carol Francis (Bunsey) C. BS in Radio-TV-Film, Miami U., Oxford, Ohio, 1973; JD, DePaul U., 1996. Bar: Ill. 1996. Ops. mgr. Sta. WOXR, Oxford, 1973-74; writer-producer El-Bee Advt, Inc., Dayton, Ohio, 1974-75, Byer and Bowman Advt., Columbus, Ohio, 1975-78; radio-TV dir. Fessel, Siegfriedt and Moeller Advt., Louisville, 1978-80; writer Price Weber Mktg. Communications, Louisville, 1980-86; pres. Charles K. Cowdery, Inc., Louisville, 1986-87, Chgo., 1987-90; exec. creative dir. Rogers Merchandising, Inc., Chgo., 1987; freelance writer, cons. Chgo., 1990—; pvt. practice lawyer, 1996—. Pub. The Bourbon Country Reader. Author: Blues Legends, 1995. Mem. Maxwell St. Historic Preservation Coalition.

COWELL, MARION AUBREY, JR., lawyer; b. Wilmington, N.C., Dec. 25, 1934; s. Marion Aubrey and Alice Saunders (Hargett) C.; m. Norma Hearne; children: Lindsay G., Mark P., Kathryn Huffman, Graham Shannonhouse, Elizabeth Shannonhouse, Mary Robbins Whisnant. BSBA, U. N.C., 1958, LLB, 1964. Bar: N.C. 1964. Pvt. practice law, Durham, N.C., 1964-72; assoc. Bryant, Lipton, Bryant and Battle, 1964-69, ptnr., 1971-72; pvt. practice law Durham, 1969-70; gen. counsel Cameron Brown Co., Raleigh, N.C., 1972-78; exec. v.p., gen. counsel, sec. First Union Corp., Charlotte, N.C., 1978-99, Kilpatrick-Stockton LLP, Charlotte, N.C., 1999—. Office: Kilpatrick Stockton LLP 214 N Tyron St Ste 2500 Charlotte NC 28202-6001 Office Fax: 704-371-8279.*

COWEN, WILSON, judge; b. nr. Clifton, Tex., Dec. 20, 1905; s. John Rentz and Florence Juno (McFadden) Cowen; m. Florence Elizabeth Walker, Apr. 18, 1930; children: W. Walker, John E. LLB, U. Tex., 1928. Bar: Tex. 1928. Pvt. practice, Dalhart, Tex., 1928—34; judge Dallam County, Tex., 1935—38; Tex. dir. Farm Security Adminstrn., 1938—40, regional dir., 1940—42; commr. U.S. Ct. Claims, Washington, 1942—43, 1945—59, chief commr., 1959—64, chief judge, 1964—77, sr. judge, 1977—82; sr. judge fed. cir. U.S. Ct. Appeals, Washington, 1982—98. Asst. adminstr. War Food Adminstrn., 1943—45; spl. asst. to sec. agr., 1945; mem. Jud. Conf. U.S., 1964—77. Mem.: FBA, ABA, State Bar Tex., Cosmos Club (Washington), Delta Theta Phi, Order of Coif. Presbyterian. Home: 2512 Q St NW Apt 205 Washington DC 20007-4310 Office: US Ct Appeal Federal Circuit 717 Madison Pl NW Washington DC 20439-0002

COWIN, JUDITH A. state supreme court judge; m. William; 3 children. Grad., Wellesley Coll., Harvard U. Prosecutor, Norfolk County; judge Mass. Superior Ct.; assoc. justice Mass. Supreme Judicial Ct., Boston, 1999—. Office: Mass Supreme Judicial Ct 1300 New Courthouse Pemberton Sq Boston MA 02108

COWLES, ROBERT LAWRENCE, lawyer; b. Jacksonville, Fla., Feb. 5, 1942; m. Barbara Bearden; children: Robert L., Kelli R. McMullin. BS, U. N.C., 1964; JD, Emory U. Law Sch., 1969. Bar: Fla. 1969, Ga. 1969. Claims adjuster, supr. Travelers Ins. Co., Jacksonville, Atlanta, N.Y.C., 1964-68; assoc. Neely, Freeman & Hawkins, Atlanta, 1968-69, Swift, Currie, McGhee & Hiers, Atlanta, 1969-71; dir. Howell, Kirby, Montgomery, D'Aiuto, Dean & Hallowes PA, Jacksonville, 1971-76; pres. Cowles, Coker & Myers, Jacksonville, 1976-83, Cowles, Coker, Myers, Schickel & Pierce PA, Atlanta, 1982-83, Cowles, Hayden, Facciolo, McMorrow & Barfield PA, Jacksonville, 1984-87; judge Fourth Jud. Cir. Ct., Atlanta, 1987-90; comdr. Legler, Werber, Dawes, Sadler & Howell PA, Jacksonville, 1990-91; pvt. practice Law Offices of Robert L. Cowles, 1991-93; ptnr. Cowles & Shaughnessy PA, Jacksonville, 1993-2000; pvt. practice The Cowles Law Firm, Jacksonville, 2000—01; assoc. Wood Atter & Assocs., Jacksonville, 2001—. Bd. dirs. Boys Home of Jacksonville, 1989—. Mem. Am. Bd. Trial Advocacy, Fla. Bar Assn. (chmn. bd. cert. civil trial lawyers com. 1998-00, chmn. 1998-99), State Bar Ga. Avocations: golfing, gardening, travel. State civil litigation, Product liability, Professional liability. Office: Wood Atter & Assocs 333-1 E Monroe St Jacksonville FL 32202-2834 E-mail: rcowles@woodatter.com.

COWNIE, WILLIAN GARRY, lawyer; b. Sioux City, Iowa, Oct. 4, 1958; s. William Garry and Marie Francis (Hanna) C.; m. Louanne Marie Junck, Dec. 16, 1978; children: Amanda, Abigail, Ashley. BA, Morningside Coll., 1980; JD, U. Mo., 1982. Bar: Mo. 1982, Kans. 1992, U.S. Dist. Ct. Mo. 1982. Assoc. Neiwald, Waldeck & Brown, Kansas City, 1982-84; claims atty. Amoco Corp., Kansas City, 1984-92; atty. pvt. practice, Lees Junction, Mo., 1992—. Mem. Kansas City Met. Bar Assn. Avocations: exercising, reading, reading, travel. Personal injury (including property damage). Office: PO Box 1276 Lees Summit MO 64063-8276 E-mail: lslaw@sound.net.

COWPERTHWAIT, LINDLEY MURRAY, lawyer; b. Abington, Pa., Mar. 13, 1933; s. Lindley Murray Cowperthwait and Ruth Bronde Nicholas; m. Suzanne Dewees, Nov. 26, 1955 (div. July 1976); children: Murray, Mary Ruth, Edward, Linda, Tom, Suzanne; m. Karin Schmid Cowperthwait, Apr. 1, 1989. BA, Calif. State U., 1957; LLB, U. Pa., 1960, JD, 1970. Assoc. Wisler, Pearlstine, Talone Craig & Garrity, Norristown, Pa., 1960-68, ptnr., 1968-80; pvt. practice Norristown, 1980-96; of counsel High, Swartz, Roberts & Seidel, LLP, Norristown, 1997—. Prodr., author, dir. (video) Medicine for Lawyers, 1980-93; author: Damages-Delay and Punitive 1999, 2000, 2001, Scrivener Med-Leg Code of Ethics, 1960, 75, 94, 2001. Bd. dirs. ARC, Norristown, 1993-95, Big Bros./Big Sisters, Norristown, 1985-92. Recipient Citizenship award Big Bros./Big Sisters, 1992. Mem. Pa. Trial Lawyers Assn. (pres. 1974-75), Montgomery County Trial Lawyers (founder, sec. 1965-74), Assn. Trial Lawyers of Am., Pa. Bar Assn., Pa. Soc. Republican. Episcopalian. Avocation: sailing. Federal civil litigation, General civil litigation, State civil litigation. Office: High Swartz Roberts & Seidel LLP 40 E Airy St Norristown PA 19401-4803

COWSER, DANNY LEE, lawyer, mental health specialist; b. Peoria, Ill., July 7, 1948; s. Albert Paul Cowser and Shirley Mae (Donaldson) Chatten; m. Nancy Lynn Hatch, Nov. 11, 1976; children: Kimberly Catherine Hatch Cowser, Dustin Paul Hatch Cowser. BA, No. Ill. U., 1972, MS, 1975; JD, DePaul U., 1980. Bar: Ill. 1980, Wis. 1981, U.S. Dist. Ct. (no. dist.) Ill. 1981, U.S. Ct. Appeals (7th cir.) 1983, U.S. Dist. Ct. (ea. and we. dists.) Wis. 1984, U.S. Supreme Ct. 1984, Ariz. 1985, U.S. Ct. Appeals (9th cir.) 1987, U.S. Dist. Ct. Ariz. 1989, U.S. Tax Ct. 1990, U.S. Ct. Claims 1990, Colo. 2000. Adminstr. Ill. Dept. Mental Health, Elgin, 1972-76, psychotherapist, 1976-79; assoc. Slaby, Deda & Henderson, Phillips, Wis., 1982-83; ptnr. Slaby, Deda & Cowser, Phillips, 1983-86; asst. atty. City of Flagstaff, Ariz., 1986-88; pub. defender Coconino County, Flagstaff, 1988-89; pvt. practice Flagstaff, 1989-97. Atty. City Park Falls, Wis., 1983-86; spl. dep. Mohave County capital def., 1989-90; instr. speech comms. No. Ariz. U., 1992-93; adminstrv. law judge Ariz. Dept. Econ. Security, 1997—. Bd. dirs. DeKalb County (Ill.) Drug Coun., 1973-75, Counseling and Personal Devel., Phillips, 1985-86, Northland YM-WYCA, 1990-91. Reginald Heber Smith fellow, 1980-81; C.J.S. legal scholar, 1979. Mem. NRA, Nat. Assn. Criminal Def. Lawyers, Ariz. Bar Assn., State Bar Ariz. (cert. specialist in criminal law 1993-98), State Bar Wis., Nat. Assn. of Criminal Def. Lawyers. Democrat. Avocations: skiing, photography, bicycling. Administrative and regulatory, Bankruptcy, Criminal. Office: PO Box 22329 Flagstaff AZ 86002-2329

COX, CHAPMAN BEECHER, lawyer, corporate executive; b. Dayton, Ohio, July 31, 1940; s. Charles Benjamin and Jewel Lorene (Nicholson) C.; m. Jeannette Gail Korody, Aug. 28, 1964; children: Charles Benjamin, Andrew David. BA, U. So. Calif., 1962; JD, Harvard U., 1965. Bar: Calif. 1966, Colo. 1972, U.S. Ct. Mil. Appeals 1966, U.S. Supreme Ct. 1986. Assoc. Adams, Duque & Hazeltine, Los Angeles, 1968-72, Sherman & Howard, Denver, 1972-74, ptnr., 1974-80, mng. ptnr., 1980-81, ptnr., 1987-90; dep. asst. sec. U.S. Dept. Navy, Washington, 1981-83, asst. sec., 1983-84; gen. counsel Dept. Def., Washington, 1984-85, asst. sec., 1985-87; pres., CEO United Svc. Orgns., Inc., 1990-96; sr. v.p. Lockheed Martin IMS, 1996-2000; ret., 2000. Vis. lectr. U. Colo. Sch. Law, Boulder, 1977-78; mem. def. policy bd. U.S. Dept. Def., 1988-90; mem. comml. space transp. adv. com. U.S. Dept. Transp., 1989-91; chmn. Colo. Commn. Space Sci. and Industry, 1988-90. Gen. counsel Colo. Reps., Denver, 1977-81; del. U.S. Dept. State cultural exch. mission to Syria and Jordan, 1979; ruling elder Presbyn. Ch., 1976—; bd. dirs. United Svc. Orgns., 1985-96, Colorado Springs Symphony Orch., 1988-90, MicroLithics Corp., 1989-91, Presbyn. Ch. U.S.A. Found., 1990-99, Freedoms Found., 1994-99, Fund for Am. Studies, 1995—, New Covenant Trust Co., 1996-99, Presbyn. Lay Com., 1997-2000, Alliance Def. Fund, 2002—; bd. govs. Army-Navy Club Washington, 1998-2000. Col. USMCR, 1962-93, ret. Fellow: Am. Coll. Trust and Estate Counsel; mem.: ABA (standing com. law and nat. security 1988—2002), Colo. Bar Assn. (bd. govs. 1977—79, chmn. probate and trust law sect. 1978—79), Calif. Bar Assn., Army-Navy Club of Washington. E-mail: chapmancox@att.net.

COX, EMMETT RIPLEY, judge; b. Cottonwood, Ala., Feb. 13, 1935; s. Emmett M. Jr. Cox and Myra E. (Ripley) Stewart; m. Ann MacKay Haas, May 16, 1964; children: John Haas, Catherine MacKay. BA, U. Ala., 1957, JD, 1959. Bar: Ala. 1959, U.S. Ct. Appeals (5th, 8th and 11th cirs.), U.S. Supreme Ct. Assoc. Mead, Norman & Fitzpatrick, Birmingham, Ala., 1959—64; assoc. then ptnr. Gaillard, Wilkins, Smith & Cox, Mobile, Ala., 1964—69; ptnr. Nettles, Cox & Barker, 1969—81; judge U.S. Dist. Ct. (so. dist.) Ala., Mobile, 1981—88, U.S. Ct. Appeals (11th cir.), Mobile, 1988—2000, sr. judge, 2000—. Mem. def. svcs. com. Jud. Conf. U.S., 1992—98, chair, 1995—98, mem. jud. br. com., 2001—. Mem.: FBA, Maritime Law Assn. of the U.S., Mobile Bar Assn., Ala. Bar Assn., Alpha Tau Omega (past pres.), Phi Delta Phi, Omicron Delta Kappa. Office: US Courthouse 11th Circuit 113 Saint Joseph St Ste 433 Mobile AL 36602-3624 also: 56 Forsyth St NW Atlanta GA 30303

COX, GILBERT W., JR., lawyer; b. Stoneham, Mass. s. Gilbert W. and Verna O. (Linscott) C.; m. Helen Pillsbury, June 6, 1959; children: Gilbert, David, Carol, Elizabeth. BA, Northeastern U., 1955; JD, Boston U., 1962. Pvt. practice law, Needham, Mass., 1962—. Elected legislator, Mass., 1968-76. Comdr. USN. Estate planning, Probate (including wills, trusts). Office: 60 Dedham Ave Needham MA 02492-3061

COX, HEADLEY MORRIS, JR., lawyer, educator; b. Mt. Olive, N.C., July 25, 1916; s. Headley Morris and Frank (English) C.; m. Irene Todd, June 26, 1940; children: John Morris, Deborah English, Thomas Headley; m. Elizabeth Shelton Smith, Dec. 30, 1994. AB, Duke, 1937, AM, 1939; postgrad., U. Colo., 1944-45; PhD, U. Pa., 1958; JD, U. S.C., 1984.

Successively instr., asst. prof., assoc. prof., prof. English Clemson (S.C.) U., 1939-82, head dept., 1950-69, dean Coll. Liberal Arts, 1969-80; of counsel Olson, Smith, Jordan & Cox, P.A., 1984—. Sr. Fulbright lectr. in Am. lit. Universitat Graz, Austria, 1958-59 Served with USNR, 1944-46. Mem. Phi Beta Kappa. Methodist. Home: 213 Riggs Dr Clemson SC 29631-1427 Office: PO Box 1633 Clemson SC 29633-1633

COX, JAMES TALLEY, lawyer; b. Temple, Tex., Sept. 22, 1921; s. George Allan and Jane (Talley) C.; m. Alice Tarver, Jan. 12, 1945; children: Martha Cox Daniels, Louise Cox McGuire, Anne Cox, Allan. BBA, U. Tex., 1943; LL.B., 1947. Bar: Tex. 1947, U.S. Supreme Ct. 1951. Spl. atty. Justice Dept., Washington, 1947-48; staff atty. Tax Ct. U.S., Washington, 1948-50; trial atty. Treasury Dept., Phila., 1950-51; tax counsel Schlumberger Well Services, Houston, 1951-65; ptnr. Hoover, Cox & Shearer, Houston, 1965-86; sole practice Houston, 1986-90; pres. James T. Cox, P.C., Houston, 1990—, Advent Trust Co., 1991-99. V.p., bd. dirs. Westchase Travels, Inc., 1972-82; bd. dirs. Paradigm Valve Svcs. Inc., Embedded Sys. Products Inc. Contbr. articles to profl. publs. Bd. dirs. Houston Met. YMCA, 1972-78, Pin Oak Charity Horse Show Assn., 1972—, Retina Rsch. Found., 1977—. Served to lt. USNR, 1943-46. Mem. Am., Tex., Houston Bar Assns., Tax Rsch. Assn. (exec. com. 1950-67), Delta Theta Phi, Phi Kappa Psi. Republican. Presbyterian. Estate planning, Probate (including wills, trusts), Taxation, general. Home: 11701 Forest Glen St Houston TX 77024-6433 Office: 908 Town and Country Blvd Ste 225 Houston TX 77024

COX, JOHN THOMAS, JR., lawyer; b. Shreveport, La., Feb. 9, 1943; s. John Thomas and Gladys Virginia (Canterbury) C.; m. Tracey L. Tanquary, Aug. 27, 1966; children: John Thomas, III, Stephen Lewis. BS, La. State U., 1965; JD, 1968. Bar: La. 1968, U.S. Dist. Ct. (we., mid. and ea. dist.) La., U.S. Dist. Ct. (ea. dist.) Tex., U.S. Ct. Appeals (5th and 8th cir.), U.S. Tax Ct., U.S. Supreme Ct. Assoc. Sanders, Miller, Downing & Keene, Baton Rouge, 1968-70, Blanchard, Walker, O'Quin & Roberts, Shreveport, La., 1970-71; ptnr., 1971—. Tchr. bus. law Centenary Coll. La., La. State U., Shreveport. Lt. USAR, 1963—69. Recipient George Washington Honor medal Valley Forge Freedoms Found. Mem. ABA, La. Bar Assn., Caddo parish Bar Assn., Am. Assn. Def. Counsel, La. Assn. Def. Counsel, Com. of 100, Shreveport Club. Presbyterian. Banking, Corporate, general, Labor (including EEOC, Fair Labor Standards Act, labor-management relations, NLRB, OSHA). Address: 555 Dunmoreland Dr Shreveport LA 71106-6124 E-mail: jcox@bwor.com.

COX, KENNETH ALLEN, lawyer, communications consultant; b. Topeka, Dec. 7, 1916; s. Seth Leroy and Jean (Sears) C.; m. Nona Beth Fumerton, Jan. 1, 1943; children— Gregory Allen, Jeffrey Neal, Douglas Randall. BA, U. Wash., 1938, LL.B., 1940; LL.M., U. Mich., 1941; LL.D., Chgo. Theol. Sem., 1969. Bar: Wash. bar 1941. Law clk. Wash. Supreme Ct., 1941-42; asst. prof. U. Mich. Law Sch., 1946-48; with firm Little, LeSourd, Palmer, Scott & Slemmons (and predecessor), Seattle, 1948-61, partner, 1953-61; spl. counsel com. interstate and fgn. commerce charge TV inquiry U.S. Senate, 1956-57; chief broadcast bur. FCC, Washington, 1961-63, commr., 1963-70; counsel to comm. law firm Haley, Bader & Potts, 1970-99; sr. v.p., dir. MCI Comm. Corp., 1970-87; cons. MCI, 1987—2000. Lectr. U. Washington Law Sch., part-time 1954, 60; adj. prof. Georgetown U. Law Center, 1971, 72. Vice pres. Municipal League Seattle and King County, 1960, Seattle World Affairs Council, 1960; pres. Seattle chpt. Am. Assn. UN, 1957; chmn. one of five citizen subcoms. Legis. Interim Com. Edn., 1960; Bd. dirs. Nat. Pub. Radio, 1971-80; bd. dirs. Nat. Advt. Rev. Bd., 1971-74, chmn. bd., 1976-96 . Served to capt. Q.M.C. AUS, 1943-46, 51-52. Recipient Alfred I. duPont award in broadcast journalism Columbia U., 1970 Mem. Am., Fed. Communications, Wash. State, D.C. bar assns., Order of Coif, Phi Beta Kappa, Phi Delta Phi. Democrat. Congregationalist. Administrative and regulatory, Communications. Home: 5836 Marbury Rd Bethesda MD 20817-6076 Office: MCI Comm Corp 1133 19th St NW Washington DC 20036 E-mail: coxk1o@cs.com., 100-4689@mcimail.com.

COX, MELVIN MONROE, lawyer; b. Omaha, Jan. 31, 1947; s. Monroe M. Cox and Wilma Grace (Prickett) McPherson. BA with high honors, U. Wyo., 1969; JD, Harvard U., 1972. Bar: Pa. 1972, U.S. Dist. Ct. (we. dist.) Pa. 1972, N.J. 1987, U.S. Dist. Ct. (N.J.) 1987. Assoc. Rose, Schmidt & Dixon, Pitts., 1972-78; atty. Chgo. Pneumatic Tool Co., N.Y.C., 1978-81, asst. sec., 1981-88; asst. gen. counsel Sun Chem. Corp., Ft. Lee, N.J., 1989-93, asst. gen. counsel and asst. sec., 1993-97, v.p., gen. counsel, sec., 1997—. Adj. prof. engring. law The Cooper Union, N.Y.C., 1984-91; asst. sec. DIC Ams., Inc., Ft. Lee, 1993-97; mng. dir. Sun Chem. B.V., Soest, The Netherlands; bd. dirs. Polychrome Corp., Ft. Lee, Kodak Polychrome, Graphics Co. Ltd., Barbados; bd. visitors U. Wyoming, Coll. Arts and Scis., 1997—, vice chmn., 1998-2001. Bd. dirs. Good Shepherd Cmty. Svcs., Inc., Ft. Lee, 1999-2001; bd. trustees U. Wyoming Found., 2001-. Recipient Outstanding Alumnus award, U. Wyo., 2002. Mem. ABA, Am. Corp. Counsel Assn., Phi Beta Kappa, Phi Kappa Phi. Corporate, general, Private international, Mergers and acquisitions. Office: Sun Chem Corp 222 Bridge Plz S Fort Lee NJ 07024-5703

COX, MIKE, state attorney general; m. Laura Cox; 4 children. BA in Polit. Sci. with distinction, U. Mich., 1986, JD, 1989. Asst. pros. atty. Office Pros. Atty. Oakland County, Pontiac, Mich., 1989—90; asst. pros. atty. spl. crimes sect. Office Pros. Atty. Wayne County, Detroit, 1990—2001, dep. chief homicide unit, 2001—03; atty. gen. State of Mich., Lansing, 2003—. With USMC, 1980—83. Mem.: Inc. Soc. Irish/Am. Lawyers, State Bar Mich. (criminal law sect.), Pros. Attys. Assn. Mich. (instr. Basic Sch.). Republican. Office: G Mennen Williams Bldg 7th Fl PO Box 30212 525 W Ottawa St Lansing MI 48909*

COX, PAUL L. lawyer; b. Cleve., Aug. 27, 1946; s. Paul Langdon and Jean Cox; m. Nancy Joan Miller, Sept. 3, 1977. BA, Johns Hopkins U., 1968; JD, Cleve. State U., 1974. Bar: Ohio 1975, U.S. Dist. Ct. (no. and so. dists.) Ohio 1976, U.S. Supreme Ct. 1980, U.S. Ct. Appeals (6th cir.) 1986. Clk. Ohio Ct. Appeals (9th dist.), Akron, Ohio, 1975-76; asst. atty. gen. State of Ohio, Columbus, Ohio, 1977-82; chief counsel Fraternal Order of Police of Ohio, Columbus, 1982—; pvt. practice, Columbus, 1982—; exec. dir. Fraternal Order of Police, Ohio Labor Coun., Columbus, 1984-87, chief counsel, 1984—, Law Enforcement Legal Assn., Inc., Columbus, 1992—. Adminstrv. law judge Rehab. Svcs. Commn. Ohio, Columbus, 1982-92 negotiator numerous pub. sector labor agreements. Writer: Ohio Police mag.; contbr. articles to profl. jours. Chief counsel FOP Polit. Action Com., Columbus, 1982—; del. Moscow Conf. on Law and Bilateral Econ. Rels. With USN, 1968-72. Mem. ABA, Ohio Bar Assn., Johns Hopkins Alumni Assn., Tau Epsilon Phi, Alpha Phi Omega. Administrative and regulatory, General practice, Labor (including EEOC, Fair Labor Standards Act, labor-management relations, NLRB, OSHA). Office: 222 E Town St Columbus OH 43215-4611

COX, ROGER FRAZIER, lawyer; b. Phila., Sept. 11, 1939; s. Roger Newcomb and Ethel May (Frazier) C.; m. Lucy Jakstas, June 24, 1967. BA, Amherst Coll., 1962; LLB, U. Pa., 1966. Bar: D.C. 1967, Pa. 1967, Calif. 1970. Law clk. to presiding judge U.S. Dist. Ct., N.Y.C., 1966-67; asst. dist. atty. Phila. Dist. Atty.'s Office, 1967-69; staff atty. Alameda County Legal Aid Soc., Oakland, Calif., 1969-71; from assoc. to ptnr. Blank Rome LLP, Phila., 1971—. Mem. ABA, Am. Judicature Soc., Pa. Bar Assn., Phila. Bar Assn., Order of Coif. Environmental, Federal civil litigation, State civil litigation. Home: 303 Delancey St Philadelphia PA 19106-4208 Office: Blank Rome LP One Logan Sq Philadelphia PA 19103-6998 E-mail: cox@blankrome.com.

COX, ROGER STEPHEN, lawyer; b. Ft. Smith, Ark., Nov. 6, 1957; s. Thomas R. and Rhoda (Rosenthal) C.; m. Susan Zimmer, May 18, 1985. BS in Edn., S.W. Tex. State U., 1980; JD, St. Mary's Sch. of Law, 1983. Bar: Tex. 1983, U.S. Dist. Ct. (no. dist.) Tex. 1984, U.S. Ct. Appeals (5th cir.) 1984, U.S. Dist. Ct. (ea. dist. 1994), U.S. Dist. Ct. (we. and so. dists 1995); bd. cert. bus. bankruptcy law and comml. real estate law Tex. Bd. Legal Specialization. Ptnr. Ham, Irwin & Cox, Amarillo, 1989-94; shareholder Sanders, Baker P.C., Amarillo, 1995—. Faculty Tex. Tech. Farm, Ranch and Agribus. Law Inst., 1996-98, 99, 2003, Univ. of Texas Bankruptcy Conf. 2001-03. Contbr. articles to profl. jours., including So. Meth. U. Law Rev. Ann. Survey of Tex. Law, 1994-2003. Trustee Nat. Multiple Sclerosis Soc., Amarillo, 1986-94, chmn., 1989-90, nat. co-chair chmn.'s adv. coun.,1992-94; dir. Amarillo YMCA, pres., 2001; appt. by Gov. George Bush to Tex. Commr. Canadian River Interstate Compact Commn., 1998—. Fellow Tex. Bar Found.; mem. Tex. Bar Assn. (faculty advanced consumer bankruptcy course 1993, advanced bus. bankruptcy course 1998), Panhandle Bankruptcy Bar Assn. (pres. 1995-97), Am. Bankruptcy Inst., Amarillo Area Young Lawyers (pres. 1989-90), Bar Assn. Fifth Fed. Cir., Tex. Assn. Bank Counsel, Amarillo C. of C. (exec. com. and chair, govtl. affairs coun. 2002—, state affairs com. chair 1999-2000), Federalist Soc., Amarillo Country Club, United Way of Amarillo, Major Gifts (co-chair, governing bd. dirs.). Republican. Avocations: golf, motorcycles, youth sports. Banking, Bankruptcy, Commercial, contracts (including sales of goods; commercial financing). Office: Sanders Baker Law Firm 700 One Maxor Plaza 320 S Polk St Amarillo TX 79101-1426

COX, SANFORD CURTIS, JR., lawyer; b. El Paso, Tex., July 31, 1929; s. Sanford Curtis Sr. and Iva M. (Richardson) C.; m. Helen A. Thurston, Sept. 27, 1958; children: Sanford Curtis III, Christopher Thurston. BA, Tex. Western Coll., 1951, MA, 1952; LLB, U. Tex., 1957. Bar: Tex. 1957, U.S. Dist. Ct. (we. dist.) Tex. 1960, U.S. Ct. Appeals (5th cir.) 1964, U.S. Ct. Appeals (D.C. cir.) 1975. Assoc. Andress, Lipscomb, Peticolas & Fisk, El Paso, 1957-61; ptnr. Lipscomb, Fisk & Cox, El Paso, 1961-74, Fisk & Cox, El Paso, 1974-79; sole practice El Paso, 1979-81; pres./shareholder Sanford C. Cox Jr. P.C., El Paso, 1981-93, mem., 1993—. Mem. bd. editors U. Tex. Law Rev. Mem. adv. bd. Booth Meml. Home, 1963-79, Pleasant View Home, 1979-91. Served with U.S. Army, 1952-54. Mem. ABA, Tex. Bar Assn. (admissions com. 17th dist. 1976), El Paso Bar Assn. (ethics com. 1965-69, fee arbitration com. 1973-75), Order of Coif, Phi Delta Phi. Republican. Episcopalian. General civil litigation, Probate (including wills, trusts), Property, real (including real estate development, water). Office: 6006 N Mesa St El Paso TX 79912-4659

COX, WILLIAM DONALD, JR., lawyer; b. Haverhill, Mass., Nov. 26, 1957; s. William Donald, Sr. and Beatrice Mary (Denzin) Cox. BA, Bradford Coll., 1979; postgrad., Am. U., 1979-80; JD, New Eng. Sch. Law, 1987. Bar: Mass. 1987, U.S. Dist. Ct. Mass. 1989, Maine 1990. Pers. dir. City of Haverhill, 1984-88; asst. dist. atty. Dist. Atty.'s Office County of Essex, Salem, Mass., 1988; pvt. practice Haverhill, 1988—; asst. city solicitor City of Haverhill, 1994—. Chmn. Haverhill Dem. City Com., 2002—. Mem.: ABA, Essex County Bar Assn., Boston Bar Assn., Mass. Bar Assn., Bradford Coll. Alumni Assn. (treas.). Avocation: politics. Family and matrimonial, General practice, Probate (including wills, trusts). Home: 8 Richmond St Haverhill MA 01830-6010 Address: 145 S Main St Bradford MA 01835-7438

COX, WILLIAM MARTIN, lawyer, educator; b. Bernardsville, NJ, Dec. 26, 1922; s. Martin John and Nellie (Fotens) Cox; m. Julia Sebastian, June 14, 1952; children: Janice Cox Trautman, William Martin, Joann Cox Cahoon, Julieann Cox Allen. AB, Syracuse U., 1947; JD, Cornell U., 1950. Bar: NJ, US Dist. Ct. Mem. Dolan & Dolan, Newton, NJ, 1950—; mem. faculty, tchr. zoning admintrn. Rutgers U., New Brunswick, NJ, 1968-98. Gen. counsel emeritus N.J. Planning Ofcls.; pres. N.J. Inst. Mcpl. Attys., 1982—84; mem. Land Use Law Drafting Com., 1970—, chmn., 1993—98; dir. Equip, Inc., Marion, NC; bd. dirs. Newton Cemetery Co., v.p., 2000—. Author: Zoning and Land Use Administration in New Jersey, 22nd edit., 2003. With U.S. Army, 1943—45. Named Citizen of Yr., Town of Newton, 2002; recipient Resolution of Appreciation award, N.J. Senate and Gen. Assembly, 1994, Pres.'s Disting. Svc. award, N.J. League Municipalities, 1999, Excellence in Land Use Law award, N.J. Inst. Mcpl. Attys., 1999. Mem.: NJ Bar Assn., Sussex County Bar Assn., NJ Planning Ofcls., Am. Planning Assn., VFW, Rotary (pres. 1978—79, Vocat. award 1996), Monarchist League, Am. Legion. Baptist. Land use and zoning (including planning). Office: 1 Legal Ln Newton NJ 07860-1827

COX, WILLIAM VAUGHAN, lawyer; b. Jersey City, Nov. 12, 1936; s. Walter Miles and Emily (McNenney); divorced; children: Millicent S., Jennifer V. BA, Princeton U., 1958; LLB, Yale U., 1964. Bar: Colo. 1965, N.Y. 1974. Law clk. Holland & Hart, Denver, 1963; atty. Conoco Inc., Denver, 1966-72, asst. to v.p., gen. counsel Stamford, Conn., 1972-73; v.p., gen. counsel Stromberg-Carlson Corp., Rochester, N.Y., 1974-78; mng. ptnr. Bader & Cox, Denver, 1979-86, of counsel, 1986-88; pres. William V. Cox, P.C., Denver, 1988—, also bd. dirs.; project and planning dir. Interwest Comm. Corp., 1995-97. Pres., bd. dirs. New West Indies Trading Co., Denver, 1984—; pres. Coll. Football Ltd., Denver, 1990—. Sportswriter/editor: Colorado Springs (Colo.) Free Press, 1960-61. Football coach Cheyenne Mountain H.S., Colorado Springs, 1961; founder, bd. dirs., v.p., com. chmn., editor Colo. chpt. Nat. Football Found., 1992-2001; mem. adv. bd. Downtown Denver Dist., 1991-93; bd. dirs., com. chmn. Downtown Denver Residents, 1990-93; pres., bd. dirs. Barclay Towers Condominiums, Denver, 1990-92, sec., bd. dirs., 1998-99, pres. bd. dirs., 1999-2000, 2001—, sec. bd. dirs., 2000-2001; dist. capt. Rep. Com., Cherry Hills, Colo., 1980-85; bd. dirs. Monroe County Humane Soc., Rochester, 1975-78. With inf., intelligence USAR, 1959—65. Mem.: Am. Arbitration Assn. (arbitrator 2002—), Denver Bar Assn., Colo. Bar Asn., Law Club Denver (com. chmn. 1971), Rocky Mountain Club (com. chmn. 1972), Univ. Club Denver (bd. dirs. 1997—2000), Am. Legion, Corbey Ct., Phi Delta Phi. Roman Catholic. Avocations: running, politics, college football history, military history, animal rights. Alternative dispute resolution, State civil litigation, Commercial, contracts (including sales of goods; commercial financing). Office: 1625 Larimer St Ste 2707 Denver CO 80202-1538 E-mail: wvcsq@mduonline.net.

COYLE, MARTIN ADOLPHUS, JR., lawyer, consultant; b. Hamilton, Ohio, June 3, 1941; s. Martin Adolphus and Lucille (Baird) C.; m. Sharon Sullivan, Mar. 29, 1969 (div. Dec. 1991); children: Cynthia Ann, David Martin, Jennifer Ann; m. Linda J. O'Brien, July 31, 1993 (div. July 1996); m. Sandra C. Lund, July 1998. BA, Ohio Wesleyan U., 1963; JD summa cum laude, Ohio State U., 1966. Bar: N.Y. 1967, Ohio 1966. Assoc. Cravath, Swaine & Moore, N.Y.C., 1966-72; chief counsel securities and fin. TRW Inc., Cleve., 1972-73, sr. counsel, asst. sec., 1973-75, asst. gen. counsel, asst. sec., 1976, asst. gen. counsel, sec., 1976-80, v.p., gen. counsel, sec., 1980-89, exec. v.p., gen. counsel, sec., 1989-97, exec. v.p., 1997-99; sec. TRW Found., Cleve., 1975-80, trustee, 1980-88. Sec. TRW Found., 1975-80, trustee, 1980-98. Co-inventor voting machine. Pres. Judson Retirement Cmty., 1986-88, trustee, 1986-90; chmn., sec. Martin A. Coyle Found.; trustee Berea Coll. 1989—, Chautauqua Found., 1999-, Chautauqua Inst., 1990-2000, Ohio Wesleyan U., 1992-2001, Gebbie Found., 2001-. Mem. ABA, Am. Soc. Corp. Secs. (pres. Ohio regional group 1978-80, nat. dir. 1981-87, nat. chmn. 1985-86), Assn. Gen. Counsel (exec. com. 1992-99, pres. 1995-97), Harbour Club. Corporate, general. Home: 26 Cormorant Island Ln Kiawah Island SC 29455-5808 E-mail: coyle@cecomet.net.

COYLE, MICHAEL LEE, lawyer; b. Mechanicsburg, Pa., Oct. 2, 1944; s. Patrick G. and Bertha M. C.; m. Kathleen J. West, July 15, 1967; children: Patrick M., Darren W. BS in Acctg., Utica Coll., 1966; JD, Syracuse U., 1971; LLM in Taxation, Georgetown U., 1975. Bar: N.Y. 1972, Conn. 1975, U.S. Tax Ct. 1975. Acct. Peat, Marwick, Mitchell & Co., Syracuse, N.Y., 1966, tax acct., 1969-71; atty., adviser interpretive div. Office Chief Counsel IRS, Washington, 1971-73; atty. adviser to judge U.S. Tax Ct., Washington, 1973-75; mem. firm Reid & Riege, P.C., Hartford, Conn., 1975—. Trustee U. Hartford Tax Inst., 1982-86; bd. dirs. adv. coun. Nat. Inst. State & Local Taxation, Old Lyme, Conn., 1987—. Mem., v.p., pres. St. Paul's Luth. Ch. Coun., Wethersfield, Conn., 1976-82, 87-92, 97-2000; bd. dirs. Children's Home Cromwell, Inc., Conn., 1980-88; mem. leadership Greater Hartford, 1978, Conn. Task Force Corp. Taxation; pres. Wethersfield Bus. & Civic Assn., 1978-80. With U.S. Army, 1966-68. Named one of Best Lawyers in Am., 1987—. Mem. ABA (chmn. sales and fin. transaction com., tax sect. 1983-85), Conn. Bar Assn. (tax exec. com., ltd. liability subcom. 1991—), Conn. Bus. & Industry Assn. (tax com. 1987—), Hartford Tax Study Group, Tax Club Hartford (pres.). Avocations: tennis, reading. Corporate, general, Corporate taxation, State and local taxation. Home: 144 Stonehill Dr Rocky Hill CT 06067 Office: Reid & Riege PC 1 State St Ste 18 Hartford CT 06103-3185 E-mail: mcoyle@reidandriege.com.

COYLE, ROBERT EVERETT, federal judge; b. Fresno, Calif., May 6, 1930; s. Everett LaJoya and Virginia Chandler C.; m. Faye Turnbaugh, June 11, 1953; children— Robert Allen, Richard Lee, Barbara Jean BA, Fresno State Coll., 1953; JD, U. Calif., 1956. Bar: Calif. Ptnr. McCormick, Barstow, Sheppard, Coyle & Wayte, 1958-82; chief judge U.S. Dist. Ct. (ea. dist.) Calif., 1990-96, sr. judge, 1996—. Former chair 9th Cir. Conf. of Chief Dist. Judges, chair 9th Cir. space and security com., mem. com. on state and fed. cts. Mem. Calif. Bar Assn. (exec. com. 1974-79, bd. govs. 1979-82, v.p. 1981), Fresno County Bar Assn. (pres. 1972). Office: US Dist Ct 5116 US Courthouse 1130 O St Fresno CA 93721-2201

COYNE, CHARLES COLE, lawyer; b. Abington, Pa., Dec. 3, 1948; s. James Kitchenman Jr. and Pearl (Black) Coyne; m. Paula J. Latta, May 15, 1976; 1 child, Anna Elizabeth. BS in Econs., U. Pa., 1970; JD, Temple U., 1973. Bar: Pa. 1973, U.S. Supreme Ct. 1982, N.J. 1985. Intern Gen. Svcs. Adminstrn., Washington, 1971; counsel Hepburn Willcox Hamilton & Putnam, Phila., 1994—. Bd. dirs. George S. Coyne Chem. Co., Inc., Croydon, Pa., sec., 1973—, chmn., 2000—; dir. Kitchenman Terminal Co. LLC; mng. dir. Cygnet Leasing Co. LLC. Assoc. editor: Temple Law Rev., 1972—73, columnist: Life in the Country, Ledger Newspaper Group, 1993—99. Chester County (Pa.) rep. Delaware Valley Regional Planning Commn., 1982—; mem. Chester County Health and Edn. Facilities Authority, 1982—, chmn., 1996—2000; bd. suprs. East Fallowfield Twp., Chester County, 1982—83; mem. panel U.S. Bankruptcy Trustees, 1991—93; mem. Chester County Pk. and Recreation Bd., 1998—; mem. racing com. Pa. Hunt Cup, 1992—; chmn. Greater Phila. Young Reps., 1975—76; Rep. candidate Pa. State Legislature, 1976; Phila. Rep. City Policy Com., 1975—77. Recipient Disting. Young Rep. award, 1976; Assn. Internat. Etudantes Scis. Econ. Comml. exch. awardee, U. Melbourne, Australia, 1968. Mem.: ABA, S.R. (bd. mgrs. 2000—03), Nat. Steeplechase Assn., Phila. Bar Assn., Pa. Bar Assn., Pa. Soc., U. Pa. Gen. Alumni Soc. (exec. bd. organized classes, pres. class of 1970), Temple Law Sch. Alumni Assn. (chmn. 10th reunion com.), Quaker City Farmers Club, Union League, Capitol Hill Club, Lawyers Club Phila., Masons (master), Kappa Alpha Soc. Home: Sycamore Run Farm PO Box 155 Unionville PA 19375-0155 Office: Hepburn Willcox Hamilton & Putnam 1100 One Penn Ctr 1617 John F Kennedy Blvd Philadelphia PA 19103-1979 E-mail: cccoyne@aol.com.

COYNE, JOHN COUGHLIN, lawyer; b. Lakewood, Ohio, Mar. 16, 1966; s. John Irwin and Margaret Mary Coyne. BA, John Carroll U., 1988; MA in Philosophy, Cleve. State U., 1991, JD, 1998. Bar: Ill. 1998, Ohio 2001. Adj. instr. philosophy Cuyahoga CC, Parma, Ohio, 1992—97; law clk. Nuremburg, Plevin, Heller & McCarthy, LPA, Cleve., 1997—98; asst. state's atty. Cook County, Chgo., 1998—2001; lawyer Reminger & Reminger, Attys.-at-law, Cleve., 2001—. Mem.: Ill. Prosecutors Bar Assn. (charter mem.). Criminal, Personal injury (including property damage). Office: Reminger & Reminger 101 Prospect Ave W Cleveland OH 44115 Fax: 216-687-1841. E-mail: jcoyne@reminger.com.

COYNE, WILLIAM JOSEPH, judge; b. Cleve., Dec. 3, 1934; s. Anthony Joseph and Mary (Irwin) C.; m. Patricia Ann Ward, Nov. 26, 1959; children: Karen A. Coyne McLaughlin, William Joseph Jr., Daniel P., Timothy J., Patrick J. BS in Social Sci., John Carroll U., 1958; JD, Cleve.-Marshall Law Sch., 1964. Bar: Ohio 1964, U.S. Dist. Ct. (no. dist.) Ohio 1971, U.S. Ct. Appeals (6th cir.) 1971. Asst. pros. atty. Cuyahoga County, Cleve., 1965-72; assoc. Rhoa & Follen, Cleve., 1972-73; prin. Rhoa, Follen & Coyne Co. LPA, Cleve., 1973-79; prin., pres. William J. Coyne & Assocs. Co., LPA, Cleve., 1979—; judge Cuyahoga County Ct. Common Pleas, 1995—. Mem., pres. Cuyahoga County Pub. Defenders Commn., Cleve., 1984—. With U.S. Army, 1958-59. Fellow Am. Coll. Trial Lawyers; mem. ABA, Ohio Bar Assn., Cleve. Bar Assn. Avocations: reading, golf, jogging. Office: Justice Ctr 15-D Cleveland OH 44113

CRABB, BARBARA BRANDRIFF, federal judge; b. Green Bay, Wis., Mar. 17, 1939; d. Charles Edward and Mary (Forrest) Brandriff; m. Theodore E. Crabb, Jr., Aug. 29, 1959; children: Julia Forrest, Philip Elliott. AB, U. Wis., 1960, JD, 1962. Bar: Wis. 1963. Assoc. Roberts, Boardman, Suhr and Curry, Madison, Wis., 1962-64; legal rschr. Sch. Law, U. Wis., 1968-70, Am. Bar Assn., Madison, 1970-71; U.S. magistrate Madison, 1971-79; judge U.S. Dist. Ct. (we. dist.) Wis., Madison, 1979—, chief judge, 1980-96, dist. judge, 1996—. Mem. Gov. Wis. Task Force Prison Reform, 1971-73 Membership chmn., v.p. Milw. LWV, 1966-68; mem. Milw. Jr. League, 1967-68. Mem. ABA, Nat. Assn. Women Judges, State Bar Wis., Dane County Bar Assn., U. Wis. Law Alumni Assn. Office: US Dist Ct PO Box 591 120 N Henry St Madison WI 53701-0591*

CRABTREE, VALLERI JAYNE, real estate executive, lawyer; b. Columbus, Ohio, Feb. 22, 1957; d. Ralph Dale and Ida Mae (Call) C. BS in Bus. Adminstrn., Ohio State U., 1979; JD, Capital U., 1983. Bar: Ohio 1983; lic. real estate broker, Ohio, Fla.; CLU; FLMI. Various mgmt. positions Nationwide Life Ins. Co., Columbus, 1980-87, dir. group annuity underwriting, adminstr., 1987-91; pvt. practice Columbus, 1991-95, 99—; real estate salesperson Metro II Realty, Henderson Realty, Columbus, 1991-94; pres., broker Onyx Real Estate Svcs., Inc., Columbus, 1994—2003, Condos to Castles Realty, Inc., 2003—; atty., owner Crabtree & Assocs., Attys. at Law, Columbus, 1995-99; owner Crabtree Jocularities, 2002—, Quixtar IBO, 2003—. Mem. adj. faculty Columbus State C.C., 1995-2002; instr. IFREC, 2003—; mem. equal opportunity com. Columbus Bd. Realtors, 1996-98, 2000-2002. Chair various coms. Welsh Hills Sch. Parent Orgn., 2000—02; asst. leader Brownie Girl Scout Troop 72, 2002—03; pres. Royal Ballet Parents Orgn., 2002—; trustee Unity Ch. Christianity, Columbus, 1991—94, 1999—2000, usher, 1990—2000, chair devel. com., 1996—99; vol. bus. mgr. Light in the Woods Ch., 2000—; bd. dirs. Royal Celebration Ballet, Inc., 2003—. Mem. AAUW, ACLU, Nat. Assn. Realtors, Ohio Assn. Realtors, Columbus Bd. Realtors, Osceola County Assn. Realtors, Rotary Club of Celebration. Democrat. Avocation: toy collecting. Office: Condos to Castles Realty Inc 215 Celebration Pl Ste 500 Celebration FL 34747

CRADDOCK, JOHN DURRETT, III, lawyer; b. Louisville, May 22, 1942; s. John Durrett Jr. and Dorothy Bowles (Patterson) C.; m. Gloria Nevellen Clark, Apr. 16, 1966; children: Clark, Jay, Carter. BS in Commerce, U. Ky., 1964, BS in Agr., 1965, JD, 1967. Pvt. practice, Munfordville, Ky., 1967; county atty. Hart County, Munfordville, 1978—2002. Mem. ABA, Ky. Bar Assn. Democrat. Methodist. Office: 200 Caldwell St S Munfordville KY 42765-9033

CRAFT, ROBERT HOMAN, JR., lawyer; b. N.Y.C., Sept. 24, 1939; s. Robert Homan and Janet Marie (Sullivan) C.; m. Margaret Jamison Ford, Feb. 6, 1971; children: Robert H. III, Gerard Ford. AB, Princeton U., 1961; BA, Oxford U., 1963; LLB, Harvard U., 1966. Bar: N.Y. 1973, U.S. Dist. Ct. (so. and ea. dists.) N.Y. 1977, U.S. Ct. Appeals (D.C. cir.) 1977, U.S. Dist. Ct. D.C. 1978, U.S. Ct. Appeals (2nd cir.) 1974, U.S. Supreme Ct. 1977. Assoc. Sullivan & Cromwell, N.Y.C., 1966-74; spl. asst. to under sec. of state for security assistance U.S. Dept. State, Washington, 1974-76; exec. asst. to chmn. SEC, Washington, 1976; ptnr. Sullivan & Cromwell, Washington, 1977—. Bd. trustees Washington Opera, 1978—, pres. 1992-98; dir. Coun. for Excellence in Govt., 1989—. Mem. ABA, D.C. Bar Assn., N.Y. State Bar Assn., Assn. Bar City of N.Y., Am. Soc. Internat. Law, Met. Club (Washington), Chevy Chase (Md.) Club. Corporate, general, Securities. Home: 5010 Millwood Ln NW Washington DC 20016-2620 Office: Sullivan & Cromwell 1701 Pennsylvania Ave NW Washington DC 20006-5866

CRAGIN, CHARLES LANGMAID, lawyer; b. Portland, Maine, Oct. 9, 1943; s. Charles Langmaid and Ruth (Meriam) C.; m. Maureen Patricia Ford, Oct. 8, 1994; children: Christine, Jean, Cathleen. BS, U. Maine, 1967, JD, 1970. Bar: Maine 1970, U.S. Dist. Ct. Maine 1970, U.S. Supreme Ct. 1974, U.S. Ct. Appeals (D.C. cir.) 1989, U.S. Ct. Vet. Appeals 1997. Assoc. Verrill & Dana, Portland, Maine, 1970-74, ptnr., 1974-90; chmn. U.S. Bd. of Vet.'s Appeals, Washington, D.C., 1991-97; counselor to undersec. U.S. Dept. VA, 1997, prin. dep. asst. sec. of def., Res. affairs, 1997-98, acting asst. sec. of def., res. affairs, 1998-2001; prin. dep. under sec. defense, personnel & readiness U.S. Dept. Defense, 1998-2001, acting under sec. def., personnel and readiness, 2001; ptnr. Blank Rome LLP, Washington, 2001—03; sr. v.p. nat. intelligence, security and response Sys. Planning Corp., Arlington, Va., 2003—. Contbr. articles to legal publs. Rep. candidate for gov. Maine, 1982; bd. dirs., v.p. Margaret Chase Smith Found., Skowhegan, Maine, 1986—, Potomac divsn. AAA, 1992—; chmn. budget com. Rep. Nat. Com., 1984-90; mem. MaineCommn. on Govt. Ethics and Elections, 1986-88, Def. Adv. Com. on Women in Svcs.,1986-88; bd. dirs. U.S. Navy Meml. Found., 1989—, vice chmn., 2002--. Capt. USNR; ret. Decorated Legion of Merit; named Outstanding Young Man Maine, Maine Jaycees, 1976; recipient Disting Svc. award U. So. Maine Alumni Assn., 1986, Exceptional Svc. award U.S. Dept. Vets. Affairs, 1997, Disting. Pub. Svc. award USCG, 2000, Nat. Pres.'s award Naval Res. Assn., 2000, Minuteman award Res. Officers Assn., 2000, Outstanding Svc. award Nat. Mil. Family Assn., 2000, Disting. Pub. Svc. medal Dept. Def., 2001, Decoration for Exceptional Civilian Svc., USAF, 2001, U.S. Army, 2001, Disting. Pub. Svc. medal U.S. Navy, 2001. Fellow Am. Acad. Hosp. Attys. (bd. dirs. 1979-82); mem. ABA, Maine Bar Assn. (Disting. Svc. award 1986), DC Bar Assn., Capitol Hill Club (Washington), Army and Navy Club (Washington). Roman Catholic. Avocations: skiing, wine collecting, ham radio, gardening. Veteran. Office: Sys Planning Corp 1000 Wilson Blvd Arlington VA 22209-2211 E-mail: ccragin@sysplan.com.

CRAGNOLIN, KAREN ZAMBELLA, real estate developer, lawyer; b. Boston, May 19, 1949; d. John T. Zambella and Corrine M. (Feeney) Zenga; m. Robert Louis Cragnolin, Sept. 8, 1974; 1 child, Nikki Josephine. BA, Georgian Ct. Coll., 1971; JD, New Eng. Sch. Law, 1974. Bar: N.Y. 1974, D.C. 1981. Sr. tax editor Prentice-Hall, Englewood Cliffs, N.J., 1974-76; dir. pub. affairs Am.-Arab Affairs Coun., Washington, 1981-83; founder, dir. Am. Bus. Coun., Dubai, United Arab Emirates, 1983-86; dir. River Link, Inc., Asheville, N.C., 1987—. Bd. trustees Clean Water Mgmt. Trust Fund, WNC Tommorrow. Pres. Young Dems., Georgian Court, N.J., 1970-71; chair Greenway Commn., Asheville, N.C., 1990—; pres., bd. dirs. Leadership Asheville, 1993—, Asheville Area C. of C., 1992-96; bd. dirs. Hand Made Am., Asheville, 1994—, Handi-Skills, Asheville, 1986-90, chmn., 1986-88. Recipient Downtown Hero award Asheville Downtown Assn., 1991, Cir. Excellence Leadership Asheville, 1995, Friend of River award Land Regional Coun., 1995, Athena award Asheville C. of C., 1999. Mem. D.C. Bar Assn., N.Y. Bar Assn. Avocations: gardening, cooking, paddling. Home: 7 Cedarcliff Rd Asheville NC 28803-2905 Office: RiverLink Inc PO Box 15488 Asheville NC 28813-0488 E-mail: Karen@riverlink.org.

CRAIG, DAVID J. lawyer; b. Kaikohe, New Zealand, Feb. 1, 1967; B of Commerce and Adminstrn., LLB with honors, Victoria U., Wellington, New Zealand, 1989. Bar: New Zealand 1990. Solicitor Bell Gully, Wellington, 1990—93, sr. assoc., 1995—98, ptnr., 1999—; atty. Cravath, Swaine & Moore, N.Y.C., 1994—95. Mem. editl. bd.: Capital A$IA, 1998—. Mem.: Inst. Fin. Profls. New Zealand. Banking, Commercial, contracts (including sales of goods; commercial financing). Office: Bell Gully 171 Featherston St Wellington New Zealand

CRAIG, JAMES WILLIAM, lawyer; b. Manchester, N.H., June 2, 1951; s. William Henry and Felicia Agnes Craig; m. Sharon Elizabeth Moher, June 22, 1973; children: Molly, William. BA, Keene State Coll., N.H., 1973; MA, U. So. Calif., 1980; JD, Franklin Pierce Law Ctr., Concord, N.H., 1983. Bar: N.H. 1973, U.S. Ct. Appeals (1st cir.) 1983. From assoc. to ptnr. Craig, Wenners Craig and Capuchino P.A., Manchester, NH, 1983—; chair Manchester Conduct Bd., 1998—2002; rep. N.H. Ho. of Reps., Concord, 1998—. Pres. Serenity Pl. D&A Rehab., Manchester, 2000—; commr. Manchester Water Wks., 2001—; bd. dirs. Easter Seals, Manchester, 1999—, Greater Manchester Mental Health Ctr., 1999—. Sgt. U.S. Army, 1977—80. Mem.: N.H. Trial Lawyers Assn., Manchester Bar Assn. (past pres.), N.H. Bar Assn., Queen City Rotary. Democrat. Avocations: golf, long distance running. General practice, Personal injury (including property damage), Landlord-tenant, Civil rights. Home: 233 Linden St Manchester NH 03104 Office: Craig Wenners Craig and Capuchino 84 Bay St Manchester NH 03104

CRAIG, L. CLIFFORD, lawyer; b. Ohio, Aug. 29, 1938; Student, Stanford U., 1957-59; BA, Duke U., 1961, LLB, 1964. Bar: Ohio. Ptnr. Taft, Stettinius & Hollister, Cin., 1971—. Fellow Am. Coll. Trial Lawyers; mem. ABA, Ohio Bar Assn., Cin. Bar Assn. Office: 425 Walnut St Ste 1800 Cincinnati OH 45202-3957

CRAIG, PAUL MAX, JR., retired lawyer; b. Munich, Aug. 8, 1921; came to U.S., 1941; naturalized, 1944; s. Paul Max and Helen A. Craig; m. Leonie R. Hildebrand, June 26, 1962: children: Anthony P., Claudine A., Stephen P. BS in Elec. Engring., Worcester (Mass.) Poly. Inst., 1946; LLB, Georgetown U., 1950; LLM, George Washington U., 1952. Bar: D.C. 1950. Patent examiner U.S. Patent Office, Washington, 1946-50; patent advisor Office Chief Ordnance, Dept. Army, Washington, 1950-52; pvt. practice Washington, 1952—; ptnr. Craig & Antonelli (and predecessor firm), Washington, 1967-82, Craig & Burns, Washington, 1982-86, Barnes & Thornburg, Washington, 1986-88, Paul M. Craig, P.C., Washington, 1989-97; of counsel Dow, Lohnes & Albertson, 1989-92, affiliated with, 1992-95; of counsel Birch, Stewart, Kolasch & Birch, Falls Church, Va., 1995-97; pvt. practice Silver Spring, Md., 1998—. With USNR, 1944-46. Mem. Am., Inter-Am. bar assns., Am. Patent Law Assn., Assn. Internat. Pour la Protection de la Propriete Indsl., Licensing Execs. Soc., Am. Soc. Internat. Law, Assn. Trial Lawyers Am. Home: 207 Quaint Acres Dr Silver Spring MD 20904-2715 Fax: 301-622-3980. E-mail: pmcraig@starpower.net.

CRAIG, ROBERT MARK, III, lawyer, educator; b. Mpls., Sept. 21, 1948; s. Robert Mark Jr. and Shirley A. (Collier) C.; m. Suzanne Bartlett, Aug. 22, 1970; children: Shannon Michelle, Scott Collier. BA in Journalism, Tex. Christian U., 1970; JD, U. Va., 1973. Bar: Va. 1973, U.S. Ct. Mil. Appeals 1974, Tex. 1975, U.S. Dist. Ct. (no. dist.) Tex. 1976, U.S. Dist. Ct. (so. dist.) Tex. 1980, U.S. Dist. Ct. (we. dist.) 1985, U.S. Ct. Appeals (5th and 11th cirs.) 1981, U.S. Supreme Ct. 1981, U.S. Ct. Appeals (9th and 10th cir.) 1984. Assoc. Judin, Ellis & Barron, McAllen, Tex., 1979-80, ptnr., 1980-81; sr. atty. Tenneco Oil Co., Houston, 1981-88; sr. v.p., assoc. gen. counsel First City, Tex., Houston, 1988-93; assoc. gen. counsel Am. Gen. Corp., Houston, 1993-99; v.p., gen. counsel A.G. Fin. Svc. Ctr., Inc., Evanville, Ind., 1999; assoc. gen. counsel Waste Mgmt., Inc., Houston, 1999—. Staff atty. Presdl. Clemency Bd., Washington, 1975; mem. faculty Vernon Regional Jr. Coll., Sheppard AFB, 1975-76; instr. paralegal tng., Houston, 1982-85; instr. USAF Acad., 1976-77, asst. prof. law, 1977-79; councilman City of Oak Ridge North, Tex., 1988-94, also mayor pro tem; dir. Oak Ridge N.Mcpl. Utility Dist., 1994-96; pres. Oak Ridge N.Econ. Devel. Corp., 1994-96, 2003—. Vice pres. Upper Rio Grande Valley Heart Assn., McAllen, 1980-81; ruling elder Timber Ridge Presbyn. Ch., 1983-88; pres. Montgomery County Assn. for Gifted and Talented, Conroe, Tex., 1985; chmn. Permanent Jud. Commn., New Covenant Presbytery, 1986-92; legal counsel Tex. Jaycees, 1981-82. Capt. USAF, 1973-79. Mem.: ABA (vice chair com. corp. counsel litigation sect.), Internat. Assn. Def. Coun., Tex. Bar Found., Tex. Bar Assn. (coun. mem. antitrust and bus. litig. sect. 1999—2002), Va. Bar Assn. (assoc.), Clark Soc. and Alumni Bd. of Tex. Christian U., McAllen Jaycees (sec., bd. dirs. 1979—81). Republican. Avocation: golf. Federal civil litigation, State civil litigation, Corporate, general. Home: 27122 Wells Ln Conroe TX 77385-9080 Office: Waste Mgmt Inc 1001 Fannin St Ste 4000 Houston TX 77002-6711 E-mail: rcraig@wm.com., rmcraig@swbell.net.

CRAMER, ALLAN P. lawyer; b. Norwich, Conn., Mar. 8, 1937; s. E.L. and Dorothy N. (Pasnik) C.; children: Peter Alden, Alison Jane. BA cum laude, U. Pa., 1958; JD, U. Conn., 1964. Bar: Conn. 1964, U.S. Dist. Ct. Conn. 1965, U.S. Ct. Appeals (2d cir.) 1965. Atty. HEW, Washington, 1964-65; ptnr. Cramer & Ahern, Westport, Conn., 1966— . Chmn. Westport Dem. Town Com., 1972-73; J.P., Town of Westport, 1973-77; bd. dirs. Westport Pub. Libr., 1975-82; mem. Westport Zoning Bd. Appeals, 1984-88 . Mem. Conn. Bar Assn., Westport Bar Assn. General practice, Personal injury (including property damage), Property, real (including real estate development, water). Home: Yankee Hill Rd Westport CT 06880 Office: Cramer & Ahern 38 Post Rd W Westport CT 06880-4207 Business E-Mail: cramer.ahern@snet.net.

CRAMER, EDWARD MORTON, lawyer, music company executive; b. N.Y.C., May 27, 1925; s. Israel and Elsie (Neuman) C.; m. Henrietta Pantel, 1973 (div.); children: Evin Joyce, Marjorie Sue Cramer Gmelin, Charles Harris; m. Ethel Metzger, June 13, 1982. BA, Columbia U., 1947; LLB with distinction, Cornell U., Ithaca, N.Y., 1950; LLM, NYU, 1953; HHD (hon.), Lincoln (Ill.) Coll., 1982; LHD (hon.), Five Towns Coll., N.Y., 1998. Bar: N.Y. 1950, U.S. Supreme Ct 1953. Teaching fellow NYU Sch. Law, 1950-51; assoc. Rosenman & Colin, N.Y.C., 1951-58; ptnr. Cramer & Hoffinger, N.Y.C., 1958-68; pres., CEO, Broadcast Music, Inc. (BMI), 1968-86; pvt. practice, N.Y.C., 1986—. Treas. Copyright Soc. U.S., 1963-68, 78-79, bd. edits bull., 1953-63; former mem. Peabody Awards Selection Com.; editor Cornell Law Quar. Trustee Congregation Adas Emuno; former trustee Tony Martell Found., Ford's Theater. lt. USNR, 1943-46 Recipient Spl. award Songwriters Guild Am., 1986, Spl. award Am. Composers Alliance, 1987, Spl. Peabody award, 1991; named Personality of Yr. Nat. Arts Club, 1972; Ed Cramer Day named in his honor, N.Y.C., 1979. Mem.: ABA (copyright com.), Practising Law Inst., Nat. Acad. Popular Music (trustee, bd. dirs. 1969—93, founding mem. Songwriters Hall of Fame, adv. com.), Internat. Confedn. Authoral Socs. (adminstrv. coun.), Broadcast Pioneers (pres. 1984, officer, bd. dirs. 1984—97), Nat. Music Coun. (v.p. 1968—86), Assn. Bar City NY (copyright com.), B'nai B'rith (pres. 1989—90, trustee, officer, pres. music and performing arts unit, Man of Yr. award 1979), Order of Coif. Jewish. Entertainment, Trademark and copyright. Home: 254 Chestnut St Englewood NJ 07631-3134 Office: 110 E 59th St New York NY 10022-1304

CRAMER, HAROLD, lawyer; b. Phila., June 16, 1927; s. Aaron Harry and Blanche (Greenberg) C.; m. Geraldine Hassuk, July 14, 1957; 1 dau., Patricia Gail. AB, Temple U., 1948; JD cum laude, U. Pa., 1951. Bar: Pa. 1951. Law clk. to judge Common Pleas Ct. No. 2, 1953; mem. law faculty U. Pa., 1954; assoc. firm Shapiro, Rosenfeld, Stalberg & Cook, 1955-56, ptnr., 1956-67, Meslrov, Gelman, Jaffe & Levin, 1967-74, Mesirov, Gelman, Jaffe & Cramer, Phila., 1974-77, Mesirov, Gelman, Jaffe, Cramer & Jamieson, Phila., 1977-89, of counsel, 1996-2000; ret. ptnr. Schnader, Harison Segal & Lewis, 2000—; CEO Grad. Health System, Phila., 1989-96. Instr. Nat. Inst. Trial Advocacy, 1970-78; pres. Jewish Exponent, 1987-89, Times., 1987-89. Co-author: Trial Advocacy, 1968; contbr. articles to profl. jours. Chmn. bd. Eastern Pa. Psychiat. Hosp., 1974-81, Grad. Hosp., 1975-91; trustee Fedn. Jewish Agys., Jewish Publ. Soc., pres., 1996-98, chmn., 1998-2001. 1st lt. U.S. Army, 1951-53. Decorated Bronze Star. Fellow Am. Bar Found.; mem. ABA, Am. Law Inst., Pa. Bar Assn. (ho. of dels. 1966-75, 78—, bd. govs. 1975-78), Phila. Bar Found. (pres. 1988, trustee, pres. elect), Phila. Bar Assn. (bd. govs. 1967-69, chmn. 1969, vice chancellor 1970, chancellor 1972, editor The Shingle 1970-72), U. Pa. Law Alumni Soc. (bd. mgrs. 1959-64, pres. 1968-70), Order of Coif (past chpt. pres., nat. exec. com. 1973-76), Tau Epsilon Rho (chancellor Phila. grad. chpt. 1960-62), Philmont Country Club, Pyramid Club, Greate Bay Golf Club. Mergers and acquisitions, Family and matrimonial, Health, Federal civil litigation. Home: 728 Pine St Philadelphia PA 19106-4005 Office: Schnader Harrison Segal & Lewis 1600 Market St Ste # 34 Philadelphia PA 19103-7501 E-mail: hcramer@schnader.com.

CRAMER, JEFFREY ALLEN, lawyer; b. Kansas City, Mo., Mar. 16, 1951; s. Robert Donald and Betty Jane (Leventhal) C.; m. Melinda Gail Segal, Nov. 18, 1993. BA, Vanderbilt U., 1972; JD, U. Fla., 1974. Bar: Fla. 1975, U.S. Dist. Ct. (no. dist.) 1975, U.S. Dist. Ct. (so. dist.) Fla. 1980, U.S. Dist. Ct. (mid. dist.) Fla. 1981, U.S. Ct. Appeals (5th cir.) 1975, U.S. Ct. Appeals (11th cir.) 1981. Assoc. Levin, Warfield, Middlebrooks, Graff, Mabie & Rosenbloum, Pensacola, Fla., 1975-76; mem. Carlton, Fields, Ward, Emmanuel, Smith & Cutler, Pensacola and Tampa, Fla., 1976-84; prin. Law Offices of Jeffrey A. Cramer, P.A., Pensacola, 1984-93; pvt. practice The Cramer Law Firm, Jacksonville, Fla., 1993—. Mem. Leadership Pensacola, 1985-86; pres. Five Flags Sertoma, Pensacola, 1985-86; dist. gov., Gulf Coast Dist. Sertoma Internat., 1986-87; bd. dirs. Speech-Hearing Bd. Bapt. Health Care Found., Pensacola, 1987, Etz Chaim Synagogue, 2002-. Mem. Fla. Bar Assn., Am. Bd. Trial Advocates (N.W. Fla. chpt. sec. 1990, v.p. 1991, pres. 1992, nat. bd. dirs. 1993-94), Escambia-Santa Rosa Bar Assn. (treas. 1988-89, v.p. 1989-90, pres.1990-91), Fla. Bar (cert. civil trial lawyer, workers' compensation lawyer, cir. ct. mediator). Labor (including EEOC, Fair Labor Standards Act, labor-management relations, NLRB, OSHA), Personal injury (including property damage), Workers' compensation. Office: 1 Independent Dr Ste 3300 Jacksonville FL 32202-5027 E-mail: cramerlf@bellsouth.net.

CRAMER, JOHN MCNAIGHT, lawyer; b. Lewistown, Pa., Sept. 23, 1941; s. John Mumma and Elaine Elizabeth (McNaight) C.; m. Susan Oakman, Nov. 26, 1966 (div. Mar. 1989); children: Natalie, Daniel, Melinda; m. Kay Stephenson, Apr. 8, 1989; children: Julia, Maria. AB, Juniata Coll., 1963; LLB, Harvard Law Sch., 1966. Bar: Pa. 1968. Law clk. U.S. Dist. Ct. So. Dist. N.Y., 1966-67; assoc. Reed Smith Shaw & McClay, Pitts., 1967-76, ptnr., 1976—2002, of counsel, 2002. Advocacy fellow Dickinson Sch. Law, Pa. State U., Carlisle, Pa., 1987-2002. Mem. editl. staff: Harvard Law Rev. Trustee Juniata Coll., Huntingdon, Pa., 1981—, sec., 1983—96, vice chair, 1996—97, chair, 1997—2001; bd. dirs. Ctrl. Pa. Food Bank, 1996—2001. Mem. ABA, Cumberland County Bar Assn. Democrat. General civil litigation, Computer, Environmental. Home: Box 17 Old Trail Rd New Buffalo PA 17069 E-mail: crmfrm@aol.com.

CRAMER, ROBERT W. lawyer; b. Monticello, Ind., Nov. 10, 1957; s. James Robert and Doris Pace Cramer; m. Ann Ashley Hollowell, May 30, 1981; children: Ashley Pace, Robert Wayne Jr., David McKinnie. BA, U. NC, 1980, MBA, JD, U. NC, 1984. Bar: NC 1984, U.S. Dist. Ct. (we. dist.) NC 1984, U.S. Supreme Ct. 2001. Atty. Helms, Mulliss & Wicker, PLLC (and predecessor firms), Charlotte, NC, 1984—. Bd. dirs. U. NC Law Found., Inc., Chapel Hill, 2001—. Finance. Office: Helms Mulliss & Wicker PLLC 201 N Tryon St Charlotte NC 28202 Office Fax: 704-343-2300. E-mail: bob.cramer@hmw.com.

CRAMP, JOHN FRANKLIN, lawyer; b. Ridley Park, Pa., Mar. 14, 1923; s. Alfred Charles and Mildred Frances (Cummins) C.; m. Suzanne Surrick, Sept. 15, 1951 (div.); children: John F., Catherine T., David B., Andrew H., Daniel E.; m. Gloria C. Maddox, Jan. 29, 1972. BS, Pa. Mil. Coll. (now Widener U.), 1943; LLB, Dickinson Sch. Law, 1948. Bar: Pa. 1949, U.S. Dist. Ct. (ea. dist.) Pa. 1951, U.S. Ct. Appeals (3d cir.) 1951. Assoc. Hodge, Hodge & Balderston, Chester, Pa., 1949-53; sr. ptnr. Cramp, D'Iorio, McConchie & Forbes, P.C., Media, Pa., 1954-75, pres., 1975-90; founding counsel Beatty, Cramp, Kauffman & Lincke, 1996—. Gen. counsel, bd. dirs. Bryn Mawr Group (name now Dixon Ticonderoga Inc.), 1965-79, pres. 1973-74; gen. counsel Widener U., 1968-91; bd. dirs. Phila. Subtransp. Co. Trustee Williamson Sch., 1968-91; bd. dirs., chmn. Crozer Chester Med. Ctr.; Elwyn Inst.; bd. dirs. Chester Hosp., Crozer-Keystone Health System; chmn. bd. dirs. Am. Inst. Mental Studies, Jerusalem Elwyn, Can. Friends of Elwyn; Rep. county chmn., 1957-61; del. Rep. Nat. Conv., 1960; state chmn. Citizens for Scranton, 1962. Mem. ABA, Del. County Bar Assn., Pa. Bar Assn., Internat. Soc. Barristers, Nat. Assn. Coll. and Univ. Attys., Def. Rsch. Inst., Wildcat Run Country Club, Masons. Episcopalian. State civil litigation, Corporate, general, Insurance. Office: 215 N Olive St Media PA 19063-2810

CRAMTON, ROGER CONANT, law educator, lawyer; b. Pittsfield, Mass., May 18, 1929; s. Edward Allen and Dorothy Stewart (Conant) C.; m. Harriet Cutter Haseltine, June 29, 1952; children: Ann, Charles, Peter, Cutter. AB, Harvard U., 1950; JD, U. Chgo., 1955; LLD, Nova U., 1980; MA (hon.), Oxford U., 1987. Bar: Vt. 1956, Mich. 1964, N.Y. State 1979. Law clk. to Hon. S.R. Waterman U.S. Ct. of Appeals (2d cir.), 1955-56; law clk. to justice Harold H. Burton U.S. Supreme Ct., 1956-57; asst. prof. U. Chgo., 1957-61; assoc. prof. U. Mich. Law Sch., 1961-64, prof., 1964-70; chmn. Adminstrv. Conf. of U.S., 1970-72; asst. atty. gen. Justice Dept., 1972-73; dean Cornell U. Law Sch., Ithaca, N.Y., 1973-80, Robert S. Stevens prof. emeritus, 1982—. Mem. U.S. Commn. on Revision Fed. Ct. Appellate Sys., 1973-75; bd. dirs. U.S. Legal Svcs. Corp., 1975-79, chmn. bd., 1975-78; mem. U.S. Commn. on Jud. Discipline and Removal, 1991-93. Co-author: Conflict of Laws, 5th rev. edition, 1993, Law and Ethics of Lawyering, 3d rev. edit., 1999; editor Jour. Legal Edn., 1981-87; contbr. articles to profl. jours. Guggenheim fellow, 1987-88; recipient Rsch. award Am. Bar Found., 2000. Mem. ABA, Am. Law Inst. (council mem.), Assn. Am. Law Schs. (pres. 1985), Am. Acad. Arts and Scis., Order of Coif, Phi Beta Kappa. Congregationalist. Home: 49 Highgate Cir Ithaca NY 14850-1486 Office: Cornell Law Sch Myron Taylor Hall Ithaca NY 14853-4901

CRANE, BENJAMIN FIELD, lawyer; b. Holden, Mass., May 5, 1929; s. Frederick Turner and Gertrude (Stange) C.; m. Sarah Anne Molloy, Feb. 8, 1959; children: Michael Turner, Elizabeth Loring, Susan Field. BA, U. Iowa, 1951; LL.B., NYU, 1954. Bar: N.Y. 1955. Assoc. Cravath, Swaine & Moore, N.Y.C., 1954-63, ptnr., 1963-94. Served with U.S. Army, 1946-47. Mem. Assn. of Bar of City of N.Y. Private international, Mergers and acquisitions, Securities. Office: Cravath Swaine & Moore LLP Worldwide Plz 825 8th Ave New York NY 10019-7475

CRANE, MARK, lawyer; b. Chgo., Aug. 27, 1930; s. Martin and Ruth (Bangs) C.; m. Constance Bird Wilson, Aug. 18, 1956; children: Christopher, Katherine, Stephanie. AB, Princeton U., 1952; LLB, Harvard U., 1957. Bar: U.S. Dist. Ct. (no. dist.) Ill. 1957, U.S. Ct. Appeals (7th cir.) 1968, U.S. Ct. Appeals (9th cir.) 1972, U.S. Supreme Ct. 1978, U.S. Ct. Appeals (10th cir.) 1982, U.S. Ct. Appeals (fed. cir.) 1983, U.S. Ct. Appeals (6th cir.) 1995, U.S. Ct. Appeals (8th cir.) 1998. Assoc. Hopkins & Sutter, Chgo., 1957-63, ptnr., 1963-2001; of counsel Foley & Lardner, Chgo., 2001—. Adj. prof. Loyola U. Law Sch., 2000—; comml. arbitrator, mediator complex case panel Am. Arbitration Assn., Chgo., 1997—. Served to lt. (j.g.) USNR, 1952-54. Fellow Am. Bar Found., Am. Coll. Trial Lawyers (chmn. upstate Ill. com. 1997-99); mem. ABA (chmn. antitrust sect. 1986-87), Ill. Bar Assn. (chmn. fed. jud. appointments com. 1978-79, chmn. antitrust sect. 1970), Chgo. Bar Assn., 7th Cir. Bar Assn. (pres. 1984-85). Republican. Episcopalian. Antitrust, Federal civil litigation, Criminal. Home: 520 Hoyt Ln Winnetka IL 60093-2623 Office: 321 N Clark St Chicago IL 60610

CRANFORD, PAGE DERONDE, lawyer; b. West Chester, Pa., Nov. 20, 1935; s. Joseph D. and Dorothy (Griffith) C.; m. Virginia Langen, Nov. 21, 1965; children: Elizabeth, Courtenay. BS, Washington and Lee U., 1958; JD, George Washington U., 1964; postgrad. in banking, Rutgers U., 1981. Bar: Md. 1964, D.C. 1965, Va. 1974, U.S. Ct. Appeals (D.C. cir.) 1965. Asst. v.p. Nat. Bank Washington, 1958-65; staff counsel U.S. Comptr. of Currency, Washington, 1965-66, regional adminstr. nat. banks Richmond, Va., 1966-72; sr. v.p., sec., gen. counsel Fidelity Am. Bank, Lynchburg, Va., 1972-75; assoc. Boothe, Prichard & Dudley, Fairfax, Va., 1975-76; corp. gen. counsel Va. Nat. Bankshares, Norfolk, Va., 1976-89; exec. v.p., gen. counsel Sorvan Fin. Corp, Norfolk, 1989-90, sr. exec. v.p., gen. counsel, 1990-91; sr. exec. v.p., gen. counsel, sec. C&S/Sovran Corp., Norfolk and Atlanta, 1990-92; ptnr. McGuire Woods Battle & Boothe, Norfolk, 1992-99, ptnr. in charge, 1992-96; of counsel McGuire Woods LLP, Norfolk, 2000—. Adj. prof. Sch. Law Regent U., Va. Beach, 1995-99, Sch. Law Coll. William and Mary, Williamsburg, Va., 1997-98. Trustee Richmond Montessori Sch., 1970-72, Lynchburg Montessori Sch., 1972-75, James River Day Sch., Lynchburg, 1973-75, Va. Symphony, Norfolk, 1984— . Served to capt. U.S. Army, 1958-66 Recipient Arthur S. Fleming award Jaycees, 1972 Mem. ABA (banking law subcom, corp. counsel subcom., bus. law sect.), Va. Bar Assn., Md. Bar Assn., D.C. Bar Assn., Town Point Club (Norfolk). Republican. Episcopalian. Office: McGuire Woods LLP 9000 World Trade Ctr 101 W Main St Ste 9000 Norfolk VA 23510-1655

CRANGLE, ROBERT D. lawyer, management consultant, entrepreneur, manufacturing executive; b. Putnam, Conn., May 5, 1943; s. Dale E. and Libbie S. (Krepela) C.; m. S. Jeanne Rose, June 6, 1968; children: Rob, Scott, Elenor, Bill, Kimball, Susan, Sara, Paul, Hally. BS in Nuclear Engring., Kans. State U., 1966; JD, Harvard U., 1969. Bar: Mass. 1969, Ill. 1974, Kans. 1987, U.S. Dist. Ct. Kans. 1987. Sr. v.p. Harbridge House, Inc., Boston, 1969-84; pres., dir. Rose & Crangle, Ltd., Lincoln, 1984—; dir. Helisys Inc., L.A., 1985-99; ptnr. Metz and Crangle, Chartered, Lincoln, Kans., 1987—; elected Lincoln County Atty., 1997—2001. Mem. faculty Bus. Sch., Ill. Inst. Tech., Chgo., 1984-87, dir. Ctr. Rsch. on Indsl. Strategy and Policy, Chgo., 1984-87. Bd. dirs. Lake Bluff (Ill.) Sch. Bd., 1982-87, Farmers Nat. Bank, 1992—; mem. Kans. Sci. and Tech. Coun., 1992-96; mem. Natural History Mus. Bd., 1995-98, Kans. Geol. Survey Adv. Com., 1995-2002. Recipient Meritorious Pub. Service award NSF, 1985. Fellow AAAS; mem. ABA, Kans. Bar Assn. (officer bus. law sect. 1993-97), N.W. Kans. Bar Assn., Kans. Math and Sci. Edn. Coalition (bd. dirs.), Inst. Mgmt. Cons. (cert. 1980). Republican. Mem. Soc. Of Friends. Avocations: science policy, entrepreneurship. Corporate, general, Non-profit and tax-exempt organizations, Commercial, contracts (including sales of goods; commercial financing). Office: Metz and Crangle Chartered PO Box 36 116 S 4th St Lincoln KS 67455-0036 also: Rose & Crangle Ltd PO Box 285 102 E Lincoln Av Lincoln KS 67455-0285 E-mail: rcltd@nckcn.com., mcc@nckcn.com.

CRANK, PAT, state attorney general; m. Anna Crank; children: Abbigail, Jerry, Zachary, Noah. B in Acctg., U. Wyo., 1982, JD, 1985. With Wyo. Atty. Gens. Office, 1985—86, Natrona County Dist. Attys. Office,

1987—90, U.S. Attys. Office for Dist. Wyo., 1990—2002; atty. gen. State of Wyo., Cheyenne, 2003—. Democrat. Avocations: hunting, fishing, camping. Office: Atty Gens Office 123 Capitol Bldg 200 W 24th St Cheyenne WY 82002*

CRANMER, THOMAS WILLIAM, lawyer; b. Detroit, Jan. 13, 1951; s. William Eugene and Betty Lee (Orphal) C.; children: Jacqueline, Taylor, Chase. BA, U. Mich., 1972; JD, Ohio No. U., 1975. Bar: Mich. 1975, U.S. Dist. Ct. (ea. dist.) Mich. 1978, U.S. Ct. Appeals (6th cir.) 1978, U.S. Supreme Ct. 1982, U.S. Tax Ct. 1986. Asst. pros. atty. Oakland County, Mich., 1975-78; asst. atty. U.S. Dist. Ct. (ea. dist.) Mich., 1978-80, asst. chief criminal div., 1980-82; assoc. Miro, Miro & Weiner, Bloomfield Hills, Mich., 1982-84, ptnr., 1984—. Mem. faculty Atty. Gen's. Adv. Inst., Washington, 1980-82, Nat. Inst. Trial Adv., Northwestern Chicago, Ill., 1987—, trial adv. workshop Inst. Continuing Legal Edn., 1988—, local rules adv. com. U.S. Dist. Ct. (ea. dist.) Mich., 1989-92; hearing panelist Atty. Discipline Bd., 1987—. Fellow Am. Coll. Trial Lawyers, Oakland County Bar Found. (charter, trustee 1994—, pres. 2002-), Mich. State Bar Found., Internat. Acad. Trial Lawyers; mem. ABA (chair litigation sect., Detroit graphic subcom. of com. on complex crimes litigation 1990), FBA (exec. bd. dirs. Detroit chpt. 1988-96, pres. 1995-96, Leonard R. Gilman award 1995), Am. Bd. Trial Advocates, Am. Arbitration Assn. (mem. hearing panel 1990), State Bar Mich. (rep. assembly 1986-92, mem. grievance com. 1990—, chair 1993-97, bd. commrs. 1998—, treas. 2001-02, sec. 2002-), Oakland County Bar Assn. (chair CLE com. 1992, bd. dirs. 1994—, Disting. Svc. award 1996, chair membership com. 1997). Republican. Presbyterian. General civil litigation, Criminal, Labor (including EEOC, Fair Labor Standards Act, labor-management relations, NLRB, OSHA). Office: Miro Weiner & Kramer PC 38500 Woodward Ave Ste 100 Bloomfield Hills MI 48304-5047 Home: 4739 Sandpiper Ln West Bloomfield MI 48323-2063 E-mail: tcranmer@mirolaw.com.

CRANNEY, MARILYN KANREK, lawyer; b. Bklyn., June 18, 1949; d. Sidney Paul and Aurelia (Valice) Kanrek; m. John William Cranney, Jan. 22, 1970 (div. June 1975); 1 child, David Julian. BA, Brandeis U., 1970; MA in History, Brigham Young U., 1975; JD, U. Utah, 1979; LLM in Tax Law, NYU, 1984. Bar: N.Y. 1980, U.S. Dist. Ct. (so. and ea. dists.) N.Y. 1992. Assoc. Cravath Swaine & Moore, N.Y.C., 1979-81; 1st v.p., asst. gen. counsel Morgan Stanley Investment Advisors Inc., N.Y.C., 1981—. Mem. Order of the Coif. Democrat. Jewish. Avocations: travel, reading. Corporate, general, Securities. Office: Morgan Stanley Investment Advisors Inc 22nd Fl 1221 Ave of the Americas New York NY 10020 E-mail: marilyn.cranney@morganstanley.com.

CRANSTON, HOWARD STEPHEN, lawyer, management consultant; b. Hartford, Conn., Oct. 20, 1937; s. Howard Samuel and Agnes (Corvo) C.; m. Karen Youngman, June 16, 1962; children: Margaret, Susan. BA cum laude, Pomona Coll., 1959; LLB, Harvard U., 1962. Bar: Calif. 1963. Assoc. MacDonald & Halsted, L.A., 1964-68; ptnr. MacDonald, Halsted & Laybourne, L.A., 1968-82, of counsel, 1982-86; pres. Knapp Comm., L.A., 1982-87, S.C. Cons. Corp., 1987—. Bd. dirs. Boys Republic. Author: Handbook for Creative Managers, 1987. 1st lt. U.S. Army, 1962—64. Republican. Episcopalian. Corporate, general, General practice, Private international. Office: 1613 Chelsea Rd # 252 San Marino CA 91108-2419 E-mail: hscran@earthlink.net.

CRAPO, MICHAEL DEAN, senator, former congressman, lawyer; b. Idaho Falls, Idaho, May 20, 1951; s. George Lavelle and Melba (Olsen) C.; m. Susan Diane Hasleton, June 22, 1974; children: Michelle, Brian, Stephanie, Lara, Paul. BA Polit. Sci. summa cum laude, Brigham Young U., 1973; postgrad., U. Utah, 1973-74; JD cum laude, Harvard U., 1977. Bar: Calif. 1977, Idaho 1979. Law clk. to Hon. James M. Carter U.S. Ct. Appeals (9th cir.) San Diego, 1977-78; assoc. atty. Gibson, Dunn & Crutcher, L.A., 1978-79; atty. Holden, Kidwell, Hahn & Crapo, Idaho Falls, 1979-92, ptnr., 1983-92; mem. Idaho State Senate from 32A Dist., 1984-93, asst. majority leader, 1987-88; pres. Pro Tempore, 1989-92; congressman U.S. House of Reps., 2d Idaho dist., Washington, 1992-98; mem. commerce com., new mem. leader 103rd Congress, sophomore class leader 104th Congress, co-chair Congl. Beef Caucus, dep. whip western region U.S. House of Reps., Washington, vice chair energy and power subcom., strategic planning leader House Leadership 105th Congress, mem. house resources com., mem. commerce com., mem. resources com.; senator from Idaho U.S. Senate, 1999—. Precinct committeeman Dist. 29, 1980-85; vice chmn. Legislative Dist. 29, 1984-85; Mem. Health and Welfare Com., 1985-89, Resources and Environ. Com., 1985-90, State Affairs Com., 1987-92; Rep. Pres. Task Force, 1989. Leader Boy Scouts Am., Calif., Idaho, 1977-92; mem. Bar Exam Preparation, Bar Exam Grading; chmn. Law Day.; Bonneville County chmn. Phil Batt gubernatorial campaign, 1982. Named one of Outstanding Young Men of Am., 1985; recipient Cert. of Merit Rep. Nat. Com., 1990, Guardian of Small Bus. award Nat. Fedn. of Ind. Bus., 1990, 94, Cert. of Recognition Am. Cancer Soc., 1990, Idaho Housing Agy., 1990, Idaho Lung Assn., 1985, 86, 89, Friend of Agr. award Idaho Farm Bur., 1989-90, medal of merit Rep. Presdl. Task Force, 1989, Nat. Legislator of Yr. award Nat. Rep. Legislators Assn., 1991, Golden Bulldog award Watchdogs of the Treas., 1996, Thomas Jefferson award Nat. Am. Wholesale Grocers Assn.-Ind. Food Distbrs. Assn., 1996, Spirit of Enterprise award U.S. C. of C., 1993, 94, 95, 96. Mem. ABA (antitrust law sect.), Idaho Bar Assn., Rotary. Republican. Mem. Lds Ch. Avocations: sports, backpacking, hunting, skiing. Office: US Senate 111 Russell Senate Ofc Bldg Washington DC 20510-0001

CRARY, MINER DUNHAM, JR., lawyer; b. Warren, Pa., Sept. 8, 1920; s. Miner D. and Edith (Ingraham) C.; m. Mary Chapman, Jan. 23, 1943; children: Edith Crary Howe, James G., Laura Crary Hall, Harriet Crary, Miner A. BA, Amherst Coll., 1942; MA, Harvard U., 1943, LLB, 1948. Bar: N.Y. 1949. Assoc. Curtis, Mallet-Prevost, 1949-61, ptnr., 1961-96, coun., 1996—. Trustee Am. U. in Cairo, 1959—, Heckscher Art Mus., Huntington, N.Y., 1968—; trustee Sterling and Francine Clark Art Inst., Williamstown, Mass., 1974—; bd. dirs. Robert Sterling Clark Found., N.Y.C., 1972—; chmn. exec. com. alumni coun. Amherst Coll., 1961-68; chmn. Huntington Bd. Edn. and Ctrl. Sch. Dist. 2, 1961-67; acting village justice Village of Asharoken, Northport, N.Y., 1987-2002. Lt. USNR, 1942-45. Mem. ABA (real property and probate com.), N.Y. State Bar Assn. (taxation and estate com. 1973), Assn. of Bar of City of N.Y. (surrogate ct. com. 1969-73), Union League Club, Century Assn. Club. (N.Y.C.), Huntington Country Club. Estate planning, Probate (including wills, trusts), Estate taxation. Office: Curtis Mallet-Prevost Colt 101 Park Ave Fl 34 New York NY 10178-0061 E-mail: mdcrary@aol.com., mcrary@cm-p.com.

CRAVEN, GEORGE W. lawyer; b. Louisville, Mar. 11, 1951; s. Mark Patrick and Doris Ann Craven; m. Jane A. Gallery, Aug. 16, 1980; children: Charles, Francis. Student, Sophia U., Tokyo, Japan, 1970-71; BA, U. Notre Dame, 1973; JD, Harvard U., 1976. Bar: Ill. 1976, U.S. Dist. Ct. (no. dist.) Ill. 1976, U.S. Tax Ct. 1977. Assoc. Sidley & Austin, Chgo., 1976—80; ptnr. Ogden & Robertson, Louisville, 1980—81; assoc. Mayer, Brown, Rowe & Maw, Chgo., 1981—82, ptnr., 1983—. Sec., United Way/Crusade of Mercy, Inc., 1997—, bd. dirs., 2001-. Mem. ABA (sect. taxation), Coun. on Fgn. Rels. (Chgo. com. 1996—), Econ. Club Chgo. Roman Catholic. Corporate, general, Corporate taxation, Taxation, general. Office: Mayer Brown Rowe & Maw 190 S La Salle St Ste 3100 Chicago IL 60603-3441 E-mail: gcraven@mayerbrown.com.

CRAVEN, THOMAS ARTHUR, lawyer; b. Portland, Oreg., June 13, 1941; s. Leavitt Homer and Maude (Galloway) C.; m. Patricia Hope Wong, Feb. 2, 1974; 1 child, Kelly Wong. B.A., Stanford U., 1963, J.D., 1966. Bar: Calif. 1966, U.S. Dist. Ct. (ea. dist.) Calif. 1968. Assoc., Diepenbrock, Wulff, Plant & Hannegan LLC, Sacramento, Calif., 1969-75, ptnr., 1975-98, pres., 1988—; of counsel Pillsbury Madison & Sutro LLP, 1999-2000; solo practice Law Office of Thomas A. Craven, 1999—. Bd. dirs. Ctr. for Civic Edn., Calabasas, Calif., 1974— ; pres. Sacramento Estate Planning Council, 1980-81; chmn. Sacramento Law-Related Edn. Conf., 1980— ; pres., chmn. bd. Ctr. Youth Citizenship, 1984-94. Served to capt. U.S. Army, 1966-68. Mem. Sacramento County Bar Assn. (pres. 1978). Democrat. Estate planning, Probate (including wills, trusts), Estate taxation. Office: 400 Capitol Mall 17th Floor Sacramento CA 95814

CRAWFORD, DEWEY BYERS, lawyer; b. Saginaw, Mich., Dec. 22, 1941; s. Edward Owen and Ruth (Wentworth) C.; m. Nancy Elizabeth Eck, Mar. 24, 1973. AB in Econs., Dartmouth Coll., 1963; JD with distinction, U. Mich., 1966. Bar: Ill. 1967, U.S. Dist. Ct. (no. dist.) Ill. 1969. Assoc. Gardner, Carton & Douglas, Chgo., 1969-74, ptnr., 1975—. Adj. prof. law, ITT, Kent Sch. Law, 1992—. Contbr. articles to profl. jours. Chmn. Winnetka (Ill.) Caucus Coun., 1988-89; governing mem. Chgo Symphony, Chgo. Bot. Garden. With U.S. Army, 1966-68, Vietnam. Mem. ABA, Chgo. Bar Assn., Am. Coll. Investment Counsel, Lawyers Club Chgo., Legal Club Chgo., Exec. Club Chgo. Republican. Congregationalist. Avocations: running, reading, music. Finance, Mergers and acquisitions, Securities. Office: Gardner Carton & Douglas LLC 191 N Wacker Dr Ste 3700 Chicago IL 60606-1698 E-mail: dcrawford@gcd.com.

CRAWFORD, HOWARD ALLEN, lawyer; b. Stafford, Kans., Aug. 4, 1917; s. Perry V. and Kate (Allen) C.; m. Millie Houseworth, Oct. 9, 1948; children: Catherine, Edward BS, Kans. State U., 1939; JD, U. Mich., 1942. Bar: Kans. 1942, Mo. 1943, U.S. Ct. Appeals (8th, 10th and D.C. cirs.), U.S. Supreme Ct. Mem. firm Lathrop and Gage, Kansas City, Mo., 1950-91; mng. ptnr. Lathrop and Norquist, Kansas City, Mo., 1970-85, ret., 1991. Dir. various cos. Mem. coun. City of Mission Hills, Kans., 1965-70 Mem. Lawyers Assn. Kansas City, Kansas City Club, Mission Hills Country Club. Corporate, general, Probate (including wills, trusts), Estate taxation. Home: 3103 W 67th Ter Shawnee Mission KS 66208-1857 Office: Lathrop and Gage 2345 Grand Blvd Fl 25 Kansas City MO 64108-2603

CRAWFORD, JOHN FORT, lawyer; b. N.Y.C., Sept. 23, 1937; s. Alfred Ross and Barbara (Fort) C.; m. Elisabeth Tjerneld, June 6, 1962 (div.); 1 child, Alexander Olaf; m. Anne-Gabrielle Laurent, May 19, 1989; children: Cyril David, William Franklin. BA, Haverford Coll., 1958; MA, Fletcher Sch., 1959; postgrad., Inst. d'Etudes Politiques, Paris, 1959-61; JD, Columbia U., 1964. Bar: D.C. 1965, U.S. Ct. Appeals D.C. 1965, Paris 1970. Assoc. Surrey & Morse, Washington, 1964-68; spl. asst. to dir. gen. ILO, Geneva, 1968-70; assoc. Surrey & Morse, Paris, 1970-71, ptnr., 1971-85, Jones, Day, Reavis & Pogue, Paris, 1986—, vice chmn. Bd. govs. Am. Hosp. Paris, 1983—; vice chmn. internat. bd. overseers Tufts U., 1988—; chmn. Haverford Internat. Coun., 2002—; mem. adv. coun. U.S. and fgn. comml. svc. U.S. Dept. Commerce, 1988-91; bd. dirs. Aspen Inst. France, 1985—; trustee Carnegie Instn., Washington, 1994—. Decorated chevalier Legion of Honor (France); L.J. Palmer scholar, 1957-58; Noble Found. fellow, 1958-60. Mem. ABA, Bar Assn. D.C., Assn. Bar City N.Y., Internat. Bar Assn., Am. C. of C. in France (dir. 1976—, pres. 1985-88), European Coun. Am. C. of C. (chmn. 1987-90), Internat. C. of C. (coun. 1976—), U.S. Coun. for Internat. Bus. (trustee 1988—), Institut pour l'Arbitrage Internat. (treas., dir. 1985—), Coun. Fgn. Rels., Cercle de l'Union Interalliee (Paris; bd. dirs.), Polo de Paris, Nouveau Cercle de l'Union, Maxim's Bus. Home: 9 Ave Emile Deschanel 75007 Paris France Office: 120 Rue Faubourg St Honore 75008 Paris France

CRAWFORD, JOHN RICHARD, lawyer; b. St. Petersburg, Fla., Sept. 18, 1951; s. Robert Ray and Mary Lorraine (Allen) C.; m. Barbara S. Dula, June 9, 1973 (div. Nov. 1997); children: Daniel E., Neil P. BA, U. Fla., 1973, JD, 1975. Bar: Fla. 1976, U.S. Dist. Ct. (mid. dist.) Fla. 1976, U.S. Tax Ct. 1979, Ga. 1995. Atty. Jennings, Watts, Clarke & Hamilton, Jacksonville, Fla., 1976-78, Kent, Watts & Durden, Jacksonville, Fla., 1978-86; mng. atty. Kent & Crawford, Jacksonville, Fla., 1986—. Bd. dirs. Tom Coughlin Jay Fund Found.; past chmn. Catholic Found. St. Augustine. Mem. Estate Planning Coun. N.E. Fla., Planned Giving Coun. N.E. Fla. Republican. Roman Catholic. Office: Kent & Crawford 225 Water St Ste 900 Jacksonville FL 32202-5142 E-mail: JRC@FirstCoastLaw.com.

CRAWFORD, LINDA SIBERY, lawyer, educator; b. Ann Arbor, Mich., Apr. 27, 1947; d. Donald Eugene and Verla Lillian (Schenck) Sibery; m. Leland Allardice Crawford, Apr. 4, 1970; children: Christina, Lillian, Leland. Student, Keele U., 1969; BA, U. Mich., 1969; postgrad., SUNY, Potsdam, 1971; JD, U. Maine, 1977. Bar: Maine 1977, U.S. Dist. Ct. Maine 1982, U.S. Ct. Appeals (1st cir.) 1983. Tchr. Pub. Sch., Tupper Lake, N.Y., 1970-71; asst. dist. atty. State of Maine, Farmington, 1977-79, asst. atty. gen. Augusta, Maine, 1979-95; prin. Litigation Consulting Firm, N.Y.C. & Hallowell, Maine, 1986—, Linda Crawford and Assoc. Law Firm, Hallowell, Maine, 1995-2000. Legal adv. U. Maine, Farmington, 1975; legal counsel Fire Marshall's Office, Maine, 1980-83, Warden Svc., Maine, 1981-83, Dept. Mental Health, 1983-90, litigation divsn. 1990-95; mem. tchg. team trial advocacy Law Sch., Harvard U., 1987—; lectr. Sch. Medicine Harvard U., 1991; counsel to Bd. of Registration in Medicine, 1994-95; chmn. editl. bd. Mental and Physical Disability Law Reporter, 1993-95; arbitrator Am. Arbitration Assn., 1995—; facilitator Nat. Constrn. Task Force, St. Louis, 1995. Contbg. editor: Med. Malpractice Law and Strategy, 1997—, Managed Care Law Strategist, 1999—2002. Bd. dirs. Diocesan Human Rels. Coun., Maine, 1977-78, Arthritis Found., Maine, 1983-88; atty. expert commn. experts UN War Crime Investigation in the former Yugoslavia, 1994. Named one of Outstanding Young Women of Yr. Jaycees, 1981. Mem. ABA (com. on disability 1992-95), Nat. Assn. State Mental Health Attys. (treas. 1984-86, vice chmn. 1987-89, chmn. 1989-91), Nat. Health Lawyers Assn. State civil litigation, Health, Personal injury (including property damage). Home and Office: 1643 Cambridge #77 Cambridge MA 02138 also: 45 Rockefeller Plz Fl 20 New York NY 10111-2099 E-mail: lscrawford@aol.com.

CRAWFORD, MURIEL LAURA, lawyer, author, educator; d. Mason Leland and Pauline Marie (DesIlets) Henderson; m. Barrett Matson Crawford, May 10, 1959; children: Laura Joanne, Janet Muriel, Barbara Elizabeth. BA with honors, U. Ill., 1973; JD with honors, Ill. Inst. Tech., 1977; cert. employee benefit splst., U. Pa., 1989. Bar: Ill. 1977, Calif. 1991, U.S. Dist. Ct. (no. dist.) Ill. 1977, U.S. Dist. Ct. (no. dist.) Calif. 1991, U.S. Ct. Appeals (7th cir.) 1977, U.S. Ct. Appeals (9th cir.) 1991; CLU; chartered fin. cons. Atty. Washington Nat. Ins. Co., Evanston, Ill., 1977-80; sr. atty., 1980-81; asst. counsel, 1982-83; asst. gen. counsel, 1984-87; assoc. gen. counsel, sec., 1987-89; cons. employee benefit splst., 1989-91; assoc. Hancock, Rothert & Bushoft, San Francisco, 1991-92. Author: (with Beadles) Law and the Life Insurance Contract, 1989, (sole author) 7th edit., 1994, Life and Health Insurance Law, 8th edit., 1998; co-author: Legal Aspects of AIDS, 1990; contbr. articles to profl. jours. Recipient Am. Jurisprudence award Lawyer's Coop. Pub. Co., 1975, 2nd prize Internat. LeTourneau Student Med.-Legal Article Contest, 1976, LOMA FLMI Ins. Edn. award, 1999. Fellow Life Mgmt. Inst.; mem. Ill. Inst. Tech./Chgo.-Kent Alumni Assn. (bd. dirs. 1983-89, Bar and Gavel Soc. award 1977). Democrat.

CRAWFORD, ROBERT F. lawyer; b. Wahpeton, N.D., Apr. 21, 1948; s. William F. and Maryann Crawford; children: William, Courtney. BA, U. N.D., 1970; JD, Ariz. State U., 1973, MBA, 1983. Bar: Ariz. 1973, N.D. 1973, Minn. 1973, U.S. Dist. Ct. Ariz. 1975. Asst. prosecutor City of Phoenix, Phoenix, 1974—84, asst. city counsel Civil divsn., 1984—85, ct. adminstr. mcpl. ct., 1985—86; pvt. practice Scottsdale, Ariz., 1986—. Mem. Ariz. Com. on Profl. Responsibility, 1984—94; judge pro-tem Mesa Mcpl. Ct., 2001—. Pres. Broadmor PTA, Tempe, Ariz., 1993—95; mem. budget adv. com. Tempe Elem. Sch. Dist., Tempe, 1999. Mem.: ABA, Scottsdale Bar Assn., Maricopa County Bar Assn. (Vol. of Month Vol. Lawyer Program 2002), State Bar Ariz. Assn., Ariz. Bar Found. Avocations: coaching youth softball, coaching youth baseball. Criminal, Personal injury (including property damage), Probate (including wills, trusts). Office: 7509 E First St Scottsdale AZ 85251

CRAWFORD, ROY EDGINGTON, III, lawyer; b. Topeka, Dec. 23, 1938; s. Roy E. and Ethel Trula (Senne) C.; children: Michael, Jennifer. BS, U. Pa., 1960; LL.B., Stanford U., 1963. Bar: Calif. 1964, U.S. Ct. Mil. Appeals 1964, U.S. Tax Ct. 1969, U.S. Dist. Ct. (no. dist.) Calif. 1971, U.S. Ct. Claims 1974, U.S. Supreme Ct. 1979. Assoc. Brobeck Phleger & Harison, San Francisco, 1967-73, ptnr., 1973—2003; spl. counsel Heller, Ehrman, White & McAuliffe, San Francisco, 2003—. Bd. dirs. Sqauw Valley Ski Corp. Contbr. chpts. to books; bd. editors: Stanford U. Law Rev., 1962-63. Served to capt. AUS, 1964-67. Recipient award of merit U.S. Ski Assn., 1980 Mem. ABA (chmn. com. on state and local taxes 1979-81), Calif. State Bar Assn., San Francisco Bar Assn., Calif. Trout (bd. dirs. 1970-1992, v.p. 1975-94, sec.-treas. 1994-2001), The Nature Conservancy of Idaho (bd. dirs. 1994—), Yosemite Inst. (bd. dirs. 1997—), Beta Gamma Sigma. State and local taxation. Office: Heller Ehrman White & McAuliffe 333 Bush St San Francisco CA 94104

CRAWFORD, SUSAN JEAN, federal judge; b. Pitts., Apr. 22, 1947; d. William Elmer Jr. and Joan Ruth (Bielau) C.; m. Roger W. Higgins; 1 child, Kelley S. BA, Bucknell U., 1969; JD, New Eng. Sch. Law, 1977. Bar: Md. 1977, D.C. 1980, U.S. Ct. Appeals for Armed Forces 1985, U.S. Supreme Ct. 1993. Tchr. history, coach Radnor (Pa.) H.S., 1969-74; assoc. Burnett & Eiswert, Oakland, Md., 1977-79; ptnr. Burnett, Eiswert and Crawford, Oakland, 1979-81; prin. dep. gen. counsel U.S. Dept. Army, Washington, 1981-83, gen. counsel, 1983-89; insp. gen. U.S. Dept. Def., Arlington, Va., 1989-91; judge U.S. Ct. Appeals for the Armed Forces, Washington, 1991-99, chief judge, 1999—. Asst. states atty. Garrett County, Md., 1978-79; instr. Garrett County C.C., 1979-81. Del. Md. Forestry Adv. Commn., Garrett County, 1978-81, Md. Commn. for Women, Garrett County, 1980-83; chair Rep. State Cen. Com., Garrett County, 1978-81; trustee Bucknell U., 1988—, New England Sch. Law, 1989—. Mem. FBA, Md. Bar Assn., D.C. Bar Assn., Edward Bennett Williams Am. Inn of Ct. Presbyterian. Office: US Ct Appeals Armed Forces 450 E St NW Washington DC 20442-0001

CRAWFORD, THOMAS HARDY, lawyer, publisher; b. Covina, Calif., Aug. 18, 1937; s. Glenn A. and Ruth Lee (Hardy) C.; m. Caroline Canfield Cooley, Mar. 24, 1962; children: Hardy, Martha, Caitlin. BA, Stanford U., 1959; JD, George Washington U., 1964. Bar: D.C. 1964, Calif. 1969. Fgn. Svc. officer USIA, 1964-68; atty. Crawford & Haskins, San Francisco, 1969-76; country dir. Ea. Caribbean, Peace Corps, Barbados, 1979-82; counsel, v.p. Am. Learning Corp., Huntington Beach, 1982-84; atty. Continuing Edn. of Bar, Berkeley, 1985-89, Bay Area Air Quality Mgmt. Dist., San Francisco, 1976-79, 89—. Owenr, pub. Green Trees Press, San Francisco, 1994— Contbr. articles to legal publs., chpt. to book. Lt. (j.g.) USN, 1959-61. Democrat. Home: 67 7th Ave San Francisco CA 94118-1204

CRAWFORD, WILLIAM WALSH, retired consumer products company executive; b. Clearwater, Fla., Oct. 7, 1927; s. Francis Marion and Frances Marie (Walsh) C. BS, Georgetown U., 1950; LL.B., Harvard, 1954. Bar: N.Y. 1955, Ill. 1972. Assoc. Sullivan & Cromwell, N.Y.C., 1954-58; counsel Esso Standard Oil, N.Y.C., 1958-60; ptnr. Alexander & Green, N.Y.C., 1960-71; v.p., gen. counsel Internat. Harvester Co., Chgo., 1971-76, v.p., gen. counsel, sec., 1976-80; sr. v.p. gen. counsel Kraft, Inc., Glenview, Ill., 1980-81; sr. v.p., gen. counsel, sec. Dart & Kraft, Inc., 1981-86, Kraft, Inc., 1986-88, sr. v.p., sec., 1988-89, ret., 1989. Mem. ABA, Ill. Bar Assn., Assn. Bar City N.Y., Am. Judicature Soc., Am. Law Inst., Assn. Gen. Counsel, Chgo. Club, River Club (N.Y.C.), Beach Club, Everglades Club, Old Guard Soc. Palm Beach Golfers.

CREAMER, ROBERT ALLAN, lawyer; b. Sept. 25, 1941; m. Joy A. Blakslee. BA, Northwestern U., 1963; LLB, Harvard U., 1967. Bar: Ill. 1967, U.S. Dist. Ct. (no. dist.) Ill. 1967, U.S. Ct. Appeals (7th cir.) 1969, U.S. Supreme Ct. 1976. Assoc. Keck, Mahin & Cate, Chgo., 1967—73, ptnr., 1974—93; v.p., loss prevention counsel Attys.' Liability Assurance Soc., Inc., Chgo., 1994—. Adj. prof. John Marshall Law Sch., Chgo., 1969—75, Northwestern U. Sch. Law, Chgo., 2000—. Mem.: ABA, Am. Law Inst., Ill. Bar Assn. (chmn. standing com. profl. conduct 1990—91, 1997—98), Chgo. Bar Assn., Northwestern U. Alumni Assn. (pres. 1990—94), Univ. Club (Chgo.), Cliff Dwellers Club (Chgo.), Lawyers Club Chgo. Democrat. Episcopalian. General civil litigation, Insurance. Home: 1500 Oak Ave Evanston IL 60201-4279 Office: Attys' Liability Assurance Soc Inc 311 S Wacker Dr Ste 5700 Chicago IL 60606-6629 Fax: 312-697-6901. E-mail: racreamer@alas.com.

CREATURA, MARK ANTHONY, lawyer; b. Conn., 1959; AB, Harvard U., 1980; JD, U. Calif., Berkeley, 1985. Bar: Calif. 1985. Atty. Troy & Gould, L.A., 1985-93; v.p., gen. counsel Urethane Technologies, Inc., Santa Ana, Calif., 1993-96; sr. v.p., gen. counsel Consumer Portfolio Svcs., Inc., Irvine, Calif., 1996—. Finance, Securities. Office: Consumer Portfolio Svcs Inc 16355 Laguna Canyon Rd Irvine CA 92618-3801 E-mail: markc@consumerportfolio.com.

CREBBIN, ANTHONY MICEK, lawyer, retired military officer; b. Columbus, Neb., Sept. 10, 1952; s. Harry and Donna Mae (Micek) C. BA, Rockhurst Coll., 1974; JD, St Louis U., 1977; LLM, JAG Sch., 1989; M in Jud. Studies, U. Nev., Reno, 2000. Bar: Mo. 1977, U.S. Ct. Mil. Appeals 1980, Hawaii 1987, U.S. Supreme Court 1989. Commd. 2d lt. USMC, 1978, advanced through grades to maj., 1986, trial counsel, 1979, officer legal assistance, def. counsel, 1980, chief trial counsel, 1982, chief def. counsel Kaneohe Bay, Hawaii, 1986-87, chief legal assistance, 1987-88, staff judge adv. marine amphibious unit, 1980—81, 1984—85, mil. judge Camp Pendleton, Calif., 1989-92; dep. staff judge adv. Camp Pendleton, Calif., 1992-95; judge adv. 3d Marine Air Wing, Miramar, Calif., 1995-97; law clk. to Hon. John A. Borron, Jr., Probate Ct., Jackson County, Mo., 2000—. Mem. ABA, Mo. Bar Assn., Hawaii Bar Assn. Democrat. Roman Catholic. Avocations: marathoning, scuba diving, snow skiing.

CREEL, LUTHER EDWARD, III, lawyer; b. Huntsville, Ala., Sept. 23, 1937; s. Luther Edward and June (Oldacre) C.; m. Nan Dee McHalek, Apr. 11, 1974; children by previous marriage: Scott Mitchell, Todd Oldacre. AB in Psychology, George Washington U., 1959; JD, So. Methodist U., 1963. Bar: Tex. 1963. Pvt. practice, Dallas, 1963—; chmn. Creel & Atwood (and predecessors), Dallas, 1971-96; of counsel Malouf, Lynch, Jackson, Kessler & Collins, Dallas, 1996-98; chmn. Creel, Susman & Moore, Dallas, 1998—. Chmn. The Pines Camp, 1999—2001; lectr. in bankruptcy and reorgn. law. Contbr. articles to profl. jours. Chmn. Ford Debtor Assistance Program, 1995-98. Mem. Dallas Bar Assn. (chmn. bankruptcy sect. 1972), State Bar Tex. (cert. bus. bankruptcy specialist 1989, chmn. bankruptcy com. 1979-81), Am. Bankruptcy Inst. (co-founder, pres. 1982-87, vice-chmn. 1987-96, bd. dirs. 1982-2000, chmn. 1996-98, chmn. emeritus 1998-2000), Am. Coll. Bankruptcy (co-founder, fellow, pres. 1996-97), John C. Ford Inn of Ct. (master, exec. com. 1999—), Park Cities Club, GTG Tex. Longhorn Assn. (pres. 1998-2000), Internat. Tex. Longhorn Assn. (bd. dirs.). Republican. Baptist. Bankruptcy. Home: 7214 Desco Dr Dallas TX 75225-2003 Office: Creel Susman & Moore 8235 Douglas Ave Ste 1100 Dallas TX 75225-6011

CREEL, THOMAS LEONARD, lawyer; b. Kansas City, Mo., June 21, 1937; s. Thomas Howard and Elizabeth Alberta (Sharon) C.; m. Carol M. Plaisted, Nov. 26, 1992; children: Charles, Andrew, Andrea, Thomas. BS, U. Kans., 1960; LLB, U. Mich., 1963. Bar: Mich. 1963, N.Y. 1967, D.C. 1983, U.S. Supreme Ct. 1973, Ct. Mil. Appeals, 1964, U.S. Patent and Trademark Office 1965. Assoc. Kenyon and Kenyon, N.Y.C., 1966-74, ptnr., 1974-92, Kaye, Scholer, Fierman, Hayes & Handler, N.Y.C., 1992—2001, Goodwin Procter LLP , N.Y.C., 2001—. Faculty lectr. Columbia U. Sch. Law, N.Y.C., 1984-2001. Editor: Guide to Patent Arbitration, 1987. Capt., U.S. Army, 1963-66. Mem. ABA, Fed. Bar Coun., N.Y. Intellectual Property Law Assn. (past pres.), Am. Intellectual Property Assn. Intellectual property, Patent, Alternative dispute resolution. Home: 104 Cedar Cliff Rd Riverside CT 06878-2606 Office: Goodwin Procter LLP 599 Lexington Ave New York NY 10022

CREELMAN, ANN VIRGINA, lawyer; b. Sommerset, NJ, Nov. 23, 1952; d. William Kitchell Creelman and Janet Margaret Fitch; m. Nabil Abboud, June 14, 1975 (div. Nov. 4, 1998); children: Catherine Abboud, Christopher Abboud. ML, Univ. Paris, 1981. Bar: Paris (conseil juridique) 1982. Assoc. Willkie Farr & Gallagher, Paris, 1981—88, ptnr., 1988—91; ptnr. head of corp. Frere Cholmey Bischoff, Paris, 1991—98, Watson Farley Williams, Paris, 1998—2000; sole practioner Paris, 2000—01; ptnr. Granrut Vatier Baudelot et Associes, Paris, 2001, Vatier & Associés, Paris, 2002—. Mem.: Internat. Bar Assn. Home: 107 bd Murat 75016 Paris France Office: Vatier et Associés 12 rue d'Astorg 75008 Paris France

CREENAN, KATHERINE HERAS, lawyer; b. Elizabeth, N.J., Oct. 7, 1945; d. Victor Joseph and Katherine Regina (Lederer) Petervary; m. Edward James Creenan; 1 child, David Heras. BA, Kean Univ., 1968; JD, Rutgers U., 1984. Bar: N.J. 1984, Maine, 1996, U.S. Dist. Ct. N.J. 1984, U.S. Ct. Appeals (3d cir.), 1998. Various tchg. positions including, Union and Stanhope, N.J., 1968-81; law clk. to presiding judge Superior Ct. of N.J. Appellate Div., Newark, 1984-85; assoc. Lowenstein, Sandler, Kohl, Fisher & Boylan, Roseland, N.J., 1985-88, Kirsten, Simon, Friedman, Allen, Cherin & Linken, Newark, 1988-89, Whitman & Ranson, Newark, 1989-93; sr. atty. Whitman Breed Abbott & Morgan LLP, Newark, 1993-99; assoc. Skadden, Arps, Slate, Meagher & Flom LLP, Newark, 1999—. Mem. ABA, N.J. State Bar Assn. General civil litigation, Corporate, general. Office: Skadden Arps Slate Meaghar & Flom LLP 1 Newark Ctr Newark NJ 07102-5297 E-mail: kcreenan@skadden.com.

CREGAN, MARK THOMAS, academic administrator, lawyer, priest; b. Jersey City, May 24, 1957; s. William Patrick and Bernice Cregan. AB, Stonehill Coll., 1978; MDiv, U. St. Michael's Coll., Toronto, Ont., Can., 1984; JD, Bklyn. Law Sch., 1990. Bar: N.Y. 1990, Mass. 1990, U.S. Ct. Appeals (1st cir.) 1990, DC 1991, U.S. Dist. Ct. P.R. 1992, U.S. Supreme Ct. 1994, U.S. Dist. Ct. (so. and ea. dists.) N.Y. 1996, U.S. Dist. Ct. Mass. 2001. Assoc. pastor Punnoquia Santa Cruz, Chiorbote, 1983—84, Our Lady Gen Counsel Ch., Bklyn., 1984—89; law clk. U.S. Dist. Ct. Paentohuo, San Juan, PR, 1990—92; pvt. practice Bronx, NY, 1992—, Easton, Mass., 1992—; pastor Sacred Heart Parish, Bronx, 1992—2000; pres., gen. counsel Stonehill Coll., Easton, 2000—. Cons., 1992—. Office: Stonehill Coll 320 Washington St North Easton MA 02357

CREHAN, JOSEPH EDWARD, lawyer; b. Detroit, Dec. 8, 1938; s. Owen Thomas and Marguerite (Dunn) C.; m. Sheila Anderson, Nov. 6, 1965; children: Kerry Marie, Christa Ellen. AB, Wayne State U., Detroit, 1961; JD, Ind. U., 1965. Bar: Ind. 1965, Mich. 1966, U.S. Supreme Ct. 1984. Pvt. practice, Detroit, 1966-68; assoc. Louisell & Barris (P.C.), 1968-72; ptnr. Fenton, Nederlander, Dodge, Barris & Crehan (P.C.), 1972-74, Barris & Crehan (P.C.), 1975-88; pvt. practice Bloomfield Hills, Mich. and Naples, Fla., 1977—. Mem. Am. Trial Lawyers Assn. Roman Catholic. Federal civil litigation, General practice, Personal injury (including property damage). Home and Office: 827 Bentwood Dr Naples FL 34108-8204

CREHORE, CHARLES AARON, lawyer; b. Lorain, Ohio, Sept. 15, 1946; s. Charles Case and Catherine Elizabeth Crehore; 1 child, Charles Case II. BA, Wittenberg U., 1968; postgrad., U. Mich., 1968-69, Cleve. State U., 1972-73; JD, U. Akron, 1976; diploma mgmt. mgrs. program, Pa. State U., 1983. Bar: US Patent Office 1975, Ohio 1976, US Dist Ct (no dist) Ohio 1976, US Ct Appeals (DC cir) 1977, US Tax Ct 1977, US Supreme Ct 1980, US Ct Appeals (fed cir) 1982. Assoc. chemist B.F. Goodrich Co., Akron, 1969-70, chemist, 1970-72, sr. chemist, 1972, patent atty. trainee, 1972-74, sr. patent atty. trainee, 1974-75, patent assoc., 1975-76, patent atty., 1976-79; atty. regulatory affairs The Lubrizol Corp., Wickliffe, Ohio, 1979-81, corp. counsel environment, health and safety, 1981-85, sr. corp. counsel, 1985-94, counsel, 1994-99; patent atty. Hudak and Shunk Co., L.P.A., 2000; of counsel Ulmer & Berne, LLP, 2000—. Guest lectr, moot ct judge Case Western Res Univ, 1983—; spkr. Calif Inst Bus Law, Ohio, 1991, Northeast Ohio Software Asn, 2001—, Lakeland Cmty. Coll., 2001—, Media Profls. Conf., 2002—; adv bd applied environ mgmt program Lake Erie Col, 1991—94. Grantee, Kennedy Found, 1968—69; scholar, Delta Sigma Phi Found, 1968—69. Mem.: ABA, Cleve. Intellectual Property Law Assn., Am. Intellectual Property Law Assn., Greater Cleve. Intellectual Lawyers Group, Phi Alpha Delta. Intellectual property, Patent, Trademark and copyright. Home: PO Box 466 Wickliffe OH 44092-0466 Office: Penton Meda Bldg 1300 E 9th St Ste 900 Cleveland OH 44114 E-mail: ccrehore@aol.com.

CREIGHTON, WILLIAM BREEN, lawyer, educator; b. Belfast, No. Ireland, June 18, 1947; s. Robert John and Evelyn Margaret (Henderson) C.; m. Carolynn Muir Mackie, Sept. 3, 1976 (div.); children: Katharine Mackie, Rebecca Breen. LLB, Queens U., Belfast, 1969; PhD, Cambridge (Eng.) U., 1975; LLB, U. Melbourne, 1998. Sr. lectr., reader in law U. Melbourne, 1977-88; legal officer Australian Coun. Trade Unions, Melbourne, 1986-88; prin. legal officer Internat. Labour Orgn., Geneva, 1988-91; cons. Dept. Indsl. Rels., Commonwealth of Australia, Canberra, 1991-92; prof. law and legal studies La Trobe U., Melbourne, 1992-96; professorial fellow U. Melbourne, 1998—; spl. counsel Corrs Chambers Westgarth, Melbourne, 1997-99, ptnr., 1999—. Mem. Adminstrv. Rev. Coun., Canberra, 1987-88; adv. com. on distbn. of powers Constl. Commn., Canberra, 1986-88; com. on indsl. legislation Nat. Labour Coun., Canberra, 1986-88; mem. Occupational Health and Safety Commn. of Victoria, Melbourne, 1985-86. Co-author: Labour Law: An Introduction, 3d edit., 2000, Labour Law: Text and Materials, 2d edit., 1993; joint editor Australian Jour. Labour Law, 1992-2002; author acad. study. Avocations: food, wine, bush walking, reading. Labor (including EEOC, Fair Labor Standards Act, labor-management relations, NLRB, OSHA). Home: 544 Park Street Carlton North VIC 3054 Australia Office: Corrs Chambers Westgarth 600 Bourke St Melbourne VIC 3000 Australia E-mail: breen_creighton@corrs.com.au.

CREIM, JERRY ALAN, lawyer; b. Chattanooga, Oct. 20, 1956; s. James Mond and Claire Sylvia Creim; m. Sarah McNeel Hrobsky, Mar. 25, 1983; children: Daniel, Elizabeth. BA, Emory U., 1978; JD cum laude, U. Puget Sound, Tacoma, 1981. Bar: Wash. 1981, U.S. Dist. Ct. Wash. 1984, U.S. Ct. Appeals (9th cir.) 1984. Law clk. to chief judge Wash. State Ct. Appeals, Seattle, 1981-83; assoc. Williams, Kastner & Gibbs PLLC, Seattle, 1983-89, ptnr., 1990—. Named Top Lawyer, Seattle Mag., 2003, Wash. Super Lawyer, Wash. Law and Politics, LLC, 2003. Fellow Am. Coll. Mortgage Attys.; mem. Bldg. Owners and Mgrs. Assn. (assoc., bd. trustees, course instr. 1993-95, trustee 2002—). Avocations: fly fishing, fly tying, golf. Corporate, general, Mergers and acquisitions, Property, real (including real estate development, water). Office: Williams Kastner & Gibbs PLLC 601 Union St Ste 4100 Seattle WA 98101-1368

CREMER, LEON EARL, federal agent, lawyer; b. Cin., Dec. 30, 1945; s. Walter H. and Beatrice (Campbell) C. BS, Calif. State U., 1973; MA, George Washington U., 1976; JD, Rutgers U., 1982. Bar: Pa. 1982. Officer U.S. Secret Svc., Washington, 1975-77; spl. agt. U.S. Bur. Alcohol Tobacco and Firearms, U.S. Dept. Treasury, Phila., 1977-83, FBI, U.S. Dept. Justice, N.Y.C., 1983—. With U.S. Army, 1968-69. Mem. ABA, FBI Agts. Assn., Phila. Bar Assn., Pa. Bar Assn., Am. Trial Lawyers Assn., Internat. Platform Assn., Am. Mensa Soc. Avocations: yachting, aviation, skiing, tennis, long-distance running. Office: FBI 26 Federal Plz New York NY 10278-0127

CREMINS, WILLIAM CARROLL, lawyer; b. Virginia Beach, Va., Nov. 13, 1957; s. James Smyth and Mary Louise (Gallagher) C.; m. Kelly Robin Knapp, July 6, 1985; children: William Carroll Jr., Robert Gallagher. BA, BJ, U. Mo., 1980; JD, St. John's U., 1984. Bar: Tenn. 1984, N.Y. 1985, U.S. Dist. Ct. (ea. dist.) Tenn., U.S. Ct. Appeals (6th cir.). Assoc. Law Offices of J.D. Lee, Knoxville, Tenn., 1984-85; pvt. practice, Knoxville, 1986—. Dep. nat. organizer Ancient Order of Hibernians in Am., Inc., Tenn., 1985, pres. James Dardis divsn., 1997, 98; bd. dirs. Florence Crittenton Agy. of Knoxville, Inc., 1989-96, 2002—, pres., 1995; Little League baseball coach, 1993-97, football coach, 1987, 1993-94, soccer coach, 1992, 1995. Recipient Pro Bono award Knoxville Bar Assn. Vol. Legal Assistance Program, 1992. Mem. ATLA (Advocate recognition 1994), ABA, Tenn. Bar Assn., Knoxville Bar Assn., Tenn. Trial Lawyers Assn. Roman Catholic. General civil litigation, Family and matrimonial, Personal injury (including property damage). Home: 710 Saint John Ct Knoxville TN 37922-1556 Office: 810 Henley St Knoxville TN 37902-2901 Fax: 865 546-7151. E-mail: wmcremins@aol.com.

CRENSHAW, FRANCIS NELSON, retired lawyer; b. Washington, Dec. 9, 1922; s. Russell Sydnor and Sally Nelson (Robins) C.; m. Jane Elizabeth Treadwell, Aug. 20, 1949 (dec. June 1993); children: Elizabeth, Page, Marian; m. Anne Bolling Alfriend, July 12, 1997. Grad., St. George's Sch., 1939; BA, U. Va., 1943, LLB, 1948. Bar: Va. 1948. Ptnr. Baird, White & Lanning, Norfolk, 1952-55, Baird, Crenshaw & Lanning, Norfolk, 1955-60, Baird, Crenshaw & Ware, Norfolk, 1960-68, Crenshaw, Ware & Johnson, Norfolk, 1968-89, Crenshaw, Ware & Martin, Norfolk, 1989-99; ret., 1999. Mem. Va. Bd. Bar Examiners, 1973-90, pres., 1983-90. Mem. Norfolk City Sch. Bd., 1955-64, chmn., 1962-64; bd. visitors Old Dominion U., 1968-76, rector, 1972-76; mem. bd. commrs., Ea. Va. Med. Authority, 1966-68. Served with USNR, 1943-46. Decorated Bronze Star. Fellow ABA, Va. Law Found.; mem. Va. Bar Assn. (chmn. exec. com. 1988-89), Va. State Bar (chmn. sr. lawyers sect. 1998-99; editor sr. lawyers newsletter 1999-2002), Norfolk-Portsmouth Bar Assn. (pres. 1967), Maritime Law Assn. Home: 305 Brooke Ave Unit 208 Norfolk VA 23510 Office: 1200 Bank Am Bldg Norfolk VA 23510

CREPEAU, DEWEY LEE, lawyer, educator; b. Richmond Heights, Mo., June 3, 1956; s. Dewey Lee and Floy Evelyn (Lacefield) Crapo; m. Susan Jane Stonner, July 15, 1978; children: Elizabeth, Courtney, Luke. AB, U. Mo., 1977, JD, 1980. Bar: Mo. 1980, U.S. Dist. Ct. (we. dist.) Mo. 1980, U.S. Ct. Appeals (8th cir.) 1984, U.S. Tax Ct. 2000. Assoc. William Johnson, P.C., Versailles, Mo., 1980-81; asst. prosecutor Morgan County, Mo., 1980; legal aid atty. Mid-Mo. Legal Services Corp., Columbia, 1981; pvt. practice Columbia, 1982—. Adj. prof. criminal justice Columbia Coll., 1983-84; adj. prof. bus. law U. Mo., 1988-90. Active Christian Fellowship of Columbia. Mem. Nat. Lawyers Assn., Mo. Bar Assn., Boone County Bar Assn., Nat. Orgn. Social Security Claimants' Reps., Order Barristers. Pension, profit-sharing, and employee benefits, Workers' compensation. Home: 212 Bright Star Dr Columbia MO 65203-0279 Office: 2501 W Ash St Columbia MO 65203-4609

CREWE, TRENTON GUY, JR., lawyer; b. Portsmouth, Va., June 22, 1950; s. Trenton Guy Sr. and Celia Lois (Conner) C.; m. Maetta H. Newman, May 14, 1988; 1 child, John Tyler Lee; 1 stepchild, Christopher David Newman. BA, Marshall U., 1972; JD, Washington & Lee U., 1975. Bar: W.Va. 1975, Va. 1976. Assoc. Campbell, Young & Hodges, Wytheville, Va., 1975-78, ptnr., 1978-85, Campbell, Young & Crewe, Wytheville, 1985-89; pres. Crewe & Davis, P.C., Wytheville, 1989-92, Trenton G. Crewe Jr., P.C., Wytheville, 1992—. Substitute judge Juvenile, Domestic Rels. and Gen. Dist. Cts., Va., 1983-90, pres. Va. Municiple League, 2000-2001. Mem. Town Council, Wytheville, 1983-89; pres. Wytheville Baseball Club, 1985—1987; mayor Town of Wytheville, 1990—. Mem. ABA, Va. Bar Assn., 27th Jud. Cir. (v.p. 1983-85, pres. 1985—), Wytheville Jaycees (internal v.p. 1979). Democrat. Presbyterian. Avocations: flying, jogging, fishing, hunting. Criminal, Personal injury (including property damage), Property, real (including real estate development, water). Home: View Pointe 895 S Main St Wytheville VA 24382 Office: 210 W Main St # 200 Wytheville VA 24382-2332

CRICHTON, THOMAS, IV, lawyer; b. Shreveport, La., Dec. 2, 1947; Student, Vanderbilt U.; BS, La. State U., 1969, JD, 1972. Bar: Tex. 1972, La. 1972, D.C. 1988. Mem. Vinson & Elkins, LLP, Dallas. Adj. prof. sch. law U. Houston, 1978-86. Mem. Order of Coif, Beta Alpha Psi, Beta Gamma Sigma, Omicron Delta Kappa, Phi Kappa Phi. Corporate taxation, Taxation, general, Personal income taxation. Office: Vinson & Elkins LLP 3700 Trammell Crow Ctr Dallas TX 75201-2975 also: Vinson & Elkins LLP 2500 First City Tower 1001 Fannin St Ste 3300 Houston TX 77002-6706 also: Vinson & Elkins LLP 1455 Pennsylvania Ave NW Fl 7 Washington DC 20004-1008

CRIGLER, B. WAUGH, US magistrate judge; b. Charlottesville, Virginia, July 17, 1948; s. Bernard Weaver and Jayne (Waugh) C.; m. Anne (Kendall), June 20, 1970; children: C. Kendall, Jason C., and Anne Stuart. BA in history, Washington and Lee U., 1970; JD, U. Tenn., 1973. Bar: Tenn., 1973, U.S. Dist. Ct. (ea. dist.) Tenn., 1973, Va., 1974, D.C., 1974, U.S. Dist. Ct. (we. and ea. dist.) Va., 1975, U.S. Ct. Appeals (4th cir.) 1978, U.S. Supreme Ct., 1979. Law clk. to presiding judge U.S. Dist. Ct. Tenn., Knoxville, Tenn., 1973-74; ptnr. Lea and Crigler, Culpeper, Va., 1974-75, Lea, Davies, Crigler, and Barrell, Culpeper, Va., 1975-79, Davies, Crigler, Barrell, and Will, PC, Culpeper, Va., 1979-81; magistrate judge U.S. Dist. Ct., Charlottesville, Va., 1981—. Instr. Trial Practice Sch. Law, U. Va., 1986—; mem. criminal rules adv. com. Jud. Conf. U.S., 1992-97; mem. Fed. and State Jud. Coun., Va., 1992-2001. Mem.: ABA (criminal law com. young lawyers divsn. 1974—80), Tenn. Bar Assn., Va. Bar Assn. (chmn. criminal law corrections young lawyers divsn. 1979—80), Va. State Bar (standing com. on professionalism 1997—2003, chmn. and moderator VSB Professionalism for Law Students. 2000—), Thomas Jefferson Inn of Ct. (pres. 1991—92), Order of Coif, Phi Kappa Phi. Avocations: landscaping, swimming, biblical studies. Home: 100 Peterson Pl Charlottesville VA 22901-3175 Office: US Magistrate Judge 255 W Main St Rm 328 Charlottesville VA 22902-5058

CRINION, GREGORY PAUL, lawyer; b. Eau Claire, Wis., Feb. 19, 1959; s. Harlan D. and Shirley P. (Paff) C. BBA cum laude, U. Wis., Eau Claire, 1981; MBA, U. Minn., 1982; JD cum laude, U. Wis., 1985. Bar: Wis. 1985, Tex. 1985, U.S. Dist. Ct. (we. dist.) Wis. 1985, U.S. Dist. Ct. (so. dist.) Tex. 1985, U.S. Ct. Appeals (5th cir.) 1985, U.S. Dist. Ct. (ea. dist.) Tex. 1986, U.S. Ct. Appeals (7th cir.) 1986, D.C. 1987, Colo. 1994, U.S. Supreme Ct. 1989, U.S. Dist. Ct. (we. dist.) Tex. 1989, U.S. Dist. Ct. (no. dist.) Tex. 1990; cert. ski instr. Atty. Exxon Co., U.S.A., Houston, 1985-87, Exxon Corp., N.Y.C., 1987; from assoc. to ptnr. Jackson Walker, LLP (and predecessor firms), Houston, 1987-97; ptnr. Citti & Crinion, L.L.P., Houston, 1997-99, Ashby & Whitmire, LLP, Houston, 1999—. Bd. dirs., pres. Innovative Alternatives, Inc., 2000-02. Apptd. NORM (Naturally Occurring Radioactive Material) Adv. Com., 1996-99, sign ordinance rev. com. City of Friendswood, 1996-98, cmty. and econ. devel. com., 2000—, chair, 2002—; mem. Galveston County Mediation Svcs. Bd., 2000-02; mem. Leadership Friendswood Class I, 2001-02. Recipient Scroll of Appreciation U.S. Army, Europe, 1984. Mem. ABA, Houston Bar Assn., Tex. Petroleum Marketers and Convenience Store Assn. Federal civil litigation, State civil litigation, Environmental. Office: Ashby & Whitmire LLP 1002 Gemini St Ste 116 Houston TX 77058-2746

CRISER, MARSHALL M. lawyer, retired university president; b. Rumson, N.J., Sept. 4, 1928; s. Marshall and Louise (Johnson) C.; m. Paula Porcher, Apr. 27, 1957; children: Marshall III, Edward, Mary, Glenn, Kimberly, Mark. BSBA, U. Fla., 1951, LLB, 1951 (replaced by J.D., 1967). Bar: Fla. 1951. Pvt. practice, Palm Beach, 1953-84; ptnr. Gunster, Yoakley, Criser & Stewart, 1955-84; atty. Palm Beach County Sch. Bd., 1958-64; pres. U. Fla., Gainesville, 1984-89, pres. emeritus, 1989—; shareholder Mahoney, Adams & Criser, Jacksonville, Fla., 1989-97; of counsel McGuire, Woods Battle, & Boothe, LLP, Jacksonville, 1998-2000, ret. ptnr., 2000—. Dept. chmn. Rinker Group Ltd., 2003—; chmn. bd. dirs. Rinker Materials, Corp.; mem. pres.'s coun. NCAA, 1986-87; chmn. Installment Land Sales Bd., 1963-64, chmn. Acad. Task Force rev. tort and ins. law, Fla., 1986-88, The Emerald Funds; chmn. bd. trustees Emerald Fund, 1997-98. Bd. dirs. Univ. Med. Ctr., Jacksonville, 1989-96, Shands at Jacksonville Hosp., 1999-2003, M.E. Rinker Found., 1998—; bd. dirs. Shands Tchg. Hosp., Gainesville, Fla., pres., 1984-89, bd. govs., 1996-2001; bd. govs. Good Samaritan Hosp., West Palm Beach, pres., 1979-84; mem. Fla. Bd. Regents, 1965, 71-81, chmn., 1974-77, Bus.-Higher Edn. Forum, 1987-89; trustee Collins Ctr., 1989-99; pres. Alliance for World Class Edn., Duval County, 1998-2001; chmn. Fed. Crt. Adv. Group Mid. Dist. of Fla., 1991-96; trustee U. Fla., 2001—, chmn., 2001-; mem. Fla. Fed. Jud. Nominating Com., 2001—; mem. Gov.'s Med. Malpractice Task Force, 2002—. With U.S. Army, 1951-53. Fellow Am. Bar Found.; mem. Fla. Coun. 100 (chmn. 1979-80), ABA (ho. dels. 1968-72), Fla. Bar (gov. 1960-68, pres. 1968-69), Fla. Blue Key, Phi Delta Phi, Sigma Nu. Office: McGuire Woods Et Al 3400 Bank of America Ctr Jacksonville FL 32201

CRISLIP, STEPHEN RAY, lawyer; b. Oak Hill, W.Va., Apr. 23, 1948; s. Raymond Brooks and Virginia Lucille Crislip; m. Melinda Lee White, Mar. 6, 1976; children: Brooks H., Seth M. BA in Polit. Sci., W.Va. U., 1970, JD, 1973. Bar: W.Va. 1973, U.S. Dist. (no. and so. dists.) W.Va. 1973, U.S. Dist. Ct. (ea. dist.) Ky. 1974, U.S. Ct. Appeals (4th cir.) 1987. Assoc. Jackson, Kelly, Holt & O'Farrell, Charleston, W.Va., 1973-80; ptnr. Jackson Kelly PLLC, Charleston, 1980—. Mem. vis. com. W.Va. Coll. Law, 1997-2000. Bd. dirs. Greater Kanawha Valley Found., Charleston, 1996—, chmn., 2001—; chmn. bd. dirs. YMCA, Charleston, 1997-98. Mem. ABA, Assn. Def. Trial Attys. (exec. coun. 1992-95, nat. membership chair 1998—), Def. Trial Attys. W.Va. (pres. 1997), W.Va. Bar Assn., Kanawha County Bar Assn., Def. Rsch. Inst. Republican. Methodist. General civil litigation, Personal injury (including property damage), Professional liability. Office: Jackson Kelly PLLC 1600 Laidley Tower Charleston WV 25301-2189 E-mail: scrislip@jacksonkelly.com.

CRISPINO, JERRY L. judge; b. N.Y.C., Apr. 17, 1930; s. Louis Crispino and Nina Fucci; m. Marguerite Probo; children: Nina, Louis. BA, Manhattan Coll., 1952; postgrad., NYU; LLB, Fordham U., 1955. Bar: N.Y. 1955, U.S. Supreme Ct. 1959. Adminstrv. asst. to U.S. Congressman Alfred E. Santangelo, 1962—63; assoc. counsel joint legis. com. Study N.Y. State Alcoholic Beverage Laws, 1964; mem. Cmty. Planning Bd. No. 11, 1965—67; arbitrator Am. Arbitration Assn., 1969—75; coun. mem. N.Y.C., 1975—91, chmn. health com., mem. com. pub. safety, 1st chmn. new land use com.; judge Supreme Ct. State of N.Y., 1992—. Dem. candidate State Senator 33d S.D., Bronx, 1968, 1970; dep. commr. City Dept. of Real Estate, 1974; mem. Bronx County Cath. Interracial Coun., Allerton Ave. Homeowners Assn.; past bd. dirs. Victory Day Care Ctr., Inc., Bronx Found. Sr. Citizens, Nat. Multiple Sclerosis Soc.; mem. Chester Civic Assn. With N.Y. N.G., 1955—58, maj. N.Y. N.G. Named Legislator of the Yr., Evander Childs HS, 1984, Disting. Humanitarian, Am. Jewish Congress, 1984, Dedicated Svc. award, Boston Secor Tenants Assn., 1985; recipient Distng. Svc. Arbitrator award, Am. Arbitrator Assn., 1969, cert. Appreciation, U.S. Pres., 1972, Hon. citizenship, Boys Town Rome, 1978, Cmty. Support award, Decatur Dem. Club, 1980, Cmty. Svc. award, Woodlawn Taxpayers Assn., 1980, Winthrop Tenants Assn., 1983, Mindbulder Creative Arts Ctr., 1986, Cmty. Svc. & Support award, Edenwald/Gunhill Com. Ctr., 1983, Dedicated Svc. award, 1985, Distng. Leadership award, Alcoholism Coun. Greater N.Y., 1984, Svc. & Support to Youth award, Cmty. Sch. Bd. #11, 1987, others. Fellow: No. Bronx Dem. Club; mem.: NAACP (life), Colombia Lawyers Assn., Bronx County Bar Assn., N.Y. State Bar Assn., La Salle Alumni Assn., Fordham Law Sch. Alumni Assn., Columbus-Esca Alliance, Order Sons of Italy. Avocations: tennis, swimming, reading, politics. Office: 851 Grand Concourse Bronx NY 10451-2937

CRIST, CHARLES (CHARLIE CRIST), state attorney general; b. Altoona, Pa., July 24, 1956; Student, Wake Forest U., 1974-76; BS in Govt., minor in edn., Fla. State U., 1978; JD, Samford U., 1981. Mem. Fla. State Senate, Tallahassee, 1992—98; dep. sec. Fla. Dept. Bus. and Profl. Regulation, 1999—2000; atty. gen. State of Fla., 2003—. Mem. Subcom. D. Criminal Justice Ways and Means Com., 1996-98, Judiciary Com., 1996-98, Govtl. Reform and Oversight Com., 1996-98, Criminal Justice Com., 1996-98; chmn. Exec. Bus., Ethics and Elections Com., 1996-98; former state dir. U.S. Sen. Connie Mack; chmn. anti-trust adv. com. Sen. Connie Mack's Baseball Anti-Trust Adv. Com.; mem. Sen. Connie Mack's Fed. Jud. Adv. Com.; mem. ethics com. Fla. Bar. Mem. Pinellas County Rep. Exec. Com., Area Agy. on Bay Mgmt.; mem. adminstrv. bd. First United Meth. Ch.; mem. Booster Fla. State U.; bd. dirs. Found. for Fla.'s Future, Op. PAR, Police Athletic League; mem. adv. com. Tampa Bay MDA. Recipient Phil Piton award for svc. Major League Baseball, Leadership St. Petersburg, Roll Call award Fla. C. of C., 1993, PACE award, 1993, Legis. award Pinellas Sch. Adminstrs., 1993, Fla. Assn. Sch. Adminstrs., 1993, Fla. Sheriffs Assn., 1994, 96, Govt. award Urban League, 1995, Senatorial Leadership award Fla. Prosecuting Attys. Assn., 1995, Legis. Conservation award Fla. Conservation Assn., 1996, Disting. Legislator award Fla. Police Benevolent Assn., 1996; named Conservationist Legislator of Yr. Fla. Wildlife Fedn., 1995, Legislator of Yr. Police Benevolent Assn., 1995, Hon. Sheriff, 1995. Fellow Am. Swiss Assn.; mem. ABA, Am. Lung Assn. (mem. pres.'s coun. Pinellas County), Fla. Conservation Assn., St. Petersburg C. of C., Pinellas Pk. C. of C., Hillsborough Bar Assn., St. Petersburg Bar Assn., Rep. Nat. Lawyers Assn. (bd. govs.), Suncoasters Civic Club, Rotary, Suncoast Tiger Bay Club (bd. dirs., True Grit award). Republican. Methodist. Avocations: water skiing, reading, jogging. Office: Office of Atty Gen State of Fla The Capitol Tallahassee FL 32399*

CRIST, PAUL GRANT, lawyer; b. Denver, Sept. 9, 1949; s. Max Warren and Marjorie Raymond (Catland) C.; m. Christine Faye Clements, June 4, 1972; children: Susan Christine, Benjamin Warren, John Willis. BA, U. Nebr., 1971; JD cum laude, NYU, 1974. Bar: Ohio 1974, U.S. Ct. Mil. Appeals 1975, Calif. 1976, U.S. Dist. Ct. (no. dist.) Ohio 1979, U.S. Ct. Appeals (6th cir.) 1982. Assoc. Jones, Day, Reavis & Pogue, Cleve., 1974, 78-83, ptnr., 1984—. Rsch. editor NYU Law Rev., 1972-74. Capt. JAGC, USAF, 1974-78. Decorated Meritorious Svc. medal. Fellow Am. Coll. Trial Lawyers; mem. Ohio State Bar Assn., Cleve. Bar Assn., State Bar Calif., Order of Coif, Am. Inns of Ct. Democrat. Presbyterian. Federal civil litigation, General civil litigation, State civil litigation. Home: 6565 Canterbury Dr Hudson OH 44236-3484 Office: Jones Day Reavis & Pogue N Point 901 Lakeside Ave E Cleveland OH 44114-1190

CRISTOL, A. JAY, federal judge; b. Fountain Hill, Pa., Feb. 25, 1929; s. Samuel and Mae (Stein) C.; m. Eleanor Rubin; children: Stephen Michael, David Alan. BA, U. Miami, 1958, LLB, 1959, PhD, 1997. Bar: Fla. 1959. Spl. asst. to Atty. Gen. of Fla., Tallahassee, 1959-65; sr. ptnr. Cristol,

Mishan, Sloto, Miami, 1959-85; judge U.S. Bankruptcy Ct., Miami, 1985-93, chief judge, 1994-99, trustee, 1982-84, chief judge emeritus, 1999—. Adj. prof. U. Miami Law Sch.; bd. govs. 11th cir. Nat. Conf. Bankruptcy Judges; bankruptcy rules adv. com. Jud. Conf. of U.S., 1995-2001; bankruptcy com. U.S. Ct. Appeals (11th cir.), 1996-2002; tchr. bankruptcy law to judges in Czech Republic, Slovenia, Thailand, Russia, India, Malaysia, Hong Kong, South Africa. Bd. trustees U. Miami, 1988-90, Coral Gables; bd. dirs. ARC, Miami, 1989—, Wings Over Miami Aviation Mus., 2001—. Capt. USNR, 1951-89. Fellow Am. Coll. Bankruptcy; mem. ABA, Am. Bankruptcy Inst., Nat. Conf. Bankruptcy Judges, Bankruptcy Bar Assn. (so. dist. of Fla.), Fla. Bar Assn., Dade County Bar Assn. Avocations: water skiing, windsurfing, flying, reading. Office: US Bankruptcy Ct 1412 Fed Bldg 51 SW 1st Ave Miami FL 33130-1669

CRITCHLOW, CHARLES HOWARD, lawyer; b. Morristown, NJ, Nov. 23, 1950; s. George F. and Florence Critchlow; m. Mary Ellen Donnelly (dec.); children: Katharine F., Mary E.G. BA, Yale U., 1972; JD, Columbia U., 1975. Bar: N.Y. 1976, U.S. Dist. Ct. (so. and ea. dists.) N.Y. 1976, U.S. Ct. Appeals (2d cir.) 1982, U.S. Ct. Appeals (3d and 10th cirs.) 1991, U.S. Supreme Ct. 1993, U.S. Ct. Appeals (5th cir.) 1994, U.S. Ct. Appeals (4th cir.) 1995, U.S. Ct. Internat. Trade 1996, U.S. Ct. Appeals (Fed. Cir.) 1996. Assoc. Lord, Day & Lord, N.Y.C., 1975-85, ptnr., 1985-86, Coudert Bros. LLP, N.Y.C., 1986—. Contbr. to Antitrust Law Developments; contbr. articles to profl. jours. Active Yale Alumni Fund; mem. Yale Alumni Schs. Com. Mem.: ABA. Antitrust, Federal civil litigation, Private international. Office: Coudert Bros LLP 1114 Avenue of the Americas New York NY 10036-7703 E-mail: critchlowc@coudert.com., ccbk91@aol.com.

CRITCHLOW, RICHARD H. lawyer; b. Pitts., Mar. 28, 1947; s. John Park and Ruth Lauderbaugh C.; m. Deirdre Lynn Flower, Feb. 18, 1979; children: Courtney Leigh, Caitlin Anne. BA in Polit. Sci., Union Coll., 1969; JD, U. Miami, 1973. Bar: Fla., 1973, U.S. Supreme Ct., 1976, U.S. Tax Ct., 1978, U.S. Dist. Ct. (ea. dist.) La. 1980, U.S. Dist. Ct. (so. dist.) Fla. 1973, U.S. Dist. Ct. (mid. dist.) Fla. 1978, U.S. Ct. Appeals (5th and 11th cirs.) 1973. Assoc. Tew, Tew, Rosen & Murray, Miami, Fla., 1973-76; ptnr. Tew & Tew, Miami, Fla., 1976-77, Tew, Critchlow, Sonberg, et al, Miami, Fla., 1977-82, Finley, Kumble, Wagner, Underberg, Manley & Casey, Miami, Fla., 1982-88; mng. ptnr. McDermott, Will & Emery, Miami, Fla., 1988-91; ptnr. Kenny, Nachwalter, Seymour, Arnold & Critchow, Miami, Fla., 1991—. Arbitrator Nat. Assn. Securities Dealers, Miami, 1988—. Active United Way of Miami, 1991. Mem. ABA (vice-chmn. TIPS 1985-87), Fla. Bar Assn. (chmn. grievance com. 1987-90). Republican. Congregationalist. General civil litigation, State civil litigation, Securities. Office: Kenny Nachwalter Seymour Arnold & Critchow 201 S Biscayne Blvd Miami FL 33131-4332

CROAKE, PAUL ALLEN, lawyer; b. Janesville, Wis., Sept. 1, 1947; s. Willard m. and Dorothy R. Croake; m. Denise L. Croake; children: Katherine, John Paul, Patrick. BA, Lawrence U., 1969; JD, U. Wis., 1972. Bar: Wis. 1972, U.S. Dist. Ct. (we. dist.) Wis. 1972, U.S. Tax Ct. 1982. Lawyer DeWitt Ross & Stevens S.C., Madison, Wis., 1972-2001. Capt. U.S. Army, 1969-80. Mem. ABA, Madison Club. Roman Catholic. Avocations: tennis, golf. Commercial, contracts (including sales of goods; commercial financing), Insurance, Taxation, general. Office: 2 E Mifflin St Ste 600 Madison WI 53703-2890 E-mail: pac@dewittross.com.

CROCKER, SAMUEL SACKETT, lawyer; b. Washington, May 17, 1943; s. Reginald D. and Elizabeth (Sackett) C.; m. Dorothy Pamela Macdonald, Dec. 5, 1970; 1 child, Dorothy. BA, Williams Coll., 1965; LLB, U. Tex., 1968. Bar: Tex. 1968, Ohio 1969, Mich. 1973, N.Y. 1975. Atty., OEO/VISTA, Columbus, Ohio, 1968-69; atty. Schlumberger Ltd., Houston, 1969-73; gen. counsel Heath Co., Benton Harbor, Mich., 1973-75; corp. counsel, asst. sec. Schlumberger Ltd., N.Y.C., 1975-78; gen. counsel Schlumberger Well Services, Houston, 1978-80; v.p., sec., gen. counsel Moran Energy, Inc., Houston, 1980-84; v.p. legal affairs Baylor Coll. Medicine, 1984-97; ptnr. Gardere Wynne Sewell & Riggs, LLP, Houston, 1998-2000; v.p., gen. counsel Talent Tree, Inc., EESIS, Inc., 2000-. Mem. ABA, Forest Club. Republican. Episcopalian. Commercial, contracts (including sales of goods; commercial financing), Health, Intellectual property. Home: 3257 Huntingdon Pl Houston TX 77019-5925 Office: Talent Tree Inc 9703 Richmond Houston TX 77042 E-mail: samuel.crocker@talenttree.com.

CROFT, TERRENCE LEE, lawyer; b. St. Louis, Apr. 13, 1940; s. Thomas L. and Anita Belle (Brown) C.; m. Merry Patton, July 9, 1977; children: Michael, Shannon, Kimberly, Kristin, BethAnn, Katherine. AB, Yale U., 1962; JD with distinction, U. Mich., 1965. Bar: Mo. 1965, U.S. Dist. Ct. (ea. dist.) Mo. 1965, Ga. 1970, Fla. 1970, U.S. Ct. Appeals (5th, 8th and 11th cirs.) 1970, U.S. Supreme Ct. Assoc. Coburn, Croft & Kohn, St. Louis, 1965-69, Hansell, Post, Brandon & Dorsey, Atlanta, 1969-73; ptnr. Huie, Sterne & Ide, Atlanta, 1973-78, Kutak, Rock & Huie, Atlanta, 1978-83; shareholder Griffin, Cochrane & Marshall, Atlanta, 1983-93; ptnr. King & Croft LLP, Atlanta, 1994—. Mem. ABA (ho. of dels. 1993-99), ATLA, State Bar Ga. (bd. govs. 2002, chair alt. dispute resolution sect.), Atlanta Bar Assn. (pres., sec., treas. bd. dirs. 1986-99, chmn., bd. dirs. litigation sect. 1982-86, pres. Alt. Dispute Resolution Lawyers sect. 1996-97), Atlanta Bar Found. (pres. 1998—), Ga. Trial Lawyers Assn., Lawyers Club Atlanta, Old War Horse Lawyers Club. Episcopalian. Avocations: hiking, shooting, motorcycling, reading. Alternative dispute resolution, General civil litigation, Construction. Home: 2580 Westminster Heath NW Atlanta GA 30327-1449 Office: King & Croft LLP 707 The Candler Bldg 127 Peachtree St NE Atlanta GA 30303-1810 Fax: 404-577-8401. E-mail: tlc@king-croft.com.

CROHN, MAX HENRY, JR., lawyer; b. Asheville, N.C., Feb. 4, 1934; s. Max Henry and Edith Pearl (Hoffman) C.; m. Barbara Jean Morris, Jan. 28, 1960; children: David Michael, Edith Ann, Randal Morris. BA in Polit. Sci, U. N.C., 1955; LL.B., Georgetown U., 1961. Bar: D.C. 1961, N.C. 1977, N.Y. 1986. Practiced in, D.C., 1961-68; trial atty. Bur. Restraint of Trade, 1963-65; atty. adviser to chmn. FTC, 1965-66; asso. mem. firm Arnold & Porter, Washington, 1966-68; asso. counsel R.J. Reynolds Industries, Inc., Winston-Salem, N.C., 1968-75, asst. gen. counsel, 1975-78; sec. R.J. Reynolds Tobacco Co., 1971-81, gen. counsel, 1978-81; ptnr. Jacob, Medinger and Finnegan, 1981-95. Former chmn. bd. dirs. Forsyth County Econ. Devel. Corp., 1975-78. Served to lt. (j.g.) USNR, 1955-58. Mem. ABA. General civil litigation, Insurance, Product liability. Home: 517 Redbud Rd Chapel Hill NC 27514-1710

CROLAND, BARRY I. lawyer; b. Paterson, N.J., Jan. 11, 1938; s. Louis L. and Rae R. (Levine) C.; m. Joan Kohlreiter, Dec. 20, 1958; children: Richard, Heidi, Lizabeth, Jennifer. BA, Middlebury Coll., 1959; JD, Rutgers U., Newark, 1961. Bar: N.J. 1962, N.Y. 1983, U.S. Ct. Appeals (3d cir.) 1973. Law clk. to Hon. John Grimshaw N.J. Superior Ct., 1961, law clk. to Hon. Morris Pashman, 1961-62; assoc. Cole, Berman & Garth, Paterson, 1962-63, Shavick, Thevos, Stern, Schotz & Steiger, Paterson, 1963-68; ptnr. Shavick, Stern, Schotz, Steiger & Croland, Paterson, 1968-79, Stern, Steiger, Croland, Tanenbaum & Schielke, Paterson, 1979-95, Shapiro & Croland, Hackensack, N.J., 1995—. Asst. bar examiner State of N.J., 1965-68; mem. Fed. Ethics Com., Dist. of N.J., 1975; lectr. Inst. for Continuing Legal Edn., Trial Advocacy and Family Law, 1975—; sec. Dist. II Ethics Com. for Bergen County, 1980-81; mem. com. on civil practice N.J. Supreme Ct., 1965, matrimonial litig. com. 1980, family ct. com., 1982, family practice com., 1983-87, 2002—. Mem. bd. editors Rutgers Law Rev., 1959-61, case editor, 1960-61; sr. editor N.J. Family Lawyer, 1981-2002. Fellow Am. Bar Found., Am. Acad. Matrimonial Lawyers (N.J. bd. mgrs.); mem. ABA (family law sect.), ATLA (matrimonial trial lawyers sect. emeritus bd. 2002--), Am. Coll. Family Trial Lawyers (diplomate 1994—), Best Lawyers in U.S. (family law 1983—), Am. Inns of Ct. (master Morris Pashman 1990-95, pres.-master N.J. family law 1995-99), N.J. State Bar Assn. (mem. exec. com. family law sect. 1981-95), Bergen County Bar Assn. (chmn. jud. and prosecutorial appts. com. 1983-95, chmn. jud. performance com. 1999-2001), N.J. Supreme Ct. (mem. civil practice com. 1965, mem. matrimonial litig. com. 1980, mem. family ct. com. 1982, mem. family practice com. 1983-87, 2002—), Assn. Trial Lawyers (N.J. matrimonial trail lawyers sect. emeritus bd. 2002--). Family and matrimonial. Home: 243 Myrtle St Haworth NJ 07641-1137 Office: Shapiro & Croland 411 Hackensack Ave Fl 6 Hackensack NJ 07601-6365

CROMARTIE, ERIC ROSS, lawyer; b. Washington, Jan. 14, 1955; s. William Adrian and Dorothy Jane (Cann) C.; m. Lynn Prendergast, Sept. 12, 1981; children: William Ross, Morgan Nicole. BA, Amherst (Mass.) Coll., 1977; JD, Harvard U., 1980. Bar: Tex. 1980, U.S. Dist. Ct. (no. and ea. dists.) Tex. 1980, U.S. Tax. Ct. 1983, U.S. Ct. Appeals (5th and 11th cirs.) 1980, U.S. Ct. Appeals (8th and 10th cirs.) 1984, U.S. Supreme Ct. 1985. Assoc. Hughes and Luce, Dallas, 1980-85, ptnr., 1985-97. Mem. ABA, Dallas Bar Assn., Am. Law Inst. General civil litigation. Home: 4247 Brookview Dr Dallas TX 75220-3801

CROMER, CHARLES LEMUEL, lawyer, state legislator; b. High Point, N.C., Jan. 27, 1939; s. Charles Norman and Wilma (Duggins) C.; m. Sheila Whitlow, Oct. 8, 1966; children: Tonja Dawn, Ashley Nicole. AA, Sandhills Community Coll., Pinehurst, N.C., 1973; BA with hons., U. N.C., 1973; JD cum laude, Wake Forest U., 1975. Bar: N.C. 1975, U.S. Ct. Appeals (4th cir. 1977). Tchr. law Davidson County Community Coll., Lexington, N.C., 1975-84; prin. Charles L. Cromer, Atty. at Law, Thomasville, N.C., 1975-90; elected mem. N.C. House Reps., 1984-90; legis. counsel Gov. Jim Martin, 1990-94. Mem. various legis. study commns., 1985—; Rep. Whip Ho. ofReps., 1989—, del. Rep. Nat. Conv., 1988. Exec. mem. Republican Party, N.C., 1982—. Served with U.S. Army, 1962-65. Mem. N.C. Acad. Trial Lawyers, High Point Assn. Retarded Citizens (Legislator of Yr. 1985, Parent of Yr. 1987). Methodist. Avocation: reading. State civil litigation, Criminal, Legislative. Home and Office: 503 Center Pointe Dr Cary NC 27513-5731

CROMLEY, BRENT REED, lawyer, state senator; b. Great Falls, Mont., June 12, 1941; s. Arthur and Louise Lilian (Hiebert) C.; m. Dorothea Mae Zamborini, Sept. 9, 1967; children: Brent Reed Jr., Giano Lorenzo, Taya Rose. AB in Math., Dartmouth Coll., 1963; JD with honors, U. Mont., 1968. Bar: Mont. 1968, U.S. Dist. Ct. Mont. 1968, U.S. Ct. Appeals (9th cir.) 1968, U.S. Supreme Ct. 1978, U.S. Ct. Claims 1988, U.S. Ct. Appeals (D.C. cir.) 1988. Law clk. to presiding justice U.S. Dist. Ct. Mont., Billings, 1968-69; assoc. Hutton & Sheehy and predecessor firms, Billings, 1969-77, ptnr., 1977-78, Moulton, Bellingham, Longo & Mather, P.C., Billings, 1979—, also bd. dirs.; mem. Mont. Ho. of Reps., 1991-92, Mont. Senate, 2003—; pres. State Bar Mont., 1998-99. Contbr. articles to profl. jours. Mem. Yellowstone Bd. Health, Billings, 1972—; chmn. Mont. Bd. Pers. Appeals, 1974-80. Mem. ABA (appellate practice com.), ACLU, Internat. Assn. Def. Counsel, State Bar Mont. (chmn. bd. trustees 1995-97, trustee 1991—, pres. 1998-99), Yellowstone County Bar Assn. (various offices), Internat. Assn. Def. Counsel, Christian Legal Soc., Internat. Brotherhood of Magicians, Kiwanis. Avocations: running, magic, pub. speaking. General civil litigation, General practice. Home: 235 Parkhill Dr Billings MT 59101-0660 Office: Moulton Bellingham Longo & Mather PC 27 N 27th St Ste 1900 Billings MT 59101-2399 E-mail: Cromley@moultonlawfirm.com.

CROMLEY, JON LOWELL, lawyer; b. Riverton, Ill., May 23, 1934; s. John Donald and Naomi M. (Mathews) C; JD, John Marshall Law Sch., 1966. Bar: Ill. 1966. Real estate title examiner Chgo. Title & Trust Co., 1966-70; pvt. practice Genoa, Ill., 1970—; mem. firm O'Grady & Cromley, Genoa, 1970-96. Bd. dirs. Citizen's First Nat. Bank, 1984-92, Kingston Mut. Ins. Co., Genoa Main St., Inc. Mem.: ABA, DeKalb County Bar Assn., Chgo. Bar Assn., Ill. State Bar Assn. Estate planning, Probate (including wills, trusts), Property, real (including real estate development, water). Home: 130 Homewood Dr Genoa IL 60135-1260 E-mail: jcromley@msn.com.

CROMPTON, CHARLES SENTMAN, JR., lawyer; b. Wilmington, Del., Dec. 30, 1936; s. Charles S. and R. Eugenia (Armstrong) C.; m. Jean W. Ashe, June 15, 1958 (div. Sept. 1976); children: Rebecca Ashe, Charles S. III; m. Milbrey Warner Dean, May 21, 1977. BA, U. Del., 1958; LLB, U. Va., 1961. Bar: Del. 1962. Law clk. to presiding justice U.S. Dist. Ct. Del., Wilmington, 1961-62; ptnr. Potter, Anderson & Corroon, Wilmington, 1962—. Bd. dirs. Wilmington Trust Co. Mem. ABA, Del. Bar Assn. (treas. 1968-72, pres. 1985-86), Am. Coll. Trial Lawyers (state chmn. 1986-88), Del. Hist. Soc. (pres. 1983-84), Raven Soc., Phi Beta Kappa. Clubs: Wilmington; Vicmead Hunt (Greenville, Del). Federal civil litigation, State civil litigation, Corporate, general. Office: Potter Anderson & Corroon PO Box 951 Wilmington DE 19899-0951 Home: Campbell Rd PO Box 3946 Greenville DE 19807-0946

CROMWELL, WILLIAM M. lawyer; b. Fayetteville, Ark., July 17, 1949; s. William Jennings Cromwell and Margaret K. (Heerwagen) Tilley; m. Jan R. Rose, Mar. 11, 1972; children: Crosby K., Joseph Cash. BSBA, U. Ark., 1971, JD, 1976. Bar: Ark. 1976, U.S. Dist. Ct. (we. dist.) Ark. 1976, U.S. Ct. Appeals (8th cir.) 1978, U.S. Supreme Ct. 1979. Ptnr. Rose, Kinsey & Cromwell, Ft. Smith, Ark., 1976-87; asst. U.S. atty. Dept. of Justice, Ft. Smith, 1987-93, 1st asst. U.S. atty., 1993-2000; with U.S. Atty., 2001. Chmn. Arthritis Found., Ft. Smith, 1996; bd. dirs. Ark. Children's Hosp., Ft. Smith, 1997. Recipient Spl. Achievement award Dept. Justice, 1989, 91. Mem. Ark. Bar Assn. (del. 1977-78), Sebastian County Bar Assn. (sec. 1979), Hardscrabble Country Club (pres.), Town Club (pres. 1982). Democrat. Methodist. Avocations: golf, fly fishing. Home: 9725 Jenny Lind Rd Fort Smith AR 72908-9154*

CRON, KEVIN RICHARD, lawyer; b. Vereeniging, Transvaal, South Africa, Feb. 25, 1956; m. Barbara Cron; children: Dylan, Erin. B in Commerce, U. Witwatersrand, South Africa, 1978, BL, 1980, ML, 1985. Ptnr., dir. Deneys Reitz, South Africa, 1982—, co. law com., 1994—. Contbg. editor Trusts and Trustees; contbr. articles to profl. jours. including Internat. Fin. Law Rev., Profl. Mgmt. Rev., others; spkr. in field. Recipient Golden Arrow award Best Lawyer in S. Africa Profl. Mgmt. Rev, 1998. Mem. TVL Law Soc., Natal Law Soc., Cape Province Law Soc., Benoni Country Club, Rand Club. Avocations: reading, trout fishing, music. Banking, Commercial, contracts (including sales of goods; commercial financing), Corporate, general. Office: Deneys Reitz Inc Reitz Bldg 82 Maude St Sandton 2146 South Africa Home: PO Box 784903 Sandton 2146 South Africa

CRONE, ALAN GRADY, lawyer; b. Memphis, July 20, 1965; s. James Gerard and Dorothy Williams Crone; m. Allison S. Crone, July 8, 1989; children: James, Charles, Margaret. BA, U. Memphis, 1987, JD, 1990. Bar: U.S. Dist. Ct. (we. dist.) Tenn. 1991, U.S. Dist. Ct. (ea. and we. dists.) Ark. 1991, U.S. Dist. Ct. (ctrl. dist.) Tenn. 1995, U.S. Multi-Dist. Litigation Panel 1996, U.S. Ct. Appeals (6th cir.) 1998, U.S. Ct. Appeals (8th cir.) 2000, U.S. Supreme Ct. 2000. With Armstrong, Allen, Prewitt, Gentry, Johnston & Holmes, Memphis, 1990—91, Fisher, Avery, Yawn & Futris, Memphis, 1992—93, Apperson, Crump, Duzane & Maxwell, Memphis, 1994; apptd. chief counsel Tenn. Dept. Employment Security, 1995; asst. Shelby County atty., 1996—; co-founder, mng. mem. Crone & Mason, PLC, Memphis, 1995—. Spkr. profl. assn. convs.; panelist Nat. Fedn. Ind. Businesses Small Bus. Summit, Nashville, 1999, Am. Soc. Indsl. Security, Program on Profl. Investigations, St. Louis, 2000; campaign mgr. Salvaggio for Congress, Memphis, 1994. Frequent commentator on legal and polit. issues various local TV and radio news programs, Memphis, 1998—. Spl. judge Shelby County Gen. Sessions and City of Memphis Ct.; chmn. Rep. Party of Shelby County, 1999—; campaign counsel Congressman Ed Bryant, 1994, fin. com., 1994; steering com. Rep. Party of Shelby County, 1991—95; bd. dirs. Family Svcs. of Mid-South, 1996—98, Fire Mus. Memphis, 1998—2001, treas., 1999—2000. Mem.: ABA (litigation sect., coms. on pretrial practice and procedure and class s), Def. Rsch. Inst., Tenn. Def. Lawyers Assn., Ark. Bar Assn., Tenn. Bar Assn., Memphis Bar Assn. Roman Catholic. Labor (including EEOC, Fair Labor Standards Act, labor-management relations, NLRB, OSHA), Commercial, contracts (including sales of goods; commercial financing), Trademark and copyright. Office: Crone & Mason PLC 8 S 3d St 5th Fl Memphis TN 38103 Office Fax: 901-529-1432. E-mail: acrone@cronemason.com.

CRONIN, PHILIP MARK, lawyer; b. Boston, July 21, 1932; s. Herbert Joseph and Elizabeth Ann (Sullivan) C.; m. Paula Cook Budlong, June 8, 1957; children: Thomas B., Philip S. AB, Harvard U., 1953, LL.B., 1956. Bar: Mass. 1956. Sr. ptnr. firm Withington, Cross, Park & Groden, Boston, 1956-89, Peabody & Arnold, Boston, 1989—. Pres., pub. Harvard mag., 1971-78; city solicitor, Cambridge, Mass., 1968-72 Mng. editor: Mass. Law Rev, 1976-81; editor in chief, 1981-90; editor Mass. Legal History Jour., 1996—. Trustee Harvard Crimson, 1972—; pres. Cambridge Homes, 1991-94; overseer Mass. Supreme Jud. Ct. Hist. Soc., 1994—, editor jour., 1995—. Home: 3 Lincoln Ln Cambridge MA 02138-3351 Office: 50 Rowes Wharf Boston MA 02110-3339

CRONSON, ROBERT GRANVILLE, lawyer; b. Chgo., Dec. 23, 1924; s. Berthold A. and Ethel (Larson) C.; m. Agnes L. Diaz; children from previous marriage: Karen, Christopher, Keelyn, Morgan, Seth. AB in Econs., Dartmouth Coll., 1947; JD, U. Chgo., 1950. Bar: Ill. 1950. Atty. Daily, Dines, Ross & O'Keefe, Chgo., 1951-53; ptnr. DeBoice, Greening, Ackerman & Cronson, Springfield, Ill., 1957-60; asst. sec. of state of Ill. Springfield, 1958-64; sr. vp., sec. The Chgo. Corp., Chgo., 1965-73; assoc. prof. pub. adminstrn. Roosevelt U., 1973-74; adj. prof. adminstrn. Sangamon State U., 1983-87; auditor gen. State of Ill., 1974-92; retired, 1992. Mem. exec. com. post audit sect. Nat. Conf. State Legislatures, 1976-85, Nat. Assn. State Auditors, Comptrs. and Treasurers, 1979-81, and Nat. Intergovtl. Audit Forum, 1974-76; mem. Midwest Intergovtl. Audit Forum, 1974-92; adv. com. govt. acctg. standards Govt. Acctg. Stds. Bd. 1984-85. Chmn. Midwest Vehicle Proration Compact, 1959-61, Ill. Securities Adv. Com., 1964-73; chmn. William H. Chamberlain Scholarship Fund, Sangamon State U., 1972-85. Cpl. USMCR, 1942-46. Recipient Fin. Mgmt. Improvement (Scantlebury) award U.S. Govt., 1980 Mem. Midwest Securities Commrs. Assn. (chmn. 1959-64), Securities Industry Assn. Am. (chmn. state legislation com. 1970-72), Nat. State Auditors Assn. (pres. 1980-81), Pi Alpha Alpha (hon.), Phi Kappa Psi. E-mail: cronson@sbcglobal.net.

CROOK, DONALD MARTIN, lawyer; b. Wichita, Kans., Dec. 18, 1947; s. Leroy R. and Audrey E. (Mattiason). BA in History/Polit. Sci. with honors, U. Kans., 1970; JD, U. Chgo., 1973. Bar: N.Y. 1974, Tex. 1982. Assoc. Kramer, Levin, Nessen, Kamin & Frankel, N.Y.C., 1973-75, Layton & Sherman, N.Y.C., 1975-80; counsel LTV Corp., Dallas, 1980-85; chief counsel corp. affairs Kimberly-Clark Corp., Dallas, 1985-99, v.p., sec., 1986-99. Mem. ABA, Tex. Bar Assn., Dallas Bar Assn. (chmn. corp. counsel sect. 1986-87), Am. Soc. Corp. Secs. Banking, Corporate, general, Mergers and acquisitions.

CROOKS, N(EIL) PATRICK, state supreme court justice; b. Green Bay, Wis., May 16, 1938; s. George Merrill and Aurelia Ellen (O'Neill) C.; m. Kristin Marie Madson, Feb. 15, 1964; children: Michael, Molly, Kevin, Kathleen, Peggy, Eileen. BA magna cum laude, St. Norbert Coll., 1960; JD, U. Notre Dame, 1963. Bar: Wis. 1963, U.S. Supreme Ct. 1969. Assoc. Cohen and Parins, Green Bay, 1963; ptnr. Cohen, Grant, Crooks and Parins, Green Bay, 1966-70; sr. ptnr. Crooks, Jerry, Norman and Dilweg, Green Bay, 1970-77; judge Brown County (Wis.) Ct., 1977-78, Brown County (Wis.) Cir. Ct., 1978-96; justice Wis. Supreme Ct., Madison, 1996—. Instr. bus. law U. Wis., Green Bay, 1970-72; mem. faculty Wis. Jud. Coll., 1982. Editor Law Rev. Notre Dame, 1962-63. Pres. Brown County United Way, 1976-78; chmn. Brown County Legal Aid, 1971-73; mem. Northeast Criminal Justice Coord. Coun., 1973-85; pres. St. Joseph Acad. Sch. Bd., 1987-89. Capt. U.S. Army, 1963-66. Recipient Human Rights award Baha'i Community of Green Bay, 1971, Disting. Achievement award in Social Sci. St. Norbert Coll., 1977 award of Yr. U. Notre Dame, 1978, Brown County Vandalism Prevention Assn. award, 1982, W. Heraly MacDonald award Brown County United Way, 1983, Community Svc. award St. Joseph Acad., 1989, Alma Mater award St. Norbert Coll., 1992, Disting. Alumnus of Yr. award notre Dame Acad., 2002; named Wis. Trial Judge of the Year Wis. Chpt. Am. Bd. of Trial Advocates, 1994. Mem. ABA, FBA, State Bar Wis., Brown County Bar Assn. (pres. 1977), Wis. Acad. Trial Lawyers, Wis. Law Found. (bd. dirs., mem. exec. com.), Nat. Conf. of Appellate Ct. Judges, Assn. of Women Lawyers for Brown County, Dane County Bar Assn., James E. Doyle Am. Inn of Ct., Wis. Jud. Coun. Roman Catholic. Home: 5329 Lighthouse Bay Dr Madison WI 53704-1113 Office: PO Box 1688 State Capitol 16 E Madison WI 53701

CROOM, SAM GASTON, JR., lawyer; b. Mar. 25, 1930; s. Sam Gaston and Lola Mae (Whorton) Croom; m. Earlane Baccus, Nov. 28, 1952; children: Curtis B., Carolyn Croom Beatty. BBA, U. Tex., Austin, 1952, LLB, 1957. Bar: Tex. 1957. Ptnr. Baker & Botts, Houston, 1957—. Served to lt. USNR, 1952—54. Mem.: Am. Automobile Assn. (mem. adv. bd. dirs., chmn.), Southwest Pension Conf., Athletic of Houston, Houston Racquet (past dir.). Republican. Presbyterian. Pension, profit-sharing, and employee benefits. Office: Baker & Botts 1 Shell Plz Houston TX 77002 Home: 1421 Winrock Blvd Houston TX 77057-1729

CROSBY, THOMAS MANVILLE, JR., lawyer; b. Mpls., Oct. 9, 1938; s. Thomas M. and Ella (Pillsbury) C.; m. Eleanor Rauch, June 12, 1965; children: Stewart, Brewster, Grant, Brooke. BA, Yale U., 1960, LLB, 1965. Bar: Minn. 1965. Assoc. Faegre & Benson, Mpls., 1965-72, ptnr., 1965—. Served to lt. USNR, 1960—62. Corporate, general, Property, real (including real estate development, water). Office: Faegre & Benson 2200 Wells Fargo Ctr 90 S 7th St Ste 2200 Minneapolis MN 55402-3901

CROSBY, WILLIAM DUNCAN, JR., lawyer; b. Louisville, Ky., Sept. 1, 1943; s. William Duncan and Lucille (Edwards) C.; m. Constance Elaine Frederick, June 2, 1973; children: William Duncan III, Lelia Margaret. BA, Yale U., 1965; JD, Columbia U., 1968. Bar: Ky. 1968, U.S. Dist. Ct. D.C. 1971, U.S. Supreme Ct. 1977. Rep. chief counsel Com. on Rules U.S. Ho. of Reps., Washington, 1972-94, chief counsel Com. on Rules, 1995-99; v.p., COO The Solomon Group, Washington, 1999—2001; exec. dir. The Livingston Solomon Group, LLC, Washington, 2002—03, Livingston Group, LLC, Wash., 2003—. Chmn. Dranesville Dist., Fairfax County (Va.) Rep. Party, 1987-89; mem. Fairfax County Rep. Com., 1981—. Lt. (j.g.) USNR, 1968-71. Mem. ABA, FBA, Ky. Bar Assn., D.C. Bar, Columbia Law Sch. Alumni Assn. of Washington (pres. 1987-89). Baptist. Avocation: swimming. Home: 920 Mackall Ave Mc Lean VA 22101-1618 Office: The Livingston Solomon Group 499 South Capitol St SW Ste 600 Washington DC 20003 E-mail: billcrosby1@aol.com., bcrosby@livingstongroupdc.com.

CROSIER, DOUGLAS A. lawyer; b. Caldwell, Idaho, Oct. 4, 1948; BA, U. Hawaii, 1972, JD, 1978. Bar: Hawaii 1978. With Rush Moore Craven Sutton Morry & Beh, Honolulu. Mem.: ABA, Am. Judicature Soc., Hawaii

State Bar Assn. (pres. 2003, chair jud. adminstrn. com. 1989—95, 1999). Family and matrimonial, State civil litigation. Office: Rush Moore Craven Sutton Morry & Beh Ste 2400 Mauka Tower Pacific Guardian Ct 737 Bishop St Honolulu HI 96813*

CROSLEY, THOMAS ANDREW, lawyer; b. Freeport, Tex., Aug. 5, 1966; s. Calvin Leo and Georgia Crosley; m. Karen D. Crosley; 1 child, Andrew 1 stepchild, Julia. BBA in Fin., U. Tex., 1988; JD, U. Houston, 1992. Bar: Tex. 1992, U.S. Dist. Ct. (so. dist.) Tex. 1993, U.S. Dist. Ct. (ea. dist.) Tex. 1994, U.S. Dist. Ct. (no., we. dists.) Tex. 1996. Assoc. Brown McCarroll & Oaks Hartline, Houston, 1992—96, Branton & Hall, P.C., San Antonio, 1996—99, shareholder, 1999—. Dir. Bexar County Dispute Resolution Ctr., San Antonio, 2001—; spkr. in field. Mentor Big Bros. and Big Sisters, San Antonio, 1998—. Recipient Pres.'s award, San Antonio Bar Assn., 2001. Mem.: San Antonio Trial Lawyers Assn. (pres. 2002), San Antonio Young Lawyers Assn. (v.p. 2000), Tex. Young Lawyers Assn. (dir. 1997—2001), Am. Inn of Ct. (barrister 1996—). Avocations: reading, guitar, songwriting, water-skiing. Personal injury (including property damage), Product liability. Office: Branton and Hall PC One Riverwalk Pl # 1700 700 N Saint Marys San Antonio TX 78205 Office Fax: 210-224-1928.

CROSS, DANIEL ALBERT, lawyer; b. Moorhead, Minn., Jan. 30, 1965; s. Earl Stanley and Mary Theresa Cross; m. Michele Catherine Rini, June 6, 1992; 1 child, Siena Caterina. BA, Reed Coll., 1989; JD, Lewis and Clark Coll., 1993. Bar: Oreg. 1993. Talk show host KFXX Radio, Portland, Oreg., 1991-93; legal intern Saxon, Marquoit & Bertoni, Portland, Oreg., 1992-93; atty. Bertoni & Todd, Portland, Oreg., 1993-99; ptnr. Cross & Lurtz, Hillsboro, Oreg., 1999—2002; pvt. practice Hillsboro, Oreg., 2003—. Judge mock trial competition and appellate advocacy competition Northwestern Sch. Law, Lewis and Clark Coll., 1994-2003, mentor, 1997-99. Mem., v.p. Order of Sons of Italy in Am., Beaverton, Oreg., 1997-2000. Mem. Oreg. State Bar, Oreg. Criminal Def. Lawyers Assn. (bd. dirs. 2002—), Multnomah County Bar Assn., Washington County Bar Assn. Avocations: wine, literature (1st editions), blues and jazz, gourmet food. Appellate, Criminal, Juvenile. Office: The Law Offices of Daniel A Cross 230 NE 2d Ave Ste D Hillsboro OR 97124-3074 E-mail: crosslaw@msn.com.

CROSS, ELMO GARNETT, JR., lawyer; b. Richmond, Va., Feb. 19, 1942; m. Anne Geddy. B.S., U. Richmond, 1963; LL.B., T.C. Williams Sch. Law, 1966. Bar: Va. 1966. ptnr. Cross & Cross, Mechanicsville, Va., 1972—; mem. Va. State Senate, 1976-96. Served with U.S. Army, 1966-68. Mem. Va. State Bar Assn., Hanover Bar Assn. Methodist.

CROSS, JEFFREY D. lawyer, electric power industry executive; b. Painesville, Ohio, Apr. 28, 1956; BA summa cum laude, U. Cin., 1978, JD, 1982. Bar: Ohio 1982. Acting gen. counsel Am. Electric Power Svc. Corp., Columbus, Ohio, sr. v.p., gen. counsel, 2002—. Mem. legal com. Edison Electric. Mem.: ABA, Columbus Bar Assn., Ohio State Bar Assn., Energy Bar Assn., Ctrl. Ohio Breathing Assn. (trustee), Phi Beta Kappa. Corporate, general, Finance, Utilities, public. Office: Am Electric Power Svc Corp Legal Dept 1 Riverside Plz Columbus OH 43215-2373 Office Fax: 614-233-1687. Business E-Mail: jdcross@aep.com.*

CROSS, MILTON H. lawyer; b. Phila., July 28, 1942; s. Sidney B. and Edythe Cross; m. Joyce Volchok, June 4, 1966; children: Brian, Jonathon. BS, U. San Francisco, 1965; JD, Villanova U., 1968. Bar: Pa. 1968. Corp. counsel AEL, Inc., Phila., 1968-75; assoc. Cohen, Verlin, Sherzer & Porter, Phila., 1975-78; pvt. practice Phila., 1978-79; ptnr. Monteverde & Hemphill, Phila., 1980-96, Spector, Gadon & Rosen, Phila., 1996—. Adj. prof. Phila. Coll. Textiles and Sci., 1970-73. Chmn. Cheltenham Twp. Sch. Bd. Authority. Mem. ABA (sect. corp., banking and bus. law), Pa. Bar Assn., Phila. Bar Assn. Commercial, contracts (including sales of goods; commercial financing), Corporate, general, Property, real (including real estate development, water). Home: 251 Ironwood Cir Elkins Park PA 19027-1315 Office: Spector Gadon & Rosen 7 Penn Ctr Fl 7 Philadelphia PA 19103-2200

CROSS, ROBERT WILLIAM, lawyer, venture capital executive; b. Balt., Oct. 9, 1937; s. Rosamond and Mildred (Fowler) C.; m. Deanna Louise Deerr, Feb. 7, 1965; children Ann Elizabeth, Robert William II. BSBA, Washington U., St. Louis, 1962; JD, Washington U., 1964. Bar: N.Y. 1964. Assoc. Winthrop, Stimson, Putnam & Roberts, N.Y.C., 1964-68; gen. counsel Electronic Data Systems Corp., Dallas, 1968-69; pres. R.W. Cross & Co., Dallas and N.Y.C., 1970-90; chmn., CEO Cross Tech. Inc., N.Y.C., also Solebury, Pa., 1990—; pres., CEO Nanophase Tech. Corp., Romeoville, Ill., 1993-98; pres., COO Vcapital Inc., Chgo., 1999—2002; pres., CEO Vcapital Securities, Chgo., 2000—02; CEO DigitalWork, Inc., Chgo., 2003—. With USMC, 1957—63. Mem.: Bus. Execs. for Nat. Security, Marine Corps Assn., Univ. Club, Omicron Delta Kappa. Republican. Home: PO Box 200 Solebury PA 18963-0200 Office: Cross Tech Inc 6475 Upper York Rd Solebury PA 18963 E-mail: rcross@crosstechnologiesUS.com.

CROSS, WILLIAM DENNIS, lawyer; b. Tulsa, Nov. 7, 1940; s. John Howell and Virginia Grace (Ferrell) C.; m. Peggy Ruth Plapp, Jan. 30, 1982; children: William Dennis Jr., John Frederick. BS, U.S. Naval Acad., 1962; JD, NYU, 1969. Bar: N.Y. 1970, U.S. Dist. Ct. (so. and ea. dists.) N.Y. 1970, U.S. Ct. Appeals (2d cir.) 1970, U.S. Supreme Ct. 1974, Calif. 1977, U.S. Dist. Ct. (ctrl. dist.) Calif. 1977, U.S. Ct. Appeals (9th cir.) 1977, U.S. Ct. Appeals (5th, 10th and 11th cirs.) 1981, Mo. 1982, U.S. Dist. Ct. (we. dist.) Mo. 1982, U.S. Ct. Appeals (8th cir.) 1989, U.S. Ct. Appeals (fed. cir.) 1992, U.S. Dist. Ct. Ariz. 1997, U.S. Dist. Ct. Colo. 1997, U.S. Dist. Ct. Kans. 1998. Commd. ensign USN, 1962, advanced through ranks to lt., 1965, resigned, 1966; assoc. Cravath, Swaine & Moore, N.Y.C., 1969-76, Lillick, McHose & Charles, L.A., 1976-77; asst. gen. counsel FTC, Washington, 1977-82; of counsel Morrison & Hecker, Kansas City, Mo., 1982-83, ptnr., 1983—2002, Stinson Morrison Hecker, 2002—. Staff mem. NYU Law Rev., 1967-69, editor, 1968-69; assoc. editor Antitrust Mag. Mem. ABA, Calif. Bar Assn., Mo. Bar Assn., Assn. Bar City N.Y., Kansas City Bar Assn., Lawyers Assn. Kansas City. Administrative and regulatory, Antitrust, Federal civil litigation. Home: 1223 Huntington Rd Kansas City MO 64113-1347 Office: Stinson Morrison Hecker LLP 1201 Walnut St STe 2800 Kansas City MO 64106-2150 E-mail: dcross@stinsonmoheck.com.

CROTHERS, DANIEL J. lawyer; b. Fargo, ND, Jan. 3, 1957; BA, U. ND, 1979, JD, 1982. Law clk. NM Ct. Appeals, 1982—83; ptnr. Nilles, Hansen & Davies Ltd., Fargo. Adj. prof. Moorhead State U., 1984—90. Mem.: N.D. Bar Assn. (pres. 2001—02). General civil litigation, Appellate. Office: Nilles Hansen & Davies 1800 Radisson Tower PO Box 2626 Fargo ND 58108

CROTTY, ROBERT BELL, lawyer; b. Dallas, Aug. 16, 1951; s. Willard and Betty (Bell) C.; m. Sarah (Smith), Mar. 8, 1980; children: Robert Edwin, Rebecca Bell. BA, Va. Mil. Inst., 1973; JD, U. Tex., 1976. Bar: Tex., 1976; US Dist. Ct. (no. dist.) Tex., 1977; US Ct. Appeals (5th cir.), 1978. Assoc. Akin, Gump, Strauss, Hauer, and Feld, Dallas, 1976-82, ptnr., 1983-92, hiring ptnr., 1988-91; prin. McKool and Smith, P.C., Dallas, 1992-94; ptnr. Crotty and Johansen, LLP, Dallas, 1995—. Vis. bd. Va. Mil. Inst., 1995-99. Mem. Leadership Dallas, 1981; dir. Salesmanship Club, 1989—90, 1994—95, 2001—02, Va. Mil. Inst. Alumni Assn., 1991—95, Highland Pk. Ind. Sch. Dist. Edn. Found., 1991—97, pres., 1997—2000; chmn. bd. dir. Salesmanship Club Youth & Family Ctr., Inc., 2001—02; chmn. G.T.E. Byron Nelson Classic, 1995; bd. dir. Goodwill Industries of Dallas, Inc., 2002—; pres. Dallas Bus. League, 1983, Big Bros. Big Sisters Met. Dallas, 1987—88. First lt. U.S. Army, 1976, first lt. USAR, 1973—81. Fellow Tex. Bar Found. (sustaining); Dallas Bar Found., Fellows (pres. 1999-2000); mem. Dallas Bar Assn., Tex.; Law Rev. Assn. (life); State Bar Tex.; Northwood Club (pres. 2003). Avocations: golf, reading, hunting, hiking. General civil litigation. Office: Crotty &Johansen LLP 2311 Cedar Springs Rd Ste 250 Dallas TX 75201-7810 E-mail: bcrotty@crojolaw.com.

CROUCH, ROBERT P., JR., state agency administrator, former prosecutor; b. Mar. 28, 1948; s. Robert and Rosa Crouch; m. Clara Johnson Sept. 2, 1973; 1 child, Emily. BA, U. Md., 1971; MPA, U. N.C., 1982; JD, U. Va., 1988. Bar: Va. 1988. Aide to William B. Spong U.S. Senate, 1971-73; asst. mgr. employee benefits Fieldcrest Mills, 1973-75; adminstrv. asst. Patrick Henry Comm. Coll., 1975; adj. prof. Ferrum Coll., 1984-85; clerk circ. ct., 1976-85; assoc. McGuire, Woods, Battle & Boothe, 1988-89, Young, Haskins, Mann & Gregory, 1989-93; atty. U.S. Dept. Justice, Roanoke, Va., 1993—2001; chief dep. sec. public safety Dept. Public Safety, Va., 2002—. Mem. bd. trustees Va. Mus. Nat. History, 1989-95, pres. bd. dirs., 1990-93; mem. edn. found. Patrick Henry C.C., 1984-93; mem. bd. visitors George Mason U., 1983-91; vice chmn. Dem. Party Va., 1989-93, state party sec., 1985-89, 5th dist. com. chmn., 1981-85; chmn. statewide Wilder-Beyer-Terry Campaign Com., 1989. Mem. Va. Bar Assn., Va. Trial Lawyers Assn. Democrat. Presbyterian. Office: PO Box 1475 Richmond VA 23218*

CROUCHLEY, DANIEL GERARD, lawyer; b. Wiesbaden, Germany, Nov. 1, 1950; came to U.S., 1952; s. Edward Alfred and Mary Elizabeth (Stafford) C.; m. Maureen Therese Shanahan, Dec. 27, 1975; children: Mary Esther, Anne Maureen. BA, Creighton U., Omaha, 1973, JD cum laude, 1976. Bar: Nebr. 1976, U.S. Dist. Ct. Nebr. 1976, U.S. Ct. Appeals (8th cir.) 1980. Adminstrv. asst. Douglas County Commn., Omaha, 1976-78; dep. Douglas County atty. Omaha, 1978-81; assoc. Dwyer, O'Leary & Martin, attys., Omaha, 1981-83; atty. law dept. Met. Utilities Dist., Omaha, 1983-93, asst. gen. counsel, 1993—2001, gen. counsel, 2001—. Bd. dirs. Greater Omaha Cmty. Action, 1979-82; adult leader Boy Scouts Am., Omaha, 1993-98, trustee Mid-Am coun., 2002—. Mem. Nebr. Bar Assn. (exec. com. corp. counsel sect. 1995-97), Omaha Bar Assn. Democrat. Roman Catholic. Avocations: music, history, astronomy. Home: 4211 William St Omaha NE 68105-1749 Office: Met Utilities Dist 1723 Harney St Omaha NE 68102-1907

CROUSE, FARRELL R. lawyer; b. Portsmouth, Va., Dec. 23, 1963; s. Farrell Rondall and Grace Alice (Kenworthy) C. BA in History and Sociology, Bucknell U., Lewisburg, Pa., 1986; JD, Widener U., Wilmington, Del., 1989, LLM in Taxation, 1992. Bar: N.J. 1989, Pa. 1989, U.S. Dist. Ct. N.J. 1989. Assoc. Law Offices John William Neef, Carneys Point, N.J., 1990-91; pvt. practice Woodstown, N.J., 1991—. Mem.: ABA, Pa. Bar Assn., NJ Bar Assn. Avocations: auto racing, travel, collecting auto racing books and memorabilia. Family and matrimonial, General practice, Personal injury (including property damage). Home and Office: 36 Crimson Ct East Sewell NJ 08080-2608

CROW, NANCY REBECCA, lawyer; b. Ridgecrest, Calif., Nov. 3, 1948; d. Edwin Louis and Eleanor Elizabeth (Gish) C.; 1 child, Rebecca Ann Carr; m. Mark A.A. Skrotzki, Apr. 4, 1987. BA, Antioch Coll., 1970; JD, U. Colo., 1974; LLM in Taxation, NYU, 1977. Bars: Colo. 1974, Calif. 1977. Atty., advisor IRS, N.Y.C., 1975-77; assoc. Brawerman & Kopple, Los Angeles, 1977-80; prof. Sch. Law, U. Denver, 1980-81; of counsel Krendl & Netzorg, Denver, 1981-84; shareholder Krendl & Krendl, Denver, 1984-92, Pendleton, Friedberg, Wilson & Hennessey, P.C., Denver, 1992—. Editor estate and trust forum Colorado Lawyer, 1992-93, bd. editors, 1993-2000; contbr. chpts. to books. Mem. alumni bd. Antioch Coll., 2000—; bd. dirs. Centennial Philharmonic Orch., 1998—2001; bd. trustees Centennial Philharmonic Found., 2001—. Fellow Am. Coll. Trust and Estate Counsel; mem. ABA (chmn. Welfare Benefits subcom. of personal svcs. orgns. com. com., tax sect. 1987-92), Colo. Bar Assn. (exec. coun. tax sect. 1990-93, sec. tax sect. 1993-94, chair-elect 1994-95, chair 1995-96, bd. govs. 1996-98), Colo. Women's Bar Assn. (chair pub. policy com. 1982-83), Denver Bar Assn., Denver Tax Assn., Denver Tax Inst. Planning Com., Alliance of Profl. Women, Women's Estate Planning Coun. (bd. dirs. 1996-98), U.S.-Mex. C. of C. (bd. dirs. Rocky Mountain chpt., sec. 1998-2001), Sierra Club. Democrat. Unitarian Universalist. Avocations: skiing, backpacking, cello, running. Estate planning, Pension, profit-sharing, and employee benefits, Taxation, general. Home: 1031 Marion St Denver CO 80218-3016 Office: Pendleton Friedberg Wilson & Hennessey PC 303 E 17th Ave Ste 1000 Denver CO 80203-1263 E-mail: nrc@penberg.com.

CROW, SAM ALFRED, judge; b. Topeka, May 5, 1926; s. Samuel Wheadon and Phyllis K. (Brown) Crow; m. Ruth M. Rush, Jan. 30, 1948; children: Sam A., Dan W. BA, U. Kans., 1949; JD, Washburn U., 1952. Ptnr. Rooney, Dickinson, Prager & Crow, Topeka, 1953—63, Dickinson, Crow, Skoog & Honeyman, Topeka, 1963—70; sr. ptnr. Crow & Skoog, Topeka, 1971—75; part-time U.S. magistrate, 1973—75; U.S. magistrate, 1975—81; judge U.S. Dist. Ct. Kans., Wichita, 1981—92, Topeka, 1992—96, sr. judge, 1996—. Bd. rev. Boy Scouts Am., 1960—70, cubmaster, 1957—60; chmn. Kans. March of Dimes, 1959, bd. dirs., 1960—65, Topeka Coun. Chs., 1960—70; mem. Kans. Hist. Soc., 1960—; pres., v.p. PTA; bd. govs. Washburn Law Sch. Alumni Assn., 1993—99; mem. vestry Grace Episcopal Ch., Topeka, 1960—65. Col. JAGC USAR, ret. Named to, Topeka H.S. Hall of Fame, 2000; recipient Washburn U. Sch. Law Disting. Svc. award, 2000. Fellow: Kans. Bar Found.; mem.: ABA (del. Nat. Conf. Spl. Ct. Judges 1978), Topeka Lawyers Club (sec. 1964—65, pres. 1965—66), Wichita Bar Assn., Topeka Bar Assn. (chmn. jud. reform com., chmn. bench and bar com., chmn. criminal law com., Disting. Svc. award 2000), Nat. Assn. U.S. Magistrates (com. discovery abuse), Kans. Trial Lawyers Assn. (sec. 1959—60, pres. 1960—61), Kans. Bar Assn. (chmn. mil. law sect. 1965, 1967, 1970, trustee 1970—76, chmn. mil. law sect. 1972, 1974, 1975), Shawnee Country Club, Shriners, Am. Legion, Sigma Alpha Epsilon, Delta Theta Phi. Office: US Dist Ct 444 SE Quincy St Topeka KS 66683

CROWDER, BARBARA LYNN, judge; b. Mattoon, Ill., Feb. 3, 1956; d. Robert Dale and Martha Elizabeth (Harrison) C.; m. Lawrence Owen Taliana, Apr. 17, 1982; children: Paul Joseph, Robert Lawrence, Benjamin Owen. BA, U. Ill., 1978, JD, 1981. Bar: Ill. 1981. Assoc. Louis E. Olivero, Peru, Ill., 1981-82; asst. state's atty. Madison County, Edwardsville, Ill., 1982-84; ptnr. Robbins & Crowder, Edwardsville, Ill., 1985-87, Robbins, Crowder & Bader, Edwardsville, Ill., 1987-88, Crowder, Taliana, Rubin, and Buckley, Ill., 1988-98; assoc. judge 3d. Jud. Cir. Madison County, Ill., 1999—; presiding judge family divsn. 3d. Jud. Cir. Madison County, Ill., 2000—01, 2003—. Spkr. C.L.E. seminars Family Law Update, 1993—, 2003; co-chair 3d. Jud. Cir. Family Violence Coord. Coun., 1999—, chair ct. com., 1999—; spkr. edn. Conf. Adminstrn. Office Ill. Ct., 2002—03; mem. Spl. Supreme Ct. Com. on Child Custody Issues, Ill., 2002—03. Co-author chpts. in ISBA Family Law Handbook, 1995, Maintenance Chapter Ill. Family Law Ill. Inst. Continuing Legal Edn., 1998, supplement, 2001; contbr. articles to profl. jours. Chmn. City of Edwardsville Zoning Bd. Appeals, 1986-87; committee woman Edwardsville De, Precinct 15, 1986-98; mem. City of Edwardsville Planning Commn., 1985-87; bd. dirs. Madison-Bond County Workforce Devel. Bd., 1995-96, 96-97. Named Best Oral Advocate, Moot Ct. Bd., 1979, Outstanding Young Career Woman, Dist. XIV, Ill. Bus. and Profl. Women, 1986; recipient Alice Paul award Alton-Edwardsville NOW, 1987, Outstanding Working Woman of Ill. Ill. Fed. of Bus. and Profl. Women, 1988-89, Woman of Achievement YWCA, 1996; recipient Athena award Edwardsville/Glen Carbon C. of C., 1991. Fellow Am. Acad. Matrimonial Lawyers; mem. Ill. Bar Assn. (family law coun. sect. 1990-99, chair 1997-98, co-editor Family Law newsletter 1993, vice chair 1996-97, mem. Bench and Bar sect. coun. 2002-2003, 2003—), Ill. Judges' Assn. (bd. dirs. 2000—), Am. Judicature Soc., Ill. Fedn. Bus. and Profl. Women (parliamentaria dist. XIV 1991-92), Women Lawyers Assn. Met. East (pres. 1986), Edwardsville Bus. and Profl Women's Club (pres. 1988-89, 95-96, treas. 1989-90, Woman of Achievement award 1985, Jr. Svc. award 1987), U. Ill. Alumni Assn. (v.p. met.-east club 1994-95, bd. dirs. 1995-97). Democrat. Office: Madison County Cthse 155 N Main St Edwardsville IL 62025-1955

CROWDER, MARJORIE BRIGGS, lawyer; b. Shreveport, La., Mar. 26, 1946; d. Rowland Edmund and Marjorie Ernestine (Biles) Crowder; m. Ronald J. Briggs, July 11, 1970 (div. Nov. 2000); children: Sarah Briggs, Andrew Briggs. BA, Carson-Newman Coll., 1968; MA, Ohio State U., 1969, JD, 1975. Bar: Ohio 1975, U.S. Ct. Appeals (6th cir.) 1983, U.S. Ct. Claims 1992, U.S. Supreme Ct. 2001. Asst. dean of women Albion Coll., Mich., 1969-70; dir. residence hall Ohio State U., Columbus, 1970-71, acad. counselor, 1971-72; assoc. Porter, Wright, Morris, Arthur, Columbus, 1975—83, ptnr., 1983-2000; AmeriCorps atty. Southeastern Ohio Legal Svs., Portsmouth, Ohio, 2000—02, staff atty., 2002—. Legal aide Cmty. Law Office, Columbus, 1973—74. Co-author: (book) Going to Trial, A Step-By-Step Guide to Trial Practice and Procedure, 1989. Trustee, pres. Epilepsy Assn. Ctrl. Ohio, Columbus, 1977—84; bd. dirs. Scioto County Domestic Violence Task Force, v.p., 2001—; bd. dirs. Action Ohio Coalition Battered Women, 2002—, Columbus Speech & Hearing, 1977—82. Fellow: Columbus Bar Found. (trustee 1993—95); mem.: Scioto County Bar Assn., Columbus Bar Assn. (com. chmn. 1979—83, docket control task force 1989—91, editor 1981—83), ABA (mem. gavel awards com. 1989—96, gen. practice sect. 1983—, chair litig. com. 1987—89, mem. exec. coun. 1989—93, dir. bus. com. group 1990—91, chair program com. 1991—93, torts and ins. practice sect. 1993—, vice chair health ins. law com. 1993—96), Ohio Bar Assn. (mem. joint task force gender fairness 1991—93), Scioto County Bar Assn. Federal civil litigation, General civil litigation, Insurance. Home: 2106 Summit St Portsmouth OH 45662 Office: Southeastern Ohio Legal Svcs 800 Gallia St Ste 700 Portsmouth OH 45662-4035 E-mail: mcrowder@oslsa.org.

CROWE, DANIEL WALSTON, lawyer; b. Visalia, Calif., July 1, 1940; s. J. Thomas and Wanda (Walston) C.; m. Nancy V. Berard, May 10, 1969; children: Daniel W., Karyn Louise, Thomas Dwight. BA, U. Santa Clara, 1962; JD, U. Calif. Hastings Coll. Law, 1965. Bar: Calif. 1966, U.S. Dist. Ct. (ea. dist.) Calif. 1969, U.S. Dist. Ct. (cen. dist.) Calif. 1973, U.S. Ct. Appeals (9th cir.) 1973, U.S. Supreme Ct. 1973. Assoc. Crowe, Mitchell & Crowe, and predecessors, Visalia, Calif., 1968-74, ptnr., 1974-83; ptnr. Crowe, Williams, Jordan and Richey and predecessor firm Crowe & Williams, 1975-90, The Crowe Law Offices, 1991—; sec., treas., dir. The Exeter Devel. Co., 1969-84, Willson Ranch Co., 1983—2001. Founding mem., dir. Visalia Balloon Assn., Inc. Served to capt. U.S. Army, 1965-68. Decorated Bronze Star, Air medal, Purple Heart, Nat. Def. Svc. medal. Mem. ABA, Calif. Bar Assn., Tulare County Bar Assn., NRA, Rotary, Elks, Moose, Am. Radio Relay League, DAV. State civil litigation, Probate (including wills, trusts), Property, real (including real estate development, water). Address: PO Box 1110 Visalia CA 93279-1110

CROWE, JAMES JOSEPH, lawyer; b. New Castle, Pennsylvania, June 9, 1935; s. William J. and Anna M. (Dickson) C.; m. Joan D. (Verba), Dec. 26, 1959. BA, Pa. State U., Youngstown, Pa., 1958; JD, Georgetown U., 1963. Bar: Va. 1963, Ohio 1966. Atty. SEC, Washington, 1964-65, Gen. Tire and Rubber Co., Akron, Ohio, 1965-68; sr. atty. Eaton Corp., Cleve., 1968-72; sec. gen. counsel U.S. Shoe Corp., Cin., 1972-95, v.p., 1975-95; ptnr. Kepley, Gilligan, and Eyrich, Cin., 1996-2000; counsel Thompson Hine LLP, Cin., 2001—. Chmn. divsn. Fine Arts Fund, 1976; trustee Springer Ednl. Found., 1978-84, Cin. Music Festival Assn., 1980-86, 96—2003; group chmn. United Appeal, 1980; mem. pres. coun. Coll. Mt. St. Joseph, 1985-88; trustee Tennis for Charity Inc., 1986—, Playhouse in the Park, 1990-96, Greater Cin. Ctr. for Econ. Edn., 1992-96, Leadership Cin., Class XIV, 1990-91; trustee Cin. Nature Ctr., 1993-2000, chmn. 1996-98; bd. visitors U. Cin. Coll. Law, 1993-2002; trustee Invest in Neighborhoods, 1982-89, pres. 1984-86; trustee Cin. Hort. Soc., 1996-2002, Am. Music Scholarship Assn., 1999—. 2d lt. U.S. Army, 1958-59. Mem. Ohio Bar Assn., Cin. Bar Assn., Am. Soc. Corp. Secs., Cin. Country Club, Met. Club, Univ. Club. Corporate, general. E-mail: jcrowe7246@aol.com.

CROWE, PATRICIA MARY, family court commissioner; b. Albany, N.Y., May 6, 1946; d. James Gordon and Helen (Trenor) C.; 1 child, Adam Thimmig. MusB, U. Mo., Columbia, 1969; MusM, U. Ill., Champaign, 1971; JD, U. Wis., Madison, 1978. Bar: Wis. Assoc., shareholder Wheeler, Van Sickle, Madison, Wis., 1979-96; family ct. commr. Dane County, Madison, Wis., 1996—. Pres. bd. Madison Boychoir, 1997-98, Downtown Madison Optimist Club, 1996-97. Avocations: singing, martial arts. Office: Rm 104 210 Martin Luther King Jr Blvd 104 Madison WI 53709-0002

CROWE, ROBERT ALAN, lawyer; b. N.Y.C., Feb. 20, 1950; s. John Thomas and Annette (Korall) C.; m. Carolyn Ann Kruse, Apr. 14, 1974; children: Emily, Andrew. AB, St. Louis U., 1971, JD, 1974. Bar: Mo. 1974, U.S. Dist. Ct. Mo. 1975, U.S. Ct. Appeals (8th cir.) 1976, U.S. Ct. Appeals (7th cir.) 1977, U.S. Supreme Ct. 1977. Assoc. Law Office of Harry J. Nichols, St. Louis, 1974-76; sole practice St. Louis, 1976-83; ptnr. Kell, Kell, Custer, Weller & Crowe, St. Louis, 1983-85, Crowe & Shanahan, St. Louis, 1985—. Mem. editl. adv. bd. West's Social Security Reporting Service, 1983—; pres. U.S. Arbitration and Mediation Midwest, St. Louis, 1985-. Mem. ABA, Mo. Bar Assn., Bar Assn. Met. St. Louis, Nat. Orgn. Social Security Claimants Reps. (exec. com. 1984-92, treas. 1986-87, sec. 1987-88, v.p. 1988-89, pres. 1989-90). Pension, profit-sharing, and employee benefits. Home: 1101 Hawken Pl Saint Louis MO 63119-3911 Office: Crowe & Shanahan 720 Olive St Ste 2020 Saint Louis MO 63101-2317 E-mail: racrowe@crowe-shanahan.com.

CROWE, THOMAS LEONARD, lawyer; b. Amsterdam, N.Y., Aug. 3, 1944; s. Leonard Hoctor and Grace Agnes (O'Malley) C.; m. Barbara Ann Hauck, Aug. 2, 1969; children: Patrick, Brendan. AB, Georgetown U., 1966, JD, 1969. Law clk. to chief judge U.S. Dist. Ct. (no. dist.), Elkins, W.Va., 1969-70; trial atty. U.S. Dept. Justice, Washington, 1970-72; asst. U.S. atty. Balt., 1973-78; chief of criminal divsn. U.S. Atty.'s Office, Balt., 1977-78; ptnr. Cable, McDaniel, Bowie & Bond, Balt., 1979-91, McGuire, Woods, Battle & Boothe, Balt., 1991-95; of counsel Monshower & Miller, LLP, Columbia, Md., 1996-98; pvt. practice Balt., 1998—. Mem. jud. conf. U.S. Ct. Appeals for 4th Cir. Fellow Md. Bar Found.; mem. Fed. Bar Assn. (pres. Balt. chpt. 1981-82), Md. Bar Assn., Barristers Club (pres. 1990-91),. Democrat. Roman Catholic. Federal civil litigation, State civil litigation, Criminal. Home: 11 Osborne Ave Baltimore MD 21228-4935 Office: Law Offices of Thomas L Crowe 1622 The World Trade Ctr 401 E Pratt St Baltimore MD 21202-3117

CROWELL, ELDON HUBBARD, lawyer; b. Middletown, Conn., May 15, 1924; s. Eldon Lewis and Alice (Hubbard) C. A.B., Princeton U., 1948; LL.B., U. Va., 1951. Bar: D.C. 1951, Conn. 1951, U.S. Dist. Ct. D.C. 1951, U.S. Ct. Appeals (D.C. cir.) 1951, U.S. Ct. Appeals (3d cir.) 1956, U.S. Supreme Ct. 1958. Assoc. Cummings, Stanley et al Washington, 1951-52, ptnr., 1952-53; ptnr. Sellers, Conner & Cuneo, Washington, 1953-70, Jones, Day, Reavis, Washington, 1970-79, Crowell & Moring, Washington, 1979— ; lectr. U. Va. Law Sch., Charlottesville, 1967-80, Judge Adv. Gen. Sch., Charlottesville, 1975— , George Washington Nat. Law Sch., 1975— , Fed. Publs. Inc., Washington, 1975— . Contbr. articles to legal jours. Trustee Williston-Northampton Sch., Easthampton, Mass., 1965-75, Madeira Sch., Greenway, Va., 1970-75, Expt. in Internat. Living, Putney, Vt., 1950-60; chmn. law firm div. United Way Campaign for Met. Washington, 1983-85; bd. dirs. City Lights Sch., Washington, Procurement Round Table, 1993—. Served with U.S. Army, 1942-45. Fellow Am. Bar Found., Nat. Contract Mgmt. Assn.; mem. ABA, Internat. and Comparative Law Ctr. (bd.

advisors), D.C. Bar Assn., Nat. Security Indsl. Assn. Democrat. Episcopalian. Clubs: Metropolitan, Chevy Chase. Administrative and regulatory, Government contracts and claims. Home: 2101 Connecticut Ave NW Washington DC 20008-1728 Office: Crowell & Moring 1001 Pennsylvania Ave NW Fl 10 Washington DC 20004-2595

CROWELL, JOHN B., JR., lawyer, former government official; b. Elizabeth, N.J., Mar. 18, 1930; s. John B. and Anna B. (Trull) C.; m. Rebecca Margaret McCue, Feb. 13, 1954; children— John P., Patrick E., Ann M. AB, Dartmouth Coll., 1952; LL.B., Harvard U., 1957. Bar: N.J. bar 1958, Oreg. bar 1959. Law clk. to Judge Gerald McLaughlin U.S. Ct. Appeals, Newark, 1957-59; atty. Ga.-Pacific Corp., Portland, Oreg., 1959-72; gen. counsel La.-Pacific Corp., Portland, 1972-81; asst. sec. for natural resources and environment Dept. Agr., Washington, 1981-85; ptnr. Lane Powell Spears Lubersky, Portland, 1986-98, of counsel, 1998—. Served with USN, 1952-54. Mem. Am. Ornithologists Union, Wilson Ornithol. Soc., Cooper Ornithol. Soc., Soc. Am. Foresters, Soil Conservation Soc. Am. Clubs: Univ. (Portland). Republican. Presbyterian. Home: 1185 Hallinan Cir Lake Oswego OR 97034-4970 Office: Lane Powell Spears Lubersky 601 SW 2nd Ave # Ste #2100 Portland OR 97204-3154

CROWELL, KENNETH E. lawyer, chemical engineer; b. Kearny, N.J., Dec. 29, 1957; s. Earl L.S. and Moira Parker (Foster) C.; m. Liliana Mino, June 24, 1990. BS in Biology, Allegheny Coll., 1979; BSChemE, N.J. Inst. Tech., 1984, MS in Chem. Engring., 1992; JD, Rutgers U., 1997. Registered profl. engr., N.J.; bar: N.J., N.Y. Tech. sales rep. patent and trademark Armak divsn. Akzo N.V., Chgo., 1979-82; prodn. mgr. Drew Chem. divsn. Ashland Oil, Kearny, N.J., 1984-87; sr. chem. engr. Jacobs Engring. Group, Mountainside, N.J., 1987-92; sr. environ. engr. Schering Plough Corp., Union, N.J., 1992-94; assoc. Milbank, Tweed, Hadley & McCloy LLP, N.Y.C., 1997-2000, Hopgood, Calimafde, Judlowe & Mondolino, LLP, N.Y.C., 2000—02, Morgan Lewis & Bockius, N.Y.C., 2002—. Author: Handbook of Biotechnology, 1997. Mem. ABA, AIChE, N.Y. State Bar Assn., Bar Assn. of City of N.Y., Order of the Coif, Tau Beta Pi. Avocation: fly fishing. Home: 40 Mitchell Rd Gillette NJ 07933-1428 Office: Morgan Lewis & Bockius LLP 101 Park Ave New York NY 10166 E-mail: Kcrowell@morganlewis.com.

CROWELL, ROBERT LAMSON, lawyer; b. Tonopah, Nev., Nov. 28, 1945; s. William Jefferson and Harriet (Lamson) C.; m. Susan Asbury, Dec. 18, 1971; children: Caroline, Brad, David, Todd. AB in Econs., Stanford U., 1967; JD, U. Calif., 1973. Bar: Nev. 1973, U.S. Ct. Appeals (9th cir.) 1973, U.S. Supreme Ct. 1995. Ptnr. Crowell, Crowell & Crowell, Carson City, Nev., 1973-77; dep. atty. gen. State of Nev., Carson City, 1974-77; ptnr. Crowell, Susich, Owen & Tackes, Carson City, 1977—. Mem. Colo. River Commn., Nev., 1988-96, chmn., 1992, 94; chmn. Nev. Continuing Legal Edn. Bd., 1992-94; mem. bd. govs. State of Nev., 1990-97; trustee Carson City Sch. Bd., 1997-2002, pres. 2002. Mem. State Bar Nev. (pres. 1996-97), Masons, Rotary. Democrat. Administrative and regulatory, Corporate, general, Probate (including wills, trusts). Office: Crowell Susich Owen & Tackes 510 W 4th St Carson City NV 89703-4254

CROWLEY, JAMES WORTHINGTON, retired lawyer, business consultant, investor; b. Cookville, Tenn., Feb. 18, 1930; s. Worth and Jessie (Officer) C.; m. Laura June Bauserman, Jan. 27, 1951; children: James Kenneth, Laura Cynthia; m. Joyce A. Goode, Jan. 15, 1966; children: John Worthington, Noelle Virginia; m. Carol Golden, Sept. 4, 1981. BA, George Washington U., 1950, LLB, 1953. Bar: D.C. 1954. Underwriter, spl. agt. Am. Surety Co. of N.Y., Washington, 1953-56; adminstrv. asst., contract adminstr. Atlantic Rsch. Corp., Alexandria, Va., 1956-59, mgr. legal dept., asst. sec., counsel, 1959-65, sec., legal mgr., counsel, 1965-67, Susquehanna Corp. (merger with Atlantic Rsch. Corp.), 1967-70; pres., dir. Gen. Communication Co., Boston, 1962-70; v.p., gen. counsel E-Systems, Inc., 1970-95, sec., 1976-95; ret., 1995; ind. cons. bus. and fin., investor, 1995—. V.p., asst. sec., dir. Cemco, Inc.; v.p., dir. TAI, Inc., Serv-air, Inc., Greenville, Tex., Engring. Rsch. Assocs., Inc., Vienna, Va., HRB Systems, Inc., State Coll., Pa.; mem. adv. bd. sec. Internat. and Comparative Law Ctr.; v.p., sec., dir. Advanced Video Products, 1992-95; v.p., sec., gen. counsel E-Systems Med. Electronics, Inc., 1992-95. Mem. Am. Soc. Corp. Secs. (pres. Dallas regional group 1988-89, nat. dir. 1989-92), Inf. Mus. Assn., Nat. Security Indsl. Assn., Mfrs.' Alliance for Productivity and Innovation (mem. law coun.), Omicron Delta Kappa, Alpha Chi Sigma, Phi Sigma Kappa. Republican. Baptist. Corporate, general, Government contracts and claims, Pension, profit-sharing, and employee benefits. Home and Office: 16203 Spring Creek Rd Dallas TX 75248-3116 E-mail: jwcrowle@ix.netcom.com.

CROWN, NANCY ELIZABETH, lawyer; b. Bronx, N.Y., Mar. 27, 1955; d. Paul and Joanne Barbara (Newman) C.; children: Rebecca, Adam. BA, Barnard Coll., 1977, MA, 1978; MEd, Columbia U., 1983; JD cum laude, Nova Law Sch., 1992. Cert. tchr.; Bar: Fla. 1992. Tchr. Sachem Sch. Dist., Holbrook, N.Y., 1978-82; v.p. mail order dept. Haber-Klein, Inc., Hicksville, N.Y., 1984-88; mgr. mdse., dir. ops. Sure Card Inc., Pompano Beach, Fla., 1988-89; legal intern Office U.S. Trustee/Dept. Justice, 1992; assoc. John T. Kinsey, P.A., Boca Raton, Fla., 1993-95; pvt. practice Nancy E. Crown, P.A., Boca Raton, Fla., 1995—; owner Crystal Title, Inc., 1999—. Recipient West Pub. award for acad. achievement, 1992. Mem. NOW, Fla. Bar Assn., South Palm Beach County Bar Assn., Bus. Partnership Coun., Phi Alpha Delta. Democrat. Jewish. Avocations: theatre, walking, reading, jazz. Bankruptcy, Probate (including wills, trusts), Property, real (including real estate development, water). E-mail: necrownpa@aol.com.

CROWNOVER, WALTER PARKER, lawyer; b. Estill Springs, Tenn., Nov. 9, 1934; s. Walter Rosser and Dorothy Williams (Black) C.; m. Ellen Louise Zimmerman, Nov. 2, 1953; children— Jo Ellen, Kenneth Walter. B.A., U. Ala., 1960, J.D., 1962. Bar: Ala. 1962, U.S. Dist. Ct. (no. dist.) Ala. 1962, U.S. Ct. Appeals (5th cir.) 1970, U.S. Supreme Ct. 1971, U.S. Dist. Ct. (mid. and so. dist.) Ala. 1982, U.S. Ct. Appeals (11th cir.) 1982. Practice, Tuscaloosa, Ala., 1962— , ptnr. Crownover Standridge and Spence, and predecessors, 1988— ; bd. commrs. Ala. State Bar, 1971—99. Chmn. Tuscaloosa County Dem. Party exec. com., 1976-86. Served with USAF, 1953-57. Mem. ABA, Ala. Bar Assn., Am. Arbitration Assn., Tuscaloos Trial Lawyers Assn. (pres. 1987-88), Am. Judicature Soc. Bankruptcy, Criminal, Personal injury (including property damage). Home: 50 Beech Hls Tuscaloosa AL 35404-4929 Office: 2600 7th St Tuscaloosa AL 35401-1805

CROWSON, JAMES LAWRENCE, lawyer, financial company executive, academic administrator; b. Duncan, Okla., Aug. 3, 1938; s. George L. and Emry Elifair (McKee) C.; children from previous marriage: James Lawrence Jr., Jason Phillips, Kristan Fair Nickel; m. Linda Sue Crowson, Mar. 2, 1986; stepchildren: Chadwick Lanier Johnson, Kim Johnson Osborn. BA in English Lit., U. Okla., 1960; LLB, So. Meth. U., 1963. Bar: Tex. 1963. Legis. counsel Tex. Legis. Coun., Austin, 1966-67; dir. hearings Tex. Water Quality Bd., Austin, 1967-68, chief legal officer, 1967-68, dir. hearings and enforcement, 1969-70; adminstrv. asst. Office of Gov., Austin, 1968-69; univ. atty. U. Tex. System, Austin, 1970; asst. to pres. U. Tex., Austin, 1970-71, Dallas, 1971-74, v.p., 1974-77, exec. v.p., 1977-80; vice chancellor, gen. counsel U. Tex. System, Austin, 1980-87; sr. v.p., gen. counsel Lomas Fin. Group, Dallas, 1987-94, exec. v.p., 1994-95; pvt. investment practice Dallas, 1995-96; dep. chancellor adminstrn. Tex. Tech. Univ. System, Lubbock, 1996—2002. Sec. Tex. Higher Edn. Found., 1988-1996, Higher Edn. Legis. Polit. Action Com., 1987-1996; vice chmn. HCB Enterprises Inc., 1995—; bd. dirs. KOHM Pub. Radio Sta., 1997-99, Tex. Univs. Health Plan, 1998-2002; bd. dirs. Market Lubbock, Inc., 1997-99, v.p. 1999. Trustee Alliance for Higher Edn., 1991-96, Dallas Edn. Ctr., 1995-96. Capt. U.S. Army, 1963-66. Mem. Mortgage Bankers Assn. Am. (mem. legal issues com., mem. legis. com.), U.S. C. of C. (mem. edn. employment and tng. com., mem. labor rels. com., mem. S.W. pub. affairs task force). Bankruptcy, Corporate, general, Legislative. Office: 5109 82d St Ste 7 # 258 Lubbock TX 79424 E-mail: crowsonj@swbell.net.

CRUDEN, JOHN CHARLES, lawyer; b. Topeka, Feb. 23, 1946; s. George Harry and Agnes (Telban) C.; m. Sharon Lynn Holland, June 15, 1968; children: Kristen, Heather. BS, U.S. Mil. Acad., 1968; JD, U. Santa Clara, 1974; MA, U. Va., 1975; grad., Gen. Staff Coll., 1982; fellow, Army War Coll., 1988. Bar: Calif. 1975, D.C. 1979, U.S. Supreme Ct. 1979. Commd. 2d lt. U.S. Army, 1968, advanced through grades to col., 1987, with airborne, ranger, spl. forces, 1968-71, clk. Calif. Supreme Ct., 1974, pros., 1975-76, chief litig. br. Hdqrs. Europe, 1976-78, sr. trial atty. comml. br. litig. divsn., 1978-79, gen. counsel Def. Nuclear Agy., 1979-80; prof., chief Adminstrv. and Civil Law divsn. Judge Adv. Gen.'s Sch., Charlottesville, Va., 1982-85; staff Judge Adv. Europe, 1985-87; spl. counsel to asst. atty. gen. civil divsn. U.S. Dept. Justice, 1987-88; chief legis. counsel Dept. Army, 1988-91; chief environ. enforcement sect. Environ. & Natural Resource divsn. U.S. Dept. Justice, Washington, 1991-95, dep. asst. atty. gen., 1995—2001, acting asst. atty. gen., 2001—02, dep. asst. atty. gen., 2002—. Contbr. articles to profl. jours. Mem. Fed. Bar Assn. (chpt. pres. 1984-85, Younger Fed. Lawyers award 1981), JAG Sch. Alumni Assn. (pres. 1982-85), D.C. Bar Assn. (bd. govs. 2001—), Calif. Bar Assn., ABA (mem. coun. sect. on environment, energy and resources 2002—, vice chmn. adminstrv. law and gen. practice sect. 1985-88, vice chmn. fed. legis. com. 1989-92, adv. com., standing com. on law and nat. security 1988-94). Office: US Dept Justice 950 Pennsylvania Ave NW Washington DC 20530-0001 E-mail: john.cruden@usdoj.gov.

CRULL, JAN, JR., lawyer; s. Jan Crull and Frederika Minderop. BA honors, Dalhousie U., 1975; MA, U. Chgo., 1984; JD, Tulane U., 1990. Bar: Ill. 1990, U.S. Dist. Ct. (no. dist.) Ill. 1990. Intern GGvA, N.Y.C., 1973—74; asst. to chpt. pres. Ramah Navajo Reservation, Pinehill, N.Mex., 1979—80; profl. staff mem. U.S. Ho., Washington, 1981; asst. money mgr. Gulf and Occidental Investment Co. SA, Geneva, 1982, 1985—86, 1989, counsel, advisor, 1990—91; counsel, co-prin. SandCru, Inc., Chgo., 1992—; pres., gen. counsel Vigil Film Prodn. Co. L.A. and Sacramento, Calif., 1993—97; dir./counsel Von Quesar Holdings, OHG, Vienna, 1994—98, Beeltsnijder KG, Berlin, 1995—97. Developer (film project) Not in Fiction Only: There and Here Also, 1974, A Free People, Free to Choose, 1992—93, AIDDS: American Indians' Devastating Dilemma Soon, 1993, To Mute Them Once Again, 1994, Indian Buckaroos, 1996. Mem.: ABA, Chgo. Bar Assn., Ill. State Bar Assn., 1781 Club Netherlands Antilles, Quadrangle Club Chgo. Private international, Entertainment, Mergers and acquisitions. Office: SandCru Inc PO Box 6637 Chicago IL 60680-6637

CRUMLEY, JOHN WALTER, lawyer; b. Ft. Worth, July 20, 1944; s. Frank E. and Mary Cecilia (Gaudin) C.; m. Paulette Gavin, July 25, 1970; children: John Gavin, Brian Christopher. BS, Springhill Coll., 1967; JD, So. Meth. U., 1970, M of Comparative Law, 1973. Bar: Tex. 1970, U.S. Dist. Ct. (no. dist.) Tex. 1976, U.S. Ct. Appeals (5th cir.) 1981, U.S. Tax Ct. 1988. Assoc. McBryde & Bogle, Ft. Worth, 1973-75; ptnr. Crumley, Murphy & Shrull, Inc., Ft. Worth, 1975-85, Tracy, Crumley & Holland, Ft. Worth, 1985-92; prin. John W. Crumley, P.C., Ft. Worth, 1992—. Mem. bd. dirs. Goodrich Ctr. for the Deaf, 1995—, pres., 1998-2002; vice chair Bingo Advisor Com., 1995-96. Mem. steering com. Tarrant County Vol. Guardianship, Ft. Worth, 1986-87; bd. dirs. Camp Fire, Ft. Worth, 1985-87, Cath. Social Svcs., Ft. Worth, 1985-86. Capt. U.S. Army, 1970-72. Mem. State Bar Tex., Tarrant County Bar Assn., Tex. Assn. Def. Counsel, Tex. Assn. Diocesan Attys., U.S. Conf. Diocesan Attys. Assn., Serra Club (pres. Ft. Worth club 1985-86), KC (state adv. 1986-91, 95-96). State civil litigation, Construction, Probate (including wills, trusts). Office: 316 University Ctr 1300 S University Dr Fort Worth TX 76107-5737 E-mail: crumley1@airmail.net.

CRUMP, FRANCIS JEFFERSON, III, lawyer; b. Alexandria, Va., Dec. 4, 1942; s. Ross Gault and Pauline (DeVore) C.; m. Nancy Jo Burkle, Aug. 20, 1966; children: Tom, Laura, Elizabeth. BS in Math., Va. Mil. Inst., 1964; JD, Ind. U., 1967. Bar: Ind. 1967, U.S. Dist. Ct. (so. dist.) Ind. 1967. Gen. ptnr. Jewell, Crump & Angermeier, Columbus, Ind., 1971—. Pres. First Nat. Corp.; lectr. on estate planning and legal aspects of child abuse and neglect; bd. dirs., sec., treas. Hawpatch Corp. Past pres., bd. dirs. Columbus Boys' Club; past pres., bd. dirs., v.p., treas. Found. Youth, Inc., Babe Ruth Baseball, Inc., dir., sr. v.p. 1983-88; deacon First Presbyn. Ch. Columbus, 1972-75, elder 1977-79, 2000-03; bd. dirs. Ecumenical Assn. Barth County Chs., Inc., v.p., 2001, pres., 2002-03; dir. Presbyn. Found. Columbus, Ind., Inc., 2002—; dir. Hoosier Hills Estate Planning Coun., 2001—. Mem. Ind. State Bar Assn., Bartholomew County Bar Assn., Inc. (pres. 1983-84, treas., dir. 2001—), Rotary, Phi Alpha Delta. Republican. Estate planning, Probate (including wills, trusts), Property, real (including real estate development, water). Home and Office: PO Box 1061 Columbus IN 47202-1061

CRUMP, GERALD FRANKLIN, retired lawyer; b. Sacramento, Feb. 16, 1935; s. John Laurin and Ida May (Banta) C.; m. Glenda Roberts Glass, Nov. 21, 1959; children: Sara Elizabeth, Juliane Kathryn, Joseph Stephen. AB, U. Calif., Berkeley, 1956; JD, U. Calif., 1959; MA, Baylor U., 1966. Bar: Calif. 1960. Dep. county counsel L.A. County, 1963-73, legis. rep., 1970-73, chief pub. works div., 1973-84, sr. asst. county counsel, 1984-85, chief asst. county counsel, 1985-97; ret., 1997. Lectr. Pepperdine U., 1978, U. Calif., 1982. Former v.p. San Fernando Valley Girl Scout Coun. Served to capt. USAF, 1960-63; to maj. gen. USAFR, 1963-95, ret.; mobilization asst. to the JAG. Decorated DSM, Legion of Merit. Mem. ABA, State Bar Calif., L.A. County Bar Assn. (past chmn. trustee govtl. law sect., past mem.exec. com. litig. sect.), Air Force Assn., Res. Officers Assn., Phi Alpha Delta, Delta Sigma Phi. Home: 4020 Camino De La Cumbre Sherman Oaks CA 91423-4522

CRUMP, HARRY SEYMOUR, judge, pharmacist; b. Chgo., Dec. 20, 1937; s. Alonzo Crump and Eilee Anna Barksdale; m. Faith Esperanza, Jan. 1, 2003; children: Trina, Diane, Don, Harvey. AA in Elec. Engring., Wilson Jr. Coll. Chgo., 1962; BS in Pharmacy, U. Ill., 1967; JD, DePaul U., 1974. Fed. pub. defender, 1974; field atty., hearing officer Nat. Labor Rels. Bd., 1974—75; asst. to dir. St. Paul Civil Rights Dept., 1975—78; adminstrv. law judge Office Adminstrv. Hearings, 1979—83; commr. Minn. Pub. Utilities Commn., 1984—87; apptd. judge, 1987—. Faculty mem., cons. Washington U.; adj. prof. clin. adminstrv. law William Mitchell Coll. Law; adj. lectr. jurisprudence U. Minn. Coll. Pharmacy; faculty mem. Nat. Ctr. for State Cts.; mem. Joint County Commrs. and Bench Com., Dist. Ct. Exec. Com.; former chair security com. Hennepin County Dist. Ct.; mem. com. on probate and civil jury instrns. Minn. Dist. Judges Assn.; chief judge mental health; chair Minn. Supreme Ct. Com. on Interactive Audio-Video Comm.; Minn. rep. U.S. Transp. Commn. Conf.; co-founder Minn. Minority Lawyers Assn. Office: Hennepin County Dist Ct 300 S 6th St Minneapolis MN 55487

CRUMPTON, CHARLES WHITMARSH, lawyer; b. Shreveport, La., May 29, 1946; s. Charles W. and Frances M. (McInnis) C.; m. Thu-Huong T. Cong-Huyen, Sept. 17, 1971; children: Francesca, Ian. BA, Carleton Coll., 1968; MA, U. Hawaii, 1974, JD, 1978. Bar: Hawaii 1978, U.S. Dist. Ct. Hawaii 1978, U.S. Ct. Appeals (9th cir.) 1982. Tchr. dept. edn. State of Hawaii, Honolulu, 1972-73, 75-77; Fulbright prof. U. Can Tho, Vietnam, 1973-75; assoc. John S. Edmunds, Honolulu, 1978-80, Ashford & Wriston, Honolulu, 1980-85, David W. Hall, Honolulu, 1985-88; dir. Hall & Crumpton, Honolulu, 1988-93; dir., shareholder Stanton Clay Chapman Crumpton & Iwamura, Honolulu, 1993—. Pres./dir. Internat. Law Found., 1996—; fellow Am. Coll. Civil Trial Mediators, 2000—; barrister Am. Inn of Ct. IV, Honolulu, 1985-87; arbitrator Court-Annexed Arbitration program 1st Cir. Ct. State of Hawaii, 1987—; arbitrator, mediator Am. Arbitration Assn., 1988—, Arbitration Forums, 1990—, Mediation Specialists, 1994—, Dispute Prevention & Resolution, 1995—; mem. com. on lawyer professionalism Hawaii State Jud. Conf., 1988-89; arbitrator/mediator com. fee disputes Hawaii Bar Assn., 1990—, mem. com. jud. adminstrn., 1990—, mem. com. jud. performance, 1992-94, chair sect. on alternative dispute resolution, 1997—; prof. Hawaii Pacific U., 1995—; faculty/spkr. on ins. law, employment law, alternative dispute resolution, civil litigation, 1993—. Asst. dir. youth vols. Am. Cancer Soc., Honolulu, 1972-73. Fulbright grantee U.S. Dept. State, 1973-75. Fellow Am. Coll Civil Trial Mediators; mem. ATLA, ABA (torts and ins. practice sect., litigation sect., alt. dispute resolution sec.), Am. Coll. Civil Trial Mediators, Hawaii Bar Assn., Inter-Pacific Bar Assn. Avocations: sports, guitar. Alternative dispute resolution, Insurance, Personal injury (including property damage). Home: 1521 Alexander St # 403 Honolulu HI 96822- Office: Stanton Clay Chapman Crumpton & Iwamura 700 Bishop St Ste 2100 Honolulu HI 96813-4120 E-mail: crumpton@paclawteam.com.

CRUTCHFIELD, WILLIAM WARD, lawyer, state legislator; b. Chattanooga, Dec. 6, 1928; married; two children. Student, U. Chattanooga; JD, U. Tenn., 1951. Lawyer; mem. Tenn. Ho. of Reps. 80th-82nd Gen. Assemblies, Tenn. Senate 83rd, 84th, 94th-103rd Gen. Assemblies; chmn. senate labor com. Tenn. Senate 83rd and 84th Gen. Assemblies, former senate Dem. caucus chmn. Atty. Hamilton County Bd. Edn.; former acting atty. Hamilton County; chmn. Hamilton County Legis. Del.; former chmn. Hamilton County Dem. Party, 1970-84; Met. Govt. Charter Commn. With U.S. Army. Mem. ATLA, Tenn. Trial Lawyers Assn., Tenn. Bar Assn., Am. Legion, Temple Lodge, Scottish Rite, Alhambra Shrine Temple, High Twelve, Phi Alpha Delta. Methodist. Office: 13 Legislative Plaza Nashville TN 37243 also: Ste 301 Flatiron Bldg 707 Georgia Ave Chattanooga TN 37402-2003 E-mail: sen.ward.crutchfield@legislature.state.tn.us.*

CRYNE, ROBERT FRANCIS, lawyer, educator; b. Bklyn., Feb. 29, 1952; s. Michael Joseph Sr. and Camillus Catherine (Donnelly) C.; m. Ann L. Wright, May 21, 1978; children: Julia, Patrick. BA, Stockton State Coll., 1974; JD, Creighton U., 1978. Bar: Nebr. 1978, U.S. Dist. Ct. Nebr. 1978, U.S. Army Ct. Review 1985, U.S. Ct. Appeals Armed Forces 1979, U.S. Supreme Ct. 1982. Pvt. practice, Omaha, 1978-79, 82-87; capt., judge advocate U.S. Army, Wuerzburg, Germany, 1979-82; deputy county attorney Douglas County Attorney's Office, Omaha, 1987-95, deputy in charge narcotics divsn., 1995-2000; spl. asst. U.S. Atty. U.S. Dept. Justice, Omaha, 2000—02, asst. U.S. atty., 2002—. Adj. prof. Metropolitan Cmty. Coll., Omaha, 1990—. Scoutmaster, Boy Scouts Am., Omaha, 1999—. Capt. U.S. Army, 1979-82. Recipient Inspector Generals award U.S. Dept. Housing Urban Devel., Omaha, 1997, Meritorious Svc. award Organized Crime Drug Enforcement Task Force, West Ctrl. Region, 1997. Mem. Inns of Court (master of bench 1997—). Office: 1st Nat Bank Bldg 1620 Dodge St Ste 1400 Omaha NE 68102-1594 E-mail: robert.cryne@usdoj.gov.

CSONTOS, ALAN ARTHUR, lawyer; b. Elyria, Ohio, Dec. 1, 1943; s. Arthur George Csontos and Anne Kolopus; m. Dolores M. Novotny; children: Cindy, Kevin, Sara, Brad. BChE, U. Dayton, 1966; JD, U. Akron, 1975. Bar: Ohio 1975, S.C. 1994, U.S. Patent and Trademark Office 1975. Rsch. engr. BF Goodrich Co., Avon Lake, Ohio, 1966—70, patent agt, patent counsel Akron, Ohio, 1971—87; gen. patent counsel Uniroyal Goodrich Tire Co., Akron, 1988—93; gen.; asst. gen. counsel Michelin N.Am., Inc., Greenville, NC, 1994—. Mgr. IP Function in N.Am. Michelin Groupe, 1994—. Dir. Juvenile Diabetes Rsch. Found., We. Carolinas, 2001—. Mem.: ACPC, LES, AIPLA, ABA, INTA, Carolina Patent Trademark and Copyright Law Assn. Achievements include patents in field. Avocations: travel, golf. Intellectual property, Trademark and copyright, Patent. Office: Michelin NAm Inc 515 Michelin Rd Greenville SC 29605

CUBA, BENJAMIN JAMES, lawyer; b. Dec. 12, 1936; s. Ben and Patricia (Machalek) C.; m. Bernadette Theresa Haney, Sept. 4, 1964; children: Benjamin Courtney, Tristan Konrad. AA, Temple Coll., 1957; BBA, U. Tex., 1959; JD, Baylor U., 1963. Bar: Tex. 1964, U.S. Dist. Ct. (we. dist.) Tex. 1970, U.S. Ct. Appeals (5th and 11th cirs.) 1981, U.S. Supreme Ct. 1978. Assoc. Law Offices of Jarrard Secrest, Temple, Tex., 1964-66; ptnr. Secrest & Cuba, Temple, Tex., 1966-68; sr. ptnr. Cuba & Cuba and predecessor firms, Temple, Tex., 1968—. Dir. founding trustee, atty. Inst. for Humanities at Salado, Tex., 1980—, founding trustee, legal counsel First House, Inc., Temple, 1981-86; legal counsel, mem. cmty. adv. bd. Jr. League of Bell County, Inc. (and predecessor orgn. Svc. League of Temple, Inc.), 1976—; v.p. Temple Indsl. Devel. Corp., 1984-89; pres. Trailblazer Corp., 1973-. Fellow Tex. Bar Found. (life); mem. Bell-Lampasas-Mills Counties Bar Assn. (pres. 1973-74), State Bar Tex., U. Tex. Ex Student's Assn., Baylor Law Alumni Assn., Quarterback Club (dir. 1984, 85), Phi Delta Phi. Lutheran. General civil litigation, Corporate, general, Property, real (including real estate development, water). Office: Cuba & Cuba PLC 18 S Main St Ste 802 Temple TX 76501-7608

CUBITTO, ROBERT J. lawyer; b. Globe, Ariz., Aug. 1, 1950; s. Claude A. and Arizona C. (DiMario) C. BA, U. Ariz., 1972, BSBA, 1974; JD, Harvard Law Sch., 1976. Bar: Mass. 1977, N.Y. 1979, U.S. Dist. Ct. (so. and ea. dists.) N.Y. 1979, U.S. Tax Ct. 1979. Cons. Boston Cons. Group, 1976-78; assoc. Debevoise & Plimpton, N.Y.C., 1978-84, ptnr., 1985—. Mem. ABA, N.Y. State Bar Assn. (exec. com. tax sect. 1987-88), Assn. of Bar of City of N.Y., Harvard Club N.Y.C. (asst. treas. 1985-89, bd. mgrs. 1990-93), The Club of Turtle Bay (treas. 1994-97, pres. 1998—). Corporate taxation, Taxation, general. Office: Debevoise & Plimpton 919 3rd Ave New York NY 10022-3904

CUCIN, ROBERT LOUIS, plastic surgeon, lawyer; b. N.Y.C., Apr. 17, 1946; s. Robert and Julia C.. BA magna cum laude, Cornell U., 1967, MD, 1971; JD, Fordham U., 1985; MBA, Columbia U., 2003. Bar: N.Y. 1983, N.J. State Supreme Ct., Washington Ct. of Appeals; bd. cert. legal medicine; diplomate Am. Bd. Surgery, Am. Bd. Plastic Surgery; licensed physician, N.J., N.Y. State, Calif., Va. Intern Cornell-N.Y. Hosp., N.Y.C., 1971-72, resident in gen. surgery, 1972-76, resident in plastic surgery, 1977-79; fellow in surgery Meml.-Sloan Kettering Found., 1972-76, 77-79; practice medicine specializing in plastic surgery N.Y.C., 1979—; instr. surgery Cornell U. Med. Coll., 1980—; asst. attending plastic surgeon Beth Israel North, N.Y. Downtown Hosp., 1979—, N.Y. Hosp., 1980—, Drs. Hosp., 1987—. Pres. Esquire Cadillac Limousine Svc. Inc., 1977—93, Beaux Arts Holdings, 1979—, Rocin Labs., Inc., 1981—, Biosculpture Tech., Inc., 2001—. Author: The Kindest Cut, Keeping Face, Medical Malpractice: Handling Plastic Surgical Cases; contbr. articles to profl, jours. Mem. N.Y. County Health Svc. Rev. Orgn., 1976—; founder, dir Rocin Found. for Plastic Surg. Rsch., 1979—; Maj. M.C., USAF, 1976-77; Japan. Fellow: ACS, Am. Coll. Legal Medicine, Internat. Coll. Surgeons; mem.: ABA, ATLA, AMA (Physicians Recognition award 1978, 1981), N.Y. Acad. Scis., N.Y. County Med. Soc. (health systems, pub. rels., peer rev. coms.), N.Y. State Med. Soc., Royal Soc. Medicine, Am. Soc. Plastic and Reconstructive Surgery, Am. Mensa, Cornell Club, N.Y. Athletic Club, Le Club, Phi Beta Kappa. Republican. Office: 120 Central Park S New York NY 10019-1560

CUDAHY, RICHARD D. judge; b. Milwaukee, Feb. 2, 1926; s. Michael F. and Alice ((Dickson)) Cudahy; m. Ann (Featherston), July 14, 1956 (dec. 1974); m. Janet (Stuart), July 17, 1976; children: Richard D., Norma K., Theresa E., Daniel M., Michaela A., Marguerite L., Patrick G. BS, U.S. Mil. Acad., 1948; JD, Yale U., 1955; LLD, Ripon Coll., 1981, DePaul U., 1995, Wabash Coll., 1996, Stetson U., 1998. Bar: Conn. 1955, D.C. 1957, Ill. 1957, Wis. 1961. Commd., 2d. lt. U.S. Army, 1948, 1st. lt., 1950; law clk. to presiding judge U.S. Ct. Appeals (2d cir.), 1955—56; asst. to legal adv. Dept. State, 1956—57; assoc. Isham, Lincoln, and Beale, Chgo., 1957—60; pres. Patrick Cudahy, Inc., Wis., 1961—71, Patrick Cudahy Family Co.,

Wis., 1968—75; ptnr. firm Godfrey and Kahn, Milw., 1972; commr., chmn. Wis. Pub. Svc. Commn., 1972—75; ptnr. Isham, Lincoln, and Beale, Chgo. and Washington, 1976—79; judge U.S. Ct. Appeals (7th cir.), Chgo., 1979—94, sr. judge, 1994—. Lectr. law Marquette U. Law Sch., 1962; vis. prof. law U. Wis., 1966—67; prof. lectr. law George Washington U., Washington, 1978—79; adj. prof. DePaul U. Coll. Law, 1995—. Commr. Milw. Harbor, 1964—66; pres. Milw. Urban League, 1965—66; trustee Environ. Def. Fund, 1976—79; chmn. DePaul U., Human Rights Law Inst., 1990—98; mem. adv. com. Ctr. for Internat. Human Rights, Northwestern U., 2000—; chmn. Wis. Dem. Party, 1967—68; Dem. candidate for Wis. Atty. Gen., 1968. Mem.: ABA (spl. com. on Energy Law 1978—84, 1990—96, pub. utility sect. coun. group), Am. Inst. for Pub. Svc. (bd. selectors), Fed. Judges' Assn. (bd. dirs.), Chgo. Bar Assn., Milw. Bar Assn., Wis. Bar Assn., Am. Law Inst., Cath. Theol. Union (trustee 1997—2003), Lawyers Club, Chgo. (pres. 1992—93, spl. divsn. D.C. cir. for appt. ind. counsel 1998—2002). Office: US Ct Appeals 219 S Dearborn St Ste 2648 Chicago IL 60604-1874

CUIFFO, FRANK WAYNE, lawyer; b. Houston, Oct. 13, 1943; s. Richard and Helen (Giaco) C.; m. Barbara Joyce Streeter, Nov. 26, 1966; children: Karen, Deborah, Richard, Steven. BS, U. Notre Dame, 1964; JD, Fordham U., 1967. Bar: N.Y. 1967. Assoc. Pennie & Edmonds (formerly Pennie, Edmonds, Morton, Taylor & Adams), N.Y.C., 1967-69; sr. assoc. Emmet, Marvin, & Martin, N.Y.C., 1969-74, Golenbock & Barell, N.Y.C., 1974-78; mng. ptnr. Carro, Spanbock, Kaster & Cuiffo, N.Y.C., 1978-93; chmn. real estate dept., exec. com. Donovan, Leisure, Newton & Irvine, N.Y.C., 1993-98; ptnr. McDermott, Will & Emery, N.Y.C., 1998—. Mem. ABA, U.S. Patent Bar, N.Y. State Bar, Siwanoy Country Club, South Seas Club. Property, real (including real estate development, water). Office: McDermott Will & Emery 50 Rockefeller Plz Fl 12 New York NY 10020-1600

CULBRETH, JAMES HAROLD, JR., lawyer; b. Durham, N.C., Nov. 12, 1953; s. James Harold and Florence Rittenhouse C.; m. Kate Dickson Banks, Oct. 24, 1981; children: Julia Fairbairn, Duncan Banks. BA in Psychology, Wake Forest U., 1977; JD, George Washington U., 1980. Bar: D.C. 1981, Va. 1982, N.C. 1984. Assoc. Baylinson Kudysh & Greenberg, Washington, 1981-84; trust officer, asst. v.p. Ctrl. Carolina Bank & Trust Co., Durham, 1984-90; assoc. McGuire Woods Battle & Boothe, Richmond, Va., 1990-93, Wishart Norris Henninger & Pittman, Burlington, N.C., 1993-95; ptnr. Helms, Mulliss & Wicker, PLLC (formerly Smith Helms Mulliss & Moore LLP), Charlotte, NC, 1995—. Lectr. employee benefits Am. Bankers Assn. Nat. Trust Sch., 1987—. Chair stewardship com. and fin. com. University City United Meth., Charlotte, 1998—. Democrat. Avocations: tennis, bicycling, camping, writing. Corporate, general, Mergers and acquisitions, Pension, profit-sharing, and employee benefits. Office: Helms Mulliss & Wicker LLP 201 N Tryon St Charlotte NC 28202-2146

CULLEN, JAMES D. lawyer; b. St. Louis, May 18, 1925; s. James and Frances C. Cullen; m. Joyce Marie Jackson, Aug. 19, 1950 (div.); children: Mary Lynn Cullen Walsh, James D., Michael Parnell, Carol Cullen Bernstein. LLD, St. Louis, 1948. Bar: Mo. 1948. Pvt. practice law, St. Louis. Bd. dirs. Gen. Protestant Children's Home, Richard Greene Co. 1st lt. USAF, 1943—45. Mem.: ABA, Lawyers Assn. St. Louis, St. Louis Bar Assn., Mo. Bar Assn. Roman Catholic. Corporate, general, Entertainment, Estate planning. Office: 15 Sussex Dr Saint Louis MO 63144-2767

CULLEN, JAMES DONALD, lawyer; b. Detroit, Aug. 29, 1947; s. James W. and Eileen V. (Schneider) C.; children: Karen, Julie, James, Michael. BSBA, John Carroll U., 1969; JD, U. Pitts., 1972. Bar: Pa. 1973, U.S. Dist. Ct. (we. dist.) Pa. 1973. Assoc. MacDonald, Illig, Jones & Britton, Erie, Pa., 1972-80, ptnr., 1980—, mng. ptnr., 1988-98. Lectr. estate planning Mercyhurst Coll., 1989-91, 99-2000; mem. Erie County Estate Planning Coun. Capt. USAR, 1969-77. Mem. ABA, Erie County Bar Assn. (orphans' ct. rules com.), Pa. Bar Assn., Kahkwa Club. Republican. Estate planning, Labor (including EEOC, Fair Labor Standards Act, labor-management relations, NLRB, OSHA), Probate (including wills, trusts). Office: MacDonald Illig Jones & Britton LLP 100 State St Ste 700 Erie PA 16507-1459 Home: 4833 Thoroubred Loop Erie PA 16506-6607 E-mail: jcullen@macdonaldillig.com.

CULLEN, KATHLEEN JOY, lawyer; b. Albany, N.Y., Dec. 21, 1957; BA cum laude, Mt. Holyoke Coll., 1979; JD, Union U., Albany, N.Y., 1982. Bar: N.Y. 1983. Assoc. Tate, Bishko & Assocs., Albany, 1983-93; hearing examiner Schenectady County Family Ct., 4th Jud. Dist., Office Ct. Adminstrn., N.Y. State, 1993—. Committeewoman Albany County Dem. Com., 1993. Mem. ABA, N.Y. State Bar Assn., Womens Bar Assn., Schenectady Cty. Bar Assn. Office: Schenectady County Family Ct Schenectady NY 12305

CULLEN, RICHARD, lawyer, former state attorney general; b. N.Y.C., Mar. 10, 1948; m. Agnes Tullidge; children: Thomas, Anne Gray, Elizabeth, Richard. BS, Furman U., 1971; JD, U. Richmond, 1977. Bar: Va. Ptnr. McGuire, Woods, Battle and Boothe, Richmond, 1977-97, 98—; atty. gen. Commonwealth of Va., 1997-98. Spl. counsel Senate Iran-Contra Investigation, 1987; U.S. atty. for ea. dist. Va., 1991-93. Editor-in-chief U. Richmond Law Rev., 1976-77. Mem. Juvenile Criminal Commn.; mem. Va. Criminal Sentencing Commn.; co-chmn. Gov.'s Commn. on Parole Abolition and Sentencing Reform. Office: McGuire, Woods, Battle & Boothe One James Ctr 901 E Cary St Richmond VA 23219-4057

CULLEN, TERRANCE MICHAEL, lawyer; b. St. Paul, Aug. 11, 1953; s. Howard Anthony Sr. and Eileen Marguerite (Fenlon) C.; m. Laura Jean Vannelli, Sept. 1, 1978; children: Terrance John, Brian Patrick, Anthony Steven, Mary Margaret. BA, U. Minn., 1974, JD cum laude, 1978. Bar: Colo. 1978, U.S. Dist. Ct. Colo. 1978, U.S. Ct. Appeals (10th cir.) 1979, Minn. 1981, U.S. Dist. Ct. Minn. 1982, U.S. Ct. Appeals (8th and 7th cirs.) 1986. Atty. Gulf Oil Corp., Denver, 1978-81; ptnr. Felhaber, Larson, Fenlon & Vogt, P.A., St. Paul, 1981—. Contbr. to profl. publs. Chmn. Dist. 64B Ind. Republicans, St. Paul, 1991-98. Mem. Minn. State Bar Assn. (chmn. bar-media com. 1984-87, chmn. antitrust sect. 1997-99). Roman Catholic. Antitrust, Corporate, general, Pension, profit-sharing, and employee benefits. Office: Felhaber Larson Fenlon Vogt 601 2d Ave S Ste 4200 Minneapolis MN 55402-4302

CULLEY, PETER WILLIAM, lawyer; b. Dover-Foxcroft, Maine, Oct. 17, 1943; s. William Redfern and Kathryn (Boyle) C.; children: Courtney Little, Jonathan Redfern. BA, U. Maine, 1965; JD, Boston U., 1968. Bar: Maine 1969, U.S. Dist. Ct. Maine 1969. Asst. atty. gen. Dept. of Atty. Gen. State of Maine, 1969-72, chief, criminal divsn., 1971-72; ptnr. Hewes, Culley and Beals, Portland, Maine, 1972-85, Pierce Atwood, Portland, 1985—. Chmn. Falmouth (Maine) Town Coun., 1986-87. Fellow Am. Coll. Trial Lawyers (state chmn. 1990-92), Am. Bar Found.; mem. ABA, Maine Bar Assn., Internat. Assn. Def. Counsel, Def. Rsch. Inst. (state chmn. 1978-87), No. New Eng. Def. Counsel (pres. 1985-86), Am. Bd. Trial Advocates. Federal civil litigation, General civil litigation, Product liability. Home: 406 Chandlers Wharf Portland ME 04101-4653 Office: Pierce Atwood One Monument Sq Portland ME 04101 E-mail: pculley@pierceatwood.com.

CULLINA, WILLIAM MICHAEL, lawyer; b. Hartford, Conn., July 22, 1921; s. Michael Stephen and Margaret (Carroll) C.; m. Gertrude Evelyn Blasig, Apr. 29, 1961; children: William Gregory, Kevin Michael, John Stephen, Susan Margaret. AB, Catholic U. Am., 1942; LLB, Yale U., 1948. Bar: Conn. bar 1948. Assoc. Murtha Cullina LLP, Hartford, 1948—, ptnr., 1952-91, of counsel, 1992—. Bd. dirs. St. Francis Hosp. and Med. Ctr., 1968-2002, hon. dir., 2002—; trustee St. Joseph Coll., 1986-98, trustee emeritus, 1998—; bd. govs. The Hartford Club, 1984-89, chair, 1987-88. Served with USNR, 1942-46. Fellow Am. Bar Found.; mem. ABA, Conn. Bar Assn., Hartford County Bar Assn., Hartford Tennis Club, Country Club of Farmington, Knight of St. Gregory, Phi Beta Kappa. Roman Catholic. Office: Murtha Cullina LLP City Pl 185 Asylum St Ste 29 Hartford CT 06103-3469

CULVAHOUSE, ARTHUR BOGGESS, JR., lawyer; b. Athens, Tenn., July 4, 1948; s. Arthur Boggess and Ruth Webb (Wear) C.; m. Pamela Smith Comparato, Apr. 29, 2001; children: Sarah Abbott, Arthur Boggess (dec.), Elizabeth Louise, Anne Pierce. BS, U. Tenn., 1970; JD, NYU, 1973. Bar: Tenn. 1973, Calif. 1977, D.C. 1977. Chief legis. asst. to U.S. Sen. Howard Baker, Washington, 1973-76; assoc. O'Melveny & Myers, Washington, 1976-81, ptnr., 1982-84, 89—; chmn., 2000—; ptnr. Vinson & Elkins, Washington, 1984-87; counsel to the Pres. The White House, Washington, 1987-89. Recipient Presdl. Citizen's medal, 1989, Def. Dept. Disting. Svc. medal. 1992. Republican. Episcopalian. Office: 555 13th St NW Ste 500 Washington DC 20004-1109

CUMBERLAND, WILLIAM EDWIN, lawyer; b. Washington, Sept. 11, 1938; m. Clare Hogan, Aug. 17, 1973; children: Lisa, Joseph, Kara. AB, Georgetown U., 1960; LLB, Harvard U., 1963. Bar: D.C. 1963, Va. 1963. Law clk. to judge U.S. Dist. Ct. D.C., Washington, 1963-64; from assoc. to ptnr. Cefaratti & Cumberland, Washington, 1964-71; atty. HUD, Washington, 1971-72; counsel Mortgage Bankers Assn. Am., Washington, 1972—, gen. counsel, sr. v.p., 1988-2000. Cons. Mortgage Banks Assn., 2000—. Banking, Finance, Property, real (including real estate development, water).

CUMMINGS, ANTHONY WILLIAM, lawyer, educator, banker; b. Port Jefferson, N.Y., Dec. 3, 1962; s. Leonard and Annie (Earl) C. Student, Tulane U., 1980-81; BS in Applied Econs., Hofstra U., 1985, JD, 1988; MBA, U. N.C., 1997. Bar: N.Y. 1988, D.C. 1990, U.S. Dist. Ct. (ea. and so. dists.) N.Y. 1990, U.S. Ct. Mil. Appeals 1990, U.S. Ct. Appeals (2d, 11th and fed. cirs.) 1991, U.S. Tax Ct. 1991, U.S. Supreme Ct. 1992, N.C. 1995; diplomate Am. Bd. Forensic Examiners. Assoc. Ronald J. Rosenberg, Garden City, NY, 1988—89; of counsel Costa & Bernsten, Hauppauge, NY, 1989—92; contract atty. Bernsten & Newman, Hauppauge, 1990—93; pvt. practice Patchogue, NY, 1990—94, Raleigh, NC, 1994—97, Hauppauge, NY, 2001—; assoc. Fin. Instns. Group, First Union Securities, Inc., Charlotte, NC, 1999—2000; v.p. Hales & Co., N.Y.C., 2000—01. Adj. instr. law Suffolk County C.C., Selden, NY, 1992—94; coord. adminstrv. svcs. N.C. Biotech. Ctr., Research Triangle Park, NC, 1994—95; adj. instr. bus. Wake Tech. C.C., Raleigh, 1995—97; coord., lectr. CLE programs Suffolk Acad. Law, 1989—94; co-chmn. appellate practice com. Suffolk County Bar Assn.; judge Jessup Internat. Law Moot Ct. Competition, 1990—91; pres. Cummings Capital Advisors LLC, 2001—; adj. prof. law Hofstra U. Zarb Sch. Bus., 2001—; adj. prof. forensic exam. Touro Coll. Sch. Health Scis., 2002—. Editor-in-chief Hofstra Property Law Jour., 1988; assoc. editor Jour. Suffolk Acad. Law, 1992-94. Pres. U. N.C. MBA Student Assn., 1996-97. Recipient award of recognition Suffolk County Bar Assn., 1991, cert. of disting. merit Suffolk Acad. Law, 1991. Mem. ABA, Am. Coll. Forensic Examiners, N.C. State Bar Assn., D.C. Bar Assn., N.Y. State Bar Assn., Hofstra U. Alumni Orgn. (exec. coun. 1990-94), Scabbard and Blade, Phi Eta Sigma. Banking, Corporate, general, Finance. Office: Cummings Law Office 330 Vanderbilt Motor Pkwy Hauppauge NY 11788 also: PO Box 232 Brightwaters NY 11718 E-mail: cummingsanthony@mindspring.com.

CUMMINGS, FRANK, lawyer; b. N.Y.C., Dec. 11, 1929; s. Louis and Florence (Levine) Cummings; m. Jill Schwartz, July 6, 1958; children: Peter Ian, Margaret Anne. BA, Hobart Coll., 1951; MA, Columbia U., 1955, LLB, 1958. Bar: N.Y. 1959, D.C. 1963. Adminstrv. asst. to U.S. Senator Jacob Javits, 1969-71; minority counsel com. labor and pub. welfare U.S. Senate, Washington, 1965-67, 71-72; assoc. Cravath, Swaine & Moore, N.Y.C., 1958-63, Gall, Lane & Powell, Washington, 1967-68, ptnr., 1972-75, Marshall, Bratter, Greene, Allison & Tucker, Washington, 1976-85, Nossaman, Keurger & Knox, 1982-83, Cummings & Cummings, P.C. and predecessor firm, 1983-86, LeBoeuf, Lamb, Greene & MacRae, LLP, Washington, 1986-2000, of counsel, 2000—. Lectr. law Columbia U. Law Sch., 1970-74, U. Va. Sch. Law, 2000—; adj. prof. Georgetown U. Law Sch., 1983-86; chmn. Am. Law Inst.-ABA Ann. Course Employee Benefits Litigation, 1989—, Employment and Labor Rels. Law for Corp. Coun. and Gen. Practitioner, 1978—; mem. pub. adv. coun. employee welfare and pension benefit plans Dept. Labor, 1972-74; mem. adv. bd. Pension Reporter Bur. Nat. Affairs. Author: Capitol Hill Manual, 1976, Capitol Hill Manual, 2d edit., 1984, Pension Plan Terminations-Single Employer Plans, 3rd edit., 2002, Multiemployer Plans, 2d edit., 1986; articles editor: Columbia U. Law Rev., 1957—58. Fellow Am. Coll. Employee Benefits Counsel; mem. ABA (chmn. com. pension, welfare and related plans 1976-79), Am. Law Inst. (advisor to restatement of employment law 2002—), Bar Assn. D.C. (chmn. com. labor rels. law 1972-73), Cosmos Club, Phi Beta Kappa. Federal civil litigation, Insurance, Pension, profit-sharing, and employee benefits. Office: LeBoeuf Lamb Greene & MacRae LLP 1875 Connecticut Ave NW Washington DC 20009-5728 Home: 800 25th St NW Washington DC 20037 E-mail: fcumming@llgm.com.

CUMMINGS, JOHN PATRICK, lawyer; b. Westfield, Mass., June 28, 1933; s. Daniel Thoams and Nora (Brick) C.; m. Dorothy June D'Ingianni, Dec. 27, 1957 (div. May 1978); children: John Patrick, Mary Catherine, Michael Brick, Kevin Andrew, Colleen Elise, Erin Christine, Christopher Gerald; m. Marilyn Ann Welch, May 23, 1980. BS, St. Michael's Coll., 1955; PhD, U. Tex., 1969; JD, U. Toledo, 1973, MCE, 1977. Bar: Ohio 1973, U.S. Mil. Appeals 1974, U.S. Dist. Ct. (no. dist.) Ohio 1979. Mgr. Hamilton Mgmt., Inc., Austin, Tex., 1962-68; scientist Owens Ill., Toledo, 1968-73, risk mgr., 1974-76, staff atty., 1977-80, mgr. legis. affairs, 1981-84; pres. Hansa World Cargo Svc., Inc., Oakland, Calif., 1984-86; in-house counsel Brown Vence & Assocs., San Francisco, 1987-88; gen. counsel Pacific Mgmt. Co., Sacramento, 1986-88; pres. John P. Cummings & Assoc., Fremont, Calif., 1988—. Cons. Glass Packaging Inst., Washington, 1970-83, EPA, Washington, 1970-74. Contbr. articles to profl. jours.; patentee in field. With USAF, 1955-62, 68-69, 75-76, 84-85, col. ret. 1986. USPHS fellow, 1963-66. Fellow Royal Chem. Soc.; mem. ABA, VFW, ASTM (chmn. 1979), Am. Ceramic Soc. (chpt. chmn. 1973), Am. Indsl. Hygiene Assn., Am. Chem. Soc., Res. Officers Assn. (legis. chmn. 1979-85), Am. Legion, KC (4th degree), Amvets. Roman Catholic. Avocations: reading, travel, coin and stamp collecting. Environmental, Immigration, naturalization, and customs, Private international. Home: 843 Barcelona Dr Fremont CA 94536-2607 Office: PO Box 2847 Fremont CA 94536-0847 E-mail: epigeneint@aol.com.

CUMMINS, CHARLES FITCH, JR., lawyer; b. Lansing, Mich., Aug. 19, 1939; s. Charles F. Sr. and Ruth M. Cummins; m. Anne Warner, Feb. 11, 1961; children: Michael, John, Mark. AB in Econs., U. Mich., 1961; LLB, U. Calif., Hastings, 1966. Bar: Calif. 1966, Mich. 1976. Assoc. Hall, Henry, Oliver & McReavy, San Francisco, 1966-70, ptnr., 1971-75, Cummins & Cummins, Lansing, Mich., 1976-82, Pitto & Ubhaus, San Jose, Calif., 1982-85; prin. Law Offices Charles F. Cummins Jr., San Jose, 1985-87; ptnr. Cummins & Chandler, San Jose, 1987-92; prin. Law Offices of Charles F. Cummins, Jr., San Jose, 1992—. Bd. dirs., officer various civic orgns., chs. and pvt. schs. Lt. (j.g.) USNR, 1961-63. Mem. Rotary. Alternative dispute resolution, General civil litigation, Estate planning. Office: 224 E Jackson St Ste B San Jose CA 95112 E-mail: cfclaw@ix.netcom.com.

CUMMINS, H. E. BUD, III, lawyer; b. Enid, Okla., Aug. 6, 1959; BS, U. Ark., 1981, JD, 1989. Clk. U.S. Dist. Judge Stephen Reasoner, U.S. Magistrate John Forster Jr.; chief legal counsel Gov. Mike Huckabee; atty. Little Rock; U.S. atty. Ea. Dist. Ark. State dir. Nat. Fedn. Ind. Bus. Republican. Methodist. Office: Ea Dist Ark PO 1229 Little Rock AR 72203*

CUMMIS, CLIVE SANFORD, lawyer; b. Newark, Nov. 21, 1928; s. Joseph Jack and Lee (Berkie) C.; m. Ann Denburg, Mar. 24, 1956; children: Andrea, Deborah, Cynthia, Jessica. AB, Tulane U., 1949; JD, U. Pa., 1952; LL.M., N.Y. U., 1959. Bar: N.J. 1952. Law sec. Hon. Walter Freund, Appellate Div., Superior Ct., 1955-56; partner firm Cummis & Kroner, Newark, 1956-60; chief counsel County and Mcpl. Law Revision Commn., State of N.J., Newark, 1959-62; partner firm Schiff, Cummis & Kent, Newark, 1962-67, Cummis, Kent, Radin & Tischman, Newark, 1967-70; sr. v.p., dir. Cadence Industries, N.Y.C., 1967-70; dir. Plume & Atwood Industries, Stamford, Conn., 1969-71; chmn., chmn. emeritus Sills Cummis Radin Tischman Epstein & Gross, Newark, 1970—; exec. v.p. law and corp. affairs, sec. Park Place Entertainment corp., Las Vegas, Nev., 1999—2001, vice chmn. bd. dirs., 2000—. Dir. Essex County State Bank, Financial Resources Group; instr. Practising Law Inst. Chief counsel County and Mcpl. Revision Commn., 1959-62, N.J. Pub. Market Commn., 1961-63; counsel Bd. Edn. of South Orange and Maplewood, 1964-74, Town of Cedar Grove, 1966-70, Bd. Edn. of Dumont, 1968-72; mem. com. on rules and civil practice N.J. Supreme Ct., 1975-78. Assoc. editor NJ. Law Jour., 1961—. Trustee Newark Beth Israel Med. Ctr., 1965-75, Northfield YM-YWHA, 1968-70, U. Medicine and Dentistry N.J., 1980-84, Newark Mus., N.J. Performing Arts Ctr., Blue Cross and Blue Shield N.J.; gen. coun. N.J. Turnpike Authority, 1990-94; mem. bd. overseers U. Pa. Law Sch., 1991-96; mem. bd. govs. Daus. of Israel Home for Aged, 1968-70; mem. N.J. Commn. on Statue of Liberty; mem. pres.'s coun. Tulane U., 1992—; pres. bd. dirs. Tulane Assocs., 1994-96; mem. Pres.'s commn. on White House Fellows, 1993-2001; dir. N.J. Regional Planning Assn. Recipient 1st Ann. Judge Learned Hand award Am. Jewish Com., 1994, Fiesta Ann. Disting. Citizen award N.J. Med. Sch., 2002. Fellow Am. Bar Found.; mem. ABA, Am. Law Inst., Am. Judicature Soc., U. Pa. Law Sch. Alumni Soc. (pres.), N.J. Bar Assn., Essex County Bar Assn., City Athletic Club (N.Y.C.), Greenbrook County Club (North Caldwell, N.J.), Stockbridge Golf Club (Mass.). Democrat. Jewish. Administrative and regulatory, Federal civil litigation, State civil litigation. Office: Sills Cummis Radin Tischman Epstein & Gross One Riverfront Pl Newark NJ 07102 E-mail: ccummis@sillscummis.com.

CUNEO, DONALD LANE, lawyer, educator; b. Alameda, Calif., Apr. 19, 1944; s. Vernon Edmund and Dorothy (Lane) c.; m. Frances Susan Huze, Aug. 8, 1981; children: Kristen Marie, Lane Michael. BA, Lehigh U., 1966; JD, MBA, Columbia U., 1970. Bar: N.Y. 1971, D.C. 1992, U.S. Claims Ct. 1972, U.S. Tax Ct. 1972, U.S. Dist. Ct. (so. dist.) N.Y. 1973, U.S. Dist. Ct. (no. dist.) 1978, U.S. Dist. Ct. D.C. 1992, U.S. Ct. Appeals (2nd cir.) 1979, U.S. Ct. Appeals (D.C. cir.) 1992, U.S. Ct. Internat. Trade 1979, U.S. Ct. Appeals (fed. cir.) 1979, U.S. Supreme Ct. 1979. Assoc. Shearman & Sterling, N.Y.C., 1971-79, ptnr., 1979-93; pres., CEO Internat. House, 1993—. Sec./trustee Internat. House, N.Y.C., 1977-93; pres. Morningside Area Alliance, N.Y.C., 2000—. Author: (with others) Prevention and Prosecution of Computer and High Technology Crime, 1988; contbr. articles to profl. jours. Reginald Heber Smith Cmty. Lawyer fellow U.S. Govt., 1970-71. Mem. Coun. Fgn. Rels. Avocations: sports, travel. General civil litigation, Private international. Home and Office: Internat House 500 Riverside Dr New York NY 10027-3916

CUNHA, MARK GEOFFREY, lawyer; b. Lexington, Mass., Sept. 26, 1955; s. John Henry and Dolores (DeRosas) C.; children: Celine Yvonne, Nicholas Brian. AB magna cum laude, Cornell U., 1977; JD, Stanford U., 1980. Bar: N.Y. 1981, U.S. Dist. Ct. (so. and ea. dists.) N.Y. 1981, U.S. Ct. Appeals (2nd cir.) 1991, U.S. Tax Ct. 1992, U.S. Supreme Ct. 1996, U.S. Ct. Appeals (3d cir.) 2001. Intern The White House, Washington, 1979-80; assoc. Simpson Thacher & Bartlett, N.Y.C., 1980-88, ptnr., 1989—. Mediator comml. divsn. N.Y. State Supreme Ct., N.Y. County, 1996—; bd. dir. legal svcs. for N.Y.C., 1997—. Bd. dirs. N.Y. Lawyers for Pub. Interest, 1989—; trustee Inst. for Ednl. Achievement, 1995—, Lycee Francais N.Y., 1998—. Recipient Outstanding Vol. Lawyers award Legal Aid Soc., 1990, Pro Bono award N.Y. County Lawyers Assn., 1991. Mem.: Assn. Bar City N.Y. (chmn. exec. com., chmn. com. on legal assistance, chmn. del. to N.Y. State Bar Assn. Ho. of Dels., steering com. on legal assistance), N.Y. State Bar Assn. (exec. com. on comml. and fed. litigation sect.), Internat. Bar Assn., ABA, Phi Beta Kappa. Democrat. Insurance, Product liability, Securities. Home: 1150 Fifth Ave Apt 3A New York NY 10128-0724 Office: Simpson Thacher & Bartlett 425 Lexington Ave New York NY 10017-3954 E-mail: mcunha@stblaw.com.

CUNNINGHAM, CATHY MEYER, lawyer; b. Springfield, Ill., Oct. 29, 1957; d. William Harold and Sandra Joan (Unsell) M.; m. Blake Cunningham, July 11, 1992; 1 child, Kristen Lyn. BA, U. Ill. at Springfield, 1979; JD, St. Louis U., 1982. Assoc. George Chandler & Assoc., Baytown, Tex., 1982; asst. city atty. City of Abilene, 1983-84; sr. asst. city atty. City of Irving, 1984—. Bd. dirs. Nat. Assn. Telecomm. Officers and Advisers, 1996-98. Office: City of Irving 825 W Irving Blvd Irving TX 75060-2860

CUNNINGHAM, GARY ALLEN, lawyer; b. Seattle, July 4, 1940; s. Chester Martin and Elsie Annette (Peterson) C.; m. Marilyn Phyllis Thunman, June 13, 1964. B in Engring., Yale U., 1962; JD, U. Wash., 1965. Bar: Wash. 1965, U.S. Dist. Ct. (we. dist.) Wash. 1965, U.S. Ct. Appeals (9th cir.) 1967, U.S. Supreme Ct. 1993. Dep. prosecutor Office King County Pros. Atty., Seattle, 1965-67; ptnr. Bishop, Cunningham & Andrews, Inc., P.S., Bremerton, Wash., 1967—. Bd. dirs. Hood Canal Environ. Coun., Seabeck, Wash., 1970—, pres., 1974, 78; bd. dirs., sec. Olympic Peninsula Kidney Ctr., Bremerton, 1980—; bd. dirs. Kitsap Land Trust, Bremerton, 1989-2000, pres., 1993-2000; bd. dirs. Great Peninsula Conservancy, 2000—, pres., 2000-02. Mem. ABA, Wash. State Bar Assn., Kitsap County Bar Assn. (pres. 1975-76), Kitsap Golf and Country Club, Bremerton Rotary Club. Avocations: golf, hiking, skiing, foreign travel. Probate (including wills, trusts), Property, real (including real estate development, water). Home: 8411 Sunset Ln NW Seabeck WA 98380-9529 Office: PO Box 5060 Bremerton WA 98312-0469 E-mail: bca@silverlink.net.

CUNNINGHAM, GARY H. lawyer; b. Grand Rapids, Mich., Jan. 11, 1953; s. Gordon H. and Marilyn J. (Lookabill) C.; children: Stephanie M., Gregory H. B.Gen. Studies, U. Mich., 1975, MA, 1977; JD, Detroit Coll. Law, 1980. Bar: Mich. 1980, U.S. Dist. Ct. Mich. 1983, U.S. Ct. Appeals (6th cir.) 1986, U.S. Ct. Appeals (Fed. cir.) 1990. Law clk. and estate adminstr. U.S. Bankruptcy Ct., Ea. Dist. Mich., Detroit, 1980-83; assoc./ptnr. Schlussel, Lifton, Simon, Rands, Galvin & Jackier, Southfield, Mich., 1983-90; ptnr./shareholder Kramer Mellen, P.C., Southfield, Mich., 1990-95; prin. shareholder Strobl Cunningham Caretti & Sharp, P.C., Bloomfield Hills, Mich., 1995—. Sr. staff mem. Detroit Coll. of Law Rev., 1978-80; contbr. articles to profl. jours. Mem. ABA (bus. law sect.), Fed. Bar Assn. (chmn. bankruptcy sect. 1989-91), Oakland County Bar Assn. (bus. law com.), State Bar of Mich. (mem. corp., fin. and bus. law sect.), Am. Bankruptcy Inst. (sponsor), Comml. Law League of Am., Detroit Econ. Club, Detroit Inst. Arts, Delta Theta Phi. Avocations: sailing, skiing, tennis. Bankruptcy, General civil litigation, Corporate, general. Home: 3399 Roxbury Dr Troy MI 48084-2613 Office: Strobl Cunningham & Sharp PC 300 E Long Lake Rd Ste 200 Bloomfield Hills MI 48304-2376 E-mail: gcunningham@stroblpc.com.

CUNNINGHAM, JUDY MARIE, lawyer; b. Durant, Okla., Sept. 7, 1944; d. Rowe Edwin and Margaret (Arnott) C. BA, U. Tex., 1967, JD, 1971;

postgrad., Schiller Coll., Heidelberg, Fed. Republic Germany, 1976. Bar: Tex. 1972. Quizmaster U. Tex. Law Sch., Austin, 1969-71; rschr. Tex. Law Rev., Washington, 1970; staff atty. Tex. Legis. Coun., Austin, 1972-75; adminstrv. law judge, dir. sales tax div., assoc. counsel Comptr. of Pub. Accounts, Austin, 1975-85; owner, editor J.C. Law Publs., Austin, 1986—; pvt. practice Austin, 1986—. Author: (with others) Texas Tax Service, 1985; pub., editor, contbr. (newsletter) Tex. State Tax Update, 1986—; contbr. articles to Revenue Adminstrn.; assoc. editor Tex. Law Rev., 1968-71. State del. Dem. Party, Ft. Worth, 1990, county del., Austin, 1972, 88, 90, 92; vol. numerous Dem. campaigns, Austin, 1972-90. Mem. Industry Practitioners Liaison Group (comptr. pub. accts.), State Bar Tex. (taxation sect.), Travis County Bar (bus. corp. and taxation sect.), Tex. Taxpayers and Rsch. Assn. Avocations: traveling, cooking, reading mysteries, photography, swimming. Administrative and regulatory, Legislative, State and local taxation. Office: 4905 W Park Dr Austin TX 78731-5535

CUNNINGHAM, KEN VERNON, lawyer; b. Ottawa County, Okla., July 22, 1942; s. Henry V. and Dorothy M. (Roberts) C.; m. Jean Rea Kelley, June 12, 1968 (div. 1981); children: Vernon, Christie, Tammy, Kenny, Shirley, Nicholas. BS in Engring. Physics, U. Okla., 1966; A in Police Sci., Tulsa C.C., 1972; JD, Tulsa U., 1974; Dr. Clin. Hypnotherapy, Am. Inst. Hypnotherapy. Pros. Dist. Atty. Office, Tulsa, 1975-81; pvt. practice Tulsa, 1981—. With USN, 1961-71. Mem. ABA, Tulsa County Bar Assn. Home: RR 1 Box 177 Wyandotte OK 74370-9801

CUNNINGHAM, ROBERT JAMES, lawyer; b. Kearney, Nebr., June 27, 1942; m. Sara Jean Dickson, July 22, 1967. BA, U. Nebr., 1964; JD, NYU, 1967, LLM in Taxation, 1969. Bar: N.Y. 1967, Ill. 1969, U.S. Dist. Ct. (no. dist.) Ill. 1969, U.S. Ct. Claims 1970, U.S. Tax Ct. 1970, U.S. Ct. Appeals (D.C. cir.) 1972, U.S. Ct. Appeals (9th cir.) 1975, U.S. Ct. Appeals (7th cir.) 1979, U.S. Ct. Appeals (fed. cir.) 1982. Instr. law NYU, N.Y.C., 1967-69; assoc. Baker & McKenzie, Chgo., 1969-74, ptnr., 1974—. Spkr. in field. Contbr. articles to profl. jours. Mem. ABA, Ill. Bar Assn., Chgo. Bar Assn. Private international, Corporate taxation, Taxation, general. Office: Baker & McKenzie One Prudential Plz 130 E Randolph Dr Ste 3700 Chicago IL 60601-6342 E-mail: robert.j.cunningham@bakernet.com.

CUNNINGHAM, STANLEY LLOYD, lawyer; b. Durant, Okla., Feb. 7, 1938; s. Stanley Ryan and Hazel Dell (Dillingham) C.; m. Suzanne Yerger, Sept. 18, 1960; children: Stanley William, Ryan Yerger. BS in Geology, U. Okla., 1960, LLB, 1963. Bar: U.S. Dist. Ct. (we. dist.) Okla. 1963; U.S. Ct. Appeals (10th cir.) 1965; U.S. Supreme Ct. Okla. 1963. Atty. Phillips Petroleum Co., Oklahoma City, 1963-64, Bartlesville, Okla., 1964-71; counsel McAfee, Taft, et al., Oklahoma City, 1971—. Lectr. U. Okla. Coll. Law, Norman, 1977, 79, S.W. Legal Found., Dallas, 1986, 89. Contbr. articles to profl. jours. Layreader All Souls' Episcopal Ch., Oklahoma City, 1972-75. 1st lt. USAFR, 1963-72. Harry J. Brown scholar, U. Okla., 1960-63 Mem. ABA, Fed. Energy Bar Assn., Am. Soc. Internat. Law, Geological Soc. Am., Alumni Adv. Coun., U. Okla. Assoc., Oklahoma City Golf & Country Club, Order of Coif, Phi Alpha Delta, Sigma Gamma Epsilon. Republican. Episcopalian. Avocations: golf, reading. General civil litigation, Oil, gas, and mineral. Office: McAfee & Taft 2 Leadership Sq Fl 10 Oklahoma City OK 73102

CUNNINGHAM, THOMAS JUSTIN, lawyer; b. Hinsdale, Ill., Feb. 27, 1968; s. Thomas J. and Diane (Carlton) C.; m. Paula J. Friant, Sept. 9, 1989; children: Thomas Justin, Nicholas Joseph. BS, Ariz. State U., 1989; JD, DePaul U., 1993. Bar: Ill. 1993, U.S. Dist. Ct. (no. dist.) Ill. 1993, U.S. Ct. Appeals (7th cir.) 1993, U.S. Dist. Ct. (ctrl. dist.) Ill. 1996, U.S. Dist. Ct. (we. dist.) Mich. 2002, U.S. Supreme Ct. 1996, Trial bar 1997. Dep. clk. U.S. Bankruptcy Ct., Chgo., 1989-90; law clk. Burke, Smith & Williams, Chgo., 1990-93; assoc. Smith, Lodge & Schneider, Chgo., 1993-98, Hopkins & Sutter, Chgo., 1998-2001; ptnr. Lord, Bissell & Brook, Chgo., 2001—. Contbr. articles to profl. jours. Pres. Ill. Dist. 58 Bd. Edn. Mem. Chgo. Bar Assn. (chair moot ct. com. 1995, co-editor in chief YLS jour.). Republican. Presbyterian. Avocations: hunting, fishing. Bankruptcy, Federal civil litigation, Commercial, contracts (including sales of goods; commercial financing). Home: 5135 Fairview Ave Downers Grove IL 60515-5211 Office: Lord Bissell & Brook 115 S LaSalle 31st Fl Chicago IL 60603 E-mail: tcunningham@lordbissell.com.

CUNNINGHAM, TOM ALAN, lawyer; b. Houston, Nov. 5, 1946; s. Warren Peek and Ellen Ardelle (Benner) Cunningham; m. Jeanne Adrienne Moran, July 21, 1972; 1 child, Christopher Alan. BA, U. Tex., 1968, JD, 1974. Bar: Tex. 1974, U.S. Dist. Ct. (so. dist.) Tex. 1976, U.S. Dist. Ct. (no. dist.) Tex. 1982, U.S. Dist. Ct. (we. dist.) Tex. 1984, U.S. Ct. Appeals (5th and 11th cirs.) 1981, U.S. Ct. Appeals (8th cir.) 1919. Ptnr. Fulbright & Jaworski L.L.P., Houston, 1974—98; founding ptnr. Cunningham, Darlow, Zook & Chapoton, L.L.P., Houston, 1998—. Bd. trustee Children's Charity Fund, Houston, 1983—88; active South Tex. Ctr. Legal Responsibility; mem. exec. com., bd. dirs. Assn. for Cmty. TV. Lt. (j.g.) USNR, 1969—72. Fellow: Houston Bar Found., Tex. Trial Lawyers Assn., Am. Coll. Trial Lawyers, Am. Bd. Trial Advs., Tex. Bar Found. (life; chmn. bd. trustees, adv. bd., chair 1995—, chair Lola Wright com., chair bd. trustees 1995—, adv. bd., mem. new fellows com., mem. awards com., mem. pub. com., bd. dirs., ct. ruels com.), Am. Bar Found.; mem.: CPR Inst. for Dispute Resolution, Resolution Forum, Inc. (pres.), Tex. Empowerment Network (bd. dirs.), Tex. Ctr. Legal Ethics and Professionalism, Tex. Assn. Def. Counsel, Tex. Bd. Legal Specialization, State Bar Tex. (chmn. dist.4H grievance com. 1982—88, chmn. spl. com. on lawyer adt. and solicitation 1982, bd. dirs. 1989—92, chair bd. dirs. exec. com. 1991—92, chair com. for lawyer discipline 1992—94, chair gen. counsel adv. com., mem. exec. com., ct. rules com., Pres.'s award 1983, Pres.'s citation for meritorious svc. 1991, Pres.'s spl. recognition for meritorious svc. 1993, 1994, nominee Outstanding Young Lawyer 1981), Houston Bar Assn. (professionalism com., chmn. constn. bicentennial com., arbitration com., membership com., Pres.'s award 1988), Am. Arbitration Assn. (panel of arbitrators), ABA (litigation sect., discovery com., alternate dispute resolution com., forum com. constrn. industry, arbitration com. 1995—), Lakeside Country Club, Coronado Club, Houston Club, Phi Delta Phi. Federal civil litigation, State civil litigation. Home: 10811 Pine Bayou St Houston TX 77024-3018

CUNNINGHAM, WILLIAM FRANCIS, lawyer; b. Chgo., Feb. 24, 1945; s. Michael and Catherine B. Cunningham; m. Rae C. Cunningham; children: Kellie Marie, Kiera Megan, Michael Grant. BA, DePaul U., 1967, JD, 1971. Bar: Ill. 1971, U.S. Dist. Ct. (no. dst.) Ill. 1971. Mem. firm Gates W. Clancy, Geneva, Ill., 1971-74, O'Reilly & Quetsch, Wheaton, Ill., 1974—75; ptnr. Law Offices of Roger K. O'Reilly, 1975—78, O'Reilly & Cunningham, 1978-95, Cunningham, Meyer & Vedrine, 1995—. Lectr. in field. Mem. ABA, Ill. Bar Assn., DuPage County Bar Assn., Kane County Bar Assn., Ill. Assn. Def. Trial Counsel, Soc. Trial Lawyers, Am. Coll. Trial Lawyers, Am. Bd. Trial Advocates. Roman Catholic. State civil litigation, Insurance, Personal injury (including property damage). Home: ONO64 Forbes Dr Geneva IL 60134 Office: Cunningham Meyer & Vedrine Ste B 1050 PO Box 988 Wheaton IL 60189-0988 also: 111 W Washington Ste 937 Chicago IL 60602 Fax: (630) 260-8080.

CUNNYNGHAM, MAXINE BROWN, lawyer; b. Enid, Okla., Apr. 28, 1949; d. Max Eldon and Georgia Mae (Carter) Brown; m. O. Blair Cunnyngham; 1 child, Christopher Brown. BBA, U. Ctrl. Okla., Edmond, 1970; JD, Oklahoma City U., 1980. Bar: Okla. 1980. Bookkeeper Lamun Mock Featherly & Baer, Oklahoma City, 1970-75; office mgr. Lamun Mock Featherly Baer & Timberlake, Oklahoma City, 1975-80, assoc., 1980-84; ptnr. Lamun Mock Featherly Kuehling & Cunnyngham, Oklahoma City, 1984—. Mem. Okla. Bar Assn., Oklahoma County Bar Assn., Phi Delta Phi. General practice, Probate (including wills, trusts), Property, real (including real estate development, water). Office: Lamun Mock Cunnyngham & Davis 5900 NW Grand Blvd Oklahoma City OK 73118-1295

CUOMO, MARIO MATTHEW, lawyer, former governor; b. Queens County, N.Y., June 15, 1932; s. Andrea and Immaculata (Giordano) Cuomo; m. Matilda Raffa, June 5, 1954; children: Margaret Cuomo Maier, Andrew, Maria Cuomo Cole, Madeline Cuomo O'Donoghue, Christopher. BA summa cum laude, St. John's Coll., 1953; LLB cum laude, St. John's U., 1956. Bar: NY 1956, U.S. Dist. Ct. (no. dist.) NY 1957, U.S. Dist. Ct. (so. dist.) NY 1998, U.S. Supreme Ct. 1960, U.S. Dist. Ct. (ea. dist.) NY 1962, U.S. Ct. Appeals (2d cir.) 1967. Confidential legal asst. to Hon. Adrian P. Burke, NY State Ct. Appeals, 1956—58; assoc. Corner, Weisbrod, Froeb and Charles, Bklyn., 1958—63; ptnr. Corner, Cuomo & Charles, 1963—75; sec. of state State of NY, 1975—79, lt. gov., 1979—83, gov., 1983—94; ptnr., now of counsel Wilkie Farr & Gallagher, N.Y.C., 1995—. Mem. faculty St. John's U. Sch. Law, 1963—73; counsel to cmty. groups, including Corona Homeowners, 1966—72; charter mem. First Ecumenical Commn. of Christians and Jews for Bklyn. and Queens, NY. Author: Forest Hills Diary: The Crisis of Low-Income Housing, 1974, Diaries of Mario M. Cuomo, Campaign for Governor, 1982; co-author: Lincoln on Democracy, 1990, More Than Words, 1993, The New York Idea: An Experiment in Democracy, 1994, Reason to Believe, 1995, The Blue Spruce, 1999; contbr. articles to legal publs. Spkr. keynote address Dem. Nat. Conv., San Francisco, 1984, nominating address Dem. Nat. Conv., N.Y.C., 1992. Recipient Rapallo award, Columbia Lawyers Assn., 1976, Dante medal, Italian Govt.-Am. Assn. Tchrs. Italian, 1976, Silver medallion, Columbia Coalition, 1976, Pub. Adminstr. award, C.W. Post Coll., 1977, Theodore Roosevelt award, Internat. Platform Assn., 1984. Mem.: ABA, Am. Judicature Soc., Assn. of Bar of City of NY, Queens County Bar Assn., Nassau Bar Assn., Bklyn. Bar Assn., NY State Bar Assn., Cath. Lawyers Guild of Queens County (pres. 1966—67), St. John's U. Alumni Fedn. (chmn. bd. 1970—72), Skull and Circle. Home: 50 Sutton Pl S New York NY 10022-4167 Address: Wilkie Farr & Gallagher 787 7th Ave Rm 203 New York NY 10019-6018*

CUOZZI, WILLIAM FRANCIS, JR., lawyer; b. Kearny, N.J., Jan. 4, 1920; s. William F. and Antoinette Russo Cuozzi; m. Domenica A. Baldanza, Nov. 22, 1941; children: Carol, Jo-Ellen, William III. BSc, Seton Hall U., 1942; LLB, Rutgers U., 1945. Bar: N.Y. 1946, N.J. 1967, U.S. Dist. Ct. N.J. 1967. Counsel Dollin Corp., Irvington, N.J., 1946-61, Radiant Lamp, Newark, N.J., 1961-64, Syska Hennesy, N.Y.C., 1964-67; pvt. practice West Orange, N.J., 1967—. Mayor West Orange, N.J., 1974-78, councilman, 1964-74, mcpl. judge, 1992-2003. Mem. Essex County Bar Assn. Democrat. Roman Catholic. Avocations: tennis, golf, theatre. Bankruptcy, Estate planning, General practice. Office: 226 S Valley Rd West Orange NJ 07052-4901

CURCI-GONZALEZ, LUCY, law librarian; b. Bklyn., Sept. 15, 1955; d. Michael C. and Angela (Surace) Curci; m. Arturo B. Gonzalez-Alfonso, Apr. 29, 1990; children: Angela Grace, Monica Cecilia. BA, St. Francis Coll., 1977; MS, Columbia U., 1978. Reference libr. Fordham U., N.Y.C., 1978-79; law libr. Fed. Res. Bank N.Y. Legal div., N.Y.C., 1979-83; head libr. Morgan & Finnegan, N.Y.C., 1983—. Co-chair Practising Law Inst. Pvt. Law Librs. Program, 1989-95. Contbr. articles to profl. jours. Mem. Am. Assn. Law Librs., Spl. Librs. Assn. Roman Catholic. Home: 282 Leonia Ave Leonia NJ 07605-1617 Office: Morgan & Finnegan 345 Park Ave Fl 22 New York NY 10154-0053 E-mail: lcurcigonzalez@morganfinnegan.com.

CURLEY, ROBERT AMBROSE, JR., lawyer; b. Boston, June 5, 1949; s. Robert Ambrose and Terese M. (O'Hara) C.; m. Kathleen M. Foley, June 10, 1972; children: Christine, Elizabeth, Margaret. AB cum laude, Harvard U., 1971; JD, Cornell U., 1974. Bar: Mass. 1974, U.S. Dist. Ct. Mass. 1975, U.S. Ct. Appeals (1st. cir.) 1976. Prin. Curley & Curley, P.C., Boston, 1974—, pres. Lectr. Mass. Continuing Legal Edn., Mass. Def. Attys., Mass. Acad. Trial Attys., Flaschner Judicial Inst., Nat. Bus. Inst. Mem. ABA, ATLA (assoc.), Internat. Assn. Def. Counsel Found. (dir. 2003-), Def. Trial Acad., Mass. Bar Assn. (lectr., chmn. civil trial practice sect., civil litig. com. 1990-91, mem. ho. of dels. 2001-2002), Mass. Def. Lawyers Assn. (co-chmn. products liability sects. 1994-96, bd. dirs., sec. 1998-99, treas., v.p. 1999-2000, pres. 2001-2002), Nat. Bus. Inst., Def. Rsch. Inst. (state rep. 2002—), Harvard Club (Hingham, treas. 1983-84, v.p. 1984-85, pres. 1985-86), Clover (Boston). Roman Catholic. Federal civil litigation, State civil litigation, Personal injury (including property damage). Office: Curley & Curley PC 27 School St Ste 600 Boston MA 02108-4391 E-mail: rac@curleylaw.com.

CURNUTTE, MARK WILLIAM, lawyer; b. Vinita, Okla., May 28, 1954; s. William Elmer and Genevieve Gertrude (Fitzgerald) C.; m. Lou Ann Coffman, Aug. 4, 1979; children: Meredith Blake, Amelia Leigh. BBA in Accountancy, U. Okla., 1976, JD, 1979. Bar: Okla. 1979, U.S. Dist. Ct. (no. dist.) Okla. 1980, U.S. Dist. Ct. (ea. and we. dists.) Okla. 1984, U.S. Tax Ct. 1979, U.S. Ct. Appeals (10th and fed. cirs.) 1980, U.S. Supreme Ct. 1984. Tax staff acct. Arthur Andersen & Co., Tulsa, 1979-81; assoc. Jones, Givens, Gotcher, Doyle & Bogan, Tulsa, 1981-84, Logan & Lowry, LLP, Vinita, Okla., 1984-87, ptnr., 1987—. Bd. dirs. C&L Supply, Inc., Vinita. Trustee Craig County Law Libr., Vinita, 1984—; chmn. bd. trustees Vinita Pub. Libr., 1987-89, 91-92; treas. Vinita chpt. ARC, 1991—. Fellow: Okla. Bar Found. (trustee 2000—), Am. Coll. Trust and Estate Counsel; mem.: U. Okla. Coll. Law Assn. (bd. dirs. 1989—91), Craig County Bar Assn. (sec.-treas. 1984—91, v.p. 1995—96, pres. 1997), Okla. Bar Assn. (title stds. com. real property sect. 1988—89, clients' security fund com. 1989—91, probate code com. 1995—, legal ethics and unauthorized practice com. 1995—97), ABA (com. on estate and gift tax 1987—90, small bus. com. 1987—, com. on small law firms 1987—), Rotary (pres. Vinita 1988—89, Paul Harris fellow 1989), Shriners, Masons, Phi Delta Phi. Republican. Presbyterian. Avocations: hunting, fishing. General civil litigation, Estate planning, Probate (including wills, trusts). Office: PO Box 558 Vinita OK 74301-0558

CURRAN, J. JOSEPH, JR., state attorney general; b. West Palm Beach, Fla., July 7, 1931; s. J. Joseph Sr. and Catherine (Clark) Curran; m. Barbara Marie Atkins, 1959; children: Mary Carole, Alice Ann, Catherine Marie, J. Joseph III, William A.(dec.). LLB, U. Balt., 1959. Bar: Md. 1959, U.S. Dist. Ct. Md., U.S. Supreme Ct. 1987. State senator from Md., 1963—82; lt. gov. State of Md., 1983—87, atty. gen., 1987—. Mem. Md. Regional Planning Coun., 1963—82. Mem.: Balt. Bar Assn., Md. Bar Assn. Democrat. Office: Office of Atty Gen 200 Saint Paul Pl Baltimore MD 21202-2002*

CURRAN, MARGARET E. prosecutor; m. Michael H. Feldhunh; 1 child, Margy. BA in Biology; MS in Anthropology, Purdue U.; JD, U. Conn. Assoc. Wistow & Barylick, Providence; fed. prosecutor U.S. Atty.'s Office R.I. Dist., 1986—90, appellate chief, 1990—98, U.S. atty., 1998—. Editor-in-chief U. Conn. Law Rev. Democrat. Office: 50 Kennedy Plz Fleet Ctr 8th Floor Providence RI 02903-2018

CURRAN, MAURICE FRANCIS, lawyer; b. Yonkers, N.Y., Feb. 20, 1931; s. James F. and Mary (O'Brien) C.; m. Deborah M. Dee, May 7, 1960; children: James, Maurice, Amy, Bridget, Ceara, Sara. Student, Cathedral Coll., 1950; BA in Philosophy, St. Joseph Coll. and Sem., 1952; LLB, Fordham U., 1958. Bar: N.Y. 1958, U.S. Dist. Ct. (so. and ea. dists.) N.Y. 1960, U.S. Ct. Appeals (2d cir.) 1982, U.S. Supreme Ct. Assoc. Kelley, Drye, Newhall & Maginnes, N.Y.C., 1958-60, Wilson & Bave, Yonkers, 1960-65; divsn. counsel Merck & Co., Rahway, N.J., 1965-67; asst. gen. counsel E.R. Squibb & Sons, Inc., N.Y.C., 1967-70; corp. counsel, chief law dept. City of Yonkers, 1970-72; ptnr. Bleakley, Platt, Schmidt & Fritz, White Plains, N.Y., 1972-83, Banks, Curran & Schwam, LLP, Mt. Kisco, NY, 1983—. Past trustee, vice chmn. Westchester C.C. Capt. USMC, 1952-58. Mem. Fed. Bar Coun., N.Y. State Bar Assn., Assn. Bar City N.Y. Roman Catholic. Federal civil litigation, State civil litigation, Education and schools. Home: 388 Bronxville Rd Bronxville NY 10708-1233 Office: 61 Smith Ave Mount Kisco NY 10549-2813

CURRAN, ROBERT BRUCE, lawyer; b. Charleston, W.Va., July 2, 1948; s. Bruce Frederick and Hazel Viola (Hoy) C.; children: Michael Robert, Laura Elizabeth, Emily Ann. BA, U. Del., 1971; JD, U. Md., 1974. Bar: Md. 1974. Ptnr. Frank, Bernstein, Conaway & Goldman, Balt., 1974-92, Whiteford Taylor & Preston, Balt., 1992—. Co-author: Tax Planning Forms for Businesses and Individuals, 1985. Mem. Md. Bar Assn. (sec. and treas. taxation sect. 1985-86, chmn. taxation sect. 1987-88). Corporate, general, Pension, profit-sharing, and employee benefits, Corporate taxation. Office: Whiteford Taylor & Preston 7 Saint Paul St Baltimore MD 21202-1626 E-mail: rcurran@wtplaw.com.

CURRAN, WILLIAM P. lawyer; b. Mpls., Feb. 27, 1946; s. William P. and Margaret L. (Killoren) C.; m. Jean L. Stabenow, Jan. 1, 1978; children: Patrick, Lisa, John. BA, U. Minn., 1969; JD, U. Calif., Berkeley, 1972. Law clk. Nev. Supreme Ct., Carson City, 1973-74, state ct. adminstr., 1973-74; assoc. Wiener, Goldwater & Galatz, Las Vegas, Nev., 1974-75; chief dept. dist. atty. Clark County Dist. Atty.'s Office, Las Vegas, 1975-79; county counsel Clark County, Las Vegas, 1979-89; pvt. practice Las Vegas, 1989-94; ptnr. Curran & Parry, Las Vegas, 1994—. Co-author: Nevada Judicial Orientation Manual, 1974. Mem. Nev. Gaming Commn., Carson City, 1989-99, chmn., 1991-99. Recipient Educator Yr. award UNLV Internat. Gaming Inst., 1998. Mem. ABA (state del. 1994—), Internat. Assn. Gaming Regulators (chmn. 1992-94), Nat. Assn. County Civil Attys. (pres. 1984-85), State Bar Nev. (pres. 1988-89), Nev. Gaming Commn. (chmn. 1989-99). Democrat. Roman Catholic. Administrative and regulatory, Land use and zoning (including planning), Property, real (including real estate development, water). Office: Curran & Parry 300 S Fourth St #1201 Las Vegas NV 89101 E-mail: curranparry@curranparry.com.

CURRIE, EDWARD JONES, JR., lawyer; b. Jackson, Miss., May 23, 1951; s. Edward J. and Nell (Branton) C.; m. Barbara Scott Miller, June 26, 1976; children: Morgan E., Scott E. BA, U. Miss., 1973, JD, 1976. Bar: Miss. 1976, U.S. Dist. Ct. (no. and so. dists.) Miss. 1976, U.S. Ct. Appeals (5th cir.) 1978, U.S. Supreme Ct. 1979. Assoc. Wise, Carter, Child, Steen & Caraway, Jackson, 1976—80; ptnr. Steen, Reynolds, Dalehite & Currie, Jackson, 1980—94, Currie Johnson Griffin Gaines & Myers, P.A., Jackson, 1994—. Adj. prof. Miss. Coll. Sch. Law, Jackson, 1977-81, 84-86. Bd. dirs. Miss. chpt. Am. Diabetes Assn., Jackson, 1980-82. Mem. Fed. Bar Assn. (pres. Miss. chpt. 1989), Internat. Assn. Def. Coun. (trial acad. faculty 1992), Nat. Inst. Trial Advocacy, Nat. Lawyers Assn. (chmn. ins. sect. 1998-99), Nat. Lawyers Assn. Found. (bd. dirs. 1998-00), Miss. Jud. Coll. (model civil jury instrn. com. 1991), Miss. Def. Lawyers Assn. (bd. dirs. 2000-2003, v.p.), Miss. Bar Assn. (bd. dirs. young lawyers sect. 1981-82, chmn. litigation/gen. practice sect. 1992, mem. MDP Task Force 2000), Miss. Bd. Bar Commrs., Jackson Young Lawyers (bd. dirs. 1980-81), Hinds County Bar Assn., Phi Delta Phi, Sigma Alpha Epsilon (pres. Ctrl. Miss. alumni 1981), Omicron Delta Kappa. Presbyterian. Federal civil litigation, State civil litigation, Insurance. Home: 50 Moss Forest Cir Jackson MS 39211-2905 Office: Currie Johnson Griffin Gaines & Myers PA PO Box 750 Jackson MS 39205-0750

CURRIN, SAMUEL THOMAS, lawyer, former judge; b. Oxford, N.C., Dec. 13, 1948; s. Thomas Benjamin and Lois (Brady) C.; m. Margaret Person, June 24, 1973. BA cum laude, Wake Forest U., 1971; JD, U. N.C., 1974. Bar: N.C. 1974. Asst. U.S. atty. Eastern Dist. N.C., Raleigh, 1976-78; legis. asst. to Sen. Jesse Helms Washington, 1978-81; U.S. atty. Eastern Dist. N.C., Raleigh, from 1981; now judge Spl. Superior Ct., Raleigh; pvt. practice Raleigh, 1988—. Chmn. pub. affairs com. So. Bapt. Conv., 1983—; chmn. N.C. Rep. Com. Mem.: Lions (Raleigh). Republican. Administrative and regulatory, Federal civil litigation, Criminal. Home: PO Box 269 Raleigh NC 27602-0269 Office: Curran Law Bldg 20 Market Plz Raleigh NC 27601

CURRIVAN, JOHN DANIEL, lawyer; b. Paris; s. Gene and Rachel Currivan; m. Patrice Salley; children: Christopher, Melissa. BS with distinction, Cornell U.; MS , U Calif.-Berkeley; MS, U. West Fla.; JD summa cum laude, Cornell Law Sch., 1978. Bar: Ohio 1978. Mng. ptnr. S.W. Devel. Co., Kingsville, Tex., 1971-76; note editor Cornell Law Rev., Ithaca, N.Y., 1977-78; prosecutor Naval Legal Office, Norfolk, Va., 1978-79, chief prosecutor, 1979-81; sr. atty. USS Nimitz, 1981-83; trial judge Naval Base, Norfolk, 1983-84; tax atty. Jones, Day, Reavis & Pogue, Cleve., 1984-88, ptnr., 1989—. Adj. prof. law Case Western Res. U. Sch. Law, 1997—. Author: (with Rickert) Ohio Limited Liability Companies, 1999. Comdr. USN, 1969-84. Recipient Younger Fed. Lawyer award FBA, 1981. Mem. ABA, Nat. Assn. Bond Lawyers, Order of Coif, Tau Beta Pi, Eta Kappa Nu, Phi Kappa Phi. Municipal (including bonds), Corporate taxation, Taxation, general. Home: 12700 Lake Ave Ste 2105 Lakewood OH 44107-1506 Office: Jones Day Reavis & Pogue 901 Lakeside Ave E Cleveland OH 44114-1190

CURRY, ALTON FRANK, lawyer; b. Dallas, Aug. 21, 1933; s. William Hadley and Myrtle Estelle (Posey) McKinney; m. Carole B. Piepgrass, Feb. 14, 1960 (div. Nov. 1979); children: Robyn, Mark, John; m. Ann O. Williams, Apr. 12, 1980. BA, Baylor U., 1958, LLB, 1960. Bar: Tex. 1960. Assoc. Fulbright & Jaworski, Houston, 1960-70, ptnr., 1970-98; spl. asst. to Atty. Gen. of Tex., 1964-65, 71-72. Trustee Found. for Bus., Politics and Econs., 1979-92, A.A. White Inst.; chmn. adminstrv. bd. Methodist Ch. Cpl. U.S. Army, 1953-55. Fellow Tex. Bar Found. (sustaining life); mem. ABA, Tex. Bar Assn., Houston Bar Assn., Baylor Law Alumni Assn. (dir. 1977-79, pres. 1979-80), Phi Alpha Delta, Houstonian Club (trustee 1980-83), Coronado Club, Masons. General civil litigation, Corporate, general, Securities. Home: 2707 Weslayan St Houston TX 77027-5123 Office: Fulbright & Jaworski 1301 Mckinney St Houston TX 77010-3031

CURRY, DANIEL ARTHUR, judge; b. Phoenix, Mar. 28, 1937; s. John Joseph and Eva May (Wills) C.; m. Joy M. Shallenberger, Sept. 5, 1959. BS, Loyola U., Los Angeles, 1957, LL.B., 1960. Bar: Calif. 1961, Hawaii 1972, N.Y. 1978. Pvt. practice, L.A. County, Calif., 1964—67; counsel Technicolor, Inc., Hollywood, Calif., 1967-70; sr. v.p., gen. counsel Amfac, Inc., Honolulu and San Francisco, 1970—87; v.p., gen. counsel Times Mirror, L.A., 1987-92; judge Superior Ct. of State of Calif., 1992-98; assoc. justice Calif. Ct. Appeal 2d dist., L.A., 1998—. Served to capt. USAF, 1961-64. Office: Calif Ct Appeal 2d Dist 4th Fl North Tower 300 S Spring St Los Angeles CA 90013-1230

CURRY, J. STANTON, lawyer, educator; BA magna cum laude, Brigham Young U., 1979, JD, 1982. Bar: Ariz. 1983, U.S. Dist. Ct. Ariz. 1984, U.S. Ct. Appeals (9th cir.) 1991. Shareholder, atty. Gallagher & Kennedy, P.A., Phoenix. Adj. prof. Ariz. State U., 1987—. Assoc. editor: Brigham Young U. Law Rev., 1981—82; contbr. articles to profl. jours. Scoutmaster Boy Scouts Am.; past bishop LDS Ch. Mem.: J. Reuben Clark Law Soc., Air and Waste Mgmt. Assn., HAZwaste Soc. (founding mem., past mem. exec. bd.), Ariz. State Bar (founding mem. sect. natural resources law), Ariz. State C. of C. Environmental, Natural resources. Office: Gallagher and Kennedy PA 2575 E Camelback Rd Phoenix AZ 85016-9225 Office Fax: 602-530-8500. Business E-Mail: jsc@gknet.com.*

CURRY, ROBERT LEE, lawyer; b. Lamont, Wis., May 10, 1923; s. Irving Gregg and Emma (Zimmerman) C.; m. Muriel Clapp, July 29, 1950; children— Robert Lee J., Laura Lynne, Melinda Ann. BS, Lawrence U., 1948; LL.B., U. Wis., 1953. Bar: Wis. bar 1953. Assoc. firm Boardman, Suhr, Curry & Field, Madison, Wis., 1953-56, sr. partner, 1956-73, of counsel, 1989-94. V.p., gen. counsel CUNA Mut. Ins. Group, Madison, 1964-73, pres., 1973-88, bd. dirs., 1972-88, dir. emeritus, 1988—; dir. CUNA Credit Union, 1965-70, pres., 1968-69; bd. dirs. Cumis Ins. Soc., 1972-88, pres., 1973-88; bd. dirs. Cumis Ins. Group Can., 1972-88; pres., dir. Cudis Ins. Soc., Inc., 1972-88, C.M.C.I. Corp. Chmn., United Way of Dane County, Wis., 1981. Served with USAAF, 1942-46. Mem. Am. Law Inst., U. Wis. Law Alumni Assn. (dir. 1967-70, pres. 1969-70), Order of Coif. Home: 4805 Fond Du Lac Trl Madison WI 53705-4814

CURRY, ROBERT LEE, III, lawyer; b. New Orleans, Sept. 29, 1931; s. Robert Lee Jr. and Lydia (Sporl) C.; m. Courtney Davis, June 11, 1955; children: Robert Lee IV, Cynthia Curry Alexander, Thomas Davis, Kevin Courtney. BS, JD, La. State U., 1954; LLM in Taxation, NYU, 1958. Bar: La. 1954, U.S. Ct. Appeals (5th cir.) 1961, U.S. Supreme Ct. 1958. Judge advocate USAF, Wichita, Kans., 1954-56; teaching fellow NYU Sch. of Law, 1956-57; atty. advisor U.S. Tax Ct., Washington, 1957-60; atty. Theus, Grisham, Davis & Leigh, Monroe, La., 1960—. Coun. mem. La. Law Inst. Coun., Baton Rouge, 1978—, pres., 1995-98. Fellow Am. Coll. Trust and Estate Counsel, Am. Coll. Tax Counsel; mem. Internat. Acad. Trust and Estate Law. Episcopalian. Corporate, general, Estate planning, Taxation, general. Office: Theus Grisham Davis & Leigh 1600 Lamy Ln Monroe LA 71201-3736 E-mail: rcurry@theuslaw.com.

CURTIN, CHRISTOPHER JAMES, lawyer; b. Wilmington, Del., July 14, 1951; s. George Morrison and Margaret (Nichols) C.; m. Bonnie Louise Reid, Mar. 31, 1973; children: Laura, Andrew, Kelly. BA, U. Va., 1973; JD, N.Y. Law Sch., 1977. Bar: Del. 1977. Mgr. trainee Wilmington Trust Co., Del., 1973-74; dep. atty. gen. Del. Dept. of Justice, Wilmington, 1977-85; assoc. Sawyer & Akin P.A., Wilmington, 1985-87, ptnr., 1987-95, Erisman & Curtin, Wilmington, 1995—. Instr. writing Del. Law Sch., 1983-84; spl. asst. U.S. Atty., 1984-85; asst. Superior Ct. Jury Instrn. Rev. Com., 1997. Bd. dirs. Holy Trinity (Old Swedes) Found., Wilmington, 1986, Del. Heart Assn., Wilmington, 1987. Mem. ABA, ATLA, Del. Bar Assn., Del. Trial Lawyers Assn. (CLE com. 1993-95, chair Amicus Curiae com. 1994—). Episcopalian. Avocations: fishing, bicycling, backpacking. General civil litigation, Commercial, consumer (including collections, credit), Personal injury (including property damage). Office: Erisman & Curtin 629 Mount Lebanon Rd Wilmington DE 19803-1707

CURTIN, DANIEL JOSEPH, JR., lawyer; b. San Francisco, Jan. 7, 1933; s. Daniel Joseph and Nell Helen (Lenihan) C.; m. Myrtle Rose Wanke, Feb. 7, 1959; children: Kathleen, Mary, Patricia, Thomas, Carol. AB in Polit. Sci., U. San Francisco, 1954, JD, 1957. Bar: Calif. 1958. Asst. sec. State Senate Calif., Sacramento, 1959; cons., counsel Assembly Com. on Local Govt., Sacramento, 1959-60; dep. city atty. Richmond, Calif., 1961-65; city atty. Walnut Creek, Calif., 1965-82; with Williams, Caploe, Robbins & Curtin, Benicia, Calif., 1983-84; ptnr. McCutchen, Doyle, Brown & Enersen, Walnut Creek, 1984—2001; counsel Bingham McCutchen, 2002—. Mem. bd. advisors environ. affairs Boston Coll. Sch. of Law, 1987—; mem. State Sen. Housing Adv. Task Force, 1983-84, State Sen. Subcom. on the Redevel. of Antiquated Subdivs., 1986; instr. continuing edn. of the bar, 1975, 82, 88, U. San Francisco Sch. of Law, 1988-92, Golden Gate U. Sch. of Law, 1979-82, U. Calif. Extension, 1973—, John F. Kennedy U. Sch. of Law, Walnut Creek, 1983-90; mem. adv. com. Alcohol and Drug Abuse Coun., Pleasant Hill, Calif. Contbr. articles to profl. jours. Lt. U.S. Army, 1958, 56-64. Recipient Disting. Leadership award, Nat. Planning award Am. Planning Assn., 1988; named City Atty. of Yr., 1971 and others. Mem. ABA (sect. on state and local govt. law, coun. chair 2001-02, chmn. land use, planning and zoning com. 1976-78, vice-chair 1999), Calif. State Bar Assn. (mem. exec. com., real property law sect. 1988-91, mem. com. on environ. 1977-80), Nat. Inst. Mcpl. Law Officer (chmn. zoning and planning com. 1969-79, regional v.p. 1979-82, Lifetime Achievement in Mcpl. Law Charles S. Rhyne award), Calif. Pk. and Recreation Soc., League of Calif. Cities (pres. city atty.'s dept. 1973-74), Lambda Alpha, others. Democrat. Roman Catholic. Avocations: pub. speaking, gardening. Land use and zoning (including planning), Property, real (including real estate development, water). Office: Bingham McCutchen 1333 N Calif Blvd Ste 210 PO Box V Walnut Creek CA 94596-4534 Office Fax: 925-975-5390. E-mail: daniel.curtin@bingham.com.

CURTIN, LAWRENCE N. lawyer; b. Glen Ridge, N.J., Apr. 29, 1950; BS with honors, Fla. State U., 1972, JD with honors, 1976. Bar: Fla. 1976, U.S. Dist. Ct. (no. dist.) Fla., U.S. Ct. Appeals (4th, 5th, 11th and D.C. cirs.). Law clerk to Hon. William Stafford U.S. Dist. Ct. (no. dist.) Fla., 1976-78; mem. Holland & Knight, Tallahassee. Co-author: Surface Water Pollution Control, vol. 1, 1986-96. Mem. ABA, Fla. Bar (chmn. energy law com. 1983-84), Tallahassee Bar Assn., Beta Gamma Sigma, Sigma Iota Epsilon. Administrative and regulatory, Environmental, Legislative. Office: Holland & Knight LLP PO Drawer 810 315 S Calhoun St Ste 600 Tallahassee FL 32301-1897 E-mail: lcurtin@hklaw.com.

CURTIN, TIMOTHY JOHN, lawyer; b. Detroit, Sept. 21, 1942; s. James J. and Irma Alice (Sirotti) C.; m. B. Colleen Lindsey, July 11, 1964; children: Kathleen, Mary. BA, U. Mich., 1964, JD, 1967. Bar: Ohio 1968, Mich. 1970, U.S. Dist. Ct. (no. dist.) Ohio 1968, U.S. Dist. Ct. (we. dist.) Mich. 1970, U.S. Dist. Ct. (ea. dist.) Mich. 1980, U.S. Dist. Ct. Del. 1996, U.S. Dist. Ct. (no. dist.) Ill. 1999, U.S. Ct. Appeals (6th cir.) 1968. Assoc. Taft, Stettinius & Hollister, Cin., 1967-70, McCobb, Heaney & Van't Hof, Grand Rapids, Mich., 1970-72; ptnr. Schmidt, Howlett, Van't Hof, Snell & Vana, Grand Rapids, 1972-83, Varnum, Riddering, Schmidt & Howlett, Grand Rapids, 1983—. Contbr. articles to legal publs. Treas. Kent County Dem. Com., 1976-78, chmn. 3rd Dist. Dem. Com., 1993—. Mem. ABA, Mich. Bar Assn., Grand Rapids Bar Assn., Fed.. Bar Assn., Am. Bankruptcy Inst., Egypt Valley C.C. Roman Catholic. Avocations: travel, fishing. Bankruptcy, Commercial, contracts (including sales of goods; commercial financing). Office: Varnum Riddering Schmidt & Howlett Box 352 333 Bridge St SW Grand Rapids MI 49501-0352 E-mail: tjcurtin@varnumlaw.com.

CURTIS, CHARLES THACH, JR., lawyer; b. New Orleans, Jan. 22, 1951; s. Charles Thach and Marilyn Ellizabeth (Coons) C.; m. Marcy H. Monrose, Oct. 24, 1992; children: Sophie M., Peter T. BA, Tulane U., 1973, JD, 1976. Bar: La. 1977, U.S. Dist. Ct. (ea. dist.) La. 1979, U.S. Dist. Ct. (mid. and we. dists.) La. 1987, U.S. Ct. Apeals (5th cir.) 1981, U.S. Supreme Ct. 1983. Law clk. U.S. Dist. Ct. (ea. dist.) La., New Orleans, 1976-77; assoc. Bronfin, Heller, Feldman & Steinberg, New Orleans, 1977-79, Polack, Rosenberg, Rittenberg & Endom, New Orleans, 1979-82; ptnr. Polack, Rosenbdfg, Rittenberg & Endom, New Orleans, 1982-87; assoc. Little & Metzger, New Orleans, 1987-91; mgr. Pipeline Sys. divsn. Rinker Materials Corp., 2001—. Gen. counsel Pipe Liners Inc., 1991—. Bd. dirs. East Riverside Neighborhood Assn., New Orleans, 1983. Mem. ABA, Fed. Bar Assn., La. State Bar Assn., New Orleans Bar Assn. Democrat. Episcopalian. Corporate, general, Franchising, Intellectual property. Home: 931 Henry Clay Ave New Orleans LA 70118-5934 Office: Rinker Pipeline Systems Ste 220 1539 Jackson Ave New Orleans LA 70130-5858 E-mail: rinker@csra.com.

CURTIS, FRANK R. lawyer; b. Valley Stream, N.Y., Sept. 27, 1946; s. Frank and Rosalind (Vreeland) Curtis; m. Cynthia Mary Knapik, May 14, 1977; children: Lauren Josephine, Frank Edward, Michael Bennett. AB magna cum laude, Harvard Coll., 1968; JD, Yale U., 1971. Bar: N.Y. 1972, U.S. Dist. Cts. (so. and ea. dists.) : N.Y. 1973, U.S. Ct. Appeals (2d cir.) : 1975. Assoc. Hellerstein Rosier & Rembar, N.Y.C., 1971—73; ptnr. Rembar Wolf & Curtis, NY, 1974—77, Rembar & Curtis, N.Y.C., 1978—. Lectr. PLI, N.Y.C., 1980, N.Y.C., 88. Trustee North Salem Free Libr., NY, 1983—91. Mem.: N.Y. State Bar Assn., Copyright Soc. of the U.S.A., Assn. of Bar of City of N.Y. (sec. com. on copyright 1979—80), Harvard Club, Phi Beta Kappa. Entertainment, Libel, Trademark and copyright. Home: PO Box 908 2 Juengstville Rd Croton Falls NY 10519-0908 Office: Rembar & Curtis 19 W 44th St New York NY 10036-6070

CURTIS, GEORGE WARREN, lawyer; b. Merrill, Wis., Sept. 24, 1936; s. George Gregory and Rose E. (Zimmerman) C.; m. Judith Olson, 1956 (div. 1966); m. Mary Pelman, 1967 (dec. 1973); children: George, Catherine Schmidt, Eric, Greg, Paul, David; m. Mary Ruth Kersztyn, Dec. 27, 1973 (div. 1999); children: Emily, Benjamin; m. Suzette Bigler Whyte, July 10, 1999; stepchildren: Erika, Evan. BA, U. Minn., 1959; JD, U. Wis., 1962. Bar: Wis. 1962, Fla. 1968. Assoc. Russell & Curtis, Merrill, 1962-68; ptnr. Nolan, Engler, Yakes & Curtis, Oshkosh, Wis., 1968-74, Curtis, MacKenzie, Haase & Brown, Oshkosh, 1974-83, Curtis, Wilde & Neal, Oshkosh, 1984-96, Curtis & Neal, Oshkosh, 1997-98; with Curtis Law Offices, 1999. Host TV program It's Your Environment. Host (TV show) It's Your Law. Mem. ATLA, Am. Coll. Trial Lawyers, Am. Bd. Trial Advocates (pres. Wis. chpt.), Wis. Acad. Trial Lawyers (bd. dirs. 1978-83, treas. 1984, sec. 1985, v.p. 1986, pres. 1987), Assn. Trial Lawyers Am. (bd. govs.), Internat. Soc. Barristers. Democrat. Avocations: conservationist, dog trainer. State civil litigation, Personal injury (including property damage), Product liability. Home: 7361 Canary Rd Pickett WI 54964-9724 Office: Curtis Law Offices 2905 Universal St Oshkosh WI 54904-6341

CURTIS, JAMES THEODORE, lawyer; b. Lowell, Mass., July 8, 1923; s. Theodore D. and Maria (Souliotis) Koutras; m. Kleanthe D. Dusopol, June 25, 1950; children: Madelon Mary, Theodore James, Stephanie Diane, Gregory Theodosius, James Theodore Jr. BA, U. Mich., 1948; JD, Harvard U., 1951; ScD (hon.), U. Mass., 1972. Bar: Mass. 1951. Assoc. Adams & Blinn, Boston, 1951-52; legal asst., asst. atty. gen. Mass., 1952-53; pvt. practice law, 1953-57; sr. ptnr. firm Goldman & Curtis, and predecessors, Lowell and Boston, 1957—. Chmn. Lowell and Greater Lowell Heart Fund, 1967-68; mem. adv. bd. Salvation Army, sec., 1956-58; mem. Bd. Higher Edn. Mass., 1967-72; elected mem. Lowell charter Commn., 1969-71; del. Dem. Party State Convs., 1956-60; trustee U. Mass., Lowell, 1963-72, chmn. bd., 1968-72; bd. dirs. U. Mass. Rsch. Found., Lowell, 1965-72, Merrimack Valley Health Planning Coun., 1969-72. Served with U.S. Army, 1943-46, spl. agt. Counter Intelligence Corps., 1945-46. Decorated Knight Order Orthodox Crusade Holy Sepulcher. Mem. ABA, ATLA, Mass. Bar Assn., Middlesex County Bar Assn., Mass. Acad. Trial Lawyers, Am. Judicature Soc., Harvard Law Sch. Alumni Assn., U. Mich. Alumni Assn., Lowell Hist. Soc., DAV, Harvard Club of Lowell (pres. 1969-71, bd. dirs.), Masons, Delta Epsilon Pi. Corporate, general, General practice, Property, real (including real estate development, water). Home: 11 Rivercliff Rd Lowell MA 01852-1471 Office: Goldman & Curtis PC 144 Merrimack St Ste 444 Lowell MA 01852-1789 E-mail: law@goldman-curtis.com.

CURTIS, JOHN JOSEPH, lawyer; b. Fairmont, W.Va., Nov. 23, 1942; s. John Joseph and Marie Francis (Christopher) C.; m. Shirley Ann Slater, Oct. 15, 1971 (div. June 1993); children: Christopher, Kevin. AB, U. W.Va., 1964, JD, 1967. Bar: W.Va. 1967, Ill. 1972, Calif. 1979. Pvt. practice law, South Charleston, W.Va., 1967-68; chief counsel, asst. dir. W.Va. Tax Dept., Charleston, 1968-71; tax atty. Sears, Roebuck & Co., Chgo., 1971-73; chief tax counsel, dir. taxes Pacific Lighting, L.A., 1973-87; ptnr. Baker & Hostetler, L.A., 1987-93, Law Offices of John Curtis, L.A., 1994—. Com. mem. Pasadena Tournament Roses, 1978-93. Lt. comdr. USNR, 1968-80. Mem. ABA, L.A. County Bar Assn. (chmn. com. 1989), Calif. Bar Assn., Inst. Property Tax, So. Calif.Tax Found. (pres. 1990-96), L.A. Taxpayers Assn. (pres. 1990-95), Calif. Taxpayers Assn. (pres. 1987-88). Avocations: skiing, scuba, fishing. Legislative, Corporate taxation, State and local taxation. Office: 2 Arado Rancho Santa Margarita CA 92688-2749 E-mail: jcurtis@aol.com.

CURTIS, KAREN HAYNES, lawyer; b. Laurel, Miss., Sept. 15, 1951; d. John Travis Haynes Jr. and Jeannine Burkett Tanner; children: Laurel Elizabeth Cornell, Jaime Rodriguez Cornell. BS in Biology, Tulane U., 1973; JD summa cum laude, Nova Law Ctr., 1978. Bar: Fla. 1978; U.S. Ct Appeals (5th cir.) Fla. 1980, U.S. Ct. Appeals (11th cir.) Fla. 1981; U.S. Dist Ct. (so. dist.) Fla. 1986, U.S Dist Ct. (mid. dist.) Fla., 1986; U.S. Supreme Ct. 1994. Law clk. Steel, Hector & Davis, Miami, Fla., 1978; law clk. to Judge William M. Hoeveler U.S. Dist. Ct., Miami, Fla., 1978-80; assoc. Shutts & Bowen, Miami, Fla., 1980-84, ptnr., 1985-95; founding ptnr., pres. Gallwey Gillman Curtis & Vento, P.A., Miami, Fla., 1995—. Treas., dir. Ch. by the Sea, 1994—. Listed in Leading Fla. Attys. for Civil Appellate Law. Mem. ABA, Fla. Assn. Women Lawyers, Fed. Bar Assn., Dade County Bar Assn. (ins. law com. 1990-91, banking and corp. litigation com. 1992-93, appellate ct. com. 1991—) Fla. Bar (appellate ct. rules com. 1993-2002, grievance com. 1988-91), Fla. Bar Bd. of Legal Specialization and Edn.(cert. in appellate practice), Acad. Fla, Trial Lawyers, Assn. Trial Lawyers of Am., Supreme Ct. Historical Soc., Am. Judiciary Soc. United Ch. of Christ. Avocations: reading, piano, computer. Appellate, Federal civil litigation, General civil litigation. Home: 18720 SW 33rd Court Miramar FL 33029 Office: Gallwey Gillman Curtis & Vento PA 200 SE 1st St Ste 1100 Miami FL 33131-1912

CURTIS, ROBERT KERN, lawyer, physics educator; b. N.Y.C., June 11, 1940; s. Sargent Jackson and Phyllis (Kern) C.; m. Beverley Meadows, Dec. 26, 1971; 1 child, Phyllis. AB in Physics, Fordham U., 1964, MS in Edn., 1970; Lic. in Philosophy, Woodstock Coll., 1965; JD, Seton Hall U., 1985. Tchr. Bklyn. Prep. Sch., 1965-67; dir. Jesuit Sem. and Mission Bur., N.Y.C., 1967; tchr. Xavier High Sch., N.Y.C., 1967-69, Hackensack (N.J.) High Sch., 1969—; sole practice Hackensack, 1985—. Tchr. law Hackensack Evening Sch., 1980, law for tchrs. Hackensack Pub. Schs., 1986. Mem. Am. Phys. Soc., Assn. Trial Lawyers Am., ACLU, N.Y. Acad. Scis., Am. Assn. Physics Tchrs., Math. Assn. Am., Hackensack Edn. Assn. (pres. 1979-81, 97—). Civil rights, Education and schools, General practice. Home and Office: 287 Hamilton Pl Hackensack NJ 07601-3614 E-mail: rkc@rcurtis.com.

CURY, BRUCE PAUL, lawyer, magistrate, law educator; b. Englewood, N.J., Mar. 19, 1942; s. Beddy Galib and Violet (Maloof) C.; m. Orahdella Elizabeth Green, Oct. 14, 1972; 1 child, Lauren Elaine. BS, U. Ky., 1965; JD, U. Louisville, 1972. Bar: Fla. 1972, U.S. Dist. Ct. (mid. dist.) Fla. 1974, U.S. Ct. Appeals (5th cir.) 1980, U.S. Ct. Appeals (11th cir.) 1982, U.S. Supreme Ct. 1976. Assoc. George McDowell P.A., Tampa, Fla., 1972-73; sole practice Tampa, 1973-76; adj. prof. bus. law U. Tampa, 1977-85; adj. prof. criminal law U. South Fla., 1984-85, lectr., 1981-87; chief asst. pub. defender Office of Pub. Defender, Tampa, 1974-85; sole practice Tampa, 1985-90; gen. counsel Fla. Dept. Transportation, Bartow, 1990—. Magistrate traffic ct. Jud. 13 cir., Tampa, 1993—; chmn. Hills County Zoning Bd. Tampa, 1989-97; pres., dir. Bay Area Legal Svcs., Inc., Tampa, 1980-92; chmn. Hills County Land Use Appeals Bd. Tampa, 1997—. Legal counsel Big Bros./Big Sisters Greater Tampa, Inc., 1983-95; pres, bd. dirs. Rape Crisis Ctr., Tampa, 1982-84; bd. dirs. Hillsborough Edn. Found., Tampa, 1999—; mem. Hillsborough County City-County Planning Commn., Tampa, 1999—. Served to 1st lt. U.S. Army, 1966-69. Recipient Indigent Accused award Fla. Pub. Defender, 1985, Dirs. award Sexual Abuse Treatment Ctr. Tampa, 1986, Pres. and Dirs. award Bay Area Legal Svcs. Tampa, 1992, Sec. of Transp. Leadership award Fla. Dept. Transp., 2000. Mem. Criminal Def. Lawyers Assn. Hillsborough County, Fla. Bar Assn. (mem. several sects., chmn. 13th Jud. Circuit grievance com.), Hillsborough County Bar Assn. (mem. several coms., exec. counsel trial lawyers sect.), Fla. Leadership 2000, Am. Inn of Cts. (master). Republican. Methodist. Home: 1301 Bayshore Blvd Tampa FL 33606 Office: Fla Dept Transportation 801 N Broadway Ave Bartow FL 33830-3809 E-mail: bruce.cury@dot.state.fl.us.

CURZON, THOMAS HENRY, lawyer; b. Ft. Leonard Wood, Mo., Apr. 11, 1954; s. James E. and Vera (Roush) C.; m. Anne M. Halverhout, July 29, 1977; children: Peter Thomas, Daniel Henry. BA with highest distinction, U. Kans., 1976; JD with high honors, U. Tex., 1979. Bar: Tex. 1979, Ariz. 1980. Law clk. to Hon. James K. Logan, U.S. Ct. Appeals for 10th Circuit, Olathe, Kans., 1979-80; ptnr. Meyer, Hendricks, Osborn & Maledon, Phoenix, 1986—96, Osborn Maledon, P.A., Phoenix, 1995—2001. Bd. dirs. Ariz. Tech. Incubator; bd. dirs. Enterprise Network, Phoenix, 1989-96, pres., 1995-96. Author: Ariz. Legal Forms: Business Organizations-Corporations, 2 vols., 1990, 2d edit., 2001. Mem. exec. com. Ariz. Strategic Planning for Econ. Devel., Phoenix, 1990-91; bd. dirs. Downtown YMCA, Phoenix, 1997; chmn. troop 644 com. Boy Scouts Am., Phoenix, 1997—. Mem. Ariz. Tech. Coun. (bd. dirs. 1997—). Avocations: figure skating, Tae Kwon Do, sailing, hunting, scouting. Corporate, general, Mergers and acquisitions, Securities. Office: Osborn Maledon PA 2929 N Central Ave Phoenix AZ 85012-2727

CUSACK, JOHN THOMAS, lawyer; b. Oak Park, Ill., June 22, 1935; s. Thomas Jr. and Clare (Hock) C.; m. Mary Louise Coughlin, Nov. 1, 1969; children: John, James, Mary Helen, Cathleen. AB cum laude, U. Notre Dame, 1957; JD, U. Mich., 1960; postgrad., Harvard U., 1961-62. Bar: Ill. 1960, U.S. Dist. Ct. (no. dist.) Ill. 1961, U.S. Dist. Ct. (no. dist.) Ind. 1983, U.S. Tax Ct. 1984, U.S. Ct. Appeals (7th cir.) 1973, U.S. Ct. Appeals (5th and 9th cirs.) 1975, U.S. Ct. Appeals (3d cir.) 1986, U.S. Ct. Appeals (10th cir.) 1987, U.S. Ct. Appeals (11th cir.) 1988, U.S. Supreme Ct. 1966. Trial atty. antitrust div. U.S. Dept. Justice, 1962-70; assoc. Gardner, Carton & Douglas, Chgo., 1970-74, ptnr., 1974—, chmn. litigation dept., 1978-86, chmn. antitrust practice group, 1986—. Contbr. articles to legal jours. Trustee Fenwick H.S. 1st lt. JAGC, USAR, 1963-67. Mem. ABA (antitrust and litigation sect., health law com. 1960—), Chgo. Bar Assn., Law Club City Chgo. Roman Catholic. Antitrust, General civil litigation, Health. Home: 1030 Franklin Ave River Forest IL 60305-1340 Office: Gardner Carton & Douglas 191 N Wacker Dr Ste 3700 Chicago IL 60606-1698 E-mail: jcusack@gcd.com.

CUSICK, DANIEL FRANCIS, lawyer; b. Pitts., May 12, 1948; s. Charles S. and Ruth C. C.; m. Sheila McArdle, May 15, 1976; children: Patrick, Brian, Brendan, Timothy, Colleen. BA, U. Va., 1970; JD, U. Dayton, 1977. Bar: Pa. 1977, U.S. Dist. Ct. (we. dist.) Pa. 1977, U.S. Ct. Appeals 1983, U.S. Supreme Ct. 1987. Law clk. Hon. Joseph Ridge, Pitts., 1977-79; atty. Stein & Winters, Pitts., 1979-82, Sherry & Campbell, Pitts., 1982-88, Houston Harbaugh, Pitts., 1988-90, Mansmann & McArdle, Pitts., 1991-92; pvt. practice law Pitts., 1993—. Bd. dirs., sec., vice chair, chair South Hills Area YMCA, Pitts., 1994—, longhouse officer Indian Guides and Princesses, 1988-99. Served with U.S. Army, 1970-73. Mem. Pa. Bar Assn. (vice-chmn., chmn. dispute remution com. 1993-97, ho. of dels. 1999-2002), Allegheny County Bar Assn. (chmn. alt. dispute resolution com. 1990-95). Avocations: mediator, private pilot. Alternative dispute resolution, General civil litigation, Personal injury (including property damage). Home: 1413 Terrace Dr Pittsburgh PA 15228-1608 Office: 600 Grant St Ste 660 Pittsburgh PA 15219-2703

CUSICK, ERNEST GEORGE, lawyer; b. Worchester, Mass., Oct. 24, 1960; s. Henry Paul and Loretta Ann Cusick; m. Donna Theresa Cusick, Sept. 3, 1989; 1 child, Emily. BS in Materials Engring., Rensselaer Poly. Inst., 1982; JD, George Mason U., 1994. Bar: Va. 94, U.S. Patent and Trademark Office 94, U.S. Dist. Ct. (ea. dist.) Va. 95, U.S. Ct. Appeals 95. Primary examiner U.S. Patent and Trademark Office, Washington, 1982—94, petitions examiner, 1990—94; assoc. Oliff & Berridge, Alexandria, Va., 1994—96; patent counsel GE Global Rsch., Schenectady, NY, 1996—99, GE Power Sys., Schenectady, NY, 1999—. Recipient Bronze award, U.S. Dept. Commerce, 1990. Achievements include patents in field. Avocation: coaching youth basketball. Intellectual property, Trademark and copyright, Antitrust. Office: GE Power Sys-Energy Svcs 1 River Rd 37-568 Schenectady NY 12345 E-mail: ernest.cusick@ps.ge.com.

CUSTER, CHARLES FRANCIS, lawyer; b. Hays, Kans., Aug. 19, 1928; s. Raymond Earl and Eva Marie (Walker) C.; m. Irene Louise Macarow, Jan. 2, 1950; children: Shannon Elaine, Charles Francis, Murray Maxwell, Kelly Sue. AB, U. Chgo., 1948, JD, 1958. Bar: Ill. 1958, U.S. Dist. Ct. (no dist.) Ill. 1971, U.S. Supreme Ct. 1991. Assoc. Meyers & Matthias, Chgo., 1958-72; pvt. practice Chgo., 1972-78; ptnr. Vedder, Price, Kaufman & Kammholz, Chgo., 1978-98, of counsel, 1998—. Arbitrator, mediator. Past dir. Family Care Svcs., Chgo. Mem. ABA (mem. fed. regulation of securities and devels. in investment svcs. coms., dispute resolution sect.), Chgo. Bar Assn. (mem. securities law com., mem. investment cos. subcom., alternative dispute resolution com.), Cliff Dwellers (past officer and dir.). Avocations: music, theater . Administrative and regulatory, Corporate, general, Securities. Home: 5210 S Kenwood Ave Chicago IL 60615-4006 Office: Vedder Price Kaufman & Kammholz 222 N La Salle St Ste 2600 Chicago IL 60601-1100

CUTCHIN, JOHN FRANKS, lawyer; b. Roanoke Rapids, N.C., Dec. 19, 1949; s. Joseph Henry Jr. and Janie Priscilla (Franks) C.; m. Melissa Jane Ikerd, Dec. 22, 1979; children: Jennifer Erin, Joshua Ikerd. AB, Davidson Coll., 1972; JD, U. N.C., 1975. Bar: N.C. 1975, U.S. Dist. Ct. (we. dist.) N.C. 1975; cert. family fin. mediator. Assoc. Lefler, Gordon & Waddell, Newton, N.C., 1975-78; pvt. practice, Newton, 1978—. Mem. Catawba County Bar Assn. (pres. 1982-83), Lincoln County Bar Assn., Newton Mchts. Assn. (pres. 1978-80), Davidson Coll. Alumni Assn. (pres. Catawba County chpt. 1979-80). Episcopalian. State civil litigation, Criminal, Family and matrimonial. Office: 16 S College Ave PO Box 173 Newton NC 28658-0173 E-mail: cutchlaw@bellsouth.net.

CUTCHINS, CLIFFORD ARMSTRONG, IV, lawyer; b. Norfolk, Va., May 13, 1948; s. Clifford Armstrong III and Ann (Woods) C.; m. Jane McKenzie, Aug. 14, 1971; children: Sarah Helen, Ann Woods. BA, Princeton U., 1971; JD, MBA, U. Va., 1975. Bar: Va. 1975, U.S. Dist. Ct. (ea. dist.) Va. 1975, U.S. Ct. Appeals (4th cir.) 1975. Ptnr. McGuire, Woods, Battle & Boothe, Richmond, Va., 1975-90; sr. v.p., gen. counsel, sec. James River Corp. Va., Richmond, 1990-97, Ft. James Corp., Deerfield, Ill., 1997-2000; ptnr. McGuireWoods LLP, Richmond, 2001—. Bd. dirs. Arts Coun. Richmond, 1980-86, Richmond Heart Assn., 1980-83, St. Catherine's Sch., Richmond, 1983-86, Richmond Ballet, 1986-88, Richmond Children's Mus., 1986-94, Richmond on the James, 1986-88, Henrico Drs. Hosp., 1986—, Hist. Richmond Found., 1990-94, Richmond Met. Blood Svc., 1995-97, Kohl Children's Mus., Wilmette, Ill., 1998-2000; chmn. Fort James Found., 1997-2000, Richmond First Tee, 2001-, Nature Conservancy of Va., 2002-. Mem.: ABA, Va. Bar Assn., Commonwealth Club (bd. dirs. 1983—86, 1996—97), Kinloch Golf Club, Country Club Va. (bd. dirs. 1990—93, 2003—). Republican. Baptist. Avocations: golf, travel, reading. Corporate, general, Securities. Home: 118 Tempsford Ln Richmond VA 23226-2319 Office: McGuireWoods LLP 901 E Cary St Richmond VA 23219 E-mail: ccutchins@mcguirewoods.com.

CUTHRELL, CARL EDWARD, lawyer, educator, clergyman; b. Norfolk, Va., Aug. 13, 1934; s. Cecil Edward and Edna Catherine (Kirby) C.; m. Naomi Lorene Marshall, Dec. 23, 1960; children: Byron Eugene, Benjamin Dean. LLB, LaSalle U. Law Sch., Chgo., 1959; diploma Egyptian studies, Oriental Inst., U. Chgo., 1960; BD, Brantridge Forest Sch., Eng., 1970; MA in Med. History, Sussex (Eng.) Coll. Tech., 1972; MA in Classical Studies,

Christ Ch. Coll., Oxford, Eng., 1973; diploma Germanic langs., Heidelberg (Fed. Republic Germany) U., 1975; BA, Upper Iowa U., 1979; MA, Covington Theol. Sem., 1982; BRE, Cen. Bapt. Bicle Coll., 1989. Pvt. practice, Hampton, 1962-75; ordained to ministry Evang. Friends Ch., 1972; pastor Rescue (Va.) Friends Ch., 1968-96. Mem. faculty dept. theology, Norfolk extension Washington Bible Coll., Lanham, Md., dept. spl. programs/history Coll. William and Mary, Williamsburg, Va., dept. secular studies Cen. Bapt. Bible Coll., Hampton, Va. Author: Ancient Mummies, 1967, Paul's Voyage, 1971; Contbr.: lit. criticisms to Times Herald Newspaper; also numerous short stories. Bd. dirs. Nat. Philatelic Inst.; trustee Quincy Coll., 1970, Nat. Coll. Surgeons Hall of Fame, 1972. Served with M.C. AUS, 1950-57, Korea. Decorated Silver Star; recipient Scouter's award medal Boy Scouts Am., 1956, Silver Beaver award, 1976, Nat. Tchrs. medal Freedoms Found., 1973, Peace medal UN, 1973, Good Citizenship medal SAR, 1976 Mem. U.S. Capital, Nat. hist. socs., S.R., Sons Confederate Vets., Christian Educators Assn., Va. Herpetological Soc., Mil. Order Stars and Bars. Republican. Commercial, consumer (including collections, credit), Estate planning, General practice. Home: 307 Agusta Dr Newport News VA 23601-1436 E-mail: carloreneva@aol.com.

CUTLER, LLOYD NORTON, lawyer; b. N.Y.C., Nov. 10, 1917; s. Aaron Smith and Dorothy (Glaser) C.; m. Louise W. Howe, 1941 (dec. July 1988); children: Deborah Norton (Mrs. James Notman Jr.), Beverly Winslow (Mrs. Mark Troutman), Lloyd Norton Jr., Louisiana Winslow (Mrs. Lamar Johnson); m. Rhoda Winton Kraft, 1989. AB cum laude, Yale U., 1936, LLB magna cum laude, 1939, LLD (hon.), 1983, Princeton U., 1994; LLD (hon.) , Trinity Coll., 2000. Bar: N.Y. 1940, D.C. 1946. Pvt. practice, N.Y.C., 1940-42, Washington, 1946—; ptnr. Wilmer, Cutler & Pickering, 1962-79, 81-90, sr. counsel, 1990—; counsel to Pres. of U.S., 1979-81, 94; sec. Lawyers Com. Civil Rights Under Law, 1963-65, co-chmn., 1971-73; chmn. D.C. Com. on Adminstrn. Justice under Emergency Conditions, 1968; exec. dir. Nat. Commn. on the Causes and Prevention of Violence, 1968-69; President's spl. rep. for maritime boundary and resource negotiations with Can., 1977-79; President's spl. rep. for revision Pacific Salmon Treaty, 1999. Sr. cons. Pres.'s Commn. on Strategic Forces, 1983; vis. lectr. Yale U. Law Sch., 1973-76, Yale U. Sch. Orgn. and Mgmt., 1977-79, All Souls Coll., Oxford (Eng.) U., 1983, Nuffield Coll., Oxford, 1986; mem. U.S. Group to Permanent Ct. Arbitration, The Hague, 1984-93; mem. Quadrennial Commn. on Legis., Exec. and Jud. Salaries, 1984, chmn., 1989; mem. Pres.'s Commn. on Fed. Ethics Law Reform, 1989; co-chair Dept. Energy Task Force on Non-Proliferation Programs in Russia, 2000-01, Nat. Commn. on Fed. Election Reform, 2001—; mem. internat. adv. coun. World Bank, 2001—. Hon. trustee Brookings Instn.; chmn., mem. coun. Yale U., 1966-71, 89-94, chmn. devel. bd., 1972-77, chmn. campaign for Yale U., 1978-79; exec. bd. dirs. Met. Opera Assn., 1974-79; chmn. Salzburg Seminar, 1984-94. Recipient Jefferson medal in law U. Va., 1995, Marshall-Wythe Sch. Law medal Coll. William and Mary, 1998. Mem. Am. Law Inst. (coun.), ABA, Coun. on Fgn. Rels. (bd. dirs. 1977-79), Am. Acad. Arts and Scis., Mid. Temple of London (Hon., Bencher). Clubs: Metropolitan, Chevy Chase (Washington), Century Assn. (N.Y.C.). Administrative and regulatory, Antitrust, Private international. Home: 3115 O St NW Washington DC 20007-3117 Office: Wilmer Cutler & Pickering 2445 M St NW Washington DC 20037-1435

CUTLER, PHILIP EDGERTON, lawyer; b. Evanston, Ill., Mar. 18, 1948; s. John A. and Catherine (Hedman) C.; m. Barbara Anne Phippen, Oct. 27, 1948; children: David, Nathanael, Andrew. AB in History, Georgetown U., 1970; JD with honors, Northwestern U., 1973. Assoc. Perkins Coie, Seattle, 1973-79; ptnr. Sax and MacIver, Seattle, 1979-85; ptnr., shareholder Sax and MacIver merged Karr Tuttle Campbell, Seattle, 1986-89; shareholder, pres. Cutler, Nylander & Hayton PS (formerly Cutler & Nylander), Seattle, 1990—, also bd. dirs. Ct.-approved arbitrator King County Superior Ct., 1982—, U.S. Dist. Ct. (we. dist.) Wash., 1992—; mediator U.S. Dist. Ct. (we. dist.) Wash., 1982—; judge pro tem King County Superior Ct., 1993—; mem. comml. arbitration panel Am. Arbitration Assn., 1992—, mediator, 1997—; lectr., program chmn. numerous continuing legal edn. programs; mem. arbitration panel Nat. Assn. Securities Dealers, 1996—. Co-founder Country Dr. Cmty. Legal Clinic, Seattle, 1974—; co-pres. parents club St. Joseph Sch., Seattle, 1984-86, mem. sch. adv. bd., 1985-88; dir. St. Joseph Endowment Fund, 1986-2002, St. Joseph Parish Sch. Fund, 1990-2002, St. George Sch. Endowment Found., Seattle, 1994-2002, sec., 1996-2002; mem. sch. adv. bd. Blanchet H.S., Seattle, 1991-2000, mem. devel. com., 1992-2000; chair Georgetown Alumni Admissions Interviewing Program, 1975-2000; active St. Patrick Parish, Seattle, 1974-82, St. Joseph Parish, Seattle, 1982—, Cursillo Movement, 1975-85, Cath. Archdiocese of Seattle, 1979-82, YMCA Indian Guides/Indian Princesses program, 1980-84, chief of Husky Nation, 1982-84. Mem. ABA (antitrust, dispute resolution, and litigation sects., civil practice and procedure com. antitrust sect. 1980-90), FBA (chair ct. congestion/alt. dispute resolution com. 1985-99, mem. spl. alt. dispute resolution task force 1994 western dist. Wash.), Wash. State Bar Assn. (consumer protection, antitrust and unfair bus. practices sect., litigation sect., dispute resolution sect.), St. Thomas More Soc. Seattle (pres. 1993-95), Georgetown Alumni Assn. (bd. dirs. 1977-80, alumni sen. 1980—), King County Bar Assn. (numerous coms.), Rainier Club, Wash. Athletic Club, Col. Club Seattle, Georgetown Club Wash. (pres. 1980-86, mem. exec. com. 1986—). Roman Catholic. Avocations: swimming, downhill skiing, gourmet cooking, reading, furniture-making and woodworking. Alternative dispute resolution, Appellate, Commercial, contracts (including sales of goods; commercial financing). Office: Cutler Nylander & Hayton PS 505 Madison St Ste 220 Seattle WA 98104-1111

CUTLER, RICHARD W. lawyer; b. New Rochelle, N.Y., Mar. 9, 1917; s. Charles Evelyn and Amelia (MacDonald) C.; m. Elizabeth Fitzgerald, Oct. 18, 1947; children: Marguerite Blackburn, Alexander MacDonald, Judith Elizabeth. BA, Yale U., 1938, LLB, 1941. Bar: Conn. 1941, N.Y. 1942, Wis. 1950, D.C. 1975, U.S. Supreme Ct. 1980. Practiced in, NYC, 1941—49, Milw., 1949—87; assoc. Donovan, Leisure, Newton & Lumbard, 1941—42; atty. Legal Aid Soc., 1946—47, RCA Comm., Inc., 1947—49; ptnr. Quarles & Brady, and predecessors, 1954—87; gen. ptnr. Sunset Investment Co., Milw. Author: Zoning Law and Practice in Wisconsin, 1967, Greater Milwaukee's Growing Pains, 1950-2000: An Insider's View, 2001. Chmn. Milw. br. Fgn. Policy Assn., 1951-53; pres. Childrens Service Soc. Wis., 1961-63, Neighborhood House, 1971-74; sec. Southeastern Wis. Regional Planning Commn., 1960-84, Yale Devel. Bd., 1973-79; bd. dirs. Wis. Dept. Resource Devel., 1967-68; Met. Milw. Study Commn., 1957-61; bd. dirs. Milw. Innovation Ctr., 1985-89, pres., 1984-85, exec. v.p., 1985-89; bd. dirs. Greater Milw. Com., 1982-89. Capt. USAAF, 1943-46 and OSS, 1944-46. Recipient Disting. Leadership award Am. Planning Assn., 1992. Mem. ABA, Wis. Bar Assn., Milw. Club, Milw. Country Club, Town Club, Phi Beta Kappa. Presbyterian. Home: 938 W Shaker Cir Mequon WI 53092-6032 Office: 411 E Wisconsin Ave Milwaukee WI 53202-4461 E-mail: rwc@quarles.com.

CUTSHAW, KENNETH ANDREW, lawyer; b. Knoxville, Tenn., Sept. 2, 1953; s. Harvey Audley and Frankie Janelle (Temple) C.; m. Diane Dracos. BA, U. Tenn., 1975, JD, 1978; LLM, Am. U., 1987. Bar: Tenn. 1978, D.C. 1987, U.S. Dist. Ct. (mid. dist.) 1978, Tenn., (ea. dist.) 1978, Tenn. Supreme Ct. 1978, U.S. Supreme Ct. 1987, U.S. Fed. cir., 1991. Sr. atty. State of Tenn. Legis., Nashville, 1979-80, The 1982 World's Affair, Knoxville, 1980-83, cons., 1984; campaign mgr. for candidate U.S. Senate, 1983-84; asst. dep., asst. sec. import adminstrn. Dept. Commerce, Washington, 1985-87, chief of staff export adminstrn., 1987-89, dep. asst. sec. export enforcement, 1989-91; ptnr. Miller & Steuart, Washington, 1991-93; pres. Global Trading Ptnrs., Inc., Washington, 1991-93; of counsel Troutman Sanders, LLP, Atlanta, 1993-95, Smith Gambrell & Russell, LLP, 1995-99; ptnr. Holland & Knight, LLP, Atlanta, 1999—. Mem. U.S. Govt. Industry Adv. Com. on Customs and Trade, 1994-96; adj. fellow Hudson Inst.; adj. prof. Ga. State U., 1997—, Emory U., 2002—; hon. counsul, India. Author: Tennessee Criminal Law Statutes, 1980; co-author: Doing Business in China, 1995, Doing Business in Russia, 1999, Doing Business in India, 2001; contbr. articles to profl. jours. Vice chmn., exec. com. Tenn. Rep. Party, 1982-85; internat. chmn. Boy Scouts Am., Atlanta; mem. Bretton Woods Com.; co-chmn. Awakening Weekend. Roddy Acad. scholar U. Tenn., 1971-72. Mem. ABA, Internat. Bar Assn., Ga. Bar Assn., Atlanta Bar Assn., Tenn. Bar Assn. (com. chmn. 1983-84), D.C. Bar Assn., Am. Coun. Young Polit. Leaders (bd. dirs., co-chmn.), Coun. on Fgn. Rels., Atlanta Round Table (chmn.), World Trade Ctr. (bd. dirs.), Elks, Sigma Chi. Baptist. Avocations: flying, skiing, hiking, cultural events, golfing. Home: 4417 Dunmore Rd Marietta GA 30068-4224 Office: Holland & Knight LLP One Atlantic Center 1201 W Peachtree St NW Ste 2000 Atlanta GA 30309-3453 E-mail: kcutshaw@hklaw.com.

CYCHOLL, TASHA NICOLE, lawyer; b. Chgo., Sept. 16, 1974; d. William Gustav and Gail Ann Cycholl. BA, Ariz. State U., 1996, JD, 1999. Bar: Ariz. 1999, U.S. Dist. Ct. Ariz. 1999. Atty. Rhees Hopkins & Kreamer, Phoenix, 1999—2001, Low & Childers, PC, Phoenix, 2001—. Mem.: Ariz. Women Lawyers Assn. (young lawyers divsn., dir. Maricopa county bar, domestic violence com. 1999—). Insurance. Office: Low & Childers PC 2999N 44th St Ste 250 Phoenix AZ 85018

CYMROT, MARK ALAN, lawyer; b. Queens, N.Y., Oct. 8, 1947; s. Irwin Maurice and Anne (Kipnis) C.; children: Isaac, Erin. BA, George Washington U., 1969; JD, Columbia U., 1972. Bar: D.C. 1973, N.Y. 2000. Trial lawyer civil divsn. U.S. Dept. of Justice, Washington, 1972-77; sr. litigator Consumers Union of U.S. Inc., Washington, 1977-79; spl. litigation counsel civil divsn. U.S. Dept. of Justice, Washington, 1979-83; ptnr. Cole Corette & Abrutyn, Washington, 1983-91, Baker & Hostetler LLP, Washington, 1991—. Contbr. articles to profl. jours. Named one of 50 Best Lawyers in Washington by Washingtonian Mag., 1992. Avocations: photography, golf, tennis. Federal civil litigation, Private international, Public international. Office: Baker & Hostetler LLP 1050 Connecticut Ave NW Washington DC 20036-5304

CYPSER, DARLENE ANN, lawyer, movie producer; b. Tulsa, Jan. 3, 1958; d. Donald A. and Evelyn D. (Carrigan) Chappell; 1 child, Christopher A. BA, U. Okla., 1980, JD, 1986. Bar: N.Y. 1987, Colo. 1988. Pvt. practice, Boulder, Colo., 1988-99. Pres. The Midgard Corp., 1999—, Inferno Film Prodns., 1999—. Contbr. articles to profl. jours. Vol. Boulder County Legal Svcs., 1987-99, Legal Aid Soc. Westchester County, White Plains, N.Y., 1986-87; bd. dirs. Nyx Net, 1997--. Mem. Am. Geophys. Union, Colo. Film and Video Assn. Avocations: macrame, hiking, photography, cooking. Computer, Environmental, Non-profit and tax-exempt organizations. Office: 3410 W Bowles Ave Littleton CO 80123-6666 E-mail: darlene@milehigh.net.

CYR, CONRAD KEEFE, federal judge; b. Limestone, Maine, Dec. 9, 1931; s. Louis Emery and Kathleen Mary (Keefe) Cyr; m. Judith Ann Pirie, June 23, 1962 (dec. Mar. 1985); children: Keefe Clark, Jeffrey Louis Frederick; m. Diana Kathleen Sanborn, Sept. 25, 1987. BS cum laude, Holy Cross Coll., 1953; JD, Yale U., 1956; LLD (hon.) , Husson Coll., 1991. Bar: Maine 1956. Pvt. practice, Limestone, 1956—59; asst. U.S. atty., Bangor, Maine, 1959—61; pvt. practice Winchell & Cyr, Bangor, Maine, 1961—62; judge U.S. Bankruptcy Ct., Bangor, 1961—81, U.S. Dist. Ct., Bangor, 1981—83, chief judge, 1983—89; judge U.S. Fgn. Intelligence Surveillance Ct., 1987—89, U.S. Ct. Appeals (1st cir.), Boston, 1989—97, sr. judge, 1997—. Standing spl. master U.S. Dist. Ct., Maine, 1974—76; chief judge Bankruptcy Appellate Panel Dist., Mass., 1980—81; mem. Jud. Council (1st cir.), 1987—; com. on adminstrn. of bankruptcy sys. Jud. Conf. U.S., 1987—. Founder, editor-in-chief: Am. Bankruptcy Law Jour., 1970—81, contbg. author, editor: Collier on Bankruptcy, vol. 10. Steering com. U.S. AID Project for Assisting Bankruptcy and Reorgn. Procedures in Ctr. and Ea. Europe; treas. Limestone Rep. Com., 1958; chmn. budget com. Town of Limestone , 1959. Named one of Outstanding Young Men of Maine, 1963; recipient cert. of appreciation, Kans. Bar Assn., 1979, U. Maine, 1983, Nat. Judge's Recognition award, Nat. Conf. Bankruptcy Judges, 1979, Key to Town Limestone, 1983. Fellow: Am. Coll. Bankruptcy, Maine Bar Found. (charter); mem.: Aroostook Bar Assn., Am. Judicature Soc., Nat. Bankruptcy Conf. (exec. bd. 1974—77), Nat. Conf. Bankruptcy Judges (pres. 1976—77), Penobscot Bar Assn., Maine Bar Assn., Limestone C. of C. (pres.). Roman Catholic.*

CZAJKOWSKI, FRANK HENRY, lawyer; b. Bklyn., Jan. 7, 1936; m. Cecilia J. Artowicz, Sept. 3, 1955. BA, St. John's U., Bklyn., 1957; JD, St. John's U., 1959; LLM, George Washington U., 1966. Bar: N.Y. 1960, Pa. 1970, Conn. 1974, U.S. Supreme Ct. 1964. Claims adjustor Hartford Accident & Indemnity Ins. Co., N.Y.C., 1959-60; agt. Equitable Life Assurance Soc., N.Y.C., 1960; atty. Corp. Counsel's Office, N.Y.C., 1960-62, Fgn. Claims Settlement Commn., Washington, 1962-68, Atlantic-Richfield Co., N.Y.C., 1968-70, Phila., 1970-72; assoc. gen. counsel Unilever U.S.A. Co., Greenwich, Conn., 1972-98; pvt. practice, 1998—. Instr. Fairfield U. Ctr. Lifetime Learning, 1976, Sacred Heart U., 1983; arbitrator Am. Arbitration Assn. Mem. ABA, Conn. Bar Assn., Westchester-Fairfield Corp. Counsel Assn. Labor (including EEOC, Fair Labor Standards Act, labor-management relations, NLRB, OSHA), Pension, profit-sharing, and employee benefits, Product liability. Office: 7 Lafayette Dr Trumbull CT 06611-2751

CZARRA, EDGAR F., JR., lawyer; b. Langhorne, Pa., Oct. 4, 1928; s. Edgar F. and Mary Agnes (Copeland) C.; m. Doris Catharine Lane, June 14, 1952; children: Penelope L., Edgar F. III, Jonathan C., Melanie A. BS, Yale U., 1949, LLB, 1952. Bar: U.S. Dist. Ct. D.C. 1954, U.S. Ct. Appeals (D.C. cir.) 1954, U.S. Supreme Ct. 1959. Assoc. Covington & Burling, Washington, 1952, 55-63, ptnr., 1963-97, ret., 1997. Served to lt. (j.g.) USN, 1952-55. Mem.: DC Bar Assn. Administrative and regulatory, Federal civil litigation, Mergers and acquisitions. Office: Covington & Burling 1201 Pennsylvania Ave NW Washington DC 20004-2401

CZECH, PAUL ANDREW, lawyer; b. Queens, N.Y., Aug. 4, 1961; s. Michael and Marie Czech. BA, JD, Temple U. Bar: Pa., N.J. Assoc. Anapol Schwartz Weiss & Cohen, Phila., 1992-94; pvt. practice Phila., 1994—; CEO YB Entertainment Group Inc. , 2000—, YB420 Records, Inc., 2001—. Mem. Phila. Bar Assn. (arbitration com.). Avocation: band management. Office: 1735 Market St Ste A-428 Philadelphia PA 19103 E-mail: law@ybentertainment.com.

DABROWSKI, DORIS JANE, lawyer; b. Paterson, N.J., May 20, 1950; BA, Rutgers U., 1972, JD, 1975. Bar: Pa. 1975, U.S. Dist. Ct. (ea. dist.) Pa. 1976, U.S. Ct. Appeals (3d cir.) 1977, N.J. 1979, U.S. Dist. Ct. N.J. 1979, U.S. Ct. Appeals (fed. cir.) 1985. Staff atty. Delaware County Legal Assistance, Chester, Pa., 1975-77; assoc. Tabas, Horwitz & Furlong (later Tabas, Furlong & Roser), Phila., 1977-83; pvt. practice Phila. and Cherry Hill, N.J., 1983—. Arbitrator Nat. Assn. Securities Dealers; participant Nat. Pension Assistance Project, Patient Advocate Network; mem. adv. coun. 18th Police Dist., 1997—. Mem. editorial bd. Women's Rights Law Reporter, 1974-75. Dir. Well Woman, Phila., 1983-87, Pa. Pro Musica, Phila., 1983-84; mem. adv. bd. Clara Bell Duvall Edn. Fund, Phila.; mem. gov. bd. Health Systems Agy., S.E. Pa., 1980-86; mem. 18th Police Dist. Adv. Coun., exec. com. Phila. chpt. Nat. Police Def. Found. Recipient Cert. of Achievement Bus. Women's Network, Phila., 1984. Mem. Nat. Employment Lawyers' Assn. (pres. Ea. Pa. chpt. 1992-98), Nat. Assn. Women Lawyers (amicus com., bd. dirs. 1994-95), Phila. Bar Assn. (mem. evidence code task force 1992-93, chair support subcom. of small firm and sole practice com. 1992, exec. com. pub. interest sect., co-chair women's rights com. 2000-01), Assn. for Union Democracy, Am. Guild Organists (exec. com.). Administrative and regulatory, Labor (including EEOC, Fair Labor Standards Act, labor-management relations, NLRB, OSHA), Pension, profit-sharing, and employee benefits. Office: 1500 Walnut St Ste 900 Philadelphia PA 19102 also: 1930 Marlton Pike E Ste I48 Cherry Hill NJ 08003-4105 E-mail: dabrowskidoris@hotmail.com.

DADDARIO, EMILIO QUINCY, retired lawyer; b. Newton Centre, Mass., Sept. 24, 1918; s. Attilio Dante and Julia (Ciovacco) D.; m. Berenice Mary Carbo, Oct. 20, 1940; children: Edward, Stephen, Richard. BA, Wesleyan U., 1939; LLB, U. Conn, 1942; DSc, Wesleyan U., 1967; LLD, Rensselaer Polytech. Inst., Troy, N.Y., 1967, Phila. Coll. Osteo. Medicine, 1976. Bar: Conn., Mass., D.C., 86th-91st Congresses from 1st Conn. dist. Judge Mcpl. Ct., Middletown, Conn., 1948-50; mem. 86th, 87th, 88th, 89th, 90th and 91st Congresses, from 1st Conn. dist., 1958-71; dir. Office Tech. Assessment, Washington, 1973-77; mem. Wilkes, Artis, Hedrick & Lane, Washington, 1977-87. Vis. prof. MIT, Cambridge, 1970-71; co-chmn. ABA-AAAS Conf. of Lawyers and Scientists, Washington, 1976-88. Contbr. articles on sci. policy to profl. publs. Mayor, City of Middletown, Conn., 1946-48; mem. Commn. on Sci., Engring. and Pub. Policy, Nat. Acad. Scis., Washington, 1981—; trustee Wesleyan U., 1962—; adv. bd. Georgetown U. Sch. of Nursing. Served to maj., inf. U.S. Army, 1942-45, 50-52, ETO, PTO, Korea. Decorated Legion of Merit; Medaglia D'Argento (Italy). Mem. Silver Anniversary All-Am. Football Team, 1964; recipient Ralph Coats Roe award ASME, 1974; honor award and medal Stevens Inst. Tech., 1975; Pub. Welfare award Nat. Acad. Scis., 1976; Disting. Svc. award Nat. Sci. Found., 1990, W.R. Grace award Am. Cham. Soc., 1992. Mem. ABA, AAAS (pres. 1977, chmn. 1978, chmn. governance com. 1989-90), Inst. Medicine (bd. health sci. policy 1991-97), D.C. Bar Assn., Oak Ridge Associated Univs. (bd. dirs. 1991-97), Nat. Acad. Sci. (com. nat. forum on sci. and tech. goals 1995), Vets of OSS (v.p. 1990—). Clubs: Cosmos (Washington). Democrat. Roman Catholic. Home: #1027 3133 Connceticut Ave NW Washington DC 20008-5112

DAGENHART, LARRY JONES, lawyer; b. Taylorsville, N.C., July 20, 1932; s. Luther Jones and Louise (Icenhour) D.; m. Sarah Katheryne Petty, June 23, 1956; children: Katie Dagenhart Satterwhite, Mary Louise Dagenhart Culpepper, Larry Jones Jr. BS, Davidson (N.C.) Coll., 1953; LL.B., NYU, 1958. Bar: N.C. 1958. Pvt. practice, Charlotte, 1958—; ptnr. Helms, Mulliss & Wicker, Charlotte. Bd. dirs. So. Webbing. Trustee Davidson Coll., 1970-2002, chmn., 1998-2000; trustee U. N.C., Wilmington, 1997—, chmn., 2001—, chmn., chancellor search com., 2002—; trustee Kate B. Reynolds Trust, 1990-96; chmn. Ben Craig Incubator Ctr., 1998—; bd. dirs. N.C. Citizens for Bus. and Industry, 1995-2001; past chmn. Charlotte C. of C., 1983, Charlotte Arts and Scis. Coun., 1976-77, Mecklenburg County Bar Assn., 1974-75, Charlotte United Way, 1978, Found. for the Carolinas, 1987-89, Charlotte Country Day Sch., 1985-87, Charlotte City Club, 1979, Charlotte World Affairs Coun., 1996-98. George F. Baker scholar, 1949-53, Root-Tilden scholar, 1953-58; fellow Am. Bar Found., 1970—, Harold Josephson award, 2002. Mem. ABA, Am. Law Inst. Democrat. Lutheran. Home: 1601 Biltmore Dr Charlotte NC 28207-2611 Office: Helms Mulliss & Wicker PO Box 31247 Charlotte NC 28231-1247 E-mail: larry.dagenhart@hmw.com.

DAGGER, WILLIAM CARSON, lawyer; b. Lancaster, Ohio, May 5, 1949; s. William Carson Sr. and Thelma (Downing) D.; m. Barbara Schaeffer, Sept. 6, 1981; children: Alison Golden; Jaclyn Hedi. AB, Kenyon Coll., 1971; postgrad., Vanderbilt U., 1971-72; JD cum laude, Suffolk U., 1978. Bar: Mass. 1979, Vt. 1981, U.S. Dist. Ct. (ea. dist.) Mass. 1979, U.S. Dist. Ct. Vt. 1981, U.S. Ct. Appeals (1st cir.) 1980, U.S. Ct. Appeals (2nd cir.) 1990. Legal asst. Bernkopf, Goodman & Baseman, Boston, 1976-78; assoc. Rodick & Flavell, Weymouth, Mass., 1978-80, Dick, Hackel & Hull, Rutland, Vt., 1980-88; ptnr. Hull, Webber, Reis & Canney, Rutland, 1989-90; pvt. practice Dagger Law Offices, Woodstock, Vt., 1990—. Legal counsel The Howard Bank, Burlington, Vt., 1981-89, Vt. Indsl. Devel. Authority, Montpelier, 1982-84, Vt. Nat. Bank, 1990—, Woodstock Nat. Bank, 1993—, Vt. Housing Fin. Agy., 1990—, Ames Dept. Stores, 1990—, New London Trust Co., 1997—; trustee, treas. The Homestead, Inc., Woodstock, 1991-96. Bd. dirs. Woodstock Area Coun. Aging, 2000—, Woodstock Ctrl. Supervisory Union Cmty. Coun., 1991—; com. mem. Boy Scouts Am., 1990—. Master Sterry R. Waterman Am. Inn of Ct. (founding); mem. ABA, Vt. Bar Assn. (jud. evaluation com. 1981), Vt. Trial Lawyers Assn., Rotary Internat., Woodstock Rotary (pres. 1999-2000), Sierra Club (state rep. 1973-75). General civil litigation, Commercial, contracts (including sales of goods; commercial financing), Property, real (including real estate development, water). Home: 4702 Riverside Rd Woodstock VT 05091-9630 Office: The French Block 2 Central St PO Box 539 Woodstock VT 05091-1007 E-mail: daggrlaw@sover.net.

D'AGOSTINO, RICHARD DANIEL, lawyer; b. Sewickley, Pa., June 27, 1957; s. Joseph Dennis and Ellen Angela (Antolini) D'A.; m. Jeannie Marie Tucker, Sept. 18, 1982; children: Elena Marie, Christiana Danielle, Richard Zachary. BS in Bus. magna cum laude, U. Pitts., 1993; JD cum laude, Duquesne U. Law Sch., 2000. Bar: Pa. 2000. Realtor, 1979—; assoc. broker-appraiser Oxford Realty, Monaca, Pa., 1985—; founder, owner Ricky Dee's Pizza, Glenwillard, Pa., 1984—96; pres., founder D'Agostino Diversified Interests, Glenwillard, 1986—; legal intern Econ. Cmty. Devel. Clin., Pitts., 1998—99; law clerk Alcoa, Pitts., 1999; tipstaff Judge S. Louis Farino, Pitts., 1999—2001; law clk. Judge John McBride, Pitts., 2001—02; pres. Sheffield Lanes, Inc., Aliquippa, Pa., 2000—. Mem. Crescent Twp. Planning Commn., Glenwillard, 1987-88; co-founder Am. Water Relief, 1991. Mem. Beaver County Bd. Realtors, Am. Bar Assn., Pa. Bar Assn., Pitts. Intellectual Property Law Assn., Italian Am. Bar Assn., Sons of Italy, Mensa, Delta Psi Omega, Elks. Democrat. Roman Catholic. Avocations: musician, composer. Home: 274 Spring Run Rd Crescent PA 15046-5401 Office: 818 Raccoon St Fl 2 Aliquippa PA 15001 E-mail: rdd@dagostinolaw.com.

DAHL, TORLEIF PEDER, lawyer; b. Baerum, Norway, July 28, 1959; s. Bernt Leon and Inger Barbro Dahl; m. Marianne Dahl, May 27, 1997; children: Nora Emilie, Peder Christian, Thea Cathrine. JD, U. Oslo, 1986; LLM, Columbia U., 1991. Bar: Norway 1988. Rsch. asst. U. Oslo, 1984—85; assoc. Wikborg Rein & Co., 1986—92; asst. judge Hallingdal Dist. Ct., Nesibyen, 1986—87; ptnr. Wikborg, Rein & Co., 1993—. Mem.: Norwegian Assn. Computers and Law, Norwegian Bar Assn., Internat. Bar Assn. Communications, Corporate, general, Mergers and acquisitions. Home: Kvernveien 15 Oslo 0383 Norway Office: Wikborg Rein & Co Kronprinsesse HR 1 0117 Oslo Norway Fax: +47 22827501. E-mail: tpd@wr.no.

DAHL, TYRUS VANCE, JR., lawyer; b. Elizabeth City, N.C., July 23, 1949; s. Tyrus Vance and Emerald (Taylor) D.; m. Susan Morrow Fitzgerald, Aug. 7, 1976 (div. Apr. 1992); children: Katherine Fitzgerald, Elizabeth Sommers; m. Angela Wheelock, Aug. 8, 1998. AB, Duke U., 1971; JD, U. Tulsa, 1979. Bar: Tenn. 1979, U.S. Dist. Ct. (mid. dist.) Tenn. 1979, Okla. 1981, U.S. Dist. Ct. (no. and we dists.) Okla. 1982, U.S. Ct. Appeals (10th cir.) 1982, N.C. 1985, U.S. Dist. Ct. (ea., mid., and we. dists.) N.C. 1985, U.S. Ct. Appeals (4th cir.) 1985, U.S. Supreme Ct. 1985, U.S. Ct. Appeals (6th cir.) 1987. Law clk. to chief fed. judge, Nashville, 1979-81; assoc. Hall, Estill, Tulsa, 1981-84; ptnr. Womble Carlyle Sandridge & Rice, Winston-Salem, N.C., 1984—. Adj. prof. clin. program, adj. prof. trail practice and advanced trial practice Sch. Law, Wake Forest U. Editor and contbr. articles to law rev. Mem. ATLA, N.C. Bar Assn., Forsyth County

Bar Assn. Democrat. Methodist. Avocations: photography, music. Civil rights, Federal civil litigation, Insurance. Office: Womble Carlyle Sandridge & Rice 1 W 4th St Winston Salem NC 27101-4019 E-mail: tdahl@wcsr.com.

DAHLING, GERALD VERNON, lawyer; b. Red Wing, Minn., Jan. 11, 1947; s. Vernon and Lucille Alfrieda (Reuter) D.; m. Edell Marie Villella, July 26, 1969; children: David (dec.), Christopher, Elizabeth, Mary. BS, Winona (Minn.) State Coll., 1968; MS, U. Minn., 1970; PhD, Harvard U., 1974; JD, William Mitchell Coll. of Law, 1980. Bar: U.S. Patent Office 1979, Minn. 1980, Ind. 1980, Pa. 1997, U.S. Dist. Ct. (so. dist.) Ind. 1980. Patent atty. Eli Lilly and Co., Indpls., 1980-84, mgr. biotech. patents, 1984-86, asst. patent counsel biotech., 1986-89, asst. patent counsel biotech. and fermentation products, 1990, asst. gen. patent counsel, 1991-95; dir. intellectual property Pasteur Mérieux Connaught, Lyon, France and Swiftwater, Pa., 1995-97, corp. v.p., dir. intellectual property, 1997-98, sr. v.p. intellectual property, 1998-99, Rhone Poulenc Rorer, Collegeville, Pa., 1998-99; sr. v.p. global patents Aventis Pharms., Bridgewater, N.J., 2000—. Mem. ABA, Ind. Bar Assn., Pa. Bar Assn., Am. Intellectual Property Law Assn., Intellectual Property Owners Assn. (bd. dirs.), INTERPAT. Democrat. Roman Catholic. Federal civil litigation, Commercial, contracts (including sales of goods; commercial financing), Patent. Home: 501 Waterford Ct New Hope PA 18938 Office: Rt 202-206 PO Box 6800 Bridgewater NJ 08807-0800 also: Aventis Pasteur 13 Pont Pasteur 69348 Lyon France

DAHNK, JEAN PATRICIA, lawyer; b. 1958; BS in Bus. Adminstrn., George Washington U.; JD, Coll. William and Mary. Bar: Va. 1986. Ptnr. Glover & Dahnk, Fredericksburg, Va. Mem.: Va. State Bar (pres.-elect 2002). Office: Glover and Dahnk PO Box 207 Fredericksburg VA 22404-0207*

DAIL, JOSEPH GARNER, JR., judge; b. Elloree, S.C., June 15, 1932; s. Joseph Garner and Esther Vernette (Harbort) D.; m. Martha E. MacReynolds; children: Edward Benjamin, Mary Holyoke. BS, U. N.C., 1953, JD with honors, 1955. Bar: N.C. 1955, Va. 1976. Pvt. practice, Washington, 1959-76; ptnr. Croft, Dail & Vance (and predecessor), 1966-76; sole practitioner McLean, Va., 1976—83; counsel Gabeler, Ward & Griggs, 1983-87; judge U.S. adminstrv. law Fresno, Calif., 1987-94, San Francisco, 1994-97, Tampa, 1997-99; sr. U.S. adminstrv. law judge, 1999—. Assoc. editor: N.C. Law Rev, 1954-55. Lt. USNR, 1955-59; capt. Res. (ret.). Mem. Fed. Bar Assn., N.C. Bar Assn., Va. Bar Assn., Transp. Lawyers Assn. (Disting. Svc. award 1976), Order of Coif, Phi Beta Kappa. Republican. Home: 103 Masters Ln Safety Harbor FL 34695-3722 Office: Times Bldg 1000 N Ashley Dr Ste 200 Tampa FL 33602-3719 E-mail: macdail@aol.com.

DAILEY, COLEEN HALL, magistrate, lawyer; b. East Liverpool, Ohio, Aug. 10, 1955; d. David Lawrence and Deloris Mae (Rosensteel) Hall; m. Donald W. Dailey Jr., Aug. 16, 1980 (div. May 2001); children: Erin Elizabeth, Daniel Lester. Student, Wittenberg U., 1973-75; BA, Youngstown State U., 1977; JD, U. Cin., 1980. Bar: Ohio 1981, U.S. Dist. Ct. (no. dist.) Ohio 1981. Sr. libr. assoc. Marx Law Libr., Cin., 1979-80; law clk. Kapp Law Office, East Liverpool, 1979, 1980-81, assoc., 1981-85; pvt. practice East Liverpool, 1985-95; magistrate Columbiana County, Ohio, 1995—. Spl. counsel Atty. Gen. Ohio, 1985-92. Pres. Columbiana County Young Dems., 1985-87; bd. dirs. Big Bros./Big Sisters Columbiana County, Inc., Lisbon, Ohio, 1984-87, Planned Parenthood Mahoning Valley, Inc., 1993-97; trustee Ohio Women Inc., 1991-95; mem. Columbiana County Progress Coun., Inc. Mem. ABA, Ohio Bar Assn. (Ohio Supreme Ct. Joint Task Force on Gender Fairness, family law specialization bd.), Ohio Assn. Magistrates (chmn. domestic rels. sect. 1998-2000, 02-03), Columbiana County Bar Assn., East Liverpool Bus. and Profl. Women's Assn., Ohio Women's Bar Assn. (trustee 1997-99). Democrat. Lutheran. Office: Columbia County Common Pleas Court 105 S Market St Lisbon OH 44432-1255 E-mail: cdailey@ccclerk.org.

DAILEY, DIANNE K. lawyer; b. Great Falls, Mont., Oct. 10, 1950; d. Gilmore and Patricia Marie (Linnane) Halverson. BS, Portland State U., 1977; JD, Lewis & Clark Coll., 1982. Assoc. Bullivant, Houser, Bailey, et. al., Portland, Oreg., 1982-88, ptnr., 1988—, pres., 2002—. Contbr. articles to profl. jours. Mem.: ABA (chair task force on involvement of women 1990—93, governing coun. 1992—99, liaison to commn. on women 1993—97, vice chair tort and ins. practice sect. 1995—96, chair-elect tort and ins. practice sect. 1996—97, standing com. environ. law 1996—99, chair tort and ins. practice sect. 1997—98, chair sect. officers conf. 1998—2001, governing coun. 2003, del. 2003, property ins. law com., ins. coverage litigation com., chair task force CERCLA reauthorization, law practice mgmt. sect., comm. com.), Fedn. Ins. and Corp. Counsel, Def. Rsch. Inst., Internat. Assn. Def. Counsel, Multnomah Bar Assn. (bd. dirs. 1994—95), Oreg. State Bar, Wash. Bar Assn. General civil litigation, Environmental, Insurance. Office: Bullivant Houser Bailey 300 Pioneer Tower 888 SW 5th Ave Ste 300 Portland OR 97204-2089

DAILEY, GARRETT CLARK, publisher, lawyer; b. Bethesda, Md., Mar. 22, 1947; s. Garrett Hobart Valentine and Margaret (Clark) Dailey; m. Carolynn Farrar, June 21, 1969; children: Patrick, Steven. AB, UCLA, 1969; MA, Ariz. State U., 1974; JD, U. Calif., Davis, 1977. Bar: Calif. 1977, U.S. Dist. Ct. (no. dist.) Calif. 1969. Assoc. Stark, Stewart, Simon & Sparrowe, Oakland, Calif., 1977-80; ptnr. Davies & Dailey, Oakland, 1980-85, owner, 1986-90; ptnr. Blum, Davies & Dailey, Oakland, 1985-86; pres., pub. Attys. Briefcase, Inc., Oakland, 1989—, pres., CEO, 1989—. Lectr. U. Calif. Davis Sch. Law, 1988-90, Golden Gate U. Grad. Sch. Taxation, San Francisco, 1986—. Author: SupporTax, 2001; co-author: Attorney's Briefcase, Calif. Family Law, 1990—, Calif. Evidence, 1993—, Children and the Law, 1992—, Calif. Lawgic Marital Termination Agreements, 1996—, Calif. Divorce Guide, 1997—, Lawgic Premarital Agreements, 1997—. Bd. dirs. Amigos de las Americas, San Ramon Valley, Calif., 1980-85, Rotary 517 Found., Oakland, 1985, Kid's Turn, 1993. Recipient Hall of Fame award Calif. Assn. Cert. Family Law Specialists, 1995, Spencer Brandeis award, 2003. Fellow Am. Acad. Matrimonial Lawyers; mem. Assn. Cert. Family Law Specialists (Hall of Fame award 1995). Democrat. Congregationalist. Home: 1651 W Livorna Rd Alamo CA 94507-1018 Office: Attys Briefcase Inc 2915 McClure St Oakland CA 94609 E-mail: briefcase@aol.com.

DAILLE-DUCLOS, BRIGITTE, lawyer; b. Toulon, France; PhD in Law, U. Aix-en-Provence, France. Bar: Paris 1985. Assoc. August and Debouzy, Paris. Contbr. articles to profl. jours. Office: August & Derouzy 6 Avenue de Messine 75008 Paris France

DAILY, FRANK J(EROME), lawyer; b. Chgo., Mar. 22, 1942; s. Francis Jerome and Eileen Veronica (O'Toole) D.; m. Julianna Ebert, June 23, 1996; children: Catherine, Eileen, Frank, William, Michael. BA in Journalism, Marquette U., 1964, JD, 1968. Bar: Wis. 1968, U.S. Dist. Ct. (ea. dist.) Wis. 1968, U.S. Dist. Ct. (we. dist.) Wis. 1971, U.S. Dist. Ct. (ctrl. dist.) Ill. 1990, U.S. Dist. Ct. (ea. dist.) Mich. 1994, U.S. Ct. Appeals (7th cir.) 1977, U.S. Ct. Appeals (3d and 5th cirs.) 1985, U.S. Ct. Appeals (4th, 6th, 8th, 9th, 10th, 11th cirs.) 1990, U.S. Supreme Ct. 1998, U.S. Dist. Ct. (no. dist.) Ill. 1999. Assoc. Quarles & Brady, Milw., 1968-75, ptnr., 1975—. Lectr. in product liability law and trial techniques Marquette U. Law Sch., U. Wis., Harvard U.; lectr. seminars sponsored by ABA, State Bar Wis., State Bar S.D., State Bar S.C., Product Liability Adv. Coun., Chem. Mfrs. Assn., Wis. Acad. Trial Lawyers, Trial Attys. Am., Marquette U., Southeastern Corp. Law Inst., Risk Ins. Mgmt. Soc., Inc.; life mem. pres.'s coun. Wake Forest U., U. Dayton, Boston Coll. Author: Your Product's Life Is in the Balance: Litigation Survival-Increasing the Odds for Success, 1986, Product Liability Litigation in the 80s: A Trial Lawyer's View from the Trenches, 1986, Discovery Available to the Litigator and Its Effective Use, 1986, The Future of Tort Litigation: The Continuing Validity of Jury Trials, 1991, How to Make an Impact in Opening Statements for the Defense in Automobile Product Liability Cases, 1992, How Much Reform Does Civil Jury System Need, 1992, Do Protective Orders Compromise Public's Right to Know, 1993, Developments in Chemical Exposure Cases: Challenging Expert Testimony, 1993, The Spoliation Doctrine: The Sword, The Shield and The Shadow, 1997, Trial Tested Techniques for Winning Opening Statements, 1997, Litigation in the Next Millennium -- A Trial Lawyer's Crystal Ball Report, 1998, What's Hot and What's Not in Non-Daubert Products Liability In the Seventh Circuit, 1998. Ct. commr. Milwaukee County, Wis., 2001; bd. visitors Wake Forest U. Law Sch. Named Marquette U. Law Alumnus of Yr., 2000. Fellow Internat. Acad. Trial Lawyers; mem. ABA (past co-chair discovery com. litigation sect., vice chmn. products, gen. liability and consumer law com. of sect. tort and ins. practice, litigation sect. and mfrs. liability subcom.), ATLA, AAAS, Trial Atty. of Am., Wis. Bar Assn., Chgo. Bar Assn., Milw. Bar Assn., 7th Cir. Bar Assn., Am. Judicature Soc., Def. Rsch. Inst., Supreme Ct. Hist. Soc., Indsl. Truck Assn. (lawyers com.), Am. Law Inst., Product Liability Adv. Coun., Am. Agrl. Law Assn., Wis. Acad. Trial Lawyers, Assn. for Advancement of Automotive Medicine (life), Nat. I-Club U. Iowa, U. Ala. Nat. Alumni Assn., Circle of Champions. Roman Catholic. General civil litigation, Personal injury (including property damage), Product liability. Office: Quarles & Brady 411 E Wisconsin Ave Ste 2040 Milwaukee WI 53202-4497 E-mail: fjd@quarles.com.

DAILY, RICHARD W. lawyer; b. Boulder, Colo., Nov. 10, 1945; s. L. Donald and Lois W.; m. Patricia A. Cronin, June 30, 1986; 1 child, Samuel. BA, Antioch Coll., 1968; JD, Harvard U., 1971. Bar: Colo. 1971, U.S. Dist. Ct. Colo. 1971, U.S. Ct. Appeals (10th cir.) 1973, Fed. Cir. 1983. Assoc. Hodges, Kerwin, Otten & Weeks, Denver, 1972-73, Davis, Graham & Stubbs, Denver, 1973-79, ptnr., 1979-91; spl. counsel Burns, Wall, Smith & Mueller, P.C., Denver, 1991-93; interim staff Gt. Outdoors Colo. Trust Fund, 1993-94; shareholder Powers Phillips, P.C., 1994-99; ptnr. Hale Hackstaff Tymkovich, LLP, Denver, 1999—. Gen. counsel Colo. Dem. Party, Denver, 1987-93; bd. dirs. Goodwill Industries Denver, 1981-87; mem. Colo. Coun. on Arts and Humanities, 1983-89, Colo. Pub. Radio, 1994-2000. Capt. USAR, 1971-77. Mem. ABA, Colo. Bar Assn., Denver Bar Assn. Federal civil litigation, State civil litigation, Commercial, contracts (including sales of goods; commercial financing). Office: Hale Hackstaff Tymkovich 1430 Wynkoop St Ste 300 Denver CO 80202 E-mail: rdaily@halehackstaff.com.

DAILY, THOMAS A. lawyer; b. Ft. Smith, Ark., Jan. 8, 1946; BA, U. of the South, 1967; JD with honors, U. Ark., 1970. Bar: Ark. 1970. Ptnr. Daily & Woods PLLC, Ft. Smith, Ark. Mem.: ABA, Ark. Bar Assn. (pres.-elect 2002). Natural resources, Estate planning, Commercial, consumer (including collections, credit). Office: Daily & Woods PLLC PO Box 1446 623 Garrison Ave #600 Fort Smith AR 72902-1446*

DAISLEY, WILLIAM PRESCOTT, lawyer; b. Washington, Aug. 11, 1935; s. Gordon Walford and Augusta Greenleaf (Prescott) D.; m. Linda L. Thelin, Nov. 3, 1962; children: William Prescott Jr., Susan DeLeon. BA, Randolph Macon Coll., 1959; LL.B., George Washington U., 1962. Bar: D.C. 1962, Md. 1968, U.S. Supreme Ct. 1978. Law clk. firm King & Nordlinger, Washington, 1960-62, assoc., 1963-69, ptnr., 1969-90; prin. McChesney, Duncan & Dale, Washington, 1991-93; pres., chief exec. officer, chmn. of bd. William P. Daisley, Esq., P.C., Bethesda, Md., 1993—. Mem. Montgomery County (Md.) Juvenile Ct. Com., 1970-73; guest lectr. law George Washington U., 1972-76, 79; bd. dirs., trustee McLeod, Strasbaugh Scholarship Fund, 1984-99; bd. dirs. Citizens Bank Washington (formerly McLachlen Nat. Bank), 1982-97, chmn. audit com., 1992-94; mem. audit com. Citizens Bank of Md., 1994-97. Trustee, St. Andrew's Episc. Sch., Bethesda, Md., 1985-87. Mem. Md., Am., Montgomery County, D.C. bar assns., Phi Delta Theta, Phi Delta Phi. Clubs: Columbia Country (bd. govs. 1983-86). Republican. Episcopalian. Home and Office: 18304 Brewer House Rd Rockville MD 20852

DAITZ, RONALD FREDERICK, lawyer; b. N.Y.C., Sept. 1, 1940; s. Abraham and Anne (Birnbaum) D.; m. Linda Fay Rosenberg, Aug. 2, 1964; children: Paul Bennett, Charles Spencer. AB, Amherst Coll., 1961; LLB, Harvard U., 1964. Bar: N.Y. 1966, Colo. 1964, U.S. Dist. Ct. Colo. 1964, U.S. Ct. Appeals (10th cir.) 1964, U.S. Dist. Ct. (so. dist.) N.Y. 1979. Assoc. Henry & Adams, Denver, 1964-65; from assoc. to ptnr. Weil, Gotshal & Manges LLP, N.Y.C., 1965—. Mem. ABA (fed. regulation of securities com., bus. law sect. 1979—), Am. Coll. Comml. Fin. Lawers, N.Y. State Bar Assn. (mem. com. securities regulation, bus. law sect. 1984—, chmn. 1990-93, sec. bus. law sect. 1994-95, 2d vice-chair and fiscal officer 1995-96, mem. exec. com. 1991-2001, 1st vice chair 1996-97, chair 1997-98), Assn. Bar City N.Y. (com. corp. law 1975-77, 87-88, 95-97). Banking, Corporate, general, Securities. Office: Weil Gotshal & Manges LLP 767 5th Ave Fl Concl New York NY 10153-0119

DALE, ERWIN RANDOLPH, lawyer, author; b. Herrin, Ill., July 30, 1915; s. Henry and Lena Bell (Campbell) D.; m. Charline Vincent, Aug. 27, 1955; children: Allyson Ann (Mrs. Earl A. Samson III), Kristan Charline (Mrs. Victor L. Zimmermann). BA, U. Tex., El Paso, 1937; JD, U. Tex., 1943. Bar: Tex. 1943, D.C. 1953, Mich. 1956, N.Y. 1960. Atty. IRS, 1943-56, chief reorgn. and dividend br., 1954-56; legal staff Gen. Motors Corp., 1956-57; ptnr. firm Chapman, Walsh & O'Connell, N.Y.C. and Washington, 1957-59, Hawkins, Delafield & Wood, N.Y.C., 1959-84; of counsel Hutchison, Price, Boyle & Brooks, Dallas, 1985-86, Jenkens, Hutchison & Gilchrist, Dallas, 1986, Hutchison, Boyle, Brooks & Dansfield, Dallas, 1986-87. Lectr. tax matters; dir. Md. Electronics Mfg. Corp., 1948-58; dir., treas. The Renaissance Corp., 1968-72; dir., asst. treas. Shancom Reconstrn. Corp., 1968-72, Newhaven Corp., 1968-72 Author numerous articles on fed. tax matters; bd. editors: Tex. Law Rev., 1941-42, 42-43. Mem. ABA (chmn. com. consol. returns sect. taxation 1959-60), Tex. Bar Assn., Mich. Bar Assn., N.Y. State Bar Assn. (chmn. corp. tax com. tax sect. 1967-68, mem. exec. com. 1968-70), Tax Inst. Am. (bd. dirs. 1967-69, treas. 1966), Assn. of Bar of City of N.Y., Nat. Tax Assn., Nat. Assn. Bond Lawyers, Am. Coll. Tax Counsel, Ex-Students Assn. U. Tex., Ex-Students Assn. U. Tex., El Paso, Bronxville Field Club (N.Y.), Masons. Corporate taxation, Personal income taxation, Finance. Home: 10 Holly Ln Darien CT 06820-3303 Fax: 203-662-9386. E-mail: erdale@aol.com.

D'ALEMBERTE, TALBOT (SANDY D'ALEMBERTE), academic administrator, lawyer; b. Tallahassee, June 1, 1933; m. Patsy Palmer; children: Gabrielle Lynn, Joshua Talbot. BA in Polit. Sci. with honors, U. South, 1955; postgrad., London Sch. Econs. and Polit. Sci., U. London, 1958-59; JD with honors, U. Fla., 1962. Bar: Fla. 1962, U.S. Ct. Appeals (5th cir.) 1962, U.S. Supreme Ct. 1970. Assoc. Steel Hector & Davis, Miami, Fla., 1962-65, ptnr., 1965-84, 89-93; prof. Fla. State U., 1984—, dean Coll. Law, 1984-89, pres., 1994—2003. Lectr. U. Miami Coll. Law, 1969-71, adj. prof., 1974-76; reader Fla. Bd. Bar Examiners, 1965-67; mem. jud. nominating commn. Fla. Supreme Ct., 1975-78; chief counsel Ho. Select Com. for Impeachment of Certain Justices, 1975; mem. Fla. Law Revision Coun., 1968-74; chmn. Fla. Constl. Revision Commn., 1977-78. Articles editor U. Fla. Law Rev. Mem. Fla. Ho. Reps., 1966-72, chmn. com. on ad valorem taxation, 1968-70, chmn. judiciary com., 1970-72, mem. various coms.; chmn. Fla. Commn. on Ethics, 1974-75; trustee Miami-Dade Community Coll., 1976-84. Served with USN, 1955-58; to lt. USNR. Recipient award Fla. Acad. Trial Lawyers, 1972, 93, Fla. Patriots award Fla. Bicentennial Commn., 1976, Disting. Alumnus award U. Fla., 1977, Nelson Poynter award Fla. Civil Liberties Union, 1984, Gov.'s Emmy award Nat. Acad. TV Arts and Scis., 1985, 1st Amendment award Nat. Sigma Delta Chi/Soc. Profl. Journalists, 1986, Medal of Honor award Fla. Bar Found., 1987, Juris prudence award Anti-Defamation League of S. Fla., 1990, Fla. Acad. of Criminal Def. Lawyers Annual Justice award, 1993, Acad. of Fla. Trial Lawyers Perry Nichols award, 1993, Nat. Coun. of Jewish Women's Hannah G. Soloman award, 1996, Am. Judicature Soc. Justice award, 1996; named Outstanding First Term House Mem., 1967, Most Outstanding Mem. of House, Capital Press Corps; Rotary Found. fellowship, London Sch. Economics, 1958-59. Mem. ABA (pres. 1991-92, chmn. spl. com. on election reform 1973-76, chmn. spl. com. on resolution of minor disputes 1976-79, chmn. spl. com. on med. malpractice 1985-86, state del. from Fla. 1980-89, commn. on governance 1983-84, rules and calender com. ho. of dels. 1982-84, commn. on women in profession 1987, co-founder Ctrl. and East European Law Initiative, World Order Under Law award 1998, Robert J. Kutak award sect. legal edn. 1998), Fla. Bar Assn. (bd. govs. 1974-82), Dade County Bar Assn. (pres. young lawyers sect. 1965-66, bd. dirs.), Am. Judicature Soc. (pres. 1982-84), U. Fla. Law Ctr. Assn. (trustee 1967—), Order of Coif, Omicron Delta Kappa, Phi Beta Kappa. Office: Fla State U Coll Law 425 W Jefferson St Tallahassee FL 32306-1601 E-mail: dalember@mailer.fsu.edu.

DALENBERG, DAVID LYLE, lawyer; b. Kalamazoo, Mich., Apr. 3, 1943; s. Lyle Wilson and Hazel Maxine (Murphy) D.; m. Minerva Zivan; children: Steven David, Emily Ann. BS in Social Sci., Mich. State U., 1966; JD, Wayne State U., 1970. Bar: Mich. 1970, Fla. 1974. Assoc. Paruk & Miller, Hamtramok, Mich., 1970-74; pvt. practice North Palm Beach, Fla., 1974-75; ptnr. Shermeta, Morrissey & Dalenberg, Bloomfield Hills, Mich., 1975-76; asst. county prosecutor Macomb County, Mt. Clemons, Mich., 1976-78; asst. city atty. City of Warren, Mich., 1978-88, sr. asst. city atty., 1988—. Author, editor: Michigan Municipal Law, 1988. Pres. Mich. Epsilon Alumni Bd., Lansing, 1984-85. Mem. Mich. State Bar (sec. pub. corp. sect. 1987-88, vice chmn. 1988-89, chmn. 1989-90), Beaver Creek Golf Links. Republican. Lutheran. Avocations: sailing, golf, internet. Office: City of Warren 29500 Van Dyke Ave Warren MI 48093-6726

D'ALESSANDRO, DANIEL ANTHONY, lawyer, educator; b. Jersey City, Oct. 10, 1949; s. Donato Marino D'Alessandro and Rose Teresa (Casamassimo) Drennan; m. Beth Anne Lill, Sept. 2, 1978; children: Daniel Patrick, Eric Charles. BA, St. Peter's Coll., 1971; JD, Seton Hall U., 1974; LLM in Criminal Justice, NYU, 1981. Bar: N.J. 1975, U.S. Dist. Ct. N.J. 1975, N.Y. 1982, U.S. Supreme Ct. 1985, U.S. Dist. Ct. (so. dist.) N.Y. 1989, cert.: (ct. approved family law mediator). Law clk. to presiding judge Juvenile and Domestic Relations Ct., Hudson County, N.J., 1974-75; pub. defender City of Jersey City, 1975-76; prosecutor Town of Secaucus, NJ, 1976-77; prin. D'Alessandro & Assocs., Jersey City, 1977-82; ptnr. D' Alessandro & Tutak, Jersey City, 1982-90; pres. D'Alessandro, Tutak & Aschoff, P.C., Jersey City, 1990-92; ptnr. D'Alessandro & Aschoff, P.C., Jersey City, 1993-94; pvt. practice Jersey City, 1994—2003; ptnr. D'Alessandro & Cieckiewicz, P.C., Jersey City, 2003—. Adj. prof. Middlesex County Coll., Edison, NJ, 1981—83, St. Peter's Prep., 1981—83; arbitrator automobile arbitration program N.J. Supreme Ct., mem. ethics com. dist. VI, vice-chair fee arbitration com.; counsel Employees Retirement Sys. Jersey City, 1985—89. Vol. probation officer Hudson County Probation Dept., 1977; pro bono counsel Anthony R. Cucci Civic Assn., Jersey City, 1981—89, Battered Women's Shelter, Jersey City, 1982, Mayor's Task force for Handicapped, Jersey City, 1985—89; v.p. Jersey City Boys Club, 1991, pres., 1993—98, also trustee; baseball coach Jersey Shore Thunderbirds, N.J. AAU, 1993—2001, Mater Dei HS, 2000—02. Named Prof. of the Yr., Secaucus Patrolmen's Benevolent Assn., 1980; recipient Disting. Svc. award, Jersey City Police Dept., 1988, cert. of Merit, N.J. Supreme Ct., Meritorious Pub. Svc. award, 1990, Outstanding Bd. Mem. award, N.J. Boys and Girls Clubs Hudson County, 1998, Cmty. Svc. award, Boys & Girls Clubs, 2003. Mem.: ABA, Hudson County Bar Assn. (treas. 1991, sec. 1992, v.p. 1994, 1995, pres.-elect 1996, pres. 1997—98, past chmn., mem. various coms., trustee, Outstanding Bd. Mem. award 1998, Cmty. Svc. award 2001, 2002), N.J. State Bar Assn. Democrat. Roman Catholic. Avocations: renovating old homes, sports, renovating scholastic athletic fields. State civil litigation, General practice, Property, real (including real estate development, water). Office: 3279 John F Kennedy Blvd Jersey City NJ 07306-3418 E-mail: dadpclaw@aol.com.

D'ALESSANDRO, DIANNE MARIE, public defender; b. NYC, Apr. 20, 1952; d. Frank and Marie A. D'A.; m. John P. Foley, July 24, 1977; children: Maria, James. BA in Psychology, Upsala Coll., East Orange, NJ, 1974; JD, NY Law Sch., 1981. Bar: NJ 1981, US Dist. Ct. NJ 1981. Staff atty. Bergen City Legal Svc., Hackensack, N.J., 1981-83; sr. trial atty. Office Pub. Defender, Hackensack, 1983—. Dist. II B ethics com., Office of Atty. Ethics of the Supreme Ct. of NJ, 1992-95; bd. dir. Bergen County Legal Svc. Recipient citation from Susan Reisner, pub. advocate, for work done on State vs. Harris. Mem.: Friends of Ringwood Manor, Nat. Trust for Hist. Preservation, Nat. Assoc. Criminal Def. Lawyers. Avocations: reading, hiking, historic preservation. Office: Office of Pub Advocate/Pub Defender 60 State St Hackensack NJ 07601-5451 E-mail: dalessandro_d@opd.state.nj.us.

DALEY, PAUL PATRICK, lawyer; b. Boston, July 10, 1941; s. Patrick Joseph and Catherine Josephine (Ford) D.; m. Barbara Sabin, May 24, 1980; 1 child, Patrick. AB, Boston Coll., 1963; MBA, JD, Harvard U., 1973. Bar: Mass. 1973, U.S. Ct. Appeals (1st cir.) 1974, U.S. Ct. Appeals (5th cir.) 1980, U.S. Supreme Ct. 1980, N.Y. 1983, U.S. Ct. Appeals (2d cir.) 1998. Assoc. Hale and Dorr LLP, Boston, 1973-78; jr. ptnr. Hale and Dorr, Boston, 1978-82, sr. ptnr., 1982—. Lectr. CLE programs. Assoc. editor Mass. Law Rev., 1998—; contbr. articles to profl. jours. Trustee Mass. Sch. Profl. Psychology, Boston, 1985-2003, chair, 1994-2003; trustee St. Sebastians Sch., Needham, Mass. 1981, Naval War Coll. Found., 1996—, pres., 2000-02, chmn., 2002—; bd. dirs. Am. Sail Train Assn., Newport, R.I., 1982-86. Capt. USNR, 1963-94, Vietnam 1965-67. Decorated DFC, Air Medals (16), Vietnamese Air Gallantry Cross. Fellow Am. Coll. Bankruptcy; mem. ABA, Mass. Bar Assn. (past chmn. bus. bank com., bus. law sect., fee arbitration bd.), Boston Bar Assn. (coun.), Am. Bankruptcy Inst., Nat. Def. U. Found., Tailhook Assn., U.S. Naval Inst., Naval Res. Assn., Assn. Naval Aviation, Tailhook Assn, Comml. Law League, Navy League, Windsor Club (Waban, Mass.), Brae Burn Country Club, Wardroom Club. Democrat. Roman Catholic. Avocations: flying, scuba diving, biking, reading, theater. Bankruptcy, General civil litigation, Commercial, contracts (including sales of goods; commercial financing). Home: 9 Crofton Rd Waban MA 02468-1931 Office: Hale and Dorr LLP 60 State St Boston MA 02109-1816 Fax: (617) 526-5000. E-mail: paul.daley@haledorr.com.

DALEY, SUSAN JEAN, lawyer; b. New Britain, Conn., May 27, 1959; d. George Joseph and Norma (Woods) D. BA, U. Conn., 1978; JD, Harvard U., 1981. Bar: Ill. 1981. Assoc. Altheimer & Gray, Chgo., 1981-86, ptnr., 1986—. Mem. ABA (real property, probate and trust law sect. 1983—, chmn. welfare plans com. real property, probate and trust law sect. 1989-95, employee benefits com. taxation sect. 1984—, chmn. EEOC issues subcom. employee benefits com. taxation sect. 1990-2001, chmn. fed. securities law subcom. employee benefits com. taxation sect. 2001--), Nat. Assn. Stock Plan Profls. (pres. Chgo. chpt. 1995—), Ill. Bar Assn. (chmn. employee benefits divsn. fed. taxation sect. 1984-86, chmn. employee benefits sect., 1995-96, mem. employee benefits sect. 1990-97), Chgo. Bar Assn. (chmn. employee benefits divsn. fed. taxation com. 1985-86, chmn. employee benefits com. 1990-91, chmn. fed. taxation com. 1992-93), Chgo. Coun. on Fgn. Rels. Avocation: marathons. Pension, profit-sharing, and employee benefits. Home: 1636 N Wells St Apt 415 Chicago IL 60614-6009 Office: Altheimer & Gray 10 S Wacker Dr Ste 4000 Chicago IL 60606-7407 E-mail: daleys@altheimer.com.

DALEY, THOMAS, judge; b. Neptune, NJ, Oct. 17, 1953; s. Fredrick Daley and Winifred Carey; m. Margaret Mery Versaggi, Nov. 27, 1982; children: Bernadette, Monique. BA, Rutgers U., 1975; JD, Loyola U., New Orleans, 1978. Bar: La. 78, U.S. Supreme Ct. 80, U.S. Ct. Appeals (5th cir.) 79, DC 90. Pvt. practice, La Place, La., 1978—90; asst. dist. atty. St. John the Bapt. Parish, La Place, 1984—90; judge La. 40th Jud. Dist. Ct., Edgard, 1990—96, La. 5th Cir. Ct. Appeals, Gretna, 1996—. Adj. prof. Sch. Law La. State U., Baton Rouge, 1998—. Mem. adv. bd. St. John 4-H Found., LaPlace, 1996—, St. John Halfway Recovery House, LaPlace, 2001—; chmn. Keep St. John Beautiful, LaPlace, 1998—, St. John Shalle Tree Com., LaPlace, 1990—. Mem.: 5th Ct. Judges Assn. (bd. dirs. 1999—). Avocation: running. Home: 2037 Colonial Dr La Place LA 70068 E-mail: tdaley@fifthcircuit.org.

D'ALFONSO, MARIO JOSEPH, lawyer; b. Phila., Nov. 3, 1951; s. Albert Carmine and Yolanda (Zanfrisco) D'A.; m. Rita F. Borrelli, Apr. 26, 1975; 1 child, Mario C. BA, Villanova U., 1973; JD, Widener U., 1979. Bar: Pa. 1979, N.J. 1979, U.S. Dist. Ct. (ea. dist.) Pa. 1979, U.S. Dist. Ct. N.J. 1979, U.S. Ct. Appeals (3d cir.) 1980, U.S. Supreme Ct. 1983, U.S. Ct. Appeals (5th cir.) 1989. Assoc. Avena, Hendren & Friedman, Camden, N.J., 1979-81; ptnr. Avena, Hendren, Friedman & D'Alfonso, 1981-84, D'Alfonso & Camacho, P.A., Haddon Heights, N.J., 1984—. Cons. Marbert Construction, Haddon Heights, N.J., 1982—. Mem. Am. Arbitration Assn. (Svc. award 1984), Assn. Criminal Def. Lawyers, Camden County Bar Assn., N.J. Trial Lawyers Assn., Phi Delta Phi (pres. 1978), Phi Kappa Phi. Roman Catholic. Criminal, General practice, Personal injury (including property damage). Home: 64 Lady Diana Cir Marlton NJ 08053-3705 Office: 200 Lake Dr E Ste 203 Cherry Hill NJ 08002

DALIANIS, LINDA STEWART, BA cum laude, Northeastern U., 1970; JD, Suffolk U., 1974, JD (hon.) , 2001. Bar: N.H. 1974, U.S. Dist. Ct. N.H. 1974, U.S. Supreme Ct. 1974. Pvt. law practice, Nashua, N.H., 1974-79; marital master N.H. Superior Ct., 1979-80, assoc. justice, 1980—2000, chief justice, 2000; assoc. justice N.H. Supreme Ct., Concord, 2000—. Chair Interbranch Criminal and Juvenile Justice Com.; mem. edn. coms. N.H. Supreme and Superior Cts., Northern New Eng. Jud. Edn. Com.; mem. jud. adv. com. N.H. Dept. Corrections; mem. marital masters com., alternative dispute resolution com. N.H. Supreme Ct. Office: Supreme Ct Bldg One Noble Dr Concord NH 03301-6160

DALLAS, WILLIAM MOFFIT, JR., lawyer; b. Cedar Rapids, Iowa, May 7, 1949; s. William Moffit and Winifred Mae (Lillie) D.; m. Lynne Louise Russo, July 30, 1977 (div. July 1984); m. Janet Neustaetter, Apr. 19, 1985; children: Sarah Anne, Steven Kurt. AB, Oberlin Coll., 1971; JD, Harvard U., 1974. Bar: N.Y. 1975, U.S. Dist. Ct. (so. and ea. dists.) N.Y. 1975, U.S. Ct. Appeals (2d cir.) 1976, U.S. Ct. Appeals (3d cir.) 1983, U.S. Ct. Appeals (8th cir.) 1984. Assoc. Sullivan & Cromwell, N.Y.C., 1974-82, ptnr., 1982—. Fed. mediator U.S. Dist. Ct., 1995—. Contbr. articles on antitrust issues to law revs., 1978—, chpt. to book. Served to lt. USN, 1971-77. Mem. ABA, Assn. of Bar of City of N.Y. (chmn. com. on judicial admin., 1999—, sec. judiciary com. 1977-80, chmn. com. jud. adminstrn. 1999-2002), N.Y. County Lawyers' Assn. (chmn. com. on trade regulation 1978-81), India House Club (N.Y.C.). Antitrust, Federal civil litigation, State civil litigation. Office: Sullivan & Cromwell 125 Broad St Fl 28 New York NY 10004-2489

DALLA VEDOVA, RICCARDO, lawyer, law educator; b. Naples, Italy, Feb. 6, 1932; s. Joseph and Anna Dalla Vedova; m. Alice Maguire Dalla Vedova, Sept. 15, 1960; children: Marco, Carlo, Peter, Lorenzo. Student, Wesleyan U., 1952—53; JD maxima cum laude, U. Naples, 1954. Bar: Rome 1959. Asst. prof. U. Naples, 1955, U. Rome, 1960—63. Contbr. articles to profl. jours. Fulbright scholar, 1952—53. Private international, Public international. Office: Dalla Vedova Studio Legale Via Vittorio Bachelet 12 00185 Rome Italy

DALLEN, RUSSELL MORRIS, JR., investment company executive, lawyer, publishing company executive; b. Biloxi, Miss., Jan. 20, 1963; s. Russell Morris and Faye Annette (Werner) D.; m. Claire Lucia Hodgson, May 27, 1995; children: Allegra Julia Faye, Arabella Sarah Emma. BA in Econs. and Polit. Sci., U. Miss., 1985; M in Internat. Affairs, Columbia U., 1987; diploma in internat. law, Nottingham (Eng.) U., 1988; BA in Jurisprudence, Oxford (Eng.) U., 1990, MA in Law, 1994. Fgn. corres. Newsweek, London, 1990-91; sr. fellow, dir. UN Assn.-USA, N.Y.C., 1991-93; assoc. Morgan Stanley & Co., Inc., N.Y.C., 1994-96; ptnr. Stires, O'Donnell & Co., Inc., 1996-99, Brisbane, Mendez de Leon & Co., Fahnestock & Co. Inc., Oppenheimer & Co. Inc., 2000—; pres., editor in chief The Daily Journal. Author: Revitalizing The United Nations, 1993; (with others) Issues Before the United Nations, 1989, A Global Agenda, 1992; contbr. articles to profl. jours. Bd. govs. Harold W. Rosenthal Fellowship, Washington, 1985—; exec. com. Manhattan coun. Boy Scouts Am., N.Y.C., 1992—; vol. Big Bros./Big Sisters, N.Y.C., 1992—. Recipient Ner Tamid Leadership award Nat. Jewish Com. on Scouting, 1979, Kluwer Internat. Law award, 1990, Article of Yr. award Common Market Law Rev.; named Century III Leader, 1981; Harry S. Truman scholar, 1983, U.K. Fgn. and Commonwealth Office scholar, 1987; Harold Rosenthal fellow, 1985, Am. fellow European Communities, 1986, Ctr. fellow Ctr. for Study of Presdy., 1985. Mem. N.Y. State Bar Assn., N.Y. County Lawyers Assn. (chmn. sub-com. 1992—), Oxford and Cambridge Club, Squadron A Club, Cornell Club, Landsdowne Club. Avocations: sailing, flying, riding. Home: M-365 PO Box 3340 New York NY 10185-3340

DALLEY, GEORGE ALBERT, lawyer, consultant; b. Havana, Cuba, Aug. 25, 1941; s. Cleveland Ernest and Constance Joyce (Powell) D.; m. Pearl Elizabeth Love, Aug. 1, 1970; children: Jason Christopher, Benjamin Christian. AB, Columbia U., 1963, JD, MBA, Columbia U., 1966. Bar: N.Y. 1966, D.C. 1971, U.S. Supreme Ct. 1972. Asst. to pres. Met. Applied Rsch. Ctr., N.Y.C., 1967-69; counsel The Children's Found., Washington, 1970-71; assoc. counsel Stroock and Stroock and Lavan, Washington, 1970-71, Com. on Judiciary, U.S. Ho. of Reps., Washington, 1971-72; adminstrv. asst. to Rep. Charles B. Rangel, N.Y.C., Washington, 1973-77, counsel, staff dir., 1985-89; dep. asst. sec. for human rights and social affairs Bur. Internat. Orgns. Affairs Dept. State, Washington, 1977-80; mem. CAB, 1980-82; dep. dir. Mondale for Pres. Com., Washington, 1983-84; counsel, staff dir. Congressman Charles B. Rangel, U.S. Ho. of Reps., Washington, 1985-89; sr. v.p. Neill and Co., Washington, 1989-93; ptnr. Neill, Dalley, Carroll, Nealer and Assevero, Washington, 1992-93; sr. ptnr. Holland and Knight, Washington, 1993—. Adj. prof. Am. U. Sch. Law. Mem. legal adv. com. Dem. Nat. Com., 1975-76; bd. dirs. Africare, TransAfrica; Joint Ctr. for Polit. and Econ. Studies Internat. Inst., Jamaica Nats. Devel. Found. Mem. ABA, Nat. Bar Assn., Fed. Bar Assn., Nat. Conf. Black Lawyers, Cosmos Club, Coun. Fgn. Rels., Coun. Ams. Presbyterian. Home: 1328 Vermont Ave NW Washington DC 20005-3607 Office: Rm 2354 US House Rep Washington DC 20515

D'ALOISE, LAWRENCE T., JR., lawyer; b. Port Chester, NY, Dec. 3, 1944; s. Lawrence Thomas and Lillian Teresa D'Aloise; children: Scott, Sean, Kimberly. BS, Holy Cross Coll., 1966; JD, Villanova U., 1969. Bar: NY 1970, US Dist. Ct. (so., ea. and no. dists.) NY, US Ct. Appeals (2d cir.), US Ct. Appeals (5th cir.), US Supreme Ct. Ptnr. Clark, Gagliardi & Miller PC, White Plains, N.Y., 1970—. Contbr. Mem.: ABA, White Plains Bar Assn., Westchester County Bar Assn., NY State Bar Assn. Avocation: auto restoration. Appellate, Personal injury (including property damage), Product liability. Home: 130 Old Mamaroneck Rd White Plains NY 10605-2413 Office: Clark Gagliardi & Miller 99 Court St White Plains NY 10601-4265 E-mail: ldaloise@cgmlaw.com.

DALRYMPLE, THOMAS LAWRENCE, retired lawyer; b. Wellsburg, W. Va., May 20, 1921; s. Lawrence Chester and Ethel May (Taylor) D.; m. Marjorie May Keeler; children: Bruce Lawrence, Dale Brian. AB, U. Mich., 1943, JD, 1947. Bar: Ohio 1947, U.S. Supreme Ct. Practiced in, Toledo, 1947-96; assoc. Williams, Eversman & Morgan and successor firms, 1947-50, Welles, Kelsey, Fuller, Harrington & Seney and successor firms, 1950-52; ptnr. Fuller & Henry and predecessor firms, 1953-96. Mem. Trout Unltd., Toledo Mus. Art. Served to capt. inf. AUS, 1943-46. Decorated Combat Inf. badge, Silver Star medal, Purple Heart. Fellow Am. Coll. Trial Lawyers, Am. Bar Found., Ohio Bar Found.; mem. Order of Coif, Phi Beta Kappa. General civil litigation. Home: 4307 Stannard Dr Toledo OH 43613-3636

DAL SANTO, DIANE, writer, retired judge; b. East Chicago, Ind., Sept. 20, 1949; d. John Quentin Dal Santo and Helen (Koval) D.; m. Fred O'Cheskey, June 29, 1985. BA, U. N.Mex., 1971; cert., Inst. Internat. and Comparative Law, Guadalajara, Mex., 1978; JD, U. San Diego, 1980. Bar: N.Mex. 1980, U.S. Dist. Ct. N.Mex. 1980. Ct. planner Met. Criminal Justice Coordinating Coun., Albuquerque, 1973-75; planning coord. Dist. Atty.'s Office, Albuquerque, 1975-76, exec. asst. to dist. atty., 1976-77, asst. dir. atty. for violent crimes, 1980-82; chief dep. city atty. City of Albuquerque, 1983; assoc. firm T.B. Keleher & Assocs., 1983-84; judge Met. Ct., 1985-89, chief judge, 1988-89; judge Dist. Ct., 1989-2000. Mem. faculty Nat. Jud. Coll., 1990-95, 97-, trustee, 1995-96; adj. faculty Internat. Law Enforcement Acad., Roswell, N.Mex., 2002-. Columnist Albuquerque Jour., 1996-98. Bd. dirs. Nat. Coun. Alcoholism, 1984, S.W. Ballet Co., Albuquerque, 1982-83; mem. Mayor's Task Force on Alcoholism and Crime, 1987-88, N.Mex. Coun. Crime and Delinquency, 1987-97, bd. dirs., 1992-94, Task Force Domestic Violence, 1987-94; pres. bench, bar, media com., 1987, pres. 1992, rules of evidence com. Supreme Ct., 1993-96, chair com. access to pub. records Supreme Ct., 1988; steering com. N.Mex. Buddy Awards, 1995—; mem. Metro. Criminal Justice Coordinating Coun., 1998—. U. San Diego scholar, 1978-79; recipient Women on the Move award YWCA, 1989, Disting. Woman award U. N.Mex. Alumni Assn., 1994, Outstanding Alumnus Dept. Sociology U. N.Mex., 1995; named Woman of Yr. award Duke City Bus. and Profl. Women, 1985. Mem. ABA (Nat. Conf. State Trial Judges Jud. Excellence award 1996), LWV, AAUW, Am. Judicature Soc., N.Mex. Women's Found., N.Mex. State Bar Assn. (silver gavel award 1997), N.Mex. Women's Bar Assn. (bd. dirs. 1991-92, Power and Caring award 2000), Albuqurque Bar Assn., Nat. Assn. Women Judges (bd. dist. dirs. 1999-00), Greater Albuquerque C. of C. (steering com. 1989), N.Mex. Magistrate Judges Assn. (v.p. 1985-89), Dist. Judges Assn. (pres. 1994-95), Pennies for Homeless. Office: Dist Ct 415 Tijeras Ave NW Albuquerque NM 87102-3252 E-mail: dianedalsanto@aol.com.

DALTHORP, GEORGE CARROL, lawyer; b. Wibaux, Mont., Aug. 7, 1929; s. Henry Charles and Clara (Rud) D.; m. Lois Esther Mattson, Aug. 30, 1956; children: David Charles, Kristin Dagny Jones, Beth Helen Dalthorp Johnson, Daniel Henry. BS, Mont. State U., 1951; postgrad., Denver U., 1955-56; JD, U. Mont., 1958. Bar: Mont. 1958, U.S. Dist. Ct. Mont. 1958, U.S. Ct. Appeals (9th cir.) 1969, U.S. Supreme Ct. 1979. Law clk. to presiding judge U.S. Dist. Ct. Mont., Billings, 1958-59; assoc. Crowley, Haughey, Hanson, Toole & Dietrich, Billings, 1959-67, ptnr., 1967—99, of counsel, 2000—. Served to lt. USNR, 1952-55, Korea. Fellow Am. Coll. Trial Lawyers, Am. Bar Found.; mem. ABA, Am. Bd. Trial Advocates (assoc.), State Bar Mont. (pres. 1985-86, trustee 1982-87) (recipient William J. Jameson Professionalism Award, 2002, Yellowstone County Bar Assn., Internat. Assn. Def. Counsel, Yellowstone Kiwanis Club, Elks. Republican. Lutheran. Avocations: backpacking, racquetball, skiing, fishing. Native American, Personal injury (including property damage), Product liability. Home: 2415 Granite Ave Billings MT 59102-0537 Office: Crowley Haughey Hanson 490 N 31st St Billings MT 59101-1256

DALTON, ANNE, lawyer; b. Pitts., Dec. 6, 1951; d. Thomas John and Mary Olive (Paul) D.; m. Oliver E. Martin, Dec. 26, 1987. BA in Polit. Sci., NYU, 1973; JD, Fordham U., 1977. Bar: N.Y. 1978, U.S. Dist. Ct. (so. and ea. dists.) N.Y. 1979, Pa. 1987, Fla. 1990. Assoc. Mendes & Mount, N.Y.C., 1979-80; atty. news divsn. ABC, N.Y.C., 1980-85; TV news prodr. ABC Network, N.Y.C., 1985-86; sr. atty. Radio City Music Hall Prodns., Inc., N.Y.C., 1986-87; pvt. practice Stroudsburg, Pa., 1987-91; asst. county att., asst. port authority atty. Lee County, Ft. Myers, Fla., 1991-94; pvt. practice Ft. Myers, 1994—. Spl. hearing master 20th Jud. Cir., Fla., 1991—, ct. Commr., gen. master family civil and probate divsn., 1995—; adj. prof. Edison C.C., Ft. Myers, Barry U., Ft. Myers; Fla. family, cir. civil, dependency, county, fed. mediator, 1995; arbitrator, state ct., 1998. Recipient Clio award Internat. Clio Award Com., 1978. Mem. Pa. Bar Assn., Fla. Bar Assn., N.Y. Bar Assn., Lee County Bar Assn. Roman Catholic. Avocations: reading, gardening, swimming. Alternative dispute resolution, Computer, General practice. Office: 2044 Bayside Pkwy Fort Myers FL 33901-3102

DALY, JOHN PAUL, lawyer; b. Pitts., Aug. 6, 1939; s. John Ambrose and Cora Evelyn (Faye) D.; m. Kathleen Ellen Paul, Dec. 21, 1961. AA, Chaffey Coll., Ontario, Calif., 1959; AB, U. Calif., Riverside, 1961; JD, Loyola U., L.A., 1971. Bar: Calif. 1972. Dep. dist. atty. San Luis Obispo, Calif., 1971-78, dep. county counsel, 1978—; judge pro tem Calif. Superior Ct., 1985—. Law prof. U. Calif. Polytech., 1979-81, lectr. Calif. Jud. Coll., 1982, post doctoral forensic psychiatry curriculum U. Calif., Atascadero State Hosp., 1987—, chmn., 1996-98; lectr. probate/med. health specialists County Counsel's Assn. Calif., 1980—; lectr. for profl. credentials cert. Calif. Assn. Pub. Adminstrs., Pub. Guardians, Pub. Conservators, 1991; resident jud. radio commentator KPRL, Paso Robles, 2002—. Speaker Mental Health Dept. Social Svcs., San Luis Obispo, 1975—. Mem. AMA, San Luis Obispo Govt. Attys. Union (founder, pres. 1977-82, chief negotiator 1977-79), San Luis Obispo County Irish Bar Assn. (founder, interlocutor 1987-97), Gold Wing Road Riders Assn. Home: 10650 Colorado Rd Atascadero CA 93422-5706 Office: County Counsel Govt Ctr San Luis Obispo CA 93408

DALY, JOSEPH LEO, law educator; b. Phila., July 31, 1942; s. Leo Vincent and Genevieve Delores (McGinnis) D.; m. Kathleen Ann Dolan, July 24, 1965; children: Michael, Colleen. BA, U. Minn., 1964; JD, William Mitchell Coll. Law, 1969. Bar: Minn. 1969, U.S. Dist. Ct. Minn. 1970, U.S. Supreme Ct. 1972, U.S. Ct. Appeals (8th cir.) 1973, U.S. Ct. Appeals (D.C. cir.) 1974; cert. mediator and arbitrator alternative dispute rev. bd. Minn. Supreme Ct. Ptnr. Franke & Daly, Mpls., 1969-74; prof. law Hamline U. Sch. Law, St. Paul, 1974—. Arbitrator Am. Arbitration Assn., N.Y.C., 1980—, U.S. Fed. Mediation and Conciliation Svc., Washington, 1988—, for the states of Minn., Hawaii, Idaho, Ind., Mass., Mich., N.D., Pa., Oreg., Wisc., V.I and City of L.A.; arbitrator Bur. Mediation Svcs., St. Paul, 1978—; vis. scholar Ctr. for Dispute Resolution, Willamette U., Salem, Oreg., 1985; facilitator Minn. Internat. Health Vols., Kenya, 1985; observer Philippine Constl. Conv., Manila, 1986; participant European Arab Arbitration Congress, Bahrain, 1987; human rights investigator in the Philippines, 1989; vis. scholar U. Oslo, 1990, 91, 92, 96, 97; lectr. on trial skills for human rights lawyers, The Philippines, 1989; lectr. to leaders at Site 2 Cambodian Refugee Camp, Thai/Cambodian border, 1989; lectr. U. Cluj-NAPACA, Romania, 1991; vis. lectr. for developing countries Internat. Bar Assn., 1991-92; lectr. U. Tirana, Albania, 1992, London, 1993, Nat. Econs. U., Hanoi, Vietnam, 1993, 94, Danang (Vietnam) Poly. U., 1993, Ho Chi Minh Econs. U., Saigon, Vietnam, 1993, U. Hanoi Law Sch., 1994, U. Modena, Italy, 1994, Hanoi, Danang and Saigon, 1995, Phnom Penh, Cambodia, 1995, Hong Kong, 1996, Shenzhen, China, 1996, Oslo, Norway, 1996, Karolinska Inst., Stockholm, 1997; vis. prof. So. Cross U., Lismore, Australia, 1998, 99, U. Bergen, Norway, 1999, Tongji U., Shanghai, China, 1999, U. Saigon, Vietnam, 1999, 2000; cons. Chua U., Tokyo, 2001; team leader UN Devel. Programme mid-term evaluation of UN project, Vietnam, Hanoi, 2001; vis. prof. U. Queensland, Brisbane, Australia, 2001, 02; Fulbright scholar U. Montevideo, Uruguay, 2002, 03. Co-author: The Law, the Student and the Catholic School, 1981; co-author, editor: The Student Lawyer: A High School Handbook of Minnesota Law, 1981, rev. edit., 1986, Strategies and Exercises in Law Related Education, 1981, International Law, 1993, The American Trial System, 1994; contbr. more than 50 articles to profl. jours. Mem. Minn. Legislature Task Force on Sexual Exploitation by Counselors and Therapists, St. Paul, 1984-85, Nat. Adv. Com. on Citizen Edn. in Law, 1982-85; bd. dirs. Scenic Am., Washington, 1989-92. Recipient Spurgeon award Mayor and Citizens of St. Paul and Indianhead Scouting, 1983; named a Leading Am. Atty. in Alternative Dispute Resolution: Employment Law; fellow U. Miss. Law Sch. Mem. ABA (contbg. editor Preview of U.S. Supreme Ct. Cases mag. 1984—), Internat. Bar Assn. (London, vis. lectr. for devel. countries 1991—), Minn. State Bar Assn., Minn. Lawyers Internat. (human rights com., rep. to Philippine Constl. Conv. 1986), St. Paul Athletic Club, Phi Alpha Delta. Avocations: jogging, sailing. Office: Hamline U Sch Law 1536 Hewitt Ave Saint Paul MN 55104-1205 E-mail: jdaly@gw.hamline.edu.

DALY, WILLIAM JOSEPH, lawyer; b. Bklyn., Mar. 19, 1928; s. William Bernard and Charlotte Marie (Saunders) D.; m. Barbara A. Longenecker, Nov. 19, 1955; children: Sharon, Nancy, Carol. BA, St. John's U., 1951, JD, 1953. Bar: N.Y. 1954, U.S. Dist. Ct. (so. and ea. dists.) N.Y. 1958, U.S. Ct. Mil. Appeals 1969, U.S. Ct. Claims 1969, U.S. Tax Ct. 1969, U.S. Supreme Ct. 1973. Assoc. Garvey & Conway, Esquires, N.Y.C., 1954-55, Wing & Wing, Esquires, N.Y.C., 1955-58; ptnr. Daly Lavery & Hall, Esquires and predecessors, Ossining, N.Y., 1958—. Adj. prof. law Mercy Coll., Dobbs Ferry, N.Y. V.p. Legal Aid Soc., Westchester County, N.Y., 1983—; mem. 9th Jud. Dist. Grievance Com., 1981-89, chmn. 1988-89; spl. referee in disciplinary procs.; trustee Supreme Ct. Libr. at White Plains, 1985—. With U.S. Army, 1946-48; ret. col. JA-AUS, 1978; mem. Hall of Fame U.S. Army Officer Cand. Sch., Ft. Benning, Ga. Fellow Am. Bar Found., N.Y. Bar Found.; mem. ABA, N.Y. State Bar Assn. (ho. of dels. 1977-89, 90-96, exec. com. 1983-89, 90-96, v.p. 1985-89, 90-96), Westchester County Bar Assn. (pres. 1979-81, dirs. coun. 1981—), Westchester County Bar Inst. (bd. dirs. 1982-98), Ossinging Bar Assn. (pres. 1966-67), ATLA, N.Y. State Trial Lawyers Assn., Res. Officers Assn. U.S., Skull and Circle, Phi Delta Phi. Roman Catholic. General practice, Personal injury (including property damage), Probate (including wills, trusts). Home: 232 Hunter Ave Sleepy Hollow NY 10591-1317 Office: 73 Croton Ave Ste 209 Ossining NY 10562-4971

DALZELL, STEWART, federal judge; b. Hackensack, N.J., Sept. 18, 1943; s. Stewart V. and Jeannette (Johnson) D.; m. Kathleen Regan, Mar. 28, 1981; children: Rebecca, Andrew. BS in Economics, U. Pa., 1965, JD, 1969. Bar: Pa. 1970, U.S. Dist. Ct. (ea. dist.) Pa. 1970, U.S. Ct. Appeals (11th cir.) 1979, U.S. Ct. Appeals (9th cir.) 1977, U.S. Ct. Appeals (Fed. cir.) 1983, U.S. Ct. Appeals (5th cir.) 1984, U.S. Ct. Appeals (2d cir.) 1986, U.S. Ct. Appeals (3d cir.) 1991, U.S. Supreme Ct. 1975. Fin. analyst NBC, N.Y.C., 1965-66; assoc. Drinker, Biddle & Reath, Phila., 1970-76, ptnr., 1976-91; judge U.S. Dist. Ct. (ea. dist.) Pa., 1991—. Vis. lectr. law Wharton Sch. U. Pa., 1969-70. Contbr. articles to law revs. and profl. jours. Recipient Speiser award. Mem. Beta Gamma Sigma. Episcopalian. Avocations: movies, music. Office: US Dist Cts US Courthouse Rm 10613 601 Market St Philadelphia PA 19106-1713

DALZIEL, CHARLES MEREDITH, JR., lawyer; m. Mary Elizabeth Smith, Feb. 25, 1984. BS cum laude, Ga. So. Coll., 1977; JD magna cum laude, U. Ga., 1980. Bar: Ga. 1980, U.S. Dist. Ct. (no. and mid. dists.) Ga. 1980, U.S. Ct. Appeals (11th cir.) 1980. Assoc. Kilpatrick & Cody, Atlanta, 1980-84, Savell, Williams, Cox & Angel, Atlanta, 1984-87; ptnr. Savell & Williams, Atlanta, 1987—2001, Brock & Clay, 2001—. Co-chmn. continuing legal edn. com. younger lawyers sect. State Bar of Ga. Mem. ABA, Atlanta Bar Assn., Nat. Assn. Securities Dealers (arbitrator), Lawyers Club of Atlanta. Federal civil litigation, State civil litigation, Professional liability. Office: Brock & Clay 49 Atlanta St Marietta GA 30060

DAMASHEK, PHILIP MICHAEL, lawyer; b. N.Y.C., May 18, 1940; s. Jacob and Esther (Sassower) D.; m. Judith Ellen Gold, Dec. 3, 1967; children: Alan S., Jonathan S., Harris R. BBA, U. Miami, 1964. Bar: N.Y. 1969, U.S. Dist. Ct. (so. and ea. dists.) N.Y. 1977. Lawyer Cosmopolitan Mut. Ins. Co., N.Y.C., 1969-70, Schneider, Kleinick, Weitz & Damashek, 1971-73; sr. ptnr. Philip M. Damashek, P.C., N.Y.C., 1974-89; ptnr. Damashek, Godosky & Gentile, 1989-94; mng. ptnr. Schneider, Kleinick, Weitz, Damashek & Shoot, 1994—2000, The Cochran Firm Schneider, Kleinick, Weitz, Damashek & Shoot, 2000—02, Schneider, Kleinick, Weitz & Damashek, 2002—. Chmn. Combined Bar Assns. Jud.Screening Panel, N.Y.C., 1983—88; co-chair NYSTLA Law Pac, 1997—, trustee, 1989—91; legis. appointment mem. Com. to Rev. Audio-Visual Coverage of Ct. Procs., 1993—94; exec. apptd. to govs. N.Y. Jud. Screening Com., 1997—; adv. bd. N.Y. Israel Econ. Devel. Partnership, 1997—; apptd. Com. on Case Mgmt. Office of Ct. Adminstrn., Cts. of State of N.Y., 1993—, Task Force on Reducing Litigation Cost and Delay, 1st Jud. Dist., 1996—, Differentiated Case Mgmt. Project, Kings County, 1996—, Alt. Dispute Resolution Adv. Com. N.Y. State Unified Ct. Sys., 1999—, N.Y. State Jud. Salary Commn., 1997—, N.Y. State CLE Bd., 1997—, charter bd. mem., 1997—2000; trustee N.Y. Law Sch., 1996—; NYSTLA designated ind. jud. screening panel N.Y. County Dem. Commn., 1991—; malpractice panel Supreme Ct. of the State of N.Y. , County of N.Y., 1990—91; dir. and v.p. for govt. rels. Respect for Law Alliance, Inc., 1995—; deptl. jud. screening com. Second Dept., 1997—; adv. com. on the jud. N.Y.C. Mayor, 2002—. Named Lawyer of Yr., Inst. Jewish Humanities, 1990, Lawyer of the Yr., UJA Fedn., 1993, N.Y. Law Schs. Lifetime Achievement award, 2000. Mem. ABA, Am. Bd. Trial Advs. (advocate), Am. Judicature Soc., Am. Bar Found., Assn. Trial Lawyers Am. (life, Wiedemann Wysocki citation of excellence 1990, bd. govs. 1990-92, state rels. com. 1990-92, no-fault coordinating com. 1990-92), N.Y. State Bar Assn. (ct. adminstrn. com., com. jud. adminstrn. 1990-94), Assn. of Bar of City of N.Y., N.Y. State Trial Lawyers Assn. (pres. 1990-91, bd. dirs., trustee, Ann. Philip M. Damashek Lifetime Achievement award 2003), Assn. Trial Lawyers City N.Y. (bd. dirs.), N.Y. County Lawyers Assn., Jewish Lawyers Guild (bd. govs.). State civil litigation, Personal injury (including property damage). Office: Schneider Kleinick Weitz & Damashek 233 Broadway Fl 5 New York NY 10279-0599

D'AMICO, ANDREW J. lawyer; b. Phila., Feb. 18, 1953; s. Joseph J. and Alice H. (Falotica) D'A.; m. Georgiana R. Etheridge, Feb. 25, 1978; children: Andrew J. Jr., Joseph W., Jennifer T., Theresa J. BA, St. Joseph's U., Phila., 1975; JD, Villanova U., 1978. Bar: Pa. Supreme Ct. 1978, U.S. Dist. Ct. (ea. dist.) Pa. 1979, U.S Ct. Appeals (3d Cir.) 1981, U.S Supreme Ct. 1982. Sole practitioner Law Offices Andrew J. D'Amico, Media, Pa., 1979—. Coach Llanerch Hills Little League, Drexel Hill, Pa., 1986-96, St. Bernadette CYO Basketball, 1996-2000. Mem.: ATLA, Guy G. deFuria Am. Inn of Ct., Delaware County Bar Assn. (bd. dirs. 1991—92, chmn. ADR com. 1996—, bd. dirs. 1997—98, chmn. civil trial practice com. 2001), Pa. Trial Lawyers Assn., Alpha Sigma Nu. Roman Catholic. Avocations: music, coaching sports, reading. General civil litigation, Personal injury (including property damage), Property, real (including real estate development, water). Office: PO Box 605 115 N Monroe St Media PA 19063-3037

DAMICO, NICHOLAS PETER, lawyer; b. Chester, Pa., June 29, 1937; s. Ralph A. and Mary C. (Ametrane) D.; m. Patricia Ann Swatek, Aug. 26, 1967; children: Christine, Gregory. BS in Acctg., St. Joseph's U., 1960; LLB, U. Pa., 1963; LLM, Georgetown U., 1967. Bar: Pa. 1963, D.C. 1967, Md. 1986. Tax law specialist IRS, Washington, 1963-66; assoc. Silverstein & Mullens, Washington, 1966-72, ptnr., 1972-76; prin. Damico & Assocs.,

Washington, 1976—. Adj. prof. Georgetown U. Law Ctr., Washington, 1973-75. Mem. ABA. Estate planning, Pension, profit-sharing, and employee benefits, Probate (including wills, trusts). Office: 1101 17th St NW Ste 820 Washington DC 20036-4731

DAMICO, PAUL ANTHONY, lawyer, educator; b. Rockville Centre, N.Y., July 3, 1960; s. Anthony and Connie Ida Damico; m. Jennifer Lynn Damico, Sept. 26, 1992; children: Alec Anthony, Kyle James. BS, Fla. State U., 1983, JD, 1986. Bar: Fla. 1983, U.S. Ct. Appeals (11th cir.), U.S. Ct. Appeals (D.C. cir.), U.S. Dist. Ct. (so., mid. and no. dists.) Fla., U.S. Supreme Ct.; bd. cert. in criminal trial. Atty. Palm Beach County State Atty.'s Office, West Palm Beach, Fla., 1986—2001; chief asst. Palm Beach County Pub. Defender's Office, 1996—2001; cty. criminal ct. judge, 2001—. Adj. prof. legal studies Barry U., 1991—; bd. dirs. Weed/Seed Orgn., West Palm Beach, Cmty. Ct. Task Force, West Palm Beach, Anti-Drug Grant Com. Mem. Republican Exec. Com., West Palm Beach, 1998—, asst. vice chmn. campaign endorsement committeeman dist. 6; bd. dirs. 2001—, re-elected rep. com. dist. 6, Lake Worth Criminal Justice Acad., 1998—. Mem. Kiwanis (pres.-elect Ctrl. Palm Beach County 1998, pres. 1999, Pres. award 1991), Masons. Christian. Avocations: scuba diving, golf. Office: WPB Courthouse 205 N Dixie Hwy West Palm Beach FL 33401

DAMOOSE, GEORGE LYNN, lawyer; b. Grand Rapids, Mich., Feb. 2, 1938; s. George G. and Geneva J. (Joseph) D.; m. Carol Sweeney, Dec. 7, 1968; children: Alison Dana, George Christopher. AB cum laude, Harvard U., 1959, JD cum laude, 1965. Bar: Calif. 1966, U.S. Tax Ct., 1973. Assoc. O'Melveny and Myers, L.A., 1965-72; ptnr. Jennings, Engstrand, Henrikson, P.C., San Diego, 1972-76, Procopio, Cory, Hargreaves, and Savitch, San Diego, 1976—. Bd. dirs. San Diego Civic Light Opera Assn., 1984-90, 92; trustee The Bishops Sch., LaJolla, 1987-90, La Jolla Chamber Music Soc., 1988-89; commr. San Diego Crime Commn., 1987-90. Served to lt. (j.g.) USN, 1959-62. Mem. Am. Bar Found., San Diego County Bar Assn. (chmn. tax sect. 1974-75, 86-87), Calif. Bar Assn. (ind. inquiry and rev. panel, program for certifying legal specialists 1986-87), State Bar Calif. (exec. com., taxation sect. 1990-95, chair 1994-95, chair CEB joint adv. com. taxation 1996-98), San Diego C. of C. (bd. dirs. 1994-96), La Jolla Country Club, La Jolla Beach and Tennis Club. Republican. Episcopalian. Avocations: tennis, music, reading, golf. Home: 208 Avenida Cortez La Jolla CA 92037-6502 Office: Procopio Cory et al 530 B St Ste 2100 San Diego CA 92101-4496

DAMPEER, JOHN LYELL, retired lawyer; b. Cleve., June 3, 1916; s. James W. and Felicia (Gressitt) D.; m. Lucie Augustin Kennerdell, June 30, 1950 (dec. July 1990); children: Lyell B., David K., G. Geoffrey. S.B., Harvard U., 1938, LL.B., 1942; student, New Coll., Oxford (Eng.) U., 1938-39. Bar: Ohio 1946. Practiced in, Cleve.; ptnr. Thompson Hine LLP, Cleve., 1955—97; ret., 1997. Trustee Family Svc. Assn. Cleve., 1951-70; trustee, chmn. bd. trustees Kelvin and Eleanor Smith Found., 1984-96; trustee, treas. Sea Rsch. Found., 1984-96. Henry fellow, 1938-39 Mem. ABA, Ohio Bar Assn. (chmn. corp. law com. 1960-62), Greater Cleve. Bar Assn. (exec. com. 1958-61), Phi Beta Kappa. Clubs: Union (Cleve.), Kirtland Country (Cleve.). Corporate, general, Non-profit and tax-exempt organizations, Securities. Home: 44 Laurel Lake Dr Hudson OH 44236-2159 Office: Thompson Hine LLP 3900 Key Ctr 127 Public Sq Cleveland OH 44114-1216

DAMSEL, CHARLES H., JR., lawyer; b. Columbus, Ohio, Apr. 30, 1929; s. Charles H. and Dorothy Mae (Carter) D.; m. Margaret W. Damsel, Aug. 25, 1951; children— Charles H. III, Cherie Damsel Boone. B.S. in Bus. Adminstrn., U. Fla., 1950, J.D., 1956. Bar: Fla. 1956, U.S. Dist. Ct. Fla. 1956, U.S. Ct. Appeals (5th cir.) 1958, U.S. Supreme Ct. 1969, U.S. Ct. Appeals (11th cir.) 1981; cert. civil trial lawyer Fla., adv. Nat. Bd. Trial Advocacy, civil mediator Fla. Supreme Ct. Assoc. Gurney, McDonald & Handly, Orlando, Fla., 1956-58; mem. Jones & Foster, P.A., West Palm Beach, Fla., 1958-86, Damsel & Gelston, P.A., 1987-98; sole practitioner, 1999—. Contbr. articles to legal jours. Served with U.S. Army, 1951-53. Diplomate Am. Bd. Trial Advs., Nat. Bd. Trial Advocacy. Mem. Palm Beach County Bar Assn. (pres. 1971), Palm Beach County Trial Lawyers Assn., Am. Trial Lawyers Assn., Fla. Def. Lawyers Assn. (pres. 1976-77), Fed. Bar Assn. (pres. local chpt. 1977), Fla. Bar (bd. of legal specialization; exec. council trial lawyers sect.), ABA, Fedn. Ins. Counsel (v.p. 1978-79), Def. Research Inst. (area chmn.), Am. Arbitration Assn., Palm Beach County Econ. Council, Fla. Blue Key (pres. 1954), Masons, Phi Delta Phi, Alpha Kappa Psi, Alpha Phi Omega, Pi Epsilon Delta, Kappa Sigma. Republican. Presbyterian (ruling elder United Presbyn. Ch.). Federal civil litigation, General civil litigation, Product liability. Office: 601B N Dixie Hwy West Palm Beach FL 33401-3913 E-mail: cdamsel@aol.com.

DAMSGAARD, KELL MARSH, lawyer; b. Darby, Pa., May 16, 1949; s. Kjeld and Dorothy (Fanck) D.; m. Katherine Elizabeth Stark, June 17, 1972; children: Peter Kjeld, Christopher William, David Zentner. BA cum laude, Yale U., 1971; JD, U. Pa., 1974. Bar: Pa. 1974, U.S. Dist. Ct. (ea. dist.) Pa. 1975, U.S. Ct. Appeals (3d cir.) 1984, U.S. Ct. Appeals (D.C. cir.) 1989, U.S. Ct. Appeals (8th cir.) 1990, U.S. Ct. Appeals (10th cir.), 1991, U.S. Supreme Ct. 1991. Law clk. to judge Superior Ct. of Pa., Phila., 1974-75; assoc. Morgan, Lewis & Bockius LLP, Phila., 1975-81; ptnr. Morgan, Lewis & Bockius, Phila., 1981—, firm adminstrv. ptnr., 1996—. Fellow Am. Coll. Trial Lawyers; mem. ABA, Phila. Bar Assn. Avocations: skiing, jogging, tennis, antiques. General civil litigation, Computer, Product liability. Home: PO Box 141 Birchrunville PA 19421-0141 Office: Morgan Lewis & Bockius LLP 1701 Market St Philadelphia PA 19103-2903 E-mail: kdamsgaard@morganlewis.com.

DAMSTRA, DANIEL LOUIS, lawyer; b. N.Y.C., Jan. 22, 1964; s. David Arthur and Evelyn Rogers Damstra; m. Ingeborg Krompholz, Oct. 12, 1991; children: John, Conrad, Ella. AB, Williams Coll., Williamstown, Mass., 1986; MBA, NYU, 1989; JD, Rutgers U., Newark, 1992. Bar: N.Y. 1993, N.J. 1992, Pa. 1993. Acct. Arthur Young & Co., N.Y.C., 1986—88; law clk. Ernst & Young, N.Y.C., 1990—91; assoc. Dechert Price & Rhoads, N.Y.C. and Phila., 1992—96, Pepper Hamilton LLP, Berwyn, Pa., 1996—2001, ptnr., 2002—. Mem.: ABA, Chester County Bar Assn., Phila. Bar Assn. Mergers and acquisitions, Corporate, general, Securities. Office: Pepper Hamilton LLP 400 Berwyn Pk 899 Cassatt Rd Berwyn PA 19312

DANA, HOWARD H., JR., state supreme court justice; Assoc. justice Supreme Jud. Ct. of Maine, Portland, 1993—. Office: Cumberland County Courthouse PO Box 368 142 Federal St Portland ME 04112-0368

DANA, LAUREN ELIZABETH, lawyer; b. Hollywood, Calif., Sept. 30, 1950; d. Franklin Eugene and Margaret Elizabeth (Nixon) D.; m. Andrew Russell Willing, May 25, 1986; 1 child, Matthew Barkan Willing. BA cum laude, Calif. State U., Northridge, 1973; JD cum laude, Southwestern U., 1982. Bar: Calif. 1982, U.S. Dist. Ct. (cen. dist.) Calif. 1983, U.S. Ct. Appeals (9th cir.) 1983, U.S. Supreme Ct. 1987. Assoc. Law Office Andrew R. Willing, L.A., 1982-84; dep. atty. gen. Calif. Dept. Justice-Atty. Gen., L.A., 1984—. Temporary judge L.A. Mcpl. Ct. Assoc. editor legal update Police Officer Law Report, 1986-87. Recipient Am. Jurisprudence Book award Lawyers Coop. Pub. Co., 1980, Am. Jurisprudence Book award in Evidence, 1980. Mem.: ABA, Los Angeles County Bar Assn. (conf. of dels. 1998—), L.A. World Affairs Coun., Women Lawyers Assn. L.A., U.S. Supreme Ct. Hist. Soc., Selden Soc., Constnl. Rights Found., Am. Judicature Soc., Alliance for Children's Rights, Women of Pasadena, The Da Camera Soc., Town Hall, Phi Alpha Delta. Avocations: reading, music, collecting books on english history, travel, french, nutrition. Office: Calif Dept Justice 300 S Spring St Los Angeles CA 90013-1230

DANAHER, JOHN ANTHONY, III, prosecutor; b. New Haven, Conn., Aug. 22, 1950; s. John Anthony Jr. and Grace Elizabeth (Burkett) D.; m. Anne Elizabeth Morrison, May 11, 1985; children: Ceara Morrison Danaher, Brendan Ahearn, Austin Spellman, Mary Kate Shea. Awd, Fairfield U., 1972; MA, U. Hartford, 1977; JD, U. Conn., 1980. Bar: Conn. 1980; U.S. Dist. Ct. Conn. 1980; U.S. Ct. Appeals (2d cir.) 1982; U.S. Supreme Ct. 1987. Law clk. to hon. judge T. Emmet Clarie U.S. Dist. Ct. Conn., Hartford, Conn., 1980-81; trial atty. Day, Berry & Howard, Hartford, Conn., 1981-86; prosecutor U.S. Atty.'s Office, Hartford, Conn., 1986—; former U.S. atty. U.S. Atty.'s Office Ct. Dist. Editor Conn. Law Rev. 1978-80. Mem. Red Cross blood svcs. com., Hartford, 1981-85; active Long Rivers Coun., Boy Scouts Am., 1994—. Recipient Disting. Svc. award Atty. Gen. of U.S., Washington, 1990; 10 Superior Achievement awards Dept. of Justice, Hartford, 1988, 90-97. Mem. Fed. Bar Assn. (pres. Hartford County chpt. 1985-86). Office: US Attys Office Ct Fin Ctr 157 Church St PO Box 1824 New Haven CT 06508*

DANAS, ANDREW MICHAEL, lawyer; b. Redwood City, Calif., Apr. 25, 1955; s. Michael George and Marjorie Jean (Bailey) D.; m. Barbara C. Matthews. BA in Polit. Sci. and History, U. Conn., 1977; JD, George Washington U., 1982. Bar: D.C. 1982, U.S. Dist. Ct. (D.C. cir.) 1985, U.S. Dist. Ct. Md. 1987, U.S. Ct. Appeals (Fed. cir. 1984), U.S. Ct. Appeals (11th cir. 1987), U.S. Ct. Appeals (3d and 4th cirs.) 1988, U.S. Ct. Appeals (6th cir.) 1990, U.S. Ct. Appeals (2d cir.) 1998, U.S. Ct. of Claims 1984, U.S. Supreme Ct. 1994. Atty. Assn. Am. R.R.s, Washington, 1983-84; assoc. Grove Jaskiewicz & Cobert, Washington, 1984-90, Ptnr., 1991—. Contbg. author: Freewheeling; author legal column Intermodal Reporter, 1986-94; contbr. articles to profl. jours. Exec. com. Friends Assisting the Nat. Symphony, Washington, 1996-97. Mem.: ABA, Transp. Lawyers Assn. (chmn. legis. com. 1995—98, co-chmn. 1999—2001, Disting. Svc. award 1996), Transp. Law Inst. (chair 1993—94), Euro-Am. Lawyers Group (mgmt. com. 2000—, sec. 2002—), Internat. Bar Assn., Mensa, Univ. Club (Washington), Phi Alpha Theta. Avocations: skiing, music, travel. Administrative and regulatory, Federal civil litigation, Private international. Home: 621 Tivoli Psge Alexandria VA 22314-1932 Office: Grove Jaskiewicz and Cobert 1730 M St NW Ste 400 Washington DC 20036-4579

DANE, STEPHEN MARK, lawyer; b. Chillicothe, Ohio, Mar. 27, 1956; s. Clyde and Rita M. (Murray) D.; m. Kim P. Piatt, July 7, 1979; children: Tara, Adam, Shannon, Alexandra, Courtney. BS with honors, U. Notre Dame, 1978; JD magna cum laude, U. Toledo, 1981. Bar: Ohio 1981, U.S. Ct. Appeals (6th and 10th cirs.) 1982, U.S. Dist. Ct. (no. dist.) Ohio 1983, U.S. Dist. Ct. (no. dist.) Tex. 1983, U.S. Ct. Appeals (5th cir.) 1984, U.S. Supreme Ct. 1985, U.S. Ct. Appeals (7th cir.) 1993. Law clk. U.S. Ct. Appeals (6th cir.), Cin., 1981-82; ptnr. Cooper & Walinski , Toledo, 1986—. Judge pro tempore Perrysburg Mcpl. Ct., 1990—. Recipient Fair Housing award HUD, 1996, Spirit of Wood County award, 1988, Pub. Interest Law award Equal Access to Justice Com., 2000, Fair Housing award Oho Civil Rights Comm. 2001; named Lawyer of Yr. Lawyers Weekly, 1998; named to St. John's Jesuit H.S. Hall of Fame, 1991. Mem. ABA, Ohio State Bar Assn., Toledo Bar Assn. (chmn. fed. ct. com. 1987-89, trustee 2001--), Wood County Bar Assn.. Roman Catholic. Civil rights, Federal civil litigation, Labor (including EEOC, Fair Labor Standards Act, labor-management relations, NLRB, OSHA). Home: 501 Hickory St Perrysburg OH 43551-2206 Office: Cooper & Walinski 900 Adams St Toledo OH 43624-1505

DANG, MARVIN S. C. lawyer; b. Honolulu, 1954; s. Brian K.T. and Flora Dang. BA with distinction, U. Hawaii, 1974; JD, George Washington U., 1978. Bar: Hawaii 1978, U.S. Dist. Ct. Hawaii 1978, U.S. Ct. Appeals (9th cir.) 1979. Atty. Gerson, Steiner & Anderson and predecessor firms, Honolulu, 1978-81; owner, atty. Law Offices of Marvin S.C. Dang, Honolulu, 1981—. Sr. v.p., bd. dirs. Rainbow Fin. Corp., Honolulu, 1984-95; bd. dirs. Foster Equipment Co. Ltd., Honolulu, 1986—, Hawaii Cmty. Reinvestment Corp., 1994-96; vice chmn. Hawaii Consumer Fin. Polit. Action Com., 1988-95, sec./treas., 1999—; hearings officer (per diem) Adminstrv. Drivers License Revocation Office, Honolulu, 1991-95. State rep., asst. minority floor leader Hawaii State Legislature, Honolulu, 1982-84; chmn., vice chmn., mem. Manoa Neighborhood Bd., Honolulu, 1979-82, 84-87; pres., v.p., mem. Hawaii Coun. on Legal Edn. for Youth, Honolulu, 1979-86; mem. Hawaii Bicentennial Commn. of U.S. Constn., Honolulu, 1986-88. Recipient Cert. of Appreciation award Hawaii Speech-Lang.-Hearing Assn., Honolulu, 1984; named one of Ten Outstanding Young Persons of Hawaii, Hawaii State Jaycees, 1983. Mem. ABA (standing com. on group and prepaid legal svcs. 2000—, coun. of fund for justice and edn. 1993-99, standing com. on law and electoral process 1985-89, spl. com. on youth edn. for citizenship 1979-85, 89-92, Hawaii membership chmn. 1981-93, exec. coun. young lawyers divsn. 1986-88), Hawaii State Bar Assn. (chair collection law sec. 1999—, bd. dirs. young lawyers divsn. 1990), Am. Prepaid Legal Svcs. Inst. (bd. dirs. 2000—), Hawaii Fin. Svcs. Assn. (sec. 1991, 2002—, treas. 1992, v.p. 1993, prs. 1994, lobbyist 1996—). Avocations: family, law, politics. Commercial, consumer (including collections, credit), Probate (including wills, trusts), Property, real (including real estate development, water). Office: PO Box 4109 Honolulu HI 96812-4109 E-mail: dangm@aloha.net.

D'ANGELO, GEORGE A. lawyer; b. Phila., Dec. 7, 1926; s. Dominic S. and Lillian (Alessi) D'A.; children: Marc Scott, Christopher Scott, David Steven, Victoria Scott. BA, U. Pa., 1947, LLB, 1950. Bar: Pa. 1950. Sr. ptnr. D'Angelo and Eurell, Phila., 1970—; mem. faculty Temple U. Law Sch., 1954-69. Pres., Phila. Art Alliance, Ch. Club of Phila., Episcopal Diocese of Pa. Mem. Phila. Bar Assn., ABA, Pa. Bar Assn. Clubs: Rittenhouse, Phila. Club, Phila. Lawyers (dir. 1982—), Merion Cricket. Federal civil litigation, Personal injury (including property damage), Probate (including wills, trusts). Office: D'Angelo & Eurell Land Title Bldg 22d Floor Philadelphia PA 19110

D'ANGELO, ROBERT WILLIAM, lawyer; b. Buffalo, Nov. 10, 1932; s. Samuel and Margaret Theresa Guercio D'A.; m. Ellen Frances Neary, Sept. 17, 1959; children: Christopher Robert, Gregory Andrew. BBA, Loyola U. Los Angeles, 1954; JD, UCLA, 1960. Bar: Calif. 1960; cert. specialist taxation law. Practiced in L.A., 1960-89; mem. firm. Myers & D'Angelo, Pasadena, Calif., 1967—. Adj. prof. law, taxation Whittier Coll. Sch. of Law., 1981 Served to capt. USAF, 1954-57. Mem. ABA, AICPA, State Bar Calif., L.A. County Bar Assn., Wilshire Bar Assn., Pasadena Bar Assn., Calif. Soc. CPAs, Am. Assn. Atty. CPAs, Calif. Assn. Atty. CPAs (pres. 1980), Phi Delta Phi, Alpha Sigma Nu. Estate planning, Probate (including wills, trusts), Taxation, general. Home: 1706 Highland Ave Glendale CA 91202-1265 Office: 301 N Lake Ave Ste 800 Pasadena CA 91101-4108 E-mail: m-dlaw@pacbell.net.

D'ANGELO-MAYER, IDA, lawyer; b. Long Island City, N.Y., Aug. 22, 1967; d. Fileno Domenico and Nicoletta D'Angelo; m. Robert Michael Mayer, May 6, 1995; children: Robert Mayer, Ariana Nicole Mayer. BS, Fordham U. at Lincoln Ctr, 1988; JD, St. John's U., Jamaica, N.Y., 1992. Bar: N.Y. 1992, N.J. 1993, U.S. Dist. Ct. (ea. and so. dists.) N.Y. 1993. Assoc. atty. Law Offices of Peter T. Roach, Westbury, N.Y., 1992-94, Ida D'Angelo & Assocs., P.C., Melville, NY, 1994—. Mem. ABA, N.Y. State Bar Assn., Suffolk County Bar Assn. Property, real (including real estate development, water). Office: 555 Broadhollow Rd Melville NY 11747-5078

DANIEL, J. REESE, lawyer; b. Sanford, N.C., Dec. 24, 1924; AB, U. S.C., 1949, JD cum laude, 1956. Bar: S.C. 1955, U.S. Dist. Ct. S.C. 1956, U.S. Tax Ct. 1959, U.S. Ct. Appeals (4th cir.) 1959. Sr. ptnr. Daniel & Daniel, Litchfield, S.C. Mem. S.C. Supreme Ct. Bd. Commrs. on Grievances and Discipline, 1970-73, Columbia Zoning Bd. of Adjustment, 1970-79. Contbg. author 7 South Carolina Law Quarterly; contbr. articles to profl. jours. With USNR, 1943-46. Mem. ABA, S.C. Bar Assn. (assoc. editor S.C. Bar Assn. News Bull. 1957, editor 1958-59), Phi Delta Phi. General civil litigation, Personal injury (including property damage), Probate (including wills, trusts). Office: Daniel & Daniel PO Box 857 10B Pawleys Sta Hwy 17 S Pawleys Island SC 29585 E-mail: reesedaniel@email.msn.com.

DANIEL, JAMES EDWARD, lawyer; b. Danville, Va., Dec. 27, 1955; s. Edward Hudson and Betty Jean (Riddle); m. Patricia Ann Anderson, June 21, 1980; children: William Thomas, Margaret Rose, Katharine Elisabeth. BS, U. N.C., 1978; MBA, Emory U., 1979, JD, 1982. Bar: N.C. 1982, U.S. Dist. Ct. (mid. dist.) N.C. 1983, U.S. Dist. Ct. (we. dist.) 1996. Ptnr. Womble Carlyle Sandridge & Rice, Winston-Salem, Charlotte, N.C., 1982—. Mem. ABA (employee benefits com. tax sect., employee benefits and exec. compensation com. bus. sect.), N.C. Bar Assn., Order of Coif, Phi Beta Kappa, Beta Gamma Sigma, Phi Eta Sigma. Pension, profit-sharing, and employee benefits. Office: Womble Carlyle Sandridge & Rice 3300 One Wachovia Ctr 301 S College St Ste 3300 Charlotte NC 28202-6025

DANIEL, LANCE, lawyer; b. St. Louis, Sept. 12, 1960; s. Robert Edward and Arlene Franklin Leber. BSBA, San Diego State U., 1985; JD, U. of the Pacific, 1988. Bar: Calif. 1989. Dep. dist. atty. Dist. Attys. Office, Sacramento, 1989; assoc. David Allen & Assocs., Sacramento, 1989-91; pvt. practice law Sacramento, 1991—. Instr. paralegal studies Humphrey's Coll., Sacramento, 1996-99; bd. dirs. Chai Found., Phoenix; judge pro-tem sml. claims and traffic court. Mem. State Bar Calif., Inns of Ct. (barrister). Avocations: collecting fountain pens, autographs, antique watches. General civil litigation, Criminal, Personal injury (including property damage). Office: 1028 2nd St 3rd Fl Sacramento CA 95814-3235 E-mail: deucedefender@aol.com.

DANIEL, ROBERT MICHAEL, lawyer; b. Rocky Mount, NC, Aug. 21, 1947; s. Harvey Derby and Edna Lois (McCullen) D.; m. Kaye Ruth Coates, Aug. 31, 1968; children: Robert M. Jr., John Matthew. AB in Econs., U. N.C., 1968, JD, 1971. Bar: N.C. 1971, Pa. 1976; U.S. Dist. Ct. (we. dist.) Pa. 1976; U.S. Tax Ct. 1979. Judge adv. U.S. Marine Corps., 1971-74; ptnr. Smith & Daniel, Pittsboro, N.C., 1974-75; trust officer Mellon Bank, N.A., Pitts., 1975-78; assoc. Buchanan Ingersoll, Pitts., 1978-82, ptnr., 1982—2001; dir. Cohen & Grigsby PC, Pitts., 2002—. Bd. dirs. Cohen & Grigsby, Pitts., 2002. Pres. Greater Pitts. coun. Boy Scouts Am., 1996-99, bd. dirs. N.E. region. Col. USMCR, 1966-98, ret. Fellow Am. Coll. Trust and Estate Coun.; mem. Pa. Bar Assn. (past chmn. real property, probate and trust law sect. 1998-99), Duquesne Club. Presbyterian. Avocations: travel, reading military history. Estate planning, Probate (including wills, trusts), Estate taxation. Home: 1491 Redfern Dr Pittsburgh PA 15241-2956 Office: Cohen & Grigsby PC 11 Stanwix St 15th Flr Pittsburgh PA 15222-1319

DANIEL, ROYAL THOMAS, III, lawyer, engineer, accountant; b. Portsmouth, Va., July 30, 1956; s. Royal Thomas Daniel, Jr. and Lillian Martha (Ellis) Daniel; m. Holly Ann Walsh, Oct. 30, 1993; children: Andrew Joseph, Royal Thomas IV, James David. BS in Nuclear Engring., N.C. State U., 1978, MS in Indsl. Mgmt., 1980; MS in Acctg., Bentley Coll., 1985, MS in Computer Info. Systems, 1986; JD, Suffolk U., 1990. Bar: N.C. 1991, Mass. 1991, D.C. 1992, N.Y. 2003, N.J. 2003, U.S. Tax Ct. 1993; registered profl. mech. and indsl. engr., Mass., N.C.; CPA, Md., N.C.; cogeneration profl. Assn. Energy Engrs. Sr. proposal engr. Combustion Engring. Power Systems, Inc., Windsor, Conn., 1979-80; coordinating specialist Boston Edison Co., 1980-85, power supply coord., 1985-92; prin. Daniel Law Offices, P.A., Raleigh, N.C., 1992-94; v.p. PSEG Asia, Ltd., Hong Kong, 1994—2000; bd. dirs., v.p. Meiya Power Co. Ltd., Hong Kong, 1995-98, 2002—; pres., bd. dirs. Energy Infrastructure Devel., Bangkok, 1998-2000; vice chmn. ops. and fin. Sri U-Thong, Bangkok, 1998-2000; corp. devel. PSEG Global Inc., NJ, 2000—01, U.S. bus. mgr., 2001—. Contbr. chapters to books. Mem. NSPE, ABA, Am. Inst. Certification of Computer Profls., Am. Arbitration Assn. (panel arbitrators), Nat. Assn. Accts. (cert. Inst. Cert. Mgmt. Accts.), N.C. Assn. CPA's, N.C. Bar Assn., D.C. Bar Assn., Inst. Cert. Computer Profls. (cert. data processor, systems profl.), Rotary, Order St. Patrick, Phi Delta Phi, Tau Beta Pi. Baptist. Construction, Corporate, general. Home: 333 Boulevard Mountain Lakes NJ 07046-1517 E-mail: royal_daniel@hotmail.com.

DANIEL, WILLIAM LARUE, II, lawyer; b. Louisville, Ky., July 11, 1968; s. William LaRue and Mary Lois Daniel; m. Karen Elaine Ball, Apr. 24, 1999. BA, Centre Coll., 1991; JD, Univ. Louisville, 1995; MBA, Duke U., 2002. Bar: Ky. 1995, U.S. Dist. Ct. (ea. dist.) Ky. 1997, U.S. Dist. Ct. (we. dist.) Ky. 1997, U.S. Dist. Ct. (no. dist.) Ind. 2003, U.S. Ct. Appeals (6th cir.) 1997, U.S. Supreme Ct. 1999. Assoc. Sheffer, Hoffman, Louisville, 1995—96; asst. atty. gen. Office of the Atty. Gen., Commonwealth of Ky., Frankfort, 1997—2003; gen. counsel Davis Electronics, Louisville, 2003—. Editor (co-author): (legal manual) Post Conviction Manual. Commr. City of Moorland, Ky., 2000—03; mem. Leadership Ky., Frankfort, 2000—02; del. Am.-German Young Leaders Conf., 2003. Mem.: ABA, Louisville Bar Assn., Ky. Bar Assn. Methodist. Avocations: travel, sports, reading. Appellate, Corporate, general, Communications. Home: 1802 Ashmoor Ln Louisville KY 40223 Office: Davis Electronics 2211 Brownsboro Rd Louisville KY 40206 Office Fax: 502-897-6093. Personal E-mail: willlarue@earthlink.net. E-mail: bdaniel@twoway.com.

DANIELS, BRUCE JOEL, lawyer; b. Denver, Apr. 16, 1935; s. Daniel Lester and Lillian Daniels; children: Julia K., Marya L., Jade A., Gregory R.S., Brenna J. AB, Ohio State U., 1957; JD, U. Mich., 1961. Bar: Fla. 1961, U.S. Dist. Ct. (middle dist.) Fla. 1962, U.S. Dist. Ct. (so. dist.) Fla. 1988. Pvt. practice, Fla., 1961—, 1987—. Co-author: (book) Eminent Domain, 1971. Mem.: AARP (regional advocacy team leader). Probate (including wills, trusts), Property, real (including real estate development, water). Home: 336 Golfview Rd Apt 1018 North Palm Beach FL 33408-3513 Office: PO Box 14806 North Palm Beach FL 33408-0806 E-mail: brucedan@juno.com.

DANIELS, JAMES WALTER, lawyer; b. Chgo., Oct. 13, 1945; s. Ben George and Delores L. (Wolanin) D.; m. Gail Anne Rihacek, June 14, 1969; children: Morgan, Abigail, Rachel. AB, Brown U., 1967; JD, U. Chgo., 1970. Bar: Calif. 1970, U.S. Dist. Ct. (ctrl. dist.) Calif. 1970, U.S. Tax Ct., 1972, U.S. Supreme Ct. 1979. Assoc. firm Latham & Watkins, L.A. and Newport Beach, Calif., 1970-77, ptnr., 1977—2003. Arbitrator Orange County Superior Ct., Santa Ana, Calif., 1978-88, judge pro tem, 1979-87. Fin. dir. St. Elizabeth Ann Seton Parish, Irvine, Calif., 1975-82; sec. Turtlerock Tennis Com., Irvine, 1981-83, 86—, pres., 1985-86; bd. dirs. Turtlerock Terr. Homeowners Assn., 1983-85, 87-89. Mem. ABA, Internat. Coun. Shopping Ctrs., Center club, Irvine Racquet Club, Palm Valley Country Club. Democrat. Roman Catholic. Corporate, general, Landlord-tenant, Property, real (including real estate development, water). Home: 19241 Beckwith Ter Irvine CA 92612-3503 Office: Latham & Watkins 650 Town Center Dr Ste 2000 Costa Mesa CA 92626-7135

DANIELS, JOHN DRAPER, lawyer; b. Bklyn., Feb. 11, 1939; s. Draper L. and Louise Parker-Lux (Cort) D.; m. Sara Josephine Sears, Dec. 27, 1962; children: Stephen Draper, Elizabeth Marie, Rebecca Cort. AB, Princeton U., 1961; JD, U. Chgo., 1964. Bar: Ill. 1964, U.S. Dist. Ct. (no. dist.) Ill. 1967. Assoc. Jacobs & McKenna, Chgo., 1964-70, Law Offices Dale L. Schlafer, Chgo., 1970-73; assoc. then ptnr. Jacobs, Williams & Montgomery, Chgo., 1973-87; ptnr. Sanchez & Daniels, Chgo., 1987—. Arbitrator Cir. Ct. of Cook County. Mem. admissions screening panel Princeton Alumni Coun. Capt. U.S. Army, 1964-66. Mem. ABA, Ill. Bar Assn. (chmn. ins. sect. coun. 1985), Chgo. Bar Assn., Am. Arbitration Assn.

(arbitrator 1977—), Internat. Assn. Def. Counsel, Soc. Trial Lawyers (bd. dirs. 1990, '92), Am. Bd. Trial Advs., Ill. Assn. Defense Trial Counsel, Trial Lawyers Club of Chgo., Tower of Chgo. Club (bd. trustees. 1985-87), East Bank Club. Roman Catholic. Avocations: guitar, musical composition, tennis, fishing, golf. General civil litigation, Insurance, Personal injury (including property damage). Home: 1611 Wilmette Ave Wilmette IL 60091-2424 Office: Sanchez & Daniels 333 W Wacker Dr Chicago IL 60606-1220 E-mail: jdaniels@sanchezdaniels.com.

DANIELS, JOHN HILL, lawyer; b. Albany, N.Y., Oct. 17, 1928; s. David Samuel and Sadie (Davidson) D.; m. Helen R. Marcus, May 24, 1952; children: Marc, Scott, Seth. Grad., L.I. U., 1949; LLB, Bklyn. Law Sch., 1952; LLM, NYU, 1958. Bar: N.Y. 1954, U.S. Dist. Ct. (ea. and so. dists.) N.Y. 1954, U.S. Supreme Ct. 1958. Assoc. Friedman & Friedman, Bklyn., 1954, Finkelstein, Benton & Soll, N.Y.C., 1955-58, Levy & Kornblum, Bklyn., 1959; ptnr. Kamen & Daniels, Bklyn., 1959-61; sr. ptnr. Different people & Different Firm, Law offices of John H. Daniels & Marc A. Daniels, Mineola, N.Y., 1983—; sole practice Roosevelt, N.Y., 1960-88, Mineola, 1975—. Lectr. in field. Candidate for judge Nassau County Dist. Ct., Mineola, 1960-63; bd. dirs. Mental Health and Alcohol, Roosevelt, 1980-92; past pres. Civic Assn. of Woodbury. Sgt. U.S. Army, 1952-54. Mem. N.Y. State Bar Assn., Nassau County Bar Assn., Nassau Lawyers Assn. L.I. (dir. 1970—, pres. 1984), Jewish Lawyers Assn. Nassau County (bd. dirs. 1964—, pres. 1985-86), Yankee Sports and Gun Club (Roosevelt) (past pres.), Lions (dir. 1960-84), Kiwanis (dir. 1978-84), epsilon Phi Alpha, Iota Theta. Criminal, Probate (including wills, trusts), Property, real (including real estate development, water). Home: 29 Kodiak Dr Woodbury NY 11797-2706 Office: 114 Old Country Rd Mineola NY 11501-4400

DANIELS, JOHN PETER, lawyer; b. N.Y.C., Feb. 5, 1937; s. Jack Brainard and Isabelle (McConachie) D.; m. Lynn Eldridge, Aug. 28, 1978 (div. Jan. 1980); m. Susan Gurley, Apr. 1, 1983. AB, Dartmouth Coll., 1959; JD, U. So. Calif., 1963. Bar: Calif. 1964; diplomate Am. Bd. Trial Advocates. Assoc. Bolton, Groff and Dunne, L.A., 1964-67, Jones and Daniels, L.A., 1967-70, Acret and Perrochet, L.A., 1971-81; ptnr. Daniels, Baratta and Fine, L.A.Angeles, 1982-99, Daniels, Fine, Israel & Schonbuch, L.A.Angeles, 1999—. Mem. Assn. So. Calif. Def. Counsel (bd. dirs. 1975-80), Fedn. Ins and Corp. Counsel. Clubs: Wilshire Country (Los Angeles). Avocations: scuba diving, golf, hunting. Federal civil litigation, State civil litigation. Office: Daniels Fine Israel & Schonbuch 1801 Century Park E Fl 9 Los Angeles CA 90067-2302

DANIELS, MICHAEL PAUL, retired lawyer; b. Maplewood, N.J., Apr. 22, 1930; s. Samuel and Lena E. (Oxman) D.; m. Lora Lee, June 23, 1949 (div. Aug. 1964); children: Lisa J., Rachel L., Aaron N.; m. Elaine Makris, Sept. 1, 1964; children: Anthony P., Maria, Alexander P. BA, U. Chgo., 1949, JD, 1952; student, U. Tokyo Sch. Law, 1958-59. Bar: U.S. Ct. Appeals (D.C. cir.) 1955, U.S. Supreme Ct., U.S. Ct. Internat. Trade; U.S. Ct. Appeals (fed. cir.). Atty. U.S. Congl. Reference Service, Washington, 1955-56; assoc. Becker & Maguire, Washington, 1956-57, Stitt & Hemendinger, Washington, 1958-63; ptnr. Stitt, Hemindinger & Daniels, Washington, 1963-67, Daniels, Houlihan & Palmeter, Washington, 1968-84; ptnr., internat. dept. head Mudge, Rose, Guthrie, Alexander & Ferdon, Washington, 1984-95; ptnr. Graham & James, Washington, 1995-97, Powell Goldstein Frazer & Murphy, Washington, 1997—2000; ret., 2000. Cons. Fasturn Inc., 2000—03. Served with U.S. Army, 1952-54, Korea. Decorated Meritorious Bronze Star; fellow Fulbright fellow. Mem. ABA, D.C. Bar Assn. Administrative and regulatory, Private international. Home: 5615 Bent Branch Rd Bethesda MD 20816-1049 E-mail: mpemd@erols.com.

DANIELS, WILLIAM ANTHONY, lawyer, writer; b. San Francisco, Aug. 29, 1956; s. William Edward and Violetta (Remedios) D.; m. Cheryl Ann Cureton, June 21, 1986; children: William Anthony, Jennifer Ann. BA in Radio and TV, San Francisco State U., 1982; JD, Loyola U., L.A., 1994. Bar: Calif. 1994, D.C. 1994. Bus. reporter Daily Variety, Hollywood, Calif., 1984-90; sr. v.p. Near North Nat. Group, Beverly Hills, Calif., 1991-92; assoc. Paul & Janofsky, Santa Monica, Calif., 1994—99, Mazursky Schwartz & Angelo, 1999—2002, Mazursky & Schwartz, 2003. Recipient 1st prize Nathan Burkan Competition, ASCAP, N.Y.C., 1994. Mem. Am. Trial Lawyers Assn., Consumer Attys. Calif., Consumer Attys. L.A. (bd. govs. 2001—, editor-in chief CAALA Advocate 2002-03), Cowboy Lawyer Assn. (bd. govs. 1998—, pres. 2002-03). Democrat. Roman Catholic. Insurance, Personal injury (including property damage), Product liability. Office: Mazursky Schwartz & Angelo 10990 Wilshire Blvd # 1200 Los Angeles CA 90024

DANIELSON, GARY R. lawyer; b. Detroit, June 8, 1953; s. Ronald Gregory and Catherine (Gibson) D. BA in Psychology, Oakland U., Rochester, Mich., 1976; JD cum laude, Wayne State U., 1983. Bar: Mich. 1983, U.S. Dist. Ct. (ea. dist.) Mich., 1985, U.S. Supreme Ct. 1987. Sr. job placement counselor Ferndale (Mich.) Sch. Dist., 1976-79; employment and tng. adminstr. Oakland County Govt., Pontiac, Mich., 1979-82; sr. corp. labor rels. rep. Harper-Grace Hosps., Detroit, 1982-83; corp. labor rels. mgr. Vis. Nurse Assn., Detroit, 1983-85; atty., v.p., cons. Indsl. Rels., Inc., Detroit, 1985-90; pres. The Danielson Group, P.C., St. Clair Shores, 1989—. Bd. dirs. Henry Ford Village, Dearborn, Mich., 2002—. Mem. ABA, Mich. Bar Assn., Indsl. Rels. Rsch. Assn. Republican. Avocation: sailing. Civil rights, Labor (including EEOC, Fair Labor Standards Act, labor-management relations, NLRB, OSHA). Office: Danielson Group PC 27735 Jefferson Ave Saint Clair Shores MI 48081-1309

DANILSON, DAVID RAY, lawyer; b. Perry, Iowa, Mar. 10, 1954; s. Dale and Edna LaRue (McMorris) D.; m. Jane Fitzgerald, Nov. 30, 1996; children: Elizabeth, Sarah, Jennifer. BS, Iowa State U., 1976; JD, Creighton U., 1979. Bar: Nebr. 1979, Iowa 1980, U.S. Dist. Ct. (so. dist.) Iowa 1980. Asst. trust officer Omaha Nat. Bank, 1979-80; sole practice Boone, Iowa, 1980-87; mgistrate, 1981-87; dist. assoc. judge, 1987-96; dist. judge, 1997—. Jud. hospitalization referee State of Iowa, Boone, 1981; faculty mem. Iowa Magistrate Conf., Des Moines, 1985-87; bd. dirs. Jud. Dist. 2B, Iowa; chmn. Boone Estate and Fin. Planners, 1984. Bd. dirs. Boone County Fair Bd., 1984-90, Boone County Prevention and Cmty. Svcs., 1985-86; bd. trustees Nat. Ct. Rpts. Found., 2001—. Mem. ABA, Iowa Bar Assn., Boone County Bar Assn. (pres. 1982-83), Am. Judicature Soc., Boone C. of C. (chmn. legis. com. 1986-87, chmn. agril. com. 1984), Boone Jaycees (bd. dirs. 1983), Assn. Ltd. Jurisdiction Judges (bd. dirs. 1985, Iowa Judges Assn. (bd. dirs. 1998-2002). Democrat. Family and matrimonial, General practice. Home: 1704 Timberlane Dr Boone IA 50036-5234

DANKNER, JAY WARREN, lawyer; b. Bklyn., June 15, 1949; s. Morris and Frances Dankner; m. Iris Rose Terens, May 15, 1983; children: Danielle Renee, Nicole Beth. BA cum laude, Bklyn. Coll., 1970, JD cum laude, 1973. Bar: N.Y. 1974, Fla. 1974, U.S. Dist. Ct. (ea. and so. dists.) N.Y. 1974, U.S. Ct. Appeals (2d cir.) 1974, U.S. Supreme Ct. 1977, U.S. Dist. Ct. (no. dist.) N.Y. 1986. From assoc. to ptnr. Sullivan & Liapakis P.C., N.Y.C., 1974-94; ptnr. Dankner & Milstein, P.C., N.Y.C., 1994—. Lectr. Practicing Law Inst., N.Y.C., 1983-87, N.Y. State Trial Lawyers Inst., 1985—, continuing legal edn. program Bklyn. Law Sch., 1986—, N.Y. State Bar Assn. CLE Programs, Nassau County Bar Assn., Queens Bar Assn.; mem. Bklyn. Law Rev., 1972-73; bd. dirs. Atty's Info. Exchange Group, Inc., 1981—. Author: Products Liability Practice Guide, 1988, Masters of Trial Practice, 1988, Deposing Corporate Defendants in Products Liability Actions, 1988, Trial Strategy - Plaintiffs View, 1988; contbr. articles to profl. jours. Named one of Best Trial Lawyers in the U.S., Town & Country, 1985. Mem. ABA, N.Y. State Bar Assn. (spl. com. on procedures for jud. discipline 1987-90), Assn. of Bar of City of N.Y. (mem. products liability com. 1993-94), Fla. Bar Assn., Assn. Trial Lawyers Am., N.Y. State Trial Lawyers Assn. (chair products liability com. 1991, 93-94), N.Y. County Lawyers Assn. General civil litigation, Personal injury (including property damage), Product liability. Home: 524 E 72nd St New York NY 10021-9801 Office: Dankner & Milstein PC 41 E 57th St New York NY 10022-1908

DANNHAUSER, STEPHEN J. lawyer; b. N.Y.C., May 23, 1950; s. Frank A. and Irene (Tinney) Dannhauser; m. Mary Elizabeth Robinson, July 1, 1973; children: Benjamin, Todd, Jess. BA with honors, SUNY, Stonybrook, 1972; JD with honors, Bklyn. Law Sch., 1975. Bar: NY 1976. Atty. Weil Gotshal & Manges LLP, N.Y.C., 1975—, exec. ptnr., 1989—2001, chmn., 2002—. Decisions editor: Bklyn. Law Rev., 1974—75. Pres. N.Y. Police and Fire Widows' and Children's Benefit Fund, N.Y.C., 1985—; chair, mem. various coms. Nat. Minority Bus. Coun., N.Y.C., 1993; chmn., bd. dirs. Boys and Girls Harbor, Inc., East Harlem, NY. Mem.: ABA. Avocations: running, golf. Office: Weil Gotshal & Manges LLP c/o Grace F Lopez 767 5th Ave 10th Flr New York NY 10153-0119

DANOWSKY, PETER, lawyer; b. Solna, Sweden, Sept. 15, 1949; s. Simon and Rita Danowsky; m. Lotti Helström; m. Marita Danowsky; children: Robert, Sandra. LLM, Uppsala (Sweden) U., 1972; diploma, Coll. Europe, Brügge, 1974; LLM, Columbia U., 1975. Bar: Sweden. Assoc. Advokatfirman Göran Luterkort, Malmö, Sweden, 1976—83; ptnr. Advokatfirmn Chrysander, Uppsala, 1983—88, Lagerlöf & Leman, Stockholm, 1988—93, Danowsky & Ptnrs. Advokatbyrå KB, Stockholm, 1993—. Author: Vardagslagen, 1974; co-author: Bildrätt, 1980, Pressen inför rätta, 1982, CAD i byggandet - Ansvar avtal och upphovsrätt, 1989, International Protection of Intellectual Property - Swedish Report, 1995, Upphovsrätt på redaktioner, 1995, Kommentarer till immaterialrättslagarna, 1999, Medier, Internet och Juridik, 2000. Intellectual property, Communications, Entertainment. Office: Danowsky & Ptnrs Advokatbyrå KB Hovslagargatan 5 PO Box 16097 103 22 Stockholm Sweden

D'ANTONIO, JAMES JOSEPH, lawyer; b. Tucson, Jan. 13, 1959; s. Lawrence Patrick and Rosemary Catherine (Kane) D'A. Student, Tufts U., 1978-79; BA, U. Ariz., 1981, JD, 1984. Bar: Ariz. 1984, U.S. Dist. Ct. Ariz. 1984, U.S. Ct. Appeals (9th cir.) 1993. Assoc. Law Office of D'Antonio and D'Antonio, Tucson, 1984-93; pvt. practice law Law Offices of James J. D'Antonio, Tucson, 1993—. Chmn. bd. govs. U. Ariz. Coll. Law, 1983-84; mem. Pima County Teen Ct. Adv. Bd; mem. Health South Rehab. Inst., Tucson Cmty. Adv. Bd.; bd. dirs. Coyote Task Force. Named Outstanding Pro Bono Lawyer Pima County Vol. Lawyers Program, 1993. Fellow Ariz. Bar Found.; mem. ABA, Assn. Trial Lawyers Am., Ariz. Bar Assn., Ariz. Trial Lawyers Assn., Pima County Bar Assn. General civil litigation, Personal injury (including property damage), Property, real (including real estate development, water). Office: 751 N Country Club Rd Tucson AZ 85716

DANZIGER, JOEL BERNARD, lawyer; b. N.Y.C., Oct. 17, 1932; AB, Columbia Coll., 1953; LLB, Yale U., 1956. Bar: N.Y. 1958, Conn. 1958, U.S. Dist. Ct. (so. and ea. dists.) N.Y. 1963, U.S. Ct. Appeals (2d cir.) 1958, U.S. Supreme Ct. 1964. Ptnr. Danziger & Markhoff, White Plains, N.Y., 1958—. Adj. prof. law Bridgeport (N.Y.) Law Sch., 1982-85. Mem. ABA, N.Y. Bar Assn., Westchester County Bar Assn., Yale Club. Estate planning, Pension, profit-sharing, and employee benefits, Corporate taxation. Office: Danziger & Markhoff 123 Main St White Plains NY 10601-3104

DANZIS, COLIN MICHAEL, lawyer; b. Newark, May 3, 1938; s. Sidney and Selma (Colin) D.; m. Jo-Ann Fine, Nov. 16, 1963; children: Mitchell, Nicholas. BA, Wesleyan U., 1960; LLB, NYU, 1962, LLM in Taxation, 1963. Bar: N.J. 1962. Mem., dir. Lum, Danzis, Drasco & Positan LLC, Roseland, NJ, 1970—. Dir. Pottermeter Corp. Pres. bd. govs. Newark Acad., 1971-75, trustee, 1973-96, vice chair, 1991-96. Mem. ABA, N.J. Bar Assn., Essex County Bar Assn., West Orange Tennis Club, Beta Theta Pi. Corporate, general, Corporate taxation, Taxation, general. Office: 103 Eisenhower Pky Roseland NJ 07068-1029 E-mail: cdanzis@lumlaw.com.

DARIOTIS, TERRENCE THEODORE, lawyer; b. Chgo., Feb. 28, 1946; s. Theodore S. and Dorothy Mizzen D.; m. Jeanne Elizabeth Gibbons, Oct. 24, 1970; children: Sara, Kristin, Jennifer. BA in Philosophy, St. Joseph's Coll., Rensselaer, Ind., 1969; JD, Loyola U., Chgo., 1973. Bar: Ill. 1973, Fla. 1975, U.S. Tax Ct. 1993, U.S. Supreme Ct., 1978. Law clk. to presiding justice Appellate Ct. of Ill. (2d dist.), Waukegan, 1973-74; assoc. Keith Kinderman, Tallahassee, 1975-76; sole practitioner Tallahassee, 1976-82; ptnr. Kahn and Dariotis, P.A., Tallahassee, 1982-96, Warfel, Goldberg, Dariotis, Waldoch & Olive, P.A., Tallahassee, 1996-00; sole practice Tallahassee, 2000—. Adj. prof. Fla. State U. Coll. Bus., 1987-93. Estate planning, Probate (including wills, trusts). Office: 1695 Metropolitan Cir Ste 6 Tallahassee FL 32308-3731

DARLING, SCOTT EDWARD, lawyer; b. Los Angeles, Dec. 31, 1949; s. Dick R. and Marjorie Helen (Otto) D.; m. Cynthia Diane Harrah, June 1970 (div.); 1 child, Smokie; m. Deborah Lee Cochran, Aug. 22, 1981; children: Ryan, Jacob, Guinevere. BA, U. Redlands, 1972; JD, U.S.C., 1975. Bar: Calif. 1976, U.S. Dist. Ct. (cen. dist.) Calif. 1976. Assoc. atty. Elver, Falsetti, Boone & Crafts, Riverside, 1976-78; ptnr. Falsetti, Crafts, Pritchard & Darling, Riverside, 1978-84; pres. Scott Edward Darling, A Profl. Corp., Riverside, 1984—. Grant reviewer HHS, Washington, 1982-88; judge pro tem Riverside County Mcpl. Ct., 1980, Riverside County Superior Ct., 1987-88; bd. dirs. Tel Law Nat. Legal Pub. Info. System, Riverside, 1978-80. Author, editor: Small Law Office Computer Legal System, 1984. Bd. dirs. Youth Adv. Com. to Selective Svc., 1968-70, Am. Heart Assn. Riverside County, 1978-82, Survival Ministries, 1986-89; atty. panel Calif. Assn. Realtors, L.A., 1980—; pres. Calif. Young Reps., 1978-80; mem. GI Forum, Riverside, 1970-88; presdl. del. Nat. Rep. Party, 1980-84; asst. treas. Calif. Rep. Party, 1981-83; Rep. Congl. candidate, Riverside, 1982; treas. Riverside Sickle Cell Found., 1980-82, recipient Eddie D. Smith award; pres. Calif. Rep. Youth Caucus, 1980-82; v.p. Riverside County Red Cross, 1982-84; mem. Citizen's Univ. Com., Riverside, 1978-84, World Affairs Council, 1978-82, Urban League, Riverside, 1980-82. Calif. Scholarship Fedn. (life). Named one of Outstanding Young Men in Am., U.S. Jaycees, 1979-86. Mem. ABA, Riverside County Bar Assn., Speaker's Bur. Riverside County Bar Assn., Riverside Jaycees, Riverside C. of C. Lodges: Native Sons of Golden West. Avocations: skiing, swimming, reading. Personal injury (including property damage), Property, real (including real estate development, water), Estate taxation. Office: 3697 Arlington Ave Riverside CA 92506-3938

DARLOW, JULIA DONOVAN, lawyer; b. Detroit, Sept. 18, 1941; d. Frank William Donovan and Helen Adele Turner; m. George Anthony Gratton Darlow (div.); 1 child, Gillian; m. John Corbett O'Meara. AB, Vassar Coll., 1963; postgrad., Columbia U. Law Sch., 1964-65; JD cum laude, Wayne State U., 1971. Bar: Mich. 1971, U.S. Dist. Ct. (ea. dist.) Mich. 1971. Assoc. Dickinson, Wright, McKean, Cudlip & Moon, Detroit, 1971-78; ptnr. Dickinson, Wright, Moon, Van Dusen & Freeman and predecessor, Detroit, 1978—2001; sr. v.p. Detroit Med. Ctr., 2001—01; cons. mem. Dickinson, Wright PLLC, Detroit, 2002—. Adj. prof. Wayne State U. Law Sch., 1974-75, 96; commr. State Bar Mich., 1977-87, mem. exec. com., 1979-83, 84-87, sec. 1980-81, v.p., 1984-85, pres.-elect 1985-86, pres. 1986-87, coun. corp. fin. and bus. law sect. 1980-86, coun. computer law sect. 1985-88; mem. State Officers Compensation Commn., 1994-96; chair Mich. Supreme Ct. Task Force on Gender Issues in the Cts., 1987-89. Reporter: Mich. Nonprofit Corp. Act, 1977-82. Bd. dirs. Hutzel Hosp., 1984—, chair, 2002-03; bd. dirs. Mich. Opera Theater, 1985—, Mich. Women's Found., 1986-91, Detroit Med. Ctr., 1990-2003, Marygrove Coll., 1996—; trustee Internat. Inst. Met. Detroit, 1986-92, Mich. Met. coun. Girl Scouts U.S., 1988-91, Detroit coun. Boy Scouts Am., 1988—; mem. exec. com. Mich. Coun. for Humanities 1988-92; mem. Blue Cross-Blue Shield Prospective Reimbursement Com., Detroit, 1979-81; v.p., mem. exec. com. United Found., 1988-95; mem. Mich. Gov.'s Bilateral Trade Team for Germany, 1992-98. Fellow Am. Bar Found. (Mich. State chairperson 1990-96; mem. state officers compensation commn., 1994-96); mem. Detroit Bar Assn. Found. (treas. 1984-85, trustee 1982-85), Mich. Bar Found. (trustee 1987-94), Am. Judicature Soc. (bd. dirs. 1985-88), Internat. Women's Forum (global affairs com. 1994—), Women Lawyers Assn. (pres. 1977-78), Mich. Women's Campaign Fund (charter), Detroit Athletic Club. Democrat. Non-profit and tax-exempt organizations, Corporate, general, Private international. Office: Dickinson Wright PLLC 500 Woodward Ave Ste 4000 Detroit MI 48226-3416

DARMODY, STEPHEN JEROME, lawyer; b. Worcester, Mass., Nov. 28, 1957; s. Jeremiah and Anna Mae (Tangney) D.; m. Maureen Adelaide Miller, June 4, 1983; children: Caroline Marie, James Edward, Mary Grace. BS in Mgmt., USCG Acad., 1979; MBA in Fin./Investments, George Washington U., 1984, JD with honors, 1988, LLM with highest honors in Environ. Law, 1993. Bar: Va. 1988, D.C. 1989, U.S. Ct. Mil. Appeals 1989, U.S. Ct. Appeals (4th cir.) 1988, U.S. Ct. Appeals (D.C. cir.) 1994, U.S. Supreme Ct. 1994, N.C. 1996, Fla. 2001, U.S. Ct. Appeals (11th cir.) 2001. Commd. officer USCG, advanced through grades to comdr.; shipboard ops. officer USCG Cutter Acushnet, Gulfport, Miss., 1979-81; planning, programming and budgeting analyst USCG Hdqs., Washington, 1981-85, law clk., 1986-87; asst. dist. legal officer 8th Coast Guard Dist., New Orleans, 1988-92; staff atty. Coast Guard Environ. Law divsn., Coast Guard Hdqrs., Washington, 1993-95; asst. chief Coast Guard Office of Regulations and Adminstrv. Law, 1995-97; regional counsel Great Lakes U.S. Coast Guard, Cleve., 1997—, ret., 2001; atty. Shook, Hardy & Bacon, Miami, Fla., 2001—. Apptd. mil. judge for trials by court-martial, 1995. Contbr. articles to profl. jours. Mem. sch. bd. St. Andrew's Elem. Sch., New Orleans, 1991-92, religion tchr., 1989-91. Recipient 2 Meritorious Svc. medals, 2 Commendation medals U.S. Coast Guard, 2 Achievement medals, Commandants's Letter of Commendation, 2 Vice Presdl. award for reinventing govt. Mem. ABA (Outstanding Young Coast Guard lawyer 1990-91), Va. State Bar, D.C. Bar Assn., Fla. Bar (mem. admiralty com. 2002—), Judge Advocates Assn. (bd. dirs. 1994-95, Outstanding Career Lawyer of Yr. 1996). Office: One Miami Ctr Ste 2400 201 Biscayne Blvd Miami FL 33132 E-mail: sdarmody@shb.com.

DARNA, PABLO, lawyer; b. Barcelona, Mar. 6, 1976; s. Javier Darna Piera and Lourdes Galobart Satrustegui. LLM, Escuela de Administracion y Direccion de Empresas, Barcelona, 1999. Spanish Abogado: Ilustre Colegio de Abogados de Barcelona 1999. Assoc. lawyer Uria & Menendez, Barcelona, 1999—. Mem.: Circulo de Economia (assoc.), Circulo Ecuestre (assoc.), Asociacion de Antiguos Alumnos de ESADE (assoc.). Corporate, general, Finance, Computer. Office: Uria & Menendez Diagonal 514 08006 Barcelona Spain Office Fax: + 34 416 55 60. E-mail: pdg@uria.com.

DARNELL, ALAN MARK, lawyer; b. N.Y.C., Dec. 6, 1946; s. Sidney and Serene (Rackow) D.; m. Joan Silverman, Sept. 5, 1971. B.A., U. Rochester, 1968; J.D., U. Pa., 1971. Bar: N.J. 1971. Assoc. Wilentz, Goldman & Spitzer, Woodbridge, N.J., 1971-79, ptnr., 1980— . Named Trial Lawyer of the Yr., Trial Lawyers for Pub. Justice, 1983. Mem. Assn. Trial Lawyers Am., Def. Research Assn., Middlesex County Bar Assn., N.J. Bar Assn. Democrat. Jewish. Federal civil litigation, State civil litigation, Personal injury (including property damage). Home: 8 Old Weathersfield Rd Asbury Park NJ 07712-3325

DAROSA, RONALD ANTHONY, lawyer; b. Joliet, Ill., June 28, 1943; s. Edmund A. and Claire L. (Turner) DaR.; m. Cynthia E. Ohlenkamp; children: Ronald II, Laurel Anne, Ryan, Samantha. BS, No. Ill. U., 1965; JD, John Marshall Law Sch., 1970. Bar: Ill. 1970, U.S. Dist. Ct. (no. dist.) Ill. 1970. Asst. state's atty. DuPage County, Wheaton, Ill., 1970-71; ptnr. Mountcastle & DaRosa, P.C., Wheaton, 1971-93; sr. ptnr. DaRosa & Miller, Wheaton, 1993—. Co-chmn. DuPage County Criminal Justice Council, 1979-80. Chmn. Zoning Bd. Appeals, Glen Ellyn, Ill., 1975-77; mayor Village of Glen Ellyn (cert. appreciation 1981), 1977-81; pres. Mayors and Mgrs. Conf. (cert. appreciation 1981), DuPage County, 1980-81; commr. Du Page Airport Authority, 1987-90. Recipient 10-Yr. cert. appreciation Dupage County Child Conciliation Oversight Com., 1998. Fellow Am. Acad. Matrimonial Lawyers; mem. ABA, Ill. Bar Assn., DuPage County Bar Assn. (chmn. matrimonial law com. 1981-82, bd. dirs. 1984-85). Clubs: Medinah Country. Republican. Roman Catholic. Family and matrimonial. Office: DaRosa & Miller 208 N West St Wheaton IL 60187-5098

DARRELL, NORRIS, JR., lawyer; b. Berlin, May 10, 1929; s. Norris and Doris Clare (Williams) D. (parents Am. citizens); m. Henriette Maria Haid, July 31, 1962; 1 child, Andrew. AB, Harvard U., 1951, LL.B. cum laude, 1954. Bar: N.Y. 1955, U.S. Supreme Ct. 1965. Assoc. Sullivan & Cromwell, N.Y.C., 1956-65, ptnr., 1965-92, sr. ptnr. European office Paris, 1968-71, sr. counsel, 1993—. Bd. dirs. Lumina Found. for Edn., Inc., Indpls., Ind. Trustee Cold Spring Harbor Lab., Inc., 1974-81, United Student Aid Funds, Inc., Fishers, Ind., 1974-94, USA Group Inc., Fishers, Ind., 1993-2000, East Woods Sch., Oyster Bay, N.Y., 1974-79; hon. trustee Heckscher Mus., Huntington, N.Y. With U.S. Army, 1954-56. Fellow Am. Bar Found.; mem. Am. Law Inst., ABA, Assn. Bar City N.Y., Harvard Club N.Y., Pilgrims Club, River Club (bd. govs. 1978-98), Cold Spring Harbor Beach Club, Edgartown Yacht Club. Home: 44 Walnut Tree Ln Cold Spring Harbor New York NY 11724 E-mail: norrisd482@aol.com.

DARROW, JILL E(LLEN), lawyer; b. N.Y.C., Jan. 6, 1954; d. Milton and Elaine (Sklarin) D.; m. Michael V.P. Marks, May 14, 1987. AB in English, Barnard Coll., 1975; JD, U. Pa., 1978; LLM in Tax Law, NYU, 1983. Bar: Pa. 1978, N.Y. 1979, U.S. Tax Ct. 1982. Assoc. Shearman & Sterling, N.Y.C., 1978-79, Rosenman & Colin, N.Y.C., 1979-86, ptnr., 1987—2002, Katten Muchin Zavis Rosenman, N.Y.C., 2002—. Mem. ABA, N.Y. State Bar Assn., Pa. Bar Assn., Phi Beta Kappa. Taxation, general, Personal income taxation, Partnership taxation. Home: 860 5th Ave New York NY 10021-5856 Office: Katten Muchin Zavis Rosenman 575 Madison Ave Fl 12 New York NY 10022-2511 E-mail: jill.darrow@kmzr.com.

DAS, KALYAN, lawyer; b. Calcutta, India, June 23, 1956; s. Amulyaratan and Chaitaly (Mitra) D.; m. Pia Mukherjee, Feb. 18, 1986; children: Sabrina, Rahul. Barrister-at-Law, The Lincoln's Inn, London, 1979; diploma, Assoc. of the Chartered Inst. of Arbitrators, London, 1980; LLM, NYU, 1989. Bar: Eng. 1979, Wales 1979, N.Y. 1983; advocate Supreme Ct. India, 1981; barrister and solicitor Melbourne, Australia, 1984. Barrister-at-law Fountain Ct. Temple, London, 1980-81; assoc. Malcolm A. Hoffmann, N.Y.C., 1981-82, White & Case, LLP, N.Y.C., 1983-88, Milbank, Tweed, Hadley & McCloy, LLP, N.Y.C., 1988-90, Seward & Kissel LLP, N.Y.C., 1990-93, ptnr., head global banking and instl. fin. restructuring/workout group, 1993—. Editor: Company Law, 1980. Internat. life v.p. Internat. Students' Trust, London, 1987—. Fellow Am. Coll. Investment Counsel (co-chair ann. meeting 1998); mem. ABA, N.Y. State Bar Assn., Assn. Bar City of N.Y., Am. Arbitration Assn. (panel mem.), Hon. Soc. Lincoln's Inn, Wine Soc. London, Met. Club (N.Y.C.). Avocation: travel. Banking, Commercial, contracts (including sales of goods; commercial financing), Finance. Home: Penthouse A and B 107 W 89th St New York NY 10024-1944 Office: Seward & Kissel LLP 1 Battery Park Plz Fl 23 New York NY 10004-1485 E-mail: das@sewkis.com.

DASH, ADAM S. lawyer; b. Pitts., Aug. 12, 1965; BA, Brandeis U., 1987; JD, George Washington U., 1990. Bar: Mass. 1990, U.S. Dist. Ct. Mass. 1991. Assoc. Mitchell Garabedian, Boston, 1991-93; pvt. practice Adam Dash & Assoc., Somerville, Mass., 1993—. Instr. Nat. Acad. Paralegal Studies, Framingham, Mass., 1993-94; lectr. City of Boston, 1994, Minuteman Tech. Sch., Lexington, Mass., 1994. Pres. Somerville Homeless Coalition, 1993—; chmn. Somerville C. of C., 2002-. Recipient Hazel Hughes award of distinction Somerville Cmty. Corp., 1994. Mem. Mass. Bar Assn., Somerville C. of C. (bd. dirs., chmn. 1995—). General civil litigation, Corporate, general, Personal injury (including property damage). Office: 1 Davis Sq Ste 200 Somerville MA 02144-2904

DASILVA, WILLARD H. lawyer, educator; b. Freeport, N.Y., Oct. 17, 1923; BA, NYU, 1946; LLB, Columbia U., 1949. Bar: N.Y. 1949, U.S. Tax Ct. 1969, U.S. Supreme Ct. 1969. Pvt. practice, N.Y.C., 1969-70, Carle Place, N.Y., 1973-76, Garden City, NY, 1978—91; ptnr. Goodman & DaSilva, N.Y.C., 1970-73, DaSilva & Samuelson, Garden City, 1977, DaSilva & Keidel, Garden City, 1992—97, DaSilva, Garson & Hilowitz LLP, Garden City, 1998-99, DaSilva, Hilowitz & McEvily LLP, Garden City, 1999—. V.p. Marcus Bros. Textile Corp., N.Y.C., 1961-63; pres. Cortley Fabrics subs. Cone Mills Corp., N.Y.C., 1964-65; lectr. Columbia U. Law Sch., Bklyn. Law Sch., St. John's Law Sch., Cardozo Law Sch., Hofstra U. Law Sch., Touro Law Sch.; mem. faculty Practising Law Inst., N.Y.C., 1972—; mem. nat. panel arbitrators Am. Arbitration Assn., 1965-2001. Author: N.Y. Matrimonial Practice, 1980—; editor Matrimonial Law Jour., 1977-85, Fair Share mag., 1985-99, N.Y. Matrimonial Case Law, 1985—; editor-author Family Law Practice Systems Manual, 1982—; editor-in-chief N.Y. Domestic Rels. Reporter, 1992—; editor NY Bar Jour., 1999—; contbr. articles to law jours. Trustee NAFA Found., 1977-85; trustee North Shore U. Hosp., 1988=95, chmn. adv. bd. family in transition program, 1991—; atty. Edn. and Assistance Corp., 1992-97. 2d lt. USAAF, 1942-46. Fellow ABA (coun. family law sect. 1992—, editor-in-chief Family Adv. 1981—), N.Y. State Bar Found. (former mem.); mem. Am. Coll. Family Trial Lawyers (diplomate), Am. Acad. Matrimonial Lawyers (pres. 1982-84, bd. mgrs. 1977—), N.Y. State Trial Lawyers Assn., Am. Bar Found., N.Y. State Bar Assn. (CLE com. 1980-90, program chmn. family law sect. 1978-82, sec. gen. practice sect. 1994-95, chmn. matrimonial com. 1989—, coun. 1992—, chmn.-elect 1995-96, chmn. 1996-97, editor Jour. 2000—), Nassau County Bar Assn., Suffolk County Bar Assn. (chmn. family law sect. 1982-84), N.Y. Family Law Am. Inn of Ct. (master 1995—, sec. 1999-2000, counsel 2001-02, pres. 2003—), Internat. Soc. on Family Law, Am. Soc. Writers on Legal Subjects, Phi Beta Kappa. General civil litigation, Family and matrimonial, Property, real (including real estate development, water). Office: 585 Stewart Ave Garden City NY 11530-4783

DATTOLO, ALPHONSE ROBERT, lawyer, engineering consultant; b. Bklyn., Aug. 5, 1946; s. Carmine Louis and Anna (Cardile) D.; m. Virginia Eileen Lensch, Feb. 14, 1970; children: Bonnie Lynn, Jennifer Ann, Dianne Mari. BS in Indsl. Engring., Poly. Inst. Bklyn., 1968; MS in Indsl. Engring., Ga. Inst. Tech., 1977; JD, Woodrow Wilson Coll. Law, 1980; LLM in Taxation, Woodrow Wilson Coll. Law, 1987. Bar: Ga. 1980. Indsl. engr. JFD Electronics, Bklyn., 1968-69; safety engr. Gen. Services Adminstrn., Atlanta, 1972-80; ptnr. Davis & Dattolo, Riverdale, Ga., 1980—; asst. regional counsel GSA, Atlanta, 1982—; pres. S&D Assocs., Ltd., Ellenwood, Ga., 1977—; v.p., dir. Concepts VI, Inc., Doraville, Ga., 1984—. Coordinator ARC, Atlanta, 1984. Served to capt. U.S. Army, 1969-72. Mem. Am. Soc. Safety Engrs., ABA, Assn. Trial Lawyers Am., Ga. Bar Assn. Democrat. Roman Catholic. Lodge: Kiwanis (bd. dirs. 1984—, treas. 1988-89). Government contracts and claims, Taxation, general. Home: 111 Panther Woods Dr Jackson GA 30233 Office: GSA Office Regional Counsel 77 Forsyth St Atlanta GA 30303 E-mail: a.dattolo@att.net.

DAUDT, MICHAEL D. lawyer; b. Weiser, Idaho, Jan. 14, 1967; BA in Govt., Abilene Christian U., 1989; JD, U. Calif., Berkeley, 1996. Bar: Calif. 1992, Wash. 1996. Assoc. Neumiller & Beardslee, Stockton, Calif., 1992—95, Askew & Archbold, Stockton, Calif., 1995—96, Tousley Brain Stephens PLLC, Seattle, 1996—2002, mem., 2002—. Galt Boys and Girls Club Galt, Calif., 1994—96; bd. govs. San Joaquin County Bar, Stockton, 1995—96. Condemnation (eminent domain), Construction, Property, real (including real estate development, water). Office: Tousley Brain Stephens 56th fl Key Tower 700 Fifth Ave Seattle WA 98104 E-mail: mdaudt@tousley.com.

DAUER, EDWARD ARNOLD, law educator; b. Providence, Sept. 28, 1944; s. Marshall and Shirley (Moverman) D.; m. Carol Jean Egglestone, June 16, 1966; children: E. Craig, Rachel P. AB, Brown U., 1966; LLB cum laude, Yale U., 1969; MPH, Harvard U., 2001. Bar: Conn. 1978, Colo. 1986. Asst. prof. law sch. U. Toledo, 1969-72; assoc. prof. law U. So. Calif., L.A., 1972-74, Yale U., New Haven, Conn., 1975-85, assoc. dean, 1978-83, dep. dean law sch., 1983-85; dean, prof. law U. Denver, 1985-90, dean emeritus, prof. law, 1991—. Vis. scholar Harvard U. Sch. Pub. Health, 1996-2003; of counsel Popham, Haik, Schnobrich and Kaufman, 1990-97; pres. CEJAD Aviation Corp.; assoc. Health Care Negotiation Assocs., Inc. Author: Materials on a Nonadversarial Legal Process, 1978, Conflict Resolution Strategies in Health Care, 1993, Manual of Dispute Resolution: ADR Law and Practice, 1994 (CPR Book award 1994), Health Care Dispute Resolution, 2000; contbr. articles to profl. jours. Bd. dirs. New Haven Cmty. Action Agy., 1978-81, Cerebral Palsy Found. Denver, 1989—, pres., 1992-95; founder, pres. Nat. Ctr. Preventive Law; mem. Colo. Commn. Higher Edn., 1987-91; commr. Colo. Advanced Tech. Inst., 1989-91. Recipient W. Quinn Jordan award Nat. Blood Found., 1994, Paella award Harvard Sch. Pub. Health, 1996, Sanbar award Am. Coll. Legal Medicine, 1999. Mem. Am. Law Inst. (life), Order of Coif, Cherry Creek Athletic Club, Met. Club. Republican. Home: 127 S Garfield St Denver CO 80209 Office: U Denver Coll Law 1900 Olive St Denver CO 80220 E-mail: edauer@du.edu., edauer@hcna.net.

DAUGHERTY, FREDERICK ALVIN, federal judge; b. Oklahoma City, Aug. 18, 1914; s. Charles Lemuel and Felicia (Mitchell) D.; m. Marjorie E. Green, Mar. 15, 1947 (dec. Feb. 1964); m. Betsy F. Amis, Dec. 15, 1965. LL.B., Cumberland U., 1933; postgrad., Oklahoma City U., 1934-35, LL.B. (hon.), 1974; postgrad., Okla. U., 1936-37; HHD (hon.), Okla. Christian Coll., 1976. Bar: Okla. 1937. Practiced, Oklahoma City, 1937-40; mem. firm Ames, Ames & Daugherty, Oklahoma City, 1946-50, Ames, Daugherty, Bynum & Black, Oklahoma City, 1952-55; judge 7th Jud. Dist. Ct., Oklahoma City, 1955-61; U.S. dist. judge Western, Eastern and No. Dists. Okla., Oklahoma City, 1961—; chief judge Western Dist. Okla., Oklahoma City, 1972-82. Mem. Fgn. Intelligence Surveillance Ct., 1981-88, Temporary Emergency Ct. Appeals, 1983-93, Multi dist. Litigation panel, 1980-90; mem. codes of conduct com. U.S. Jud. Conf., 1980-87. Active local ARC, 1956—, chmn., 1958-60, nat. bd. govs., 1963-69, 3d nat. vice chmn., 1968-69; active United Fund Greater Oklahoma City, 1957—, pres., 1961, trustee, 1963—; pres. Community Coun. Oklahoma City and County, 1967-69; exec. com. Okla. Med. Rsch. Found., 1966-69. With AUS, 1940-45, 50-52. Decorated Legion of Merit with 2 oak leaf clusters, Bronze Star with oak leaf cluster, Combat Infantrymans badge; recipient award to mankind Okla. City Sertoma Club, 1962, Outstanding Citizen award Okla. City Jr. C. ofC., 1965, Disting. Alumni citation Samford U., 1974, Disting. Svc. citation Okla. U., 1973, Constn. award Rogers State Coll., 1988, Pathmakers award Oklahoma County Hist. Soc., 1991; named to Okla. Hall of Fame, 1969, Okla. Mil. Hall of Fame, 2000. Mem. Fed. Bar Assn., Okla. Bar Assn., Am. Bar Found., Sigma Alpha Epsilon, Phi Delta Phi, Men's Dinner Club (Oklahoma City) (pres. 1966-69), Kiwanis (pres. 1957, lt. gov. 1959), Masons (33 degree, sovereign grand insp. gen. in Okla. 1982-86), Shriners, Jesters, Order of Coif (hon. mem. Okla. chpt.). Episcopalian (sr. warden 1957).

DAUGHERTY, KENDRA LEA, lawyer; b. Cin., July 11, 1956; d. Clifford Brooks and Viola (Mills) D. BA, U. Cin., 1978, JD, 1982. Bar: Ohio 1982, U.S. Dist. Ct. (fed. dist., so. dist., we. dist.) Ohio. Pvt. practice, Cin., 1982—. Part-time asst. pub. defender Clermont County Pub. Defender's Office, Batavia, Ohio, 1987—; former adj. prof. bus. law U. Cin.; former adj. prof. real estate law Cin. Tech. Coll; pres. bd. of Trustees, U. Cin. Coll. of Law Alumni Assoc. Mem. ABA (former mem. awards of achievement com., young lawyers divsn.), Ohio State Bar Assn. (former chair young lawyers bd. govs., dist. 1 rep. to coun. of dels.), Cin. Bar Assn. (mem. continuing edn. bd., past chair, sec. ethics and profl. responsibility com., bd. trustees 1987-88, former chmn. young lawyers sect.), Clermont County Bar Assn. (sec., treas., past pres.), Greater Cin. Criminal Def. Lawyers Assn., Greater Cin. Women Lawyers Assn. (former co-chair programming), Ohio Assn. Criminal Def. Lawyers Assn., Ohio Women Lawyers Assn., Phi Alpha Delta (former dist. justice). Democrat. Methodist. Home: 3846 Field Ln Cincinnati OH 45255-4919 Office: 4529 Aicholtz Rd Cincinnati OH 45245-1001

DAUGHTREY, MARTHA CRAIG, federal judge; b. Covington, Ky., July 21, 1942; d. Spence E. Kerkow and Martha E. (Craig) Piatt; m. Larry G. Daughtrey, Dec. 28, 1962; 1 child, Carran. BA, Vanderbilt U., 1964, JD, 1968. Bar: Tenn. 1968. Pvt. practice, Nashville, 1968; asst. U.S. atty., 1968—69; asst. dist. atty., 1969—72; asst. prof. law Vanderbilt U., Nashville, 1972—75; judge Tenn. Ct. Appeals, Nashville, 1975—90; assoc. justice Tenn. Supreme Ct., Nashville, 1990—93; circuit judge U.S. Ct. Appeals (6th cir.), Nashville, 1993—. Lectr. law Vanderbilt Law Sch., Nashville, 1975—82, adj. prof., 1988—90; mem. faculty NYU Appellate Judges Seminar, N.Y.C., 1977—90, N.Y.C., 1994—. Contbr. articles to profl. jours. Pres. Women Judges Fund for Justice, 1984—85, 1986—87; active various civic orgns. Recipient Athena award, Nat. Athena Program, 1991. Mem.: ABA (chmn. appellate judges conf. 1985—86, ho. of dels. 1988—91, chmn. jud. divsn. 1989—90, standing com. on continuing edn. of bar 1992—94, commn. on women in the profession 1994—97, bd. editors ABA Jour. 1995—2001), Lawyers Assn. for Women (pres. Nashville 1986—87), Nat. Assn. Women Judges (pres. 1985—86), Am. Judicature Soc. (bd. dirs. 1988—92), Nashville Bar Assn. (bd. dirs. 1988—90), Tenn. Bar Assn. Office: US Ct Appeals 300 Customs House 701 Broadway Nashville TN 37203-3944

DAUSTER, WILLIAM GARY, lawyer, economist; b. Sacramento, Nov. 25, 1957; s. William Joe and Marianne Dauster; m. Ellen Lisa Weintraub, May 10, 1986; children: Matthew Isaac, Natanya Miriam, Emma Sophia. BA in Econs., Polit. Sci. and Internat. Rels., U. So. Calif., 1978, MA in Econs., 1981; JD, Columbia U., 1984. Bar: N.Y. 1985, U.S. Dist. Ct. (so. and ea. dists.) N.Y. 1985, D.C. 1986, U.S. Supreme Ct. 1997. Assoc. Cravath, Swaine & Moore, N.Y.C., 1984-86; chief counsel com. on budget U.S. Senate, Washington, 1986-94, acting staff dir., chief counsel, 1994, Dem. chief of staff, chief counsel, 1995-97, Dem. dep. staff dir., gen. coun. com. labor/human resources, 1997, Dem. chief of staff, chief counsel, 1997-98; counselor Wellstone Pres. Exploratory Com., Washington, 1998-99; dep. asst. to the Pres. for econ. policy, dep. dir. Nat. Econ. Coun., The White House, Washington, 1999-2000; sr. counselor to Senator Russ Feingold U.S. Senate, Washington, 2000—01, legis. dir., 2001—03, Dem. gen. counsel com. on fin., 2003—. Author: Congressional Budget Act Annotated, 1990, Budget Process Law Annotated, 1991, 1993; contbr. articles to profl. jours. Bd. visitors Columbia Law Sch., 1992—2000. Recipient Order of Palm, 1978, trustee scholarship, U. So. Calif., 1974, Harlan Fiske Stone scholar, 1982—84. Mem.: N.Y. Bar Assn., D.C. Bar Assn. Democrat. Jewish. Home: 9713 Connecticut Ave Kensington MD 20895-3528 E-mail: bill_dauster@finance-dem.senate.gov., bill_dauster@yahoo.com.

DAVENPORT, GERALD BRUCE, lawyer; b. Adrian, Mich., May 17, 1949; s. Bruce Nelson and Mildred Louise (Avis) D.; m. RoxAnn Ferguson, Dec. 27, 1975; children: Jonathan Gerald, Christopher Bruce, Timothy Charles. AB, U. Mich., 1971; JD, U. Tex., 1975. Bar: Tex. 1975, Okla. 1993. Pvt. practice Law Office of Gerald B. Davenport, Cedar Park, Tex., 1975-77; atty. Milchem Inc., Houston, 1977-81, Baker Hughes Prodn. Tools Inc., Houston, 1981-87; sr. atty. Baker Hughes Inc., Houston, 1987-88; gen. atty. environ. law Tex. Ea. Corp., Houston, 1988; atty. Browning-Ferris Industries, Houston, 1988-89, mgr. environ. law sect., 1989-92; asst. gen. counsel environ. law Mapco Inc., Tulsa, 1992-94; of counsel McKinney, Stringer & Webster, P.C., Tulsa, 1994-95; dir. Davenport & Williams, P.C., Tulsa, 1995-96; shareholder Hall, Estill, Hardwick, Gable, Golden & Nelson, P.C., Tulsa, 1996-99; of counsel Shipley, Jennings & Champlin, P.C., Oklahoma City, 1999—2002, Elias, Books, & Brown, PC, Oklahoma City, 2002—. Contbr. articles to profl. jours. Mem. ABA, State Bar Tex. (environ. law sect.), Okla. Bar Assn. (environ. law sect.). Republican. Office: Elias Books & Brown Two Leadership Sq 211 N Robinson 1300 Oklahoma City OK 73102-7114 Business E-Mail: GBDavenport@EliasBooksBrown.com.

DAVID, CHRISTOPHER MARK, lawyer; b. Buffalo, Nov. 19, 1965; s. Thomas Leonard and Anne (Nickodemus) D.; m. Elizabeth Martina Wilson, Aug. 31, 1991; 1 child, Taylor Dawn. AA, Miami Dade C.C., 1987; BA, U. Fla., 1990; JD, U. Miami, 1993. Bar: Fla. 1993, U.S. Dist. Ct. (so. dist.) Fla. 1995. Ptnr. Hall, David and Joseph, P.A., Miami, Fla., 1993—, Hall, David and Joseph, PA, Miami, Fla., 1999—. Sgt. U.S. Army, 1983-87. Mem. ATLA, ABA, Acad. Fla. Trial Lawyers, Dade County Bar Assn. General practice. Office: Hall David and Joseph P A 1428 Brickell Ave Fl 8 Miami FL 33131-3438 E-mail: cdavid@hdjlaw.com.

DAVID, ROBERT JEFFERSON, lawyer; b. New Roads, La., Aug. 10, 1943; s. Joseph Jefferson and Doris Marie (Olinde) D.; m. Stella Marie Scott, Jan. 21, 1967; children: Robert J. Jr., Richard M. BA, Southeastern La. U., 1966; JD, Loyola U., New Orleans, 1969. Bar: U.S. Dist. Ct. (ea. dist.) La. 1969, U.S. Dist. Ct. (mid. dist.) La. 1969, U.S. Dist. Ct. (we. dist.) La. 1975. Assoc. Gainsburgh, Benjamin, Fallon, David, New Orleans, 1969-74; ptnr. Gainsburgh, Benjamin, David, New Orleans, 1974—. Adj. faculty mem. Tulane U. Sch. Law, New Orleans, 1982-84, law sch. Loyola U., New Orleans, 1996; mem. hearing com. La. Atty. Disciplinary Bd.; mem. Gov.'s Commn. on Med. Profl. Liability; lectr., spkr. continuing legal edn. seminars. Staff mem. Loyola U. Law Rev., 1967-69; bd. dir Loyola Law Sch. Alumni Assn., 2001-02, vis. com. Loyola Law Sch., 2002—. Reader, recorder for La. Blind and Handicapped, 1986-91; charter mem. Lawyers for Alliance for Nuclear Arms Control, New Orleans, 1986-1990; pres. Arden Hill Acad. Parent Tchr. League, 1979-80. Fellow: Am. Coll. Trial Lawyers; mem.: ATLA, ABA, La. Trial Lawyers Assn. (bd. govs. 1981—83, 1995—96, exec. com. 1996—97, coun. of dirs. 1997—, contbg. editor Civil Trial Tactics manual 1981, chmn. sect. med. malpractice 1992—94, legis. com.), La. Bar Found., La. State Bar Assn. (asst. examiner commn. on bar admissions 1974—93, spl. inst. commn. 1974—82, med. legal interprofl. com. 1987—, co-chmn. 1991—94, contbr. La. Bar Assn. Jour. column on Profl. Liability 1989—, disciplinary com.), Am. Bd. Profl. Liability Attys., Nat. Bd. Trial Advocacy, Phi Alpha Delta, Kappa Sigma. Avocation: sports. General civil litigation, Health, Personal injury (including property damage). Home: 21 Cypress Point Ln New Orleans LA 70131-3351 Office: Gainsburgh Benjamin David 2800 Energy Ctr New Orleans LA 70163

DAVID, RONALD ALBERT, lawyer; b. Pawtucket, R.I., Mar. 24, 1951; s. Albert S. and Katherine M. David; m. Dona C. Buckner, Nov. 24, 1978; 1 child, Dana. BA in Polit. Sci., U. Fla., 1973, JD, 1975. Bar: Fla. 1975, U.S. Supreme Ct. Fla.; cert. civil mediator, civil atty. Fla. Bar Bd. Legal Specialization. Assoc. Wagner & Cunningham, Tampa, Fla., 1975-77; ptnr. Kocha, David & Houston, West Palm Beach, Fla., 1977-80, David & French P.A., Boca Raton, Fla., 1980-2000; atty. Ronald A. David & Assocs. P.A., 2000—. Past pres. U. Fla. Coll. Law Pres.'s Coun., 1990-98; trustee U. Fla. Coll. Law, 1998-2003, emeritus, 2003—. Mem. ATLA, Fla. Bar Assn., South Palm Beach County Bar Assn., Acad. Fla. Trial Lawyers, Gold Coast Gator Club (founder, past pres.), Rotary (sec., bd. dirs., v.p. 1983, Paul Harris fellow). State civil litigation, Insurance, Personal injury (including property damage). Office: 555 S Federal Hwy Boca Raton FL 33432-6312 E-mail: ron@rondavidlaw.com.

DAVIDOW, JOEL, lawyer; b. N.J., July 24, 1938; s. Isadore Davidow; m. Katherine Davidow-Lucas (div.); m. Debra Lynn Miller (div.); children: Abigail, Molly. AB, Princeton U., 1960; LLB, Columbia U., 1963; postdoctoral, U. London, Stanford U. Bar: D.C. 1965, N.Y. 1981. Legal asst. to commr. U.S. Fed. Trade Commn., Washington, 1964-65; assoc. Freeman & Hanley, Chgo., 1969-70; trial atty. Antitrust divsn. U.S. Dept. Justice, Washington, 1966-69, evaluation atty. Antitrust divsn., 1970-73, chief fgn. commerce sect. Antitrust divsn., 1973-77, dir. policy planning antitrust div., 1978-81; ptnr. Mudge, Rose, Guthrie, Alexander & Ferdon, N.Y.C., 1981-87; ptnr., head internat. sect. Dickstein, Shapiro & Morin, Washington, 1987-93; ptnr., vice chmn. Ablondi, Foster, Sobin & Davidow, Washington, 1993-2001; ptnr. Miller & Chevalier, Washington, 2001—. Del. UN Conf. Restrictive Practice, Geneva, 1974—80; adj. prof. law Columbia U., N.Y.C., 1982—87, Am. U., 1987—91, George Mason U., 1992—2003, Georgetown Law Sch., 2003; arbitrator U.S.-Can. Free Trade Agreement, Washington and Ottowa, 1991—94. Author: Antitrust Rules for International Business (Bur. Nat. Affairs 1995); fgn. antitrust editor Antitrust Bulletin, 1981; adv. bd. Bur. Nat. Affairs Antitrust Bulletin, 1981; ocntbr. articles to profl. jours. Mem. ABA. Democrat. Avocation: tennis. Antitrust, Private international. Home: 3721 39th St NW Apt B194 Washington DC 20016 Office: Miller & Chevalier 655 15th St NW Washington DC 20005

DAVIDSON, DANIEL MORTON, lawyer; b. Lynbrook, N.Y., July 9, 1950; BA summa cum laude, Williams Coll., 1972; JD magna cum laude, Harvard U., 1975. Bar: D.C. 1975, Calif. 1977, U.S. Tax Ct. 1979, U.S. Supreme Ct. 1992. Law clk. Mass. Supreme Ct., 1975-76; ptnr. Sidley & Austin, Washington, 1985-98, Hogan & Hartson, L.L.P., Washington, 1998—. Contbr. articles to profl. jours. Mem. ABA, D.C. Bar Assn., State Bar Calif., Phi Beta Kappa. Corporate taxation, Taxation, general, Personal income taxation. Office: Hogan & Hartson LLP 555 13th St NW Ste 900W Washington DC 20004-1109 E-mail: dmdavidson@hhlaw.com.

DAVIDSON, DUNCAN MOWBRAY, lawyer, management consultant, entrepreneur; b. Houston, Jan. 6, 1953; s. Alexander Norman and Elsie Dorothy (Baumann) D.; m. Jean Ann Kunkel, Feb. 16, 1980; children: James Cameron, Claire Amanda, Julie Logan. BS in Physics/Math with honors, Brown U., 1975; JD magna cum laude, U. Mich., 1978. Bar: N.Y. 1979, Calif. 1980, Colo. 1984. Assoc. Cleary, Gottlieb, Steen & Hamilton, N.Y.C., 1978-80, Irell & Manella, Los Angeles, 1980-83; ptnr. Cambridge Venture Ptnrs., Denver, 1983-85; mgr. Strategic Planning Assocs., Inc., Washington, 1986-88; v.p. Gemini Consulting, San Francisco, 1989-95; mng. ptnr. The McKenna Group, 1995-96; founder, chmn. Covad Comm. Group, 1997—97; sr. v.p. InterTrust Tech. Corp., Santa Clara, Calif., 1997-00; CEO Sky Pilot Network, Redwood Shores, Calif., 2001—. Bd. dirs. Genuity, Inc. Author: (with others) Advanced Legal Strategies for Buying and Selling Computers and Software, 1986; editor Mich. Law Rev., 1977-78; mem. editorial bd. Computer Law and Practice, London, 1984-89, Computer Lawyer, 1984-88, Computer Law Reporter, 1987-90; contbr. articles on software, fin., and computers to profl. jours. Mem. ABA (com. chmn. sci. and tech. sect. 1982-87), Computer Law Assn. (bd. dirs. 1984-88). Presbyterian. Avocation: chess. Home: 47 Linda Vista Ave Atherton CA 94027-5428 E-mail: dd@davi.net.

DAVIDSON, FRANK PAUL, macroengineer, lawyer; b. N.Y.C., May 20, 1918; s. Maurice Philip and Blanche (Reinheimer) D.; m. Izaline Marguerite Doll, May 19, 1951; children: Roger Conrad, Nicholas Henry, Charles Geoffrey. BS, Harvard U., 1939, JD, 1948; DHL (hon.), Hawthorne Coll., 1987; D in macro-eng. and diplomacy (hon.) , Roger Williams U., 2003. Bar: NY 1953, U.S. Dist. Ct. (so. dist.) NY 1953. Dir. mil. affairs, gen. counsel Houston C. of C., 1948-50; contract analyst Am. Embassy, Paris, 1950-53; assoc. Carb, Luria, Glassner & Cook, N.Y.C., 1953-54; pvt. practice law N.Y.C., 1955-70; founding pres., counsel, bd. dirs. The Inst. for the Future, 1967-70; rsch. assoc. MIT, Cambridge, Mass., 1970-96, also chmn. system dynamics steering com. Sloan Sch. Mgmt., coord. macro-engring. Sch. Engring. Pres., gen. counsel Tech. Studies Inc., N.Y.C., 1957-96, vice chmn. Inst. for Ednl. Svcs., Bedford, Mass., 1980-84, spl. lectr. Société des Ingénieurs et Scientifiques de France, 1991, NAS del. to Renewable Resources Workshop, Katmandu, Nepal, 1981, governing bd. Channel Tunnel Study Group, 1957-85, co-founder Channel Tunnel Study Group, London, Paris, 1957, apptd. to NASA Exploration Task Force, Washington, 1989, mem. internat. sci. and tech. com. Ocean Cities Symposium, Monaco, 1995. Author: Macro: A Clear Vision of How Science and Technology Will Shape Our Future, 1983, Macro: Big is Beautiful, 1986; editor: series of AAAS books on macroengring., Tunneling and Underground Transport, 1987; co-editor: Macro-Engineering, Global Infrastructure Solutions, 1992, Solar Power Satellites, 1993, 2nd edit., 1998, A Festschrift, Essays in Honor of Frank Davidson, Macro-Engineering and The Earth: World Projects for the Year 2000 and Beyond, 1998; mem. editl. bd. Interdisciplinary Sci. Revs., 1985—; mem. adv. bd. Tech. in Soc., 1979—, Mountain R&D, 1981-2000, Project Appraisal, 1986-98. Bd. dirs. Internat. Mountain Soc., Boulder, Colo., 1981-2000, Assn. Prospective 2100, Paris, 1997; trustee Norwich (Vt.) Ctr., 1980-83, mem. steering com. Am. Trails Network, 1986-88, bd. dirs. Am. Trails Washington, 1988-90. RCAC, 1941-46, ETO; Troop Leader 10th Cdn., Armoured Rgt. (Fort Garry Horse), Intelligence Officer and Squadron Leader, GSO III (Intelligence) Second Armoured Brigade Group, maj. Tex. State Guard; apptd. to Senate Ft. Garry Horse, 1995. Decorated chevalier Legion of Honor (France), 1999, Bronze Star medal; recipient Key to City Osaka, Japan, 1987, Twice the Citizen award Royal Mil. Inst., Manitoba, Can., 1999, William James award Rensselaerville Inst., 2001; elected Mem. Honoraire, Pres. d'Honneur Assn. Louis Armand, Paris, 1996-99; Lewis Mumford Fellow Rensselaerville Inst., 1982. Mem. ABA, Internat. Assn. Macro-Engring. Socs. (bd. dirs. 1987—, hon.chmn. 1997-2000), Am. Soc. Macro-Engring. (bd. dirs. 1982—, vice chancellor 1983-97, pres. 1997-98, chmn. 1998), Assn. Bar of City of N.Y. (internat. law com. 1959-62), Major Projects Assn. (mem. overseas adv. com. U.K. 1995—), Knickerbocker (N.Y.C.) Club, St. Botolph (Boston) Club, MIT Quarter Century Club. Home: 151 Main St Concord MA 01742

DAVIDSON, GEORGE ALLAN, lawyer; b. N.Y.C., Apr. 6, 1942; s. George Roger and Jean Allan (McKaig) D.; m. Annette L. Richter, Sept. 4, 1965; children: Emily, Charlotte. AB, Brown U., 1964; LLB, Columbia U., 1967. Bar: N.Y. 1967, U.S. Dist. Ct. (so. and ea. dists.) N.Y. 1969, U.S. Ct. Appeals (2d cir.) 1970, U.S. Supreme Ct. 1974, U.S. Tax Ct. 1974, U.S. Ct. Appeals (D.C. cir.) 1976, U.S. Dist. Ct. (no. dist.) Calif. 1980, U.S. Ct. Appeals (9th cir.) 1981, U.S. Ct. Appeals (5th cir.) 1982, U.S. Dist. Ct. (no. dist.) N.Y. 1982, U.S. Ct. Appeals (11th cir.) 1983, U.S. Ct. Appeals (1st cir.) 1986, U.S. Ct. Appeals (7th cir.) 1992. Law clk., 1967-68; assoc. Hughes Hubbard & Reed, N.Y.C., 1968-74, ptnr., 1974—; dir. P.R. Legal Def. and Edn. Fund, Inc., 1980-84. Dir. Legal Aid Soc., 1979-92, pres. 1987-89, N.Y. Lawyers for Pub. Interest, Inc., 1984-86, Columbia Law Sch. Alumni Assn., 1987-91, Practicing Attys. for Law Students, 1989—, VIP Cmty. Svcs., 1994—, Greenwich House, Inc., 2002—. Contbr. writings to legal publs. Fellow Am. Coll. Trial Lawyers; mem. ABA, Internat. Bar Assn., Fed. Bar Coun., Am. Law Inst., N.Y. Sci. Policy Assn., N.Y. State Bar Assn., Assn. Bar City N.Y., Nat. Assn. Coll. and Univ. Attys., Union Internationale des Avocats, Century Assn. General civil litigation, Constitutional, Non-profit and tax-exempt organizations. Office: Hughes Hubbard & Reed LLP 1 Battery Park Plz Fl 12 New York NY 10004-1482 E-mail: davidson@hugheshubbard.com.

DAVIDSON, GLEN HARRIS, federal judge; b. Pontotoc, Miss., Nov. 20, 1941; s. M. Glen and Lora (Harris) D.; m. Bonnie Payne, Apr. 25, 1973; children: Glen III, Gregory P. BA, U. Miss, 1962, JD, 1965. Bar: Miss. 1965, U.S. Ct. Appeals (5th cir.) 1965, U.S. Supreme Ct. 1971. Asst. dist. atty. First Jud. Dist., Tupelo, Miss., 1969-74, dist. atty., 1975; U.S. atty. U.S. Dist. Ct. (no. dist.) Miss., Oxford, 1981-85; U.S. district judge U.S. Ct. House, Aberdeen, Miss., 1985—; chief judge U.S. Dist. Ct. (no. dist.) Miss., 2000—. Atty. Lee County Sch. Bd., Miss., 1974-81. Bd. dirs. Community Devel. Found., Tupelo, 1976-81; exec. bd. Yocona Council Boy Scouts Am., 1972—. Maj. USAF, 1966-69. Mem. Fed. Bar Assn. (v.p. 1984), Miss. Bar Found., Lee County Bar Assn. (pres. 1974), Assn. Trial Lawyers Am., Miss. Prosecutors Assn., Kiwanis (pres. Tupelo 1978). Presbyterian. Office: US Dist Ct PO Box 767 Aberdeen MS 39730-0767 E-mail: Davidson@msnd.uscourts.gov.

DAVIDSON, GORDON BYRON, lawyer; b. Louisville, June 24, 1926; s. Paul Byron and Elizabeth (Franz) D.; m. Geraldine B. Geiger, Dec. 21, 1948; children: Sally Burgess, Stuart Gordon. AB, Centre Coll., 1949; JD, U. Louisville, 1951; LL.M., Yale U., 1952. Law clk. Supreme Ct. U.S., 1954; of counsel Wyatt, Tarrant & Combs, Louisville, 1955-92, mng. ptnr., 1978-92. Bd. dirs. DNP Select Income, Inc., Warner L. Jones Farm, Inc., Norton Healthcare, Inc., Warben, Inc. Pres. Louisville Ctrl. Area, Inc., 1971-73; chmn. River City Mall Com., 1973-74, Louisville Devel. Com., Ky. Ctr. for Arts, 1980-95, Louisville Area C. of C., 1986, trustee; bd. dirs., chmn. Norton Childrens Hosps., 1973-75, Louisville Fund for Arts, 1987-93; trustee emeritus Centre Coll. Recipient Louisville Citizen of Yr. award, 1973-74, Mayor's Fleur de Lis award, 1974, Louisville Man of Yr. award, 1981, Outstanding Lawyer of Ky. award, 1984, Disting. Alumnus award U. Louisville Law Sch., 1982, Disting. Citizen award City of Louisville, 1987, Man of Vision award, 1991, Ky. Commonwealth award, 1995, Caritas Found. award, 1998; named to Louisville Male High Sch. Hall of Fame, 1989. Mem. Harmony Club, Landing Country Club, Jefferson Louisville Country Club, Dennbarr Club, Lawyers Club, Gulf Stream Bath and Tennis Club (Fla.), Gulf Stream Golf Club (Fla.). Democrat. Presbyterian. Home: 435 Lightfoot Rd Louisville KY 40207-1853 also: 1102 Vista Del Mar Dr N Delray Beach FL 33483-7146 Office: Wyatt Tarrant & Combs Citizens Plz Louisville KY 40202-2823

DAVIDSON, JAMES JOSEPH, III, lawyer; b. Lafayette, La., July 27, 1940; s. James Joseph and Virginia Lee (Dunham) D.; m. Kay Cecile Holloway, Aug. 7, 1962; children: Kimberly Kay, James Joseph IV, Lynda Leigh, Virginia Holland. BA, U. SW La., 1963; JD, Tulane U., 1964. Bar: La. 1964, U.S. Dist. Ct. (we. dist.) La. 1965, U.S. Dist. Ct. (ea. dist.) La. 1979, U.S. Dist. Ct. (mid. dist.) La. 1986, U.S. Ct. Appeals (5th cir.) 1972 Us. Supreme Ct. 1975, U.S. Ct. Appeals (11th cir.) 1981. Ptnr. Davidson, Meaux, Sonnier & McElligott, Lafayette, La., 1964—. Mem. exec. bd. Evangeline Area coun. Boy Scouts Am., 1969-80; trustee U. La. Lafayette Found., 1980—, pres., 1988-91. Fellow Am. Bar Found. (life); mem. ABA (ho. of dels. 2002--), La. State Bar Assn. (del. 1970-96), La. Bar Found., La. State Law Inst. (coun. 2002--), La. Assn. Def. Counsel (dir. 1975-77), Nat. Assn. R.R. Trial Counsel, Am. Bd. Trial Advocates (adv. bd.), Am. Counsel Assn., Internat. Assn. Def. Counsel, Assn. Def. Trial Attys., Assn. Transp. Practitioners. Republican. Baptist. Federal civil litigation, State civil litigation, Condemnation (eminent domain). Home: 539 Girard Park Dr Lafayette LA 70503-2601 Office: PO Box 2908 Lafayette LA 70502-2908

DAVIDSON, JEFFREY H. lawyer; b. Brookline, Mass., Apr. 7, 1952; s. Jacob and Bernice (Beckerman) D.; m. Cynthia J. Cohen, June 11, 1972; 1 child, Clifford. BA cum laude, Harvard U., 1973, JD cum laude, 1976. Bar: Calif. 1977, U.S. Dist. Ct. (cen. dist.) Calif. 1977, U.S. Dist. Ct. (so. dist.) Calif. 1981, U.S. Ct. Appeals (9th cir.) 1983, U.S. Dist. Ct. (no. dist.) Calif. 1986. Shareholder Stutman, Treister & Glatt, P.C., L.A., 1976—. Fellow Am. Coll. Bankruptcy; mem. ABA (sect. bus. law, bus. bankruptcy com., UCC com.), FBA (bankruptcy sect.), Fin. Lawyers Conf. (bd. govs. 1988-91, 2001—, exec. com. 1990-91), State Bar Calif. (exec. com. bus. law sect. 1987-90, treas. bus. law sect. 1989-90, chmn. UCC com. 1986-87), L.A. County Bar Assn. (chmn. comml. law and bankruptcy sect. 1987-88, exec. com. 1985—, chmn. bankruptcy com. 1984-86, mem. nominating com. for trustees and officers 1988), Phi Beta Kappa. Bankruptcy, Commercial, contracts (including sales of goods; commercial financing). Office: Stutman Treister & Glatt PC 1901 Ave of the Stars 12th Fl Los Angeles CA 90067 E-mail: jdavidson@stutman.com.

DAVIDSON, KENNETH LAWRENCE, lawyer, educator; b. Tulsa, Feb. 4, 1945; s. Joe and Elsie (Hutchens) D.; m. Anne Devine; children: Rebecca Marie, Deborah Shannon. BSBA, U. Tulsa, 1968, JD, 1970; LLM, Georgetown U., 1975. Bar: Okla. 1970, U.S. Dist. Ct. (no. dist.) Okla. 1970, U.S. Ct. Mil. Appeals 1971, U.S. Supreme Ct. 1976, U.S. Dist. Ct. (no. dist.) Ill. 2003, D.C. Ct. Appeals 1978, Ill. 1990. Assoc. CEO, assoc. legal counsel Bd. Regents Okla. State U. and A&M Colls., Stillwater, 1976-90; gen. counsel Regency Univs. System Ill. Bd. Regents, Springfield, 1990-96; parliamentarian, counsel, bd. trustees No. Ill. U., DeKalb, 1995-97, parliamentarian counsel for governance, risk mgmt., equity svcs., 1997-2000, corp. counsel, bd. parliamentarian, 2000—02, assoc. v.p. and gen. coun., bd. trustees parliamentarian, 2002—. Adj. assoc. prof. Coll. Edn. Okla. State U., 1986-90; adminstrv. law judge Okla. Dept. Edn., Oklahoma City, 1978-90. Bd. dirs. YMCA Aquatic Club, Stillwater, 1985-86, Judith Karman Hospice, Stillwater, 1987. Capt. JAGC, USAF, 1970-76. Decorated Meritorious Svc. medal, Commendation medal. Mem. AAUP, Ill. Bar Assn., DeKalb County Bar Assn., Okla. Bar Assn., D.C. Bar Assn., Nat. Assn. Coll. and Univ. Attys., Am. Soc. Parliamentarians, Univ. Risk Mgmt. Assn., Univ. Club (Chgo.), Kappa Sigma. Democrat. Education and schools, Insurance, Labor (including EEOC, Fair Labor Standards Act, labor-management relations, NLRB, OSHA). Office: No Ill U 302 Lowden Hall Dekalb IL 60115-3080 E-mail: kdavidso@niu.edu.

DAVIDSON, MICHAEL, lawyer; b. Louisville, July 27, 1954; s. M. and Sonia Davidson; m. Kris Davidson, Dec. 19, 1987; children: Tess, Zachary. Bachelors Degree, U. Ky., 1981, JD, 1986. Bar: Ky. 1986, U.S. Dist. Ct. (ea. dist.) Ky. 1986, U.S. Bankruptcy Ct. 1986. Assoc. Reuff, Alexander & Shriner, Lexington, 1986—87, Summers, Fox, Dixon & McGinty, Lexington, 1987—90, Cleve., 1987—90; prin. Law Offices of Michael Davidson, Lexington, 1990—. Spkr. in field. Editor: Collection Practice in Domestic Relations Matters, 2002. U. Ky. family law plannig com. U. Ky. Law Sch., Lexington, 1997—. With USN, 1972—76. Mem.: ABA (custody com. vice chair 1998—2000), Fayette County Bar Assn. (chair family law 2001—02, Pro Bono award 1995), Ky. Bar Assn. (chair family law 2001—02). Avocations: tennis, swimming, Karate, fishing, golf. Family and matrimonial, Juvenile, Military. Office: 135 W Short St Lexington KY 40507

DAVIDSON, ROBERT BRUCE, lawyer; b. N.Y.C., May 6, 1945; BS in Econs. cum laude, U. Pa., 1967; JD, Columbia U., 1972. Bar: NY 1973, US Dist Ct (so and ea dists) NY 1973, US Ct Appeals (2d cir) 1975, US Ct Appeals (DC cir) 1981, US Supreme Ct 1979, US Tax Ct 1984, US Ct Appeals (fed cir) 1989, US Ct Appeals (3d cir) 1990. Assoc. Baker & McKenzie, N.Y.C., 1972-79, ptnr., 1979—. Mem adv bd World Arbit Inst, New York, NY, 1984—. Author (with others): (book) Voting Laws and Procedures, 1973; contbr. articles to profl jours. Vol US Peace Corps, The Philippines, 1968—70. Mem.: ABA, Am. Arbitration Assn. (panels for large complex cases and for internat. cases 1997—), Fed. Bar Coun., Maritime Law Assn. U.S., Am. Fgn. Law Assn. (bd. dirs.), Assn. Bar City N.Y. (com. internat. law 1986—89, com. arbitration 1999—, chair com. arbitration 1982—85). Alternative dispute resolution, Federal civil litigation, Private international. Office: Baker & McKenzie 805 3d Ave New York NY 10022-7513 E-mail: robert.b.davidson@bakernet.com.

DAVIDSON, SHEILA KEARNEY, lawyer; b. Paterson, N.J., Dec. 16, 1961; d. John James and Rita Barbara (Burke) Kearney; m. Anthony H. Davidson, Oct. 5, 1996; children: Andrew John, Patrick Kearney. BA cum laude, Fairfield U., 1983; JD, George Washington U., 1986. Bar: N.Y. 1987, U.S. Dist. Ct. (so. dist.) N.Y. 1987, D.C. 1989. Assoc. Shearson Lehman Bros., Inc., N.Y.C., 1986-87; staff atty. Nat. Assn. Securities Dealers, N.Y.C., 1987-89, regional atty., 1989-90, sr. regional atty., 1990-91; regional counsel N.Y. Life Ins. Co., N.Y.C., 1991-93, assoc. counsel, 1993-94, asst. gen. counsel, 1994-95, v.p., assoc. gen. counsel, 1995-97, sr. v.p. in charge of corp. compliance dept., 1998-00, sr. v.p./gen. counsel, 2000—. Mem. D.C. Bar Assn., Fairfield U. Alumni Club (pres. 1988-90, exec. com. 2001—), Phi Delta Phi. Republican. Roman Catholic. Administrative and regulatory, Corporate, general, Securities. Office: NY Life Ins Co 51 Madison Ave New York NY 10010-1603

DAVIDSON, TOM WILLIAM, lawyer; b. Madison, Wis., Oct. 10, 1952; s. Alvin William and Louise Elizabeth (Zeratsky) D.; m. Linda Mary Greiber, July 27, 1974; children: Jessica, Heather, Thomas. BA, U. Wis., 1977, JD, 1974. Bar: Wis. 1977, U.S. Dist. Ct. (we. dist.) Wis. 1977, U.S. Ct. Appeals (D.C. cir.) 1986, U.S. Supreme Ct. 1986, Va. 2001. Gen. atty. FCC, Washington, 1977-79, trial atty., 1979; assoc. Sidley & Austin, Washington, 1980-84, ptnr., 1985-91, Akin, Gump, Struass, Hauer & Feld, LLP, Washington, 1992—. Active Burke (Va.) Ctr. Cmty. Assn., 1977-79; chmn. Bass Pond Cluster Bd., 1977-78. Mem. ABA, FBA, Fed. Comm. Bar Assn., Lowe's Island Club, Tournament Players Club at Avenal, Phi Beta Kappa, Phi Eta Sigma, Phi Kappa Phi. Avocations: golf, softball, soccer, basketball, racquetball. Administrative and regulatory, Communications, Trademark and copyright. Office: Akin Gump Strauss Hauer & Feld Ste 400 1333 New Hampshire Ave NW Washington DC 20036-1564

DAVIDSON, WHITNEY L. paralegal; b. Knoxville, Mar. 12, 1979; d. William A. and Rozan G. Davidson. AAS, Pellissippi State Tech. C.C., 2000. With The Davis Law Firm, Knoxville, 2000—. Mem.: Tenn. Trial Lawyers Assn., Am. Trial Lawyers Assn. Office: The Davis Law Firm 1341 Branton Blvd Ste 105 Knoxville TN 37922 Fax: 865-691-6214. E-mail: wdavidson@tnlaw-knox.com.

DAVIES, CHARLES R. lawyer; BS, Duquesne U., 1964; JD, Georgetown U., 1967. Bar: D.C. 1968. Asst. v.p., asst. gen. counsel Geico Corp., Washington, 1978, v.p., gen. counsel, 1992—, group v.p., gen. counsel, 1999, sr. v.p., gen. counsel, 2000—. Office: Geico Corp Gelco Plz Washington DC 20076-0001

DAVIES, DAVID GEORGE, lawyer, educator; b. Waukesha, Wis., July 19, 1928; s. David Evan and Ella Hilda (Degler) D.; m. Elaine Kowalchik, May 12, 1962; children: Thea Kay, Bryn Ann, Degler Evan. BS, U. Wis., 1950, JD, 1953. Bar: Wis. 1953, Ariz. 1959. Trust rep. First Nat. Bank of Ariz., Phoenix, 1957-58, asst. trust officer, 1958-62, trust officer, head bus. devel. in trust dept., 1962-66, v.p., trust officer, 1966; practice in Phoenix, 1967—; assoc. Wales & Collins, 1967-68; ptnr. Wales, Collins & Davies, 1968-75, Collins, Davies & Cronkhite, Ltd., 1975-85, David G. Davies, Ltd., 1986—. Instr. bus. law local chpt. C.L.U.s, 1965; instr. estate and gift taxation, 1973— ; instr. estate planning Phoenix Coll., 1968— ; past instr. Maricopa County Jr. Coll. Pres. Central Ariz. Estate Planning Council; pres., bd. dirs. Vis. Nurse Service, United Fund Agy.; chmn. bd. Beatitudes Campus of Care; bd. dirs. Phoenix chpt. Nat. Hemophilia Found.; bd. dirs., treas. trusteeship St. Luke's Hosp. Med. Ctr., Phoenix, 1982—; mem. adv. bd. planned giving com. Salvation Army, 1997—. Served to capt. JAGC, AUS, 1953-57. Mem. Central Assn. Life Underwriters (asso.), ABA, Wis. Bar Assn., State Bar Ariz., Am. Assn. Homes for Aged (legal affairs com., future com.) Congregationalist (chmn. bd. trustees, moderator). Office: 5110 N 40th St Ste 236 Phoenix AZ 85018-2151

DAVIES, GILLIAN, judge, writer, educator; b. Abersoch, Wales, U.K., Apr. 5, 1940; d. Ninian Rhys and Gweneth Elizabeth (Griffith) D. Grad., Grenoble (France) U., 1958; Barrister at Law, Inns of Ct., London, 1961; PhD, U. Wales, 1997. Barrister-at-law Lincoln's Inn, Inn of Ct., London, 1962-63; legal asst. The De La Rue Co. Ltd., London, 1963-65; head legis. and periodicals sect. United Internat. Bur. Protection Intellectual Property, Geneva, 1965-70; legal asst., 1970-80; asst. dir. gen., chief legal advisor Internat. Fedn. Phonog. Industry, London, 1980-91; judge, mem. bd. appeals European Patent Office, Munich, 1991-97; presiding judge, chmn. bd. appeals EPO, Munich, 1997—. Dir. Snowdon Mountain Railway, Llanberis, U.K., 1970-99; hon. prof. U. Wales, Aberystwyth, 1994—; dep. lt. County of Gwynedd, Wales, 2001—. Author: Piracy of Phonograms, 1981, 2d edit., 1986, Private Copying of Sound and Audiovisual Recordings, 1984, 2d edit., 1993, Copyright and The Public Interest, 1994, 2d edit., 2002; co-author: Challenges to Copyright and Related Rights in the European Community, 1983, Copinger and Skone James on Copyright, 14th edit., 1999, supplement, 2002. Avocations: travel, golf, painting. Office: European Patent Office Erhardstrasse 27 D-80331 Munich Germany Fax: 0 89/23 99-30 14.

DAVIES, GREGORY LANE, lawyer; b. Seattle, Aug. 21, 1951; s. Cynric C. Davies and Marilyn R. (Baker) Amdal; m. Julia M. Dent, Apr., 1973 (div. 1975); m. Barbara A. Hess, Sept. 2, 1978; children: Andrea M., Susan E. AA, Edmonds Community Coll., 1975; BA, Cen. Wash. State U., 1977; JD, U. Puget Sound, 1980. Bar: Wash. 1980, U.S. Dist. Ct. (we. dist.) Wash. 1980, U.S. Tax Ct. 1981, U.S. Ct. Appeals (9th cir.) 1988, U.S. Supreme Ct. 1988. Legal intern Thurston County, Olympia, Wash., 1979-80; assoc. Rudolf Mueller, Everett, Wash., 1980-81; pvt. practice law Everett, 1981-84; ptnr. Cooper, Lyderson, Cooper & Davies, Everett, 1984-87, Lyderson & Davies, Everett, 1987-91; pvt. practice law Everett, Wash., 1991—. Arbitrator, ct. commr., arbitrator Snohomish County Superior Ct., Everett, 1987—. Tchr. community schs., Everett, 1981—; bd. dirs. Mental Health Snohomish County, 1987—; mem. Everett Citizen's Adv. Bd., 1988; treas. Arden Bedle for judge, Everett, 1988. With U.S. Army, 1971-73. Dean's scholar Cen. Wash. State U., 1977. Mem. Wash. State Bar Assn., Snohomish County Bar Assn. (bd. trustees), Phi Theta Kappa. Democrat. Avocations: outdoor sports, golf, hiking, jogging. General civil litigation, Family and matrimonial. Office: 3721 Colby Ave Everett WA 98201-4910 E-mail: gldavies@silvernet.net.

DAVIES, PAUL LEWIS, JR., retired lawyer; b. San Jose, Calif., July 21, 1930; s. Paul Lewis and Faith (Crummey) D.; m. Barbara Bechtel, Dec. 22, 1955 (dec. June 2001); children: Laura (Mrs. Segundo Mateo), Paul Lewis III. AB, Stanford U., 1952; JD, Harvard U., 1957. Bar: Calif. 1957. Assoc. Pillsbury, Madison & Sutro, San Francisco, 1957-63, ptnr., 1963-89; gen. counsel Chevron Corp., 1984-89. Bd. dirs. FMC Corp., 1965—2001. Hon. trustee Calif. Acad. Scis., trustee, 1970-83, chmn., 1973-80; pres. Herbert Hoover Found.; bd. overseers Hoover Instn., chmn., 1976-82, 91-93; hon. regent U. of Pacific, regent, 1959-90. Lt. U.S. Army, 1952-54. Mem. Bohemian Club, Pacific-Union Club, Villa Taverna, World Trade Club (San Francisco), Claremont Country Club, Cypress Point (Pebble Beach, Calif.), Sainte Claire (San Jose, Calif.), Collectors, Explorers, Links (N.Y.C.), Met. Club (Washington), Chgo. Club, Phi Beta Kappa, Pi Sigma Alpha. Republican. Office: 3470 Mt Diablo Blvd Ste A210 Lafayette CA 94549-3985 E-mail: pauldaviesjr@yahoo.com.

D'AVIGNON, ROY JOSEPH, lawyer; b. Dallas, July 20, 1942; s. Roy J. and Ann (Ham) D'A.; m. Tania M. Mychajlyshyn, Nov. 29, 1969; children: Larissa A., Markian W. BSS, Loyola U., New Orleans, 1964; LLB, Harvard U., 1967. Bar: Tex. 1967, Mass. 1969. Assoc. Hutchins & Wheeler, Boston, 1969-77; counsel Raytheon Co., Lexington, Mass., 1977-86, div. counsel, 1986-90, asst. gen. counsel, 1990-99; v.p., sect. and gen. counsel Simplex Time Recorder Co., Gardner, Mass., 1999—2001; sole practitioner, 2001—. Capt. M.I., U.S. Army, 1967-69. Mem. ABA, Mass. Bar Assn., Tex. Bar Assn., Boston Bar Assn. Corporate, general, Private international, Mergers and acquisitions.

DAVIS, ANDREW NEIL, lawyer, educator; b. Boston, Nov. 7, 1959; s. Gerald Stanley and Sarah Lee D.; m. Suzanne Frances DiBenedetto, Oct. 11, 1992; children: David R. Bray, Hannah M., Zachary G. BS in Biology, Trinity Coll., 1981; MS in Botany, U. Mass., 1983, PhD in Botany, 1987; JD, George Washington U., 1990. Bar: Conn. 1990, U.S. Dist. Ct. Conn. 1991, Mass. 1998. Atty. Pepe & Hazard, Hartford, Conn., 1990-93, Brown, Rudnick, Freed & Gesmer, Hartford, 1993-94; ptnr. LeBoeuf, Lamb, Greene & MacRae LLP, Hartford, 1994—. Adj. prof. environ. studies Conn. Coll., 1994—. Sr. author/co-author: The Home Environmental Sourcebook, 1996, ISO 14001: Meeting Business Goals Through An Effective Environmental Management System, 1998; contbr. articles to profl. jours. Mem. Leadership Greater Hartford, 1997; chmn. lake adv. commn. Town Marlborough, 1992—, zoning commn., 1993-95. Recipient Hon. Sci. award Bausch & Lomb, 1977; Albert L. Deslisle Botany fellow, 1982. Mem. Am. Arbitration Assn. (environ. adv. com. 1993-95), Conn. Bar Assn. (exec. com. environ. law sect. 1996-2000), Conn. Bus. and Industry Assn. (environ. policies coun. 1991—), Internat. Coun. Shopping Ctrs. Avocations: photography, sailing, scuba diving, arctic travel, reading. Environmental, Land use and zoning (including planning), Mergers and acquisitions. Office: LeBoeuf Lamb Greene & MacRae LLP 225 Asylum St Fl 13 Hartford CT 06103-1529 E-mail: adavis@llgm.com.

DAVIS, ARNOLD, lawyer; s. Harry and Helen Davis; m. Violet C. Markowitz, June 23, 1951; children: Sanford M., Robyn A. LLB, Bklyn Law Sch., 1948; LLM, Bklyn. Law Sch., 1954. Bar: N.Y. 1951, U.S. Dist. Ct. (so. dist.) N.Y. 1951, U.S. Dist. Ct. (ea. dist.) N.Y. 1952, U.S. Ct. Appeals (2d cir.) 1953, U.S. Supreme Ct. 1959, U.S. Ct. Appeals (6th cir.) 1980. Atty. pvt. practice, N.Y.C., 1951—2002. Mem.: Am. Acad. Matrimonial Lawyers, United Bros. (pres. 1980—85). Family and matrimonial, Appellate, Probate (including wills, trusts). Office: Arnold Davis Esq 40 Exchange Place New York NY 10005 Office Fax: 212-785-4425. E-mail: arndavlex@yahoo.com.

DAVIS, BONNIE CHRISTELL, judge; b. Petersburg, Va., July 13, 1949; d. Robert Madison and Margaret Elizabeth (Collier) D. BA, Longwood Coll., 1971; JD, U. Richmond, 1980. Bar: Va. 1980, U.S. Dist. Ct. (ea. dist.) Va. 1980, U.S. Ct. Appeals (4th cir.) 1982. Tchr. Chesterfield County Schs., Chesterfield, Va., 1971-77; pvt. practice, Chesterfield, 1980-83; asst. commonwealth atty. Chesterfield County, 1983-93; judge Juvenile and Domestic Rels. Ct. for 12th Jud. Dist. Va., 1993—. Adviser Youth Svcs. Commn., Chesterfield, 1983-93; cons. Task Force on Child Abuse, 1983-93, Met. Richmond Multi-Discipline Team on Spouse Abuse, 1983-93, Va. Dept. of Children for handbook "Step by Step Through the Juvenile Justice System in Virginia, 1988; mem. nat. adv. com. for prodn. on missing and runaway children Theatre IV; mem. adv. group to set stds. and tng. for Guardians Ad Litem, Supreme Ct. Va., 1994; chmn. jud. adminstrn. com. Jud. Conf. Va. for Dist. Cts., 1995-97; mem. state adv. com. for CASA and children's Justice Act, 1998-2002. Co-author: Juvenile Law and Practice in Virginia, 1994. Mem. Chesterfield County Pub. Schs. Task Force on Core Values, 1999. Mem.: Chesterfield-Colonial Heights Bar Assn., Met. Richmond Women's Bar Assn., Va. Trial Lawyers Assn., Va. Bar Assn., Va. State Bar (bd. govs. family law sect. 1997—2001), State-Fed. Jud. Coun. Va. Home: 415 Lyons Ave Colonial Heights VA 23834-3154 Office: Chesterfield Juvenile and Domestic Rels Dist Ct 7000 Lucy Corr Blvd Chesterfield VA 23832-6717

DAVIS, BRITTON ANTHONY, retired lawyer; b. Highland Park, Ill., Jan. 2, 1936; s. James Archie and Anita (Blanke) D.; m. Lynn Marriott Wegner, 1958 (dec. 1975); children: Hilary, Shepard; m. Peggy M. Swint, 1986; children: Stephen Swint, Thomas Swint. Student, Denison U., 1954-57; BS in Law, Northwestern U., 1959, LLB, 1960. Bar: Ill. 1960. Assoc. Haight & Hofeldt, Chgo., 1959-89; pvt. practice Winnetka, Ill., 1989-96. Vol. Children's Spl. Edn. Programs, Winnetka. Mem.: ABA, Patent Law Assn. Chgo., Bar Assn. 7th Fed. Cir., Chgo. Curling Club, Indian Hill Club (Winnetka). Home: 285 Linden St Winnetka IL 60093-3826

DAVIS, C. VANLEER, III, lawyer; b. Camden, N.J., 1942; AB summa cum laude, Princeton U., 1964; LLB magna cum laude, Harvard U., 1967. Bar: Pa. 1969. Law clk. to Hon. Abraham L. Freedman U.S. Ct. Appeals (3d cir.), 1967-68; ptnr. Dechert, LLP, Phila. Lectr. Pa. State U. Tax Conf., 1980, mem. planning com., 1986—, chair, 1991-92; lectr. grad. tax program Temple U., 1988-89. Author: (with Jay Zagoren) Pennsylvania Limited Liability Company Forms and Practice Manual, 1996; co-editor (with Patrick Dolan) Securitization Handbook, 2000. Mem. Phi Beta Kappa. Corporate taxation. Office: Dechert LLP 4000 Bell Atlantic Tower 1717 Arch St Philadelphia PA 19103-2713

DAVIS, CLAUDE-LEONARD, lawyer, university official; s. James and Mary Davis; m. Margaret Earle Crowley; 1 child, Margaret Michelle. BA in Journalism, U. Ga., 1966, JD, 1974. Bar: Ga. 1974. Broadcaster Sta. WKLE Radio, Washington, Ga., 1958-62; realtor Assocs. Realty, Athens, Ga., 1963-66; bus. cons. Palm Beach, Fla., 1970-71; asst. to dir. Ga. Coop. Extension Svc., Athens, 1974-81; atty. Office of Pres. U. Ga., Athens, 1981—; mem. faculty, regent Ga. Athletics Inst., 1988-98; broadcaster Leonard's Losers.com, Athens, Ga., 2000—. Cons. numerous agrl. chem. industry groups nationwide, 1977—, Congl. Office Tech. Assessment, Washington, 1978-79, USDA, Washington, 1979-80; del. Kellogg Nat. Leadership Conf., Pullman, Wash., 1980. Editor and contbr. Ga. Jour. of Internat. and Comparative Law, 1972-74; contbr. articles on agr. and fin. planning to profl. jours.; author and editor: DAWGFOOD: The Bulldog Cookbook, 1981, Touchdown Tailgates, 1986. Del. So. Leader Forum, Rock Eagle Ctr., Ga., 1976-99; trainer Ga. 4-H Vol. Leader Assn., 1979—; coordinator U. Ga. Equestrian Team, Athens, 1985-87; mem. Clarke County Sheriff's Posse, 1985-2000. Capt. U.S. Army, 1966-70. Chi Psi Scholar, 1965; Recipient Outstanding Alumnus award Chi Psi, 1972, Service to World Community award Chi Psi, 1975. Mem. Nat. Assn. Coll. and Univ. Attys., DAV, Poets Soc., Am. Legion, Rotary, The President's Club (Athens), Gridiron Secret Soc., Chi Psi (advisor 1974). Baptist. Avocations: martial arts, creative writing, music. Corporate, general, Education and schools, Labor (including EEOC, Fair Labor Standards Act, labor-management relations, NLRB, OSHA). Home: 365 Westview Dr Athens GA 30606-4635 Office: U Ga Peabody Hall Ste 3 Athens GA 30602

DAVIS, CRESWELL DEAN, lawyer, consultant; b. Abilene, Tex., Sept. 12, 1932; s. Emmett Dean and Marye (Creswell) D.; m. Mollie Villeret, Aug. 9, 1958; children: Addison Dean Davis, Kevin Tucker Davis. BA with honors, U. North Tex., 1953; JD, U. Tex., 1958. Bar: Tex. 1958. Asst. atty. gen. State of Tex., Austin, 1958-61; sr., mng. ptnr. Davis & Davis, P.C., Austin, 1961—. Dir. Tex. Jr. Bar Conf., 1964-65. Author: Texas Legal and Consent Manual for Texas Hospitals, 1967-90; contbr. articles to profl. jours. Mem. U. North Tex. bd. regents, 1967-88, chmn., 1988; mem. U. North Tex. Health Sci. Ctr. and Tex. Coll. Osteopathic Medicine, 1967-88, chmn. 1988; adj. prof. hosp. law, Trinity U., San Antonio, 1967-90; adj. prof. pharmacy jurisprudence, U. Tex., 1969—. Recipient Disting. Svc. award Tex. Pharm. Assn., 1973, Outstanding Achievement award Tex. Assn. Life Underwriters, 1986, Outstanding Svc. award Tex. Assn. Child Care Facilities, 1984, Disting. Alumnus award U. North Tex., 1990. Mem. Rotary, Masons, Phi Alpha Delta. Episcopalian. Avocations: ranching, horses, education. Administrative and regulatory, General civil litigation, Health. Office: Davis & Davis PC 9442 N Capital Of Texas Hwy Austin TX 78759-7262

DAVIS, CYNTHIA D'ASCENZO, lawyer; b. Galveston, Tex., Dec. 6, 1953; d. Austin Christofer and Leah (Ellis) D'Ascenzo; 1 child, Field. BA, Sam Houston State U., 1975; JD cum laude, South Tex. Coll. Law., 1985. Bar: Miss. 1987, U.S. Dist. Ct. (no. dist., so. dist.) Miss. 1987, U.S. Ct. Appeals (5th cir.). Actuarial policy analyst Am. Nat. Ins. Co., Galveston, 1975-76; tchr. ESL Texas City (Tex.) Indep. Sch. Dist., 1976-83; legal asst. Law Offices of Darrel D. Ryland, Marksville, La., 1985; pvt. practice Gloster, Miss., 1987—; municipal judge Town of Crosby, 1993—; prosecutor and municipal atty. Town of Gloster, 1993—. Atty. Town of Crosby, Miss., 1993—; 2000-03, mcpl. judge, Town of Gloster, 1994—; prosecutor Amite County Youth Ct., 1994—; atty. Amite County Sch. Bd., 1995—; mem. Jud. Coll. Juvenile Justice curriculum com. Treas. Amite County Hist. Soc., 1988—; mem. Miss. Animal Rescue League, Jackson, 1987—, Am. Cancer Soc., 1980—, past bd. dirs., past pub. relations chmn. Mem. ABA, Miss. Trial Lawyers Assn., S.W. Miss. Bar Assn., Miss. Bar Assn. (child advocacy com. 1990—, alternative dispute resolution com. 1991—, Pres.'s award 1990, 91, assoc. pro bono project), Miss. Women Lawyers Assn., Assn. Trial Lawyers Am., Miss. Mcpl. Judges Assn. (v.p. and pres.-elect, pres. 1999-2001, past pres. 2001—, bd. dirs. curriculum com. Miss. Judicial Coll. 1998—), Miss. Capital Def. Resource Ctr. (sec., exec. com. bd. dirs.), Gloster C. of C. (sec.), Jr. League. Avocations: antiques, water skiing. Criminal, Family and matrimonial, General practice. Home: PO Box 940 Gloster MS 39638-0940 Office: 349 E North St Gloster MS 39638-9795

DAVIS, DEBORAH LYNN, lawyer; b. N.Y.C., Apr. 23, 1948; d. Melvin Jerome and Beatrice (Greenapple) D. BS, Case Western Res. U., 1970, JD, 1973. Bar: N.Y. 1974, U.S. Dist. Ct. (ea. and so. dists.) N.Y. 1974. Staff atty., dir. litigation Community Action for Legal Svcs., Inc., Bklyn., 1974-77, 78-81; atty. BLS Legal Svcs., N.Y.C., 1977-78; assoc. Gallet & Dreyer, N.Y.C., 1981-86; ptnr. Wagner, Davis & Gold, P.C., N.Y.C., 1986-99, of counsel, 1999—; ptnr. El-Baz Gallery N.Y. Ltd., N.Y.C., 1999-2000; pres., owner Deborah Davis Fine Art Inc., Hudson, N.Y., 2000—. Contbg. author chpts. in book. Incorporator, officer, bd. dirs. N.Y. Svc. Program for Older People, Inc., 1978-91; mem. Family Ct. Panel Screening and Oversight com. 1st Jud. Dept., 1985-88, vice-chair screening applicants, 1985-87. Mem. N.Y. State Bar Assn., N.Y. County Lawyers Assn., N.Y. Women's Bar Assn. General civil litigation, Landlord-tenant, Property, real (including real estate development, water). Office: Deborah Davis Fine Art Inc 345 Warren St Hudson NY 12534 E-mail: deborahdavisfineart@earthlink.net.

DAVIS, DON LAWRENCE, lawyer; b. San Antonio, Oct. 30, 1939; s. A.F. and Esther Davis; m. Patricia Ann Davis, May 6, 1960; children: Dana Leslie, Derek Lawrence. BS, Abilene Christian Coll., 1962; LLB, U. Tex., 1965. Bar: Tex., Colo., U.S. Dist. Ct. (we. dist.) Tex., U.S. Ct. Appeals (5th, 9th and 11th cirs.), U.S. Supreme Ct. Briefing atty. Supreme Ct. Tex., Austin, 1965—66; ptnr. Byrd, Davis, Eisenberg, Walter & Furman, Austin, 1967—. Editor: legal articles; sculpture, Children's Hosp. of Austin , PGA of Am. Chmn. Austin Smiles, Tex., 1980—85. Fellow: Tex. Bar Found., Am. Bar Found.; mem.: Fed. Bar Assn. Democrat. Mem. Ch. Of Christ. Aviation, Personal injury (including property damage), Product liability. Home: 3917 Balcones Dr Austin TX 78731 Office: Byrd Davis Eisenberg Walter & Furman 707 W 34th Austin TX 78705 Fax: 512-451-3751. E-mail: dondavis@byrddavis.com.

DAVIS, DONALD GLENN, lawyer; b. San Gabriel, Calif., Sept. 15, 1954; BS in Acctg., Calif. State U., Pomona; JD, U. So. Calif. Assoc. Adams, Duque & Hazeltine, L.A., O'Melveny & Meyers, L.A.; prof. of law Southwestern U. Law Sch., L.A., 1972-80; gen. counsel Republic Corp., L.A., 1973; ptnr. Danielson, St. Clair & Davis, L.A., 1974-77; mng. ptnr. Davis & Assocs., L.A., 1980—, DGD Enterprises P.V., L.A., 1980—, DGD Investment Banking, L.A., 1980—. Exec. editor Law Rev. jour., U. So. Calif., 1968-69. Vice-pres. student body, Calif. State U., Pomona, 1964-65; candidate 42nd Congl. Dist., Calif., 1988. Mem. ABA, L.A. Bar Assn. (chmn. securities cooperative seminar 1988, chmn. bus. lawyers sect. 1986-87), Order of Coif, Calif. Club, L.A. Yacht Club. Entertainment, Public international, Securities.

DAVIS, EDMOND RAY, lawyer; b. Glendale, Calif., Sept. 4, 1928; s. Archie Allen and Eve Mae (Hoover) D.; m. Ruby Evelyn Davis, Oct. 17, 1954; children: Phillip A., Sandra A. Ed., Pepperdine Coll.; JD, U. Calif., San Francisco, 1952. Bar: Calif. 1952, U.S. Dist. Ct. (cen. dist.) Calif. 1952. Assoc. Bailie, Turner & Sprague, 1955-60; trust counsel Security Pacific Nat. Bank, 1960-67; ptnr. Overton, Lyman & Prince, L.A., 1967-87, Brobeck, Phleger & Harrison, L.A., 1987-99, Davis & Whalen, Pasadena, Calif., 1999—. Chmn. legal adv. com. San Marino Unified Sch. Dist., 1981—; mem. legal com. Music Ctr. Found., Performing Arts Council, Los Angeles County, 1980—; trustee WM Group of Funds. Chmn., pub. adminstr. Pub. Guardian Adv. Commns., Los County Bd. Suprs., 1974-76; bd. dirs. Braille Inst. Am., Inc., 1974—, Children's Bur. So. Calif., Children's Bur. Found., WM Group of Funds, Mut. Funds; pres. Calif. Jaycees, 1962. With U.S. Army, 1952-54. Recipient Alumni award Pepperdine Coll., 1962. Fellow Am. Coll. Trust and Estate Counsel (chmn. Calif. chpt. 1981-86); mem. Internat. Acad. Estate and Trust Law (academician), State Bar of Calif. (chmn. estate planning, trust and probate law sect. 1977-78), L.A. County Bar Assn. (exec. com., probate and trust law sect. 1986-89, Arthur K. Marshall award Probate and Trust Law sect. 1991), Order of Coif, Calif. Club, Chancery Club. Estate planning, Probate (including wills, trusts), Estate taxation. Office: Davis & Whalen LLP 553 S Marengo Ave Pasadena CA 91101-3114 E-mail: edavis@daviswhalen.com.

DAVIS, EDWARD BERTRAND, retired federal judge, lawyer; b. W. Palm Beach, Fla., Feb. 10, 1933; s. Edward Bertrand and Mattie Mae (Walker) D.; m. Patricia Lee Klein, Apr. 5, 1958; children: Diana Lee Davis, Traci Russell, Edward Bertrand, III. JD, U. Fla., 1960; LLM in Taxation, N.Y. U., 1961. Bar: Fla. 1960. Pvt. practice, Miami, 1961-79; counsel High, Stack, Lazenby & Bender, 1978-79; U.S. dist. judge So. Dist. Fla., 1979-2000; assoc. Ackerman Senterfitt, 2000; chair state wide litig. practice. Served with AUS, 1953-55. Mem. Fla. Bar Assn., Dade County Bar Assn. Office: Akerman Senterfitt Suntrust Internat Ctr One SE 3d Ave 28th Fl Miami FL 33131 Fax: 305-374-5095. E-mail: edavis@akerman.com.

DAVIS, E(DWARD) MARCUS, lawyer; b. Atlanta, Nov. 24, 1951; s. Edward Martin and Marcine (McConnell) D.; m. Sue Fouquet; children: Edward Clark, Hannah Morgan. AB in Econs., Duke U., 1973; JD, U. Ga., 1976. Bar: U.S. Supreme Ct. 1981. Ptnr. Davis, Zipperman, Kirschenbaum & Lotito, Atlanta, 1983—. Contbr. articles to profl. jours. Mem. ABA, ATLA, Ga. Trial Lawyers Assn., Ga. Criminal Def. Lawyers Assn., Nat. Bd. Trial Advocacy (cert.), Am. Bd. Profl. Liability Attys. (cert.), Lawyers Club of Atlanta. Presbyterian. Avocations: boating, painting, horses. Personal injury (including property damage). Office: Davis Zipperman Kirschenbaum & Lotito 918 Ponce De Leon Ave NE Atlanta GA 30306-4212 E-mail: marc@dzkl.com.

DAVIS, EGBERT LAWRENCE, III, lawyer; b. Winston-Salem, N.C., Dec. 30, 1937; s. Egbert Lawrence Jr. and Eleanor (Layfield) D.; m. Alexandra Holderness, Aug. 25, 1962; children: Alexandra Davis Hipps, Egbert L. IV, Lucinda Davis, Pamela Davis. AB, Princeton U., 1960; LLB, Duke U., 1963; MBA, George Washington U., 1966. Bar: N.C. 1963. Assoc. Womble, Carlyle, Sandridge & Rice, Winston-Salem, N.C., 1965-70, ptnr., 1970-82, Raleigh, N.C., 1982-97, of counsel, 1997—. Mem. editl. bd. Duke U. Law Jour., 1963. Sec. Wachovia Realty Investments, Winston-Salem, 1969-82; rep. N.C. Ho. of Reps., Raleigh, 1970-74; sen. N.C. Senate, Raleigh, 1974-78; chmn. N.W. Environ. Preservation Com., Inc., Winston-Salem, 1980; chmn. trustees N.C. Bapt. Hosp., Winston-Salem, 1981-82, Family Bus. Forum, 1993-94; N.C. Prison Fellowship State coun., 1994-97; exec. com. N.C. Found. for Econ. Edn., 1996—, Ea. Ctr. for Regional Devel., 1996-97; bd. dirs. N.C. chpt. Coastal Conservation Assn., 1997—. Named Citizen of Yr. Winston-Salem Mayor's Com. on Employment of the Handicapped, 1971, Young Man. of Yr. Winston-Salem Jaycees, 1972; recipient Freedom Guard award N.C. Jaycees, 1973, U.S. Jaycees, 1973. Mem. N.C. Bar Assn. (bd. govs. 1979-82), Raleigh Rotary Club (pres. 1986-87). Presbyterian. Avocations: reading, writing, tennis, biking, fishing. Office: Womble Carlyle Sandridge PO Box 831 Raleigh NC 27602-0831

DAVIS, FERD LEARY, JR., law educator, lawyer, consultant; b. Zebulon, N.C., Dec. 4, 1941; s. Ferd L. and Selma Ann (Harris) D.; m. Joy Baker Davis, Jan. 25, 1963; children: Ferd Leary III, James Benjamin, Elizabeth Joy. BA, Wake Forest U., 1964, JD, 1967; LLM, Columbia U., 1984. Bar: N.C. 1967. Editor Zebulon (N.C.) Record, 1958; tchr. Davidson County Schs., Wallburg, N.C., 1966; ptnr. Davis & Davis and related law firms, Zebulon and Raleigh, N.C., 1967-76; asst. pros. Wake County Dist. Ct., Raleigh, 1968-69; town atty. Town of Zebulon, 1969-76; founding dean Campbell U. Sch. Law, Buies Creek, N.C., 1975-86, prof. law, 1975—. Dir. Inst. to Study Practice of Law and Socioecon. Devel., 1985—; chmn. The Davis Cons. Group, Inc., Buies Creek, 1987—; pres. LAWLEAD/NIELLP, 1998—; cons. U. Charleston, W.Va., 1979; vis. scholar Ctr. for Creative Leadership, 1993. Assoc. editor Wake Forest U. Law Rev. Trustee Wake County Pub. Librs., 1971-75, Olivia Raney Trust, 1969-71; mem. N.C. State Dem. Exec. Com., 1970-72, N.C. Gen. Statutes Commn., 1977-79, Commn. on the Future of N.C., 1980-83; dir., Howard Meml. Christian Edn. Fund, Raleigh Bus. and Tech. Ctr., NC BarCares. 1st Lt. USAR, 1959-66. Babcock scholar Wake Forest U., 1963-67; Dayton Hudson fellow Columbia U., 1982-83. Fellow Coll. Law Practice Mgmt.; mem. ABA, N.C. Bar Assn., N.C. State Bar, Rotary, Phi Delta Phi, Delta Theta Phi, Omicron Delta Kappa. Democrat. Office: LAWLEAD/NIELLP PO Box 4280 Buies Creek NC 27506-4280

DAVIS, FRANK WAYNE, lawyer; b. Ada, Okla., Aug. 24, 1936; s. Roscoe Gladstone and Neva Dell (Peck) D.; m. Kay Diane Higginbotham, Aug. 12, 1961; children: David, Paul. Student, U. Ill., Urbana, 1956-57; BA, East Cen. U., 1958; LLB, U. Okla., Norman, 1959. Bar: Okla. 1959, U.S. Dist. Ct. (we. dist.) Okla. 1965, U.S. Ct. Appeals (10th crct.) 1976. Acting postmaster U.S. Postal Service, Ada, 1959-61; assoc. Denny W. Falkenburg, Medford, Okla., 1961; atty. Logan County, Guthrie, Okla., 1961-65; sole practice Guthrie, 1965—83, 1988—; ptnr. Davis and Hudson, Guthrie, 1985-88. Mcpl. judge City of Guthrie, 1974-78; rep. State of Okla., Oklahoma City, 1978—; vice chmn. judiciary com. Okla. Ho. of Reps., 1981-82, 89, 91—; minority fl. leader, 1982-86, asst. minority fl. leader, 1986-90. Del. gen. conf. United Meth. Ch., Portland, Oreg., 1976; del. Rep. Nat. Convs., 1984, 96, alt. del., 2000; scoutmaster Boy Scout Troop # 850, Guthrie, 1961-2000; chmn. Logan County Reps., Guthrie, 1964-69. Recipient Silver Beaver award Boy Scouts Am., 1978. Mem. Okla. Bar Assn., Logan County Bar Assn. (pres. 1972-73), Gideons. Lodges: Lions, Masons. Methodist. Avocations: fishing, stamp collecting, farming, oil and gas production. General practice, Probate (including wills, trusts), Property, real (including real estate development, water). Office: 115 N Division St Guthrie OK 73044-3240 also: 509 State Capitol Bldg Oklahoma City OK 73105 Home: 17300 Valley Crst Edmond OK 73003-6770

DAVIS, FRANK TRADEWELL, JR., lawyer; b. Atlanta, Feb. 2, 1938; s. Frank T. and Sue (Burnett) D.; m. Winifred Storey, June 23, 1961; children: Frank, Frederick, Gordon. AB, Princeton U., 1960; JD, George Washington U., 1963; LLM, Harvard U., 1964. Bar: Ga. 1963, D.C. 1966, U.S. Ct. Appeals (5th cir.) 1963, U.S. Ct. Appeals (11th cir.) 1982, U.S. Supreme Ct. 1968. Assoc. Hansell, Post Brandon & Dorsey, Atlanta, 1964-67; ptnr. Hansell & Post, Atlanta, 1968-77, 79-86, Long, Aldridge & Norman, Atlanta, 1986—. Ptnr., gen. counsel Pres.'s Reorgn. Project Office of Pres., 1977-79; vis. instr. U. Ga. Law Sch., 1964-66, Ga. State U. Law Sch., 1988-90; vis. prof. Emory U. Law Sch., 1992—. Author: Business Acquisitions, 1977, (2d edit.), 1982; contbr. articles to legal jours. Bd. dirs. Nat. Inst. Justice, 1980—81, Westminster Schs., 1969—, chmn. bd. dirs., 1984—89; bd. dirs.. Va. Sem., 1980—94, exec. com., 1985—89; mem. Atlanta Charter Commn.; chmn. Atlanta Crime Commn., 1977; mem. bd. councilors Carter Presdl. Ctr., 1988—; chmn. Rotary Ednl. Found. Atlanta; commr. Atlanta Regional Commn., 1999—; sr. warden All Saints' Episcopal Ch., 1982, 2002, vestry, 2000—. Lt. USN, 1960—62. Fellow Am. Bar Found.; mem. Am. Law Inst., Atlanta C. of C. (bd. dirs. 1975-77), Piedmont Driving Club (Atlanta), Capital City Club (Atlanta), Cedar Creek Racquet Club (Cashiers, N.C.), The Army and Navy Club (Washington), Rotary (pres. Atlanta chpt. 1990-91, bd. dirs., sec. 1988-89, chmn. bd., 1991-92, chmn. Ednl. Found. 1997—). Corporate, general, Libel. Home: 2500 Peachtree Rd Atlanta GA 30305-5609 Office: 303 Peachtree St NE Ste 5300 Atlanta GA 30308-3264 E-mail: ftdjr@earthlink.net.

DAVIS, FREDERICK BENJAMIN, law educator; b. Bklyn., Aug. 21, 1926; s. Clifford Howard and Anne Frances (Forbes) D.; m. Mary Ellen Saecker, Apr. 21, 1956; children: Judith, Robert, James, Mary. AB, Yale U., 1948; JD, Cornell U., 1953; LLM with honors, Victoria U. of Wellington, New Zealand, 1955. Bar: N.Y. 1953, Mo. 1970, Ohio 1981. Assoc. Engel Judge & Miller, N.Y.C., 1953-54; instr. U. Pa. Law Sch., 1955-56; asst. prof. NYU, 1956-57, U. S.D., 1957-60, assoc. prof., 1960-62, Emory U., 1962-63, prof., 1963-66, U. Mo.-Columbia, 1966-70, Edward W. Hinton prof. law, 1970-81, Edward W. Hinton prof. emeritus, 1981—; dean, prof. law U. Dayton Sch. Law, 1981-86; dean, prof. Memphis State U., 1987-92, prof., 1992-98, prof., dean emeritus, 1998—. Cons. adminstrv. procedure Mo. Senate, 1974-77; vis. prof. Wake Forest U. Sch. Law, 1980, 86-87, U. Wis., 1960, George Washington U., 1965, Tulane U., 1966, U. Mo.-Kansas City, 1973, U. Ky., 1977. Contbr. numerous articles, comments, revs., notes to profl. jours. Served with USNR, 1944-46. Mem. ABA (coun. sect. adminstrv. law 1969-75), Am. Law Inst., Rotary Club (Memphis Ctrl. chpt.), Summit Club. Republican. Episcopalian. E-mail: freddyandmary@aol.com.

DAVIS, GREGORY R. lawyer; b. Lexington, Va., Aug. 22, 1961; s. James B. and Joyce O. Davis; m. Elizabeth Fletcher, Aug. 4, 1984; 1 child, Sarah. BA, U. Va., Charlottesville, 1983; JD, Coll. of William & Mary Sch. Law, Williamsburg, 1986. Bar: Supreme Ct. of Va. 1986, U.S. Dist. Ct., Eastern Dist. 1992, U.S. Bankruptcy Ct. of Va., Eastern Dist. 1992. Summer assoc. Steptoe & Johnson, Clarksburg, Va., 1985; adj. prof. Marshall-Wythe Sch. Law, Williamsburg, Va., 1986—98; atty. Anderson, Franck & Davis, P.C., Williamsburg, Va., 1986—98, Kaufman & Canoles, P.C., Williamsburg, Va., 1999—. Trustee, bd. mem. Walsingham Acad., Williamsburg, Va., 1998—; bd. dirs. chmn., atty. divsn. United Way of Greater Williamsburg, Va., 1990—99; adv. bd. mem. Suntrust Bank, Williamsburg, Va., 1999—. Named Top 40 Under Forty, Inside Bus. Mag., 2000. Avocations: golf, duck hunting, boating, astronomy, music. Office: Kaufman & Canoles PC 1200 Old Colony Ln Williamsburg VA 23185 Fax: 757-259-3867.

DAVIS, HENRY BARNARD, JR., lawyer; b. East Grand Rapids, Mich., June 3, 1923; s. Henry Barnard and Ethel Margaret (Turnbull) D.; m. Margaret Lees Wilson, Aug. 27, 1946; children: Caroline Dellenbusch, Laura Davis, George B. BA, Yale U., 1945; JD, U. Mich., 1950; LLD, Olivet Coll., 1983. Bar: Mich. 1951, U.S. Dist. Ct. (we. dist.) Mich. 1956, U.S. Ct. Appeals (6th cir.) 1971, U.S. Supreme Ct. 1978. Assoc. Allaben, Wiarda, Hayes & Hewitt, 1951-52; ptnr. Hayes, Davis & Dellenbusch PLC, Grand Rapids, Mich., 1952—2002, Davis & Davis Law Office PLC, Grand Rapids, 2002—. Mem. Kent County Bd. Commrs., 1968-72; mem. Cmty. Mental Health Bd., 1970-94, past chmn.; trustee, sec. bd. Olivet Coll., 1965-91, trustee emeritus, 1991—; bd. dirs. Jr. Achievement Grand Rapids, 1960-65; chair Grand Rapids Historic Preservation Com., 1977-79; trustee East Congregational Ch., 1979-81. Served with USAAF, 1943-46, Philippines. Mem. ABA, Mich. Bar Assn., Grand Rapids Round Table (pres. 1969), Masons. Republican. Estate planning, Probate (including wills, trusts), Property, real (including real estate development, water). Home: 30 Mayfair Dr NE Grand Rapids MI 49503-3831 Office: 535 Fountain St NE Grand Rapids MI 49503-3421 E-mail: hbdavis@mac.com.

DAVIS, HERBERT OWEN, lawyer; b. Washington, June 11, 1935; s. Owen Stier and Claudie Lea (Pointer) D.; children: Herbert O. Jr., Ann P., Paul B. BA, U. N.C., 1957; JD, Duke U., 1960. Bar: N.C. 1960, U.S. Dist. Ct. (mid. dist.) N.C. 1960. Assoc. Smith Moore Smith Schell & Hunter, Greensboro, NC, 1960—66, ptnr., 1966—86, Smith Helms Mulliss & Moore, Greensboro, 1986—2002, Smith Moore LLP, Greensboro, 2002—. Editor in chief Duke Law Jour., 1959—60. Mem. ABA, N.C. Bar Assn., Greensboro Country Club, Greensboro City Club (bd. dirs.), The Carolina Club, Phi Beta Kappa. Banking, Corporate, general, Mergers and acquisitions. Home: 2303 Danbury Rd Greensboro NC 27408-5123 Office: Smith Moore LLP 300 N Greene St Ste 1400 Greensboro NC 27401-2171 E-mail: bert.davis@smithmoorelaw.com.

DAVIS, JAMES HORNOR, III, lawyer; b. Clarksburg, W.Va., Oct. 9, 1928; s. James Hornor II and Martha (Maxwell) D.; m. Ouida Caldwell, July 1, 1950; children— James Hornor IV, Lewis Caldwell. AB, Princeton U., 1950; LL.B., U. Va., 1953. Bar: W.Va. 1953. Ptnr. firm Preston & Davis, Charleston, 1953-65, Spilman, Thomas, Battle & Klostermeyer, Charleston, 1965-86; of counsel Campbell, Woods, Bagley, Emerson McNeer & Herndon, Charleston, 1987—. Mem. W.Va. Ho. of Dels., 1961-62, W.Va. Senate, 1963-66; pres. Dingess-Rum Properties, Inc. Hon. trustee Ea. Mineral Law Found. Served with USAF, 1953-55. Fellow ABA (life); mem. Am. Law Inst. (life), Am. Judicature Soc. (dir. 1978-81), W.Va. Jud. Coun. (chmn. 1973-81), W.Va. Bar Assn. (pres. 1985-86), Kanawha County Bar Assn., Nat. Coun. Coal Lessors (chmn. 1980—), W.Va. Mfrs. Assn. (chmn. 1973-75, hon. dir.) Democrat. Episcopalian. Corporate, general. Office: Campbell Woods Bagley et al PO Box 2393 Charleston WV 25328-2393

DAVIS, JAMES THOMAS, lawyer; b. Uniontown, Pa., Oct. 17, 1951; s. Norman J. and Thelma (Solomon) D.; m. Martha Russin, Sept. 4, 1976; children: Cara Catherine, Jeremy James, Adina Ann, Jacob Jamail, Kalie Marie. BA, California (Pa.) State Coll., 1973; JD, Duquesne U., 1976. Bar: Pa. 1976, U.S. Dist. Ct. (we. dist.) Pa. 1976, U.S. Supreme Ct. 1984; cert. criminal and civil trial advocate Nat. Bd. Trial Advocacy. Asst. dist. atty. Fayette County, Pa., 1977-83; ptnr. firm Davis & Davis, Uniontown, 1976—. Adj. faculty California (Pa.) U. Mem. ATLA, Pa. Trial Lawyers Assn. Democrat. Eastern Orthodox. Criminal, Personal injury (including property damage), Probate (including wills, trusts). Office: Davis & Davis PO Box 1163 Uniontown PA 15401-1163 E-mail: jdavis@davisanddavislaw.com.

DAVIS, JIMMY FRANK, assistant attorney general; b. Lubbock, Tex., June 14, 1945; s. Jack and Fern Lisemby D.; M. Joyce Zelma Hart, Nov. 6, 1976; children: Jayme Leigh, Julee Ellen. BS in Edn., Tex. Tech. U., 1968; JD, U. Tex., 1972. Bar: Tex. 1972, U.S. Supreme Ct. 1975, U.S. Dist. (no dist.) Tex. 1976, U.S. Ct. Appeals (5th cir.) 1976, U.S. Ct. Appeals (11cir.) 1981. Asst. criminal dist. atty. Lubbock County, 1973—77, adminstrv. asst., 1976-77; county and dist. atty. Castro County, Tex., 1977-92; asst. atty. gen. State of Tex., 1993—; mem. forms com. Atty. Gen. Office, 1999—2001. Mem. State Bar of Tex. (com. admissions dist. 16 1974-78, dist. 13 1983-92, govt. lawyers sect., coun. mem. 1991-92), Tex. Dist. and County Attys. Assn., Lubbock County Jr. Bar Assn. (pres. 1977), Tex. Tech. Ex Students Assn. (dist. rep. 1981-84, bd. dirs. 1985-90), Coll. of State Bar of Tex. (continuing legal edn. 1984-93), Kiwanis of Lubbock (pres. 1977), Kiwanis of Dimmitt (pres. 1981), Delta Theta Phi. Office: PO Box 2747 916 Main St Suite 900 Lubbock TX 79408

DAVIS, JOHN CHARLES, lawyer; b. Kansas City, Mo., Mar. 4, 1943; s. Ralph B. Jr. and Helen M. (Schneider) D.; m. C. Jane Reusser, June 18, 1966; children: Tracy A., Matthew S. BA, U. Kans., 1965; JD, U. Mich., 1968. Bar: Mo. 1968, Kans. 1983. Ptnr. Stinson, Mag & Fizzell, P.C., Kansas City, 1968—. Chmn. Fed. Estate Tax Symposium, 1986-87. Chmn. Bacchus Found., Kansas City, 1974; bd. dirs. Crittenten, Kansas City, 1988-94, vice chmn., 1990-92; trustee Schutte Found., Kansas City, 1986—, U. Kansas City, 1989—, treas., 1994-96, counsel, 1996—; trustee Village Presbyn. Ch. Found., chmn., 1991-93; elder Village Presbyn. Ch., 1994-97; bd. dirs. Gamma O Edn. Found., 1991—, Heart of Am. Counsel, Boy Scouts Am., 1995—, exec. com., 1996—; dir. John Cty. C.C. Found., 2000—. Fellow Am. Coll. Trust and Estate Counsel (by-laws com. 1987-96, chmn. 1996-99, 2002-, program com. 1993-96); mem. ABA, Mo. Bar Assn., Kans. Bar Assn., Estate Planning Soc. Kansas City (pres. 1990-91), Nelson-Atkins Mus. Soc. Fellows, Kansas City Club (v.p. 1989-90), Indian Hills Country Club (Mission Hills, Kans.), Rotary, Gamma Omicron (pres., bd. dirs. 1979-85). Presbyterian. Avocations: squash, hopi art, marklin trains, travel, photography. Estate planning, Estate taxation. Home: 6421 High Dr Shawnee Mission KS 66208-1935 Office: Stinson Morrison Hecker LLP 1201 Walnut St Kansas City MO 64106

DAVIS, JOHN MACDOUGALL, lawyer; b. Seattle, Feb. 20, 1914; s. David Lyle and Georgina (MacDougall) D.; m. Ruth Anne Van Arsdale, July 1, 1939; children: Jean, John, Bruce, Ann, Margaret, Elizabeth. BA, U. Wash., 1936, LLB, JD, 1940. Bar: Wash. 1940. Assoc. Poe, Falknor, Emory & Howe, Seattle, 1940-45; pvt. practice Seattle, 1945-46; ptnr. Davis & Riese, Seattle, 1946-48, Emory, Howe, Davis & Riese, Seattle, 1948-50, Howe, Davis & Riese, Seattle, 1951-53, Howe, Davis, Riese & Aiken, Seattle, 1953-58, Howe, Davis, Riese & Jones, Seattle, 1958-68, Davis, Wright, Todd, Riese & Jones, Seattle, 1969-85; of counsel Davis, Wright & Jones, Seattle, 1985-89, Davis Wright Tremaine, Seattle, 1990—. Lectr. U. Wash. Law Sch., 1947-52. Bd. dirs. Virginia Mason Hosp., Seattle, 1952-79, pres., 1970-72; bd. dirs. Pacific Sci. Ctr., 1971-90, dir. emeritus, 1991—, past pres., past chmn.; trustee Whitman Coll., 1971-86, chmn., 1983-86; bd. dirs. Blue Cross Wash. and Alaska, 1982-89, Diabetic Trust Fund, 1954—, Wash. Student Loan Guaranty Assn., 1978-83; mem. adv. bd. Chief Seattle council Boy Scouts Am.; mem. Mercer Island Sch. Bd., 1956-66. Served with USNG, 1931-34. Recipient Disting. Eagle Scout award, 1982 Mem. ABA, Wash. State Bar Assn. (merit award 1965), Seattle-King County Bar Assn. (pres. 1960-61), Order of Coif, Rainier Club (Seattle), The Mountaineers Club, Phi Delta Phi, Alpha Delta Phi. Clubs: Rainier (Seattle). Presbyterian. Avocation: mountain climbing. Home: 9104 Fortuna Dr #3305 Mercer Island WA 98040-3166 Office: Davis Wright Tremaine 2600 Century Sq 1501 4th Ave Ste 2600 Seattle WA 98101-1688

DAVIS, KENNETH BOONE, JR., dean, law educator; b. Louisville, Sept. 1, 1947; s. Kenneth Boone and Doris Edna (Gordon) D. m. Arrietta Evoline Hastings, June 2, 1984; children: Peter Hastings, Mary Elizabeth, Kenneth Boone III. AB, U. Mich., 1969; JD, Case Western Res. U., 1974. Bar: D.C. 1975, Ohio 1974. Law clk. to chief judge U.S. Ct. Appeals (9th cir.), San Francisco, 1974-75; assoc. Covington & Burling, Washington, 1975-78; prof. law U. Wis., Madison, 1978—, dean Law Sch., 1997—. Contbr. numerous articles on corp. and securities law to profl jours. Mem. ABA, Am. Fin. Assn., Am. Law Inst., Wis. Bar Assn. (reporter, corp. and bus. law com.). Office: U Wis Law Sch 975 Bascom Mall Madison WI 53706-1399

DAVIS, KIRK STUART, lawyer; b. Olean, N.Y., Dec. 30, 1957; s. Robert DeWitt and Joan Gracie Davis; m. Aileen Stewart, Dec. 24, 1982. BS, Stetson U., 1979, JD, 1982. Bar: Fla. 1983, U.S. Dist. Ct. (mid. dist.) Fla. 1983. Lawyer Greene, Mann, Rowe, St. Petersburg, Fla., 1983-84, Greene & Mastry, P.A., St. Petersburg, 1984-91, Elias & Davis, P.A., Clearwater, Fla., 1991-94, Annis, Mitchell, Tampa, Fla., 1995-97, Akerman Senterfitt, Tampa, 1997—. Mem. Fla. Bar Assn. (chair health law sect. 1992-93, chair health law cert. com. 1998-99), Bayou Club (mem. adv. bd. 1991-98, chair adv. bd. 1994-98). Avocation: golf. General civil litigation, Health. Office: Akerman Senterfitt 100 S Ashley Dr Ste 1500 Tampa FL 33602-5314

DAVIS, MARGUERITE HERR, judge; b. Washington, Nov. 12, 1947; d. Norman Phillip and Margaretha Joanna Herr; m. James Riley Davis, June 20, 1970; children: Amy Marguerite, Christine Riley. AA with honors, St. Petersburg J. Coll., Clearwater, Fla., 1966; BA with honors, U. of South Fla., 1968; JD with honors, Fla. State U., 1971. Bar: Fla. 1971, U.S. Dist. Ct. (no. dist.) Fla. 1971, U.S. Dist. Ct. (mid. dist.) Md. 1985, U.S. Ct. Appeals (11th cir.) 1985, U.S. Supreme Ct. 1986. Atty. workers compensation div. U.S. Dept. Labor, Tallahassee, 1971; sr. legal aide Fla. Supreme Ct., Tallahassee, 1971-85, exec. asst. to Hon. Chief Justice Alderman, 1982-84; ptnr. Swann & Haddock, Tallahassee, 1985-87, Katz, Kutter, Haigler, Alderman, Davis & Marks, Tallahassee, 1987-93; judge Dist. Ct. of Appeal (1st dist.) Fla., Tallahassee, 1993—. Mem. editl. bd. Trial Advocate Quar., 1991-93; contbr. chpts. to books. Mem. ABA, Fla. Bar Assn. (Tallahassee chpt., appellate ct. rules com. 1995—, appellate ct. rules com. chair, 1995-97, grievance com., disciplinary rev. com., chmn. supreme ct. local rules adv. com., jud. cir. grievance com., rules of jud. adminstrn. 1995-99, chair 1997-98, chair jud. evaluation com. 1999-2000, chair 2001-03, exec. coun. appellate advocacy sect.), Fla. State Fed. Jud. Coun. (exec. dir. 1985—), Tallahassee Women Lawyers, Fla. Def. Lawyers Assn. (amicus curiae com.), Fla. Supreme Ct. Hist. Soc., Am. Arbitration Assn. (ad hoc com. stds. for appellate practice cert.), Altrusa Club of Tallahassee (treas. 1971-76), Fla. State U. Alumni Assn. (bd. dirs. 1975-76), Jud. Mgmt. Coun. (appellate ct. workload and jurisdiction com. 1996—, chair appellate rules liaison com., appellate practice and advocacy sect. 1996-98), Univ. So. Fla. (bd. dirs. Alumni Assn. 1999), Phi Theta Kappa. Methodist. Avocations: quilting, sewing, knitting, running, reading.

DAVIS, MARK RICHARD, lawyer; b. Nov. 10, 1953; BA, U. N.Mex., 1975; JD, DePaul U., 1979. Asst. states atty., tax divsn. supr. Cook County States Atty. Office, Chgo., 1979-89; ptnr. O'Keefe Ashenden Lyons & Ward, Chgo., 1989—. Bd. dirs., property tax com. Civic Fedn., Chgo., 1992—; property tax adv. com. Ill. Tax Payers Fedn., Springfield, Ill., 1992—. Mem. Ill. State Bar Assn. (past chair state and local tax sect. counsel 1991—), Chgo. Bar Assn. (real estate tax com.), Phi Beta Kappa. Office: O'Keefe Ashenden Lyons & Ward 30 N Lasalle St Ste 4100 Chicago IL 60602-2507 E-mail: markdavis@okeefe-law.com.

DAVIS, MICHAEL J. judge; b. 1947; BA, Macalester Coll., 1969; JD, U. Minn., 1972; LLD (hon.) , Macalester Coll., 2001. Law clk. Legal Rights Ctr., 1971-73; with Office Gen. Counsel Dept. Health, Edn. and Welfare, Social Security Adminstrn., Balt., 1973; criminal def. atty. Neighborhood Justice Ctr., 1974, Legal Rights Ctr., 1975—78; pub. defender Hennepin County, 1978-83; judge Hennepin County Mcpl. Ct., 1983-84, Hennepin County Dist. Ct. (4th jud. dist.), 1984-94; atty., commr. Mpls. Civil Rights Commn., 1977-82; judge U.S. Dist. Ct. Minn., St. Paul, 1994—. Constnl. law instr. Antioch Mpls. C.C., 1974; criminal def. trial practice instr. Nat. Lawyer's Guild, 1977; trial practice instr. William Mitchell Coll. Law, 1977-81, Bemidji Trial Advocacy Course, 1992, 93; adj. prof. U. Minn. Law Sch., 1982—, Hubert H. Humphrey Sch. Pub. Affairs, 1990; instr. Minn. Inst. Legal Edn., Civil Trial Practice Inst., 1991-92; lectr. FBI Acad., 1991, 92. Mem. Minn. Superior Ct. Racial Bias Task Force, 1990—93, U.S. Dist. Ct.; chmn. Pretrial Release & Bail Evaluation Com., 1997—. Recipient Outstanding Alumni award Macalester Coll., 1989, Good Neighbor award WCCO Radio, 1989, Disting Svc. award William Mitchell Coll. of Law, 2000. Mem. ABA, Nat. Bar Assn., Minn. Minority Lawyers Assn., Am. Inns. of Ct., Fed. Bar Assn., Fed. Judges Assn., Hennepin County Bar Assn., Minn. State Bar Assn., Minn. Lawyers Internat. Human Rights Com. (past mem. bd. dirs.), Internat. Acad. Trial Judges, Nat. Assn. for Pub. Interest Law (bd. dirs.), 8th Cir. Jury Instruction Com., U.S. Assn. Constitutional Law. Office: US Dist Ct Minn 300 S 4th St Ste 14E Minneapolis MN 55415-2251 E-mail: mjdavis@mnd.uscourts.gov.

DAVIS, MICHAEL STEVEN, lawyer; b. Brookline, Mass., Aug. 1, 1947; s. Ralph and Beatrice (Levy) D.; m. Madelyn O. Davis, Aug. 16, 1970; children: Gregory, Adam, Bethany. AB, U. Rochester, 1969; JD cum laude, Boston U., 1972. Bar: N.Y. 1973, U.S. Dist. Ct. (so. and ea. dists.) N.Y. 1974, U.S. Ct. Appeals (2d cir.) 1974, U.S. Supreme Ct. 1979, U.S. Ct. Claims, 1980. Assoc. Chadbourne & Parke, N.Y.C., 1972-82; sr. counsel corp. litigation Am. Internat. Group, N.Y.C., 1982-88; ptnr. Zalkin, Rodin & Goodman, LLP, N.Y.C., 1988-99, Zeichner, Ellman & Krause, LLP, N.Y.C., 1999—. Asst. adj. prof. C.W. Post Ctr., L.I. U., Glen Cove, N.Y., 1975-79. Editor Boston U. Law Rev., 1970-72. Mem. Citizens Ctr. for Children of NY, Inc., 1978—87; trustee The Harvey Sch., Katona, NY, 1994—97; pres. Pelham (NY) Jewish Ctr., 1986—88; v.p. Sinai Free Synagogue, 2003—. Mem. ABA, Assn. Bar City of N.Y., Am. Arbitration Assn., Huguenot Bridge Club. Democrat. Bankruptcy, General civil litigation, Insurance. Office: Zeichner Ellman & Krause LLP 575 Lexington Ave New York NY 10022-6102 E-mail: mdavis@zeklaw.com.

DAVIS, MULLER, lawyer; b. Chgo., Apr. 23, 1935; s. Benjamin B. and Janice (Muller) D.; m. Jane Lynn Strauss, Dec. 28, 1963 (div. July 1998); children: Melissa Davis Muller, Muller Jr., Joseph Jeffrey; m. Lynn Straus, Jan. 23, 1999. Grad. with honors, Phillips Exeter (N.H.) Acad., 1953; BA magna cum laude, Yale U., 1957; JD, Harvard U., 1960. Bar: Ill. 1960, U.S. Dist. Ct. (no. dist.) Ill. 1961. Practice law, Chgo., 1960—; assoc. Jenner & Block, 1960-67; ptnr. Davis, Friedman, Zavett, Kane, MacRae, Marcus & Rubens, 1967—. Lectr. continuing legal edn., matrimonial law and litigation; legal adviser Michael Reese Med. Research Inst. Council, 1967-82. Author: (with Sherman C. Feinstein) The Parental Couple in a Successful Divorce; Illinois Practice of Family Law, 1995, 97, 98-99, (with Jody Meyer Yazici) 4th edit. 2000-2001, 5th edit., 2003-04; contbg. author Marriage, Health and the Professions; mem. editl. bd. Equitable Distbn. Jour., 1984—; contbr. articles to law jours. Bd. dirs. Infant Welfare Soc., 1975-96, hon. bd. dirs., 1996—, pres., 1978-82; co-chmn. gen. gifts 40th and 45th reunions Phillips Exeter Acad., chair class capital giving, 1994-98, 50th reunion gift com. Yale Class Council 2002—. Capt. U.S. Army, Ill. N.G., 1960-67. Fellow Am. Acad. Matrimonial Lawyers (bd. mgrs. Ill. chpt. 1996-99), Am. Bar Found.; mem. ABA, FBA, Ill. Bar Assn., Chgo. Bar Assn. (matrimonial com. 1968-83, sec. civil practice com. 1979-80, vice chmn. 1980-81, chmn. 1981-82), Am. Soc. Writers on Legal Subjects, Chgo. Estate Planning Coun., Legal Aid Soc. (vice chmn. matrimonial bar 1991-95, vice chmn. 1995-97, chmn. 1997-99), Lawyers Club Chgo., Tavern Club, Lake Shore Country Club, Chgo. Club. Republican. Jewish. Family and matrimonial. Home: 161 E Chicago Ave Apt 34 E Chicago IL 60611-2601 Office: Davis Friedman Zavett Kane MacRae Marcus & Rubens 140 S Dearborn St Ste 1600 Chicago IL 60603-5288 E-mail: mdavis@davisfriedman.com.

DAVIS, NOAH, lawyer; b. Honolulu, Sept. 5, 1971; s. Elvin R. Davis and Beverly L. Tidwell. BA in Psychology and Polit. Sci., U. Ctrl. Ark., 1995; JD, U. Ark., 1998; LLM, U. Melbourne, Australia, 2000. Bar: Wash. 2001, U.S. Dist. Ct. (we. dist.) Wash. 2002. Law clk. Judge T. Crabtree Ark. Ct. Appeals, 1998; with Treasury Funds Mgmt. Ltd., Melbourne, Australia, 1999—2000; ptnr. In Pacta PLLC, Seattle, 2001—. Chmn., CEO Aid Cambodia, Seattle. Mem.: ATLA, ABA, Wash. State Bar Assn. (fee arbiter arbitration program, chair membership com. young lawyers divsn.), Smithsonian Soc. Intellectual property, General practice, Private international. Office: In Pacta PLLC 1006 Turner Way E Seattle WA 98112 Office Fax: 206-860-0178. E-mail: nd@inpacta.com.

DAVIS, RICHARD EARL, lawyer; b. Jackson, Mich., Aug. 13, 1951; s. Richard Allen and Velva Elizabeth (England) D.; m. Paula Hurst, Dec. 9, 1972; children: Richard Seth, Tessa Rebecca. BA, U. So. Fla., 1973, MA, 1975; JD cum laude, Stetson U., 1977. Bar: Fla. 1978, U.S. Ct. Appeals (11th cir.), U.S. Dist. Ct. (mid. dist.) Fla.; bd. cert. city, county and local govt. law Fla. Bar; cert. circuit civil mediator. Asst. county atty. Hillsborough County, Fla., 1978-85; assoc. Holland & Knight, Tampa, Fla., 1985-88, ptnr., 1988-96, Richard E. Davis, P.A., Tampa, Fla., 1997—. Adj. prof. St. Leo U.; lectr. in field. Mem. ABA, Hillsborough County Bar Assn., Fla. Bar Assn., Stetson Lawyers Assn., Tampa Downtown Partnership, Phi Kappa Phi, Phi Sigma Alpha. Office: 220 E Madison St Ste 512 Tampa FL 33602-4826 E-mail: tpaland@earthlink.net.

DAVIS, RICHARD RALPH, lawyer; b. Houston, July 28, 1936; s. William Ralph and Virginia (Allison) D.; m. Christina R. Zelkoff, June 1, 1974; 1 child, Virginia Lee Allison. BA, Yale U., 1962, LLB, 1965; MBA, Columbia U., 1965. Bar: N.Y. 1966. Law clk. FAA, Washington, 1964; assoc. Chadbourne & Parke, N.Y.C., 1965-73, ptnr., 1974-83; sr. v.p., gen. counsel Inspiration Resources Corp., N.Y.C., 1983-91; sr. v.p., sec., gen. counsel Bessemer Securities Corp./Bessemer Trust Co., NA, N.Y.C., 1991—. With U.S. Army, 1956-59. Mem. ABA. Banking, Corporate, general, Finance. Home: 1185 Park Ave Apt 6-g New York NY 10128-1309 E-mail: davis@bessemer.com.

DAVIS, RICHARD WATERS, lawyer; b. Rocky Mount, Va., July 9, 1931; s. Beverly Andrew and Julia (Waters) D.; m. Mary Alice Woods; children: Debra, Julie, Richard Jr., Bob, Bev. B, Hampden-Sydney Coll., 1951; LLB, U. Richmond, 1959. Bar: Va. 1959. Pvt. practice, Radford, Va., 1959—. Dist. judge City of Radford, 1962-80; mem. Pub. Defenders Commn. Va., 1993—, chmn. 2002-; mem. Va. State Bar Coun., 1989-95; assoc. prof. bus. law Radford U.; lectr. Va. Trial Lawyers Assn. Fellow Am. Coll. Trial Lawyers, Am. Bar Found., Va. Law Found. (fellows coun. 1992-98); mem. ABA. Va. Bar Assn. State civil litigation, Insurance, Personal injury (including property damage). Home: 101 5th St Radford VA 24141 Office: PO Box 3448 Radford VA 24143-3448

DAVIS, RICHMOND T.P. lawyer; b. L.A., Sept. 30, 1945; s. Robert J. and Suzanne (Lennox) D.; m. Christine M. King; children: Timothy, Elizabeth, Katherine. BA, U. Md., 1968; JD, Georgetown U., 1977. Bar: Md. 1977, D.C. 1978, U.S. Dist. Ct. Md. 1978, U.S. Dist. D.C. 1978, U.S. Ct. Appeals (4th cir.) 1995. Editor Phillips Pub., Chevy Chase, Md., 1973-77; atty. Law Offices of Richmond Davis, Silver Spring, Md., 1977—. Contbr. articles to newspapers. Chmn. Co. Bar Bicentennial com., Mont. Co., Md., 1987, Rep. Party, Prince George's, Md., 1989-92. 1st lt. U.S. Army, 1968-71, Vietnam. Mem. Md. State Bar (character com. 1982-87). Avocations: horse racing, history reading, travel. Bankruptcy, Criminal, Personal injury (including property damage). Office: 8720 Georgia Ave Ste 700 Silver Spring MD 20910-3602 E-mail: RTPDavis@aol.com.

DAVIS, ROBERT EDWARD, state supreme court justice; b. Topeka, Aug. 28, 1939; s. Thomas Homer and Emma Claire (Hund) D.; m. Jana Jones; children: Edward, Rachel, Patrick, Carolyn, Brian. BA in Polit. Sci., Creighton U., 1961; JD, Georgetown U., 1964. Bar: Kans. 1964, U.S. Dist. Ct. Kans. 1964, U.S. Tax Ct. 1974, U.S. Ct. Mil. Appeals 1965, U.S. Ct. Mil. Review, 1970, U.S. Ct. Appeals (10th cir.) 1974, U.S. Supreme Ct. 1982. Pvt. practice, Leavenworth, Kans., 1967-84; magistrate judge Leavenworth County, 1969-76, county atty., 1980-84, judge dist. ct., 1984-86; judge Kans. Ct. Appeals Jud. Br. Govt., Topeka, 1986-93; justice Kans. Supreme Ct., Topeka, 1993—. Lectr. U. Kans. Law Sch., Lawrence, 1986-95. Capt. JAGC, U.S. Army, 1964-67, Korea. Mem. Am. Judges Assn., Kans. Bar Assn., Leavenworth County Bar Assn. (pres. 1977), Judge Hugh Means Am. Inn of Ct. Charter Orgn. Lawrence. Roman Catholic. Office: 301 W 10th Ave Topeka KS 66612

DAVIS, ROBERT LARRY, lawyer; b. Lubbock, Tex., June 6, 1942; s. R. H. and Bernice (Pray) D.; m. Peggy Saunders, Jan. 23, 1965; children: Lee Michael, Melissa Lynn. BA, Rice U., 1964; LLB (with honors), U. Tex., 1967. Bar: Tex. 1967, U.S. Dist. Ct. (We. dist.) Tex. 1969, U.S. Dist. Ct. (So. dist.) Tex. 1989. Assoc. Royston Rayzor & Cook, Houston, 1967-68; from assoc. to ptnr. Brown McCarroll, Austin, Tex., 1968—. Bus. sect. coord., mem. mgmt. com.; parliamentarian, mem. exec. com. Downtown Revitalization Task Force, Austin, 1978-80. Mem., past pres. Boys Club of Austin and Travis County, 1981—; trustee Eanes Ind. Sch. Dist., Austin, 1986-93, pres., 1990-93. Mem. Assn. Atty. Mediators (pres. Cen. Tex. chpt. 1995). Methodist. Avocations: sports, music, reading. Alternative dispute resolution, Construction, Property, real (including real estate development, water). Home: 3607-3 Pinnacle Rd Austin TX 78746 Office: Brown McCarroll 1400 One Congress Plz III Congress Austin TX 78701 E-mail: rdavis@mailbmc.com.

DAVIS, ROBERT LAWRENCE, lawyer; b. Cin., Apr. 5, 1928; s. Bryan and Henrietta Elizabeth (Weber) D.; m. Mary Lee Schulte, June 14, 1952; children: Gregory, Randy, Jenny, Bradley. BA, U. Cin., 1952; JD with honors, Salmon P. Chase Coll. Law, 1958. Bar: Ohio, 1958, U.S. Supreme Ct. 1966. Assoc. Trabert & Gay, Cin., 1958-62; ptnr. Trabert, Gay & Davis, Cin., 1962-68, Gay, Davis & Kelly, Cin., 1969-71; pvt. practice Cin., 1972—. Lectr. Mt. St. Joseph Coll, 1972-82; arbitrator Am. Arbitration Assn.; assoc. adj. prof. Salmon P. Chase Coll. Sch. Law, 1969-80; lectr. Good Samaritan Hosp. Sch. Nursing, 1960-71. Pres. bd. trustees Cmty. Ltd. Care Dialysis Ctr., 1978-86; mem. Hamilton County Ohio Hosp. Commn., 1986, Kidney Found. Greater Cin., 1989, 92. Served to capt. U.S. Army, 1946-48, 52-53. Decorated Bronze Star medal, Army Commendation medal. Fellow Am. Coll. Trial Lawyers (state chmn. 1994-95); mem. Ohio Bar Assn., Cin. Bar Assn. (John P. Kiely Professionalism award 2002), Am. Bd. Trial Advs. (adv., pres. Cin. chpt. 1996), Lawyers Club (pres. 1962-63), Order of Curia, KC, Phi Delta Theta, Phi Alpha Delta, Sigma Sigma, Omicron Delta Kappa. State civil litigation, Personal injury (including property damage), Probate (including wills, trusts). Home: 9969 Voyager Way Cincinnati OH 45252-1962 Office: 3600 Carew Tower Cincinnati OH 45202 E-mail: rdavis@choice.net.

DAVIS, ROY WALTON, JR., lawyer; b. Marion, N.C., Jan. 15, 1930; s. Roy Walton and Mildred Gertrude (Wilson) D.; m. Madeline Burch Combs, Sept. 10, 1955; children: R. Walton III, Madeline Trent, Rebekah Wilson, Sally Fielding. BS, Davidson Coll., 1952; JD with honors, U. N.C., 1955. Bar: N.C. 1955, U.S. Dist. Ct. (we. dist.) N.C. 1960, U.S. Ct. Appeals (4th cir.) 1963. Ptnr. Davis & Davis, Marion, 1959-60; from assoc. to ptnr. and pres. Van Winkle, Buck, Wall, Starnes & Davis, Asheville, N.C., 1960—. Lectr. in field. Contbr. profl. publs. Chancellor Episc. Diocese of Western N.C., 1980—. With U.S. Army, 1956-59. Fellow: Internat. Soc. Barristers, Am. Coll. Trial Lawyers (state chair 1994—96), Am. Bar Found.; mem.: ABA (Ho. of Dels. 1989—92, ins. practice and litig. sects.), N.C. Assn. Def. Attys., N.C. State Bar (pres. 1985—86, trustee IOLTA 1987—93, bd. law examiners 2002—), N.C. Bar Assn. (chmn. young lawyers divsn. 1965—66, chair adminstrn. of justice task force 1999—2002, Gen. Practice Hall of Fame), Order of the Coif. Democrat. Federal civil litigation, State civil litigation, Insurance. Home: 359 Country Club Rd Asheville NC 28804-2639 Office: Van Winkle Buck Wall Starnes & Davis 11 N Market St Ste 300 Asheville NC 28801-2932

DAVIS, SCOTT JONATHAN, lawyer; b. Chgo., Jan. 8, 1952; s. Oscar and Doris (Koller) D.; m. Anne Megan, Jan. 4, 1981; children: William, James, Peter. BA, Yale U., 1972; JD, Harvard U., 1976. Bar: Ill. 1976, U.S. Dist. Ct. (no. dist.) Ill. 1976, U.S. Ct. Appeals (7th cir.) 1977, U.S. Ct. Appeals (8th cir.) 1986. Law clk. to judge U.S. Ct. Appeals (7th cir.), Chgo., 1976—77; assoc. Mayer, Brown, Rowe & Maw, Chgo., 1977—82, ptnr., 1983—. Bd. editors: Harvard Law Rev., 1974—76; contbr. articles to profl. jours. V.p. Chgo. Police Bd. General civil litigation, Corporate, general, Mergers and acquisitions. Home: 838 W Belden Ave Chicago IL 60614-3236 Office: Mayer Brown Rowe & Maw 190 S La Salle St Ste 3100 Chicago IL 60603-3441

DAVIS, STEPHEN ALLEN, lawyer; b. Huntington, W.Va., Jan. 18, 1947; s. Allen Reed and Mary (Richardson) D.; m. Martha Helen Frazier, June 29, 1974; children: Reed Frazier, Andrew Richardson, Jeffrey Allen, Kristin Ann. BA, W.Va. U., 1968, LLD, 1974. Bar: W.Va. 1974, U.S. Dist. Ct. (so. dist.) W.Va. 1974, U.S. Ct. Appeals (4th cir.) 1983. Assoc. Law Office John B. Breckinridge, Summersville, W.Va., 1974-76; ptnr. Breckinridge, Davis & Sproles, PLLC, Summersville, 1976—. Mcpl. judge Town of Summersville, 1976-79; chmn. bd. dirs. pub. defender corp. 23d Jud. Cir., Summersville, 1980-89; asst. sec., bd. dirs. Strouds Creek & Muddlety R.R., Summersville, 1982-99; mem. bd. govs. W.Va. State Bar, 2997-2000. Chmn. exec. com. Nicholas County Dems., Summersville, 1980-86; trustee, past chmn. bd. trustees Summersville Meml. Hosp., 1976-83; trustee, chmn. Summersville Libr., 1986-2001. 1st lt. U.S. Army, 1969-71, Vietnam. Mem. ABA, W.Va. Bar Assn. (bd. govs. 1997-2000), Nicholas County Bar Asssn. (pres. 1978), Am. Assn. Hosp. Lawyers, Summersville Jaycees (pres. 1976). Presbyterian. General civil litigation, Commercial, contracts (including sales of goods; commercial financing), Property, real (including real estate development, water). Home: 211 Main St Summersville WV 26651-1315 Office: Breckinridge Davis & Sproles PLLC 509 Church St Summersville WV 26651-1493

DAVIS, SUSAN RAE, lawyer; b. Salem, Oreg., July 15, 1948; d. William Ray and Pearl E. (Lundin) Catlin; m. Donald K. Davis, June 13, 1970. BA, U. Wash., 1969, JD, 1977. Bar: Wash. 1977, U.S. Dist. Ct. (we. dist.) Wash. 1977, U.S. Ct. Appeals (9th cir.) 1977, U.S. Dist. Ct. (ea. dist.) Wash. 1989. Writer, editor AP, Seattle, 1969—70; news dir. Sta. KUUU, Seattle, 1970-71; reporter, photographer Sta. KXLY-TV, Spokane, Wash., 1971-73, Sta. KHQ-TV, Spokane, 1973-74; ptnr. Burns, Schneiderman, Davis & Finkle P.S., Seattle, 1977-86, The Davis Firm, Seattle, 1987—; writer, editor Wash. Law & Politics Super Lawyer, 2001—03. Instr. journalism Eastern Wash. State Coll., Spokane, 1973-74. Mem. tribunal Wash. State Human Rights Commn., Seattle, 1974-79; arbitrator King County Mandatory Arbitration Panel, Seattle, 1985—; bd. visitors U. Puget Sound, 1986-87. Mem. ATLA, Settlement Now (mediator 1988-97), Am. Bd. Trial Advs., Trial Lawyers for Pub. Justice, Wash. State Bar Assn., Wash. State Trial Lawyers Assn. (leadership award 1984, bd. dirs. 1980-82, treas. 1982-83, v.p. west 1983-84, v.p. pub. affairs 1984-85, pres. elect 1985-86, pres. 1986-87). Democrat. Avocation: photography. Admiralty, Personal injury (including property damage), Product liability. Office: The Davis Firm 5301 Ballard Ave NW Seattle WA 98107-4061 E-mail: thedavisfirm@seanet.com.

DAVIS, TERRY HUNTER, JR., lawyer; b. Charlottesville, Va., Mar. 19, 1931; s. Terry Hunter and Mattie May (Parsons) D.;m. Mary Jane Irwin, Sept. 3, 1960; 1 child, Terry Hunter III. BA, Va. Mil. Inst., 1953; LLB, U. Va., 1958. Bar: Va. 1958, N.Y. 1959. Assoc. Thacher, Proffitt, Prizer, N.Y.C., 1958-60; law clk. Chief U.S. Dist. Judge, Norfolk, Va., 1960-61; assoc., ptnr. Taylor, Gustin, Harris, Norfolk, 1961-88; ptnr. Harris, Fears, Davis, Lynch & McDaniel, Norfolk, 1988—. Contbg. author Virginia Lawyer's Basic Practice Handbook, 1964. Chmn. Norfolk Electral Bd., 1971-72. lst lt. U.S. Army, 1953-55. Mem. ABA, Va. Bar Assn., Va. State Bar (com. mem. 1972-73), Norfolk/Portsmouth Bar (com. chmn. 1962-63), SAR (treas. 1962-64), Kiwanis. Republican. Episcopalian. Avocations: jogging, tennis. General civil litigation, Insurance, Personal injury (including property damage). Home: 7451 N Shore Rd Norfolk VA 23505-1770 Office: Harris Fears Davis Lynch & McDaniel PO Box 12756 Norfolk VA 23541-0756 E-mail: tdavis@aol.com.

DAVIS, THOMAS HILL, JR., lawyer; b. Raleigh, NC, June 11, 1951; s. Thomas Hill and Margie Wayne (Perry) D.; m. Julia Dee Wilson, May 31, 1980; children: Thomas Hill III, Alexander Erwin, Julia Hadley, Hunter McDowell. BA, N.C. State U., 1973; JD, Wake Forest U., 1976. Bar: N.C. 1976, U.S. Dist. Ct. (ea. and middle dist.) N.C. 1976, U.S. Ct. Appeals (11th cir.) 1982, U.S. Ct. Appeals (4th cir.) 1986, U.S. Supreme Ct. 1979. Reporter Winston-Salem (N.C.) Jour., 1974-76; asst. atty. N.C. Dept. Justice, Raleigh, 1976-88; gen. ptnr. Poyner & Spruill, Raleigh, 1988—. Arbitrator Am. Arbitration Assn., Charlotte, N.C., 1990—; lectr. Campbell U. Sch. Law, Buies Creek, N.C., 1992. Supplement editor: Construction Litigation, 1992; contbg. author: Public & Private Contracting in North Carolina, 1985, North Carolina Adminstrative Law, 1996; contbr. articles to profl. jours. Active NC R.R. Legis. Study Commn., Raleigh, 1985—87; pres. Badger-Iredell Found.; bd. dirs. Juvenile Diabetes Rsch. Found. Capt. N.C. State Def. Militia, 1993—. Mem. N.C. Bar Assn. (Appreciation award 1989), Wake County Bar Assn. (VLP award 1995), North Hills Club, Lions. Democrat. Presbyterian. Avocations: fly fishing, wing shooting, photography, tennis. Condemnation (eminent domain), Construction, Labor (including EEOC, Fair Labor Standards Act, labor-management relations, NLRB, OSHA). Home: 608 Blenheim Pl Raleigh NC 27612-4943 Office: Poyner & Spruill 3600 Glenwood Ave Raleigh NC 27612-4945 E-mail: thdavis@poynerspruill.com.

DAVIS, WENDELL, JR., lawyer; b. N.Y.C., June 22, 1933; m. Penelope Case, May 17, 1969; children: Jennifer C., Virginia W. Hartung, Peter T. AB cum laude, Harvard U., 1954, LL.B. cum laude, 1961. Bar: Conn. 1961, N.Y. 1963, U.S. Dist. Ct. (so. and ea. dist.) N.Y. 1964, U.S. Dist. Ct. Conn. 1966, U.S. Ct. Appeals (2d cir.) 1966, U.S Ct. Appeals (5th cir.) 1972, U.S. Supreme Ct. 1973. Law sec. to Justice Charles D. Breitel, N.Y.C., 1964-65; ptnr. Scheuermann & Davis and predecessor firms, N.Y.C., 1975-78, 92-00, Emmet, Marvin & Martin, N.Y.C., 1978-91. Pres. Carnegie Hill-90th St. Inc., 1977-80 Bd. dirs. United Way Larchmont, 1984-91. Lt. USNR, 1957. Mem. Am. Law Inst., Assn. Bar City N.Y., Harvard Club, Univ. Club Larchmont (gov. 1991-94, pres. 1993-94). Federal civil litigation, State civil litigation, Computer. Home: 28 Huguenot Dr Larchmont NY 10538-1935

DAVIS, WILLIAM EUGENE, judge; b. Winfield, Ala., Aug. 18, 1936; s. A. L. and Addie Lee (Lenahan) Davis; m. Celia Chalaron, Oct. 3, 1963. JD, Tulane U., 1960. Bar: La. 1960. Assoc. Phelps Dunbar Marks Claverie & Sims, New Orleans, 1960—64; ptnr. Caffery Duhe & Davis, New Iberia, La., 1964—76; judge U.S. Dist. Ct., Lafayette, La., 1976—83, U.S. Ct. Appeals (5th Cir.), Lafayette, 1983—. Mem.: ABA, Maritime Assn. U.S., La. Bar Assn. Republican. Office: US Ct Appeals 800 Lafayette St Ste 5100 Lafayette LA 70501-6883

DAVIS, WILLIAM GRENVILLE, lawyer, former Canadian government official; b. Brampton, Ont., Can., July 30, 1929; s. Albert Grenville and Vera M. (Hewetson) D.; m. Helen MacPhee, 1953 (dec. 1962); children— Neil, Nancy, Catherine, Ian; m. Kathleen Mackay, 1963; 1 dau., Meg. BA, U. Toronto, 1951; grad., Osgoode Hall Law Sch., 1954; LLD (hon.), Waterloo Luth. U., 1963, Western Ont. U., 1965, U. Toronto, 1967, McMaster U., 1968, Queen's U., 1968, Windsor U., 1969; DU (hon.), Ottawa U., 1980; LHD (hon.), Yeshiva U., N.Y., Nat. U. of Ireland, U. Tel Aviv. Bar: Ont. 1955. Ptnr. Davis, Webb and Hollinrake, Brampton, 1955-59; mem. Provincial Parliament Ont. from Peel Riding, 1959, 63, Peel North Riding, 1967, 71, Brampton Riding, 1975; 2d vice-chmn. Hydro-Electric Power Commn. of Ont., 1961-62; minister of edn. Province of Ont., 1962-71, also minister of univ. affairs, 1964-71, premier, 1971-85; apptd. spl. envoy on acid rain by prime minister of Can., 1985-86; of counsel Torys, Toronto, 1986—. Apptd. mem. Privy Coun. Queen Elizabeth II, 1982—; bd. dirs. 1st Am. Title Ins. Co., Magna Internat., Inc., NIKE Can. Ltd., Power Corp. Can., Magellan Aerospace Corp., St. Lawrence Cement, 1st Am. Title Co., BPO Properties Ltd., Home Capital Group Inc., Magna Entertainment Corp. Author: Education in Ontario, 1965, Building an Educated Society, 1816-

1966, 1966, other publs. Leader Progressive Conservative Party, 1975-81. Recipient Order of Ont. award; named Companion, Order of Can. Mem. Can. Bar Assn., Ont. Bar Assn., Albany Club, Kiwanis, Masons. Mem. United Ch. Office: Torys The Maritime Life Tower Toronto ON Canada M5K 1N2

DAVIS, WILLIAM HOWARD, lawyer; b. Monmouth, Ill., May 24, 1951; s. Orville Francis and Alice Gertrude (Hennenfent) D.; m. Susan Claire Parris, April 11, 1981; children: Benjamin Patrick, Jackson Mitchell, Claire Marie. BA with honors, U. South Fla., 1974; JD with high honors, Fla. State U., 1977. Bar: Fla. 1977, U.S. Dist. Ct. (no. dist.) Fla. 1977, U.S. Dist. Ct. (mid. dist.) Fla. 1986, U.S. Ct. Appeals (11th cir.) 1986, U.S. Supreme Ct. 1993. Assoc. Thompson, Wadsworth, Messer & Rhodes, Tallahassee, 1977-80; ptnr. Wadsworth & Davis, P.A., Tallahassee, 1980—2002; of counsel Messer, Caparello and Self , PA, Tallahassee, 2003—. Instr. law Fla. State U., 1976-77; mem. Fla. Supreme Ct. Commn. on Professionalism, 2002—. Editor notes and comments Fla. State U. Law Rev., 1976-77. Bd. dirs. Legal Aid Found., Inc., 1980-81, Fla. Legal Svcs., Inc., 1988-96, pres., 1993; pres. student govt., chmn., state coun. student body pres. State U. Sys. Fla., 1973-74. Mem. Acad. Fla. Trial Lawyers, Fla. Bar (2d cir. judge nominations commn. 1986-90, chmn. 2d cir. jud. grievance com. 1988-90), Fla. Bar Found. (bd. dirs. 1993-94, 97—, sec.-treas. 2002—, chmn. legal assistance to poor grant com. 1993—, exec. com. 2000—), Tallahassee Bar Assn. (bd. dirs. 1982-88, pres. 1986-87), Nat. Assn. Criminal Def. Lawyers, Fla. Assn. Criminal Def. Lawyers (coalition juvenile justice), Am. Inns of Ct. (master of bench emeritus, exec. com. Tallahassee 1994-96), Cath. Charities (bd. dirs. Tallahassee region 1995-2002, pres. 1999-2001), Gulf Winds Track Club, Capital Tiger Bay Club, Omicron Delta Kappa, Phi Sigma Alpha. General civil litigation, Criminal, Personal injury (including property damage). Home: 914 Mimosa Dr Tallahassee FL 32312-3012 Office: 215 S Monroe St Ste 701 PO Box 1876 Tallahassee FL 32302-1876 Office Fax: 850-224-4359. E-mail: bdavis@lawfla.com.

DAVIS-MORRIS, ANGELA ELIZABETH, lawyer; b. Natchez, Miss., Feb. 21, 1967; d. Fred H. and Marie (Herring) Davis; m. Raymond Joe Morris, Sept. 14, 1996. BS, U. So. Miss., 1989; JD, U. Miss., 1992. Bar: Miss. 1992, U.S. Dist. Ct. (so. dist.) Miss. 1992, U.S. Ct. Appeals (5th cir.) 1992. Paralegal Al Shiyou, Atty. at Law, Hattiesburg, Miss., 1988-89; law clk. Hickman, Goza & Gore, Attys., Oxford, Miss., 1990-92; pvt. practice Hattiesburg, 1992—. Spkr. in field. Mem. Area Devel. Partnership, Hattiesburg, 1995—. Mem. ABA, Nat. Orgn. Social Security Claimants Reps. (sec. 5th cir.), Fifth Cir. Orgn. of Social Security Claimants Reps. (sec. 1998—), Miss. Bar Assn., South Cen. Miss. Bar Assn., Kiwanis (co-editor newsletter 1995-96). Avocations: target shooting, music performance, volleyball, travel, reading. Administrative and regulatory, Bankruptcy, Criminal. Office: 301 W Pine St Hattiesburg MS 39401-3829

DAVISON, CALVIN, retired lawyer; b. Norwood, Ohio, Jan. 9, 1932; s. Emberson and Hazel Hildreth (Jenz) D.; m. Carole Ann Sawyer, Apr. 3, 1971; 1 child, Douglas Sawyer. AB cum laude, Miami U., Oxford, Ohio, 1953; JD cum laude, Harvard U., 1959. Bar: D.C. 1959, U.S. Dist. Ct. D.C. 1959, U.S. Ct. Appeals (D.C. cir.) 1959, U.S. Ct. Appeals (6th cir.) 1973, U.S. Ct. Appeals (2d cir.) 1979, U.S. Ct. Appeals (4th cir.) 1991, U.S. Supreme Ct. 1964. Assoc. Pogue & Neal, Washington, 1959-65, ptnr., 1965-67, Jones, Day, Reavis & Pogue, Washington, 1967-79, Crowell & Moring, Washington, 1979-97. Contbr. articles to profl. jours. Lt. j.g. USN, 1953-56 Mem. ABA, D.C. Bar Assn., Univ. Club. Avocations: swimming, tennis. Administrative and regulatory, Aviation. Home: 4950 Quebec St NW Washington DC 20016-3231

DAW, HAROLD JOHN, lawyer, director; b. N.Y.C., July 6, 1926; s. Joseph and Dorothy (Dannenberg) D.; m. Meryl Kann, Sept. 25, 1960. AB, Union Coll., 1950; LL.B., Columbia U., 1954. Bar: N.Y. 1955. Assoc. Shearman & Sterling, N.Y.C., 1954-62, ptnr., 1962-89. Served with USN, 1944-46, ETO. Mem. ABA, N.Y. State Bar Assn., Bar Assn. City N.Y., Phi Beta Kappa Clubs: University. Corporate, general, Private international, Securities. Home: 15 Buena Vista Dr Westport CT 06880-6602

DAWE, JAMES ROBERT, lawyer; b. Bristol, Conn., Aug. 12, 1945; s. John Grosvenor and Madeline Rose Dawe; m. Mary Gardner, July 5, 1970; children: Emily, Jeremy, Sarah. BA, Lehigh U., 1967; M City Planning, San Diego State U., 1974; JD, U. San Diego, 1976. Bar: Calif. 1976, U.S. Dist. Ct. (so. dist.) Calif. 1976. Atty. Seltzer Caplan McMahon Vitek, San Diego, 1976—. Chair Urban Librs. Coun., Evanston, Ill., 1993-94, San Diego Pub. Libr. Commn., 1986-94; past chair Libr. Calif. Bd., Sacramento, Downtown San Diego Partnership, San Diego City Mgr. Ballot Com.; past chair San Diego Pub. Libr. Found. Mem. ABA (real property sect.), Urban Land Inst., Calif. Bldg. Industry Assn. (legal action com.). Administrative and regulatory, Environmental, Land use and zoning (including planning). Office: Seltzer Caplan McMahon Vitek 750 B St Ste 2100 San Diego CA 92101-8177

DAWSON, DENNIS RAY, lawyer, manufacturing company executive; b. Alma, Mich., June 19, 1948; s. Maurice L. and Virginia (Baker) D.; m. Marilynn S. Gordon, Nov. 26, 1971; children: Emily Lynn, Brett Thomas. AA, Gulf Coast Coll., 1968; AB, Duke U., 1970; JD, Wayne State U., 1973. Bar: Mich. 1973, U.S. Dist. Ct. (ea. dist.) Mich. 1973, U.S. Dist. Ct. (we. dist.) Mich. 1975. Assoc. Watson, Wunsch & Keidan, Detroit, 1973-75; mem. Coupe, Ophoff & Dawson, Holland, Mich., 1975-77; staff atty. Amway Corp., Ada, Mich., 1977-79; corp. counsel Meijer, Inc., Grand Rapids, Mich., 1979-82; sec., corp. counsel Tecumseh Products Co., 1982-92; corp. counsel, asst. sec. Holnam Inc., Dundee, Mich., 1992-93; v.p., gen. counsel, sec. Denso Internat. Am. Inc., Southfield, Mich., 1993-2000, sr. v.p., gen. counsel, sec., 2000—. Exec. com. Bank of Lenawee, Adrian, Mich., 1984-93, also bd. dirs.; adj. prof. Aquinas Coll., Grand Rapids, 1978-82; govt. regulation and litigation com. Outdoor Power Equipment Inst. Inc., Washington, 1982-92. Trustee Herrick Meml. Hosp., 1988-91, Tecumseh Civic Auditorium, 1986-89; mem. adv. coun. Montessori Children's House and Acad., Adrian, 1987-93. Mem. ABA, Mich. State Bar Assn., Am. Soc. Corp. Secs., Am. Corp. Counsel Assn., Mich. Mfrs. Assn. (lawyers com. 1987-92), Lenawee C. of C. (bd. dirs. 1988-92). Corporate, general. Office: Denso Internat America Inc PO Box 5133 24777 Denso Dr Southfield MI 48034-5244

DAWSON, NORMA ANN, lawyer; b. Detroit, Sept. 11, 1950; d. Emmett Chamberlain and B. Louise Dawson. BA, Pa. State U., 1971; JD, U. Mich., 1974. Bar: Calif. 1979, U.S. Dist. Ct. (cen. dist.) Calif. 1979, U.S. Ct. Appeals (9th cir.), 1979, U.S. Supreme Ct. 1984, U.S. Dist. Ct. (so. dist.) Calif. 1991, U.S. Dist. Ct. (ea. and no. dists.) Calif. 1993. Compliance atty. Penncorp Fin., Inc., Santa Monica, Calif., 1980-87; assoc. Mathon & Rosensweig, Beverly Hills, Calif., 1987-89, Stone & Hiles, Beverly Hills, 1989-94; pvt. practice L.A., 1994—. Judge pro tem L.A. Cts., 1989—. Editor: Making A Difference: Stories By and About Lawyers Who Have, 1999. Bd. dirs. Open Fist Theatre Co., Hollywood, Calif., 1991-94. Mem. Calif. State Bar (probation monitor 1984-96), Los Angeles County Bar Assn., Beverly Hills Bar Assn. (mandatory fee arbitrator 1984—), Women Lawyers Assn. L.A. General civil litigation, Personal injury (including property damage). Office: 2286 E Carson St PMB 310 Long Beach CA 90807-3044

DAWSON, STEPHEN EVERETTE, lawyer; b. Detroit, May 14, 1946; s. Everette Ivan and Irene (Dresser) D.; m. Consiglia J. Bellisario, Sept. 20, 1974; children: Stephen Everette Jr., Gina C., Joseph J. BA, Mich. State U., 1968; MA, U. Mich., 1969, JD, 1972. Bar: Mich. 1972, U.S. Dist. Ct. (ea. dist.) Mich. 1972, U.S. Supreme Ct. 1978, U.S. Ct. Appeals (6th cir.) 1980. Assoc. Dickinson, Wright, Moon, Van Dusen & Freeman, Detroit, 1972-79; ptnr. Dickinson, Wright, PLLC, Bloomfield Hills, Mich., 1979—. Adj. prof. law U. Detroit, 1986-88. Mem. ABA, Am. Coll. Real Estate Lawyers, Mich. State Bar Assn. (mem. coun. real property law sect. 1986-93, chair 1992-93, land title stds. com. 1999—), Mich. State Bar Found., Phi Beta Kappa. Republican. Avocations: jogging, reading. Commercial, contracts (including sales of goods; commercial financing), Landlord-tenant, Property, real (including real estate development, water). Office: Dickinson Wright PLLC 38525 Woodward Ave Ste 2000 Bloomfield Hills MI 48304-5092 E-mail: sdawson@dickinsonwright.com.

DAY, CHRISTIAN C. lawyer, educator; b. Rochester, N.Y., Jan. 22, 1946; s. Elmer W. and Mary Jane (Brown) D.; m. Jane D. Butzner, June 22, 1968 (div. 1970); m. Janet W. Mason, Oct. 28, 1978 (dec. 1993); children: Kimberly A. Funaro, Hilary E. Cohen; m. Ann M. Kochan, July 15, 1995. AB in Govt., Cornell U., 1967; JD, NYU, 1970. Bar: Pa. 1970, U.S. Dist. Ct. (ea. dist.) Pa. 1971. Staff atty. Comml. Legal Services, Phila., 1971-72; assoc. Morgan, Lewis & Bockius, Phila., 1970-74; sole practice Phila., 1975; asst. prof. Wharton Sch. U. Pa., Phila., 1975-82; assoc. prof. Coll. Law Syracuse (N.Y.) U., 1982—, prof., 1987—, assoc. dean, 1987-89. Rsch. alumni fellow Coll. Law, Syracuse (N.Y.) U., 1992-93, chair bldg. com. 1990-91, co-chair bldg. com., 1991-98; dir. bus. law ctr., Syracuse U., 1994-98, ctr. for law and bus. enterprise, 1998—. Editor, reviewer Am. Bus. Law Jour., 1977-81; contbr. numerous articles on real estate, fin., taxation, land use, corp. and fgn. policy to legal jours. Sec., bd. dirs. Society Hill Civic Assn., Phila., 1976-77; mem. agy. fund raising com. United Way of Ctrl. N.Y., 1993-97; task force United Way, 1997-98, fiscal mgmt. team, 1998—. Named Prof. of Yr., Wharton Evening Sch., U. Pa., 1981. Alumni fellow Syracuse U., 1992-93; mem. ABA, Phila. Bar Assn., Am. Inst. Property and Liability Underwriters (exam. com. CPCU parts 3, 4, 6), Federalist Soc., Onondaga Park Assn., Cornell Club (Phila., bd. dirs. 1972-82, sec. 1980-81). Republican. Avocations: painting, writing, model railroading, needlepoint, skiing. Home: 580 Roberts Ave Syracuse NY 13207-1639 Office: Syracuse U Coll Law 182 White Hl Syracuse NY 13244-0001 E-mail: ccday@law.syr.edu.

DAY, DAVID OWEN, lawyer; b. Long Beach, Calif., Apr. 3, 1958; s. Robert Owen and Linda Sue (Weaver) D.; m. Vicki Temple Butler, Sept. 24, 1980; children: Candi, Chad, Charles, Chase, Catelyn. BA magna cum laude, E. Tenn. State U., 1980; JD with high honors, U. Tenn., 1984. Bar: Tenn. 1984, U.S. Dist. Ct. (mid. dist.) Tenn. 1984, U.S. Ct. Appeals (6th cir.) 1990, U.S. Supreme Ct. 1990; cert. civil trial specialist, Nat. Bd. Trial Advocacy and Tenn. Commn. on Continuing Legal Edn. and Specialization. Assoc. Law Office of Donald G. Dickerson, Cookeville, Tenn., 1984-87; ptnr. Dickerson and Day Attys. at Law, Cookeville, 1987-90; pvt. practice Cookeville, Tenn., 1990—. Lectr. Bank Adminstrv. Inst., 1990, Tenn. Bankers Assn., 1993, Tenn. Consol. Ret. Sys., 1996, Am. Inst. Banking, 1996. Asst. editor Tennessee Law Review, 1982-83. Frederick T. Bonham scholar U. Tenn., 1981, Harold C. Warner scholar U. Tenn., 1982, Carl W. Miller scholar U. Tenn., 1983. Mem. ABA, ATLA, Tenn. Trial Lawyers Assn., Putnam County Bar Assn., Tenn. Bar Assn., Phi Kappa Phi, Alpha Lambda Delta. Ch. of Jesus Christ of Latter-day Saints. Avocations: song writing, singing, playing basketball, pub. speaking, traveling. General civil litigation, Commercial, contracts (including sales of goods; commercial financing), Personal injury (including property damage). Home: PO Box 704 Cookeville TN 38503-0704 Office: 19 S Jefferson Ave Cookeville TN 38501-5911

DAY, DONALD SHELDON, lawyer; b. Boston, Nov. 3, 1924; s. Israel and Frances (Goldberg) D.; m. Edythe Greenberg, July 8, 1945; children—Clifford L., Richard J., Halee Beth. BA, Bates Coll., 1946; LLB, Cornell U., 1948. Bar: N.Y. 1948. Past chmn. bd. Saperston and Day P.C., Buffalo, 1979-96; pres. World Union for Progressive Judaism, 1988-95. Bd. dirs. various corps. Gen. chmn. United Jewish Fund Campaign, Buffalo, 1971-73, 75; past co-chmn. Western N.Y. chpt. NCCJ; past pres. United Jewish Fedn. Buffalo; past chmn. bd. Childrens Hosp. Buffalo, Union Am. Hebrew Congregations; trustee Forest Lawn Cemetery and Crematory, Hebrew-Union Coll. With AUS, 1942-45. Mem. Am., N.Y. State, Erie County bar assns., Order of Coif, Phi Kappa Phi. Jewish (past pres. temple). Corporate, general, Oil, gas, and mineral, Mergers and acquisitions. Office: Hiscock & Barclay 3 Fountain Plz Buffalo NY 14203-1486

DAY, EDWARD FRANCIS, JR., lawyer; b. Portland, Maine, Nov. 4, 1946; s. Edward Francis and Anne (Rague) D.; m. Claire Ann Nicholson, June 27, 1970; children: Kelley Ann, John Edward. BA, St. Anselm Coll., 1968; JD cum laude, U. Maine, 1973; LLM in Taxation, NYU, 1976. Bar: N.J. 1973, U.S. Dist. Ct. N.J. 1973, U.S. Tax Ct. 1974, N.Y. 1981. Assoc. Hannoch, Weisman, Stern & Besser, Newark, 1973-74, Carpenter, Bennett & Morrissey, Newark, 1974-78, ptnr., 1979-93, sr. ptnr., 1994-98, of counsel, 1999—. Instr. employee benefits and comml. law The Am. Coll., Valley Forge, Pa., 1981-82; exec. v.p., gen. counsel Main Steel Polishing Co., Inc., Tinton Falls, N.J., 1999—. Editor Maine Law Rev., 1972-73. Mem., vice-chmn. Allenhurst (N.J) Bd. Adjustment, 1983-85; mem., vice-chmn. Allenhurst Planning Bd., 1985-87; mem. Nat. Ski Patrol, Denver, 1985—; scoutmaster Monmouth coun. Boy Scouts Am., Ocean Twp., 1987-90; mem. 10th Mountain Divsn. Assn., Aspen, Colo., 1996—, Appalachian Mt. Club, Boston, 2003—. Served in U.S. Army, 1968-70. Named One of Outstanding Young Men of Am., 1979; Ford Found. scholar, 1966-68. Mem.: ABA, Estate Planning Coun. No. N.J., Essex County Bar Assn., N.J. Bar Assn., Forsgate Country Club (Jamesburg, N.J.), Jersey Coast Club of Red Bank (v.p. 1976—77), Deal (N.J.) Golf and Country Club (bd. dirs. 1985—92, sec. 1991—92), Am. Legion. Roman Catholic. Avocations: golf, skiing, piano. Commercial, contracts (including sales of goods; commercial financing), Probate (including wills, trusts), Property, real (including real estate development, water). Home: 225 Spier Ave Allenhurst NJ 07711-1120 Office: Carpenter Bennett & Morrissey 3 Gateway Ctr Newark NJ 07102-4079 also: Main Steel Polishing Company Inc 2 Hance Ave Eatontown NJ 07724-2726

DAY, JAMES MCADAM, JR., lawyer; b. Detroit, Aug. 18, 1948; s. James McAdam and Mary Elizabeth (McGibbon) D.; m. Sally Marie Sterud; children: Cara McAdam, Brenna Marie, Michael James. AB, UCLA, 1970; JD magna cum laude, U. Pacific, 1973. Bar: Calif. 1973, U.S. Dist. Ct. (no. dist.) Calif. 1973, U.S. Ct. Appeals (9th cir.) 1975. Assoc. Downey, Brand, Seymour & Rohwer, Sacramento, 1973-78, ptnr., 1978—, chmn. natural resources dept., 1985—90; mng. ptnr. Downey, Brand, Seymour & Rohmer, Sacramento, 1990—94, chmn. nat. resources dept., 2002—, mng. ptnr., 1997—2001. Contbr. articles to profl. jours. Pres., bd. dirs. Sacramento Soc. for Prevention of Cruelty to Animals, 1976-79, Children's Home Soc. of Calif., Sacramento, 1979-85; bd. dirs. Sta. KXPR/KXJZ, Inc. Pub. Radio, Sacramento, 1984-94, chmn., 1990-93; bd. dirs. Calif. State Libr. Found., 1995-2000, chmn., 1995-2000. Mem. ABA (natural resources sect. 1998), Calif. Bar Assn. (exec. com. 1985-89, chmn. real property law sect. 1988), Rocky Mountain Mineral Law Found., Sacramento Petroleum Assn., Calif. Mining Assn., U. Pacific McGeorge Law Sch. Alumni Assn. (bd. dirs. 1980-83). Avocations: yacht racing and cruising, fishing. Office: Downey Brand Seymour & Rohwer 555 Capitol Mall Fl 10 Sacramento CA 95814-4504

DAY, JOHN ARTHUR, lawyer; b. Madison, Wis., Sept. 21, 1956; s. John Donald and Elinor Roletta (Heath) D. BS, U. Wis., Platteville, 1978; JD, U. N.C., 1981. Bar: Tenn. 1981, U.S. Dist. Ct. (mid. dist.) Tenn. 1981, U.S. Ct. Appeals (6th cir.) 1982; civil cert. Nat. Bd. Trial Advocacy 1991. Assoc. Boult Cummings Conners & Berry, Nashville, 1981-86, ptnr., 1987-92; shareholder Branham & Day, P.C., 1993—. Mem. Civil Justice Reform Act adv. group U.S. Dist. Ct. (mid. dist.) Tenn., 1991-95; mem. Tenn. Supreme Ct. Commn. on Continuing Legal Edn. and Specialization, 2001—. Co-author: Tennessee Law of Comparative Fault, 1997, 2d edit., 2002; founder, editor Tenn. Tort Law Letter, 1995—; contbr. articles to profl. jours. Com. mem. Cohn Roundtable, Nashville, 1988; assoc. Harry Phillips Inn of Ct., 1990-92, Tenn. John Marshall Inn of Ct., 1999—. Fellow Am. Coll. Trial Lawyers; mem. Tenn. Trial Lawyers Assn. (bd. govs. 1984-85, treas. 1985-89, v.p. 1989-93, pres. 1993-94, chair legal edn. com. 1985-86, chair legis. com. 1987-90, CLE com. 1984-97, pub. rels. com. 1986-88, long range planning com. 1991-93), Assn. Trial Lawyers Am. (Tenn. pub. rels. rep. 1986-87, people's law sch. com. co-chair 1986-88, pub. rels. com. 1986-91, chair 1988-89, edn. com. 1987-88, pub. affairs com. 1987-89, publs. com. 1990-93, vice chmn. 1991-93, co-chair 1992-93, key person com. 1987-89, nursing home litigation group 1985-89, chmn. 1987-89, mem. exec. com. 1994-95, chair pres.'s coun. 1994-95), Nashville Bar Assn. (bd. dirs. 1998-2000, circuit and chancery ct. com. chair 1989, fee disputes com. 1984-85, 87, vice chmn. 1988, chmn. 1989), Lawyers Involved for Tenn. (trustee 1988—), Tenn. Bar Assn. (mem. litigation sect. coun. 1989-90), Nat. Bd. Trial Advocacy (bd. dirs. 1998—, stds. com. 1998—, v.p. 2001-02, pres.-elect 2002-03), Tenn. Justice Ctr. (bd. dirs. 1999—). Democrat. Personal injury (including property damage). Home: 608 Good Springs Rd Brentwood TN 37027-5173 Office: Branham & Day PC PO Box 40592 Nashville TN 37204

DAY, MICHAEL GORDON, education educator; b. Madison, Wis., July 30, 1951; s. Lee Monroe and Joan (Meredith) D.; m. Donna Kay Corl, May 26, 1979 (div. Apr. 1986); children: Thomas Lee, Anne Elizabeth; m. Carol Ann Stefanko, Apr. 12, 1997. BA, Pa. State U., 1973; JD, George Washington U., 1976. Bar: Pa. 1976. Assoc. Alan Ellis, Esq., State College, Pa., 1976-77; pvt. practice State College, Pa., 1977-85; with Profl. Planning Cons., State College, Pa., 1985-86, Century Fin. Svcs., State College, Pa., 1986-96; solutions expert Netscape, 1996-99; dir. Info. Tech. Inst./Shepherd Coll., Shepherdstown, W.Va., 1999—. Instr. bus. law Pa. State U., University Park, 1978-79, instr. continuing legal edn., 2002; counsel Boccardo Law Firm, San Jose, Calif., 1983, Rees Law Firm, Washington, 1983; sr. v.p. Century Mortage Corp., 1991-96. Chmn. Com. to Elect Mel Hodes Senator, Pa., 1982, Dem. Com., State College, 1982-84; active Exec. Com. Centre County, 1982-84, United Pennsylvanians, 1982-83; gen. counsel CLEAN, 1982-85; v.p. Mt. Nittany Conservancy, 2000-02; candidate for Pa. Ho. Reps., 1980; candidate for dist. justice 49th Dist. Pa., 1977. Mem. Lions Paw Alumni Assn. (pres. 1999-2001), Parmi Nous, Omicron Delta Kappa, Delta Sigma Rho. United Ch. Of Christ. Office: 400 W Stephen St Martinsburg WV 25401 E-mail: michael@michaelday.org.

DAY, MICHAEL W. lawyer; b. Winner, S.D., July 26, 1958; BS, U. S.D., 1980, JD, 1983. Bar: S.D. 1983, U.S. Dist. Ct. S.D., U.S. Ct. Appeals (8th cir.). Mem. Day, Morris & Schreiber, Bell Fourche, SD. Mem.: Jackrabbit Bar Assn., Pennington County Bar Assn., Butte County Bar Assn. (pres. 1996—97), State Bar S.D. (pres.-elect 2000—01, pres. 2001—02, bar commr. 1990—93), S.D. Trial Lawyers Assn. (bd. govs. 1984—94, pres. 1992—93), Western Trial Lawyers Assn., Am. Judicature Soc., ATLA, ABA. Personal injury (including property damage). Office: Day Morris & Schreiber 117 Fifth Ave PO Box 370 Belle Fourche SD 57717-0370 E-mail: mikeday@westriverlaw.com.

DAY, RICHARD EARL, lawyer, educator; b. St. Joseph, Mo., Nov. 2, 1929; s. William E. and Geneva C. (Miller) D.; m. Melissa W. Blair, Feb. 2, 1951; children: William E., Thomas E. BS, U. Pa., 1951; JD with distinction, U. Mich., 1957. Bar: Ill. 1957, D.C. 1959, S.C. 1980. Assoc. Kirkland & Ellis, Chgo., 1957-58, Howrey Simon Baker & Murchison, Washington, 1958-61; asst. prof. law U. N.C., Chapel Hill, 1961-64; assoc. prof. Ohio State U., Columbus, 1964-66, prof., 1966-75, U. S.C., Columbia, 1975-76, 80-86, dean, 1977-80, John William Thurmond chair disting. prof. law, 1986-99, disting. prof. law emeritus, 1999—. Cons. U.S. Office Edn., 1964-66; course dir. Ohio Legal Ctr. Inst. Columbus, 1970-75; vis. prof. law U. Southampton (Eng.), fall 1988. Author: The Intensified Course in Antitrust Law, 1972, rev. edit., 1974; book rev. editor Antitrust Bull., 1968-71, adv. bd., 1971—; adv. bd. Antitrust and Trade Regulation Report, 1973-76, Jour. Reprints for Antitrust Law and Econs., 1974—. Ohio commr. Nat. Conf. on Uniform State Laws, 1967-75, S.C. commr., 1977-80; mem. Ohio Gov.'s Adv. Coun. Internat. Trade, 1972-74, S.C. Jud. Coun., 1977-80; chmn. S.C. Appellate Def. Coun., 1977-80, S.C. Com. Intellectual Property and Unfair Trade Practices Law, 1981-87. Lt. USNR, 1952-55. Named John William Thurmond Disting. Prof. Law. Mem. ABA, S.C. Bar Assn. (bd. govs. 1977-80), Am. Law Inst. Methodist. Home: 204 Saint James St Columbia SC 29205-3074 Office: U SC Law Ctr Main And Green Sts Columbia SC 29208-0001

DAY, ROLAND BERNARD, retired chief justice state supreme court; b. Oshkosh, Wis., June 11, 1919; s. Peter Oliver and Joanna King (Wescott) D.; m. Mary Jane Purcell, Dec. 18, 1948; 1 dau., Sarah Jane. BA, U. Wis., 1942, JD, 1947. Bar: Wis. 1947. Trainee Office Wis. Atty. Gen., 1947; assoc. mem. firm Maloney & Wheeler, Madison, Wis., 1947-49; 1st asst. dist. atty. Dane County, Wis., 1949-52; partner firm Day, Goodman, Madison, 1953-57; firm Wheeler, Van Sickle, Day & Anderson, Madison, 1959-74; legal counsel mem. staff Sen. William Proxmire, Washington, 1957-58; justice Wis. Supreme Ct., Madison, 1974-95, chief justice, 1995-96. Mem. Madison Housing Authority, 1960-64, chmn., 1961-63; regent U. Wis. System, 1972-74 Served with AUS, 1943-46. Mem. ABA, State Bar Wis., Am. Trial Lawyers Assn., Ygdrasil Lit. Soc. (pres. 1968), Madison Torske Klubben, Masons (33rd degree). Mem. United Ch. of Christ. Clubs: Madison, Madison Lit.

DAYNARD, RICHARD ALAN, law educator; b. N.Y.C., July 19, 1943; s. David M. and Sarah (Weidenbaum) D.; m. Carol S. Iskols, Aug. 9, 1975; children: David J., Gabriela C. BA, Columbia U., 1964, MA in Sociology, 1970, JD, Harvard U., 1967; PhD in Urban Studies and Planning, MIT, 1980. Bar: N.Y. 1967, U.S. Ct. Appeals (6th cir.) 1986, U.S. Supreme Ct. 1986, U.S. Ct. Appeals (11th cir.) 1987, U.S. Ct. Appeals (5th cir.) 1996. Law clk. 2d cir. U.S. Ct. Appeals, N.Y.C., 1967-68; tchg. fellow Columbia U., N.Y.C., 1968-69; asst. prof. law Northeastern U., Boston, 1969-71, assoc. prof. law, 1971-73, prof. law, 1973—. Lectr. Tufts Med. Sch., Boston, 1975-89; lectr. and cons. in field. Editor-in-chief Tobacco Products Litigation Reporter, 1985—; assoc. editor: Tobacco Control: An Internat. Jour., 1998—; contbr. articles to profl. jours. Chmn. Tobacco Products Liability Project, Boston, 1984—; pres. Group Against Smoking Pollution of Mass., Boston, 1983—, Clean Indoor Air Ednl. Found., Boston, 1983-92, Tobacco Control Resource Ctr., Inc., Boston, 1993—; pres. Stop Teenage Addiction to Tobacco, 1996-98; chair lay adv. bd. Flight Attendants Med. Rsch. Inst., 2003—. Mem. ABA, Am. Pub. Health Assn., Law and Soc. Assn., Phi Beta Kappa. Home: 90 Commonwealth Ave Boston MA 02116-3040 Office: Northeastern U Sch Law 400 Huntington Ave Boston MA 02115-5005 E-mail: r.daynard@neu.edu.

DEACHMAN, ROSS VARICK, lawyer; b. Plymouth, N.H., Mar. 13, 1942; s. W. John Deachman and H. Annie Griffin; m. Nancy L. Stone, Aug. 30, 1964; children: Amy E., William John IV. BA, U. N.H., 1964; JD, Boston U., 1967. Assoc. Burns, Bryant, Hinchey & Nadeau, Dover, N.H., 1967-70; ptnr. Murphy and Deachman, Plymouth, 1971-74; owner Deachman Law Office, Plymouth, 1974-89; ptnr. Deachman & Cowie, P.A., Plymouth, 1989—. Dir., sec. N.H. Bar Assn., 1975-80; pres. Grafton County Bar Assn., 1980. Author: Bi-Centennial of the Grafton County Bar Association, 1993; editor: 25th Reunion Class of 1964, 1989. Moderator Town of Holderness, N.H., 1988—; sch. bd. mem. Pemi-Baker Co-op Sch. Dist., Plymouth, 1989—. Estate planning, Probate (including wills, trusts), Property, real (including real estate development, water). Office: Deachman & Cowie PA PO Box 96 66 Main St Plymouth NH 03264-1451

DEACON, JOHN C. lawyer; b. Newport, Ark., Sept. 26, 1920; BA, U. Ark., 1941, JD, 1948. Bar: Ark. 1948. Ptnr. Barrett & Deacon, Jonesboro,

Ark. Commr. from Ark. to Nat. Conf. Commrs. on Uniform State Laws, 1966—, chmn. exec. com., 1977-79, pres. 1979-81. Recipient Ark. Outstanding Lawyer-Citizen award, 1973. Fellow Am. Coll. Trial Lawyers, Internat. Acad. Trial Lawyers (bd. d irs. 1978-84), Southwestern Legal Found. (trustee 1975-95, chmn. Research Fellows 1983-85); mem. Craighead County Bar Assn. (pres. 1968-69), N.E. Ark. Bar Assn. (pres. 1966-68), Ark. Bar Assn. (pres. 1970-71), ABA (chmn. sect. bar activities 1967-68, Ark. del. 1967-79, bd. govs. 1980-83, 92-93, chair sr. lawyers divsn. 1994-95), Am. Counsel Assn. (pres. 1974-75), Am. Bar Found. (pres. 1994-96), Internat. Assn. Def. Counsel, Nat. Assn. R.R. Trial Lawyers, Delta Theta Phi. General civil litigation, General practice. Office: PO Box 1700 Jonesboro AR 72403-1700 also: Barrett & Deacon PA Union Planters Bank Building 300 S Church St Jonesboro AR 72401-2911 E-mail: jdeacon@barrettdeacon.com.

DEACY, THOMAS EDWARD, JR., lawyer; b. Kansas City, Mo., Oct. 14, 1918; s. Thomas Edward and Grace (Scales) D.; m. Jean Freeman, July 10, 1943 (div. 1988); children: Bennette Kay Deacy Kramer, Carolyn G., Margaret Deacy Vickrey, Thomas, Ann Deacy Krause; m. Jean Holmes McDonald, 1988. JD, U. Mo., 1940; MBA, U. Chgo., 1949. Bar: Mo. 1940, Ill. 1946. Practice law, Kansas City, 1940-42; ptnr. Taylor, Miller, Busch & Magner, Chgo., 1946-55, Deacy & Deacy, Kansas City, 1955—. Lectr. Northwestern U., 1949-55, U. Chgo., 1950-55; dir., mem. exec. com. St. L.-S.F. Ry., 1962-80; dir. Burlington No. Inc., 1980-86; mem. U.S. team Anglo-Am. Legal Exchange, 1973, 77. Mem. Juv. Protective Assn. Chgo., 1947-55, pres., bd. dirs., 1950-53; mem. exec. bd. Chgo. coun. Boy Scouts Am., 1952-55; pres. Kansas City Philharmonic Orch., 1961-63, chmn. bd. trustees, 1963-65; trustee Sunset Hill Sch., 1963-73; trustee, mem. exec. com. u. Kansas City, 1963—; trustee Mo. Law Sch. Found., pres., 1973-77, Kans. chpt. The Nature Conservancy, 1994-99. Capt. AUS, 1942-45. Fellow Am. Coll. Trial Lawyers (regent 1968— , treas. 1973-74, pres. 1975-76), Am. Bar Found; mem. Am. Law Inst., Jud. Conf. U.S. (implementation com. on admission of attys. to fed. practice 1979-86), ABA (commn. standards jud. adminstrn. 1972-74, standing com. fed. judiciary 1974-80), Ill. Bar Assn., Chgo. Bar Assn., Mo. Bar, Kansas City Bar Assn., Lawyers Assn. Kansas City, Chgo. Club, La Jolla (Calif.) Country Club, La Jolla Beach and Tennis Club, Kansas City Club, Kansas City Country Club, River Club, Q.E.B.H. Sr. Hon. Soc. of Mo. Univ., Beta Gamma Sigma, Sigma Chi. Appellate, Banking, General civil litigation. Home: 2724 Verona Cir Shawnee Mission KS 66208-1265 Office: 920 Main St Ste 1900 Kansas City MO 64105-2010 E-mail: ted@deacylaw.com.

DEAKTOR, DARRYL BARNETT, lawyer; b. Pitts., Feb. 2, 1942; s. Harry and Edith (Barnett) D.; children: Rachael Alexandra, Hallie Sarah. BA, Brandeis U., 1963; LLB, U. Pa., 1966; MBA, Columbia U., 1968. Bar: Pa. 1966, Fla. 1980, N.Y. 1980. Assoc. firm Goodis, Greenfield & Mann, Phila., 1968-70, ptnr., 1971; gen. counsel Life of Pa. Fin. Corp., Phila., 1972; asst. prof. U. Fla. Coll. Law, Gainesville, 1972-74, assoc. prof., 1974-80; with Mershon, Sawyer, Johnston, Dunwody & Cole, Miami, Fla., 1980-81, ptnr., 1981-84, Walker Ellis Gragg & Deaktor, Miami, 1984-86, White & Case LLP, Miami, 1987-95, White & Case LLC, Johannesburg, 1995-2000, Palo Alto, Calif., 2000—01, ret. ptnr., 2002—. Mem. Dist. III (Fla.) Human Rights Advocacy Com. for Mentally Retarded Citizens, 1974-78, chmn., 1978-80; mem. adv. bd. Childbirth Edn. Assn. Alachua County, Fla., 1974-80; mem. resource devel. bd. Mailman Ctr. for Child Devel., 1981-88. Mem. Fla. Bar. Corporate, general, Mergers and acquisitions, Securities. Mailing: 5216 Sunshine Canyon Dr Boulder CO 80302-8753

DEAL, JAMES EDWARD, lawyer; b. Brazil, Ind., Oct. 25, 1957; s. Charles Edward and Margaret Ann (Evans) D.; m. Kathy Louise Wells, Sept. 18, 1982; children: Suzanne Emily, Jana Louise, Evan W. BA, Ind. State U., 1979; JD, Ind. U., 1982. Bar: Ind. 1982, U.S. Dist. Ct. (so. dist.) Ind. 1982. Assoc. Sacopulos, Crawford & Johnson, Terre Haute, Ind., 1982-83; pvt. practice Brazil, Ind., 1983—. Prosecuting atty. 13th jud. cir., 1991-94. Mem. Brazil Concert Band, 1974—. Named One of Outstanding Young Men Am., 1985. Mem. Christian Legal Soc., Ind. Bar Assn. (county contact person young lawyers sect. 1986—), Clay County Bar Assn. (pres. 2000—), Rotary. Republican. Avocations: handbell choir, reading, exercise, family activities. Property, real (including real estate development, water), General practice, Banking. Home: 5066 W State Rd 340 Brazil IN 47834-7869 Office: PO Box 186 11 W National Ave Brazil IN 47834-0186

DEAL, JOHN CHARLES, lawyer; b. Kenton, Ohio, Jan. 5, 1947; BS, Ohio State U., 1969, JD cum laude, 1974. Bar: Ohio 1974, U.S. Dist. Ct. (no. and so. dists.) Ohio 1977, U.S. Ct. Appeals (D.C. cir.) 1979, U.S. Dist. Ct. (ea. dist.) Ky. 1980, U.S. Ct. Appeals (6th cir.) 1983, U.S. Ct. Appeals (8th cir.) 1988, U.S. Supreme Ct. 1988, U.S. Ct. Appeals (4th and 5th cirs.) 1990, U.S. Ct. Fed. Claims 1993. Reg. counsel FDIC, Columbus, 1976-85; of counsel Kegler Brown Hill & Ritter, Columbus, 1988—. Contbr. articles to profl. jours. Mem. ABA (bus. law sect., chair regulatory enforcement, dir. liability subcom. of Banking Law Com. 1985-90), Ohio State Bar Assn. (chair banking, comml. and bankruptcy law com. 1992-94), Columbus Bar Assn. Administrative and regulatory, Banking, Commercial, contracts (including sales of goods; commercial financing). Office: Kegler Brown Hill & Ritter 65 E State St Ste 1800 Columbus OH 43215-4213

DEAN, BEALE, lawyer; b. Ft. Worth, Feb. 26, 1922; s. Ben J. and Helen (Beale) D.; m. Margaret Ann Webster, Sept. 3, 1948; children: Webster Beale, Giselle Liseanne. BA, U. Tex., Austin, 1943, LLB, 1947. Bar: Tex. 1946, U.S. Dist. Ct. (no., so, we. and ea. dists.), U.S. Cir. Ct. (5th and 11th cirs.) 1952, U.S. Supreme Ct. 1954. Asst. dist. atty., Dallas, 1947-48; assoc. Martin, Moore & Brewster, Ft. Worth, 1948-50; mem. Martin, Moore, Brewster & Dean, 1950-51, Pannell, Dean, Pannell & Kerry (and predecessor firms), 1951-65; ptnr. Brown, Herman, Scott, Young & Dean, Ft. Worth, 1965-71, Brown, Herman, Scott, Dean & Miles, Ft. Worth, 1971-98; 2003ptnr. Brown, Herman, Dean, Wiseman, Liser & Hart, LLP, Ft. Worth, 1998. Spl. asst. Atty. Gen. Tex., 1959-61. Regent Nat. Coll. Dist. Attys., 1985—. With AUS, 1942-45, ETO. Mem. ABA, Bar Assn. Fifth Fed. Cir., Ft. Worth-Tarrant County Bar Assn. (past pres. 1971-72, Blackstone award 1991), Am. Coll. Trial Lawyers, State Bar Tex. (dir. 1973-75), Am. Bar Found., Tex. Bar Found. (charter mem.), Ft. Worth Boat Club, Ridglea Country Club, Ft. Worth Club. Presbyterian. Labor (including EEOC, Fair Labor Standards Act, labor-management relations, NLRB, OSHA), General civil litigation, Personal injury (including property damage). Office: 200 Ft Worth Club Bldg Fort Worth TX 76102-4905

DEAN, BILL VERLIN, JR., lawyer; b. Oklahoma City, Jan. 11, 1957; s. Bill V. and Mary Lou (Dorman) D.; m. Christine Potter; children: Bill V. III, Mary Megan. BS, Cen. State U., 1978; JD, Oklahoma City U., 1981. Bar: Okla. 1982, U.S. Dist. Ct. (we. dist.) Okla. 1983, (no. dist.) Okla. 1986, (ea. dist.) Okla. 1987, Tex. 1990, N.Y. 1992, U.S. Ct. Appeals (10th cir.) 1986; US Supreme Ct., 2002; lic. real estate broker and ins. agt. Second dep. assessor Okla. County Assessor, Oklahoma City, 1978-80; atty. Struthers Oil and Gas Corp., Oklahoma City, 1980-82; cons. Bill Dean & Co., Jones, Okla., 1978—; ptnr. Dean & Assocs. P.C., Jones, Okla., 1982—; pres. Dean Ins. Agy. Ltd., 1986—, Casualty Corp. Am., Inc., 1999—. Bd. dirs. Union Mut. Ins. Co.; CEO Casualty Corp. of Am., Inc., 1999—. Mem. Okla. County Bar Assn., Okla. Bar Assn., Tex. Bar Assn., N.Y. Bar Assn., Shriners. Methodist. Banking, Insurance, Property, real (including real estate development, water). Home: 200 Cherokee St Jones OK 73049-7709 Office: Dean & Assocs P C PO Box 1060 110 W Main St Jones OK 73049-1060 E-mail: bdean@deannet.com.

DEAN, BRUCE CAMPBELL, lawyer; b. Rochester, N.Y., Apr. 10, 1958; s. David C. and Jean Lord (Butler) D.; m. Pamela Marie Prator, Feb. 14, 1987. BA, St. Lawrence U., 1980; JD, Tulane U., 1984. Bar: La. 1984, U.S. Dist. Ct. (ea. dist.) La. 1984, U.S. Ct. Appeals (5th cir.) 1984, N.Y. 1985, U.S. Dist. Ct. (mid. dist.) N.Y. 1988. Ptnr. Gauthier, Downing, LaBarre, Dean & Sulzer, Metairie, 1997—. Dir. legal assistance program Tulane U., 1983-84. Mem. ABA, ATLA, La. Bar Assn., N.Y. State Bar Assn., La. Trial Lawyers Assn., La. Assn. Def. Counsel. Democrat. Federal civil litigation, State civil litigation. Home: 1500 State St New Orleans LA 70118 Office: Gauthier Downing LaBarre Dean & Sulzer 3500 N Hullen St Metairie LA 70002-3420 E-mail: bcd@gauthier-downing.com.

DEAN, CHRISTINE WITCOVER, lawyer; b. Washington, May 23, 1947; d. Henry Wallace and Kate (Briggs) Witcover; m. Joseph Wayne Dean, May 22, 1977; children: Joseph Jefferson, Katherine Briggs. AB, Sweet Briar Coll., 1968; JD, Duke U., 1971. Bar: N.C. 1971, U.S. Dist. Ct. (ea. dist.) N.C., 1972, U.S. Ct. Appeals (4th cir.) 1973, U.S. Supreme Ct. 1983, Fed. Cir. Ct. Appeals 1986. Assoc. attorney N.C. Dept. Justice, Raleigh, 1971-72; asst. U.S. attorney U.S. Attorney Office, Raleigh, 1973-78, 87—; partner Dean & Dean, Raleigh, 1978-85; pvt. practice Raleigh, 1985-87. Judge Siegal Moot Court Competition, Durham, N.C., 1993-95. Vice chmn. Govs. Council Drug Abuse, Raleigh, 1986-92. Mem. Braxton Craven Inn of Court (master attorney 1993-97, master attorney emeritus 1998). Republican. Episcopalian. Avocations: horseback riding, tap dancing. Office: US Attorneys Office EDNC 310 New Bern Ave Rm 800 Raleigh NC 27601-1461 E-mail: Christine.Dean2@usdoj.gov.

DEAN, J. THOMAS, lawyer; b. Cleve., Feb. 22, 1933; s. John Ladd and Margaret Caroline (Blakely) D.; m. Patricia Jean Whitmore, Aug. 6, 1960; children: Thomas W., Carol M., Joan G. BA, Ohio Weslyan U., 1956; JD, Western Res. U., 1959. Bar: Ohio 1959. Asst. pros. atty. Lake County, Ohio, 1960; assoc. Blakely, Rand, Painesville, Ohio, 1961-67; ptnr. Blakely & Dean, 1967-76, Blakely, Dean, Wilson & Klingenberg, Painesville, 1975-90, Blakely, Dean & Klingenberg, 1990-92, Blakely, Dean & Wagner, 1992-97; law dir. North Perry Village, Ohio, 1970-90. Mem. Painesville Bd. Zoning Appeals, 1971-76; mem. Planning Commn., 1967-79, chmn., 1970-77; pres. Painesville Sr. Citizens, 1982-84; mem. Lake County Found. Bd., 1978-2000, sec., 1978-90; mem. Lake County Bd. Elections, 1964-84, 88-90; chmn. Lake County Rep. Com., 1970-74, 82-84; mem. Ohio Rep. Cen. Com., 1980-88; clk. Painesville Twp. Park, 1962—/ mem. Lake County Planning Commn., 1997-2000; bd. trustees Lake County Vis. Bur., 1996—. Mem. Lake County Bar Assn. (pres. 1979-80), Ohio State Bar Assn. Republican. Methodist. Lodge: Kiwanis (pres. 1980-81). Avocation: swimming. State civil litigation, Corporate, general, Probate (including wills, trusts). Office: Blakely & Dean PO Box 526 Painesville OH 44077-0526 E-mail: jtdean222@aol.com.

DEAN, LAURA HANSEN, lawyer, foundation administrator; b. Toledo, Feb. 9, 1951; d. Roy Edgerton and Geraldine Ann (Bogart) Hansen; m. Michael Lee Dean, Mar. 2, 1970 (div. Apr. 1995); m. Kenneth L. Ruff, Jan. 5, 2001. BA, Ball State U., 1972; JD magna cum laude, Ind. Univ., 1979. Bar: Ind. 1979, U.S. Dist. Ct. (so. dist.) Ind. 1979. Cons. atty., reporter Ind. Ct. Appeals, Supreme Ct., Indpls., 1980; legal editor and dir. of seminars R&R Newkirk Assocs., Indpls., 1980; dir. of planned giving Ball State U. Found., Indpls., 1981-87, acting exec. dir., 1987, exec. dir., 1988-90; assoc. dir. Ind. U. Ctr. on Philanthropy, Indpls., 1990; pvt. practice law Indpls., 1991—; pres. Laura Hansen Dean and Assocs., 1991—2001; of counsel Barnes & Thornburg, 2002—. Cons. to numerous univs., hosps., United Way agys., 1981—. Mem. editl. rev. panel Jour. Gift Planning, 1997—. Bd. dirs., 1st v.p. Wapehani coun. Girl Scouts U.S., Daleville, Ind., 1982-90; mem. Riley-Jones Hist. Found., pres., 1988-92; bd. dirs. Nat. Com. Planned Giving, 1990-92; sr. legal counsel, dir. gift planning Ctrl. Ind. Cmty. Found., Inc., 1995-2001; pres. Planned Giving Group Ind., 1995-97. Mem. ABA, Nat. Soc. Fund Raising Execs. (treas. 1992, pres. Ind. chpt. 1994), East Ctrl. Ind. Estate Planning Coun. (pres. 1987-88), Estate Planning Coun. of Indpls., Ind. State Bar Assn. (real property, probate and estate planning sects.), Indpls. Bar Assn., Rotary, Riley-Jones Club. Corporate, general, Estate planning, Taxation, general. Office: PO Box 8428 Fort Wayne IN 46898-8428

DEANE, RICHARD HUNTER, JR., lawyer, former federal judge; b. Oct. 18, 1952; BA, U. Ga., 1974, JD, 1977; LLM, U. Mich., 1979. Bar: Ga. 1977. Asst. U.S. atty. No. Dist. Ga., 1980-88; chief gen. crimes sect. U.S. Attys. Office, 1988-91, chief criminal divsn., 1991-94; magistrate judge U.S. Dist. Ct. (no. dist.) Ga., Atlanta, 1994-98; U.S. atty. No. Dist. Ga., Atlanta, 1998—2002; with Jones Day, Atlanta, 2002—. Office: Jones Day 303 Peachtree St Ste 3500 Atlanta GA 30308

DEASON, HEROLD MCCLURE, lawyer; b. Alton, Ill., July 24, 1942; s. Ernest Wilburn and Mildred Mary (McClure) D.; m. Wilma Lee Kaemmerle, June 18, 1966; children: Sean, Ian, Whitney. BA, Albion Coll., 1964; JD, Northwestern U., 1967. Bar: Mich. 1968. Assoc. Bodman, Longley & Dahling, LLP, Detroit, 1967-74, ptnr., 1975—. City atty. Grosse Pointe Pk., Mich., 1978—. Vice chmn. Detroit, Windsor Freedom Festival, 1978-92; bd. dirs. Spirit of Detroit Assn., 1980—. Recipient Spirit of Detroit award, Detroit City Coun., 1986. Mem. ABA, Mich. Assn. Mcpl. Attys. (pres. 1995-97), Detroit Bar Assn., Can.-U.S. Bus. Assn. (v.p. 1997—), Grosse Pointe Yacht Club (commodore 1992-93), Detroit Racquet Club, Windsor Club, Clinton River Boat Club. Corporate, general, Mergers and acquisitions, Municipal (including bonds). Home: 1044 Kensington Ave Grosse Pointe Park MI 48230-1437 Office: Bodman Longley & Dahling 100 Renaissance Ctr 34th Fl Detroit MI 48243-1001 E-mail: hdeason@bodmanlongley.com.

DEATHERAGE, WILLIAM VERNON, lawyer; b. Drumright, Okla., Apr. 17, 1927; s. William Johnson and Pearl Mae (Watson) D.; m. Priscilla Ann Campbell, Sept. 16, 1932; children: Thomas William, Andrea Susan. BS, U. Oreg., 1952, LLB with honors, 1954. Bar: Oreg. 1954, U.S. Dist. Ct. Oreg. 1956. Ptnr. Frohnmayer, Deatherage, Pratt, Jamieson & Clarke & Moore, Medford, Oreg., 1954—. Bd. dirs. Oreg. Law Inst., U. Oreg. Found. With USN, 1945-48. Mem. Am. Coll. Trial Lawyers, Internat. Acad. Trial Lawyers, Delta Theta Phi, Rogue Valley Country Club (pres. 1988), Rogue River Valley Univ. Club. Democrat. Episcopalian. Federal civil litigation, State civil litigation, Insurance. Address: 2592 E Barnett Rd Medford OR 97504-8345

DEATON, CHRIS HAROLD, lawyer; b. Laurel, Miss., Apr. 15, 1960; s. Harold Eugene and Mary Gwendolyn Deaton; m. Dana Gail Dew, July 17, 1991; children: Sara Kathryn, Eric Chris, Luke Christian;children from previous marriage: Mary Christina, James Robert. BA, Miss. State U., 1982; JD, U. Miss., 1991. Bar: Miss. 1991, U.S. Dist. Ct. (no. and so. dists.) Miss. 1991, U.S. Ct. Appeals (5th cir.) 1991, U.S. Supreme Ct. 1996. Assoc. Holcomb Dunbar Connell Chaffin & Willard, Oxford, Miss., 1991—93, Webb McLaurin & O'Neal, Tupelo, 1993—94; ptnr. Webb, Sanders Deaton Balducci & Smith, Tupelo, 1994—98, Deaton & Deaton, Tupelo, 1998—. Dist. appeals bd. mem. Selective Svc. System, Jackson, 2001—; legis. advisor Miss. Swimming, Inc., 2001—. With U.S. Army, 1984—86. Mem.: Internat. Assn. Arson Investigators, Miss. Fire Investigators Assn. (bd. dirs. 1996—, legal counsel 1997—, instr. 1997—), Am. Legion. Insurance, Personal injury (including property damage), Toxic tort. Office: Deaton & Deaton 113 Clark St Ste 5 Tupelo MS 38801 Fax: 662-840-6039. E-mail: chrisd@deatonanddeaton.com.

DEAVER, PHILLIP LESTER, lawyer; b. Long Beach, Calif., July 21, 1952; s. Albert Lester and Eva Lucille (Welton) D. Student, USCG Acad., 1970-72; BA, UCLA, 1974; JD, U. So. Calif., 1977. Bar: Hawaii 1977, U.S. Dist. Ct. Hawaii 1977, U.S. Ct. Appeals (9th cir.) 1978, U.S. Supreme Ct. 1981. Assoc. Carlsmith, Wichman, Case, Mukai & Ichiki, Honolulu, 1977-83, ptnr., 1983-86, Bays, Deaver, Lung, Rose & Baba, Honolulu, 1986, mng. ptnr., 1986-95. Contbr. articles to profl. jours. Bd. dirs. Parents and Children Together, 1993—, v.p. 1999-2003, chmn. bd., 2003-. Mem. ABA (forum com. on the Constrn. Industry), AIA (affiliate Hawaii chpt.), Am. Arbitration Assn. (arbitrator). Alternative dispute resolution, Construction, Commercial, contracts (including sales of goods; commercial financing). Home: 2471 Pacific Heights Rd Honolulu HI 96813-1029 Office: Bays Deaver Lung Rose and Baba PO Box 1760 Honolulu HI 96806-1760 E-mail: pdeaver@legalhawaii.com.

DEBEAUBIEN, HUGO H. lawyer; b. Detroit, Sept. 20, 1948; s. Phillip Frances and June (Hesse) deB.; m. Mary Lazenby, Apr. 30, 1977; 1 child, Hugo Samuel. BS in Bus., Fla. State U., 1970; JD, Stetson U., 1973. Bar: Fla. 1973, U.S. Dist. Ct. (mid. dist.) Fla. 1974, U.S. Supreme Ct. 1978, U.S. Ct. Appeals (11th cir.) 1981. Asst. state atty. Fla. 9th Jud. Cir. Ct., Orlando, 1973-76; ptnr. Drage, deBeaubien, Orlando, 1976-79; ptnr., pres. Drage, deBeaubien, Knight & Simmons, Orlando, 1980-87, Drage, deBeaubien, Knight, Simmons, Romano and Neal, Orlando, 1987-98; ptnr. Drage, deBeaubien, Knight, Simmons, Mantzaris and Neal, Orlando, 1999—; pres. deBeaubien, Knight, Simmons, Mantzaris and Neal LLP, 2002—. Lectr. Fla. Bar Assn., 1981-83; bd. dirs. Fla. Citrus Sports Assn., 1996—; dir. Princeton Charter Sch., 2000-02. Mem. ATLA, Nat. Assn. Criminal Def. Lawyers, Fla. State U. Alumni Assn. (bd. dirs. 1986-93, sec. 1993-94, treas. 1995-96, v.p. 1996-97, chmn.-elect 1997-98, chmn. 1998-99), Univ. Center Club Tallahassee, Country Club Orlando. Republican. Methodist. Avocations: golf, tennis. State civil litigation, Criminal, Family and matrimonial. Home: 1125 Belleaire Cir Orlando FL 32804-6703 Office: deBeaubien Knight Simmons Mantzaris & Neal LLP 322 N Magnolia Ave Orlando FL 32801-1609 E-mail: hdeBeaubien@dbksmn.com.

DEBEVOISE, DICKINSON RICHARDS, federal judge; b. Orange, N.J., Apr. 23, 1924; s. Elliott and Josephine (Richards) D.; m. Katrina Stephenson Leeb, Feb. 24, 1951; children: Kate, Josephine Debevoise Davies, Mary Debevoise Rennie, Abigail D. Byrne. BA, Williams Coll., 1948; LLB, Columbia U., 1951. Bar: N.J. 1953, U.S. Supreme Ct. 1956. Law clk. to Hon. Phillip Forman, chief judge U.S. Dist. Ct. for Dist. N.J., 1952-53; assoc. firm Riker, Emery & Danzig, Newark, 1953-56; partner firm Riker, Danzig, Scherer, Debevoise & Hyland, Newark, 1957-79; judge U.S. Dist. Ct. for N.J., 1979—; adj. prof. constitutional law Seton Hall U., 1992-94. Pres. Newark Legal Services Project, 1965-70; chmn. N.J. Gov.'s Workmen's Compensation Study Commn., 1972-73; mem. N.J. Supreme Ct. Adv. Com. on Jud. Conduct, 1974-78; chmn. N.J. Disciplinary Rev. Bd., 1978-79; mem. Lawyers Adv. Com. for 3d Circuit, 1975-79, chmn., 1979; chmn. N.J. Legal Services Adv. Council, 1976-78 Asso. editor: N.J. Law Jour, 1959-79. Trustee Ramapo Coll., N.J., 1969-73, chmn. bd., 1971-73; trustee Williams Coll., 1969-74, Fund for N.J., 1985—; trustee Hosp. Ctr. at Orange, N.J., v.p., 1975-79; pres. Democrats for Good Govt., 1956-60, active various presdl., senatorial, gubernatorial campaigns; active St. Stephens Episcopal Ch. Sgt. U.S. Army, WWII, 1st lt. Korean War. Decorated Bronze Star. Fellow Am. Bar Found.; mem. ABA, N.J. Bar Assn., Fed. Bar Assn. (v.p. 1976), Assn. Fed. Bar State N.J. (v.p. 1977-79), Essex County Bar Assn. (treas. 1960-64, trustee 1968-71), Am. Law Inst., Judicature Soc., Columbia Law Sch. Assn. (bd. dirs., pres. 1992-94). Office: US Dist Ct PO Box 999 Newark NJ 07101-0999

DE BRIER, DONALD PAUL, lawyer; b. Atlantic City, Mar. 20, 1940; s. Daniel and Ethel de B.; m. Nancy Lee McElroy, Aug. 1, 1964; children: Lesley Anne, Rachel Wynne, Danielle Verne. BA in History, Princeton U., 1962; LL.B. with honors, U. Pa., 1967. Bar: N.Y. 1967, Tex. 1977, Utah 1983, Ohio 1987. Assoc. firm Sullivan & Cromwell, N.Y.C., 1967-70, Patterson, Belknap, Webb & Tyler, N.Y.C., 1970-76; v.p., gen. counsel, dir. Gulf Resources & Chem. Corp., Houston, 1976-82; v.p. law Kennecott Corp. (former subs. BP America Inc.), Salt Lake City, 1983-89; assoc. gen. counsel BP America Inc., Cleve., 1987-89; gen. counsel BP Exploration Co. Ltd., London, 1989-93; exec. v.p., gen. counsel Occidental Petroleum Corp., L.A., 1993—. Bd. dirs. L.A. Philham., L.A., 1995—; mem. adv. bd. govs. Riveria Country Club, 2002—. Lt. USNR, 1962—64. Mem. Calif. Club, Adv. Bd. Gov., Riviera Tennis Club. Corporate, general, General practice, Private international. Home: 699 Amalfi Dr Pacific Palisades CA 90272-4507 Office: Occidental Petroleum Corp 10889 Wilshire Blvd Los Angeles CA 90024-4201

DEBUNDA, SALVATORE MICHAEL, lawyer; b. Phila., June 17, 1943; s. Salvatore and Marie Ann (Carilli) DeB.; children: Lauren, David. BS in Econs., U. Pa., 1965, JD, 1968. Bar: Pa. 1968, U.S. Supreme Ct. 1977. Law clk. to justice Phila. Ct. of Common Pleas, 1968-69; asst. gen. counsel ARA Services, Inc., Phila., 1969-74; sr. assoc. Cohen, Verlin, Sherzer & Porter, Phila., 1974-75; v.p., sec., gen. counsel AEL Industries, Inc., Montgomeryville, Pa., 1975-80; v.p., gen. counsel Cooper Assocs., Inc., Marlton, N.J., 1980-81; v.p. cable TV devel. Greater Media, Inc., East Brunswick, N.J., 1981-85; ptnr., chmn. media/entertainment law group Fox, Rothschild, O'Brien & Frankel, Phila., 1985-91; shareholder, dir. Pelino & Lentz, PC, Phila., 1991—. Mem. ABA, Pa. Bar Assn., Phila. Bar Assn., Fed. Comm. Bar Assn. Avocations: sports, owning thoroughbred horses. Communications, Corporate, general, Entertainment. Office: Pelino & Lentz PC 1650 Market St One Liberty Pl 32d Fl Philadelphia PA 19103-7393

DECARLO, DONALD THOMAS, lawyer, insurance company executive; BA in Econs., Iona Coll., 1960; JD, St. John's U., 1969. Bar: N.Y. 1970, U.S. Dist. Ct. (so. and ea. dists.) 1972, U.S. Supreme Ct. 1973; cert. reins. arbitrator. Asst. regional sales dir. Govt. Employees Ins. Co., 1962-71; lawyer, counsel Lee, McCarthy & Derosa, 1971-72; v.p., gen. counsel Nat. Coun. on Compensation Ins., 1972-86; sr. v.p. Am. Ins. Assn., N.Y.C., 1986-87; sr. v.p., gen. counsel Comml. Ins. Resources, Inc., N.Y.C., 1987-96; dep. gen. counsel Travelers Corp., 1991-96; gen. counsel Travelers Ins. Cos., 1994-96; exec. v.p., gen. counsel Gulf Ins. Co., N.Y.C., 1987-97; ptnr. Lord, Bissell & Brook, 1997—. Apptd. master arbitrator N.Y. Inst. Supt.; adj. prof. NYU, Coll. Ins.; mem. Def. Rsch. Inst.; mem. N.Y. State commrs. N.Y. State Fund, 1997—. Author: (with D.J. Gruenfeld) Stress in the American Workplace--Alternatives for the Working Wounded, 1989, (with M. Minkowitz) Workers Compensation Insurance and Law Practice--The Next Generation, 1989; contbr. articles to profl. jours. Mem. ABA (past chmn. workers' compensation com., chair corp. counsel com. 1992-93), Assn. of Bar of City of N.Y. (ins. com.), Queens County Bar Assn. (past chmn. ins. com.), N.Y. State Bar Assn. (worker's compensation), N.Y. County Lawyers Assn. (chair workers' compensation com. 1993). Alternative dispute resolution, Insurance, Workers' compensation. Home: 200 Manor Rd Douglaston NY 11363-1130 Office: Lord Bissell & Brook 1 Penn Plz New York NY 10119-0002

DECARVALHO, KAS R. lawyer; b. NY, Dec. 24, 1970; s. Job Joao Miguel Decarvalho and Mary Norman; m. Kathleen Brendan Jarrell, May 1, 1999. BA, U. NC, 1994, JD, 1999. Bar: RI. Assoc. Legal Svcs. Blue Ridge, Boone, NC, 1997, Hinckley, Allen & Snyder, Providence, 1998—2001; counsel Harrison Law Assocs., Providence, 2001—. Bd. fin. com. Internat. Inst. RI, Providence; bd. dirs. Internat. Charter Sch., Providence; corporator Providence Libr. Sys. Mem.: ABA. Land use and zoning (including planning), Corporate, general, Entertainment. Office: Harrison Law Assocs 807 Broad St Ste 100 Providence RI 02907

DE CASTELLAN, ELISABETTA FERRUTA, lawyer; b. Milan, Oct. 27, 1960; d. Ferdinando Carl and Stephania Negri Ferruta; m. de Castellan, Sept. 10; 1 child, Edouard. JD, U. Milan, 1984; student, Hague Acad., Holland. Cert.: lawyer, Milan 1990, lawyer, Paris 1995. Lawyer internat. law firm Grippo Law Firm, Milan, 1985—87, Danoli Law Firm, Milan, 1988—97, Mavro and Ptnrs. Law Firm, Paris, 1994—98, K and G Law Firm, Paris, 1999—2003. Contbr. articles to profl. jours. Mem.: Milan and Paris Bar, Camera Commercio Italiania, Assn. Giuristi Lingua Italiana.

Avocations: sports, tennis, jogging, sailing, golf. Commercial, contracts (including sales of goods; commercial financing), Intellectual property, Trademark and copyright, Corporate, general. Office: K&G 18 Ave Kléber 75116 Paris France Office Fax: 0033-1-45012684.

DE CASTRO, HUGO DANIEL, lawyer; b. Panama City, Panama, Sept. 12, 1935; came to U.S., 1947; s. Mauricio Fidanque and Armida Rebecca (Salas) de C.; m. Isabel Shapiro, July 25, 1958; children: Susan M., Teresa A., Andrea L., Michele L. BSBA in Econs. cum laude, UCLA, 1957, JD summa cum laude, 1960. CPA Calif.; bar: Calif. 61. Prin. de Castro, West, Chodorow, Glickfeld & Nass Inc., L.A., 1961—. Lectr. UCLA, 1962-67, 68, counsel to dean Law Sch., 1963—; commr. tax adv. com. State Bar Calif. Editor UCLA Law Rev., 1959-60, Taxation for Lawyers, 1971-88; contbr. articles to profl. jours. Trustee Stephen S. Wise Temple, Jewish Fedn. Cmty. Found.; trustee, bd. dirs., chmn. fin. com. UCLA Found.; bd. dirs. Western L.A. Found.; bd. dirs. Hebrew Union Coll.; bd. govs. Trustee Endowment Trusts. Mem. ABA chmn. taxation subcom.), ACLU, L.A. County Bar Assn., Beverly Hills Bar Assn. (bd. dirs. Law Found.), L.A. C. of C. (former chmn., dir.), L.A. World Affairs coun., Am. Jewish Com., Del Rey Yacht Club (Calif., former dir., officer), Founders of Music Ctr., Las Hadas Country Club (Mex.), Pi Lambda Phi. Corporate, general, Mergers and acquisitions, Property, real (including real estate development, water). Office: de Castro West Chodorow et al 10960 Wilshire Blvd Ste 1400 Los Angeles CA 90024-3702

DECHENE, JAMES CHARLES, lawyer; b. Petaluma, Calif., May 14, 1953; s. Harry George and Domenica Theresa (Cuffia) D.; m. Teresa Marie Caserza, Aug. 2, 1975; children: Michelle, Mark, Sabrina, Diane. BS summa cum laude, Santa Clara U., 1975; JD magna cum laude, AM in Econs., U. Mich., 1978, PhD in Econs., 1980. Bar: Ill. 1979, U.S. Dist. Ct. (no. dist.) Ill. 1980, U.S. Ct. Appeals (7th cir.) 1993, U.S. Dist. Ct. (ea. dist.) Wis. 1996. Assoc. Sidley & Austin, Chgo., 1980-86; ptnr. Sidley Austin Brown & Wood, Chgo., 1986—2001, 2001—. Adj. prof. Health Law Inst. DePaul U. Coll. of Law, 1987—; bd. dirs. Med. Sci. Labs., Wauwatosa, Wis., 1991-95. Author: Establishing a Physician Organization, 1993; author: (with others) Health Law Practice Guide, 1993-2002, Financing and Liability, 1994, Health Law Handbook, 1989, 90, 91, 93, Managed Care, 1996; contbr. articles to profl. jours. Mem. Ill. Bar Assn., Am. Health Lawyers Assn., Am. Econs. Assn. Roman Catholic. Administrative and regulatory, Antitrust, Health. Office: Sidley Austin Brown and Wood Bank One Plz 10 S Dearborn St Chicago IL 60603-2000

DECKELBAUM, NELSON, lawyer; b. Washington, Apr. 1, 1928; s. Fred and Rose (Egber) D.; m. Louann Jacobs, Oct. 19, 1952; children: David Alan, Todd Stuart. BS, Georgetown U., 1950, JD, 1952. Bar: D.C. 1952, Md. 1957, U.S. Supreme Ct. 1966. Practice law, Washington, 1952—; sr. ptnr. Deckelbaum Ogens & Raftery, Chartered, 1974—. Staff mem. Commn. on Govt. Security, 1956; dir. Independence Savs. Bank. Chmn. Democratic precinct, Montgomery County, Md., 1958. Served with USAF, 1952-54. Named in Best Lawyers in Am. Fellow Am. Coll. of Bankruptcy; mem. Am., Md., D.C. bar assns., Am. Judicature Soc., Georgetown Univ. Alumni Assn., Woodmont Country Club, Univ. Club (pres. 1994-95), D.C. Real Estate Commn. Home: 4200 Massachusetts Ave NW Apt 115 Washington DC 20016 Office: Deckelbaum Ogens & Raftery 3 Bethesda Metro Ctr Bethesda MD 20814-5330 E-mail: ndeckelbaum@deckelbaum.com.

DECKER, JOHN ROBERT, lawyer; b. Milw., Apr. 29, 1952; s. John Anthony and Margaret Eleanor (Cook) D.; m. Sandra Jean Kuelz, May 25, 1974; 1 child: Jennifer. BA, U. Wis., 1974; JD, Marquette U., 1977. Bar: Wis. 1977, U.S. Ct. Appeals (7th cir.) 1978, U.S. Supreme Ct. 1990. Assoc. Michael, Best & Friedrich, Madison, Wis., 1977-80, Milw., 1980-84, ptnr., 1984-91; pvt. practice law Milw., 1991-92; pres. Decker & Gunta, S.C., Milw., 1992-98, Decker Corp., Milw., 1998—2002, Evansville, Wis., 2002—. Instr. Milw. Sch. Engring., 1987—; mem. Wis. Jud. Coun., 1989-90, Wis. Bd. of Attys. Profl. Responsibility, 1989-90; hearing examiner, 1991—; mem. Wis. Equal Justice Task Force, 1989-91. Author: Construction Claims Under Wisconsin Law, 1988; co-author: Special Verdict Formulation in Wisconsin, 1977; exec. editor Marquette U. Law Rev., 1976-77. Trustee Mt. Zion Luth. Ch., 1986-89, pres., 1988-89. Mem. ABA (ho. of dels. 1984-88, 93, 95-96, governing com. of forum on constrn. industry 1987-89, 91-95, achievement award 1985), Wis. Bar Assn. (bd. govs. 1984-92, exec. com. 1984-85, 87-92, chmn. bd. 1987-88, pres. 1990-91, chmn. constrn. and pub. contract law sect. 1992-94, chmn. constrn. lien law revision com. 1994-99). General civil litigation, Construction, Property, real (including real estate development, water). Home and Office: 143 W Main St Evansville WI 53536

DECKER, MICHAEL LYNN, lawyer, judge; b. Oklahoma City, May 5, 1953; s. Leroy Melvin and Yvonne (Baird) D. BA, Oklahoma City U., 1975, JD, 1978; grad., Nat. Jud. Coll., U. Nev., Reno, 1990. Bar: Okla. 1978, U.S. Ct. Appeals (10th cir.) 1979, U.S. Dist. Ct. (we. dist.) Okla. 1985, U.S. Supreme Ct. 1994. Assoc. Bay, Hamilton, Lees, Spears, and Verity, Oklahoma City, 1978-80; assoc. dir. devel. Oklahoma City U., 1980-81, asst. dean, Sch. of Law, 1981-82; sr. oil and gas adminstrv. law judge Okla. Corp. Commn., Oklahoma City, 1982-92, sr. asst. gen. counsel oil and gas conservation, 1992-95, deputy gen. counsel oil and gas conservation, 1995—. Campaign staff intern U.S. Senator Henry Bellmon's Re-election Campaign, 1974; mem. Civil Arbitration Panel, U.S. Dist. Ct. (we. dist.) Okla., 1985—; seminar spkr. Am. Inst. Profl. Geologists (Okla. sect.), 1985, Conf. on Consumer Fin. Law, Oil and Gas Law Inst., 1999-2001; mem. dean's adv. com. Oklahoma City U. Law Sch., 1986; mem. sys. rev. bd. Okla. Corp. Commn., 1990-93, mem. process mgmt. rev. team, 1995-96; lectr. adminstrv. law Vanderbilt U. Sch. Law, 1993, lectr. oil and gas regulatory practice Okla. U Coll. Law, 2003; mem. legal and regulatory affairs com. Interstate Oil and Gas Compact Commn., 2000—, mem. coun. state oil and gas attys., 2001-, chair, 2003, mem. revision subcom. Model Oil and Gas Conservation Act, Interstate Oil and Gas Compact Commn., 2003. Trustee Oklahoma City U., 1989—91, mem. alumni bd. dirs., 1986—2000; mem. com. of twenty Oklahoma City Art Mus., 1987—95, co-chair omelette party, 1990; vol. Contact Teleminister, Oklahoma City, 1986—91; Okla. Corp. Commn., 1990; mem. Class XI Leadership Oklahoma City, 1993; area rep. Okla. Mozart Festival, Bartlesville, 1988—; pres. alumni assn. Oklahoma City U., 1988—92; mem. adminstrv. bd. St. Luke's United Meth. Ch., 1988—92, chair missions com., 1993—94; mem. nat. alumni bd. dirs. Oklahoma City U., 2000—, also mem. devel. com., long range planning com., adminstrv. liaison com., and student rels. com.; bd. dirs. Eldercare Access Ctr., Inc., 2001—, Contact Teleminister, Oklahoma City, 1987—90, March of Dimes Western Okla., 1990—93. Mem.: Oklahoma City Mineral Lawyers Soc., Okla. County Bar Assn. (exec. com. young lawyers sect. 1978—82, mem. law day com. 1979—88, chmn. law day luncheon spkr. com. 1979—88), Okla. Bar Assn. (mineral law sect., environ. law sect.), Raymer Soc. for the Arts (bd. dirs., Lindsborg, Kans. 1999—, sec. 2002—), Lions, Lambda Chi Alpha (Outstanding Alumnus award 1983, treas. bldg. corp. 1984—89, pres. 1989—91), Phi Alpha Delta. Republican. Administrative and regulatory, Oil, gas, and mineral. Home: 2008 NW 44th St Oklahoma City OK 73118-1902 Office: Okla Corp Commn State Capitol Complex Jim Thorpe Bldg PO Box 52000 Oklahoma City OK 73152-2000 E-mail: bloomin2@cox.net.

DECKER, RICHARD KNORE, lawyer; b. Lincoln, Nebr., Sept. 15, 1913; s. Fred William and Georgia (Kilmer) D.; m. Fern Iona Steinbaugh, June 12, 1938. AB, U. Nebr., 1935, JD, 1938. Bar: Nebr. 1938, U.S. Supreme Ct. 1941, D.C. 1948, Ill. 1952. Trial atty. antitrust div. Dept. Justice, 1938-52; ptnr. Lord, Bissell & Brook, Chgo., 1953-84, of counsel, 1984—. Trustee Village of Clarendon Hills (Ill.), 1960-64; chmn. bd. elders Community Presbyn. Ch., Clarendon Hills, 1963-66; mem. Union Ch. of Hinsdale; chmn. bd. Community House, Hinsdale, Ill., 1976, Robert Crown Ctr. for Health Edn., Hinsdale, Ill., 1981-83, also bd. dirs, 1976—. With USNR, 1942-45, lt. comdr. ret. Mem. ABA (chmn. antitrust sect. 1971-72), Ill. Bar Assn. (gov. 1969-73, chmn. antitrust sect. 1964-66), Chgo. Bar Assn. (chmn. antitrust law com. 1956-59), The Lawyers Club Chgo., Hinsdale Golf Club (pres. 1968). Republican. Home: 196 Pheasant Hollow Dr Burr Ridge IL 60527 Office: 115 S La Salle St Ste 2900 Chicago IL 60603-3801

DECOTIIS, MICHAEL R. lawyer; m. Amy DeCotiis; 3 children. BA, Clarion U.; JD, Seton Hall U. Bar: N.J. 1991, Pa. 1991. Mng. ptnr. DeCotiis, Fitzpatrick, Gluck & Cole LLP, NJ, 1991—2001; dep. exec. dir. Port Authority N.Y. & N.J., N.Y.C., 2002—03; chief counsel to gov. Office Gov. State of N.J., Trenton, 2003—. Office: Office Gov State Ho 125 State St, PO Box 001 Trenton NJ 08625*

DECROW, KAREN, lawyer, author, lecturer; b. Chgo., Dec. 18, 1937; d. Samuel Meyer and Juliette (Abt) Lipschultz; m. Alexander Allen Kolben, 1960 (div. 1965); m. Roger DeCrow, 1965 (div. 1972, dec. 1989). BS, Northwestern U., 1959; JD, Syracuse U., 1972; DHL (hon.), SUNY, Oswego, 1994. Bar: N.Y., U.S. Dist. Ct. (no. dist.) N.Y. Resorts editor Golf Digest mag., Evanston, Ill., 1959-60; editor Am. Soc. Planning Ofcls., Chgo., 1960-61; writer Ctr. for Study Liberal Edn. for Adults., Chgo., 1961-64; editor Holt, Rinehart, Winston, Inc., N.Y.C., 1965; textbook editor L.W. Singer, Syracuse, N.Y., 1965-66; writer Ea. Regional Inst. for Edn., Syracuse, 1967-69, Pub. Broadcasting System, 1977; tchr. women and law, 1972-74; nat. bd. mem. NOW, 1968-77, nat. pres., 1974-77, also nat. politics task force chair; cons. affirmative action; pvt. practice, 1974—. Lectr. topics including law, gender, internat. feminism to corps., polit. groups, colls. and univs., U.S., Can., Mex., Finland, China, Greece, former USSR; nat. coord. Women's Strike for Equality, 1970; moot ct. judge, 1974--; N.Y. State del. Internat. Women's Yr., 1977; originator Schs. for Candidates; participant DeCrow-Schlafly ERA Debates, from 1975; founder (with Robert Seidenberg, MD) World Woman Watch, 1988; gender issues advisor Nat. Congress for Men; mem. Task Force on Gender Bias. Author: (with Roger DeCrow) University Adult Education: A Selected Bibliography, 1967, American Council on Education, 1967, The Young Woman's Guide to Liberation, 1971, Sexist Justice, 1974, First Women's State of the Union Message, 1977, (with Robert Seidenberg) Women Who Marry Houses: Panic and Protest in Agoraphobia, 1983, Turkish edit., 1988, 2d Turkish edit., 1989, United States of America vs. Sex: How the Meese Commission Lied About Pornography, 1988, (with Jack Kammer) Good Will Toward Men: Women Talk Candidly About the Balance of Power Between the Sexes, 1994; editor: The Pregnant Teenager (Howard Osofsky), 1968, Corporate Wives, Corporate Casualties (Robert Seidenberg, MD), 1973; contbr. articles to USA Today, N.Y. Times, L.A. Times, Chgo. Tribune, Nat. Law Jour., Women Boston Globe, Vogue, Mademoiselle, Ingenue, Newsday, Chgo. Sun Times, Penthouse, Washington Post, L.A. Times Mag., Policy Review, Miami Herald, Internat. Herald Tribune, Social Problems, Houston Chronicle, Pitts. Press, Nat. NOW Times, Syracuse U. Mag., San Francisco Chronicle, Civil Rights Quar., Women Lawyers Jour., other newspapers, mags.; regular columnist: Syracuse New Times; columnist N.Y. Times Spl. Features; recording: Opening Up Marriage, 1980. Hon. trustee Elizabeth Cady Stanton Found.; active Hon. Com. to Save Alice Paul's Birthplace; Liberal party candidate for Mayor of Syracuse, 1969. Recipient Profl. Recognition award for best newspaper column Syracuse Press Club, 1990, 94, 95, 96, 2000, Best Column award, 1994-95, 99, 2001, 02, Best Column award N.Y. Press Assn., 1991-92, 95, award Barnard Coll., Vet. Feminists of Am. and the Barnard Ctr. for Rsch. on Women, Woman of Achievement/Distinction award Gov. George E. Pataki, 1998; Svc. to Soc. award Northwestern U. Alumni Assn., 2002, Achievement award The Post-Standard, Syracuse, 2003, Joan L. Ellenbogen Founders award Women's Bar Assn. State of N.Y., 2003. Mem. NOW (pres.), Onondaga County Bar Assn. (profl. ethics com.), N.Y. Women's Bar Assn. (ctrl. N.Y. chpt. pres. 1989-90, jud. screening com.), N.Y. Bar Assn., ACLU (Ralph E. Kharas Disting. Svc. in Civil Liberties award 1985), Elizabeth Cady Stanton Found. (trustee), Working Women's Inst. (bd. advisors), Syracuse Friends Chamber Music, Atlantic States Legal Found., Yale Polit. Union (hon. life), Nat. Congress Men (gender issues advisor), Mariposa Edn. and Rsch. Found., Nat. Coun. Children's Rights (adv. panel), Wilderness Soc., Northwestern U. Alumni Assn., Women's Inst. Freedom Press, Art Inst. Chgo., Nat. Women's Polit. Caucus, Theta Sigma Phi. Address: 7599 Brown Gulf Rd Jamesville NY 13078-9636

DE DAMPIERRE, MARIE-AIMEE, lawyer; b. Paris, July 31, 1964; d. Olivier and Marie-Beatrice La Fouchardiere; m. Henri Dampierre, Dec. 10, 1988; children: Gabrielle, Eric. LLM, 1986; DESS in Indsl. Property, U. Paris II, 1987. Bar: Paris 1990, cert.: Paris Bar (advs. specialization cert.) 1996. Trade mark agt. Novamark, Paris, 1988—91; advocate Duclos, Thorne and Mollet-Vieville Law Firm, Paris, 1991—99; sr. adv. Lovell White Durrant, Paris, 1999; ptnr. Lovells (formerly Lovell White Durrant), Paris, 2000. Mem.: AFPPI, AIPPI, INTA, APRAM. Home: 112 Bd Exelmans 75016 Paris France Office: Lovells 28 rue Hamelin 75116 Paris France

DEDERICK, DAVID, lawyer; b. Point Pleasant, N .J., Oct. 9, 1962; s. William L. and Phyllis P. Dederick; m. Yvonne P. Morcz, May 1, 1993; children: Christopher R., Catherine A. BS in Econs., Cornell U., 1985; JD, George Washington U., 1988. Bar: D.C. 1988, N.J. 1988, cert.: Budapest Bar (Fgn. Legal Advisor) 1999. Assoc. Weil, Gotshal & Manges, LLP, Washington, 1988—94, mng. ptnr. Budapest, 2000—; seconded as in ho. counsel Hungarian-Am. Enterprise Fund, Budapest, Hungary, 1992—93; counsel Arent Fox Kintner Plotkin & Kahn, Budapest, 1994—96, ptnr., 1998—2000; v.p., gen. counsel COFINEC, NV, Vienna, 1996—98. Mem. supervisory bd. Krkonosské Papírny Packaging A.S., Czech Republic, 1994—2000, Kner Printing Co., Hungary, 1995—2000, COFINEC Bohemia A.S., Czech Republic, 2000—; guest lectr. Eötvös Loránd U. Law Sch., Budapest, Ctrl. European U. Legal Studies Program, Budapest. Contbr. articles to profl. jours. Mem. sch. bd. Am. Internat. Sch., Budapest, 1998—2000. Named Dealmaker of the Month, European Corp. Lawyer; named one of World's Leading Corp. and M&A Lawyers, Chambers Global. Roman Catholic. Mergers and acquisitions, Corporate, general, Finance. Office: Weil Gotshal & Manges LLP Szabadság tér 7 H-1054 Budapest Hungary Office Fax: +36 1 302 9110. E-mail: david.dederick@weil.com.

DEDERICK, RONALD OSBURN, lawyer; b. Chgo., Aug. 26, 1935; s. Clint Goddard and Isabel Lucille (Osburn) D.; m. Dorothy Hope Spence; children: Cynthia Rae Dederick Stroili, Kenneth Scott. BA, U. Va., 1957, JD, 1962. Bar: N.Y. 1962, U.S. Dist. Ct. (so. dist.) N.Y. 1964, Conn. 1969, U.S. Dist. Conn. 1970, U.S. Supreme Ct. 1990. Assoc. Sullivan & Cromwell, N.Y.C., 1962—69; ptnr. Durey & Pierson, Stamford, Conn., 1969—79, Day, Berry & Howard, Stamford and Greenwich, 1979—. Bd. dirs. Vol. Action Coun., Stamford, 1972-79, Guardianship Advocacy Resource Program, Inc., Stamford, 1984-2000; trustee, sec. West Conn. Multiple Sclerosis Soc., 1985-99; chair Greenwich (Conn.) Arts Coun., 1990-94. Capt. USNR, ret. Fellow Am. Bar Found.; mem. ABA (chair multistate com. 1984-87), Conn. Bar Assn. (chair probate sect. 1988-90), Conn. Bar Found. (James W. Cooper fellow), Stamford Regional Bar Assn. (bd. dirs. 1982-88), Internat. Bar Assn., Internat. Acad. Estate and Trust Law, Rotary (pres. Stamford 1980-81, Paul Harris fellow 1984), Milbrook Club (pres. 1980-81). Republican. Presbyterian. Avocations: golf, fishing. Office: Day Berry & Howard LLP One E Putnam Ave Greenwich CT 06830 Home: 1440 Laurel View Dr Virginia Beach VA 23451 E-mail: rdederick@dbh.com.

DEEDS, ROBERT CREIGH, lawyer, state legislator; b. Richmond, Va., Jan. 4, 1958; s. Robert Livingston Deeds Jr. and Emma Lewis (Tyree) Hicklin; m. Pamela Kay Miller, Feb. 10, 1981; children: Amanda Jane, Rebecca Lewis, Austin Creigh, Susannah Kemper. BA, Concord Coll., Athens, W.Va., 1980; JD, Wake Forest U., 1984. Bar: Va. 1984, U.S. Dist. Ct. (we. dist.) Va. 1988. Assoc. Carter, Craig & Bass, P.C., Danville, Va., 1984-85, John C. Singleton, Warm Springs, Va., 1985-87; ptnr. Singleton & Deeds, Warm Springs, Va., 1988-99; mem. Va. Ho. of Dels., 1992—2001, Va. Senate, 2001—; sole practice R. Creigh Deeds, P.C., Hot Springs, Va., 2000—. Commonwealth atty. Bath County, Va., 1988-92; chmn. Dem. Caucus, Va. Ho. Dels., 2000-01. Bd. dirs. Va. Mus. Frontier Culture. Mem. Va. State Bar, Allegheny-Bath Bar Assn., Va. Trial Lawyers Assn., Va. Assn. Commonwealth's Attys. (bd. dirs. 1989-91). Democrat. Presbyterian. Avocation: fishing. Criminal, General practice, Personal injury (including property damage). Office: R Creigh Deeds PC Drawer D Hot Springs VA 24445 E-mail: rcdeeds@tds.net.

DEEG-DABROWSKA, AGNIESZKA, lawyer, consultant; b. Warsaw, Mar. 27, 1968; d. Jerzy Deeg and Barbara Szumik; m. Tomasz Dabrowski, Oct. 26, 1990; 1 child, Bartek Dabrowski. LLM, Warsaw U., 1992. Bar: Warsaw 1996. Lawyer Nabarro Nathanson, Poland, 1991—93; lawyer, ptnr. Weil, Goisual & Manges, Poland, 1993—2000, Salans, Hertzfeld & Hellbronn, Poland, 2000—02; legal counsel Eli Lilly, Poland, 1997. Mem. supervisory bd. Ceaseplan, Warsaw, 2002—. Author: The Environmental Liability, 1993; contbr. articles to profl. jours. Avocations: theater , literature, movies, tennis, yoga. Mergers and acquisitions, Securities, Corporate, general. Home: Szeroka 31 05-092 Lomianki Poland

DEENER, LARRY COLBY, lawyer; b. Campbellsville, Ky., Sept. 15, 1950; s. Colby Velmer and Gloria Mae (Reynolds) D.; m. Martha Jean Strnad, Dec. 28, 1971; 1 child, Elizabeth Anna. BA, U. Ky., 1971; JD, No. Ky. U., 1979. Bar: Ky. 1979, U.S. Dist. Ct. (ea. dist.) Ky. 1980, U.S. Ct. Appeals (6th cir.) 1982, U.S. Supreme Ct. 1987. Law clk. to assoc. justice Supreme Ct. Ky., Frankfort, 1979-80; ptnr. Landrum & Shouse, Attys., Lexington, Ky., 1980—. Capt. USAF, 1972-76, lt. col. USAFR, 1976-99. Mem. Order of Curiae. Republican. Presbyterian. General civil litigation, Personal injury (including property damage), Transportation. Office: Landrum & Shouse Attys PO Box 951 106 W Vine St Ste 800 Lexington KY 40507-1688 E-mail: ldeener@landrumshouse.com.

DEER, DWAYNE GENE, lawyer; b. Brookhaven, Miss., Apr. 24, 1963; s. Gene Conerly and Charolett Ann Deer; m. Paula Michel Deer, Feb. 20, 1998; children: Jason, Jessica, Zachary, Elisabeth, Eli. BA, Miss. Coll., Clinton, 1992; JD, Miss. Coll., Jackson, 1995. Bar: Miss., U.S. Dist. Ct. (so. and no. dists.) Miss., U.S. Ct. Appeals (5th cir.). Office: PO Box 1361 Mccomb MS 39649

DEERSON, ADELE SHAPIRO, lawyer, educator; b. N.Y.C., July 14, 1924; d. Samuel and Marion (Pestreich) Shapiro; m. Nathan Deerson, Sept. 8, 1946 (dec. 1992); children: Bruce Alan, Jayne Ellen; m. Paul Berg, Oct. 23, 1999. BA, Hunter Coll., 1944; JD magna cum laude, Bklyn. Law Sch., 1946, JSD magna cum laude, 1949. Bar: N.Y. 1946. Atty. Henry H. Salzberg, N.Y.C., 1946-49; trial counsel Cosmopolitan Mut., N.Y.C., 1959-78; sole practice Nassau County, N.Y., 1949—; asst. prof. N.Y. Inst. Tech., 1968, assoc. prof., 1969-78, prof. law, 1978—. Profl. no-fault arbitrator, N.Y., 1990—; arbitrator Am. Arbitration Assn., Small Claims Ct., Civil Ct., Dist. Ct. Nassau, N.Y. Author: Learning Manual Business Law, 1978; staff editor Jour. Legal Svcs. Edn. Recipient Cert. of Appreciation Judges Civil Ct., Queens, 1977, N.Y.C. Family Ct. 1977. Mem. Queens County Bar Assn., Nassau County Bar Assn., Nat. Bus. Law Tchrs., Assn. Arbitrators, Nassau-Suffolk Women's Bar Assn., B'nai B'rith (v.p. 1956-58), Philonomic, Delta Mu Delta. Alternative dispute resolution, Commercial, contracts (including sales of goods; commercial financing), General practice. Home: 7612 176th St Flushing NY 11366-1514 E-mail: ADeerson@aol.com.

DEFEIS, ELIZABETH FRANCES, law educator, lawyer; b. N.Y.C. d. Francis Paul and Lena (Amendola) D. BA, St. John's U., 1956, JD, 1958, JSD (hon.), 1984; LLM, NYU, 1971; postgrad., U. Milan, Italy, 1963-64, Inst. Internat. Human Rights, 1991. Bar: N.Y. 1959, U.S. Dist. Ct. (fed. dist.) 1960, U.S. Dist. Ct. (so. dist.) N.Y. 1961, U.S. Supreme Ct. 1965, U.S. Dist. Ct. (ea. dist.) N.Y. 1978, N.J. 1983. Asst. U. S. atty. So. Dist. N.Y., Dept. Justice, 1961-62; atty. RCA Corp., 1962-63; assoc. Carter, Ledyard & Milburn, N.Y.C., 1963-69; atty. Bedford Stuyvesant Legal Svcs. Corp., 1969-70; prof. law Seton Hall U., Newark, 1971—, dean Sch. Law, 1983-88. Vis. prof. St. Louis U. Sch. Law, 1988, St. John's U. Sch. Law, 1990, 2001, U. Milan, Italy, 1996; Fulbright-Hays lectr., Iran, India, 1977-79; lectr. Orgn. Security and Cooperation in Europe, Russia, Turkmenistan, Tajikistan, Azerbaijan; vis. scholar Ctr. Study of Human Rights, Columbia U., 1989; project dir. TV series Women and Law, 1974-80; narrator TV series Alternatives to Violence, 1981; mem. com. women and cts. N.J. Supreme Ct., 1982-95; trustee Legal Svcs. N.J., 1983-88; mem. 3rd Cir. Task Force on Equality in the Cts., 1995-98; tech. cons. on Constitution of Armenia, 1992-95; project dir. T.V. series Pub. Internat. Law.; legal expert Armenia election OSCE, 1998. Chair Albert Einstein Inst., Boston, 1995—2001. Fulbright-Hays scholar Milan, Italy, 1963-64, Fulbright-Hays, Orgn. for Security and Cooperation in Europe scholar, Armenia, Russia, Italy, 1996; Ford Found. fellow, 1970-71. Mem. ABA, Nat. Italian Am. Bar Assn., Columbian Lawyers Assn., Assn. of Bar of City of N.Y. (internat. law com., coun. internat. affairs), N.J. Bar Assn., Nat. Italian Am. Found. Office: Seton Hall U Law Sch One Newark Ctr Newark NJ 07102 E-mail: defeisel@shu.edu.

DEFFNER, ROGER L. lawyer, investment counselor, chef; b. Merrill, Wis., Aug. 17, 1945; s. Oscar A. and Elsie E. (Liebers) D. BSChemE, U. Wis., Madison, 1968, JD, 1973. Bar: Wis. 1973, U.S. Dist. Ct. (we. dist.) Wis. 1973. Chem. engr. prodn. and rsch., spl. products divsn. NCR, Portage, Wis., 1968-69; chem. engr. plant modernization Olin Chem., Baraboo, Wis., 1969-70; pres., owner Deffner Law Firm, S.C., Wausau, 1973—; gen. ptnr. D&D Investments, Wausau, 1974—. Advisor N. Central Tech. Inst., Wausau, 1977-98; dir. Wausau Kayak/Canoe Corp., 1992—, Crossroads Mental Health Svcs., Inc., Abbotsford State Bank; pres., owner Outdoor Gourmet, L.L.C. Co-author: Legal Systems Inc., 1977-78. Mem. Wausau C. of C., Jaycees (life, bd. dirs. Portage 1969, pres. 1970, state v.p. Madison 1971, dir. Wausau 1974), Wausau Noon Optimists (life, internal v.p. 1985-86, pres. 1986-87), Elks, Fraternal Triangle. Republican. Lutheran and Polish Catholic. Estate planning, General practice, Property, real (including real estate development, water). Address: Deffner Law Firm 1803 Stewart Ave Wausau WI 54401-5374 E-mail: chefdeff@dwave.net.

DEFOOR, J. ALLISON, II, lawyer; b. Coral Gables, Fla., Dec. 6, 1953; s. James Allison Sr. and Marjorie (Keen) DeF.; m. Terry Ann White, June 24, 1977; children: Melissa Anne, Mary Katherine, James Allison III. BA, U. So. Fla., 1976; JD, Stetson U., 1979; MA, U. So. Fla., 1979; postgrad., Harvard U., 1989; STD, So. Fla. Ctr. Theol. Studies, 1999, MDiv, 2001, postgrad., 2002—. Bar: Fla. 1979, U.S. Dist. Ct. (so. dist.) Fla. 1980, U.S. Ct. Appeals (5th cir.) 1981, U.S. Ct. Appeals (11th cir.) 1982. Asst. pub. defender, 1979—80; asst. state's atty. 16th Cir., Key West, Fla., 1980—83, dir. narcotics task force, 1981—83; judge Monroe County, Plantation Key, Fla., 1983—87; assoc. Cunningham, Albritton, Lenzi, Warner, Bragg & Miller, Plantation Key, 1987—89; sheriff Monroe County, Fla., 1989—90; sr. v.p. CEO Wackenut Monitoring Systems Inc., Coral Gables, Fla., 1991—92; gen. counsel, sec. HEM Pharm. Corp., Phila. and Key Largo, 1992—93; ptnr. Hershoff, Lupino DeFoor & Gregg, Tavernier, Fla., 1993—99; Everglades policy coord. State of Fla., Office of Gov., Tallahassee, 1999—2002; gen. counsel Tidewater Cons, Inc., Tallahassee, 2000—02; state coord. EarthBalance, Inc., Tallahassee and North Port,

2002—; of counsel Hershoff, Lupino & Mulick, Tavernier, Fla., 2000—. Adj. faculty St. Leo Coll., Key West, 1980-81, U. So. Fla., Ft. Myers, 1981-82, Fla. Internat. U., Miami, 1985, U. Miami Law Sch., 1985-99, Fla. A&M U., 1999-2001; faculty Nat. Jud. Coll., Reno, Nev., 1985-86; lectr. Yale U., 2000, U. Pa. Law Sch., 2000. Editor U. Miami Law Rev., 1985; author: DeFoor & Schultz, Fla. Civil Procedure Forms with Practice Commentary, 1989, Odet Philippe, Peninsular Pioneer, 1997 (Safety Harbor Mus., Fla.). Trustee Coun. for Sustainable Fla., 2000—, Fla. Dispute Resolution Consortium, Kairos Horizon, Collins Ctr. for Pub. Policy, Fla. C. of C.; pres. Mus. of Fla. History Found., 2000—01, Coun. for Sustainable Fla., 2001—; chmn. Monroe County Rep. Exec. Com., 1987—88, 1994, state committeeman, 1994—99; mem. Fla. Rep. Exec. Com., 1995—99; del. Rep. Nat. Conv., 1992; Rep. nominee Lt. Gov. of Fla., 1990; chmn. Wakulla County Rep. Exec. Com., 2001—; vice chmn. Rep. Party of Fla., 2003—. Named one of Five Outstanding Young Men in Fla., Jaycees, 1984, Ten Outstanding Young Men in Am., Jaycees, 1985; recipient Merit award Fla. Crime Prevention Commn., 1982, Leadership Fla. Class V, Chmn.'s award Fla. Audubon, 1997. Mem. ABA, Fla. Bar (bd. govs. 1995-97), Mensa, Ocean Reef Club (Key Largo, Fla.), Islamorada Fishing Club, Key West Yacht Club, Explorer's Club (New York), Gov.'s Club. Republican. Episcopalian. Avocations: scuba diving, sailing, golf. Environmental, Technology. Home: 359 River Plantation Rd Crawfordville FL 32327-1517 Office: Earth Balance 200 W College Ave Ste 311-D Tallahassee FL 32301

DEFOREST, WALTER PATTISON, III, lawyer; b. Ft. Sill, Okla., Dec. 4, 1944; s. Walter P. Jr. and Mary E. (Miller) DeF.; m. Anna Thun. BA, U. Pitts., 1966; JD, Harvard U., 1969. Bar: Pa. 1970, U.S. Ct. Appeals (2d and 3d cirs.) 1973, U.S. Ct. Appeals (4th, 5th and D.C. cirs.) 1978, U.S. Ct. Appeals (10th cir.) 1981, U.S. Ct. Appeals (11th cir.), U.S. Ct. Appeals (7th cir.) 1986, U.S. Ct. Appeals (fed. cir.) 1995, U.S. Supreme Ct. 1974, W.Va. 1997, Ohio 2001. Assoc. Reed, Smith, Shaw & McClay, Pitts., 1969—77, ptnr., 1978—93, DeForest Koscelnik Yokitis & Kaplan, Pitts., 1994—2003, 2003—. Instr. Grad. Sch. Indsl. Adminstrn. Carnegie Mellon U., Pitts., 1974-75. Mem. adv. com. Big Bros. and Big Sisters Western Pa., Pitts., 1984—; bd. dirs. Pa. Small Bus. Advocacy Coun., Harrisburg, 1984-89, 92. Mem. ABA (litigation, labor sects.), Pa. Bar Assn. (litigation, labor sects.), Allegheny County Bar Assn. (litigation sect., fed. ct. sect.). Administrative and regulatory, General civil litigation, Labor (including EEOC, Fair Labor Standards Act, labor-management relations, NLRB, OSHA). Office: DeForest Koscelnik Yokitis & Kaplan 3000 Koppers Bldg 436 7th Ave Pittsburgh PA 15219-1826

DE GARCIA VILLEGAS, OLGA SANCHEZ CORDERO, judge; b. Mexico City; Grad., Nat. Autonomous U. Mexico; postgrad., U. Coll. Swansea, 1973—74. Prof. Nat. Autonomous U. Mexico, 1975—; notary pub. Fed. Dist., 1984—93; min. Supreme Ct. Justice, Mexico City, 1995—. Office: Suprema Corte de Justicia de la Nacion Pino Suarez No 2 Col Centro 06065 Mexico City Mexico*

DEGNAN, JOHN MICHAEL, lawyer; b. Mpls., Apr. 2, 1948; s. John F. and Lorraine A. Degnan; m. Barbara B. Degnan; children: Michael Gene Carland, John Patrick, Amy Marie, David Charles. BA, U. Minn., 1970; JD, William Mitchell Coll. Law, 1976. Bar: Minn. 1976, U.S. Dist. Ct. Minn. 1976, U.S. Ct. Appeals (8th cir.) Minn. 1976, U.S. Supreme Ct. 1976. Ins. underwriter Marsh & McLennan, Mpls., 1973-76; lawyer Bassford, Lockhart, Truesdell & Briggs, P.A., Mpls., 1976—2003, Murnane, Conlin, White & Brandt, St. Paul, 2003—. Lectr. in field. Bd. dirs. Hennepin County Pub. Libraries, 1980-84, Storefront Youth Action, 1981-83, Mediation Ctr., 1991—. 1st lt. U.S. Army, 1971-72, Vietnam. Fellow: Am. Bd. Trial Advocates, Am. Coll. Trial Lawyers; mem.: ABA, Am. Soc. Law and Medicine, Def. Rsch. Inst., Minn. Def. Lawyers Assn. (bd. dirs. 1986—, pres. 1990—91), Am. Bd. Trial Advocates, Nat. Bd. Trial Advocacy (cert. civil trial specialist), Hennepin County Bar Assn. (professionalism com.), Minn. State Bar Assn. (ins. com., lectr. convs. 1984—85, civil trial cert. governing coun., cert. trial specialist), Richfield Jaycees (past pres.). Avocations: running, tennis, golf, boating, sports. State civil litigation, Insurance, Personal injury (including property damage). Office: Murnane Conlin White & Brandt 1800 US Bank Corp Piper Jaffray Tower 444 Cedar St Saint Paul MN 55101

DEHE, RICHARD, lawyer; b. Paris, June 11, 1952; m. Mia Hindle, Dec. 23, 1996; m. Charlotte Davidson, Sept. 8, 1979 (div. Dec. 14, 1989); children: Henry, Caroline, Constance, James. Licence en Droit Pub., U. Paris, Paris France, 1970—74, Des de Droit Fiscal Et Des Affaires, 1974—76; M Comparative Law, Georgetown U., Washington D.C., 1978—79. Bar: (Paris) 1983. Assoc. S.G. Archibald, Paris, 1979—85; European counsel Paul, Weiss, Rifkind, Wharton & Garrison, Paris, 1985—99; ptnr. C.L.& A, Paris, 1999—2001, Cournot Avocats, Paris, 2001—02, Altheimer & Gray, Paris, 2002—. Dir. Nus Consulting Group, Paris, 2001—. Mem.: Am. Hosp. Paris (assoc.), Automobile Club De France (assoc.), Am. Club Paris (assoc.). Mergers and acquisitions, Corporate, general, Finance. Office: Altheimer & Gray 24 Rue De Prony Paris 75017 France Office Fax: 33 1 44293371. E-mail: rdehe@24rueprony.fr.

DE HOYOS, DEBORA M. lawyer; b. Monticello, N.Y., Aug. 10, 1953; d. Luis and Marion (Kinney) de Hoyos; m. Walter C. Carlson, June 20, 1981; children: Amanda, Greta, Linnea. BA, Wellesley Coll., 1975; JD, Harvard U., 1978. Bar: Ill. 1978, U.S. Dist. Ct. (no. dist.) Ill. 1980. Assoc. Mayer, Brown & Platt, Chgo., 1978—84, ptnr., 1985—, mng. ptnr., 1991—. Bd. dirs. Evanston Northwestern Healthcare; bd. trustees Providence St. Mel. Sch. Contbr. chpt. to Securitization of Financial Assets. Trustee Chgo. Symphony Orch. Office: Mayer Brown & Platt 190 S La Salle St Ste 3100 Chicago IL 60603-3441

DEITRICK, WILLIAM EDGAR, lawyer; b. N.Y.C., July 30, 1944; s. John English and Dorothy Alice (Geib) D.; m. Emily Jane Posey, June 22, 1968; children: William Jr., Elizabeth, Peter. BA, Johns Hopkins U., 1967; JD, Cornell U., 1971. Bar: Ill. 1972, U.S. Dist. Ct. (no. dist.) Ill. 1972, U.S. Ct. Appeals (7th cir.) 1976, D.C. 1981. Ptnr. Gardner, Carton and Douglas, Chgo., 1972—85; sr. v.p., dep. gen. counsel, mgr. litigation divsn. Continental Bank N.A., 1985—91; ptnr. Mayer, Brown, Rowe & Maw, Chgo., 1991—. Contbr. articles to profl. jours. Trustee North Shore Country Day Sch., 1992-97; gov. mem. Shedd Aquarium; With U.S. Army, 1968-70. Mem. ABA, Ill. Bar Assn., Chgo. Bar Assn., Johns Hopkins U. Alumni Assn. (class agt. 1967-95), Cornell Law Sch. Chgo. Alumni Assn. (chmn. 1985-87), Legal Club, Univ. Club Chgo. (bd. dirs.), Indian Hill Club (Winnetka, Ill.). Federal civil litigation, State civil litigation. Home: 365 Greenwood Ave Glencoe IL 60022-2045 Office: Mayer Brown Rowe & Maw 190 S La Salle St Ste 3100 Chicago IL 60603-3441

DEJOHN, MICHAEL ANTHONY, defender; b. Erie, Pa., Apr. 28, 1975; s. Anthony Samuel and Kathleen Rose DeJohn; m. Kara Christine Lesonik, Oct. 25, 2002; 1 child, Samuel David. BA in Criminal Justice, Gannon U., 1997; JD, U. Dayton, 2000. Bar: Pa. 2003. Prosecutor's aide, hearing office City of Dayton Prosecutor's Office, Dayton, 1999—2000; clk. Erie County Ct. Common Pleas, Erie, 2000—02; asst. pub. defender Office of Pub. Defender, Meadville, Pa., 2002—. Mem.: Phi Delta Phi (magister 1999—2000). Avocations: guitar, piano, karaoke, computers, art. Home: 632 W 7th St Erie PA 16502 Office: Office Pub Defender 903 Diamond Sq Meadville PA 16335 E-mail: gcutti@msn.com.

DE JONG, DAVID JOHN, lawyer, physician; b. Grand Rapids, Mich., July 17, 1951; s. Alexander Cornelius and Joanne Minnie (Vander Baan) De J.; m. Gwen Rachel Prins, May 25, 1974; children: Connor David, Caleb Ijmen, Samuel Nicholas. Student, Trinity Christian Coll., 1969-72; MD, Loyola U., Maywood, Ill., 1975; JD, Northwestern U., 1980. Bar: Ill. 1980, U.S. Dist. Ct. (no. dist.) Ill. 1980. Physician emergency dept. Morris (Ill.) Hosp., 1976-77; assoc. John D. Hayes & Assocs., Ltd., Chgo., 1980-84; prin. David J. De Jong & Assocs., Ltd., Chgo., 1984—. Bd. dirs. Elim Christian Sch. Fellow Am. Coll. Legal Medicine; mem. Chgo. Acad. Legal Medicine, Ill. Trial Lawyers Assn. (med. malpractice com. 1985—), Chgo. Bar Assn. Mem. Christian Reformed Ch. State civil litigation, Personal injury (including property damage). Home: 2042 N Orleans St Chicago IL 60614-4715 Office: 20 N Clark St Ste 2700 Chicago IL 60602

DE JONG, DAVID SAMUEL, lawyer, educator; b. Washington, Jan. 8, 1951; s. Samuel and Dorothy (Thomas) De J.; m. Tracy Ann Barger, Sept. 23, 1995; children: Jacob Samuel, Franklin Joseph. BA, U. Md., 1972; JD, Washington and Lee U., 1975; LLM in Taxation, Georgetown U., 1979. Bar: Md. 1975, U.S. Dist. Ct. Md. 1977, U.S. Tax Ct. 1977, U.S. Ct. Appeals (4th cir.) 1978, U.S. Supreme Ct. 1979, D.C. 1980, U.S. Dist. Ct. D.C. 1983, U.S. Ct. Claims, U.S. Ct. Appeals (fed. cir.) 1983; CPA, Md.; cert. valuation analyst. Atty. Gen. Bus. Svcs., Inc., Rockville, Md., 1975-80; ptnr. Stein Sperling Bennett De Jong Driscoll & Greenfeig, PC, Rockville, 1980—. Adj. prof. Southea. U., Washington, 1979-85, Am. U., Washington, 1983-2002; instr. U. Md., College Park, 1986-87, Montgomery Coll., Rockville, 1983; mem. character com. 7th Appeals Cir. Md. Ct. of Appeals. Co-author: (ann. book) J.K. Lasser's Year-Round Tax Strategies, 1989—; editor Notes and Comments, Washington and Lee U. Law Rev., 1974-75. V.p. Seneca Whetstone Homeowners Assn., Gaithersburg, Md., 1981-82, pres. 1982-83. Mem. ABA, AICPA, Am. Assn. Atty.-CPAs (bd. dirs. 1997—, sec. 1998-99, treas. 1999-2000, v.p. 2000-02, pres. elect 2002-2003, pres. 2003—), Md. Bar Assn., Montgomery County Bar Assn. (chmn. tax sect. 1991-92, treas. 1996-97), D.C. Bar Assn., Md. Assn. CPAs, D.C. Inst. CPAs, Nat. Assn. Cert. Valuation Analysts, Inst. Bus. Appraisers, Md. Soc. Accts., Phi Alpha Delta. Corporate taxation, Estate taxation, Personal income taxation. Office: 25 W Middle Ln Rockville MD 20850-2214

DEKIEFFER, DONALD EULETTE, lawyer; b. Newport, R.I., Nov. 8, 1945; s. Robert and Melissa (Hibberd) deK.; m. Nancy Kishida, June 27, 1970; 1 child, Nathan Hiroyuki. BA, U. Colo., 1968; JD, Georgetown U., 1971. Bar: U.S. Supreme Ct. 1982, U.S. Ct. Appeals (D.C. cir.) 1971, U.S. Dist. Ct. D.C. 1971, U.S. Ct. Claims 1971, U.S. Ct. Internat. Trade 1971. Mem. profl. staff Senate Rep. Policy Com., 1969-71; assoc. Collier, Shannon, Rill & Edwards, 1971-74; ptnr. Collier, Shannon, Rill, Edwards & Scott, 1974-80, deKieffer, Berg & Creskoff, 1980; gen. counsel U.S. Trade Rep., Washington, 1981-83; ptnr. Plaia, Schaumburg & deKieffer, Washington, 1983-84, Pillsbury, Madison & Sutro, Washington, 1984-92, deKieffer Dibble & Horgan, Washington, 1992—. Author: How to Lobby Congress, 1981, Doing Business with the USA, 1984, Doing Business with Romania, 1985, Doing Business in the United States, 1985, Doing Business With the New Romania, 1991, International Business Travellers Companion, 1992, How Lawyers Screw Their Clients, 1996, The Citizens Guide to Lobbying Congress, 1997. Mem. Presdl. Transition Team, 1980-81. Mem. ABA, D.C. Bar, Bar Assn. D.C., Fed. Bar Assn., Am. Soc. Internat. Law, Internat. Antitrust Soc. E-mail: ddekieffer@dhlaw.com. Antitrust, Private international, Public international. Office: deKieffer & Horgan 729 15th St NW Ste 800 Washington DC 20005-2105

DE KOSTER, JOHN G. lawyer; b. Berea, Ohio, May 23, 1950; s. Lucas J. and Dorothea L. De Koster; m. Glenda F. Alons, Aug. 19, 1972; children: Lucas, Philip. BS in Polit. Sci., Iowa State U., 1972; JD, U. Colo., 1975. Bar: Iowa 1975, U.S. Supreme Ct. 1978. Atty., advisor U.S. Dept. of Interior, Washington, 1975-79; ptnr. De Koster & De Koster, Hull, Iowa, 1979—. Bd. dirs. Iowa State Bank, Hull, Mut. Fire and Auto Ins. Co., Cedar Rapids. Pres. Hull Cmty. Found., 1999—. Named Citizen of Yr. Hull Bus. and Profl. Club, 1997, Employer of Yr., 2002; recipient Cmty. Svc. award Modern Woodmen, Hull, 1987. Fellow Iowa State Bar Found.; mem. Iowa State Bar Assn. (bd. govs. 1994-99), Sioux County Bar Assn. (pres. 1996-98), Kiwanis. Office: De Koster & De Koster 1102 Main St PO Box 801 Hull IA 51239-0801

DE LA CALLE, JOSÉ ANTONIO, lawyer; b. Madrid, July 25, 1972; s. Sixto de la Calle and Matilde Peral; m. Sanna Erika Teresia Orkan, Aug. 17, 2002. Law Degree magna cum laude, U. Madrid, 1995; EU Law Degree magna cum laude, San Pablo U., Madrid, 1996; LLM with grand distinction, U. Brussels, 1996; diploma in U.S. law, U. Calif., Berkeley, 2001, U. Calif., Davis, 2001. Bar: Madrid 1998. In-house lawyer Spanish Brandy Assn., Jerez, Spain, 1996—97; jr. assoc. Baker & McKenzie, Madrid, 1998—2001, fgn. lawyer London, 2002, sr. assoc. Madrid, 2003—. Contbr. articles to profl. jours. Mem.: Madrid Bar Assn. Avocations: sailing, wine, movies, travel. Corporate, general, Commercial, contracts (including sales of goods; commercial financing), Communications. Home: 6th Fl P Castellana 33 28046 Madrid Spain Office: Baker & McKenzie Law Firm P Castellana 33 6th Fl 28046 Madrid Spain

DELACERDA, MELISSA GRINER, lawyer; b. St. Petersburg, Fla., Mar. 17, 1952; d. Joseph Henry and Dorothy Jean (Stephens) G.; m. Fred G. DeLacerda, June 17, 1972. BS, Memphis State U., 1973; JD, U. Tulsa, 1979. Bar: Okla. 1979. Tchr., elem. sch., Crowley, La., 1974-75; sports reporter Daily Advertiser, Lafayette, La., 1974-75; assoc. firm Bird & Hochderffer, Stillwater, Okla., 1979-80; sole practice law, Stillwater, 1980— . Bd. dirs. Alcoholism Council Area Okla., 1981-82, Stillwater Domestic Violence Svcs., 1979—. Mem. Okla. Bar Assn. (pres. elect, 2002-03, pres. 2003-), Payne County Bar Assn. (sec. 1984), Am. Trial Lawyers Assn., Bus. and Profl. Women Stillwater (pres. 1985), Stillwater C. of C. (ambassador 1982-84). Office: Law Office of Melissa DeLacerda 301 S Duck St PO Box 1252 Stillwater OK 74076*

DELA CRUZ, JOSE SANTOS, retired state supreme court justice; b. Saipan, Commonwealth No. Mariana Islands, July 18, 1948; s. Thomas Castro and Remedio Sablan (Santos) Dela C.; m. Rita Tenorio Sablan, Nov. 12, 1977; children: Roxanne, Renee, Rica Ann. BA, U. Guam, 1971; JD, U. Calif., Berkeley, 1974; cert., Nat. Jud. Coll., Reno, 1985. Bar: No. Mariana Islands, 1974, U.S. Dist. Ct. No. Mariana Islands 1978. Staff atty. Micro. Legal Svcs. Corp., Saipan, 1974-79; gen. counsel Marianas Pub. Land Corp., Saipan, 1979-81; liaison atty. CNMI Fed. Laws Commn., Saipan, 1981-83; ptnr. Borja & Dela Cruz, Saipan, 1983-85; assoc. judge Commonwealth Trial Ct., Saipan, 1985-89; state supreme ct. chief justice Supreme Ct. No. Mariana Islands, 1989-95; retired, 1995. Mem. Conf. of Chief Justices, 1989-95, Adv. Commn. on Judiciary, Saipan, 1980-82; chmn. Criminal Justice Planning Agy., Saipan, 1985-95. Mem. Coun. for Arts, Saipan, 1982-83; chmn. Bd. of Elections, Saipan, 1977-82; pres. Cath. Social Svcs., Saipan, 1982-85. Mem. No. Marianas Bar Assn. (pres. 1984-85). Roman Catholic. Avocations: golf, reading, walking.

DE LACY, RICHARD MICHAEL, arbitrator; b. Kingston upon Hull, Eng., Dec. 4, 1954; m. Sybil del Strother; children: Barbara, Edward, Philippa. MA, Clare Coll., Cambridge, 1975. Bar: Eng. 1976, Wales 1976. Comml. barrister Chambers of C. Symons QC & J.Jarvis QC, London, 1976—. Editor: Bullen & Leake & Jacob, Precedents of Pleading, 2000. Fellow Chartered Inst. of Arbitrators; mem. Queen's Counsel Eng. Avocations: music, equestrianism, wine. Office: Chambers C Symons J Jarvis 3 Verulam Bldgs London WC1R 5NT England Office Fax: 44-2078318479. E-mail: rdelacy@3vb.com.

DELAFIELD, JOSEPH LIVINGSTON, III, lawyer; b. Fayetteville, N.C., June 27, 1940; s. Joseph Livingston and Anna Shippen (Howe) D.; m. Audrey Ayrault Sawtelle, Nov. 27, 1965; children: Katharine Ayrault, MIchael Ross, Joseph Egerton. AB magna cum laude, Princeton (N.J.) U., 1962; LLB cum laude, Harvard U., 1965. Bar: Calif. 1966, U.S. Dist. Ct. (no. dist.) Calif. 1966, U.S. Mil. Appeals 1966, U.S. Ct. Appeals (9th cir.) 1966, Maine 1970, U.S. Dist. Ct. Maine 1970. Assoc. Heller, Enrman, White & McAuliffe, San Francisco, 1965-66; assoc., shareholder Drummond Woodsum & MacMahon, Portland, 1970—2000, of counsel, 2000—. Chancellor, Episcopal Diocese of Maine. Capt. U.S. Army, 1966-70. Fellow Maine Bar Found. Corporate, general, Mergers and acquisitions, Securities.

DELAMOTHE, CASSANDRA MACON, lawyer; b. Trenton, NJ, Mar. 8, 1958; d. Mary Harris and Paul Macon; m. Jean Martin DeLaMothe, June 8, 1985; children: Danielle C., Phillipe A., Rachelle M., Justin D. BA, The Coll. of NJ., Trenton, New Jersey, 1980; JD, Fordham U. Sch. of Law, N.Y.C., 1996. Bar: NY 1997, NJ 1997, U.S. Dist. Ct. (so. dist. NY) 1999. Atty. Law Office of Cassandra M. DeLaMothe, Cortlandt Manor, NY, Law Office of Carolyn Minter, Ossining, NY, Law Office of Leonard Buddington, Jr., Yonkers, NY. Contbr. articles to profl. jours. Mem.: ABA, Westchester County Bar Assn., NY State Bar Assn. Avocations: writing, swimming, fitness, travel. Family and matrimonial, Probate (including wills, trusts), Estate planning. Office: Law Office of Cassandra M DeLaMothe 2117 Crompond Road Suite 25 Cortlandt Manor NY 10567 E-mail: delamothelaw@aol.com.

DELANEY, TIMOTHY QUINN, lawyer, engineer; b. Evergreen Park, Ill., Sept. 25, 1960; s. William Ellis and Jean Marie (Quinn) D.; m. Marjorie Lee Schack, Dec. 1, 1981; children: Quinn, Mark, Stephen. BS in Gen. Engring., U. Ill., 1983; JD with honors, George Washington U., 1988. Bar: Ill. 1988; U.S. Dist. Ct. (no. dist.) Ill. 1989, (we. dist.) Mich. 1992; U.S. Ct. Appeals (fed. cir.) 1991, (10th cir.) 1999 (6th cir.) 2001; registered with U.S. Patent and Trademark Office. Shareholder Brinks, Hofer, Gilson & Line, Chgo., 1988—. Mem. Fed. Cir. Bar Assn. (chmn. writing contest 1993-99, bd. govs. 1999-2002), ABA, Intellectual Property Law Assn. Chgo. (chmn. dinner com. 1999), Am. Intellectual Property Law Assn. Democrat. Roman Catholic. Avocations: baseball, golf, reading, creative writing. Intellectual property. Office: Brinks Hofer Gilson & Lione Ste 3600 455 N Cityfront Plaza Dr Chicago IL 60611-5599

DELANIS, JAMES ALFRED, lawyer; b. Parma, Ohio, Oct. 4, 1953; s. John Joseph and Irene Ann (Harm) DeL. AB, Dartmouth Coll., 1975; JD, Vanderbilt U., 1978. Bar: Tenn. 1978, Ohio 1979, U.S. Dist. Ct. Tenn. 1978, U.S. Ct. Appeals (6th cir.) 1981), U.S. Supreme Ct. 1996. Law clk. Cir. Ct. for Davidson County, Nashville, 1978-79; asst. atty. gen. Atty. Gen. Office State of Tenn., Nashville, 1979-81; assoc. atty. Baker Worthington Law Firm, Nashville, 1981-88, ptnr., 1988-95; shareholder Baker Donelson Law Firm, Nashville, 1995—. Bd. dirs. Nashville Pro Bono, Inc., 1994-98, chmn. 1996-97; bd. dirs. Nashville Humane Assn., 1996-2002, pres., 1999-2000. Recipient Tutor of Yr. award YMCA Cmty. Action Program, 1995. Mem. ABA (litig., antitrust and intellectual property sects. 1995—), Tenn. Bar Assn., Nashville Bar Assn. Avocations: handball, tennis, reading, gardening. Federal civil litigation, General civil litigation, State civil litigation. Office: Baker Donelson Ste 1000 211 Commerce St Nashville TN 37201

DE LASA, JOSÉ M. lawyer; b. Havana, Cuba, Nov. 28, 1941; came to U.S., 1961; s. Miguel and Conchita de Lasa; m. Maria Teresa Figueroa, Nov. 23, 1963; children: Maria Teresa, José, Andrés, Carlos. BA, Yale U., 1968, JD, 1971. Bar: N.Y. 1973. Assoc. Cleary, Gottlieb, Steen & Hamilton, N.Y.C., 1971-76; legal dept. Bristol-Myers Squibb Co., N.Y.C., 1976-94; sr. v.p., sec. and gen. counsel Abbott Labs., 1994—. Lectr. internat. law, various locations. Bd. dirs. Am. Arbitration Assn., Chgo. Children's Mus., The Resource Found., Chgo. Coun. Fgn. Rels., The Stovir Found. Mem. ABA, Assn. of Bar of City of N.Y., Assn. Gen. Counsel, North Shore Gen. Counsel Assn., Ill. State Bar Assn. Roman Catholic. Corporate, general, Health, Private international. Office: Abbott Laboratories D-364 AP6D-2 100 Abbott Park Rd North Chicago IL 60064-3500

DEL BONO, IRENE LILLIAN (IRENE STONE GUILD DEL BONO), lawyer; b. Milford, Mass., May 27, 1949; d. Roy Prescott and Sara Lucretia (Snyer) Stone; children: Gregory Howe Jr., Daniel David. BS in Criminal Justice, Westfield State Coll., 1989; JD, Boston U., 1991, MA in Hist. Preservation, 1992. Bar: Mass. 1991, U.S. Supreme Ct. 1996, U.S. Dist. Ct. Mass. 2000. Asst. atty. gen. Office Atty. Gen., Boston, 1992-2001; dir. land acquisition and protection State Mass. Dept. Environ. Mgmt., 2001—. Active Framingham Hist. Soc. Mem. Mass. Bar Assn. (property law sect.), Mass. Conveyancer's Assn., Nat. Trust Hist. Preservation, N.E. Legal Preservation Network, U.S. Supreme Ct. Hist. Soc., Danvers Alarm List Co. Avocations: writing, bicycling, hiking, internet. Home: 24 Nern St Natick MA 01760-3527 Office: State Mass Dept Environ Mgmt Land Acquisition/Protection 251 Causeway St Boston MA 02114 E-mail: delbonoandlaw@hotmail.com.

DELEON, PATRICK HENRY, lawyer; b. Waterbury, Conn., Jan. 6, 1943; s. Patrick and Catherine (Dzubay) D.; m. Jean Louise Murphy; children: Patrick Daniel Nainoa, Katherine Malia Malie. BA, Amherst Coll., 1964; MS, Purdue U., 1966, PhD in Clin. Psychology, 1969; MPH, U. Hawaii, 1973; JD, Catholic U., 1980. Bar: Hawaii 1981, U.S. Dist. Ct. Hawaii 1983, U.S. Ct. Appeals (9th cir.) 1983; diplomate Am. Bd. Profl. Psychology, Am. Bd. Forensic Psychology. Tng. psychologist Peace Corps Tng. Ctr., Hilo, Hawaii, 1969-70; staff psychologist Diamond Head Mental Health Ctr., Hawaii State Hosp., Honolulu and Kaneohe, Hawaii, 1970-73; adminstrv. asst. U.S. Senator Daniel K. Inouye, Washington, 1973—. Fellow APA (pres. 2000, assoc. editor Am. Psychologist Jour. 1981—, editor Profl. Psychology Rsch. and Practice 1995-2000), Hawaii Psychol. Assn. (Disting. Svc. award 1981), Hawaii Bar Assn. Democrat. Home: 5701 Wilson Ln Bethesda MD 20817 Office: care Senator D K Inouye Us Senate Washington DC 20510-0001

DE LEON, SYLVIA A. lawyer; b. Corpus Christi, Tex., Mar. 2, 1950; BA, Briarcliff Coll., 1972; JD, U. Tex., 1976. Bar: Tex. 1976, D.C. 1977. Ptnr. Akin, Gump, Strauss, Hauer & Feld LLP, Washington. Adj. prof. law Georgetown U. law ctr., 1988-90; bd. dirs. Amtrak, Nat. Railroad Passenger Corp., 1994—, chair corp. strategy com. Bd. dirs. U. Tex. Law Sch. Found. 2002-, U. Tex. Law Assn., 1985-89, 92-96, 2000-, U. Tex. Devel. Bd., 1996—, Washington Ballet, 2001-; coord. issues transp. Clinton-Gore Presdl. Transition Team, 1992; presdl. appointee Nat. Commn. Ensure Strong Competitive Airline Industry, 1993, White House Conf. on Travel and Tourism. Mem. Bar Assn. D.C., State Bar Tex. (chmn. fed. law and regulations com. 1984-87), Nat. Civil Aviation Rev. Commn. Office: Akin Gump Strauss Hauer & Feld Ste 400 1333 New Hampshire Ave NW Washington DC 20036-1564

DELGADILLO, ROCKARD J. (ROCKY DELGADILLO), lawyer; b. L.A., July 15, 1960; m. Michelle Delgadillo; 1 child, Christian. B with honors, Harvard U.; JD, Columbia U. Tchr., coach L.A. Unified Sch. Dist.; sr. atty. O'Melveny and Myers, L.A.; dir. bus. devel. Rebuild L.A.; dep. mayor econ. devel. City of L.A., city atty., 2001—. Bd. dirs. Arnold's All-Stars, Para Los Niños, Cath. Big Bros., 1st AME Ch. Renaissance Program, Franklin HS Scholarship Found., Friends Jordan HS, Workforce L.A.; leader L.A. ann. salute to Latino Heritage Month, 1993—. Named Disting. Young Alumnus, Columbia U., 1998, Alumnus of the Yr., 2002; named an All-Am. Football Player; recipient medal of excellence, Columbia U. Office: City Hall E 200 N Main St Rm 1800 Los Angeles CA 90012-4131*

DELHOMME, BEVERLY ANN, lawyer; b. New Orleans, Sept. 24, 1954; s. August Nevle and Shelby (Bourgeois) DelH.; m. Bertis Little. Cert. in radiologic tech., Charity Hosp. Sch., New Orleans, 1972-74; BS magna cum laude in Biology, William Carey Coll., 1980; JD, U. Houston, 1984. Bar: Tex. 1984, La. 1985, U.S. Dist. Ct. (no. dist.) Tex. 1985. X-ray technician

VA Hosp., New Orleans, 1974-79; assoc. Richard Martin PC, Dallas, La., 1985, Paul A. Lockman PC, Dallas, 1986-88; ptnr. DelHomme & Skrepnek (name now DelHomme & Assocs.), Dallas, 1986—, 1986—. Editor Houston Jour. Internat. Law, 1983-84. Vol. ARC, 1970-81. Prudential Life Ins. Health Law scholar U. Houston Law Ctr., 1983; recipient 10 Yrs. Svc. award ARC, Chalmette, La., 1980. Mem. ABA, Am. Trial Lawyers Assn., Tex. Trial Lawyers Assn., La. Bar Assn., Dallas Bar Assn., Dallas Trial Lawyers Assn. Episcopalian. Avocation: water skiing. Personal injury (including property damage), Entertainment, Alternative dispute resolution. Office: DelHomme & Assocs 415 Oakwood Tower 3626 N Hall St Dallas TX 75219-5107 E-mail: tjtnsly@aol.com.

DE LIO, ANTHONY PETER, lawyer; b. Bklyn., 1928; s. David V. and Margaret M. De L.; m. Marie DiTrani, 1952; children: Anthony P., Donna Marie Maistros, Lois Anne Cromwell. BS in Physics, Poly Inst. Bklyn., 1953; JD with honors, George Washington U., 1957. Bar: D.C. 1957, Conn. 1958, U.S. Dist. Ct. Conn. 1958. With patent dept. Bendix Corp., Washington, 1954-56; patent advisor U.S. Navy Dept., Washington, 1957; assoc. Blair & Spencer, Stamford, Conn., 1957-60; ptnr. Spencer, Rockwell & Bartholow, Stamford, 1960-62, Rockwell & De Lio, New Haven, 1962-64, De Lio & Montgomery, New Haven, 1964-81, De Lio and Libert, New Haven, 1981-84, De Lio & Assocs., New Haven, 1984-91, De Lio & Peterson, New Haven, 1991—. Lectr. in field. Contbr. articles to legal jours. Chmn. Hamden Planning and Zoning Commn., 1969-81; alt. commr. Hamden Zoning Bd. Appeals, 1981-85. Served with USMC, 1946-48. Mem. ABA, Am. Intellectual Property Law Assn., Conn. Intellectual Property Law Assn., Internat. Intellectual Property Law Assn., New Haven Country Club, Amity Club (New Haven), Alpha Phi Delta. Democrat. Roman Catholic. Intellectual property, Patent, Trademark and copyright. Office: 121 Whitney Ave New Haven CT 06510-1242 E-mail: delpet@delpet.com.

DE LISIO, STEPHEN SCOTT, lawyer, director, pastor; b. San Diego, Dec. 30, 1937; s. Anthony J. and Emma Irving (Cheney) DeL.; m. Margaret Irene Winter, June 26, 1964; children: Anthony W., Stephen Scott, Heather E. Student, Am. U., 1958-59; BA, Emory U., 1959; LLB, Albany Law Sch., 1962; LLM, Georgetown U., 1963. Bar: N.Y. 1963, D.C. 1963, Alaska 1964. Practice law, Fairbanks, Alaska, 1963-71, Anchorage, 1972-96; asst. dist. atty. Fairbanks, 1963-65; assoc. McNealy & Merdes, 1965-66; lectr. U. Alaska, 1965-67; ptnr. Staley, DeLisio & Cook, 1966-93, DeLisio, Moran, Geraghty & Zobel, Inc., 1994—2003. Bd. dirs. Woodstock Property Co., Inc., Pasit Inc., Challenger Films Inc.; vice chmn. Crosstown CBMC, 1986—87, chmn., 1987—88, 1990—91, area coord., 1987—92; city atty., Fairbanks, 1967—70, Barrow, 1969—72, Ft. Yukon and North Pole, 1970—72; past sec. U. Alaska Heating Corp., Inc.; past sec.-treas. Trans-Alaska Electronics, Inc., Baker Aviation, Inc.; former arbitrator, mem. Alaska regional coun. Am. Arbitration Assn. Author: (with others) Law and Tactics in Federal Criminal Cases, 1964. Past pres. Tanana Valley State Fair Assn.; past v.p. Fairbanks Mental Health Assn., Fairbanks United Good Neighbors Fund; bd. dirs. Anchorage Cmty. Chorus, 1975—77, Common Sense for Alaska, 1987—94, Alaska chpt. Lupus Found., 1989—96; chmn. bd. Alaska Voluntary Health Assn., 1993—96; former bd. dirs. Greater Fairbanks Cmty. Hosp. Found.; met. dir. Christian Businessmen's Outreach, 1993—94, bd. dirs. Anchorage, 1985—92; met. dir. Alaska Christian Businessmen's Com. U.S.A., 1994—2000; rep. precinct committeeman, 1970—76; chmn. Alaska Rep. Rules Com. Anchorage Rep. Com, 1973; v.p. We the People, 1977—79; vice chmn. Alaska Libertarian Party, 1983—84; mem. nat. com. Libertarian Party, 1982—85; deacon Anchorage Bible Fellowship, 1986—90, elder, pastor, 1990—; Alaska coord. Crown Ministries, 1991—93. Recipient Jaycee Disting. Service award, 1968 Mem. Am. Trial Lawyers Assn., Am. Judicature Soc., Alaska Bar Assn., D.C. Bar Assn., Anchorage Bar Assn., Spenard Bar Assn. (pres. 1975-77), U.S. Jaycees (past dir.), Alaska Jaycees (past pres.), Fairbanks Jaycees (past pres.), Chi Phi, Pi Sigma Phi, Woodstock Golf Inc. Club (pres. 1984—). Home: 5102 Shorecrest Dr Anchorage AK 99502-1329 Office: Anchorage Bible Fellowship 7348 Abbott Loop Rd Anchorage AK 99507 Office Fax: 907-522-9079. E-mail: cbmcak@alaska.net.

DELIZIA, CAROLYN, lawyer; b. Staten Island, N.Y. d. Edward Joseph and Carol Ann Delizia. BA, Tulane U., 1996, JD, 1999. Assoc. Henderson, Franklin, Starnes & Holt, P.A., Ft. Myers, Fla., 1999—. Adv. bd. mem. Friends of Six Mile Cypress Slough, Ft. Myers. Mentor Teen Ct., Ft. Myers, 1999—. Mem.: Lee County Bar Assn. (vice chair young lawyers com. 2001—), Fla. Assn. Women Lawyers (pres. 2002—), Assn. Family Law Profls. (bd. dirs.), Lee County Assn. Women Lawyers (pres. 2002—). Roman Catholic. Family and matrimonial. Office: Henderson Franklin Starnes & Holt PA PO Box 280 1715 Monroe St Fort Myers FL 33902-0280

DELKOUSIS, JIM, lawyer; b. Melbourne, Australia, Apr. 9, 1965; s. George and Angela Delkousis; m. Pota Delkousis; children: Eleanor, George, Nikita. LLB with hons., U. Melbourne, 1988; LLM in Comml. Law, U. London, 1993. Solicitor Baker & McKenzie, Melbourne, 1989—90; from solicitor to ptnr. Mallesons Stephen Jaques, Melbourne, 1991—99, ptnr., 1999—. Construction. Office: Mallesons Stephen Jaques Rialto 525 Collins St Melbourne 3000 Australia Fax: 613 9643 5999. E-mail: jim.delkousis@mallesons.com.

DELL, ROBERT MICHAEL, lawyer; b. Chgo., Oct. 4, 1952; s. Michael A. and Bertha Dell; m. Ruth Celia Schiffman, May 29, 1976; children: David, Michael, Jessica. BGS, U. Mich., 1974; JD, U. Ill., 1977. Bar: U.S. Dist. Ct. (no. dist.) Ill. 1977, U.S. Ct. Appeals (7th cir.) 1977, U.S. Dist. Ct. (no. dist.) Calif. 1990. Law clk. to justice U.S. Ct. Appeals (7th cir.), Chgo., 1977—79; assoc. Latham & Watkins, Chgo., 1982—85, ptnr., 1985—, mng. ptnr. San Francisco office, 1990—94, firm chmn. and mng. ptnr., 1995—. Antitrust, Federal civil litigation, State civil litigation. Home: 19 Tamal Vista Ln Kentfield CA 94904-1005 Office: Latham & Watkins 505 Montgomery St Ste 1900 San Francisco CA 94111-2552

DELLAGLORIA, JOHN CASTLE, city attorney, educator; b. NYC, June 29, 1952; s. Arthur A. and Marianne Dellagloria; divorced; 1 child, Rebecca; m. Marilyn Castle Dellagloria, Sept. 25, 1988; 1 child, Caitlin. BA in English Lit., SUNY, Binghamton, 1976; JD, U. Miami, 1979. Bar: Fla. 1979, N.Y. 1986, U.S. Ct. Appeals (11th cir.) 1981, U.S. Dist. Ct. (so. dist.) Fla. 1980, U.S. Supreme Ct. Rsch. asst. 3rd Dist. Ct. Appeal, Miami, Fla., 1980-81; assoc. Cassel & Cassel PA, Miami, 1981-82; dep. city atty. City of North Miami Beach, Fla., 1983-86; city atty. City of South Miami, Fla., 1986-90; chief dep. city atty. City of Miami Beach, Fla., 1990-96; city atty. City of North Miami, Fla., 1995—; gen. counsel Miami Beach Housing Authority, 1997-2000, South Miami Cmty. Redevel. Agy., 1998—2002. Lectr. Sch. Profl. Devel., U. Miami, 1982-88, dir. paralegal program, 1984-86, lectr. Sch. Bus., 1989—, lectr. real property program; lectr. govt. law sect. Fla. Bar; moderator Rachlin, Cohen & Holtz, Ann. Govt. Law Symposium, 1996—. Com. person Parrot Jungle Com., Pinecrest, Fla., 1998. Mem. Eugene P. Spellman Am. Inn of Ct. (alumnus). Democrat. Jewish. Avocation: long distance running. Office: City of North Miami 776 NE 125th St North Miami FL 33161-5654 E-mail: catdel@hotmail.com.

DELLA ROCCO, KENNETH ANTHONY, lawyer; b. Bridgeport, Conn., Sept. 5, 1952; BA, Sacred Heart U., Fairfield, Conn., 1974; JD, U. Bridgeport, 1982. Bar: Conn. 1983, U.S. Dist. Ct. Conn. 1985, N.Y. 1988, U.S. Supreme Ct. 1991. Assoc. Cummings & Lockwood, Stamford, Conn., 1982-88; from asst. gen. counsel to v.p. Melville Corp., Rye, NY, 1988—93, v.p. legal affairs, gen. counsel, 1993—95; counsel Cacace, Tusch & Santagata, Stamford, 1996—2002; ptnr. Martin, Lucas & Chioffi LLP, Stamford, 2003—. Mem. Conn. Bar Assn., Regional Bar Assn. Office: Martin Lucas and Chioffi LLP 1177 Summer St Stamford CT 06905

DELL'ATTI, SILVIA, lawyer; b. Bari, Italy, June 1, 1972; Grad. in law, U. Bari, 1996; PhD, Scuola Superiore di Studi san Anna, Pisa, Italy, 2000. Qualified lawyer: Italy. Assoc. Andersen Legal, Milan, 2000—01, Allen and Overy, Milan, 2001—. Contbr. book, articles to profl. jours. Office: Allen & Overy Via Manzoni 41/43 20121 Milan Italy Home: Viale Tunisia 24 20100 Milan Italy also: Via Dante 155 70121 Bari Italy

DELLINGER, MARK WAYNE, lawyer; b. Newport News, Va. s. Gerald W. and Mary Anne Dellinger; m. Jane N. Dellinger, Mar. 25, 2000. BA, U. Richmond, 1991, JD, 1994. Assoc. Gentry, Locke, Rakes and Moore, Roanoke, Va., 1994—2001, Bersch, Rhodes and Butler PC, Roanoke, 2002—. Recipient Eagle Scout, Boy Scouts Am. Mem.: Roanoke Jaycees Found. (treas. 2000—, bd. dirs.), ABA, Roanoke Bar Assn., Va. State Bar Assn., Va. Bar Assn., Omicron Delta Kappa. Estate planning, Corporate, general, Probate (including wills, trusts). Office: Bersch Rhodes and Butler PC 10 Franklin Rd Ste 640 Roanoke VA 24011

DELLOFF, STEFAN T. lawyer; b. N.Y.C., Apr. 15, 1942; AB, Rutgers U., 1963; JD, NYU, 1972. Bar: N.J. 1972. Revenue officer IRS, N.Y.C., 1966-72; exec. asst. Motivation and Tng. Programs, Fair Lawn, N.J., 1972—; pvt. practice, Fair Lawn, 1972—. Construction. Office: 518 Essex Pl Fair Lawn NJ 07410-1012

DELMAS, CALIXTE, legal executive; b. Montauban, Pyrenees, France, Sept. 10, 1934; s. Jean and Germaine (Rasse) D.; m. Colette Terrailmon, Apr. 1, 1960; children: Bruno, Sophie. Ingeniuer degree, Arts and Metiers, Paris, 1957. Ingenieur Elf, Paris and Africa, 1957-62, Daumas Enterprise, Aix, 1962-70, Cegos Cons., Paris, 1970-85; chmn. Comia Fao, Vitre, 1976-80, Sechoir Ohnium, Orleans, 1980-81, Law, Senlis, France, 1985—. Office: Law S Ave Giniral Gaulle F-60304 Senlis France

DEL NEGRO, JOHN THOMAS, lawyer; b. Springfield, Mass., Oct. 2, 1948; s. Angelo Antonio and Marguerite (Garofalo) Del N.; m. Linda Anne Mayberry, July 6, 1973. BA, George Washington U., 1970; JD, Cornell U., 1975. Bar: Conn. 1975, U.S. Dist. Ct. Conn. 1978, U.S. Tax Ct. 1981. Assoc. Murtha, Cullina, Richter & Pinney, Hartford, Conn., 1975-81, ptnr., 1982-95, Del Negro & Feldman, LLC, Hartford, 1995—. Author: (with Levenson) Depreciation and Investment Tax Credits, 1983. Bd. dirs. Conn. Opera Assn., 1990-2003, Watkinson Sch., 1992-2000. Mem. ABA, Conn. Bar Assn. (tax exec. com. 1992-2002). Corporate, general, Health, Taxation, general. Office: Del Negro & Feldman LLC Goodwin Sq 225 Asylum St Hartford CT 06103-1524 E-mail: jdelnegro@dfctlaw.com.

DELO, ELLEN SANDERSON, lawyer; b. Nassawadox, Va., Nov. 29, 1944; d. Robert G. and Daisy B. (Hitchens) Sanderson; m. Arthur C. Delo Jr., Mar. 20, 1971; 1 child, Marjorie Cotton Delo. BA, U. Richmond, 1966; JD, Rutgers U., 1977; LLM, NYU, 1985. Bar: N.J., 1977, U.S. Dist. Ct. N.J., 1977, U.S. Tax Ct., 1987, U.S. Ct. Appeals (2nd cir.) 1997, D.C. 1999, N.Y. 1999. Law clk. to Hon. John J. Geronimo N.J. Superior Ct., 1977-78; assoc. Lamb Hutchinson Chappell Ryan & Hartung, Jersey City, 1978-80, Chasan Leyner Holland & Tarrant, Jersey City, 1980-84, Stryker Tams & Dill, Newark, 1985-92, ptnr., 1993-98; exec. compensation assoc. Bachelder Law Offices, N.Y.C., 1998—2002, of counsel, 2002—. Lectr. on tax issues. Contbr. articles to profl. jours. Lay reader Ch. St. Andrew and Holy Communion, South Orange, N.J. Democrat. Episcopalian. Avocation: animal welfare organizations and activities. Pension, profit-sharing, and employee benefits, Personal income taxation, Taxation, general. Home and Office: 340 Montrose Ave South Orange NJ 07079-2439 E-mail: esdelo1@aol.com.

DELONG, DEBORAH, lawyer; b. Louisville, Sept. 5, 1950; d. Henry F. and Lois Jean (Stepp) D.; children: Amelie DeLong, Samuel Prentice. BA, Vanderbilt U., 1972; JD, U. Cin., 1975. Bar: Ohio 1975, Ky. 1999, U.S. Dist. Ct. (so. dist.) Ohio 1975, U.S. Ct. Appeals (Fed. cir.) 1990, (11th cir.), 1995, U.S. Ct. Appeals (6th cir.) 1991, U.S. Supreme Ct. 1982. Assoc. Paxton & Seasongood, Cin., 1975-82, ptnr., 1982-88, Thompson, Hine & Flory, 1989—2001. Contbr. articles to profl. jours. Bd. dirs. Cin. Opera, Cin. Shakespeare Festival, Clovernook Ctr. for the Blind. Mem. ABA, Ohio State Bar Assn., Cin. Bar Assn., Arbitration Tribunal U.S. Dist. Ct., Ohio, 1984. Republican. Episcopalian. Federal civil litigation, State civil litigation, Labor (including EEOC, Fair Labor Standards Act, labor-management relations, NLRB, OSHA). Office: Dinsmore & Shohl LLP 1900 Chemed Ctr 255 E Fifth St Cincinnati OH 45202-4089

DELONG, DONALD ALAN, lawyer; b. Detroit, Apr. 29, 1957; s. Dean Oliver and Marjorie Nell (Jones) DeL.; m. Leslie Carol Fleming, Oct. 18, 1981. BA with high honors, Mich. State U., 1979; student, U. Tex., 1979-80; JD cum laude, Wayne State U., 1985. Bar: Mich. 1985, U.S. Dist. Ct. (so. dist.) Mich. 1985. Assoc. Rockwell & Kotz, P.C., Detroit, 1985-90, Frank & Stefani, P.C., Troy, Mich., 1990-91; shareholder Kotz & Sangster, P.C., Detroit, 1991-94, Donald A. DeLong, P.C., Birmingham, Mich., 1994-96, Thompson, Morello, FeKaris, Radner & DeLong, P.C., Farmington Hills, Mich., 1996—98; sole practitioner Southfield, Mich., 1998—. Mem. ABA, State Bar Mich., Oakland County Bar Assn. Avocations: running, soccer, chess, reading. Estate planning, Taxation, general. Office: Ste 380 25899 W 12 Mile Rd Southfield MI 48034-8315

DE LOUSANOFF, OLEG, lawyer; b. Frankfurt am Main, Germany, June 14, 1952; s. Oleg and Marianne (Idel) de L.; children: Nadejda, Nikolaj, Anatol, Victor. First Legal State Exam, U. Freiburg, Breisgau, Germany, 1976, Dr. iur. utriusque summa cum laude, 1978; 2nd Legal State Exam, Stuttgart, 1980; 2nd, London Sch. Econs., 1974—75, Keio U., Tokyo, 1979; LLM, U. Calif., Berkeley, 1981. Bar: Frankfurt 1981. Asst. prof. Law Faculty U. Freiburg, 1976-80; assoc. Hengeler Mueller, Frankfurt am Main, Germany, 1981-83, ptnr., 1984—. Pres. supervisory bd. OTIS Escalator GmbH, 1993—99; spkr. in field of mergers and acquisitions and corp. law. Author (and co-author) 4 books; contbr. over 60 articles to profl. jours. Trustee Dr. M. Lee Pearce Found., Lichtenstein, 1996—, Vorontzov Palace and Corps of Pages Meml. Trust, 1995—. Mem. Internat. Bar Asn., Union Internat. Avocats., Union de la Noblesse Russe, German-French Soc. Frankfurt am Main. Russian Orthodox. Avocations: classical guitar, tennis, old books, bordeaux wines. Home: Tannenwaldallee 11 61348 Bad Homburg vdH Germany Office: Hengeler Mueller Bockenheimer Landstr 51 60325 Frankfurt am Main Germany E-mail: oleg.delousanoff@hengeler.com.

DELP, WILBUR CHARLES, JR., lawyer; b. Cedar Rapids, Iowa, Oct. 26, 1934; s. Wilbur Charles and Irene Frances (Flynn) D.; m. Patricia Lynn Vesely, June 22, 1963; children: Marci Lynn, Melissa Kathryn, Derek Charles. BA, Coe Coll., 1956; LL.B., NYU, 1959. Bar: Ill. 1960, U.S. Supreme Ct. 1962. Assoc. Sidley Austin Brown & Wood, Chgo., 1959—68, ptnr., 1968—. Lectr. securities law seminars With USAF, 1959-65. Mem. ABA (securities com.), Chgo. Bar Assn., Lawyers Club (Chgo.), Mid-Day Club (Chgo.), Phi Beta Kappa, Phi Kappa Phi. Corporate, general, Utilities, public, Securities. Home: PO Box 97 Wayne IL 60184-0097 Office: Sidley Austin Brown & Wood Bank One Plz Chicago IL 60603-0001 E-mail: wdelp@sidley.com.

DEL PAPA, FRANKIE SUE, former state attorney general; b. 1949; BA, U. Nev.; JD, George Washington U., 1974. Bar: Nev. 1974. Staff asst. U.S. Senator Alan Bible, Washington, 1971—74; assoc. Law Office of Leslie B. Grey, Reno, 1975—78; legis. asst. to U.S. Senator Howard Cannon, Washington, 1978—79; ptnr. Thornton & Del Papa, 1979—84; pvt. practice Reno, 1984—87; sec. of state State of Nev., Carson City, 1987—91, atty. gen., 1991—2002. Active Nev. Women's Fund; bd. dirs. Sierra Arts Found.; adv. com. Trust for Pub. Land. Democrat.*

DEL RASO, JOSEPH VINCENT, lawyer; b. Phila., Dec. 21, 1952; s. Vincent and Dolores Ann (D'Adamo) Del R.; m. Anne Marie McGloin, Apr. 17, 1982; children: Joseph Vincent Jr., Katherine Anne, Marianna. BS in Acctg., Villanova U., 1974, JD, 1983. Bar: Pa., 1983, Fla. 1988. Exec. v.p. Belgrade Constrn., Inc., Wayne, Pa., 1974-80; atty. SEC, Washington, 1983-85; assoc. Dechert, Price & Rhoads, Washington, 1986-88; ptnr. Holland & Knight, Ft. Lauderdale, Fla., 1988-92, Stradley, Ronon, Stevens & Young, Phila., 1992-98, Pepper Hamilton LLP, Phila., 1998—. Gen. counsel, bd. dirs. Nat. Italian-Am. Found.; chair bd. Am. U., Rome. Co-editor-in-chief Villanova Jour. Law and Investment Mgmt. Sec. of bd. consultors Villanova U. Sch. Law; bd. dirs. Justinian Found.; mem. Columbus Citizens Found., N.Y. Mem. ABA, Villanova U. Alumni Assn. (class agt. 1974-97), Aronimink Golf Club. Republican. Roman Catholic. Corporate, general, Securities. Office: Pepper Hamilton LLP 18th & Arch Sts 3000 Two Logan Sq Philadelphia PA 19103

DEL RUSSO, ALESSANDRA LUINI, retired law educator; b. Milan, Jan. 2, 1916; d. Avvocato Umberto and Candita (Recio) Luini; m. Carl R. del Russo, Apr. 12, 1947; children: Carl Luini, Alexander David. PhD in History with honors, Royal U., Milan, 1939; SJD summa cum laude, Royal U., Pavia, Italy, 1943; LLM in Comparative Law, George Washington U., Washington, 1949. Bar: Md. 1956, Md. Ct. Appeals, Ct. of Appeals (Milano) 1947, U.S. Ct. Appeals (D.C. cir.) 1950, U.S. Supreme Ct. 1955. Legal adviser Allied Mil. Govt. and Ct., Milan, 1945-46, U.S. Consulate Gen., Milan, 1946-47; pvt. practice Washington, Bethesda, Md., 1950-58; atty. adviser Legis. Ref. Libr. of Congress, Washington, 1958-59; atty. U.S. Commn. on Civil Rights, Washington, 1959-61; prof. Howard U. Sch. Law, Washington, 1961-81, dir. grad. program, 1972-74, prof. emerita, 1981—; adj. prof. Stetson U. Coll. Law, St. Petersburg, Fla., 1980-95, adj. prof. emerita, 1995—. Professorial lectr. George Washington U. Law Ctr., 1970-80; mem. legal cons. com. U.S. Commn. on Status of P.R., Washington, 1965-66; lectr. in field. Author: International Protection of Human Rights, 1971; editor and chmn. of symposium on International Law of Human Rights, Howard U. Sch. of Law, Washington, 1965; contbr. numerous articles to internat. and Am. profl. jours. Rsch. grant Howard U., 1963. Mem. ABA, Brit. Inst. Internat. and Comparative Law, Am. Soc. Internat. Law. Republican. Roman Catholic. Achievements include 1st woman to receive LLM in Comparative Law from George Washington U. Home: 400 Ocean Trail Way Apt 908 Jupiter FL 33477-5527

DELSAUT, PHILIPPE PATRICK, lawyer; b. Veurne, West Vlaanderen, Belgium, Dec. 23, 1969; s. Jean-Luc and Erna (Coucke) D. Law Degree, Vrye U. Brussels, 1995, U. Fribourg, Switzerland, 1995; tax law, Fiscale Hogesch., Brussels, 1998'. Bar: Brussels. Assoc. Caestecker & Ptnrs., Brussels, 1995-98, McKenna & Cuneo LLP, Brussels, 1998-2000, Washington, 2000, Eversheds, Brussels, London, 2000—. Contbr. articles to profl. jour. Avocations: cooking, reading, sports. Corporate, general, Banking, Bankruptcy. Office: Eversheds 75 Ave Cortenberg 1000 Brussels Belgium

DEL TUFO, ROBERT J. lawyer, former US attorney, former state attorney general; b. Newark, Nov. 18, 1933; s. Raymond and Mary (Pellecchia) Del T.; m. Katherine Nouri Hughes; children: Barbara, Ann, Robert, David. BA cum laude in English, Princeton U., 1955; JD, Yale U., 1958. Bar: N.J. 1959. Law sec. to chief justice N.J. Supreme Ct., 1958-60; assoc. firm Dillon, Bitar & Luther, Morristown, N.J., 1960-62, ptnr., 1962-74; asst. prosecutor Morris County, N.J., 1963-65; 1st asst. prosecutor, 1965-67; 1st asst. atty. gen., 1974-77; dir. criminal justice, 1976-77; U.S. atty. Dist. of N.J., Newark, 1977-80; prof. Rutgers U. Sch. Criminal Justice, 1979-81; ptnr. firm Stryker, Tams & Dill, 1980-86, Hannoch Weisman, 1986-90; atty. gen. State of N.J., 1990-93; ptnr. Skadden, Arps, Slate, Meagher & Flom, N.Y.C. and Newark, 1993—; commr. N.J. State Commn. of Investigation, 1981-84. Instr. bus. law Fairleigh-Dickinson U., 1964; mem. N.J. State Bd. Bar Examiners, 1967-74; mem. criminal law drafting com. Nat. Conf. Bar Examiners, 1972-2002; bd. dirs. Nat. Ctr. for Victims of Crime, 1995-2003; Nat. Italian Am. Found., 1995-2003, Integrity Inc., 1995—, John Cabot U. in Rome, 1997—, Legal Svcs. N.J., 2000—, IOLTA, 1994-99, N.J. Pub. Interest Law Ctr., 1996-99, Daytop Village Found., 1998—, Planned Parenthood, 1998-99; mem. com. on character N.J. Supreme Ct., 1982-84; spl. master, fed. jail overcrowding litigation, Essex County, 1989-90; trustee Boys and Girls Clubs of Am., 2000—. Bd. editors Yale U Law Jour; contbr. articles to profl. jours. Mem. law enforcement adv. com. County Coll. of Morris, 1970-85; mem. Morris County Ethics Com., 1968-71, Morris County Jud. Selection Com., 1970-72, Essex County Jud. Selection Com., 1982-84; v.p., mem. exec. com. United Fund of Morris County, 1966-70; chmn. Morris Twp. Juvenile Conf. Com., 1963-74; bd. dirs. Nat. Found. March of Dimes, 1966-68, Vis. Nurse Assn. Morris County, 1963-70, Morristown YMCA, 1970-74; trustee Boys & Girls Club Am., 1999—, Atty.'s Fund for Client Protection, 1999—; trustee Newark Acad., 1976-95, 97—2002, pres. bd. dirs. 1983-87; bd. regents St. Peter's Coll., 1979-85. Fellow Am. Bar Found.; mem. Am., N.J., Morris County bar assns., Nat. Dist. Attys. Assn., Yale Law Sch. Assn. (exec. com. 1978-84), Order of Coif. Home: 13 Ober Rd Princeton NJ 08540-4917 Office: Skadden Arts Slate Meagher & Flom One Newark Ctr Newark NJ 07102 also: 4 Times Sq New York NY 10036-6522 E-mail: rdeltufo@skadden.com.

DE LUCA, THOMAS GEORGE, lawyer; b. Jersey City, Dec. 28, 1950; s. Michael Anthony and Estelle Theresa (Wickiewicz) De L.; m. Annette Catherine Pandolfo, Aug. 16, 1975; children: Michele, Thomas, Rachel. BS in Econs., St. Peters Coll., Jersey City, 1972; JD, Seton Hall U., 1978. Bar: N.J. 1978, U.S. Dist. Ct. 1978, N.Y. 1981, U.S. Dist. Ct. (so. and ea. dists.) N.Y. 1981, U.S. Ct. Appeals (2d cir.) 1986, U.S. Ct. Appeals (3d cir.) 1987, U.S. Claims Ct. 1989, U.S. Dist. Ct. (we. dist.) N.Y. 1990, U.S. Dist. Ct. (no. dist.) N.Y. 1991, U.S. Supreme Ct. 1987. Supervising underwriter Fireman's Fund Ins. Cos., Newark, 1972-77; assoc. Sellar, Richardson & Stuart, Newark, 1978-80, Postner & Rubin, N.Y.C., 1980-84, ptnr., 1985-93, De Luca & Forster, Cranford, N.J., 1994—. Mem. ABA, N.J. Bar Assn., N.Y. County Lawyers Assn. Roman Catholic. Federal civil litigation, State civil litigation, Construction. Home: 14 Kilmer Dr Colonia NJ 07067-1213 Office: De Luca and Forster 11 Commerce Dr Cranford NJ 07016-3501 also: 1 N Broadway White Plains NY 10601-2310 E-mail: delucafor@aol.com.

DEL VALLE, TERESA JONES, lawyer; b. Dayton, Ohio, July 20, 1965; BS, Ariz. State U., 1988; JD, U. Houston, 1993. Bar: Tex. 1993, U.S. Dist. Ct. (so. and ea. dists.) Tex. 1994. Underwriter Prudential Property and Casualty Ins. Co., Scottsdale, Ariz., 1988-90; assoc. Doyle, Rider, Restrepo, Harvin & Robbins, LLP, Houston, 1993-97, Cash, Jones & Springhetti, LLP, Houston, 1997—99, Rios & Bain, P.C., 1999—2002; atty. The Del Valle Law Firm, Houston, 2002—. General civil litigation. Office: The Del Valle Law Firm 3200 SW Fwy # 3300 Houston TX 77027

DEMAPAN, MIGUEL S. judge; b. Saipan, Northern Marianas; m. Frances Tenorio; 5 children. BS in Chemistry, Seattle U., 1975; MBA with honors, Golden Gate U., 1983; JD, Santa Clara U., 1985. Gen. counsel J. C. Tenorio Enterprises, Inc.; pvt. practice; ptnr. Demapan and Atalig; assoc. judge Commonwealth Superior Ct., 1992—98; assoc. justice Commonwealth Supreme Ct., 1998—99, chief justice, 1999—. Judge pro tem Superior Ct. Guam, Supreme Ct. Guam; pres. Pacific Jud. Coun., 2000—02. Chmn. Commonwealth Law Revision Commn.; mem. CNMI Tax Task Force. Trust Ter. scholar, Seattle U. Mem.: U.S. Conference Chief Justices (bd. dirs. 2002—03), World Jurist Assn., CNMI Fed. Bench Coun., Asia Pacific Conf. Chief Justices, U.S. Conf. Chief Justices, Nat. Inst. Trial Advocacy, Nat. Jud. Coll. Office: Supreme Ct Commonwealth Northern Mariana Islands PO Box 502179 Saipan MP 96950-2165 Office Fax: 670-236-9702.

DEMARIA, JOSEPH ANGELO, lawyer; b. Rochester, N.Y., Mar. 22, 1957; s. Joseph G. and Jacqueline (Rose) DeM.; m. Sandra Mary LaRusch, Feb. 19, 1983; 1 child, Peter Joseph. BA magna cum laude, St. Bonaventure U., 1979; JD cum laude, SUNY, Buffalo, 1982. Bar: N.Y. 1983, U.S. Dist. Ct. (ea. and so. dists.) N.Y. 1983, Fla. 1988, U.S. Ct. Appeals (11th cir.) 1986, U.S. Dist. Ct. (so. dist.) Fla. 1988, U.S. Dist. Ct. (mid. dist.) Fla. 1991; bd. cert. bus. litigation. Assoc. Kelley Drye & Warren, N.Y.C., 1982-85; spl. atty. Miami Strike Force, U.S. Dept. Justice, Miami, 1985-89; ptnr. Greer, Homer & Bonner, P.A., Miami, 1989-93, Tew, Cardenas, Rebak, Kellogg, Lehman, DeMaria, Tague, Raymond & Levine, LLP, Miami, 1993—. Adj. faculty trial skills program U. Miami Sch. Law, 1993—; instr. Nat. Inst. Trial Advocacy, 1996; lectr. Advanced Constrn. Law Inst., 1999-2001. Mng. editor Buffalo Law Review. Recipient Spl. Commendation for outstanding svc. Criminal div. U.S. Dept. Justice, 1987. Mem. ABA (litigation sect.). Republican. Roman Catholic. Federal civil litigation, Construction, Criminal. Office: 2600 Miami Ctr 201 S Biscayne Blvd Miami FL 33131-4332 E-mail: jad@texlaw.com.

DE MARIE, ANTHONY JOSEPH, lawyer; b. Buffalo, May 10, 1928; s. Joseph and Josephine (Radice) DeM.; m. Rose Galluzzo, July 23, 1955; children— Michael, Janice, Gregory, Lynda. J.D., U. Buffalo, 1955. Bar: N.Y. 1956, U.S. Dist. Ct. (we. dist.) N.Y. 1960, U.S. Ct. Appeals (2d cir.) 1982. Ptnr., Dixon & De Marie, Buffalo, 1956— . Dir., Neighborhood Legal Services of Erie County, Buffalo, 1971-74. Served with AUS, 1946-48, 50-51. Mem. Erie County Bar Assn. (past bd. dirs.), Trial Lawyers Assn. Erie County (past pres., gov.) N.Y. State Bar Assn., Fla. Bar Assn., N.Y. State Trial Lawyers Assn., Assn. Trial Lawyers Am., Western N.Y. Trial Lawyers Assn. Republican. Roman Catholic. Club: Transit Valley Country. State civil litigation, Insurance, Personal injury (including property damage). Office: De Marie & Schoenborn PC 800 Convention Tower Buffalo NY 14202-3174

DEMATTEO, CHRISTINA M. lawyer; b. Ridgewood, N.J., Jan. 7, 1974; AB in Econs., Coll. William & Mary, 1995; JD, Villanova U., 1998. Bar: N.J. 1999, Pa. 1999. Law clk. Office of Adminstrv. Law Judges, U.S. Dept. Labor, Camden, NJ, 1998—99; atty. Wolf Block Schorr & Solis-Cohen, Norristown, Pa., 1999—. Mem.: Montgomery Bar Assn. (co-chair practicum com. family law sect. 2001, co-chair legis com. family law sect. 2001—02). Family and matrimonial. Office: Wolf Block Schorr & Solis-Cohen 325 Swede St Norristown PA 19404 Fax: 610-272-6976.

DEMBLING, PAUL GERALD, lawyer, former government official; b. Rahway, N.J., Jan. 11, 1920; s. Simon and Fannie (Ellenbogen) D.; m. Florence Brotman, Nov. 22, 1947; children: Ross Wayne, Douglas Evan, Donna Stacy. BA, Rutgers U., 1940, MA, 1942; JD, George Washington U., 1951. Bar: D.C. 1952. Grad. asst., teaching fellow Rutgers U., 1940-42; economist Office Chief Transp., Dept. Army, 1942-45; since practiced in Washington; indsl. relations NACA, 1945-51, spl. counsel, legal adviser, gen. counsel, 1951-58; asst. gen. counsel NASA, 1958-61, dir. legis. affairs, 1961-63, dep. gen. counsel, 1963-67, gen. counsel, 1967-69, chmn. bd. contract appeals, 1958-61, vice chmn. inventions and contbns. bd., 1959-67; mem. and alt. rep. U.S. del. UN Legal Subcom. Com. on Outer Space, 1964-69; gen. counsel GAO, 1969-78; partner Schnader, Harrison, Segal & Lewis, Washington, 1978-93, sr. counsel, 1994—2002. Prin. author NASA Act, 1958; professorial lectr. George Washington U. Law Sch., 1965-86. Co-author: Federal Contract Management, 1988, Essentials of Grant Law Practice, 1991; editor in chief Fed. Bar Jour., 1962-69; contbr. articles to profl. jours. Recipient Meritorious Civilian Service award War Dept., 1945; Disting. Service medal NASA, 1968; Nat. Civil Service League award, 1973 Fellow: AIAA (chmn. com. law and sociology 1969—71), Nat. Acad. Pub. Adminstrn., Nat. Contract Mgmt. Assn. (bd. advisers 1973—98), Fed. Bar Found. (life); mem.: FBA (nat. coun. 1963—, pres. Capitol Hill chpt. 1977—78, nat. sec. 1978—79, pres.-elect 1981—82, nat. pres. 1983—84, bd. dirs. bldg. corp. 1989—, fellow (life)), ABA (coun., pub. contract law sec. 1983—84, vice chmn. 1984—85, chmn. elect 1985—86, chmn. 1986—87), Internat. Inst. Space Law (pres. Am. assn. 1970—72, Internat. Astronaut. Fedn. award 1992), Procurement Roundtable (bd. dirs. 1984—, vice chmn. 1988—), D.C. Bar (mem. steering com. govt. contracts and litigation sect. 1989—95), Nat. Lawyers Club, Cosmos Club, Phi Delta Phi. Government contracts and claims, Public international. Home: 11625 Pamplona Blvd Boynton Beach FL 33437-4077 Office: Schnader Harrison Segal & Lewis 1300 I St NW Washington DC 20005-3314 E-mail: pfdemb@webtv.net.

DE MENT, IRA, judge; b. Birmingham, Ala., Dec. 21, 1931; s. Ira J. and Helen (Sparks) De M.; m. Ruth Lester Posey; 1 child, Charles Posey. AS, Marion Mil. Inst., 1951; AB, U. Ala., 1953, LLB, 1958, JD, 1969. Bar: Ala. 1958, U.S. Dist. Ct. (mid. dist.) Ala. 1958, U.S. Ct. Appeals (5th cir.) 1958, U.S. Supreme Ct. 1966, U.S. Dist. Ct. (so. dist.) Ala. 1967, U.S. Dist. Ct. D.C. 1972, U.S. Ct. Appeals (D.C.) 1972, U.S. Tax Ct. 1972, U.S. Customs and Patents Appeals 1976, U.S. Dist. Ct. (no. dist.) Ala. 1977, U.S. Ct. Appeals (11th cir.) 1981, U.S. Ct. Mil. Appeals 1972. Law clk. Sup. Ct. Ala., 1958-59; asst. atty. gen. State of Ala., 1959, spl. assty. atty. gen., 1966-69, 81-92; asst. U.S. atty. Montgomery, Ala., 1959-61; pvt. practice, 1961-69, 77-92; U.S. dist. judge (mid. dist.) Ala., 1992—. Acting U.S. atty. Mid. Dist. Ala. 1969, U.S. atty., 1969-77; asst. atty., legal advisor to police and fire depts. City of Montgomery, 1965-69; inst. Jones Law Sch., 1962-64; instr. Montgomery Police Acad., 1964-77; lect. constl. Ala. Police Acad., 1971-75; instr. law enforcement U. Ala., 1967, mem. adj. faculty New Coll., 1974-75, adj. prof. psychology, 1975-92; spl. counsel to Gov. State Ala., 1980-88, gen. counsel Commn. on Aging, 1980-82. Lt. col. USAR, 1953-74; maj. gen. USAFR ret. Decorated Legion of Merit, DSM, others; recipient Disting. Svc. award Internat. Assn. Firefighters, 1975, Rockefeller Pub. Svc. award Woodrow Wilson Sch. Pub. and Internat. Affairs Princeton U., 1976; named Alumnus of Yr. Marion Mil. Inst., 1988, Significant Sig award Sigma Chi Fraternity, 1998, Judicial Award of Merit Ala. State Bar, 1998, Marion Mil. Inst. Disting. Alumnus award, 2003. Mem. ABA, Fed. Bar Assn., D.C. Bar Assn., Ala. Bar Assn. (mem. editl. adv. bd. The Alabama Lawyer 1966-72), Am. Judicature Soc., Nat. Assn. Former U.S. Attys., Phi Alpha Delta. Republican. United Methodist. Clubs: Masons, Shriners. Address: PO Box 2149 Montgomery AL 36102-2149 also: 1 Church St Montgomery AL 36104 Fax: 334-954-3681. E-mail: Ira_DeMent@almd.uscourts.gov.

DEMENT, JAMES ALDERSON, JR., lawyer; b. Clinton, Okla., Sept. 11, 1947; s. James Alderson and Ruby (Weaver) DeM.; m. Sally Anne Wylder, June 6, 1970; children: Stephen, Suzanne, Jonathan. BA summa cum laude, Tex. Christian U., 1969; JD in Internat. Affairs, Cornell U., 1972. Bar: N.Y. 1973, Tex. 1974. Assoc. Alexander & Green, N.Y.C., 1972-73, Baker Botts, LLP, Houston, 1977-85, ptnr., 1998—; ptnr., chmn. corp. tax and internat. sect. Butler & Binion, LLP, Houston, 1985-97. Adj. prof. U. Houston, 1987-88; dir. Houston World Affairs Coun. 2002—. Mem. edtl. rev. bd. The Internat. Lawyer, 1987-94. Trustee Houston Ballet Found., 1989-96, Brazos Presbyn. Homes, Inc., 1990-96. Capt. USAF, 1973-77. Fellow Tex. Bar Found.; mem. State Bar Tex. (internat. law sect., chmn. 1989-90), Internat. and Comparative Law Ctr. Southwestern Legal Found. (adv. coun. 1986—), Houston Bar Assn. (internat. law sect., pres. 1989-90). Presbyterian. Private international. Office: Baker Botts LLP 910 Louisiana St Houston TX 77002-4995 E-mail: james.dement@bakerbotts.com.

DEMER, MARGARET ELIZABETH, lawyer; b. Cleve. BS in Edn., Kent State U., 1941; LLB, JD, Ind. U., 1958. Bar: Ind. 1958, Ohio 1959. Pvt. practice law, Cleve., 1958—. Pers. specialist U.S. Govt., Washington, 1979-82. Sgt. Women's Army Corps, 1942—46. Mem. Garfield Heights Womens Club. Republican. Mem. United Ch. of Christ. Mem. United Ch. Of Christ. Family and matrimonial, Probate (including wills, trusts), Property, real (including real estate development, water). Home and Office: 11429 Bradwell Rd Garfield Heights OH 44125-3505

DEMITCHELL, TERRI ANN, law educator; b. San Diego, Apr. 10, 1953; d. William Edward and Rose Annette (Carreras) Wheeler; m. Todd Allan DeMitchell, Aug. 14, 1982. AB in English with honors, San Diego State U., 1975; JD, U. San Diego, 1984; MA in Edn., U. Calif., Davis, 1990; EdM, Harvard U., 1997. Bar: Calif. 1985, U.S. Dist. Ct. (so. dist.) Calif. 1985; cert. elem. tchr., Calif. Tchr. Fallbrook (Calif.) Union Elem. Sch. Dist., 1976-86; adminstrv. asst. gen. counsel San Diego Unified Sch. Dist., 1984; assoc. Biddle and Hamilton, Sacramento, 1986-88; instr. U. N.H., 1990-93. Teaching asst. U. Calif., Davis, 1987. Author: The California Teacher and the Law, 1985, The Law in Relation to Teacher, Out of School Behavior, 1990, Censorship and the Public School Library: A Bicoastal View, 1991; Satues and Standards: Has the Door to Educational Malpractice Been Opened?, contbr. chpt. Statutes and Standards: Has the Door to Educational Malpractice Been Opened?, 2003. Mem. Calif. Bar Assn., Am. Bar Assn. Office: Apt 2207 10 Chestnut St Exeter NH 03833-1878

DEMMLER, JOHN HENRY, retired lawyer; b. Pitts., June 20, 1932; s. Ralph Henry and Catherine (Hollinger) D.; m. Janet Rice, July 20, 1957; children: Richard H., Ralph W., Carol L. BA, Princeton U., 1954; LLB cum laude, Harvard U., 1959. Bar: Pa. 1960, U.S. Dist. Ct. (we. dist.) Pa. 1960. Assoc. Reed Smith Shaw & McClay, Pitts., 1959-65, ptnr., 1966-93, of counsel, 1994—. Dir. Duquesne Light Co., Pitts., 1977-90. Trustee Shady Side Acad., Pitts., 1969-75, 77—, vice chmn., 1980-84, chmn., 1984-87; chmn. Fox Chapel Borough Zoning Hearing Bd., 1993—. Mem. Pa. Bar Assn. (pub. utility law sect. 1976—), Fox Chapel Golf Club, HYP-Pittsburgh Club. Republican. Episcopalian. Corporate, general, Municipal (including bonds), Utilities, public. Home: 102 Foxtop Dr Pittsburgh PA 15238-2202 Office: Reed Smith LLP 435 6th Ave Pittsburgh PA 15219-1886

DEMOFF, MARVIN ALAN, lawyer; b. L.A., Oct. 28, 1942; s. Max and Mildred (Tweer) D.; m. Patricia Caryn Abelov, June 16, 1968; children: Allison Leigh, Kevin Andrew. BA, UCLA, 1964; JD, Loyola U., L.A., 1967. Bar: Calif. 1969. Asst. pub. defender Los Angeles County, 1968-72; ptnr. Steinberg & Demoff, L.A., 1973-83, Craighill, Fentress & Demoff, L.A. and Washington, 1983-86; of counsel Mitchell, Silberberg & Knupp, L.A., 1987—2002; mng. dir. Neuberger Berman LLC, L.A., 2002—. Mem. citizens adv. bd. Olympic Organizing Com., L.A., 1982-84; bd. trustees Curtis Sch., L.A., 1985-94, chmn. bd. trustees, 1988-93; sports adv. bd. Constitution Rights Found., L.A., 1986—. Mem. ABA (mem. forum com. on entertainment and sports), Calif. Bar Assn., UCLA Alumni Assn., Phi Delta Phi. Avocations: sports, music, art. Entertainment, Sports. Office: Neuberger Berman LLC 1999 Ave of the Stars Los Angeles CA 90067

DEMOND, WALTER EUGENE, lawyer; b. Sacramento, Oct. 15, 1947; s. Walter G. and Laura (Bartlett) D.; m. Kari Demond; 1 child, William. BA, U. Tex., 1969, JD with honors, 1976. Bar: Tex. 1976. With Clark, Thomas & Winters, Austin, 1976—, CFO, 1984—, sr. ptnr. energy and telecomm. sect. Mem. mgmt. com. Clark, Thomas & Winters, 1984-94, 97-99, 01—. Capt. USAF, 1970-74. Fellow: Tex. Bar Found., Am. Bar Found.; mem.: ABA (vice chmn. gas com. pub. utility, comm. and transp. law sect. 1986—91, chmn. gas com. 1991—93, vice chmn. gas com. pub. utility, comm. and transp. law sect. 1997—2003, vice chair corp. governance com. 2003—, pub. utility comm. and transp. law sect.), State Bar of Tex. (adminstrv. law com. 1984—87). Avocations: skiing, jogging. Administrative and regulatory, Utilities, public. Office: Clark Thomas & Winters Box 1148 Austin TX 78767 E-mail: wed@ctw.com.

DEMOPULOS, HAROLD WILLIAM, lawyer; b. Providence, R.I., Jan. 14, 1924; s. George K. and Grace (Loures) D.; m. Frances Scorzoni, June 10, 1967; children— Amelia Hannah, Abigail Mary. BA, Brown U., 1948; JD, U. Miami, 1952. Bar: Fla. 1952, R.I. 1953, U.S. Dist. Ct. (so. dist.) Fla. 1952, U.S. Dist. Ct. R.I. 1953. Sole practice, Providence and Bristol, R.I., 1953—; Patentee in field. Clk. R.I. State Senate Jud. Com., 1953-54; atty. labor rels. bd. R.I. Dept. Labor, 1968-70; mem. dist. adv. coun. SBA, 1970-78, mem. adv. bd. State of R.I. Briston County Cable Area; probate judge Town of Bristol (R.I.), 1973-74; bd. dirs. Bristol Land Trust Corp. Pres., Bristol C. of C., 1970s; mem. corp. Roger Williams Coll., Bristol; v.p. Bristol Art Mus., 1970s; treas., bd. dirs. Coggeshall Farm Mus. Inc.; incorporator, bd. dirs. Prepaid Legal Service Corp. R.I. With U.S. Army, 1942-46. Mem. R.I. Bar Assn. (pres. 1984—), ABA, Fla. Bar Assn., R.I. Law Inst. (bd. dirs.), R.I. Law Found., Order of Ahepa (pres. Sophocles chpt. 1958, dist. gov. 1966-67). Rotary, Brown Club (pres. R.I. 1975). Republican. Greek Orthodox. General practice, Personal injury (including property damage), Probate (including wills, trusts). Office: Westminster Square Bldg 10 Dorrance St Ste 634 Providence RI 02903-2018

DEMOREST, MARK STUART, lawyer; b. Chambley, France, Mar. 14, 1957; came to U.S., 1960; s. Raymond Phillip and Maud Jane (Dahle) D.; m. Patricia Louise Button, July 28, 1979; children: Melissa, Matthew, Kristin, Kevin, Ryan. AB magna cum laude, Harvard U., 1979; JD magna cum laude, U. Mich., 1983. Bar: Mich. 1983, U.S Dist. Ct. (ea. dist.) Mich. 1983, U.S. Ct. Appeals (6th cir.) 1984, U.S. Ct. Appeals (7th cir.) 1986, U.S. Supreme Ct. 1993, U.S. Dist. Ct. (cen. dist.) Ill. 1995, U.S. Ct. Appeals (4th cir.) 1995, U.S. Dist. Ct. (we. dist.) Mich. 1996, U.S. Dist. of (east dist.) WI 2003. Assoc. Dykema Gossett, Detroit, 1983-85, Simpson & Moran, Birmingham, Mich., 1985-87; ptnr. The Robert P. Ufer Partnership, Bloomfield Hills, Mich., 1987-92, Hainer, Demorest & Berman, P.C., Troy, Mich., 1993-98; pvt. practice, 1998—. Mem. ABA, State Bar Mich., Harvard Club of Ea. Mich. (schs. com.), Order of Coif. Methodist. Avocations: lacrosse, other sports. General civil litigation, Corporate, general, Labor (including EEOC, Fair Labor Standards Act, labor-management relations, NLRB, OSHA). Office: Ste 100 19853 W Outer Dr Dearborn MI 48124-2066 E-mail: mdemorest@rileyhurley.com.

DEMOSS, HAROLD RAYMOND, JR., federal judge; b. Houston, Tex., Dec. 30, 1930; s. Harold R. and Jessy May (Cox) DeMoss; m. Judith Phelps; children: Harold R. III, Louise Holland. BA, Rice U., 1952; LLB, U. Tex., 1955. Bar: Tex. Assoc. Bracewell & Patterson, Houston, 1957—61, ptnr., 1961—91; judge U.S. Ct. of Appeals (5th cir.), Houston, 1991—. Chmn. bd. Tex. Bill of Rights Found., Houston, 1969—70; pres. Tanglewood Homeowners Assn., 1987; area chmn. Bush Congl. Campaign, 1968; mem. platform group Bush for Pres., Washington, 1988; rsch. analyst Bush/Quayle campaign, 1988; dist. del.-at-large Rep. Nat. Conv., Houston, 1980, alt. del.-at-large, 1984, 1988; Harris County vice chmn. Tower Senate campaign, Houston, 1972, Ford/Dale campaign, 1976; Harris County chmn. Loeffler for Gov. Primary, 1986; Harris County co-chair Regan/Bush campaign, 1980, 1984; Tex. state chmn. Bush for Pres. Primary, 1979—80, Tex. vice chmn., 1988; del. Rep. State Conv., Houston, 1968; vestryman St. Martin's Episcopal Ch., Houston, 1968—72; mem. exec. bd. Episcopal Diocese Tex., 1983—86, chmn. planning com., 1985—88, del. Diocesan Conv., 1976—88; bd. dirs. Amigos de las Americas, 1974—76. Sgt. U.S. Army, 1955—57. Fellow: Tex. Bar Assn. (life); mem.: ABA, Tex. Assn. Def. Counsel (bd. dirs. 1972—74), Houston Bar Assn. (bd. dirs. 1969—71, 1st v.p. 1972—73), Maritime Law Assn. U.S., Am. Judicature Soc., Internat. Bar Assn., The Houston Club. Avocations: fishing, waterskiing. Office: Bob Casey US Courthouse 515 Rusk St Ste 12015 Houston TX 77002-2605

DEMOSS, JON W. insurance company executive, lawyer; b. Kewanee, Ill., Aug. 9, 1947; s. Wendell and Virginia Beth DeMoss; m. Eleanor T. Thornley, Aug. 9, 1969; 1 child, Marc Alain. BS, U. Ill., 1969, JD, 1972. Bar: Ill. 1972, U.S. Dist. Ct. (cen. dist.) Ill. 1977, U.S. Supreme Ct. 1978, U.S. dist. Ct. (no. dist., trial bar) Ill. 1983. In house counsel Assn. Ill. Electric Coop., Springfield, 1972-74; registered lobbyist Ill. Gen. Assembly, Springfield, 1972-74; asst. dir. Ill. Inst. for CLE, Springfield, 1974-85; exec. dir. Ill. State Bar Assn., 1986-94; pres., CEO ISBA Mut. Ins. Co., Chgo., 1994—. Bd. dirs. Bar Plan Surety & Fidelity Co., St. Louis, 1999-. Bd. dirs. Springfield Symphony Orch., 1982-87, Ill. Inst. for CLE, 1986-89, Nat. Assn. of Bar Related Ins. Cos., 1989, pres., elect., 1998-99, pres. 1999-2000; bd. dirs. Lawyers Reins. Co., 1997—; bd. visitors John Marshall Law Sch., 1990—. Capt. U.S. Army, 1972. Fellow Am. Bar Found. (life, co-chmn. projects to prepare Appellate Handbook 1978, 90), Ill. Bar Found. (life, bd. dirs. 1983-85); mem. ABA (ho. of dels. 1979-85, 89, 91, 93-94), Nat. Conf. Bar Pres., Am. Judicature Soc. (bd. dirs. Ill. state chpt., treas. 2002-), Ill. State Bar Assn. (pres. 1984-85, bd. govs. 1975-85, chmn. com. on scope and correlation of work 1982-83, chmn. budget com. 1983-85, chmn. legis. com. 1983-84, 85, chmn. com. on merit selection of judges 1977, del. long-range planning conf. 1972, 78, liaison to numerous coms. and sects.), Chgo. Bar Assn., Lake County Bar Assn., U. Ill. Coll. Dean's Club, La Chaine des Rotisseurs (Chgo.), Ordre Mondial des Gourmet Degustateurs (Chgo.), Les Gourmets (Chgo.). Home: 180 Norwich Ct Lake Bluff IL 60044-1914 Office: ISBA Mutual Ins Co 223 W Ohio St Chicago IL 60610-4101

DEMPSEY, BERNARD HAYDEN, JR., lawyer; b. Evanston, Ill., Mar. 29, 1942; s. Bernard H. and Margaret C. (Gallagher) D.; m. Cynthia T. Dempsey; children: Bernard H. III, Matthew B., Kathleen N., Rose Maureen G., Alexandra C., Anastasia M. BS, Coll. Holy Cross, 1964; JD, Georgetown U., 1967. Bar: Fla. 1968, D.C. 1979. Law clk. to chief judge U.S. Dist. Ct. (mid. dist.) Fla., 1967-69; asst. U.S. Atty. Mid. Dist. Fla., 1969-73; pvt. practice Orlando, Fla., 1973—; spl. asst. to U.S. Atty. Mid. Dist. Fla., 1974. Lectr. in field. Contbr. articles to profl. jours. Recipient John Marshall award U.S. Dept. Justice, 1972, U.S. Atty's Outstanding Performance award 1970-73. Mem.: Fla. Bar Found., Am. Judicature Soc., Fla. Bar Assn., Nat. Employment Lawyers Assn., U.S. Attys. Assn. for the Mid. Dist. Fla., Fla. Assn. Criminal Def. Lawyers, Nat. Assn. Criminal Def. Lawyers, ATLA, ABA, Winter Park (Fla.) Racquet Club, Univ. Club (Orlando), Delta Theta Phi. Republican. Roman Catholic. Federal civil litigation, State civil litigation, Criminal. Office: Dempsey & Sasso Bank of America Ctr 390 N Orange Ave Ste 2700 Orlando FL 32801-1643 E-mail: bhd@dempseyandsasso.com.

DEMPSEY, EDWARD JOSEPH, lawyer; b. Lynn, Mass., Mar. 13, 1943; s. Timothy Finbar and Christine Margaret (Callahan) D.; m. Eileen Margaret McManus, Apr. 15, 1967; children: Kristen A. Stolfi, Katherine B. Aydin, Shelagh E., James P. AB, Boston Coll., 1964; JD, Cath. U. Am., 1970. Bar: D.C. 1970, Conn. 1982. Assoc. Arent, Fox, Kintner, Plotkin & Kahn, Washington, 1970-72, Akin, Gump, Strauss, Hauer & Feld, Washington, 1972-75; supervisory trial atty. EEOC, Washington, 1975-79; assoc. Whitman & Ransom, Washington, 1979-81, Farmer, Wells, McGuinn & Sibal, Washington, 1981-82; ptnr. Farmer, Wells, Sibal & Dempsey, Washington, Hartford, Conn., 1983-84; dir. indsl. rels. and labor counsel United Technologies Corp., Hartford, 1985—. Capt. USNR (ret.). Mem. ABA. Civil rights, Federal civil litigation, Labor (including EEOC, Fair Labor Standards Act, labor-management relations, NLRB, OSHA). Office: United Techs Bldg Hartford CT 06101

DE MUNIZ, PAUL J. state supreme court justice; Judge Oreg. Ct. Appeals, 1990—2001; justice Oreg. Supreme Ct., 2001—. Author (with others): Immigrants in Courts, 1999. Office: Supreme Ct 1163 State St Salem OR 97301

DEMURO, PAUL ROBERT, lawyer; b. Aberdeen, Md., Mar. 21, 1954; s. Paul Robert and Amelia C. DeMuro; m. Susan Taylor, May 26, 1990; children: Melissa Taylor, Natalie Lauren, Alanna Leigh. BA summa cum laude, U. Md., 1976; JD, Washington U., 1979; MBA, U. Calif., Berkeley, 1986. Bar: Md. 1979, U.S. Dist. Ct. Md. 1979, D.C. 1980, U.S. Dist. Ct. D.C. 1980, U.S. Dist. Ct. (ea. dist.) Calif. 1986, U.S. Ct. Appeals (4th cir.) 1981, U.S. Tax Ct. 1981, Calif. 1982, U.S. Dist. Ct. (no. dist.) Calif. 1982; CPA, Md.; cert. med. practice exec. Assoc. Ober, Grimes & Shriver, Balt., 1979-82; ptnr. Carpenter et al, San Francisco, 1982-89, McCutchen, Doyle, Brown & Enerson, San Francisco, 1989-93, Latham & Watkins, San Francisco, 1993—. Author: The Financial Managers Guide to Managed Care and Integrated Delivery Systems, 1995, The Fundamentals of Managed Care and Network Development, 1999; co-author: Health Care Mergers and Acquisitions: The Transactional Perspective, 1996, Health Care Executives' Guide to Fraud and Abuse, 1998; editor, contbg. author Integrated Delivery Systems, 1994; article and book rev. editor Washington U. Law Qrtly., St. Louis, 1975-76. Mem. San Francisco Mus. Modern Art, 1985—. Fellow Healthcare Fin. Mgmt. Assn. (bd. dirs. No. Calif. chpt. 1990-93, 99—, sec. 1999-2001, pres.-elect 2001-02, pres. 2002-03, nat. principles and practices bd. 1992-95, vice chair 1993-95, nat. bd. dirs. 1995-97, exec. com. 1996-97, chair compliance officers forum adv. coun. 1998-2000, nominating com. 2001-02, governance com. 2002-03); mem. ABA (health law sect., chair transactional and bus. health care interest group 1998-2000, chair programs com. 2000-02, governing coun. 2000—, chmn. mem. and mktg. com. 2002—, vice chair coord. com. on diversity 2002—, finance officer 2003-), AICPA, L.A. County Bar Assn. (health law sect.), Calif. Bar Assn., San Francisco Bar Assn., Am. Health Lawyers Assn. (fraud and abuse and self-referral substantive law com. 1998—, task force on best practices in advising clients 1998-99, task force on ENRON 2002), The IPA Assn. Am. (mem. legal adv. coun. 1996—), Med. Group Mgmt. Assn. Republican. Administrative and regulatory, Health, Mergers and acquisitions. Office: Latham & Watkins 505 Montgomery St Ste 1900 San Francisco CA 94111-2552 E-mail: paul.demuro@lw.com.

DENACO, PARKER ALDEN, state official, lawyer, arbitrator; b. Bangor, Maine, Apr. 19, 1943; s. Alden F. and Pauline N. Denaco; m. Gayle Gernert Denaco, May 23, 1989. BA in History and Govt., U. Maine, 1965, MBA, 1975; JD, Washington and Lee Univ., 1968; postgrad., Air Command and Staff Coll., 1981. Bar: Maine 1968, U.S. Dist. Ct. Maine 1968, U.S. Ct. Mil. Appeals. Assoc. atty. Eaton & Peabody, Bangor, Maine, 1968—69; exec. officer and adj. 100 MP Bn, Ft. Bragg, NC, 1969—70; provost marshal US Army, Inchon, Republic of Korea, 1970—71; exec. dir. Maine Labor Rels. Bd., Augusta, 1972—88; adj. grad. instr. Thomas Coll., Waterville, Maine, 1977—80; state staff judge advocate Maine Air N.G., Augusta, ME, 1973-86; vis. prof. in constl. law U. Maine, 1990—91; hon. fac. mem. USAF Judge Advocate Gen. Sch., Maxwell AFB, Ala.; exec. dir. N.H. Pub. Employee Labor Rels. Bd., 1991—2003. Contbr. articles to profl. jours. Bd. dirs. Acad. Collective Bargaining Info. Svc., 1979-82; bd. dirs., founding mem. and dir. Pub. Employment Rels. Svcs., 1978-81; bd. dirs. New Eng. Consortium of State Labor Rels. Agys., 1978-2003; neutral pub. mem. Com. on Pub. Sector Bargaining, ABA, 1974—; neutral chair, 1987-01, mem. Alternate Dispute Resolution Section, ABA, 1998—; mem. Boston Adv. Coun., Am. Arbitration Assn., 1978—; elected Nat. Acad. Arbitrators, 1987; Judicial Divsn., ABA, 1998—, Nat. Conf. of Admin. Law Judges; corporator Maine Savs. Bank, 1982-84; law coun. Washington and Lee Univ., 1988-92. Served to capt. U.S. Army, 1969-73, to col. Air NG and USAFR, 1973-95. Recipient Harmon award. USAF, 1986, Legion of Merit, 1990, Disting. Svc. award ABA, 2001. Fellow Coll. Labor and Employment Lawyers (chmn. First Circuit Com., 2003); mem. ABA (Disting. Svc. award 2001), Assn. Labor Rels. Agys. (pres. 1978-79), Maine Bar Assn. (labor sect. co-chmn. 1980-85), N.H. Bar Assn. (chmn. labor and employment law sect. 2002-03) Soc. Profls. in Dispute Resolution (charter), Indsl. Rels. Rsch. Assn., Nat. Acad. Arbitrators, Res. Ofcrs. Assn. (life), N.G. Assn. of U.S. (life), Phi Delta Phi, Beta Gamma Sigma. Address: 1465 Hooksett Rd Unit 11 Hooksett NH 03106-1861 also: PO Box 227 Lincolnville ME 04849-0227 Fax: 603-268-0914. E-mail: denaco4adr@yahoo.com.

DENARO, GREGORY, lawyer; b. Rochester, N.Y., Dec. 10, 1954; m. Nancy Cardiff; children: Adrienne, Gregory, Madeline. BA, U. Rochester, 1976; JD, U. Miami, 1979. Bar: Fla. 1979, U.S. Dist. Ct. (so. dist.) Fla. 1979, U.S. Ct. Appeals (5th and 11th cirs.) 1981, U.S. Supreme Ct. 1984, N.Y. 1985, U.S. Dist. Ct. (mid. dist.) Fla. 1986, U.S. Ct. Appeals (D.C. cir.) 1989, U.S. Dist. Ct. (we. dist.) Tex. 1990, U.S. Ct. Appeals (4th cir.) 1992. Pub. defender Dade County, Miami, Fla., 1979-82; sr. ptnr. Gregory C. Denaro P.A., Miami, 1982—. Advisor nat. mock trial U. Miami Law Sch., 1984—. Mem. ABA (criminal law sect.), Dade County Bar Assn., Assn. Trial Attys., Nat. Assn. Criminal Def. Lawyers, Fla. Assn. Criminal Def. Lawyers (bd. dirs.). Criminal. Office: Coconut Grove Bank Bldg 2701 S Bayshore Dr Ste 605 Coconut Grove FL 33133-5360 E-mail: gdenaro@bellsouth.net.

DE NATALE, ANDREW PETER, lawyer; b. Bklyn., July 7, 1950; s. Peter E. and Mary (Tamberino) DeN.; m. Lynn Susan Kennedy, July 28, 1973; children: Andrew, Christopher. BS in Econs., U. Pa., 1972; JD, Fordham U., 1975. Bar: N.Y. 1976, U.S. Dist. Ct. (so. dist.) N.Y. 1976, U.S. Dist. Ct. (ea. dist.) N.Y. 1977, U.S. Ct. Appeals (2d cir.) 1978, U.S. Supreme Ct. 1979, U.S. Dist. Ct. (no. dist.) N.Y. 1982. Assoc. Krause, Hirsch & Gross, N.Y.C., 1975-79, Stroock & Stroock & Lavan, N.Y.C., 1980-83, ptnr., 1984-91, White & Case, N.Y.C., 1991—. Contbr. numerous articles to newspapers and profl. jours. Mem. ABA, N.Y. Yacht Club, Seawanhaka Corinthian Yacht Club. Bankruptcy, Commercial, contracts (including sales of goods; commercial financing). Office: White & Case LLP 1155 Avenue Of The Americas New York NY 10036-2787

DENCE, EDWARD WILLIAM, JR., lawyer, banker; b. Newport, R.I., Feb. 25, 1938; s. Edward William and Dorothea Margaret (Conway) D.; m. Claire A. Guertin, Nov. 14, 1970; children: Suzanne Lynn, Christine Anne. AB summa cum laude, Providence Coll., 1959; LL.B., Harvard U., 1963. Bar: Mass. 1963, R.I. 1965. Atty. New Eng. Electric System, 1963-68; sec., gen. counsel Fleet Boston Fin. Corp., Providence, 1968-85, v.p., mem. mgmt. com., 1980-85, Ropes & Gray, Providence, 1985-92, Edwards & Angell, Providence, 1992—. Mem. stockholders' adv. com. Fed. Res. Bank, Boston, 1976-77 Mem. R.I. Commn. Inter-Govtl. Rels., 1970-71; chmn. Sargent Rehab. Ctr., 1991-92; bd. dirs. R.I. Pub. Expenditure Coun., 1969-85, R.I. Bar Found.; mem. Providence Roman Cath. Diocesan Bd. Edn., 1970-73; trustee, chmn. audit com., chmn. compensation com. St. Joseph Hosp.; trustee So. New Eng. Rehab. Ctr. Named One of Outstanding Young Men in Am., 1972 Mem. R.I. Bar Assn., Boston Bar Assn. (program chmn. banking com.). Home: 1485 High Hawk Rd East Greenwich RI 02818-1364 E-mail: edence@ealaw.com.

DENEEN, DANIEL GUY, lawyer; b. Bloomington, Ill., Aug. 25, 1957; s. Robert Gregory and Hazel Jean (Sloan) D. BS in Fin., U. Ill., 1979, JD, 1982. Bar: Ill. 1982. Ptnr. Deneen and Deneen, Bloomington, 1982—; mem. profl. adv. com. Home Care divsn. OSF/St. Joseph's Med. Ctr2002. Founding dir. Beyond Normal Films, 1996-97. McLean County Ctr. for Human Svcs., Bloomington, 1987-94. Mem. Ill. Bar Assn. (mental health law com. 1983-89, 91-99), McLean County Bar Assn., Mental Health Assn. (pres. 1994-95), K.C. Roman Catholic. Avocations: sports activities, lit. Commercial, consumer (including collections, credit), Commercial, contracts (including sales of goods; commercial financing), General practice. Office: 202 S Eldorado Rd Bloomington IL 61704-4471

DENEGRE, GEORGE, lawyer; b. New Orleans, Oct. 10, 1923; s. Thomas Bayne and Alma (Baldwin) D.; m. Gayle Stocker, Oct. 4, 1950; children: Stanhope Bayne-Jones, Gayle Stocker Felchlin, George, John Gayle. BA, Yale U., 1943; LLB, Tulane U., 1948. Bar: La. 1948. With firm Chaffe, McCall, Toler & Philips, 1948-49; assoc. Jones, Walker Waechter, Poitevent, Carrère & Denègre, New Orleans, 1949-52; ptnr. Jones, Walker, Waechter, Poitevent, Carrère & Denègre, 1951—2002. Sec., dir. Canal Barge Co., Inc., 1951-2002; sec., dir. Cen. Gulf Lines, Inc., 1958-99; sec. Internat. Shipholding Corp., 1978-99; dir. G.H. Tichenor Antiseptic Co., 1966-2002. Bd. dirs. Met. Crime Commn., 1966-02, Eugenie and Joseph Jones Family Found., 1963-93, Bus. Task Force for Edn., New Orleans Neighborhood Devel. Found., 1989-90, New Orleans Regional Med. Ctr., La. Assn. Mental Health, 1953-77, pres., 1960-61; bd. dirs., sec., exec. com., pres. World Trade Ctr.; bd. govs. Tulane Med. Ctr., 1969-83, vice-chmn., 1977-82, chmn., 1983; vice-chmn., bd. adminstrs. Tulane U., 1980-93; bd. dirs. Chamber New Orleans and River Region, chmn., 1991; vice-chmn. bd. dirs. Met. Arts Fund, 1989-90, New Orleans Coun.-Navy League U.S.; bd. dirs., sec. Bus. Coun., 1986-2001; mem. bd., exec. com. Pub. Affairs Rsch. Coun.; sec. La. Coun. for Fiscal Reform, 1987-96; bd. commrs. Downtown Devel. Dist., 1989-95, chmn., 1992; co-chmn. Mayor's Found. for Edn., 1987-91; chmn. Mayor's Com. for Charity Hosp.; founding mem. La. Partnership for Innovation and Tech. Metrovision Partnership; sec. bd. dirs. Orleans Intercmty. Coun.; vice-dean Consular Corps, 1988-91; Com. 100, 1993-95, Select Com. on Revenues and Expenditures in La. Future (SECURE), 1993-95; adv. bd. Coll. Bus. Adminstrn., U. New Orleans, 1994-96; mem. Com. for Better New Orleans. Lt. USNR, 1943-46. Hon. Consul of India, 1977-2002; Rex, King of Carnival, 1986. Mem. La. Bar Assn., New Orleans Bar Assn., Maritime Bar Assn., Boston Club of New Orleans, Pickwick Club, La. Club, New Orleans Country Club, Stratford Club. Home: 1525 Webster St New Orleans LA 70118-6134 Office: Jones Walker Waechter Poitevent Carrere Denegre 201 Saint Charles Ave New Orleans LA 70170-5100 E-mail: gdenegre@joneswalker.com.

DENGER, MICHAEL LOUIS, lawyer; b. Davenport, Iowa, Sept. 8, 1945; s. Ralph Henry and Bernice Marie (Cederberg) D.; m. Mary Elizabeth Colbert, Aug. 30, 1969; children: Lorna Marie, Mary Catherine, Rachel Anne. BS with highest distinction, Northwestern U., 1967; JD cum laude, Harvard U., 1970. Bar: D.C. 1970, U.S. Ct. Appeals (D.C. cir.) 1971, U.S. Supreme Ct. 1978. Assoc. atty. Sutherland, Asbill & Brennan, Washington, 1970-76, ptnr., 1976-92, Gibson, Dunn & Crutcher LLP, Washington, 1992—. Adj. prof. law Washington and Lee U., 2000—; speaker on antitrust, trade regulation numerous groups. Bd. editors Antitrust Report, 1992—; contbr. articles to profl. jours. Mem. nat. adv. coun. Northwestern U. Sch. Comm., Evanston, Ill., 1990—. 2nd lt. USAR, 1970. Mem. ABA (vice chair antitrust law sect. 1985-86, sec. antitrust law sect. 1988-91, chair-elect antitrust law sect. 1991-92, chair antitrust law sect. 1992-93, chair edit. bd. antitrust sect. Federal and State Price Discrimination Law 1991, co-editor in chief antitrust sect. State Antitrust Practice and Statutes 3 vols. 1990, vice chair edit. bd. antitrust sect. Antitrust Law Devels. 2d edit. 1984), Columbia Country Club (Chevy Chase, Md.). Republican. Roman Catholic. Avocations: tennis, collecting military miniatures, military history, bridge. Antitrust, Federal civil litigation. Home: 5802 Kirkside Dr Chevy Chase MD 20815-7118 Office: Gibson Dunn & Crutcher LLP 1050 Connecticut Ave NW Ste 900 Washington DC 20036-5306

DENHAM, EARL LAMAR, lawyer; b. Biloxi, Miss., July 1, 1947; s. Earl Lamar and Ruby (Young) D.; children: Katherine Elizabeth, Rachel Ann, Israel Anderson, Nathan Levi, Earl Lamar III; m. N.A. Hema Malini; children: Judith Jaya, Sachika Braka, Arya Tova. BS, U. Miss., 1969, JD, 1972. Bar: Miss. 1972, U.S. Dist. Ct. (no. and so. dists.) Miss. 1972, U.S. Ct. Appeals (5th cir.) 1978, U.S. Supreme Ct. 1978. Assoc. Hurlbert & O'Barr, Biloxi, 1972-73; ptnr. Levi & Denham, Ltd., Ocean Springs, Miss., 1973—99. Capt. USAR, 1970-78. Mem. ABA, ATLA (sustaining), Nat. Assn. Criminal Def. Lawyers, Miss. Trial Lawyers Assn., Miss. Bar Assn., Ocean Springs Yacht Club (bd. govs. 1988), Southern Trial Lawyers Assn. Democrat. Jewish. Avocations: sailing, hunting. Criminal, Family and matrimonial, Personal injury (including property damage). Office: Denham Backstrom & Assoc Ltd 424 Washington Ave PO Box 596 Ocean Springs MS 39566-0596

DENISON, MARY BONEY, lawyer; b. Wilmington, N.C., June 8, 1956; d. Leslie Norwood Jr. and Lillian (Bellamy) Boney; children: Mary Catesby Bellamy, James Wholley IV. AB, Duke U., 1978; JD, U. N.C., 1981. Bar: N.Y. 1982, U.S. Dist. Ct. (so. and ea. dists.) N.Y. 1983, U.S. Ct. Appeals (2d cir.) 1984, DC 1988, U.S. Dist. Ct. DC 1988, U.S. Ct. Appeals (DC cir.) 1988. Assoc. Law Office William G. Kaelin, N.Y.C., 1981-82, Smith, Steibel, Alexander & Saskor, N.Y.C., 1982-86, Graham & James, Washington, 1986-91, ptnr., 1992-96, Farkas & Manelli PLLC, Washington, 1996-2000, Manelli, Denison & Selter, PLLC, Washington, 2001—. Vol. Legal Aid Soc., N.Y.C., 1983—86. Mem.: ABA, Internat. Trademark Assn. (vice chair treaty analysis com. 2000—01, chair treaty analysis com. 2001—, bd. dirs. 2003—), French Am. C. of C. Washington (treas. 1991—97). Democrat. Episcopalian. General civil litigation, Private international, Trademark and copyright. Office: Manelli Denison & Selter 2000 M St NW Ste 700 Washington DC 20036-3364 E-mail: mdenison@mdslaw.com.

DENIUS, FRANKLIN WOFFORD, lawyer; b. Athens, Tex., Jan. 4, 1925; s. S.F. and Frances (Cain) D.; m. Charmaine Hooper, Nov. 19, 1949; children: Frank Wofford, Charmaine. BBA, LL.B., U. Tex. Bar: Tex. 1949. Pvt. practice, Austin, 1949—. Past pres., chief exec. officer, chmn. bd., dir. So. Union Co.; past legal counsel Austin Better Bus. Bur.; dir., chmn. bd. emeritus So. Union Co., 1991—; advt. dir. JPMorgan Chase Bank, Austin, Tex. Chmn. spl. schs. div. United Fund, 1960, Pacesetters div., 1961, Schs. div., 1964; 1st v.p. United Fund; chmn. steering com. sch. bond campaign, past trustee Austin Ind. Sch. Dist., 1964; past pres. Young Men's Bus. League Austin; past pres., exec. council Austin Ex-Students Assn. U. Tex.; past co-chmn. LBJ U Tex. Library Found.; chmn., mem. chancellor's council, mem. pres.'s assos. U. Tex.; advisory trustee Schreiner Coll.; chmn. capital planning com. Longhorn Adv. Coun., U. Tex., mem. Longhorn Legacy Com; chmn. Austin Leadership Coun., U. Tex. Devel. Office; mem. U. Tex. Devel. bd. Decorated Silver Star medal with 3 oak leaf clusters, Purple Heart; recipient Outstanding Young Man of Austin award Jr. C. of C., 1959; named Disting. Alumnus U. Tex. Ex-Students Assn., 1991. Mem. ABA, Tex. Bar Assn., Travis County Bar Assn., Tex. Philos. Soc., Longhorn Club (past pres.), West Austin Optimists (past dir.), Headliners (pres., sec. bd. trustees, exec. com.), Masons. Presbyterian (deacon, elder). Home: 3703 Meadowbank Dr Austin TX 78703-1025 Office: Chase Bank Bldg 700 Lavaca St Ste 700 Austin TX 78701-3108

DENKER, JAMES MITCHELL, solicitor, lawyer; b. Mar. 7, 1947; BA with hons. magna cum laude, U. Pa., 1969; BA with hons., Cambridge (Eng.) U., 1971, MA, 1976. Bar: Law Soc. England & Wales 1976. Solicitor Rowe & Maw, Solicitors, London, 1976—80, ptnr., 1980—99, Bircham Dyson Bell, Solicitors, London, 1999—. Co-author: European Succession Law, 2002; contbr. articles to profl. jours. Mem.: The Law Soc. of Eng. and Wales, Internat. Bar Assn., Internat. Acad. Estate and Trust Law, The Athenaeum. Estate planning, Private international, Probate (including wills, trusts). Office: Bircham Dyson Bell 50 Broadway Westminster London SW1H 0BL England Fax: 44 20 7222 3480.

DENMARK, WILLIAM ADAM, lawyer; b. N.Y.C., July 30, 1957; s. Jerome and Frieda (Pollack) D.; m. Carol J. Sack, Apr. 20, 1986; children: Andrea K., Julie E. AB, Cornell U., 1979; JD, U. Pa., 1982. Bar: Pa. 1982, U.S. Dist. Ct. (ea. dist.) Pa. 1982. Assoc. Ballard, Spahr, Andrews & Ingersoll, Phila., 1982-86, Jacoby Donner, P.C., Phila., 1986-89, shareholder, 1989—. Contbr. articles to profl. jours. Mem. ABA, Nat. Assn. Demolition Contractors (assoc.), Phila. Bar Assn. (vice chair mergers and acquisitions com. bus. law sect. 1994-95, constrn. law and comml. leases com. real property sect.), Delaware Valley Soc. Assn. Execs. (bd. dirs. 2001—), Phi Beta Kappa. Avocations: jogging, tennis, reading. Commercial, contracts (including sales of goods; commercial financing), Estate planning, Property, real (including real estate development, water). Office: Jacoby Donner PC 1515 Market St Ste 2000 Philadelphia PA 19102-1920 E-mail: wdenmark@jacobydanner.com.

DENN, MATTHEW P. lawyer; b. 1966; B with high distinction, U. Calif., Berkeley; JD, Yale U. Atty. Young Conaway, 1994—2001; legal counsel to gov. Office Gov. State of Del., Dover, 2001—. Chmn. Child Protection Accountability Commn., Del.; vice chmn. Del. Dems. Office: Office Gov Legis Hall Dover DE 19901 Business E-Mail: matthew.denn@state.de.us.*

DENNEEN, JOHN PAUL, lawyer; b. N.Y.C., Aug. 18, 1940; s. John Thomas Denneen and Pauline Jane Ludlow; m. Mary Veronica Murphy, July 3, 1965 (dec. Dec. 2000); children: John Edward, Thomas Michael, James Patrick, Robert Andrew, Daniel Joseph, Mary Elizabeth. BS, Fordham U., 1963; JD, Columbia U., 1966. Bar: N.Y. 1966, U.S. Ct. Appeals (2d cir.) 1974, U.S. Dist. Ct. (so. and ea. dists.) N.Y. 1975, Mo. 1987. Assoc. Seward & Kissel, N.Y.C., 1966-75; sr. v.p., gen counsel, sec. GK Techs., Inc., Greenwich, Conn., 1975-83; exec. v.p., gen. counsel, sec. Chromalloy Am. Corp., St. Louis, 1983-87; ptnr. Bryan Cave LLP, St. Louis, 1987-99; exec. v.p. corp. devel. and legal affairs, sec. NuVox, Inc., St. Louis, 1999—. Mem. ABA, Internat. Bar Assn., N.Y. State Bar Assn., N.Y.C. Bar Assn., Bar Assn. Met. St. Louis. Communications, Mergers and acquisitions, Securities. Office: NuVox Inc Ste 500 16090 Swingley Ridge Rd Chesterfield MO 63017-6029

DENNEY, JAMES ALLEN, lawyer; b. Youngstown, Ohio, Nov. 2, 1949; s. Vergil Herold and Mary (Maropoulakis) D.; m. Mary Lou Thomas, Aug. 7, 1970; children: Theodore, Jesse, Louis, Athena, Daniel. AB in Polit. Sci., Youngstown State U., 1974; JD, Capital U., 1977. Bar: Ohio 1977, U.S. Dist. Ct. (no. dist.) Ohio 1978. Pvt. practice Office of Atty. James A Denney, Girard, Ohio. Trustee N.E. Ohio Legal Svcs., Youngstown, 1979-80, U.S. Internat. Peace Race, Youngstown, 1985-89. Treas. 17th congl. dist. Jesse Jackson Campaign, Mahoning/Trumbull County, Ohio, 1984; mgr. 64th state dist. Robert Hagan State Rep. Campaign, Youngstown, 1986-93; chmn. Mahoning Valley Friends, NRA, 1997-2003. Mem. Mahoning County Bar Assn., Pan Cretan Assn. Am. (pres. Manolakakis/Theodorakis chpt. 2003), Mahoning County Fedn. Sportsmens Clubs (pres. 2003). Ea. Orthodox. Avocations: track coach (middle school), hunting, target shooting, gardening. Criminal, Family and matrimonial, General practice. Office: Atty James A Denney 1631 S State St Girard OH 44420-3370

DENNIS, ANTHONY JAMES, lawyer; b. Manchester, Conn., Feb. 11, 1963; BA cum laude, Tufts U., 1985; JD, Northwestern U., Chgo., 1988. Bar: Conn. 1988, DC 1989, US Dist. Ct. Conn. 1988. Assoc. Robinson & Cole, Hartford, Conn., 1988-89; atty. Aetna, Inc., Hartford, 1989-92, counsel, 1992—. TV and radio talk show guest. Author: The Rise of the Islamic Empire and the Threat to the West, 1996, Letters to Khatami: A Reply to the Iranian President's Call for a Dialogue Among Civilizations, 2001, Osama Bin Laden: A Psychological and Political Portrait, 2002; co-author: Healthcare Antitrust: Strategies for Changing Provider Organizations, 1994; contbr. articles to profl. jours. Mem. Conn. Bar Assn. (subcom. chmn. 1990-93, exec. com. 1990—, com. chmn. 1990—, treas. 1993-94, vice-chmn. 1994-95, chmn. 1995-99), D.C. Bar Assn., Am. Health Lawyers Assn., KC (past grand knight). Antitrust, Corporate, general, Health. Office: Aetna Inc 151 Farmington Ave Hartford CT 06156-3124 E-mail: dennisaj@aetna.com.

DENNIS, JAMES LEON, judge; b. Monroe, La., Jan. 9, 1936; s. Jenner Leon and Hope (Taylo) Dennis; children: Stephen James, Gregory Leon, Mark Taylo, John Timothy. BS in Bus. Adminstrn, La. Tech. U., Ruston, 1959; JD, La. State U., 1962; LLM, U. Va., 1984. Bar: La. 1962. Assoc. firm Hudson, Potts & Bernstein, Monroe, 1962—65, ptnr., 1965—72; judge 4th Dist. Ct. La. for Morehouse and Ouachita Parishes, 1972—74, La. 2d Circuit Ct. Appeals, 1974—75; assoc. justice La. Supreme Ct., 1975—95; coord. La. Constnl. Revision Commn., 1970—72; del., chmn. judiciary com. La. Constnl. Conv., 1973; judge U.S. Ct. Appeals Fifth Cir., New Orleans, 1995—. Chmn. La. Commn. on Bicentennial U.S. Constn.; mem. La. Ho. of Reps., 1968—72. With U.S. Army, 1955—57. Mem.: ABA (com. on appellate practice), 4th Jud. Bar Assn., La. Bar Assn., Rotary. Methodist. Office: US Courthouse 600 Camp StRm 219 New Orleans LA 70130-3425

DENNISTON, BRACKETT BADGER, III, lawyer; b. Oak Park, Ill., July 23, 1947; s. Brackett Badger Jr. and Frances Ann (Jones) D.; m. Kathleen Foley, Aug. 2, 1975; children: Alexandra, Brackett Badger IV, Elizabeth. AB, Kenyon Coll., 1969; JD, Harvard U., 1973. Bar: Mass. 1974, U.S. Dist. Ct. Mass. 1975, U.S. Dist. Ct. (we. dist.) Tex. 1987, U.S. Ct. Appeals (1st cir.) 1975, U.S. Ct. Appeals (D.C. cir.) 1976, U.S. Ct. Appeals (7th cir.) 1978, U.S. Ct. Appeals (10th cir.) 1981, U.S. Supreme Ct. 1981. Law clk. to judge U.S. Ct. Appeals for 9th Cir., Honolulu, 1973-74; assoc. Goodwin, Procter & Hoar, Boston, 1974-81, ptnr., 1981-82, 86-93, mem. exec. com., 1990-93; chief major frauds unit U.S. Atty.'s Office, Boston, 1982-86; chief legal counsel Gov. of Mass., Boston, 1993-96; v.p., sr. counsel litigation GE, Fairfield, Conn., 1996—, also chmn. policy compliance rev. bd. Class chmn. Kenyon Coll., Gambier, Ohio, 1979-90, trustee, 2000—; mem. Duxbury (Mass.) Zoning Bd. Appeals, 1980-92, chmn., 1984-90. Recipient Dir.'s award for superior achievement U.S. Dept. Justice, 1986, alumni award Kenyon Coll., 1991-96. Mem. Mass. Bar Assn. (chmn. coun. jud. adminstrn. sect. 1989-90, jud. adminstrv. coun. 1987-90, 95-96, criminal justice sect. 1986—, litig. sect. 1988—), trustee, Boston Bar Found., 2002-. General civil litigation, Criminal, Securities. Office: GE Co 3137 Easton Tpke Fairfield CT 06432-1008 E-mail: brackett.denniston@corporate.ge.com.

DENNISTON, JEANNIE L. lawyer; b. Jackson, Miss., May 3, 1951; d. Verne Leroy Culbertson and Mabel Jean Bunge; m. Michael Edward Denniston, (div. Aug. 1999); 1 child, Sara Elizabeth. BS, U. Ozarks, 1973; JD, U. Ark., Little Rock, 1994. Office mgr. McGuire-Smith, Little Rock, 1976-79; mortgage banker Worthen Bank & Trust, Little Rock, 1979-84; constrn. loan officer City Nat. Bank, Ft. Smith, Ark., 1984; adminstrv. asst. ERC properties, Ft. Smith, 1984-91; pvt. practice law Morrilton, Ark., 1994-98; dep. prosecuting atty. Conway County, Morrilton, 1997-98; assoc. Gordon, Caruth & Virden, Morrilton, 1998—. Instr. 100 Proof Inc., Morrilton, 1997-2000. Mem. Morrilton Planning and Zoning Commn., 1996-99; bd. dirs. Safe Place Inc., Morrilton, 1995-96, Main St. Morrilton Inc., 1996-97. Mem. ABA, Ark. Bar Assn., Ark. Trial Lawyers Assn., Ark. Assn. Women Lawyers, Conway County Bar Assn., Morrilton Area C. of C. (treas. 1999, 2d v.p. 2000, 1st v.p. 2001, bd. dirs. 1997-98), Kiwanis. Baha'I. Avocations: scuba diving, needlework. Alternative dispute resolution, Criminal, Probate (including wills, trusts). Office: Gordon Caruth & Virden PLC PO Box 558 105 S Moose St Morrilton AR 72110-3425

DENNY, COLLINS, III, lawyer; b. Richmond, Va., Dec. 5, 1933; s. Collins Jr. and Rebecca (Miller) Denny; m. Anne Carples, June 28, 1957; children: Collins IV, William R., Katharine D. Joyce. AB, Princeton U., 1956; LLB, U. Va., 1961. Bar: Va. 1961, U.S. Dist. Ct. (ea. dist.) Va. 1962, U.S. Ct. Appeals (4th cir.) 1962, U.S. Tax Ct. 1971, U.S. Ct. Claims 1976. Assoc. Denny, Valentine & Davenport, Richmond, 1961-67; ptnr. Mays & Valentine LLP, Richmond, 1967-2000, mng. ptnr., 1992-93; gen. counsel, corp. sec. Coastal Lumber Co., Weldon, NC, 1980—2003; ptnr. Troutman, Sanders, Mays & Valentine LLP, Richmond, 2001. Gen. counsel Bear Island Timberlands Co., LLC, Ashland, Va., 1985—99, Bear Island Paper Co., LLC, 1989—2000. Contbr. chapters to books, articles to profl. jours. Lt. USNR, 1956—66. Mem.: ABA (chmn. exempt orgns. subcom., tax. sect. 1971—86), Richmond Feeder Cattle Assn. (pres. 1972—77), Va. Forestry Assn., Va. Tax Rev. (adv. bd. 1978—2002), Va. State Bar (com. chmn. 1981—83), Va. Bar Assn. (chmn. jr. bar 1965—66), Princeton Alumni Assn. Va. (pres. 1974—78), Va. Country Club, Deep Run Hunt Club (pres. 1987—88), Richmond-First Club (pres. 1969—70). Episcoplian. Avocations: horse sports, tree farming, agriculture. Corporate, general, Natural resources, Taxation, general. Office: TroutmanSanders 1111 E Main St PO Box 1122 Richmond VA 23218-1122

DENNY, RICHARD ALDEN, JR., retired lawyer; b. Atlanta, Oct. 13, 1931; s. Richard Alden and Maybeth Sullivan (Graham) D.; m. Margaret Hunt, Aug. 1954; children: Margaret Denny Dozier, Richard Alden III, Dallas Hunt, Lee Denny Griffith. BA, Washington and Lee U., 1952; LLB, Emory U., 1954. Bar: Ga. 1954. Assoc. King & Spalding, Atlanta, 1954-60, ptnr., 1960-92. Chmn. bd. Met. Atlanta Crime Commn., 1972-73; bd. dirs. Woodruff Arts Ctr., 1991-97, life trustee, 1997—; bd. dirs. High Mus. of Art, Atlanta, 1971—, chmn., 1991-94; bd. dirs. Lovett Sch., Atlanta, 1969—, chmn., 1980-83, emeritus trustee, 1999—. Mem. Lawyers Club Atlanta (pres. 1972-73), Atlanta Lawyers Found. (chmn. 1976-77), Washington and Lee Alumni Assn. (pres. 1980-81), Piedmont Driving Club (pres. 1982-84), Peachtree Golf Club, Omicron Delta Kappa. Episcopalian. Office: King & Spalding Ste 4900 191 Peachtree St NE Atlanta GA 30303-1740

DENSMORE, DOUGLAS WARREN, lawyer; b. Jan. 30, 1948; s. Warren Orson and Lois Martha (Ery) D.; m. Janet Roberta Broadley, Oct. 26, 1973; children: Bradley Wythe, Andrew Fitz Douglas. AB, Coll. of William and Mary, Williamsburg, Va., 1970; JD cum laude, U. Toledo, 1975. Bar: Ohio 1976, US Dist. Ct. (no. and so. dist.) Ohio, Va. 1980, US Dist. Ct. (ea. and we. dist.) Va. 1980, US Ct. Appeals (4th cir.) 1980, US Supreme Ct., 1997, US Bankruptcy Ct. (we. dist.) Va., 2002. Assoc. Gertner, Barkan & Robon, Toledo, 1975-77, Shumaker, Loop & Kendrick, Toledo, 1977-79; corp. counsel Dominion Bankshares Corp., Roanoke, Va., 1979-80; assoc. Woods, Rogers, Muse, Walker & Thornton, Roanoke, Va., 1980-84; ptnr. Woods, Rogers & Hazlegrove, Roanoke, Va., 1984-96, Flippin, Densmore, Morse and Jessee, Roanoke, Va., 1996—. Co-author: Examining the Increase in Federal Regulatory Requirements and Penalties: Is Banking Facing Another Troubled Decade?, 1995; contbr. articles to profl. jour. Decorated Venerable Order St. John (Eng.), Companion of the O'Conor Don (Ireland), knight grand cross Royal Order of Don Carlos I (Portugal), knight grand cross Order of St. Catherine, knight comdr. of justice Order of St. Lazarus, first class Order of Polonia Restituta (Poland), knight grand cross Order St. Stanislas (Poland), knight grand cross Order of the Temple, knight comdr. Order of Crown of Thorns, knight grand cross Order of St. Michael and St. George, knight grand cross Orthodox Order St. John, knight Order of St. John, Knights of Malta, knight grand cross Order of Holy Cross of Jerusalem, knight grand cross with collar Order of St. Gregory, knight grand cross Order of St. Stephen, Royal Ukranian Order of St. Vladimir the Great, knight grand cross Greek Order of St. Denis of Zante, Order of the White Eagle. Master: Masons (jr. deacon 1992, 32 degree); fellow: Baskerville Soc. (U.K.); mem.: ABA (banking law com. 1988—, Uniform Comml. Code com. 1988—), The Business Leadership Fund (bd. of dir. 2003), Roanoke Bar Assn. Found. (pres. 2002—), Bar Assn. City of Roanoke (bd. dirs. 1998—, pres. 2001—02), Va. Bar Assn. (Corp. Code com. 1984—), New Century Venture Ctr., Scottish Soc. Va. Highlands (bd. dir. 1992—2000), Roanoke Regional C. of C., New Century Tech. Coun. (bd. dir. 1997—), Vet. Corps Art NY, English Speaking Union, Augustan Soc., Army-Navy Union, Brit. Manorial Soc. (Lord of Stratford St. Andrew), Soc. of St. George, Royal Overseas Club (London), Farmington Country Club (Charlottesville, Va.), Roanoke Country Club, Shenandoah Club (Roanoke), Rotary, Royal Order of Scotland, Shriners, Kiwanis Internat. Episcopalian. Avocations: golf, gardening, reading. Banking, General civil litigation, Corporate, general. Office: Flippin Densmore Morse & Jessee Ste 1800 First Union Tower Roanoke VA 24011-3315 E-mail: densmore@flippindensmore.com.

DENT, EDWARD DWAIN, lawyer; b. Ft. Worth, Dec. 23, 1950; BA, Tex. Christian U., 1973; JD, St. Mary's U., Tex., 1976. Bar: Tex., U.S. Dist. Ct. (no. and so. dists.) Tex., U.S. Supreme Ct. Atty., ptnr. Kugle, Stewart, Dent, Frederick, Ft. Worth, 1979-89; founder Dent Law Firm, Ft. Worth, Dallas, 1990—. Bd. dirs. West Side Little League. Recipient Hist. Preservation Award, Tarrant County Hist. Soc., 1992. Mem. ATLA, Pres.'s Club (life), U.S. Supreme Ct. Hist. Soc., Tex. Trial Lawyers (bd. dirs. 1989-2002, Tarrant County Trial Lawyers (bd. dirs. 1988-89, officer 1989), Trial Lawyers for Pub. Justice, Ft. Worth Club, Colonial Country Club, Million Dollar Advocacy Soc. (life). Democrat. Insurance, Personal injury (including property damage). Office: Dent Law Firm 1120 Penn St Fort Worth TX 76102-3417

DENT, JOHN ROBERT, lawyer; b. L.A., July 21, 1963; m. Patricia A McBride. BA, UCLA, 1984; JD., U. of Chgo., 1990. Bar: Calif. 1990. Assoc. Tuttle & Taylor, L.A., 1990—97, shareholder, 1997—2000; v.p. and sr. counsel Hilton Hotels Corp., Beverly Hills, Calif., 2000—. General civil litigation, Alternative dispute resolution, Hotel Development & Operations. Office: Hilton Hotels Corp 9336 Civic Center Dr Beverly Hills CA 90210 Office Fax: 310-205-7878. E-mail: john_dent@hilton.com.

DENTEN, CHRISTOPHER PETER, lawyer; b. Oakland, Calif., Apr. 23, 1964; s. Richard and Waltraud Denten; m. Mary McLaughlin, May 18, 1996; 1 child, Aiden. BA, U. Calif., Berkeley, 1986; JD, U. San Francisco, 1990; LLM in Tax, Golden Gate U., 2003. Bar: Calif. 1991, U.S. Dist. Ct. (no. dist.) Calif. 1991, U.S. Ct. Appeals (9th cir.) 1991; CPA, Colo.; notary public. Tax profl. KPMG Peat Marwick, Oakland, 1988-92; sr. tax analyst Cisco Sys., Inc., San Jose, Calif., 1992-97; assoc. gen. counsel, dir. legal affairs and taxation Network Assocs., Inc. (formerly McAfee, Inc.), Santa Clara, Calif., 1997—2002; pvt. practice cons., 1991—. Bd. dirs. Network Assocs. fgn. subs., 2000-02; gen. counsel iManage, Inc., Foster City, Calif., 2003—. Named to Outstanding Young Men of Am., 1982; Brother Gary Stone Meml. scholar, 1982. Mem. AICPA, Santa Clara Bar Assn., Nat. Notary Assn., U. Calif. Berkeley Alumni Assn., U. San Francisco Law Sch. Alumni Assn., Network Assocs. Pres. Club. Republican. Roman Catholic. Avocations: marathons, golf, art, travel. Corporate, general, Mergers and acquisitions, Corporate taxation. Home and Office: PO Box 117932 Burlingame CA 94011-7932

DENVER, THOMAS H. R. lawyer; b. N.Y.C., Oct. 29, 1944; s. Thomas H. Rorke and Eileen Ann Boland; m. Barbara Ann Denver, Dec. 19, 1987; children: Rorke, Nate. BS, Syracruse U., 1966; MS, U. Wash., 1967; JD, U. Calif., San Francisco, 1973. Bar: Calif. 1973, U.S. Dist. Ct. (no. dist.) Calif. 1973. From assoc. to mng. ptnr. Hoge, Fenton, Jones & Appel, Inc., San Jose, Calif., 1973—99. Judge pro tem Santa Clara County Superior Ct., San Jose, 1980—; instr. Stanford U. Law Sch. Advocacy Program; mem. faculty Hastings Coll. of Advocacy; mediator, arbitrator. Contbr. articles to profl. jours. Fellow Am. Coll. Trial Lawyers; mem. Am. Bd. Trial Advocates, Santa Clara County Civil Litigation Com., Santa Clara County Bar Assn. (chmn. fast track com.). Avocations: running, fishing, reading. General civil litigation, Intellectual property, Product liability. Office: Mediation Masters 96 N Third St # 300 San Jose CA 95112

DENYS, SYLVIA, lawyer, researcher; d. Joseph and Louise D. BA in Philosophy and English with honors, Duquesne U., 1970, MA in English, 1977, JD, 1979. Bar: Pa. 1979, U.S. Dist. Ct. (we. dist.) Pa. 1979, U.S. Ct. Appeals (3d cir.), 1994. Atty. Neighborhood Legal Svcs. Assn., Pitts., 1979-81; jud. law clk. Superior Ct. Pa., Pitts., 1981-82; asst. prof. Duquesne U. Grad. Sch. Bus. and Sch. Bus., 1982-89; pvt. practice, Pitts., 1982-91, 93—; tchr. Acad. for Advancement Sci., Pecs, Hungary, 1992-93. Adj. prof. Duquesne U. Sch. Bus., 1990-91; vis. prof. Sch. Medicine, Pecs, 1991-92; adj. prof. Janus Pannonius Sch. Law, Pecs, Hungary, 1991-92lectr. and presenter in field. Mem. editl. bd. Duquesne Law Rev., 1978-79; contbr. articles to profl. jours. Legal coun., bd. dirs. Pitts. Deaf Theatre, Pitts., 1984-85; bd. dirs. YWCA, Pitts., 1984, Blind Outdoor Leisure Devel., Pitts., 1994-95; rev. com. United Way, Pitts., 1982-86; citizens assembly mem. Health and Welfare Planning Allegheny County, Pitts., 1982-85; v.p. UN Assn. Pitts., 1984-85, bd. dirs., 1982-85; vol. atty. Legal Resources for Women, Pitts., 1997, Neighborhood Legal Svcs. Assn., Pitts., 1994—; adv. bd. Radio Info. Svc., Pitts., 1994-95, vol. atty., 1996-97; govtl. activities com. United Cerebral Palsy, Pitts., 1994-96; dir. legal project for deaf and hard of hearing Pitts. Hearing, Speech and Deaf Svcs., 1995-96; tutor goodwill literacy program Allegheny County Jail, Pitts., 1995-96; membership com. World Affairs Coun., Pitts., 1983-85. Hunkele Found. grantee, Brussels, 1988, U.S. Info. Agy. grantee U. Pitts., 1992-93; Fulbright-Hayes fellow Coun. for Internat. Exch. of Scholars, 1990; selected mem. Team '92 Delegation of Commn. of European Communities, 1989-91. Mem. ABA (editor-in-chief Internat. Aspects of Antitrust Law newsletter 1984-86, del. to European Union 1989), ACLU (lawyers com. 1994-98), Fed. Bar Assn. (steering com., Western Pa. chpt. 1995—, sec., steering com., editor newsletter), Nat. Employment Lawyers Assn., Nat. Alliance for Mental Illness (nat. profl. diversity group), Am. Inns of Ct., Pa. Bar Assn. (legal svcs. to persons with disabilities com. 1994—, civil and equal rights com. 1994-98), Allegheny County Bar Assn. (antitrust and class action com., court rules com., editl. bd. Pitts. Legal Jour. 1982-88, pub. svc. com., civil rights com., internat. twinning com. 1994-98), Womens Bar Assn. Allegheny County, Amnesty Internat., Pitts. Aids Task Force (legal com., buddy program, spkr's. bur.), Lawyers Com. for Human Rights, Sierra Club. Avocations: hiking, reading, arts, nature, gourmet cooking. Civil rights, Labor (including EEOC, Fair Labor Standards Act, labor-management relations, NLRB, OSHA). Office: 1220 Grant Bldg 330 Grant St Pittsburgh PA 15219-2257 E-mail: civright@telerama.com.

DE NYS BIK, WILLEM WYNANCL, lawyer; b. Amsterdam, Netherlands, Apr. 16, 1963; m. Clarian Bottinga; children: Willem Wynand Jan Nys Bik, Francÿn Anne Jet Nys Bik. ML, U of Utrecht, 1988; officer, Royal Dutch Navy, 1988—89. Bar: 1992. Trainee Trenité Va Doorne, 1989—97; ptnr. Simmons & Simmons, 1997—. Mem. body delegates Dutch Bar. Author: (articles) Corp. Law, 1990—; lecturer (seminars) Corp. Law, 1990—. Lt Navy, 1988—89, Amsterdam. Office: Simmons & Simmons Weena 666 3000AD Rotterdam Netherlands

DEORCHIS, VINCENT MOORE, lawyer; b. NYC, Aug. 25, 1949; s. Mario E. and Frankie (Moore) DeO.; children: Vincent Scott, Dana Lauren. BA, Fordham Coll., 1971, JD, 1974. Bar: N.Y. 1975, U.S. Dist. Ct. (so. and ea. dists.) N.Y. 1975, U.S. Ct. Appeals (2d cir.) 1975, U.S. Supreme Ct. 1985, U.S. Ct. Appeals (3d cir.) 1989, U.S. Dist. Ct. (so. dist.) Tex. 1992, U.S. Ct. Appeals (4th cir.) 1996. Assoc. Haight, Gardner, Poor & Havens, N.Y.C., 1974-84; ptnr. DeOrchis, Walker & Corsa, LLP, N.Y.C., 1997—2002, DeOrchis & Ptnrs. LLP, NYC, 1984—. Co-author: Attorney's Practice Guide to Negotiations, 1985. Pres. North Stratmore Civic Assn., Manhasset, N.Y., 1978-82. Mem. ATLA, ABA (com. on maritime litig.), Inter-Pacific Bar Assn., Maritime Law Assn. (bd. dirs., rep. to Comite Maritime Internat.), Assn. Transp. Practitioners, N.Y. County Lawyers Assn. (com. on maritime and admiralty law), Propeller Club U.S. Avocation: sailing. Admiralty, Commercial, contracts (including sales of goods; commercial financing), Insurance. Office: DeOrchis and Ptnrs LLP 61 Broadway Fl 26 New York NY 10006-2802

DEPALMA, GIUSEPPE, lawyer; b. La Spezia, Italy, Oct. 17, 1968; s. Vincenzo De Palma and Bianca Di Giovanni; m. Cristina Trivella Mallery, July 27, 1998; children: Matteo, Marco. LLD, U. Rome, 1991, PhD, 1997; LLM, U. London, 1995. Bar: Italy 1994. Assoc. Grimaldi & Associati, Rome, 1995—2000, ptnr., 2000—01, Clifford Chance, Rome-Milan, 2001—02. Contbr. articles to profl. jours. Oil, gas, and mineral. Office: Clifford Chance Via Clerici 7 20121 Milan Italy

DEPAUL, ANTHONY KENNETH, lawyer; b. Chester, Pa., Feb. 9, 1938; s. Samuel DePaul and Lucille DiNicola; m. Joanne J. Machristie, June 30, 1984. BA, Widener U., 1959; JD, Georgetown U., 1962. Bar: Pa., U.S. Dist. Ct. D.C. 1964, U.S. Ct. Mil. Appeals 1968, U.S. Supreme Ct. 1975. Pub. defender, Media, Pa., 1970-75; pro bono def. counsel for indigent accused Phila., 1970—90. Instr. U.S. Mil. Acad., West Point, N.Y., 1965-70; prof. law Widener U., Chester, Pa., 1970-90, St. Joseph's U., Phila., 1972-92; solicitor mcpl. fire cos., 1970-90. With JAGC U.S. Army, 1966—70. Recipient Alumni Achievement award, Widener U. Mem.: Pa. Trial Lawyers Assn., Pa. Bar Assn., Phila. Bar Assn. General practice, Juvenile, Property, real (including real estate development, water). Home: Gen Delivery Honey Brook PA 19344

DEPEW, HARRY LUTHER, retired lawyer; b. Neodesha, Kans., Nov. 18, 1923; s. Clarence William and Dorothy J. (Bushaway) D.; m. Frances Allene Crisp, Mar. 27, 1951; children— Douglas D., Dennis D. B.S. in Bus., Kans. U., 1948, LL.B., 1951. Bar: Kan. 1951. County atty. County of Wilson (Kans.), 1955-58; ptnr. Depew Law Firm, Neodesha, Kans., 1952—; ret. Served with U.S. Army, 1942-45, 51-52; Korea. Mem. C. of C., Kans. Bar Assn. (various coms.), S.E. Kans. Bar Assn. (past pres.), Wilson County Bar Assn. (past pres.), Lions Club. Republican. Bankruptcy, General practice, Probate (including wills, trusts). Home: PO Box 313 Neodesha KS 66757-0313 Office: 620 Main St Neodesha KS 66757-1633

DEPEW, SPENCER LONG, lawyer; b. Wichita, Kans., June 6, 1933; s. Claude I. and Frances Ann (Bell) D.; m. Donna Wolever, Dec. 28, 1957; children: Clifford S., Sally F. AB, U. Wichita, 1955; LLB, U. Mich., 1960. Bar: Kans.; U.S. Dist. Ct. Kans.; U.S. Supreme Ct. Mem. Depew and Gillen, LLC, Wichita. Mem. Interstate Oil and Gas Compact Commn., Oklahoma City. With U.S. Army, 1955-57, Germany. Mem. IPAA, Kans. Ind. Oil and Gas Assn. Corporate, general, Oil, gas, and mineral, Estate planning. Home: 6322 E English St Wichita KS 67218-1802 Office: Depew and Gillen LLC 151 N Main St Ste 800 Wichita KS 67202-1409

DE PFYFFER, ANDRE, lawyer, director; b. Lucerne, Switzerland, Nov. 3, 1928; s. Leodegar and Anna (Carvalho) de P.; children by previous marriage: Corinne, Francois; m. Francoise Garnier del Campo, 1983. Baccalaureat, U. Berne, 1947; postgrad., U. Geneva, 1947-50. Admitted to Geneva Lawyers Assn., 1952; since practiced in Geneva; sr. ptnr. firm de Pfyffer & Assocs. Vice chmn. Pargesa Holding, S.A.; past consul gen. of Sweden in Geneva. Decorated comdr. Royal Order of the Polar Star (Sweden). Mem. Internat. Law Assn., Circle de la Terrasse. Banking, Commercial, contracts (including sales of goods; commercial financing), Corporate, general. Home: 6 Rue Eynard Geneva Switzerland Office: 6 Rue Bellot Geneva Switzerland E-mail: andre.depfyffer@depfyffer.ch.

DE RAISMES, JOSEPH NAPOLÉON, lawyer; b. Summit, N.J., Apr. 26, 1944; s. Joseph Napoléon and Elena Brewerton (Barron) de R.; m. Esther Smith Quinlan, Dec. 21, 1969 (div. 1973); m. Jaird Byrne, May 1, 1982; 1 child, Joseph Napoléon. AB magna cum laude, Yale U., 1967; JD, Harvard U., 1970. Bar: Colo. 1970, U.S. Dist. Ct. Colo. 1970, U.S. Ct. Appeals (10th cir.) 1971, U.S. Supreme Ct. 1981. Assoc. Holland & Hart, Esquires, Denver, 1970-73; regional counsel ACLU, Boulder, Colo., 1973-75; 1st asst. atty. gen. human resources sect. State of Colo., Denver, 1975-79; city atty. City of Boulder, 1979—. Interim city mgr. City of Boulder, 1990-91; adj. prof. law U. Colo., 1994-95; asst. Bur. du Contentieux, City of Paris, 1988; appt. to task force on takings legis. Nat. Conf. State Legislatures; lectr. mcpl. law profl. and ednl. instns.; CLE presenter various profl. confs. Contbr. articles to legal publs. Chairperson ad hoc tech. rev. com. on TABOR (amendment 1, 1992) implementation, mem. various coms. Colo. Mcpl. League; mem. Colo. Mental Health Planning Adv. Coun., 1989—, chairperson, 1991-96; founding mem., pres. Nat. Assn. Mental Health Planning and Adv. Couns., 1994-2000; bd. dirs. Mental Health Ctr. Boulder County, 1982—, mem. exec. com., 1991—. Recipient Fletcher Gaylord Advocacy award Colo. Mental Health Assn., 1995, extraordinary cert. of appreciation Colo. Mcpl. League, 1996. Mem. ABA, Internat. Mcpl. Lawyers Assn. (formerly Nat. Inst. Mcpl. Law Officers, trustee 1988-97, pres. 1995-96, past chairperson antitrust com., past chairperson strategic planning com.), Colo. Bar Assn. (past v.p., mem. state civil commitment task force, mem. mental health com., now disability law com. 1977—, mem. ethics com. 1987-2002, mem., now chairperson polit. edn. com., writer, performer assn. shows 1987, 89), Colo. City Attys. Assn. (past pres.), Boulder Bar Assn., Metro City Attys. Assn. (founding, past pres., sec.-treas. 1985—, 3 Outstanding City Atty. awards, 2 Spl. Accomplishment awards, Spl. Recognition award, Ethics award), Order of Coif. Democrat. Avocations: a cappela singing, russian music, french language and literature, mental health/disability law. Home: 544 University Ave Boulder CO 80302-5807 Office: Office of City Atty PO Box 791 Boulder CO 80302

DERBES, ALBERT JOSEPH, III, lawyer, accountant; b. New Orleans, Mar. 18, 1940; s. Albert Joseph Jr. and Marcelle (Jourdan) D.; m. Shirley Brown, June 8, 1963; children: Albert Joseph IV, Eric Joseph. BBA, Tulane U., 1963, JD, 1966. Bar: La., Tex., U.S. Tax Ct., U.S. Supreme Ct., U.S. Ct. Appeals (5th cir.), U.S. Dist. Ct. (ea., mid. and we. dists.) La., U.S. Dist. Ct. (ea. dist.) Tex.; CPA, La., Miss., Ga., Fla. Ptnr. Derbes & Derbes, CPAs, New Orleans, 1964-69, Trahan, Kernion, & Derbes, CPAs, New Orleans, 1970-78, Hurdman & Cranston, CPAs, New Orleans, 1978-79, Main, Hurdman, CPAs, New Orleans, 1979-82, Windhorst, Pastorek & Gaundry, Attys. at Law, Harvey, La., 1982-88, Derbes & Co., CPAs, Metairie, La., 1982—2002; pvt. practice, 1988-95; with The Derbes Law Firm, LLC, Metairie, 1995—. Capt. USAF, 1966-69. Mem. ABA, AICPAs, La. State Bar Assn., La. Soc. CPAs, Miss. Soc. CPAs, Nat. Assn. State Bds. of Accountancy (bd. dirs. 1983-84, v.p. 1984-85, pres. 1986-87). Republican. Roman Catholic. Avocations: fishing, reading. Corporate, general, Probate (including wills, trusts), Taxation, general. Office: 3027 Ridgelake Dr PO Box 8176 Metairie LA 70011-8176 E-mail: ajderbesiii@derbeslaw.com.

DERBY, ERNEST STEPHEN, federal judge; b. Boston, July 10, 1938; s. Elmer Goodrich and Lucy (Davis) D.; m. Gretel Hanauer, June 10, 1961 (dec. Oct. 2000); children: Anne Gray, Michael Stephen; m. Carolyn Schwenk, May 11, 2002. AB with distinction, Wesleyan U., 1960; LLB cum laude, Harvard U., 1965. Bar: Md. Ct. Appeals 1965, U.S. Dist. Ct. Md. 1966, U.S. Ct. Appeals (4th cir.) 1968, U.S. Supreme Ct. 1973. Law clk. to presiding justice U.S. Dist. Ct. Md. and U.S. Ct. of Appeals 4th cir., 1965-66; assoc. Piper & Marbury, Balt., 1966-71, ptnr., 1973-87; asst. atty. gen. Atty. Gen. Md., 1971-73; judge U.S. Bankruptcy Ct., Balt., 1987—. Adj. faculty U. Md. Sch. Law, 1987, 90-99. Pres. Dismas Ho., Balt. Inc., 1969—; trustee Enoch Pratt Free Libr., Balt., 1977-93. Fellow Am. Coll. Bankruptcy, Md. Bar Found.; mem. Md. State Bar Assn., Anne Arundel County Bar Assn., Paca/Brent Am. Inn of Ct. (pres. 1993-94). Office: US District Court US Courthouse 101 W Lombard St Ste 9442 Baltimore MD 21201-2906

DE RHAM, CASIMIR, JR., lawyer; b. N.Y.C., Sept. 5, 1924; s. Casimir and Lucy Lathrop (Patterson) de Rham; m. Elizabeth Moran Evarts, June 9, 1945; children: Elizabeth Morgan, Henry Casimir, Rufus Patterson, Jeremiah Evarts. Student, Yale U., 1943-44; AB, Harvard U., 1946, JD, 1949. Bar: Mass. 1949, U.S. Dist. Ct. Mass. 1949. Assoc. Palmer & Dodge, Boston, 1949-51, 52-55, ptnr., 1956-94, of counsel, 1994—. Dir. Cambridge Trust Co., Cambridge Bancorp, 1967-99, hon. dir., 1999-2002. Trustee Mount Auburn Hosp., Cambridge, Mass., 1962-93, pres., 1966-77, chmn. bd. dirs., 1977-80, treas., 1993—, The Mount Auburn Found., Inc., 1985-91, 93-96, Commonwealth Sch., Boston, 1958-2002, chmn. bd. dirs., 1966-87, bd. advisers, 2002—, St. Mark's Sch., Southborough, Mass., 1962-74, Cambridge Cmty. Found., 1985—; overseer, dir. Boys and Girls Clubs of Boston Inc., 1956-93, sec., 1973-93, sr. adv. bd., 1993—; dir. Ctr. for Blood Rsch. Inc., Boston, 1964-90, clk., 1964-84, hon. trustee, 1990—; trustee, sec. Sterling and Francine Clark Art Inst., Williamstown, Mass., 1973-95, hon. trustee, 1995—; dir. Women's Ednl. and Indsl. Union, Boston, 1975-98; dir., treas. Florence Evans Bushee Found., Boston, 1982-94; trustee Campbell & Hall Charity Fund, Boston, 1981—; dir. Olivetti Found. Inc., Boston, 1960—, treas., 1983-94, clk., 1960-94; trustee Little Harbor Chapel, Portsmouth, N.H., 1959—; fin. adv. com. Cambridge Hist. Soc., 1980-91, chmn., 1988-90; chmn. Cambridge Rep. City Com., 1954-58; mem. Mass. Rep. State Com., 1960-69; alt. del. Rep. Nat. Conv., 1964, 68; mem. exec. com. Permanent Fund Soc., The Boston Found., 1993-94. Capt. USMCR, 1943-46, 51-52. Mem. ABA, Mass. Bar Assn., Boston Bar Assn., Cambridge-Arlington-Belmont Bar Assn. (pres. 1982-83), Am. Bar Found., St. Botolph Club (Boston), The Country Club (Brookline, Mass.), Masons (Harvard Lodge), Am. Legion. Episcopalian. Avocations: reading, tennis, politics. Estate planning, Probate (including wills, trusts), Estate taxation. Home: 47 Lakeview Ave Cambridge MA 02138-3255 Office: Palmer & Dodge Prudential Ctr 111 Huntington Ave Boston MA 02199-7613 E-mail: cderham@palmerdodge.com.

DERMAN, EMRE, lawyer; b. Istanbul, Turkey, Aug. 9, 1967; s. Mehmet Ugur and Emine Gul Derman; m. Sebnem Durhan, June 25, 1994; children: Ege, Yunus. LLB, Istanbul U., 1988; LLM, Harvard U., 1989. Assoc. White & Case, N.Y.C., 1988—90, Istanbul, 1990—94; counsel EBRD, England, 1994—95; assoc. White & Case, England, 1995—96, 1996—98, ptnr., 1998—. Mergers and acquisitions, Banking, Corporate, general.

DE ROECK, MARTINE M. lawyer; b. Antwerp, Belgium, Dec. 7, 1965; Cand. Jur., UFSIA, Antwerp, 1985; Lic. Jur., UIA, Antwerp, 1988; LLM, U. Chgo., 1989. Bar: Brussels 1989, Antwerp 1997. Assoc. De Bandt, Van Hecke & Lagae, Brussels, 1989—96, ptnr., 1997—2001, Loyens, Brussels, 2001—. Contbr. articles to profl. jours. Scholar, Rotary Found., Belgium, 1988. Corporate, general, Commercial, contracts (including sales of goods; commercial financing), Banking. Office: Loyens Frankrylei 38 2000 Antwerp Belgium

DE ROE DEVON, The Marchioness See GERRINGER, ELIZABETH

DERON, EDWARD MICHAEL, lawyer; b. Detroit, Dec. 18, 1945; m. Jana Lene Berlenbach, Aug. 12, 1977. BS, Wayne State U., 1968, JD cum laude, 1972; LLM in Taxation, NYU, 1973. Bar: Mich. 1972, U.S. Ct. Appeals (6th cir.) 1973, U.S. Tax Ct. 1974. Assoc. Evans & Luptak, Detroit, 1973-79, ptnr., 1980—. Contbr. chpt. to book. With U.S. Army, 1969-71, ETO, Germany. Mem.: ABA, Fin. and Estate Planning Coun. Met. Detroit, Detroit Met. Bar Assn. (co-chmn. taxation com. 1984—86), Mich. Bar Assn. (taxation sect., chmn. estates and trusts com. 1994—96, taxation sect. coun. 1996—99, editor Mich. Tax Lawyer 1998—99, sec. 1999—2000, treas. 2000—01, vice-chmn. 2001—02, chmn. 2002—03), KC, Rotary, Detroit Athletic Club. Corporate, general, Estate planning, Taxation, general. Office: Evans & Luptak 7457 Franklin Rd Ste 250 Bloomfield Hills MI 48301 also: 18720 Mack Ave Ste 220 Grosse Pointe Farms MI 48236 E-mail: ederon@evansluptak.com.

DERRICK, GARY WAYNE, lawyer; b. Enid, Okla., Nov. 3, 1953; s. John Henry and Leota Elaine (Glenn) D.; m. Susan Adele Goodwin, Dec. 22, 1979 (div. June 1981); m. Francys Hollis Johnson, May 3, 1986; children: Meghan, Drew, Jane. BA in History, English, Okla. State U., 1976; JD, U. Okla., 1979. Bar: Okla. 1979. Assoc. Andrews, Davis, Legg, Bixler, Milsten & Price, Oklahoma City, 1979-84, ptnr., 1985-90; of counsel McKinney, Stringer & Webster, P.C., Oklahoma City, 1990-93; ptnr. Derrick & Briggs, LLP, Oklahoma City, 1994—. Active Securities Law and Acctg. Group, Oklahoma City, 1979—; chmn. Gen. Corp. Act Commn., Okla., 1984—, chmn. Securities Liaison Com., Okla., 1985-86; lectr. sem. Okla. Corp. Act, 1986—. Conbg. author: Oklahoma Business Organizations. Mem. Okla. State U. Found., Stillwater, 1983—89, Univ. Found., Norman, 1982—; mem. condr.'s cir. Okla. Symphony Orch., 1981—88; chmn. constn. and canons com. Episcopal Diocese of Okla., 1999—; bd. dirs. Historic Preservation, Inc., 1990—. Mem.: ABA (taxation and corp. sect. , banking and bus. law sect.), Am. Soc. Corp. Secs. (pres. Okla.-Ark. chot. 1994—95), Oklahoma County Bar Assn. (bd. govs. young lawyers divsn. 1981—82), Okla. Bar Assn. (chmn. bus. assn. sect. 1985—87, outstanding contbn. to continuing legal edn., Earl Sneed award 1997), Oklahoma City Boat Club, Oklahoma City Golf and Country Club. Republican. Episcopalian. Avocations: sailing, violin. Securities, Corporate, general. Home: 500 NW 15th St Oklahoma City OK 73103-2102 Office: Derrick & Briggs LLP Bank One Ctr 20th Fl 100 N Broadway Ave Oklahoma City OK 73102-8606 E-mail: derrick@derrickandbriggs.com.

DERRICK, RAYMOND TODD, lawyer; b. Delhi, La., Mar. 1, 1967; AA, Enterprise State Jr. Coll., Enterprise, Ala., 1988; BA magna cum laude, U. Ala., 1990, JD, 1994. Bar: Ala. 1994, U.S. Dist. Ct. (mid. dist.) Ala. 1994, U.S. Ct. Appeals (11th cir.) 1995, U.S. Dist. Ct. (no. dist.) Ala. 1998. Ptnr. Cobb, Shealy, Crum & Derrick, Dothan, Ala., 1994—. Served with U.S. Army, 1985-92, with USNGR, 1985-92. Mem. Ala. Def. Lawyers, Ala. Trial Lawyers, Houston County Bar (pres. elect), Phi Beta Kappa. General civil litigation. Office: Cobb & Shealy PO Box 6346 Dothan AL 36302-6346

DERSHOWITZ, ALAN MORTON, lawyer, educator; b. Bklyn., Sept. 1, 1938; s. Harry Dershowitz and Claire Dershowotz; m. Carolyn Cohen; children: Elon Marc, Jamin Seth, Ella Kaille Cohen Dershowitz. BA magna cum laude, Bklyn. Coll., 1959, LLD, 2001; LLB magna cum laude, Yale U., 1962; MA (hon.) , Harvard Coll., 1967; LLD (hon.) , Yeshiva U., 1989; PhD (hon.) , Haifa U., 1993; LLD (hon.) , Syracuse U., 1997, Hebrew Union Coll., Monmouth Coll., Bklyn. Coll., 2001. Bar: D.C. 1963, Mass. 1968, U.S. Supreme Ct. 1968. Law clk. to chief judge David L. Bazelon, U.S. Ct. Appeals, 1962—63; to justice Arthur J. Goldberg, U.S. Supreme Ct., 1963—64; mem. faculty Harvard Law Sch., 1964—, prof. law, 1967—, Felix Frankfurter Prof. of Law, 1993—; fellow Ctr. for Advanced Study of Behavioral Scis., 1971—72. Cons. to dir. NIMH, 1967—69, Pres.'s Commn. Civil Disorders, 1967, Pres.'s Com. Causes Violence, 1968, NAACP Legal Def. Fund, 1967—68, NIMH's Pres.'s Commn. Marijuana and Drug Abuse, 1972—73, Coun. on Drug Abuse, 1972—, Ford Found. Study on Law and Justice, 1973—76; rapporteur Twentieth Century Fund Study on Sentencing, 1975—76. Author (with others): Psychoanalysis, Psychiatry and the Law, 1967, Criminal Law: Theory and Process, 1974, The Best Defense, 1982, Reversal of Fortune: Inside the von Bulow Case, 1986, Taking Liberties: a Decade of Hard Cases, Bad Laws and Bum Raps, 1988, Chutzpah, 1991, Contrary to Popular Opinion, 1992, The Abuse Excuse, 1994, The Advocate's Devil, 1994, Reasonable Doubts, The Vanishing American Jew, 1997, Sexual McCarthyism: Clinton, Starr and the Emerging Constitutional Crisis, 1998, Just Revenge, 1999, The Genesis of Justice, 2000, Supreme Injustice, 2001, Letters to a Young Lawyer, 2001, Shouting Fire, 2002; contbr. articles to profl. jours., with others: America Declares Independence, 2003, with others: America Declares Independence, 2003; editor-in-chief: Yale Law Jour., 1961—62. Chmn. civil rights com. New England region Anti-Defamation League, B'nai B'rith, 1980—85; bd. dirs. ACLU, 1968—71, 1972—75, Assembly Behavioral and Social Scis. at NAS, 1973—76. Fellow Guggenheim, 1978—79. Mem.: Order of Coif, Phi Beta Kappa. Jewish. Office: Harvard Law Sch 1575 Massachusetts Ave Cambridge MA 02138-2801

DERZAW, RICHARD LAWRENCE, lawyer; b. N.Y.C., Mar. 6, 1954; s. Ronald Murray and Diana (Diamond) D.; m. Susan Katz, 1993. BA magna cum laude, Fairleigh Dickinson U., 1976; JD, Ohio No. U., 1979. Bar: Fla. 1979, U.S. Dist. Ct. (so. dist.) Fla. 1981, U.S. Ct. Appeals (5th cir.) 1981, U.S. Ct. Appeals (11th cir.) 1981, U.S. Ct. Appeals (2d cir.), 1988, N.Y. 1982, N.C. 1995, U.S. Dist. Ct. (so. dist.) N.Y. 1985, U.S. Dist. Ct. (ea.

dist.) N.Y., 1986, U.S. Tax Ct. 1986, U.S. Supreme Ct., 1988. Sole practice, Boca Raton, Fla., 1979-82, N.Y.C., 1982—. Mem. ABA, N.Y. State Bar Assn., N.C. Bar Assn., Fla. Bar Assn., Am. Arbitration Assn., Assn. of Bar of City of N.Y., Fed. Bar Coun., Lions of Boca Raton (treas. 1981-82), Phi Alpha Delta, Phi Zeta Kappa, Phi Omega Epsilon. General civil litigation, Commercial, contracts (including sales of goods; commercial financing), Corporate, general. Office: 477 Madison Ave New York NY 10022 E-mail: derzlaw@aol.com.

DE SALVA, CHRISTOPHER JOSEPH, lawyer, consultant; b. Milw., June 16, 1950; s. Salvatore Joseph and Elaine Mae De S.; m. Erika Marie De Salva, May 24, 1975; 1 child, Jessica Anne. BA in Polit. Sci., St. Vincent Coll., 1972; JD summa cum laude, Am. Coll. Law, 1987; MBA, Calif. Coast U., 1993, postgrad., 1994. Bar: Calif. 1994, U.S. Dist. Ct. (ctrl. dist., so. dist.) Calif. 1995, U.S. Ct. Fed. Claims 1995, U.S. Tax Ct. 1995, U.S. Supreme Ct., 2000. Founder, owner C.J. De Salva & Assocs. Investment and Mktg. Svcs. of La Quinta (now C.J. De Salva & Assocs., La Quinta, 1979—; pvt. practice La Quinta, Calif., 1994-98, Indio, Calif., 1994—, San Diego, 1996-98. Ceo, pres. The Kings Vault Gallery, Inc., 1985; adj. faculty property law Am. Coll. Law, Brea, Calif., 1989-90, 92-95; life and disability ins. agent C.J. De Salva Ins. Agency 1978—; real estate broker De Salva Realty Calif., 1980—, realtor, 1985-94; tax cons., preparer Christopher De Salva Tax Cons.; cons. Christopher De Salva Bus. and Mgmt. Cons.; lectr. property law. Am. Coll. Law. Author: NAFTA, The Hidden Agenda, 1995. 1st lt. USMC, 1974-77. Recipient Am. Jurisprudence scholarship award Am. Coll. Law. Mem. ABA, Assn. Trial Lawyers, Vietnam Era Vet., Vet. of Latin Am., Nat. Soc. Pub. Accts (cert. 1984), Calif. Bar Assn. Avocations: music, sports, writing songs, flying. General civil litigation, Criminal, Estate taxation. Office: 45-902 Oasis St Ste D Indio CA 92201

DESANTO, JAMES JOHN, lawyer; b. Chgo., Oct. 12, 1943; s. John Joseph and Erminia Asunda (Cassano) DeS.; m. Denise Clare Caneva, Feb. 3, 1968; children: Carrie Ann, James Thomas, John Joseph. BA, U. Ill., 1965; JD, DePaul U., 1969. Bar: Ill. 1969, U.S. Dist. Ct. (no. dist.) Ill. 1969, U.S. Ct. Appeals (7th cir.) 1972, U.S. Supreme Ct. 1974; cert. mediator 19th Jud. Circuit, Ill., 1996. Asst. state's atty., Waukegan, Ill., 1969-72; assoc. Finn, Geiger & Rafferty, Waukegan, 1972-74; ptnr. Rawles, Katz & DeSanto, Waukegan, 1975-80; pvt. practice, Waukegan, 1980-88; sr. ptnr. DeSanto & Bonamarte, Waukegan, 1988-91; pvt. practice, Libertyville, Ill., 1991—, James J. DeSanto and Assocs., 1992-99; ptnr. DeSanto, Morgan & Mittelman, Libertyville, 1999—. Lectr. in trial technique and practice Ill. Inst. for CLE and Ill. Bar Assn.; lectr. in bus. law Coll. of Lake County, 1974-84; bd. dirs. Ill. State Bar Assn. Mut. Ins. Co., 1989—, chair com. on fin. and investment 1995-97, 2000-01, sec./treas., 1999—, 2d v.p., 2001-02, 1st v.p., 2002—, chmn. bd. dirs., 2003—. Co-editor Tort Trends newsletter, 1988-91. Trustee Village of Libertyville, 1991-93; chairperson parish pastoral coun. St. Joseph's Ch., Libertyville, 2000-02. Fellow Ill. Bar Inst.; mem. ATLA, State Bar Assn. (mem. ad hoc com. profl. quality in practice of law, 1995—, ins. law sect. coun., 2001—), Ill. State Bar Assn., Lake County Bar Assn. (sec. 1979-80, 2d v.p. 1991-92, pres. 1993-94), Lake County Trial Lawyers Assn. (sec. 1985—), Jefferson Inns of Ct., Libertyville Rotary (pres. 1990-91). Avocations: golf, fishing. Federal civil litigation, State civil litigation, Personal injury (including property damage). Home: 1209 St William Dr Libertyville IL 60048-1275 Office: 712 Florsheim Dr Libertyville IL 60048-5270 E-mail: desanto@iconnect.net.

DESCHAMPS, DELPHINE, lawyer; b. Nevilly sur Seine, France, Sept. 25, 1964; d. Andre Deschamps and Georgette Catelan; m. Jean Pierre Claude Marcel Martel. Grad., Dauphine Bus. Sch., Paris. Lawyer Rambaud Martel, Paris, 1991—, ptnr., 1996—. Mem.: Paris Bar Assn. (registered lawyer), Juristes Associes, Euronext, Cercle Foch, Paris Polo Club. Office: Rambaud Martel 25 Blvd de L Amiral Bruix 75782 Paris France

DESCHAMPS, MARIE, judge; b. Repentigny, Que., Can., Oct. 2, 1952; d. Jean Deschamps and Gisele Gagnon; 2 children. LLL, U. Montreal, 1974; LLM, McGill U., 1983. Bar: Que. 1975. With Martineau, Walker, 1975—76, Sylvestre & Matte, 1976—77, Rouleau, Rumanek & Sirois, 1977—80; apptd. Que. Supreme Ct., 1990; with Byers Casgrain, 1980—90; apptd. Que. Ct. Appeal, 1992—2002; justice Supreme Ct. Can., Ottawa, Canada, 2002—. Bd. dirs. U. Montreal, 1989—91, U. Montreal Alumni Assn., 1986—91. Office: Supreme Ct Can 301 Wellington St Ottawa ON Canada K1A 0J1

DE SEAR, EDWARD MARSHALL, lawyer; b. Bradenton, Fla., Oct. 27, 1946; s. Robert Ashland and Shirley Ethelwyne (Griffin) De S.; m. Patricia Gail Healy, Aug. 8, 1970; children: Emily, Andrew. AB, Columbia Coll., 1968; JD, U. Va., 1973. Bar: N.Y. 1974. Ptnr. Brown & Wood, N.Y.C., 1973-82; v.p. Salomon Bros., Inc., N.Y.C., 1982-88; ptnr. Milbank, Tweed Hadley & McCloy, N.Y.C., 1988-93, Orrick, Herrington & Sutcliffe, LLP, N.Y.C., 1993—, head structured fin. group, 1998—. Mem. secondary schs. com. Columbia U., N.Y.C., 1984—. Mem. ABA, Phi Gamma Delta. Republican. Episcopalian. Finance, Municipal (including bonds), Securities. Office: Orrick Herrington Sutcliffe LLP 666 5th Ave New York NY 10103-1798

DESMOND, SUSAN FAHEY, lawyer; b. Greenville, Miss., Feb. 24, 1961; d. Richard Paul and Bonnie Jean (Williams) Fahey; m. John Michael Desmond; May 28, 1994; children: Meghan, Kelsey. BA in English and History, U. Miss., 1982; JD, U. Tenn., 1985. Bar: Miss. 1985, Colo. 1996, La. 1998. Assoc. Robertshaw, Terney & Noble, Greenville, Miss., 1985-86, Miller, Milam & Moeller, Jackson, Miss., 1986-89, Phelps Dunbar, Jackson, Miss., 1989-92, ptnr., 1992-97, New Orleans, 1998—2003; shareholder Watkins, Ludlam, Winter and Stennis, P.A., Gulfport, Miss., 2003—. Author: Employment Issues for Hospital Supervisors, 1996; editor: Mississippi Pro Bono Material, 1989. Bd. dirs. Am. Cancer Soc. Hinds County Unit, Jackson, Miss., 1990-96, YMCA Greater New Orleans, 2002-03. Mem. Jackson Young Lawyers (dir. 1991-93, merit award 1988), Am. Bar Assn./Young Lawyers (labor com. chmn., Chgo., 1990-92), Miss. Bar Assn. (dir. 1990-92, Outstanding Young Lawyer 1997). Republican. Roman Catholic. Avocations: tennis, reading. Civil rights, Immigration, naturalization, and customs, Labor (including EEOC, Fair Labor Standards Act, labor-management relations, NLRB, OSHA). Office: Watkins Ludlam Winter Stennis PA 2510 14th St Ste 1010 Gulfport MS 39502 E-mail: sdesmond@watkinsludlam.com.

DESO, ROBERT EDWARD, JR., lawyer; b. Albany, N.Y., Mar. 20, 1943; s. Robert Edward and Mary Audrey (Donahue) D.; m. Alice Rae Jones, Oct. 28, 1967; children: Robert, Susan, Karen, Kathleen. BSFS, Georgetown U., 1965; JD, U. Va., 1968. Bar: Va. 1968, D.C. 1973, U.S. Ct. Mil. Appeals 1968, U.S. Dist. Ct. D.C. 1977, U.S. Dist. Ct. (ea. dist.) Va. 1981, U.S. Ct. Claims 1975, U.S. Ct. Appeals (D.C. cir.) 1988, U.S. Ct. Appeals (4th cir.) 2003, U.S. Tax Ct. 2003. Spl. asst. to Judge Advocate Gen. U.S. Army-Pentagon, Washington, 1972-73; asst. gen. counsel Met. Police Dept., Washington, 1973-75, dep. gen. counsel, 1975-78; ptnr./prin. Deso & Greenberg, P.C., Washington, 1978-90; ptnr., prin. Deso, Thomas, Stien & Weitzman, Washington, 1990—2001. Researcher/author: Law at War, 1975. Scoutmaster Boy Scouts Am., Falls Church, Va., 1981-84; legis. chmn. PTA, McLean, Va., 1985-88. Capt. U.S. Army. 1968-73. Decorated Bronze Star medal. Mem. ABA, Va. Bar Assn., Bar Assn. of D.C. Lodges: Fraternal Order of Police. Roman Catholic. General civil litigation, General practice, Labor (including EEOC, Fair Labor Standards Act, labor-management relations, NLRB, OSHA). Office: Deso Thomas Buckley & Stien PC 1828 L St NW Ste 660 Washington DC 20036-5112 E-mail: redeso@dtswlaw.com.

DE SOUZA, WILLIAM JEREMY, solicitor; b. London, Feb. 26, 1945; s. Guilherme Chambers and Vera Constance (Hayter) de S.; m. Caroline Lilian Elsie Adams, Jan. 30, 1988; 1 child, Amelia Cara Vera. MA in Jurisprudence, Oxford (Eng.) U., 1966. Articled clk. Farrer & Co., London, 1967-69, asst. solicitor, 1970-73, assoc., 1974-76, ptnr., 1976-96, cons., 1996-99, White & Bowker, Winchester, Eng., 1999—. Co-author: The Property Investor & VAT, 1990, The Conveyancer's Tax Primer, 1999; editor: (loose leaf series) Land Taxation, 1991—; contbr. articles to profl. jours. including The Brit. Tax Rev., Pvt. Client Bus., Taxation, The Tax Jour., The Estates Gazette, Trusts & Estates Tax Jour., Environ. Law Rev. Mem. The Law Soc. (corp. tax subcom. 1989-92), City of Westminster and Holborn Law Soc. (revenue com. 1984—, chmn. 1995-), Royal Inst. Internat. Affairs, Brooks Club. Conservative. Anglican. Office: White & Bowker 19 St Peter St Winchester SO23 8BU England E-mail: jeremy.desouza@wandb.co.uk.

D'ESPOSITO, JULIAN C., JR., lawyer; b. N.Y.C., Aug. 6, 1944; BS, Loyola U., 1966; JD cum laude, Northwestern U., 1969. Bar: Ill. 1969, U.S. Dist. Ct. (no. dist.) 1969. Counsel to Gov. Ill., 1977-81; ptnr. in charge Chgo. office Mayer, Brown, Rowe & Maw. Chmn. Winnetka Plan Commn., 1985-89; mem. Ill. Med. Ctr. Commn., 1987-94; dir. Ill. Capital Devel. Bd., 1994-95; chmn. Ill. State Toll Hwy. Authority, 1995-99. Co-editor-in-chief Jour. Criminal Law, Criminology & Police Sci., Northwestern U., 1968-69. Mem. ABA. Office: Mayer Brown Rowe & Maw 190 S La Salle St Ste 3100 Chicago IL 60603-3441

DESPRES, LEON MATHIS, lawyer, former city official; b. Chgo., Feb. 2, 1908; s. Samuel and Henrietta (Rubovits) D.; m. Marian Alschuler, Sept. 10, 1931; children— Linda Baskin, Robert Leon. PhB, U. Chgo., 1927, JD, 1929; DLitt, Columbia Coll., 1990, U. Ill., 2000. Bar: Ill. 1929. Ptnr. Despres, Schwartz and Geoghegan, Chgo.; trial examiner NLRB, Chgo., 1935-37; instr. U. Chgo., 1936, U. Wis., summers 1946-49; alderman 5th Ward Chgo. City Council, 1955-75, parliamentarian, 1979-87. Mem. Chgo. Plan Commn., 1979-89. Mem. Am., Ill., Chgo. bar. assns., Chgo. Council Lawyers, Order of Coif, Phi Beta Kappa. Home: 5830 S Stony Island Ave Apt 10A Chicago IL 60637-2024 Office: 77 W Washington St Chicago IL 60602-2801 E-mail: DSG777@aol.com.

DETERMAN, SARA-ANN, lawyer; b. Palmerton, Pa., Aug. 17, 1938; d. Albert H. and Evelyn (Tucker) Heimbach; m. Dean W. Determan, July 28, 1957 (div. Nov. 1981); children: Dann, David, Steven (dec.); m. Gary Sellers, May 21, 1988. Student, Conn. Coll., 1956-57, Stanford U., 1958; AB, U. Del., 1960; LLB, George Washington U., 1967. Bar: U.S. Dist. Ct. D.C. 1968. Law clk. to sr. judge U.S. Ct. Appeals (D.C. cir.), Edgerton, 1967-68; assoc. Hogan & Hartson, Washington, 1968-75, ptnr., 1975—. Trustee Lawyers Com. for Civil Rights Under Law, Washington, 1982-94, co-chmn., 1994—. Bd. dirs. Mex.-Am. Legal Def. and Ednl. Fund, 1983-88, Women's Legal Def. Fund, 1980-2002. Fellow Am. Bar Found.; mem. ABA (chmn. individual rights sect. 1985-86, commr. legal programs for elderly 1983-89, com. on delivery of legal svcs. 1989-93, mem. consortium on legal svcs.), ACLU (bd. dirs. 1975-92), D.C. Bar (pres. 1990-91). Democrat. Unitarian Universalist. Estate planning, Probate (including wills, trusts), Estate taxation. Office: Hogan & Hartson Columbia Square 555 13th St NW Ste 800E Washington DC 20004-1161

DETHOMASIS, CRAIG CONSTANTINE, lawyer, educator; b. Glen Cove, N.Y., Oct. 2, 1958; AA, U. Fla., 1978, BS, 1980, JD, 1983. Bar: Fla. 1983. Asst. pub. defender Pub. Defender's Office, Gainesville, Fla., 1983-87; atty. Silverman, Wilkov, DeThomasis & Buchanan, Gainesville, 1987-90, DeThomasis & Buchanan P.A., Gainesville, 1990—. Adj. prof. law U. Fla. Coll. Law, Gainesville, 1990—; chmn. grievance com. Fla. Bar 8th Jud. Cir., Gainesville, 1994-97. Bd. dirs. Children's Home Soc.-Mid. Fla. Divsn., Gainesville, 1994—; mem. Leadership Gainesville, Gainesville Co. of C., 1996. Mem. Fla. Assn. Criminal Def. Lawyers (treas., v.p., pres. 1994-96), Eighth Jud. Cir. Assn. Criminal Def. Lawyers, Eighth Jud. Cir. Bar Assn., J.C. Adkins Inn of Ct. (emeritus 1995—). Criminal. Office: DeThomasis & Buchanan PA 1800 N Main St Gainesville FL 32609-8606

DETJEN, DAVID WHEELER, lawyer; b. St. Louis, Jan. 25, 1948; s. Don Wheeler and Shirley (Pence) Detjen; m. Barbara Louise Morgan, Jan. 6, 1973; children: Andrea Marlene, Erika Alexandra. AB magna cum laude, Washington U., 1970, JD with honors, 1973; postgrad., Eberhard-Karls-Universitaet, Tuebingen, Germany, 1969-70. Bar: Mo. 1973, U.S. Ct. Appeals (8th cir.) 1976, U.S. Supreme Ct. 1976, N.Y. 1981. Law clk. to chief judge U.S. Ct. Appeals (8th cir.), St. Louis, 1973-75; assoc. Lewis, Rice, Tucker, Allen & Chubb, St. Louis, 1975-80, Walter, Conston, Alexander & Green, P.C., N.Y.C., 1980-83; ptnr. Walter, Conston, Alexander & Green, N.Y.C., 1983-2000, Alston & Bird LLP, N.Y.C., 2001—, co-chmn. internat. practice group, 2001—. Lectr. law Washington U., St. Louis, 1975—80; bd. dirs. Felix Schoeller Tech. Papers, Inc. Author: (book) Distributorship Agreements in the U.S., 1983, 2d edit., 1989, The Germans in Missouri, 1900-1918: Prohibition, Neutrality and Assimilation, 1985, Licensing Technology and Trademarks in the United States, 1988, 2d edit., 1997, Establishing a United States Joint Venture with a Foreign Partner, 1988, 3d edit., 1993, United States Joint Ventures with International Partners, 2000. Sec. German Forum, N.Y.C., 1988—, bd. dirs., 1995—; co-pres. King=Merritt cmty. Assn., Greenwich, Conn., 1997—; mem. Am. Coun. Germany, N.Y.C., Atlantik-Bruecke, Berlin, St. Louis County Rep. Ctrl. Com., 1976—83, Rep. Town Meeting, Greenwich, 2000—, vice-chmn. labor contracts com., 2002—; mem. nat. coun. Washington U. Law Sch., St. Louis, 1989—; trustee Am. Inst. Contemporary German Studies, Johns Hopkins U., 1999—, corp. sec., 2000—. Recipient Disting. Alumnus award, Washington U. Law Sch., 1998. Mem.: ABA, Order of Coif, German Am. Law Assn., Assn. Bar City of N.Y., N.Y. State Bar Assn. (exec. editor Interant. Law Practicum 1988—, mem. exec. com. internat. law and practice sect. 1999—), German-Am. C. of C. (bd. dirs. 2003—), William G. Eliot Soc. Washington U. (N.Y. chmn. 1993—), German Am. Round Table, Deutscher Verein Club N.Y.C. (bd. dirs. 1994—97, 1999—, v.p., sec. 2000—03), Delta Phi Delta. Presbyterian. Corporate, general, Private international, Mergers and acquisitions. Home: 35 Stonehedge Dr Greenwich CT 06831-3220 Office: Alston & Bird LLP 90 Park Ave Fl 14 New York NY 10016-1301 Fax: 212 210-9444. E-mail: ddetjen@alston.com.

DETTINGER, WARREN WALTER, lawyer; b. Toledo, Feb. 13, 1954; s. Walter Henry and Elizabeth Mae (Zoll) D.; m. Patricia Marie Kasper, June 21, 1975; children: John Robert, Laura Marie. BS cum laude, U. Toledo, 1977, JD magna cum laude, 1980. Bar: Ohio 1980, U.S. Dist. Ct. (no. dist.) Ohio 1980, U.S. Ct. Appeals (6th cir.) 1980, U.S. Tax Ct. 1981. Law clk. to presiding judge U.S. Ct. Appeals (6th cir.), Grand Rapids, Mich., 1980-81; assoc. Fuller & Henry, Toledo, 1981-84; atty. Sheller-Globe Corp., Toledo, 1984-87; v.p., gen. counsel Diebold, Inc., Canton, Ohio, 1987—. Mem. ABA, Ohio Bar Assn., Stark County Bar Assn., Am. Corp. Counsel Assn., Mfr.'s Alliance (law coun. II), Brookside Country Club, Phi Kappa Phi. Roman Catholic. Avocations: golf, travel, photography, tennis. Corporate, general, Private international, Mergers and acquisitions. Home: 5237 Birkdale St NW Canton OH 44708-1825 Office: Diebold Inc 5995 Mayfair Rd PO Box 3077 North Canton OH 44720-8077 E-mail: dettinw@diebold.com.

DETTMANN, DAVID ALLEN, lawyer; b. Milw., Mar. 30, 1949; s. Karl F. and Beverly J. (Rusdal) D.; m. Jenee A. Nelson, June 26, 1971; children: Justin, Lisa, Jacob. BA in Acctg./Econs., Luther Coll., 1971; MBA, JD, Drake U., 1974. Bar: Iowa 1974, U.S. Dist. Ct. (so. dist.) Iowa 1974, U.S. Tax Ct. 1974, U.S. Ct. Appeals (8th cir.) 1989, Ill. 1993; CPA, Iowa; accredited estate planner, Am. Coll. Real Estate Lawyers, 1994. Ptnr. Lane & Waterman, Davenport, Iowa, 1974—. Former mem. and pres. ch. coun. Redeemer Luth. Ch.; trustee, vice chair, chair Miss. Valley Regional Blood Ctr., Davenport, 1984—; bd. dirs. Am. Inst. Commerce, Davenport, 1986—1998, Quad-City Estate Planning Coun., Quad Cities, Iowa, Ill., pres., 1990-91. Mem. ABA, AICPA, Am. Coll. Trust and Estate Counsel, Iowa Bar Assn. (title stds. com. 1985-94, real estate & title law sect. coun. 1993—96, 2001-, chair 1994—95, chmn. title guaranty subcom. 1990-94), Real Estate Modernization Com.(chmn. 2002-), Iowa Soc. CPAs, Scott County Bar Assn. (chmn. abstract/real estate com. 1985-95). Avocations: travel, photography, golf. Estate planning, Pension, profit-sharing, and employee benefits, Property, real (including real estate development, water). Office: Lane & Waterman 600 Norwest Bank Bldg 220 N Main St Ste 600 Davenport IA 52801-1987

DETTMER, MICHAEL HAYES, lawyer, former prosecutor; b. Detroit, June 6, 1946; s. Frank Arthur and Mary Frances (Conway) D.; m. Teckla Ann Getts, Aug. 15, 1969; children: Bryn Patrick, Janna Hayes. BS, Mich. State U., 1968; JD, Wayne State U., 1971. Bar: Mich. 1971, U.S. Dist. Ct. (we. dist.) Mich. 1992. Atty. Dettmer Thompon Parsons, Traverse City, Mich., 1972-90; pres., CEO Mich. Lawyer Mutual Ins. Co., Southfield, Grand Rapids, Mich., 1990-93; U.S. atty. we. dist. Mich. U.S. Dept. Justice, Grand Rapids, 1994—2001; sole practice Traverse City, Mich., 2002—; prin. Dettmer, Thompson & Parsons, P.C., Traverse City, Mich., 1987—93; assoc. Parsons, Ringsmuth, Traverse City, Mich., 2003—. Lectr. in field. Contbr. articles to profl. jour. Pres. Traverse City Montessori Ctr., 1978-83; commr. Traverse City Human Rights Commn.; chmn. Grand Traverse County Dem. Party, 1986. Fellow Am. Bar Found., Mich. State Bar Found.; mem. ABA, State Bar of Mich. (pres. 1993-94, commr. No. Mich. and Upper Peninsula 1986-94, exec. com. bd. commrs. 1988-94, com. on legislation 1990-91, task force on professionalism 1988-90, co-chair standing com. on professionalism 1992-94, chair Upper Mich. lawyers com. 1986-94, rep. assembly 1977-80, 88-94, atty. discipline bd. hearing panelist 1980-88), Am. Bd. Trial Advocates, Nat. Bd. Trial Advocacy (cert. 1981-1993). Democrat. Presbyterian. Office: Old Munson Hall 921 W 11th St Ste 2E Traverse City MI 49684*

DEUKMEJIAN, GEORGE, lawyer, former governor; b. Albany, N.Y., June 6, 1928; s. C. George and Alice (Gairdan) D.; m. Gloria M. Saatjian, 1957; children: Leslie Ann, George Krikor, Andrea Diane. BA, Siena Coll., 1949; JD, St. John's U., 1952. Bar: N.Y. 1952, Calif. 1956, U.S. Supreme Ct. 1970. Mem. Calif. Assembly, 1963-67, Calif. Senate, 1967-79, minority leader; atty. gen. State of Calif., 1979-82, gov., 1983-91; former dep. county counsel Los Angeles County.; former ptnr. Sidley & Austin, 1991-2000. Served with U.S. Army, 1953-55. Republican. Episcopalian. Office: 5366 E Broadway Long Beach CA 90803-3549

DEUTSCH, DAVID, lawyer; b. Bklyn., Sept. 9, 1952; s. Morris and Frieda (Rosenblatt) D.; m. Deborah Auerbach, Aug. 21, 1977. BA, SUNY, Buffalo, 1973, JD, 1977; M Pub. Adminstrn., U. Wis., 1974. Bar: N.Y., D.C., U.S. Dist. Ct. D.C., U.S. Ct. Appeals (2d, 5th, 11th, D.C. and 7th cirs.). Law clk. to judge, Buffalo, 1977; jud. clk. CAB, Washington, 1978-79; sr. trial atty. HUD, Washington, 1979-86; sr. assoc. Haley, Bader & Potts, Washington, 1986-87; sr. trial atty. civil rights div. U.S. Dept. Justice, Washington, 1987—. Instr. continuing legal edn. programs Dept. Justice, 1982—, George Washington U., 1984-87; mediator U.S. Dist. Ct., D.C., 1991—; arbitrator D.C. Superior Ct., 1991—. Mem. U.S. Pub. Housing Desegregation Task Force, Washington, 1982-85. Mem. Assn. Trial Lawyers Am., ABA, N.Y. State Bar Assn., D.C. Bar Assn., Phi Beta Kappa. Avocation: Karate. Administrative and regulatory, Civil rights, Federal civil litigation. Home: 11605 W Hill Dr Rockville MD 20852-3750 Office: US Dept Justice Civil Rights Div Spl Litigation 601 D St NW Rm 5630 Washington DC 20004

DEUTSCH, DAVID M. lawyer; b. Dayton, Ohio, July 28, 1943; s. Jacob and Mary Deutsch; m. Joanne Deutsch. BS, Ohio State U., 1965; JD, Samford U., 1969. Bar: Ohio 1969, U.S. Ct. Appeals (4th, 6th cirs.) 1970, U.S. Ct. Appeals (11th cir.) 2000. Pvt. practice, Dayton, 1969—. Mem. head injury re-entry program adv. bd. Miami Valley Hosp., Dayton, 1991—. Chmn. Cmty. Rels. Coun., 1982-87, Supreme Ct. Ohio Commn. Continuing Legal Edn., 1994-99; bd. dirs. Greater Dayton Jewish Fedn., 1982-87; pres. govt. affairs com. Ohio Jewish Cmtys., 1986-88; bd. dirs., v.p. Temple Israel, Dayton, 1989-91. Mem. Ohio State Bar Assn. (sec. 1981-82), Ohio Acad. Trial Lawyers (governing trustee 1984-90), Dayton Bar Assn. Democrat. Avocations: skiing, jogging. Office: David M Deutsch Co LPA 208 W Monmument Ave Dayton OH 45402 E-mail: david@deutschatlaw.com.

DEUTSCH, STEPHEN B. lawyer; b. N.Y.C., Jan. 3, 1944; s. A. William and Rose (Berkowitz) D.; m. Jane M. Burnat, Nov. 23, 1986; children: Nancy, Jeffrey, Elizabeth. SB, MIT, 1965, PhD, 1969; JD, Harvard U., 1974. Bar: Mass. 1975, U.S. Dist. Mass., U.S. Ct. Appeals (1st cir.), U.S. Supreme Ct., U.S. Patent Office. Law clk. Supreme Judicial Ct. Mass., Boston, 1974-75; assoc. Foley, Hoag & Eliot, Boston, 1975-80, ptnr., 1981—. Mem. ABA, Mass. Bar Assn., Boston Bar Assn. Intellectual property, Labor (including EEOC, Fair Labor Standards Act, labor-management relations, NLRB, OSHA), Patent. Office: Foley Hoag LLP 155 Seaport Blvd Boston MA 02210

DEVANEY, DONNA BROOKES, lawyer; b. Orlando, Fla., Sept. 7, 1972; d. Edward Nolan and Carolyn (Jessen) B.; m. David Brooks DeVaney, Jr., May 24, 1997; children: Megan Kate, Sarah Grace. BS, Auburn U., 1993; JD cum laude, Stetson U., 1997. Bar: Fla. 1997, U.S. Dist. Ct. (mid. dist.) Fla. 1997, U.S. Dist. Ct. (so. and no. dists.) Fla. 1999, U.S. Ct. Appeals (11th cir.) 1999. Atty. Carlton Fields PA, Tampa, Fla., 1997—. Vol. Hillsborough Reads, Tampa, 1998-2000. Mem. ABA, Fed. Bar Assn., Fla. Bar Assn., Hillsborough County Bar Assn. (bd. dirs. young lawyers divsn.), Ferguson White Inn of Ct., Alpha House of Tampa, Inc. (bd. dirs.). Avocations: boating, swimming, running. Federal civil litigation, State civil litigation, Condemnation (eminent domain). Office: Carlton Fields One Harbour Pl Tampa FL 33602-5729 E-mail: ddevaney@carltonfields.com.

D'EVEGNEE, CHARLES PAUL, lawyer; b. Liege, Belgium, Aug. 4, 1939; came to U.S., 1959; s. Charles Clement and Fernande Francoise (Godet) Devignez; m. Marie-Therese L. Barnich, Apr. 17, 1962; children: Chantal E., Charles D. BA, Brigham Young U., 1966; MA, U. Conn., Storrs, 1969; JD, U. Conn., West Hartford, 1974. Bar: Va. 1991, U.S. Banktuptcy Ct. (ea. dist.-Richmond divsn.), U.S. Dist. Ct. 9ea. dist.) Va., U.S. Ct. Appeals (4th cir.), U.S. Supreme Ct. Group pension underwriter Conn. Gen. Life Ins. Co., Bloomfield, 1969-72; legal cons. Frank B. Hall & Co., N.Y.C., 1974-76; regional counsel Meidinger & Assocs., Richmond, Va., 1976-78; dir. Office Benefits Devel., Commonwealth of Va., Richmond, 1978-91; pvt. practice, Ashland, Va., 1991—. Co-author: European Antitrust Law, 1976. Mem. Va. Gov.'s U.S. Savs. Bond Com., Richmond, 1986; rep. exec. bd. State's United Appeals of Greater Richmond Community Chest, 1989. With U.S. Army, 1960-63. Mem. ABA, Va. State Bar Assn., Hanover Bar Assn., Richmond Bar Assn. Avocations: travel, landscaping, sports. General practice, Private international, Workers' compensation. Home: 6034 Northfall Creek Pkwy Mechanicsville VA 23111-7522 Office: 6034 Northfall Creek Pkwy Mechanicsville VA 23111 E-mail: cdevegnee@aol.com.

DEVENS, PAUL, lawyer; b. Gary, Ind., June 8, 1931; s. Zenove and Anna (Brilla) Dewenetz; m. Setsuko Sugihara, Aug. 14, 1955; children: Paula, Vladimir, Mignon. BA in Econs. cum laude, Ind. U., 1954; LLB, Columbia U., 1957. Bar: N.Y. 1958, U.S. Dist. Ct. Hawaii 1960, Hawaii 1961, U.S. Ct. Appeals (9th cir.) 1962, U.S. Ct. Internat. Trade 1963, U.S. Supreme Ct. 1970. Pvt. practice law, N.Y.C., 1958-60; ptnr. Lewis, Saunders & Key, Honolulu, 1960-69; corp. counsel City and County of Honolulu, 1969-72, mng. dir., 1973-75; ptnr. Devens, Nakano, Saito, Lee, Wong & Ching,

Honolulu, 1975-94, of counsel, 1994—2002; ret., 2002. Judge Nuclear Claims Tribunal, Majuro, Republic of the Marshall Islands, 1988-90. Mem. Japan-Hawaii Econ. Coun., 1975-95, Honolulu Charter Reorgn. Com., 1979-80, Pacific and Asian Affairs Coun., 1983; trustee Japan-Am. Soc. Honolulu, 1981—, pres., 1987-89; chmn. bd. dirs. Nat. Assn. Japan-Am. Socs., 1989-91; mem. bd. govs. Japanese Cultural Ctr., Hawaii, 1989-94, mem. bd. dirs., v.p., 1994-96, chmn. bd. dirs., 1996-97. Decorated Imperial Order of the Sacred Treasure, Gold Rays with Neck ribbon Govt. of Japan, 1993. Democrat. Eastern Orthodox. Federal civil litigation, State civil litigation, Property, real (including real estate development, water). Office: Devens Nakano Saito Lee Wong & Ching 220 S King St Ste 1600 Honolulu HI 96813-4597

DEVGUN, DHARMINDER SINGH, lawyer; b. Dudley, U.K., Nov. 27, 1967; came to U.S., 1990; s. Mohan Singh and Kirpal Kaur Devgun; m. Amrit Bhooi, May 4, 1994; 1 child, Kavya Devgun. LLB with honors, U. Birmingham, 1990; JD with high distinction, U. Iowa, 1993. Bar: Minn. 1993, U.S. Ct. Internat. Trade 1997, Eng./Wales 2003. Assoc. Faegre & Benson, Mpls., 1993-96, Doherty, Rumble & Butler, St. Paul, 1996-98; sr. corp. counsel The St. Paul Cos., Inc., 1998-99; assoc. Dorsey & Whitney, Mpls., 1999—2003; ptnr. Lindquist & Vennum P.L.L.P., Mpls., 2003—. Lectr., adj. prof. William Mitchell Coll. of Law, St. Paul, 1994—. Author: Doing Business in the United Kingdom, 1998, Cooperatives, 2000; editor-in-chief Transnational Law and Contemporary Problems, 1992-93; contbr. articles to profl. jours. Mem. Minn. State Bar Assn., Order of Coif. Avocations: writing, computers. Corporate, general, Private international, Mergers and acquisitions. Office: Lindquist & Vennum PLLP 80 S 8th St Minneapolis MN 55402

DEVINE, DICK See DEVINE, RICHARD

DEVINE, DONN, lawyer, genealogist, former city official; b. South Amboy, NJ, Mar. 30, 1929; s. Frank Edward and Emily Theresa (DeRevere) D. m. Elizabeth Cecilia Baldwin, Nov. 23, 1951; children: Edward (dec.), Mary Elizabeth, Martin Joseph. BS, U. Del., 1949; JD (hon.) , Widener U., 1975. Bar: Del. 1975, US Dist. Ct. Del. 1976, US Supreme Ct. 1997; cert. genealogist and cert. genealogy instr. Bd. for Cert. Genealogists; cert. Am. Inst. Cert. Planners. Devel. chemist Allied Chem. Corp., Claymont, Del., 1950-52; newspaper writer, editor corp. publs. Atlas Powder Co., Wilmington, Del., 1952-60; mgmt. cons., 1960-68; dir. renewal planning City of Wilmington, 1968-79, dep. dir. planning, 1979-80, dir. planning, 1981-85; cons. Wilmington City Coun., 1985-01; pvt. practice, 1985-00; archival cons. Cath. Diocese Wilmington, 1989—; of counsel City of Wilmington Law Dept., 2001—. Spl. counsel Del. Div. Alcoholism, Drug Abuse and Mental Health, 1990-93; trustee Bd. for Cert. Genealogists, 1992—; mediator Del. Superior Ct., 1998—. Author: Delaware National Guard, A Historical Sketch, 1968, DeRevere Family of Peekskill, NY, 1982; editor Del. Geneal. Soc. Jour., 1980-81, Cultural Resources Survey of Wilmington, Del., 1982-84; assoc. editor Del. Jour. Corp. Law, 1974-75; assoc editor Professional Genealogy: A Manual for Researchers, Writers, Editors, Lecturers and Librarians, 2001. Past bd. dir. Wilmington Small Bus. Devel. Corp., Wilmington Econ. Devel. Corp.; past officer Delmarva Ecumenical Agy.; emeritus bd. dirs., past officer Generations Home Care (formerly Geriatric Svcs. Del.); past officer Christina Cultural Arts Ctr., Cath. Interracial Coun., Del. chpt. ACLU, Maplewood Housing for Elderly, St. Mary's-St. Patrick's Parish Coun. With USAR, 1950-54; brig. gen. Del. Army N.G., 1954-84, ret. Decorated Meritorious Svc. medal. Mem. Am. Planning Assn. (Peter Larson Achievement award 2002), Am. Chem. Soc., Del. Bar Assn., Del. Soc. SAR (past pres.), Nat. Geneal. Soc. (bd. dir. 1994-2002), Assn. Cath. Diocesan Archivists (bd. dir. 1993-95), Del. Geneal. Soc. (past pres.), Ft. Delaware Soc. (recognition award), Old Bohemia Hist. Soc. (bd. dirs. 1992—), Univ. and Whist Club, Chemists Club NYC, Ancient Order Hibernians, Phi Kappa Phi, Delta Theta Phi. Democrat. Intellectual property, Land use and zoning (including planning). Home: 2004 Kentmere Pkwy Wilmington DE 19806-2014 E-mail: donndevine@aol.com.

DEVINE, EDMOND FRANCIS, lawyer; b. Ann Arbor, Mich., Aug. 9, 1916; s. Frank B. and Elizabeth Catherine (Doherty) DeV.; m. Elizabeth Palmer Ward, Sept. 17, 1955; children: Elizabeth Palmer, Stephen Ward, Michael Edmond, Suzanne Lee. AB, U. Mich., 1937, JD, 1940; LLM, Cath. U. Am., 1941. Bar: Mich. 1940, U.S. Dist. Ct. (ea. dist.) Mich. 1940, U.S. Ct. Appeals (6th cir) 1974, U.S. Supreme Ct. 1975. Spl. agt. FBI, 1941-43; chief asst. prosecutor Washtenaw County (Mich.), Ann Arbor, 1947-53, prosecuting atty., 1953-58; ptnr. DeVine & DeVine, Ann Arbor, 1958-74, DeVine, DeVine, Kantor & Serr, Ann Arbor, 1974-84; sr. ptnr. Miller, Canfield, Paddock & Stone, Ann Arbor, 1984-92, of counsel, 1992—. Asst. prof., adj. prof. U. Mich. Law Sch., 1949-79. Co-author: Criminal Procedure, 1960. Lt. USNR, 1943—46, PTO. Decorated Bronze Star with combat v. Fellow Am. Bar Found. Am. Coll. Trial Lawyers, Mich. Bar Found.; mem. ABA, State Bar Mich. (bd. commrs., chmn. judiciary com. 1976-85, mem. rep. assembly, chmn. rules and calendar com.1971-76, co-chair U.S. Cts. com. 1986-87), Internat. Assn. Def. Counsel, U.S. Supreme Ct. Hist. Soc., Ann Arbor C. of C. (chmn. bd. 1971), Detroit Athletic Club, Barton Hills Country Club, Pres.'s Club. U. Mich., Varsity M Club, Order of Coif, Barristers, Phi Delta Phi, Phi Kappa Psi. Republican. Roman Catholic. Avocations: golf, running, reading. Home: 101 Underdown Rd Ann Arbor MI 48105-1078 Office: Miller Canfield Paddock & Stone 101 N Main St Fl 7 Ann Arbor MI 48104-5507

DEVINE, EUGENE PETER, lawyer; b. Albany, N.Y., Oct. 14, 1948; s. Eugene Peter and Phyllis Jean (Albanese) D.; m. Debra Ann Ziamandanis, Apr. 11, 1992; children: Kimberly, Tracy, Adrianne, Madeline. JD, Union U., 1975. Bar: N.Y. 1975, U.S. Dist. Ct. (no. dist.) N.Y. 1975, U.S. Supreme Ct. 1980. Asst. N.Y. Pub. Defender, Albany County, 1976-85; ptnr. Cooper, Erving & Savage, Albany, 1975-85, Devine, Piedment & Rutnik, 1985-91; chief pub. defender Albany County, 1994—; of counsel Ruberti Girvin & Ferlazzo, 2000—; chief atty. Albany County Dept. Social Svcs., 1985-88. Bd. dirs. Ronald McDonald House, Albany, 1980—, founding mem.; committeman Albany County Dem. Com., 1979—; treas. com. to elect Jim Tully N.Y. State Compt. N.Y. State Compt., 1980, vice chmn. Albany Med. Ctr. Found., 1994—. Mem. Woolferts Roost Country Club, Steuben Athletic Club, Albany Sons of St. Patrick (pres. 1984). Criminal, General practice, Labor (including EEOC, Fair Labor Standards Act, labor-management relations, NLRB, OSHA). Office: Girvin & Ferlazzo 20 Corporate Woods Blvd Albany NY 12211-2362

DEVINE, JAMES I. lawyer; b. Darby, Pa., July 31, 1958; s. Martin J. and Gabrielle M. Devine. BS, U. Notre Dame, 1980; JD, Widener U., 1983. Bar: Pa. 1983, U.S. Dist. Ct. (ea. dist.) Pa. 1983, U.S. Ct. Appeals (3d cir.) 1985. Jud. law clk. Hon. Joseph L. McGlynn Jr. U.S. Dist. Ct. (ea. dist.) Pa., Phila., 1983—84; atty. Dilworth Paxson, 1984—85; ptnr. O'Brian & Ryan, Plymouth Meeting, 1985—91; shareholder James I. Devine & Assocs., 1991—96; atty. pvt. practice, Phila., 1996—2000, Norristown, 2000—. Personal injury (including property damage), Product liability, Professional liability. Office: 509 Swede St Norristown PA 19401

DEVINE, MICHAEL BUXTON, lawyer; b. Des Moines, Oct. 25, 1953; s. Cleatie Hiram, Jr., and Katherine Ann (Buxton) D. Student, St. Peter's Coll., Oxford U., Eng., 1975; BA cum laude, St. Olaf Coll., 1976; MPA, JD, Drake U., 1980; diploma in Advanced Internat. Legal Studies, U. Pacific, Salzburg, Austria, 1986; LLM in Internat. Bus. Legal Studies, U. Exeter, Eng., 1988, postgrad., 1997—; LLM Internat. Comml. Law, Aberdeen Bus. Sch; LLM, Robert Gordon U., Aberdeen, Scotland, 2001—. Bar: Iowa 1980, U.S. Dist. Ct. (no. and so. dists.) Iowa 1980, U.S. Ct. Appeals (8th cir.) 1980, Nebr. 1985, Supreme Ct. 1985, Minn. 1986, D.C. 1986., N.Y. 1987, Wis. 1987, Colo. 1988, N.Y. 1990, U.S. Ct. Appeals (fed. cir.) 1990, U.S. Ct. Internat. Trade 1990, Eng. and Wales, 1995, U.K. Ho. of Lords, 1995, Ct. Justice of the European Com., 1995, No. Ireland, 2000. Assoc. Bump & Haesemeyer, P.C., Des Moines, 1980-85; jud. law clk. Jud. Dept. State of Iowa, 1987-88; assoc. Christianson, Hohnbaum & George, Des Moines, 1989, Pavelic & Levites, P.C., N.Y.C., 1989-92; with chambers Alan Tyrrell, Q.C., London, 1993-94; with legal dept. Philips Electronics U.K., Ltd., London, 1994; with Lafili, Van Crombrugghe & Ptnrs., Brussels, 1995; pvt. practice Des Moines/N.Y.C./London, 1997—; of counsel Pavelic & Levites, P.C., N.Y.C., 1997—. Internat. legal intern Herbert Oppenheimer, Nathan & Vandyk, London, 1986; lectr. in law U. Kent, Canterbury, Eng., 2000-2001. Contbr. articles to profl. jours. Nat. alt. U.S. Presdl. Mgmt. Intern Program, 1980. Scholar St. Olaf Coll., 1972-76 Mem. ABA (sect. internat. law), Fed. Bar Assn. (chmn. state of Iowa SBA export assistance program 1983-85, treas. Iowa chpt. 1984-85, exec. com. 1985-87), N.Y. State Bar Assn. (sec. internat. law), Assn. of Bar of City of N.Y. (coun. internat. affairs 1990-92), Phi Alpha Theta, Pi Alpha Alpha. Presbyterian. Commercial, contracts (including sales of goods; commercial financing), Corporate, general, Private international. Home: 2611 40th St Des Moines IA 50310-3949 Office: 865 3rd Ave New York NY 10022-6202 E-mail: mde1009767@aol.com.

DEVINE, RICHARD A. (DICK DEVINE), lawyer; b. Chgo., Ill., July 5, 1943; m. Charlene DeVine; children: Matt, Karen, Tim, Pete. BA cum laude, Loyola U., 1966; JD cum laude, Northwestern U., 1968. Bar: Ohio 1968, Ill. 1969, U.S. Dist. Ct. (no. dist.) Ill. 1973, U.S. Ct. Appeals (7th cir.) 1983, U.S. Supreme Ct. 1983. Assoc. Squire, Sanders & Dempsey, Cleve., 1968-69; adminstrv. asst. to mayor of Chgo., 1969-72; assoc. Pope, Ballard, Shepard & Fowle, 1972-74; assoc., ptnr. Foran, Wiss & Schultz, 1974-80, ptnr., 1983-85; 1st asst. state's atty. Cook County State's Atty.'s Office, 1980-83; ptnr. Phelan, Pope, Cahill, DeVine & Ouinlan, Ltd., 1985-95, Shefsky Froelich & DeVine Ltd., 1995-96; state's atty. Cook County, 1996—. Lectr. continuing legal edn. IIT Kent Coll. Law, John Marshall U.; co-chair courses on damages in bus. litigation Law Jour. Seminar; judge moot ct. programs Northwestern Law Sch., John Marshall Law Sch.; appointed mem. State Commn. on Accreditation of Criminal Justice; appointed mem. Spl. Commn. on Adminstrn. of Justice in Cook County, chmn. task force on misdemeanor and preliminary hearing cts., chmn. task force on jud. adminstrn.; appointed mem. profl. adv. com. Office of State's Atty. of Cook County, 1984-89; bd. dirs. Cook County Criminal Justice Project; mem. Chgo.-Cook County Criminal Justice Commn., 1971-78; hearing officer Chgo. Bd. Election Commrs., 1984. Mem. editl. bd. Northwestern U. Law Rev., 1966-68, mng. editor, 1967-68; contbr. to law jours. Bd. commrs. Chgo. Park Dist., 1989-93, pres. bd., 1990-93; bd. trustees Loyola Acad., 1982-88, St. Scholastica H.S.; bd. dirs. Chgo. Hist. Soc., 1990-93, Adler Planetarium; pro bono mem., pres. Chgo. Park Dist, 1989-93. Russell Sage fellow in law and social scis. Mem. ABA, Am. Coll. Trial Lawyers (elected), Ill. State Bar Assn., Chgo. Bar Assn. (com. jud. evaluation 1983-88, chmn. legis. assistance and evaluation com., young lawyers sect. 1973-74, vice-chmn. 1974-76, chmn. 1976-77, urban affairs com., mem. local govt. com. 1974-76, faculty young lawyers sect. trial advocacy program, lectr. on continuing legal edn.), Northwestern Law Sch. Alumni Assn. (bd. dirs. 1993—), Ill. State Attys. Assn. (bd. dirs.), Nat. Dist. Attys. Assn. (bd. dirs.). Office: Cook County State Atty 500 Richard J Daley Ctr Chicago IL 60602*

DEVINS, ROBERT SYLVESTER, retired lawyer; b. N.Y.C., Mar. 19, 1949; s. Arthur Sylvester and Judith Delores (Whelan) D. BA, Tulane U., 1971; JD, Emory U., 1978. Bar: Ga. 1978, Fla. 1981, U.S. Dist. Ct. (no. dist.) Ga. 1978, U.S. Tax Ct. 1978, U.S. Ct. Appeals (5th cir.) 1978, U.S. Supreme Ct. 1982, U.S. Dist. Ct. (mid. dist.) Ga. 1994. Pvt. practice, Atlanta, 1978-99; ret., 1999. Lt. USN, 1971-75. Mem. ABA, Internat. Bar Assn. (vice chmn. criminal law sect. 1985-87, chmn. 1987-89. rep. UN Conf. 1987, 89), Inter Am. Bar Assn., Nat. Assn. Criminal Def. Lawyers, Ga. Assn. Criminal Def. Lawyers, Assn. Trial Lawyers Am., Ga. Trial Lawyers Assn., Union International des Avocats. Avocation: reading. General civil litigation, Criminal, Family and matrimonial. Home: Casa Ventosear 2335 S Ocean Blvd Palm Beach FL 33480-5368

DEVLIN, FRANCIS JAMES, lawyer; b. N.Y.C., Apr. 12, 1943; s. Francis James and Marie A. D.; m. Patricia Ann Scheid; children: Christopher James, Kimberley Ann. BA magna cum laude, Providence Coll., 1964; JD, Fordham U., 1967. Bar: N.Y. 1968, Tex. 1979, U.S. Ct. Appeals (5th and 11th cirs.) 1981, U.S. Supreme Ct. 1993. Assoc. Rogers and Wells, N.Y.C., 1967-72; counsel Standard Oil Co. N.J., N.Y.C., 1972, Exxon Corp., N.Y.C., 1973-78, Exxon Co., U.S.A., Houston, 1978-90, sr. counsel, 1990-99, coord. gen. comml. practice group, 1996-99; sr. counsel Exxon Mobil Corp., Fuels Mktg. Co., 1999—, coord. mktg., 1999—2002; spl. counsel Duane Morris, LLP, Houston, 2003—. Articles editor Fordham Law Rev., 1966-67. Bd. dirs. Our Lady of Guadalupe Sch., Houston, 1994-2000, chmn., 1998-2000. Fellow Coll. State Bar Tex.; mem. ABA (vice-chmn. petroleum mktg. com., environment, energy and resources sect.), Tex. State Bar (Bar Jour. com. 1995-98, unauthorized practice of law com. 1989-92), Am. Petroleum Inst. (chmn. subcom. on mktg. law, gen. com. law, chmn. 1990-92, 97-98, vice-chmn. 1992-94, 98-99), Tex. Mid-Continent Oil and Gas Assn. (chmn. mktg. subcom. legal com. 1982-2000), Soc. Friendly Sons of St. Patrick in City N.Y. Republican. Roman Catholic. Antitrust, Franchising, Legislative. Home: Townhouse 112 12625 Memorial Dr Houston TX 77024-4889 Office: Duane Morris LLP 1 Greenway Plz Ste 500 Houston TX 77046 E-mail: fjdevlin@duanemorris.com.

DEVLIN, JAMES RICHARD, lawyer; b. Camden, N.J., July 7, 1950; s. Gerald William and Mary (Hand) D.; children: Grace, Jennifer, Kristen. BS in Indsl. Engring., N.J. Inst. Tech., 1972; JD, Fordham U., 1976. Bar: N.J. 1976, N.Y. 1977, Kans. 2002, U.S. Ct. Appeals (D.C. cir.) 1982. Various mgmt. positions in Long Lines Sect. AT&T, N.Y.C., 1972-76, counsel Long Lines Sect. Bedminster, N.J., 1976-82, counsel N.Y.C., 1982-83, gen. atty. comm. sect. Basking Ridge, N.J., 1983-86; v.p., gen. counsel telephone United Telecomm., Inc., Westwood, Kans., 1987-88; exec. v.p. gen. counsel and external affairs Sprint Corp., Westwood, 1989—. Past pres., bd. dirs. Ctr. for Mgmt. Assistance, Kansas City, Mo., 1993-96 Mem. ABA (past chmn. comm. com. pub. utility law sect.), Am. Arbitration Assn., Fed. Comm. Bar Assn. Administrative and regulatory, Communications, Corporate, general. Home: 12300 Catalina St Leawood KS 66209-2220 Office: Sprint Corp Eisenhower A 6200 Sprint Pkwy Overland Park KS 66251

DEVORE, PAUL CAMERON, lawyer; b. Great Falls, Mont., Apr. 25, 1932; s. Paul Theodore and Maxine (Cameron) DeV.; m. Roberta Humphrey, Feb. 3, 1962; children: Jennifer Ross, Andrew Cameron, Christopher Humphrey. BA, Yale U., 1954; MA, Cambridge U., 1956; JD, Harvard U., 1961. Bar: Wash. 1961. Assoc. Wright, Innis, Simon & Todd, Seattle, 1961-66; ptnr. Davis Wright Tremaine, Seattle, 1967—, chmn. exec. com., 1983-95. Mem. adv. bd. BNA Media Law Reporter, 1978—. Chmn. Seattle C.C., 1967-68, Bush Sch., Seattle, 1976-79, Virginia Mason Med. Found., 1984-85, Virginia Mason Rsch. Ctr., 1983-84, Seattle Found., 1985-87, Children's Hosp. Found., 1993-95; trustee Lakeside Sch., 1995—; chmn. bd. visitors U. Wash. Sch. Comm., 1989-98; pres. A Contemporary Theatre, Seattle, 1972-74; sec. Seattle Art Mus., 1973-2000. Mem. ABA (chmn. forum on comm. law 1981-84), Wash. State Bar Assn. (chmn. sect. corp. bus. and banking law 1981-82, bench, bar, press com. 1984-90), Seattle-King County Bar Assn. (trustee 1975-76), Seattle Tennis Club, Phi Beta Kappa, Beta Theta Phi. Home: 5740 27th Ave NE Seattle WA 98105-5512 Office: Davis Wright Tremaine 2600 Century Sq 1501 4th Ave Ste 2600 Seattle WA 98101-1688 E-mail: camdevore@dwt.com.

DEVRIES, DONALD LAWSON, JR., lawyer; b. Phila., May 1, 1947; s. Donald Lawson and Jeanne (Coleman) DeV.; m. Nancy Shafer, Aug. 10, 1977; children: Donald Lawson III, Emily Shafer; stepdaughter: Alison Brady Beale. BA with honors, Dartmouth Coll., 1969; JD with honors, U. Md., 1973. Bar: Md. 1973, U.S. Dist. Ct. Md. 1973, U.S. Ct. Appeals (4th cir.) 1976, U.S. Ct. Appeals (D.C. cir.) 1989, U.S. Dist. Ct. D.C. 1991. Assoc. Semmes, Bowen & Semmes, Balt., 1973-80, ptnr., chmn. med. malpractice dept., 1980-88; founding and mng. ptnr. Goodell, DeVries, Leech & Dann, Balt., 1988—. Chmn. dept. med. malpractice Semmes, Bowen & Semmes, 1980-88; mem. faculty Md. Inst. Continuing Profl. Edn. for Lawyers, 1984-95; gov.'s task force on Med. Malpractice Ins., 1985; master Am. Inns of Court, 1986-90. Contbr. Md. Law Rev., 1973. Trustee Roland Pk. Country Sch., 1987-94, Woodbourne Ctr., 1981-88; trustee, exec. com. South Balt. Gen. Hosp., 1983-88; mem. Canons and Other Bus. Coms. of Episcopal Diocese Md., 1984-95; vestryman St. David's Ch., 1982-85; bd. dirs. Md. affiliate Am. Heart Assn., 1986-90, co-chmn. Heart Ball, 1986, 87, 88, chmn. solicitation com. Shock Trauma Gala, 1988, 89, co-chmn., 1990, 91, bd. visitors Shock Trauma, 1989-93, chmn. 1990-93; chmn. Emergency Med. Svcs. Bd., Md., 1992—; mem. joint exec./legis. task force on med. malpractice ins., Md., 1985; mem. com. on uninsured persons Gov.'s Commn. on Health Care Policy and Financing, 1988-90. Fellow Am. Coll. Trial Lawyers; mem. ABA (spkr. ann. meeting 1984, moderator, program planner ann. meeting medicine and law com. 1986, 88, vice chmn. medicine and law com. torts and ins. practice sect. 1982-89, med. adv. panel medicine and law com. 1986-87, forum com. health law 1984—, faculty nat. inst. on med. malpractice 1987, 88, 89, 90, chmn. medicine and law com., torts and ins. practice sect. 1988-89), Internat. Assn. Ins. Counsel, Internat. Assn. Def. Counsel (faculty trial acad. 1991, moderator, program planner 1992, vice chmn. med. malpractice com. for newsletters 1989-90, program chmn. 1990-92, chmn. med. malpractice com. 1992-94, chmn. def. counsel com. 1997-99, exec. com. 1999-2002, George W. Yancey Meml. award 1998), Internat. Soc. Barristers, Assn. Def. Trial Attys., Am. Bd. Trial Advocates (pres. Md. chpt. 1993-95, nat. bd. dirs. 1993—), Md. State Bar Assn. (spl. com. on health claims arbitration 1983), Md. Trial Lawyers Assn. (faculty 1983, 85), Md. Assn. Def. Trial Counsel, Def. Rsch. Inst., Wednesday Law Club, Maryland Club, Chesapeake Bay Yacht Club, Center Club, Annapolis Yacht Club. Republican. Personal injury (including property damage), Product liability, Professional liability. Office: Goodell DeVries Leech & Dann LLP 1 South St Ste 2000 Baltimore MD 21202-7314

DEW, THOMAS EDWARD, lawyer; b. Detroit, Feb. 13, 1947; s. Albert Nelson and Irene Theresa (Morris) D.; m. Gail Ruth Tuesink, June 27, 1970. BA, U. Mich., 1969; JD, Detroit Coll. Law, 1974. Bar: Mich. 1974, U.S. Dist. Ct. (ea. dist.) Mich. 1974, U.S. Tax Ct. 1980. Agt. IRS, Detroit, 1969-74; trust officer Ann Arbor (Mich.) Trust Co., 1974-75, asst. v.p., 1975-78; ptnr. Conner, Harbour, Dew, Ann Arbor, 1978-83, Harris, Lax, Guenzel & Dew, Ann Arbor, 1983-87; private practice Thomas E. Dew Profl. Corp., Ann Arbor, 1987-88; prin. Dever and Dew Profl. Corp., Ann Arbor, 1988-99, Wise & Marsac, Detroit, 1999-2001, Berry Moorman, PC, Detroit, 2001—. Lectr. Am. Coll., Bryn Mawr, Pa., 1979-82, Am. Inst. Paralegal Studies, Detroit, 1982; adj. prof. Ave Marie Sch. Law, 2003—. Mem. Ann Harbor Housing Commn., 1979-81, pres. 1981; trustee Ann Arbor Area Cmty. Found. Named Law scholar, Sigma Nu Phi, 1974. Fellow Mich. State Bar Found.; mem. State Bar Mich., Washtenaw County Bar Assn., Washtenaw Estate Planning Coun. (pres. 1979-80), New Enterprise Forum. Republican. Presbyterian. Corporate, general, Probate (including wills, trusts), Estate taxation. Office: Berry Moorman PC 455 E Eisenhower Pky #210 Ann Arbor MI 48108 E-mail: tdew@berrymoorman.com.

DEWALT, DEBORAH N. lawyer; b. Bismarck, ND, Oct. 18, 1954; BA summa cum laude, U. ND, 1976; JD cum laude, U. Minn., 1983. Bar: ND 83, Minn. 83. Law clk. U.S. Dist. Ct. (we. dist.) ND, Bismarck, 1983—84; assoc. Horvei & Krueger, Roseville, Minn., 1984—85, Reidenberg & Ormond, Mpls., 1985—87; ptnr. Ormond & Dewalt, Mpls., 1987—96; pvt. practice Dewalt Law Office, Burnsville, Minn., 1996—. Fellow: Acad. Matrimonial Lawyers; mem.: Minn. Assn. Conflict Resolution, Nat. Assn. Conflict Resolution, Dakota County Bar Assn., Hennepin County Bar Assn., Minn. State Bar Assn., Collaborative Law Inst. (bd. dirs. 1999—2003). Alternative dispute resolution, Family and matrimonial. Office: Dewalt Law Office 2412 117th St Ste 100 Burnsville MN 55337

DEWELL, JULIAN C. lawyer; b. San Antonio, Feb. 13, 1930; s. Julian and Hope (Correll) D.; m. Alice Jane Palmer, Aug. 28, 1954; children: Gwen A. Dewell Brown, Jane H., Laura M. BS, Trinity U., 1952; LLD, U. Wash., Seattle, 1957. Bar: Wash. 1957, Calif. 1958, U.S. Ct. of Appeals (9th cir.) 1958. Trial lawyer (anti trust) U.S. Dept. Justice, San Francisco, 1957-59; assoc. Howe, Davis, Riese & Jones, Seattle, 1959-63; ptnr. Anderson Hunter Law Firm, Everett, Wash., 1963-99, of counsel, 2000—. Freeholder City of Everett, Wash., 1966—67, mem. growth mgmt. com., 1982, mem.shoreline mgmt. rev. com., 1998—2000; bd. dirs. Everett Sch. Dist., 1966—71, U. Wash. Law Sch. Found., 1981—84, Snohomish County Land Trust, 1989—93; Law Fund, 1992—98, Sno-Isle Natural Foods Co-Op, 2000—02; Wash. Trails Assn., 2001—. Named to Law Sch. Honor Grad. Program, U.S. Dept. Justice, San Francisco, 1957. Fellow Am. Coll. Trial Lawyers; mem. ABA, Wash. Bar Assn. (disciplinary bd. 1974-77, bd. govs. 1980-83, advt. task force, access to justice bd. 1998—, professionalism award 1991, merit award 1998), Calif. Bar Assn. Democrat. Unitarian Universalist. Avocations: sailing, hiking, tennis. Alternative dispute resolution, Non-profit and tax-exempt organizations, Property, real (including real estate development, water). Home: 609 Maulsby Ln Everett WA 98201-1031 Office: Anderson Hunter Firm PO Box 5397 Everett WA 98206-5397

DEWEY, CHARLES NICHOLS, JR., lawyer; b. Worcester, Mass., Apr. 3, 1935; s. Charles Nichols and Barbara Plum (Bruske) D.; m. Martha Sperry; children: David S., Dale N., Carolynn. BS, Williams Coll., 1957; LLB, JD, U. Mich., 1960. Bar: Mich. 1961, U.S. Dist. Ct. (we. dist.) Mich. 1961, U.S. Ct. Appeals (6th cir.) 1964, U.S. Supreme Ct. 1980. Ptnr. Dilley & Dewey, Grand Rapids, Mich., 1960—. Pres. West Mich. Guidance Ctr., Grand Rapids, 1994-96; mem. campaign cabinet Transitions Bldg. Campaign, Grand Rapids, 1989, 90. Bd. dirs. Mental Health Found. of West Mich., 1994-96, Life Guidance Svs., 1997-2003, Tres, 1997, 98, Wailea Ekolu Village, 2002-03, pres. 2003-. Mem. ABA, State Bar Mich. Finance, Commercial, contracts (including sales of goods; commercial financing), Property, real (including real estate development, water). Office: Dilley & Dewey Ste 400 77 Monroe Center NW Grand Rapids MI 49503

DEWEY-BALZHISER, ANNE ELIZABETH MARIE, lawyer; b. Balt., Mar. 16, 1951; d. George Daniel and Elizabeth Patricia (Mohan) Dewey; m. Richard J. Balzhiser; children: Brendan M. Barnett, Andrew P. Barnett, Meghan E. Barnett. BA, Mich. State U., 1972; JD, U. Chgo., 1975; grad., Stonier Grad. Sch. Banking, East Brunswick, N.J., 1983. Bar: D.C. 1976. Legal clk. and atty. FTC, Washington, 1975-78; atty. and sr. atty. Comptr. of Currency, Dallas and Washington, 1978-86; assoc. gen. counsel, gen. counsel, spl. counsel Farm Credit Adminstrn., McLean, Va., 1986-92; counsel, closed bank litig. and policy sect. FDIC, Washington, 1993-94; gen. counsel, spl. advisor Office of Fed. Housing Enterprise Oversight, HUD, Washington, 1994—. Mem. D.C. study devel. coun. Mich. State U., 1999—. Mem.: FBA (bd. dirs. D.C. chpt. 1988—91, banking law com. exec. coun. 1995—2001), ABA (coun. 2002—, coun. mem. adminstrv. law and regulatory practice sect., coun. mem. govt. and pub. sect. law divsn., bus. law sect., banking law com.), D.C. Bar Assn., Women in Housing and Fin. (bd. dirs. 1982—83, gen. counsel 1991—93, co-chair, profl. devel. com. 2002—), Exchequer Club. Roman Catholic. Office: Office Fed Housing Enterprise Oversight 1700 G St NW Fl 4 Washington DC 20552-0003

DEWITT, CHARLES BENJAMIN, III, lawyer, educator; b. Glendale, Calif., Nov. 29, 1952; s. Charles Benjamin Jr. and Lucille Ann (Johnston) deW.; m. Karen Denise Blackwood, Dec. 29, 1979. BA magna cum laude, Pacific Union Coll., 1973; JD, U. So. Calif., 1976; MA, U. Memphis, 1995. Bar: Tenn. 1984, U.S. Dist. Ct. (we. dist.) Tenn. 1984, D.C. 1989. Atty., agy. mgr., v.p. SAFECO/Chgo. Title Ins., Memphis, 1980-91; regional underwriting counsel Commonwealth Land Title Ins. Co., 1991-93. Asst. prof., instr. U. Memphis, 1986—, asst. dean paralegal, 1993-96., asst. dean law sch., 1996—; judge adv. U.S. Army Gen. Corps, ILT (Reserves). Contbr. articles to profl. jours. Registrar gen. Washington Family Descendants Mem. ABA, Memphis Bar Assn., Tenn. Land Title Assn. (sec.-treas. 1983-87), U. S.C. Alumni Assn. (life), Order Crown of Charlemagne, Kiwanis, Mensa, Phi Alpha Theta, Phi Kappa Phi, Phi Alpha Delta. Education and schools, Property, real (including real estate development, water). Home: 2488 Cedarwood Dr Germantown TN 38138-5802 Office: U Memphis Sch Law 107 Law School Memphis TN 38152-0001 E-mail: cdewitt@memphis.edu.

DEWOSKIN, ALAN ELLIS, lawyer; b. St. Louis, Sept. 10, 1940; s. Samuel S. and Lillian (Sachs) DeW.; m. Iris Lynn Shapiro, Aug. 15, 1942; children: Joseph, Henry, Franklin. BA, Washington U., St. Louis, 1962, JD, 1965; postgrad., U.S. Army Command & Gen. Staff Coll., 1978, U.S. Army War Coll., 1985. Bar: Mo. 1968, Ill. 1999, U.S. Dist. Ct. (ea. dist.) Mo. 1968, U.S. Ct. Appeals (8th cir.) 1969, U.S. Ct. Appeals (Armed Forces) 1976, U.S. Supreme Ct. 1990, U.S. Ct. Claims 1997. Pvt. practice, St. Louis, 1968-82; prin. Alan E. DeWoskin, PC, St. Louis, 1982—. Active Boy Scouts Am. Col. JAGC, USA Ret. Col. JAGC U.S. Army, ret. Recipient U.S. Legion of Merit, 1992. Fellow Am. Bar Found., Mo. Bar Found., St. Louis Bar Found. (disting.); mem. ABA (chmn., gen. practice sect. 1985-86, ho. of dels. 1986-87, assembly del., standing com. mil. law, standing com. assembly resolutions 1988-91, vice-chmn. task force solo and small firm practitioners), ATLA, Mo. Bar Assn. (chmn. gen. practice com. 1987-90, chmn. computer interest groups 1988-90), Bar Assn. Met. St. Louis (exec. com. 1993-94, bd. govs. 1994-95, chmn. solo and small firm sect. 1993-95), Mo. Assn. Trial Attys., Res. Officers Assn. (Mo. Dept. pres. 1979), Masons (past master, dir. 1972—), Am. Legion. Federal civil litigation, State civil litigation, General practice. Home: 14030 Deltona Dr Chesterfield MO 63017-3311 Office: 225 S Meramec Ave Ste 426 Saint Louis MO 63105-3511 E-mail: aedewoskin@cs.com.

DEXTER, DEIRDRE O'NEIL ELIZABETH, lawyer; b. Stillwater, Okla., Apr. 15, 1956; d. Robert N. and Paula E. (Robinson) Maddox; m. Terry E. Dexter, May 14, 1977; children: Daniel M. II, David Maddox. Student, Okla. State U., 1974-77; BS cum laude, Phillips U., 1981; JD with highest honors, U. Okla., 1984. Bar: Okla. 1984, U.S. Dist. Ct. (no. and ea. dists.) Okla. 1985, U.S. Dist. Ct. (we. dist.) Okla. 1987, U.S. Ct. Appeals (10th cir.) 1987; grad. Nat. Inst. Trial Advocacy Advanced Trial seminar. Jud. intern Supreme Ct. Okla., Oklahoma City, summer 1983; assoc. Conner & Winters, Tulsa, 1984-90, ptnr., 1991, shareholder, 1991-2000; assoc. dist. judge Tulsa County Dist. Ct., 2000—03; assoc. Frederic Dorwart, Lawyers, Tulsa, 2003—. Article editor Okla. U. Law Rev., 1982-84. U. Okla. scholar, 1983. Mem. Okla. Bar Assn. (advising atty. state champion H.S. mock trial team competition 1992), Tulsa County Bar Assn., Order of Barristers, Order of Coif, Am. Inns of Ct. (master), Delta Theta Phi. Republican. Baptist. Appellate, General civil litigation, Labor (including EEOC, Fair Labor Standards Act, labor-management relations, NLRB, OSHA). Office: Old City Hall 124 E 4th St Tulsa OK 74103 E-mail: Ddexter@fdlaw.com.

DEXTER, ROBERT PAUL, lawyer; b. Halifax, N.S., Can., Dec. 11, 1951; s. Carl Edmund and Jean Rankin (Collins) D.; 1 child, Angela Elizabeth. BComm, Dalhousie U., 1973, LLB, 1976. With firm Stewart McKelvey Stirling Scales, Halifax, 1977—; CEO Maritime Travel, Halifax, Canada, 1978—. Vice chmn. N.S. Bus. Devel. Corp., 1992-94; bd. dirs. Empire Co. Ltd., Wajax Ltd., Sobeys Inc., High Liner Foods Inc., Maritime Life Assurance Co., Corpora Tel, Aliant Inc.; pres. Halifax Bd. Trade, 1993-94. Chmn. Metro United Way Campaign, 1997. I.W. Killam scholar, 1973, Sir James Dunn scholar, 1976. Mem. N.S. Barristers Soc., Can. Bar Assn., Young Pres. Orgn. Avocations: sailing, skiing, tennis. Home: 1028 Ridgewood Dr Halifax NS Canada B3H 3Y4 Office: Maritime Travel 2000 Barrington St Ste 202 Halifax NS Canada B3J 2X2

DE YOE, DAVID P. lawyer; b. Muskegon, Mich., July 18, 1948; s. Frank A. and Mildred E. (Jensen) DeY.; m. Ilene L. Nevel, May 26, 1979; children: Andrew, Mary, Emily, Peter. BA in Econs., U. Mich., 1970; JD, Stanford U., 1973. Bar: Ill. 1973, U.S. Dist. Ct. (no. dist.) Ill. 1973, Cal. 1975. Assoc. McDermott, Will & Emery, Chgo., 1973-79, ptnr., 1979—. Contbr. articles to profl. jours. Property, real (including real estate development, water). Office: McDermott Will & Emery 227 W Monroe St Ste 4700 Chicago IL 60606-5096

DIAMANT, AVIVA F. lawyer; b. N.Y.C., Mar. 13, 1949; d. Herman and Anni (Silbermann) D.; m. Steven Kaufman, May 31, 1976; 2 children. BS cum laude, CCNY, 1969; JD, Columbia U., 1972. Bar: N.Y. 1973, U.S. Ct. Appeals (2d cir.) 1975, U.S. Dist. Ct. (so. dist.) 1976. Assoc. Fried, Frank, Harris, Shriver & Jacobson, N.Y.C., 1972-79, ptnr., 1979—. James Kent scholar, 1972. Mem. Assn. of Bar of City of N.Y. (com. on corps. 1982-85), Phi Beta Kappa. Jewish. Corporate, general, Securities. Office: Fried Frank Harris Shriver & Jacobson 1 New York Plz Fl 22 New York NY 10004-1980

DIAMOND, BERNARD ROBIN, lawyer; b. Bronx, N.Y., July 3, 1944; m. Elizabeth Heimbuch, Oct. 20, 1976; children: Jessica, Carey, Erin. BA, Rutgers U., 1966; JD, Bklyn. Law Sch., 1972. Bar: N.Y. 1973, U.S. Dist. Ct. (so. and ea. dists.) N.Y. 1973, U.S. Ct. Appeals (2d cir.) 1974. Gen. counsel The Trump Orgn., N.Y.C., 1995—. Mem. Assn. of the Bar of the City of N.Y. Property, real (including real estate development, water). Office: Trump Orgn 725 5th Ave Fl 26 New York NY 10022-2520

DIAMOND, EUGENE CHRISTOPHER, lawyer, hospital administrator; b. Oceanside, Calif., Oct. 19, 1952; s. Eugene Francis and Rosemary (Wright) D.; m. Mary Theresa O'Donnell, Jan. 20, 1984; children: Eugene John, Kevin Seamus, Hannah Rosemary, Seamus Michael, Maeve Therese. BA, U. Notre Dame, 1974; MHA, St. Louis U., 1978, JD, 1979. Bar: Ill. 1979. Staff atty. AUL Legal Def. Fund, Chgo., 1979-80; adminstrv. asst. Holy Cross Hosp., Chgo., 1980-81, asst. adminstr., 1981-82, v.p., 1982-83, counsel to adminstr., 1980—, exec. v.p., 1983-91; exec. v.p., COO, St. Margaret Mercy Healthcare Ctrs., Hammond, Ind., 1991-93, pres., CEO, 1993—, regional COO, 2001—. Cons. Birthright of Chgo., 1979—, mem. benefit com., 1981—; bd. dirs. Hammond C. of C., 1993, North West Ind. Forum. Mem. Ill. State Bar Assn., Chgo. Bar Assn. Roman Catholic. Health. Office: St Margaret Mercy Healthcare Ctrs 5454 Hohman Ave Hammond IN 46320-1999

DIAMOND, GUSTAVE, federal judge; b. Burgettstown, Pa., Jan. 29, 1928; s. George and Margaret (Solinsky) D.; m. Emma L. Scarton, Dec. 28, 1974; 1 dau., Margaret Ann; 1 stepdau., Joanne Yoney. AB, Duke U., 1951; JD, Duquesne U., 1956. Bar: Pa. bar 1958, U.S. Ct. Appeals bar 1962. Law clk. to judge U.S. Dist. Ct., Pitts., 1955-61; 1st asst. U.S. atty. Western Dist. Pa., 1961-62, U.S. atty., 1963-69; partner firm Cooper, Schwartz, Diamond & Reich, Pitts., 1969-75; formerly individual practice law Washington, Pa.; former solicitor Washington County, Pa.; judge U.S. Dist. Ct. Western Dist. Pa.; chief judge U.S. Dist. Ct. (we. dist.) Pa., 1992-94, sr. judge, 1994—. Chmn. Jud. Conf. Com. on Defender Svcs. Mem. ABA, Fed. Bar Assn., Pa. Bar Assn., Allegheny County Bar Assn., Washington County Bar Assn. Office: US Dist Ct 821 US Courthouse 7th St Rm 2 Pittsburgh PA 15219

DIAMOND, JOSEF, lawyer; b. L.A., Mar. 6, 1907; s. Michael and Ruby (Shifrin) D.; m. Violett Diamond, Apr. 2, 1933 (dec. 1979); children: Joel, Diane Foreman; m. Ann Dulien, Jan. 12, 1981 (dec. 1984); m. Muriel Bach, 1986. BBA, U. Wash., 1929, JD, 1931. Bar: Wash. 1931, U.S. Dist. Ct. (we. dist.) Wash. 1932, U.S. Ct. Appeals (9th cir.) 1934, U.S. Supreme Ct. 1944. Assoc. Caldwell & Lycette, Seattle, 1931-35; ptnr. Caldwell, Lycette & Diamond, Seattle, 1935-45, Lycette, Diamond & Sylvester, Seattle, 1945-80, Diamond & Sylvester, Seattle, 1980-82, of counsel, 1982-88, Short, Cressman & Burgess, Seattle, 1988—2002; pvt. practice Seattle, 2002—. Chmn. bd. Diamond Parking Inc., Seattle, 1945-70; cons. various businesses. Bd. dirs. Am. Heart Assn., 1960; chmn. Wash. Heart Assn., 1962. Col. JAGC, U.S. Army, WWII. Decorated Legion of Merit. Mem. Wash. Bar Assn., Assn. Trial Lawyers Wash., Seattle Bar Assn., Mil. Engrs. Soc., Wash. Athletic Club, Bellevue Athletic Club, Harbor Club. Office: Diamond Bldg Ste 200 3161 Elliott Ave Seattle WA 98121 Office Fax: 206-285-5598.

DIAMOND, M. JEROME, lawyer, former state official; b. Chgo., Mar. 16, 1942; s. Leo and Sonya (Pevsner) D.; m. Carol English Robinson; 8 children. AB, George Washington U., 1963; MA, U. Tenn., 1965, JD, 1968. Bar: Vt. 1968, U.S. Supreme Ct. 1975. Law clk. U.S. Dist. Judge Ernest Gibson, 1968-69; assoc. Kristensen, Cummings & Price, Brattleboro, Vt., 1969-70; state's atty. Windham County, Vt., 1970-74; atty. gen. State of Vt., 1975-81; atty., sr. ptnr. Diamond & Robinson, P.C., Montpelier, Vt., 1981—. Trustee Brooks Meml. Library, 1970-73; chmn. Putney Zoning Bd. Adjustment, 1971-74; mem. Vt. Criminal Justice Tng. Council, 1974-81, Vt. Commn. Adminstrn. of Justice, 1975-81; mem. Vt. Adv. Group, U.S. Civil Rights Commn.; gen. campaign chmn. United Way Washington County, 1986-87, 88-89; bd. dirs. Nat. Coun. on Aging, 1990-93, Vt. Bar Found., 1997—, Vt. State Employees Credit Union, 1997—; internat. commr. Anti-Defamation League, 1988-93. Mem. Vt. State's Attys. Assn. (past pres.), Vt. Bar Assn., Vt. Bar Found. (bd. dirs. 1997—), Washington County Bar Assn., Nat. Assn. Atty. Gens. (v.p. 1978-79, pres. 1980), Ea. Regional Conf. Attys. Gen. (chmn. 1975-76), B'nai B'rith (internat. commr. anti-defamation league 1988-93, internat. bd. govs. 1990-92), Jewish Inst. for Nat. Security Affairs (bd. dirs. 1993—), Am. Judicature Soc. (bd. dirs., Vt. rep. 1994-00), Vt. State Employees Credit Union, 1997 (bd. dirs., v.p. of bd. VSECU 2000—), Shriners, Masons, Montpelier Rotary Club (bd. dirs. 1998—, v.p. 2001-02, pres.-elect 2002-03, pres. 2003-04). Democrat. Jewish. General civil litigation, Family and matrimonial, Personal injury (including property damage). Office: Diamond & Robinson PC PO Box 1460 Montpelier VT 05601

DIAMOND, PAUL STEVEN, lawyer, educator; b. Bklyn., Jan. 2, 1953; s. George and Anna (Jaeger) D.; m. Robin Nilon. BA magna cum laude, Columbia U., 1974; JD, U. Pa., 1977. Bar: Pa. 1977, U.S. Dist. Ct. (ea. dist.) Pa, 1979, U.S. Ct. Appeals (3d cir.) 1979, U.S. Supreme Ct. 1983. Asst. dist. atty. Phila. Dist. Atty. Office, 1977-83; law clk. Supreme Ct. Pa., Phila., 1980; assoc. Dilworth, Paxson, Kalish & Kauffman, Phila., 1983-85, ptnr., 1986-91, Obermayer, Rebmann, Maxwell & Hippel, Phila., 1992—. Lectr. Temple U. Sch. Law, Phila., 1990—92; mem. civil procedural rules com. Supreme Ct. Pa., 1995—98, treas. Pa. lawyers fund for client security bd., 1999—; mem. civil procedural rules com. fed. jud. nominating commn., 1993, 1995—2000; vice chmn., chmn. Amicus Curiae Briefs Com., 1995—99. Author: Federal Grand Jury Practice and Procedure, 1990, rev. 4d edit., 2001. Mem. ABA (criminal justice sect., Amicus Curiae briefs subcom. 1984-99, grand jury subcom. 1991-93), Am. Law Inst., Pa. Bar Assn., Phila. Bar Assn. Republican. Jewish. General civil litigation, Constitutional, Criminal.

DIAMOND, RICHARD S. lawyer; b. Newark, June 26, 1960; BA in Econs./Bus. Adminstrn., Rutgers U., 1981; JD, Seton Hall U., 1985. Bar: N.J. 1985, Fla. 1991, U.S. Dist. Ct. N.J. 1991; cert. matrimonial trial, Laywer by the N.J. Supreme Ct. cert. divorce mediator; ct. apptd. econ. mediator N.J. Supreme Ct. Law sec. to Hon. Burton J. Ironson State of N.J., Union County, N.J., 1985-86; assoc. Law Firm of Robert Diamond, Springfield, N.J.; ptnr. Diamond Hodes & Diamond, Springfield, Gourvitz, Diamond, Hodes, Braun & Diamond, Springfield, Diamond & Diamond P.A., Millburn, N.J. Spkr., guest lectr. TV and radio broadcasts. Contbr. articles to profl. jours. Mem. Union County Bar Assn.), Essex County Bar (matrimonial practice), N.J. Bar Assn. (lectr., speaker). Avocations: racquetball, running. General civil litigation, Family and matrimonial. Office: Diamond & Diamond PA 225 Millburn Ave Ste 208 Millburn NJ 07041-1712 Fax: 973-379-9210. E-mail: njdivorcelawyer@aol.com.

DIAMOND, STANLEY JAY, lawyer; b. Los Angeles, Nov. 27, 1927; s. Philip Alfred and Florence (Fadem) D.; m. Lois Jane Broida, June 22, 1969; children: Caryn Elaine, Diana Beth. BA, UCLA, 1949; JD, U. So. Calif., 1952. Bar: Calif. 1953. Practiced law, Los Angeles, 1953—; dep. Office of Calif. Atty. Gen., Los Angeles, 1953; ptnr. Diamond & Tilem, Los Angeles, 1957-60, Diamond, Tilem & Colden, Los Angeles, 1960-79, Diamond & Wilson, Los Angeles, 1979—. Lectr. music and entertainment law UCLA; Mem. nat. panel arbitrators Am. Arbitration Assn. Bd. dirs. Los Angeles Suicide Prevention Center, 1971-76. Served with 349th Engr. Constrn. Bn. AUS, 1945-47. Mem. ABA, Calif. Bar Assn., Los Angeles County Bar Assn., Beverly Hills Bar Assn., Am. Judicature Soc., Calif. Copyright Conf., Nat. Acad. Rec. Arts and Scis., Zeta Beta Tau, Nu Beta Epsilon. Entertainment. Office: 12304 Santa Monica Blvd Fl 3D Los Angeles CA 90025-2551

DIAZ, JOSEPH MICHAEL, lawyer; b. Camp Pendleton, Calif., Mar. 23, 1956; s. Alex and Barbara Ann (Rodarme) D.; m. Lauren Michelle Nathan, June 20, 1982 (div. Aug. 1985); m. Valentina Bocanegra, July 1, 1989; children: Eliséo Ramon, De Vonté Manuel. BA, Boise State U., 1978, U. Wash., 1981; JD, U. Puget Sound, 1985. Bar: Wash. 1986, U.S. Dist. Ct. (we. dist.) Wash. 1986, U.S. Ct. Appeals (9th cir.) 1992, U.S. Dist. Ct. (ea. dist.) Wash. 2000. City prosecutor City of Tacoma, Wash., 1984-87, asst. city atty., 1988-98; assoc. atty. Law Office of J. Angus Coghill, Seattle, 1987-88; shareholder Davies Pearson P.C., Tacoma, 1998—. Mem. law and justice com. Wash. Traffic Safety Commn., 1991-92. Bd. dirs. Tacoma Cmty. House, 1990-2002, pres., 1998-2001; bd. dirs. Centro Latino SER, Tacoma, 1995-99. Named Tacoma-Pierce County MESA Pacific Luth. U., 1993. Fellow Grad. Am. Leadership Forum Assn. (sec., v.p., pres. 1994-97). Avocations: hiking, camping, alpine skiing. Home: 4406 N 7th St Tacoma WA 98406-3508 Office: Davies Pearson P C 920 Fawcett St Tacoma WA 98402 E-mail: jdiaz@dpearson.com.

DIAZ, NELSON, lawyer; b. NYC, May 23, 1947; s. Luis Diaz and Maria (Cancel) Rodriguez; children: Vilmarie, Nelson M.V., Delia Lee. AAS, St. John's U., 1967, BS, 1969; JD, Temple U., 1972; LLD (hon.) , LaSalle Coll., 1982, St. John's U., 1987, Temple U., 1990, Albright Coll., 1995, Lincoln U., 1996. Bar: Pa. 1972, D.C. 1978, U.S. Supreme Ct. 1978, N.Y. 1998. Legal intern Camden (N.J.) Regional Legal Svcs., 1970-71; asst. defender Defender Assn. Phila., 1972-73; asoc. counsel Temple U. Legal Aid Office, Phila., 1973-75; assoc. Fell, Spalding, Goff & Ruben, Phila., 1976-77; exec. dir. Spanish Mchts. Assn., Phila., 1973-77; White House fellow v.p. of U.S., 1977-78; assoc. Wolf, Block, Schorr & Solis-Cohen, Phila., 1978-81; adminstrv. judge Phila. Ct. of Common Pleas, 1981-93; gen. counsel HUD, Washington, 1993-97; ptnr. Blank, Rome, Comisky & McCauley, Phila., 1997—2001; city solicitor City of Philadelphia, Pa., 2001—. Lectr. Sch. Law Temple U., Phila., 1983—. Columnist Phila. Sun and Evening Bull., 1973-75; contbr. articles on Japanese, Peruvian legal system to various publs. Founder Phila. Leadership Prayer Breakfast, 1984-93; bd. dirs., com. chmn. Revitalized Neighborhood, 1983-87; participant, hon. chair Soviet Jewry Coun., 1985; com. mem. Charter Rev. Phila., 1986; chmn. Nat. Assn. Hispanic Elderly, L.A., 1978-93; trustee Young Life, 1989-93, Temple U., 1997—, Phila. Mus. Art; bd. govs. Temple Hosp., Phila., 1975-93; founder, bd. dirs. Nat. P.R. Coalition, 1978-86; co-chmn., bd. dirs. Urban Affairs Partnership, Phila., 1984-90; bd. dirs. USHLI, Chgo., 1982-93, 97—, World Affairs Coun., 1997—; chair Greater Phila. Billy Graham Crusade; active Found. Improvement Justice, 1992, Nat. Bar Assn. Jud. Coun., 1993, Frederick Douglass Soc. Found., 1995, Salvation Army, 1995, Boricua Coll., 1995. Recipient Life Achievement award Nat. Puerto Rican Coalition, Washington, 1988, Judge of the Yr. award Pa. Trial Lawyers Assn., 1989, Man of the Yr., NAACP, North Phila., 1990, Cesar Chavez award, 1995, Spirit of Excellence award ABA, 2001, William Hall award Barristers, 2003, Lifetime Achievement award Minority Bar, 2003, Learn Hand award Am. Jewish Com., 2003; named Grand Marshall, P.R. Milburne (Fla.) Parade; Japan Soc. fellow, Fulbright fellow, 1990. Mem. Pa. Bar Assn. (chair DNC Hispanic Caucus, exec. com., bylaws and rules com., Martin Luther King Barrister award 2003), Phila. Bar Assn., D.C. Bar Assn., Pa. Trial Lawyers Assn., State Conf. Trial Judges, Mayor's St. Police Discipline Task Force. Democrat. Avocation: sports. Office: City Solicitor One Parkway 1515 Arch St 17th Fl Philadelphia PA 19103 E-mail: nelson.a.diaz@phila.gov.

DIAZ, OLIVER E., JR., judge; b. Biloxi, Miss., Dec. 16, 1959; s. Oliver E. Sr. and Sylvia (Fountain) D. AA, Miss. Gulf Coast Jr. Coll., 1979; BA, U. S. Ala., 1982; JD, U. Miss., 1985. Bar: Miss., U.S. Dist. Ct. (no. and so. dists.) Miss., U.S. Ct. Appeals (5th cir.). Assoc. Holkins Logan Vaughn & Anderson, Gulfport, Miss., 1985-86, Gerald R. Emil PA, Gulfport, 1986-88; ptnr. Diaz Davis & Emil, Gulfport, 1988—95; judge Miss. Ct. of Appeals, Jackson, 1995—2000; justice Miss. Supreme Court, Jackson, 2000—. Miss. state rep., 1988-94; mem. Harrison County Rep. exec. com., 1987—; treas. Miss. State Young Reps., 1987-88; pres. Miss. Gulf Coast Young Reps., Harrison County, 1987-88. Mem. Assn. Trial Lawyers Am., Miss. Trial Lawyers Assn., Am. Legis. Exchange Com., Jaycees. Office: Mississippi Supreme Ct Gartin Justice Bldg 450 High St Jackson MS 39201-1006 also: PO Box 450 Jackson MS 39205*

DIAZ-ARRASTIA, GEORGE RAVELO, lawyer; b. Havana, Cuba, Aug. 20, 1959; came to U.S., 1968; s. Ramon Fuentes and Elihut (Ravelo) D.-A.; m. Maria del Carmen Gomez, Aug. 6, 1983. BA in History, Rice U., 1980; JD, U. Chgo., 1983. Bar: Tex. 1983, U.S. Dist. Ct. (so. dist.) Tex. 1985, U.S. Ct. Appeals (5th and D.C. cirs.) 1985, U.S. Supreme Ct. 1992, U.S. Dist. Ct. (no., we. and ea. dists.) Tex. 1994. Assoc. Baker & Botts, Houston, 1983-88, Deaton & Briggs (formerly Deaton, Briggs & McCain), Houston, 1988-90; ptnr. Gilpin, Paxson & Bersch, LLP, Houston, 1991-98, Schirrmeister Ajamie LLP, Houston, 1998—. Fellow Tex. Bar Found., Houston Bar Found.; mem. ABA, Am. Judicature Soc., Am. Soc. Internat. Law, State Bar of Tex., Houston Bar Assn., Coll. of State Bar Tex. Republican. Roman Catholic. Commercial, consumer (including collections, credit), Construction, Education and schools. Home: 3794 Drake St Houston TX 77005-1118 Office: Schirrmeister Ajamie LLP 711 Louisiana St Ste 2150 Houston TX 77002-2720 E-mail: gdarrastia@salawfirm.com.

DIBBLE, FRANCIS DANIEL, JR., lawyer; b. Holyoke, Mass., Mar. 1, 1947; s. Francis Daniel and Rita (Egan) D.; m. Mary Harris Dibble, June 26, 1971. AB, Amherst Coll., 1971; JD magna cum laude, Suffolk U., 1974. Bar: Mass. 1974, U.S. Dist. Ct. Mass. 1975, U.S. Dist. Ct. Conn. 1978, U.S. Dist. Ct. (ea. dist.) Mich. 1984, U.S. Ct. Appeals (1st cir.) 1987, U.S. Ct. Appeals (D.C. cir.) 1981, U.S. Supreme Ct. 1984. Law clk. to justice Supreme Jud. Ct. of Mass., Boston, 1974-75; from assoc. to mng. ptnr. Bulkley, Richardson and Gelinas, Springfield, Mass., 1975-94, chmn., exec. com., 1997—. Instr. Western New Eng. Law Sch., Springfield, 1979. Contbr. articles to profl. jours. Mem. civil justice adv. bd. U.S. Dist. Ct. Mass.; spl. counsel. Fellow Mass. Bar Found. (life); mem. ABA (antitrust law sect.), Mass. Bar Assn., Hampden County Bar, Boston Bar Assn., The Colony Club, Longmeadow Country Club, East Chop Assn., East Chop Yacht Club, East Chop Tennis Club. Antitrust, General civil litigation, Family and matrimonial. Home: 180 Eton Rd Longmeadow MA 01106-1516 Office: Bulkley Richardson and Gelinas LLP 1500 Main St Ste 2700 Springfield MA 01115-0001 E-mail: fdibble@bulkley.com.

DIBBLE, ROBERT WIGHTMAN, JR., lawyer; b. Berwyn, Ill., Mar. 29, 1940; s. Robert Wightman and Saluda (Reese) R.; m. Nancy Britton; children— Nancye Leigh, Robert Wightman, III. B.S., U. So. Carolina, 1963; J.D. cum laude, U. S.C., 1966; student U. N.Mex. Bar: S.C., U.S. Dist. Ct. S.C. 1967, U.S. Ct. Claims 1994, U.S. Ct. Appeals (4th cir.) 1972, U.S. Ct. Appeals (5th cir.) 1989, U.S. Ct. Appeals (11th cir.), U.S. Supreme Ct. 1978; Shareholder McNair Law Firm; ptnr. loss prevention Atty.'s Liability Assurance Soc., ethics ptnr., 1986-, counsel, 1995-; chmn. litig. Columbia office, 1995-; mem. U. S.C. Law Rev.; Fellow Am. Coll. Trial Lawyers, Com. Fed. Rules of Evidence; mem. U.S. Dist. Ct. Adv.Com. Fed. Rules and Civil Procedure, S.C. Bar Assn., Jud. Qualifications Com. Com., 4th Cir. Jud. Conf., Order of Wig and Robe. Antitrust, Federal civil litigation, Environmental, General civil litigation. Office: Bank of Am Tower 18th Floor McNair Law Firm PA 1301 Gervais St Columbia SC 29201 Office Fax: 803-799-9804.

DIBIAGIO, THOMAS M. prosecutor; BA, Dickinson Coll.; JD U. Richmond. Assoc. Semmes, Brown and Semmes, Balt., 1986—91; asst. U.S. atty. Dist. Md, U.S. Dept. Justice, 1991—2000; ptnr. Dyer, Ellis and Joseph, Washington, 2000—01; U.S. atty. U.S. Dept. of Justice, Md., 2001—. Office: 6625 US Courthouse 101 W Lombard St Baltimore MD 21201*

DIBLASI, GANDOLFO VINCENT, lawyer; b. Bklyn., July 7, 1953; s. Rudolph Francis and Theresa (Restivo) DiB.; m. Roberta Wilson, Sept. 13, 1980; children: Richard, William. BA, Yale Coll., 1975, JD, 1978. Bar: N.Y., 1979, U.S. Ct. Appeals (2d cir.), 1982, U.S. Ct. Appeals (4th cir.), 1991, U.S. Ct. Appeals (9th cir.), 1981, U.S. Supreme Ct., 1990, U.S. Dist. Ct. (so. dist.) N.Y., 1979, U.S. Dist. Ct. (ea. dist.) N.Y., 1982, U.S. Dist. Ct. (no. dist.) Calif., 1989. Assoc. Sullivan & Cromwell, N.Y.C., 1978-85, ptnr., 1985—. Antitrust, General civil litigation, Securities. Home: 200 E End Ave Apt 15I New York NY 10128-7887 Office: Sullivan & Cromwell 125 Broad St Fl 28 New York NY 10004-2489

DICARA, LAWRENCE S. lawyer; b. Boston, Apr. 30, 1949; s. Salvatore Vincent and Concetta Claire (Alibrandi) DiC. BA, Harvard Coll., 1971; JD, Suffolk U., 1976; M of Pub. Adminstrn., J.F. Kennedy Sch. of Govt., 1977. Bar: Mass., U.S. Dist. Ct. Mass., U.S. Ct. Appeals (1st cir.), U.S. Supreme Ct. At large mem. Boston City Coun., 1972-81, pres., 1978; ptnr. Nixon Peabody, Boston, 1990—. Bd. dirs. Harvard Coop. Soc., Cambridge, Mass., 1975—. Contbr. various articles to jours. and mags. Mem. ABA, Mass. Bar Assn., Boston Bar Assn., Harvard Club of Boston, Harvard Club of N.Y. Democrat. Roman Catholic. Avocations: squash, reading. Administrative and regulatory, Land use and zoning (including planning), Property, real (including real estate development, water). Home: 35 Burroughs St Jamaica Plain MA 02130-4015 Office: Nixon Peabody 101 Federal St Fl 13 Boston MA 02110-1832

DICHTER, MARK S. lawyer; b. Phila., Jan. 22, 1943; s. Harry B. and Mollie (Silverstein) D.; m. Tobey Gordon, Aug. 17, 1969; children: Aliza, Melissa. BSEE, Drexel U., 1966; JD magna cum laude, Villanova U., 1969. Bar: Pa. 1969, U.S. Ct. Appeals (3d cir.) 1969, U.S. Supreme Ct. 1979. Assoc. Morgan, Lewis & Bockius, LLP, Phila., 1969-76, ptnr., 1976—, chmn. labor and employment law practice group. Co-author: Employee Dismissal Law: Forms and Procedures, 1986-91; editor-in-chief Ann. Supplement Employment Discrimination Law, 1984-89; co-editor: Employment-at-will, 1985, 86, State-by-State Survey, 1984-89; adv. bd. Disability Law Reporter. Bd. dirs. Urban League Phila.; bd. dirs., chmn. Wilma Theater; bd. consultors Villanova U. Sch. Law; bd. dirs. Pub. Interest Law Ctr. Phila. Mem. ABA (labor and employment law sect., chmn.

2000-01, mem. governing coun. 1991-2000, co-chmn. equal opportunity com. 1986-89, employment law com. litigation sect.), FBA (vice chmn. equal employment com. 1983-86), Nat. Employment Law Inst. (adv. bd. 1984—), Am. Employment Law Counsel (bd. dirs.), Am. Coll. Employment Lawyers, Def. Rsch. Inst. (chmn. employment law com. 1989-93). Labor (including EEOC, Fair Labor Standards Act, labor-management relations, NLRB, OSHA). Home: 1017 Clinton St Philadelphia PA 19107-6016 Office: Morgan Lewis & Bockius LLP 1701 Market St Philadelphia PA 19103-2903 Fax: 215-963-5001. E-mail: mdichter@morganlewis.com.

DICICCO, MARGARET C. lawyer; b. Bklyn., Mar. 22, 1961; d. Vincent Richard and Margaret Josephine (Ciullo) DiC.; m. James Louis O'Rourke, Sept. 18, 1994. BA in Polit. Sci., Bklyn. Coll., CUNY, 1983; JD, U. Bridgeport, 1987. Bar: N.Y. 1989, Conn. 1994, U.S. Dist. Ct. (so. dist.) N.Y. 1989, U.S. Dist. Ct. (ea. dist.) N.Y. 1990, U.S. Dist. Ct. Conn. 1995, U.S. Supreme Ct., 1998. Assoc. Ginsberg & Caesar, N.Y.C., 1988-89, Abrams & Martin P.C., N.Y.C., 1989-93, Chesney, Murphy & Moran, Westbury, N.Y., 1993-94, Law Offices of James L. O'Rourke, 1994—. Mem. ABA, NYSBA, Greater Bridgeport Bar Assn. Roman Catholic. Home: 221 Nells Rock Rd Shelton CT 06484-3831 Office: Law Offices James L O'Rourke 1825 Barnum Ave Ste 201 Stratford CT 06614-5333

DICKERMAN, JOHN MELVIN, lawyer; b. Hope, Ark., Aug. 21, 1914; s. Charles and Dorothy W. (Schultz) D.; m. Serafina Peoria, Oct. 26, 1956; 1 child, Dorothea W. BA, U. Ill., 1938, JD, 1940. Bar: Ill. 1940, Ohio 1942, U.S. Supreme Ct. 1944, U.S. Dist. Ct. (D.C. dist.) 1964. Atty. Rep. Steel Corp., Massillon, Ohio, 1940-42, U.S. Alien Property Custodian, Chgo., 1942-43; atty., Washington rep. Airline Pilot's Assn., 1943-47; legis. dir. Nat. Assn. Home Builders, Washington, 1947-52, exec. v.p., 1952-64; pres. John Dickerman & Assocs., Washington, 1964—. Mem. Nat. Assn. Home Builders (life, bd. dirs. 1964, named to Hall of Fame 1980), Am. Soc. Assn. Execs., Chgo. Bar Assn., D.C. Bar Assn., Lambda Alpha. Republican. Administrative and regulatory, Land use and zoning (including planning), Property, real (including real estate development, water).

DICKERSON, CLAIRE MOORE, lawyer, educator; b. Boston, Apr. 1, 1950; d. Roger Cleveland and Ines Idelette (Roullet) Moore; m. Thomas Pasquali Dickerson, May 22, 1976; children: Caroline Anne, Susannah Moore. AB, Wellesley Coll., 1971; JD, Columbia U., 1974; LLM in Taxation, NYU, 1981. Bar: N.Y. 1975, U.S. Dist. Ct. (ea. and so. dists.) N.Y. 1975, U.S. Ct. Appeals (2d cir.) 1975, U.S. Supreme Ct. 1980. Assoc. Coudert Brothers, N.Y., 1974-82, ptnr., 1983-86, Schnader, Harrison, Segal & Lewis, N.Y., 1987-88, of counsel, 1988—; assoc. prof. law St. John's U., Jamaica, N.Y., 1986-88, prof., 1989-2000; prof law Rutgers U., Newark, 2000—. Author: Partnership Law Adviser; contbr. articles to profl. jours. Scholar Arthur L. Dickson scholar. Mem.: ABA, Soc. for Advancement of Socio-Econs., Law and Soc. Assn., Assn. of Bar of City of N.Y., Shenorock Club. Democrat. E-mail: cmdckrsn@rci.rutgers.edu.

DICKERSON, MICHELLE MOODY, lawyer; b. Chester, S.C., Feb. 9, 1975; d. John Marion and Elaine Robinson Moody; m. Michael Lewis Dickerson, Nov. 7, 1998. BA, Wofford Coll., 1997; JD, U. S.C., 2000. Bar: S.C. 2000, U.S. Dist. Ct. S.C. 2002. Staff atty. S.C. Adminstrv. Law Divsn. Judge, Columbia, 2000—01; assoc. Setzler & Scott, PA, West Columbia, SC, 2001—. Assoc. editor S.C. Environ. Law Jour., 1999—2000. Family and matrimonial, Probate (including wills, trusts), General civil litigation. Office: Setzler & Scott PA 1708 Augusta Rd West Columbia SC 29171

DICKEY, DAVID HERSCHEL, lawyer, accountant; b. Savannah, Ga., Dec. 31, 1951; s. Grady Lee and Sara (Leon) D.; children: David Bradford, Carolyn Amanda. BBA in Acctg. and Fin., Armstrong State Coll., 1974; M in Accountancy, JD, U. Ga., 1977. CPA; bar: Ga. 1978, U.S. Dist. Ct. (no. dist.) Ga. 1980, U.S. Ct. Claims 1978, U.S. Tax Ct. 1978, U.S. Ct. Appeals (5th and 11th cirs.) 1978, U.S. Supreme Ct. 1981. Assoc., acct. Thompson and Benken, Attys., Savannah, 1977-79; pub. acct. Arthur Andersen & Co., Atlanta, 1979-81; assoc. Oliver Maner & Gray, Attys. LLP, Savannah, 1981-82; ptnr. Oliver Maner & Gray, Attys., Savannah, 1982—. Pres. Savannah Estate Planning Coun., 1986-87, chmn. bd., 1987-88; bd. dirs. Chatham-Savannah Citizen's Advocacy; mem. legal adv. bd. Small Bus. Coun. Am., Inc., 1989—; pres. Seminar Group, Inc., 1989—, Hist. Investment Properties, Inc., 1991—. Pres. L'Alliance Francaise de Savannah, 2001—03; bd. dirs. Savannah Theatre Co., 1984, Savannah chpt. Am. Cancer Soc., 1986—91, Hist. Savannah Found., Inc., 1988—94, Chandler Hosp. Found., 2003; chmn., trustee Armstrong State Coll. Alumni Endowment Fund, Inc., 1991; chmn. lawyers divsn. Chatham County United Way, 1992; dir., v.p. Armstrong Atlantic State U. Found., 2001—03; bd. trustees The Candler Found., 2001—03. Recipient Outstanding Svc. award Am. Cancer Soc., 1987, Outstanding Alumni Svc. award Armstrong State Coll., 1992; named to Leadership Savannah, Savannah C. of C., 1984-86. Fellow: Am. Coll. Trust and Esttae Coun.; mem.: ABA (estate and give tax com. taxation sect. 1990—), AICPA, SAR (pres. Ga. 2001—03), Am. Assn. Atty.-CPAs, Ga. Soc. CPAs, Savannah Bar Assn., Ga. Bar Assn., Sons Confederate Vets (commdr. Francis S. Bartow camp no. 93 1997—98), Chatham Club, First City Club (bd. dirs. Savannah 1987—90). Avocations: history, genealogy, music, computers, historic rehab. Estate planning, Probate (including wills, trusts), Taxation, general. Home: 4 Springfield Pl Savannah GA 31411 Office: Oliver Maner & Gray 218 W State St Savannah GA 31401-3232

DICKEY, JOHN HARWELL, lawyer; b. Huntsville, Ala., Feb. 22, 1944; s. Gilbert McClain and Marjorie Loucille (Harwell) D.; m. Nancy Margaret Eagar, Nov. 24, 1984; children: Marjorie Ruth, Gilbert Charles. BA, Samford U., 1966; JD, Cumberland Sch. of Law, 1969. Bar: Tenn. 1971, U.S. Dist. Ct. (ea. dist.) Tenn. 1972. Adminstrv. asst. Dist. Atty.'s Office, Huntsville, 1969-70; law clerk domestic and juvenile divsn. Cir. Ct., Huntsville, 1970-72; trial lawyer Legal Aid Soc., Chattanooga, 1972-75; pvt. practice Chattanooga, 1975-77, Fayetteville, Tenn., 1977-89; dist. pub. defender 17th jud. cir. State of Tenn., Fayetteville, 1989-98; pvt. practice, Fayetteville, Tenn., 1998—. Mem. continuing edn. com. Pub. Defenders Conf., Tenn., 1990-92, mem. long range planning com., 1991-93, mem. legis. com., 1990-93, mem. exec. com., Mid. Tenn. rep., 1993-94. Lectr. Fayetteville-Lincoln County Leadership Tng. Program, 1989—; mem. adv. bd. Community Correction South Ctrl. Tenn., Fayetteville, 1989—; mem. Bedford County Dem. Club, 1989—. Mem. Nat. Assn. Criminal Def. Lawyers, Tenn. Bar Assn., Tenn. Assn. Criminal Def. Lawyers (membership com. 1989—, juvenile law com. 1988—, Disting. Svc. award 1990, 91, 92), Marshall County Bar Assn., Fayetteville-Lincoln County Bar Assn. (treas. 1977, sec. 1978, v.p. 1979, pres. 1980), Fayetteville-Lincoln County C. of C., Elks, Masons (jr. steward 1991, sr. steward 1992, jr. deacon 1993, jr. warden 1994, sr. warden 1995, worshipful master 1996), York Rite Mason, Scottish Rite Mason (32d degree), Shriners (sgt.-at-arms 1993, v.p. 1994, dir. pub. rels. 1994, 96—, pres. 1995), Internat. Platform Assn., Order of Ea. Star (chaplain 1993-94), Tenn. 4-H Found., Gideons Internat. Democrat. Methodist. Avocations: hunting, fishing, canoeing, kayaking. Constitutional, Criminal, Juvenile. Home: 122 Brookmeade Dr Fayetteville TN 37334-2046 Office: 105 Main Ave S Fayetteville TN 37334-3057

DICKEY, JOHN W. lawyer; b. Springfield, Mo., 1927; AB, U. Mo., 1950; BA, Oxford (Eng.) U., 1952, MA, 1956; LLB, Harvard U., 1954. Bar: Mo. 1954, N.Y. 1955, Eng. and Wales 1999. Sr. counsel Sullivan & Cromwell, London. Mem. Am. Coll. Trial Lawyers. Alternative dispute resolution, General civil litigation, Private international. Office: Sullivan & Cromwell 1 New Fetter Ln London EC4A 1AN England

DICKIE, ROBERT BENJAMIN, lawyer, consultant, educator; b. Glendale, Calif., Sept. 10, 1941; s. John A. and Dorothy C. Dickie; m. Susan J. Williams, Jan. 28, 1967 (div. 1987); children: Amy, John, Thomas. BA, Yale U., 1963; JD, U. Calif., Berkeley, 1967. Bar: Calif. 1967, N.Y. 1970, Mass. 1971. Assoc. Shearman & Sterling, N.Y.C., 1969-71, Sullivan & Worcester, Boston, 1971-77; asst. prof. mgmt. policy Boston U., 1977-83, tenured assoc. prof., 1983-94; prin The Dickie Group, 1994—. Cons. World Bank, Washington, Fortune 100 Cos., leading law firms in U.S., Europe and Asia. Author: Financial Statement Analysis and Business Valuation for the Practical Lawyer, ABA, 1999; contbr. numerous articles to Nat. Law Jour., Strategic Mgmt. Jour., Columbia Jour. World Bus., others. Mem.: N.Y. Bar Assn., Calif. Bar Assn., Boston Bar Assn., Longwood Cricket Club, Yale Club Boston. Corporate, general, Securities, Finance. Office: The Dickie Group Reservoir Pl 1601 Trapelo Rd Waltham MA 02451

DICKINSON, NANCY, lawyer; b. Denver, Oct. 25, 1965; d. Martin Brownlow and Mary Ann Mize Dickinson. AB in Econs., U. Kans., 1987; JD, Yale Law Sch., 1991. Bar: Ill. 1991, D.C. 1994, Colo. 1999. Trial atty. antitrust divsn. U.S. Dept. Justice, Wash., 1991—94; assoc. atty. Covington and Burling, Wash., 1994—98; atty. advisor, policy planning FTC, Wash., 1998—99; assoc. atty. Faegre and Benson, LLP, Boulder, 1999—2002. Sec. Social Venture Ptnrs., Denver, 2001—03. Corporate, general, Finance, Antitrust. Home: 2675 Irving St Denver CO 80211 Office: Faegre & Benson LLP 1900 15th St Boulder CO 80302

DICKSEN, DENNIS JOHANSSON, lawyer; b. Gothenburg, Sweden, Oct. 19, 1975; s. Tommy and Ulla Johansson; m. Sara Johanna Kristin Dickson, June 29, 2002; 1 child, Frida Christina Celine. M of Laws, Uppsala U., 1999. Assoc. Advokatfirman Vinge KB, Stockholm, 1999—2001, Advokatfirman Lindahl KB, Uppsala, 2001—02, Orebro, 2002—. Avocations: golf, exercise, cooking, wine, interior decorating. Commercial, contracts (including sales of goods; commercial financing), Landlord-tenant, General civil litigation. Office: Advokatfirman Lindahl KB PO Box 143 SE-70142 Orebro Sweden Fax: +46 19104445. E-mail: dennis.dicksen@lingdahl.se.

DICKSON, BRENT E(LLIS), state supreme court justice; b. July 18, 1941; m. Jan Aikman, June 8, 1963; children: Andrew, Kyle, Reed. BA, Purdue U., 1964; JD, Ind. U., Indpls., 1968; LittD, Purdue U., 1996. Bar: Ind. 1968, U.S. Ct. Appeals (7th cir.) 1972, U.S. Supreme Ct. 1975; cert. civil trial adv., NBTA. Pvt. practice, Lafayette, Ind., 1968-85; sr. ptnr. Dickson, Reiling, Teder & Withered, 1977-85; assoc. justice Ind. Supreme Ct., Indpls., 1986—. Adj. prof. Sch. of Law Ind. U., 1992—. Past pres. Tippecanoe County Hist. Assn.; mem. dean's adv. coun. Sch. Liberal Arts Purdue U., 1990-94; mem. adv. bd. Heartland Film Festival, 1995-2000. Mem. Am. Inns Ct. (founding pres. Sagamore chpt.), Am. Law Inst. Office: Ind Supreme Ct 306 Statehouse Indianapolis IN 46204-2213

DICKSON, CONSTANCE PIERCE, law librarian; b. Boston; d. Lorin Edward and Kathryn (Josephs) Pierce; m. William Simmonds Dickson; children: Mark Pierce, Carol Anne. AB, Tufts U., 1956; MLS, U. Md., 1973. Law librarian Dow, Lohnes & Albertson, Washington, 1973-74, Dewey Ballantine Bushby Palmer & Wood, Paris, 1974-78, Y.B. Kim & Assocs., Seoul, 1978-81, Brownstein Zeidman & Schomer, Washington, 1982-84, Gibson, Dunn & Crutcher, Washington, 1984—. Mem. Am. Assn. Law Librs. (membership com. 1987-88, stats. com. 1988-89, PLL survey 1989-91, CRIV 1993-95, gov. rels. com. 1996-98, AMPS com. 1999-2001, AMPS spl. com. 2001-03, salary survey rev. 2002-03), PLL program com. 1996-99), Law Librarians Soc. Washington (PLL sec. 1984-85, v.p. 1989-90, pres. 1990-91, chair bylaws com. 1992-93), Internat. Assn. Law Librs., Brit. and Irish Assn. Law Librarians, Phi Kappa Phi, Beta Phi Mu. Office: Gibson Dunn & Crutcher 1050 Connecticut Ave NW Washington DC 20036

DICKSON, GREGORY JOHN, lawyer; b. Sydney, Australia, Dec. 8, 1958; s. Alexander and Margaret Dawn (Jennings) D.; m. Sharon Harcourt Jones, Apr. 26, 1990. BJuris, U. NSW, 1981; LLB, U. NSW, Australia, 1982, LLM, 1996. Accredited specialist in family law, Law Soc. of NSW; Appointed solictor Cmty. Panel for Young Offenders, NSW. Solicitor J.J. Cullen & Assoc., NSW, 1982-83, Warren & Co., NSW, 1983-84; ptnr. Warren, McKeon Dickson, NSW, 1984—, Waters Solicitors, NSW, 1996—, J.J. Francis & Co., NSW, 1994—, Shannon, Danieletto, Adler, NSW, 1995—, W.J. Barclay & Co., NSW, 1997—, Phillip Wood & Co., NSW, 1997—, Peter Saxton & Co., NSW, 1997—, Ian M. Genge & Co., 1996—, J.W. Orrell & Assoc., 1994—, Graeme V. Collins & Assocs., 1998—. Chmn. North Cronulla Precinct Com., 1992-95; pres., capt. U. NSW Australian Football Club, 1980-84. Mem. Law Soc. NSW, Royal Automobile Club Australia, Royal Motor Yacht Club of New South Wales. Avocations: Australian football, sailing, military history, travel, reading and collecting books. Office: Warren McKeon Dickson 20-24 Gibbs St/Miranda 2228 Sydney Australia

DICKSON, ROBERT JAY, lawyer; b. Waukegan, Ill., Sept. 20, 1947; s. Robert Jay and Suzanne Elizabeth (Smith) D.; m. J. Alyson Younghusband, June 21, 1969; children: Peter M., Joshua H., Theodore F., Ian A. BA, Northwestern U., 1969; JD, U. Ill., Champaign, 1972. Bar: Alaska 1972, U.S. Dist. Ct. Alaska 1972, U.S. Ct. Appeals (9th cir.) 1972, U.S. Supreme Ct. 1973. Assoc. Atkinson, Conway & Gagnon, Anchorage, 1972—, ptnr., 1974—. Mem. Forum Com. Constrn. Industry, 1978—. Co-author: AK Construct.. Law, 6th rev. edit., 1986, AK Construct. Law, 1998, Advanced Construct. Law in AK, 1999, State Pub. Construct. Law Source book (CCH2002); listed in the Best Lawyers in Am., 1997—. Mem. cmty. adv. bd. Providence Health Sys. Ala., Anchorage; bd. dir. Alaskan Scottish Club, Alaska, 1973—88, Meier Lake Conf. Ctr., Wasilla, Alaska, 1979—88, Homer Soc. Natural History, Alaska, 1985—89, AK Ctr. for the Performing Arts, Alaska, 1990—91, Anchorage Sch. Bus. Partnerships, Alaska, 1995—, AK Support Industry Alliance, Alaska, 1997—, Gov.'s Prayer Breakfast, 1997—, Anchorage Symphony Orch., Alaska, 1987—, pres., 1989—91, 1999—2001; bd. dir., chmn. Russian AK Acad. Fine Arts, 1996—; chmn. bd. trustees Robert E. and Margaret E. Lyle Trust, 1996—. Mem. ABA, Alaska Bar Assn., Anchorage Bar Assn., Am. Acad. Healthcare Attys., Assoc. Gen. Contractors (legal affairs com. Alaska chpt.), Def. Rsch. Inst., Anchorage C. of C., Commonwealth North Club, Capt. Cook Athletic Club (Anchorage). Episcopalian. Avocations: piano, boating. General civil litigation, Construction, Health. Office: Atkinson Conway & Gagnon 420 L St Anchorage AK 99501-1937

DICKSON, ROBERT LEE, lawyer; b. Hot Springs, Ark., Sept. 3, 1932; s. Constantine John and Georgia Marie (Allen) D.; m. Christina Farrar, Oct. 29, 1978; children— Robert Lee, Geoffrey, Alexandra, Christopher, George, John. BBA, U. Tex., 1959, LLB, 1960. Bar: Tex. 1960, Calif. 1965, U.S. Dist. Ct. (no. dist.) Tex. 1960, U.S. Dist. Ct. (ea. dist.) Wis. 1979, U.S. Supreme Ct. 1980, U.S. Dist. Ct. (ea. dist.) Calif. 1983, U.S. Ct. Appeals (7th cir.) 1983, U.S. Dist. Ct. (no. and so. dists.) Calif. 1984, U.S. Ct. Appeals (9th cir.) 1987, U.S. Ct. Appeals (1st and 10th cirs.) 1989. Assoc. to ptnr. Eplen, Daniel & Dickson, Abilene, Tex., 1960-65; assoc. to sr. ptnr. Haight, Dickson, Brown & Bonesteel, Santa Monica, Calif., 1965-88; sr. ptnr. Dickson, Carlson & Campillo, Santa Monica, 1988-98; ptnr. Arter & Hadden, L.A., 1998—2001, Musick, Peeler & Garrett, 2001—. Contbr. articles to profl. jours. Fellow Am. Coll. Trial Lawyers; mem. Ind. Bar Com., Def. Rsch. Inst. (steering com. of drug and device litigation com.), Fedn. Ins. and Corp. Counsel (chmn. pharm. liability litigation sect. 1984-87, v.p. 1986-89, bd. dirs. 1989-95, sec.-treas. 1991-92, pres.-elect 1992-93, pres. 1993-94, chmn. 1994-95), Am. Bd. Trial Advocates, Assn. So. Calif. Def. Counsel (pres. 1976), Bel Air Country Club, Bel Air Bay Club (Pacific Palisades). Republican. Roman Catholic. Federal civil litigation, General civil litigation, State civil litigation. Home: 14952 Alva Dr Pacific Palisades CA 90272-4401 E-mail: rdickson@mpglaw.com.

DICKSON, VICTOR PAUL, lawyer; b. Pensacola, Fla., Aug. 20, 1950; s. Victor Lewis and Mary (Sasnette) D.; m. Paige Stenstrom, May 14, 1988. BA, U. West Fla., 1973; JD, Stetson U., 1976. Bar: Fla. 1976, Tex. 1979; bd. cert. criminal law splist. Tex. Bd. Legal Splization, 1988, bd. cert. Criminal Trial Adv. Nat. Bd. Trial Advocacy, 1992. Asst. pub. defender 20th Cir. Pub. Defenders Off., Naples, Fla., 1977—78; asst. city atty. City Atty.'s Office, Ft. Worth, 1979—84; asst. dist. atty. Tarrant County Criminal Dist. Atty.'s Off., Ft. Worth, 1984—94; pvt. practice Ft. Worth, 1994—. Criminal. Office: PO Box 11611 Fort Worth TX 76110-0611

DICKSTEIN, MICHAEL ETHAN, lawyer; b. Montreal, Sept. 8, 1959; s. Joseph and Barbara Dickstein AB, Harvard U., 1981, JD, 1985. Bar: Calif. 1985. Assoc. Heller, Ehrman, White & McAuliffe, San Francisco, 1985-91, ptnr., 1992; atty., mediator, arbitrator, cons. in pvt. practice, 1993—. Judge pro tem/mediator San Francisco and Alameda Superior and Mcpl. Cts., 1992—; adj. prof., U. San Francisco, 2003; mediation and negotiation instr. Stitt, Feld, et al, 1996—; lectr. in appellate advocacy Boalt Law Sch., U. Calif., Berkeley, 1990; co-chair workplace sect., Assn. for Conflict Resolution, 2001-. Alternative dispute resolution, General civil litigation, Labor (including EEOC, Fair Labor Standards Act, labor-management relations, NLRB, OSHA).

DICKSTEIN, SIDNEY, lawyer; b. Brooklyn, May 13, 1925; s. Charles and Pearl (Stahl) D.; m. Barbara H. (Duke), Sept. 20, 1953; children: Ellen Simeon, Matthew Howard, Nancy Joy. BA, Franklin and Marshall Coll., Lancaster, Pa., 1947; JD, Columbia U., 1949; LLD (hon.) , Franklin and Marshall Coll., Lancaster, Pa., 2003. Bar: N.Y., 1949; D.C., 1959. Law clk. Joseph Richter, N.Y.C., 1949-50; assoc. law office Herman E. Cooper, 1950-53; founder Dickstein and Shapiro, N.Y.C., 1953; sr. ptnr. successor firm Dickstein, Shapiro, Morin, and Oshinsky, Washington, 1953-97, sr. counsel, 1998—. Mem. bd. advisors and article contbr., Jour. of Wealth Mgmt. Contbr. articles to profl. jours including Jour. Wealth Mgmt. Trustee Franklin and Marshall Coll., 1978—. Served with AUS, 1943-44; USNR, 1944-46. Mem.: Am. Jewish Com. (pres. Washington chpt., 1999-2001, mem. nat. bd. gov.), Bar Assn., D.C., ABA. Antitrust, Corporate, general, Securities. Office: 9050 Bradgrove Dr Bethesda MD 20817-3003 also: Dickstein Shapiro Morin & Oshinsky 2101 L St NW Washington DC 20037-1526 E-mail: dicksteins@dsmo.com.

DICLERICO, JOSEPH ANTHONY, JR., federal judge; b. Lynn, Mass., Jan. 30, 1941; s. Joseph Anthony and Ruth Adel (Cummings) DiC.; m. Laurie Breed Thomson, July 27, 1975; 1 child, Devon Thomson. BA, Williams Coll., Williamstown, Mass., 1963; LLB, Yale U., 1966. Bar: N.H. 1967, U.S. Dist. Ct. N.H. 1967, U.S. Ct. Appeals (1st cir.) 1973, U.S. Supreme Ct. 1975. Law clk. to presiding justice U.S. Dist. Ct. N.H., Concord, 1966-67, N.H. Supreme Ct., Concord, 1967-68; assoc. Cleveland Waters & Bass, Concord, 1968-70; asst. atty. gen. State of N.H., Concord, 1970-77; assoc. justice N.H. Superior Ct., Concord, 1977-91, chief justice, 1991-92; chief judge U.S. Dist. Ct. N.H., Concord, 1992-97. Chmn. Superior Ct. sentence rev. disvn., 1987-92. Fellow Am. Bar Found. (life), N.H. Bar Found. (jud.); mem. N.H. Bar Assn (nat. conf. state trial judges 1986-92, nat. conf. fed. trial judges, 1992-96, mem. com. on codes of conduct jud. conf. of U.S. 1994-2002, dist. judge rep. from 1st cir. to Jud. Conf. of U.S. 1997—), Phi Beta Kappa. Republican. Roman Catholic. Avocation: gardening. Office: 55 Pleasant St Concord NH 03301-3954

DICUS, STEPHEN HOWARD, lawyer; b. Kansas City, Mo., Mar. 3, 1948; s. Clarence Howard and Edith Helen (George) D.; m. Jolene Purcell; children: Brett S., Adam J. AB, U. Mo., 1970; JD, U. Mo., Kansas City, 1973. Bar: Mo. 1973, U.S. Dist. Ct. (we. dist.) Mo. 1973. Ptnr. Armstrong Teasdale, Schlafly, Davis & Dicus (formerly Dietrich, Davis, Dicus, Rowlands, Schmitt & Gorman), Kansas City, 1979-91; shareholder Dicus Davis Sands & Collins, P.C., Kansas City, 1991—. Mem. Kansas City Met. Bar Assn., The Missouri Bar, Estate Planning Soc. Kansas City, Rotary Club, Mission Hills Country Club. Presbyterian. Avocations: tennis, golf. Estate planning, Probate (including wills, trusts), Property, real (including real estate development, water). Home: 12019 Ensley Ln Shawnee Mission KS 66209-1069 Office: Dicus Davis Sands & Collins PC 1100 Main St Ste 1930 Kansas City MO 64105-5175

DIDZEREKIS, PAUL PATRICK, lawyer; b. Chgo., Mar. 17, 1939; s. Louis Joseph and Estelle (Traczyk) D.; m. Judith V. Wright, June 30, 1962 (div. 1968); children: Ann Frances, Paul Patrick; m. Heather Joy Izod, Aug. 1969 (dec. 1993); children: Alexandria, Alexis; m. Kathleen A. Breier, Mar. 31, 1994. BBA, Loyola U., Chgo., 1963; JD, Loyola U., 1964. Bar: Ill. 1964, U.S. Supreme Ct. 1971. Atty. govt. affairs law and tax depts. Sears, Roebuck & Co., 1960-65; mem. Ashcraft & Ashcraft, Chgo., 1965-72; sole practice Chgo., 1972-74; pres., ptnr. Didzerekis & Douglas Ltd., Chgo., 1972-74; sole practice Chgo., Wheaton, Ill., 1978—. Mem. paraprofl. adv. bd. Lewis U. Coll. Law, Glen Ellyn, Ill., 1975, adj. prof. legal ethics in action program, 1976-77; chmn. bd., pres. Real Estate Profls. Am. Inc., 1989—; bd. dirs., gen. counsel The Eleanor Assn., 1970-88, pres., 1983-84; commr. DuPage County Bd., 1998-2002. Pres. United Way, Wheaton, 1987-88; chmn. Milton Twp. Rep. Cen. Com., 1996-98; park dist. commr. Wheaton, 1991-98, pres., 1995-97; pub. adminstr. DuPage County, Ill., 01998—; commr. DuPage County Forest Preserve, 1998-2002. Recipient David. C. Hilliard award Chgo. Bar Assn., 1973-74. Fellow Am. Acad. Matrimonial Lawyers; mem. DuPage County Bar Assn., Kiwanis (dir. 1989-93, 2d v.p.). State civil litigation, Family and matrimonial, Probate (including wills, trusts). Home: 411 Hevern Dr Wheaton IL 60187-7395 Office: 610 W Roosevelt Rd Ste 2B Wheaton IL 60187-2303

DIEFENBACH, DALE ALAN, retired law librarian; b. Cleve., Aug. 14, 1933; s. Walter Ewald and Alice Naomi (Austin) D.; m. Olga Maspaitella, Jan. 20, 1973; 1 stepson, Andrew Ivan Ward. BA, Baldwin-Wallace Coll., 1955; MLS, U. Hawaii, 1970. Fgn. svc. officer U.S. Dept. State, 1961-68; reference libr. Cornell U. Law Libr., Ithaca, N.Y., 1970-87; sr. reference libr. Harvard U. Law Libr., Cambridge, Mass., 1987-97, ret., 1997; reference libr., adj. assoc. prof. law libr. Barry U. Sch. Law Euliano Law Libr., 1998—2003. Lt. (j.g.) USNR, 1956-60, Philippines. Recipient Ficken Meml. award Baldwin-Wallace Coll., Berea, Ohio, 1988. Mem. ALA, Am. Assn. Law Librs. Democrat. Home: 500 Windmeadows St Altamonte Springs FL 32701-3572 E-mail: deepbrook@earthlink.net.

DIEHL, BARBARA ROHRMAYER, lawyer, educator; b. West Chester, Pa., June 4, 1945; d. Francis Peter and Mabel Emma (Anderson) Rohrmayer; m. David Waring Diehl, Aug. 28, 1965; children: David, Nathaniel, Deborah. AB, Bryn Mawr Coll., 1967; JD, Pace U., 1981. Bar: N.Y. 1982, Fla. 1982, Calif. 1983. Tchr. Ossining (N.Y.) H.S., 1967-68; instr. The Kings Coll., Briarcliff Manor, N.Y., 1968-81; pvt. practice law Yorktown Hgts., N.Y. Instr. Nyack (N.Y.) Coll., 1992—. Pres. Sch. Bd. Yorktown Hts., mem., 1976-97; gen. counsel Am. Bible Soc., 1994-1998; sr. gift planning officer ARC, 2000-. Mem. ABA, N.Y. State Bar Assn., Christian Legal Soc. Office: 2074 Crompond Rd Yorktown Heights NY 10598-4232

DIEHL, DEBORAH HILDA, lawyer; b. Troy, N.Y., Feb. 13, 1951; d. Warren S. and Norma K. (Apple) D.; 1 child, Alexandra Ellen. Student, U. de Rouen, France, 1971-72; BA, St. Lawrence U., 1973; JD, Syracuse U., 1976; postdoctoral, George Washington U., 1978-79. Bar: N.Y. 1977, D.C. 1981, Ohio 1982, Md. 1987. Atty. USDA, Washington, 1976-81; assoc. Thompson, Hine & Flory, Columbus, Ohio, 1981-87, Semmes, Bowen & Semmes, Balt., 1987-90, ptnr., 1990-95, Whiteford, Taylor & Preston, Balt., 1995—. Pres. Mt. Royal Improvement Assn., 1995—97; chair Midtown Cmty. Benefits Dist. Mgmt. Authority, 1998—2000, dir., 1995—2001, Midtown Devel. Corp., 2000—; participant Leadership Md., 1997; mem. U.

Md. Balt. County Tech. Ctr. Adv. Bd., 2001—. Mem.: ABA, Bar Assn. City Balt., Md. State Bar Assn. (bus. law sect. coun. 1998—, chair 2002—03). Avocations: bicycling, travel, economic development. Corporate, general, Finance, Mergers and acquisitions.

DIEHL, RICHARD PAUL, lawyer; b. Toledo, Dec. 25, 1940; s. Clair Bertrand and Josephine Frances (Kwiatkowski) D.; m. Laura Gean Carpenter, Mar. 26, 1966; children: Michelle, Michael. BSME, U. Mich., 1963; MBA, Tulane U., 1972; JD, U. Detroit, 1983. Bar: Mich. 1983, U.S. Dist. Ct. (ea. dist.) Mich. 1983, U.S. Supreme Ct. 1988, U.S. Ct. Fed. Claims 1990, U.S. Ct. Appeals (6th cir.) 1991, U.S. Ct. Appeals (fed., D.C. cirs.) 1992), U.S. Dist. Ct. (we. dist.) Mich. 1996. Commd. 2d lt. U.S. Army, 1963, advanced through grades to col., ret., 1986; pres. Diehl & Sobczak, PC, Troy, Mich., 1986-99; with Inst. for Def. Analyses, Alexandria, Va., 1999—. Adj. prof. bus. Am. Tech. U., Killeen, Tex., 1977-78; adj. prof. law U. Detroit, 1987-89. Contbr. articles to profl. jours. Decorated 2 Silver stars, five Bronze stars, 2 Purple Hearts, 2 Legions of Merit Meritorious Svc. medal, Army Commendation medal, 3 Air medals, Cross of Gallantry. Mem. Am. Def. Preparedness Assn., Assn. U.S. Army, U. Mich. Alumni Assn., Elks. Avocations: hunting, fishing, sports. General practice, Government contracts and claims. Office: 1105 Kingsview Ave Rochester Hills MI 48309-2510 E-mail: rpdiehl@aol.com.

DIEHM, JAMES WARREN, lawyer, educator; b. Lancaster, Pa., Nov. 6, 1944; s. Warren G. and Verna M. (Hertzler) D.; m. Cathleen M. Hohmeier; children: Elizabeth Ann, Rebecca Jane. BA, Pa. State U., 1966; JD, Georgetown U., 1969. Bar: D.C. 1969, V.I. 1975, Pa. 1988. Asst. U.S. atty., Washington, 1970-74; asst. atty. gen. Atty. Gen.'s Office U.S. V.I., St. Croix, 1974-76; from assoc. to ptnr. Isherwood, Hunter & Diehm, St. Croix, 1976-83; U.S. atty. U.S. V.I., 1983-87; prof. law Widener U., 1987—. Bar examiner U.S. V.I. Bar, 1979-87. Mem. ABA. Republican. Lutheran. Office: Widener U Sch Law 3800 Vartan Way PO Box 69382 Harrisburg PA 17106-9382

DIEKMANN, GILMORE FREDERICK, JR., lawyer; b. Evansville, Ind., Jan. 14, 1946; s. Gilmore Frederick Sr. and Mabel Pauline (Daniel) K.; children: Anne Westlake, Andrew Gilmore, Matthew Frederick. BSBA, Northwestern U., 1968, JD, 1971. Bar: Calif. 1972, U.S. Dist. Ct. Calif. (no., ea., cen. and so. dists.) Calif. 1972, U.S. Ct. Appeals (9th cir.) 1972, U.S. Supreme Ct. 1978. Assoc. Bronson, Bronson & McKinnon, San Francisco, 1971-78, ptnr. labor and employment law, 1979-99, chmn., mng. ptnr., 1991-93, chmn. labor, employment dept., 1993-99; ptnr. Seyfarth Shaw, San Francisco, 1999—, chmn. no. Calif. labor dept., 1999—. Author and speaker in field. Mem. ABA, Def. Rsch. Inst., Am. Employment Law Coun., Order of Coif. Republican. Lutheran. General civil litigation, Labor (including EEOC, Fair Labor Standards Act, labor-management relations, NLRB, OSHA). Home: 901 Powell St # 6 San Francisco CA 94108 Office: Seyfarth Shaw 101 California St Ste 2900 San Francisco CA 94111-5858 E-mail: gdiekmann@sf.seyfarth.com.

DIENES, LOUIS ROBERT, lawyer; b. New Brunswick, N.J., Apr. 17, 1966; s. Louis S. and Rosemary T. D. AB, U. Calif., Berkeley, 1990; JD, Stanford U., 1994. Bar: Calif. 1994. Assoc. Baker & McKenzie LLP, Palo Alto, Calif., 1994-96, Pennie & Edmonds LLP, 1996-99, Gibson Dunn & Crutcher LLP, N.Y.C., 1999—2001, Christensen Miller, L.A., 2001—. Bd. dirs. Hollywood Bowl Soc., Calif., 2002—; mem. adv. bd. L.A. Bus. Tech. Ctr., L.A., 2002—. Mem. Santa Clara Bar Assn. (co-chmn. high tech law sect. 1998-99), Phi Beta Kappa. Commercial, contracts (including sales of goods; commercial financing), Corporate, general, Intellectual property. Office: 2121 Ave of the Stars Los Angeles CA 90067 E-mail: l_dienes@msn.com.

DIENST, ARMIN, lawyer; b. Herzberg, Lower Saxony, Germany, Sept. 27, 1965; s. Joachim Siegfried and Maria Sophie Dienst. 1st exam, Georgia Augusta U., 1992; 2d exam, Ct. Appeals Braunschweig, 1997. Bar: Regional Cts. Germany. Legal asst. Tech. U., Clausthal, Germany, 1992—94; assoc. Feddersen Laule Scherzberg Ohle Hansen Ewerwahn, Frankfurt/Main, Germany, 1997—2000, Schulte Lawyers, Frankfurt/Main, 2000—01, ptnr., 2002—. Mem.: Rechtsanwaltskammer, Atlantik Bruecke. Corporate, general, Mergers and acquisitions. Office: Schulte Lawyers Hochstrasse 49 60313 Frankfurt Hessen Germany

DIESELHORST, JOCHEN, lawyer; b. Hannover, Germany, Mar. 18, 1966; married. JD, U. Hamburg, Germany, 1992. Communications, Computer, Intellectual property. Office: Freshfields Bruckhaus Deringer Alsterarkaden 27 20354 Hamburg Germany Fax: 49-40-36 90 61 55. E-mail: jochen.dieselhorst@freshfields.com.

DIETEL, JAMES EDWIN, lawyer, consultant; b. Dallas, Sept. 14, 1941; s. Bernhard Herman and Gladys Ellen D.; m. Elizabeth Nathan, May 9, 1964; 1 child, Elizabeth Lindsay. BSME, So. Meth. U., 1964; JD, George Washington U., 1969; LLM in Internat. Trade, Georgetown U., 1977; MBA, U. Pa., 1992. Bar: D.C. 1971, U.S. Dist. Ct. D.C. 1971, U.S. Ct. Appeals (D.C. cir.) 1975, U.S. Supreme Ct. 1975, Va. 1990. Engr. CIA, Washington, 1964-70, program evaluation officer, 1970-73, assoc. gen. counsel, 1979-80, assoc. dep. gen. counsel, 1980—82, dep. gen. counsel, 1982—90, insp. and with office exec. dir., 1990—94, counsel for info. policy, 1994-95; pvt. practice, 1995—. Participant ann. jud. conf. U.S. Ct. Appeals (D.C. cir.), 1986; speaker, ltr. and presenter in field. Author: Leading a Law Practice to Excellence, 1992, Sustaining Law Practice Excellence, 1992, Designing Effective Records Retention Compliance Program, 1993, Leaders' Digest: A Review of the Best Books on Leadership, 1995; chmn. bd. Law Practice Quar.; contbr. articles to profl. jours. Mem. ABA (coun. mem. law practice mgmt. sect., chmn. govt. and pub. sector lawyers divsn.), Coll. Law Practice Mgmt., Cosmos Club, Pi Tau Sigma, Kappa Mu Epsilon, Kappa Alpha.

DIETRICH, JOSEPH EDWARD, III, lawyer; b. Buffalo; s. Joseph Edward and Kathleen Nora Dietrich; m. Colleen Patricia Dietrich, Dec. 21, 1997; children: Grace Marie, Liesl Monica, Joseph Edward III. BBA, Temple U., Phila., 1991; JD, SUNY, Buffalo, 1995. Bar: N.Y. 1996, U.S. Dist. Ct. (we. dist.) N.Y. 1997. Asst. dist. atty. Erie County Dist. Atty., Buffalo, 1996—98; 1st asst. dist. atty. Cattaraugus County Dist. Atty., Little Valley, NY, 1998—99; ptnr. Cellino & Barnes, P.C., Buffalo, 1999—. Legal counsel Dietrich Funeral Homes, Inc., Amherst, NY, 1996—. Mem.: ATLA, Bar Assn. Erie County. Avocations: skiing, water-skiing, windsurfing, Telemark skiing. Personal injury (including property damage). Home: 120 Wood Acres Dr East Amherst NY 14051 Office: Cellino & Barnes PC 17 Court St 7th Flr Buffalo NY 14202

DIETRICH, WILLIAM GALE, lawyer, real estate developer, consultant; b. Kansas City, Mo., Mar. 6, 1925; s. Roy Kaiser and Gale (Gossett) D.; m. Marjorie Nell Reich, July 14, 1945; children: Meredith G. Dietrich Steinhaus, Ann. E. Dietrich Cooling, Walter R. AB with high honors, Yale U., 1948, LLB, 1951. Bar: Mo. 1951. Ptnr. Dietrich, Davis, Dicus, Rowlands, Schmitt & Gorman (and predecessors), 1953-73; project dir., gen. counsel Blue Ridge Shopping Ctr., Inc., Kansas City, 1955-73, pres., gen. mgr., 1964-73, Blue Ridge Tower, Inc., Kansas City, 1967-73; sec.-treas. A. Reich & Sons, Inc., Kansas City, 1973-88, chmn., 1988—; pvt. practice law Kansas City, 1973—; sec., treas. A. Reich & Sons Gardens, Inc., 1973-89; pres. J&D Devel., Inc., 1987—; gen. ptnr. J & D Enterprises, 1986—; gen. mgr. The Farm Shopping and Office Ctr., 1994-98; pres. BBJ Treats, L.L.C., 1994-98; mem. WGD Properties, LLC, 1999—. Sec., bd. dirs. Rsch. Med. Ctr., Kansas City, 1977, vice-chmn., 1980-83, chmn., 1983-87; bd. dirs. The Rsch. Found., 1980-91, vice-chmn., 1989-91; bd. dirs. Rsch. Health Svcs., 1980-81, vice chmn., 1983-87, chmn. 1987-89; bd. dirs. Mahana Condominium Assn., Maui, Hawaii, 1977-96, Blue Ridge Bank and Trust Co., Kansas City, 1982-94; vestry mem. Grace & Holy Trinity Cathedral, Kansas City, 1972-95, former treas. 1st lt. AUS, 1943-46, PTO. Recipient Army Commendation Ribbon, 1946. Mem. ABA, Mo. Bar Assn., Kansas City Bar Assn., Blue Ridge Mall Mchts. Assn. (dir. 1958-73), Internat. Coun. Shopping Ctrs. (past dir. for Mo., Kans, Iowa, cert. shopping ctr. mgr.), Lawyers Assn. Kansas City, Mission Hills Country Club, Yale Club, Kansas City (Mo.) Club, Rotary (bd. dirs., sec. found. Kansas City 1978—), Phi Beta Kappa (pres. Kansas City chpt. 1989-91), Phi Delta Phi. Home: 1000 Huntington Rd Kansas City MO 64113-1346 Office: 6155 Oak St Profl Bldg Ste A Kansas City MO 64113-2266 E-mail: wgdlo@aol.com.

DIETZ, CHARLTON HENRY, lawyer; b. LeMars, Iowa, Jan. 8, 1931; s. Clifford Henry and Mildred Verna (Eggensperger) D.; m. Viola Ann Lange, Aug. 17, 1952; children: Susan (Mrs. Jay Kakuk), Robin (Mrs. Jack Mayfield), Craig. BA, Macalester Coll., 1953; JD, William Mitchell Coll. Law, 1957, LLD, 1993. Bar: Minn. 1957. Mem. pub. rels. staff 3M, St. Paul, 1952-58, atty., 1958-70, assoc. counsel, asst. sec., 1970-72, asst. gen. counsel, 1972-75, sec., 1972-76, gen. counsel, 1975-92, v.p. legal affairs, 1976-88, sr. v.p., 1988-93. Bd. dirs. Mairs & Power Mutual Funds; instr. William Mitchell Coll. Law, 1960-74, trustee, 1974-86, 87-96, pres., 1980-83. Bd. dirs. St. Paul Area YMCA, 1973-80, chmn. 1978-80, Minn. Citizens Coun. on Crime and Justice, 1976-88, 2002—, pres., 1982-84, St. Paul United Way, 1980-95, Ramsey County Hist. Soc., 1979-86, 2002—, St. Paul Lowertown Redevel. Corp., 1988-94, Minn. Hist. Soc., 1993-2002, Supreme Ct. Hist. Soc., 1991—, Children's Hosps. and Clinics, 1994-2002; trustee United Theol. Sem., 1976-82, Macalester Coll., 1983-89, Wilder Found., 1989-2003, chmn., 1996-2000; mem. Conferees of Minn. Citizens Conf. on Cts.; bd. dirs. Masonic Cancer Ctr. Fund, 1984—, pres. 1994-97; exec. bd. Indianhead Coun., Boy Scouts Am., 1986—, pres., 1992-93; bd. dirs. Historic St. Paul, 2002—. Fellow Am. Bar Found.; mem. ABA, Minn. Bar Assn., Ramsey County Bar Assn., Assn. Gen. Counsel, Am. Judicature Soc. (bd. dirs. 1989-95), Am. Law Inst., Masons, Shriners, Jesters. Republican. Mem. United Ch. of Christ. Corporate, general. Home: 1 Birch Ln Saint Paul MN 55127-6402

DIETZ, ROBERT BARRON, lawyer; b. San Diego, May 14, 1942; s. J. Thomas and Mary Agnes (Barron) D.; m. Grace Louise Purcell, Aug. 19, 1967; children: Thomas E., Michael B., Denis P., M. Alison. AB, Coll. Holy Cross, 1964; JD, Cornell U., 1968. Bar: N.Y. 1968, U.S. Dist. Ct. (no. dist.) N.Y. 1968, U.S. Dist. Ct. (so. and ea. dists.) N.Y. 1973, U.S. Supreme Ct. 1974. Asst. dist. atty. County of Dutchess, Poughkeepsie, N.Y., 1969-70, confidential law clk. to surrogate of Dutchess County, 1970-73; corp. counsel City of Poughkeepsie, 1973-75; assoc. Garrity & Dietz, Poughkeepsie, 1969-73, ptnr., 1973-75; assoc. Gellert & Cutler, P.C. and predecessor firms, Poughkeepsie, 1975-78, ptnr., 1978-86; pvt. practice law Poughkeepsie, 1986-94; ptnr. Dietz & Dietz LLP, Poughkeepsie, 1995—. Lectr. Dutchess C.C., Poughkeepsie, 1985-98, practical skills course N.Y. State Bar Assn. Bd. dirs. Mid Hudson Workshop for Disabled; former mem. Sports Mus. Dutchess County; chmn. Mid Hudson adv. bd. Salvation Army, 1998-2000; bd. trustees Vassar-Warner Home, 1997-2001; bd. counsellors The Children's Home of Poughkeepsie, Inc., 1997—; past bd. dirs. Dutchess County coun. Boy Scouts Am., 1997; former mem. City of Poughkeepsie Recreation Commn.; bd. dirs. Greystone Programs, Inc., 1999—; mem. Pastoral Coun. Ch. Holy Trinity, 1999-2001. Fellow Dist. 721 Rotary, Poughkeepsie, 1964-65. Mem. ABA, N.Y. State Bar Assn. (lectr. practical skills course, probate, elder), Dutchess County Bar Assn., Poughkeepsie C. of C., Kiwanis (pres. Poughkeepsie club 1974-75). Republican. Roman Catholic. Avocations: golf, tennis, reading, baseball card collecting. General practice, Probate (including wills, trusts), Property, real (including real estate development, water). Office: 2 Cannon St Poughkeepsie NY 12601-3224 E-mail: rdietz@dietzllp.com.

DIEZ, MAITE, lawyer; b. Bilbao, Spain, Jan. 13, 1963; Diploma in Econs., Law Degree, U. of Deusto, Madrid, 1986; LLM in Internat. Bus., Legal Studies, U. of Exeter, Eng., 1987. Assoc. Baker & McKenzie, Madrid, 1988—93, N.Y.C., 1993—94, Madrid, 1994—96, 1996—2000, internat. ptnr., 2000—, mng. ptnr., 2001—. Communications, Corporate, general, Mergers and acquisitions. Office: Baker & McKenzie Paseo de la Castellana 33 Madrid 28046 Spain Office Fax: 34 91 391 51 45.

DIFRONZO, MICHAEL A. lawyer, accountant; b. Billings, Mont., Sept. 23, 1968; s. Michael J. and Ashlea C. DiFronzo. BS in Acctg., Mont. State U., 1991; JD, U. Mont., 1994; LLM in Tax, NYU, 1997. Mont. 1994, Nev. 1995, DC 1998, U.S. Ct. Appeals (fed. cir.) 1998, U.S. Tax Ct. 1998. Sr. tax cons. Deloitte & Touche, Reno, 1994-96, internat. tax mgr. Washington, 1997-99, internat. tax sr. mgr., 2000—; assoc. Weil Gotshal & Manges, Washington, 1999-2000. Contbr. articles to profl. jours. Mem. ABA, Mont. Bar Assn., Nev. Bar Assn., D.C. Bar Assn., Mont. Bd. CPAs. Public international, Corporate taxation, Taxation, general.

DIGGES, EDWARD S(IMMS), business management consultant; b. Pitts., June 30, 1946; AB, Princeton U., 1968; JD, U. Md., 1971. Bar: Md. 1972, U.S. Supreme Ct. 1975. With staff of gov. State of Md., Annapolis, 1973; ptnr. Piper & Marbury, Washington and Balt., 1977-84; founding ptnr. Digges, Wharton & Levin, Annapolis, 1984-89; corp. cons. various corps., Towson, Md., 1989—. Bd. dirs. Televest, LLC, Intervest, LLC, Corp. Comms. Mgmt. Group, LLC, Interlude, LLC, ITMG, LLC, DTC Telecom, LLC, Spindrift, LLC, Antiques News Group, LLC; instr. advanced bus. law Johns Hopkins U., 1975—78; lectr. civil procedure U. Balt. Law Sch., 1976—78; mem. govs. commn. to revise Md. code, 1978—90. Contbr. articles to profl. jours. Mem. Alumni Council Mercersburg Acad., 1982-88, pres. 1987-88; bd. advisors Indian Creek Sch., 1982-88, chmn. 1986-88; pres. Beacon Hill Community Assn., 1978-86. ROTC, U.S. Army, 1970-71. Mem. Md. State Bar Assn. (bd. govs. 1972-84), Am. Law Inst., Am. Bd. Trial Adv. (pres. Md. chpt. 1984-89), Inn XIII, Am. Inns of Ct. (Master of the Bench 1986-89), Scribes. Clubs: So. Md. Soc. (bd. govs., pres. 1988), Mid Ocean (Bermuda), Princeton Club of N.Y. Democrat. Roman Catholic. Home: PO Box 42737 Baltimore MD 21284-2737 E-mail: diggesy@aol.com.

DI GIULIAN, BRUNO L. lawyer; b. West Palm Beach, Fla., Dec. 24, 1933; s. Angelo and Teresita Irma Di Giulian; m. Patsy R. Sammons, July 30, 1960; children: Teri, Bee Gee, Angelo. BA, Stetson U., 1954; JD, Yale U., 1957. Bar: Fla. 1957, U.S. Dist. Ct. (no. dist.) Fla. 1959, U.S. Dist. Ct. (so dist.) Fla. 1965, U.S. Ct. Appeals (11th cir.) 1981; cert. mediator. Assoc. Coe, Richardson & Broberg, Palm Beach, 1957-58; rsch. assoc. to chief justice Glenn Terrell Fla. Supreme Ct., Tallahassee, 1958-60; city atty. City of Pompano Beach, Fla., 1960-63; pvt. practice law Ft. Lauderdale, Fla., 1964-94; of counsel Ruden, McClosky, Smith, Schuster & Russell, P.A., Ft. Lauderdale, 1994—. Bd. dirs. BankAtlantic; chmn. 17th Cir. Trial Ct. Nominating Coun., 1971-76. Trustee St. Thomas Aquinas Found., 1979-81; pres., bd. dirs. St. Thomas More Soc. South Fla. Recipient Young Man of the Yr. award Pompano Beach Jaycees, 1963. Mem. Fla. Bar (vice-chmn. com. on econs. 1966-71, chmn. group legal svc. com. 1975, real property and probate law sect. 1976-90, family law sect. 1978-94), Broward County Bar Assn. (chmn. 17th cir. grievance com. A 1969, treas. 1969-70, pres. 1971-72, Professionalism in Practice award 2000, Fla. bar grievance com. A 2000-2003, chmn. 2002), Phi Delta Phi. Roman Catholic. Avocations: travel, languages, computers. Home: 12045 NW 62d Ct Coral Springs FL 33076-1906 Office: Ruden McClosky Smith Schuster & Russell PA 200 E Broward Blvd Fort Lauderdale FL 33301-1963 E-mail: bld@ruden.com., bdigiulian@cs.com.

DIGNAN, THOMAS GREGORY, JR., lawyer; b. Worcester, Mass., May 23, 1940; s. Thomas Gregory and Hester Clare (Sharkey) D.; m. Mary Anne Connor, Sept. 16, 1978; children: Kellyanne E., Maryclare E. BA, Yale U., 1961; JD, U. Mich., 1964. Bar: Mass. 1964, U.S. Supreme Ct. 1968. Assoc. firm Ropes & Gray, Boston, 1964-74, ptnr. firm, 1974-2000, of counsel, 2001—. Spl. asst. atty. gen. State of Mass., 1974-76; trustee NSTAR. Asst. editor: Mich. Law Rev., 1963-64; contbr. articles to profl. jours. Bd. dirs. Family Counseling and Guidance Ctrs., Inc., 1967-76, 78-94, v.p., 1983-87, pres., 1987-89; trustee Cath. Charitable Bur. of Boston, Inc., 1994-97, Dana Hall Sch., 1994—; bd. dirs. Gov.'s Mgmt. Task Force, 1979-81, Mass. Moderator's Assn., 1994-2000; mem. fin. com. Town of Sudbury, 1982-85, moderator, 1985—; bd. advisors Environ. Law Ctr., Vt. Law Sch., 1981—; mem. vis. com. U. Mich. Law Sch.; corporator Emerson Hosp., 1989—. Mem. Nashawtuc Country Club, Shadow Wood Country Club, Order of the Coif, Phi Delta Phi. Republican. Roman Catholic. Federal civil litigation, Nuclear power, Environmental. Home: 8 Saddle Ridge Rd Sudbury MA 01776-2772 E-mail: tdignanjr@aol.com.

DIKEOU, GEORGE DEMETRIOS, lawyer, educator; b. Denver, Sept. 2, 1938; s. James George and Minnie A. (Girk) D.; m. Debby E. Wing, June 12, 1960 (div. June 1975); children: Erica, Carissa; m. Yonnie Kay Bell, June 18, 1977; 1 child, Damara. BA in Econs., Colo. Coll., 1960; cert. completion, U. Edinburgh, 1961; JD, Stanford U., 1964. Bar: Colo. 1965, Calif. 1965, U.S. Dist. Ct. Colo. 1965, U.S. Ct. Appeals (10th cir.) 1965, U.S. Ct. Claims 1980, U.S. Supreme Ct. 1980. Assoc. Holland & Hart, Denver, 1964-66; ptnr. Davies, St. Veltrie & Dikeou, Denver, 1966-72; asst. atty. gen. State of Colo., Denver, 1972-81, spl. asst. atty. gen., 1981-85; mng. ptnr. Roan & Grossman, Denver, 1981-82; ptnr. Gorsuch, Kirgis, Denver, 1982-85, Faegre & Benson, Denver, 1985-89; pvt. practice Englewood, Colo., 1989—. Asst. atty. gen. Colo. Dept. Hwys., Denver, 1966-72; gen. counsel Health Scis. Ctr. U. Colo, 1972-77, instr. Dept. Preventative Medicine, 1972-80, clin instr., 1980-82, asst. prof. sch. nursing, 1978-80, adj. asst. prof. health adminstrn. Grad. Sch. Bus. Adminstrn., 1982-98, vice chancellor for legal affairs and risk mgmt., 1980-81, mem. trust adv. bd., 1976-84, asst. Univ. counsel, 1972-77; instr. Webster U. Grad. Sch., Denver, 1983-88; bd. dirs. COPIC Trust, Denver; exec. v.p. COPIC Ins. Co., Denver. Pres. Wellshire Homeowner's Assn., 1969-71; chmn. adv. com. Regional Cancer Ctr., Denver, 1977-79; bd. dirs. for Neurologic Diseases, Rocky Mountain Multiple Sclerosis Found., Denver, 1979-92; bd. dirs. Family Support Svcs., Inc., Denver., 1982-84, Timber Ridge Homeowners Assn., Dillon, Colo., 1986-92, Wilderness Homeowners Assn., Dillon, 1986-92; bd. vis. Stanford U. Sch. Law, 1985-91; bd. dirs. Mountain Med. Affiliates, 1992-96, Case Med. Found., Denver, 1992—, Colo. Personalized Edn. for Physicians, Denver, 1990—, Colo. Physicians Health Program, Denver, 2003—. Recipient Mack Easton Distinguished Svc. award U. Colo., 1987, Outstanding Faculty MHA program award U. Colo., 1997. Mem. ABA, Colo. Bar Assn. (interprofl. com. 1987-89) Calif. Bar Assn., Denver Bar Assn. (interprofl. com. 1987-89), Soc. Law and Medicine. Health, Insurance, Legislative.

DIKTAS, CHRISTOS JAMES, lawyer; b. June 17, 1955; s. Christos James and Elpiniki (Angelou) D. Student, U. Salonika, Greece, 1976, U. Copenhagen, Denmark, 1976; BA, Montclair State U., 1977; JD, Calif. Western Sch. Law, 1981; diplomate, Rutgers U., 1992. Bar: N.J. 1982, U.S. Dist. Ct. N.J. 1982, N.Y. 1989, U.S. Supreme Ct. 1989. Law sec. to Hon. James F. Madden Superior Ct., Hackensack, N.J., 1981-82; sr. assoc. Klinger, Nicolette, Mavroudis & Honig, Hackensack, 1982-85; ptnr. Montecallo & Diktas, Hackensack, 1985-86, Biagiotti, Marino, Montecallo & Diktas, Hackensack, 1986-89, Diktas & Habeeb, North Bergen, N.J., 1989-94, Diktas Gillen, 1995-99; pvt. practice Diktas & Assocs., Cliffside Park, N.J., 2000—. Asst. counsel Bergen County, 1986-87; atty. zoning bd. adjustment Borough of Cliffside Park, 1986-94, borough atty., 1994—; planning bd. Borough of Ridgefield, N.J., 1987-99, 2001—, borough atty., 2000-01; borough atty., Bogota, N.J., 1989-91, Fairview, N.J., 1994-95; bd. edn. atty., Bogota, 1992-95; labor counsel Bergen County, N.J., 1990-2001; atty. planning bd. City of Garfield, N.J., 1994-2003; atty., sec. Garfield Redevel. Agy., 2002—; adj. prof. law Montclair (N.J.) State U., 1988—. Editor lead articles Calif. Western Internat. Law Jour., 1980-81. Campaign dir. Kingman for Senate Com., Bergen County, N.J., 1983; mcpl. coord. Kean for Gov. campaign, 1985; asst. treas. Arthur F. Jones for Congress, 9th Congl. Dist., 1986. Mem. ABA, N.J. Bar Assn., Bergen County Bar Assn., Order of Am. Hellenic Edn. Progressive Assn., Phi Alpha Delta (parliamentarian Campbell E. Beaumont chpt. 1978-81), Sons of Pericles (5th dist. gov. 1976-77, supreme gov. 1977-78). Greek Orthodox. Commercial, contracts (including sales of goods; commercial financing), General practice, Property, real (including real estate development, water). Home: 445 Oncrest Ter Cliffside Park NJ 07010-2814 Office: Diktas & Assocs 596 Anderson Ave Cliffside Park NJ 07010-1831 E-mail: diktasesqs@aol.com.

DILG, JOSEPH CARL, lawyer; b. Dallas, Apr. 1, 1951; s. Millard John and Helen Mary (Gill) D.; m. Alexandra Gregg, Aug. 5, 1972; children: Helen Lane, Mary Saunders. BA, So. Meth. U., 1973; JD with high honors, U. Tex., 1976. Bar: Tex. 1976. Assoc. Vinson & Elkins, Houston, 1976-83, ptnr., 1983—. Editor U. Tex. Law Rev., 1976. Named Outstanding Editor U. Tex. Law Rev., 1976. Mem. ABA, Tex. Bar Assn., Houston Bar Assn., Chancellors, Order of Coif. Corporate, general, Private international. Office: Vinson & Elkins 3401 First City Tower 1001 Fannin St Houston TX 77002-6760 E-mail: jdilg@velaw.com.

DILKS, PARK BANKERT, JR., lawyer; b. Phila., Mar. 25, 1928; s. Park Bankert and Gertrude Scott (Hilton) D.; children: Jonathan Park, Jennifer Robin. AB, U. Pa., 1948, JD, 1951. Bar: Pa. 1952, D.C. 1951, U.S. Supreme Ct. 1962. Asst. dist. atty., Phila., 1952; assoc. firm Souser & Schumacker, Phila., 1953-60, Morgan, Lewis & Bockius, Phila., 1961-63, ptnr., 1964-95, of counsel, 1996—. Chmn. bd. U.S. Investment Fund, 1973-2001; bd. dirs. Pri Mentia, Inc. Served as 1st lt. USAR, 1952-58. Mem. ABA, Pa. Bar Assn., Phila. Bar Assn., D.C. Bar Assn., Fed. Bar Assn., Assn. Bar City N.Y., Union League, Phi Beta Kappa. Banking, Private international. Home: 140 Lakeside Ln Media PA 19063-2047 Office: 1701 Market St Philadelphia PA 19103-2903 E-mail: pbdilks@worldnet.att.net., pdilks@morganlewis.com.

DILLARD, JOHN MARTIN, lawyer, pilot; b. Long Beach, Calif., Dec. 25, 1945; s. John Warren and Clara Leora (Livermore) D.; m. Patricia Anne Yeager, Aug. 10, 1968; children: Jason Robert, Jennifer Lee. Student, U. Calif., Berkeley, 1963-67; BA, UCLA, 1968; JD, Pepperdine U., 1976. Bar: Calif. 1976. Instr. pilot, Norton AFB, Calif., 1973-77; assoc. Magana, Cathcart & McCarthy, L.A., 1977-80, Lord, Bissell & Book, L.A., 1980-85; of counsel Finley, Kumble, Wagner, 1985-86, Schell & Delamer, 1986-94, Law Offices of John M. Dillard, 1986—; v.p., gen. counsel, dir. Resort Aviation Svcs., Inc., Calif., 1988-93; mng. ptnr. Natkin & Weisbach, So. Calif., 1988-89; arbitrator Orange County Superior Ct. Atty. settlement officer U.S. Dist. Ct. Ctrl. Dist. Calif.; trained mediator Straus Inst. Active Am. Cancer Soc.; bd. dirs. Placentia-Yorba Linda Ednl. Found., Inc. Capt. USAF, 1968-73, Vietnam. Mem. ATLA (aviation litigation com.), Am. Bar Assn. (aviation com.), Orange County Bar Assn., Fed. Bar Assn., L.A. County Bar Assn. (aviation com.), Century City Bar Assn., Internat. Platform Assn., Res. Officers Assn., Orange County Com. of 100, Sigma Nu. Home: 19621 Verona Ln Yorba Linda CA 92886-2858 Office: 313 N Birch St Santa Ana CA 92701-5263

DILLARD, JOHN ROBERT, lawyer; b. Sylva, N.C., Mar. 14, 1955; s. George Washington and Ethel Thomasine (Freeman) Dillard; m. Olga M. Dillard, Feb. 3, 1998. BSBA cum laude, Western Carolina U., 1977; JD, Samford U., 1980; postgrad., Western Carolina U., 1986-88; PhD in Bus. Adminstr. with honors, S.W. U., 1989. Bar: N.C. 1980, U.S. Dist. Ct. (we. dist.) N.C. 1981. Sole practice, Cashiers, N.C., 1980-81; ptnr. Alley, Killian, Kersten & Dillard, Waynesville, N.C., 1981-85; sr. v.p., atty. Commonwealth Land Title Co., Asheville, N.C., 1985-93; pres., state mgr. Stewart Title of N.C., Asheville, 1993—. Legal counsel Woodmen of World Ins.,

Waynesville, 1982-85, bd. dirs.; sec. Beta-Zeta Ltd., Waynesville, 1982-84, bd. dirs.; cons. Nereus Inc., Greenville, Tenn., 1986-88; adj. faculty Asheville-Buncome Tech. Coll., 1990-93, Mars Hill Coll., 1992; instr. Nat. Bus. Inst., 1996. Legal counsel, bd. dirs. Lambda Chi Alpha, Cullowhee, N.C., 1983-85; adv. Jr. Achievement, Clyde, N.C., 1984. Recipient Unsung Brother award, Lambda Chi Alpha, 1974. Mem.: ATLA, ABA (cert. arbitrator), N.C. Land Title Assn., N.C. Real Property Assn., Am. Land Title Assn., N.C. Coll. Advocacy, N.C. State Bar (mem. constl. law com. 1996—2000), N.C. Acad. Trial Lawyers, Woodsmen (trustee 1982—99), Masons. Democrat. Episcopalian. Corporate, general, Property, real (including real estate development, water). Home: 4 Wagner Branch Dr Asheville NC 28804-1000 Office: 53 Asheland Ave Ste 101 Asheville NC 28801-3522

DILLARD, STEPHEN C. lawyer; b. Tyler, Tex., Nov. 1, 1946; BA, Baylor U., 1968, JD, 1971. Bar: Tex. 1971. Mem. Fulbright & Jaworski L.L.P., Houston. Fellow Am. Coll. Trial Lawyers (life), Tex. Bar Found. (life), Internat. Assn. Def. Counsel, Am. Bd. Trial Advocates; mem. ABA, State Bar Tex., Tex. Assn. Def. Counsel, Houston Bar Assn., Phi Alpha Delta (v.p. 1984-87). Office: Fulbright & Jaworski LLP 1301 Mckinney St Ste 5100 Houston TX 77010-3031 E-mail: sdillard@fulbright.com.

DILLARD, W. THOMAS, lawyer; b. Dothan, Ala., Nov. 28, 1941; s. William T. and Gladys (Harris) D.; m. Susan Jean Jakuboski, Oct. 26, 1974. BA, U. Tenn., 1963, JD, 1964. Bar: Tenn. 1965; cert. criminal trial specialist Nat. Bd. Trial Advocacy. Asst. U.S. atty. Dept. Justice, Knoxville, Tenn., 1967-76, chief asst. U.S. atty., 1978-83, U.S. atty., 1981, Tallahassee, 1983-86; ptnr. Ritchie, Fels, and Dillard, P.C., Knoxville, Tenn., 1987—; U.S. magistrate, 1976-78. Adj. prof. East Tenn. State U., Knoxville, 1979-80, U. Tenn. Coll. Law, 1993—; instr. Knoxville Police Acad., 1979-82, Nat. Inst. Trial Advocacy, Chapel Hill, N.C. and Boulder, Colo., 1985-2001, U. Tenn. Trial Advocacy Program, 1992-2001 mem. Tenn. Bar Profl. Stds. com.; pres. Fed. Def. Svcs., 2001. Deacon Presbyn. Ch., Knoxville, 1972-76, elder, 1978-82, 88-91, 95-98, 2000—; mem. Mayor's Commn. on Police; mem. Leadership Knoxville, 1998. Fellow Am. Coll. Trial Lawyers, Tenn. Bar Found.; mem. ABA, Am. Judicature Soc., Knoxville Young Lawyers (pres. 1972-73), Nat. Assn. Criminal Def. Lawyers, Tenn. Assn. Criminal Def. Lawyers (bd. dirs.), Nat. Assn. Former U.S. Attys. (bd. dirs.), Knoxville Bar Found. (bd. govs.). Avocations: reading, hiking, travel. Criminal, Government contracts and claims. Home: 8667 Ellijay Way Strawberry Plains TN 37871 Office: Ritchie Fels & Dillard 606 W Main St Knoxville TN 37902-2617 E-mail: dillard@rfdlaw.com.

DILLING, KIRKPATRICK WALLWICK, lawyer; b. Evanston, Ill., Apr. 11, 1920; s. Albert W. and Elizabeth (Kirkpatrick) D.; m. Betty Ellen Bronson, June, 1942 (div. July 1944); m. Elizabeth Ely Tilden, Dec. 11, 1948; children: Diana Jean, Eloise Tilden, Victoria Walgreen, Albert Kirkpatrick (dec.). Student, Cornell U., 1939-40; BS in Law, Northwestern U., 1942; postgrad., DePaul U., 1946-47, L'Ecole Vaubier, Montreux, Switzerland; Degré Normal, Sorbonne U., Paris. Bar: Ill. 1947, U.S. Dist. Ct. (no. dist.) Ill., Ind., Mich., Md., La., Tex., Okla., Wis., Idaho, U.S. Ct. Appeals (2nd, 3rd, 5th, 7th, 8th, 9th, 10th, 11th, fed. and D.C. cirs.), U.S. Supreme Ct. Ptnr. Dilling and Dilling, 1948—. Counsel Cancer Control Soc., Nat. Coun. for Improved Health; bd. dirs. Nutradelle Labs., Ltd., V.E. Irons, Inc.; v.p. Midwest Medic-Aide, Inc.; spl. counsel Herbalife (U.K.) Ltd., Herbalife Australasia Pty., Ltd.; lectr. on pub. health law. Contbr. articles to pub. health publs. Bd. dirs. Adelle Davis Found., Liberty Lobby. 1st lt. AUS, 1943-46. Recipient Humanitarian award Nat. Health Fedn. Mem. ABA, Ill. Bar Assn., Chgo. Bar Assn., Assn. Trial Lawyers Am., Stalwart Cornell Soc. Engrs., Am. Legion, Air Force Assn., Pharm. Advt. Club, Rolls Royce Owners' Club, Tower Club, Cornell U., Chicago Club, Delta Upsilon. Republican. Episcopalian. Administrative and regulatory, Federal civil litigation, Health. Home: 1120 Lee Rd Northbrook IL 60062-3816 E-mail: dilling1@juno.com.

DILLON, CLIFFORD BRIEN, retired lawyer; b. Amarillo, Tex., Oct. 25, 1921; s. Clifford Newton and Leone (Brien) D.; m. Audrey Catherine Johnson, Jan. 16, 1945; children: Audrey Catherine Dillon Peters (dec. Nov. 1997), Robert Brien, Douglas Johnson. BBA, U. Tex., 1943, LL.B. with honors, 1947. Bar: Tex. 1947. Practiced in, Houston, 1947—87; ptnr. Baker Botts LLP, 1957—87, ret. ptnr., 1987—. Mem. faculty Southwestern Legal Found., 1968-87. Author articles in field. Life mem., bd. dirs. U. Tex. Health Sci. Ctr., Houston; past mem. antitrust adv. bd. Bur. Nat. Affairs; past bd. dirs. Houston Vis. Nurses Assn.; bd. visitors, life mem. Mc Donald Obs. and Astronomy, 1986—. Fellow ABA (chmn. sect. antitrust law 1975-76, Ho. of Dels. 1974-75, 85-87, bd. govs. 1985-87), State Bar Tex., Am. Judicature Soc., Tex. Bar Found., Houston Bar Found.; mem. Houston Bar Assn., Houston C. of C., U.S. C. of C. (past mem. adv. coun. antitrust policy), Houston Country Club (Houston), Petroleum Club (Houston), Riverhill Country (Kerrville, Tex.), Old Baldy (Saratoga, Wyo.), Comanche Trace Country Club (Kerrville), Phi Kappa Psi, Phi Delta Phi. Presbyterian. Antitrust. E-mail: mardillon@compuserve.com.

DILLON, JAMES JOSEPH, lawyer; b. Rockville Ctr., N.Y., June 18, 1948; s. James Martin and Rosemary (Peter) D.; m. Martha Stone Wiske, Mar. 19, 1977; 1 child, Eleanor. BA, Fordham U., 1970, Oxford U., 1972; JD, Harvard U., 1975; MA, Oxford U., 1982. Bar: Mass. 1975, U.S. Dist. Ct. Mass. 1976, N.Y. 2000, U.S. Ct. Appeals (1st cir.) 1978, U.S. Ct. Appeals (5th cir.) 1986, U.S. Ct. Appeals (6th cir.) 1996, U.S. Ct. Appeals (11th cir.) 1995, U.S. Supreme Ct. 1990. Assoc. Goodwin Procter LLP, Boston, 1975-83, ptnr., 1983—2002. Dir. Beth Israel Deaconess Med. Ctr. Obstetrics and Gynecology Found., Inc.; trustee Huntington Theatre Co. Mem. ABA, Boston Bar Assn. Democrat. Federal civil litigation, General civil litigation, State civil litigation. Office: Foley Hoag LLP 155 Seaport Blvd Boston MA 02210 E-mail: jjdillon@foleyhoag.com.

DILLON, JOSEPH FRANCIS, lawyer; b. Bklyn., Oct. 15, 1938; s. Joseph and Elizabeth (Sullivan) D.; m. Pamela Margaret Higbee, May 15, 1966 (div. Feb. 1972); children: Elizabeth Margaret, J. Alexander; m. Diane K. Long, Mar. 17, 1978. BBA, St. John's U., 1960; LLB, U. Va., 1963. Bar: Va. 1963, N.Y. 1964, U.S. Tax Ct. 1965, Mich. 1968, Ohio 1975, Fla. 1983. Tax trial atty. IRS, Washington and Detroit, 1963-68; mem. Raymond & Dillon, P.C., Detroit, 1969-93, Dykema Gossett PLC, Detroit, 1993-97, Cox, Hodgman & Giarmarco, P.C., Detroit, 1997—. Adj. prof. taxation U. Detroit Law Sch., 1977-87; spkr., planning chmn. Inst. CLE Programs; mem. magistrates merit selection panel and profl. assistance com. U.S. Dist. Ct. for Ea. Dist. Mich.; mem. U.S. Ct. Internat. Trade. Bd. dirs., exec. com. Met. Ctr. for High Tech., Detroit, 1993-96. Cpl. USAR, 1958-64. Fellow Mich. State Bar Found.; mem. ABA (taxation and internat. sects. 1963—), FBA (officer, pres. Detroit chpt. 1978-82), Mich. Bar Assn. 1988—, (taxation counsel 1979-82, internat. sec. 1990—), Detroit Bar Assn. (taxation com. 1973—), Ohio Bar Assn., Fla. Bar Assn., Am. Judicature Soc., Am. C. of C. in Japan, London Ct. of Internat. Arbitration, Inter-Pacific Bar Assn., Internat. Bar Assn., Greater Detroit-Windsor Japan Am. Soc. (bd. dirs. 1992—, exec. com. 1999—), Japanese Bus. Soc. Detroit Found. (v.p. 1992—), Detroit Regional Chamber (nominating com. for dirs.), French-Am. C. of C. of Detroit (bd. dirs. 1997-2000), Detroit Athletic Club, Lochmoor Club, Vineyards Country Club, World Trade Club, Econ. Club (Detroit). Republican. Roman Catholic. Avocations: golf, squash, skiing. Corporate, general, Private international, Taxation, general. Office: Cox Hodgman & Giarmarco PC 10th Fl Columbia Ctr 101 W Big Beaver Rd Troy MI 48084-5280 Fax: 248-457-7001. E-mail: jdillon@chglaw.com.

DILORENZO, LOUIS PATRICK, lawyer; b. Waterloo, N.Y., Nov. 3, 1952; s.Luigi and Theresa Marie (Grieco) D.; m. Deborah Joan Boudreau, Aug. 18, 1973; children: Louis Patrick, Lisa Marie, Laura Gabriel. Student, U.S. Mil. Acad., West Point, 1970-72; BA, Syracuse U., 1973; JD, SUNY, Buffalo, 1976. Bar: N.Y. 1977, U.S. Dist. Ct. (no. dist.) N.Y. 1977, U.S. Supreme Ct. 1988. Assoc. Bond, Schoeneck & King, Syracuse, 1976-84, ptnr., 1985—, chair recruiting com., chair labor and employment law dept.; co-chair employment law litigation group, adj. prof. Syracuse U. Sch. Mgmt., 1988—. Participant NYU Ann. Conf. on Labor, 1989. Author: Syracuse Law Jour., 1978, Jour. of Coll. and U. Law Jour., 1980, N.Y. State Bar Jour., 1982; author: (with others) Corporate Counseling, 1988, Public Sector Labor Law, 1988, Duke Journal of Gender Law and Policy, 1999; mem. editl. bd. N.Y. State Bar Jour., 1998—; mem. editl. bd., N.Y. Civil Practice Before Trial, 2001. Bd. dirs. Syracuse Opera Co., 1986. Fellow Am. Coll. Employment and Labor Law Lawyers; mem. ABA, Nat. Assn. Coll. and Univ. Attys., Fedn. Def. and Corp. Counsel, N.Y. State Bar Assn. (mem. ho. of dels. 1984-90, 99—, chmn. young lawyers sect. 1987, chmn. labor rels. com. 1988, chmn. CLE com. 1990-93, chmn. labor and employment law sect. 1994). Republican. Roman Catholic. Avocations: golf, gardening, reading. Federal civil litigation, Labor (including EEOC, Fair Labor Standards Act, labor-management relations, NLRB, OSHA). Office: Bond Schoeneck & King 1 Lincoln Ctr Fl 18 Syracuse NY 13202-1324

DILTS, JON PAUL, law educator; b. Monterey, Ind., Sept. 7, 1945; s. Charles Albert and Janet Cecilia (Keitzer) D.; m. Anne Williams Avirett, Aug. 21, 1971; children: Christopher, Andrew. BA, Saint Meinrad Coll., 1967; MA, Ind. U., 1974; JD, Valparaiso U., 1981. Bar: Ind. 1981, U.S. Dist. Ct. (so. dist.) Ind. 1981, U.S. Supreme Ct. 2000. Reporter Peru (Ind.) Daily Tribune, 1972-73, wire editor, 1973-76, city editor, 1976-78; law clk. Ind. Ct. Appeals, Indpls., 1981-82; asst. prof. Ind. U., Bloomington, 1982-88, assoc. prof., 1988—, assoc. dean, 1985-2000. Author: The Magnificent 92 Indiana Courthouses, 1992; co-author: Media Law, 1994, 97; mem. editl. bd. Comms. Law & Policy, 1998—. Bd. overseers St. Meinrad Coll. Sch. Theology, 1992—, trustee 1996-98, vice chmn., 2002; exec. bd. dirs. Hoosier Trails Coun., Boy Scouts Am., Bloomington, 1992-93. With U.S. Army, 1968-71. Nat. Press Club First Amendment fellow, 2002. Mem. Assn. for Edn. in Journalism and Mass Comm. (head law divsn. 1987-88), Internat. Comms. Assn., Soc. Profl. Journalists, AP Mng. Editors Assn., Rotary. Democrat. Roman Catholic. Avocations: skiing, hiking, backpacking, canoeing, sailing. Office: Ind U Sch Journalism 940 E 7th St Bloomington IN 47405-7108 E-mail: dilts@indiana.edu.

DIMASCIO, JOHN PHILIP, lawyer; b. Bklyn., Feb. 4, 1944; s. Eugenio and Stella (Scheuermann) DiM.; m. Angela Piccininni, Apr. 2, 1967 (div. 1980); children: John Philip, Jr., Christine Pagano, Thomas; m. Linda Nick, Oct. 19, 1997. BA, C.W. Post Coll., 1975; MA, L.I. U., 1976; postgrad., NYU, 1976-79; JD, St. John's U., 1983. Bar: N.Y. 1984, U.S. Dist. Ct. (ea. and so. dists.) N.Y. 1984, U.S. Ct. Appeals (2d cir.) 1984, U.S. Supreme Ct. 1997, U.S. Ct. Appeals for Armed Forces 1997, U.S. Ct. of Fed. Claims, 1997, U.S. Ct. Appeals (fed. cir.) 1997. Sr. ct. officer N.Y. State Supreme Ct., Mineola, 1970-82; assoc. Joel R. Brandes, PC, Garden City, N.Y., 1984; pvt. practice N.Y., 1984-87; ptnr. Di Mascio, Meisner & Koopersmith, Carle Place, 1987-93; pvt. practice Garden City, 1993—. Lectr. Nassau Acad. Law. With USN, 1962—69. Recipient acad. awards. Mem.: ABA (family law sect.), Am. Inns of Ct. (N.Y. family law chpt.), Nassau County Bar Assn. (chmn. matrimonial com., ethics com., family ct. com. 1984—, editor Recent Decisions, contbg. author), N.Y. State Bar Assn. (family law com. 1982). Avocations: photography, boating. Appellate, Family and matrimonial, General practice. Office: 300 Garden City Plz Garden City NY 11530-3302 E-mail: jpdlawoff@msn.com.

DIMENTO, CAROL A.G. lawyer; b. Salem, Mass., Dec. 5, 1942; B in Edn., Salem State Coll., 1965, M in Edn., 1967; JD, Suffolk U., 1977. Bar: Mass. 1977. Tchr. Town of Hamilton, 1965—67, Town of Marblehead, 1967—74; ptnr. DiMento & DiMento, Swampscott, Mass., 1977—. Mem.: ABA (house of delegates 1995—), Essex County Bar Assn. (pres. 1992—94), Mass. Bar Assn. (sec. 1996—97, v.p. 1997—98, treas. 1998—99, 1st v.p. 1999—2000, pres.-elect 2000—01, pres. 2001—02). Family and matrimonial.

DIMES, EDWIN KINSLEY, lawyer; b. Hartford, Conn., Apr. 13, 1923; s. Alfred Eustace and Charlotte (Miller) D.; m. Edwina May Adams, Feb. 3, 1945 (div. 1981); chldren: Martha, Deborah, Kimberley; m. S. Antoinette Morton, Dec. 29, 1990. BA, Conn. Wesleyan U., Middletown, 1947; JD, Yale U., 1950. Bar: Conn. 1950, U.S. Tax Ct. 1960, U.S. Supreme Ct. 1960. From assoc. to ptnr. Wake, See, Dimes and Bryniczka, Westport, Conn., 1950—. State trial referee State of Conn., 1985—. Chmn. bd. fin. City of Westport, 1979-97. 2d lt. USAF, 1943-45. Mem. ABA, Westport Bar Assn., Conn. Bar Assn. (bd. govs.). Republican. Congregationalist. Avocations: boating, tennis. Estate planning, General practice, Property, real (including real estate development, water). Home: 70 Morningside Dr S Westport CT 06880-5415 Office: Wake See Dimes and Brynicza 27 Imperial Ave Westport CT 06880-4303 E-mail: edimes@wsdb.com.

DIMITRY, THEODORE GEORGE, retired lawyer; b. New Orleans, Jan. 15, 1937; s. Theodore Joseph and Ouida Marion (Seiler) D.; m. S. Elizabeth Warren; children: Mary Elizabeth Hyry, Theodore Warren. BS, Tulane U., 1958, JD, 1960. Bar: La. 1960, Tex. 1964. Assoc. firm Phelps, Dunbar, Marks, Claverie & Sims, New Orleans, 1965-69, ptnr., 1969-75; ptnr. firm Vinson & Elkins, Houston, 1975-98; ret., 1998; pvt. arbitrator and mediator, 1999—. Rsch. fellow Southwestern Legal Found., Dallas, 1973-98; spkr. on maritime law, offshore contracting, ins. and resource devel. at profl. seminars, 1975— Contbr. articles to profl. jours. Mem. permanent adv. bd. Tulane U. Admiralty Law Inst., 1985—2000. Served with USN, 1960—64. Mem.: Maritime Law Assn. U.S. Admiralty, Insurance, Private international. Fax: 713-467-7153. E-mail: dimitry@net1.net.

DIMMICK, CAROLYN REABER, federal judge; b. Seattle, Oct. 24, 1929; d. Maurice C. and Margaret T. (Taylor) Reaber; m. Cyrus Allen Dimmick, Sept. 10, 1955; children: Taylor, Dana. BA, U. Wash., 1951, JD, 1953; LLD, Gonzaga U., 1982, CUNY, 1987. Bar: Wash. 1953. Asst. atty. gen. State of Wash., Seattle, 1953-55; pros. atty. King County, Wash., 1955-59, 60-62; sole practice Seattle, 1959-60, 62-65; judge N.E. Dist. Ct. Wash., 1965-75, King County Superior Ct., 1976-80; justice Wash. Supreme Ct., 1981-85; judge U.S. Dist. Ct. (we. dist.) Wash., Seattle, 1985-94, chief judge, 1994-97, sr. judge, 1997—. Chmn. Jud. Resources Com., 1991-94, active, 1987-94. Recipient Matrix Table award, 1981, World Plan Execs. Council award, 1981, Vanguard Honor award King County of Washington Women Lawyers, 1996, Disting. Alumni award U. Wash. Law Sch., 1997. Mem. ABA, Am. Judges Assn. (gov.), Nat. Assn. Women Judges, World Assn. Judges, Wash. Bar Assn., Am. Judicature Soc., Order of Coif (Wash. chpt.). Office: US Dist Ct 407 US Courthouse 1010 5th Ave Seattle WA 98104-1189 E-mail: carolyn_dimmick@wawd.uscourts.gov.

DIMMITT, LAWRENCE ANDREW, retired lawyer, educator; b. Kansas City, Kans., July 20, 1941; s. Herbert Andrew and Mary (Duncan) D.; m. Lois Kinney, Dec. 23, 1962; children: Cynthia Susan, Lawrence Michael. BA, Kans. State U., 1963, MA, 1967; JD, Washburn U., 1968. Bar: Kans. 1968, U.S. Dist. Ct. Kans. 1968, U.S. Ct. Appeals (10th cir.) 1969, Mo. 1973, N.Y. 1975, U.S. Supreme Ct. 1986. Atty. Southwestern Bell Telephone Co., Topeka, 1968-73, St. Louis, 1973-74, gen. atty. regulation, 1979; atty. AT&T, N.Y.C., 1974-79; gen. atty. Kans. Southwestern Bell Telephone Co., Topeka, 1979-94; ret., 1994. Adj. prof. telecom. law Washburn U. Sch. Law, 1996—. Bd. dirs. First United Meth. Ch., Topeka, 1979-84, mem. nominating com., 1985-87; bd. dirs. Sunflower Music Festival, 1993-94; mem. master planning com. Historic Ward-Meade Park, 1998—; mem. Jayhawker Lit. Club, 2003—. Recipient commendation Legal Aid Soc. Topeka, 1986, 90, 93. Mem. Kans. Bar Assn. (pres. adminstrv. law sect. 1985-86, bd. editors newsletter), Topeka Bar Assn., Phi Alpha Delta (alumni bd. 1986-88, 1993-97), Rotary (bd. dirs., 1st v.p. 2000, pres. 2001, asst. gov. 2003—). Administrative and regulatory, Communications. Home: 3123 SW 15th St Topeka KS 66604-2515 E-mail: LLDimmitt@aol.com.

DIMONTE, VINCENT A. lawyer; b. Providence, R.I., Jan. 20, 1951; BA magna cum laude, Providence Coll., 1973; JD, Villanova U., 1976. Bar: R.I. 1976, U.S. Dist. Ct. R.I. 1977. Of counsel Lovett Schefrin Harnett, Providence. Master: R.I. Family Law Inns of Court; fellow: Am. Acad. Matrimonial Lawyers; mem.: R.I. Bar Assn. (sec. 1986—92, chair 1992—96, treas. 1998—99, sec. 1999—2000, pres. elect 2000—01, pres. 2001—02). Family and matrimonial. Office: Lovett Schefrin Harnett 155 S Main St Providence RI 02903

DIMURO, BERNARD JOSEPH, lawyer; b. Boston, Mar. 3, 1954; s. Bernard P. and Katherine (Deuce) D. BA, Northwestern U., 1976; JD, George Washington U., 1979. Bar: Va. 1979, U.S. Dist. Ct. (ea. dist.) Va. 1979, U.S. Ct. Appeals (4th cir.) 1979, Ill. 1980, D.C. 1985, U.S. Ct. Appeals (9th cir.) 1986, U.S. Ct. Appeals (8th cir.) 1987. Ptnr. Hirschkop, DiMuro & Mook, Alexandria, Va., 1979—89; found. ptnr. Dimuro, Ginsberg & Mook PC, Alexandria, Va., 1990—. Founder, pres. The Civil Workplace, 1996—. Mem. ABA, Va. State Bar Assn. (mem. com. to implement pro bono report, chmn. 8th dist. grievance com., disciplinary bd. 1988-95, chair 1993-95, exec. com. 1995-97, 2000-, chair task force on public access to the disciplinary system, mem. task force on corp. counsel 2001-, Va. model rules com. 1995-99, lawyers serving as fiduciaries com. 1993-94, vice chair publications/public info. com. 1996-2001, faculty for the professsionalism course 1995-98, pres. 2002-03), Ill. State Bar Assn., D.C. Bar, Va. Trial Lawyers Assn. (bd. govs. 1997-2000), Assn. Trial Lawyers Am.; fellow Va. Law Found. 1995, ABA 1998 Roman Catholic. Civil rights, Federal civil litigation, Personal injury (including property damage). Home: 7705 Northdown Rd Alexandria VA 22308-1333 Office: DiMuro Ginsberg & Mook PC 908 King St Ste 200 Alexandria VA 22314-3018

DINAN, CHRISTOPHER CHARLES, lawyer, mediator; b. Winchester, Mass., May 27, 1955; s. Edward Joseph and Catherine Marie Dinan; m. Judy Ann Parlin, Sept. 10, 1989; children: Sean Christopher, Elyse Catherine. BA, Harvard Coll., 1977; JD, U. Maine, 1982. Bar: Maine 1982, U.S. Dist. Ct. Maine 1982. Ptnr. Monaghan Leahy, LLP, Portland, Maine, 1982—. Mem. Zoning Bd. Appeals, Portland, Maine, 1986-89. Mem. Maine State Bar Assn., Maine Trial Lawyers Assn. (bd. govs. 2001--). Avocations: golf, skiing, running. General civil litigation, Insurance, Personal injury (including property damage). Office: Monaghan Leahy LLP 95 Exchange St Ste 300 Portland ME 04101-5044

DINAN, DONALD ROBERT, lawyer; b. Nashua, N.H., Aug. 28, 1949; s. Robert J. and Jeanette F. (Farland) D.; m. Amy Littlepage, June 24, 1978; 1 child: Emma. BS in Econs., U. Pa., 1971; JD, Georgetown U., 1974; LLM, London Sch. Econs., 1975. Bar: Mass. 1976, D.C. 1977, N.Y. 1986, U.S. Ct. Appeals (1st, 2d, D.C. and fed. cirs.), U.S. Supreme Ct. 1979, U.S. Ct. Internat. Trade 1982. Atty. advisor U.S. Internat. Trade Commn., Washington, 1976-81, chief patent br., 1981-82, chief unfair imports investigation div., 1981-82; ptnr. Adduci Dinan & Mastriani, Washington, 1982-88, Fitzpatrick, Cella, Harper & Scinto, Washington, 1988-90, O'Connor & Hannan, Washington, 1990-98, Hall Estill, 1998—. Prof. internat. trade Georgetown U., Wharton Econs. Soc.; prin. Coun. for Excellence in Govt. Mem. Mayor's Internat. Adv. Coun., Washington, D.C. Regulatory Reform Com.; mem. Washington Dem. State Com., gen. counsel, 1988-92, 94-2000; chmn. D.C. Affirmative Action Com. for Dem. Conv. 2004; chmn. D.C. Dem. Campaign Victory Fund, 2004. Mem. ABA, Fed. Bar Assn., ITC Trial Laywers Assn., Am. Intellectual Property Law Assn. (chmn. internat. trade com., export lic. com.). Democrat. Roman Catholic. Federal civil litigation, Intellectual property, Private international. Home: 221 9th St SE Washington DC 20003-2112 Office: Hall Estill Hardwick Gable Goldin & Nelson 1120 20th St NW Ste 700N Washington DC 20036-3485

DINICOLA, JOHN W., II, lawyer; b. Malden, Mass., Oct. 5, 1969; s. John William and Kathleen Rose DiNicola. BS in Fin., Fairfield U., 1991; JD cum laude, Cath. U. Am., 1995. Bar: Mass. 95, Md. 1995, U.S. Dist. Ct. Md. 1995, NJ 1998, U.S. Dist. Ct. NJ 1998, U.S. Dist. Ct. Mass. 2003. Assoc. Ober, Kaler, Grimes & Shriver, Balt., 1995—98, McElroy, Deutsch & Mulvaney, Morriston, NJ, 1998—2000, Holland & Knight LLP, Boston, 2000—03, ptnr., 2003—. Mem.: ABA (mem. forum on constrn. industry 1995—), Boston Bar Assn., NJ Bar Assn., Mass. Bar Assn., Md. Bar Assn. Construction. Office: Holland & Knight LLP 10 St James Ave Boston MA 02116 Fax: 617-523-6850. E-mail: jwdinicola@hklaw.com.

DINKINS, CAROL EGGERT, lawyer; b. Corpus Christi, Tex., Nov. 9, 1945; d. Edgar H. Jr. and Evelyn S. (Scheel) Eggert; m. Bob Brown; children: Anne, Amy. BS, U. Tex., 1968; JD, U. Houston, 1971. Bar: Tex. 1971. Prin. assoc. Tex. Law Inst. Coastal and Marine Resources, Coll. Law U. Houston, Tex., 1971-73; assoc., ptnr. Vinson & Elkins, Houston, 1973-81, 83-84, 85—, mem. mgmt. com., 1991-96; asst. atty. gen. environ. and natural resources Dept. Justice, 1981-83, U.S. dep. atty. gen., 1984-85. Chmn. Pres.'s Task Force on Legal Equity for Women, 1981-83; mem. Hawaiian Native Study Commn., 1981-83; dir. Nat. Consumer Coop. Banks Bd., 1981, chmn. Gov.'s conservation task force, 2000. Contbr. articles to profl. jours. Chmn. Gov.'s Conservation Task Force, 2000, Tex. Gov.'s Flood Control Action Group 1980-81; commr. Tex. Parks and Wildlife Dept., 1997-2001; bd. govs. The Nature Conservancy, 1996—, vice chmn. 2002-2004, Oryx Energy Co., 1990-95, U. Houston Law Ctr. Found., 1985-89, 96-98, Environ. and Energy Study Inst., 1986-98, Houston Mus. Natural Sci., 1986-98, 2000—, Tex. Nature Conservancy, 1985—, chmn., 1996-99., chair com. on fed. judiciary, 2002-03. Mem. ABA (ho. of dels., past chmn. state and local govt. sect., past chair sect. nat. resources, energy, and environ. law, standing com. on Fed. Judges 1997-98, bd. editors ABA Jour.), Fed. Bar Assn. (bd. dirs. Houston chpt. 1986), State Bar Tex., Houston Bar Assn., Tex. Water Conservation Assn., Houston Law Rev. Assn. (bd. dirs. 1978). Republican. Lutheran. Environmental. Office: Vinson & Elkins 2300 First City Tower 1001 Fannin St Houston TX 77002-6706

DINNING, WOODFORD WYNDHAM, JR., lawyer; b. Demopolis, Ala., Aug. 15, 1954; s. Woodford W. and Gladys (Brown) D.; m. Tammy E. Cannon, May 27, 1994. AS, U. Ala., 1976, JD, 1979. Bar: Ala. 1979, U.S. Dist. Ct. (so. dist.) Ala. 1980. Mcpl. judge City of Demopolis, 1980-93, 98—; ptnr. Lloyd & Dinning, LLC, Demopolis, 1979—; mcpl. judge City of Linden, Ala., 1997—. Pres. and bd. dirs. Tenn. Tom Motel, Inc.; atty. Marengo County Commn. and City of Linden, Ala. Mem. Ala. Alumni Assn. (chmn. 1985-86). Avocations: water skiing, marathon running. State civil litigation, Commercial, contracts (including sales of goods; commercial financing), Family and matrimonial. Office: Lloyd & Dinning LLC PO Drawer Z Demopolis AL 36732

DINSE, JOHN MERRELL, lawyer; b. Rochester, N.Y., June 26, 1925; s. Frank John and Lois Vanlora (Merrell) D.; m. Ann Thompson (Goodenough), Dec. 27, 1948; children— Jeffrey P., Pamela D. Johnston AB, U. Rochester, 1947; LL.B., Cornell U., 1950. Bar: N.Y. 1950, Vt. 1951, U.S. Dist. Ct. Vt. 1952, U.S. Ct. Appeals (2d cir.) 1957. Assoc. firm Austin & Edmunds, Burlington, Vt., 1950-57; ptnr. Dinse, Erdmann, & Clapp (and predecessor firms), Burlington, 1957-90; of counsel Dinse, Knapp, & McAndrew (and predecessor firms), Burlington, 1990—. Mem. Med. Ctr.Hosp. Assocs.; dir. Vt. Mcpl. Bond Bank, 1980—83; past trustee Burlington (Vt.) YWCA; past bd. govs. Med. Ctr. Hosp. Vt.; past bd. dirs. Vt. Diabetes Assn., Arthritis Found.; bd. dirs. Vt. Symphony Orch., v.p., 1995—2001, chmn. bd., 2001—; mem. Vt. Waterways Commn., 1962—63;

chmn. Jud. Nominating Bd., 1967—77; campaign chmn. Gov. Deane C. Davis, 1968, 1970; mem. Waterways Commn. on Champlain Basin. With USAR, 1943—46. Decorated Bronze Star U.S. Army. Fellow Am. Coll. Trial Lawyers, Am. Bar Found., Am. Coll. Trust and Estate Counsel; mem. ABA, New Eng. Bar Assn. (bd. dirs. 1977-80), Chittenden County Bar Assn., Vt. Bar Assn. (bd. mgrs. 1974— , pres. 1978-79), Am. Bd. Trial Advs. (bd. dirs. 1990-92), Am. Judicature Soc. (dir. 1975-79), Am. Acad. Hosp. Attys., No. New Eng. Def. Counsel Assn. (pres. 1971-72), Assn. Def. Attys., Internat. Assn. Def. Counsel, Def. Research Inst. (dir. 1975-81, pres. 1980, chmn. bd. 1981), Am. Law Inst., Nat. Assn. Coll. and Univ. Attys. Clubs: Lake Champlain Yacht (commodore 1961-62); Malletts Bay Boat (master 1957-58). Home: Harbor Rd Shelburne VT 05482 Office: Dinse Knapp & McAndrew PO Box 988 209 Battery St Burlington VT 05402

DINSMOOR, ROBERT DAVIDSON, lawyer, judge; b. El Paso, Tex., May 19, 1955; s. William Bell Jr. and Mary (Higgins) D. BA in Polit. Sci., Brigham Young U., 1979, JD, 1982. Bar: Tex. 1983, U.S. Dist. Ct. (we. dist.) Tex. 1985, U.S. Ct. Appeals (5th cir.) 1986, U.S. Supreme Ct. 1987. Rsch. assoc. J. Reuben Clark Law Sch., Brigham Young U., Provo, Utah, 1981-82; asst. dist. atty. El Paso (Tex.) Dist. Atty., 1983-90; dist. ct. judge State of Tex., El Paso, 1991—2002; ptnr. Roy, Valdez, Mc Christian, Jeans, 2003—. Spkr. in field; co-founder El Paso Criminal Law Study Group. Contbr. articles to profl. jours. Bd. dirs. S.W. Repertory Orgn., El Paso, 1994-95; Sunday Sch. pres. Latter Day Saints Ch., 5th ward, El Paso, 1993-95; exec. sec. to bishop, 1995—. Recipient Outstanding Achievement award El Paso Young Lawyers Assn., 1990, Outstanding Jurist award, 1999, 2001. Mem.: El Paso Mex.-Am. Bar Assn. (bd. dirs. 2001—), El Paso Bar Assn. (mem. Law Day com., libr. com., criminal law com., others 1996—, bd. dirs. 1993—96, sec. 1996—97, treas. 1997—98, v.p. 1998—99, pres.-elect 1999—2000, pres. 2000—01, Professionalism award 2002), State Bar Tex. (mem. indigent representation com. 1994—98, 1999—, victim/witness com. 1992—95, 1997—98, 1999—, chmn. victim/witness com. 1999—2000). Democrat. Avocations: playing piano, writing music, bicycle riding, basketball, accordion playing. State civil litigation, Criminal, Family and matrimonial. Office: 5822 Cromo Dr El Paso TX 79912

DIODOSIO, CHARLES JOSEPH, lawyer; b. Pueblo, Colo., Apr. 27, 1951; s. Warren Joseph and Lucille Julia Diodosio. BSChemE, U. Colo., 1973; JD, Northwestern U., 1976. Assoc. McDermott, Will & Emery, Chgo., 1976-80; internat. counsel Beatrice Co., Chgo., 1980-84, v.p. Asia devel., 1984-88; chmn. TMGC Ltd., Chgo., 1988—, Meadow Gold Investment Holding Co., Beijing, 1993—; chmn. L&D International Corp., Beijing, 1993—. Chmn. L&D Internat. Corp., Beijing, China, 1993—. Mem. ABA, Ill. Bar. Home: 1387 Calle de Maria Palm Springs CA 92264-8503 Fax: 760-327-1200. E-mail: meadgo@aol.com.

DIORIO, ROBERT MICHAEL, lawyer, public official; b. Phila., Aug. 5, 1947; s. Carl and Yolanda D. (DiJohn) DiO.; m. Bianka M. Chojnacki; children: Danielle, Stephanie Lauren. BA in Polit. Sci., Pa. State U., 1969; JD, Temple U., 1973. Cert. elem. tchr., Pa. Pvt. practice, Media, Pa., 1973—; asst. pub. defender Delaware County, Media, 1974-76, asst. dist. atty., 1976-79, support master, 1980, custody conciliator, 1980-97, solicitor, controller, 1985-90; ptnr. DiOrio & Sereni LLP, Media, Pa., 1989—. Spl. solicitor City of Springfield, Pa., Upper Darby Sch. Dist.; solicitor County Svcs. for Aging, Delaware County Bd. Prison Insps., S.E. Delco Sch. Dist. Commr. Springfield Twp. Bd. of Commrs., 1977-87, pres. 1981-87; bd. dirs. Deaf Hearing Comm. Ctr., Springfield, Immaculata (Pa.) Coll. Pres. Council, Met. Hosp., Phila., Delaware County Regional Water Quality Control Authority, 1987-89; mem. Delaware County Leadership Adv. Bd., Delaware County Bur. Elections; mem. liberal arts coun. Pa. State U. Mem. ATLA, Pa. Bar Assn., Pa. Assn. Trial Lawyers, Delaware County Bar Assn. (sect. dir. 1976, 93-95), Delaware County C. of C. (chmn. family bus. com.), Pa. State U. Alumni Assn. (pres.), Lions. Republican. Roman Catholic. Avocations: golf, skiing. General civil litigation, Family and matrimonial, Personal injury (including property damage). Home: 3 Springton Pointe Dr Newtown Square PA 19073-3931 Office: DiOrio & Sereni LLP Front and Plum Sts Media PA 19063 Fax: (610) 891-0652. E-mail: rdiorio@diorioserení.com.

DI PALMA, JOSEPH ALPHONSE, investment company executive, lawyer; b. N.Y.C., Jan. 17, 1931; s. Gaetano and Michela May (Ambrosio) Di P.; m. Joycelyn Ann Engle, Apr. 18, 1970; children: Joycelyn Joan, Julianne Michelle. BA, Columbia U., 1952; JD, Fordham U., 1958; LLM in Taxation, NYU, 1959. Bar: N.Y. 1959. Tax atty. CBS, N.Y.C., 1960-64; v.p. tax dept. TWA, N.Y.C., 1964-74; pvt. practice law N.Y.C., 1974-87; investor, exec. dir. Di Palma Family Holdings, Las Vegas and N.Y.C., 1987—. Cons. in field; head study group Comprehensive Gaming Study, N.Y.C. and Washington, 1990—; think tank exec. dir. Di Palma Position Papers; founder Di Palma Forum, U. Nev., Las Vegas; established The Di Palma Ctr. for Study of Jewelry and Precious Metals at Cooper-Hewitt, Nat. Design Mus., Smithsonian Instn., N.Y.C. Contbr. articles to profl. jours.; author: Di Palma Postion Papers. Bd. dirs. Friends of the Henry St. Settlement, N.Y.C., 1961-63, Outdoor Cleanliness Assn., N.Y.C., 1961-65; chmn. Air Transport Assn. Taxation Com., 1974. With U.S. Army, 1953-54. Recipient Disting. Svc. and Valuable Counsel commendation award, Air Transport Assn., 1974, spl. commendation, NYC mayor Rudolph Giuliani, 1997, U. Nev., Las Vegas, 1999, Tiffany Smithsonian Benefactors Circle award, 2001, WNET/Thirteen Pub. Spirit award, 2002. Mem. Internat. Platform Assn., N.Y. State Bar Assn., N.Y. Athletic Club. Roman Catholic. Home: 3111 Bel Air Dr Apt 21B Las Vegas NV 89109-1506 Office: PO Box 72158 Las Vegas NV 89170-2158 also: 930 5th Ave # 4 J&H New York NY 10021-2651

DISENHAUS, HELEN ELIZABETH, lawyer; b. Washington, Nov. 2, 1948; d. Nathan and Henrietta (Weiss) D.; m. Brian Girard Driscoll, Sept. 11, 1977; children: Daniel Benjamin Driscoll, David Michael Driscoll. AB, Mt. Holyoke Coll., 1970; MAT, Wesleyan U., Conn., 1972; JD, Yale U., 1977. Bar: D.C. 1977. Tchr. English Glastonbury (Conn.) H.S., 1971-74; atty. Dow, Lohnes & Albertson, Washington, 1977-87; of counsel Swidler & Berlin, Washington, 1987-94, counsel, 1994, mem., 1995-98, Swidler, Berlin, Shereff, Friedmen LLP, Washington, 1998—. Pres. D.C. chpt. Am. Women in Radio and TV, 1982-83, bd. dirs., 1983-84, nat. v.p. govt. industry affairs, 1984-86, nat. sec.-treas., 1986-88. Sarah Williston scholar, 1968; recipient Leadership award Am. Women in Radio and TV, 1995. Mem. ABA, D.C. Bar Assn., Womens Bar Assn. D.C., Fed. Comm. Bar Assn. (chair continuing legal edn. com. 1991-93, transactional practice com. 1994-96), Yale Law Sch. Assn. D.C. (pres. 1982-83, exec. com. 1983-84), Mt. Holyoke Club, Phi Beta Kappa. Jewish. Administrative and regulatory, Communications. Office: Swidler, Berlin Shereff Friedman LLP 3000 K St NW Ste 300 Washington DC 20007-5116 E-mail: hedisenhaus@swidlaw.com.

DISHER, DAVID ALAN, lawyer, consultant; b. Chgo., Apr. 15, 1944; s. Hugh George and Beatrice Rose (Selmanovitz) D.; children: Karl Theodore, Carol Ann, Kathy; m. Clara Hoffman, Sept. 17, 1991. BS in Elec. Engring., MIT, 1965, MS in Elec. Engring., 1966; JD, U. Houston, 1983. Bar: Tex. 1984, U.S. Ct. Appeals (5th cir.) 1984, U.S. Tax Ct. 1984, U.S. Dist. Ct. (so. dist.) 1986, U.S. Supreme Ct. 1987. Mathematician Shell Devel., Houston, 1966-68; sr. engr. Tex. Instruments, Stafford, 1968; dir. rsch. GEOCOM, New Orleans, 1969-70; cons., inventor Disher Consulting Svc., Houston, 1970-73; pres., chmn. bd. Seismic Programming Internat., 1973-84, 1974-84; pvt. practice law LaMarque, Tex., 1984-99; pvt. practice Houston, 1999—. Ind. geophys. rsch. cons. Contbr. articles to Geophysics. Mem. crime control com. Houston C. of C., 1974—76. Mem. ACLU, Coll. State Bar Tex., Tex. Criminal Def. Lawyers Assn., Galveston County Bar Assn., Harris County Bar Assn., Harris County Criminal Lawyers Assn., Houston Geophys. Soc., Houston Bar Assn. Criminal, Family and matrimonial, Personal income taxation. Office: 3318 Mercer St Houston TX 77027-6020 Fax: 713-961-9402. E-mail: disherdave@aol.com.

DISHEROON, FRED RUSSELL, lawyer; b. Hot Springs, Ark., Nov. 21, 1931; s. Andrew Russell and Ruth Fayrene (Bearden) D.;children: Terri Suzanne, John Frederick; m. Diane L. Donley, Apr. 8, 1989; 1 child, Travis William. AB, Hendrix Coll., 1953; JD, So. Meth. U., 1956; LLM in Environ. Law, George Washington U., 1976. Bar: Tex. 1956, U.S. Ct. Appeals (1st, 5th, 6th, 8th, 9th, 10th, 11th D.C. and fed. cirs.), U.S. Supreme Ct. 1964, Va. 1974. Atty. Superior Ins. Co., Dallas, 1960-64; claims atty. Sentry Ins. Co., Dallas, 1964-67; litigation counsel Stigall, Maxfield & Collier, Dallas, 1967-69; sole practice Dallas, 1969-70; asst. gen. counsel for litigation C.E. U.S. Army, Washington, 1970-75; spl. litigation counsel Dept. Justice, Washington, 1975—. Instr. environ. law U. Ala.-Huntsville, 1979-82; lectr. law George Washington U., 1981-86; vis. rsch. specialist U. Calif., Davis, 1990. Co-author: Sustainable Environmental Law, 1993, Water Law, Trends, Policies and Practice, 1995; editor Southwestern Law Jour., 1955-56. Col. JAGC, USAR. Recipient numerous outstanding performance awrds U.S. Army, Dept. Justice, Sr. Exec. Svc. meritorious award Dept. Justice, 1984, Outstanding Civilian Svc. medal Dept. Army. Mem. Sr. Execs. Assn. Home: 3508 Riverwood Rd Alexandria VA 22309-2720 Office: Dept Justice Environ & Natural Resources Divsn 601 D St NW Washington DC 20004 E-mail: fred.disheroon@usdoj.gov.

DISKANT, GREGORY L. lawyer; b. Phila., June 7, 1948; s. Robert and Eda (Grunberg) D.; m. Sandra S. Baron, Feb. 29, 1980; children: Edward, Benjamin. AB, Princeton U., 1970; JD, Columbia U., 1974. Bar: N.Y. 1975. Law clk. to Hon. J. Skelly Wright, U.S. Ct. Appeals for D.C. Cir., Washington, 1974-75; law clk. to Hon. Thurgood Marshall, U.S. Supreme Ct., Washington, 1975-76; asst. U.S. atty. for so. dist. N.Y., Dept. Justice, N.Y.C., 1976-80, chief appellate atty., 1980; assoc. Patterson, Belknap, Webb & Tyler, N.Y.C., 1981—82, ptnr., 1982—, co-chmn., 1997—2002, chmn., 2003—. Editor-in-chief Columbia Law Rev., 1973-74. Kent scholar, 1972, Stone scholar, 1973, 74. Fellow Am. Coll. Trial Lawyers; mem. ABA, N.Y. State Bar Assn., Assn. Bar of City of N.Y. Federal civil litigation, Communications, Pharmaceuticals. Office: Patterson Belknap Webb & Tyler Rm 2400 1133 Avenue Of The Americas Fl 22 New York NY 10036-6731

DISSEN, JAMES HARDIMAN, lawyer; b. Pitts., Jan. 26, 1942; s. William Paul and Kathryn Grace (Reilly) D.; m. Shirley Ann Stark, Dec. 17, 1976; children: Elizabeth Ann, William Stark, Anna Kathryn. BS, Wheeling (W.Va.) Jesuit U., 1963; MBA, Xavier U., Cin., 1966; JD, Duquesne U., Pitts., 1972. Bar: Pa. 1972, U.S. Dist. Ct. (we. dist.) Pa. 1972, W.Va. 1973, U.S. Dist. Ct. (so. dist.) W.Va. 1973, U.S. Supreme Ct. 1976. Spl. agent Counter Intelligence U.S. Army Intelligence Corps, 1963-66; personnel mgr. Columbia Gas of Pa., Inc., Uniontown, 1969-73; dir. labor rels. Columbia Gas Transmission Corp., Charleston, W.Va., 1973-84, dir. personnel and labor rels., 1984-87, dir. employee rels., 1987-96; v.p. Columbia Nat. Resources, Charleston, W.Va., 1996-2001; v.p., ptnr. Triana Energy, Charleston, W.Va., 2001—. Bd. dirs. Fourth Venture Investment Group, Inc.; adj. prof. W.Va. Grad. Coll., 1996-97, Wheeling Jesuit U., 1997, U. Charleston, 1998; chmn., exec. com., bd. dirs. Star U.S.A. Fed. Credit Union. V.p., bd. trustees Highland Hosp., 1991—; chmn. bd. dirs. Inroads/W.Va., 1995-2001, Christmas in April, 2000-2001. Mem. ABA, W.Va. State Bar, Soc. Human Resource Mgmt., W.Va. C. of C. (chmn. human resource com., bd. dirs.), St. Thomas Moore Soc., Berry Hills Country Club. Republican. Roman Catholic. Avocation: golf. Labor (including EEOC, Fair Labor Standards Act, labor-management relations, NLRB, OSHA). Home: 1501 Brentwood Rd Charleston WV 25314-2307 Office: Triana Energy 300 Summers St Ste 300 BB&T Bldg Charleston WV 25301 E-mail: jdissen@trianaenergy.com.

DITKOWSKY, KENNETH K. lawyer; b. Chgo., July 12, 1936; s. Samuel J. and Lillian (Plavnik) D.; m. Judith Goodman, Aug. 9, 1959; children—Naomi, Deborah, R. Benjamin. B.S., U. Chgo.; J.D., Loyola U., Chgo. Bar: Ill. 1961, U.S. Dist. Ct. (no. dist.) Ill. 1962, U.S. Ct. Apls. (7th cir.) 1973, U.S. Tax Ct. 1973, U.S. Sup. Ct. 1975. Ptnr., Ditkowsky & Contorer, Chgo., 1961— . Mem. Ill. Bar Assn. Federal civil litigation, State civil litigation, General practice. Office: Ditkowsky & Contorer 2626 W Touhy Ave Chicago IL 60645-3110 E-mail: kenditkowsky@yahoo.com.

DITTMAN, STEVAN CRAIG, lawyer; b. Hampshire, Ill., Dec. 7, 1949; s. Lawrence F. and Barbara J. (Anderson) D.; m. Nathalie Margaret Walker, Apr. 26, 1975; children: Anderson Walker, Christian Walker. BA, U. Wis., 1971; postgrad., U. Mich., 1972-77, MA, 1973; JD, Tulane U., 1985. Bar: La. 1985, U.S. Dist. Ct. (ea. and mid. dists.) La. 1986, U.S. Ct. Appeals (5th cir.) 1986, U.S. Supreme Ct. 1989, U.S. Dist. Ct. (we. dist.) La. 1994. Teaching fellow U. Mich., Ann Arbor, 1973-77; instr. English U. New Orleans, 1977-82; jud. clk. U.S. Dist. Ct. (ea. dist.) La., New Orleans, 1985-86; assoc. Gainsburgh, Benjamin, Fallon & David, New Orleans, 1986-89; ptnr. Gainsburgh, Benjamin, David, Meunier & Warshauer, 1990—. Mem. adj. faculty U. New Orleans Paralegal Inst., 1987-90, Loyola U. Sch. Law, 1990-96, Tulane U. Sch. Law, 1994-96. Sr. articles editor Tulane Law Rev., 1984-85; contbr. articles to profl. jours. Rackham fellow U. Mich., 1976-77. Mem.: ATLA (officer admiralty law sect. 1996—2002, chair 1999—2000), ABA, Fed. Bar Assn. (bd. dirs. New Orleans chpt. 2000—), La. Bar Found., Maritime Law Assn. (proctor), La. Trial Lawyers Assn. (bd. govs. 2002), La. Bar Assn., Trial Lawyers Pub. Justice, Phi Kappa Phi, Order of Coif. Democrat. Episcopalian. Avocations: tennis, baseball, travel, literature. Admiralty, General civil litigation, Personal injury (including property damage). Home: 832 Topaz St New Orleans LA 70124-3626 Office: Gainsburgh Benjamin et al 2800 Energy Centre New Orleans LA 70163 E-mail: sdittman@gainsben.com., walkerdittman@cox.net.

DITTRICH, STEVEN MICHAEL, lawyer; b. Winona, Minn., Apr. 23, 1969; s. Daniel Willard Dittrich and Kathy Mary Chafos; m. Andrea Turner; 1 stepchild, Jasmine Chantel Bush. BA, Gustavus Adolphus Coll., 1991; JD, U. Ark., 1999. Bar: Minn. 1999. Assoc. atty. Lawrence Downing & Assocs., Rochester, Minn., 1999—. Family and matrimonial. Home: 4107 4 Pl NW Rochester MN 55901 Office: Lawrence Downing and Assocs 330 Wells Fargo Ctr 21 1st Ave SW Rochester MN 55902 Office Fax: 507-282-9259.

DIVIER, PIERRE-FRANÇOIS, lawyer; b. Boulogne-Billancourt, France, Aug. 18, 1946; s. Robert D. and Véra Lilienthal. Diploma Econ. and Fin. Sect., Inst. D'Etudes Politiques de Paris, 1968; Diploma Superior Studies Penal Law, Faculté de Droit, Paris, 1971; Cert. d'Aptitude, U. Droit, Paris, 1971; brevet de terminologie anglo-am., Inst. Droit Comparé, 1990. Bar: Paris. 1971. Chief publicity Ted Bates Grey, 1970-71; assoc. Law Office of Bruno Boccara, 1972-75; pvt. practice Paris, 1977—. Author: The Lie of Publicity, 1972, The Frustrated Consumer, 1973, Ralph Nader in 33 Lessons or How to Become a Lawyer in the Public Interest, 1974, The Transparent Administration: the American Citizens' Access to Official Documents, 1975, 50 Cases of Lying Publicity, 1978, Le Guide Bordas des particuliers, 1983, Votre bail commercial et vous, 1995, L'héritage et vous, 1990, Le permis à points Et vous, 1992, Lettre recommandée à François Mitterrand sur l'affaire Urba-Gracco, 1992, Le Jacques Pote, 2002, "et mourir à l'Elysée", 2003. Lt. Intendance de l'armée de Terre, 1968-70. Mem. Racing Club France. Mem. Ecologist Party. Avocations: tennis, photography, writing, piano, reading. Civil rights, Commercial, consumer (including collections, credit), Communications. Home and Office: 31 Rue de L'Assomption 75016 Paris France Fax: 01 42 15 20 13. E-mail: pierre-divier@wanadoo.fr.

DIX, MARTIN ROBERT, lawyer; b. Daytona Beach, Fla., Feb. 24, 1955; s. Everett Stewart and Natalie (True) Dix; m. Linda Louise Grotendorst, June 6, 1982; children: Patrick Robert, Natalie Louise Xiae Mei. B, Fla. State U., 1977, JD, 1985. Assoc. Swann and Haddock PA, Tallahassee, 1985—87, Katz, Kutter, Aldevntau, Bryant and Yon PA, Tallahassee, 1987—. Contbr. Bd. dirs. Legal Svcs. North Fla., Tallahassee, pres., 2003; pres., bd. dirs. Tallahassee Families with Asian Children. Recipient Outstanding Svc. award, Fla. Pharmacy Assn., 2001, Judy Florence Outstanding Achievement award, Environ. and Land Use Law Sect. Fla. Bar Assn., 1987—88. Mem.: Tallahassee Bar Assn., Am. Soc. Pharmacy Law. Avocations: swimming, fishing, bicycling. Health, Environmental, Land use and zoning (including planning). Office: Katz Kutter Alderman Bryan and Yon 106 E College Ave Ste 1200 Tallahassee FL 32301

DIXON, E. A., JR., lawyer; b. Bryn Mawr, Pa., Dec. 12, 1939; m. Margaret Kennedy Cortright; children: Thomas W.W., Abigail C., Marion W., Meghan. AB, Princeton U., 1962; JD with honors, George Washington U., 1967. Bar: Pa. 1968, U.S. Dist. Ct. (ea. dist.) 1968. Assoc. Montgomery, McCracken, Walker & Rhoads, Phila., 1967-69; assoc. resident counsel Industrial Valley Bank, Phila., 1970-73; ptnr. Hepburn, Ross, Wilcox & Putnam, Phila., 1974-78; owner wholesale nursery business, 1979-85; atty. Monumental Title Corp., Severna Park, Md., 1985-86; mgr. comml. divsn. The Sentinel Title Corp., Balt., 1987-89; regional underwriting counsel Nations Title Ins. (formerly Nat. Attys and TRW Title), Trevose, Pa., 1989-96; sr. title counsel Lawyers Title Ins. Corp., Phila., 1996, N.J. area counsel Iselin, 1997; counsel Stewart Title Guaranty Co., Wayne, Pa., 1998—. Seminar spkr. Nat. Bus. Inst., N.J., 1995-96, Title Acad. N.J., 1995—. Contbr. articles to co. publs., 1990—. 2d lt. USAF, 1963—64. Mem. Pa. Land Title Assn. (exec. com. 1993-96), Pa. Bar Assn., The Phila. Club, Rittenhouse Club, St. Andrew's Soc. (Phila.), Montrose Club. Libertarian. Episcopalian. Avocations: horticulture, sailing, fly fishing, tennis. Office: 900 W Valley Rd Wayne PA 19087-1830

DIXON, HARRY D., JR., (DONNIE DIXON), former prosecutor; b. Waycross, Ga., Nov. 6, 1953; s. Harry D. Sr. and Ruth (Starling) D.; m. Elizabeth Tonning, Apr. 19, 1980; 2 children. AB in History, Valdosta State Coll., 1974; JD, U. Ga., 1977. Bar: Ga. 1977, U.S. Dist. Ct. Ga. 1978, U.S. Ct. Appeals 1979. Law clk. to Hon. Marvin Hartley, Jr. Superior Ct. for Mid. Jud. Cir., 1977-78; asst. dist. atty. Waycross Jud. Cir. 1977-79, dist. atty., 1983-94; atty. Bennett, Pedrick and Bennett, 1979-83; U.S. atty. for so. dist. Ga. U.S. Dept. Justice, Savannah, 1994—2001; atty. Oliver Maner & Gray LLP, Savannah, Ga., 2002—. His profl. assoc. include the Nat. Assoc. of Former US Atty., the Nat. Assoc. of Criminal Defense Lawyers, the fGa. Assoc. of Criminal Defense Lawyers, the Savannah Bar Assoc. and the Savannah Assoc. of Criminal Defense Lawyers. Office: Oliver Maner & Gray 218 W State St PO Box 10186 Savannah GA 31412*

DIXON, PAUL EDWARD, lawyer, metal products and manufacturing company executive; b. Bklyn., Aug. 27, 1944; s. Paul Stewart and Bernice (Mathisen) D.; m. Kathleen Constance Kayser, Sept. 23, 1967; children: Jennifer Pyne, Paul Kayser, Meredith Stewart. BA, Villanova U., 1966; JD, St. Johns U., 1972. Bar: N.Y. 1972, U.S. Supreme Ct. 1976. Assoc. mem. firm Rogers & Wells, N.Y.C., 1972-77; sec., asst. gen. counsel Volvo of Am. Corp., Rockleigh, N.J., 1977-79, v.p., gen. counsel, 1979-81; v.p., gen. counsel, sec. Reichhold Chems. Inc., 1981-88; sr. v.p., gen. counsel, sec. The Warnaco Group Inc., 1988-91; v.p., gen. counsel, sec. Handy & Harman, Rye, N.Y., 1992-97, sr. v.p., gen. counsel, sec., 1997—. Chmn. Teeches Ltd., Bermuda. Mem. ABA, Assn. Bar City N.Y., N.Y. State Bar Assn., U.S. Supreme Ct. Hist. Soc., Am. Corp. Counsel Assn., Bedford Golf and Tennis Club. Corporate, general. Office: Handy & Harman 555 Theodore Fremd Ave Rye NY 10580-1451

DIXON, PHILLIP RAY, SR., lawyer; b. Wake Forest, N.C., Mar. 26, 1949; s. Milton R. Dixon and Lottie Belle (Tippett) Larson; m. Candace (Mamie) Cicerone, Nov. 26, 1977; children: Phillip Ray Jr., Joseph David, Jonathan Scott. BSBA, East Carolina U., 1971; JD, U. N.C., 1974. Bar: N.C. 1974, U.S. Dist. Ct. (ea. dist.) N.C. 1976, U.S. Ct. Appeals (4th cir.) 1981, U.S. Supreme Ct. 1981. Law clk. to assoc. justice N.C. Ct. Appeals, Raleigh, 1974-75; assoc. Gaylord & Singleton, Greenville, N.C., 1975-78; ptnr. Dixon, Duffus & Doub, Greenville, 1978-90; N/A Dixon Doub Conner and Foster P.L.L.C, Greenville, 1990—. Instr. police sci. paralegal program Pitt Community Coll. and Pitt Tech. Inst., 1975-79, advisor 1982—; 981; bd. dirs., counsel PBC Ctr. Bank and Trust Co., Greenville, bd. dirs. RBC Centura Bank. Editor-in-chief N.C. Law Record, 1972-73, assoc. editor 1973-74. Atty. Greenville City Schs. and Greenville City Bd. Edn., 1978-86, Pitt County Schs. and Bd. of Edn., 1978—; local and state hearing officer N.C. Dept. Pub. Instrn.; atty. Greenville Utilities Commn., 1981—; mem. Pitt County Area Mental Health Mental Retardation and Substance Abuse Bd., 1983-87, chmn. bd. dirs. 1984-86; chancel choir mem. 1st Christian Ch. of Greenville, 1975-77, Sunday sch. supt., 1977, deacon, 1978-82, elder, 1983-87, guest minister, 1984, vice chmn. bd. dirs. 1981, chmn. 1982; bd. dirs., trustee Pitt-Greenville Arts Council, Inc., 1979-81; exec. bd. Pitt County United Way, Inc., 1981, sec., campaign chmn., pres. 1982, 1986; mem. Downtown Greenville Assn., 1980—, Greenville Mus. of Art, 1980—, treas. 1986-87, v.p., 1987-88, trustee, 1986—; pres. 1988—; bd. dirs. Greenville Jaycees 1975-77; immediate past pres. East Carolina U. Ednl. Founds., Inc., 1987; del. county, dist. and state Dem. Convs., 1984, del. N.C. State Dem. Conv., Pitt. County campaign chmn. lt. gov.'s race, 1983-84. Named Outstanding Young Men of Am., 1974-83. Mem. ABA, N.C. Bar Assn. (sustaining mem., family law sect., criminal law sect., real estate sect., probate sect., practical tng. com., instr. and seminar speaker on topic appeals, practical skills course 1975-81) bd. gov., Pitts County Bar Assn. (sec. law library com. 1976-77, chmn. 1976-82), N.C. Acad. Trial Lawyers, N.C. Coll. of Advocacy, N.C. Council Sch. Bd. of Attys. (bd. dirs. 1982—, chmn. 1984-85, v.p. 1983-84, chmn. ins. com. 1983-84, disting. svc. award, 2003), Nat. Council Sch. Bd. Attys., Greenville C. of C. (chmn.), Greenville-Pitt County Home Builders Assn. (chmn.), East Carolina Univ. Alumni Assn. (Outstanding Alumnus award 1984), Phi Sigma Pi. Clubs: Greenville Sports (chartered, sec., treas. 1975-77, pres. 1979-80). Lodges: Rotary (chartered, bd. dirs. Greenville chpt. 1981-83, dist. sec. 1982, v.p. 1983, pres. 1986-87, Paul Harris Fellow 1982). Democrat. Corporate, general, Education and schools, Estate planning. Home: 1510E 5th St Greenville NC 27858-2803 Office: Dixon Doub and Conner PO Box Drawer 8668 110 Arlington Blvd Greenville NC 27835

DIXON, RICHARD DEAN, lawyer, educator; b. Columbus, Ohio, Nov. 6, 1944; s. Dean A. and Katherine L. (Currier) D.; m. Kathleen A. Manfrass, June 17, 1967; children: Jennifer, Lindsay. BSEE, Ohio State U., 1967, MSEE, 1968; MBA, Fla. State U., 1972, JD, 1974. Bar: Fla. 1975, Colo. 1985, Mich. 1992, U.S. Dist. Ct. (mid. dist.) Fla., U.S. Dist. Ct. Colo. 1985, U.S. Patent and Trademanrk Office 1975. Telemetry sys. engr. Pan Am. World Airways, Patrick AFB, Fla., 1968-72; sole practice Melbourne and Orlando, Fla., 1975-80; sr. counsel Harris Corp., Melbourne, 1980-85; corp. counsel, dir. strategic and bus. planning Ford Microelectronics, Inc., Colorado Springs, Colo., 1985-89; mgr. strategic alliances electronics divsn. Ford Motor Co., Dearborn, Mich., 1989-90, assoc. counsel intellectual property, 1991-93, dep. chief patent counsel, 1994—2000; with Dixon Mediation Svcs., 2001—. Adj. prof. bus. law U. Cen. Fla., Cocoa, 1977, Fla. Inst. Tech., Melbourne, 1980-84. Cooper Industries Engring. scholar Ohio State U., 1964-67. Mem. ABA, Licensing Execs. Soc., Am. Intellectual Property Law Assn., Am. Corp. Counsel Assn., Sigma Iota Epsilon, Eta Kappa Nu, Phi Eta Sigma. Commercial, contracts (including sales of goods; commercial financing), Intellectual property, Patent. Home and Office: 8162 Old Tramway Dr Melbourne FL 32940-2183

DIXON, STEWART STRAWN, lawyer, consultant; b. Chgo., Nov. 5, 1930; s. Wesley M. and Katherine (Strawn) D.; m. Romayne Wilson, June 24, 1961 (dec. July 1993); children: Stewart S. Jr., John W., Romayne W. Thompson; m. Ann Wilson Grozier, Sept. 15, 1997. BA, Yale U., 1952; JD, U. Mich., 1955. Bar: Ill. 1957, U.S. Dist. Ct. 1957, U.S. Ct. Appeals 1974, U.S. Supreme Ct. 1974. Ptnr. Kirkland & Ellis, Chgo., 1957-67, Wildman, Harrold, Allen & Dixon, Chgo., 1967—. Dir. Lord, Abbett & Co. Managed Mut. Funds, N.Y.C., 1976-2002, ret. Dec. 31, 2002; dir. Otho Sprague Inst., Chgo. Trustee, past chmn. Chgo. Hist. Soc., 1982-87. 1st lt. U.S. Army, 1955-60. Mem. Am. Bar Assn., Am. Law Inst., Ill. Bar Assn., Chgo. Bar Assn. Clubs: Chgo., Commonwealth, Commercial, Met., Univ., Old Elm, Onwentsia, Rolling Rock. Republican. Episcopalian. Antitrust, Federal civil litigation, Probate (including wills, trusts). Office: Wildman Harrold Allen & Dixon 225 W Wacker Dr Chicago IL 60606-1224

DIXON, WILLIAM, lawyer; BA, Tufts U., 1990; JD magna cum laude, Boston U., 1997. Bar: N.Y. Assoc. Cravath, Swaine & Moore, LLP, N.Y.C., 1997—. Fellow John S. Nolan fellow, ABA Taxation Sect., 2001—02. Corporate taxation, Taxation, general. Office: Cravath Swaine & Moore LLP 825 8th Ave New York NY 10019-7416

DIXON, WRIGHT TRACY, JR., retired lawyer; b. Raleigh, N.C., Oct. 7, 1921; s. Wright T. and Marion Jefferson (Homes) D.; m. Elizabeth Prince Nufer, June 3, 1950; children: Wright III, William N., Elizabeth Prince. AB, Duke U., 1947; LLB, U. N.C., 1951. Bar: N.C. 1951, U.S. Dsit. Ct. (ea., mid. and we. dists.), N.C. 1951, U.S. Ct. Appeals (4th cir.) 1956. Ptnr. Bailey & Dixon, Raleigh, N.C., 1956-99; ret. Mem. Bd. of Adjustments, Raleigh, 1960-74, chmn., 1969-74. Jr. warden, sr. warden, mem. vestry St. Michael's Episcopal Ch., Raleigh; trustee So. Sem. Va., 1961-81, N.C. Client Security Fund, 1986-91. With USMC, 1943-59. Fellow Am. Bar Found.; mem. ABA (del. 1984-88), N.C. State Bar (counselor 1979-86, pres. 1985-86, Gen. Practice Hall of Fame 1997), Wake County Bar Assn. (pres. 1976, mem. N.C. commn. on code recodification 1979-81, hon. bd. mem. 1995, Joseph Branch professionalism award 1996), Raleigh Kiwanis Club (pres.), Sphinx Club (pres.), Carolina Country Club, Capital City Club. Avocations: golf, woodworking, genealogy, tennis, reading. Administrative and regulatory, General civil litigation, Insurance. Home: 414 Marlowe Rd Raleigh NC 27609-7018 Office: Bailey & Dixon PO Box 1351 2 Hannover Sq Raleigh NC 27602 E-mail: WDixon@BDixon.com.

DJEMAT, HUMPHREY RITHAN, lawyer; b. Jakarta, Indonesia, Oct. 17, 1956; s. Gani Djemat and Louise Farida Simanjuntak; married, June 20, 1978; children: Pricilla Irena, Reldy Garisi, Patricia Irene. Grad., Indonesia U., 1983, U. Calif., 1986; LLM, So. Meth. U., 1988. Atty. Gani Djemat & Ptnrs., Jakarta, 1983—2001, chmn., 2001—. Banking, Civil rights, Criminal. Office: Gani Djemat & Ptnrs Jl Imam Bonjol 76-78 Jakarta 10310 Indonesia Fax: 62-021 3902908. E-mail: gdp@ganidjemat.com.

DJINGOV, ASSEN ALEXANDROV, lawyer; b. Sofia, Bulgaria, Apr. 29, 1965; s. Alexander Ivanov Djingov and Maya Kostova Djingova; m. Biliyana Hristova Djingova, Dec. 15, 1996; children: Maya Assenova, Niya Assenova. LLM, U. Sofia, 1991; diploma (hon.) , Acad. Am. and Internat. Law, Dallas, Tex., 1993. Bar: Sofia 92. Legal counsel Ministry of Justice, Sofia, Bulgaria, 1992—93; fgn. atty. Gibson, Dunn & Crutcher, Washington, 1993; mng. ptnr. Dijongov, Gouginski, Kyutchukov & Velichkov, Sofia, 1994—. Mem.: Sofia Bar Assn., Internat. Bar Assn. Avocations: jazz, skiing. Mergers and acquisitions, Finance, Corporate, general. Office: Djingov Gouginski Kyutchukov & Velichkov 10 Tsar Osvobodital Blvd 1000 Sofia Bulgaria Fax: 00359 2 980 35 86. E-mail: assen.djingov@dgkv.com.

DJOKIC, WALTER HENRY, lawyer; b. Schwaforden, Germany, Sept. 12, 1947; came to U.S., 1951, naturalized, 1959; s. Radovan and Martha (Schulenburg) D.; married; 1 child, Joshua David. B.A., U. Ill., 1969; J.D., DePaul U., 1972. Bar: Ill. 1972, Ariz. 1980. Fla. assoc. Wachowski & Wachowski, Chgo., 1972-73; atty. Pretzel & Stouffer, Chartered, Chgo., 1973-79, ptnr., 1979-85; ptnr. Wood, Lucksinger & Epstein, Chgo., 1985-86, Finley Kumble Wagner, Heine, Underberg, Manley, Myerson & Casey, Chgo., 1986-88; of counsel McCullough, Campbell & Lane, 1988-93, Conrad, Scherer & James, 1994-965 Miller, Kagan, Rodriguez & Silver, 1995-2000; atty. McIntosh, Sawran Peltz & Cargaya, 2000-02, ptnr., 2002—. Mem. Chgo. Bar Assn., Ill. State Bar Assn., State Bar of Ariz., State Bar of Fla. Federal civil litigation, State civil litigation, Personal injury (including property damage). Office: 625 N Flagler Dr Ste 502 West Palm Beach FL 33401 E-mail: wdjokic@mspcesq.com.

DLUGOFF, MARC ALAN, lawyer; b. N.Y.C., Oct. 6, 1955; s. Arnold M. and Ruth B. (Schnall) D. AB, Colgate U., 1976; JD, Hofstra U., 1980; LLM in Taxation, NYU, 1981. Bar: N.Y. 1981, D.C. 1985, Calif. 1988. Law clk. to presiding justice U.S. Tax Ct., Washington, 1981-83; assoc. Mudge, Rose, Guthrie, Alexander & Ferdon, N.Y.C., 1983-85, Milbank, Tweed, Hadley & McCloy, N.Y.C., 1985-89, ptnr., 1989—92; counsel Roberts & Holland, N.Y.C., 1993-94; pres., CEO, Atlantic Adv. Corp., N.Y.C., 1995—. Fundraiser lawyers divsn. United Jewish Appeal, N.Y.C. chpt., 1986-90. Charles Dana scholar Colgate U., 1976. Mem. ABA, N.Y. State Bar Assn., Assn. Bar City N.Y., State Bar Calif., Phi Beta Kappa. Jewish. Corporate, general, Private international, Taxation, general. Home and Office: 130 Water St Ste 5-G New York NY 10005-1625 E-mail: marcnyc130@hotmail.com.

DOAN, GERALD XUYEN VAN, lawyer; b. Hadong, Vietnam, Apr. 1, 1949; came to U.S., 1975; s. Quyet V. Doan and Binh T. Kieu; m. Binh Thanh Tran, 1980; children: Quy-Bao, Ky-Nam. Licence en droit, U. Saigon Law Sch., Vietnam, 1971; MBA, U. Ark., 1977; JD, U. Calif., Hastings, 1982. Bar: Saigon 1972, Calif. 1982. Sole practice, Costa Mesa and San Jose, Calif., 1982-84; ptnr. Doan & Vu, San Jose, 1984-90; prin. Law Offices of Xuyen V. Doan, 1990-95; ptnr. Doan & Tran, San Jose, 1995—. Author: Of the Seas and Men, 1985, other publs. in English and Vietnamese. Named Ark. Traveler Ambassador of Good Will, State of Ark., 1975. Corporate, general, Immigration, naturalization, and customs, Private international. Office: PO Box 14117 Irvine CA 92623-4117 E-mail: jd@vietlawyers.com.

DOAN, KIRK HUGH, lawyer; b. Independence, Iowa, Jan. 30, 1953; s. Arthur Nelson and Kathlyn (Kingsley) D.; m. Laura Leah Brown, Sept. 24, 1982. BS, Iowa State U., 1975; JD, U. Iowa, 1978. Bar: Mo. 1978, Kans. 1998, U.S. Dist. Ct. (we. dist.) Mo. 1978, U.S. Dist. Ct. Kans., 1998, U.S. Ct. Appeals (8th cir.) 1989, U.S. Supreme Ct. 1990. Assoc. Stinson Morrison Hecker, LLP, Kansas City, Mo., 1978-83, ptnr., 1983—. Contbr. articles to profl. jours. Advisor Heart of Am. coun. Boy Scouts Am., 1982—; counsel Met. Med. Soc. Greater Kansas City; capt. U.S. CAP. Mem. Mo. Bar Assn., Kansas City Met. Bar Assn., Lawyers Assn. Kansas City (pres. young lawyers sect. 1984-85, treas. sr. sect. 1991-94), Order of Coif, Lakewood Oaks Country Club. Republican. Methodist. Health, Commercial, contracts (including sales of goods; commercial financing), Property, real (including real estate development, water). Home: 4300 NW Lake Dr Lees Summit MO 64064-1425 Office: Stinson Morrison Hecker LLP 1201 Walnut Ste 2600 Kansas City MO 64106-2150 E-mail: kdoan@stinsonmoheck.com.

DOBBINS, CARYL DEAN, lawyer; b. Indpls., July 3, 1947; s. Caryl L. and Janet (Matlock) D.; m. Amanda M. Cline, Nov. 22, 1972 (div. Jan. 1977); 1 child, Heather Lynn; m. Barbara J. Perry, Nov. 10, 1977; 1 child, Jason Dean. BS, Purdue U., 1969; postgrad., Valparaiso (Ind.) U., 1969-70; spl. med. student, Ind. U. Med. Sch., 1970-72; JD, Ind. U., Indpls., 1972; postgrad., Oxford (Eng.) U. and Brunel U., 1971. Bar: Ind. 1972, U.S. Dist. Ct. (so. dist.) Ind. 1972, U.S. Ct. Appeals (7th cir.) 1973, U.S. Supreme Ct. 1987. Chief law clk. to chief judge U.S. Dist. Ct. for So. Dist. Ind., Indpls., 1972-74; pros. atty. 18th jud. cir. State of Ind., 1975-78, dir. child support, 1979; pvt. practice, Greenfield, Ind., 1979—. Dir. Ind. Law Enforcement Asst. Adminstrn., 1976-78; bd. dirs. Ind. Pros. Atty. Coun., 1976-78. Recipient Am. Farmer degree Future Farmers Am., 1967, Preservation award Greenfield Hist. Landmarks, 1984. Mem. ABA (gen. practice link bar leader award 1997), Ind. Bar Assn. (del. 1988-98, 2001—, chair gen. practice, solo and small firm sect. 1996-97, chair, law practice mgmt. 1998-2001, bd. govs. 2002—), Ind. Bar Found. (master fellow), Hancock County Bar Assn. (pres. 1999-2000), C. of C. Greater Hancock County and Greenfield (bd. dirs. 2d v.p. 1990, 1st v.p. 1991, pres. 1992, chmn. bd. dirs. 1993), Rotary (bd. dirs. 1991-94, 99—, v.p. 1999-2000, pres. elect 2000-01, pres. 2001-02, chmn. bd. 2002-03, Paul Harris fellow), Sertoma (treas. Greenfield 1982-84, sec. 1984-85, pres. 1985-86, chmn. bd. dirs. 1986-87, internat. del. 1983-86, Cmty. Achievement award 1986), Farm House, Phi Alpha Delta. Avocations: gardening, travel. Criminal, Personal injury (including property damage), Probate (including wills, trusts). Home: 4392 E 100 S Greenfield IN 46140-9758 Office: 19 W Main St Greenfield IN 46140-2340 Office Fax: 317-462-4903. E-mail: dobbinsd@iquest.net.

DOBRANSKI, BERNARD, law educator; b. Sept. 3, 1939; s. Walter John and Helen Dolores (Rudnick) Dobranski; m. Caroll Sue Wood, Aug. 31, 1963; children: Stephanie, Andrea, Christopher. BBA in Fin., U. Notre Dame, 1961; JD, U. Va., 1964. Bar: Va. 64, U.S. Supreme Ct. 68, U.S. Ct. Appeals (DC cir.) 71. Legal advisor to bd. Nat. Labor Rels. Bd., 1964—67; profl. staff mem. Pres.'s Adv. Commn. on Civil Disorders, 1967—68; adminstrv. asst. U.S. Ho. of Reps., 1968—71; gen. counsel Washington Met. Area Transit Commn., 1971—72; mem. faculty Creighton U. Sch. of Law, Omaha, 1972—77, U. Notre Dame, 1977—83; prof., dean U. Detroit Sch. of Law, 1983—95; dean Cath. U. Am. Sch. of Law, 1995—99; pres., dean Ave Maria Sch. of Law, Ann Arbor, Mich., 1999—. Labor arbitrator Fed. Mediation and Conciliation Svc.; active Mich. Commn. on Death and Dying. Contbr. articles to profl. jours. Mem.: ABA, Am. Law Inst., Am. Arbitration Assn., Detroit Athletic Club, Hurlingham Club, Frank Murphy Honor Soc. Roman Catholic. Office: Ave Maria Sch of Law 3475 Plymouth Rd Ann Arbor MI 48105 E-mail: bdobranski@avemarialaw.edu.

DOBSON, ROBERT ALBERTUS, III, lawyer, executive, volunteer; b. Greenville, S.C., Nov. 27, 1938; s. Robert A. Jr. and Dorothy (Leonard) D.; m. Linda Josephine Bryant, Nov. 18, 1956; children: Robert, William, Michael, Daniel, Jonathan, Laura (dec.); m. Catherine Elizabeth Cornmesser, Sept. 17, 1983; children: Andrew, Thomas, Juana. BS in Acctg. summa cum laude, U. S.C., 1960, JD magna cum laude, 1962; DPS, Limestone Coll., 2002. Asst. dean of students U. S.C., 1960-62; pvt. practice pub. acctg. Greenville, 1962-64; ptnr. Dobson & Dobson, Greenville, 1964-93. Chmn., bd. trustees Limestone Coll., 1987-89, founder Christian edn. and leadership program; trustee The King's Coll., 2003—. Contbr. articles on tax and acctg. to profl. jours. Lay minister St. Francis Episcopal Ch., Greenville; chmn. bd. Dobson Tape Ministry, Homeless Children Internat., Inc.; bd. dirs. A Child's Haven, Inc., Found. for the Multihandicapped, Deaf and Blind, Spartanburg, S.C.; mem. adv. bd. Salvation Army, Greenville; chmn. bd. Sch. Ministries, Inc.; mem. History's Handful Campus Crusade for Christ; founder Dobson Vol. Svc. Program, U. S.C. Mem. ABA, S.C. Bar Assn., AICPAs, Am. Assn. Attys. and CPAs, S.C. Assn. Pub. Accts., Block C Assn. The Group, U. S.C. Alumni Assn. (cir. v.p.), Kappa Sigma (chmn. legal com. 1989-93, dist. grand master 1971—, Nat. Dist. Grand Master of the Yr. 1986, John G. Tower Disting. Alumni award 1997, Stephen Alonzo Jackson award 1998), Phi Beta Kappa. Lodges: Sertoma Internat. (dist. treas.), Sertoma Sunrisers (pres. Greenville club). Episcopalian. Corporate, general, Estate planning, Taxation, general. Home: 1207 Pelham Rd Greenville SC 29615-3643 Office: 1306 S Church St Greenville SC 29605-3814

DOCKENS, ELAINE BILLINGSLEA, law librarian, lawyer; b. Cleve., ; d. William Charles Billingslea; 1 child, Michael. BA, Ohio State U.; MS in Libr. Sci., Syracuse U.; JD, U. Calif., Berkeley, 1975. Bar: Pa. 1992, Ill. 1994. Law libr. Broad Shultz Larson, San Francisco, 1988—89, Weston Hurd Fallon Paisley & Howley, Cleve., 1989—94; libr. mgr. Burditt & Radzius, Chgo., 1994—98; dir. libr. bur. Ill. Attys. Gens. Office, Chgo., 1999—2000; dir. libr. svcs. Rooks Pitts, Chgo., 2000—01, Tressler Soderstrom Maloney & Priess, Chgo., 2001—. Chair person, cmty. services com. Chgo. Assn. of Law Libraries, Chicago, 1999—2002. Mem.: Ill. State Bar Assn., Chgo. Assn. Law Librs. (chairperson cmty. svcs. com. 1999—2002), Spl. Librs. Assn., Am. Assn. Law Librs. Office: Tressler Soderstrom Maloney & Priess 233 S Wacker Dr 22nd Flr Sears Tow Chicago IL 60606 Office Fax: 312-627-1717.

DOCKING, THOMAS ROBERT, lawyer, former state lieutenant governor; b. Lawrence, Kans., Aug. 10, 1954; s. Robert Blackwell and Meredith (Gear) D.; m. Jill Sadowsky, June 18, 1977; children: Brian Thomas, Margery Meredith BS, U. Kans., 1976, MBA, JD, 1980. Bar: Kans. 1980. Assoc. Regan & McGannon, Wichita, Kans., 1980-82, ptnr., 1983-90, Ayesh, Docking, Herd & Theis, Wichita, 1990, Morris, Laing, Evans, Brock & Kennedy, Wichita, 1990—; lt. gov. State of Kans., Topeka, 1983-87. Dem. nominee for Gov. of Kans., 1986; chmn. adv. bd. Docking Inst. Pub. Affairs, Ft. Hays State U. Mem. steering com. Campaign Kans.; chmn. campaign com. Coll. Liberal Arts and Sci., 1988-91; bd. dirs. Kans. Easter Seals-Goodwill Industries, 1987-93, chmn. 1989 Telethon, vice-chair, 1991-93; bd. dirs. Wichita Conv. and Visitors Bur., 1988-2002; chmn., bd. dirs. St. Francis Found., 1988-94; trustee Emporia State U. Sch. Bus.; chmn. Wichita Water Conservation Task Force, 1991—; mem. Wichita/Brookes Water Task Force, 1997; chmn. allocation com. United Way of the Plains, 2003; mem. bd. govs. U. Kans. Sch. Law, 1998—2000; bd. dirs. Wichita Downtown Devel. Corp., 2001—, bd. Fin. Fitness Found., 1999—. Recipient Bob Brock award, Kansas City Dem. Party, 2003. Mem. ABA, Kans. Bar Assn., Pi Sigma Alpha, Beta Gamma Sigma, Beta Theta Pi. Presbyterian. Home: 125 S Crestway St Wichita KS 67218-1309 Office: Morris Laing Evans Brock & Kennedy 200 W Douglas Ave Fl 4 Wichita KS 67202-3013

DOCKSEY, JOHN ROSS, lawyer; b. Milw., Sept. 4, 1951; s. John Warren and Marilyn Ruth (Skinner) D.; m. D. Christine Bjorum, May 21, 1988; children: John Thomas, Adam Christopher. BS, U.S. Mil. Acad., 1973; JD, U. Minn., 1981. Bar: Ill. 1981, U.S. Dist. Ct. (no. dist.) Ill. 1981. Assoc. Sonnenschein Nath & Rosenthal, Chgo., 1981-88, ptnr., 1988—, chmn. corp. practice group, 1998—2002; chmn. tech. and outsourcing group Lex Mundi internat. assn. law firms. Bd. dirs. Daubert Industries, Oak Brook, Ill., Gullikson Found., Chgo., United Svcs. Orgn. of Ill., Chgo.; chmn. tech. and outsourcing practice group Lex Mundi, 2003—. Contbr. articles to profl. jours. Capt. U.S. Army, 1973-78. Mem. Met. Club, West Point Soc. Chgo. (v.p. 1984-86), Royal Melbourne Country Club, Human Resoures Outsourcing Assn. Avocations: skiing, family, golf. Corporate, general, Private international, Mergers and acquisitions. Office: Sonnenschein Nath & Rosenthal 8000 Sears Tower Chicago IL 60606 E-mail: jdocksey@sonnenschein.com.

DODD, JERRY LEE, lawyer; b. Bakersfield, Calif., Nov. 16, 1953; s. James Luther and Juanita Louise (Holmes) D.; m. Phena Fite, Jan. 9, 1972; children: Jody, Kimberly, Kristy, Julie, Timothy, Andrew, Matthew, Lindsey, Allison, Daniel. BS magna cum laude, U. Ark., 1975; MBA, Monmouth Coll., 1978; JD, Rutgers U., 1979. Bar: N.J. 1979, Pa. 1983, Minn. 1988; CPA. Commd. 2d. lt. USAF, 1975, advanced through grades to capt., auditor A.F. Audit Agy., 1975-78, base counsel Alexandria, La., 1979-81, def. counsel, 1981-82, contract trial atty. A.F. Contract Law Ctr. Dayton, Ohio, 1982-86, ret., 1986; govt. contracts counsel U.S. Army 7th Signal Command, Ft. Richie, Md., 1986-87; group counsel Honeywell, Mpls., 1987-90; divsn. counsel Harsco-BMY Wheeled Vehicles Divsn., Marysville, Ohio, 1990—. Mem.: ABA (com. mem.), Ark. Soc. CPAs, Ohio Bar Assn. (com. mem.), Assn. Corp. Counsels Am. (bd. dirs.). Corporate, general, Government contracts and claims, Corporate taxation. Home: 700 Kirkpatrick Rd Malvern AR 72104 Office: Harsco BMY Wheeled Vehicles 3735 Grantz Rd Grove City OH 43123 E-mail: jerryleedodd@yahoo.com.

DODD, ROGER J. lawyer; b. Sewickley, Pa., Sept. 15, 1951; s. Carl Roger and Dorothy Maude (Barley) Dodd; m. Marcia J. Dodd; children: Matthew A., Andrew J., Kristin. BA in Econs., Bucknell U., 1973; JD, U. Pitts., 1976, Ga., 1976, Fla., 1977. Ptnr. Blackburn, Bright, Edwards Dodd & Joseph, Valdosta, Ga., 1976-87; prin. Roger J. Dodd Lawyers, P.C., Valdosta, 1987—; spl. asst. atty. gen. State of Ga., 1979-85; mem. faculty Ga. Inst. Trial Advocacy, 1986—92, chmn. of bd., 1988—91; mem. faculty Nat. Coll. Criminal Def., 1986—. Mem. faculty Nat. Coll. Criminal Def., 1986—, Advance Cross Exam., Advance Trial Inst.; adj. prof. Valdosta State Coll.; guest lectr. sch. law Mercer U. Ga. State U.; mem. family law sect. exec. com., 1985-88, criminal law sect., mem. family law sect., exec. com. 1985-88; mem. ABA family law sect., criminal law sect. exec. coms., 1992—; internat. lectr. in field. Co-author: Cross Examination: Science and Techniques, 1993; guest commentator on Court TV; peer rev. lawyer Trial Mag., 1991—; contbr. articles to profl. jours., newspapers; videos: Killer Cross-Examination (6 hrs. of audio & video tapes) The Art and Science of Cross Examination, 2 parts, 1990, How to Dominate a Courtroom on Cross Examination, 4 parts, 1994. Bd. dirs. Lowndes Country Assn. Retarded Citizens, Valdosta, 1977, Valwood Sch., Valdosta, 1984-86, Nat. Bd. Trial Advocacy, 1989, civil trial specialist, criminal trial specialist, 1990; peer rev. lawyer Trial Mag., 1991; mem. Boy Scouts Am., sustaining mem. Alapaha Coun. Mem.: Am. Acad. Matrimonial Lawyers, Internat. Acad. Matrimonial Lawyers. Libertarian. Presbyterian. Criminal, Family and matrimonial, Personal injury (including property damage). Home: 5634 Danieli Dr N Lake Park GA 31636 Office: PO Box 1066 613 N Patterson St Valdosta GA 31601-4609 E-mail: doddlaw@doddlaw.com.

DODDS, MICHAEL BRUCE, lawyer; b. Spokane, Wash., June 27, 1952; s. Bruce Alison and Janet Lorraine (Swanbeck) D.; m. Karen Lynn Sifford, Jan. 5, 1972; children: Jennifer Ann, Stephanie Marie, Alexander Michael, Matthew Tyler. BA, Gonzaga U., 1974, JD, 1979. Bar: Wash. 1980, U.S. Dist. (ea. dist.) Wash. 1983, U.S. Dist. Ct. (we. dist.) Wash. 1987, U.S. Ct. Appeals (9th cir.) 1994, U.S. Supreme Ct. 1987. Dep. prosecutor Okanogan (Wash.) County, 1980-87, Clark (Wash.) County, 1987—. Served to 2d lt. U.S. Army, 1974-76. Recipient Excellence in Performance award Clark County, 1995. Mem. Clark County Bar Assn., Wash. State Bar Assn., Nat. Dist. Attys. Assn., Phi Alpha Delta. Lodges: Eagles, Moose. Republican. Home: 2104 NE Cranbrook Dr Vancouver WA 98664-2960 Office: Clark County Prosecuter's Office PO Box 5000 Vancouver WA 98666-5000

DODDS, ROBERT JAMES, III, lawyer; b. San Antonio, Sept. 19, 1943; s. Robert James Jr. and Kathryn (Bechman) D.; m. Deborah N. Detchon, June 25, 1966 (div. Mar. 1989); children: Zachary Bechman, Seth Detchon; m. D.J. Knowles, Dec. 27, 1990. BA, Yale U., 1965; LLB, U. Pa., 1969. Assoc. Reed Smith Shaw & McClay, Pitts., 1969-77, ptnr., 1978-91; ptnr. Davenport & Dodds, LLP, Santa Fe, 1992—; of counsel Strassburger, McKenna, Gutnick & Potter, Pitts., 1991—. Bd. dirs. ATP Inc., Davison Sand & Gravel Co., Pitts.; pres. Homewood Cemetery, Pitts., 1980-91, bd. dirs. Trustee Mus. Art, Carnegie Inst, 1974-84, Westmoreland Mus. Art, Greensburg, Pa., YMCA of Pitts., Carnegie-Mellon U.; dir., pres. Pitts. Plan for Art, 1981-85; dir., chmn. West Pa. Hosp. Found., Carnegie Mellon Art Gallery; bd. dirs. Western Pa. Hosp., Western Pa. Healthcare Systems Inc., Pitts. Athletic Assn., Inst. Am. Indian Arts Found., Santa Fe; mus. panel Pa. Coun. on the Arts. Mem.: Rolling Rock Club (Ligonier, Pa.), Duquesne Club (Pitts.). Democrat. Episcopalian. Home: 3101 Old Pecos Trl Unit 687 Santa Fe NM 87505-9547 Office: Davenport & Dodds LLP 721 Don Diego Ave Santa Fe NM 87505

DOERHOFF, DALE CHARLES, lawyer; b. St. Elizabeth, Mo., Dec. 13, 1946; s. Leonard Joseph and Cyrilla Anna (Tellman) D.; m. Ruth Ann Wilde, Jan. 29,. 1971; children: Heidi, Erica, Stephen. AB, U. Mo., 1968, JD cum laude, 1971. Bar: Mo. 1971, U.S. Dist. Ct. (we. and ea. dists.) Mo. 1975, U.S. Ct. Appeals (8th cir.) 1985, U.S. Supreme Ct. 2000. Assoc., then ptnr. Smith, Lewis & Rogers, Columbia, Mo., 1971-76; ptnr. Cook, Vetter & Doerhoff, Jefferson City, Mo., 1976-95, Cook, Vetter, Doerhoff & Landwehr, Jefferson City, Mo., 1995—. Mem. com. on rules Mo. Supreme Ct., 1995—; mem. faculty Mo. Jud. Coll., 1985-2000; chmn. tort law com. Mo. Bar, 1988-92. Recipient Lon O. Hocker Trial Lawyer's award, Mo. Bar Found., 1981. Fellow Am. Coll. Trial Lawyers; mem. The Mo. Bar (pres. 2002—, bd. govs.), Cole County Bar Assn. (pres. 1983), Mo. Assn. Trial Attys., U. Mo. Law Sch. Alumni Assn. (pres. 1983-84), KC, Rotary (pres. Jefferson City chpt. 1987-88). Roman Catholic. Avocations: photography, fishing, music, hunting. General civil litigation. Office: Cook Vetter Doerhoff and Landwehr 231 Madison St Jefferson City MO 65101-3202 E-mail: ddoerhoff@cvdl.net.

DOGGRELL, HENRY PATTON, lawyer; b. Memphis, July 3, 1948; s. Frank Ernest Doggrell Jr. and Martha (Patton) Brown; m. Beverly Gay Rhoda, Jan. 22, 1983; children: Henry Patton Jr., Dana Scott, Adrian Edward. BS in Commerce, U. Va., 1970; JD, Vanderbilt U., 1976. Bar: U.S. Dist. Ct. (mid. dist.) Tenn. 1977, U.S. Ct. Appeals (6th cir.) 1977, U.S. Dist. Ct. (we. dist.) Tenn. 1978, U.S. Ct. Appeals (fed. cir.) 1985. Law clk. to Judge Harry W. Wellford, U.S. Dist. Ct., 1975; assoc. Boult, Cummings, Conners & Berry, Nashville, 1976-78; ptnr. Burch, Porter & Johnson, Memphis, 1978-88, Baker, Donelson, Bearman & Caldwell, Memphis, 1988—96; gen. counsel Buckeye Techs., Inc., 1996—97, sr. v.p. corp. devel., 1998—2001; gen. coun., sec. GTx, Inc., Memphis, 2001—. Chmn. ad hoc com. Citizens on Govtl. Consolidation, Memphis, 1978; chmn. Brooks Mus. Art, 2000-02; bd. dirs. Calvary St. Ministry, 1996—. lt. (j.g.) USN, 1970-71. Mem. ABA, Tenn. Bar Assn. (chmn. real estate sect., sec. com. on real estate 1988-90). Republican. Unitarian. Avocations: backpacking, fishing, hiking, skiing, reading. Mergers and acquisitions, Property, real (including real estate development, water), Securities. Home: 1657 Peabody Ave Memphis TN 38104-3829 Office: GTx Inc 3 N Dunlap 3rd FL Memphis TN 38163

DOHERTY, DAVID P. lawyer; b. Boston, June 28, 1962; s. David E. and C. Laura Doherty; m. Christine M. Noody, Aug. 22, 1987; 1 child, Emily C. BA in Polit. Sci., BA in Econs., SUNY, Fredonia, 1984; JD, Syracuse U., 1987. Bar: N.Y. 1988, U.S. Dist. Ct. (no. dist.) N.Y. 1988, Mass. 2000, N.J. 2001. Ptnr. Ali Pappas and Cox PC, Syracuse, NY, 1987—. Mem.: Onandaga County Bar Assn., N.Y. State Bar Assn. Roman Catholic. Avocations: golf, basketball, music. Office: Ali Pappas and Cox PC 614 James St Syracuse NY 13203 Office Fax: 315-472-8299 . E-mail: davidd@alipappascox.com.

DOHERTY, ROBERT CHRISTOPHER, lawyer; b. Elizabeth, N.J., Sept. 3, 1943; s. Christopher Joseph and Marie Veronica (McLaughlin) D.; m. Sarajane Frances Doherty, June 12, 1965; children: Dennis Michael, Amy Elizabeth, Tracey Carolan. AB, St. Peter's Coll., 1965; JD, Seton Hall U., 1970. Bar: N.J. 1970, U.S. Ct. Appeals (3d cir.) 1982, U.S. Supreme Ct. 1977. Asst. prosecutor Union County, Elizabeth, 1971-72; mem. firm Schumann, Hession, Kennelly & Dorment, Jersey City, 1972-73, Robert D. Younghans, Westfield, N.J., 1973-76; ptnr. Doherty & Kopnicki, Westfield, 9176-87; county counsel, Union County, 1981-88; assoc. Nelinson, Roche & Carter, East Orange, N.J., 1988-92, Stanley Marcus, Newark, 1992-98, Weiner Lesniak, Parsippany, N.J., 1998-2000; dep. atty. gen. N.J. Divsn. Law, Trenton, 2000—. Mem. ABA, N.J. Bar Assn., Union County Bar Assn., Essex County Bar Assn., N.J. Assn. County Counsels. Republican. Roman Catholic. State civil litigation, General practice, Personal injury (including property damage). Home: 771 Fairacres Ave Westfield NJ 07090-2027 Office: RJ Hughes Justice Complex PO Box 112 Trenton NJ 08625-0112

DOKE, MARSHALL J., JR., lawyer; b. Wichita Falls, Tex., June 9, 1934; s. Marshall J. and Mary Jane (Johnson) D.; m. Betty Marie Orsini, June 2, 1956; children: Gregory J., Michael J., Laetitia Marie. BA magna cum laude, Hardin-Simmons U., 1956; LLB magna cum laude, So. Meth. U., 1959. Bar: Tex. 1959. Founding ptnr. Rain Harrell Emery Young & Doke, Dallas, 1965-87; assoc. Thompson, Knight, Wright & Simmons, Dallas, 1959, 62-65; founding ptnr. Doke & Riley, Dallas, 1987-92; ptnr. McKenna & Cuneo, 1993-96, Gardere Wynne Sewell L.L.P., Dallas, 1996—. Gen. counsel Tex. Rep. Party, 1976-77; mem. adv. coun. U.S. Ct. Fed. Claims, 1982—. Author: Ann. Procurement Rev., Govt. Contractor Briefing Papers, Contract Changes, Fed. Contract Mgmt., 1982—, also articles; editor-in-chief: Southwestern Law Jour., 1958-59. Pres. Hope Cottage-Children's Bur., Inc., 1969-70, Hope Cottage Found., 1997-2002, pres., 1998-2002; bd. visitors Law Sch., So. Meth. U., 1966-69, McDonald Obs., U. Tex., 1990—; dir. Tex. Hist. Found., 1993—, v.p., 1996-98, pres. 2000—; law com., bd. trustees So. Meth. U., 1977-78; bd. dirs., pres. World Trade Assn., Dallas-Ft. Worth, 1979-80; chmn. bd. dirs. Internat. Trade Assn. Dallas/Ft. Worth, 1993-94; bd. dirs., sec. Theater Trustees Am., 1983-93; chmn. Mayor's Internat. Com., City of Dallas, 1984-87, mem. Judicial Nominating Commn., 1997—, vice chair, 1998-2000, chair, 2000—. 1st lt. JAGC, U.S. Army, 1959-62. Fellow Am. Bar Found., Tex. Bar Found.; mem. ABA (chmn. sect. pub. contract law 1969-70, ho. of dels. 1970-72, 74—, bd. govs. 1980-82, nominating com. 1988-91, 2000—, chmn. conf. sect. dels. 1991—), Tex. Bar Assn., U.S. Ct. of Fed. Claims Bar Assn. (bd. govs. 1987-2001, pres. 1996), Bd. of Contract Appeals Bar Assn. (pres. 1988-90, bd. govs. 1988—), Am. Bar Retirement Assn. (bd. dirs., trustee 1980-84, pres 1982-84), Nat. Conf. Lawyers and CPAs (co-chmn. 1983-85), Nat. Contract Mgmt. Assn. (nat. bd. advisors 1983—), Dallas C. of C. (chmn. internat. com. 1979-83). Construction, Government contracts and claims, Private international. Home: 6910 Dartbrook Dr Dallas TX 75254-7926 Office: Gardere Wynne Sewell LLP Thanksgiving Tower Ste 3000 Dallas TX 75201-7254 E-mail: mdoke@gardere.com.

DOKURNO, ANTHONY DAVID, lawyer; b. Gardner, Mass., Mar. 14, 1957; s. Anthony Chester and Damey Anteena (Aleson) D. BA, Holy Cross Coll., 1979; JD, Vt. Law Sch., 1982; postgrad., Johns Hopkins U., 1993-94. Bar: Mass. 1982, U.S. Ct. Appeals for the Armed Forces 1986, U.S. Supreme Ct. 1987. Pvt. practice, Fitchburg, Mass., 1982-86; appellate counsel Navy-Marine Corps Appellate Rev. Activity, Navy JAG, Washington, 1986-88; atty. admiralty law divsn. Navy JAG, Washington, 1988-90, atty. ops. and mgmt., 1991-93. Assoc. counsel, bd. vets. appeals Dept. Vets. Affairs, 1994-96; analyst Dept. of Def., 1996—. Comdr. USNR, 1998—. Mem.: Nat. Cryptologic History Found., Maritime Law Assn., Mensa, Naval Res. Assn., Amnesty Internat., Navy League, Am. Legion, Phi Beta Kappa.

DOLAN, BRIAN THOMAS, lawyer; b. Springfield, Ill., Dec. 27, 1940; s. William Stanley and Dorotha Caroline (Battles) D.; m. Kathleen Lois Smith, Sept. 14, 1963; children: Elizabeth Beaumont, Leslie Caroline. AB, Stanford U., 1963, JD, 1965. Bar: Calif. 1966, Colo. 1966, D.C. 1980. Capt. USAF, 1966-70; ptnr. Davis, Graham & Stubbs LLP, Denver, 1970—2001; prin. Resource Capital Funds, Denver, 2000—. Finance, Natural resources. Office: Resource Capital Funds 1400 16th St Ste 200 Denver CO 80202 E-mail: btd@rcflp.com.

DOLAN, DENNIS JOSEPH, airline pilot, lawyer; b. St. Louis, Mar. 19, 1946; s. Robert Glennon and Lucille Anne (Stanley) D.; m. Aura Maritza Vargas, June 8, 1974; children: Dennis J. Jr., Rebecca and Robert (twins). BSC, Spring Hill Coll., Mobile, Ala., 1967; JD cum laude, St. Louis U., 1985. Bar: Mo., 1985, U.S. Dist. Ct. (ea. dist.) Mo. 1987. Commd. 2nd lt. USMC, 1967, advanced through grades to capt., 1970, resigned, 1976; served to maj. USMCR; flew in numerous combat missions, 2 combat tours Vietnam; airline pilot Western Air Lines, L.A., 1976-87, Delta Air Lines, Inc., Atlanta, 1987—; pvt. practice law Clayton, Mo., 1985-88. Mem. ABA, Assn. Trial Lawyers Am., Air Line Pilots Assn. (bd. dirs. 1992-94, exec. v.p. 1994-96, chmn. Delta Master exec. coun. 1996-98, 1st v.p. 1999—), Internat. Fedn. Airline Pilot Assns. (prin. v.p. profl. affairs 2000—). Roman Catholic. Avocations: skiing, woodworking. Home: PO Box 906 Roswell GA 30077-0906

DOLAN, JAMES VINCENT, lawyer; b. Washington, Nov. 11, 1938; s. John Vincent and Philomena Theresa (Vance) D.; m. Anne McSherry Reilly, June 18, 1960; children: Caroline McSherry, James Reilly. AB, Georgetown U., 1960, LLB, 1963. Bar: U.S. Dist. Ct. 1963, U.S. Ct. Appeals (D.C.) cir. 1964, U.S. Ct. Appeals (4th cir.) 1976. Law clk. U.S. Ct. Appeals D.C., 1963-64; assoc. Steptoe & Johnson, Washington, 1964-71, ptnr., 1971-82; mem. Steptoe & Johnson Chartered, Washington, 1982-83; v.p. law Union Pacific R.R., Omaha, 1983—2002, vice chmn., 2002—. Co-author: Construction Contract Law, 1981; contbr. articles to legal jours.; editor-in-chief: Georgetown Law Jour., 1962-63. Mem.: ABA, Barristers, D.C. Bar Assn., Nebr. Bar Assn., Omaha Country Club, Congl. Country Club (v.p. 1982, pres. 1983). Republican. Roman Catholic. Federal civil litigation, Corporate, general, Utilities, public. Home: 1909 County Road 8 Yutan NE 68073-5013 Office: Union Pacific RR 1416 Dodge St Omaha NE 68179

DOLAN, JOHN F. lawyer; b. Cleve., Oct. 19, 1925; s. John Francis and Lillian Marie (Courtad) D.; m. Rose M. Fitzsimmons, June 13, 1953 (dec.); children: Patricia Ann, John Patrick, Mary Bridget, Margaret Mary, Ann Marie, Kathleen Marie, Michael Anthony, Daniel Joseph. AB, Harvard U., 1947; JD, LLB, Western Res. U., 1949. Asst. dir. law City of Cleve., 1951-56, chief of litigation, 1955-56; dir. law City of Shaker Heights, Ohio, 1956-57; asst. gen. atty. N.Y.C., Penn Cen. Conrail, Cleve., 1957-78; sole practice Cleve., 1978—. Served to lt. (j.g.) USN, 1943-46. Mem. Ohio State Bar Assn., Cleve. Bar Assn. Democrat. Roman Catholic. Federal civil litigation, General civil litigation, State civil litigation.

DOLAN, MICHAEL WILLIAM, lawyer; b. Kansas City, Mo., Dec. 13, 1942; s. William Michael and Vivian (Bush) D.; m. Laurel C. Cummings, June 13, 1964 (div. 1984); children: Matthew, Abigail. BA, U. Kans., 1964; JD with honors, George Washington U., 1969; LLM, Georgetown U., 1981. Bar: Va. 1969, D.C. 1970, U.S. Ct. Claims 1981, U.S. Tax Ct. 1981, U.S. Supreme Ct. 1973. Atty. Dept. Justice, Washington, 1971-73, dep. legis. counsel, 1973-79, dep. asst. atty. gen., 1979-85; with Fed Exec. Devel. Program, 1978-79; assoc. Winthrop, Stimson, Putnam & Roberts, Washington, 1985-94; chief Article III Judges divsn. Adminstrv. Office of U.S. Ct., Washington, 1994—2002; atty. Michael W. Dolan, PLLC, 2003—. Contbr. numerous articles to profl. jours. 1st lt. U.S. Army, 1964-66. Recipient John Marshall award Dept. Justice, 1978 Democrat. Taxation, general, Federal civil litigation, Administrative and regulatory. Office: 2021 L St NW 2d Fl Washington DC 20036 E-mail: mwdolan@att.net.

DOLAN, PETER BROWN, lawyer; b. Bklyn., Mar. 25, 1939; s. Daniel Arthur and Eileen Margaret (Brown) D.; m. Jacqueline Elizabeth Gruning, Sept. 9, 1961; children: Kerry Anne, Peter Brown Jr. BS, U.S. Naval Acad., 1960; JD, U. So. Calif., 1967. Bar: Calif. 1967, U.S. Ct. Appeals (9th cir.) 1968, U.S. Dist. Ct. (no. and ctrl. dists.) Calif. 1967, U.S. Dist. Ct. (ea. dist.) Calif. 1972, U.S. Dist. Ct. (so. dist.) Calif. 1973, U.S. Claims Ct. 1982, U.S. Supreme Ct. 1986. Dep. L.A. County counsel, 1967-69; assoc. Macdonald, Halsted & Laybourne, L.A., 1969-71, ptnr., 1972-77, Overton, Lyman & Prince, L.A., 1977-87, Morrison & Foerster, L.A., 1987-93, Morgan, Lewis & Bockius LLP, L.A., 1993-99; prin. The Dolan Law Firm, L.A., 1999—. Active Pasadena (Calif.) Tournament of Roses Assn., 1973—; pres. West Pasadena Residents Assn., 1979-81. Served to lt. USN, 1960-64, comdr. USNR, 1964-86. Mem.: ABA, L.A. County Bar Assn., Assn. Bus. Trial Lawyers, State Bar Calif., Chancery (LA), Bel-Air Bay Club, Phi Delta Phi. Roman Catholic. Federal civil litigation, State civil litigation, General civil litigation. Fax: 213-680-9889. E-mail: dolanlaw@earthlink.net., jacquiedol@aol.com.

DOLAN, ROBERT E. defender; b. N.Y.C., Sept. 19, 1955; s. James and Catherine Dolan; m. Martha Hesse, June 16, 1984. AS, Nassau C.C., Garden City, N.Y., 1975; BA, C.W. Post U., 1977; JD, St. Johns U., 1980. Bar: N.Y. 1981, D.C. 1983, Nev. 1997. Dir. Internat. Youth Yr. Commn., Washington, 1982—83; chmn. Young Ams. for Freedom, Sterling, Va., 1983—85, Am. Citizens for Polit. Action, Washington, 1986—92; pvt. practice Washington, 1984—93, Houston, 1994—97; dep. pub. defender Nev. Pub. Defender, Winnemucca, 1998—. Chmn. Humboldt County Rep. Party, Winnemucca, 2001—. Office: Nev Pub Defender PO Box 309 Winnemucca NV 89446

DOLE, ROBERT J. lawyer, former senator; b. Russell, Kans., July 22, 1923; s. Doran R. and Bina Dole; m. Elizabeth Hanford, Dec. 1975. Student, U. Kans., 1941—43, U. Ariz.; AB, LLB, Washburn Mcpl. U., Topeka, 1952; LLD (hon.) , Washburn U., Topeka, 1969. Bar: Kans. 1952. Mem. Kans. Ho. of Reps., 1951—53; sole practice Russell, Kans., 1953—61; Russell County atty., 1953—61; mem. 87th Congress from 6th Dist. Kans., 1961—63, 88th-90th Congresses from 1st Dist. Kans., 1963—69; U.S. senator from Kans., 1969—96; Senate majority leader, 1985—87, 1995—96; Senate minority leader, 1987—95; chmn. Rep. Nat. Com., 1971—73; of counsel Verner, Liipfert, Bernhard, McPherson & Hand, 1999—, Alston & Bird, 2003—. Rep. vice-presdl. candidate, 1976; Rep. presdl. candidate, 96. Author: Great Political Wit, Great Presidential Wits. Chmn. Int.. Commn. on Missing Persons, Nat. WWII Meml., Dole Found. Served with U.S. Army, WW II. Decorated Purple Heart (2), Bronze Star with 2 clusters; recipient Horatio Alger award, Horatio Alger Assn. Disting. Ams., 1988, Presdl. medal of Freedom. Mem.: DAV, VFW, 4-H Fair Assn., Am. Legion, Kiwanis, Elks, Shriners, Masons, Kappa Sigma. Methodist. Office: Office of Sen Dole c/o Alston & Bird 601 Pennsylvania Ave NW Washington DC 20004

DOLEAC, CHARLES BARTHOLOMEW, lawyer; b. New Orleans, Sept. 20, 1947; s. Cyril Bartholomew and Emma Elizabeth (St. Clair) D.; m. Denise Kilfoyle, Feb. 2, 1972; children: Keith Gabriel, Jessa Lee. BS cum laude, U. N.H., 1968; JD, NYU, 1971. Bar: Mass. 1972, N.H. 1972, Maine 1973. Law clk. to Justice Grimes N.H. Supreme Ct., Concord, 1972-73; assoc. Boynton, Waldron, Dill & Aeschliman, Portsmouth, N.H., 1973-76; ptnr. Boynton, Waldron, Doleac, Woodman & Scott, Portsmouth, 1977—. Apptd. mediator N.H. Superior Ct., 1992—; del. to tour Chinese legal system Chinese Ministry Justice, 1982; del. to People's Republic of China/U.S. joint session on trade investments and econ. law Chinese Ministry Justice/U.S. Dept. Justice, Beijing, 1987; propr. Portsmouth Athenaeum; moderator seminars on ethics for Leaders & Comparative Cultures and Values/East & West and Exec. Seminar Aspen Inst., 1990-95; moderator exec. sem. Aspen Inst., 1997-2000; mem. faculty Southwestern Legal Found. Internat. & Comparative Law Ctr., 1997—; ofcl. guest Fgn. Ministry Japan, Tokyo, 1998; developed Asian Seminar, Aspen Inst., 2000; spkr. ethics Ann. Nat. Conf. Appellate Ct. Clks., 1999-2000. Contbr. articles to profl. jours. Mem. citizens adv. coun. Portsmouth Cmty. Devel. Program, 1976-77; incorporator N.H. Charitable Found.; pres., bd. dirs. Seacoast United Way; chmn. Portsmouth Bd. Bldg. Appeals, 1976-77; chmn. stewardship com. Soc. Preservation New Eng. Antiquities, 1980-84, also trustee; pres. bd. trustees Strawbery Banke Mus., 1985-88; founder Daniel Webster Inn of Ct., 1993, Charles C. Doe Inn of Ct., 1994, Portsmouth Peace Treaty Forums I-IV, 1994-2000; founder, pres. Japan-Am. Soc. N.H., 1988; develop Asian seminar, Aspen Inst., 2000. Named Citizen of Yr., Portsmouth, N.H., 1991; recipient John E. Thayer III award, Japan Soc. Boston, Inc., 2001. Fellow N.H. Bar Found; mem. ATLA, Mass. Bar Assn., Maine Bar Assn., N.H. Bar Assn., N.H. Trial Lawyers Assn., Maine Trial Lawyers Assn. Avocation: masters swimming. General civil litigation, Commercial, contracts (including sales of goods; commercial financing). Home: Little Harbor Rd Portsmouth NH 03801 Office: Boynton Waldron Doleac Woodman & Scott PA 82 Court St Portsmouth NH 03801-4414 E-mail: cdoleac@nhlawfirm.com.

DOLIN, MITCHELL F. lawyer; b. Augusta, Ga., Feb. 6, 1956; s. Martin and Harriet Dolin. m. Monica C. Tuo. BA, Tufts U., 1978; JD, NYU, 1981. Bar: D.C. 1982, U.S. Supreme Ct. 1986. Clk. to chief judge U.S. Ct. Appeals (5th cir.), 1981-82; assoc. Covington & Burling, Washington, 1982-89, ptnr., 1989—. Mem. adv. com. Lawyers Com. for Human Rights. Mem. ABA, Am. Law Inst., Am. Judicature Soc. (bd. dirs.), Lawyers Com. for Human Rights (bd. dirs.). Alternative dispute resolution, General civil litigation, Insurance. Office: Covington & Burling 1201 Pennsylvania Ave NW Washington DC 20004

DOLINER, NATHANIEL LEE, lawyer; b. Daytona Beach, Fla., June 28, 1949; s. Joseph and Asia (Shaffer) D.; m. Debra Lynn Simon, June 5, 1983. BA, George Washington U., 1970; JD, Vanderbilt U., 1973; LLM in Taxation, U. Fla., 1977. Bar: Fla. 1973. Assoc. Smalbein, Eubank, Johnson, Rosier & Bussey, PA, Daytona Beach, Fla., 1973-76; vis. asst. prof. law U. Fla. Law Sch., Gainesville, 1977-78; assoc. Carlton, Fields, Ward, Emmanuel, Smith & Cutler, PA, Tampa, Fla., 1978-82; shareholder Carlton Fields, PA, Tampa, 1982—, chair bus. transactions practice group, 1998—. Co-chmn. ABA Presdl. Showcase Programs, N.Y.C., 1996, ABA Nat. Inst. Negotiating Bus. Acquisitions, Chgo., 1997, New Orleans, 98, New Orleans, 2001, Newport Beach, Calif., 1999, Boca Raton, Fla., 2000, Chgo., 02; spkr. Internat. Inst. Mergers and Acquisitions, Paris, 2002, Internat. Inst. on mergers and acquisitions, Paris, 2002. Adv. bd. Mergers and Acquisitions Law Report, pub. Bur. Nat. Affairs. Dist. commr. Gulf Ridge coun. Boy Scouts Am., 1983—84; bd. dirs. Big Bros./Big Sisters Greater Tampa, Inc., 1980—82, Child Abuse Coun., Inc., 1986—95, asst. treas., 1987—88, treas., 1988—89, pres.-elect, 1989—90, pres., 1990—91; bd. dirs. Tampa Jewish Fedn. Bd., 1988—91, Mus. Sci. and Industry, Tampa, 1994—, exec. com., 1994—, sec., 1995—97, first vice-chmn., 1997—99, chair, 1999—2001; mem. alumni bd. Vanderbilt Law Sch., 1999—2000; bd. dirs., exec. com. Hillel Sch., Tampa, 1998—, first v.p., 1999—2000, pres.-elect, 2000—01, pres., 2001—03. Fellow: Am. Coll. Tax Counsel, Am. Bar Found.; mem.: Com. Negotiated Acquisitions, Tampa C. of C. (chmn. Ambassadors Target Task Force of Com. of 100 1984—85, 1987—88, vice-chmn. govt. fin. and taxation coun. 1987—88, chmn. 1988—89, chair geographic task force 1989—90, bd.govs. 1991—93, exec. com. 1992, chmn. govtl. affairs com. 1992), Greater Tampa C. of C., Fla. Bar Assn. (exec. coun. tax sect. 1980—82, tax cert. com. 1987—88, vice-chmn. 1988—89, chmn. 1989—90), Am. Law Inst., ABA (vice-chmn. cont. legal edn. com. 1986—88, chmn. 1988—90, chmn. task force preliminary and ancillary agreements 1992—95, acquisition rev. task force 1992—95, chmn. 1993, chmn. programs subcom. 1995—98, vice-chmn. 1997—98, chmn. 1998—2002, coun. mem. bus. law sect. 2002—), Anti-Defamation League (regional bd. dirs. 1986—90, exec. com. 1987—90), Tampa Club (sec. 1987—89, bd. dirs. 1987—92, pres. 1990—91). Corporate, general, Mergers and acquisitions, Taxation, general. Home: 13341 Golf Crest Cir Tampa FL 33624-4648 Office: Carlton Fields Ward Emmanuel Smith & Cutler PA Ste 500 777 S Harbour Island Blvd Tampa FL 33602-5729

DOLPH, WILBERT EMERY, lawyer; b. Palatka, Fla., Dec. 29, 1923; s. Wilbert Emery and Ophelia (Reynolds) D.; m. Roberta Hundley; children: Wilbert Emery III, Kenneth Alan, Scott Marshall, Cheryl Karlsson. Student, U. Ariz., 1941-42, LL.B., 1949. Bar: Ariz. 1949. Asst. city atty., Tucson, 1949-50; asst. atty. gen., 1950-51; pvt. practice, 1951—93; counsel. jud. com. Ariz. Senate, 1952; shareholder Bilby & Shoenhair, P.C., 1953-89; ptnr. Snell & Wilmer, Tucson, 1989-93, of counsel, 1992-93; ret., 1993. Pres. Pima County Young Dems., 1952-53; v.p. Ariz. Young Dems., 1952-53; trustee Tucson Med. Ctr., pres., 1973-75; mem. U. Ariz. Found., U. Ariz. Pres.'s Club; past chmn. bd. dirs. Friends of Libr., U. Ariz., 1995-97; past bd. visitors U. Ariz. Law Coll.; past bd. dirs. Ariz. Sonora Desert Mus., Ariz. Heart Assn., So. Ariz. Heart Assn., Tucson Festival Soc., Ariz. Children's Home Assn., Tucson YMCA, Ariz. Coun. Econ. Edn.; past vestryman, parish warden St. Phlips in the Hills Episcopal Ch., 1974-76. With USNR, 1942-44, to capt. USMCR, 1944-46. Decorated Air medal. Mem. ABA, Ariz. Bar Assn., Pima County Bar Assn. (exec. com., pres. 1974-75), Phi Delta Phi, Sigma Chi, Coronado Yacht Club.

DOLT, FREDERICK CORRANCE, lawyer; b. Louisville, Oct. 10, 1929; s. O. Frederick and Margaret A. (Corrance) D.; m. Lucy M. Voelker, Dec. 8, 1960; 1 child, Frederick C. Jr. JD, U. Louisville, 1952. Bar: Ky. 1952, U.S. Ct. Appeals (6th cir.) 1965, U.S. Supreme Ct. 1972, La. 1982. Assoc. Morris & Garlove, Louisville, 1955-59; sole practice Louisville, 1959-70, 79—; ptnr. Leibson, Dolt & McCarthy, Louisville, 1970-73. Mem. Inner Circle Advocates, 1981. Served with U.S. Army, 1953-55. Mem. Ky. Bar Assn. (chmn. ins. negligence sect. 1968-70, mem. Ho. of Dels. 1970-80), Ky. Trial Lawyers Assn. (pres. 1970). Republican. Presbyterian. Avocation: golf. Federal civil litigation, State civil litigation. Home: 7216 Heatherly Sq Louisville KY 40242-2847 Office: 310 Starks Bldg Louisville KY 40202

DOMALAKES, PAUL GEORGE, lawyer; b. Frackville, Pa., Mar. 21, 1951; s. John George and Sara Jane (Wetzel) D.; m. Patricia Marie Kiefer, Oct. 5, 1985; children: Meredith Ann, Ann Patricia, Paul Luke, Madeline Claire. BA, Allentown Coll., 1973; JD, Dickinson Coll., 1976. Bar: Supreme Ct. Pa. 1976, U.S. Dist. Ct. (ea. dist.) Pa. 1977, U.S. Supreme Ct. 1992. Ptnr. Rubright, Domalakes, Troy & McDonald, Frackville, 1980—. Pres. bd. dirs. Intermediate Unit No. 29 Bldg. Authority, Marlin, Pa., 1983—; dir. Annunciation B.V.M. Ch. Choir, Frackville, 1984—; bd. dirs., founding mem. Pa. Shakespeare Festival. Mem. Pa. Bar Assn. Republican. Roman Catholic. Criminal, General practice, Workers' compensation. Office: Rubright Domalakes Troy & McDonald PO Box 9 Frackville PA 17931-0009

DOMANSKIS, ALEXANDER RIMAS, lawyer; b. Chgo., June 3, 1952; s. Van and Alina Alexandra (Tamasauskas) Domanskis; m. Frances Laucka, May 6, 1978; children: Maria Laucka, John Joseph Laucka. AB, U. Mich, 1973; JD, U. Mich., 1977. Bar: Ill. 1977, U.S. Dist. Ct. (no. dist.) Ill. 1977, U.S. Ct. Appeals (7th cir.) 1978, U.S. Supreme Ct. 1985. Law clk. U.S. Dist. Ct. (no. dist.) Ill., Chgo., 1977—79; assoc. Ross & Hardies, Chgo., 1979—84, ptnr., 1985—87, 1993—94, of counsel, 1987—92; ptnr. Shaw, Gussis, Domanskis, Fishman & Glantz, 1994—2002, Boodell & Domanskis, LLC , 2002—. Assoc. gen. counsel and v.p. Intercounty Title Co. of Ill., 1987—91, bd. dir., 1990—91. Editor (adminstrv.): (jour.) U. Mich Jour. Law Reform, 1976—77. Pres. Lithuanian World Ctr., 1988—92, bd. dir., 1988—95, chmn. bd., 1994—95; bd. dir. Intercounty Credit Corp., Chgo., 1988—91, Lithuanian Montessori Soc., Chgo., 1987—90. Mem.: Lithuanian Roman Cath. Fedn. Am. (bd. dir. Chgo. 1980—87), Lithuanian Am. Coun. (bd. dir. Chgo. 1981—88), Chgo. Bar Assn., ABA. Corporate, general, Land use and zoning (including planning), Property, real (including real estate development, water). Home: 4236 Hampton Ave Western Springs IL 60558-1310 Office: Boodell & Domanskis LLC 205 N Michigan #4307 Chicago IL 60601 Fax: 312-540-1162.

DOMIANO, JOSEPH CHARLES, lawyer; b. Cleve., Oct. 21, 1928; s. Charles Joseph and Mary Grace (Santora) D.; m. Julie Ann Birinyi, Sept. 9, 1950; children: Joseph, Jr., Laura, John. BBA, Case Western Reserve U., 1951; LLD, Cleve. State U., 1956. Bar: Ohio 1957. Ptnr. Mandanici & Domiano, Cleve., 1957-84, Sindell, Rubenstein, Cleve., 1984-87, Friedman, Domiano & Smith, Cleve., 1987—. Prosecutor City of Maple Heights (Ohio), 1963-65; solicitor Village of Bentleyville (Ohio), 1974-94; law dir. City of Olmsted Falls (Ohio), 1992-93; mem. (life) 8th Dist. Jud. Law Conf., Cleve., 1994—. Contbr. articles to law jours.; presenter in field. Bd. dirs. Maple Heights Little Theatre, 1962-65, Transitional Housing, Cleve., 1994—; mem. parish coun. Ch. of Resurrection, Solon, Ohio, 1992-94, mem. fin. coun., 1996—. Mem. Assn. Trial Lawyers Am., Ohio State Bar Assn., Ohio Acad. Trial Lawyers, Cleve. Bar Assn., Cleve. Acad. Trial Lawyers, Cuyahoga County Bar Assn. (pres. 1993-94, torts personal injury, employer intentional torts, product liability), KC (mem. exec. com. 1985-86). Avocations: snow skiing, water skiing, sailing, golf, scuba diving. Personal injury (including property damage), Professional liability. Office: Friedman Domiano & Smith 600 Standard Bldg 1370 Ontario St Fl 6 Cleveland OH 44113-1701

DOMINIK, JACK EDWARD, lawyer; b. Chgo., July 9, 1924; s. Ewald Arthur and Gertrude Alene (Crotzer) D.; children: Paul, David, Georgia Lee, Elizabeth, Sarah, Clare. BSME with distinction, Purdue U., 1947; JD, Northwestern U., 1950. Bar: Ill. 1950, U.S. Patent Office 1953, Wis. 1959, Fla. 1964, U.S. Dist. Ct. (ea. dist.) Wis. 1959, U.S. Supreme Ct. 1965, U.S. Dist. Ct. (no. dist.) Ohio 1962, U.S. Dist. Ct. (so. dist.) Ill. 1965, U.S. Ct. Appeals (7th and 9th cirs.) 1965, U.S. Ct. Appeals (4th cir.) 1973, U.S. Dist. Ct. (so. dist.) Fla. 1974, U.S. Ct. Appeals (5th cir.) 1977, U.S. Dist. Ct. (mid. dist.) Fla. 1979, U.S. Ct. Appeals (fed. cir.) 1983, U.S. Ct. Appeals (11th cir.) 1984, U.S. Ct. Appeals (2d cir.) 1987. Assoc. Carlson, Pitzner, Hubbard & Wolfe, Chgo., 1950—54; ptnr. Ooms and Dominik, Chgo., 1954—59, White & Hirshboeck, Milw., 1959—62, Dominik, Knechtel, DeMeur & Samlan, Chgo., 1962—78, Dominik & Assocs., Miami, Fla., 1978—. Served to 1st lt., C.E. AUS, 1943-46, ETO. Mil. govt. judge, 1945-46. Mem. ABA, Wis. Bar Assn., Fla. Bar Assn., Chgo. Bar Assn., Am. Patent Law Assn., Chgo. Patent Law Assn. (chmn. taxation com. 1966, 69-70), Milw. Patent Law Assn., Patent Law Assn. So. Fla. (founder, dir. 1982—, past pres.), Chgo. Yacht Club, Union League Club, Tau Beta Pi, Pi Tau Sigma, Tau Kappa Alpha. Avocation: flying. Federal civil litigation, Intellectual property, Private international. Home: 14751 Lewis Rd Miami Lakes FL 33014-2731 Office: 6175 NW 153rd St Miami Lakes FL 33014-2435

DOMZALSKI, KENNETH STANLEY, lawyer; b. Phila., May 6, 1949; s. Stanley Z. and Helen (Papuga) D.; m. Mary Christine Brennan, June 19, 1971; children: Meredith, Kyle. BA in Polit. Sci., LaSalle Coll., 1971; JD, Rutgers U., 1974. Bar: N.J. 1975, U.S. Dist. Ct. N.J. 1975. Assoc. Hartman, Schlesinger, Schlosser & Faxon, Mt. Holly, N.J., 1974-81, Forkin & Eory, Cherry Hill, N.J., 1981-82, Toll, Forkin, Sullivan & Luthman, Cherry Hill, 1982-83; ptnr. Bookbinder, Guest & Domzalski, Burlington, N.J., 1983-90; mng. ptnr. Guest, Domzalski, Kurts, Landgraf & McNeill, Burlington, N.J., 1990-93, Domzalski & Tals, Burlington, N.J., 1993-97; pvt. practice Burlington, N.J., 1997—. Mem. Medford Twp. Bd. Edn., 1986-2001, YMCA, 1984—, Maple Shade Dem. County Com., 1975-76, Cinnaminson Dem. County Com., 1976-78, vice chmn., 1977-78, Medford Dem. County Com., 1979—, vice chmn., 1984-86, chmn., 1980-81, treas., 1979-80; campaign mgr. Carmel Fischer for Cinnaminson Twp. Com., 1977; baseball coach Cinnaminson Police Athletic League, Lenape Youth Athletic Assn.; mem. by-laws com. Sherwood Forest Homeowners Assn.; chmn. Heart Fund Cinnaminson Twp., 1977; bd. dirs. Mt. Laurel Regional Ballet Co., 1984-88, pres., 1985, v.p., 1984-85; active Medford Twp. Bd. Edn., 1986-2001. Recipient award Cinnaminson Dem. County Com., 1978, Profl. Lawyer of Yr. award, 1998, Wells Civility award, 1998. Mem. ABA (family law and young lawyers sects.), N.J. Bar Assn. (exec. com. family law sect., young lawyers sect., trustee 1990-94), N.J. State Bar Found. (trustee 1992-2000), Burlington Bar Assn. (sec. 1986-87, pres.-elect 1988-89, pres. 1989-90—, v.p. 1987-88, treas. 1985-86, trustee 1982-85, various coms., Robert W. Criscuolo Meml. award 1980, Boss Yr. award 1986), Am. Acad. Matrimonial Lawyers, N.J. Fedn. Planning Ofcls., N.J. Inst. Mcpl. Attys., Rutgers Sch. Law Alumni Assn., LaSalle Coll. Alumni Assn., Burlington

County and City C. of C., Sigma Beta Kappa, Alpha Epsilon. Lodges: KC. Roman Catholic. Avocations: sports, music. Family and matrimonial, Probate (including wills, trusts). Home: 24 Summit Pass Medford NJ 08055-9757 Office: 235 High St # 429 Burlington NJ 08016-4409

DONAHO, TIMOTHY LAWRENCE, JR., lawyer; b. Rantoul, Ill., Aug. 31, 1964; s. Timothy Lawrence Donaho Sr. and Peggy Jo Donaho; m. Maureen Ann Donaho, Sept. 28, 1991; children: Bridjet Elizabeth, Katherine Theresa, Timothy L. III. B, Ill. Coll., 1982; JD summa cum laude, So. Ill. U., 1990. Atty. Cavanaugh Sudly, Peoria, Ind., 1990—92, Campbell & Coyne, St. Louis, 1992—94, The Durey Law Firm, Belleville, Ill., 1994—98, pvt. practice, Collinsville, 1998—99; trial atty. The Robbins Law Firm, St. Louis, 1997—. Bd. dirs. Nu-Ritepy Ill., Inc., Collinsville, Rusler Transport Svcs., Inc., Nationwide Flag Car, Inc., Woodriver. Mem.: Assn. Trial Lawyers Am. Corporate, general, Personal injury (including property damage), Product liability. Home: 130 Hilltop Pl Collinsville IL 62234 Office: The Robbins Law Firm 2030 Delmar Ste 100 Saint Louis MO 63103 E-mail: tdonaho@cheatre.net.

DONAHUE, CHARLOTTE MARY, lawyer; b. Columbus, Ohio, Sept. 29, 1954; d. Patrick Henry and Helen Dillon (Meany) D. AB, Holy Cross Coll., 1976; JD, U. Toledo, 1983. Bar: Pa. 1984, D.C. 1985, U.S. Dist. Ct. (ea. dist.) Pa. 1985, U.S. Ct. Appeals 3d cir.) 1985, U.S. Supreme Ct. 1990, Mass. 1992. Jud. clk. to presiding justice Commonwealth Ct. Pa., Phila., 1983-84; spl. asst. U.S. atty. U.S. Dist. Ct. (ea. dist.) Pa., Phila., 1987-90; atty. HUD, Phila., 1984-93, Boston, 1993—. Mem. Fed. Bar Assn., Pa. Bar Assn., Mass. Bar Assn., D.C. Bar Assn., Order of Barristers, Internat. Platform Assn., Supreme Ct. Hist. Soc. Home: 40 Meredith Cir Milton MA 02186-3916 Office: HUD Thomas P O'Neill Jr Fed Bldg 10 Causeway St Boston MA 02222-1092

DONAHUE, JOHN EDWARD, lawyer; b. Milw., Aug. 22, 1950; s. Joseph Robert and Helen Ann (Kelly) D.; m. Maureen Dolores Hart, Sept. 20, 1974; children: Timothy Robert Hart, Michael John Hart. BA with honors, Marquette U., 1972; JD, U. Wis., Madison, 1975. Bar: Wis. 1975, U.S. Dist. Ct. (we. and ea. dists.) Wis. 1975. Assoc. Weiss, Steuer, Berzowski and Kriger, Milw., 1975-80; ptnr. Weiss, Berzowski, Brady & Donahue LLP, Milw., 1981-2001; shareholder Godfrey & Kahn, S.C., Milw., 2001—. Guest lectr. Marquette U. Law Sch., Milw., 1976-90; presenter programs Wis. Inst. CPAs, 1984—, Minn. Soc. CPAs, 1992-97; expert witness.. Past chmn. bd. trustees, past chmn. bd. dirs., past chmn. bd. govs., trustee, exec. com., com. chmn. Mt. Mary Coll., Milw., 1984-2001, past pres., bd. dirs. com. chmn. Met. Milw. Civic Alliance, 1980—, Children's Hosp. Found., Milw., 1984—; mem. steering com. Greater Milw. Initiative, 1989-92; v.p., bd. dirs. Future Milw., 1984-88; v.p., coun. bd., com. chmn., scoutmaster Boy Scouts Am., 1990—. Recipient citation Milw. County Bd. Suprs., 1990, spl. svc. award Met. Milw. Civil Alliance, 1990, silver beaver award Boy Scouts Am., 1995; named outstanding instr. AICPA, 1991. Mem. ABA, Wis. Bar Assn., Milw. Bar Assn. (program chmn. employee benefits sect.), Wis. Retirement Plan Profls., Greater Milw. Employee Benefits Coun., Kiwanis Club (pres. Milw. unit 1989-90, Outstanding Kiwanian 1989-97, Kiwanian of Yr. 1993). Corporate, general, General practice, Pension, profit-sharing, and employee benefits. Office: Godfrey & Kahn SC 780 N Water St Milwaukee WI 53202-3590 Business E-Mail: jdonahue@gklaw.com.

DONAHUE, MICHAEL JOSEPH, lawyer; b. Manchester, N.H., Dec. 28, 1947; s. Francis Lawler and Laura (Veroneau) D.; m. Diane Landry, May 26, 1973; children: Sarah, Kerry. AB, Holy Cross Coll., Worcester, Mass., 1970; JD, U. Pa., Phila., 1973. Bar: N.H. 1973, U.S. Dist. Ct. N.H. 1977, U.S. Ct. Appeals (1st cir.) 1982, U.S. Ct. Mil. Appeals 1991. Ptnr. Kearns, Colliander, Donahue & Tucker, P.A., Exeter, N.H., 1977-85, Donahue, Tucker & Ciandella, Exeter, 1985—. Bd. dirs. Greater Seacoast United Way, 1985-92; v.p., sec., bd. trustees Strawbery Banke Mus., 1992-98. Capt. JAGC, USNR, 1970-98. Mem. ABA, N.H. Bar Assn. (bd. dirs. mcpl. law sect. 1984-86). Roman Catholic. Environmental, Land use and zoning (including planning), Property, real (including real estate development, water). Home: 8 Old Locke Rd North Hampton NH 03862-2236 Office: Donahue Tucker & Ciandella PO Box 630 Exeter NH 03833-0630 E-mail: mjdesq@attbi.com., MDonahue@DTCLAWYERS.com.

DONAHUE, TIMOTHY PATRICK, lawyer; b. Phila., Sept. 7, 1955; s. Joseph Thomas and Margaret Teresa (Golden) D.; m. Diane Gilbert, June 26, 1982; children: Timothy Patrick Jr., Elizabeth O'Reilly. BA, U. Ala., 1977, JD, 1981. Bar: Ala. 1982. Assoc., then ptnr. Clark & Scott, P.A., Birmingham, Ala., 1982-87; assoc. then ptnr. Edmond & Vines, Birmingham, 1987-91; ptnr. Clark & Scott P.C., Birmingham, 1991—; shareholder Bradford & Donahue P.C., 1995—2001, Donahue & Assocs. LLC, 2002—. Mem. Ala. Bar Assn., Ala. Trial Lawyers Assn., Birmingham Bar Assn. (exec. com. young lawyers sect. 1986-89). Roman Catholic. General civil litigation, Personal injury (including property damage), Workers' compensation. Home: 2044 Magnolia Rdg Birmingham AL 35243-2018

DONALDSON, DAVID HOWARD, JR., lawyer; b. Midland, Tex., Oct. 1, 1951; s. David Howard and Joan (Steinberger) D.; m. Susan Arleen Kepple, Aug. 13, 1971; children: Matthew, Shannon. BA summa cum laude, Tex. A&M U., 1973; JD with high honors, U. Tex., 1976. Bar: U.S. Dist. Ct. (we. dist.) Tex. 1978, U.S. Ct. Appeals (5th and 11th cirs.) 1981, U.S. Dist. Ct. (so. dist.) Tex. 1983, U.S. Dist Ct. (ea. dist.) Tex., U.S. Supreme Ct. 1984. Law clk. to presiding judge U.S. Ct. Appeals (5th cir.), New Orleans, 1976-77; assoc. Graves, Dougherty, Hearon & Moody, Austin, Tex., 1977-83, ptnr., 1983-92, George & Donaldson, LLP, Austin, 1992—. Recipient James Madison award Tex. Freedom of Info. Found., 1991; named Tex. Friend of 1st Amendment, Soc. Profl. Journalists, 1986; named to Outstanding Young Men of Am., 1983, 84; Pres.'s scholar Tex. A&M U., 1970. Mem. ABA, Tex. Bar Assn. Democrat. Federal civil litigation, State civil litigation, Libel. Home: 106 Oak Terr Austin TX Office: 114 W 7th St Ste 1100 Austin TX 78701-3000

DONALDSON, JOHN WEBER, lawyer; b. Lebanon, Ind., Oct. 13, 1926; s. Fred R. and Esther Ann (Coombs) D.; m. Sara Jane Rudolph, Nov. 22, 1953; children: Carmen Donaldson Cumbee, Catherine Donaldson Buckaller, J. Bradford. AB, DePauw U., 1951; JD, Ind. U., 1954. Bar: Ind. 1954, U.S. Dist. Ind. 1954, U.S. Supreme Ct. 1973. Sole practice law, Lebanon, Ind., 1958-76; ptnr. Hutchinson & Donaldson, Lebanon, 1954-58, Donaldson & Andreoli, Lebanon, 1976-81, Donaldson, Andreoli & Truitt, Lebanon, 1982—. City atty. City of Lebanon, 1965-66; mem. Ind. Gen. Assembly, 1956-58, 60-92, criminal law study commn., 1969-89, commn. on trial cts., 1987-90; chmn. Gov.'s Task Force on Drunk Driving, 1982-88. Served with USN, 1944-49; ATO. Recipient Disting. Svc. award Jaycees, 1958, Boone County Citizen of Yr. award, 1992. Mem. ABA, Ind. Bar Assn., Boone County Bar Assn., Ind. Criminal Law Study Commn., Lebanon Jaycees, Ind. Def. Lawyers Assn., DAV, Am. Legion, Elks, Kiwanis (pres. 1964). Republican. Presbyterian. Avocation: tennis. State civil litigation, Criminal, Family and matrimonial. Address: 129 N Meridian St Lebanon IN 46052-2263

DONALDSON, MICHAEL CLEAVES, lawyer; b. Montclair, N.J., Oct. 13, 1939; s. Wyman C. and Ernestine (Greenwood) D.; m. Diana D., Sept. 12, 1969 (div. 1979); children: Michelle, Amy, Wendy. BS, U. Fla., 1961; JD, U. Calif., Berkeley, 1967. Bar: Calif. 1967, U.S. Dist. Ct. (cen. dist.) Calif. 1967, U.S. Ct. Appeals (9th cir.) 1967. Assoc. Harris & Hollingsworth, L.A., 1969-72; ptnr. McCabe & Donaldson, L.A., 1972-79; pvt. practice Law Office of M.C. Donaldson, L.A., 1979-90; ptnr. Dern & Donaldson, L.A., 1990-94, Donaldson & Hart (formerly Berton & Donaldson), Beverly Hills, Calif., 1994—. Lectr. in field; judge, preliminary and finalist judge Internat. Emmys; preliminary judge Night Time Emmys; gen. counsel Ind. Feature Project West, Writers Guild Found.; pres. Internat. Documentary Assn. Author: EZ Legal Guide to Copyright and Trademark, 1995, (booklet) A Funny Thing Happened on the Way to Dinner, 1976; contg. author: Conversations with Michael Landon, 1992, Negotiating for Dummies, 1996, Clearance & Copyright What the Independent Filmmaker Needs to Know, 1997, 2d edit., 2003, Film Secrets, 2003. Bd. dirs. Calif. Theatre Coun., L.A. 1st lt. USMC, 1961-64. Mem. ABA (entertainment and sports sect.), NATAS, Nat. Acad. Cable Broadcasting, Beverly Hills Bar Assn. (chmn. entertainment sect.), L.A. Copyright Soc., pres. Internat. Documentary Assoc. Republican. Avocations: photography, writing, gardening, hiking, skiing. Entertainment, Intellectual property. Home: 1057 20th St Santa Monica CA 90403 Office: Donaldson & Hart 9220 W Sunset Blvd Ste 224 Los Angeles CA 90069-3501 E-mail: mcd@donaldsonhart.com.

DONALDSON, STEVEN BRYAN, lawyer; b. Vincennes, Ind., Sept. 23, 1963; s. Steve Donaldson and Lynne Raye (Wilson) Murray. BA, Ind. U., 1985, JD, 1988. Bar: Ind. 1988, U.S. Dist. Ct. (no. and so. dists.) Ind. 1988. Assoc. Berry Capper & Tulley, Crawfordsville, Ind., 1988-94; ptnr. Berry Capper Donaldson & Tulley, Crawfordsville, Ind., 1995-96; prin. S. Bryan Donaldson, Crawfordsville, Ind., 1997—. Judge teen ct. Youth Svc. Bur., Crawfordsville, 1993, 2001—; mem. Montgomery County Cultural Found., Crawfordsville, 1994—; chmn. bd. trustees 1st United Meth. Ch., Crawfordsville, 1994—97, chmn. endowment com., 1999—2000, chmn. adminstrv. bd., 2001—02. Mem. Ind. Bar Assn., Montgomery County Bar Assn., Kiwanis (bd. dirs. Crawfordsville 1992-94, pres. 2001-2002). Republican. Avocations: bowling, golf, spectator sports, reading. Commercial, consumer (including collections, credit), Family and matrimonial, General practice. Home: 180 Shayne Dr Crawfordsville IN 47933-2149 Office: 134 W Main St Crawfordsville IN 47933-1718 E-mail: sbdlawoff@hotmail.com.

DONDANVILLE, JOHN WALLACE, lawyer; b. Moline, Ill., Nov. 29, 1937; s. Laurence A. and Eva C. (Ender) D.; m. Maureen C. Ryan, Apr. 16, 1966; children: Edward John, Julie Ann. AB in History, Holy Cross Coll., 1959; JD, Northwestern U., 1962. Bar: Ill. 1962. Ptnr. Baker & McKenzie, Chgo., 1965-97; ret., 1997. Author: Product Liability Trends & Implications, 1970. Mem.: Ill. Bar Assn. Avocation: hiking. General civil litigation, Construction, Insurance.

DONEGAN, CHARLES EDWARD, lawyer, educator; b. Chgo., Apr. 10, 1933; s. Arthur C. and Odessa (Arnold) D.; m. Patty Lou Harris, June 15, 1963; 1 son, Carter Edward. BSC., Roosevelt U., 1954; MS, Loyola U., 1959; JD, Howard U., 1967; LL.M., Columbia, 1970. Bar: N.Y. 1968, D.C. 1968, Ill. 1979. Pub. sch. tchr., Chgo., 1956-59; with Office Internal Revenue, Chgo., 1959-62; labor economist U.S. Dept. Labor, Washington, 1962-65; legal intern U.S. Commn. Civil Rights, Washington, summer 1966; asst. counsel NAACP Legal Def. Fund, N.Y.C., 1967-69; lectr. law Baruch Coll., N.Y.C., 1969-70; asst. prof. law State U. N.Y. at Buffalo, 1970-73; assoc. prof. law Howard U., 1973-77; vis. assoc. prof. Ohio State U., Columbus, 1977-78; asst. regional counsel U.S. EPA, 1978-80; prof. law So. U., Baton Rouge, 1980—; sole practice law Chgo. and Washington, 1984—. Arbitrator steel industry, 1972, U.S. Postal Svc., New Orleans, D.C. Superior Ct., 1987—, Fed. Mediation and Conciliation Svc., 1985—, N.Y. Stock Exch.; vis. prof. law La. State U., summer 1981, N.C. Cen. U., Durham, 1988—, So. U., Baton Rouge, spring 1992; real estate broker; mem. bd. consumer claims Dist. D.C., 1988—; mem. Mayor's Transition Task Force, Washington, 1995; moot ct. judge Georgetown U. Law Sch., Washington, 1987—, Howard U. Law Sch., Washington, 1987—, Balsa, 1987—; spkr., participant nat. confs. on law, edn. and labor rels. Author: Discrimination in Public Employment, 1975; Contbr. articles to profl. jours., to Dictionary Am. Negro Biography. Active Ams. for Dem. Action; mc. adv. com. D.C. Bd. of Edn. Named one of Top 42 Lawyers in Washington Area, Washington Afro-Am. Newspaper, 1993, 94, 95, 96' Ford Found. scholar, 1965-67. Columbia U., 1972-73, NEH Postdoctoral fellow in Afro-Am. studies Yale U., 1972-73. Mem. ABA (vice chmn. edn. and curriculum com. local govt. law sect. 1972-80, pub. edn. com. sect. local govt. 1974-84, chmn. liaison com. AALS, 1984, chair arbitration sect.), Nat. Bar Assn. (labor and employment law sect., steering com.), D.C. Bar Assn., Washington Bar Assn. (chmn. legal edn. com.), Chgo. Bar Assn., Fed. Bar Assn., Cook County Bar Assn., Am. Arbitration Assn. (arbitrator), D.C. Fee Arbitration Bd. (bd. govs. 1990—), Nat. Conf. Black Lawyers (bd. organizers), Nat. Futures Assn. (arbitrator), Nat. Assn. Securities Dealers (arbitrator), Assn. Henri Capitant, Roosevelt U. Alumni Assn. (rep. at George Washington U. 175th anniversary charter day convocation 1996), Loyola U. Alumni Assn. (v.p. Washington), Howard U. Alumni Assn. (rep. at Hunter Coll. Centennial 1970), Columbia U. Alumni Assn. (v.p. law Washington), Alpha Phi Alpha, Phi Alpha Kappa, Phi Alpha Delta. Alternative dispute resolution, General practice, Labor (including EEOC, Fair Labor Standards Act, labor-management relations, NLRB, OSHA). Home: 4315 Argyle Ter NW Washington DC 20011-4243 Office: 601 Pennsylvania Ave NW Ste 900 Washington DC 20004-3615 also: 311 S Wacker Dr Ste 4550 Chicago IL 60606-6622

DONEGAN, JOSEPH MICHAEL, lawyer; b. Englewood, N.J., Sept. 17, 1961; s. James J. and Mary C. Donegan; m. Darlene A. Donegan, Nov. 17, 1993; children: Lindsay A., Joseph S. BA in Acctg., Pace U., 1983; JD, Widener Sch. of Law, 1987. Bar: N.J. 1987, Pa. 1987, N.Y. 1993, U.S. Tax Ct., 1993. Atty. Courter, Kobert, Laufer, Purcell & Cohen, Morristown, N.J., 1987-93; pvt. practice Morristown, 1993-96; ptnr. Purcell, Ries, Shannon, Mulcahy & O'Neill, Bedminster, NJ, 1996—2002, Scarinci and Hollenbeck, LLC, 2002—. Editor Del. Jour. of Corp. Law, 1986-87. Commn. N.J. Commn. on Aging, Trenton, 1995-97, N.J. Nat. Conf. Commrs. on Uniform State Laws, Trenton, 1998—. Mem. N.J. Bar Assn. (chair corp. and individual tax sect. 1995-97). Republican. Avocations: golfing, marathon running. Estate planning, Probate (including wills, trusts), Estate taxation. Home: 1511 Long Hill Rd Millington NJ 07946-1813 Office: Scarinic & Hollenbeck LLC One Valley Brook Ave Lyndhurst NJ 07071 E-mail: jdonegan@prsmo.com.

DONER, GARY WILLIAM, lawyer; b. Louisville, Nov. 3, 1951; s. Charles and Billie (Miller) D.; m. Cynthia Ann Herman, July 7, 1973; 1 child, Laura. BS, Wright State U., 1974; JD cum laude, U. Toledo, 1990. CPA, Ohio. Tax analyst NCR Corp., Dayton, Ohio, 1975-80; tax mgr. Dayco Corp., Dayton, 1980-85; tax dir. Cooper Tire & Rubber Co., Findlay, Ohio, 1985-99; mgr. fed. taxes Dana Corp., Toledo, Ohio, 1999—. Part-time instr. Ownes Coll., Toledo, 1985-86, acctg. adv. com., 1985—; officer Tax Execs. Inst.; pres. Tax Forum, Toledo, 1993. Named Ky. Col. Mem. AICPA, Ohio Soc. CPAs, Tax Execs. Inst., Ohio Bar Assn., Ohio C. of C. (tax com., adv. on taxes). Roman Catholic. Avocations: tennis, weightlifting. Corporate, general, Corporate taxation, Taxation, general. Home: 26065 Edinborough Cir Perrysburg OH 43551-9545 Office: DANA Corp PO Box 1000 Toledo OH 43697-1000

DONLEVY, JOHN DEARDEN, lawyer; b. Chgo., May 29, 1933; s. Frank and Alice Genevieve (O'Connor) D.; m. Kristin Bach Minnick, Apr. 20, 1963 (div. Sept. 1985); 1 son, John Dearden. Student, Stanford U., 1950-52; BS, Northwestern U., 1954; JD, U. Chgo., 1957; postgrad., Northwestern U., 1958. Bar: Ill. 1957, U.S. Dist. Ct. (no. dist.) 1957, U.S. Ct. Appeals (7th cir.) 1969, U.S. Supreme Ct. 1972. Asst. state's atty. Cook County Criminal Divsn., Chgo., 1958-61; city prosecutor City of Evanston, Ill., 1961; assoc. Mayer, Brown & Platt, Chgo., 1962-73, ptnr., 1973-90; pvt. practice law Chgo., 1990—. Participant Hinton Moot Ct. Competition U. Chgo., 1955-56, judge, 1972. Bd. dirs. English-Speaking Union, Chgo., 1964-65; active Rep. Orgn., 1958-60. Recipient Disting. Legal award Am. Legion, Chgo., 1960; named spl. prosecutor-labor racketeering Cook County State's Atty., Chgo., 1959-61; profiled in Lindberg "Summerdale--35 Year Anniversary", 1995. Mem. ABA, Ill. Bar Assn., Chgo. Bar Assn. (criminal law com., chair def. of prisoners com., criminal law and in-court criminal def. panels), Chgo. Athletic Assn. Criminal, State civil litigation. Office: Ste 2040 30 N La Salle St Chicago IL 60602-2506

DONLEY, DENNIS W. lawyer; b. Denver, Mar. 20, 1974; s. Dennis W. and Linda Jo D. BS summa cum laude, U. Mary Hardin-Baylor, 1995; JD, U. Tex., 1997. Bar: Tex. Clk. to Judge Paul Davis 200 Dist. Ct., Austin, Tex., 1996; intern/clk. to Justice James A. Baker Tex. Supreme Ct., Austin, 1997; ptnr. Naman, Howell, Smith & Lee, Austin, 1997—. Assoc. gen. counsel Rep. Party of Tex. Campaign vol. Gov./Pres. Bush, Austin; vol. Habitat for Humanity, Austin, Meals on Wheels, Austin. Mem. Tex. Young Lawyer Assn. (com. on voter edn., com. dropout prevention), Austin Young Lawyer Assn. (com. teen ct., cmty. svcs. com.). Republican. Avocations: boxing, reading, running, power lifting. Administrative and regulatory, General civil litigation, Corporate, general. Office: Naman Howell Smith & Lee PC 8310 Capital of Texas Hwy N # 490 Austin TX 78731

DONLON, WILLIAM JAMES, retired lawyer; b. Colorado Springs, Colo., Apr. 22, 1924; s. John Andrew and Kathleen M. D; m. Josephine A. Janssen, July 19, 1946; children: William James, Gregory A., Michele, Dru Ann Gazelle. Student, Colo. Coll., 1941-43; BS, U. Denver, 1949, JD, 1950. Bar: Colo. 1950, Ohio 1964, Ill. 1969, U.S. Dist. Ct. Colo. 1956, U.S. Dist. Ct. (no. dist.) Ill. 1974, U.S. Ct. Appeals (10th cir.) 1957, U.S. Ct. Appeals (5th cir.) 1970, U.S. Ct. Appeals (7th cir.) 1974, U.S. Ct. Appeals D.C. 1979, U.S. Supreme Ct. 1965. Dep. clk. Dist. Ct., Denver, 1949-50; pvt. practice Denver, 1953-63; gen. counsel Brotherhood Ry. Airline & S.S. Clks., Freight Handlers, Express & Sta. Empl., Rosemont, Ill., 1963-84, Rockville, Md., 1963-86; ret., 1985. Instr. labor U. Ill., 1972-78. With USAAF, 1942-45. Decorated Air medal with 2 oak leaf clusters; named Ky. Col. Mem. ABA (coun. sect. labor and employment law 1977-86), Ill. Bar Assn., D.C. Bar Assn., Am. Legion, VFW, KC (Grand Knight coun. 10329 1991-93), 34th Bomb Group Assn., Phi Alpha Delta, Phi Delta Theta. Democrat. Roman Catholic. Labor (including EEOC, Fair Labor Standards Act, labor-management relations, NLRB, OSHA). Office: PO Box 2212 Pineland FL 33945-2212

DONNELL, BRIAN JAMES, lawyer; b. Glen Cove, N.Y., Oct. 27, 1955; s. John Francis and Margaret (Grosek) D.; m. Karen Wachtell, June 20, 1981. BA in Polit. Sci. & Econs, Trinity Coll., 1977; JD cum laude, Boston Coll., 1980. Bar: Conn. 1980, U.S. Dist. Ct. Conn. 1981, U.S. Supreme Ct. 1991, U.S. Ct. Appeals (2nd cir.) 1994. From assoc. to ptnr. Halloran & Sage LLP, Hartford, Conn., 1980—. Editor-in-chief Boston Coll. Law Sch., 1979, Uniform Comml. Code Reporter-Digest, 1980. Mem. U. Hartford Constrn. Inst., 1987—. Mem. ABA, Conn. Bar Assn. (sects. on antitrust, constrn. law exec. com., comml. and bankruptcy law), Hartford County Bar Assn., Am. Arbitration Assn. (panel arbitrators constrn. industry), Pi Gamma Mu. Republican. General civil litigation, Commercial, contracts (including sales of goods; commercial financing), Construction. Office: Halloran & Sage LLP 1 Goodwin Sq Hartford CT 06103-4300 E-mail: donnell@halloran-sage.com.

DONNELLY, FREDERICK JAMES, lawyer; b. Utica, N.Y., Apr. 4, 1953; s. Frederick J. and Shirley (Woodruff) D. BA, St. Lawrence U., 1974; JD, Vanderbilt U., 1977. Bar: N.Y. 1977, S.D. 1981, Colo. 1982. Judge adv. U.S. Army, Stuttgaart, Fed. Republic Germany, 1978-81; assoc. David Stanton Law Offices, Rapid City, S.D., 1981-82, Stutz, Dyer, Miller & Delap, Denver, 1982-85, ptnr., 1985-86, Slavin & Donnelly, Denver, 1986. Rep. precinct capt., Denver, 1984-85; mem. 1st Congl. com. Rep. Party, Denver, 1986. Mem. Denver Bar Assn., Colo. Bar Assn. Unitarian Universalist. Federal civil litigation, State civil litigation, Construction. Home: 6076 S Chester Way Greenwood Village CO 80111-5230 Office: Slavin & Donnelly 825 Logan St Denver CO 80203-3114

DONNELLY, JAMES CORCORAN, JR., lawyer; b. Newton, Mass., June 10, 1946; s. James C. and Margery J. (MacNeil) D.; m. Carol R. Burns, June 28, 1968; children: James C. IV, Sarah Y. BA, Dartmouth Coll., 1968; JD, Boston Coll., 1973. Bar: Mass. 1973, U.S. Dist. Ct. Mass. 1974, U.S. Ct. Appeals (7th cir.) 1979, U.S. Ct. Appeals (1st cir.) 1983, U.S. Tax Ct. 1988, U.S. Dist. Ct. (no. dist.) Ohio 1991, U.S. Ct. Appeals (2d cir) 1994, U.S. Ct. Appeals (3d cir.) 1999. From assoc. to ptnr. Hale & Dorr, Boston, 1973-84; sr. ptnr. Mirick, O'Connell, DeMallie & Lougee, Worcester, Mass., 1985—, chmn. litigation dept., 1993-97. Editor-in-chief 1972 Annual Survey of Mass. Law. Corporator Greater Worcester Cmty. Found., 1986—, mem. monitoring and evaluation com., 1997—; trustee Higgins Armory Mus., Worcester, 1985—, pres. 1994-97; corporator Worcester Art Mus., 1986—, pres., mem. coun., 1987-88; councilor Am. Antiquarian Soc., 1996—, treas., 1997—; mem. club officers exec. com. Dartmouth Coll., 1997—, pres., 1999-2002, mem. alumni coun., 2000—, mem. com. on alumni orgns., 2000-2003, exec. com., 2002-03, chmn., 2003-03, coll. rels. group, 2002—, com. on alumni orgn., 2000—, chmn. 2002-03. Lt. U.S. Army, 1968-70. Decorated Army Commendation medal for meritorious svc., 1970. Fellow Mass. Bar Found. (life); mem. ABA, Mass. Bar Assn., Worcester County Bar Assn. (co-chmn. fed. ct. com. 1995-98), Dartmouth Lawyers Assn., Worcester Club (bd. dirs. 1995-98), Worcester Fire Soc., Dartmouth Club Ctrl. Mass. (exec. com. 1996—, pres. 1997—2002). Avocations: sailing, bicycling, hiking, history. General civil litigation, Corporate, general, Health. Home: 285 Salisbury St Worcester MA 01609-1661 Office: Mirick O'Connell 100 Front St Worcester MA 01608-1425

DONNEM, ROLAND WILLIAM, retired lawyer, real estate owner, developer; b. Seattle, Nov. 8, 1929; s. William Roland and Mary Louise (Hughes) D.; m. Sarah Brandon Lund, Feb. 18, 1961; children: Elizabeth Donnem Sigety, Sarah Madison. BA, Yale U., 1952; JD magna cum laude, Harvard U., 1957. Bar: N.Y. 1958, U.S. Dist. Ct. (ea. and so. dists.) N.Y. 1959, U.S. Ct. Appeals (2d cir.) 1959, U.S. Ct. Claims 1960, U.S. Tax Ct. 1960, U.S. Supreme Ct. 1963, U.S. Ct. Appeals (3d cir.) 1969, D.C. 1970, U.S. Ct. Appeals (D.C. cir.) 1970, Ohio 1976, U.S. Dist. Ct. (no. dist.) Ohio 1980, U.S. Ct. Appeals (7th cir.) 1980, U.S. Ct. Appeals (6th cir.) 1984. With Davis Polk & Wardwell, N.Y.C., 1957-63, 64-69; law sec. appellate divsn. N.Y. Supreme Ct., N.Y.C., 1963-64; dir. policy planning antitrust divsn. Justice Dept., Washington, 1969-71; v.p., sec., gen. counsel Standard Brands Inc., N.Y.C., 1971-76; from v.p. law to sr. v.p. law and casualty prevention Chessie System, Cleve., 1976-86; ptnr. Meta Ptnrs., real estate devel., 1984—2002, mng. ptnr., 1989—2002, registered security rep., 1985-90; bd. dirs., gen. counsel Acorn Properties, Inc., Cleve., 1985—2002, pres., 1989—2002; bd. dirs., gen. counsel Meta Devel. Corp., Cleve., 1985—2002, pres., 1989—2002; bd. dirs., gen. counsel Meta Properties, Inc., Cleve., 1988—2002, pres., 1989—2002. Founding mem., bd. dirs. Assn. Sheraton Franchisees N.Am., 1997—2002. Mem. editl. bd. Harvard Law Rev., 1955-57. Bd. dirs., fin. v.p. Presbyn. Home for Aged Women, N.Y.C., 1972-76; bd. dirs., treas. James Lenox Ho., Inc., 1972-76; trustee Food and Drug Law Inst., 1974-76; trustee, sec. Brick Presbyn. Ch., N.Y.C., 1974-76; sec. class of 1952, Yale U., 1992-97; bd. dirs. Yale Alumni Fund, 1990-95; chmn. Cleve. Area Yale Campaign, 1991-97. Lt. (j.g.) USNR, 1952-54. Fellow Timothy Dwight Coll., Yale U., 1987—. Mem. D.C. Bar Assn., Greater Cleve. Bar Assn., Am. Law Inst. (life), Am. Arbitration Assn. (nat. panel arbitrators), Def. Orientation Conf. Assn. (bd. dirs. 1996-99), Yale U. Alumni Assn. Cleve. (treas. 1982-84, del. 1984-87, trustee 1984-93, adv. coun. 1993—), Yale U. Alumni Assn. (bd. govs. 1987-90), Union Club (N.Y.C. and Cleve.), Capitol Hill Club (Washington), Washington Chevy Chase Club, Cleve. Racquet Club, Kirtland Club (Cleve.), Met. Club (Washington), Mory's Assn. (New Haven), Phi Beta Kappa. Republican. Presbyterian. Home: 2945 Fontenay Rd Shaker Heights OH 44120-1726 Home (Winter): Ft Sumter Ho 1 King St Spt 307 Charleston SC 29401

DONNER, HENRY JAY, lawyer; b. Atlantic City, N.J., Sept. 1, 1944; s. Harry and Sylvia (Payes) D.; m. Katherine Weiner, Dec. 20, 1969; children: Benjamin James, Melissa Faith. BA, Am. U., 1966; JD, Villanova U., 1969. Bar: Pa. 1969, U.S. Dist. Ct. (ea. dist.) Pa. 1969, U.S. Ct. Appeals (3d cir.) 1983. Staff mem. U.S. Senator Joseph A. Clark, Washington, 1965-68; assoc. Dilworth, Paxson, Kalish and Levy, Phila., 1969-74; ptnr. Jacoby, Donner & Jacoby, Phila., 1974-82; sr. mem. Jacoby Donner, P.C., Phila., 1982—. Lectr. Nat. Home Builders Assn., Pa. State U., State Coll., 1989-90. Author: West Legal Forms: Specialized Forms, Vol. 27, Chpt. 8, Building Agreements. Mem. sch. com. Germantown Friends Sch., 1993—; bd. dirs. Germantown Jewish Ctr., 1989-91. Mem. ABA, Phila. Bar Assn. (exec. com. real property sect. 1987-96, chmn. constrn. law com., real property sect. 1986-89, chmn. real property sect. 1993, bd. govs. 1993), Constrn. Fin. Mgmt. Assn. (bd. dirs. Phila. chpt 1990-95), Union League Phila., Germantown Cricket Club. Construction, Estate planning, Pension, profit-sharing, and employee benefits. Office: Jacoby Donner PC 1515 Market St Ste 2000 Philadelphia PA 19102-1920 E-mail: hdonner@jacobydonner.com.

DONNER, TED A. lawyer; b. N.Y.C., Nov. 22, 1960; s. Robert A. and Barbara (Wood) D.; m. Leslie Lynn Wasserman, Sept. 16, 1990; children: Alexandra Sofia, Samuel Joseph. BA, Roosevelt U., 1987; JD, Loyola U., 1990. Bar: U.S. Dist. Ct. Ill. 1990. Assoc. Rock, Fusco, Reynolds & Garvey, Chgo., 1990-94; of counsel Altheimer & Gray, Chgo., 1994-2000; ptnr. Bischoff Ptnrs. LLC, Chgo., 2000—02; mgr. Donner & Co. Law Offices LLC, 2002—. Instr. Loyola U. Chgo. Sch. Law, 1990—96, lectr., 1996—. Author: Attorney's Practice Guide to Negotiations, 2d edit., 1995-2003, Jury Selection Strategy & Science, 3d edit., 2000-03, Jury Selection Handbook, 1999. Mem. ATLA, ABA, Am. Soc. Trial Consultants, Am. Soc. Legal Writers, Internat. Platform Assn., DuPage County Bar Assn., Chgo. Bar Assn., Alpha Sigma Nu. Antitrust, General civil litigation, Insurance. Office: 203 N LaSalle St # 2100 Chicago IL 60601 also: 1131 Wheaton Oaks Ct Wheaton IL 60187 E-mail: email@donnerco.com.

DONOHOE, JEROME FRANCIS, lawyer; b. Yankton, S.D., Mar. 17, 1939; s. Francis A. and Ruth D. Donohoe; m. Elaine Bush, Jan. 27, 1968; 1 child, Nicole Elaine. BA, St. John's U., 1961; JD cum laude, U. Minn., 1964. Bar: Ill. 1964, S.D. 1964. Atty. Atchison, Topeka & Santa Fe Ry. Co., Chgo., 1967-73, gen. atty., 1973-78; gen. counsel corp. affairs Santa Fe Industries Inc., Chgo., 1978-84; v.p. law Santa Fe Industries, Inc., Chgo., 1984-90, Santa Fe Pacific Corp., Chgo., 1984-94; ptnr. Mayer, Brown, Rowe & Maw, Chgo., 1990-99, sr. counsel, 1999—. Bd. dirs. Evanston Cmty. Found., 2000—. Capt. JAGC U.S. Army, 1964—67. Fellow: Ill. Bar Found.; mem.: ABA (sect. officer, pub. utility, comm. and transp. law sect.), Northwestern U. Assocs., Mich. Shores Club (Wilmette, Ill.), Chgo. Athletic Assn., Chgo. Club. Administrative and regulatory, Corporate, general, Securities. Office: Mayer Brown Rowe & Maw 190 S La Salle St Ste 3100 Chicago IL 60603-3441 E-mail: jdonohoe@mayerbrown.com.

DONOHUE, JOHN PATRICK, lawyer; b. N.Y.C., Sept. 16, 1944; s. Joseph Francis and Catherine Elizabeth (Feeney) D.; m. Patricia Ann Holly, June 11, 1977; children: Eileen Mary, Anne Catherine. BA, Providence Coll., 1966; JD, Catholic U. Am., 1969. Bar: N.Y. 1973, U.S. Ct. Appeals (2d cir.) 1973, U.S. Ct. Appeals (fed. cir.) 1974, N.J. 1975, U.S. Dist. Ct. N.J. 1975, U.S. Dist. Ct. (so., ea. dists.) N.Y. 1975, U.S. Supreme Ct. 1978, D.C. 1981, Pa. 1986. Spl. agt. FBI, Washington, 1969-71; assoc. Donohue & Donohue, N.Y.C., 1971-74, ptnr., 1974—. Adj. prof. law internat. bus. transactions Seton Hall U. Sch. Law, Newark, 1986-94, 2002—. Author book sect. Customs Fraud Section on Business Crimes, 1982; co-author: The Prevention and Prosecution of Computer and High Technology Crime. Bd. dirs. Maritime Exch. Delaware River and Bay, 1989—; mem. bd. regents Cath. U. Am., 1990-2000, chmn., 1997-2000; trustee Rosemont (Pa.) Sch., 1995—, chmn., 1996-2001; mem. bd. visitors Cath. U. Sch. Law, 1998—; mem. Congress of Fellows, Ctr. for Internat. Legal Studies, Salzburg, Austria. Named Man of Yr., Phila. Customs, Brokers and Forwarders Assn., 1984. Mem. Customs and Internat. Trade Bar Assn., Pa. State Bar Assn., Congress of Fellows, Ctr. Internat. Legal Studies. Republican. Roman Catholic. Federal civil litigation, Immigration, naturalization, and customs, Private international. Office: Donohue & Donohue 232 S 4th St Philadelphia PA 19106-3704 E-mail: jdonohue@donohueanddonohue.com.

DONOHUE, MARY, lieutenant governor; b. Rensselaer County, N.Y. children: Sara, Justin. B.Edn., Coll. New Rochelle, 1968; MS in Edn., Russell Sage Coll., Troy, N.Y., 1973; JD, Union U., 1983. Bar: N.Y. 1983. Tchr. elem., jr. h.s. Rensselaer and Albany County (N.Y.) sch. dists., Albany, 1969-78; law clk., intern U.S. Atty.'s Office, Albany, 1980-83; assoc. O'Connell & Aronowitz, Albany, 1983-88; pvt. practice Troy, 1988-92; asst. county atty. Rensselaer County, 1990-92, dist. atty., 1992-96; justice N.Y. Supreme Ct., 3rd Jud. Dist., 1996-98; lt. gov. State of N.Y., Albany, 1998—. Chair Capital Dist. Women's Adv. Coun., 1996; mem. Gov.-elect Pataki's Transition Team for Criminal Justice, 1994-96. Republican. Office: Office of Lt Governor State Capitol Rm 246 Albany NY 12224

DONOVAN, CHARLES STEPHEN, lawyer; b. Boston, Feb. 28, 1951; s. Alfred Michael and Maureen (Murphy) D.; m. Lisa Marie Dicharry, Apr. 21, 1979; children: Yvette, Martine, Neal. BA, Haverford Coll., 1974; JD, Cornell U., 1977. Bar: Mass. 1977, La. 1977, Calif. 1982, U.S. Supreme Ct. 1988. Atty. Phelps, Dunbar, Marks, Claverie & Sims, New Orleans, 1977-81, Dorr, Cooper & Hays, San Francisco, 1981-84, Walsh, Donovan & Keech LLP, San Francisco, 1984-2000, Schnader Harrison Segal & Lewis, LLP, San Francisco, 2000—03, co-chmn. internat. practice group, 2002—03, Sheppard Mullin Richter & Hampton LLP, San Francisco, 2003—. Instr. maritime law Calif. Maritime Acad., Vallejo, 1982—; spl. advisor U.S. State Dept., 1993-96. Contbr. numerous articles to profl. jours. Recipient Gustavus H. Robinson prize Cornell Law Sch., 1977. Mem.: ABA (chmn. admiralty and maritime law com. Chgo. 1989—90), Marine Exch. (bd. dirs. San Francisco Bay region 1993—96), Tulane Admiralty Inst. (permanent adv. bd.), Maritime Law Assn. U.S. (chmn. com. on maritime criminal law 1998—2001, chmn. subcom. on maritime liens and mortgages 1994—2001), Internat. Bar Assn. Avocations: skiing, hiking, mandolin, guitar, soccer. Admiralty, General civil litigation, Private international. Office: Sheppard Mullin Richte & Hampton LLP 17th Fl Embascader Ctr San Francisco CA 94111 E-mail: cdonovan@sheppardmullin.com.

DONOVAN, CRAIG THOMAS, lawyer; b. S.I., Apr. 19, 1966; s. John Maurice and Arlene Frances Donovan; m. Yukie Eguchi, Dec. 4, 1999; children: Lintaro, Kie. BA, NYU, 1988; MA, Columbia U., 1991; postgrad., Internat. Christian U., Tokyo, 1991—92; JD, Miss. Coll., 1997. Bar: N.Y. 1999, N.J. 1999, U.S. Dist. Ct. (so., ea. dists.) N.Y. 1999, U.S. Dist. Ct. N.J. 1999, DC 2000. Tokyo liaison, registration Daiwa Securities Am., Inc., N.Y.C., 1992—93; assoc. Arnberger, Kim, Buxbaum & Choy, Beijing, 1995; compliance Bears Stearns & Co., Inc., Whippany, NJ, 1998; assoc. atty. Assadi & Marks, LLP, N.Y.C., 1999—2001, Law Offices Nolan Cheng, N.Y.C., 2001—. Legis. liaison Nature Conservancy, Jackson, Miss., 1997; pro bono atty. Natural Resources Def. Coun., N.Y.C., 2001; mem. moot ct. bd. Miss. Coll. Sch. Law, 1995—97. Contbr. articles to profl. jours.; editor: Public Lands and Land Use Com. Newsletter, 2003—. Vice chair Public Lands and Land Use Com., 2003. Named winner Environ. Law Writing Competition, S.E. Assn. Fish & Wildlife Agys., 1997. Mem.: ABA (mem. Pacific law com. 1999—), N.Y. County Lawyers Assn. (mem. internat. com. 1999—, vice chair environmental law com. 2003—, Pro Bono Svc. award 2002), N.Y. State Bar Assn. (mem. environ. law sect. 1999—), Omicron Delta Epsilon. Avocations: reading, East Asian studies, music, art, American Civil War. Private international, General practice, Federal civil litigation. Office: Law Office Nolan Cheng 11 E Broadway Ste 7C New York NY 10038

DONOVAN, MICHAEL JOSEPH, lawyer; b. Dubuque, Iowa, June 3, 1948; s. Joseph Francis and Dorothea Adelaide (Eilers) D.; m. Jean Ann Hoppmann, June 13, 1970; children: Jon Michael, Jodi Jean. BA cum laude, Loras Coll., Dubuque, 1970; JD with distinction, U. Iowa, 1973. Bar: Iowa 1973, Wis. 1973, U.S. Dist. Ct. (ea. dist.) Wis. 1973, U.S. Supreme Ct. 1992; cert. civil trial advocate Nat. Bd. Trial Advocacy. Assoc. Borgelt, Powell, Peterson & Frauen, S.C., Milw., 1973-77; shareholder Hausmann-McNally, S.C., Milw., 1977—. Mem., pres. athletic bd. Christ King Sch., Wauwatosa, Wis. Mem. Wis. Acad. Trial Lawyers (bd. dirs. 1989-91), Am. Trial Lawyers Assn., State Bar Wis., State Bar Iowa. General civil litigation, Personal injury (including property damage), Product liability. Office: Hausmann-McNally SC 633 W Wisconsin Ave Ste 2000 Milwaukee WI 53203-1957

DONOVAN, RICHARD EDWARD, lawyer; b. Cleve., Dec. 3, 1952; s. Richard A. and Eileen (Karthaus) D.; m. Ellen Brode, June 16, 1979; children: Colin, Ryan Michael, Patrick. BS, U. Notre Dame, 1974; JD, Rutgers U., 1977. Bar: N.Y. 1978, U.S. Dist. Ct. (ea. dist.) N.Y. 1978, N.J. 1985, U.S. Dist. Ct. N.J. 1985, U.S. Ct. Appeals (2d cir.) 1987, U.S. Supreme Ct. 1990. Assoc. Breed, Abbott & Morgan, N.Y.C., 1977-80, Kelley, Drye & Warren LLP, N.Y.C., 1980-86, ptnr., 1987—. Mem. ABA, Assn. Bar City N.Y. (com. prof. and jud. ethics 1996-99), N.J. Bar Assn., Rutgers Alumni Coun., N.Y. State Bar Assn. (sec. comml. and fed. litigation sect. 1988-90), Fed. Bar Coun., Assn. Fed. Bar N.J. Antitrust, General civil litigation, Health. Home: 61 Oak Ridge Ave Summit NJ 07901-4306 Office: Kelley Drye & Warren LLP 101 Park Ave New York NY 10178 E-mail: rdonovan@kelleydrye.com.

DOOLEY, JOHN AUGUSTINE, III, state supreme court justice; b. Nashua, N.H., Apr. 10, 1944; s. John A. and Edna Elizabeth (Elwell) D.; m. Sandra C. Sapp, Dec. 19, 1970 BS, Union Coll., 1965; LLB, Boston Coll., 1968. Bar: Vt. 1968. Law clk. to presiding judge U.S. Dist. Ct. Vt., 1968-69; asst. dir. Vt. Legal Aid, 1969-72, dir., 1972-78; legal counsel to gov. of Vt., 1985; sec. of adminstrn. State of Vt., 1985-87; assoc. justice Vt. Supreme Ct., 1987—. Part-time U.S. magistrate for Vt., from 1971. Co-author: Cases and Materials on Urban Poverty Law, 1974. Mem. Vt. Bar Assn. Office: Vt Supreme Ct 109 State St Montpelier VT 05609-0001

DOOLITTLE, JESSE WILLIAM, JR., lawyer; b. Wheaton, Ill., May 19, 1929; s. Jesse William and Selma Caroline (Schacht) D.; m. Annette Danforth Bush, May 5, 1962; children: Danforth Bush, Alice Walters. AB, DePauw U., 1951; LLB magna cum laude, Harvard, 1954. Bar: D.C. 1954. Law clk. to U.S. Supreme Ct. Justice Felix Frankfurter, 1957-58; assoc. firm Covington & Burling, Washington, 1958-61; asst. to solicitor gen. of U.S. Dept. Justice, Washington, 1961-63, 1st asst. civil div., 1963-66; gen. counsel Dept. Air Force, Washington, 1966-68, asst. sec. for manpower and res. affairs, 1968-69; partner firm Prather Seeger Doolittle & Farmer, Washington, 1969-94. Editl. cons. Lexis-Nexis, 1995-98; comml.arbitrator, 1992-. Mem.: Harvard Law Rev, 1952-54. Pres. bd. trustees Nat. Child Rsch. Ctr., Washington, 1972-74; mem. bd. overseers com. to visit ROTC programs Harvard, 1967-69; com. to visit Law Sch., 1969-75; mem. governing bd. Nat. Cathedral Sch. for Girls, Washington, 1979-85, vice-chmn., 1981-82, chmn., 1982-85; mem. chpt. Washington Nat. Cathedral, 1982-85; mem. policy bd. Legal Counsel for the Elderly, Washington, 1992-97; bd. dirs. Westchester Corp., Washington, 2000-2003. 1st lt. AUS, 1954-57. Recipient Career Service award Nat. Civil Service League, 1968, Exceptional Civilian Service award Dept. Air Force, 1969 Mem. Am. Law Inst., Harvard Law Sch. Assn. (coun. 1964-68), Harvard Law Rev. Assn. (bd. overseers 1967-72, 92-98), Phi Beta Kappa, Delta Chi. Democrat. Episcopalian (sr. warden 1973-75, past vestryman). Clubs: Metropolitan, Chevy Chase. Administrative and regulatory, Corporate, general, General practice. Home: 4000 Cathedral Ave NW Apt 444B Washington DC 20016-5282

DOPF, GLENN WILLIAM, lawyer; b. N.Y.C., June 6, 1953; s. William Bernard and Doris Virginia (Roxby) D. BS cum laude, Fordham Coll., 1975; JD, Fordham U., 1979; LLM, NYU, 1983. Bar: N.J. 1979, U.S. Dist. Ct. N.J. 1979, N.Y. 1980, U.S. Dist. Ct. (so. and ea. dists.) N.Y. 1980, U.S. Ct. Appeals (2d cir.) 1980, U.S. Ct. Internat. Trade 1981, U.S. Supreme Ct. 1983. Assoc. Martin, Clearwater & Bell, N.Y.C., 1980-81; ptnr. Kopff, Nardelli & Dopf LLP, N.Y.C., 1982—. Mem. ABA, Assn. Bar City N.Y. Federal civil litigation, State civil litigation, Insurance. Office: Kopff Nardelli & Dopf LLP 440 9th Ave Fl 15 New York NY 10001-1688

DOPKIN, MARK DREGANT, lawyer; b. Balt., Jan. 14, 1943; s. Wilford and Beverly (Dregant) D.; m. Ilene Kleinman, Mar. 21, 1967 (div.); children: Rebecca, Peter; m. Deborah Cohn, May 28, 1984. BA, Union Coll., Schenectady, 1964; JD, U. Md., 1967. Bar: Md. 1967, U.S. Dist. Ct. Md. 1968, U.S. Supreme Ct. 1974. Assoc. Blades & Rosenfeld, Balt., 1968-71, Kaplan, Heyman, Greenberg, Engelman & Belgrd, P.A., Balt., 1971-76, ptnr., 1977-98, Tydings & Rosenberg LLP, Balt., 1998—. Mem. Real Property Records Improvement Fund Oversight Com., 1995—. Mem. Gov.'s Salary Rev. Com., Md., 1980-85, Balt. County Charter Rev. Com., 1977-79; treas. Congressman Benjamin L. Cardin, Balt., 1985—; 1st v.p. Har Sinai Cong., Balt., 1987-89, pres., 1989-91, trustee, 1973-75, 77-80, 86—; active various charitable orgns. With U.S. Army, 1967-73. Fellow Md. Bar Found.; mem. ABA, Bar Assn. Balt. City, Md. Bar Assn. (chair real property sect. 2000-01). Democrat. Jewish. Corporate, general, Land use and zoning (including planning), Property, real (including real estate development, water). Office: Tydings & Rosenberg LLP 100 E Pratt St Fl 26 Baltimore MD 21202-1009 E-mail: mdopkin@tydingslaw.com.

DORADO, MARIANNE GAERTNER, lawyer; d. Wolfgang Wilhelm and Marianne L. Gaertner; m. Richard Manuel Dorado, Oct. 1, 1982; children: Marianne Christine, Kathleen Gina. BA, Yale U., 1978; JD, U. Mich., 1981. Bar: N.Y. 1982, U.S. Supreme Ct. 1993. Ptnr. The Dorado Law Group, LLC, N.Y.C., 1998—. Contbr. Extern office legal advisor U.S. Dept. State, Washington, 1980. Republican. Roman Catholic. Corporate, general, Mergers and acquisitions, Securities. Office: The Dorado Law Group LLC 74 Trinity Pl Ste 1204 New York NY 10006 E-mail: mdorado@doradolaw.com.

DORAN, KENNETH JOHN, lawyer; b. Janesville, Wis., Feb. 10, 1950; s. Henry James and Alice Elizabeth (Fanning) D.; m. Dianne Marie Carlson, Feb. 28, 1987; children: Taylor, Olivia. BA, U. Wis., 1974, JD, 1977. Atty. The Legal Clinic, Madison, Wis., 1978-79, Doran Law Offices, Madison, 1980-84, Smoler & Albert, S.C., Madison, 1984-88, Kassner Law Offices, Middleton, Wis., 1988-92, Doran Law Offices, 1993—. Author: Personal Bankruptcy and Debt Adjustment, 1991, 2d edit., 1996. Bd. dirs. Wis. Madison chpt. Civil Liberties Union, Wis., 1983-85. Mem. Dane County Bar Assn., Western Dist. Wis. Bankruptcy Bar Assn. (pres. 2000-01). Democrat. Bankruptcy, General civil litigation, Commercial, consumer (including collections, credit). Home: 2101 Fox Ave Madison WI 53711-1920 E-mail: kendoran@execpc.com.

DORAN, KENNETH M. lawyer; b. June 10, 1955; AB with distinction, Stanford U., 1977; JD, U. So. Calif., 1981. Bar: Calif. 1981. With Gibson, Dunn, & Crutcher, L.A., 1981—2002, ptnr., mng. ptnr., 2002—. Co-chair corp. practice group Dunn & Crutcher LLP, L.A. and Century City, Calif.; lectr. in field. Exec. articles editor: So. Calif. Law Rev., 1979—81. Mem.: Order of Coif. Office: Gibson Dunn & Crutcher LLP 333 S Grand Ave Los Angeles CA 90071-3197

DORAN, WILLIAM MICHAEL, lawyer; b. Albany, N.Y., May 26, 1940; s. James R. and Lorene Tinsley (Nees) D.; m. Susan Coryell Lloyd; children: Melissa, Heather, Leigh. BS in Journalism, Northwestern U., 1962; LLB, U. Pa., 1966. Assoc. Morgan, Lewis & Bockius, Phila., 1967-76, ptnr., 1976—. Dir. SEI Investments Co.; trustee SEI Liquid Asset Trust, SEI Daily Income Trust, SEI Tax Exempt Trust, SEI Instl. Managed Trust, SEI Index Funds, SEI Internat. Trust, The Advisors Inner Cir. Fund, The Arbor Fund, Inventor Funds, Incs.; chmns. adv. coun. Eisenhower Exchange Fellowships, Phila. Vice chmn. World Affairs Coun. Phila. Mem. ABA, Pa. Bar Assn., Phila. Bar Assn. Corporate, general, Finance, Private international. Home: 27 Druim Moir Ln Philadelphia PA 19118-4134 Office: Morgan Lewis & Bockius LLP 1701 Market St Philadelphia PA 19103-2903 E-mail: wdoran@morganlewis.com.

DORCHAK, THOMAS J. lawyer; b. Cleve., Aug. 31, 1940; s. Joseph J. and Julia H. D.; m. Eileen C. Coakley, June 27, 1964; children: Joshua, Andrew, Claire Marie, Sarah T. BA with honors, Xavier U., 1962; JD, Boston Coll., 1965. Bar: Ohio 1966, U.S. Dist. Ct. (no. dist.) Ohio 1970, U.S. Ct. Appeals (6th cir.) 1981. In house def. atty. Allstate Ins. Co., Cleve., 1969-73; assoc. Bertsch Edelman & Fludine, Cleve., 1973-76; pvt. practice Cleve., 1976-92; assoc. The Crombie Law Firm, North Olmsted, Ohio, 1993—. Actor cmty. theater. General civil litigation, Family and matrimonial, General practice. Office: The Crombie Law Firm 4615 Great Northern Blvd North Olmsted OH 44070-3426

DORDELL, TIMOTHY PAUL, lawyer; b. Mpls., June 26, 1962; BA summa cum laude, St. Olaf Coll., Northfield, Minn., 1984; student, Cambridge (Eng.) U., 1983; JD cum laude, U. Minn., 1987. Bar: Ariz. 1987, Minn. 1989, U.S. Dist. Ct. Ariz. 1987, U.S. Dist. Ct. Minn. 1991. Atty. Streich Lang, Phoenix, 1987-89; v.p., gen. counsel Twin Star Prodns., Inc., Scottsdale, Ariz., 1989-91; atty. Fredrikson & Byron, Mpls., 1992-96; assoc. gen. counsel Ecolab Inc., St. Paul, 1996—2002. Bd. dirs. Minn. AIDS Project, Mpls., 1996—. Mem. Phi Beta Kappa, Phi Alpha Theta. Private international, Mergers and acquisitions. Office: Ecolab Inc 370 Wabasha St N Saint Paul MN 55102-1390 E-mail: tim.dordell@ecolab.com., timdordell@yahoo.com.

DOREMUS, OGDEN, lawyer; b. Atlanta, Apr. 23, 1921; s. C. Estes and Mary (McAdory) D.; m. Carolyn Wooten Greene, Aug. 30, 1947 (dec. Aug. 1989); children: Celia Jane, Frank O., Dale Marie Doremus; m. Linda Parker, Dec. 4, 1992. BA, Emory U., 1946, JD, 1949. Bar: Ga. 1947; cert. U.S. postal mediator, 1999. Asst. solicitor gen., Atlanta, 1947-49; ptnr. firm Smith Field Doremus & Ringel, Atlanta, 1949-60, Falligant, Doremus and Karsman, Savannah, Ga., 1960-72, Doremus, Jones & Smith, P.C., Metter, Ga., 1972-94; of counsel Karsman, Brooks & Callaway, 1994—2000. Prof. Woodrow Wilson Sch. Law, Atlanta, 1948-50; judge State Ct. Candler County, Ga., 1985—, chair uniform rules com. Coun. State Cts., 1990—; pres. Ga. Coun. State Ct. Judges, 1990-91, chair legis. com., 1997-99; mem. Jud. Coun. State of Ga., 1989-91, Unified Trial Ct. Commn., 1997; mem. ct. futures com. State Bar Ga., 1996—; bd. dirs. Ctr. for Law in the Pub. Interest, 1996—; judge Mcpl. Ct., Metter, Ga., 1997-2001; mem. commn. on judiciary Supreme Ct. Ga., 1999—. Mem. editorial adv. bd. Environ. Law. Reporter, 1969-80. Scoutmaster Boy Scouts Am., Atlanta, 1951-60, commn., 1961-70; chmn. Ga. Day and Savannah Arts Festival, 1968-72; mem. Atlanta City Coun., 1950-53; mem. Savannah Govtl. Reorgn. Commn., 1960-61, Ga. Ct. Futures Commn., 1991-93, 97—; adv. com. Nat. Coastal Zone Mgmt. Coun., 1978-86; trustee Ga. Conservancy; bd. dirs. Legal Environ. Assistance Found., 1983-86, Ga. Hazardous Waste Authority, 1989—, Chatham Environ. Forum, 1990-93; mem. strategic planning com. Coun. State Cts. Ga., 1996—; bd. dirs. Coastal Environ. Orgn. Ga., 1998—, Cancochee Riverkeeper. Served with USAAC, 1942-46, ETO. Named Young Man of Yr. Atlanta, 1951; recipient Thomas H. gignilliat award Cultural Progress of Savannah, 1969, Tradition of Excellence award Ga. State Bar, 1988, 1st Ann. Coun. of State Cts. award named Ogden Doremus in his honor, 1993. Mem.: ABA (chmn. environ law com., gen. practice 1976—77), Atlanta Soc., Ga. Inst. Trial Advocacy (chmn. 1984—89), Savannah Bar Assn., State Bar Ga. (chmn. ins. law sect. 1963—67, 1977—83, mediator for U.S. Postal Svc. 1999—, cert. mediator Ga. commn. on dispute resolution), Izaak Walton League (founder Ga. chpt. 1950), Willow Lake Country Club, Chatham Tennis Club, Chatham Club, Sierra Club (exec. com. Chattahoochee chpt. 1965—75, chair legal com. Ga. chpt. 1997—2001, Lifetime Achievement Ga. environ. coun. Citizenship award 1997, 1999, Conservation Leadership award Ga. chpt. 1999, Common Cause Citizenship award 1998). Alternative dispute resolution, General civil litigation, Environmental. Home: RR 2 Box 188A Metter GA 30439-9570 Office: Doremus and Assocs Courthouse Sq PO Box 702 Metter GA 30439-0702 E-mail: odoremus@excite.com.

DOREN, ROBERT ALAN, lawyer; b. Buffalo, Mar. 11, 1949; m. Teri B. Shaffer, Aug. 27, 1978; children: Lee Michael, Lindsey Maria. BS, SUNY, Buffalo, 1972; JD, U. Buffalo, 1975. Bar: N.Y. 1976, Ohio 2002, Pa. 2002, U.S. Dist. Ct. (we. dist.) N.Y. 1976, U.S. Ct. Appeals (2d cir.) 1978. Assoc. Brizdle & Hankin, P.C., Buffalo, 1975-76; ptnr. Flaherty, Cohen, Grande, Randazzo & Doren, Buffalo, 1976—97, Bond, Schoeneck & King, LLP, Buffalo, 1997—. Labor (including EEOC, Fair Labor Standards Act, labor-management relations, NLRB, OSHA). Home: 252 Ranch Trl Buffalo NY 14221-2340 Office: Bond Schoeneck & King PLLC 40 Fountain Plz Ste 600 Buffalo NY 14202-2200 E-mail: rdoren@bsk.com.

DORIS, ALAN S(ANFORD), lawyer; b. Cleve., June 18, 1947; s. Sam E. and Rebecca (Sunshine) D.; m. Nancy Rose Spitzer, Jan. 10, 1976; children: Matthew, Lisa. AB and BS in Bus. cum laude, Miami U., Oxford U., 1969; JD cum laude, Harvard U., 1972. Bar: Ohio 1972, U.S. Dist. Ct. (no. dist.) Ohio 1972, U.S. Tax Ct. 1972, U.S. Ct. Appeals (6th cir.) 1972. Assoc. Stotter, Familo, Cavitch, Elden & Durkin, Cleve., 1972-77; ptnr. Elden & Ford, Cleve., 1978-79, Benesch, Friedlander, Coplan & Aronoff, Cleve., 1980-2000, Squire, Sanders & Dempsey, 2000—. Editor: Ohio Transaction Guide. Treas. Hawthorne Valley Country Club, Cleve., 1984-85; chmn. Cleve. Tax Inst., 1994. Mem. ABA (chmn. capital recovery com. taxation sect. 1994-96). Avocation: golf. Corporate taxation, Taxation, general, Personal income taxation. Office: Squire Sanders & Dempsey LLP 4900 Key Tower Cleveland OH 44114

DORKEY, CHARLES E., III, lawyer; b. Phila., June 23, 1948; s. Charles Edward and Peggy O'Neal D.; children: Charles Edward IV, John Hilliard, Marjorie Lyddon. AB cum laude, Dartmouth Coll., 1970; JD, Univ. Pa., 1973. Bar: Pa. 1974, N.Y. 1975, D.C. 1977. Law clk. to hon. Samuel J. Roberts Supreme Ct. of Pa., 1973-74; assoc. Sullivan & Cromwell, N.Y.C., 1975-81; ptnr. Reboul, MacMurray, Hewitt, Maynard & Kristol, N.Y.C., 1981-84, Richards & O'Neil, N.Y.C., 1984-91, Haythe & Curley, N.Y.C., 1992-99, Torys LLP, N.Y.C., 1999—. Approved mediator U.S. Dist. Ct. (so. dist.), N.Y. Panel Disting. Neutrals for Ctr. for Pub. Resources; mediator Supreme Ct., N.Y. County, Banking Dept., Jud. Hearing Office, State of N.Y.; chair Hudson River Park Trust. Trustee Citizens Budget Commn., 1993—98, N.Y. Hist. Soc., 1998—; mem. mayor's adv. com., housing ct. adv. coun. 1st Dept. Jud. Screening Com., 1995—99; mem. State Ct. of Claims Jud. Screening Com., 1995—99; mem. Departmental Disciplinary Com. 1st Jud. Dept.; trustee N.Y. Interest Lawyers Acct. Fund; overseer U. Pa. Law Sch., 1993—99; nat. chmn. Law Annual Giving, 1991—93; trustee Hist. Hudson Valley; chair Hudson River Park Trust; bd. dirs. Empire State Devel. Corp., N.Y.C. Water Fin. Authority, N.Y. State Job Devel. Authority, Harlem Cmty. Devel. Corp., 42d St. Devel. Project, N.Y. State Mortgage

Loan Enforcement and Adminstrn. Corp., N.Y. Parks and Conservation Assn., Liberty Devel. Corp.; mem. alumni coun. Dartmouth Coll., 1990—93, pres. class 1970, 1991—95. Mem. ABA, N.Y. State Bar Assn. (exec. com. comml. and fed. litigation sect. 1986—, fed. judiciary com. 1989—, internat. law and practice sect., com. internat. dispute resolution 1987—) Assn. of Bar of City of N.Y. (products liability com. 1983-86. fed. legis. com. 1990-93, state cts. of superior jurisdiction 1993-96, coun. jud. adminstrn. 1996-99, fed. judiciary 2000—), N.Y. Athletic Club. Republican. Congregationalist. General civil litigation, Private international, Product liability. Home: 205 E 69th St Apt 6C New York NY 10021-5431 also: 74 Pascal Ave Rockport ME 04856-5919 Office: Torys LLP 237 Park Ave Fl 19 New York NY 10017-3161 E-mail: cdorkey@torys.com.

DORNAN, DONALD C., JR., lawyer; b. Columbus, Miss., Oct. 26, 1952; s. Donald C. and Virginia (Shelley) D.; children: Gloria Diana, Donald Patrick. BA, Miss. State U., 1974; JD, U. Miss., 1976. Bar: Miss. 1977, U.S. Dist. Ct. (no. and so. dists.) Miss. 1977, U.S. Ct. Appeals (5th and 11th cirs.) 1981, cert. civil trial advocate Nat. Bd. of Trial Advocacy. Atty. Page, Mannino & Peresich, Biloxi, Miss., 1976-80; ptnr. Dornan Law Office, Biloxi, 1980-87; sole practice Biloxi, 1987—; asst. city prosecutor City of Biloxi, 1977-80, city judge pro tem, 1982—; bd. dirs. Gulf Law Inst., 1981—. Mem. ABA, Fed. Bar Assn., Miss. Bar Assn. (pres. elect 2001, pres. 2002-03), Harrison County Bar Assn., Harrison County Young Lawyers (treas. 1980-81, v.p. 1981-82, pres. 1982-83), Miss. Trial Lawyers Assn., Assn. Trial Lawyers Am., Southeastern Admiralty Law Inst., Phi Delta Phi. Methodist. Alternative dispute resolution, Insurance, Personal injury (including property damage). Office: PO Box 154 771 Water St Biloxi MS 39530-4219

DORNBUSCH, ARTHUR A., II, lawyer; b. Peru, Ill., Nov. 8, 1943; s. Arthur A. Sr. and Genevieve C. (Knudtson) D.; children: Kimberly, Brendan, Courtney, Eric; m. Jacqueline Bahrs Montanus, Feb. 10, 1996. BA, Yale U., 1966; LLB, U. Pa., 1969. Bar: N.Y. 1970, U.S. Ct. Appeals. (2d cir.) 1971, U.S. Dist. Ct. (so. and ea. dists.) N.Y. 1971. Assoc. Dewey, Ballantine, Bushby, Palmer & Wood, N.Y.C., 1969-72; asst. gen. counsel Boise Cascade Corp., N.Y.C., 1972-75; asst. gen counsel Teleprompter Corp., N.Y.C., 1975-76; asst. gen. counsel Engelhard Industries div. Engelhard Minerals and Chem. Corp., Edison, N.J., 1976-80; v.p., gen. counsel minerals and chems. divsn. Engelhard Corp., Edison, 1980—84, v.p., gen. counsel, sec. Iselin, NJ, 1984—. Mem. Pelham (N.Y.) Union Free Sch. Bd., 1979-82. Mem. ABA, N.Y. State Bar Assn., Assn. Bar City N.Y., Am. Corp. Counsel Assn., Am. Intellectual Property Law Assn., Am. Soc. Corp. Secs., Mfrs. Alliance for Productivity and Innovation. Antitrust, Corporate, general, Patent. Office: Engelhard Corp PO Box 770 101 Wood Ave S Iselin NJ 08830-0770 E-mail: arthur.dornbusch@engelhard.com.

DORNE, DAVID J. lawyer; b. Chgo., Dec. 9, 1946; BS magna cum laude, U. Ill., 1969; MSc, London Sch. Econs., 1970; JD cum laude, Boston U., 1973. Bar: N.Y. 1973, U.S. Ct. Appeals (2d cir.) 1973, U.S. Tax Ct. 1973, U.S. Dist. Ct. (so. dist.) N.Y. 1975, Calif. 1978. Mem. Seltzer Caplan McMahon Vitek P.C., San Diego. Mem. City of San Diego Charter Rev. Commn., 1989—. Mem. ABA (taxation sect., corp., banking and bus. law sect.), State Bar Calif. (taxation sect., real property law sect., chmn. personal income tax subcom. 1982-84), San Diego County Bar Assn., Assn. of Bar of City of N.Y. (taxation sect.), Beta Gamma Sigma. Corporate, general, Property, real (including real estate development, water), Taxation, general. Office: Seltzer Caplan McMahon Vitek PC 2100 Symphony Tower 750 B St San Diego CA 92101-8114

DORNETTE, W(ILLIAM) STUART, lawyer, educator; b. Washington, Mar. 2, 1951; s. William Henry Lueders and Frances Roberta (Hester) D.; m. Martha Louise Mehl, Nov. 19, 1983; children: Marjorie Frances, Anna Christine, David Paul. AB, Williams Coll., 1972; JD, U. Va., 1975. Bar: Va. 1975, Ohio 1975, U.S. Dist. Ct. (so. dist.) Ohio 1975, D.C. 1976, U.S. Ct. Appeals (6th cir.) 1977, U.S. Supreme Ct. 1980. Assoc. Taft, Stettinius & Hollister, Cin., 1975-83, ptnr., 1983—. Instr. law U. Cin., 1980-87, adj. prof., 1988-91. Co-author: Federal Judiciary Almanac, 1984-87. Mem. Ohio Bd. Bar Examiners, 1991-93, Hamilton County Rep. Exec. Com., 1982—; bd. dirs. Zool. Soc. Cin., 1983-94, Cin. Parks Found., 1995—; bd. visitors U. Cin. Law Sch., 2002—. Mem. FBA, Ohio State Bar Assn., Cin. Bar Assn., Am. Phys. Soc. Methodist. Federal civil litigation, State civil litigation, Sports. Home: 329 Bishopsbridge Dr Cincinnati OH 45255-3948 Office: 1800 US Bank Tower 425 Walnut St Cincinnati OH 45202-3923 E-mail: dornette@taftlaw.com.

DOROCKE, LAWRENCE FRANCIS, lawyer; b. Chgo., Oct. 4, 1946; s. Walter P. and Effie M. (Gillis) D.; m. Diane L. Roberts, June 22, 1968; children: Todd D., Rob L., Jill A. BS in Econs., Purdue U., 1968, MS in Indsl. Relations, 1970; JD magna cum laude, Ind. U., 1973. Bar: Ind. 1973, U.S. Dist. Ct. (so. dist.) Ind. 1973, Iowa 1974, U.S. Ct. Appeals (7th cir.). Asst. mgr. personnel Comml. Solvents Corp., Terre Haute, Ind., 1970-71; law clk. to chief justice U.S. Dist. Ct. (so. dist.) Iowa, Des Moines, 1973-75; ptnr. Dann, Pecar, Newman & Kleiman P.C., Indpls., 1975—. Mem. ABA, Ind. Bar Assn., Indpls. Bar Assn. Roman Catholic. Corporate, general, Landlord-tenant, Property, real (including real estate development, water). Office: Dann Pecar Newman & Kleiman PO Box 82008 Indianapolis IN 46282-2008 E-mail: ldorocke@dannpecar.com.

DORR, ROBERT CHARLES, lawyer; b. Denver, Jan. 7, 1946; s. Owen and Rose Esther (Tudek) D.; m. Sandra Leah Gehlsen, Feb. 26, 1972; children: Bryan, Aric. BSEE, Milw. Sch. Engring., 1968; MSEE, Northwestern U., 1970; JD, U. Denver, 1975. Bar: Colo. 1975, U.S. Dist. Ct. Colo. 1975, U.S. Patent Office 1975. Mem. tech. staff Bell Labs, Naperville, Ill., 1968-72, mem. patent staff Denver, 1975-76; ptnr. Dorr, Carson, Sloan & Birney, P.C., Denver, 1976-86, sr. ptnr., 1986—. Ptnr. Internat. Practicum Inst., Denver, 1979—; seminar speaker various profl. orgns. Co-author: Protecting Trade Secrets, Patents and Copyrights, 1995, 3d edit., 2003; contbr. articles to profl. jours. Mem. IEEE, AAAS, Sigma Xi. Roman Catholic. Intellectual property, Patent, Trademark and copyright. Home: 6101 Muddy Creek Rd Pueblo CO 81004-9747 Office: Dorr Carson Sloan & Birney PC 3010 E 6th Ave Denver CO 80206-4328 E-mail: bobdorr@patnet.com.

DORRIER, LINDSAY GORDON, JR., lawyer; b. Scottsville, Va., Aug. 27, 1943; s. Lindsay Gordon and Anne Shirley (Bruce) D.; m. Jane Ikenberry, Feb. 14, 1982; children: Margaret Anne, Lindsay Gordon III. BA, Trinity Coll., 1966; JD, U. Va., 1972; MBA, James Madison U., 1987; LLM, U. Va., 1989. Bar: Va. 1972, U.S. Dist. Ct. (we. dist.) Va. 1972. Law clk. to presiding judge U.S. Dist. Ct. (we. dist.) Va., Roanoke, 1972-73; assoc. Paxson, Smith, Boyd, Gilliam & Gouldman, Charlottesville, Va., 1973-76; sole practice Charlottesville, 1976-80; commonwealth atty. Albemarle County, Charlottesville, 1980-90; dir. Va. Dept. Criminal Justice Svcs., Richmond, 1990-94; pvt. practice Scottsville, Va., 1994—2003; ptnr. Dorrier, Warthen and Clementson, Scottsville, 2003—. Pres. Charlottesville-Albemarle Mental Health Assn., 1974-75, bd. dirs., 1973-76; pres. Jefferson Area Community Corrections Resources Bd., 1981-83, bd. dirs., 1981-90; mem. Albemarle County Bd. Suprs., 1976-80. 2000-, chmn. 2003; Dem. candidate for Congress from 7th dist. Va., 1982; bd. dirs. Charlottesville-Albemarle United Way, 1983-90, Tandem Sch., 1987-91, James River Alcohol Safety Action Program, 1988-90; mem. Va. Dem. Leadership Com., 1989-93; co-chair Richmond One-to-One Partnership, 1992-94. Lt. col. JAGC, USAR, 1966-95. Mem. Nat. Criminal Justice Assn. (bd. dirs. 1990-94), Va. Bar Assn., Va. Assn. Local Exec. Constl. Officers (bd. dirs. 1982-86, pres. 1986-87), Va. Assn. Comml. Attys. (bd. dirs. 1984-90), Albemarle Hist. Soc. (pres. 1976-78), Fraternal Order Polic, Am. Legion. Criminal, Probate (including wills, trusts).

DORSEN, NORMAN, lawyer, educator; b. N.Y.C., Sept. 4, 1930; s. Arthur and Tanya (Stone) D.; m. Harriette Koffler, Nov. 25, 1965; children: Jennifer, Caroline Gail, Anne. BA, Columbia U., 1950; LLB magna cum laude, Harvard U., 1953; postgrad., London Sch. Econs., 1955-56; LLD (hon.), Ripon Coll., 1981, John Jay Coll. Criminal Justice, 1992. Bar: D.C. 1953, N.Y. 1954. Law clk. to chief judge Calvert Magruder U.S. Ct. Appeals, Boston, 1956-57; law clk. to Justice John Marshall Harlan U.S. Supreme Ct., Washington, 1957-58; assoc. Dewey, Ballantine, Bushby, Palmer & Wood, N.Y.C., 1958-60; prof. law NYU Sch. Law, N.Y.C., 1961-81, Stokes prof., 1981—, dir. Hays civil liberties program, 1961—, dir. global law sch. program, 1994-96, chmn., 1996—2002; counselor to pres. NYU, 2002—. Vis. prof. law London Sch. Econs., 1968, U. Calif., Berkeley, 1974-75, Harvard U., 1980, 83, 84; cons. U.S. Commn. on Violence, 1968-69, Random House, 1969-73, B.B.C., 1969-73, U.S. Commn. on Social Security, 1979-80, Native Am. Rights Fund, 1978-89; exec. dir. spl. com. on courtroom conduct Assn. Bar N.Y.C., 1970-73; chmn. Com. for Pub. Justice, 1972-74; vice chmn. HEW sec.'s rev. panel on new drug regulation, 1975-76, chmn., 1976-77; mem. N.Y.C. Commn. on Status of Women, 1978-80; chmn. Sec. of Treasury's Citizen Rev. Panel on Good O' Boy Round-up, 1995-96. Author (with others): Political and Civil Rights in U.S., 3rd edit., 1967, Political and Civil Rights in U.S., 4th edit., Vol. I, 1976, Political and Civil Rights in U.S., 4th edit., Vol. II, 1979, Frontiers of Civil Liberties, 1968, Discrimination and Civil Rights, 1969, Comparative Constitution, 2003; author: (with L. Friedman) Disorder in the Court, 1973; author: (with S. Gillers) Regulation of Lawyers, 1985, Regulation of Lawyers, 2d edit., 1989; editor: The Rights of Americans, 1971; editor: (with S. Gillers) None of Your Business, 1974; editor: Our Endangered Rights, 1984, The Evolving Constitution, 1987; editor: (with others) Human Rights in Northern Ireland, 1991, The Unpredictable Constitution, 2001, with P. Gifford: Democracy and the Rule of Law, 2001; ; editor: (with others) Constitutionalism Cases and Materials, 2003; editl. dir. Internat. Jour. Constl. Law, 2002—. 1st lt. JAGC, U.S. Army, 1953-55. Recipient medal French Minister of Justice, 1983, Eleanor Roosevelt Human Rights award 2000; Fulbright Disting. Prof., Argentina, 1987, 88. Fellow Am. Acad. Arts and Scis.; mem. ABA (chmn. com. free speech and press 1968-70), ACLU (gen. counsel 1969-76, pres. 1976-91), Am. Law Inst., Coun. on Fgn. Rels., Lawyers Com. Human Rights (chmn. bd. dirs. 1995-2000), Lawyer Com. Civil Rights, Internat. Assn. Constnl. Law (exec. com.), U.S. Assn. Constnl. Law (pres. 1996—), Soc. Am. Law Tchrs. (pres. 1972-74, Tchg. award 1997), Thomas Jefferson Ctr. for Free Expression (trustee). Home: 146 Central Park W New York NY 10023-2005 Office: NYU Sch Law 40 Washington Sq S New York NY 10012-1005 E-mail: norman.dorsen@nyu.edu.

DORSETT, JAMES K., III, lawyer; b. Raleigh, N.C., Nov. 10, 1951; BA, Davidson Coll., 1974; JD, Wake Forest U., 1977. Bar: N.C. 1977. Atty. Smith, Anderson, Blount, Dorsett, Mitchell & Jernigan, LLP, Raleigh, NC. Fellow: Internat. Soc. Barristers (bd. govs., chair N.C. fellowship); mem.: ABA, Wake County Bar Assn. (bd. dirs. 1982—84, 1988—90, vol. lawyers program 1990—93), Am. Bd. Trial Advs., N.C. Assn. Def. Attys., Am. Counsel Assn. (bd. govs.), N.C. State Bar (councilor 1992—, pres. 2002—, chmn. grievance com.), N.C. Bar Assn., Phi Delta Phi. Federal civil litigation, State civil litigation, Product liability. Office: Smith Anderson Blount Dorsett et al PO Box 2611 2500 First Union Capitol Ctr Raleigh NC 27602-2611*

DORSEY, MARY ELIZABETH, lawyer; b. Florissant, Mo., July 4, 1962; d. Richard Peter Jr. and Dolores Irene (McNamara) D. BA in Acctg., Benedictine Coll., 1984; JD, St. Louis U., 1987. Bar: Mo. 1989, U.S. Dist. Ct. (we. dist.) Mo. 1989, U.S. Dist. Ct. (ea. dist.) Mo. 1990, U.S. Supreme Ct. 1994, U.S. Ct. Appeals (8th cir.) 1997. Rschr. Ind. Legal Rsch., Florissant, 1987-89; atty. assoc. Deeba Sauter Herd, St. Louis, 1989-98; ptnr. Ahlheim & Dorsey, LLC, St. Charles, 1998—. Bd. dirs. North County, Inc. Merit badge counselor St. Louis Area coun. Boy Scouts Am., 1988—, mem. com. Troop 748, mem. Order of the Arrow, 1992, Brotherhood, 1994; corr. sec. Florissant Twp. Open Dem. Club, 1989-91, sgt. at arms, 1991-2000; treas. Friends of Rick Dorsey, St. Louis, 1988, 90, 92, 96; mem. Dem. Com., Florissant Twp., 1996—. Mem.: ATLA, ABA, St. Charles County Bar Assn., Bar Assn. Met. St. Louis (lectr. law related edn. com. 1988—96), Mo. Assn. Trial Attys., Mo. Jaycees (state legal counsel 1997—99, dist. dir. 1998—99, region dir. 2000, membership v.p. 2001, state legal counsel 2002—03), Florissant Valley Jaycees (dir. 1993—94, treas. 1994—95, state dir. 1995—97, v.p. 1997—98), U.S.Jaycees (regional coord. 2002, Nat. Resource Team 2003). Democrat. Roman Catholic. Avocations: golf, camping, theatre. General civil litigation, Corporate, general, Family and matrimonial. Office: Ahlheim & Dorsey LLC 2209 1st Capitol Dr Saint Charles MO 63301-5809 E-mail: med@ahlheimdorsey.com.

DORSEY, PETER COLLINS, federal judge; b. New London, Conn., Mar. 24, 1931; s. Thomas F., Jr. and Helen Mary (Collins) D.; m. Cornelia McEwen, June 26, 1954; children: Karen G., Peter C., Jennifer S., Christopher M. BA, Yale U., 1953; JD, Harvard U., 1959. Ptnr. Flanagan, Dorsey & Flanagan, New Haven, 1963-74; U.S. atty. Dept. Justice, New Haven, 1974-77; ptnr. Flanagan, Dorsey & Mulvey, New Haven, 1977-83; judge U.S. Dist. Ct. Conn., New Haven, 1983-99, chief judge, 1994-98, now sr. judge. Mem. Jud. Conf. of U.S. Cts., 1995-98; adj. prof. Quinnipiac Coll. Sch. Law, 1999—. Councilman Town of Hamden, Conn., 1961-69; town atty., 1973-74; commr. Bd. of Police, Hamden, 1977-81. Served to lt. comdr., USNR, 1953-56 Fellow Am. Coll. Trial Lawyers; mem. ABA (mem. house of dels. 1974-78), Conn. Bar Assn. (bd. govs. 1968-70, 74-78, pres. 1978), Am. Coll. Trial Lawyers, Conn. Def. Lawyers Assn. (pres. 1974), Am. Inns of Ct. Hartford (pres. 1991-93). Roman Catholic. Office: US Dist Ct 141 Church St New Haven CT 06510-2030

DORSI, STEPHEN NATHAN, b. Bklyn., June 2, 1947; s. Stephen Nathan and Fannie (Christopher) D.; m. Phyllis Elizabeth Blastervold, Aug. 12, 1976; 1 child, Michael. AA, Pasadena City Coll., 1968; BA, Calif. State U., L.A., 1970; JD, Golden Gate U., 1973. Bar: Calif. 1973, U.S. Dist. Ct. (no. dist.) Calif. 1973, U.S. Dist. Ct. (cen. dist.) Calif. 1974, U.S. Ct. Appeals (9th cir.) 1973. Sole practitioner, San Luis Obispo, Calif., 1974—. Bd. dirs. Sta. KCBX Pub. Radio, San Luis Obispo. Author: Horse Trader's Guide, 1987. Bd. bldg. trustee San Luis Obispo Art Ctr., 1976—; bd. dirs. KCBXNET (formerly SLONET), non-profit ISP, 1997. Avocations: mock trial coach, speech and debate judge. Estate planning, Property, real (including real estate development, water), Trademark and copyright. Home: PO Box 1253 San Luis Obispo CA 93406-1253 Office: Ste 6 1026 Chorro St San Luis Obispo CA 93401-3230 E-mail: trusts@DorsiLaw.com., trademark@DorsiLaw.com., RealProperty@DorsiLaw.com.

DORWART, DONALD BRUCE, lawyer; b. Zanesville, Ohio, Dec. 12, 1949; s. Walter G. and Katherine (Kachmar) D.; children: Claire Lauren, Hillary Beth. BA, Vanderbilt U., 1971; JD, Washington U., St. Louis, 1974. Bar: Mo. 1974, U.S. Dist. Ct. (ea. dist.) Mo. 1974. Assoc. Thompson Coburn LLP, St. Louis, 1974-79, ptnr., 1980—; dir. New Energy Corp. Ind., 1992-95. Contbr. articles to profl. jours. Mem.: ABA, FOCUS St. Louis (mem. selection com. 1990—91, mem. fin. com. 1990—2002, mem. cmty. policy com. 2000—, bd. dirs. 2000—, treas. 2001—02, pres. 2002—), Bar Assn. Met. St. Louis (chair securities regulation com. 1979), Maritime Law Assn. U.S. (mem. maritime fin. com. 1980—, proctor), Noonday Club. Admiralty, Corporate, general, Mergers and acquisitions. Office: Thompson Coburn LLP One US Bank Plz Ste 3300 Saint Louis MO 63101-1643 E-mail: ddorwart@thompsoncoburn.com.

DOSA, ANDREW ALEXANDER, lawyer; b. Aberdeen, Md., July 27, 1958; s. Thomas Dosa and Patricia G. Ketcham; m. Lisa Dosa; children: Joshua, Rebekah. AB, Univ. Calif., 1980; JD, Univ. San Francisco, 1983. Lawyer Law Offices of Andrew Dosa, Alameda, Calif., 1989—. Adj. faculty Nat. Hispanic U., Oakland, 1988-89, instr. paralegal program Calif. State U., Hayward, 1988-89. Chair Alamada County Adv. Bd. on Alcohol Problems, Oakland, 1986-92; judge pro term Alameda Judical Mcpl. Ct., 1993—, Fremont Newark Union City Jud. Dist. Mcpl. Ct., 1989-96. Mem.: Alameda County Bar Assn., Christian Legal Soc., Consumer Attys. Calif., Calif. State Bar Assn., Phi Delta Phi. Protestant. General civil litigation, Estate planning, Personal injury (including property damage). Office: 1516 Oak St Ste 310 Alameda CA 94501-2958

DOSS, THERESA, judge; b. Murtlewood, Ala., Oct. 8, 1939; d. Eddie Edison and Ida (Richards) Doss; m. James T. Wahls, Aug. 15, 1981; 1 child, James Christopher Doss Wahls. AB, Ohio U., 1961; JD, Ohio State U., 1964; MA, Wayne State U., 2000. Tchr. Cleve. Pub. Schs., 1961; law libr. State Law Libr., Lansing, Mich., 1964—65; program developer Archdiocesan Opportunity Org., Detroit, 1965—66; asst. atty. gen. Mich. Atty. Gen., 1966—76; judge Common Pleas Ct., 1976—81, 36th Dist. Ct., 1981—. Mem. Mich. Jud. Tenure Commn., Detroit, 1995—2001. Bd. dirs. Mich. Met. Girl Scouts Coun., Detroit, 1979—84, Neighborhood Svc. Orgn., 1971—87. Mem.: ABA, Wolverine Bar Assn. (sec., bd. dirs.), Detroit Bar Assn. (com. mem.), Nat. Bar Assn. (bd. dirs.), Women Lawyers Assn. Mich. (pres. 1973), Mich. Dist. Judges Assn. (pres. 1991), State Bar Mich. Office: 36th Dist Ct 421 Madison Detroit MI 48226

DOST, MARK W. lawyer; b. Attleboro, Mass., May 22, 1955; s. Raymond and A. Louise (Fraser) D.; m. Karen M. Sullivan, Aug. 1976; children: Christopher, Stephen, Gregory, Isaac. AB summa cum laude, U. Mass., 1978; JD cum laude, Boston Coll., 1981. Bar: Conn. 1981, U.S. Dist. Ct. Conn. 1986, U.S. Tax Ct. 1985. Atty. Gager & Henry, Waterbury, Conn., 1981-95; ptnr. Tinley, Nastri, Renehan & Dost, Waterbury, 1995—. Author: (with John V. Galiette) Planning for Retirement Benefit Distributions, 1995, 2d revised edit., 1999. Fellow Am. Coll. Trust and Estate Counsel; mem. ABA, Conn. Bar Assn. (exec. com., elder law sect. 1991—, exec. com., estates and probate sect. 1991—, chair elder law sect. 1994-96, chair publs. com. 1997-2000), Nat. Acad. Elder Law Attys. Estate planning, Probate (including wills, trusts), Estate taxation. Office: Tinley Nastri Renehan Dost 60 N Main St Waterbury CT 06702-1403

DOSTART, PAUL JOSEPH, lawyer, investor and director; b. Iowa, Nov. 12, 1951; s. Leonard A. and Lois M. Dostart; m. Joyce A. Dostart; children: Zachariah Paul, Samuel Paul. BS, Iowa State U., 1973; JD, U. Houston, 1977; LLM in Taxation, NYU, 1978. Bar: Tex, 1977, Calif. 1978; CPA, Ill. Mng. ptr. Dostart, Clapp & Coveney LLP. Adj. prof. U. San Diego, 1986—90; bd. dirs. Q3DM Inc. Editor Houston Law Rev. Founder U. Houston Tax Law Soc.; bd. dirs. Neuroscis. Rsch. Found. Lasker scholar, NYU, Nat. Merit scholar. Fellow Am. Bar Found. (life), Am. Coll. Tax Counsel; mem. ABA (chmn. various subcoms. sect. taxation 1982—, exempt orgns. com. 1977—), Calif. Bar Assn. (tax and bus. sects.), San Diego County Bar Assn. (chmn. tax sect. 1989), San Diego Tax Practitioners Group, Am. Electronics Assn. (San Diego coun. exec. com. 1993-95), World Trade Assn. (bd. dirs.). Presbyterian. Corporate, general, Non-profit and tax-exempt organizations, Taxation, general. Office: Dostart Clapp & Coveney LLP Ste 970 4370 La Jolla Village Dr San Diego CA 92122-1249 E-mail: pdostart@sdlaw.com.

DOTSON, DONALD L. lawyer; b. Rutherford County, N.C., Oct. 8, 1938; s. Herman A. and Lottie E. (Hardin) D. AB, U. N.C., 1960; JD, Wake Forest U., 1968. Bar: N.C., Pa., D.C., U.S. Supreme Ct. Atty. NLRB, 1968-73, chmn., 1983-87; labor counsel Westinghouse Electric Corp., 1973-75; labor atty. Western Electric Co., 1975-76; chief labor counsel Wheeling-Pitts. Steel Corp., 1976-81; asst. sec. labor, 1981-83, 2001—; pvt. practice law, 1987-91; sr. v.p. Beverly Enterprises, 1991—2001; pvt. practice, 2001—. Served with USN, 1960-65. Republican. Episcopalian. Home: RD Louisa VA Office: 6914 W Grace St Richmond VA 23226

DOTTEN, MICHAEL CHESTER, lawyer; b. Marathon, Ont., Can., Feb. 23, 1952; came to U.S., 1957; s. William James and Ona Adelaide (Sheppard) D.; m. Kathleen Curtis, Aug. 17, 1974 (div. July 1991); children: Matthew Curtis, Tyler Ryan; m. Cheryl Calvin, Apr. 16, 1994. BS in Polit. Sci., U. Oreg., 1974, JD, 1977. Bar: Idaho 1977, Oreg. 1978, U.S. Dist. Ct. Idaho 1977, U.S. Dist. Ct. Oreg. 1978, U.S. Ct. Appeals (9th cir.), U.S. Ct. Appeals (D.C. cir.) 1987, U.S. Ct. Claims 1986, U.S. Supreme Ct. 1996. Staff asst. to Senator Bob Packwood, U.S. Senate, Washington, 1973-74; asst. atty. gen. State of Idaho, Boise, Idaho, 1977-78; chief rate counsel Bonneville Power Adminstrn., Portland, Oreg., 1978-83; spl. counsel Heller, Ehrman, White & McAuliffe, Portland, 1983-84, ptnr., 1985-98, 99—; gen. counsel PG&E Gas Transmission, N.W. Corp., Portland, 1998-99; co-chair Energy Nat. Practice Group, 2003—. Utility com. mem. Ctr. for Pub. Resources, N.Y.C., 1992—. Coun. Emanual Hosp. Assocs., Portland, 1988-92; bd. dirs. William Temple House, 1995-99, chmn. devel. com., 1996-98, v.p., 1997-98, pres., 1998-99; active Portland Interneighborhood Trans. Rev. Commn., 1986-88; vestryman Christ Episcopal Ch., Lake Oswego, Oreg., 1999-2003, sr. warden, 2001-03. Hunter Leadership scholar U. Oreg., 1973, Oreg. scholar, 1970. Mem. ABA (chmn. electric power com. sect. natural resources 1985-88, coun. liaison energy com. 1990-93, coordinating group on energy law 1992-96), Fed. Bar Assn. (pres. Oreg. chpt. 1989-90, Chpt. Activity award 1990, Pres. award 1988-89), Oreg. State Bar (chmn. dispute resolution com. 1986-87), U. Oreg. Law Sch. Alumni Assn. (pres. 1989-92), Arlington Club, Multnomah Athletic Club. Democrat. Episcopalian. Avocations: snow skiing, golf, hiking, travel, racquetball. Administrative and regulatory, FERC practice, Utilities, public. Office: Heller Ehrman White & McAuliffe 200 SW Market St Ste 1750 Portland OR 97201-5722

DOTY, DAVID SINGLETON, federal judge; b. Anoka, Minn., June 30, 1929; BA, JD, U. Minn., 1961; LLD (hon.) , William Mitchell Coll. Law. Bar: Minn. 1961, U.S. Ct. Appeals (8th and 9th cirs.) 1976, U.S. Supreme Ct. 1982. V.p., dir. Popham, Haik, Schnobrich, Kaufman & Doty, Mpls., 1962-87, pres., 1977-79; instr. William Mitchell Coll. Law, Mpls., 1963-64; judge U.S. Dist. Ct. for Minn., Mpls., 1987—. Mem. Adv. Com. on Civil Rules, 1992-98, Adv. Com. on Evidence Rules, 1994-98; trustee Mpls. Libr. Bd., 1969-79, Mpls. Found., 1976-83. Fellow ABA Found.; mem. ABA, Minn. Bar Assn. (gov. 1976-87, sec. 1980-83, pres. 1984-85), Hennepin County Bar Assn. (pres. 1975-76), Am. Judicature Soc., Am. Law Inst. Home: 23 Greenway Gables Minneapolis MN 55403-2145 Office: US Dist Ct 14 W US Courthouse 300 S 4th St Minneapolis MN 55415-1320 E-mail: dsdoty@mnd.uscourts.gov.

DOTY, ROBERT WALTER, lawyer; b. Aliquippa, Pa., Sept. 19, 1942; s. David Lucien and Iona (Fox) D.; m. Joyce Marie Shaffalo, Sept. 10, 1961; children: Genie, Merrie Beth. BA cum laude, Wheaton Coll., 1963; JD, Vanderbilt U., 1966. Bar: Pa. 1966, U.S. Supreme Ct. 1982. Assoc. Eckert Seamans Cherin & Mellot, Pitts., 1966-74, ptnr., 1975-91; dir. Cohen & Grigsby, P.C., Pitts., 1991—. Solicitor Crescent Township, Allegheny County, Pa., 1969—; arbitrator Am. Arbitration Assn., nat. panel, 1978—, speaker at seminars; lectr. Westinghouse Internat. Sch. Environ. Mgmt., Ft. Collins, Colo., 1980-82. Mem. nat. com. on wills and trusts centennial campaign Vanderbilt U., 1977-81. Recipient Archie B. Martin Meml. scholarship medal Vanderbilt U., 1964, Robert F. Jackson Meml. scholarship prize, 1965, Founder's medal, 1966; 3 Am. Jurisprudence awards in contracts, civil procedure and criminal law The Lawyers Co-operative Pub. Co., Rochester, N.Y., 1964, 65; Mark Woodworth Walton scholar Vanderbilt U., 1965. Mem. Pa. Bar Assn., Allegheny County Bar Assn. (governing coun. civil litigation sect.), Wheaton Club (past pres.), Fox Chapel Racquet Club, Breckenridge Golf & Tennis Club, Vines Country Club, Racquet Club

Memphis, Order of Coif, Phi Kappa Delta, Phi Alpha Delta. Avocations: swimming, tennis. General civil litigation, Construction, Libel. Office: 11 Stanwix St 15th Floor Pittsburgh PA 15222

DOUAIHY, TONI PATRICIA, lawyer; b. St. Louis, Jan. 27, 1967; d. Lynn Louis and Mary Gail Surrett; m. Thomas Zakhia Douaihy, Dec. 3, 1987; children: Salim Zakhia, Noah Zakhia. BA in History, BA in Spanish, U. Mo., 1991; JD, Washington U., St. Louis, 1994. Bar: Mo. 1994, Ill. 1995. Counsel The May Dept. Stores Co., St. Louis, 1993—. Vol. lawyer Legal Svcs. Eastern Mo., St. Louis, 1994—; mem. Compton Heights Assn., St. Louis, 1996—. Mem. Bar Assn. Metro. St. Louis. Republican. Avocations: reading, gourmet cooking, gardening. Federal civil litigation, State civil litigation, Labor (including EEOC, Fair Labor Standards Act, labor-management relations, NLRB, OSHA). Office: The May Dept Stores Co 611 Olive St Ste 1750 Saint Louis MO 63101-1721 E-mail: toni-douaihy@may-co.com.

DOUB, WILLIAM OFFUTT, lawyer; b. Cumberland, Md., Sept. 3, 1931; s. Albert A. and Fannabelle (Offutt) D.; m. Mary Graham Boggs, Sept. 12, 1959; children: Joseph Peyton, Albert A., II. AB, Washington and Jefferson Coll., 1953; LLB, U. Md., 1956. Bar: Md. 1956, D.C. 1974. With law dept. B. & O. R.R., 1955-57; assoc. Bartlett Poe & Claggett, Balt., 1957-61; ptnr. Niles Barton & Wilmer, Balt., 1961-71; commr. AEC, 1971-74; ptnr. LeBoeuf, Lamb, Leiby & MacRae, Washington, 1974-77, Doub, Muntzing and Glasgow, Washington, 1977-91, Newman & Holtzinger, P.C., Washington, 1991-94, Morgan Lewis & Bockius, Washington, 1995-2000. Chmn. Minimum Wage Commn., Balt., 1964-66; peoples' counsel Md. Pub. Service Commn., 1967-68, chmn., 1968-71; vice chmn. Washington Met. Area Transit Commn., 1968-71; mem. President's Air Quality Adv. Bd., 1970-71; mem. exec. adv. com. FPC, 1969-71, Nat. Gas Survey, 1975-78; pres. Great Lakes Conf. Pub. Utility Commrs., 1971; mem. nat. adv. bd. Am. Nat. Standards Inst., 1975-80; mem. Md. Adv. Com. Retardation, 1969-71 Mem. Adminstrv. Conf., U.S., 1973-75; chmn. U.S. Energy Assn., Inc., World Energy Conf., 1978-80, U.S. del., 1974, 77, 80, 83, 86, 89, 92, 95, 98; vice chmn. World Energy Conf., 1986-88, hon. vice chmn., 1988—; mem. adv. groups Nat. Acad. Pub. Adminstrn., NSF; presdl. appointee as rep. to So. States Energy Bd., 1983-90; bd. govs. Mid. East Inst. of U.S., 1982-86, 88-94, 95-2000; mem. exec. com. Thomas Alva Edison Found., 1983-90, 85-90; presdl. appointee 33d Ann. Conf. of Internat. Atomic Energy Agy., 1989. Recipient Nat. Energy award U.S. Energy Assn., 1998. Mem. Met. Club. Nuclear power, Legislative, Utilities, public. Home (Summer): 512 Neapolitan Lane Naples FL 34103 E-mail: fudoub@aol.com.

DOUBEK, JOHN C. lawyer, educator; b. St. Louis, Apr. 30, 1951; s. John C. and Mary E. Doubek; m. John N. Doubek, Mar. 11, 1954; children: Andrew, Jake, Anna. BA in Polit. Sci., Carroll Coll., 1973; JD, U. Mont., 1976. Bar: Mont. 1976, U.S. Ct. Appeals (9th cir.) 1976. Trial atty. Mont. Consumer Counsel, Helena, 1976—78; ptnr. Small Hutch Doubke & Pyter, Helena, 1978—. Sec. Mont. Irrigators, 1981—93; assoc. prof. Carroll Coll., Helena, 1984—. Mem.: ATLA, Mont. Trial Attys. Achievements include over 12 cases with verdicts or settlements in excess of $1 million. Personal injury (including property damage), Product liability. Home: 640 S Harris Helena MT 59601 Office: Small Hutch Doubek & Pyter 307 N Jackson Helena MT 59601 Fax: 406-442-7839. E-mail: jdoubek@uswest.net.

DOUCETTE, JODI LEAZOTT, lawyer; b. Eau Claire, Wis., June 5, 1962; d. Lawrence George and Sylvia Elaine Leazott; m. Dennis Joseph Doucette, March 26, 1988; children: Lauren E., Chanelle N., Lucas L. Cert. interpreter, U. Sampere, Madrid, 1983; BA, Pepperdine U., 1984; postgrad., Oxford U., 1985; JD, U. San Diego, 1987. Bar: Calif., U.S. Dist. Ct. (so. dist.) Calif. Dep. county counsel County San Diego, 1988-93; dep. city atty. City of Oceanside (Calif.), 1993—. Author: (model ordinance) League of California Cities Sign Ordinance, 1999; contbr. to handbook. Big sister Vol. in Parole, San Diego, 1988—93; chair, mem. Commn. Children and Youth, San Diego County, 1989—93; bd. dirs., treas. Hanna Fenichel Pre-Sch., 1994—; bd. mem., com. chair U. San Diego Law Sch., 1995—99; bd. dirs., v.p., sec. Lawyers Club, 1994—97; classroom vol. Del Mar (Calif.) Heights Elem. Sch., 1995—; Sunday sch. tchr. St. James Ch., Solana Beach, Calif., 1995—97; mem. bd. dirs., chmn. project rev. Torrey Pines Planning, 2001—. Mem. Bar Assn. No. San Diego (bd. dirs., com. chair, v.p., sec.). Roman Catholic. Avocations: running, skiing, reading, crafts. Office: City Attys Office 300 N Coast Hwy Oceanside CA 92054-2824

DOUCHKESS, GEORGE, lawyer; b. N.Y.C., Apr. 19, 1911; s. Frank A. and Dorothy (Grunberg) D.; m. Sonia Sloshay; children: Donald, Barbara. BBA in Acctg., CCNY, 1937; JD, Bklyn. Law Sch., 1939. Bar: N.Y. 1940, U.S. Dist. Ct. (ea. and so. dists.) N.Y. 1951, U.S. Supreme Ct. 1991. Claim supr. Aetna Casualty and Surety Co., N.Y.C., 1940-44; compensation hearing atty. Liberty Mut. Ins. Co., N.Y.C., 1944-47; compensation atty. Preferred Accident and Ins. Co., N.Y.C., 1947-51; U.S. supt. divsn. compensation claims, compensation atty. Gen. Fire and Casualty Co., N.Y.C., 1951-65; compensation atty. Zurich Am. Ins. Co., N.Y.C., 1965-96. Mem. Torch and Scroll. Republican. Administrative and regulatory, Workers' compensation. Home: 715 Park Ave New York NY 10021-5047

DOUGALL-SIDES, LESLIE K. lawyer; b. Washington, Sept. 5, 1953; d. George Malcolm Richardson and Kathleen (Cahill) Dougall; m. Kenneth Jacob Sides, Feb. 19, 1994. BA, New Coll., Sarasota, Fla., 1975; JD cum laude, Florida State U., Tallahassee, 1978. Bar: Fla. 1981, DC 1981, Oreg. 1986, cert.: in city, county and local govt. law 1996, cert. profl. human resources 2001, bar: U.S. Dis. Ct. (middle and southern dist.) Fla., U.S. ct. appeals (11th cir.). Staff atty. Ctrl. Fla. Legal Svcs., Cocoa, 1982—85, dir. atty. Handicapped Law Ctr., 1985—87; asst. city atty., acting city atty. City of Key West (Fla.), 1987—95; asst. city atty. City of Clearwater (Fla.), 1995—; bd. dirs. IRRA, 2000—02; sec. West Ctrl. Fla. Chpt., Indsl. Rels. Rsch. Assn., 2003. Mem.: Indsl. Rels. Rsch. Assn. (sec. West Ctrl. Fla. chpt. 2003, bd. dirs. 2000—02), Soc. Human Resources, Clearwater Bar Assn., ABA. Avocation: sailing. Office: City of Clearwater City Atty's Office PO Box 4748 Clearwater FL 33758 Office Fax: 727-562-4021. E-mail: lsides@clearwater-fl.com.

DOUGHERTY, JOHN CHRYSOSTOM, III, retired lawyer; b. Beeville, Tex., May 3, 1915; s. John Chrysostom and Mary V. (Henderson) D.; m. Mary Ireland Graves, Apr. 18, 1942 (dec. July 1977); children: Mary Ireland, John Chrysostom IV; m. Bea Ann Smith, June 1978 (div. 1981); m. Sarah B. Randle, 1981 (dec. June 1997). BA, U. Tex., 1937; LLB, Harvard U., 1940; diploma, Inter-Am. Acad. Internat. and Comparative Law, Havana, Cuba, 1948. Bar: Tex. 1940. Atty. Hewit & Dougherty, Beeville, 1940-41; ptnr. Graves & Dougherty, Austin, Tex., 1946-50, Graves, Dougherty & Greenhill, Austin, 1950-57, Graves, Dougherty & Gee, Austin, 1957-60, Graves, Dougherty, Gee & Hearon, Austin, 1961-66, Graves, Dougherty, Gee, Hearon, Moody & Garwood, Austin, 1966-73, Graves, Dougherty, Hearon, Moody & Garwood, Austin, 1973-79, Graves, Dougherty, Hearon & Moody, Austin, 1979-93, sr. counsel, 1993—; ret., 1997. Spl. asst. atty. gen., 1949-50; Hon. French Consul, Austin, 1971-86; lectr. on tax, estate planning, probate code, community property problems; mem. Tex. Submerged Lands Adv. Com., 1963-72, Tex. Bus. and Commerce Code Adv. Com., 1964-66, Gov.'s Com. on Marine Resources, 1970-71, Gov.'s Planning Com. on Colorado River Basin Water Quality Mgmt. Study, 1972-73, Tex. Legis. Property Tax Com., 1973-75; adv. com. Mex. Ctr. Inst. of Latin-Am. Studies U. Tex., 1997—. Co-editor: Texas Appellate Practice, 1964, 2d edit., 1977; contbr. Bowe, Estate Planning and Taxation, 1957, 65; Texas Lawyers Practice Guide, 1967, 71, How to Live and Die with Texas Probate, 1968, 7th edit., 1995, Texas Estate Administration, 1975, 78; mem. bd. editors: Appellate Procedure in Tex., 1964, 2d edit., 1982; contbr. articles to profl. jours. Bd. dirs. Tex. Beta Students Aid Fund, 1949-84, Grenville Clark Fund at Dartmouth Coll., 1976-90, Umlauf Sculpture Garden, Inc., 1990-91, New Life Inst., 1993-2001; past bd. dirs. Advanced Religious Study Found., Holy Cross Hosp., Sea Arama, Inc., Nat. Pollution Control Found., Austin Nat. Bank; trustee St. Stephen's Episcopal Sch., Austin, 1969-83, Tex. Equal Access to Justice Found., 1986-90, U. Tex. Law Sch. Found., 1974-2002; mem. adv. com. Legal Assts. Tng. Inst., U. Tex., 1990-98; mem. vis. com. Harvard Law Sch., 1983-87. Capt. C.I.C., AUS, 1941-44, JAGC, 1944-46, maj. USAR. Decorated Medaille Française, France, Medaille d'honneur en Argent des Affairs Etrangeres, France, chevalier l'Ordre Nat. du Merite; recipient Wm. Reece Smith Spl. Svcs. to Pro Bono award Nat. Assn. of Pro Bono Coords., 2000. Fellow Am. Bar Found., Tex. Bar Found., Am. Coll. Trust and Estate Counsel, Am. Coll. Tax Counsel; mem. ABA (ho. of dels. 1982-88, standing com. on lawyers pub. responsibility 1983-85, spl. com. on delivery legal svcs. 1987-91, com. legal problems of the elderly 1997-2000, Sr. Lawyers divsn. Pro Bono Lawyer of 1999), Am. Arbitration Assn. (nat. panel arbitrators 1958-90), Travis County Bar Assn. (pres. 1979-80), Internat. Acad. Estate and Trust Law (exec. coun. 1988-90), State Bar Tex. (chmn. sect. taxation 1965-66, pres. 1979-80, com. legal svcs. to the poor 1986-94), Am. Judicature Soc. (bd. dirs. 1985-87), Am. Law Inst. (adv. com. project law governing lawyers 1990-97), Tex. Supreme Ct. Hist. Soc. (trustee 1997—, chmn. 1999-2002), Philos. Soc. Tex. (pres. 1989, bd. dirs. 1989—), Harvard Law Sch. Assn. (com. on pub. svc. law 1990-95, chmn. 1990-95, coun. 1991-95, exec. com. 1992-95), Tex. Appleseed, Inc. (bd. dirs. 1996—), The Austin Project (bd. dirs. 1999—), Rotary. Presbyterian. Home: 1801 Lavaca St Apt 5J Austin TX 78701 Office: Bank of America Center 515 Congress Ave Ste 2300 Austin TX 78701-3508 also: PO Box 98 Austin TX 78767-0098 Home Fax: 512-476-8186. E-mail: cdougherty@gdhm.com.

DOUGHTY, MARK ANTHONY, lawyer; b. Pasadena, Calif., Aug. 18, 1951; s. Lawrence Richard and Bertha Lou D.; children: Matthew James, Luke Anthony. BA in Bus. Law, Calif. State U., Chico, 1976; JD, U. Pacific, Sacramento, Calif., 1979. Bar: Calif. 1979, U.S. Dist. Ct. (ea. dist.) Calif. 1979; lic. real estate broker. Law clk. Calif. Ct. Appeals (5th cir.), Fresno, Calif., 1979-80; assoc. Ashby and Guth, Yuba City, Calif., 1980-82; ptnr. Ashby, Guth and Doughty, Yuba City, 1982-86, Ashby & Doughty, Yuba City, 1986-92; prin. Law Offices of Mark A. Doughty, Yuba City, 1992—. Pres. Russian Radio Bible Inst. Mem. Sutter Buttes Rotary, Consumer Attys. of Calif. (bd. govs. 19th dist.), Fellowship of Christian Businessmen, Yuba Sutter Bar Assn. (pres. 2001), Consumer Attys. Gold Country (pres. 1999—). Republican. Avocations: fathering, golf, private pilot, hunting, boating. General civil litigation, Estate planning, Personal injury (including property damage). Office: Law Offices of Mark A Doughty PO Box 3420 1528 Poole Blvd Ste A Yuba City CA 95992-3420 Fax: 530-674-1180. E-mail: mark@golaw.com.

DOUGLAS, ANDREW, retired state supreme court justice; b. Toledo, July 5, 1932; 4 children JD, U. Toledo, 1959. Bar: Ohio 1960, U.S. Dist. Ct. (no. dist.) Ohio 1960. Former ptnr. Winchester & Douglas; judge Ohio 6th Dist. Ct. Appeals, 1981-84; ret. justice Ohio Supreme Ct., 1985—2002. Mem. nat. adv. bd. Ctr. for Informatics Law John Marshall Law Sch., Chgo.; former spl. counsel Atty. Gen. of Ohio; former instr. law Ohio Dominican Coll. Served with U.S. Army, 1952-54 Recipient award Maumee Valley council Girl Scouts U.S., 1976, Outstanding Service award Toledo Police Command Officers Assn., 1980, Toledo Soc. for Autistic Children and Adults, 1983, Extra-Spl. Person award Central Catholic High Sch., 1981, Disting. Service award Toledo Police Patrolman's Assn., 1982, award Ohio Hispanic Inst. Opportunity, 1985, Disting. Merit award Alpha Sigma Phi, 1988, Gold "T" award U. Toledo, First Amendment award Cen. Ohio Chpt. Soc. Profl. Journalists Sigma Delta Chi, 1989; named to Woodward High Sch. Hall of Fame. Mem. Toledo Bar Assn., Lucas County Bar Assn., Ohio Bar Assn., Toledo U. Alumni Assn., U. Toledo Coll. Law Alumni Assn. (Disting. Alumnus award 1991), Internat. Inst., North Toledo Old Timers Assn., Old Newsboys Goodfellow Assn., Pi Sigma Alpha, Delta Theta Phi. Office: Ohio Supreme Ct 30 E Broad St Fl 3 Columbus OH 43215

DOUGLAS, JAMES MATTHEW, law educator; b. Onalaska, Tex., Feb. 11, 1944; s. Desso D. and Mary L. (Durden) D.; div.; children: DeLicia, Renee. BA in Math., Tex. So. U., 1966, JD, 1970; MS Law, Stanford U., 1971. Bar: Tex. 1970. Programmer analyst Singer Gen. Precision Co., Houston, 1966-70, 71-72; asst. prof. law Tex. So. U., Houston, 1971-72; asst. prof. Cleve. State U., Cleve.-Marshall Coll. Law, Ohio, 1972-75, asst. prof., asst. dean student affairs, 1974-75; assoc. prof. law, assoc. dean Coll. of Law Syracuse U., NY, 1975-80; prof. law Northea. U., Boston, 1980-81; dean, prof. law Tex. So. U., Houston, 1981-95, provost, v.p. acad. affairs, 1995, pres., 1995-99, prof., 1995—. Mem. Law Sch. Admissions Coun.; cons. computer law and computer contracts; bd. dir. Civil Ct. Legal Svcs., Gulf Coast Legal Found.; bd. dir. Boy Scouts Am., mem. exec. com., 1998—. Mem. editl. bd. The Tex. Lawyer. Mem. ABA (mem. affirmative action com.), Tex. Bar Assn., Houston Bar Assn., Hiscock Legal Soc. (dir.), Houston C. of C. (mem. chmns. club), Greater Houston Partnership (bd. dir.). Home: 5318 Calhoun Rd Houston TX 77021-1714 Office: Tex U Thurgood Marshall Law Sch Bldg 3100 Cleburne St Houston TX 77004-4501 E-mail: sdouglas@tsulaw.edu.

DOUGLAS, JAMES MCCRYSTAL, lawyer; b. Wantagh, N.Y., 1956; Student, Bucknell U.; BA, SUNY, Binghamton, 1978; JD cum laude, Fordham U., 1981. Bar: N.Y. 1982. Ptnr., co-head banking group Skadden, Arps, Slate, Meagher & Flom LLP, N.Y.C. Mem. Fordham Law Rev., 1980-81. Banking. Office: Skadden Arps Slate Meagher & Flom LLP 4 Times Sq New York NY 10036-6595 E-mail: jdouglas@skadden.com.

DOUGLAS, JOHN WOOLMAN, lawyer; b. Phila., Aug. 15, 1921; s. Paul H. and Dorothy S. (Wolff) D.; m. Mary Evans St. John, July 14, 1945; children: Katherine D. Torrey, Peter R. AB, Princeton U., 1943; LLB, Yale U., 1948; DPhil, Oxford U., 1950. Bar: N.Y. 1948, D.C. 1953. Law clk. to justice Harold H. Burton U.S. Supreme Ct., 1951—52; asst. atty. gen. U.S. Dept. Justice, 1963—66; lawyer Covington & Burling, Washington, 1950—51, 1952—63, ptnr., 1966—. Chmn. Carnegie Endowment for Internat. Peace, 1978-86. Served to lt. (j.g.) USNR, 1943-46, MTO, PTO. Trustee Deerfield Acad., 1972-77; co-chair Citizens for McGovern com., 1972; chmn. Robert F. Kennedy Meml. Found., 1980-83. Rhodes scholar, 1948-50. Fellow Am. Coll. Trial Lawyers; mem. ABA, D.C. Bar Assn. (pres. 1974-75), Nat. Lawyers Com. for Civil Rights Under Law (co. chmn. 1969-71), Nat. Legal Aid and Defender Assn. (pres. 1970-71), Yale Law Sch. Assn. (pres. 1975-77). Democrat. Presbyterian. Federal civil litigation. Home: 5700 Kirkside Dr Bethesda MD 20815-7116 Office: Covington & Burling 1201 Pennsylvania Ave NW PO Box 7566 Washington DC 20044-7566

DOUGLASS, FRANK RUSSELL, lawyer; b. Dallas, May 29, 1933; s. Claire Allen and Caroline (Score) D.; m. Carita Calkins, Feb. 5, 1955 (div. 1983); children: Russell, Tom, Andrew, Cathy; m. Betty Elwanda Richards, Dec. 31, 1983. BBA, Southwestern U., 1953; LLB, U. Tex., 1958. Bar: Tex. 1957, U.S. Dist. Ct. (we. dist.) Tex. 1960, U.S. Dist. Ct. (so. dist.) Tex. 1981, U.S. Dist. Ct. (no. dist.) Tex. 1985, U.S. Dist. Ct. (ea. dist.) Tex. 1987, U.S. Supreme Ct. 1964, U.S. Ct. Appeals (5th cir.) 1985; cert. in civil trial law, and oil, gas and energy law. Various positions to ptnr. McGinnis, Lochridge & Kilgore, Austin, Tex., 1957-76; sr. ptnr. Scott, Douglass & McConnico, Austin, 1976—. Bd. dirs. Pierce Energy Co., Amarillo, Tex., Pierce Energy Corp., Amarillo; trustee Southwestern U., Georgetown, Tex. Contbr. articles to profl. jours. City atty., Westlake Hills, Tex., 1968. Served as airman USAF, 1953-55. Named Dist. Alumus Southwestern U., 1999. Fellow Am. Coll. Trial Lawyers; mem. ABA (natural resources law sect., coun. 1987-90, Am. Bar Found.), Am. Inns of Ct., State Bar of Tex., Tex. Bar Found., The Tex. Ctr. for Legal Ethics and Professionalism (founding), Dallas Bar Assn., The Littlefield Soc. U. Tex. (charter). Administrative and regulatory, General civil litigation, Oil, gas, and mineral. Home and Office: 10424 Woodford Dr Dallas TX 75229-6317 Fax: 214-352-4588.

DOUGLASS, JOHN JAY, lawyer, educator; b. Lincoln, Nebr., Mar. 9, 1922; s. Edward Lyman and Edna Marie (Ball) D.; m. Margaret Casteel Pickering, Aug. 31, 1946; children: Carrie Bess, Timothy Pickering, Margaret Marie. AB with distinction, U. Nebr., 1943; JD with distinction, U. Mich., 1952; MA, George Washington U., 1963; LLM, U. Va., 1973; postgrad., Army War Coll., 1963. Bar: Nebr. 1952, Mich. 1952, Tex. 1975. Infantry officer U.S. Army, 1943-52, advanced through grades to col., 1966, judge adv., 1952-74, 1968-69, mil. judge Ft. Riley, Kans., 1969-70; comdt. U.S. Army JAG Sch., Charlottesville, Va., 1970-74; ret. U.S. Army, 1974; dean Nat. Coll. Dist. Attys., Houston, 1974-94; prof., dir. trial advocacy U. Houston, 1974—. Advisor on criminal law to Albania, 1991; advisor on elections to Ukraine, 1993; advisor Russian procuracy, 1994, Ukraine procuracy, 1995; named dist. mem. JAGC, 1994. Author: Ethical Concerns in Prosecution, 1988, 93; contbr. articles to profl. jours. Judge Harris County Absentee Voting, Houston, 1980-92. Decorated D.S.C., Legion of Merit, Bronze Star; recipient U. Nebr. Alumni Achievement award, 2003. Fellow Am. Bar Found. (life); mem. ABA (ho. of dels. 1980-96, chmn. standing com. on law and electoral process 1987-90, Nelson award 2001), Tex. Bar Assn. (penal code and criminal process com. 1988-90), Houston City Club, Army and Navy Club, Order of Coif, Alpha Tau Omega. Avocation: tennis. Home: 25 T 14 E Greenway Plz Houston TX 77046-1406 Office: Univ Houston Law Ctr 100 Law Center Houston TX 77204-6060 E-mail: jdouglass@UH.edu., jjdouglass@earthlink.net.

DOUGLASS, KEVIN K. lawyer; b. Pitts., Oct. 4, 1961; s. Samuel L. and Judith K. Douglass; m. Pamela W. Douglass, June 30, 1984; children: Kathryn, Julia, Margaret. BA, Mt. Union Coll., Alliance, Ohio, 1983; JD, Duquesne U., 1986. Bar: Pa. 1986, W.Va. 2000, U.S. Dist. Ct. (we. dist.) Pa. 1986. Assoc. Buchanan Ingersoll, Pitts., 1986—92, Babst Celland Clements & Zommer, PC, Pitts., 1992—95, shareholder, 1996—; vice chair ct. rules com. Allegheny County Ct., 2002—. Co-chair wine-tasting event Children's Hosp., Pitts., 2002—03; bd. dirs., Pitts. br. Brit.-Am. Bus. Coun., 2002—03. Mem.: ABA, Allegheny County Bar Assn., Pa. Bar Assn. General civil litigation, Product liability, Construction. Office: Babst Calland Clements & Sommir 2 Gateway Ctr Pittsburgh PA 15222

DOUGLAS-TALLEY, RITA FAYE, lawyer; b. Oct. 29, 1957; BA in Journalism, U. Okla., 1979; M of Criminal Justice Adminstrn., Okla. City U., 1981, JD, 1985. Bar: Okla. 1985, U.S. Dist. Ct. (we. dist.) Okla. 1985, U.S. Supreme Ct. 1997. Newspaper reporter Daily Oklahoman Times, Oklahoma City, 1980-82; law clk. City Oklahoma City, 1982-84, legal intern, 1984-85, asst. city atty., 1985—. Mem. Assn. Black Lawyers. Office: City of Oklahoma City 200 N Walker Ave Rm 309 Oklahoma City OK 73102-2232

DOUMENGE, ARNAUD, lawyer; b. Sept. 10, 1970; M in Tax and Bus. Law, U. Paris II, 1992, KKN ub Kabir Kaw, 1993, Doctor of Law, 1996. Bar: France 1998. Bus. counsel CNPF, Paris, 1994-95, Fedn. Francaise des Courtiers d'Assurance, Paris, 1995-97; lawyer Coopers & Lybrand, CLC Juridique et Fiscal, Paris, 1997-99, Magellan, Paris, 1999—, ptnr., 2003—. Author: Droit Commercial, 1998. Labor (including EEOC, Fair Labor Standards Act, labor-management relations, NLRB, OSHA), Labor Litigation. Office: Magellan Tour Areva 1 Place Coupole 92084 Paris France

DOWBEN, CARLA LURIE, lawyer, educator; b. Chgo., Jan. 22, 1932; d. Harold H. and Gertrude Lurie; m. Robert Dowben, June 20, 1950; children: Peter Arnold, Jonathan Stuart, Susan Laurie. AB, U. Chgo., 1950; JD, Temple U., 1955. Bar: Ill. 1957, Mass. 1963, Tex. 1974, U.S. Supreme Ct. 1974. Assoc. Conrad and Verges, Chgo., 1957-62; exec. officer MIT, Cambridge, Mass., 1963-64; legal planner Mass. Health Planning Project, Boston, 1964-69; assoc. prof. Life Scis. Inst. Brown U., Providence, 1970-72; asst. prof. health law U. Tex. Health Sci. Ctr., Dallas, 1973-78, assoc. prof., 1978-93; ptnr. Choate & Lilly, Dallas, 1989-92; head health law sect. Looper, Reed, Mark & McGraw, Dallas, 1992-95, of counsel, 1995-99. Adj. assoc. prof. health law U. Tex., 1993-95; cons. to bd. dirs. Mental Health Assn., 1958-86, Ft. Worth Assn. Retarded Citizens, 1980-90, Advocacy, Inc., 1981-85; dir. Nova Health Systems, 1975—, Tockwotton Home, 1994-98. Contbr. articles to profl. jours. Active in drafting helath and mental health legis., agy. regulation in several states and local govts. Mem. ABA, Tex. Bar Assn., Dallas Bar Assn., Am. Health Lawyers Assn., Hastings Inst. Ethics, Tex. Family Planning Assn. Mem. Soc. Of Friends. Administrative and regulatory, Health, Government contracts and claims.

DOWD, EDWARD L., JR., lawyer, former prosecutor; s. Edward L. Dowd; m. Jill Goessling; 3 children. JD with distinction, St. Mary's Univ. With Dowd, Dowd & Dowd; from asst. U.S. atty. to chief narcotics sect., regional dir. south cen. region Pres.'s Organized Crime Drug Enforcement Task Force U.S. Atty.'s Office, 1979-84; pvt. practice, 1984-93; U.S. atty. ea. dist. of Mo. U.S. Dept. Justice, St. Louis, 1993-99; dep. spl. counsel to John C. Danforth Spl. Counsel Waco Investigation, 1999; ptnr. Bryan Cave, LLP, St. Louis, 1999—. Office: Bryan Cave LLP One Metropolitan Square 211 N Broadway Ste 3600 Saint Louis MO 63102-2733 Office Fax: 314-259-2020. E-mail: eldowd@bryancave.com.

DOWD, MICHAEL PATRICK, lawyer; b. Los Alamitos, Mar. 25, 1970; s. Owen Joseph and Geraldine Ann Dowd; m. Dorena Joann Dominguez, Feb. 14, 1999. BA, Calif. State U., Long Beach, 1992; JD, U. of Houston Law Ctr., 1995. Prosecutor Ft. Bend Cty Dist. Atty, Richmond, Tex., 1994—95; atty. Law Offices of John Guerin, Huntington Beach, 1995—96; dep. dist. atty. San Bernardino Cty Dist. Atty., Rancho Cucamonga, 1996—. Com. mem. U. of La Verne Adv. Com., 2000—; legal advisor, cons. Gt. Western Gun Shows, Pomona, 1998—2001; com. mem. U. of La Verne Curriculum Devel. Com., 2000—. Campaign advisor Rep. Lawyers Assn., Orange, 1999—2000; founder San Bernardino Cty Dep. Dist. Atty. Assn., 2002; co-founder San Bernardino Cty Pub. Attorneys Assn., 2000. Mem.: ABA, Fed. Bar Assn., Orange Cty Rep. Lawyers Assn., Federalist Soc., Kiwanis Club. Republican. Roman Catholic. Avocations: baseball, reading, polit.activities. Office: San Bernardino Cty Dist Atty 8303 Haven Ave 4th Fl Rancho Cucamonga CA 91730-3848

DOWDLE, PATRICK DENNIS, lawyer; b. Denver, Dec. 8, 1948; s. William Robert and Helen (Schraeder) D.; m. Eleanor Pryor, Mar. 8, 1975; children: Jeffery William, Andrew Peter. BA, Cornell Coll., Mt. Vernon, Iowa, 1971; JD, Boston U., 1975. Bar: Colo. 1975, U.S. Dist. Ct. Colo. 1975, U.S. Ct. Appeals (10th cir.) 1976, U.S. Supreme Ct. 1978. Acad. dir. in Japan Sch. Internat. Tng., Putney, Vt., 1974; assoc. Decker & Miller, Denver, 1975-77; ptnr. Miller, Makkai & Dowdle, Denver, 1977—. Designated counsel criminal appeals Colo. Atty. Gens. Office, Denver, 1980-81; guardian ad litem Adams County Dist. Ct., Brighton, Colo., 1980-83; affiliated counsel ACLU, Denver, 1980—. Mem. Colo. Bar Assn., Denver Bar Assn. (various coms.), Porsche Club of Am. Avocations: scuba diving, photography, wine making, travel, skiing. Bankruptcy, General civil litigation, Property, real (including real estate development, water). Home: 3254 Tabor Ct Wheat Ridge CO 80033-5367 Office: Miller Makkai & Dowdle 2325 W 72nd Ave Denver CO 80221-3101 E-mail: pdowdle@rm.ince.net.

DOWDY, JOHN VERNARD, JR., lawyer, educator, arbitrator, mediator; b. Malakoff, Tex., July 3, 1942; s. John Vernard Sr. and Johnnie Dena (Riley) D.; m. Sarah Ellen Chambers, June 13, 1964; children: Rebekah Anne, Susannah Lynn. BSc in Phys. Edn., Baylor U., 1966, JD, 1968. Bar: Tex. 1968, U.S. Dist. Ct. (no. dist.) Tex. 1972, U.S. Dist. Ct. (ea. dist.) Tex. 1980. Assoc. Warwick, Jenkins Law Firm, Waxahachie, Tex., 1968-69,

Atkins, Carpenter & Dowdy, Arlington, Tex., 1969-72, Duke, Rosenberry & Dowdy, Arlington, 1972-74; pvt. practice law Arlington, 1974—; lectr. bus. law U. Tex., Arlington, 1974—. Mem. ptnrs. in search of ednl. excellence Arlington Ind. Sch. Dist., 1989-90; pres., bd. dirs. AWARE Found., Inc., Arlington, 1989-90, 92. Mem. ABA, Assn. Atty.-Mediators (bd. dirs. 2002-03, pres.-elect 2003—), Christian Legal Soc., State Bar Tex., Arlington Bar Assn., Tarrant County Bar Assn., Tarrant County Probate Bar Assn. (bd. dirs. 2001-2003). Baptist. Avocations: scuba diving, backpacking, running, physical fitness, handball. Alternative dispute resolution, Corporate, general, Probate (including wills, trusts). Home: 3706 Shadycreek Dr N Arlington TX 76013-1017 Office: Ste A 2400 Garden Park Ct Arlington TX 76013-1339 Fax: 917-460-8366. E-mail: jdowdy1@mindspring.com.

DOWDY, WILLIAM CLARENCE, JR., retired lawyer; b. McKinney, Tex., Feb. 27, 1925; s. William C. and Emily Harryette (Gilson) D.; m. Ann Atkinson, Aug. 31, 1947; children: William Clarence III, Jill Ann, Daniel Andrew. Student, North Tex. Agrl. Coll., Arlington, 1942-43; BBA, U. Tex., Austin, 1949, JD, 1951. Bar; Tex. 1951, U.S. Supreme Ct. 1957, U.S. Dist. Ct. (no. dist.) Tex. 1960, U.S. Ct. Appeals (5th cir.) 1974. Asst. dist. atty. Dallas County, 1951-54; atty. Tex. & Pacific Ry. Co., Dallas, 1954-59; gen. atty. Tex. & Pacific Ry. Co./Mo. Pacific R.R. Co., Dallas, 1959-82; gen. solicitor Mo. Pacific R.R. Co./Union Pacific R.R. Co., Dallas, 1982-86, sr. counsel, 1986-87; ret., 1987. Dir. Great S.W. R.R.; v.p., asst. sec., dir. Weatherford, Mineral Wells & Northwestern R.R. Elder, trustee Presbyn. Ch. With field arty., 24th divsn. AUS, 1943-46; PTO. Mem. Tex. Bar Assn., Dallas Bar Assn., Collin County Bar Assn., Nat. Assn. R.R. Trial Counsel (exec. com., regional v.p.), Tower Club (Dallas), Eldorado Club (McKinney, Tex.), Phi Alpha Delta, Kappa Sigma. Administrative and regulatory, Corporate, general, Personal injury (including property damage). Home: 510 Tucker St Mc Kinney TX 75069-2714

DOWELL, JAMES DALE, lawyer; b. Goose Creek, Tex., July 17, 1932; s. James Dale and Margaret (King) D.; m. Patricia Jo Skaggs, Feb. 2, 1957; children: Terry Dowell Owens, James Dale III. BA, Tex. A&M U, 1954; LLB, U. Tex., 1957. Bar: Tex. 1956, U.S. Dist. Ct. (ea. dist.) Tex. 1958, U.S Ct. Appeals (5th cir.) 1964, U.S. Supreme Ct. 1969. Assoc. King, Sharfstein & Rienstra, Beaumont, Tex., 1957-63, ptnr., 1963-68, Rienstra, Rienstra & Dowell, Beaumont, 1968-85, Rienstra, Dowell & Flatten, Beaumont, 1985—. Mem. Tex. Dem. Exec. Com., 1966-68, del. Nat. Conv., 1976—. Mem. ABA, State Bar Tex., Tex. Bar Found., Jefferson County Bar Assn. (pres. 1978-79, Blackstone award 2000), Def. Rsch. Inst., Tex. Assn. Def. Counsel, Beaumont Country Club, Beaumont Club (bd. dirs. 1975-77), Rotary (Paul Harris fellow 2000), Phi Gamma Delta. Methodist. Avocation: reading. General civil litigation, Insurance, Personal injury (including property damage). Home: 6275 Wilchester Ln Beaumont TX 77706-4328 Office: 595 Orleans St Beaumont TX 77701-3214

DOWERY-RODRIQUEZ, BRENDA, judge; b. Shelbyville, Ky., Feb. 5, 1946; d. Robert Dowery and Laetitia Miller; m. Peter Rodriquez, Sept. 21, 1993; 1 child, Paige L. Dowery Rodriquez. BA, St. Augustine's Coll., Raleigh, N.C., 1967; LLD, Santa Clara (Calif.) U., 1975. Bar: N.Y. 1977. Dist. atty. City of Bronx, NY, 1975—78; pvt. practice Westchester, NY, 1978—86; judge City Ct. Mt. Vernon, NY, 1986—. Office: Roosevelt Sq Mount Vernon NY 10552

DOWIS, LENORE, lawyer; b. N.Y., Nov. 7, 1934; d. Thomas and Julianna (Csitkovits) Esteves; children: Daniel, Lenore, Denise, Jonathan. AAS, Suffolk County Community Coll., 1981; BA, SUNY, Stony Brook, 1983; JD, Touro Coll., 1987. Bar: N.Y. 1988, N.J. 1988, U.S. Dist. Ct. N.J. 1988, U.S. Dist. Ct. (so. and ea. dists.) N.Y. 1992, U.S. Ct. Mil. Appeals 1993, U.S. Ct. Claims 1993, U.S. Ct. Appeals (fed. cir.) 1993, U.S. Supreme Ct. 1993. Tel. operator N.Y. Tel. Co., L.I., 1951-58; real estate sales agt. Gen. Devel. Corp., Hauppauge, N.Y, 1974-75; student law clk. to assoc. judge appellate div. U.S. Supreme Ct. N.Y., Bklyn., 1986; staff atty. Nassau/Suffolk Law Svcs., Bay Shore, N.Y., 1988; pvt. practice, Smithtown, N.Y., 1988—. Mem. ABA, Suffolk County Bar Assn., N.Y. State Bar Assn., Phi Theta Kappa, Alpha Beta Gamma. Republican. Administrative and regulatory, Family and matrimonial, General practice. Home and Office: 33 Beverly Rd Smithtown NY 11787-5324

DOWLING, NICOLA CHRISTINA, solicitor; b. Linericu, Ireland, May 1, 1973; d. Nicholas and Bridget Dowling. Student, U. Wales, Dublin, Ireland, 1992—95. Bar: 2001. Solicitor Mason, Hayes & Curran, Dublin, 2001—. Office: Mason Hayes and Curran 6 Fitzwilliam Sq Dublin Ireland

DOWLING, VINCENT JOHN, retired lawyer; b. NYC, Dec. 20, 1927; s. Victor Hurlin and Joan Agnes (Reardon) D.; m. Jane Cooney, Apr. 16, 1958; children: Vincent John Jr., Douglas J., S. Colin, Joseph G. BS, Lehigh U., 1949; JD, U. Conn., 1957. Bar: Conn. 1957, Mass. 1985, Fla. 1986, U.S. Dist. Ct. Conn. 1958, U.S. Ct. Appeals (2d cir.) 1960, U.S. Ct. Claims 1986. Chief mfg. engr. Veeder-Root, Inc., Hartford, Conn., 1949-58; ptnr. Dowling & Dowling, Hartford, Conn., 1958-65, Cooney, Scully & Dowling, Hartford, Conn., 1965—2001; ret., 2001. Lectr. constrn. law. Capt. U.S. Army, 1951-53. Mem. ASME, ABA, Conn. Bar assn. (liaison com. with ctrs., constrn. law com., alt. dispute resolution com., chmn. specialization com.), Am. Arbitration Assn., Nat. Panel Constrn. Arbitrators and Mediators, Nat. Arbitration and Mediation (panel), Fed. Bar Assn., Mass. Bar Assn., Fla. Bar Assn., Internat. Bar Assn., Diocesan Attys. Assn., Hartford Golf Club, Hartford Club, John's Island Club (Vero Beach, Fla.), Quail Valley Club (Vero Beach), Kappa Alpha Soc. Roman Catholic. Alternative dispute resolution, Federal civil litigation, Construction. Address: 111 Stoner Dr West Hartford CT 06107 E-mail: vin@dowling.com.

DOWNER, ROBERT NELSON, lawyer; b. Newton, Iowa, July 15, 1939; s. Lowell William and Mabel Mary (Hannon) Downer; m. Jane Alice Glafka, May 29, 1971; children: Elise Michele, Andrew Nelson. BA, U. Iowa, 1961, JD, 1963. Bar: Iowa 1963, U.S. Dist. Ct. (so. dist.) Iowa 1963, U.S. Dist. Ct. (no. dist.) Iowa 1964, U.S. Supreme Ct. 1995, U.S. Ct. Appeals (8th cir.) 2001. Assoc. Meardon Law Office, Iowa City, 1963-68; mem. Meardon, Sueppel & Downer PLC and predecessor firms, Iowa City, 1969—. Dir., sec. KZIA, Inc., Cedar Rapids, Iowa, 1975—, Iowa City Tennis & Fitness Ctr., 1987—93; trustee The Oaknoll Found., Iowa City, 1990—98, Herbert Hoover Presdl. Libr. Assn., West Branch, Iowa, 2000—; dir. Christian Retirement Svcs., Inc., Iowa City, 1967—82, Iowa State Bar Found., 1996—2002, Iowa Law Sch. Found., 2000—; bd. regents State of Iowa, 2003—. Mem. Iowa Supreme Ct. Task Force on Domestic Abuse, 1993—94; bd. dirs. Iowa City Area Devel. Group, 1993—2001, chmn., 1996—97, co-chair, 2000—01; dir., sec. Cmty. Found. Johnson County, Iowa, 2000—; del. Rep. Nat. conv., New Orleans, 1988; mem. Iowa Supreme Ct. comm. Continuing Legal Edn., 1975—83; chair adminstrv. bd. First United Meth. Ch., Iowa City, 1985—87; pres. Greater Iowa City Area C. of C., 1979; bd. trustees Iowa City Pub. Libr., 1971—75, chair, 1973—74. Recipient Excellence in Svc. award, Legal Svcs. Corp. Iowa, 1996. Fellow: Iowa State Bar Found., Am. Bar Found., Am. Coll. Trust and Estate Counsel (state chair 2000—); mem.: ABA, Johnson County Bar Assn. (pres. 1988—89), Iowa State Bar Assn. (chair probate sect. 1990—93, v.p. 1993—94, pres.-elect 1994—95, pres. 1995—96, Merit award 2001), Rotary (pres. 1989—90). Republican. Methodist. Banking, Corporate, general, Probate (including wills, trusts). Home: 2029 Rochester Ct Iowa City IA 52245-3246 Office: Meardon Sueppel & Downer PLC 122 S Linn St Iowa City IA 52240-1830 E-mail: bobd@meardonlaw.com.

DOWNES, WILLIAM F. judge; b. 1946; BA, U. North Tex., 1968; JD, U. Houston, 1974. Ptnr. Clark and Downes, Green River, Wyo., 1976-78; mem. Brown & Drew, Casper, Wyo., 1978-94; dist. judge U.S. Dist. Ct. Wyo., Casper, Wyo., 1994—; chief judge. Capt. USMC, 1968-71. Mem. Wyo. State Bar, Natrona County Bar Assn., Casper Petroleum Club, Wyo. Athletic Club. Office: US Dist Ct 111 S Wolcott St Rm 210 Casper WY 82601-2534

DOWNEY, ARTHUR HAROLD, JR., lawyer, mediator; b. N.Y.C., Nov. 21, 1938; s. Arthur Harold Sr. and Charlotte (Bailey) D.; m. Gwen Vanden Berg, May 28, 1960; children: Anne Leigh, Neal Arthur, Drew Thomas. BA, Cen. Coll., Pella, Iowa, 1960; LLB, Cornell U., 1963. Bar: Colo. 1963, Wyo. 1991, U.S. Dist. Ct. Colo. 1963, U.S. Dist. Ct. Wyo. 1993, U.S. Ct. Appeals (10th cir.) 1963; diplomate Am. Bd. Forensic Examiners. From assoc. to ptnr. Weller, Friedrich, Ward & Andrew, Denver, 1963-82; ptnr., chief exec. officer Downey Law Firm P.C., Denver, 1982—. Trustee panel Colo. Hosp. Assn., 1988-93; del. Nat. Congress Hosp. Trustees, Am. Hosp. Assn., 1988-93. Contbr. articles to profl. jours. Vice moderator Presbytery of Denver, 1972; past pres. Columbine Village Homeowners Assn., Trails End Homeowners Assn., Upper Village Homeowners Assn., Powderhorn Condominium Homeowners Assn., Breckenridge, Colo.; chmn bd. trustees Bethesda Psychealth Sys., Inc., 1990-93. Fellow Internat. Soc. Barristers (emeritus); mem. ABA, Colo. Bar Assn., Larimer County Bar Assn., Wyo. Bar Assn., Def. Rsch. Inst. (disting. svc. award), Nat. Inst. Trial Advocacy (teaching faculty, team leader 1973—), Colo. Def. Lawyers Assn. (pres. 1977-78), Am. Coll. Legal Medicine (assoc. in law), Nat. Bd. Trial Advocacy (cert.), Am. Arbitration Assn. Republican. Mem. Christian Reformed Ch. In Am. Avocations: photography, woodworking, skiing. General civil litigation, Insurance, Personal injury (including property damage). Office: Downey Law Firm PC 7688 Promontory Dr Fort Collins CO 80528-9305 E-mail: downeypc@attbi.com.

DOWNEY, BRIAN PATRICK, lawyer; b. Pitts., Sept. 1, 1964; s. Edmond John and Mary Elizabeth (Wallace) D.; m. Linda Alice McKay, Oct. 9, 1993. BA, Dartmouth Coll., 1987; JD, Dickinson Sch. of Law, 1990. Bar: Pa. 1990, U.S. Dist. Ct. (we. dist.) Pa. 1991, U.S. Dist. Ct. (ea. and mid. dists.) Pa. 1994, U.S. Ct. Appeals (3rd cir.) 1994. Assoc. counsel Eckert Seamans Cherin & Mellott, Pitts., 1990-92; asst. counsel Pa. Dept. of Labor, Harrisburg, 1992-94; ptnr. Pepper Hamilton, LLP, Harrisburg, 1994—. Mem. Friends of Tom Foley Com., Harrisburg, 1994; bd. dirs., v.p. Open Stage Harrisburg, 2001—. Mem. ABA, Pa. Bar Assn., Dauphin County Bar Assn. Democrat. Roman Catholic. Avocations: creative writing, golf, reading fiction. General civil litigation, Environmental, Product liability. Office: Pepper Hamilton LLP 200 One Keystone Plz Harrisburg PA 17108 E-mail: downeyb@pepperlaw.com.

DOWNEY, MICHAEL PATRICK, lawyer; b. St. Louis; m. Elizabeth R. Downey. BA, Georgetown U., 1992; JD, Washington U., St. Louis, 1998. Bar: Mo. 98, U.S. Ct. Appeals (8th cir.) 98, Ill. 99, U.S. Dist. Ct. (ea. dist.) Mo. 99, U.S. Dist. Ct. (so. dist.) Ill. 1999, U.S. Dist. Ct. (cen. dist.) Ill. 2003. Law clk. to Chief Judge Pasco M. Bowman U.S. Ct. Appeals (8th cir.), Kansas City, Mo., 1998—99; sr. assoc. Fox Galvin LLC, St. Louis, 2001—. Adj. prof. Washington U. Sch. of Law, 2000—. Sr. articles editor: Washington U. Law Quar., 1997—98. Mem.: Bar Assn. Metro St. Louis (chmn. ethics com. 2003—). General civil litigation, Product liability, Professional liability. Office: Fox Galvin LLC 1 Memorial Dr Saint Louis MO 63102 Fax: 314-588-1965.

DOWNEY, RICHARD LAWRENCE, lawyer; b. Washington, Apr. 3, 1948; s. William G. and Laufey A. D.; m. Pamela L. Drewry, July 10, 1971; children: Anna Christine, Laura Michele, Richard Lawrence, Patricia Kathleen. BA, Randolph-Macon Coll., 1970; JD, Hamline U., 1977. Bar: Va. 1978, U.S. Dist. Ct. (ea. dist.) Va. 1978, U.S. Ct. Appeals (4th cir.) 1978, U.S. Supreme Ct. 1983, U.S. Tax Ct. 1990, U.S. Claims Ct. 1990; diplomate Nat. Bd. Trial Advocacy; bd. cert. civil trial adv. Assoc. Downey & Lennhoff, Springfield, Va., 1978-80; pvt. practice Fairfax, Va., 1980-82; sr. ptnr. Duvall, Blackburn, Hale & Downey, Fairfax, Va., 1982-92; prin. Richard L. Downey & Assocs., 1992—. Served to lt. col. USAR. Named Outstanding Young Man of Am. U.S. Jaycees, 1982. Mem. ABA, ATLA, Va. State Bar Assn., Va. Trial Lawyers Assn., Fairfax Bar Assn. (gen. dist. cts. com. 1984-86, cir. ct. com. 1988-89), Nat. Lawyers Assn., Christian Legal Soc., Fairfax County C. of C. (internat. trade com., planning and land use com., legis. com. 1984), Phi Alpha Delta, Rotary. Republican. General civil litigation, Commercial, contracts (including sales of goods; commercial financing), Corporate, general. Address: 4126 Leonard Dr Fairfax VA 22030-5118 Office Fax: 703-273-8800.

DOWNIE, ROBERT COLLINS, II, lawyer; b. Panama Canal Zone, Feb. 18, 1965; s. Robert Wahl Downie and Margaret Brandon Ausley; m. Robyn Elizabeth McGuire, Sept. 1, 1994. BA in English, Davidson Coll., 1987; JD, Fla. State U., 1989. Bar: Fla. 1990, U.S. Dist. Ct. (mid. and no. dists.) Fla. 1996, U.S. Ct. Appeals (11th cir.) 1996. Assoc. Oertel, Hoffman, Fernandez & Cole, Tallahassee, Fla., 1990-94; shareholder Mathews & Downie, P.A., Tallahassee, 1994-97; assoc. Brown, Ward et al, Orlando, 1997-99; sr. atty. Fla. Dept. Transp., 1999—. Administrative and regulatory, Environmental, Transportation. Office: Dept Transp 605 Suwannee St # MS58 Tallahassee FL 32399-0458 E-mail: robert.downie@dot.state.fl.us.

DOWNING, LAWRENCE DEWITT, lawyer; b. McPherson, Kans., Aug. 2, 1936; s. Wayne Curtis and Waneta Corinne (DeWitt) D.; m. Kristi Karen Anderson, June 19, 1960 (div. 1983); children: Kyia, Christopher; m. Ann Marie Lucke, June 2, 1985. BS, Iowa State U., 1958; JD, U. Minn. 1962. Bar: Minn. 1962, U.S. Dist. Ct. Minn. 1962, U.S. Supreme Ct. 1978. Chemist Procter & Gamble, Cin., 1958-59; ptnr. O'Brien, Ehrick, Wolf, Deaner & Downing, Rochester, Minn., 1962-90; pvt. practice Rochester, 1990—. Owner Lawrence Downing & Assocs., Rochester, 1990—. Trustee John Muir Trust, U.K., 1988—, Esalen Inst., 2002—; past mem. Minn. Gov.'s Task Force on Environ. Compact of the States; mem. hon. com. Earth Day, 1990; past mem., chmn. subcom. Minn. Gov.'s Task Force on Energy Policy; past mem. Minn. Gov.'s Power Plan Sitting Adv. Com., Olmsted County Environ. Quality Commn. Fellow Am. Acad. Matrimonial Lawyers, 1977—; mem. ABA (family law sect.), Minn. Bar Assn. (bd. dirs. family law sect. 1978-79), 3d Dist. Bar Assn., Olmsted County Bar Assn. (pres. 1985-86), Sierra Club (mem. exec. com. 1984-88, 5th officer 1984-85, sec. 1985-86, v.p. for adminstv. law 1988-92, bd. dirs. 1983-89, pres. 1986-88, pres. Sierra Club Found. 1989-92, mem. numerous nat. coms. and task forces). Achievements include co-inventor Mr. Clean liquid cleaner. Family and matrimonial. Office: Lawrence Downing & Assocs 330 Wells Fargo Ctr 21 1st Ave SW Rochester MN 55902 E-mail: LDowning@Downinglaw.net., LDD@LDowning.com.

DOWNING, ROBERT ALLAN, lawyer; b. Kenosha, Wis., Jan. 6, 1929; s. Leo Vertin and Mayme C. (Kennedy) D.; m. JoAnn C. Cramton, Apr. 14, 1951 (div. Sept. 1977); children: Robert A., Kevin C., Tracey Downing Clark, Gregory E.; m. Joan Govan, Oct. 29, 1977; 1 child, Charles E. Reiter III. BS, U. Wis., 1950, JD, 1956. Bar: Wis. 1956, Ill. 1956, U.S. Supreme Ct. 1965. Assoc. Sidley & Austin, Chgo., 1956-64, ptnr., 1964-94, counsel, 1994-97, Ruff, Weidenaar & Reidy, Ltd., Chgo., 1997—. Trustee (life), former pres. Episcopal Charities and Cmty. Svcs., Chgo. Diocese. Served to lt. USN, 1950-53, Korea. Fellow Am. Coll. Trial Lawyers; mem. ABA, Soc. Trial Lawyers, Ill. Bar Assn., Chgo. Bar Assn., Wis. Bar Assn., 7th Cir. Bar Assn., Union League Club, Law Club, Legal Club, MidDay Club, Westmoreland Country Club. Republican. Episcopalian. General civil litigation, Insurance, Antitrust. Office: Ruff Weidenaar & Reidy Ltd 222 N Lasalle St Ste 1525 Chicago IL 60601-1003

DOWNS, CLARK EVANS, lawyer; b. Boston, July 30, 1946; s. Willis A. and Josephine Joyce (Evans) D.; m. Emilie Louise Hartnett, Aug. 17, 1968; children: Elizabeth Morgan, Julia Clark. AB in English Lit., Boston U., 1968, JD cum laude, 1973. Bar: Ill. 1973, D.C. 1981. Assoc. Isham Lincoln & Beale, Washington, 1973-80, ptnr., 1981-87, Jones Day, Washington, 1988—. Trustee, sec. Found. Energy Law Jour., Washington, 1989-93; trustee Mt. Ida Coll., Newton Centre, Mass., 1989-98, chair, 1994-98; trustee Nat. Presbyn. Sch., Washington, 1986-90, Nat. Presbyn. Ch., Washington, 1991-93, Chevy Chase Presbyn. Ch., Washington, 1981-84; bd. visitors Boston U. Sch. Law, 2000-02. Fellow Am. Bar Found.; mem. ABA (ho. of dels. 1995-97), Energy Bar Assn. (chmn. program com. 1985-86, bd. dirs. 1986-89), FERC (Practice Procedure Manual editl. adv. bd. 1996—), D.C. Bar (chmn. lawyers counseling com. 1989), Order St. John (serving brother 2000—). Avocations: cello, folk music, choral music. FERC practice, Finance, Utilities, public. Office: Jones Day 51 Louisiana Ave NW Washington DC 20001-2113

DOWNS, THOMAS EDWARD, IV, lawyer; b. South Amboy, N.J., Sept. 27, 1950; s. Thomas Edward III and Theresa Mary (Jaje) D.; m. Marie Popik, Oct. 6, 1979; children: Thomas Edward V, Lauren Ann. BA, St. Peter's Coll., 1972; JD, Seton Hall U., 1975. Bar: N.J. 1975, U.S. Dist. Ct. N.J. 1975, U.S. Dist. Cts. (so. and ea. dists.) N.Y. 1981. Law clk. to presiding judges Middlesex County, N.J., 1975; assoc. Irving Tabman, Old Bridge, N.J., 1975-76; ptnr. Tabman, Downs & McDonnell, Old Bridge, 1976-77, Tabman & Downs, Old Bridge, 1978-82; pvt. practice Old Bridge, 1982—; South Amboy Mcpl. prosecutor, 1977—; Sayreville Mcpl. prosecutor, 1987—90, 1994—2000; Carteret Mcpl. prosecutor, 2002. Atty. Old Bridge Econ. Devel. Bd., 2002—. Sec. South Amboy Shade Tree com., 1974; co-chmn. South Amboy Blood Bank; pres. South Amboy Young Dem. Orgn.; dep. chmn. Sayreville Dem. Orgn., 1992—; bd. dirs. Middlesex County Social Svcs., 2001-. Mem. Assn. Trial Lawyers Am., N.J. State Trial Lawyers Assn., Middlesex County Bar Assn., N.J. State Bar Assn., Lions (pres. South Amboy chpt. 1984). Roman Catholic. Criminal, Family and matrimonial, Property, real (including real estate development, water). Home: 26 Carter Pl Sayreville PO Box Parlin NJ 08859 Office: PO Box 498 Old Bridge NJ 08857-0498

DOYLE, AUSTIN JOSEPH, lawyer; b. Atlanta, Aug. 2, 1941; s. Austin Joseph Sr. and Marguerite Clare (Sheridan) D.; m. Marian Frances Murphy, June 24, 1980; children: Kelly, Deborah. BBA, U. Notre Dame, 1963; JD, Am. U., 1973. Bar: D.C. 1974, U.S. Dist. Ct. D.C. 1974, U.S. Tax Ct. 1974, U.S. Ct. Appeals (D.C. cir.) 1986, U.S. Ct. Appeals (9th cir.) 1990, U.S. Ct. Appeals (5th cir.), 1994; CPA, D.C. CPA Williams & Connolly, Washington, 1967-73; sole practice Washington, 1973—. Served to 1st lt. U.S. Army, 1963-65. Mem. ABA, D.C. Bar Assn., Am. Assn. Atty. CPAs, Greater Washington Soc. CPAs, Fin. Planning Assn. Roman Catholic. Estate planning, Corporate taxation.

DOYLE, DAVID PERRIE, lawyer; b. Orange, N.J., May 11, 1960; s. Ralph Thomas and Dorothy (Trevorrow) D.; m. Ana Linda Day, Mar. 7, 1987. BA, Emory U., 1982; JD, Rutgers U., 1985; LLM in Taxation, N.Y.U., 1990. Bar: N.J. 1986, U.S. Dist. Ct. N.J. 1986, U.S. Tax Ct. 1988, U.S. Dist. Ct. (so. dist.) N.Y. 1998. Law clk. to presiding judge Tax Ct. N.J., Trenton, 1985-86; assoc. Pitney, Hardin, Kipp & Szuch, Morristown, N.J., 1986-92, counsel, 1993-94, ptnr., 1995—. Mem. ABA (tax sect., mem. employee benefits com.), N.J. State Bar Assn. (tax sect., past chair employee benefits com.). Pension, profit-sharing, and employee benefits, Taxation, general. Office: Pitney Hardin Kipp & Szuch LLP PO Box 1945 Morristown NJ 07962-1945 E-mail: ddoyle@pitneyhardin.com.

DOYLE, DENNIS T. lawyer; b. White Plains, N.Y., Apr. 9, 1943; BA, Boston Coll., 1965; JD, Fordham U., 1968. Bar: N.Y. State 1968, U.S. Dist. Ct. (so. and ea. dists.) N.Y. 1978, U.S. Supreme Ct. 1978. Ptnr. O'Connor, McGuiness, Conte, Doyle & Oleson, White Plains, 1969—. Author: You Haven't Got a Prayer. Mem. ABA, Am. Trial Lawyers Assn., N.Y. State, Fedn. Ins. and Corp. Counsel, Trial Lawyers Assn., Appalachian Mountain Club, Adirondeck Mountain Club, Adirondeck Coun. Avocations: bicycling, religious education, hiking, golf. Federal civil litigation, General civil litigation, State civil litigation. Office: O'Connor McGuiness Conte Doyle & Oleson One Barker Ave Ste 675 White Plains NY 10601-1517 Fax: 914 948-0645. E-mail: ddoyle@omcdoc.com.

DOYLE, DUANE LYNN, lawyer, writer; b. Erie, Pa., Jan. 24, 1942; s, Vernon Charles and Lynnette Shirley (Otto) D.; m. Kathleen M. Doyle, July 10, 1976 (div. Feb., 1995); children: Amber Melanie, Sean Patrick, Christopher Matthew, Daniel Casey. BA, Gannon U., 1965; spl. agt. tng., Military Intelligence, Fort Holabird, Balt., 1966; JD, Case Western Reserve U., 1971. Bar: Ohio 1971, U.S. Dist. Ct. (no. and so. dists.) Ohio 1972. Announcer WWGO Radio, Erie, Pa., 1961-65; spl. agt. mil. intelligence Columbia, S.C., 1965-68; dir., producer news WOLO-TV, Columbia, 1966-67; staff atty. Cuyahoga County Pub Defenders Office, Cleve., 1971-72; pvt. practice Cleve., 1972-94; ins. defense atty. Baran, Piper & Tarkowski, Twinsburg, Ohio, 1994-96; pvt. practice Twinsburg, 1996—. Instr. in law Adult Edn. Classes, Various Cleve. H.S., 1968—; bd. dirs. Revenue Generator Industries, Inc., Twinsburg, 1993—, Internat. Antifreeze Recycling Assn., 1995—. Columnist: Dukes Law, Akron Bus. Jour., 1996-97; contbr. articles to Akron Beacon Jour., Cleve. Plain Dealer. Rep. state legis. cand., Cleve. Hghts., Ohio, 1972; speaker various bar assns. N.E. Ohio, 1991-93. With U.S. Army (mil. intelligence) 1965-68. Recipient Citation from DAV, Columbia, S.C., 1967; named Disting. Alumnus, Phi Delta Alpha, 1979, 82. Avocations: martial arts, rustic camping, game photography, astronomy. General civil litigation, Criminal, General practice, State civil litigation, Criminal, Personal injury (including property damage). Office: Tower Park 8413 Tower Dr Twinsburg OH 44087 Home: 9962 Chamberlin Rd Twinsburg OH 44087

DOYLE, GERARD FRANCIS, lawyer; b. Needham, Mass., Oct. 25, 1942; s. John Patrick and Catherine Mary (Lawler) D.; m. Paula Marie Dervay, may 14, 1983; children: Laura Dervay, Meredith Lawler, Philip John. BS in Indsl. Adminstrn., Yale U., 1966; JD, Georgetown U., 1972. Bar: D.C. 1973, U.S. Dist. Ct. D.C. 1973, U.S. Ct. Fed. Claims 1976, U.S. Ct. Appeals (fed. cir.) 1982, U.S. Supreme Ct. 1982, Va. 2000. Group head for operating submarine reactors and reactor tech Div. Naval Reactors AEC, Washington, 1970-72; atty. Morgan, Lewis & Bockius, Washington, 1972-76; legal counsel Am. Nuclear Energy Coun., Washington, 1975-76; ptnr. Cotten, Day & Doyle, Washington, 1976-87, Doyle & Savit, Doyle, Simmons & Bachman, Doyle & Bachman LLP, Washington, 1987-99, Arlington, Va., 1999—. Legal counsel Assn. Fed. Data Peripheral Suppliers, Washington, 1979; dir. M Internat., Inc.; author and lectr. in field; columnist Federal Computer Week, 1989. Served in USN, 1966-71. Recipient outstanding young man of yr. award, 1976. Mem. ABA (coun. publ. contract law sect. 1989-92), D.C. Bar Assn., Fed. Bar Assn., Am. Arbitration Assn. (panel arbitrators), Nat. Contract Mgmt. Assn., Met. Club (Washington), Yale Club (Washington), Washington Golf & Country Club. Republican. Roman Catholic. Computer, Government contracts and claims. Home: 901 Whann Ave Mc Lean VA 22101-1570 Office: Doyle & Bachman LLP 4245 Fairfax Dr Arlington VA 22203-1637 E-mail: gdoyle@doylebachman.com.

DOYLE, JAMES E(DWARD), governor; b. Washington, Nov. 23, 1945; s. James E. and Ruth (Bachhuber) Doyle; m. Jessica Laird, Dec. 21, 1966; children: Augustus, Gabriel. Student, Stanford U., 1963—66; AB in History, U. Wis., 1967; JD cum laude, Harvard U., 1972. Bar: Ariz. 1973, Wis. 1975, U.S. Dist. Ct. N.Mex. 1973, U.S. Dist. Ct. Ariz. 1973, U.S. Dist. Ct. Utah 1973, U.S. Dist. Ct. (we. dist.) Wis. 1975, U.S. Dist. Ct. (ea. dist.) Wis. 1976, U.S. Ct. Appeals (10th cir.) 1974, U.S. Ct. Appeals (7th cir.) 1985, U.S. Supreme Ct. 1989. Vol. Peace Corps, Tunisia, 1967—69; atty. DNA Legal Svcs., Chinle, Ariz., 1972—75; ptnr. Jacobs & Doyle, Madison, Wis., 1975—77; dist. atty. Dane County, Madison, 1977—83; ptnr. Doyle & Ritz, Madison, 1983—90; of counsel Lawton & Cates, Madison, 1990—91; atty. gen. State of Wis., Madison, 1991—2002, gov., 2003—. Mem.: ABA,

7th Cir. Bar Assn. (chmn. criminal law sect. 1988—89), Wis. Bar Assn. (bd. dirs. criminal law sect. 1988). Democrat. Roman Catholic. Office: 115 E State Capitol Madison WI 53702

DOYLE, JOHN ROBERT, lawyer; b. Chgo., May 12, 1950; s. Frank Edward and Dorothy (Bolton) D.; m. Kathleen Julius, June 14, 1974; children: Melissa, Maureen. BA magna cum laude, St. Louis U., 1971; JD summa cum laude, DePaul U., 1976. Bar: Ill. 1976, U.S. Dist. Ct. 1976, U.S. Dist. Ct. (no. dist.) Ill. 1982, Ill. Trial Bar 1982, U.S. Ct. Appeals (7th cir.) 1982. Ptnr. McDermott, Will & Emery, Chgo., 1976—. Mem. ABA, Chgo. Bar Assn. (jud. investigative hearing panel 1986-88), Phi Beta Kappa. Construction, Insurance, Personal injury (including property damage). Office: McDermott Will & Emery 227 W Monroe St Ste 3100 Chicago IL 60606-5096

DOYLE, JOSEPH ANTHONY, retired lawyer; b. N.Y.C., June 13, 1920; s. Joseph A. and Jane (Donahue) D.; m. Eugenie A. Fleri, Aug. 19, 1944; children: Christopher, Stephen, Eugenie, Jane, Richard. BS, Georgetown U., 1941; LLB, Columbia U., 1947. Bar: N.Y. 1948. Assoc. Shearman & Sterling, N.Y.C., 1947-57, ptnr., 1957-79, 81-97; asst. sec. for manpower, res. affairs and logistics USN, Washington, 1979-81. Bd. dirs. The Fuji Bank and Trust Co. Bd. dirs. USO of Met. N.Y., 1982-90. Lt. USNR, 1941-45. Decorated Navy Cross, D.F.C. with 3 gold stars, Air medal with 7 gold stars; recipient Disting. Pub. Service award Sec. of Navy, 1980. Mem. Met. Club (Washington). Democrat. Roman Catholic. Banking, Corporate, general, Finance. Home: 32 Washington Sq W New York NY 10011-9156

DOYLE, JUSTIN P. lawyer; b. Rochester, N.Y., Oct. 26, 1948; s. Justin Joseph and Jane Martha (Kreag) Doyle; children: Mary, Joe. BA, Dartmouth Coll., 1970; JD, Cornell U., 1974. Bar: N.Y. 1974. From assoc. to ptnr. Nixon, Hargrave, Devans & Doyle, Rochester, 1974-99; ptnr. Nixon Peabody LLP (formerly Nixon, Hargrave, Devans & Doyle), Rochester, 1999—. Mem.: Monroe County Bar Assn., N.Y. Bar Assn. Corporate, general, Mergers and acquisitions, Securities. Home: 252 Overbrook Rd Rochester NY 14618-3648 Office: Nixon Peabody LLP Clinton Sq PO Box 31051 Rochester NY 14603-1051

DOYLE, MICHAEL ANTHONY, lawyer; b. Atlanta, Nov. 4, 1937; s. James Alexander and Wilma (Summersgill) D.; children: John, David, Peter.; m. Bernice H. Winter, Nov. 12, 1977. BA, Yale U., 1959, LLB, 1962. Bar: Ga. 1961, D.C. 1967, U.S. Dist. Ct. D.C. 1967, U.S. Dist. Ct. (no. dist.) Ga. 1962, U.S. Ct. Appeals (5th cir.) 1962, U.S. Ct. Appeals (11th cir.) 1982, U.S. Ct. Appeals (D.C. cir.) 1968, U.S. Supreme Ct. 1972, U.S. Ct. Appeals (4th cir.) 1985. Assoc. Alston, Miller & Gaines, Atlanta, 1962-67; ptnr. Alston & Bird and predecessor, Atlanta, 1967—. Bd. dirs. Atlanta Legal Aid Soc., 1969-84, pres., 1975-76; bd. dirs. Ga. Legal Services Program; mem. Leadership Atlanta, 1974. Served to lt. USNR, 1964-69. Mem. ABA, State Bar Ga., Atlanta Lawyers Club, Master, Bleckley Inn of Court, Assn. Yale Alumni, Yale Law Sch. Assn. (nat. v.p. 1982-85, mem. exec. com. 1978-85, chmn. planning com. 1988-90, pres. 1991-92, chmn. exec. com. 1992-94). Piedmont Driving Club, Commerce Club, Yale Club Ga. (pres. 1982-84), Yale Club N.Y. Roman Catholic. Antitrust, Federal civil litigation, State civil litigation. Office: Alston & Bird 4200 One Atlantic Ctr 1201 W Peachtree St NW Atlanta GA 30309-3424

DOYLE, PAUL FRANCIS, lawyer; b. N.Y.C., Sept. 3, 1946; s. Paul Francis and Rita Lilian (Mulcahy) D.; m. Margaret Mary Sullivan, Aug. 23, 1969; children: Karen, Lynn. BA in English, Holy Cross Coll., 1968; JD cum laude, NYU, 1973. Bar: Mass. 1973, N.Y. 1975, U.S. Dist. Ct. (so. and ea. dists.) N.Y. 1975, U.S. Ct. Appeals (2d and 3d cirs.) 1975, U.S. Supreme Ct. 1991, U.S. Dist. Ct. Mass. 1992, U.S. Dist. Ct. (no. dist.) N.Y. 1995. Law clk. Superior Ct. Commonwealth of Mass., Boston, 1973-74; assoc. Kelley, Drye & Warren, N.Y.C., 1974-82, ptnr., 1983—. Instr. Nat. Inst. Trial Advocacy, 1994—95; mem. departmental disciplinary com. Supreme Ct. of N.Y., 1st Jud. Dept., 2003—. Assoc. editor Ann. Survey Am. Law, 1972-73. Mem. Planning Bd., Croton-on-Hudson, N.Y., 1989-92, mem. Comprehensive Plan Com., 1999—; mem. pres.'s coun. Holy Cross Coll. With U.S. Army, 1968-70, Vietnam. Mem. Am. Inns of Ct., Order of Coif. Roman Catholic. Federal civil litigation, General civil litigation, State civil litigation. Office: Kelley Drye & Warren LLP 101 Park Ave New York NY 10178-0062

DOYLE, RICHARD, lawyer; b. 1954; BA, Calif. State U., Chico; JD, McGeorge Sch. Law, 1979. Bar: Calif. 1979. Ptnr. Jensen & Doyle, San Francisco, 1979—89; atty. City of San Jose, Calif., 1989—95, chief mcpl. counsel, 2001—. Office: 151 W Mission St San Jose CA 95110 Business E-Mail: richard.doyle@ci.sj.ca.us.*

DOYLE, RICHARD HENRY, IV, lawyer; b. Elgin, Ill., Aug. 8, 1949; s. Richard Henry and Shirley Marian (Ohms) D.; m. Debbie Kay Cahalan, Aug. 2, 1975; children: John Richard, Kerry Jane. BA, Drake U., 1971, JD, 1976. Bar: Iowa 1976, U.S. Dist. Ct. (no. and so. dists.) Iowa 1977, U.S. Ct. Appeals (8th cir.) 1977, U.S. Supreme Ct. 1986. Asst. atty. gen. Iowa Dept. Justice, Des Moines, 1976-77; assoc. Lawyer, Lawyer & Jackson, Des Moines, 1977-79, Law Offices of Verne Lawyer & Assocs., Des Moines, 1979-93, Reavely, Shinkle, Bauer, Scism, Reavely & Doyle, Des Moines, 1993, Michael J. Galligan Law Firm, P.C., Des Moines, 1994-96, Galligan, Tully, Doyle & Reid, P.C., Des Moines, 1996—2003, Gulligan, Doyle & Reid PC, 2003. Lawyer; b. Elgin, Ill., Aug. 8, 1949; s. Richard Henry and Shirley Marian (Ohms) D.; m. Debbie Kay Cahalan, Aug. 2, 1975; children: John Richard, Kerry Jane. BA, Drake U., 1971, JD, 1976. Bar: Iowa 1976, U.S. Dist. Ct. (no. and so. dists.) Iowa 1977, U.S. Ct. Appeals (8th cir.) 1977, U.S. Supreme Ct. 1986. Asst. atty. gen. Iowa Dept. Justice, Des Moines, 1976-77; assoc. Lawyer, Lawyer & Jackson, Des Moines, 1977-79; assoc. Law Offices of Verne Lawyer & Assocs., Des Moines, 1979-93, Reavely, Shinkle, Bauer, Scism, Reavely & Doyle, Des Moines, 1993, Michael J. Galligan Law Firm, P.C., Des Moines, 1994-96. Contbr. articles to profl. jours. With U.S. Army, 1971-73. Fellow Iowa Acad. Trial Lawyers; mem. ABA, ATLA, Iowa Trial Lawyers Assn., Iowa Bar Assn., Iowa State Bar Assn., Polk County Bar Assn., SAR (registrar Iowa 1983-94, v.p. 1994-97, chancellor 1997-99), Order of the Founders and Patriots of Am., Phi Alpha Delta (chpt. pres. 1975). Contbr. articles to profl. jours. With U.S. Army, 1971-73. Fellow Iowa Acad. Trial Lawyers; mem. ABA, ATLA, SAR (registrar Iowa 1983-94, 2001—, v.p. 1994-97, chancellor 1997-2001), Iowa Trial Lawyers Assn., Iowa Bar Assn., Iowa State Bar Assn., Polk County Bar Assn., Order of the Founders and Patriots of Am., Phi Alpha Delta (chpt. pres. 1975). State civil litigation, Personal injury (including property damage). Home: 532 Waterbury Cir Des Moines IA 50312-1316 Office: Galligan Doyle & Reid PC The Plaza 300 Walnut St Ste 5 Des Moines IA 50309-2233 E-mail: rdoyle@galliganlaw.com.

DRABKIN, MURRAY, lawyer; b. N.Y.C., Aug. 3, 1928; s. Max Drabkin and Minnie Masin; m. Mary Elizabeth Hooper, Nov. 27, 1971. AB, Hamilton Coll., 1950; LLB, Harvard U., 1953. Bar: D.C. 1953, U.S. Ct. Appeals (D.C. cir.) 1954, N.Y. 1966, U.S. Supreme Ct. 1972. Counsel com. on judiciary U.S. Ho. of Reps., Washington, 1957-66; spl. asst. to mayor City of N.Y., 1966-68; pvt. practice N.Y.C. and Washington, 1968-82; ptnr. Cadwalader, Wickersham & Taft, Washington, 1983-92; ret., 1992; of counsel Hopkins & Sutter, Washington, 1992-2000. Dir. Conn. State Revenue Task Force, 1969-71; mem. adv. com. FRS, Washington, 1970-71, D.C. Tax Revision Com., 1976-77. Contbr. articles to profl. jours. Served with USN, 1953-57, to lt. comdr. USNR. Fellow Phi Beta Kappa (bd. dirs. 1996—, pres. 2001—); mem. Nat. Bankruptcy Conf. (chmn. com. on RR reorgn. 1984-2000, chmn. com on bankruptcy crimes, 1994-98), D.C. Bar Assn., Harvard Club of Washington (pres. 2000-02, bd. dirs. 1996—), Harvard Club of N.Y.C., Chesapeake Bay Bermuda 40 Assn., Cosmos Club, Nat. Press Club, Delta Sigma Rho. Bankruptcy, State and local taxation.

DRAGON, ALBERT, lawyer; b. Phila., June 2, 1937; m. Barbara Joan Meinster, June 25, 1970. BS, Temple U., 1958, JD, 1961, postgrad. Bar: Pa. 1962, U.S. Dist. Ct. (ea. dist.) Pa., U.S. Ct. Appeals (3d cir.), U.S. Supreme Ct. Ptnr. Dragon, Verlin & Galfand, Phila., 1968-71; pvt. practice Phila., 1971-82; pres. A. Dragon Assocs., Phila., 1982-94; of counsel Litvin, Blumberg, Matusow & Young, Phila., 1994—. Mem. Am. Trial Lawyers Assn., Pa. Trial Lawyers Assn., Phila. Bar Assn. (fee disputes com., state civil jud. procedures com., co-chair sole practitioners and small firms com. 1992, co-planner, panel mem. seminars), Phila. Trial Lawyers Assn. (bd. dirs.), Tau Epsilon Rho Law Soc. (bursar Phila. chpt., historian nat. soc., chmn. long range planning com., vice chancellor 1992, chancellor 1994-96, chmn. Pa. Supreme Ct. Disciplinary bd. hearing com.). Personal injury (including property damage), Product liability. Office: Litvin Blumberg Matusow & Young The Widener Bldg 18th Fl Philadelphia PA 19107

DRAGOO, DENISE ANN, lawyer; b. Colorado Springs, Mar. 28, 1952; d. Harold E. and Irma A. D.; m. Craig W. Anderson, Nov. 25, 1977. BA in History, U. Colo., 1973; cert. planning, JD, U. Utah, 1976; LLM in Environ./Land Use Law, Washington U., 1977. Bar: Utah 1978. Staff Environ. Law Inst., Washington, 1977; shareholder Fabian and Cleudenin, 1981—95; spl. asst. atty. gen. energy & natural resources State of Utah, Salt Lake City, 1978-81; shareholder VanCott Bagley Corwall & McCarthy, 1995-98; ptnr. Snell & Wilmer, LLP, 1998—. Mem. coal com. We. States Policy Office, 1980—81; bd. bar commrs. Utah State Bar, 1991—2002, jud. conduct com., 1993—2002. Named Woman Lawyer of Yr., Woman Lawyers Utah, 1997; recipient Dorothy Brothers Merrill award for advancement of women in law Utah State Bar, 2003. Fellow: Am. Bar Found.; mem.: ABA (mem. mining com. 1999—, chair SONREEL pub. lands com.), Utah Mining Assn. (bd. dirs. 2002—), Utah Bar and Gavel Soc., Rocky Mtn. Mineral Law Assn. (trustee 1987, mem. exec. com. 2002—). Environmental, Natural resources, Property, real (including real estate development, water). Home: 1826 Hubbard Ave Salt Lake City UT 84108-1362 Office: Snell & Wilmer 15 W South Temple Ste 1200 Salt Lake City UT 84101-1547

DRAKE, EDWIN P. lawyer; b. Battle Creek, Mich., Mar. 18, 1960; s. Ross Burton and Mary (Smith) D.; m. Janet Anne Van Dongen, May 9, 1981; children: Caleb, Rachel, Bethany, Hannah. BS, Olivet Nazarene U., Kankakee, Ill., 1981; JD, MBA, U. Tenn., Knoxville, 1984. Bar: Pa. 1984. Atty. Alcoa Inc., Pitts., 1985-90, counsel, 1991—. Student materials editor U. Tenn. Law Rev., Knoxville, 1982-84. Mem. Order of Coif. Avocations: dramatic musical theatre acting, slot car collecting. Antitrust, Corporate, general, Mergers and acquisitions. Office: Alcoa Inc 201 Isabella St Ste 6014 Pittsburgh PA 15212-5859

DRAKE, FRANCIS LEBARON, law librarian; b. Pitts., Aug. 17, 1944; s. Francis LeBaron Sarah Jane (Fultz) D. BA, Oberlin Coll., 1966; MMus, U. Tex., 1973, MLS, 1978. Info. specialist Telemedia, Inc., Chgo., 1979-83; dir. libr. svcs. Arnstein & Lehr, Chgo., 1983—. Profl. mem. Chgo. Symphony Chorus, 1980—. Mem. Chgo. Assn. Law Librs. (sec. 1992-93, pres. 2000-01, chair nominations com. 2002-03, chair relations with Information Vendors Com. 1994-96), Am. Assn. Law Librs. (chair coun. of chpt. presidents, 2001-02) Office: Arnstein & Lehr Ste 1200 120 S Riverside Plz Rm 1200 Chicago IL 60606-3910

DRAKE, JAMES FREDERICK, barrister; b. Adelaide, Australia, Mar. 13, 1959; s. Frederick George and Palmira Rose Drake; m. Karen Jane Falcocchio, Mar. 27, 1993; children: Sophie, Hannah, Thomas. BA, U. South Australia, 1979; LLB with honors, U. Adelaide, 1984; LLM, Columbia U., 1992. Acct. KPMG, Adelaide, Australia, 1980—81; solicitor Reilly Ahern & Kerin, 1985—86, Baker & McKenzie, Sydney, 1987—93; barrister 7 King's Bench Walk, London, 1998—. Mem.: Am. Australian Assn. (exec. dir. 1994—98), Bar Assn. City of N.Y. (mem. com. internat. trade 1995—98), Wentworth Club. Avocation: golf.

DRAKE, WILLIAM FRANK, JR., lawyer; b. St. Louis, Mar. 29, 1932; s. William Frank and Beatrice Drake; m. Martha Minohr Mockbee. BA, Principia Coll., 1954; LLB, Yale U., 1957. Bar: Pa. 1958. Practice, Phila., 1958-68, 84—; mem. firm Montgomery, McCracken, Walker & Rhoads, 1958-68, 87-96, of counsel, 1984-87, 96—; sr. v.p., gen. counsel Alco Std. Corp., 1968-79, 96-98, sr. v.p. adminstrn., 1979-83; chmn., CEO Alco Health Svcs. Corp., 1983-84, vice chmn., 1984-98, also bd. dirs.; vice chmn., gen. counsel Alco Standard Corp. (now Ikon Office Solutions Inc.), 1996-98. Trustee Peoples Light & Theatre Co., Malvern, Pa. With U.S. Army, 1957-58. Mem. ABA, Phila. Bar Assn., Union League (Phila.), Roaring Fork Club (Basalt, Colo.), Wilmington (Del.) Country Club, First Troop, Phila. City Calvary. Corporate, general, Pension, profit-sharing, and employee benefits, Securities. Office: Montgomery McCracken Walker & Rhoads 123 S Broad St Fl 24 Philadelphia PA 19109-1099

DRAKEMAN, DONALD LEE, biotechnology company executive, lawyer; b. Camden, N.J., Oct. 21, 1953; s. Fred J. and Jean (Faucett) D.; m. Lisa Natale Drakeman, Aug. 23, 1975; children: Cynthia, Amy. AB magna cum laude, Dartmouth Coll., 1975; JD, Columbia U., 1979; MA, Princeton U., 1984, PhD, 1988. Bar: N.J. 1979, U.S. Dist. Ct. N.J. 1979, N.Y. 1980, U.S. Supreme Ct. 1984. Assoc. Milbank, Tweed, Hadley & McCloy, N.Y.C., 1979-82; gen. counsel Essex Chem. Corp., Clifton, N.J., 1982-89, v.p., 1987-89; pres. Essex Med. Products, Clifton, 1988-89; pres., CEO Medarex, Inc., Annandale, N.J., 1987—. Adj. prof. polit. sci. Montclair State Coll., NJ, 1984; rsch. cons. Lilly Found., Inc., 1989—90; lectr. dept. politics Princeton U., 1990—93, 1995—; bd. dirs. Mannkind, Inc., Oxford; chmn. adv. coun. James Madison Program in Am. Ideals and Instn., Princeton U., 2000—; co-chair adv. coun. dept. religion Princeton U. Author: Church-State Constitutional Issues, 1990; co-editor Church and State in American History, 2d edit., 1986, 3d edit., 2003; contbr. articles to profl. jours. Chmn. Montclair Bd. Adjustment, 1984; trustee, chair Biotech. Coun. N.J., 1996-98; trustee U. Charleston, 1999-2003, Drew U., 2002—; adv. coun. Rutgers Bus. Sch., 2002—. Harlan Fiske Stone scholar, Columbia U., 1976-79; inducted N.J. High Tech Hall of Fame, 2000. Mem.: AAAS, ABA, John Maclean Soc., Asssn. Bar City N.Y., Yale Club, Princeton Club, Princeton Alumni Coun. Home: 49 Rolling Hill Rd Skillman NJ 08558-2319 Office: Medarex Inc 707 State Rd Princeton NJ 08540-1437 E-mail: ddrakeman@medarex.com.

DRAPER, DANIEL CLAY, retired lawyer; b. Boston, June 7, 1920; s. John W. and Lulu H. (Clay) D.; m. Marcia Humphreys, Nov. 25, 1989. BA, W.Va. U., 1940, MA, 1941; LLB, Harvard U., 1947. Assoc. Kelly, Drye & Warren, N.Y.C., 1947-55; ptnr. Cadwalader, Wickersham & Taft, N.Y.C., 1962-91, ret. Bd. dirs. Union Devel., Montclair, N.J.; adj. prof. history Bloomfield Coll., 1991. Contbr. articles to profl. jours. Mgr. campaign Montclair's Cmty. Com. Candidates, 1964; trustee Montclair Art Mus., 1966-71, Bloomfield Coll., 1974-81, 87-95. With USN, 1942-46. Decorated Bronze Star, European Service Ribbon (3 stars). Mem. N.Y. State Bar Assn. (chmn. banking com. 1981-85), N.Y. County Lawyers Assn. (sec. 1979-81, pres. 1984-87, chmn. banking com. 1968-78, housing and urban affairs and real property coms., chmn. investment com.), St. George Soc., Harvard Club, N.Y.C. Episcopalian. Home: 14 Houston Rd Little Falls NJ 07424-2406

DRAPER, GERALD LINDEN, lawyer; b. Oberlin, Ohio, July 14, 1941; s. Earl Linden and Mary Antoinette (Colloto) Draper; m. Barbara Jean Winter, Aug. 26, 1960; children: Melissa Leigh Price, Stephen Edward. BA, Muskingum Coll., 1963; JD, Northwestern U., 1966. Bar: Ohio 1966, US Dist Ct (so dist) Ohio 1966, US Ct Appeals (6th cir) 1975, US Supreme Ct 1980, US Dist Ct (no dist) Ohio 2000. Ptnr. Bricker & Eckler, Columbus, Ohio, 1966-88, Thompson, Hine & Flory, Columbus, 1989-95, Draper, Hollenbaugh, Briscoe, Yashko & Carmany, Columbus, 1996-99, Roetzel & Andress, Columbus, 1999—. Trustee Ohio Bd. Bar Examiners, 1996—99; trustee bd. commns. on unauthorized practice of law Ohio Supreme Ct., 2002—; mem. Ohio Commn. on Unauthorized Practice of Law, 2002—, Ohio Med. Malpractice Commn., 2003—. Trustee, pres Wesley Glen Retirement Ctr, Columbus, Ohio, 1979—95; trustee Meth Elder Care Servs, Inc, 1995—, Muskingum Coll., New Concord, Ohio, 1988—92, 1993—, vice chair, 1994—; trustee, pres Wesley Ridge Retirement Ctr, 1995—2000, treas, 2001—. Fellow: Am Bd Trial Advs (trustee Ohio chpt. 2001), Am Col Trial Lawyers; mem.: ABA (House Dels 1991—97, 1999—2001), Def Research Inst, Ohio Asn Hosp Attys, Ohio Continuing Legal Educ Inst (trustee 1992—98, chair 1997—98), Nat Conf Bar Found (trustee 1987—90, 1991—94), Columbus Bar Found (pres 1984—86), Columbus Bar Asn (pres 1982—83, Bar Serv Medal 1998), Ohio State Bar Found (trustee 1992—97), Ohio State Bar Asn (pres 1990—91). Avocations: travel, golf, photography. General civil litigation, Insurance, Professional liability. Office: Roetzel & Andress 155 E Broad St Columbus OH 43215-3609 E-mail: gdraper@ralaw.com.

DRAPER, STEPHEN ELLIOT, lawyer, engineer; b. Columbus, Ga., Mar. 17, 1942; s. Philip Henry and Ethel Illges (Woodruff) D.; m. Lucy Leila Hargrett, June 20, 1970; 1 child, Jessie Roxanne. BS, U.S. Mil. Acad., 1964; MBA, C.W. Post/L.I. U., 1976; JD, Ga. State U., 1992; MSCE, PhD, Ga. Inst. Tech., 1971, 81. Registered profl. engr., Ga., Fla. Commd. 2d. lt. U.S. Army, 1964, advanced through grades to col., retired, 1984; forensic engr. Atlanta, 1984-86; pres. and tech. dir. Draper Engring. Rsch., Atlanta, 1986-93, The Draper Group, Atlanta, 1993-98; mil. policy advisor, water policy advisor Gov. of Ga., Brig. Gen., 1999—2002. Apptd. mem. Clean Water Initiative, Met. Atlanta C. of C., 2000; rep. to gov. Ga. Joint Sturdy Com. Statewide Comprehensive Water Mgmt., 2001—02. Editor, prin. author: Model Water Sharing Agreements for the 21st Century, 2002; contbr. articles to profl. jours. Bd. dirs. J.W. & E.I. Woodruff Found., Columbus, Ga., 1991—, Met. Boys Club, Columbus, 1981-84; mem. long-range planning com. Atlanta Area Coun., Boys Scouts Am., 1972; trustee the Foxcroft Sch., Middleburg, Va., 1994; bd. visitors U. Ga. Libr., 1997—; mem. svc. acad. selection bd. U.S. Senate, 1998—. Decorated Gallantry Cross with Palm and Silver Star, Legion of Merit, Bronze Star (2), Soldier's medal, Purple Heart (3), Air medal (2), Army Commendation medal (4), others; recipient Am. Jurisprudence award Ga. State U., 1992, Spl. Actions award Women's Equity Action League, 1976. Mem. ABA, ASCE, NSPE, Am. Water Resources Assn., Nat. Acad. Forensic Engrs., Nature Conservancy of Ga. (bd. dirs. 1998—), Ga. Conservancy (bd. dirs. 1999—), Capital City Club, Commerce Club, Sea Island Beach Club. Avocations: travel, history, sports, phys. fitness. Office: The Draper Group 1401 Peachtree St NE Ste 500 Atlanta GA 30309-3000

DRASCO, DENNIS J. lawyer; b. Hoboken, N.J., July 15, 1948; s. John S. and Helen (Maher) D.; m. Janet O'Leary, Aug. 8, 1970. BA, Fordham Coll., 1970; JD, Rutgers U., 1973. Bar: N.J. 1973, U.S. Ct. Appeals (3rd cir.) 1975, N.Y. 1982, U.S. Dist. Ct. N.J. 1973, U.S. Dist. Ct. (so. dist.) N.Y. 1985, U.S. Tax Ct. 1978, U.S. Supreme Ct. 1985, U.S. Dist. Ct. (ea. dist.) N.Y. 1989, U.S. Ct. Appeals (2nd cir.) 1991. Assoc. Lum, Biunno & Tompkins, Newark, 1973-80, ptnr., 1980-83, Lum, Hoens, Abeles, Conant & Danzis, Roseland, N.J., 1984-88, Lum, Hoens, Conant, Danzis & Kleinberg, Roseland, 1989-94, Lum, Danzis, Drasco, Positan & Kleinberg, Roseland, 1995—2002, Lum Danzis Drasco & Positan LLC, Roseland, 2003—. Author: (with others) Condemnation Trial Manual, 1983, Bad faith Condemnation, ABA Trial Notebook, 1992, How to Get From the War Room to the Courtroom: The Basics for Civil Trial Preparation, 1993, Construction Contracts: Arbitration as a Means of Dispute Resolution in New Jersey, 2003; mem. editl. bd. N.J. Lawyer, 1992-94. Trustee, bd. dirs. United Way of North Essex, 1991-97; trustee Assn. Fed. Bar of N.J., 2001—; active Charter Study Com., Verona, N.J. Mem. ABA (ho. of dels. 2002—, chair condemnation land use and zoning litig. 1987-90, chair constrn. litig. com. 1990-93, divsn. dir. litig. sect. 1993-94, coun. litig. sect. 1994-97, vice chair litig. sect. 2002-03), N.J. State Bar Assn. (pub. contract law com., civil trial com., co-chair task force for minority trial lawyer 1997-99, co-chair coordinating com. of diversity 1997-99, dir. divsn. 1997-99), N.J. Civil Trial Atty. Bd. (cert.), Essex County Bar Assn. (chair jud. selection com., 2001—, co-chair joint med. legal com.), Essex County Legal Svcs. Found. (bd. dirs.), Seton Hall Law Sch. Inn of Ct. (master 1992—), Verona Jaycees (pres. Disting. Svc. award 1979-80), Essex Fells Country Club, La Chaine des Rotisserurs (vice charge de Mission 1987-89, de Argentier 1990—), Verona Lions Club (v.p. 1994-97, pres. 1997-98). Democrat. Roman Catholic. Avocations: golf, wine. General civil litigation, Condemnation (eminent domain), Construction. Office: Lum Danzis Drasco & Positan LLC 103 Eisenhower Pkwy Roseland NJ 07068-1029

DRAUGHON, SCOTT WILSON, lawyer, social worker, educator; b. Muskogee, Okla., June 17, 1952; s. Arthur Eugene and Helen Carrie (Vanhooser) D. AA, Tulsa Jr. Coll., 1972; BA, Okla. State U., 1974; JD, U. Tulsa, 1977; postgrad., Oxford U., Eng., 1978; MSW, U. Okla, 1992. Bar: Okla. 1979, U.S. Dist. Ct. (no. dist.) Okla. 1980, U.S. Claims Ct., U.S. Tax Ct. 1979, U.S. Ct. Appeals (10th cir.) 1984, U.S. Supreme Ct. 1984; lic. social worker with clin. splty. cert.; lic. tchr. social studies, sch. counselor. Sole law practice, Tulsa, 1979—; stockbroker, 1983-93; pvt. practice fin. planning, 1984—; aftercare dept. coord. Tulsa Boys' Home, 1992-94; pvt. practice social worker, 1994—; legal counsel Tulsa City-County Health Dept., 1996-97; clin. social worker Cushing (Okla.) Regional Hosp., 1996-99; social worker Hospice of Green Country, Inc., 2000—. Founder, exec. dir. The Fin. Hotline, Tulsa, 1984—; adj. faculty Tulsa Jr. Coll., 1986-87; v.p. govtl. and pub. affairs Okla. Credit Union League, Inc., 1988-90, dir. rsch./info. Okla. Credit Union Affiliates, 1991; founder Internat. Family Providers Alliance, 2000—. Mem. Indian Affairs Commn. City of Tulsa, 1989-91, 20th Anniversary Com. Leadership Tulsa, Inc., 1992—, class IX grad.; mem. exec. bd. Tulsa Assn. Vol. Adminstrs., 1994-95; bd. dirs. Arts and Humanities Coun., Tulsa, 1982-83, Ea. Okla. chpt. March of Dimes, 1989-90, Internat. Coun. Tulsa, 1987-91, Tulsa County Regional Planning Coord. Bd. Svcs. to Children and Youth, 1992-95; mem. exec. com. Corp. Vol. Coun. Greater Tulsa, 1990; chmn. pub. rels. com., exec. com. Tulsa Human Rights Commn., 1987-88; registered lobbyist Okla. Credit Union League Affiliate, 1988-90; grad. Okla. Aging Advocacy Leadership Acad., 2000; vol. docent Tulsa 2000, 1999—; mem. Okla. Human Rights Commn., 1997-2000, vice chmn., 1999. Mem. NASW (past chmn. internat. activities com., Okla. chpt.), Okla. Bar Assn., Masons, Shriners, Phi Delta Phi. Republican. Methodist. Avocations: travel, photography, reading, gardening, cooking. Estate planning, Health, Labor (including EEOC, Fair Labor Standards Act, labor-management relations, NLRB, OSHA). Address: 9071 E 28th St Tulsa OK 74129-6806

DRAYTON, WILLIAM, social entrepreneur, lawyer, management consultant; b. N.Y.C., June 15, 1943; s. William A. and Joan (Bergere) D. BA, Harvard, 1965; MA, Oxford (Eng.) U., 1967; JD, Yale, 1970. Bar: N.Y. 1971, D.C. 1976. Cons. McKinsey and Co., Inc., N.Y.C., 1970-77, of counsel, 1981-87; vis. assoc. prof. law Stanford, 1975-76; lectr. John F. Kennedy Sch. of Govt., Harvard U.; also dir. Harvard Regulatory and Mgmt. Group, 1976-77; cons. White House Domestic Coun., 1977; asst. adminstr. for planning and mgmt. EPA, 1977-81; pres. Environ. Safety, Washington, 1981-89, chair, 1989—; pres., founder Ashoka: Innovators for the Pub., Arlington, Va., 1980-2001, chair, CEO, 2001—. Nat. staff mem. Hubert H. Humphrey Presdl. Campaign, Washington, 1968; dir. Corp. for Fiscal Policy, 1971-75; founder, chmn. Yale Legis. Svcs.; mem. adv. coun. Carnegie Commn. Sci., Tech. and Govt., 1990-96. Contbr. articles to mgmt., devel. and legal jours. Pres. Ams. in India for McGovern, 1972; mem. Carter-Mondale Policy Planning, 1976, Carter-Mondale Govt. Reorgn. Transition Group, 1976-77; dep. dir. for issues Mondale-Ferraro campaign, 1984; mem. energy and environment com. Dem. nat. Com., 1982-86; bd. dirs. Oxfam Am., 1985-89, Appropriate Tech. Internat., 1988-97, chmn. bd. dirs., 1989-97; trustee Black Rock Forest (formerly Harvard Forest), N.Y.; chmn. bd. dirs. Youth Venture, 1994—; founder, chair Get Am. Working!, 1997—; pres. Save EPA, Washington, 1981-83; chair Cmty. Greens, 2000—; founder, dir. Social Entrepreneur Assocs., 1998—. Recipient Ann. award for Entrepreneurial Excellence Yale U. Sch. Mgmt., 1987, Nat. Pub. Svc. award Nat. Acad. Pub. Adminstrn. and Am. Soc. for Pub. Adminstrn., 1995, Pub. Svc. Achievement award Common Cause, 1999, Vanguard Nonprofit Lawyers award ABA, 2002, Edward A. Smith Award for Excellence in Nonprofit Leadership, 2002; Henry fellow, 1965-67, MacArthur Prize fellow, 1984-89. Mem. AAAS (com. on sci. pub. policy 1973-76), Assn. Bar City N.Y., Friends of India Soc. (chmn. 1974-75), Coun. Fgn. Rels., Nat. Acad. Pub. Adminstrn., Am. Acd. Arts and Scis., Asia Soc. (contemporary affairs com. 1987—2000), India Internat. Ctr. (New Delhi), Yale Club N.Y., Harvard Club N.Y., Phi Beta Kappa. Home: 1200 N Nash St Arlington VA 22209-3616 Office: 1700 N Moore St Ste 2000 Arlington VA 22209-1921

DREBSKY, DENNIS JAY, lawyer; b. N.Y.C., Sept. 28, 1946; s. Benjamin and Ronnie (Penso) D.; m. Norma Louise Linschitz, Aug. 16, 1970; children: Richard Michael, Joshua William Evan. BBA magna cum laude, CCNY, 1967; JD, Cornell U., 1970. Bar: N.Y. 1971, U.S. Dist. Ct. (so. dist.) N.Y. 1972, U.S. Ct. Appeals (2d cir.) 1971, U.S. Ct. Appeals (5th cir.) 1980, U.S. Ct. Appeals (9th cir.) 1982, U.S. Ct. Appeals (1st cir.) 1981, U.S. Ct. Appeals (10th cir.) 1984, U.S. Ct. Appeals (4th cir.) 1986, U.S. Ct. Appeals (D.C. cir.) 1998. Assoc. Skadden, Arps, Slate, Meagher & Flom, N.Y.C., 1970-77, ptnr., 1978-91, Clifford, Chance, Rogers & Wells, 1991—. Trustee Community Law Offices, N.Y.C., 1980—. Mem. Assn. of Bar of City of N.Y. (mem. com. on corp. reorgn. 1985—). Jewish. Avocations: reading, jogging, theater. Bankruptcy, General civil litigation, Corporate, general. Home: 7 Glen Hill Ct Dix Hills NY 11746-4819 Office: Clifford Chance Rogers & Wells 200 Park Ave Fl 8E New York NY 10166-0800 E-mail: dennis.drebsky@cliffordchance.com.

DRECHSEL, ROBERT EDWARD, journalism educator; b. Fergus Falls, Minn., Aug. 7, 1949; BA, U. Minn., 1971, MA, 1976, PhD, 1980. Reporter, city editor Daily Jour., Fergus Falls, 1971-74; instr. dept. journalism S.D. State U., Brookings, 1976-77; asst. prof. dept. tech. journalism Colo. State U., Ft. Collins, 1979-83; from asst. prof. to assoc. prof. Sch. Journalism and Mass Comm. U. Wis., Madison, 1983-91, prof., 1991—, dir., 1991-98; affiliated prof. law U. Wis., Madison, 2000—. Author: News Making in the Trial Courts, 1983; contbr. articles to profl. jours. Mem. Assn. Edn. Journalism and Mass Comm. (Krieghbaum Outstanding Achievement Rsch., Teaching & Pub. Svc. award 1989), Am. Judicature Soc., Wis. Freedom Info. Coun., Internat. Comm. Assn. Office: U Wis Sch Journalism & Mass Comm 821 University Ave Madison WI 53706-1412 E-mail: drechsel@wisc.edu.

DREIER, WILLIAM ALAN, lawyer; b. N.Y.C., Sept. 18, 1937; s. Henry M. and Mildred R. Dreier; m. Sandra F. Hollander, June 12, 1960; children: Susan Dreier Wishnow, David H. BS, MIT, 1958; JD, Columbia U., 1961. Bar: N.J. 1961, N.Y. 1988, U.S. Dist. Ct. N.J. 1961, U.S. Dist. Ct. (so. dist.) N.Y. 1999, U.S. Ct. Claims 1972, U.S. Ct. Appeals (3d cir.) 1972, U.S. Ct. Appeals (2d cir.) 1999, U.S. Ct. Appeals (fed. cir.) 2000, U.S. Supreme Ct. 1969. Law clk. to Hon. Sidney Goldmann Superior Ct. N.J., Trenton, 1961-62, judge law divsn., 1973—80, judge chancery divsn., 1980-83, judge appellate divsn. Springfield, 1983-84, presiding judge, 1984-98; assoc. Gordon, Mackenzie & Welt, Elizabeth, 1962-65; ptnr. Mackenzie, Welt & Dreier, Elizabeth, 1965-73, Norris, McLaughlin & Marcus, Somerville, N.J., 1998—. Lectr. N.J. Inst. for CLE, 1978, 80, 82-96, 98, Nat. Jud. Coll., U. Nev., Reno, 1982-90, N.J. Jud. Coll., 1977—, N.J. Inst. Mcpl. Attys., 1969-72, Seton Hall Law Sch., 1992—, Rutgers U. Law Sch., 1995, U. Mich. Law Sch., 1996, U. Tex. Law Sch., 1998, also numerous others; corp. counsel City of Plainfield, N.J., 1969-73; arbitrator, mediator Graduate Ctr. Dispute Settlement, Washington; panel Distinguished Neutrals CPR Inst. Dispute Resolution; arbitrator Am. Arbitration Assn. Author: Secured Financing under the Uniform Commercial Code, 1963, 8th edit., 1989, Products Liability and Toxic Torts Law in New Jersey—A Practitioner's Guide, 1978, 6th edit., 1988, Chancery Practice in New Jersey, 1983, 4th edit., 1997, New Jersey Products Liability and Toxic Torts Law, 1995, 96, 98-; mem. editl. bd. N.J. Law Jour., 1998—; contbr. articles to law jours. Mem. bd. visitors Columbia U. Law Sch., N.Y.C., 1993—; mem. com. on continuing profl. edn., product liability adv. group Am. Law Inst.-ABA, 1985—97; mem. standing com. on evidence N.J. Supreme Ct., 1981—, civil practice, 1979—90; mem. Plainfield City Coun., 1966—69; treas., dist. committeeman Plainfield Rep. City Com., 1963. Named Plainfield's Outstanding Citizen, Plainfield Jaycees, 1972; recipient Jud. Achievement award Nat. Inst. for Child Custody and Divorce Awareness, 1979, Alfred C. Clapp award for excellence N.J. Inst. CLE, 1993. Fellow Am. Bar Found. (life); mem. ABA, Am. Law Inst., N.J. Bar Assn., Plainfield P.B.A. (hon. life), Twin Brooks Country Club (pres. bd. govs. 1997), Richard J. Hughes Am. Inn Ct. (master 1988—). Avocations: golf, classical music. Alternative dispute resolution, General civil litigation, Product liability. Home: 48 Skyline Dr Warren NJ 07059-6718 Office: Norris McLaughlin & Marcus 721 Rts 202-206 Somerville NJ 08876-1018 Fax: 908-722-0755. E-mail: wadreier@nmmlaw.com.

DRELL, LEA ARMSTRONG, lawyer; b. Chgo., Oct. 6, 1934; d. Sidney Citron and Mollie Rose Armstrong; m. Ronald Edward Drell, Mar. 28, 1953 (div. Mar. 28, 1978); children: Sydney Reiner, Michael, Murray; m. George McCarter Stuhr, Jan. 18, 1987. BA, Nat. Coll. Edn., 1970, MEd, 1978; JD, John Marshall Law Sch., 1985. Bar: Ill. 85. 7th grade sci. tchr. Wilmette (Ill.) Jr. H.S., 1975—76, 1977—85; 8th grade math. tchr. Red Oak Jr. H.S., Northbrook, Ill., 1976—77; assoc. Stuhr Law Offices, Joliet, Ill., 1985—86; ptnr. Stuhr & Drell, Joliet, 1986—. Bd. dirs. Will County Legal Assistance, Joliet. Bd. dirs. Joliet Jewish Congregation. Recipient Pro Bono award, Will County Legal Assistance, 1990, 2000. Family and matrimonial, Juvenile, General practice. Office: Stuhr and Drell 54 N Ottawaw St Joliet IL 60432 Fax: 815-722-3809. E-mail: stuhr_drell@earthlink.net.

DRENGLER, WILLIAM ALLAN JOHN, lawyer; b. Shawano, Wis., Nov. 18, 1949; s. William J. and Vera J. (Simmonds) D.; m. Kathleen A. Hintz, June 18, 1983; children: Ryan, Jeffrey, Brittany. BA, Am. U., 1972; JD, Marquette U., 1976. Bar: Wis. 1976, U.S. Dist. Ct. (ea. and we. dists.) Wis. 1976. Assoc. Herrling, Swain & Drengler, Appleton, Wis., 1976-78; dist. atty. Outagamie County, Appleton, 1979-81; corp. counsel Marathon County, Wausau, Wis., 1981-96, Drengler Law Firm, Wausau, Wis., 1997—. Vice chmn. Wis. Equal Rights Coun., 1978-83, Wis. Coun. on Criminal Justice, Madison, 1983-87. Nat. pres. Future Bus. Leaders Am., 1967-68; mem. nat. Dem. delegation, 1974-76; mem. adminstrv. com. Wis. Dems., Madison, 1977-81, 86-88; chmn. local Selective Svc. Bd., Wausau, 1982-89; mem. adv. bd. Wausau Salvation Army, 1986—; judge adv. officer Wis. Army N.G., 1989-96; bd. dirs. Wausau Youth/Little League Baseball, 1988—, team mgr., 1994-2002. Mem. ABA (chair com. on govt. lawyers, sect. state and local govt. 1991-93, bylaws com. govt. and pub. sect. lawyers divsn. 1993-98), KC, Nat. Assn. County Civil Attys. (dir. 1986-88, v.p. 1988-91, pres. 1991-92), Nat. Assn. Counties (bd. dirs. 1991-92, taxation and fin. steering com. 1991-93, deferred compensation adv. com. 1993-95, justice and pub. safety steering com. 1993-94), State Bar Wis. (govt. lawyers divsn., bd. dirs. 1982-86, sec. 1986-87, pres. 1989-91, professionalism com. 1987-91, 92-2000, solo and small firm practice com. 2001--), Kiwanis (lt. gov. 1985-86, club pres. 1989-90, chair past lt. govs. coun. 1990-91), Wausau Elks (parliamentarian 2000-03), Kiwanis Internat. Found. (Hixon Fellowship Award 2001). Roman Catholic. Avocations: baseball, camping, fishing, gardening, tennis. Criminal, Family and matrimonial, General practice. Office: PO Box 5152 609 Scott St Wausau WI 54402-5152

DRESCHER, JOHN WEBB, lawyer; b. Norfolk, Va., May 13, 1948; s. Otto Charles and Anne Best (Webb) D.; m. Dale McKeithan Moore, June 13, 1970; 1 child, Ryan. BA, Hampden-Sydney Coll., 1970; JD, U. Richmond, 1973. Bar: Va. 1973, U.S. Supreme Ct. 1980, U.S. Ct. Appeals (4th cir.) 1985, U.S. Dist. Ct. (ea. dist.) Va. 1976. Assoc. Brydges, Hammers & Hudgins, Virginia Beach, 1973-74; asst. atty. Office of Commonwealth Atty., Virginia Beach, 1974-75; assoc. Pickett, Spain & Lyle, P.C., Virginia Beach, 1976-78; ptnr. Pickett, Lyle , Siegel, Drescher & Croshaw P.C., Virginia Beach, 1979-87, Breit, Drescher & Imprevento, P.C., Norfolk, 1988—. Trustee Hampden-Sydney Coll., 2003—. Named among best lawyers in Am. Naifch & Smith, 1995—. Fellow Am. Bd. Trial Advocates; mem. ATLA, Va. Trial Lawyers Assn. (bd. govs. 1990—), Am. Inns Ct., Norfolk-Portsmouth Bar Assn., Hampden-Sydney Alumni Assn. (pres. 1990), U. Richmond Law Sch. Alumni Assn., Virginia Beach Bar Assn. (pres. 1990). Democrat. Episcopalian. Avocations: physical fitness, golf. Civil rights, Personal injury (including property damage), Product liability. Home: 925 Holladay Pt Virginia Beach VA 23451-3912 Office: Breit Drescher & Imprevento 1000 Dominion Twr 999 Waterside Dr Ste 1000 Norfolk VA 23510-3304 E-mail: jdrescher@breitdrescher.com.

DRESNER, BYRON, lawyer; b. N.Y.C., Nov. 13, 1927; s. Leo and Minnie (Plisner) D.; m. Irene Helen Dresner, Nov. 18, 1956; children: Lisa, Cheryl, Andrea. BSS, CCNY, 1949; LLB, NYU, 1951. Bar: N.Y. 1952, U.S. Supreme Ct. 1961, U.S. Ct. Appeals (2d cir.), U.S. Dist. Ct. (no., so., ea. dists.) N.Y. Assoc. Alexander Rockmore, N.Y.C., 1952-57; ptnr. Kronish, Dresner & Henle, 1957-66, Dresner & Henle, N.Y.C., 1966—; spl. master N.Y. State Supreme Ct., 1977—. Chmn., Anti-Defamation League Young Adults, 1954-55; treas. Maspeth Jewish Ctr., 1959-71; pres., trustee Flushing Jewish Ctr., 1971—; exec. v.p. Queens Jewish Community Council, 1981-84, pres., 1984-85; pres. Flushing Jewish Community Coun., 1986-89, 92—, v.p., 1991-92; bd. dirs. YMHA-YWHA, Flushing, 1979-91, v.p., 1990-91. With AUS, 1946-47. Mem. ABA, Bankruptcy Lawyers Bar Assn., N.Y. County Lawyers Assn., Brandeis Assn., Comml. Law League Am. Clubs: Camera, B'nai B'rith. Bankruptcy, Corporate, general, Property, real (including real estate development, water). Home: 45-57 189th St Flushing NY 11358-3430 Office: 276 Fifth Ave # 712 New York NY 10001 Personal E-mail: bdresner@nyc.rr.com. Business E-Mail: bdresner@dresnerhenle.com.

DRESSLER, ROBERT A. lawyer; b. Fort Lauderdale, Fla., Aug. 20, 1945; s. R. Philip and Elisabeth (Anthony) D.; children: James Philip, Kathryn S. AB cum laude, Dartmouth Coll., 1967; JD cum laude, Harvard U., 1973. Bar: Mass. 1973, Fla. 1974, D.C. 1980, U.S. Dist. Ct. (so. dist.) Fla., U.S. Dist. Ct. Mass., U.S. Ct. Appeals (1st cir.), U.S. Ct. Appeals (5th cir.), U.S. Supreme Ct. Assoc. Goodwin, Proctor & Hoar, Boston, 1973-75; ptnr. Dressler & Dressler, Ft. Lauderdale, 1975-82; mayor City of Ft. Lauderdale, 1982-86; pvt. practice law Ft. Lauderdale, 1982—. Bd. regents State Univ. System, 1987-93; mem. Estate Planning Coun. Broward County; adv. com. Fla. Atlantic U., Broward, 1989—; exec. com. Tchr. Edn. Alliance, 1991-2000. Capt USMC, 1969-72. Named Person of Yr. Fla. Atlantic U., 1993. Mem. ABA, Greater Ft. Lauderdale C.of C. (bd. govs. 1982-89), Broward County Bar Assn., Fla. Bar Assn., D.C. Bar Assn., Vietnam Vets. Am., Rotary Internat., Tower Forum (bd. govs. 1983--), Phi Beta Kappa. Presbyterian. Avocations: jogging, scuba diving, hiking. Estate planning, Probate (including wills, trusts), Estate taxation. Home: 1215 E Broward BlvdSuite 201 Fort Lauderdale FL 33301 Office: PO Box 2425 Fort Lauderdale FL 33303-2425

DRETZIN, DAVID, lawyer; b. N.Y.C., July 24, 1928; s. Isadore and Clara Yohalem D.; m. Joanna Merlin, Mar. 1, 1964; children: Rachel Dretzin Goodman, Julie Y. BA, Reed Coll., 1951; MA, U. Chgo., 1952; JD, Yale U., 1959. Bar: N.Y.; U.S. Dist. Ct. (so. and ea. dists.) N.Y, U.S. Supreme Ct. Asst. gen. counsel ILGWU, N.Y.C., 1959-62; assoc. Finkelstein, Benton & Soll, N.Y.C., 1962-66; ptnr. Heller & Dretzin, N.Y.C., 1966-68; pvt. practice N.Y.C., 1968-70; ptnr., counsel Dretzin, Kauff, McClain & McGuire, N.Y.C., 1970-90; ptnr. Stroock & Stroock & Lavan, N.Y.C., 1990-93; pvt. practice N.Y.C., 1994—. Bd. dirs. Floating Hosp., N.Y.C. Author: PLI Publs. on Employment Law. Pvt. U.S. Army, 1954-56. Mem. Bar Assn. of City of N.Y. (mem. com. on labor and employment law 1995-97), Phi Beta Kappa. Entertainment, Labor (including EEOC, Fair Labor Standards Act, labor-management relations, NLRB, OSHA). Office: 1251 Avenue Of The Americas New York NY 10020-1104

DREVVATNE, DAG, lawyer; b. Oslo, Oct. 10, 1955; s. Tor and Randi D.; m. Elizabeth Christensen Drevvatne, June 19, 1993; children: Catherine Elizabeth, Camilla Charlotte. JD, U. Oslo, Norway, 1983. Lawyer Tax Office, Barum, Norway, 1984-86; atty. Arthur Andersen, Oslo, Norway, 1986-88, Vogt & Co., Oslo, Norway, 1989-94, Sander, Truyen & Co., Oslo, Norway, 1994-99; lawyer pvt. practice Oslo, Norway, 1999—. Avocations: boating, skiing, travel. Corporate, general, Franchising, General practice. Home: Asfaret 8 1362 Barum Norway Office: Advokat Dag Drevvatne Fossumveien 70 1332 Osteras Norway

DREW, STEPHEN RICHARD, lawyer; b. Detroit, May 25, 1949; s. Richard Theodore and Gwendolyn (Johnson) D.; m. Clarice Y. Smith, Apr. 22, 1989; children: Richard, Stephen, Anthony, Thomas, Sahara. BA, U. Mich., 1971, JD, 1974. Bar: Mich. 1974, U.S. Dist. Ct. (we. and ea. dists.) Mich. 1974, U.S. Ct. Appeals (6th cir.) 1979, U.S. Supreme Ct. 1989. Assoc. Reamon, Williams, Klukowski & Craft, Grand Rapids, Mich., 1974-77; ptnr. Williams, Klukowski, Drew & Fotieo, P.C., Grand Rapids, 1977-90, Drew, Cooper & Anding, Grand Rapids, 1991—. Spl. investigator Saginaw (Mich.) Police Dept., 1985-86; mem. jud. selection panel U.S. Ct. Appeals (6th cir.), Cin., 1986-87. Chmn. Grand Rapids Community Relations Comm., 1984-85; mem. legal redress com. Grand Rapids NAACP, 1987-89; bd. dirs. Hugh Michael Behan Fund, Grand Rapids, 1987-88; mem. U.S. Dist. Ct. Jud. Rev. com., 1990-91. Recipient Floyd Skinner Justice Giant award Grand Rapids Jr. Coll., 1988, Patriotic Service award U.S. Treasury, 1986, Giant of Giants award 1999. Fellow: Am. Coll.Trial Lawyers, Inns of Ct., Mich. State Bar; mem.: ACLU, ATLA (Civil Libertarian of Yr. 1989), ABA, Floyd Skinner Bar Assn. (pres. 1989—91), Grand Rapids Bar Assn. (trustee 1987—88, jud. selection com. 1990, pres. elect 1991—92, pres. 1992—93), Mich. Trial Lawyers Assn., Sigma Pi Phi. Democrat. Episcopalian. Avocations: golf, basketball. Civil rights, General civil litigation, Personal injury (including property damage). Office: Drew Cooper & Anding 125 Ottawa Ave NW Grand Rapids MI 49503-2898 E-mail: sdrew@dcadvocate.com.

DREXEL, RAY PHILLIPS, lawyer; b. Cleve., Aug. 28, 1949; s. Gordon Arthur and Jean Elizabeth (Phillips) D.; m. Beverly Lynn Beall, June 26, 1971; children: Kate Phillips, Alexander Ray. BS, Ohio State U., 1971; JD, Capital U., 1974. Bar: Ohio 1974, U.S. Dist. Ct. (so. dist.) Ohio 1975, U.S. Supreme Ct. 1978. Staff atty. Buckeye Fed. Savs. & Loan Assn., Columbus, Ohio, 1974-82; ptnr. Hilliard, Ramsey & Drexel, Columbus, 1982-85, Hilliard, Ramsey, Drexel & DePew, Columbus, 1985-86, Hilliard, Drexel & DePew, Columbus, 1986-89, Hilliard & Drexel, 1989-93, Buckley King, Columbus, 1994—. E2 v.p. Annehurst Village Residents Assn., Westerville, Ohio, 1983-86. Arnold Cohn Meml. scholar, 1970-71. Mem. Columbus Bar Assn., Mid Ohio Lenders Counsel Assn. (pres. 1978-80), Franklin County Trial Lawyers, Nat. Mgmt. Assn. (pres. Buckeye Fed. chpt. 1980-81), Masons. Republican. Methodist. State civil litigation, Commercial, consumer (including collections, credit), General practice. Office: Buckley King 10 W Broad St Ste 1300 Columbus OH 43215-3419

DREXLER, KENNETH, lawyer; b. Aug. 2, 1941; s. Fred and Martha Jane (Cunningham) D. BA, Stanford U., 1963; JD, UCLA, 1969. Bar: Calif. 1970. Assoc. David S. Smith, Beverly Hills, Calif., 1970, McCutchen, Doyle, Brown and Enersen, San Francisco, Calif., 1970-77, Chickering & Gregory, San Francisco, Calif., 1977-80, ptnr., 1980-82, Drexler & Leach, San Rafael, Calif., 1982—. Served with AUS, 1964-66. Mem. Calif. State Bar (resolutions com. conf. of dels. 1979-83, chmn. 1982-83, adminstrn. justice com. 1983-89, chmn. 1987-88, adv. mem. 1990-2000), Marin County Bar Assn. (bd. dirs. 1985-87), Bar Assn. San Francisco (bd. dirs. 1980-81), San Francisco Barristers Club (pres. 1976, dir. 1975-76), Marin Conservation League (bd. dirs. 1985-97, 98—, treas. 2001—). Estate planning, General practice. Office: 1330 Lincoln Ave Ste 300 San Rafael CA 94901-2143 E-mail: kdrexler@svn.net.

DREYER, JOHN EDWARD, lawyer; b. Feb. 22, 1929; s. Felix Edward and Marie Ann (Bungert) D.; m. Shirley Ann Fenhaus, May 29, 1954 (div.); children: Thomas, Laura, Gregory, Michael; m. Nancy A. Mickelson; stepchildren: Karen Mickelson Ortiz, Kevin W. Mickelson. BS, Loyola U., Chgo., 1951; JD, DePaul U., 1953. Bar: Ill. 1953, U.S. Dist. Ct. (no. dist.) Ill. 1953, U.S. Ct. Appeals (7th cir.) 1953, U.S. Ct. Mil. Appeals 1954. Jr. ptnr. Sears Streit, Tyler & Dreyer, Chgo. and Aurora, Ill., 1961-63; sr. ptnr. Dreyer, Foote & Streit, Assocs., Aurora, 1963-84, Dreyer, Foote, Streit, Furgason & Slocum, PA, 1984-94, of counsel, 1994—. Dir. Valley Nat. Bank Aurora, 1975-86. Bd. editors DePaul Law Rev., 1952-53. Bd. dirs. Family Support Ctr., Aurora, 1975-86. 1st lt. JAGC, U.S. Army, 1953-56. Mem. ABA, Ill. State Bar Assn. (assembly 1972-78), Kane County Bar Assn., Am. Judicature Soc., Ill. Soc. Trial Lawyers, Nat. Assn. R.R. Trial Counsel, Moose, Phi Alpha Delta, Pi Gamma Mu. State civil litigation, Labor (including EEOC, Fair Labor Standards Act, labor-management relations, NLRB, OSHA). Home: 3 S 611 Finley Rd Sugar Grove IL 00554 Office: 1999 W Downer Pl Aurora IL 60506

DRIGGS, CHARLES MULFORD, lawyer; b. East Cleveland, Ohio, Jan. 26, 1924; s. Karl Holcomb and Lila Vandeveer (Wilson) D.; children: Ruth, Rachel, Carrie, Karl H., Charles M.; m. Ann Eileen Zargari, Oct. 25, 1991. BS, Yale U., 1947, JD, 1950. Bar: Ohio 1951. Assoc. Squire, Sanders & Dempsey, Cleve., 1950-64, ptnr., 1964-88, of counsel, 1988-91; pvt. practice civil law Cleve., 1991-95; ptnr. Driggs, Lucas, Brubaker & Hogg Co., LPA, Mentor, Ohio, 1995—. Pres. Bratenahl (Ohio) Sch. Bd., 1958-62; mem. adv. coun. Cleve. Ctr. for Theol. Edn., 1978—. Mem. ABA, Ohio Bar Assn., Lake County Bar Assn., Cleve. Bar Assn., Greater Cleve. Growth Assn., Cleve. Law Libr. Assn. (trustee 1977-91), Ct. Nisi Prius (judge 2000), Citizens League Greater Cleve., Geauga County Bar Assn., Phi Delta Phi, Tau Beta Pi, Phi Gamma Delta. Estate planning, Probate (including wills, trusts), Estate taxation. Home: 9181 Hidden Glen Dr Mentor OH 44060-7359 Office: 8522 East Ave Mentor OH 44060 E-mail: Charles@DriggsLaw.com.

DRIKER, EUGENE, lawyer; b. Detroit, Feb. 24, 1937; s. Charles and Frances (Hoffman) D.; m. Elaine Carol Zeidman, June 17, 1959; children: Elissa Ruth, Stephen Joel. AB, Wayne State U., 1958, JD, 1961; LL.M., George Washington U., 1962; LLD (hon.) , Wayne State U., 2002. Bar: Mich. 1962, U.S. Ct. Appeals (5th and 6th cirs.), U.S. Supreme Ct. Trial atty. antitrust div. U.S. Dept. Justice, Washington, 1961-64; ptnr. Friedman, Meyers & Keys, Detroit, 1964-68, Barris, Sott, Denn & Driker, Detroit, 1968—. Lectr. law Wayne State U., Detroit, 1964-68; lectr. in field; arbitrator Am. Arbitration Assn. Commr. City of Detroit Bldg. Authority, 1974-79; mem. City of Detroit Bd. Police Commrs., 1979-83; chmn. Wayne State U. Law Sch. Fund, 1972-74, 87-88; bd. dirs. Jewish Vocat. Sch., 1983-92, pres., 1993-95; bd. dirs. Detroit Symphony Orch. Hall, Inc., 1983—; v.p. Am. Jewish Com., Detroit, 1988-90. Fellow Am. Coll. Trial Lawyers, Internat. Acad. Trial Lawyers, Am. Bar Found.; mem. Wayne State Law Sch. Alumni Assn. (pres. 1971-72), Am. Law Inst., Order of Coif, Detroit Club, Renaissance Club. Democrat. Jewish. Avocations: biking, reading, walking. Antitrust, General civil litigation, Corporate, general. Office: Barris Sott Denn & Driker 211 W Fort St Lbby 15 Detroit MI 48226-3244

DRINKO, JOHN DEAVER, lawyer; b. St. Marys, W.Va., June 17, 1921; s. Emery J. and Hazel (White) D.; m. Elizabeth Gibson, May 14, 1946; children: Elizabeth Lee Sullivan, Diana Lynn Drinko, John Randall, Jay Deaver. AB, Marshall U., 1942; JD, Ohio State U., 1944; postgrad., U. Tex. Sch. Law, 1944; LLD (hon.), Marshall U., 1980, Ohio State U., 1986, John Carroll U., 1987, Capital U., 1988, Cleve. State U., 1990; DHL (hon.), David N. Myers Coll., 1990, U. N.H., 1992, Baldwin-Wallace Coll., 1993, Ursuline Coll., 1994, Notre Dame Coll., 1997, U. Rio Grande, 1999, Marietta Coll., 2001. Bar: Ohio 1945, D.C 1946, U.S. Dist. Ct. (no. dist.) Ohio 1958. Assoc. Baker & Hostetler, Cleve., 1945-55, ptnr., 1955-69, mng. ptnr., from 1969, sr. adviser to mng. com. Chmn. bd. Cleve. Inst. Electronics Inc., Double D Ranch Inc., Ohio; bd. dirs. Cloyes Gear and Products Inc., McGean-Rohco Worldwide Inc., Orvis Co. Inc., Preformed Line Products Inc. Trustee Elizabeth G. and John D. Drinko Charitable Found., Orvis-Perkins Found., Thomas F. Peterson Found., Mellen Found., The Cloyes-Myers Found., Marshall U. Found.; founder Consortium of Multiple Sclerosis Ctrs., Mellen Conf. on Acute and Critical Care Nursing, Case Western Res. U. Disting. fellow Cleve. Clinc Found., 1991; Ohio State Law Sch. Bldg. named in his honor, 1995, libr. at Marshall U. named in his honor, 1997; inducted into Bus. Hall of Fame, Marshall Univ., 1996. Mem. ABA, Am. Jud. Assn., Bar Assn. Greater Cleve., Greater Cleve. Growth Assn., Ohio State Bar Assn., Jud. Conf. 8th Jud. Dist. (life), Soc. Benchers, Case Western Res. U. Law Sch. Assn., Cleve. Play House, Cleve. Civil War Round-table, Mayfield Country Club, Union Club, The Club at Soc. Ctr., O'Donnell Golf Club, Order of Coif, 33o Scottish Rite Mason, Knight Templar, York Rite, Euclid Blue Lodge No. 599 (Jesters, Shrine, Grotto). Republican. Presbyterian. Home: 4891 Middledale Rd Cleveland OH 44124-2522 also: 1245 Otono Dr Palm Springs CA 92264-8445 Office: Baker & Hostetler LLP 1900 E 9th St Ste 3200 Cleveland OH 44114-3475

DRIVER, WALTER W., JR., lawyer; b. El Paso, Tex., Apr. 10, 1945; s. Walter Williamson and Carolyn Bonds (Mayfield) D.; m. Bettie Townsend Willerson, Dec. 27, 1970; children: Eleanor, Anna, Walter III. AB, Stanford U., 1967; JD, U. Tex., 1970. Bar: Ga. 1970. Ptnr. King & Spalding, LLP, Atlanta, 1976—, chmn. policy com., 1992-94, 98-99, mng. ptnr., chmn., 2000—. Mem. exec. com. Children's Mus. Atlanta, 1990-95; bd. dirs. Ctrl. Atlanta Progress, 1993—; chair Celebration of Life Cancer Soc., 1993. Mem. ABA, State Bar Ga., U.S. Golf Assn. (gen. counsel 1997-99, mem. exec. com. 1999—, treas. 2000-01, v.p. 2001—), Ga. State Golf Assn. (gen. coun., exec. com. 1988-97), Atlanta C. of C. (exec. com., bd. dirs.), Piedmont Driving Club, Peachtree Golf Club (bd. dirs.), Pine Valley Golf Club, Seminole Golf Club. Banking, Commercial, contracts (including sales of goods; commercial financing). Office: King & Spalding LLP 191 Peachtree St Atlanta GA 30303-1763 E-mail: wdriver@kslaw.com.*

DRONEY, CHRISTOPHER F. judge; b. June 22, 1954; m. Elizabeth Kelly, Oct. 13, 1979. BA, Coll. Holy Cross, 1976; JD, U. Conn., 1979. Ptnr. Reid & Riege, P.C., Hartford, Conn., 1983-93; U.S. atty. for dist. of Conn. U.S. Dept. Justice, New Haven, 1993-97; judge U.S. Dist. Ct., Conn., 1997—. Notes and comments editor Conn. Law Rev., 1978-79. Mem. U.S. atty. gen. adv. com., 1996-97. Office: 450 Main St Hartford CT 06103-3022

DROPKIN, CHARLES EDWARD, lawyer; b. N.Y.C., Dec. 17, 1951; s. Harry and Jeanette Dropkin; m. Jeanine Deborah Love, Nov. 5, 1983; children: Melissa Emily, Rebecca Allyson. BA, Williams Coll., 1974; JD, Harvard U., 1977. Bar: N.Y. 1978, U.S. Dist. Ct. (so. and ea. dist.) N.Y. 1978, U.S. Ct. Appeals (2d cir.) 1981, U.S. Supreme Ct. 1981. With Milbank Tweed Hadley & McCloy, N.Y.C., 1977-94; chair banking and fin. instns. dept. Proskauer Rose LLP, N.Y.C., 1994—. Editl. adv. bd. Banking

Policy Report, 1994—; contbg. author: Securities Lending and Repurchase Agreements, 1997; contbr. articles to profl. jours. Fellow Am. Coll. of Investment Counsel; mem. Assn. of the Bar of the City of N.Y. (uniform state laws com. 2000—), N.Y. State Bar Assn. (exec. com. comml. and fed. litigation sect. 1989-91, creditors rights and banking litigation com. 1995—), B'Nai B'rith. Avocation: golf. Banking, General civil litigation, Securities. Home: 177 Laurel Dr Oradell NJ 07649-2422 Office: Proskauer Rose LLP 1585 Broadway New York NY 10036-8299 E-mail: cdropkin@proskauer.com.

DROWOTA, FRANK F., III, state supreme court chief justice; b. Williamsburg, Ky., July 7, 1938; married; 2 children. BA, Vanderbilt U., 1960, JD, 1965. Bar: Tenn. 1965, U.S. Dist. Ct. Tenn. 1965. Pvt. practice, 1965-70; chancellor Tenn. Chancery Ct. Div. 7, 1970-74; judge Tenn. Ct. Appeals, Middle Tenn. Div., 1974-80; assoc. justice Tenn. Supreme Ct., Nashville, 1980-89, chief justice, 1989-93, assoc. justice, 1993-2001; chief justice, 2001—. Served with USN, 1960-62. Office: Admin Office Cts 511 Union St Ste 600 Nashville TN 37219*

DRUCKER, JACQUELIN F. lawyer, arbitrator, educator, author; b. Celina, Ohio, Oct. 15, 1954; d. Jack Burton and Dorothea (Eckenstein) Davis; m. John H. Drucker, Sept. 8, 1990. BA with distinction and honors, Ohio State U., 1977, JD with honors, 1981. Bar: Ohio 1981, N.Y. 1992, U.S. Supreme Ct. 1989. Legis. asst. Speaker of Ohio Ho. of Reps., Columbus, 1974-78; rsch. asst., lobbyist United Auto Workers, Columbus, 1978-81; labor and employment atty. Porter, Wright, Morris & Arthur, Columbus, 1981—84; gen. counsel Ohio Employment Rels. Bd., Columbus, 1984-86, exec. dir., 1986-88, vice chmn., 1988-90; pvt. practice arbitration and mediation nationwide and the Caribbean, 1990—; dir. labor mgmt. programs sch. indsl. and labor rels. Cornell U., 1994-97. Dir. programs for neutrals Cornell U. Sch. of Indsl. and Labor Rels., 1996—; dir. for ednl. svcs. Cornell Inst. on Conflict Resolution, 1998—; cons. to W.J. Usery Ctr. for Workplace, Ga. State U.; counsel to Gov.'s Task Force on Collective Bargaining, Columbus, 1983-84; adj. prof. labor law Franklin U., Columbus, 1988-89; mem. panel of labor arbitrators Fed. Mediation and Conciliation Svc., Am. Arbitration Assn., Employment ADR Roster of Neutrals of Am. Arbitration Assn., N.Y. State Employment Rels. Bd.; mem. roster of neutrals N.Y.C. Office of Collective Bargaining; mem. panel V.I. Pub. Employment Rels. Bd., N.J. Pub. Employment Rels. Commn., N.Y. Pub. Employment Rels. Bd., Port Authority Employment Rels. Panel; mem. permanent arbitration panel United Mine Workers and Bituminous Coal Operators Assn., Am. Postal Workers Union, U.S. Postal Svc., Off-Track Betting Corp. and Local 32E, State of N.Y. and Pub. Employees Fedn., State of N.Y. and Civil Svc. Employees Assn., Consolidated Edison and Utility Workers Local 1-2, U. Cin. and Dist. 925, Beth Israel Med. Ctr. and 1199 Nat. Health and Human Svcs. Employees Union, Infineum and Teamsters Local 877; cons. labor mgmt. cooperation, 1996—; lectr., spkr. in field. Author: Collective Bargaining Law in Ohio, 1993; editor L.I. Indsl. Rels. Quar.; contbg. editor Pub. Sector Law and Employment Law supplement, 1995, Pub. Sector Labor and Employment Law, 2d edit.; assoc. editor Discipline and Discharge in Arbitration, 1998; contbg. editor: Public Sector Labor and Employment Law, 2nd edit., 1998; contbr. numerous articles to profl. jours. Mem. ABA (labor and employment law sect., neutral chmn. employment and labor law com. 2001—, co-chair tng. devel. sub-com. of ADR com., 1998-2001), Nat. Acad. Arbitrators, Ohio State Bar Assn., Assn. of Bar of City of N.Y., N.Y. State Bar Assn. (labor and employment law sect., chmn.-elect 2002—, sec. 1997-98, co-chair ADR in employment com. 1998-2001, continuing legal edu. chair, 2001-2002), N.Y. County Lawyers Assn. (employment law and labor rels. com., chmn.), Nassau County Bar Assn., Suffolk County Bar Assn., Indsl. Rels. Rsch. Assn. (N.Y. chpt., Cleve. chpt., L.I. chpt.), Soc. Fed. Labor Rels. Profls. Jewish. Alternative dispute resolution, Commercial, contracts (including sales of goods; commercial financing), Labor (including EEOC, Fair Labor Standards Act, labor-management relations, NLRB, OSHA). Office: 432 E 58th St Suite 2 New York NY 10022-2331 E-mail: jdrucker@aol.com.

DRUCKER, MICHAEL STUART, lawyer; b. Brookline, Mass., May 14, 1968; s. C. Gerard and Marjorie (Epstein) Drucker; m. Laura Ann Sugar, June 14, 1997; children: Samuel Evan, Maxwell Rubin. BA, U. Mich., 1990; JD, Suffolk U., 1993. Bar: Ga. 1993, Mass. 1993. Sr. dir., assoc. counsel The Collegiate Licensing Co., Atlanta, 1993—. Avocations: travel, sports, american literature, dining. Corporate, general, Sports, Trademark and copyright. Office: The Collegiate Lic Co 290 Interstate North Ste 200 Atlanta GA 30339-2205 E-mail: mdrucker@clc.com.

DRUEN, WILLIAM SIDNEY, lawyer; b. Farmville, Va., May 5, 1942; s. William Gills and Minnie (Kessler) D.; m. Janet Elizabeth Ward, Dec. 21, 1969; children— Courtney Paige, William Sidney II. B.A., Hampden Sydney Coll., 1964; LL.B., U. Va., 1968. Bar: Va. 1968, Ohio 1970. Spl. counsel Govs. Office State of Va., Richmond, 1968-70; with legal dept. Nationwide Ins. Co., Columbus, Ohio, 1970-82, v.p., assoc. gen. counsel, 1982-89; v.p., dep. gen. counsel, 1989-94, sr. v.p., gen. counsel, asst. sec., 1994—; asst. sec. Employer Mutual Ins. Wausau, Wis., 1986-94, sr. v.p., gen. counsel, 1994—; ptnr. Wagner, Schmidt, McCutchan, Hank & Birkhimer, 1970-76, McCutchan, Schmidt, Birkhimer & Druen, 1976-85, McCutchan, Schmidt & Druen, 1986-88, McCuthan, Druen, Maynard, Rath and Dietrich, 1988-93, McCutchan, Druen, Rath & Dietrich, 1993-94, Druen, Rath & Dietrich, 1994-97, Druen, Dietrich, Reynolds & Koogler, 1997—. Pres. bd. trustees German Village Found., 1983-86; bd. housing appeals City of Columbus, 1988-90; mem. Franklin County Alcohol, Drug Addiction and Mental Health Svcs. Bd., 1993-97; trustee Direction for Youth, 1989-93. Mem. Nat. Assn. Mutual Ins. Cos. Bd., Ohio Ins. Inst., Ohio Bar Assn., Va. Bar Assn., Columbus Bar Assn., Ohio C. of C. (bd. dirs.), Univ. Club (pres. 1992-93), Coun. Ethics in Econs. 1990-94. Republican. Corporate, general, Insurance. Home: 85 Deshler Ave Columbus OH 43206 Office: Nationwide Mut Ins Co 1 Nationwide Plz Columbus OH 43215-2239

DRUKE, WILLIAM ERWIN, lawyer, judge; b. Phoenix, Dec. 5, 1938; s. Erwin J. and Mary Nell (Hadden) D.; m. Shirley Jean Robinson, Aug. 12, 1978 (div. 1990); children: John E., Michael C.; m. Barbara L. Ross, Mar. 4, 1995. BS, Ariz. State U., 1961; JD, U. Ariz., 1969. Bar: Ariz. 1969, U.S. Dist. Ct. Ariz. 1969. Law clk. Ct. of Appeals, Phoenix, 1969-70; prosecutor Pima County Atty., Tucson, 1970-72; magistrate Tucson City Ct., 1972-74; judge Pima County Superior Ct., Tucson, 1975-85, presiding judge, 1980-85; ptnr. Druke, Feulner & Cornelio P.C., Tucson, 1985-86; assoc. Fred R. Esser, P.C., Sedona, Ariz., 1986-88; pvt. practice Tucson, 1988-92; judge Ariz. Ct. Appeals, Tucson, 1992—, chief judge, 1994-99. Mem. Commn. on Jud. Conduct, 1992-96; mem. Ariz. Jud. Coun., 1993-99; mem. Ariz. Supreme Ct. Appellate Study Com., 1994-95; chair bench/bar ad hoc criminal com., 1994-95; chair Ariz. Supreme Ct. Ct. Reporters Com., 1995-97; dean Ariz. Jud. Coll., 1999-2001. Mem. Juvenile Pro Bon Task Force, Tucson, 1991-92; bd. dirs. The Haven, Am. Heart Assn., Tucson, 1984-85, Alcoholism Counsel of Tucson, 1980-83; mem. Ariz. Criminal Justice Commn., Phoenix, 1983-85; judge Teen Ct.; vol. U. Med. Ctr. Fellow Ariz. Bar Found.; mem. Ariz. Judges Assn. (pres. 1984), Pima County Bar Assn. (bd. dirs. 1981-85). Avocations: rollerblading, travel, reading, tap dancing. Office: Ariz Ct of Appeals 400 W Congress St Tucson AZ 85701-1352 E-mail: druke@alptwo.ct.state.az.us.

DRUMKE, MICHAEL WILLIAM, lawyer; b. Chgo., Mar. 29, 1966; s. Ronald Alfred and Sandra Drumke; m. Jody L. Pabst, Jan. 2, 1993. BA cum laude, Tufts U., 1988; JD, U. Wis., 1991. Bar: Wis. 1991, Ill. 1992; U.S. Dist. Ct. (we. dist. Wis.) 1991, U.S. Dist. Ct. (no. dist. Ill.) 1992, U.S. Dist. Ct. (ea. dist. Wis.) 1995, U.S. Dist. Ct. (no. and so. dists. Ind.) 1995, U.S. Dist. Ct. (ctrl. dist.) Ill. 1999, Tex. 2001. Intern to chief justice Supreme Ct. of Wis., Madison, 1991; law clk. to presiding judges Dane County Cir. Ct., Madison, Wis., 1991-92; assoc. Taylor, Miller, Sprowl, Hoffnagle & Merletti, Chgo., 92-94, Segal McCambridge Singer & Mahoney, Ltd., Chgo., 1994-2000, Freeborn & Peters, Chgo., 2001—02; ptnr. Schiff Hardin & Waite, Chgo., 2002—. Spkr. in field. Contbr. articles to profl. jours. Fellow Am. Bar Found.; mem. ABA (past chair toxic tort and environ. law com. Tort and Ins. Practice sect., coord. nat. CLE programs), Ill. Bar Assn., State Bar Wis., State Bar Tex. General civil litigation, Product liability, Toxic tort. Office: Schiff Hardin & Waite 6600 Sears Tower 233 S Wacker Dr Chicago IL 60606

DRUMMOND, GERARD KASPER, lawyer, retired minerals company executive; b. N.Y.C., Oct. 9, 1937; s. John Landells and Margaret Louise (Kasper) D.; m. Donna J. Mason, Sept. 14, 1957 (div. 1976); children: Alexander, Jane, Edmund; m. Sandra Hamilton, Aug. 31, 1985 BS, Cornell U., 1959, LL.B. with distinction, 1963. Bar: Oreg. 1963. Assoc. Davies, Biggs, Strayer, Stoel & Boley, Portland, Oreg., 1963-64; assoc., ptnr. Rives, Bonyhadi, Drummond & Smith, Portland, 1964-77; pres. Nerco, Inc., Portland, from 1977-87, chmn. bd. dirs., CEO, 1987-93; mem. corp. policy group PacifiCorp, 1979-93, exec. v.p., 1987-93, also bd. dirs.; of counsel Stoel Rives, Portland, 1993-98. Pres., chmn. bd. dirs. Tri-County Met. Transit Dist., Portland, 1974-85; Oreg. Investment Coun., 1987-98, 2001— chmn., 1990-98, 2001—; bd. dirs. Oreg. Bus. Coun., 1987—; trustee Reed Coll., 1982-99; bd. dirs. Oreg. Symphony, 1987-93, pres., 1990-92; cmty. bd. dirs. Providence Hosp., 1986-95, chmn., 1993; mem. adv. coun. Cornell U. Law Sch., 1991-95; bd. dirs. Oreg. Shakespeare Festival Assn., 1992-98, Oreg. chpt. Nature Conservancy, 1992-93; trustee Oreg. Symphony Found., 1996—; chmn. bd. dirs. N.W. Bus. Commn. for Arts, 1992-94; trustee Oreg. Shakespeare Festival Found., 1999—, chmn. 2000—. 1st lt. USAR, 1959-67. Mem. Am. Mining Congress (bd. dirs. 1986-92), Arlington Club. Home: 28815 S Needy Rd Canby OR 97013-9570

DRUMMOND, WINSLOW, lawyer; b. Phila., Jan. 29, 1933; s. Winslow Shaw and Dorothy (Moore) D.; m. Katherine Pace, June 18, 1983; children: Judith L., Kathryn W., Winslow Shaw II. AB, Coll. of Wooster, Ohio, 1954; LLB, Duke U., 1957. Bar: Ark. 1957, U.S. Dist. Ct. Ark. 1957, U.S. Ct. Appeals (8th cir.) 1958, U.S. Supreme Ct. 1992; diplomate Am. Bd. Trial Advs. Mem. firm Wright, Lindsey & Jennings, Little Rock, 1957-82, ptnr., 1962-82, McMath Woods P.A., Little Rock, 1982—. Mem. faculty Coll. Advocacy, Hastings Coll. Law, 1974-89, Nat. Inst. Trial Advocacy, 1979-92; chmn. com. on jury instrns. Ark. Supreme Ct., 1980-89. Co-author: Arkansas Model Jury Instructions-Civil, 1965, 3d edit., 1989. Pres., bd. dirs. Urban League Greater Little Rock; bd. dirs. Little Rock Sch. Dist; trustee U. Ozarks, 1991-99. With U.S. Army, 1957-58. Named Outstanding Lawyer, Pulaski County Bar Assn., 1998, Ark. Bar Assn., 1999. Fellow Am. Coll. Trial Lawyers, Am. Bar Found., Ark. Bar Found., ABOTA Found; mem. ABA, ATLA, Ark. Bar Assn. (past chmn. exec. com., ho. of dels.), Pulsaki County Bar Assn., Am. Judicature Soc., Ark. Trial Lawyers Assn. (pres. 1985-86), Am. Inn of Ct. (master of the bench), Order of Coif, Phi Alpha Theta. Democrat. Presbyterian. Federal civil litigation, State civil litigation, Personal injury (including property damage). Home: 1 Tree Tops Ln Little Rock AR 72202-1676 Office: McMath Woods PA 711 W 3rd St Little Rock AR 72201-2201

DRYDEN, MARY ELIZABETH, law librarian, writer, actress; b. Chgo., Oct. 18, 1952; d. James Heard and Hazel Anne (Potts) Rule; m. Ian Dryden, Nov. 22, 1975 (div. 1990); m. Stephen Quadros, Sept. 12, 1992 (div. 1996); m. Larry Borkin, Jan. 3, 2003. Student, U. London, 1969, Bath U., 1970; BA, Scripps Coll., 1971; postgrad., U. Edinburgh, 1971-74. Libr. dir. Hahn, Cazier & Leff, San Diego, 1980, Fredman, Silverberg & Lewis, San Diego, 1980-83, Riordan & McKinzie, L.A., 1983—. Freelance photog. model, 1973—. Theatrical appearances include Antony and Cleopatra, London, 1984, Table Manners, L.A., 1985, Julius Caesar, L.A., 1986, Witness for the Prosecution, L.A., 1987, Come and Go, L.A., 1988, The Actor's Nightmare, L.A., 1989, The Dresser, L.A., 1989, Absent Friends, Long Beach, Calif., 1990, Run For Your Wife!, Long Beach, 1991, The Hollow, Long Beach, 1992, Cock and Bull Story, Hollywood, 1993, Towards Zero, Long Beach, 1993, Angel Street, L.A., 1994, Bedroom Farce, L.A., 1995, Postmortem, L.A., A Weekend with Sam Beckett, L.A., 1997, Deathtrap, 1998, Angel Street, 1999, Fortinbras, L.A., 1999, Othello, Hollywood, 2000, Sweet Bird of Youth, 2000, Walt Whitman's Song of Myself, Edinburgh Festival, 2000, Frankie & Johnny in the Clair de Lune, 2001, Richard III, 2002; (film) Private Collections, 1989, Eye Opener, 1992, A Situation, 1994, Porn Queens of the Seventies, 1994, The Nutty Professor, 1996, The Sophia Replacement, 1996; (TV) War Stories, 2002; also music videos and TV commls.; book critic L.A. Times; contbr. articles to newspapers. Mem. ABA, Brit. Equity, So. Calif. Soc. Law Librs., Brit. Assn. Film and TV Arts, SAG, Mensa, Phi Beta Kappa. Avocations: photography, wine, architecture, fine art, languages. Office: Riordan & McKinzie 300 S Grand Ave Ste 2900 Los Angeles CA 90071-3139 Address: 2450 Hunter St Los Angeles CA 90021

DRYDEN, ROBERT EUGENE, lawyer; b. Chanute, Kans., Aug. 20, 1927; s. Calvin William and Mary Alfreda (Foley) D.; m. Jetta Rae Burger, Dec. 19, 1953; children: Lynn Marie, Thomas Calvin. AA, City Coll., San Francisco, 1947; BS, U. San Francisco, 1951, JD, 1954. Bar: Calif. 1955; diplomate Am. Bd. Trial Advocates (pres. San Francisco chpt. 1997). Assoc. Barfield, Dryden & Ruane (and predecessor firm), San Francisco, 1954-60, jr. ptnr., 1960-65, gen. ptnr., 1965-89; sr. ptnr. Dryden, Margoles, Schimaneck & Wertz, San Francisco, 1989—. Lectr. continuing edn. of the bar, 1971-77; evaluator U.S. Dist. Ct. (no. dist.) Calif. Early Neutral Evaluation Program; master atty. San Francisco Am. Inn of Ct. Mem. bd. counsellors U. San Francisco, 1993—. With USMCR, 1945-46. Fellow Am. Coll. Trial Lawyers, Am. Bar Found., Internat. Acad. Trial Lawyers; mem. ABA, San Francisco Bar Assn., Assn. Def. Counsel (bd. dirs. 1968-71), Def. Rsch. Inst., Internat. Assn. Ins. Counsel, Fedn. Ins. Counsel, U. San Francisco Law Soc. (mem. exec. com. 1970-72), U. San Francisco Alumni Assn. (mem. bd. govs. 1977), Phi Alpha Delta. Alternative dispute resolution, Personal injury (including property damage), Product liability. Home: 1320 Lasuen Dr Millbrae CA 94030-2846 Office: Dryden Margoles Schimaneck & Wertz 101 California St Ste 2050 San Francisco CA 94111-5427

DRYDEN, WILLIAM GEORGE, lawyer; b. Los Angeles, Jan. 24, 1953; s. Lowell Leroy and Oral (Robertson) D.; m. Debrha Jo Carnahan, June 15, 1985. BA, Stanford U., 1975; JD, Willamette U., 1978. Bar: Idaho 1979, U.S. Dist. Ct. Idaho 1979. Law clk. to presiding justice Idaho Supreme Ct., Boise, 1978-79, Fed. Dist. Ct., Boise, 1979-80; assoc. Elam, Burke & Boyd, Boise, 1978-85, ptnr., 1985—. Bd. dirs. YMCA, Boise, 1990-99. Mem.: Fedn. Def. and Corp. Counsel, Def. Research Inst., Idaho Def. Counsel. Democrat. Avocations: triathalons, snow skiing, water skiing, golf, hunting. General civil litigation, Personal injury (including property damage), Product liability. Office: Elam & Burke PA 201 W Front St PO Box 1539 Boise ID 83701-1539

DRYVYNSYDE, GEOFFREY BERESFORD, lawyer, law educator, utilities commission counsel; b. Vancouver, B.C., Can., Oct. 27, 1964; came to U.S. 1981; s. Beresford O'Neil and Ann Christine D. AB, Stanford U., 1985; JD, Yale U., 1988. Assoc. Cooley, Godward LLP, San Francisco, 1991-92; staff counsel Calif. Pub. Utilities Commn., San Francisco, 1993—; prof. law New Coll. Law Sch., San Francisco, 1994—. Achievements include surviving the Calif. electrician crisis and representing the state in complex $11 billion bond transaction. Administrative and regulatory, Appellate. Office: State Pub Utility Commn 505 Van Ness Ave Fl 5 San Francisco CA 94102-3214

DU, HARRY HUILI, lawyer; b. Pingdingshan, Henan, China, Nov. 12, 1965; s. Yunliang Du and Fanyu Meng; m. Wei Zang, Oct. 18, 1995; 1 child, Yudu Zang. LLB, China U. Polit. Sci. and Law, Beijing, 1988, LLM, 1991, UCLA, 2001. Bar: China 1988. Legal counsel Am. Woolworth Overseas Corp., Guangzhou City, China, 1991—93; assoc. Da Cheng Law Office, Beijing, 1993—94; ptnr. King & Wood, Beijing, 1994—. Office: King and Wood LLP 30 F North Tower Kerry Ctr Beijing 100020 China

DUARTE COPPEL, LUIS A. lawyer; b. Mexico, D.F., Mexico, Dec. 20, 1964; s. Jose Luis Duarte Martinez and Martha Coppel; m. Rebeca Herrera, Feb. 13, 1966; children: Lenika Duarte Herrera, Pablo Duarte Herrera. JD, Escuela Libre de Derecho, Mexico City, 1990. Bar: Sec. Pub. Edn., Mex. (Mexico) 1991. Fgn. assoc. Mayer, Brown, Rowe & Maw, Chicago, Ill., 1997—98; ptnr. Jauregui, Navarrete, Nader y Rojas, Mex. City DF, Mexico, 2000—. Author: The Effects Doctrine in International Monopolistic Practices: Treatment in Mexico, Casinos in Mexico: New Gambling Law. Mem.: Nat. Lawyers Assn., Nat. Assn. of Corp. Counsels, Mexican Acad. of Pvt. Internat. and Comparative Law, Internat. Bar Assn. Antitrust, Civil rights, Mergers and acquisitions. Office: Jauregui Navarrete Nader y Rojas Paseo Tamarindos # 400-B Piso 9 Mexico DF Bosques de las Lomas 05120 Mexico Office Fax: (52-55) 5258-0351. E-mail: ldc@jnnr.com.mx.

DUBACK, STEVEN RAHR, lawyer; b. Washington, Sept. 4, 1944; s. Paul Hewitt and Natalie (Rahr) D.; children: David, Peter, Andrew. BA, Princeton U., 1966; JD, U. Mich., 1969. Bar: Wis. 1969, U.S. Dist. Ct. (ea. dist.) Wis. 1969, U.S. Ct. Claims 1969, U.S. Tax Ct. 1969. Ptnr. Quarles & Brady LLP, Milw., 1969—. Bd. dirs. Oshkosh (Wis.) B'Gosh, Inc., Commerce Indsl. Chems., Inc. Dir. Ctr. for the Deaf and Hard of Hearing, Milw. Estate Planning Coun. Mem. Estate Counselors Forum, Town Club, Milw. Athletic Club, Wis. State and Local Tax Club, Am. Soc. Corp. Secs., Order of Coif, Phi Beta Kappa. Avocations: golf, tennis. Corporate, general, Estate planning, Taxation, general. Office: Quarles & Brady LLP 411 E Wisconsin Ave Ste 2550 Milwaukee WI 53202-4497 E-mail: srd@quarles.com.

DUBÉ, LAWRENCE EDWARD, JR., lawyer; b. Chgo., Sept. 25, 1948; s. Lawrence Edward and Rosemary Nora (Cooney) D.; m. Paula Ann Goodgal, Jan. 10, 1982; 1 child, Charles Bernard. BA in Polit. Sci. cum laude, Knox Coll., 1970; JD with distinction, U. Iowa, 1973. Bar: Ill. 1973, Md. 1982, Pa. 1982, D.C. 1983, U.S. Supreme Ct., 1987. Field atty. NLRB, Chgo., 1973-80, supr. atty., 1980-81; sole practice Balt., 1981-85; assoc. Grove, Jaskiewicz, Gilliam & Cobert, Washington, 1985-87; ptnr. Dubé & Goodgal, P.C., Balt., 1987—. Author: Management on Trial-The Law of Wrongful Discharge, 1987, New Employment Issues: How to Shield your Business from Costly Lawsuits, 1988, Employment References and the Law, 1989; co-author: The Maryland Employer's Guide, 1984. Mem. Nat. Assn. Securities Dealers (arbitrator). Federal civil litigation, Labor (including EEOC, Fair Labor Standards Act, labor-management relations, NLRB, OSHA), Pension, profit-sharing, and employee benefits. Home: 622 W University Pky Baltimore MD 21210-2908 Office: Dubé & Goodgal PC 2400 Boston St Ste 407 Baltimore MD 21224-4787

DUBER, MICHAEL JOSEPH, lawyer; b. Columbus, Ohio, Mar. 3, 1947; s. Herbert Charles and Pauline Selma (Yaross) D.; m. Cindy A. Roller, Feb. 29, 1976; children: Herbert, Brandon, Craig. BS in Bus. Adminstrn., Ohio State U., 1970; JD, U. Cin., 1973. Bar: Ohio 1973, U.S. Dist. Ct. (no. dist.) Ohio 1973. Assoc. F.J. Bentoff Co., L.P.A., Cleve., 1973-79; ptnr. Bentoff & Duber Co., L.P.A., Cleve., 1979—. Instr. Ohio Paralegal Inst., Cleve., 1984. Mem. Holden Arboretum, Cleve., 1978—. Mem. Ohio Bar Assn., Cleve. Bar Assn. (past chmn. workers' compensation sect.), Cuyhoga County Bar Assn., Cleve. Law Library Assn., Ohio Acad. Trial Lawyers, Tau Epsilon Phi., mem. Nat. Orgn. Social Security Claimants' Reps. Democrat. Jewish. Workers' compensation. Home: 3952 White Oak Trl Cleveland OH 44122-4722 Office: Bentoff and Duber Co LPA 526 Superior Ave Ste 230 Cleveland OH 44114

DUBIN, CHARLES THOMAS, accountant, consultant; b. Balt., Sept. 20, 1952; s. Charles Thomas and Margaret Louise Dubin; m. Karen Frances Stys, Mar. 30, 1977 (div.). BS, Towson U., 1974; postgrad., U. Md., 2002. Legal arbitrator Md. Exec. Dept. Med. Bds., Balt., 1990—95. Cons. in field. With U.S. Army, 1980—86. Mem.: D.C. Bar Assn. Democrat. Avocation: sports. Mailing: 3016 E Northern Pky Baltimore MD 21214-1418 E-mail: ctdubin@abanet.org.

DUBIN, JAMES MICHAEL, lawyer; b. N.Y.C., Aug. 20, 1946; s. Benjamin and Irene (Wasserman) D.; m. Susan Hope Schraub, Mar. 15, 1981; children: Alexander Philip, Elizabeth Joy. BA, U. Pa., 1968; JD, Columbia U., 1974. Bar: N.Y. 1975, D.C. 1984, U.S. Dist. Ct. (so. and ea. dists.) N.Y. 1975, U.S. Ct. Appeals (2d cir.) 1975. Assoc. Paul, Weiss, Rifkind, Wharton & Garrison, N.Y.C., 1974-82, ptnr., 1982—, chmn. corp. dept., 1995—. Bd. dirs. Conair Corp., Carnival Corp., CTPI Group, Inc., European Capital Ventures, PLC; internat. bd. govs. Tel-Aviv U., 2001—; chmn. bd. govs. Tel-Aviv U. Law Sch., 2001—. Mem. bd. editors Columbia Law Rev., 1973-74. Trustee Solomon Schechter Sch. Westchester, 1991—, vice chmn., 1997—; bd. dirs. Nat. Found. Advancement in Arts, 1991—, vice chmn., 1994—; bd. dirs. Jewish Guild for the Blind, 1989—, chmn., 1995—99, chmn. exec. com., 2000—; bd. dirs. YM-YWHA of Mid-Westchester, Scarsdale, NY, 1983—86. With U.S. Army, 1969—71. Mem.: ABA, Am. Arbitration Assn. (comml. panel arbitrators 1989—), Assn. Bar City N.Y., Snowmass Club, The Dukes Golf Club, Indian Harbor Yacht Club, Sunningdale Country Club (bd. govs. 1989—, pres. 2000—), Queenwood Golf Club, Colony Club, Phi Delta Phi. Corporate, general, Mergers and acquisitions, Securities. Office: Paul Weiss Rifkind Wharton & Garrison 1285 Avenue Of The Americas New York NY 10019-6064 E-mail: jdubin@paulweiss.com.

DUBIN, LEONARD, lawyer; b. Trenton, N.J., July 30, 1934; s. Isadore and Selma (Lotman) D.; m. Marlene B. Bronstein, July 12, 1962; children: Elisa K., David I., Michael B. BS, Temple U., 1956, LLB, 1961. Bar: Pa. 1962. Law clk. Ct. Common Pleas, Phila., 1961-62; assoc. Blank Rome Comisky & McCauley LLP, Phila., 1962-69; ptnr. Blank Rome LLP and predecessor cos., Phila., 1969—. Contbr. articles to profl. jours. Bd. dirs. Juvenile Diabetes Found., 1974-95. 1st lt. U.S. Army, 1956-58. Fellow Am. Bar Found., Pa. Bar Found., Am. Coll. Trial Lawyers, Am. Acad. Matrimonial Lawyers; mem. ABA (ho. of dels. 1988-96), Pa. Bar Assn. (house of dels. 1977— , bd. govs. 1981-84, v.p. 1987-88, pres.-elect 1988-89, pres. 1989-90, chair family law sect. 1991-92), Phila. Bar Assn. (bd. govs. 1975-77). Democrat. Jewish. Alternative dispute resolution, General civil litigation, Family and matrimonial. Office: Blank Rome LLP One Logan Sq Philadelphia PA 19103 E-mail: dubin@blankrome.com.

DUBIN, STEPHEN VICTOR, lawyer, holding company executive; b. Bklyn., June 17, 1938; s. Herman E. and Rhoda (Fogel) D.; m. Paula L. Dubin, June 28, 1959; children: Jeffrey D., Michelle L. BA, CUNY, 1961; JD, Boston U., 1961. Bar: N.Y. 1961, Ill. 1975, Pa. 1984, U.S. Dist. Ct. (so. and ea. dists.) N.Y. 1966, U.S. Dist. Ct. (no. dist.) Ill. 1975, U.S. Ct. Appeals (2d cir.) 1975, U.S. Supreme Ct. 1970, U.S. Dist. Ct. (ea. dist.) Pa. 1993, U.S. Ct. Appeals (3d cir.) 1993. Assoc. Kronish, Lieb, Weiner & Hellman, N.Y.C., 1965-67; counsel corp. sec Seligman & Latz, N.Y.C., 1967-72; gen. atty. Montgomery Ward & Co., Inc., N.Y.C., 1972-75, regional counsel, asst. sec. Chgo., 1975-78; gen. counsel, exec. v.p., sec. dir. CSS Industries, Inc., Phila., 1978—. Lectr. consumer law Am. Mgmt. Assn., 1974, 79, 81, Practicing Law Inst., 1982, 88. Nassau County Dem. committeeman, 1967-75, mem. county jud. screening com., 1972-75, del. Nat. Dem. Issues Conv., 1974; pres. Phila. chpt. Am. Jewish Com., 1995-97, chmn. 1997-99, nat bd. govs., 1997—, nat. v.p., 2002—. Capt. JAGC AUS, 1961-65. Mem. ABA, N.Y. State Bar Assn., Pa. Bar Assn., Ill. Bar Assn., Chgo. Bar Assn., Phila. Bar Assn., Bar Assn. Nassau County, N.Y. County Lawyers Assn., Am. Soc. Corp. Secs., Masons (master 1982). Corporate, general, Mergers and acquisitions, Property, real (including real estate development, water). Office: CSS Industries Inc 1845 Walnut St Philadelphia PA 19103-4708 E-mail: steve.dubin@cssindustries.com.

DUBINA, JOEL FREDRICK, federal judge; b. Elkhart, IN, 1947; BS, U. Ala., 1970; JD, Cumberland Sch. Law, 1973. Pvt. practice law Jones, Murray, Stewart & Yarbrough, 1974—83; law clk. to Hon. Robert E. Varner U.S. Dist. Ct. (mid. dist.) Ala., Montgomery, 1973—74, U.S. magistrate, 1983—86, U.S. Dist. judge, 1986—90; judge U.S. Ct. Appeals (11th cir.), 1990—. Mem.: FBA (pres. Montgomery chpt. 1982—83), Montgomery County Bar Assn. (chmn. Law Day com. 1975, constrn. and bylaws com. 1977—80, grievance com. 1981—83), 11th Cir. Hist. Soc., Ala. State Bar Assn., Supreme Ct. Hist. Soc., Fed. Judges Assn., Nat. Coun. U.S. Magistrate Judges, Cumberland Sch. Law Alumni Assn., Am. Inn of Cts. (pres. Montgomery chpt. 1993—94), Lions, Phi Delta Phi. Office: US Cir Ct Appeals 11th Cir PO Box 867 Montgomery AL 36101-0867 also: US Courthouse Ste C5 1 Church St Montgomery AL 36104

DUBOFF, LEONARD DAVID, lawyer; b. Bklyn., Oct. 3, 1941; s. Rubin Robert and Millicent Barbara (Pollach) DuB.; m. Mary Ann Crawford, June 4, 1967; children: Colleen Rose, Robert Courtney, Sabrina Ashley. JD summa cum laude, Bklyn. Law Sch., 1971. Bars: N.Y. 1974, Oreg. 1977, U.S. Dist. Cts. (so. and ea. dists.) N.Y. 1974, U.S. Ct. Appeals (2d cir.) 1974, U.S. Ct. Appeals (9th cir.) 1990, U.S. Customs Ct. 1975, U.S. Supreme Ct. 1977, U.S. Fed. Dist. Ct. 1990. Teaching fellow Stanford (Calif.) U. Law Sch., 1971-72; mem. faculty Lewis & Clark Coll. Northwestern Sch. Law, Portland, Oreg., 1972-94, prof. law, 1977-94; ptnr. DuBoff & Ross, PLLC, Portland, 1994-99, mng. mem. DuBoff, Dorband, Cushing, & King, PLLC, 2000-01, The DuBoff Law Group, LLC, 2001—; instr. Hastings Coll. Law Coll. Civil Advocacy, San Francisco, summers 1978, 79. Founder, past pres. Oreg. Vol. Lawyers for Arts; mem. lawyers' com. ACLU, 1973-78, bd. dirs. Oreg., 1974-76; mem. Mayor's Adv. Com. Security and Privacy, 1974; bd. dirs. Portland Art Mus. Asian Art Council, 1976-77, Internat. Assn. Art Security, N.Y.C., 1976-80; pres. Arts Commn. of Tigard Tualatin and Sherwood, 1990-92; Gov. Oreg. Com. Employment of Handicapped, 1978-81; cons., panelist spl. projects Nat. Endowment for Arts, 1978-79; mem. Mayor's Adv. Com. on Handicapped, 1979-81; mem. Wash. State Atty. Gen's. Com. to Reorganize Maryhill Mus.; Oreg. Commn. for Blind, 1987-93; Oreg. Com. for Humanities, 1981-87. Recipient Bklyn. Law Sch. Stuart Hirschman Property, Jerome Prince Evidence, Donald W. Matheson Meml. awards, 1st scholarship prize; Hofstra U. Lighthouse scholar 1965-71; recipient Hauser award, 1967, Howard Brown Pickard award, 1967-69, Oreg. Govs. Arts award, 1990, Dist. award of merit Pioneer Dist., Boy Scouts Am., 1995, Silver Beaver award Boy Scouts Am., 1996, Vigil mem. Order of the Arrow, 1996. Mem. Am. Soc. Internat. Law, Assn. Alumni and Attenders of Hague Acad. Internat. Law, Assn. Am. Law Schs. (standing com. sect. activities 1975, chmn. sect. law and arts 1974-80, 91-93, spl. com. on disabilities 1989-91), ABA, N.Y. State Bar Assn., Oreg. Bar Assn., Delta Kappa Phi, Sigma Pi Sigma, Sigma Alpha. Spl. columnist on craft law, The Crafts Report, 1973-87; editor, contbr. materials to legal and art textbooks; author textbooks and articles for legal and art jours. Corporate, general, Securities, Art. Office: The DuBoff Law Group LLC 6665 SW Hampton St Ste 200 Portland OR 97223-8357

DU BOFF, MICHAEL H(AROLD), lawyer; b. N.Y.C., June 27, 1945; s. Rubin Robert and Millicent Barbara (Pollack) Du B.; widowed; children: Jill Bonnie, Robert Evan. BBA, Pace U., 1967; JD, Bklyn. Law Sch., 1970. Bar: N.Y. 1971, U.S. Dist. Ct. (so. and ea. dists.) N.Y. 1972, U.S. Supreme Ct. 1974, U.S. Tax Ct. 1973, U.S. Ct. Internat. Trade 1973. Sr. trial asst. dist. atty. Bronx County, N.Y.C., 1970—73; ptnr. Gainesburg, Gottlieb, Levitan & Cole, N.Y.C., 1974—81; counsel Hahn & Hessen, N.Y.C., 1981-84; ptnr. Salon, Marrow & Dyckman, N.Y.C., 1985-97, Davidoff & Malito LLP, N.Y.C., 1997—. Dir., cons. Harwell Group, Inc., N.Y.C., 1982— ; mem. panel of arbitrators NASD, 1991--, N.Y. Stock Exch., 1991--; v.p. Classic Antique & Restored Spls., Ltd., N.Y.C., 1980—; bd. trustees, gen. coun. Soundview Preporatory Acad., 1993—; bd. trustees The Harvey Sch. 1997—. Contbr. article to Bklyn. Law Sch. Law Review, 1969, Patron Children's Art Workshop, Mamaroneck, N.Y., 1979—. Sponsor Children's Med. Ctr., Lake Success, N.Y., 1979—; mem. Westchester Coun. Arts., N.Y., 1980—; assoc. chmn. fin. industries div. Nat. Asthma Ctr., Denver, 1981. Recipient award for disting. svc. Bronx Dist. Atty., 1973. Mem. ABA, Am. Arbitration Assn. (panel of arbitrators 1979—, guest spkr. 1983), Assn. Bar City of N.Y. (com. uniform state laws 1972-81), Fed. Bar Coun., N.Y. State Bar Assn. (arbitration com.), Lawyers Assn. Textile and Apparel Industries (pres.), Alpha Phi Omega (v.p. N.Y.C. chpt. 1964-67). Commercial, contracts (including sales of goods; commercial financing), Alternative dispute resolution, Securities. Home: 7 Mckenna Pl Mamaroneck NY 10543-2112

DUBOSE, CHARLES WILSON, lawyer; b. Sumter, S.C., Mar. 2, 1949; s. Frank Elsivan and Fannie Louise (Wilson) DuB.; m. Patricia Holman Rayle, Dec. 5, 1987; children: Charles Wilson Jr., Margaret Louise Rayle, Frank Elsivan IV. AB magna cum laude, Harvard U., 1971; JD, U. Va., 1974. Bar: Ga. 1974, S.C. 1992, U.S. Dist. Ct. (no. dist.) Ga. 1974, U.S. Ct. Appeals (5th cir.) 1976, U.S. Ct. Appeals (4th cir.) 1978, U.S. Supreme Ct. 1979, U.S. Ct. Appeals (11th cir.) 1981, U.S. Dist. Ct. (mid. dist.) Ga. 1982, U.S. Dist. Ct. S.C. 2000. Assoc. Kutak, Rock & Huie and predecessor firms, Atlanta, 1974-79; ptnr. Kutak, Rock & Huie, Atlanta, 1979-84; of counsel Griffin, Cochrane & Marshall, P.C., Atlanta, 1985-86, ptnr., 1986-89, mng. ptnr., 1989-92; ptnr. Schnader, Harrison, Segal & Lewis, Atlanta, 1992—2000, Atlanta mng. ptnr., 1995-2000; ptnr. Winkler, DuBose & Davis LLC, Atlanta and Madison, Ga., 2000—. Mem. Chief Justice's Commn. on Indigent Def., 2000—. Elder Peachtree Presbyn. Ch., Atlanta, Madison (Ga.) Presbyn. Ch.; mem. adv. bd. Atlanta's Table, 1991—, chmn., 1995; exec. vice chmn. Atlanta Billy Graham Crusade. Fellow Found. Ga.; mem. ABA (ho. of dels. 2000—), Am. Law Inst., State Bar Ga. (bd. govs. 1998—, chair ind. def. com. 1997—), Atlanta Bar Assn. (bd. dirs. 1992-97, 2000—, sec. 1993-94, v.p., pres.-elect 1994-95, pres. 1995-96, bd. dirs. litigation sect. 1988-94, chmn. litigation sect. 1992-93), Lawyers Com. for Civil Rights Under Law (Atlanta steering com.), Atlanta Bar Found. (bd. dirs. 1995-96, 2000—), Atlanta Vol. Lawyers Found. (bd. dirs. 1995-96), Inst. Continuing Legal Edn. in Ga. (bd. trustees 1995-96), Am. Arbitration Assn. (comml. arbitration panel, constrn. industry arbitration panel), Lawyers Club of Atlanta, World Trade Ctr. Atlanta. Avocations: photography, piano, architecture, historic preservation. Federal civil litigation, Construction, Corporate, general. Home: 1050 East Ave Madison GA 30650-1467 Office: 300 Hancock St Madison GA 30650-1380 also: Ste4540 303 Peachtree St NE Atlanta GA 30308-3263 E-mail: wdubose@wddlaw.com.

DUBROW, JON B. lawyer; b. Riverside, NJ, Aug. 5, 1966; s. Walter and Nancy Lee Dubrow; m. Karen Bunning, Oct. 9, 1993; children: Bryan Charles, Eric Brett, Matthew Bunning. BA, U. Va., 1988; JD cum laude, U. Pa., Phila., 1992. Bar: DC 1994, US Dist. Ct. DC 1998. Assoc. Howrey & Simon, Washington, 1992—97, McDermott Will & Emery, Washington, 1997—98, ptnr., 1999—. Mem.: ABA (antitrust law and litigation sects.). Avocations: tennis, reading, camping, jogging. Antitrust, Mergers and acquisitions. Office: McDermott Will & Emery 600 13th St NW Washington DC 20005 E-mail: jdubrow@mwe.com.

DUBUC, CARROLL EDWARD, lawyer; b. Burlington, Vt., May 6, 1933; s. Jerome Joachim and Rose (Bessette) D.; m. Mary Jane Lowe, Aug. 3, 1963; children; Andrew, Steven, Matthew. BS in Acctg., Cornell U., 1955; LLB, Boston Coll., 1962; postgrad., NYU, 1963-64. Bar: N.Y. 1963, D.C. 1972, Va. 1999; U.S. Dist. Ct. (so. and ea. dists.) N.Y. 1964, U.S. Ct. Appeals (2d cir.) 1965, U.S. Supreme Ct. 1970, D.C. 1972, U.S. Ct. Appeals (D.C. cir.) 1972, U.S. Dist. Ct. D.C. 1973, U.S. Ct. Claims 1975, U.S. Ct. Appeals (4th cir.) 1977, U.S. Ct. Appeals (7th cir.) 1984, U.S. Ct. Appeals (9th cir.) 1985, U.S. Ct. Appeals (5th cir.) 1986, U.S. Ct. Appeals (fed. cir.) 1988, U.S. Ct. Internat. Trade 1988, U.S. Ct. Appeals (6th cir.) 1989, Va. 1999; cert. ct. mediator 1998. Assoc. Haight, Gardner, Poor & Havens, N.Y.C., 1962-70, ptnr., 1970-75; resident ptnr. Finley Kumble Wagner Heine Underberg Manley Myerson & Casey, Washington, 1983-87, Laxalt, Washington, Perito & Dubuc, Washington, 1988-90, Washington, Perito & Dubuc, 1990-91; ptnr. Graham & James, 1991-95, of counsel, 1996-98, Cohen Gettings & Dunham, 1998—. Capt. AC USN, 1954-59. Mem.: ABA (chmn. aviation and space law com. 1985—86, subcom. aviation ins., subcom. internat. practice 1985—87, vice chmn. alternative resolution com., mktg. legal svcs. com. 1991—92, vice chmn. ins. com. 1982—84), ATLA, Internat. Soc. Air Safety Investigators, Internat. Bar Assn. (vice chmn. travel and tourism com. 1998—), Def. Assn. N.Y., Def. Rsch. Inst. (vice chmn. alternative dispute resolution com. 2002—), Fed. Ins. and Corp. Counsel (chmn. alternative dispute resolution sect. 1996—99, aviation transp. 1996—), Internat. Assn. Def. Counsel (past chmn. alternative dispute resolution com.), Maritime Law Assn. U.S., Fed. Bar Coun., Fed. Cir. Bar Assn., Assn. Bar of City of N.Y. (aeroav. com.), Va. Bar Assn., D.C. Bar Assn., N.Y. State Bar Assn. (past chmn. aviation law com.), French-Am. C. of C., Nat. AEro. Assn., Boston Coll. Law Sch. Alumni (pres. Washington chpt. 1992—96), Naval Aviation Command (vice comdr.), Congrl. Country Club, Internat. Aviation Club, Wings Club, Cornell Club, Washington chpt. Aero Club, Sigma Chi. Alternative dispute resolution, Aviation, Federal civil litigation.

DUCANTO, JOSEPH NUNZIO, lawyer, educator; b. Utica, N.Y., Mar. 18, 1927; s. Joseph and Martha (Purchine) D'Acunto; m. Connie Davis (div. May 1990); children: Anthony D. DuCanto, James C. DuCanto; m. Patricia Naegle; children: 1 adopted child, William P. Heiman-DuCanto. BA, Antioch Coll., 1952; JD, U. Chgo., 1955. Bar: Ill. 1955, U.S. Tax Ct. 1960, U.S. Ct. Mil. Appeals 1960, U.S. Supreme Ct. 1960. Rsch. asst. Law and Behavioral Sci. Rsch. Project U. Chgo., 1954-55; assoc. Cotton, Fruchtman & Watt, Chgo., 1955-62; ptnr. Bentley, Campbell, DuCanto & Silvestri, Chgo., 1962-80; prin. Schiller, DuCanto & Fleck, Ltd., Chgo., 1981—; chmn., CEO Securatex, 1982—. Adj. prof. family law Loyola U., Chgo., 1968-2003, vis. prof., 2003; frequent lectr. on family law, taxation, fin. planning and estate planning in connection with divorce. Author: Tax Aspects of Litigation, 1979; contbr. articles, essays on family law and fed. taxation, trusts and estates to profl. publs.; editor, pub. Tax, Fin. and Estate Planning Devels. in Connection with Divorce and Family Law, 1970-85; mem. editl. bd. Fair Share, 1981—, Equitable Distbn. Reporter, 1981—, Matrimonial Lawyer Strategist, 1982—. Served with USMCR, 1944-47, PTO, Guam, Iwo Jima, China. Fellow Am. Acad. Matrimonial Lawyers (nat. pres. 1977-79, chmn.-dir. Inst. Matrimonial Law 1976-85), Am. Coll. Trust and Estate Counsel; mem. Ill. State Bar Assn. (bd. govs. 1983-89, Laureate 2003), Scribes, Cliff Dwellers Club, Union League Club. Republican. Unitarian Universalist. Family and matrimonial. Office: 200 N LaSalle 27th Floor Chicago IL 60601-1089 E-mail: jducanto@sdflaw.com.

DUCKSTAD, JON ROBERT, lawyer, educator; b. Beaver Creek, Minn., June 4, 1934; s. Norman Brown and Mary Josephine (Holbert) D.; children: Julie, Patricia, Marjorie Duckstad Coluccio. BA, Luther Coll., 1956; LLB, JD, William Mitchell Coll. Law, 1962. Bar: Minn. 1962, U.S. Dist. Ct. Minn. 1967, U.S. Ct. Appeals (8th cir.) 1968. Asst. St. Paul City Atty., 1963-70; asst. pub. defender Ramsey County, St. Paul, 1973—; pvt. practice St. Paul, 1962—; adj. prof. William Mitchell Coll. Law, St. Paul, 1983—. Mem., atty. civil commitment def. panel Probate Ct., Ramsey County, Minn., 1971—; mental illness and dangerous def. atty. jud. appeal panel Minn. Supreme Ct., 1973—. Mem. St. Paul Charter Commn., 2000—, vice chair, 2002—; mem. St. Paul Zoning Bd. Appeals, 2000—, sec., 2002—; co-chair safe and drug-free schs. St. Paul Pub. Schs., 2000—. With M.C., U.S. Army, 1956-58, Germany. Mem. ABA (del. 1995-99), Ramsey County Bar assn. (pres. 1995-96), Minn. State Bar Assn. (pres. 2002-03). Avocations: hunting, fishing. Criminal, Personal injury (including property damage), Health. Office: 2334 University Ave W #190 Saint Paul MN 55114

DUCKWORTH, MARVIN E. lawyer, educator; b. Aug. 16, 1942; s. Marvin E. and Maryann Duckworth; children: Matthew, Brian, Jennifer, Jeffrey. BS in Indsl. Engring., Iowa State U., 1964; JD, Drake U., 1968. Bar: Iowa 1968, U.S. Dist. Ct. (no. and so. dists.) Iowa 1969. Assoc. Davis, Huebner, Johnson & Burt, Des Moines, 1968-70; asst. prof. Drake U., 1970-71, lectr. law, 1971-85, assoc. dean clin. programs, 1986-87, adj. prof., 1987—; shareholder Hopkins & Huebner, P.C., Des Moines, 1971—. Spkr. in field. Pres. Drake Law Bd. Counselors, 1991-92, Drake Law Endowment Trust, 1995-96. Named Alumnus of Yr. Drake Law Sch., 1997. Fellow Iowa Bar Found.; mem. ABA (chmn. workers compensation and employers liability law 1986-87, vice hmn. toxic and hazardous substances and environ. law com. 1989-93), Iowa Bar Assn. (pres. young lawyers sect. 1977-78, Merit award 1982, chair workers compensation sect. 1992-93), Def. Rsch. Inst., Fedn. Ins. and Corp. Counsel (workers compensation com.), Iowa Assn. Workers Compensation Lawyers (pres. 1988-89), Iowa Acad. Trial Lawyers, Order of Coif. State civil litigation, Insurance, Workers' compensation. Office: 2700 Grand Ave Ste 111 Des Moines IA 50312-5215

DUDEN, PAUL RUSSELL, lawyer, managing partner; b. Portland, Oreg., Sept. 1, 1940; s. Harold Pennoyer Duden and Helen Pearson Campbell; m. Martha Anderson, Nov. 9, 1985 (dec.); children: Emily, Andrew, Lessie, Gurney. BS, U. Oreg., 1963, LLB, 1966. Bar: Oreg. 1966, U.S. Dist. Ct. Oreg. 1966, U.S. Ct. Appeals (5th cir.) 1966, U.S. Supreme Ct. 1977. Assoc. Tooze, Kerr, Tooze & Peterson, Portland, 1966-70, ptnr., 1970-72; mng. ptnr. Tooze, Duden, Creamer, Frank & Hutchinson, Portland, 1972—2002; ptnr. Duden Neiman LLP, Portland, 2003—. Bd/. dirs. Riverdale Sch. Dist., Portland, 1972-80; commr. Palatine Hill Water Act, Portland, 1982—; bd. dirs. Easter Seal Soc. Oreg., 1967—. Fellow Am. Coll. Trial Lawyers; m. Am. Bd. Trial Advocates, Internat. Assn. Def. Counsel, Def. Rsch. Inst. General civil litigation, Product liability, Toxic tort. Home: 250 SW Carey Ln Portland OR 97219-7973 Office: Duden Neiman LLP 333 SW Taylor St Portland OR 97204-2413 E-mail: pduden@duden-neiman.com.

DUDLEY, GEORGE ELLSWORTH, lawyer; b. Earlington, Ky., July 14, 1922; s. Ralph Emerson and Camille (Lackey) D.; m. Barbara J. Muir, June 28, 1950 (dec. Feb. 1995); children: Bruce K., Camille Dudley McNutt, Nancy S., Elizabeth Dudley Stephens. BS in Commerce, U. Ky., 1947; JD, U. Mich., 1950. Bar: Ky. 1950, D.C. 1951, U.S. Dist. Ct. (we. dist.) Ky. 1962, U.S. Ct. Appeals (6th cir.) 1987. Assoc. Gordon, Gordon & Moore, Madisonville, Ky., 1950-51; pvt. practice law Louisville, 1952-59; ptnr. Brown, Ardery, Todd & Dudley, Louisville, 1959-72, Brown, Todd & Heyburn, Louisville, 1972-92, of counsel, 1992—, mem. mgmt. com., 1972-90, chmn., 1989-90. Pres. Ky. Easter Seal Soc., Louisville, 1971-72; treas. Ky. Dem. Party, Frankfort, 1971-74; bd. dirs. Alliant Adult Health Svcs., Louisville, 1976—; 1st v.p. Nat. Easter Seal Soc., Chgo., 1981. Capt. inf. U.S. Army, 1943-46, ETO; capt. JAGC, U.S. Army, 1951-52. Mem. ABA, Ky. Bar Assn., Louisville Bar Assn., U.S. 6th Cir. Jud. Conf. (life), Harmony Landing Country Club (pres. 1978-79), Tavern Club, Barristers Soc., Omicron Delta Kappa. Presbyterian. Avocations: golf, tennis, travel, sports spectator. Home: 1905 Crossgate Ln Louisville KY 40222-6405 Office: Frost Brown Todd 3200 Aegon Cepter Louisville KY 40202

DUDLEY, TODD STEVEN, lawyer; b. Dallas, Apr. 17, 1970; s. Charles Dudley and Rebecca Chenoweth. BA in Polit. Sci., BA in Sociology, So. Meth. U., 1992; JD, St. Mary's U., San Antonio, 1995. Bar: Tex. 1995. Pvt. practice, Ft. Worth, 1995-98; with Dunham Law Firm, Austin, Tex., 1998—. Mem. Tex. Criminal Def. Lawyers Assn., Austin Criminal Def. Lawyers Assn. Criminal, Juvenile. Office: 400 W 15th St Ste 1410 Austin TX 78701-1648

DUESENBERG, MARK HUGO, lawyer; b. NYC, Jan. 17, 1962; s. Richard William and Phyllis Evelyn (Buehner) D. BA, Valparaiso U., 1984; JD, Harvard U., 1987. Bar: Mo. 1988, D.C. 1991, U.S. Dist. Ct. D.C. 1992, U.S. Ct. Appeals (8th cir.) 1989, U.S. Ct. Appeals (5th cir.) 1991, U.S. Ct. Appeals (D.C. cir.) 1991, U.S. Ct. Appeals (4th cir.) 1993, U.S. Supreme Ctr. 1995. Jud. clk. to hon. Pasco M. Bowman U.S. Ct. Appeals (8th cir.), Kans. City, Mo., 1987-89; atty. Civil div. U.S. Dept. Justice, Wash., 1989-90, Hughes Hubbard & Reed, Wash., 1990—98; v.p., gen. counsel Vision Aire Corp., St. Louis, 1998—99; group sr. counsel Invensys PLC, London, 1999—2002; v.p. Group Legal Invensys PLC, 2002—. Editor Harvard Environ. Law Rev., 1986-87. Corporate, general, General civil litigation, Private international. Office: Invensys PLC Carlisle Pl London SWIP1BX England

DUESENBERG, RICHARD WILLIAM, lawyer; b. St. Louis, Dec. 10, 1930; s. (John August) Hugo and Edna Marie (Warmann) D.; m. Phyllis Evelyn Buehner, Aug. 7, 1955; children: Karen, Daryl, Mark, David. BA, Valparaiso U., 1951, JD, 1953, LLD, 2001; LLM, Yale U., 1956. Bar: Mo. 1953. Prof. law NYU, N.Y.C., 1956-62, dir. law ctr. publs., 1960-62; sr. atty. Monsanto Co., St. Louis, 1963-70, asst. gen. counsel, asst. sec., 1975-77, sr. v.p., sec., gen. counsel, 1977-96. Dir. law Monsanto Textiles Co., St. Louis, 1971-75; corp. sec. Fisher Controls Co., Marshalltown, Iowa, 1969-71, Olympia Industries, Spartanburg, S.C., 1974-75; vis. prof. law U. Mo., 1970-71; faculty Banking Sch. South, La. State U., 1967-83; vis. scholar Cambridge U., England, 1996; vis. prof. law St. Louis U., 1997-98. Author: (with Lawrence P. King) Sales and Bulk Transfers Under the Uniform Commercial Code, 2 vols, 1966, rev., 1984, New York Law of Contracts, 3 vols, 1964, Missouri Forms and Practice Under the Uniform Commercial Code, 2 vols, 1966; editor: Ann. Survey of Am. Law, NYU, 1961-62; mem. bd. contbg. editors and advisors: Corp. Law Rev, 1977-86; contbr. articles to law revs., jours. Mem. lawyers adv. coun. NAM, Washington, 1980, Adminstrv. Conf. U.S., 1980-86, legal adv. com. N.Y. Stock Exch., 1983-87, corp. law dept. adv. coun. Practising Law Inst., 1982; bd. dirs. Bach Soc., St. Louis, 1985-86, pres., 1973-77; bd. dirs. Valparaiso U., 1977—, chmn. bd. visitors law sch., 1966—, Luth. Charities Assn., 1984-87, vice chmn., 1986-87; bd. dirs. Luth. Med. Ctr., St. Louis, 1973-82, vice chmn., 1975-80; bd. dirs. Nat. Jud. Coll., 1984-90, St. Louis Symphony, 1988-2002, Opera Theatre St. Louis, 1988—, Luth. Brotherhood, Mpls., 1992-2000, Liberty Fund, Inc., Indpls., 1997—. Served with U.S. Army, 1953-55. Decorated officer's cross Order of Merit (Germany); named Disting. Alumnus, Valparaiso U., 1976. Fellow Am. Bar Found.; mem. ABA (chmn. com. uniform comml. code 1976-79, coun. sect. corp., banking and bus. law 1979-83, sec. 1983-84, chmn. 1986-87), Mo. Bar Assn., Am. Law Inst., Mont Pelerin Soc., Nat. Jud. Coll. (bd. dirs. 1984-90), Order of Coif, Bach Soc., Am. Soc. Corp. Sec. (bd. chmn. 1987-88), Assn. Gen. Coun., Am. Arbitration Assn., St. Louis Club. Commercial, contracts (including sales of goods; commercial financing), Corporate, general, General practice. Home: 1 Indian Creek Ln Saint Louis MO 63131-3333 E-mail: rwduesenberg@worldnet.att.net.

DUESENBERG, ROBERT H. retired lawyer; b. St. Louis, Dec. 10, 1930; s. Hugo John August and Edna Marie (Warmann) D.; m. Lorraine Freda Hall, July 23, 1938; children: Lynda Renee, Kirsten Lynn, John Robert. BA, Valparaiso (Ind.) U., 1951, LLB, 1953; LLM, Harvard U., 1956. Bar: Mo. 1953, U.S. Supreme Ct. 1981, Va. 1993. Pvt. practice, St. Louis, 1956-58; atty. Wabash R.R. Co., St. Louis, 1958-65, Norfolk & Western Ry. Co., St. Louis, 1962-65; atty., assoc. gen. counsel Pet Inc., St. Louis, 1965-77, v.p., assoc. gen. counsel, 1977-80, v.p., gen. counsel, 1980-83, Gen. Dynamics Corp., Falls Church, Va., 1984-91, sr. v.p. and gen. counsel, 1991-93; ret., 1993. Bd. dirs. Valparaiso (Ind.) U.; adv. bd. ELawForum, Inc., Washington. Contbr. numerous articles to profl. jours. Sec., treas., legal advisor Am. Kantorei, St. Louis, 1970-75; mem. Coun. on World Affairs, St. Louis, 1975—, Mo. Coordinating Bd. for Higher Edn., Jefferson City, 1976-83, chmn., 1978-81; mem. pres.'s coun. Valparaiso (Ind.) U., 1979—, bd. dirs., 1995—; bd. dirs. Higher Edn. Loan Authority, 1982-84; mem. adv. bd. Northwestern U. Corp. Counsel Ctr., 1988—, chmn. adv. bd., 1992; bd. dirs. Opera Theatre of St. Louis, 1988—; bd. dirs. Luther Inst., Washington, 1999—, chair, 2000-03; mem. adv. bd. ELawForum, Washington. Cpl. U.S. Army, 195355. Recipient Disting. Alumnus award Valparaiso U., 1982. Mem. ABA, Va. Bar Assn., Mo. Bar Assn., St. Louis Bar Assn. (chmn. antitrust com. 1971-73, v.p. bus. law sect. 1972-73, chmn. 1973-74), Am. Law Inst., Gen. Counsels Assn., Machine and Allied Products Inst. (legal counsel 1986—), Am. Corp. Counsel Assn., S.W. Legal Found. (adv. bd.), Aerospace Industry Assn. (legal com. 1981-88), Bach Soc. of St. Louis (bd. dirs.). Republican. Lutheran. Corporate, general, Government contracts and claims. Home: 10171 Castlewood Ln Oakton VA 22124-3027

DUFF, BRIAN S. lawyer; b. Sunbury, Pa., Mar. 9, 1975; s. David A. and Bonnie L. Duff; m. Valerie A. Kropa, Oct. 17, 1998. BA, Dickinson Coll., 1997; JD, U. Pitts., 2000. Bar: Pa. 2000. Assoc. Owlett & Lewis, P.C., Wellsboro, 2000—. Mem.: Tioga County Bar Assn. Commercial, consumer (including collections, credit), Estate planning, Taxation, general. Home: RR 7 Box 287 Wellsboro PA 16901 Office: Owlett and Lewis PC PO Box 878 Wellsboro PA 16901-0878

DUFF, WILLIAM BRANDON, lawyer; b. Flushing, N.Y., June 1, 1949; s. Daniel Vincent and Priscilla (Booth) D.; m. Terri Ann Sherman, June 16, 1985; children: Elizabeth, Madeleine. AB, Coll. of Holy Cross, 1971; JD, Georgetown U., 1975. Bar: D.C. 1975, U.S. Dist. Ct. (D.C.) 1975, U.S. Ct. Appeals (D.C. cir.) 1975, N.Y. 1983. Assoc. McChesney & Pyne, Washington, 1975-78, Carter, Ledyard & Milburn, N.Y.C., 1980-84; pvt. practice, N.Y.C., 1984-86; ptnr., dept. head DeForest & Duer, N.Y.C., 1986-96, Baer, Marks & Upham, N.Y.C., 1996-2000; ptnr. Jenkens & Gilchrist Parker Chapin LLP, N.Y.C., 2000—02, KMZ Rosenman, N.Y.C., 2002—. Instr. fed. employee benefit plans law Georgetown U. Sch. Continuing Edn., Washington, 1977, 78. Mem. legislature City of Greenwich, Conn., 1994-98. Labor (including EEOC, Fair Labor Standards Act, labor-management relations, NLRB, OSHA), Pension, profit-sharing, and employee benefits. Office: KMZ Rosenman 575 Madison Ave New York NY 10022- E-mail: william.diff@kmzr.com.

DUFFEY, WILLIAM SIMON, JR., lawyer; b. Phila., May 9, 1952; s. William Simon and Elinor (Daniluk) D.; m. Betsy Byars, Dec. 17, 1977; children: Charles, Scott. BA in English, honors, Drake U., 1973; JD cum laude, U. S.C., 1977. Bar: S.C. 1977, Ga. 1982, U.S. Dist. Ct. (no., mid. and so. dists.) Ga. 1982, U.S. Ct. Appeals (llth cir.) 1983, U.S. Supreme Ct., 1992. Atty. Nexson, Pruet, Jacobs & Pollard, Columbia, S.C., 1977-78, King & Spalding, Atlanta, 1982-94, ptnr., 1995—2001; dep. ind. counsel Office of the Ind. Counsel, Little Rock, 1994-95; U.S. Atty. No. Dist. Ga., Atlanta, 2002—. Adj. prof. U. S.C. Law Sch., 2000—01. Articles editor S.C. Lawyer, 1990-94. Pres. Pine Hills Civic Assn., Atlanta, 1984-88; trustee Drake U.; Ga. Rep. Found., Leadership Atlanta; bd. dirs. Ga. Wilderness Inst., 1992-2001; mem. Peachtree Rd. Race Com., 1993-2002, chmn. Ga. Good Govt. Com.; chmn. bd. advisors Coverdell Leadership Inst., 1995-2002; bd. mem. North Ga. Walk to Emmaus, Camp Hope; founder New Century Forum. Mem. Atlanta Bar Assn. (chmn. alt. dispute resolution com. 1984-88), Lawyers Club, Atlanta Track Club (gen. counsel 1993—), Nat. Practitioners Advisory Coun. The Fed. Soc. Republican. Avocations: running, cooking, wood turning. Federal civil litigation, State civil litigation, Criminal. Home: 4825 Franklin Pond NE Atlanta GA 30342-2765 Office: Office US Atty US Courthouse Ste 600 75 Spring St Atlanta GA 30303*

DUFFY, JOHN LEONARD, lawyer; b. Oelwein, Iowa, Feb. 8, 1947; s. Leonard Francis and Margaret Elizabeth (Miller) D.; m. Paula Ann Rundle, June 7, 1969; children: Adam, Bridget, Alex. BA maxima cum laude, Loras Coll, l969; JD with distinction, U. Iowa, 1973. Bar: Iowa 1973, U.S. Dist. Ct.

(no. and so. dists.) Iowa 1973, U.S. Ct. Appeals (8th cir.) 1985. Mem. Laird, Heiny, McManigal, Winga, Duffy & Stambaugh, P.L.C., Mason City, Iowa, 1973--. Author: (with others) Iowa Land Title Standards, 1984. Bd. dirs. North Iowa Area Community Coll. Found., Mason City, 1977-83, Mason City Devel. Assn., 1983--; pres. YMCA, Mason City, 1980; pres. Newman High Sch. Bd. Edn., Mason City, 1990-91. With U.S. Army, 1970-71. Mem. Iowa Bar Assn. (com. on title standards), VFW, K.C. Roman Catholic. Avocations: racquetball, golf, bicycling, baseball, photography. Commercial, consumer (including collections, credit), Probate (including wills, trusts), Property, real (including real estate development, water). Office: Laird Heiny McManigal Winga Duffy & Stambaugh 10 N Washington Ave Mason City IA 50401-3252

DUFFY, MARTIN PATRICK, lawyer; b. Louisville, Feb. 2, 1942; s. Martin Joseph and Elsie (Shrader) D.; m. Virginia Schoo, Mar. 20, 1970; children: Timothy Brian, Kathleen Kelly. AB in English, U. Notre Dame, 1964; JD, U. Louisville, 1975. Bar: Ky. 1975, U.S. Tax Ct. 1980. Ptnr. Olson, Baker, Henriksen & Duffy, Louisville, 1978-79, Wyatt, Tarrant & Combs, Louisville, 1979--. Bd. dirs. Bellarmine Coll. Overseers, Louisville, 1974-80; trustee St. Mary & Elizabeth Hosp., Louisville, 1980-86, chmn. bd. 1982-85. With U.S. Army, 1964-65, 68-69. Mem. ABA, Ky. Bar Assn., Louisville Bar Assn. Democrat. Roman Catholic. Avocations: running, golf. Estate planning, Probate (including wills, trusts), Estate taxation. Office: Wyatt Tarrant & Combs 2700 Citizens Plz Louisville KY 40202 Fax: 502-589-0309. E-mail: pduffy@wyattfirm.com.

DUFFY, SHIRLEY KATHLEEN, lawyer; b. Pitts., July 24, 1955; d. John and Mary Shabatura; m. Michael Joseph Duffy, May 26, 1984. BS in Biology cum laude, U. Pitts., 1977, MS in Biol. Scis., 1979; JD, Duquesne U., 1984; MS in Environ. Sci., SUNY, Syracuse, 1996. Bar: Pa. 1984, N.Y. 2000. Instr. biology U. Pitts., 1979—84; environ. toxicologist Syracuse Rsch. Corp., 1985—87; assoc. Birnbaum & Rojas, P.C., Syracuse, 1987—88, Law Firm Michael Duffy, Syracuse, 1991—93, Vincler Knoll & Assocs., Pitts., 1997—99; environ. scientist Baker Environ., Inc., Caraopolis, Pa., 1994—96; sr. atty. Hiscock Legal Aid Soc., Syracuse, 1999—. Adj. prof. SUNY, Morrisville, 1993. Contbr. articles to profl. jours. Vol. law clk. Legal Svcs. City of N.Y., Syracuse, 1985; vol. atty. Neighborhood Legal Svcs., Pitts., 1997; atty. Vera Ho., Syracuse, 2000—. Mem.: ABA, Lake Ontario Soc. Toxicology, Onondaga County Bar Assn. (CLE com. mem. 2000—01, bar reporter, mem. editl. bd. 2001—). Avocations: reading, writing, walking. Appellate, Environmental, Criminal. Office: Hiscock Legal Aid Soc 351 S Warren St Syracuse NY 13202-2057 Office Fax: 315-472-2819. Business E-Mail: sduffy@wnylc.com.

DUGAN, JOHN R. lawyer; b. Washington, Apr. 5, 1943; s. Thomas J. and Mary A. (McDevitt) D.; divorced; children: John Jr., Joseph, Katherine, Christina, David, Matthew. AB, Coll. Holy Cross, 1965; JD, George Washington U., 1968. Bar: Md. 1968, D.C. 1968, Va. 1972, U.S. Dist. Ct. (D.C.) 1968. Law clk. to Hon. Judge Matthew McGuire U.S. Dist. Ct., Washington, 1968-69; asst. U.S. atty. D.C., 1969-78; assoc. atty. Levitan, Ezrin, Cramer, West & Weinstein, Chevy Chase, Md., 1978-80; pvt. practice Rockville, Md., 1980—. Mem. D.C. Bar Assn., Md. State Bar Assn. Roman Catholic. Federal civil litigation, State civil litigation, Insurance. Office: 27 Wood Ln Rockville MD 20850-2228

DUGAN, KEVIN F. lawyer; b. Kingston, N.Y., Oct. 30, 1959; s. Owen F. and Helen A. (Frost) D.; m. Diane Tremaine, Dec. 30, 1988; children: Molly, Brighid, Owen. BS, Fla. State U., 1981; JD, Stetson Coll. Law, 1985. Bar: Fla. 1985, U.S. Dist. Ct. (mid. dist.), Fla., 1986, U.S. Ct. Appeals (11th cir.) 1987, N.H. 1991, U.S. Supreme Ct. 1991. Lawyer Woodworth & Dugan, St. Petersburg, Fla., 1985-90, Abramson, Brown & Dugan, Manchester, N.H., 1990—, Masterson, Rogers, Masterson & Gustafson, St. Petersburg, 1998—. Mem. ATLA, N.H. Trial Lawyers Assn. (Bd. Govs. award 1997, bd. govs. 1995—, pres. 1999-2000, chair legis. com. 1999—), N.H. Bar Found., Inns of Ct. Democrat. Roman Catholic. Personal injury (including property damage). Office: Abramson Brown & Dugan 1819 Elm St Manchester NH 03104-2910 E-mail: kdugan@arbd.com.

DUGAS, DAVID ROY, lawyer; b. New Iberia, La., July 4, 1953; s. Claude Anthony and Gladys Marie (Hippler) D.; m. Dolores Ann Broussard, Mar. 22, 1974; children: Brandy Nicole, Kelly Ann, Mary Katherine. JD, La. State U., 1978. Bar: La. 1978, U.S. Dist. Ct. (mid. dist.) La. 1978, U.S. Dist. Ct. (we. dist.) 1980, U.S. Ct. Appeals (5th cir.) 1981, U.S. Dist. Ct. (ea. dist.) 1984. Assoc. Sanders, Downing, Kean & Cazedessus, Baton Rouge, 1978-80; from assoc. to ptnr. Caffery, Oubre, Dugas & Campbell, New Iberia, 1980—2000; US atty. middle dist. U.S. Dept. of Justice, La., 2001—. Editor La. State U. Law Rev., 1977. Chmn. Iberia Parish Reps., 1984, Dist. H delegation to Rep. State Convention, 1984. Mem. ABA, La. Bar Assn., Iberia Parish Bar Assn., La. Assn. Def. Counsel (bd. dirs. 1985—), Order of Coif, Phi Kappa Phi, Omicron Delta Kappa. Lodges: Kiwanis. Republican. Roman Catholic. Avocations: golf, sailing. Federal civil litigation, State civil litigation, Insurance. Office: 777 Florida St Ste 208 Baton Rouge LA 70801*

DUGGAN, JAMES E., JR., state supreme court justice; b. 1942; Prof. Franklin Pierce Law Ctr., 1977—2001, interim dean, 1992—93; chief appellate defender State of NH, 1981—2001; assoc. justice NH Supreme Ct., 2001—. Office: Supreme Ct Bldg One Noble Dr Concord NH 03301-6160

DUGGAN, JAMES EDGAR, law librarian; b. Roanoke, Va., Mar. 24, 1961; s. Daniel David Sr. and Margaret Candler (Mallonee) D. BA, Va. Tech., 1983; JD, U. Miss., 1986; MLIS, La. State U., 1987. Bar: Miss. 1987, U.S. Dist. Ct. (so. dist.) Miss., U.S. Ct. Appeals (5th cir.). From asst. prof. to assoc. prof. So. Ill. U. Sch. Law, Carbondale, 1988-98, prof., 1998—. Ref. libr. So. Ill. U. Sch. Law, Carbondale, 1988-90, computer svcs. libr., 1990-98, dir. info. tech., 1998—. Bd. trustees, mem., Carbondale Pub. Libr., Carbondale, Ill., 1998-, pres. bd. trustees Carbondale Pub. Libr, 2001-, Carbondale, 1998—; bd. trustees Shawnee Libr. Sys., 2001—. Scholar West Pub. Co., 1987. Mem. Miss. State Bar Assn., Am. Assn. of Law Librs. (grant 1987, grant New Orleans chpt. 1987, Call for Papers Competition award 1990, chair coun. chpt. pres. 1999, exec. bd. 2001—), Mid-Am. Assn. of Law Librs. (pres. 1997-98), Phi Alpha Delta, Pi Kappa Delta, Beta Phi Mu. Roman Catholic. Home: PO Box 605 Carbondale IL 62903-0605 Office: So Ill U Law Sch Carbondale IL 62901 E-mail: duggan@siu.edu.

DUGGAN, KEVIN, lawyer, inventor; b. Rockville Centre, NY, Dec. 9, 1953; s. John and Nancy Duggan; 1 child, Patrick. AA, Nassau CC, Garden City, NY, 1975; BA, SUNY, Albany, 1977; JD, South Tex. Coll., 1986. Bar: Tex. 1987, Fla. 1990, U.S. Dist. Ct. (mid. dist.) Fla. 1992. Pvt. practice, Houston, 1987—90; asst. pub. defender Pub. Defender's Office, Sarasota, Fla., 1990—92; pvt. practice Ruskin, Fla., 1992—97, Sarasota, 1992—97. Mem.: Profl. Assn. Diving Instrs., Aircraft Owners and Pilots Assn. Achievements include patent pending for car stabilizer. Avocations: skiing, flying, scuba diving (cert.), motorcycling, car collecting. Personal injury (including property damage). Office: 3111 N Tamiami Trail Sarasota FL 34234 Fax: 941-351-8614.

DUGGAN, MICHAEL E. prosecutor; BA, U. Mich., grad., 1983. COO Wayne County Mich., Detroit, pros., 2000—. Co-chair Detroit/Wayne County Stadium Authority. Founder, former pres. Wayne County Kidspace, Inc. Office: 1200 Frank Murphy Hall Justice 1441 St Antoine Detroit MI 48226*

DUGGAN, PATRICK JAMES, federal judge; b. 1933; BS in Econs., Xavier U., 1955; LLB, U. Detroit, 1958. Pvt. practice Brashear, Duggan & Tangora, 1959-76; judge Wayne County Cir. Ct., 1977-86, U.S. Dist. Ct. (ea. dist.) Mich., Detroit, 1987—. Adj. prof. Madonna U., Livonia, Mich., 1975-93. Chmn. Livonia Family YMCA, 1970-71; bd. trustees Madonna U., 1970-79; pres. Livonia Bar Assn., 1975-76. Mem. Mich. Jaycees (pres. 1967-68), Am. Inn of Ct. U. Detroit Law Sch. (pres.) Office: US Dist Ct 867 Theodore Levin Cthouse 231 W Lafayette Blvd Detroit MI 48226-2700

DUGGAN, TIMOTHY E. lawyer; b. Springfield, Ill., Oct. 9, 1952; BA in History, So. Ill. U., 1974, JD, 1980. Law clk. Ill. Appellate Ct., Springfield, 1980-82; assoc. atty. Peter F. Ferracutti, Ottawa, Ill., 1983; law clk. to judge Ben Miller Ill. Appellate Ct., 1984; hearing examiner Ill. Commerce Commn., Springfield, 1984-87; pvt. practice Timothy E. Duggan, Springfield, 1987—. Avocation: musician. Bankruptcy, Personal injury (including property damage), Transportation. Office: Timothy E Duggan 426 S 5th St Springfield IL 62701-1820

DUKE, GEORGE F. lawyer; b. N.Y.C., Aug. 21, 1935; s. David S. and Marlene D.; m. Eugenie Arnold (div. 1985); children: Jonas, Nina; m. Shirley Kison, Sept. 4, 1988. BA magna cum laude, Tufts U., 1956; JD, Harvard U., 1959. Law clk. Calif. Ct. of Appeal, 1960-61; assoc. Leonard, Dole & Formichelli, San Francisco, 1961-66; directing atty. Calif. Rural Legal Assistance, Santa Rosa, 1966-67; dir. Calif. Indian Legal Svcs., Berkeley, 1968-71; cons. Carnegie Endowment for Internat. Peace, Geneva, Switzerland, 1972; pvt. practice law San Francisco, 1973—. Lectr. Boalt Hall Law Sch., Berkeley, 1975-78, U. Calif., Davis, 1980. Ford Found. grantee, 1971-72. Mem. Calif. Bar Assn., Bar Assn. of San Francisco, Phi Beta Kappa. Avocations: music, hiking. Antitrust, Banking, Health. Office: 31 Maywood Way San Rafael CA 94901-1100 Office Fax: 415-456-6078. Business E-Mail: dukelaw@svn.net.

DUKES, KATHARINE LEE, lawyer; b. Washington, July 31, 1968; d. Mack Gerald and Elizabeth (McClellan) Fleming; m. Glenn Edward Dukes, Sept. 4, 1993. BA in History, Rice U., 1990; JD, U. Tex., 1993. Bar: Tex. 1993, U.S. Dist. Ct. (ea. dist.) Tex. 1994, U.S. Ct. Appeals (5th cir.) 1994, U.S. Dist. Ct. (we. dist.) Tex. 1995, U.S. Supreme Ct. 1998. Jud. law clk. U.S. Dist. Ct. (ea. dist.) Tex., Marshall, Tex., 1993-94, U.S. Ct. Appeals (5th cir.), Tyler, Tex., 1994-95, Austin, 1995-96; assoc. Cantilo Maisel & Hubbard LLP, Austin, 1996-98; staff atty. 3d Ct. Appeals, Austin, 1998-99; jud. law clk. U.S. Magistrate Ct. (we. dist.) Tex., Austin, 1999—2003; assoc. Clark, Thomas & Winters, P.C., Austin, 2003—. Mem. Travis County Bar Assn., Austin Young Lawyers Assn. Democrat. Presbyterian. Avocations: musical theater, vocal ensemble. Office: Clark Thomas & Winters PC 300 W 6th St 15th Fl Austin TX 78701 E-mail: kld@ctw.com.

DULANEY, RICHARD ALVIN, lawyer; b. Charlottesville, Va., Oct. 18, 1948; s. Alvin Tandy and Susie Lucille (Sims) D. BA, Yale U., 1971; JD, Coll. William and Mary, 1977. Bar: Va. 1977, U.S. Dist. Ct. (ea. dist.) Va. 1978. V.p. Christian Ctr., Charlottesville, Va., 1972-73; rsch. asst. Marshall-Wythe Sch. Law, Williamsburg, Va., 1975; assoc. Niles & Chapman, Remington, Va., 1977-79; gen. ptnr. Niles, Dulaney & Parker, Culpeper, Va., 1980-92; of counsel Chandler, Franklin, and O'Bryan, Culpeper, Va., 1988—; ptnr. Niles Dulaney Parker and Lauer LLP, Culpeper, 1992-98, Dulaney, Parker, Lauer & Thomas LLP, Culpeper, 1999-2001, Dulaney, Lauer & Thomas LLP, Culpeper, 2001—. Bd. dirs. Rappahanock Legal Svcs., Fredericksburg, Va., 1981-83. Bd. dirs. Christian Ctr., Syria, Va., 1974-89, U. Sci. and Philosophy Swannanoa, Waynesboro, Va., 1985-2002, The Quest Inst., Charlottesville, Va., 1986-87; mem. Bd. Zoning Appeals, Culpeper County, Culpeper, Va., 1983-90. Mem. Piedmont Bar Assn., Va. Bar Assn., Va. Trial Lawyers Assn., Am. Trial Lawyers Assn., Culpeper Bar Assn. (pres. 1985-86), New Haven chpt. Pierson Fellowship Club, Omicron Delta Kappa. Home: PO Box 511 Culpeper VA 22701-0511 Office: Dulaney Lauer & Thomas LLP PO Box 190 Culpeper VA 22701-0190 E-mail: dulaneylaw@aol.com.

DULANY, WILLIAM BEVARD, lawyer; b. Sykesville, Md., Sept. 4, 1927; s. William Washington and Helen Marie (Bevard) D.; m. Anna Winifred Spencer, Aug. 16, 1952; children: William Bryant, Thomas Patrick, Anne French. AB, McDaniel Coll., 1950, LLD (hon.) , 1989; postgrad., U. Mich., 1950—51; JD, U. Md., 1953. Bar: Md. 1953, U.S. Dist. Ct. Md. 1954, U.S. Tax Ct. 1979, U.S. Supreme Ct. 1990. Assoc. Baldwin, Jarman & Norris, Balt., 1953-59; sr. ptnr. Dulany & Leahy LLP, Westminster, Md., 1959—. Mem. character com. Md. Ct. Appeals, Annapolis, 1974—93; chmn. bd. dirs. Mut. Fire Ins. Carroll County. Mem. Md. Ho. of Dels., Annapolis, 1962-66, Md. Constl. Conv., Annapolis, 1967-68, Md. Regional Planning Coun., 1964-66; chmn. Md. Fair Campaign Practices Commn., 1975-78; chmn. adv. com. Carroll County C.C., 1976; trustee McDaniel Coll., Westminster, Md., 1976—; bd. dirs. nat. office Am. Heart Assn., Dallas, 1982-89, chmn., 1987-88; bd. dirs. Episcopal Ministries to Aging, Inc., Fairhaven, 1982—, chmn., 1986—; former commr. Md. Human Rels. Commn.; vice chmn. Md. Spl. Com. on Gen. Equality, 1989-91; mem. commn. on Racial and Ethnicity Fairness in Judicial Process, 2002—; trustee Md. Hist. Soc., 1991-2001; past pres. Hist. Soc. Carroll County; former mem. Vestry Ascension Episc. Ch. Named one of Outstanding Young Men of Am., Westminster chpt. Jaycees, 1961, Alumnus of Yr., McDaniel Coll., 1986; recipient Outstanding Citizen award Westminster chpt. Rotary, 1985, Trustee of Yr. award Am. Assn. Homes and Svcs. for the Aging, 2002. Fellow Md. Bar Found. (pres. 1986-88, bd. dirs.); mem. ABA, Md. Bar Assn. (v.p. 1970-71), Carroll County Bar Assn. (pres. 1966-67), Am. Judicature Soc., Am. Bar Found., Bachelor's Cotillon Club (Balt.), Phi Alpha Delta. Avocations: travel, volunteer work in non-profit organizations. Administrative and regulatory, General practice, Probate (including wills, trusts). Home: 1167 Old Taneytown Rd Westminster MD 21158-3605 Office: Dulany & Leahy LLP 127 E Main St Westminster MD 21157-5012 E-mail: dulany@dulany.com.

DULAUX, RUSSELL FREDERICK, lawyer; b. West New York, N.J., Dec. 30, 1918; s. Frederick and Theresa A. (Noble) L.; m. Ann deFriedberg, Aug. 22, 1962 (dec.); m. Eva DeLuca, Dec. 24, 1985. Student, Drake's Bus. Sch., 1937, Pace Inst., 1938-40, Fordham U., 1946-48; LLB summa cum laude, N.Y. Law Sch., 1950; postgrad., Pace Coll., 1951, Columbia U., 1955; DBA (hon.), Adam Smith U. Am., 2001. Bar: N.Y. 1951, U.S. Dist. (so. dist.) N.Y. 1951, U.S. Ct. Appeals (2d cir.) 1951, U.S. Ct. Claims 1952, U.S. Tax Ct. 1952, U.S. Dist. Ct. (ea. dist.) N.Y. 1953, U.S. Ct. Customs and Patent Appeals 1963, U.S. Ct. Mil. Appeals 1963, U.S. Supreme Ct. 1963. Mem. staff N.Y. State Dept. Law, Richmond County Investigations, 1951-54, N.Y. State Exec. Dept. Office of Commr. of Investigations, 1954-57; comptroller-counsel Odyssey Productions, Inc., 1957-59; ptnr. Ryan, Murray & Laux, N.Y.C., 1951-61, Ryan & Laux, N.Y.C., 1961; pvt. practice N.Y.C., 1961—; prof. of bus. law and legal studies Adam Smith Univ., 2001. Served with AUS, 1940-46; capt. JAG, vet. corps. of arty. State of N.Y., 1975-92, maj., 1992—; spl. agt. counter intelligence corps and security intelligence corps; col. U.S. Army. Recipient Eloy Alfaro Grand Cross Republic of Panama, Cert. of World Leadership for Leadership and Achievement, 1987, Cert. of Merit for Disting Achievement, 1984, Cert. for Internt. Contemporary Achievement for Outstanding Contbr. to Soc., 1984, Disting. Leadership award for Contbns. to the Legal Profession, Award of Merit for Outstanding Profl. and Pub. Svc., Guglielono Marconi Bronze award, 1987, 1st Century award for achievements in bus. adminstrn. and law, 2001; inducted Hall of Fame for Contbn. to Legal Profession, recipient, Am. Medal of Honor, ABA, 2002., Outstanding People of 21st Century award, England Internat. Bar Assn., 2002. Mem. NATAS, Bronx County Bar Assn. (Townsend Wandell Gold medal), Met. Opera Guild, Internat. Platform Assn., VFW (adjutant Floyd Gibbons Post 500, Cert. of Recognition and Appreciation Polit. Action Com. 1990, Cert. of Svc. on Pres. Rehab. Com. Vets. sect.), Order of Lafayette, Am. Def. Preparedness Assn., Sons Union Vets. Civil War, Soc. Am. Wars, Nat. Sojourners, Heroes of '76, Navy League, St. Andrews Soc. N.Y., St. George Soc. N.Y., Soc. Friendly Sons St. Patrick, English Speaking Union, Asia Soc., China Inst. Am., Army and Navy Union USA, Am. Legion (past post comdr. admen's post 209), Mid Manhattan C. of C., Res. Officers Assn. U.S. (col.), Humanity Against Hatred, Delta Theta Phi, Lambs Club, Knights Hospitaller of St. John of Jerusalem, Grand St. Boys' Club, Soldiers' Club, Sailors' and Airmen's Club, Order Ea. Star, Masons (past comdr. N.Y. Masonic War Vets), Shriners, Knights of Malta, Knights of St. George, Sovereign Mil. Order of Temple of Jerusalem. Probate (including wills, trusts), Property, real (including real estate development, water), Estate taxation. Office: FDR Station PO Box 477 New York NY 10150-0477

DULCHINOS, PETER, lawyer; b. Chicopee Falls, Mass., Feb. 2, 1935; s. George and Angeline D.; children: Matthew George, Paul Constantine, Gregory Peter. BSEE, MIT, 1956, MSEE, 1957; MS in Engring. Mgmt., Northeastern U., 1965; JD, Suffolk U., 1984. Bar: Mass. 1984, U.S. Dist. Ct. (Mass.) 1984, U.S. Ct. Appeals (1st cir.) 1985, U.S. Supreme Ct. 1988, U.S. Patent and Trademark Office 1989, U.S. Claims Ct. 1989. With Sylvania Co., Waltham, Mass., 1957-61, Needham, Mass., 1963-66, Tech Ops, Burlington, Mass., 1961, RCA, Burlington, 1962-63, Raytheon Co., Lexington, Mass., 1966—. Computer ops. mgr. tactical software devel. facility Patriot Ground Computer System, 1977-86, intellectual property mgr., 1986—; lectr. Fitchburg State Coll., 1985-90; corporator Ctrl. Savs. Bank, Lowell, Mass., 1980-92; sec.-treas. U. Lowell Bldg. Authority, 1974-85; mem. statewide adv. coun. Dept. Mental Health, 1996—. Mem. statewide adv. coun. Dept. Mental Retardation, 1993-96; mem. human studies subcom. Bedford VA Hosp., 1987-90; pres. Chelmsford Rep. Club, 1964-70; chmn. Chelmsford Rep. Town Com., 1972-76, 80—, chmn., 2000—; assoc. town counsel Tyngsborough, Mass., 1985-87; mem., chmn. Chelmsford Bd. Health, 1972-87, 93—; mem. Nashoba Tech. High Sch. Com., 1970-71; trustee, chmn. Medfield State Hosp., 1993-2003; v.p. Greater Lowell Comprehensive Cmty. Support Systems Bd. Dept. Mental Health, 1994-99; mem. State Mental Health Planning Coun., 1999—. 2d lt. U.S. Army, 1957-58. Mem. Mass. Bar Assn., Boston Patent Law Assn., Raytheon Employees Profl. Assn. (treas. 1998, pres. 1999). Republican. Greek Orthodox. Intellectual property, Probate (including wills, trusts), Trademark and copyright. Home: 17 Spaulding Rd Chelmsford MA 01824-1021 Office: Raytheon Co 141 Spring St Lexington MA 02421-7899 E-mail: peter_dulchinos@raytheon.com.

DULIN, THOMAS N. lawyer; b. Albany, N.Y., May 26, 1949; s. Joseph Paul and Mary Carol (Keane) D.; m. Pamela Lee Kendall, May 14, 1983; children: Chelsea K., Danielle Y. Boshea, Amanda L. Boshea, Thomas M. Boshea. BA, Siena Coll., 1972; JD, Western New England U., 1976. Bar: N.Y. 1977, U.S. Dist. Ct. (no. dist.) N.Y. 1977, U.S. Supreme Ct. 1984. Asst. dist. atty. Albany County, 1977-81; assoc. McCarthy & Evanick, Albany, 1981-83; sole practice Albany, 1983-88; sr. ptnr. Dulin, Harris & Bixby, Albany, 1988-92; ptnr. Gerstenzang, Weiner & Gerstenzang, Albany, 1992-93, The Dulin Law Firm, Albany, 1993—. Staff atty. Albany County Pub. Defender's Office, 1983—. Bd. dirs. Big Bros. and Sisters of Albany County, Inc., 1983-92, pres., bd. dirs. , 1988-90. Mem.: N.Y. State Trial Lawyers Assn., Assn. Trial Lawyers Am., Albany County Bar Assn., Capital Dist. Trial Lawyers Assn., N.Y. State Assn. Criminal Def. Lawyers, N.Y. State Bar Assn. Democrat. Avocations: skiing, golfing, swimming. Criminal, Personal injury (including property damage). Office: 1761 Central Ave Albany NY 12205

DULLES, FREDERICK HENDRIK, lawyer; b. NYC, Mar. 12, 1942; s. William Winslow and Joanna (deLeu) D.; m. Martine Pred'homme, Aug. 26, 1977; 1 child, Emilie Pred'homme. AB cum laude, Harvard U., 1964; JD, MBA, Columbia U., 1968. Bar: D.C. 1971, N.Y. 1972. Assoc. Shearman & Sterling, N.Y.C. and Paris, 1971-80; counsel Philip Morris Inc., N.Y.C., 1980, asst. gen. counsel, 1981-83; dir. regional counsel EFTA-Eastern Europe-Middle East-Africa region, Lausanne, Switzerland, 1983-92; counsel Pirenne Python Schifferli Peter & Ptnrs., Geneva, 1993-94; ptnr. McDermott, Will & Emery, Chgo., 1994-96; of counsel Jackson & Nash, LLP, N.Y.C., 2000; ptnr. McFadden, Pilkington & Ward, LLP, London, N.Y.C., 1997—. Trustee Mass. Fin. Svcs.-Sun Life Compass mut. funds, 2001--; internat. exec. Assn. Internat. des Etudiants en Sciences Economiques et Commerciales, 1961-66, U.S. gen. counsel, 1977-80. Trustee Am. U. of Paris, 2001--. Lt. Security Group Command, USNR, 1968-71. Decorated Navy Achievement medal. Mem. Am. Bar Assn., Assn. Bar City N.Y., Swiss Arbitration Assn., Am. Mgmt. Assn., Internat. Bar Assn., Harvard Club (N.Y.C., Boston). Republican. E-mail: dulles@post.harvard.edu.

DUMANIS, BONNIE M. prosecutor; Dist. atty., San Diego, 2003—; dep. dist. atty. San Diego Dist. Attys. Office. Instr. U. Calif. San Diego Sch. Law, Nat. and Calif. Jud. Colls. Recipient Tribute to Women award, YWCA, Calif. Women in Govt. Law and Justice award, Aux. award for women of dedication, Salvation Army, Belva Lockwood award, Lawyers Club. Mem.: San Diego Bar Assn. (bd. dirs.), Lawyers Club San Diego (past pres.). Office: Hall of Justice 330 W Broadway San Diego CA 92101*

DUMONTIER, CLARISSA WILLIAMS, lawyer; b. Jefferson City, Mo., Apr. 13, 1957; d. James Albert and Ann Marguerite (Dyer) Williams; m. Bruce John DuMontier, July 19, 1980; children: Benjamin John, Clark William. BS in Edn., U. Mo., 1977, JD, 1982. Bar: U.S. Dist. Ct. (we. dist.) Mo. 1982. Assoc. atty. Harlan, Harlan, and Still, Boonville, Columbia, Mo., 1982-84; asst. pros. atty. Cooper County, Mo., 1986-2000, Howard County, Fayette, Mo., 1994-2000, Randolph County, Moberly, Mo., 1994-2000, Chariton County, Keytesville, Mo., 1994-2000. Mem. Child Support Adv. Com. Child Support Enforcement divsn., Jefferson City, 1991-94, Child Support Guidelines Com. Mo. Supreme Ct., Jefferson City, 1993, Pros. Atty's. Adv. Com. Child Support Enforcement divsn., Jefferson City, 1998-2000, Change Ctl. bd. Child Support Enforcement, Jefferson City, 1999-2000. Chmn. Mo. River Festival Arts, Boonville, 1993-94; pres. SS. Peter and Paul Home and Sch., Boonville, 1997-98. Recipient Cert. of Appreciation Mo. Child Support Enforcement Assn., 1997. Mem. Mo. Bar Assn., Wis. Bar Assn., Cooper County Assn. (treas. 1992, 98, v.p. 1998-2000, pres. 2000-01). Republican. Roman Catholic. Avocations: piano, watercolor painting, writing, being a church organist.

DUMVILLE, S(AMUEL) LAWRENCE, lawyer; b. Richmond, Va., Mar. 14, 1953; m. Frances Adair Davis, Oct. 24, 1981; 2 children. BA, Washington and Lee U., 1975; JD, Coll. William and Mary, 1978. Bar: Va. 1978, U.S. Dist. Ct. (ea. dist.) Va. 1978, U.S. Ct. Appeals (4th cir.) 1979, U.S. Dist. Ct. (we. dist.) Va. 1981, U.S. Supreme Ct. 2002. Assoc. Breeden, Howard & MacMillan, Norfolk, Va., 1978-85; ptnr. Breeden, MacMillan & Green, PLC, Norfolk, 1985-95; atty. Norris & St. Clair, P.C., Virginia Beach, Va. Bd. dirs. Breeden Adams Found., 1992-95. Mem. adv. bd. Back Bay Restoration Found., Virginia Beach, 1982-87; fin. chair, mem. adminstrn. bd. St. Andrew's United Meth. Ch., Virginia Beach, 1992—, del. to ann. conf., 1989-92, pres., 1995-97; treas., bd. dirs. Larkspur Civic League, 1989-92, 94-2000; pres. Norfolk Law Libr. Found., 1989; bd. dirs. Norfolk Law Libr., 1986-91; mem., chaplain troop com. Boy Scouts Am., 1998—. Mem. Va. Bar Assn., Norfolk-Portsmouth Bar Assn. (bd. dirs. 1988-89), Virginia Beach Bar Assn., Va. Assn. Def. Counsel. Republican. Avocations: deep sea sport fishing, sporting clays. Federal civil litigation, General civil litigation, Insurance. Office: Norris & St Clair PC 2840 S Lynnhaven Rd Virginia Beach VA 23452-6715 E-mail: sdumville@norrisstclair.com.

DUNAGAN, WALTER BENTON, lawyer, educator; b. Midland, Tex., Dec. 11, 1937; s. Clinton McCormick and Allie Mae (Stout) D.; m. Tera Childress, Feb. 1, 1969; children: Elysha, Sandi. BA, U. Tex., 1963, JD, 1965, postgrad., 1965-68. Bar: Tex. 1965, Fla. 1970, U.S. Dist. Ct. (mid.

dist.) Fla. 1971, U.S. Ct. Appeals (11th cir.) 1982. Corp. atty. Gulf Oil, New Orleans, 1968-69, Getty Oil Co., L.A., 1969—, Westinghouse/Econocar, Internat., Daytona Beach, Fla., 1969-72; assoc. Becks & Becks, Daytona Beach, 1973-75; prin. Walter B. Dunagan, Daytona Beach, 1975—. Cons. Bermuda Villas Motel, Daytona Beach, Buccanneer Motel, Daytona Beach, Pelican Cove West Homeowners Assn., Edgewater, Fla. Organizer Interfaith Coffee House, New Orleans; tchr., song leader various chs.; chief Indian guide/princess program YMCA, Daytona Beach; bd. dirs. Legal Aid, Daytona Beach. Lance cpl. USMC. Mem. Volusia County Bar Assn., Lawyers Title Guaranty Fund, Phi Delta Phi. Avocations: reading, languages. Commercial, consumer (including collections, credit), Commercial, contracts (including sales of goods; commercial financing), Corporate, general. Home and Office: 714 Egret Ct Edgewater FL 32141-4120 Fax: 386-409-3710. E-mail: wbdunfla@msn.com.

DUNCAN, ALLYSON K. lawyer; b. Sept. 1951; BA, Hampton U., 1972; JD, Duke U., 1975. Bar: N.C. 1975, D.C. 1977. With Kilpatrick Stockton LLP, Raleigh, NC. Mem.: Wake County Bar Assn. (pres. 2002—03), N.C. Bar Assn. (pres.-elect 2002). Labor (including EEOC, Fair Labor Standards Act, labor-management relations, NLRB, OSHA), Sports. Office: Kilpatrick Stockton LLP Ste 400 3737 Glenwood Ave Raleigh NC 27612*

DUNCAN, ED EUGENE, lawyer; b. Gary, Ind., Dec. 10, 1948; s. Attwood and Freddie Leon (Ballard) D.; m. Patricia Louise Revado, Sept. 8, 1973 (div.); children: Kristin, Anika, Gregory. BA, Oberlin Coll., 1970; JD, Northwestern U., 1974. Bar: Ohio 1974, U.S. Dist. Ct. (no. dist.) Ohio 1977, U.S. Supreme Ct. 1977. Assoc. Arter & Hadden, Cleve., 1974-82, ptnr., 1982—. Bd. mem. Glenville br. YMCA, Cleve., 1979—, Ohio Bd. of Bldg. Standards, Columbus, 1986-89; trustee Legal Aid Soc., Cleve., 1990-91. Mem.: Cleve. Bar Assn., Ohio Bar Assn. Avocations: writing, reading. General civil litigation, Insurance, Personal injury (including property damage). Home: 935 Roland Rd Cleveland OH 44124-1033 Office: Arter & Hadden 925 Euclid Ave Ste 1100 Cleveland OH 44115-1475 E-mail: ed.duncan1@arterhadden.com.

DUNCAN, JOHN PATRICK CAVANAUGH, lawyer; b. Kalamazoo, Mich., Jan. 25, 1949; s. James H. and Colleen Patricia (Cloney) D.; children: Sarah Ellen, James Patrick Cloney. BA cum laude, Yale U., 1971; JD, U. Chgo., 1974. Bar: Ill. 1974, U.S. Dist. Ct. (no. dist.) Ill. 1974, U.S. Ct. Appeals (7th cir.) 1975, U.S. Supreme Ct. 1979. Assoc. firm Holleb & Coff, Chgo., 1974-79; mem., 1979-87; ptnr. Jones, Day, Reavis & Pogue, Chgo., 1987-99; leader banking and investment practice area, 1996-99; prin. Duncan Assocs., LLC, 2000—. Adj. prof. IIT Chgo.-Kent Coll. Law Fin. Svcs. LLM Program, 1988—; mem. Fulbright Vis. Scholar Adv. Bd., 1995—98; mem. Chgo. com. Chgo. Coun. on Fgn. Rels., 1998—2000; author fed. and state trust co. laws. Contbr. articles to profl. jours. Fellow NSF, 1970. Fellow: Ill. Bar Found.; mem.: ABA (chmn. securities activities banks subcom. 1995—98, privacy task force 1998—2001, banking com.), Ill. Bankers Assn. (legal affairs com. 1986—87), Chgo. Bar Assn. (chmn. fin. insts. com. 1985—86), Yale Club (Chgo., N.Y.). Banking, Finance, Mergers and acquisitions. Home: 3814 N Paulina St Chicago IL 60613-2716 Office: Duncan Assocs LLC 180 N LaSalle Ste 2410 Chicago IL 60601-2704 E-mail: jpcd@jpcdlaw.com.

DUNCAN, RICHARD ALAN, lawyer; b. Mpls., July 8, 1963; BA in Econs. summa cum laude, Yale U., 1985, JD, 1988. Bar: Minn. 1988, U.S. Ct. Appeals (8th cir.) 1988, U.S. Ct. Appeals (9th cir.) 1990, U.S. Ct. Appeals (10th cir.) 1998, U.S. Ct. Appeals (fed. cir.) 2000 , U.S. Ct. Appeals (11th cir.) 2001, U.S. Supreme Ct. 1991. Assoc. Faegre & Benson, LLP, Mpls., 1988-95, ptnr., 1996—. Adj. prof. law U. Minn. Law Sch., 1998—. Mem. exec. com. North Star chpt. Sierra Club, 1988-91, 95-98, 2001—. Mem. Phi Beta Kappa. Antitrust, Environmental, Native American. Office: Faegre & Benson LLP 90 S 7th St Ste 2200 Minneapolis MN 55402-3901 E-mail: rduncan@faegre.com.

DUNCOMBE, RAYNOR BAILEY, lawyer; b. Washington, July 17, 1942; s. Raynor Lockwood and Avis Ethel (Bailey) D.; m. Janice Assunta Rini, Apr. 12, 1969; children: Christina Luccioni, Raynor Luccioni. AB, Franklin and Marshall Coll., 1965; JD, Syracuse U., 1968. Bar: N.Y. 1972, U.S. Dist. Ct. (no. dist.) N.Y. 1972. Staff atty. State of N.Y., Albany, 1968-70; mgmt. trainee State Bank Albany, 1970-72; staff atty. Vibbard, Donaghy & Wright, Schoharie, N.Y., 1972-73, F. Walter Bliss, Esq., Schoharie, 1973-74; pvt. practice Schoharie, 1974—. Chmn. bd. dirs. Fulmont Mut. Ins. Co., Mohawk Minden Ins. Co.; town atty. seven towns two villages and one water dist. in Schoharie County, 1975—; adminstr. Assigned Counsel Program, 1975—; sch. atty. Middleburgh (N.Y.) Schs., 1981—85, 1997—; atty. Schoharie County, 1982—87, 1990—91, Schoharie County Hist. Soc., 1975—; mem. Tax Cons. Tech. Adv. Group Catskill Watershed Corp., 1998—. Dist. commr. Boy Scouts Am., 1987—92, asst. scoutmaster, 1988—91, Explorer advisor, 1991—99, dist. chmn., 1992—95, asst. coun. commr., 1995—96, coun. commr., 1996—99, coun. pres., 1999—2002; mem. Area 3 commn., 2002—03; Rep. committeeman Schoharie county, 1984—92; chmn. Middleburgh Rep. Town Com., 1995—2000; elder Presbyn. Ch., 1992—98, 2001—; mem. pers. com. Albany Presbytery of Presbyn. Ch., 1998—2001. Mem. ABA, N.Y. State Bar Assn., Schoharie County Bar Assn. (sec.-treas. 1975—), Rotary (past pres.), Masons (past master), Lions. Avocations: camping, cross country skiing, collecting stamps. General practice. Home: 190 Main St Middleburgh NY 12122-9415 Office: PO Box 490 283 Main St Schoharie NY 12157

DUNDAS, PHILIP BLAIR, JR., lawyer; b. Middletown, Conn., Apr. 29, 1948; s. Philip Blair and Madolyn Margaret Dundas; m. Elizabeth Anne Adorno, Aug. 9, 1969; children: Philip Blair III, Chapman P. BA, Wesleyan U., Conn., 1970; JD, Washington and Lee U., 1973. Bar: N.Y. 1974. Assoc. Shearman & Sterling, N.Y.C., 1973-81, ptnr., 1981—, ptnr. in charge of Abu Dhabi, United Arab Emirates Office, 1981—. Mem. ABA, Internat. Bar Assn., N.Y. State Bar Assn., Assn. Bar City N.Y., Union Internationale des Avocats, Clinton Country Club. Corporate, general, Finance, Private international. Home: 599 Lexington Ave New York NY 10022-6030

DUNE, STEVE CHARLES, retired lawyer; b. Vithkuqi, Korca, Albania, June 15, 1931; s. Costa Pappas and Evanthia (Vangel) D.; m. Irene Duff Boudreau, Sept. 4, 1955; children: Michelle Dune Gesky, Christopher Michael. AB, Clark U., 1953; JD, NYU, 1956. Bar: N.Y. 1957. Law clk. U.S. Ct. Appeals 1st Cir., 1956-57; from assoc. to ptnr. Cadwalader, Wickersham & Taft, N.Y.C., 1957-95; counsel Albanian-Am. Enterpise Fund, 1995-96. Trustee Clark U., Worcester, Mass., 1974-86, 93-97, hon. trustee, 1997-2001, vice-chmn. bd. dirs., 1980-84, chmn. bd. dirs., 1984-86, chmn. presdl. search com., 1983-84, mem. pres.'s coun., 1987-90; dir. Albanian Children Fund, 1998-2002, chmn. Albanian-Am. C. of C., 1995-96. Recipient Disting. Svc. award, Clark U. Alumni Assn., 2003; Root-Tilden scholar, 1953—56. Mem.: ABA (divsn. sr. lawyers), Assn. Bar City NY, NY State Bar Assn. (com. on Ea. European affairs 1992—95, admiralty com. 1976—79, 1987—90), India House, Phi Beta Kappa. Admiralty, Commercial, contracts (including sales of goods; commercial financing), Corporate, general. Home and Office: PO Box 456 98 Barrett Hill Rd Brooklyn CT 06234-1500 E-mail: scdune@snet.net.

DUNHAM, CHRISTOPHER COOPER, lawyer; b. N.Y.C., Jan. 29, 1937; s. Robert Secrest and Elizabeth Walls (Cooper) D.; m. Marjorie Jean Corliss, June 14, 1958; children: Douglas Webber, William Sigler, Anne Corliss. BA, Wesleyan U., 1958; JD, Columbia U., 1961. Bar: N.Y. 1961, U.S. Dist. Cts. (so. and ea. dists.) N.Y. 1963, U.S. Patent and Trademark Office 1964, U.S. Ct. Appeals (2d cir.) 1964. Assoc. Cooper, Dunham, Dearborn & Henninger, N.Y.C., 1961-68; ptnr. Cooper & Dunham LLP and predecessor firms, N.Y.C., 1968—. Chmn. Westport Democratic Town Com., Conn., 1965-66, 67-70, 80-86; mem. Conn. Dem. Ctrl. Com., 1978-80; del. Conn. Dem. Conv., Conn., 1966, 68, 74, 80, 82, 84, 90, 98; alt. Westport Planning and Zoning Com., 1965; mem. Westport Bd. Fin., 1975, Conn. Safety Commn., 1977-78, Westport Rep. Town Meeting, 1986-93. Mem. N.Y. Intellectual Property Law Assn., Gamma Psi, Phi Beta Kappa. Congregationalist. Patent. Home: 277 Compo Rd S Westport CT 06880-6513 Office: Cooper and Dunham 1185 Ave of the Americas New York NY 10036

DUNHAM, CORYDON BUSHELL, lawyer, broadcasting executive; b. Yonkers, N.Y., Nov. 14, 1927; s. Corydon Bushell and Marion (Howe) D.; m. Janet Burke, Oct. 29, 1966; children: Corydon B. III, Christopher B. BA, Bowdoin Coll., 1948; LL.B., Harvard U., 1951. Bar: N.Y. 1951, D.C. 1990. Assoc. Cahill, Gordon & Reindel, N.Y.C., 1951-65, counsel, 1990—; asst. gen. atty. NBC Inc., N.Y.C., 1965-68, v.p., gen. counsel, 1971-76, exec. v.p., gen. counsel, 1976-89, exec. v.p., sr. counsel to pres., 1989-90. Guest scholar Woodrow Wilson Internat. Ctr. for Scholars, 1995. Author: Fighting for the First Amendment, Stanton of CBS vs. Congress and the Nixon White House, 1997. Served to 2d lt. Arty AUS, 1944-46, Japan. Mem. Am. Arbitration Assn., Nat. Acad. TV Arts and Scis. (treas.). Office: Cahill Gordon & Reindel 80 Pine St Fl 20 New York NY 10005-1702

DUNHAM, KENNETH FRANKLIN, law educator; b. Lebanon, Tenn., Sept. 17, 1948; s. Albert and Winnie (Jackson) Dunham; m. Linda Faye Darby, Mar. 16, 1969; children: Laurie, Mark. BS, David Lipscomb Coll., 1970; JD, Atlanta Sch. Law, 1982; M Dispute Resolution, Pepperdine U., 2000; LLM, Pepperdine U. Sch. Law, 2003. Bar: Ga. 82, U.S. Dist. Ct. (no. dist.) Ga. 84. Assoc. Costanzo, Krischer and Spearman, Atlanta, 1982—84; shareholder Spearman, Dunham and Gaughen, P.C., Atlanta, 1984—88; trial counsel Aetna Ins. Co., Atlanta, 1988—92; pvt. practice Atlanta, 1992—96; prof. law, dir. clin. and alternative dispute resolution programs Faulkner U., Montgomery, Ala., 1996—. Pvt. practice mediator, Atlanta, 1982—96; arbitrator Am. Arbitration Assn., Atlanta, 1987—96; ct. approved mediator, Ga., Calif., Ala.; presenter in field; mediation trainer Ala. Adminstrv. Office Cts. Author: District Court Mediation Training Manual, 1999; contbr. articles to profl. jours. Mem. Laubach Literacy Coun., Montgomery, 2000—01. Named Pepperdine fellow, Pepperdine U. Sch. Law, 1996—97. Mem.: ABA, Ala. State Bar (mem. com. on dispute resolution 2000—), Assn. Conflict Resolution. Mem. Church Of Christ. Avocations: golf, boating, music. Office: Faulkner U Thomas Goode Jones Sch Law 5345 Atlanta Hwy Montgomery AL 36109 Fax: 334-386-7223. E-mail: kdunham@faulkner.edu.

DUNHAM, SCOTT H. lawyer; b. Seattle, May 7, 1950; BA with highest honors, Wash. State U., 1972; JD, U. Wash., 1975. Bar: Calif. 1975, U.S. Dist. Ct. (ctrl. dist.) Calif. 1976, U.S. Supreme Ct. 1977. Mem. O'Melveny & Myers, LLP, L.A. Author: Avoiding and Defending Wrongful Discharge Claims, 1987, Designing an Effective Fair Hiring and Termination Compliance Program, 1992; contbr. chpts. to books; editor-in-chief Wash. Law Rev., 1974-75. Mem. ABA (mem. com. occupational safety and health labor and employment law sect.), L.A. County Bar Assn. (tchr., lectr. Calif. Bus. Law Inst., ABA nat. Inst., Pers. and Indsl. Rels. Assn., Japan Bus. Assn., Inst. Applied Mgmt. and Law, Inc., Calif. Continuing Edn. Bar and various other employer assns.), Order of Coif, Phi Beta Kappa, Phi Kappa Phi, Omicron Delta Kappa, Phi Delta Phi (magister Ballinger inn chpt. 1974). Banking, General civil litigation, Labor (including EEOC, Fair Labor Standards Act, labor-management relations, NLRB, OSHA). Office: O'Melveny & Myers LLP 400 S Hope St Los Angeles CA 90071-2899

DUNHAM, WOLCOTT BALESTIER, JR., lawyer; b. N.Y.C., Sept. 14, 1943; s. Wolcott Balestier and Isabel Caroline (Bosworth) D.; m. Joan Scott Findlay, Jan. 26, 1974; children: Mary Findlay, James Wolcott. AB magna cum laude, Harvard U., 1965, LLB cum laude, 1968. Bar: N.Y. 1969. Vol. VISTA, 1968-69; assoc. Debevoise & Plimpton and predecessor Debevoise, Plimpton, Lyons & Gates, N.Y.C., 1969-76, ptnr., 1977—. Exec. dir. N.Y. State Exec. Adv. Commn. on Ins. Industry Regulatory Reform, 1982; spkr. in field. Co-author: Insurance M&A, 1997—; contbr. articles to profl. jours.; gen. editor and chpt. author, New York Insurance Law, 1991, and ann. supplements. Treas., trustee Fund for Astrophys. Rsch., N.Y.C., 1970—, sec., 1970-84, pres., 1984—; bd. dirs. UN Assn., N.Y.C., 1973-79, vice chmn., 1975-79, adv. coun., 1992—; vestry mem. St. James Ch., N.Y.C., 1987-93, clk., 1988-93, jr. warden, 1993-94, sr. warden, 1994-95, chancellor, 1994—; bd. dirs. Neighborhood Coalition for Shelter, Inc., 1983—; pres., bd. dirs. East Side Cmty. Ctr., Inc., 1988—; bd. dirs. Dutchess Land Conservancy, 1996—; bd. mgrs. Shekomeko Valley Farm Assn., LLC, 1996-2003. Fellow Am. Coll. Investment Counsel; mem. ABA (chmn. com. on ins. sect. adminstrv. law 1979-83), Assn. Bar City N.Y. (com. on ins. 1981-87, chmn. com. 1984-87), Assn. Life Ins. Counsel, Union Internationale des Avocats, Am. Soc. Internat. Law, Harvard Law Sch. Assn. N.Y.C. (dir. 1978-81) Episcopalian. Corporate, general, Insurance, Securities. Office: Debevoise & Plimpton 919 Third Ave New York NY 10022-3904

DUNIPACE, IAN DOUGLAS, lawyer; b. Tucson, Dec. 18, 1939; s. William Smith and Esther Morvyth (McGeorge) D.; m. Janet Mae Dailey, June 9, 1963; children: Kenneth Mark, Leslie Amanda. BA magna cum laude, U. Ariz., 1961, JD cum laude, 1966. Bar: Ariz. 1966, U.S. Supreme Ct. 1972, Nev. 1994, Colo. 1996. Reporter, critic Long Branch (N.J.) Daily Record, 1963; assoc. firm Jennings, Strouss, Salmon & Trask, Phoenix, 1966-69; assoc. Jennings, Strouss & Salmon, PLC, Phoenix, 1969-70, ptnr., 1971-93, mem., 1993—, chmn. comml. practice dept., 1998—2001. Comments editor Ariz. Law Rev., 1965-66. Reporter Phoenix Forward Edn. Com., 1969-70; mem. Phoenix Arts Commn., 1990-93, chmn., 1992-93; bd. mgmt. Downtown Phoenix YMCA, 1973-80, chmn. 1977-78; bd. dirs. Phoenix Met. YMCA, 1976-87, 88—, chmn. 1984-85; bd. mgmt. Paradise Valley YMCA, 1979-82, chmn. 1980-81; bd. mgmt. Scottsdale/Paradise Valley YMCA, 1983, mem. legal affairs com. Pacific Region YMCA, 1978-81; chmn. YMCA Ariz. State Youth and Govt. Com., 1989-95; bd. dirs. The Schoolhouse Found. 1990-96, pres. 1990-94, Kids Voting, 1990-94, Beaver Valley Improvement Assn. 1977-79, Pi Kappa Alpha Holding Corp., 1968-72, The Heard Mus. 1993-94, Ariz. Bar Found., 1996-2003, pres., 2001-02, Phoenix Kiwanis Charitable Found, 2001—, Phoenix Ctr. Cmty. Devel., 2002-; trustee Paradise Valley Unified Dist. Employee Benefit Trust, 1980-93, chmn. 1987-93, Sch. Theology, Claremont, Calif. 1994—, vice chmn., 2002-; trustee First Meth. Found. of Phoenix, 1984-93, 99—, pres., 2002—; mem. Greater Paradise Valley Cmty. Coun., 1985-87; bd. dir. Heard Mus. Coun., 1990-95, pres. 1993-94; mem. Ariz. Venture Capital Conf. Planning Com., 1994—, mem. exec. com. 1997—, chmn., 2000; mem. Assn. for Corp. Growth, 1995-96, Ariz. Bus. Leadership Assn., 1996—, bd. dirs., 2001—, sec.-treas., 2002—, Ariz. Town Hall, 2003-; bd. visitors U. Ariz. Law Coll., 1996—; mem. met. Phoenix commn., Meth. Ch., 1968-71, lay leader, 1975-78, trustee, 1979-81, pres., 1981; mem. Pacific S.W. ann. Meth. Conf., 1969-79, lawyer commn., 1980-85, chancellor Desert S.W. ann. conf. 1985—; bd. mgrs. Desert Schs. Financial Svcs. 2003; Capt. AUS, 1961-63. Mem. State Bar Ariz. (securities regulation sect. 1970—, chmn. 1991-92, mem. com. unauthorized practice of law 1972-84, chmn. 1975-83, mem. bus. law sect. 1981—, chmn. 1984-85), State Bar Nev., State Bar Colo., Am., Fed. (pres. Ariz. chpt. 1980-81), Maricopa County Bar Assns. (bd. dirs. Corp. Coun. divsn. 1996-99), U. Ariz. Law Coll. Assn. (bd. dirs. 1983-90, pres. 1985-86), U. Ariz. Alumni Assn. (bd. dirs. 1985-86), Orange Tree Club, Masons, Kiwanis (pres. Phoenix 1984-85, disting. lt. gov. 1986-87, S.W. dist. cmty. svc. chmn. 1987-88, dist. activity com. coord. 1988-89, dist. laws and regulation chmn. 1989-90, 92-93, 95-96, 2002—, asst. to dist. gov. for club svcs. 1990-91, field dir. 1991-92, dist. conv. chmn. 1993-94, pub. rels. chmn. 1996-98, mem. internat. com. on Project 39, 1988-89, internat. com. On to Anaheim 1990-91, internat. com. on leadership tng. and devel. 1991-92, 93-94, trustee SW dist. found. 1987-92, 1st v.p. 1990-92), Phi Beta Kappa, Phi Kappa Phi, Phi Delta Phi, Phi Alpha Theta, Sigma Delta Pi, Phi Eta Sigma, Pi Kappa Alpha (nat. counsel 1968-72). Democrat. Methodist. Corporate, general, Non-profit and tax-exempt organizations, Mergers and acquisitions. Home: 2527 E Vogel Ave Phoenix AZ 85028-4729 Office: Jennings Strouss & Salmon PLC 201 E Washington Ste 1100 Phoenix AZ 85004-2383 E-mail: dunipace@jsslaw.com.

DUNKUM, BETTY LEE, lawyer; b. Farmville, Va., Jan. 23, 1968; d. Wesley Earl Jr. and Elizabeth Burnette D. BA magna cum laude, Williams Coll., 1990; JD cum laude, Harvard U., 1995. Bar: Calif. 1995, D.C. 1998, Fla., 2001, U.S. Supreme Ct. 1999. Intern Office of U.S. Congressman L.F. Payne, Washington, 1989, budget com. assoc., 1990-92; legal asst. U.S. Nat. Labor Rels. Bd., Washington, 1993; assoc. McDermott, Will & Emery, Washington, 1994; atty. Howarth & Smith, L.A., 1995-96; law clk. Sr. U.S. Dist. Judge Jackson Kiser, Danville, Va., 1996-97; atty. Preston, Gates, Ellis & Rouvelas Meeds, Washington, 1997-99; legal counsel Christian Legal Soc., Annandale, Va., 1999-2001; founder, pres. Alive in Jesus Ministries, 2001—; atty. Christine D. Hanley & Assocs., West Palm Beach, Fla., 2001—03, Carlton Fields, West Palm Beach, Fla., 2003—. Cons. Mass. Mus. Contemporary Art, North Adams, 1988-90. Mem. ABA, Christian Legal Soc., Harvard Law Sch. Christian Fellowship Alumni Assn. (founder, pres. 1995-2000, chmn. bd. dirs. 2000-02), Phi Beta Kappa. Avocations: swimming, photography, travel. Bankruptcy, General civil litigation, Labor (including EEOC, Fair Labor Standards Act, labor-management relations, NLRB, OSHA). Office: Carlton Fields 227 Lakeview Ave Ste 1400 West Palm Beach FL 33401 E-mail: bldunkum@post.harvard.edu.

DUNLAP, F. THOMAS, JR., lawyer, electronics company executive; b. Pitts., Feb. 7, 1951; s. Francis Thomas and Margaret (Hubert) D.; m. Kathy Dunlap; children: Bridgette, Katie. BSE.E., U. Cin., 1974; JD, U. Santa Clara, Calif., 1979. Bar: Calif., 1979, U.S. Dist. Ct. (no. dist.) Calif. 1979. Mgr. engring. Intel Corp, Santa Clara, Calif., 1974-78, adminstr. tech. exchange, 1978-80, European counsel, 1980-81, sr. atty., 1981-83, gen. counsel, sec., 1983-87, v.p., gen. counsel, sec., 1987—. Drafter, lobbyist Semiconductor Chip Protection Act, 1984 Republican. Roman Catholic. Avocation: jogging. Office: Intel Corp 2200 Mission College Blvd Ste 4 Santa Clara CA 95054-1549*

DUNLAP, JEFFREY SCOTT, lawyer; b. Warren, Ohio, Aug. 17, 1963; s. Harry Sanford and Patricia Ann (Walker) D.; m. Amy Margaret Lyden, Sept. 5, 1993; children: Erin, Casey. BS, Cornell U., 1986; JD, Harvard U., 1989. Bar: Ill. 1989, Ohio 1997, U.S. Dist. Ct. (no. dist.) Ill. 1989, U.S. Dist. Ct. (ea. dist.) Mich. 1995, U.S. Dist. Ct. (no. and so. dists.) Ohio 1997, U.S. Ct. Appeals (6th cir.) 1998, U.S. Supreme Ct. 1998. Assoc. Ross & Hardies, Chgo., 1989-97, Ulmer & Berne, Cleve., 1997—99, ptnr., 2000—. Mem. ABA, Ohio State Bar Assn., Cleve. Bar Assn., Am. Inns of Ct. Democrat. Avocations: softball, golf. Federal civil litigation, State civil litigation, Labor (including EEOC, Fair Labor Standards Act, labor-management relations, NLRB, OSHA). Home: 2880 Chippendale Dr Hudson OH 44236-2406 Office: Ulmer & Berne LLP 1300 E 9th St Ste 900 Cleveland OH 44114-1503

DUNLAY, CATHERINE TELLES, lawyer; b. Cin., Apr. 5, 1958; d. Paul Albert and Donna Mae Telles; m. Thomas Vincent Dunlay, July 10, 1981; children: Christine Jennifer, Thomas Paul, Brian Patrick. Student, Ind. U., 1976-78; BA in English Lit. summa cum laude, U. Cin., 1981; JD summa cum laude, Ohio State U., 1984. Bar: Ohio 1984. Teaching asst., legal rsch. and writing Ohio State U. Coll. of Law, Columbus, 1982; law clk. Brownfield, Bowen & Bally, Columbus, 1983; assoc. Schottenstein, Zox & Dunn, LPA, Columbus, 1984-91, atty., principal, 1991—. Mng. editor Ohio State Law Jour., 1983-84; co-author Health Span, 1993, Akron Law Rev., Fall 1993; co-editor Health Law Jour. of Ohio, 1994-95. Grad. Columbus Leadership Program, 1991; mem. admissions/inclusiveness com. United Way of Franklin County, Columbus, 1991-94, 96; bd. dirs. Ctrl. Ohio chpt. Arthritis Found., 2003—. Recipient C. Simeral Bunch award for Acad. Excellence, Ohio State U., 1984, Law Jour. Past Editors award, 1984. Mem. ABA, Ohio State Bar Assn. (chair healthcare law com. 2000-02), Columbus Bar Assn., Ohio Women's Bar Assn., Women Lawyers of Franklin County (trustee, treas. 1990-93, 91-92), Am. Health Lawyers Assn., Soc. of Ohio Hosp. Attys., Order of the Coif. Roman Catholic. Avocations: cooking, hiking, camping, reading. Corporate, general, Health, Securities. Office: Schottenstein Zox & Dunn 41 S High St Ste 2600 Columbus OH 43215-6109 E-mail: cdunlay@szd.com.

DUNLEVY, WILLIAM SARGENT, lawyer; b. Burbank, Calif., June 5, 1952; s. Roy William and Zella LaVerne (Singleton) D.; m. Margaret Joy Lehman Dunlevy, June 22, 1974; children: Thomas William, Gregory Michael. BA, U. Calif., Davis, 1974; JD, UCLA, 1977. Bar: Calif. 1977. Lawyer Law office of Robert Silver, Ventura, Calif., 1977-80, Taylor, Churchman & Lingl, Camarillo, Calif., 1980-84, Liebmann & Dunlevy, Camarillo, Calif., 1984-88, James P. Lingl & Assoc., Camarillo, Calif., 1988-97, Knopfler & Robertson, Camarillo, Calif., 1998-2001; pvt. practice, 2001—. Editor Inst. Channel Islands chpt. Cmty. Assn., Ventura, Calif., 1984—, pres., 1986-87. Pres. Ventura (Calif.) Downtown Lions Club, 1985-86; bd. mem. Am. Youth Soccer Orgn., Ventura, Calif., 1986-88, 90-96. Mem. Community Assn. Inst., Poinsetta Lodge. Republican. Baptist. Avocations: photography, hiking. Estate planning, Property, real (including real estate development, water). Office: Law Offices William S Dunlevy 1200 Paseo Camarillo Ste 255 Camarillo CA 93010-6085 Fax: 805-383-6227. E-mail: dunlevylaw@aol.com.

DUNN, DONALD JACK, law librarian, law educator, dean, lawyer; b. Tyler, Tex., Nov. 9, 1945; s. Loren Jack and Clara Inez (Milam) Dunn; m. Cheryl Jean Sims, Nov. 24, 1967; 1 child, Kevin. BA., U. Tex.-Austin, 1969, MLS, 1972; JD, Western New Eng. Coll., 1983. Asst. to law libr. U. Tex., 1969-72, supervising libr. Criminal Justice Reference Libr., 1972-73; law libr., prof. law Western New Eng. Coll., Springfield, Mass., 1973-96, interim dean, 1996-98, dean, 1998—2001, assoc. dean for libr. and info. resources, prof. law, 2002—03; dean, prof. law U. LaVerne Coll. Law, 2003—. Editor (with Flynn): Immigration and Nationality Law Rev., vols. 3-7, 1979—84; editor: (with Mersky) Fundamentals of Legal Research, 8th edit., 2002. Bd. dirs. Pioneer Valley chpt. ARC; pres. Scribes, 2001—. Fellow: Am. Bar Found.; mem.: ABA (chair law librs. com. 1988—92), ALA, Am. Law Inst., Law Librs. New Eng. (pres. 1982—83), Spl. Libr. Assn., Am. Assn. Law Librs. (chair acad. law librs. spl. interest sect. 1989—90), Scribes (pres. 2001—03). Democrat. Episcopalian. Office: U LaVerne Coll Law 320 E D St Ontario CA 91764 E-mail: ddunnd@ulv.edu.

DUNN, EDWIN RYDELL, lawyer; b. Boston, July 24, 1942; s. Richard Joseph and Clara Hudson (Rydell) D.; m. Kathleen Lynch, July 23, 1966; children— Jeanne, Kathleen, Anne, Daniel. B.A., U. Notre Dame, 1964; J.D. cum laude, Northwestern U., Chgo., 1967. Bar: Ill. 1967. Assoc., Baker & McKenzie, Chgo., 1967-73, ptnr., 1973— . Mem. law bd. Northwestern U. Law Sch., 1996-; bd. dirs. Near West Side Cmty. Devel. Corp., 1991-; mem. bd. advisors Cath. Charities, Chgo., 1999-. Mem. ABA, Ill. Bar Assn., Chgo. Bar Assn. Corporate, general, Mergers and acquisitions, Securities. Office: Baker & McKenzie 1 Prudential Pla 130 E Randolph St Ste 3700 Chicago IL 60601-6342

DUNN, FREDERICK LOUIS, III, lawyer, investor; b. Ft. Worth, Jan. 29, 1941; s. Frederick Louis, Sr. and Virginia (Goss) Dunn; m. Jeannette Lee Dashiell, July 3, 1962; children: Kathryn Aileen Dunn Jackman, James Dashiell. BA, Washington U., St. Louis, 1963; JD, U. Okla., 1966. Bar: Okla. 1966, U.S. Dist. Ct. (we. dist.) Okla. 1967, U.S. Dist. Ct. (no. dist.) Okla. 1979, U.S. Ct. Appeals (10th cir.) 1990. Asst. trust officer 4th Nat. Bank, Tulsa, 1966—70; asst. dist. atty. Dist. Atty.'s Office, Tulsa County,

1970—79, 1st asst., chief prosecutor, 1982—85; pvt. practice Tulsa, 1979—82, 1985—91, 1997—; 1st asst. U.S. atty., acting U.S. atty. U.S. Atty.'s Office, Tulsa, 1991—97. Chmn. civil svc. commn. City of Tulsa, 1986—95; Dem. candidate dist. atty. Tulsa County, 1997. Mem.: ATLA, Tulsa County Bar Assn., Okla. Bar Assn. Presbyterian. General practice, Criminal, Personal injury (including property damage). Office: 403 S Cheyenne Ste 302 Tulsa OK 74103 Office Fax: 918-584-5479. E-mail: fldunniii@aol.com.

DUNN, HUBERT GLENN TOLSON, lawyer; b. New Bern, N.C., Sept. 11, 1944; s. Mark Stevenson and Genevieve (Tolson) Dunn; m. Ann Reed, Feb. 12, 1977; children: Nancy Reed, Helen Tolson. B in Design, U. Fla., 1966; M in City and Regional Planning, JD, U. N.C., 1976. Bar: N.C., U.S. Dist. Ct. (ea. dist.) N.C. Bd. dirs. N.C. Beautiful, Raleigh, 1996—; bd. visitors Trinity Ctr., Carteret County, NC, 1995—. Mem.: N.C. Bar Assn. (councillor environ. law sect. 1998—, councillor adminstrv. law sect. 2001—). Avocations: music, boating, golf. Administrative and regulatory, Natural resources, Environmental. Home: 2347 Lyon St Raleigh NC 27608 Office: Poyner & Spruill LLP 3600 Glenwood Ave Raleigh NC 27612

DUNN, JOHN BENJAMIN, lawyer; b. Washington, July 12, 1948; s. Read P. and Barbara (Butts) D.; m. Virginia Ann Hughes, July 3, 1983; children: Lily Conti, Noah Benjamin. BA, Ohio Wesleyan U., Delaware, Ohio, 1970; JD, George Washington U., 1973. Bar: D.C. 1973, Md. 1974. Assoc. Schultz & Overby, Washington, 1973-76, Law Offices of Daniel E. Schultz, Washington, 1976-80; prin. Schultz & Dunn Chartered to Schultz Dunn & Murray Chartered, Washington, 1980-85; sole practice Takoma Park, Md., 1985—. Estate planning, Family and matrimonial, Probate (including wills, trusts). Office: 7030 Carroll Ave Ste 2 Takoma Park MD 20912-4448 E-mail: jbdunn@erols.com.

DUNN, JOHN FRANCIS, lawyer, state representative; b. Logansport, Ind., Dec. 24, 1936; s. John Francis and Bertha (Newman) D.; m. Barbara Burke, Feb. 10, 1962; children: John F. III, Robert E., William M., Nancy L. BS in Chem. Engring., U. Notre Dame, 1958, JD, 1961. Bar: Ill. 1961, Ind. 1961, U.S. Dist. Ct. (so. dist.) Ill. 1961, U.S. Ct. Appeals (4th cir.) 1962. Atty. Standard Oil Ind. (now Amoco), Chgo., 1961-64; assoc. Morey and Dunn, Attys., Decatur, Ill., 1964-74; ptnr. Dunn and Fichter, Attys., Decatur, Ill., 1975-85; pvt. practice Decatur, Ill., 1986—. State rep. Ill. Gen. Assembly, Springfield, 1974-94, asst. majority leader; city councilman City of Decatur, 1971-74. Democrat. Roman Catholic. Avocations: bicycling, jogging. General practice. Office: 301 Millikin Ct Decatur IL 62523-1399

DUNN, LARRY K. lawyer; b. Oaha, Hawaii, Apr. 3, 1948; s. Norman Dunn and Anne Martin; m. Kathleen Lillo, March 23, 1968; children: Jennifer, Karena, Jeffrey, Lindsay. AA, Western Nev. Cmty. Coll., 1977; BA, U. Nev., 1980; JD, McGeorge Sch. Law, 1984. Bar: Nev. 1984. Law clerk County Pub. Defenders Office, Sacramento, Calif., 1982-84; deputy dist. attorney Washoe County Dist. Attorney, Reno, Nev., 1984-86; criminal defense attorney Larry K. Dunn Chartered, Reno, Nev., 1986—. Lectr. High Sierra Police Acad., Reno, 1994—. With U.S. Army, 1967-72. Mem. Am. Legion. Republican. Episcopalian. Avocations: golf, ocean fishing, guitar. Criminal. Office: Larry K Dunn Chartered 1385 Haskell St Reno NV 89509-2843 E-mail: lkdesq@aol.com.

DUNN, M(ORRIS) DOUGLAS, lawyer; b. Ionia, Mich., Nov. 1, 1944; s. Morris Frederick and Lola Adella (Gee) D.; m. Jill Lynn Fasbender, July 22, 1967; children: Brooks, Gillian, Joshua. BSME, U. Mich., 1967; JD, Vanderbilt U., 1970. Bar: U.S. Dist. Ct. (so. dist.) N.Y. 1972, U.S. Ct. Appeals (2d cir.) 1973, U.S. Supreme Ct. 1978. Assoc. Winthrop Stimson, Putnam & Roberts, N.Y.C., 1970-78, ptnr., 1978-84; sr. v.p., mng. dir. Shearson Lehman Bros., Inc., N.Y.C., 1984-85; ptnr. Milbank, Tweed, Hadley & McCloy, N.Y.C, 1985—. Contbr. articles to profl. jours. Fellow: Am. Bar Found.; mem.: ABA (fed. regulation of securities com. bus. law sect. 1981—, chair pub. utility, comms. and transp. law sect. 1997—98, bd.govs. 1998—2001), Internat. Bar Assn. (com. chmn. 1990—94), Assn. Bar City NY, Grey Oaks Country Club, Loch Lomond Golf Club, Canoe Brook Country Club, Down Town Assn. Mergers and acquisitions, Utilities, public, Securities. Office: Milbank Tweed Hadley & McCloy LLP 1 Chase Manhattan Plz Fl 47 New York NY 10005-1413

DUNN, RANDY EDWIN, lawyer; b. Hutchinson, Kans., Oct. 8, 1954; s. Roy Edwin and Joan Irene (Farney) D.; m. Michelle Renee Sandwith, Dec. 18, 1976 (div. Aug. 1979); 1 child, Brandi Dawn Sandwith; m. Rosalind O'Nita Heiman, Dec. 22, 1990. BA magna cum laude, Wichita State U., 1977; JD, U. Colo., 1983. Bar: Colo. 1983, U.S. Dist. Ct. Colo. 1986. Store and sales mgr. Pop Shoppe, Inc., Wichita, Kans., 1976-77; sales rep. Lifesavers, Inc., Wichita, 1977-80; asst. mgr. Quik Trip, Inc., Wichita, 1980; assoc. McIntyre & Varallo, P.C., Greeley, Colo., 1983-85; pvt. practice law Denver, 1985-87; ptnr. Dean & Dunn, P.C., Denver, 1987-89; assoc. Lau & Choi, P.C., Denver, 1989-90, Baker & Hostetler, Denver, 1991, Hopper & Kanouff, P.C., Denver, 1991-95; pvt. practice law Denver, 1995—; assoc. Clanahan, Tanner, Downing, and Knowlton P.C., 1997—2002, Ireland, Stapleton, Pryor, & Pascoe, P.C., 2002—. Mem. ABA, Colo. Bar Assn., Denver Bar Assn., Masons. Democrat. General civil litigation, Commercial, contracts (including sales of goods; commercial financing), Corporate, general. Office: Ireland Stapleton Pryor & Pascoe PC 1675 Broadway Ste 2600 Denver CO 80202

DUNN, ROBERT LAWRENCE, lawyer; b. Westerly, R.I., Jan. 2, 1938; m. Sammie Louise Sanford (dec. Sept. 1999); children: Christopher Jon, Geoffrey Robert; m. Linda Elizabeth Barry, 2003. BA, Cornell U., 1958; JD magna cum laude, Harvard U., 1962. Bar: N.Y. 1962, Calif. 1966, U.S. Dist. Ct. (no. dist.) Calif. 1966, U.S. Ct. Appeals (9th cir.) 1966, U.S. Dist. Ct. (ea. dist.) Calif. 1970, U.S. Supreme Ct. 1984, U.S. Dist. Ct. (cen. dist.) Calif. 1987. Law clk. to cir. judge U.S. Cir. Ct., Hartford, Conn., 1962-63; assoc. Paul, Weiss, Rifkind, Wharton & Garrison, N.Y.C., 1963-65, Bancroft, Avery & McAlister, San Francisco, 1965-71; ptnr. Bancroft & McAlister, San Francisco, 1971-93, Cooper, White & Cooper, San Francisco, 1993-99; corp. counsel Real Restaurants, Sausalito, Calif., 1999—. Author: Recovery of Damages for Lost Profits, 1978, rev. edit., 1998, Recovery of Damages for Fraud, rev. edit., 1995, Expert Witnesses: Law and Practice, 1996, rev. edit., 2003; contbr. articles to profl. jours. Mem. planning commn. Town of Corte Madera, Calif. 1974-78, mem. town coun., 1978-84, mayor, 1979, 82; bd. dirs. Merola Opera Program, 1995—, Philharmonia Baroque Orch., San Francisco, 1991-94. 1st lt. U.S. Army, 1958-59. Avocations: travel, scuba diving, opera, literature. Corporate, general.

DUNN, WARREN HOWARD, retired lawyer, brewery executive; b. Omaha, Sept. 25, 1934; s. John Ralph and Frances (Liddell) D.; m. Nancy Ann Nolan, July 2, 1955; children— Kathleen, Erin, Theresa, Maureen. BS in Bus. Adminstrn, Creighton U., Omaha, 1956, JD, 1958. Bar: Nebr. 1958, Wis. 1967. Claims adjuster U.S. Fidelity & Guarantee Co., Omaha, 1958-59; spl. agt. FBI, 1959-66; with Miller Brewing Co., Milw., 1966-94, v.p., gen. counsel, 1973-84, sr. v.p. adminstrn., 1984-90, exec. v.p., 1990-91, pres., CEO, 1991-92, chmn., CEO, 1992-93; ret., 1994. Mem.: Nebr. Bar Assn., Wis. Bar Assn.

DUNN, WILLIAM BRADLEY, lawyer; b. Newark, Dec. 2, 1939; s. Ernest William and Ruth Harriet (Bradley) D.; m. Judy Ann Shepherd, Aug. 2, 1988; children: John, Peter, Brian, Kelly. AB, Muskingum Coll., 1961; JD, U. Mich., 1964. Bar: Mich. 1964. Mem. Clark Hill PLC (formerly Clark, Klein & Beaumont), Detroit, 1964—. Mem. subcom. on profl. ethics State Bar of Mich., 2002—; lectr. in field. Contbr. articles to legal jours. Mem.: ABA (chair sect. real property, probate and trust law 1989—90, mem. ho. of dels. 1990—98, mem. standing com. on professionalism 1993—96, mem. standing com. on ethics and profl. responsibility 1998—2001, spl. adv. standing com. on ethics and profl. responsibility 2001—02), Internat. Assn. Attys. and Exec. Corp. Real Estate, Urban Land Inst., Am. Coll. Real Estate Lawyers (pres. 1983—84). Episcopalian. Commercial, contracts (including sales of goods; commercial financing), Property, real (including real estate development, water). Home: 6398 Catalpa Ct Troy MI 48098-2231 Office: Clark Hill PLC 500 Woodward Ave Ste 3500 Detroit MI 48226-3435 E-mail: wdunn@clarkhill.com.

DUNNE, FREDERICK R., JR., lawyer; b. Kearny, N.J., Mar. 27, 1944; s. Frederick R. and Agnes M. (Lynch) D.; m. Donna M. Polc, Nov. 17, 1973; children: Kelly Anne, Jaime Elizabeth, Frederick R. III. BA, Niagara U., 1966; JD, Seton Hall U., 1970. Bar: N.J. 1972, U.S. Dist. Ct. N.J. 1972, N.Y. 1984, U.S. Dist. Ct. Colo. 1997, U.S. Ct. Appeals (3rd cir.) 1998, U.S. Dist. Ct. (so. and ea. dists.) N.Y. 2000; cert. tchr. N.J. Tchr. St. Benedict's Prep. Sch., 1966-68, Essex Coll. Bus., 1968-69, East Orange (N.J.) H.S., 1969-73; atty. N.J. Office Pub. Defender, 1973; ptnr. Harrington & Dunne, Kearny, 1973-77; sole practice Kearny, 1977-81; ptnr. Dunne & Waller, Kearny, 1981-86, Dunne & Thompson PC, 1987—; atty. Arco Globus Internat. Co. Inc., 2001—. Examining atty. Chgo. Title Ins. Co., 1973—, Chelsea Title & Guaranty Co., 1973-93; atty. Kearny Bd. Edn., 1978-95; pub. defender Borough of North Arlington, 1984-2003, spl. prosecutor ABC violations, 1985-2003; alpine official USSA Ski Racing, 1994—. V.p. Immaculate Heart of Mary Sch. Bd., Wayne, N.J., 1981-82; bd. trustees Pioneer Boys Am., 1976-78; chmn. St. Benedict's Alumni Fund, 1978-92. Recipient Svc. and Citizenship award, Pioneer Boys Am., 1978, Outstanding Performance Resolution, Kearny Bd. Edn., 1980, Cert. of Appreciation, Supreme Ct. N.J., 1985, 1986, 1989, 1990, 1991, 1992, 1999, 2000, 2001, 2002. Mem. ABA, N.J. Bar Assn., West Hudson Bar Assn. (v.p. 2003), Hudson County Bar Assn. Family and matrimonial, General practice, Property, real (including real estate development, water). Home: 81 Hemlock Ter Wayne NJ 07470-4341 Office: 683 Kearny Ave Kearny NJ 07032-3004 Home (Summer): 304 Lincoln Ave Avon By The Sea NJ 07717

DU PASQUIER, SHELBY ROBERT, lawyer; b. Le Havre, France, Dec. 9, 1960; s. Christian Maurice du P. and Sally Love (Humphreys) Lusseyran; m. Silvia Maria Tevini, Aug. 3, 1987; children: Federica, Cosima. Licence es sc. commerciales, U. Geneva Bus. Sch., 1981; LLB, U. Geneva, 1983; LLM, Columbia U., 1988. Bar: N.Y., Geneva. Grad. asst. U. Geneva Bus. Sch., 1981-82; law clk. Lalive Budin and Ptnrs., Geneva, 1984-86; assoc. Sullivan & Cromwell, N.Y.C., 1987; ptnr. Lenz & Staehelin, Geneva, 1988—. Mem. ABA, Swiss Bar Assn., Geneva Bar Assn., Columbia Alumni Assn. Home: 2 Place Claparede 1205 Geneva Switzerland Office: Lenz & Staehelin 25 Grand Rue 1204 Geneva Switzerland

DUPLANTIER, ADRIAN GUY, federal judge; b. New Orleans, Mar. 5, 1929; s. F. Robert and Amelie (Rivet) D.; m. Sally Thomas, July 15, 1951; children: Adrian G., David L., Thomas, Jeanne M., Louise M., John C. JD cum laude, Loyola U., New Orleans, 1949; LLD, Loyola U., 1993; LLM, U. Va., 1988. Bar: La. 1950, U.S. Supreme Ct. 1954. Pvt. practice law, New Orleans, 1950-74; judge Civil Dist. Ct. Parish of Orleans, 1974-78, U.S. Dist. Ct., New Orleans, 1978-94, sr. judge, 1994—. Part-time prof. code of civil procedure Loyola U., 1951—, lectr. dental jurisprudence, 1960-67, lectr. English dept., 1948-50, chmn. law sch. vis. com., 1995-97, adj. prof. law, 1952—; prof. summer sch. abroad Tulane Law Sch., Rhodes, Greece, 1992, Cambridge, England, 1993, Loyola Law Sch., Vienna, Austria, 1996; mem. La. State Senate, 1960-74; 1st asst. dist. atty. New Orleans, 1954-56; mem. Jud. Conf. of U.S. Bankruptcy Rules Adv. Com., 1994-96, chmn. 1997—; elected La. State Senate, 1960-74; 5th cir. dist. judge rep. Jud. Conf. U.S., 1993-94, com. bicentennial of constn., 1986-91; chmn. Bill of Rights Bicentennial Conf. Fed. Judges, 1991. Editorial bd.: Loyola Law Rev, 1947-48; editor-in-chief, 1948-49. Del. Democratic Nat. Conv., 1964; pres. Associated Cath. Charities New Orleans, Social Welfare Planning Council Greater New Orleans; mem. adv. bd. St. Mary's Dominican Coll., 1970-71, Ursuline Acad., 1968-73, Mt. Carmel Acad., 1965-69; chmn. pres.'s adv. coun. Jesuit H.S., 1980-81, mem., 1976—; chmn. bd. dirs. Boys Hope, 1980—, nat. bd. dirs., 1982-92, coun., 1992—; active Assn. Retarded Children. Recipient Meritorious award New Orleans Assn. Retarded Children, 1965, Gov.'s Cert. of Merit, 1970, Outstanding Alumnus award Loyola U., 1985, Vol. Activist award Outstanding Vol. Svc., 1986. Mem. ABA (award 1960), La. Bar Assn., New Orleans Bar Assn., Loyola Law Sch. Vis. Com. (chmn. 1993-96), Jud. Conf. of U.S., Loyola Law Sch. Alumni Assn. (St. Ives award 1998), U.S. Adv. Com. (jud. conf. on bankruptcy rules 1993—, chmn. 1996—), Order of Coif, Alpha Sigma Nu. Office: US Dist Ct C-205 US Courthouse 500 Camp St New Orleans LA 70130-3313

DUPLECHIN, D. JAMES, lawyer; b. Rayne, La., Aug. 1, 1967; s. Kermit Joseph and Neva (Boudreaux) D.; m. Deborah Lynn McEachern, Oct. 13, 1990; children: Ryan James, Andrew David. BS, Troy State U., 1990, MPA, 1991; JD, Birmingham U. Sch. Law, 1996. Bar: Ala. 1997, U.S. Dist. Ct. (mid. dist.) Ala. 1997, U.S. Dist. Ct. (so. dist.) Ala. 2001. Case mgr. Norris & Assocs., Birmingham, 1991-95; intern McCallum & Assocs., Birmingham, 1996; from law clk. to assoc. Powell, Powell & Powell, Crestview, Fla., 1996—2002; atty. D. James Duplechin LLC, Florala, Ala., 2002—. Adv. coun. USAF Tactical Air Warfare Ctr., Eglin AFB, Fla., 1988-91, 8th Tactical Fighter Wing, Kunsan Air Base, South Korea, 1987-88. Mem. ABA, Ala. State Bar Assn., ATLA, Acad. Fla. Trial Lawyers. Roman Catholic. State civil litigation, Personal injury (including property damage), Workers' compensation. Office: 24147 Fifth Ave Florala AL 36442

DUPONT, ANTOINETTE LOIACONO, judge; b. N.Y.C., Jan. 10, 1929; d. Albert J. Loiacono and Helen Utano; m. Albert W. Cretella Jr., Aug. 24, 1990; children: Ellen, Antonia, William. AB, Brown U., 1950; JD, Harvard U., 1954; LLD (hon.), Conn. Coll., 1998. Judge Hartford (Conn.) Superior Trial Ct., 1977-83; chief judge Appellate Ct. of Conn., Hartford, 1984-98, sr. judge, 1998—. Office: Appellate Ct of Conn 95 Washington St Hartford CT 06106-4431

DUPREE, DAVID H. lawyer; b. Knoxville, Tenn., Aug. 18, 1959; s. William Franklin and Eloise (Edwards) D. BBA, Howard U., 1981, JD, 1984. Bar: Pa. 1985, D.C. 1986, U.S. Tax Ct. 1986. Asst. econ. analyst TVA, Knoxville, 1973-77; rsch. asst. acad. computing Howard U., Washington, 1978-84; evaluation specialist Howard U. Cancer Ctr., Washington, 1985; programmer-analyst Acad. Computing Howard U., 1985-87; self-employed rsch. methodologist Washington, 1980—; pvt. practice law, 1985—; instr. Howard U. Sch. Bus., Washington, 1990-94. Bd. dirs. Achievement Scholarship Program, Washington, 1987—; trustee Howard U., 1979-80, Greater Mt. Calvary Holy Ch., Washington, 1988—. Mem. ABA, Pa. Bar Assn., D.C. Bar Assn., Computer Law Assn., D.C. Computer Law Forum, EDP Audit Assn. Democrat. Mem. Pentacostal Ch. Avocations: swimming, playing piano, choral singing. Computer, Personal injury (including property damage), Trademark and copyright. E-mail: attydupree@aol.com.

DUPRIEST, DOUGLAS MILLHOLLEN, lawyer; b. Ft. Riley, Kans., Dec. 28, 1951; s. Robert White and Barbara Nadine (Millhollen) DuP. AB in Philosophy with high honors, Oberlin Coll., 1974; JD, U. Oreg., 1977. Bar: Oreg. 1977, U.S. Dist. Ct. Oreg. 1977, U.S. Ct. Appeals (9th cir.) 1977. Assoc. Coons & Anderson and predecessors, Eugene, Oreg., 1977—81, Hutchinson, Harrell et al, 1981; ptnr. Hutchinson, Cox, Coons, DuPriest , Orr, and Sherlock and predecessors, 1982—. Adj. prof. sch. law U. Oreg., 1986; mem. task forces Wetlands Mgmt., 1988-89, 92-93. Author: (with others) Land Use, 1982, 2000, Administrative Law, 1985; contbg. editor Real Estate & Land Use Digest, 1983-86; articles editor, mng. bd. mem. U. Oreg. Law Rev., 1976-77. Bd. dirs. Home Health Agy., Eugene, 1977-79, pres., 1978-79; bd. dirs. Oreg. Environ. Coun., Portland, 1979-84, pres., 1980-81, McKenzie River Trust, 1998—; bd. dirs., McKenzie River Trust, 1998—; chair voters pamphlet com. Eugene City Club, 1993. Recipient Disting. Svc. award Oreg. Environ. Coun., 1988. Mem. Oreg. Bar Assn. (exec. com. real estate and land use sect. 1978-81). General practice, Land use and zoning (including planning), Property, real (including real estate development, water). Home: 225 Dartmoor Dr Eugene OR 97401-6620 Office: Hutchinson Cox Coons DuPriest Orr & Sherlock 777 High St Ste 200 Eugene OR 97401-2750

DUPUIS, DELPHINE MARIE, lawyer; b. Boulogne-Billancourt, France (incl. Monaco), July 24, 1971; LLM, U. of Paris II, 1994. Bar: EFB Paris 1995. Lawyer Latham & Watkins, Paris, 1999—2003; atty. Shearman & Sterling, Paris, 1996—99. Alternative dispute resolution, Private international, General practice, General civil litigation. Office: Latham & Watkins 154 rue de l'Université Paris 75007 France Office Fax: 33-1-40-62-23-93. E-mail: delphine.dupuis@lw.com.

DUQUETTE, DONALD NORMAN, law educator; b. Manistique, Mich., Apr. 3, 1947; s. Donald Francis and Martha Adeline (Rice) D.; m. Kathy Jo Loudenbeck, June 17, 1967; 1 child, Gail Jean. BA, Mich. State U., 1969; JD, U. Mich., 1974. Bar: Mich. 1975. Children's caseworker Mich. Dept. Social Svcs., Muskegon, 1969-72; asst. prof. pediatrics and human devel. Mich. State U. Coll. Human Medicine, East Lansing, 1975-76; clin. prof., dir. child advocacy law clinic U. Mich., Ann Arbor, 1976—, co-dir. interdisciplinary project on child abuse and neglect, 1979-89, dir. permanency planning legal svcs., 1984—, dir. interdisciplinary grad. edn. in child abuse-neglect, 1986-92, dir. Kellogg child welfare law program, 1995-98. Bd. visitors U. Ariz. Sch. of Law, 1995-99; legal cons. U.S. Children's Bur., Pres. Clinton's Initiative on Adoption and Foster Care, 1997-98; bd. dirs. Nat. Assn. Counsel for Children, 1999—. Author: (non-fiction) Advocating for the Child, 1990, Michigan Child Welfare Law, 1990, Michigan Child Welfare Law, rev. edit., 2000; editor (mem. editl. bd.): (jour.) Child Abuse and Neglect Internat. Jour., 1985—90; contbr.: articles to profl. jours. Mem. Washtenaw County Bd. Commrs., 1981-88; bd. dirs. Children's Trust Fund for Prevention of Child Abuse, 1983-85; mem. Permanency Planning Com. Mich. Supreme Ct., 1982-85, Probate Ct. Task Force, 1986-87, Govs. Task Force on Children's Justice, 1992—; trustee Bay Vierw Assn., 1998--. Named Citizen of Yr. Huron Valley NASW, Ann Arbor, 1985; recipient Rsch. in Advocacy award Nat. Ct. Apptd. Spl. Advocate Assn., Seattle, 1985, Outstanding Legal Advocacy award Nat. Assn. of Counsel for Children, 1996, Hicks Child Welfare Leadership award Mich. Fedn. Children's Agys., 1998. Mem. Am. Profl. Soc. on Abuse of Children, Mich. State Bar (co-chair Children's Task Force 1993-95). Democrat. Unitarian Universalist. Avocations: piano, sailing. Home: 1510 Linwood Ave Ann Arbor MI 48103-3659 Office: U Mich Sch Law Child Advocacy Law Clinic 625 S State St Ann Arbor MI 48109-1215 E-mail: duquette@umich.edu.

DURANT, JAMES MELBOURNE, III, judge; b. San Bernardino, Calif., Dec. 21, 1964; s. James Melbourne Durant, II and Turner Mae Thompson; 1 child, James Melbourne IV. BA, Howard U., 1987, JD, 1990. Bar: Pa. 1990, U.S. Armed Forces Ct. Appeals 1991, U.S. Supreme Ct. 1997. Advanced through grade to maj., 1998; asst. staff judge adv. 63 Air Lift Wing, Norton AFB, Calif., 1991—93, 7 Bomb Wing, Dyess AFB, Tex., 1993—96; spl. asst. U.S. atty. U.S. Dist. Ct. (ctrl. dist.) Calif., San Bernardino, 1991—93, U.S. Dist. Ct. (no. dist.) Tex., Abilene, 1993—96; chief judge adv. accessions Hdqs. USAF Judge Adv., Pentagon, Washington, 1996—99; staff judge adv. Def. Threat Reduction Agy., Ft. Belvoir, Va., 1999—2001; dep. staff judge adv. 2d Bomb Wing, Barksdale AFB, La., 2001—. Editor, author: Successful Interviewing, 1999. Mentor Abilene Elem. Sch., 1993—96; chmn. AFA Scott Edn. Found., San Bernardino, 1991—93; v.p. east ctrl. chpt. Tuskegee Airmen, Washington, 2000—01. Fellow: ABA (dir. young lawyers divsn. 2000—01, coun. gen. practice, solo and small firm sect. 2001—, chmn. standing com. armed forces law 2002—, chmn. tort and ins. pvt. sector 2002—, chmn. govt. liability com. 2002—). Avocations: poetry, golf, mentoring. Office: 2BW JA 334 Davis Ave Ste 100 Barksdale Afb LA 71110

DURANT, MARC, lawyer; b. N.Y.C., Jan. 17, 1947; s. Sidney Irwin and Estelle (Haas) D.; m. Karen Rose Baker, June 9, 1968 (div. 1975); children: Lauren, Elyssa; m. Rita Mary Tatar, Dec. 31, 1979; children: David, Alexander. BS, Cornell U., 1968; JD, Harvard U., 1968-71. Bar: Pa. 1972, U.S. Dist. Ct. (ea. dist.) Pa. 1972, U.S. Supreme Ct. 1980, U.S. Ct. Appeals (3d cir.) 1981, N.Y. 1991. Law clk. U.S. Dist. Ct., Wilmington, Del., 1971-72; assoc. Schnader, Harrison, Segal & Lewis, Phila., 1972-75; asst. U.S. Atty. U.S. Dept. Justice, Phila., 1975-77; dep. chief criminal divsn.v. U.S. Atty.'s Office, Phila., 1977-81; ptnr. Durant and Durant, Phila., 1981—. Mem.: ABA, Phila. Bar Assn., Pa. Bar Assn., Nat. Assn. Criminal Def. Lawyers, Fed. Bar Assn. Federal civil litigation, Criminal. Office: Durant & Durant 325 Chestnut St Philadelphia PA 19106-2614 E-mail: mdurant@durantlaw.com.

DURBIN, RICHARD LOUIS, JR., lawyer; b. Gary, Ind., Dec. 23, 1955; s. Richard Louis and Carolyn Martha (Bohrer) D.; m. Diana Cabaza Durbin, June 2, 1979; children: Louis Eloy, Laura Elena. Student, Rutgers U., 1973-75; BA, U. Chgo., 1977; JD, U. Tex., 1980. Bar: Tex. 1980. Law clk. to presiding judge U.S. Dist. Ct. (we. dist.) Tex., San Antonio, 1980-82; assoc. Susman, Godfrey & McGowan, Houston, 1982-83; asst. U.S. atty. U.S. Atty.'s Office (we. dist.) Tex., San Antonio, 1983—, chief criminal sect., 1988-90, 98—, chief narcotics sect., 1990-92, 97-98, chief appellate sect., 1992-98; adj. prof. law St. Mary's U. Sch. of Law, 1995—. Instr. U.S. Atty. Gen. Adv. Inst., Washington, 1987—; Dept. of Justice Nat. Advocacy Ctr., 1998—; speaker San Antonio Bar Assn. Criminal Law Inst. 1999— Editor Tex. U. Law Rev., 1979-80. Interviewer U. Chgo. Alumni Schs. Com., San Antonio, 1984—. Recipient Dir.'s award Tex. Dept. Pub. Safety, Austin, 1985. Mem. Tex. State Bar, Coll. State Bar Tex., Order of Coif, Phi Beta Kappa. Office: US Attys Office 601 NW Loop 410 Ste 600 San Antonio TX 78216-5512 E-mail: richard.durbin@usdoj.gov.

DURCHSLAG, STEPHEN P. lawyer; b. Chgo., May 20, 1940; s. Milton Lewis and Elizabeth (Potovsky) D.; m. Ruth Florence Mayer, Nov. 21, 1976; children: Rachel Beth, Danielle Leah. BS, U. Wis., 1963; LLB, Harvard U., 1966. Bar: Ill. 1966. Assoc. Sidley & Austin, Chgo., 1966-72, ptnr., 1972-89, Winston & Strawn, Chgo., 1989—. Contbr. articles to profl. jours. Mem. bd. Anshe Emet, Chgo., 1983—, pres., 2000—02; bd. trustee Nathan Cummings Found., 1996—. Mem. ABA (AAF legal com.), Promotion Mktg. Assn. (bd. dirs.), Am. Standard Club, East Bank Club. Jewish. Avocations: skiing, running, tennis, rare books. Administrative and regulatory, Corporate, general, Entertainment. Office: Winston & Strawn 35 W Wacker Dr Ste 3600 Chicago IL 60601-1695 E-mail: sdurchsl@winston.com.

DURHAM, CHRISTINE MEADERS, state supreme court chief justice; b. L.A., Aug. 3, 1945; d. William Anderson and Louise (Christensen) Meaders; m. George Homer Durham II, Dec. 29, 1966; children: Jennifer, Meghan, Troy, Melinda, Isaac. AB, Wellesley Coll., 1967; JD, Duke U., 1971. Bar: N.C. 1971, Utah 1974. Sole practice law, Durham, N.C., 1971-73; instr. legal medicine Duke U., Durham, 1971-73; adj. prof. law Brigham Young U., Provo, Utah, 1973-78; ptnr. Johnson, Durham & Moxley, Salt Lake City, 1974-78; judge Utah Dist. Ct., 1978-82; assoc. justice Utah Supreme Ct., 1982—2002, chief justice, 2002—. Pres. Women Judges Fund for Justice, 1987-88. Fellow Am. Bar Found.; mem. ABA (edn. com. appellate judges' conf.), Nat. Assn. Women Judges (pres. 1986-87), Utah Bar Assn., Am. Law Inst. (coun. mem.), Nat. Ctr. State Courts (bd. dirs.), Am. Inns of Ct. Found. (trustee). Office: Utah Supreme Ct PO Box 140210 Salt Lake City UT 84114-0210*

DURHAM, HARRY BLAINE, III, lawyer; b. Denver, Sept. 16, 1946; s. Harry Blaine and Mary Frances (Oliver) Durham; m. Lynda L. Durham, Aug. 4, 1973; children: Christopher B., Laurel A. BA cum laude, Colo. Coll., 1969; JD, U. Colo., 1973. Bar: Wyo. 1973, U.S. Tax Ct. 1974, U.S. Ct. Appeals (10th cir.) 1976. Assoc. Brown, Drew, Apostolos, Massey & Sulllivan, Casper, Wyo., 1973-77; ptnr. Brown & Drew, Casper, 1977-98, Brown, Drew & Massey, LLP, Casper, 1998—. Articles editor: U. Colo. Law Rev., 1972—73. Bd. dirs. Natrona County United Way, 1974—76, pres., 1975—76; mem. City of Casper Pks. and Recreation Commn., 1985—94, vice chmn., 1987—94; Rep. precinct committeeman, 1999—2002; bd. dirs. Casper Symphony Assn., 1974—88, vice chmn., 1979—82, pres., 1983—87. Named Permanent Class Pres., Class of 1969, Colo. Coll., Mem. Nat. Alumni Coun.; recipient State Heroes award, Sporting Goods Mfg. Assn., 1997. Mem.: ABA, Nat. Assn. R.R. Trail Counsel, Natrona County Bar Assn., Wyo. Bar Assn., Wyo. Amateur Hockey Assn. (bd. dirs., sec. 1974—85, pres. 1985—88), Casper Amateur Hockey Club (bd. dirs. 1970—77, sec. 1974—77), Phi Beta Kappa. Commercial, consumer (including collections, credit), Oil, gas, and mineral, Probate (including wills, trusts). Home: 3101 Hawthorne Ave Casper WY 82604-4975 Office: 159 N Wolcott St Ste 200 Casper WY 82601-7009

DURHAM, JAMES W. lawyer; b. Nov. 18, 1937; m. Kathleen B. Wollman; children: Linda, Cynthia, Andrea. BSBA, Pa. State U., 1959; MBA in Bus. Adminstrn., U. Portland, 1962; JD, Pa. State U., 1965. Bar: Oreg. 1965, U.S. Dist. Ct. Oreg., U.S. Ct. Appeals (9th cir.), U.S. Supreme Ct. Assoc. Davies, Biggs, Strayer, Stoel & Boley, Portland, Oreg., 1965—68; ptnr. Durham, Smith, Todd & Ball, Portland, 1968—70; atty. Oreg. Dept. Justice, Salem, Oreg., 1970—78; sr. v.p., gen. counsel, sec. Portland Gen. Electric Co., 1978—87; sr. v.p., gen. counsel Phila. Electric Co. (now Exelon Corp.), Phila., 1988—2001, mediator, arbitrator, 2001—. Chmn. bd. dir. Oreg. Pub. Broadcasting Found., 1984—88; chmn. Oreg. Pub. Defender Com., 1984—85. Chmn., bd. dir. Columbia-Willamette YMCA; bd. dir., trustee Franklin Inst., 1991—2001; bd. dir. Del. Valley Citizens Crime Commn., vice chmn., 2000—02, chmn., 2002—; mem. legal adv. com. Rep. Com. Oreg., 1984—86. Mem.: ABA, Phila. Bar Found. (trustee 1991—94), Del. Valley Corp. Counsel Assn. (bd. dir. 1989—, pres. 1998), Phila. Bar Assn., Pa. Electric Assn. (chmn. 1993—94), Pa. Bar Assn., Oreg. Law Found. (bd. dir. 1986—88, pres. 1988), Oreg. State Bar (bd. govs. 1983—86, pres. 1985—86), Rotary, Tau Kappa Epsilon (fraternity alumnus of yr. 1987). Administrative and regulatory, Alternative dispute resolution, Nuclear power. Office: 2620 N Providence Rd Media PA 19063

DURHAM, J(OSEPH) PORTER, JR., lawyer, educator; b. Nashville, May 11, 1961; AB in Polit. Sci. and History cum laude, Duke U., 1982, JD, 1985. Bar: Tenn. 1985, Md. 1988. Ptnr. Miller & Martin, Chattanooga, 1990-96, Baker, Donelson, Bearman & Caldwell, Chattanooga, 1997—, chmn. corp. dept., 1998—. Adj. prof. dept. acctg. and fin. U. Tenn., Chattanooga, 1992-98; participant Russian tax code adv. group, 1999. Editor Duke Law Mag., 1984-85; contbr. articles to legal publs. Mem. Balt. Citizens Planning and Housing Assn., 1988-90; career edn. spkr. Explorer Scout program Boy Scouts Am., 1985, 88, 90-92; mem., v.p. bd. dirs., chmn. fin. com. Waxter Ctr. Found., 1989-91; mem., sec. bd. dirs. Assn. for Visual Artists, 1993-96; trustee Good Shepherd Sch., 1992-93; chmn. spl. mgmt. com. Nashville Rehab. Hosp., 1995; trail maintenance vol. U.S. Pk. Svc., 1993-95; mem. adv. com. Chattanooga State Tech. C.C.; bd. dirs. Sr. Neighbors, Inc., 2001—. Recipient Outstanding Svc. award Waxter Ctr. Found., 1991. Mem. ABA, Tenn. Bar Assn., Md. Bar Assn., Duke U. Law Sch. Alumni Assn. (bd. dirs. 1994-97), Duke U. Gen. Alumni Assn. (bd. dirs. 1986-92, exec. com. 1989-92). Corporate, general, Mergers and acquisitions, Securities. Home: 600 W Brow Rd Lookout Mountain TN 37350-1118 Office: Baker Donelson Bearman & Caldwell 1800 Republic Ctr 633 Chestnut St Chattanooga TN 37450-4000

DURHAM, ROBERT DONALD, JR., state supreme court justice; b. Lynwood, Calif., May 10, 1947; s. Robert Donald Durham and Rosemary Constance (Brennan) McKelvey; m. Linda Jo Rollins, Aug. 29, 1970; children: Melissa Brennan, Amy Elizabeth. BA, Whittier Coll., 1969; JD, U. Santa Clara, 1972; LLM in the Judicial Process, U. Va., 1998. Bar: Oreg. 1972, Calif. 1973, U.S. Dist. Ct. Oreg. 1974, U.S. Ct. Appeals (9th cir.) 1980, U.S. Supreme Ct. 1987. Law clk. Oreg. Supreme Ct., Salem, 1972-74; ptnr. Bennett & Durham, Portland, Oreg., 1974-91; assoc. judge Oreg. Ct. Appeals, Salem, 1991-94; state supreme ct. assoc. justice Oreg. Supreme Ct., Salem, 1994—. Adv. com. Joint Interim Judiciary Com., 1984-86; chmn. Oreg. Commn. on Adminstrv. Hearings, 1988-89; faculty Nat. Jud. Coll., Reno, Nev., 1992; mem. Case Disposition Benchmarks Com., 1992-93, Coun. on Ct. Procedures, 1992-93, 95—; mem. Oreg. Rules of Appellate Procedure Com., 1998-2002; bd. dirs. Oreg. Law Inst.; chmn. commn. on jud. rule 4 Oreg. Supreme Ct., 1995-97, 2002— Mem. ACLU Lawyer's Com., Eugene and Portland, Oreg., 1978-91. Recipient award for civil rights litigation ACLU of Oreg., 1988, Ed Elliott Human Rights award Oreg. Edn. Assn., Portland, 1990. Mem. Am. Acad. Appellate Lawyers (ninth cir. screening com. 1991—, rules com. 1994, co-chair appellate cts. liaison com. 1994), Oreg. Appellate Judges Assn. (pres. 1996-97), Oreg. State Bar (chair labor law sect. 1983-84, adminstrv. law com. govt. law sect. 1986), Willamette Valley Inns of Ct. (master of bench, team leader 1994—). Office: Oreg Supreme Ct 1163 State St Salem OR 97310-1331

DURHAM, WILLIAM ANDREW, lawyer; b. Paris, Tex., Mar. 21, 1956; s. James David and Ruby (Bartlett) D.; m. Susan Margaret Gallagher, Sept. 30, 1982; children: Andrew Gallagher, Margaret Rudyard. BA cum laude, Tex. A&M U., 1978; JD cum laude, U. Houston, 1981. Bar: Tex. 1981, U.S. Dist. Ct. (so. and ea. dists.) Tex. 1981, U.S. Ct. Appeals (5th cir.) 1982, U.S. Dist. Ct. (no. dist.) Tex. 1983, U.S. Supreme Ct. 1990. Assoc. Eastham, Watson, Dale & Forney, Houston, 1981-84, ptnr., 1984-98, mng. ptnr., 1998—. Bd. dirs. Casa Juan Diego, Houston, 1986—. Mem. State Bar Tex., Houston Bar Assn., Maritime Law Assn. Republican. Episcopalian. Admiralty, Federal civil litigation, Insurance. Office: Eastham Watson Dale & Forney Niels Esperson Bldg 20th 808 Travis St Houston TX 77002-5706 E-mail: wdurham@aol.com.

DURIO, WILLIAM HENRY, lawyer; b. Crowley, La., May 15, 1947; s. Lennard Edwin and Helen Hazel (Miller) D.; m. Rita Jane Putch, June 6, 1971; children: Matthew, Caroline. BS, U. La., Lafayette, 1970; JD, La. State U., 1975. Pvt. practice, Lafayette, La., 1976-78, 83-89; ptnr. Hughes Durio & Grant, Lafayette, 1978-83; gen. counsel Global Industries Ltd., Maurice, La., 1990-91; pvt. practice. Lafayette, 1991—. Adj. prof. mineral law U. La., Lafayette, 1983-84. With U.S. Army, 1970-72. Mem. La. Bar Assn., Lafayette Town House Club, Order of Troubadours. Avocations: running, fishing, scuba diving, hunting, traveling. Oil, gas, and mineral, Natural resources, Probate (including wills, trusts). Home: 608 Claymore Dr Lafayette LA 70503-4020

DURNEY, MICHAEL CAVALIER, lawyer; b. Piedmont, Calif., May 20, 1943; s. James Joseph and Camille (Cavalier) D.; m. Ann E. Belanger, Nov. 27, 1971 (dec. Oct. 2001); 1 child, Christine Cavalier; m. Carla Voetsch, June 6, 2002; 1 child, James McIvor. BA, U. Calif., Berkeley, 1965; JD, U. Calif.-Hastings Coll. of Law, 1968. Bar: Calif. 1969, D.C. 1972, U.S. Supreme Ct. 1972. Trial atty. Tax div. Dept. Justice, Washington, 1968-72, dep. asst. atty. gen. Tax div., acting asst. atty. gen., 1986-88; assoc. Hamel and Park, Washington, 1972-78, ptnr., 1978-86, Myerson, Kuhn & Sterrett, Washington, 1988-89, Law Offices of Michael C. Durney, Washington, 1990—. Chmn. bd. trustees St. Patrick's Episcopal Day Sch., Washington, 1989-92. Mem. ABA (tax and litigation sects.), Fed. Bar Assn. (chmn. tax sect. 1982-84), Calif. Bar Assn., D.C. Bar Assn. Clubs: Metropolitan (Washington), Burning Tree. Republican. Episcopalian. Avocation: golf. Federal civil litigation, Criminal, Taxation, general. Home: 6732 Selkirk Dr Bethesda MD 20817-4955 Office: 1072 Thomas Jefferson St NW Washington DC 20007-3832 E-mail: mcd@mdurney.com.

DURNIL, GORDON KAY, lawyer, diplomat, arbitrator, political party official; b. Indpls., Feb. 20, 1936; s. J. Ray and E. Merle Durnil; m. Lynda L. Powell, Mar. 1, 1963; children: Guy S., Cynthia L. BS, Ind. U., 1960, JD, 1965. Bar: Ind. 1965. Sales rep. Franklin Life Ins. Co., 1956; v.p. Ind. Ornamental Iron Works, Inc., 1960-65; sales rep. Moore Bus. Forms, Inc., 1960; pvt. practice, Indpls., 1965—. Dep. atty. gen. State of Ind., 2001—; dep. prosecutor Marion County, Ind., 1965—66; legal counsel Ind. Fedn. Young Reps., 1965—68; spl. asst. Office Bus. Svc. U.S. Dept. Commerce, 1971; profl. arbitrator, mediator, Indpls., 1993—; chmn. Internat. Joint Commn. U.S. and Can., 1989—; head del. UN Conf. on Environ. and Devel., Rio de Janeiro, 1992, v.p. Author: The Making of a Conservative Environmentalist, 1995, Is America Beyond Reform?, 1997, Soft Money, 1998, Throwing Chairs and Raising Hell, 1999; editor: Marion County Rep. Reporter, 1966—71. Justice of peace Washington Twp., Ind., 1967—70; bd. dirs. Our House Inc. (Ind. Ronald McDonald House); mem. exec. coun. Rep. Nat. Com., 1985—89; active Rep. Party, 1960—; mem. publicity com. Marion County Rep. Com., 1966—67; mem. campaign coordinating com. Ind. Rep. Com., 1968—80, mem. congl. coordinating com., 1972—74, campaign dir., 1978, state chmn., 1981—89; campaign mgr. for numerous candidates; chmn. Midwestern Rep. State Chairmen Assn., 1988—89; chmn. Ind. del., del. Rep. Nat. Conv., 1984, 1988; chmn. Marion County Election Bd., 1978—81. With U.S. Army, Korea. Mem.: Ind. Bar Assn., Soc. Profls. in Dispute Resolution, Am. Assn. Polit. cons., Emmerich Manual H.S. Alumni Assn. (pres. 1968, named Alumnus of Yr. 2000). Administrative and regulatory, Environmental. Office: Internat Joint Commn 1250 23d St NW Ste 100 Washington DC 20037-1100 E-mail: gdurnil@aol.com.

DU ROCHER, JAMES HOWARD, lawyer; b. Racine, Wis., Aug. 4, 1945; s. Howard James and Frances Ann (Rasmussen) Du R.; m. Rosalyn Ann, Sept. 2, 1972; children: Jessica Lynn, James Howard, Emily Rosalyn. Student, U.S. Mil. Acad., 1963-65, Ripon Coll., 1965-66; JD, U. Wis., 1969. Bar: Wis. Assoc. Stewart, Peyton, Crawford & Josten, Racine, 1969-78; pres. Du Rocher, Murphy, Murphy & Schroeder, S.C., Racine, 1978-96, Du Rocher Law Offices, S.C., 1996—. Bd. dirs., Careers Industries, Inc., pres., 1988-89. Bd. dirs. Racine Area United Way, 1973-79, v.p., 1977-79; chmn. Park Trails Dist. Boy Scouts Am., 1979-82; bd. dirs. Careers for Retarded Adults, Inc., 1982, pres., 1983, 90; bd. dirs. A-Center of Racine, Inc., 1978-85, pres., 1985; bd. dirs. Careers Industries Support Found., Inc., 1993-2000; deacon Atonement Luth. Ch., Racine, 1978-81; mem. adv. bd. Children's Svc. Soc. Wis.; treas. Faith Cmty. Ch., Racine, 2002—. Capt. JAGC, U.S. Army, 1969-73. Decorated Bronze Star. Mem. State Bar Wis., Mason, Rotary (pres. Racine-West club 1998-99). Corporate, general, Probate (including wills, trusts), Property, real (including real estate development, water). Home: 5531 Whirlaway Ln Racine WI 53402-1865 Office: 827 Main St Racine WI 53403 E-mail: durlaw@execpc.com.

DURR, WILLIAM SCOTT, lawyer; BA, U. Rochester, 1987; JD, Washington U., 1990. Bar: N.Y. 1991, U.S. Dist. Ct. (no. dist.) N.Y. 1991, N.C. 2001, U.S. Dist. Ct. (ea. dist.) N.C. 2001. Assoc. Chernin & Gold, Binghamton, 1990—96; acting village justice Village of Johnson City, NY, 1993—96, village justice, 1997—2001; ptnr. Durr & Sacco, Binghamton, 1998—2000; of counsel Pearis, Resseguie, Kline & Barber, LLP, Binghamton, 2000—01; ptnr. Ward and Smith, P.A., New Bern, NC, 2001—. Mem. Tryon Civitan Club, New Bern, 2001—03; judge N.C. Regional Mock Trial Competition, New Bern, 2001—03; vestry mem. All Saints Episcopal Ch., Johnson City, 1995—98; bd. dirs. Partners in Edn., New Bern, 2002—03. Named to Order of Barristers, Washington U. Sch. Law, 1990. Family and matrimonial, General civil litigation. Office: Ward and Smith PA 1001 College Ct New Bern NC 28562 Office Fax: 252-672-5477. E-mail: wsd@wardandsmith.com.

DURRANT, MATTHEW B. state supreme court justice; JD, Harvard U., 1984. Adj. prof. Brigham Young U., Salt Lake City; law clerk U.S. Supreme Ct. Appeals (10th cir.), Salt Lake City; shareholder Parr, Waddoups, Brown & Gee, Salt Lake City; judge Third Dist. Ct., Salt Lake City, 1997-2000; justice Utah Supreme Ct., 2000—. Office: Utah Supreme Ct PO Box 140210 Salt Lake City UT 84114-0210

DURRETT, JAMES FRAZER, JR., retired lawyer; b. Atlanta, Mar. 23, 1931; s. James Frazer and Cora Frazer (Morton) D.; m. Lucretia McPherson, June 9, 1956; children: James Frazer III, William McPherson, Lucretia Heston Miller, Thomas Ratcliffe. AB, Emory U., 1952; postgrad., Princeton U., 1952-53; LLB cum laude, Harvard U., 1956. Bar: Ga. 1955. Ptnr. Alston & Bird (and predecessor firm), Atlanta, 1956-97, retired, 1997. Adj. prof. Emory U. Law Sch., 1961-77. Trustee emeritus Student Aid Found., The Howard Sch. Mem. Am. Law Inst. (life, adv. estate and gift tax project, restatement, second. property, Fed. Income Tax project), Capital City Club, Harvard Club (Atlanta). Presbyterian. Corporate, general, Estate planning, Taxation, general. Home: 3483 Ridgewood Rd NW Atlanta GA 30327-2417 Office: Alston & Bird 1 Atlantic Ctr Atlanta GA 30309-3400

DURST, MICHAEL C. lawyer; b. Perth, N.J., Feb. 24, 1951; s. Wallace J. and Alice B. Durst; m. Carol A. Emig, May 1, 1983; children: Claire, Rebecca. BA, Williams Coll., 1975; MS, MIT, 1978; JD, U. Calif. Berkeley, 1981; LLM, Harvard U., 1985. Bar: D.C. Ptnr. King and Spalding, Washington, 2000—. Dir. Advance Pricing Agreement Program Internal Revenue Svc., 1994—97. Contbr. Estate taxation. Office: King and Spalding 1730 Pennsylvania Ave NW Washington DC 20006

DURST, ROBERT JOSEPH, II, lawyer; b. Pitts., Jan. 23, 1943; s. Robert J. and Catherine (Thomas) D.; m. Sandra A. Cattani; children: Thomas Sandberg, Eric Francis. BA, Gettysburg Coll., 1964; JD, Villanova U., 1967. Bar: Pa. 1967, N.J. 1968, U.S. Dist. Ct. (we. dist.) Pa. 1967, U.S. Dist. Ct. (N.J.) 1968, U.S. Supreme Ct. 1973. Corp. staff atty. Alcoa, Pitts., 1967; assoc. Herr & Fisher, Flemington, N.J., 1967-76; ptnr. Bernhard, Durst & Dilts, Flemington, 1976-89, Stark & Stark, Princeton, N.J., 1989—. Board cert. matrimonial atty. N.J. Supreme Ct., 1982— ; lectr., author on divorce and family law. With USMC, 1960—64. Fellow Am. Acad. Matrimonial Lawyers (pres. N.J. chpt. 1998-99); mem. ABA, Am. Trial Lawyers Assn., N.J. Bar Assn. (mem. exec. com. family law sect., Saul Tiscu;er award Lifetime Contbn. Family Law 2003), Hunterdon County Bar Assn., Mercer County Bar Assns., Am. Coll. Family Trial Lawyers (diplomate). Family and matrimonial. Home: 28 Marvin Ct Lawrenceville NJ 08648-2112 Office: Stark & Stark PO Box 5315 Princeton NJ 08543-5315

DU SARTEL, ALEXANDRE, lawyer; b. St. Saulve, Nord, France, Sept. 19, 1972; arrived in USA, 1998; s. Hubert Fremin Du Sartel and Nancy Vieillescazes. Degree in law, Universite Rene Descartes, Paris, 1996; M in Bus. Law, Universite Montesquieu, Bordeaux, France, 1998; LLM in Internat. and Comparative Law, U. Chgo., 1999. Bar: NY 1999, Paris, France 2003. Clk. Mirieu de Labarre Law Firm, Bordeaux, 1996—98; corp. counsel Bioméríeux, Inc., St. Louis, 2000—01, atty. Durham, NC, 2001—. Mem.: ABA, N.Y. State Bar Assn. Avocations: winemaking, sailing, rock climbing, martial arts. Corporate, general, Health, Private international. Home: 1804 Oak Tree Dr Chapel Hill NC 27514 Office: Bioméríeux Inc 100 Rodolphe St Durham NC 27712 Office Fax: 919-620-2519. Business E-Mail: alex.dusartel@law.com.

DUTILE, FERNAND NEVILLE, law educator; b. Lewiston, Maine, Feb. 15, 1940; s. Wilfred Joseph and Lauretta Blanche (Cote) D.; m. Brigid Dooley, Apr. 4, 1964; children: Daniel, Patricia. AB, Assumption Coll., 1962; JD, U. Notre Dame, 1965. Bar: Maine 1965. Atty. U.S. Dept. Justice, Washington, 1965-66; prof. law Cath. U. Am., Washington, 1966-71, U. Notre Dame Law Sch., Ind., 1971—. Bd. dirs. Ind. Lawyers Commn., Indpls., 1975-85, Legal Svcs. No. Ind., South Bend, 1975-83; dir. South Bend Work Release Ctr., 1973-75, Ind. Criminal Law Study Commn., 1991-99. Editor: Legal Education and Lawyer Competency, 1981; author: Sex, Schools and the Law, 1986; co-editor: Early Childhood Interventiion and Juvenile Delinquency, 1982, The Prediction of Criminal Violence, 1987; co-author: State and Campus, 1984. Democrat. Roman Catholic.

DUTKO, MICHAEL EDWARD, lawyer; b. Memphis, Jan. 18, 1954; s. Edward James and Norma Dean (Sparks) D.; m. Bettie Ballowe, Mar. 14, 1981; children: Michael, Christina, Ashley. BA, Biscayne Coll., 1978; JD, Nova U., 1984. Police officer, detective Ft. Lauderdale (Fla.) Police Dept., 1976-81; pros., asst. state atty. Broward State Atty.'s Office, Ft. Lauderdale, 1984-86; assoc. Kay & Bogenschutz, P.A., Ft. Lauderdale, 1986-90; ptnr. Kay, Bogenschutz & Dutko, Ft. Lauderdale, 1990-92, Bogenschutz & Dutko, P.A., Ft. Lauderdale, 1992—. Mem. Broward Assn. Criminal Def. Lawyers, Fla. Assn. Criminal Def. Lawyers, Nat. Assn. Criminal Def. Lawyers, St. Thomas More Soc. South Fla. (bd. govs.), Canon Law Soc. Am. (assoc.). Democrat. Roman Catholic. Avocations: golf, boxing, motorcycles. Criminal. Office: Bogenschutz & Dutko PA 600 S Andrews Ave Ste 500 Fort Lauderdale FL 33301-2851

DUTTON, CLARENCE BENJAMIN, retired lawyer; b. Pitts., May 31, 1917; s. Clarence Benjamin and Lillian (King) D.; m. Marian Jane Stevens, June 21, 1941; children: Victoria Lynn Dutton Sheehan, Barbara King Dutton Morgan. BS with distinction, Ind. U., 1938, JD with high distinction, 1940, LLD, 1970. Bar: Ind. 1940. Instr. bus. law Ind. U. Sch. Bus., 1940-41; atty. E.I. duPont de Nemours & Co., Inc., Wilmington, Del., 1941-43; asst. prof. law Ind. U. Sch. Law, 1946-47; pvt. practice Indpls., 1947—2000; ret. Bd. dirs. Sarkes Tarzian, Inc.; mem. Ind. Jud. Study Commn., 1965-74; regional adv. group Ind. U. Sch. Medicine, 1966-75; mem., sec. Ind. Civil Code Study Commn., 1967-73; mem. Ind. Commn. on Uniform State Laws, 1970—, chmn., 1980-91, life mem., Nat. Conf. Commrs., 1991. Author: (bus. law sect.) Chemical Business Handbook, 1954; contbr. articles to profl. jours. Bd. dirs. Found. Ind. U. Sch. Bus., Found. Econ. and Bus. Studies; mem. bd. visitors Ind. U. Sch. Law, 1971—, chmn., 1974-75; bd. dirs. Soc. for Advanced Study, Ind. U., 1984—, pres., 1985-87; mem. Acad. Alumni Fellows, Ind. U. Sch. Law, 1988. Comdr. USNR, 1943-45. Recipient Ind. Bar Found. 50-Yr. award, 1992, Ind. U. Disting. Alumni Svc. award, 1995. Mem. ABA (ho. of dels. 1960-62, state del. 1967-72, bd. govs. 1971-74, chmn. gen. practice sect. 1971-72), Ind. State Bar Assn. (bd. mgrs. 1957-63, pres. 1961-62), Indpls. Bar Assn. (v.p. 1957), Lawyers Club (pres. 1959-60), Indpls. Country Club (pres. 1955), Columbia Club, Woodstock Club, Wilderness Country Club (Naples, Fla., dir. 1991-94). Republican. Presbyterian. Home: 1402 W 52d St Indianapolis IN 46228-2317 E-mail: JLisher@ohllaw.com.

DUTTON, DIANA CHERYL, lawyer; b. Sherman, Tex., June 27, 1944; d. Roy G. and Monett D.; m. Anthony R. Grindl, July 8, 1974; children: Christopher, Bellamy. BS, Georgetown U., 1967; JD, U. Tex., 1971. Bar: Tex. 1971. Regional counsel U.S. EPA, Dallas, 1975-79, dir. enforcement div., 1979-81; ptnr., head firm-wide environ. practice, mem. Dallas practice com. Akin, Gump, Strauss, Hauer & Feld, L.L.P., Dallas, 1981—. Bd. dirs. Dallas Nature Ctr., 2001-02; chair Greater Dallas Chamber Environ. Com., 2001. Named One of Best Lawyers in Dallas D Mag., 2001, Best Laswyers in Am., 2003, Leading Bus. Lawyers Chambers USA Am., 2003-. Mem. ABA, Tex. Bar Assn. (chmn. environ. and natural resources law sect. 1985-86), Dallas Bar Assn. (chmn. environ. law sect. 1984). Episcopalian. Administrative and regulatory, Environmental. Office: Akin Gump Strauss Hauer & Feld LLP 1700 Pacific Ave Ste 4100 Dallas TX 75201-4675 E-mail: ddutton@akingump.com.

DUTTON, DOMINIC EDWARD, lawyer; b. New Orleans, Aug. 21, 1944; s. Lee M. and Fara C. Dutton. BS, Lamar Coll. Tech., 1968; JD, U. Houston, 1973. Bar: Tex. 1973, N.Mex., U.S. Dist. Ct. (we. dist.) Tex., U.S. Dist. Ct. N.Mex., U.S. Tax Ct., U. S. Ct. Appeals (10th cir.). Assoc. Bivins, Wienbrenner P.A., Las Cruces, N.Mex., 1973—76; ptnr. Dutton, Wincheste Las Cruces, N.Mex., 1976—81, Underwood & Dutton Ltd., Ruidoso, N.Mex., 1982—85, Underwood, Dutton & Griffin, Ltd., Ruidoso, N.Mex., 1985—91, Dutton, Griffin & Hakanson, Ltd., Ruidoso, N.Mex., 1991—94, Dutton & Hakanson, Ltd., Ruidoso, N.Mex., 1994—96, The Dutton Firm, Ltd., Ruidoso, N.Mex., 1997—. Village atty., Ruidoso Downs, N.Mex., 1982—86, Carrizozo, N.Mex., 1983—85, Capitan, N.Mex., 1987—2002; bd. mem. N.Mex. Gaming Control Bd., 2003—. Del. Dem. State Conv., 1980, 1984; bd. dirs. Open Door Ctr., Inc., Las Cruces, 1976—80. Mem.: N.Mex. State Bar Assn. (chmn. ethics com. 1976—77), Lincoln County Bar Assn. (sec.-treas. 1983—84, pres. 1985—87), Dona Ana County Bar Assn., Tex. State Bar Assn., Alto Lakes Country Club (Alto, N.Mex.), Cree Meadows Country Club (Ruidoso), Lions (past bd. dirs. Las Cruces club). Banking, Personal injury (including property damage), Property, real (including real estate development, water). Home: 200 Racquet Ct Ruidoso NM 88345-1668 Office: The Dutton Firm Ltd 1096 Mechem Dr Ste 229 Ruidoso NM 88345-7068

DUTTON, MARK ANTHONY, lawyer; b. Moulton, Ala., Jan. 24, 1964; s. William B. and Judith C. (Barrett) D. BA, Huntingdon Coll., Montgomery, Ala., 1987; JD, Samford U., 1990. Bar: Ala. 1991, U.S. Dist. Ct. (no. dist.) Ala. 1991, U.S. Ct. Appeals (11th cir.) 1991. Pvt. practice, Moulton, Ala., 1991—. Exec. committeeman Dem. Party, Lawrence County, Ala., 1993-, former pres. of Lawrence Continental, Al. Bar Assn.. Mem. Ala. Bar Assn., Ala. Trial Lawyers Assn., Masons, The Players Club (N.Y.C.). Democrat. Baptist. Avocations: racquetball, politics, reading. General civil litigation, State civil litigation, Criminal. Home: 14220 Market St Moulton AL 35650-1442 Office: 714 East St Moulton AL 35650-1668

DUTTON, STEPHEN JAMES, lawyer; b. Chgo., Sept. 20, 1942; S. James H. and Marjorie C. (Smith) D.; m. Ellen W. Lee; children: Patrick, Mark. BS, Ill. Inst. Tech., 1965; JD, Ind. U., 1969. Bar: Ind. 1969, U.S. Dist. Ct. (so. dist.) Ind. 1969, U.S. Ct. Appeals (7th cir.) 1972, U.S. Ct. Appeals (D.C. cir.) 1980, U.S. Supreme Ct. 1978. With McHale, Cook & Welch, P.C., Indpls., 1969-86, Dutton & Overman, P.C., 1986-91, Dutton & Bailey, P.C., 1991-94, Locke, Reynolds, Boyd & Weisell, 1994-99, Leagre Chandler & Millard LLP, Indpls., 1999—. Mem. Com. on Law of Cyberspace Bus. Law Sect. Mem. ABA. Computer, Corporate, general, Securities. Home: 3705 Spring Hollow Rd Indianapolis IN 46208-4169 Address: 135 N Pennsylvania St Ste 1400 Indianapolis IN 46204-2489 E-mail: sdutton@lcmlaw.com.

DUUS, GORDON COCHRAN, lawyer; b. Ridley Park, Pa., Oct. 17, 1954; s. Frank Martin and Shirley (Cochran) D.; m. Mary Ellen Moses, Nov. 9, 1985; children: Alexander, Hannah, Julianne. BA in Aquatic Biology magna cum laude, U. Pa., 1977; JD with honors, George Washington U., 1981. Bar: D.C. 1981, N.J. 1982, Calif. 1987, U.S. Dist. Ct. N.J. 1982, U.S. Supreme Ct. 1989. Assoc. Previti, Todd, Gemmel, Fitzgerald & Nugent, Linwood, N.J., 1982-87; ptnr., chmn. environ. law dept. Margolis, Chase, Kosicki, Aboyoun & Hartman, Verona, N.J., 1987-90, Cole, Schotz, Meisel, Forman & Leonard, Hackensack, N.J., 1990—. Mem. faculty Cook Coll. of Rutgers U., New Brunswick, N.J., 1991-2002, Nat. Bus. Insts., Saddlebrook, N.J., 1992, Govt. Inst., Atlantic City, 1995; spkr. in field. Contbr. articles to profl. jours. Mem. ABA, N.J. Bar Assn., Bergen County

Bar Assn. Environmental, Land use and zoning (including planning), Property, real (including real estate development, water). Office: Cole Schotz Meisel Forman & Leonard 25 Main St Hackensack NJ 07601-7015 E-mail: gduus@coleschotz.com.

DUVAL, STANWOOD RICHARDSON, JR., judge; b. New Orleans, Feb. 8, 1942; m. Deborah Barnes, Jan. 20, 1979. BA, La. State U., 1964, JD, 1966. Assoc. Duval, Arceneaux & Lewis, 1966-94; ptnr. Duval, Funderburk, Sundberry & Lovell, L.L.P., 1966-94; asst. city atty. Terrebonne Parish Consol. Govt., 1970-72, parish atty., 1988-92; dist. judge U.S. Dist. Ct. (ea. dist.), New Orleans, 1994—. Mem. Indigent Def. Bd., 1976-82; elected La. Constnl. Conv., 1973, mem. exec. br. com., com. to write rules of procedure. Mem. Terrebone Parish. Mem. ABA (adv. com. appellate rules 1997-2003), La. Law Inst. (coun. 1996-2001), La. State Bar Assn., Terrebonne Parish Bar Assn., Tulane Inns of Ct. Avocations: traveling, scuba diving, fishing, performing arts. Office: US Dist Ct Ea Dist 500 Camp St Rm C-368 New Orleans LA 70130-3313

DUVALL, JOHN EDWARD, law librarian; b. Washington, July 18, 1947; s. John Bernard and Barbara Annette (Bangham) D. BA in French, U. Md., 1970, MA in French, 1972, MLS, 1974. Bibliographic searcher George Washington U. Library, Washington, 1975; libr. Nat. Press Club, Washington, 1975-77, Washington Met. Area Transit Authority, 1975-79; adminstrv. analyst Hogan & Hartson, Washington, 1979—. Mem. ALA, Spl. Librs. Assn., Phi Beta Kappa, Kappa Delta Pi. Republican. Methodist. Home: 14605 Dowling Dr Burtonsville MD 20866-1711 Office: Hogan & Hartson 555 13th St NW Ste 9w100G Washington DC 20004-1109 E-mail: jeduvall@hhlaw.com.

DUVIN, ROBERT PHILLIP, lawyer; b. Evansville, Ind., May 18, 1937; s. Louis and Henrietta (Hamburg) D.; m. Darlene Chmiel, Aug. 23, 1961; children: Scott A., Marc A., Louis A. BA with honors, Ind. U., 1958, JD with highest honors, 1961; LLM with highest honors, Columbia U., 1963. Bar: Ohio 1964. Since practiced in, Cleve.; pres. Duvin, Cahn & Hutton, 1972—. Lectr. law schs.; labor adviser corps., cities and hosps. Contbr. to books and legal jours.; bd. editors: Ind. Law Jour., 1961, Columbia Law Rev., 1963. Served with AUS, 1961-62. Mem. ABA, FBA, Ohio Bar Assn., Cleve. Bar Assn., Cleve. Racquet Club, Beechmont Country Club, Soc. Club, Canterbury Golf Club, Sanctuary Golf Club. Jewish. Labor (including EEOC, Fair Labor Standards Act, labor-management relations, NLRB, OSHA). Home: 2775 S Park Blvd Cleveland OH 44120-1669 Office: Duvin Cahn & Hutton Erieview Tower 1301 E 9th St Ste 2000 Cleveland OH 44114-1886 E-mail: rduvin@duvin.com.

DUVIVIER, KATHARINE KEYES, lawyer, educator; b. Alton, Ill., Jan. 1, 1953; d. Edward Keyes and Marjorie (Attebery) DuVivier; m. James Wesley Perl, Mar. 30, 1985 (div. Aug. 1997); children: Alice Katharine Perl, Emmett Edward Perl. BA in Geology and English cum laude, Williams Coll., 1975; JD, U. Denver, 1982. Bar: Colo. 1982, U.S. Dist. Ct. Colo. 1982, U.S. Ct. Appeals (10th cir.) 1982. Intern-curator Hudson River Mus., Yonkers, N.Y., 1975; geologist French Am. Metals Corp., Lakewood, Colo., 1976-79; assoc. Sherman & Howard, Denver, 1982-84, Arnold & Porter, Denver, 1984-87; atty. Office of City Atty., Denver, 1987-90; sr. instr. sch. law Univ. Colo., 1990-00; reporter of decisions Colo. Ct. of Appeals, Denver, 2000; asst. prof., dir. Lawyering Process Program U. Denver Coll. Law, 2000—. Chair Appellate Practice Subcom., 1998—2000, vice-chmn., 1996—98, 2000—. Contbr. Mem. Denver Botanic Gardens, 1981—88; vol. Outdoor Colo., Denver, 1985—87, 1998—. Mem.: ABA (vice chmn. subcom. 1985—91), Boulder Women's Bar Assn. (pres. 1991—93), Colo. Bar Assn., Alliance Profl. Women (bd. dirs. 1985—90, pres. 1988—89), Work and Family Consortium (bd. dirs. 1988—90), St. Ives, William Coll. Alumni Assn. (co-pres. Colo. chpt. 1984—86), Phi Beta Kappa. Avocation: Avocations: geology, skiing, dancing, swimming. Home: 4761 McKinley Dr Boulder CO 80303-1142 E-mail: kkduvivier@law.du.edu.

DUZEY, ROBERT LINDSEY, lawyer; b. Long Beach, Calif., Nov. 15, 1960; s. Donald Bohdan and Noreen (Rosen) D.; m. Susan Misook Yoon, Mar. 14, 1987; children: Dylan Grey, Zenon Drake. BA, U. Calif., Irvine, 1984; JD, Western State U., Fullerton, Calif., 1994. Bar: Calif. 1994., U.S. Dist. Ct. (so., ctrl., ea. and no. dists.) Calif., U.S. Ct. Appeals (9th cir.), U.S. Supreme Ct. Claims rep., mgr. Farmers Ins. Group, Santa Ana, Calif., 1985-89; risk mgr. Dollar Rent A Car, Irvine, 1989-93; law clk. Callahan, McCune & Willis, Tustin, Calif., 1994-96; atty. Madigan, Evans & Boyer, Costa Mesa, Calif., 1996-98, Law Offices of Robert Lindsey Duzey, Downey, Calif., 1998—. Recipient Am. Jurisprudence award. Mem. ATLA, ABA, Orange County Bar Assn., Fed. Bar Assn., Orange County Barristers, L.A. County Bar Assn., Delta Theta Phi. Avocations: bicycling, badminton, home decorating. Commercial, consumer (including collections, credit), Commercial, contracts (including sales of goods; commercial financing), Insurance. Office: Law Offices Robert Lindsey Duzey 9900 Lakewood Blvd Ste 250 Downey CA 90240-4038 Fax: (562) 862-7721. E-mail: RDuzey@earthlink.net.

DWORETZKY, JOSEPH ANTHONY, lawyer, city official; b. N.Y.C., Sept. 17, 1951; s. Lawrence H. and Grace W. (Jackson) D.; m. Amy L. Banse; children: Lydia Light, Adam Eliot, Alex John, Anna Grace. BA with distinction, Purdue U., 1972; JD summa cum laude, Villanova U., 1977. Bar: Pa. 1977, D.C. 1978. Law clk. to judge U.S. Ct. Appeals 2d Cir., N.Y.C., 1977-78; assoc. Drinker Biddle & Reath, Phila., 1978-84, ptnr., 1984-93, mng. ptnr., 1992-93; chmn. corp. group law dept. City of Phila., 1993, city solicitor, 1994-96; shareholder Hangley Aronchick Segal & Pudlin, 1997—, exec. com., 1998—. Adj. prof. Rutgers U. Sch. Law, Camden, 1986-93. V.p., bd. dirs. Phila. Vol. Lawyers for Arts, 1981-84, Phila. Bd. Pensions, 1994-96, Phila. Indsl. Devel. Corp., 1994-96, Phila. Theatre Co., 1998-2000, William Penn Found., 2001—, Moore Coll. Art and Design, 2003—; sec.-treas., bd. dirs. Consumer Bankruptcy Assistance Project, 1992—, Acad. for Law, Pub. Adminstrn. and Criminal Justice, 1995-98; chair East Dist. Pa. Bankruptcy Conf., 2001. Fellow Am. Coll. Bankruptcy (regent); mem. ABA, Pa. Bar Assn., Phila. Bar Assn., Order of Coif, Phi Beta Kappa. Home: 7801 Huron St Philadelphia PA 19118-4218 E-mail: jad@hangley.com.

DWORKIN, MICHAEL LEONARD, lawyer; b. Bridgeport, Conn., Oct. 10, 1947; s. Samuel and Frances (Stein) D.; m. Christina Lyn Hildreth, Sept. 25, 1977; children: Jennifer Hildreth, Amanda Hildreth. BA in Govt. with honors, Clark U., 1969; JD with honors, George Washington U., 1973. Bar: D.C. 1973, Calif. 1975, U.S. Supreme Ct. 1978, U.S. Ct. Appeals (9th cir.) 1982, U.S. Claims Ct. 1983. Atty. FAA, Washington, L.A., 1973-77, United Airlines, San Francisco, 1977-81; pvt. practice San Francisco, 1981-95, San Mateo, Calif., 1995—. Instr. Embry Riddle Aeronautical U., San Francisco, 1980-81; dir. Poplar Ctr., San Mateo, Calif., 1979-86. Benefactor Hiller No. Calif. Aviation Mus. Jonas Clark scholar Clark U., 1966-69. Mem. ABA, Lawyer Pilots Bar Assn., Nat. Transp. Safety Bd. Bar Assn. (regional v.p. 1986-87, 90-99, chmn. rules com. 1985-99, pres. 2000-02), Aircraft Owners and Pilots Assn., Conn. Aviation Hist. Assn., Benefactor-Hiller Aviation Mus., San Mateo County Bar Assn., Bar Assn. San Francisco, Internat. Soc. Air Safety Investigators (bd. dirs. San Francisco regional chpt. 1988-89), State Bar Calif., D.C. Bar Assn., Regional Airline Assn., Commonwealth Club of Calif., New England Air Mus., Aero Club of No. Calif. Jewish. Aviation, Commercial, contracts (including sales of goods; commercial financing), Insurance. Office: 465 California St Ste 210 San Francisco CA 94104 E-mail: law@avialex.com.

DWORKIN, RONALD MYLES, legal educator; b. Worcester, Mass., Dec. 11, 1931; s. David and Madeline (Taber) D.; m. Betsy Ross, July 18, 1958; children; Anthony Ross, Jennifer. BA, Harvard U., 1953, LLB, 1957; BA, Oxford U., 1955; MA; LLB (hon.), Yale U., 1965. Bar: N.Y. 1959. Law clk. to Judge Learned Hand, 1957-58; assoc. firm Sullivan & Cromwell, 1958-62; faculty Yale Law Sch., 1962-69, master Trumbull Coll., 1966-69, Hohfeld prof. jurisprudence, 1968-69, Oxford, Eng., 1969-98; Quain prof. jurisprudence Univ. Coll., London, 1998—; prof. law NYU, 1975—. Prof.-at-large Cornell U., 1976—; vis. prof. philosophy Princeton (N.J.) U., 1963, 74-75, Gauss seminarian, 1966; vis. prof. law Stanford U., 1967; vis. prof. law and philosophy Harvard U., Cambridge, Mass., 1977, vis. prof. philosophy, 1979; acad. freedom lectr. U. Witwatersrand, 1976. Author: Taking Rights Seriously, 1977, A Matter of Principle, 1985, Law's Empire, 1986, A Bill of Rights for Britain, 1990, Life's Domain, 1993, Freedom's Law, 1996, Sovereign Virtue, 2000; editor: Philosophy of Law, 1977, A Badly Flawed Election, 2002; contbr. articles to profl. jours. Chmn. Dems. Abroad, 1972-74; del. Dem. Nat. Conv., 1972, 76; mem. Dem. Charter Commn., 1974. Fellow Brit. Acad., Am. Acad. Arts and Scis. Office: NYU Law Sch 40 Washington Sq S New York NY 10012-1099

DWORSKY, CLARA WEINER, lawyer, former merchandise brokerage executive; b. N.Y.C., Apr. 28, 1918; d. Charles and Rebecca (Becker) Weiner; m. Bernard Ezra Dworsky, Jan. 2, 1944; 1 child, Barbara G. Goodman. BS, St. John's U., N.Y.C., 1937, LLB, 1939, JD, 1968. Bar: N.Y. 1939, U.S. Dist. Ct. (ea. dist.) N.Y. 1942, U.S. Dist. Ct. (so. dist.) Tex. 1993, U.S. Ct. Appeals (9th cir.) 1994, U.S. Ct. Appeals (5th cir.) 1995. Pvt. practice, N.Y.C., 1939-51; assoc. Bessie Farberman, N.Y.C., 1942; clk., sec. U.S. Armed Forces, Camp Carson, Colo., Camp Claiborne, La., 1944-45; abstractor, dir. Realty Title, Rockville, Md., 1954-55; v.p. Kelley & Dworsky Inc., Houston, 1960—. Appeals agt. Gasoline Rationing Apls. Bd., N.Y.C., 1942; bd. dirs. Southlan Sales Assocs., Houston. Co-editor: Senior Citizens Handbook. Vol. ARC, N.Y.C.; vice chmn. War Bond pledge drive, Bklyn.; vol. Houston Legal Found., 1972-73; pres. Women's Aux. Washington Hebrew Acad., 1958-60, v.p. bd. trustees, 1959-60; co-founder, v.p. S. Tex. Hebrew Acad. (now Hebrew Acad.), Houston, 1970-75, hon. pres. women's divsn., 1973. Recipient Cert. award Treas. of U.S., 1943; Commendation Office of Chief Magistrate of City N.Y., 1948; Pietas medal St. Johns U., 1985. Mem.: ABA (chmn. social security com., sr. lawyers divsn. 1989—93, mem. sr. lawyers divsn. coun. 1989—95, chairsubcom. 1993—95, chmn. social security com., sr. lawyers divsn. 1995—, mem. editl. bd. sr. lawyers divsn. pub. Experience), Nat. Assn. Women Lawyers (chmn. organizer Juvenile Delinquency Clinic N.Y. 1948—51), Houston Bar Assn. (sec. social secutiry sect. 1995—96), Fed. Bar Assn. (vice chair programs, sr. lawyers divsn. 1994—96, dep. chair 1996—97, chmn. 1997—98, chair sr. lawyers com. south Tex. chpt. bd. 1998—, chmn. soc. sec. com., sen. lawyers divsn., co-editor sr. citizens handbook), N.Y. State Bar Assn., St. Johns U. Alumni Assn. (coord. Houston chpt. 1983—, pres. 1986), Amit Women Club, Delphians Past Pres.'s Club, Hadassah. Jewish. Pension, profit-sharing, and employee benefits. Home: 9726 Cliffwood Dr Houston TX 77096-4406

DWYER, CORNELIUS J., JR., lawyer; b. New Rochelle, N.Y., Sept. 3, 1943; s. Cornelius John and Mary Cecelia (McDonough) D.; m. June Forsythe Sonnekalb, Sept. 14, 1968; children: Cornelius William, Colin Micheal. BA, Yale U., 1965; LLB, Harvard U., 1968. Bar: N.Y. 1968, U.S. Dist. Ct. N.Y. 1969. Assoc. Shearman & Sterling, N.Y.C., 1968-76, ptnr., 1976—. Democrat. Roman Catholic. Banking, Commercial, contracts (including sales of goods; commercial financing), Corporate, general. Office: Shearman & Sterling 599 Lexington Ave Fl C2 New York NY 10022-6069 E-mail: cdwyer@sharman.com.

DWYER, DIANE MARIE, lawyer, judge; b. Amityville, N.Y., Nov. 5, 1958; d. Joseph R. and Geraldine (Burchell) D. BA, Molloy Coll., 1980; JD, St. John's U., 1983. Bar: N.Y. l983, U.S. Supreme Ct. 1991. Assoc. Deutsch & Schneider, Bklyn., 1983—84; pvt. law practice Wantagh, NY, 1984—91; dist. ct. judge, 1999; hearing examiner Nassau County Family Ct., 2000—. Dep. county atty. Nassau County, 1984—91; advisor cmty. legal instrn. program St. John's U., Jamaica, NY, 1984. Mem. ABA, N.Y. State Bar Assn., Nassau County Bar Assn. (com. mem. 1987—), Nassau County Women's Bar Assn. (bd. dirs. 1993—, pres. 2000-01), Molloy Coll. Alumni Assn. (v.p. 1986-89, pres. 1989-92, admissions recruiter 1988-94). General civil litigation, Criminal, Family and matrimonial. Office: 1200 Old Country Rd Westbury NY 11590-5630

DYE, ALAN PAGE, lawyer; b. Eustis, Fla., Apr. 4, 1946; s. Harlan Page and Maryse Jean (Tyre) D.; m. Rebecca Deen Comer, June 11, 1972; children: Katherine Ann, Andrew. AB in Econs., Duke U., 1968; JD, U. Fla., 1971; LLM, NYU, 1973. Bar: Fla. 1971, U.S. Ct. Claims 1974, U.S. Tax Ct. 1974, D.C. 1975, U.S. Ct. Appeals (10th cir.) 1975, U.S. Dist. Ct. D.C. 1976, U.S. Supreme Ct. 1976. Dir. Ea. Water Law Ctr., Gainesville, Fla., 1971—72; clk. U.S. Tax Ct., 1973—75; assoc. Webster, Chamberlain & Bean, Washington, 1975—79, ptnr., 1979—. Author: Association Legal Check List, 1983; contbr. articles to profl. jours. Bd. dirs. United Children's Fund, Washington, 1987—, Cancer Rsch. Found. Am., Washington, 1986—, chmn., 1994-96, Capitol Hill Restoration Soc., Washington, 1975-79, Am. Franklin Friends Com., 1991-95, Lee-Fendall House, 1992—, Freedom House, 1996—, Barracks Row Mainstreet, 2000—. Capt USAR, 1972-80. Mem. ABA, Am. Coll. Tax Counsel. Republican. Presbyterian. Avocations: golf, skiing, tennis. Corporate, general, Non-profit and tax-exempt organizations, Taxation, general. Office: Webster Chamberlain & Bean Ste 1000 1747 Pennsylvania Ave NW Washington DC 20006-4693 E-mail: adye@wc-b.com.

DYE, STUART S. lawyer; b. Ogden, Utah, 1939; BS cum laude with honors, U. Utah, 1961; LLB, U.Va., 1967. Bar: Va. 1967, D.C. 1967. Sec. Navy staff Deep Submergence Systems Rev. Group; Office of Legis. Affairs, 1963-64; spl. asst. on Law of the Sea matters internat. law divsn. Office of Judge Advocate Gen., 1965-66; ptnr. Holland & Knight, Washington. Adv. bd. Latin Am. Law and Bus. Report, 1994—. Mem. editl. bd. Va. Jour. Internat. Law, 1966-67; contbg. editor Oil and Gas Regulations Analyst, 1976-82. Mem. nat. adv. coun. U. Utah, 2001--. Lt. comdr. USNR. Mem. ABA (natural resources law sect., adminstrv. law sect.), Maritime Law Assn. (exec. com.), U.S., Maritime Adminstrv. Bar Assn., U.S.-Mex. C. of C. (chmn., bd. dirs. 1998—, chmn. transp. task force), Caribbean-Ctrl. Am. Action (bd. trustees, sec. 2003-), Phi Alpha Delta. Office: Holland & Knight LLP 2099 Pennsylvania Ave NW Washington DC 20006-6801 E-mail: sdye@hklaw.com.

DYEKMAN, GREGORY CHRIS, lawyer; b. Ft. Collins, Colo., Aug. 2, 1955; s. Elmer Clifford and Patsy Joyce (Hill) D. BS with honors, U. Wyo., 1977, JD, 1980. Bar: Wyo. 1980, U.S. Dist. Ct. Wyo. 1980, U.S. Ct. Appeals (10th cir.) 1980, U.S. Tax Ct. 1981, U.S. Supreme Ct. 1988, U.S. Claims Ct. 1990. Assoc. Dray, Madison & Thomson, P.C., Cheyenne, Wyo., 1980-82, shareholder, 1983-96; Dray, Thomson & Dyekman, P.C., 1996—. Adj. prof. law U. Wyo., 1993, 98, 2000, 2002; chmn. law sch. liaison com., 1998—; bd. visitors Univ. Wyo. Coll. Arts and Scis., 1999—, v. chair, 1999-2001, chair, 2001—; ex-officio mem. U. Wyo. Coll. of Law Bd. Visitors, 2001—; mem. Leadership Wyo. Class of 2003. Editor-in-chief Land and Water Law Rev., 1978-79. Mem. dist. com. Boy Scouts Am., Cheyenne, 1980-83, 87-88, dist. chmn., 1987-88, fin. chmn., 1995-96; bd. counsel Symphony and Choral Soc. of Cheyenne, 1983-88; pres. Cheyenne Family YMCA, 1984-85, bd. dirs., 1982-88, YMCA Endowment Bd., 1993—; pres., elder 1st Presbyn. Ch., Cheyenne, 1983-85, treas., 1986—; bd. dirs. Meals on Wheels Found., 1993-99, 2002—, v.p., 1995, pres.-elect, 1996, pres., 1997-98; cabinet mem. United Way, 1997; trustee Long's Peak coun. Boy Scouts Am., 1998—, v.p. endowment; bd. dirs. Cheyenne Schs. Found., 2001—; mem. Leadership Wyo Class of 2003. Mem. ABA, Laramie County Bar Assn. (sec., treas. 1985-86), Wyo. Trial Lawyers Assn. (editor newsletter 1983—), Kiwanis Found. (bd. dirs. 1993-95, pres. 1995), Cheyenne Kiwanis Club (bd. dirs. 1998-2000). Republican. Avocations: music composition, sports, internet. Banking, Federal civil litigation, State civil litigation. Home: 5010 McCue Dr Cheyenne WY 82009-4815 E-mail: Greg.Dyekman@draylaw.com.

DYER, CHARLES ARNOLD, lawyer; b. Blairstown, Mo., Aug. 29, 1940; s. Arnold and Mary Charlotte (West) D.; children: Kristine, Erin, Kathleen, Kerry. BJ, U. Mo., 1962; JD, U. Calif., 1970. Bar: Calif. 1971, U.S. Supreme Ct. 1976. Ptnr. Dyer & White, Menlo Park, Calif.; judge Pro Tem Mcpl. and SuperiorCt., San Mateo County, Calif., Pro Tem Superior Ct., Santa Clara County, Calif., arbitrator, mediator. Lectr. in field. Bd. dirs. Boys Club of San Mateo, 1971-83, pres., 1975; mem. exec. coun. Boys Clubs of Bay Area, 1977-83; mem. Dem. Nat. Fin. Com., 1978. Served to capt. USNR, 1963-93, ret. Mem. Calif. Bar Assn., San Mateo County Bar Assn., Santa Clara County Bar Assn., Palo Alto Bar Assn., Consumer Attys. Calif., Consumer Attys. San Mateo County, Assn. Atty. Mediators, Trial Lawyers Pub. Justice, Am. Bd. Trial Advs., Nat. Bd. Trial Advocacy. Roman Catholic. Federal civil litigation, State civil litigation. Office: Dyer & White 800 Oak Grove Ave Menlo Park CA 94025-4477

DYER, CHARLES RICHARD, law librarian, law educator; b. Richmond Heights, Mo., Aug. 20, 1947; s. Helmuth Kinner and Sue Anne (Stone) D.; m. Cecelia Ann Duncan, Dec. 20, 1969 (div. June 1982); m. Roberta Sharlyn Monroe, June 2, 1984; 1 child, Christina L. Floyd. BA, U. Tex., 1969; MA, Northwestern U., 1971; JD, U. Tex., 1974, MLS, 1975. Bar: Tex. 1974. Assoc. law libr., asst. prof. law St. Louis U., 1975-77; law libr., assoc. prof. U. Mo., Kansas City, 1977-87; dir. librs. San Diego County Pub. Law Libr., 1987—. Cons. in field. Editor Law Libr. Jour., 1972-74. Mem. Centre City adv. com. City of San Diego, 2000—02; chair relocation appeal bd. City of San Diego Redevel. Agy., 2001—. Mem. Am. Assn. Law Librs., Mid-Am. Assn. Law Librs (sec.-treas. 1976-78), Southwestern Assn. Law Librs. (v.p. 1981-82, pres. 1982-83), So. Calif. Assn. Law Librs. (mem. exec. bd. 1991-93), Coun. Calif. County Law Librs. (pres. 1998-2000). Democrat. Unitarian Universalist. Home: 2323 Montclair St San Diego CA 92104-5344 Office: San Diego County Pub Law Library 1105 Front St San Diego CA 92101-3904 E-mail: cdyer@sdcll.org.

DYER, CROMWELL ADAIR, JR., lawyer, international organization official; b. St. Louis, Sept. 9, 1932; came to The Netherlands, 1973; s. Adair and Tompie Leora (Giles) D.; m. Margaret Copeland Peickert, June 12, 1958 (div. Aug. 1976); children: Gretchen, Jack, Julie, Stephen; m. Susan Aynesworth, Aug. 20, 1977; stepchildren: Carol Godso, Amanda McDonough, Donnella Railsback. BA, U. Tex., 1954; JD, 1961; LLM, Harvard U., 1971. Bar: Tex. 1961, U.S. Dist. Ct. (no dist.) Tex. 1965, U.S. Dist. Ct. (ea. dist.) Tex. 1966, U.S. Dist. Ct. (we. dist.) Tex. 2003, U.S. Ct. Appeals (5th cir.) 1965, U.S. Ct. Appeals (11th cir.) 1982, U.S. Ct. Appeals (9th cir.) 1999. Law clk. FTC, Washington, 1960; assoc. Branscomb, Gary, Thomasson & Hall, Corpus Christi, Tex., 1961-62; staff atty. So. Union Gas Co., Dallas, 1962-64; assoc. Dedman & May, Dallas, 1964-65, White, McElroy & White, Dallas, 1965-67; sole practice, 1967-73; sec. Hague Conf. on Pvt. Internat. Law, The Hague, The Netherlands, 1973-78; 1st sec., 1978-93; dep. sec. gen., 1993-97; observer, cons. to intergovtl. orgns., 1976-97. Lectr. Asser Coll. Europe, 1992-96, Davis Sch. Law U. Calif. Davis, 1996, Brigitte M. Bodenheimer Meml. Lecture on the Family, 1996; ; moderator Common Law Jud. Conf. on Internat. Child Custody, Washington, 2000; condr. seminars. Honoree of symposium: Globalization of Child Law The Role of the Hague Conventions, 1999; co-author: Report on Trusts and Analogous Institutions, 1982; contbr. articles to profl. jours. Mem. adv. com., faculty internat. kidnapping program Nat. Jud. Coll., Reno, 2003; dir. studies Hague Acad., 1985, course on Unfair Competition in Pvt. Internat. Law, 1988, jury for award of Diploma in Internat. Law, 1980, 1984, 1985, 1986, 1987, 1991, 1994, 1995, 1996. Mem.: ABA (law sect. internat. law and practice, chair com. on internat. family law 2002—03, Leonard J. Theberge award for pvt. internat. law), Internat. Law Assn. (Am. br.), Inter-Am. Bar Assn., Internat. Bar Assn., Assn. Louis Chatin pour la Def. des Droits de l'Enfant (Paris), Internat. Soc. Family Law, Dallas Bar Assn., Travis County Bar Assn., Am. Fgn. Law Assn., Club du jeudi (The Hague) (pres. 1983—85). Private international, Public international. Office: PO Box 30020 Austin TX 78755-3020 Fax: 512-343-7299. E-mail: adyer@jump.net.

DYER, DUSTIN WALLACE, lawyer; b. Richmond, Va., May 17, 1972; s. Charles Gravley Jr. and Carole Williams Dyer. BA, U. Richmond, 1994; JD, Temple U., 1997. Bar: Ky. 1997, Va. 2000. Asst. dist. defender Louisville-Jefferson County Pub. Defender, 1997—98; staff atty. Ctrl. Am. Resource Ctr., Washington, 1999, mng. atty., 1999—2000; assoc. Boleman Law Firm, PC, Richmond, Va., 2000—01; ptnr. McDonald Dyer, PC, Richmond, Va., 2001—. Mem. Va. Hispanic C. of C., Richmond, 2001; pro bono atty. Capital Area Immigrants Rights Coalition, Washington, 1999; legal advisor United Food and Comml. Workers Union Local 400, Lanham, Md., 2002. Mem.: ABA, Richmond Bar Assn., Va. Trial Lawyers Assn., Am. Immigration Lawyers Assn. (ct. liaison 2001—02). Immigration, naturalization, and customs. Office: McDonald Dyer PC 1320 W Main St Richmond VA 23220 E-mail: dwdyer@mcdonalddyer.com.

DYER, GREGORY CLARK, lawyer, mediator; b. Stanford, Calif., May 29, 1947; s. Allen Clayton (dec.) and Mary Louise (Sutter) D.; m. Karyne Lee Clough, June 28, 1980; children: Ash, Chelsea. BA, Stanford U., 1970, JD, 1971. Bar: Calif. 1972, U.S. Ct. Appeals (9th cir.) 1972, U.S. Dist. Ct. (no. dist.) Calif. 1972; cert. specialist estate planning, trust and probate law, Bd. Legal Specialization of State Bar of Calif. Pvt. practice, Marin County, Calif., 1972—. Referee, arbitrator, mediator Marin County Superior Ct. Bd. dirs. Legal Aid Soc., Marin, 1979-81; past coach Mill Valley Soccer Club; basketball coach YMCA, Cath. Youth Orgn.; mgr. Mill Valley Little League. Mem. Marin County Bar Assn. (bd. dirs. 1980-82, treas. 1985, pres. 1987), Rotary (pres. local club 1984-85, area rep. 1986-87, leader fgn. exch. team 1981, 87, dist. treas. 1991-92), Scott Valley Swim and Tennis Club (bd. dirs. 1976-80). Avocations: travel, tennis, scuba diving, photography. Alternative dispute resolution, Estate planning, Probate (including wills, trusts). Office: 103 E Blithedale Ave Ste 3 Mill Valley CA 94941-2062

DYESS, BOBBY DALE, lawyer; b. Waxahachie, Tex., Jan. 27, 1935; s. Robert Olin and Rubie Lee (Odom) D.; m. Janet Lee Hassell, Jan. 30, 1960 (dec. 1973); children: Robert Dale, Jonathan David, Julianna Whitfield; m. Sharon Erwin Saylor, June 6, 1974. BA, U. N. Tex., Denton, 1956; JD, So. Methodist U., 1959. Bar: Tex. 1959. Ptnr. Elliott, Churchill, Hansen, Dyess & Maxfield, 1965-82, DeHay & Blanchard, 1983-92, Payne & Blanchard, Dallas, 1992—. Chmn. bd. Rainbow Sound, Inc., 1975-85. Editor: Bests, Life and Health Ins. Edit., 1973-85. Mem. bd. mgmt. East Dallas YMCA, 1970, 1976, campaign chmn., 1976, chmn. bd. mgmt., 1977—79; chief Indian Guides, 1971; chmn. Cub Scout pack com. Boy Scouts Am., 1970; mem./sponsor Dallas Mus. Art; trustee Baylor Med. Ctr., Ellis County, 2002—; bd. dirs. Waxahachie Found., 1999—2003. Mem.: Am. Counsel Assn. (membership chmn. 1976, pres. 1979—80, sec.-treas. 1984—87, membership chmn. 1996—98), Coll. State Bar Tex. (dir. 1996—, chmn. 1999—2001), Scribes (bd. dirs. 1976), Am. Soc. Legal Writers, Dallas Bar Found. (charter), Tex. Bar Assn. Presbyterian. Estate planning, Insurance, General civil litigation. Home: 110 Magnolia Dr Waxahachie TX 75165 Office: Payne and Blanchard 500 N Tower Plz of America Dallas TX 75201 E-mail: bdyess@msn.com.

DYK, TIMOTHY BELCHER, federal judge, educator; b. Boston, Feb. 14, 1937; s. Walter and Ruth (Belcher) Dyk; m. Inga Shirer, June 18, 1960 (div. 1970); children: Deirdre, Caitlin; m. Sally Katzen, Oct. 31, 1981; 1 child, Abraham Benjamin. AB, Harvard U., 1958, LLB magna cum laude, 1961. Bar: DC, NY. Law clk. to Justices Reed and Burton U.S. Supreme Ct., Washington, 1961—62, law clk. to Chief Justice Earl Warren, 1962—63;

spl. asst. to asst. atty. gen. U.S. Dept. Justice, Washington, 1963—64; assoc. Wilmer Cutler & Pickering, Washington, 1964—69, ptnr., 1969—90, Jones, Day, Reavis and Pogue, Washington, 1990—2000; cir. ct. judge U.S. Ct. of Appeals Fed. Cir., 2000—. Adj. prof. Georgetown U. Law Ctr., Washington, 1983, Washington, 86, Washington, 89, Washington, 91, U. Va. Law Sch., Charlottesville, 1984—85, Charlottesville, 1987—88, Yale U. Law Sch., 1986—87, 1989. Mem.: Harvard Law Rev., 1959—61; contbr. articles to profl. jours. Office: US Court Appeals Fed Cir 717 Madison Pl NW Ste 915 Washington DC 20439

DYKES, OSBORNE JEFFERSON, III, lawyer; b. L.A., Dec. 3, 1944; s. Osborne J. Jr. and Frances (Fox) D.; m. Ann Dennis, Dec. 29, 1973; children: Barbara Nell, Osborne J. IV. BA, Stanford U., 1966, MA, 1968; JD, U. Tex., 1972. Bar: Tex. 1973, U.S. Supreme Ct. 1977, U.S. Ct. Appeals (5th cir.) 1973, U.S. Ct. Appeals (11th cir.) 1981, U.S. Dist. Ct. (so. dist.) Tex. 1975, U.S. Dist. Ct. (ea. dist.) Tex. 1976, U.S. Dist. Ct. (no. dist.) Tex. 1994. Law clk. to Hon. Homer Thornberry U.S. Ct. Appeals 5th Cir., Austin, Tex., 1972-73; ptnr. Fulbright & Jaworski, Houston, 1973—. Contbr. articles to profl. publs. With U.S. Army, 1969-71. Fellow Am. Bar Found., Tex. Bar Found. (life), Houston Bar Found. (life); mem. ABA (chmn. property ins. law com. 1983-84, tort and ins. practice sect.), Fed. Bar Assn. (bd. dirs. South Tex. chpt. 2002), Energy Bar Assn., Bar Assn. of Fifth Fed. Cir., Am. Bd. Trial Advs., Tex. Assn. Civil Trial Specialists (pres. 2002-2003). Republican. Episcopalian. Avocations: tennis, bicycling. General civil litigation, Oil, gas, and mineral, Insurance. Home: 5135 Holly Terrace Dr Houston TX 77056-2125 Office: Fulbright & Jaworski 1301 Mckinney St Houston TX 77010-3031 E-mail: jdykes@fulbright.com.

DYKSTRA, DANIEL D. lawyer; b. Patterson, N.J., Oct. 29, 1955; s. H. Allan and Evelyn M. (Brown) D.; m. Sharon R. Leensvaart, June 4, 1976; children: Josiah, Jesse, Jordan, Shantelle. BA, Dordt Coll., 1977; JD with distinction, U. Iowa, 1980. Bar: Iowa 1980, U.S. Dist. Ct. (no. dist.) Iowa 1980. Assoc. Gleysteen, Harper, Eidsmoe, Heidman & Redmond, Sioux City, Iowa, 1980-83; ptnr. Heidman, Redmond, Fredregill, Patterson, Plaza, Dykstra & Prahl LLP, Sioux City, 1983—. Adj. prof. bus. law Dordt Coll., 1990-93; lectr. various orgns. Author: Practical Financial Stewardship Handbook, 2000. Mem. Siouxland Com. for Handicapped, Sioux City, 1980-98; mem. subcom. on governance State of Iowa Edn. Task Force, 1988-90; mem. funds allocation com. Siouxland United Way, 1988-92; mem. cmty. rels. com. Marion Health Ctr., 1987-90; elder, past v.p. Morningside Reformed Ch.; pres., dir. G.I.F.T.S. Found., 1988-94; mem. Siouxland Regional Cncer Ctr. Found., 2000—; bd. dirs. Sioux City Symphony, 2002—. Recipient Gov's. Disting. Svc. award Siouxland Com. for Handicapped, 1990 Mem. ABA (spl. com. problems of farmers and ranchers real property probate and trust div.), Iowa Bar Assn. (chair legal forms com. 1991-93, real estate practice manual com., profl. corps. com.), Woodbury County Bar Assn. (probate com.), Estate Planning Coun. Greater Siouxland Inc. (past pres.), Planned Giving Coun. of Siouxland, Dordt Coll. Alumni Assn. (coord. 1985-2000, pres. 1994-97). Mem. Reformed Ch. Am. Avocations: gardening, photography, travel. Corporate, general, Probate (including wills, trusts), Property, real (including real estate development, water). Home: 2515 Mcdonald St Sioux City IA 51104-3740 Office: Heidman Redmond Fredregill Plaza Dykstra & Prahl LLP PO Box 3086 Sioux City IA 51102-3086

DYKSTRA, PAUL HOPKINS, lawyer; b. Chgo., July 13, 1943; s. Paul C. and Frances Marie (Hopkins) D. Student, Exeter Coll. Oxford U., Eng., 1964; AB, Princeton U., 1965; LLB, Yale U., 1968. Bar: Ill. 1968, D.C. 1977. Assoc. Gardner, Carton & Douglas, Chgo., 1968-74, ptnr., 1975—2003, ptnr. Washington office, 1977-79, fin. ptnr., 1985-89, chmn., 1989-95; mem. Bell, Boyd & Lloyd LLC, Chgo., 2003—. Adj. prof. law Northwestern U. Sch. Law, 2001—. Contbr. articles to profl. jours. Trustee Chgo. Theatre Group, Inc. (Goodman Theatre), 1975—, pres., 1983-85, vice chmn., 1988-92, pres., 1992-97; mem. aux. bd. Art Inst. Chgo., 1973-77, 79-88, exec. com., 1976-77, 82-87, 2000—; chmn. Orange and Black Club of Princeton Club of Chgo., 1987-90; chmn. maj. gifts Princeton U. Class of 1965, 1982-85; mem. cultural affairs adv. bd. City of Chgo., 1990—, Blue Skies for Kids, Chgo. Cmty. Trust, Chgo. Pub. Libr. Bd., 1991-97, chmn. adminstrn. and fin. com., 1996—; trustee Chgo. Pub. Libr. Found., 1999—. Mem. ABA (fed. and regulation of securities com.), Chgo. Bar Assn. (sec. 1976-77), Chgo. Hist. Soc. (trustee 1999—, mem. Making History awards com. 1994—, chmn. 2000-2002), Econ. Club of Chgo. (reception com. 1982-85), Legal Club of Chgo., Law Club Chgo., Racquet Club of Chgo. (bd. govs., vice chmn. membership com. 1980-83), Chgo. Club (bd. dirs., sec. 1996-2000), Shoreacres, Chgo. Commonwealth Club, The Comml. Club of Chgo. (sec., mem. exec. com. 2001—), Chgo. Coun. Fgn. Rels. (Chgo. com.). Episcopalian. Avocations: travel, golf, bicycling. Corporate, general, Securities. Office: Bell Boyd & Lloyd LLC 70 W Madison St Chicago IL 60602-4207 Office Fax: 312-569-3112. E-mail: pdykstra@gcd.com.

DYWAN, JEFFERY JOSEPH, judge; b. Hammond, Ind., Apr. 26, 1949; s. Joseph Michael and Florence Marie (Buda) D.; m. Jacque Ann Shulmistras, June 20, 1971; children: Dina, Abigail, Kathryn. BS in Indsl. Engring., Purdue U., 1971; JD, Valparaiso U., 1974. Bar: Ind. 1974, U.S. Dist. Ct. (no. and so. dists.) Ind. 1974, U.S. Ct. Appeals (7th cir.) 1975, Ill. 1984, U.S. Dist. Ct. (no. dist.) Ill. 1986. Assoc. Breclaw & Dywan, Griffith, Ind., 1974-77; sole practice Griffith, 1977-81; dep. prosecuting atty. Lake County, Crown Point, Ind., 1978-80, pub. defender, 1981-83; assoc. Chudom & Meyer, Schererville, Ind., 1981-89; ptnr. O'Drobinak, Dywan & Austgen, Crown Point, 1989-91; judge Lake Superior Ct., Crown Point, 1991—, chief judge, 1998-2000. Instr. Calumet Coll., Hammond, Ind., 1974-76, Ind. Vocat. and Tech. Coll., Gary, Ind., 1978-79. Mem. Ind. State Bar Assn., Lake County Bar Assn., Am. Judicature Soc., KC. Roman Catholic. Office: Lake Superior Ct 2293 N Main St Crown Point IN 46307

EAGAN, CLAIRE VERONICA, judge; b. Bronx, N.Y., Oct. 9, 1950; d. Joseph Thomas and Margaret (Lynch) E.; m. M. Stephen Barrett, Aug. 25, 1978 (div. 1984); m. Anthony J. Loretti, Jr., Feb. 13, 1988. Student, U. Fribourg, Switzerland, 1970-71; BA, Trinity Coll., Washington, 1972; postgrad., U. Paris, 1972-73; JD, Fordham U., 1976. Bar: N.Y. 1977, Okla. 1977, U.S. Dist. Ct. (no. dist.) Okla. 1977, U.S. Ct. Appeals (10th cir.) 1978, U.S. Supreme Ct. 1980, U.S. Dist. Ct. (we. dist.) Okla. 1981, U.S. Ct. Appeals (5th cir.) 1982, U.S. Dist. Ct. (ea. dist.) Okla. 1988, U.S. Ct. Appeals (Fed. cir.) 1990. Mem. Hall, Estill, Hardwick, Gable, Golden & Nelson, Tulsa, 1978-98, shareholder, 1981-98, also bd. dirs., exec. com.; magistrate judge U.S. Dist. Ct. (no. dist.) Okla., Tulsa, 1998—2001, dist. judge, 2001—. Mem. Jud. Conf. Com. on Defender Svcs., 2002—. Editor: Fordham Law Rev., 1975—76. Bd. dirs. Okla. Med. Rsch. Found., 2003—, Cath. Charities, Tulsa, 1983-98, Cystic Fibrosis Found., Tulsa, 1982-84; mem. Jr. League Tulsa, Inc., 1983—; trustee Gannon U., Erie, Pa., 1995-98; bd. dirs. Okla. Sinfonia, Tulsa, 1982-86; adj. settlement judge, Tulsa County, 1990-97. Fellow Am. Bar Found.; mem. Tulsa County Bar Assn., 10th Cir. Jud. Conf., Am. Inns of Ct. (chpt. pres. 1999-2000). Republican. Roman Catholic. Office: US Dist Ct No Dist Okla 333 W 4th St Ste 411 Tulsa OK 74103-3819

EAGAN, DAVID EUGENE, lawyer; b. Oil City, Pa., June 23, 1956; s. Robert Francis Eagan and Margaret Agnes Kirshner; m. Mary Ann McCaffrey, May 16, 1980. BA with History magna cum laude, SUNY, Geneseo, 1979; JD cum laude, SUNY, Buffalo, 1982. Bar: N.Y. 1983. Assoc. Chadbourne & Parke LLP, N.Y.C., 1982—94; ptnr. Bittle, Fouler LLP, N.Y.C., 1994—2000, Fulbrith & Jaworski LLP, N.Y.C., 2000—. Mem. Wainscott Citizens Adv. Com. Sea Grant Law scholar, 1981. Mem.: Met. Club, N.Y. Athletic Club (mem. law com.). Avocation: horse farm. Corporate, general, Finance, Mergers and acquisitions. Home: PO Box 249 Roosevelt NY 11575 Office: Fulbrigh and Jaworski LLP 666 5th Ave Fl 31 New York NY 10103-0001 Office Fax: 212-319-3400. Business E-Mail: degan@fulbright.com.

EAGAN, MICHELE, lawyer; b. Berwick, Pa., Sept. 20, 1971; d. Robert M. and Anna Marie Stawinski; m. Michael A. Eagan, Apr. 26, 1997. BA in Journalism, BA in Sociology, Pa. State U., 1993; JD, Dickinson Sch. Law, 1996. Bar: Pa. 1996, N.J. 1996, U.S. Dist. Ct. N.J. 1996, U.S. Dist. Ct. (ea. dist.) Pa. 1999, U.S. Dist. Ct. (mid. dist.) Pa. 1999, U.S. Ct. Appeals (3rd cir.) 1999. Law clk. Monroe County Courthouses, Stroudsburg, Pa., 1996—98; assoc. Roda & Nast, P.C., Lancaster, Pa., 1998—. Vol. Project Linus, Lancaster, Pa., 2001—. Mem.: ATLA, ABA, Lancaster Bar Assn., Pa. Bar Assn., Pa. State Alumni Assn. (bd. mem. Lancaster County chpt. 2000—, v.p. membership 2001—). Democrat. Avocations: yoga, crafts. Labor (including EEOC, Fair Labor Standards Act, labor-management relations, NLRB, OSHA), Insurance, class actions and complex litigation. Office: Roda & Nast PC 801 Estelle Dr Lancaster PA 17601

EAGAN, WILLIAM LEON, lawyer; b. Tampa, Fla., Feb. 10, 1928; s. John Robert and Margaret (Williams) E.; m. Marjorie Young, Mar. 6, 1949; children: Barbara Anne, Rebecca Elizabeth, Laurel Lea. Student, U. Tampa, 1959; LLB, U. Fla., 1961. Bar: Fla. 1961, U.S. Dist. Ct. (mid. dist.) Fla. 1959, U.S. Dist. Ct. (so. dist.) Fla. 1962, U.S. Ct. Appeals (5th cir.) 1972; bd. cert. civil trial lawyer, Fla. Assoc. Dexter, Conlee & Bissell, Sarasota, Fla., 1961-62; ptnr., v.p. Arnold, Matheny & Eagan, P.A., Orlando, 1962—. Mem. Fla. Bar Ninth Circuit Grievance Com., 1982-84; mediator Family Law Mediation Program. Articles editor U. Fla. Law Rev., 1961. Chmn. bd. trustees First Bapt. Ch., Winter Park, Fla., 1970-72, chmn. bd. deacons, 1967-69; active Indsl. Devel. Commn. Mid-Fla., Orlando, 1979-84. Served to seaman 2d class USN, 1945-46. Mem. ATLA, Acad. Fla. Trial Lawyers, Lawyers Title Guaranty Assn., Orange County Bar Assn. (exec. coun.), Univ. Club, Order of Coif, Phi Alpha Delta, Phi Kappa Phi. Republican. Baptist and Methodist. Federal civil litigation, State civil litigation, Property, real (including real estate development, water). Office: Arnold Matheny & Eagan PA 801 N Magnolia Ave Ste 201 Orlando FL 32803-3842 E-mail: Weagan@ameorl.com.

EAGLES, SIDNEY SMITH, JR., judge; b. Asheville, N.C., Aug. 5, 1939; s. Sidney Smith Sr. and Mildred Truman (Brite) E.; m. Rachel Phillips, May 22, 1965; children: Virginia Brite, Margaret Phillips. BA, Wake Forest U., 1961, JD, 1964. Bar: N.C. 1964. Revisor Gen. Statutes Commn., Raleigh, N.C., 1967-70; asst. atty. gen. legis. drafting service Office Atty. Gen. N.C., Raleigh, 1970-74, dep. atty. gen. spl. prosecution divsn., 1974-76; counsel to speaker N.C. State Legislature, Raleigh, 1976-80; ptnr. Eagles Hafer & Hall, Raleigh, 1977-82; judge N.C. Ct. Appeals, Raleigh, 1983—, chief judge, 1998—. Adj. prof. Campbell U. Sch. Law, 1977—; chmn. N.C. Jud. Stds. Commn., 1994—96; mem. faculty Appellate Judges Sch. Law Sch. NYU, N.Y.C., 1993—99; mem. Uniform Laws Conf., 1968—83, 1992—, life mem., 2000. Co-author: North Carolina Criminal Procedure Forms, 1975, 3d edit., 1989; contbr. articles to profl. jours. V.p. Raleigh Jaycees, 1972-73; mem. Senatorial Dist. Dem. Com., 1979-81; bd. dirs. Wake County (N.C.) Symphony Soc., 1980-81, Women's Aid of Wake County, 1978—; bd. elders, bd. deacons, trustee, tchr. Sunday sch. Hillyer Meml. Christian Ch., 1980—, chmn bd., 1989; bd. visitors Wake Forest U. Sch. Law; vice chair bd. trustees Barton Coll., 1999, chair, 2002—. Served to capt. USAF, 1964-67; col., ret. 1991. Named Disting. Law Alumnus, Wake Forest U., 1981; N.C. Justice Found. fellow, 1972. Mem. ABA (chmn. appellate judges conf. 1993-94, mem. appellate jud. edn. com. 1994-98, ho. of dels. 1992—, mem. legal edn. 2002—), Am. Law Inst. (life), N.C. Bar Assn. (v.p. 1989-90), Wake county Bar Assn. (chmn. exec. com. 1975), N.C. State Bar, Execs. Club (pres. 1985), Kiwanis (disting. pres. Raleigh 1986-87, disting. lt. gov. 1995, Kiwanian of Yr. award 1989), Phi Delta Phi, Phi Alpha Delta (James Iredell award 1990). Avocations: politics, reading. Office: NC Ct of Appeals PO Box 888 Raleigh NC 27602-0888

EAGLETON, EDWARD JOHN, lawyer; b. Tulsa, Jan. 22, 1932; s. William L. and Pauline (Dellinger) E.; m. Norma Lee, Oct. 6, 1956; children: Courtney Jean, Richard John. BA, Okla. U., 1954, JD, 1956. Bar: Okla. 1955, U.S. Dist. Ct. (ea., we. and no. dists.) Okla. 1956, U.S. Tax Ct. 1958, U.S. Supreme Ct. 1964; CPA, Tex., Okla. Acct. Peat Marwick Mitchell, Dallas, 1956-58; with IRS, Dallas and New Orleans, 1958-62; assoc. Houston & Klein, Tulsa, 1962-65; ptnr. Kothe & Eagleton, Tulsa, 1965-74, Houston & Klein Inc., Tulsa, 1974-94, Eagleton Eagleton & Harrison Inc., Tulsa, 1994—. Served with U.S. Army, 1956. Named one of Best Tax Lawyers in Am., Bar Register of Preeminent Lawyers, 1983—2001. Republican. Unitarian Universalist. Probate (including wills, trusts), Corporate taxation, Taxation, general. Home: 3210 E 65th St Tulsa OK 74136-1225 Office: Eagleton, Eagleton & Harrison Inc 320 S Boston Ave Ste 1700 Tulsa OK 74103-4706

EAKELEY, DOUGLAS SCOTT, lawyer; b. Morristown, NJ, Mar. 2, 1946; m. Priscilla Van Tassel, June 2, 1973. BA, Yale U., 1968, JD, 1972; BA in Jurisprudence, MA in Jurisprudence, Oxford (England) U., 1970. Bar: N.Y. 1973, U.S. Ct. Appeals (2nd cir.) 1974, N.J. 1978, U.S. Ct. Appeals (3rd cir.) 1980, U.S. Supreme Ct. 1981. Law clk. to judge Harold R. Tyler, Jr. U.S. Dist. Ct. (so. dist.) N.Y., N.Y.C., 1972-73; assoc. Debevoise, Plimpton, N.Y.C., 1973-80; ptnr. Riker, Danzig, Scherer, Hyland & Perretti, Newark and Morristown, N.J., 1980-90, 91-94; first asst. atty. gen. State of N.J., 1990-91; ptnr. Lowenstein Sandler, PC, Roseland, N.J., 1994—. Chmn. Legal Svcs. N.J., North Brunswick, 1981-90, Legal Svcs. Corp., Washington, 1993-2003; pres. Legal Svc. Found. Essex County, Newark, 1981-90; chmn. N.J. Sentencing Policy Study Commn., 1992-93; trustee Practising Law Inst., N.Y.C., 1994—; trustee Boys and Girls Clubs of Newark, 1993-2003. Chmn. bd. editors N.J. Law Jour., 1984-90. Trustee N.J. Network Found., 1994—, N.J. Inst. for Social Justice, 1996—; pres. N.J. Shakespeare Festival, Madison, 1982-86. Rhodes scholar Oxford U., 1968. Fellow Am. Bar Found.; mem. ABA (John Minor Wisdom award, litigation sect. 1997), N.J. Bar Assn., Essex County Bar Assn., Fed. Bar Assn. N.J. (v.p. 1983-90), Urban League of Essex County (trustee 1987-88), Assn. Am. Rhodes Scholars (bd. dirs. 1995-2002), Phi Beta Kappa. Democrat. Antitrust, Federal civil litigation, General civil litigation. Office: Lowenstein Sandler PC 65 Livingston Ave Roseland NJ 07068-1725 E-mail: deakeley@lowenstein.com.

EAKEN, BRUCE WEBB, JR., lawyer; b. Cleve., Mar. 23, 1938; s. Bruce Webb and Kathryn (Peacock) E.; m. Wilhelmina Murray Martin, Oct. 23, 1971; children: Amanda, Webb. BA, Dartmouth Coll., 1960; JD, U. Mich., 1964. Bar: Ohio 1964, N.Y. 1965. Atty. Allied Chem. Co., N.Y.C., 1966-72; assoc. counsel U.S. Filter Corp., N.Y.C., 1972-81; prin. atty. N.Y. Power Authority, N.Y.C., 1981—95. Bd. dirs. East Harlem Little League, N.Y.C., 1970-73; pres. St. Bartholomews Players, N.Y.C., 1972-74; bd. dirs., treas. Media Ctr. for Children, N.Y.C., 1982-90. Mem. Assn. Bar City NY (adminstrv. law com. 1983-86, inter-Am. Affairs com. 1988-2001, corp. law dept. com. 1989-92, second century com. 1990-94, Africa affairs 2003—), UN Assn. NYC (v.p. 2000—), Dartmouth Alumni Assn. NYC (pres. 2000—). Nuclear power, Utilities, public, Property, real (including real estate development, water). E-mail: eaken@aol.com.

EAKIN, J. MICHAEL, judge; b. Mechanicsburg, Nov. 18, 1948; m. Heidi Eakin; children: Michael, Zachary, Chase. BA in Govt., Franklin & Marshall Coll., 1970; JD, Pa. State U., 1975. Asst. dist. atty. Cumberland County, 1975—83, dist. atty., 1984—95; pvt. practice, 1980—83; judge Superior Ct. Pa., 1995—2001; justice Supreme Ct. Pa., 2001—. Lectr. Nat. Coll. Dist. Attys. Contbr. articles to profl. jours. With Pa. Army N.G., 1971—77. Recipient Sweetheart of the Yr. award, MADD, 1988, Best Catch award, Mid-Penn Anglers, 1991, Career Achievement award, Dickinson Sch. Law, 2000. Mem.: ABA, Pa. Dist. Atty.'s Inst. (bd. dirs. 1987—95, pres. 1994—95), Pa. Dist. Atty.'s Assn. (mem. exec. com., chmn. edn. 1987—95, pres. 1992—93), Pa. Bar Inst. (faculty, mem. criminal law sypmosium planning com.), Am. Inns Ct., Cumberland County Bar Assn., Dauphin County Bar Assn., Lancaster County Bar Assn., Pa. Bar Assn. (mem. plain English com.), Am. Judges Assn., Brehon Soc. Office: Pa State Supreme Ct 4720 Old Gettysburg Rd #405 Mechanicsburg PA 17055

EAKIN, MARGARETTA MORGAN, lawyer; b. Ft. Smith, Ark., Aug. 27, 1941; d. Ariel Thomas and Oma (Thomas) Morgan; m. Harry D. Eakin, June 7, 1959; 1 child, Margaretta E. BA with honors, U. Oreg., 1969, JD, 1971. Bar: Oreg. 1971, U.S. Dist. Ct. Oreg. 1973, U.S. Ct. Appeals (9th cir.) 1977. Law clk. to chief justice Oreg. Supreme Ct, Salem, 1971-72; Reginald Heber Smith Law Reform fellow, 1962-73; house counsel Hyster Co., 1973-75; assoc. N. Robert Stoll, 1975-77; pvt. practice, Margaretta Eakin, P.C., Portland, Oreg., 1977—. Tchr. bus. law Portland State U., 1979-80; spkr.; mem. bd. profl. responsibility Oreg. State Bar, 1979-82; mem. bd. visitors U. Oreg. Sch. Law, 1986-93, vice chair, 1989-91, chair, 1992-93; mem. Oreg. State. Bar Com. on Uniform State Laws, 1989-93; vol. lawyer Fed. Emergency Mgmt. Assn., 1995—. Mem. ann. fund com. Oreg. Episcopal Sch., 1981; chmn. subcom county fair, 1981; sec. bd. Parent Club St. Mary's Acad., 1987. Paul Patterson fellow. Mem. ABA, ATLA, Oreg. Trial Lawyers Assn., Oreg. Bar Assn., Multnomah County Bar Assn. (jud. selection com. 1992-94), 1000 Friends of Oreg., City Club. Federal civil litigation, State civil litigation, Commercial, contracts (including sales of goods; commercial financing). Office: 1001 SW 5th Ave 13th Fl Portland OR 97204 E-mail: ME71051@aol.com.

EAKINS, WILLIAM SHANNON, lawyer; b. Glen Cove, N.Y., July 22, 1951; s. William Shannon and Jean (Pickup) E.; 1 child, Amelia Moore. BA, Yale U., 1974; JD, Cornell U., 1977. Lawyer, trust adminstr. J.P. Morgan Bank, N.Y.C., 1977-81; counsel com. on taxation and investigations N.Y. State Senate, Albany, 1981-84; assoc. Gelberg & Abrams, N.Y.C., 1981-84, Phillips, Nizer, Benjamin, Krim & Ballon, N.Y.C., 1984-88, ptnr., 1989-92; ptnr., chair trusts and estates dept. Olshan, Grundman, Frome & Rosenzweig, N.Y.C., 1993-98; of counsel Forsythe, Patton, Ellis, Lipsett & Savage, N.Y.C., 1998—. Bd. dirs. Asphalt Green Inc.; mem. estate planning com. Arthritis Found. Contbr. articles to profl. jours. Vice chmn. N.Y. Rep. County Com., N.Y.C., 1985-89, exec. com., 1979-87, dist. leader, 1979-87; vice chmn. Manhattan Cmty. Bd. No. 8, N.Y.C., 1980-84, 93-97; Rep., Ind. Neighbors and Conservative candidate for N.Y. State Assembly, 1992; bd. dirs. Homecrest Cmty. Svcs., Inc.; sec. Hellgate Hill-Highgate Cmty. Assn.; elder, mem. session, mem. planned giving com. Brick Presbyn. Ch. Mem. N.Y. State Bar Assn., Assn. Bar City N.Y. (mem. com. on estate and gift taxation, mem. com. on N.Y. state legislation), Yale Club, St. Andrews Soc. State of N.Y. (bd. mgrs.). Republican. Presbyterian. Office: Forsythe Patton Ellis Lipsett & Savage 420 Lexington Ave New York NY 10170-0002 E-mail: wmeakins@rcn.com.

EARLY, ALEXANDER RIEMAN, III, judge; b. Phila., Sept. 22, 1917; s. A.R. Jr. and Elizabeth Frances (Dence) Early; m. Celeste Worland, Aug. 15, 1959; children: A.R. IV, Lucia C. Stroh, Elizabeth V., John Drennan, V. BA, Cornell U., 1938; LLB, Harvard U., 1941. Bar: Calif. 1946. Pvt. law practice, L.A., 1946—50; sr. atty. Divsn. of Hwys., State of Calif., 1950-55; asst. U.S. atty. Lands divsn. U.S. Dept. Justice, L.A., 1955-57; asst. county counsel Los Angeles County, Calif., 1957-72; judge Superior Ct., L.A., 1972-87, chmn. Exec. Com., Rules Com., BAJI Com.; judge by assignment, 1987—; ret., 1987. Adj. prof. Southwestern Law Sch., L.A., 1970-79. Contbr. articles to profl. jours. Mgr. internat. fedn. rels. boxing venue 1984 Olympics. Comdr. USNR, 1941-46. Served U.S. Navy in Destroyers, Pacific (earned nine battle stars); dir. sinking I.J.N. sub. RO-38, 1943. Decorated comdr. Order Polonia Restituta (Poland); knight grand cross Order of Holy Sepulchre (Vatican), Law Enforcement medal SAR, 1981. Fellow: Samuel Victor Constant Soc.; mem.: Nat. Conf. State Tax Judges, Am. Bd. Trial Adv., Navy League, Aztec Club, U.S. Naval Inst. (hon. mem. crew USS Canberra), Md. Hist. Soc., Soc. Cincinnati, Soc. War of 1812 (v.p. gen., Disting. Svc. award), Calif. Soc. Colonial Wars (dep. gov. gen., Disting. Svc. medal), Calif. Soc. Sons of Revolution (pres., Disting. Svc. award). Roman Catholic. Avocations: American history, genealogy, camellia seedlings. Home: 3017 Kirkham Dr Glendale CA 91206-1127

EARLY, BERT HYLTON, lawyer, consultant; b. Kimball, W.Va., July 17, 1922; s. Robert Terry and Sue Keister (Hylton) E.; m. Elizabeth Henry, June 24, 1950; children— Bert Hylton, Robert Christian, Mark Randolph, Philip Henry, Peter St. Clair Student, Marshall U., 1940-42; AB, Duke U., 1946; JD, Harvard U., 1949. Bar: W.Va. 1949, Ill. 1963, Fla. 1981. Assoc. Fitzpatrick, Marshall, Huddleston & Bolen, Huntington, W.Va., 1949-57; asst. counsel Island Creek Coal Co., Huntington, W.Va., 1957-60, assoc. gen. counsel, 1960-62; dep. exec. dir. ABA, Chgo., 1962-64, exec. dir., 1964-81; sr. v.p. Wells Internat., Chgo., 1981-83, pres., 1983-85, Bert H. Early Assocs. Inc., Chgo., 1985-94, Early Cochran & Olson, Chgo., 1994-98, of counsel, 1999—. Dir. Am. Bar Found., Chgo., 1993-95; instr. Marshall U., Huntington, W.Va., 1950-53; legal search cons. and lectr. in field. Bd. dirs. Morris Meml. Hosp. for Crippled Children, 1954-60, Huntington Pub. Libr., 1951-60, W.Va. Tax Inst., 1961-62, Huntington Mus. Art, 1961-62; mem. W.Va. Jud. Coun., 1960-62, Huntington City Coun., 1961-62; bd. dirs. Cmty. Renewal Soc., Chgo., 1965-76, United Charities Chgo., 1972-80, Hinsdale (Ill.) Hosp. Found., 1987-93, Internat. Bar Assn. Found., 1987-89; bd. dirs. Am. Bar Endowment, 1983-95, sec., 1987-89, treas., 1989-91, v.p., 1991-93, pres., 1993-95, dir. emeritus, 1995-2000; mem. vis. com. U. Chgo. Law Sch., 1975-78; trustee Davis and Elkins Coll., 1960-63; mem. Hinsdale Plan Commn., 1982-85. 1st lt. AC, U.S. Army, 1943-45. Fellow Am. Bar Found., Ill. Bar Found. (charter); mem. ABA (ho. of dels. 1958-59, 84-93, chmn. young lawyers divsn. 1957-58, Disting. Svc. award young lawyers divsn. 1983), Am. Law Inst. (life), Internat. Bar Assn. (asst. sec. gen. 1967-82), Nat. Legal Aid and Defender Assn., Legal Aid Soc. Chgo., Am. Judicature Soc. (bd. dirs. 1981-84), Fla. Bar, W.Va. Bar Assn., Chgo. Bar Assn. Presbyterian. Office: Early Cochran & Olson LLC 401 N Michigan Ave Ste 2010 Chicago IL 60611-4206

EARLY, JAMES H., JR., lawyer; b. Henderson, N.C., May 6, 1939; s. James Howard and Nettie Anna (Hicks) E.; children from previous marriage: James H. III, Anna Elizabeth, Mary Elizabeth. AA, Mars Hill Coll., 1960; BA, Wake Forest U., 1962, LLB, 1964, JD, 1970. Bar: N.C. 1964, U.S. Dist. Ct. (mid. dist.) N.C. 1970, U.S. Ct. Appeals (4th cir.) 1995; cert. mediator Superior Cts. of N.C., 1992. Pvt. practice, Winston-Salem, 1964—; mediator Adminstrv. Office of the Cts. of N.C., 1992—. Mediator Am. Arbitration Assn., 1992—. Contbr. articles to profl. jours. With U.S. Army, 1957. Chmn. fundraising Cub Scouts/Boy Scouts Am., Little League, Pop Warner, Indian Guides, March of Dimes, others. Mem. ABA, ATLA, N.C. Bar Assn. (chmn. continuing legal edn. subcom., mem. effectiveness and quality of life com., moderator skills course com.), , Forsyth County Bar Assn. (sec. 1970-71), N.C. Acad. Trial Lawyers, Phi Alpha Delta (alumni advisor 1969-84, Outstanding Alumnus award 1967), Kiwanis (pres. 1989-90, 91-92), Masons. Baptist. Avocations: hunting, fishing, walking horses, bird dogs, racing. Corporate, general, Labor (including EEOC, Fair Labor Standards Act, labor-management relations, NLRB, OSHA), Personal injury (including property damage). Home: 144 Sterling Pt Ct Winston Salem NC 27104 Office: 1320 Westgate Center Dr Winston Salem NC 27103-2933

EASLEY, CHARLES D., JR., state supreme court justice; b. Port of Spain, Trinidad, Apr. 8, 1949; (parents Am. citizens); s. Charles D. and Doris B. Easley; m. Pamela Robinson; children: Christopher, Lindsey, Ali Mara. BBA, U. Miss., 1972, JD, 1979; MBA, Miss. State U., 1976. Asst. dist. atty. 3d Jud. Cir. Ct. Dist., 1980—83; pvt. practice Columbus, Miss.,

1983—2000; prosecutor Caledonia, 1999, judge, 2000; assoc. justice Miss. Supreme Ct., 2001—. Mem.: Lowndes County Bar Assn., Miss. Mcpl. Judges Assn., ABA, NRA, Masons, Shriners. Office: Miss Supreme Ct Gartin Justice Bldg 450 High St Jackson MS 39201 also: PO Box 249 Jackson MS 39205

EASLEY, MICHAEL F. governor; b. Rocky Mount, N.C., 1950; m. Mary Pipines; 1 child, Michael F., Jr. BA in Polit. Sci. cum laude, U. N.C., 1972; JD cum laude, N.C. Ctrl. U. Dist. atty. 13th Dist., N.C., 1982-91; pvt. practice Southport, N.C., 1991-93; atty. gen., 1993-2000; gov. State of N.C., 2000—. Contbr. numerous articles in field. Recipient Pub. Svc. award U.S. Dept. Justice, 1984. Pres. N.C. Conf. Dist. Attys.; mem. N.C. Dist. Attys. Assn. (past pres., legis. chmn.). Democrat. Avocations: hunting, sailing, woodworking. Office: Office of the Gov 20301 Mail Service Ctr Raleigh NC 27699-0303

EASTAUGH, ROBERT L. state supreme court justice; b. Seattle, Nov. 12, 1943; BA, Yale U., 1965; JD, U. Mich., 1968. Bar: Alaska 1968. Asst. atty. gen. State of Alaska, 1968—69, asst. dist. atty., 1969—72; lawyer Delaney, Wiles, Hayes, Reitman & Brubaker, Inc., 1972—94; assoc. justice Alaska Supreme Ct., 1994—. Office: Alaska Supreme Ct 303 K St Anchorage AK 99501-2013

EASTERLING, CHARLES ARMO, lawyer; b. Hamilton, Tex., July 22, 1920; s. William Hamby and Jennie (Arilla) E.; m. Irene A. Easterling, Apr. 25, 1943; children: Charles David, Danny Karl, Jan Easterling Petty. BBA, LLB, Baylor U., 1951, JD, 1969. Bar: Tex. 1950, U.S. Supreme Ct. 1954. Sr. asst. city atty. City of Houston, 1952-64; pvt. practice Houston, 1964-70; city atty. Pasadena, Tex., 1970-82; of counsel Easterling and Easterling, Houston, 1982—. Instr. So. Tex. Coll. Law, 1954-69. Lt. col. (ret.) USAFR. Mem. Houston-Harris County Bar Assn., Masons (33d degree, inspector gen. hon.), Shriners, Jesters, Arabia Temple Shrine (past potentate), Red Cross Constantine (past sovereign) Phi Alpha Delta. Democrat. Medthodist. Estate planning, General practice, Probate (including wills, trusts). Fax: 713-228-4072. E-mail: cae20@swbell.net.

EASTMAN, HOPE BETH, lawyer; b. Chgo., Nov. 4, 1943. BA with highest honors, UCLA, 1964; LLB cum laude, Harvard U., 1967. Bar: Calif. 1968, D.C. 1970, U.S. Supreme Ct. 1972, Md. 1982. Atty. office legal adv., Dept. State, Washington, 1967-69; assoc. dir. nat. office ACLU, Washington, 1969-77; ptnr. Morgan Assocs., P.C., Washington, 1977-86; ptnr. Paley, Rothman, Goldstein, Rosenberg & Cooper, Chartered, Bethesda, Md., 1987—; gen. counsel, bd. dirs. Israel Tennis Ctrs. Assn., Inc.; bd. dirs. Washington Coun. Lawyers, 1971-74; co-chmn. Md. del. White House Conf. on Small Bus., 1986. Founder, bd. dirs. Women's Legal Def. Fund, 1971-74, mem. steering com. jud. selection project, 1978; bd. dirs. Am. Employment Law Coun., 1993—, Learning and Leadership in Families, 1998—, Nat. Small Bus. United. Mem. ABA (co-chair com. rights for women 1976—; mem. spl. com. on delivery legal svcs. 1977-81, mem. labor sect. EEO com.), Fed. Bar Assn. Md. Bar Assn., Calif. Bar Assn., D.C. Bar Assn., Nat. Assn. Women Bus. Owners (bd. dirs.1984-88, v.p. gov. affairs). Contbr. articles to legal jours. Estate planning, General practice, Labor (including EEOC, Fair Labor Standards Act, labor-management relations, NLRB, OSHA). Office: Paley Rothman Goldstein Rosenberg & Cooper 4800 Hampden Ln Ste 700 Bethesda MD 20814-2922

EASTMENT, THOMAS JAMES, lawyer; b. N.Y.C., Mar. 3, 1950; s. George Thomas and Grace Anne (Manning) E. BChemE, Manhattan Coll., 1972; JD, U. Mich., 1975. Bar: N.Y. 1976, D.C. 1977. Assoc. Morton, Bernard, Brown, Washington, 1975-77, Baker Botts LLP, Washington, 1977-84, ptnr., 1985—. Mem. D.C. Bar Assn., Fed. Energy Bar Assn. Republican. Roman Catholic. General civil litigation, FERC practice, Oil, gas, and mineral, Administrative and regulatory. Office: Baker Botts LLP The Warner 1299 Pennsylvania Ave NW Washington DC 20004-2400 E-mail: Tom.Eastment@BakerBotts.com.

EASTON, REED W. lawyer, law educator; b. Newark, Jan. 16, 1950; m. Janet W. Wilde, Sept. 4, 1971 (div. Dec., 1994); children: Christian, Kurt; m. Elise E. Polinak, June 18, 1999. BS in Acctg. cum laude, Seton Hall U., 1971; JD, Coll. William and Mary, 1975; LLM in Tax, NYU, 1982. Bar: N.J. 1976, U.S. Dist. Ct. N.J. 1976, U.S. Tax Ct. 1978, D.C. 1979, N.Y. 1986; CPA, N.J. Staff acct. Price Waterhouse & Co., Morristown, N.J., 1971-72, Deloitte & Touche, Parsippany, N.J., 1976-79; assoc. Crummy, Del Deo, Dolan, Griffinger & Vecchione, Newark, N.J., 1979-80, Jeffer, Hopkinson, Vogel & Peiffer, Hawthorne, N.J., 1980-83; ptnr. Reed W. Easton, P.C., N.Y.C., Chester, N.J., 1983—; assoc. prof. Seton Hall U., South Orange, N.J., 1989—. Gen. counsel MONA Industries, Inc., Paterson, N.J., 1979-2000; lectr. in field. Contbr. articles to profl. jours. including The Tax Adviser, Taxation for Accountants, Taxation for Lawyers, Practical Tax Strategies, Jour. of Tax Practice and Procedure, Valuation Strategies, CCH Fin. and Estate Planning. Coord. Vol. Income Tax Assistance Program, South Orange, N.J., 1989—. With N.J. N.G., 1971-77. Mem. AICPA, N.J. Bar Assn., D.C. Bar Assn., N.Y. Bar Assn. Republican. Avocation: athletics. State civil litigation, Corporate, general, Taxation, general. Home: PO Box 368 Chester NJ 07930-0368 Office: 230 Park Ave New York NY 10169 E-mail: eastonre@shu.edu., REa1607227@aol.com.

EATON, J(AMES) TIMOTHY, lawyer; b. Decatur, Ill., Sept. 2, 1951; s. Edward Loftus and Helen Christine (Carlson) E.; m. Jane Katzenberg, Dec. 10, 1983. BA, Miami U., Oxford, Ohio, 1973; JD, So. Ill. U., 1977; LLM, Washington U., 1979. Bar: Ill. 1977. Law clk. to presiding justice Ill. Supreme Ct., Decatur, Ill., 1977-79; ptnr. Baird, Latendresse, McCarthy & Rowden, Decatur, 1979-83, Hinshaw, Culbertson, Moelmann, Hoban & Fuller, Chgo., 1983-86, Ungaretti & Harris and predecessor firms, Chgo., 1986—. Contbr. articles to profl. jours. Dept. legal counsel Ill. campaign Mondale for Pres., 1983-84; mem. St. Matthews Episc. Ch., Evanston. Fellow Ill. Bar Found.; mem. Ill. Bar Assn. (active various coms., pres. 2001-02), Lawyers Trust Fund Ill., Appellate Lawyers Assn. (bd. dirs. 1982-84), Miami U. Alumni Assn. (pres. elect 1986—). State civil litigation, Product liability. Home: 1029 Chestnut Ave Wilmette IL 60091-1731 Office: Ungaretti & Harris 3500 3 First Nat Plaza 70 W Madison Chicago IL 60602

EATON, JOE OSCAR, federal judge; b. Monticello, Fla., Apr. 2, 1920; s. Robert Lewis and Mamie (Gireadeau) E. AB, Presbyn. Coll., 1941, LLD (hon.), 1979; LLB, U. Fla., 1948. Pvt. practice law, Miami, Fla., 1948-51, 55-59; asst. state atty. Dade County, Fla., 1953; circuit judge Miami, 1954-55, 59-67; mem. Fla. Senate, 1956-59; mem. law firm Eaton & Achor, Miami, 1955-58, Sams, Anderson, Eaton & Alper, Miami, 1958-59; judge U.S. Dist. Ct. (so. dist.) Fla., 1967-83, chief judge, 1983-85, sr. judge, 1985—. Instr. law U. Miami Coll. Law, 1954-56 Served with USAAF, 1941-45; Served with USAF, 1951-52. Decorated D.F.C., Air medal. Mem.: Kiwanian. Methodist.

EATON, JOEL DOUGLAS, lawyer; b. Miami, Fla., Oct. 31, 1943; s. Joe Oscar and Patricia (MacVicar) E.; m. Mary Benson, June 24, 1967; children: Douglas, Darryl, David. BA, Yale U., 1965; JD, Harvard U., 1975. Bar: Fla. 1975, U.S. Dist. Ct. (so. dist.) Fla. 1976, U.S. Ct. Appeals (5th cir.) 1976, U.S. Supreme Ct. 1978, U.S. Ct. Appeals (11th cir.) 1981, U.S. Ct. Appeals (Fed. cir.) 1996. Ptnr. Podhurst Orseck, P.A. and predecessors, Miami, 1975—. With USN, 1965-71. Decorated Air medal with Bronze Star and numeral 14, Navy Commendation medal with 2 gold stars, Cross of Gallantry (Viet Nam). Mem. ABA, ATLA, Am. Law Inst., Acad. Fla. Trial Lawyers, Fla. Bar Assn. (appellate rules com. 1981-2002, chmn. 1989-90, jud. evaluation com. 1995-98, Fla. std. jury instn. com. 1998—), Am. Acad. Appellate Lawyers. Democrat. Appellate, Federal civil litigation, State civil litigation. Office: Podhurst Orseck PA 25 W Flagler St Ste 800 Miami FL 33130-1720 E-mail: jeaton@podhurst.com.

EATON, LARRY RALPH, lawyer; b. Quincy, Ill., Aug. 18, 1944; s. Roscoe Ralph and Velma Marie (Beckett) E.; m. Janet Claire Rosen, Oct. 28, 1978. BA, Western Ill. U., 1965; JD, U. Mich., 1968. Bar: Ill. 1968, U.S. Dist. Ct. (no. dist.) Ill. 1978, U.S. Ct. Appeals (D.C. cir.) 1984, U.S. Ct. Appeals (7th cir.) 1989, N.Y. 1997. Vol., instr. law U. Liberia Sch. Law, U.S. Peace Corps, Monrovia, 1968-70; lawyer Forest Park Found., Peoria Heights, Ill., 1970-71; asst. atty. gen. State of Ill., Springfield, 1971-75; ptnr. Peterson & Ross and predecessors, Chgo., 1975-94; founder Blatt, Hammesfahr & Eaton, Chgo., 1994-2000; sr. mem. Cozen O'Connor, Chgo., 2000—. Instr. environ. law Quincy Coll., Ill., 1973-75. Bd. dirs. Edgewater Cmty. Coun., Chgo., 2000—; pres. Lakewood Balmoral Residents' Coun., Chgo., 2000—02; bd. dirs. Near North Montessori Sch., 1989—95, vice chmn., 1992—95; bd. dirs., v.p. Edgewater Devel. Corp., 2000—, v.p., 0002—. Contbg. writer Chgo. Daily Law Bull., 1975-77; field editor Pollution Engring., 1976. Fellow: Ill. Bar Found. (charter); mem.: ABA (environ. ins. litig. task force 1990), Bar Assn. for 7th Jud. Cir., Chgo. Bar Assn., Ill. Bar Assn. (editor sect. newsletter 1972—77, coun. 1973—77, chmn. environ. control law sect. 1976—77, assembly 1980—86, 1989—92, coun. 1990—94, coun. jud. evaluation Cook County 2000—), Atticus Finch Inn of Ct., Lawyers Club Chgo., Law Club Chgo. Federal civil litigation, Environmental, Insurance.

EAVIS, KATHARINE NAOMI, lawyer; b. England, Dec. 31, 1966; d. Patrick Portnell and Dorothy Ritson Eavis; m. Joseph Charles Pillman; 1 child, Lucy Charlotte Pillman. BA with honors, Cambridge U., 1988, MA, 1991. Solicitor Cole & Cole, Oxford, England, 1990—98; ptnr. Morgan Cole, 1998—2000, Brobeck Hale and Dorr, 2000—. Mem.: The Law Soc. Office: Hale and Dorr Park Gate 25 Milton Park Abingdon OX14 4SH England E-mail: Kate.Eavis@haledorr.com.

EBEL, DAVID M. federal judge; b. 1940; BA, Northwestern U., 1962; JD, U. Mich., 1965. Law clk. assoc. justice Byron White U.S. Supreme Ct., 1965—66; pvt. practice Davis, Graham & Stubbs, Denver, 1966—88; judge U.S. Ct. Appeals (10th cir.), Denver, 1988—. Adj. prof. law U. Denver Law Sch., 1987—89; sr. lectr. fellow Duke U. Law Sch., 1992—94. Mem.: Jud. Conf. U.S. (com. on codes of conduct 1991—98, co-chair 10th cir. gender bias task force 1994—99), Colo. Bar Assn. (v.p. 1982), Am. Coll. Trial Lawyers. Office: US Ct Appeals 1823 Stout St Rm 109L Denver CO 80257-1823 E-mail: david_m_ebel@ca10.uscourts.gov.

EBELL, C(ECIL) WALTER, lawyer; b. Baker, Oreg., June 26, 1947; s. Cecil John and Sylvia Jean (Malone) E.; m. Dianna Rae Gentry, June 2, 1980; children: Anne, Erik, Michael. BS, Oreg. State U., 1970; MS, U. No. Colo., 1973; JD, Lewis and Clark Coll., 1977. Bar: Oreg. 1977, Alaska 1978, U.S. Ct. Appeals (9th cir.) 1981, U.S. Supreme Ct. 1985, Wash. 1990. Pvt. practice, Portland, Oreg., 1977-78; ptnr. Hartig, Rhodes, Norman & Mahoney, Anchorage, 1978-84, Jamin, Ebell, Bolger & Gentry, Kodiak, Alaska, 1984-90, Seattle, 1990-2000, Jamin, Ebell, Schmitt & Mason, Anchorage, Alaska, 2000—. Press sec., Clay Myers for Gov. campaign, Oreg., 1974. Capt. USMC, 1970-73. Mem. ABA, Assn. Trial Lawyers Am., Rotary. Democrat. Avocations: photography, fishing, skiing. Admiralty, Corporate, general, Native American. Office: Jamin Ebell Schmitt Mason 1007 W 3rd Ave Ste 201 Anchorage AK 99501 E-mail: webell@jesmanc.com.

EBERHARDT, DANIEL HUGO, lawyer; b. Milw., Feb. 19, 1938; s. Erwin M. and Hazel M. (Daley) E.; m. Josephine E. Jeka, Sept. 10, 1960; children: Daniel Hugo Jr., Mark John. BS, Colo. State U., 1962; JD, Marquette U., 1968. Bar: Wis. 1968, U.S. Dist. Ct. (ea. dist.) Wis. 1968. Assoc. Morrissy, Morrissy, Sweet & Race, Elkhorn, Wis., 1968-70; ptnr. Sweet & Eberhardt, Elkhorn, 1970-76; sole practice Elkhorn, 1976—. Commr. Walworth County Cir. Cts., 1975—. Served to 1st lt. U.S. Army, 1962-65, AUS. Mem. ABA, Wis. Bar Assn., Walworth County Bar Assn. (sec., treas. 1983-85, v.p. 1985-86, pres. 1986-87), VFW (comdr. 1980-81). Lodges: Rotary (pres. 1980-81). Republican. Roman Catholic. Family and matrimonial, Probate (including wills, trusts), Property, real (including real estate development, water). Home: N6601 Peck Station Rd Elkhorn WI 53121-3247 Office: 18 S Broad St PO Box 258 Elkhorn WI 53121-0258

EBERT, GARY ANDREW, lawyer; b. Sandusky, Ohio, May 15, 1950; s. Harry J. and Virginia M. Ebert; m. Pamela M. Wentz, Aug. 5, 1972; children: Caroline, Amanda, Brian. BS in Bus. Adminstrn., Ashland U., 1972; JD, Cleveland Marshall U., 1975. Bar: Ohio 1978, U.S. Dist. Ct. (no. dist.) Ohio 1978. Ptnr. Coltman, Ebert & Valore, Fairview Park, Ohio, 1978-91, Seeley, Savidge & Ebert, Cleve., 1991—. Law dir. City of Bay Village, 1986—. Councilman City of Bay Village, Ohio, 1981-86. Mem. Ohio State Bar Assn., Cuyahoga County Law Dir. Assn., Internat. Mpcl. Lawyers Assn. Avocation: golf. Corporate, general, Estate planning, Municipal (including bonds). Home: 153 Kensington Cir Bay Village OH 44140-1060 Office: Seeley Savidge & Ebert 800 Bank One Ctr Cleveland OH 44114 E-mail: gaebert@sse-law.com.

EBINER, ROBERT MAURICE, lawyer; b. L.A., Sept. 2, 1927; s. Maurice and Virginia (Grand) E.; m. Paula H. Van Sluyters, June 16, 1951; children: John, Lawrence, Marie, Michael, Christopher, Joseph, Francis, Matthew, Therese, Kathleen, Eileen, Brian, Patricia, Elizabeth, Ann. JD, Loyola U., L.A., 1953. Bar: Calif. 1954, U.S. Dist. Ct. (cen. dist.) Calif. 1954. Pvt. practice, West Covina, Calif., 1954—. Judge pro tem L.A. Superior Ct., 1964-66, 90—, arbitrator, 1979—; arbitrator San Bernardino Superior Ct., 1990—; judge pro tem Citrus Mcpl. Ct., 1966-70, 1990—, El Monte Mcpl. Ct., 1998—, Whittier Mcpl. Ct., 2001—, mediator, 2000-; mem. disciplinary hearing panel Calif. State Bar, 1968-75. Bd. dirs. West Covina United Fund, 1958-61, chmn. budget com., 1960-61; organizer Joint United Funds East San Gabriel Valley, 1962, bd. dirs., 1961-68; bd. dirs. San Gabriel Valley Cath. Social Svcs., 1969—, pres., 1969-72; bd. dirs. Region II Cath. Social Svc., 1970—, pres., 1970-74; trustee L.A. Cath. Welfare Bur. (now Cath. Charities), 1978—; charter bd. dirs. East San Gabriel Valley Hot Line, 1969-74, sec., 1969-72; charter bd. dirs. N.E. L.A. County unit Am. Cancer Soc., 1973-78, chmn. by-laws com., 1973-78; bd. dirs. Queen of the Valley Hosp. Found., 1983-89; organizer West Covina Hist. Soc., 1982—; active Calif. State Dem. Cen. Com., 1963-68; mng. meet dir. Greater La Puente Valley Spl. Olympics, 1985-88, Bishop Amat Relays, 1981-96; mem. MSAC Relays Com., 1978—; campaign mgr. Congressman Ronald B. Cameron, 1964. With U.S. Army, 1945-47. Recipient L.A. County Human Rels. Commn. Disting. Svc. award, 1978, Thomas A. Kiefer Humanitarian award, 1993; named West Covina Citizen of Yr., 1986, San Gabriel Valley Daily Tribune's Father of Yr., 1986. Mem. ABA, Calif. Bar Assn., L.A. County Bar Assn. (arbitrator 1975—), Fed. Ct. So. Dist. Calif. Assn., Consumer Attys. LA, Ea. Bar Assn. L.A. County (pres. Pomona Valley 1965-66), West Covina C. of C. (pres. 1960), Am. Arbitration Assn. (arbitrator 1965-98), KC, Bishop Amat H.S. Booster Club (bd. dirs. 1973-96, pres. 1978-80), Kiwanis (charter West Covina, pres. 1976-77, 2002-2003, lt. gov. divsn. 35 1980-81, Kiwanian of Yr. 1978, 82, Disting. Lt. Gov. 1980-81, bd. dirs. Cal-Nev-Ha Found. 1986-98, pres. 1994-96). Avocation: collector western U.S. historical olympic and political memorabilia. State civil litigation, Personal injury (including property damage), Probate (including wills, trusts). Office: 100 N Citrus St Ste 520 West Covina CA 91791-1694

EBITZ, ELIZABETH KELLY, lawyer; b. LaPorte, Ind., June 9, 1950; d. Joseph Monahan and Ann Mary (Barrett) Kelly; m. David MacKinnon Ebitz, Jan. 23, 1971 (div. 1981). AB with honors, Smith Coll., 1972; JD cum laude, Boston U., 1975. BAr: Maine 1979, Mass. 1975, U.S. Dist. Ct. Mass. 1976, U.S. Dist. Ct. Maine 1979, U.S. Ct. Appeals (1st cir.) 1976, U.S. Supreme Ct. 1982. Law clk. Boston Legal Assistance Project, 1973-75; law clk., assoc. Law Offices John J. Thornton, Boston, 1974-76; ptnr. Ebitz & Zurn, Northampton, Mass., 1976-79; assoc. Gross, Minsky, Mogul & Singal, Bangor, Maine, 1979-80; pres. Elizabeth Kelly Ebitz P.A., Bangor, 1980-92, Ebitz & Thornton, P.A., 1993—. Pres. Greater Bangor Rape Crisis Bd., 1983-85; bd. dirs., sec., legal counsel Bangor Area Homeless Shelter, 1985-92, 93-99; bd. dirs. Maine Women's Lobby, 1986-89, No. Maine Bread for the World, 1987-90; bd. dirs., sec. Machias River Clinic for Mental Health and Substance Abuse, 2000—; bd. dirs. Am. Heart Assn., Maine, 1989—, sec., 1989-91, chair, 1993-95; mem. various peace, feminist and hunger orgns., Bangor, 1982—. Named Young Career Woman of Hampshire County, Nat. Bus. and Profl. Women, Northampton, 1979. Mem. Maine State Bar Assn., Nat. Orgn. Social Security Claimants (rep. 1994—), Sigma Xi. Democrat. Roman Catholic. Family and matrimonial, Pension, profit-sharing, and employee benefits, Personal injury (including property damage). Home: 111 Maple St Bangor ME 04401-4031 Office: 329 Wilson St Brewer ME 04412-1504 E-mail: bgrlegal@aol.com.

EBLIN, ROBERT L. lawyer; b. Columbus, Ohio, Apr. 21, 1963; AB cum laude, Harvard U., 1985; JD summa cum laude, Ohio State U., 1991. Bar: Ohio 1991, U.S. Dist. Ct. (so. dist.) Ohio 1991, U.S. Ct. Appeals (6th cir.) 1992, U.S. Supreme Ct. 1997. Assoc. Schwartz Warren & Ramirez, Columbus, 1991-96, Arter & Hadden LLP, Columbus, 1997-99, ptnr., 2000—. Adj. prof. law Ohio State U., Columbus, 1997. Contbg. author: Looking at Law School, 3d edit., 1990, 4th edit., 1997, Liability of Corporate Officers and Directors, 6th edit., 1999, 7th edit., 2002. Mem. Ohio Human Rights Bar Assn. (trustee 1989-93, 99—, pres. 2000—), Profl. Liability Underwriting Soc., Order of Coif. General civil litigation, Insurance, Labor (including EEOC, Fair Labor Standards Act, labor-management relations, NLRB, OSHA). Office: Arter & Hadden LLP 10 W Broad St Ste 2100 Columbus OH 43215-3422 E-mail: Robert.Eblin@ArterHadden.com.

EBNER, ELIZABETH MARIE, prosecutor; b. Easton, Pa., Aug. 7, 1968; d. Rose Marie and William Joseph Shannon(Stepfather); life ptnr. Amy Michelle Fazzari; 1 child, David Michael Fazzari. AA, Northampton Area C.C., Bethlehem, Pa., 1992; BA, Moravian Coll., Bethlehem, 1998; JD, Temple U., Phila., 2001. Bar: Pa. 2001. Law clk. Ramy I. Djerassi, Esquire, Atty., Phila., 2000—01; asst. pub. defender Berks County Pub. Defender, Reading, Pa., 2001—. With Army N.G., 1990—96. Office: Berks County Public Defenders 633 Court St Reading PA 19601 E-mail: eebner@countyofberks.com.

EBNER, I. NOAM, mediator, educator; b. N.Y.C., June 5, 1973; arrived in Israel, 1982; s. David and Rachel Ebner; m. Yifat Winkler, Feb. 7, 2002; 1 child, Etelle. LLB, Hebrew U., Jerusalem, 1999, LLM with honors, 2000. Bar: Israel 2000. Lectr. law and mediation Tel-Hai Coll., Israel, 2000—; dir. Tachlit Mediation Ctr., Jerusalem, 2000—; staff dir. Campus Mediation Ctr. Bar Ilan Univ., Israel, 2001—. Profl. cons. Gesharim Cmty. Mediation Ctr., Israel, 2000—; mem. adv. bd. Mosaica Jerusalem Cmty. Mediation Ctr., Israel, 2002—. Co-editor: Introduction to Israeli Law, 1998. 1st sgt. Israeli Infantry, 1991—95. Mem.: Israeli Bar Assn. (com. on consumer oriented legislation 2000—, com. on mediation 2000—). Office: Tachlit Mediation Ctr 1 Mishmar Ha'am St 93226 Jerusalem Israel E-mail: noam@tachlit.net.

ECHOHAWK, JOHN ERNEST, lawyer; b. Albuquerque, Aug. 11, 1945; s. Ernest V. and Emma Jane (Conrad) E.; m. Kathryn Suzanne Martin, Oct. 23, 1965; children: Christopher, Sarah. BA, U. N.M., 1967, JD, 1970. Bar: Colo. 1972, U.S. Dist. Ct. Colo. 1972, U.S. Appeals (8th cir.) 1976, U.S. Ct. Appeals (9th cir.) 1980. Research assoc. Calif. Indian Legal Services, Escondido, 1970, Native Am. Rights Fund, Berkeley Calif. and Boulder, Colo., 1970-72, dep. dir. Boulder, 1972-73, 1975-77, exec. dir., 1973-75, 1977—. Mem. task force Am. Indian Policy Rev. Commn., U.S. Senate, Washington, 1976-77; bd. dirs. Am. Indian Lawyer Tng. Program, Oakland, Calif., 1975—; bd. dirs. Assn. Am. Indian Affairs, 1980—, Nat. Com. Responsive Philanthropy, Washington, 1981-2000; mem. Clinton Adminstrn. Transition Team for Interior Dept., 1992-93. Presdl. appointee Western Water Policy Rev. Adv. Commn., 1995-97; Ind. Sector, Washington, 1986-92; mem. Natural Resources Def. Coun., N.Y.C., 1988—; bd. dirs. Nat. Ctr. Enterprise Devel., 1988—, Keystone Ctr., 1993-99, Environ. and Energy Study Inst., 1994—. Recipient Disting. Service award Ams. For Indian Opportunity, 1982, Pres. Indian Service award Nat. Congress Am. Indians, 1984, Annual Indian Achievement award Indian Council Fire, 1987; named one of most influential attys. Nat. Law Jour., 1988, 91, 94, 97, 2000. Mem. Native Am. Bar Assn., Colo. Indian Bar Assn. Democrat. Avocations: fishing, skiing. Civil rights, Native American. Office: Native Am Rights Fund 1506 Broadway St Boulder CO 80302-6217

ECHOLS, ROBERT L. federal judge; b. 1941; BA, Rhodes Coll., 1962; JD, U. Tenn., 1964. Law clk. to Hon. Marion S. Boyd U.S. Dist. Ct. (we. dist.) Tenn., Nashville, 1965-66; legis. asst. Congressman Dan Kuykendall, 1967-69; ptnr. Baily, Ewing, Dale & Conner, Nashville, 1969-72, Dearborn & Ewing, Nashville, 1972-92; fed. judge U.S. Dist. Ct. (mid. dist.) Tenn., Nashville, 1992—, chief judge, 1998—. Mem. exec. com. 6th Cir. Jud. Coun.; mem libr. com. 6th Cir. Ct. Appeals; mem. ann. conf. planning com. 6th Cir.; mem. Tenn. State-Fed. Jud. Coun.; mem. jud. br. com. U.S. Jud. Conf. With U.S. Army, 1966; brig. gen. Tenn. Army N.G., 1969-2001 Mem. ABA, Am. Bar Found., Fed. Judges Assn. (mem. exec. com.), Tenn. Bar Found., Tenn. Bar Assn., Nashville Bar Assn., Nashville Bar Found., Harry Phillips Am. Inn of Ct. Office: US Dist Ct 801 Broadway Ste 824 Nashville TN 37203-3868

ECK, GEORGE GREGORY, lawyer; b. Evanston, Ill., Sept. 3, 1950; s. George F. and Dorothy E. (Frake) E.; m. Margaret K. Gorman, Sept. 1, 1973; children: Jessica Elizabeth, Michelle Margaret. BS, No. Ill. U., 1972; JD cum laude, U. Minn., 1977. Bar: Minn. 1977, U.S. Dist. Ct. Minn. 1977, U.S. Ct. Appeals (8th cir.) 1977. Assoc. Dorsey & Whitney, Mpls., 1977-83, ptnr., 1983—. Mem. editorial bd. U. Minn. Law Rev., 1977. With U.S. Army, 1972—74. General civil litigation, Construction, Personal injury (including property damage). Home: 6413 Mendelssohn Ln Hopkins MN 55343-8424 Office: Dorsey & Whitney 220 S 6th St Ste 2200 Minneapolis MN 55402-1498

ECK, JOHN TERRENCE, lawyer; b. Mpls., Jan. 4, 1969; s. Terrence J. and Nancy Eck; m. Tammy L. Eck. BA in Polit. Sci., BS in Econs., So. Meth. U., 1991; JD, U. Okla., 1994. Assoc. Law Offices Robert T. Stites, Ft. Worth, 1994—. Office: Law Offices of Robert T Stites 933 W Weatherford St Fort Worth TX 76102-1800

ECKER, HOWARD, lawyer; b. N.Y.C., June 10, 1946; s. David and Sylvia (Goldstein) E.; children: David, Ashley. BA, U. Mich., 1967; JD, NYU, 1971. Bar: Nev. 1973, U.S. Dist. Ct. Nev. 1974, U.S. Ct. Appeals (9th cir.) 1976, U.S. Supreme Ct. 1976. Pub. defender Clark County Pub. Defender's Office, Nev., 1973-77; ptnr. Ecker & Standish, Chtd., Clark County, Nev., 1977—. Guest lectr. in field. Mem. Nev. Employee Mgmt. Rels. Bd., Las Vegas, 1990-94. Mem.: Am. Acad. Matrimonial Lawyers, Am. Inns of Ct. (barrister 1990—93, master 1993—), Nev. Trial Lawyers Assn. (bd. govs. 1977—89, pres. 1985—86), Clark County Bar Assn., State Bar Nev. (bd. govs. 1984—90), ATLA. Avocations: travel, golf, reading. Family and matrimonial. Office: Ecker & Standish Chtd 300 S 4th St Ste 901 Las Vegas NV 89101-6025

ECKERT, STEPHEN PAUL, lawyer; b. Ft. Wayne, Ind., Jan. 15, 1955; s. Aldhelm Joseph and Evangeline Betty (Hodson) E.; m. Diane Lynn Arend, Aug. 2, 1980; children: Jennifer Christine, Matthew Stephen, Katelin

Diane, Andria Lynn. BA, Ind. U., Bloomington, 1978; JD, Ind. U., Indpls., 1981. Bar: Ind. 1981, U.S. Dist. Ct. (so. dist.) Ind. 1981, U.S. Ct. Mil. Appeals 1983. Rschr. Civil Liberties Union, Indpls., 1979, Legal Services Orgn., Indpls., 1979-80; assoc. George Clyde Gray, P.C., Indpls., 1981-83; ptnr. Gray, Robinson, Eckert & Ryan, P.C., Indpls., 1984-95, Eckert Eckert & Craven, P.C., Indpls., 1996—. Mem. ABA, Ind. Bar Assn., Indpls. Bar Assn., Assn. Trial Lawyers Am., Ind. Trial Lawyers Assn., Johnson County Bar Assn. Roman Catholic. Personal injury (including property damage), Product liability, Workers' compensation. Office: 7550 S Meridian St # C-1 Indianapolis IN 46217-2920

ECKHARDT, WILLIAM RUDOLF, III, lawyer; b. Houston, Dec. 14, 1915; s. William Rudolf and Ura (Link) E.; m. Elra Hodges, Oct. 11, 1940; 1 son, Donald Kent. BA, Rice Inst., 1937; LL.B., U. Tex., 1940. Bar: Tex. 1940. Asst. U.S. atty. Dept. Justice, So. Dist. Tex., 1940-44, 46-52; assoc. McGregor & Sewell, Houston, 1952-56, Vinson & Elkins, Houston, 1956—91. Served to lt. (j.g.) USN, 1944-46. Fellow Am. Coll. Trial Lawyers; mem. ABA, Tex. Bar Assn., Maritime Law Assn., Tex. Def. Attys. Assn., Chancellors, Order of Coif, Phi Delta Phi, Chi Phi Clubs: Houst. Republican. Baptist. Admiralty, Personal injury (including property damage). Home: 25 Robinlake Ln Houston TX 77024-7121 Office: Ste 111 7880 San Felipe Houston TX 77063

ECKL, WILLIAM WRAY, lawyer; b. Florence, Ala., Dec. 2, 1936; s. Louis Arnold and Patricia Barclift (Dowd) E.; m. Mary Lynn McGough, June 29, 1963; children: Eric Dowd, Lynn Lacey. BA, U. Notre Dame, 1959; LLB, U. Va., 1962. Bar: Va. 1962, Ala. 1962, Ga. 1964. Law clk. Supreme Ct. of Ala., 1962; ptnr. Gambrell, Harlan, Russell & Moye, Atlanta, 1965-68, Swift, Currie, McGhee & Hiers, Atlanta, 1968-82, Drew, Eckl & Farnham, Atlanta, 1983—. Served to capt. JAGC, USAR, 1962-65. Mem. Am. Bd. Trial Advocates, Trial Attys. Am., Lawyers Club of Atlanta, Brookwood Hills Club. Roman Catholic. Insurance, Personal injury (including property damage), Product liability. Home: 348 Camden Rd NE Atlanta GA 30309-1513 Office: Drew Eckl & Farnham 880 W Peachtree St PO Box 7600 Atlanta GA 30357-0600

ECKLAND, JEFF HOWARD, lawyer; b. Warren, Ohio, Jan. 17, 1957; s. William Howard and Barbara Ann (Hirsch) E.; m. Deborah Pauline Causey, May 27, 1989. BA summa cum laude, U. Minn., 1979; JD, U. Chgo., 1982. Bar: Minn. 1982, U.S. Dist. Ct. Minn. 1982, U.S. Ct. Appeals (8th cir.) 1987, U.S. Ct. Appeals (9th cir.) 1990, U.S. Ct. Appeals (fed. cir.) 1993, U.S. Ct. Fed. Claims 1993, U.S. Supreme Ct. 1997. Ptnr. Faegre & Benson, Mpls., 1982—. Vol. Lawyer Network. Mem. ABA, Minn. Bar Assn., Hennepin County Bar Assn., Fund for the Legal Aid Soc., Nat. Contract Mgmt. Assn., Phi Beta Kappa. Avocations: sailing, tennis. Federal civil litigation, Government contracts and claims, Trademark and copyright. Office: Faegre & Benson LLP 2200 Wells Fargo Ctr 90 S 7th St Ste 2200 Minneapolis MN 55402-3901 E-mail: jeckland@faegre.com.

ECKSTEIN, MICHAEL LEHMAN, lawyer; b. New Orleans, June 18, 1954; s. Robert E. and Ernestine (Lehman) E. B in Gen. Studies, U. Ky., 1976; JD, Tulane U., 1979; LLM in Taxation, Georgetown U., 1980. Bar: U.S. Dist. Ct. (ea. dist.) La. 1979, U.S. Ct. Claims 1980, U.S. Tax Ct. 1980; cert. estate planning and adminstrn. specialist; cert. tax atty. Assoc., tax atty. Molony, Nolan, North & Riess, Metairie, La., 1980-84; pvt. practice New Orleans, 1984-86; tax atty., head bus. sect. Gelpi, Sullivan, Carroll & Laborde, New Orleans, 1986-90; sole practitioner New Orleans, 1990—. Contbr. articles to profl. jours. Fund raiser Boy Scouts Am., New Orleans, 1981, Children's Hosp., New Orleans, 1985, Rep. Nat. Conv.; vol. Ron Faucheaux Mayorial Campaign, New Orleans, 1982; bd. dirs. Big Brothers/Big Sisters S.E. La., past pres.; vol. La. Tax Free Shopping Program, Inc., Catholic Charities Archdiocese New Orleans, past pres. adv. bd. Mem. ABA (taxation, real property, probate, trust, corporations and business law sects., com. on depreciation and investment tax credit 1982—), New Orleans Bar Assn., Sports Lawyers Assn., Assn. Employee Benefit Planners of New Orleans, Estate Planning Coun., Tulane Alumni Assn. (past dir., past dir. Tulane Law Sch. CLE adv. bd.), New Orleans Lawn Tennis Club. Clubs: Audubon Tennis, World Trade Ctr. (New Orleans). Republican. Avocations: tennis, scuba diving, fishing, swimming, horses. Mergers and acquisitions, Estate taxation, Corporate taxation. Home: 7035 Birch St New Orleans LA 70118-5547 Office: 1515 Poydras St Ste 2195 New Orleans LA 70112-3753

EDELMAN, ALAN IRWIN, lawyer; b. Poughkeepsie, N.Y., June 14, 1958; s. Edwyn Herman and Shirley Frances (Kandel) E.; m. Erica Joy Schwartz, Aug. 16, 1981; children: Leah Hanit, Avram Natan, Samuel Aaron. BA, Cornell U., 1980; JD, Boston U., 1983. Bar: D.C. 1983, U.S. Dist. Ct. D.C. 1985, U.S. Supreme Ct. 1991. Atty. enforcement div. SEC, Washington, 1983-86, atty. Office of Gen. Counsel, 1986-87; counsel U.S. Senate Permanent Subcom. on Investigations, Washington, 1987-97, U.S. Senate Com. on Govtl. Affairs, 1997-99; trial atty. divsn. enforcement Commodity Futures Trading Commn., Washington, 1999—. Edward F. Hennessy scholar Boston U., 1983. Mem. ABA, Fed. Bar Assn. Office: Commodity Futures Trading Commn Three Lafayette Centre 1155 21st St NW Washington DC 20581-0001

EDELMAN, ALVIN, lawyer; b. Chgo., Dec. 12, 1916; m. Rose Marie Slossy, Sept. 22, 1940; children: Marilyn Frances Edelman Snyder, Stephen D., Leon F. BS in Law, Northwestern U., 1938, JD, 1940. Bar: Ill. 1940. Practiced in Chgo., 1940—; pres. Edelman & Edelman, Chartered and predecessors, 1973—; gen. counsel Internat. Coll. Surgeons. Lectr. Internat. Mus. Surg. Sci. and Hall of Fame; chmn. wills and gifts com. Medinah Temple of Masonic Shrine, Chgo., 1975-79; pres. Lawyers Shrine Club of Medinah Temple, 1971-73. Contbr. articles to profl. jours. Fellow Am. Coll. Trust and Estate Counsel; mem. ABA, Ill. Bar Assn., Chgo. Bar Assn. (chmn. grievance com. 1971-72), Phi Beta Kappa (pres. Chgo. area assn. 1975-85), Phi Beta Kappa Fellows (bd. dirs. 1985—, nat. v.p. 1986-95, nat. pres. 1996-2001), Elks (past exalted ruler). Corporate, general, Probate (including wills, trusts), Property, real (including real estate development, water). Office: 100 W Monroe St Chicago IL 60603-1967

EDELMAN, PAUL STERLING, lawyer; b. Bklyn., Jan. 2, 1926; s. Joseph S. and Rose (Kaminsky) E.; m. Rosemary Jacobs, June 15, 1951; children: Peter, Jeffrey. AB, Harvard U., 1946, JD, 1950. Bar: N.Y. 1951, U.S. Dist. Ct. (so. and ea. dists.) N.Y. 1954, U.S. Ct. Appeals (2d cir.) 1965, U.S. Supreme Ct. 1967. Ptnr. Kreindler & Kreindler, N.Y.C., 1953-95, counsel, 1996—. Legal advisor Andrea Doria TV show, 1984, QE2 TV show, 1995; cons. Slave Ship TV Program, April, 2001. Author: Maritime Injury and Death, 1960; editor: Maritime Law Reporter, 1987-99, Marine Laws, 1993, 94; columnist N.Y. Law Jour. With U.S. Army, 1944-46. Fellow N.Y. Bar Found.; mem. ABA (past chmn. admiralty com., toxic and hazardous substances litigation com., mem. long range planning com. 1982-84, mem. TIPS coun. 1984-88, Soviet-Am. lawyers conf. Moscow 1987, 94, TIPS lawyer conf. Russia 1993), ATLA (past chmn. admiralty coms.), Maritime Law Assn. (rep. to law of the sea seminar Moscow 1994), N.Y. State Bar Assn. (TICL award 1980, 90, 93, chmn. INCL sect. 1982-83, editor Ins. Jour. 1973—), Maritime Law Assn., Hastings Hist. Soc., Oliver Wendell Holmes Soc. of Harvard Law Sch., Supreme Ct. Hist. Soc., World Peace Through Law Ctr., Hudson Valley Tennis Club, Hastings on Hudson (past chmn., planning bd.), Supreme Ct. Hist. Soc., Hastings Hist. Soc. Democrat. Jewish. Admiralty, Private international, Personal injury (including property damage). Home: 57 Buena Vista Dr Hastings On Hudson NY 10706-1103 Office: 100 Park Ave New York NY 10017-5516 E-mail: pedelman@kreindler.com.

EDELSON, GILBERT SEYMOUR, lawyer; b. N.Y.C., Sept. 15, 1928; s. Saul and Sarah (Sunshine) E.; m. Jane Barbara Levin, Sept. 6, 1953; children: Martha Jane, Paula Topal, Dorothy Rachel. BS, NYU, 1948; LLB, Columbia U., 1955. Bar: N.Y. 1955, U.S. Dist. Ct. (so. dist.) N.Y. 1959, U.S. Ct. Appeals (2nd cir.) 1959, U.S. Dist. Ct. (ea. dist.) N.Y. 1960, U.S. Ct. Appeals (9th cir.) 1995. Assoc. Rosenman Goldmark Colin & Kaye, N.Y.C., 1955-63; ptnr. Rosenman & Colin, N.Y.C., 1963-97, counsel, 1997—2002, Katten, Muchin, Zavis, Rosenman, NYC, 2002—. Adminstrv. v.p., counsel Art Dealers Assn. Am., N.Y.C., 1985—. Editor Columbia Law Rev., 1955. Bd. dirs. Coll. Art Assn. Am., N.Y.C., 1969-88, High Five Tickets for the Arts, N.Y.C., 1999-2001; sec., trustee Am. Fedn. Arts, N.Y.C., 1984-94; trustee Internat. Found. for Art Rsch., 1986-99, N.Y. Studio Sch., 1989—, Archives Am. Art, N.Y.C., 1989—. With U.S. Army, 1950-52, JLC. Mem. ABA, N.Y. Bar Assn., Assn. Bar of N.Y.C. (chmn. com. on art law 1992-95), Columbia U. Law Sch. Alumni Assn. (bd. dirs. 1981-84), Century Assn. Jewish. Avocation: collecting art. Federal civil litigation, State civil litigation, Art. Home: 580 W End Ave New York NY 10024-1723 Office: Katten Muchin Zavis Rosenman 575 Madison Ave New York NY 10022-2585 E-mail: gilbert.edelson@kmzr.com.

EDEN, NATHAN E. lawyer; b. Key West, Fla., Mar. 24, 1944; s. Delmar M. and Lois (Archer) E.; m. Cindy Pike, Jan. 4, 1964 (div. Mar. 1984); 1 child, Jennifer S. BA, U. Fla., 1966; JD magna cum laude, Stetson U., 1969. Bar: Fla. 1969, U.S. Dist. Ct. (so. and mid. dists.) Fla. 1969, U.S. Ct. Appeals (5th cir.) 1969, U.S. Ct. Appeals (11th cir.) 1982. Assoc. Nelson, Stinnett, Surfus, et al, Sarasota, Fla., 1969; ptnr. Feldman & Eden & predecessors, Key West, 1970-84; pvt. practice Key West, 1984—99, 2002—; of counsel Lazzara and Paul, P.A., Tampa, 1982—; ptnr. Browning, Eden, Sireci & Klitenick, 1999—2002. Bd. atty. Utility Bd. of Key West, 1974—; asst. pub. defender State of Fla., Key West, 1970, county solicitor State of Fla., Key West, 1970-72; chief asst. state atty State of Fla., Key West, 1972-74; U.S. magistrate, U.S. Dist. Ct. (so. dist.) Fla., 1974-78. Mem. jud. nominating com. 16th Jud. Cir. State of Fla., 1995, bd. dirs. Hospice Monroe County, Hospice-VNA of Fla. Keys, 1998—. Mem. Acad. Trial Lawyers, Fla. Acad. Trial Lawyers, Nat. Assn. Criminal Def. Lawyers, Fla. Bar Assn. (bd. govs. 1976-80), North Am. Hunt Club, NRA. Democrat. Avocations: hunting, softball, jogging, basketball. Office: 402 Applerouth Ln Key West FL 33040-6535 also: Lazzara and Paul PA 606 E Madison St Ste 2001 Tampa FL 33602-4017

EDENFIELD, BERRY AVANT, federal judge; b. Bulloch County, Ga., Aug. 2, 1934; s. Perry and Vera E.; m. Vida Melvis Bryant, Aug. 3, 1963. BBA U. Ga, 1956, LL.B., 1958. Bar: Ga. 1958. Partner firm Allen, Edenfield, Brown & Wright (and predecessors), Statesboro, Ga., 1958-78; judge U.S. Dist. Ct. (so. dist.) Ga., Savannah, 1978-90, chief judge, 1990-97, judge, 1997—. Mem. Ga. Senate, 1965-66. Office: US Dist Ct PO Box 9865 Savannah GA 31412-0065

EDENHOFER, CARL R. lawyer; b. Oak Park, Ill., Aug. 12, 1958; BS in History, No. Ariz. U., 1980; JD, Hamline U., 1983. Bar: Wis. 1983—, U.S. Dist. Ct. (ea. dist.) 1983—, U.S. Dist. Ct. (we. dist.) 1983—, 7th Cir. Ct. Appeals 1983—. Atty. Joling Rizzo & Willems S.C., Kenosha, Wis., 1983-86; atty., mng. ptnr. Joling Edenhofer & Van Cura, Kenosha, 1986-88, Joling Edenhofer & Assoc. S.C., Kenosha, 1988-95; atty., CEO Edenhofer Law Offices, S.C., Salem, Wis., 1995—. Prof. Carthage Coll., Kenosha, 1988—, mem. adv. bd. paralegal program, 1988-95. Contbr. articles to profl. jours. Bd. dirs. Plan Commn., Brighton, 1995—. Mem. Assn. Trial Lawyers Am. 1985—, Inadequate Security Litigation Group (treas. 1996—), State of Wis. Bar Assn. (sole small firm com. 1995—). Avocations: fishing, hiking, softball. Estate planning, General practice, Product liability. Office: Edenhofer Law Offices SC 23042 75th St Salem WI 53168-9465

EDGAR, R(OBERT) ALLAN, federal judge; b. Munising, Mich., Oct. 6, 1940; s. Robert Richard and Jean Lillian (Hansen) E.; m. Frances Gail Martin, Mar. 30, 1968; children: Amy Elizabeth, Laura Anne. BA, Davidson Coll., 1962; LLB, Duke U., 1965. Bar: Tenn. 1965. From assoc. to ptnr. Miller & Martin, Chattanooga, 1967-85; judge U.S. Dist. Ct. (ea. dist.) Tenn., Chattanooga, 1985—. Mem. com. ct. adminstrn. and case mgmt. Jud. Conf. of the U.S. Mem. Tenn. Ho. of Reps., Nashville, 1970-72, Tenn. Wildlife Resources Commn., Nashville, 1979-85. Served to capt. U.S. Army, 1966-67, Vietnam. Decorated Bronze Star, 1967. Mem. Fed. Bar Assn., Chattanooga Bar Assn. Episcopalian. Office: US Dist Ct PO Box 1748 960 Georgia Ave Chattanooga TN 37402-2220

EDGETT, WILLIAM MALOY, lawyer, labor arbitrator; b. Balt., Feb. 26, 1927; s. Eugene Albert and Priscilla Ruff (Streett) E.; m. Bronwen Winifred Reese, Nov. 25, 1950. AA, Towson State Coll., 1949; BA, U. Md., 1951, JD, 1959; LL.M., Georgetown U., 1970. Bar: Md. bar 1959. Asst. personnel mgr. Am. Sugar Refining Co., Balt., 1951-55; supr. indsl. relations Westinghouse Electric Co., Balt., 1955-61; sr. labor relations specialist Martin Co., Balt., 1961-64; asst. mgr. indsl. relations Md. Shipbuilding and Drydock Co., Balt., 1964-67; pvt. practice law, 1967—. Asst. prof. Towson State U., 1971-72 Mem. Md. Commn. Nursing, 1974-76; chmn. pub. law bds. Nat. Mediation Bd., 1971— ; neutral mem. Nat. R.R. Adjustment Bd., 1971— . Served to staff sgt. USAAF, 1944-46. Mem. ABA. Nat. Acad. Arbitrators, Am. Arbitration Assn., Am., Roster Arbitrators Fed. Mediation and Conciliation Service. Home: 3 Beechmere Ln Cockeysville Hunt Valley MD 21030-1101 Office: PO Box 203 Cockeysville Hunt Valley MD 21030-0203

EDGINTON, JOHN ARTHUR, lawyer; b. Kingsburg, Calif., July 23, 1935; s. Arthur George and Pochantas Clementina (Ball) E.; m. Jane Ann Simmons, June 25, 1960. AA, U. Calif., Berkeley, 1955, AB in Econs., 1957, JD, 1963. Bar: Calif. 1964, No. Marianas 1969, U.S. Ct. Claims 1969, U.S. Ct. Appeals (9th cir.) 1969, U.S. Supreme Ct. 1969. Assoc. Graham & James, San Francisco, 1964-71, ptnr., 1971-94, Dezurick Edginton & Harrington LLP, Emeryville, Calif., 1994-98, Booth Banning LLP, San Francisco, 1999-2000; pvt. practice Point Richmond, Calif., 2000—. Author: Maritime Bankruptcy, 1989, Benedict on Admiralty, vol. 3B and 3C; editor-in-chief Maritime Practice and Procedure, vol. 29 Moore's Federal Practice, 1997, Maritime Desk Reference, Benedict on Admiralty, vol. 8, 2001; editor Benedict's Maritime Bull., 2003; contbr. articles to profl. jours. With USN, 1957—60. Disting. U. Calif. alumni Order of Golden Bear. Mem.: East Bay Model Engrs. Soc. (bd. dirs. 1996—2002, pres. 2000—02), Swedish-Am. C. of C. (bd. dirs. 1971—, pres. Western Nat. 1988—90, nat. vice chmn. 1988—90, pres. Western Nat. 1998—2000, bd. dirs. 1998—, CFO 1999—2000, corp. sec. 2000—), Maritime Law Assn. (chmn. practice and procedure com. 1991—95, bd. dirs. 1993—96), Golden State Model R.R. Mus. (corp. sec., bd. dirs. 1995—), Sierra Club (nat. outing com. 1964—, chmn. ins. com. 1991—, internat. trips 1992—95, outing governance com. 1992—). Democrat. Methodist. Avocations: mountaineering, hiking, photography, model railroads. Admiralty, Bankruptcy, General civil litigation. Office: Law Office of John A Edginton 124 Washington Ave Ste A-1 Point Richmond CA 94801-3979 Fax: (510) 235-4427. E-mail: jedginton@edg-law.com.

EDH, STAFFAN, lawyer; b. Uppsala, Sweden, Dec. 16, 1959; s. Thorolf and Ulla Edh; m. Veronica Wingstedt, July 12, 1986; children; Rebecka, Mathilda. LLM, U. Uppsala, Sweden, 1986. Chief clk. dist. ct. Gothenburg Dist. Ct., Sweden, 1986—88; chmn. bd. Facit AB (publ.), Stockholm, 1997—98; bd. mem. Hamilton & Co., AB, 1999—2002. With Swedish Mil., 1978-79. Mem. Bd. Mems. Acad. Western Sweden. Corporate, general, Mergers and acquisitions. Office: Hamilton & Co Lawfirm Stora Nygatan 33 S-411 08 Gothenburg Sweden Fax: 46 31 743 20 61. E-mail: staffan.edh@hamilton-adv.se.

EDIN, CHARLES THOMAS, lawyer; b. Williston, N.D., Mar. 23, 1955; s. Charles Crane and A. Borgni (Skorpen) E.; children: Charles, Taylor Marie. BA summa cum laude, Concordia Coll., 1978; JD with honors, U.N.D., 1983. Bar: N.D. 1984, U.S. Dist. Ct. N.D. 1984, U.S. Ct. Appeals (8th cir.) 1984. With Landman Westex Petroleum Corp., Bismarck, N.D., 1980-82; ptnr. Zuger Kirmis & Smith, Bismarck, 1984-94; pvt. practice Bismarck, 1995—; spl. asst. atty. gen. State of N.D., Bismarck, 1998—. Precinct committeeman Rep. Party, Bismarck, 1990. Burtness scholar U. N.D., 1983. Mem. N.D. Bar Assn. (mineral title stds. com. real property sect.), Burleigh County Bar Assn., Rocky Mountain Mineral Law Found. (N.D. case law reporter Mineral Law Newsletter 1988-96). Lutheran. General civil litigation, Insurance, Property, real (including real estate development, water). Office: PO Box 2391 Bismarck ND 58502-2391

EDLES, GARY JOEL, lawyer; b. N.Y.C., Feb. 27, 1941; s. Allen Irving and Helen (Hurowitz) E.; m. Nadine Cohen, Feb. 15, 1973. BA, Queens Coll., 1962; JD, NYU, 1965; LLM, George Washington U., 1966, DJuridical Sci., 1975. Bar: N.Y. 1966, U.S. Ct. Appeals (D.C. cir.) 1970. Staff atty. Civil Aeronautics Bd., Washington, 1967-75, assoc. gen. coun., 1975-77, dep. gen. coun., 1977-80; dir. office of procs. Interstate Commerce Commn., Washington, 1980-81; adminstrv. appeals judge Nuclear Regulatory Commn., Washington, 1981-87; gen. coun. Adminstrv. Conf. U.S., Washington, 1987-95; fellow Am. U., 1995—. Faculty Dept. Justice Legal Edn. Inst., 1982-97; vis. prof. U. Sheffield, Eng., 1994, U. Hull, Eng., 1997—. Co-author: Federal Regulatory Process, 2d edit., 1989; contbr. articles to profl. jours. Mem. ABA, Fed. Bar Assn. (chmn. adminstrv. law sect. (1989-91). Home: 10 Keldgate Beverley HU17 8HY England E-mail: G.J.Edles@hull.ac.uk., Gedles@wcl.american.edu.

EDLUND, LARS HARALD, lawyer; b. Linkoping, Sweden, July 20, 1952; s. Stig and Ingrid Edlund; m. Gunilla Ardwidsson, Feb. 25, 1984; children: Anders, Asa, Gunnar. B of Law, Uppsala U., 1976. Sr. judge Swedish Cts., Stockholm, 1976—82; assoc. various law firms, 1982—86, Advokatfirman Vinge, 1986—88, ptnr., 1988—2002, Coudert Bros., 2002—. Bd. dirs. Mediation Inst. Stockholm C. of C. Contbr. articles to profl. jours. Professional liability, Alternative dispute resolution. Office: Coudert Bros Birger Jarlsg 16 Stockholm Sweden Fax: +46 86110404.

EDMONDS, THOMAS LEON, lawyer, management consultant; b. Borger, Tex., May 10, 1932; s. Cline Azel and Flora (Love) E.; m. Virginia Marguerite Leon, June 20, 1960; 1 child, Stephanie Lynn. BSChemE, Tex. Tech. U., 1953, JD, 1973. Bar: Tex. 1974, U.S. Tax Ct. 1975, U.S. Ct. Appeals (5th cir.) 1975, U.S. Dist. Ct. (no. dist.) Tex. 1976, U.S. Supreme Ct. 1996; registered profl. engr., Tex. Engr. computers-exec. dept. Phillips Petroleum, Bartlesville, Okla., 1953-67; mktg. specialist Control Data, Dallas, 1967-68; exec. v.p. CUI, Austin, Tex., 1968-70; mgmt. cons. Mcauto, St. Louis, 1970-71; sr. ptnr. Edmonds & Assocs., Borger, 1973—. City atty. City of Borger, 1991—; treas., dir. Ram Biochems., Inc. Mem. chancellor's coun. Tex. Tech. U.; bd. dirs. Can. River Mcpl. Water Authority, Hutchinson County Tex. Hist. Commn., chmn. 1992-00. Mem. 5th Cir. Bar Assn. (charter), Borger Bar Assn. (pres. 1998-2002). Oil, gas, and mineral, Estate planning, Intellectual property. Home: 210 Broadmoor St Borger TX 79007-8210 Office: PO Box 985 Borger TX 79008-0985

EDMONDSON, FRANK KELLEY, JR., lawyer, legal administrator; b. Newport, R.I., Aug. 27, 1936; s. Frank Kelley Sr. and Margaret (Russell) E.; m. Christiane Semirot, Mar. 5, 1959 (div. Sept. 1969); children: Mylene Anne, Yvonne Marie, Catherine May; m. Elaine Sueko Kaneshiro, Aug. 17, 1970 (div. June 1992); m. Karen Louise Bishop, Feb. 27, 1993 (div. Feb. 1996). BBA, Ind. U., 1958; MBA, So. Ill. U., 1978; JD, U. Puget Sound, 1982. Bar: Wash. 1982, U.S. Dist. Ct. (we. dist.) Wash. 1983. Commd. 2d lt. USAF, 1959, advanced through grades to maj., 1969, ret., 1979; contracts specialist Wash. State Lottery, Olympia, 1982-85, asst. contracts adminstr., 1985-87; contracts officer 1989 Washington Centennial Commn., 1987-90; fin. svc. officer Office of the Adminstr. for the Cts., 1990-92; contracts officer, office of adminstr. for the cts. State of Wash. Supreme Ct., Olympia, 1992-99. Mem. Seattle U. Sch. Law, Law Alumni Soc. Nat. Coun., 1997—, scholarship com. Wash. State Employees Credit Union, 1995-2001. Bd. dirs. Friends of Chambers Creek, Tacoma, 1981-90; mem. pro bono panel Puget Sound Legal Assistance Found., Olympia, 1985-90; mock trial program com. Youth and Govt. YMCA, 1994-96. Mem. Wash. State Bar Assn. (spl. dist. counsel 1993-95), Thurston County Bar Assn., Ind. U. Soc. Advanced Study, Govt. Lawyers Bar Assn. (sec. 1985-86, 1st v.p. 1986-87, pres. 1987-89, liaison to Wash. State Bar Assn. 1989-93), Beta Gamma Sigma, Coll. Club. Home: 6600 Miner Dr SW Tumwater WA 98512-7282 E-mail: fkedmon@aol.com.

EDMONDSON, WILLIAM ANDREW, state attorney general; b. Washington, D.C., Oct. 12, 1946; m. Linda Larason; children: Mary Elizabeth, Robert Andrew. BA in Speech Edn., Northeastern State U., Tahlequah, Okla., 1968; JD, U. Tulsa, 1978. Mem. Okla. Legislature, 1974—76; intern Office Dist. Atty., Muskogee, Okla., 1978—, asst. dist. atty., 1979, chief prosecutor, 1982—, dist. atty., 1982—92; pvt. practice atty. Muskogee, 1979—82, Green & Edmondson, 1992—94; atty. gen. State of Okla., 1994—. With USN, 1968—72. Named Outstanding Dist. Atty., State of Okla., 1985. Mem.: Okla. Dist. Attys. Assn. (pres. 1983—85), Okla. Bar Assn. Democrat. Office: Office Atty Gen 2300 N Lincoln Blvd Rm 112 Oklahoma City OK 73105-4894

EDMUNDS, JOHN SANFORD, lawyer; b. L.A., Jan. 3, 1943; s. Arthur Edmunds and Sarah Bernadine (Miles) E.; m. Virginia Maejan Ching, Nov. 30, 1975; children: Laura, Shauna. AB, Stanford U., 1964; JD, U. So. Calif., 1967. Bar: Hawaii 1972, U.S. Dist. Ct. Hawaii, U.S. Ct. Appeals (9th cir.), U.S. Supreme Ct. Chief dep. pub. defender State of Hawaii, 1970-72, spl. dep. atty. gen., 1974-75; acting chief justice Supreme Ct., Republic of Marshall Islands, 1980-81; ptnr. Edmunds & Verga, Honolulu, 1981-97, Edmunds, Maki, Versa and Thorn, Honolulu, 1997—. Adj. prof. law U. Hawaii, 1976-77, 85-89; counsel Hemmeter Investment Co., Obayashi Corp., Shell Oil Co., Nestle, U.S.A., Inc., Bank of Am. Bd. dirs. Legal Aid Soc. Hawaii, 1974-75; vice-chair selection commn. Hawaii State Jud., 2000-. Fellow Internat. Acad. Trial Lawyers, Am. Coll. Trial Lawyers (state chmn. 1991-92, nat. com. legal ethics and profl. responsibility 1994), Internat. Soc. Barristers, Am. Bar Found.; mem. ABA, ACLU (bd. dirs. 1969-73, pres. 1971-73, adv. counsel 1974-75), Hawaii Bar Assn., Assn. Trial Lawyers Am., Hawaii Acad. Plaintiffs Attys (bd. govs. 1995—), Master of Bench, Am. Inns. of Ct. General civil litigation, Criminal, Personal injury (including property damage). Office: Edmunds Maki Verga & Thorn 841 Bishop St Ste 2104 Honolulu HI 96813-3921 E-mail: jedmunds@emut.com.

EDMUNDS, ROBERT H., JR., state supreme court justice; Student, Williams Coll., Williamstown, Mass., 1967—69; BA in English, Vassar Coll., 1971; JD, U. N.C., Chapel Hill, 1975. Bar: NC 1975, Va. 1977. Asst. dist. atty. 18th Judicial Dist., Guilford County, NC, 1978—82; asst. U.S. atty. Mid. Dist. N.C. U.S. Dept. Justice, Greensboro, 1982—86, U.S. atty. Mid. Dist. N.C., 1986—93; ptnr. Stern & Klepfer, 1993—98; assoc. judge N.C. Ct. Appeals, 1999—2001; assoc. justice N.C. Supreme Ct., 2001—. Contbr. articles to profl. jours. Office: PO Box 1841 Raleigh NC 27602

EDWARDS, BLAINE DOUGLASS, lawyer; b. Borger, Tex., Sept. 30, 1961; s. Charles Afton and Harriett (Hauser) E.; m. Jill Summers Hendrickson. Sept. 1, 1984; children: Audrey Summers, Cole Douglass. BBA in Acctg. and Fin., Tex. A&M U., 1984; JD magna cum laude, St. Mary's U., 1990. Bar: Tex. 1990, U.S. Dist. Ct. (so., no., and ea. dists.) Tex. 1991, 96, U.S. Ct. Appeals (5th and 11th cirs.). Oil and gas/real estate lending officer InterFirst Bank, San Antonio, 1984-87; participating assoc. Fulbright &

Jaworski, LLP, Houston, 1990-95; ptnr. Shook, Hardy & Bacon, LLP, Houston, 1995—. Adj. prof. law South Tex. Coll. Law , Houston. Co-author: Texas Environmental Law Handbook, 1990, 92; editor St. Mary's Law Jour., 1989-90; contbr. articles to profl. jours. Mem. Phi Delta Phi. Avocations: reading, snow skiing, golfing. General civil litigation, Environmental, Toxic tort. Office: Shook Hardy & Bacon Ste 1600 600 Travis St Houston TX 77002

EDWARDS, CARL NORMAN, lawyer; b. Norwood, Mass., Jan. 22, 1943; s. Wilfred Carl and Cecile Marie-Anne (Pepin) E.; m. Mary Louise Buyse, Jan. 22, 1982. MEd, Suffolk U., 1969; postgrad., Harvard U.; JD, Boston Coll., 1998; PhD, U. So. Calif., 1997. Cons. dept. social rels. Harvard U., Cambridge, Mass., 1966-69, rsch. fellow, 1969-71, lectr. social rels., 1971-72; cons. rsch. psychologist Cambridge Computer Assocs., Mass., 1966—; rsch. social psychologist Tufts-New Eng. Med. Ctr., 1969—; assoc. clin. prof. psychiatry Tufts U. Sch. Medicine, 1971—. Dir. Four Oaks Research Inst., Norfolk, Mass., 1974—; sr. assoc. for policy planning and research Justice Resource Inst., 1971—; field faculty grad. program Goddard Coll., Plainfield, Vt., 1972-82; chmn. bd. dirs. MEDx Systems, Ltd., Dover, Mass., 1985—; chmn. bd. trustees Ctr. for Birth Defects Info. Services, Inc., Dover, 1984—; tchr. seminars; cons. to major corps., govt. agys. and pub. instns. in human dynamics and pub. policy; lectr., thesis adviser, program devel. cons. schs., colls., insts. Author: Responsibilities and Dispensations: Behavior, Science and American Justice, 2001; contbr. articles to profl. jours., monographs, revs. Mem. USNG, 1963-64. Mem. ABA, APA, Mass. Psychol. Assn. (bd. dirs.), Am. Acad. Forensic Scis., Nat. Trust for Hitoric Preservation, Harvard Club, Appalachian Mt. Club, Norfolk Hunt Club, Blue Ridge Hunt Club. Home: Four Oaks PO Box 1776 Dover MA 02030-0279

EDWARDS, CHRISTINE ANNETTE, retired lawyer, securities firm executive; b. Ft. Monmouth, N.J., Aug. 30, 1952; d. Harry W. Jr. and Elizabeth Power; m. John H. Edwards, Aug. 24, 1974; children: Lindsey, John. BA, U. Md., College Park, 1974; JD with honors, U. Md., Balt., 1983. Bar: Md. 1983, D.C. 1984, Ill 1990. With Sears, Roebuck and Co., Md., 1971-81, sr. paralegal, staff asst., 1981-83, atty. govt. affairs, 1983-87; asst. v.p., dir. govt. affairs Dean Witter Fin. Svcs. Group, Washington, 1987-88, v.p., gen. counsel Lincolnshire, Ill., 1988-89, sr. v.p., 1989-91, exec. v.p., sec., chief legal officer N.Y.C., 1991-97; exec. v.p., chief legal officer, corp. sec. Morgan Stanley Dean Witter & Co. (merger Dean Witter Discover & Co. with Morgan Stanley & Co. Inc.), N.Y.C., 1997—99; legal dept. ABN AMRO, 1999—2000; v.p., gen. counsel Bank One Corp., 2000—03. Mem. bd. Fin. Svcs. Coun., Washington, 1990—; bd. trustees Nat. Found. for Consumer Credit Counseling Svcs., Silver Spring, Md., 1990-92; mem. Women in Housing and Fin., Washington, 1982—, SAI Letigation Com., 1995—, N.Y. Stock Exchange Legal Adv. Com., 1992-95; bd. dirs. Chgo. Bd. of Options Exchange, SPS Transaction Svcs. Inc.; exec. v.p., chief legal officer, corp. sec. CLO Roundtable, 1995—. Recipient Disting. Mem. award Women in Housing and Fin., Washington, 1988; named 1 of 50 Top Women Lawyers Nat. Law Journal, 1998. Mem. ABA, Securities Industry Assn. (mem. fed. regulation com. 1990—). Securities.*

EDWARDS, DANIEL PAUL, lawyer; educator; b. Enid, Okla., Apr. 15, 1940; s. Daniel Paul and Joye Virginia (van Horn) E.; m. Virginia Lee Kidd, Mar. 27, 1976; children: Austin Daniel, David Paul, Anne Marie. BA, U. Okla., 1962; JD, Harvard Law Sch., 1965. Bar: Colo. 1965, Hawaii, 1987, Ariz. 1988. Ptnr. Beltz, Edwards & Sabo, Colorado Springs; lectr. law Colo. Coll., 1976-87. Pres. Springs Area Beautiful Assn., 1978. Mem. ABA, Colo., Ariz. and Hawaii Bar Assn., Harvard Law Sch. Assn. Colo. (pres. 1986-87), El Paso Club, Broadmoor Golf Club, Cheyenne Mt. Club, Garden of the Gods Club, Kapalua Tennis Club, Phi Beta Kappa, Phi Delta Theta. Republican. Presbyterian. Estate planning, Property, real (including real estate development, water), Securities. E-mail: dpedwards@bestlawllp.com.

EDWARDS, DANIEL WALDEN, lawyer; b. Vancouver, Wash., Aug. 7, 1950; s. Chester W. Edwards and Marilyn E. Russell; m. Joan S. Heller, Oct. 18, 1987; children: Nathaniel, Matthew, Stephen, Alexander. BA in Psychology magna cum laude, Met. State Coll., Denver, 1973, BA in Philosophy, 1974; JD, U. Colo., 1976. Bar: Colo. 1977, U.S. Dist. Ct. Colo. 1977. Dep. pub. defender State of Colo., Denver, 1977-79, Littleton, 1979-81, Pueblo, 1981-86, head office pub. defender Brighton, 1987-89, mem. jud. faculty, 1988-91; sole practitioner Denver, 1991-93; magistrate Denver Juvenile Ct., 1993-99; sole practice law Denver, 1999—. Instr. sch. of law U. Denver, 1988-91, adj. prof., 1991—, coach appellate advocacy team, 1991-99; adv. coun. Colo. Legal Svcs., 1989—; adj. mem. Colo. Supreme Ct. Grievance Com., 1991-95. Author: Basic Trial Practice: An Introduction to Persuasive Trial Techniques, 1995, Principles of Persuasion: Basic Appellate Advocacy Techniques, 1999. Mem. visual arts com. City Arts III, 1989-90, com. chmn., mem. adv. coun., 1991; bd. dirs. Metropolitan State Coll., Alumni Assn., 1991-92; vol. lectr. CSE Thursday Night Bar Pro Se Divorce Clinic, 1991-95. Named Pub. Defender of Yr. Colo. State Pub. Defender's Office, 1985, Outstanding Colo. Criminal Def. Atty., 1989. Mem. ABA, Assn. Trial Lawyers Am., Colo. Bar Assn., Adams County Bar Asss., Denver Bar Assn., Met. State Coll. Alumni Assn. (bd. dirs. 1991-94). Home: 2335 Clermont St Denver CO 80207-3134 Office: 1733 High St Denver CO 80218-1320 E-mail: edwards_dan_atty@msn.com.

EDWARDS, EDITH MARTHA, lawyer; b. Great Neck, N.Y., Mar. 7, 1945; d. Paul Walter and Alice Matilda (Hansen) Steen; m. Thomas Murray Edwards Sr., Dec. 27, 1966; children: Janice Audrey, Thomas Murray Jr. BS, Coker Coll., 1967; JD, Olgethorpe U., 1981. Bar: Ga. 1982, U.S. Dist. Ct. (no. dist.) Ga. 1983, U.S. Supreme Ct. 1986. Atty. Ga. Legal Svcs., Nashville, 1983-84; asst. dist. atty. Alapaha Cir., Ga., 1984-86; asst. dist. Cherokee Jud. Cir., Ga., 1987; atty. pvt. practice, Valdosta, Ga., 1988—. Mem.: AAUW. Republican. Episcopalian. Avocation: art. Criminal, Family and matrimonial. Home and Office: 508 Gornto Rd Valdosta GA 31602-1602

EDWARDS, HARRY T. judge; b. N.Y.C., Nov. 3, 1940; s. George H. Edwards and Arline Ross Lyle; m. Pamela Carrington; children: Brent, Michelle. BS, Cornell U., 1962; JD, U. Mich., 1965. Assoc. firm Seyfarth, Shaw, Fairweather & Geraldson, Chgo., 1965—70; prof. law U. Mich., 1970—75; vis. prof. law Harvard U., 1975—76, prof., 1976—77; judge U.S. Ct. Appeals (D.C. cir.), Washington, 1980—; vis. prof. Free U. Brussels, 1974; dir. AMTRAK, 1977—80, chmn. bd., 1979—80; disting. lectr. law Duke U., 1983—89; lectr. law Georgetown Law Ctr., 1985—86; chief judge U.S. Ct. Appeals (D.C. cir.), Washington, 1994—2001; prof. law U. Mich., 1977—80. Adj. prof. law NYU Law Sch., 1989—; lectr. Harvard Law Sch., 1982—88, Mich. Law Sch., 1988—89; mem. Adminstrv. Conf. of U.S., 1976—80. Co-author: Labor Relations Law in the Public Sector, 1974, 1979, 1985, Lawyer as a Negotiator, 1977, Collective Bargaining and Labor Arbitration, 1979, Higher Education and the Law, 1979. Mem.: ABA (sec. sect. labor law 1976—77), Am. Law Inst., Am. Arbitration Assn. (dir. 1979—80), Am. Acad. Arts and Scis., Nat. Acad. Arbitrators (dir. 1975—80, v.p. 1978—80), Order of Coif. Office: US Ct Appeals 333 Constitution Ave NW Washington DC 20001-2866

EDWARDS, HARRY LAFOY, lawyer; b. Greenville, SC, July 29, 1936; s. George Belton and Mary Olive (Jones) E.; m. Suzanne Copeland, June 16, 1956; 1 child, Margaret Peden. LLB, U. S.C., 1963, JD, 1970. Bar: S.C. 1963, U.S. Dist. Ct. S.C. 1975, U.S. Ct. Appeals (4th cir.) 1974. Assoc. Edwards and Edmunds, Greenville, 1963; v.p., sec., dir. Edwards Co., Inc., Greenville, 1963-65; atty. investment legal dept. Liberty Life Ins. Co., Greenville, 1965-67, asst. sec., asst. v.p., head investment legal dept., 1967-70; asst. sec. Liberty Corp., 1970-75; asst. v.p. Liberty Life Ins. Co., 1970-75; sec. Bent Tree Corp., CEL, Inc., 1970-75; sec., dir. Westchester Mall, Inc., 1970-75; asst. sect. Libco, Inc., Liberty Properties, Inc., 1970-75; pvt. practice, Greenville, 1975—. Editor U. S.C. Law Rev., 1963. Com. mem. Hipp Fund Spl. Edn., Greenville County Sch. Sys.; mem. Boyd C. Hipp II Scholarship Com., Wofford Coll. Spartanburg, S.C.; scholarship com. Liberty Scholars, U. S.C., 1984, 86-2003. With USAFR, 1957-63. Mem. ABA, S.C. Bar Assn., Greenville County Bar Assn., Phi Delta Phi, Greenville Lawyers, Poinsett Club (Greenville). Baptist. Corporate, general, Estate planning, Property, real (including real estate development, water). Home: 106 Ridgeland Dr Greenville SC 29601-3017 Office: PO Box 10350 Greenville SC 29603-0350 E-mail: hle106@aol.com.

EDWARDS, JAMES ALFRED, lawyer; b. Orlando, Fla., Feb. 18, 1954; BA in Psychology with high honors, Auburn U., 1976; JD with high honors, U. Fla., 1979. Bar: Fla. 1979, U.S. Dist. Ct. (no. dist.) Fla. 1979, U.S. Dist. Ct. (mid. and so. dists.) Fla. 1981, U.S. Ct. Appeals (5th cir.) 1979, U.S. Ct. Appeals (11th cir.) 1982, U.S. Supreme Ct. 1984; bd. cert. civil trial lawyer Fla. Bar Assn.; cert. mediator cir. ct. Ptnr. Rumberger, Kirk & Caldwell, Orlando, Fla., 1979-89, Roth, Edwards & Smith, P.A., Orlando, Fla., 1989-2000, Cabaniss, Conroy & McDonald, LLP, Orlando, 2000, Law Office James A. Edwards, PA, Maitland, Fla., 2001—. Mem. Fla. Bar Assn. (cert. civil trial lawyer, mem. trial lawyers, appellate practice sects.), Orange County Bar Assn. (mem. jud. rels. com.). Avocations: fishing, water skiing, snow skiing. Alternative dispute resolution, Personal injury (including property damage), Product liability. Office: 100 E Sybelia Ave # 375 Maitland FL 32751 Fax: 407-647-9735. E-mail: JEdwards@bigfishlaw.com.

EDWARDS, JAMES MALONE, lawyer; b. Champaign, Ill., Aug. 15, 1931; s. Harold Mortimer and Marion Bell (Scarlett) E.; m. Veronica Marianne Greeven, Mar. 2, 1968; children: Nina Scarlett, Philip Mortimer. BA, U. Ill., 1953; postgrad., Inst. des Sci. Politiques, 1955; LLB, Yale U., 1960. Bar: N.Y. 1961. Law clk. to justice Charles E. Whittaker U.S. Supreme Ct., Washington, 1960-61; assoc. Cravath, Swaine & Moore, N.Y.C., 1961-69, ptnr., 1969—. 1st lt. USAF, 1955-56. Corporate, general, Private international, Mergers and acquisitions.

EDWARDS, JEROME, lawyer; b. N.Y.C., July 5, 1912; s. Philip and Anna (Hollinger) E.; m. Mildred Kahn, Dec. 7, 1941 (dec.); children: Susan, Bruce (dec.). BS, NYU, 1931, JD, 1933. Bar: N.Y. State 1934, Calif. 1975. Asso. firm T.J. Lesser, 1934-36; pvt. practice N.Y.C., 1936-42; sr. partner Phillips, Nizer, Benjamin, Krim & Ballon, N.Y.C., 1942-62; v.p., gen. counsel 20th Century Fox Film Corp., N.Y.C. and Los Angeles, 1962-77; of counsel Kaplan, Livingston, Goodwin, Berkowitz & Selvin, Beverly Hills, Calif., 1977-81, Musick, Peeler & Garrett, Los Angeles, 1982-83, Phillips, Nizer, Benjamin, Krim & Ballon, Los Angeles, 1985-89. Mem. ABA, Am. Film Mktg. Assn. (arbitrator panel), Am. Arbitration Assn. (nat. pnel neutral arbitrators 1960-2000). Fax: 310-475-6328. E-mail: JerEdwards1903@aol.com.

EDWARDS, JOHN DUNCAN, law educator, librarian; b. Louisiana, Mo., Sept. 15, 1953; s. Harold Wenkle and Mary Elizabeth (Duncan) E.; m. Beth Ann Rahm, May 21, 1977; children: Craig, Martha, Brooks. BA, Southeast Mo. State U., 1975; JD, U. Mo., Kansas City, 1977; MALS, U. Mo., Columbia, 1979. Bar: Mo. 1978, U.S. Dist. Ct. (we. dist.) Mo. 1978. Instr. legal research and writing U. Mo., Columbia, 1978, dir. legal research and writing, librarian, 1979-80; pub. svcs. librarian Law Sch., U. Okla., Norman, 1980-81, assoc. librarian, 1981-84, adj. instr. sch. library sci., 1983-84; prof. law, dir. law library law sch. Drake U., Des Moines, 1984—. Adj. instr. Columbia Coll., 1979-80; cons. Cleveland County Bar Assn., 1984. Author: Emerging Solutions in Reference Services: Implications for Libraries in the New Millennium, 2001; editor: Iowa Legal Research Guide, 2003; contbr. articles to profl. jours. Cons. Friends Drake U. Libr., 1985—; coach, mgr. Westminster Softball Team. Des Moines, 1987-94; pres. Crestview Parent-Tchr. Coun., Des Moines, 1988-90; trustee Westminster Presbyn. Ch., Des Moines, 1988-89, treas., 1990, pres., 1991; mem. Clive City Coun., 1995—, mayor pro tem, 1998—; trustee Des Moines Metro Transit Authority, 1996—, chmn. bd. dirs., 1997-98, 2003—, sec.-treas., 1996, 2001-02. Recipient Presdl. award Drake U. Student Bar Assn., 1987; named Outstanding Vol., Crestview Elem. Sch., 1989-90. Mem. Am. Assn. Law Librs. (chmn. awards com. 1987-88, chmn. grants com. 1996-97, chmn. scholarship com. 1998-99), Mid-Am. Assn. Law Librs. (chmn. resource sharing 1986-93, v.p. 1994-95, pres. 1995-96), Mid-Am. Law Sch. Librs. Consortium (pres. 1986-88), Delta Theta Phi, Beta Phi Mu. Avocations: softball, tennis. Office: Drake U Libr Law Sch 27th & Carpenter Sts Des Moines IA 50311

EDWARDS, JOHN WESLEY, II, lawyer; b. Williamsport, Pa., Nov. 29, 1948; s. Robert Wesley Edwards and Jean Eleanor (Seitzer) Leprohon; m. Lee Ellen Berliner, May 22, 1971; children: Wesley David, Katherine Lee, Meredith Jean. BA, Colgate U., 1970; JD, Duke U., 1974. Bar: Ohio 1974, Calif. 2001, U.S. Dist. Ct. (no. dist.) Ohio 1974, U.S. Dist. Ct. (no. dist.) Calif. 2001, U.S. Ct. Appeals (6th cir.) 1974, U.S. Ct. Appeals (9th cir.) 2001. Assoc. Jones, Day, Reavis & Pogue, Cleve., 1974-82, ptnr., 1982—. Served to cpl. USMCR, 1970-76. Mem. Cleve. Bar Assn. (Fed. ct. com.), Order of Coif, Phi Beta Kappa. Clubs: Mayfield Country (Lyndhurst, Ohio). Republican. Presbyterian. Federal civil litigation, State civil litigation. Office: Jones Day 2882 Sand Hill Rd Ste 240 Menlo Park CA 94025 Home: 1272 San Raymundo Rd Hillsborough CA 94010-6653

EDWARDS, NINIAN MURRY, judge; b. St. Louis, Jan. 11, 1922; s. N. Murry and Mabel E. (Dailey) E.; m. Mary Catherine McKeown, May 12, 1944; children: Katherine S. Edwards Burckhalter, Barbara Edwards Perkins. JD, U. Mo., 1947. Trial lawyer, St. Louis area, 1947-65; cir. judge St. Louis County, Clayton, Mo., 1965-66, 70-88, sr. judge, arbitrator, mediator, 1988—. Coun. mem. City of Kirkwood, Mo., atty., 1968-70. Maj. USAFR, 1950-90, ret. Mem. Mo. Bar Assn. (past bd. govs.), Bar Assn. Met. St. Louis, St. Louis County Bar Assn. (Disting. Svc. award 1970), Nat. Coun. Juvenile and Family Ct. Judges (bd. trustees, past sec., treas., v.p., pres. elect 1990, pres. 1991-92), Phi Delta Phi. Democrat.

EDWARDS, PRISCILLA ANN, paralegal, business owner; b. Orlando, Fla., Sept. 28, 1947; d. William Granville and Bernice Royster; m. Charles R. King, Apr. 2, 1981. Paralegal cert., U. Calif., Berkeley, 1994. Paralegal Charles R. Garry Esquire, San Francisco, 1989-90; owner, mgr. Fed. Legal Resources, San Francisco, 1991—. Speaker Sonoma State U., Santa Rosa, Calif., 1993. Publisher: (book) Zero Weather, 1981. Recipient Wiley W. Manuel award for pro bono legal svcs. Bd. Govs. State Bar of Calif., 1994, 95, 96, 97, 98. Episcopalian. Avocations: horseback riding, mountain biking.

EDWARDS, RICHARD LANSING, lawyer; b. Wilmington, Del., Apr. 16, 1944; s. Robert Wilson Jr. and Eleanor (Inscho) E.; m. Betsey Ann Barney, Aug. 24, 1980; children: Beth, Melissa, Jeffrey, Jason, Karen. BS in Indsl. Engring., Lehigh U., 1966; JD, Northeastern U., 1980. Bar: Mass. 1980, U.S. Dist. Ct. Mass. 1981, U.S. Ct. Appeals (1st cir.) 1983, U.S. Supreme Ct. 1985, U.S. Dist. Ct. Conn. 1998. Lawyer Craig & Macauley, Boston, 1980-83; lawyer, shareholder Campbell, Campbell, Edwards & Conroy P.C., Boston, 1983—. Faculty Internat. Assn. Def. Counsel Trial Acad., 1994, ABA TIPS Nat. Trial Acad., 2000. Contbr. articles to profl. jours. Capt. USAF, 1966—70. Decorated Bronze star. Mem. ABA (tort and ins. practice and litigation sect. 1984—, faculty torts and ins. sect. Nat. Trial Acad. 2000), Mass. Bar Assn. (civil litigation sect. 1983—), Def. Rsch. Inst. (bd. dirs. 1999-2002, products liability com., chmn. 1997-99, chmn. duty to warn and labeling subcom. 1985-88, steering com. 1988—), Internat. Assn. of Def. Counsel (chmn. advocacy practice and procedure com. 1993-95, faculty Trial Acad. 1994), Mass. Def. Lawyers Assn., Product Liability Adv. Coun., Boston Bar Assn. Construction, Personal injury (including property damage), Product liability. Office: Campbell Campbell Edwards & Conroy PC One Constitution Plaza Boston MA 02129 E-mail: redwards@campbell-trial-lawyers.com.

EDWARDS, ROBIN MORSE, lawyer; b. Glens Falls, N.Y., Dec. 9, 1947; d. Daniel and Harriet Morse; m. Richard Charles Edwards, Aug. 30, 1970; children: Michael Alan, Jonathan Philip. BA, Mt. Holyoke Coll., 1969; JD, U. Calif., Berkeley, 1972. Bar: Calif. 1972. Assoc. Donahue, Gallagher, Thomas & Woods, Oakland, Calif., 1972—77, ptnr., 1977—89, Sonnenschein, Nath & Rosenthal, San Francisco, 1989—, mgmt. com., 1998—. Bd. dirs. Temple Sinai, 1997-2002. Mem. ABA, Calif. Bar Assn., Alameda County Bar Assn. (bd. dirs. 1978-84, v.p. 1982, pres. 1983), Alameda County Bar Found. (bd. dirs. 1998-2000). Jewish. Avocations: skiing, cooking. Corporate, general, Property, real (including real estate development, water), Securities. Office: Sonnenschein Nath Rosenthal 685 Market St 6th Flr San Francisco CA 94105-4202 E-mail: redwards@sonnenschein.com.

EDWARDS, SAMUEL HOLLIS, lawyer, urban/regional planner; b. Lebanon, Tenn., Apr. 13, 1950; s. Hollis Elverton and Aggie Rhea Edwards; m. Debra Joyce Edwards, Aug. 19, 1972; children: Rebecca Joyce Sellars, Samantha Leigh Granstaff. BS, Mid. Tenn. State U., 1972; MPA, U. Tenn., 1976; JD, Nashville Sch. Law, 1991. Bar: Tenn., 1991, U.S. Dist. Ct. (middle dist.), Tenn., 1992. Transp. planner Dept. Transp., Nashville, 1972-76; planning dir. Wilson County/Lebanon Planning Office, 1977-86; dep. exec. dir. Greater Nashville Regional Coun., 1986—, legal counsel, 1991—. Mem. ABA, Am. Inst. Cert. Planners, Am. Planning Assn., Tenn. Bar Assn., Nashville Bar Assn. Home: 208 Oakdale Dr Lebanon TN 37087 Office: Greater Nashville Regional Coun 501 Union St 6th Fl Nashville TN 37219 E-mail: sedwards@gnrc.org.

EDWARDS, WILLIAM THOMAS, JR., lawyer, consultant; b. Eglin AFB, Fla., Feb. 8, 1956; s. William Thomas and Josephine (Fabian) E.; children: Jennifer, Ali. BA, Fla. State U., 1977, JD, 1980. Bar: Fla. 1980, U.S. Dist. Ct. (mid. dist.) Fla. 1981, U.S. Ct. Claims 1981, U.S. Tax Ct. 1981, U.S. Ct. Appeals (11th cir.) 1983. Assoc. William T. Lassiter Jr., P.A., Jacksonville, Fla., 1980-82; sole practice Middleburg, Fla., 1982-93, 95-98, The Edwards Law Firm, P.A., Orange Park, Fla., 1999—; owner Edwards Internat., Orange Park, 1994—. Pres. Middleburg Bus. Coun., 1985, 87, v.p., 1984. Mem. Am. Acad. Estate Planning Attys., Fla. Bar Assn., Clay County Bar Assn., Jacksonville Bar Assn., Clay County C. of C. (bd. dirs. 1985, 87-90, chmn. film liaison com. 1990-91, chmn. mil. affairs com. 1990, v.p. membership svcs. 1990), Cath. Lawyers Guild, KC. Republican. Roman Catholic. Avocations: travel, reading, walking. Estate planning, Probate (including wills, trusts).

EFFEL, LAURA, lawyer; b. Dallas, May 9, 1945; d. Louis E. and Fay (Lee) Ray; m. Marc J. Patterson, Sept. 19, 1992 (dec. July 30, 2002); 1 child, Stephen Patterson. BA, U. Calif., Berkeley, 1971; JD, U. Md., 1975. Bar: N.Y. 1976, U.S. Dist. Ct. (so. and ea. dists.) N.Y. 1976, U.S. Ct. Appeals (2d cir.) 1980, U.S. Supreme Ct. 1980, D.C. 1993, N.C. 1998, Va. 2001. Assoc. Burns Jackson Miller Summit & Jacoby, N.Y.C., 1975-78, Pincus Munzer Bizar & D'Alessandro, N.Y.C., 1978-80; v.p., sr. assoc. counsel Chase Manhattan Bank, N.A., N.Y.C., 1980-96; counsel Baker & McKenzie, N.Y.C., 1996-99; gen. counsel Garban Cos., 1999-2000; counsel Flippin Densmore Morse & Jessee, Roanoke, Va., 2000—02, ptnr., 2002—. Bd. dirs. Blue Ridge Pub. TV, 2001—. Treas. Workforce Devel. Com., New Century Tech. Coun.; bd. dirs. Bklyn. Legal Svcs. Corp. A, 1992-2000. Mem.: ABA (com. pretrial practice 2000—03, litig. sect. co-chair, subcom. atty. client privilege), Roanoke Bar Assn., Va. Bar Assn., NC Bar Assn., Am. Corp. Counsel Assn. (dir. emeritus, pro bono svc. award 1989). General civil litigation, Labor (including EEOC, Fair Labor Standards Act, labor-management relations, NLRB, OSHA), Alternative dispute resolution. Office: Flippin Densmore Morse & Jessee Drawer 1200 Roanoke VA 24006 E-mail: effel@flippindensmore.com.

EFFINGER, CYNTHIA LYNN, lawyer; b. New Haven, Nov. 21, 1972; d. Paul Joseph and Dorothy Lucille Hackbarth; m. Joseph Meredith Effinger, Nov. 5, 1999; 1 child, Caroline Rose. BA in History, U. Ga., 1994; JD, U. Louisville, 1998. Bar: Ky. 98. Assoc. Seiller & Handmaker, LLP, Louisville, 1998—. Mem.: Ky. Acad. Trial Attys., Louisville Bar Assn. Democrat. Civil rights, Labor (including EEOC, Fair Labor Standards Act, labor-management relations, NLRB, OSHA), Personal injury (including property damage). Office: Seiller & Handmaker LLP 462 S 4th Ave Ste 2200 Louisville KY 40202 Fax: 502-583-2100. E-mail: effinger@derbycitylaw.com.

EFRON, MORTON LEON, lawyer; b. N.Y.C., Jan. 10, 1938; s. Frank S. and Mary (Freedman)E.; m. Anita Schwartz, June 7, 1964; children: Jessica M., Matthew L. BA in Econs., U. Mich., 1959, JD, 1962; postgrad., U. Chgo., 1963. Bar: Ind. 1962, U.S. Dist. Ct. (no. dist.) Ind. 1962. Ptnr. Efron and Efron, P.C., Hammond, Ind., 1962—. Chmn. bd. dirs., Western State Bank, Howard City, Mich. Bd. dirs., Hammond Legal Aid Soc., 1962-88. Mem. Ind. State Bar Assn., Hammond Bar Assn., Lake City Bar Assn. Office: Efron and Efron PC 5246 Hohman Ave Fl 5 Hammond IN 46320-1733

EGAN, CHARLES JOSEPH, JR., lawyer, greeting card company executive; b. Cambridge, Mass., Aug. 11, 1932; s. Charles Joseph and Alice Claire (Ball) E.; m. Mary Bowersox, Aug. 6, 1955; children: Timothy, Sean, Peter, James. AB, Harvard U., 1954; LLB, Columbia U., 1959. Bar: N.Y. 1960, Mo. 1973. Assoc. Donovan, Leisure, Newton & Irvine, N.Y.C., 1959-62; ptnr. Hall, McNicol, Marett & Hamilton, N.Y.C., 1962-68; v.p., gen. counsel Thomson & McKinnon Securities, N.Y.C., 1969-70, Hallmark Cards, Inc., Kansas City, Mo., 1972—. Bd. dirs. Am. Multi Cinema, Inc., Kansas City, Mo. Trustee Notre Dame de Sion Sch., Kansas City, 1973-77, Pembroke Country Day Sch., Kansas City, 1976-82, Kansas City Art Inst., 1995—; bd. dirs. Kansas City YMCA, 1976-80; mem. dean's coun. Columbia Law Sch., 1991—; vice chmn. Harvard Coll. Fund, 1994-99, co-chmn., 2000—. Served to 1st lt. USMC, 1954-56. Mem. Mo. Bar Assn., Kansas City Lawyers Assn., Harvard Alumni Assn. (pres. 1989-90, exec. com. 1987—), Century Assn., Somerset Club, Harvard Club of N.Y., Harvard Club of Kansas City (pres. 1985-87). Roman Catholic. Antitrust, Corporate, general, Taxation, general. Office: Hallmark Cards Inc 2501 Mcgee St Kansas City MO 64108-2600

EGAN, KEVIN JAMES, lawyer; b. Chgo., June 24, 1950; s. Raymond Basil and Harriet Olene (Landbo) E.; children: Ryan, Daniel. BA, U. Ill., 1972; JD, Northwestern U., 1975. Bar: Ill. 1975, U.S. Dist. Ct. (no. dist.) Ill. 1975, U.S. Ct. Appeals (7th cir.) 1976, U.S. Ct. of Customs and Patent Appeals 1978. Law clk. to judge U.S. Dist. Ct. (no. dist.) Ill., Chgo., 1975-77; assoc. Pattishall, McAuliffe & Hofstetter, Chgo., 1977-78; asst. U.S. atty. No. Dist. of Ill., 1978-82; assoc. Winston & Strawn, Chgo., 1982-84, ptnr., 1984-93, Sonnenschein, Nath & Rosenthal, Chgo., 1993-98, Foley & Lardner, Chgo., 1998—. Article editor Jour. Criminal Law and Criminology, 1974-75. Bd. trustees Village of Frankfort, 1991—. Mem. ABA, Chgo. Bar Assn. (com. mem.), Bar Assn. of 7th Cir., Prestwick Country Club (Frankfort, Ill.). Roman Catholic. Avocation: hockey. Health. Home: 904 Huntsmoor Dr Frankfort IL 60423-8747 Office: Foley & Lardner 321 N Clark St Ste 2800 Chicago IL 60610

EGAN, MICHAEL JOSEPH, retired lawyer, state legislator; b. Savannah, Ga., Aug. 8, 1926; s. Michael Joseph and Elise (Robider) E.; m. Donna Cole, Apr. 14, 1951; children: Moira Elizabeth, Michael Joseph, Donna, Cole, Roby, John Patrick. BA, Yale U., 1950; LL.B., Harvard U., 1955. Bar:

Ga., D.C. Assoc. Sutherland, Asbill & Brennan, Atlanta, 1955-61, ptnr., 1961-77, 79-97, ret. ptnr., 1998; mem. Ga. Ho. of Reps., 1966-77, minority leader, 1971-77; assoc. atty. gen. U.S. Dept. Justice, Washington, 1977-79; mem. Ga. Senate, 1989-2001. Served with U.S. Army, 1945-47, 50-52. Mem. ABA, Atlanta Bar Assn., State Bar Ga., Am. Law Inst., Am. Coll. Trust and Estate Counsel. Republican. Roman Catholic. Home: 3145 Argonne Dr NW Atlanta GA 30305-1949 Office: Sutherland Asbill & Brennan 999 Peachtree St NE Atlanta GA 30309-3915 also: 1275 Pennsylvania Ave NW Washington DC 20004-2404

EGENOLF, ROBERT F. lawyer; b. San Francisco, Jan. 23, 1946; s. John D. and Virginia (Kirkland) Butler; m. Judy Wish, Jan. 23, 1970; children: Cristi Michelle, Jonah Wish. BA, U.S. Internat. U., San Diego, 1970; JD, Calif. Western U., San Diego, 1973; LLM, U. Miami, Fla., 1974. Bar: Calif. 1973, U.S. Tax Ct. 1974. Assoc. Blum & Blum, Oakland, Calif., 1974-75; ptnr. Westwick & Collison, Santa Barbara, Calif., 1976-80, Egenolf & Moore, Santa Barbara, 1980-94. Pres., founder Calif. Exchange Corp., Santa Barbara, 1984-90, Santa Barbara Exch. Corp., 1984-90, 97—, First Exch. Corp., Santa Barbara, 1988-90, Amherst Exch. Corp., Santa Barbara, 1989—; instr., lectr. Santa Barbara City Coll., 1987—; lectr. in real estate exch. seminars Lawyers Throughout the U.S., 1987—. Bd. dirs. Tri Counties Devel. Disabilities Bd., Santa Barbara, 1977-78, Child Abuse Listening Mediation, Santa Barbara, 1979-80, Ensemble Theatre Project, Santa Barbara, 1981-83, Santa Barbara City Coll. Theatre Group, 1983-84; dir., Anti-Defamation League, Santa Barbara, 2000-; trustee Laguna Blanca Sch., 1997-2003; dir. Am. Inst. Food and Wine, 1991-93, Santa Barbara Wine Auction, 1993-94, Semana Nautica Masters Volleyball Tournament, 1993-97; mem. polit. action com. Planned Parenthood, 1995; mem. fin. devel. steering com. Santa Barbara Contemporary Arts Forum, 1995-96; dir. Santa Barbara Bd. ACLU, 2002—. With USN, 1963-69. Recipient Disting. Cmty. Svc. award, Anti-Defamation League, 2002. Mem. Calif. Bar Assn. (co-chair joint tax subsect. 1990-95), Santa Barbara Bar Assn. (bd. dirs. 1978, 95-2001, pres. 2000), Barristers Santa Barbara (pres. 1976-77). Avocations: pilot, volleyball, sailing. Estate planning, Property, real (including real estate development, water), Taxation, general. Office: Egenolf Assocs LLP 130 E Carrillo St Santa Barbara CA 93101-2111 E-mail: egenolf@egenolf.com.

EGER, JOHN MITCHELL, lawyer, educator; b. Chgo., Jan. 16, 1940; s. Elvin William and Elizabeth (Kleinman) E.; m. Judith Prescott, June 16, 1962 (div. Sept. 1982); children: Mark, Laura; m. Mary Ann Jackson, Dec. 23, 1982; children: John, Matthew. BA in English, Va. Mil. Inst., 1962; JD, John Marshall Law Sch., 1970. Bar: Ill. 1970, U.S. Ct. Appeals (7th cir.) 1970, D.C. 1972. Exec. mgr. AT&T, Chgo., 1965-70; assoc. Menk, Johnson & Bishop, Chgo., 1970; legal advisor gen. counsel FCC, Washington, 1971, legal advisor chmn., 1971-73; dep. dir. White House Office of Telecommunications Policy, Washington, 1973-74, dir., 1974-76; sole practice Washington, 1976-81; sr. v.p. CBS, Inc., N.Y.C., 1981-86; sole practice N.Y.C., 1986—; Van Deerlin endowed prof. communications and pub. policy San Diego State U., 1990—, dir. Internat. Ctr. for Communications, 1990—. Trustee Internat. Inst. Communications, London, 1986—; adviser Fletcher Sch. Law and Diplomacy, 1984—. Mem. editorial bd. The Info. Soc., 1988—; contbr. articles to profl. jours. Served to 1st lt. U.S. Army, 1962-65. Trustee Internat. Inst. Communications, London, 1986—; adviser Fletcher Sch. Law and Diplomacy, 1984—; pres. San Diego Communications Coun., 1991—. Clubs: Cosmos (Washington). Lodges: Masons. Republican. Episcopalian. Communications, Private international, Public international. Home: 2717 Caminito Prado La Jolla CA 92037-4010 Office: San Diego State U San Diego CA 92182-0412

EGGERT, RUSSELL RAYMOND, lawyer; b. Chgo., July 28, 1948; s. Ralph A. and Alice M. (Nischwitz) E.; m. Patricia Anne Alegre, 1998. AB, U. Ill., 1970, JD, 1973; postgrad., Hague Acad. Internat. Law, The Netherlands, 1972. Bar: Ill. 1973, U.S. Supreme Ct. 1979. Assoc. U. Ill., Champaign, 1973-74; asst. atty. gen. State of Ill., Chgo., 1974-79; assoc. O'Connor, Karaganis & Gail, Chgo., 1979-83; legal counsel to Ill. atty. gen., Chgo., 1983-87; ptnr. Mayer, Brown, Rowe & Maw, Chgo., 1987—. Contbr. articles to profl. jours. Mem. ABA. Democrat. Administrative and regulatory, General civil litigation, Environmental. Office: Mayer Brown Rowe & Maw 190 S La Salle St Chicago IL 60603-3441 E-mail: reggert@mayerbrownrowe.com.

EGGLETON, GLENN DAVID, lawyer; b. Sydney, NSW, Australia, Feb. 15, 1949; s. George Travers and Madeleine Helen Eggleton; life ptnr. Jane Forster, Oct. 24, 1956; children: Crystal, Elise, Amy. BA, LLB, LLM, U. Sydney. Ptnr. Clayton Utz Solicitors, Sydney, 1979—, mng. ptnr., 1985—87, Clayton Utz, Solicitors, Sydney, 1995—2000. Product liability, Alternative dispute resolution, Toxic tort. Office: Clayton Utz Solicitors Lvls 22-35 No 1 O'Connell St NSW Sydney 2000 Australia Home Fax: (612)8220 6700; Office Fax: (612) 8220 6700. Personal E-mail: geggleton@claytonutz.com. E-mail: geggleton@claytonutz.com.

EGHBAL, MORAD, geologist, lawyer; b. Tehran, Iran, June 7, 1952; s. Mohammad Ali and Fari Eghbal; m. Niloofar Sadjadi, July 17, 1983; children: Elaheh, Aria. BA, George Washington U., 1975, MA, 1977; JD, Howard U., 1989; LLM, U. Pacific, 1991. Asst. George Washington U., Washington, 1972; asst. to dir. Smithsonian Instn., Washington, 1972-75; spl. advisor to dir. Georgetown U., Washington, 1975; cons. Leo A Daly, Washington, 1975, Kodak, Rochester, N.Y., 1976; ofcl. del. 2d Circum-Pacific Energy and Mineral Resources conf., Honolulu, 1978; CEO MERE Enterprises, Washington, 1976—87; fgn. assoc. Pestalozzi, Gmuer & Heiz, Zurich, 1989; law clk. to Hon. William B. Bryant, U.S. Dist. Ct. D.C., Washington, 1990-91; trustee, CFO Riess Inst., Washington, 1983—. Dir., pres. The Grail Corp., 1983—; dir., v.p. exploration GASCO, Inc.; judge oral arguments and memls. regional and internat. semi-finals, finals Jessup competition Internat. Law Students Assn., 1990—2003, past mem. bd. dirs.; adj. prof. legal and ethical studies U. Balt., 1994—95, adj. prof. law, 1995—99, adj. prof. internat. mgmt., 1998—99, vis. asst. prof. law, internat. mgmt. and legal, ethical and hist. studies, 1999—2001, vis. assoc. prof. law, 2001—, asst. dir. Ctr. for Internat. and Comparative Law, 2000—; guest spkr. Tulane U., 1994, New Eng. Sch. Law, 1995, Mercer U. Sch. Law., 1997, U. Balt., 1999, Middle East Inst., 1999, Howard Law Sch., 2001. Rschr. The Divining Hand (E.P. Dutton), 1973-79; keynote spkr. symposium Dickinson Sch. Law, Carlisle, Pa., 1991, 1st Conf. Expeditionary Learning/Outward Bound, Greenbelt, Md., 2000; author: 1995 Philip C. Jessup Internat. Law Moot Ct. Competition Problem, 1995. Trustee Capital City Pub. Charter Sch., 2000—03. Recipient Cert. Achievement, Circum-Pacific Energy & Mineral Resources conf., 1978, Ga. U., 1980, 2d Place Nat. Roscoe Hogan Environ. Law Essay contest award ATLA, 1988, Outstanding Student Adv. award Met. Trial Lawyers Assn., 1989, Citizen Citation City and mayor of Balt., 2000, Spirit of Excellence award U. Balt. Alumni Assn., 2002, John May Faculty award U. Balt. Student Bar Assn., 2003. Mem. ABA, Nat. Bar Assn., Internat. Law Assn., Am. Assn. Petroleum Geologists (founding mem. energy minerals divsn.), Geol. Soc. Am., Soc. Econ. Paleontologists and Mineralogists, Potomac Appalachian Trails Club, Nat. Capital Area Paralegal Assn., Internat. Law Students Assn. (past mem. bd. dirs.), Nat. Lawyers Club, U.S. Japan Trade Coun., Am. Inns Ct. (Prettyman/Leventhal chpt.), Phi Delta Phi. Office: Riess Inst 9555 Friendship Station Washington DC 20016-9555 E-mail: eghbal@riess.org.

EGINTON, WARREN WILLIAM, federal judge; b. Bklyn., Feb. 16, 1924; AB, Princeton U., 1948; LLB, Yale U., 1951. Bar: N.Y. 1952, Conn. 1954. Assoc. Davis Polk & Wardwell, N.Y.C., 1951-53; ptnr. Cummings & Lockwood, Stamford, Conn., 1954-79; judge U.S. Dist. Ct., Bridgeport, Conn., 1979—. Editor-in-chief Products Liability Law Jour., 1988-93. Mem. ABA, Am. Judicature Soc., Am. Bar Found., Am. Law Inst., Conn. Bar Assn., Fed. Bar Coun., Fed. Bar Assn., Ins. Jud. Adminstrn., Jud. Leadership Devel. Coun., Internat. Jud. Acad., Fgn. Policy Assn., Raymond E. Baldwin Am. Inn of Ct. (founder, pres.). Office: US Dist Ct 915 Lafayette Blvd Ste 335 Bridgeport CT 06604-4765

EHLINGER, RALPH JEROME, lawyer; b. Oconto, Wis., Mar. 22, 1941; s. Jerome Nicholas and Margaret Ann (Otradovec) E.; m. Nancy L. McKinley, Dec. 26, 1966 (div. Oct. 1986); children: Nicholas Joseph, Martha Johanna; m. Mary Verstegen, Sept. 25, 1987; children: Autumn V., Andrea V., Jessa V., Jenna V. BA in Philosophy, St. Paul Sem., 1963; JD, Georgetown U., 1968. Bar: Wis. 1968, U.S. Dist. Ct. (ea. dist.) Wis. 1969, U.S. Dist. Ct. (we. dist.) Wis. 1977, U.S. Ct. Appeals (7th cir.) 1983, U.S. Supreme Ct. 1986, D.C. 1988, U.S. Ct. Appeals (4th cir.) 1988. Ptnr. Meissner, Tierney, Ehlinger & Whipp, Milw., 1968-86; pvt. practice Milw., 1986-87; counsel Casson, Harkins & LaPallo, Washington, 1987-88; pres. Ehlinger & Krill, SC, Milw., 1988-99, Ehlinger Law Office, Milw., 2000—; adj. prof. law Marquette U. Law Sch., 1999—. Dir. Milw. Bar Assn., 1990-93. Articles editor: The Georgetown Law Jour., 1967-68 (Outstanding Editor 1968); editor-in-chief: The Milwaukee Lawyer, 1982-84. Trustee Wis. Sch. Profl. Psychology, Milw., 1990-93; bd. pres. Grand Ave Club, Milw., 1990-92, Mental Health Assn., Milw., 1992-93; dir. Centro Legal Por Derechos Humanos, 1996-2001; mem. planning commn. Town of Richfield, 2002—. Mem. Am. Judicature Soc., Milw. Bar Assn. Found. (pres. 1994-97), Nordic Ski Club (life), Milw. Bar Assn. (Lawyer of Yr. award 1997). Democrat. Roman Catholic. Avocations: instrumental and vocal music, cross-country skiing, backpacking, canoeing, poetry. General civil litigation, Corporate, general, Health. Office: Ehlinger Law Office W175 N 11117 Stonewood Dr Germantown WI 53022 E-mail: ehlinger@execpc.com.

EHMANN, ANTHONY VALENTINE, lawyer; b. Chgo., Sept. 5, 1935; s. Anthony E. and Frances (Verweil) E.; m. Alice A. Avina, Nov. 27, 1959; children: Ann, Thomas, Jerome, Gregory, Rose, Robert. BS, Ariz. State U., 1957; JD, U. Ariz., 1960. Bar: Ariz. 1960, U.S. Tax Ct. 1960, U.S. Supreme Ct. 1968; CPA, Ariz.; cert. tax specialist, trusts and estates specialist. Spl. asst. atty. gen., 1961-68; mem. Ehmann and Hiller, Phoenix, 1969—. Rep. dist. chmn. Ariz., 1964; pres. Grand Canyon coun. Boy Scouts Am., 1987-89, mem. exec. com., 1981—, v.p. western region, 1991-99; bd. dirs. Nat. Cath. Com. on Scouting, 1995—. Recipient Silver Beaver award Boy Scouts Am., 1982, Bronze Pelican award Cath. Com. on Scouting, 1981, Silver Antelope award Boy Scouts Am., 1994. Fellow Am. Coll. Trusts and Estate Counsel; mem. State Bar Ariz. (chmn. tax sect. 1968, 69), Ctrl. Ariz. Estate Planning Coun. (pres. 1968, 69), KC (grand knight Glendale, Ariz. 1964, 65), Serra Internat. (pres. Phoenix 1992-93, dist. gov. ariz. 1993-95), Knight of Holy Sepulchre, Knight of Malta, Legatus. Republican. Roman Catholic. Estate planning, Pension, profit-sharing, and employee benefits, Corporate taxation. Office: Ehmann & Hiller 2525 E Camelback Rd Ste 720 Phoenix AZ 85016-4229 E-mail: ehmann@ehpclaw.com.

EHRENHAFT, PETER DAVID, lawyer; b. Vienna, Aug. 16, 1933; came to U.S., 1940, naturalized, 1945; s. Bruno B. and Ann J. (Polacek) E.; m. Charlotte Kennedy, May 4, 1958; children: Elizabeth Ann, James Bruno, Daniel Parker. AB with honors, Columbia Coll., 1954; LLB, M Internat. Affairs with honors, Columbia U., 1957. Bar: (N.Y.) 1958, (D.C.) 1961. Motions law clk. to U.S. Ct. Appeals (D.C. cir.), 1957—58; sr. law clk. to Chief Justice U.S. Supreme Ct., 1961—62; assoc. Cox, Langford & Brown, Washington, 1962—66, ptnr., 1966—68, Fried, Frank, Harris, Shriver & Kampelman, Washington, 1968—77; dep. asst. sec., spl. counsel tariff affairs U.S. Dept. Treasury, Washington, 1977—79; ptnr. Hughes Hubbard & Reed, Washington, 1980—83, Bryan Cave, Washington, 1984—95; mem. Ablondi, Foster, Sobin & Davidow, P.C., Washington, 1995—2001, Miller & Chevalier, Chartered, Washington, 2001—. Professorial lectr. law George Washington U., 1965-72, U. Pa., 1980-85; mem. faculty Salzburg (Austria) Seminar in Am. Studies Law Session, 1973; mem. Fed. Jud. Ctr. Study Group on Workload of Supreme Ct., 1971-74; mem. adv. com. U.S. Ct. Appeals (fed. cir.), 1992-96; mem. industry sector adv. com. on trade in svcs. Dept. Commerce and U.S. Trade Rep., 1999—. Contbr. articles and revs., primarily on internat. trade, to law jours.; mem. adv. bd. Jour. Law and Policy in Internat. Bus., 1967—, Patent, Trademark and Copyright Jour., 1970—; mem. editl. bd. Internat. Legal Materials, 1977-87. Pres. bd. trustees Nat. Child Rsch. Ctr., Washington, 1976-77; mem. adv. coun. George Washington U. Med. Ctr., 1990-96. With USAF, 1958-61, USAFR, 1962-88; judge Ct. Mil. Rev., 1987-88. Mem.: ABA (mem. coun. internat. law sect. 1983—85, 1989—97, chmn. task force on legal svcs. in Japan 1991—98, liaison to Gen. Agreement on Tariffs and Trade 1992—94, vice chair 1993—94, internat. legal scholar 1994—97, vice chair transnat. practice com. 1998—, commn. on multijurisdictional practice 2000—02), Am. Arbitration Assn. (corp. counsel com. 1993—), Washington Fgn. Law Soc. (bd. govs. 1982—92, pres. 1986—87), Am. Soc. Internat. Law, Am. Law Inst. (mem. various cons. coms.). Administrative and regulatory, Corporate, general, Private international. Home: 2510 Virginia Ave NW Washington DC 20037-1904 Office: Miller & Chevalier Chartered 655 15th St NW Washington DC 20005-5701 E-mail: pehrenhaft@milchev.com.

EHRENKRANZ, JOEL S. lawyer; b. Newark, Mar. 25, 1935; s. George J. and Hilda (Schreiber) E.; m. Anne Bick, June 9, 1963; children: Alissa, John, Jeanne. BS in Econs., U. Pa., 1956, MBA, 1957; LLB, NYU, 1961, LLM in Taxation, 1964. Bar: N.Y. 1961; CPA, N.Y. Acct. Peat, Marwick, Mitchell & Co., N.Y.C., 1957-62; sr. ptnr. Ehrenkranz & Ehrenkranz, N.Y.C., 1962—. Chmn. investment com. NYU Law Sch., 2000—; trustee Lincoln Ctr. for Performing Arts, 2003—; trustee, mem. distbn. com. Fedn. Jewish Philanthropies, N.Y.C., 1979—83, United Jewish Appeal/Fedn. Jewish Philanthropies, N.Y.C., 1982—92, pres., 1987—92; trustee Archives Am. Art, 1973—, pres., 1984—86; trustee Whitney Mus. Am. Art, 1973—, v.p., 1973—, pres., 1998—2002; trustee NYU Law Sch., 1992—; mem. grad. bd. Wharton Sch. U. Pa., 1985—; trustee, vice chmn., mem. exec. com. Mt. Sinai Med. Ctr., N.Y.C., 1987—92, chmn. fin. budgets and accts. com., 1992—95; trustee NYU, 1998—2001; mem. bd. overseers Calif. Inst. Arts, 2001—; trustee Lincoln Ctr. for Performing Arts. Mem. Century Club (White Plains, N.Y.). Office: 375 Park Ave Ste 2800 New York NY 10152-0002 also: Keeler Ln North Salem NY 10560 also: Mayfly Dr Wilson WY 83014

EHRENWERTH, DAVID HARRY, lawyer; b. Pitts., Apr. 22, 1947; s. Ben and Beatrice Lee (Schwartz) E.; m. Judith B. Ehrenwerth; children: Justin Reid, Lindsey Royce. BA, U. Pitts., 1969; JD, Harvard U., 1972. Bar: Pa. 1972, U.S. Dist. Ct. (we. dist.) Pa. 1972, U.S. Ct. Appeals (3d cir.) 1976. Asst. atty. gen. Commonwealth of Pa., Pitts., 1972-74; assoc. Kirkpatrick & Lockhart LLP, Pitts., 1974-79, ptnr., 1979—. Pres. Pitts. chpt. Am. Jewish Com., 1988-90, nat. bd. govs., 1991-95, 2001—, chmn. Pitts. chpt., 1996-98; mem. nat. adv. coun. Fed. Nat. Mortgage Assn., 1984-85; bd. dirs. Pa. Bd. Vocat. Rehab., Harrisburg, 1983-88, United Jewish Fedn., Pitts., 1991-93, Presbyn. U. Hosp., Pitts., 1993-94, Riverview Ctr. for Jewish Srs., 1991-93, U. Pitts. Cancer Inst., 1995-99, Pitts. Symphony, 2001--; bd. mem. Am. Israel Pub. Affairs Com., 1995-99, 2001—; bd. dirs. Montefiore Hosp., Pitts., 1985-93, treas., 1989, vice chmn., 1990-92, chmn., 1992-93; bd. govs. Pa. Econ. League, Western Region, 1999—. Recipient Human Rels. award Am. Jewish Com., 1999; named Pittsburgher to Watch Pitts. Mag., 1980. Mem. Pa. Bar Assn. (chmn. real estate fin. com. 1985-87), Allegheny County Bar Assn. (bar fellow, 2000—, chmn. real property sect. 1989, fellow 2000—), Harvard U. Law Alumni Assn. Western Pa. (pres. 1986-87), Concordia Club, Westmoreland Country Club, Heinz Fifty-Seven Club (chmn. 1974-91), Duquesne Club, Phi Beta Kappa. Jewish. Avocations: tennis, golf. Finance, Property, real (including real estate development, water), Securities. Home: 413 Windmere Dr Pittsburgh PA 15238-2440 Office: Kirkpatrick & Lockhart LLP 1500 Oliver Building Bldg Pittsburgh PA 15222-2312 E-mail: dehrenwerth@kl.com.

EHRLICH, STEPHEN RICHARD, lawyer; b. Rockville Centre, N.Y., Dec. 28, 1949; s. Harry Simon and Ida G. (Lable) E. BA, U. Pa., 1971; JD, U. Denver, 1977. Bar: Colo. 1977, U.S. Dist. Ct. Colo. 1977. Pvt. practice, Denver, 1977—. Mem. Assn. Trial Lawyers Am., Colo. Bar Assn., Colo. Trial Lawyers Assn., Denver Bar Assn. Avocations: skiing, tennis, bicycling. Criminal, Personal injury (including property damage), State civil litigation.

EIBERGER, CARL FREDERICK, lawyer; b. Denver, Jan. 17, 1931; s. Carl Frederick and Madeleine Anastasia (Ries) E.; children: Eileen, Carl III, Mary, James. BS in Chemistry magna cum laude, U. Notre Dame, 1952, JD magna cum laude, 1954; MBA, Denver U., 1959. Sole practice, 1954-55; ptnr. Rovira, DeMuth & Eiberger, Denver, 1957-69, Eiberger, Stacy, Smith & Martin, Denver, 1979-96; prin. Carl F. Eiberger & Assocs., Denver, 1996—. Chmn. CBA/DBA/Econs. of Law Practice Coms.; co-founder CBA/Steering Com. Labor Law Com., Denver; arbitrator Am. Arbitration Assn.; asst. bar examiner, 1963-68; lectr. on continuing legal edn. Contbr. articles to legal jours. Bd. dirs. Colo. Assn. Commerce and Industry; pres. Prospect Recreation and Park Dist.; founder Applewood Athletic Club, Jefferson County; gen. counsel Denver Symphony Orch. Recipient merit award Jefferson County Commrs., merit cert. Jefferson County Homeowners, McCafferty Disting Svc. award U. Notre Dame Law Sch.; named Man of the Yr. Notre Dame Club of Denver, Vol. of Yr. Channel 9TV, Denver., Citizen of Yr., Lions Club Internat; Prospect Dist. Pk. named in his honor. Mem. ABA, Colo. Bar Assn. (bd. govs.), Denver Bar Assn. (nominated pres.), Notre Dame Law Assn. (bd. dirs. 1965—, exec. com. 1998—), Gov. Adv. Coun. to Colo dept. of labor, Notre Dame Club (pres., bd. dirs.), Athletic Club (Denver). Roman Catholic. General civil litigation, Labor (including EEOC, Fair Labor Standards Act, labor-management relations, NLRB, OSHA). Home: 14330 Fairview Ln Golden CO 80401-2050 Office: 14330 Fairview Ln Golden CO 80401-2050

EICHENBERGER, JERRY ALAN, lawyer; b. Columbus, Ohio, Apr. 16, 1947; m. Candace R. Roberson, Jan. 17, 1971; 1 child, Sara Marie. BS, Ohio State U., 1970; JD, Capital U., 1975. Bar: Ohio 1975, U.S. Supreme Ct. 1978, U.S. Dist. Ct. (no. and so. dists.) Ohio 175, U.S. Ct. Appeals (6th cir.) 1976. Ptnr. Martin & Eichenberger, Columbus, 1975-90, Crabbe, Brown, Jones, Potts & Schmidt, Columbus, 1990-2000, Eichenberger & Assocs., Columbus, 2001—. Adj. prof. aviation law Ohio State U., Columbus, 1988-90. Author: General Aviation Law, 1990, 2d edit., 1998, Your Pilot's License, 1998, Cross Country Flying, 1996, Handling In-Flight Emergencies, 2001; contbr. articles to bus. and comml. aviation jours. Lt. col. CAP, chief check pilot 1980-84, legal officer, 1986-90. Named Ky. Col. Commonwealth Ky., 1972. Mem. ABA, Lawyer-Pilots Bar Assn., Ohio State Bar Assn., Aviation Ins. Assn., Aircraft Owners and Pilots Assn., Exptl. Aircraft Assn., Gen. Aviation Operators Assn., Columbus Maennerchor Club, Masons, Shriners. Republican. Baptist. Avocations: aviation, bicycling. Aviation, Construction, Product liability. Office: Eichenberger & Assocs 6099 Frantz Rd Columbus OH 43017 E-mail: JEichenberger@ehlawyers.com.

EICHER, DONALD E., III, lawyer; b. Vicksburg, Miss., July 26, 1969; s. Donald E. Jr. and Rosemary E. Eicher; m. Amy Christine Carlson, May 30, 1998. BBA cum laude, U. Miss., 1991, JD, 1994. Bar: Miss. 1994, U.S. Dist. Ct. (no. and so. dists.) Miss. 1994, U.S. Ct. Appeals (5th cir.) 1994, Ala. 1996, U.S. Dist. Ct. (ctrl. dist.) Ala. 1999, U.S. Ct. Appeals (11th cir.) 1999. Assoc. McTeer Assocs., Greenville, Miss., 1994-96, William L. Bambach, Columbus, Miss., 1996; atty. Malone Law Firm PLLC, Ridgeland, Miss., 1996-97; assoc. McDavid Noblin & West PLLC, Jackson, Miss., 1997—. Mem. ABA, Miss. Oil and Gas Lawyers Assn., Hinds County Bar Assn. Commercial, consumer (including collections, credit), Oil, gas, and mineral, Property, real (including real estate development, water). Home: 204 Barkley Ln Brandon MS 39047-7664 Office: McDavid Noblin West PLLC 248 E Capitol St Ste 840 Jackson MS 39201-2505 E-mail: mnwlaw@msn.com.

EICHHORN, FREDERICK FOLTZ, JR., retired lawyer; b. Gary, Ind., Oct. 16, 1930; s. Frederick Foltz and Adele D. (DeLano) E.; m. Julia Abel, Aug. 27, 1955; children: Jill, Thomas, Timothy, Linda. BS, Ind. U., 1952, JD, 1957. Bar: Ind. 1957, U.S. Ct. Appeals (7th cir.) 1957, U.S. Dist. Ct. (no dist.) Ind. 1957, U.S. Supreme Ct. 1973. Assoc. Gavit, Eichhorn, Gary, 1957-62; ptnr. Eichhorn, Eichhorn & Link, and predecessor firm, 1963-76; sr. ptnr. Eichhorn, Eichhorn & Link and predecessor firm, 1977-96; ret., 1996. Mem. Ind. Sesquicentennial Commn.; chmn. Lake County Cmty. Devel. Com., 1984; commr. Conf. Uniform State Law; bd. dirs. Gary Housing Authority, 1972—75, Planned Parenthood, Gary Police Civil Svc. Commn., 1975—82; bd. dirs., founder Miller Citizens Corp., 1971; bd. dirs. N.W. Ind. Symphony; trustee Ind. U., 1990—, bd. pres., 2002—; chmn. N.W. Ind. Forum, World Affairs Coun., Gary Regional Airport Task Force, 1989—94. With USAF, 1952—54. Fellow: Ind. Bar Found., Am. Bar Found.; mem.: ABA (membership chmn. for Ind. ho. of dels.), Ind. Soc. Chgo. (trustee 1989—92), Midwest Gas Assn. (legal affairs sect. 1982), Am. Gas Assn. (state rate litigation com. 1982, regulation of gas supplies com., state regulatory matters com.), Ind. Bar Assn. (inst. chmn. white collar crime 1979, treas. 1977—78, bd. mgr. 1979—80, v.p. 1983—84, pres. 1985—86), Delta Tau Delta, Phi Delta Phi. Corporate, general, Utilities, public, Securities.

EICHLER, BURTON LAWRENCE, lawyer; b. Newark, Mar. 1, 1933; s. Philip and Anna (Kessler) E.; children— Betsy, Peter, Thomas. BS, Ohio State U., 1954; LLB, Rutgers U., 1957. Bar: NJ 1958, N.Y. 1983, U.S. Dist. Ct. NJ 1958, U.S. Ct. Appeals (3d cir.) 1981. Assoc., ptnr. Zucker, Brach & Eichler and predecessor, Newark, 1958-59, ptnr., 1959-67; ptnr. Eichler, Rosenberg & Silver, Newark, 1967-69, Brach, Eichler, Rosenberg, Silver, Newark, 1969-72, Brach, Eichler, Rosenberg, Silver, Bernstein & Hammer PA, East Orange, NJ, 1972-81, Brach, Eichler, Rosenberg, Silver, Bernstein, Hammer & Gladstone PC, Roseland, NJ, 1981— ; chmn. dist. fee arbitration com. for Essex County, Dist. V-C, NJ Sup. Ct., 1983-86. Pres., chmn. bd. United Cerebral Palsy, East Oarnge, 1967-69; mem. South Orange/Maplewood Bd. Edn., 1979-83, v.p., 1981-83, 99--; bd. dirs. YM-YWHA Met. NJ, West Orange, 1970-74, 99-2002; former trustee Congregation B'nai Jeshurun, Short Hills, NJ Recipient J.H. Cohn Outstanding Young Leadership award Jewish Cmty. Fedn. Met. NJ, East Orange, 1961; named Outstanding Citizen, NJ Acad. Medicine, 1998, one of Best Lawyers in NJ, NJ Monthly. Mem. Eseex County Bar Assn. (chmn. med.-legal affairs com. 1985-86), NJ Bar Assn., ABA, Am. Health Lawyers Assn. Administrative and regulatory, Health, Property, real (including real estate development, water). Office: Brach Eichler Rosenberg Silver Bernstein Hammer & Gladstone PC 101 Eisenhower Pkwy Roseland NJ 07068 E-mail: beichler@bracheichler.com.

EICKMEYER, EVAN, lawyer; BA, U. So. Calif., 1990; JD, U. of the Pacific, 1993. Bar: Calif. 1993, U.S. Dist. Ct. (ea. dist.) Calif. 1993, U.S. Ct. Appeals (9th cir.) 1996, U.S. Dist. Ct. (ctrl. dist.) Calif. 1998, U.S. Supreme Ct. 1999. Dep. dist. atty. Sacramento (Calif.) County Dist. Atty.'s Office, 1994-95. Mem. Nat. Eagle Scout Assn. (life). Toxic tort, Environmental, Appellate. Office: Miller & Sawyer 1651 Response Rd 2nd Fl Sacramento CA 95815-5253

EIGNER, WILLIAM WHITLING, lawyer; b. Dover, Ohio, Feb. 4, 1959; s. Stanley Spencer and Jeraldine (Lippy) E.; m. Jeanne Beach, May 24, 1987. BA, Stanford U., 1981; JD, U. Va., 1986. Bar: Calif. 1986, U.S. Dist. Ct. (so. dist.) Calif. 1986. Jud. intern U.S. Supreme Ct., Washington, 1981; assoc. Higgs, Fletcher & Mack, San Diego, 1986-89, Procopio, Cory, Hargreaves & Savitch, LLP, San Diego, 1989-95, ptnr., 1995—. Mem. bd. advisors QuantumThink Group, Inc. (QThink), Sky River Comms., Inc.; mem. San Diego Venture Group; mem. San Diego Telecom Coun. and chmn. policy com. Contbr. articles to profl. jours. Trustee, La Jolla (Calif.) Town Coun., 1988-92. chmn. landuse com., 1988-90. Recipient spl. commendation San Diego City Coun. Mem. ABA, State Bar Calif., San Diego County Bar Assn. (bus. sects.), Greater San Diego C. of C. (bd. dirs. 1998-2001, 03—, chmn. bus. recognition and awards com. 1989-98, chmn. emerging bus. com. 1998-2000, energy com. nominations com. and pub. policy com.). Republican. Jewish. Avocations: tennis, civil war history. Corporate, general, Legislative, Mergers and acquisitions. Office: Procopio Cory Hargreaves & Savitch LLP 530 B St Ste 2100 San Diego CA 92101-4496 E-mail: wwe@procopio.com.

EILAND, GARY WAYNE, lawyer; b. Houston, Apr. 25, 1951; s. William N. and Louise A. (Foltin) E.; m. Sandra K. Streetman, Aug. 4, 1973; children; Trina L. Wuensche, Peter T. BBA, U. Tex., 1973, JD, 1976. Bar: Tex. 1976, U.S. Ct. Claims 1977, U.S. Ct. Appeals (5th cir.) 1978, U.S. Ct. Appeals (11th cir.) 1981, U.S. Supreme Ct. 1989. Assoc. Wood, Lucksinger & Epstein, Houston, 1976-81, ptnr., 1981-91, Vinson & Elkins L.L.P., Houston, 1991—; ptnr., co-chair health industry group, 1996—. Lectr. Aspen Health Care Industry seminars, Aspen Pubs., Inc., Rockville, Md., 1978-89, HLO Health Care seminars, 1990-91; charter mem. health law exam. commn. Tex. State Bd. Legal Specialization, 2002—. Mem. Tex. Bar Assn. (chmn. health law sect. 1991-92), Am. Acad. Healthcare Attys. (bd. dirs. 1991-97, pres. 1996-97), Am. Health Lawyers Assn. (past pres., exec. com. 1997-98), Healthcare Fin. Mgmt. Assn. (pres. Tex. Gulf Coast chpt. 1992-93, Region 9 chpt. liaison rep. 1994-95, compliance officers forum adv. coun. 2000-02, Founders medal of honor 1999), Assn. Am. Med. Colls., Houston Ctr. Club, Bentwater Yacht and Country Club. Administrative and regulatory, Government contracts and claims, Health. Home: 23319 Holly Hollow Tomball TX 77377-3684 Office: Vinson & Elkins LLP 1001 Fannin St Ste 2300 Houston TX 77002-6760 E-mail: geiland@velaw.com.

EILEN, HOWARD SCOTT, lawyer, mediator; b. N.Y.C., Mar. 28, 1954; m. Sharon R. Kornbluth, Oct. 21, 1979; children: Michael, Jeffrey. BA summa cum laude, MA, CUNY, 1975; JD, St. John's U., 1979. Bar: N.Y. 1980, U.S. Tax Ct. 1980, U.S. Dist. Ct. (so., ea. dists.) N.Y. 1980, U.S. Dist. Ct. (ea. dist.) Mich. 1982. Assoc. Bloom & Tese, N.Y.C., 1980-83; ptnr. Bloom & Eilen, N.Y.C., 1983-86, 87-94; of counsel Spengler, Carlson, Gubar, Brodsky & Frischling, N.Y.C., 1986-87; ptnr. Lehman & Eilen, Uniondale, N.Y., 1994—. Arbitrator Nat. Assn. Securities Dealers, Inc., Nat. Futures Assn., Am. Arbitration Assn., U.S. Arbitration and Mediation, Inc., N.Y. Stock Exch., Inc.; mediator Nat. Assn. Securities Dealers, Inc.; spl. master N.Y. Supreme Ct.; mem. faculty securities arbitration program Practising Law Inst.; lectr. securities arbitration program Nassau Acad. Law. Contbg. editor Futures Tribune Mag., Japan. Mem. N.Y. County Lawyers Assn. (com. on securities and exchs. 1983—, chmn. subcom. on commodities regulation, com. on arbitration and conciliation 1990—), Nassau County Bar Assn. (securities law com.). Alternative dispute resolution, General civil litigation, Securities. Office: Lehman & Eilen LLP Ste 505 50 Charles Lindbergh Blvd Uniondale NY 11553-3650 E-mail: heilen@lehmaneilen.com.

EIMER, NATHAN PHILIP, lawyer; b. Chgo., June 26, 1949; s. Irving A. and Charlotte Eimer; m. Kathleen L. Roach; children: Micah Jacob, Noah Joseph, Daniel Jordan, Anna Beatrice. AB in Econs. magna cum laude, U. Ill., 1970; JD cum laude, Northwestern U., 1973. Bar: Ill. 1973, U.S. Supreme Ct. 1978, N.Y. 1985, Tex. 1998. Assoc. Sidley & Austin, Chgo., 1973-80, ptnr., mem. exec. com., 1980—2000; founding ptnr. Eimer Stahl Klevorn & Solberg, Chgo., 2000—. Adj. prof. Law Sch., Northwestern U., Chgo., 1989-96. Note and comment editor Northwestern U. Law Rev., 1972-73. Bd. dirs. Chgo. Lawyers Com. for Civil Rights, 1991—, pres., 1993-94; bd. dirs. UNICEF, 1992-93, Infant Welfare Soc., Chgo., exec. v.p., 1992-96, pres., 1996-98; mem. adv. bd. Children & Family Justice Ctr., Northwestern U. Legal Clinic, 1996—. Mem. ABA, Univ. Club. Antitrust, General civil litigation. Office: Eimer Stahl Klevorn & Solberg Ste 1100 224 S Michigan Ave Chicago IL 60604 E-mail: neimer@eimerstahl.com.

EINHORN, DAVID ALLEN, lawyer; b. Bklyn., Dec. 11, 1961; s. Harold and Jane Ellen (Wiener) Einhorn. BA in Computer Sci. magna cum laude, Columbia U., 1983, JD, 1986. Bar: N.Y. 1987, DC 1988, U.S. Dist. Ct. (so. and ea. dists.) N.Y. 1989, U.S. Ct. Appeal (fed. cir.) 1992, U.S. Dist. Ct. (no. dist.) Calif. 1994, U.S. Dist. Ct. Conn. 2003. Assoc. Kaye, Scholer, Fierman, Hays & Handler, N.Y.C., 1986-89; ptnr. Anderson Kill & Olick, PC, N.Y.C., 1989—. Lectr. Am. Conf. Inst. Co-author: (2-vol. treatise) Patent Licensing Transactions; editor-in-chief: Intellectual Property for the New Millenium, 1997—; contbr. articles to profl. jours.; columnist: Grapevine. Lt. col. JAGC, N.Y. Guard, 1987—. Named to Order of Merit, Les Amis du Vin, 1982; recipient Nat. prize, Nathan Burkan Copyright Essay Competition, 1985, Off Off Broadway Rev. award for producing Ionesco Fest.; Fiske Stone scholar, Columbia U., 1985. Mem.: ABA (chmn. software patent subcom. 1988—91, software licensing subcom. 1991—95, software copyright subcom. 1995—96, chmn. broadcasting, sound recordings, and performing artists com. 2000—02, chmn. com. trademarks and internet 2002—), Licensing Execs. Soc. (lectr.), DC Bar Assn. (computer law sect.), Internat. Trademark Assn., N.Y. Intellectual Property Law Assn., Am. Intellectual Property Law Assn. (chmn. software copyright subcom. 1999—), Intellectual Property Owners Assn. (chmn. cybersquatting com. 2003—), Untitled Theater Co. #61, Ltd. (chmn. bd. dirs., producing dir., treas. 1994—), Tasters Guild (v.p., bd. dirs. 1997—), N.Y. Soc. Mil. and Naval Officers (v.p. 1995—). Democrat. Jewish. Avocations: tennis, racquetball, wine tasting, theater . Computer, Intellectual property, Military. Home: 2373 Broadway Apt 802 New York NY 10024-2835 Office: Anderson Kill & Olick PC 1251 Ave of the Americas New York NY 10020-1182 E-mail: deinhorn@andersonkill.com.

EINSTEIN, STEVEN HENRY, investment banker, lawyer, accountant; b. N.Y.C., Aug. 14, 1954; s. Ralph Gunther and Beatrice (Katz) E. BS, Lehigh U., 1976; JD, Seton Hall U., 1979; LLM in Taxation, NYU, 1985. Lic. CPA, N.Y., N.J.; Bar: N.J. 1979, N.Y. 1985, U.S. Dist. Ct. N.J. 1979, U.S. Tax Ct. 1982, U.S. Ct. Appeals (3d cir.) 1983, U.S. Supreme Ct. 1985. Judicial law clk. to presiding justice Superior Ct., Hackensack, NJ, 1979—80; assoc. Wacks, Hirsch, Ramsey & Berman Esqs., Morristown, NJ, 1980—81; sr. tax mgr. Touche Ross & Co., Newark, 1981—86; v.p., investment banking, mergers & acquisitions dept. Paine Webber Capital Mkts., N.Y.C., 1986—88; v.p., merchant banking/pvt. equity Kluge, Subotnick, Perkowski & Co., N.Y.C., 1988—90; mng. dir. Price Waterhouse Corp. Fin. Group, N.Y.C., 1991—98; ptnr. & mng. dir. Pricewaterhouse Coopers Securities LLP, N.Y.C., 1998—99, ptnr., chmn.'s office, global leader, corp. devel., 1999—. Mem. editl. bd. Corp. Taxation Mag.; contbr. articles to profl. jours. Mem. ABA, AICPAs, N.J. State Bar Assn., N.Y. State Bar Assn., Essex County Bar Assn. (taxation divsn.), N.J. Soc. CPAs, Beta Gamma Sigma, Phi Eta Sigma. Jewish. Corporate taxation, Estate taxation, Personal income taxation. Home: 174 Carter St New Canaan CT 06840-5007 Office: Pricewaterhouse Coopers Securities LLP 1177 Avenue of the Americas New York NY 10036-2714

EISEMAN, NEAL MARTIN, lawyer; b. Perth Amboy, N.J., Dec. 13, 1955; s. Lawrence and Ethel (Goldenberg) E.; m. Lynda Bolnick, Sept. 4, 1988. BA in Journalism, Polit. Sci., George Washington U., 1978; JD, St. John's U., 1981. Bar: N.Y. 1982, N.J. 1981, U.S. Dist. Ct. N.J. 1981, U.S. Dist. Ct. (ea. dist., so. dist.) N.Y. 1982, U.S. Ct. Appeals (2d cir.) 1984, U.S. Supreme Ct. 1985. Assoc. Goetz, Fitzpatrick & Flynn, N.Y.C., 1981-86, ptnr., 1987—, mng. ptnr., 1999—. Panel of arbitrators, Am. Arbitration Assn., N.Y.C., 1987—; arbitrator small claims dept. N.Y. Civil Ct., 1990—; prof. masters program in real estate and constrn. mgmt. Real Estate Inst. NYU, 1990—. State civil litigation, Construction, Corporate, general. Office: Goetz Fitzpatrick LLP 1 Penn Plz Ste 4401 New York NY 10119-0196

EISEN, ERIC ANSHEL, lawyer; b. N.Y.C., Apr. 9, 1950; s. Morton and Victoria (Goldstein) E.; m. Claire L. Shapiro, Jan. 6, 1979; children: Rebecca, Jennifer, Melissa. AB, U. Mich., 1971, JD magna cum laude, 1975. Bar: Alaska 1976, D.C. 1977, Md. 1988. Law clk. to presiding justice Alaska Supreme Ct., Fairbanks, 1975-76; assoc. Covington & Burling, Washington, 1976-81, Birch, Horton, Bittner, Washington, 1981-85, ptnr., 1985-93, Eisen Law Offices, Bethesda, Md., 1993—. Prin. speaker various seminars and colloquia on energy and bus. matters. Contbr. articles to legal publs. Pres. Wildwood Hills Citizens Assn., Bethesda, Md., 1987—; sec. N. Bethesda Cong. Citizens Assns., 1989-90. Mem. ATLA, Energy Bar Assn. (antitrust com.), D.C. Bar Assn., Montgomery County Bar Assn. (chmn. bus. sect., mem. intellectual property and litig. sects.), Toastmasters, Order of Coif. Avocation: woodworking. Labor (including EEOC, Fair Labor Standards Act, labor-management relations, NLRB, OSHA), General civil litigation, FERC practice. Office: Eisen Law Offices 10028 Woodhill Rd Bethesda MD 20817-1218 also: 1101 30th St NW Ste 500 Washington DC 20007-3708

EISEN, SAUL, lawyer; b. Cleve., July 26, 1935; s. Ben and Manya (Parsons) E.; m. Hermine Beth Greene, Dec. 16, 1961; children: Barbara, Brian, Abigail. BA, Case Western Res. U., 1957, LLb, 1959. Bar: Ohio 1960, U.S. Dist. Ct. (no. dist.) Ohio 1960, U.S. Supreme Ct. 1960. Ptnr. Blane, Eisen & Wasserman, Cleve., 1960-63, Starkoff, Yelsky & Eisen, Cleve., 1963-73, Yelsky, Eisen & Singer, Cleve., 1973-80, Javitch & Eisen Co., L.P.A., Cleve., 1981-92, Javitch, Block, Eisen & Rathbone, Cleve., 1992—. U.S. trustee Region 9, 2002—. Bd. dirs., pres. Beachwood (Ohio) Sch. Bd., 1972—; pres. Friends of Beachwood Library, 1982-87; acting judge Shaker Heights Ohio Mcpl. Ct., 1994—. Mem. Nat. Assn. Bankruptcy Trustees (chmn. membership com. 1988—, past pres.), Cleve. Bar Assn. (sec. bankruptcy sect. 1988—), Cuyahoga County Bar Assn. (chmn. bankruptcy sect. 1988—, trustee, 1st v.p., pres. 2000-01), Masons (pres. 1969). Bankruptcy, Commercial, consumer (including collections, credit). Home: 25010 Duffield Rd Cleveland OH 44122-3263 Office: US Trustee 200 Public Sq Ste 20-3000 Cleveland OH 44114 E-mail: saul.eisen@usdoj.gov.

EISEN, STEVEN JEFFREY, lawyer; b. Nashville, May 14, 1958; s. Harvey and Ann Eisen; m. Gay Lisa Levine, June 26, 1988. BA in Econs., Northwestern U., 1979; MBA, Vanderbilt U., Nashville, 1983; JD, Vanderbilt U., 1983. Bar: Tenn 1983, U.S. Dist. Ct. (mid. dist.) Tenn., U.S. Ct. Appeals (6th cir.). Assoc. Bone, Langford & Armistead, Nashville, 1983-87; ptnr. Baker, Donelson, Bearman & Caldwell, Nashville, 1988—. European Inst. scholar, 1980, Owen scholar, 1979. Mem. ABA, Tenn. Bar Assn., Nashville Bar Assn. Avocations: tennis, boating. Banking, Corporate, general, Securities. Office: Baker Donelson Bearman & Caldwell 211 Commerce St Ste 1000 Nashville TN 37201

EISENBERG, THEODORE, law educator; b. Bklyn., Oct. 26, 1947; s. Abraham Louis and Esther (Waldman) E.; m. Lisa Wright, Nov. 27, 1971; children: Katherine Wright, Ann Marie, Thomas Peter. BA, Swarthmore Coll., 1969; JD, U. Pa., 1972. Bar: Pa. 1972, N.Y. 1974, U.S. Ct. Appeals (2d cir.) 1974, Calif. 1977. Law clk. U.S. Ct. Appeals, D.C. Cir., 1972-73; law clk. to U.S. Supreme Ct. Justice Earl Warren, 1973; assoc. Debevoise & Plimpton, N.Y.C., 1974-77; prof. law UCLA Law Sch., 1977-81, Cornell U. Law Sch., Ithaca, N.Y., 1981-96, Henry Allen Mark prof. law, 1996—. Vis. prof. law Harvard U. Law Sch., 1984-85; vis. prof. Law, Stanford U. Law Sch., 1987. Author: Civil Rights Legislation, 1981, 4th edit., 1996, Bankruptcy and Debtor-Creditor Law, 1984, 2d edit., 1988; editor Jour. Empirical Legal Studies; mem. adv. bd. Law and Soc. Rev., Am. Law and Econ. Rev.; contbr. articles to profl. jours. Am. Bar Found grantee, NSF grantee. Fellow Royal Statis. Soc.; mem. ABA, Assn. Bar City N.Y., Law and Soc. Assn., Am. Law and Econ. Assn., Am. Bankruptcy Inst. Office: Cornell U Law Sch Myron Taylor Hall Ithaca NY 14853 E-mail: te13@cornell.edu.

EISENMENGER, KATHY L. arbitrator, mediator, lawyer; b. Salt Lake City, May 20, 1952; d. Cletus J. Eisenmenger and Beverly J. Howell; m. Ernest J. Duarte, June 13, 1970 (div.); 1 child, Karey L. Duarte; m. William J. Drasky, Mar. 2, 1985. AA, Barstow (Calif.) C.C., 1976; BSBA, U. of Redlands, 1981; JD, Tex. Wesleyan U., 1995. Bar: Tex. 1995, U.S. Supreme Ct. 2002. Labor rels. specialist Dept. of Navy/Marine Corps, Hawaii, 1976—83; labor rels. advisor Office of Civilian Pers. Mgmt., Pacific Region, Pearl Harbor, Hawaii, 1983—85; labor rels. specialist/officer USAF Acad., Colorado Springs, 1985—87; hearing examiner/factfinder Air Force Civilian Appellate Rev. Agy., Denver, 1987—89; labor rels. dir. Phila. Naval Shipyard, Phila., 1989—91; labor arbitrator-mediator-attorney Dispute Resolution Svcs., Highland Village, Tex., 1992—. Factfinder-mediator Delany, Siegel, Zorn & Assoc., Inc., Boston, 1991—2002. Mediator Tarrant County Dispute Resolution Ctr., Fort Worth, Tex., 1992—94; arbitrator Ford Motor Co. Dispute Settlement Bd., Dallas, 1997—2001. Mem.: Assn. for Conflict Resolution (assoc.), State Bar of Tex. (assoc.; com. for pro bono 1995—2002, labor and employment sect.), Indsl. Rels. Rsch. Assn. (assoc.; v.p., sec./treas. of chpt. 1992—2002). Avocations: long-distance cycling, tennis, golf, creative writing, cooking. Office: 2530 Rosedale St Highland Village TX 75077 Fax: 972-317-9020. E-mail: keisenmenger@attbi.com.

EISERT, EDWARD GAVER, lawyer; b. N.Y.C., May 26, 1948; s. Israel Jay and Bess (Gaver) E.; div.; children: Carolyn B., Stephen J. AB, Cornell U., 1969; JD, NYU, 1973. Bar: N.Y. 1974. Law clk. to Judge Charles L. Brieant U.S. Dist. Ct. (so. dist.) N.Y., N.Y.C., 1973-74; assoc. Simpson Thacher & Bartlett, N.Y.C., 1974-76, Schulte Roth & Zabel, N.Y.C., 1976-80, ptnr., 1981—2002; sr. v.p., gen. corp. counsel Fiduciary Trust Co. Internat., N.Y.C., 2002—. Bd. dirs. N.Y. Small Bus. Venture Fund LLC., 1998—. Note and comment editor NYU Law Rev., 1972-73. Mem. ABA (com. on fed. regulation of securities 1983—, subcom. on ann. rev. fed. regulation of securities 1983-89, subcom. on mcpl. and govtl. obligations 1984-92, subcom. on investment cos. and investment advisors 1992—), Internat. Bar Assn., N.Y. Stat Bar Assn., Assn. Bar City N.Y., Univ. Club N.Y.C. Corporate, general, Finance, Securities. Home: 302 Church St White Plains NY 10603-3525 Office: Fiduciary Trust Co International 600 Fifth Avenue New York NY 10020

EITTREIM, RICHARD MACNUTT, lawyer; b. Neptune, N.J., Feb. 10, 1945; s. Wilbur Lawrence and Leta Blanch (MacNutt) E.; m. Margaret Anne Nolan, June 11, 1967; children: Theodore Scott, Elisabeth Marie, Samantha Leta. AB, Yale U., 1967; JD, U. Va., 1973. Bar: N.J. 1973, U.S. Dist. Ct. N.J. 1973, U.S. Ct. Appeals (3d cir.) 1984, (11th cir.) 1996, U.S. Supreme Ct. 1998. Assoc. McCarter & English, Newark, N.J., 1973-80, ptnr., 1980—. Trustee Children's Psychiat. Ctr., Eatontown, N.J., 1977-87, Riverview Hosp. Found., Red Bank, N.J., 1988-93. Mem. ABA, N.J. State Bar Assn., Essex County Bar Assn., Phi Alpha Delta, Sea Bright Lawn Tennis and Cricket Club (pres. 2000—, bd. govs. 1994—), Monmouth Boat Club (treas. 1983-86), Essex Club, Yale Club (pres. 1986-87). Democrat. Presbyterian. Federal civil litigation, Insurance, Libel. Home: 100 Woodland Dr Fair Haven NJ 07704 Office: McCarter & English 4 Gateway Ctr 100 Mulberry St Newark NJ 07102-4004 E-mail: reittreim@mccarter.com.

EKDAHL, JON NELS, lawyer, association executive; b. Topeka, Nov. 15, 1942; s. Oscar S. and Dorothy O. (Ekdahl) M.; m. Marcia Opp, May 24, 1975; children: Kirsten, Erika, Kristofer. AB magna cum laude, Harvard U., 1964, LLB, 1968; MS in Econs., London Sch. Econs., 1965. Bar: Ill. 1969, U.S. Ct. Appeals (7th cir.) 1981, U.S. Supreme Ct. 1981. Assoc. Sidley & Austin, Chgo., 1968—73, ptnr., 1973—75; mng. ptnr., gen. counsel Andersen Worldwide SC, Chgo., 1975—2000; sr. v.p., gen. counsel AMA, Chgo., 2001—. With USAR, 1968-74. Mem. ABA, Chgo. Bar Assn., Mid-Am. Club, Chgo. Club. Office: Am Med Assn 515 N State St Chicago IL 60610 E-mail: jon_ekdahl@ama-assn.org.

EKLUND, CLAUDIA RIETH, lawyer; b. Cleve., Nov. 9, 1951; s. Carlton E. and Mildred (Olson) R.; m. Paul D. Eklund, Dec. 16, 1978; children—Craig, Kristen. B.A., Cleve. State U., 1974; J.D., Cleve.-Marshall U., 1979. Bar: Ohio 1979, U.S. Dist. Ct. (no. dist.) Ohio 1981, U.S. Ct. Appeals (6th cir.) 1983; cert. civil trial lawyer (Best Lawyers in Am. award). Ptnr. Lowe, Eklund, Wakefield & Mulvihill, Cleve., 1979—. Mem. ABA, ATLA, Ohio State Bar Assn., Greater Cleve. Bar Assn. General civil litigation, Personal injury (including property damage). Home: 29232 Regency Cir Westlake OH 44145-6701 Office: Lowe Eklund Wakefield 610 Skylight Office Tower 1660 W 2nd St Ste 610 Cleveland OH 44113-1497

ELA, WILLIAM MACHARG, judge, mediator, arbitrator; b. Grand Junction, Colo., May 11, 1923; s. Wendell Dennett and Lucy Ferril Ela; m. Shirley P. Phillips, Oct. 3, 1946; children: Beth Ela Wilkens, Wendell Phillips, Thomas Nelson, Daniel Dennett, Steven Dean. LLB, Harvard U., 1949; D for Pub. Svc., Mesa State Coll., 1993. Bar: Colo. 1949, U.S. Dist. Ct. Colo. 1949. Pvt. practice Adams, Heckman, Traylor & Ela, Grand Junction, 1949-65; dist. ct. judge, chief judge State of Colo., Grand Junction, 1965-87, sr. dist. judge, 1987-99. Faculty, faculty advisor Nat. Jud. Coll., Reno, 1966-75. Contbr. articles to profl. jours. Mem. Grand Junction Lion's Club, 1955-98; trustee, pres. Goodwin Found., Grand Junction, 1975-98; founding co-chmn. Grand Junction Mesa County Riverfront Commn., 1988-96. Lt. (j.g.) USN, 1944-46, ATO, PTO. Fellow Am. Coll. Trust and Estates Coun.; mem. ABA, Colo. Bar Assn. (sect. chmn., v.p. 1958), Mesa County Bar Assn. (pres. and numerous coms. 1949-88) Avocations: cross country skiing, bicycling, fishing, gardening, astronomy. Home and Office: 3051 L Rd Hotchkiss CO 81419-9407 E-mail: silvers@acsol.net.

ELBERGER, RONALD EDWARD, lawyer; b. Newark, Mar. 13, 1945; s. Morris and Clara (Denes) Elberger; m. Rena Ann Brodey, Feb. 15, 1975; children: Seth, Rebecca. AA, George Washington U., 1964, BA, 1966; JD, Am. U., 1969. Bar: Md. 1969, D.C. 1970, Ind. 1971, U.S. Ct. Appeals (7th cir.) 1971, U.S. Supreme Ct. 1973. Atty. Balt. Legal Aid Bur., 1969-70; chief counsel Legal Services Orgn., Indpls., 1970-72; ptnr. Elberger & Stanton, Indpls., 1974-76; assoc. Bose, McKinney & Evans, LLP, Indpls., 1972—74, ptnr., 1976—; asst. sec. Chip Ganassi Racing Teams, Inc., 1998—. V.p. Worldwide Slacks, Inc., 1984—92, Cardboard Shoe Prodns., Inc., 1989—93; asst. sec., v.p., litig. counsel Emmis Comm. Corp., 1986—2002. Mem., v.p. Med. Licensing Bd., Ind., 1982—98; pres., chmn. bd. dirs. Ind. Civil Liberties Union, Indpls., 1972—77, bd. dirs., 1972—77, 1980—82; mem. nat. coun. media and pub. affairs George Washington U., 2000—; bd. dirs. Jewish Cmty. Rels. Coun., 1997—2000, ACLU, N.Y.C., 1972—77; trustee Children's Mus. Indpls., 1994—2003, Disting. advisor, 2003—; bd. dirs. Flanner Ho. Indpls., Inc., 1999—. Fellow Reginald Heber Smith, U. Pa., 1969—71. Fellow: Ind. Bar Found., Indpls. Bar Found.; mem.: ABA, Ind. Bar Assn. Democrat. Jewish. Avocations: fishing, music, gardening. Federal civil litigation, State civil litigation, Entertainment. Office: Bose McKinney & Evans LLP 2700 First Indiana Pla 135 N Pennsylvania St Indianapolis IN 46204-2400

ELBERT, CHARLES STEINER, lawyer; b. St. Louis, May 18, 1950; s. Harold I. and Carol B. (Steiner) E.; m. Karen Berry, Dec. 9, 1979; children: Matthew Berry, Lisa Beth. AB, Washington U., 1972; JD cum laude, St. Louis U., 1976. Bar: Mo. 1976, Ill. 1977, U.S. Dist. Ct. (ea. and we. dists.) Mo. 1977, U.S. Ct. Appeals (8th cir.) 1977, U.S. Supreme Ct. 1985. Assoc. Kohn, Shands, Elbert, Gianoulakis & Giljum, LLP, St. Louis, 1976-81, ptnr., 1982—. Spl. rep. 22d Jud. Bar Com., St. Louis, 1978-88; spk. labor and employment law CLEs. Contbr. articles to profl. jours. Trustee Clayton Gardens Neighborhood Assn., Mo., 1983-84, 85-86, pres., 1984-85; bd. dirs. St. Louis chpt. Am. Diabetes Assn., 1998—, St. Louis chpt. Am. Jewish Com., 1984-97, mem. nat. legal com., 1997—; sec., 1994-97; v.p. Nursery Found., St. Louis, 1988-89, bd. dirs., Mo. Coalition Against Censorship, 1986-92, sec., 1988-92; mentor Dunbar Sch., 1995-2001. Mem. ABA (labor law sect. 1984—, corp. banking and bus. law sect. 1987—), Mo. Bar Assn. (labor law com. 1977—), Ill. State Bar Assn., Bar Assn. Met. St. Louis (labor law com. 1977—, grievance com. 1978-87, Clayton Hockey Club (pres. 2001-02). Jewish. Corporate, general, Labor (including EEOC, Fair Labor Standards Act, labor-management relations, NLRB, OSHA), General civil litigation. Home: 8137 University Dr Saint Louis MO 63105-3726 Office: Kohn Shands Elbert et al Ste 2410 One US Bank Plaza Saint Louis MO 63101 E-mail: celbert@ksegg.com.

ELBERY, KATHLEEN MARIE, lawyer, accountant, cartoonist; b. Boston, Nov. 30, 1959; d. Norman F. and June E. (Ramsay) E. BSBA with high honors, Northeastern U., 1983; JD cum laude, Suffolk U., 1990. Bar: Mass. 1990, U.S. Ct. Appeals (1st cir.) Mass. 1991, U.S. Dist. Ct. Mass. 1991; CPA, Mass, 1986. CPA, supr. Gately & Assocs., P.C., Wellesley, Mass., 1983-87; sr. tax mgr. and multi-state income and franchise tax practice leader KPMG Peat Marwick LLP, Boston, 1988-96; tax mgr. state taxes Arthur Andersen LLP, Boston, 1996—98; pvt. practice Boston, 1998—. Mem. Mass. Dept. Revenue Practitioner Liaison Com.; instr., panel mem. state taxation seminars and profl. devel. courses; spkr. in field. Creator: Funny Bone Cartoons; Funny Bone Cartoons; creator Funny Bone Cartoons. Merit scholar Northeastern U., 1978; recipient Outstanding Achievement award in Appellate Brief Writing, 1988. Mem. AICPAs, ABA, Mass. Soc. CPAs (chair multi-state tax sub-com. 1996-97), Mass. Bar Assn., Beta Alpha Psi (elected recording sec. 1981-82), Beta Gamma Sigma, Phi Kappa Phi, Phi Delta Phi.

ELCANO, MARY S. lawyer; BA cum laude, Lynchburg Coll., 1971; JD, Cath. U., Washington, 1976. Litigation atty. Balt. Legal Aide Bur., 1976; staff atty. Office Solicitor Dept. Labor, 1979; gen. trial and appellate atty. Office Labor Law U.S. Postal Svc., 1982, exec. dir. Office EEO, 1984, regional dir. human resources N.E. region, 1987, sr. v.p., gen. counsel, 1992-99, exec. v.p., gen. counsel, 1999-2000; ptnr. Sidley Austin Brown & Wood LLP, Washington, 2000—03; gen. counsel, corp. sec. ARC, Washington, 2003—. Alternative dispute resolution, Corporate, general, Labor (including EEOC, Fair Labor Standards Act, labor-management relations, NLRB, OSHA). Office: ARC 430 17th St NW Washington DC 20006 E-mail: ElcanoM@usa.redcross.org.

ELDEN, GARY MICHAEL, lawyer; b. Chgo., Dec. 11, 1944; s. E. Harold and Sylvia Arlene (Diamond) E.; m. Phyllis Deborah Mandler, Apr. 20, 1975; children: Roxanna Mandler, Erica Mandler. BA, U. Ill., 1966; JD, Harvard U., 1969. Bar: Ill. 1969, U.S. Dist. Ct. (no. dist.) Ill. 1969, U.S. Ct. Appeals (7th cir.) 1973, U.S. Supreme Ct. 1973, U.S. Dist. Ct. (ea. dist.) Mich. 1985, U.S. Ct. Appeals (8th cir.) 1988, U.S. Ct. Appeals (6th and 10th cirs.) 1990, U.S. Dist. Ct. (ea. dist.) Wis. 1992. Ptnr. Kirkland & Ellis, Chgo., 1969-78, Reuben & Proctor, Chgo., 1978-86, Isham, Lincoln & Beale, Chgo., 1986-88, Grippo & Elden, Chgo., 1988—. Contbr. articles to profl. jours. Fellow Am. Coll. Trial Lawyers; mem. ABA, Chgo. Bar Assn. (sec. com. appellate procedures 1975-77), Chgo. Coun. Lawyers, Appellate Lawyers Assn. (bd. dirs. 1975-77), Met. Club. Federal civil litigation, General civil litigation, Insurance. Home: 3750 N Lake Shore Dr Chicago IL 60613-4238 Office: Grippo & Elden 227 W Monroe St Ste 3600 Chicago IL 60606-5098

ELDER, JAMES CARL, lawyer; b. Detroit, Mar. 11, 1947; s. Carl W. and Alta M. (Bradley) E.; m. Margaret Ford, Apr. 6, 1974; children: James B., William J., Michael L., Samuel F. BA, U. Okla, 1969, JD, 1972. Bar: Okla. 1972, U.S. Dist. Ct. (we. dist.) Okla. 1972. Ptnr., dir. Crowe & Dunlevy, Oklahoma City, 1972-82; dir., mem. Mock, Schwabe, Waldo, Elder, Oklahoma City, 1982-96, 98—; ptnr. Gable Gotwals Mock Schwabe Kihle Gaberino, 1996-98. Nat. coun. rep. Last Frontier Coun. Boy Scouts Am., 1989—, pres., 1997-99; trustee Norman (Okla.) Pub. Sch. Found., 1988-97, pres., 1995-97; elder Meml. Presbyn. Ch., Norman, clk. of session, 1992-95; dir. Cmty. Coun. Ctrl. Okla., 1999-2003, v.p., 2002-03. Capt. 95th Inf. Div. (tng) USAR, 1972—78, Capt. 95th inf. divsn. USAR, 1970—78. Recipient Silver Beaver award Boy Scouts Am., Oklahoma City, 1989, Silver Antelope award, 1999. Fellow Okla. Bar Found. (life), Baden Powell World Fellowship; mem. ABA (mem. title ins. com. real property, probate and trust law sect. 1993—, chmn. closing issues subcom. 1995—), Rotary, Beta Theta Pi Corp. of Okla. (trustee, v.p., chpt. counselor 1975-86, 95—, pres. 1995-2002). Avocations: scouting, skiing, reading. Banking, Commercial, contracts (including sales of goods; commercial financing), Property, real (including real estate development, water). Office: Mock Schwabe Waldo et al 211 N Robinson 2 Leadership Sq 14th Fl Oklahoma City OK 73102

ELDRIDGE, DAVID P. lawyer, military officer; b. Chester, Ill., May 16, 1973; s. Wayne Allen and Myrna Mahnken Eldridge; m. Sara Shipley Shipley, June 10, 2000. BS, U. Ill., 1995; JD, Tulane U., 1998. Bar: Miss. 2000, U.S. Dist. Ct. (no. dist.) Miss. 2000, U.S. Dist. Ct. (so. dist.) Miss. 2000, U.S. Ct. Appeals (5th cir.) 2000, D.C. 2001. Assoc. Steven H. Smith, PLLC, Jackson, Miss., 2002—02; staff atty. Butler, Snow, O'Mara, Stevens & Cannada, PLLC, 2000—01; jud. law clk. Miss. Supreme Ct., 1998—99; ensign USNR, New Orleans, 2002—. Profl. divsn. nat. v.p. FBLA-PBL, Inc., Reston, 2002—. Contbr. articles to profl. jours. Civil rights, General civil litigation, Appellate. Personal E-mail: dpeldridge@usa.net.

ELDRIDGE, JOHN COLE, judge; b. Balt., Nov. 13, 1933; s. Arthur Clement and Bertha Jean (Klitch) E.; m. Dayne S. Worsham, July 15, 1961; children: Kathryn Chandler, John Cole. BA, Harvard U., 1955; LL.B., U. Md., 1959. Bar: Md. 1960, D.C. 1961. Law clk. to chief judge U.S. Ct. Appeals 4th Circuit, 1959-61; trial atty. appellate sect., civil div. Dept. Justice, 1961-67, asst. chief appellate sect., 1967-69; chief legis. officer, counsel Staff of Gov. of Md., 1969-74; judge Ct. Appeals Md, Annapolis, Md., 1974—. Chmn. Md. Adv. Bd. Correction, 1969-70; dir. Annapolis Fine Arts Found., 1974-77 Mem. Anne Arundel County Bar Assn., Annapolis Yacht Club. Democrat. Methodist. Office: Ct Appeals Md Robert Murphy Cts Appeal Bldg 361 Rowe Blvd Annapolis MD 21401-1672

ELDRIDGE, RICHARD MARK, lawyer; b. Okmulgee, Okla., June 20, 1951; s. H.G. and Marcheta (Barnes) E.; m. Nellene Jane Mark, Aug. 20, 1971; children: Richard Mark Jr. (dec.), Christopher Bryan, Ryan Matthew, Michael Jonathan. BA, Okla. State U., 1973; JD, U. Tulsa, 1975. Bar: Okla. 1976; U.S. Dist. Ct. (no. dist.) Okla. 1976, U.S. Dist. Ct. (ea. dist.) Okla. 1989; U.S. Ct. Appeals (10th cir.) 1977, U.S. Dist. Ct. (we. dist.) Okla. 1991, U.S. Dist. Ct. (ea. dist.) Ark. 2001. Ptnr. Jacobus, Green & Eldridge, Tulsa, 1976-78; spl. judge Dist. Ct., Tulsa, 1979-81; ptnr. Rhodes, Hieronymus, Jones, Tucker & Gable, Tulsa, 1981—2001, Eldridge Cooper Steichen & Leach, PLLC, Tulsa, 2001—. Adj. prof. Oral Roberts U., Tulsa, 1985. Tchr. Couples for Christ, Asbury United Meth. Ch., Tulsa, 1979—; pres., sec. Christian Businessmen's Com., Tulsa, 1981-93; chmn. Asbury Presch. Bd., Tulsa, 1985-95; trustee Metro. Christian Acad., 1998—, 1st v.p., 2001-02, chmn., 2002-03. Recipient Cert. of Achievement, Am. Acad. Jud. Edn., 1979. Mem.: ABA, Okla. Assn. Def. Coun., Am. Judicature Soc., Def. Rsch. Inst., Tulsa County Bar Assn., Okla. Bar Assn. Republican. Avocation: coaching baseball and basketball. Federal civil litigation, State civil litigation, Product liability. Home: 2985 E 45th Pl Tulsa OK 74105 Office: Eldridge Cooper Steichen & Leach PLLC 110 W 7th St Ste 200 Tulsa OK 74119

ELDRIDGE, TRUMAN KERMIT, JR., lawyer; b. Kansas City, Mo., July 27, 1944; s. Truman Kermit and Nell Marie (Dennis) E.; m. Joan Ellen Jurgeson, Feb. 9, 1965; children: Christina Joanne, Gregory Truman. AB, Rockhurst Coll., 1966; JD, U. Mo., Kansas City, 1969. Bar: Mo. 1969, U.S. Dist. Ct. (we. dist.) Mo. 1969, U.S. Ct. Appeals (8th cir.) 1977, (10th cir.) 1995, U.S. S. Ct., 1992, U.S. Dist. Ct. Kans. 1998. Assoc. Morris, Foust, Moudy & Beckett, Kansas City, 1969-70, Dietrich, Davis, Dicus, Rowlands & Schmitt, Kansas City, 1971-74, ptnr., 1975, Armstrong, Teasdale, LLP, Kansas City, 1989-2000; sr. counsel Schlee, Huber McMullen & Krause, 2001—. Author: (with othrs) Missouri Environmental Law Handbook, 1990, 2d edit., 1993, 3d edit., 1997; contbr. articles to profl. jours. Chmn. bd. dirs. Loretto Sch., Kansas City, 1981-83; mem. Energy and Environ. Commn. City of Kansas City, 1990-91, 1994, bd. dirs. Sheffield Pl., 1997—, vice chair, 1998-99, chair, 1999-2000. Master Ross T. Roberts Inn of Ct.; mem. ABA, Def. Rsch. Inst., Mo. Bar Assn., Kansas City Met. Bar Assn. (fed. ct. com., vice chair 1989-90, chair 1990-91), Am. Arbitration Assn. (arbitrator), Nat. Arbitration Forum (arbitrator), Kansas City Club (athletic com. 1990—2001, chair 199-2001, house com. 1993-96, 98-99, long range planning com. 1993-97, bd. dirs. 1997-2001). Roman Catholic. Avocations: sailing, reading, photography, raquetball. General civil litigation, Environmental, Product liability. Home: 448 W 68th Ter Kansas City MO 64113-1933 Office: PO Box 32430 4050 Pennsylvania Ste 300 Kansas City MO 64171-5430 E-mail: truman_eldridge@hotmail.com., teldridge@schleehuber.com.

ELFVIN, JOHN THOMAS, federal judge; b. Montour Falls, N.Y., June 30, 1917; s. John Arthur and Lillian Ruth (Dorning) E.; m. Peggy Pierce, Oct. 1, 1949. B.E.E., Cornell U., 1942; JD, Georgetown U., 1947. Bar: D.C. 1948, N.Y. 1949. Confidential clk. to U.S. Circuit Ct. Judge E. Barrett Prettyman, 1947-48; asst. U.S. atty., Buffalo, 1955-58; U.S. atty. Western Dist. N.Y., 1972-75; with firm Cravath, Swaine & Moore, N.Y.C., 1948-51, Dudley, Stowe & Sawyer, Buffalo, 1951-55, Lansdowne, Horning & Elfvin, Buffalo, 1958-69, 70-72; justice N.Y. Supreme Ct., 1969; judge U.S. Dist. Ct., Buffalo, 1975—, now sr. judge. Mem. bd. suprs. Erie County, N.Y., 1962-65, mem. bd. ethics, 1971-74, chmn., 1971-72; mem., minority leader Buffalo Common Council Delaware Dist., 1966-69. Mem.: Tech. Socs. Niagara Frontier (pres. 1960—61), Engring. Soc. Buffalo (pres. 1958—59), Erie County Bar Assn., Am. Judicature Soc., Saturn Club, Buffalo Country Club, Cornell Club (pres. 1957—58), Phi Kappa Tau. Republican. Office: US Dist Ct 716 US Courthouse 68 Court St Buffalo NY 14202-3405

ELIAS, RAYMON TODD, lawyer; b. Corpus Christi, Aug. 3, 1968; s. Raymon K. and Susan Elias; m. Rose Sabrina Elias, Nov. 19, 1998; children: Raymon Andrew, Rose Alyssa. BSBA The Citadel, 1990; JD, Tex. Tech. U. Sch. of Law, 1993. Bar: Tex., (Licensed in all Tex. State Courts, Fed. Cts. Ea. and So. Dist. of Tex.). Of counsel Law Offices of J. Michael Black, Houston, 1993—95, Green, Downey and Black, LLP, Houston, 1995—98; ptnr. Black and Elias, 1998—2000, Gordon and Elias, LLP, Tex., 2000—. Mem.: Houston Trial Lawyers Assn., Am. Trial Lawyers Assn. Admiralty, Personal injury (including property damage), Product liability. Office: 5821 SW Frwy Ste 422 Houston TX 77057

ELIASON, RUSSELL ALLEN, judge; b. Mpls., Jan. 28, 1944; s. Walter Joseph and Hazel Agnes Pearl (Jensen) E.; m. Karen L. Stevens; children: Nathaniel, Heidi, Justine, Danielle. Student U. Minn., 1964-65, JD, 1970; BA, Yale U., 1967; student Wake Forest U. Sch. Law, 1967-68. Bar: Minn. 1970, Iowa 1971, N.C. 1973, Nebr. 1975, U.S. Dist. Ct. (no. dist.) Iowa 1971, U.S. Dist. Ct. (mid. dist.) N.C. 1974, U.S. Dist. Ct. Nebr. 1975, U.S. Ct. Appeals (8th cir.) 1971, U.S. Ct. Appeals (4th cir.) 1976. Law clk. to judge U.S. Ct. Appeals 8th Cir., 1970-71; asst. U.S. atty. Dept. Justice, Sioux City, Iowa, 1971-72; law clk. to judge U.S. Dist. Ct. Mid. Dist. N.C., 1972-74; assoc. Ryan, Scoville & Uhlir, South Sioux City, Nebr., 1974-75; asst. U.S. atty. Dept. Justice, Greensboro, N.C., 1975-76; U.S. magistrate judge U.S. Dist. Ct. Mid. Dist. N.C., Winston-Salem, 1976—; lectr. in field; active law-sch. skills programs. Trumpeter Salem Band, Old Salem Band. Mem. ABA, N.C. Bar Assn., Forsyth County Bar, Minn. Bar Assn., Nebr. Bar Assn., Sons of Norway, Phi Alpha Alpha Delta. Mem. Moravian Ch. Office: 224 Fed Bldg 251 N Main St Winston Salem NC 27101-3914

ELIBOL, DAVID HAKAN, lawyer; b. LI, May 31, 1968; s. Tarik Elibol and Karen Elizabeth Andersen; m. Lynn Marie Price, Aug. 8, 1998; children: Cassidy Marie, Hannah Elisabeth. BS, Fla. State U., 1986; JD, Thomas M. Cooley Law Sch., 1995. Bar: NY 1996, U.S. Dist. Ct. (we. dist.) NY 1997, U.S. Supreme Ct. 2001. Assoc. Lipsitz, Green, Fahringer et. al., Buffalo, 1997—98; shareholder Gross, Shuman, Brizdle & Gilfillan, P.C., Buffalo, 1998—. Mem.: ATLA, Sports Lawyer's Assn., Erie County Bar Assn., W. N.Y. Trial Lawyers Assn., N.Y. State Bar Assn. Personal injury (including property damage), State civil litigation. Office: Gross Shuman Brizdle and Gilfillan PC 465 Main St Ste 600 Buffalo NY 14203 Office Fax: 716-854-2787. Business E-Mail: delibol@gross-shuman.com.

ELIOT, THEODORE QUENTIN, lawyer; b. Tulsa, Mar. 18, 1954; s. Theodore Quentin and Norma Jo (Jones) E.; m. Judith Rae Seymour, May 16, 1954. BA, Drake U., 1976; JD, U. Okla., 1979. Bar: Okla. 1979, U.S. Dist. Ct. (no., we. and ea. dists.), U.S. Ct. Appeals (10th cir.). Assoc. Gable & Gotwals, Inc., Tulsa, 1979-85, ptnr., 1985—. Mem. ABA, Okla. Bar Assn., Tulsa Bar Assn., Summit Club. Avocations: hunting, sports, reading. Bankruptcy, Federal civil litigation, General civil litigation. Office: Gable & Gotwals 100 W 5th St 1100 Oneok Plz Tulsa OK 74103-4217

ELJURI, ELISABETH, lawyer; b. Caracas, Venezuela, Jan. 13, 1970; d. Elias Rafael and Sabeth (Ramirez) E. JD cum laude, U. Catolica, Venezuela, 1991; LLM, Harvard U., 1992. Bar: Venezuela 1991, NY 1993. Law clk. Baker & McKenzie, Caracas, 1988-91, assoc. N.Y.C., summer 1990, San Francisco, 1992-93, Caracas, 1993-98; ptnr. Macleod Dixon, Caracas, 1998—. Prof. U. Ctrl., Venezuela, 1994-1996; nat. adminstr. Philip Jessup, Venezuela, 1994—. Recipient scholarhip Fundayacucho, Venezuela, 1991. Mem. Assn. Internat. Petroleum Negotiators, Colegio de Abogados del Distrito Federal, Caracas. Commercial, contracts (including sales of goods; commercial financing), Oil, gas, and mineral, General practice. Office: Macleod Dixon Torre Copérnico Piso 8 Ctr San Ignacio La Castellana Caracas 1060 Venezuela

ELKINS-ELLIOTT, KAY, law educator; b. Dallas, Nov. 21, 1938; d. William Hardin and Maxidine (Sadler) E.; m. Michael Gail Hodgson, July 7, 1960 (div. Dec. 1974); children: Michael Brett, Ashley Kim, Samantha; m. Frank Wallace Elliott, Aug. 15, 1983. AA with honors, Stephens Coll., 1958; JD, U. Okla., 1964; LLM, So. Meth. U., 1984; MA, U. Tex., Dallas, 1990. Bar: Okla. 1964, Tex. 1982, U.S. Dist. Ct. (no. dist.) Tex. 1982, U.S. Supreme Ct. 1984, U.S. Dist. Ct. (we. dist.) Okla. 1989. Assoc. Ben Hatcher and Assocs., Oklahoma City, Okla., 1964-65; dir., gen. counsel Take-A-Tour Swaziland, Mbabane, Swaziland, 1966-74; atty. Dept. Health and Human Svcs., Dallas, 1975-80; hearing officer EEOC, Dallas, 1980-84; atty. pvt. practice, Dallas, 1984-92; vis. assoc. prof. Tex. Wesleyan U. Sch. Law, Dallas, 1992-95; arbitrator State Farm Ins., Dallas, 1991-96. Adj. prof. Wesleyan U. Sch. Law, 1995—, coach nat. ABA champion negotiation team, 1998; mediator pvt. practice, Dallas, Granbury, 1991—; coord. cert. in conflict resolution program Tex. Woman's U., 1996—; coach internal champion negotiation team ICOD, 2002-; coach internat. champion online dispute resolution competition; cons. in field. Author: (with others) West Texas Practice, 1995, (with Frank Elliott) State Bar of Texas ADR Handbook, 2002. Dir. diversity tng. State Bar Tex. 9/11 project. Mem. ABA (negotiation and tng. coms., alternative dispute resolution sect.), Tex. Bar Assn. (ADR sect. coun. mem. 1998-2001, chair publs. com.), Tex. Bar Found., Tex. Initiatives for Mediation in Edn. (founder, planning com. 1993-95), Assn. for Conflict Resolution (pres. Dallas region 1995-97), Tex. Assn. Mediators, Dallas Bar Assn. (coun. mem. 1993-94), Inst. for Responsible Dispute Resolution (charter), Granbury C. of C. and Historic Merchants Assn., Toastmasters (v.p. 1993-94, pres. 1996-97), Optimist Internat. Avocations: singing, public speaking. Home: 2120 N Rough Creek Ct Granbury TX 76048-2903 Office: 2401 Turtle Creek Blvd Dallas TX 75219-4712 E-mail: k4mede8@swbell.net.

ELLENBERGER, JACK STUART, law librarian; b. Lamar, Colo., Sept. 5, 1930; s. Emmert C. and Ruby F. (Overstreet) E. BS, Georgetown U., 1957; M.L.S., Columbia U., 1959. Law libr. HEW, 1957; libr. Carter, Ledyard & Milburn, N.Y.C., 1957-60, Jones, Day, Reavis & Pogue (and predecessor firm), Cleve., 1960, Bar Assn. of D.C., Washington, 1961-63, Covington & Burling, Washington, 1963-78, Shearman & Sterling, N.Y.C., 1978-93, law libr. emeritus, 1994-95; ret., 1995. Editor: (with Mahar) Legislative History of the Securities Act of 1933 and the Securities Exchange Act of 1934, 1973. Served with USAF, 1951-54. Mem. Am. Assn. Law Libraries (pres. 1976-77, M.G. Gallagher Disting. Svc. award 1994), Spl. Libraries Assn.

ELLER, LESLIE ROBERT, lawyer; b. Denver, Aug. 30, 1949; s. Burton and Eileen E. BA cum laude, Claremont (Calif.) Men's Coll., 1971; JD, U. Denver, 1975. Bar: Colo. 1976, Calif., 1999, U.S. Dist. Ct. Colo. 1976, U.S. Ct. Appeals (10th cir.) 1976. Assoc. Neil C. King, Atty. at Law, Boulder, Colo., 1976-80; dir., v.p., shareholder King & Eller, P.C., Boulder, 1980—97, also bd. dirs. V.p. First Colo. Title Corp., Boulder, 1987-97; v.p. Mesa Moving and Storage Co., Grand Junction, Colo., 1981-97. Mem. Nat. Assn. Realtors, Calif. Bar Assn., Calif. Assn. Realtors, Am. Immigration Lawyers Assn. Corporate, general, Estate planning, Property, real (including real estate development, water). Home: 10 El Rose Dr Petaluma CA 94952-4009 Office: 10 El Rose Dr Petaluma CA 94952-4009 E-mail: leseller@attbi.com.

ELLETT, JOHN SPEARS, II, retired taxation educator, accountant, lawyer; b. Richmond, Va., Sept. 17, 1923; s. Henry Guerrant and Elizabeth Firmstone (Maxwell) E.; m. Mary Ball Ruffin, Apr. 15, 1950; children: John, Mary Ball, Elizabeth, Martha, Henry. BA, U. Va., 1948, JD, 1957, MA, 1961; PhD, U. N.C., 1969. CPA, Va., La.; bar: Va. 1957. Lab. instr. U. Va., Charlottesville, 1953-58; instr. Washington and Lee U., 1958-60; asst. prof. U. Fla., 1967-71; assoc. prof. U. New Orleans, 1971-76, prof. taxation, 1976-94, prof. emeritus, 1994—. Trainee Va. Carolina Hardware Co., Richmond, 1948-51; acct. Equitable Life Assurance Soc., Richmond, 1951-52; staff acct. Musselman & Drysdale, Charlottesville, 1952-54; staff acct. R.M. Musselman, Charlottesville, 1957-58; mem. U. New Orleans Oil and Gas Acctg. Conf., 1973-92; bd. dirs., publicity chmn. U. New Orleans Energy Acctg. and Tax Conf., 1993-94, bd. dirs. publicity com.; pres. Maxwelton Farm and Timber Corp., 1994—; treas. U. New Orleans Estate Planning Seminar, 1975-78, lectr. continuing edn.; CPCU instr. New Orleans Ins. Inst., 1975-78. Author books; contbr. articles to profl. jours. Served with AUS, 1943-46. Mem. AICPA (40 yr. hon. mem. 2000—), Am. Acctg. Assn., Am. Assn. Atty.-CPAs (chmn. ptnrship. taxation continuing edn. com. 1989, ptnrship. taxation com. 1990, organized La. chpt., v.p. 1991-93), Va. Soc. CPAs, Soc. La. CPAs, Va. Bar Assn. (40 yr. hon. mem. 2000—). Democrat. Episcopalian. Home: 177 Maxwelton Rd Charlottesville VA 22903-7859

ELLICKSON, ROBERT CHESTER, law educator; b. Washington, Aug. 4, 1941; s. John Chester and Katherine Heilprin (Pollak) Ellickson; children: Jenny, Owen. AB, Oberlin Coll., 1963; LLB, Yale U., 1966. Bar: D.C. 1967, Calif. 1971. Atty. adviser Pres.'s Com. Urban Housing, Washington, 1967-68; mgr. urban affairs Levitt & Sons Inc., Lake Success, N.Y., 1968-70; prof. law U. So. Calif., L.A., 1970-81; prof. Stanford U., Calif., 1981-85, Robert E. Paradise prof. natural resources law, 1985-88; Walter E. Meyer prof. property and urban law Yale U., New Haven, 1988—, dep. dean, 1991-92. Author: (with Tarlock) Land-Use Controls, 1981, Order Without Law, 1991 (Triennial award Order of the Coif), (with Rose & Ackerman) Perspectives on Property Law, 3d edit., 2002, (with Been) Land Use Controls, 2d edit., 2000. Mem. Am. Acad. Arts and Scis., Am. Law and Econs. Assn. (pres. 2000-01), Am. Law Inst. Office: Yale U Law Sch PO Box 208215 New Haven CT 06520-8215 E-mail: robert.ellickson@yale.edu.

ELLICOTT, JOHN LEMOYNE, lawyer; b. Balt., May 26, 1929; s. Valcoulon LeMoyne and Mary Purnell (Gould) Ellicott; m. Mary Lou Ulery, June 19, 1954 (dec. Jan. 1995); children: Valcoulon, Ann; m. Beatrice Berle Meyerson, Sept. 14, 1996. AB summa cum laude, Princeton U., 1951; LLB cum laude, Harvard U., 1954. Bar: D.C. 1957, U.S. Supreme Ct. 1959. Assoc. Covington & Burling, Washington, 1958-65, ptnr., 1965-98, chmn. mgmt. com., 1986-90, sr. counsel, 1998—. Pres. Fairfax County Fedn. Citizens Assn., Va., 1964; mem. governing bd. Nat. Cathedral Sch., Washington, 1973—80, 1989—90, chmn., 1978—79; trustee Landon Sch., Bethesda, Md., 1972—76; bd. dirs. Protestant Episc. Cathedral Found., Washington, 1980—88. Mem.: ABA (sect. internat. law and practice), Washington Inst. Fgn. Affairs, Am. Bar Found. (life), Phi Beta Kappa. Democrat. Administrative and regulatory, Corporate, general, Private international. Home: 5117 Macomb St NW Washington DC 20016-2611 Office: Covington & Burling 1201 Pennsylvania Ave NW Washington DC 20004

ELLIN, MARVIN, lawyer; b. Balt., Mar. 6, 1923; s. Morris and Goldie (Rosen) E.; children: Morris, Raymond, Elisa; m. Marta I. Quintana, Aug. 15, 2001. JD, U. Balt., 1953. Bar: Md. 1953, U.S. Supreme Ct. 1978; diplomate Am. Bd. Forensic Examiners. Practice law, Balt., 1953—; mem. firm Ellin & Baker, 1957—; specialist in med. malpractice law. Cons. on med. and legal trial matters; lectr. ACS, U. Md. Law Sch., U. Balt. City, Yale U. Sch. Medicine, Johns Hopkins Hosp., U. Calif., San Francisco, U. N.J.; former mem. cmtn.'s adv. coun. com. on judiciary U.S. Senate. Mem. editl. adv. bd.: Ob/Gyn Malpractice Prevention; contbr. chpts. on med. malpractice to various profl. publs. including Radiation Therapy of Benign Diseases. Fellow Internat. Acad. Trial Lawyers; mem. ABA, Am. Soc. Law and Medicine. General civil litigation, Personal injury (including property damage). Home: 13414 Longnecker Rd Glyndon MD 21136-4839 Office: 1101 Saint Paul St Baltimore MD 21202-2662 E-mail: EllinLaw@aol.com.

ELLIOT, CAMERON ROBERT, lawyer; b. Portland, Oreg., Jan. 6, 1966; s. James Addison and Dianne Louise (Youngblood) Elliot. BS, Yale U., 1987; JD, Harvard U., 1996. Bar: Calif 1996, DC 1999. Jud. clk. U.S. Dist. Ct., Reno, 1996-98; atty. civil divsn. U.S. Dept. Justice, Washington, 1998—2001; asst. U.S. atty. So. Dist. Fla., 2001—. Editor-in-chief: jour Harvard Environ Law Rev, 1995—96. Mem Reno Environ Bd, 1996—97. Lt USN, 1987—92. Home: 1717 N Bayshore Dr Apt 1250 Miami FL 33132 Office: US Atty's Office 99 NE 4th St Miami FL 33132 E-mail: cameron@justice.com.

ELLIOT, RALPH GREGORY, lawyer; b. Hartford, Conn., Oct. 20, 1936; s. K. Gregory and Zarou (Manoukian) E. BA, Yale U., 1958, LLB, 1961. Bar: Conn. 1961, U.S. Dist. Ct. Conn. 1963, U.S. Ct. Appeals (2d cir.) 1966, U.S. Ct. Appeals (Fed. cir.) 1993, U.S. Ct. Appeals (1st cir.) 1997, U.S. Supreme Ct. 1967. Law clk. to assoc. justice Conn. Supreme Ct., Hartford, 1961-62; assoc. Alcorn, Bakewell & Smith, Hartford, 1962-67, ptnr., 1967-83, Tyler, Cooper & Alcorn, Hartford, 1983—. Adj. prof. law U. Conn., Hartford, 1973—; sec. Superior Ct. Legal Internship Com., Conn., 1971—; chmn. Superior Ct. Legal Specialization Screening Com., Conn., 1981—, U.S. Dist. Ct. Panel Spl. Masters, Hartford, 1983-88. Chmn. bd. editors Conn. Law Tribune, 1986-87. Chmn. Constn. Bicentennial Commn., Conn., 1986-91; mem. Criminal Justice Commn. Conn., 1991-95. Recipient Fenton P. Futtner award Conn. Reps., 1993. Conn. Law Tribune Pub. Award, 2003, Fellow Am. Bar Found.; mem. ABA (standing com. on ethics and profl. responsibility 1989-95, standing com. on profl. discipline 1998-2001, ho. of dels. 1983-87), Conn. Bar Assn. (officer, bd. govs. 1971-79, 83-87, pres. 1985-86, John Eldred Shields Disting. Profl. Svc. award 1993), Am. Law Inst., Yale Law Sch. Assn. (pres. 1988-90, chmn. exec. com. 1990-92), Yale Club (pres. 1977-79, Nathan Hale award 1984, Betty McCallip Meml. award 1991), Hartford, Grad. Club (New Haven), Phi Beta Kappa. Republican. Episcopalian. Federal civil litigation, State civil litigation, Libel. Home: 27 Brookline Dr West Hartford CT 06107-1265

ELLIOTT, BRADY GIFFORD, judge; b. Harlingen, Tex., Nov. 26, 1943; s. Clyde Andres Elliott and Mildred (Parker) Bounds; m. Rhea Elizabeth Ricks, May 15, 1967; children: Adrian Winthrope, Jason Lawrence. BBA, McMurray Coll., 1970; JD, South Tex. Coll. Law, 1973. Bar: Tex. 1973, U.S. Dist. Ct. (so. dist.) Tex. 1974, U.S. Tax Ct. 1974, U.S. Ct. Appeals (5th cir.) 1974, U.S. Supreme Ct. 1979, U.S. Ct. Appeals (11th cir.) 1981. Asst. sec., asst. treas., asst. gen. counsel Gordon Jewelry Corp., Houston, 1970-79; sec., gen. counsel Oshman's Sporting Goods, Inc., Houston, 1979-82; sole practice, Sugar Land, Tex., 1982-88; legal counsel Ft. Bend C. of C., Sugar Land, Tex., 1982-88; mcpl. judge Missouri City, Tex., 1983-88; judge 268th Dist. Ct., Fort Bend County, Tex., 1988—. Bd. dirs. Ft. Bend chpt. Texans' War on Drugs, Sugar Land, 1981-94; bd. dirs. Ft. Bend Boys Choir, 1984-94. Mem. ABA, Houston Bar Assn., Fort Bend County Bar Assn., Masons, Rotary (treas. 1983-85). Republican. Methodist. Office: County Ct House Richmond TX 77469

ELLIOTT, DIANE VOLLWEILER, lawyer; b. June 28, 1952; AB in Psychology, Lafayette Coll., 1974; JD, U. Miami, 1977; MS in Environtl. Sci., N.J. Inst. and Tech., 1995. Atty., 1977-96; dir. cmty. devel. Northampton County Devel. Corp., Easton, Pa., 1996-98; dir. Lehigh Valley Recycling Intiative, Allentown, Pa., 1999; dir. found., corp. rels. Lafayette Coll., 1999—2002, assoc. dir. for pub. svc. Meyner Ctr. for Study of State and Local Govt., 2002—. Cons. Brownfields Redevel., 1999—. Mem. Northampton County Coun., 1994-96. E-mail: elliottd@lafayette.edu.

ELLIOTT, EDWARD SPORL, lawyer; b. San Francisco, Calif., Nov. 9, 1971; s. William Terry and Myrtle Sporl Elliott; m. Erika Fortune Litchfield, June 6, 1999. BA, Wash. and Lee U., Lexington, VA, 1990—94; J.D., U. San Francisco Sch. of Law, San Francisco, 1994—97. Bar: Calif. 1997. Ceo Jobscience, Inc., San Francisco, Calif., 1999—2003; gen. counsel & corp. sec. Zarix, Inc., Malvern, Pa., 1997—99; ptnr. OPV Lifescience Partners, San Francisco, Calif., 1995—97; cons. Maczkov Biosciences, San Francisco, Calif., 1994—95. Dir. Jobscience, Inc., San Francisco, 1990. Mem. Town Sch. Alumni Coun., San Francisco, 1995—99. Mem.: St. Francis Yacht Club (life). R-Consevative. Episcopal. Avocations: sailing, hunting. Corporate, general, Finance, Securities. E-mail: legal@ureach.com.

ELLIOTT, FRANK WALLACE, lawyer, educator; b. Cotulla, Tex., June 25, 1930; s. Frank Wallace and Eunice Marie (Akin) E.; m. Winona Trent, July 3, 1954 (dec. 1981); 1 child, Harriet Lindsey; m. Kay Elkins, Aug. 15, 1983. Student, N.Mex. Mil. Inst., 1947-49; BA, U. Tex., 1951, LLB, 1957. Bar: Tex. 1957, U.S. Supreme Ct. 1962, U.S. Ct. Mil. Appeals 1974, U.S. Dist. Ct. (no. dist.) Tex. 1987, U.S. Ct. Appeals (5th cir.) 1988. Asst. atty. gen. State of Tex., 1957; briefing atty. Supreme Ct. Tex., 1957-58; prof. U. Tex. Law Sch., 1958-77; dean, prof. law Tex. Tech U. Sch. Law, 1977-80; pres. Southwestern Legal Found., 1980-86; ptnr. Baker, Mills & Glast, Dallas, 1987-88; of counsel Ramirez & Assocs., 1988—; dean Dallas/Ft. Worth Sch. Law, 1989-92; dean Sch. Law Tex. Wesleyan U., 1992-94, prof., dean emeritus, 1994—. Parliamentarian Tex. Senate, 1969-73; dir. rsch. Tex. Constl. Revision Commn., 1973 Author: Texas Judicial Process, 2d edit., 1977, Texas Trial and Appellate Practice, 2d edit., 1974, Cases on Evidence, 1980, West's Texas Forms, 20 vols., 1977—, West's Texas Practice, vol. 11, 1990, vol. 14, 1996. Served with U.S. Army, 1951-53, 73-74. Decorated Purple Heart. Mem. ABA, Judge Advs. Assn., Am. Judicature Soc., Am. Bar Found., Tex. Bar Found., Dallas Bar Found., Am. Law Inst., N.Mex. Mil. Inst. Alumni Hall of Fame. Federal civil litigation, State civil litigation, Private international. Home: 2120 N Rough Creek Ct Granbury TX 76048-2903 Office: 1515 Commerce St Fort Worth TX 76102-6572 E-mail: felliott@law.txwes.edu.

ELLIOTT, JAMES SEWELL, lawyer; b. Augusta, Ga., Dec. 20, 1922; s. Lester Franklin and Frances (Sewell) E.; m. Mary Jones Grace, June 25, 1947; children: James Sewell Jr., Lester Franklin II, Walter Grace, Randolph Squire, Robert Bruce. BS, The Citadel, 1943, U.S. Mil. Acad., 1946; JD, Mercer U., 1952. Bar: Ga. 1952, U.S. Dist. Ct. (mid. dist.) Ga. 1953, U.S. Ct. Appeals (11th cir.) 1953, U.S. Supreme Ct. 1959. Asst. U.S. atty. U.S. Dist. Ct. (mid. dist.) Ga., Macon, 1953-57; prin. Law Offices of J. Sewell Elliott, Macon, Ga., 1957. Mem. Ga. Ho. of Reps. 107th dist., Atlanta, 1966; chmn. exec. com. Bibb County Republicans, Macon, 1985. Maj. USAR, 1946-58. Mem. ABA, Ga. Bar Assn., Macon Bar Assn., Kiwanis (pres. Macon chpt.). Episcopalian. State civil litigation, Corporate, general, General practice. Office: 544 Mulberry St Ste 100 Macon GA 31201-2770

ELLIOTT, JOHN MICHAEL, lawyer; b. Girardville, Pa., July 8, 1941; s. John T. and Clair C. E.; children: John P., Heather D., Kirwan B., Kyle M. AB in Econs. magna cum laude, St. Vincent Coll., 1963, LL.D. (hon.), 1985; LL.B. cum laude, Georgetown U., 1966. Bar: Pa. 1966, U.S. Dist. Ct. (ea., we. and mid. dists.) Pa. 1967, U.S. Ct. Appeals (3d cir.) 1967, U.S. Supreme Ct. 1968,. Chmn. Elliott, Reihner, Siedzkowski & Egan, Phila., 1990—. Pa. counsel Del. River Port Authority, 1987-95; mem. Phila. Coal Rail Task Force, Rockefeller Commn., White House Coal Adv. Commn., 1980; bd. dirs. James A. Finnegan Fellowship Found., 1976-90; bd. dirs. Irish Edn. Devel. Found., Inc., chmn., 2002; mem. Pa. Citizens Adv. Coun. Dept. Environ. Resources, 1970-78, chmn. urban com.; mem. environ. quality bd. Commonwealth of Pa., 1970-78; commr. Del. River Port Authority; rep. auditor Gen. Robert P. Casey; mem. Phila. City Planning Commn., 1970-75, Del. Valley Citizens Coun. for Clean Air; chmn. Disciplinary Bd. Supreme Ct. Pa., 1985-86, vice chmn., 1985, chmn. rules com., 1982, Pa. Bar Inst., 1988-94; mem. Commn. on Security and Coop. in Europe Conf. on the Human Dimension, Paris, 1989, Conf. on Dem. Instns., Oslo, 1991; mem. coun. of advisors Sch. of Humanities and Fine Arts, Georgetown U., 2002. Contbr. articles to profl. jours. Bd. dirs. Mann Music Ctr., 1988-91, Walnut St. Theatre, 1988-93, Internat. League for Human Rights, 1988-95. Recipient St. Patrick's Coll. Maynooth Ireland Salamanaca Archives Dedication, Cahal B. Cardinal Daly, 1995, Gold medal St. Patrick Desmond Cardinal Connell Dublin, 2001; Williston rsch. fellow, 1965. Fellow Pa. Bar Found.; mem. ABA (lectr. on trial practice), Pa. Bar Assn. (ho. of dels. 1983-91, task force on civil ct. rules), Pa. Bar Inst. (bd. dirs. 1987-93, course planner, faculty), Am. Law Inst. (ABA appelate practice program), Nat. Inst. Trial Advocacy (lectr.), Phila. Bar Assn., Nat. Lawyers Com. for Civil Rights Under Law, Braehon Law Soc., Mil. History Soc. Ireland. Antitrust, State civil litigation, Constitutional. Home: 1202 Penllyn Blue Bell Pike Blue Bell PA 19422-2108 Office: Elliott Reihner Siedzkowski & Egan 925 Harvest Dr Blue Bell PA 19422-1956

ELLIOTT, RICHARD HOWARD, lawyer; b. Astoria, N.Y., Apr. 30, 1933; m. Judith A. Kessler, Dec. 26, 1956; children: Marc Evan, Jonathan Hugh, Eve; m. 2d, Diane S. Schaefer, Nov. 18, 1978; children: Alexis, Sara Jane, Benjamin, David. BS, Lehigh U., 1954; JD cum laude, U. Pa., 1962. Bar: U.S. Dist. Ct. (ea. dist.) Pa. 1962, Pa. Supreme Ct. 1962, U.S. Ct. Appeals (3d cir.) 1963, U.S. Dist. Ct. (mid. dist.) Pa. 1976. Assoc. Clark, Ladner, Fortenbaugh & Young, Phila., 1962-69, ptnr., 1970-75, Elliott & Magee, Doylestown, Pa., 1976—. Moderator Permanent Jud. Commn., Presbytery of Phila.; v.p., dir. Bucks County Soc. Prevention Cruelty to Animals; former pres., dir. Pa. Soc. for Prevention of Cruelty to Animals; gen. counsel, dir. Pa. Fedn. Humane Socs., adj. faculty Bucks County Cmty. Coll.; mem. Pa. Navigation Commn., 1977-80. Lt. USN, 1954-59. Mem. ABA, Pa. Bar Assn., Phila. Bar Assn., Bucks County Bar Assn. Republican. General civil litigation, General practice, Probate (including wills, trusts). Home: 1205 Victoria Rd Warminster PA 18974-3923 Office: Elliott & Magee 11 Duane Rd PO Box 885 Doylestown PA 18901-2837 E-mail: relli59360@aol.com.

ELLIOTT, R(OY) FRASER, lawyer, holding and management company executive; b. Ottawa, Ont., Can., Nov. 25, 1921; B.Comm., Queen's U., Kingston, Ont., Can., 1943; LLB, Osgoode Hall Law Sch., 1946; grad., Harvard U. Sch. Bus. Adminstrn., 1947. Bar: Ont. 1946, Que. 1948; created queen's counsel. Ptnr. Stikeman, Elliott, Toronto, Ont., 1952—. Bd. dirs. CAE Inc., Toronto; lectr. co. law McGill U., Montreal, 1951. Contbg. author, editor: Que. Corp. Manual, 1948-53; co-editor: Doing Business in Canada. Mem. Montreal Bar Assn., Can. Bar Assn., Law Soc. Upper Can. Home: 22 St Thomas St Ste 17B Toronto ON Canada ON M5S 3E7 Office: Commerce Ct W Ste 5300 Toronto ON Canada M5L 1B9 E-mail: felliott@stikeman.com.

ELLIOTT, SCOTT, lawyer, theatre artistic director, critic; b. San Jose, July 26, 1957; s. Roland Meredith and Sandra Gale (Deem) E.; m. Nancy Marie Oller, Apr. 6, 1979; children: Tristan Robin, Jordan Brook, Robin Sage, Forest Dream. BA in Drama magna cum laude, Calif. State U. Stanislaus, Turlock, 1979; JD, U. Oreg., 1987. Bar: Oreg. 1987, U.S. Dist. Ct. Oreg. 1988, U.S. Ct. Appeals (9th cir.) 1992. Assoc. Larry O. Gildea, Eugene, Oreg., 1987-88, Thorp, Dennet, Purdy & Golden, Springfield, Oreg., 1988; law clk. U.S. Dist. Ct. Nev., Las Vegas, 1988-89; ptnr. Green & Elliott, Lincoln City, Oreg., 1989-95; assoc. Thorp, Purdy, Jewett, Urness & Wilkinson, Springfield, Oreg., 1995-96, Wine, Weller, Ehrlich and Green, Lincoln City, 1996-98; pvt. practice Lincoln City, 1998—. Theatre critic: Lincoln City News Guard. Founder, artistic dir. Cmty. Family Players, 1997—2003; mem. choir Congl. Ch., 1997—2003; founder, artistic dir. Lincoln City Congl. Ch. Choir, 1997—2003. Recipient Commitment to Excellence in Art award, 4Cs, 2001; grad. tchg. fellow, U. Oreg. Theatre, 1979—80. Mem. Kiwanis. Mem. Congl. Ch. Avocations: family, theology, gardening, theatre, singing. Civil rights, General civil litigation, Commercial, consumer (including collections, credit). Office: 2137 NW Highway 101 Ste B Lincoln City OR 97367-4214 also: Lincoln City Congl Ch 1760 NW 25th St Lincoln City OR 97367-4151 E-mail: lawyer_elliott@yahoo.com.

ELLIOTT, TIMOTHY B. lawyer; BS in Acctg., Fla. State U ., 1973; JD, Fla. State U., 1975. Bar: Fla. 1976, U.S. Ct. Appeals (11th cir.) 1984, U.S. Ct. Appeals (5th cir.) 1977, U.S. Dist. Ct. (no. dist.) Fla. 1977, U.S. Dist. Ct. (ctrl. dist.) Fla. 1985, U.S. Dist. Ct. (so. dist.) Fla. 1996, U.S. Tax Ct. 2001. Assoc. Ausley & McMullen, PA, Tallahassee, 1976—81, ptnr., shareholder, 1981—99; solo practitioner Tallahassee, 2000—. Apptd. bus. and fin. subcom. Tallahassee Improvement Authority, 1998—2000; organizer, presenter various seminars. Contbr. chapters to books. Mem.: ABA, Fla. Def. Lawyers Assn., Def. Rsch. Inst., Tallahassee Bar Assn. (ann. pro bono representation), Fla. Bar (cert. spl. recognition 1988), Phi Delta Phi. Appellate, Banking, Insurance. Office: 1350 E-4 Mahan Dr Box 301 Tallahassee FL 32308

ELLIOTT, WARREN G. lawyer; b. Pueblo, Colo., Jan. 3, 1927; s. Wallace Ford and Hazel (Ellsworth) E.; m. Martha McCabe, June 20, 1953 (div. Sept. 1980); children: Mark, Winthrop, Carolyn, Byron. Student, U. Nebr., 1944-45, U. Colo., 1947-49, AB, 1973; JD, U. Mich., 1952. Bar: Colo. 1952, Conn. 1976, D.C. bar 1978. Asst. city mgr., city atty., Pueblo, 1952-55; adminstrv. asst., legislative counsel U.S. Senator Gordon Allott, 1956-61; asst. gen. counsel Life Ins. Assn. Am., Washington, 1961-68; gen. counsel Aetna Life & Casualty Co., Hartford, Conn., 1968-78; mem. firm Hedrick & Lane, Washington, 1978-79; ptnr. Nossaman, Guthner, Knox & Elliott, Washington, 1979-85, of counsel, 1986—, Epstein, Becker & Green, P.C., Washington, 1986—. Bd. dirs. Friends of the Hopkins Ctr.; trustee Opera North. Served with USAAC, 1944-46. Mem. ABA, Fed. Bar Assn., Phi Gamma Delta, Phi Alpha Delta. Office: 3703 Magnolia Ln Santa Barbara CA 93105 E-mail: warrengelliott@hotmail.com.

ELLIS, ALFRED WRIGHT (AL ELLIS), lawyer; b. Cleve., Aug. 26, 1943; s. Donald Porter and Louise (Wright) E.; m. Kay Genseke, June 1965 (div. 1976); 1 child, Joshua Kyle; m. Sandra Lee Fahey, Feb. 11, 1989. BA with honors, U. Tex., Arlington, 1965; JD, So. Meth. U., 1971. Bar: Tex., U.S. Dist. Ct. (no., so., ea. and we. dists.) Tex., U.S. Ct. Appeals (5th cir.), U.S. Supreme Ct.; cert. personal injury and civil trial lawyer, Best Lawyers in Am. 2003-04. Atty. Woodruff, Kendall & Smith, Dallas, 1972; ptnr. Woodruff & Ellis, Dallas; pvt. practice Dallas, 1983-96; of counsel Howie & Sweeney, 1996—2003; of coun. Sommerman, Moore, & Quesada, 2003—. Instr. So. Meth. U. Law Sch. Trial Advocacy; past pres. Law Focused Edn., Inc. Past mem. City of Dallas Urban Rehab. Standards Bd., Dallas Assembly, Salesmanship Club, Dallas; bd. dirs. Dallas Habitat for Humanity, 1998-2002; trustee Hist. Preservation League, 1992-94; tournament dir. Dallas Regional Golden Gloves Tournament, 1976-96; pres., bd. dirs. Dallas Coun. on Alcoholism, 1980. Capt. U.S. Army, 1965-69, Dallas All Sports Assn. (pres. 1980). Fellow Roscoe Pound Found.; named one of Outstanding Young Mem of Am., 1977, named Boss of Yr. Dallas Assn. Legal Secs., 1978; recipient Certs. of Recognition (8) D.I.S.D., 1971-83, Wall St. Jour. award So. Meth. U. Law Sch., 1972, Hayward McMurray award Dallas Jaycees, 1975-76, Spl. Recognition award All Sports Assn., 1977, Cert. of Appreciation for Exceptional and Disting. Vol. Svc. Gov. Mark White, 1983, Community Spirit award Dallas Bus. Jour., 1993, Disting. Svc. award Dallas All Sports Assn., 1993,award Nancy Garms Meml. for outstanding Contr. to Law Focus Edn., 1996-Leon Jaworski award (Internat. Acad. of Trial Lawyers, Al Ellis Award by Dallas Minority Bar Assn. 2002, D Mag., Best Lawyers in Dallas (personal injury) 2003. Fellow Tex. Bar Found. (sustaining life, Dan R. Price Meml. award 2003), Dallas Bar Found., Dallas Assn. Young Lawyers Found. (life); mem. ATLA, Am. Bd. Trial Advocates (diplomate, sec.-treas. Dallas chpt. 1998, pres. 1999), Am. Coll. Legal Medicine (assoc.), Million Dollar Advocates Forum, Legal Svcs. of North Tex. (bd. dirs., Outstanding Svc. award 1990), State Bar Tex. (lectr. seminars, bd. dirs. 1991-94, Excellence in Diversity award 1994, Outstanding 3d Yr. Dir. award, Judge Sam Williams Local Bar Leadership award), Internat. Acad. Trial Lawyers, Dallas Bar Assn. (bd. dirs. 1978, chmn. bd. dirs. 1986, v.p. 1987-88, pres. 1990), Dallas Trial Lawyers Assn. (pres. 1977, Disting. Cmty. Svc. award 1990), Million Dollar Advocates, Tex. Trial Lawyers Assn., Tex. Equal Access to Justice Found. (bd. dirs. 1994-96), Am. Coll. Barristers, Coll. State Bar of Tex. (bd. dirs. 1997-1999), Tex. Commn. Lawyer Discipline, Tex. Ctr. for Legal Ethics and Professionalism (bd. dirs. 1999—, chmn. 2002-), Tex. Legal Svcs. Ctr. (bd. dirs. 1999-2002), William Mac Taylor Inn of Ct. Avocations: tennis, skiing. General civil litigation, Insurance, Personal injury (including property damage). Office: 3232 McKinney Ste 1160 Dallas TX 75204

ELLIS, ANDREW JACKSON, JR., lawyer; b. Ashland, Va., June 23, 1930; m. Dorothy L. Lichliter, Apr. 24, 1954; children: Elizabeth E. Attkisson, Andrew C., William D. BA, Washington and Lee U., 1951, LLB, 1953. Bar: Va. 1952. Ptnr. Campbell, Ellis & Campbell, Ashland, 1955-70, Mays, Valentine, Davenport & Moore, Richmond, Va., 1970-88, Mays & Valentine, Richmond, 1988-96, sr. counsel, 1998—2002, Troutman & Sanders, Richmond, 2002—. Substitute judge County of Hanover (Va.) Ct., 1955—63, 15th Jud. Dist., 1990—96; commr. chancery cir. ct. Hanover County, 1955—96; commonwealth atty., 1963—70; county atty., 1970—78; judge 15th Dist. Juvenile and Domestic Rels. Ct., 1996—98; capital adv. bd. NationsBank Va., 1960—93. Mem. Ashland Town Coun., 1956—63; mayor Town of Ashland, 1958—63; trustee J. Sargent Reynolds CC, 1972—80. 1st lt. U.S. Army, 1953—55. Fellow: Va. Law Found., Am. Coll. Trial Lawyers; mem.: S.R., Hanover Bar Assn. (past pres.), 15th Jud. Cir. Bar Assn. (past pres.), Richmond Bar Assn., Va. Trial Lawyers Assn., Va. State Bar (coun. 1968—74), Va. Bar Assn., Kiwanis. Episcopalian. General civil litigation, Condemnation (eminent domain), Insurance. Home: 15293 Old Ridge Rd Beaverdam VA 23015-1610 Office: PO Box 1122 Richmond VA 23218-1122

ELLIS, COURTENAY, lawyer; b. Cottingham, Eng., Jan. 4, 1946; came to the U.S., 1970; BA, Oxford U., Eng., 1967, MA, 1974; LLM, George Washington U., 1972. Bar: D.C. 1973; cert. solicitor, Eng. Solicitor's articled clk. Field, Fisher & Co., London, 1968-69; solicitor Farrer & Co., London, 1970; assoc. atty. Covington & Burling, Washington, 1972-76, Akin, Gump, Strauss, Hauer & Feld, 1976-78, ptnr., 1979-98, Oppenheimer Wolff Donnelly Bayh, Washington, 1998-99, Murphy Ellis Weber, 2000—. Bd. dirs. The Episcopal Ctr. for Children, Washington, 1986-92. Mem. ABA, Law Soc. London, Brit. Am. Bus. Assn. (bd. dirs., program chair 1997-98, pres. 1999-2001), Washington Fgn. Law Soc. (bd. govs., membership coord. 1993-95, program coord. 1995-96, pres. 1997-98), Fed. Bar Assn. (internat. law sect., chair 1996-98), Globalscot (founder 2002), The Law Soc., London, Met. Club, Annapolis Yacht Club. General civil litigation, Oil, gas, and mineral, Private international. Office: Murphy Ellis Weber Ste 1200 818 Connecticut Ave NW Washington DC 20006 E-mail: cellis@murphyellisweber.com.

ELLIS, DONALD LEE, lawyer; b. Oct. 2, 1950; s. Truett T. and Rosemary (Tarrant) Ellis; children: Angela Nicole, Laura Elizabeth, Natalie Dawn, Donald Lee II. BS, U. Tulsa, 1973; JD, Okla. City U., 1976. Bar: Tex. 1979, Okla. 1977, U.S. Dist. Ct. (ea. dist.) Tex. 1978, U.S. Dist. Ct. (we. dist.) Okla. 1978, U.S. Ct. Appeals (5th cir.) 1984, U.S. Ct. Appeals (11th cir.), U.S. Supreme Ct. 1984. Spl. agt. FBI, Washington, 1976—78; asst. dist. atty. Smith County, Tyler, Tex., 1979—80; mem. firm Barron & Ellis, Tyler, 1980—85; pvt. practice, 1985—. Bd. dir. Mental Health Assn. Mem.: Lawyers-Pilot Bar Assn., FBI Agents Assn., Tex. Trial Lawyers Assn., Soc. Former Spl. Agts. FBI, Smith County Bar Assn., Okla. Bar Assn., Tex. Bar Assn., Assn. Trial Lawyers Am. Personal injury (including property damage). Home: PO Box 131221 Tyler TX 75713-1221 Office: 217 W Houston St Tyler TX 75702-8137

ELLIS, DORSEY DANIEL, JR., lawyer, educator; b. Cape Girardeau, Mo., May 18, 1938; s. Dorsey D. and Anne (Stanaland) E.; m. Sondra Wagner, Dec. 27, 1962; children: Laura Elizabeth, Geoffrey Earl. BA, Maryville Coll., 1960; JD, U. Chgo., 1963; LLD, Maryville Coll., 1998. Bar: N.Y. 1967, U.S. Ct. Appeals (2d cir.) 1967, Iowa 1976, U.S. Ct. Appeals (8th cir.) 1976. Assoc. Cravath, Swaine & Moore, N.Y.C., 1963-68; assoc. prof. U. Iowa, Iowa City, 1968-71, prof., 1971-87, v.p. fin. and univ. svcs., 1984-87, spl. asst. to pres., 1974-75; dean Washington U. Sch. Law, St. Louis, Mo., 1987-98, prof. law, 1998-99; disting. prof. law, 1999—. Vis. mem. sr. common room Mansfield Coll., Oxford U., Eng., 1972-73, 75; vis. prof. law Emory U., Atlanta, 1981-82, Victoria U., New Zealand, 1999; vis. sr. rsch. fellow Jesus Coll. Oxford U., Eng., 1998; bd. dirs. Maryville Coll., 1989-98, 99—, vis. scholar U. Va., 2003. Contbr. articles to profl. jours. Trustee Mo. Hist. Soc., St. Louis, 1995-2000. Nat. Honor scholar U. Chgo., 1960-63; recipient Joseph Henry Beale prize, 1961, Alumni award Maryville Coll., 1988. Mem. ABA, Am. Law Inst., Bar Assn. Metro St. Louis, Mound City Bar Assn., Iowa Bar Assn., AALS Acad. Resource Corps., Order of Coif. Home: 6901 Kingsbury Blvd Saint Louis MO 63130 Office: Box 1120 1 Brookings Dr Saint Louis MO 63130-4862 E-mail: ellis@wulaw.wustl.edu.

ELLIS, DOUGLASS N., JR., lawyer; BA, U. Va., 1965; JD, Boston U., 1972. Bar: Mass. 1972. With Ropes & Gray, Boston, 1972—81, mng. ptnr., 1981—. Office: Ropes & Gray 1 International Pl Boston MA 02110-2646

ELLIS, JAMES D. communications executive, corporate lawyer; b. 1943; BBA, U. Iowa, 1965; JD, U. Mo., 1968. Bar: Mo. 1968, U.S. Ct. Appeals (D.C. cir.) 1977, Tex. 1980. Atty. AT&T, 1972-74, AT&T Long Lines, 1974-77; atty. gen. depts. AT&T, 1977-79; gen. atty. Southwestern Bell Telephone Co., San Antonio, 1979-83; v.p., gen. counsel Bellcore, 1983-84, Southwestern Bell Telephone Co., Tex., 1984-86, v.p., gen. counsel, sec., 1986-88; sr. v.p., gen. counsel Southwestern Bell Corp., 1988-89; sr. exec. v.p., gen. counsel SBC Comm., San Antonio, 1989—. With U.S. Army, 1968-72. Office: SBC Communications Inc 175 E Houston St San Antonio TX 78205-2255*

ELLIS, LESTER NEAL, JR., lawyer; b. Washington, Aug. 1, 1948; s. Lester Neal and Marie (Brooks) E. BS, U.s. Mil. Acad., 1970; JD, U. Va., 1975. Bar: Va. 1975, U.S. Ct. Appeals (5th cir.) 1977, D.C. 1978, U.S. Ct. Appeals (4th and D.C. cirs.) 1979, U.S. Ct. Appeals (11th cir.) 1982, N.C. 1985, U.S. Supreme Ct. 2000, U.S. Dist. Ct. (ea., mid., we. dists.) N.C., U.S. Dist. Ct. (ea., we. dists.) Va., U.S. Ct. Claims. Trial atty. litigation divsn. Office of JAG, U.S. Dept. Army, Washington, 1975-78; assoc. Hunton & Williams, Richmond, Va., 1978-84, ptnr. Raleigh, 1984—. Maj. U.S. Army, 1970-78, col. USAR, 1993-99. Recipient Judge Paul Brosman award U.S. Ct. Mil. Appeals, 1975. Mem.: D.C. Bar Assn. (Wake County bd. elections 1986—93, chmn. 1987—93, ct. rules com.), Va. Bar Assn. (spl. issues com. 1982), ABA (chair tort and trial practice steering com., editor-in-chief Tort Source, chair comml. torts commn., chair trial techniques com., tort and ins. practice sect., editor-in-chief Tort and Ins. Law Jour., coun. mem.), Phi Kappa Phi. Republican. Episcopalian. General civil litigation, Environmental. Home: 1116 Wagon Ridge Rd Raleigh NC 27614 Office: Hunton & Williams One Hanover Sq PO Box 109 Raleigh NC 27602-0109

ELLIS, ROBERT BRYAN, JR., lawyer; b. Rome, Ga., June 9, 1957; s. Robert Bryan and Ferris Opal (Everett) E. BA cum laude, Mercer U., 1978, JD, 1981. Bar: Ga. 1981, U.S. Dist. Ct. (no. dist.) Ga. 1981, U.S. Ct. Appeals Ga. 1981, U.S. Dist. Ct. (mid. dist.) Ga. 1986. Law clk. to presiding judge Rome Jud. Cir. Ct., Ga., 1981-82; asst. dist. atty. Alapaha Jud. Cir. Ct., 1982-86; pvt. practice Nashville, Ga., 1986-88; dist. atty. Alapaha Jud. Cir. Ct., Ga., 1989—. Judge City of Nashville, 1986-88, City of Alapaha, 1986-88. Mem. ABA, Jaycees (v.p. Berrrien County chpt. 1984-85). Democrat. Baptist. Avocations: hunting, fishing, running. General civil litigation, Criminal, Family and matrimonial. Office: PO Box 125 115 N Davis St Nashville GA 31639-2161

ELLISON, PATRICIA LEE, lawyer; b. Elizabeth, N.J., Oct. 17, 1943; d. Harry C. and Leila D. Ellison. Student, U. Paris, France, 1963-64; BA, Denison U., France, 1965; MA, U. Calif., Riverside, 1967; JD cum laude, U. San Diego, 1973. Bar: Calif. 1973, N.Y. 1983. Fin. analyst NASA, Greenbelt, Md., 1967-68; rsch. atty. Dist. Atty.'s Office, San Diego, 1973-74; assoc. atty. Butler Ruff & Harrigan, San Diego, 1974-75; ptnr. Ellison Eichten & Bell, San Diego, 1975-82; pvt. practice Kingston, N.Y., 1983—. Bd. dirs. Ulster County YWCA, Kingston, 1988-91, pres. bd. dirs., 1992; chair Dem. Com. Town of Shandaken, N.Y., 1993—; mem. Ulster County Youth Bd., 2002—; mem. panel surrogate decision-making com. N.Y. State Commn. on Quality of Care, 2001—. Recipient Internat. Acad. Trial Lawyers Advocacy award, 1973. Mem. Alpha Chi Omega. Avocations: piano, gardening. Family and matrimonial, Pension, profit-sharing, and employee benefits, Probate (including wills, trusts). Office: 175 Clinton Ave PO Box 1717 Kingston NY 12402-1717

ELLMANN, DOUGLAS STANLEY, lawyer; b. Detroit, July 15, 1956; s. William Marshall and Sheila Estelle E.; m. Claudia Joan Roberts, Feb. 16, 1985. AB, Occidental Coll., 1978; JD, U. Mich., 1982. Bar: Mich. 1982, U.S. Dist. Ct. (ea. dist.) Mich. 1982, U.S. Ct. Appeals (6th cir.) 1982. Prin. Ellmann & Ellmann, P.C., Ann Arbor, Mich., 1989—. Spl. asst. atty. gen., 1986; trustee U.S. Panel, 1989-, sec. bankruptcy trustee assoc. U.S. Bankruptcy Ct. (ea. dist.) Mich., 1993—. Author: Selected Issues in Asset Protection, 1994, My Advice: Next Time Go Solo, 1994, LWUSA; co-author: Winning Labor Arbitrations, 1987. Mem. U. Mich. Law Sch. Fund, 1986-87. Mem. ABA (vice chair bankruptcy com. 1995—), Mich. Bar Assn. (rep. assembly 1983-89, 90-92, 98—, exec. counsel young lawyers sect. 1985-87, mem. client security fund com. 1987-95), State Bar Mich. (mem. manditory CLE com. 1989-96, chmn. 1995-96, judicial qualifications com. 2000—), Washtenaw County Bar Assn. (chmn. banking, bus., bankruptcy com. 1995-2000). Bankruptcy, General civil litigation, Commercial, contracts (including sales of goods; commercial financing). Office: 308 W Huron St Ann Arbor MI 48103-4204

ELLSWORTH, JOHN DAVID, lawyer; b. Clarion, Iowa, Nov. 13, 1944; s. John Alfred and Marjorie Eileen (Smith) E.; m. Jane Porteous, July 9, 1975; children: John P., Charles G. AB, Carleton Coll., 1966; JD, Harvard U., 1969; LLM, Georgetown U., 1974. Bar: Nebr. 1969, D.C. 1972, U.S. Ct. Appeals (8th cir.) 1972. Law clk. to judge U.S. Ct. Appeals (8th cir.), St. Louis, 1971-72; atty., advisor SEC, Washington, 1972-74; from assoc. to ptnr. Ober, Kaler, Grimes & Shriver, Washington, 1974-80; ptnr. Kutak, Rock & Campbell, Omaha, 1980-81; pvt. practice Omaha, 1981-90; prin. Lieben, Whitted, Houghton, Slowiaczek & Cavanagh, Omaha, 1990—. Pres. Broker-Dealer Communications Ltd., Omaha, 1983—. Author: How to Register the DPP Broker-Dealer, 1982, How to Operate the DPP Broker-Dealer, 1984, Real Estate Syndication Handbook, 1984. Capt. USAR, 1970—78. Mem. Real Estate Securities and Syndication Inst. (chmn. various coms.), Nat. Assn. Securities Dealers (real estate com.), Nebr. Environ. Trust, Audubon Soc. Nebr., Nebr. Land Trust, Happy Hollow Club. Presbyterian. Avocations: hunting, fishing. Securities, Corporate taxation, Personal income taxation. Office: 2027 Dodge St Ste 100 Omaha NE 68102-1229 E-mail: jellsworth@liebenlaw.com.

ELLWANGER, THOMAS JOHN, lawyer; b. Summit, N.J., Feb. 26, 1949; s. James Warren and Lorean (Nicholson) E.; children: James Hunter, Margaret Lorean. BA, Northwestern U., 1970; JD, U. Fla., 1974. Bar: Fla. 1975, U.S. Dist. Ct. (mid. dist.) Fla. 1976, U.S. Ct. Appeals (11th cir.) 1976, U.S. Dist. Ct. (so. dist.) Fla. 1977, U.S. Tax Ct. Mem. Fowler, White, Gillen, Boggs, Villareal & Banker P.A. (now Fowler, White, Boggs, Banker P.A.), Tampa, Fla., 1975—. Instr. law U. Fla., Gainesville, 1975; adj. prof. Stetson U. Coll. Law, 1997-2000. Editor: Gadsden County Times, 1970-72. Pres. Neighborhood Housing Services Hyde Park, Tampa, 1978. Fellow Am. Coll. Trust and Estate Counsel, Fla. Bar (cert. tax lawyer), Hillsborough County Bar Assn. (chmn. com. probate liaison 1985-86, real property probate and trust law sect. 1987-89), Tampa Bay Estate Planning Counsel (pres. 1994-95). Democrat. Avocations: music. lit., sports. Estate planning, Probate (including wills, trusts), Estate taxation. Office: Fowler White Boggs Banker PA 501 E Kennedy Blvd Ste 1700 Tampa FL 33602-5239 E-mail: tellwang@fowlerwhite.com.

ELLWOOD, SCOTT, lawyer; b. Boston, July 8, 1936; s. William Prescott and Doris (Cook) E.; m. Suzanne M. Timble; children: Victoria, William Prescott II, Marjorie. Student, Williams Coll., 1954-56; AB, Eastern Mich. U., 1958; LLB, Harvard U., 1961. Bar: Iowa 1961, Ill. 1961, U.S. Dist. Ct. (no. dist.) Ill., 1961. Assoc. McBride & Baker, Chgo., 1961-67, ptnr., 1968-84, McDermott, Will & Emery, Chgo., 1984-99. Pres. Miller Investment Co., 1973-93, bd. dirs.; pres. SMI Investment Corp., 1978—. Pres., bd. dirs. 110 N Wacker Dr Found., 1974-84, Northfield Found., 1978-84, Leadership Found., 1979-84, Woodbine Found., 1980-84, The Cannon River Found., 1982-84, L.M. McBride Found., 1982-84, Bellarmine

Found., 1982-84, Mark Morton Meml. Fund, 1982—. Mem. Iowa Bar Assn., Ill. State Bar Assn., Harvard Law Soc. Ill. (bd. dirs. 1983-98, treas. 1987-88, sec. 1988-89, v.p. 1989-93, pres. 1993-95), Harvard Club Chgo. (bd. dirs. 1993-95), Monroe Club (bd. dirs. 1988-98), Skokie Country Club (Glencoe, Ill.). Republican. Episcopalian. Estate planning, Corporate taxation, Personal income taxation. Home: 1296 Hackberry Ln Winnetka IL 60093-1606 Office: McDermott Will & Emery 227 W Monroe St Ste 3100 Chicago IL 60606-5096

ELMA, MAGDANGAL BORJA, lawyer, educator; b. Lucban, Quezon, The Philippines, Jan. 2, 1939; s. Medardo and Hiwaga (Borja) E.; m. Elsa Kimhoko, Feb. 2, 1963; children: Lorelei, Gerardo, Enrique, Daniel. BS in Jurisprudence cum laude, LLB cum laude, U. of The Philippines, 1961; LLM, Yale U., 1962. Editor Lawyers Coop. Pub. Co., Rochester, N.Y., 1962—; assoc. justice Ct. Appeals, The Philippines, 1987; undersec. Dept. Environ. and Natural Resources, The Philippines, 1987; dep., acting exec. sec. Office of the Pres. of The Philippines, 1988-91, presdl. asst. for legal and jud. affairs, 1990-93, chief Presdl. Legal Counsel, 1998—; sr. and mng. ptnr. Belo Gozon Elma Parel Asuncion and Lucila, Makati, Philippines, 1993—. Spl. lectr., prof. Law Ctr. U. of The Philippines; chmn. Presdl. Commn. on Good Govt., 1998—. Author: The Aquino Presidency and the Constitution, 1993; contbg. editor to legal ency. American Jurisprudence and American Law Reports, 1962-67; mem. bd. editl. cons. Supreme Ct. Reports Annotated. Mem. Philippine Bar Assn. (bd. dirs. 1994-96), Philippine Constl. Assn., Philippine Soc. Internat. Law, Integrated Bar of the Philippines, U.P.-Yale Club Alumni Assn, Phi Kappa Phi, Pi Gamma Mu. Office: Sagittarius Condos 15th Fl HV dela Costa Salcedo Manila Philippines

ELMER, BRIAN CHRISTIAN, lawyer; b. Washington, Apr. 18, 1936; s. Arthur Christian and Kathryn Aleen (O'Brien) E.; m. Sonja Kay Glass, Sept. 3, 1966; children: Mark Christian, Kimberly Kay, Robin Ann. BA in Arts and Sci., Cornell U., 1960; JD, U. Mich., 1962. Bar: D.C. 1963. Law clk. U.S. Ct. Appeals for D.C. Cir., Washington, 1962-64; ptnr. Jones, Day, Reavis and Pogue, Washington, 1964-79, Crowell and Moring, LLP, Washington, 1979—. Author: Fraud in Government Contracting, 1985; contbr. articles to profl. jours. Mem. ABA, D.C. Bar Assn., Met. Club. Office: Crowell & Moring LLP 1001 Pennsylvania Ave NW Washington DC 20004-2595 E-mail: belmer@crowell.com.

ELMORE, EDWARD WHITEHEAD, lawyer; b. Lawrenceville, Va., July 15, 1938; s. Thomas Milton and Mary Norfleet (Whitehead) E.; m. Gail Harmon, Aug. 10, 1968; children: Mary Jennifer, Edward Whitehead Jr. BA, U. Va.-Charlottesville, 1959, JD, 1962. Bar: Va. 1962. Assoc. firm Hunton & Williams, Richmond, Va., 1965-69; staff atty. Ethyl Corp., Richmond, 1969-78, asst. gen. counsel, 1978-79, gen. counsel, 1979-80, gen. counsel., sec., 1980-83, v.p., gen. counsel, sec., 1983-94, spl. counsel to exec. com., corp. sec., 1994-97; sr. v.p., gen. counsel, sec. Albemarle Corp., Richmond, 1994-2001, exec. v.p., sec., 2001—02, exec. v.p., 2002—. Served to capt. AUS, 1962-65. Decorated Army Commendation medal Mem. ABA, Va. Bar Assn., Internat. Bar Assn., Va. State Bar, Am. Corp. Counsel Assn., Bar Assn. Richmond, Am. Soc. Corp. Secs., Raven Soc., Phi Beta Kappa Corporate, general. Office: Albemarle Corp 330 S 4th St Richmond VA 23219-4350

ELROD, EUGENE RICHARD, lawyer; b. Roanoke, Ala., May 14, 1949; s. James Woodrow and Selma Fromer (Steinbach) E. AB, Dartmouth Coll., 1971; JD, Emory U., 1974. Bar: Ga. 1974, D.C. 1976, U.S. Ct. Appeals (D.C. cir.) 1985, U.S. Ct. Appeals (5th cir.) 1987, U.S. Dist. Ct. D.C. 1987, U.S. Ct. Appeals (11th cir.) 1987, U.S. Supreme Ct. 1987, U.S. Ct. Appeals (10th cir.) 1997. Trial atty. Fed. Power Com., Washington, 1974-76; atty.-advisor Fed. Energy Adminstrn., Washington, 1977; assoc. Sidley & Austin, Washington, 1977-80, ptnr., 1981—. Mem. adv. bd. The Keplinger Cos., Houston. Mem. selection com. for Woodruff scholars Emory U. Law Sch., Dartmouth '71 Exec. Com. Mem. ABA, D.C. Bar Assn., Ga. Bar Assn., Energy Bar Assn. (chmn. oil pipeline com. 1982-83, tax com. 1980-81, 92-95, liaison with adminstrv. law judges 1986-87, ethics com. 1997-2001, bd. dirs. 2000—), Dartmouth Club (exec. com. class of 1971), Book Club of Calif. Avocations: running, book collecting, gardening. Administrative and regulatory, FERC practice. Home: 4300 Hawthorne St NW Washington DC 20016-3571 Office: Sidley Austin Brown & Wood 1501 K St NW Ste 900 Washington DC 20005

ELROD, LINDA DIANE HENRY, lawyer, educator; b. Topeka, Kans., Mar. 6, 1947; d. Lyndus Arthur Henry and Marjorie Jane (Hammel) Allen; divorced; children: Carson Douglas, Bree Elizabeth. BA in English with honors, Washburn U., 1969, JD cum laude, 1971. Bar: Kans. 1972. Instr. U. S.D., Topeka, 1970-71; research atty. Kans. Jud. Council, Topeka, 1972-74; asst. prof. Washburn U., Topeka, 1974-78, assoc. prof., 1978-82, prof. law, 1982-93, disting. prof., 1993—, dir. Children and Family Law Ctr. ;vis. prof. law U. San Diego, Paris Summer Inst., 1988, 90, Washington U. Sch. Law, St. Louis, 1990, 98, summer 1991, 93, Fla. State U. Law Sch., spring, 2000. Author: Kansas Family Law Handbook, 1983, rev. edit., 1990, supplement, 1993, Child Custody Practice and Procedure, 1993, supplements, 1994-97, 99, 2000, 01, 02; co-author: Principles of Family Law, 1999, 5th edit., 2003, Kansas Family Law Guide, 1999, supplement, 2000, 01, 02; editor Family Law Quar., 1992—; contbr. articles to profl. jours. Pres. YWCA, Topeka, 1982-83; vice-chair Kans. Commn. on Child Support, 1984-87, Supreme Ct. Commn. on Child Support, 1989—; chair Kans. Cmty. Svc. Orgn., 1986-87; adv. bd. CASA, 1997—; bd. dirs. Appleseed, 2000—. Recipient Disting. Service award Washburn Law Sch. Assn., 1986; named YWCA Woman of Distinction, 1997. Mem. ABA (coun. family law sect. 1988-92, sec. 1998, vice-chair, 1999, chair-elect 1999-2000, chair 2000-01, chair Schwab Meml. Grant Implementation 1984-87, co-chair Amicus Curiae com. 1987-92, steering com. on unmet legal needs of children 2002—), Topeka Bar Assn. (sec. 1981-85, v.p. 1985-86, pres. 1986-87), Kans. Child Support Enforcement Assn. (bd. dirs. 1988—, Child Support Hall of Fame 1990), Kans. Bar Assn. (sec.-treas. 1988-89, com. ops. and fin. 1988, pres. family law sect. 1984-86, Disting. Svc. award 1985), NONOSO, Phi Kappa Phi, Phi Alpha Delta Alumni Assn. (justice 1976-77), Phi Beta Delta, Kappa Alpha Theta (pres. alumnae chpt. 1995-97). Presbyterian. Avocations: bridge, reading, quilting. Office: Washburn U Law Sch 17th and College Topeka KS 66621 E-mail: linda.elrod@washburn.edu.

ELSEN, SHELDON HOWARD, lawyer; b. Pitts., May 12, 1928; m. Gerri Sharfman, 1952; children: Susan Rachel, Jonathan Charles. AB, Princeton U., 1950; AM, Harvard U., 1952, JD, 1958. Bar: N.Y. 1959, U.S. Supreme Ct. 1971. Ptnr. Orans, Elsen & Lupert LLP, N.Y.C., 1965—. Adj. prof. law Columbia U. Law Sch., 1969—; chief counsel N.Y. Moreland Act Commn. on UDC, 1975-76; asst. U.S. atty. So. Dist. N.Y., 1960-64; cons. Pres.'s Commn. Law Enforcement Adminstrn. Justice, 1967; mem. faculty Nat. Inst. Trial Advocacy, 1973; panel chair 1st dept. disciplinary com. N.Y., 1992-96. Contbr. articles to profl. jours. Fellow Am. Coll. Trial Lawyers; mem. Assn. of Bar of City of N.Y. (v.p. 1988-89, chmn. com. on fed. legislation 1969-72, chmn. com. on fed. cts. 1983-86, chmn. nominating com. 1986-87, chmn. com. amenities in land use process for N.Y.C. 1987-88), Am. Law Inst. (adviser Transnat. Rules of Civil Procedure 1999—), Phi Beta Kappa. General civil litigation, Securities, Criminal. Office: 1 Rockefeller Plz New York NY 10020-2102 Office Fax: 212-765-3662. Business E-Mail: selsen@oellaw.com.

ELSENER, G. DALE, lawyer; b. Frederick, Okla., Mar. 26, 1951; s. Gordon Lee and Anita Lois (Vaughan) Elsener; children: Hayley Lynn, Garrett Dale. BS, Okla. State U., 1973; JD, Okla. U., 1976. Bar: Okla. 1976, U.S. Dist. Ct. (ea. and we. dists.) Okla. 1984. Assoc. Richard S. Roberts, Wewoka, Okla., 1976-78; ptnr. Roberts & Elsener, Wewoka, 1979-86; sole practice, 1986-90. City atty. City of Wewoka, 1986—. Chmn. bd. trustees Seminole County Law Libr., 1986; chmn. Seminole County Econ. Devel. Adv. Com., 1986; bd. dirs. Rural Water Dist. 3, Cromwell, Okla., 1982—90; mem. Seminole Econ. Devel. Coun., 1997—2000. Mem.: Seminole County Bar Assn., Okla. Bar Assn. (real property and mineral law sects.), Seminole State Coll. Edn. Fund (bd. dirs.), Seminole C. of C. (pres. 1998). Oil, gas, and mineral, Probate (including wills, trusts), Property, real (including real estate development, water). Office: Elsener & Cadenhead PO Box 2067 Seminole OK 74818-2067 E-mail: delsener@swbell.net.

ELSMAN, JAMES LEONARD, JR., lawyer; b. Kalamazoo, Sept. 10, 1936; s. James Leonard and Dorothy Isabell (Pierce) E.; m. Janice Marie Wilczewski, Aug. 6, 1960; children— Stephanie, James Leonard III. BA, U. Mich., 1958, JD, 1962; postgrad., Harvard Div. Sch., 1958-59. Bar: Mich. 1963. Clk. Mich. Atty. Gen.'s Office, Lansing, 1961; atty. legal dept. Chrysler Corp., Detroit, 1962-64; founding ptnr. Elsman, Young, O'Rourke, Bruno & Bunn, Birmingham, Mich., 1964-72; pvt. practice Elsman Law Firm, Birmingham, 1972—. Owner Radio Sta. WOLY, Battle Creek, Mich. Author: The Seekers, 1962; screenplay, 1976, 200 Candles to Whom?, 1973; contbr. articles to profl. jours.; Composer, 1974, 76; talk show host Citizen's Court, TV-48, Detroit. Mem. Regional Export Expansion Coun., 1966-73, Mich. Ptnrs. for Alliance for Progress, 1969-80; cand. U.S. Senate, 1966, 76, 94, 96, U.S. Ho. of Reps., 1970. Rockefeller Bros. Found. fellow Harvard Div. Sch., 1959. Mem. ABA, Am. Soc. Internat. Law, Econ. Club Detroit, World Peace Through Law Center, Full Gospel Businessmen, Bloomfield Open Hunt Club, Pres. Club (U. Mich.), Circumnavigators Club, Naples Bath and Tennis, Rotary. Republican. Mem. Christian Ch. Private international, Personal injury (including property damage), Product liability. Home: 4811 Burnley Dr Bloomfield Hills MI 48304-3781 Office: 635 Elm St Birmingham MI 48009-6768

ELSON, ALEX, lawyer, educator, arbitrator; b. nr. Kiev, Russia, Apr. 17, 1905; came to U.S., 1906, naturalized, 1913; s. Jacob and Rebecca (Brodsky) E.; m. Miriam Almond, July 6, 1933; children: Jacova Silverthorne (dec.), Karen O'Neil. PhB, U. Chgo., 1925, JD, 1928. Bar: Ill. 1928. Bill drafter Legislative Reference Bur., Springfield, Ill., 1929; atty. Legal Aid Bur., Chgo., 1929-34; assoc. atty. Tolman, Chandler & Dickinson, 1934-38; regional atty. Wage-Hour Div., Chgo., 1938-41; regional atty., asst. gen. counsel OPA, 1941-45; sr. ptnr. Elson, Lassers & Wolff, 1952—79. Of counsel Rosenthal & Schanfield, 1979-99; lectr. U. Chgo., intermittently 1933-48, 79-99, Yale Law Sch., 1946, seminar-labor rels. Northwestern U. Sch. Law, 1961-65; seminar constl. law Ariz U., 1971 Author: Civil Practice Forms, 1934; co-author: Civil Practice Forms, Illinois-Federal, 1952, rev., 1965; contbr.: articles to profl. jours., also to Ency. Brit. Former pub. mem. Regional War Labor Bd.; former chmn. Chgo. Rent Commn.; pres. Fund for Justice, 1972-76; former chmn. Ill. divsn. ACLU (hon. mem. bd. dirs. Ill. divsn.); former vice chmn. Ill. Commn. on Children; former chmn. Bd. Mental Health Commrs. State Ill., 1960-69; v.p. Law in Am. Soc. Found.; pres. Nat. Acad. Arbitrators Rsch. and Edn. Found., 1987-90; bd. govs. Orthogenic Sch., U. Chgo.; mem. instnl. rev. bd. divsn. social sci. U. Chgo., 1994-97; cons. Ford Found., 1963-68; bd. dirs. Hull House Assn., 1955-65. Fellow Am. Bar Found., Emeritus fellow Coll. of Labor and Employment Lawyers, 1998—; mem. ABA, Ill. Bar Assn., Chgo. Bar Assn. (bd. mgrs.), Am. Law Inst. (life), Nat. Acad. Arbitrators (hon. life mem., v.p. 1983-85), Inst. Psychoanalysis (pres. 1976-79) Home: 5550 South Shore Dr Chicago IL 60637

ELSON, CHARLES MYER, law educator; b. Atlanta, Nov. 12, 1959; s. Edward Elliott and Suzanne (Goodman) E.; m. Aimee F. Kemker, Dec. 18, 1993; children: Caroline Kemker, Charles MacKenzie. AB magna cum laude, Harvard U., 1981, postgrad., 1981—82; JD, U. Va., 1985. Bar: N.Y. 1987, D.C. 1988, U.S. Dist. Ct. (so. and ea. dists.) N.Y. 1987, U.S. Ct. Appeals (11th cir.) 1987. Law clk. to judge U.S. Ct. Appeals (11th cir.), Atlanta, 1985-86; assoc. Sullivan & Cromwell, N.Y.C., 1986-90; asst. prof. Stetson U. Coll. Law, St. Petersburg, Fla., 1990-93, assoc. prof., 1993-96, prof., 1996-2001; Edgar S. Woolard Jr. prof. corp. governance U. Del., 2000—, dir. John L. Weinberg Ctr. for Corp. Governance, 2000—. Vis. prof. law U. Ill., Champaign-Urbana, 1995, Cornell U. Law Sch., Ithaca, N.Y., 1996, U. Md. Law Sch., Balt., 1998; cons. Holland & Knight, 1995—, Towers, Perrin, 1998; bd. dirs. Alderwoods Group, Inc., Auto Zone, Inc., Nuevo Energy Co., Investor Responsiblity Rsch. Ctr. Bd. dirs. Big Apple Circus, Ltd., N.Y.C., 1987-93, Circon Corp., 1997-99, Sunbeam Corp., 1996-2002; trustee Talladega Coll., 1994-2001, Tampa Bay Performing Arts Ctr., 2000—, Tampa Mus. Art, 1993-99, Del. Mus. Natural History, 2003—. Salvatori fellow Heritage Found., 1993-94. Mem.: ABA (vice chair com.on corp. governance, mem. com.on corp. laws), Nat. Assn. Corp. Dirs. (adv. coun. 1997—, commn. dir. compensation 1995, commn.dir. professionalism 1996, com.on securities litig. reform and fraud detection 1997, com.on succession planning 1998, com. on audit coms. 1999, com on role of bd. in strategic planning 2000, com. on dir. evaluation 2001), Assn. of Bar of City of N.Y., Am. Law Inst., Univ. Club N.Y.C., Down Town Assn., Harvard Club N.Y.C., Chevaliers du Tastevin. Home: 906 Cecil Rd Wilmington DE 19807 Office: U Del Coll Bus and Econs 104 MBNA America Hall Newark DE 19716 E-mail: elson@be.udel.edu.

ELWIN, JAMES WILLIAM, JR., lawyer; b. Everett, Wash., June 28, 1950; s. James William Elwin and Jeannette Georgette (Zichy-Litscheff) Sherman; m. Regina K. McCabe, Oct. 25, 1986. BA, U. Denver, 1971, MA, 1972; JD, Northwestern U., 1975. Bar: Ill. 1975, U.S. Dist. Ct. (no. dist.) Ill. 1975, U.S. Ct. Appeals (7th cir.) 1977, U.S. Supreme Ct. 1980, U.S. Ct. Fed. Claims 1989. Trial atty. antitrust divsn. U.S. Dept. Justice, Chgo., 1975-77; asst. dean Sch. Law Northwestern U., Chgo., 1977-82, assoc. dean, 1982-2000; dir. profl. devel. and tng. Shearman & Sterling, N.Y.C., 2000—. Exec. dir. Corp. Counsel Ctr., 1984-2000; planning dir. Corp. Counsel Inst., Garrett Corp. and Securities Law Inst., Chgo., 1983-2000; dir. Short Course for Pros. Attys., 1981-2000, Short Course for Def. Lawyers in Criminal Cases, Chgo., 1979-2000. Bd. dirs. Legal Assistance Found. of Chgo., 1985-97; vice chmn. Gov.'s Adv. Coun. on Criminal Justice Legis., 1986-91. Fellow German Acad. Exch. Svc., 1986; Fulbright scholar, Germany, 1990. Mem. Chgo. Coun. Fgn. Rels. (mem. Chgo. com.), Chgo. Bar Assn. (bd. mgrs. 1983-85), Chgo. Bar Found. (bd. dirs. 1985-93, pres. 1989-91), Ill. Inst. Continuing Legal Edn. (bd. dirs. 1978-90, chmn. 1987-88), Am. Law Inst., Legal Club (pres. 1991-92), Univ. Club, Law Club City of Chgo., Phi Beta Kappa, Pi Gamma Mu. Antitrust, Corporate, general. Office: Shearman & Sterling 599 Lexington Ave Ste N721 New York NY 10022-6030

ELWING, CARL MAGNUS, law educator; b. Helsingborg, Sweden, Sept. 8, 1921; m. Elisabeth Helen, July 28, 1945; children: Margareta, Fredrik. Juris Kandidat, U. Lund, Sweden, 1949, JD, 1961. Asst. prof. law U. Lund, 1961-67, assoc. prof. law, 1967-69, prof. of law, 1969-86; assoc. prof. law U. Stockholm, Sweden, 1964-66; expert Swedish Dept. Justice, Stockholm, 1961-72. Sgt. Royal Swedish Flight Artillery, 1949-52. Mem. World Fedn. Protection Animals/Zurich, Switzerland (coun. mem. 1960-81). Office: Juridiska Institutionen PO Box 207 S-22100 Lund Sweden

ELWOOD, H. PHILIP, lawyer; b. Wichita, Kans., June 22, 1946; s. Harold Campbell and Mary Elizabeth Elwood; m. Darlene Jo Werner, June 8, 1968; 1 child, Denise J.(Elwood) Walsh. BA in Polit. Sci., Wichita State U., 1968; JD, Washburn U., 1971. Bar: Kans. 1971, U.S. Dist. Ct. Kans. 1971, U.S. Tax Ct., 1998. Assoc. Goodell, Stratton, Edmonds & Palmer LLP, Topeka, 1971-74, ptnr., 1975—, mng. ptnr., 1993—. Sr. warden Grace Episc. Cathedral, Topeka, 1986-89, jr. warden, 1985-86, vestry mem. 1982-85, mem. budget com., 1982—, mem. fin. com., 1982—, mem. exec. com., 1982-89, fin. com. chmn., 2000-01; trustee, mem. investment com., mem. ins. com. Episcopal Diocese, Kans., Topeka, 1986-89; mem., benefactor Topeka Symphony Soc., 1968—; bd. dirs. Kans. Health Lawyers Sect., 1988-94, Topeka Performing Arts Ctr., 1990—, treas., 1991-93, pres. 1993-95, search com. chmn., 1995-96; mem. United Way Greater Topeka, 1985-89, fin. com. 1991-98, chmn. fin. com., 2000-01, bd. dirs. 1995—; exec. coun. Kans. Law Related Edn. Project, 1987-90. Recipient Disting. Pres. award Civitan Internat., 1978. Mem. ABA, Kans. Bar Assn. (mem. continuing legal edn. program devel. com. 1981-95), Kans. Health Lawyers Bd., Topeka Bar Assn. (bd. dirs. 1984-90, mem. ethics and grievance com. 1987-93, co-chmn. set. com. bar show 1988, chmn. legal aid and lawyer referral com. 1983-89), Phi Alpha Delta Alumni Assn. (bd. dirs. 1987-93), Topeka Lawyers Club (sec., treas. 1995-96, pres. 1996-97), Rotary (bd. dirs. 1991-94, 2d v.p. 2000-01, first v.p. 2001-02, pres. 2002—), Paul Harris Fellow, 1993, Topeka Country Club, Topeka MG-T Club, Topeka Gun Club. Republican. Episcopalian. Avocations: reading, running, antique sports cars and planes restoration, community svc, hiking. Corporate, general, Corporate taxation, Commercial, contracts (including sales of goods; commercial financing). Office: Goodell Stratton Edmonds & Palmer LLP 515 S Kansas Ave Topeka KS 66603-3999

ELY, JOHN HART, lawyer, university dean; b. N.Y.C., Dec. 3, 1938; s. John H. and Martha Foster (Coyle) E.; children: John Duff, Robert Allan Duff, m. Gisela Cardonne, 2002. AB summa cum laude, Princeton U., 1960; LL.B. magna cum laude, Yale U., 1963, MA (hon.), 1971, Harvard U., 1973; LLD, U. San Diego, 1988, Ill. Inst. Tech., 1991. Bar: D.C. 1965, Calif. 1967. Atty. Warren Commn., 1964; law clk. to Chief Justice Warren, 1964-65; Fulbright scholar London Sch. Econs., 1965-66; atty. Defenders, Inc., San Diego, 1966-68; asso. prof., then prof. law Yale U. Law Sch., 1968-73; prof. Harvard U. Law Sch., 1973-1982, Ralph S. Tyler, Jr. prof. constl. law, 1981-1982; Richard E. Lang prof. law Stanford U. Law Sch., Calif., 1982-87, dean, 1982-87; Robert E. Paradise prof. Stanford (Calif.) U. Law Sch., 1987-96; Richard A. Hausler prof. U. Miami (Fla.) Law Sch., 1996—. Gen. counsel U.S. Dept. Transp., 1975-76 Author: Democracy and Distrust, 1980, War and Responsibility, 1993, On Constitutional Ground, 1996. Served with USAR, 1963-69. Fellow Woodrow WIlson Internat. Ctr. scholars (1978-79), Am. Acad. Arts and Scis., Coun. on Fgn. Rels. Office: U Miami Law Sch PO Box 248087 Coral Gables FL 33124-8087

ELY, JOHN P. lawyer; b. Lubbock, Tex., Apr. 21, 1945; s. John O. and Laverne (Barton) Ely; m. Julie McCall Sherman, Dec. 27, 1967. BA, U. N.H., 1967; JD, Boston U., 1976. Bar: Mass. 1977, U.S. Dist. Ct. Mass. 1977, U.S. Dist. Ct. Conn. 1980, U.S. Supreme Ct. 1980. Sole practice, Agawam, Mass., 1977-78; assoc. Laming, Smith, et al., Springfield, Mass., 1978-80; jr. ptnr. Auchter, Bozenhard & Socha, Springfield, 1980-83, ptnr., 1984-85, Bozenhard, Socha, Ely & Kolber, Springfield, 1985-92, Bozenhard, Socha & Ely, Springfield, 1992—. 1st lt. USMC, 1968—71. Mem.: Mass. Conveyancers Assn., Hampden County Bar Assn., Mass. Bar Assn., 3d Marine Divsn. Assn., Marine Corps Assn. General practice, Probate (including wills, trusts), Property, real (including real estate development, water). Office: Bozenhard Socha & Ely 1242 Elm St Ste 12 West Springfield MA 01089-1890 E-mail: bsejpe@aol.com.

EMANUEL, WILLIAM JOSEPH, lawyer; b. Oct. 31, 1938; s. Lawrence John and Henrietta (Moser) Emanuel; m. Elizabeth Wolfe, Mar. 14, 1964; children: Christina, Michael, Steven. AB, Marquette U., 1960; JD, Georgetown U., 1963. Bar: Nebr. 1963, Calif. 1965, U.S. Supreme Ct. 1976. Assoc. Musick, Peeler & Garrett, L.A., 1963—70, ptnr., 1970—76, Morgan, Lewis & Bockius, L.A., 1976—97, Jones, Day, Reavis & Pogue, L.A., 1998—. Mem. labor rels. com. Am. Hosp. Assn., also mem. spl. subcom. to analyze report of Nat. Commn. on Nursing, Comparable Worth Task Force; mem. adv. com. NLRB, 1994—. Author (with Michael L. Wolfram): California Employment Law, A Guide to California Laws Regulating Employment in the Private Sector, 1989; contbr. articles to profl. jours. Mem.: ABA (com. on devel. of law under Nat. Labor Rels. Act, sect. on labor and employment law), State Bar Nebr., Am. Soc. Hosp. Attys., So. Calif. Labor Law Symposium (founding chmn. 1980, 1981), Los Angeles County Bar Assn. (chmn. labor law sect. 1983—84, exec. com. 1974—86), State Bar Calif. (labor and employment law sect.). Labor (including EEOC, Fair Labor Standards Act, labor-management relations, NLRB, OSHA). Home: 345 17th St Santa Monica CA 90402 Office: Jones Day 555 W 5th St Ste 4600 Los Angeles CA 90013-1025

EMBRY, STEPHEN CRESTON, lawyer; b. Key West, Fla., Feb. 13, 1949; s. Jewell Creston and Julia Martine (Taylor) E.; m. Priscilla Mary Brown, Aug. 21, 1971; children: Nathaniel, Julia, Jessamyn. BA, Am. U., 1971; JD, U. Conn., 1976. Bar: Conn. 1976, U.S. Dist. Ct. Conn. 1976, U.S. Ct. Appeals (2d, 5th and 9th cirs.). Staff aide to Pres. The White House, Washington, 1969-72; assoc. Turner & Hensley, Great Bend, Kans., 1976, O'Brien, Shafner, Bartinik, & Stuart, Groton, Conn., 1976-85, Embry and Neusner, Groton, Conn., 1985—. Editor: Longshore and Harborworkers Textbook; mem. editl. bd. Matthew Bender, BRB Reporter; contbr. articles to profl. publs. Mem. Groton Rep. com., 1976-83, North Stonington Rep. com., 1984-88; chmn. Groton Housing Authority, 1979-80; mem. dean's adv. coun. Am. U. Sch. Internat. Svc., 2002—. Mem. ATLA (chair workers compensation sect. 1984-85, bd. dirs. workplace injury litigation group, sec. 1999-2000, pres.-elect 2001-02, pres. 2002—), Maritime Claimants Attys. Assn. (bd. dirs.), Conn. Trial Lawyers, Conn. Bar Assn. (exec. bd.), Thames Club, Grange. Democrat. Personal injury (including property damage), Product liability, Workers' compensation.

EMENS, J. RICHARD, lawyer; b. Jackson, Mich., May 3, 1934; s. John R. and Aline (Brainerd) E.; m. Mary Francis, July 31, 1957 (div. Aug. 1980); children: Anne, John D., Alaine, Elizabeth; m. Beatrice Wolper, Aug. 31, 1983; children: Renee, Jennifer. BA, DePauw U., 1956; JD, U. Mich., 1959. Bar: Mich. 1959, Ohio 1964. Ptnr. McInally, Rosenfeld & Emens, Jackson, 1959-64, Emens and Ashworth, Marion, Ohio, 1964-68; dir. Emens, Kegler, Brown, Hill & Ritter, Columbus, Ohio, 1968-97, mng. dir., 1984-95; ptnr. Chester, Willcox & Saxbe LLP, Columbus. Trustee Ea. Mineral Law Found., pres., 1982-83. Co-author: Family Business Basics: The Guide to Family Business Financial Success; contbr. articles to law jours. Co-founder Emens scholars program Ball State U. Muncie, Ind., 1977—; trustee, chmn. bd. trustees Franklin U., Columbus, 1995-96; past chmn. fin. com. Franklin County Rep. Com.; former trustee and pres. Friends of Librs. Ohio State U. Mem. Internat. Bar Assn., Ohio Audubon (pres.), Rotary, Phi Beta Kappa. Avocations: travel, reading, fishing. Corporate, general, Estate planning, Private international. Office: Chester Willcox & Saxbe Llp 65 East State St Ste 1000 Columbus OH 43215

EMERSON, CARTER WHITNEY, lawyer; b. Oak Park, Ill., Mar. 18, 1947; s. Garner P. and Daisy M. (Carter) E.; m. Susan D. Emerson, June 28, 1969. BS in Fin., Miami U., Oxford, Ohio, 1969; JD magna cum laude, Northwestern U., 1972. Law clk. to judge U.S. Dist. Ct. (no. dist.) Ill., 1972-73; assoc. Kirkland & Ellis, Chgo., 1974-78, ptnr., 1978—. Mem. ABA (business corps. and banking sect.), Order of Coif. Clubs: Mid-Am. (Chgo.). Mergers and acquisitions, Securities, Venture capital. Office: Kirkland & Ellis 200 E Randolph St Fl 54 Chicago IL 60601-6636

EMERSON, WILLIAM HARRY, lawyer, retired, oil company executive; b. Rochester, N.Y., Jan. 13, 1928; s. William Canfield and Alice Sarah (Adams) E.; m. Jane Anne Epple, Dec. 27, 1956; children: Elizabeth Anne, Carolyn Jane. BA, Cornell U., 1951, LLB, 1956. Bar: Ill. 1974. Atty. Amoco Corp., 1956-91; sec., dir. Amoco Gas Co., 1979-91. Pres., dir. Undercroft Montessori Sch., Tulsa, 1965-67, Tulsa Figure Skating Club, 1969; bd. dirs. Lake Forest (Ill.) Found. for Hist. Preservation, 1983-2001; mem. vestry Ch. Holy Spirit, Lake Forest, 1988-91. Federal civil litigation, State civil litigation, FERC practice. Home: 593 Greenvale Rd Lake Forest IL 60045-1526

EMERY, HERSCHELL GENE, lawyer; b. Hobart, Okla., Oct. 19, 1923; s. W. Herschell and L. Norean (Lewis) E.; m. Charlotte Chrisney, Oct. 29, 1948; children— Kathy Emery Miller, Steve . A.B., U. Ill., 1945; LL.B., Harvard U., 1948. Bar: Ind. 1949, Tex. 1955, U.S. Tax Ct. 1956, U.S. Ct. Appeals (5th cir.) 1980, U.S. Ct. Claims, 1980. Assoc., Ross McCord Ice & Miller, Indpls., 1948-55; assoc., ptnr. Thompson Knight Wright & Simmons, Dallas, 1955-65; ptnr. Rain Harrell Emery Young & Doke, Dallas, 1965-87, ptnr. Locke Purnell Rain Harrell, 1987-98, Locke Liddell & Sapp, 1999-2001, of counsel, 2002-; lectr. various tax and legal insts. Former pres. Dallas Estate Council, North Tex. chpt. Arthritis Found. Served with U.S. Army, 1943. Fellow Am. Coll. Tax Counsel, Am. Coll. Trust and Estate Counsel; mem. ABA, Tex. Bar Assn., Dallas Bar Assn., Phi Beta Kappa. Presbyterian. Clubs: Dallas Country (pres. 1993), Dallas Petroleum, Birnam Wood. Probate (including wills, trusts), Corporate taxation, Estate taxation. Office: Locke Liddell & Sapp 2200 Ross Ave Ste 2200 Dallas TX 75201-6776

EMERY, NANCY BETH, lawyer; b. Shawnee, Okla., July 9, 1952; d. Paul Dodd Finefrock and Kathryn Jo (Saling) Hutchens; m. Lee Monroe Emery, May 18, 1974. BA with highest honors, U. Okla., 1974; JD, Harvard U., 1977. Bar: D.C. 1981. Atty. advisor Office Gen. counsel, USDA, Washington, 1977-79; legal advisor Fed. Energy Regulatory Commr. Matthew Holden, Jr., Washington, 1979-81; assoc. Pierson, Ball & Dowd and predecessor Sullivan & Beauregard, Washington, 1981-83, Paul Hastings, Janofsky & Walker, Washington, 1983-87, ptnr., 1987-93, Sutherland, Asbill & Brennan, Washington, 1993-97; v.p., gen. counsel, corp. sec. Calif. Ind. Sys. Operator Corp., 1997-99; ptnr. Hopkins & Sutter, Washington, 1999-2001, Ballard, Spahr, Andrews & Ingersoll, LLP, Washington, 2001—. Nat. adv. bd. USAID Tng. Program, 1994—98. Bd. dirs., sec. Park Place Condominium Assn., Inc., Washington, 1982—84; page Continental Congress DAR, 1978—82, chpt. del., 1981, 1984; chmn. Strategic Planning Comm., 2002—; bd. dirs. New Hope Housing, Inc., Alexandria, Va., 2001—, chair strategic planning com., 2002—. Mem.: ABA (natural resources energy and eviron. law sect. 1990—98, bd. editors Natural Resources & Environment 1990—98, pub. utility law sect., vice chmn. electricity com. 1998—, chmn. program com. 2000—01, chmn. mem. com. 2001—02, chmn. strategic planning com. 2001—02, chmn. cmty. outreach com. 2002—, mem. coun. 2002—, chmn. Cmty. involvment 2002—), Soc. Profl. Journalists, Fed. Energy Bar Assn. (chair tax com. 1986—87, chair FERC ops. and adminstrn. com. 1991—93, chair elec. utility regulation com. 1995—97, chair program com. 1997—98), Mortar Bd., Phi Beta Kappa. Democrat. FERC practice, Finance, Utilities, public. Office: Ballard Spahr Andrews & Ingersoll LLP 601 13th St NW Washington DC 20005 E-mail: bemery@ballardspahr.com.

EMISON, EWING RABB, JR., lawyer; b. Vincennes, Ind., Feb. 3, 1925; s. Ewing and Tuley (Sheperd) E.; m. Kathleen M. Crowley, Nov. 28, 1952; children: Susan, Anne Emison Wishard. AB, DePauw U., 1947; LLB, Ind. U., 1950. Bar: Ind. 1950. Of counsel Emison Doolittle Kolb & Roellgen, Vincennes; dep. atty. gen. State of Ind., 1968-69. Lectr. CLE seminars, ABA Nat. Conf. for Diversity, 2002. Contbg. columnist Res Gestae, Ind. State Bar mag., 1987—. Mem. Wabash Valley Interstate Commn., 1959-62, Ind. Flood Control and Water Resources Commn., 1961-65; mem. bd. visitors Ind. Univ. Sch. Law, 1984-87. With USN, 1943-46, 52-53. Mem. ABA (sects. on litigation, econs. of law practice, Spirit of Excellence award commn. on racial and ethnic diversity in the profession 2003), Nat. Bar Assn., Ind. State Bar Assn. (bd. of mgrs. 1975-77, chmn. ho. of dels. 1979, pres. 1986-87), Columbia Club, Phi Delta Phi, Phi Kappa Psi. Republican. Presbyterian. Avocations: golf, assistance to minority law students, military history. General civil litigation, Alternative dispute resolution, Condemnation (eminent domain). Office: Emison Doolittle Kolb & Roellgen PO Box 215 8th and Busseron Sts Vincennes IN 47591

EMRICH, EDMUND MICHAEL, lawyer; b. N.Y.C., Apr. 12, 1956; s. Edmund and Mary Ann (Picarella) E. BA, SUNY, Albany, 1978; JD, Hofstra U., 1981. Bar: N.Y. 1982, U.S. Dist. Ct. (so. and ea. dists.) N.Y. 1982, U.S. Ct. Appeals (2d cir.) 1987. Law clk. to presiding justice U.S. Bankruptcy Ct. (ea. dist.) N.Y., Westbury, 1982-83; assoc. Levin & Weintraub & Crames, N.Y.C., 1983-90, Kaye, Scholer, Fierman, Hays & Handler, N.Y.C., 1990-92, ptnr., 1993—. Local rules com. U.S. Bankruptcy Ct. (ea. dist.) N.Y., 1985-86; mem. local rules drafting subcom. U.S. Bankruptcy Ct. (so. dist.) N.Y., 1985-86, 95-98. Mem. Hofstra U. Law Rev., 1981-82. Mem. ABA, N.Y. State Bar Assn., Am. Bankruptcy Inst. Avocations: golf, tennis, wine collecting. Bankruptcy. Home: 300 E 85th St New York NY 10028-4500 Office: Kaye Scholer LLP 425 Park Ave New York NY 10022-3506 E-mail: eemrich@kayescholer.com.

ENDIEVERI, ANTHONY FRANK, lawyer; b. Syracuse, N.Y., May 21, 1939; s. Santo and Anne Rose (Zeolla) Endieveri; m. Arlene Rita McDonald, May 20, 1967; children: Anne C., Steven A. BA, Syracuse U., 1961, LLB, 1965, JD, 1968. Bar: N.Y. 1967, U.S. Dist. Ct. (no. dist.) N.Y. 1967, U.S. Ct. Appeals (2d cir.) 1969, U.S. Supreme Ct. 1970; cert. civil trial lawyer Nat. Bd. Trial Advocacy. Assoc. Ronald Crowley, Atty., North Syracuse, N.Y., 1965-67, Love, Balducci & Scacciz, Syracuse, 1967; pvt. practice law Camillus, N.Y., 1968—; appellate counsel Hiscock Legal Aid, Syracuse, 1968-70; asst. corp. counsel, housing code prosecutor City of Syracuse, 1970-74. Participant Nat. Coll. Advocacy, 1981-83, 86; lectr. Melvin Belli seminar, San Francisco, 1987, 93, Kansas City, Mo., 1988, Boston, 1989, San Diego, 1990; spkr. in field. (spkr.) in field. Mem. ministry program Syracuse Diocese Pre-Deacon Study, 1980-82. Maj. USMCR, 1972-88, ret. Mem. ATLA (spkr. nat. conv. 1990, seminar 1990, ultimate trial advocacy course 1 991), Assn. Trial Lawyers Am. Coll. Advocacy, N.Y. Bar Assn., N.Y. State Bar Assn., Onondaga County Bar Assn., N.Y. Trial Lawyers Assn., Nat. Brain Injury Assn., N.Y. Brain Injury Assn; mem. Phi Delt Phi. Democrat. Roman Catholic. Personal injury (including property damage), Product liability, Professional liability. Home: 205 Emann Dr Camillus NY 13031-2009

ENGEBRETSON, ANDREW, lawyer; b. Starbuck, Minn., Aug. 21, 1932; s. Herman Ferdinand and Agnes Serina (Knutson) E.; m. Fay Louise Amundson, Nov. 28, 1959 (div. Apr. 1970); children: Peter, Sarah; m. Rachel Waynne Warrick, June 16, 1970; 1 child, Margaret. BA cum laude, St. Olaf Coll., 1954; JD, U. Minn., 1959. Assoc. Rudolph L. Swore, Alexandria, Minn., 1959-61, Ernest H. Steneroden, St. Paul, 1968-69; ptnr. Engebretson Law Offices, St. Paul, 1969-94, pvt. practice, 1995—. Conv. del. Ramsey County Republicans, St. Paul, 1974-90, congrl. candidate, St. Paul, 1976. With U.S. Army, 1955-56. Mem. ABA, Minn. Bar Assn., Minn. Trial Lawyers Assn., Am. Trial Lawyers Assn., Mason. Republican. Lutheran. Avocations: fishing, chess, fgn. lang. studies, non-fiction books. Personal injury (including property damage), Workers' compensation. Office: Engebretson Law Offices 5 N 3d Ave W Ste 300 Duluth MN 55802

ENGEL, ALBERT JOSEPH, retired federal judge; b. Lake City, Mich., Mar. 21, 1924; s. Albert Joseph and Bertha (Bielby) Engel; m. Eloise Ruth Bull, Oct. 18, 1952; children: Albert Joseph III, Katherine Ann, James Robert, Mary Elizabeth. Student, U. Md., 1941—42; AB, U. Mich., 1948, LLB, 1950. Bar: Mich. 1951. Administrative asst. to U.S. Rep. Ruth Thompson, 1951; ptnr. firm Engle & Engel, Muskegon, Mich., 1952—67; judge Mich. Circuit Ct., 1967—71; judge U.S. Dist. Ct. Western Dist. Mich., 1971—74; circuit judge U.S. Ct. Appeals, 6th Circuit, Grand Rapids, Mich., 1974—88, chief judge, 1988—89, sr. judge, 1989—2002; ret., 2002. With U.S. Army, 1943—46, ETO. Fellow: Am. Bar Found.; mem.: FBA, Am. Judicature Soc., Grand Rapids Bar Assn., Cin. Bar Assn., Mich. Bar Assn., Grand Rapids Torch Club, Am. Legion, Phi Delta Phi, Phi Sigma Kappa. Episcopalian.*

ENGEL, DAVID CHAPIN, lawyer; b. N.Y.C., Oct. 6, 1931; s. Robert Albert and Mabel Gretchen (Eshbaugh) E.; children: Karen, Kathleen, Julie, Peter, Rebekah; m. Priscilla Gail Stevens, May 26, 1972; 1 adopted child, Terri, 1 child, Heidi. BA, St. Lawrence U., 1954; LLB, NYU, 1956. Bar: N.H. 1956, U.S. Dist. Ct. N.H. 1957, Mass. 1969, U.S. Dist. Ct. Mass. 1969, U.S. Ct. Appeals (1st cir.) 1969, U.S. Supreme Ct. 1993. Law clk. Atty. Gen. Office, Concord, N.H., 1956-58; ptnr. Shute, Engel & Morse, Exeter, N.H., 1958-84, Engel & Morse, Exeter, 1984-88, Engel & Gearreald, Exeter, 1988-92, Engel, Gearreald & Gardner, Exeter, 1992-96, Engel & Gearreald, Exeter, 1996—98, Engel & ASsocs., P.A., Exeter, 1998—. Arbitrator Am. Arbitration Assn., 1962—; chmn. Gov's. Commn. on Child Support Enforcement, 1985-87. Del. Rep. Nat. Conv., 1964, Rep. State Conv., 1965, 67, 69, Nat. Conf. State Legis., Charleston, South Carolina, 1985; bd. dirs. Greenland (N.H.) Community Congl. Ch., 1975-78, deacon 1980-83; mem. Greenland Planning Bd., 1980-92, Greenland Budget Com., 1986-87. Mem. N.H. Bar Assn. (legis. com. 1963-64, chmn.). Federal civil litigation, State civil litigation, Personal injury (including property damage). Home: PO Box 15 Greenland NH 03840-0015 Office: # 1 21 Hampton Rd Exeter NH 03833-4831

ENGEL, DAVID LEWIS, lawyer; b. N.Y.C., Mar. 31, 1947; s. Benjamin and Selma (Fruchtman) Engel; m. Edith Greetham Smith, June 9, 1973; children: Richard William, Jonathan Martin. AB in Gen. Studies in Econ. cum laude, Harvard U., 1967, JD magna cum laude, 1973; Disting. Naval grad., U.S. Naval Officer Candidate Sch., 1969. Bar: Mass. 1975. Law clk. to Judge Henry J. Friendly U.S. Ct. Appeals (2d cir.), N.Y.C., 1973-74; assoc. Goodwin, Procter & Hoar, Boston, 1974-76, 79-80; asst. prof. law Stanford U., Calif., 1976-79; ptnr. Berman, Dittmar & Engel, P.C., Boston, 1980-84, Bingham McCutchen LLP, Boston, 1984—. Pres. Harvard Law Rev., 1972—73. Mem. bd. visitors Stanford U. Law Sch., 1982—84; bd. dirs. Project Joy, 1995—2001. Lt. j.g. USNR, 1969—71. Recipient Sears prize, 1968, John Bingham Hurlbut award, 1979; John Harvard scholar, Harvard Coll. scholar, Nat. Merit scholar, 1964—67. Mem.: ABA, Boston Bar Assn. (working group of task force on revision of Mass. corp. statute 1987—2001), Phi Beta Kappa. Corporate, general, Securities. Office: Bingham McCutchen LLP 150 Federal St Boston MA 02110-1713 E-mail: david.engel@bingham.com.

ENGEL, PAUL BERNARD, lawyer; b. Balt., Feb. 6, 1926; s. Robert and and Ida (L) E.; m. Lorraine Goodman, Sept. 7, 1947; children— Seena Engel Kling, Cindy Engel Dubansky, Lon Craig. AA, U. Balt., 1947, JD, 1950. Bar: Md.1950, DC 1950. Ptnr. Engel and Engel P.A., Balt., 1950—. Bd. govs. Boca Highland Ctr. Assn., gov., 1992-, also treas., pres., chmn. legal com.; v.p. Aberdeen Arms Condos. With AUS, 1944-45. With USAR, 1944—45. Mem. ABA, Md. Plaintiffs Bar Assn., Balt. City Bar Assn., Bonnie View C. of C. (bd. dirs. 1964-67, 69-72). Clubs: Bonnie View Country (bd. dirs.). Lodges: Masons. Home: 3409 Deep Willow Ave Baltimore MD 21208-3116 Office: 11 E Lexington St Ste 200 Baltimore MD 21202-1733 E-mail: pb.e2626@aol.com.

ENGEL, RALPH MANUEL, lawyer; b. N.Y.C., May 13, 1944; s. Werner Herman and Ruth Fredericke (Friedlander) E.; m. Diane Linda Weinberg, Aug. 10, 1968; children— Eric M., Daniel C., Julie R. BA in Econs. with highest honors, NYU, 1965, JD, 1968. Bar: N.Y. 1968, U.S. Supreme Ct. 1972. Assoc. Gilbert, Segall and Young, N.Y.C., 1968-71, Trubin Sillcocks Edelman & Knapp, N.Y.C., 1971-76; assoc., then ptnr. Summit Rovins & Feldesman and predecessor firms, N.Y.C., 1976—91; ptnr. Rosen & Reade, LLP, N.Y.C., 1991-2001, Sonnenshein Nath & Rosenthal, N.Y.C., 2001—. Lectr. Sch. Law, Fordham U., 1990-91. Contbr. articles to legal and other publs.; editor-in-chief The Commentator, NYU, 1968 Mem. Planning Com., Larchmont, N.Y., 1992—. Fellow Am. Coll. Trust and Estate Counsel; mem. N.Y. State Bar Assn. (trust and estate law sect. com. on practice and ethics 1991—, elder law sect., com. on guardianships and fiduciaries 1991-97, com. on estates and tax planning 1997—), Assn. Bar City of N.Y. (com. on estate and gift taxation 1992-95, chmn. subcom. on splitting and combining trusts 1994-95, chmn., subcom. on spousal rights 1994-95, com. on trusts, estates and surrogate's cts. 1997-2000), Estate Planning Coun. Westchester County (bd. dirs. 1985-91). Estate planning, Probate (including wills, trusts), Estate taxation. Home and Office: 6 Rockwood Dr Larchmont NY 10538-2537 Office: 1221 Ave of the Americas New York NY 10020 Business E-Mail: engelesq@yahoo.com. E-mail: rengel@sonnenschein.com.

ENGEL, TALA, lawyer; b. N.Y.C. d. Volodia Vladimir Boris and Risia (Modelevska) E.; m. James Colias, Nov. 22, 1981 (dec. Nov. 1989). AA, U. Fla., 1952; BA in Russian and Spanish, U. Miami, 1954; JD, U. Miami, Coral Gables, 1957; postgrad., Middlebury Coll., 1953. Bar: Fla. 1957, D.C. 1982, U.S. Dist. Ct. (so. dist.) Fla. 1957, Ill. 1962, U.S. Dist. Ct. (no. dist.) Ill. 1962, U.S. Supreme Ct., 1965. Pvt. practice, Miami, Fla., 1957—61, Chgo., 1966—86, Washington, 1987—89, Chgo., 1990—93, Washington, 1993—2002, Miami, Fla., 2002—. Atty. Immigration and Naturalization Service, Chgo., 1961-62; parole agt. Ill. Youth Commn., Chgo., 1963-66. Editor The Lawyer, 1956; mem. editl. bd. Miami Law Quar., 1955-57, 10 ML Q 110 Criminal Law, 10 ML Q 608 Ins. Law, 1955-56. Bd. dirs. Cordi-Marian Settlement, Chgo., 1977-93. Named One of 2000 Outstanding Women of 20th Century, Dictionary Internat. Biography, 2000. Mem.: Fla. Bar Assn., Fed. Bar Assn., Chgo. Bar Assn. (devel. of law com. 1985—87, entertainment com. 1971—72), Ill. Bar Assn. (gen. assembly 1984—86), Chgo. Bar Found. (life), Nu Beta Epsilon, Alpha Lambda Delta. Achievements include Sued Chgo. Bar Assn. in 1970 for right of women lawyers to participate in activities of Bar Assn. Avocations: travel, reading, theater , singing, Russian and Spanish languages. Immigration, naturalization, and customs. Address: PO Box 221432 Hollywood FL 33022 also: 509 N Federal Hwy Hollywood FL 33020 E-mail: talaengel@aol.com.

ENGELHARDT, JOHN HUGO, lawyer, banker; b. Houston, Feb. 3, 1946; s. Hugo Tristram and Beulah Lillie (Karbach) E.; m. Jasmin Inge Nestler, Nov. 12, 1976; children: Angelique D., Sabrina N. BA, U. Tex., 1968; JD, St. Marys U., San Antonio, 1973. Tchr. history Pearsall H.S., Tex., 1968-69; pvt. practice New Braunfels, Tex., 1973-75, 82—; examining atty. Comml. Title Co., San Antonio, 1975-78, San Antonio Title Co., 1978-82. Adv. dir. M Bank Brenham, Tex., 1983-89. Fellow Coll. State Bar Tex.; mem. ABA, Pi Gamma Mu. Republican. Roman Catholic. Probate (including wills, trusts), Property, real (including real estate development, water), Estate taxation.

ENGELHARDT, THOMAS FRANCIS, lawyer, consultant; b. May 24, 1926; s. William Fredrick and Norma Agnes Engelhardt; m. Elizabeth Lina Blais, Sept. 24, 1954. BA, U. Wis., Madison; JD, George Washington U., 1958. Bar: Va. 1959, U.S. Dist. Ct. D.C. 1963, U.S. Ct. Appeals (D.C. cir.) 1963, U.S. Supreme Ct. 1964. Intelligence officer CIA, Washington, 1952—59; chief trial counsel AEC, Washington, 1959—65, chief counsel, 1966—74; chief dept. contract law Westinghouse Electric, Pitts., 1965—66; dep. legal dir. Nuclear Regulatory Commn., Washington, 1974—82; cons. Sun City, Ariz., 1982—2000, Peoria, Ariz., 2000—. Chmn. adv. com. Battelle Meml. Inst. , Columbus, Ohio, 1983—86. Pres. Sun City United Way, Sun City Cmty. Coun., Montgomery Cmty. Assn., Montgomery County, Md., 1976, Sumner Cmty. Assn., Bethesda, Md., 1982; v.p. Cath. Social Svc. Ariz. Served with U.S. Army, 1944—46. Recipient Disting. Svc. award, Nuclear Regualatory Commn., 1980. Mem.: D.C. Bar Assn., Va. Bar Assn. Roman Catholic. Home and Office: 20554 N 101st Ave Apt 2018 Peoria AZ 85382-5501

ENGELS, PATRICIA LOUISE, lawyer; b. Joliet, Ill., July 2, 1926; d. Fred Bridges and Loretta Mae (Fisk) B.; m. Henry William Engels, Feb. 1, 1947; children: Patrick Henry, Michael Bruce, Timothy William. BS in Edn., Olivet Nazarene Coll., 1970, MEd, 1971; JD, John Marshall Law Sch., 1979. Bar: Ill. 1979, Ind. 1979; cert. elem. and high sch. tchr., edn. adminstrn., Ill. Tchr. Bourbonnais (Ill.) and Momence (Ill.) Unit Schs., 1970-76; instr. Kankakee (Ill.) Community Coll., 1975; sole practice Ind. and Ill., 1979—. Qualified divorce mediator, 1991—. Active Lake Village (Ind.) Civic Assn., 1980—; edn. coord. St. Augusta Ch., Lake Village, 1985-89. Avocations: exercise, swimming, sewing, country dancing, reading. Mem. ABA, Ind. Bar Assn., Ill. Bar Assn., Pub. Defender Bar Assn., Theta Chi Sigma, Kappa Delta Pi. Roman Catholic. Avocations: exercise, swimming, sewing, dancing, reading. Estate planning, Family and matrimonial, Property, real (including real estate development, water). Home and Office: 33 Brittany Ln Bourbonnais IL 60914-1640

ENGLAND, GORDON R. federal agency administrator; B in Elec. Engring., U. Md.; MBA, Tex. Christian U. With Gen. Dynamics, 1966—, v.p. engring. to divsn. pres. land sys. unit, 1986, pres. aircraft sys. Ft. Worth divsn., exec. v.p., 1991, pres. Lockheed Ft. Worth, 1993-95; owner consulting co., 1995-97; exec. v.p. combat sys. group Gen. Dynamics, Falls Church, Va., 1997—2001; sec. Navy Dept. Def., Washington, 2001—03; dep. sec. dept. Homeland Security, Washington, 2003—. Mem. Def. Sci. Bd. Vice-chmn. Goodwill Internat.; bd. govs. USO; bd. visitors TCU. Recipient award, Boy Scouts Am., Nat. Def. Indsl. Assn., Nat. Mgmt. Assn., Centennial award, IEEE, inductee, Aviation Hall of Fame. Mem.: Beta Gamma Sigma, Omicron Delta Kappa, Eta Kappa Nu. Office: Dept Homeland Security 3801 Nebraska Ave NW Washington DC 20016*

ENGLAND, JOHN MELVIN, lawyer, clergyman; b. June 29, 1932; s. John Marcus and Frances Dorothy (Brown) E.; m. Jane Cantrell, Aug. 2, 1953; children: Kathryn Elizabeth, Janette Evelyn, John William, Kenneth Paul, James Andrew, Samuel Robert. Student, Ga. State U., 1951-53; JD, U. Ga., 1956; BD magna cum laude with honors Theology, Columbia Theol. Sem., Decatur, Ga., 1964. Bar: Ga. 1959, U.S. Dist. Ct. (no. dist.) Ga. 1967, U.S. Ct. Mil. Appeals 1976, U.S. Ct. Appeals (5th cir.) 1967, U.S. Ct. Appeals (11th cir.) 1981, U.S. Supreme Ct. 1977, U.S. Dist. Ct. (mid. dist.) Ga. 1986, U.S. Dist. Ct. (so. dist.) Ga. 1991, U.S. Dist. Ct. (no. dist.) Tex. 1991; ordained to ministry Presbyn. Ch., 1964. Spl. agt. FBI, Washington, 1956-57, Indpls., 1957-59, Charlotte, N.C., 1959, Greenville, S.C., 1959-60; student supply pastor Bethel and Buford Presbyn. Chs., Atlanta, 1960-63; pastor Mullins (S.C.) Presbyn. Ch., 1964-67; asst. dist. atty. Fulton County, Ga., 1967-75; sr. ptnr. England and Weller, Atlanta, 1975-88, England, Weaver & Kytle, 1988-94, England & McKnight, 1994-2000, England & England, 2000—. Legal seminar lectr. and spkr. throughout the country under auspices of Christian orgns.; spl. pros. for gov. Ga., 1976-79; spl. cons. on appellate reform Supreme Ct. Ga., 1979-80; state bar rep. to Superior Ct. Uniform Rules Com. Coun. Superior Ct. Judges, 1984, Uniform Rules Com. State Bar Ga., 1993—. Elder, tchr., evangelism coord. Presbyn. Ch. USA; chmn. Christian Bus. Men's Coms. of U.S.A., Atlanta, 1971-73, chmn. internat. conv., Atlanta, 1979, bd. dirs., 1971-81. Mem. ABA, ATLA, State Bar Ga., Atlanta Bar Assn., Lawyers Club Atlanta, Ga. Trial Lawyers Assn., Nat. Assn. Criminal Def. Lawyers, Ga. Assn. Criminal Def. Lawyers, North Fulton Bar Assn. General civil litigation, Criminal, Personal injury (including property damage). Office: England & England 201 Bombay Ln Roswell GA 30076 E-mail: england_england_11p@hotmail.com.

ENGLAND, LYNNE LIPTON, lawyer, speech pathologist, audiologist; b. Youngstown, Ohio, Apr. 11, 1949; d. Sanford Y. and Sally (Kentor) Lipton; m. Richard E. England, Mar. 5, 1977. BA, U. Mich., 1970; MA, Temple U., 1972; JD, Tulane U., 1981. Bar: Fla. 1982, U.S. Dist. Ct. (mid. dist.) Fla. 1982, U.S. Ct. Appeals (11th cir.) 1982; cert. clin. competence in speech pathology and audiology. Speech pathologist Rockland Children's Hosp., N.Y., 1972-74, Jefferson Parish Sch., Gretna, La., 1977-81; audiologist Rehab. Inst. Chgo., 1974-76; assoc. Trenam, Simmons, Kemker, Scharf, Barkin, Frye & O'Neill, Tampa, Fla., 1981-84; asst. U.S. atty. for Middle Dist. Fla. Tampa, 1984-87; asst. U.S. trustee, 1987-91; ptnr. Stearns, Weaver, Miller, Weissler, Alhadeff & Sitterson, P.A., 1991-94, Prevatt, England & Taylor, Tampa, Fla., 1994-99; pvt. practice Brandon, Fla., 1999—. Editor Fla. Bankruptcy Casenotes, 1983. Recipient clin. assistantship Temple U., 1972-74. Mem. ATLA, Comml. Law League, Am. Speech and Hearing Assn., Tampa Bay Bankruptcy Bar Assn. (dir. 1990-95), Am. Bankruptcy Inst., Fla. Bar Assn., Hillsborough County Bar Assn., Order of Coif. Jewish. Avocations: tennis, golf, playing french horn and piano. Bankruptcy, Commercial, consumer (including collections, credit). Office: 1463 Oakfield Dr Ste 125 Brandon FL 33511-0802 E-mail: englandlawoffice@aol.com.

ENGLERT, ROY THEODORE, lawyer; b. Nashville, Sept. 11, 1922; s. Roy T. and Ruth Rowe (Tindall) E.; m. Helen Frances Wiggs, Sept. 25, 1948; children: Lee Ann, Roy Jr. BA, Vanderbilt U., 1943; JD, Columbia, 1951; LLM, George Washington U., 1953. Bar: Tenn. 1951, U.S. Dist. Ct. D.C. 1951, U.S. Supreme Ct. 1955, Internat. Trade 1975. Asst. counsel Office Comptroller of Currency, U.S. Treasury Dept., 1951-58, chief counsel, 1958-62, asst. gen. counsel of dept., 1962-66, dep. gen. counsel, 1966-73; sole practice Washington, 1973-96. Bd. dirs., sec. Walker/Potter Assocs., Inc., Washington, 1973-96; mem. Sr. Seminar in Fgn. Policy, Dept. State, 1963-64, U.S. Assay Commn., 1975; lectr., writer on banking law. Contbr. articles to profl. jours. Judo tech. ofcl. Atlanta Olympics; bd. dirs. Westminster Ingleside Found. Lt. USNR, 1943—46. Recipient Exceptional Service award U.S. Treasury, 1972, Gen. Counsel's award, 1973; named US Track Nat. Masters Champion 10,000 meter run, 1998. Mem. ABA, Tenn. Bar Assn. Presbyterian. Banking. Home: 12183 Cathedral Dr Woodbridge VA 22192-2227 Office: 6720 Bellamy Ave Springfield VA 22152-3023 E-mail: frodo49@juno.com.

ENGLISH, JERRY FITZGERALD, lawyer, educator; b. Houston, Dec. 18, 1934; d. William Edward Michael and Viola Catherine (Christopherson) Fitzgerald; m. Alan Taylour English, July 23, 1955; children: Holly, Christopher, Anderson, Eric. BA, Stanford U., 1956; JD, Boston Coll., Harvard Law Sch., 1963. Bar: N.J. 1965, U.S. Dist. Ct. N.J. 1965. Clk., assoc., ptnr. Moser, Griffin, Kerby & Cooper, Summit, N.J., 1964-74; mem. N.J. Senate, 1971-72, asst. counsel to, 1972-74; legis. counsel Gov. N.J., Trenton, 1974-79; commr. N.J. Dept. Environ. Protection, 1979-82; of counsel Kerby, Cooper, English, Schaul & Garvin, Summit, 1982—85, ptnr., 1985, Cooper Rose & English, Summit, NJ. Adj. prof. N.J. Inst. Tech., 1983—; lectr. nationally for many orgns. Assoc. editor, vice chmn., editl. bd. N.J. Law Jour. Commr. Port Authority of N.Y. and N.J., 1979-88; trustee N.J. Ctr. for Visual Arts, N.J. Harvard Law Sch. Assn., 1973-; bd. dirs. Regional Plan Assn.; mem. Gateway Nat. Recreation Area Adv. Commn., 1981; mem. exec. coun. Dem. Nat. Com., 1978-84; mem. chem. events com. Nat. Acads. Sci., 2001-03. Mem. ABA (co-chair subcom. hazardous waste & CERCLA), Internat. Bar Assn., N.J. Bar Assn., Summit Bar Assn.; fellow ABA, Harvard Club. Unitarian Universalist. Environmental, Private international. Office: Cooper Rose & English 480 Summit Ave Summit NJ 07901

ENGLISH, JOHN DWIGHT, lawyer; b. Evanston, Ill., Mar. 28, 1949; s. John Francis English and Mary Faye (Taylor) Butler; m. Claranne Kay Lundeen, Apr. 22, 1972; children: Jennifer A., Katharine V., Margaret E. BA, Drake U., 1971; JD, Loyola U., 1976. Bar: Ill. 1976, U.S. Dist. Ct. (no. dist.) Ill. 1976, U.S. Tax Ct. 1977. Assoc. Bentley DuCanto Silvestri & Forkins, Chgo., 1976-79; ptnr. Silvestri Mahoney English & Zdeb, Chgo., 1979-81; assoc. Coffield Ungaretti Harris & Slavin, Chgo., 1981-83; ptnr. Ungaretti & Harris, Chgo., 1983—. Instr. estate planning Loyola U., Chgo., 1982-87; instr. Ill. Inst. Continuing Edn. Estate Planning Short Course, 1998, 2001. Bd. dirs. Prince of Peace Luth. Sch., Chgo., 1977-83, Bethesda Home for the Aged, Chgo., 1981-89, 2000—, Luth. Family Mission, Chgo., 1985-91; alderman Park Ridge (Ill.) City Coun., 1991-95. Mem.: Chgo. Bar Assn. (former chmn. divsn. II probate practice com.), Ill. State Bar Assn.,

Phi Beta Kappa. Lutheran. Estate planning, Probate (including wills, trusts), Estate taxation. Home: 631 Wisner St Park Ridge IL 60068-3428 Office: Ungaretti & Harris 3500 Three 1st Nat Bank Plz Chicago IL 60602

ENGLISH, NICHOLAS CONOVER, lawyer; b. Elizabeth, N.J., Apr. 12, 1912; s. Conover and Sara Elizabeth (Jones) E.; m. Agnes N. Perry, Mar. 18, 1939 (div. 1947); children— Henry H. P., Anne Whitall (Mrs. Edward J. Wardwell); m. Eleanor Morss, May 1, 1948; children— Priscilla English Vincent, Sara (dec.), Sherman, Eleanor English Folta. Grad., Pingry Sch., 1929; AB magna cum laude, Princeton, 1934; LL.B., Harvard, 1937. Bar: N.J. 1937. Since practiced in, Newark; partner firm McCarter & English, 1947-77, of counsel, 1978—. Bd. dirs. Summit (N.J.) YMCA, 1950-57, pres., 1953-55; bd. dirs. Newark YMWCA, also pres.; chmn. exec. com. Ctrl. Atlantic Area YMCA, 1957-63; mem. nat. coun. YMCA, 1954, 58-81, v.p., 1959-60, mem. nat. bd., 1960-71, 73-81, vice chmn., 1969-71, treas., 1977-81; trustee N.J. Nat. Land Trust, 1983-93, Kent Place Sch., 1959—, pres., 1961-72, Pingry Sch., 1954-73; bd. dirs. Nat. Legal Aid Assn., 1953-56. Lt. USNR, 1943—45. Mem. ABA (ho. of dels. 1957-58), N.J. Bar Assn., Essex County Bar Assn., Am. Bible Soc. (bd. trustees 1964-93, sr. trustee 1993—), Am. Law Inst. Congregationalist. Home: 46 Meadow Lks Apt 04L Hightstown NJ 08520-3332 Office: McCarter & English 4 Gateway Ctr 100 Mulberry St Newark NJ 07102-0652

ENGLISH, RICHARD D. lawyer, mediator, diplomat, government official; b. Beaumont, Tex., Jan. 11, 1948; s. Richard Wilfred and Clara Elizabeth (Dunshie) E. BA, U. Tex., 1970, JD, 1974. Bar: Tex. 1974, U.S. Dist. Ct. (so. dist.) Tex. 1975, U.S. Supreme Ct. 1987. Law clk. to U.S. judge U.S. Dist. Ct., Laredo, Tex., 1975-76; atty. Tenneco Inc., Houston, 1976-80; policy asst. Gov. of Tex., Austin, 1980-81; dep. asst. dir. ACTION, Washington, 1981-83; dep. asst. sec. Dept. State, Washington, 1983-87; spl. counsel to sec. of state State of Tex., 1987-88; dep. dir. policy devel. Office of Pres.-Elect, 1988-89; policy advisor White House Office Policy Devel., 1989; sr. policy advisor on Europe Dept. State, Washington, 1989-91, dep. asst. sec. for East Asian and Pacific affairs, 1991-92; gen. counsel, sr. v.p. United Am. Export, Inc., San Diego, 1992-93; pvt. practice law, mediator, Houston, 1993—99; atty., sr. policy analyst Office of Comptroller of Pub. Accounts, 1999—. Contbr. articles to profl. jours. Assoc. Tex. Lyceum Assn., 1984; del. Rep. Nat. Conv., Detroit, 1980; pres. World Affairs Coun., Austin, Tex. Mem.: Mensa, World Affairs Coun. Austin (founding pres.). Corporate, general, Immigration, naturalization, and customs, Public international.

ENGLISH, WILLIAM DESHAY, lawyer, director; b. Piedmont, Calif., Dec. 25, 1924; s. Munro and Mabel (Michener) E.; m. Nancy Ames, Apr. 7, 1956; children: Catherine, Barbara, Susan, Stephen. AB in Econs., U. Calif., Berkeley, 1948, JD, 1951. Bar: Calif. 1952, D.C. 1972. Trial atty., spl. asst. to atty. gen. U.S. Dept. Justice, Washington, 1953-55; sr. atty. AEC, Washington, 1955-62; legal advisor U.S. Mission to European Communities, Brussels, 1962-64; asst. gen. counsel internat. matters COMSAT, Washington, 1965-73; counsel Internat. Telecomm. Satellite Orgn., 1965-73; v.p., gen. counsel, dir. COMSAT Gen. Corp., 1973-76; sr. v.p. legal and govtl. affairs Satellite Bus. Sys., McLean, Va., 1976-86; v.p., gen. counsel Satellite Transponder Leasing Corp. (IBM), McLean, Va., 1986-87; pvt. practice Washington, 1987—; counsel Am. Space Transp. Assn., 1987-93, Washington Space Bus. Roundtable; gen. counsel Iridium, LLC, 1992-96, spl. counsel, 1996-2000. With USAAF, 1943-45. Decorated Air medal. Fellow Coun. on Econ. Regulation, 1985-91; mem. ABA, AIAA (chmn. com. legal aspects aeronautics and astronautics,1993-2000, chmn. allocation space launch risks subcom. 1987, chmn. orbital debris legal subcom.), Am. Competitive Telecomm. Assn. (bd. dirs. 1976-84, pres. 1983), D.C. Bar Assn., Fed. Comm. Bar Assn., State Bar Calif., Fgn. Policy Discussion Group, Met. Club, Chevy Chase Club. Administrative and regulatory, Private international, Legislative. Home: 7420 Exeter Rd Bethesda MD 20814-2352 E-mail: w.english2@verizon.net.

ENGORON, ARTHUR FREDERICKS, judge; b. NYC, May 22, 1949; s. Malcolm Wilson and Edna June (Fredericks) E.; 1 child, Ian Abbie Intrator Engoron. BA, Columbia Coll., 1972; JD, NYU, 1979. Bar: N.Y., U.S. Dist. Ct. (so. and ea. dists.) N.Y. 1980, U.S. Supreme Ct. 1996. Assoc. Olwine, Connelly, Chase, O'Donnell & Weyher, N.Y.C., 1979-81, Pryor, Cashman, Sherman & Flynn, N.Y.C., 1981-83; prin. law clk. for Hon. Martin Schoenfeld N.Y. State Supreme Ct., N.Y.C., 1991—2002; judge N.Y.C. Civil Ct., 2003—. Author: Manual for Small Claims Arbitrators, 2001. Newsletter editor Park River Ind. Dems., N.Y.C., 1994-96. Mem. Assn. of the Bar of the City of N.Y. (chairperson civil ct. com.), Coun. Jud. Adminstrn., Assn. Small Claims Arbitrators (pres.). Democrat. Avocations: politics, computers, chess, art, physical fitness. Home: 255 W 84th St Apt 11E New York NY 10024-4325 Office: NYC Civil Ct Rm 527D 851 Grand Concourse Bronx NY 10451 E-mail: artengoron@aol.com., aengoron@courts.state.ny.us.

ENGSBERG, MARK DAVID, law librarian; b. St. Louis, Mo., Sept. 25, 1962; s. David Arthur and Evelyn Sue Engsberg; m. Rebecca Baldwin, May 23, 1987; children: Caleb David, Elizabeth Virginia. BA, Drury Coll., 1980—84; JD, Willamette U. Coll. of Law, 1984—87; MA, U. of Ill., 1991—94, PhD, 1994—99, MSLIS, 1999—2000. Bar: Idaho State 1988. Reference libr. Lillian Goldman Law Libr. , Yale Law Sch., 2000—01; internat. law libr. Lillian Goldman Law Libr., Yale Law Sch., 2001—. Contbg. author, contbg. editor, bd. mem. Gale Ency. of Everyday Law. Contbr. Law Libr. Jour.; Oxford Ency. of Am. Law. Capt. US Army, 1988—91. Mem.: Internat. Assn. of Law Libraries, Spl. Libraries Assn., Conn. Libr. Assn., Am. Libraries Assn., Am. Assn. of Law Libraries. Office: Goldman Law Library / Yale Law School PO Box 208215 New Haven CT 06520-8215 Office Fax: 203-432-4604. E-mail: mark.engsberg@yale.edu.

ENNIS, EDGAR WILLIAM, JR., lawyer; b. Macon, Ga., May 20, 1945; s. Edgar W. and Nelle (Branan) E.; m. Judith Anne Godfrey, June 29, 1974; children: William, Branan. BS in Engring. Sci., USAF Acad., Colorado Springs, Colo., 1967; JD, U. Ga., 1971. Bar: Ga. 1971. Commd. 2d lt. USAF, 1967, advanced through ranks to capt., 1970, resigned, 1975; asst. U.S. atty. U.S. Atty.'s Office-Mid. Dist. of Ga., Macon, 1975-88; U.S. atty. U.S. Dept. Justice, Macon, 1988-93; of counsel Haynsworth, Baldwin, Johnson & Harper, Macon, 1993-97; ptnr. Haynsworth, Baldwin, Johnson & Greaves LLC, Macon, 1998-99, Constangy, Brooks & Smith LLC, Macon, 1999—. Federal civil litigation, Environmental, Labor (including EEOC, Fair Labor Standards Act, labor-management relations, NLRB, OSHA). Office: Constangy Brooks & Smith LLC 577 Mulberry St Ste 710 Macon GA 31201-8588 E-mail: eennis@constangy.com.

ENOCH, CRAIG TRIVELY, state supreme court justice; b. Wichita, Kans., Apr. 3, 1950; BA, So. Meth. U., 1972, JD, 1975; LLM, U. Va., 1992. Bar: Tex. 1975, U.S. Dist. Ct. (no. dist.) Tex. 1976, U.S. Ct. Appeals (5th cir.) 1979; cert. Civil Trial Law. Assoc. Burford, Ryburn & Ford, Dallas, 1975-77; ptnr. Moseley, Jones, Enoch & Martin, Dallas, 1977-81; judge 101st Dist. Ct., Dallas, 1981-87; chief justice Tex. Ct. Appeals (5th dist.), 1987-92; justice Tex. Supreme Ct., Austin, 1993—. Mem. exec. bd. Dedman Sch. Law So. Meth. U., 1990—. Capt. USAFR, 1973-81. Recipient Outstanding Young Lawyer in Dallas, 1985, Disting. Alumni award for judicial svc. So. Meth. U. Dedman Sch. Law, 1999, J. Edward Finch Law Day Speech award, 2001. Fellow: Dallas Bar Found., Tex. State Bar Found., Am. Bar Found.; mem.: ABA (past chair exec. bd. appellate judges conf. jud. divsn.), Tex. Supreme Ct. (liaison to State Bar of Tex. 1999—), Am. Law Inst. Episcopalian.

ENSENAT, DONALD BURNHAM, ambassador, lawyer; b. New Orleans, Feb. 4, 1946; s. A.G. and Genevieve (Burnham) E.; m. Taylor Harding, June 5, 1976; children: Farish, Will. BA, Yale U., 1968; JD, Tulane U., 1973. Bar: La. 1973, U.S. Ct. Appeals (5th cir.) 1974, U.S. Supreme Ct. 1975, U.S. Ct. Appeals (11th cir.) 1982, Tex. 1991. Legis. asst. Congressman Hale Boggs, U.S. Ho. of Reps., Washington, 1969-70, legis asst. Congresswoman Lindy Boggs, 1973-74; personal aide Hon. George Bush, Houston, 1970; asst. atty gen. State of La., New Orleans, 1975-80; assoc., dir., mng. dir. Carmouche, Gray, & Hoffman, A.P.L.C., New Orleans, 1981-89; mng. dir. Hoffman Sutterfield Ensenat, A.P.L.C., New Orleans, 1989-92, sr. dir., 1994-97; of counsel Locke Liddell & Sapp, PC, New Orleans, 1997-2001; U.S. Chief of Protocol Washington, 2001—. U.S. amb. to Brunei, 1992-93. Bd. dirs. World Trade Ctr., New Orleans, chmn. fin. com., 1990-92, exec. com., 1993-2001, pres.-elect, 1995, pres., 1996, chmn. bd. dirs., 1997. With USAR, 1968-74. Mem. State Bar Tex., La. State Bar Assn., Maritime Law Assn. U.S., Yale Alumni Assn. La. (bd. dirs. 1976-92, 94—, pres. 1980-82), Assn. Yale Alumni (rep. 1976-79). Republican. Roman Catholic. Avocation: sports. Home: 5527 Hurst St New Orleans LA 70115 Office: US State Dept S/CPR 2201 C St NW Washington DC 20520

ENSLEN, RICHARD ALAN, federal judge; b. Kalamazoo, May 28, 1931; s. Ehrman Thrasher and Pauline Mabel (Dragoo) E.; m. Pamela Gayle Chapman, Nov. 2, 1985; children— David, Susan, Sandra, Thomas, Janet, Joseph, Gennady. Student, Kalamazoo Coll., 1949-51, Western Mich. U., 1955; LL.B., Wayne State U., 1958; LL.M., U. Va., 1986. Bar: Mich. 1958, U.S. Dist. Ct. (we. dist.) Mich. 1960, U.S. Ct. Appeals (6th cir.) 1971, U.S. Ct. Appeals (4th cir.) 1975, U.S. Supreme Ct. 1975. Mem. firm Stratton, Wise, Early & Starbuck, Kalamazoo, 1958-60, Bauckham & Enslen, Kalamazoo, 1960-64, Howard & Howard, Kalamazoo, 1970-76, Enslen & Schma, Kalamazoo, 1977-79; dir. Peace Corps, Costa Rica, 1965-67; judge Mich. Dist. Ct., 1968-70; U.S. dist. judge Kalamazoo, 1979—; chief judge, 1995-2001. Mem. faculty Western Mich. U., 1961-62, Nazareth Coll., 1974-75; adj. prof. polit. sci. Western Mich. U., 1982— Co-author: The Constitutional Law Dictionary: Volume One, Individual Rights, 1985; Volume Two, Governmental Powers, 1987, Constitutional Deskbook: Individual Rights, 1987, (with Mary Bedikian and Pamela Enslen) Michigan Practice, Alternative Dispute Resolution, 1998. Served with USAF, 1951-54. Named Person of the Century-Law and Courts, The Kalamazoo Gazette, 1999; recipient Disting. Alumni award, Wayne State Law Sch., 1980, Western Mich. U., 1982, Outstanding Practical Achievement award, Ctr. Pub. Resources, 1984, award for Excellence and Innovation in Alternative Dispute Resolution and Dispute Mgmt., Legal Program; scholar, Jewel Corp., 1956—57, Lampson McElhorne, 1957. Mem. ABA (standing com. on dispute resolution 1983-90), Mich. Bar Assn., Am. Judicature Soc. (bd. dirs. 1983-85), Sixth Cir. Jud. Coun. Office: US Dist Ct 410 W Michigan Ave Kalamazoo MI 49007-3757

ENZEL, DAVID HOWARD, lawyer; b. Pitts., Jan. 21, 1955; s. Abram and Dora Enzel. BA, U. Pitts., 1976, JD, 1979. Bar: Pa. 1979, D.C. 1981. Chief atty. for fair housing enforcement HUD, Washington, 1979-91; spl. counsel Office of Thrift Supervision, Washington, 1991-2000; dep. asst. sec. for enforcement and programs HUD, Washington, 2000—. Mem. Phi Beta Kappa. Avocations: running, photography. Office: HUD Dep Asst Sec for Enforcement and Programs 451 7th St SW Washington DC 20410

EPLEY, LEWIS EVERETT, JR., lawyer; b. Ft. Smith, Ark., Apr. 28, 1936; s. Lewis Everett and Evelyn (Wood) E.; m. Donna Louise Swopes, Feb. 24, 1962. BS, JD, U. Ark., 1961. Bar: Ark. 1961. Formerly practiced in Eureka Springs, Ark.; city atty., 1969-71; chmn. bd. Bank of Eureka Springs, Ark., 1990-93, vice-chmn., 1993—, also bd. dirs. Del. Ark. Constl. Conv., 1969-70; apptd. spl. assoc. justice Ark. Supreme Ct., 1984. Mem. Ark. Bldg. Svcs. Coun., 1975-80, chmn., 1976-78; mem. Carroll County Cen. Dem. Com., 1964-68; bd. dirs. Eureka Springs Ozark Folk Festival, 1964-69, Ark. Cancer Rsch. Ctr., N.W. Ark. Radiation Therapy Inst., 1984-91, pres. bd. dirs., 1989; chmn. adv. bd. Eureka Springs Mcpl. Hosp., 1963-71; mem. Beaver Lake Adv. Com., 1982-89; trustee U. Ark., 1989-99, chmn. bd. trustees, 1996-98; bd. dirs. U. Ark. Found., 1994—, Mashburn Scholarship Found., 1993-2002; past dir. Washington Regional Med. Found.; past chmn. Carroll County adv. com. Ark.; mem. Carroll County Com. for Study of Long-Term Health Care Needs, 1990-93; mem. devel. coun. Eureka Springs Hosp., 1997-2001. Fellow Ark. Bar Assn. (del. 1975-78), Am. Inns of Ct. (mem. emeritus W. B. Putnam chpt. 1990-97), Carroll County Bar Assn. (past pres.), Eureka Springs C. of C. (dir., past pres.), Fayetteville Rotary Club, Phi Alpha Delta, Kappa Kappa Psi. Baptist. General practice, Probate (including wills, trusts), Property, real (including real estate development, water). Home: 2805 Brandon Cir Fayetteville AR 72703

EPLING, RICHARD LOUIS, lawyer; b. Waukegan, Ill., Aug. 16, 1951; s. Carrol Franklin and Mary Teresa Epling; m. Suzanne Braley, Aug. 4, 1973. BA in English and History magna cum laude, Duke U., 1973; JD, U. Mich., 1976. Bar: Ill. 1977, U.S. Dist. Ct. (no. dist.) Ill. 1977, U.S. Ct. Appeals (7th cir.) 1979, Ariz. 1981, U.S. Dist. Ct. Ariz. 1981, U.S. Ct. Appeals (9th cir.) 1982, N.Y. 1988, U.S. Ct. Appeals (2d cir.) 1988, U.S. Dist. Ct. (ea. and so. dists.) N.Y. 1989. Law clk. to presiding justice Mich. Supreme Ct., Southfield, 1976-77; assoc. Katten, Muchin & Zavis, Chgo., 1977-81; ptnr. Brown & Bain, P.A., Phoenix, 1981-88, Sidley & Austin, N.Y.C., 1988-92, Pillsbury Winthrop LLP and predecessor firm, N.Y.C., 1992—. Assoc. conferee Nat. Bankruptcy Conf., Washington, 1985-93. Contbr. articles to profl. jours. Mem. Am. Bankruptcy Inst., Phi Beta Kappa. Bankruptcy, Commercial, consumer (including collections, credit), Commercial, contracts (including sales of goods; commercial financing). Office: Pillsbury Winthrop LLP One Battery Park Plz New York NY 10004

EPPERSON, JOEL RODMAN, lawyer; b. Miami, Fla., Aug. 29, 1945; s. John Rodman and Ann Louise (Barrs) E.; m. Gretchen Jean Meyer, Apr. 16, 1968; children: Joel Rodman, David Michael, Sandra Elizabeth. BS, U. South Fla., 1967; JD, South Tex. Coll., 1976. Bar: Fla. 1976, U.S. Dist. Ct. (mid. dist.) Fla. 1976, U.S. Ct. Appeals (5th cir.) 1976, U.S. Supreme Ct. 1979, U.S. Ct. Appeals (11th cir. 1991. Asst. state's atty. State of Fla., Tampa, 1976-79; ptnr. Bryant & Epperson, Tampa, 1979-86; assoc. Bruce L. Scheiner, Ft. Myers, Fla., 1987-88; ptnr. Epperson & Stahl, Ft. Myers, 1988-90, Epperson & DeMinico, Tampa and Ft. Myers, 1991-92, Epperson & Assocs., P.A., Tampa and Ft. Myers, 1993-99, Tampa, 1999—. Capt. USMC, 1968-72. Mem. ABA, ATLA, Acad. Fla. Trial Lawyers Assn., Hillsborough County Bar Assn. Democrat. Personal injury (including property damage). Home: 1306 Anglers Ln Lutz FL 33548-5040 Office: Epperson & Rich PA 8401 JR Manor Dr Tampa FL 33634

EPPERSON, KRAETTLI QUYNTON, lawyer, educator; b. Ft. Eustis, Va., May 2, 1949; s. Dimpster Eugene Sr. and Helen Walter (Davidson) E.; m. Kay Lawrence, Aug. 22, 1970; children: Kraettli L., Kristin J., Kevin Q., Keith W. BA in Polit. Sci., U. Okla., 1971; MS in Urban and Policy Scis., SUNY, Stony Brook, 1974; JD, Oklahoma City U., 1978. Bar: Okla. 1979, U.S. Dist. Ct. (we. dist.) Okla. 1984, Fed. Claims Ct. 1997. Urban planner Gov.'s Office of Community Affairs and Planning, Oklahoma City, 1974-75; adminstr. of pub. transp. planning Okla. Dept. of Transp., Oklahoma City, 1975-79; title examiner Lawyers Title of Oklahoma City, Inc., 1979-80; gen. counsel, v.p. Am. First Land Title Ins. Co., Oklahoma City, 1980-82; assoc. Ferguson & Litchfield, Oklahoma City, 1982-85; of counsel Ames & Ashabranner, Oklahoma City, 1986-88, ptnr., 1989-93, Cook & Epperson, Oklahoma City, 1994-97, Oklahoma City, 1997—2002, Rolston, Hamill, Epperson, Myles & Nelson, 2002—. Adj. prof. law Okla. land titles Oklahoma City U., 1982—; instr. real property Okla. Bar Rev., 1998—; instr. real property titles Grad. Realtors Inst., 1998-99. Author: Basye Clearing Land Titles, 1998-2000, contbr., 2001-; contbg. author, editor: Vernon's Oklahoma Forms 2d-Real Estate, 2000—; contbr. articles to profl. jours. Asst. scoutmaster Boy Scouts Am., Oklahoma City, 1984-88, 1993-2000, asst. cubmaster, 1989-90, cubmaster, 1990-91, webelos leader, 1991-95, dist. vice-chair, 2000-01, dist. chair, 2001—. 2d lt. USAR, 1971. Recipient Dist. Svc. award, Boy Scouts Am., 2001. Mem. ABA (vice-chmn. conveyancing com. 1987-88, 93-94, chmn. 1991-93, chmn. state customs and practice subcom. 1987-88, project chmn. title exam. standards nat. survey 1988—), Am. Land Title Assn. (legis. com. 1981-82, jud. com. 1981-82), Okla. Bar Assn. (real property sect. 1979—, dir. 1982-88, 94-95, chmn. 1985-86, project chmn. Okla. Title Exam. Standards Handbook project 1982-85, mem. title exam. standards com. 1980—, chmn. 1992—, legis. liaison com. 1986-92, co-chmn. abstracting standards com. 1982-84), Oklahoma City Real Property Lawyers Assn. (dir. 1985-91, pres. 1990-91), Oklahoma City Commml. Law Attys. Assn. Republican. Episcopalian. Avocations: skeet, storytelling, camping. State civil litigation, Land use and zoning (including planning), Property, real (including real estate development, water). Home: 3029 Rock Ridge Ct Oklahoma City OK 73120-5731 Office: 4334 NW Expressway St Ste 174 Oklahoma City OK 73116-1574 E-mail: kqelaw@aol.com.

EPPS, JAMES HAWS, III, lawyer; b. Johnson City, Tenn., Sept. 15, 1936; s. James Haws and Anne Lafayette (Sessoms) E.; m. Jane Mahoney, Oct. 9, 1976; children from previous marriage--James Haws IV, Sara Stuart. BA, U.N.C., 1955-59; JD, Vanderbilt U., 1962. Bar: Tenn. 1962, U.S. Dist. Ct. Tenn. 1962, U.S. Ct. Appeals (6th cir.) 1971, Interstate Commerce Commn. Bar 1962, U.S. Supreme Ct. 1967. Prin. Epps & Epps, Johnson City, Tenn. City atty. Johnson City, 1967—, Johnson City Bd. Edn., 1967-86; spl. counsel State of Tenn., 1966-70; former gen. counsel Appalachian Flying Svc. Inc., ET&WNC Transp. Co., Inc. First bd. govs. Transp. Law Jour. Past bd. dirs. Washington County Mental Health Assn., East Tenn. and Western N.C. Transp. Co., East Tenn. and Western N.C. R.R., Tennolina Corp., Appalachian Air Lines, Inc., Appalachian Flying Svc., Inc., Farmers and Mchts. Bank, Limestone, Tenn., budget com. United Fund of Johnson City, 1964-68, Assault Crime Counsel Early Support Svcs. Inc., Safe Passage Inc., Johnson City Homeless Coalition, Home Base Adv. Coun., Johnson City/Washington County Health Coun. adv. com.; former legal adviser Appalachian coun. Girl Scouts U.S.A.; mem. Tenn. Law Revision Commn., 1970-71; legal counsel Salvation Army, mem. adv. bd. 1974—, exec. com. 1977—, 1st v.p. adv. bd. 1991, pres. adv. bd. 1993, 94, mem. property com.; chmn. Family Violence Coun.; legal counsel Washington County Humane Soc., Inc.; mem. Civil Def., 1967—; chmn. Washington County for Tenn. Leukemia Soc., 1991; mem. exec. com. Washington County Dem. Party, Tenn. Bicentennial Commn., exec. and fin. coms.; past mem. bd. dirs. Tenn. Mental Health ASsn. Fellow Tenn. Bar Found.; mem. ABA, Fed. Bar Assn., Nat. Orgn. Legal Problems Edn., Am. Counsel Assn., Nat. Assn. R.R. Trial Counsel, Internat. Mcpl. Lawyers Assn. (bd. dirs. 1982—, state chmn. Tenn. 1988-89, ethics and environ. coms. 1989—, regional v.p. 1989-92, chmn. resolutions com. 1989-90, lectr., trustee, 1992—, chmn. dues and alternatives revenue 1996-97, budget and fin., federalism com. 1996—, state league counsel rev. com. 1997, awards com., 1999—, bd. mem. policy adv. com. 2000, 1st v.p. 2001, pres. 2002-03), Nat. Legal Aid Defender Assn., Tenn. Bar Assn., Am. Judicature Soc., Washington County Bar Assn. (past pres.), Tenn. Mcpl. Attys. Assn., Assn. ICC Practitioners (past com. profl. ethics and grievences), Transp. Lawyers Assn., Motor Carrier Lawyers Assn., Johnson City C. of C. (Disting. Service award 1968), Internat. Platform Assn., Lawyers Com. for Civil Rights Under Law, World Peace Through Law Ctr., Tenn. Lung Assn., Tenn. Correctional Assn., Tenn. Taxpayers Assn. (past bd. dirs.), Tennesseans for Better Transp., U.S. Supreme Ct. Hist. Soc., Def. Rsch. Inst., Tipton Haynes Hist. Assn. (past dir.), Hurstleigh Club, Unaka Rd. and Gun Club, Highland Stable Club, North Johnson City Bus. Club (dir., past pres. 1966-67), Nat. Lawyers Club, East Tenn. State U. Century Club, Boys'Club (charter, Johnson City/Washington County), Masons, Elks (legal counsel 1963-67), Phi Delta Phi, Phi Delta Theta. Episcopalian. Administrative and regulatory, General practice. Office: 115 E Unaka Ave Johnson City TN 37601-4623 also: PO Box 2288 Johnson City TN 37605-2288

EPSTEIN, ALAN BRUCE, lawyer; b. Passaic, N.J., Sept. 20, 1944; s. Jerome P. and Stella M. (Goldfinger) E.; m. Eve Teichholz, June 21, 1966; children: Jason, Dylan. BA, Temple U., 1967, JD, 1969. Bar: Pa. 1970, U.S. Dist. Ct. (ea. dist.) Pa. 1970, U.S. Ct. Appeals (3d cir.) 1972, U.S. Ct. Appeals (5th cir.) 1977, U.S. Dist. Ct. (cen. and we. dists.) Pa. 1987, U.S. Supreme Ct. 1988, U.S. Ct. Appeals (9th cir.) 2000. Assoc. firm Freedman, Borowsky & Lorry, Phila., 1969-77; ptnr. firm Jablon, Epstein, Wolf & Drucker, Phila., 1977-99; shareholder Spector, Gadon & Rosen, Phila., 1999—. Pres. Judicate Nat. Pvt. Ct. System, Phila., 1983-88. Fellow Pa. Bar Found., Coll. Labor and Employement Lawyers; mem. ABA, ATLA, Pa. Trial Lawyers Assn. (bd. govs. 1984-86), Phila. Trial Lawyers Assn., Pa. Bar Assn., Phila. Bar Assn., Temple Am. Inn Ct. (bd. dirs. 1994—, pres. 2001—, nat. edn. chair 2000—). Jewish. Civil rights, Federal civil litigation, Labor (including EEOC, Fair Labor Standards Act, labor-management relations, NLRB, OSHA). Home: 404 S Camac St Philadelphia PA 19147-1112 Office: Spector Gadon & Rosen PC Seven Penn Ctr 1635 Market St Fl 7 Philadelphia PA 19103-2217 E-mail: aepstein@lawsgr.com.

EPSTEIN, EDWARD LOUIS, lawyer; b. Walla Walla, Wash., Jan. 10, 1936; s. Louis and Marie (Barger) E.; m. Marilyn K. Young, Dec. 29, 1962; children: Lisa Marie, Rachel Ann. BA with great distinction, Stanford U., 1958; LLB magna cum laude, Harvard U., 1961. Bar: Oreg. 1962, U.S. Dist. Ct. Oreg. 1962, U.S. Ct. Appeals (9th cir.) 1963. Assoc. Stoel Rives LLP, Portland, Oreg., 1962-67, ptnr., 1967—. Past sec., bd. dirs. Portland Hosp. Facilities Authority; trustee Good Samaritan Hosp. and Med. Ctr., Portland, 1972-78, pres., 1978; past trustee Morrison Ctr. for Youth and Family Svcs., Oreg. Assn. Hosps. Found. Mem. ABA, Am. Bar Found., Am. Health Lawyers Assn., Oreg. Bar Assn., Multnomah County Bar Assn., Multnomah Athletic Club, Univ. Club, Harvard Law Rev., Phi Beta Kappa. Corporate, general, Health, Corporate taxation. Office: Stoel Rives LLP 900 SW 5th Ave Ste 2600 Portland OR 97204-1268 E-mail: elepstein@stoel.com.

EPSTEIN, GARY MARVIN, lawyer; b. Bklyn., Nov. 28, 1946; s. Arthur and Juliett (Winick) E.; m. Jeralyn Needel, June 29, 1969; children: Daniel, Deborah. BSEE, Lehigh U., 1968; JD, Harvard U., 1971. Bar: D.C. 1971, U.S. Ct. Appeals (3d cir.) 1973, U.S. Supreme Ct. 1975, U.S. Ct. Appeals (9th cir.) 1988. Engr. Gordon Engring. Co., Wakefield, Mass., 1967-70; assoc. Arent, Fox, Kinter, Plotkin & Kahn, Washington, 1971-79, ptnr., 1979-81; chief Common Carrier Bur. FCC, Washington, 1981-83; ptnr., head telecom. group Latham & Watkins, Washington, 1983—. Pub. mem. Adminstrv. Conf. U.S., 1983-86; chmn. adv. com. reduced orbital spacing FCC, 1983-86; chmn. adv. Com. World Radiocomms. Conf., FCC, 1994-96; dir. D.C. Appleseed Ctr., 2001—, vice chair, 2002—, vice chair, 2003-, Appleseed Found., 2002—, v.p., 2002-. Bd. dirs. Appleseed Found., 2002—. Mem. ABA, D.C. Bar Assn., Eta Kappa Nu, Tau Beta Pi. Administrative and regulatory, Computer, Private international. Home: 1111 23d St NW Apt PH1F Washington DC 20037-2809 Office: Latham & Watkins 555 11th St NW Washington DC 20004-2585 E-mail: Gary.Epstein@lw.com.

EPSTEIN, JEREMY G. lawyer; b. Chgo., Sept. 28, 1946; s. Joseph and Gayola (Goldman) E.; m. Amy Kallman, Sept. 15, 1968; children: Joshua, Abigail. BA summa cum laude, Columbia U., 1967; BA, Cambridge U., Eng., 1969, MA, 1973; JD, Yale U., 1972. Bar: N.Y. 1973. Law clk. to judge Arnold Bauman U.S. Dist. Ct. (so. dist.) N.Y., 1972-74; asst. U.S. atty. So. Dist. N.Y., 1974-78; ptnr. Shearman & Sterling, N.Y.C., 1982—. Vol. Lawyers for the Arts; bd. dirs. Fund for Modern Cts. Fellow Am. Coll. Trial Lawyers, Phi Beta Kappa. Office: 599 Lexington Ave Fl C2 New York NY 10022-6030

EPSTEIN, JON DAVID, lawyer; b. Starkville, Miss., Dec. 25, 1942; s. Martin Epstein; m. Elizabeth A. B.S., U. Ill., 1965, J.D., 1967. Bar: Ill. 1970, Tex. 1974, D.C. 1978. Assoc. counsel Blue Cross Assn., Chgo., 1969-74; assoc. Wood, Lucksinger & Holland, Houston, 1974-75; ptnr. Wood, Lucksinger & Epstein, Houston, 1975-91, Vinson & Elkins LLP, 1991—; mem. faculty Aspen System Health Care Seminars, 1974—; adj. prof. U. Houston Coll. Law, 1982—, St. Louis U. Health Sci. Ctr., 1981-91. Contbr. articles to profl. jours. Chmn. bd. dirs. Gulf Coast chpt. March of Dimes, 1994-95; mem. devel. bd. U. Tex. Med. Br., 2000—; mem. bd. visitors U. Ill. Coll. Law, 2002—. Served as officer U.S. Army, 1967. Mem. Am. Soc. Hosp. Attys. (dir. 1980—, pres.-elect 1985, pres. 1986), ABA, Houston Bar Assn., Tex. Bar Assn., D.C. Bar Assn., Hosp. Fin. Mgmt. Assn. (dir. Gulf Coast chpt. 1977-79), Fed. Bar Assn., Houston Touchdown Club (pres. 1981). Administrative and regulatory, Federal civil litigation, Health. Home: 19039 Kahala Dr Galveston TX 77554 Office: 1001 Fannin St Ste 2500 Houston TX 77002-6706 E-mail: jepstein@velaw.com.

EPSTEIN, JUDITH ANN, lawyer; b. L.A., Dec. 23, 1942; d. Gerald Elliot and Harriet (Hirsh) Rubens; m. Joseph I. Epstein, Oct. 4, 1964; children: Mark Douglas, Laura Ann. AB, U. Calif., Berkeley, 1964; MA, U. San Francisco, 1974, JD, 1977. Bar: Calif. 1978, U.S. Dist. Ct. (no. dist.) Calif 1978, U.S. Supreme Ct. 1983, U.S. Ct. Appeals (9th cir.) 1984. With social svcs. dept. Sutter County, Yuba City, Calif., 1964-66; bus. devel. assoc. Yuba County C. of C., Marysville, Calif., 1968-70; rsch. clk. Calif. Supreme Ct., San Fransisco, 1977; ptnr. Crosby, Heafey, Roach & May, Oakland, Calif., 1978-91; gen. counsel and sec. Valent USA Corp., 1991-98; fellow The Commonwealth Club of Calif., 1999—2001; appellate judge Calif. State Bar Ct., 2002—. Lectr. U. Calif. Grad. Sch. Journalism in Media Law, Berkeley, 1987-91; bd. dirs. Sierra Pacific Steel, Hayward, Calif.; adj. prof. U. San Francisco, 1999—. Bd. dirs., v.p. Oakland Ballet, 1980-92; mem. bd. counselors U. San Francisco Sch. Law, 1994; trustee U. San Francisco, 1996—; bd. dirs. San Francisco Bay area Girl Scouts U.S., 1998—, East Bay Cmty. Found. Recipient Pres.'s award Oakland Ballet, James Madison Freedom of Info. award Soc. Profl. Journalists, 1992; award for Disting. Achievement, Girl Scouts U.S., 1995. Fellow Am. Bar Found.; mem. Calif. Women Lawyers Assn., Alameda Bar Assn., Berkeley Tennis Club. Antitrust, Corporate, general, Libel.

EPSTEIN, MELVIN, lawyer; b. Passaic, N.J., Jan. 4, 1938; s. Hyman and Lillian (Rozenblum) E.; m. Rachel Judith Stein, Dec. 20, 1964; children: Jonathan Andrew, Emily E. Landau. AB, Harvard U., 1959, LLB, 1962. Bar: N.Y. 1963. Assoc. Stroock & Stroock & Lavan, L.L.P., N.Y.C., 1962-71, ptnr., 1972—. Bd. dirs. Hillel of N.Y.C.; mem. schs. com. Harvard U., 1984—. Mem. N.Y. State Bar Assn., Assn. of Bar of City of N.Y. Democrat. Jewish. Corporate, general, Private international, Securities. Office: Stroock & Stroock & Lavan LLP 180 Maiden Ln New York NY 10038-4925 E-mail: mepstein@stroock.com.

EPSTEIN, MICHAEL ALAN, lawyer; b. N.Y.C., June 26, 1954; s. Herman and Lillian (King) E. BA, Lehigh U., 1975; JD, NYU, 1979. Bar: N.Y., 1980, US. Dist. Ct. (so., ea. dists.) N.Y., 1980. Ptnr. Weil, Gotshal & Manges, N.Y.C., 1979—. Lectr. in field. Author: Modern Intellectual Property, 1984, 3d edit., 1994, International Intellectual Property, 1992, Epstein on Intellectual Property, 4th edit., 2001; editor: Corporate Counsellors Deskbook, 1982, 3d edit., 1990, Biotechnology Law, 1988, The Trademark Law Revision Act, 1989, Trade Secrets, Restrictive Covenants and Other Safeguards, 1986, Online-Internet Law, 1997; co-editor, mem. editl. bd. Jour. Proprietary Rights, The Computer Lawyer, The Intellectual Property Strategist, The Cyberspace Lawyer; contbr. articles to profl. jours. Trustee Jonas Salk Found., Am. Health Found. Donald L. Brown fellow in trade regulation NYU Sch. Law, 1978-79. Mem. ABA, N.Y. State Bar Assn. Antitrust, Computer, Trademark and copyright. Home: 1020 Park Ave New York NY 10028-0913 Office: Weil Gotshal & Manges 767 5th Ave Fl Concl New York NY 10153-0119

EQUEY, ROBERT, lawyer; b. Bucharest, Romania, June 10, 1949; s. Jérôme Equey and Aurelia Razus; m. Anne-France Eskenazi, Mar. 24, 1977; children: Alexandre, Raphaël, Coralie. B in Philosophy and Math., Inst. Florimont Coll. St. Maurice, Switzerland, 1969; degree, U. Lausanne, Switzerland, 1975. Bar: Geneva 1978. Legal counsel Banque de Paris and Pays-Bas, Geneva, 1981—86; gen. counsel, head of compliance, gen. mgr. United European Bank, Geneva, 1985—98; freelance legal and fin. advisor, cons. Geneva, 1998—2000; ptnr. Keppeler & Assocs., Geneva, 2000—. Bd. dirs. Israel Discount Bank, Geneva; pres. ORT Switzerland; bd. govs., mem Ben Gurion Univ. of the Negev, Beer-Sheva, Israel; bd. govs., mem. Weizmann Inst. of Sci., Rehovot, Israel. Pres. French chpt. Suisse-Israel C. of C., Switzerland, 2000—; pres. kindergarten, Geneva, 2001—; mem. Radical Party, Geneva, 2001—. Avocations: cycling, golf, skiing. Banking, Finance, Commercial, contracts (including sales of goods; commercial financing). Office: Keppeler & Assocs 15 rue Ferdinand-Hodler 1207 Geneva Switzerland Office Fax: (41-22) 718 61 71. E-mail: equey@keplaw.ch.

ERENS, JAY ALLAN, lawyer; b. Chgo., Oct. 18, 1935; s. Miller S. and Annette (Goodman) R.; m. Patricia F. Brett, Aug. 21, 1960 (div. May 1985); children: Pamela B., Bradley B.; m. Patrice K. Franklin, June 15, 1985; 1 child, Cameron Jay. BA, Yale U., 1956; LLB, Harvard U., 1959. Bar: Ill. 1960. Law clk. to Justice John M. Harlan U.S. Supreme Ct., Washington, 1959-60; pvt. practice Chgo., 1960-64; founding and sr. ptnr. Levy and Erens (name changed to Erens and Miller 1985), Chgo., 1964-86; sr. ptnr. Hopkins & Sutter, Chgo., 1986-2001; with Foley & Lardner, Chgo., 2001—. Lectr. law Northwestern U., Chgo., 1961-63; spl. asst. atty. gen. State Ill., Chgo., 1964-70. Trustee Latin Sch. Chgo., 1975-80. Mem. ABA, Chgo. Bar Assn. Office: Foley & Lardner 321 N Clark St Chicago IL 60610 E-mail: jerens@foleylaw.com.

ERGAZOS, JOHN WILLIAM, lawyer; b. Canton, Ohio, Nov. 26, 1924; s. Manso Aristidis and Ella (Wongler) E.; m. Margaret Berbeles, Oct. 22, 1950; children: John William Jr., Veronica. BA, Kent State U., 1948; LLB, McKinley Law Sch., 1952. Bar: Ohio 1952, U.S. Dist. Ct. 1954. Pvt. practice, Canton, Ohio, 1952—. Bd. dirs. Factory Indsl. Maintenance Co., Kimdot Travel, Inc. Com. mem. Greater Canton C. of C., 1981-91. 2d lt. U.S. Army, 1943-46, ETO. Named Man of the Yr., St. Haralambos Men's Club, Canton, 1979. Mem. Am. Trial Lawyers Assn., Ohio State Bar Assn., Stark County Bar Assn., Order of Ahepa (pres. 1985-89), Eagles, Elks. Office: 315 Tuscarawas St W Canton OH 44702

ERHART, JOHN JOSEPH, lawyer; b. Rush City, Minn., May 20, 1952; m. Debra Elaine Borris, Oct. 22, 1988; children: Laura Frances, Jenna Rae. BA, St. John's U., 1974; JD, Georgetown U., 1977. Bar: Minn. 1977, U.S. Dist. Ct. Minn. 1977, U.S. Ct. Appeals (8th cir.) 1978. Law clk. Judge Gerald W. Heaney U.S. Ct. Appeals (8th cir.), Duluth, Minn., 1977-79; shareholder Fredrikson & Byron, Mpls., 1979—. Corporate, general, Mergers and acquisitions, Taxation, general. Office: Fredrikson & Byron 4000 Pillsbury Ctr 200 S 6th St Minneapolis MN 55402-1425 E-mail: jerhart@fredlaw.com.

ERICHSEN, KIELD-GUSTAV, lawyer; b. Copenhagen, May 20, 1951; Cand. Jur., U. Copenhagen, 1977. Asst. prof. U. Copenhagen, 1978—81; rschr. European U. Inst., Florence, 1981—83; lectr. Bus. Sch. Copenhagen, 1983—87; ptnr. Konig, Homann, Erichsen Law Office, 1987—. Office: Konig Homann Erichsen 21 Amagertorv DK1160 Copenhagen Denmark

ERICKSON, DIANE QUINN, lawyer, artist, small business owner; b. La Grange, Ill., Oct. 8, 1959; d. Stanley Brittian Sr. and Marilyn Agnes (Miller) Quinn; m. Russell Lee Erickson, Mar. 9, 1985. BS in Psychology, U. Ill., 1981; JD, Valparaiso U., 1984. Bar: Ill. 1985. Assoc. Dreyer, Foote, et al Aurora, Ill., 1984-87; trust officer, atty. 1st Nat. Bank Des Plaines, Ill., 1987-89; owner Erickson Art & Frame, Naperville, Ill., 1988—. Mem. Brain Rsch. Found. Mem. NAFE, Ill. Bar Assn., DuPage County Bar Assn., N.W. Suburban Bar Assn., Chgo. Bar Assn. Lutheran. Avocations: tennis, travel, dance, skiing. Home: 6413 Greene Rd Woodridge IL 60517-1485 Office: 6804 Hobson Valley Rd Ste 118 Woodridge IL 60517

ERICKSON, ROBERT STANLEY, lawyer; b. Kemmerer, Wyo., Apr. 17, 1944; s. Stanley W. and Dorothy Marie (Johnson) E.; m. Alice Norman, Dec. 27, 1972; children: Robert Badger, Erin Elizabeth, Andrew Carl, Scott Stanley, Courtney Ellen, Brennan Marie. BS in Bus., U. Idaho, 1966; JD, U. Utah, 1969; LLM in Taxation, George Washington U., 1973. Bar: U.S. Supreme Ct. 1973, U.S. Ct. Appeals (9th cir.) 1980, U.S. Dist. Ct. Idaho 1973, U.S. Tax Ct. 1969, Idaho 1973, Utah 1969. Assoc. atty. Office of Chief Counsel, Dept. Treasury, Washington, 1969-73; assoc. Elam, Burke, Jeppesen, Evans & Boyd, Boise, Idaho, 1973-77; ptnr. Elam, Burke, Evans, Boyd & Koontz, Boise, 1977-81; spl. counsel Holme Roberts & Owen, Salt Lake City, 1981-83; ptnr. Hansen & Erickson, Boise, 1983-85, Hawley Troxell Ennis & Hawley, Boise, 1985—. Contbr. articles to profl. jours. Named Citizen of Yr., Boise Exch. Club, 1980. Fellow Am. Coll. of Trust and Estate Counsel (past Idaho chmn. 1993—); mem. ABA (sect. on taxation, com. state and local taxes), IRS/Western Region Bar Assn. (mem., past chmn. liaison com. Idaho co-chair local task force IRS non-filer program 1993), Idaho State Bar (founding chmn. taxation, probate and trust law sect.), Utah State Bar (tax and estate planning sect.), Boise Estate Planning Council, Idaho State Tax Inst. (exec. com., numerous other local and nat. coms.). Mem. Lds Ch. Estate planning, Probate (including wills, trusts), Corporate taxation. Office: Hawley Troxell Ennis & Hawley First Interstate Ctr 877 Main St Ste 1000 Boise ID 83702-5884

ERICKSON, WILLIAM HURT, retired state supreme court justice; b. Denver, May 11, 1924; s. Arthur Xavier and Virginia (Hurt) E.; m. Doris Rogers, Dec. 24, 1953; children: Barbara Ann, Virginia Lee, Stephen Arthur, William Taylor. Degree in petroleum engring., Colo. Sch. Mines, 1947; student, U. Mich., 1949; LLB, U. Va., 1950; PhD in Engring. (hon.) , Colo. Sch. of Mines, 2002. Bar: Colo. 1951. Pvt. practice, Denver; state supreme ct. justice Colo. Supreme Ct., 1971-96, state supreme ct. chief justice, 1983-86; faculty NYU Appellate Judges Sch., 1972-85. Mem. exec. Commn. on Accreditation of Law Enforcement Agys., 1980-83; chmn. Pres.'s Nat. Commn. for Rev. of Fed. and State Laws Relating to Wiretapping and Electronic Surveillance, 1976. Chmn. Erickson Commn., 1997, Owens Columbine Rev. Commn., 2000-01; chmn. gov.'s Columbine Rev. Commn., 1999-2001. With USAAF, 1943. Recipient Disting. Achievement medal Colo. Sch. Mines, 1990. Fellow Internat. Acad. Trial Lawyers (former sec.), Am. Coll. Trial Lawyers, Am. Bar Found. (chmn. 1985), Internat. Soc. Barristers (pres. 1971); mem. ABA, (bd. govs. 1975-79, former chmn. com. on standards criminal justice, former chmn. coun. criminal law sect., former chmn. com. to implement standards criminal justice, mem. long-range planning com., action com. to reduce ct. cost and delay), Colo. Bar Assn. (award of merit 1989), Denver Bar Assn. (past pres., trustee), Am. Law Inst. (coun. 1973—), Practising Law Inst. (nat. adv. coun., bd. govs. Colo.), Freedoms Found. at Valley Forge (nat. coun. trustees, 1986—), Order of Coif, Scribes (pres. 1978). Home: 10 Martin Ln Englewood CO 80110-4821

ERICSON, ROGER DELWIN, lawyer, forest resource company executive; b. Moline, Ill, Dec. 21, 1934; s. Carl D. and Linnea E. (Challman) E.; m. Norma F. Brown, Aug. 1, 1957; children: Catherine Lynn, David. AB, JD, Stetson U., DeLand, Fla., 1958; MBA, U. Chgo., 1971. Bar: Fla. 1958, Ill. 1959, Ind. 1974. Atty. Brunswick Corp., Skokie, Ill., 1959-62; asst. sec., asst. gen. counsel Chemetron Corp., Chgo., 1962-73; asst. v.p. Inland Container Corp., Indpls., 1973-75, v.p., gen. counsel, sec., 1975-83, Temple-Inland, Inc., 1983-94, of counsel, 1994—. V.p., sec. bd. dirs. Inland Container Corp.; dir., pres., co-CEO Kraft Land Svcs., Inc., Atlanta, 1978-88; bd. dirs., v.p. Guaranty Holdings Inc., Dallas; v.p. Temple-Inland Fin. Svcs., Inc., Austin, 1990-94; bd. dirs. Temple-Inland Forest Products, Temple-Inland Real Estate Investment, Inc., Temple-Inland Realty Inc. Trustee Chgo. Homes for Children, 1971-74; mem. alumni coun. U. Chgo., 1972-76; mem. Palatine Twp. Youth Commn., 1969-72; sect. chmn. Chgo. Heart Assn., 1972, 73; alumni bd. dirs. Stetson U.; bd. dirs. Temple-Inland Found; mem. Safe and Drug-Free Comm. Collier County Sch. Bd., 1996—. Mem. ABA, Am. Arbitration Assn. (nat. panel comml. arbitrators), Am. Soc. Corp. Secs., Am. Forest Products Assn. (past mem. govt. affairs com. and legal com.), Am. Corp. Counsel Assn., Ind. Bar Assn., Fla. Bar Assn., Chgo. Bar Assn., Indpls. Bar Assn. (chmn. corp. counsel sect., mem. profl. responsibility com. 1982), Collier County Bar Assn., Indpls. C. of C. (govt. affairs com.), Plum Grove Club (pres. 1967), The Club at Olde Cypress, Omicron Delta Kappa, Phi Delta Phi. Administrative and regulatory, Antitrust, Corporate, general. Office: PO Box 110218 Naples FL 34108-0104

ERKENBRACK, STEPHEN KENNETH, lawyer; b. Washington, June 28, 1952; s. Phillip Frederick and Irene (Brady) E.; m. Lysa Marie Loew, Aug. 18, 1979; children: Kenneth, Elizabeth, Daniel. BA, Washington & Lee U., 1974; JD, U. Colo., 1978. Bar: Colo. 1978, U.S. Dist. Ct. Colo. 1978. Clk. Colo. Supreme Ct., Denver, 1979; dep. dist. atty. Mesa County, Grand Junction, Colo., 1979-82; assoc., office mgr. Tipping & Beckner, Grand Junction, 1982; v.p. Beckner & ErkenBrack, Grand Junction, 1983—87; dist. atty. Mesa County, Grand Junction, 1987—93; chief dep. atty. gen. Denver, 1993—97; pvt. practice, 1997; ptnr. Hale, Hackstaff, Tymkovich, ErkenBrack, 1998—2001; v.p. Rocky Mountain Health Plans, Grand Junction, 2002—. Vice chmn. Attention to Youth, Grand Junction, 1979-84; bd. govs. Colo. Dist. Atty's. Coun., 1987-93, pres., 1992-93; bd. law examiners Colo. Supreme Ct. Bd., 1989-99, chmn., 1989-99. Mem. Colo. Bar Assn (bd. govs. 1989-93), Mesa County Bar Assn. Republican. Avocations: music, history, philosophy, skiing, camping. State civil litigation, Criminal. Office: PO Box 10600 Grand Junction CO 81502

ERLEBACHER, ARLENE CERNIK, retired lawyer; b. Chgo., Oct. 3, 1946; d. Laddie J. and Gertrude V. (Kurdys) Cernik; m. Albert Erlebacher, June 14, 1968; children: Annette Doherty, Jacqueline. BA, Northwestern U., 1967, JD, 1973. Bar: Ill. 1974, U.S. Dist. Ct. (no. dist.) Ill. 1974, U.S. Ct. Appeals (7th cir.) 1974, Fed. Trial Bar 1983, U.S. Supreme Ct. 1985. Assoc. Sidley & Austin, Chgo., 1974-80, ptnr., 1980-95, ret., 1996. Fellow Am. Bar Found.; mem. Order of Coif. Federal civil litigation, State civil litigation, Product liability. E-mail: Erlebacher@attbi.com.

ERLENBORN, JOHN NEAL, lawyer, educator, former congressman; b. Chgo., Feb. 8, 1927; s. John H. and Veronica M. (Moran) E.; m. Dorothy C. Fisher, May 10, 1952; children: Debra Lynn, Paul Nelson, David John. Student, U. Notre Dame, 1944, U. Ill., 1945-46; JD, Loyola U., Chgo., 1949. Bar: Ill. 1949. With law office Joseph S. Perry, Wheaton, 1949-50; partner firm Erlenborn & Bauer, Elmhurst, 1952-63, Erlenborn, Bauer and Hotte, 1963-71; mem. 89-97th congresses from 14th Dist., Ill., 1965-83, 98th congress from 13th dist., Ill., 1983-85; asst. states atty. DuPage County, Ill., 1950-52; mem. Ill. Ho. of Reps. from DuPage County, 1956-64; ptnr. Seyfarth, Shaw, Fairweather & Geraldson, Washington, 1985-92, of counsel, 1993-94. Bd. dirs. Custodial Trust Co., Princeton, N.J.; mem. U.S. Dept. Labor Employee Retirement Income Security Act Adv. Coun., 1985-89, chmn., 1985-86; adj. prof. Georgetown U. Law Ctr., 1994-2002; mem., vice chair Legal Svcs. Corp., 1989-90, 1996—, pres. 2001-03. Trustee The Aerospace Corp., 1990-99, chair audit and fin. com., 1999; advisor U.S. Delegation to ILO 78th and 79th Session, Geneva. With USNR, 1944-46. Mem.: Former Mems. of Congress (bd. dirs. 1993—, sec. 1995—96, treas. 1996—97, v.p. 1998—2000, pres. 2000—02). Labor (including EEOC, Fair Labor Standards Act, labor-management relations, NLRB, OSHA), Legislative, Pension, profit-sharing, and employee benefits. E-mail: JErlenborn@aol.com.

ERMA, REINO MAURI, lawyer, university chancellor emeritus; b. Tampere, Finland, Apr. 8, 1922; s. Edvin Eugen and Ida Irene (Haapala) E.; m. Hilkka Marjatta Ahjo, Jan. 5, 1946; children: Juhani, Sinikka, Anneli, Tapio. LLM, Helsinki U., 1944, Licentiate in Laws, 1948, LLD, 1955. With KOP Bank, Helsinki, 1947-70, dir., 1960-70; prof. bus. law Faculty Econs. and Administrn. U. Tampere, 1970-84, rector, 1976-81, chancellor, 1984-90. Author: Contract of Work, 1955, General Conditions for the Building Contracts, 1974, 91, Legal Aspects of Subcontracting, 1975, General Conditions for the Delivery of Goods between Finland and CMEA Countries, 1980, Banking Laws, 1986, Legal Handbook of Foreign Trade, 1989, 94; co-author: (with A. Guttorm and L. Lehtinen) Arbitration in Finland and in Russia, 1999. Served with Finnish Army, 1940-44. Decorated Comdr. Order first cl. Finnish White Rose, Cross of Freedom, Medal of Freedom. Mem. Internat. Law Assn., Arbitration Assn. Finland, Rotary (past pres.). Home: Mustanlahdenkatu 1 B 87 33210 Tampere Finland Office: Law Office Erma Toimisto Mustanlahdenkatu 1 B 95 33200 Tampere Finland

ERNO, TORKEL, lawyer; b. Oslo, Dec. 5, 1956; s. Ernst Lars and Else Omholt Erno; m. Kristin Ostensen Erno, June 2, 1979; children: Kine, Ingrid. Degree in law, U. Oslo, 1983. Bar: Norway 1985. Atty. Norsk Hydro Asa, Oslo, 1983—85, mgr., 1985—87, sr. in-house atty., 1987—96; gen. counsel Postbanken AS, 1996—2000; ptnr. Wiersholm, Mellbye & Bech, 2000—. Mem.: Norwegian Lawyers Assn. Avocations: sailing, windsurfing, bicycling, skiing, photography. Corporate, general, Commercial, contracts (including sales of goods; commercial financing), Finance. Home: Trudvangveien 33 Stabekk 1368 Norway Office: Wiersholm Mellbye & Bech Ruseloulveien 26 Oslo 0115 Norway Fax: +47 210210001. E-mail: ter@wiersholm.no.

ERNST, CHRISTOPHER MARK, lawyer; b. Cleve., Dec. 1, 1966; s. Chalmer Mark and Helen Elizabeth (Gibson) E. BA, Tufts U., 1988; JD, Case Western Res. U., 1991. Bar: Ohio 1991, U.S. Dist. Ct. Ohio 1992, U.S. Ct. Appeals (6th cir.) 1995, U.S. Supreme Ct. 2001. Law clk. Cuyahoga County Ct. of Common Pleas, Cleve., 1992; ptnr. Ernst & Dowling, 1992-96; prin. Ernst & Co., LPA, 1996-97; assoc. Weston Hurd Fallon Paisley & Howley, 1997—99, ptnr., 2000—. Vol. in-house counsel Call For Action, WJW TV-8, 1993-96; vol. counsel Legal Aid Soc. Mem. Playhouse Square Ptnrs., Cleve., 1992-2000, trustee, 1995-2000, mem. exec. com., 1995-98, chair activities com. 1995-96, chair fiduciary com. 1996-97, chair leadership devel., 1997-98; trustee Cuyahoga County Corrections Planning Bd., 1996—. Mem. ABA (Cyberspace Com. 2002-), Ohio State Bar Assn., Cuyahoga County Bar Assn. (trustee 1996-2001, mem. judicial selection com., 1997-98, co-chair judicial selection com., 1998-99, cert. grievance com., 1997-2001), Cuyahoga County Young Democrats (pres. 1999-2000), Mensa. Avocation: jazz trombone. Computer, Corporate, general, General civil litigation. Office: 50 Public Sq Cleveland OH 44113-2201

ERNST, DANIEL PEARSON, lawyer; b. Des Moines, Sept. 30, 1931; s. Daniel Ward and Thea Elaine (Pearson) E.; m. Ann Robinson, April 14, 1956; children: Ellen, Daniel R., Ruth Ann. BA, Dartmouth Coll., 1953; JD, U. Mich., 1956. Bar: Iowa 1956, Ill. 1964, Mich. 1980. Assoc. Clewell Cooney & Fuerste, 1960-64; ptnr. Nelson Stapleton & Ernst, Stapleton & Ernst, Stapleton Ernst & Sprengelmeyer, East Dubuque, Ill., Nelson Stapleton & Ernst & Sprengelmeyer, Dubuque, Iowa, 1964-79; pvt. practice Dubuque, 1979-80; ptnr. Ernst & Cody, Dubuque, 1981-84, Daniel P. Ernst, P.C., Dubuque, 1984-90, Vincent Roth & Ernst, P.C., Galena, Ill., 1991; pub. defender State of Iowa, Dubuque, 1991-96; pvt. practice Dubuque, 1997—. U.S. trustee 1979-91. Capt. USAF, 1957-60, U.S. Coast Guard Aux. Mem. ABA, Iowa State Bar Assn. (bd. govs. 1985-89), Dubuque County Bar Assn. (2d v.p. 1979-80, 1st v.p. 1980-81, pres. 1981-82), Ill. State Bar Assn., Jo Daviess County Bar Assn., State Bar Assn. Mich., Grand Traverse-Leelanau-Antrim Bar Assn. Democrat. Avocations: swimming, boating. Office: Attorney-at-Law 899 Mount Carmel Rd Dubuque IA 52003-7946 Fax: 563-582-0324. E-mail: ernstdan@mchsi.com.

ERRICO, MELISSA, lawyer; b. Waterbury, Conn., Mar. 14, 1969; d. John and Carol Ann (Summa) E. BA, U. Ariz., 1991; JD, Washburn U., 1994. Bar: Ariz., U.S. Dist. Ct. Ariz. Assoc. Virgelli & Errico, Tucson, 1994—. Republican. Roman Catholic. Appellate, Family and matrimonial, Personal injury (including property damage). Office: Vingelli & Errico 33 N Stone Ave Ste 1800 Tucson AZ 85701-1429 E-mail: merricoesq@aol.com.

ERSEK, GREGORY JOSEPH MARK, lawyer, business administrator; b. Cleve., Aug. 30, 1956; s. Joseph Francis and Mary H. (Hurchanik) E. AB, Columbia U., 1977; MBA, U. Pa., 1979; JD, U. Fla., 1984; cert. cir. civil mediator, Fla. Internat. U., 1998. Bar: Fla. 1986, U.S. Dist. Ct. (so. dist.) Fla. 1987. Cons. fin. valuation Am. Appraisal Co., Princeton, N.J., 1979-80; mgr. import-export Marie L. Veslie Co., Coral Gables, Fla., 1980-85; assoc. Lunny, Tucker, Karns & Brescher, Ft. Lauderdale, Fla., 1986; dir. legal dept. Horizons Rsch. Labs. Inc., Ft. Lauderdale, 1986-89, sr. corp. planner, 1988-89; gen. counsel Unisco Corp., Ft. Lauderdale, 1989-93, TRICORD Corp., Ft. Lauderdale, 1990-93, Irish Times, Inc., Ft. Lauderdale, 1993-97; dir. corp. fin. dept. & sr. corp. counsel Canton Fin. Svcs. Corp., subs. Cyber Am. Corp., Salt Lake City, 1995-96; gen. counsel Greenstreet Capital Corp., Investment Bankers, Las Vegas, 1996-99, Gaelic Pub. Devel., Inc., Ft. Lauderdale, 1998—, Premier Fin. Corp., Jacksonville, 1998—. Sec.-treas. Sorkar Group, Inc., Ft. Lauderdale, 1987-89; CEO Am. CompuShopper, Inc., 1989-98; with legal dept. Pfizer Inc., N.Y.C., 1983; co-founder, mgr. Poland/U.S. Trade and Mktg. Consortium, 1989—; pres. Corp. Execs. with Spinal Cord Injury, 2002—; sec. Dirs. Cos. with Spinal Cord Injury, 2002—; mem. Philip C. Jessup Internat. Moot Ct. team, 1983; gen. counsel Biltmore Vacation Resorts, Inc., f/k/a Cyber Info., Inc., Las Vegas, 1997-99, Avalon Group, Inc., Cedar Rapids, Iowa, 1997-99. Editor Medscanner, med. industry newsletter, 1987-89. Mem. venture coun. forum; alumnus Internat. House, N.Y.C., 1984. Mem. Fla. Bar Assn., Nat. Assn. Securities Dealers (nat. arbitration com. 1991-98), Assn. Attys. with Disabilities (exec. dir. 2002—), Coun. on Fgn. Rels. (local com.), Corp. Execs. with Spinal Cord Injury (pres. 2002—), Dirs. Pub. Co. with Spinal Cord Injury (sec. 2002—), Wharton Club South Fla. Avocations: travel, books. Health, Estate planning, Securities. Home and Office: 17820 NW 18th Ave Miami FL 33056-4949

ERTEL, ALLEN EDWARD, lawyer, former congressman; b. Williamsport, Pa., Nov. 7, 1936; s. Clarence and Helen (Froehner) E.; m. Catharine Bieber Klepper, June 20, 1959; children: Taylor John (dec.), Edward Barnhardt, Amy Sara. BA, Dartmouth Coll., 1958, MSBA, MS, 1959; LL.B., Yale U., 1965. Bar: Pa., Del., U.S. Supreme Ct. Law clk. U.S. Dist. Ct. of Del., 1965-66; ptnr. Candor, Youngman, Gibson & Gault, Williamsport, 1967-72, Ertel & Kieser, Williamsport, 1972-76; dist. atty. Lycoming County, Pa., 1967-76; mem. 95th-97th Congresses from 17th Pa. Dist.; ptnr. Reed Smith Shaw & McClay, Williamsport, 1985-88; pvt. practice Williamsport, 1988—. Del. Democratic. Nat. Conv., 1972; Dem. nominee for gov. of Pa., 1982, for atty. gen. of Pa., 1984. Served with USN, 1959-62. Mem. Pa. Bar Assn., Del. Bar Assn., Dartmouth Soc. Engrs., Lions. Lutheran. Corporate, general, Environmental, Personal injury (including property damage). Home: 2245 Heim Hill Rd Montoursville PA 17754-9699 Office: 800 W 4th St Williamsport PA 17701-5901

ERVIN, ROBERT MARVIN, lawyer; b. near Ocala, Fla., Jan. 19, 1917; s. Richard William and Carrie (Phillips) E.; m. Frances Anne Cushing, Dec. 25, 1941; children: Anne Cushing (Mrs. Henry Lamar Rowe), Robert

Marvin. BSBA, U. Fla., 1941, LLB, 1947. Bar: Fla. 1947. Of counsel Ervin, Chapman & Ervin, Tallahassee, 1947—; U.S. referee in bankruptcy No. Dist. Fla., part time, 1952-72. Mem. Fla. Constn. Revision Commn., 1966-68; Trustee U. Fla. Law Center Assn.; mem. founders com., mem. bd. visitors Fla. State U. Coll. Law. Served with USMC, 1941-45, PAO; col. ret. Recipient Disting. Svc. award for legal edn. John B. Stetson U., 1966, Disting. Svc. award Armed Forces League, 1966, Medal of Hon. award Fla. Bar Found., 2003; named to Fla. Housing Hall of Fame, 1993. Fellow Am. Bar Found. (chmn. 1989-90); mem. ABA (ho. of dels. 1966-91, bd. govs., 1979-82, chmn. sect. criminal justice 1975-76, mem. resource devel. coun., audit com., vice chmn. sr. lawyers div., chmn. special com. on fiscal policy 1984-85), Am. Coll. Trial Lawyers (bd. regents 1983-84), Am. Law Inst., Am. Judicature Soc., Fla. Bar (pres. 1965-66, Disting. Svc. award 1966), Fla. Supreme Ct. Hist. Soc. (pres. 1986-87, chmn. trustees 1987-98), Am. Bar Retirement Assn. (pres. 1980-82), Nat. Conf. Referees in Bankruptcy (pres. 1963-64), Ret. Officers Assn., Elks, Fla. Blue Key, Phi Alpha Delta, Alpha Kappa Psi. Baptist. Federal civil litigation, State civil litigation, General practice. Home: 530 N Ride Tallahassee FL 32303-5127 Office: PO Box 1170 223 S Gadsden St Tallahassee FL 32301-1811

ERVIN, SPENCER, lawyer; b. Bala, Pa., Nov. 25, 1932; s. Spencer and Miriam Williams (Roberts) E.; m. Florence Wetherill Schroeder, Sept. 12, 1964; children: Margaret, Mary, Miriam, Helen. AB, Harvard U., 1954, JD, 1959. Bar: Pa. 1960, Maine 1995, U.S. Supreme Ct. 1963. Staff counsel Philco Corp., Phila., 1959-62; assoc. Ringe & Dewey, Phila., 1962-64; ptnr. Ringe, Tate & Ervin, Phila., 1964-72, Gratz, Tate, Spiegel, Ervin & Ruthrauff, Phila., 1972-92, Hepburn, Willcox, Hamilton & Putnam, Phila., 1992-96, Largay Law Offices, Bangor, Maine, 1996-97; pvt. practice, Bass Harbor, Maine, 1998—. Bd. dirs. Mt. Desert Island Biol. Lab. Bd. dirs., officer Neighborhood Club, Bala Cynwyd, Pa., 1969-89. Lt. USNR, 1954-56. Republican. Episcopal. Bankruptcy, General civil litigation, General practice. Home and Office: PO Box 383 Bass Harbor ME 04653-0383 E-mail: law@spencerervin.com.

ERWIN, GREGORY SCOTT, lawyer; b. Baton Rouge, May 10, 1949; s. Scott Wilson and Anne (Sanders) E.; m. Terry Williams, May 7, 1971; children— Amy, Gregory Scott. B.A., La. State U., 1971, J.D., 1974. Bar: La. 1974, U.S. Dist. Ct. (we., mid. and ea. dists.) La. 1974, U.S. Ct. Appeals (5th cir.) 1974, U.S. Ct. Appeals (11th cir.) 1981, U.S. Supreme Ct. 1984. Ptnr. Bolen & Erwin, Ltd., Alexandria, La., 1974—99; sole practitioner, 1999—; mem. products liability com. Def. Rsch. Inst., Chgo., 1984— . Profl. liaison United Givers of Rapides Parish, Alexandria, La., 1982; mem. Indsl. Devel. Bd. of Cenla, Alexandria, 1984. Served to capt. U.S. Army, 1967-74. Mem. La. Assn. Def. Counsel (bd. dirs. 1982-84), La. State Bar Assn., La. Trial Lawyers Assn. (Robert Lee Tullos Meml. award 1974), Alexandria Bar Assn., Alexander/Pineville C. of C. (city govt. liaison com. 1983), Lions (bd. dirs. 1981-82), Rotary Internat. Republican. Baptist. Insurance, Personal injury (including property damage), Workers' compensation.

ERWIN, H. ROBERT, lawyer; b. L.A., May 19, 1945; s. Howard R. and Nina B. Erwin; m. Nancy Smick, Sept. 9, 1967; children: Meghan, Kate, Benson, Carter. BA, Purdue U., 1967; JD, Georgetown U., 1972. Bar: Md. 1973, D.C. 1972, U.S. Dist. Ct. Md. 1973, U.S. Ct. Appeals (4th cir.) 1985. Dir. Consumer Law Ctr. Legal Aid Bur., Balt., 1972-78; cons., Office of Consumer Affairs U.S. Dept. Energy, Washington, 1978; chief Consumer Protections Divsn. Office of Atty. Gen., Balt., 1979-82; ptnr. Pretl & Erwin, P.A., Balt., 1983-95, The Erwin Law Firm, P.A., Balt., 1996—. Guest lectr., moot ct. judge U. Md. Sch. Law, Balt., 1988, 91-94; adv. bd. St. Ambrose Legal Svcs., Balt., 1994—. Contbr. chpt. to book. Pres., bd. mem. League for the Disabled, Balt., 1989-98; chpt. mem. Cathedral of the Incarnation, Balt., 1987-89. With U.S. Army, 1969-71. Mem. Am. Trial Lawyers Assn., Md. Trial Lawyers Assn., Md. State Bar Assn., Nat. Assn. Consumer Advocates, Engring. Soc. Commercial, consumer (including collections, credit), Product liability. Office: The Erwin Law Firm PA Side 10 W Madison St Baltimore MD 21201-2398

ERWIN, JUDITH ANN (JUDITH ANN PEACOCK), writer, photographer, lawyer; b. Decatur, Ga., Jan. 4, 1939; d. Milo Eugene and Lucy Isabelle (Simpson) Peacock; m. William Wofford Erwin, Sept. 5, 1959 (div. Mar. 1982); children: William Wofford Jr., Allison Sheridan (Norton). AA, Fla. C.C., 1987; BA summa cum laude, Jacksonville U., 1989; JD, U. Fla., 1993. Cert. mediator, custody evaluator. Photography instr., freelance writer, Jacksonville, Fla., 1986-91; freelance dance photographer, 1984-91; theater and dance critic Folio Weekly, Jacksonville, Fla., 1987-89; writer dance VUE mag.; founder On Our Own, 1991; pvt. practice lawyer. Pres. Ballet Guild, Jacksonville, 1973—75, Ballet Repertory Jacksonville, 1979—80; freelance costume designer, Jacksonville, 1981—86; mem. grand rev. dance panel Fla. Dept. Cultural Affairs, 1996—97, 2002; seminar spkr. in field; child custody evaluator. Mem. editorial staff Kalliope, Jour. Women's Art, 1989-91; editor-in-chief U. Fla. Jour. of Law and Pub. Policy, fall 1993; editor Jacksonville Trial Lawyers Newsletter. Mem. del.'s council Art's Assembly Jacksonville, 1979-80. Mem. AAUW, ATLA, Nat. Soc. Arts and Letters, Nat. League Am. Pen Women, Fla. Bar Assn., Phi Kappa Phi, Phi Theta Kappa. Republican. Episcopalian.

ESCARRAZ, ENRIQUE, III, lawyer; b. Evergreen Park, Ill., Aug. 30, 1944; s. Enrique Jr. and Mary Ellen (Bandy) E.; children from previous marriage: Erin Christine, Martina Mary; m. Patricia Jane Escarraz; children: Sarah Ellen, James Lee, Jason F. BA, U. Fla., 1966, JD, 1968. Bar: Fla. 1969, U.S. Dist. Ct. (so. and mid. dists.) Fla. 1969, U.S. Ct. Appeals (5th cir.) 1971, U.S. Ct. Appeals (11th cir.) 1981. VISTA atty. Community Legal Counsel, Chgo., 1968-69; mng. atty. Fla. Rural Legal Services, Ft. Myers, 1969-71; pvt. practice law St. Petersburg, Fla., 1971-82, 85-87, 88—; ptnr. Anderson & Escarraz, St. Petersburg, 1982-85; asst. gen. counsel U. South Fla., 1987-88; assoc. James L. Eskald Law Office, Largo, Fla., 1988. Part-time atty. Pub. Defender's Office Fla. 6th Cir., St. Petersburg, 1973-74; bd. dirs. Gulf Coast Legal Svcs., Inc., 1989—, pres., 1994-96. Vol. Cmty. Law Prog., Inc.; coord. James B. Sanderlin for Judge, Pinellas County, Fla., 1972-76; mem. ACLU Legal Panel, St. Petersburg, 1972—; cooperating atty. NAACP Legal Def. Edn. Funds, Inc., N.Y.C., 1973—; pres. Creative Care, Inc., Clearwater, Fla., 1974-80; mem. allocations com. United Way, Pinellas County, 1976, 1978-81; pres., treas. Cmty. Youth Svcs., Inc., St. Petersburg, 1977-82; co-chmn. Blue Ribbon Com. Pinellas County Dem. Exec. Com., 1977-82; mem. Fla. HRS Dist. V Adv. Coun., Pinellas County, 1982, St. Petersburg Human Rels. Rev. Bd., 1984, 90—, St. Petersburg Adult Cmty. Band, 1989-2003, Greater St. Petersburg Second Time Around Marching Band, 1990-92; mem. adv. bd. Jacquelyn Elvera Hodges Johnson Fund, 1990—. Mem.: FBA, ATLA, ABA, St. Petersburg Bar Assn. (pro bono com. 1988, 1995—2001, diversity com. 2000—), Nat. Assn. Social Security Claimant Reps., Show Me the Money Investment Club Pinellas (founding mem., 1st pres. 2002), Greater Pinellas County Dem. Club (sec.-treas. 1989—97, bd. dirs. 1997—2001). Civil rights, Pension, profit-sharing, and employee benefits, Workers' compensation. Office: 2121 5th Ave N Saint Petersburg FL 33713-8013 also: PO Box 847 Saint Petersburg FL 33731-0847

ESHELMAN, DAVID RICHARD, lawyer; b. West Reading, Pa., Aug. 12, 1949; s. William Richard and Mary Prudence (Mackie) E.; m. Elizabeth Josephine Hayes, Aug. 24, 1974; children: Sarah Elizabeth, Suzanne Chandler. BA, Dickinson Coll., 1971, JD, 1974. Bar: Pa. 1974, U.S Dist. Ct. (ea. dist.) Pa. 1975, U.S. Dist. Ct. (cen. dist.) Pa. 1980, U.S. Ct. Appeals (3d cir.) 1980, U.S. Supreme Ct. 1980, U.S. Tax Ct. 1981. Asst. pub. defender Berks County, Reading, Pa., 1975-78; assoc. Stevens & Lee, Reading, 1975-79, ptnr., 1980-83; sole practice Reading, 1983-91; prin. Eshelman & Shucker, Reading, Pa., 1991—. Active Mohnton Reps., Pa., 1980-84, Berks County Reps., Reading, 1980-84, exec. com., 1980-81; pres. Berks County Prison Soc., Inc., Reading, 1984-87. YMCA Leaders fellow, 1977. Mem. ABA, Pa. Bar Assn., Pa. Trial Lawyers Assn., Nat. Assn. Criminal Def. Lawyers, Pa. Assn. Criminal Def. Lawyers (bd. dirs. 1990—, pres. 2001-03), Assn. of Trial Lawyers Am., Berks County Bar Assn. (chmn. criminal law com. 1979, 82, 84, 90-91). Methodist. State civil litigation, Criminal, Family and matrimonial. Office: Eshelman & Shucker 424 Walnut St PO Box 142 Reading PA 19603-0142 E-mail: esh@epix.net.

ESHER, JACOB AARON, lawyer, mediator; b. Boston, Oct. 25, 1950; s. Eli Abraham and Irma (Hoffman) Etscovitz; m. Susan Riedle Foucault, June 1975 (div. Sept. 1979); m. Linda Ann Robinson, May 9, 1984; children: Joel Harry Robinson, Samantha Blihn Robinson. BA, Brandeis U., 1972; JD magna cum laude, U. San Francisco, 1977. Bar: Calif. 1977, Mass. 1985, U.S. Dist. Ct. (no. dist.) Calif. 1977, U.S. Dist. Ct. (ea. dist.) Calif. 1979, U.S. Dist. Ct. Mass. 1985. Assoc., Murphy, Weir & Butler, San Francisco, 1977-79; assoc. counsel, legal dept. Bank of Am., San Francisco, 1979-82; pvt. practice Law and Mediation Offices of Jacob Aaron Esher, Petaluma, Calif., 1982-84; ptnr. Riemer & Braunstein, Boston, 1984-90, Rubin and Rudman, Boston, 1990-99; sr. mediator JAMS, Boston, 1996—; ptnr. Riley & Esher, Cambridge, 1999—. Author: Mediation Manual, ABI, 1996, (songs) Blindspot, 1998; contbr. chpts. to books. Mem. Am. Bankruptcy Inst. (chair ADR subcom. 1994—), Boston Bar Assn. (chair ADR subcom. 1995-98). Alternative dispute resolution, Bankruptcy, Commercial, contracts (including sales of goods; commercial financing). Office: Riley & Esher LLP 69 Thorndike St Cambridge MA 02141 E-mail: jesher@rileyesher.com.

ESKIN, BARRY SANFORD, court investigator; b. Pitts., Mar. 6, 1943; s. Saul and Dorothy (Zaron) E.; m. M. Joyce Rosalind, Sept. 12, 1965; 1 child, David. AA, L.A. City Coll., 1963; BA, Calif. State U., L.A., 1965; JD, Citrus Belt Law Sch., 1976. Bar: Calif. 1976. Social service worker San Bernardino (Calif.) Dept. Pub. Social Services, 1965-77; assoc. Law Office of Lawrence Novack, San Bernardino, 1978; ct. investigator San Bernardino Superior Ct., 1978, supervising investigator, 1978—2003. Pro bono atty. Mex. Am. Commn., 1977-78. Mem. ARC Svc. Ctr. Advising Bd., San Bernardino, 1980-82; bd. dirs. Golden Valley Civ. Assn., San Bernardino, 1978-81, Congregation Emanuel, San Bernardino, 1984-87, bd. dirs. 1994-96. Mem. ABA, Calif. Assn. of Superior Ct. Investigators (pres. 1980-81, treas. 1984-85, bd. dirs., chmn. guardianship legis. com.), San Bernardino County Bar Assn., B'nai B'rith (pres. Paradise Lodge 1988), Alpha Phi Omega. Democrat. Jewish. Avocations: reading, photgraphy, baseball. Office: San Bernardino Superior Ct 351 N Arrowhead Ave Rm 200 San Bernardino CA 92415-0240

ESKIN, JEFFREY LAURENCE, lawyer; b. N.Y.C., May 10, 1952; s. Jordan Harlan Eskin and Charlette (Davies) Krane; m. Darla Lynn Gugel, Aug. 5, 1977; children: Jennifer, Jonathan, Emily, Lindy. BA, Yale U., 1974; JD, Emory U., 1978. Bar: Nev. 1978, U.S. Dist. Ct. Nev. 1979, U.S. Ct. Appeals (9th cir.) 1980, U.S. Supreme Ct. 1982. Assoc. Vargas, Bartlett & Dixon, Las Vegas, Nev., 1978-79; dep. atty. gen. State of Nev., Las Vegas, 1979-81; atty. Law Offices of Jeffrey L. Eskin, 1981—89, 1992—, Keefer, O'Reilly, Ferrario and Eskin, Las Vegas, 1989-92; law clk. Northern Ky. Legal Aid Soc., 1977. Spl. prosecutor State of Nev., Las Vegas, 1982-84. Moderator Sun Youth Forum; vol. VISTA; coach Clark County Basketball League, 1989—93; baseball coach, 1990, 1991, 1994; softball coach, 1995—97; All-Stars coach, 1995—97; coach Silver State Girls Soccer League, 1989—97, 2003—; mem. Employee Mgmt. Rels. Bd., Las Vegas, 1983—89, chmn., 1986—87. Mem. ABA, ATLA, Clark County Bar Assn., Assn. Yale Alumni (assembly 1980-83, class treas. 1989-94, alumni interviewer 1982-97). Democrat. Jewish. State civil litigation, Commercial, contracts (including sales of goods; commercial financing), Property, real (including real estate development, water). Home: 2431 Greens Ave Henderson NV 89014-3736 Office: 1389 Galleria Dr Ste 200 Henderson NV 89014-6686 E-mail: jeskin007@aol.com.

ESPERON, ROSARIA RODRIGUEZ, lawyer; b. N.Y.C., Nov. 17, 1950; BA, Fordham, U., 1976; JD, Hofstra U., 1980. Bar: N.Y. 1981. Pub. info. specialist N.Y. Divsn. Human Rights, N.Y.C., 1976-77; vis. atty., staff counsel P.R. Legal Def. Fund, N.Y.C., 1980-85; adminstrv. law judge N.Y. Workers' Compensation, N.Y.C., 1985-87; asst. gen. counsel AFSCME, Inc., Dist. Council 37, N.Y.C., 1987-90; asst. dep. comptroller N.Y. Comptroller's Office, N.Y.C., 1990-94, dep. comptroller, claims and contracts, 1994—. Co-editor: (brochurs) How to Become a Lawyer, 1990. Treas., vice-chmn. MFY Legal Svcs., Inc., N.Y.C., 1972-90; vice-chmn. Grand St. Guild Housing Co., N.Y.C., 1973-90; chmn. Joint Planning Coun. on Housing, N.Y.C., 1976-80; mem. Ctr. Social Welfare, Policy and Law, Washington, 1980-85, N.Y. Civil Liberties Union, N.Y.C., 1987-90. Recipient Cmty. Activist award Kings County Dist. Atty., 1995; named to Celebrating Women, N.Y. Women's Found., 1992, 50 Successful Women, El Diario-La Presena, 1996. Mem. P.R. Bar Assn., Hispanic Nat. Bar Assn. Jehovah'S Witness. Avocations: reading, sewing, teaching and preaching about jehovah's kingdom. Office: NY City Office of the Comptroller 1 Centre St Rm 1200 New York NY 10007-1602

ESPOSITO, JOHN VINCENT, lawyer; b. Logan, W.Va., Dec. 25, 1946; s. Vito T. and Mary Frances (Lamp) E. BA magna cum laude, W.Va. U., 1968, JD, 1971. Bar: W.Va. 1971, S.C. 1980, D.C. 1994, W.Va., S.C., Legis. aide to Congressman Ken Hechler, 4th Dist. W.Va., 1971; counsel to Hans McCourt, Pres. W.Va. State Senate, 1972; instr. So. W.Va. Community Coll., 1972-; founder, sr. ptnr. Esposito & Esposito, Logan, W.Va. and Hilton Head Island, S.C., formerly in Wash., D.C. and NY, 1972—; arbitrator United Mine Workers Am.-Coal Operators Assn.; spl. judge Cir. Ct. Logan County (W.Va.); commr. in chancery Cir. Ct. Logan County; judge Mcpl. Ct. City of Chapmanville (W.Va.); spl. pros. atty., W. Va.; Citizen Ambassador to People's Republic of China and Soviet Union for U.S. Legal Del.; Founder, Citizens Environ. Quality, 1983.; of coun. to several Nat. & Internat. law firms; coun. to various Internat., Nat., State, and Local leaders; Citizen's Amb. relative to U.S. Legal Sys.; spkr. for Nat. & Internat. Forums; fashion model for Elite Knot; 2d lt. U.S. Army. U. Calif.; Hastings Coll. Law Coll. Advocacy scholar; Mem. ABA, Assn. Trial Lawyers Am., Am. Judicature Soc., W.Va. State Bar, S.C. Bar, D.C. State Bar, U.S. Supreme Ct. Bar, Internat. Platform Assn., Acad. Am. Poets; assisted in formation of Internat. War Crimes Amb., in Democracies establishing their gov., including Solvenia, Bosnia, Romania; Co-author: Laws for Young Mountaineers, 1973-74; Author: Law & Sex Come Together in the 90's; featured in a coll. textbook, Public Speaking/Theory Into Practice by Dr. John Makay; Creator, Dir. & Host of TV program, Law USA. Criminal, General civil litigation, General practice. Office: Ste 303 WatersEdge at Shelter Cove Harbour PO Drawer 5705 Hilton Head Island SC 29938

ESPOSITO, JOSEPH ANTHONY, lawyer; b. Spokane, Wash., Oct. 4, 1941; s. Charles Esposito and Angela (Migliuri) E.; m. Joyce A. Chastek, July 7, 1966; children: Kate, Molly, Jill, Sara, Amy. BBA, Gonzaga U., 1963, JD, 1969. Bar: Wash., U.S. Dist. Ct. Wash., U.S. Ct. Appeals (9th cir.). Law clk. to presiding justice Wash. State Ct. Appeals, Spokane, 1969-70; lawyer in prin. Dellwo, Rudolph and Grant, Spokane, 1970-73; ptnr. Trezona Lorenz and Esposito, Spokane, 1973-85; prin. Esposito, Tombari and George, Spokane, 1985—. Trustee St. Joseph's Children's Home, Spokane, 1970-85, Gonzaga Preparatory Sch., 1982-88; legal counsel, bd. dirs. Spokane Jr. C. of C., 1969-75; bd. dirs. Spokane Legal Svcs. Bd., 1970-75. Recipient svc. award Spokane Jr. C. of C., 1973. Mem.: Wash. Bar Assn., Rotary, Manito Golf and Country Club. Roman Catholic. Avocations: golf, fly fishing, hunting. Bankruptcy, Commercial, contracts (including sales of goods; commercial financing), Property, real (including real estate development, water). Office: Esposito Tombari and George 960 Paulsen Bldg Spokane WA 99201

ESPOSITO, JOSEPH J. protective services official; b. Bklyn. BA in Criminal Justice, SUNY. Police trainee N.Y.C. Police Dept., 1968—71, patrolman, 1971—83, sgt., 1983—86, lt., 1986—89, capt., 1989—93, dep. insp., 1993—94, insp., 1994—96, dep. chief, 1996—97, asst. chief, 1997—2000, dept. chief, 2000—. Office: One Police Plaza New York NY 10038*

ESPOSITO, JOSEPH LOUIS, lawyer; b. New Haven, Conn., Nov. 2, 1941; s. Joseph Henry and Camille (Carrano) E.; m. Nancy Giller, June 17, 1967 (div. 1973); m. Maddalena Fiorillo, Dec. 17, 1977 (div. 1986); 1 child, Giulio; m. Katherine Valenzuela, Oct. 26, 1996. BS, Fairfield U., 1964; MA, NYU, 1968, PhD, 1970; JD, U. Ariz., 1986. Bar: Ariz. 1987, U.S. Dist. Ct. (9th cir.) Ariz. 1987, U.S. Supreme Ct. 1991, U.S. Ct. Appeals (fed. cir.) 1998. Assoc. prof. philosophy Bradley U., Peoria, Ill., 1968-70, prof. philosophy, 1970-76; editor, 1974-80; with various bus. ventures, 1981-88; assoc. Smitherman and Sacks, Tucson, 1987-88; ptnr. Smitherman, Sacks and Esposito, Tucson, 1988-89, Smitherman & Esposito, Tucson, 1989-91; pvt. practice Tucson, 1992—. Rsch. prof. Inst. for Studies in Pragmatism, Tex. Tech. U., Lubbock, 1975-84; vis. scholar U. Ariz., 2001-03. Author five philosophy books; contbr. articles to profl. jours. Mem. Am. Philos. Assn. Avocation: travel. Civil rights, Constitutional, Labor (including EEOC, Fair Labor Standards Act, labor-management relations, NLRB, OSHA). Office: 630 N Craycroft Rd Ste 250 Tucson AZ 85711-1456 E-mail: jespo@earthlink.net.

ESRICK, JERALD PAUL, lawyer; b. Moline, Ill., Oct. 1, 1941; s. Reuben and Nancy (Parson) E.; m. Ellen Feinstein, June 18, 1966; children: Sara Elizabeth, Daniel Michael. BA, Northwestern U., 1963; JD, Harvard U., 1966. Bar: Ill. 1966, U.S. Dist. Ct. (no. dist.) Ill. 1967, U.S. Supreme Ct. 1974, U.S. Ct. Appeals (9th cir.) 1985, U.S. Ct. Appeals (7th cir.) 1967. Law clk. U.S. Dist. Ct. (no. dist.) Ill., 1966-68; assoc. Wildman, Harrold, Allen & Dixon, Chgo., 1968-73, ptnr., 1973—, also chmn. firm mgmt. com., 1987-90. Lectr. Northwestern U., 1984-93, Coll. Arts and Scis. bd. visitors, 1993—, Nat. Panel Comml. Arbitrators, Am. Arbitration Assn. Pres. bd. trustees Nat. Lekotek Ctr., Evanston, Ill., 1989-93, U.S. Toy Libr. Assn., 1987-88; bd. dirs. Evanston Mental Health Assn., 1984-86, Fund for Justice, 1969-95, Lawyers' Com. for Civil Rights, 1974-84. Fellow Am. Coll. Trial Lawyers; mem. ABA, Ill. State Bar Assn., Chgo. Coun. Lawyers (bd. dirs., sec., founding mem.), Chgo. Bar Assn., Lawyers Club Chgo. Avocations: running, skiing, sailing, windsurfing, classical music. Antitrust, General civil litigation, Corporate, general. Home: 1326 Judson Ave Evanston IL 60201-4720 Office: Wildman Harrold Allen & Dixon 225 W Wacker Dr Ste 3000 Chicago IL 60606-1229 E-mail: esrick@wildmanharrold.com.

ESSA, DANIEL F. lawyer; b. Houston, Feb. 25, 1958; s. Fred Alex and Doris Cecil Essa; m. Julie Lawton, Mar. 29, 1997; children: Elena, Elizabeth. BBA, S.W. Tex. State U., 1982; BS, U. Houston, 1989; JD, Thomas M. Cooley Law Sch., Lansing, Mich., 1994; LLM in Taxation, Wayne State U., Detroit, 2001. Bar: Mich. 1995, U.S. Ct. Appeals (6th cir.) 2000. Review appraiser Resolution Trust Corp., Houston, 1989—91; appraiser/staff appraiser Mich. Nat. Bank, Lansing, 1991—94; owner Profl. Title & Mortgage, East Lansing, Mich., 2001—; appraiser/owner Profl. Appraisal Svcs., East Lansing, 1994—; atty./owner Essa & Barrett PLC, East Lansing, 2001—. Named to Pro Bono Hall of Fame, Legal Aid of Ctrl. Mich., Lansing, 1998. Mem.: Appraisal Inst. MAI designation. Property, real (including real estate development, water), Corporate taxation. Office: Professional Appraisal Svcs 610 Abbott Rd East Lansing MI 48823

ESSLINGER, JOHN THOMAS, lawyer; b. Ephrata, Pa., Aug. 11, 1943; s. Doster Alvin and Lucy Mildred (Ream) E.; m. Patricia Lynn Smith, Aug. 15, 1970; 1 child, John David. BA, Yale U., 1965; JD, Georgetown U., 1973. Bar: D.C. 1973, U.S. Dist. Ct. D.C. 1974, U.S. Supreme Ct. 1974, U.S. Ct. Appeals (D.C. cir.) 1974. Assoc. Morgan, Lewis & Bockius, Washington, 1973-76; ptnr. Schmeltzer, Aptaker & Shepard, P.C., Washington, 1976—. Capt. USMC, 1966-70, Vietnam. Decorated Purple Heart, Bronze Star, Gold Star. Mem. ABA, Bar Assn. D.C., D.C. Bar Assn., Maritime Adminstrv. Bar Assn. Episcopalian. Avocations: golf, wine, baseball. Federal civil litigation, Labor (including EEOC, Fair Labor Standards Act, labor-management relations, NLRB, OSHA), Transportation. Home: 9102 Brierly Rd Chevy Chase MD 20815-5655 Office: Schmeltzer Aptaker & Shepard PC 2600 Virginia Ave NW Ste 1000 Washington DC 20037-1922

ESSMYER, MICHAEL MARTIN, lawyer; b. Abilene, Tex., Dec. 6, 1949; s. Lytle Martin Essmyer and Roberta N. Essmyer Nicholson; m. Cynthia Rose Piccolo, Dec. 27, 1970; children: Deanna, Mike, Brent Austin. BS in Geology, Tex. A&M U., 1972; postgrad., Tex. Christian U., 1976; JD summa cum laude, South Tex. Coll. Law, 1980. Bar: Tex. 1980, U.S. Dist. Ct. (no., so., ea. we. dists) Tex. 1982, U.S. Ct. Appeals (5th cir.) 1981, U.S. Ct. Appeals (9th cir.) 1990, U.S. Ct. Appeals (1st cir.) 1993, U.S. Ct. Appeals (7th cir.) 1995, U.S. Ct. Appeals (fed. cir.) 1985, U.S. Ct. Claims, 1981, U.S. Supreme Ct. 1991. Briefing atty. Supreme Ct. Tex., Austin, 1980-81, Haynes & Fullenweider, Houston, 1981-89, Essmyer & Hanby, Houston, 1989-92; atty. Essmyer & Assocs., Houston, 1992-94; pres. Essmyer & Tritco, LLP, Houston, 1994-95, Essmyer, Tritco & Clary, LLP, Houston, 1995-99, Essmyer & Tritco, LLP, Houston, 1999—. Lead article editor South Tex. Law Jour., 1979. Dem. candidate for state rep., Bryan, Tex., 1972; del. Dem. Party, Houston, 1982, 84; precinct chmn. Harris County Dem. Exec. Com., Houston, 1983-86. Capt. USAF, 1972-78. Nat. Merit Scholar, 1968-72. Mem. ABA, Houston Bar Assn., Tex. Trial Lawyers Assn. (dir. 1996—), Harris County Trial Lawyers Assn. (dir. 1997—), Assn. Trial Lawyers Am., Tex. Criminal Def. Lawyers Assn., Tex. Bar Found., Harris County Criminal Lawyers Assn. (dir. 1986-87), Fed. Bar Assn., Houstonian Club, The Petroleum Club of Houston. Roman Catholic. Federal civil litigation, Criminal, Personal injury (including property damage). Home: 1122 Glourie Dr Houston TX 77055-7506 Office: Essmyer & Tritico LLP 4300 Scotland St Houston TX 77007-7328 E-mail: essmyer@flash.net.

ESTEP, ARTHUR LEE, lawyer; b. Forsyth, Mo., Dec. 4, 1932; s. Raymond B. and Nancy Mabel (Melton) E.; m. Joan Marie Hayes, June 16, 1956; 1 child, Sallie Ann Estep Warren. BS, U. Mo., 1954; JD, U. Ariz., 1959, honors grad., 1989. Bar: Ariz. 1959, Calif. 1959. Trust officer 1st Nat. Bank, San Diego, 1959-60; dep. city atty. City of San Diego, 1960-61; pvt. practice San Diego, 1961—. Bd. visitors U. Ariz., Tucson, 1986-96. 1st lt. USMC, 1950-56, Korea. Recipient Outstanding Svc. to Legal Profession award San Diego Bar Assn., 1986. Diplomate Am. Bd. Trial Advs. (pres. San Diego chpt. 1991, mem. nat. bd. dirs. 1990-96). General civil litigation. Office: Hughes & Nunn 450 B St Ste 2000 San Diego CA 92101

ESTEP, ROBERT LLOYD, lawyer; b. Marion, Va., Dec. 20, 1939; s. Lanson Eugene and Clara Nell (White) E.; m. Elizabeth Grayson Werth, July 10, 1971; 1 child, Laura White. BA with Honors, U. Va., 1962, JD, 1973. Bar: Ill. 1973, U.S. Dist. Ct. (no. dist.) Ill. 1973, Tex. 1984. From assoc. to ptnr. Isham, Lincoln & Beale, Chgo., 1973-83; ptnr. Jones, Day, Reavis & Pogue, Dallas, 1983—. Served to capt. U.S. Army, 1966-70, Vietnam.. Woodrow Wilson fellow, U. Va., 1962. Mem. Tex. Bar Assn., Law Club Chgo., Spl. Forces Assn., Phi Beta Kappa. Republican. Lutheran. Corporate, general, Securities. Home: 6331 Park Ln Dallas TX 75225-2108 Office: Jones Day Reavis & Pogue 2727 N Harwood St Dallas TX 75201-1515

ESTES, ANDREW HARPER, lawyer; b. Pecos, Tex., Dec. 16, 1956; s. Bobby Frank and Gayle (Harper) E.; m. Deidre Dement, Mar. 19, 1976; children: Andrew Kimble, Jada Catherine. BA, Tex. Tech U., 1977; JD, Baylor Sch. Law, 1979. Bar: Tex. 1980, U.S. Dist. Ct. (no. dist.) Tex. 1980,

U.S. Dist. Ct. (we. dist.) Tex. 1981, U.S. Ct. Appeals (5th cir.) 1982, U.S. Supreme Ct. 1983, U.S. Tax Ct., U.S. Ct. Appeals (10th cir.) 1987. Ptnr. Lynch, Chappell & Alsup P.C., Midland, Tex., 1980—. Mem. admissions com. Dist. 16, State Bar Tex., 1982-85, bd. dirs., 1999-2002. Mem. Tex. Tech. U. Coll. Edn. Devel. Coun., Lubbock, 1986-87; vol. Big Bros., Midland, 1983—, bd. dirs., 1985-89; bd. dirs. Hearthstone Temporary Children's Shelter, 1988-92; mem. bd. dirs. Tex. Book Festival, 2001-. Named Big Brother of Yr., Big Bros./Big Sisters of Midland, 1985; recipient Trimble Vol. Svc. award, Leadership Midland Alumni, 1986, Pro Bono Atty. award West Tex. Legal Svcs., 1991. Mem. ABA, Midland County Young Lawyers Assn. (sec., treas. 1987-88, Outstanding Young Lawyer of Midland County 1992), Midland County Bar Assn. (sec., treas. 1987-88, v.p. 1992-93, pres. elect. 1993-94, pres. 1995-96), State Bar Tex. (Dist. 16B grievance com. 1990-93, chmn. 1992-93, bd. dirs. 1999-2002), Tex. Young Lawyers Assn. (bd. dirs. 1987-89), Tex. Bd. Legal Specialization (cert.), Phi Delta Phi. Presbyterian. Federal civil litigation, State civil litigation. Home: 1404 Princeton Ave Midland TX 79701-5760 Office: Lynch Chappell & Alsup PC The Summit Bldg 300 N Marienfeld St Fl 7 Midland TX 79701-4345

ESTES, CARL LEWIS, II, lawyer; b. Ft. Worth, Feb. 9, 1936; s. Joe E. and Carroll E.; m. Gay Gooch, Aug. 29, 1959; children: Adrienne Virginia, Margaret Ellen. BS, U. Tex., 1957, LL.B., 1960. Bar: Tex. 1960. Law clk. U.S. Supreme Ct., 1960-61; assoc. firm Vinson & Elkins, Houston, 1961-69, ptnr., 1970—2002. Bd. dirs. Houston Grand Opera Assn., Houston Arboretum. Fellow Am. Bar Found., Tex. Bar Found.; mem. ABA, Internat. Bar Assn., Am. Law Inst., Am. Coll. Probate Counsel, Tex. Bar Assn., Internat. Fiscal Assn., Internat. Acad. Estate and Trust Law. Fellow Am. Bar Found., Tex. Bar Found.; mem. ABA, Internat. Bar Assn., Am. Law Inst., Am. Coll. Probate Counsel, Tex. Bar Assn., Internat. Fiscal Assn., Internat. Acad. Estate and Trust Law, Asia Soc. (bd. dirs.). Private international, Corporate taxation, Personal income taxation.

ESTEVE, EDWARD V. lawyer; b. N.Y.C., May 29, 1937; m. Mildred Briand, June 10, 1961; children: Greg, Christopher, Kimberly. Grad., NYU, 1959; LLB, JD, N.Y. Law Sch., 1962. Ptnr. Taitz, Bernard & Esteve, Patchogue, N.Y., to 1997, Pelletreau & Pelletreau, Patchogue, 1997—98, Roe Wallace Esteve Taroff & Taitz, 1999—. Adj. prof. Touro Coll. Law, Huntington, N.Y., 1995—; mem. com. on character and fitness, 2d dept. N.Y. Appellate Divsn., 1991—. Bd. dirs. Brookhaven Meml. Hosp., Patchogue, 1995—; v.p., officer Suffolk Acad. Law, 1977-89. Mem. N.Y. State Bar Assn. (gen. practice sect. 10th and 11th jud. dist. v.p. 1981-82, pres. com. access justice 1990-96), Suffolk County Bar Assn. (pres. 1989-90, bd. dirs. and exzc. com. 1977-93). Avocation: aviation. General civil litigation, Criminal, Property, real (including real estate development, water). Office: Roe Wallace Esteve Taroff & Taitz LLP 31 Oak St PO Box 352 Patchogue NY 11772 Fax: 631-475-9882.

ESTIS, DENNIS ARNOLD, lawyer; b. Newark, May 4, 1947; s. Harold and Anne (Rosenweig) E.; m. Ann Haiet, Aug. 29, 1976 (div. Mar. 1982); m. Rebecca D. Perkins, May 30, 1982 (div. Aug. 1999); m. Phyllis J. Kessler, March 19, 2000; children: Sara Rebecca, Jonathan Harold. BA in Polit. Sci., Johns Hopkins U., 1969; JD, NYU, 1972. Bar: N.J. 1972, U.S. Dist. Ct. N.J. 1972, U.S. Ct. Appeals (3d cir.) 1982, N.Y. 1983, U.S. Supreme Ct. 1984. Law sec. appellate div. N.J. Judiciary, Newark, 1972-73; assoc. Greenbaum, Greenbaum, Rowe & Smith, Newark, 1973-79; ptnr. Greenbaum, Rowe, Smith, Ravin Davis & Himmel LLP, Woodbridge, 1979—. Atty. Borough of Keansburg, N.J., 1983-84, Borough of Roselle Park, N.J., 1984-86, Borough of Fanwood, N.J., 1988-2000, Rahway Valley Sewerage Authority, 1987-96; lectr. in constrn. law and condominium law. Co-author: N.J. Condominium and Community Association Law, 2002. Active Roselle Park Coun., 1976-81; chmn. Union County (NJ) Dem. Com., 1980-81, Fanwood (NJ) Dem. Com., 1986-87, Warren (NJ) Dem. Com., 1988-96; co-chair N.J. chpt. Johns Hopkins U., 1985-2002, alumni coun., 1990-96; mem. NYU Alumni Coun., 1988-96, vice-chair, 1995-96; bd. dirs. Jewish Fedn. Ctrl. NJ, 1992-96; bd. trustees Philharmonic Orch. NJ, 2001-. Mem. ABA (co-chair constrn. litig. com., litig. sect. 1996-99), NJ Bar Assn. (co-chmn. alt. dispute resolution subcom., products liability and toxic torts sect. 1991-2000, chmn. equity com. 1985-86), Middlesex County Bar Assn. (trustee 1994-98, chair chancery practice com. 1994-2000, co-chair professionalism com. 1999-2003, pres. 2003—), NYU Alumni Assn. (bd. dirs. 1984-88, pres. NJ chpt. 1983-85, coun.), Coll. Cmty. Assn. Lawyers. Jewish. Avocations: politics, comic book collecting. State civil litigation, Construction. Office: Greenbaum Rowe Smith Ravin Davis & Himmel LLP PO Box 5600 Woodbridge NJ 07095-0988

ESTOCK, HOWARD GORDON, lawyer; b. Erie, Pa., Nov. 13, 1943; s. Gordon Andrew and Ethel (Buman) E.; m. Sarah Williamson, Aug. 9, 1969; children— Emily, Katherine. B.S., Pa. State U., 1965; M.A., Gannon Coll., 1970; J.D., U. Pitts., 1973. Bar: N.Y. 1974, U.S. Dist. Ct. (ea. and so. dists.) N.Y. 1975, U.S. Ct. Appeals (2d cir.) 1975, U.S. Supreme Ct. 1980. Project engr. Midland Ross Corp., Sharon, Pa., 1965-68; mgr., indsl. engr. Singer Corp., Erie, Pa., 1968-70; assoc. Clifton, Budd, Burke & DeMaria, N.Y.C., 1973-79, ptnr., 1979— ; lectr. in field. Author: Supervisor's Guide to Labor Law, 1980. Mem. ABA, N.Y. State Bar Assn., Assn. Bar City N.Y. Roman Catholic. Club: N.Y. Athletic. Civil rights, Labor (including EEOC, Fair Labor Standards Act, labor-management relations, NLRB, OSHA), Pension, profit-sharing, and employee benefits. Home: Old North Rd Colebrook CT 06021 Office: Clifton Budd & DeMaria 420 Lexington Ave Rm 420 New York NY 10170-0089

ESTREICHER, SAMUEL, lawyer, educator; b. Bergen, Democratic Republic Germany, Sept. 29, 1948; came to U.S., 1951; s. David and Rose (Abramowicz) E.; m. Aleta Glaseroff, Aug. 10, 1969; children: Michael, Hannah. BA, Columbia U., 1970, JD, 1975; MS in Labor Rels., Cornell U., 1974. Bar: N.Y. 1976, D.C. 1978, U.S. Dist. Ct. (so. and ea. dists.) N.Y., U.S. Ct. Appeals (2d and 11th cirs.), U.S. Supreme Ct. Law clk. to assoc. judge U.S. Ct. Appeals (D.C. cir.), 1975-76; assoc. Cohn, Glickstein, Lurie, Ostrin & Lubell, N.Y.C., 1976-77; law clk. to assoc. justice Lewis F. Powell Jr. U.S. Supreme Ct., Washington, 1977-78; prof. law NYU, 1978—; of counsel Cahill, Gordon & Reindel, N.Y.C., 1984-98; labor and employment counsel O'Melveny & Myers LLP, N.Y.C., 1998—2002; spl. counsel Morgan Lewis & Bockius LLP, N.Y.C., 2002—. Vis. prof. law Columbia U., 1984-85; dir. NYU-Inst. Jud. Adminstrn., 1991—, Ctr. for Labor and Employment Law at NYU Sch. Law, 1996—. Author: Redefining the Supreme Court, 1986, Labor Law and Business Change, 1988, The Law Governing the Employment Relationship,1990, 2d edit., 1992, Labor Law: Text and Materials, 4th edit., 1996, Procs. of 49th NYU Annual Conference on Labor, 1997, Employee Representation in the Emerging Workplace: Alternatives/Supplements to Collective Bargaining, 1999, Sexual Harassment in the Workplace, 1999, Foundations of Labor and Employment Law, 2000, Employment Discrimination and Employment Law, 2000, Global Competition and The American Employment Landscape, 2000; contbr. articles to profl. jours.; editor-in-chief Columbia U. Law Rev., 1974-75. Pulitzer Fund scholar, 1966-70; Herbert H. Lehman fellow, 1970-72. Mem. ABA (labor and employment law sect. 1978—), N.Y. State Bar Assn. (labor and employment law sect. 1980—), Assn. Bar City N.Y. (chmn. labor and employment law com. 1984-87), Am. Law Inst. (reporter Restatement of Employment Law 2000—). Office: NYU Sch Law 40 Washington Sq S New York NY 10012

ETHRIDGE, LARRY CLAYTON, lawyer; b. Houston, Feb. 27, 1946; s. Robert Pike and Gladys Jeannette (Grant) E.; m. Edith Kirkbride Gilbert, May 21, 1977; children: Elizabeth Kirkbride, Grant Harbin. BA, Duke U., 1968; JD cum laude, U. Louisville, 1975. Bar: Ky. 1975, U.S. Dist. Ct. (we. dist.) Ky. 1980, U.S. Ct. Appeals (6th cir.) 1981, U.S. Dist. Ct. (ea. dist.) Ky. 2003. Intern Adv. Commn. on Intergovtl. Rels., Washington, 1975-76; asst. dir. model procurement code project ABA, Washington, 1976-80; ptnr. Mosley, Clare & Townes, Louisville, 1980-97, Ackerson Mosley & Yann, 1998—2003, Ackerson & Yann, Louisville, 2003—. Cons. ABA model procurement code project, Washington, 1980-82; panel mem. N.Y. State Procurement Rev., 1984—. Co-author: Supplement to Annotations on the Model Procurement Code, 1991, Annotations, 3d edit., 1996. Elder Highland Presbyn. Ch., Louisville, clk. of session, 1989-90, 96-2001; vol. Am. Cancer Soc.; gen. counsel Mobile Riverine Force Assn., 1995—. Lt. USNR, 1969, Vietnam, Cambodia, and Japan. Recipient Disting. Svc. award Nat. Inst. Govtl. Purchasing, 1987. Fellow Am. Bar Found. (life); mem. ABA (chmn. coord. com. on a model procurement code 1985-96, co-chmn. model procurement code revision project steering com. 1997—, coun. mem., state and local govt. law sect. 1988—, sect. publs. dir. 1990-93, comms. dir. 1993-95, sec. 1995-96, vice-chmn. 1996-97, chmn. elect 1997-98, chmn. 1998-99, Donald M. Davidson award), AAA Ky. (bd. dirs. 1990-96, sec., gen. counsel 1996—) , Ky. Bar Assn., Louisville Bar Assn., Jefferson Fordham Soc., U. Louisville Law Alumni Assn. (pres. 1990-92), U. Louisville Alumni Assn. (exec. com., pres.-elect —, Alumni Svc. award), Duke Club Ky. (pres. 1992-94), Waggener H.S. Alumni Assn. (pres. 1996-97), Univ. of Louisville Club (bd. dirs. 1997—, treas. 2000—, v.p. 2002—). Republican. Presbyterian. Avocations: gardening, travel, golf, bicycling, reading. General civil litigation, Construction, Government contracts and claims. Home: 2402 Longest Ave Louisville KY 40204-2125 Office: Ackerson & Yann 401 W Main St Ste 1200 Louisville KY 40202-2806 E-mail: lethridge@amy-law.com.

ETIENNE, MARGARETH, law educator; b. Jan. 31, 1969; m. Patrick James Keenan. Bachelor's Degree, Yale U., 1991, JD, 1995. Bar: N.Y. 1996, U.S. Ct. Appeals (4th cir.) 1996, Ga. 1997, U.S. Dist. Ct. (no. dist.) Ga. 1998, U.S. Supreme Ct. 2001. French tchr. Brookhaven (Miss.) H.S., 1991—92; law clk. to Judge D. Motz U.S. Ct. Appeals 4th Cir., Balt., 1995—96; staff atty. U. Ga. Leagal Aid Clinic, Athens, 1996—97; fed. pub. defender Fed. Defender Program, Inc., Atlanta, 1997—2001; asst. prof. law U. Ill., Champaign, 2001—. Mem.: ABA (family law sect., criminal justice sect.). Office: Univ Ill Coll Law 504 E Pennsylvania Ave Champaign IL 61820

ETIENNE, MYRON E., JR., lawyer; b. Pasadena, Calif., May 19, 1924; s. Myron E. Etienne and Lucile B. McClung; m. Charlene A. Pinder; children: Victor, Dirk. BS, U.S. Merchant Marine Acad./U. Calif., Berkeley, 1945; JD, Hastings Coll., 1952. Bar: Calif., D.C. Legal rsch. aide, dist. ct. appeal 1st Appellate Dist., Divsn. I, 1953—54; dep. dist. atty. Monterey County, Calif., 1954—55; mem. Noland, Hamerly, Etienne & Hoss, Salinas, Calif., 1955—. Mem. alumni coun. exec. com. U. Calif., Berkeley, 1969—75; v.p. exec. coun., mem. Coun. Barristers, 1960—61; past mem. Center City Authority, Salinas; pro bono counsel Salinas River Channel Coalition; mem. pro bono referral panel Legal Svcs. for Srs.; vice chmn., bd. dirs. Hastings Coll. Law, 1981—88; past bd. dirs. Hastings Law Ctr. Found.; past pres., bd. dirs. 1066 Found. Hastings Coll. Law; bd. trustees Med. Ctr. Found. Monterey County; bd. dirs. Friends of Historic San Antonio Mission; past bd. dirs. Joe Gheen Found., Salinas, Salvation Army, Salinas, Salinas Valley Fair, King City, Calif., 1968—91; past pres., bd. dirs. Salinas Jr. C. of C.; past pres., bd. dirs., gen. counsel Monterey Jazz Festival, Calif. Rodeo, Salinas; past. pres., bd. trustees Rodeo Info. Found., 1966—70; chmn. humane adv. com. Profl. Rodeo Cowboys Assn.; chmn. bd. harbor commrs. Moss Landing Harbor Dist., Calif., 1957—64. Lt. (j.g.) U.S. Maritime Svc. USNR. Named Outstanding Young Man of Yr., Salinas Jr. C. of C., Citizen of Yr., Salinas C. of C., 2002; named to, Profl. Rodeo Cowboys Hall of Fame, 2001; recipient Alumnus of Yr. award, Hastings Coll. Law, 1982, Chief Justice Phil Gibson award, Monterey County, 1989, Std. of the West award, Outstanding Rodeo Committeeman, 1991. Mem.: ABA, Calif. Trial Lawyers Assn., Monterey County Bar Assn., Profl. Rodeo Cowboys Assn. (hon.). General practice, Estate planning, Property, real (including real estate development, water). Office: Noland Hamerly Etienne & Hoss 333 Salinas St Salinas CA 93901 Office Fax: 831-424-1975.

ETTER, ORVAL, b. Appleton, Colo., July 30, 1915; s. Wayne and Laura (Carpenter) E.; m. Mary Field, Aug. 11, 1939; children: John, Kristina, Hanya, Ted. BS, U. Oreg., 1937, JD with honors, 1939. Rsch. asst. Bur. Mcpl. Rsch., U. Oreg., Eugene, 1939-45, rsch. atty., 1960-65, assoc. prof. pub. affairs and adminstrn., 1968-80; ret., 1980. Sec. Far West, Fellowship of Reconciliation, Berkeley, Calif., 1946-57; pub. adminstrn. analyst bur. pub. adminstrn., U. Calif., Berkeley, 1957-60; legal adviser numerous county charter coms., Oreg., 1962-78; gen. counsel Portland Area Met. Study Commn., 1965-71; of counsel Harrang, Long, Watkinson and Arnold, Eugene, 1971-81. Author: Municipal Home Rule On and Off: Unconstitutional Law in Oregan Now and Then, 1991, Municipal Home Rule in Oregon: Unfulfilled Revolution, 1993; Oreg. corr., Nat. Civic Rev., 1968-81; contbr. articles Oreg. Law Rev., 1940-82, Fellowship (monthly jour.), 1947-55, Nat. Civic Rev. (monthly of Nat. Mcpl. League), 1970-80, We. City (monthly of We. Leagues of Mcpltys.), 1942-45, (monthly jour.) Human Quest, 2001-03. Pres., Eugene Symphony Assn., 1965-72. Mem. Phi Beta Kappa. Democrat. Home: 3080 Potter St Eugene OR 97405-4277

ETTERS, RONALD MILTON, lawyer, former government official; b. San Antonio, Nov. 6, 1948; s. Milton William and Ilse Charlotte (Ostler) E.; m. Anna Colleen Wesson, Feb. 12, 1977; children: William Lawrence, Elizabeth Charlotte, Margaret Lawreen. BA magna cum laude, Am. U., 1971, JD, 1976. Bar: Va. 1976, U.S. Ct. Appeals (D.C. cir.) 1977, U.S. Dist. Ct. (ea. dist.) Va. 1978, U.S. Ct. Appeals (4th and 9th cirs.) 1978, U.S. Supreme Ct. 1979, D.C. 1980, U.S. Dist. Ct. D.C. 1980, U.S. Ct. Appeals (1st and 2d cirs.) 1980, U.S. Ct. Appeals (7th cir.) 1981, U.S. Ct. Appeals (3rd, 11th and fed. cirs.) 1982, U.S. Ct. Appeals (5th cir.) 1983. Intern to gen. counsel Adminstrv. Office of U.S. Cts., Washington, 1970-71; fed. mgmt. intern IRS, Washington, 1971-72, labor rels. officer, 1972-75; ptnr. Nusbaum & Etters, Burke, Va., 1976-80; gen. counsel Nat. Mediation Bd., Washington, 1980—2002; ret., 2002. With Sigma Alpha, 1971; justice Phi Alpha Delta, 1975; professorial lectr. Am. U., Washington, 1978-83; adj. prof. law Georgetown U., Washington, 1985-88; vis. prof. George Mason U. Sch. Law, Arlington, Va., 1999, dir. Ctr. Advanced Study of Law and Dispute Resolution Processes, Arlington, 2000-2002. Sr. bd. editors The Railway Labor Act, 1991-2002. Mem. ABA (co-chmn. com. on railway and airline labor law 1987-93, 1999-2002), Christian Legal Soc., Nat. Lawyers Assn., Fed. Bar Assn. Home: PO Box 2374 Centreville VA 20122-2374 E-mail: etters5@etters.net.*

ETTINGER, JOHN RICHE, lawyer; b. N.Y.C., June 12, 1951; s. Austen A. and Shirley (Riche) E.; m. Linda A. Simpson, Apr. 19, 1986; children: Katharine Simpson, John Tyler, William Riche. BA, Yale U., 1973; JD, Harvard U., 1978. Bar: N.Y. 1979. Ptnr. Davis Polk & Wardwell, N.Y.C., 1986—. Rhodes scholar Oxford (Eng.) U., 1975. Office: Davis Polk & Wardwell 450 Lexington Ave Fl 31 New York NY 10017-3982*

EUBANK, J. THOMAS, lawyer; b. Port Arthur, Tex., Mar. 17, 1930; s. J.T. and Ada (White) E.; m. Nancy Moore, Feb.10, 1956; children: John, Marshall, Stephen, Laura. BA, Rice U., 1951; JD, U. Tex., 1954. Bar: Tex. 1954, U.S. Supreme Ct. 1960. With Baker Botts L.L.P., Houston, 1954-90, sr. ptnr., 1979-90, sr. counsel, 1999—; dir. Sentinel Trust Co., L.B.A., 1997—. Mem. joint editorial bd. Uniform Probate code, 1972-86. Bd. govs. Rice U., 1985-91. Mem. ABA (chmn. sect. real property, probate and trust law 1978-79), Am. Coll. Trust and Estate Counsel (pres. 1984-85, pres. Found. 1986-89, Trachtman lectr. 1986), State Bar Tex. (chmn. sect. real estate, probate and trust law 1972-73, Lifetime Achievement award 2003), Am. Bar Found., Tex. Bar Found., Houston Philos. Soc., Rice U. Alumni Assn. (pres. 1979-80, Rice Gold medal 1992), Am. Law Inst., Internat. Acad. Estate and Trust Law, Houston Country, Coronado, Allegro, Thalia, Chevaliers du Tastevin. Probate (including wills, trusts), Estate taxation, Personal income taxation. Home: 26 Liberty Bell Cir Houston TX 77024-6303 Office: 910 Louisiana St Houston TX 77002-4995 E-mail: tom.eubank@bakerbotts.com.

EULAU, PETER H. lawyer; b. Basel, Switzerland, June 17, 1946; s. Werner and Marlise (Levaillant) E.; m. Miriam J. Bachner; children: Thomas M., Liliane A., Florence R. Lic. iur., U. Basel, 1970, dr. iur. magna cum laude, 1976; postgrad., Harvard Law Sch., 1976-77. Bar: Basel 1972; cert. notary public 1973. Asst. to prof. Basel U., 1973-74; trainee A. Sarasin & Cie., Baupiers, 1976; assoc. Csaplar & Bok, Boston, 1977-78; ptnr. Eulau Kaufmann Giavarini & Recher, Basel, 1978—. Bd. dirs. numerous cos. Author: Verleitung zum Vertragsbruch und Ausnutzung fremden Vertragsbruches, Zurich, 1976, Inducing Breach of Contract, 1978, A Comparison of Laws of the United States, France, the Federal Republic of Germany and Switzerland, 1978. Mem. parliament Canton Basel-Stadt, 1980-91; vicechair Freisinnig-Demokratische Partei, Basel-Stadt, 1988-92; with constl. coun. Canton of Basel-Stadt, 1999—. Scholar Swiss Nationalfonds, 1976-77. Mem. ABA (internat. assoc.), Bar Assn. Basel-Stadt, Internat. Bar Assn., Internat. Fiscal Assn., Harvard Law Sch. Assn. Corporate, general, Finance, Mergers and acquisitions. Office: Eulau Kaufmann Giavarini & Recher Marktplatz 18 CH-4001 Basel Switzerland

EUSTICE, FRANCIS JOSEPH, lawyer; b. LaCrosse, Wis., Feb. 2, 1951; s. Frank R. and Cecelia T. (Babler) E.; m. Mary J. McCormick, July 28, 1971; children: Cristen L., Tara L. BS in Chemistry, Kansas Newman Coll., 1976; JD, U. Wis., 1980. Bar: Wis. 1980, U.S. Dist. Ct. (ea. and we. dists.) Wis. 1980, U.S. Tax Ct. 1981, U.S. Ct. Appeals (7th cir.) 1990, U.S. Dist. Ct. (no. dist.) Ill. 1993. With Eustice, Laffey & Sebranek, S.C. and predecessor firms, Sun Prairie, Wis., 1980—. Bd. dirs., pres. Sun Prairie Devel. Corp., 1989—. Bd. dirs. Exch. Ctr. for Prevention of Child Abuse, Inc., Dane County, Wis., 1984-95. Sgt. USAF, 1973-77. Mem. Wis. Bar Assn., Dane County Bar Assn., Sun Prairie C. of C. (bd. dirs., pres., amb. 1987—), Sun Prairie Exch. Club (sec., pres., bd. dirs. 1980—). Alternative dispute resolution, Banking, Commercial, contracts (including sales of goods; commercial financing). Office: PO Box 590 100 Wilburn Rd Ste 202 Sun Prairie WI 53590-0590 E-mail: f.eustice@els-law.com.

EUSTICE, JAMES SAMUEL, legal educator, lawyer; b. Chgo., June 9, 1932; s. Burt C. and Julia (Bohon) E.; m. LaVaun Schild, Jan. 29, 1956 (dec. 1994); m. Carol Fonda, Nov. 1995; children: Cynthia, James M. BS, U. Ill., 1954, LLB, 1956; LLM in Taxation, NYU, 1958. Bar: Ill. 1956, N.Y. 1958. Assoc. White & Case, N.Y.C., 1958-60; prof. law NYU, 1960—; counsel Kronish Lieb, N.Y.C., 1970—. Author: (with Kuntz) Federal Income Taxation of Subchapter S Corporations, 2001, (with Bittker) Federal Income Taxation of Corporations and Shareholders, 2000. Mem. ABA, N.Y. State Bar Assn., Am. Coll. Tax Counsel, Order of Coif. Club: University (N.Y.C.). Republican. Presbyterian. Office: NYU Sch Law 40 Washington Sq S New York NY 10012-1005

EUSTIS, RICHMOND MINOR, lawyer; b. New Orleans, Nov. 24, 1945; s. David and Molly Cox (Minor) E.; m. Catherine Luise Baños, Apr. 15, 1971; children: Richmond Minor Jr., Julie Bransford, Joshua Leeds, Molly Minor. BA in Econs., U. Va., 1967; JD, Tulane U., 1970. Bar: La. 1970. Assoc. Phelps Dunbar, New Orleans, 1970-75; ptnr. Monroe and Lemann, New Orleans, 1975-96; founder, ptnr. Eustis, O'Keefe & Gleason LLC, New Orleans, 1996—. Bd. dirs. New Orleans Bd. of Trade. Bd. dirs. Children's Bur., 1976-88, treas., 1984. Mem. La. Bar Assn., New Orleans Bar Assn. (chmn. torts and ins. com. 1992-95), Maritime Law Assn., S.E. Admiralty Law Inst., Am. Inns of Ct., Boston Club, La. Club. Republican. Episcopalian. Avocation: fishing. Admiralty, General civil litigation, Insurance. Home: 289 Audubon St New Orleans LA 70118-4841 Office: Eustis & O'Keefe 228 Saint Charles Ave Ste 1010 New Orleans LA 70130-2686

EVANICH, KEVIN R. lawyer; b. 1956; BA, U. Wis., 1976; JD, Northwestern U., 1980. Bar: Ill. 1980. Ptnr. Kirkland & Ellis, Chgo., 1986—. Named one of World's Leading Lawyers in Corp. M&A, Chambers Global, 2002—03. Mem.: Phi Beta Kappa. Office: Kirkland & Ellis 200 E Randolph Dr Chicago IL 60601

EVANS, CHARLES GRAHAM, lawyer; b. Charlottesville, Va., Sept. 13, 1949; s. Kerr Stewart and Josephine (Smith) E.; m. Nancy M. Lee, Dec. 29, 1984; children: Charles G. IV, Elizabeth Q. BA with distinction, U. Va., 1972, JD, 1976. Bar: Va. 1976, U.S. Dist. Ct. (we. dist.) Va. 1976, Alaska 1977, U.S. Ct. Appeals (4th cir.) 1977, U.S. Dist. Ct. Alaska 1978, U.S. Ct. Appeals (9th cir.) 1978, U.S. Supreme Ct. 1993. Assoc. Law Offices J. Anthony Smith, Anchorage, 1977-78; partner Smith & Gruening, Anchorage, 1978-84, Smith Robinson & Greuning, Anchorage, 1984-85, Smith Robinson Gruening & Brecht, Anchorage, 1985-86, Smith Gruening Brecht Evans & Spitzfaden, Anchorage, 1986-87, Wohlforth Flint & Gruening, Anchorage, 1987-88; pvt. practice Law Offices Charles Evans, Anchorage, 1988—. Dir. Post-Conviction Assistance Project, Charlottesville, Va., 1974-76; mem. Anchorage Hazardous Materials Commn., 1990-92. Dir. Anchorage Audubon Soc., 1979-92, Nat. Audubon Soc., N.Y.C., 1987-92. Mem. ABA (fidelity & surety law section legis reporter), Va. State Bar, Alaska Bar Assn. (arbitrator 1989-92). Avocations: birding, fishing, wilderness recreation. General civil litigation, Commercial, consumer (including collections, credit), Construction. Office: 8401 Brayton Dr Ste 123 Anchorage AK 99507-3433 E-mail: locge@gci.net.

EVANS, DOUGLAS HAYWARD, lawyer; b. Providence, July 21, 1950; s. Jerrold Merton and Gladys Jean (Snelgrove) E.; m. Sarah Edwards Cogan, May 28, 1983; children: Anne Morrill, Thomas Taylor Seelye, Elizabeth Hayward. AB, Franklin and Marshall Coll., 1972; JD, Cornell U., 1975. Bar: N.J. 1975, U.S. Dist. Ct. N.J. 1975, N.Y. 1976, U.S. Dist Ct. (so. dist.) N.Y. 1991. Assoc. Windels, Marx, Davies & Ives, N.Y.C., 1975-85, Sullivan & Cromwell, N.Y.C., 1985-90, spl. counsel, 1990—. Faculty NYU Inst. Fed. Taxation, N.Y.C., 1984; counsel, treas., pres. St. David's Soc. State of N.Y., N.Y.C., 1985—; bd. dirs. Friends of Washington Sq. Park, 1989—, Washington Sq. Assn., 1992—, 1st Presbyn. Ch. Nursery Sch., 1999—. Co-Author: Estate Accounting, 1980, Probate and Estate Administration, 1982, Administration of Estates, 1985, Settling An Estate, 1989; editor-in-chief, co-author: Probate and Administration of New York Estates, 1995, 2d edit., 2001; also articles. Trustee Franklin and Marshall Coll., 1994—, Grace Ch. Sch., N.Y.C., 1997—, vice chmn., 2000-01, chmn., 2001—; mem. Ch. Club of N.Y., Salmagundi Club, N.Y.C. Fellow: Am. Coll. of Trust and Estate Coun.; mem.: ABA, Assn. of the Bar of the City of N.Y. (com. on estate and gift taxation), N.Y. County Lawyers Assn. (not-for-profit com.), N.Y. State Bar Assn. (estate litig. and adminstrn. of trusts and estates com., com. on CLE, chmn. 1991—94), N.J. Bar Assn., Pi Gamma Mu, Phi Alpha Theta, Phi Delta Phi, Phi Beta Kappa. Episcopalian. Estate planning, Probate (including wills, trusts), Estate taxation. Home: 43 Fifth Ave New York NY 10003-4368 Office: Sullivan & Cromwell 125 Broad St Fl 28 New York NY 10004-2489

EVANS, LAWRENCE E. lawyer, educator; b. Houston, Mar. 30, 1950; s. Lawrence Edgar and Edith (Kinzy) E.; m. Nancy Campbell, Aug. 20, 1977; children: Christopher, Laura. BA, Washington & Lee U., 1973; JD, South Tex. Coll., 1977. Bar: Tex. 1977, Mo. 1989; registered patent atty. Lawyer Gunn, Lee & Miller, Houston, 1977-88, Herzog, Crebs & McGhee, St. Louis, 1988-2000, Blackwell, Sanders, Peper, Martin LLP, St. Louis, 2000—. Adj. prof. Washington Univ. Sch. of Law, St. Louis. Mem. Metro. Bar Assn. St. Louis (chmn. Patent, Trademark and Copyright sect. 1994),

Internat. Trademark Assn., Am. Intellectual Property Law Assn. Intellectual property, Patent, Trademark and copyright. Office: Blackwell Sanders Peper Martin LLP 720 Olive St Ste 2400 Saint Louis MO 63101 E-mail: levans@blackwellsanders.com.

EVANS, MARTIN FREDERIC, lawyer; b. Nashville, June 12, 1947; s. Robert Clements and Adelaide Hawkins (Roberts) E.; m. Margaret Carroll Kidder, Apr. 17, 1982. BA, U. Va., 1969; JD, Yale U., 1972. Bar: N.Y. 1973, U.S. Dist. Ct. (so. dist.) N.Y. 1973, U.S. Ct. Appeals (2d cir.) 1974, U.S. Ct. Appeals (D.C. cir.) 1981, U.S. Supreme Ct. 1981, D.C. 1982. Assoc. Debevoise & Plimpton, N.Y.C., 1972-80, ptnr., 1981—. Researcher Nat. Commn. for Rev. of Antitrust Laws and Procedure, Washington, 1978. Mem. ABA (sect. for antitrust law), Assn. of Bar of City of N.Y., Phi Beta Kappa. Antitrust, Federal civil litigation, Insurance. Office: Debevoise & Plimpton 919 Third Ave New York NY 10022-6225

EVANS, NOLLY SEYMOUR, lawyer; b. Augusta, Ga., Sept. 16, 1927; s. Nolly Seymour and Laura (Taylor) E.; m. Judith Anne Leach, Feb. 18, 1965; children: Samantha, Meredydd, Clelia, Nolly. BFA in Music, U. Ga., 1948, MA in English Lit., 1950; LLB, Yale U., 1956; LLD, Yale Law Sch., 1971. Bar: N.Y. 1956. Assoc. firm Milbank, Tweed, Hadley & McCloy, N.Y.C., 1956-64; fin. counsel Amax, Inc., N.Y.C., 1964-70; gen. counsel Gilman Paper Co., N.Y.C., 1970-74; gen. counsel, sec. Crouse-Hinds Co., Syracuse, N.Y., 1976-82; counsel Hancock & Estabrook, Syracuse, N.Y., 1982-83; prin. Nolly S. Evans Law Offices, Syracuse, 1983-93. Docent Homewood House Mus., Balt. With U.S. Army, 1947—48. Mem. Confrerie des Chevaliers du Tastevin, Grand Officier of Sous Commanderie de Etats-Unis, N.Y., Commanderie de Bordeaux, Le Grand Conseil de Bordeaux, Jurade de St. Emilion, Connetable de Guyenne, Royal Over-Seas Club (London), and others. Home: 647 W University Pkwy Baltimore MD 21210-2907

EVANS, PAUL VERNON, lawyer; b. Colorado Springs, Colo., June 19, 1926; s. Fred Harrison and Emma Hooper (Austin) Evans; m. Patricia Gwyn Davis, July 27, 1964 (dec. Dec. 2001); children: Bruce, Mike, Mark, Paul, Paula Jean; m. Betty J. Haynes, 2002; m. Frances Irene Pool, Sept. 7, 1947 (dec.). BA cum laude, Colo. Coll., 1953; JD, Duke U., 1956. Bar: Colo. 1956, U.S. Dist. Ct. Colo. 1956, U.S. Supreme Ct. 1971, U.S. Ct. Appeals (10th cir.) 1974. Field mgr. Keystone Readers Service, Dallas, 1946-50; sole practice Colorado Springs, 1956-60; ptnr. Goodbar, Evans & Goodbar, 1960-63; sr. ptnr. Evans & Briggs Attys., Colorado Springs, 1963-95; ret., 2001. City atty. City of Fountain, Colo., 1958—62, City of Woodland Park, Colo., 1962—78; atty. Rock Creek Mesa Water Dist., Colorado Springs, 1963—2002. Author instruction materials. Precinct com. man Republican Com., Colorado Springs, 1956-72. Served with USNR, 1944-46, PTO. Recipient Jr. C. of C. Outstanding Achievement award, 1957. Mem. Colo. Mining Assn., Am. Jud. Soc., ABA, Colo. Bar Assn. (com. chmn. 1966-67, 84), El Paso County Bar Assn. (com. chmn. 1956—0, Assn. Trial Lawyers Am., Colo. and Local Trial Lawyers, Tau Kappa Alpha (pres.), Phi Beta Kappa. Clubs: Optimist (pres. 1966-67). Republican. Family and matrimonial, General practice, Personal injury (including property damage). Home: 244 Cobblestone Dr Colorado Springs CO 80906-7624 E-mail: paulvevans@msn.com.

EVANS, ROBERT DAVID, legal association executive; b. Vergennes, Vt., Mar. 1, 1945; BA, Yale U., 1966; JD, U. Mich., 1969. Bar: Ill. 1969. Assoc. Sachnoff Schrager Jones & Weaver, Chgo., 1969-72; asst. dir. divsn. pub. svc. activities ABA, Chgo., 1972-73, asst. dir. govtl. rels. office Washington, 1973-78, assoc. dir. govtl. rels. office, 1978-82, dir. govtl. affairs office, 1982—, assoc. dir., dir. Washington Office, 1988—. Mem. Washington Grove (Md.) Town Coun., 1977-81, 98—, Washington Grove Town Planning Commn., 1977-81, 98—; mayor Washington Grove, 1981-83; vice chmn. assns. divsn. Nat. Capital Area United Way, 1986, chmn., 1987. Recipient Spl. Achievement award Nat. Legal Aid and Defender Assn., 1990. Fellow ABA (life), Am. Bar Found.; mem. Am. Law Inst. Home: PO Box 332 Washington Grove MD 20880-0332 Office: ABA 740 15th St NW Fl 8 Washington DC 20005-1019

EVANS, ROGER, lawyer; b. Syracuse, Apr. 18, 1951; s. David Longfellow and Louise Maude (Crawford) Evans; children: Jonathan Longfellow, Gillian Crawford, Catherine Leigh, Skylar Elizabeth, Valerie Lynn, Joel Brian. AB, Cornell U., 1974; postgrad., Columbia U., 1976-77; JD, Harvard U., 1977. Bar: Ohio 1977, U.S. Dist. Ct. (no. dist.) Ohio 1978, Tex. 1981, U.S. Dist. Ct. (no. dist.) Tex. 1981, U.S. Dist. Ct. (so. dist.) Tex. 1997, U.S. Ct. Appeals (5th, 6th and 11th cirs.) 1981, U.S. Ct. Appeals (10th cir.) 1982, U.S. Tax Ct. 1989, U.S. Dist. Ct. (we. and ea. dists.) Tex. 1998. Assoc. Jones, Day, Reavis & Pogue, Cleve., 1977-81, Dallas, 1981-84; ptnr. Shank, Irwin & Conant, Dallas, 1985, Gardner, Carton & Douglas, Dallas, 1986-88, Vinson & Elkins, Dallas, 1988-91; pvt. practice Dallas, 1991-2001; ptnr. Mathis & Donheiser, Dallas, 2001—. Bd. dirs., gen. counsel Equest, Inc., Dallas, 1986—88; instr. trial advocacy, instr. law and econs. So. Meth. U. Sch. Law; instr. labor law Baylor U.; mem. faculty Nat. Inst. Trial Advocacy. Gen. counsel, bd. dirs. Freedom Ride Found., Dallas, 1985-86; cmty. svcs. bd. mgmt. YMCA, 1990-92; bd. dirs. Legal Svcs. Corp. North Tex., 1991-92; adv. bd. dirs. Providence Christian Sch. Tex., Inc., 1995-2000. Recipient Advocacy award, Dallas Epilepsy Assn., 1995. Mem. Tex. Bar Assn., Dallas Bar Assn., Cornell U. Alumni Assn. (class pres. 1984-89), Harvard U. Law Sch. Alumni Assn. No. Ohio (sec. 1978-81), Harvard Club. Federal civil litigation, State civil litigation, Labor (including EEOC, Fair Labor Standards Act, labor-management relations, NLRB, OSHA). Office: 2001 Ross Ave Ste 4600 Dallas TX 75201 E-mail: revans@mathisdonheiser.com.

EVANS, THOMAS STEVEN, lawyer; b. Coral Gables, Fla., July 27, 1943; s. Robert C. and Wilma A. Evans; m. Cynthia P. Faigle, Aug. 1, 1970; children: Elizabeth S., David T. BA, Duke U., 1965, JD, 1969; postgrad., U. Ceylon, 1965-66. Bar: Mich. 1969, N.Y. 1971, Fla. 1977, U.S. Dist. Ct. (no. dist.) N.Y. 1971, U.S. Ct. Appeals (2d cir.) 1977, U.S. Supreme Ct. 1980. Assoc. Warner, Norcross & Judd, Grand Rapids, Mich., 1969-70; from assoc. to sr. ptnr. Bond, Schoeneck & King, LLP, Syracuse, N.Y., 1971—. Mem. adv. bd. law tech. and mgr. program, Syracuse U. Coll. of Law, 1985-90. Bd. dirs., pres. Friends of Burnet Park Zoo, Syracuse, 1984-90; trustee Manlius Pebble Hill Sch., syracuse, 1992-98, Syracuse U. Theatre, Syracuse, 1986-92, 98—. Mem. ABA, N.Y. State Bar Assn., Onondaga County Bar Assn., Nat. Assn. of Col./Univ. Attys., Greater Syracuse C. of C. (bd. dirs. 1992—). Republican. Avocations: golf, racquetball, cross-country skiing, hunting, fishing. Corporate, general, Intellectual property, Non-profit and tax-exempt organizations. Office: Bond Schoeneck & King LLP One Lincoln Ctr Syracuse NY 13202

EVANS, THOMAS WILLIAM, lawyer; b. N.Y.C., Dec. 9, 1930; s. William J. and R. Helen (Stenvall) E.; m. Lois deBaun Logan, Dec. 22, 1956; children: Heather, Logan, Paige. BA, Williams Coll., 1952; JD, Columbia U., 1958; EdD, Piedmont Coll., 1993. Bar: N.Y. 1958, U.S. Supreme Ct. 1961. Assoc. Simpson, Thacher & Bartlett, N.Y.C., 1958-64; asst. coun. to spl. state commn. of investigation, spl. dep. asst. N.Y. Atty. Gen., 1964-65; assoc. Mudge Rose Guthrie Alexander & Ferdon, N.Y.C., 1965-66, ptnr., 1967-93, of counsel, 1993-94. Founder MENTOR, nat. law-related edn. program for pub. sch. students, 1983; mem. Pres.'s Pvt. Sector Initiative Adv. Coun. Author: The School in the Home, 1973, Admissions Practices (Center for Public Resources), 1986, Mentors, 1992. Chmn. Nat. Symposium on Partnerships in Edn., 1983-90; chmn. bd. trustees Columbia U. Tchrs. Coll., 1991-98, trustee, 1985—, adj. prof. of ednl. adminstrn., 1992-95; co-chmn. N.Y. Korean Vets. Meml. Commn.; chmn. The Mentor Ctr., L.C., 1998-2003. With USMC, 1952-54. Mem. ABA, Fed. Bar Coun. (pres. 1989-90, trustee 1981—), Century Assn. Republican. Episcopalian. Federal civil litigation, State civil litigation. Home: 9660 W Bay Harbor Dr Apt PHE Miami FL 33154 E-mail: thoswevans@aol.com.

EVANS, WAYNE LEWIS, lawyer; b. Bluefield, W.Va., Mar. 30, 1954; s. Douglas Evan and Wanda (Shrewsberry) E.; m. Cheryl Jane Richardson, June 28, 1980; children: Lisa Marie, Jason Lloyd. BA summa cum laude, U. N.C., Greensboro, 1976; MS, Radford U., 1978; diploma, Roanoke Police Acad., 1980; JD, Wake Forest U., 1984. Bar: W.Va. 1984, U.S. Dist. Ct. (so. dist.) W.Va. 1984, U.S. Ct. Appeals (4th cir. 1989); cert. Va. Cert. Bds. Zoning Appeals Programs. Probation/parole officer Va. Dept. Corrections, Tazewell, Va., 1976-77; dep. sheriff Roanoke County Sheriff Dept., Salem, Va., 1979-81; summer assoc. Katz Kantor & Perkins, Bluefield, W.Va., 1982; ptnr. Katz, Kantor & Perkins, Bluefield, 1985—; summer assoc. Gardner, Moss, Brown & Rocovich, Roanoke, 1983; assoc. Law Office of John H. Shott, Bluefield, 1984-85; sec. Bandy Minerals Corp., 2001—. V.p., sec. WELD Enterprises, 1989-95; mem. Campaigning With Lee-Civil War Roundtable, Va. Tech., 1994, 95, 96, 97; mem. mentoring program W.Va. State Bar, 2002—; speaker at seminars. Mem. Bd. Zoning Appeals, Bluefield, 1991—, chmn., 2000—; participant Career Awareness, Mercer County (W.Va.) Schs., 1989, 92; coach Odyssey of the Mind, Tazewell County (Va.) Schs., 1994, 95, 96, 97, judge, 1999; vol. United Way, Mercer and Tazewell Counties, 1989; chmn. com. PTA, Dudley Primary Sch; leader Boy Scouts Am., Bluefield, Va., 1996-99, 2000—; pres. Graham Middle Sch. PTA, Bluefield, 1997-98; pres. Graham H.S. Band Boosters, 1999-00. Mem. ATLA, W.Va. Trial Lawyers Assn., Fincastle Country Club, Phi Beta Kappa, Psi Chi, Phi Kappa Phi. Avocations: golf, tennis, civil war history. General civil litigation, Health, Personal injury (including property damage). Home: 45 College Dr Bluefield VA 24605-1736 Office: Katz Kantor and Perkins 307 Federal St Bluefield WV 24701-3005

EVANS, WILLIAM DAVIDSON, JR., lawyer; b. Memphis, Jan. 20, 1943; s. William D. and Maxey (Carter) Evans; m. Eileen McKenna, June 19, 1971; children: William D., Carter M., Alexander B. BA, Vanderbilt U., 1965; JD, U. Tenn., 1968; LLM, Georgetown U., 1985. Bar: Tenn. 1968, D.C. 1988, Md. 1996. Spl. agt. FBI, N.Y.C., 1968-72; ptnr. Glankler, Brown, Gilliland, Chase, Robinson & Raines, Memphis, 1972-82; trial atty. environ. enforcement sect. U.S. Dept. of Justice, Washington, 1982-86; of counsel Washington, Perito & Dubuc, Washington, 1986-91, Graham & James, Washington, 1991-93; ptnr. Rich and Henderson, P.C., Annapolis, Md., 1993-98; sr. asst. county atty. Anne Arundel County Office of Law, Annapolis, 1998—. Editor: Digest Environ. Law of Real Property, 1986—90, Environ. Hazards, 1989—90; contbr. Mem. environ. issues group George Bush for Pres. Campaign, Washington, 1987—88, Robert Dole for Pres. Campaign, Washington, 1995—96. Mem.: ABA, Environ. Law Inst., Md. Bar Assn., D.C. Bar Assn. Republican. Roman Catholic. Home: Apt 111A 3900 Cathedral Ave NW Washington DC 20016 Office: Anne Arundel County Office Law 2660 Riva Rd Annapolis MD 21401-7305 E-mail: billevansjr@hotmail.com.

EVANS, WILLIAM ELLIS, lawyer; b. Starkville, Miss., June 8, 1952; s. Leslie Lee Evans and Beth (York) Fisher; m. Kathleen Thurmond, June 1, 1974 (div. Apr. 1979); m. Pamela Sue Marlin; children: Blake Ellis, Kyle William. BA, So. Meth. U., 1974, LLM in Taxation, 1980; JD, U. Mo., 1977. Jr. ptnr. Bryan, Cave, St. Louis, 1977-79; assoc. Woolsey, Fisher, Whiteacre, McDonald and Ansley, Springfield, Mo., 1980-81; prin. Carnahan, Evans, Cantwell and Brown, P.C., Springfield, 1981—. Lectr. various programs Ark. Fed. Tax Inst., Mo. Assn. Tax Practitioners. Mem. bd. editors Mo. Bus. Law Quar. Mem. ABA (com. on civil and criminal tax penalties, past chmn. subcom. on important developments civil), Mo. Bar Assn. (taxation sect., continuing legal edn. com.), Greene County Bar Assn., Bar Assn. Met. St. Louis, U.S. Tax Ct. Bar Assn., Am. Coll. Tax Counsel, Acad. Magical Arts, Internat. Brotherhood of Magicians, Soc. Am. Magicians, Am. Coll. of Tax Counsel. Avocations: magic, guitar, golf, fishing, canoeing. Entertainment, Property, real (including real estate development, water), Corporate taxation. Office: Carnahan Evans Cantwell & Brown PC 2805 S Ingram Mill Rd Springfield MO 65804-1680

EVANS, WINTHROP SHATTUCK, retired lawyer; b. Santa Monica, Calif., June 21, 1939; s. Clifford E. and Luella (Wyble) E.; m. Carlene D. Buschena, June 26, 1965; children: Theresa, Shalene, Shanna, Michelle. AA, Fullerton Coll., 1969; BA, Calif. State U., Fullerton, 1973; JD, Western State U., Fullerton, 1980. Bar: Calif. 1980. Enlisted U.S. Navy, 1957, commd. ensign, 1961, advanced through grades to lt. comdr., 1969; served with U.S. Naval Res., 1965-76, ret. lt. comdr., 1976; airline capt. Am. Airlines, L.A., 1965-97; pvt. practice law Placentia, Calif., 1980—2001; ret., 2001. Mem. Calif. Bar Assn., Orange County Bar Assn., Aircraft Owners and Pilots Assn. Republican. Roman Catholic. Landlord-tenant, Personal injury (including property damage), Probate (including wills, trusts). Office: PO Box 532 Placentia CA 92871-0532 E-mail: winevans@juno.com.

EVE, ROBERT MICHAEL, JR., lawyer; b. Charlotte, N.C., Apr. 26, 1953; s. Robert Michael and Carolyn Elizabeth (Roesel); m. Kimberly Denise Davenport, June 9, 1984. BA with honors, U. N.C.; JD cum laude, Samford U. Bar: Ala. 1978, N.C. 1979, U.S. Dist. Ct. (mid. dist.) N.C. 1979, U.S. Ct. Appeals (4th cir.) 1980. Dep. clk. Superior Ct., Mecklenburg County, N.C., 1972-73, dep. sheriff, 1974-75; law clk. to justice Supreme Ct. of Ala., Montgomery, 1978-79; assoc. Justice, Eve & Edwards, P.A., Charlotte, prin., 1984—; law clk. U.S. Dist. Ct. (no. dist.) Ala., 1978. Editor-in-chief Cumberland Law Rev., 1977-78; contbr. articles to profl. jours. Mem. Mechlenburg County Eagle Scout Rev. Bd., Boy Scouts Am. Recipient Order of the Old Well, U. N.C., 1975. Mem. N.C. Bar Assn., N.C. Acad. Trial Lawyers, Mecklenberg County Bar Assn. (bd. dirs. exec. com.), Order of the Arrow. Lutheran. State civil litigation, Commercial, contracts (including sales of goods; commercial financing), Personal injury (including property damage). Home: 2000 Brandon Cir Charlotte NC 28211-1615 Office: 1801 East Blvd Charlotte NC 28203-5825

EVELAND, THOMAS SHAW, judge; b. Detroit, Nov. 24, 1941; s. De Forest H. and Florence May E. BA, U. Mich., 1963, JD, 1965. Bill drafter Legis. Svc. Bur., Lansing, Mich., 1966-69; pvt. practice Lansing, 1969-88; judge cir. ct. Eaton County, Charlotte, Mich., 1989—. Pres. Eaton (Mich.) Shelter/Siren, Charlotte, Mich., 1994—, Eaton Area Habitat for Humanity, Charlotte, 1995—, Eaton County Cmty. Found., 1996—, Eaton County Comty. Corrections, 1998—; elder First Presbyn. Ch., 1991. Mem. Mich. Judges Assn. (head com. 1995), Eaton County Bar Assn. (pres. 1995). Avocations: gardening, reading, guilding. Office: Courthouse Charlotte MI 48813

EVELETH, JANET STIDMAN, law association administrator; b. Balt., Sept. 6, 1950; d. John Charles and Edith Janet (Scales) Stidman; m. Donald P. Eveleth, May 11, 1974. BA, Washington Coll., 1972; MS, Johns Hopkins U., 1973. Counselor Office of Mayor, Balt., 1973-75; asst. dir. Gov. Commn. on Children, Balt., 1975-78; lobbyist Balt., 1978-80; comm. specialist Med. Soc., Balt., 1980-81; dir. pub. affairs Mid-Atlantic Food Dealers, Balt., 1981-84; dir. comm. Home Builders Assn., Balt., 1984-87, Md. Bar Assn., Balt., 1987—. Contbr. articles to profl. jours. Recipient Gov. citation State of Md., 1993, Citizen citation City of Balt., 1993. Mem.: NAFE, Nat. Assn. Bar Execs. (chmn. pub. rels. sect. 1994—95, Achievement award 1995, E.A. Wally Richter award 1997, Luminary award 1999, 2001), Md. Soc. Assn. Execs. (pres. 1992—93), Am. Soc. Profl. Women, Pi Lambda Theta, Alpha Chi Omega. Office: Md Bar Assn 520 W Fayette St Baltimore MD 21201-1781 E-mail: jeveleth@msba.org.

EVEN, FRANCIS ALPHONSE, lawyer; b. Chgo., Sept. 8, 1920; s. George Martin and Cecilia (Neuman) E.; m. Margaret Hope Herrick, Oct. 16, 1945; children: Janet Beth, Dorothy Elizabeth. BS in Mech. Engring, U. Ill., 1942; JD, George Washington U., 1949. Bar: D.C. bar 1949, Ill. bar 1950. Engr. GE, 1945-49; ptnr. Fitch, Even, Tabin & Flannery (patent and trademark law), Chgo., 1952—. Mem. bd. edn., River Forest, Ill., 1963-69; trustee West Suburban Hosp., Oak Park, Ill., 1974-77; mem. bd. Ill. State Hist. Soc., 2000-03. With combat engrs., U.S. 3d inf. divsn., 1942-45. Fellow Am. Coll. Trial Lawyers (emeritus); mem. ABA, Am. Intellectual Property Law Assn. (bd. mgrs. 1963-66), Ill. Bar Assn., Chgo. Bar Assn., Intellectual Property Law Assn. Chgo. (bd. mgrs. 1972-73, pres. 1984), No. Ill. Ct. Hist. Assn. (pres.), Union League Club (Chgo.), Oak Park (Ill.) Country Club, Chgo. Literary Club. Republican. Home: 1018 Park Ave River Forest IL 60305-1308 Office: 120 S La Salle St Chicago IL 60603-3403

EVERARD, GERALD WILFRED, lawyer, trust company executive; b. Green Bay, Wis., Sept. 25, 1952; s. Wilfred A. and Regina P. (Arendt) E.; m. Paula M. Devroy, Sept. 17, 1977. BA, St. Norbert Coll., 1974; JD, U. Wis., 1977. Bar: Wis. 1977. Assoc. Boaroman, Suhr, Curry & Field, Madison, Wis., 1977-81; trust officer 1st Wis. Nat. Bank, Madison, 1981—. Law instr. U. Wis., Madison, 1985. Bd. dirs. Cen. YMCA, Madison, 1983-86. Mem. Wis. Bar Assn., Dane County Bar Assn., ABA. Probate (including wills, trusts). Office: US Bank PO Box 7900 Madison WI 53707-7900 E-mail: jay.everard@usbank.com.

EVERBACH, OTTO GEORGE, lawyer; b. New Albany, Ind., Aug. 27, 1938; s. Otto G. and Zelda Marie (Hilt) E.; m. Nancy Lee Stern, June 3, 1961; children: Tracy Ellen, Stephen George. BS, U.S. Mil. Acad., 1960; LLB, U. Va., 1966. Bar: Va. 1967, Ind. 1967, Calif. 1975, Mass. 1978. Counsel CIA, Langley, Va., 1966-67; corp. counsel Bristol-Meyers Co., Evansville, Ind., 1967-74, Alza Corp., Palo Alto, Calif., 1974-75; sec., gen. counsel Am. Optical Corp., Southbridge, Mass., 1976-81; assoc. gen. counsel Warner-Lambert Co., Morris Plains, N.J., 1981-83; v.p. Kimberly-Clark Corp., Neenah, Wis., 1984-86, sr. v.p., gen. counsel, 1986—, sr. v.p. law & govt. affairs, 1988—. Served with U.S. Army, 1960-63. Mem. Am. Bar Assn., Mass. Bar Assn., Ind. Bar Assn., Calif. Bar Assn. Office: Kimberly-Clark Corp DFW Airport Sta PO Box 619100 Dallas TX 75261-9100

EVERETT, C(HARLES) CURTIS, retired lawyer; b. Omaha, Aug. 9, 1930; s. Charles Edgar and Rosalie (Cook) E.; m. Joan Rose Bader, Sept. 7, 1951; children: Jeffrey, Ellen, Amy, Jennifer. BA cum laude, Beloit Coll., 1952; JD, U. Chgo., 1957. Bar: Ill. 1957. Pvt. practice, Chgo., 1957-91; ptnr. Bell, Boyd, Lloyd, Haddad & Burns, 1965-81, successor firm Bell, Boyd & Lloyd, 1981-91; v.p. law, sec., gen. counsel AMRE, Inc., Dallas, 1991-96; v.p. law, sec., gen. counsel, bd. dirs. Am. Remodeling, Inc., Dallas, 1992-96; v.p. Canre Remodelling, Inc., Dallas, 1992-94. V.p., sec. Hans Bader, Cons., Inc., Clearwater, Fla., 1954-99, also bd. dirs.; vis. com. U. Chgo. Law Sch., 1986-89; lectr. Ill. Inst. CLE. Mem. editl. bd. U. Chgo. Law Rev., 1956-57; contbr. articles to profl. jours. Chmn. So. Suburban area Beloit Coll. Ford Found. challange program, 1964-65; pres. The Players, Flossmoor, 1970-71; bd. govs. Lake Shore Dr. Condominium Assn., 1986-91. With AUS, 1952-54. Mem. ABA, Ill. Bar Assn., Chgo. Bar Assn. (mem. securities law com. 1960-91), U. Chgo. Law Sch. Alumni Assn. (dir. 1973-76, pres. Chgo. chpt. 1979-80), Legal Club, Law Club, Monroe Club (bd. govs. 1976-97), Univ. Club Chgo., Order of DeMolay (past master counselor Rock River chpt.), Order of Coif, Sigma Chi, Phi Alpha Delta. Mem. Cmty. Ch. (deacon). Corporate, general, Mergers and acquisitions, Securities. Home: 532 Long Reach Dr Salem SC 29676-4214

EVERETT, JAMES JOSEPH, lawyer; b. San Antonio, May 7, 1955; BA, St. Mary's U., San Antonio, 1976; JD, Tex. So. U., 1980. Bar: U.S. Dist. Ct. Ariz. 1987, U.S. Tax Ct. 1980, U.S. Ct. Appeals (9th cir.) 1988. Sr. trial atty. IRS, Phoenix, 1980-87; ptnr. Brnilovich & Everett, Phoenix, 1987-89; owner Law Offices of James J. Everett, Phoenix, 1989—; of counsel Broadbent, Walker & Wales, 1991-95. Mem. ATLA, ABA (bus. and tax sects.), Fed. Bar Assn., Tex. Bar Assn., Ariz. Bar Assn., State Bar Ariz. (cert. tax specialist), Maricopa County Bar Assn., Ariz. Tax Controversy Group, Valley Estate Planners (Phoenix), Ctrl. Ariz. Estate Planners, Ariz. Soc. Boutiques, St. Thomas Moore Soc. Corporate taxation, Estate taxation, Personal income taxation. Office: Ste 225 2999 N 44th St Phoenix AZ 85018 E-mail: james.everett@azbar.org.

EVERETT, MIKE, lawyer; b. McCrory, Ark., Mar. 12, 1948; s. John Grant and Mary Lucille (Pohnka) E.; m. Betsy Ann Milwre, Jan. 19, 1968 (div. July 1975); m. Laurel Casey, Dec. 27, 1977; children: Michael Wayne, Casey Toye. BA, Ark. State U., 1970; JD, U. Ark., 1973. Pvt. practice, Marked Tree, Ark., 1973—; mem. Ark Senate from 23rd dist., Little Rock, 1971—2002. Maj. U.S. Army res. Fellow Ark. Bar Found.; mem. Ark. Bar Assn. Democrat. Avocations: cooking, reading. Address: 412 Broadway St Marked Tree AR 72365-1406*

EVERETT, RALPH BERNARD, lawyer; b. Orangeburg, S.C., June 23, 1951; s. Francis G.S. and Alethia (Hilton) E.; m. Gwendolyn Harris, June 22, 1974. BA, Morehouse Coll., 1973; JD, Duke U., 1976. Bar: N.C. 1977, D.C. 1979. Adminstrv. asst. N.C. Dept. Labor, 1976-77; legis. asst. Office of Sen. Ernest F. Hollings, Washington, 1977-82; minority chief counsel, staff dir. U.S. Senate Com. on Commerce, Sci., Transp., Washington, 1983-87, chief counsel, staff dir., 1987-89; ptnr. Paul, Hastings, Janofsky and Walker, LLP, Washington, 1989—. Bd. dirs. Shenandoah Life Ins. Co., Cumulus Media Inc.; mem. adv. bd. Norfolk So. Corp., Washington, 1991—; life mem. bd. visitors Duke U. Sch. Law; former mem. Pres.'s Bd. Advisors on Historically Black Colls. and Univs.; head U.S. Del. to World Telecomm. Conf., 1998; U.S. amb. to 1998 Internat. Telecomm. Union Plenipotentiary Conf. Former trustee Nat. Urban League, N.Y.C., 1990, 92; senate liaison Clinton/Gore Presdl. Campaign, Washington, 1992; former mem. Congl. Award Found., McLean, Va., 1993—; former mem. Fed. City Coun. Mem.: Econ. Club Washington, Phi Beta Kappa, Alpha Phi Alpha. Office: Paul Hastings Janofsky & Walker LLP 10th Fl 1299 Pennsylvania Ave NW Washington DC 20004-2400 E-mail: ralpheverett@paulhastings.com.

EVERETT NOLLKAMPER, PAMELA IRENE, legal management company executive, educator; b. L.A., Dec. 31, 1947; d. Richard Weldon and Alta Irene (Tuttle) Bunnell; m. James E. Everett, Sept. 2, 1967 (div. 1973); 1 child, Richard Earl; m. Milton Nollkamper, Dec. 20, 2000. Cert. Paralegal, Rancho Santago Coll., Santa Ana, Calif., 1977; BA, Calif. State U.-Long Beach, 1985; MA, U. Redlands, 1988. Owner, mgr. Orange County Paralegal Svc., Santa Ana, 1979—; pres. Gem Legal Mgmt. Inc., Fullerton, Calif., 1986—; co-owner Bunnell Publs., Fullerton, Calif., 1992-96. Instr. Rancho Santiago Coll., 1979-96, chmn. adv. bd., 1980-85; instr. Fullerton Coll., 1989-2002, Rio Hondo Coll., Whittier, Calif., 1992-94; advisor Saddleback Coll., 1985—, North Orange County Regional Occupational Program, Fullerton, 1986-99, Fullerton Coll. So. Calif. Coll. Bus. and Law; bd. dirs. Nat. Profl. Legal Assts. Inc., editor PLA News. Author: Legal Secretary Federal Litigation, 1986, Bankruptcy Courts and Procedure, 1987, Going Independent--Business Planning Guide, Fundamentals of Law Office Management, 1994. Republican. Avocation: reading. Office: 940 Manor Way Corona CA 92882 E-mail: 2Pan@attbi.com.

EVERS, WILLIAM DOHRMANN, lawyer; b. San Francisco, May 6, 1927; s. Albert John and Sepha (Pischel) E.; m. Edwina Bigelow Benington, Aug. 26, 1950 (div. May 1978); children: Elliot B., Anne B., Albert John II, William Dohrmann Jr.; m. Britte-Marie Emblad, May 27, 1978. BA, Yale U., 1949; LLB, JD, U. Calif., Berkeley, 1952. Bar: Calif. 1952. Assoc. Chickering & Gregory, San Francisco, 1953-56; legal asst. to commr. SEC,

1956-57; assoc. atty. Allen, Miller, Groezinger, Keesling & Martin, San Francisco, 1957-60; ptnr. Pettit, Evers & Martin, San Francisco, 1960-78; chmn. On-Line Bus. Sys., Inc., 1980-82; chmn., CEO Precision Techs., 1982-87; ptnr. Chickering & Gregory, San Francisco, 1986-89, Sullivan, Roche & Johnson, San Francisco, 1989-95, Miller, Mailliad & Culver LLP, San Francisco, 1995-96, Evers & Andelin LLP, San Francisco, 1996-97, Evers & Hendrickson LLP, 1997-2000, Foley & Lardner, 2000—. Pres. Econ. Devel. Council City and County of San Francisco, 1978-80; chmn. San Francisco Bay Conservation and Devel. Commn., 1972-75; pres. Calif. Roadside Council, 1959-60; chmn. SPUR, San Francisco, 1975-78; chmn. assistance and adv. council Calif. Gov.'s Office Planning and Research, 1977-78; founder, pres. Planning and Conservation League, 1965-68; mem. air quality adv. bd. EPA, 1970-73; vice chmn. San Francisco Republican County Central Com., 1959-63; trustee Marin County Day Sch., 1967-70, 79-82, Katherine Branson Sch., 1976-78; bd. dirs. Yosemite Nat. Inst., 1981—, chmn. 1988-90; mem. governing council Wilderness Soc., Washington, 1984-96; chmn. Calif. Capital Access Forum, 1996—; vice chmn. TechVentures Network, 2002—. With USN, 1944-45. Mem. ABA, San Francisco Bar Assn., State Bar Calif., Bohemian Club (San Francisco). Corporate, general, Mergers and acquisitions, Securities. Home: 2019 Lyon St San Francisco CA 94115-1609 E-mail: wevers@foleylaw.com.

EVERSON, STEVEN LEE, lawyer, real estate executive; b. Philippi, W.Va., June 16, 1950; s. Billie Lee and Mildred Ann (Hill) E.; m. Donna Janine Chmielarz, May 29, 1976; 1 child, Michael. BA in Math. magna cum laude, W. Va. U., 1972; JD, Northwestern U., 1979. Bar: Colo. 1979. Tax sr. acct. Deloitte, Haskins & Sells, Colorado Springs, Colo., 1979-82; v.p., sec., treas. The Schuck Corp., Colorado Springs, 1982—. Instr. real estate U. Colo. Project bus. instr. Jr. Achievement, 1985—87; treas. Steve Schuck for Gov. Com., 1988—98; bd. dirs. Silver Key Sr. Svcs., Inc., 2000—, Boys and Girls Club of Pikes Peak Region, Colorado Springs, 1987—90, UCCS Exec. Club, Colorado Springs, 1988—90; bd. dirs., past chmn. Pikes Peak Found. Mental Health, Colorado Springs, 1986—2001, treas., 2001—; past chmn. Pikes Peak Mental Health Ctr. Sys., Inc., treas., 2001—. Capt. USAF, 1972—76. Named Vol. of Yr., Pikes Peak Mental Health Ctr., 1999, 2002. Mem. Phi Beta Kappa. Republican. Mem. Ch. of Christ. Avocations: racquetball, skiing, softball, golf, tennis, vol. coaching youth sports teams. Property, real (including real estate development, water), Taxation, general, Personal income taxation. Home: 1690 Colgate Dr Colorado Springs CO 80918-8106 Office: The Schuck Corp 2 N Cascade Ave Ste 1280 Colorado Springs CO 80903-1601

EWAN, DAVID E. lawyer; b. Camden, N.J., June 23, 1959; s. Eugene H. and Catherine T. (Stannard) E.; m. Lisa J. Draves, Sept. 12, 1998. BA, Dickinson Coll., 1981; JD, Rutgers U., 1991. Bar: N.J. 1991, Pa. 1991, Fla. 1992, Colo. 1994, U.S. Dist. Ct. N.J. 1991, U.S. Ct. Appeals (3d cir.) 1992. Legal intern Camden County Prosecutor, 1989; law clk. U.S. Ct. Appeals (3d cir.), Phila., 1990-91; assoc. Begley, McCloskey & Gaskill, Moorestown, NJ, 1991—2001; pres. Computer Network SOS, Inc., 2002—. Cons. N.J. Land Title Assn., 2000—; sr. adj. prof. paralegal program Burlington County Coll., Pemberton, N.J., 1996—. Mem.: Assn. for Info. and Image Mgmt. Internat., Property Records Industry Assn., Am. Ednl. Rsch. Assn. Property, real (including real estate development, water). Home: 400 N Haddon Ave Unit 50 Haddonfield NJ 08033-1731 Office: PO Box 102 Haddonfield NJ 08033

EWAN, WILLIAM KENNETH, lawyer; b. Riverdale, Md., May 15, 1943; s. Richard Kenneth and Dorothy Alice (Spencer) E.; m. Naomi Ruth Browne, July 31, 1971; 1 child, Andrea Sue. BS, Ind. U., 1964, JD, 1967. Bar: Ind. 1967, U.S. Dist. Ct. (so. dist.) Ind. 1967, U.S. Ct. Mil. Appeals 1976. Pvt. practice law, Lawrenceburg, Ind., 1974—. Unit sec. Salvation Army, chmn. kettle drive. Capt. USNR, 1967-99, ret. Decorated Meritorious Svc. Medal USN. Mem. Ind. State Bar Assn., Dearborn-Ohio County Bar Assn. (pres. 1976-78), Ind. U. Alumni Assn., Ind. U. Alumni Club Dearborn County (pres. 1976), Am. Legion. Methodist. Avocations: photography, hiking Appalachian Trail, sailing, golf. Utilities, public, Probate (including wills, trusts), Property, real (including real estate development, water). Home: 9636 Old State Road 350 Aurora IN 47001-9343 Office: 210 W High St Lawrenceburg IN 47025-1910 E-mail: bewan@one.net.

EWBANK, THOMAS PETERS, lawyer, retired banker; b. Indpls., Dec. 29, 1943; s. William Curtis and Maxine Stuart (Peters) E.; m. Alice Ann Shelton, June 8, 1968; children: William Curtis, Ann Shelton. Student, Stanford U., 1961-62; AB, Ind. U., 1965, JD, 1969. Bar: Ind. 1969, U.S. Tax Ct. 1969, U.S. Dist. Ct. (so. dist.) Ind. 1969, U.S. Supreme Ct. 1974; cert. trust & fin. advisor. Legis. asst. Ind. Legis. Coun., 1966-67; estate and inheritance tax adminstr. Mchts. Nat. Bank, Indpls., 1967-69; assoc. Hilgedag, Johnson, Secrest and Murphy, Indpls., 1969-71; asst. gen. counsel Everett I. Brown Co., Indpls., 1971-72; with Mchts. Nat. Bank & Trust Co. (now Nat. City Bank), Indpls., 1972-95; from probate adminstr. to sr. v.p. & sr. trust officer, pres. Mechants Capital Mgmt., Inc., Ind., 1990-93; ptnr. Krieg DeVault LLP, Indpls., 1995—. Contbr. articles to profl. jours. Asst. treas. Ruckelshaus for U.S. Senator Com., 1968; candidate for Ind. Legislature, 1970, 74; bd. dirs. Noble Found. Ind., 1997-99, Indpls. Art Ctr., 1997-2002, Ruth Lilly Found., 1997-2002, Ctr. Philanthropy, Ind. U., Indpls., 1998-2002, Benjamin Harrison Home Found., 1994—, v.p., 1996-98, pres., 1998-2000; chmn. adv. com. ARC, 1987—. Fellow: Ind. Bar Found. (life); mem.: ABA, Indpls. Bar Found. (treas. 1976-81), Ind. Bar. Assn., Indpls. Bar Assn., Estate Planning Coun. Indpls. (pres. 1982—83), English Speaking Union Indpls., Kiwanis (Circle K Internat. trustee 1963-64, pres. 1964-65, chmn. internat. com. 1988-90, George Hixson Diamond fellow, past treas. Indpls. club) (Career Achievement award 2001), Meridian Hills Country Club, Blue Key. Republican. Baptist. Estate planning, Probate (including wills, trusts), Estate taxation. Office: One Indiana Sq Ste 2800 Indianapolis IN 46204-2017 E-mail: tewbank@kdlegal.com.

EWELL, A. BEN, JR., lawyer, businessman; b. Elyria, Ohio, Sept. 10, 1941; s. Austin Bert and Mary Rebecca (Thompson) E.; m. Suzanne E.; children: Austin Bert III, Brice Ballantyne, Harrison Dale, Jonathan Eli, Tucker Benjamin. BA, Miami U., Oxford, Ohio, 1963; JD, Hasting Coll. Law, U. Calif., San Francisco, 1966. Bar: Calif. 1966, U.S. Dist. Ct. (ea. dist.) Calif. 1967, U.S. Supreme Ct. 1982, U.S. Ct. Appeals (9th cir.) 1967. Pres. A.B. Ewell, Jr., A. Profl. Corp., Fresno, 1984-98, The Clarksfield Co., Inc., Fresno, 1989—; formerly gen. counsel to various water dists. and assn.; gen. counsel, chmn. San Joaquin River Flood Control Assn., 1984-88; CEO Millerton New Town Devel. Co., 1988-94, chmn., 1994-96; pres. Millerton Open Space and Natural Resource Plan, 1999—; regional v.p. Western Water Co., Fresno, 2001—; pres. Lake Millerton Marinas, LLC. Mem. task force on prosecution, cts. and law reform Calif. Coun. Criminal Justice, 1971-74; columnist, The Willington Enterprise; mem. Fresno Bulldog Found., Calif. State U.; mem. San Joaquin Valley Agrl. Water commn., 1979-88; co-chmn. nat. adv. coun. SBA, 1981, 82, mem. 1981-87; bd. dirs. Fresno East Cmty. Ctr., 1971-73; mem. Fresno County Water Adv. Com., 1989; chmn. various area polit. campaigns and orgns., including Reagan/Bush, 1984, Deukmejian for Gov., 1986; mem. adv. com. St. Agnes Med. Ctr. Found., 1983-89; trustee U. Calif. Med. Edn. Found., 1989-90, Fresno Met. Mus. Art, History and Sci., active, 1989—, mem. adv. coun., 1993-94; bd. dirs. Citizens for Cmty. Enrichment, Fresno, 1990-93; mem. Police Activities League, 1995—. Bd. dirs. Fresno Conv. and Visitors Bur., 1997—, pres. 2003-04. Mem. Millerton Lake C. of C., Brighton Crest Country Club (pres. 1989-96), Copper River Country Club, Phi Alpha Delta, Brighton Crest Golf and Country Club, Sigma Nu. Congregationalist. Corporate, general, Utilities, public, Property, real (including real estate development, water). Office: 410 W Fallbrook Ave Ste 102 Fresno CA 93711-5830

EWEN, MICHAEL, lawyer; b. Emden, Germany, Apr. 11, 1960; 1st exam, U. Erlangen and Gottingen, 1986; 2d exam, Ct. Appeals Celle, 1989; MBL-HSG, U. St. Gallen , 1999. Bar: 1990. Assoc. Parigger and Schluchtmann, Hannover, Germany, 1990—93; reporter German Fed. Cartel Office, Berlin, 1993—96; ptnr. Feddersen Laule Scherzberg Ohle Hansen Ewerwahn, Frankfurt/Main, Germany, 1996—2000, Schulte Lawyers, Frankfurt/Main, 2000—. Contbr. Mem.: Studienvereinigung Kartellrecht. Antitrust. Office: Schulte Lawyers Hochstrasse 49 60313 Frankfurt/Main Hessen Germany

EWEN, PAMELA BINNINGS, lawyer; b. Mar. 22, 1944; d. Walter James and Barbara (Perkins) Binnings; m. Jerome Francis Ayers, Aug. 22, 1965 (div. July 1974); 1 child, Scott Dylan Ayers; m. John Alexander Ewen, Dec. 13, 1974. BA, Tulane U., 1977; JD cum laude, U. Houston, 1979. Bar: Tex. 79, U.S. Dist. Ct. (so. dist.) Tex. 81, U.S. Ct. Appeals (5th cir.) 81. Law clk. Harris, Cook, Browning & Barker, Corpus Christi, Tex., 1977—79; assoc. Kleberg, Dyer, Redford & Weil, Corpus Christi, 1979—80; atty. law dept. Gulf Oil Corp., Houston, 1980—84; assoc. Baker & Botts, L.L.P., Houston, 1980—84, ptnr., 1988—. Author: Faith On Trial, 1999. La. Legis. scholar, New Orleans, 1976—77. Mem.: ABA (forum com. on franchising 1983—85, law practice mgmt. sect., subcom. Women Rainmakers Assn.), Tex. Assn. Bank Coun., Tex. State Bar (bd. dirs. 1994—97), Am. Petroleum Inst. (com. on product liability 1982—85, spl. subcom. to gen. com. on law), Order of Barons, Jr. Achievement S.E. Tex. (bd. dirs. 1997—2001, bd. dirs. Inprint, Inc. 2002—). Commercial, contracts (including sales of goods; commercial financing), Corporate, general, Finance. Office: Baker & Botts 3000 1 Shell Plz Houston TX 77002

EWING, CHARLES PATRICK, lawyer, educator; b. Binghamton, N.Y., Aug. 2, 1949; s. Charles Joseph and Pauline Margurite (Rogers) E.; m. Sharon Harris, June 20, 1976; children: Elaine, Benjamin. BA magna cum laude, Syracuse U., 1971; PhD, Cornell U., 1975; JD cum laude, Harvard U., 1983. Bar: N.Y. 1984; diplomate Am. Bd. Profl. Psychology. Postdoctoral fellow Yale U., New Haven, 1976-77; dir. children's services Genesee Hosp., Rochester, N.Y., 1977-78; pvt. practice clin. and forensic psychology Rochester, 1978-80, Buffalo, 1983—; asst. prof. law SUNY, Buffalo, 1983-85, assoc. prof., 1985-87, prof., 1988—, dist. svc. prof., 2003—. Author: Crisis Intervention as Psychotherapy, 1978, Battered Women Who Kill, 1987, When Children Kill, 1990, Kids Who Kill, 1990, Fatal Families, 1997; editor: Psychology, Psychiatry and the Law, 1985; assoc. editor: Encyclopedic Handbook of Private Practice, 1988; editor Behavioral Scis. and the Law, 1987—; contbr. articles to profl. jours. Magavern fellow, 1986; recipient Disting. Achievement award, Western N.Y. Psychol. Assn., 1990, Outstanding Achievement award, N.Y. Bar Assn., 2001. Fellow Am. Psychol. Assn.; mem. ABA, Am. Psychol. Assn. Am. Psychology-Law Soc., Am. Acad. Forensic Psychology (Disting. Contbn. Forensic Psychology award 1993), Am. Soc. Law and Medicine, Am. Acad. Forensic Scis. Democrat. Avocations: physical fitness, baseball. Criminal, Juvenile. Home: 10 Greencastle Ln Buffalo NY 14221-1764 Office: SUNY Buffalo Law School 723 Obrian Hall Buffalo NY 14260-1100 E-mail: cewing@acsu.buffalo.edu.

EWING, CHRISTOPHER HAIG, lawyer; b. Johannesburg, Gauteng, South Africa, Feb. 23, 1949; s. Ernest Haig and Ethne Ewing; m. Susan Elizabeth Whitford, Mar. 30, 1974; children: Timothy, Graeme, Jonathan. B in Commerce, U. Witwatersrand, Johannesburg, 1971, LLB, 1975. Staff fin. dept. South AFrican Breweries, Isando, 1970—73; articled clk. Cliffe Dekker Inc., Johannesburg, 1974—75, profl. asst., 1976—77, ptnr., 1979—98, dir., 1998—2001, chmn., 2001—; legal advisor Credit Guarantee Corp. Ltd., Johannesburg, 1978. Mem.: Law Soc. Western Cape, Law Soc. No. Provinces. Mergers and acquisitions. Office: Cliffe Dekker Inc Pvt Bag x7 Benmore 2010 South Africa

EWING, JOSEPH NEFF, JR., retired lawyer; b. Bryn Mawr, Pa., Nov. 10, 1925; s. Joseph Neff and Anne (Ashton) E.; m. Margaret Converse Howe, Dec. 22, 1951; children: Margaret E. Lloyd, Anne A., Elizabeth M. Peifer AB, Princeton U., 1947; JD, U. Pa., 1953. Bar: Pa. 1954, U.S. Tax Ct. 1992, U.S. Supreme Ct. 1978. Assoc. Saul, Ewing, Remick & Saul, Phila., 1953-63, ptnr., 1963-95, of counsel, 1996—. Bd. govs. Main Line Health, Inc., 1988-95; trustee The Bryn Mawr Hosp., 1969-96, Bryn Mawr Hosp. Found., 1981-98, Hist. Sugartown, Inc., Malvern, Pa., 1990-98; trustee Dunwoody Village, Inc., 1997--, 2d vice chmn. 1999--; chancellor Clan Ewing in Am., 1998—. Chmn. Willistown Twp. Planning Commn., Malvern, 1960-69, chmn. bd. suprs., 1970-82, chmn. zoning hearing bd., 1985-95, East Goshen Twp., chmn. Zoning Hearing Bd., 1996—; pres. bd. trustees Embreeville (Pa.) State Hosp., 1965-72, chmn. spl. contacts divsn. Phila. United Fund, 1965-66; mem. hosp. coun. Mental Health Assn., Southeastern Pa., Phila., 1967-68; elder Paoli (Pa.) Presbyn. Ch., 1970-72. Mem. ABA, Phila. Bar Assn. (med.-legal com. 1962-76, chmn. 1971), Phila. Assn. Def. Counsel (pres. 1973), Nat. Assn. R.R. Trial Counsel, Pa. Soc. Healthcare Attys. (pres. 1975-77), Waynesborough Country Club (v.p. 1965-69), Hershey's Mill Golf Club. Avocations: sailing, photography, gardening, fox hunting, skiing. General civil litigation, Condemnation (eminent domain), Health. Home: 1109 Lincoln Dr West Chester PA 19380-5721

EWING, KY PEPPER, JR., lawyer; b. Victoria, Tex., Jan. 7, 1935; s. Ky Pepper and Sallie (Dixon) E.; m. Almuth Rott, Apr. 6, 1963; children: Kenneth Patrick, Kevin Andrew, Kathryn Diana. BA cum laude, Baylor U., 1956; LLB cum laude, Harvard U., 1959. Bar: D.C. 1959, U.S. Supreme Ct 1963. Assoc. firm Covington & Burling, Washington, 1959-64; partner firm Prather, Seeger, Doolittle, Farmer & Ewing, Washington, 1964-77; dep. asst. atty. gen. antitrust div. Dept. Justice, Washington, 1978-80; ptnr. Vinson & Elkins, Washington, 1980—2001, of counsel, 2002—. Mem. Washington Inst. Fgn. Affairs. Author: Competition Rules for the 21st Century: Principles from America's Experience, 2003; co-editor-in-chief: State Antitrust Practice and Statutes, 3 Vols., 1990; mem. antitrust adv. bd. Antitrust and Trade Regulation Report Bur. Nat. Affairs, 1990—; mem. edit. bd. Antitrust Report Matthew Bender & Co., 1993—. Pres. Potomac Valley League, 1977, Carderock Springs Citizens Assn., 1975-78. Fellow: Am. Bar Found. (life); mem.: ABA (chmn. legis. com. antitrust sect. 1987—91, coun. antitrust sect. 1991—94, fin. officer antitrust sect. 1994—96, chmn. FTC/Dept. Justice working group 1994—97, mem. Ho. of Dels. 1996—98, vice chair antitrust sect. 1998—99, chair-elect antitrust sect. 1999—2000, chair antitrust sect. 2000—01, chmn. nominating com. antitrust sect. 2002—03), D.C. Bar Assn., Inter-Am. Bar Assn., Internat. Bar Assn. (editl. bd. Bus. Law Internat.), Am. Soc. Internat. Law, Met. Club. Democrat. Episcopalian. Antitrust, Federal civil litigation, Environmental. Home: 8317 Comanche Ct Bethesda MD 20817-4561 Office: Vinson & Elkins 1455 Pennsylvania Ave NW Washington DC 20004-1013 E-mail: kewing@velaw.com.

EWING, MARY, lawyer; b. Shreveport, La., Feb. 21, 1948; d. George and Christine (Cocek) Hengy; m. Robert Craig Ewing, Aug. 30, 1981; 1 child, Kyle Ross. BA, U. Colo., 1972; JD, U. Denver, 1975. Bar: Colo. 1975, U.S. Supreme Ct. 1979. Assoc. Johnson & Mahoney, Denver, 1975-80; ptnr. Branney, Hillyard, Ewing & Barnes, Englewood, Colo., 1980-85, Bucholtz, Bull & Ewing, Denver, 1985-96, Ewing & Ewing PC, Englewood, Colo., 1996—. Asst. prof. law U. Denver, 1977-78, part time prof. 1978—; mem. faculty Nat. Inst. Trial Advocacy, 1984-89; instr. nat. session 1984, 85, 87, Nat. Bd. Trial Advocacy, regional session, 1984-89; bd. trustees Lowell Whiteman Sch., Steamboat Springs, Colo., 2001—. Chmn. Denver County Task Force, 1976—77, mem., 1990; treas. Cen. Com. 1st Congl. Dist., 1976—77; v.p. Young Rep. League Denver, 1975, pres., 1976; mem. govt. rels. com. Jr. Symphony Guild, 1978—; mem. legal com. County Horse Assn., 1990—; mem. bd. trustee The Lowell Whiteman Sch., Steamboat Springs, Colo., 2000—; mem. capital campaign com. Denver Dumb Friends League; bd. dirs. Steamboat Springs Arts Coun., Emerald City Opera Guild, 2003. Mem. ABA, Colo. Bar Assn. (ethics com.), Denver Bar Assn. (vice chmn. new lawyers assistance com. 1977), Colo. Women's Bar Assn., Rocky Mountain Dressage Soc. (sec. High Plains chpt. 1979-80, chmn. constn. and by-laws com. 1988—), Assn. Trial Lawyers Am., Colo. Trial Lawyers Assn. (bd. govs., chmn. interprofl. com. 1980—, bd. dirs. polit. action com. 1989—, exec. bd. 2000—), Douglas County Bar Assn., Am. Arbitration Assn., Nat. Bd. Trial Advocacy (cert. 1983), Am. Trakehner Assn., Rocky Mountain Trakehner Assn. (v.p. 1987), Arapahoe Hunt Club, Greenwood Athletic Club, Kappa Beta Pi (pres. 1977-78). Labor (including EEOC, Fair Labor Standards Act, labor-management relations, NLRB, OSHA), Personal injury (including property damage), Workers' compensation. Home: Nonesuch Farm 4256 S Perry Park Rd Sedalia CO 80135-8207 Address: 3601 S Pennsylvania St Englewood CO 80110-3753 E-mail: MaryEwingEsq@aol.com.

EXLEY, PAUL MARCUS, lawyer; b. Dewsbury, May 27, 1963; s. Donald Barrie and June Exley; m. Anna Monika Kowalska, Aug. 14, 1998. LLB with honors, U. Coll., London, 1984. Solicitor Simmons & Simmons, London, 1985—. Editor: (book) Tolley's Company Law, 1990. Mem.: U.K. Energy Lawyers Group, Law Soc. Eng. and Wales. Corporate, general, Mergers and acquisitions, Oil, gas, and mineral. Office: Simmons & Simmons One Ropemaker St London EC2Y 9SS England

EY, ROBERT M. law librarian; JD, U. of Denver, 1979. Project editor Shepard's/McGraw-Hill, Colorado Springs, Colo., 1980—96; edit. editor Vox Juris Inc., Pennington, NJ, 1997—2000; ref. libr. Wolf, Block, Schorr and Solis-Cohen LLP, Phila., 2001—. Office: Wolf Block Schorr and Solis-Cohen LLP 1650 Arch St Philadelphia PA 19103-2097

EYMANN, RICHARD CHARLES, lawyer; b. Hanover, N.H., June 6, 1945; BS, U. Oreg., 1968; JD, Gonzaga U., 1976. Bar: Wash. 1976, U.S. Dist. Ct. (ea. dist.) Wash. 1978, U.S. Ct. Appeals (9th cir.) 1987, U.S. Dist. Ct. (we. dist.) Wash. 1989, U.S. Supreme Ct. 1995. Ptnr. Eymann, Allison, Fennessy, Hunter Jones, P.S., Spokane, Wash. Mem. ABA (founder, chmn. nat. appellate advocacy competition 1975-84, bd. advs. 1985-93), ATLA, Wash. State Bar Assn. (bd. govs. 1997-98, pres. elect 1998-99, pres. 1999-2000), Wash. State Trial Lawyers Assn. (bd. govs. 1984-86, 88-95, legis. steering com. 1990-96, membership chair 1984-85, v.p. East 1991-92, fin. com. 1994-95, Trial Lawyer of Yr. 1995, pres. 1996-97), Wash. Trial Lawyers for Pub. Justice (bd. dirs. 1994-98), Am. Bd. Trial Advocates, Spokane County Bar Assn., Am. Inns of Ct. (barrister 1986, master of the bench 1990, Charles L. Powell & Inn pres. 1991-93), Damage Attys. Round Table. Personal injury (including property damage), General civil litigation. Office: Eymann Allison Fennessy Hunter & Jones PS 601 W Main Ave Ste 801 Spokane WA 99201 E-mail: eymann@eahjlaw.com.

EYRE, PAUL P. lawyer; b. Dublin, Mar. 13, 1947; BA, U. Wis., 1971, JD, 1975. Bar: Wis. 1975, Ohio 1982. Asst. regional dir. FTC, Washington, 1977-79, regional dir., 1979-82; ptnr. Baker & Hostetler, Cleve. With USN, 1967-69. Mem. Ohio Bar Assn. Office: Baker & Hostetler 3200 Nat City Ctr 1900 E 9th St Ste 3200 Cleveland OH 44114-3475

FABE, DANA ANDERSON, state supreme court chief justice; b. Cin., Mar. 29, 1951; d. George and Mary Lawrence (Van Antwerp) F.; m. Randall Gene Simpson, Jan. 1, 1983; 1 child, Amelia Fabe Simpson. BA, Cornell U., 1973; JD, Northeastern U., 1976. Bar: Alaska 1977, U.S. Supreme Ct. 1981. Law clk. to justice Alaska Supreme Ct., 1976-77; staff atty. pub. defenders State Alaska, 1977-81; dir. Alaska Pub. Defender Agy., Anchorage, 1981—. Judge Superior Ct., Anchorage; justice Alaska Supreme Ct., Anchorage, 1996—, chief justice, 2000—. Named alumna of yr. Northeastern Sch. Law, 1983, alumni pub. svc. award, 1991. Office: Alaska Supreme Ct 303 K St Fl 5 Anchorage AK 99501-2013

FABENS, ANDREW LAWRIE, III, lawyer; b. Washington, Apr. 8, 1942; s. Andrew Lawrie Jr. and Alicia Gordon (Hail) F.; m. Martha Leigh Leingang, June 24, 1966; children: Andrew Lawrie IV, Jennie Leigh. AB, Yale U., 1964; JD, U. Chgo., 1967. Bar: Ohio 1967. Assoc. Thompson, Hine and Flory, Cleve., 1967-74; ptnr. Thompson Hine LLP (formerly Thompson, Hine and Flory), Cleve., 1974—, chmn. estate planning and probate area, 1988-94. Contbr. articles on estate planning and related topics to profl. publs. Pres. Family Health Assn., Cleve., 1978-80, 83-84; trustee A.M. McGregor Home, East Cleveland, Ohio, 1991—, chmn., 2001—; trustee Bascom Little Fund, Cleve., 1985—, Great Lakes Basin Conservancy, 1999—; vestryman Christ Episcopal Ch., Shaker Heights, Ohio, 1972-77. Fellow Am. Coll. Trust and Estate Counsel; mem. Ohio State Bar Assn. (bd. govs. estate planning, trust and probate law sect. 1983—, treas. 1997-99, sec. 1999-2001, vice-chmn. 2001—), Probate Law Jour. Ohio (adv. bd.), Cleve. Bar Assn. (speaker, com. mem. 1976—), Cleve. Skating Club, Rowfant Club (fellow 2000-03), The Novel Club (sec. 1986-88, pres. 1995-97), The Union Club. Estate planning, Probate (including wills, trusts), Estate taxation. Home: 2280 Woodmere Dr Cleveland OH 44106-3604 Office: Thompson Hine LLP 3900 Key Ctr 127 Public Square Cleveland OH 44114-1216

FABER, DAVID ALAN, federal judge; b. Charleston, W.Va., Oct. 21, 1942; s. John Smith and Wilda Elaine (Melton) F.; m. Deborah Ellayne Anderson, Aug. 24, 1968; 1 dau., Katherine Peyton. BA, W.Va. U., 1964; JD, Yale U., 1967; LLM, U. Va., 1998. Bar: W.Va. 1967, U.S. Ct. Mil. Appeals 1970, U.S. Supreme Ct. 1974. Assoc. Dayton, Campbell & Love, Charleston, W.Va., 1967-68, Campbell, Love, Woodroe, 1972-74; ptnr. Campbell, Love, Woodroe & Kizer, Charleston, 1974-77, Love, Wise, Robinson & Woodroe, Charleston, 1977-81; U.S. atty. U.S. Dept. Justice, Charleston, 1982-86; ptnr. Spilman, Thomas, Battle & Klostermeyer, Charleston, 1987-91; judge U.S. Dist. Ct. (so. dist.) W.Va., Bluefield, 1991—. Counsel to ethics commn. W.Va. State Bar, Charleston, 1974-76 Served to capt. USAF, 1968-72, to col. W.Va. Air N.G., 1978-92. Nat. law scholar Yale Law Sch. New Haven, 1964-65 Mem. W.Va. State Bar, W.Va. Bar Assn., Phi beta Kappa. Republican. Episcopalian. Office: US Dist Ct PO Box 5009 110 N Heber St Beckley WV 25801 Fax: (304) 253-6811.

FABER, MICHAEL WARREN, lawyer; b. N.Y.C., June 7, 1943; s. Carl Faber and Harriet Ruth Cohen; m. Adele Zolot, Apr. 16, 1975; children: Evan, Jenna. AB, Hunter Coll., 1964; JD, Fordham U., 1967. Bar: N.Y. 1967, D.C. 1972, U.S. Ct. Claims, 1972, U.S. Supreme Ct. 1972, Colo. 1993. Gen. atty. FCC, Washington, 1967-69, trial atty., 1969-71, atty. advisor to Commr. T.J. Houser, 1971; assoc. Peabody, Rivlin, Lambert & Meyers, Washington, 1971-73; ptnr. Peabody, Lambert & Meyers, Washington, 1973-84, Reid and Priest, Washington, 1984-93, mem. exec. com., 1986-92; prin. The Faber Group, Cascade, Colo., 1993-94; pres. USA Volleyball Ctrs. LLC, Colorado Springs, Colo., 1995-96; owner The Pantry Restaurant, Green Mountain Falls, Colo., 1996—2001; prin. Crossroads Cons., LLC, Cascade, Colo., 2001—. Cons. White House Office Telecomm. Policy, 1976; chmn. organizing com. Nat. Volleyball League. Bd. dirs. Washington Very Spl. Arts, 1986-93; mem. Telecom. Policy Adv. Com., Colo. Springs, 2002-, SAFE Com., Colo. Springs, 2002-; pres. Manitou Springs Edn. Assn., Manitou Springs, 2002-; dir. Workforce Partnership Project, Pikes Peak, Workforce Investment Bd., Colorado Springs, Colo. Mem. N.Y. Bar Assn., D.C. Bar Assn., Fed. Communications Bar Assn., Colo. Bar Assn. Administrative and regulatory, Communications. E-mail: mwfaber@aol.com.

FABER, PETER LEWIS, lawyer; b. N.Y.C., Apr. 29, 1938; s. Alexander W. and Anne L. Faber; m. Joan Schuster, June 14, 1959; children: Michael, Julia, Thomas. AB, Swarthmore Coll., 1960; LLB, Harvard U., 1963. Bar: N.Y. 1964. Assoc. Wiser, Shaw, Freeman, Ickes & Williams, Rochester,

N.Y., 1963-65, Parker, Chapin & Flattau, N.Y.C., 1965-66; ptnr. Harter, Secrest & Emery, Rochester, N.Y., 1966-82, Winthrop, Stimson, Putnam & Roberts, N.Y.C., 1982-84, Kaye, Scholer, Fierman, Hays & Handler, N.Y.C., 1984-95, McDermott, Will & Emery, N.Y.C., 1995—. Mem. adv. com. NYU Ann. Inst. on State & Local Taxation; mem. N.Y. State Coun. on Fiscal and Econ. Priorities, 1991-95. Contbr. articles to profl. jours. Chmn. Rochester Econ. Devel. Com., 1979-82; pres. Rochester Philharm. Orch., Inc., 1980-82; bd. dirs. Met. Rochester Devel. Coun., Harley Sch., 1978-81; mem. fin. com. Monroe County Dem. Party, 1979-82; active N.Y.C. Partnership. Fellow Am. Bar Found., Am. Coll. Tax Counsel; mem. ABA (chmn. tax sect. 1991-92, vice chmn. 1986-88, chmn.-elect 1990-91, chmn. com. corp. stockholder relationships tax sect. 1980-82, liaison to IRS for North Atlantic region, vice chmn. spl. com. on integration 1979-81, sec. tax sect. 1984-86), N.Y. State Bar Assn. (chmn. sect. taxation 1976-77, exec. com. sect. taxation 1969—), N.Y. C. of C. (chmn. tax com. 1988—, trustee 1989—, exec. com. 1990—), Monroe County Bar Assn., Am. Law Inst. (tax project adv. group), Rochester Area C. of C. (trustee 1980-82). Corporate taxation, State and local taxation. Home: 300 Central Park W New York NY 10024-1513 Office: McDermott Will & Emery 50 Rockefeller Plz Fl 12 New York NY 10020-1600

FABER, ROBERT CHARLES, lawyer; b. N.Y.C., June 26, 1941; s. Sidney G. and Beatrice (Siebert) F.; m. Carol Z. Zimmerman, Aug. 15, 1965; 1 child, Susan Faber. BA, Cornell U., 1962; JD, Harvard Law Sch., 1965. Bar: N.Y. 1966; U.S. Dist. Ct. (so. dist.) N.Y. 1967; U.S. Ct. Appeals (2nd cir.); U.S. Ct. Appeals (fed. cir.) 1982; U.S. Supreme Ct. 1971; U.S. Patent and trademark Office 1967. Atty., ptnr. Ostrolenk, Faber, Gerb & Soffen, LLP, N.Y.C., 1965—. Lecturer Practicing Law Inst., N.Y.C., 1974—. Author: Landis on Mechanics of Patent Claim Drafting, 3d edit. 1990, 4th edit. 1996. Mem. Am. Intellectual Property Law Assn., N.Y. Intellectual Property Law Assn., Harvard Club of N.Y. Intellectual property, Patent, Trademark and copyright. Office: Ostrolenk Faber Gerb & Soffen LLP 1180 Ave of Americas New York NY 10036-8401

FACEMIRE, RICHARD ALLEN, judge; b. Sutton, W.Va., June 17, 1955; s. Russell Allen and Carol Joy Facemire; m. Patricia Facemire, July 29, 1989; children: Andrew, Patrick, Christian. BA, W.Va. Wesleyan Coll., 1978; MA, Marshall U., 1979; JD, Antioch Sch. Law, Washington, 1982. Bar: W.Va. 1983, U.S. Dist. Ct. (no. and so. dists.) W.Va. 1983, U.S. Ct. Appeals (4th cir.) 1983, U.S. Supreme Ct. 1986. Law clk. U.S. Bankruptcy Ct. W.Va., Wheeling, 1982, U.S. Dist. Ct. W.Va., Clarksburg, 1982—85; asst. atty. gen. Atty. Gen. W.Va., Charleston, 1985; pros. atty. Clay County, Clay, W.Va., 1985—92; pvt. practice, 1985—2000; child adv. atty. W.Va. Dept. Health and Human Resources, Sutton, 1992—99; judge 14th cir. W.Va. Supreme Ct., Sutton, 2000—. Mem.: Lions, Masons, Rotary. Democrat. Methodist. Office: Braxton County Courthouse 300 Main St Ste 204 Sutton WV 26601 Office Fax: 304-765-5496.

FACEY, JOHN ABBOTT, III, lawyer; b. Springfield, Mass., June 14, 1950; s. John Abbott Jr. and Mary Agnes (Murphy) F.; m. Patricia Marie Otto, Sept. 27, 1975; children: Justin Abbott, Christopher John, Michael Edward. BA, Coll. of the Holy Cross, 1972; JD, Suffolk U., 1975. Bar: Mass. 1975, Vt. 1976, U.S. Dist. Ct. Vt. 1977. Assoc. Bishop & Crowley, Rutland, Vt., 1975-81; ptnr. Keyser, Crowley, Banse & Facey, Rutland, 1981-90, Reiber Kenlan Schwiebert & Facey, P.C., Rutland, 1990—. Corporator Rutland Regional Med. Ctr.; trustee Rutland Free Libr., 1988-94, pres., 1989-90; bd. dirs. Downtown Devel. Corp., 1990-94; mem. Rutland City Planning Commn., 1994—, chair, 1996—. Mem. ABA, Mass. Bar Assn., Vt. Bar Assn. (title stds. subcom.), Rutland County Bar Assn., New Eng. Land Title Assn., Rotary (bd. dirs. 1989-95, pres. 1991-92). Republican. Roman Catholic. Avocations: skiing, tennis, travel. Land use and zoning (including planning), Municipal (including bonds), Property, real (including real estate development, water). Home: 82 Davis St Rutland VT 05701-3308 Office: Reiber Kenlan Schwiebert & Facey 71 Allen St Rutland VT 05701-4570 E-mail: jfacey@reiberlaw.com.

FACTOR, MAX, III, mediator, arbitrator; b. L.A., Sept. 25, 1945; s. Sidney B. and Dorothy (Levinson) F.; BA in Econs. magna cum laude, Harvard U., 1966; JD, Yale U., 1969. Bar: Calif. 1970, U.S. Ct. Appeals (6th cir.) 1971, U.S. Dist. Ct. (cen. dist.) Calif. 1971. Law clk. U.S. Ct. Appeals (6th cir.), 1969-71; exec. dir. Calif. Law Ctr., Los Angeles, 1973-74; dir. Consumer Protection Sect., Los Angeles City Atty., 1974-77; pvt. practice Factor & Agay, Beverly Hills, Calif, 1978—. expert witness numerous state and fed. bds., 1974-78; guest lectr. UCLA, U. So. Calif., Los Angeles County Bar Assn., Calif. Dept. Consumer Affairs, 1974-76; hearing examiner City of Los Angeles, 1975. Contbr. articles to profl. jours. Bd. dirs. Western Law Ctr. for the Handicapped, Los Angeles, 1977-79, Beverly Hills Unified Sch. Dist., 1979-83; pres. Beverly Hills Bd. Edn., 1983; bd. councilors U. So. Calif. Law Ctr., Los Angeles, 1983— ; chmn. Beverly Hills Visitors Bur., 1989-90. Recipient scholarship award Harvard Coll., 1965; Max Factor III Day proclaimed in his honor Beverly Hills City Council, 1979; recipient Disting. Service to Pub. Edn. award Beverly Hills Bd. Edn., 1979. Mem. Los Angeles County Bar Assn. (chmn. various coms. 1976-78), Beverly Hills C. of C. (pres. 1987-88), Beverly Hills Edn. Found. (pres. 1977-79). Office: 345 N Maple Dr Ste 294 Beverly Hills CA 90210-3878

FADELEY, EDWARD NORMAN, retired state supreme court justice; b. Williamsville, Mo., Dec. 13, 1929; m. Nancie Peacocke, June 11, 1953; children: Charles, Shira; m. Darian Cyr, Sept. 12, 1992. AB, U. Mo., 1951; JD cum laude, U. Oreg., 1957. Bar: Oreg. 1957, U.S. Supreme Ct. 1968. Practice law, Eugene, Oreg., 1957-88; mem. Oreg. Ho. of Reps., 1961-63, Oreg. Senate, 1963-87, pres., 1983-85; justice Oregon Supreme Ct., 1989-98; ret., 1998. Mem. jud. working group Internat. Water Tribunal, Amsterdam, The Netherlands 1991-95; invitee Rio Environ. Conf., 1992, Indigenous Peoples of World Conf., New Zealand, 1993; adj. prof. law U. Oreg.; formerly gen. couns., bd. officer for rsch. corp., fin. instn.; founder, dir. World Wide Hollis Internat. Law Ctr., 2001—. Advisor to past Pres.; chmn. Oreg. Dem. party, 1966-68; chmn. law and justice com. Nat. Conf. Legislators, 1977-78; adv. com. to State and Local Law Initiative., Washington; participants com. Washington Pub. Power Supply System, 1982-88; candidate for nomination for gov., 1986; bd. dirs. Wayne Morse Hist. Park; mgr. Stille Nacht Found., 1990—. Lt. USNR, 1951-54. Recipient First Pioneer award U. Oreg., 1980, Assn. Oreg. Counties award for leadership in the reform of state ct. system, 1982; named to the Order of Coif. Mem. ABA (internat. law, pub. utility law), Oreg. State Bar Assn. (chmn. uniform laws com. 1962-64), Alpha Pi Zeta, Phi Alpha Delta. Methodist. Avocations: canoeing, backpacking, hunting, riding, poetry.

FAGAN, PETER LEDFORD, lawyer, naval officer; b. Key West, Fla., Sept. 11, 1951; s. Monroe Eriskine and Corene Polly (Ledford) F.; m. Pamela Ann Pettitt, May 21, 1977; children: Justin, Nicole, Christie, Sean, Ian, Amy. BS, Ind. U., 1972; JD, U. San Diego, 1976, LLM, 1988; MS, Nat. War Coll., 1994. Bar: Iowa 1976, Calif. 1995, U.S. Dist. Ct. (so. dist.) Iowa 1976, U.S. Dist. Ct. (we. dist.) Wash. 1981, U.S. Ct. Mil. Appeals 1976. Commd. ensign USN, 1973, advanced through grades to capt., 1994; internat. law atty./trial and def. counsel Naval Legal Svc. Office, Subic Bay, Philippines, 1977-79; legal officer USN, San Diego, 1979-81; staff judge advocate/spl. asst. U.S. atty. Naval Submarine Base Bangor, Seattle, 1981-84; sr. trial counsel Naval Legal Svc. Office, San Diego, 1984-87; spl. asst. to vice chief naval ops. USN, Washington, 1988-89, spl. asst. to Sec. of Navy for legal/legis. affairs, 1989-94, force judge advocate, Commdr. Naval Air Forces Pacific, 1994-97; commanding officer Naval Legal Svc. Office S.W., 1997—99; cir. judge, 1999—. Mem. Naval War Coll. Internat. Law Adv. Bd., 1989—. Mem. ABA, ATLA, Iowa Bar Assn., Calif. Bar Assn., Judge Advs. Assn. Republican. Episcopalian. Avocations: racquetball, skiing, squash, camping, jogging. Home: 379 F Ave Coronado CA 92118-1230 Office: Naval Legal Svc Office SW Naval Sta Box 368138 3205 Senn Rd San Diego CA 92136-5090

FAGEN, LESLIE GORDON, lawyer; b. N.Y.C., Apr. 12, 1950; s. Herman and Estelle (Garber) F. BA, Yale U., 1971; JD, Columbia U., 1974. Bar: N.Y. 1975, D.C. 1985, U.S. Dist. Ct. (so. and ea. dists.) N.Y. 1975, U.S. Ct. Appeals (2d cir.) 1975, U.S. Ct. Appeals (3d cir.) 1991, U.S. Ct. Appeals (7th and fed. cirs.) 1993; U.S. Supreme Ct. 1978. Law clk to judge U.S. Dist. Ct. (ea. dist.) N.Y., Bklyn., 1975; assoc. Milbank, Tweed, Hadley & McCloy, N.Y.C., 1975-76; from assoc. to ptnr. Paul, Weiss, Rifkind, Wharton & Garrison, N.Y.C., 1976—. Former adj. faculty Cardozo Law Sch., CCNY. Vice-chmn., pres. and trustee The Ednl. Alliance, Inc., 1993—. Mem. N.Y. State Bar Assn., Assn. Bar City N.Y. Federal civil litigation, State civil litigation. Office: Paul Weiss Rifkind Wharton & Garrison Ste 2330 1285 Avenue Of The Americas Fl 21 New York NY 10019-6028

FAGEN, PETER KIRK, lawyer; b. Sigourney, Iowa, Dec. 5, 1960; s. Walter Jr. and Charlotte Louise (Kirkpatrick) F.; m. Sarah Ann Mitchell, Aug. 10, 1985; 1 child, Andrew Mitchell. BA in Polit. Sci. and History, U. No. Iowa, 1983; JD, U. Iowa, 1988. Bar: Calif. 1989, U.S. Dist. Ct. (ea. dist.) Calif. 1989, U.S. Dist. Ct. (no., so. and cen. dists.) Calif. 1990, U.S. Ct. Appeals (9th cir.) 1994. Law clk. Phelan Tucker Boyle & Mullen, Iowa City, 1986-88, McCormick Barstow Sheppard Wayte & Carruth, Fresno, Calif., summer 1987, assoc., 1988-92, Lozano Smith Smith Woliver & Behrens, Fresno, 1992-95, shareholder, 1996—; mng. shareholder Lozano Smith, San Diego and L.A., Calif., 1998—. Mem. adv. bd. Fresno City Coll. Paralegal Program, 1997-98; spkr. and presenter in field. Contbr. articles to legal jours. Bd. dirs. Northside Christian Early Childhood Devel. Ctr., Fresno, 1995-98, Northside Christian Ch., Fresno, 1994-95; legis. field dir. Rep. Party of Iowa, Des Moines, 1984, cons., 1985; mem. attendence boundary task force Oceanside Unified Sch. Dist., 2002-03. Stipendee U. No. Iowa, 1982. Avocations: travel, sports, reading. General civil litigation, Education and schools, Labor (including EEOC, Fair Labor Standards Act, labor-management relations, NLRB, OSHA). Office: Lozano Smith 2800 28th St Ste 240 Santa Monica CA 90405 also: Lozano Smith 450 S Melrose Dr Ste 100 Vista CA 92083

FAGERBERG, ROGER RICHARD, lawyer; b. Chgo., Dec. 11, 1935; s. Richard Emil and Evelyn (Thor) F.; m. Virginia Fuller Vaughan, June 20, 1959; children: Steven Roger, Susan Vaughan, James Thor, Laura Craft. BS in Bus. Adminstrn., Washington U., St. Louis, 1958, JD, 1961, postgrad., 1961-62. Bar: Mo. 1961. Grad. teaching asst. Washington U., St. Louis, 1961-62; assoc. firm Rassieur, Long & Yawitz, St. Louis, 1962-64; ptnr. Rassieur, Long, Yawitz & Schneider and predecessor firms, St. Louis, 1965-91; pvt. practice St. Louis, 1991—. Mem. exec. com. Citizens' Adv. Council Pkwy. Sch. Dist., 1974—, pres.-elect, 1976-77, pres., 1977-78; bd. dirs. Parkway Residents Orgn., 1969—, v.p., 1970-73, pres., 1973—; scoutmaster Boy Scouts Am., 1979-83; Presbyn. elder, 1976—, pres. three local congs. 1968-70, 77-78, 83-84. Mem. ABA, Mo. Bar Assn., St. Louis Bar Assn., Christian Bus. Men's Com. (bd. dirs. 1975-78, 87-91), Full Gospel Bus. Men's Fellowship, Order of Coif, Omicron Delta Kappa, Beta Gamma Sigma, Pi Sigma Alpha, Phi Eta Sigma, Phi Delta Phi, Kappa Sigma. Lodges: Kiwanis (bd. dirs. 1988-91), Masons, Shriners. Republican. Corporate, general, Probate (including wills, trusts), Taxation, general. Home and Office: 13812 Clayton Rd Chesterfield MO 63017-8407

FAGG, GEORGE GARDNER, federal judge; b. Eldora, Iowa, Apr. 30, 1934; s. Ned and Arleene (Gardner) Fagg; m. Jane E. Wood, Aug. 19, 1956; children: Martha, Thomas, Ned, Susan, George, Sarah. BSBA, Drake U., 1965, JD, 1958. Bar: Iowa 1958. Ptnr. Cartwright, Druker, Ryden & Fagg, Marshalltown, Iowa, 1958—72; judge Iowa Dist. Ct., 1972—82, U.S. Ct. Appeals (8th cir.), 1982—99, sr. judge, 1999—. Faculty Nat. Jud. Coll., 1979. Mem.: Iowa Bar Assn., Order of Coif. Office: US Ct Appeals US Courthouse Annex 110 E Court Ave Ste 455 Des Moines IA 50309-2044

FAHEY, WILLIAM THOMAS, II, lawyer; b. Dec. 27, 1949; s. William T. and Mildred K. (Flood) F.; m. Elizabeth Ann Acord, May 3, 1975; children: William T., Sean E., Erin E. BBA, U. Notre Dame, 1970; JD, Duke U., 1973. Bar: W.Va. 1973, U.S. Dist. Ct. (no. dist.) W.Va. 1978, U.S. Ct. Appeals (4th and 6th cirs.) 1981, U.S. Tax Ct. 1985. Spl. counsel W.Va. State Auditor, Charleston, 1973-77; assoc. Pinsky, Barnes, Watson, Cuomo & Hinerman, Weirton, W.Va, 1977-79; ptnr. Barnes, Watson, Cuomo, Hinerman & Fahey, Weirton, W.Va, 1980-84, Hinerman, Fahey & Risovich, Weirton, 1984-85, Hinerman and Fahey, Weirton, 1985-98; pvt. practice Weirton, 1998—2000; ptnr. Fahey & Risovich Law Office, Weirton, 2001—. Asst. pros. atty. Hancock County, Weirton, 1977-78, 90—; spl. counsel Weirton City mgr., 2001—; dist. character com. W.Va. Supreme Ct., 1985—; pres. Hancock County Civil Service, New Cumberland, W.Va., 1978-81; city solicitor City of New Cumberland, 1978-89; commr. State Delinquent Lands, Charleston, 1977-95; mem. water bd. City of Weirton, 1978-89; bd. dirs. Hancock County Sr. Citizens, Inc., New Cumberland, 1978-89; spl. pros. atty. Brooke County, Ohio County, W.Va., 1998—. Mem. ABA, W.Va. State Bar, W.Va. Trial Lawyers Assn. (bd. govs. 1989—), Assn. Trial Lawyers Am., Williams Country Club, Notre Dame Monogram Club, K.C. (adv. 1979—), Am. Quarter Horse Assn. (World Champion Stallion award 1998), Weirton Rotary Club (pres. 2003). Republican. Roman Catholic. State civil litigation, Personal injury (including property damage), Probate (including wills, trusts). Home: 1480 Cove Rd Weirton WV 26062-3820 Office: Fahey & Risovich 2116 Pennsylvania Ave Weirton WV 26062-3526 E-mail: wfahey@prodigy.net.

FAHEY SANDELL, JACQUELYN MARIE, lawyer; b. Boston, Aug. 12, 1968; arrived in Italy, 2000; d. Joseph Clarke and June Carole Fahey. BA, Duke U., 1990; JD magna cum laude, Boston U., 1995. Bar: N.Y. 1996, Mass. 1996. Assoc. Shearman & Sterling, NYC, 1995—98, London, 1998—2000, Allen & Overy, Rome, 2000—. Securities, Corporate, general, Mergers and acquisitions. Office: Allen & Overy Corso Vittorio Emanuele II 284 00186 Rome Italy

FAHLBECK, REINHOLD HANS, legal studies educator; b. Stockholm, July 9, 1938; s. Erik and Gertrud F.; m. Marie Christine Anckarsvard, June 8, 1963. BA, U. Lund, 1963, LLB, 1967, LLM, 1972, LLD, 1974. Faculty dept. bus. econs. U. Lund (Sweden) Law Sch., 1963-66, asst. prof. pvt. law, 1974-78, assoc prof., 1978-80; pvt. practice Stockholm, 1967-77; prof. labor law Stockholm Sch. Econs., 1980—. Chmn. India-Bangladesh sect. Emmaus-Swallos, Caritas Lund; vis. prof. Sophia U., Tokyo, 1989, 94, Stanford Law Sch., 1990, Jagiellonian U., Crakow, Poland, 1992. Mem. editl. bd. Internat. Jour. Comparative Labour Law and Indsl. Rels., Holland, Comparative Labor Law and Policy Jour. Recipient Pro Ecclesie et Pontifice medal, 2001; Zorn fellow, 1981. Fellow Am. Coun. Learned Socs., Japan Found.; mem. U.S. Nat. Acad. Arbitrators (fgn. corr.). Home: 26 Nyckelkroken S226 47 Lund Sweden Office: Stockholm Sch Econs Box 6501 S113 83 Stockholm Sweden E-mail: reinhold.fahlbeck@jur.lu.se.

FAHRENKOPF, FRANK JOSEPH, JR., lawyer; b. Bklyn., Aug. 28, 1939; s. Frank J. and Rose (Freeman) F.; m. Mary Ethel Bandoni, Aug. 25, 1962; children: Allison Marie, Leslie Ann, Amy Michelle. BA, U. Nev., 1962; JD, U. Calif., Berkeley, 1965. Bar: Nev. 1965, D.C. 1983. Assoc. atty. Breen & Young, Reno, 1965-67; ptnr., atty. Sanford, Sanford, Fahrenkopf & Mousel, Reno, 1967-75, Fahrenkopf, Mortimer, Sourwine, Mousel & Sloane, Reno, 1976-85, Hogan & Hartson, Washington, 1985—; pres., CEO Am. Gaming Assn., 1995—. Instr. criminal law U. Nev., 1967-82; panelist reporter Citizens Conf. on Nev. Cts., 1968; mem. Nev. Bd. Bar Examiners, 1971-85; judge pro tem Reno Municipal Ct., 1972-85; mem. faculty Nat. Jud. Coll., Reno, 1974-83; chmn. Coun. for the Future, Nat. Jud. Coll., 1990-94, bd. trustees, 1995-2000. Chmn. lawyers divsn. United Fund, 1969-70; chmn. Rep. Nat. Com., 1983-89; chmn. Nev. Rep. Com., 1975-83, gen. counsel, 1972-75; No. Nev. co-chmn. Com. for Re-election of Pres., 1972; mem. exec. bd. Nev. Rep. Cen. Com., 1969; nat. committeeman Nev. Young Reps., 1969-73; mem. Rep. Nat. Com., 1975-89; del. Rep. Nat. Conv., 1972, 76, 80, 84, 88; chmn. Western States Rep. Chmn.'s Assn., 1978-83; nat. chmn. Rep. State Chmn.'s Assn., 1981-83; bd. dirs. Nev. Cancer Soc., chmn., 1978-87; bd. dirs. Washoe County Legal Aid Soc., Babe Ruth Baseball League, Nev. Opera Guild, Reno YWCA, Sierra Sage coun. Camp Fire Girls, 1974-76, Nat. Endowment Democracy, 1938-93, Am. Coun. Young Polit. Leaders, 1983-89; co-chmn. Nat. Commn. on Presdl. Debates, 1987—, Commn. on Nat. Polit. Conv., 1989-93; vice chmn. Ctr. Democracy, 1995-98; dep. chmn. Internat. Dem. Union, 1983-98; chmn. Pacific Dem. Union, 1983. With AUS, 1957. Recipient Disting. Service award U.S. Jaycees, 1973, Humanitarian award NCCJ, 1981 Mem. Am. Judicature Soc., Comml. Law League Am., ABA (mem. gov. coun. gen. practice sect., internat. law com., chmn. Coalition for Justice 1993-95), Am. Trial Lawyers Assn., No. Nev. Trial Lawyers Assn. (v.p. 1969), State Bar Nev., Washoe County Bar Assn. (pres. 1973-74), Execs. Assn. Reno (dir. 1973-74), Nat. Assn. Gaming Attys. (v.p. 1981, pres. 1982-83), Barristers Club Nev. (v.p. 1969-73), Alpha Tau Omega. Administrative and regulatory, Commercial, contracts (including sales of goods; commercial financing). Office: 555 13th St NW Ste 1010E Washington DC 20004-1147 E-mail: agafjf@aol.com.

FAHRNBRUCH, DALE E. retired state supreme court justice; b. Lincoln, Nebr., Sept. 13, 1924; s. Henry and Bessie M. (Osborne) F.; m. Margaret L. Hunt, July 4, 1952; children: Rebecca Kay Fahrnbruch Braymen, Daniel D. (dec.). AD in Journalism, U. Nebr., 1948, BS in Law, 1950; JD, Creighton U., 1951; LLM, U. Va., 1986. Bar: Nebr. 1951, U.S. Ct. Appeals (8th cir.) 1969. City editor Jour. Newspaper, Lincoln, 1951-52; asst., then dep. county atty. Lancaster County, Lincoln, Nebr., 1952-55, chief dep. county atty., 1955-59; ptnr. Beynon, Hecht & Fahrnbruch, Lincoln, 1959-73; dist. judge Nebr. Lincoln, 1973-87; justice Nebr. Supreme Ct., Lincoln, 1987-97.

FAIGNANT, JOHN PAUL, lawyer, educator; b. Proctor, Vt., Mar. 24, 1953; s. Joseph Paul and Ann (DeBlasio) F.; children: Janelle, Melissa. BA, U. New Haven, 1974; JD, George Mason U., 1978. Bar: Va. 1978, Vt. 1979, U.S. Dist. Ct. Vt. 1979, U.S. Ct. Appeals (4th cir.) 1979, U.S. Supreme Ct. 1992. Assoc. Griffin & Griffin, Rutland, Vt., 1978-79, Miller, Norton & Cleary, Rutland, 1979-84, ptnr., 1984-87, Miller, Cleary and Faignant PC, Rutland, 1988-91, Miller & Faignant, Ltd., Rutland, 1991-97, Miller Faignant & Whelton PC (now Miller Faignant & Behrens), Rutland, 1997—. Adj. prof. Coll. St. Joseph, Rutland, 1982-90. Mem. Rutland Town Fire Dept., 1989—; mem., pres. No. New England Def. Counsel, 1995-96. Mem. Va. Bar Assn., Vt. Bar Assn., Assn. Trial Lawyers Am., Def. Rsch. Inst., Am. Bd. Trial Advocates. Roman Catholic. Avocation: antique trucks. General civil litigation, Insurance, Personal injury (including property damage). Home: RR 1 Box 3762 Rutland VT 05701-9214 Office: Miller Faignant & Behrens PC 36 Merchants Row PO Box 6688 Rutland VT 05702-6688

FAIN, JOEL MAURICE, lawyer; b. Miami Beach, Fla., Dec. 11, 1953; s. William Maurice and Carolyn Genievive (Baggett) F.; m. Moira Joan Slocum, June 15, 1974; children: Hannah Ruth, Dylan Michael, Rachel Joan. BA, Yale U., 1975; JD, U. Conn., 1978. Bar: Conn. 1978, U.S. Dist. Ct. Conn. 1978, U.S. Ct. Appeals (2d cir.) 1989, U.S. Supreme Ct. 1999. Assoc. Kahan, Kerensky, Capossela, Levine & Breslau, Vernon, Conn., 1978-83, ptnr., 1984-90, mng. ptnr., 1990-91; ptnr. Morrison, Mahoney & Miller, Hartford, Conn., 1992—. Chmn. Youth Adv. Bd., Tolland, Conn., 1983-92; chmn. Tolland Town Coun., 1995-97. Mem. ABA, Conn. Bar Assn., Tolland County Bar Assn. (pres. 1991-92), Assn. Trial Lawyers Am., Conn. Trial Lawyers Assn., Lions (pres. 1987-88). Democrat. Congregationalist. Insurance, Professional liability, Personal injury (including property damage). Home: 140 Huyshope Ave Hartford CT 06106-2857 Office: Morrison Mahoney & Miller 1 Constitution Plaza Hartford CT 06103-4506

FAIRBAIRN, SYDNEY ELISE, lawyer; b. Fullerton, Calif., Feb. 20, 1963; d. Robin H. and Yvonne A. Fairbairn. BA in Rhetoric, BA in Anthropology, U. Calif., Berkeley, 1982; JD, Golden Gate U., 1985. Bar: Calif. 1986. Pvt. practice, San Rafael, Calif., 1986—. Atty. YWCA, San Anselmo, Calif., 1995—. Mem. Marin County Bar Assn. (chair ins. sect. 1999—), Marin County Women's Bar Assn. (pres. 2002-03), Mission San Rafael, Rotary. Democrat. General civil litigation, Personal injury (including property damage), Property, real (including real estate development, water). Office: Ste A-110 Seven Mt Lassen Dr San Rafael CA 94903 E-mail: s.e.fairbairn@att.net.

FAIRBANK, ROBERT HAROLD, lawyer; b. Northampton, Mass., Mar. 4, 1948; s. William Martin and Jane (Davenport) F.;children: Sarah Julia, David Kivy. AB in Polit. Sci., Stanford U., 1972; MLS, U. Calif.-Berkeley, 1973; JD, NYU, 1977. Bar: Calif. 1977, U.S. Dist. Ct. (cen. and no. dists.) Calif. 1978, U.S. Dist. Ct. (so. dist.) Calif. 1993. Assoc. Gibson, Dunn & Crutcher, L.A., 1977-84, ptnr., 1985-96; co-founding ptnr. Fairbank & Vincent, 1996—. Lawyer rep., co-chair 9th cir. Jud. Conf. Ctrl. Dist., 2000—02; bd. dirs. 9th Jud. Cir. Hist. Soc., 2003—. Author: Effective Pretrial and Trial Motions, 1983, California Practice Guide: Civil Trials and Evidence (The Rutter Group 1993, with yearly updates); mem. editl. bd. NYU Law Rev., 1975-76. Named One of Top 100 Bus. Lawyers in L.A., L.A. Bus. Jour., 1995. Mem. Assn. Bus. Trial Lawyers (co-founder San Francisco and Orange County chpts., bd. govs. 1984-85, treas. 1986-87, sec. 1987-88, v.p. 1988-89, pres. 1989-90), L.A. County Bar Assn. (fed. cts. com. 1983-85), Jud. Coun. Calif. Adv. Com. on Local Rules (subcom. chair on civil trial rules). Federal civil litigation, State civil litigation, Securities. Office: Fairbank & Vincent 11755 Wilshire Blvd Ste 2320 Los Angeles CA 90025-1501 E-mail: rfairbank@fairbankvincent.com.

FAIRBANKS, ROBERT ALVIN, lawyer; b. Oklahoma City, July 9, 1944; s. Albert Edward and Lucille Imogene (Scherer) F.; m. Linda Gayle Geer, Aug. 26, 1967; children: Chele Lyn, Kimberly Jo, Robert Alvin II, Michael Albert, Richard Alan, Joseph Alexander. BS in Math., U. Okla., 1967, JD, 1973; MBA, Oklahoma City U., 1970, MCJA, 1975; LLM, Columbia U., 1976; MA, Stanford U., 1984; MEd, Harvard U., 1993. Bar: Okla. 1974, U.S. Dist. Ct. (we. dist.) Okla. 1974, U.S. Ct. Customs and Patent Appeals 1974, U.S. Ct. Mil. Appeals, 1974, U.S. Tax Ct. 1974, U.S. Claims Ct. 1975, U.S. Customs Ct. 1975, U.S. Ct. Appeals (10th cir.) 1975, U.S. Supreme Ct. 1977, U.S. Dist. Ct. (ea. dist.) Okla. 1984, Minn. 1993. Commd. 2d lt. USAF, 1967, advanced through grades to capt., 1970; col. USAFR, 1986; asst. staff judge adv., chief of claims div. Office of Staff Judge Adv., Tinker AFB, Okla., 1974-75; legal asst. to Justice William A. Berry, Okla. Supreme Ct., 1977; pvt. practice Norman, Okla., 1974—; v.p. St. Gregory's U., Shawnee, Okla., 1997—. Instr. bus. adminstrn. U. Md. Far East div., Nha Trang, Viet Nam, 1970-71, Rose State Coll., Midwest City, Okla., 1974; rsch. assoc. in law U. Okla., Norman, 1974, spl. lectr., 1974-75, vis. asst. prof., 1976-77, adj. prof. law, 1984—; vis. asst. prof. law Oklahoma City U., 1977; asst. prof. law U. Ark., Fayetteville, Arks., 1977-81; assoc. prof. law La. State U., Baton Rouge, 1981; rsch. asst. dept. family, community and preventative medicine Stanford (Calif.) Med. Sch., 1981-82; adj. asst. prof. govt. contract law Air Force Inst. Tech., Wright-Patterson AFB, Ohio, 1985—; v.p. St. Gregory's U., Shawnee, Okla.; prof. bus. adminstrn. U. Phoenix; adj. prof. law and mgmt. Okla. Christian U. Coll. Bus.; cons. Cheyenne Tribe, Clinton, Okla., 1977-81, 90, Citizens Band of Pottawatomie Tribe, Shawnee, Okla., 1977-79, Inst. for Devel. of Indian Law, Washington, 1976-81; dir. Native Am. Coll. Prep. Ctr. Bemidji State U., Minn., 1993—. Editor-in-chief Am. Indian Law Rev., 1973; editor Okla. Law Rev., 1971-73; producer, dir.: (with Barbara P. Ettinger) "Aa-Niin" film, 1994; author book revs.; contbr. articles to profl. jours. Mem. bd. control Fayetteville (Ark.) City Hosp., 1977-81; cubmaster Boy Scouts Am., Norman, 1982-83, asst. scoutmaster, Stanford, 1981, scoutmaster, Norman, 1990-91, com. mem., den leader, 1988; softball coach Jr. High Girls League, Fayetteville, 1977-81; mem. adv. bd. Native Am. Prep. Sch., Santa Fe; pres., chmn. bd. Native Am. Coll. Prep. Ctr., Bemidji, Minn.; mem. exec. adv. bd. Aerospace Sci. and Tech. Edn. Ctr. of Okla., Okla. City Univ.; mem. legal edn. com., Okla. Bar Assn. U.S. Dept. Edn. fellow Stanford U. Med. Sch.; Charles Evans Hughes fellow Columbia U. Law Sch., 1976; Sequoyah fellow Assn. Am. Indian Affairs, 1975-76; Mellon fellow Harvard U. Sch. Edn., 1993; nominee Pulitzer prize for Disting. Commentary, 1997. Mem. ABA, Okla. Bar Assn., Fed. Bar Assn., Am. Trial Lawyers Assn., Okla. Trial Lawyers Assn., Okla. Indian Bar Assn., Oklahoma County Bar Assn., Assn. Am. Law Schs., N.G. Assn. U.S., Air Force Assn. (life), Res. Officers Assn. (life), Nat. Contract Mgmt. Assn., Soc. Logistics Engrs., Phi Alpha Delta, Phi Delta Epsilon, Phi Delta Kappa. Republican. Roman Catholic. Entertainment, Personal injury (including property damage). Office: 2212 Westpark Dr Norman OK 73069-4012 E-mail: ojibwe@oklahoma.net., robert.fairbanks@oc.edu.

FAIRCHILD, THOMAS E. federal judge; b. Milw., Dec. 25, 1912; s. Edward Thomas and Helen (Edwards) Fairchild; m. Eleanor E. Dahl, July 24, 1937; children: Edward, Susan, Jennifer, Andrew. Student, Princeton, 1931—33; AB, Cornell U., 1934; LLB, U. Wis., 1938. Bar: Wis. 1938. Practiced, Portage, Wis., 1938—41, Milw., 1945—48, 1953—57; atty. OPA, Chgo., Milw., 1941—45; hearing commr. Chgo. Region, 1945; atty. gen. Wis., 1948—51; consultant Office of Price Stabilization, 1951; U.S. atty. for Western Dist. Wis., 1951—52; justice Supreme Ct. Wis., 1957—66, U.S. Ct. Appeals for 7th Circuit, 1966—75; chief judge, 1975—81; sr. judge, 1981—. Dem. candidate Senator from Wis., 1950, 1952. Mem.: KP, FBA, ABA, Am. Law Inst., Am. Judicature Soc., Dane County Bar Assn., 7th Cir. Bar Assn., Milw. Bar Assn., Wis. Bar Assn., Phi Delta Phi. Democrat. Mem. United Church Of Christ. Office: US Courthouse Rm 2764 219 S Dearborn St Chicago IL 60604-1702

FAIRHURST, MARY E. judge; BA in Polit. Sci. cum laude, Gonzaga U., 1979, JD magna cum laude, 1984. Jud. clk. to Hon. William H. Williams U.S. Supreme Ct., 1984, jud. clk. to Hon. William C. Goodloe, 1986; with Wash. Atty. Gen.'s Office, chief revenue, bankruptcy and collections divsn.; justice Wash. State Supreme Ct., Olympia, 2003—. Mem. pacific peak coun. Girls Scouts U.S. Bd.; fundraiser YMCA Youth and Govt. Program; mem. Supreme Ct.'s Gender and Justice Commn., Access Justice Bd. Com.; mem. bd. advisors Gonzaga Law Sch. Recipient Myra Bradwell award, Gonzaga U., 1999. Mem.: Wash. Women Lawyers (pres., Passing the Torch award 1999), Wash. State Bar Assn. (pres., mem. bd. govs.). Office: Wash Supreme Ct PO Box 40929 415 12th Ave SW Olympia WA 98504-0929 Office Fax: 360-357-2067. Business E-Mail: supreme@courts.wa.gov.

FALBAUM, BERTRAM SEYMOUR, law educator, investigator; b. N.Y.C., July 28, 1934; s. Abraham and Shari (Greenfield) Falbaum; m. Roberta Jessie Oberstone, Sept. 1, 1957; children: Vance Leonard, Stacy Lynn. AA, L.A. City Coll., 1961; BS with honors, Calif. State U., L.A., 1962; postgrad., George Washington U., 1966—68; MPA, Syracuse U., 1972. Lic. pvt. investigator Va., Washington, Ariz. Agt. U.S. Customs Svc., L.A. and Nogales, Ariz., 1961—66, spl. agt. Washington, 1969—73; instr. Treasury Law Enforcement Sch., Washington, 1966—69; dep. chief law enforcement U.S. Fish & Wildlife Svc., Washington, 1973—78, spl. projects officer, 1978—79; sr. criminal investigator U.S. Dept. Justice (office spl. investigations), Washington, 1979—86; v.p. The Investigative Group, Inc., Washington, 1986—92; pres. Investigative Dynamics, Inc., Tucson, 1992—. Adj. prof. Am. U., 1977—78, 1990—91; bd. dirs. Forensic Scis. Corp.; adv. bd. Found. Genetic Medicine, Inc. Chmn. troop com. Nat. Capital Area coun. Boy Scouts Am., Centreville, Va., 1974—77; bd. dirs. 88-CRIME, 1998, pres., 2002. Served with USAF, 1953—57. Recipient commendations, U.S. Customs Svc., U.S. Dept. Justice. Fellow: Am. Bd. Forensic Examiners; mem.: INTELNET (adv. bd. 1997—), Vidocq Soc., Customs Spl. Agt. Assn. (pres. 1994—), Internat. Assn. Law Enforcement Intelligence Analysts, Global Investigators Network, World Investigators Network, Calif. Assn. Licensed Investigatons, Pvt. Investigators Assn. of Va., Pvt. Investigators and Security Assn., Nat. Assn. Chief of Police, Fraternal Order of Police, Fraternal Order of Border Agts., Fed. Law Enforcement Officers Assn., Ariz. Assn. Lic. Pvt. Investigators (bd. dirs. 1994—96, pres. 1997, 2000), Nat. Coun. Investigation and Security Svcs. (bd. dirs. 1998), Assn. of Former Intelligence Officers, So. Ariz. Counter Intelligence Corps Assn., Am. Criminal Justice Assn. (life; chpt. pres. 1959—61), Internat. Assn. Chiefs of Police (life), Am. Coll. Forensic Examiners (life; cert.), Internat. Narcotic Enforcement Officers Assn., Nat. Assn. Legal Investigators, World Assn. Detectives, Coun. Internat. Investigators (treas. 2002—, cert.), Nat. Dist. Attys. Assn., Am. Soc. Indsl. Security (cert. protection profl.), Assn. Cert. Fraud Examiners (cert.), Am. Law Enforcement Officers Assn., Am. Fedn. Police, Fed. Criminal Investigators Assn., Am. Judicature Soc., Assn. Fed. Investigators (bd. dirs. 1979—86, cert. profl. investigator), 88-CRIME (bd. dirs. 1998—, pres. 2002—), La Paloma Country Club (golf com. and handicap chmn. 1994—95, vice chmn. 1996—98, chmn. 1999—2000, vice chmn. 2002), Chantilly Country Club (v.p. for golf 1978, 1980, 1981, 1983, bd. dirs. 1984, chmn. bd. 1985—89), Lambda Alpha Epsilon (life). Home: 4921 N Fort Verde Trl Tucson AZ 85750-5903 E-mail: bertfalbaum@compuserve.com.

FALES, HALIBURTON, II, lawyer; b. N.Y.C., Aug. 7, 1919; s. DeCoursey and Dorothy Mildred (Mitchell) F.; m. Katharine Ladd, Dec. 27, 1941; children: Nancy, Haliburton, Priscilla, Lucy, William E. Ladd. Student, Harvard U., 1938-41; LLB, Columbia U., 1947. Bar: N.Y. 1948, U.S. Supreme Ct. 1957. Assoc. firm White & Case, N.Y.C., 1947-58, ptnr. firm, 1959-88, of counsel, 1988-90, ret. ptnr., 1991—. Spl. master Appellate div. 1st dept. N.Y. State Supreme Ct., 1983—, chmn. departmental discipline com., 1991—96, special counsel, 1997—; nat. ctr. for state courts Warren Burger Assoc., 2002. Author: Trying Cases A Life in the Law, 1997; contbr. articles to profl. jours. Trustee, pres. emeritus Pierpont Morgan Libr.; trustee St. Barnabas Hosp., 1949-96, trustee emeritus, 1996—; sr. warden St. Luke's Ch., 1967-93; bd. dirs. Union Theol. Sem., 1986-94; bd. visitors Columbia Law Sch., 1993-98, emeritus, 1998—. Lt. comdr. USNR, 1941-45. Recipient Columbia U. medal, 1994. Fellow Am. Bar Found., N.Y. Bar Found., Inst. Judicial Adminstrn., Am. Coll. Trial Lawyers; mem. ABA, Albert Gallatin Assocs., Am. Judicature Soc., Am. Law Inst. (life), Assn. of Bar of City of N.Y., N.Y. County Lawyers Assn. (William Nelson Cromwell award 1998), N.Y. State Bar Assn. (pres. 1983-84, chair task force on the prof., 1994-96), Columbia Law Sch. Assn., Inc. (pres. 1991-92), St. Paul's Sch. Alumni Assn. (v.p. 1988-92), Alumni Fedn. Columbia U. Home: 560 Pottersville Rd Gladstone NJ 07934-2046 Office: c/o White & Case 1155 Ave of Americas New York NY 10036-2711

FALEY, R(ICHARD) SCOTT, lawyer; b. Trenton, N.J., Aug. 18, 1947; s. Henry and Winifred (Goeke) F.; m. Josepha Ann Bartlett, Aug. 29, 1970; children: Scott Joseph, Zachary Lorin, Katherine Winifred. BA, Georgetown U., 1969, JD, 1972; LLM, George Washington U., 1975. Bar: D.C. 1973, U.S. Tax Ct. 1973, U.S. Dist. Ct. D.C. 1973, Mont. 1996. Assoc., ptnr. Danzansky, Dickey, Tydings, Quint & Gordon, Washington, 1972-78; prin. R. Scott Faley, P.C., Washington, 1978—. Bd. dir. Fed. Employees News Digest, Inc., Fairfax, Va., 1980—; bd. dir., pres. NCC Trout Unltd., 1985—; del. Mid Atlantic Coun. Trout Unltd., 1985—, v.p., 1992—; bd. dirs. Falling Springs Greenway, Inc., Chambersburg, Pa. Inst. for Safety Analysis, Inc., Rockville, Md., 1980-89. Contbr. articles to profl. jours. Mem. instnl. rev. com. Sibley Meml. Hosp., Washington, 1980—. Capt. USAF, 1974. Mem. ABA, FBA, Univ. Club, Boca Bay Pass Club, The Williams Club, Alpha Phi Omega, Phi Alpha Delta. Roman Catholic. Estate planning, Pension, profit-sharing, and employee benefits, Taxation, general. Home: 25 Primrose St Chevy Chase MD 20815-4228 Office: Ste 401 5100 Wisconsin Ave NW Washington DC 20016-4119 Fax: 202-363-7355. E-mail: faleyfish@aol.com.

FALGOUR, TILMAN JOSEPH, III, lawyer; b. Galveston, Tex., Feb. 4, 1949; s. Tilman J. Falgout, Jr. and Estelle Holste; m. Melanie A. Falgout, Nov. 20, 1976; children: Kiley E. Falgout, Beau Falgout. BA, Tulane U., 1972, JD, 1974. Bar: Tex. Atty. Childs, Fortenbach, Beck & Guerton, Houston, 1974—78, Stumpf & Falgout, Houston, 1978—95; CEO, gen. counsel America's Car Mart, Dallas, 1995—. Mem.: Dallas Bar Assn., Tex. Bar Assn. Avocations: tennis, golf. Corporate, general. Office: Americas Car Mart Inc 4040 N MacArthur Blvd #100 Irving TX 75038

FALKNER, WILLIAM CARROLL, lawyer; b. Baird, Tex., Mar. 26, 1954; s. Vernon Lee and Eunice Vera (Fore) F.; m. Linda May (Tilley), May 23, 1987; children: Heather Lynn, Holly Ann. BA in Govt., Tarleton State U., Stephenville, Tex., 1976; JD, Stetson U., Gulfport, Fla., 1984. Bar: Fla. 1984, U.S. Dist. Ct. (mid. dist.) Fla. 1985, U.S. Ct. Appeals (11th cir.) 1985. Asst. co. atty., sr. asst. co. atty. Pinellas County Atty.'s Office, Clearwater, Fla., 1985—. Editor Res Ipsa, Clearwater, Fla., 1992-93; contbr. articles to profl. jours. Col. U.S. Army Res., 1976—. Mem. ABA, Fla. Bar Assoc., Clearwater Bar Assoc. Baptist. Avocations: reading, writing, sports, biblical studies. Office: Pinellas County Atty's Office 315 Court St Clearwater FL 33756-5165 E-mail: bfalkner@co.pinellas.fl.us.

FALL, ROBERT J. lawyer; b. Homestead, Pa., July 22, 1955; s. Philip J. and Alice A. Fall; m. Patricia A. Hammerton, Oct. 16, 1982; children: Meghan, Kelsey. BS in Sociology, St. Joseph's Coll., Rensselaer, Ind., 1977; JD, Ohio No. U., 1980. Bar: Pa. 1980, U.S. Dist. Ct. (we. dist.) Pa. 1980. Atty. Neighborhood Legal Svcs. Assn., Pitts., 1980-82, Wymard, Dunn, Gordon, Fall, Pitts., 1982-90, Babb, Fall & Assocs. P.C., Pitts. and Wexford, Pa., 1990-96; sole practitioner Pitts. and Wexford, 1996-2000; atty. Raphael, Ramsden & Behers, P.C., 2000—. Bd. dirs. St. Nicholas Ch., Homestead, Pa., 1980-85, Cmty. Alcoholism Svcs. of Beaver County, Beaver, Pa., 1981-90; mem. McCandless (Pa.) Rep. Com., 1990—; vol. firefighter Ingomar Vol. Fire Co., McCandless, 1998—; mgr., coach McCandless Athletic Assn., 1992-2000; pres. Western Pa. Children's Charities, Inc., 2000—. Family and matrimonial, General practice, Probate (including wills, trusts). Office: 1200 Frick Bldg 437 Grant St Pittsburgh PA 15219

FALLEK, ANDREW MICHAEL, lawyer; b. Bklyn., Aug. 15, 1956; m. Elaine Friedman, June 4, 1984. BA, U. Pa., 1978; JD, Vanderbilt U., 1981. Bar: N.Y. 1982, U.S. Dist. Ct. (so. and ea. dists.) N.Y. 1985, U.S. Ct. Appeals (2d cir.) 1991, U.S. Ct. Appeals (D.C. cir.) 1993. Assoc. Belson, Connolly & Belson, N.Y.C., 1981-84; pvt. practice Bklyn., 1984—. Dir. Bklyn. Bar Found. Editor in-chief Bklyn. Barrister. Mem. N.Y. State Bar Assn., Bklyn. Bar Assn. (judiciary com., continuing legal edn. com., trustee), Def. Rsch. Inst., Assn. Bar of City N.Y. (adj. mem. judiciary com.). General civil litigation, Labor (including EEOC, Fair Labor Standards Act, labor-management relations, NLRB, OSHA), Product liability. Office: One Whitehall St 16th Flr New York NY 10004

FALLER, RHODA, lawyer; b. N.Y.C., Dec. 21, 1946; d. Benjamin and Marion (Mediasky) Sragg; m. Stanley Grossberg, Apr. 12, 1973 (div. Oct. 1983); children: Joseph Seth, Daniel Benjamin; m. Bernard Martin Faller, May 31, 1987. BS, SUNY, Stony Brook, 1967; MS, Pace U., 1973; JD, N.Y. Law Sch., 1978. Bar: N.Y. 1979, N.J. 1979, U.S. Dist. Ct. N.J. 1979, Fla. 1980, U.S. Dist. Ct. (ea. and so. dists.) N.Y. 1982, Ky. 1996, U.S. Dist. Ct. (ea. dist.) Ky. 1997. Assoc. Fuchsberg & Fuchsberg, N.Y.C., 1982-91, DeBlasio & Alton, P.C., N.Y.C., 1991-95, Rhoda Grossberg Faller, Esq., Teaneck, 1995-96, Becker Law Office, Louisville, Ky., 1997-2000; pvt. practice Louisville, 2000—. Mem.: Women Lawyers Assn., Louisville Bar Assn., Fla. Bar Assn., N.Y. State Bar Assn., Ky. Bar Assn., Ky. Acad. Trial Attys., Nat. Assn. Women Bus. Owners, Assn. Trial Lawyers Am., Million Dollar Advocates Forum. Democrat. Jewish. Personal injury (including property damage). Home: 213 Mockingbird Gardens Dr Louisville KY 40207-5718 Office: Law Office of Rhoda Faller PLLC 455 S 4th St Ste 310 Louisville KY 40202

FALLER, SUSAN GROGAN, lawyer; b. Cin., Mar. 1, 1950; d. William M. and Jane (Eagen) Grogan; m. Kenneth R. Faller, June 8, 1973; children: Susan Elisabeth, Maura Christine, Julie Kathleen. BA, U. Cin., 1972; JD, U. Mich., 1975. Bar: Ohio 1975, Ky. 1989, U.S. Dist. Ct. (so. dist.) Ohio 1975, U.S. Ct. Claims 1982, U.S. Ct. Appeals (6th cir.) 1982, U.S. Supreme Ct. 1982, U.S. Tax Ct. 1984, U.S. Dist. Ct. (ea. dist.) Ky., 1991. Assoc. Frost & Jacobs, Cin., 1975-82; ptnr. Frost & Jacobs LLP, Cin., 1982-2000; mem. Frost Brown Todd LLC, Cin., 2000—. Assoc. editor Mich. Law Rev., 1974-75; contbg. author: MLRC 50-State Survey of Media Libel and Privacy Law, 1982-93, MLRC 50-State Survey of Media Libel Law, 1999-, MLRC State Survey of Employment Libel and Privacy Law, 1999-. Bd. dirs. Summit Alumni Coun., Cin., 1983-85; trustee Newman Found., Cin., 1980-86, Cath. Social Svc., Cin., 1984-93, nominating com., 1985-88, sec., 1990; mem. Class XVII Leadership Cin., 1993-94; mem. exec. com., def. counsel sect. Media Law Resource Ctr., 1998-2002; pres., def. counsel sect. Libel Def. Resource Ctr., 2001; mem. parish coun. St. Monica-St. George Ch., 1996-2000. Recipient Career Women of Achievement award YWCA, 1990. Mem. ABA (co-editor newsletter media litig. 1993-97), FBA, Ky. Bar Assn., No. Ky. Bar Assn., No. Ky. Women's Bar Assn., Ohio Bar Assn. (chair media law com.), Cin. Bar Assn. (com. mem.), Potter Stewart Inn of Ct., U. Cin. Alumni Assn., Arts & Scis. Alumni Assn. (bd. govs. U. Cin. Coll. 1988-2000), U. Mich. Alumni Assn., Mortar Bd., Leland Yacht Club, Coll. Club, Clifton Meadows Club, Phi Beta Kappa, Theta Phi Alpha. Roman Catholic. Appellate, General civil litigation, Libel. Home: 5 Belsaw Pl Cincinnati OH 45220-1104 Office: Frost Brown Todd LLC 2200 PNC Ctr 201 E 5th St Cincinnati OH 45202-4182

FALSGRAF, WILLIAM WENDELL, lawyer; b. Cleve., Nov. 10, 1933; s. Wendell A. and Catherine J. F.; children: Carl Douglas, Jeffrey Price, Catherine Louise. AB cum laude, Amherst Coll., 1955, LLD (hon.), 1986; JD, Case Western Res. U., 1958. Bar: Ohio 1958, U.S. Supreme Ct. 1972. Ptnr. Baker & Hostetler, Cleve., 1971—2002; ret., 2002. Chmn. vis. com. Case Western Res. U. Law Sch., 1973-76; trustee Case Western Reserve U., 1978-90, chmn. bd. overseers, 1977-78; trustee Cleve. Health Mus., 1975-90, Hiram Coll., 1989—; chmn. bd. trustees Hiram Coll., 1990-99. Recipient Disting. Service award; named Outstanding Young Man of Year Cleve. Jr. C. of C., 1962. Fellow Am. Bar Found., Ohio Bar Found.; mem. ABA (chmn. young lawyers sect. 1966-67, mem. ho. of dels. 1967-68, 70—, bd. govs. 1971-75, pres. 1985-86, bd. dirs. Am. Bar Endowment 1974-84, 87-97), Am. Bar Ins. Plans Cons. (pres. 1991—), Ohio Bar Assn. (mem. coun. of dels. 1968-70), Cleve. Bar Assn. (trustee 1979-82), Amherst Alumni Assn. (pres. N.E. Ohio 1964), The Country Club, LaPaloma Country Club. Corporate, general, Environmental, Probate (including wills, trusts). Home: 616 North St Chagrin Falls OH 44022-2514 Office: Baker & Hostetler LLP 3200 National City Ctr Cleveland OH 44114-3485 E-mail: wfalsgraf@bakerlaw.com.

FALSTROM, KENNETH EDWARD, lawyer; b. San Luis Obispo, Calif., June 25, 1946; s. William and Irene (Carroll) F.; children: Kenneth Todd, Tricia Karen. BA, UCLA, 1967; JD, U. Calif., Berkeley, 1970. Bar: Calif. 1971, U.S. Dist. Ct. (cen. dist.) Calif. 1977. Rsch. asst. Ctr. Study Dem. Insts., Santa Barbara, Calif., 1971; atty. Law Office Christopher Zayic, Santa Barbara, Calif., 1972; pvt. practice Santa Barbara, Calif., 1973—. Bd. dirs. Hope Sch. Dist. Santa Barbara, 1972-80. General practice. Office: 1530 Chapala St Santa Barbara CA 93101-3017

FALVEY, PATRICK JOSEPH, lawyer; b. Yonkers, N.Y., June 29, 1927; s. Patrick J. Falvey and Nora Rowley Falvey; m. Eileen Ryan, June 29, 1963; 1 child, Patrick James. Student, Iona Coll., 1944-47; JD cum laude, St. John's U., Jamaica, N.Y., 1950. Bar: N.Y. 1951, U.S. Supreme Ct. 1972. Law asst. Port Authority of N.Y. and N.J., 1951, atty., 1951-65, chief condemnation and litigation, 1965-67, asst. gen. counsel, 1967-72, gen. counsel, 1972-91, gen. counsel, asst. exec. dir., 1979-87, dep. exec. dir., 1987-91, spl. counsel, 1991—. Advisor U.S. del. to UN Com. on Internat. Trade Law, U.S. State Dept. Pvt. Trade Law; advisor to U.S. del. UN diplomatic confs. on treaty on liability of ops. of transport terminals, N.Y. County Lawyers Assn., 1992—. With USN, 1945-46. Recipient Howard S. Cullman Disting. Svc. medal Port Authority of N.Y. and N.J., 1982, 91; Loftus award and Trustee's Honoree Iona Coll., 1982. Fellow Am. Bar Found.; mem. ABA (chmn. urban state and local govt. law sect. 1983-84, vice-chmn. model procurement code project 1979—, sect. del. 1987-90, Award for Lifetime Achievement in Local Law 2000), Assn. Bar City N.Y., N.Y. County Lawyers Assn., Internat. Assn. Ports and Harbors (hon., legal counsellors com., arbitrator, mediator trade and comml. matters, cons. transp. and trade studies). Address: PMB 81 Pondfield Rd Ste 338 Bronxville NY 10708-3818 E-mail: woodlawnfalvey@aol.com.

FALVEY, W(ILLIAM) PATRICK, judge; b. Penn Yan, N.Y., Aug. 31, 1946; s. William Jennings and Thelma Rosetta (Hall) F.; m. Suzanne G. Christensen, Sept. 14, 1968; children: Scott P., Jennifer G. BA, Hobart Coll., 1968; JD, John Marshall Law Sch., 1975; postgrad., U. Nev., 1994. Bar: N.Y. 1976, U.S. Dist. Ct. (we. dist.) N.Y. 1979, U.S. Supreme Ct. 1984. Confidential law clerk N.Y. State Supreme Justice, Penn Yan, 1976-77; atty. Dept. Social Svcs. Yates County, Penn Yan, 1976-77, pvt. practice, 1976-88, asst. pub. defender, 1977-80, acting dist. atty., 1980-81, dist. atty., 1981-88, judge surrogate and family ct., acting Supreme Ct. Justice, 1988—. Mem. alternatives to incarceration com. Yates County; mem. Yates County Custody and Visitation Mediation Bd., 1995—; adv. com. Finger Lakes Vol. Lawyer's Svc., Geneva, N.Y., 1989-91; chair bd. trustees Yates County Law Libr.; jud. adv. coun. Seventh Jud. Dist. Mem., sec. Yates County Republican Com., Penn Yan, 1977-81; mem. Yates County Coop. Farm & Craft Market, Penn Yan, 1976-79; bd. dirs. Lit. Vols., Penn Yan, 1979-83; mem., pres. Yates County Profl. & Health Adv. Com., Penn Yan, 1980-88. 1st lt. U.S. Army, 1969-71, Vietnam. Recipient N.Y. State Conspicuous Svc. Cross, Hon. Hugh R. Carey Gov. N.Y., 1979. Ctr. for Dispute Settlement's Disting. Jurist award, 1996. Mem. Am. Judges Assn., Am. Judicature Soc., Ontario/Yates Magistrates Assn., N.Y. Bar Assn., N.Y. State, County, Family and Surrogate Judges Assn. (exec. com.), Yates County Bar Assn. (past pres.), VFW, Am. Legion (post comdr. 1981). Office: Yates County Cts 415 Liberty St Penn Yan NY 14527-1102 Fax: 315-536-5197.

FAMULARO, JOSEPH L. former prosecutor; b. Mt. Olivet, Ky., Nov. 6, 1942; BA, Loyola U., New Orleans, 1964; JD, U. Ky., 1967. Clk. to Hon. Mac Swinford U.S. Dist. Ct. Ky.; atty. Ky. Atty. Gen. Office, 1971—74; legal adviser Ky. State Police, 1970—72; 1st asst. and U.S. atty. for ea. dist. Ky. Office U.S. Atty., 1977-81; chief dep. atty. gen. Office Atty. Gen. Ky., 1982—88; 1st asst. county atty. Fayette County Attys. Office, 1988-89; commr. pub. safety Lexington Fayette Urban County, Ky., 1990-93; US atty. for ea. dist. Ky., formerly US Dept. Justice, Lexington, Ky., 1993—2001; dep. sec. for legal affairs Ky. Transport Cabinet, Frankfurt, Ky., 2002—. Office Fax: 502-564-4809.*

FANCHER, RICK, lawyer; b. Tucson, July 27, 1953; s. James Richard and Margaret Mae (Gum) F.; m. Cecelia Francis Baney, July 12, 1975; children: Jeffery Reed, Ashley Kristin. BA, Trinity U., 1975; JD, U. Tex., 1978. Bar: Tex. 1979, U.S. Dist. Ct. (we. and so. dists.) Tex. 1981, U.S. Ct. Appeals (5th cir.) 1981. Law clk. U.S. Dist. Ct., Corpus Christi, Tex., 1978-80; asst. atty. City of Corpus Christi, 1980; assoc. Gibbins, Burrow & Bratton, Austin, Tex., 1981, John L. Johnson, Corpus Christi, 1982-85; ptnr. Thornton, Summers, Biechlin, Dunham & Brown, Corpus Christi, 1985-99, Barker, Leon, Fancher & Matthys, Corpus Christi, 2000—. Mem. Tex. Bar Assn., Tex. Bd. Legal Specialization (cert. personal injury trial law). Democrat. Avocations: jogging, bicycling, hunting, golf. Insurance, Personal injury (including property damage), Product liability. Home: 4502 Lake Bistineau Dr Corpus Christi TX 78413-5261 Office: Barker Leon Fancher & Matthys 1200 First City Tower II 555 N Carancahua St Corpus Christi TX 78478-0002 E-mail: rfancher@blfmlaw.com.

FANCIULLO, WILLIAM PATRICK, lawyer; b. S.I., N.Y., Nov. 20, 1953; s. Gilbert Louis and Betty Elaine (Beyer) F.; m. Gunilla G. Fanciullo, July 25, 1981 (dec.); children: Chirstina Marie, Matthew William, James Eric. BA magna cum laude, SUNY, Albany, 1975; JD, SUNY, Buffalo, 1979. Bar: N.Y. 1980, U.S. Dist. Ct. (no. dist.) N.Y. 1980, U.S. Ct. Appeals (9th cir.) 1980, U.S. Ct. Appeals (2d cir.) 1981, U.S. Dist. Ct. (we. dist.) N.Y. 1990, U.S. Supreme Ct. 1992. Trial atty. honor grads. program U.S. Dept. Justice, Washington, 1979-80, asst. U.S. atty. Albany, 1980-89; pvt. practice, Albany, 1989—. Speaker in field. Recipient commendation FBI, 1985, 87, Dir.'s award for superior performance U.S. Dept. Justice, 1988. Mem. ABA (sects. on litigation and criminal justice), N.Y. State Bar Assn. (trial lawyers and criminal law sect.), Nat. Assn. Criminal Def. Lawyers, Albany County Bar Assn. (former chmn. fed. practice com.), Capital Dist. Trial Lawyers Assn. General civil litigation, Criminal, Personal injury (including property damage). Home: 214 Woodscape Dr Albany NY 12203-5604 Office: 61 Columbia St Albany NY 12210-2736

FANECA, CY T. lawyer; b. New Orleans, Mar. 1, 1941; s. Cyril Thomas Faneca and Mary Lucy Famiglio; m. Georgia Anne Thatcher, Mar. 28, 1972; children: Robert, Michael. BA, U. Miss., 1964, JD, 1967. Bar: Miss. 1967, U.S. Dist. Ct. (so. dist.) Miss. 1971, U.S. Ct. Appeals (5th cir.) 1972, U.S. Supreme Ct. 1976, U.S. Dist. Ct. D.C. 1982. Field officer CIA, 1967—71; ptnr. Daniel, Coker, Horton, Bell & Dukes, Gulfport, Miss., 1974—79; project dir. South Miss. Legal Svcs., Biloxi, 1979—82; chief of staff Congressman Larkin Smith, Washington, 1989; ptnr. Dukes, Dukes, Keating & Faneca, Gulfport, 1988—. Legal counsel mem. jud. com. U.S. Ho. of Reps., Washington, 1989; gen. counsel Gulfport-Biloxi Regional Airport Authority, Gulfport, 1977—2002, Harrison County Sheriff's Dept., Gulfport, 2000—02, Harrison County Emergency Comm. Commn., Gulfport, 2000—02, Long Beach Water Mgmt. Dist., Long Beach, Miss., 1999—2002; adv. bd. Union Planters Bank, Gulfport; adj. instr. Embry Riddle U., Biloxi; spl. master Harrison County Chancery, Gulfport. Pres. Babe Ruth Baseball League, Gulfport, 1995—97; campaign mgr. Congressman Paul Larkin Smith, 1988; mem. Harrison County Rep. Exec. Com., Gulfport, 1990—2002; sr. warden St. Peters Episcopal Ch., Gulfport, 1986—88; bd. dirs. South Miss. Legal Svcs., Biloxi, 1977—97; pres., bd. dirs. Westminster Acad., Gulfport, 1973—75. Paul Harris fellow, Rotary, Gulfport, 1988. Fellow: Miss. Bar Assn.; mem.: Miss. Def. Lawyers Assn., Great Southern Club, Gulfport Yacht Club (fleet capt. 1987). Republican. Episcopalian. Avocations: offshore fishing, hunting, boating. Home: 1526 Bert Ave Gulfport MS 39501 Office: Dukes Dukes Keating and Faneca PA 2909 13th St 6th Fl Gulfport MS 39501

FANGANELLO, JOSEPH MICHAEL, lawyer; b. Denver, Nov. 16, 1941; s. Anthony and Imogene (Baskett) F.; m. JoAnne Craig, Aug. 13, 1966; children: Joseph Duffy, Anne, Joan. BA, Regis Coll., 1963; JD, U. Colo., 1968. Bar: Colo. 1968. Law clk. Denver Dist. Ct., 1968-69; sole practice Denver, 1968-82; ptnr. Joseph M. Fanganello, P.C., Denver, 1982—. Officer, dir. numerous Colo. cos., 1968—. Bd. dirs., counsel Denver Opera Co., 1977-80. Mem. Denver Bar Assn., Colo. Bar Assn. Corporate, general, General practice, Property, real (including real estate development, water). Office: Joseph M Fanganello PC 1650 Washington St Denver CO 80203-1407

FANIZZA, JOANNE, lawyer; b. Bklyn., Jan. 22, 1957; d. John Carmelo and Mary Carmela (Spadafora) F. BA, U. Fla., 1981, JD, 1987. Bar: Fla., U.S. Dist. Ct. (so. dist.) Fla. 1988, U.S. Ct. Appeals (5th and 11th cirs.) 1988, U.S. Dist. Ct. (mid. dist.) Fla. 1989, U.S. Supreme Ct. 1997. Newspaper editor and reporter Ft. Lauderdale (Fla.) News/Sun-Sentinel, 1977-79, 1981-85; newspaper reporter, editor Gainesville (Fla.) Sun, 1979-81, 1985-86; assoc. Ferrero & Middlebrooks, P.A., Ft. Lauderdale, 1988-94, Law Offices of Joanne Fanizza, P.A., Ft. Lauderdale, 1995—. Adj. prof Broward C.C., Coconut Creek, Fla., 1988-91; Broward County Commn. on Status of Women, 2000-02. Rsch. editor U. Fla. Jour. of Law and Pub. Policy, 1986-87. Mem. city coun. City of Wilton Manors, 1998—2002, mem. bd. adjustment, 1992—98, chair bd. adjustment, 1993—98; mem. Wilton Manors Bus. Assn., Tropical Pines Civic Assn.; bd. dirs., sec. Abandoned Pet Rescue, Inc., 1996—. Recipient Am. Jurisprudence award constitutional law AmJur, 1986, spl. citation John Marshall Bar Assn., 1987; named one of Outstanding Young Women of Am., 1982, Atty. of Yr., 1998, 2003, Broward Lawyers Care. Mem. ABA, ATLA, FBA, Broward County Trial Lawyers Assn. (bd. govs. 1993-), Broward County Bar Assn. (young lawyers div. 1988-92), Broward Lawyers Care (pro bono), Broward County Gators Club, Phi Delta Phi. Democrat. Roman Catholic. Avocations: sports, cooking, traveling. General civil litigation, General practice, Probate (including wills, trusts). Office: Law Offices Joanne Fanizza PA 2700 E Oakland Park Blvd Ste D Fort Lauderdale FL 33306-1623 Fax: (954) 565-1941. E-mail: jfanizza@netzero.net.

FANNING, BARRY HEDGES, lawyer; b. Olney, Tex., Dec. 5, 1950; s. Robert Allen and Carolyn (Parker) F.; m. Rebecca Sue Cobbs, May 24, 1975 (dec. Mar. 1997); m. Sherri Winn Perry, Mar. 6, 1999. BBA, Baylor U., 1972, LL.B., 1973. Bar: Tex. 1973, Fla. 1974, U.S. Dist. Ct. (no., ea. we. and so. dists.) Tex. 1974, U.S. Ct. Appeals (5th and 11th cirs.) 1974. Mem. firm Fanning, Harper & Martinson, Dallas, 1974—. Social v.p. Dallas Symphony Orch. Guild, 1975-77; mem. Dallas Regional Young Life Bd., 1977—, fund raising chmn., 1982-84, 86-88, 97—; bd. dirs., membership/mktg. com., Downtown YMCA, 1997—, chmn. cmty. svcs. fund dr., 2003; mem. Russell Perry Free Enterprise Banquet Com., Dallas Bapt. U.; mem. Miss Tex. Pageant Bd., 2003. Mem. ABA (vice chmn. young lawyers com. 1980, pub. rels. com. torts sect.), Baylor U. Student Found. (steering com. 1971-72), Baylor Alumni Assn. (bd. dirs. 1978-82, 95), Tryon Coterie (pres. 1971), Highland Park Forensics Found. (pres. 1993-95), Preston Ctr. Legal Assn. (sec. 1993-94, bd. dirs. 1994-95), Dervish Club, Calyx Club, Dallas Baylor Club (bd. dirs. 1976-84, pres. 1981-82), Christian Men's Club, Phi Eta Sigma, Omicron Kappa Delta, Phi Delta Theta. Baptist. Federal civil litigation, State civil litigation, Insurance. Home: 3404 Centenary Ave Dallas TX 75225-4850 Office: Fanning Harper & Martinson 4849 Greenville Ave Ste 1300 Dallas TX 75206

FANNING, FRANCIS GERARD, lawyer; b. Chgo., Nov. 20, 1947; s. Francis Joseph and Catherine Beatta (Heatherly) F.; m. Muriel Anne Knoblauch, Aug. 22, 1970; children: Michael G., Christopher J., Patrick D. BA, U. Ill., 1970; MEd, U. Ariz., 1974; JD, Ariz. State U., 1978. Bar: Ariz. 1978, U.S. Dist. Ct. Ariz. 1978, U.S. Ct. Appeals (9th cir.) 1992, U.S. Supreme Ct. 1995, U.S. Ct. Appeals (10th cir.) 1996. Prosecutor intern City Atty., Tempe, Ariz., summer 1977; law clk. Justice William Holohan Ariz. Supreme Ct., Phoenix, 1978-79; assoc. atty. Law Office of Carl Divelbiss, Phoenix, 1979-81; pvt. practice Tempe and Mesa, Ariz., 1981-88, 90—; assoc. Bill Stephens & Assocs., Phoenix, 1988-90. Judge pro tempore Maricopa County Superior Ct., Phoenix, 1991-96, commr. pro tempore, 1982-83; mem. local bd. Supreme Ct. Foster Care Rev. Bd., Phoenix, 1981-85. Vol. Maricopa County Bar Assn. Vol. Lawyers Assn., Phoenix, 1981—; mem. troop com. Troop 7 Boy Scouts Am., Tempe, 1993-98; vol. coach YMCA, Tempe, 1989-93. Named Atty. of Yr., Maricopa County Bar Assn. Vol. Lawyers Program, Phoenix, 1987. Mem. Ariz. Employment Lawyers Assn. (bd. dirs. 1996-97), Nat. Employment Lawyers Assn. Democrat. Avocations: piano, choral music, backpacking. General civil litigation, Labor (including EEOC, Fair Labor Standards Act, labor-management relations, NLRB, OSHA). Home: 1941 E Los Arboles Dr Tempe AZ 85284-2586 Office: 500 E Southern Ave Ste B Tempe AZ 85282-5210 E-mail: fanning@azbar.org.

FANNING, ROBERT ALLEN, lawyer; b. Dallas, Nov. 3, 1931; s. Charles Allen and Beryl Julia (Buckner) F.; m. Carolyn Parker Hedges, Aug. 6, 1960; children: Barry H., Marc H. BBA, Baylor U., 1953; JD, So. Meth. U., 1960. Bar: Tex. 1959, U.S. Supreme Ct. 1964, U.S. Ct. Appeals (5th cir.) 1967, U.S. Ct. Appeals (11th cir.) 1981, U.S. Dist. Ct. (no., so., we. and ea. dists.) Tex. Chmn. bd. dirs. Fanning, Harper & Martinson P.C., Dallas, 1961—. Mem. bd. visitors So. Meth. U. Law Sch., 1969-72; trustee Annuity Bd. So. Bapt. Conv., 1971-79, past vice chmn.; mem. Nat. Bd. Fellowship Christian Athletes; past chmn. bd. trustees San Marcos Bapt. Acad.; mem. devel. coun. Baylor U.; mem. found. bd. Dallas Bapt. U. Recipient Disting. Svc. medal San Marcos Acad., 1970; named Outstanding Young Texan, 1975. Fellow Tex. Bar Found., Dallas Bar Found.; mem. ABA, Am. Judicature Soc., Tex. Bar Assn., Dallas Bar Assn., S.W. Legal Found., Tex. Assn. Def. Counsel, Park City Club, Delta Theta Phi (life). Office: Fanning Harper & Martinson Preston Commons W 8117 Preston Rd Fl 3 Dallas TX 75225-6332

FANONE, JOSEPH ANTHONY, lawyer; b. Sharon, Pa., Apr. 14, 1949; s. Anthony and Nancy Fanone; children: Michael, Kathleen, Peter. AB, Georgetown U., 1971, JD, 1974. Bar: Pa. 1974, D.C. 1980. Asst. atty. gen. Pa. Dept. of Justice, 1974-77; assoc. Squire, Sanders & Dempsey, Washington, 1977-81, Ballard, Spahr, Andrews & Ingersoll, Washington, 1981-83, ptnr., 1983-94, Piper & Marbury, Washington, 1994-95, Ballard, Spahr, Andrews & Ingersoll, Washington, 1996—. Mem. ABA. Finance. Office: Ballard Spahr Andrews & Ingersoll 601 13th St NW Ste 1000 Washington DC 20005-3807

FANTINO, LISA MARIA, lawyer, reporter; b. NYC; d. Alfred Anthony and Theresa (Lo Presti) F. BA in Lit. and Comm., Pace U., 1980; MS in Telecomm., Syracuse U., 1983; JD, Pace U., 1997. Reporter, writer Sta. WINS-AM, NYC, 1982-92; reporter United Artists UA-Columbia Cablevision, Mamaroneck, NY, 1985-87, 90-93; news anchor, reporter NBC Radio Network, 1988-90; reporter, writer WCBS-AM, NYC, 1994—2001; host, prodr. Face to Face with Lisa Fantino TCI Cable of Westchester, 1993-97; litigation assoc. Hashmall, Sheer, Bank & Geist, White Plains, NY, 1997; pvt. practice, 1998—. Media curriculum advisor Westchester C.C., 1986-96; pres. Juris Media Strategies, 2002-. Contbr. articles and photographs to various publs. Recipient Silver medal for best entertainment mag. Internat. Radio Festival, 1989, Bronze medal, 1990. Mem. AFTRA, NATAS, Writers Guild Am., NY State Bar Assn. Entertainment, Estate planning, Intellectual property.

FARBER, BERNARD JOHN, lawyer; b. London, Feb. 27, 1948; came to U.S., 1949; s. Solomon and Regina (Wachter) F.; m. Mary Lee Mueller, Feb. 14, 1987; children: Zachary, Anne. BS, U. of State of N.Y., Albany, 1978; JD, Ill. Inst. Tech., 1983. Bar: Ill. 1983, U.S. Dist. Ct. (no. dist.) Ill. 1983, U.S. Ct. Appeals (7th cir.) 1985, U.S. Tax Ct. 1986, U.S. Ct. Mil. Appeals 1986, U.S. Supreme Ct. 1987, U.S. Ct. Appeals (6th cir.) 1988, U.S. Ct. Appeals (4th cir.) 1989, U.S. Ct. Appeals (11th cir.) 1990. Instr. legal writing Chgo.-Kent Law Sch. Ill. Inst. Tech., 1983-85, computer rsch. atty., 1985-86, adj. prof. law, 1987—; legal editor Longman Fin. Svcs., Chgo., 1986-87; rsch. counsel publs. Ams. for Effective Law Enforcement, Chgo., 1987—. Instr. Law Scholastic Aptitude Test; preparation course BAR/BRI, Chgo., 1984-88; v.p. Brickton Montessori Sch., Chgo., 1992-93; sec. bd. dirs., 1993-95. Mng. editor: Chgo.-Kent Law Rev., 1981-82, editor-in-chief, 1982-83; co-author: Protective Security Law, 1996; editor: (with others) Dow Jones-Irwin Handbook of Micro Computer Applications in Law, 1987, Illinois Law of Criminal Investigation, 1986; contbr. articles to profl. jours. Elected mem. Local Sch. Coun., Agassiz Elem. Sch., Chgo., 1996—, chmn., 1999-2002, vice-chmn. 2002—. Mem. ABA, Ill. State Bar Assn., Chgo. Bar Assn., Sci. Fiction Rsch. Assn., Mensa. Avocations: history, computers, science fiction. Civil rights, Criminal, General practice. Home and Office: 1126 W Wolfram St Rear Chicago IL 60657-4330 E-mail: bernfarber@aol.com., bernardjfarber@voyager.net.

FARBER, DONALD CLIFFORD, lawyer, educator; b. Columbus, Nebr., Oct. 19, 1923; s. Charles and Sarah (Epstein) F.; m. Ann Eis, Dec. 28, 1947; children: Seth, Patricia. BS in Law, U. Nebr., 1948, JD, 1950. Bar: N.Y. 1950. Assoc. Newman, Hauser & Teitler, N.Y.C., 1950-58; pvt. practice, N.Y.C., 1958-80; of counsel Conboy, Hewitt, O'Brien & Boardman, N.Y.C., 1980-84; ptnr. Tanner Propp Fersko & Sterner, N.Y.C., 1984-95, Farber & Rich LLP, N.Y.C., 1995-98; of counsel Hartman & Craven LLP, N.Y.C., 1998—2000, Jacob Medinger & Finnegan LLP, N.Y.C., 2000—. Prof. law York U., Toronto, Ont., Can., 1970, 72-73; prof. theatre law Hofstra Law Sch., Hempstead, N.Y., 1974-75; prof. New Sch. for Social Rsch., N.Y.C., 1972—, Hunter Coll., 1978. Author: From Option to Opening, 1968, 4th edit., 1st Limelight edit., 1988, Producing on Broadway, 1969, Actor's Guide: What You Should Know About the Contracts You Sign, 1971, Producing, Financing and Distributing Film, 1973, 2d edit., 1991, The Amazing Story of the Fantasticks: America's Longest Running Play, 1991, Producing Theatre: A Comprehensive Legal and Business Guide, 1981, 3d Limelight edit., 1997, Common Sense Negotiation-The Art of Winning Gracefully, 1996; gen. editor (10 vol. series, author theatre vol.) Entertainment Industry Contracts-Negotiating and Drafting Guide. With AUS, 1941-44, ETO. Mem. Order of Coif. Home: 14 E 75th St New York NY 10021-2657 Office: Jacob Medinger & Finnegan LLP 1270 Ave of Americas New York NY 10020 E-mail: donaldc14@aol.com., dcfarber@jmfnylaw.com.

FARBER, HOWARD, lawyer; b. N.Y.C., Dec. 7, 1931; m. June R. Polinger, Dec. 20, 1953; children: Shelly G., Carol R. BBA, CCNY, 1953; MS, Columbia U., 1957; JD, Temple U., 1972. Bar: Pa. 1972, U.S. Dist. Ct. (ea. dist.) Pa. 1972, U.S. Ct. Appeals (3d cir.) 1975, U.S. Supreme Ct. 1975, N.Y. 1980. Ptnr. Farber & Halligan, P.C., Media, Pa., 1972-80; pvt. practice law Media, 1980-89; ptnr. Farber & Farber, Media, 1989—. Solicitor Twp. of Marple, Pa., 1975-78. Bd. dirs. Marple-Newton Sch. Dist., Newton Square, Pa., 1972-75. Served with U.S. Army, 1954-56. Recipient Disting. Service to Community award Marple Township Bd. Coms., 1978, Outstanding Service to Edn., Pa. Sch. Bds. Assn., 1976. Mem. ABA, Pa. Bar Assn., Pa. Trial Lawyers Assn., Delaware County Bar Assn. Personal injury (including property damage), Probate (including wills, trusts), Workers' compensation. Office: 1 Veterans Sq Media PA 19063-3216

FARBER, STEVEN GLENN, lawyer; b. Phila., July 20, 1946; s. Isadore Irving and Sylvia (Galperin) F.; children: Jamie, Daniel, Zoey, Avi. BBA, Temple U., 1968, JD, 1972. Bar: Pa. 1972, U.S. Dist. Ct. (ea. dist.) Pa. 1972, U.S. Dist. Ct. Appeals (3d cir.) 1972, N.Mex. 1975, U.S. Dist. Ct. N.Mex. 1975, U.S. Ct. Appeals (10th cir.) 1979, U.S. Supreme Ct. 1980. Asst. defender Pub. Defender Assn. Phila., 1972-74; acting dist. pub. defender State of N.Mex., Santa Fe, 1975-76, asst. atty. gen., 1976-78; pvt. practice Santa Fe, 1978—. Mem. N.Mex. Bd. Legal Specialization, 1986-90, chmn., 1991-93. Mem. Santa Fe Mcpl. Home Rule Charter Commn., 1997; bd. dirs. Ptnrs. in Edn., 1997—2002, Santa Fe County United Way, 1998—2002; elected city councilor City of Santa Fe, 1992—96; bd. dirs. Temple Beth Shalom, 1997—, v.p., 2000—01, pres., 2002—03. Mem. Nat. Assn. Criminal Def. Lawyers (vice-chmn. continuing legal edn. com. 1990-91), N.Mex. Lawyers Guild (pres. 1980-81), N.Mex. State Bar Assn. (bd. dirs. criminal law sect. 1980-83, chmn. 1981-82), N.Mex. Criminal Def. Lawyers Assn. (bd. dirs. 1991, treas. 1996), First Jud. Dist. Criminal Def. Lawyers Assn. (sec. 1999). Democrat. Jewish. Civil rights, Criminal, Personal injury (including property damage). Office: PO Box 2473 306 Catron St Santa Fe NM 87504-2473 E-mail: sgfsaf@aol.com.

FARENTHOLD, FRANCES TARLTON, lawyer; b. Corpus Christi, Tex., Oct. 2, 1926; d. Benjamin Dudley and Catherine (Bluntzer) Tarlton; children: Dudley Tarlton, George Edward, Emilie, James Dougherty, Vincent Bluntzer (dec.). AB, Vassar Coll., 1946; JD, U. Tex., 1949; LLD, Hood Coll., 1973, Boston U., 1973, Regis Coll., 1976, Lake Erie Coll., 1979, Elmira Coll., 1981, Coll. Santa Fe, 1985. Bar: Tex. 1949. Pvt. practice, 1949-65, 67-76, 80—; mem. Tex. Ho. of Reps., 1968-72; dir. legal aid Nueces County, 1965-67; pres. Wells Coll., Aurora, N.Y., 1976-80; asst. prof. law Tex. So. U., Houston, Thurgood Marshall disting. vis. prof., 1994-95. Lawyer; b. Corpus Christi, Tex., Oct. 2, 1926; d. Benjamin Dudley and Catherine (Bluntzer) Tarlton; children: Dudley Tarlton, George Edward, Emilie, James Dougherty, Vincent Bluntzer (dec.). AB, Vassar Coll., 1946; JD, U. Tex., 1949; LLD, Hood Coll., 1973, Boston U., 1973, Regis Coll., 1976, Lake Erie Coll., 1979, Elmira Coll., 1981, Coll. of Santa Fe, 1985. Bar: Tex. 1949. Pvt. practice, 1949-65, 67-76, 80—; mem. Tex. Ho. of Reps., 1968-72; dir. legal aide Nueces County, 1965-67; asst. prof. law Tex. So. U., Houston; pres. Wells Coll., Aurora, N.Y., 1976-80; disting. vis. prof. Thurgood Marshall Tex. So. U., Houston, 1994-95. Mem. Human Relations Com., Corpus Christi, 1963-68, Corpus Christi Citizen's Com. Community Improvement, 1966-68; mem. Tex. adv. com. to U.S. Commn. on Civil Rights, 1968-76; mem. nat. adv. council ACLU; mem. Orgn. for Preservation Unblemished Shoreline, 1964—; Dem. candidate for Gov. of Tex., 1972; del. Dem. Nat. Conv., 1972, 1st woman nominated to be candidate v.p. U.S., 1972; nat. co-chmn. Citizens to Elect McGovern-Shriver, 1972; chmn. Nat. Women's Polit. Caucus, 1973-75; mem. Dem. platform com., 1988; trustee Vassar Coll., 1975-83; bd. dirs. Fund for Constl. Govt., Ctr. for Devel. Policy, 1983—, Mexican Am. Legal Def. and Ednl. Fund, 1980-83; chmn. Inst. for Policy Studies, 1986-91; mem. bd. dirs. Rothko Chapel, 1997—. Recipient Lyndon B. Johnson Woman of Year award, 1973. Mem. State Bar Tex. Mem. Human Rels. Com., Corpus Christi, 1963-68, Corpus Christi Citizens Com. Cmty. Improvement, 1966-68; mem. Tex. adv. com. to U.S. Commn. on Civil Rights, 1968-76; mem. nat. adv. coun. ACLU; mem. Orgn. for Preservation Unblemished Shoreline, 1964—; Dem. candidate for Gov. of Tex., 1972; del. Dem. Nat. Conv., 1972, 1st woman nominated to be candidate v.p. U.S., 1972; nat. co-chair Citizens to elect McGovern-Shriver, 1972; chmn. Nat. Women's Polit. Caucus, 1973-75; mem. Dem. Platform Com., 1988; trustee Vassar Coll., 1975-83; bd. dirs. Fund for Constl. Govt., Ctr. for Devel. Policy, 1983—, Mexican Am. Legal Def. and Ednl. Fund, 198--83; chmn. Inst. for Policy Studies, 1986-91; bd. dirs. Rothko Chapel, 1997—, chmn., 2001—. Recipient Lyndon B. Johnson Woman of Yr. award, 1973, Lifetime Svc. award Dem. Party of Tex., 1998. Mem. State Bar Tex. Office: 2929 Buffalo Speedway Apt 1813 Houston TX 77098-1710

FARHA, ALFRED SAM, lawyer, consultant; b. Kansas City, Mo., Oct. 13, 1933; arrived in Switzerland, 1973; s. Sam Albert and Raifa Said Farha; m. Klara Emma Perner, Aug. 22, 1959; children: Alfred Jr., Arthur, Philip, Mark. AB in Internat. Rels., U. Kans., 1955, JD, 1961. Bar: Kans. 1961, Mo. 1962, Mich. 1965. Atty. at law Shughart, Thomson & Kilroy, Kansas City, Mo., 1961-65; legal counsel Dow Chem. Co., Midland, Mich., 1965-73; dir. basic hydrocarbons Dow Chem. Europe SA, Zurich, Switzerland, 1973-82; gen. mgr. Dow Chem. Mid. East, Geneva, Switzerland, 1982-88; dir. regulatory affairs Dow Europe SA, Zurich, 1988-93; counselor at law Zurich, 1993—. Bd. advisors Northwestern U. Law Jour., Chgo., 1989—; chmn. Swiss Corp. Capital at Lloyd's Ltd., London, 1994—; mem. adv. bd. N.Y. State Bar Assn. Internat. Law Rev., 1990—. Contbr. articles to law jours. Chmn. Reps. Abroad, Zurich, 1994—. With U.S. Army, 1956-58. Named Tchr. of Yr., City U., 1994. Mem. ABA, Swiss-Am. C. of C., Am. Club Zurich (pres. 1991-92). Roman Catholic. Avocations: piano, hiking, swimming, gardening. Home: Säumerstrasse 55 8800 Thalwil Zurich Switzerland Office: Bahnhofstrasse 71 8001 Zurich Switzerland E-mail: alfarha@aol.com.

FARINA, JOHN, lawyer; b. Rockville Center, N.Y., Oct. 20, 1959; s. Joseph P. Farina and Marilyn A. Echkoff; m. Julia Pressly, May 30, 1987; children: Matthew, Timothy, Nicholas. BA, Villanova U., 1981; JD, Suffolk U., 1985. Bar: Mass. 1985, Fla. 1986. Law clk. U.S. Ct. Appeals (4th dist.), West Palm Beach, Fla., 1985-86; assoc. Winthrop Stimson Putnam & Roberts, Palm Beach, Fla., 1986-90, Edwards & Angell, Palm Beach, 1990-94; ptnr. Boyes & Farina, West Palm Beach, 1994—. Mem. Fla. Probate Rules Com., Fla. Bar Greivance Com., 1998—. Mem. Palm Beach County Bar Assn. Avocations: trap and skeet shooting, running, tennis. State civil litigation, Probate (including wills, trusts). Home: 131 Thornton Dr Palm Beach Gardens FL 33418-8089 Office: Boyes & Farina PA 1601 Forum Pl Ste 900 West Palm Beach FL 33401-8105

FARINA, MARIO G. lawyer; b. Newark, Nov. 1, 1927; s. Gerardo and Marianna F.; m. Lois R. Wachman, Apr. 11, 1955; children: Jay E., Wendy D., F. William. BS in Edn., Montclair State U., 1949; MA in Adminstrn., Seton Hall U., 1955, JD, 1960. Bar: N.J. 1963, N.Y. 1982, U.S. Dist. Ct. N.J. 1963, U.S. Supreme Ct. 1977. Atty. N.J. Pub. Defenders Office, Elizabeth, 1968-86; pvt. practice Clark, N.J., 1963—. Sgt. U.S. Army, 1950-52. Mem. Union County Bar Assn. Democrat. Roman Catholic. Avocation: writing. State civil litigation, Criminal, Juvenile. Office: 990 Raritan Rd Clark NJ 07066-1740 E-mail: mariogfarina@aol.com.

FARKAS, STEPHEN GERARD, lawyer; b. Troy, N.Y., June 13, 1960; s. Joseph Farkas and Mary Francis (Welch) Kalil; m. Lynn Elizabeth Schultz, Aug. 15, 1987. AS in Gen. Mgmt., N.H. Coll., 1985, BS in Bus. Mgmt., 1987; postgrad., Mass. Sch. Law, 1989-92. Bar: Mass. 1992, N.H. 1996, U.S. Dist. Ct. Mass. 1993, U.S. Dist. Ct. N.H. 1996, U.S. Ct. Appeals (1st cir.) 1993. With Lockheed Sanders Inc., Nashua, N.H., 1982-86; program adminstr. Sanders Assoc., Inc., Nashua, N.H., 1986-87, contracts adminstr., 1987—92; pvt. practice Tyngsboro, Mass., 1992—. Mng. editor Imprimatur newspaper Mass. Sch. Law; exec. editor Mass. Sch. Law Law Rev. Chmn. bd. dirs. Meadowview Condo Assn., Nashua, 1989-2001; mem. Nashua city planning bd., 2002-; commnr. Nashua Regional Planning Commn., 2002-. Sgt. USAF, 1978-82. Recipient Ambassadors Commendation award U.S. Embassy, 1982. Republican. Methodist. Avocations: skiing, golf, swimming. Computer, Corporate, general, Public international. Office: 150 Westford Rd Ste 26 Tyngsboro MA 01879-2513

FARLEY, ANDREW NEWELL, lawyer, consultant; b. Brownsville, Pa., Oct. 31, 1934; s. Andrew Polycarp and Sarah Theresa (Landymore) F.; m. Marta Olha Pisetska, May 5, 1963; children— Andrew Daniel, Mark Landymore. AB, Washington and Jefferson Coll., 1956; MPA, U. Pitts., 1962, JD, 1961; diploma, U.S. Army Command and Gen. Staff Coll., 1972, Indsl. Coll. Armed Forces, 1967; grad., U.S. Army War Coll., 1976. Bar: Pa. 1962, U.S. Supreme Ct. 1965. Assoc. Reed Smith Shaw & McClay, Pitts., 1961-65, ptnr., 1966-91; cons. Pitts., 1992—. Bd. dirs. Corp. Devel. USAM Mid-Atlantic and Ohio; mng. dir. USAM-Nat., 1992-95; Am. Arbitration Assn. Nat. Panel Comml. Disputes, 1995—; mediator JAMS-Endispute, 1996—; sec.-treas. Internat. Acad. Mediators, 1996-2000; lectr. in fed. jurisprudence and adminstrv. law U. Pitts.; adminstrv. asst. Pa. Atty. Gen., 1959; counsel to Pa. Constl. Conv., 1968; mem. Pa. Atty. Gen.'s Task Force on Adminstrn., 1970. Assoc. editor Pitts Legal Jour., 1963— (mem. exec. com.); contbr. articles to profl. jours. Bd. dirs. Ind. Sch. Chmn. Assn., World Affairs Coun., Pitts., Pitts. Opera, 1986-95; sec., bd. dirs. Found. for Calif. U. Pa.,; mem. adv. bd. Western Pa. Advanced Tech. Ctr., Internat. Resuscitation Rsch. Ctr., U. Pitts. Med. Sch., Mon Valley Renaissance; mem. bd. visitors U. Pitts. Grad. Sch. Pub. and Internat. Affairs; trustee Thiel Coll., 1989-95. Brig. gen. U.S. Army. Decorated Meritorious Svc. medals, Dept. Def. and U.S. Army, Army Commendation medals; recipient Gubernatorial citation Commonwealth of Pa., 1978, Omicron Delta Kappa award, 1960; Nat. Def. Transp. Assn. fellow, 1956; named Mon Valley Renaissance MVP, 1987. Mem. Internat. Acad. Mediators, Pa. Bar Assn. (chmn. sect. internat. law, bd. editors, jud. adminstrn. com., statewide computer com. for the cts., alternative dispute resolution com.), Allegheny County Bar Assn. (fee determination com.), Am. Law Inst., Nat. Health Lawyers Assn., Am. Arbitration Assn., Soc. for Profls. in Dispute Resolution, Assn. U.S. Army (pres. Ft. Pitt chpt., pres. Pa.), Sr. Army Res. Comdrs. Assn. (exec. com.), Pitts. Athletic Assn., Duquesne Club, Pa. State Grange, Masons. Corporate, general, Health, Construction. Home: Gen Del Box 196 Cowansville PA 16218-0196 Office: 942 N Highland Ave Pittsburgh PA 15206-2108

FARLEY, BARBARA SUZANNE, lawyer; b. Salt Lake City, Dec. 13, 1949; d. Ross Edward Farley and Barbara Ann (Edwards) Farley Swanson; m. Arthur Hoffman Ferris, Apr. 9, 1982 (div. 1995); children: Barbara Whitney, Taylor Edwards; m. Michael L. Levine, Aug. 7, 1999. BA with honors, Mills Coll., 1972; JD, U. Calif.-Hastings, San Francisco, 1976. Bar: Calif. 1976. Extern law clk. to justice Calif. Supreme Ct., San Francisco, 1975; assoc. Pillsbury, Madison & Sutro, San Francisco, 1976-78, Bronson, Bronson & McKinnon, San Francisco, 1978-80, Goldstein & Phillips, San Francisco, 1980-84; ptnr., head litigation Rosen, Wachtell & Gilbert, San Francisco, 1984-89; of counsel Lempres & Wulfsberg, Oakland, Calif., 1989—99; pvt. practice, 2000—. Founder, pres. and CEO Fiducety Tech. Inc.; arbitrator U.S. Dist. Ct. (no. dist.) Calif., San Francisco, 1981—, Calif. Superior Ct., San Francisco, 1984—89; judge pro tem San Francisco Mcpl. Ct., 1983—; probation monitor Calif. State Bar, 1990—2002; del. to the Calif. Bar San Francisco Bar Assn., 2003; spkr. , author Nat. Bus. Inst. Estate Adminstrn., 2000; spkr. Lorman Edn. Svcs. Tax Exempt Orgns. Contbg. author Calif. Continuing Edn. of the Bar, Nat. Bus. Inst., Lorman Edn. Svcs.; mng. editor Hastings Coll. of Law-U. Calif.-San Francisco Constl. Law Quar., 1975-76; civil litigation reporter. Mills Coll. scholar, 1970-72, U. Calif.-Hastings, San Francisco scholar, 1973-76. Mem. ATLA, San Francisco Bar Assn., Calif. Trial Lawyers Assn., San Francisco Bar Assn. (del. Calif. State Bar 2003), Alameda Bar Assn. General civil litigation, Probate (including wills, trusts).

FARLEY, JOHN JOSEPH, III, federal judge; b. Hackensack, N.J., July 30, 1942; s. John Joseph and Patricia (Earle) F.; m. Kathleen Mary Wells, June 27, 1970; children: Maura, Brendan, Thomas, Caitlin. AB in Econs., Holy Cross Coll., 1964; MBA, Columbia, 1966; JD cum laude, Hofstra U., 1973. Bar: N.Y. 1974, D.C. 1975, U.S. Supreme Ct. 1977. Trial atty. torts sect. civil div. U.S. Dept. Justice, Washington, 1973-78, asst. dir. torts br. civil div., 1978-80, dir. torts br. civil div., 1980-89; judge U.S. Ct. of Appeals for Vets. Claims, Washington, 1989—. Mem. faculty OPM Exec. Seminar Ctrs., Denver, 1980—, Columbus Sch. Law Catholic U. Am., 2003; lectr. Atty. Gen's Advocacy Inst., Washington, 1976-89, FBI Acad., Quantico, Va., 1978-88; lectr. Columbus Sch. Law, Cath. U. Am., 2003. Editor-in-chief Hofstra Law Rev., 1971-73; contbr. articles to profl. jours. Vice-chmn. bd. dirs. Amputee Coalition of Am., 1997—. Served to capt. U.S. Army, 1966-70, Vietnam. Decorated Bronze Star with V device and 3 oak leaf clusters, Purple Heart with oak leaf cluster; recipient Sr. Exec. Service Spl. Achievement award U.S. Dept. Justice, 1984, Civil Div. Spl award U.S. Dept. Justice, 1980; Samuel Bronfman fellow, 1964-65, Dean's award for Disting. Hofstra Law Sch. Alumni, 1995, Disting. Alumni medal Hofstra U. Sch. of Law, 1986; inducted into Massapequa H.S. Hall of Fame, 1999. Mem. Fed. Bar Assn. (1st chmn. vets. law sec. 1990-91). Roman Catholic. Avocations: skiing, tennis, bicycling, reading. Office: US Court Of Appeals for Vets Claims 625 Indiana Ave NW Ste 900 Washington DC 20004-2917

FARLEY, JOSEPH MCCONNELL, lawyer; b. Birmingham, Ala., Oct. 6, 1927; s. John G. and Lynne (McConnell) F.; m. Sheila Shirley, Oct. 1, 1958 (dec. July 1978); children: Joseph McConnell, Thomas Gager, Mary Lynne. Student, Birmingham-So. Coll., 1944-45; BSME, Princeton U., 1948; student, U. Ala., 1948—49; LLB, Harvard U., 1952; LHD (hon.) , Judson Coll., 1974; LLD (hon.) , U. Ala. at Birmingham, 1983. Bar: Ala. 1952. Assoc. Martin, Turner, Blakey & Bouldin, Birmingham, 1952-57; ptnr.

successor firm Martin, Balch, Bingham & Hawthorne, 1957-65; exec. v.p., dir. Ala. Power Co., 1965-69, pres., dir., 1969-89; v.p. So. Electric Generating Co., 1970-74, pres., dir., 1974-89; exec. v.p. nuclear, bd. dirs. The So. Co., Birmingham, 1989-90; pres., CEO So. Nuclear Oper. Co., Birmingham, 1990-91, chmn., CEO, 1991-92, also bd. dirs.; exec. v.p., corp. counsel So. Co., 1991-92; of counsel Balch & Bingham, LLP, Birmingham, 1993—. Bd. dirs. N.A., Torchmark Corp., SVI Corp.; mem. exec. bd. Southeastern Electric Reliability Coun., chmn., 1974-76; bd. dirs. Edison Electric Inst.; bd. dirs. Southeastern Electric Exch., pres., 1984; adv. dir. So. Co., 1992-97; bd. dir. emeritus Am. South Bancorp. Mem. Jefferson County Republican Exec. Com., 1953-65; counsel, mem. Ala. Rep. Com., 1962-65; permanent chmn. Ala. Rep. Conv., 1962; alternate del. Rep. Nat. Conv., 1956; bd. dirs. Ala. Bus. Hall of Fame, Birmingham Area YMCA (hon. dir.); chmn. bd. trustees So. Rsch. Inst., 1970-99; trustee Tuskegee U., 1981-2002; trustee Children's Hosp. Birmingham, pres. bd. trustees 1983-85; mem. Pres.'s Cabinet U. Ala.-Tuscaloosa; bd. visitors U. Ala. Sch. Commerce, chmn., 1991-93. Served with USNR, 1948; now lt. ret. Mem. ABA, NAM (bd. dirs. 1987-92), Ala. Bar Assn., Birmingham Bar Assn., Inst. Nuclear Power Ops. (bd. dirs. 1982-89, chmn. 1987-89), U.S. Coun. for Energy Awareness (bd. dirs. 1985-92), Am. Nuclear Energy Coun. (chmn. bd. dirs. 1987-92), Newcomen Soc. N.Am., Birmingham Country Club, Shoal Creek Club, The Club, Mountain Brook Club, Summit Club, Rotary, Phi Beta Kappa, Kappa Alpha, Tau Beta Pi, Beta Gamma Sigma (hon.). Episcopalian. Home: 3333 Dell Rd Birmingham AL 35223-1319 Office: Balch & Bingham LLP PO Box 306 Birmingham AL 35201-0306

FARLEY, THOMAS T. lawyer; b. Pueblo, Colo., Nov. 10, 1934; s. John Baron and Mary (Tancred) F.; m. Kathleen Maybelle Murphy, May 14, 1960; children: John, Michael, Kelly, Anne. BS, U. Santa Clara, 1956; LLB, U. Colo., 1959. Bar: Colo. 1959, U.S. Dist. Ct. Colo. 1959, U.S. Ct. Appeals (10th cir.) 1988. Dep. dist. atty. County of Pueblo, 1960-62; pvt. practice Pueblo, 1963-69; ptnr. Phelps, Fonda & Hays, Pueblo, 1970-75, Petersen & Fonda, P.C., Pueblo, 1975—. Bd. dirs. Pub. Svc. Co. Colo., Wells Fargo Pueblo, Wells Fargo Sunset, Health Net, Inc., Colo. Pub. Radio. Minority leader Colo. Ho. of Reps., 1967-75; chmn. Colo. Wildlife Commn., 1975-79, Colo. Bd. Agr., 1979-87; bd. regents Santa Clara U., 1987—; commr. Colo. State Fair; trustee Cath. Found. Diocese of Pueblo, Great Outdoors Colo. Trust Fund. Recipient Disting. Svc. award U. So. Colo., 1987, 93, Bd. of Regents, U. Colo., 1993. Mem. ABA, Colo. Bar Assn., Pueblo C. of C. (bd. dirs. 1991-93), Rotary. Democrat. Roman Catholic. Administrative and regulatory, Education and schools, Health. Office: Petersen & Fonda PC 215 W 2d St Pueblo CO 81003-3251

FARMER, CORNELIA GRIFFIN, lawyer, consultant, hearings official; b. NYC, Mar. 3, 1945; d. John Bastin and Elizabeth McCue (Sussman) Griffin; m. William Paul Farmer, Jan. 8, 1972; children: Suzanne Elizabeth, John Paul. BA, Mt. Holyoke Coll., 1967; M in Regional Planning, Cornell U., 1970; JD, Marquette U., 1978. Bar: Wis. 1978, Pa. 1981, Minn. 1996, Oreg. 1999, Ill. 2001. Planner Frederick P. Clark Assoc., Rye, N.Y., 1970-71, Tri State Regional Planning Com., N.Y.C., 1971-72, State of Wis. and City of Milw., 1973-75; assoc. Friebert & Finerty, Milw., 1978-80, Baskin & Sears, Pitts., 1981-82; adj. faculty U. Pitts., 1986-94; jud. law clk. Commonwealth Pa., Pitts., 1992-95; pvt. practice Mpls., 1996—99; staff atty., hearings ofcl. Lane Coun. Govts., Eugene, Oreg., 1999—2001. Cons. County of Allegheny, Pitts., 1983; vic-chmn. loan monitoring com. Pitts. Countywide Corp., 1981—87; child adv. Allegheny County Pro Bono Program, Pitts., 1986—92; mediator Dispute Resolution Ctr., St. Paul, 1998—99; adj. faculty U. Wis., Milw., 1978—79. Book rev., referee books, articles. Vol. polit. campaigns Milw., Pitts. and Eugene, 1972-2000; bd. trustees Folk Sch. Fund; v.p. PTA Falk Lab. Sch. U. Pitts., 1985-89; ct. monitor abuse cases WATCH, Mpls., 1996-99; pres. Class of 1967 Mt. Holyoke Coll., 1992-97, reunion co-chair, 1987, 2000-02, head class agt., 2002—; vol., WITS tutoring and mentoring program, 2002-, SMART, Eugene, Oreg., WITS, Chgo. Mem. ABA, APA, Chgo. Bar Assn., Silver Bay Assn. Coun., Mt. Holyoke Coll. Alumnae Assn. (alumnae vol.). Mt. Holyoke Club Pitts. (pres., treas.).

FARMER, JOHN J. state commissioner, former state attorney general; b. June 24, 1957; m. Beth Gates. BA, Georgetown U., 1979, JD, 1986. Law clk. hon. Alan B. Handler N.J. Supreme Ct. Justice; assoc. Riker, Danzig, Scherer, Hyland and Perretti, Morristown, 1988—90; asst. U.S. atty. Dist. N.J. , 1990—94; dep. chief counsel, sr. assoc. counsel to the Gov., 1994—97; chief counsel to the Gov., chief law enforcement officer State of N.J., Trenton, 1997—99, atty. gen., 1999—2002; Commr. State of N.J. Comm. on Investigation, Trenton, 2002—. Adj. prof. law Seton Hall U. Law Sch., 1993—97; chmn. Juvenile Justice Commn. Mem.: Nat. Assn. Attys. Gen. (co-chair health care fraud, abuse and adv. com.). Republican. Office: 28 W State St 10th Fl Trenton NJ 08625-0045*

FARMER, ROBERT LINDSAY, lawyer; b. Portland, Oreg., Sept. 29, 1922; s. Paul C. and Irma (Lindsay) F.; m. Carmen E. Engebretson, Sept. 8, 1943; children: Cort W., Scott L., Eric C. BS, UCLA, 1946; LLB, U. So. Calif., 1949. Bar: Calif. 1949. Since practiced in, L.A.; mem. Farmer & Ridley, L.A., 1949—. Trustee Edward James Found., West Dean Estate, Chichester, Eng. Served with AUS, 1943-46. Mem. ABA, Los Angeles County Bar Assn., Order of Coif, Beta Gamma Sigma, Kappa Sigma, Phi Delta Phi, Annandale Golf Club (Pasadena, Calif.). Home: 251 S Orange Grove Blvd Apt 1 Pasadena CA 91105-1766 Office: 444 S Flower St Los Angeles CA 90071-2901

FARMER, TERRY D(WAYNE), lawyer; b. Oklahoma City, May 1, 1949; s. Gayle V. and Allene (Edsall) F.; children: Grant L., Tyler M. BA, U. Okla., 1971, JD, 1974. Bar: Okla. 1974, N.Mex. 1975, U.S. Dist. Ct. N.Mex. 1976, U.S. Ct. Claims 1975, U.S. Ct. Appeals (10th cir.) 1977, U.S. Supreme Ct. 1980. Asst. trust officer First Nat. Bank of Albuquerque, 1974-75; assoc. Nordhaus, Moses & Dunn, Albuquerque, 1975-78, ptnr., 1978-80; dir. Moses, Dunn, Farmer & Tuthill, P.C., Albuquerque, 1980—. Pres. Albuquerque Lawyers Club, N. Mex., 1982-83. Fellow N.Mex. Bar Found.; mem. N.Mex. Bar Assn. (pres. Young Lawyers div., 1978-79), Okla. Bar Assn., N.Mex. Trial Lawyers. General civil litigation, Commercial, contracts (including sales of goods; commercial financing), Property, real (including real estate development, water). Office: Moses Dunn Farmer & Tuthill PC PO Box 27047 Albuquerque NM 87125-7047

FARNAM, THOMAS CAMPBELL, lawyer, educator; b. Indpls., Feb. 13, 1945; s. Frederick Dean Farnam and Isabelle (Campbell) Fearheiley; m. Naomi M. Morales; children: Rachel Anne Stujenske, Thomas Matthews; m. Naomi Maddox Morales, Oct. 6, 2001. BS, Butler U., 1966; JD, Ind. U., Indpls., 1970; LLM in Taxation, Georgetown U., 1973. Bar: Ind. 1970, U.S. Dist. Ct. (so. dist.) Ind. 1970, U.S. Ct. Appeals (7th cir.) 1970, U.S. Tax Ct. 1970, Mo. 1983, U.S. Supreme Ct 1991. Asst. dir. advanced underwriting Indpls. Life Ins. Co., 1970-72; tax atty., employee benefits specialist Emerson Electric Co., St. Louis, 1973-78; benefits cons. Alexander & Alexander, St. Louis, 1978-79; asst. v.p. pension profit sharing Centerre Trust, St. Louis, 1979-82; dir. of pensions St. Louis Home Builders Assn., St. Louis, 1982-83; v.p., gen. counsel, benefits cons. Pension Assocs., Inc., St. Louis, 1983-84; pvt. practice T.C. Farnam & Assocs., St. Louis, 1984-92; adj. prof. Webster U., St. Louis, 1984-93; pvt. practice The Farnam Law Firm, St. Louis, 1993—. Bd. dirs. Small Bus. Coun. Am., Washington; exec. com. Employee Benefits Assn. of St. Louis, 1985-99, Art St. Louis, Inc.; steering com. WEB, St. Louis, 1987-90. Contbr. chpt. to book and articles to profl. jours. Trustee Eugene Field Found., St. Louis, 1986—; pres. of trustee Wydown Terr., Clayton, Mo., 1982-93; com. chmn. troop 21 Boy Scouts Am., Clayton, 1989-92, asst. scoutmaster, 1992-98, post advisor Explorer Post 9021, Clayton, 1996-97; mem. parish coun. St. Joseph's Ch., Clayton, 1982-85. Fellow Am. Coll. Tax Counsel; mem. ABA (taxation, bus. & labor sect., employee benefit coms.), Mo. State Bar Assn., Ind. State Bar Assn., Bar Assn. Met. St. Louis (chair employee benefits com. 1986-93), Noonday Club. Republican. Avocations: restoring 356 porsches, photography, computers, cooking. Pension, profit-sharing, and employee benefits, Corporate taxation, Personal income taxation. Office: The Farnam Law Firm One Metropolitan Sq 211 N Broadway Ste 2940 Saint Louis MO 63102-2733 E-mail: tcf@farnamlaw.com.

FARNHAM, CLAYTON HENSON, lawyer; b. New Brunswick, N.J., Aug. 18, 1938; s. Richard Bayles and Naomi Shropshire (Henson) F.; m. Katharine Gross, Sept. 16, 1967; children: Julia Kernan, Richard Bayles II. BA, U. of the South, 1961; LLB, U. Ga., 1967. Bar: Ga. 1968, U.S. Dist. Ct. (no., so. and mid. dists.) Ga. 1968, U.S. Supreme Ct. 1978, U.S. Dist. Ct. (no. dist.) Miss. 1978, U.S. Ct. Appeals (5th. cir., 11th cir.) 1968, (4th cir.) 1980, U.S. Ct. Appeals (8th cir.) 1992. Law clk. to judge U.S. Dist. Ct., Atlanta, 1967-69; from assoc., to ptnr. Swift, Currie, McGhee & Hiers, Atlanta, 1969-82; ptnr. Drew, Eckl & Farnham, Atlanta, 1983—. Contbr. articles to profl. jours. Lt. (j.g.) USNR, 1961-64. Mem. ABA (coun. TIPS sect. 1989-92), Internat. Assn. Def. Counsel (com. chmn. 1987-89), Ansley Golf Club, Lawyer's Club Atlanta, Old War Horse Lawyer's Club. Federal civil litigation, State civil litigation, Insurance. Home: 30 Inman Cir NE Atlanta GA 30309 Office: Drew Eckl & Farnham 800 W Peachtree St NW PO Box 7600 Atlanta GA 30357 E-mail: cfarnham@deflaw.com.

FARNSWORTH, E(DWARD) ALLAN, lawyer, educator; b. Providence, June 30, 1928; s. Harrison Edward and Gertrude (Romig) F.; m. Patricia Ann Nordstrom, May 30, 1952; children: Jeanne Scott, Karen Ladd, Edward Allan (dec.), Pamela Ann. BS, U. Mich., 1948; MA, Yale U., 1949; JD (Ordronaux prize 1952), Columbia U., 1952; LLD (hon.), Dickinson Law Sch., Pa. State U., 1988; Docteur en Droit (hon.), U. Paris, 1988, U. Louvain, 1989. Bar: D.C 1952, N.Y. 1956. Mem. faculty Columbia U., N.Y.C., 1954—, prof. law, 1959—, Alfred McCormack prof. law, 1970—. Vis. prof. U. Istanbul, U. Dakar, 1964, U. Paris, 1974-75, 90, 93, Harvard Law S ch., 1970-71, Stetson Coll. Law, 1991, 94, U. Mich., 1994; mem. faculty Salzburg Seminar Am. Law, 1963, Columbia-Leyden-Amsterdam program on Am. law, 1964, 69, 73, 85, San Diego Inst. Internat. and Comparative Law, Paris, 1982, 94, Tulane Summer Inst., Paris, 1995, 98, 99, 00, Rhodes, 1996, China Ctr. for Am. Law Study, Beijing, 1986; dir. orientation program on Am. law Assn. Am. Law Schs., 1965-68; U.S. rep. UN Commn. on Internat. Trade Law, 1970-81; reporter Restatement of Contracts 2nd, 1971-80; cons. N.Y. State Law Revision Commn., 1956, 58, 59, 61, P.R. comml. code revision, 1988-91; mem. coms. validity and agy. internat. sales contracts Internat. Inst. Unification Pvt. Law, Rome, 1966-72, mem. governing coun., 1978-98; mem. adv. com. on pvt. internat. law Sec. of State, 1985-89; spl. counsel city reorgn. N.Y.C. Coun., 1966-68; U.S. del. Vienna Conf. on Internat. Sales Law, 1980, Bucharest and Geneva Conf. on Internat. Agy., 1979, 83. Author: Changing Your Mind: The Law of Regretted Decisions, 1998, An Introduction to the Legal System of the United States, 3d edit., 1993; (with J. Honnold, S. Harris, C. Mooney, and C. Reitz) Cases and Materials on Commercial Law, 5th edit., 1993; (with W.F. Young and C. Sanger) Cases and Materials on Contracts, 6th edit., 2001, Cases and Materials on Negotiable Instruments, 4th edit., 1993, Treatise on Contracts, 1982, 3d edit., 1999; (with V. Mozolin) Contract Law in the USSR and the United States, 1987, Farnsworth on Contracts, 3 vols., 1990, 2nd edit., 1998, United States Contract Law, 1992, 2d revised edit, 1999. Capt. USAAF, 1952-54. Fellow British Acad.; mem. ABA (Theberge award for pvt. internat. law 1996), Am. Philos. Soc., Am. Law Inst., Assn. of Bar of City of N.Y. (chmn. com. on fgn. and comparative law 1967-70, chmn. spl. com. on products liability 1979-82), Phi Beta Kappa, Phi Delta Phi. Unitarian Universalist. Home: 201 Lincoln St Englewood NJ 07631-3158 Office: Columbia U 435 W 116th St New York NY 10027-7201 E-mail: allan@law_columbia.edu.

FARNSWORTH, T. BROOKE, lawyer; b. Grand Rapids, Mich., Mar. 16, 1945; s. George Llelwyn and Gladys Fern (Kennedy) Farnsworth; m. Connie D. Hedblom, June 15, 1996; children: Leslie Erin, T. Brooke. BS in Bus., Ind. U., 1967; JD, Ind. U., Indpls., 1971. Bar: Tex. 1971, U.S. Dist. Ct. (so. dist.) Tex. 1972, U.S. Tax Ct. 1972, U.S. Ct. Appeals (5th cir.) 1977, U.S. Ct. Appeals D.C. Cir. 1977, U.S. Supreme Ct. 1978, U.S. Ct. Appeals (11th cir.) 1982, U.S. Dist. Ct. (we. dist.) Tex. 1988, U.S. Dist. Ct. (no. dist.) Tex. 1994. Adminstrv. asst. to treas. of State of Ind., Indpls., 1968-71; assoc. Butler, Binion, Rice, Cook & Knapp, Houston, 1971-74; counsel Damson Oil Corp., Houston, 1974-78; prin. Farnsworth & Assocs., Houston, 1978-90, Farnsworth & von Berg, Houston, 1990—. Contbr. articles on law to profl. jours. Mem.: ATLA, ABA, Tex. Trial Lawyers Assn., Fed. Energy Bar Assn., Houston Bar Assn., State Bar Tex., Fed. Bar Assn., Champions Golf Club, Loch Lomond Golf Club, Olympic Club. Republican. General civil litigation, Commercial, contracts (including sales of goods; commercial financing), Oil, gas, and mineral. Home: 6038 Pebble Beach Dr Houston TX 77069 Office: Farnsworth and von Berg 333 N Sam Houston Pkwy E Ste 300 Houston TX 77060-2414

FARON, ROBERT STEVEN, lawyer; b. N.Y.C., Jan. 10, 1947; s. Jack and Ceil Faron; m. Linda A. Baumann, May 18, 1975; children: Gregory Andrew, Douglas James, Daniel Scott. BS in Engring., Princeton U., 1968; JD, Columbia U., 1975. Bar: D.C. 1975, U.S. Ct. Appeals (D.C. cir.) 1978, U.S. Ct. Appeals (4th cir.) 1986, U.S. Ct. Claims 1986. Systems engr. IBM Corp., Holmdel, N.J., 1968-69; atty. U.S. Dept. of Commerce, Washington, 1975-76; fgn. svc. officer U.S. Dept. of State, Washington, 1976-77; assoc. LeBoef, Lamb, Leiby & MacRae, Washington, 1977-82; of counsel Lane & Mittendorf, Washington, 1982-84, Brown, Roady, Bonvillian & Gold, Washington, 1984-85; ptnr. Alagia, Day, Marshall, Mintmire & Chauvin, Washington, 1986-90; dep. asst. gen. counsel for environ. Dept. of Energy, Washington, 1990-93; asst. gen. counsel Amerada Hess Corp., 1993-97; sr. advisor PHB Hagler Bailly, Inc., Washington, 1997-2000; pvt. practice, 2001—. Chair energy com. D.C. Bar sect. environ. energy and nat. resources. Contbr. articles to profl. jours. Capt. USAF, 1969—72. Mem. ABA (chmn. TIPS energy resources law com. 1988-89, 91-97, mem. TIPS profl. issues com. 1989-92, coordinating group energy law 1989-94), Assoc. Internat. de Droit des Assurances (chmn. U.S. pollution law working party 1986-89). Environmental, Insurance, Private international. Office: Law Offices Ste 708 1330 New Hampshire Ave NW Washington DC 20036 E-mail: rsfaron@verizon.net.

FARQUHARSON, GORDON MACKAY, lawyer, director; b. Charlottetown, P.E.I., Can., July 12, 1928; s. Percy Alfred and Rachel Lillian (MacKay) F.; m. Judy Lynne Bridges, Oct. 10, 1980; children: Trevor, Jordan; children by previous marriage: Douglas, Tanyss, Rob, Caryn. BA, U. Toronto, 1950; LL.B., Osgoode Hall Law Sch., 1954. Bar: Called to Ont. bar 1954; Queen's Counsel 1965. Pvt. practice, Toronto, 1954—; ptnr. Lang Michener, 1964—. Dir. Valleydene Corp. Ltd., Doverhold Investments Ltd. Mem. University Club (Toronto), Craigleigh Ski Club, Phi Gamma Delta (pres. 1950). Home: 419 Brunswick Ave Toronto ON Canada Office: BCE Pl 181 Bay St Ste 2500 Toronto ON Canada M5J 2T7

FARR, G(ARDNER) NEIL, lawyer; b. L.A., Jan. 9, 1932; s. Gardner and Elsie M. (Schuster) F.; m. Lorna Jean, Oct. 26, 1957; children: Marshall Clay, Jennifer T., Thomas M. BA, U. Calif., Berkeley, 1957; JD, U. Calif., San Francisco, 1960. Bar: Calif. 1961, U.S. Supreme Ct. 1977; cert. specialist family law Calif. Bd. Specialization. Dep. dist. atty. Solano County, 1961-66; recreation commr. City of Fairfield, 1964-66; dep. dist. atty. Kern County, 1966-69; ptnr. Law Offices Young Wooldridge, Bakersfield, Calif., 1969—. Judge protem Kern County Superior Ct. Chmn. Kern County Juvenile Justice Commn. With USNR, 1949-53. Mem. ABA, Calif. Bar Assn., Kern County Bar Assn. (pres. 1984, past pres. family law sect.). Family and matrimonial. Office: Young Wooldridge 1800 30th St Fl 4 Bakersfield CA 93301-1919 Fax: 661-327-1087.

FARRAGUT-HEMPHILL, SANDRA, judge; BS, Spelman Coll., 1975; JD, U. Fla., 1979. Bar: Mo. 1982, U.S. Dist. Ct. (ea. dist.) Mo. 1982. Law clk. Jacksonville Area Legal Aid, Inc., Fla., 1979—81; asst. prof. Edward Waters Coll., Jacksonville, Fla., 1981—82; staff atty. Legal Svcs. of Ea. Mo., St. Louis; asst. adj. prof. Sch. Law, St. Louis U. Bd. dirs. Jacksonville Urban League, Fla., 1980—81, N. Fla. Coun. Camp Fire Girls Am., 1980—81, Children's Home Soc. Fla., Jacksonville, 1980—81, St. Louis Neighborhood Mediation Ctr., 1984. Grantee, Coun. on Legal Edn. Opportunity, U. Fla., 1976—79, Bd. Regents, U. Fla., 1978—79; Reginald Herber Smith fellow, 1979—81. Mem.: ABA, Nat. Assn. Women Judges, Women Lawyers Assn. St. Louis, Mound City Bar Assn., Met. Bar Assn. St. Louis, Phi Alpha Delta, Alpha Kappa Alpha. Office: St Louis Cty Cir Ct 7900 Carondelet Divsn 42 Clayton MO 63105

FARRAR, FRANK LEROY, lawyer, former governor; b. Britton, S.D., Apr. 2, 1929; s. Virgil William and Venetia Soule (Taylor) F.; m. Patricia Jean Henley, June 5, 1953; children— Jeanne Marie, Sally Ann, Robert John, Mary Susan, Ann M. BS, U. S.D., 1951, LL.B., 1953; LL.D., Huron Coll. Bar: S.D. 1953. Practiced law, Britton, 1957-63; agt. IRS, 1955-57; judge Marshall County, S.D., 1958, state's atty., 1959-62; atty. gen. State of S.D., 1963-69, gov., 1969-70; ptnr. Farrar & Spiry, Britton, S.D., 1970—. Chmn. Cardinal and Gold Ins. Co., Frank L. Farrar & Assocs., Performance Bankers, Inc., Capital, Fulda, Beresford, Wanbay, Sidney, Uptown, Versailles, Glenrock, Wolf Point Bancorps., Inc., NW Investment Inc., Carlton Agy., Inc., 1st Agy. Hasting, Cairo, First, Inc., Peoples Holding Co.; adv. bd. dirs. Citicorp, Correspondent Resources Inc. Past pres. Pheasant council Boy Scouts Am.; past chmn. S.D. March of Dimes; past fund raising chmn. S.D. Mental Health Assn.; bd. dirs. Rural Coalition Am.; chmn. Marshall County Republican Party, 1959; asst. sgt.-at-arms Rep. Nat. Conv., 1960. Served to capt. U.S. Army Recipient Alumnus Achievement award U. S.D., 1981, named Alumnus of Yr. Sch. Bus., 1979; named Sr. Olympics Athlete of the Yr. for S.D., 4th All Am. for Triathlon, 1999; named to Hall of Fame Sr. Olympics, S.D. Mem. S.D. Bar Assn., Ind. Bar Assn., Wash. Bar Assn., S.D. States Attys. Assn. (asst. pres.), Nat. Dist. Attys. Assn., Alpha Tau Omega, Phi Delta Phi. Lodges: Masons, Shriners, Jesters, Lions, Elks, Odd Fellows, Sportsmen. Address: PO Box 936 Britton SD 57430-0936

FARRAR, STANLEY F. lawyer; b. Santa Ana, Calif., 1943; BS, U. Calif., Berkeley, 1964, JD, 1967. Bar: Calif. 1968, N.Y. 1969. Mem. Sullivan & Cromwell LLP, L.A. Mem. ABA (chmn. subcom. on bank holding cos. and nonbank activities banking law com. 1980-85, chmn. letters credit subcom. uniform comml. code com. 1982-88, sect. bus. law), State Bar Calif. (chmn. fin. instns. com. 1981-82). Banking, Mergers and acquisitions, Securities. Office: Sullivan & Cromwell LLP 1888 Century Park E Los Angeles CA 90067-1725 E-mail: farrars@sullcrom.com.

FARRELL, LYNNE S. lawyer; b. New Haven; BA in History, Albertus Magnus Coll.; MS in Edn., So. Conn. State U.; PhD, Fordham U.; JD, Quinnipiac U.; MS in Adminstrn., Fairfield U. Bar: Conn. Pub. sch. prin. Bd. Edn., West Haven, Conn.; adj. prof. Fordham U., N.Y.C., U. New Haven; ptnr. Farrell, Leslie & Grachowski, Wallingford, Conn. Mem.: ABA, West Haven Bar Assn., New Haven County Bar Assn., Conn. Bar Assn. Avocation: golf. Education and schools, Juvenile, Criminal. Office: Farrell Leslie & Grachowski 375 Center St Wallingford CT 06492

FARRELL, MICHAEL W. state supreme court justice; Grad., U. Notre Dame; MA, Columbia U.; JD, Am. U. Law clerk to Assoc. Judge John P. Moore Md. Ct. Spl. Appeals, 1973; atty. criminal divsn. U.S. Dept. Justice; chief appellate divsn. Office U.S. Atty. D.C., 1982-89; assoc. judge D.C. Ct. Appeals, 1989—. Chmn. Eng. dept. Georgetown Prep. Sch. Office: Ct Appeals 500 Indiana Ave NW Rm 6000 Washington DC 20001-2131*

FARRELL, TERESA JOANNING, lawyer; b. L.A., Sept. 17, 1958; d. Harold T. and Helen Dolores Joanning; m. Michael P. Farrell, Oct. 18, 1986. BA, U. Calif., San Diego, 1980; JD, U. Calif., 1986. Bar: Calif. 1986, U.S. Dist. Ct. (ctrl. dist.) Calif. 1987. Assoc., spl. counsel Gibson, Dunn & Crutcher LLP, Irvine, Calif., 1986-98, ptnr., 1999—. Bd. dirs. Second Harvest Food Bank, Orange, Calif., 1993—, The Harvesters, Newport Beach, Calif., 1993—, Pretend City--The Children's Mus. of Orange County, Newport Beach, Calif., 2001—. Mem. Calif. State Bar Assn. (real property sect.), Internat. Coun. Shopping Ctrs. Finance, Landlord-tenant, Property, real (including real estate development, water). Office: Gibson Dunn & Crutcher LLP 4 Park Plz Ste 1400 Irvine CA 92614-8557

FARRIS, JEROME, federal judge; b. Birmingham, Ala., Mar. 4, 1930; s. William J. and Elizabeth (White) Farris; 2 children. BS, Morehouse Coll., 1951, LLD, 1978; MSW, Atlanta U., 1955; JD, U. Wash., 1958. Bar: Wash. 1958. Mem. Weyer, Roderick, Schroeter and Sterne, Seattle, 1958—59; ptnr. Weyer, Schroeter, Sterne & Farris and successor firms, Seattle, 1959—61, Schroeter & Farris, Seattle, 1961—63, Schroeter, Farris, Bangs & Horowitz, Seattle, 1963—65, Farris, Bangs & Horowitz, Seattle, 1965—69; judge Wash. State Ct. of Appeals, Seattle, 1969—79, U.S. Ct. of Appeals (9th cir.), Seattle, 1979—95, sr. judge, 1995—. Lectr. U. Wash. Law Sch. and Sch. Social Work, 1976—; mem. faculty Nat. Coll. State Judiciary, U. Nev., 1973; adv. bd. Nat. Ctr. for State Cts. Appellate Justice Project, 1978—81; founder First Union Nat. Bank, Seattle, 1965, dir., 1965—69; mem. U.S. Supreme Ct. Jud. Fellows Commn., 1997—; mem. Jud. Conf. Com. on Internat. Jud. Rels., 1997—2000. Del. The White House Conf. on Children and Youth, 1970; mem. King County (Wash.) Youth Commn., 1969—70; vis. com. U. Wash. Sch. Social Work, 1977—90; mem. King County Mental Health-Mental Retardation Bd., 1967—69; past bd. dirs. Seattle United Way; mem. Tyee Bd. Advisers, U. Wash., 1984—88, bd. regents, 1985—97, pres., 1990—91; trustee U. Law Sch. Found., 1978—84, Morehouse Coll., 1999—; mem. vis. com. Harvard Law Sch., 1996—. With Signal Corps U.S. Army, 1952—53. Recipient Disting. Svc. award, Seattle Jaycees, 1965, Clayton Frost award, 1966. Fellow: Am. Bar Found. (chair of fellows 2000, bd. dirs. 1987, exec. com. 1989—97); mem.: ABA (exec. com. appellate judges conf. 1978—84, chmn. conf. 1982—83, exec. com. appellate judges conf. 1987—88, del. jud. adminstrn. coun. 1987—88, sr. lawyers divsn. coun. 1998—), State-Fed. Jud. Coun. State Wash. (vice-chmn. 1977—78, chmn. 1983—87), Wash. Coun. on Crime and Delinquency (chmn. 1970—72), U. Wash. Law Sch., Order of Coif (mem. law rev.). Office: US Ct Appeals 9th Cir 1030 US Courthouse 1010 5th Ave Seattle WA 98104-1181

FARRIS, SPENCER EDWARD, lawyer; b. Great Bend, Kans., June 23, 1964; children: Spencer Edward II, Mason Gabriel. BA, Okla. State U., Stillwater, 1986; JD, Washington U., St. Louis, 1992. Bar: Mo. 1991, Ill. 1992, U.S. Dist. Ct. (ea. dist.) Mo. 1992. Buyer Ft. Howard Corp., Muskogee, Okla., 1986-87; v.p. purchasing Ctrl. Paper Stock, St. Louis, 1987-89; assoc. Hullverson Law Firm, St. Louis, 1992—2002; pvt. practice, 2002—. Trustee Kirkwood (Mo.) Bapt. Ch., 1993-95. Recipient Am. Jurisprudence award, 1991, Lawyers award Internat. Acad. Trial Lawyers, 1992. Mem. ATLA, Mo. Bar Assn., Ill. Bar Assn., Mo. Assn. Trial Attys. (bd. govs. 1999-). Democrat. Avocations: weight training, computers. Product liability, Personal injury (including property damage), Workers' compensation. Office: SE Farris Law Firm 734 N Harrison Saint Louis MO 63122

FARTHING, EDWIN GLENN, lawyer; b. Greensboro, N.C., July 2, 1947; s. Edwin Harold Glenn and Martha Rachel (Harris) F.; 1 child, Lyle Britton. BA, U. N.C., 1969, JD, 1972. Bar: N.C 1972, U.S. Dist. Ct. (we. dist.) N.C. 1976, U.S. Ct. Appeals (4th cir.) 1982. Assoc. Smathers & Ferrell, Hickory, N.C., 1972; ptnr. Smathers, Ferrell & Farthing, Hickory, 1973, Smather & Farthing, Hickory, 1973-78, Farthing & Cheshire, Hickory, 1978-81, Tate, Young, Morphis, Bach & Farthing, Hickory,

1982-94; pvt. practice Law Office Edwin G. Farthing, Hickory, 1995—. Bd. dirs. N.C. Legal Edn. Assistance Fund, Raleigh, 1990-98. Elder Northminster Presbyn. Ch., Hickory, 1982-85, 89-92; precinct chmn. Catawba County Rep. Com., Hickory, 1993—; bd. dirs. N.C. Pride Polit. Action Com., Raleigh, 1993-97, N.C. Equality PAC, 2001—; mem. Hickory Cmty. Rels. Coun., 1995-2001, Hickory Bus. Task Force, 2002--. Mem. Mem. N.C. State Bar, N.C. Assn. Def. Attys. (sec.-tras. 1989-92), N.C. Bar Assn., Catawba County Bar Assn., N.C. Gay and Lesbian Attys. (pres. 1996-97). Avocations: politics, reading, boating, snow skiing. Alternative dispute resolution, Civil rights, General practice. Office: PO Box 9294 Hickory NC 28603-9294

FARUKI, CHARLES JOSEPH, lawyer; b. Bay Shore, N.Y., July 3, 1949; s. Mahmud Taji and Rita (Trownsell) F.; m. Nancy Louise Glock, June 5, 1971 (div. Oct. 1995); children: Brian Andrew, Jason Allen, Charles Joseph Jr.; m. Michelle F. Zalar, June 15, 1996. BA summa cum laude, U. Cin., 1971; JD cum laude, Ohio State U., 1973. Bar: Ohio 1974, U.S. Dist. Ct. (no. and so. dists.) Ohio 1975, U.S. Ct. Appeals (9th cir.) 1977, U.S. Tax Ct. 1977, U.S. Supreme Ct. 1977, U.S. Ct. Appeals (6th cir.) 1978, U.S. Dist. Ct. (no. dist.) Tex. 1979, U.S. Dist. Ct. (ea. dist.) Ky. 1982, U.S. Ct. Appeals (D.C. cir.) 1982, U.S. Ct. Customs and Patent Appeals 1982, U.S. Ct. Appeals (4th cir.) 1986, U.S. Ct. Appeals (2d cir.) 1989, U.S. Ct. Appeals (fed. cir.), 1991, U.S. Ct. Appeals (8th cir.) 1997. Assoc. Smith & Schnacke, Dayton, Ohio, 1974—78, ptnr., 1979—89; founder, mng. ptnr. Faruki Ireland & Cox PLL, Dayton, 1989—. Lectr. in field. Contbr. articles in field. Trustee Dayton Bar Assn. Found., 1997—, pres., 2002-03. Served to capt. U.S. Army Res., 1971-79. Fellow Am. Bar Found., Am. Coll. Trial Lawyers (complex litigation com. 1993-98, Ohio state com. 1998--); mem. ABA, Fed. Bar Assn. (officer and exec. com. Dayton chpt. 1988-93, pres. 1991-92), Ohio State Bar Assn. (bd. govs. Antitrust sect. 1992—), Dayton Bar Assn. (officer 1992-94, pres. 1994-95, 2002-03, trustee 1997—), Def. Rsch. Inst., Human Factors and Ergonomics Soc. (affiliate mem.), Fed. Cir. Bar Assn. Avocation: numismatics. Antitrust, Federal civil litigation, General civil litigation. Home: 300 Fairforest Cir Dayton OH 45419-1308 Office: Faruki Ireland & Cox PLL 500 Courthouse Plz SW Dayton OH 45402 E-mail: cfaruki@fgilaw.com.

FASCETTA, CHRISTOPHER MICHAEL, lawyer; b. N.Y.C., Apr. 27, 1966; s. Salvatore Charles and Mary Barbara Fascetta; m. Patricia Ann Salloum, July 25, 1998. BA, Washington Coll., 1988; JD, Widener U., 1991. Bar: Md. 1991, U.S. Dist. Ct. Md., 1992. Assoc. Rodgers and Dickerson, P.C., Timonium, Md., 1991-95, Law Offices Robert Grossbart, Balt., 1995-97; sr. assoc. Rodgers and Dickerson, P.C., Lutherville, Md., 1997—. Mem. Harford County Rep. Com., Bel Air, Md., 1998—, Balt. County Rep. Com., Towson, Md., 1995-98. Mem. Bankruptcy Bar Assn. (adv. bd. 1992—), Kappa Alpha (alumni advisor 1990—). Roman Catholic. Avocations: golf, camping. Bankruptcy, Commercial, consumer (including collections, credit), Corporate, general. Home: 481 Copeland Rd Fallston MD 21047-2924 Office: Rodgers and Dickerson PC 1301 York Rd Ste 500 Heaver Plaza Lutherville MD 21093

FASMAN, ZACHARY DEAN, lawyer; b. Chgo., Oct. 27, 1948; s. Irving D. and Lillian V. (Vilatzer) F.; children: Jonathan, Benjamin, Rebecca. BA, Northwestern U., 1969; JD, U. Mich., 1972. Bar: Ill. 1972, D.C. 1977, N.Y. 2001, U.S. Supreme Ct. 1977. Assoc., then ptnr. Seyfarth, Shaw et al, Chgo. and Washington, 1972-81; ptnr. Wald, Harkrader et al, Washington, 1981-83, Crowell & Moring, Washington, 1983-88, Paul, Hastings, Janofsky & Walker, Washington, 1988—2000, N.Y.C., 2000—. Author: Equal Employment Audit Handbook, 1983, Employment Law Compliance Manual, 1988, What Business Must Know About The ADA, 1992. Mem. ABA (labor law sect., litig. sect.), Coll. Labor and Employment Lawyers, Order of Coif. Federal civil litigation, Labor (including EEOC, Fair Labor Standards Act, labor-management relations, NLRB, OSHA), Civil rights. Home: 201 E 79th St Apt 15B New York NY 10021 Office: Paul Hastings Janofsky & Walker 75 E 55th St New York NY 10022 Office Fax: 212-318-6837. E-mail: zacharyfasman@paulhastings.com.

FASON, RITA MILLER, lawyer; b. Fargo, ND, July 12, 1935; d. John Maurice Miller and Mary Dullea; divorced; children: Catherine, John, William, Richard. BA in History, Rice Inst., 1957; JD, U. Houston, 1979. Bar: Tex. 1979. Pvt. practice John Graml & Assocs., Houston, 1979—; ptnr. Brady & Fason, Houston, 1981-82; pvt. practice Houston, 1982—. Eucharistic min. St. Anne's Cath. Ch., Houston, 1988—; pres. bd. dirs. Wellsprings, Houston, 1989-95. Mem. Assn. Women Attys. (com. 1979—). Avocations: gardening, traveling. Family and matrimonial, Probate (including wills, trusts). Home: 2121 Peckham St Houston TX 77019-6431 Office: 3212 Smith St Ste 202 Houston TX 77006-6622

FASS, PETER MICHAEL, lawyer, educator; b. Bklyn., Apr. 11, 1937; s. Irving and Bess (Fordin) F.; m. Deborah K. Orshan, May 6, 1989; 1 child, Olivia Jae; children from previous marriage: Brian Samuel, Lyle Williams. BS in Econs. with honors, U. Pa., 1958; JD cum laude, Harvard U., 1961; LLM, NYU, 1964. Bar: N.Y. 1965; CPA. From assoc. to ptnr. Carro, Spanbock, Fass, Geller, Kaster & Cuiffo, N.Y.C., 1968-86; ptnr. Kaye, Scholer, Fierman, Hayes & Handler, N.Y.C., 1988-95, Battle Fowler LLP, N.Y.C., 1995-2000, Proskauer Rose LLP, N.Y.C., 2000—. Adj. asst. prof. real estate NYU; lectr. Practising Law Inst., N.Y. Law Jour., Instl. mag., Ill. Inst. Continuing Legal Edn.; spl. cons. Calif. Commr. of Corps Real Estate Adv. Com.; mem. ad hoc com. Real Estate Securities and Syndication Inst., chmn. regulatory legis and taxation com., 1975-76; mem., dir. participant/real estate com. NASD, 1991-94. Co-author: Tax Advantaged Securities, 1977—, Real Estate Syndication Handbook, 1985-87, Tax Aspects of Real Estate Investments, 1988—, Blue Sky Practice Handbook, 1987—, Real Estate Investment Trusts Handbook, 1987—, S Corporation Handbook, 1985—, Tax Advantaged Securities Handbook, 1979—; contbr. articles to profl. jours. Recipient Haskins award for outstanding achievement in N.Y. State C.P.A.s exam., 1964 Mem. ABA (chmn. real estate investment com., real property, probate and trust sect.), N.Y. State Bar Assn., Am. Inst. CPA's, N.Y. State Soc. CPA's, Pi Lambda Phi, Beta Gamma Sigma, Beta Alpha Psi. Securities, Taxation, general, Corporate, general. Home: 115 Central Park W New York NY 10023-4153 Office: Proskauer Rose LLP 1585 Broadway New York NY 10036-8299 E-mail: pfass@proskauer.com., reitman411@aol.com.

FASSLER, CHARLES, lawyer; b. Bklyn., May 22, 1946; s. Meyer Sam and Esther (Genberg) F.; m. Marcia Belle Goldstein, July 3, 1971; children: Jacqueline I., Lauren S., Michael S. BS in Acctg., Bklyn. Coll., 1967; JD, U. Wis., 1970; LLM in Taxation, NYU, 1974. Bar: N.Y. 1971, Ky. 1976. Mem. staff Laventhal & Horwath, N.Y.C., 1963-68, Arthur Young & Co., N.Y.C., 1969; assoc. Marshall, Bratter, Greene, Allison & Tucker, N.Y.C., 1970-75; ptnr. Greenebaum Doll & McDonald PLLC, Louisville, 1976—. Author: Kentucky Mineral Law, Kentucky Limited Liability Company Forms and Practice Manual; contbr. numerous articles to profl. jours. Bd. dirs. Jewish Edn. Assn., Louisville, 1982-86, Congregation Adath Jeshurun, 1985-93. Mem. ABA, Ky. Bar Assn. Democrat. Jewish. Corporate, general, Corporate taxation, Taxation, general. Office: Greenebaum Doll Et Al 3300 National City Tower Louisville KY 40202

FAST, KENNETH H. lawyer; b. Newark, Apr. 1929; s. Moe M. and Eva H. Fast; m. Judith Nicholson, Nov. 23, 1969; children: Jonathan Nicholson, Madelaine M. BA, Lafayette Coll., 1951; LLB, Yale U., 1954. Bar: N.J. 1954, D.C. 1954, U.S. Ct. Appeals (3d cir.) 1958, U.S. Supreme Ct. 1960. Ptnr. Fast & Fast, East Orange, N.J., 1957-86, Fox & Fox, Livingston, N.J., 1987—. Trustee Weisberger Fund for Age, Poor and Needy, Raritan, N.J., 1969—. 1st lt. USAF, 1955-57. Mem. N.J. State Bar Assn., Essex County Bar Assn. Commercial, contracts (including sales of goods; commercial financing), Landlord-tenant, Property, real (including real estate development, water). Home: 91 Fairfield Dr Short Hills NJ 07078-1718

FATE, AARON ALAN, lawyer; b. Royal Oak, Mich., Sept. 19, 1973; s. Gary Alan and Patricia Andrews Fate. BA, Grinnell (Iowa) Coll., 1996; MA, U. Iowa, 2001; JD, U. Mich., 2001. Bar: Va., D.C., U.S. Ct. Appeals (4th cir.) 1979. Rsch. and speechwriting cons. Iowans for Jim Leach, Bettendorf, 1996; staff asst. Congressman Jim Leach, Washington, 1996—97; field dir. Iowans for Jim Leach, Bettendorf, 1998; rsch. asst. U. Mich. Law Sch., Ann Arbor, 1999; summer assoc. Baker Botts LLP, Washington, 2000; law clk. Verner Lijpfert, Washington, 2000—01; atty. Piper Rudnick LLP, Washington, 2001—. Mem.: ABA, Va. State Bar Assn. Administrative and regulatory, Private international, Public international. Home: 13005 Collingwood Ter Silver Spring MD 20904 Office: Piper Rudnick LLP 901 15th St NW Washington DC 20005

FAUCHIER, DAN R(AY), mediator, arbitrator, educator, construction management consultant; b. Blackwell, Okla., Sept. 27, 1946; s. Wallace Monroe and Betty Lou F.; m. Sylvia Stephanie Chan Fauchier, Mar. 15, 1969; 1 child, Angele Calista Fauchier; m. Jonah Keri, 1997. BA cum laude, Southwestern Coll., 1964-68; student, Sch. Theology, Claremont, Calif., 1968-69, Claremont Grad. Sch., 1969-70. Lic. bldg. contractor, Calif.; cert. arbitrator and mediator. Min. of youth First United Meth. Ch., Winfield, Kans., 1964-68, First Congl. Ch., Riverside, Calif., 1968-69; adminstr. Calif. Youth Authority, Chino and Paso Robles, Calif., 1969-76; tchr. Chaffey Coll., Rancho Cucamonga, Calif., 1971-74; dir. Pacific Fin. Svcs., Beverly Hills, Calif., 1977-81; pres. Littlefields Corp., Santa Maria and Corona del Mar, Calif., 1978-81; cons. Hughes Helicopters, Oasis Oil, Jakarta, Indonesia, 1981; systems designer Teltrans Corp., L.A., 1982-85; project mgr. Pacific Sunset Builders, L.A., 1985-87, DW Devel., Fontana, Calif., 1987-90; owner Fauchier Group Builders, San Diego, 1988—; pres. Empire Bay Devel. Corp., San Bernardino, Calif., 1991-92; project mgr. White Sys. L.A. Ctrl. Libr., 1993; dir. project mgmt. White Sys. divsn. Pinnacle Automation, Inc., San Diego, 1993-95; dir. project mgmt.; dir. design logistics White Systems divsn. Pinnacle Automation, Inc., San Diego, 1995-97; v.p. SDC & Assocs., San Diego and Washington, 1997-2000; tchr. Power Summit, 2000—, dir., bd. advisors, 2001—. Founding dir. Neighborhood Restoration Project, San Bernardino, Calif., 1991-92; cons. project mgr. White Sys., Inc., Cin. Pub. Libr., 1997, FCC Document Mechanization Project, 1998; instr. U. Calif. San Diego, 1998-2001; Inst. Constrn. Mgmt., arbitrator and mediator Arbitration Works, 1999—, Saddle Island Inst., 1999—; instr. San Diego State U., 2001—, mediator panelist La Jolla Ctr. Dipsute Resolution, 2003-. Contbr. cons.: President's Commission on Criminal Justice, 1972; co-author: Consumer Credit, 1984. Deputy Registrar Voters San Bernardino, Calif., 1975; mem. Skid Row Mental Health Adv. Bd., L.A., 1986, Chaffey Coll. Adv. Bd. Rancho Cucamonga, Calif., 1991-95, chmn. Bus. Security Alliance, San Bernardino, Calif., 1992. Named Nat. fellow Woodrow Wilson Fellowship, Princeton, N.J., 1968-69; Grad. scholar State of Calif., Claremont, 1969. Mem. Associated Gen. Contractors (chmn. edn. com. 1999-2001), Am. Subcontractor Assn. (chmn. mktg. com. 1999-2000), Associated Builders and Contractors, Nat. Elec. Contractors Assn., Forensics Cons. Assn., Nat. Found. for Dispute Rev. Bds., Engring. Gen. Contractors Assn. (pub. works advocate), ABA Constrn. Industry Forum, Self-Realization Fellowship, Christmas in April (bd. dirs., v.p. 1999-2000), Habitat for Humanity, Internat. Platform Assn., Inst. for Cmty. Econ., Homeless Coalition, People for Ethical Treatment of Animals, Rainforest Alliance. Avocations: painting, photography, writing. Home: PMB249 9921 Carmel Mountain Rd San Diego CA 92129-2813 E-mail: dan@danzpage.com.

FAULK, MICHAEL ANTHONY, lawyer; b. Kingsport, Tenn., Sept. 10, 1953; s. Loy Glade and Rosella E. (Dykes) F.; m. Janet Lynn McLain, Aug. 31, 1974; children: Katherine Lea, Andrew McLain. BS, U. Tenn., 1975; M in Pub. Adminstrn., Memphis State U., 1978, JD, 1979. Bar: U.S. Dist. Ct. (we. dist.) Tenn. 1980, U.S. Dist. Ct. (ea. dist.) Tenn. 1985, U.S. Supreme Ct., 1998; cert. civil trial specialist, Nat. Bd. Trial Advocacy. Dep. clk. to presiding justice Shelby County Chancery Ct., Memphis, 1977-79; assoc. Weintraub & Dehart, Memphis, 1980-82; ptnr. Frazier & Faulk, Church Hill, Tenn., 1982-83; sole practice Church Hill, 1983-93; ptnr. Law Offices of Faulk, May & Coup, Church Hill, Tenn., 1993-96; sole practice Church Hill, 1996—. Commr. Tenn. Human Rights Commn., Nashville, 1985-92, vice chmn. 1988-92; referee Hawkins County Juvenile Ct., Rogersville, Tenn., 1985-96; bd. commrs. Hawkins County, 1998-2002; bd. dirs. Legal Services Inc., Johnson City, Tenn. Bd. dirs. Upper East Tenn. Div. Am. Heart Assn., Blountville, 1984-86. Named one of Outstanding Young Men in Am. U.S. Jaycees, 1977. Mem. ABA, Hawkins County Bar Assn. (pres. 1987-88), Assn. Trial Lawyers Am., Ducks Unltd. (chmn. Holston River chpt. 1984-98). Lodges: Moose. Republican. Baptist. Avocation: outdoors. State civil litigation, General practice. Office: 112 E Main Blvd Church Hill TN 37642-2080 E-mail: mfaulk@chartertn.net.

FAURI, ERIC JOSEPH, lawyer; b. Lansing, Mich., Feb. 16, 1942; s. Fedele Fauri and Iris M. Petersen; m. Sherrill Lynn Nurenberg, July 15, 1969; children— Lauren, Nadia, Kirk. B.A., U. Del., 1963; J.D. with distinction, U. Mich., 1966. Bar: Mich. 1967, U.S. Dist. Ct. (ea. dist.) Mich. 1967, U.S. Dist. Ct. (we. dist.) Mich. 1972, U.S. Ct. Appeals (6th cir.) 1974. Assoc. Dykema, Gossett, Spencer, Goodnow & Trigg, Detroit, 1966-71; Parmenter Forsythe, Rude et al, Muskegon, Mich., 1971-73; ptnr. Parmenter, Forsythe, Rude et al, Muskegon, 1973—; Parmenter O'Toole, 1992—. Served to capt. U.S. Army, 1967-68. Mem. ABA, State Bar Mich. Banking, Commercial, contracts (including sales of goods; commercial financing). Office: Parmenter O'Toole 175 W Apple Ave PO Box 786 Muskegon MI 49443-0786

FAWCETT, CHARLES WINTON, lawyer; b. Long Beach, Calif., May 26, 1946; s. Phillip Nimmons and Beatrice Stricker (Winton) F.; m. Kathleen Gloria Mayes, Dec. 15, 1975; children: Reid Charles, Tracie Diane, Ryan Mayes, Marni Taylor. BA, U. Calif., Santa Barbara, 1968; JD, U. Calif., Berkeley, 1971. Bar: Idaho 1971, Wash. 1975, U.S. Tax Ct. 1982. Staff atty. Idaho Legal Aid Services, Lewiston, 1971-73, Caldwell, 1973-74; adminstrv. law judge State of Wash., Seattle, 1974-76; asst. atty. gen. State of Idaho, Boise, 1976-77; sr. ptnr. Skinner Fawcett, Boise, 1977—. Contbr. articles to law jour. Mem. Idaho Bar Assn., Boise Bar Assn., Nat. Assn. Bond Lawyers, Comml. Law League Am. Commercial, consumer (including collections, credit), Corporate, general, Municipal (including bonds). Office: Skinner Fawcett PO Box 700 Boise ID 83701-0700

FAWCETT, DWIGHT WINTER, lawyer; b. Springfield, Ohio, Sept. 24, 1927; s. Dwight Ansley and Hazel (Winter) F.; m. Anne N. Langfitt, Apr. 27, 1957; children: Dwight P., Jane F. Dearborn, Donald N. B.S., Ind. U., 1948; J.D., Harvard U., 1951. Bar: Ill. 1951, U.S. Supreme Ct. 1975. Assoc. Mayer, Brown & Platt, Chgo., 1951-61, ptnr., 1961-91. Served with USN, 1945-46. Republican. Episcopalian. Clubs: Law; Indian Hill (Winnetka, Ill.); Lost Tree (North Palm Beach, Fla.). Administrative and regulatory, Banking, Commercial, contracts (including sales of goods; commercial financing). Home: 711 Locust St Winnetka IL 60093-2013

FAWSETT, PATRICIA COMBS, federal judge; b. 1943; BA, U. Fla., 1965, MAT, 1966, JD, 1973. Pvt. practice law Akerman, Senterfitt & Edison, Orlando, Fla., 1973-86; commr. 9th Cir. Jud. Nominating Commn, 1973-75, Greater Orlando Crime Prevention Assn., 1983-86; judge U.S. Dist. Ct. (mid. dist.) Fla., Orlando, 1986—. Trustee Legal Aid Soc., 1977-81, Loch Haven Art Ctr., Inc., Orlando, 1980-84, U. Fla. Law Sch., 2001—; hon. trustee Reago Spiritual Scholarship Found., 1999—; commr. Orlando Housing Authority, 1976-80, Winter Park (Fla.) Sidewalk Festival, 1973-75; bd. dirs. Greater Orlando Area C. of C., 1982-85. Mem. ABA (trial lawyers sect., real estate probate sect.), Am. Judicaturs Soc., Assn. Trial Lawyers Am., Fla. Bar Found. (bd. dirs. grants com.), Commn. on Access to Cts., Fla. Coun. Bar Assn. Pres.'s (pres., bd. dirs. 9th cir. grievance com.) Osceola County Bar Assn., Fla. Bar (bd. govs. 1983-86, budget com., disciplinary rev. com., integration rule and bylaws com., com. on access to legal system, bd. of cert., designation and advt., jud. adminstrn., selection and tenure com., jud. nominating procedures com., pub. rels. com., ann. meeting com., appellate rules com., spl. com. on judiciary-trial lawyer rels., chairperson midyr. conv. com., bd. dirs. trial lawyers sect.), Orange County Bar Assn. (exec. coun. 1977-83, pres. 1981-82), Order of Coif, Phi Beta Kappa. Office: US Dist Ct Federal Bldg 80 N Hughey Ave Ste 611 Orlando FL 32801-2231

FAWWAL, AUDEH EDWARD, lawyer; b. Washington, Nov. 15, 1953; s. Mansur J. and Zahia M. Fawwal; m. Cynthia Blackwell Fawwal, July 2, 1997; 1 child, Dorelle Victoria. BS in Journalism, U. Fla., 1975, JD, 1978. Bar: Ala. 1979, Fla. 1979, 11th cir. 1982. Asst. dist. atty. Jefferson County, Bessemer, Ala., 1979—81; pvt. practice Fawwal & Fawwal PC, Bessemer, 1981—. Bd. mem. Govs. Ala. Trial Lawyers Assn., 1989—91. Mem.: Bessemer Bar, Ala. State Bar. Avocation: music. Family and matrimonial, Workers' compensation, Pension, profit-sharing, and employee benefits. Office: Fawwal & Fawwal PC 312 N 18th St Bessemer AL 35020

FAX, CHARLES SAMUEL, lawyer; b. Balt., Sept. 12, 1948; s. David Hirsch and Eleanor Shirley (Lobe) F.; m. Nancy Lee Gruenberg, 1980 (div. 1995); children: Joanna May, Benjamin Zachary; m. Michele Weil, 1996. BA, Johns Hopkins U., 1970; JD with honors, George Washington U., 1973. Bar: D.C. 1974, N.Y. 1974, Md. 1990. Office of dist. atty. N.Y.C. (Bronx county), 1973-74; assoc. Truitt & Fabrikant, Washington, 1974-75, Chapman, Duff & Paul, Washington, 1975-79, ptnr., 1979-84, Porter, Wright, Morris & Arthur, Washington, 1985-89; sr. ptnr., co-chmn. lit. dept. Shapiro Sher Guinot & Sandler (formerly Shapiro and Olander), Balt., 1989—; mem. exec. com. Shapiro Sher Guinot & Sandler, Balt., 1999—; gen. counsel Parents and Children Together, Inc., 1992-98; apptd. mediator Cir. Ct. for Balt. City, 1994-98; spl. outside litigation counsel Commonwealth P.R. Dept. Justice, 1998-2001, Balt. City Mayor, 1994—95. Mem. faculty Exec. Enterprises, Inc., N.Y.C., Chgo., 1985-86; lectr. fed. personnel litigation Adminstrv. Law Inst., Washington, Chgo., San Francisco, 1982-83; lectr. Md. Mcpl. League, 1990-98; book rev. Cleve. Plain Dealer. Contbr. articles to newspapers and mags. Mem. Washington com. Sch. Arts and Scis., Johns Hopkins U., 1987—89; class agent Johns Hopkins U class of '70, 1995—, Johns Hopkins U. Class of 1970, 1995—; bd. dirs. Md. region Jewish Nat. Fund, 2002—, chmn. exec. com., 2002—, chmn. Md. region ann. campaign, 2002; bd. dirs. Am. Friends of Haifa Music Festival, 2002—. Mem. Johns Hopkins U. Soc. for 2d Decade, Tudor and Stuart Club, Johns Hopkins Club, Alpha Delta Phi. Democrat. Jewish. Appellate, Federal civil litigation, General civil litigation. Home: 10720 Gloxinia Dr North Bethesda MD 20852-3404 Office: Shapiro Sher Guinot & Sandler 36 S Charles St Ste 2000 Baltimore MD 21201-3147 E-mail: csfax@shapirosher.com., csf@aol.com.

FAXON, THOMAS BAKER, retired lawyer; b. Des Moines, Oct. 15, 1924; s. Ralph Henry and Prue (Baker) Faxon; m. Virginia Webb Johnson, Sept. 8, 1949; 1 child, Thomas Baker;1 child, Rebecca Webb Osgood. BA, Princeton U., 1949; LLB, Harvard U., 1952. Bar: Colo. 1953. Asst. prof., asst. dir. Inst. Govt. U. N.C., Chapel Hill, 1952-53; assoc. Pershing, Bosworth, Dick & Dawson, Denver, 1953-57; ptnr. Dawson, Nagel, Sherman & Howard, Denver, 1957-84; of counsel Sherman & Howard, Denver, 1984-92. Bd. trustees Colo. Legal Aid Found., Denver, 1984-91. Bd. dirs. Urban League Colo., Denver, 1964-67, Colo. chpt. UN Assn. of U.S.A., 1980-81, Recording for the Blind Colo., 1988-94; pres. bd. trustees 1st Unitarian Ch., Denver, 1960; mem. Denver Equality of Edn. Com., 1969. USAAF, 1943-46. Mem. Harvard Law Sch. Assn. Colo. (pres. 1968), Cactus Club Denver. Democrat. Address: 830 Race St Denver CO 80206-3734

FAY, REGAN JOSEPH, lawyer; b. Cleve., Sept. 19, 1948; s. Robert J. and Loretta Ann (Regan) F.; married; children: John, Mary, Matthew, Jessica, Samantha. BS in Chem. Engring., MIT, 1970; JD with honors, George Washington U., 1974. Bar: Ohio 1974, U.S. Dist. Ct. (no. dist.) Ohio 1974, U.S. Patent Office 1973, U.S. Ct. Appeals (fed. cir.) 1974, U.S. Ct. Appeals (9th cir.) 1975, U.S. Dist. Ct. (ea. dist.) Wis. 1976, U.S. Dist. Ct. (no. dist.) Tex. 1986, U.S. Supreme Ct. 1988. Patent examiner U.S. Patent and Trademark Office, Washington, 1970-72; law clk. to presiding justice U.S. Ct. Customs and Patent Appeals, Washington, 1973-75; assoc. Yount & Tarolli, Cleve., 1975-79; assoc., then ptnr. Jones, Day, Reavis & Pogue, Cleve., 1979—. Lectr. patent and trademark law Case Western Res. U., Cleve., 1976-86. Mem. Cleve. Intellectual Property Law Assn (pres. 1996-97). Republican. Roman Catholic. Avocation: skiing. Federal civil litigation, Patent, Trademark and copyright. Office: Jones Day Reavis & Pogue 901 Lakeside Ave E Cleveland OH 44114-1190 E-mail: rjfay@jonesday.com.

FAZIO, PETER VICTOR, JR., lawyer; b. Chgo., Jan. 22, 1940; s. Peter Victor and Marie Rose (LaMantia) F.; m. Patti Ann Campbell, Jan. 3, 1966; children: Patti-Marie, Catherine, Peter. AB, Coll. of Holy Cross, Worcester, Mass., 1961; JD, U. Mich., 1964. Bar: Ill. 1964, U.S. Dist. Ct. (no. dist.) Ill. 1965, U.S. Ct. Appeals (7th cir.) 1972, U.S. Supreme Ct. 1977, D.C. 1981, U.S. Ct. Appeals (D.C. cir.) 1988, Ind. 1993. Assoc. Schiff, Hardin & Waite, Chgo., 1964-70, ptnr., 1970-82, 84-95, mng. ptnr., 1995—2000, chmn., 2001—; exec. v.p. Internat. Capital Equipment, Chgo., 1982-83, also bd. dirs., 1982-85, sec., 1982-87; exec. v.p., gen. counsel NiSource Inc., 2000—. Bd. dirs. Planmetrics Inc., Chgo., 1984-92, Chgo. Lawyers Commn. for Civil Rights Under Law, 1976-82, co-chmn., 1978-80; bd. dirs. Seton Health Corp. No. Ill., Chgo 1987-90, vice chmn., 1989-90. Trustee Barat Coll., Lake Forest, Ill., 1977-82; bd. dirs. St. Joseph Hosp., Chgo., 1990-95, mem. exec. adv. bd., 1984-89, chmn., 1986-89; vice chmn. bd. dirs. Cath. Health Ptnrs., 1995-99, chmn., 1999—; dir. exec. com. Ill. Coalition, 1994—, N.W. Ind. Forum, 1994-98. Mem. ABA (coun. 1991-94, chmn. sect. pub. utility, transp. and comm. law 2000-01), FBA, Ill. Bar Assn., Chgo. Bar Assn., Fed. Energy Bar Assn., Edison Electric Inst. (chmn. legal com. 1999-2001), Am. Gas Assn. (legal com.), Am. Soc. Corp. Secs., Met. Club, Econ. Club Chgo., Comml. Club Chgo. Commercial, contracts (including sales of goods; commercial financing), FERC practice, Utilities, public. Office: Schiff Hardin & Waite 6600 Sears Tower 233 S Wacker Dr Chicago IL 60606-6473

FEAGLEY, MICHAEL ROWE, lawyer; b. Exeter, N.H., Feb. 1, 1945; s. Walter Charles and Laura (Rowe) F. BA, Wesleyan U., 1967; JD, Harvard U., 1973. Bar: Mass., Ill., U.S. Dist. Ct. (no. dist.) Ill., U.S. Dist. Ct. (ctrl. dist.) Ill., U.S. Ct. Appeals (6th, 7th, 8th and 10th cirs.), U.S. Supreme Ct. Assoc. Mayer Brown & Platt, Chgo., 1973-79, ptnr., 1980—. Instr. Nat. Inst. Trial Advocacy, Chgo., 1977--, John Marshall Law Sch., Chgo., 1980-85. Served to 1st lt. U.S. Army, 1968-71, Vietnam. Fellow Am. Coll. Trial Lawyers; mem. ABA, Chgo. Coun. Lawyers, Chgo. Bar Assn., Union League Club (Chgo.). Federal civil litigation, General civil litigation, State civil litigation. Office: Mayer Brown & Platt 190 S La Salle St Ste 3100 Chicago IL 60603-3441

FEAZELL, VIC, lawyer; b. Monroe, La., June 8, 1951; 1 child, Gregory Victor. BA, Mary Hardin Baylor Coll., 1972; JD, Baylor U., 1979. Bar: Tex. 1979, U.S. Dist. Ct. (5th cir.) 1988, U.S. Dist. Ct. (no. dist) 1988, U.S. Dist. Ct. (so. dist), 1989. Dir. drug abuse treatment program Mental Health-Mental Retardation, Waco, Tex., 1975-79; pvt. practice Waco, 1979-82; dist. atty. McLennan County, Tex., 1983-88; pvt. practice Austin, Tex., 1989-94; of counsel Rosenthal and Watson, Austin, 1995-2000; ptnr. Feazell, Rosenthal and Watson, Austin, 2001—. Pres. McLennan County

Peace Officers Assn., Waco, 1984-87; pro bono def. counsel Henry Lee Lucas, 1989-94; expert legal corr. O.J. Simpson Trial, KTBC TV. Primary character: Careless Whispers, 1986 (Edgar award 1986); exec. prodr. Rhinos the Movie, Natural Selection, Final Redemption, Blood Sweat and Teeth, Rage in the Cage; pres. One Horn Prodns.; contbr. articles to profl. jours. Del. State Dem. Conv., Houston, 1988. Named Outstanding Young Alumni, U. Mary Hardin Baylor, Belton, Tex., 1985, Peace Officer of Yr., Waco JC's, 1986. Fellow Tex. Bar Found. (life); mem. ATLA, Nat. Assn. Criminal Def. Lawyers (life), Tex. Trial Laywers Assn., Tex. Criminal Def. Lawyers Assn., State Bar Tex., Bar of U.S. Fifth Cir. Avocation: flim making. General civil litigation, Criminal, Personal injury (including property damage). Office: Feazell Rosenthal & Watson PC 6601 Vaught Ranch Rd Ste 200 Austin TX 78730 E-mail: vic@vicfeazell.com.

FECHTEL, VINCENT JOHN, legal administrator; b. Leesburg, Fla., Aug. 10, 1936; s. Vincent John and Annie Jo (Hayman) F.; m. Dixie Davenport, Feb. 1992; children: John, Katherine, Elizabeth D., MaryKatherine. BSBA, U. Fla., 1959. Mem. Fla. Ho. of Reps., 1972-78, Fla. Senate, 1978-80; parole commr. U.S. Dept. Justice, Chevy Chase, Md., 1983-96. Served with USNR and Fla. Nat. Guard. Mem. Alpha Tau Omega. Republican. Methodist. Home: 609 Cascade Ave Leesburg FL 34748-6323

FEDDE, G(ABRIEL) BERNHARD, retired lawyer; b. Bklyn., Mar. 7, 1909; s. Bernhard Andreas and Anna Mathea (Heggelund) F.; m. Johanna Borrevik, Aug. 14, 1957; m. Elizabeth Amy Ralston, Oct. 9, 1938 (div. 1955). AB, Williams Coll., 1930; postgrad., U. Munich, 1930-31, Columbia U., 1933-35; JD, U. Oreg., 1936; AM, Oreg. State U., 1964. Bar: Oreg. 1936. Pvt. practice law, Eugene, Oreg., 1938-43, Portland, Oreg., 1955-90; with forest svc. Civil Pub. Svc., Cascade Locks, Oreg., 1943-46; head relief mission Am. Friends Svc. Com., Oberhausen, Germany, 1946-48; lawyer Luth. World Fedn., Palestine, 1949-50. Adj. prof. Portland State U., 1955-90. Author: Norwegian-Swedish Crisis of 1905, 1964, also monographs. Mem. Scandinavian Heritage Found. (pres. 1985-90, 2001-02, bd. dirs. 1990-), Oreg. UN Assn. (bd. dirs. 1954-00), Norsemen's Fedn. Oreg. (pres. 1982-91), Scandinavian Club of Portland (pres. 1977-82). Lutheran. Home: 1919 NW Ramsey Crest Portland OR 97229-4209

FEDDERS, JOHN MICHAEL, lawyer; b. Covington, Ky., Oct. 21, 1941; s. Aloysius Henry and Mary Margaret (Schmidt) F.; m. Barbara E. Baxter; children: Luke D., Mark A., Matthew C., Andrew M., Peter J. BA in Journalism, Marquette U., 1963; LL.B., Cath. U. Am., 1966. Bar: N.Y. 1967, D.C. 1967. Assoc. Cadwalader, Wickersham & Taft, N.Y.C., 1966-71; exec. v.p. Gulf Life Holding Co., Dallas, 1971-73; with firm Arnold & Porter, Washington, 1973-81; ptnr., 1975-81; dir. Div. of Enforcement, SEC, 1981-85; ptnr. Miller, Cassidy, Larroca & Lewin, 1985-87; sole practice Washington, 1987—. Lectr. corp. securities and fin. Contbr. articles to legal jours. Recipient Service award Marquette U., 1977, Achievement award Cath. U. Am. Alumni Assn., 1982, Chmn.'s award for excellence SEC, 1982, Supervisory Excellence award, SEC, 1983 Mem. ABA, Assn. Bar City N.Y., Sigma Delta Chi, Phi Alpha Delta. Republican. Roman Catholic. General civil litigation, Corporate, general, Securities. Office: 1914 Sunderland Pl NW Washington DC 20036-1608 E-mail: jfedders@erols.com.

FEDER, ARTHUR A. lawyer, business executive; b. N.Y.C., Mar. 23, 1927; s. Leo and Bertha (Franklin) F.; m. Ruth Musicant, Sept. 4, 1949; children: Gwen Lisabeth, Leslie Margaret, Andrew Michael. BA, Columbia Coll., 1949; LLB, Columbia U., 1951. Bar: N.Y. 1951. Assoc. Fulton Walter & Halley, 1951-53; rsch. asst. Am. Law Inst. Fed. Income, Estate and Gift Tax Project, 1953-54; assoc., ptnr. Roberts & Holland, N.Y.C., 1954-66; ptnr. Willkie, Farr & Gallagher, N.Y.C., 1966-69, Fried, Frank, Harris, Shriver & Jacobson, N.Y.C., 1970-94, of counsel, 1994—; sr. adv. to exec. com. Herzog, Heine, Geduld Inc., N.Y.C., 1996—2001; counsel Geduld & Co., LLC , N.Y.C., 2002—, Cougar Trading, 2002—. Lectr. in law Columbia U., 1961-63; lectr. Am. Law Inst., NYU Inst. on Fed. Taxation, Practicing Law Inst., various profl. groups. Editor Columbia Law Rev., 1949-51; contbr. articles to profl. jours. With USN, 1945-46. Fellow Am. Coll. Tax Counsel; mem. ABA (taxation sect., chmn. com. on real property tax problems 1964-66, com. on legis. drafting 1968-84), Assn. of Bar of City of N.Y. (various coms.), N.Y. State Bar Assn. (taxation sect., co-chmn. various coms. 1982-86, sec. 1987-88, 2d vice chmn. 1988-89, vice chmn. 1989-90, chmn. 1990-91), Internat. Fiscal Assn. (coun. U.S.A. br. 1984-91), Am. Law Inst. (tax adv. group fed. income tax project), Univ. Club, Phi Beta Kappa. Democrat. Corporate taxation, Estate taxation, Taxation, general. Home: 25 W 81st St New York NY 10024-6023 Office: Cougar Trading 535 Madison Ave New York NY 10022 Home Fax: 212-877-2489; Office Fax: 212-319-8066. E-mail: afeder@nyc.rr.com., afeder@gedulddco.com.

FEDER, BRUCE, lawyer; b. N.Y.C., May 9, 1950; s. Morton A. and Ruth Leah (Baker) F.; married; two children. BA, U. Ariz., 1972; JD, George Washington U., 1976. Bar: Ariz. 1977, Washington 1982; U.S. dist. Ct. Ariz. 1977, U.S. Ct. Appeals (9th cir.) 1980; U.S. Supreme Ct., 1994. Prin. Feder Law Office PA, Phoenix, 1977—. Mem. Ariz. State Bar (com. on rules of profl. responsibility 1987—, now emeritus), Ariz. Attys. for Criminal Justice (pres. 1993, bd. dirs. 1988-95). Criminal, Juvenile, Personal injury (including property damage). Office: 2930 E Camelback Rd Ste 205 Phoenix AZ 85016

FEDER, GARY HAROLD, lawyer; b. Cin., Dec. 12, 1948; s. Max Henry and Marian Alice (Blumenthal) F.; m. Robin Melman; Aug. 19, 1973; children: Jessica, Amy. AB, Washington U., 1970, JD, 1974, LLM in Taxation, 1980. Bar: Mo. 1974, U.S. Dist. Ct. (we. and ea. dists.) Mo., U.S. Tax Ct., U.S. Ct. Appeals (8th cir.), U.S. Supreme Ct. Assoc. Team Four, Inc., St. Louis, 1974-78, Shifrin & Treiman, St. Louis, 1978-84, ptnr., 1984-88, Ziercher & Hocker, P.C., St. Louis, 1988-2000; mem. Husch & Eppenberger, LLC, 2000—. Sec. Sta. KWMU, St. Louis, 1984-86. Co-author: Tax Abatement Alternatives, 1978; editor in chief urban law annual Washington U. Law Rev., 1974. Treas. Clayton (Mo.) Sch. Dist., 1986-90; chmn. City of Clayton Bd. of Adjustment, 2000—. Federal civil litigation, Property, real (including real estate development, water). Office: Husch & Eppenberger LLC 190 Carondelet Plz Ste 600 Saint Louis MO 63105-1925

FEDER, ROBERT, lawyer; b. N.Y.C., Nov. 29, 1930; BA cum laude, CCNY, 1953; LLB, Columbia U., 1953. Bar: N.Y. 1953, U.S. Tax Ct. 1956, U.S. Dist. Ct. (so. dist.) N.Y. 1973. V.p., gen. counsel Presdl. Realty Corp., White Plains, N.Y., 1953-71; ptnr. Cuddy & Feder LLP, White Plains, 1971—. Bd. dirs. Westchester County (N.Y.) Legal Aid Soc., 1972—, pres., 1974—78; adj. prof. sch. bus. Columbia U., N.Y.C., 1988—89; bd. dirs. Presdl. Realty Corp. (Amex), Interplex Industries, Inc., Stellaris Health Network, Inc., vice chmn., 2001—; adj. prof. Pace U. Law Sch., 1985—87. Pres. White Plains Cmty. Action Program, 1967—69; bd.. dirs. White Plains Hosp. Ctr., 1978—, also sec., treas., chmn., 1992—97, 2002—; commr. White Plains Housing Authority, 1984—2002; chmn. White Plains Jud. Rev. Com., 2003; trustee SUNY-Purchase Coll. Found., 1988—, vice-chmn., 1995—. Mem. ABA, N.Y. State Bar Assn., White Plains Bar Assn., Westchester County Bar Assn., Am. Coll. Real Estate Lawyers. Corporate, general, Environmental, Property, real (including real estate development, water). Home: 9 Oxford Rd White Plains NY 10605-3602 Office: Cuddy & Feder LLP 90 Maple Ave White Plains NY 10601-5105 E-mail: rfeder@pipeline.com., rfeder@cfwlaw.com.

FEDER, SAUL E. lawyer; b. Bklyn., Oct. 8, 1943; s. Joseph Robert and Toby Feder; m. Marcia Carrie Weinblatt, Feb. 25, 1968; children: Howard Avram, Fayge Miriam, Tamar Miriam, Michael Elon, David Ben-Zion Aaron, Alexandra Rachel, Evan Daniel, Sarah Lily, Maya Malka. BS, NYU, 1965; JD, Bklyn. Law Sch., 1968. Bar: N.Y. 1969, U.S. Ct. Appeals (2d cir.) 1969, U.S. Ct. Claims 1970, U.S. Customs Ct. 1972, U.S. Supreme Ct. 1972, U.S. Ct. Customs and Patent Appeals 1974. Mng. lawyer Queens Legal Svcs., Jamaica, N.Y., 1970-71; ptnr. Previte-Glasser-Feder & Farber, Jackson Heights, N.Y., 1972-73, Hein-Waters-Klein & Feder, Far Rockaway, N.Y., 1973-78, Regosin-Edwards-Stone & Feder, N.Y.C., 1979—. Spl. investigator Bur. Election Frauds, Atty. Gen.'s Office, N.Y.C., 1976-77, spl. dep. atty. gen., 1969-70; arbitrator, consumer counsel small claims div. Civil Ct. City of N.Y., 1974—. Pres. Young Israel Briarwood, Queens, N.Y., 1978; chmn. polit. affairs com. Young Israel Staten Island, 1985—; rep. candidate State of N.Y. Assembly, Queens, 1976; chmn. Stat Pac Polit. Action Com. Mem. N.Y. Bar Assn., Queens County Bar Assn., Nassau County Bar Assn., Am. Judges Assn., N.Y. Trial Lawyers Assn., Richmond County Bar Assn., Com. on Law and Pub. Affairs, Internat. Acad. Law & Sci., Am. Jud. Soc., Soc. Med. Jurisprudence, Am. Arbitration Assn. Republican. State civil litigation, Commercial, contracts (including sales of goods; commercial financing), General practice. Home: 259 Ardmore Ave Staten Island NY 10314-4349 Office: Regosin Edwards Stone & Feder 225 Broadway Ste 613 New York NY 10007-3059 E-mail: sfeder@resflaw.com.

FEDERLE, KATHERINE HUNT, lawyer; b. Alton, Ill., Aug. 5, 1958; d. George Davis and Sarah Spence (Richards) F.; m. John Paul Haynes Jr., July 12, 1986. BA, Pomona Coll., 1980; JD cum laude, Seattle U., 1983; LLM, Georgetown U., 1986. Bar: Wash. 1983, U.S. Dist. Ct. (we. dist.) Wash. 1983, D.C. 1984, Hawaii 1986, Ohio 1998. Asst. pub. defender Snohomish County Pub. Defender's Office, Everett, Wash., 1983—84; Prettyman fellow Georgetown U. Law Ctr., Washington, 1984—86; rschr. Ctr. for Youth Rsch., Honolulu, 1988—90; asst. prof. law U. Hawaii, Honolulu, 1986—90; assoc. prof. law Tulane U., New Orleans, 1990—97; assoc. prof. law, dir. Justice Children Project Ohio State U. Coll. Law, Columbus, 1998—2002, prof. law, 2002—. Supervising atty. U. Hawaii Juvenile Def. Clinic, Honolulu, 1986-90. Mem. adv. bd. Internat. Jour. Children's Rights, 1999—; contbr. articles to profl. jours. Chmn. state legis. com. 2d Pub. Defender, Honolulu, 1987; mem. Hawaii Permanency Planning Task Force, Honolulu, 1987, Hawaii Continuing Legal Edn. for Youth, 1986-90; mem. Am. Inns of Ct.; bd. dirs. Dave Thomas Ctr. for Adoption Law, 1999—. Recipient Outstanding Pub. Svc. award Office of the Mayor, Washington, 1986, Felix Frankfurter Disting. Tchrs. award, Tulane Sch., 1996. Mem. ABA (chair juvenile law com. 1993-97, family law sect. 1989—, co-chair conclave subcom. 1995-96), Ct. Apptd. Spl. Advocates for Children (bd. dirs. 1993-96), Assn. Am. Law Schs. (sect. on clin. legal edn., subcom. on polit. interference 1988-90, co-chair stds. for practice for representing children in abuse and neglect cases com., family law sect. 1994-95), Nat. Coun. Juvenile & Family Courts (liaison 1995-97), Legal Aid Soc. Hawaii (bd. dirs. 1988-90), Ohio State Bar Assn. (juvenile justice com. 2002-), Columbus Bar Assn. (task force on domestic violence and the cts.). Avocations: hiking, swimming, fencing. Office: Ohio State Univ Coll Law 55 W 12th Ave Columbus OH 43210-1338 E-mail: federle.1@osu.edu.

FEENER, DONALD EDWARD, lawyer; b. Boston, Sept. 4, 1950; m. Elaine M. Feener; 1 child, Donald. BA, Boston State Coll., 1972; JD, New Eng. Sch. Law, 1976. Bar: Mass. 1977, U.S. Dist. Ct. 1977, U.S. Supreme Ct. 1982. Legal counsel, spl. asst., corp. counsel City of Boston, 1977-81; asst. dist. atty. Suffolk County Dist. Attys., Boston, 1981-87; sr. trial atty. Law Offices of Robert Noonan, Boston, 1987-94; mng. trial counsel Donald E. Feener & Assocs., Worcester, Mass., 1994—. Arbitrator Am. Arbitration Assn., Boston, 1991—. General civil litigation, Insurance, Personal injury (including property damage). Office: Donald E Feener & Assocs 120 Front St Worcester MA 01608-1425

FEENEY, DAVID WESLEY, lawyer; b. Phila., Nov. 1, 1938; s. William James McKay and Mary Catherine (Watkins) Feeney; m. Elizabeth Butler Shamel, Aug. 15, 1959; children: Shawn, Shari, David, Darryl. BS, Cornell U., 1960, LLB with distinction, 1963. Bar: U.S. Tax Ct. 1966, U.S. Dist. Ct. (so. dist.) N.Y. 1976, U.S. Ct. Claims 1976, U.S. Ct. Appeals (2d cir.) 1976. Assoc. Cadwalader, Wickersham & Taft, N.Y.C., 1963-64, 66-71, ptnr., 1971—. Served to 1st lt. U.S. Army, 1964-66. Mem. N.Y. State Bar Assn. (tax sect.), Cornell Club of N.Y.C. Republican. Presbyterian. Corporate taxation. Home: 1 Black Point Horseshoe Rumson NJ 07760-1500 Office: Cadwalader Wickersham et al 100 Maiden Ln New York NY 10038-4818

FEENKER, CHERIE DIANE, law librarian; b. Birmingham, Ala., Nov. 14, 1950; d. Marshall Ross and Joy (Martin) F. BA, U. Montevallo, 1971; MLS, U. Ala., 1979; JD with honors, Birmingham Sch. Law, 1989. Periodical libr. sci. and tech. dept. Birmingham Pub. Library, 1971-73, br. head, 1973-80, reference libr. tech. and bus. dept., 1980-84; law libr. Lange, Simpson, Robinson & Somerville, Birmingham, 1984—2003; libr. Cumberland Sch. Law, Birmingham, 2003—. Firm rep. Exec. Women Internat., 1990-2003, historian, 1991, bd. dirs., 1993, 96-97, pub. dir., 1993, scholarship dir., 1995, dir. at-large, 1996, sgt.-at-arms, 1997, sustaining mem. liaison, v.p./pres. elect, 1998, pres. 1999, past-pres. 2000. Mem. bd. trustees St. Martin's in the Pines, 1995-2000, bd. dirs. 1999, 2000; mem. vestry St. Andrew's Parish, Birmingham, 1985-87; bd. visitors Coll. Comms. and Info. Scis. U. Ala., 1997-. Mem. ABA, Ala. Bar Assn. (faculty CLE 1987), Birmingham Bar Assn. (pub. rels. project com. 1992-93, pub. svc. com. 1994, econ. practice law com. 2002), Ala. Libr. Assn. (faculty roundtable 1986-88, moderator 1987-88), Am. Assn. Law Librs., Libr. Sch. Assn. (bd. dirs. 1991-94, pres.-elect 1995-97, pres. 1997-2000, past pres. 2000-02, bd. dirs. 2002—), Law Libr. Assn. Ala., Spl. Librs. Assn., Beta Phi Mu. Episcopalian. Home: 4052 Brentwood Dr Irondale AL 35210-3505 Office: Samford U Law Sch 800 Lakeshore Dr Birmingham AL 35229 E-mail: cdfeenke@samford.edu.

FEERICK, JOHN DAVID, law educator; b. N.Y.C., July 12, 1936; s. John D. and Mary J. F.; m. Emalie Platt, Aug. 25, 1962; children: Maureen, Margaret, Jean, Rosemary, John, William. BS, Fordham U., 1958, LL.B., 1961; hon. degree, Coll. New Rochelle, 1991. Bar: N.Y. 1961. Assoc. Skadden, Arps, Slate, Meagher & Flom, N.Y.C., 1961-68, partner, 1968-82; prof. law Fordham U. Sch. Law, 1982—, dean, 1982—2002. Author: From Failing Hands: The Story of Presidential Succession, 1965, The 25th Amendment, 1976; co-author: The Vice Presidents of the United States, 1967, NLRB Representation Elections-Law, Practice and Procedure, 1980; also articles; editor-in-chief Fordham Law Rev., 1960-61. Chmn. N.Y. State Commn. Govt. Integrity, 1987-90. Recipient Eugene J. Keefe award Fordham U. Law Sch., 1975, 85, spl. award Fordham U. Law Rev. Assn., 1977. Fellow Am. Bar Found.; mem. ABA (chmn. spl. com. election law and voter participation 1976-79, spl. award 1966), N.Y. State Bar Assn. (chmn. com. fed. constrn. 1979-83, exec. com. 1985-87), Assn. Bar City N.Y. (v.p. 1986-87, pres. 1992-94), Am. Arbitration Assn. (chair exec. com. and bd. dirs. 1995, chair Fund for Modern Cts. 1995—), Fordham U. Law Sch. Alumni Assn. (dir. 1972—, medal of achievement 1980), chair of Homeless Panel of N.Y. and Comn. on Jud. Elections, 2000, Phi Beta Kappa. Office: Fordham U Sch Law 33 W 60th St 2nd Fl New York NY 10023

FEFFER, GERALD ALAN, lawyer; b. Washington, Apr. 24, 1942; s. Louis Charles and Elsie (Glick) F.; children: Andrew, John, Keith. BA with honors, Lehigh U., 1964; JD, U. Va., 1967. Bar: N.Y. 1968, D.C. 1980. Assoc. Mudge, Rose, Guthrie & Alexander, N.Y.C., 1967-71; asst. U.S. atty. So. Dist. N.Y., 1971-76, asst. chief criminal div., 1975-76; ptnr. Kostelanetz & Ritholz, N.Y.C., 1976-79; dep. asst. atty. gen. tax div. Dept. Justice, Washington, 1979-81; ptnr. Steptoe & Johnson, Washington, 1981-86, Williams & Connolly, Washington, 1986—. Mem. editl. bd. Busniess Crimes Bulletin: Compliance and Litigation; contbr. articles to profl. jours. Fellow Am. Coll. Tax Counsel, Am. Coll. Trial Lawyers; mem. ABA (criminal justice litigation and taxation sects.), Nat. Assn. Criminal Def. Lawyers, Nat. Inst. on Criminal Tax Fraud (chmn.). Criminal. Office: Williams & Connolly 725 12th St NW Washington DC 20005-5901 Home: 3000 Garrison St NW Washington DC 20008-1032 also: # 306 2512 Q St NW Washington DC 20007-4310

FEIBLEMAN, GILBERT BRUCE, lawyer; b. Portland, Oreg., Jan. 29, 1951; s. Herbert Frank and Bernice Feibleman; m. Ellen M. McDowell, June 20, 1981; 1 child, Benjamin David. BS, U. Oreg., 1972; JD, U. Pacific, 1976. Bar: Oreg. 1976, U.S. Dist. Ct. Oreg. 1976, U.S. Ct. Appeals (9th cir.). Assoc. Goodenough & Pierson, Salem, Oreg., 1976-78; mng. ptnr. Ramsay, Stein, Feibleman & Myers P.C., Salem, 1978-89, Ramsay, Stein & Feibleman P.C., Salem, 1989-94, Feibleman & Assocs. P.C., 1995—. Adj. prof. trial law and negotiation skills Willamette U.; adj. prof. bus. law Chemeketa Community Coll., Marion County, Oreg., 1977; arbitrator Marion County Ct., Salem, 1985—; referee juvenile ct., 1985; judge pro tem Oreg. Dist. Cts., 1982—, Oreg. Cir. Cts., 1987—; reference judge Marion County, 1989—. Fellow Am. Acad. Matrimonial Lawyers; mem. Assn. Trial Lawyers Am., Oreg. Trial Lawyers Assn., Oreg. Bar Assn. (arbitrator), Oreg. State Bar Assn. (bar counsel 1989—, sec. joint chiropractic com. 1989—, chair family juvenile law sect). Democrat. Avocations: skiing, gourmet cooking. State civil litigation, Family and matrimonial, Personal injury (including property damage). Home: 552 Stagecoach Way SE Salem OR 97302-3925 Office: 1815 Commercial St SE Salem OR 97302-5203 E-mail: gil@feibleman-law.com.

FEIERSTEIN, MARK ERROL, retired lawyer; b. N.Y.C., May 22, 1948; s. Lester and Rose (Feingersh) F. BA, Miami U., Oxford, Ohio, 1970; MS in Bus., L.I. U., 1975; JD, N.Y. Law Sch., 1979. Bar: N.Y. 1979, U.S. Tax Ct., 1988. Assoc. Olvaney, Eisner and Donnelly, N.Y.C., 1977-79, Oppenheim, Appel and Co., N.Y.C., 1981-82; law guardian Family Ct. of N.Y., Westchester; atty. Article 18-B Panel, Westchester; of counsel Thomas and Sykes, Yonkers, N.Y., 1985-86; ret., 1996. Adminstrv. law judge N.Y.C. Taxi and Limousine Commn., N.Y.C. Parking Violations Bur., 1984-93, N.Y.C. Environ. Control Bd., 1987-99; arbitrator Civil Ct. of N.Y.C., N.Y. Stock Exch., 1988, Nat. Assn. Securities Dealers, 1989; hearing officer N.Y.C. Transit Adjudication Bur., Bklyn., 1987-88; expert in credit card fraud Tech. Adv. Svc. for Attys., Blue Bell, Pa. Author: Emergency Guidelines to Assist Individuals and Businesses Counter Credit Card Fraud, 1992. Mem. Bronx Citizens Com., N.Y., 1986. Mem. ABA, N.Y. State Bar Assn., N.Y. Law Sch. Alumni Assn., Am. Arbitration Assn. Jewish. Avocations: movies, theater, reading.

FEIGEN, BRENDA S. lawyer, film producer, author; b. Chgo., July 7, 1944; d. Arthur Paul Feigen and Shirley (Bierman) Feigen Kadison; children: Alexis Feigen Fasteau. BA in Math. cum laude, Vassar Coll., 1966; JD, Harvard U., 1969. Bar: Mass. 1970, N.Y. 1971, Calif. 2001. Chief analyst Boston Redevel. Authority, 1969; assoc. firm Rosenman, Colin, Kaye, Petschek, Freund & Emil, N.Y.C., 1970; pvt. practice N.Y.C., 1970—, L.A., 2001—. Founder, coordinating dir. Women's Action Alliance, N.Y.C., 1970—72; co-founder Ms. Mag., 1971; dir. Nat. Women's Rights project ACLU, N.Y.C., 1972—74; ptnr. Fasteau and Feigen, N.Y.C., 1974—80; assoc. Hess, Segall, Guterman, Pelz & Steiner, N.Y.C., 1980—81; atty., motion picture agt. William Morris Agy., N.Y.C., 1982—87; pres. Brenda Feigen Prodns., N.Y.C. and L.A., 1987—97; ptnr. Baxter/Feigen Prodns., 1991—92, Berton & Feigen, Beverly Hills, 1992—94; of counsel Berton & Donaldson, Beverly Hills, 1994—96; gen. counsel Feigen/Parrent Lit. Mgmt., Bel Air, Calif., 1995—; co-pres. and gen. counsel Reel Life Women Prodn. Co., Bel Air, 1996—; chair Nat. Breast Cancer Edn. and Legal Ctr., Bel Air, 2001—; prof. UCLA Ext., 1990; guest spkr., panelist numerous confs., seminars; panelist Harvard Law Sch. seminar, 1999, Yale Law Sch. seminar, 1999, Calif. Lawyers for Arts, 1999—, L.A. Times Book Festival, 2001, Vassar Coll., 2001; co-chair Practicing Law Inst. Seminars on Entertainment Law, 1987, 88, Harvard Law and Harvard Bus. Schs. Entertainement Law Conf., 1999, Vassar Coll. Symposium on Entertainment Industry, 1998; practicing Law Inst., 1987, 88; bd. dirs. Calif. Lawyers for the Arts, 1996—, Population Media Ctr., 2003—; emerita mem. bd. dirs. Women's Action Alliance; adv. com. Am. Friends of Israel Mus., 2002—; moderator panel on employment law Harvard Law Sch., Celebration 50, 2003. Prodr.: (films, Orion Pictures) NAVY SEALS, 1990; author: Not One of the Boys: Living Life as a Feminist, 2000; contbr. Mem. adv. bd. Working Women United, nat. adv. bd. Take Our Daughters to Work, 1993—; bd. dirs. Film Forum, 1986-90; mem. Pen Ctr. USA West, 1996—, Authors' Guild, 1996—, Harvard Com. Entertainment, Sports and Cyberspace Law, 1997—; candidate for N.Y. State Senate, 1978; panelist L.A. Times Book Festival, 2001; adv. com. Am. Friends of Israel Mus., 2002—. Hon. Pres.'s fellow Columbia U., 1977, 78; participant Exec. Seminar, Aspen Inst., 1979. Mem. ABA, ATLA, NOW (nat. legis. v.p., bd. dirs. 1970-71), Show Coalition (bd. govs. 1990-92), Calif. State Bar Assn., Los Angeles County Bar Assn., Nat. Employment Law Assn., N.Y. Civil and Criminal Cts. Bar Assn., N.Y. Women in Film (bd. dirs. 1985-86), Women's Action Alliance (co-founder, dir.), Nat. Women's Polit. Caucus (co-founder, nat. adv. com.), Nat. Employment Law Assn. Democrat. Entertainment, Labor (including EEOC, Fair Labor Standards Act, labor-management relations, NLRB, OSHA), Civil rights. Office: Law Office of Brenda S Feigen 11150 W Olympic Blvd Ste 860 Los Angeles CA 90064 E-mail: bfeigen@feigenlaw.com.

FEIKENS, JOHN, federal judge; b. Clifton, N.J., Dec. 3, 1917; s. Sipke and Corine (Wisse) F.; m. Henriette Dorothy Schulthouse, Nov. 4, 1939; children: Jon, Susan Corine, Barbara Edith, Julie Anne, Robert H. AB, Calvin Coll., Grand Rapids, Mich., 1938; JD, U. Mich., 1941; LL.D., U. Detroit, 1979, Detroit Coll. Law, 1981. Bar: Mich. 1942. Gen. practice law, Detroit; dist. judge Ea. Dist. Mich., Detroit, 1960-61, 70-79, chief judge, 1979-86, sr. judge, 1986—. Past co-chmn. Mich. Civil Rights Commn.; past chmn. Rep. State Central Com.; past mem. Rep. Nat. Com.; mem. com. visitors U. Mich. Law Sch. Past bd. trustees Calvin Coll. Fellow Am. Coll. Trial Lawyers; mem. ABA, Detroit Bar Assn. (dir. 1962, past pres.), State Bar Mich. (commr. 1965-71), U. Mich. Club (com. visitors). Office: US Dist Ct 851 Theodore Levin US Ct 231 W Lafayette Blvd Detroit MI 48226-2700

FEIN, RONALD LAWRENCE, lawyer; b. Detroit, Aug. 26, 1943; s. Lee Allen and Billie Doreen (Thomas) F.; m. Rosemary Heath, Sept. 2, 1966 (div. 1997); children: Samantha, Mark. AB with honors, UCLA, 1966; JD with honors, U. San Diego, 1969. Bar: Calif. 1970, U.S. Dist. Ct. (cen. dist.) Calif. 1970. Assoc. Gibson, Dunn & Crutcher, Los Angeles, 1969-75; chief dep. commr. of corps. State of Calif., Los Angeles, 1975-78; ptnr., mem. firmwide adv. com., chmn. corp. fin./mergers and acquisitions sect. Jones, Day, Reavis & Pogue, Los Angeles, 1978-87; ptnr., mem. exec. com., chmn. gen. bus. dept. Wyman, Bautzer, Kuchel & Silbert, L.A., 1987-91; sr. ptnr. Stutman, Treister & Glatt, 1991—. Bd. dirs. Executours, Inc., Los Angeles, Lottery Info., North Hollywood, Calif., Malibu Grand Prix, Woodland Hills, Calif.; adj. prof. law Loyola U., Los Angeles, 1978—; mem. Commr.'s Circle Adv. Com. to the Calif. Commr. of Corps., Fin. Lawyers Conf.; mem. adv. bd. U. S.C. Inst. for Corp. Counsel. Articles editor San Diego Law Rev., 1969; contbr. articles to profl. jours. Co-dir. protocol for boxing Los Angeles Olympic Organizing Com., 1984. Lt. USAF, to 1966-69. Mem. ABA (corp., banking and bus. law sect., mem. ad hoc com. on merit regulation, mem. fed. regulation of securities com., mem. ad hoc com. on the Uniform Limited Offering Exemption, com. on Counsel Responsibility, mem. ad hoc com. on Regulation D, mem. subcom. on Registration Statements—1933 Act, vice chmn. state regulation securities com., chmn. pvt. offering exemption and simplification of capital formation subcom.), Calif. Bar Assn. (bus. law sect.), Los Angeles County Bar Assn. (mem. exec. com. bus. and corps. law sect.), Nat. Assn. of Securities Dealers, Inc. (mem. subcom. on indemnification, mem. arbitration panel). Clubs: Regency. Avocations: athletics, reading, theater. Corporate, general, Mergers and acquisitions, Securities. Office: Stutman Treister & Glatt 3699 Wilshire Blvd Ste 900 Los Angeles CA 90010-2766 Home: 455 N Oakhurst Dr Beverly Hills CA 90210-3911

FEIN, SHERMAN EDWARD, lawyer, psychologist; b. June 17, 1928; s. Samuel L. and Mildred B. (Sherman) F.; m. Myra N. Becker, Nov. 13, 1955; children: Dina, Julia, Sara. BA, Bowdoin Coll., 1949; JD, Boston U., 1953; MS, Springfield Coll., 1962; EdD, U. Mass., 1969; Sc.MD, Sch, Medicine, Ross U., Portsmouth, Dominica, West Indies, 1983; PhD, Kensington U., 1993. Bar: Maine 1952, Mass. 1953, U.S. Dist. Ct. Mass., 1957, U.S. Supreme Ct. 1965; diplomate Am. Bd. Med. Psychotherapists. Ptnr. Fein, Pearson & Emond, P.C., Springfield, 1953—; pvt. practice psychology Springfield, 1962—; hon. consul Republic of Nicaragua, 1999—. Author: Selected Cases on Shoplifting, 1975; Divorce Handbook, 1978. Sgt. USAF, 1950-52; to lt. col. CAP, 1953-77. Mem. ABA, Hampden County Bar Assn., Mass. Bar Assn., Assn. Trial Lawyers Am., N.Y. Acad. Scis., Am. Psychology-Law Assn., Masons, Shriners. Republican. Jewish. Health, Personal injury (including property damage), Workers' compensation. Home: 224 Longmeadow St Longmeadow MA 01106 Office: Fein Pearson Emond & Fein 52 Mulberry St Springfield MA 01105-1410

FEINBERG, PAUL H. lawyer; b. Newark, Aug. 24, 1951; s. Frederick H. and Ruth S. Feinberg; m. Nancy S. Greenberg, Sept. 3, 1972; children: Jacob L., David R. BA, Rutgers U., 1973; JD, U. Toledo, 1976. Bar: N.J. 1976, U.S. Dist. Ct. N.J. 1976, U.S. Supreme Ct. 1986, U.S. Ct. Appeals (3rd cir.) 1998, cert.: (criminal trial atty.) 1989. Law clk. Superior Ct. Essex County, Newark, 1976—77; atty. Freeman & Bas, Newark, 1977, Leibowitz & Corradino, East Orange, NJ, 1978—79; ptnr. Feinberg & Feinberg, South Orange, NJ, 1979—. Pub. defender Town of South Orange, 1991—. Mem.: ATLA, Essex County Bar Assn., Assn. Criminal Trial Lawyers N.J., Nat. Assn. Criminal Trial Lawyers. Jewish. Criminal, Juvenile, Personal injury (including property damage). Office: Feinberg & Feinberg 7690 Orange Ave South Orange NJ 07079

FEINBERG, WILFRED, judge; b. N.Y.C., June 22, 1920; s. Jac and Eva (Wolin) Feinberg; m. Shirley Marcus, June 23, 1946; children: Susan Stelk, Jack, Jessica Twedt. BA, Columbia U., 1940, LLB, 1946, LLD (hon.) , 1985, Syracuse U., 1985; LLD (hon.) , Bklyn. Law Sch., 1998. Bar: N.Y. 1947. Law clk. Hon. James P. McGranery U.S. Dist. Ct. (ea. dist.) Pa., 1947—49; assoc. Kaye, Scholer, Fierman & Hays, N.Y.C., 1949—53; ptnr. McGoldrick, Dannett, Horowitz & Golub, N.Y.C., 1953—61; dep. supt. N.Y. State Banking Dept., N.Y.C., 1958; judge U.S. Dist Ct (so. dist.), N.Y.C., NY, 1961—66, U.S. Ct. Appeals (2nd cir.), N.Y.C., NY, 1966—, chief judge, 1980—88, sr. judge, 1991—. Mem. U.S. Jud. Conf. U.S., 1980—88, chmn. exec. com., 1987—88, mem. Devitt award com., 1989, 90, mem. long-range planning com., 1991—96; Madison lectr. NYU Law Sch., 1983; Sonnett lectr. Fordham U. Law Sch., 1984; Inaugural Howard Kaplan Meml. lectr. Hofstra U. Law Sch., 1986; The Future of Justice lectr. Inst. of Comparative Law, Chuo U., Japan, 1991. Editor-in-chief: Columbia Law Rev., 1946; contbr. With U.S. Army, 1942—45. Recipient Learned Hand medal for excellence in fed. jurisprudence, 1982, Gold medal, award for disting. svc. in the law, N.Y. State Bar Assn., 1990, medal for excellence, Columbia Law Alumni Assn., 1990, Pursuit of Justice award, Internat. Assn. Jewish Lawyers and Jurists, 1993, Disting. Pub. Svc. award, N.Y. County Lawyers Assn., 1994, Edward Weinfeld award, 1995, Ann. Wilfred Feinberg prize named in his honor for best student work at Columbia Law Sch. related to fed. cts., 1998. Mem.: ABA, Am. Law Inst., Am. Judicature Soc., N.Y. County Lawyers Assn., Assn. of Bar of City of N.Y., Phi Beta Kappa. Office: US Ct Appeals 2nd Cir Room 2004 US Court House Foley Sq New York NY 10007-1501

FEINGOLD, MARK HOWARD, lawyer; s. Earl and Irma Feingold; m. Irene Elizabeth Cross, June 4, 1988; children: Emma Louise, Julia Elizabeth. BA, Pa. State U., 1976; JD, Am. U., 1980. Bar: Pa. 1980, U.S. Ct. Appeals (3rd cir.) 1980, N.J. 1981, D.C. 1982. Atty.-advisor U.S. Dept. Labor, Washington, 1981—82; dep. atty. gen. Office of the N.J. Atty. Gen., Trenton, 1982—85; assoc. Shapiro & Shapiro, Hackensack, NJ, 1985—87; staff counsel U. Pa. Health Sys., Phila., 1988—95; corp. counsel Aventis, Bridgewater, NJ, 1995—. Arbitrator Phila. Ct. Common Pleas, 1990—95, U.S. Dist. Ct. (ea. dist.) Pa., Phila., 1990—94; chmn. Non-Profit Corp. Law Com., Phila. Bar Assn., Philadelphia, 1992—94; chmn. non-profit corp. law com. Phila. Bar Assn., 1992—94; mem. N.J. Tech. Coun., Mt. Laurel, 2002—. Contbr. articles to profl. jours. Chief local tribe Indian Princesses, Doylestown, Pa., 2001—03. Mem.: ABA (assoc.), Computer Law Assn., Am. Corp. Counsel Assn. (assoc.), Pa. Bar Assn. (assoc.), Doyleston Fitness Ctr. (assoc.), Phila. Folksong Soc. (assoc.), Bucks County Folk Song Soc. (assoc.), Phi Kappa Phi. Health, Computer, Transactions. Office: Aventis 200 Crossing Blvd Mail Code BX2-71 Bridgewater NJ 08807-0800 Office Fax: 908-231-2243. E-mail: mark.feingold@aventis.com.

FEINGOLD, RUSSELL DANA, senator, lawyer; b. Janesville, Wis., Jan. 2, 1953; s. Leon and Sylvia (Binstock) Feingold; m. Susan Levine, Aug. 21, 1977; children: Jessica, Ellen; m. Mary Speerschneider, Jan. 20, 1991; stepchildren: Sam Speerschneider, Ted Speerschneider. BA with honors, U. Wis.-Madison, 1975; postgrad., Magdalen Coll., Oxford U., Eng., 1975—77; JD with honors, Harvard U., 1979. Bar: Wis. 1979. Assoc. Foley & Lardner, Madison, 1979—82, LaFollette, Sinykin, Anderson & Munson, Madison, 1983—85, Goldman & Feingold, 1985—88; mem. Wis. Senate, 1983—92; U.S. senator from Wis., 1993—; mem. aging com., budget com., fgn. rels. com., judiciary com., senate Dem. policy com. U.S. Senate. Scholar, Wis. Honors scholar, 1971, Rhodes scholar, 1975. Mem.: Phi Beta Kappa. Democrat. Jewish. Office: US Senate 506 Hart Senate Office Bldg Washington DC 20510-0001 also: US Senators Office 1600 Aspen Commons Rm 100 Middleton WI 53562-4626

FEINSMITH, PAUL LOWELL, lawyer; b. N.Y.C., July 30, 1941; s. Sydney William and Esther (Gell) Feinsmith; m. Sherry Raphael Feinsmith, May 28, 1967 (div. 1972); children: Jeremiah R., Deborah Gardner; m. Alicia Goldstein, Nov. 18, 1979; 1 child, Sylvie G. BA, U. Pa., 1962; JD, NYU, 1965. Bar: N.J. 1965, Ill. 1969, Fla. 1981. Assoc. Platoff Heftler Harker & Nashel, Esqs., Union City, NJ, 1965—69; v.p., gen. counsel Elgin & Waltham Watch Cos., Chgo., 1969—79, N.Y.C., 1972—76, Miami, Fla., 1979—82; ptnr. Hoffman Larin & Feinsmith, North Miami Beach, Fla., 1982—88; sole practice Miami, 1990—. Mem. Broward County Dem. Exec. Com., Fla., 1994—2000; pres. Nat. Kidney Found. Fla., 1981—85; mem. exec. com. Renal Network, 1982—; pres. NAPHT, 1984—86; co-founder, former chmn. Nat. Renal Coalition, Fla. Renal Coalition. Mem.: ABA, Fla. Bar Assn., B'nai B'rith. Democrat. Jewish. Corporate, general, Landlord-tenant, Property, real (including real estate development, water). Home: 1730 N 55th Ave Hollywood FL 33021-3934 Office: 1111 Lincoln Rd Miami FL 33139-2452 also: 19098 W Dixie Hwy Aventura FL 33180

FEINSTEIN, ALLEN LEWIS, lawyer; b. N.Y.C., Apr. 18, 1929; s. Jacob and Kate (Goldberg) F.; m. Charlesa Joan Wolfe, Dec. 14, 1957. AB, CCNY, 1949; LLB, Columbia U., 1952. Bar: N.Y. 1952, U.S. Supreme Ct. 1958, Ariz. 1960, U.S. Dist. Ct. Ariz. 1960, U.S. Ct. Appeals (9th cir.) 1960. Assoc. Proskauer Rose Goetz & Mendelsohn, N.Y.C., 1955-59; law clk. to justice Supreme Ct. Ariz., Phoenix, 1959-61, 1st adminstrv. dir., 1961-64; pvt. practice law Phoenix, 1964-72, 1995—; ptnr. Daughton Feinstein & Wilson, Phoenix, 1972-86; sr. ptnr. Rawlins, Burrus, Lewkowitz & Feinstein, P.C., Phoenix, 1986-95. Mem. Phoenix Housing Code Com., 1968; vice-chmn. adv. com. State Legislative com. on Medicaid; mem. Phoenix Charter Review Com., 1969; mem. exec. com. Phoenix Sister City Commn., 1973-75 Author: First, Second and Third Reports of Courts of Arizona, 1962, 63, 64. Bd. dirs. Meml. Hosp. Phoenix, chmn., 1973-76, Community Coun., 1970-76, Ariz. Jewish Hist. Soc.; chmn. Meml. Hosp. Found., 1980-82; bd. dirs., chmn. coun. trustees, mem. exec. com. Ariz. Hosp. Assn., 1981-87, chmn. 1986-87, Ariz. del. to nat. conf. governing bds.; chmn. PMH Health Resources, Inc., 1983-89, Ariz. Voluntary Hosp. Fedn., 1984-88; chmn. Phoenix chpt. Am. Jewish Com., 1989-91; legal advisor Salt River Pima-Maricopa INdian Cmty. Police Commn., 1997-2002. 2d lt. USAF, 1952-53. Mem. Ariz. Bar Assn., Maricopa County Bar Assn., State Bar Ariz. (chmn. com. civil practice and procedure 1971-74, chmn. long-range com. 1980, peer rev. com., sole practitioner com. sect., alternate dispute resolution sects., mentor-mentee com.), Univ. Club Phoenix (pres. 1971-72), Phi Beta Kappa, Phi Delta Phi. Democrat. Jewish. Alternative dispute resolution. Address: 2110 Encanto Dr SW Phoenix AZ 85007-1526 E-mail: alfeinstein@cox.net.

FEINSTEIN, FRED IRA, lawyer; b. Chgo., Apr. 6, 1945; s. Bernard and Beatrice (Mines) F.; m. Judy Cutler, Aug. 25, 1968; children: Karen, Donald. BSC, DePaul U., 1967, JD, 1970. Bar: Ill. 1970, U.S. Supreme Ct. 1977. Ptnr. McDermott, Will & Emery, Chgo., 1976—; lectr. in field. Pres., Skokie/Evanston (Ill.) Action Council, 1981-84; bd. dirs. Temple Judea Mizpah, Skokie, 1982-84, 2000-2002, Deborah Goldfine Meml. Cancer Research, 1968—, YMCA of Chgo., 1985—. Mem. Ill. Bar Assn., Am. Coll. Real Estate Lawyers, Union League, Blue Key, Beta Gamma Sigma, Beta Alpha Psi, Pi Gamma Mu, Lambda Alpha. Contbr. articles to profl. jours. Bankruptcy, Environmental, Property, real (including real estate development, water). Office: McDermott Will & Emery 227 W Monroe St Ste 3100 Chicago IL 60606-5096

FEINSTEIN, MILES ROGER, lawyer; b. Camden, N.J., June 25, 1941; s. Louis Emory and Sylvia K. (Jacobs) F.; m. Margaret Bott, Oct. 3, 2000; children: Bari, Matthew, Elizabeth. BA, Rutgers U., 1963; JD, Duke U., 1966. Bar: N.J. 1966, U.S. Dist. Ct. N.J. 1966, U.S. Ct. Appeals (3d cir.) 1967, U.S. Ct. Appeals (2d cir.) 1971. Pvt. practice, Clifton, N.J., 1967—. Mem. Passaic Criminal Justice commn.; mem. com. on drugs and cts. N.J. Supreme Ct.; mem. speedy trial com. N.J. Supreme Ct.; expert commentator Nat. Courtroom TV; lectr. N.J. Inst. of Continuing Legal Edn., Trial Lawyers Assn. Author: Historical Development of Pineys of Southern New Jersey. Trustee Passaic County Heart Fund, 1970-93, Passaic County Cancer Soc.; chmn. Passaic County March of Dimes, 1989. Named Man of Yr., Passaic County Heart Fund, 1976, Passaic County Cancer Soc., 1978, Passaic County coun. Boy Scouts Am., 1978, Passaic County Bad Guys Charitable Orgn., 1974; recipient award Passaic Civic Orgn., Humanitarian award Unico, 1976, Nationwide Bail Bonds award Policeman's Benevolent Assn., Disting. Svc. award, 1980, 84, 85, History prize Soc. Colonial Wars; subject of numerous legal articles. Mem. ABA, Assn. Trial Lawyers Am., Nat. Assn. Criminal Def. Lawyers, Fed. Bar Assn., N.J. Bar Assn. (criminal law com. 2000-2002), N.J. Assn. Criminal Def. Lawyers (former trustee, treas., v.p., pres. 1990-91; lectr.), N.J. Assn. of Trial Lawyers (bd. govs. 1992-93), Passaic County Bar Assn. (chmn. criminal law com. 1990-93), Phi Beta Kappa, Phi Delta Phi, Phi Alpha Theta (Henry Rutgers scholar). Avocations: sports, theatre, collecting stamps. Criminal. Office: 1135 Clifton Ave Clifton NJ 07013-3642

FEINSTEIN, PAUL LOUIS, lawyer; b. Chgo., Jan. 5, 1955; s. Sherman C. and Sara (Steinman) F.; m. Andrea Lee Albaum, June 26, 1983; 1 child, Glen Joseph. BA, Tulane U., 1977; JD, Emory U., 1980. Bar: Ga. 1980, Ill. 1980, U.S. Dist. Ct. (no. dist.) Ill. 1980, U.S. Supreme Ct. 1997. Assoc. Jones, Baer & Davis, Chgo., 1980-81; sr. assoc. Marshall Auerbach and Assocs., Chgo., 1981-84, 86-91; sr. ptnr. Chausow & Feinstein, Chgo., 1984-86; ptnr. Kaufman, Litwin & Feinstein, Chgo., 1991—2003; pvt. practice Chgo., 2003—. Chmn. programming Tulane U. Chgo. Alumni Coun., 1984-86, pres., 1986-89; bd. dirs. 3600 Lake Shore Dr. Condominium Assn., Chgo., 1986-88; active Ill. Marriage and Family Therapy Licensing and Disciplinary Bd., 1998-2002. Fellow Am. Acad. Matrimonial Lawyers; mem. ABA, Ill. Bar Assn., Ga. Bar Assn., Pi Sigma Alpha, Phi Alpha Delta, Tau Epsilon Phi. Appellate, Family and matrimonial. Office: 100 N La Salle St Ste 2400 Chicago IL 60602-2410 E-mail: pfeinlaw@aol.com.

FEINTUCH, RICHARD DAVID, lawyer; b. Passaic, N.J., July 11, 1952; s. Jack Loeb and Lee (Kurlander) F.; m. Merry E. Henig, June 15, 1974; children: Jason, Jonathan. BS in Econs., U. Pa., 1974; JD, NYU, 1977. Bar: N.Y. 1978. Assoc. Wachtell, Lipton, Rosen & Katz, N.Y.C., 1977-83, ptnr., 1984—. Contbg. author (treatise) Collier Bankruptcy Practice Guide, 1984. Mem. ABA, N.Y. State Bar Assn., Assn. of Bar of City of N.Y. Clubs: Fenway Golf (Scarsdale, N.Y.). Banking, Bankruptcy, Commercial, contracts (including sales of goods; commercial financing). Office: Wachtell Lipton Rosen & Katz 51 W 52nd St Fl 29 New York NY 10019-6150

FEIRSON, STEVEN B. lawyer; b. Bklyn., June 6, 1950; s. Aaron M. and Gertrude F. BA, U. Pa., 1972; JD, U. Chgo., 1975. Bar: Pa. 1975, U.S. Dist. Ct. (ea. dist.) Pa. 1975, U.S. Ct. Appeals (3d cir.) 1976, U.S. Ct. Appeals (2d cir.) 1990, U.S. Ct. Appeals (9th cir.) 1990, U.S. Ct. Appeals (8th cir.) 1992, U.S. Ct. Appeals (6th cir.) 1994, U.S. Ct. Appeals (5th cir.) 2003, U.S. Supreme Ct. 1980, U.S. Dist. Ct. (ea. dist.) Mich. 1996. Assoc. Dechert, Price & Rhoads, Phila., 1975-83, ptnr., 1983—. Mem. Phila. Bar Assn. Constitutional, Labor (including EEOC, Fair Labor Standards Act, labor-management relations, NLRB, OSHA), Mergers and acquisitions. Office: Dechert Price & Rhoads 4000 Bell Atlantic Tower 1717 Arch St Lbby 3 Philadelphia PA 19103-2713

FEIT, GLENN M. lawyer; b. Elizabeth, N.J., Oct. 16, 1929; s. Charles Theodore and Beatrice (Esther) F.; m. Rona F. Gottlieb, June 14, 1953 (div. 1974); children: Glenn M., John Paul, Adam Gibbs (dec.); m. Barberi Platt Paull. BS in Econ., U. Pa., 1951; JD magna cum laude, Harvard U., 1957. Bar: N.Y. 1958, U.S. Dist. Ct. (2d dist.) 1959). Assoc. Cravath, Swaine & Moore, N.Y.C., 1957-64; ptnr. London, Buttenwieser & Chalif, N.Y.C., 1965-70, Feit & Ahrens, N.Y.C., 1970-88, Feit & Shor, N.Y.C., 1988-89, Proskauer Rose LLP, N.Y.C., 1989—. Bd. dirs. Blair Industries, Inc., Scott City, Mo.; sec. Charterhouse Group Internat., Inc., N.Y.C. Mem. editl. bd. Harvard Law Rev., 1955-57. Bd. dirs. Friends of the IDF, N.Y.C. Lt. USN, 1951-54. Mem. ABA, Assn. Bar City N.Y., Aircraft Owners and Pilots Assn., Exptl. Aircraft Assn., Tailhook Assn., Harvard Club, Seaplane Pilots Assn., N.Y. Yacht Club, Doubles. Corporate, general, Mergers and acquisitions, Securities. Office: Proskauer Rose LLP 1585 Broadway New York NY 10036-8299 E-mail: gfeit@proskauer.com.

FELD, ALAN DAVID, lawyer; b. Dallas, Nov. 13, 1936; s. Henry R. and Rose (Scissors) F.; m. Anne Sanger, June 1, 1957; children: Alan David, Elizabeth S., John L. BA, So. Methodist U., 1957, LL.B., 1960. Bar: Tex. 1960. Since practiced in Dallas; from ptnr. to chmn. bd. Akin, Gump, Hauer, Strauss & Feld, Dallas, 1960-96, sr. exec. ptnr., 1996—. Lectr. Southwestern U. Med. Sch.; chmn. Tex. State Securities Bd.; bd. dirs. Clear Channel Comms., Inc., Ctr. Point Properties, Inc. Contbr. articles to legal jours. Trustee AMR Advaantage Funds, So. Meth. U.; bd. dirs. Dallas Day Nursery Assn., Timberlawn Found., Dallas Symphony Orch. Mem.: ABA, Dallas Bar Assn., D.C. Bar Assn., Tex. Bar Assn., Dallas Country Club, Royal Oaks Country Club (corr.), Salesmanship Club, Phi Delta Phi. Corporate, general, Mergers and acquisitions, Securities. Home: 4235 Bordeaux Ave Dallas TX 75205-3717 Office: Akin Gump Strauss Hauer & Feld 1700 Pacific Ave Ste 4100 Dallas TX 75201-4675

FELDER, RAOUL LIONEL, lawyer; b. N.Y.C., May 13, 1934; s. Morris and Millie (Goldstein) F.; m. Myrna Felder, May 26, 1963; children: Rachel, James. BA, NYU, 1955; JD, NYU, Switzerland, 1959; postgrad., U. Bern, Switzerland, 1955-56; hon. degree of fellow in jurisprudence, Oxford U., 1995. Bar: N.Y. 1959, U.S. Dist. Ct. (so. and ea. dists.) N.Y. 1962, U.S. Ct. Appeals (2d cir.) 1962, U.S. Supreme Ct. 1970. Pvt. practice, N.Y.C., 1959-61, 64—; asst. U.S. atty., 1961-64. Mem. faculty Practicing Law Inst., 1979, Marymount Coll., 1982-85, Ethical Culture Sch., 1981, 82; moderator Nat. Conf. on Child Abuse, 1989; apptd. to N.Y.C. Cultural Affairs Adv. Commn., 1995-2001, State Commn. on Child Abuse, 1996. Author: Divorce: The Way Things Are, Not the Way Things Should Be, 1971, Lawyers Practical Handbook to the New Divorce Law, 1981, Raoul Felder's Encyclopedia of Matrimonial Clauses, 1990, updated, 1991, Getting Away with Murder, 1996, Restaurant Guide to Los Angeles and New York, 1996, Survival Guide to New York, 1997, Bare Knuckle Negotiations, 2003; columnist Fame mag., 1988-92, Am. Women Mag., 1994, N.Y. Daily News Sundays, 1995; contbr. articles on law to profl. jours. and N.Y. Times; editorials to Newsweek mag., Harper's Bazaar mag., Newsday newspaper, N.Y. Post, The Guardian (London),Jerusalem Post, Penthouse mag., Cosmopolitan mag., N.Y. Times; columnist Am. Spectator Mag, 1999-2001, Washington Times, 1999-2002; commentator Cable News Network, 1989, BBC World Wide, 1994, 95, 97, Crossing the Line (pub. TV series), 1997-99, The Felder Report (pub. TV series), 1998-99, guest commentator Court TV, 1992, bd. advisors, 1992-95, editl. contbr.; (documentary) Survival Guide to New York, 1998; host (TV series) Metrolaw, 1995-97; host (radio talk show) The Felder Report, 1997-2002, TalkAmerica. Mem. Gov.'s Commn. on Child Abuse, 1989; chmn. Nat. Kidney Found. Auction, N.Y. Fund; chmn. dinner Jerusalem Reclamation Project; bd. dirs. Big Apple Greeters, 1997—99, Cop Care, Hosp. Audiences Inc., Nat. Kidney Found., N.Y.C. Econ. Devel. Corp., 2000—, Kidney and Urology Found. Am., N.Y. Cops Found.; hon. police commr. N.Y. City Police Comms., 2000—; grand marshall U.S.A. Day Washington, Israel Day Parade, N.Y.C.; apptd. Cultural Adv. Commn., N.Y.C., 1994—2001, 2001—02. Named Man of Yr. Bklyn. Sch. for Spl. Children, Met. Geriatric Ctr., Shield Inst., 1997; recipient Defender of Jerusalem medal, 1990, Crimebusters award Take Back N.Y., 1996, Child Abuse Prevention Svc. award, Child Safety Inst. 1998. Mem. ABA (judge nat. finals client counseling competition), Assn. of Bar of City of N.Y. (spl. com. matrimonial law 1975-77), N.Y. State Trial Lawyers Assn. (past chmn. matrimonial law 1974-75), Am. Arbitration Assn., N.Y. Women's Bar Assn., Minion of the Stars (chmn. bd. 1993). Appellate, Family and matrimonial, General practice. Home: 60 Sutton Pl S New York NY 10022-4168 Office: 437 Madison Ave New York NY 10022-7001 E-mail: raoulfelder@raoulfelder.com.

FELDERSTEIN, STEVEN HOWARD, lawyer; b. Rochester, NY, Oct. 28, 1946; s. Lester and Ruth (Tatelbaum) Felderstein; m. Sandra Lynn Goldman, Aug. 24, 1969; 1 child, Janis. BA, SUNY, 1968; JD, U. Calif., San Francisco, 1973. Bar: Calif. Law clk. U.S. Dist. Ct., Sacramento, 1973-75; ptnr. Felderstein Rosenberg & McManus, Sacramento, 1978-86, Diepenbrock, Wulff, Plant & Hanmegan, LLP, Sacramento, 1986-98, Felderstein Fitzgerald Willoughby & Pascuzzi LLP, Sacramento, 1999—. Adj. prof., U. the Pacific McGeorge Sch. Law, 2003—. Contbr. articles to profl. jours. Bd. trustees Jewish Fedn. Sacramento Region, 1990-95. Mem.: Anthony M. Kennedy Inn of Ct. (master of the Bar 1999—2001), Calif. Bankruptcy Forum (v.p. 1998, pres. 1998—99), Am. Coll. Bankruptcy, Practicing Law Inst. (lectr. 1995—), Calif. Continuing Edn. of Bar (lectr. 1987—), Calif. Bar Assn. (uniform comml.code com. bus. sect. 1983—85, insolvency com. bus. sect. 1999—2003). Bankruptcy, Commercial, contracts (including sales of goods; commercial financing). Office: Felderstein Fitzgerald Willoughby & Pascuzzi LLP 400 Capitol Mall Ste 1450 Sacramento CA 95814-4434 Fax: 916-329-7435. E-mail: sfelderstein@ffwplaw.com.

FELDHAUS, STEPHEN MARTIN, lawyer; b. Lawrenceburg, Tenn., Jan. 12, 1945; s. Lawrence Bernard and Margaret Martha (Holthouse) F.; m. Allis Rennie, Aug. 18, 1968 (div. 1980); 1 child, Rennie Elizabeth; m. Marcia Virginia Hughes, Dec. 30, 1980; stepchildren: Matthew Rankin FitzSimmons, Ryan Ford FitzSimmons. AB, U. Notre Dame, 1967; JD, Stanford U., 1973. Bar: Tex. 1973, D.C. 1984. Law clk. to Hon. Eugene A. Wright U.S. Ct. Appeals (9th cir.), Seattle, 1972-73; assoc. Fulbright & Jaworski, Houston, 1973-76, London, 1976-79, ptnr., 1979-81, Washington, 1981—. Bd. dirs. Foundation, Vaduz, Liechtenstein. Bd. dirs. D.C. Downtown Partnership, Washington, 1988-92 Mem.: ABA, D.C. Bar, Internat. Fiscal Assn., Internat. Bar Assn., City Club of Washington. Republican. Avocations: tennis, squash, skiing, chess, reading. Corporate, general, Private international, Taxation, general. Office: Fulbright & Jaworski 801 Pennsylvania Ave NW Fl 3-5 Washington DC 20004-2623 E-mail: sfeldhaus@fulbright.com.

FELDKAMP, JOHN CALVIN, lawyer, educational administrator; b. Milw., Sept. 5, 1939; s. Leroy Lyle and Dorothea Arpke (Reineking) F.; m. Barbara Joan Condon, June 30, 1962; children: John Calvin, Stephen Patrick, Amy Genevieve. BA, U. Mich., 1961, JD, 1965. Bar: Mich. 1970, N.J. 1980, D.C. 1983. Asst. to v.p. U. MIch., Ann Arbor, 1964-66, dir. housing, 1966-77; gen. mgr. svcs. Princeton U., N.J., 1977-82; pvt. practice law Ann Arbor, 1970-77, Princeton, 1977-82; assoc. Caplin & Drysdale, Washington, 1982-85; exec. dir. Brown & Wood, N.Y.C., 1985—2001; exec. dir. N.Y. office Sidley, Austin, Brown & Wood, 2001—. Councilman, City of Ann Arbor, 1967-69; hearing referee Mich. Civil Rights Commn., Lansing, 1975-77. Mem. Rotary (bd. dirs. Ann Arbor 1970-77, Princeton 1978-82). General practice. E-mail: jfeldkamp@sidley.com.

FELDMAN, CLARICE ROCHELLE, lawyer; b. Milw., Dec. 2, 1941; d. Harry and Beatrice (Hiken) Wagan; m. Howard J. Feldman, July 11, 1965; 1 child, David Lewis. BS, U. Wis., 1963, LL.B., 1965. Bar: Wis. 1965, D.C. 1969, Md. 1984. Appellate atty. NLRB, Washington, 1965—69; co-counsel to Joseph A. Yablonski, Washington, 1969; atty. Washington research project Clark Coll., 1970-72; asso. gen. counsel United Mine Workers Am., Washington, 1972-74; partner Becker, Channell, Becker & Feldman, Washington, 1974-76, Becker & Feldman, 1976-77; gen. counsel Ams. for Energy Independence, Washington, 1978-80; atty. Office of Spl. Investigations, Dept. Justice, 1980-84; pvt. practice law Washington, 1984-98; atty. pro bono, 1999—. Trustee Washington Internat. Sch., 1987-98; advisor Assn. Union Democracy. Mem. Wis., D.C., Md. bar assns. Democrat. Jewish. Federal civil litigation, Family and matrimonial, Immigration, naturalization, and customs. Home: 4455 29th St NW Washington DC 20008-2307

FELDMAN, FRANKLIN, lawyer, printmaker; b. N.Y.C., Nov. 12, 1927; s. Reuben and Anne (Schulman) F.; m. Naomi Goldstein, June 3, 1956; children: Sarah, Eve, Jacob. BA, NYU, 1948; LLB, Columbia U., 1951. Bar: N.Y. 1952. Mem. office Gen. Counsel, USAF, Dept. Def., Washington, 1951-53; atty. office gen. counsel to gov. State of N.Y., Albany, 1954; assoc. Stroock & Stroock & Lavan, N.Y.C., 1955-64, ptnr., 1965-88, counsel, 1989—. Cons. Temp. N.Y. Commn. on Constl. Conv., 1967; lectr. in law Columbia Law Sch., 1979-2001. Editor-in-chief Columbia U. Law Rev., 1950-51; author: (with Stephen E. Weil) Art Works: Law, Policy and Practice, 1974, Art Law, 1986 (Best Law Book Published in 1986, Scribes); contbr. articles to profl. jours. Trustee Am. Jewish Hist. Soc., Waltham, Mass., 1987-96. 1st lt., USAF, 1951-53. Yaddo Fellow, Saratoga Springs, 1983. Fellow Am. Bar Found. (life); mem. N.Y. State Bar Assn., Assn. of Bar of City of N.Y. (chmn. art com. 1968-71), Internat. Found. Art Rsch. (pres. 1971-76, bd. dirs. 1976-96), Ltd., Soc. Am. Graphic Artists, Century Assn., Pvt. Art Dealers Assn., Inc. (counsel, dir. 1993—), Grolier Club. Jewish. Corporate, general, Intellectual property, Art Law. Home: 15 W 81st St New York NY 10024-6022 Office: Stroock & Stroock & Lavan 180 Maiden Ln Fl 17 New York NY 10038-4937 E-mail: feldmanf@aol.com.

FELDMAN, LARRY, JR., lawyer; b. Shreveport, La., Aug. 7, 1950; BA, La. State U., 1972, JD, 1974. Bar: La. 1974. Atty. Wiener, Weiss & Madison, PC, Shreveport, La. Capt. JAGC U.S. Army, 1974—77. Mem.: ABA, Shreveport Bar Assn., Fedn. Def. and Corp. Counsel, La. Assn. Def.

Counsel, La. State Bar Assn. (bd. govs. 1994—97, sec. 1997—99, past chair continuing legal edn. program com., pres.-elect 2002—03). Commercial, consumer (including collections, credit), Workers' compensation. Office: Wiener Weiss and Madison PO Box 21990 333 Texas St Ste 2350 Shreveport LA 71120-1990*

FELDMAN, MARTIN L. C. federal judge; b. St. Louis, Jan. 28, 1934; s. Joseph and Zelma (Bosse) F.; m. Melanie Pulitzer, Nov. 26, 1958; children: Jennifer Pulitzer, Martin L.C. Jr. BA, Tulane U., 1955, JD, 1957. Bar: La., Mo. 1957. Law clk. to Hon. J.M. Wisdom, U.S. Ct. Appeals, 1958-59; assoc. Bronfin, Heller, Feldman & Steinberg, New Orleans, 1959-60, ptnr., 1960-83; judge U.S. Dist. Ct., New Orleans, 1983—. Trustee, former chmn. Sta. WYES-TV; spl. counsel to Gov. of La., 1979-83. Contbr. articles to profl. jours. Former nat. sec. Anti-Defamation League; former pres. bd. mgrs. Touro Infirmary; bd. dirs. Public Broadcasting Service, 1978-84, Fed. Jud. Ctr., 1991-95; bd. dirs. Fed. Jud. Ctr., 1991-95. Mem. ABA (chair nat. conf. of fed. trial judges 1996-97), La. Bar Assn. (chmn. law reform com. 1981-82), Mo. Bar Assn., Am. Law Inst., Order of Coif. Republican. Jewish. Home: 12 Rosa Park New Orleans LA 70115-5044 Office: US Dist Ct Chambers of Judge Feldman 500 Camp St New Orleans LA 70130-3313

FELDMAN, PHILLIP, lawyer; b. N.Y.C., Apr. 26, 1932; BS, Calif. State U., 1956; MBA, U. So. Calif., 1963, JD, 1966. Bar: Calif. Expert witness Law Offices of Phillip Feldman, Sherman Oaks, Calif., 1967—. Fellow Am. Bd. Profl. Liability Attys. (chair cert. com. legal). Professional liability. Office: 15250 Ventura Blvd Ste 610 Sherman Oaks CA 91403-3218

FELDMAN, ROGER DAVID, lawyer; b. N.Y.C., Apr. 7, 1943; s. Louis and Dora (Goldsmith) F.; m. Gail Steg, May 31, 1969; children: Rebecca, Seth. AB, Brown U., 1962; LLB, Yale U.; MBA, Harvard U. Bar: N.Y. 1966, D.C. 1977. Ops. rsch. analyst Office Asst. Sec. Def., Washington, 1967-68; staff asst. Office of Pres. U. S., Washington, 1968-69; assoc. LeBoeuf Lamb Leiby & MacRae, 1969-75; ptnr. Le Boeuf Lamb Leiby & MacRae, 1977-83; dep. asst. adminstr. FEA, Washington, 1975-77; mng. ptnr. project fin. group Nixon Hargrave Devans & Doyle, Washington, 1983-89; head ptnr. project fin. group McDermott Will & Emery, Washington, 1989-97; chair project fin. group Bingham McCutchen LLP, 1997—. Mem. fin. adv. bd. EPA, 1989-92; bd. dirs. R.J. Rudden & Assocs. Inc., Cogeneration Inst., pub.-pvt. venture divsn. Am. Road and Transp. Builders, 1991-93, Water Industry Coun.; bd. dirs. N.E. Energy and Commerce Assn., also chair fin. com.; pres. Nat. Coun. for Pub. Pvt. Partnerships, 1983-98, chair, 1998—. Author: (with others) Infrastructure Finance: Tools for the Future, 1988, Public-Private Ventures in Transportation, 1990, Comprehensive Guide to Water and Wastewater Finance, 1991, Privatization of Public Utilities, 1995, Privatization, 1995; mem. bd. editors Yale Law Jour., 1964-65, Jour. Structured and Project Fin., 1995—, Constrn. Bus. Rev., 1992—; Washington editor Cogeneration Monthly Letter, 1987-98, Mcht. Power Monthly, 1998—, Strategic Planning for Energy and the Environment, 1992— (Author of the Yr. 1998), Power Marketers Assn. On Line Mag., 1999—, Power Exec., 2002-; contbr. articles to profl. jours. Mem. ABA (chmn. energy law com. 1980-83, alt. energy sources com. 1981-84, 86-90, chmn. environ. values com. 1983-89, com. on privatization 1985-90, chmn. energy fin. 1990-91), Fed. Energy Bar Assn. (chmn. cogeneration com. 1981-82), Nat. Coun. for Pub.-Pvt. Partnerships (Outstanding Contbn. to Privatization award), N.Y. Bar Assn., D.C. Bar Assn. (chair internat. fin. and investment com. 1998—), Assn. Energy Engrs. (Cogeneration Profl. of Yr. 1990), Phi Beta Kappa. Finance, Utilities, public, Government contracts and claims. Office: Bingham Dana LLP 1120 20th St NW Ste 800 Washington DC 20036-3406 E-mail: r.feldman@bingham.com.

FELDMAN, SCOTT MILTON, lawyer; b. N.Y.C., July 31, 1942; s. Abe and Lilian F.; m. Susan Lauer, July 13, 1968; children: James W., Mark A. BA, Amherst Coll., 1964; JD, Harvard U., 1967. Bar: NY 1968, Ill. 1978. Instr. UCLA Law Sch, 1967-68; lt. Judge Advocate Gen's. Corp. U.S. Navy, Washington, 1968-71; assoc. Sullivan & Cromwell, N.Y.C., 1971-77; ptnr. Winston & Strawn, Chgo., 1978-2001; assoc. gen. counsel Bank of Am. N.A., Chgo., 2001—. Trustee Village of Glencoe, Ill., 1983-91. Mem. ABA, Chgo. Bar Assn., Assn. Bar City N.Y., Amherst Alumni Assn. Commercial, contracts (including sales of goods; commercial financing), Finance, Securities. Office: Bank of America NA Mail Code ILI-231-07-17 231 S LaSalle St 7th Fl Chicago IL 60697 E-mail: scott.m.feldman@bankofamerica.com.

FELDMAN, STANLEY GEORGE, lawyer; b. N.Y.C., N.Y., Mar. 9, 1933; s. Meyer and Esther Betty (Golden) F.; m. Norma Arambula; 1 dau., Elizabeth L. Student, U. Calif., Los Angeles, 1950-51; LL.B., U. Ariz., 1956. Bar: Ariz. 1956. Practiced in, Tucson, 1956-81; ptnr. Miller, Pitt & Feldman, 1968-81; justice Ariz. Supreme Ct., Phoenix, 1982—2002, chief justice, 1992-97; of counsel Haralson, Miller, Pitt & McAnnally. Lectr. Coll. Law, U. Ariz., 1965-76, adj. prof., 1976-81, 2000, 03. Bd. dirs. Tucson Jewish Community Council, U. Ariz. Found., 1999—. Mem. ABA, Am. Bd. Trial Advocates (past pres. So. Ariz. chpt.), Ariz. Bar Assn. (pres. 1974-75, bd. govs. 1967-76), Pima County Bar Assn. (past pres.), Am. Trial Lawyers Assn. (dir. chpt. 1967-76), U. Ariz. Law Coll. Assn. Democrat. Jewish. Insurance, Personal injury (including property damage), Product liability. Office: 1 S Church Ave Tucson AZ 85701-1620

FELLER, URS P. lawyer; b. Uzwil, Switzerland, June 21, 1967; s. Hans-Ulrich and Hedi Feller; m. Rita Kaegi Feller, Aug. 26, 1995; children: Lea Kathrin, Kilian Cyrill, Anna Noemi. Lic. Law, U. Zurich, Switzerland, 1997, PhD in Law, 1998. Bar: St. Gall 1999, Zurich 2000, Eng. and Wales 2002. Tchr. Canton of St. Gall, Switzerland, 1989—93; law clk. Dist. Ct., St. Gall, 1997—98, High Ct., St. Gall, 1998—99; atty.-at-law Prager Dreifuss, Zurich, 2000—. Rsch. asst. U. Zurich, Zurich, Switzerland, 1995; substitute judge Dist. Ct. Obertoggenburg, Nesslau, 1995—97, single judge, 1997—99, 1st v.p., 1999—. Mem.: Brit.-Swiss C. of C. (com. mem. tax and legal chpt. 2002—). Banking. Office: Prager Dreifuss Muhlebachstr 6 8008 Zurich Switzerland Office Fax: 41 1 254 55 99. E-mail: urs.feller@prager-dreifuss.com.

FELLERS, RHONDA GAY, lawyer; b. Gainesville, Tex., July 20, 1955; d. James Norman and Gaytha Ann (Sanders) F.; m. Bruce C. Hinton, Oct. 15, 1981 (div. Oct. 1985). BA, U. Tex., 1977, JD, 1980; LLM in Taxation, U. Denver, 1987. Bar: Tex. 1981, Colo. 1981, U.S. Dist. Ct. (no. dist.) Tex. 1982, U.S. Dist. Ct. Colo. 1985, U.S. Tax Ct. 1985, U.S. Ct. Appeals (5th cir.) 1986, U.S. Ct. Appeals (10th cir.) 1989, U.S. Supreme Ct. 1993, U.S. Ct. Claims 1993. Assoc. Walters & Assocs., Lubbock, Tex., 1981-83; gen. counsel Security Nat. Bank, Lubbock, 1983; sole practice Lubbock, 1983-87; assoc. Melvin Coffee & Assocs., P.C., Denver, 1984-85, 87-90; atty. adviser U.S. Tax Ct., Washington, 1990-94; pvt. practice Pinehurst, Tex., 1994-98; with Arthur Andersen LLP, Houston, 1998—2002; sole practice, 2002—. Mem. ABA, State Bar Tex., Colo. Bar Assn., Houston Bar Assn. Avocations: golf, tennis, photography. E-mail: rgfellers@starband.net.

FELLMAN, RICHARD MAYER, lawyer; b. Omaha, May 30, 1935; s. Leon E. and Frances (Green) F.; m. Beverly Bloom, Jan. 12, 1964; children: Susan, Deborah, Jonathan, Daniel. BA in Polit. Sci., U. Nebr., 1957, JD, 1959. Bar: Nebr. 1959, U.S. Dist. Ct. Nebr. 1959. Farm editor, reporter Lincoln (Nebr.) Star, 1956-58; state capitol reporter AP, Lincoln, 1958; assoc. Marks, Clare, Hopkins & Rauth, Omaha, 1960-64; ptnr. Fellman & Stern, Omaha, 1965-73, Fellman Law Offices, Omaha, 1973-86, Fellman, Moylan, Natvig, Wilke & Wik, Omaha, 1987—. Chair jud. subcom. Nebr. State Legis. on No Fault Divorce, 1973-74; bd. dirs. Vol. Bur., 1965-67; bd. dirs. NCCJ, 1968-72, Omaha-Douglas County Health Dept., 1977-80; mem. Omaha-Douglas Bldg. Commn., 1977-80; bd. dirs. Metro Area Planning Agy., Omaha, 1979; founding bd. dirs. Omaha Coun. on Domestic Violence, current chair of legis. com.; hon. bd. dirs. Alzheimer's Assn., Omaha, 1997-98; governing authority Omaha Symphony Assn.; bd. dirs., officer Beth El Synagogue, Omaha; chmn. Omaha com. Anti-Defamation League, 1967-70; mem. Nat. Civil Rights Com. and Law Com., 1965—; bd. dirs. Jewish Fedn. Omaha, 1969-72; founding pres. Omaha Jewish Day Sch. (now Friedel Acad.), 1970; gen. men's chair United Jewish Appeal, 1968; bd. dirs. Omaha Jewish Press, J.C.C. Libr. Br., Nebr. Jewish Hist. Soc., Jewish Coll. Learning; organizer, chair Nebr. Dem. State Reform Commn., 1971; mem. Douglas County Bd. Commrs., 1977-80, chair of bd., 1980; senator State of Nebr., 1973-74, mem. jud. com. and govt., mil. and vets. affairs com.; mem. Mid-Am. coun. adv. bd. Boy Scouts Am., 1983—, cub and scout troop committeeman, 1980-87, chair coun. Jewish cmty. relationships com., 1985-96. Capt. USAR, 1959-66. Recipient Humanitarian of the Yr. award Sons of Italy, 1977. Mem. Nebr. Trial Lawyers Assn. (bd. dirs. 1971-72, legis. com. 1992-95), Nebr. Bar Assn. (chmn. family law com. 1971-72, 75-76), Omaha Bar Assn. (chair com. on domestic violence 1996, Pro Bono Publico award 1972), Rotary, Delta Sigma Rho, Zeta Beta Tau. Democrat. Jewish. Family and matrimonial, Personal injury (including property damage), Criminal. Home: 12206 Leavenworth Rd Omaha NE 68154 Office: Fellman Moylan Natvig Wilke & Wik 100 Continental Bldg 209 S 19th St Omaha NE 68102-1755 Fax: 402-341-8159. E-mail: fellmanrm@aol.com.

FELLOWS, HENRY DAVID, JR., lawyer; b. N.Y.C., Dec. 17, 1954; s. Henry D. Sr. and Mary (Stecko) F.; m. Pam Neal Fellows, May 15, 1982; children: Christopher, Suzanne, Thomas. BSBA, Bucknell U., 1975; JD, Georgetown U., 1978. Bar: Ga. 1978, U.S. Dist. Ct. (no. dist.) Ga. 1978, U.S. Ct. Appeals (11th cir.) 1978, U.S. Supreme Ct. 1997. Law clk. to hon. judge Charles A. Moye Jr. U.S. Dist. Ct. (no. dist.) Ga., Atlanta, 1978-80; assoc. Hurt, Richardson, Garner, Todd & Cadenhead, Atlanta, 1981-87, ptnr., 1987-92, Fellows, Johnson & LaBriola, LLP (and predecessor firm), Atlanta, 1993—. Mem. ABA, Ga. Bar Assn., Atlanta Bar Assn. (chmn. ct. com. 1992-98, bd. dirs. litigation sect. 1999—, CLE com. bd. dirs. 2001--, bd. dirs. 2002--), Lawyers Club of Atlanta, Indsl. Rels. Rsch. Assn. (bd. dirs. Atlanta chpt.), Fulton Indsl. Bus. Assn. (gen. counsel). Avocations: tennis, piano. Federal civil litigation, General civil litigation. Office: Fellows Johnson & LaBriola LLP Peachtree Ctr # 2300 South 225 Peachtree St NE Atlanta GA 30303-1701 E-mail: hfellows@fjl-law.com.

FELLOWS, JERRY KENNETH, lawyer; b. Madison, Wis., Mar. 19, 1946; s. Forrest Garner and Virginia (Witte) F.; m. Patricia Lynn Graves, June 28, 1969; children: Jonathon, Aaron, Daniel. BA in Econs., U. Wis., 1968; JD, U. Minn., 1971. Bar: U.S. Dist. Ct. (no. dist.) Ill. 1971. Ptnr. McDermott, Will & Emery, Chgo., 1971—2002; with Bell, Boyd & Lloyd LLC, Chgo., 2002—. Speaker Bur. Nat. Affairs, Washington, 1985—. Contbr. articles to profl. jours. Bd. dirs. Midwest Benefits Coun., 1998. Mem. U. Minn. Law Alumni Assn. (bd. visitors), Gamma Eta Gamma. Avocations: coaching track, basketball, baseball. Administrative and regulatory, Labor (including EEOC, Fair Labor Standards Act, labor-management relations, NLRB, OSHA), Pension, profit-sharing, and employee benefits. Home: 4541 Middaugh Ave Downers Grove IL 60515-2761 Office: Bell Boyd & Lloyd LLC 70 West Madison St Ste 3100 Chicago IL 60602-4207 E-mail: jfellows@bellboyd.com.

FELLRATH, RICHARD FREDERIC, lawyer; b. Dearborn, Mich., Nov. 30, 1940; s. Jerome John and Jane Elizabeth (Ayers) F.; m. Barbara Ann Osani, Oct. 14, 1966; children: Richard F., Jr., Christina Joyce Devlin. BA, U. Notre Dame, 1963; JD, U. Detroit, 1966. Bar: Mich. 1967, D.C. 1969, U.S. Ct. Mil. Appeals 1967, U.S. Supreme Ct. 1970, U.S. Ct. Appeals (6th cir.) 1984, U.S. Ct. Claims 1987. Judge adv. U.S. Army, Balt., 1967-71; ptnr. Milmet & Vecchio P.C., Detroit, 1971-85; sr. atty. Miller, Canfield, Paddock & Stone, Detroit, 1985-91, Fitzgerald & Dakmak, P.C., Detroit, 1991-96; pvt. practice Detroit, 1996—. Contbr. articles to profl. jours. Capt. U.S. Army, 1967-71. Mem. Fed. Bar Assn. (Detroit bankruptcy chmn. 1985-87), SAR, Sons Union Vets Civil War. Republican. Roman Catholic. Avocations: stamps, windsurfing, ancient coins, military miniatures, genealogy. Bankruptcy, Government contracts and claims. Home: 4056 Middlebury Dr Troy MI 48085-3620 Office: 600 Ford Bldg 615 Griswald Detroit MI 48226 Fax: 313-961-3132.

FELNER, RICHARD M. real estate consultant, lawyer; b. N.Y.C., Mar. 27, 1936; s. Theodore I. and Sylvia L. Felner; m. Linda Marks Vogel, Dec. 15, 1963 (div. May 1994); children: Andrew, David, Julie. AB, Cornell U., 1958; LLB, Columbia U., 1961. Bar: N.Y. Supreme Ct. 1962. Intern Senator Jacob Javits U.S. Senate, Washington, 1958, spl. asst. to Senator Jacob Javits N.Y.C., 1958-61; assoc. Hays, Sklar & Hertzberg, N.Y.C., 1961-62, Cole and Dietz, N.Y.C., 1962-65; assoc. counsel N.Y. State Joint Legis. Com. to Revise the Banking Law, N.Y.C. and Albany, 1962-65; co-chief exec. The Fabric Tree Ind., N.Y.C., 1966-77; gen. counsel, sec. Brooks Fashion Stores, Inc., N.Y.C., 1978-85; exec. v.p., dir. Worths Stores, Inc., N.Y.C. and St. Louis, 1985-91; chmn. Richard M. Felner Assocs., N.Y.C., 1991—. Bd. dirs. Ames Dept. Stores, Inc., Rocky Hill, Conn. Active Westchester (N.Y.) County Rep. Com., 1968-85; mem. various adv. coms. Town of Mamaroneck, N.Y., 1970-85. Mem. Internat. Coun. Shopping Ctrs., Assn. Bar City N.Y. Office: 200 E 57th St New York NY 10022-2860

FELPER, DAVID MICHAEL, lawyer; b. Springfield, Mass., Dec. 17, 1954; s. Lawrence Allen and Edith Charlotte (Flesher) F.; m. Kimberlee White, May 19, 1979; children: Andrew Martin, Evan Matthew, Scott Tyler. BA in Polit. Sci., George Washington U., 1976; JD cum laude, Western New Eng. Coll., 1980. Bar: Mass. 1980, U.S. Dist. Ct. Mass. 1981, U.S. Ct. Appeals (1st cir.) 1987. Assoc. Michelman & Feinstein, Springfield, 1980-82; asst. regional counsel Dept. Social Services, Commonwealth of Mass., Springfield, 1982-83; labor relations counsel Sprague Electric Co., Lexington, Mass., 1983-87; assoc. Bowditch & Dewey, Framingham, Mass., 1987-92, ptnr., 1992—. Lectr. various human resource orgns. throughout U.S., 1984—; pres. Valley Tech. Ednl. Found. Inc., 1998—; corporator Milford-Whitinsville Regional Hosp. Bd. dirs. Horace Mann Ednl. Assocs., Inc. Mem.: Worcester County Bar Assn., Mass. Bar Assn. (labor law com.), Blackstone Valley C. of C. (dir.). Avocations: golf, running, reading. Labor (including EEOC, Fair Labor Standards Act, labor-management relations, NLRB, OSHA), Pension, profit-sharing, and employee benefits, Workers' compensation. Office: Bowditch & Dewey 311 Main St Worcester MA 01608 E-mail: DFelper@bowditch.com.

FELS, NICHOLAS WOLFF, lawyer; b. White Plains, N.Y., Mar. 19, 1943; s. Lawrence P. and Fredericka (Gaines) F.; m. Susan T. McEwan, Dec. 28, 1968; 1 child, Sarah. BA, Harvard U., 1964; MA, U. Calif., Berkeley, 1965; LLB, Harvard U., 1968. Bar: N.Y. 1968, Calif. 1970, U.S. Dist. Ct. (cen. dist.) Calif. 1970, D.C. 1971, U.S. Dist. Ct. D.C. 1971, U.S. Ct. Appeals (10th cir.) 1976, U.S. Ct. Appeals (D.C. cir.) 1977, U.S. Supreme Ct. 1978, U.S. Ct. Appeals (4th cir.) 1979, U.S. Ct. Appeals (8th cir.) 1981, U.S. Ct. Appeals (5th cir.) 1982. Law clk. to Hon. John Minor Wisdom U.S. Ct. Appeals, New Orleans, 1968-69; atty. OEO Legal Services, Los Angeles, 1969-70; assoc. Covington & Burling, Washington, 1970-76, ptnr., 1976—. Mem. Nat. Com. on U.S.-China Relations, N.Y.C., 1982—. Contbr. articles to profl. jours. Mem. Fed. Energy Bar Assn., D.C. Appleseed Ctr. (bd. dirs. 1994—, pres. 1996-2000). FERC practice. Home: 3534 Edmunds St NW Washington DC 20007-1431 Office: Covington & Burling 1201 Pennsylvania Ave NW Washington DC 20004-2401 E-mail: nfels@cov.com.

FELSENTHAL, STEVEN ALTUS, lawyer, educator; b. Chgo., May 21, 1949; s. Jerome and Eve (Altus) F.; m. Carol Judith Greenberg, June 14, 1970; children: Rebecca Elizabeth, Julia Alison, Daniel Louis Altus. AB, U. Ill., 1971; JD, Harvard U., 1974. Bar: Ill. 1974, U.S. Dist. Ct. (no. dist.) Ill. 1974, U.S. Ct. Claims 1975, U.S. Tax Ct. 1975, U.S. Ct. Appeals (7th cir.) 1981. Assoc. Levenfeld, Kanter, Baskes & Lippitz, Chgo., 1974-78; ptnr. Levenfeld & Kanter, Chgo., 1978-80, Levenfeld, Eisenberg, Janger, Glassberg & Lippitz, Chgo., 1980-84; sr. ptnr. Sugar, Friedberg & Felsenthal, Chgo., 1984—. Lectr. Kent Coll. Law, Ill. Inst. Tech., Chgo., 1978-80. Mem. ABA, Ill. Bar Assn., Chgo. Bar Assn., Chgo. Coun. Lawyers, Harvard Law Soc. Ill., Standard Club, Harvard Club, Phi Beta Kappa. Corporate, general, Estate planning, Taxation, general. Office: Sugar Friedberg & Felsenthal 30 N La Salle St Ste 3000 Chicago IL 60602-3327 E-mail: saf@sff-law.com.

FELTER, EDWIN LESTER, JR., judge; b. Washington, Aug. 11, 1941; s. Edwin L. Felter and Bertha (Peters) Brekke; m. Yoko Yamauchi-Koito, Dec. 26, 1969. BA, U. Tex., 1964; JD, Cath. U. of Am., 1967. Bar: Colo. 1970, U.S. Dist. Ct. Colo. 1970, U.S. Ct. Appeals (10th cir.) 1971, U.S. Supreme Ct. 1973, U.S. Tax Ct. 1979, U.S. Ct. Claims 1979, U.S. Ct. Internat. Trade 1979. Dep. pub. defender State of Colo., Ft. Collins, 1971-75; asst. atty. gen. Office of the Atty. Gen., Denver, 1975-80; state adminstrv. law judge Colo. Divsn. of Adminstrv. Hearings, Denver, 1980-83, chief adminstrv. law judge, 1983-98, sr. adminstr., law judge, 1998—. Disciplinary prosecutor Supreme Ct. Grievance Com., 1975-78; mem. faculty Nat. Jud. Coll., 1999—; mem. Coun. Can. Adminstrv. Tribunals, 2002--. Contbg. editor Internat. Franchising, 1970. Mem. Colo. State Mgmt. Cert. Steering Com., 1983-86; No. Colo. Criminal Justice Planning Coun., Ft. Collins, 1973-75; bd. dirs., vice chmn. The Point Cmty. Crisis Ctr., Ft. Collins, 1971-73; mem. Denver County Dem. Party Steering Com., 1978-79, chmn. 12th legis. dist., 1978-79; bd. dirs., pres. Denver Internat. Program, 1989-90. Mem.: Colo. Bar Assn. (chmn. grievance policy com. 1991—94, interprofl. com. 1995—), Nat. Assn. Adminstrv. Law Judges (pres. Colo. chpt. 1982—84, chair fellowship com. 1996—, Fellowship winner 1994), Denver Bar Assn., Arapahoe County Bar Assn., Nat. Conf. Adminstrv. Law Judges (chair 2000—01), ABA, Am. Inns of Ct. (master level 1996—). Office: Colo Divsn Adminstrv Hearings 1120 Lincoln St Ste 1400 Denver CO 80203-2140 Fax: 303-764-1401. E-mail: ed.felter@state.co.us.

FELTER, JOHN KENNETH, lawyer; b. Monmouth, N.J., May 9, 1950; s. Joseph Harold and Rosanne (Bautz) F. BA magna cum laude, MA in Econs., Boston Coll., 1972; JD cum laude, Harvard U., 1975. Bar: Mass. 1975, N.Y. 2003, D.C. 2003, U.S. Dist. Ct. Mass. 1976, U.S. Ct. Appeals (1st cir.) 1977, U.S. Ct. Appeals (2nd cir.) 2002, U.S. Ct. Appeals (DC cir.) 2002, U.S. Supreme Ct. 1982, U.S. Tax Ct. 1993, U.S. Ct. Appeals (2d cir.) 2002, D.C. Ct. Appeals 2002. Assoc. Goodwin, Procter LLP, Boston, 1975-83, ptnr., 1983—. Spl. asst. gen. Commonwealth of Mass., 1982-84, 94-95; spl. counsel Town of Plymouth, Mass., Town of Salisbury, Mass., Town of Edgartown, Mass.; spl. outside counsel City of Boston, 1990-92; mem. devel. com. Greater Boston Legal Svcs., 1980—, bd. dirs., 1982—, mem. exec. com., 1989-93; mem. faculty Mass. Continuing Legal Edn., Inc., Boston. Mem. adv. com. The Boston Plan for Excellence in Pub. Schs.; mem. elem. edn. com. Blue Ribbon Commn. on Cmty. Learning Ctrs.; VIP panelist Easter Seals Telethon, Boston, 1978-79. Fellow: Am. Coll. Trial Lawyers, Mass. Bar Assn. (co-chmn. edn. com. pub. law sect.); mem.: ABA (litigation sect., gen. practice sect., mem. personal rights litigation com. environ. law sect., mem. ABA-Am. Law Inst. com. on cont. edn.), Greater Boston C. of C. (mem. edn. com., mem. health care com.), Boston Bar Assn. (bd. dirs. law firm resources project 1985—, mem. coll. and univ. law com. 1986—, chmn. fed. rules com. litigation sect. 1994), Mass. Bar Assn., Am. Arbitration Assn. (comml. arbitrator). Federal civil litigation, State civil litigation, Education and schools. Office: Goodwin Procter LLP Exchange Pl 53 State St Ste 17 Boston MA 02109-2881

FELTES, CHARLES VICTOR, lawyer; b. St. Charles, Ill., Apr. 9, 1947; s. Victor P. and Ramona R. (Nagle) F.; m. Susan Joyce Seidelman, Nov. 21, 1975; children: Jennifer, Katherine, Victor, Laura. BS, U. Wis., 1969; JD, U. Ill., 1973. Bar: Ill. 1973, Wis. 1975, U.S. Dist. Ct. (no. dist.) Ill. 1973, U.S. Dist. Ct. (we. dist.) Wis. 1976. Assoc. Tyler, Peskind & Solomon, Aurora, Ill., 1973-75, Kostner, Ward & Koslo, Osseo, Wis., 1975-84, ptnr., 1984-94; atty. pvt. practice, Osseo, Wis., 1995—. Mem. Wis. Bar Assn., Ill. Bar Assn., Tri-County Bar Assn. (pres. 1996), Osseo Comml. Club (pres. 1983). Republican. Roman Catholic. General civil litigation, General practice, Personal injury (including property damage). Home: N51061 Ward Rd PO Box 54 Osseo WI 54758-0054 Office: PO Box 485 Osseo WI 54758-0485

FELTON, WILLIAM RAYMOND, lawyer; b. New Brunswick, N.J., Dec. 1, 1956; s. W. Raymond and Joan Campilongo Felton; m. Deborah I. Lynch, Jan. 9, 1982; children: Patrick, Lauren, Christopher. BA, Rutgers U., 1978, JD, 1981. Bar: N.J. 1981, U.S. Dist. Ct. N.J. 1981, U.S. Tax Ct. 1983. Assoc. Greenbaum, Rowe, Smith, Ravin, Davis & Bergstien, Woodbridge, NJ, 1981—87; ptnr. Greenbaum, Rowe, Smith, Ravin, Davis & Himmel LLP, Woodbridge, NJ, 1988—. Author: Organization and Sale of Small Businesses, 1995. Mem.: N.J. State Bar Assn. (bd. dirs. corp. and bus. law sect. 1990—, chair 2002—). Avocation: running. Commercial, contracts (including sales of goods; commercial financing), Corporate, general, Securities. Home: 38 William Penn Rd Warren NJ 07059-5038 Office: Greenbaum Rowe Smith Ravin Davis & Himmel PO Box 5600 Woodbridge NJ 07095-0988 Office Fax: 732-549-1881. E-mail: rfelton@greenbaumlaw.com.

FELTY, KRISS DELBERT, lawyer; b. Cleve., May 5, 1954; s. John Gilbert and Stephanie (Kriss) F. BA in Psychology, Case Western Res. U., 1976; postgrad., Cleve. State U., 1977-79; JD, U. Akron, Ohio, 1983. Bar: Ohio 1983, Tex. 1988, Wis. 1989, U.S. Dist. Ct. Ohio 1983, U.S. Ct. Appeals (6th cir.) 1984, Fla. 1985, U.S. Supreme Ct. 1986. Assoc. Dennis Reimer Co., LPA, Twinsburg, Ohio, 1983-87; mng. ptnr. Shapiro & Felty, Independence, Ohio, 1987--. Mem. ABA, Fla. Bar Assn., Ohio Bar Assn., Greater Cleve. Bar Assn., Cuyahoga County Bar Assn., Mortgage Bankers Assn. Am., Ohio Mortgage Bankers Assn., Mortgage Bankers Assn. Met. Cleve., Phi Kappa Theta (trustee 1973-74). Avocations: golf, swimming, reading, music, leaded glass lamps. Bankruptcy, Commercial, consumer (including collections, credit), Property, real (including real estate development, water). Office: Shapiro & Felty 1500 W 3d St Ste 400 Cleveland OH 44113

FENECH, JOSEPH CHARLES, lawyer; b. London, May 28, 1950; came to U.S., 1953; s. Carmel John and Elizabeth Frances (Borg) F.; m. Cynthia A. Rennie, June 14, 1980 (div. 1998); children: Paul C., Peter J., Elizabeth F. BA with honors, Mich. State U., 1972; JD, U. Mich., 1975. Bar: Mich. 1975, U.S. Dist. Ct. (ea. dist.) Mich. 1975, U.S. Ct. Appeals (6th cir.) 1977, Ill. 1980, U.S. Dist. Ct. (no. dist.) Ill. 1980, U.S. Dist. Ct. (ctrl. dist.) Ill. 1993, U.S. Dist. Ct. (ea. dist.) Wis. 1993, U.S. Ct. Appeals (7th cir.) 1980, U.S. Supreme Ct. 1993, U.S. Tax Ct. 1993. Law clk. Washtenaw Cir. Ct., Ann Arbor, Mich., 1975-76; asst. atty. gen. State of Mich., Detroit, 1976-80; labor rels. counsel McDonald's Corp., Oak Brook, Ill., 1980-82, sr. internat. atty., 1982-84; sr. mem. Fenech & Assoc., Oak Brook, Ill., 1985—. Contbr. articles to profl. jours. Bd. dirs. Cath. Charities Diocese of Joliet, Ill.; active Family Focus, Mich., 1979-80, Internat. Found. Employee Benefit Plans, Brookfield, Wis., 1980-83, Chmns. Club Ctrl.; mem. bd. govs. DuPage Hosp., Ctrl. DuPage Hosp. Tree Life, Ctrl., Glen Oaks Med. Ctr., Tree of Life, Rep. Campaign Coun., 1995; supt. adv. com. Naperville Cmty. Sch. Dist. 203; improvement com. Mill St. Sch., Naperville; charter mem. Marklund Children's Home Endowment; bd. govs. Ctrl. DuPage Hosp. Named Regents scholar U. Mich., 1973, 74, 75, Trustees scholar Mich. State U., 1969-72. Mem. ABA, Ill. State Bar Assn., Mich. Bar assn., DuPage Estate Planning Coun., U. Mich. Lawyers Club, Ill. Bankers Assn., Ill. Mortgage Bankers Assn., Internat. Platform Assn. Am. Hosp. Assn. (sr.

mem.), Am. Acad. Healthcare Attys. (sr. mem.). Commercial, contracts (including sales of goods; commercial financing), Corporate, general, Private international. Office: Fenech & Pachulski PC PO Box 5996 Naperville IL 60567

FENG, PAUL YEN-HSIUNG, lawyer, chemist; s. Chih-Chung and Pao-Ru Hu Feng; m. Marie Rose Rysiejko, Feb. 14, 1976; m. Mary Stella Pao-Ching Pai, Oct. 2, 1947 (dec. May 25, 1975); children: Joseph, Dorothy Feng Hamamura, Alphonso. BS, Fu-Jen Cath. U., Beijing, 1947; grad. fellow, Nat. Beijing U., 1947—48; PhD, Wash. U., 1954; JD, DePaul U., 1986; MBA, U. Chgo., 1991. CPA U. of Ill. Bd. Examiners, 1996; bar: U. S. Dist. Ct. (no. dist.) Ill. 1986, U. S. Tax Ct. 1994, U. S. Patent and Trademark Office 1989, U. S. Ct. Appeals (7th cir.) 1986, U. S. Supreme Ct. Tchr. Wen-Hua H.S., Beijing, 1945—47; tech. dir. Manu-Mine R & D Co., Reading, Pa., 1953—55; mgr. IIT Rsch. Inst. (formerly Armour Rsch. Found.), Chicago, 1955—66, sci. advisor, 1962—66; assoc. prof. Marquette U., Milw., 1966—70, prof., 1970—88; of counsel Lamet Kanwit & Davis, Brezina & Ehrlich, Chicago, Ill., 1990—2000; fulbright lectr. Nat. Taiwan U., Taipai, 1965; nrc prof. and dean Nat. Tsinghua U., Hsinchu, Taiwan, 1973—74; pvt. practice Wilmette, Ill., 1986—. Tech. advisor U. S. Del. to 2nd UN Conf. Peaceful Uses Atomic Energy, Geneva, 1958; cons. U.S. Army Natick Labs., Natick, Mass., 1966—74, Apollo Program - NASA, Washington, 1968, Chung Shan Inst. Tech., Taoyuan, Taiwan, 1970—74; sr. advisor NRC, Taipai, Taiwan, 1973—74; pres. North Suburban Bar Assn., Glenview, Ill., 1996—97. Contbr. articles, chapters to books; author: (book) Dividend Reinvestment Handbook. Dir. Chinese Refugee Relief, Washington, 1962; mem. Chinese Adv. Com. Cultural Rels. in Am., Washington; dir. Neighborhood Assistance Found., Chgo., 1992—96. Recipient Achievement award, Nat. Youth Commn. , Taiwan, 1971; Rsch. grantee, USAF, U. S. Army, U.S. AEC, 1955 - 74. Mem.: Phoenix Soc., ACS (career cons. 1992—), Overture Soc., Elliott Soc. (life), Sigma Xi (pres., marquette chpt. 1973—74). Achievements include patents for method of making fluorinated compounds; a hot-atom cation defixation method for the production of high specific activity isotopes; research in method for specific tritiation of organic compounds. Avocations: linguistics, musicology, geographic archaeology. Intellectual property, Immigration, naturalization, and customs, Taxation, general. Mailing: PO Box 424 Kenilworth IL 60043 Personal E-mail: paulfeng@att.net.

FENNING, LISA HILL, lawyer, mediator, former federal judge; b. Chgo., Feb. 22, 1952; d. Ivan Byron and Joan (Hennigar) Hill; m. Alan Mark Fenning, Apr. 3, 1977; 4 children. BA with honors, Wellesley Coll., 1971; JD, Yale U., 1974. Bar: Ill. 1975, Calif. 1979, U.S. Dist. Ct. (no. dist.) Ill., U.S. Dist. Ct. (no., ea., so. & cen. dists.) Calif., U.S. Ct. Appeals (6th, 7th & 9th cirs.), U.S. Supreme Ct. 1989. Law clk. U.S. Ct. Appeals 7th cir., Chgo., 1974-75; assoc. Jenner and Block, Chgo., 1975-77, O'Melveny and Myers, L.A., 1977-85; judge U.S. Bankruptcy Ct. Cen. Dist. Calif., L.A., 1985-2000; mediator JAMS, Orange, Calif., 2000-01; ptnr. Dewey Ballantine LLP, L.A., 2001—. Bd. govs. Nat. Conf. Bankruptcy Judges, 1989-92; pres. Nat. Conf. of Women's Bar Assns., N.C., 1987-88, pres.-elect, 1986-87, v.p., 1985-86, bd. dirs.; lectr., program coord. in field; bd. govs. Nat. Conf. Bankruptcy Judges Endowment for Edn., 1992-97, Am. Bankruptcy Inst., 1994-2000; mem., bd. advisors Nat. Jud. Edn. Program to Promote Equality for Women and Men in the Cts., 1994—. Mem., bd. advisors: Lawyer Hiring & Training Report, 1985-87; contbr. articles to profl. jours. Durant scholar Wellesley Coll., 1971; named one of Am's. 100 Most Important Women Ladies Home Jour., 1988, one of L.A.'s 50 Most Powerful Women Lawyers, L.A. Bus. Jour., 1998. Fellow Am. Bar Found., Am. Coll. Bankruptcy (bd. regents 1995-98); mem. ABA (standing com. on fed. jud. improvements 1995-98, mem. commn. on women in the profession 1987-91, Women's Caucus 1987—, Individual Rights and Responsibilities sect. 1984—, bus. law sect. 1986—, bus. bankruptcy com.), Nat. Assn. Women Judges (nat. task force gender bias in the cts. 1986-87, 93-94), Nat. Conf. Bankruptcy Judges (chair endowment edn. bd. 1994-95), Am. Bankruptcy Inst. (nominating com. 1994-95, bd. steering com. stats. project 1994-96), Calif. State Bar Assn. (chair com. on women in law 1986-87), Women Lawyers' Assn. L.A. (ex officio mem., bd. dirs., chmn., founder com. on status of women lawyers 1984-85, officer nominating com. 1986, founder, mem. Do-It-Yourself Mentor Network 1986-96), Phi Beta Kappa. Democrat. Office: Dewey Ballantine LLP 333 S Grand Ave 26th Fl Los Angeles CA 90071 E-mail: Lfenning@deweyballantine.com.

FENSOM, JAMES B. lawyer; b. Port St. Joe, Fla., Feb. 25, 1950; s. Paul Sherwood and Elizabeth (Ball) F.; m. Jan Lehman, July 14, 1973; children: Meredith, Stuart. BS, Auburn (Ala.) U., 1972; JD, Fla. State U., 1975. Bar: Fla. 1975, U.S. Dist. Ct. (no. dist.) Fla. 1978, U.S. Ct. Appeals (11th cir.) 1979. Legis. asst. U.S. Congress, Washington, 1975-76; with felony divsn. State Atty.'s Office, Panama City, Fla., 1976-78; ptnr. Barron, Redding, Hughes, Fite, Bassett, Fensom & Sanborn, PA, Panama City, 1979—. Bd. dirs. SouthTrust Bank, Panama City; bd. govs. 14th Jud. Cir. Grievance Com., Panama City, 1990-91; commr. First Dist. Ct. of Appeal Jud. Nominating Commn., 1999—. Mem. Gulf of Mex. Fishery Mgmt. Coun., 1999—. Mem. Bay County Bar Assn. (prs. 1980), Fla. Bar (bd. govs. 1992-96, exec. com. 1995), St. Andrews Yacht Club (bd. dirs. 1996-98). Avocations: cruising, fishing. General civil litigation, Insurance, Personal injury (including property damage). Office: Barron Redding et al 220 Mckenzie Ave Panama City FL 32401-3129

FENSTER, ROBERT DAVID, lawyer; b. N.Y.C., Sept. 25, 1946; BA, Queen's Coll., 1968; JD, Bklyn. Law Sch., 1973. Bar: N.Y. 1974, U.S. Dist. Ct. (so. and ea. dists.) N.Y. 1974, U.S. Supreme Ct. 1977. Investigator, prosecutor N.Y. Stock Exch., N.Y.C., 1972-73; ptnr. law firms Rockland County, 1974—80; prin. Robert D. Fenster, Atty. at Law, P.C., 1980—2001; ptnr. Fenster & Kurland LLP, New City, 2002—. Bd. dirs. Brit. Pub. Corp., various other corps. Advisor Clarkstown Youth Ct., New City, NY, 1982; bd. dirs. Legal Aid Soc., Rockland County, 1974—78, Nyack Hosp. Found., 1995—2000, Good Samaritan Hosp. Found. Mem. ABA, N.Y. State Bar Assn., Rockland County Bar Assn., Am. Arbitration Assn. (arbitrator), Police Chiefs Found., Internat. Bus. Network of Greater N.Y. General civil litigation, Corporate, general, Property, real (including real estate development, water). Office: Fenster & Kurland LLP Attys at Law 337 N Main St Ste 11 New City NY 10956-4310 Fax: 845-638-4767.

FENTON, ELLIOTT CLAYTON, lawyer; b. Oklahoma City, Nov. 26, 1914; s. Edgar R. and Mary (Gaddo) F.; m. LeNoir Massey, July 6, 1939; children: Mike, Ann Wallis; m. Ruby L. Simpson, Aug. 21, 2002. BA, U. Okla., 1935, LLB, 1937. Bar: Okla. 1937, U.S. Dist. Ct. (no., ea. and we. dists.) Okla., U.S. Ct. Appeals (10th cir.), U.S. Supreme Ct., U.S. Ct. Mil. Appeals. Atty. Looney & Fenton, Oklahoma City, 1937-38; atty., claims rep. Nat. Mut. Casualty Co., Tulsa, 1938-40, Hartford Ins. Group, Oklahoma City, 1940-47; atty. Fenton & Fenton, Oklahoma City, 1947—. Chmn. bd. trustees United Meth. Found., Oklahoma City, 1973-83; chancellor United Meth. Found., Oklahoma City, 1983-89. Ret. comdr. USNR. Fellow Am. Bar Found; mem. Internat. Assn. Def. Counsel, Def. Research Inst. (state chmn. 1978-83), Okla. Assn. Def. Counsel (pres. 1972), Okla. County Bar Assn. (bd. dirs.). Republican. United Methodist. Avocation: golf. Federal civil litigation, State civil litigation, Personal injury (including property damage). Home: 14901 N Penn Ave Duplex 4A Oklahoma City OK 73134-6079 Office: Fenton Fenton Smith et al 1 Leadership Sq Ste 800 Oklahoma City OK 73102 E-mail: elbeau88@cox.net., ecfenton@fentonlaw.com.

FENTON, LEWIS LOWRY, lawyer; b. Palo Alto, Calif., Aug. 20, 1925; s. Norman and Jessie (Chase) F.; m. Gloria J. Palmieri, Aug. 21, 1978; children: Lewis Lowry, Juanita F. Donnelly, Daniel Norman, Pamela Chase. BA, Stanford U., 1948, LL.B., 1950. Bar: Calif. 1950, U.S. Dist. Ct. (no. dist.) Calif. Atty. Calif. Dept. Pub. Works, 1950-52; chmn., bd. dirs. Hoge, Fenton, Jones & Appel, Inc., Monterey, San Luis Obispo and San Jose; counsel Fenton & Keller, P.C., Monterey, 1993—, Hoge, Fenton, Jones & Appel, Inc., San Jose, 1993—. Bd. dirs. 1st Nat. Bank Monterey County, 1984—, chmn., 1987-90. Mem. bldg. com. Community Hosp. Monterey Peninsula, Carmel, 1961-62; found. dir. Monterey Jazz Festival, 1958; past bd. dirs. Monterey Peninsula Coll., pres. 1971-72, Monterey Inst. Fgn. Studies; past pres. and bd. dirs. York Sch., Monterey, Calif., 1960-74, chmn. bd., 1992—; bd. dirs. Monterey Bay Aquarium, Community Found. Monterey County, chmn., 1998—; bd. visitors Stanford Law Sch. Served to 2d lt. USAAF, 1942-46. Fellow Am. Coll. Trial Lawyers, Internat. Acad. Trial Lawyers; mem. ABA, Calif. Bar Assn., Santa Clara Bar Assn., Monterey County Bar Assn. (pres. 1963, 1st Chief Justice Gibson award), Assn. Def. Counsel (pres. 1969), Nat. Bd. Trial Advocacy, Nat. Assn. R.R. Counsel, Internat. Assn. Def. Counsel, Def. Research Inst., Am. Judicature Soc., Am. Acad. Hosp. Attys., Am. Bd. Trial Advs. (adv.), Stanford U. Alumni Assn. (pres. 1966-67), Calif. Med. Legal Nat. Health Lawyers Assn. Episcopalian (vestryman, sr. warden 1956-58). Clubs: Cypress Point, Old Capital, Pacheco, Pacific Union. Home and Office: PO Box 791 Monterey CA 93942-0791 E-mail: LFenton@fentonkeiler.com., llf@hogefenton.com.

FENTON, THOMAS CONNER, lawyer; b. Cin., Feb. 9, 1954; S. William Conner and Virginia (Rawnsley) F.; m. Karen Lois Haswell, Oct. 20, 1979; children: Margaret Lois, Rebecca Conner, Robert Ellis. BA, Centre Coll., 1976; JD, Ohio State U., 1979. Bar: Ky. 1979, U.S. Dist. Ct. (we. dist.) Ky. 1979, U.S. Ct. Appeals (D.C. cir.) 1981, U.S. Dist. Ct. (ea. dist.) Ky. 1985, U.S. Ct. Appeals (6th cir.) 1986. Assoc. Greenebaum, Treitz, Brown & Marshall, Louisville, 1979-85, ptnr., 1985-88; v.p., counsel Nat. City Bank Ky., Louisville, 1989-93; counsel Nat. City Corp., Cleve., 1989-93; v.p. human resources Nat. City Processing Co., Louisville, 1993-95; of counsel Morgan & Pottinger PSC, Louisville, 1996-2001, mem., 2001—. Lectr. Ohio Bankers Assn. Sch. of Human Resources Adminstrn., 1989-91. Author: Affirmative Action Relevant to Bankers, 1996. Bd. trustees St. Matthew's United Meth. Ch., 2001—, chmn., 2002—; bd. dirs. Elder Serve Inc., Louisville, 1983—91, 1995—2001, sec., 1984—86, v.p., 1986—87, pres., 1987—90; bd. dirs. Louisville Youth Choir, Inc., 1996—2002, chmn., 1997—2002. Mem. Ky. Bar Assn. (chmn. labor rels. law sect. 1981-83), Louisville Bar Assn. Methodist. Banking, Commercial, contracts (including sales of goods; commercial financing), Labor (including EEOC, Fair Labor Standards Act, labor-management relations, NLRB, OSHA). Home: 11003 Fox Moore Ct Louisville KY 40223-5531 Office: Morgan & Pottinger PSC 601 W Main St Louisville KY 40202-2976

FERENCZ, BENJAMIN BERELL, lawyer; b. Soncuta Mare, Romania, Mar. 11, 1920; came to U.S., 1921, naturalized, 1933; s. Joseph Ference and Sarah (Legman) Ference Schwartz; m. Gertrude Fried, Mar. 29, 1946; children— Carol, Robin Eve, Donald Martin, Nina Dale. B.S.S., CCNY, 1940; J.D., Harvard U., 1943. Bar: N.Y. 1943, U.S. Supreme Ct. 1943, U.S. Dist. Ct. (so. and ea. dists.) N.Y. 1958. Exec. counsel U.S. Chief of Counsel for War Crimes, Nuremberg, Fed. Republic Germany, 1946-48; dir. gen. Jewish Restitution Orgn., Frankfurt, Fed. Republic Germany, 1948-56; ptnr. Taylor, Ferencz & Simon, N.Y.C., 1956— ; adj. prof. Pace U. Sch. Law, N.Y.C.; dir. United Restitution Orgn., London, Frankfurt and N.Y.C., 1948— . Author: Less Than Slaves, 1979 (Nat. and Present Tense Lit. awards 1980); Defining International Aggression, 2 vols., 1975; An International Criminal Court, 2 vols., 1980; Enforcing International Law, 2 vols., 1983, Common Sense Guide to World Peace, 1985. Mem. Human Rights Commn., New Rochelle, N.Y., 1975— . Served with inf. U.S. Army, 1943-45, ETO. Mem. Am. Soc. Internat. Law (v.p. 1979-80), Internat. Law Assn., Internat. League for Human Rights, Amnesty Internat., World Peace Through Law Ctr. Democrat. Jewish. Club: Harvard (N.Y.C.). Lodge: B'nai B'rith (local pres. 1960's, counsel supreme lodge 1966-70). Private international, Public international. Home: 14 Bayberry Ln New Rochelle NY 10804-3402

FERENCZ, ROBERT ARNOLD, lawyer; b. Chgo., Sept. 10, 1946; s. Albert and Frances (Reiss) F.; m. Marla J. Miller, May 20, 1973; children: Joseph, Ira. BS in Acctg., U. Ill., 1968; JD magna cum laude, U. Mich., 1973. Bar: Ill. 1973. From assoc. to ptnr. Sidley, Austin, Brown & Wood, Chgo., 1973—. Mem. ABA, Ill. Bar Assn. Pension, profit-sharing, and employee benefits, Corporate taxation. Office: Sidley Austin Brown & Wood Bank One Plz 10 S Dearborn St Chicago IL 60603-2000

FERGUS, GARY SCOTT, lawyer; b. Racine, Wis., Apr. 20, 1954; s. Russell Malcolm and Phyl Rose (Muratore) F.; m. Isabelle Sabina Beekman, Sept. 28, 1985; children: Mary Marckwald Beekman Fergus, Kirkpatrick Russell Beekman Fergus. AB, Stanford U., 1976; JD, U. Wis., 1979; LLM, NYU, 1981. Bar: Wis. 1979, Calif. 1980. Assoc. Brobeck, Phleger & Harrison, San Francisco, 1980-86, ptnr., 1986—2001, mng. ptnr. products liability, ins. coverage, environ. and antitrust/appellate practices, 1996-2000, sr. ptnr. e-commerce anti-trust group, 2000—01; founder law firm Fergus, San Francisco, 2002—. Mem. ABA. FERC practice, Toxic tort, Antitrust. Home: 3024 Washington St San Francisco CA 94115-1618 Office: Fergus a law firm 595 Market St Ste 2430 San Francisco CA 94105 E-mail: gfergus@ferguslegal.com.

FERGUSON, CLEVE ROBERT, lawyer, educator; b. Long Beach, Calif., Dec. 31, 1938; s. Frank H and Ruth S Ferguson; m. Kathryn Jane Weaver, Apr. 10, 1965 (div. June 25, 1995); children: Sharon Anne, Robert Timothy; m. Peggy Burke Daniell, Nov. 19, 1995. AB in Econs., U. So. Calif., 1961, JD, 1965. Bar: Calif 1966, US Dist Ct (cent dist) Calif 1966, US Ct Appeals (9th cir) 1987, US Supreme Ct 1975. Assoc. Musick, Peeler & Garrett, L.A., 1965-69, Hayes & Hume, Beverly Hills, Calif., 1969-74; pvt. practice Pasadena/Claremont, Calif., 1974—; adj. prof. physics and astronomy U. La Verne (Calif.), 1993—; pres., CEO Mars Manned Mission Corp.; adj. prof. Coll. Law U. La Verne (Calif.), 1994—2001. Mem. alcohol and drug abuse com. Calif. State Bar, 1990—91; instr. astronomy and bus. law Chapman U., 1992—93; arbitrator Am. Arbitration Assn., Nat. Arbitration Forum; lectr. in field. Editor: (book) Tall Tales and Memories, 1987. Mem. Stony Ridge Obs., 1985—, pres., 1994—97; co-founder, trustee Mt. Wilson Inst., Calif., 1987, 2003—; lectr., cons. Mcpl. Officers for Redevel. Reform, Calif., 1996—; mem. L.A. Opera League; bd. dirs. Clan Fergusson Soc. N.Am., 1987—2000. With U.S. Army, 1961—62. Decorated knight, Knights Templar of Jerusalem, Grand Priory of the Scots. Fellow: Soc. Antiquaries Scotland; mem.: SAR, Univ. Club Claremont, Univ. Club Pasadena, Beta Theta Pi (past pres). Avocations: astronomy, mountaineering, dry fly fishing, skiing. General civil litigation, Corporate, general, Land use and zoning (including planning). Office: C Robert Ferguson Atty at Law 237 W 4th St Claremont CA 91711-4710 Office Fax: 909-624-7291. E-mail: crflawyer@earthlink.net., crf@marsmannedmission.org.

FERGUSON, GERALD PAUL, lawyer; b. Teaneck, N.J., Oct. 17, 1951; s. James Richard and Ilene Veronica (Meyer) F.; m. Nancy Ivers, Aug. 20, 1977; 1 child, James Ralph. BA, Fairleigh Dickinson U., 1974; JD, Capital U., 1979. Bar: Ohio 1979, U.S. Dist. Ct. (so. dist.) Ohio 1980, U.S. Ct. Appeals (6th cir.) 1986, U.S. Supreme Ct. 1990. Ptnr. Vorys, Sater, Seymour and Pease, Columbus, 1979—; mem. rules adv. com. Ohio Supreme Ct., Columbus, 1993. Mem. ABA (litigation sect., mem. trial evidence subcom. 1985-86), Ohio State Bar Assn. (mem. jud. adv. and legal reform com., unauthorized practice law com. 1985-90), Columbus Bar Assn. (chmn. juror subcom. 1979-86). Republican. Roman Catholic. Avocations: tennis, golf, fishing. Federal civil litigation, State civil litigation, Intellectual property. Office: Vorys Sater Seymour & Pease 52 E Gay St Columbus OH 43215-3161 E-mail: gpferguson@vssp.com.

FERGUSON, GORDON DOUGLAS, lawyer; b. Santa Ana, Calif. s. Gordon Theodore and Eleanor (Bosshard) F.; m. Robin Eve Gillespie, Oct. 9, 1976. BS, U. Wash., 1966, MBA, 1967, JD, 1973. Bar: Wash. 1973, U.S. Dist. Ct. (we. dist.) Wash. 1974, U.S. Ct. Appeals (9th cir.) 1975. Assoc. Anderson, Hunter, Denell, Baker & Collins, Everett, Wash., 1973-77; mng. shareholder, dir. Anderson Hunter Law Firm, Everett, 1977—. With Wash. State Commn. on Jud. Conduct, Olympia, 1991-97; pres. United Way Snohomish County, Everett, 1983, Everett Drug Abuse Coun., 1976; chmn. Gen. Hosp. Found., Everett, 1992. Recipient Edna Davert award Everett Drug Abuse Coun., 1977. Mem. Wash. State Bar Assn. (chmn. disciplinary bd. 1983-86), Wash. Coun. Sch. Attys. (pres. 1983), Wash. Soc. Hosp. Attys. (pres. 1988-89), Everett Golf & Country Club, Milltown Sailing Assn. Health, Labor (including EEOC, Fair Labor Standards Act, labor-management relations, NLRB, OSHA), Municipal (including bonds). Office: Anderson Hunter Law Firm 2707 Colby Ave Ste 1001 Everett WA 98201-3566

FERGUSON, JO MCCOWN, lawyer; b. Central City, Ky., Apr. 5, 1915; s. Jo Marvin and Willie Mae (Cain) F.; m. Margarita Hauser, July 12, 1947; children— Rita, Diane, Jo Frances. AB, U. Ky., 1937, LL.B., 1939. Bar: Ky. 1938. Practiced in, Central City, 1939-42; asst. atty. gen., 1948-56; atty. gen., 1956-60; commr. econ. security, 1960-61; partner firm Harper, Ferguson & Davis. Mcpl. bd. counsel, 1961-91. Chmn. Gov.'s Com. on Constl. Revision, 1961-62; chmn. Gov.'s Task Force on Fin., 1976-77; pres. Ky. Hist. Soc., 1988-90; chief Property Control br. Mil. Govt., Bavaria, 1946-47. Capt. AUS, 1944-47, ETO. Decorated Brigadier d'Honneur 3eme Regiment Anjou, French Army. Mem. ABA, Ky. Bar Assn., VFW, So. Attys. Gen. (chmn. 1957-58). Democrat. Episcopalian. Home: 403 Duff Ln Louisville KY 40207-1524

FERGUSON, JOHN MARSHALL, retired federal judge; b. Marion, Ill., Oct. 14, 1921; s. John Marshall and Vessie (Widdows) F.; m. Jeanne Harmon, Sept. 23, 1950; children: Marcia Ferguson Velde, Mark Harmon, John Scott, Mary Sue Holley. Student, So. Ill. U., 1939-41, S.E. Mo. Tchrs. Coll., 1941; LLB, JD, Washington U., St. Louis, 1948. Bar: Ill. 1949, U.S. Ct. Appeals (7th cir.) 1956, U.S. Supreme Ct. 1960. Asst. mgr. I.W. Rogers Theaters, Inc., Anna, Ill., 1934-42; atty. U.S. Fidelity & Guaranty Co., St. Louis, 1948-51; assoc. Baker, Kagy & Wagner, East St. Louis, Ill., 1951-56, ptnr., 1956-59, Wagner, Conner, Ferguson, Bertrand & Baker, East St. Louis and Belleville, Ill., 1959-72; magistrate judge U.S. Dist. Ct. (so. dist.) Ill., 1990-94. Pres. bd. Arch Aircraft, Inc., 1966-68; disciplinary commr. Ill. Supreme Ct., 1957-90, mem. joint com. on revision disciplinary rules, 1972-74; mem. hearing bd. Ill. Registration and Disciplinary Commn., 1974-90; pres. 1st Dist. Fedn. Bar Assns. Precinct committeeman Stookey Twp., St. Clair County (Ill.) Republican Com., 1958-62; Bd. dirs., v.p. East St. Louis chpt. ARC. Capt. AUS, 1942-45. Mem. ABA, Ill. Bar Assn. (prof. responsibility com. 1975-86, chmn. 1983-84), St. Clair County Bar Assn., 7th Fed. Cir. Bar Assn. (bd. govs.), Ill. Club (govs., pres. 1966-67), East St. Louis City Club (pres. 1960-61), Ill. Club (gov. pres. 1966-67), St. Clair Country Club (Belleville, pres. 1972-73), Masons, Elks, Delta Theta Phi. Home: 12 Oak Knoll Pl Belleville IL 62223-1817 E-mail: jferg7@juno.com.

FERGUSON, MILTON CARR CARR, JR., lawyer; b. Washington, Feb. 10, 1931; s. Milton Carr and Gladys (Emery) F.; m. Marian Evelyn Nelson, Aug. 21, 1954; children: Laura, Sharon, Marcia, Sandra. BA, Cornell U., 1952; LL.B., 1954; LL.M., N.Y. U., 1960. Bar: N.Y. State 1954. Trial atty. tax div. Dept. Justice, Washington, 1954-60, asst. atty. gen., 1977-81; asst. prof. law U. Iowa, 1960-62; assoc. prof. N.Y.U., 1962-65; prof. N.Y. U., 1965-77; vis. prof. law Stanford (Calif.) U., 1972-73; of counsel Wachtell, Lipton, Rosen & Katz, N.Y.C., 1969-76; ptnr. Davis Polk & Wardwell, N.Y.C., 1981—2001, sr. counsel, 2002—. Spl. cons. to Treasury Dept., Commonwealth P.R., 1974 Author: (with others) Federal Income Taxation Legislation in Perspective, 1965, Federal Income Taxation of Estates and Beneficiaries, 1970, 2d edit., 1994. Trustee NYU Law Ctr. Found., Lewis and Clark Coll. Mem. ABA (chmn. tax sect. 1993-94), N.Y. State Bar Assn., Soc. Illustrators. Corporate taxation, Taxation, general. Home: 32 Washington Sq W New York NY 10011-9156 Office: Davis Polk & Wardwell 450 Lexington Ave New York NY 10017-3982

FERGUSON, RALPH ALTON, JR., (SONNY FERGUSON), circuit court judge; b. St. Louis, Mar. 23, 1948; s. Ralph Anderson and Mary P. Ferguson; m. Pennye Michelle Boackle, Oct. 8, 1972; children: Trey, Lorie, Jamie. BS in Bus., Auburn (Ala.) U., 1970; JD, Cumberland Sch. Law, Birmingham, Ala., 1973. Bar: Ala. 1974, U.S. Dist. Ct. (all dists.) Ala. 1974, U.S. Ct. Appeals (11th cir.) 1978. Sales clk., security Yeildings, Birmingham, 1970; lumber sales Southeastern Treated, Birmingham, 1971; head coach all sports Briarwood Christian, Birmingham, 1971-73; lawyer Lindberg, Lindberg & Leach, Birmingham, 1974-76, Leach, Dillard & Ferguson, Birmingham, 1976-80, Hampe, Dillard & Ferguson, Birmingham, 1980-88, Dillard & Ferguson, Birmingham, 1988-95; circuit judge State of Ala., Birmingham, 1995—. Student/adult leader Fellowship of Christian Athletes, Birmingham, 1966—; mem. Monday Morning Quarterback, Birmingham, 1988—. Sgt. Air N.G., 1966-72. Named Nat. Lineman/Southeastern, Sports Illus./SEC, 1969. Mem. Ala. Bar Assn., Birmingham Bar Assn. (exec. com. 1994-97), Birmingham Bar Found., Am. Acad. Adoption Lawyers. Republican. Roman Catholic. Avocations: handball, football, basketball, boating. Office: Domestic Rels Cts Bldg 2124 7th Ave N Birmingham AL 35263-0001

FERGUSON, STEVEN EDWARD, lawyer; b. Oklahoma City, Apr. 26, 1955; m. Shelly J. Smith, Aug. 5, 1977; children: Steven E. Jr., Cicely J. BA, U. Okla., 1977; JD, Oklahoma City U., 1980. Bar: Okla. 1980, U.S. Dist. Ct. (we. dist.) Okla. 1980. Sole practice Crabb, Ferguson & Riesen, PA, Oklahoma City, 1980—. Criminal, Family and matrimonial, Personal injury (including property damage). Office: Crabb Ferguson & Riesen 5101 N Classen Blvd Ste 404 Oklahoma City OK 73118-4433

FERGUSON, WARREN JOHN, judge; b. Eureka, Nev., Oct. 31, 1920; s. Ralph and Marian (Damele) Ferguson; m. E. Laura Keyes, June 5, 1948; children: Faye F., Warren John, Teresa M., Peter J. BA, U. Nev., 1942; LLB, U. So. Calif., 1949; LLD (hon.) , Western State U., San Fernando Valley Coll. Law. Bar: Calif. 1950. Mem. firm Ferguson & Judge, Fullerton, Calif., 1950—59; city atty. for cities of Buena Park, Placentia, La Puente, Baldwin Park, Santa Fe Springs, Walnut and Rosemead, Calif., 1953—59; mcpl. ct. judge Anaheim, Calif., 1959—60; judge Superior Ct., Santa Ana, Calif., 1961—66, Juvenile Ct., 1963—64, Appellate Dept., 1965—66; U.S. dist. judge Los Angeles, 1966—79; judge U.S. Circuit Ct. (9th cir.), Los Angeles, 1979—86; sr. judge U.S. Ct. Appeals (9th cir.), Santa Ana, 1986—; faculty Fed. Jud. Ctr., Practising Law Inst., U. Iowa Coll. Law, N.Y. Law Jour. Assoc. prof. psychiatry (law) Sch. Medicine, U. So. Calif.; assoc. prof. Loyola Law Sch. With U.S. Army, 1942—46. Decorated Bronze Star. Mem.: Theta Chi, Phi Kappa Phi. Democrat. Roman Catholic. Office: US Courthouse 411 W 4th St Ste 10-80 Santa Ana CA 92701-4500 E-mail: judge_ferguson@ca9.uscourts.gov.

FERNANDEZ, FERDINAND FRANCIS, federal judge; b. 1937; BS, U. So. Calif., 1958, JD, 1963; LLM, Harvard U., 1963. Bar: Calif. 1963, U.S. Dist. Ct. (cen. dist.) Calif. 1963, U.S. Ct. Appeals (9th cir.) 1963, U.S. Supreme Ct. 1967. Elec. engr. Hughes Aircraft Co., Culver City, Calif., 1958-62; law clk. to dist. judge U.S. Dist. Ct. (cen. dist.) Calif., 1963-64; pvt. practice law Allard, Shelton & O'Connor, Pomona, Calif., 1964-80; judge Calif. Superior Ct. San Bernardino County, Calif., 1980-85, U.S. Dist. Ct. (cen. dist.) Calif., L.A., 1985-89, U.S. Ct. Appeals (9th cir.), L.A., 1989—2002, sr. judge, 2002—. Lester Roth lectr. U. So. Calif. Law Sch., 1992. Contbr. articles to profl. jours. Vice chmn. City of La Verne Commn. on Environ. Quality, 1971-73; chmn. City of Claremont Environ. Quality Bd., 1972-73; bd. trustees Pomona Coll., 1990—. Fellow Am. Coll. Trust and Estate Counsel; mem. ABA, State Bar of Calif. (fed. cts. com. 1966-69, ad hoc com. on attachments 1971-85, chmn. com. on adminstrn. of justice 1976-77, exec. com. taxation sect. 1977-80, spl. com. on mandatory fee arbitration 1978-79), Calif. Judges Assn. (chmn. juvenile cts. com. 1983-84, faculty mem. Calif. Jud. Coll. 1982-83, faculty mem. jurisprudence and humanities course 1983-85), L.A. County Bar Assn. (bull. com. 1974-75), San Bernardino County Bar Assn., Pomona Valley Bar Assn. (co-editor Newsletter 1970-72, trustee 1971-78, sec.-treas. 1973-74, 2d v.p. 1974-75, 1st v.p. 1975-76, pres. 1976-77), Estate Planning Coun. Pomona Valley (sec. 1966-76), Order of Coif, Phi Kappa Phi, Tau Beta Pi, Eta Kappa Nu. Office: US Ct Appeals 9th Cir 125 S Grand Ave Ste 602 Pasadena CA 91105-1621

FERNANDEZ, FRANK L. lawyer, retail executive; BBA, St. Bonaventure U.; JD, Albany Law Sch.; ML in Taxation, NYU. CPA. With Haskins & Sells, N.Y.C.; ptnr. Fernandez Burstein Tuczinski & Collura, P.C., 1982—2001; pres. Saratoga Equine Sports Ctr.; sec., gen. counsel, exec. v.p. Home Depot, Inc., Atlanta, 2001—. Office: Home Depot Inc 2455 Paces Ferry Rd Atlanta GA 30339-4024 Office Fax: 770-384-2356.*

FERNANDEZ, HERMES A., III, lawyer; b. Queens, N.Y., Aug. 22, 1955; s. Hermes Alexander and Helen Gloria (Hall) F.; m. Theresa Anne Dehm, Sept. 10, 1977; children: Holly Kathryn, Amy Elizabeth, Daniel Dehm. BA with honors, LeMoyne Coll., 1977; JD magna cum laude, Syracuse U., 1981. Bar: N.Y. 1982, U.S. Dist. Ct. (no. dist.) N.Y. 1991, U.S. Ct. Appeals (2d cir.) 1991, U.S. Ct. Appeals (5th cir.) 1984. Jud. clk. Hon. John MacKenzie U.S. Dist. Ct. (ea. dist.) Va., Norfolk, 1981-82; trial atty. civil divsn. U.S. Dept. Justice, Washington, 1982-86; asst. counsel to gov. State of N.Y., Albany, 1986-90; assoc., ptnr. Bond, Schoeneck & King, LLP, Albany, 1990—. Author articles. Mem. Citizens Budget Adv. Com., Albany, 1996-99; past pres. Homeless and Travelers Aid Soc., Albany; chair legis. com. MS Soc. N.E. N.Y., Albany, 1997-2000, mem. clin. adv. com., 2000—; past mem. bd. dirs. Capitol Region chpt. N.Y. Civil Liberties Union. Mem. N.Y. State Bar Assn. (health law sect., chair profl. discipline com., legis. policy com.), Am. Health Lawyers Assn., Univ. Club., Pine Haven Country Club. Avocations: golf, history. Administrative and regulatory, Government contracts and claims, Health. Office: Bond Schoeneck & King PLLC 111 Washington Ave Albany NY 12210-2202 E-mail: fernanh@bsk.com.

FERNANDEZ, JOSE WALFREDO, lawyer; b. Cienfuegos, Cuba, Sept. 19, 1955; arrived in U.S., 1967; s. Jose Rigoberto and Flora (Gomez) Fernandez; m. Andrea Gabor, June 22, 1985. BA, Dartmouth Coll., 1977; JD, Columbia U., 1980. Bar: N.Y. 1981, N.J. 1981, U.S. Dist. Ct. (so. dist.) N.Y. 1981, U.S. Dist. Ct. N.J. 1981. Assoc. Curtis, Mallet, Prevost, Colt & Mosle, N.Y.C., 1981-84, Baker & McKenzie, N.Y.C., 1984-89, ptnr., 1989-96, O'Melveny & Myers, L.L.P., N.Y.C., 1996—, mng. ptnr. N.Y. office, 2002—. Adj. prof. N.Y. Law Sch., 1984—87. Contbr. Bd. dirs. Ballet Hispanico, Ceiba Prodns., WBGO-FM Newark Pub. Radio; mem. adv. bd. Coun. of Ams., 2001—; bd. of trustees Dartmouth Coll., 2002—. Mem.: ABA (Inter-Am. law com. 1955—, Ctrl. Am. task force 1985—92, presdl. commn. L.Am. 1986—91), N.Y.C. Bar Assn. (fgn. and comparative law com., Inter-Am. affairs com. 1996—98, city bar fund 1999—), Brazilian-U.S. C. of C. (bd. dirs. 1994—99,), U.S.-Spain C. of C. (bd. dirs.). Avocation: Avocations: sports, non-fiction writing, travel. Banking, Commercial, contracts (including sales of goods; commercial financing), Private international. Home: 508 E 87th St New York NY 10128-7602 Office: O'Melveny & Myers LLP Citicorp Ctr 153 E 53rd St Fl 53D New York NY 10022-4611

FERNANDEZ, PATRICIA S. lawyer; b. Middletown, N.Y., Mar. 21, 1961; BA, Wellesley Coll., 1983; JD, Yale U., 1986. Bar: Mass. 1986, U.S. Dist. Ct. Mass. 1987. Atty. Brown, Rudnick, Freed & Gesmer, Boston, 1986-96; pvt. practice North Andover, Mass., 1996—. Contbr. articles to profl. jours. Fellow: Am. Acad. of Matriomonial Lawyers; mem.: Mass. Prolate and Family Inn of Ct., Wellesley Alumnae Assn., Mass. Bar Assn. Family and matrimonial. Office: 401 Andover St North Andover MA 01845-5076

FERNANDEZ, RODOLFO, lawyer; b. Barcelona, Catalunya, Spain, Jan. 9, 1964; s. Alvaro and Juana Fernandez; m: Diana Marly; children: Sandra, Rodolfo. LLB, U. Barcelona, Spain, 1988, postgraduate E-Commerce Law, 2000. Assoc. Marti and Assoc., Barcelona, 1994-98, Pedro Brosa and Assoc., Barcelona, 1998—; ptnr., dir. IT Law Dept. BROSA. Lctr. U. Barcelona, 1995-2001. Contr. articles to profl. jours. Avocations: skiing, diving. Communications, Computer, Corporate, general. Office: Brosa Abogados y Economistas A V Diagonal 598 08021 Barcelona Lata Lunya Spain Fax: 93-2022907. E-mail: rodolfo.fernandez@ben.brosa-assiados.com.

FERNANDEZ, WILLIAM WARREN, SR., lawyer; b. Washington, Aug. 31, 1943; s. Gumersindo Alonso and Kathryn Naomi (Nycum) F.; m. Linda J.; children: William Warren, James Robert, Rosemarie Patricia. AA, U. Fla., 1964, BA, 1967, JD, 1969. Bar: Fla. 1969, U.S. Dist. Ct. (mid. dist.) Fla. 1970, U.S. Ct. Claims 1973, U.S. Tax Ct. 1973, U.S. Ct. Appeals (5th cir.) 1972, U.S. Ct. Appeals (11th cir.) 1981, U.S. Supreme Ct. 1972. Staff atty. Law, Inc. Hillsborough County, Fla., 1969-70; assoc. Pope & Burton, P.A., Tampa, 1970-71; ptnr. Fernandez & Scarito, Orlando, 1971-79; sole practice Orlando, 1979-98, Winter Springs, Fla., 1999—. Fla. Bar Study and Standardization of Disciplinary Enforcement com., 1972-73, client security fund, 1993-99. Chmn. Winter Springs Beautification Bd., 1994-95, planning and zoning bd. and local planning agy., 1995—, chmn., 1996-98, 2001-02, vice chair, 2000—01; treas. Citrus coun. Girl Scouts U.S., 1997-98; mem. Seminole County Greenways and Trails Adv. Com., 1999—; chmn. Altamonte Springs Code Enforcement Bd., 1982-88; mem. Altamonte Springs Charter Revision Commn., 1974, 79, 85; citizens adv. com., sec. Seminole County Expressway Auth., 1984-88; bd. dirs. Fla. Symphony Youth Orch., 1988-89; bd. dirs. Muscular Dystrophy Assn. Am., 1972-77, pres., 1975-76; bd. dirs. Seminole County Mental Health Ctr., Inc., 1979-84, pres., 1982-83; bd. dirs. Coun. of 100 Seminole County, 1975-85, pres., 1979-80, 83-85; bd. dirs. The Wayfarer Inc. Orlando, 1976-79, treas., 1977-79; bd. dirs. Easter Seals Soc., Orange, Seminole and Osceola, 1978-79. Served with U.S. Army, 1968-69. Recipient numerous civic awards, including certs. of appreciation from Muscular Dystrophy Assn., Easter Seals, YMCA, The Wayfarer Inc., Seminole County Mental Health Ctr.; recipient svc. award City Altamonte Springs, 1974, 83, City Winter Springs, 1999-02. Mem. ABA, Fla. Bar Assn., Aircraft Owners and Pilots Assn., Ranchlands Homeowner's Assn. (v.p. 1994-95, pres. 1995—). Democrat. Roman Catholic. Alternative dispute resolution, Probate (including wills, trusts). Office: 250 Panama Rd E Winter Springs FL 32708-3516 E-mail: fernandez@justice.com.

FERNANDEZ AGUADO, JUAN IGNACIO, lawyer, educator; b. Madrid, Aug. 13, 1970; s. Enrique Fernandez-Pena and Carmen Aguado Marin; m. Maria Jesús Garrido, July 28, 2001. With firm Despacho Albinana & Suarez de Lezo SL, Madrid. Bankruptcy, General civil litigation, Alternative dispute resolution. Office: Despacho Albinana & Suarez De Lezo SL José Abascal 61-3 Izda 28003 Madrid Spain E-mail: jifernandez@dasl.es.

FERRANDO, ENRIQUE, lawyer; b. Lima, Peru, July 21, 1961; s. Enrique Guillermo and Carmela (Gamarra) Ferrando; m. Martha Patricia Bauer, May 2, 1992; 1 child, Alex. BA, Catholic U of Perú, Lima, Perú, 1987. Bar: Coll. of Abogados of Lima 1989. Counsel Commn. apptd. to prepare the Peruvian Environ. Law, Lima, Peru, 1986, Legis. Assembly, Lima, Peru, Can. Agy. for the Internat. Desarrollo, Lima, Peru, 1989; ptnr. Estudio Osterling, Lima, Peru, 1989—2003; counsel United Nat. Program for the Medio Ambiente - ORPALC, 1992, Banco Interamericano de Desarrollo, Lima, 1994—95, Consejo Asesor del Plan Dir. del Sistema Nacional de Areas Protegidas del Peru-GTZ, Lima, Peru, 1994—96, Inst. of Minor Econ. Study of the Nat. Soc. of the Industries of Peru, Lima, Peru, 1994, Global Environ. Facility for the Prevention of smog, Lima, Peru, 1994; arbitrator Coll. de Abogados de Lima and Arbitration Ctr., Lima, Peru, 1995—2003. Prof. U. Lima, 1988—90. Author: (essay) Civil Responsibilty for Daño Ambiental in Responsibity for the Daño Ambiental in Perú, Reflexion and Debate, 2000, The Responsibility for Environmental Damages in Peru, 1996; co-author: (report) Diagnostic Legis. Situation and Gestión Ambiental in Panama, 1994. Mem.: Tribunal Arbitral of the Coll. of Abogados of Lima, Ctr. for Nat. and Internat. Arbitration of the Lima Chamber of Commerce, Environ. Comm., Nat. Mining Soc., Peruvian Soc. of Environ. Law (v.p., founder). Avocations: hunting, photography, horseback riding. Office: Piso 8 Av Pardo & Aliaga 640 Lima 27 Peru

FERRANTI, THOMAS, JR., lawyer; b. S.I., N.Y., Mar. 14, 1969; s. Thomas and Janet Rose (Giordano) F.; m. Renée Esposito, July 11, 1998. BA, St. John's U., N.Y.C., 1991, JD, 1994. Bar: N.Y. 1995, N.J. 1995, D.C. 1995. Dietary aide S.I. (N.Y.) U. Hosp., 1987-1993; intern Dept. of Investigation, N.Y.C., 1990, Justice Finnegan, N.Y. State Supreme Ct., Queens, 1990; legal intern Macy's Northeast, N.Y.C., 1991, N.Y.C. Coun., S.I., 1992; intern Supreme Ct. trial divsn. Richmond County Dist. Atty., S.I., 1993-94; tchr. law Monsignor Farrell H.S., S.I., 1994-95; pvt. practice, S.I., 1995—. Lawyer, witness Criminal Trial Inst., St. John's U., 1991-94, Civil Trial Inst., 1991-94; tutor, counselor Student Network Accessing Counselor Program, 1991-94; fire fighter N.Y.C. Fire Dept., 1993—. Gen. mgr., pres. Sta. WMOC, S.I., 1989-91. St. John's U. scholar, 1988-91. Mem. ABA, N.Y. State Bar Assn., Nat. Italian-Am. Bar Assn., Golden Key, Lambda Kappa Phi, Kappa Gamma Pi, Iota Alpha Sigma (pres. 1990-91). Roman Catholic. Avocations: aquarium hobbyist, weight training, science fiction, coin collecting, travel. General practice, Probate (including wills, trusts), Property, real (including real estate development, water). Home and Office: 99 Pitney Ave Staten Island NY 10309-1918 Fax: 718-317-5294. E-mail: tofesq@aol.com.

FERRARA, RALPH C. lawyer; b. Gloversville, N.Y., June 16, 1945; s. Rufus Ferrara and Clara F. Riccitiello. BSBA, Georgetown U., 1967; JD, U. Cin., 1970; LLM in Corp. Law summa cum laude, George Washington U., 1972. Bar: D.C. 1970, U.S. Ct. Appeals, U.S. Supreme Ct.; cert. ind. assessor Ins. Marketplace Stds. Assn. Profl. asst. to law libr. Nat. Law Ctr., Washington, 1970-72; mem. faculty George Washington U. Nat. Law Ctr., Washington; atty. divsn. enforcement SEC, Washington, 1971-72, trial atty. divsn. trading and markets, 1972-73, spl. counsel to chief enforcement atty., 1973-74, supervisory trial atty., 1974-75, spl. counsel to chmn., 1975, asst. gen. counsel, 1975-76, exec. asst. to legal counsel, 1976-77, exec. asst., 1977-78, gen. counsel, 1978-81; ptnr. Debevoise & Plimpton, Washington, 1981—. Co-chmn. PLI Ann. Inst. on Securities Law, 1994-98; mem. bd. visitors U. Cin. Coll. Law, 1995—, bd. advisors, D & O Advisor, 2003-. Author: Takeovers II: A Strategists' Manual for Business Combinations in the 1990s, 1993, Shareholder Derivative Litigation: Beseiging the Board, 1995, Ferrara on Insider Trading the Wall, 1995, Managing Marketeers: Supervisory Responsibilities of Broker-Dealers and Investment Advisors, 2000, Takeovers: A Strategic Guide to Mergers and Acquisitions, 2001; contbr. articles on topics related to fed. securities law to profl. jours. With USAR. Recipient John L. Sayler award, Am. Jurisprudence award, Judge Alfred Mack award. Mem. ABA (planning rev. com. sect. on corp. and banking bus. law, fed. regulation of securities com.), FBA (exe. coun. securities law com., nat. coun., gen. counsels' com.), Southwestern Legal Found. (adv. com.). Administrative and regulatory, Federal civil litigation, Corporate, general. Office: Debevoise & Plimpton 555 13th St NW Ste 1100E Washington DC 20004-1163 Address: 919 3rd Ave New York NY 10022

FERRARI, GARY JOHN, lawyer; b. Ill., Oct. 14, 1958; s. John Joseph and Geraldine May F. AA, Ill. Valley C.C., 1978; BA, U. Ill., 1980, JD, 1983. Bar: Ill. 1983, U.S. Ct. Mil. Appeals 1986, U.S. Dist. Ct. (cen. dist.) Ill. 1987, U.S. Dist. Ct. (no dist.) Ill. 1990. Atty. Goldsworthy, Fifield & Hasselberg, Peoria, Ill., 1987-90, John E. Mitchell Law Offices, Peoria, Ill., 1990—. Pres. Peoria Italian-Am. Soc., 1998-2000; sec. Peoria Area Ethnic Assn., 1997-2001. Lt.USNR, 1983-86. Mem. KC, Am. Legion. Roman Catholic. Workers' compensation. Home: 6710 N Fawndale Dr Peoria IL 61615-2315 Office: Law Offices John Mitchell 415 NE Jefferson Ave Peoria IL 61603-3725 E-mail: gjf445peo@aol.com., wclaw@mtco.net.

FERRARO, GERALDINE ANNE, lawyer, former congresswoman; b. Newburgh, N.Y., Aug. 26, 1935; d. Dominick and Antonetta L. (Corrieri) F.; m. John Zaccaro, 1960; children: Donna, John, Laura. BA, Marymount Manhattan Coll., 1956, hon. degree, 1982; JD, Fordham U., 1960; postgrad., NYU Law Sch., 1978, hon. degree, 1984, Hunter Coll., 1985, Plattsburgh Coll., 1985, Coll. Boca Raton, 1989, Va. State U., 1989, Muhlenberg Coll., 1990, Briarcliffe Coll. for Bus., 1990, Potsdam Coll., 1991. Bar: N.Y. 1961, U.S. Supreme Ct. 1978. Pvt. practice, N.Y.C., 1961-74; asst. dist. atty. Queens County, N.Y., 1974-78; chief spl. victims bur., 1977-78; mem. 96th-98th Congresses from 9th N.Y. Dist.; sec. House Democratic Caucus; 1st woman vice presdl. nominee on Democratic ticket, 1984; fellow Harvard Inst. of Politics, Cambridge, Mass., 1988; mng. ptnr. Keck Mahin Cate & Koether, N.Y., 1993-94. Appointed Amb. to UN Human Rights Commn., 1994-95; co-host Crossfire, CNN, 1996-97; pres. G&L Strategies Golin Harris Internat., 1999—, Fox News Nightly, 1999—. Author: Ferraro, My Story, 1985, Changing History: Women, Power, and Politics, 1993, Framing a Life, 1998. Chair Dem. Platform Com., Bertarelli Found.; Dem. candidate U.S. Senate, 1992, 98; U.S. President Clinton's appointee to UN Human Rights Commn. Conf., Geneva, 1993, World Conf., Vienna, Austria, 1993, World Conf. on Women, 1995; bd. dirs. Fordham Law Sch. Bd. Visitors; bd. advocates Planned Parenthood Fedn. Am.; bd. dir. Nat. Women's Health Rsch. Ctr., Nat. Dem. Inst. Mem. Queens County Women's Bar Assn. (past pres.), Coun. Fgn. Rels., Internat. Inst. Women's Polit. Leadership (former pres.), Assn. Bar City NY. Roman Catholic.

FERREIRA, ANABELA GONÇALVES, lawyer; b. Lisbon, Portugal, July 16, 1972; parents Manuel Ferreira Antunes and Silvina Goncalves Ferreira; m. Luis Miguel Pinto Raposo, Mar. 22, 1997; 1 child, Luis Manuel Goncalves Ferreira Raposo. Law Degree, Lisbon U., 1995. Bar: Lisbon 1995. Lawyer PLMJ Law Office, Lisbon, 1995—. Prof. Lisbon Law Sch., Lisbon, 1995—99, Ind. Law Sch., Lisbon, 1997—2001; cons. Min. Agr., Lisbon, 1997—98. Avocations: sports, travel, teaching music. Commercial, contracts (including sales of goods; commercial financing), Corporate, general, Banking. Office: PLMJ Law Office Av Liberdade 224 1250-148 Lisbon Portugal

FERRELL, MILTON MORGAN, JR., lawyer; b. Coral Gables, Fla., Nov. 6, 1951; s. Milton M. and Annie (Blanche) Bradley; m. Lori R. Sanders, May 22, 1982; children: Milton Morgan III, Whitney Connolly. BA, Mercer U., 1973, JD, 1975. Bar: Fla. 1975. Asst. state's atty. State's Atty.'s Office, Miami, 1975-77; ptnr. Ferrell & Ferrell, Miami, 1977-84; sole practice Miami, 1985-87; ptnr. Ferrell & Williams, P.A., Miami, 1987-90, Ferrell & Fertel, P.A., Miami, 1990-98, Ferrell Schultz Carter & Fertel P.A., 1999-2000, Ferrell Schultz Carter Zumpano & Fertel, P.A., 2000—. Bd. dirs. Isotag Tech., Inc. Trustee Mus. Sci. and Space Transit Planetarium, 1977-82, Mt. Sinai Med. Ctr. Found., The Founders, Founder, 2002-; mem. Ambs. of Mercy, Mercy Hosp. Found., Inc., 1985-94, ARC, 2001; trustee, mem. legal com., chair com. U. Miami Project to Cure Paralysis, 1985-94; trustee Eaglebrook Sch., 1995-98, ARC Greater Miami and The Keys, mem. bd. dirs., 2001-, Robinson Charitable Found., 1993—, United Way of Miami-Dade, 2000—; bd. dirs. Jackson Meml. Found., 1999—, Greater Miami and the Keys chpt. ARC, 2001—, Performing Arts Ctr. Found., 1998—. Fellow Nat. Assn. Criminal Def. Lawyers, Am. Bd. Criminal Lawyers (bd. govs. 1981-82, sec. 1983-84, v.p. 1984-86, pres. 1987-88); mem. ABA (grantee 1975), Fla. Bar Assn. (jury instrns. com. 1987-88, chmn. grievance com. 11-L 1989-91), Dade County Bar Assn. (bd. dirs. 1977-80), Assn. Trial Lawyers Am., Bath Club (bd. govs. 1992-95), Miami City Club, Univ. Club, Banker's Club, Cat Cay Yacht Club, Inc. (bd. dirs. 1997-2000, treas. 1998-99, pres. 1999-2000), Am. Bar Found., Internat. Bar Assn., Indian Creek Country Club, LaGorce Country Club, Fisher Island Club, Univ. Club, Farmington Country Club. Federal civil litigation, State civil litigation, Criminal. Home: Bay Point 4511 Lake Rd Miami FL 33137-3372 Office: Ferrell Schultz Carter Zumpano & Fertel PA 201 S Biscayne Blvd Fl 34 Miami FL 33131-4332 E-mail: mmf@ferrellschultz.com.

FERRELL, SUSAN R. lawyer; b. Muncy, Pa., Jan. 13, 1959; d. Robert Walton and Lorma Rae (Egli) Ferrell; m. David Edward Troller, Aug. 31, 1985; children: Katharine Troller, Andrew Troller, Robert Troller. BA, Pa. State U., 1980; JD, Coll. William and Mary, 1983. Bar: Pa. 1983, Ohio 1986. Assoc. Mitchell, Mitchell & Gray, Williamsport, Pa., 1983-85; asst. dist. atty. Lycoming County, Williamsport, 1984; assoc. Hollingsworth & Sunderland, Cin., 1986-89; law clk. to judge U.S. Dist. Ct. (so. dist.) Ohio, Cin., 1990—. Adj. prof. U. Dayton Sch. Law, 1997, Chase Sch. Law, N. Ky. U., 2001—. Pres. Jr. League Cin., 2000—01; bd. sec. Family Nurturing Ctr. Ky., Edgewood, 1993—96; bd. dirs. Village Views, Terrace Park, Ohio, 1994—98; mem. outreach coun. Armstrong Chapel United Meth. Ch., Cin., 2002—. Mem.: ABA. Avocations: volunteer work, music, writing. Office: 801 Potter Stewart US Courthouse 100 E 5th St Cincinnati OH 45202-3927 E-mail: sftroller@aol.com., susan_ferrell@ohsd.uscourts.gov.

FERREN, JOHN MAXWELL, judge; b. Kansas City, Mo., July 21, 1937; s. Jack Maxwell and Elizabeth Anne (Hansen) Ferren; m. Ann Elizabeth Speidel, Sept. 4, 1961 (div.); children: Andrew John, Peter Maxwell; m. Linda Jane Finkelstein, June 17, 1994. AB magna cum laude, Harvard U., 1959, LLB, 1962. Bar: Ill. 1962, Mass. 1967, D.C. 1970. Assoc. Kirkland, Ellis, Hodson, Chaffetz & Masters, Chgo., 1962—66; dir. Neighborhood Law Office Program, Harvard U. Law Sch., Cambridge, Mass., 1966—68; tchg. fellow, dir. Neighborhood Law Office Program, Harvard Law Sch., Cambridge, 1968—69, lectr. law, dir., 1969—70; ptnr. Hogan & Hartson, Washington, 1970—77; assoc. judge D.C. Ct. Appeals, 1977—97, sr. judge, 1999—, disciplinary bd., 1972—76; corp. counsel D.C., 1997—99; fellow Woodrow Wilson Internat. Ctr. for Scholars, 2000—01; exec. com., bd. dirs. Council on Legal Edn. for Profl. Responsibility, 1970—80. Exec. com. Washington Lawyers Com. for Civil Rights Under Law, 1970—77. Contbr. articles to profl. jours. Exec. com. of legal adv. com. Nat. Com. Against Discrimination in Housing, 1974—77; steering com. Nat. Prison Project ACLU Found., 1975—77; legis. subcom. on consumer credit Chgo. Commn. on Human Rels. Com. on New Residents, 1964—66; originator, chmn. Neighborhood Legal Advice Clinics, Ch. Fedn. Greater Chgo., 1964—66; treas., bd. dirs. Firman Neighborhood House, Chgo., 1964—66; bd. dirs. Frederick B. Abramson Meml. Found., 1991—97, People's Devel. Corp., Washington, 1970—74, George A. Wiley Meml. Fund, 1974—84, Nat. Resource Ctr. for Consumers of Legal Svcs., 1973—77, Ctr. for Law and Edn., Cambridge, Mass., 1989—94. Fellow: Am. Bar Found.; mem.: ABA (commn. on nat. inst. justice 1972—80, consortium on legal svcs. and pub. 1972—73, 1976—79, chmn. 1979—82, chmn. spl. com. on pub. interest practice 1976—78), Am. Law Inst., Phi Beta Kappa. Presbyterian. Office: Dist Columbia Ct Appeals 500 Indiana Ave NW Washington DC 20001-2131

FERRER, RAFAEL DOUGLAS PAUL, lawyer; b. Seattle, Apr. 12, 1957; s. Rafael George and Barbara (Gould) F. BA in Acctg., U. Wash., 1979; JD, U. Puget Sound, 1982. Bar: Wash. 1985, U.S. Ct. Appeals (9th cir.) 1986. Acct. Lallman & Feldman, Ketchum, Idaho, 1980; tax profl. Touche Ross & Co., Seattle, 1981-82; securities syndicator Brouner Securities, Seattle, 1983; legal intern Davies Pearson, Tacoma, Wash., 1984; Ferrer Law Offices P.C. Seattle, 1985—. Bd. dirs. Paisans on First, Seattle, Ferrer Law Offices. Mem. Poncho Arts Found., Seattle, 1982, Madrona Community Group, Seattle, 1985; bd. dirs. Westboro Assn., Federal Way, Wash., 1981. Served with U.S. Marine Corps, 1975-80. Recipient Mr. Seattle 1st Place award IFBB Affiliate, 1978, Mr. Wash. 2d Place award IFBB Affiliate, 1978. Mem. ACLU, Wash. State Bar Assn., Assn. Trial Lawyers Am., Seattle King County Bar Assn., Wash. State Trial Lawyers Assn., Constrn. Fin. Mgmt. Assn., Phi Delta Phi. Republican. Congregationalist. Avocations: skiing, skydiving, scuba diving, mountain climbing, sailing. General civil litigation, Commercial, contracts (including sales of goods; commercial financing), Corporate, general. Home: 710 Lakeside Ave S Apt 118 Seattle WA 98144-3335 Office: Interurban Bldg Ste 606 157 Yesler Way Seattle WA 98104

FERRIS, WILLIAM MICHAEL, lawyer; b. Jackson, Mich., May 1, 1948; s. Franklyn C. and Betty J. (Dickerson) F.; m. Cynthia L. Muffitt, June 26, 1970 (div.); 1 child, Christina M.; m. Kathleen S. Santacroce, Mar. 21, 1987; stepchildren: Michael W. Santacroce, Megan D. Santacroce. BS with distinction, U.S. Naval Acad., 1970; JD summa cum laude, U. Balt., 1978, LLM in Taxation, 1994. Commd. ensign USN, 1970, advanced through grades to lt., 1974, resigned active duty, 1977; staff atty. Md. Legis., Annapolis, 1977-78, 80-81; assoc. Semmes, Bowen & Semmes, Balt., 1978-80; ptnr. Ferris & Robin, Annapolis, 1981-83, Krause & Ferris, Annapolis, 1983-87, Michaelson, Krause & Ferris, PA, Annapolis, 1987-91, Krause & Ferris, Annapolis, 1991—. Adj. faculty Anne Arundel C.C., 1988—, U. Balt. Sch. Law, 1997—. Author: Maryland Style Manual for Statutory Law, 1985; article supr. Md. Annotated Code, 1981-84. Elder Woods Meml. Presbyn. Ch., Severna Park, Md., 1980—; temporary zoning hearing officer Anne Arundel County, Annapolis, 1984—87; hearing officer Anne Arundel County Bd. Edn., Annapolis, 1990—98; pres. Md. Bd. Dental Examiners, Balt., 1987—88; mem. inquiry com. Md. Atty. Grievance Commn., 1987—2001; mem. Md. Commn. on Jud. Disabilities, 1995—; treas. Bay Hills Cmty. Assn., 1990—96. Comdr. USNR, 1984—91. Mem. ABA, Md. State Bar Assn., Maritime Law Assn., Anne Arundel County Bar Assn. Republican. Avocations: golfing, running, tennis. General civil litigation, Family and matrimonial, Military. Home: 115 Terrapin Ln Stevensville MD 21666 Office: Krause & Ferris 196 Duke Of Gloucester St Annapolis MD 21401-2515 E-mail: wferris@krauseferris.com.

FERRITER, MAURICE JOSEPH, lawyer; b. Holyoke, Mass., Aug. 14, 1930; s. John J. and Aldea F.; m. Margaret; children: Maurice J., John J., Mary M., Joseph P. AA, Holyoke Jr. Coll., 1952; BA, U. Mass., 1979; JD, Western New Eng. Law Sch., Springfield, Mass., 1957. Bar: Mass. 1957, U.S. Dist. Ct. Mass. 1960, U.S. Supreme Ct. 1967, U.S. Ct. Appeals (1st cir.) 1980. Of counsel Lyon, Ferriter & Fitzpatrick, LLP, Holyoke, 1957—. Chmn. bd. dirs. emeritus Ferriter, Scobbo, Sikora, Singal, Caruso & Rodophele, P.C., Boston; gen. counsel emeritus Mass. Mcpl. Wholesale Electric Co.; arbitrator AAA. Pres. emeritus Holyoke Heritage Park R.R.; trustee Providence Health Sys., former chmn. bd. Holyoke C.C., Providence Ministries Needy; former city solicitor, Holyoke. With U.S. Army, 1948-51. Recipient Outstanding Servant of Pub. award Springfield TV Sta. WWLP Channel 22, 1976, Spl. Svc. award Mcpl. Electric Assn. Mass., 1981, award of merit Bur. Exceptional Children, 1979, Cmty. Svc. award YMCA, 1989, Disting. Alumni award Holyoke C.C., 1987, Disting. Svc. award, 2002, Outstanding Significant Achievement award Rotary, 1996; named Person of Yr., N.E. Pub. Power Assn., 1992, Peace and Justice award Providence Ministries, 1999. Fellow Mass. Bar Found.; mem. ATLA, Am. Pub. Power Assn. (Individual Achievement award 1998), Mass. Bar Assn., Hampden County Bar Assn., Holyoke Bar Assn., Mass. Acad. Trial Lawyers, Holyoke C. of C. (past pres., Bus. Man of Yr. award 1990, Appreciation award 1975).

Administrative and regulatory, Corporate, general, Municipal (including bonds). Home: 31 Longfellow Rd Holyoke MA 01040-1290 Office: Whitney Place 14 Bobala Rd Holyoke MA 01040-9632 E-mail: mferriter@lyonferriter.com.

FERRO, ELIZABETH KRAMS, lawyer; b. Cheverly, Md., Oct. 14, 1948; d. Harry Francis and Jeanne Elizabeth (Edwards) Krams; children: Stephen Christopher, Elizabeth Juliet, Alexander Eli; m. Jose M. Ferro, Oct. 7, 1994. BS magna cum laude, U. Md., 1977; JD, George Washington U., 1982. Bar: D.C. 1983. Adminstr. Raleigh Stores Corp., Washington, 1973-83; atty. Lansfam Mgmt. Corp., Balt., 1983-2000, corp. sec., 1986-2000. V.p., dir. Sidney Lansburgh III Found., 1989—; bd. dirs. Debel Foods Corp., Elizabeth, N.J., 1986. Mem.: D.C. Bar Assn., Phi Kappa Phi, Alpha Sigma Lamda. Roman Catholic. Estate planning, General practice. Home: 10210 Riggs Rd Hyattsville MD 20783-1213 Office: Elizabeth K Ferro Esq 300 E Lombard St Ste 1800 Baltimore MD 21202-6739 E-mail: eferro1048@aol.com.

FERSHTMAN, JULIE ILENE, lawyer; b. Detroit, Apr. 3, 1961; d. Sidney and Judith Joyce (Stoll) F.; m. Robert S. Bick, Mar. 4, 1990. Student, Mich. State U., 1979-81, James Madison Coll., 1979-81; BA in Philosophy and Polit. Sci., Emory U., 1983, JD, 1986. Bar: Mich. 1986, U.S. Dist. Ct. (ea. dist.) Mich. 1986, U.S. Ct. Appeals (6th cir.) 1987, U.S. Dist. Ct. (we. dist.) Mich. 1993. Assoc. Miller, Canfield, Paddock and Stone, Detroit, 1986-89; assoc. Miro, Miro & Weiner P.C., Bloomfield Hills, Mich., 1989-92; pvt. practice, Bingham Farms, Mich., 1992—; of counsel Fink, Zausmer & Kaufman, P.C., Farmington Hills, Mich., 2002—. Adj. prof. Schoolcraft Coll., Livonia, Mich., 1994—; lectr. in field. Author: Equine Law & Horse Sense, 1996, More Equine Law and Horse Sense, 2000; contbr. article to Barrister Mag. Bd. dirs. Franklin Cmty. Assn., 1989-92, sec., 1991-92; mem. Franklin Planning Commn., 1993-94. Recipient Nat. Ptnr. in Safety award Assn. for Horsemanship Safety and Edn., 1997, Outstanding Achievement award Am. Riding Instrs. Assn., 1998, Catalyst award, 2002; named one of Crain's Detroit Bus. "40 Bus. Leaders Under 40", 1996. Mem. ABA (planning bd. litigation sect. young lawyers divsn., honoree Barrister mag., 1995, FBA (courthouse tours com. Detroit chpt., featured in Barrister mag. in 21 Young Lawyers Leading US and the 21st Century 1995), State Bar Mich. (exec. coun. young lawyers sect. 1989-96, chmn. 1995-96, bd. commrs. 1994-96, 1999-2003, grievance com. 1997-99, structure and governance com. 1997-98, strategic planning action group 2001, rep. assn. 1997—, chmn. rep. assembly 2001-2002), Oakland County Bar Assn. (profl. com. 1995—, chmn. 1998-99 Inns of Ct. com. 1995—, chair 1998-99, bd. dirs. 2001–, Professionalism award 2000), Markel Equestrian Safety Bd., Women Lawyers Assn., Soc. Coll. Journalists, Phi Alpha Delta, Omicron Delta Kappa, Phi Sigma Tau, Pi Sigma Alpha. Avocations: horse showing, writing, music, art. Bus. General civil litigation, Insurance, Labor (including EEOC, Fair Labor Standards Act, labor-management relations, NLRB, OSHA). Office: 31700 Middlebelt Rd Ste 150 Farmington Hills MI 48334 Home: 31700 Briarcliff Franklin MI 48025 E-mail: fershtman@aol.com.

FESSENDEN, ANN T. law librarian; b. Norman, Okla., Oct. 4, 1951; d. Wayne B. and Tula D. (McCarty) F.; m. Ronald F. Bock, June 6, 1992; 1 child, Michael F. Bunnell. BA in Jour., U. Okla., 1974, MLS, 1977; JD magna cum laude, U. Miss., 1984. Acquisitions asst. U. Okla., Norman, 1974-77; tech. svcs. libr. U. Miss., University, 1978-84, co-acting law libr., 1982; cir. libr. U.S. Ct. Appeals (8th cir.), St. Louis, 1984—. Contbg. author (book) Judicial Opinion Writing Manual, 1991; contbr. articles to profl. jours. Mem. Am. Assn. Law Librs. (exec. bd. 2002-.), Mid-Am. Assn. Law Librs. (v.p., pres. 1992-94), Beta Phi Mu. Office: US Ct Appeals Libr 111 S 10th St Rm 22300 Saint Louis MO 63102

FETTERMAN, JAMES CHARLES, lawyer; b. Charleston, W.Va., Apr. 13, 1947; s. Kenneth Lee and Sara Jane (Shaffer) F.; children: Janet, Paula, Kenneth, David. BA, Miss. State U., 1969, MA, 1970; JD, U. Miss., Oxford, 1972; MBA, St. Louis U., 1985. Bar: Miss. 1972, Sarasota County, U.S. Dist. Ct. (no. dist.) Miss. 1972, U.S. Ct. Mil. Appeals 1972, U.S. Dist. Ct. (mid. dist.) Fla. 1986, U.S. Tax Ct. 1986, U.S. Ct. Appeals (11th cir.) 1986. Staff atty. First Miss. Corp., Jackson, 1976-77; cert. of need adminstr. Office of Gov. State of Miss., Jackson, 1977-78; administrator, prin. investigator Miss. Bd. Nursing, Jackson, 1978-79; asst. prof., head dept. fin. Jackson State U., 1979-82; asst. prof. dept. mgmt sci. St. Louis U., Mo., 1982-86; ptnr. Borza Fetterman, Sardelis, Chartered, Sarasota, 1986-89, James C. Fetterman, P.A., Sarasota, Fla., 1989-2000; pres., ptnr. Fetterman & Zitani, P.A., 2001—03; prin., owner James C. Fetterman Chartered, 2003—. Sr. res. adviser to gen. counsel and assoc. gen. counsel Def. Logistics Agy., 1993-94; assoc. prof. U. Sarasota, 1987—; judge advocate I.M.A. USAF, 1987; spl. master for zoning and code enforcement Sarasota County, 1991-2000; vol. counsel Am. Radio Relay League, 1995—; legal advisor Family Forum, CompuServe, 1996—. Editor Midwest Law Review U. Kans., 1984-86, also textbooks. Asst. scoutmaster Boy Scouts Am., 1991—95, 1999—, scoutmaster, 1995—98, scoutmaster nat. jamboree troop, 1998, dist. com., 1998—, venture crew advisor, 2001—; mem. sch. adv. coun. McIntosh Mid. Sch., 1999—2000; mem. Sarasota chpt. Eagles Club, 1999—, chaplain, 2001—02, v.p., 2002—03; active Incarnation Ch. Folk Group, 1986—90, 2000—; bd. dirs., v.p., chaperone Sarasota Boy's Choir, 1992—93; bd. dirs. Fla. Inst. Traditional Chinese Medicine, 1998—2002, chmn. bd. dirs., 1998—2002. Capt. USAF, 1972—76, ETO, col. res. USAF, 1972—. Named one of Outstanding Young Men of Am., Jaycees, 1982; recipient award of merit Boy Scouts Am., 1998, Order of the Bronze Pelican, Nat. Cath. Com. on Scouting, 2001, Silver Beaver award Boy Scouts Am., 2003. Mem. Am. Bus. Law Assn., Res. Officer Assn. (Sarasota chpt. pres. 1989-91, v.p. 1991-92), Fla. Bar (vice chmn. mil. law com. 1991-94, chmn. 1994-95), Ret. Officer's Assn. (bd. dirs. Sarasota chpt. 1991-93), Am. Legion, Nat. Eagle Scout Assn., Loyal Order Moose. Republican. Roman Catholic. Avocations: running, swimming, ham radio. Bankruptcy, Corporate, general, Education and schools. Office: 4521A Bee Ridge Rd Sarasota FL 34233-2517 E-mail: jfetterman@compuserve.com.

FETZER, MARK STEPHEN, lawyer; b. Louisville, Oct. 10, 1950; s. Sherrill Lee and Betty Ann (Meyer) F.; m. Pamela Ferrell, May 8, 1982; children: Martha Meyer, John Mark. Student, Purdue U., 1968-70; BA, U. Ky., 1973; JD, U. Denver, 1976. Bar: Colo. 1979, U.S. Dist. Ct. Colo. 1979. Sr. landman Minerals Svc. Co., Grand Junction, Colo., 1976-79; mgr. land & pub. affairs Marline Oil Corp., Danville, Va., 1980-85; mgr. R.R., utility & govtl. acquisition Dallas Area Rapid Transit, 1986-88; environ. counsel Cura, Inc., Dallas, 1989-91; dir., environ. counsel Terra-Mar, Inc., Dallas, 1991-92; environ. counsel Infodata Systems, Inc., Falls Church, Va., 1992-94; project mgr. Walcoff & Assocs., Inc., Fairfax, Va., 1994; sr. regulatory analyst Ecology and Environment, Inc., Idaho Falls, Idaho, 1995-99, Portage Environ., Inc., Idaho Falls, 2000—. Mem. ABA, Colo. Bar Assn., Rocky Mountain Mineral Law Found., Air and Waste Mgmt. Assn. Evangelist. Avocation: bicycling. Nuclear power, Environmental, Property, real (including real estate development, water). E-mail: msfetzer@hotmail.com.

FEUERSTEIN, ALAN RICKY, lawyer; b. Buffalo, Oct. 24, 1950; s. Aaron Irving and Doris Jean (Davis) F.; m. June, 1973 (div. Jan. 1984); children: Marni Lauren, Jami Lynn; m. Susan T. Skop, Dec. 31, 1986; children: Christopher Borkowski, Philip Borkowski. BS cum laude, SUNY, Buffalo, 1974; LLB, U. Toledo, 1977. Bar: N.Y. 1978, Territorial and Dist. Ct. V.I. 1989, U.S. Supreme Ct. 1992, Fed. Ct. Puerto Rico 1993. Assoc. Law Offices of Salvatore Martoche, Buffalo, 1977-79; ptnr. Martoche & Feuerstein, Buffalo, 1979-81; lectr. Erie County Cen. Police Svcs. Acad., Buffalo, 1981-82; pvt. practice Buffalo, 1981-93; ptnr. Feuerstein & Santapia, Buffalo, 1993-94; prin. Law Offices of Alan R. Feuerstein, Buffalo, 1994-97; ptnr. Feuerstein & Smith, LLP, Buffalo, 1998—. Lectr. Daemen Coll. Consortium, Buffalo, 1980-81; cons. in field. Mem. Erie County Reps., Buffalo, 1979—. Mem. Niagara Club, St.Thomas Yacht Club, The Buffalo Launch Club, Confrérie de la Chȃne des Rôtisseurs (chevalier). Republican. Jewish. Civil rights, General civil litigation, Personal injury (including property damage). Office: 17 St Louis Pl Buffalo NY 14202-1502 also: Woods & Woods 1 Comptroller Plz San Juan PR 00917 also: PO Box 502008 Saint Thomas VI 00805-2008

FEUERSTEIN, HOWARD M. lawyer; b. Memphis, Sept. 16, 1939; s. Leon and Lillian (Kapell) F.; m. Tamra Lynn Saperstein, May 19, 1968; children: Laurie, Leon. BA, Vanderbilt U., 1961, JD, 1963. Bar: Tenn. 1963, Oreg. 1965. Law clk. to justice U.S. Ct. Appeals (5th cir.), Montgomery, Ala., 1963-64; teaching fellow Stanford U., 1964-65; assoc. Davies, Biggs et al (now Stoel Rives LLP), Portland, Oreg., 1965-71; ptnr. Stoel Rives LLP, Portland, 1971—. Mem. Oreg. Gov.'s Task Force on Land Devel. Law, 1974; bd. realtors Condominium Study Com., Oreg., 1975-76. Editor-in-chief Vanderbilt Law Rev., 1962-63. Trustee Congregation Beth Israel, Portland, 1977-83; bd. dirs. Jewish Family & Child Service, Portland, 1975-81, Young Musicians and Artists Inc., 1991-96. Recipient Founder's medal Vanderbilt Law Sch., 1963. Mem. ABA, Oreg. State Bar, Community Assn. Inst. (bd. dirs. Oreg. chpt. 1980-86), Am. Coll. Real Estate Lawyers. Property, real (including real estate development, water). Office: Stoel Rives LLP 900 SW 5th Ave Ste 2600 Portland OR 97204-1268 E-mail: hmfeuerstein@stoel.com.

FEUERZEIG, HENRY LOUIS, lawyer; b. Chgo., Dec. 12, 1938; s. Samuel Alexander Feuerzeig and Esther Fleeger; m. Penny Zweigenhaft, Apr. 8, 1967; children: Paul Lawrence, Darcy Elizabeth. BS, U. Wis., 1962; JD, George Washington U., 1970. Bar: D.C., V.I., Fla., Md. Reporter various newspapers, Dubuque, Iowa, Chgo., Madison, Wis., Cin. and Washington, 1962-64, 65-67; assoc. Sachs, Greenebaum, Frohlich & Tayler, Washington, 1970-72; asst. atty. gen. V.I. Dept. Law, St. Thomas, 1972-73, chief civil and adminstrv. law divsn., 1973-74, 1st asst. atty. gen., 1974; ptnr. Feuerzeig & Zebedee, St. Thomas, 1974-76; judge Territorial Ct. V.I., St. Thomas, 1977-87; del., chmn. jud. powers and functions com. 4th V.I. Constl. Conv., 1981; ptnr. Dudley, Topper and Feuerzeig, St. Thomas, 1987—. Mem. supervisory bd. V.I. Law Enforcement Planning Commn., 1978-87, Juvenile Justice and Delinquency Prevention, 1988—; mem. V.I. Juvenile Code Revision Task Force, 1978-83, V.I. Criminal Code Revision Task Force, 1978-87. Mem. Montgomery County (Md.) Dem. State Ctrl. Com., 1970-72; mem. V.I. Indsl. Devel. Commn., 1976; bd. dirs. Environ. Studies Program, St. Thomas, 1977-80, United Way, 1986-92; bd. reps. Hebrew Congregation of St. Thomas, 1983-90, 96-2002, co-chair Bicentennial Campaign com., 1993-97; trustee Antilles Sch., St. Thomas, 1983-91; mem. adv. coun. Youth Multi-Svc. Ctr., 1989-94; dir. Cmty. Found. of V.I., 1992—, pres., 1993-94. Sigma Delta Chi scholar, 1962; Congressional fellow Am. Polit. Sci. Assn., 1964-65; named Person of Yr. Hebrew Congregation of St. Thomas, 2003. Mem. ABA (lawyers conf. jud. performance and conduct com. 1984—), D.C. Bar Assn., Fla. Bar Assn., V.I. Bar Assn. (pres. 1976), Am. Law Inst. (life, cons. group for principles of family dissolution, 1992-2000, cons. group for restatement of law governing lawyers, 1992-99), Am. Judicature Soc., Assn. Trial Lawyers Am., Internat. Soc. of Barristers, Order of Coif, Sigma Delta Chi, Phi Delta Phi. Lodges: Rotary, Harmonic Lodge No. 356, E.C. Jewish. Office: Dudley Topper and Feuerzeig 1A Frederiksberg Gade PO Box 756 Charlotte Amalie VI 00804-0756 E-mail: hfeuerzeig@dtflaw.com., hfeuer@attglobal.net.

FEUILLE, RICHARD HARLAN, lawyer, director; b. Mexico City, June 10, 1920; s. Frank and Margaret (Levy) F.; m. Louann Johnston Hoover, Oct. 20, 1948; children: Louann H., Richard H., Robert R., Joseph L. (dec.), James M., Patrick F. (dec.), Margaret J. BA, U. Va., 1947, LL.B., 1948; JD, 1970. Bar: Tex. 1948. Assoc. Jones, Hardie, Grambling & Howell, El Paso, Tex., 1948-53; ptnr. Hardie, Grambling, Sims & Feuille, El Paso, 1953-57; sr. ptnr. Scott, Hulse, Marshall & Feuille, El Paso, 1957—. Bd. dirs. El Paso Nat. Bank (now known as Chase Bank of Tex., N.A.), 1964-93. Active United Fund El Paso, 1963—, founder, v.p. trust fund, 1969—, pres., 1968, 75—, bd. dirs., 1966-72; pres. El Paso Cmty. Concert Assn., 1961-67; mem. adv. coun. U. Tex. at El Paso, 1968—, mem. exec. com., 1968-70; bd. dirs. Providence Meml. Hosp., 1986-92; bd. dirs. St. Clement's Episcopal Parish Sch., El Paso, pres., 1993-95; trustee YWCA, El Paso; bd. dirs. El Paso Cmty. Found., 1980—, pres., 1983-84. Served to maj. USAAF, 1941-46, PTO. Decorated bronze star; recipient Disting. Svc. award City of El Paso and Rotary Club, 2002. Mem. ABA (estate and gift tax com.), El Paso County Bar Assn. (pres. 1972-73), Tex. Bar Assn., Greater El Paso Tennis Assn. (bd. dirs.), Rotary Club of El Paso, Order Coif, Phi Beta Kappa, Omicron Delta Kappa. Episcopalian (vestryman, sr. warden). Clubs: Coronado Country (El Paso), El Paso Tennis (El Paso) (pres. 1973). Estate taxation, Estate planning, Probate (including wills, trusts). Home: 1021 Broadmoor Dr El Paso TX 79912-2003 Office: Scott Hulse Marshall & Feuille 201 East Main Dr 1100 Chase Tower El Paso TX 79901 E-mail: rfeu@scotthulse.com.

FEVURLY, KEITH ROBERT, educational administrator; b. Leavenworth, Kans., Oct. 30, 1951; s. James R. Fevurly and Anne (McDade) Barrett; m. Peggy L. Vosburg, Aug. 4, 1978; children: Rebecca Dawn, Grant Robert. BA in Polit. Sci., U. Kans., 1973; JD, Washburn U. of Topeka Sch. Law, 1976; postgrad., U. Mo. Sch. Law, 1984; MBA, Regis U., 1988; LLM, U. Denver, 1992. Bar: Kans. 1977, Colo. 1986; cert. fin. planner. Pvt. practice, Leavenworth, 1977; atty. estate and gift tax IRS, Wichita and Salina, Kans., Austin, Tex., 1977-83; atty., acad. assoc. Coll. for Fin. Planning, Denver, 1984-91, program dir., 1991-95, v.p. edn., 1995-98; COO, U. St. Augustine (Fla.) for Health Scis., 1998-2000; exec. dir. fin. planning edn. program Kaplan Coll., Denver, 2000—. Adj. prof. taxation Met. State Coll., Denver; adj. faculty in retirement planning and estate planning Coll. Fin. Planning. Contbg. author tng. modules, articles on tax mgmt., estate planning. Mem. Colo. Bar Assn., Toastmasters Internat., Rotary Internat., Delta Theta Phi, Pi Sigma Alpha. Republican. Presbyterian. Avocations: softball, racquetball. Home: 3007 E Otero Pl Littleton CO 80122-3666 Office: Kaplan Coll 1401 19th St Denver CO 80202 E-mail: KFevurly@KaplanCollege.edu.

FEWELL, CHARLES KENNETH, JR., lawyer; b. Washington, Jan. 26, 1943; s. Charles Kenneth and Mary Amanda (Hunt) F.; m. Christine Baker Huff, Jan. 23, 1971; children: Anna Catherine, John Maenner. BA magna cum laude, Dartmouth Coll., 1964; JD, Harvard U., 1967. Bar: N.Y. 1968, U.S. Dist. Ct. (so. dist.) N.Y. 1970, U.S. Ct. Appeals (2d cir.) 1975. Law clk. U.S. Dist. Ct. (so. dist.) N.Y, N.Y.C., 1967-68; assoc. White & Case, N.Y.C., 1968-75; v.p., counsel Nat. Westminster Bank, N.Y.C., 1975-80; sr. counsel, sr. v.p. Deutsche Bank AG, N.Y.C., 1980-92; chief counsel, mng. dir. Deutsche Bank N.Am., 1992-97; ptnr. Eaton & Van Winkle, N.Y.C., 1998—. Bd. dirs. Deutsche Bank Trust Co., Deutsche Fin. Svcs. Can. Corp.; v.p., sec. Deutsche Bank Fin., Inc., N.Y.C., 1980-97; v.p. DB Alumni Inc., 2003—. Mem. mediation panel U.S. Dist. Ct. (so. dist.) N.Y., 2001—; mem. vestry Grace Episc. Ch., Hastings-on-Hudson, N.Y., 2000-02. Mem. ABA (banking com. 1980—, co-chair internat. banking and fin. com. 1995-98), Am. Fgn. Law Assn. (v.p. 2000—), Inst. Internat. Bankers (legis. and regulatory com. 1988-97), German Am. Law Assn. (dir. 1982—), N.Y. State Bar Assn. (internat. banking and securities markets 1987—, internat. employment law 1992—, publ. com., editl. bd. 2001—), Assn. Bar City N.Y. (banking law sect. 1992-95), Phi Beta Kappa. Banking, Corporate, general, Private international. Office: Eaton & Van Winkle Three Park Ave New York NY 10016-2078 E-mail: cfewell@evw.com.

FICEK, GARY A. lawyer; b. Waukesha, Wis., Oct. 23, 1956; s. Anton Vincent and Elizabeth Ficek; m. Rhonda Kay Janes, Aug. 3, 1984; children: Anton, Daniel, Andrew. BA, U. N.D., 1978, JD, 1981. Bar: N.D., Minn., U.s. Dist. Ct. N.D. 1981, U.S. Ct. Appeals (8th cir.) 1981. Assoc. Howe, Hardy, Galloway & Maus, Dickinson, N.D., 1981-87, Kennelly Law Office, Fargo, N.D., 1987-88; pvt. practice Fargo, 1990—. Recipient Advocacy Achievement award Legal Svcs. of N.W. Minn., 1995. Mem. ATLA, N.D. Trial Lawyers Assn., Cass County Bar Assn., Clay County Bar Assn. Pension, profit-sharing, and employee benefits, Personal injury (including property damage), Workers' compensation. Office: 15 Broadway Ste 505 Fargo ND 58102

FICHERA, LEWIS CARMEN, lawyer; b. Woodbury, N.J., July 16, 1949; s. Paul Benjamin and Mary (Cristaudo) F. BSBA, Villanova U., 1971; JD, Widener U., 1982. Bar: N.J. 1984, Pa. 1984. Cost analyst Catalytic, Inc., Phila., 1974-76, field cost analyst Balt., 1976-77, cost analyst London, 1977-78, chief cost analyst Phila., 1978-82; ptnr. Cristaudo & Fichera, West Deptford, N.J., 1984-86; pvt. practice West Deptford, 1987—. Pres. Diversified Funding Svcs., Inc. Active Cristaudo for N.J. Ho. of Reps. campaign, 1988. With USANG, 1971-77. Mem. Am. Cash Flow Assn., Cash Flow Profls. Network (sec.), N.J. State Bar ASsn., Pa. Bar Assn., Gloucester County Bar Assn., Fitness Unltd., Nat. Orgn. of Social Security Claimant's Reps., Nat. Orgn. of Vet.'s Advocates, Cherry Hill Regional C. of C. Republican. Roman Catholic. General practice, Probate (including wills, trusts), Pension, profit-sharing, and employee benefits. Home: 773 Atlantic Ave Sewell NJ 08080-1502 Office: 773 W Atlantic Ave Sewell NJ 08080-1502 Fax: 856-468-3089. E-mail: lcfichera@yahoo.com.

FICKLER, ARLENE, lawyer; b. Phila., Apr. 21, 1951; BA cum laude, U. Pa., 1971, JD cum laude, 1974. Bar: Pa. 1974, D.C. 1980, U.S. Supreme Ct. 1989. Ptnr. Hoyle Morris & Kerr LLP, Phila. Staff atty. Commn. on Revision of Fed. Ct. Appellate System, 1974-75; exec. asst. Bicentennial Com. Jud. Conf. of U.S., 1975-76. Comment editor U. Pa. Law Rev., 1973-74; contbr. articles to law jours. Pres. U. Pa. Law Sch. Alumni Bd. Mgrs., 1997-99; trustee Jewish Fedn. of Greater Phila., 1981-88, 89-93, 94-98, 99—, Phila. Bar Found., 1993-98, Jewish Cmty. Rels. Coun. Greater Phila., 1983-94, 98-00; trustee Jewish Cmty. Ctrs. of Phila., 1997—, asst. treas., 1999-2000, v.p., 2000-02, chair-designate 2001—, chair-elect, 2002—; trustee HIAS Immigration Svcs. Phila., 1998—, treas., 1999—; mem. United Jewish Appeal Nat. Young Women's Leadership Cabinet, 1982-87; v.p. Phila. chpt. Am. Jewish Congress, 1995-2001; co-chmn. Phila. Maccabi Games, 2001. Recipient Mrs. Isidore Kohn Young Leadership award Jewish Fedn. Greater Phila., 1981, Next Generation Leadership award Jewish Cmty. Ctrs. Assn., 2000, award of merit U. Pa. Law Sch. Alumni, 2001. Mem. ABA, Am. Law Inst., Am. Bar Found., Pa. Bar Assn., D.C. Bar, Phila. Bar Assn. (chmn. fed. cts. com. 1992), Fed. Bar Coun. of Second Cir., U. Pa. Am. Inn of Ct. General civil litigation, Product liability, Toxic tort. Office: Hoyle Morris & Kerr LLP 1650 Market St Ste 1 Philadelphia PA 19103-7301 E-mail: afickler@hoylemk.com.

FIEBACH, H. ROBERT, lawyer; b. Paterson, N.J., June 7, 1939; s. Michael M. and Silvia Irene (Nadler) F.; m. Elizabeth D. Carlton, Mar. 17, 1984; children: Michael, Emma; children by previous marriage: Jonathan, Rachel. BS, U. Pa., 1961, LLB cum laude, 1964. Bar: Pa. 1965, U.S. Supreme Ct. 1971. Law clk. to Chief Judge Biggs U.S. Ct. Appeals for 3d Cir., 1964-65; assoc. Wolf, Block, Schorr and Solis-Cohen, Phila., 1965-71, ptnr., 1971-79, sr. ptnr., 1979-95; sr. mem., shareholder Cozen O'Connor, Phila., 1995—. Permanent mem. U.S. Jud. Conf. for 3d cir., 1967—; mem. Pa. Supreme Ct. Adv. Com. on Appellate Rules, 1987-93, Commn. on Jud. Elections, 1997-98; arbitrator, mediator U.S. Dist. Ct. (ea. dist.) Pa., 1966—. Contbg. author: Business and Commercial Litigation in the Federal Courts, 1998; rsch. editor U. Pa. Law Rev., 1964-65; contbr. articles to legal jours. Past mem. Phila. adv. bd. Anti-Defamation League of B'nai Brith, Greater Phila. Regional Commn. on Law and Social Action, Am. Jewish Congress; bd. dirs. Greater Phila. chpt. ACLU, past chmn. criminal justice and police practices com.; past bd. dirs. Pa. chpt. ACLU; bd. dirs. Congregation Rodeph Shalom. Fellow: Am. Coll. Trial Lawyers; mem.: ABA (past chmn. jud. performance and conduct com., jud. adminstrn. divsn. 1986—91, nat. conf. bar pres. 1991—95, ho. of dels. 1991—2000, pres. nat. caucus state bar assns. 1994—95, chmn. standing com. on lawyers profl. liability 1994—95, bd. govs. 1997—2000, ho. of dels. 2001—, state del. 2001—, litigation sect., 1988 and 2002 midyear meeting host com.), Am. Bar Found., Soc. of Fellows, Phila. Trial Lawyers Assn. (bd. dirs. 1989—90, past chmn. bus. litig. com.), Am. Judicature Soc. (state membership chmn. 1988), Defender Assn. Phila. (bd. dirs.), Pa. Bar Inst. (pres. bd. dirs. 1984—90, 2000—), Phila. Bar Assn. (chmn. spl. com. on ins. 1983—84, bd. govs. 1983—87, past chmn. fed. cts. com., spkr. various panels, past vice-chmn. arbitration com., civil jud. procedures com., past mem. spl. com. to study appellate cts.), Pa. Bar Assn. (past vice-chmn. jud. selection com., chmn. jud. retention election com 1980—83, chmn. polit. action com. for merit retention of judges 1980—83, ho. of dels. 1983—, chmn. com. on profl. liability 1984—87, bd. govs. 1987—95, pres.-elect 1992—93, pres. 1993—94, Pa. Bar Trust 1996—, Spl. Achievement award 1986), Order of Coif (past dir. U. Pa. chpt.). Federal civil litigation, State civil litigation. Home: 301 Delancey St Philadelphia PA 19106-4208 Office: Cozen & O'Conner 1900 Market St Fl 3 Philadelphia PA 19103-3572 E-mail: rfiebach@cozen.com.

FIEDEROWICZ, WALTER MICHAEL, lawyer; b. Hartford, Conn., Aug. 23, 1946; s. Michael and Sylvia Christine (Ramunno) F.; m. Gerry Prattson, June 1, 1968; children: Michael, Catherine. BA, Yale U., 1968; JD (DuPont fellow), U. Va., 1971. Bar: Conn. 1971, U.S. Supreme Ct. 1977. Mem. firm Cummings & Lockwood, Stamford, Conn., 1971-76, ptnr. firm, 1979-88, of counsel, 1989-91; pres. Covenant Mut. Ins. Co., Hartford, 1985-92; White House fellow U.S. Dept. Justice, Washington, 1976-77; spl. asst. to Atty. Gen., Dept. Justice, Washington, 1976-77; assoc. dep. Atty. Gen., 1977-79. Bd. dirs. Photronics, Inc., First Albany Corp., Hematech; chmn. CDT Corp., Meacock Capital, Heritage Underwriting Agy. Mem. editl. Va. Law Rev., 1969-71. Mem. grad. coun. Loomis-Chaffee Sch. Bd.; trustee Conn. Trust for Hist. Preservation. Mem. ABA, Conn. Bar Assn., Order of the Coif, Hartford Golf Club, Univ. Club. Roman Catholic. Banking, Commercial, contracts (including sales of goods; commercial financing), Corporate, general. Home: 102 North St PO Box 939 Litchfield CT 06759-0939 E-mail: fiederowicz@juno.com.

FIEDLER, LAURIE W. lawyer; b. N.Y.C., Aug. 1, 1960; d. Merle William and Dorothy (Hutt) Wynn; m. Alan Wayne Fiedler, June 12, 1982; children: Amber Joy Wynn, Andrew Wynn, Adam Wynn. BA, Gordon Coll., 1982; MA, Drew U., 1983; JD, Seton Hall U., 1989. Bar: N.J. 1989. Law clk. A.J. Fusco, Passaic, N.J., 1988-89, assoc., 1989-91; pvt. practice Wayne, N.J., 1991—. Bd. dirs. Christian Homes for Children. Mem. N.J. Bar Assn., Passaic County Bar Assn., Am. Ctr. for Law and Justice (affiliate), C. of C. Mem. Assembly of God. Family and matrimonial, Personal injury (including property damage), Property, real (including real estate development, water). Office: 324 Valley Rd Wayne NJ 07470-3953

FIEGER, GEOFFREY NELS, lawyer; b. Detroit, Dec. 23, 1950; s. Bernard Julian and June Beth (Oberer) F.; m. Kathleen Janice Podwoiski, June 25, 1983. BA, U. Mich., 1974, MA, 1976; JD, Detroit Coll. Law, 1979. Bar: Mich. 1979, U.S. Dist. Ct. (ea. dist.) Mich. 1979, Fla. 1980, U.S. Dist. Ct. (mid. dist.) Fla. 1980, Ariz. 1980. Ptnr. Fieger Fieger Kenney & Johnson, P.C., Southfield, Mich., 1979—. V.p. Orgn. United to Save Twp., West Bloomfield, Mich., 1987; dem. nominee for gov. of Mich., 1998. Mem. ABA, Detroit Bar Assn., Assn. Trial Lawyers Am. Unitarian Universalist. Avocations: running, swimming. Federal civil litigation, State civil litigation, Personal injury (including property damage). Office: Fieger Fieger Kenney & Johnson PC 19390 W 10 Mile Rd Southfield MI 48075-2463

FIELD, ARTHUR NORMAN, lawyer; b. N.Y.C., Sept. 28, 1935; s. Harry and Rose (Lemberg) F.; m. Doris Helen Rabbiner, Sept. 1, 1957; children: Michael, Karen. BBA, CCNY, 1955; LLB, Harvard U., 1958. Bar: (N.Y.) 1959, (Fla.) 1975. Assoc. Shearman & Sterling, N.Y.C., 1959-68, ptnr., 1968-2000; pres. GXG Mgmt., LLC , N.Y.C., 2000—; mem. Field Cons. LLC; of counsel Shearman & Sterling, N.Y.C., 2001. Author: Legal Opinions in Business Transactions, 2003; co-editor (with M. Moskin): Transactional Lawyers Deskbook, 2001. Chmn., bd. dirs. Community Action for Legal Svcs., 1972-77 (chair 78-79); bd. dirs. Brookdale Found., 1983—, Wave Hill Inc., N.Y.C., 1968-80, Washington Square Legal Svcs., 1979-95, Historic House Trust of N.Y., 2000-; trustee Ramapo Trust, 1983; dir. Preservation League N.Y., 2003-, Brookdale Inst. on Aging, 2003-. Fellow Am. Bar Found., N.Y. Bar Found., N.Y. County Lawyers Assn. (pres. 1990-92); mem. ABA (ho. of dels. 1990-92), N.Y. State Bar Assn. (v.p. 1992-97), Assn. Bar City N.Y., Am. Law Inst., Assn. of Arbitrators (dir. N.Y. 1998-2002, chair Tribar Opinion Com.1985-90, chair ABA Bus. Sect. Opinion Com. 2002—). Banking, Bankruptcy, Corporate, general. E-mail: anfield@igxg.com.

FIELD, HENRY AUGUSTUS, JR., lawyer; b. Wisconsin Dells, Wis., July 8, 1928; s. Henry A. and Georgia (Coakley) F.; m. Patricia Ann Young, Nov. 30, 1957 (dec. 1980); children: Mary Patricia (dec. 1992), Thomas Gerard, Susan Therese (Mrs. Thomas Hempel); m. Molly Kelly Martin, Apr. 13, 1985. Student, Western Mich. Coll., 1946-47; PhD, Marquette U., 1950; LLB (cum laude), U. Wis., 1952. Bar: Wis. 1952, U.S. Dist. Ct. (we. and ea. dists.) Wis. 1952, U.S. Ct. Appeals (7th cir.) 1957, U.S. Supreme Ct. 1980. Asst. U.S. atty. Western Dist. of Wis., 1956-57; assoc. Roberts, Boardman, Suhr, Bjork & Curry, 1957-62; jr. ptnr. Roberts, Boardman, Suhr & Curry, 1962-70; ptnr. Boardman, Suhr, Curry & Field, Madison, Wis., 1970—, chmn. exec. com., 1985-95; mem. Wis. Jud. Council, 1974-79. Dir. Family Service Soc., 1969-75, treas., 1971-72, pres., 1973-74; trustee Dane County Bar Pro Bono Trust Found., 1995-99. Served with C.I.C., AUS, 1952-55. Fellow: Wis. Bar Found., Am. Bar. Found., Am. Coll. Trial Lawyers (state chmn. 1982—83); mem.: ABA (Wis. chmn. legis. com. 1975—76), Wis. Law Found. (trustee 2003), Wis. Bar Assn. (chmn. litigation sect. 1971—72), Milw. and Dane County Bar Assn. (pres. 1971—72), 7th Fed. Cir. Bar Assn., Madison Club, Order of Coif, Sigma Tau Delta, Phi Delta Phi. Republican. Roman Catholic. State civil litigation, Insurance, Product liability. Home: 3310 Valley Creek Cir Middleton WI 53562-1988 Office: Boardman Suhr Curry & Field 1 S Pinckney St Madison WI 53703-2892

FIELD, NOEL MACDONALD, JR., lawyer; b. Providence, May 15, 1934; s. Noel Macdonald and Ellen DeWolf (Preston) F.; m. Phyllis Campbell, Nov. 10, 1962; children: Ellen, Noel III, Campbell, Margaret. AB summa cum laude, Brown U., 1956; LLB cum laude, Harvard U., 1961. Bar: R.I. 1962. Ptnr. Hinckley, Allen & Snyder and predecessors, Providence, 1961—. Former v.p. and sec. bd. dirs. U.S. Yacht Racing Union, Newport, R.I.; former trustee Rocky Hill Sch., Providence Country Day Sch.; v.p., trustee Lincoln Sch., Providence; bd. dirs., former mem. Arthritis Found. (Southern New Eng. chpt.). Fellow Am. Coll. Trust and Estate Counsel (state chmn. 1986-91); mem. Phi Beta Kappa (pres. R.I. Alpha). Avocations: sailing, bicycle riding. Probate (including wills, trusts), Personal income taxation. Office: Hinckley Allen & Snyder LLP 1500 Fleet Ctr Providence RI 02903-2319

FIELD, ROBERT EDWARD, lawyer; b. Chgo., Aug. 21, 1945; s. Robert Edward and Florence Elizabeth (Aiken) F.; m. Jenny Lee Hill, Aug. 5, 1967; children: Jennifer Kay, Kimberly Anne, Amanda Brooke. BA, Ill. Wesleyan U., 1967; MA, Northwestern U., 1969, JD, 1973. Bar: Ill. 1973, U.S. Dist. Ct. (no. dist.) Ill. 1974, U.S. Supreme Ct. 1979. Exec. dir. Winnetka (Ill.) Youth Orgn., 1969-73; assoc. Seyfarth, Shaw, Fairweather & Geraldson, Chgo., 1973-79, ptnr., 1979-93, Field & Golan, Chgo., 1993—. Bd. dirs. Gt. Lakes Fin. Resources, Matteson, Ill., 1983—, vice chmn., 1988-91, chmn. 1991—; bd. dirs. Gt. Lakes Trust Co., 2001--, chmn., 2001--; bd. dirs. Chgo. chpt. Ill. Wesleyan U. Assocs., Great Lakes Ins. Svcs., Alsip, Ill., 2001--; chmn. bd. dirs. 1st Nat. Bank of Blue Island, 1989-2001, Great Lake Bank, 2001—, Bank of Homewood, 1988-2001; bd. dirs. Winchester Mfg. Co., Wood Dale, Ill., Ludell Mfg. Co., Milw., Comml. Resources Corp., Naperville, Ill., 1984-93; dir., sec. Ellis Corp., Itasca, Ill., 1980—; chmn. bd. dirs. Cmty. Bank of Homewood-Flossmoor, Ill., 1983-92, Bank of Matteson, Ill., 1992-99; bd. dirs. Grand Prairie Svcs., Inc., 1999--, sec., 2001--; mem. State Banking Bd. Ill., 1993-97. Bd. dirs. Ctr. for New Beginnings, 1997—, Svcs. Exch., 1998—, Family Svc. Ctrs. Cook County, Matteson, 1979-99, treas., 1981-82, pres., 1986-88, chmn., 1988-93; pres. Lakes of Olympia Condominium Assn., 1987-89; trustee Village of Olympia Fields, Ill., 1981-89, pres., 1991-97; trustee Ill. Wesleyan U., 1990—, treas., 1994—; bd. dirs. Northwestern U. Sch. Law Alumni Assn., 1990-94. Mem. ABA, Ill. Bar Assn., Am. Bankers Assn., Ill. Bankers Assn., United Meth. Bar Assn. (v.p. Chgo. chpt. 1989), Chgo. Bar Assn., Bankers Club Chgo., Union League Club Chgo., Calumet Country Club. Banking, Commercial, contracts (including sales of goods; commercial financing), Property, real (including real estate development, water). Office: Field & Golan 3 1st National Plz Ste 1500 Chicago IL 60602 E-mail: refield@fieldgolan.com.

FIELDING, FRED FISHER, lawyer; b. Phila., Mar. 21, 1939; s. Fred P. and Ruth Marie (Fisher) F.; m. J. Maria Dugger, Oct. 21, 1967; children: Adam Garrett, Alexandra Caroline. AB, Gettysburg Coll., 1961; LL.B, JD, U. Va., 1964; LittD (hon.), U. Detroit, 1986, Pepperdine U., 1986. Bar: Pa. 1965, D.C. 1974. Assoc. Morgan, Lewis & Bockius, Phila., 1964-65, 67-70, ptnr. Washington, 1974-81; asst. counsel to Pres. of U.S. The White House, Washington, 1970-72, dep. counsel, 1972-74, counsel to Pres. of U.S., 1981-86; ptnr. Wiley, Rein & Fielding, Washington, 1986—; pres. Gilmore Broadcasting Corp., 1988-90. Mem. Jud. Conf. D.C. Cir. Ct., 1976—; mem. internat. adv. bd. Credit Internat. Bank, 1990-96; bd. dirs. Gilmore Broadcasting Corp., Coun. for Excellence in Govt.; spl. counsel Adminstrv. Conf. U.S., 1982-86, pub. mem., 1987-94, chmn. spl. com. on ethics in govt., 1988-92, com. on regulation, 1992-94; presdl. appointment to panel arbitrators Internat. Ctr. for Settlement Investment Disputes, 1987-95, 2002--; mem. CPR panel Disting. Neutrals, 2000—, bd. dirs. Pediat. AIDS Foundn, 1998—, mem. standing com. Fed. Judiciary ABA, 1996-2002; bd. dirs., vice chmn. Nat. Legal Ctr., 2002—; clearance counsel Bush-Cheney transition team, 2000-2001. Mem. Commn. on White House Fellowships, 1981-86, Pres.'s Commn. for German-Am. Tricentennial, 1983-84; mem. presdl. del. to observe Philippine presdl. elections, 1986, pres.'s personal rep. Australia/Am. Friendship Week, 1986; spl. counsel to Rep. vice presdl. campaign, 1988, sr. legal advisor Bush-Quayle campaign, 1992; conflict-of-interest counsel Office of Pres.-Elect, 1980; gen. counsel 50th presdl. inaugural, 1984-85; dep. dir. presdl. transition, 1988-89; mem. Pres.'s Commn. on Fed. Ethics Law Reform, 1989; U.S. designated arbitrator Arbitration Tribunal on U.S.-U.K. Air Treaty Dispute, 1989-94, Sec. of Transp. Task Force on Air Disaster Victims, 1996-98; mem. bd. visitors Sch. Law Pepperdine U., 1989-92; bd. dirs. Coun. for Excellence in Govt., 1989-95; bd. fellows Gettysburg Coll., 1992—, also trustee; bd. dirs. USAir Shuttle, 1992—, Ethics Resource Ctr., 1993; sec.-treas., bd. dirs. Arlington Va. Hosp. Found., 1994—; mem. commn. on selection fed. judges U. Va. Miller Ctr., 1994-97; bd. dirs. Washington Scholarship Fund, 1994-97, Ctr. Democracy, 1995-98, vice-chmn. 1996-97, chmn., 1997; commr. Nat. Commn. Terrorism Attack, 2002-. Served to capt. AUS, 1965-67. John McKee Found. fellow. Fellow ABA (life, standing com. on fed. judiciary), CEELI, FBA, D.C. Bar Assn. (bd. govs. 1996-98), Pa. Bar Assn., Am. Arbitration Assn. (nat. panel), Lawyer's Club of Washington, Fed. City Club, Washington Golf and Country Club, 1925 F Street Club, Univ. Club, Phi Gamma Delta, Pi Delta Epsilon, Omicron Delta Kappa, Pi Lambda Sigma, Phi Delta Phi. Republican. Lutheran. Office: Wiley Rein & Fielding 1776 K St NW Washington DC 20006-2304

FIELDS, BERTRAM HARRIS, lawyer; b. Los Angeles, Mar. 31, 1929; s. H. Maxwell Fields and Mildred Arlyn (Ruben); m. Lydia Ellen Minevitch, Oct. 22, 1960 (dec. Sept. 1986); 1 child, James Eldar; m. Barbara Guggenheim, Feb. 21, 1991. BA, UCLA, 1949; JD magna cum laude, Harvard U., 1952. Bar: Calif. 1953. Practiced in, LA, 1955—; assoc. firm Shearer, Fields, Rohner & Shearer, and predecessor firms, 1955—57, mem. firm, 1957—82; ptnr. Greenberg, Glusker, Fields, Claman, Machtinger and Kinsella, 1982—. Author (as D. Kincaid): The Sunset Bomber, 1986; author: The Lawyer's Tale, 1992; author: (as B. Fields) Royal Blood Richard III and the Mystery of the Princes, 1998; mem. bd. editors: Harvard Law Rev., 1953—55. Bd. dirs. U. So. Calif. Annenberg Sch. Comm. 1st lt. USAF, 1953—55, Korea. Mem.: ABA, Coun. Fgn. Rels., LA County Bar Assn. Achievements include being the subject of profiles Calif. Mag., Nov. 1987; Avenue Mag., Mar. 1989; Am. Film Mag., Dec. 1989; Vanity Fair Mag., Dec. 1993; Harvard Law Sch. Bull., spring 1998; London Sunday Telegraph, June 1999; Sunday New York Post, July 1999; W Mag., Apr. 2002; L.A. Times, Apr. 2003; London Sunday Times, Apr. 2003. Office: Greenberg Glusker Fields Claman & Machtinger Ste 2000 1900 Avenue Of The Stars Los Angeles CA 90067-4590

FIELDS, WENDY LYNN, lawyer; b. N.Y.C., Sept. 22, 1946; d. Sidney and Helen (Silverstein) F. BA, George Washington U., 1968, JD, 1976. Bar: D.C. 1976. Assoc. Arent, Fox, Kintner, Plotkin & Kahn, Washington, 1976-78; ptnr. Weissbard & Fields, Washington, 1978-83, Wilkes, Artis, Hedrick & Lane, Washington, 1983-86, Foley & Lardner, Washington, 1986-97, Katten Muchin Zavis Rosenman, Washington, 1997—. Mem. George Washington Law Rev., 1973-75. Mem. D.C. Bar. Assn. Office: Katten Muchin Zavis Rosenman 1025 T Jefferson St NW East Lobb Ste 700 Washington DC 20007-5214

FIELDS, WILLIAM ALBERT, lawyer; b. Parkersburg, W.Va., Mar. 30, 1939; s. Jack Lyons and Grace (Kelley) F.; m. Prudence Brandt Adams, June 26, 1964. BS magna cum laude, Ohio State U., 1961; postgrad., Harvard Law Sch., 1961-64. Bar: Ohio bar 1964. Since practiced in, Marietta; city prosecutor, 1964-65; acting Judge Marietta Mcpl. Ct.; dir. elections Washington County, 1967-74; profl. bass-baritone soloist. Bd. dirs. Bank One, Marietta, N.A.; lectr. on estate planning and probate matters. Mem. editl. bd. Probate Law Jour. of Ohio. Chmn. Washington County Heart Assn., 1965-67; mem. dist. exec. com. Boy Scouts Am., 1967-74; Treas. County Republican Exec. Com., 1966—; trustee YMCA, Salvation Army; pres. bd. trustees Washington State Community Coll., Marietta; exec. com., trustee Coll. Adminstrv. Scis., Ohio State U.; trustee Appalachian Bible Coll., Bradley, W.Va., 1974-77, Marietta Meml. Hosp., also treas.; bd. dirs. Ohio Valley Port Authority. Recipient Wall St. Jour. award, 1961; named Outstanding Young Man of Marietta, 1968, Outstanding Citizen of Marietta, 1992; named to Ohio Valley Sports Hall of Fame, 2001. Fellow Am. Coll. Trust and Estate Counsel; mem. Ohio Bar Assn. (chmn., bd. govs., probate and trust law sect., mem. splty. bd. Ohio Supreme Ct.), Washington County Bar Assn., Marietta Area C. of C. (v.p., trustee), Am. Mensa, Nat. Soc. of Arts and Letters (bd. trustees), Sigma Chi, Beta Gamma Sigma. Clubs: Rotarian (pres. 1970-71), Marietta Country (trustee). Home: 129 Hillcrest Dr Marietta OH 45750-9321 Office: 217 2nd St Marietta OH 45750-2916 E-mail: WAF125@wirefire.com.

FIER, ELIHU, lawyer, educator; b. N.Y.C., Mar. 25, 1931; s. Charles H. and Helen N. (Nadel) F.; m. Jane Lee Saltser, Jan. 10, 1956 (dec. Jan. 1964); children— Jennifer, Michael, Carlyn. BA, Dartmouth Coll., 1952; LL.B., Harvard U., 1958. Bar: N.Y. 1959, U.S. Dist. Ct. (so. and ea. dists.) N.Y. 1960 U.S. Tax Ct. 1961, U.S. Ct. Appeals (2d cir.) 1961, Fla. 1997. Ptnr. Weil, Gotshal & Manges, N.Y.C., 1969-80, Morgan, Lewis & Bockius, N.Y.C., 1980-83, Finley, Kumble, Wagner, Heine, Underberg, Manley & Casey, Beverly Hills, Calif., 1983-88, N.Y.C., 1983-88; of counsel Pryor, Cashman, Sherman & Flynn, N.Y.C., 1988-93, Blum & Fier P.C., N.Y.C., 1993-97, Gillespie & Allison, P.A., Boca Raton, Fla., 1995-97; mgr. Realty Cons. LLC. Adj. assoc. prof. NYU, N.Y.C., 1969-76; lectr. N.Y. Law Jour., Law and Bus., Practicing Law Inst. Served to lt. (j.g.) USNR, 1952-60 Mem.: ABA (com. creditors' rights in real estate financing 1983—90). Commercial, contracts (including sales of goods; commercial financing), Finance, Property, real (including real estate development, water). Home: 240 NW 70th St Boca Raton FL 33487-2391 Office: 50 Vanderbilt Ave New York NY 10017

FIERKE, THOMAS GARNER, lawyer; b. Boone, Iowa, Nov. 12, 1948; s. Norman Garner and Mary Margaret (Mullen) F.; m. Susan Marie Butler, July 17, 1976 (div. Mar. 1983); m. Debra Lynn Clayton, Sept. 17, 1988; children: Veronica Helen, Caroline Margaret. BSMetE, Iowa State U., 1971; JD, U. Minn., 1974; LLM, Boston U., 1978; M in Strategic Studies, U.S. Army War Coll., 1999. Bar: Ill. 1974, U.S. Dist. Ct. Mass. 1976, U.S. Dist. Ct. (no. dist.) Ill. 1976, U.S. Ct. Appeals (1st cir.) 1976, U.S. Tax Ct. 1978, U.S. Supreme Ct. 1978, Mass. 1980, N.Y. 1981, U.S. Ct. Appeals (fed. cir.) 1989. Commd. 2nd lt. U.S. Army, 1971, advanced through grades to col., 1980, ret., 2002; trial ct. prosecutor Ft. Devens, Mass., 1974-77; group judge adv. 10th Spl. Forces Group, 1975-78; chief adminstrv. law sect., 1977-78; chief legal counsel, contracting officer U.S. Def. Rep., Am. Embassy, Tehran, Iran, 1979; chief adminstrv. law Ft. Devens, 1979-80; judge adv. gen. corps, 1974-80; atty.-advisor Army Materiel Command, 1980-82; mgr. contracts policy and review Martin Marietta Michoud Aerospace, Martin Marietta Corp., New Orleans, 1982; gen. counsel Lockheed Martin Manned Space Sys., Lockheed Martin Corp., New Orleans, 1984—. Apptd. to La. Gov.'s Mil. Adv. Commn., 1991; bd. dirs. La. Orgn. for Jud. Excellence, 1988—; mem. La. state com. Employer Support of Guard and Res., 1988—92, dep. state ombudsman, 1992—94, state ombudsman, 1994—2001, state chmn., 2001—; mem. Mil. Adv. Com. of Greater New Orleans, 1993—, vice chair internat. rels., 2002—. Recipient Most Valuable Employer Support for the Guard and Res. award, NASA Pub. Svc. medal, 1992, La. Cross Merit award State of La., 1994, 5 Outstanding Vol. Svc. medals Dept. Def., 1994, 96, 97, 99, 2001, Legion of Merit, 1998, 2001, USN Superior Pub. Svc. medal, 1999, USCG commendation, 2001. Mem. Am. Corp. Counsel Assn. (bd. dirs. New Orleans chpt. 1987—, v.p. 1989-90), Internat. Assn. Def. Counsel, New Orleans C. of C. (bd. dirs.), Metro-Vision Econ. Devel. Orgn. (bd. dirs., mayor's mil. adv. com. 1993—, vice chair internat. rels. 2002—), French-Am. C. of C. (bd. dirs.). Republican. Episcopalian. Avocations: snow skiing, reading, running. General civil litigation, Corporate, general, Government contracts and claims. Office: Lockheed Martin Michoud Space Sys PO Box 29304 New Orleans LA 70189-0304 E-mail: tom.fierke@lmco.com.

FIERST, FREDERICK UDELL, lawyer; b. Washington, July 12, 1948; s. Herbert Abner and Edith Udell Fierst; m. Eva Christiana Lauber, Apr. 17, 1981; children: Benjamin Thomas, Daniel Lauber, Sonya Elene. BA magna cum laude, Tufts Coll., 1970; JD, Columbia U., 1976. Bar: NY 1977, Mass. 1981. Assoc. Peter Eikenberry, N.Y.C., 1976—78; jr. ptnr. Parcher and Herbert, N.Y.C., 1978—79; ptnr. Fierst & Neiman, Northampton, Mass., 1981—94, Fierst & Pucci LLP, Northampton, 1995—. Watson fellow, 1971. Entertainment, Licensing, Intellectual property, Corporate, general. Home: 10 Park St Florence MA 01062-1206 Office: Fierst Pucci and Kinder LLP 64 Gothic St Northampton MA 01060-3042 E-mail: fred@ent-atty.com.

FIFIELD, GUY, lawyer; LLB, U. West England, 1981. Ptnr. Denton Wilde Sapte, London, 1984—. Mem. City of London Solicitors Co., Inst. Dirs. I.B.A. Labor (including EEOC, Fair Labor Standards Act, labor-management relations, NLRB, OSHA). Office: Denton Wilde Sapte 1 Fleet Place London EC4M 7WS England Office Fax: 02072467777.

FIFIELD, WILLIAM O. lawyer; b. Crown Point, Indiana, May 25, 1946; BS(hon.) , Purdue U., 1968; JD (hon.) , Harvard U., 1971. Bar: Ill., 1971; Tex., 1998. Assoc. Sidley and Austin, Dallas, 1971-77, ptnr., 1977—, mng. ptnr. Dallas office, 1996—. Bd. dirs. Kimberly-Clark Corp., 1995—2003. Office: Sidley Austin Brown & Wood LLP 717 N Harwood St Ste 3400 Dallas TX 75201-6534

FIFLIS, TED JAMES, lawyer, educator; b. Chgo., Feb. 20, 1933; s. James P. and Christine (Karakitsos) F.; m. Vasilike Pantelakos, July 3, 1955; children: Christina Eason, Antonia Fowler, Andreanna Lawson. BS, Northwestern U., 1954; LLB, Harvard U., 1957. Bar: Ill. 1957, Colo. 1975, U.S. Supreme Ct. 1984. Pvt. practice law, Chgo., 1957-65; mem. faculty U. Colo. Law Sch., Boulder, 1965—, prof., 1968—. Vis. prof. NYU, 1968, U. Calif., Davis, 1973, U. Chgo., 1976, U. Va., 1979, Duke U., 1980, Georgetown U., 1982, U. Pa., 1983, Am. U., 1983, Harvard U., 1988; Lehmann disting. vis. prof. Washington U., St. Louis, 1991; cons. Rice U.; arbitrator AT&T divesture disputes, 1984-87. Author: (with Homer Kripke, Paul Foster) Accounting for Business Lawyers, 1970, 3rd edit., 1984, Accounting Issues for Lawyers, 1991; editor-in-chief Corp. Law Rev., 1977-88; contbr. articles to profl. jours. Mem. ABA, Am. Assn. Law Schs. (past chmn. bus. law sect.), Colo. Bar Assn. (mem. coun. sect. of corp., banking and bus. law 1974-75), Am. Law Inst. (chmn. com. on rsch. proposed fed. securities code), Colo. Assn. Corp. Counsel (pres. 1998-99). Greek Orthodox. Home: 1602 Columbine Ave Boulder CO 80302-7832 Office: Univ Of Colo Law Sch Boulder CO 80309-0001 E-mail: ted.fiflis@colorado.edu.

FIGARI, ERNEST EMIL, JR., lawyer, educator; b. Navasota, Tex., Feb. 18, 1939; s. Ernest Emil and Louise (Campbell) F.; children: Alexandra Caroline, Audrey Elizabeth. BS, Tex. A&M U., 1961; LLB, U. Tex., 1964; LLM, So. Meth. U., 1970. Bar: Tex. 1964, U.S. Ct. Appeals (5th cir.) 1965, U.S. Dist. Ct. (no. dist.) Tex. 1964, U.S. Supreme Ct. 1967. Law clk. to judge U.S. Dist. Ct. (no. dist.) Tex., Dallas, 1964-65; assoc. Coke & Coke, Dallas, 1965-70, ptnr., 1970-75, Johnson & Swanson, Dallas, 1975-86, Figari Davenport & Graves, Dallas, 1986—. Adj. prof. law So. Meth. U., Dallas, 1974-79, 81-82, U. Tex., 1980. Contbr. articles to profl. jours. Fellow ABA Found., Tex. Bar Found., Dallas Bar Found.; mem. State Bar Tex. Roman Catholic. Federal civil litigation, State civil litigation. Office: Figari Davenport & Graves Bank of Am Plz 901 Main St Ste 3400 Dallas TX 75202-3796

FILDES, RICHARD JAMES, lawyer; b. N.Y.C., Nov. 9, 1952; s. Edgar E. and Lucille (Sanna) F.; m. Deborah D. Davenport, June 21, 1979; children: Matthew, Melissa, Heather. BS in Psychology and Econs. magna cum laude, Duke U., 1974; JD cum laude, U. Fla., 1977. Bar: Fla. 1977. Ptnr. Lowndes, Drosdick, Doster, Kantor & Reed, Orlando, Fla., 1977—, also bd. dirs., mem. mgmt. com. Gen. counsel Fla. Citrus Sports; trustee, dir. at large Fla. Citrus Sports Found., Inc. Mem. Lake Nona Club. Democrat. Roman Catholic. Avocations: golf, working out, fishing, reading, running. Commercial, contracts (including sales of goods; commercial financing), Finance, Property, real (including real estate development, water). Office: Lowndes Drosdick Doster et al 215 N Eola Dr Orlando FL 32801-2095

FILIPPINE, EDWARD LOUIS, federal judge; b. 1930; AB, St. Louis U., 1951, JD, 1957. Bar: Mo. 1957. Pvt. practice law, St. Louis, 1957—77; spl. asst. atty. gen. State of Mo., 1963—64; dist. judge U.S. Dist. Ct. (ea. dist.) Mo., St. Louis, 1977—, chief judge, 1990—95; U.S. sr. dist. judge U.S. Dist. Ct. for Ea. Dist. Mo., 1995—. Served with USAF, 1951-53 Mem. ABA, Mo. Bar Assn., Bar Assn. Met. St. Louis, Lawyers Assn. of St. Louis. Office: US Dist Ct Thomas F Eagleton US Cthse 111 S 10th St Rm 10 137 Saint Louis MO 63102

FILLER, RONALD HOWARD, lawyer; b. St. Louis, Apr. 11, 1948; s. Leon Isaac and Jeanette Frances (Sanofsky) F.; m. Paula; children: Stephen Paul, Lindsay Ann. BS, U. Ill., 1970; JD, George Washington U., 1973; LLM in Taxation, Georgetown U., 1976. Bar: D.C. 1973, Ill. 1976, N.Y. 1993. Atty. SEC, Washington, 1973-76; assoc. Abramson & Fox, Chgo., 1976-77; assoc. counsel Conti Cmty. Svc., Chgo., 1977-78, dir. mgmt. accounts, 1978-80; mng. ptnr. Filler Zaner & Assocs., Chgo., 1980-85; ptnr. Vedder, Price, Kaufman & Kammholz, Chgo., 1985-93, corp. practice leader, 1989-91, mem. exec. com., 1991-93; dir. futures adminstrn. Lehman Bros., Inc., 1993—. Dir. Commodities Law Inst., Ill. Inst. Tech./Chgo-Kent Law Sch., 1978-97, adj. prof. law, 1977-93, bd. overseers, 1982-97; lectr. Commodities Ednl. Inst., 1977-89; adj. prof. law Bklyn. Law Sch., 1994-96; vice chmn. Broker Tec Clearing Corp., 2002—. Contbr. articles to jours. and futures mags. Named one of top 315 lawyers State of Ill., 1991. Mem. ABA (chmn. sub futures commn. mchts. 1986—), Nat. Futures Assn. (bd. dirs. 1984-87), Am. Arbitration Assn. (arbitrator), Mid Am. Commodity Exch. (bd. dirs. 1984-86), Chgo. Bar Assn. (chmn. commodities law com. 1981-82, vice chmn. fin. and legal svcs. com. 1988-89, co-vice chmn. large law firm com. 1991-92), Nat. Assn. Futures Traders Assn., Futures Industry Assn. (bd. dirs. 1990-92, exec. com. Chgo. divsn. 1986-88, exec. com. Law and Comp. divsn. 1985-90, 92—, sec. 1995-98, pres. 1998—), N.Y. State Bar Assn., Ill. State Bar Assn. Democrat. Jewish. Commercial, contracts (including sales of goods; commercial financing), Securities, Commodities. Home: 54 Collinwood Rd Maplewood NJ 07040-1038 Office: Lehman Bros Inc 745 7th Ave 5th Fl New York NY 10019 Office Fax: 212-526-6193. E-mail: RFiller@LEHMAN.com.

FINA, PAUL JOSEPH, lawyer; b. Chgo., Mar. 1, 1959; s. Paul Emil and Vera Christiane (Mutzbauer) F.; m. Robyn Leann Hughes, May 24, 1986; 1 child, Paul George. BA in Econs., U. Ill., 1982, MA, 1983; JD, DePaul U., Chgo., 1987. Bar: Ill. 1988, U.S. Dist. Ct. (no. dist.) Ill. 1990, U.S. Ct. Appeals (7th cir.) 1990, U.S. Supreme Ct. 1991. Assoc. Haskin, Taylor & McDonough, Wheaton, Ill., 1988-90, Komessar & Wintroub, Chgo., 1990-94; pvt. practice Law Offices of Paul J. Fina, Chgo., 1994—2001, Law Offices of Fina & Huner, Chgo., 2001—. Mem. bus. faculty Coll. of DuPage, Glen Ellyn, Ill., 1986—, Aurora (Ill.) U., 1997—. Gen. counsel Housing Helpers, Inc., Riverside, Ill., 1991—. DePaul law grantee, 1985. Mem. ABA, Ill. Bar Assn., Assn. Trial Lawyers Am., DuPage County Bar Assn. (civil practice com.), Million Dollar Advocates Forum (life), Phi Alpha Delta. Roman Catholic. Avocations: music performance, athletics. State civil litigation, Personal injury (including property damage). Home: 509 Bent Tree Ct Oswego IL 60543-8734 Office: 940 W Adams St Ste 300 Chicago IL 60607 E-mail: pjfinalawyer@aol.com.

FINBERG, JAMES MICHAEL, lawyer; b. Balt., Sept. 6, 1958; s. Laurence and Harriet (Levinson) Finberg; m. Melanie Piech; children: Joseph, John. BA, Brown U., 1980; JD, U. Chgo., 1983. Bar: Calif. 1984, U.S. Dist. Ct. (no. dist.) Calif. 1984, U.S. Dist. Ct. (ea. dist.) Calif. 1987, U.S. Ct. Appeals (9th and fed. cirs.) 1987, U.S. Dist. Ct. Hawaii, 1988, U.S. Supreme Ct. 1994. Law clk. to assoc. justice Mich. Supreme Ct., 1983-84; assoc. Feldman, Waldman and Kline, San Francisco, 1984-87, Morrison and Foerster, 1987-90; ptnr. Lieff, Cabraser, Heimann & Bernstein, L.L.P., San Francisco, 1991—. Lawyer rep. to 9th Jud. Conf., 1999-2001 (chair No. Calif. del. 2000-01); adv. com. local rules for securities cases U.S. Dist. Ct., Calif., 1996. Exec. editor U. Chgo. Law Rev., 1982-83. Mem.: ACLU (bd. dirs. No. Calif. chpt. 1995), ABA (chmn. securities subcom. class and derivative action com. 1998—, plaintiff's program chair equal employment opportunity com. 1999—2001), Lawyers Com. for Civil Rights of San Francisco Bay Area (fin. chmn. 1992—95, bd. dirs. 1992—98, sec. 1996, co-chmn. 1997—98), Calif. Bar Assn. (mem. standing com. on legal svcs. to poor 1990—94, vice-chmn. 1993—94), Bar Assn. San Francisco (jud. evaluation com. 1994, bd. dirs. 1999—2000, sec. 2001—02, treas. 2002—03). Federal civil litigation, Securities. Office: Lieff Cabraser Heimann & Bernstein LL 275 Battery St Fl 30 San Francisco CA 94111-3305

FINCH, EDWARD RIDLEY, JR., lawyer, diplomat, author, lecturer; b. Westhampton Beach, N.Y., Aug. 31, 1919; AB with Atwater honors, Princeton U., 1941; JD, NYU, 1947; LLD (hon.), Mo. Valley Coll., 1963; DSc (hon.), Cumberland Coll., 1985. Bar: N.Y. 1948, U.S. Supreme Ct. 1953, D.C. 1978, Fla. 1980, Pa. 1992. Ptnr. Finch & Schaefler, N.Y.C., 1950-85; of counsel Le Boeuf, Lamb, Leiby & MacRae, N.Y.C., 1986-88; commr. City of N.Y., 1955-58. V.p. gen. counsel, dir. St. Giles Found., 1964—, Am. Internat. Petroleum Corp., 1988-92; U.S. del. 4th UN Congress, Geneva, 1970, 5th UN Congress, Japan, 1975; U.S. spl. ambassador to Panama, 1972; legal advisor, mem. U.S. Del. UNISPACE II, 1982, UNISPACE III, Vienna, Austria, 1999; lectr. in field. Author: Holes in Your Pockets, 3rd edit., Astro Business-A Guide to Commerce and Law of Outer Space, Judicial Politics; contbr. articles to profl. jours. Pres., bd. dirs. St. Nicholas Soc. N.Y., 1948—; past pres. N.Y. Inst. Spl. Edn., 1950—; bd. govs. Nat. Space Soc., 1984—; mem. faculty adv. com. dept. politics Princeton U.; treas. Jessie Ridley Found., N.Y.C., Finch Trusts; pres. Adams Meml. Fund Inc.; v.p. St. Giles Found.; trustee St. Andrew's Dune Ch., Southampton, Cathedral of St. John the Divine, 1989-92, Whittell Trust; bd. dirs. Am. Found. Cancer Rsch.; life trustee Met. Mus. of Art, N.Y.C.; mem. Coun. Am. Ambs. Col. JAG, USAFR, 1941-72. Decorated U.S. Legion of Merit with oak leaf cluster; order Brit. Empire; Knight Order St. John; officer French Legion of Honor, Disting. Eagle Scout, Coun. of Am. Ambassadors. Fellow Am. Bar Found. (chmn. aerospace coun. sect. sci. and tech 1986-92); mem. ABA (ho. of dels. 1971-72, chmn. corp. lawyers sr. lawyer divsn., chmn. aerospace law divsn. internat. law sect.1973-79), AIAA (sr.), Fed. Bar Assn., Inter-Am. Bar Assn. (Hallgartern telecommunications award 1991), N.Y. State Bar Assn. (internat. law and practice sec., chmn. arms control and nat. security com.), Pa. Bar Assn., Fla. Bar Assn., Assn., Bar City of N.Y., Internat. Bar Assn., Judge Advs. Assn. U.S. (past pres.), Am. Law Inst., Am. Judicature Soc. (sr.), Internat. Astronautical Acad. (full elected mem.), Internat. Inst. Space Law (Lifetim Disting. Svc. award 1997), Am. Arbitration Assn. (panelist), Univ. Clubs of Wash. and N.Y., Union League Club, Union Club, Princeton Club (bd. govs. 1982—), L.I. Club, Bathing Corp. of Southampton, Westhampton Country Club, Hillsboro Club (sr.). Non-profit and tax-exempt organizations, Securities, Estate taxation. Office: 862 Park Ave New York NY 10021-1831 Fax: 212-327-0593. E-mail: erfinchjr@aol.com.

FINCH, FRANK HERSCHEL, JR., lawyer; b. Mpls., Mar. 13, 1933; s. Frank H. and Louise A. (Henry) F.; children: Frank H. III, Lani D.L. BA, Harvard U., 1953; LLB, Harvard U. Law Sch., 1959. Bar: Conn. 1959, U.S. Supreme Ct. 1967, U.S. Dist. Ct. Conn. 1997. Assoc. Howd & Lavieri, Winsted, Conn., 1959-61; ptnr. Howd, Lavieri & Finch, Winsted, 1961—. Pros. atty. Conn. Cir. Ct., 1961-78; bd. dirs. Northwest Conn. Health Corp. Chmn., bd. dirs. Winsted Meml. Hosp., 1975-77; mem. regional adv. coun. N.W. Conn. C.C.; chmn. bd. trustees N.W. Conn. YMCA. Lt. USNR, 1953-59. Mem. ABA, Conn. Bar Assn. (bd. govs. 1985-99, pres. 1998-99), Litchfield County Bar Assn. (pres. 1974-76, grievance com. 1982-86, state trial referee 1984—), Am. Arbitration Assn. (arbitrator 1975—), Nat. Assn. Dist. Attys., N.W. Conn. C. of C. (bd. dirs. 1978-93, chmn. 1980-81, sec. 1985-89, v.p. 1989—), Rotary (pres. Winsted club 1967-68), Univ. Club (exec. com. 1985—, v.p. 1998—). Corporate, general, General practice, Property, real (including real estate development, water). Office: Howd Lavieri & Finch LLP PO Box 1080 682 Main St Winsted CT 06098-1515

FINCH, MICHAEL PAUL, lawyer; b. Galveston, Tex., Jan. 4, 1946; s. Albert Lynn and Ila Belle (Robertson) Finch; m. Rebecca Jean Minnear, Dec. 27, 1969; children: Michael Paul, Rachelle Jean. BA cum laude, MEE, Rice U., 1969; JD magna cum laude, U. Houston, 1972. Bar: Tex. 1973. Petroleum engr. Exxon Corp., Houston, 1969-72; assoc. Vinson & Elkins, Houston, 1972-79, ptnr., 1980—. Bd. dirs. Rice Engring. Alumni, 1994—98; dir. Houston Pops Orch., 1988—89. Master: Am. Contact Bridge League (life); mem.: ABA, Houston Bar Assn., Tex. Bar Assn. Republican. Methodist. Avocations: electronics, woodworking, skiing, piano. Corporate, general, Mergers and acquisitions, Securities. Home: 12531 Overcup Dr Houston TX 77024-4915 Office: Vinson & Elkins 2300 First City Tower 1001 Fannin St Houston TX 77002-6706

FINCH, RAYMOND LAWRENCE, chief judge; b. Christiansted, St. Croix, V.I., Oct. 4, 1940; s. Wilfred Christopher and Beryl Elaine (Bough) F.; m. Anne Marie Mohammed, May 8, 1996; children: Allison, Mark, Jennifer. AB, Howard U., 1962, JD, 1965. Bar: V.I. 1971, Third Circuit Ct. of Appeals 1976. Law clk. Judge's Municipal Ct. of V.I., 1965-66; partner firm Hodge, Sheen, Finch & Ross, Christiansted, 1970-75; judge Territorial Ct. of V.I., Charlotte Amalie, 1975-86, Ct. of Appeals, V.I., Charlotte Amalie, 1986-94, U.S. Dist. Ct. of V.I., 1994—, chief judge, 1999—. Instr. Grad. div., Coll. of V.I., Am. Inst. Banking, 1976— Bd. dirs. Boy Scouts Am., Boys Club Am. Served to capt. U.S. Army, 1966-69. Decorated Army Commendation medal, Bronze Star medal. Mem. Am. Judges Assn., Am., Nat. bar assns., Internat. Assn. Chiefs of Police. Democrat. Lutheran. Office: PO Box 24051 Christiansted VI 00824-0051

FINCK, KEVIN WILLIAM, lawyer; b. Whittier, Calif., Dec. 14, 1954; s. William Albert and Ester (Gutbub) F.; m. Kathleen A. Miller, Oct. 7, 1989. BA in History, U. Calif., Santa Barbara, 1977; JD, U. Calif., San Francisco, 1980. Bar: Calif. 1980. Pvt. practice, Orinda, Calif. Lectr. Internat. Bar Assn., Learning Annex. Author: California Corporation Start Up Package and Minute Book, 1982, 9th edit., 1998; contbr. articles to various profl. jours. Avocations: hiking, golf, skiing. Commercial, contracts (including sales of goods; commercial financing), Corporate, general, Private international. Office: Ste 1670 Two Embarcadero Ctr San Francisco CA 94111 E-mail: kevin@kevinfinck.com.

FINE, A(RTHUR) KENNETH, lawyer; b. N.Y.C., June 29, 1937; s. Aaron Harry and Rose (Levin) F.; m. Ellen Marie Jensen, July 11, 1964; children: Craig Jensen, Ricki-Barie, Desiree-Ellen. AB, Hunter Coll., 1959; JD, Columbia U., 1963; CLU, Coll. Ins., 1973; diploma, Command and Gen. Staff Coll., 1978. Bar: N.Y. 1974; registered rep. and limited prin. Nat. Assn. Securities Dealers, Inc. Joined U.S. Army N.G., 1955, advanced through grades to maj., 1973, ret., 1980. Cons. U.S. Life Ins. Co., N.Y.C., 1970-74, atty., 1975-78, asst. gen. counsel, 1978; asst. counsel USLIFE Corp., N.Y.C., 1978-79, assoc. counsel, 1979-93; v.p., sr. counsel Western Res. Life Assurance Co. Ohio, Clearwater, Fla. Mem. ABA, Soc. Fin. Svc. Profls., N.Y. State Bar Assn., N.G. Assn. U.S., Militia Assn. N.Y. (chmn. vet. officers com. 1981-90), Am. Legion (7th regt. post), Ret. Officers Club St. Petersburg, Fla. Republican. Lutheran. Administrative and regulatory, Corporate, general, Insurance. Home: 5953 36th Ave N Saint Petersburg FL 33710-1835 Office: Western Res Life Assurance Co of Ohio PO Box 5068 Clearwater FL 33758-5068 E-mail: kfine@aegonusa.com.

FINE, BARRY KENNETH, lawyer; b. N.Y.C., May 15, 1938; s. Harry Harold and Annn Fine; m. Rho Joy Stengel, Sept. 3, 1965; children: Scott Jefferson, Jill Ashley. BS, SUNY Empire State Coll., 1986; JD, Touro Coll., 1990. Jr. civil engr. N.Y.C. Transit Authority, 1957-58; pres. Active Industries (formerl Active Steel Drum Co.), L.I., N.Y., 1958-93; founder, pres. Glass Tint Svcs., Inc., L.I., N.Y., 1985-93; founding ptnr. Fine Hummel, P.C., Huntington, NY, 1990—2002; founding mem. Fine, Fine & Berman, LLP, Melville, NY, 2003—. Patentee in field. Project bus. cons. Queens Jr. Achievement, Queens, N.Y., 1984-88. With USAR, 1957-63. Mem. ABA, Suffolk County Bar Assn. (former co-chair Environ. law com., lectr., environ. law writer Suffolk Lawyer), Nassau County Bar Assn., N.Y. State Bar Assn., Masons (past master). Republican. Jewish. Avocations: boating, cabinetmaking, gardening. Office: Fine Fine & Berman LLP 445 Broad Hollow Rd Ste 200 Melville NY 11747-3448 E-mail: bkf@ffbllp.com.

FINE, LAWRENCE B. lawyer; b. June 20, 1951; BA, BS, U. Pa., 1973; JD, U. Va., 1976. Bar: Pa. 1976. Ptnr. Morgan, Lewis & Bockius, Phila. Labor (including EEOC, Fair Labor Standards Act, labor-management relations, NLRB, OSHA). Office: Morgan Lewis & Bockius 1701 Market St Philadelphia PA 19103-2903

FINE, ROBERT PAUL, lawyer; b. Buffalo, June 10, 1943; s. Leonard and Sylvia (Wagner) Finkelstein; m. Eileen Joyce Levitsky, Nov. 26, 1967; children: Lisa Robin, Julie Beth. BA, SUNY, Buffalo, 1965, JD, 1968. Bar: NY 1968, US Dist. Ct. (we. dist.) NY 1969, U.S. Tax Ct. 1973, Fla. 1985. Intern US Dept. Justice, Washington, 1967; law asst. appellate divsn. 4th jud. dept. NY Supreme Ct., Rochester, NY, 1968-69, chief law asst., 1969-70; assoc. Williams, Stevens, McCarville & Frizzell, P.C., Buffalo, 1970-74, ptnr., 1974-77; co-founder, sr. ptnr. Hurwitz & Fine, P.C., Buffalo, 1977—. Participant, panelist Fed. Tax Inst. Western N.Y., 1976—85; chmn. inst. Fed. Tax Inst. Western NY, 1978—81; dir. Buffalo and Erie County Pvt. Industry Coun., 1988—95; exec. com., counsel local organizing com. World Univ. Games, Buffalo, 1993; adj. prof. SUNY Buffalo Sch. Law, 1996—; bd. dir. Roswell Pk. Cancer Inst., 1998—, chair fin. com. Bd. dirs. United Jewish Fedn., 1979-84, treas., 1982-84, v.p., 1986-88; chmn. exec. bd. We. NY Israel Bonds, 1980-82; mem. Dean's Adv. Coun., SUNY Buffalo Law Sch., mem. dean search com., 1986-87; mem. dept. jud. screening com. 4th dept. appellate divsn. state of NY, 1999—, Magistrate Judge, merit selection panel we. dist. NY, 1990—, chair, 2000—. Mem. ABA, NY State Bar Assn. (exec. com. bus. law sect.), Fla. Bar Assn., Erie County Bar Assn. (chmn. tax com. 1978-81, chmn. corp. law com. 1981-84, bd. dirs. 1985-88), Fin. Planning Counselors We. NY (pres. 1986-87), Estate Analysts We. NY, Nat. Health Lawyers Assn., SUNY Sch. Law Alumni Assn. (pres. 1976-77), Mid-Day of Buffalo Club, Westwood Country Club (Williamsville, NY), Buffalo Club (dir. 2001-). Corporate, general, Health, Estate planning. Office: Hurwitz & Fine PC 1300 Liberty Building Buffalo NY 14202-3670

FINE, ROGER SETH, pharmaceutical executive, lawyer; b. Bklyn., Sept. 22, 1942; s. Jack F. and Mildred (Perlmutter) F.; m. Rebecca Gold, June 14, 1964; children: David, Adam. BA, Columbia Coll., 1963; LLB, NYU, 1966. Bar: N.Y. 1966, U.S. Dist. Ct. (so. dist.) N.Y. 1967, U.S. Ct. Appeals (2d cir.) 1967. Assoc. Cahill, Gordon & Reindel, N.Y.C., 1966-74; gen. atty. Johnson & Johnson, New Brunswick, N.J., 1974-78, asst. gen. counsel, 1978-84, assoc. gen. counsel, 1984-91, v.p. adminstrn., mem. exec. com., 1991-95, v.p., gen. counsel, mem. exec. com., 1996—. Mem. ABA. Home: 26 Brook Dr Milltown NJ 08850-1932 Office: Johnson & Johnson 1 Johnson And Johnson Plz New Brunswick NJ 08933-0002*

FINE, TONI MICHELE, law educator; b. N.Y.C., Feb. 7, 1961; d. Seymour and Wilma Gangel Fine. BA, SUNY, Binghamton, 1983; JD, Duke U., 1986. Bar: Pa. 1986, D.C. 1988, U.S. Ct. Appeals (D.C. cir.) 1988. Assoc. Crowell & Moring, Washington, 1986-93; assoc. professorial lectr. in law George Washington U. Law Ctr., Washington, 1992-93; lawyering instr. NYU Law Sch., N.Y.C., 1993-95, coord. Master Comparative Jurisprudence program, 1995-98, assoc. dir. global law sch. program, 1998-2000, acting dir. LLM (CJ) program, 1999-2000; dir. grad. and internat. programs Benjamin N. Cardozo Sch. Law, 2000—. Author: Americal Legal Systems: A Resource and Reference Guide, 1997; contbr. articles to profl. jours. Mem.: Am. Assn. Law Schs. (chair sect. on grad. programs for fgn. students 2001, sect. internat. legal exch. chair 2002), Phi Beta Kappa, Pi Sigma Alpha. Office: Cardozo Sch Law 55 Fifth Ave New York NY 10003 Fax: 212-790-0232. E-mail: tfine@ymail.yu.edu.

FINE, WILLIAM IRWIN, lawyer; b. Hammond, Ind., Feb. 2, 1951; s. Leonard and Sylvia (Appleman) F.; m. Adele Barbara Hult; children: Rachel, Sarah, Rebecca. AB, Ind. U., 1973, JD, 1976; MA, Purdue U., 1996. Bar: Ind. 1976, U.S. Dist. Ct. (no. dist.) Ind. 1987. Assoc. Efron, Efron & Komyatte, Hammond, 1977-79, Efron and Efron, Hammond, 1979-88; pvt. practice, Highland, Ind., 1988—. Fellow Anglo-Zulu War Hist. Soc.; mem. Ind. State Bar Assn., Lake County Bar Assn., Phi Beta Kappa. Commercial, contracts (including sales of goods; commercial financing), Probate (including wills, trusts), Property, real (including real estate development, water). Home: 1341 Fitzgerald Dr Munster IN 46321-4203 Office: 2833 Lincoln St Ste F Highland IN 46322-1924

FINEBERG, ROBERT ALAN, lawyer; b. Portland, Maine, May 29, 1948; s. Samuel and Lillian (Smith) F.; m. Virginia June Brealey, Aug. 22, 1970; children: Cynthia Joy, Daniel Harwood. BA, U. Conn., 1970; JD, Temple U., 1975. Bar: Pa. 1976, N.J. 1976, U.S. Dist. Ct. (ea. dist.) Pa. 1976, U.S. Dist. Ct. N.J. 1976, U.S. Supreme Ct. 1981; cert. civil trial atty. Assoc. Charles Blasband, Norristown, Pa., 1975-76, Perskie & Callinan, Wildwood, N.J., 1976-79; sole practice Wildwood, 1979-81; ptnr. Fineberg & Rodgers, North Wildwood, N.J., 1981-89; sole practice Cape May Courthouse, 1989—. Solicitor Borough of Avalon, N.J., 1979-87, Borough of Wildwood Crest, N.J., 1985-89, Bd. of Edn. of City of Cape May, N.J., 1983-91, City of Cape May, 1991-99, City of Cape May Hist. Preservation Commn., 1999—. Bd. dirs. Assn. for Retarded Citizens of Cape May County, Rio Grande, N.J., 1982-87, Cape May Jazz Festival; pres. Wildwood Crest Civic Assn., 1985-87; mem. Bd. Edn. Middle Township, N.J., 1990—. Mem. ATLA, ABA, N.J. State Bar Assn., Assn. N.J. Trial Lawyers, Cape May County Bar Assn., N.J. Inst. Mcpl. Attys., Phi Beta Kappa, Phi Kappa Phi, Delta Sigma Rho, Pi Sigma Alpha. Clubs: Union League (Cape May County, N.J.). Lodges: Lions. Democrat. Jewish. State civil litigation, Personal injury (including property damage). Home: 24 Chestnut Ave Cape May Court House NJ 08210-2623 Office: 208 N Main St Cape May Court House NJ 08210-2122 E-mail: courtlaw@bellatlantic.net.

FINELSEN, LIBBI JUNE, lawyer; b. Encino, Calif., Apr. 14, 1968; BA in Polit. Sci. summa cum laude, U. Nev., 1990; JD magna cum laude, Lewis and Clark Coll., 1993. Bar: D.C. 1996, U.S. Ct. Appeals (9th, 11th and D.C. cirs.) 1996, U.S. Ct. Appeals (4th cir.) 1999, U.S. Ct. Appeals (fedl. cir.) 2001, Ct. Fed. Claims 2001, Ct. Fed. Claims 2001. Jud. law clk. Gen. Svcs. Bd. Contract Appeals, Washington, 1993-94; assoc. McAleese & Assocs. P.C., McLean, Va., 1994-96; atty. USDA, Washington, 1996-99; trial atty. U.S. Dept. Air Force, Wright Patterson AFB, Ohio, 2000—01; atty./adv. U.S. Dept. Air Force, L.A. AFB, 2001—. V.p. edn. Hadassah Young Profls. Group, Washington, 1998-99; mem. hospitality com. Kesher Israel Synagogue, Washington, 1998-99. Mem. ABA, Phi Alpha Delta, Phi Kappa Phi. Avocations: cooking, handicrafts, travel, art exhibitions.

FINEMAN, S. DAVID, lawyer; b. Phila., Oct. 23, 1945; BA, Am. U., 1967; JD with honors, George Washington U., 1970. Bar: Pa. 1971, U.S. Dist. Ct. (ea. dist.) Pa., U.S. Ct. Appeals (3d cir.) Pa. 1980. Trial atty. Defender Assn., Phila., 1971-72; law clk. Superior Ct. Commonwealth, Pa., 1972-73; mng. ptnr. Fineman & Bach, P.A., Phila., 1981—, Fineman & Bach, Phila., 1987—. Instr. bus. law Temple U., 1974-83; mem. Phila. Planning Commn., 1989-91; mem. Industry Policy Adv. Com. to Advise Sec. of Commerce on Internat. Trade Issues, 1994-98. Bd. govs. U.S. Postal Svc., 1995—, chmn. compensation com., 1997-2000, vice chmn., 2001-03, chmn., 2003—, chmn. strategic planning com., 2001-03. Mem. ABA, Phila. Bar Assn., Pa. Bar Assn., Pa. State Trial Lawyers Assn., Def. Rsch. Inst. Administrative and regulatory, General civil litigation, Insurance. Home: 335 Woodley Rd Merion Station PA 19066-1430 Office: 1608 Walnut St Ste 19 Philadelphia PA 19103-5443 E-mail: sdfineman@finemanbach.com.

FINK, EDWARD MURRAY, lawyer, educator; b. N.Y.C., Mar. 11, 1934; s. Nathaniel and Elsa Charlotte (Lenrow) F.; divorced; children: Jeffrey Neil, Andrea Sue; m. Rita Toby Cohen, Aug. 11, 1985. BS in Chemistry, CCNY, 1955; JD, Georgetown U., 1959. Bar: D.C. 1960, U.S. Dist. Ct. D.C. 1960, U.S. Ct. Appeals (D.C. cir.) 1960, N.Y. 1962, N.J. 1970, U.S. Dist. Ct. N.J. 1970, U.S. Patent and Trademark Office 1960. Patent examiner U.S. Patent Office, Washington, 1955-60; atty. Bell Labs., Murray Hill, N.J., 1960-83, Bell Comm. Rsch. Inc., Livingston, N.J., 1984-91, Edward M. Fink, P.A., Edison, N.J., 1991—; v.p., gen. counsel Eastern R.R. Investment Corp., Bridgewater, N.J., 2000—, chmn. bd. dirs., 2001—, Somerset Terminal R.R. Corp., 2001—02. Adj. prof. torts, bus. law and civil litigation Middlesex County Coll., Edison, N.J., 1980-2000; adj. prof. partnerships and corps, contract law Montclair State U., Upper Montclair, N.J., 1984-2000. Mem. ABA, Am. Intellectual Property Assn., N.J. Patent Law Assn., N.J. State Bar Assn., Middlesex County Bar Assn., D.C. Bar Assn., N.Y. State Bar Assn. Democrat. Jewish. General practice, Patent, Property, real (including real estate development, water). Home and Office: 51 Jamaica St Edison NJ 08820-3726 E-mail: patemf@aol.com.

FINK, JEROLD ALBERT, lawyer; b. Dayton, Ohio, July 16, 1941; s. Albert Otto and Marjorie Carolyn (Scheidt) F.; m. Mary Jo McHone, Dec. 31, 1961 (div. July 1978); children: Marjorie, Kathryn, Erick; m. 2d, Deborah Lynn Bailey, Dec. 25, 1980 (div. Oct. 1986); 1 child, Justin. AB, Duke U., 1963, LLB, 1966. Bar: Ohio 1966. Assoc. Taft, Stettinius & Hollister, Cin., 1966-73, ptnr., 1973—. Bd. dirs. The Wm. Powell Co., Cin., 1974—, Great Trails Broadcasting Co., Cin., 1974-79. Co-author: (with Judy Cohn) Power Defensive Carding, 1988, (with Joe Lutz) The American Forcing Minor Bidding System, 1995, (with Joe Lutz) Defensive Carding in the 21st Century, 2001. Pres. Cin. Musical Festival Assn., 1978-79; trustee Cin. Playhouse, 1976-95, New Life Youth Svcs., Cin., 1971—. Republican. Presbyterian. Pension, profit-sharing, and employee benefits, Corporate taxation. Office: 1800 Firstar Tower 425 Walnut St Cincinnati OH 45202-3923 E-mail: fink@taftlaw.com.

FINK, JOSEPH ALLEN, lawyer; b. Lexington, Ky., Oct. 4, 1942; s. Allen Medford and Margaret Ruth (Draper) F.; m. Marcia L. Horton; children: Alexander Mentzer, Justin McGranahan. Student, Wayne State U., 1960-61; BA, Oberlin Coll., 1964; JD, Duke U., 1967. Bar: Mich. 1968, U.S. Dist Ct. (ea. dist.) Mich. 1968, U.S. Dist. Ct. (we. dist.) Mich. 1974, U.S. Ct. Appeals (6th cir.) 1987, U.S. Supreme Ct. 1998. Assoc. Dickinson, Wright, McKean & Cudlip, Detroit, 1967—72, Lansing, Mich., 1972—75; ptnr. Dickinson Wright PLLC, Lansing, 1976—. Instr. U.S. Internat. U. Grad. Sch. Bus., San Diego, 1971; adj. prof. trial advocacy Thomas M. Cooley Law Sch., Lansing, 1984-85; mem. com. on local rules U.S. Dist. Cts., 1985; chmn. trial experience subcom. U.S. Dist. Ct. (we. dist.) Mich., 1981; bd. dirs. Universal Holding Co.. Contbg. author: Construction Litigation, 1979, Legal Considerations in Managing Problem Employees, 1988, Michigan Civil Procedure During Trial, 2d edit., 1989; contbr. articles to profl. jours. Bd. dirs. Lansing 2000 Inc., 1985-92; bd. trustees Olivet (Mich.) Coll., 1985-94; mem. bd. advisors Mich. State U. Press, 1993-96. Lt. JAGC, USNR, 1968-72. Fellow Mich. State Bar Found.; mem. State Bar of Mich. (chmn. local disciplinary com. 1983—, com. for US Cts. 1984), Profls. Direct (bd. dirs.), Assn. Life Ins. Counsel, Internat. Assn. Ins. Episcopalian. Avocations: writing, reading, golf. Administrative and regulatory, General civil litigation, Insurance. Home: 6302 W Lake Dr Haslett MI 48840-8930 Office: Dickinson Wright PLLC 215 S Washington Sq Ste 200 Lansing MI 48933-1816

FINK, NORMAN STILES, lawyer, educational administrator, fundraising consultant; b. Easton, Pa., Aug. 13, 1926; s. Herman and Yetta (Hyman) F.; m. Helen Mullen, Sept. 1, 1956; children: Hayden Michael, Patricia Carol. AB, Dartmouth Coll., 1947; JD, Harvard U., 1950. Bar: N.Y. 1951, U.S. Dist. Ct. (ea. and so. dists.) N.Y. 1954, U.S. Supreme Ct. 1964. Mem. legal staff Remington Rand, Inc., N.Y.C., Washington, 1949-54; ptnr. Lans & Fink, N.Y.C., 1954-68; counsel devel. program U. Pa., Phila., 1969-80; v.p. devel. and univ. rels. Brandeis U., Waltham, Mass., 1980-81; dep. v.p. devel., alumni rels., assoc. gen. counsel devel. Columbia U., N.Y.C., 1981-89; sr. counsel John Grenzebach & Assocs., Inc., Chgo., 1989-91. Cons. v.p. Engle Consulting Group, Inc., Chgo. Editor: Deferred Giving Handbook, 1977; author: (with Howard C. Metzler) The Costs and Benefits of Deferred Giving, 1982. V.p. Am. Australian Studies Found.; mem. bd. visitors Brevard (N.C.) Coll., 1995-99, life trustee, 1999; Warren Wilson Coll., 1997—, Killough Trustee, N.Y.C. With U.S. Army, 1945-46. Recipient Alice Beeman award for excellence in devel. writing Coun. Advancement and Support of Edn., 1984, Silver medal for fundraising comms., Coun. Advancement and Support of Edn., 1988; Lilly Endowment grantee, 1979-80. Master Mason; mem. ABA (mem. com. on exempt orgns. sect. taxation and com. estate planning and drafting, charitable givint), Coun. Advancement and support of Edn. (various coms.), Am. Arbitration Assn. (panelist), Assn. of Bar of City of N.Y.C. (com. on tax-exempt orgns. 1987-90), Dartmouth Lawyers Assn., Harvard Law Sch. Assn., Nat. Assn. Fundraising Profls. (Contbn. to Knowledge award 1985), Harvard Club Western N.C., Elks. Democrat. Jewish.

FINK, THOMAS MICHAEL, lawyer; b. Huntington, Ind., Oct. 6, 1947; s. Francis Anthony and Helen Elizabeth (Hartman) F.; m. Sheila Ann Jeffers, Aug. 11, 1973; children: Mark, Matthew, Megan. BBA, U. Notre Dame, 1970; JD, Northwestern U., 1973. Bar: Ind. 1973, U.S. Dist. Ct. (no. dist.) Ind. 1973. Assoc. Barrett & McNagny, Ft. Wayne, Ind., 1973-78, ptnr., 1979—. Speaker Estate Planning Coun., Ft. Wayne, 1987—. Pres. Bishop Luers H.S. Bd. Edn., Ft. Wayne, 1992-93; bd. dirs. Ft. Wayne Cmty. Found. Bus. Edn. Fund, 1990—; bd. dirs., treas. Planned Giving Coun. N.E. Ind., 1995—. Mem. Am. Coll. Trust and Estate Counsel, Ft. Wayne Country Club, Notre Dame Club of Ft. Wayne, Beta Gamma Sigma. Roman Catholic. Avocations: coaching basketball, golf, tennis, travel. Estate planning, Probate (including wills, trusts), Estate taxation. Home: 1302 Sunset Dr Fort Wayne IN 46807-2952 Office: Barrett & McNagny 215 E Berry St Fort Wayne IN 46802-2705 E-mail: tmf@barrettlaw.com.

FINK, VELLA MARY, lawyer; b. Niles, Mich., Aug. 29, 1947; d. Boyd L. and Betty (Frucci) F.; m. Austin R. Kessler, May 7, 1983; children: Benjamin D. Kessler, David B. Kessler. BA, U. Mich., 1969; JD, George Washington U., 1975. Bar: D.C. 1975, U.S. Ct. Appeals (4th cir.) 1976, U.S. Ct. Appeals (5th and 9th cirs.) 1977, U.S. Ct. Appeals (10th and D.C. cirs.) 1978, U.S. Ct. Appeals (1st cir.) 1979, U.S. Supreme Ct. 1980, U.S. Ct. Appeals (11th cir.) 1981, Tex. 1991, U.S. Dist. Ct. (we. dist.) Tex. 1992, U.S. Dist. Ct. (no., ea. and so. dists.) Tex. 1994, U.S. Dist. Ct. (no. dist.) Tex. 1995. Law clk. to Hon. Julia Copper Mack Ct. Appeals, D.C., 1975-76; atty. EEOC, Washington, 1976-80, asst. gen. counsel, 1981-90; assoc. Van Os, Deats & Owen, P.C., Austin, Tex., 1992-93; shareholder Van Os, Pittman & Fink, P.C., Austin, 1994, Pittman & Fink, P.C., Austin, 1994—. Bd. dirs. Live Oak Unitarian Universalist Ch., Austin, 1992-93. Fellow Tex. Bar Found.; mem. State Bar Tex., Travis County Bar Assn. (chair labor and employment law sect. 1995-96), Travis County Women Lawyers' Assn. (treas. 1992-94). Labor (including EEOC, Fair Labor Standards Act, labor-management relations, NLRB, OSHA), Pension, profit-sharing, and employee benefits, Probate (including wills, trusts). Office: Pittman & Fink PC 4601 Spicewood Springs Rd Bldg 3 Ste 100 Austin TX 78709

FINKE, ROBERT FORGE, lawyer; b. Chgo., Mar. 11, 1941; s. Robert Frank and Helen Theodora (Forge) Finke. AB, U. Mich., 1963; JD, Harvard U., 1966. Bar: Ill. 1966, U.S. Dist. Ct. (no. dist.) Ill. 1966, U.S. Ct. Appeals (7th cir.) 1966, U.S. Supreme Ct. 1970, U.S. Ct. Appeals (9th cir.) 1980, U.S. Ct. Appeals (4th and 6th cirs.) 1982, (18th cir.), 1998. Law clk., 1966—67; assoc. Mayer, Brown Rowe & Maw, Chgo., 1967—71, ptnr., 1972—. Pres., bd. dirs. Lyric Opera Guild; trustee Rush Presbyn. St. Luke's Med. Ctr. Mem. ABA (sects. litigation, bus., antitrust, legal edn. and admissions to the bar, vice chmn. 1974-75), Lawyers Club Chgo., Univ. Club, Econ. Club. Antitrust, General civil litigation, Corporate, general. Office: Mayer Brown Rowe & Maw 190 S La Salle St Ste 3100 Chicago IL 60603-3441

FINKEL, EUGENE JAY, lawyer; b. Phila., June 21, 1931; BA, Swarthmore (Pa.) Coll., 1952; MA, George Washington U., 1961, JD, 1965. Bar: U.S. Dist. Ct. D.C. 1966, U.S. Ct. Appeals (D.C. cir.) 1972, U.S. Supreme Ct. 1980. Various positions U.S. Dept. Treasury, Washington, 1952-74; dep. dir. Office Internat. Fin. Policy Coordination and Ops., Washington, 1963-67; dir. Office Latin Am., Washington, 1967-70, Multilateral Instns. Program Office, 1970-74, Developing Nations Fin., 1974-75; asst. exec. sec. World Bank-IMF Devel. Com., 1975-77; alt. U.S. exec. dir. Inter-Am. Devel. Bank, Washington, 1977-81; ptnr. Porter Wright Morris & Arthur, Washington, 1981—. Lt. comdr. USNR ret. Office: Porter Wright et al 1919 Pennsylvania Ave NW Washington DC 20006-3434 E-mail: jfinkel@porterwright.com.

FINKEL, SANFORD NORMAN, lawyer; b. Troy, N.Y., Oct. 19, 1946; s. Max and Mildred (Fares) F.; m. Amy Lynn Gordon, Oct. 13, 1974 (div. July 1984); children: Marcy Jennifer, Melanie Gordon. BA, SUNY, Buffalo, 1968; JD, Union U., 1974. Bar: N.Y 1975, U.S. Dist. Ct. (no. dist.) N.Y. 1975. Tchr. sci. Enlarged City Sch. Dist. of Troy, N.Y., 1968-71; pvt. practice Troy, 1975—; counsel to dem. study group N.Y. State Assembly, Albany, 1977-78; instr. paralegal studies Jr. Coll. Albany divsn. Russell Sage Coll., 1977-81; dep. corp. counsel City of Troy, 1990-94. Mem. Rensselaer County Bar Assn. Avocations: reading, numismatics, philately, travel. General civil litigation, Family and matrimonial, Personal injury (including property damage). Home: 19 Capitol Pl Rensselaer NY 12144-9658 Office: 68 2nd St Troy NY 12180-3932

FINKELSTEIN, ALLEN LEWIS, lawyer; b. N.Y.C., Mar. 19, 1943; s. David and Ella (Miller) F.; m. Judith Elaine Stutman, June 20, 1964 (div. Mar. 1980); children: Jill, Jennifer; m. Shelley Gail Barone, June 15, 1980; 1 child, Amanda. BS, NYU, 1964; JD, Bklyn. Law Sch., 1967; MBA, L.I. U., 1969. Bar: N.Y. 1968, U.S. Dist. Ct. (ea. and so. dists.) N.Y. 1973, U.S. Ct. Appeals (2d cir.) 1973, U.S. Supreme Ct. 1976, U.S. Tax Ct. 1979. Ptnr. Finkelstein, Bruckman, Wohl, Most & Rothman, N.Y.C., 1974-97; sr. ptnr. Pressman Finkelstein, N.Y.C., 1997-99; ptnr. Ganfer & Shore LLP, N.Y.C., 1999—. Asst. prof. L.I. U., N.Y.C., 1969-73, adj. assoc. prof., 1973-74; bd. dirs. Amyotrophic Lateral Sclerosis Assn. Mem. ABA (bus. law and family law sect.), N.Y. State Bar Assn., Assn. of Bar of City of N.Y., Queens County Bar Assn. Lodges: Masons. Jewish. Corporate, general, Family and matrimonial, Property, real (including real estate development, water). Home: 425 E 63rd St New York NY 10021-7804 Office: Ganfer & Shore LLP 360 Lexington Ave New York NY 10017-6502 E-mail: afinkelstein@ganshore.com.

FINKELSTEIN, BERNARD, lawyer; b. N.Y.C., Jan. 21, 1930; s. Irving and Sadie (Katz) F.; m. Adele S. Levine, June 29, 1952; children: Sharon Ann, Marcia Lyn. BA, NYU, 1951; LLB, Yale U., 1954. Bar: N.Y. 1954, D.C. 1970. Assoc. Paul, Weiss, Rifkind, Wharton & Garrison, LLP, N.Y.C., 1956-64, ptnr., 1965-95, of counsel, 1996—. Mem. wills and trusts adv. com. Practicing Law Inst. Trustee, mem. Altman Found., N.Y.C., 1985—. Named one of the Best Lawyers in N.Y., N.Y. Mag., 1995. Fellow Am. Coll. of Trust and Estate Counsel (estate and gift tax com. 1987-93); mem. ABA (com. on pre-death planning, probate and trust div. of sect. on real property, probate and trust law 1985-88), N.Y. State Bar Assn. (chmn. gift and tax com. of tax sect. 1978-80), Assn. of Bar of City of N.Y. (trusts, estate and surrogate's ct. com. 1986-89), N.Y. Bar Found., Yale Law Sch. Assn. (exec. com. 1983-86), Phi Beta Kappa, Phi Alpha Delta, Order of Coif. Clubs: Elmwood Country (White Plains, N.Y.). Estate planning, Probate (including wills, trusts). Home: 1 Tory Ln Scarsdale NY 10583-2314 Office: Paul Weiss Rifkind Wharton & Garrison LLP 1285 Avenue of the Americas New York NY 10019-6064

FINKELSTEIN, IRA ALLEN, lawyer; b. N.Y.C., Oct. 7, 1946; s. Louis and Lillian (Reiser) F.; m. Madelyn Kay Hoffman, May 30, 1982; 1 child, Sarah Rebekah. BA, CCNY, 1967; JD, Harvard U., 1973. Bar: N.Y. 1974, U.S. Dist. Ct. (ea. and so. dists.) N.Y. 1974, U.S. Ct. Appeals (2d cir.) 1976, U.S. Supreme Ct. 1978. Assoc. firm Cahill, Gordon & Reindel, N.Y.C., 1972-81, Tenzer, Greenblatt, Fallon & Kaplan, N.Y.C., 1981-83, ptnr., 1983-99, Blank Rome Tenzer Greenblatt LLP, N.Y.C., 2000—02, Harnik & Finkelstein, N.Y.C., 2002—. Mem. Harvard Law Rev., 1970-72. Mem. N.Y. State Bar Assn., Assn. Bar City N.Y. General civil litigation, Trademark and copyright, Sports. Office: Harnik & Finkelstein LLP 405 Lexington Ave New York NY 10174-2210 E-mail: finkelstein@harnik.com.

FINKELSTEIN, JAY GARY, lawyer; b. Riverdale, Md., July 22, 1953; s. Harry and Gertrude Finkelstein; m. Susan Carole Slatkin, Oct. 4, 1980; children: Jeffrey, Rachel, Andrew. AB, Princeton U., 1975; JD, Harvard U., 1978. Bar: D.C. 1978, U.S. Dist. Ct. Md. 1978. Law clk. to hon. Frank A. Kaufman U.S. Dist. Ct. Md., Balt., 1978-79; assoc. Bergson Borkland, Margolis & Adler, Washington, 1979-82, Piper Rudnick LLP, Washington, 1982-85, ptnr., 1986—. Contbg. editor: How to Keep Your Company Out of Court, 1984. Dir. Charles E. Smith Jewish Day Sch., Rockville, Md., 1995-2001. Avocation: travel. Corporate, general, Finance, Securities. Office: Piper Rudnick LLP 1200 19th St NW Washington DC 20036-2430 Office Fax: 202-689-7479. E-mail: jay.finkelstein@piperrudnick.com.

FINKELSTEIN, JESSE ADAM, lawyer; b. Rochester, N.Y., Mar. 25, 1955; s. Nisson A. and Rona G. (Glassman) F.; m. Elizabeth Bowman, Aug. 20, 1978; 2 daus., Sarah Moir, Danielle Bowman. BA cum laude, U. Rochester, 1977; JD cum laude, Boston Coll., 1980. Bar: Del. 1980. assoc. Richards, Layton & Finger, Wilmington, Del., 1980-86, ptnr., 1986—. chmn. Del. Supreme Ct. Rules Com., 1990-96. Author: Corporation Law Review, 1982, The Business Lawyer, 1983, 90, 97, Revue Internationale de Droit Comparé, 1982, The Delaware Law of Corporations and Business Organizations, 1986, Meetings of Stockholders, 1987, Review of Securities and Commodities Regulation, 1985-87; contbr. the Securities Regulation Law Jour., 1986-87; bd. editors BNA Corp. Practice Series, Corp. Governance Law Reporter. Mem. ABA, Del. State Bar Assn. (chmn. supreme ct. rules com. 1990-96, mem. coun. corp. sect.). General civil litigation, Corporate, general, Mergers and acquisitions. Office: Richards Layton & Finger 10th And King St Wilmington DE 19899

FINKELSTEIN, JOSEPH SIMON, lawyer; b. Vineland, N.J., Feb. 28, 1952; s. Absalom and Goldie (Cukier) Finkelstein; m. Sara M. Green, May 30, 1976; children: Adam, Julia, Seth. BA, Rutgers U., 1973; JD, U. Pa., 1976. Bar: Pa. 1976, N.J. 1976, U.S. Supreme Ct. 1982. Assoc. Wolf, Block, Schorr and Solis-Cohen, Phila., 1976-85, ptnr., 1985—. Pres. Perelman Jewish Day Sch., 1996—99; mem. Wexner Heritage Found., 1991—95; mem. exec. com., bd. dirs., chair funds distbn. United Way Southeastern Pa., 1997—99; exec. bd. young leadership coun. bd. Fedn. Jewish Agys., Phila., 1986—88; mem. nat. young leadership cabinet United Jewish Appeal, 1987—91; bd. dirs. Temple Beth Hillel Beth El, Beth Am Israel; trustee Jewish Fedn. Greater Phila., 1996—2000; bd. dirs. State of Israel Bonds, Phila., SCRUB Found. Recipient New Life/New Leadership award, State of Israel, 1989, Hearts of Gold award, United Way Southeastern Pa., 1999. Mem.: ABA, Pa. Land Title Assn., Phila. Bar Assn., N.J. Bar Assn., Pa. Bar Assn., Internat. Coun. Shopping Ctrs. Commercial, contracts (including sales of goods; commercial financing), Property, real (including real estate development, water). Home: 716 Oxford Rd Bala Cynwyd PA 19004-2112 Office: Wolf Block Schorr & Solis-Cohen LLP 1650 Arch St Fl 22D Philadelphia PA 19103-2097 E-mail: jfinkelstein@wolfblock.com.

FINKELSTEIN, STUART M. lawyer; b. N.Y., 1960; BBA with distinction, U. Mich., 1982, JD cum laude, 1985. Bar: N.Y. 1986. Assoc. Skadden, Arps, Slate, Meagher & Flom LLP, N.Y.C., 1985-93, ptnr., 1993—. Corporate taxation, Taxation, general. Office: Skadden Arps Slate Meagher & Flom LLP 4 Times Sq New York NY 10036-6595

FINLEY, CHANDLER R. lawyer; b. Miami Beach, Fla., Oct. 2, 1963; BA, B of Music Performance/Polit. Sci., Emory U., 1985, JD, 1988. Bar: Fla. 1988, U.S. Dist. Ct. (so. dist.) Fla. 1989. Ptnr. Stuber & Finley, West Palm Beach, Fla., 1988-92; talent agt. Miami Beach, Fla., 1992—; ptnr. Finley & Assocs., West Palm Beach, 1992—2001, Chandler Finley & Assocs., West Palm Beach, 2001—02, Finley & Bologna Internat., 2003—; sports agt. Internat. Polo & Equestrian Sports Agy., West Palm Beach, 1994—. Legal counsel, state bd. Fla. Motion Picture T.V. Assn., Palm Beach County, 1995-2000, Finley Music and Entertainment, 1998—. Legal counsel Palm Beach County Work Force Devel. Bd., 1988—, Workforce Alliance, Inc., 2002—; bd.dirs. Fla. Philharmonic, West Palm Beach, 1997-2000. Mem.: Am. Immigration Lawyers Assn., Nat. Italian Am. Bar Assn., Italy Am. C. of C. (treas/. bd. dirs. 2002—). Entertainment, Immigration, naturalization, and customs, Private international. Office: Finley & Bologna Internat Ste 460 1645 Palm Beach Lakes Blvd West Palm Beach FL 33401-2217 also: 150 SE 2d St # 1010 Miami FL 33131 also: 1515 N Federal Hwy Ste 300 Boca Raton FL 33432-1994 E-mail: finleybologna@aol.com.

FINLEY, JOSEPH MICHAEL, lawyer; b. Mpls., Oct. 21, 1952; s. Joseph Moore and Lillian (Manzavrakos) F.; m. Mary Cecilia Morrissey, May 14, 1983; children: Bridget McCann, Joseph William, Brenna Kathleen. BA, Harvard U., 1974, M City Planning, 1977; JD, U. Minn., 1980. Bar: Minn. 1980, U.S. Ct. Appeals (8th cir.) 1980. Exec. intern Met. Transit Commn., St. Paul, 1977; assoc. Leonard, Street and Deinard, Mpls., 1980-85, ptnr., 1986—, chair real estate dept., 1990-95, chair bus. divsn., 1996-99; head of St. Paul office/ real estate law, 2000—. Co-author: Minnesota's Groundwater Protection Act: A Response to Federal Inaction, 1990; articles editor Minn. Law Rev., 1979-80; contbr. West's Minn. Real Estate Law and Practice, articles to legal and trade jours. Mem. transp. adv. bd. Mpls.-St. Paul Met. Coun., 1986-94; mem. Mpls.-St. Paul Airport Adequacy Study Task Force, 1987-88, Mpls.-St. Paul Airport Planning Task Force, 1990-91, Mpls.-St. Paul Airport Site Selection Study Task Force, 1992-94; pres. Edgcumbe Hockey Booster Club 1992-97. Mem. ABA, Minn. Bar Assn., Urban Land Inst., Sensible Land Use Coalition, Am. Planning Assn., Am. Coll. Real Estate Lawyers, Irish-Am. Cultural Inst., Harvard Club Minn. (chair schs. and scholarships com. 1994-01), Town and Country Club. Avocations: ice hockey, genealogy, environ. causes, golf, map and atlas collecting. Finance, Land use and zoning (including planning), Property, real (including real estate development, water). Office: Leonard Street & Deinard Ste 500 380 St Peter St Saint Paul MN 55102 Fax: (651) 222-7644. E-mail: joe.finley@leonard.com.

FINMAN, SHELDON ELIOT, lawyer, mediator; b. Tampa, Fla., Aug. 25, 1943; s. Oscar E. and Shirley E. Finman; m. Bonnie I. Finman, Jan. 16, 1966 (div. Sept. 1976); 1 child, Seth; m. Lynn E. Finman, June 18, 1978; children: Jennilynn, Julia Lynn. BA, U. Fla., 1965, JD, 1971. Bar: Fla. 1971; cert. family law mediator and arbitrator, cert. marital and family lawyer Fla. Bar Assn. Assoc. Robinson, Ginsburg et al, Sarasota, Fla., 1971-73, Allen Knudsen et al, Ft. Myers, Fla., 1973-75, ptnr., 1975-77; pvt. practice Ft. Myers, 1977—. Family law mediator Sheldon E. Finman Mediation Svcs., Ft. Myers, 1983—; mem. family steering com. Fla. Supreme Ct., 2000—02. Pro bono atty. Guardian Ad Litem Program, Ft. Myers, 1996—; exec. bd. Lee County YMCA, Ft. Myers, 1976-80, S.W. Fla. Sports Assn., Inc., Ft. Myers, 1976-2000. Capt. U.S. Army, 1966-68. Master: Calusa Inn of Ct.; mem.: AFCLC (pres. Fla. chpt. 2003, bd. dirs. 2000—), Assn. of Family Law Profls. (charter pres. 1995—97, exec. bd.), Assn. for Conflict Resolution, Fla. Bar Assn. (advanced practitioner). Avocations: health and fitness, racquetball, hiking, reading. Family and matrimonial. Office: 2215 1st St Fort Myers FL 33901-2901 E-mail: sfinman@attglobal.net.

FINNEY, ERNEST ADOLPHUS, JR., retired state supreme court chief justice; b. Smithfield, Va., Mar. 23, 1931; s. Ernest A. Sr. and Collen (Godwin) F.; m. Frances Davenport, Aug. 20, 1955; children: Ernest A. III, Lynn Carol (Nikky) Finney, Jerry Leo. BA, Claflin Coll., 1952; JD, S.C. State U., 1954, LHD (hon.), 1996; HHD (hon.), Claflin Coll., 1977; LLD, U. S.C., 1991, The Citadel, 1995, Johnson C. Smith U., 1995, Morris Coll., 1996; LHD (hon.), Coll. of Charleston, 1995; LLD, Morris Coll., 1996. Bar: S.C. 1954, U.S. Dist. Ct. S.C. 1957, U.S. Ct. Appeals (4th cir.) 1964. Pvt. practice law, Conway, S.C., 1954-60, Sumter, S.C., 1960-66; with Finney and Gray, Attys. at Law, Sumter, 1966-76; mem. S.C. Ho. of Reps., Columbia, 1973-76; judge SC Cir. Ct., Columbia, SC, 1976-85; assoc. justice SC Supreme Ct., Columbia, SC, 1985-94, chief justice, 1994-2000; interim pres. SC State U., 2003—. Chmn. S.C. Legis. Black Caucus, Columbia, 1973-75; chmn. bd. dirs. Buena Vista Devel. Corp., Sumter, 1967—; mem. S.C. State Elections Commn., Columbia, 1968-72; trustee Claflin Coll., Orangeburg, S.C., 1986—, chmn. bd. trustees, 1987-95; sch. law minority adv. com. U. S.C., 1988—. Recipient Disting. Alumni of Yr. award Nat. Assn. Equal Opportunity Edn., 1986, Achievement award C. of C., Sumter, 1986, Presdl. Citation Morris Coll., Sumter, 1986, Wiley A. Branton award NBA, 1998, Afro Am. Achievement award Turner Broadcasting Sys., 1998, Pub. Servant of Yr. S.C. C. of C., 1999, David P. Richardson Jr. Nation Builder award The Nat. Black Caucus of State Legislators, 1999; named 1987 Citizen of Yr. Charleston (S.C.) Med. Soc., 1987; inductee Nat. Black Coll. Alumni Hall of Fame, 1988. Mem. ABA, Am. Judges Assn., Am. Law Inst. (bd. dirs.), Conf. Chief Justices (bd. dirs.), Sumter County Bar, S.C. Bar, Assn. Trial Lawyers Am., Nat. Bar Assn. (appellate com.), S.C. Trial Lawyers Assn. (hon.), Masons, Shriners. Methodist. Avocations: reading, fishing, golf. Home: 24 Runnymede Blvd Sumter SC 29153-8742 Office: SC State U 300 College St NE Orangeburg SC 29117*

FINSTAD, SUZANNE ELAINE, writer, producer, lawyer; b. Mpls., Sept. 14, 1955; d. Harold Martin and Elaine Lois (Strom) F. Student, U. Tex., 1973-74; BA in French, U. Houston, 1976, JD, 1980; postgrad., London Sch. Econs., 1980, U. Grenoble, France, 1979. Bar: Tex. 1981. Legal asst. Butler & Binion, Houston, 1976-78, law clk., 1978-81, assoc., 1982; spl. counsel Ad Litem in the Estate of Howard Hughes Jr., Houston, 1981; mng. ptnr. Finstad & Assoc., Houston, 1990—93. Author: Heir Not Apparent, 1984 (Frank Wardlaw award, 1984), Ulterior Motives, 1987, Child Bride, 1997, Sleeping With the Devil, 1991, Natasha: The Biography of Natalie Wood; co-prodr. (TV films) Sleeping with the Devil; exec. prodr.: (TV series) Natasha, 2003. Named to Order of Barons, Bates Coll. Law, 1980; recipient Am. Jurisprudence award in criminal law. Office: care Alan Nevins 9465 Wilshire Beverly Hills CA 90210

FINSTON, FELICIA A. lawyer; b. Jan. 2, 1961; d. Howard V. and Phyllis H. (Moeller) F. BS magna cum laude, Ariz. State U., 1982; MS with honors, U. Utah, 1983; JD with honors, U. N.Mex., 1986. Bar: Ariz. 1986, Tex. 1990. Student asst. field examiner NLRB, Phoenix, 1980-82; legal asst. Kelcher & McLeod, Albuquerque, 1985; assoc. Snell & Wilmer, Phoenix, 1986-89, Johnson & Gibbs, P.C., Dallas, 1989-91, jr. shareholder, 1992, shareholder, 1993-94; ptnr. Gardere & Wynne, Dallas, 1994—98, Vinson & Elkins, Dallas, 1998—. Co-author: BNA Portfolio on Pension and Profit Sharing Plans, 1995, 98, 2002 (BNA Disting. Author award 2002); contbr. articles to profl. jours. Mem. ABA, State Bar Tex. (labor sect. and tax sect., chair employee benefits com. tax sect. 2000-02), State Bar Ariz., Dallas Bar Assn. (employee benefits sect., sec. 2002, vice chair employee benefits sect. 2003), S.W. Benefits Assn., Worldwide Employee Benefits Network, Phi Beta Kappa, Beta Gamma Sigma, Sigma Iota Epsilon. Avocations: running, cycling. Labor (including EEOC, Fair Labor Standards Act, labor-management relations, NLRB, OSHA), Pension, profit-sharing, and employee benefits, Workers' compensation. Office: Vinson & Elkins LLP 3700 Trammell Crow Ctr 2001 Ross Ave Dallas TX 75201-2916

FINZEN, BRUCE ARTHUR, lawyer; b. Mpls., Mar. 11, 1947; s. Floyd Arthur and Lorraine Jeannette (Offerdahl) F.; children: Margaret, Sara, Stephanie. BA, U. Minn., 1970; JD, U. Kans., 1973. Bar: Minn. 1973, U.S. Dist. Ct. Minn. 1973, Calif. 1988, U.S. Ct. Appeals (8th cir.) 1973, U.S. Ct. Appeals (7th cir.) 1983, U.S. Ct. Appeals (2d cir.) 1986, U.S. Ct. Appeals (4th cir.) 1994, U.S. Ct. Appeals (9th cir.) 1994, U.S. Supreme Ct. 1996. D.C., 2002, U.S. Dist. Ct. D.C. 2003. Law clk. to presiding justice Minn. Supreme Ct., St. Paul, 1973-74; assoc. Robins, Kaplan, Miller & Ciresi, Mpls., 1974-79; ptnr. Robins, Kaplan, Miller & Ciresi LLP, Mpls., 1979—. Mem. adv. bd. Ctr. for Pub. Integrity, 2001—; trustee Ho. of Hope Presbyn. Ch., 1988—94; bd. dirs. Union Gospel Mission, St. Paul, 1983—89; sec. bd. dirs. Boys and Girls Clubs St. Paul, 1984—91. Mem. ABA, Minn. Bar Assn., ATLA, Minn. Trial Lawyers Assn., Consumer Attys. Calif., Assn. Personal Injury Lawyers. Avocations: hunting, fishing. Federal civil litigation, State civil litigation, Product liability. Office: Robins Kaplan Miller & Ciresi LLP 2800 LaSalle Plz 800 Lasalle Ave Ste 2800 Minneapolis MN 55402-2015

FIORE, WILLIAM JOSEPH, lawyer; b. Passaic, N.J., Feb. 8, 1951; s. Samuel W. and Mary A. (Fazio) F.; m. Patrice M. Moore, July 19, 1975; children: Kelly, Daniel. BA, Fordham Coll., 1973; JD, Rutgers U., 1977. Bar: N.J. 1977, U.S. Dist. Ct. N.J. 1977, U.S. Ct. Appeals (3d Cir.) 1987. Law clk. N.J. Appellate Div., Trenton, 1977-78; ptnr. Meyner and Landis, Newark, 1978—. Mem. Summit Zoning Bd. of Adjustment, 1992-99. Mem. ABA, N.J. State Bar Assn., Essex County Bar Assn. (chmn. young lawyers div. 1983-84). Bankruptcy, Pension, profit-sharing, and employee benefits. Office: Meyner and Landis 1 Gateway Ctr Ste 2500 Newark NJ 07102-5315 E-mail: wfiore@meyner.com.

FIORETTI, ROBERT WILLIAM, lawyer; b. Chgo., Mar. 8, 1953; s. Edward E. and Helene (Krypcio) F. BA, U. Ill., 1975; JD, No. Ill. U., 1978. Bar: Ill. 1978, U.S. Dist. Ill. 1978, N.Y. 1981, U.S. Supreme Ct. 1981. Asst. corp. counsel City of Chgo., 1978-82, sr. supervising atty., 1982-86; litigation chief Shain, Firsel & Burney, Chgo., 1986-88; ptnr. Fioretti & Des Jardins Ltd., Chgo., 1989—99, Fioretti, Des Jardins & Reda, Ltd., 1999—. Adj. prof. law No. Ill. U., 2000—; appointed Ill. Supreme Ct. com. on character and fitness, 2000—; mem. bus. adv. com. Sec. of STate, 1999—. Contbr. articles to law rev. Bd. dirs. Historic Pullman Found., Chgo., 1992-00, pres., 1995—, mem. exec. com.; mem. pres.'s coun. U. Ill. Found., Champaign, 1993—; mem. bd. visitors No. Ill. U., DeKalb, 1992—, mem. alumni coun. Coll. law, 1991-00, pres. alumni coun., 1994-98; bd. dirs. Chgo. Vol. Legal Svcs., 1997—, v.p. devel., 1999—; mem. adv. bd. St. Mary Nazareth Hosp., 1998—; bd. dirs. One Historic Blvd., treas., 1999-2000, pres., 2000—; mem. Friends of 5 Hosp.; appointed spl. asst. states atty. of Cook County, 1992-95, spl. asst. atty. gen., 1990—; pres. Historic Pullman Found., 1995-2000; alumni mem. search com. for pres. No. Ill. U., 1999-00; bd. visitors No. Ill. Coll. Law, 1996—; appointed ethics commns. vice-chair State of Ill. Office of Treas., 2000—; mem. Bus. Adv. Coun., Sec. of State, 1999—. Named Outstanding Young Alumni No. Ill. U., 1994, Outstanding Alumni, 1999, Disting. Svc. award, 1999. Mem. FBA (bd. dirs.), Chgo. Bar Assn. (mem. jud. evaluation com. 1996—, co-chair hearing divsn. jud. evaluation com.), Chgo. Athletic Assn. (bd. dirs. 1993-97, v.p. 1995-97), No. Ill. U. Alumni Assn. (bd. dirs. 1997—, exec. com. 1999—, v.p. 1999, pres. 2000—), Jostinian Soc., Italian American Political Action (bd. dirs). Office: Fioretti Des Jardins & RedaLtd 8 S Michigan Ave Chicago IL 60603-3357

FIORITO, EDWARD GERALD, lawyer; b. Irvington, N.J., Oct. 20, 1936; s. Edward and Emma (DePascale) F.; m. Charlotte H. Longo; children— Jeanne C., Kathryn M., Thomas E., Lynn M., Patricia A. BSEE, Rutgers U., 1958; JD, Georgetown U., 1963. Bar: U.S. Patent and Trademark Office 1960, Va. 1963, N.Y. 1964, Mich. 1970, Ohio 1975, Tex. 1984. Patent staff atty. IBM, Armonk, N.Y., 1958-69; v.p. patent and comml. relations Energy Conversion Devices, Troy, Mich., 1969-71; mng. patent prosecution Burroughs Corp., Detroit, 1971-75; gen. patent counsel B.F. Goodrich Corp., Akron, Ohio, 1975-83; dir. patents and licensing Dresser Industries, Inc., Dallas, 1983-93. Alt. mem. Dept. Commerce Adv. Commn. on Patent Law Reform, 1991-92; spl. master, arbitrator, neutral evaluator, expert providing opinion testimony in intellectual property litigation, 1986—; U.S. del. to World Intellectual Property Orgn. Diplomatic Conf., 1991. Bd. dirs. Akron's House Extending Aid on Drugs, 1976. Mem. ABA (chmn. sci. and tech. sect. 1984-85, chair intellectual property law sect. 2000-2001), IEEE, Tex. Bar Assn. (chmn. intellectual property law sect. 1990-91), Internat. Assn. for Protection Indsl. Property (exec. bd. 1989—), Assn. Corp. Patent Counsel (exec. com. 1982-84), Tau Beta Pi. Roman Catholic. Avocations: music, running. Intellectual property, Patent, Trademark and copyright. E-mail: ipconsulting@msn.com.

FIRESTONE, BRUCE MICHAEL, lawyer, educator; b. N.Y.C., June 20, 1946; s. Frederick and Sophie (Witzling) F. BA, Colgate U., 1968; MA, U. N.C., 1970, PhD, 1975; JD, Duke U., 1984. Bar: Wash. 1984. Instr. U. N.C., Chapel Hill, 1974-75; asst. prof. Clemson (S.C.) U., 1975-81; assoc. Perkins & Coie, Seattle, 1984-91; ptnr. Firestone, Landsman, Fleming, Dixon & Matson LLP, Seattle, 1991—. Editor Carolina Quar., Chapel Hill, 1973-75, S.C. Rev., 1976-80. Mem. Seattle Arts commn., 1986—92; pres. bd. dirs. Seattle Arts and Lectures, 1990—, Friends of Magnuson Pk. Mem. ABA, Wash. State Bar Assn., Seattle-King county Bar Assn., Order of Coif. Corporate, general, Mergers and acquisitions, Securities.

FIRESTONE, GARY, lawyer; b. Montreal, Quebec, Can., May 27, 1952; came to U.S., 1984; s. E. Harvey Firestone and Dorothy F. McCauley; m. M. Jane Burns, June 8, 1976; 1 child, Elliot T. BA, McGill U., 1974, MA, 1979; JD, U. Ariz., 1987. Bar: Oreg. 1987, Wash. 1994, U.S. Dist. Ct. Oreg. 1991, U.S. Dist. Ct. (We. Dist.) Wash. 1995, U.S. Ct. Appeals (9th and D.C. cirs.) 1990. Atty. Heller Ehrman White & McAuliffe, Portland, Oreg., 1989-93, Ramis, Crew, Corrigan & Bachrach, Portland, 1993—. Editor Ariz. J. Internat. Comp. Law, 1986-87. Land use and zoning (including planning), Municipal (including bonds). Office: Ramis Crew Corrigan & Bachrach 1727 NW Hoyt St Portland OR 97209-2226 E-mail: garyf@rccb.com.

FIRESTONE, GREGORY, mediator; b. N.Y.C., Feb. 25, 1950; s. Frederick and Bobbie S. Firestone; children: Beryl, Garrett, Lindsay. BS in psychology, Trinity Coll., Hartford, Conn., 1972; MA in psychology, U. South Fla., 1976, PhD in clinical and community psychology, 1978. Cert.: Fla. Supreme Ct. (Family, Dependency and County Ct. Mediator). Asst. prof., dept. psychiatry U. South Fla., Tampa, 1980—87, affiliate assoc. prof., dept. psychiatry, 1987—; pvt. practice psychologist and mediator Tampa, 1983—; dir. U. South Fla. Mediation Inst., 1994—2003, U. South Fla. Conflict Resolution Collaborative, 2003—. Vice chair, alternative dispute resolution rules com. Fla. Supreme Ct., Tallahassee, 2002—, mem. mediation and arbitration tng. com., 1993—2001; official observer Nat. Conf. Commrs. Uniform State Laws Uniform Mediation Act drafting com. Co-author: (video) Mediation Works: Make It Work For You, 1995; mem. editl. bd.: Family Ct. Rev., 1998—; co-guest editor (jour.) Family and Conciliation Ct. Rev., 2002. Mem.: APA, Fla. Acad. Profl. Mediators (diplomate), Assn. Conflict Resolution (adv. practitioner mem.), Acad. Family Mediators, Acad. Family Mediators (bd. dirs. 1999—2001), Assn. Family and Conciliation Cts. (bd. dirs. 1996—2001, pres. Fla. chpt. 2000—02), Phi Beta Kappa. Office: 2901 W Busch Blvd # 707 Tampa FL 33618 Office Fax: 813-908-6248. E-mail: firestoneg@aol.com.

FIRKSER, ROBERT MICHAEL, lawyer; b. Phila., Mar. 16, 1953; s. Benjamin and Agnes V. Firkser; m. Judith J. Farrell, June 24, 1978; children: Stephen, Ryan, David, Carolyn. BA, St. Joseph's Coll., 1975; JD, U. Miami, 1978. Bar: Pa. 1979, U.S. Dist. Ct. (ea. dist.) Pa. 1979, U.S. Ct. Appeals (3rd cir.) 1981, U.S. Supreme Ct. 1982, Ct. Common Pleas. Assoc.

Thomas R. Kimmel, Folcroft, Pa., 1978-80; ptnr. Kimmel & Firkser, Springfield, Pa., 1980-92, DelSordo, Firkser & Donze, Media, Pa., 1992-2000, DelSordo & Firkser, Media, 2000—. Editor: Del. County Legal Jour., 1985. Dir. Wallingford-Swarthmore (Pa.) Sch. Bd., 1991—, pres., 1996-97; founder, co-commr. daniel e. Murtaugh, Jr. Young Lawyers' Sect. Softball League; past bd. dirs. Child Guidance and Mental Health Clinic of Del. County, Inc., Del. County Immediate Unit. Mem. Pa. Bar Assn. (ho. of dels. 1983-86, real property and probate sect., civil litigation sect.), Pa. Trial Lawyers' Assn., Delaware County Bar Assn. (chmn. citizens' conf. com. 1985, jud. retention com. 1990, arbitration com. 1993—, civil trial practices com., civil rules com., civil justice adv. com., real estate practices com., civil legal edn. com., bd. dirs. 2001-), Delaware County Trial Lawyers Assn., Guy G. deFuria Am. in of Ct. (pres. 1993-94). General civil litigation, Personal injury (including property damage), Probate (including wills, trusts). Office: DelSordo & Firkser 333 W Baltimore Ave Media PA 19063-5625 Fax: 610-565-9853. E-mail: rfirkser@barristersclub.com.

FISCH, EDITH L. lawyer; b. N.Y.C., Mar. 3, 1923; d. Hyman and Clara L. Fisch; m. Steven Ludwig Werner, Dec. 14, 1963 (dec.). BA, Bklyn. Coll., 1945; LLB, Columbia U., 1948, LLM, 1949, J.Sc.D, 1950. Bar: N.Y. 1948, U.S. Supreme Ct. 1957. Grad. asst. Columbia U. Law Sch., N.Y.C., 1948, fellow in law, 1949-50; assoc. firm Conrad & Smith, N.Y.C., 1951-57; pvt. practice N.Y.C., 1957-62, 65—. Asst. prof. law N.Y. Law Sch., 1963-65; counsel firm Brodsky, Lenett & Altman, N.Y.C., 1973-75; pres. Lond Publs., 1958—; ednl. dir. Found. for CLE, 1964-95; editor N.Y.C. Charter and Adminstrv. Code, 1965-81; presenter lectures, seminars and courses for profl. groups. Author: The Cy Pres Doctrine in the U.S., 1950, (with others) State Laws on the Employment of Women, 1953, Lawyers in Industry, 1956, Fisch on New York Evidence, 1959, 2d edit., 1977, supplements, 1978—, (with others) Charities and Charitable Foundations, 1974; contbr. numerous articles to legal publs. County committeewoman 7th Dist. N.Y. Dem. Party, 1949-52; bd. dirs., treas. nat. women's com. Brandeis U., 1964-68. Mem. AAUW, N.Y. Women's Bar Assn. (pres. 1970-71, bd. dirs. 1971-73, adv. coun. 1974—), Nat. Assn. Women Lawyers, Assn. Bar City N.Y. (chmn. libr. com. 1991-94), Bklyn. Coll. Lawyers Group (rec. sec. 1961-63, bd. govs. 1963-65), Am. Arbitration Assn. (nat. panelist), Acad. Polit. Sci., Alumni Assn. Columbia U., Bklyn. Coll. Alumni Assn. Appellate, Probate (including wills, trusts). Home: 250 W 94th St New York NY 10025-6954 Office: PO Box D-3300 Pomona NY 10970

FISCH, JOSEPH, lawyer; b. N.Y.C., Apr. 7, 1939; s. Israel Ben Zion and Esther Leah (Spielvogel) F.; m. Norma Potter, Aug. 7, 1960; children: Adam Jeffrey, Jennifer Anne, Rachel Lynne. BA, Tufts U., 1960; JD, NYU, 1963, LLM in Taxation, 1969. Bar: N.J. 1964, U.S. Dist. Ct. N.J. 1964, U.S. Tax Ct. 1966, U.S. Supreme Ct. 1969, U.S. Ct. Appeals (3d cir.) 1971. Law clk. to judge N.J. Superior Ct., Jersey City, 1963-64; assoc. Hannock, Wiseman, Stern and Besser, Newark, 1964-65, Blume and Kalb, Newark, 1965-66; sole practice Somerset, N.J., 1966-87, Kendall Park, N.J., 1987—. Asst. prof. Rutgers U., New Brunswick, N.J., 1971-81; arbitrator Am. Arbitration Assn., 1969-97, N.J. Superior Ct., Somerville, 1985-89; atty. Franklin Twp. Rent Leveling Bd., Somerset, 1980-91; mem. malpractice panel N.J. Supreme Ct., 1980-84; atty. Franklin Twp. Bd. Adjustment, Somerset, 1991-2001. Contbr. articles to law jours. Pres. Franklin Twp. Jaycees, 1967-68, Franklin Housing and Neighborhood Devel. Corp., Somerset, 1975-78, Temple Beth El Men's Club, Somerset, 1971-72, trustee, 1970, 97—. Mem. ABA, N.J. Bar Assn. (chair gen. practice sect. 1990-91, Gen. Practitioner of Yr. 1992), Somerset County Bar Assn., Rotary (Franklin Twp. bd. dirs. 1987-88), Franklin Twp. Rep. Club (pres. 1999-2001). Republican. Jewish. Avocations: tennis, golf, skiing, sailing. State civil litigation, General practice, Property, real (including real estate development, water). Office: 3084 State Route 27 Ste 7 Kendall Park NJ 08824-1657 E-mail: fischjos@aol.com.

FISCHBACH, CHARLES PETER, railway executive consultant, lawyer, arbitrator, mediator; b. Apr. 3, 1939; s. Howard C. and Pauline Lillian (Wasserman) F.; m. Paula Rae Steinhorn, July 15, 1973. BS, U. Wis., 1960, JD, 1967; MA, Rutgers U., 1962. Bar: Wis. 1967, U.S. Supreme Ct. 1974. Pvt. practice, Madison, Wis., 1967-68; labor rels. rsch. analyst and cons. N.Y.C., 1968-70; asst. to exec. officer labor rels. and pers. N.Y.C. Transit Authority, 1970; labor rels. rsch. analyst N.Y.C., 1970-72; exec. dir. Classified Mcpl. Employees Assn. Balt. City, 1972-74; labor rels. cons./arbitrator Balt., 1974-77; dir. labor rels., chief labor rels. officer, spl. labor counsel Chgo., Rock Island and Pacific R.R. Co., 1977-81, dir. pers. and employee rels., spl. labor counsel, 1981-84; dir. adminstrn. and human resources Chgo. Pacific Corp., 1984-85. V.p. Rock Island Improvement Co., 1984—85; dir., arbitrator, mediator Peoria and Bureau Valley R.R. Co., 1985—; lectr. Am. Mgmt. Assn., Am. Arbitration Assn. Collective Bargaining Inst.; mem. editl. adv. panel Labor Rels. Bull. Aspen Pubs., Inc., 1999—; referee Nat. R.R. Adjustment Bd. Contbg. editor: The Railway Labor Act, 1995; mem. editl. adv. panel Labor Rels. Bull., 1999—; contbr. articles on labor rels. and arbitration to profl. jours. Mem. pub. sector labor rels. conf. bd. U. Md., 1973—77, Ill. Econ. Bd., 1988—90; mem. landlord-tenant law study commn. State of Md., 1976—77; mem. gov.'s commn. on sci. and tech. State of Ill., 1990—98; advisor Balt. City Charter Revision Commn., 1974—75, Balt. City Commn. on Aging, 1973—74; mem. Chgo. Workforce Bd. City of Chgo., 1999—, mem. Mayor's Task Force on Employment of People with Disabilities, 2002—; mem. coll. edn. adv. coun. Roosevelt U., 1990—93; mem. Chgo. postal customer adv. coun. U.S. Postal Svc., 1994—95; mem. bd. visitors dept. polit. sci. and LaFolette Sch. Pub. Affairs U. Wis., Madison, 2001—, vice chair, 2002—03; chair Com. on Support for Tchg. and Rsch., 2002—. Recipient Am. Jurisprudence prize in corp. law Joint Pubs. of Annotated Reports Sys., 1966, cert. for encouragement of vol. dispute settlement procedures Am. Arbitration Assn., 1981-84; named hon. fellow Harry S. Truman Libr. Inst., 1976. Mem.: ABA, Rutgers Alumni Assn., Wis. Alumni Assn., Am. Found. Automation and Employment, Friends of the Nat. Baseball Hall of Fame and Mus., Soc. Am. Baseball Rsch., Statue of Liberty -Ellis Island Found. (charter), Warner-Lambert (arbitration panel), Montgomery Ward Holding Corp. (alternative dispute resolutiion panel), Loewen Group Internat. (alternative dispute resolution panel), Herzog Transit Svcs./Transport Workers Union Am. (arbitration panel), Am. Airlines (Am. Eagle) and Air Line Pilots Assn. (mem. sys. bd. adjustment), United Air Lines and Internat. Assn. Machinists and Aerospace Workers Am. (mem. sys. bd. adjustment), Ill. Bd. Edn. Panel of Hearing Officers, Indsl. Rels. Rsch. Assn., Nat. Assn. R.R. Referees (regional v.p. 1996—2000), Ill. Pub. Employee Arbitration Mediation Panel, Nat. Mediation Bd. Register of Arbitrators, Fed. Mediation and Conciliation Svc. Roster of Arbitrators, State Bar Wis., Nat. Hist. Soc. Avocations: collecting commemorative coin series and first day medallic covers, collecting commemorative stamps, reading, baseball history and research, art. Office: 1122 N Clark St Ste 2303 Chicago IL 60610-2866 also: Ste 305-PMB 110 3455 Peachtree Industrial Blvd Duluth GA 30096-6501 Fax: 312-943-2539.

FISCHER, CÉDRIC HENRI, lawyer; s. Albert and Monique (Delmonte) Fischer; m. Thérence de Verdalle-La Romagère, Sept. 4, 1982; children: Marine, Quentin, Albéric, Clémence, Pierre-Céols. Law degree, U. Paris II, 1979, LLM, 1980, DEA law, 1982. Bar: Paris 1980. Assoc. Sur & Martin, Paris, 1980—81, Jacques Toutain's Law Office, Paris, 1982—84; founding ptnr. Fischer, Tandeau de Marsac Sur & Assocs, Paris, 1985—. Mem. Town Coun., Saint Céols, 1983—89. Master: Les Sorbonicoles; mem.: Cir. Union Interallied, New Cir. Union. Avocations: sailing, hunting. Corporate, general, Labor (including EEOC, Fair Labor Standards Act, labor-management relations, NLRB, OSHA), Commercial, consumer (including collections, credit). Office: Fischer Tandeau Marsac Sur & Assocs 46 Ave d'Léna Paris 75116 France Office Fax: 0033147239053. E-mail: cfischer@ftms-a.com.

FISCHER, DALE SUSAN, judge; b. East Orange, N.J., Oct. 17, 1951; d. Edward L. and Audrey (Tenner) F. Student, Dickinson Coll., 1969-70; BA magna cum laude, U. So. Fla., 1977; JD, Harvard U., 1980. Bar: Calif. 1980. Ptnr. Kindel & Anderson L.L.P., L.A., 1980-96; spl. counsel Heller Ehrman White & McAuliffe, L.A., 1996-97; judge L.A. Mcpl. Ct., 1997, L.A. Superior Ct., 2000. Faculty Nat. Inst. Trial Advocacy; lawyer in classroom Constl. Rights Found.; moderator, panelist How to Win Your Case with Depositions. Recipient Lawyer in Classroom award Constl. Rights Found. Mem. Nat. Assn. Women Judges, Am. Judicature Soc., Calif. Assn. Judges, So. Calif. Litigation Inn of Ct. (past pres.). Office: LA Superior Ct Dept 120 210 W Temple St Dept 120 Los Angeles CA 90012-3210 E-mail: dfischer@lasuperiorcourt.org.

FISCHER, DAVID CHARLES, lawyer; b. Columbia, S.C., Oct. 10, 1952; s. Emeric and Bernice (Cooper) F.; m. Vicki Joyce Stoller, Nov. 9, 1985; children: Adam, Jeremy. BA, Vanderbilt U., 1975; JD, Coll. William & Mary, 1978. Bar: Mich. 1978, N.Y. 1980. Lawyer GM, Detroit, 1978-79, N.Y.C., 1979-80; assoc. Finley Kumble Wagner Heine Underberg & Casey, N.Y.C., 1980-82, Burns Summit Rovins & Feldesman, N.Y.C., 1982-86; ptnr. Summit Rovins & Feldesman, N.Y.C., 1986-90, Loeb & Loeb, LLP, N.Y.C., 1990—; sec. Standard Microsystems Corp., 1998—2002. Achievements include patents in field. Corporate, general, Mergers and acquisitions, Securities. E-mail: dfischer@loeb.com.

FISCHER, DAVID JON, lawyer; b. Danville, Ill., July 27, 1952; s. Oscar Ralph and Sarah Pauline (Pomerantz) F. BA, U. Miami, 1974, JD, 1977. Bar: Fla. 1977, Iowa 1978, (mid. dist.) Fla. 1993, U.S. Ct. Appeals (8th cir.) 1978, U.S. Ct. Appeals (D.C. cir.) 1979, U.S. Ct. Appeals (llth cir.) 1984, U.S. Tax Ct. 1987, Ga. 1989, U.S. Dist. Ct. (no. dist.) Ga. 1990, U.S. Supreme Ct. 1990, U.S. Dist. Ct. (mid. dist.) Fla., 1993. Atty. Iowa Dept. Social Svcs., Des Moines, 1978; assoc. Parrish & Del Gallo P.C., Des Moines, 1978-79, Donald M. Murtha & Assocs., Washington, 1979-80; assoc. editor Lawyers Coop. Pub. Co., Washington, 1980-82; pvt. practice law Washington, 1982-83, Des Moines, 1983-84, Atlanta, 1984-93; pvt. practice Tampa, Fla., 1993; asst. dist. legal counsel Fla. Dept. Health and Rehab. Svcs., Largo, 1993-95; pvt. practice law Atlanta, 1995-2000; case law editor LexisNexis Group, 2001—. Part-time atty. Fla. Dept. of Children and Families, 1996-2000; prof. John Marshall Law Sch., Atlanta, 1986-88; instr. legal studies program dept. ins. and risk mgmt. Ga. State U., 1988-93, instr. aviation adminstrn. program Coll. Pub. and Urban Affairs, 1989-93; apptd. gen. counsel Techwerks, Inc., Mo., 1990-92; instr. Bridge the Gap seminar, Inst. CLE in Ga., 1993; presenter State of Fla. Dept. Health and Rehabilitative Svcs. Dist. Legal Counsel Workshop, 1994, 96, 97; spkr. Clearwater Bar Assn., 1993, 94, 95. Author: The Aeronaut's Law Handbook, 1986, (with others) Georgia Corporate Practice Forms for the Small Business Attorney, 1992; contbg. editor Balloon Life mag., 1986-96; editor: (suppl.) Georgia Corporate Forms, 1993—, Florida Criminal Sentencing, 1997-99; editor: Georgia Corporate Forms, 2d edit., 1999. Vol. liaison Atlanta Com. for the Olympic Games, 1991-92. Mem. ABA (sect. com. 1980-82), Fed. Bar Assn., Iowa Bar Assn., State Bar Ga., Atlanta Bar Assn., Fla. Bar Assn., D.C. Bar Assn., Polk County Bar Assn., Pros. Attys. Coun. Ga. (tech. editor Computer Crime Jour.), U. of Miami Alumni Assn., Balloon Fedn. Am. (chmn. com. 1986-91), Carolinas Balloon Assn., Ga. Balloon Assn. (chmn. com. 1985-90), Chesapeake Balloon Assn., Great Ea. Balloon Assn., Alpha Epsilon Pi (hon., faculty advisor). Jewish. Avocations: hot air balloon pilot, writing, competitive sports. General civil litigation, Computer, Corporate, general. E-mail: schnauzers@mindspring.com., davidjon.fischer@lexisnexis.com.

FISCHER, ERIC ROBERT, lawyer, educator; b. N.Y.C., Aug. 22, 1945; s. Maurice and Pauline (Pilcer) F.; m. Anita Ellen Cohen, July 31, 1977; children: Joshua, Lauren BA, U. Pa., 1967; MBA, JD, Stanford U., 1971; LLM in Taxation, Boston U., 1982. Bar: N.Y. 1975, Mass. 1977. Assoc. Fried, Frank, Harris, Shriver & Jacobson, N.Y.C., 1971-76; v.p., asst. gen. counsel, asst. sec. First Nat. Bank of Boston, 1976-86; exec. v.p., gen. counsel, corp. sec. UST Corp., Boston, 1986-2000; sr. counsel Goodwin Procter LLP, Boston, 2000—02, ptnr., 2002—. Lectr. on law Boston U. Law Sch., 1984— Trustee Boston Lyric Opera, Inc., 1989-2001; bd. dirs. Boston Area Youth Soccer, 1989-90, Spirit of Mass. Boys Soccer Club, 1991-97. Mem. ABA (banking law com., chmn. cmty. banking subcom., banking law com.), Bank Capital Markets Assn. (chmn. banking law subcom. 1984-90), UN Assn. Boston (treas. 1978-91), New Eng. Legal Found. (bd. dirs. 1990-92). Jewish. Banking, Corporate, general, Securities. Home: 205 Waban Ave Waban MA 02468-2101 Office: Goodwin Procter Exchange Pl Boston MA 02109 E-mail: efischer@goodwinprocter.com.

FISCHER, MARK ALAN, lawyer, law educator; b. Evanston, Ill., Sept. 28, 1950; s. Lee Earle and Zelda (Dlugo) F. BA magna cum laude, Emerson Coll., 1975; JD, Boston Coll., 1980. Bar: Mass. 1980, U.S. Dist. Ct. Mass. 1980, U.S. Ct. Appeals (1st cir.) Mass. 1985. Sole practice, Cambridge, Mass., 1980-83; mem. Cohen & Burg, Boston, 1983-86; ptnr. Wolf, Greenfield & Sacks, Boston, 1986-96, Palmer & Dodge, Boston, 1996—2002, Fish & Richardson, Boston, 2002—. Lectr. copyright and trademark law Boston Coll. Law Sch., 1985—87; lectr. entertainment law New Eng. Sch. Law, Boston, 1983—93; assoc. prof. music law Berklee Coll. Music, 1989—90, 1994—95; lectr. intellectual property Northeastern Sch. Law, Boston, 1986; mem. adj. faculty advanced copyright law Suffolk U. Law Sch., 1999—2002. Contbr. articles to profl. jours.; columnist New Eng. Entertainment Digest, 1982-90; co-editor: Perle & Williams on Publishing Law, (3rd edit.). Mem. ABA, Mass. Bar Assn., Boston Patent Law Assn. (chmn. copyright law com., 1985-96), Copyright Soc. U.S.A. (trustee 1997-2000), Copyright Soc. New Eng. (co-founder). Computer, Entertainment, Trademark and copyright. Office: Fish & Richardson 225 Franklin St Boston MA 02110

FISCHER, MARK DAVID, lawyer; b. Manhasset, NY, May 2, 1961; s. Martin Joseph and Greta Priscilla Fischer; m. Marlene Kern, Aug. 16, 1987; children: Eric, Jonah, Isaac. BA, Brandeis U., 1983; JD, Boston U., 1987. Bar: Mass. 1987, N.Y. 1988, U.S. Dist. Ct. (so. and ea. dists.) N.Y. 1988. Assoc. Nixon. Hargrave, Devans & Doyle, N.Y.C., 1987—89, Rosenman & Colin, N.Y.C., 1989—96, ptnr., 1996—99; v.p., gen. counsel, sec. Phllips-Van Heusen Corp., N.Y.C., 1999—. V.p. Whippoorwill Hills Home Owners Assn., Armonk, NY, 2001—02; mem. nat. alumni bd. Brandeis U., Waltham, Mass., 2001—; coach Am. Youth Soccer Assn., Armonk, 1998—. Mem.: ABA, Am. Soc. Corp. Secs. (mem. securities law com. 2001—), Am. Corp. Counsel Assn. Corporate, general, Securities, Mergers and acquisitions. Office: Phillips-Van Heusen Corp 200 Madison Ave New York NY 10016 Fax: 212-381-3970. E-mail: markfischer@pvh.com.

FISCHER, NORA BARRY, lawyer; b. Pitts., June 13, 1951; d. Michael T. and Olga G. (Stipetich) Barry; m. Donald R. Fischer, Jan. 3, 1976; children: Erin, Lauren, Adam. BA magna cum laude, St. Mary's Coll., Notre Dame, Ind., 1973; JD, U. Notre Dame, 1976. Bar: Ill. 1976, Pa. 1977, U.S. Dist. Ct. (no. dist.) Ill. 1977, U.S. Dist. Ct. (we. dist.) Pa. 1977, U.S. Ct. Appeals (3rd cir.) 1981, U.S. Supreme Ct. 1982, W.Va. 1990, U.S. Dist. Ct. (so. dist.) W.Va. 1990, U.S. Dist. Ct. (no dist.) W.Va. 2002. Legal editor Callaghan's, Chgo., 1976-77; assoc. Meyer, Darragh, Buckler, Bebenek & Eck, Pitts., 1977-80, jr. ptnr., 1980-82, ptnr., 1983-92, mem. exec. com., 1987-89; ptnr. Pietragallo Bosick & Gordon, Pitts., 1992—, mem. practice mgmt. com., 1996—2001. Mem. Pitts. Allegheny Co. Pvt. Industry Coun., 1982-84. Mem.: ABA, Acad. Trial Lawyers (v.p.), Allegheny County Bar Assn. Found., Exec. Womens Coun., Ins. Women Pitts., Allegheny County Bar Assn, (med.-legal com. 1984—89, interprofl. code com. 1985—86, judiciary com. 1985—88, health law sect. 1990—92, civil litigation coun. 1990—93, health law sect. vice chair 1992—93, health law sect chair 1994, bd. govs., women in law com., edn. subcom.), Pa. Bar Assn. (civil litigation coun. 1985—87, ins. and surety law com. 1991), Am. Inns of Court (pres. 1999—2001). Democrat. Roman Catholic. Federal civil litigation, State civil litigation. Office: Pietragallo Bosick & Gordon 3800 The Oxford Ctr Pittsburgh PA 15219

FISCHER, RICHARD SAMUEL, lawyer; b. Buffalo, July 31, 1937; s. Richard D. and Isabel B. (Van Dorn) F.; m. Malinda Berry, June 3, 1960; children: Richard B., Van D. AB, Harvard U., 1959, JD, 1963. Bar: N.Y. 1963, Okla. 1996. Law clk N.Y. Ct. Appeals, Albany, 1963-65; assoc. Nixon, Hargrave, Devans & Doyle, Rochester, N.Y., 1965-71, ptnr., 1972-95, mem. policy com., 1991-95, head Rochester office, 1992-95; mem. faculty Okla. State U., Stillwater, 1997—2002. Bd. dirs. Cowboy Golf, Inc. Past chair, trustee Highland Hosp.; past pres. Harley Sch.; past bd. dirs. Rochester Area Hosp. Corp., Primary Mental Health Project; bd. dirs. United Way, Stillwater; past pres. Friends of Music and Allied Arts, 2000-01, bd. United Way. Mem. ABA, N.Y. State Bar Assn. (past chmn. com. ins. programs and retirement plans), Monroe County Bar Assn., NYU Inst. Fed. Taxation (adv. com.), Okla. Bar Assn. Clubs: Genessee Valley, Country Club of Rochester (N.Y.), Stillwater Country Club, Karsten Creek Golf Club (dir.). Health, Pension, profit-sharing, and employee benefits, Personal income taxation. Office: PO Box 1897 Stillwater OK 74076-1897

FISCHER, SUSANNA FREDERICK, law educator; b. Balt. d. David Hackett and Judith (Hummel) Fischer; m. Erik Mueller, Dec. 29, 1997. AB, Princeton U., 1983; BA, U. Oxford, Eng., 1987; LLM, U. Va., 1995. Bar: Eng. 1988, Wales 1988, N.Y. 1996. Pupil barrister Queen Elizabeth Bldgs., London, 1988—89, Brick Ct. Chambers, London, 1989; barrister 5 Raymond Bldgs., London, 1989—94; assoc. Skadden, Arps, Slate, Meagher & Flom, N.Y.C., 1996, Paul, Hastings, Jarofsky & Walter, N.Y.C., 1997—99; asst. prof. Cath. U. Am., Washington, 1999—. Contbr. articles to profl. jours. Mem.: ABA, N.Y. State Bar Assn., Lansdowne Club. Episcopalian. Office: Cath U Am Cardinal Station Washington DC 20064

FISCHER, THEODORE DAVID, retired lawyer; b. Pitts., Pa., Oct. 21, 1933; s. Samuel M. and Beatrice (Stewart) Fischer; m. Joan F. Friedman, Aug. 29, 1954; children: Bruce, Steven, Sandra, Betsy. BA, U. Pitts., 1955, LLB, 1958, SJD (hon.) , 1962. Bar: Pa. 1959, Fla. 1978, U.S. Dist. Ct. (we. dist.) Pa. 1959. Ptnr. Markel, Markel, Levenson & Fischer, Pitts., 1961—69, Motor Inn Investors, Pitts., 1971—91, Guren, Merritt, Fischer, Udell, Lasky, Sogg & Cohen, Miami, Fla., 1979—82; counsel Bercuson, Cahan, Weksler & Lasky, Miami, Fla., 1982—87; prin. In-Rel Group of Cos., 1987—2002; ret., 2002. Editor: U. Pitts. Law Rev., 1958; contbr. articles to profl. jours. Bd. dirs. Marion-Citrus Mental Health Ctr. and Mental Health Found. Mem.: Score, Order of Coif. Office: 3180 N Pinelake Village Pt Lecanto FL 34461-8139 E-mail: tfische2@tampabay.rr.com.

FISCHOFF, GARY CHARLES, lawyer; b. Manhasset, N.Y., Nov. 23, 1954; s. Harold and Ann (Yablon) F.; m. Linda Lee Sacca, Nov. 22, 1985 (div. Nov. 2002); 1 child, Lisa Frances. BA, U. Buffalo, 1976; JD, St. John's U., Jamaica, N.Y., 1983. Bar: N.J. 1983, U.S. Dist. Ct. N.J. 1983, N.Y. 1984, U.S. Dist. Ct. (so. and ea. dists.) N.Y. 1985, U.S. Dist. Ct. (no. and we. dist.) N.Y., U.S. Ct. Appeals (2d cir.) 1988. Asst. treas. IAP, Inc., Lyndhurst, N.J., 1980-82; assoc. Hannoch Weisman, Roseland, N.J., 1983-85; ptnr. Fischoff Gelberg & Director, Garden City, N.Y., 1985-96, Fischoff & Assocs., Garden City, 1996—, Steinberg, Fineo, Berger, Barone & Fischoff, Garden City, NY, 2003—. Lectr. seminar Nat. Bus. Inst., Westbury, N.Y., 1990, 91, Practicing Law Inst., 1992, 93, N.Y. State Bar Assn., 1995. Rep. Greentree Homeowners Assn., Northport, N.Y., 1988-89; trustee Suffolk County Vanderbilt Mus., 1994-2002, corp. sec., 1995-97, treas. 1997-99, 1st v.p., 1999-2002. Mem. Am. Bankruptcy Bd. Cert. (cert. bus. bankruptcy and consumer bankruptcy), N.Y. State Bar Assn. (real property sect., seminar lectr. 1995, Practicing Law Inst., continuing legal edn. lectr. 1992, 93), Nassau County Bar Assn. (mem. bankruptcy com., jud. liaison 1988-89). Jewish. Avocation: bicycling. Bankruptcy, General civil litigation, Property, real (including real estate development, water). Office: Steinberg Fineo Berger Barone & Fischoff 1001 Franklin Ave Garden City NY 11530

FISH, PAUL MATHEW, lawyer; b. N.Y.C., Sept. 27, 1947; s. Louis and Shirley (Aaronowitz) F.; m. Patrice Ellen Schooley, Nov. 27, 1976. BA, Drake U., 1969; JD, Harvey U., 1972. Bar: N.Mex. 1972, U.S. Dist. Ct. N.Mex. 1972, U.S. Ct. Appeals (10th cir.) 1972, U.S. Ct. Appeals (fed. cir.) 1999, Ct. of Fed. Claims, 1995, U.S. Supreme Ct. 1993. Assoc. Cotter, Atkinson, Campbell, Kelsey & Hanna, Albuquerque, 1972-74; ptnr. Modrall, Sperling, Roehl, Harris & Sisk, P.A., Albuquerque, 1974—. Chmn. Chpt. 11 Local Rules Com., Albuquerque, 1981, bankruptcy law sect. N.Mex. State Bar, Albuquerque, 1983. Mem. ABA, N.Mex. Bar Assn., Albuquerque Bar Assn., Am. Coll. Bankruptcy. Avocation: raising wine grapes. Banking, Bankruptcy, Commercial, contracts (including sales of goods; commercial financing). Home: 50 Tunnel Springs Rd Placitas NM 87043 Office: Modrall Law Firm PO Box 2168 Albuquerque NM 87103-2168 E-mail: pmf@modrall.com.

FISHBEIN, PETER MELVIN, lawyer; b. N.Y.C., June 20, 1934; s. Arthur L. and Lotta (Chary) F.; m. Bette Klinghoffer, June 16, 1957; children: Stephen, Bruce, Gregory. BA magna cum laude, Dartmouth Coll., 1955; JD, Harvard U., 1958. Bar: N.Y. 1959, U.S. Supreme Ct. 1973. Note editor Harvard Law Rev., Cambridge, Mass., 1956-58; law clk. to Justice William J. Brennan, Jr. U.S. Supreme Ct., Washington, 1958-59; dep. sec. gen. Internat. Peace Corps., Washington, 1962-64; ptnr. Kaye, Scholer LLP, N.Y.C., 1967—2002, mng. ptnr., 1984-91; chief counsel N.Y. State Constl. Conv., Albany, 1967; mem. Presdl. Commn. to Nominate Candidates for Fed. Ct. of Appeals, N.Y.C., 1980. Adj. prof. constl. law NYU Law Sch., 1970-84. Contbr. articles to profl. jours. Trustee Goddard Coll., 1967—75, Fedn. Jewish Philanthropies, N.Y.C., 1975—81, Citizen's Budget Comm., 1995—99; mem. N.Y. State Gov.'s Bd. Pub. Disclosure, Albany, 1975—77; mgr. Justice Arthur J. Goldberg's Campaign for Gov., 1970; bd. dirs. Health Care Chaplaincy, 1993—99, Brennan Ctr. for Justice, 1995—, I Have A Dream Found., 2001—, White Plains Hosp., 2002—. Recipient Disting. Cmty. Svc. award Brandels U., Jurisprudence award Am. Ort. Fellow Am. Coll. Trial Lawyers, Am. Bar Found.; mem. ABA, Assn. of Bar of City of N.Y., Harvard Club (N.Y.), Beach Point Club (bd. govs. 1981-86), Phi Beta Kappa General civil litigation. Home: 101 Woodlands Rd Harrison NY 10528-1423 Office: Kaye Scholer LLP 425 Park Ave New York NY 10022-3506

FISHBURNE, BENJAMIN P., III, lawyer; b. South Bend, Ind., Nov. 14, 1943; s. Benjamin Postell and Peggy (Gahan) F.; m. Edith E., Aug. 5, 1983. BA cum laude, U. Notre Dame, 1965; JD, U. Va., 1968. Bar: U.S. Ct. Mil. Appeals 1968, U.S. Army Ct. Mil. Rev. 1968, D.C. 1971. Capt. JAG Corps US Army, 1968-72; atty. Surrey & Morse, Washington, 1968, ptnr., 1975, mng. ptnr., 1981-84; ptnr. Jones, Day, Reavis & Pogue, 1986, ptnr.-in-charge Hong Kong office, 1986-91, ptnr., 1991-93, Winston & Strawn, Washington, 1993—. Gen. counsel Nat. Coun. U.S.-China Trade, 1981—87, assoc. coun., 1987—89, chmn. legal com., 1994—2001; mem. adv. com. China-U.S. Conciliation Ctr., 1993—; mem. Am. Arbitration Assn. spl. corp. com. East-West trade arbitration, 1973—79; mem. nat. coun. U.S.-China Trade Investment Del. to China; alt. mem. UN Assn.'s Nat. Policy panel study U.S.-China Rels., 1979; spkr. in field. Contbr. articles to profl. jours. Co-chmn. Am. C. of C. Hong Kong legal com., 1990, mem. bd. govs., 1991; mem. bd. advisors Johns Hopkins Nanjing Ctr., 1986-97. Mem.: Order of Coif. Alternative dispute resolution, Private international, Mergers and acquisitions. Home: 5535 Nevada Ave NW Washington DC 20015-1768 Office: Winston & Strawn 1400 L St NW Washington DC 20005-3508 E-mail: bfishbur@winston.com.

FISHER, ANN LEWIS, judge; b. Reading, Pa., Mar. 31, 1948; d. William E. and Florence (Makowiecki) Lewis; m. Donald E. Fisher, Dec. 27, 1965 (div. July 1986); children: Caroline E., Catherine E., John Michael (dec.); m. David H. DeBlasio, May 28, 1988; 1 child, Michael Joseph DeBlasio. BS in Liberal Studies, Oreg. State U., 1975; JD, Willamette U., 1983. Bar: Oreg. 1984, U.S. Dist. Ct. Oreg. 1984, U.S. Ct. Appeals (9th cir.) 1984, Wash. 1987, U.S. Dist. Ct. (we. dist.) Wash. 1987, U.S. Dist. Ct. (ea. dist.) Wash. 1996, U.S. Ct. Appeals (fed. cir.) 1996. Atty. Spears, Lubersky, Portland, Oreg., 1983-85, Greene & Markley, Portland, Oreg., 1985-89; asst. gen. counsel Portland GE, 1988-93; atty. Schwabe, Williamson & Wyatt, Portland, 1993-96; founder Ann L. Fisher Legal and Consulting Svcs., Portland, 1996—. Pro tem judge Multnomah County Cir. Ct., Portland, 1995—; spkr. on corp. ethics, 1993-95; spkr. on energy issues, 1997—. Contbg. author: (treatise) ABA Year in Review, 1994, 95, Fed. Energy Bar Yr. Rev., 1997, 2000. Recipient Mem. of Yr. award, Bldg. Owners and Mgrs., Portland, 2001. Mem.: FBA (vice chair gas pipelines com. 1994—96, vice chair electric power com. sect. natural resources, energy and env), ABA, Builder Owners and Mgrs., N.W. Energy Assn. (sec.-treas. 1999—2000, Mem. of Yr. award 2001), Fed. Energy Bar Assn. (electric utility regulation com. 1996—99, ethics com. 1999—), Multnomah Bar Assn. (membership com. 1987—89, Multnomah Lawyer publ. com. 1994—96, chair 1995—96, professionalism com. 1997—99), Oreg. Bar Assn. (ins. and bar sponsored program com. 1985—87, sec. 1986—87, chair 1987—88, MCLE bd. 1991—94, Disciplinary bd. Region 5 1991—97, sec. 1992—93, chair 1993—94, 1996—97, ethics com. 1998—2001, chair utility sect. 2001—03), Oreg. State Bar (legis. exec. com. on adminstrv. law sect. 2002—03), Wash. State Bar Assn. Avocations: reading, writing, computers, golf, family activities. Office: Ann L Fisher Legal and Cons Svcs 1425 SW 20th Ave Ste 202 Portland OR 97201-2485 Fax: (503) 223-2305. E-mail: afisher1@qwest.net., annfisher@annfisherlaw.com.

FISHER, BARRY ALAN, lawyer; b. L.A., May 15, 1943; s. Harry Benjamin and Fay Doris (Sternfeld) F.; m. Susan E. Landman, June 16, 1968; children: J. Benjamin, Jonathan J., Robert A. A.B., UCLA, 1965, J.D., 1968. Bar: Alaska 1969, R.I. 1969 (spl.), Calif. 1971, U.S. Supreme Ct. 1972. law clk. to chief justice Alaska, 1968-69; Reginald Heber Smith fellow U. Pa., Law Sch., 1969-71; staff counsel Sierra Club Legal Def. Fund, San Francisco, 1972-74; mem. Fleishman, Brown, Weston & Rhode, Beverly Hills, Calif., 1974-77; ptnr. Fleishman, Fisher & Moest (now Fleishman & Fisher), L.A., 1977—; v.p. Human Rights Advs. Internat.; justice of peace, R.I., 1971; speaker profl. confs. Bd. dirs. Constitutions Rsch. Ctr., Gypsy Lore Soc., West side Urban Forum. Contbr. articles to profl. jours. Mem. ABA (co-chair first amendment com., co-chair nat. inst. on tort and religion, chair religious freedom subcom., vice chair 1st Ammendment com.), Calif. Acad. Appellate Lawyers, World Assn. Lawyers, Judges. Contbg. author Government Intervention in Religious Affairs, 1982; mem. adv. bd. Religious Freedom Reporter. Federal civil litigation, Constitutional, Environmental. Office: Fleishman & Fisher 1875 Century Park E Ste 2130 Los Angeles CA 90067-1736

FISHER, BENJAMIN CHATBURN, lawyer; b. Coos Bay, Oreg., Feb. 6, 1923; s. Benjamin S. and Catherine Selina (Chatburn) F.; m. Jean L. Whiting, June 30, 1951; children: John, Richard, Robert. AB with honors, U. Ill., 1948; JD magna cum laude, Harvard U., 1951. Bar: D.C. 1951. Law clk. to Hon. Learned Hand U.S. Ct. Appeals 2d cir., N.Y.C., 1951-52; with Fisher, Wayland, Cooper, Leader & Zaragoza, Washington, 1952-2000; sr. counsel Shaw, Pittman, Washington, 2000—. Mem. edn. appeal bd. U.S. Office Edn., 1973-83; mem. Adminstrv. Conf. U.S., 1970-76; U.S. del. Plenipotentiary Conf. Internat. Telecomm. Union, Nice, France, 1989, Geneva, 1992, Kyoto, Japan, 1994, Mpls., 1998, Marrakesh, Morocco, 2002; mem. U.S. del. World Radio Conf., Torremolinos, Spain, 1992, Geneva, 1995, 97; mem. nat. com. radio comm. sect., 1989—; chmn. bd. dirs. U.S. Internat. Telecomm. Union Assn., 2000—. Bd. dirs. Boys and Girls Clubs of Greater Washington, 1990—; bd. govs. Sigma Chi Found., 1991—. Mem. ABA (chmn. sect. adminstrv. law 1968-69, mem. ho. of dels. 1970-72, 73-75), Fed. Commn. Bar Assn. (pres. 1967-68), D.C. Bar Assn., Am. Law Inst., Soc. Satellite Profls. (chmn. 1983-85, bd. dirs. 1986-93, gen. counsel 1993—), Rotary (bd. dirs. Washington Club 1980-85, pres. 1983-84), Phi Beta Kappa, Phi Kappa Phi. Administrative and regulatory, Communications, Private international. Home: 5118 Cammack Dr Bethesda MD 20816-2902 Office: 2300 N St NW Washington DC 20037-1128 E-mail: ben.fisher@shawpittman.com.

FISHER, CHERYL SMITH, lawyer; b. Corning, N.Y., Sept. 4, 1951; d. Norman Albert and Betty (Manzella) Smith; 1 child: Daniel Terence. BA cum laude, SUNY, Oswego, 1973; JD cum laude, SUNY, Buffalo, 1976. Bar: N.Y. 1977, U.S. dist. Ct. (we. dist.) N.Y. 1977, U.S. Ct. Appeals (2d cir.) 1980, U.S. Supreme Ct. 1992. Assoc. Runfola, Birzon & Renda, Buffalo, 1976-77, Kavinoky Cook et al, Buffalo, 1977-79; asst. U.S. Atty. Western Dist. N.Y., Buffalo, 1979-84; assoc. Cohen Swados Wright Hanifin Bradford & Brett, Buffalo, 1984-86, Magavern & Magavern, Buffalo, 1986-87; ptnr. Magavern, Magavern & Grimm, 1988—. Spl. asst. U.S. atty. Dept. Justice, Buffalo, 1984. Pres. Cathedral Park Counseling Svc., Inc., Buffalo, 1979—83; mem. Civil Justice Reform Act, 1993—96, adv. panel, 1993—98; chmn. Lord of Life Adult and Child Svcs., 1999—2002; mem. vestry St. Paul's Cathedral, Buffalo, 1979—82, 1984—87, 2002—05; mem. bd. dirs. Child and Family Svc. Erie County, Buffalo, 1982—, chmn. bd. dirs., 1993—96; bd. dirs. Lord of Life Adult and Child Svcs., 1997—. Recipient Bishop Lauriston Scaife award, Episcopal Cmty. Svcs., 1999, John N. Walsh Jr. award, Child & Family Svcs. of Erie County, 2000. Mem. N.Y. State Bar Assn. (com. on profl. ethics), Erie County Bar Assn. (bd. dirs. 1996-99), N.Y. State Women's Bar Assn., Women Lawyers Assn., Alpha Psi Omega. Democrat. Episcopalian. Bankruptcy, Federal civil litigation, General civil litigation. Home: 306 Highland Ave Buffalo NY 14222-1751 Office: Law Offices 1100 Rand Building Bldg Buffalo NY 14203-1911 E-mail: cfisher@magavern.com.

FISHER, D. MICHAEL, state attorney general; b. Pitts., Nov. 7, 1944; s. C. Francis and Dolores (Darby) Fisher; m. Carol Hudak, Aug. 15, 1973; children: Michelle Lynn, Brett Michael. AB, Georgetown U., 1966; JD, Georgetown Law Ctr., 1969. Bar: Pa. 1970. Asst. dist. atty. Allegheny County, Pitts., 1970—74; rep. Pa. Ho. of Reps., Harrisburg, 1974—80; mem. Pa. Senate, Harrisburg, 1980—97; ptnr. Houston Harbaugh, Pitts., 1984—97; atty. gen. Commonwealth of Pa., Harrisburg, 1997—. Chmn. House Subcom. on Crime and Corrections, 1979—80, Senate Environ. Resources & Energy, 1981—90, Senate Majority Policy Com., 1988—90, Senate Rep. Caucus, 1992—; vice-chmn. Senate Jud. Com., 1981—90; mem. Majority Whip, 1990—96. Contbr. articles to profl. jours. Active Environ. Quality Bd., 1980—90, Pa. Commn. on Crime and Delinquency, 1979—; mem. Pa. Security Task Force, 2001—; chmn. Office of Nat. Drug Control Policy's Phila./Camden High Intensity Drug Trafficking Area, 2003—; mem. exec. working group for fed., state and local prosecutorial rels. U.S. Dept. Justice, 2001—; v.p. Nat. Assn. Attys. Gen. Exec. Bd., 2000—01; Rep. candidate for lt. gov. State of Pa., 1986; active Pa. Gov.'s Energy Coun., 1981—86, Pa. Energy Devel. Authority, 1984—86; del. Rep. Nat. Conv., 1988, 1992; Rep. nominee for gov. State of Pa., 2002; bd. dirs. Am. Legacy Found., 2003. Named Man of Yr., Upper St. Clair Rep. Club, 1980, Vector's Law & Govt., 1991; named one of Outstanding Young Men Am., 1977—79. Mem.: Pa. Bar Assn., Bethel Park Chamber, Rotary, Am. Legion, Elks. Republican. Roman Catholic. Avocations: golf, hockey, football. Office: Atty Gen 16 Strawberry Sq Harrisburg PA 17120

FISHER, EDWIN H. lawyer; b. York, Pa., Apr. 8, 1946; s. Gordon H. and Lucy (Warner) F.; m. Sara Rankey, May 23, 1973 (wid. Jan. 1994). BSBA, Pa. State U., 1968; JD, South Tex. Coll. of Law, Houston, 1976. Acct./tax acct. M.W. Kellogg Co., Houston, 1969-72; tax acct. Storm Drilling & Marine, Houston, 1972-74; tax mgr. Oceaneering Internat., Inc., Houston, 1974-78, Raymond Internat. Builders, Houston, 1978-79; pvt. practice Houston, 1979-81, Brenham, Tex., 1981—. V.p., sec. Brenham Abstract & Title Co., 1991—. 1st vice-chmn. Vol. Svcs. Coun., Brenham, 1994—; mem. ethics com. Brenham State Sch., 1996—. Recipient Star award Tex. Dept. Mental Health, 1996, cert. recognition Tax Execs. Inst., Bloomington, Ind., 1972. Mem. Lions (treas. Chappell Hill club 1994—), Exch. Club of Brenham (sec., bd. dirs. 1982-92). Probate (including wills, trusts), Property, real (including real estate development, water), Taxation, general. Office: 205 N Market St Brenham TX 77833-3215

FISHER, JAMES R. lawyer; b. South Bend, Ind., Apr. 15, 1947; s. Russell Humphries and Virginia Opal (Maple) F.; m. Cynthia Ann Winters, Aug. 14, 1971; children: Gabriel Christopher, Cory Andrew. AB in Psychology, Ind. U., 1969, JD summa cum laude, 1972. Bar: Ind. 1972, U.S. Dist. Ct. (so. dist.) Ind. 1972. Ptnr. Ice Miller, Indpls., 1971—. Co-author: Personal Injury Law and Practicesol. 23 of Indiana Practico series; contbr. articles to legal publs. Mem. ATLA, Ind. Bar Assn., Ind. Trial Lawyers Assn., Order of Coif. Federal civil litigation, State civil litigation, Personal injury (including property damage). Office: Ice Miller 1 Am Sq PO Box 82001 Indianapolis IN 46282 E-mail: james.fisher@icemiller.com.

FISHER, JOSEPH FREILER, lawyer; b. Highland Park, Ill., Dec. 25, 1955; s. Milton Leonard and Jean (Freiler) F. BA, Lake Forest Coll., 1978; JD, Northwestern U., 1981; MBA, U. Chgo., 1990. Bar: Ill. 1982, U.S. Dist. Ct. (no. dist.) Ill. 1982, U.S. Ct. Appeals (7th cir.) 1982, U.S. Tax Ct. 1985; lic. real estate broker, Ill. 1986. Assoc. Frankel, McKay & Orlikoff, Chgo., 1981-82, Altheimer & Gray, Chgo., 1983-85, Schwartz & Freeman, 1985; sole practice Chgo., 1985—. Mem. ABA, Ill. Bar Assn. Chgo. Bar Assn. Clubs: Cliffdwellers (Chgo.). Democrat. Jewish. Bankruptcy, Commercial, consumer (including collections, credit).

FISHER, JOY DEBORAH, lawyer; b. Chgo., Mar. 15, 1952; d. J. Barry and Rochelle Barbara (Levin) F.; m. Arthur Walter Stawinski, Nov. 2, 1979; 1 child, Steven Lee Fisher-Stawinski; step children: Kathryn, Elizabeth Kline. BA, U. Ill., 1973, JD, 1976. Bar: Ill. Supreme Ct. 1976, Fed. Dist. Ct. (no. dist.) Ill. 1976. With Fisher & Sherman, Chgo., 1976-78; ptnr. J.B. Fisher & J.D. Fisher, Chgo., 1978-87; pvt. practice Chgo., 1987—99, Buffalo Grove, Ill., 1987—99, Long Grove, Ill., 1999—. Contract atty. Ill. Sec. State, Chgo., 1981-83; mem. real estate panel Am. Arbitration Assn., Chgo., 1982-92; v.p. for legal counsel Discovery Sci. Edn. Found.; spkr. in field. Contbr. articles to profl. jours. Vol. atty. Free Women's Legal Clinic, Chgo., 1976-79; mem. steering com. Com. for ERA, Chgo., 1976-78; pro bono legal counsel for misc. non-profit orgns. and abused women, Cook County, Ill., 1976—; v.p. for legal counsel Discovery Learning Found., 1990-94; elected mem., sec. Bd. Edn. Wheeling (Ill.) Dist. 21, 1985-93; family sponsor JCC Family to Family, Cook County, 1990; elected mem. Wheeling Twp. Bd. Trustees, 2001—. Recipient cert. appreciation Decalogue Soc. Lawyers, Chgo., 1980. Mem. Women's Bar Assn., Greenpeace, Ill. State Bar Assn., Northwest Suburban Bar Assn. (chair estate planning com. 1999-2001, Cert. of Appreciation), Indian Trail Pub. Lib. Dist., Lavisso Sch., Internat. Alliance of Holistic Lawyers, Women in Real Estate. Avocations: mothering, sewing soft furnishings, singing in shir shalom choir, reading popularized science. Estate planning, Probate (including wills, trusts), Property, real (including real estate development, water). Home: 567 Weidner Rd Buffalo Grove IL 60089-3232 Office: Long Grove Executive House Suite 208 4180 Rfd Long Grove IL 60047-9582 E-mail: joyfisher@voyager.net.

FISHER, KATHLEEN V. lawyer; b. Aug. 9, 1948; AB, UCLA, 1971; JD, U. Calif., Davis, 1976. Bar: Calif. 1976. Extern to Hon. Raymond Sullivan Calif. Supreme Ct., 1975; mem. Morrison & Foerster, San Francisco. Mem. Order of Coif. Office: Morrison & Foerster 425 Market St San Francisco CA 94105

FISHER, LLOYD EDISON, JR., lawyer; b. Medina, Ohio, Oct. 23, 1923; s. Lloyd Edison and Wanda (White) F.; m. Twylla Dawn Peterson, Sept. 11, 1949 (dec. Apr. 1996); children: Karen S., Kirk P. BS, Ohio State U., 1947, JD, 1949. Bar: Ohio 1950. Mem. gen. hearing bd. Ohio Dept. Taxation, 1950-53; trust officer Huntington Nat. Bank, Columbus, 1953-62; ptnr. Porter, Wright, Morris & Arthur and predecessor firm, Columbus, 1962—. Adj. prof. law Ohio State U., Columbus, 1967-69, 84-91. Bd. dirs Wesley Glen Retirement Ctr., 1974-80, 88-95; bd. dirs. Grant/Riverside Hospice, 1997—. Served with AUS, 1943-45. Fellow Am. Coll. Trust and Estate Counsel; mem. ABA, Ohio Bar Assn., Columbus Bar Assn., Order of Coif. Probate (including wills, trusts), Estate taxation, State and local taxation. Home: 6478 Strathaven Ct E Worthington OH 43085-2985 Office: 41 S High St Columbus OH 43215-6101 E-mail: lfisher@porterwright.com.

FISHER, LLOYD KENT, prosecutor; b. Baker City, Oreg., Feb. 10, 1960; s. Lloyd Kent and Shirley May Fisher; m. Mignonette Valerie Price, Jan. 19, 1984; children: L. Zane, H. Karson. BA in History, Ea. Oreg. U., 1985; JD, U. Oreg., 1991. Bar: Oreg. 1991. Dep. pub. defender Unatilla/Morrow Pub. Defender, Pendleton, Oreg., 1992; dep. dist. atty. Unatilla County Dist. Atty.'s Office, Pendleton, 1992—97; assoc. Garland Law Offices, Hillsboro, Oreg., 1997—98; dep. pub. defender Intermantain Pub. Defender, Pendleton, 1998—99; sr. dep. dist. atty. Unatilla County Dist. Atty.'s Office, Pendleton, 1999—. Chmn. Unatilla County Multi-disciplinary Team, Pendleton, 1999—; supr. Guardian Care Ctr., Pendleton, 1999—. Editor (reference book): A Surveyor's Guide to Oregon Revised Statutes, 1993. Dir. Unafilla County ESD/Pendleton Round-up, Pendleton, 2002—03. Mem.: 6th Jud. Bar Assn., Oreg. State Bar Assn. Avocations: horseback riding, disc golf. Office: Unatilla County Juvenile Svcs 817 SE 13th St Pendleton OR 97801

FISHER, MICHAEL ERNEST, lawyer; b. Heidelberg, Germany, Jan. 23, 1960; came to U.S., 1960; s. Ernest Ebenezer and Linda Arlene (Berg) F.; m. Deborah Elizabeth Matthews, Aug. 9, 1986; children: Carter, Grace. BA, Spring Arbor Coll., 1981; JD, Harvard U., 1984. Bar: Mich. 1984. Assoc. Miller Canfield Paddock and Stone, Detroit, 1984-87; v.p. Hibbs and Fisher, P.C., Detroit, 1988-94; asst. city attorney City of Livonia, Mich., 1994—. Coop. attorney Fair Housing Ctr. Metropolitan Detroit, 1991-95. Author: Mike's Guide to the Motor City, 1993. Recipient Spirit of Detroit award Mayor Coleman A. Young, Detroit, 1992, Christian Man of Yr. award Trinity Faith United Meth. Ch., Detroit, 1992. Democrat. Avocations: studying, teaching the bible. Office: City of Livonia 33000 Civic Center Dr Livonia MI 48154-3097

FISHER, MORTON POE, JR., lawyer; b. Balt., Aug. 17, 1936; s. Morton Poe Sr. and Adelaide (Block) F.; m. Ann P. Fisher, Aug. 12, 1962; children: Stephen N., Marjorie P. AB, Dartmouth Coll., Hanover, N.H., 1958; LLB, Yale U., 1961. Bar: Md. 1961, D.C. 1961. Law clk. to presiding justice U.S. Dist. Ct. Md., Balt., 1961-62; assoc. Piper & Marbury, 1962-68; asst. gen. counsel Rouse Co., 1968-73; ptnr. Frank, Bernstein, Conaway & Goldman, Balt., 1973-92; mng. ptnr. Balt. office Ballard Spahr Andrews & Ingersoll, Balt., 1992—2002. Faculty mem. U. Md. Law Sch., 1978-87. Mem. Balt. County Econ. Devel. Commn., 1988-90, Mayor's Adv. Commn., Balt. City, Risk Mgmt. Com. Balto City, 1999; bd. dirs. Balt. Downtown Partnership, 1998-2003; dean U. of Shopping ctrs., 1998-99; bd. trustees U. of Md. Balt. Found., 2003—. Mem. ABA (vice chmn. real property divsn 1990-92, chmn. sect. real property, probate and trust law 1993-94), Am. Coll. Real Estate Lawyers (pres. 1988-89), Am. Coll. Constrn. Lawyers, Am. Law Inst., Anglo-Am. Real Property Inst., Internat. Coun. Shopping Ctrs. (co-chmn. law conf. 1995-97). Environmental, Property, real (including real estate development, water). Office: Ballard Spahr Andrews & Ingersoll LLP 300 E Lombard St Ste 1800 Baltimore MD 21202-6739 E-mail: fisher@ballardspahr.com.

FISHER, MYRON R. lawyer; b. Chgo., Aug. 13, 1935; BA, Calif. State U., Long Beach, 1964; JD, Southwestern U., 1969. Bar: Calif. 1970, U.S. Dist. Ct. (cen. dist.) Calif. 1970, U.S. Supreme Ct. 1974. Dep. pub. defender San Bernardino County (Calif.), 1970-71; assoc. Anderson, Adams & Bacon, Rosemead, Calif., 1971-74; sole practice San Clemente, Calif., 1974—. Judge pro tem South Orange County Mcpl. Ct., 1978— . Mem. State Bar Calif., South Orange County Bar Assn. (bd. dirs. 1978-83), Orange County Bar Assn., Los Angeles Trial Lawyers Assn., Orange County Trial Lawyers Assn., Calif. Trial Lawyers Assn., Assn. Trial Lawyers Am. Insurance, Personal injury (including property damage), Probate (including wills, trusts). Office: Fisher Profl Bldg 630 S El Camino Real San Clemente CA 92672-4200 Fax: 949-498-2673. E-mail: mrfisher@sbcglobal.net.

FISHER, RAYMOND CORLEY, judge; b. Oakland, Calif., July 12, 1939; s. Raymond Henry and Mary Elizabeth (Corley) Fisher; m. Nancy Leigh Fairchilds, Jan. 22, 1961; children: Jeffrey, Amy. BA, U. Calif., Santa Barbara, 1961; LLB, Stanford U., 1966. Bar: Calif. 1967, U.S. Supreme Ct. 1967. Law clk. to Hon. J. Skelly Wright U.S. Ct. Appeals (D.C. cir.), Washington, 1966—67; law clk. to Hon. William J. Brennan U.S. Supreme Ct., Washington, 1967—68; ptnr. Tuttle & Taylor, L.A., L.A., 1968—88, Heller, Ehrman, White & McAuliffe, L.A., 1988—97; assoc. atty. gen. U.S. Dept. of Justice, Washington, 1997—99; judge U.S. Ct. Appeals (9th cir.), 1999—. Pres.: Stanford Law Rev., 1965—66. Dir. Constl. Rights Found., L.A., 1978—, pres., 1983—87, L.A. City Bd. Civil Svc. Commn., 1987—88; dep. gen. counsel Christopher Commn., L.A., 1991—92; pres. L.A. City Bd. Police Commrs., 1996—97; dir. Western Justice Ctr. Found., 2000—; spl. asst. to Gov. of Calif., 1975. With USAR, 1957—64. Fellow: Am. Bar Found., Am. Coll. Trial Lawyers; mem.: ABA, Am. Law Inst., L.A. County Bar Assn., Calif. State Bar, Fed. Bar Assn. (exec. com. 1990—96), Chancery Club, Order of Coif. Office: US Ct Appeals 125 S Grand Ave Rm 400 Pasadena CA 91105

FISHER, ROBERT I. lawyer; b. Bklyn., July 10, 1939; s. Sidney B. and Jeanette (Talisman) F.; m. Debra Kram Fisher, June 30, 1974; children: Daniel I., Elizabeth R. BA, Columbia U., 1960; JD cum laude, Harvard U., 1963; LLM, N.Y.U., 1967. Bar: N.Y. 1964. Assoc. Dewey, Ballantine, Bushby, Palmer & Wood, N.Y.C., 1964-67, Sullivan & Cromwell, N.Y.C., 1967-72; ptnr. Greenbaum, Wolff & Ernst, N.Y.C., 1972—82, Katten Muchin Zavis Roseman, N.Y.C., 1982—. Lectr. Practicing Law Inst. Fulbright fellow, Israel, 1963-64. Mem. ABA, N.Y. State Assn., Assn. Bar. City of N.Y., Corporate, general, Private international, Securities. Home: 150 Factory Pond Rd Locust Valley NY 11560-1416 Office: Katten Muchin Zavis Rosenman 575 Madison Ave Fl 11 New York NY 10022-2585 E-mail: robert.fisher@kmzr.com.

FISHER, ROBERT SCOTT, lawyer; b. Detroit, July 16, 1960; s. Alvin Fisher and Beverly (Raider) Levin. BA, U. Mich., 1982; JD, U. Colo., 1985. Bar: Colo. 1985, U.S. Dist. Ct. Colo. 1985, Mich. 1987, U.S. Ct. Appeals (10th cir.) 1989, U.S. Supreme Ct. 1989, U.S. Ct. Appeals (D.C. cir.) 1999. Prin. Law Office of Robert S. Fisher, Colorado Springs, Colo., 1985—. Mem. Colo. Bar Assn., El Paso County Bar Assn., Criminal Def. Bar Assn., Phi Delta Phi. Avocations: scuba diving, ice hockey, skiing, racquetball. Criminal, Family and matrimonial, Personal injury (including property damage). Home: 5185 Engleman Ct Colorado Springs CO 80906 Office: 924 N Wahsatch Ave Colorado Springs CO 80903-2915

FISHER, ROGER DUMMER, lawyer, educator, negotiation expert; b. Winnetka, Ill., May 28, 1922; s. Walter Taylor and Katharine (Dummer) F.; m. Caroline Speer, Sept. 18, 1948; children: Elliott Speer, Peter Ryerson. AB, Harvard U., 1943, LLB magna cum laude, 1948; LHD, Conn. Coll., 1994; DHL, Bay Path Coll., 1999. Bar: Mass. 1948, D.C. 1950. Asst. to gen. counsel, then asst. to dep. U.S. spl. rep. ECA, Paris, 1948-49; with firm Covington & Burling, Washington, 1950-56; asst. to solicitor gen. U.S., 1956-58; lectr. law Harvard Law Sch., Cambridge, Mass., 1958-60, prof. law, 1960-76, Samuel Williston prof. law, 1976-92, prof. emeritus, 1992—, dir. Harvard negotiation project, 1980—. Vis. prof. internat. rels. dept. London Sch. Econs., 1965-66; cons. pub. affairs editor WGBH-TV, Cambridge, 1969; tech. advisor Found. for Internat. Conciliation, Geneva, 1984-87. Originator, 1st exec. editor: (pub. TV series) The Advocates, 1969-70, moderator, 1970-71; co-originator, exec. editor: (pub. TV series) Arabs and Israelis, 1975; author: International Conflict for Beginners, 1969, Dear Israelis, Dear Arabs, 1972, International Mediation: A Working Guide, 1978, International Crises and the Role of Law: Points of Choice, 1978, Improving Compliance with International Law, 1981; co-author: Getting to Yes: Negotiating Agreement Without Giving In, 1981, 2d edit., 1991, Getting Together: Building Relationships as We Negotiate, 1988, Beyond Machiavelli: Tools for Coping with Conflict, 1994, Getting Ready to Negotiate: The Getting to Yes Workbook, 1995, Coping with International Conflict: A Systematic Approach to Influence in International Negotiation, 1997, Getting It Done: How to Lead When You're Not in Charge, 1998; co-author, editor: International Conflict and Behavioral Science--The Craigville Papers, 1964; lectr., contbr. articles on internat. rels., negotiation, internat. law and TV. Bd. dirs. Coun. for Livable World; trustee Hudson Inst., 1962-95. 1st lt. USAF, 1942-46. Recipient Szilard Peace award 1981, Peace Advocate award Lawyers Alliance for Nuclear Arms Control, 1988, Spl. Contbn. award Ctr. Pub. Resources, 1993, Steve Brutschè award Assn. Atty. Mediators, 1994, D'Alemberte-Raven Outstanding Achievements and Contributions to Dispute Resolution award, 1995, Honorato Vasquez Nat. Order Insignia Great Cross Republic Ecuador, 1999, Lifetime Achievement award Am. Coll. Civil Trial Mediators, 1999, Pioneer award New Eng. Soc. Profls. Dispute Resolution, 1999, St. Thomas More award St. Mary's U. Law Sch., 1999; named Guggenheim fellow 1965-66. Fellow Am. Acad. Arts and Scis.; mem. ABA (sect. dispute resolution), Am. Soc. Internat. Law (exec. coun. 1961-64, 66-69, v.p. 1982-84), Mass. Bar Assn., Commn. to Study Orgn. of Peace, Coun. Fgn. Rels., Phi Beta Kappa. Clubs: Metropolitan (Washington); Harvard (N.Y.C.). Office: Harvard U Law Sch Harvard Negotiation Project Pound Hall # 524 Cambridge MA 02138 also: Conflict Mgmt Group 9 Waterhouse St Cambridge MA 02138-3607

FISHER, RUTH E. lawyer; b. Frankfurt, Germany, Dec. 12, 1955; BA, Scripps Coll., 1976; JD, UCLA, 1980. Law clk. to Judge Malcolm M. Lucas U.S. Dist. Ct. (cen. dist.) Calif., 1980—82; with Munger, Tolles & Olson LLP, L.A., 1982—87, corp. ptnr., 1987—. Lectr. in field. Mem.: ABA (chair subcom. of bus. law sect.), Women Lawyers' Assn., L.A. County Bar Assn. Office: Munger Tolles & Olson LLP 35th Fl 355 S Grand Ave Los Angeles CA 90071

FISHER, STEWART WAYNE, lawyer; b. Phila., Mar. 5, 1950; s. Frederick and Evalyn (Wilson) F.; m. Melinda Ruley, Oct. 1, 1994; children: Henry J., Isabel Rose; children from previous marriage: Kira H., Amos N., Emily E. BA magna cum laude, Duke U., 1972; MA, Yale U., 1974; JD with honors, U. N.C., 1982. Bar: N.C. 1982, U.S. Dist. Ct. (ea. and ctrl. dists.) N.C. 1982, U.S. Dist. Ct. (we. dist.) N.C. 1997, U.S. Ct. Appeals (4th cir.) 1993, U.S. Supreme Ct. 1997, bd. cert. Civil Trial Advocate: Nat. Bd. Trial Advocacy 1998. Atty. Haywood, Denny & Miller, Durham, N.C., 1982-85; ptnr. Glenn, Mills & Fisher, PA, Durham, 1985—. Faculty Nat. Inst. for Trial Advocacy, Durham, 1988—. Coop. atty. ACLU, Raleigh, 1992—. Mem. ABA, ATLA, Nat. Employment Lawyers, N.C. Acad. Trial Lawyers, N.C. Bar Assn., Phi Beta Kappa. Democrat. Avocations: fishing, gardening.

Civil rights, Labor (including EEOC, Fair Labor Standards Act, labor-management relations, NLRB, OSHA), Personal injury (including property damage). Office: Glenn Mills & Fisher PA PO Box 3865 Durham NC 27702-3865

FISHER, THOMAS EDWARD, lawyer; b. Cleve., Sept. 29, 1926; s. McArthur and Ruth Morgan (Dissette) F.; m. Virginia Moore, June 29, 1957; children: Laura, Linda, John. BS in Naval Sci. and Tactics, Purdue U., 1947, BS in Engring. Law, 1950; JD, Ind. U., 1950. Bar: Ohio 1951, U.S. Dist. Ct. (no. dist.) Ohio 1954, U.S. Supreme Ct. 1955, U.S. Ct. Appeals (Fed. cir.) 1973. Asst. to v.p. Lempco Products, Bedford, Ohio, 1950-51; house counsel Willard Storage Battery Co., Cleve., 1951-54; assoc. Schram & Knowles, Cleve., 1954-55; ptnr. Watts, Hoffmann, Fisher & Heinke Co. (predecessor firms), Cleve., 1955—. Mem. adv. bd. BNA Patent Trademark and Copyright Jour., 1972—; mem. adv. panel Franklin Pierce Law Sch., 1987—. Councilman Mentor (Ohio) on the Lake, 1955-57; chmn. ARC, Painesville, Ohio, 1956. Lt. USN, 1944. Mem. ABA (divsn. chair), Cleve. Bar Assn. (trustee), Am. Intellectual Property Law Assn. (chair com., bd. dirs.), Cleve. Intellectual Property Law Assn. (pres.), Cleve. World Trade Assn., Nat. Inventors Hall of Fame (pres.), Nat. Coun. Patent Law Assns. (chair). Avocations: woodworking, fishing, travel, gardening. Federal civil litigation, Patent, Trademark and copyright. Home: 617 Falls Rd Chagrin Falls OH 44022-2560 Office: Watts Hoffmann Fisher & Heinke Co 1100 Superior Ave Ste 1750 Cleveland OH 44114-2518 E-mail: tfisher@wattshoff.com.

FISHER, THOMAS GEORGE, lawyer, retired media company executive; b. Debrecen, Hungary, Oct. 2, 1931; came to U.S., 1951; s. Eugene J. and Viola Elizabeth (Rittersporn) F.; m. Rita Knisley, Feb. 14, 1960; children: Thomas G. Jr., Katherine F. Vaaler. BS, Am. U., 1957, JD, 1959; postgrad., Harvard U., 1956. Bar: D.C. 1959, Iowa 1977. Atty. FCC, Washington, 1959-61, 65-66; pvt. law practice, 1961-65, 66-69; asst. counsel Meredith Corp., N.Y.C., 1969-72, assoc. gen. counsel Des Moines, 1972-76, gen. counsel, 1976-80, v.p. gen. counsel, 1980-94, corp. sec., 1988-94, ret., 1994. Comml law liaison ABA Ctr. and East European Law Initiative, Krakow, Poland, 1994—95; atty. Iowa Legal Aid, 1996—. Contbr. articles to profl. jours. Bd. dirs. Des Moines Met. Opera Co., Indianola, 1980-94, pres., 1990-91; bd. dirs. Civic Music Assn., Des Moines, 1982-92, pres., 1987-88; chmn. legis. com. Greater Des Moines C. of C., 1976-77; bd. dirs. Legal Aid Soc. Polk County, 1986-93, pres., 1993. With U.S. Army, 1952-54. Mem. ABA, Iowa State Bar Assn. (chmn. corp. counsel subcom. 1979-82), Polk County Bar Assn., Embassy Club. Communications, Intellectual property. Office: Iowa Legal Aid 1111 9th St Ste 380 Des Moines IA 50314-2527

FISHER, THOMAS GEORGE, JR., lawyer; b. Washington, June 1, 1961; s. Thomas George and Rita (Knisley) F.; m. Susan Jane Koenig, June 23, 1990. BA, Iowa State U., 1983; JD with high distinction, U. Iowa, 1986. Bar: Iowa 1986, U.S. Dist. Ct. (so. dist.), Iowa 1987, U.S. Ct. Appeals (8th cir.) 1987, U.S. Dist. Ct. (no. dist.) Iowa 1993. Jud. clk. Iowa Supreme Ct., Davenport, 1986-87; assoc. Duncan, Jones, Riley & Finley, P.C., Des Moines, 1987-91; asst. atty. gen. State of Iowa, Justice Dept., Des Moines, 1991-95; counsel Am. Mut. Life Ins. Co., Des Moines, 1995-96; ptnr. Hogan & Fisher, PLC, Des Moines, 1997—. Precinct chair Polk County Dem. Party, Des Moines, 1988-90, 94-96, 98-2000, 02--; candidate Iowa Ho. of Reps. Dists. 73, 1994; mem. Des Moines Leadership Inst., 1998-99; bd. dirs. Anawim Housing; bd. dirs., mem. exec. com. Metro Arts Alliance of Greater Des Moines. Mem. Blackstone Inn of Ct. Democrat. Roman Catholic. Communications, Utilities, public, Property, real (including real estate development, water). Office: Hogan & Fisher PLC 3101 Ingersoll Ave Des Moines IA 50312-3918 E-mail: Tom@Hogan-Fisher.com.

FISHMAN, CRAIG L. lawyer; b. Phila., Nov. 14, 1962; m. Lorrie K. Albert, Esq.. BA, U. Pa., 1982; postgrad., U. Pitts., 1983—86, JD, 1990; MPH in Health Care Adminstrn., Northwestern U., Chgo., 1988. Bar: Pa. 1990, U.S. Dist. Ct. (we. dist.) Pa. 1990, U.S. Ct. Appeals (3d and 4th cir.) 1990. Assoc. atty. Feldstein, Grinberg, Stein & McKee, P.C., Pitts., 1990—96; assoc. atty., jr. ptnr. Tarasi Law Firm, P.C., Pitts., 1996—2001; ptnr. Tarasi, Tarasi & Fishman, P.C., Pitts., 2001—. Contbr. articles to profl. jours. Mem.: Allegheny County Bar Assn. (mem. bench-bar com. 1994—, v. chair 2003), Western Pa. Trial Lawyers Assn. (bd. govs. 1997—2002), Million Dollar Advs. Forum (life). Personal injury (including property damage), Professional liability, General civil litigation. Office: Tarasi Tarasi and Fishman PC 510 3d Ave Pittsburgh PA 15219 Office Fax: 412-471-2673. Business E-Mail: clf@tarasilaw.com.

FISHMAN, EDWARD MARC, lawyer; b. Cambridge, Mass., Apr. 28, 1946; s. Eli Manuel and Marian (Goldberg) F.; m. Barbara Ellen Stern, June 29, 1969 (div. Sept. 1982); children: Andrea Stern, Bradley Craig; m. Tracy Ann Lind, July 13, 1985; children: Alison Leigh, Kendall Paige. AB, Bowdoin Coll., 1968; JD, Columbia U., 1972. Bar: Tex. 1972. Assoc. Akin, Gump, Strauss, Hauer & Feld, Dallas, 1972-73, Luce, Hennessy, Smith & Castle, Dallas, 1973-76; corp. counsel Centex Corp., Dallas, 1976-78; from assoc. to ptnr. Brice & Barron, Dallas, 1978-82; v.p. Baker, Smith & Mills, Dallas, 1982-86; pres. Fishman, Jones, Walsh & Gray, Dallas, 1986-99; v.p. Clements, Allen, Fishman, Woods & Walsh, P.C., Dallas, 1999-2000; with Glast, Phillips & Murray, P.C., Dallas, 2000—. Bd. dirs. Space Found. Roundtable, Dallas, 1985-87, Hope Cottage, Dallas, 1990-96; officer local pub. TV sta., Dallas, 1976—. Mem. ABA, Tex. Bar Assn., Dallas Bar Assn. Avocations: reading, bicycling, swimming, running, skiing. Corporate, general, Landlord-tenant, Property, real (including real estate development, water). Home: 4723 Stonehollow Way Dallas TX 75287-7525 Office: Glast Phillips & Murray PC Ste 2200 13355 Noel Rd Dallas TX 75240-6657 E-mail: efishman@gpm-law.com.

FISHMAN, FRED NORMAN, lawyer; b. N.Y.C., Aug. 21, 1925; s. Arthur Elihu and Frederica (Greenspan) F.; m. Claire S. Powsner, Sept. 19, 1948; children: Robert J., Nancy K. S.B. summa cum laude, Harvard U., 1946, LL.B. magna cum laude, 1948; postgrad., Yale U., 1945-46. Bar: N.Y. State 1950, U.S. Supreme Ct. 1954. Law clk. to Chief Judge Calvert Magruder, U.S. Ct. Appeals, 1st Circuit, Boston, 1948-49; to Asso. Justice Felix Frankfurter, Supreme Ct. U.S., 1949-50; assoc. firm Dewey Ballantine LLP (and predecessors), N.Y.C., 1950-57; with Freeport Minerals Co., N.Y.C., 1957-61, asst. sec., 1958-59, asst. v.p., 1959-61; partner firm Kaye Scholer LLP, N.Y.C., 1962-92, mem. exec. com., 1970-87, chmn. exec. com., 1981-83, spl. counsel, 1993-95. Editor, officer: Harvard Law Rev. Chmn. Harvard Law Sch. Fund, 1977—79; mem. bd. overseers' com. to visit Harvard Law Sch., 1975—81, 1988—94; chmn. com. Harvard Law Sch. Class of 1948 Twenty-Fifth Anniversary Gift, Forty-Fifth Anniversary Gift; mem. bd. overseers' com. to visit Grad. Sch. Edn., Harvard U., 1971—77, bd. overserrs' Com. on Univ. Resources, 1991—, permanent class com. Harvard Class of 1946; mem. bd. overseers' com. to visit Med. Sch. and Sch. of Dental Medicine Harvard U., 1997—2003; trustee Pub. Edn. Assn., N.Y.C., 1956—73, chmn. bd., 1970—71; dir. Harvard Alumni Assn., 1981—83; trustee Hosp. for Joint Diseases and Med. Ctr., 1971—73, Lawyers' Com. for Civil Rights under Law, 1979—, bd. dirs., 1983—, co-chmn., 1983—85; mem. steering com. Campaign for Harvard Law Sch., 1991—95; mem. dean's adv. bd. Harvard Law Sch., 2001—. Fellow: Am. Bar Found.; mem.: ABA, Harvard Law Sch. Assn. (trustee N.Y.C. assn. 1966—69, v.p. N.Y.C. assn. 1974—75, coun. 1978—82, exec. com. 1980—82, 1st v.p. 1984—86, pres. 1986—88, exec. com. 1988—90, pres. N.Y.C. assn. 1988—89), Legal Aid Soc. (bd. dirs. 1991—94), Am. Law Inst. (adviser corp. governance project 1980—92), Assn. of Bar of City of N.Y. (chmn. com. fed. legis. 1963—66, exec. com. 1966—70, chmn. com. corp. law 1980—82, treas. 1993—94), Harvard Club N.Y.C., Phi Beta Kappa. Home: 650 Park Ave Apt 3D New York NY 10021-6115 Office: Kaye Scholer LLP 425 Park Ave New York NY 10022-3598 E-mail: ffishman@kayescholer.com.

FISHMAN, KENNETH JAY, judge; b. Roslyn, N.Y., Nov. 12, 1950; s. George Norman and Eudys Sonia (Goldstein) F.; m. Nancy Ellen Santos, Sept. 22, 1984; children: Jason Edward, Hayley Alissa. BS in Econs., U. Pa., 1972; JD cum laude, Suffolk U., 1976. Bar: Mass. 1977, U.S. Dist. Ct. Mass. 1977, U.S. Dist. Ct. (no. dist.) Calif. 1982, U.S. Ct. Appeals (4th and 3rd cirs.) 1980, (6th cir.) 1982, (1st cir.) 1983, (5th and 10th cirs.) 1985, (8th cir.) 1985, U.S. Tax Ct. 1981, U.S. Ct. Mil. Appeals 1981, U.S. Dist. Ct. (ea. dist.) Wis. 1991, U.S. Ct. Appeals (2d cir.) 1993, U.S. Fed. Claims Ct. 1997, U.S. Supreme Ct. 1980. Assoc. Law Offices F. Lee Bailey, Boston, 1976-84; ptnr. Law Offices Bailey & Fishman, Boston, 1984-91, Law Offices Bailey, Fishman & Leonard, Boston, 1991-97, Law Offices Fishman, Ankner & Horstmann, Boston, 1997—2002; pvt. practice, 2002; assoc. justice Mass. Superior Ct., 2002—. Former instr. Met. Coll., Boston U. Note editor Suffolk U. Law Rev., 1975—76; co-author (with F. Lee Bailey): Bailey/Fishman Criminal Law Series, 1986—. Mem. ABA, ATLA, NACDL, Mass. Assn. Criminal Def. Lawyers (treas.,1995-2002), Mass. Bar Assn. Democrat. Jewish. Office: Commonwealth of Mass - The Superior Ct John W McCormack PO and Courthouse 90 Devonshire St Boston MA 02105

FISHMAN, LEWIS WARREN, lawyer, educator; b. Bklyn., Dec. 19, 1951; BA in Polit. Sci., Syracuse U., 1972; MPA, Maxwell-Syracuse U., 1973; JD, U. Miami, 1976. Bar: Fla. 1976, U.S. Dist. Ct. (so. dist.) Fla. 1977, U.S. Dist. Ct. D.C. 1978, U.S. Ct. Appeals (5th and 11th cirs.) 1981. Assoc. Simons & Fishman P.A. (and predecessor firm), Miami, 1976-80, ptnr., 1980-81; assoc. Wood, Lucksinger & Epstein, Miami, 1981—82; pres. Lewis W. Fishman, P.A., Miami, 1982—. Adj. prof. law Fla. Internat. U., 1981, 83, 84, 91; mem. bd. legal specialization and edn. Fla. Bar, 1999—. Mem. Fla. Acad. Healthcare Attys. (bd. dirs., sec. 1986-88, pres. 1990-92), Nat. Health Lawyers Assn. (lectr. 1983, 88-89), Fla. Hosp. Assn. (lectr. 1983, 88-89), Fla. Hosp. Assn. (lectr.), Fla.Med. Record Assn. (lectr. 1982, 83, 84), Am. Acad. Hosp. Attys. (lectr. 1989, 90, 91), Nat. Health Lawyers Assn., Cath. Health Assn., Fla. Bar Assn. (mem. exec. coun. health law sect. 1988-97, chmn. health law sect. 1988-97, chmn. health law sect. 1995-96, cert. health law atty., mem. health law cert. com. 1994-99, vice chmn. 1995-96, chmn. 1996-98, bd. legal specialization and edn. 1999—). Jewish. Corporate, general, Health, Insurance. Home: 14140 SW 104th Ave Miami FL 33176-7064 Office: 9130 S Dadeland Blvd Miami FL 33156-7818 E-mail: lwfpa@aol.com.

FISHMAN, MITCHELL STEVEN, lawyer; b. N.Y.C., July 27, 1948; s. Abraham and Sylvia (Sher) F.; children: Danielle, Matthew, Jeremy. BA cum laude, Harvard U., 1970, JD cum laude, 1973. Bar: N.Y. 1974, D.C. 1984. Assoc. Breed, Abbott & Morgan, N.Y.C., 1973-74, Paul, Weiss, Rifkind, Wharton & Garrison, N.Y.C., 1975-81, ptnr., 1981-99. Exec. dir. Temp. State Commn. on Banking, Ins. and Fin. Svcs., N.Y., 1983-84; cons. Sirius Satellite Radio, Inc., N.Y.C., 2000-01. Mem. ABA, Assn. of Bar of City of N.Y. (com. on corp. law 1976-79, mem. com. on securities regulation 1998-01). Democrat. Banking, Corporate, general, Securities. Home: PO Box 1443 Washington CT 06793-0443 E-mail: mshishman@excite.com.

FISHMAN, RICHARD GLENN, lawyer, accountant; b. Orange, N.J., June 2, 1952; s. Irving and Eleanor (Tanenbaum) F.; m. Jean Goldhammer, Aug. 11, 1974; children: Neil Samuel, Peter Lawrence, Ellen Melissa. BA in Econs. with highest honors and highest distinction, Rutgers U., 1974; JD, Yale U., 1977; LLM in Taxation, NYU, 1980. Bar: N.Y. 1978, N.J. 1978, U.S. Dist. Ct. N.J. 1978, U.S. Ct. Claims 1978, U.S. Tax Ct. 1978, U.S. Dist. Ct. (so. dist.) N.Y. 1979, U.S. Ct. Appeals (3d cir.) 1994. Assoc. Stroock & Stroock & Lavan, N.Y.C., 1977-80, Roberts & Holland, N.Y.C., 1980-85; tax mgr. Spicer & Oppenheim (formerly Oppenheim, Appel, Dixon & Co.), N.Y.C., 1985-87, ptnr., 1987-88; from sr. tax. counsel to assoc. gen. tax counsel AlliedSignal Inc., Morristown, NJ, 1988—97, assoc. gen. tax counsel, 1997—99; dir. tax planning for bus. units, assoc. gen. tax counsel Honeywell Internat., Inc., Morristown, 1999—2001, dir. internat. & bus. tax planning, 2001—, assoc. gen. tax counsel, 2001—. Contbr. articles to profl. jours. Mem. ABA, AICPA, N.Y. State Bar Assn., N.J. State Bar Assn. Public international, Corporate taxation, Taxation, general. Home: 6 Tilden Ct Livingston NJ 07039-2419 Office: Honeywell Internat Inc PO Box 1057 Morristown NJ 07962-1057 E-mail: richard.fishman@honeywell.com.

FISHWICK, JOHN PALMER, retired lawyer, retired railroad executive; b. Roanoke, Va., Sept. 29, 1916; s. William and Nellie (Cross) F.; m. Blair Wiley, Jan. 4, 1941 (dec. June 1987); children: Ellen Blair (Mrs. Guyman Martin III), Anne Palmer (Mrs. Wesley Posvar), John Palmer; m. Doreen Allton, Nov. 17, 1989. AB, Roanoke Coll., 1937, DHL (hon.), 1971; LL.B., Harvard U., 1940; DL (hon.), Washington & Lee Univ., 2000. Bar: Va. 1939. Assoc. Cravath, Swaine & Moore, N.Y.C., 1940-42; asst. to gen. solicitor N. & W. Ry., Roanoke, Va., 1945-47, asst. gen. solicitor, 1947-51, asst. gen. counsel, 1951-54, gen. solicitor, 1954-56, gen. counsel, 1956-58, v.p., gen. counsel, 1958-59, v.p. law, 1959-63, sr. v.p., 1963-70, pres., chief exec. officer, 1970-80, chmn., chief exec. officer, 1980-81, also dir.; ptnr. Windels, Marx, Davies & Ives, N.Y.C., 1981-84; of counsel Fishwick, Jones and Glenn, Roanoke, Va., 1984-95; ret. Chmn., chief exec. officer Erie Lackawanna Ry. Co., 1968-70; pres., chief exec. officer Del. and Hudson Ry. Co., 1968-70; pres., dir. Dereco, Inc., 1968-81; chmn. investment com., bd. dirs. Norfolk So. Corp., 1981-89. Trustee Roanoke Coll., 1964-72; trustee Va. Theol. Sem.; former chancellor Diocese S.W. Va.; former bd. dirs. Va. Found. Humanities; former trustee Va. Mus. Fine Arts, Richmond. Served as lt. comdr. USNR, 1942—45. Mem. Met. Club (Washington). Episcopalian. Office: 110 Franklin Rd SE Roanoke VA 24042-0002

FISKE, HAROLD PARKER, lawyer; b. N.Y.C., Nov. 8, 1962; s. John Adams and Martha Cherry Fiske; m. Kim Yen Nguyen, Sept. 1, 2002. BA in Internat. Rels., Brown U., 1985; postgrad., Yale-in-China, Hong Kong, 1985; JD, Boston Coll., 1992. Bar: Calif. 1992. Assoc. Russin & Vecchi, LLP, Hanoi and Ho Chi Minh City, Vietnam, 1994—99; gen. counsel China Gen. Ltd., ShenYang, China, 1999—2000; assoc. Baker & McKenzie, Beijing, 2000—. Dir. bd. sponsors Operation Smile, Hanoi, 1998. Mem.: Am. C. of C. China (legal com. 2000—02). Democrat. Avocations: travel, languages, music, sports. Private international, Corporate, general, Commercial, contracts (including sales of goods; commercial financing). Office: Baker & McKenzie 1 Jianguomenwai Ave Beijing 100004 China

FISKE, ROBERT BISHOP, JR., lawyer; b. N.Y.C., Dec. 28, 1930; s. Robert Bishop and Lenore (Seymour) F.; m. Janet Tinsley, Aug. 21, 1954; children: Linda Goucher, Robert Bishop, Susan Williams. BA, Yale U., 1952; JD, U. Mich., 1955, LLD (hon.), 1997. Bar: Mich. 1955, N.Y. 1956, U.S. Ct. Appeals (2nd cir.) 1957, U.S. Supreme Ct. 1961. Assoc. Davis, Polk, Wardwell, Sunderland & Kiendl, 1955-57; asst. U.S. atty. So. Dist. N.Y., 1957-61; assoc. Davis Polk & Wardwell, 1961-64, ptnr., 1964—76, 1980—2002; U.S. atty. So. Dist. N.Y., N.Y.C., 1976-80; ind. counsel for Whitewater, Little Rock, 1994. Chmn. N.Y. State Jud. Commn. on Drugs and the Cts., 1999—2000; mem. Commn. for the Rev. of FBI Security Programs, 2001—02. Fellow Am. Coll. Trial Lawyers (pres. 1991-92); mem. ABA (chmn. standing com. on fed. judiciary 1984-87), Assn. of Bar of City of N.Y., Fed. Bar Coun. (pres. 1982-84), N.Y. State Bar Assn., Noroton Yacht Club, Wee Burn Country Club. Republican. Congregationalist. Federal civil litigation, State civil litigation, Criminal. Office: 450 Lexington Ave New York NY 10017-3911

FISS, OWEN M. law educator; b. 1938. BA, Dartmouth Coll., 1959; BPhil, Oxford U., 1961; LLB, Harvard U., 1964. Bar: N.Y. 1965. Law clk. to Judge Thurgood Marshall, U.S. Ct. Appeals 2d Cir., 1964-65, to Justice Brennan, U.S. Supreme Ct., 1965; spl. asst. to asst. atty. gen., civil rights div. U.S. Dept. Justice, Washington, 1966-67, acting dir. Office of Planning Coordination, 1968; prof. U. Chgo. Law Sch., 1968-74; prof. Yale U. Law Sch., New Haven, 1974-84, Alexander M. Bickel prof. pub. law, 1984-92, Sterling prof., 1992—; vis. prof. Stanford U., 1973. Mem. Harvard Law Rev.; author: Injunctions, 1972; The Civil Rights Injunction, 1978; (with R.M. Cover) The Structure of Procedure, 1979; (with D. Rendleman) Injunctions, 2d edit., 1984; (with Cover and J. Resnik) Procedure, 1988; (with Cover and Resnik) The Federal Procedural System, 1988, 3d edit., 1991, Holmes Devise History of the Supreme Ct.: Troubled Beginnings of the Modern State, 1888-1910, 1993, Liberalism Divided, 1996, The Irony of Free Speech, 1996, A Community of Equals, 1999, A Way Out, 2003; mem. editl. bd. Philosophy and Pub. Affairs and Found. Press, Yale Jour. Criticisim, Yale Jour. Law and Humanities, Law, Econs. and Orgns.

FITTERER, RICHARD CLARENCE, judge; b. Ellensburg, Wash., Jan. 22, 1946; s. L. George and Margeret H. (Lewis) F.; children: Christian C. (dec.), Zane I., Aaron G. BCS, Seattle U., 1968; JD, U. Puget Sound, 1975. Bar: Wash. 1976, U.S. Dist. Ct. (we. dist.) Wash. 1976, U.S. Dist. Ct. (ea. dist.) Wash. 1977. Assoc. Patrick R. Acres, Moses Lake, Wash., 1977; sole practice Moses Lake, 1977-79, 83-95; ptnr. Milne, Lemargie & Fitterer, Ephrata, Wash., 1979-1983; judge Grant County Dist. Ct., 1995—. Instr. Wash. State Jud. Coll. Bd. dirs. Columbia Basin Rodeo Assn. Moses Lake Roundup, 1984-91, United Way, Moses Lake, 1978-81, Moses Lake C. of C., 1979-83, 87-88. Mem. ATLA, ABA, Am. Judges Assn., Wash. State Dist. Judges Assn. (chair rules com. 1999—, bd. govs. 2001—), Grant County Bar Assn. (pres. 1993), Wash. State Trial Lawyers Assn., Moses Lake Golf and Country Club (bd. dirs. 1989-92, pres. 1991-92), Elks (bd. dirs. 1984). Avocations: skiing, boating, golfing, photography. Home: 322 N Crestview Dr Moses Lake WA 98837-1412 Office: PO Box 37 Ephrata WA 98823-0037

FITTS, MICHAEL ANDREW, law educator, dean; b. Phila., Mar. 1, 1953; s. William Thomas Jr. and Barbara Kinsey (Willits) F.; m. Renee Judith Sobel, Jan. 2, 1982; children: Alexis, Whitney. AB, Harvard Coll., 1975; JD, Yale U., 1979; MA (hon.), U. Pa., 1991. Law clk. Hon. A. Leon Higginbotham, Jr., U.S. Ct. Appeals (3d cir.), Phila., 1979-81; atty. office legal counsel Dept. of Justice, Washington, 1981-85; asst. prof. law U. Pa., Phila., 1985-90, assoc. prof., 1990-92, prof., 1992—, assoc. dean acad. affairs, 1996-98, Robert G. Fuller Jr. prof. law, 1996-2000, Bernard G. Segal prof. law, 2000—, dean Sch. of Law, 2000—. Vis. prof. dept. polit. sci. Swarthmore Coll., 1999. Editor Yale Law Jour., 1978-79; contbr. articles to profl. jours. and chpts. to books. Harvard U. scholar, 1971. Mem. Am. Polit. Sci. Assn. (law and polit. process working group), Pa. Bar Assn., Com. of Seventy, Phi Beta Kappa. Mem. Soc. Of Friends. Office: U Pa Law Sch 3400 Chestnut St Philadelphia PA 19104-6204 Office Fax: 215-573-2025. Business E-Mail: mfitts@law.upenn.edu.

FITZGERALD, JAMES PATRICK, lawyer; b. Omaha, Nebr., Nov. 30, 1946; s. James Joseph and Lorraine (Hickey) F.; m. Dianne Fager, Dec. 27, 1968; 1 child, James Timothy. BA, U. Nebr., 1968; JD, Creighton U., 1974. Bar: Nebr. 1974, U.S. Dist. Ct. Nebr. 1974, U.S. Ct. Appeals (8th cir.) 1974. Law clk. U.S. Dist. Ct. Nebr., Omaha, 1974-76; atty. McGrath, North, Mullin & Kratz, P.C., Omaha, 1976—. Sgt. U.S. Army, 1968-71. Mem. ABA, Nebr. Bar Assn., Assn. Trial Lawyers Am., Nebr. Assn. Trial Attys., Def. Rsch. Inst. General civil litigation, Commercial, contracts (including sales of goods; commercial financing). Home: 16728 Jones Cir Omaha NE 68118-2711 Office: McGrath North Mullin & Kratz 1601 Dodge St Ste 3700 Omaha NE 68102

FITZGERALD, JAMES PAUL, lawyer; b. Binghamton, N.Y., Dec. 27, 1953; s. James J. and Dawn Woodrow Fitzgerald; m. Diane L. Fitzgerald, Aug. 8, 1980. BA cum laude, Marist Coll., 1976; JD, Bklyn. Law Sch., 1980. Bar: N.Mex., U.S. Ct. Appeals (10th cir.). Asst. city atty. City of Albuquerque, 1980-85, 99—; dir. Rodey, Dickason, Sloan, Akin & Robb, P.A., Albuquerque, 1986-99. Chmn. Open Space Adv. Bd., Albuqueque, 1978-82. Author, editor: N.Mex. Environmental Law Handbook, 1998. V.p. Open Space Alliance, Albuquerque, 1999. Mem. Nat. Assn. of Indsl. and Office Properties (pres. 1997). Home: 14208 Turner Ct NE Albuquerque NM 87123-1836 Office: City Attys Office PO Box 9948 Albuquerque NM 87119-1048 Fax: 505-842-4278. E-mail: jfitzgerald@cabq.gov.

FITZGERALD, JOHN EDWARD, III, lawyer; b. Cambridge, Mass., Jan. 12, 1945; s. John Edward Jr. and Kathleen (Sullivan) FitzGerald. BCE, U.S. Mil. Acad., West Point, N.Y., 1969; JD, M in Pub. Policy Analysis, U. Pa., 1975. Bar: Pa 1975, NY 1978, Calif 1983, US Supreme Ct 1991. Commd. 2d lt. U.S. Army, 1969, advanced through grades to capt., 1971, resigned, 1972; assoc. Saul Ewing Remick & Saul, Phila., 1975-77, Shearman & Sterling, N.Y.C., 1977-78; atty., dir. govt. rels. and pub. affairs Pepsico, Inc., Purchase, N.Y., 1978-82; sr. v.p., dept. head Security Pacific Corp., Los Angeles, 1982-83; ptnr. Schlesinger, FitzGerald & Johnson, Palm Springs, Calif., 1983-87; mng. ptnr. FitzGerald & Mulé, Palm Springs, 1987—. Judge pro tem Desert Jud. Dist. Chmn, pres United Way Desert; mem Comt 25, Palm Springs; trustee, vpres Palm Springs Desert Mus; pres exec bd Coachella Valley coun Boy Scouts Am; bd dirs, chmn Palm Springs Boys and Girls Club; treas. Desert Youth Found. Named Palm Springs Disting. Citizen of Yr., 1999; recipient Friend of Youth award, Boys and Girls Clubs, 1998, Disting. Eagle award, Boy Scouts Am., 1999, Jefferson Award, 2003. Mem.: Am. Arbitration Assn. (arbitrator), Desert Bar Assn. (pres.), Calif. Bar Assn., Lincoln Club of the Coachella Valley (vice chmn. bd. dirs.), Desert Bus. Roundtable, O'Donnell Golf Club. General civil litigation, Commercial, contracts (including sales of goods; commercial financing), Labor (including EEOC, Fair Labor Standards Act, labor-management relations, NLRB, OSHA). Office: Ste 105 3001 Tahquitz Canyon Way Palm Springs CA 92262-6900 E-mail: jackfitzgerald3@aol.com.

FITZGERALD, JUDITH KLASWICK, federal judge; b. Spangler, Pa., May 10, 1948; d. Julius Francis and Regina Marie (Pregno) Klaswick; m. June 5, 1971 (div. Dec. 1982); 1 child; m. Barry Robert Fitzgerald, Sept. 20, 1986; 1 child. BSBA, U. Pitts., 1970, JD, 1973. Legal rschr. Assocs. Fin., Pitts., 1972-73; law clk. to pres. judge Beaver County (Pa.) Ct. Common Pleas, 1973-74; law clk. to judge Pa. Superior Ct., Pitts., 1974-75; asst. U.S. atty. U.S. Dist. Ct. (we. dist.) Pa., Pitts. and Erie, 1976-87, U.S. bankruptcy judge Pitts., Erie and Johnstown, 1987—, U.S. Dist. Ct. (ea. dist.) Pa., U.S. Dist. Ct. Del., 1997. Adj. prof. law U. Pitts., 1997. Co-author: Bankruptcy and Divorce, Support and Property Division, 1991; editor: Pennsylvania Law of Juvenile Delinquency and Deprivation, 1976; contbr. articles to profl. jours. Mem. Pitts. Camerata, 1978-80, Allegheny County Polit.-Legal Edn. Project, 1980, Mendelssohn Choir Pitts., 1982—; mem. coun. Program to Aid Citizen Enterprise, 1985-87. Recipient Spl. Achievement awards Dept. Justice, Spl. Recognition award Pittsburgh mag., Operation Exodus Outstanding Performance award Dept. Commerce, 1986. Mem. Internat. Women's Insolvency and Restructuring Conf., Allegheny County Bar Assn., Women's Bar Assn. of Western Pa., Nat. Conf. Bankruptcy Judges, Am. Bankruptcy Inst., Nat. Conf. Bankruptcy Clks., Comml. Law League of Am., Fed. Criminal Investigators Assn. (Spl. Svc. award 1988), Zonta. Republican. Lutheran. Avocations: singing, reading, traveling. Office: US Bankruptcy Ct 600 Grant St Ste 5490 Pittsburgh PA 15219-2805

FITZGERALD, KEVIN GERARD, lawyer; b. Milw., Aug. 1, 1963; s. Raymond E. and Virginia L. Fitzgerald; m. Jill Ann Hussinger, 1997; 1 child, Zachary J. Mitschrich. BS, Marquette U., 1984; JD, U. Wis., 1987. Bar: Wis. 1987, U.S. Dist. Ct. (ea. and we. dists.) Wis. 1987, Fla. 1994. Ptnr. Foley & Lardner, Milw., 1987—. Bd. dirs. T.E. Brennan Co., Milw. Contbr.

articles to profl. jours. Mem. ABA, Wis. Bar Assn., Milw. Bar Assn., Fedn. Regulatory Counsel. Administrative and regulatory, Insurance. Office: Foley and Lardner 777 E Wisconsin Ave Milwaukee WI 53202-5367

FITZGERALD, KEVIN MICHAEL, lawyer, mediator; b. Kansas City, Kans., May 10, 1956; s. Thomas Francis and Theresa Ann (Grosdidier) FitzG.; m. Susan Patricia Parker, June 21, 1980; children: Kathryn Ann, Shannon Elizabeth, Erin Parker. BBA, U. Tex., Arlington, 1981; JD, U. Ark., 1985. Bar: Mo. 1985, U.S. Dist. Ct. Mo. 1985, U.S. Ct. Appeals (8th cir.) 1985. Assoc. Taylor, Stafford, Woody, Cowherd and Clithero, Springfield, Mo., 1985-90; ptnr. Taylor, Stafford, Woody, Clithero and FitzGerald, Springfield, 1990-2000, Taylor, Stafford, Clithero, FitzGerald & Harris, Springfield, 2001—. Mediator, neutral U.S. Dist. Ct. (we. dist.) Mo. Atty. Roman Cath. Diocese of Springfield-Cape Girardeau. Mem. Mo. Bar Assn., Springfield Met. Bar Assn. (sec. 1997, chmn. alternative dispute com. 2000), Legal Aid Southwest Mo. (bd. dirs. 1993-96), Nat. Diocesan Attys. Assn. Alternative dispute resolution, Insurance, Product liability. Office: Taylor Stafford et al 3315 E Ridgeview St Ste 1000 Springfield MO 65804-4083 E-mail: kfitzgerald@taylorstafford.com.

FITZGERALD, PATRICK J. prosecutor; BA, Amherst Coll., 1982; JD, Harvard U., 1985. Atty. Christy & Viener, 1984—87; asst. U.S. atty. So. Dist. N.Y., 1988—2001; U.S. atty. no. dist. U.S. Dept. Justice, Ill., 2001—. Recipient Attorney General's Award for Exceptional Service, 1996, Stimson Medal, NY Bar Assoc., 1997, Attorney General's Award for Dist. Service, 2002. Office: 219 S Dearborn St 5th Fl Chicago IL 60604*

FITZGERALD, PETER GOSSELIN, senator, lawyer; b. Elgin, Ill., Oct. 20, 1960; s. Gerald Francis and Marjorie (Gosselin) F.; m. C. Nina Kerstiens, July 25, 1987; 1 child, Jake Buchanan. AB, Dartmouth Coll., 1982; cert. of attendance, Aristotelian U., Salonica, Greece, 1983; JD, U. Mich., 1986. Bar: Ill. 1986, U.S. Dist. Ct. (no. dist.) Ill. 1986. Assoc. Isham, Lincoln & Beale, Chgo., 1986-88; ptnr. Riordan, Larson, Bruckert & Moore, Chgo., 1988-92; mem. Ill. Senate, 1993-98, chmn. state govt. ops. com., 1997-98; U.S. senator from Ill., 1999-. Counsel Harris Bankmont, Inc., 1992-96. Rotary Found. internat. grad. scholar, 1982-83. Mem. Econ. Club Chgo., Inverness Golf Club, Union League Club. Republican. Roman Catholic. Office: US Senate 555 Dirksen Bldg Washington DC 20510-0001 E-mail: senator_fitzgerald@fitzgerald.senate.gov.

FITZ-GERALD, ROGER MILLER, lawyer; b. N.Y.C., July 13, 1935; s. Gerald Hartpence and Rovenia Francis (Miller) F.-G.; m. Martha Ann Odell, 1967 (div. 1985); children: Kathleen Odell, Maureen Roxanne, Arthur Thomas; m. Janice Evens, 1993. BS with honors, U. Ill., 1957, JD with honors, 1961. Bar: Ill. 1961, U.S. Dist. Ct. (no. dist.) 1961, U.S. Patent and Trademark Office, 1965, U.S. Ct. Customs and Patent Appeals, 1978, U.S. Ct. Appeals (fed. cir.) 1982, U.S. Dist. Ct. (so. dist.) Ill. 1992, U.S. Dist. Ct. (cen. dist.) Ill. 1994. Assoc. Kirkland, Ellis, Hodson, Chaffetz & Masters, Chgo., 1961-64; assoc. specializing in fgn. patent law Fitch, Even, Tabin & Luedeka, Chgo., 1964-72; patent atty. Bell & Howell Co., Chgo., 1972-74, sr. patent atty., 1974-75, group patent atty., 1975-76, group patent counsel, 1976-82, sr. patent counsel, 1982-85, sr. tech. law counsel, 1985-86, chief tech. law counsel, 1986-90; pvt. practice Urbana, Wilmette, Belleville, Ill., 1990—, St. Louis, 1990—. Author: (with Ferdinand J. Zeni) Precinct Captain's Guide, 1968; contbg. author: Materials on Legislation (Read, MacDonald, Fordham and Pierce), 1973 Constl. revision chmn. Ill. Young Republican Orgn., 1968-70. Served with AUS, 1957 Mem. ABA, Ill. Bar Assn., Chgo. Bar Assn., Champaign County Ill. Bar Assn., Intellectual Property Law Assn. Chgo., Am. Intellectual Property Law Assn., Assn. Corp. Patent Counsel, Computer Law Assn., Order of Coif, Phi Beta Kappa, Phi Eta Sigma, Phi Delta Phi, Delta Upsilon (province gov. 1969-75). Computer, Patent, Trademark and copyright. Home: 906B E Colorado Ave Urbana IL 61801-6305 Office: 1104 S Orchard St Urbana IL 61801-4852

FITZGERALD, THOMAS ROBERT, judge; b. Chgo., July 10, 1941; s. Thomas Henry and Kathryn (Touhy) F.; m. Gayle Ann Aubry, July 1, 1967; children: Maura, Kathryn, Jean, Thomas., Ann. Student Loyola U., Chgo., 1959-63; J.D., John Marshall Law Sch., Chgo., 1968. Bar: Ill. 1968, U.S. Dist. Ct. (no. dist.) Ill. 1968. Asst. state's atty. State's Atty. Cook County, Chgo., 1968-76, trial asst., 1968-72, felony trial supr., 1973-76; judge criminal div. Circuit Ct. Cook County, 1976—2000, justice Ill. State Supreme Ct., 2000-; adj. prof. law Chgo., Kent Coll. Law, 1977—2000, asst. coord. trial ad program, 1989-96, instr. Einstein Inst. for Sci., Health and Cts.; mem. faculty Nat. Inst. Trial Advs., Boulder, Colo., 1982, Ill. Jud. Conf., Chgo., 1982— . Pres. Sch. Bd. Queen of Universe Parish, Chgo., 1974-75. Served with USN. Recipient Outstanding Jud. Performance award Chgo. Crime Commn., Herman Kogan Media award for excellence in broadcast jour.; named Celtic Man of Yr. Celtic Legal Soc. Fellow Ill. Bar Found.; mem. Chgo. Bar Assn., Ill. Bar Assn., Ill. Judges Assn. (bd. dirs. 1981-84, treas. 1985, sec. 1986, 3d v.p. 1987, pres.). Office: 160 N LaSalle St Rm N-2013 Chicago IL 60601 Fax: 312-793-4579.

FITZHUGH, DAVID MICHAEL, lawyer; b. San Francisco, Nov. 24, 1946; s. William DeHart and Betty Jean (Jeffries) F.; m. Jenny Lu Conner, Dec. 22, 1967; children: Ross DeHart, Cameron Hyatt, Michael Jeffries. Student, Carleton Coll., 1964-67; BA, Coll. William and Mary, 1972; JD, U. Va., 1975. Bar: D.C. 1975, U.S. Dist. Ct. D.C. 1979, U.S. Dist. Ct. Md. 1987, U.S. Ct. Claims 1980, U.S. Ct. Appeals (fed. cir.) 1982, U.S. Ct. Appeals (D.C. cir.) 1987, U.S. Ct. Appeals (4th cir.) 1989, U.S. Supreme Ct. 1982. Assoc. McKenna & Cuneo, Washington, 1975-80, ptnr., 1980-98, chmn. litigation dept., 1984-94; assoc. counsel Office of Counsel Naval Air Systems Command, 1999—. Mem. editl. bd. Nat. Contract Mgmt. Assn. Jour., 1975-2000; contbr. articles to legal pubs. Capt. USMC, 1967-71, Vietnam. Federal civil litigation, Government contracts and claims. Home: 11140 Beacon Way Lusby MD 20657-2442 Office: AIR-11.1 NAVAIRSYSCOM HQ Office of Counsel Bldg 2272 Ste 257 47123 Buse Rd Unit Moffett Patuxent River MD 20670-1547 E-mail: fitzhughdm@navair.navy.mil.

FITZHUGH, KATHRYN CORROTHERS, law librarian; b. Little Rock, Feb. 4, 1950; d. Charles Edward and Billie Jean (Burns) Corrothers; m. Benjamin Dewey Fitzhugh, Nov. 28, 1970; 1 child, Erica Janine. BA, U. Ark., 1971; MSLS, U. Ill., 1976; JD, U. Ark., Little Rock, 1983. Bar: Ark. 1983, U.S. Dist. Ct. (ea. dist.) Ark. 1983. Sci./tech. libr. Grad. Inst. Tech., Little Rock, 1977-79; br. libr. U.S. Cts. Br. Libr., Little Rock, 1980-83, 89-92; law clk. Hon. George Howard Jr., Little Rock, 1983-84; ptnr. Fitzhugh & Fitzhugh, Little Rock, 1985-87; ref./circulation libr. U. Ark.-Little Rock/Pulaski County Law Libr., 1987-89, pub. svcs. libr., 1992-97, ref./spl. collections libr., 1997—. Contbg. author: Handbook of Law for Arkansas Women, 1987; contbr. chpt. to book; editor in field. Mem. North Little Rock NAACP, 1990—5; mem. Ouachita coun. Girl Scouts U.S., 1986-88, troop leader, 1997-98; mem. Shorter Coll. Adult Edn. Bd., 1986-87, Carver Magnet Elem. Sch. PTA, 1989-96. Co-recipient Pub. Svc. award U. Ark.-Little Rock Bowen Sch. Law, 2003; The Herbert Lehman Edn. Fund scholar, 1967-71. Mem. ALA, ABA, Am. Assn. Law Librs., Ark. Bar Assn., Ark. Assn. Women Lawyers (corr. sec. 1989-90), Soc. of Am. Archivists, Soc. Southwest Archivists, Southwestern Assn. Law Librs. (pres. 2002-03) Ark. Hist. Assn., Delta Sigma Theta. Methodist. Office: U Ark at Little Rock Pulaski County Law Libr 1203 McMath Ave Little Rock AR 72202-5142

FITZPATRICK, DENNIS JOHN, insurance company executive, lawyer; b. Milw., Dec. 10, 1948; s. John Dennis and Kathryne Leslie (Billings) F.; m. Mary Catherine Underhill, Nov. 23, 1974; children: Mary Claire, Margaret Ann. BA cum laude, Creighton U., 1971; JD cum laude, Marquette U., 1974. Bar: Wis. 1974, U.S. Dist. Ct. (ea. and we. dists.) Wis. 1974, U.S. Ct. Appeals (7th cir.) 1977, U.S. Supreme Ct. 1978; CLU; chartered fin. cons. Ptnr. Maier & Fitzpatrick, Milw., 1974-84; dir. advanced planning divsn. Northwestern Mut. Life Ins. Co., Milw., 1984—. Instr. continuing edn. Marquette U., 1977—. Contbr. articles to profl. publs. Past. pres., bd. dirs. Artreach of Milw., Ltd., 1984-94, Urban Day Sch., Milw., 1987-2001. Served to capt. USAR, 1974-82. Mem. ABA, Am. Soc. Fin. Svcs. Profls. (bd. dirs. Milw. chpt. 1995-97), Wis. Bar Assn., Milw. Bar Assn. (chmn. taxation sect. 1980-82), Advanced Assn. of Life Underwriting, Alpha Sigma Nu. Roman Catholic. Avocations: golf, reading, basketball, travel. Office: Northwestern Mut Life Ins Co 720 E Wisconsin Ave Milwaukee WI 53202-4703 E-mail: fitzlaw@execpc.com., dennisfitzpatrick@northwesternmutual.com.

FITZPATRICK, DUROSS, federal judge; b. Macon, Ga., Oct. 19, 1934; s. Mark W. and Jane L. (Duross) F.; m. Beverly O'Connor, Mar. 17, 1963; children: Mark O'Connor, Devon Hart. BS in Forestry, U. Ga., 1961, LLB, 1966. Bar: Ga. 1965. Assoc. Elliott & Davis, Macon, 1966-67; sole practice Cochran, Ga., 1967-83; ptnr. Fitzpatrick & Mullis, Cochran, 1983-86; judge U.S. Dist. Ct. (mid. dist.) Ga., Macon, 1986-95, chief judge, 1995-2001. Bd. govs. State Bar Ga., 1976-83, mem. exec. com., 1979-84, pres., 1984-85; mem. Ga. Chief Justice's Commn. on Professionalism. Legal counsel Rep. del. Gen. Assembly Ga., 1969. Served with USMC, 1954-57. Fellow Am. Bar Found., Ga. Bar Found.; mem. Oconee Bar Assn. (pres. 1970), Am. Inns Ct. (Master of the Bench, W.A. Bootle chpt. 1999—), Macon Bar Assn. Republican. Episcopalian. Home: RR 1 Box 1525 Jeffersonville GA 31044-9768

FITZPATRICK, HAROLD FRANCIS, lawyer; b. Jersey City, Oct. 16, 1947; s. Harold G. and Anne Marie F.; m. Joanne M. Merry, Sept. 22, 1973; children: Elizabeth, Kevin, Matthew, Christopher. AB, Boston Coll., 1969; MBA, NYU, 1971; JD, Harvard U., 1974. Bar: N.J. 1974, U.S. Dist. Ct. N.J. 1974, U.S. Ct. Internat. Trade, 1986, U.S. Supreme Ct. 1994. Securities analyst Chase Manhattan Bank, N.Y.C., 1970-71, Brown Bros., Harriman & Co., N.Y.C., 1971; staff asst. U.S. Senate, Washington, 1972; law clk. to assoc. justice N.J. Supreme Ct., Trenton, 1974-75; assoc. Cleary, Gottlieb, Steen & Hamilton, N.Y.C., 1975-78; mng. ptnr. Fitzpatrick & Waterman, Secaucus, N.J., 1978—, Bayonne, N.J., 1978—. Gen. counsel Housing Authority City of Bayonne, 1976—, Color Pigments Mfrs. Assn., Alexandria, Va., 1978—, N.J. Assn. Housing and Redevel. Authorities, Brick, N.J., 1979—, Housing Authority Town of Secaucus, N.J., 1980-88, Rahway (N.J.) Geriatrics Ctr. Inc., 1981-92, Housing Authority City of Englewood, N.J., 1985-91, Housing Authority City of Rahway, 1986-2000, Edgewater Mcpl. Utilities Authority, 1986-93, Housing Authority City of Woodbridge, N.J., 1988-94, Housing Authority City of Asbury Pk., N.J., 1991-94, Bd. Edn. City of Rahway, 1994-97, N.J. Pub. Housing Authority Joint Ins. Fund, 1995-2001. Mem. ABA, N.J. Bar Assn., Hudson County Bar Assn. (trustee, officer 1984-92, pres. 1993), Beta Gamma Sigma. Corporate, general, Environmental, Municipal (including bonds). Office: Fitzpatrick & Waterman 333 Meadowlands Pkwy Secaucus NJ 07096-3159

FITZPATRICK, JAMES DAVID, lawyer; b. Syracuse, N.Y., Oct. 21, 1938; s. William Francis and Margaret Mary (Shortt) F. BS, Holy Cross Coll., Worcester, Mass., 1960; JD, Syracuse U., 1963. Bar: N.Y. 1963, U.S. Dist. Ct. (no. dist.) N.Y. 1965. Assoc. Bond, Schoeneck & King, Syracuse, N.Y., 1963-76, mem., 1976-88, ptnr., 1988—. Pres. Hiscock Legal Aid Soc., Syracuse, 1975-76; faculty Nat. Bus. Inst., Eau Claire, Wis., 1990—; del. Russian Conf. on Banking-The Kremlin, Moscow, 1992, 93; spkr. Internat. Conf. on Terrorism, Madrid, 2002. Mem. presdl. Roundtable, Washington, 1991-92; founding mem. pres.'s task force Nat. Coalition Against Pornography, Common Cause; chmn. adv. bd. Rep. Nat. Coms., 1994; mem. The Studio Mus. in Harlem, Am. Mus. Nat. History; founding mem. Am. Air Mus.; nat. adv. coun. USN Meml. Found. Recipient Afghanistan Freedom Fighter award Afghan Mercy Fund, 1989, Rep. Senatorial Medal of Freedom, Honored Friend of El Salvador award, 1991, Wisdom award of Honor, Wisdom Soc. for Advancement of Knowledge, Learning and Rsch. in Edn., named to Wisdom Hall of Fame, 1999. Mem. ABA, NAACP, N.Y. State Bar Assn., Onondaga County Bar Assn. (chmn. real estate com. 1990-96), Internat. Bar Assn., Am. Land Title Assn., UN Assn. of U.S.A., Habitat for Humanity Internat., Amnesty Internat. U.S.A., Nat. Audubon Soc., Ctr. for Nat. Independence in Politics, Smithsonian Nat. Assocs., Nat. Trust for Hist. Preservation, Navy League U.S., World Future Soc., Ams. Guild, Internat. Platform Assn. (spkr. Internat. Youth Ctr., New Delhi), Inst. Global Ethics, World Jurist Assn. Republican. Roman Catholic. Avocations: housing education, reading, walking. Private international, Property, real (including real estate development, water). Home: 201 Croyden Rd Syracuse NY 13224-1917 Office: Bond Schoeneck & King 1 Lincoln Ctr Fl 18 Syracuse NY 13202-1324 E-mail: fitzpaj@bsk.com.

FITZPATRICK, JAMES FRANKLIN, lawyer; b. Bluffton, Ind., Jan. 18, 1933; s. Raymond North and Evelyn (Baughman) F.; m. Sandra McNear, July 22, 1961; children: Michael, David, Benjamin. AB, Ind. U., 1955, JD, 1959; postgrad., Cambridge U., 1956. Law clk. to chief judge U.S. Ct. Appeals, Chgo., 1959-61; assoc. Arnold & Porter, Washington, 1961-67, ptnr., 1967—. Adj. prof. law Georgetown U., Washington, 1971-75, 2003; acad. vis. London Sch. Econs., 1978-79; Trinity Coll., Dublin, Ireland, 1987-88; chmn., Internat. Human Rights Law Group, 1999—; vis. prof. law U. N.Mex., 1997. Author: Law and Roadside Hazards, 1975. Bd. dirs. ACLU, 1983-85, pres. Nat. Capital chpt., Washington, 1982-83; pres. Washington Project for the Arts, 1984-90; dir. Ctr. for Auto Safety, 1984—, The Phillips Collection, 1990—, The Shakespeare Theatre, 1991—, Site Santa Fe, 1997—, Ctr. for Arts and Culture, 1998—, Brit. Am. Arts Assn., 1999—; nat. chmn. Young Citizens for Johnson, 1964. Mem. ABA, Phi Beta Kappa Democrat. Presbyterian. Office: Arnold & Porter 555 12th St NW Washington DC 20004-1206

FITZPATRICK, JOSEPH MARK, lawyer; b. Jersey City, May 27, 1925; s. Joseph Francis Stephen and Meave (Wilson) F.; m. Elizabeth Anne Keane, June 18, 1949; children: Elizabeth A., Susan E., Christopher M., Stephen R. ME, Stevens Inst. Tech., 1945; JD, Georgetown U., 1951. Bar: Va. 1950, U.S. Patent Office 1950, N.Y. 1954. Trial atty. anti-trust divsn. Dept. Justice, 1951-53; mem. firm Ward, McElhannon, Brooks & Fitzpatrick, N.Y.C., 1954-70, Fitzpatrick, Cella, Harper & Scinto, N.Y.C., 1970—. With USNR, 1943-46. Fellow Am. Coll. Trial Lawyers; mem. ABA, Va. Bar Assn., N.Y. Bar Assn., Assn. of Bar of City of N.Y., Am. Intellectual Property Law Assn., N.Y. Intellectual Property Law Assn., Manasquan River Yacht Club. Federal civil litigation, Patent, Trademark and copyright. Home: 17 Oak Ln Scarsdale NY 10583-1628 Office: Fitzpatrick Cella Harper Scinto 30 Rockefeller Plz Fl 38 New York NY 10112-3800

FITZPATRICK, WHITFIELD WESTFELDT, lawyer; b. New Orleans, Jan. 31, 1942; s. William Harry and Frances (Westfeldt) F.; m. Jean Phipps, July 6, 1984. BA, Washington & Lee U., 1964; JD, Tulane U., 1967; LLM, Grenoble U., France, 1969, Doctorate, 1972. Bar: La. 1967, Va. 1972, N.Y. 1974, U.S. Dist. Ct. (ea. dist.) La. 1974, D.C. 1975, U.S. Dist. Ct. (we. dist.) La. 1975, U.S. Ct. Appeals (5th cir.) 1975. Law clk. Supreme Ct. Commonwealth of Va., Norfolk, 1969-70; assoc. Coudert Bros., N.Y.C., 1972-74; sr. assoc. Phelps, Dunbar, Marks, Claverie & Sims, New Orleans, 1974-76; counsel Mobil Oil Corp., New Orleans, 1976-79, Mobil North Sea Ltd., London, 1979-82; gen. counsel The Hague, Netherlands, 1982; sr. counsel, asst. sec. Mobil Exploration and Producing U.S., Inc., Midland, Tex., 1987-89; asst. sec. Mobil Producing Tex. and N.Mex., Inc., Midland, 1987-89; with direction juridique Elf Aquitaine, Europe and U.S. coord., 1989-94; spl. advisor to dir. of comml. and lic. adminstrn. divsn. ELF Petroleum Norge, 1994-97; exec. v.p. and gen. counsel Fountain Oil Inc., 1997—99; of counsel The Silecky Firm, 1999—. Contbr. articles to profl. pubs. Named Mem. Soc. of the Friends of the Legion of Honor, Ordres de Chevalerie; Grenoble U. Law Sch. scholar, 1967-69; fellow Govt. of France, 1970-72. Mem. ABA, Maritime Law Assn., Internat. Bar Assn., La. Bar Assn., Va. Bar Assn., N.Y. Bar Assn., D.C. Bar Assn., chmn. Am. Coordinating Coun. of Norway, Boston Club of New Orleans, Racquet and Tennis Club of N.Y., Royal Auto Club of London, Soc. Colonial Wars, Societé des Amis du Musée National de la Légion d'Honneur. Avocations: golf, skiing, reading, tennis. Oil, gas, and mineral, Mergers and acquisitions. Home: Camilla Collets vei No 8 0258 Oslo Norway

FITZSIMMONS, B. JOSEPH, JR., lawyer; b. Weymouth, Mass., Oct. 18, 1940; s. B. Joseph Sr. and Rita M. (Mitchell) F. AB in History cum laude, Boston Coll., 1963; JD, New Eng. Sch. Law, 1967. Bar: Mass. 1967, U.S. Dist. Ct. Mass. 1969, U.S. Ct. Appeals (1st cir.) 1969, U.S. Supreme Ct. 1979; cert. U.S. Profl. Tennis Registry instr.; PGA golf profl. Pvt. practice, Weymouth, 1967-77, 93—; spl. asst. atty. gen., asst. dist. atty. Commonwealth of Mass., Boston and Dedham, 1970—72; equity clk. Norfolk County/Commonwealth of Mass., Dedham, 1972-80; trial judge Mass. Trial Ct., Boston, 1980-93. Author: Representing the Plaintiff, 1980; contbr. articles to profl. jours. Pers. officer Town of Weymouth, 1970-73, selectman, 1973-77, chmn., 1976, chair Nike site acquisition task force. Mem. Mass. Bar Found., Mass. Bar Assn., Bar Assn. Norfolk County, Quincy Bar Assn. (bd. govs. 1967—, Alfred P. Malaney award for leadership in legal field 1991). Roman Catholic. Avocations: tennis, golf, reading. Alternative dispute resolution, Appellate, Land use and zoning (including planning). Office: Fitzsimmons Law Offices 255 Main St Weymouth MA 02188-2000 E-mail: fitzlaw@xpres.net.

FJELSTAD, PAUL, lawyer, editor; b. Northfield, Minn., Oct. 17, 1954; s. Ralph and Margaret (Haugseth) F. BA, Carleton Coll., Northfield, 1977; JD, U. Minn., 1980. Bar: N.Y. 1981, Minn. 1981, Wash. 1994. Assoc. Hall, McNicol, Hamilton & Clark, N.Y.C., 1980-83; staff atty. Gen. Instrument Corp., N.Y.C., 1983-85; legal writer Matthew Bender and Co., N.Y.C., 1986-89, database atty., analyst, 1989-91, retrieval systems devel. analyst, 1991-95; atty. Tolman & Kirk, Poulsbo, Wash., 1996-97; owner WnWin Solutions, 1997—. Chmn. Kitsap County Vol. Atty. Svc., 1998-2001; dir. Kitsap County Law Libr., 1998—; mem. steering com. Equal Justice Coalition, 2000—; dir. Kitsap Legal Svcs., 2002—. Contbr. to book Moore's Federal Practice, 1986-89. Mem. Kitsap County Bar Assn. (trustee 2000-01). Office: PO Box 1460 Silverdale WA 98383-1460 E-mail: paul@fjelstad.com.

FLADUNG, RICHARD DENIS, lawyer; b. Kansas City, Mo., Aug. 1, 1953; s. Jerome Francis and Rosemary (Voeste) F.; m. Leslie Lynn Cox, June 1, 1985; children: Daniel Edwin, Erica Anne, Derek Richard. BSCE, U. Kans., 1976, postgrad., 1977; JD, Washburn U., 1980. Bar: Kans. 1980, U.S. Dist. Ct. Kans. 1980, Ind. 1981, U.S. Dist. Ct. (so. dist.) Ind. 1981, U.S. Patent and Trademark Office 1982, Mo. 1983, Tex. 1984, U.S. Dist. Ct. (we. dist.) Mo. 1983, U.S. Dist. Ct. (so. dist.) Tex. 1984, U.S. Ct. Appeals (fed. cir.) 1984, U.S. Ct. Appeals (5th cir.) 1987, U.S. Supreme Ct. 1987, U.S. Dist. Ct. (we. dist.) Tex. 1988, U.S. Dist. Ct. (ea. and no. dists.) Tex. 2000. Engr. Black and Veatch Cons. Engrs., Kansas City, 1975—80; corp. counsel CTB Inc., Milford, Ind., 1980—82; patent atty. Chase & Yakimo and predecessor firm, Kansas City, 1982—83, Bush, Moseley, Riddle and Jackson and predecessor firm, Houston, 1983—87, Pravel, Hewitt & Kimball, Houston, 1987—88, Akin, Gump, Strauss, Hauer & Feld LLP, Houston, 1999—. Contbr. articles on patent matters and ins. coverage for intellectual property matters to profl. edn. programs. Legal aide to spkr. of Kans. Ho. of Reps., Topeka, 1980; com. chmn. Troop 1089, BSA, Houston, 2000—. Named One of Outstanding Young Men of Am., 1985. Fellow Tex. Bar Found., Houston Bar Found. (charter), Houston Young Lawyers Found.; mem. ABA (vice chmn. patent, trademark sect. young lawyer div. 1988-89), ASCE, Houston Bar Assn. (ex officio bd. dirs. 1987-88, vice chmn. profl. responsibility com. 1991—), Am. Intellectual Property Law Assn., Tex. Young Lawyers Assn. (bd. dirs. 1988), Mo. Bar Assn., Ind. Bar Assn., Houston Young Lawyers Assn. (pres. 1987-88, exec. mem. bd. dirs. 1987-88, Outstanding Com. Chmn. award 1984-86), Kansas City Bar Assn., Houston Intellectual Property Law Assn., Pi Alpha Kappa (treas. 1974-75). Roman Catholic. Avocations: tennis, jogging, biking, golf. Trademark and copyright, Intellectual property, Patent. Office: Akin Gump Strauss Hauer & Feld LLP 1900 Pennzoil Pl S Tower 711 Louisiana St Houston TX 77002-2716 E-mail: rfladung@akingump.com.

FLAHERTY, FRANCIS XAVIER, judge; b. Providence, Jan. 8, 1947; s. Eugene and Gertrude (Strong) F.; m. Donna Marie Anderson, 1969; children— Nicole, Michael, Brendan. BA, Providence Coll., 1968; JD, Suffolk U. Sch. Law, 1975. Dir., Warwick Drug Abuse Program, RI, 1971-73, dir. Fed. Program, 1973-75, labor relations administr. City of Warwick, 1975-78, asst. city solicitor, city prosecutor, 1975-78, councilman ward 6, 1978-84, mayor, 1985—1990. Litigation ptnr., Edwards & Angell, formerly mnging ptnr., Wynn & Wynn, formerly mnging ptnr., Flaherty, Orton, and Flaherty, 1995-2003; RI State Supreme Court Justice, 2003-. Chmn. Warwick Community Action Program; bd. dir. Warwick Boys and Girls Club; mem. RI Nat. League Cities. Served to 1st lt. US Army, 1968-70. Decorated 3 Bronze Stars, 3 Air medals, Vietnam Campaign medal, Vietnamese Cross for Gallantry, Combat Infantryman's award, Vietnamese Civic Action award, Vietnamese Service medal. Mem. VFW, Am. Legion, ABA, RI Bar Assn., Kent County Bar Assn., Kent County Bd. Realtors (chmn.). Roman Catholic. Office: Edward & Angell 2700 Hospital Trust Towers Providence RI 02903*

FLAHERTY, JAMES GRANT, lawyer; s, Bernard Joseph and Dorothy Janet (Longyear) F.; m. Susan Ebaugh, Sept. 27, 1980; children: Stephen Matthew, Meghan Christine. BS in Bus. Adminstrn., Miami U., Oxford, Ohio, 1980; MBA, U. Dayton, 1983, JD, 1984. Bar: Ohio 1984. Assoc. Millikin & Fitton, Hamilton, Ohio, 1984-87, Dale O. Lierman Co, LPA, Cin., 1987-89, Martin, Pergram, Browning & Parker Co., LPA, Columbus, Ohio, 1989-91, Ohio Bur. Workers' Compensation, Columbus, 1991-93; sole practice Westerville, Ohio, 1993—. Bd. dirs. Jr. Achievement, vice chmn., 1985-88; bd. dirs. United Way Hamilton, 1988-89, Butler County Litter Control, vice chmn., 1987-89; elder Presbyn. Ch.; v.p. Fairfield C. of C., bd. dirs. 1985-88; bd. dirs. Leadership Worthington, 1990-96, Ctrl. Ohio Planned Giving Coun. (pres. 2002), Leadership Westerville (sec. 2002-03), Del. City Friends of Trail (vice chair 2001). Mem. ABA (sect. of taxation com. on S corps. and small bus. com. 1990-92), Ohio State Bar Assn. (workers' compensation com. 1992-93), Columbus Bar Assn., Rotary Club Westerville (pres. 1997, asst. gov. 1999-2002), Westerville C. of C. (bd. dirs. 1995-2003, chmn. 2000). Republican. Avocations: hockey, running, woodturning, golf. Corporate, general, Estate planning, Probate (including wills, trusts). Home: 142 Baranof W Westerville OH 43081-6207 Office: James G Flaherty Co LPA Ste 100 575 Charring Cross Dr Westerville OH 43081-4901 E-mail: jim@flahertylaw.com.

FLAHERTY, JOHN PAUL, JR., state supreme court chief justice emeritus; b. Pitts., Nov. 19, 1931; s. John Paul and Mary G. (McLaughlin) F.; m. Linet Flaherty; 7 children, 2 stepchildren. BA, Duquesne U., 1953; JD, U. Pitts., 1958; LLD (hon.), Widener U., 1993. Bar: Pa. 1958. Pvt. practice, Pitts., 1958-73; mem. faculty Carnegie-Mellon U., 1958-73; judge Ct. Common Pleas Allegheny County, 1973-79, pres. judge civil divsn., 1978-79; justice Supreme Ct. Pa., 1979-96, chief justice, 1996—2001. USIA speaker in Far East, 1985-86. Mem. Pa. Hist. Soc.; chair Pa. County Records Com. Recipient Medallion of Distinction U. Pitts., 1987, Judicial award Pa. Bar Assn., 1993, Pres. award Pa. Bar Assn., 1999; Chief Justice John P. Flaherty award, Pa. Bar Assn. Conf. of Bar Leaders, 2001; named Man of Yr. in law and govt., Greater Pitts. Jaycees, 1978, named to Century Club of Disting. Alumni, Duquesne U., 1994. Mem. Pa. Acad. Sci. (chmn.

hon. exec. bd. 1978-89, Disting. Alumnus award 1977), Am. Law Inst., Pa. Soc., Pa. Bar Assn. (award 2001), Mil. History Soc. Ireland, Friendly Sons St. Patrick, Am. Legion. Office: Pa Supreme Ct Rm 810 City County Bldg Pittsburgh PA 15219

FLAHERTY, PETER, legal association administrator; m. Rose Flaherty; children: Ashleigh, Winston. Pres. Nat. Legal and Policy Ctr., Falls Church, Va., 1991—. Co-author: (book) The First Lady: A Comprehensive View of Hillary Rodham Clinton, 1996; contbr. articles to profl. jours. Chmn. Citizens for Reagan, 1984—88. Office: Nat Legal and Policy Ctr 107 Park Washington Ct Falls Church VA 22046 Office Fax: 703-237-2090.*

FLAME, ANDREW JAY, lawyer; b. Phila., Apr. 4, 1968; s. Sheldon Paul and Rita Ann Flame; m. Lori Jill Bolno, Nov. 17, 1996; 1 child, Rachel Sara. BS in Mktg., Pa. State U., 1990; JD, Temple U., 1993. Bar: Pa. 1993, N.J. 1993, U.S. Dist. Ct. N.J. 1993, U.S. Dist. Ct. (sbt. dist.) Pa. 1993, D.C. 1994, U.S. Dist. Ct. (mid. dist.) Pa. 1994. Law clk. to Hon. Louis Pollack U.S. Dist. Ct. (ea. dist.) Pa., Phila., 1992-93, law clk. to Hon. Stuart Dalzell, 1994; ptnr. Drinker Biddle & Reath LLP, Phila., 1993—. Founder, Camp 4 Happy Days, Phila., 1985-86; trainer Youth Implemented Programs, San Francisco, 1988; trustee, v.p. Reform Congregation Keneseth Israel, Phila., 1994—; mem. Golden Slipper Club Charity, Phila., 1994-2000; mem. com. Cheltenham Twp. (Pa.) Drug/Alcohol Bd., 1979-86, 91-93. Avocations: sports, travel. Bankruptcy, General civil litigation, Commercial, consumer (including collections, credit). Office: Drinker Biddle & Reath LLP 1100 N Market St Ste 1000 Wilmington DE 19801 Home: 118 Spyglass Dr Blue Bell PA 19422-3216 E-mail: andrew.flame@dbr.com.

FLAMM, LEONARD N(ATHAN), lawyer; b. Newark, May 23, 1943; s. Sydney Lewis and Lillian (Schreiber) F. Cert., London Sch. Econs., 1964; BA, Dartmouth Coll., 1965; JD, Harvard U., 1968. Bar: N.J. 1968, N.Y. 1970, U.S. Ct. Appeals (2d cir.) 1970, Fla. 1976, U.S. Dist. Ct. (so. and ea. dists.) N.Y. 1976, U.S. Ct. Appeals (7th cir.) 1986, U.S. Ct. Appeals (3d cir.) 1987, U.S. Supreme Ct. 1989. Assoc. Marshall, Bratter, Greene, Allison & Tucker, N.Y.C., 1968-70, Donovan, Leisure, Newton & Irvine, N.Y.C., 1970-72, Glass, Greenberg & Irwin, N.Y.C., 1972-75; ptnr. Hockert & Flamm, N.Y.C., 1975-90; pvt. practice N.Y.C., 1990—. Contbg. author Employee Rights Litigation: Pleadings and Practice, 1991. Named one of Best Lawyers in U.S., Town & Country Mag., 1985. Mem. Assn. Bar City N.Y. (legal referral panel 1975—), Nat. Employment Lawyers Assn. (v.p. N.Y. chpt., nat. co-chmn. Age Discrimination in Employment Act com.) Civil rights, Federal civil litigation, Labor (including EEOC, Fair Labor Standards Act, labor-management relations, NLRB, OSHA). Office: 880 3rd Ave Ste 1300 New York NY 10022-4730 E-mail: adealnf@aol.com.

FLANAGAN, DEBORAH MARY, lawyer; b. Hackensack, N.J., Sept. 17, 1956; d. Joseph Francis and Mary Agnes (Fitzsimmons) F.; m. Glen H. Koch, Aug. 27, 1983. BA summa cum laude, Fordham U., 1978, JD, 1981; LLM in Taxation, NYU, 1987. Bar: N.Y. 1982 and U.S. Dist. Ct. 1988. V.p., assoc. tax counsel The McGraw-Hill Inc. Cos., N.Y.C., 1981—. Mem. Assn. Bar City N.Y., Fordham U. Law Alumni Assn., NYU Law Alumni Assn. Corporate taxation, Personal income taxation, State and local taxation. Home: 201 Chestnut Ridge Rd Saddle River NJ 07458-2812 Office: The McGraw-Hill Cos Ste C3A 1221 Avenue Of The Americas New York NY 10020-1095

FLANAGAN, JAMES HENRY, JR., lawyer, writer, business educator; b. San Francisco, Sept. 11, 1934; s. James Henry Sr. and Mary Patricia (Gleason) F.; m. Charlotte Anne Nevins, June 11, 1960; children: Nancy, Christopher, Christina, Alexis, Victoria, Grace. AB in Polit. Sci., Stanford U., 1956, JD, 1961. Bar: Calif. 1962, U.S. Dist. Ct. (no. dist.) Calif. 1962, U.S. Ct. Appeals (9th cir.) 1962, U.S. Dist. Co. (so. dist.) Calif. 1964, U.S. Dist. Ct. (ea. dist.) Calif. 1967, Oreg. 1984. Assoc. Creede, Dawson & McElrath, Fresno, Calif., 1962-64; ptnr. Pettitt, Blumberg & Sherr and successor firms, Fresno, 1964-75; pvt. practice, Clovis, Calif., 1975—99, North Fork, Calif., 1992-98. Instr. Humprey's Coll. Law, Fresno, 1964-69; instr. bus. Calif. State U., Fresno, 1986—; instr. MBA program Coll. of Notre Dame, Belmont, 1990-91; instr. Nat. U., 1991—, Emerson Inst., 1998—; judge pro tem Fresno County Superior Ct., 1974-77; gen. counsel Kings River Water Assn., 1976-79; founder, CEO Bus. and Non-profit Devel. Ctr. Author: California Water District Laws, 1962; columnist. Choir mem. Our Lady of Sierra, 1998—; exec. com. parish coun. St. Helen's Ch., 1982-85, chmn. exec. com., 1985; pres. parish coun. St. John's Cathedral, 1974-82; pres. bd. dirs. 3d Floor Ctrl. Calif.; bd. dirs. Fresno Facts Found., 1969-70, Fresno Dance Repertory Assn., St. Anthony's Retreat Ctr., Three Rivers, Calif.; sec. Coarsegold Resource Conservation Dist.; co-founder Clovis Big Dry Creek Hist. Soc.; co-chmn. Sierra Vista Nat. Scenic Byway Assn.; judge advocate Mountain Detachment, Marine Corps League. Recipient President award Fresno Jaycees, 1964. Mem. Calif. Bar Assn., Oreg. Bar Assn. (inactive), Fresno County Bar Assn., Calif. Trial Lawyers Assn. (chpt. pres. 1975, 83, state bd. govs. 1990-94), Fresno Trial Lawyers Assn., Am. Arbitration Assn., Stanford Alumni Assn. (life, svc. award), Fresno Region Stanford Club (pres. 1979-80), Celtic Cultural Soc. Ctrl. Calif. (pres. 1977-78), Fresno County and City C. of C. (chmn. natural resources com. 1977-78), Clovis C. of C., North Fork C. of C. (pres. 1993-96, sec. 1998-2000, exec. dir. 2000—), Serra Club (pres. Fresno chpt. 1980-81, v.p. 1986-87), Rotary, Elks, KC (4th degree dep. grand knight), Superchex, Western Assn. Chamber Exec. Republican. Roman Catholic. Avocations: writing, music, gardening, sailing, fishing. Office: PO Box 1555 North Fork CA 93643-1555 E-mail: jayflanagan@netptc.net.

FLANAGAN, JOHN ANTHONY, lawyer, educator; b. Sioux City, Iowa, Nov. 29, 1942; s. J. Maurice and Lorna K. (Fowler) F.; m. Martha (Lang), May 8, 1982; children: Sean, Kathryn, Molly. BA, Iowa State U., 1964; JD, Georgetown U., 1968. Bar: Iowa, 1968; D.C., 1975; Ohio, 1977. Law clk. to judge U.S. Tax Ct., Washington, 1968-70; trial atty. U.S. Dept. Justice, Washington, 1970-74; prof. law U. Ohio, Cin., 1974-78; sr. tax ptnr. Graydon, Head, and Ritchey, Cin., 1978—. Adj. prof. U. Ohio, (Cin.), 1978--. Contbr. articles to profl. jour. Corp. mgr. United Way, Cin., 1988; head lawyers div. Fine Arts Fund, Cin., 1987-88; mem. Downtown Cin. Inc., 1995-2000. Mem. D.C. Bar Assn., Cin. Bar Assn.; Order of Coif. Roman Catholic. Avocations: gardening, golf, fly fishing. Corporate, general, Corporate taxation, Taxation, general. Home: 5 Walsh Ln Cincinnati OH 45208-3435 Office: Graydon Head & Ritchey 1900 5th-3rd Ctr PO Box 6464 Cincinnati OH 45202

FLANAGAN, JOSEPH PATRICK, JR., lawyer; b. Wilkes-Barre, Pa., Sept. 18, 1924; s. Joseph P. and Grace B. F.; m. Mary Elizabeth Mayock, Aug. 5, 1950; children: Maureen Elizabeth, Joseph P. III. BS, U.S. Naval Acad., 1947; JD, U. Pa., 1952. Bar: Pa. 1953, U.S. Dist. Ct. (ea. dist.) Pa. 1953, U.S. Ct. Appeals (3d cir.) 1953, U.S. Supreme Ct. 1997. Assoc. Saul, Ewing, Remick & Saul, Phila., 1952-56; ptnr. Ballard, Spahr, Andrews & Ingersoll, Phila., 1956-94, chmn. pub. fin. dept., 1961-90. Editor: Practicing Law Inst., Health Facilities Financing, 1976; co-author: In Search of Capital-A Trustee's Guide to Hospital Financing; reviewing editor Disclosure Roles of Counsel in State and Local Government Securities Offerings. editor-in-chief: U. Pa. Law Rev., 1951-52; contbr. articles to profl. jours. Bd. dirs. Phila. Com. of 70, 1952-56; former trustee Wyoming Sem., Kingston, Pa.; former mem. bd. visitors U. Pa. Law Sch.; bd. dirs. John Bartram Assn.; adv. coun. of federalism Nat. Govs. Assn., 1988. Served to lt. (j.g.) USN, 1946-49. Fellow Am. Bar Found.; mem. ABA (past chmn. urban, state and local govt. sect.), Nat. Assn. Securities Dealers (regulation arbitrator 1998—), Phila. Bar Assn. (past chmn. bus. law sect., bd. govs., past founding chmn. tax exempt fin. com., past chmn. profl. edn. com., client's security fund com., fee disputes com.), Pa. Bar Assn., Pa. Bar Inst. (pres. 1983, chmn. curriculum and course planning com. 1976-88), Phila. Club, Racquet Club, Phila. Cricket Club, Chesapeake Bay Yacht Club, Army Navy Country Club of Va. Republican. Roman Catholic. Finance, Health. Home: 401 E Mill Rd Flourtown PA 19031-1631 Office: Ballard Spahr Andrews & Ingersoll 1735 Market St Fl 49 Philadelphia PA 19103-7501

FLANAGAN, KATHLEEN, lawyer; b. Chickasha, Okla., Oct. 10, 1942; d. Funston Pershing and Frances Rita (Novotny) F.; m. Ralph Curtis Collins, Mar. 15, 1986 (dec. July 1993); children: Matthew, Margaret, Mariah. BS, Okla. State U., 1964, JD, 1976. Bar: Okla. 1976, U.S. Dist. Ct. (we. dist.) Okla. 1976, U.S. Ct. Appeals (10th cir.) 1978, U.S. Supreme Ct. 1980. Asst. U.S. atty. West. Dist. Okla. U.S. Atty. Office, Oklahoma City, 1978-81; asst. dist. Dist. Atty. Comanche County, Lawton, Okla., 1981-82; pvt. practice Walters, Okla., 1981—. Mem. Okla. Bar Assn., Cotton County Bar Assn. Democrat. Roman Catholic. Avocations: horseback riding, reading, silversmithing, cooking. Criminal, Family and matrimonial, Probate (including wills, trusts). Office: 310 N 5th PO Box 36 Walters OK 73572-0036

FLANAGAN, NORMAN PATRICK, lawyer; b. Pitts., Feb. 3, 1953; s. Norman Patrick and Janice (Smith) F.; m. Caroline E.E. Reverdin, Aug. 2, 1975; children: Erin Elizabeth, Sean Patrick. BS in Edn., Duquesne U., 1975; JD, Calif. Western U., 1978. Bar: Pa., Nev., U.S. Dist. Ct. Nev., U.S. Ct. Appeals (9th cir.), U.S. Supreme Ct. Dep. pub. defender Washoe County Pub. Defender's Office, Reno, 1979-81; asst. pub. defender Pub. Defender's Office, Reno, 1982—90; atty. Hale, Lane, Peek, Dennison & Howord, 1990—. Mem. Nev. State Bar Assn. (continuing legal edn. sect., pres-elect, 2002-), Legal Def. Fund (capital litigation sect.). Republican. Roman Catholic. Avocations: tennis, cross-country skiing. Office: 100 W Liberty St 10th Fl Reno NV 89505 Office Fax: 775-786-6179. E-mail: pflanagan@halelane.com.*

FLANARY, DONALD HERBERT, JR., lawyer; b. Texarkana, Ark., July 27, 1949; s. Donald Herbert and Tenney-Margaret (Webb) Flanary; m. Gina Lynn Rexrod; children: Donald Herbert III, Shannon Gail, Lauren Paige, David Tyler, John Paul, Noah Toliver. BS with honors, Tex. A&M U., 1971; JD, U. Houston, 1974. Bar: Tex. 1974, U.S. Dist. Ct. (no. dist.) Tex. 1975, U.S. Dist. Ct. (ea. dist.) Tex. 1976, U.S. Dist. Ct. (so. dist.) Tex. 1982, U.S. Tax Ct. 1982, U.S. Ct. Appeals (5th cir.) 1976, U.S. Ct. Appeals (11th cir.) 1984, U.S. Supreme Ct. 1983. Law clk. Hon. Mary Lou Robinson U.S. Dist. Ct., Amarillo, Tex., 1974—75; asst. dist. atty. Dallas County, Tex., 1975—76; ptnr. Henderson Bryant & Wolfe, Sherman, Tex., 1976—87, Vial Hamilton Koch & Knox, Dallas, 1988—99, Arter and Hadden, Dallas, 1999—2002, Flanary & Carter, Dallas, 2002—. Lectr. for bar assns. on tort law, 1981—84. Bd. dirs. Texoma Valley coun. Boy Scouts Am., Cancer Soc., Sherman. Named one of Outstanding Young Men Am., Jaycees, 1981. Fellow: Tex. Bar Found. (life); mem.: Am. Bd. Trial Advocates (cert.), Am. Bd. Profl. Liability Attys. (cert.), State Bar Assn. Tex. (bd. dirs. 1986—89, pres.-elect 1999), Nat. Bd. Trial Adv., Bd. Legal Specialization (civil trial law), Internat. Assn. Ins. Counsel (bd. cert. personal jury trial law), Grayson County Bar Assn. (pres. 1983—84), Tex. Assn. Def. Counsel (bd. dirs. 1981 1984, bd. dirs. 1986—88). Democrat. Roman Catholic. Federal civil litigation, State civil litigation, Insurance. E-mail: dflanary@flanarycarter.com.

FLANDERS, ROBERT G., JR., state supreme court justice; b. Freeport, N.Y., July 9, 1949; m. Ann I. Walls, May 29, 1971; children: Danielle, Heather, Zachary. AB magna cum laude, Brown U., 1971; JD, Harvard Law Sch., 1974. Bar: N.Y. 1975, Mass. 1976, R.I. 1976, U.S. Ct. of Appeals (1st and 2d cir.), U.S. Dist. Ct. (so. dist., ea. dist.) N.Y., R.I., Mass. Assoc. Paul, Weiss, Rifkind, Wharton & Garrison, N.Y.C., 1974-75; ptnr., chmn. litig. dept. Edwards & Angell, Providence, 1975-87; founding ptnr. Flanders & Medeiros Inc., 1987-96; assoc. justice R.I. Supreme Ct., 1996—. Mem. Am. Law Inst., 2000—; bd. dirs. Rsch. Engring. and Mfg., Inc. Contbr. articles to profl. publ. Bd. dirs. Brown Sports Found., 2000, Greater Providence YMCA, 1995—, Providence Performing Arts Ctr., 1997—, Vets. Meml. Auditorium, 1999—, Women and Infants Hosp., 1996—. Mem. ABA, Phi Beta Kappa. Avocations: tennis, clarinet, jazz, poetry, cigars. Office: Rhode Island Supreme Ct 250 Benefit St Providence RI 02903-2719 E-mail: rflanders@courts.state.ri.us.*

FLANNERY, ELLEN JOANNE, lawyer; b. Bklyn., Dec. 13, 1951; d. William Rowan and Mary Jane (Hamilla) Flannery. AB cum laude, Mount Holyoke Coll., 1973; JD cum laude, Boston U., 1978. Bar: Mass. 1978, D.C. 1979, U.S. Ct. Appeals (D.C. cir.) 1979, U.S. Dist. Ct. D.C. 1980, U.S. Ct. Appeals (4th cir.) 1981, U.S. Supreme Ct. 1983. Spl. asst. to commr. of health Mass. Dept. Pub. Health, Boston, 1973-75; law clk. U.S. Ct. Appeals D.C. cir., Washington, 1978-79; assoc. Covington & Burling, Washington, 1979-86, ptnr., 1986—. Lectr. ins. U. Va. Sch. Law, 1984—90, Boston U. Law Sch., 1993; bd. visitors Boston U. Sch. Law, 1995—; lectr. ins. U. Md. Sch. Law, 1994; mem. Nat. Conf. Lawyers and Scientists, AAAS-ABA, 1989—92; chair Fellows Adv. Rsch. Commn., 2002—. Contbr. to articles to profl. jours. Fellow: Am. Bar Found. (chair fellows adv. rsch. com. 2002—); mem.: ABA (chmn. life scis. divsn. 1982—84, chmn. com. med. practice 1987—88, chmn. life scis. divsn. 1988—91, vice chair food and drug law com. 1991—97, chmn. sect. sci. and tech. 1992—93, del. of sci. and tech. sect. to ho. of dels. 1993—, chmn. coordinating group on bioethics and the law 1998—2000, vice chair Ho. Tech. Com. 2002—), Cosmos Club. Administrative and regulatory, Health, Product liability. Office: Covington & Burling 1201 Pennsylvania Ave NW Washington DC 20004-2401

FLANNERY, HARRY AUDLEY, lawyer; b. New Castle, Pa., June 11, 1947; s. Wilbur Eugene and Ruth (Donaldson) F.; m. Maureen Louise Flaherty, June 28, 1969; children: Preston Wilbur, Courtney Lilyan. BA, Wesleyan U., 1969; JD, Ohio No. U., 1972; LLM in Taxation, Boston U., 1973. Bar: Pa. 1972, Ohio 2000, U.S. Tax Ct. 1973, U.S. Dist. Ct. (we. dist.) Pa. 1975, U.S. Supreme Ct. 1976, U.S. Ct. Appeals 1984. Sr. gen. svcs. specialist Pitts. Nat. Bank, 1973, asst. trust officer, 1974-75, trust legal officer, 1976; atty. Pa. Power Co., New Castle, 1977-98, FirstEnergy Corp., 1998—2002, FirstEnergy Svc. Co., 2002—; sec. fed. and state polit. coms. Pa. Power Co., New Castle, 1983-2000. V.p. Euclid Manor Corp.; mem. panel arbitrators Bur. Mediation Dept. Labor and Industry. Assoc. editor Pitts. Legal Jour., 1981-99; contbr. numerous articles to legal publs. Bd. dirs. Lawrence County chpt. Pa. Assn. for Blind, 1st v.p., 1994-96, pres. 1996-98; mem. Highland Presbyn. Ch., New Castle, Estate Planning Coun. of Pitts., 1975-77; sec. Lil Maur Found., 1989—, v.p., 1999—; elected mem. sch. bd. dirs. Neshannock Twp. Sch. Bd. Lawrence County, Pa., 1993—, v.p., 1997-99, pres., 1999-2001; mem. Pearson Park Commn., 1993-95; mem. oper. com. Lawrence County Area Vocat. Tech. Sch., 1997-2001; elected mem. Rep. Com., 3d Dist. Neshannock Twp., 2000. Mem. ABA (labor and employment law sect. com. on labor arbitration and law of collective bargaining agreements to 2002, tax sect. 1973-92, com. excise and employment taxes, subcom. payroll tax issues 1978-80), Pa. Bar Assn. (workmen's compensation sect., adminstrv. law sect., labor and employment law sect., pub. utility law sect., in house counsel com. 1995-98, 99-2000, dispute resolution com. 1989-91, 99-2000), Allegheny County Bar Assn. (coun., taxation sect. 1975-77, workmen's compensation sect., coun. labor and employment law sect. 2000—), Pitts. Legal Jour. Com., Lawrence County Bar Assn., Allegheny Tax Soc., Pennsylvania Soc. (life), The Supreme Ct. Pa. Hist. Soc. (life, trustee 1994—, sec. 1995-99, v.p. 1999-2002), Duquesne Club, Lawrence Club, New Castle Country Club, Lions (bd. dirs. 1982-91, tailtwister 1983-84, 3rd v.p. 1984-85, 2nd v.p. 1985, 1st v.p. 1986-87, pres. 1987-88), New Castle Lions Charities, Inc. (Lion of Yr. 1988-89), Iroquois Boating and Fishing Club, Phi Alpha Delta. Republican. Avocations: family, writing, tennis, boating. Labor (including EEOC, Fair Labor Standards Act, labor-management relations, NLRB, OSHA), Utilities, public, Workers' compensation. Home: 116 Valhalla Dr New Castle PA 16105-1037 Office: FirstEnergy Corp 76 S Main St Akron OH 44308-1425 E-mail: flanneryh@firstenergycorp.com.

FLANNERY, JOHN PHILIP, lawyer; b. N.Y.C., May 15, 1946; s. John Philip and Agnes Geraldine (Applegate) F.; 1 child by a previous marriage: Diana Elizabeth; m. Holly Lynne Smith, Mar. 1, 2003. BS in Physics, Fordham Coll., 1967; BS in Engring., Columbia U., 1969, JD, 1972; student, Art Students League, 1972-73; MS in Info. Sci., George Washington U., 2002. Bar: N.Y. 1973, U.S. Dist. Ct. (so. dist.) N.Y. 1973, U.S. Ct. Appeals (2d cir.) 1973, Va. 1983, U.S. Ct. Appeals (4th cir.) 1985, U.S. Ct. Appeals (D.C. cir.) 1985, U.S. Dist. Ct. (ea. dist.) Va. 1985, U.S. Supreme Ct. 1985. Mem. staff Ford Found. Project to Restructure Columbia U., N.Y.C., 1968; news rep. nat. press rels. IBM, 1970; law clk. Adminstrv. Conf. U.S., 1971, U.S. Ct. Appeals (2d cir.), 1972-74; asst. U.S. atty. Narcotics and Ofcl. Corruption units, So. Dist. N.Y., N.Y.C., 1974-79; sr. assoc. Poletti Freidin Prashker Feldman & Gartner, N.Y.C., 1979-82; spl. counsel U.S. Senate Judiciary Com., 1982, U.S. Senate Labor Com., 1982-83; Dem. candidate U.S. Congress from Va. 10th Dist., 1983-84; pvt. practice in civil and criminal litigation, 1984—. Spl. counsel Sen. Howard Metzenbaum, 1985-87; asst. dist. atty., Bronx, N.Y., 1986-87; counsel, bd. dirs. Washington Internat. Horse Show Assn., 1989-91; legal expert "Crime in D.C.", Fox TV, 1993, "Crime Bill" Wis. Pub. Radio, 1994, "People vs. O.J. Simpson" ABC Network Radio, 1994-95, "Va.'s No Parole" Larry King Live CNN, 1994, "Imprisonment" CBS Morning Show, 1994, Habeas Reform Court TV, 1996, Terrorism, 1996; spl. counsel U.S. House Judiciary Com., 1996-97; project dir., spl. counsel U.S. Edn. and Work Force Com., 1997-98; spl. counsel (impeachment proceedings) U.S. Rep. Zoe Lofgren, 1998-99, Washington staff chief, spl. counsel, 1999-2001; vis. exec. George Washington U. Sch. Bus. and Pub. Mgmt., 2002--; of counsel, Campbell, Miller, Zimmerman, P.C., 2002—; lectr. in field. Author: Commercial Information Brokers, 1973, Habeas Corpus Bores Hole in Prisoners' Civil Rights Action, 1975, Pro Se Litigation, 1975, Prison Corruption: A Mockery of Justice, 1980, Conspiracy: A Primer, 1988, Is Innocence Relevant to Execution? If Not, Isn't that Murder?, 1994, Equal Justice For All, 1995, Virginia Governor Allen's No-Parole Plan: A Billion Dollar Wasteland of Prisons, 1995; tech. columnist, Londoun Times Mirror, May 2002—. Mem. legis. commn. Citizen's Union, 1971—72; mem. Arlington Transp. Commn., 1983—85; chmn. bus. coun. Va. Gov.'s War on Drugs Task Force, 1983—84; pres. Franklin Soc., 1979—80; committeeman Dem. Party N.Y. County, 1979—80, Dem. Party Arlington County, 1983—84; coord. N.Y. State Lawyers Com. for Sen. Edward M. Kennedy, 1979—80; dir. Citizens for Sen. M. Kennedy, 1980; del. Dem. Nat. Conf., 1988, Va. Assembly Univ. W.Va., 1990; committeeman Loudoun County Dem. Com., 1995—, sec., 1995—, chmn., 1995—97; del. 10th Congress and Dist. Com., 1997—; mem. Ctrl. State (Va.) Com., 1997—; del. Dem. Nat. Conv., 2000; v.p. Loudoun County Dem. Com., 2001. Recipient U.S. Justice Dept. award for Outstanding Contbns. in Field of Drug Law Enforcement, 1977, U.S. Atty. Gen.'s Spl. Commendation for Outstanding Svc., 1979, FLEOA award, Fed. Law Enforcement Officer's Assn., 1984, NACDL's Marshall Stern award Outstanding Legis. Achievement, 1997. Mem. ABA, Bar Assn. of City of N.Y., N.Y. County Lawyers Assn., Arlington County Bar Assn., Loudon County Bar Assn., Nat. Assn. Criminal Def. Lawyers (chair briefbank com. 1990-91, legis. co-chair 1991—, dir. 1993—, President's commendation 1991, 92, 95), Acad. Polit. Sic., Va. Coll. Criminal Def. Attys. (bd. dirs. 1993-96). Democrat. Home: Ithaca Journey 21005 Stanford Sq Ste 406 Dulles VA 20166 E-mail: jonflan@aol.com.

FLANNERY, THOMAS AQUINAS, federal judge; b. Washington, May 10, 1918; s. John J. and Mary (Sullivan) C.; m. Rita Sullivan, Mar. 3, 1951; children: Thomas Aquinas, Irene M. LL.B., Cath. U., 1940. Bar: D.C. 1940. Practice in, Washington, 1940-42, 45-48; trial atty. Dept. Justice, Washington, 1948-50; asst. U.S. Atty. Washington, 1950-62; ptnr. Hamilton and Hamilton Washington, 1962-69; U.S. atty for D.C. Washington, 1969-71; U.S. dist. judge for D.C., 1971-85; now sr. judge U.S. Dist. Ct. for D.C., 1985—. Served as combat intelligence officer USAF, 1942-45, ETO. Fellow Am. Coll. Trial Lawyers; Mem. Am., D.C. bar assns. Office: US Dist Ct US Courthouse 333 Constitution Ave NW Washington DC 20001-2802

FLATTERY, THOMAS LONG, lawyer, legal administrator; b. Detroit, Nov. 14, 1922; s. Thomas J. and Rosemary (Long) F.; m. Gloria M. Hughes, June 10, 1947 (dec.); children: Constance Marie, Carol Dianne Lee, Michael Patrick, Thomas Hughes, Dennis Jerome, Betsy Ann Sprecher m. Barbara J. Balfour, Oct. 4, 1986; Laura B. Lundquist, Linda B. Flint, William D. Balfour III. BS, U.S. Mil. Acad., 1947; JD, UCLA, 1955; LLM, U. So. Calif., 1965. Bar: Calif. 1955, U.S. Patent and Trademark Office 1957, U.S. Customs Ct. 1968, U.S. Supreme Ct. 1974, Conn. 1983, N.Y. 1984. With Motor Products Corp., Detroit, 1950, Equitable Life Assurance Soc., Detroit, 1951, Bohn Aluminum & Brass Co., Hamtramck, Mich., 1952; mem. legal staff, asst. contract adminstr. Radioplane Co. (divsn. Northrop Corp.), Van Nuys, Calif., 1955-57; successively corp. counsel, gen. counsel, asst. sec. McCulloch Corp., L.A., 1957-64; sec., corp. counsel Technicolor, Inc., Hollywood, Calif., 1964-70; successively corp. counsel, asst. sec., v.p., sec. and gen. counsel Amcord, Inc., Newport Beach, Calif., 1970-72; v.p., sec., gen. counsel Schick Inc., L.A., 1972-75; counsel, asst. sec. C.F. Braun & Co., Alhambra, Calif., 1975-76; sr. v.p., sec., gen. counsel Automation Industries, Inc. (now PCC Tech. Industries Inc. a unit of Penn Cen. Corp.), Greenwich, Conn., 1976-86; v.p., gen. counsel G&H Tech., Inc. (a unit of Penn Cen. Corp.), Santa Monica, Calif., 1986-93; temp. judge Superior. Ct. Calif. L.A. Jud. Dist. and Santa Monica Unified Cts., 1987—; settlement officer L.A. Superior Ct., 1991—; pvt. practice, 1993—. Panelist Am. Arbitration Assn., 1991—; jud. arbitrator and mediator Alternative Dispute Resolution Programs L.A. Superior Ct., 1993—, Calif. Ct. Appeals 2d Appellate Dist., 1999—; mem. L.A. Supr. Ct. Alternative Dispute Resolution com., 2001—. Contbr. articles to profl. jours. Served to 1st lt. AUS, 1942-50. Mem. ABA, Nat. Assn. Secs. Dealers, Inc (bd. arbitrators 1996, mediators 1997), State Bar Calif. (co-chmn. corp. law dept. com. 1978-79, lectr. continuing legal edn. program), L.A. County Bar Assn. (chmn. corp. law dept. com. 1966-67), Century City Bar Assn. (chmn. corp. law dept. com. 1979-80), Conn. Bar Assn., Santa Monica Bar Assn. (trustee 1999—, chmn. alt. dispute resolution sect. 2000—), N.Y. State Bar Assn., Am. Soc. Corp. Secs. (L.A. regional group pres. 1973-74), L.A. Intellectual Property Law Assn., Am. Ednl. League (trustee 1988—, sec. 1998—), Am. Legion (life), West Point Alumni Assn., Army Athletic Assn., Friendly Sons St. Patrick, Jonathan Club (dir. 1996-99), Braemar Country Club, Phi Alpha Delta. Roman Catholic. Alternative dispute resolution, Corporate, general, Intellectual property. Home and Office: 439 Via De La Paz Pacific Palisades CA 90272-4633 E-mail: flatterytl@earthlink.net.

FLAUM, JOEL MARTIN, judge; b. Hudson, N.Y., Nov. 26, 1936; s. Louis and Sally (Berger) Flaum; m. Delilah Brummet, June 4, 1989. BA, Union Coll., Schenectady, 1958; JD, Northwestern U., 1963, LLM, 1964; LLD, John Marshall Law Sch., 2002. Bar: Ill. 1963. Asst. state's atty. Cook County, Ill., 1965—69, 1st asst. atty. gen. Ill., 1969—72; 1st asst. U.S. atty. Chgo., 1972—75; judge U.S. Dist. Ct. (no. dist.) Ill., Chgo., 1975—83, U.S. Ct. Appeals (7th cir.), 1983—. Mem. Ill. Law Enforcement Commn., 1970—72; cons. U.S. Dept. Justice, Law Enforcement Assistance Adminstrn., 1970—71; lectr. DePaul U. Coll. Law, 1987—88; adj. prof. Northwestern U. Sch. Law, 1993—2000. Mem.: Northwestern U. Law Rev., 1962—63; contbr. articles to legal jours. Mem. vis. com. U. Chgo. Law Sch., 1983—86, Northwestern U. Sch. Law, 1983—; mem. adv. com. USCG Acad., 1990—93. Lt. comdr. JACG USNR, 1981—92. Fellow Ford Found. fellow, 1963—64. Fellow: Am. Bar Found. (licentiate); mem.: FBA, ABA, Am. Judicature Soc., Navy-Marine Corps Ret. Judges Advs. Assn.,

Maritime Law Assn., Chgo. Bar Assn., Chgo. Inn of Ct., 7th Cir. Bar Assn., Ill. Bar Assn., Chgo. Bar Found. (licentiate), Naval Res. Assn., Lawyers Club Chgo. Jewish. Office: US Ct Appeals 7th Ct 219 S Dearborn St Chicago IL 60604-1702

FLECK, WILLIAM RODNEY, lawyer; b. Mt. Vernon, Wash., July 13, 1967; s. Gordon Clifford Fleck and Janis Beth Knechtel; m. Cheri Ann Tinker, Oct. 25, 1986; children: Anastasia, Emma-Grayce, William. AA, Boise State U., 1988; BA, U. Wash., 1991; JD, U. Puget Sound, 1994. Bar: Wash. 94, U.S. Dist. Ct. (we. dist.) Wash. 98. City atty., planner City of Forks, Wash., 1994—. Mem. U.S. Sen. Murray's Rural Working Group, Wash., 1999—; apptd. to adv. bd. Olympic Nat. Resources Ctr., Forks, 2002—. Mem. rev. commn. Callam County, Port Angeles, Wash., 2002—03, mem. econ. devel. coun., 1994—. With USAF, 1985—89. Recipient Heritage award, Clallam County Hist. Soc., 2000. Mem.: Sons of Union Vets. of Civil War (camp comdr. 1995—2001), Seattle Geneal. Soc. (interest group leader 1991—2001). Democrat. Lutheran. Avocations: genealogy, quilting, gardening. Office: City of Forks 500 E Division Forks WA 98331 Fax: 360-374-9430. E-mail: rodf.forks@centurytel.net.

FLEDDERMANN, STEPHEN ROY, lawyer; b. St. Louis, Apr. 30, 1956; s. Roy O. and Louise (Harris) F.; m. Victoria Lynn Bartnett, May 4, 1985. AA, St. Louis Community Coll., 1976; BA, U. Mo., 1978, JD, 1981. Bar: Mo. 1981, U.S. Dist. Ct. (ea. dist.) Mo. 1983. Assoc. Cundiff, Turken & Londoff, St. Charles, Mo., 1981-85, ptnr., 1986-97; pvt. practice St. Charles, 1997—. Recipient Legal Svcs. Ea. Mo. Lawyer Svc. award, 1993. Mem. ABA, Mo. Bar Assn., St. Louis Met. Bar Assn., St. Charles Bar Assn. (pres. 1993—), Order of Barristers. Republican. Avocations: tennis, scuba diving. State civil litigation, Family and matrimonial, Personal injury (including property damage). Home: 12270 Prince Towne Dr Saint Louis MO 63141-6635 Office: Fleddermann Law Office 320 N 5th St Saint Charles MO 63301-1854

FLEENOR, ANN, lawyer; b. San Francisco, Dec. 31, 1941; BA, Dominican Coll., San Rafael, Calif., 1963; JD with great distinction, McGeorge Sch. of Law, Sacramento, 1998. Bar: Calif. 1998. Staff atty. Sr. Legal Hotline, Legal Svcs. of No. Calif., Sacramento, 1999—. Mem. sch. bd. Twin Ridges Elem. Sch. Dist., North San Juan, Calif., 1981—90. Mem.: Traynor Honor Soc., Order of the Coif. Office: Senior Legal Hotline Legal Svcs of No Calif 515 12th St Sacramento CA 95814

FLEGLE, JIM L. lawyer; b. Paducah, Ky., Dec. 3, 1951; s. J.L. and Alice M. (Goodman) F.; m. Ophelia Flegle Camina; children: Lauren Tyler, Brittanie Len, James Brendan, Alexandra Carlisle, James Armand. BA, U. Ky., 1974; JD, U. Va., 1977. Bar: Tex. 1977, U.S. Dist. Ct. (so. dist.) Tex. 1977, U.S. Dist. Ct. (no. dist.) Tex. 1984, U.S. Dist. Ct. (we. dist.) Tex. 1988, U.S. Dist. Ct. (ea. dist.) Tex. 1989, U.S. Dist. Ct. Colo. 2002, U.S. Ct. Appeals (5th and 11th cirs.) 1981, U.S. Ct. Appeals (9th cir.) 1991, U.S. Ct. Appeals (fed. cir.) 1994, U.S. Supreme Ct. 1993. Assoc. Bracewell & Patterson, Houston, 1977-83, ptnr., 1983-89, Dallas, 1989—2002, head Dallas office, 1992-98; adv. com. Bracewell & Patterson , Dallas, 1996-98; ptnr. Loewinsohn & Flegle, LLP, 2002—. Mem. Coll. of the State Bar of Tex., 2003-, criminal justice act vol. atty. panel U.S. Dist. Ct. (no. dist.) Tex. Vol. Houston Pro Bono Program; active Tex. Lawyers and Accts. for Arts, Houston, 1982-85, St. Paul's Chamber Music Soc.; mem. corp. campaign com. Dallas Mus. Art, 1994-95, Dallas Hist. Soc., 1991-92. Mem. ABA, Tex. Bar Assn. (grievance com. 1996-99), Houston Bar Assn., Dallas Bar Assn., Houston Bar Found., Tex. Bar Found., Dallas Bar Found., Am. Bd. Trial Advocates (assoc.), Higginbotham Inn of Ct. (barrister), Raven Soc., Phi Beta Kappa, Omicron Delta Kappa, Sigma Nu. Methodist. Federal civil litigation, State civil litigation. Office: Loewinsohn & Flegle 18383 Preston Rd ste 100 Dallas TX 75252-5476 E-mail: jimf@texasverdict.com.

FLEISCHER, ARTHUR, JR., lawyer; b. Hartford, Conn., Jan. 27, 1933; s. Arthur and Clare Lillian (Katzenstein) F.; m. Susan Abby Levin, July 6, 1958; children: Elizabeth, Katherine. BA, Yale U., 1953, LLB, 1958. Bar: N.Y. 1959. Assoc. Strasser, Spiegelberg, Fried & Frank, N.Y.C., 1958-61; legal asst. SEC, Washington, 1961-62, exec. asst. to chmn., 1962-64; assoc. Fried, Frank, Harris, Shriver & Jacobson, N.Y.C., 1964-67, ptnr., 1967—, chmn., 1989-97, sr. ptnr., 1997—. Vis. lectr. law Columbia U., N.Y.C., 1972-73; adviser to adv. com. Fed. Securities Code Project, Am. Law Inst., 1970-78; adviser to com. to consider new issue proposals Nat. Assn. Securities Dealers, 1973-75, mem. com. corp. financing, 1976-80; bd. dirs. Haleakala Inc. (The Kitchen), N.Y., 1987-2002; chmn. Ann. Inst. on Securities Regulation, Practising Law Inst., 1969-81; mem. indsl. issuers adv. com. SEC, 1972-73; mem. adv. com. corp. disclosure, 1976-77; bd. govs. Am. Stock Exch., 1977-83; legal adv. com, bd. dirs. N.Y. Stock Exch., 1987-91. Co-author: Tender Offers, 1978, 6th edit., 1995, Board Games, 1988; co-editor: Annual Institute on Securities Regulation, 1970-81; contbr. articles to profl. jours. Mem. adv. coun. Ctr. for study of fin. instns. U. Pa.; trustee, mem. photography com. of Whitney Mus.; trustee Ind. Curators Internat., 1990-2002. Recipient Disting. Cmty. Svc. award Brandeis U., 1983, Judge Learned Hand Human Rels. award Am. Jewish Com., 1983, Harold P. Seligson award Practicing Law Inst., 1988, Judge Joseph W. Proskauer award UJA Fedn., 1994. Mem. ABA (mem. com. on fed. regulation of securities regulation 1969—), Assn. Bar City N.Y. (mem. spl. com. on lawyers role in securities transactions 1973-77, chmn. com. securities regulation 1972-74), Century Country Club (N.Y.C.). Home: 1050 Park Ave New York NY 10028-1031 Office: Fried Frank Harris 1 New York Plz Fl 27 New York NY 10004-1980

FLEISCHER, CARL AUGUST, law educator, consultant; b. Oslo, Aug. 26, 1936; s. Carl Johan and Marie (Mathiesen) F.; m. Eva Sylvia Funder, Sept. 15, 1967. Legal exam. laudabilis, U. Oslo, 1960, LLD, 1964. 1st sec. legal divsn. Ministry Fgn. Affairs, 1960-61; spl. cons. internat. law, 1962—. Lectr. law U. Oslo Faculty Law, 1961-69, prof., 1969—; adviser in internat. law Ministry Fgn. Affairs, 1986—; lectr., cons., mem. dels. internat. confs.; mem. Internat. Council Environ. Law, Norwegian Petroleum Soc., Norwegian Soc. Int. Law. Author: Jurisdiction on Fisheries, 1963, International Law, 7th edit., 2000, Constitutional Limitations, 1969, The Law on Building and Regulation of Property, 4th edit., 1983, Commentary to the Act of Expropriation and Compensation, 1974, The Economic Zone, 1976, The Law of Expropriation, 1978, Expropriation Procedure, 1980, Application and Interpretation of Judgements, 1981, Petroleum Law, 1983, La pêche (The Fisheries), 1985; co-author: Traitè du Nouveau Droit de la Mer, 1985, Compensation to Fisheries for Offshore Devel. Report, 1986, The New Regime of Maritime Fisheries, 1989, Environment and Resources Management, 1991, 99; co-author: A Handbook on the Law New of the Sea, 1991, Environmental Law, 1992-96, Planning Building Law, 1992, Landlease Contracts, 1992, Sources of Law, 1995, Private Law Subjects, 1995, Studies in International Law, 1997, Sources of Law and Legal Method, 1998; contbr. articles to profl. jours. Home: 13 Thomas Heftyes Oslo 2 Norway Office: U Oslo Karl Johans gt 47 Oslo N-0162 Norway

FLEISCHLI, GEORGE ROBERT, lawyer; b. Springfield, Ill., Aug. 23, 1940; s. Edward Constantine and Margaret Dorothy Fleischli F.; m. Ann Elizabeth Malmer, Nov. 5, 1966; children: Mary Elizabeth, Margaret Ann. BS, U. Ill., 1962, JD with honors, 1965, MA in Labor Rels., 1970. Bar: Ill. 1965, Wis. 1971. Rsch. asst. U. Ill., Urbana, 1965-66, 69-70; mediator, examiner employee rels. commn. State of Wis., Madison, 1970-75, gen. counsel employee rels. commn., 1976-81; pvt. practice Madison, 1981—. Guest spkr. U. Wis., Madison. Contbr. articles to profl. jours. Capt. USAF, 1966—69. Mem. Ill. Bar Assn., Wis. Bar Assn., Nat. Acad. Arbitrators (chmn. legal affairs com. 1978-90, bd. govs. 1990-93, chmn. com. profl. responsibility and grievance 1994-97, v.p. 1997-99), Order of Coif. Administrative and regulatory, Labor (including EEOC, Fair Labor Standards Act, labor-management relations, NLRB, OSHA). Office: 131 W Wilson St Ste 1100 Madison WI 53703-3245

FLEISCHMAN, EDWARD HIRSH, lawyer, consultant; b. Cambridge, Mass., June 25, 1932; s. Louis Isaac and Jean (Grossman) F.; m. Joan Barbara Walden, Dec. 27, 1953 (dec. 1993), m. Judy Vernon, Sept. 27, 1998. BA, Harvard U.; LLB, Columbia U., 1959. Bar: N.Y. 1959, U.S. Supreme Ct. 1980. Assoc. Beekman & Bogue, N.Y.C., 1959-67, ptnr., 1968-86; commr. SEC, Washington, 1986-92; ptnr. Rosenman & Colin, 1992-94; sr. counsel Linklaters, N.Y.C., 1994—. Bd. dirs. Soundview Tech. Group, Inc. (formerly Wit Capital Corp.), 1998—. Served with U.S. Army, 1952-55. Mem.: ABA (chmn. bus. law subcom. rule 144 1970—72, subcom. broker-dealer matters 1973—78, subcom. model simplified indenture 1980—83, adminstrv. law com. on securities, commodities and exchs. 1981—84, bus. law com. on devels. in bus. financing 1987—91, com. on counsel responsibility 1995—99, internat. law com. on internat. securities transactions 1999—2002), Security Traders Assn. (bd. govs. 1997—2000), Internat. Law Assn. (chmn. com. on internat. securities regulation 1998—), Internat. Bar Assn., Am. Soc. Corp. Secs., Am. Coll. Investment Counsel (pres. 1990—91), Am. Law Inst. Republican. Jewish. Administrative and regulatory, Private international, Securities. Office: Linklaters 1345 6th Ave New York NY 10105-0302 Home: 897 Franklin Lake Rd Franklin Lakes NJ 07417-2115 E-mail: edward.fleischman@linklaters.com., edward@fleischman.org.

FLEISCHMAN, HERMAN ISRAEL, lawyer; b. Bklyn., Aug. 30, 1950; s. Boris and Bella (Weisbrot) F.; m. Francine Moskowitz, Feb. 3, 1973; children: Meredith, Brandon, Gary. BA, Bklyn. Coll., 1972; JD, Bklyn. Sch. Law, 1976; MPA, NYU, 1974. Bar: N.Y. 1977, U.S. Dist. Ct. (ea., so., we. and no. dists.) N.Y. 1977, U.S. Ct. Appeals (D.C. cir.) 1979, U.S. Tax Ct. 1982. Asst. counsel Amalgamated Ins. Fund, N.Y.C., 1976; spl. asst. atty. gen. State of N.Y., N.Y.C., 1977-79; asst. counsel N.Y. State Dept. Mental Hygiene, Staten Island, N.Y., 1979; assoc. Ackerman, Salwen & Glass, N.Y.C., 1979-80; sole practice N.Y.C., 1980—. Mem. Thomas Jefferson Dem. Club, Bklyn., 1983-85; chmn. B'nai Brith Youth Orgn., 1980-82; bd. dirs. Big Apple Region, vice chmn., 1986-88, bd. dirs. Nassau and Suffolk Counties, N.Y., 1990-2001. Recipient Citation, Town of Hempstead, 1986, Dist. Key award, B'nai B'rith Youth Org., 1979, Man of Yr. award, B'nai B'rith Youth Org., 1980; named Coach of Yr., North Merrick-North Bellmore Basketball League, 1998. Mem. ABA, N.Y. State Bar Assn., Bklyn. Bar Assn., United Mut. Industries, Inc. (pres. 1983—). General civil litigation, General practice, Personal injury (including property damage). E-mail: HFleischma@aol.com.

FLEISCHMAN, KEITH MARTIN, lawyer; b. Newark, June 13, 1958; BA, U. Vt., 1980; JD, Calif. Western U., 1984. Bar: N.Y. 1985, U.S. Dist. Ct. (so. dist.) N.Y. 1986, U.S. Ct. Appeals (2d cir.) 1989, U.S. Ct. Appeals (11th cir.) 1995, U.S. Ct. Appeals (4th cir.) 1999, U.S. Supreme Ct. 2000. Asst. dist. atty. Bronx (N.Y.) County Dist. Atty., Rackets and Maj. Offense, 1984-88; trial atty. U.S. Dept. Justice, Dallas Bank Fraud Task Force, Washington, 1988-90; asst. U.S. atty. U.S. Atty. Office, Dist. Conn., 1990-92; trial lawyer, ptnr. Milberg Weiss Bershad Hynes & Lerach LLP, N.Y.C., 1992—2002; sr. ptnr. Bernstein Liebhard & Lifshitz, N.Y.C., 2003—. Inst., lectr. trial practice U.S. Dept. Justice, Washington, 1990-91. Coord. com. mem. New England Bank Fraud Task Force, Dist. Conn., 1990-92, ptnr. mgmt. com., 1997-2002. Avocations: skiing, climbing. Civil rights, General civil litigation, Securities. Office: Bernstein Liebhard & Lifshitz 10 E 40th St New York NY 10016

FLEISHER, STEVEN M. lawyer; b. Chgo., Feb. 5, 1945; s. Max M. and Meta J. (Shifris) F.; m. Marilyn J. Eto, Sept. 2, 1984. AB cum laude, Yale U., 1966; JD cum laude, Harvard U., 1969. Bar: Calif. 1970, U.S. Ct. Appeals (9th cir.) 1970, U.S. Dist. Ct. (no. dist.) Calif. 1970, D.C. 1973, U.S. Ct. Appeals (D.C. cir.) 1973, U.S. Supreme Ct. 1973. Law clk. U.S. Dist. Ct., San Francisco, 1969-70; atty. Calif. Rural Legal Assistance, Gilroy, 1970-72; gen. counsel Food Advocates, Davis, Calif., 1973-74; dir. Drew Health Rights Project, San Francisco, 1974-76; counsel Calif. Dept. Consumer Affairs, Sacramento, 1976-78; ptnr. Fleisher & Neckritz, Oakland, Calif., 1978-82; shareholder Burnhill, Morehouse, Burford, Schofied & Schiller, Walnut Creek, Calif., 1982-87; ptnr. McNichols, McCann & Inderbitzen, Pleasanton, Calif., 1987-91, Hallgrimson, McNichols, McCann & Inderbitzen, Pleasonton, Calif., 1991-95; assoc. gen. counsel Calif. Med. Assn., San Francisco, 1995-2000; v.p., gen. counsel Medepass, Inc., San Francisco, 2000—02; prin. Fleisher & Assocs., 2002—. Bd. dirs. Nat. Health Law Program, L.A., 1988-94; arbitrator U.S. Dist. Ct., San Francisco, 1984-91. Contbg. author Advising California Partnerships, 1988, California Sole Proprietorships & Partnerships, 1992; contbg. editor Calif. Ltd. Liability Cos. Reginald H. Smith fellow Office Legal Svcs., Calif., 1970-72. Mem. ABA (bus. law sect., sci. and tech. sects. chair health info. privacy and security protection subcom. info. security com. 2000—), Am. Health Lawyers (health info. tech. com.), Am. Soc. Med. Assn. Counsel (pres. 2001), D.C. Bar Assn., Calif. State Bar (exec. com. bus. law sect. 1993-96, nonprofits orgn. com. bus. law sect. 1996-2000, chair 1998-99). Corporate, general, Health, Non-profit and tax-exempt organizations. Office: Fleisher & Assocs 35 Corwin Dr Alamo CA 94507-1906 E-mail: steven@fleisherlaw.com.

FLEIT, MARTIN, lawyer; b. Bklyn., Apr. 5, 1926; s. Samuel and Nellie (Greenfield) F.; m. Lois Lenefsky, Dec. 29, 1979; children— Julie, Pam, Douglas, Lauren, David. Student Tufts U., 1944-45; BSChemE, U. N.H., 1948, JD, Georgetown U., 1952. Bar: D.C., 1952, Fla., 1974, N.Y., 1980. Ptnr., Stevens, Davis, Miller & Mosher, Washington, 1948-69, sr. ptnr. Fleit, Jacobson, Cohn & Price, Washington, 1969-92; of couns. Keck, Mahin & Cate, Washington, 1992-97, Evenson, McKeown, Edwards & Lenahan, 1997-99, Fleit, Kain, Gibbons, Gutman & Bongini, 2000—; pres. Martin Fleit P.A., Miami, Fla., 1992—. Mem. adv. bd. Patent, Trademark and Copyright Jour., Bur. Nat. Affairs Inc. With USNR, 1943-46. Mem. ABA, FBA, ATLA, Am. Intellectual Property Law Assn., Patent and Trademark Inst. Can., Internat. Assn. Protection Indsl. Property, Inter-Am. Assn. Indsl. Property, Fedn. Internat. Des Conseils en Propriete Industrielle, Internat. PAT-GOT Assn. (founder). Fax: 305-574-8241. Federal civil litigation, Patent, Trademark and copyright. Home and Office: 520 Brickell Key Dr Ste 201 Miami FL 33131-2607 E-mail: mfleit@fleitkain.com.

FLEMIING, JOSHUA MICHAEL, lawyer; b. Teaneck, N.J., Sept. 22, 1971; s. Joseph Michael and Barbara Fleming; 1 child, Mackenzie Skye Starling-Fleming. BA in Econs., Stanford U., 1993; JD, Vanderbilt U., 1996. Bar: Fla. 1996. Assoc. Fleming, Haile & Shaw, North Palm Beach, Fla., 1996—2002, Watterson & Hyland, Palm Beach Gardens, 2002—. Republican. Probate (including wills, trusts), Estate taxation, Estate planning. Office: Watterson & Hyland 4100 RCA Blvd Palm Beach Gardens FL 33410 Fax: 561-627-5600. E-mail: joshfleming@wattersonlaw.com.

FLEMING, JOSEPH CLIFTON, JR., dean, law educator; b. Atlanta, July 24, 1942; s. Joseph Clifton Sr. and Claudia Leola (Duncan) F.; m. Linda Wightman, May 27, 1964; children: Allison, Erin, Anne, Matthew Clifton, Stephen Joseph, Michael Grant. BS, Brigham Young U., 1964; JD, George Washington U., 1967. Bar: Wash. 1967, U.S. Dist. Ct. (we. dist.) Wash. 1967, U.S. Tax Ct. 1969, U.S. Ct. Appeals (9th cir.) 1970, Utah 1979. Assoc. Bogle & Gates, Seattle, 1967-73; assoc. prof. Law Sch. U. of Puget Sound, Tacoma, 1973-74, Brigham Young U., Provo, Utah, 1974-76, prof. Law sch., 1976-98, assoc. dean Law Sch., 1986—. Ernest L. Wilkinson prof. Law Sch., 1998—; Fulbright prof. faculty law U. Nairobi, Kenya, 1977-78; prof. in residence Office of Chief Counsel IRS, Washington, 1985-86. Vis. prof. U. Queensland, Brisbane, Australia, 1997, 99, Ctrl. European U., Budapest, Hungary, 2001—03; James J. Freeland eminent vis. scholar U. Fla. Law Sch., 2002. Author: Estate and Gift Tax, 1975, Tax Aspects of Buying and Selling Corporate Businesses, 1984, Tax Aspects of Forming and Operating Closely Held Corporations, 1992, Federal Income Tax: Doctrine, Structure and Policy, 1995, 2nd edit., 1999; notes editor George Washington U. Law Rev., 1966-67; contbr. numerous articles to scholarly and profl. jours. Bishop Ch. of Jesus Christ of LDS, Orem, Utah, 1981-85. Mem. ABA (subcom. chair tax sect. corp. tax com. 1979-83, chair tax sect. com. on teaching taxation 1992-94), Am. Law Inst. (tax adv. group 1988-94, 98-2001). Office: Brigham Young U J Reuben Clark Law Sch PO Box 28000 Provo UT 84602-8000

FLEMING, JOSEPH Z. lawyer; b. Miami, Fla., Jan. 30, 1941; s. Richard Marion and Lenore C. Fleming; m. Betty Corcoran, Feb. 12, 1947; 1 child, Katherine Anne. BA in English, U. Fla., 1958; postgrad., U. Chgo., 1959, Hague Acad. Internat. Law, 1966; JD, U. Va., 1965; LLM in Labor Law, NYU, 1966. Bar: Fla. 1965, D.C. 1981. Assoc. Paul & Thomson, Miami, 1966-72, ptnr., 1972-74, Fleming & Neuman, 1974-81, Fleming & Huck, Miami, 1981-86; pvt. practice Miami, 1986-87; with Fleming & Klink, 1987-88; pvt. practice, 1988—96; with Ford & Harrison, Greenberg Traurig PA, 2001—. Lectr. in field. Author: Airline and Railroad Labor Law, 1981-2003; editor, contbg. author Environmental Regulation and Litigation in Florida, 1980, 82, 84, 85, 87, 88, 90, 91, 93-95, 97, 99, 2000, 03; editor, contbg. author: Environmental Pollution and Individual Rights, 1978, Reporter's Handbook, 1979—, Historic Preservation Law, 1984-87, 89, 99, 2001, 02, Entertainment Arts and Sports Law, 1989-91, 97-99, 2001, 03. Trustee Met. Dade County Ctr. for Fine Arts, 1982-86; mem. Biscayne Bay Environ. Task Force Subcom., 1982-83, well field protection adv. com. Dade County Task Force, 1984-87; mem. Noguchi-Bayfront Park Trust, Miami, 1983-89; pres., bd. dirs. Fla. Rural Legal Svcs., 1967-78, Pres.'s Water Policy Implementation Workshops, Dept. of Interior Water Task Force, 1979; bd. dirs. Miami chpt. Am. Jewish Com. Recipient conservation award Fla. Audubon Soc., 1981, 89, Tropical Audubon Soc., 1979, award Dade County Mental Health Assn., 1974, award Miami Design Preservation League, 1982, 83, award Progressive Architecture, 1982, Am. Jewish Com. award. Mem. Am. Law Inst., ABA (continuing profl. edn. com. 1985—), Fla. Bar Assn. (past chmn. environ. and land use law sect., labor law and employment discrimination law sect., entertainment, arts and sports law sect., cert. labor and employment law). Administrative and regulatory, Environmental, Labor (including EEOC, Fair Labor Standards Act, labor-management relations, NLRB, OSHA). Home: 34 LaGorce Cir Miami Beach FL 33141-4520 Office: 1221 Brickell Ave Miami FL 33131 E-mail: flemingj@gtlaw.com.

FLEMING, JULIAN DENVER, JR., lawyer; b. Rome, Ga., Jan. 12, 1934; s. Julian D. and Margaret Madison (Mangham) F.; m. Sidney Howell, June 28, 1960; 1 dau., Julie Adrianne. Student, U. Pa., 1951-53; BChemE, Ga. Inst. Tech., 1955, PhD, 1959; JD, Emory U., 1967. Bar: Ga. 1966, D.C. 1967; registered profl. engr., Ga., Calif. Rsch. engr., prof. chem. engring. Ga. Inst. Tech., 1955-67; ptnr. Sutherland, Asbill & Brennan, Atlanta, 1967—. Contbr. articles to profl. jours.; patentee in field. Bd. dirs. Mental Health Assn. Ga., 1970-80; bd. dirs. Mental Health Assn. Met. Atlanta, 1970-80, pres., 1974-75; mem. coun. legal advisors Rep. Nat. Com., 1981-85. Fellow: Am. Bar Found., Am. Coll. Trial Lawyers, Am. Inst. Chemists; mem.: AIChE, AAAS, ABA (coun. sect. sci. and tech. 1980—82, vice chmn. 1982—84, chmn. 1985—86, ho. dels. 1990, bd. govs. 1994—95, ho. dels. 1994—96, chmn. spl. citation issues com. 1995—96, coord. commn. legal tech. 1995—97, standing com. tech. and info. sys. 1997—2001), Bleckley Inn of Ct. (master of bench), Nat. Conf. Lawyers and Scientists (chmn. ABA del. 1988—90, standing com. nat. conf. groups 1990, ABA liaison 1990—93, chmn. 1992—93). Achievements include patent for data apparatus. Federal civil litigation, State civil litigation, Intellectual property. Home: 1248 Oxford Rd NE Atlanta GA 30306-2610 Office: Sutherland Asbill & Brennan 999 Peachtree St NE Ste 2300 Atlanta GA 30309-3996

FLEMING, MICHAEL PAUL, lawyer; b. Orlando, Fla., June 25, 1963; s. Joseph Patrick and Therese (Eccles); m. Natalie Jackson, Oct. 15, 1988; children: Shannon Isabel, Nicholas Patrick, Patrick Edward, Michael Paul, Eamon John, Celeste Natalie. BA, U. St. Thomas, 1984; JD, U. Houston, 1987. Bar: Tex. 1987; U.S. Dist. Ct. (so. dist.) Tex. 1988; U.S. Ct. Appeals (5th cir.) 1988, U.S. Supreme Ct. 1991; cert. personal injury. Ptnr. Fleming & Fleming, Houston, 1987-91; asst. county atty. Harris County, Houston, 1991-96, elected Harris county atty., 1996-2001; ptnr. Bracewell & Patterson, Houston, 2001—02; gen. counsel LGI Devel., Conroe, Tex., 2002—; vice chair Harris County Housing Authority, 2003—. Bd. dirs. U. St. Thomas, 2002—. Named Irish Person of Yr., 2000. Mem. State Bar of Tex., Houston Bar Assn., Ancient Order of Hibernians, KC, KHS, Equestrian Order of Holy Sepulchre of Jerusalem, Phi Delta Phi, 100 Club of Houston, Irish Soc. Roman Catholic. Avocations: genealogy, castlemahon history. Home: 643 W Forest Dr Houston TX 77079-6915 Office: 19221 I-45 South Conroe TX 77385

FLEMING, TOMMY WAYNE, lawyer; b. Canyon, Tex., Nov. 13, 1941; s. Benjamin Dalby and Willie Mildred (Vineyard) F.; m. Sally Ann Moore, Nov. 30, 1968; children: Benjamin Dalby II, Hunter Leah. Student, West Tex. State U., 1960-61; BBA, U. Tex., 1964, JD, 1966. Bar: Tex. 1969, U.S. Dist. Ct. (so. dist.) Tex. 1971, U.S. Supreme Ct. 1978, U.S. Ct. Appeals (5th cir.) 1983. Asst. dist. atty. Office Dist. Atty., Amarillo, Tex., 1969-70; asst. criminal dist. atty. Cameron County Criminal Dist. Atty.'s Office, Brownsville, Tex., 1970-72; ptnr. Wiech, Lewis & Fleming, Brownsville, 1972-74, Wiech, Fleming, Hamilton & Uribe, Brownsville, 1974-82, Wiech & Black, Brownsville, 1982-89, Atlas & Hall, Brownsville, 1989-94, Fleming, Hewitt & Olvera, Brownsville, 1994-98, Fleming & Olvera, Brownsville, 1998-2001, Fleming & Hernandez, Brownsville, 2001—. Mem. Supreme Ct. Grievance Oversight Com., 1983-2000. Chmn. Brownsville Cmty. Health Clinic, 1978-79. 1st lt. U.S. Army, 1966-69. Fellow Tex. Bar Found. (life, bd. dirs. 1984-87); mem. Tex. Assn. Bank Counsel, State Bar Tex. (bd. dirs. 1981-84), Cameron County bar Assn. (bd. dirs. 1972-79, pres. 1979-80), Brownsville Hist. Assn. (bd. dirs. 1977-80). Banking, Commercial, contracts (including sales of goods; commercial financing), General practice. Home: 915 Santa Ana Ave Rancho Viejo TX 78575-9749 Office: Fleming & Hernandez 1650 Paredes Line Rd Ste 102 Brownsville TX 78521-1665

FLESCH, MARCOS RAFAEL, lawyer; b. São Paulo, Brazil, Dec. 17, 1970; s. Jorge and Hannelore Struca Flesch; m. Cristiane Naomi Kaneko, Nov. 20, 1994. LLB, U. São Paulo, 1992; LLM, Cornell U., 1996. Bar: Brazil 1992, N.Y. 1996. Internat. assoc. Brown & Wood, N.Y.C., 1995, Simpson Thacher & Bartlett, N.Y.C., 1996—97; assoc. Machado, Meyer, Sendacz e Opice, São Paulo, 1997—2000, ptnr., 2000—01, Souza, Cescon Avedissian, Barrieu e Flesch, São Paulo, 2001—. Mergers and acquisitions, Corporate, general, Commercial, contracts (including sales of goods; commercial financing). Office: Souza Cescou Avedissian Barrieu e Flesch Rua Funchal 263 04551-060 São Paulo Brazil

FLESSNER, MARK ALAN, lawyer; s. Donald John and Patricia Ann Flessner; m. Diane Marie Butterfield, July 7, 1984; children: Max, Christian, Eleanor. BA, U. Ill., 1976; MDiv, U. Notre Dame, 1980; JD, DePaul U., 1986. Bar: Ill. 1987, U.S. Dist. Ct. (no. dist.) Ill. 1987, U.S. Ct. Appeals (7th cir.) 1987. Assoc. Kovar Nelson & Brittian, Chgo., 1987; asst. U.S. atty. U.S. Attys. Office, 1987—2000; ptnr. Altheimer & Gray, 2000—02. Bd. dirs. Appleseed Fund Justice, Chgo., 2000—01. With Transp. Adv. Bd., Naperville, Ill., 1996—, 2002—; bd. dirs. Naperville Lightning Soccer Club, 2002—; mem. com. Greater Chgo. Food Depository Fin. and Legal Cmty. Luncheon, 2000—01, co-chmn., 2000—03. Fellow: Leadership-Greater Chgo. (bd. dirs. 1996—98); mem.: Chgo. Coun. Lawyers (bd. dirs. 1994—98, 2000—02), Com. Greater Chgo. Food Depository Finance and Legal Community (co-chair 2002—03). Roman Catholic. Avocations: running, swimming, bicycling, reading. Criminal. Office: Altheimer & Gray 10 S Wacker Dr Ste 4000 Chicago IL 60606 Fax: 312-715-4800. E-mail: flessner@altheimer.com.

FLETCHER, ANTHONY L. lawyer; b. Washington, Dec. 12, 1935; s. Robert J. and Lyndell (Pickett) F.; m. Juliana Schump, Sept. 3, 1960 (div. 1977); children: Leigh Anne Grinstead, Kristin Marie Giffin, Julie Bowen Cimino; m. Zelda L. Fletcher, Mar. 30, 1986. BA, Princeton U., 1957; JD, Harvard U., 1962. Bar: N.Y. 1963, U.S. Ct. Appeals (2d cir.) 1966, U.S. Ct. Appeals (7th cir.) 1966, U.S. Supreme Ct. 1966, U.S. Ct. Appeals (3d cir.) 1969, U.S. Ct. Appeals (5th cir.) 1973, U.S. Ct. Appeals (1st cir.) 1981, U.S. Ct. Appeals (9th cir.) 1983. Assoc. Simpson Thacher & Bartlett, N.Y.C., 1962-71, Conboy, Hewitt, O-Brien & Boardman, N.Y.C., 1971-74, ptnr., 1974-86, Hunton & Williams, N.Y.C., 1986-97; prin. Fish & Richardson P.C., N.Y.C., 1997—2002, sr. counsel, 2003—. Editor-in-chief Trademark Reporter, 1982-84; contbr. articles to profl. jours. With U.S. Army, 1957-59. Mem. Internat. Trademark Assn. (bd. dirs. 1983-85), Princeton Club. Episcopalian. Federal civil litigation, State civil litigation, Trademark and copyright. Office: Fish & Richardson PC 45 Rockefeller Plz Fl 28 New York NY 10111-0100

FLETCHER, BETTY BINNS, judge; b. Tacoma, Mar. 29, 1923; BA, Stanford U., 1943; LL, U. Wash., 1956. Bar: Wash. 1956. Mem. firm Preston, Thorgrimson, Ellis, Holman & Fletcher, Seattle, 1956—79; judge U.S. Ct. Appeals (9th cir.), Seattle, 1979—, sr. judge, 1998—. Mem.: ABA (Margaret Brent award 1992), Fed. Judges Assn. (past pres.), Am. Law Inst., Wash. State Bar Assn., Phi Beta Kappa, Order of Coif. Office: US Ct Appeals 9th Cir 1010 5th Ave Ste 1000 Seattle WA 98104-1196

FLETCHER, DOUGLAS CHARLES, lawyer; b. Rockford, Ill., Mar. 5, 1943; s. Fred Leland and Dorothy Edwards Fletcher; m. Adele Ann Pinkerton, Aug. 20, 1964 (div. Apr. 1985); children: Adrian, Lauren, Robin. BA in Econs. and Engring., U. Nev., Reno, 1969, MBA in Fin. cum laude, 1972; JD, U. of Pacific, 1975; postgrad., Colo. State U., 1976. Bar: Nev. 1975, U.S. Ct. Appeals (9th cir.) 1976. Exec. v.p. PanWorld Engring., 1967-68; design engr. Nev. Bell, 1968-70; economist Sierra Pacific Power Co., 1970-72, gen. counsel, 1975-78; operating trustee William Lear Motors Co., 1978-79; ptnr. Leslie Gray & Assocs., 1979-81; oper. trustee Horseshoe Club Casinos, 1981-82, Mapes Hotel and Money Tree Casinos, 1982-85; owner, ptnr. Douglas C. Fletcher, Ltd., 1985—; operating receiver Echo Summit Tahoe Ski Resort, 1989-92. Advisor U. Nev. Grad. Bus. Sch., Reno, 1976-85; mem. U.S. Trustee Panel, 1978-95; judge pro tem Reno Mcpl. Ct., 1980-82. Author: Bond Reverse Yield Gaps of Public Utilities, 1972. Mem. ctrl. planning com. Republican Party of Washoe County, 1978-82; bd. dirs. Washoe County Youth Found., Reno, 1983-92, Eagles Nest Assn., Reno, 1998; founder, bd. dirs. Sierra League, Reno, 1989-99; bd. dirs., pres. ski team advisors U. Nev., Reno, 1982—. Mem. No. Nev. Bankruptcy Bar Assn. (founding mem.), Washoe County Bar Assn., State Bar Nev. (environ. law com. 1975—), Reno Tennis Club (pres., bd. dirs.), U.S. Ski Coaches Assn. (cert.), Reno Ski and Recreation Club (bd. dirs., pres. 1982—), Prospectors Club (bd. dirs.), Prof. Ski Instr. of Am. (cert.), Sigma Nu, Phi Kappa Phi, Beta Gamma Sigma. Bankruptcy, Corporate, general, Property, real (including real estate development, water). Office: 20 Sharps Cir Reno NV 89509-8009 E-mail: fletchlaw1@aol.com.

FLETCHER, JOHN RICHARD, lawyer; b. Chatham, N.Y., Sept. 24, 1950; s. Francis Edward and Helma Ann (Jensen) F. BA, Coll. of William and Mary, 1968-72, JD, 1975. Bar: Va. 1975, U.S. Dist. Ct. (ea. dist.) Va. 1978, U.S. Ct. Appeals (4th cir.) 1980. Assoc. Ellenson, Fox & Wittan, Newport News, Va., 1975; asst. atty. Commonwealth Atty.'s Office, Hampton, Va., 1976-78; assoc. Richard J. Tavss, P.C., Norfolk, Va., 1978-79; ptnr. Tavss, Fletcher, Maiden & Reed, PC, Norfolk, 1980—. 1st lt. U.S. Army, 1975-76. Mem. ABA, Va. Bar Assn. (mem. exec. com. young lawyers sect. 1986—, chmn. criminal law and corrections com. 1984, 85, ad hoc com. on indigent defendants), Norfolk and Portsmouth Bar Assn., Virginia Beach Bar Assn., Assn. Trial Lawyers Am., Va. Trial Lawyers Assn., Omicron Delta Kappa, Lambda Chi Alpha (pres. Epsilon Alpha chpt. 1971-72). Democrat. Roman Catholic. Avocations: golf, reading. State civil litigation, Criminal, Personal injury (including property damage). Home: 704 Linkhorn Dr Virginia Beach VA 23451-3919 Office: Tavss Fletcher Maiden & Reed PC 1st Virginia Tower Ste 1400 555 Main St Norfolk VA 23510

FLETCHER, MICHAEL S. lawyer; b. Winchester, Va., Nov. 23, 1961; s. James William and Patty Jo (Stotler) F. BS, U. Tenn., Knoxville, 1984; JD, Seton Hall U., Newark, 1988. Bar: N.J. 1988, Pa. 1988, U.S. Dist. Ct. N.J. 1988, U.S. Dist. Ct. (ea. dist.) Pa. 1989. Law sec. to Hon. Donald G. Collester Jr. Superior Ct. N.J., Morristown, 1988-89; assoc. LaBrum and Doak, P.C., Phila., 1989-90; asst. dep. pub. defender State of N.J., Morristown, 1990—. Assoc. editor Seton Hall Law Rev., 1988. Shop steward Comms. Workers Am. Local 1037, Newark, 1991—; treas. Cornerstone Evang. Free Ch., 1994—. Office: Office of Pub Defender 25 Washington St Morristown NJ 07960-3950

FLETCHER, NORMAN S. state supreme court justice; b. July 10, 1934; s. Frank Pickett and Hattie Sears Fletcher; m. Dorothy Johnson, 1957; children: Mary Kiker, Elizabeth Coan. BA, U. Ga., 1956, LLB, 1958; LLM, U. Va., 1995. Assoc. Matthews, Maddox, Walton and Smith, Rome, Ga., 1958-63; pvt. practice LaFayette, Ga., 1963-90; city atty. City of LaFayette, 1965-89; county atty. County of Walker, 1973-88; spl. asst. atty. gen. State of Ga., Atlanta, 1979-89; justice Supreme Ct. of Ga., Atlanta, 1990—, now chief judge. Mem. State Disciplinary Bd., 1984-87, chair investigative panel, 1986-87. Ruling elder Peachtree Presbyn. Ch., Atlanta; former officer First Presbyn. Ch. of Rome, Ga., LaFayette Presbyn. Ch., Cherokee Presbytery; former commr. Presbyn. Ch. USA Gen. Assembly, 1984, 85; bd. visitors U. Ga. Sch. Law, 1992-95, chmn., 1994-95. Master Joseph Henry Lumpkin Inn of Ct.; fellow Am. Bar Found., Ga. Bar Found.; mem. State Bar Ga. (chair local govt. sect. 1977-78), U. Ga. Law Sch. Alumni Assn. (pres. 1977), Rotary. Office: Supreme Ct Ga 507 State Jud Bldg Atlanta GA 30334-9007

FLETCHER, PAUL GERALD, lawyer; b. Boston, Mar. 20, 1945; m. Susan Mary Beckerman, Aug. 11, 1968; children: Lynne, Michael, Allison. BAE, U. Fla., 1967; JD, U. Miami, 1970. Bar: Fla. 1970, U.S. Dist. Ct. (so. dist.) Fla. 1970, U.S. Ct. Mil. Appeals 1971, U.S. Supreme Ct. 1973, U.S. Ct. Appeals (11th cir.) 1982. Judge Adv. USAF, 1970-74; ptnr. Peskoe, Fletcher & Cahan, Homestead, Fla., 1974-77, Fletcher & Langer, Homestead, 1977-84, Paul G. Fletcher, P.A., Coral Gables, Fla., 1984—. Instr. bus. law No. Mich. U., Marquette, 1970-72; mem. adv. bd. Amerifirst Fla. Trust Co., 1987-91. Pres. Homestead ARC, 1975. Capt. USAF, 1970-74. Recipient Service award ARC, 1977, Leadership award Jewish Fedn., 1980; named in Leading Am. Attys. in Family Law, Fla., 1997—. Mem. Fla. Bar Assn. (family law, real property probate coms.), Homestead Bar Assn. (pres. 1980-81), ATLA, Am. Arbitration Assn. (arbitrator), Kendall-South Dade Bar Assn., Coral Gables Bar Assn., First Family Law Inns of Ct. (master 1993—), Attys. Real Property Coun., Kiwanis (v.p. 1980, pres. 1983), Tau Epsilon Phi. Avocations: photography, World War II history, baseball cards. Family and matrimonial, Probate (including wills, trusts), Property, real (including real estate development, water). Office: 1500 S Dixie Hwy Ste 200 Coral Gables FL 33146-3033 Fax: 305-661-6197. E-mail: pgflaw@earthlink.net.

FLETCHER, PHILLIP DOUGLAS, lawyer; b. Bridgetown, W.I., Barbados, Sept. 16, 1957; came to U.S., 1960; s. Herbert Ernest and Mona Helga F.; m. Elena Annette Mykytiuk, Sept. 29, 1984. BSFS, Georgetown U., 1979; MA, Tufts U., 1983; JD, U. Calif., Berkeley, 1983. Bar: D.C. 1983, Calif. 1985, N.Y. 1991. Assoc. Milbank, Tweed, Hadley & McCloy, Washington, 1983-87, L.A., 1987, Hong Kong, 1987-89, N.Y.C., 1989-92, ptnr. London, 1992—. Contbr. articles to profl. jours. Avocations: tennis, hiking. Office: Milbank Tweed Hadley & McCloy Dashwood House 69 Old Broad St EC2M1QS London England

FLETCHER, ROBERT, retired lawyer, horologist; b. Birmingham, Ala., May 4, 1920; s. Robert Hall and Beatrice (Skelding) Jones; m. Florence K. Szuba, Sept. 12, 1942; children— Andrew R., William Alan. B.F.A., Ohio U., Athens, 1943; LL.B., JD, Case Western Res U., 1948. Bar: Ohio 1948. Asst. gen. counsel Cleve. Transit System, 1951-56; with firm Jamison, Ulrich, Johnson & Burt, Cleve., 1956-59, Meyers, Stevens & Rea, Cleve., 1959-61; pvt. practice Cleve., 1961-82; horologist Parma, Ohio, 1982—. Lectr. Am. Heart Assn. Served with AUS, World War II, Korea. Recipient Speakers Bur. award Am. Heart Assn., 1973-76 Mem.: Rosicrucian Order. Republican. Presbyterian. Home: 5801 Hollywood Dr Cleveland OH 44129-5220

FLICK, JOHN EDMOND, lawyer; b. Franklin, Pa., Mar. 14, 1922; s. Edmond Leroy and Mary M. (Weaver) F.; m. Lois Anna Lange, Apr. 20, 1946; children: Gregory Allan, Scott Edmond, Lynn Ellen, Ann Elizabeth. Student, Northwestern U., 1941-44, U. Pa., 1945; LLB, Northwestern U., 1948. Bar: Ill. 1948, Calif. 1971, U.S. Dist. Ct. (ctrl. dist.) Calif. 1971, U.S. Ct. Appeals (9th cir.) 1971, U.S. Supreme Ct. 1974. Commd. 1st lt. Judge Adv. Gen. Corps U.S. Army, 1950, advanced through grades to lt. col. Res., 1968; ret., 1972; faculty U.S. Mil. Acad., 1954-57, Judge Adv. Gen. Sch., U. Va., 1960-61; counsel Litton Industries, 1963-67; sr. v.p., sec., gen. counsel, dir. Bangor Punta Corp., 1967-69; sr. v.p., gen. counsel Times Mirror Co., Los Angeles, 1970-87, cons., 1987-88. Past chmn. Los Angeles adv. bd. Salvation Army; mem. adv. bd., adult rehab. ctr. corps Santa Barbara, past mem. nat. adv. bd. Salvation Army. Recipient Am. Bar Assn. Acad. award, 1961 Mem. State Bars Calif. and Ill., Wigmore Club (life benefactor, Northwestern U. Law Sch.).

FLICKINGER, DON JACOB, patent agent; b. Massillon, Ohio, Dec. 31, 1933; s. John Jacob and Elizabeth Ann (Slinger) F.; m. Sonja Loy Jersild (dec. Aug. 1987); 1 child, Packy J. Flickinger. Student, Kent (Ohio) State U., 1951-54, U. Ariz., 1958; BA, Ariz. State U., 1963, MA, 1964. Bar: U.S. Patent and Trademark Office, 1973. Apprentice tool and die maker Spun Steel Corp., Canton, Ohio, 1951-54; staff Ariz. State U., Tempe, 1963-65; law clerk, paralegal Drummond, Cahill & Phillips, Phoenix, 1966-73; reg. patent agent Drummond, Nelson & Ptak, Phoenix, 1973-77, self employed, Phoenix, 1977-94; counsel Parsons & Goltry, Phoenix, 1995—2001. Lectr., instr. Patent Seminars & Courses, Phoenix, 1977—; staff Rio Salado C.C., Phoenix, 1982-84; intellectual property counselor SCORE Phoenix Chpt. 105, 2001. Patentee Collapsible Dust Pan, Hort. Growing Unit. Comdg. officer Poolee Enrichment Program, Family Marine Force, Poolee Assistance Co., Phoenix; sponsor Thunderbird Little League, Phoenix, 1985, 86, 87; big brother Valley Big Brothers, Phoenix, 1968-70; participant, staff Valley Big Bros./Big Sisters Fish-a-Ree, 1984-87; judge Crown Royal Kinetic Contraption Compeition, 1990. With USMC, 1954-57. Am. Soc. Tool. scholar, Tucson, 1960; recipient Disting. Svc. cert. Valley Big Brothers, Phoenix,1970, Honor award Westside Area Career Project, Glendale, 1981. Mem. BBB, NRA (endowment), Nat. Wildlife Fedn. (leaders club), Am. Legion, Ariz. Heritage Alliance, Wilderness Soc., Nature Conservancy, Legal Defense Fund, Defenders of Wildlife, Am. Legion, Mensa, Svc. Corps. of Ret. Exec. (intellectual property counselor Phoenix chpt. 105 2001—), Kappa Delta Pi. Republican. Buddhist. Avocations: philosophy, reading, woodworking, arts and crafts. Patent. Office: Phoenix Score Chpt 105 2828 N Central Ave Ste 800 Phoenix AZ 85004

FLICKINGER, HARRY HARNER, organization and business executive, management consultant; b. Hanover, Pa., July 27, 1936; s. Harry Roosevelt and Goldie Anna (Harner) F.; m. Hsin Yang, May 30, 1961; children: Audrey Mae, Deborah Lynn. BS in Psychology, U. Md., 1958. Investigator U.S. Civil Service Commn., Washington, 1962-64; personnel specialist U.S. Naval Ordinance Lab., Silver Spring., Md., 1964-66; from asst. dir. to dir. personnel U.S. OMB, Washington, 1966-73; asst. dir. personnel AEC and Dept. Energy, Washington, 1973-78; dir. personnel U.S. Dept. Justice, Washington, 1978-79, dep. asst. atty. gen. adminstrn., 1979-85, assoc. asst. atty. gen., 1985-87, asst. atty. gen., 1987-92; exec. dir. Am. Consortium for Internat. Pub. Adminstrn., Washington, 1993; pres. Flickinger Enterprises, Gaithersburg, Md., 1994—. Recipient Presdl. Disting. Exec. Rank award, 1988. Office: 8730 Lochaven Dr Gaithersburg MD 20882-4464

FLINT, GEORGE SQUIRE, lawyer; b. Ft. Wayne, Ind., Oct. 28, 1930; s. A. Verne and Alberta (Minor) F.; m. Emily Gregg McLees, Nov. 23, 1968; 1 son, Alexander C.; children by previous marriage: Julia M., Melissa A., Anthony E. AB, U. Mich., 1952, JD, 1955. Bar: N.Y. 1956. Assoc., then sr. assoc. Fulton, Walter & Duncombe, N.Y.C., 1955-65; ptnr. Fulton, Duncombe and Rowe, 1983-89; with Tenneco Chems., Inc., 1965-82, v.p., sec., gen. counsel, 1969-82; counsel Jackson & Nash, N.Y.C., 1989—. Arbitrator Small Claims Part. Civil Ct., N.Y.C. With USN, 1955-57. Mem. N.Y. State Bar Assn., Assn. Bar City N.Y., Order of Coif. Clubs: Indian Harbor Yacht, Wadawanuck, Stonington. Home: 1185 Park Ave New York NY 10128-1308 Office: 330 Madison Ave New York NY 10017-5001

FLIPPEN, EDWARD L. lawyer; b. Richmond, Va., Dec. 2, 1939; s. Hannie Thomas Flippen; m. Pearcy light, Feb. 14, 1970; children: Elizabeth Hunter, Margaret Harlan. BS, Va. Commonwealth U., 1965; MBA, Coll. of William and Mary, 1967, JD, 1974. Bar: Va. 1974, N.C. 1981. Gen. atty. Va. State Corp. Commn., Richmond, 1975-78, assoc. gen. counsel, 1978-80, dep. gen. counsel, 1980; asst. gen. counsel Duke Power Co., Charlotte, N.C., 1980-81, assoc., 1981-83; ptnr. Mays & Valentine, LLP, Richmond, 1983-99, McGuireWoods, LLP, Richmond, 1999—. Lectr. U. Va. Sch. Law, 1978-82; adj. law prof. Coll. William and Mary, 1996—, Washington and Lee U., 1997-99, U. Richmond, 2000—; vis. prof. George Mason Sch. Law, 2001-02; vis. fellow U. London, 1998-99; chmn. Gov.'s Blue Ribbon Commn. Higher Edn., 1998-2000, Atty. Gen.'s Task Force on Access to Higher Edn., 2003—. Author: Practical Networking: How to Give and Get Help with Jobs, 2001. Bd. visitors Va. Commonwealth U., Richmond, 1994-2002, rector, 2000-02; adv. bd. Va. Ctr. on Aging, Richmond, 1994-98; trustee River Rd. United Meth. Ch., Richmond, 1995-98; bd. VCU Health Sys., 2000-02. With U.S. Army, 1958-61. Mem. Va. State Bar (chmn. adminstrv. law sect., 1986-87), Soc. for Advanced Legal Studies (assoc. fellow). Republican. Avocations: writing, teaching, assisting others in job placements. Utilities, public, Administrative and regulatory. Office: McGuireWoods LLP One James Ctr 901 E Cary St Richmond VA 23219-4057 E-mail: eflippen@mcguirewoods.com.

FLOM, GERALD TROSSEN, lawyer; b. Neenah, Wis., Feb. 6, 1930; s. Russell Craig and Lois Eva (Trossen) F.; m. Martha Herrington Benton, Aug. 21, 1954 (div. June 25, 1980); children— Katherine Simmons, Sarah Elizabeth Kiecker, Russell Craig. BA magna cum laude, Lawrence U., 1952; JD, Yale U., 1957. Bar: Minn. 1957, U.S. Dist. Ct. Minn. 1957. Assoc. Faegre & Benson LLP, Mpls., 1957-64, ptnr., 1964-95; retired, 1995. Adj. asst. prof. Law Sch., U. Minn., Mpls., 1966, bd. dirs., Old Republic Natl. Title Holding Co. and Old Republic Natl. Title Ins. Co., 1977-99. Mem. editorial bd. Yale Law Jour. Trustee Mpls. Soc. Fine Arts, 1970-76, Lawrence U., 1974-81, Plymouth Congl. Ch., 1978-81, William Mitchell Coll. Law, St. Paul, 1983-89; bd. dirs. Met. Med. Ctr. Research Found., Mpls., 1975-85. Served with U.S. Army, 1952-54 Mem. ABA, Minn. State Bar Assn., Hennepin County Bar Assn., Assn. Bar City of N.Y., Mace, Mpls. Club, Interlachen Country Club (Edina, Minn.), Phi Beta Kappa, Phi Delta Theta, Phi Alpha Delta. Congregationalist. Corporate, general, Mergers and acquisitions, Securities. Home: 3434 Zenith Ave S Minneapolis MN 55416-4663 Office: Faegre & Benson LLP 2200 Wells Fargo Ctr 90 S 7th St Minneapolis MN 55402-3901

FLOM, JOSEPH HAROLD, lawyer, director; b. Balt., Dec. 20, 1923; s. Isadore and Fannie (Fishman) Flom; m. Claire Cohen, Nov. 14, 1958; children: Peter Leslie, Jason Robert. Student, CCNY, 1948; LLB cum laude, Harvard U. Law Sch., 1948; LHD (hon.) , Queens Coll., 1984; LLD (hon.) , Fordham U., 1990. Practice of law, N.Y.C., 1949—. Spl. counsel subcom. on admisntrn. of internal revenue laws House Ways and Means Com. Editor Harvard Law Rev., 1947—48; co-editor: Disclosure Requirements of Public Corporations and Insiders, 1967, Texas Gulf Sulphur-Insider Disclosure Problems, 1968, Lawyer's Conflicts-The Evolving Case Law, 1991. Mem. N.Y.C. Mayor's Commn. on Status of Women, 1976—77, Mayor's Coun. Econ. Advisors, N.Y.C., 1990—93; co-chmn. task force on capital fin. and constrn. N.Y.C. Bd. Edn., 1987—89; chmn. N.Y.C. Commn. on Bicentennial of Constn., 1986—89; trustee Fedn. J ewish Philanthropies N.Y., 1977—89, Barnard Coll., 1983—93, N.Y. Hist. Soc., 1989—94; chair adv. com. Export-Import Bank of U.S., 1995; trustee Mt. Sinai-NYU Health Sys., 1978—99, Petrie Stores Liquidating Trust, Skadden Fellowship Found., Constl. Edn. Found., 1989—93, United Way N.Y.C., 1991—97; mayor's rep. Met. Mus. Art, 1990—93; mem. mayor's Mgmt. Adv. Task Force, 1991—93; chair Woodrow Wilson Internat. Ctr. for Scholars, 1994—98; mem. Archdiocesan Task Force on Crime Prevention and Youth, 1982—87. Mem.: Assn. Bar City N.Y. Office: Skadden Arps Slate 4 Times Sq Fl 41 New York NY 10036-6522

FLOM, KATHERINE S. lawyer; b. Mpls., Aug. 15, 1955; d. Floyd and Eleanore F.; m. Malcolm D. Reid. BA in Econs., Bates Coll., 1977; JD, Hamline U. Sch. Law, 1982. Bar: Minn. 1982, U.S. Dist. Ct. Minn. 1990, U.S. Ct. Appeals (8th cir.) 1995. Law clk. Judge Charles Porter Dist. Ct. Hennepin County, Mpls., 1983; asst. pub. defender Hennepin County, Mpls., 1984-90; from assoc. to ptnr. Meshbesher & Spence, Mpls., 1990—. Pres. Minn. Consumer Alliance, Mpls., 1997-98; bd. dirs. Am. Lung Assn.-Hennepin County, 1994-97, Working Opportunities for Women, St. Paul, 1991-94. Mem. Minn. Trial Lawyers Assn. (bd. govs. 1992—, v.p. 2002--, convention com. chair 2002--), Minn. State Bar Assn. (cert. civil trial specialist), Minn. Women Lawyers. Personal injury (including property damage), Product liability. Office: Meshbesher & Spence 1616 Park Ave Minneapolis MN 55404 E-mail: kflom@meshbester.com.

FLOOD, JOAN MOORE, paralegal; b. Hampton, Va., Oct. 10, 1941; d. Harold W. and Estalena (Fancher) M.; 1 child by former marriage, Angelique. B.Mus., North Tex. State U., 1963; postgrad., So. Meth. U., 1967-68, Tex. Women's U., 1978-79, U. Dallas, 1985-86. Clk. Criminal Dist. Ct. Number 2, Dallas County, Tex., 1972-75; reins. libr. Scor Reins. Co., Dallas, 1975-80; corp. ins. paralegal Assocs. Inc. Group, 1980-83; corp. securities paralegal Akin, Gump, Strauss, Hauer & Feld, 1983-89; asst. sec. Knoll Internat. Holdings Inc., Saddle Brook, N.J., 1989-90, 21 Internat. Holdings, Inc., N.Y.C., 1990-92; dir. compliance Am. Svc. Life Ins. Co., Ft. Worth, 1992-93; v.p., sec. Express Comm., Inc., Dallas, 1993-94; fin. transactions paralegal Thompson & Knight, Dallas, 1994-96; corp. transactions paralegal Jones, Day, Reavis & Pogue, Dallas, 1996-97, Weil, Gotshal & Manges, LLP, 1998—99; corp. paralegal PennCorp. Fin. Group, Inc., Dallas, 1999-2001; debt trade mgr. Patton Boggs LLP, Dallas, 2001—03, bus. transactions sr. paralegal, 2003—, sr. paralegal bus. transactions, 2003—. Mem. ABA, Tex. Bar Assn. Home: PO Box 190165 Dallas TX 75219-0165 E-mail: jflood@pattonboggs.com.

FLOOD, JOHN JOSEPH, lawyer; b. N.Y.C., Dec. 11, 1951; s. John Joseph and Margaret Mary (Madigan) F.; m. Carlo J. Melfi; children: Lauren, Kristin, Daniel, Matthew, William. Cert., U. Vienna, Austria, 1967; AB, Georgetown U., 1973, JD, 1976. Asst. dist. atty. N.Y. County Dist. Atty.'s Office, N.Y.C., 1976-79; assoc. Sedam & Herge, P.C., McLean, Va., 1979-80; trial atty. U.S. Dept. Labor, Washington, 1980-81; v.p., assoc. gen. counsel Nat. Assn. Securities Dealers Inc., Washington, 1981—. Staff mem. Law and Policy in Internat. Bus., Georgetown U. Law Ctr., 1974-76. Mem. ABA (mem. sects. on corps., banking and bus. law, litigation), D.C. Bar Assn. (mem. steering com. corp., fin. & securities law sect.), Va. Bar Assn., Phi Beta Kappa, Pi Sigma Alpha. Democrat. Roman Catholic. Avocations: art appreciation, reading, tennis. Office: Nat Assn Securities Dealers Inc 1735 K St NW Washington DC 20006-1516 E-mail: john.flood@nasd.com.

FLORSHEIM, RICHARD STEVEN, lawyer; b. Milw., Apr. 2, 1949; s. Ernst Frederick and Ingeborg Miriam Florsheim; m. Neena B. Florsheim; children: Ali Brynn, David Ira, Rebecca Lynn. BS, MIT, 1971; JD magna cum laude, Marquette U., 1974. Bar: Wis. 1974, Fla. 1983. Assoc. Foley & Lardner, Milw., 1974-81, ptnr., 1981—, leader intellectual property litigation group, 1987-97, chair intellectual property dept., 1997—. Co-author: Biotechnology Patent Practice, 1994, Inside the Minds: Leading Intellectual Property Lawyers, 2001. Pres. North Shore Libr., Milw., 1985-87, Jewish Found. Econ. Opportunity, Milw., 1992-96; bd. dirs. Milw. Jewish Fedn., 1987-93, 96-2002, NCCJ Wis. region, 1990—, Ohr Hatorah Jewish Heritage Ctr., 2002--. Mem. ABA, Am. Intellectual Property Law Assn. (subcom. chmn. 1992-97), Fed. Cir. Bar Assn., Wis. Bar Assn., Milw. Bar Assn., Marquette Law Alumni Assn. (pres. 1985-86). Office: Foley & Lardner 777 E Wisconsin Ave Ste 3800 Milwaukee WI 53202-5367 Business E-Mail: rflorsheim@foleylaw.com.

FLOWE, BENJAMIN HUGH, JR., lawyer; b. Durham, N.C., Feb. 8, 1956; s. Benjamin H. and Dorothy Amelia (Bell) F.; children: Samantha Kathleen, Andrew Benjamin. AB in Sociology and Psychology cum laude, Duke U., 1978; JD with high honors, N.C. U., 1981. Bar: U.S. Ct. Appeals (D.C. cir.) 1981, U.S. Supreme Ct. 1990. Assoc. Arent, Fox et al, Washington, 1981-84, Bowman, Conner & Touhey P.C., Washington, 1984-87, Verner, Liipfert, Bernhard, McPherson & Hand, Washington, 1987-89, ptnr., 1990-96; pvt. practice, Washington, 1996-97; ptnr. Berliner, Corcoran & Rowe, L.L.P., Washington, 1997—. Contbr. congl. testimony on export controls Ctr. for Stratetic and Internat. Studies; vice chair tech. adv. com. Commerce Dept. Author: Export Compliance Guide, 1995; contbr. articles to profl. jours. Mem.: ABA (chair export controls and econ. sanctions com.), Am. Electronics Assn. (co-chair export controls com.), Order of the Coif. Democrat. Presbyterian. Avocations: skiing, writing, golf, tennis. Admiralty, Commercial, contracts (including sales of goods; commercial financing), Private international. Home: 8120 Paisley Pl Potomac MD 20854-2748 Office: Berliner Corcoran & Rowe LLP 1101 17th St NW Ste 1100 Washington DC 20036-4798

FLOWE, CAROL CONNOR, lawyer; b. Owensboro, Ky., Jan. 3, 1950; d. Marvin C. Connor and Ethel Marie (Thorn) Smith; children: Samantha Kathleen, Andrew Benjamin. BME magna cum laude, Murray State U., 1972; JD summa cum laude, Ind. U., 1976. Bar: Ohio 1977, D.C. 1981, U.S. Dist. Ct. (so. dist.) Ohio 1977, U.S. Dist. Ct. Md. 1983, U.S. Dist. Ct. D.C. 1981, U.S. Supreme Ct. 1987, U.S. Ct. Appeals (2d, 3d, 4th, 5th, 7th and D.C. cirs.). Assoc. Baker & Hostetler, Columbus, Ohio, 1976-80, Arent Fox Kintner Plotkin & Kahn, Washington, 1980-87; deputy gen. counsel Pension Benefit Guaranty Corp., Washington, 1987-89, gen. counsel, 1989-95; ptnr. Arent, Fox, Kintner, Plotkin & Kahn, 1995—. Mem. ABA, D.C. Bar Assn., Order of Coif, Alpha Chi, Phi Alpha Delta. Avocations: computers, reading. Federal civil litigation, Labor (including EEOC, Fair Labor Standards Act, labor-management relations, NLRB, OSHA), Pension, profit-sharing, and employee benefits. Home: 8608 Aqueduct Rd Potomac MD 20854-6249 Office: Arent Fox Kintner Plotkin & Kahn 1050 Connecticut Ave NW Ste 500 Washington DC 20036-5303 E-mail: flowec@arentfox.com.

FLOWERS, BRUCE MARVIN, lawyer; b. Milw., Mar. 3, 1959; s. Marvin Percy and Joyce Jean Flowers; m. Aimee L. Flowers, Sept. 1994; children: Avery Joy, Emma Grace. BA in Prodn. & Opers. Mgmt., Tex. A&M, Commerce, 1980; JD, Tex. Tech. Sch. Law, Lubbock, 1991. Bar: Tex. State Cts., U.S. Dist. Ct. - Northern, Southern, Eastern, and Western Dists. 1991. Atty. Vial Hamilton Koch & Knox, Dallas, 1991—93, Kane Russell Coleman & Logan, Dallas, 1993—95, Reid & Flowers, Dallas, 1995—98, Guida, Slavich & Flores, Dallas, 1998—. Bd. dirs. Victory House Homeless Shelter, Dallas, 1992—95; mem. S. Poverty Law Ctr., 2002—. Named to, Million Dollar Adv.'s Forum, 2002—. Mem.: Tex. Ctr. for Legal Professionalism and Ethics, Coll. of State Bar, Tex. Bar Assn. Avocation: Tae Kwon Do. Environmental, Appellate. Office: Guida Slavich Flores PC 5949 Sherry Ste 1150 Dallas TX 75225 Fax: 214-692-6610. E-mail: flowers@guidaslavichflores.com.

FLOYD, JACK WILLIAM, lawyer; b. Columbia, S.C., May 14, 1934; s. Edward Immanuel and Edith Fletcher (Herlong) F.; m. Ruth Parker Matthews, Jan. 10, 1957; children: Connie, Cindy, Jay. BS, U. N.C., 1958, JD with honors, 1961. Bar: N.C. 1961, U.S. Supreme Ct. 1971. Assoc. Smith, Moore, Smith, Schell & Hunter, Greensboro, N.C., 1961-67, ptnr., 1967-87, Floyd, Greeson, Allen & Jacobs, Greensboro, N.C., 1988-90, Floyd, Allen & Jacobs, Greensboro, 1991-97, Floyd & Jacobs, Greensboro, 1998—. Lectr. acctg. U. N.C., 1960-61; lectr. bus. law Guilford Coll., 1962-64; speaker on jury trials Am. Bar Assn., Am. Patent Law Assn.; arbitrator U.S. Dist. Ct. Annexed Arbitration Program. Bd. editors: N.C. Law Rev, 1960-61. Mem. parents' bd. dirs. Meredith Coll., Raleigh, N.C., 1977-79, chmn., 1980-81. Served with USN, 1951-55. Mem. Am. Bar Assn., N.C. Bar Assn. (panelist on family law), Am. Law Inst., N.C. Assn. Trial Lawyers, Order of Coif. Clubs: Elks. Democrat. Baptist. General civil litigation, Family and matrimonial, Patent. Home: 1404 Valleymeade Rd Greensboro NC 27410-3938 Office: Floyd & Jacobs 401C N Eugene St Greensboro NC 27401-2644 E-mail: jackw.floyd@aol.com., jwf1404@aol.com.

FLOYD, WALTER LEO, lawyer; b. St. Louis, May 29, 1933; s. Walter L. Sr. and Estelle E. (Kiess) F.; children: Michael W., Mary Ann, Mark L.; m. Patricia A. Knapko, Sept. 3, 1994. BS, St. Louis U., 1955, LLD, 1959. Bar: Mo. 1959, Ill. 1959, U.S. Dist. (ea. dist.) Mo. 1959. Owner The Floyd Law Firm P.C., St. Louis, 1959—. Contbr. articles to profl. jours. Fellow: Orgn. Nat. Bd. Trial Advocacy; mem. Mo. Assn. Trial Attys. (sec. 1961, v.p. 1962, 85), Am. Trial Lawyers Assn. (lectr.), Mo. Bar Assn., Ill. Assn., Phi Delta Phi. Democrat. Unitarian Universalist. Personal injury (including property damage), Workers' compensation, Professional liability. Address: Floyd Law Firm 8151 Clayton Rd Ste 202 Saint Louis MO 63117-1111

FLUHR, STEVEN SOLOMON, lawyer; b. N.Y.C., Mar. 31, 1959; s. Irving Fluhr and Rita Shain; m. Elizabeth Ann Koehr, Oct. 1, 1988; children: Katherine Michelle, Alexandra Sophia. AB, Vassar Coll., 1981; JD, St. Louis U., 1984. Bar: Mo. 1984, Ill. 1985, U.S. Ct. Appeals (8th cir.) 1990, U.S. Dist. Ct. (ea. dist.) Mo. 1986. Staff atty. legal svcs. plan United Auto Workers, St. Louis, 1984-87; assoc. Dubail Judge P.C., Creve Coeur, Mo., 1987-89; ptnr. Rekowski & Collins, Collinsville, Ill., 1989-90, Gourley Sallerson & Fluhr, St. Louis, 1990-95; mng. mem. Fluhr & Moore L.L.C., Clayton, Mo., 1995—. City atty., prosecuting atty., Hanley Hills, Mo., 1989—; prosecuting atty. Olivette, Mo., 1990—; city atty. Velda Village Hills, Mo., 2001—. Mem. Bar Assn. Metro. St. Louis, Lawyers Assn. St. Louis. General civil litigation, Municipal (including bonds), Personal injury (including property damage). Home: 530 Bonhomme Forest Dr Olivette MO 63132-3108 Office: Fluhr & Moore LLC 225 S Meramec Ave Ste 532T Clayton MO 63105-3598 E-mail: FluhrStl@aol.com.

FLUM, JOSEPH, lawyer; b. June 13, 1924; BS in Pre-Law, Temple U., 1947; cert. in fgn. svc., Georgetown U., 1949; JD, Temple U., 1951; PhD, Pacific Western U., 1977. Bar: Pa. Owner, operator Flum's Dept. Store, Newtown, Pa., 1950—; pvt. practice law Newtown, 1961—. Lectr. law-related edn., world travel, exploration, and cultures; author, lectr., prof. worldwide anthropol. film documentaries and travel logs; sch. bd. rep. from U.S. to mainland China. Author: The Weave and The Woven, 1989, The Flum Atlas, 1989. Bd. dirs. Council Rock Sch. Dist., Pa., 1967-79, pres., 1971-73; chmn. legis. com. Bucks County Sch. Dirs., 1967-79, chmn. Bucks County Sch.'s legis. com., 1972—; mem. com. revision state sch. code, mem. com. on law-related edn. Pa. Dept. Edn., 1974—, mem. global edn. adv. com., 1978—, apptd. to com. for revision of state sch. code, 1974—; others. Recipient Chapel of Four Chaplains Legion of Honor award, commendation Coun. Rock Edn. Assn., 1980. Fellow Explorers Club; mem. Pa. Bar Assn. (youth-edn. com.), Bucks County Bar Assn., ABA, Northeastern Bar Assn., Phila. Anthropol. Assn., Am. Anthropol. Assn., Smithsonian Instn., Am. Legion, Newtown Hist. Assn., others. Avocations: anthropology, archeology, international travel and exploration. Office: State St at Centre Ave Newtown PA 18940

FLYNN, CHARLES P. lawyer; b. Chgo., Apr. 17, 1943; BA, Willamette U., 1965; LLB, Harvard U., 1968. Bar: Alaska 1968, U.S. Dist. Ct. Alaska 1968, U.S. Ct. Appeals (9th cir.) 1968. Lawyer Burr Pease & Kurtz, Anchorage, 1968-70, shareholder, 1970—. General civil litigation, Environmental, Labor (including EEOC, Fair Labor Standards Act, labor-management relations, NLRB, OSHA). Office: Burr Pease & Kurtz 810 N St Anchorage AK 99501-3293 E-mail: cpf@bpk.com.

FLYNN, PETER ANTHONY, judge; b. Bronxville, N.Y., July 23, 1942; s. Ralph Harold and Caroline (Lindberg) F. BA magna cum laude, Harvard U., 1963; LLB, Yale U., 1966. Bar: Ill. 1969, U.S. Dist. Ct. (no. and so. dists.) Ill. 1969, U.S. Ct. Appeals (7th cir.) 1969, U.S. Supreme Ct. 1976, U.S. Dist. Ct. (ea. dist.) Wis. 1980, U.S. Ct. Appeals (2d and 5th cirs.) 1980, U.S. Ct. Appeals (9th cir.) 1987. Asst. lect. law U. Ife, 1967-69; assoc. Jenner & Block, Chgo., 1969-75; ptnr. Cherry & Flynn, Chgo., 1976-99; judge Cir. Ct. of Cook County, Ill., 1999—; adj. prof. The John Marshall Law Sch., 2002—. Adj. prof. John Marshall Law Sch., 2002—. Mem. Olympia Fields Plan Commn., Ill., 1979-83, chmn., 1983-85; trustee Village of Olympia Fields, 1985-89; pres. Touchstone Theatre, 1990-93; active U.S. Peace Corps, 1967-69. Mem. ABA, Ill. Bar Assn., Am. Law Inst., Yale Law Sch. Assn. (nat. exec. com. 2002-), Chgo. Lincoln Inn of Ct., Chgo. Bar Assn. (vice chair, comml. litigation com., 2003). Roman Catholic. Avocations: theater, piano, poetry, guitar, choral music, sailing, history.

FLYNN, ROSEANN, lawyer; b. N.Y.C., June 3, 1957; s. Rosario John and Grace Criscione; m. Michael Francis Flynn; 2 children. AAS in Nursing, Fulton-Montgomery C.C., Johnstown, NY, 1977; BA, SUNY, Stony Brook, 1981; JD, Nova Southeastern U., 1985. Bar: Fla. 85, U.S. Dist. Ct. (so. dist.) Fla. 86, cert.: (cir. ct. mediator), Am. Arbitration Assn. (arbitrator). Staff nurse Drs. Hosp., Lake Worth, Fla., 1977—79, Brookhaven Meml. Med. Ctr., Patchogue, NY, 1979—81; assoc. Krupnick & Campbell, Ft. Lauderdale, Fla., 1985—88; mng. atty. Sams, Donato & Flynn, Ft. Lauderdale, 1988—91; of counsel Watson, Clark & Purdy, Ft. Lauderdale, 1991—93; shareholder Purdy & Flynn P.A., Ft. Lauderdale, 1993—. Vol. St. Clemens Cath. Ch., Wilton Manors, Fla., 1994—. Mem.: ATLA, ABA, Broward County Bar Assn., Acad. Fla. Trial Lawyers. Democrat. Roman Catholic. Avocations: cooking, travel, reading. Personal injury (including property damage), Insurance, Product liability. Office: Purdy & Flynn PA 1107 SE 4th Ave Fort Lauderdale FL 33316 Fax: 954-356-0017. E-mail: raflynn@purdyflynn.com.

FLYNN, THOMAS LEE, lawyer; b. Mitchell, S.D., Feb. 24, 1946; s. Melvin B. and Wilma L. (Jenks) F.; m. Kristine T. Johnson, Dec. 27, 1972; children: Ryan F., Erin M., Rory P. BA, Morningside Coll., 1968; JD, Drake U., 1972. Bar: U.S. Dist. Ct. (no. and so. dists.) Iowa 1972, U.S. Ct. Appeals (8th cir.) 1983. Ptnr. Belin, Lamson, McCormick, Zumbach & Flynn, Des Moines, Iowa, 1989—. Contbr. chpt. Am. Banker's Assn. Jour. Fellow Am. coll. Bankruptcy Law; mem. ABA, Iowa Bar Assn. (comml. and bankruptcy com. 1984-90), Polk County Bar Assn. Republican. Banking, Bankruptcy, Property, real (including real estate development, water). Office: Belin Lamson McCormick Zumbach & Flynn 2000 Financial Ctr Des Moines IA 50309-3909

FLYNN, WILLIAM FREDERICK, lawyer; b. Washington, Nov. 15, 1952; s. L. Martin and Martha Jean (Rennie) F.; m. Deborah Ann Norton, Apr. 20, 1985. AB, U. Mich., 1975, JD, 1978. Bar: Wis. 1978. Assoc. Reinhart, Boerner, Van Deuren, Norris & Rieselbach S.C., Milw., 1978-85, ptnr., 1986—. Mem. ABA, Wis. Bar Assn., Milw. Bar Assn. Banking, Commercial, consumer (including collections, credit), Municipal (including bonds). Home: 115 E Miller Dr Mequon WI 53092-6191 Office: Reinhart Boerner Et Al 1000 N Water St Ste 2100 Milwaukee WI 53202-3197

FOCHT, THEODORE HAROLD, lawyer, educator; b. Reading, Pa., Aug. 20, 1934; s. Harold Edwin and Ruth Naomi (Boyer) F.; m. Joyce Gundy, Aug. 11, 1956; children: David Scott, Eric Steven. AB in Philosophy, Franklin and Marshall Coll., 1956; JD, Coll. of William and Mary, 1959. Bar: Va. 1959. Teaching assoc. Columbia U. Sch. Law, N.Y.C., 1959-60; atty. Office of Gen. Counsel SEC, Washington, 1960-61, legal asst. to Commr., Washington, 1961-63; mem. faculty U. Conn. Sch. Law, Hartford, 1963-71 (leave of absence, 1969-71); spl. counsel on securities legislation Interstate and Fgn. Commerce Com., U.S. Ho. of Reps., Washington, 1969-71; gen. counsel Securities Investor Protection Corp., Washington, 1971-94, pres., 1984-94; adj. prof. law American U. Sch. Law, Washington, 1979-84; mem. Fla. State Comptroller's Task Force on Regulatory DeCoupling, 1995. Mem. Va. State Bar, Phi Beta Kappa. Bankruptcy, Corporate, general, Securities. Home: 8436 Pinafore Dr New Port Richey FL 34653-6739

FODEN, MARIA LUISA DE CASTRO, lawyer; b. Santiago, Chile, Mar. 4, 1947; came to U.S., 1967; d. Diego F. De Castro Reyes and Ana Eguigueren-Rozas; m. Edward Foden, Jan. 27, 1969; children: Edward, Mary, Ann. BA, Rutgers U., 1971; JD, U. Conn., 1978. Bar: Conn. 1980, U.S. Dist. Ct. Conn. 1980. Pvt. practice, Hartford, Conn., 1980—. Roman Catholic. General practice, Immigration, naturalization, and customs, Personal injury (including property damage). Office: 107 Oak St Hartford CT 06106-1551 E-mail: mldcf@lawyer.com.

FOGARTY, EDWARD MICHAEL, lawyer; b. Woonsocket, R.I., Feb. 25, 1948; s. Raymond Henry and Mary (Hogan) F.; m. Gail Higgins, Jan. 8, 1977. BA, Providence Coll., 1969; JD, Georgetown U., 1972. Bar: R.I. 1972, D.C. 1973, U.S. Supreme Ct. 1977. Law clk. U.S. Dist. Ct. R.I., Providence, 1972-73; assoc. Wilkinson, Cragun & Barker, Washington, 1973-79, ptnr., 1979-82, Baenen, Timme, De Reitzes & Middleton, Washington, 1982-83; counsel Spriggs & Hollingsworth, Washington, 1983-98. Legal counsel to speaker R.I. Ho. of Reps., Providence, 1987-93; legal counsel to majority leader R.I. Senate, Providence, 1993-2003, legal counsel to pres., 2003—; arbitrator R.I. Superior Ct., 1989—. Trustee Festival Ballet Providence, 1988—, pres., 1994—96. Mem.: ABA, Am. Arbitration Assn. (nat. panel of arbitrators 1985—96), D.C. Bar, R.I. Bar Assn. (ho. dels. 1992—94), Univ. Club Providence, Univ. Club Washington. Democrat. Roman Catholic. Home: 488 Lloyd Ave Providence RI 02906-4550 Office: 309 State House Providence RI 02903

FOGEL, RICHARD, lawyer, educator; m. Sheila Feldman; children: Bruce, Lori Ellen. BA, York Coll., CUNY, 1971; JD, N.Y. Law Sch., 1974. Bar: N.J. 1976, U.S. Dist. Ct. N.J. 1976, N.Y. 1981, U.S. Dist. Ct. (so. dist.) N.Y. 2000, U.S. Tax. Ct. 1977. Tax law specialist IRS, Newark, 1975-77; sr. pension cons., atty. N.Y. Life, N.Y.C., 1977-81; pvt. practice Franklin, N.J., 1981-85, Wayne, N.J., 1985-88, McAfee, N.J., 1988—. Lectr. Inst. for Continuing Legal Edn., Newark, 1977—; mem. adj. faculty Upsala Coll., East Orange, N.J., 1978-88; presenter 34th ann. meeting. Internat. Soc. for Systems Scis., Portland State U., 1990. Recipient Certs. of Appreciation, IRS, Newark, 1977, Inst. Continuing Legal Edn., Newark, 1981-82, 84, Cert. in Recognition of Accomplishments, Coop. Extension Cook Coll., Rutgers U., 1982, Disting. Grad. award York Coll., 1984, Founder's Day Dist. Alumni award, 1992. Estate planning, Pension, profit-sharing, and employee benefits, Property, real (including real estate development, water). Home: 28 Elizabeth Dr Sussex NJ 07461-3402 Office: Vernon Colonial Pla PO Box 737 Rt 94 Mc Afee NJ 07428

FOGLE, JAMES LEE, lawyer; b. Doniphan, Mo., June 6, 1950; s. Carter Lemuel and Leatha Sue (Logan) F.; m. Pattylynn Raymond, Sept. 18, 1982; children: Kirsten Nicole, Ryan Christopher. BA, Whitman Coll., 1972; JD, Duke U., 1975. Bar: Mo. 1975, Ill. 1976. Assoc. Coburn, Croft & Putzell, St. Louis, 1975-79; ptnr. Coburn & Croft, St. Louis, 1979-96, mng. ptnr., 1980-84, mem. mgmt. com., 1985-89; ptnr. Thompson Coburn, LLP, St. Louis, 1996—. Bd. dirs. Life Skills Found., 1991—, pres. 1996-98; adj. prof. Fontbonne Coll., St. Louis, 1991-2000. Alumni admissions rep. Whitman Coll., Walla Walla, Wash., 1980—; mem. planned giving coun. DePaul Health Ctr. Found. Nat. Merit scholar Whitman Coll., 1968. Mem. ABA, Estate Planning Coun., Mo. Bar Assn. (tax com.), St. Louis Health Lawyers Assn., Mo. Athletic Club, Racquet Club Ladue (bd. govs. 2001—), Masons, Order of Coif, Phi Beta Kappa. Republican. Baptist. Avocations: tennis, snow skiing, golf, collecting polit. memorabilia. Corporate, general, Estate planning, Pension, profit-sharing, and employee benefits. Office: Thompson Coburn LLP Ste 3500 One USBank Plz Saint Louis MO 63101-1623 E-mail: jfogle@thompsoncoburn.com.

FOGLEMAN, JOHN NELSON, lawyer; b. Memphis, Jan. 2, 1956; m. Nancy Darlene Norris, Aug. 14, 1976; children: John Nelson Jr., Adam Barrett. BS in Edn., Ark. State U., 1978; JD, U. Ark., 1981. Bar: Ark. 1981, U.S. Dist. Ct. (ea. dist.) Ark. 1981. Assoc. Hale, Fogleman & Rogers, West Memphis, Ark., 1981-85, ptnr., 1985-94; cir. judge 2d Jud. Dist. Ark., 1995—. City atty. City of Marion, 1982-94; dep. pros. atty. 2d jud. dist. Crittenden County, Marion, Ark., 1983-94. Mem. sch. bd. Marion Sch. Dist., 1985-94; pres. Marion C. of C., 1982-83. Mem. ABA, Ark. Bar Assn., Assn. Trial Lawyers Am., Ark. Trial Lawyers Assn. (mem. Ark. sentencing commn. 1998—, chair jud. resources assessment com. 1998-2002). Methodist. Avocations: golf, jogging, reading, gardening. Criminal, General practice, Personal injury (including property damage). Home: 206 Rivertrace Dr Marion AR 72364-2602 Office: 116 Military Rd Marion AR 72364-1753

FOGLEMAN, JOHN ALBERT, lawyer, retired judge; b. Memphis, Nov. 5, 1911; s. John Franklin and Julia (McAdams) F.; m. Annis Adell Appleby, Oct. 24, 1933; children: John Albert, Annis Adell Fogleman Anderson, Mary Barton Fogleman Williams. Student, U. Ark., 1927-31; LLB, U. Memphis, 1934. Bar: Ark. 1934, U.S. Supreme Ct. 1966. Dep. circuit ct. clk. , Crittenden County, 1933-34; pvt. practice law, 1934-44; ptnr. Hale & Fogleman, Marion and West Memphis, Ark., 1944-66; dep. pros. atty. Crittenden County, 1946-57; assoc. justice Ark. Supreme Ct., 1967-79, chief justice, 1980; of counsel firm Gill Skokos Simpson Buford & Owen, Little Rock, 1981-86; of counsel Gill and Elrod, 1986-92, Gill, Wallace, Clayton, Fleming, Elrod and Green, Little Rock, 1992-93, Gill, Fleming & Elrod, Little Rock, 1993, Gill Law Firm, 1994-98, Gill, Elrod, Ragon, 1999—. Mem. State Bd. Law Examiners, 1960-63; chmn. Ark. Judiciary Commn., 1963-65; mem. Ark. Constl. Revision Study Commn., 1967, Fed.-State Jud. Council, Ark., 1971-75, Ark. Criminal Code Revision Com., 1972-74; lectr. Sch. Law, U. Ark., Little Rock, 1981; assoc. justice Delta Theta Phi, 1981-93, chief justice, 1993-95. Active Ark. and Crittenden County Democratic central coms., 1937-44. Served from pvt. to 1st lt. JAGD AUS, 1944-45. Fellow Am. Coll. Trial Lawyers, Am. Bar Found., Ark. Bar Found.; mem. Ark. Bar Assn. (past pres.), NE Ark. Bar Assn. (past pres.), Crittenden County Bar Assn. (past pres.), Pulaski County Bar Assn., Masons, Rotary (charter, past pres. Marion club). Home: 8700 Riley Dr Apt 205 Little Rock AR 72205 Office: Gill Elrod Ragon 3801 TCBY Bldg Capitol at Broadway Little Rock AR 72201

FOGLEMAN, JULIAN BARTON, lawyer; b. Memphis, Apr. 17, 1920; s. John Franklin and Marie Julia (McAdams) F.; m. Melba Margaret Henderson, Aug. 11, 1950; children: Margaret Elisabeth Heath, Julian Barton, John Nelson, Jennifer Leigh Vaughan, Frances Lorie Irwin. BS, U. Ark., 1941, LL.B., 1943, JD, 1969. Bar: Ark. 1943. Practiced in Marion, 1946-54, West Memphis, 1954—; pvt. practice, 1946-52; assoc. Hale & Fogleman, 1952-66, ptnr., 1967-73, Hale, Fogleman & Rogers, 1974—2001, Fogleman & Rogers, 2002—. City atty., Marion, 1951-81, dep. pros. atty., 1957-64 Chmn. fin. dir. Crittenden dist. Chickasaw coun. Boy Scouts Am., 1969, mem. exec. bd. coun., 1970-71, 75-80; bd. dirs. Crittenden County Charities, 1994-97, v.p., 1995; bd. dirs. Ark. Good Rds. Transp. Coun., 1976-96; mem. Ark. Cmty. Based Rehab. Commn., 1978-86, Crittenden County Bd. Edn., 1987-92. With inf. AUS, 1943-45, ETO. Fellow Am. Bar Found., Ark. Bar. Found. (bd. dirs. 1989-92); mem. ABA, Ark. Bar Assn. (ho. of dels. 1972-75, 81-84, exec. council 1972-75, 81-84, outstanding lawyer citizen award 1995-96), N.E. Ark. Bar Assn. (past pres.), Crittenden County Bar Assn. (past pres.), Phi Alpha Delta, Sigma Chi. Methodist. Home: 84 Turner Ave Marion AR 72364-1932 Office: PO Box 1666 123 W Broadway West Memphis AR 72301

FOHRMAN, BURTON H. lawyer; b. Chgo., July 9, 1939; s. Max and Helen (Naparty) F.; m. Raleigh S. Newman, Dec. 12, 1975. AB cum laude, U. So. Calif., Los Angeles, 1960; JD, UCLA, 1963. Bar: Calif. 1964. Pvt. practice, Riverside, Calif., 1964-66; mng. ptnr. Redwine and Sherrill, Riverside, 1966-83; ptnr. Jones, Day, Reavis and Pogue, L.A., 1983-92, former chmn. gen. real estate sect.; ptnr. White & Case, 1992—. Editor Calif. Real Property Jour., 1978-83. Mem. State Bar Calif. (chmn. real property sect. 1983), Los Angeles County Bar Assn. (chmn. real property fin. com. 1979-80, exec. com. real property sect. 1980-83), Daini Bar Assn. Office: Three Embarcedero Ctr Ste 2210 San Francisco CA 94111-3162 E-mail: bfohrman@whitecase.com.

FOLBERG, HAROLD JAY, lawyer, mediator, educator, university dean; b. East St. Louis, Ill., July 7, 1941; s. Louis and Matilda (Ross) F.; m. Diana L. Taylor, May 1, 1983; children: Lisa, Rachel, Ross. BA, San Francisco State U., 1963; JD, U. Calif., Berkeley, 1968. Bar: Oreg. 1968. Assoc. Rives & Schwab, Portland, Oreg., 1968-69; dir. Legal Aid Service, Portland, 1970-72; exec. dir. Assn. Family and Conciliation Cts., Portland, 1974-80; prof. law Lewis and Clark Law Sch., Portland, 1972-89; clin. asst. prof. child psychiatry U. Oreg. Med. Sch., 1976-89; judge pro-tem Oreg. Trial Cts., 1974-89; dean, prof. U. San Francisco Sch. Law, 1989-99, prof. law, 1999—. Chair jud. coun. Calif. Task Force on Alternative Dispute Resolution and the Jud. Sys., 1998-99, Calif. Blue Ribbon Panel Experts on Arbitration Ethics, 2001-2002, chair jud. coun.; Rockefeller Found. scholar in residence Bellagio, Italy, 1996; vis. prof. U. Wash. Sch. Law, 1985-86; mem. vis. faculty Nat. Jud. Coll., 1975-88; mem. Nat. Commn. on Accreditation for Marriage and Family Therapists, 1984-90; cons. Calif. Jud. Coun., U.S. Dist. Ct. (no. dist.) Calif. Author: Joint Custody and Shared Parenting, 1984, 2d edit., 1991; (with Taylor) Mediation-A Comprehensive Guide to Resolving Conflicts without Litigation, 1984; (with Milne) Divorce Mediation-Theory and Practice, 1988; mem. editorial bd.Family Counts Rev., Jour. of Divorce, Conflict Resolution Quar.; contbr. articles to profl. jours. Bd. dirs. Internat. Bioethics Inst., 1989-95, Oreg. Dispute Resolution Adv. Coun., 1988-89. Recipient Bernard E. Witkin award, Jud. Coun. Calif., 2003. Mem. ABA (chmn. mediation and arbitration com. family law sect. 1980-82, chmn. ethics com. dispute resolution sect. 2002-), Oreg. State Bar Assn. (chmn. family and juvenile law sect. 1979-80), Am. Bd. Trial Advs., Multnomah Bar Assn. (chmn. bd. dirs. legal aid svc. 1973-76), Am. Arbitration Assn. (mem. panel of arbitrators), Assn. Family and Conciliation Cts. (pres. 1983-84), Assn. Marriage and Family Therapists (disting. mem.), Am. Assn. Law Schs. (chmn. alternative dispute resolution sect. 1988), Acad. Family Mediators (bd. dirs., pres. 1988), Assn. Conflict Resolution, World Assn. Law Profs. (sec.-gen. 1995-2000). Office: U San Francisco Sch Law 2130 Fulton St San Francisco CA 94117-1080 E-mail: folbergj@usfca.edu.

FOLEY, JOHN FRANCIS, retired judge, lawyer; b. Detroit, Feb. 10, 1928; s. Henry Michael and Rosemary (O'Neill) F.; m. Joan Marlow, Aug. 17, 1957; children: Sean, Patrick, Rosemary, Joan, Margaret, Ella. BS, Georgetown U., 1948; JD, U. Mich., 1957. Bar: Mich. 1957, U.S. Dist. Ct. (ea. dist.) Mich. 1961, U.S. Dist. Ct. (we. dist.) Mich. 1969, U.S. Ct. Appeals (6th cir.) 1983. Assoc. firm Wilson, Ingraham and Kavanagh, Birmingham, Mich., 1957-59; atty. NLRB, Detroit, 1959-61; ptnr. firm Swartz, O'Hare, Sharples & Foley, Detroit, 1961-66, Gergely & Foley, P.C., Vicksburg , Mich., 1969-85; judge Kalamazoo County Cir. Ct., Mich., 1985-98; ret. Commr. Mich. Ct. Appeals, Lansing, 1966-68. Mem. Dem. Exec. Com., Oakland City, Mich., 1961-64, Kalamazoo, 1980; bd. dirs. Kalamazoo ACLU, 1971-83. Lt. (j.g.) USN, 1951-55. Mem. ABA, Mich. Bar Assn., Kalamazoo County Bar Assn. Alternative dispute resolution. Home: 2846 W Y Z Ave Schoolcraft MI 49087-9744

FOLEY, MARTIN JAMES, lawyer; b. Nebr., Nov. 7, 1946; s. James Gleason and Mary Elizabeth (O'Brien) Foley; m. Linda Sivyer; children: James Gleason Foley II, Daniel Patrick, Ryan Edward, Michelle Sivyer. Cert. Completition, Cambridge U., 1967; BA in Philosophy, U. So. Calif., 1968, JD, 1974, MBA, 1975. Bar: Calif. 1975, U.S. Dist. Ct. (cen. dist.) Calif. 1980, U.S. Dist. Ct. (ea., so. and no. dists.) Calif. 1980, U.S. Ct. Appeals (9th cir.) 1980, U.S. Ct. Fed. Claims 1991, U.S. Supreme Ct. 1990. Acct. Ford Motor Co., San Jose, Calif., 1968, cost analyst, 1970-71; assoc. Adams, Duque & Hazeltine, 1975-80; sr. ptnr. Bryan, Cave, McPheeters & McRoberts, L.A., 1980-89, Sonnenschein Nath & Rosenthal, L.A., 1990—. Mem. bd. govs. Gen. Alumni Assn. U. So. Calif., 1982—84; ct. appt. settlement officer Calif. State, 1992—94, U.S. Dist. Ct. (cen. dist.), 1998—2001; lectr. groups and profl. confs. Contbr. Lt. j.g. USNR, 1968—70. Mem.: ABA (numerous coms.), L.A. County Bar Assn., Calif. Bar Assn. (conf. of dels. 1979—93), Annandale Golf Club Pasadena, Calif., Jonathan Club LA. Republican. Roman Catholic. Aviation, Intellectual property, Labor (including EEOC, Fair Labor Standards Act, labor-management relations, NLRB, OSHA). Office: Sonnenschein Nath Rosenthal 601 S Figueroa St Ste 1500 Los Angeles CA 90017-5720 E-mail: mf@sonnenschein.com.

FOLEY, RIDGWAY KNIGHT, JR., lawyer, writer; b. Portland, Oreg., Oct. 7, 1937; s. Ridgway Knight and Eunice Alberta (Ammer) F. BS magna cum laude, Lewis & Clark Coll., 1959; JD, U. Oreg., 1963. Bar: Oreg. Assoc. Mautz, Souther, Spaulding, Kinsey & Williamson, Portland, 1964-71; gen. ptnr. Schwabe, Williamson & Wyatt (and predecessor firms), Portland, 1972-84, sr. ptnr., 1985-92; ptnr., shareholder Foley & Duncan, P.C., Portland, 1993-96; of counsel Greene & Markley PC, Portland, 1997—, med. office mgr., 1999—. Com. mem. Multnomah Lawyer Com., 1964-68, 90-93, chair, 1992-93. Contbr. more than 100 articles, essays to profl. jours., 1962—; lectr. profl. orgns., 1970—. Trustee Found. Econ. Edn., Inc., Irvington-on-Hudson, N.Y., 1974-91, 93-96; founding dir. Paulist Fathers Cath. Ctr., Portland, 1978-85. Mem. ABA, Oreg. State Bar, Multnomah County Bar (dir. 1993-97), University Club (Portland), Mt. Hood Philos. Soc. (founding trustee, officer 1972-85), Lang Syne Soc., Order of Coif. Episcopalian. Avocations: writing, lecturing, genealogy, publishing, history. Office: Greene & Markley PC 1515 SW 5th Ave Ste 600 Portland OR 97201-5449

FOLEY, THOMAS JOHN, lawyer; b. Detroit, July 3, 1954; s. Thomas John and Mary Catherine (Gluekert) F.; m. Virginia Lee, Aug. 20, 1977; 1 child, Kaitlin Shea. BA, Mich. State U., 1976, JD, 1979. Bar: Mich. 1980, Ohio 1992, U.S. Dist. Ct. (ea. and we. dists.) Mich. 1980, U.S.Ct. Appeals (6th cir.) 1980. Assoc. Kitch, Drutchas, Wagner, Denardis & Valitutti, Detroit, 1980—84, assoc. prin., 1984—87, prin., shareholder, 1987—2003; founder Foley, Baron & Metzger, PLLC, Farmington Hills, Mich., 2003—. Contbr. articles to profl. jours. Mem.: Food and Drug Law Inst., Def. Rsch. Inst., Internat. Assn. Def. Counsel. Avocations: swimming, private pilot. General civil litigation, Personal injury (including property damage), Product liability. Office: Foley Baron and Metzger PLLC Ste 350 33533 W Twelve Mile Rd Farmington Hills MI 48331 Business E-Mail: tfoley@fbmlaw.com.

FOLK, THOMAS ROBERT, lawyer; b. Milford, N.J., Jan. 9, 1950; s. Conrad Frank and Isabella Ramsey (Sickels) F.; m. JoAnn Elizabeth Lo Pinto, June 21, 1975; children: Elizabeth Frances, Karina Marie. BS, U.S. Mil. Acad., 1972; JD, U. Va., 1978. Bar: Va. 1978, U.S. Ct. Mil. Appeals 1978, U.S. Ct. Appeals (4th cir.) 1978, U.S. Supreme Ct. 1983, U.S. Ct. Claims 1985, U.S. Ct. Appeals (9th and fed. cirs.) 1985, D.C. 1986., U.S. Dist. Ct. D.C. 1987, U.S. Dist. Ct. Md. 1987, U.S. Ct. Appeals (11th cir.) 2000. Commd. 2d lt. U.S. Army, 1972, advanced to maj., 1983, resigned, 1986, asst. to gen. counsel, 1980-82, atty. litigation, 1983-86; assoc. Hazel & Thomas, P.C., Fairfax, Va., 1986-88, owner, 1989-99; ptnr. Reed Smith LLP, Fairfax, 1999—. Contbr. articles to profl. jours. Mem. Com. Armed Svcs. and Vets. Affairs, 1985-88. Col. USAR, 1995, ret. Mem.: Fairfax Bar Assn. (bd. govs. 1993—97), Va. State Bar (bd. govs. constrn. and pub. contracts 1993—99), West Point Soc. D.C (bd. govs. 1993—99). Federal civil litigation, General civil litigation, Government contracts and claims. Home: 4902 Asquith Ct Fairfax VA 22032-2102 E-mail: tfolk@reedsmith.com.

FOLLICK, EDWIN DUANE, law educator, chiropractic physician; b. Glendale, Calif., Feb. 4, 1935; s. Edwin Fulfford and Esther Agnes (Catherwood) Follick; m. Marilyn K. Sherk, Mar. 24, 1986. BA, Calif. State U., LA, 1956, MA in Edn., 1961; MA in Social Sci., Pepperdine U., 1957, MPA, 1977; PhD, DTh, St. Andrews Theol. Coll., Sem. Free Prot. Episc. Ch., London, 1958; MS in LS, U. So. Calif., 1963, MEd in Instructional Materials, 1964, AdvMEd in Edn. Adminstrn., 1969; postgrad., Calif. Coll. Law, 1965; LLB, Blackstone Law Sch., 1966, JD, 1967; DC, Cleve. Chiropractic Coll., L.A., 1972; PhD, Academia Theatina, Pescara, 1978; MA in Orgnl. Mgmt., Antioch U., L.A., 1990. Tchr., libr. adminstr. L.A. City Schs., 1957-68; law librarian Glendale U. Coll. Law, 1968-69; coll. librarian Cleve. Chiropractic Coll., L.A., 1969-74, dir. edn. and admissions, 1974-84, prof. jurisprudence, 1975—, dean student affairs, 1976-92, coll. chaplain, 1985—, dean of edn., 1989—, rector, 2003—; assoc. prof. Newport U., 1982; extern prof. St. Andrews Theol. Coll., London, 1961; dir. West Valley Chiropractic Health Ctr., 1972-2000, West Valley Chiropractic Consulting, 2001—. Contbr. articles to profl. jours. Chaplain's asst. U.S. Army, 1958—60. Decorated cavaliere Internat. Order Legion of Honor of Immaculata (Italy); Knight of Malta, Sovereign Order of St. John of Jerusalem; Knight Grand Prelate, comdr. with star, Order of Signum Fidei; comdr. chevalier Byzantine Imperial Order of Constantine the Gt.; comdr. ritter Order St. Gereon; chevalier Mil. and Hospitaller Order of St. Lazarus of Jerusalem (Malta), Chaplain of the Order of St. Stanislas; numerous others. Mem. ALA, NEA, Am. Assn. Sch. Librarians, L.A. Sch. Libr. Assn., Calif. Sch. Libr. Assn., Assn. Coll. and Rsch. Librarians, Am. Assn. Law Librarians, Am. Chiropractic Assn., Internat. Chiropractors Assn., Nat. Geog. Soc., Internat. Platform Assn., Phi Delta Kappa, Sigma Chi Psi, Delta Tau Alpha. Democrat. Episcopalian. Home: 6435 Jumilla Ave Woodland Hills CA 91367-2833 Office: 590 N Vermont Ave Los Angeles CA 90004-2115 also: 7022 Owensmouth Ave Canoga Park CA 91303-2005 E-mail: follicke@cleveland.edu.

FOLTZ, MICHAEL CRAIG, lawyer; b. Chgo., June 7, 1957; s. Joseph Nicholas and Lucille (Acierno) F.; m. Kim Marie Tabor, May 18, 1985. BS, Ill. State U., 1979; JD, Ill. Inst. Tech., 1982. Bar: Ill. 1982; CPA, Ill., cert. fin. planner. Tax cons. Price Waterhouse, Chgo., 1982-84; ptnr. Dinverno & Foltz, Oak Brook, Ill., 1984—. Mem. Ill. State Bar Assn., Chgo. Bar Assn., Am. Inst. CPA's. Roman Catholic. Corporate, general, Estate planning, Personal income taxation. Home: 38 Christina Cir Wheaton IL 60187-1110 Office: Dinverno & Foltz 1301 W 22nd St Ste 602 Oak Brook IL 60523-2059

FONG, PETER C. K. lawyer, judge, company executive; b. Honolulu, Oct. 28, 1955; s. Arthur S.K. and Victoria K.Y. (Chun) F. BBA with honors, U. Hawaii, 1977; JD, Boston Coll., 1980. Bar: Hawaii 1980, U.S. Dist. Ct. Hawaii 1980, U.S. Ct. Appeals (9th cir.) 1980, U.S. Supreme Ct. 1983. Law clk. to presiding justice Supreme Ct. Hawaii, Honolulu, 1980-81; dep. pros. atty. Pros. Atty.'s Office, Honolulu, 1981-84; with Davis, Reid & Richards, Honolulu, 1984-89; chief legal counsel, chief clk. Senate jud. com. Hawaii State Legislature, 1989—; judge per diem Dist./Family Ct., Hawaii, 1989—; ptnr. Hong, Kwock & Fong, Honolulu, 1990-91, Fong & Fong, Honolulu, 1989—; pres., CEO, dir. Chun Kim Chow, Ltd., Honolulu, 1998—. Gen. legal counsel Hawaii Jr. C. of C., 1983-84; pres., bd. dirs. Legal Aid Soc. Hawaii, 1984-90; pres., 1986-87; arbitrator Hawaiian Cir. Ct., 1986—, Am. Arbitration Assn., 1989—; mediator Arbitration Forums, Inc., 1989—. Editorial staff Boston Coll. Internat. and Comp. Law Rev., 1978-80. Mem. City and County Honolulu Neighborhood Bd., 1981-83; campaign treas. for Hawaii state senator, 1981-89; mem. aux. admissions com. Boston Coll. Law Sch., 1982—, major gifts com. and sustaining membership fundraising drive com. YMCA, 1988; del. Gov.'s Congress on Hawaii's internat. role, 1988; del. Hawaii Jud. Forsight Congress, 1991; mem. hearings com. Hawaii State Atty.'s Disciplinary Bd., 1991—. Recipient Pres.'s award Hawaii Jr. C. of C., 1984; named one of ten Outstanding Persons of Hawaii, 1990, 92. Mem. ABA, ATLA, Hawaii State Bar Assn. (co-chmn. and vice-chmn., jud. salary com., mem. legis. com., coord. legis. resource bank, mem. task force on disciplinary counsel), Hawaii Developer's Coun., Am. Judicature Soc., Hawaii Supreme Ct. Hist. Soc., Hawaii Trial Judges Assn., Nat. Coun. Juvenile and Family Ct. Judges, Rsch. Bd. of Advisors, Nat. Assn. Dist. Attys., U.S. Supreme Ct. Hist. Soc., Mortar Bd., Tu Chiang Shen (past pres.), Waialae Country Club. General civil litigation, General practice, Insurance. Home: 5255 Makalena St Honolulu HI 96821-1808 Office: Fong & Fong Grosvener Ctr Makai Tower 733 Bishop St Ste 1550 Honolulu HI 96813-4003

FONSECA, GERARDO, lawyer; b. Mexico City, Nov. 23, 1974; s. Gerardo Fonseca and Maruca Pereda; m. Mónica Hernandez-Candelas, Dec. 15, 2001. Licenciado en Derecho, U. Iberoamericana, Mex. City, 1999, Cert. in Telecom., 2000; LL.M, Northwestern U., Chgo., IL, 2002; Cert. in Bus. Adminstrn., Kellogg Sch. of Mgmt., Evanston, IL, 2002. Bar: Mex. 1999. Sr. assoc. Díez & Toledo Córdova, S.C., Mex. City, Mexico, 2003—. Mem.: Illustrious and Nat. Coll. of Lawyers (assoc.). Roman Catholic. Avocations: travel, reading, music, literature. Communications, Corporate, general, Telecommunications, Foreign Investment. Home: Sierra Mojada No 405 -6 Mexico City Mexico City 11000 Mexico Office: Díez & Toledo COrdoba SC Bosque Duraznos 75-201 Col Bosques Lomas Mexico City 11700 Mexico Office Fax: +(52 55) 52515512. E-mail: gfonseca@dytc.com.

FONTAINE, VALERIE ANNE, lawyer, legal search consultant; b. Honolulu, May 17, 1955; d. Warren Tremlett Chaffey and Dorine Marks Foster. JD, Hastings Coll., San Francisco, 1979; AB, UCLA, 1976. Atty. O'Melveny & Myers, L.A., 1979-81; cons. Lee, Jackson & Bowe, Beverly Hills, Calif., 1981-83; v.p. Bench Ltd., L.A., 1983-88; ptnr. Seltzer Fontaine Beckwith, L.A., 1988—. Contbr. articles to profl. jours. and newspapers. 1st v.p., past pres., trustee Hastings 1066 Found. Mem. State Bar Calif., L.A. Bar Assn., Women Lawyers Assn. L.A. (bd. dirs., co-chair status of women lawyers com. 1989-92, co-chair legal edn. and spl. programs com., chair publ. com., co-chair mentoring and bus. devel. com., mem. adv. coun.), Hastings Alumni Assn. (bd. dirs. 1988—, pres. L.A. chpt. 1992-93), Phi Beta Kappa. Democrat. Jewish. Avocations: exercise, foreign cooking, reading, gardening. Office: Seltzer Fontaine Beckwith 2999 Overland Ave Ste 120 Los Angeles CA 90064-4243 E-mail: vfontaine@sfbsearch.com.

FONVIELLE, CHARLES DAVID, lawyer; b. Melbourne, Fla., Dec. 28, 1944; s. Charles David Fonvielle Jr. and Margaret Jordan Palmer; m. Deborah Konas, July 25, 1970; children: C. Caulley, D. Jordan. BA, U. Fla., 1968; JD, Fla. State U., 1972. Bar: Fla. 1972, U.S. Dist. Ct. (no., mid. and so. dists.) Fla. Asst. pub. defender Fla. Pub. Defender Assn., Tallahassee, 1972-74; pvt. practice Tallahassee, 1974-77; ptnr. Thompson, Wadsworth, Messer, Turner & Rhodes, Tallahassee, 1977-80, Green & Fonvielle, Tallahassee, 1980-84, Green, Fonvielle & Hinkle, Tallahassee, 1984-85, Fonvielle Hinkle & Lewis, Tallahassee, 1995—2002, Fonvielle Lewis Foote & Messer, 2002—. Bd. dirs. Fla. State U. Coll. Law, endowed prof. litigation. Mem. ATLA (sustaining), Tallahassee Bar Assn. (bd. dirs. 1978-79), Acad. Fla. Trial Lawyers (Eagle sponsor 1990—), Nat. Bd. Trial Advocacy (cert.), Fla. Bar Assn. (bd. legal specialization and edn. 1991—). Avocations: physical fitness, flying, spearfishing, sports cars. Personal injury (including property damage), Product liability, Professional liability. Office: Fonvielle Lewis Foote & Messer 3375 Capital Cir NE Ste A Tallahassee FL 32308-3778 E-mail: david@flfmlaw.com.

FOOTE, JEFFREY PAUL, lawyer; b. Portland, Oreg., Aug. 11, 1949; s. George T. and Helen J. (Rissman) F.; m. Jane B. Hall, Feb. 22, 1975 (div. Aug. 1978); m. Cynthia A. Loy, Dec. 20, 1986; 1 child, Allison Nancy. BS, U. Oreg., 1971; JD, Lewis and Clark Coll., 1974. Bar: Oreg. 1974, U.S. Dist. Ct. Oreg. 1974. Exec. dir. Natural Resources Law Inst., Portland, 1974-77; dep. city atty. City of Portland, 1977-79; assoc. Law Office John J. Haugh, Portland, 1979-82; ptnr. Haugh & Foote, P.C., Portland, 1982-88; pvt. practice Portland, 1988—. Adj. prof. Lewis & Clark Law Sch., Portland, 1974-77; Oreg. state del. Assn. Trial Lawyers Am., Washington, 1983-89; bd. dirs., founder Trial Lawyers for Pub. Justice, Washington. Contbr. articles to profl. jours. and law rev. Mem. Oreg. Trial Lawyers Assn. (bd. govs. 1981—, pres. 1990-91), Trial Lawyers for Pub. Justice (v.p. 1990-91, pres.-elect 1991—), Assn. Trial Lawyers Am. (bd. govs.). Democrat. General civil litigation, Personal injury (including property damage), Product liability. Office: Jeffrey Foote & Assocs PC 1515 SW Fifth Ave Ste 808 Portland OR 97201-5447

FORBES, ARTHUR LEE, III, lawyer; b. Houston, Sept. 3, 1928; s. Arthur Lee Jr. and Corinne (Mayfield) F.; m. Nita R. Harrison, Mar. 25, 1957; children: Dana, Tricia, Kim, Arthur Lee. BSCE, U. Tex., Austin, 1952; JD, So. Tex. Coll. Law, 1959. Bar: Tex. 1959, U.S. Ct. Appeals (5th cir.) 1960, U.S. Supreme Ct. 1967. Ptnr. Lee & Forbes, Houston, 1960-73, Shapiro, Forbes & Cox, Houston, 1974-88; gen. counsel Bay Houston Towing Co., 1989—. Lt. USMC, 1952-54. Mem. ABA, Tex. Bar Assn., Houston Bar Assn., Houston Racquet Club, Sigma Chi, Phi Delta Phi. Corporate, general, Environmental, General practice. Home: 5 Leisure Ln Houston TX 77024-5123 E-mail: artf165@earthlink.net.

FORBES, MORTON GERALD, lawyer; b. Atlanta, July 12, 1938; s. Arthur Mark and Mary Dean (Power) F.; m. Eunice Lee Haynesworth, Jan. 25, 1963; children: John, Ashley, Sarah. AB, Wofford Coll., 1962; JD, U. Ga., 1965. Bar: Ga. 1965, U.s. Dist. Ct. (mid. dist.) Ga. 1965, U.S. Dist. Ct. (so. dist.) Ga. 1968, U.S. Dist. Ct. (no. dist.) Ga. 1993, U.S. Ct. Appeals (5th cir.) 1974, U.S. Ct. Appeals (4th cir.) 1972, U.S. Ct. Appeals (11th cir.) 1981. Assoc. Pierce, Ranitz, Lee, Berry & Mahoney, 1967-70; ptnr. Pierce, Ranitz, Berry, Mahoney & Forbes, 1970-76, Pierce, Ranitz, Mahoney, Forbes & Coolidge, 1976-81; ptnr., sec. Ranitz, Mahoney, Forbes & Coolidge, P.C., 1981-91, Forbes & Bowman, Savannah, Ga., 1991—. Gen. counsel Ga. Fed. Young Rep. Clubs, 1971-72; guest lectr. dept. dental hygiene Armstrong State Coll., 1970-72. Mem. Savannah (port Authority (now Savannah Econ. Devel. Authority), 1973-2003, chmn., 1979-81; mem. Chatham County Devel. Authority, 1973-80; nat. com. Nat. Fedn. Young Reps., 1973; econ. adv. coun. Coastal Area Planning and Devel. Authority, 1980—; bd. dirs. Savannah Symphony Soc., 1971-75; Ga. del. to Japan/Southeast Trade Mission, Kyoto, Japan, 1983, S.E. Asia U.S.A./Japan Assn. meeting, Birmingham, Ala., 1984. With USN, 1965-67. Recipient Outstanding Service award Savannah Port Authority, 1981. Mem. ABA, Internat. Assn. Defense Counsel, Fedn. Def. and Corp. Counsel, State Bar Ga., Ala. Def. Lawyer Assn. (hon.), Am. Judicature Soc., Nat. Assn. Bond Counsel, Ga. Def. Lawyers Assn. (v.p. 1987—, mem. exec. com. 1988, bd. dirs., exec. v.p. 1990-91, pres. 1991-92), Savannah Bar Assn. (exec. com. 1989-94, pres. 1992-93), Libel Def. Resource Ctr., Def. Rsch. Inst. (state chmn. 1992-99, bd. dirs. 1999-2002), Savannah Econ. Devel. Action Coun. (founding), Savannah Area Wofford Coll. Alumni Club (past pres.), Soc. of the Cincinnati (Va.), St. Andrews Soc. (bd. stewards), Soc. Colonial Wars, Sons of Revolution (sec. 1988-92), Chatham Club, Savannah Yacht Club, 1st City Club, The Landings Club. Republican. Presbyterian. Federal civil litigation, Insurance, Product liability. Office: Forbes & Bowman PO Box 13929 Savannah GA 31416-0929

FORBES, THEODORE MCCOY, JR., arbitrator, mediator, retired lawyer; b. Atlanta, Oct. 28, 1929; s. Theodore M. and Mary Beatrice (Christie) F.; m. Margaret Paty, Dec. 12, 1953; children: Theodore McCoy, Margaret Paty. BS in Chemistry, Ga. Inst. Tech., 1950; LLB, U. Va., 1953. Bar: Ga., 1952, D.C. 1973, U.S. Ct. Appeals (5th cir.) 1976, U.S. Ct. Appeals (11th cir.) 1981. Instr. Culver (Ind.) Summer Naval Sch., 1950; assoc. Smith, Gambrell & Russell, and predecessor firms, Atlanta, 1953-58, ptnr., 1958-91; solo practice, 1992-95. Bd. dirs. Travelers Aid Soc., Atlanta, 1974-90, pres., 1975-76, 86-89; bd. dirs. , corp. sec. Shepherd Spinal Ctr., Atlanta, 1975-95; bd. dirs. Ga. Fund for Edn., 1986-89. Lt. (j.g.) USNR, 1950-62. Fellow Ga. Bar Found.; mem. ABA, Atlanta Bar Assn., State Bar Ga. (emeritus), Ga. C. of C. (bd. dirs. 1986-95), Capital City Club (life). Avocations: golf, american history, fishing. Corporate, general, Pension, profit-sharing, and employee benefits, Taxation, general. Home: 2520 Peachtree Rd NW Apt 202 Atlanta GA 30305-3617

FORCHELLI, CHARLES NICHOLAS, lawyer; b. Apr. 16, 1948; s. Vincent and Dorothea Maria (Downing) Forchelli; m. Mary Antoinette Sloboda, June 23, 1979; 1 child, Jennifer. BA, Syracuse U., 1969; JD, Bklyn. Law Sch., 1972. Bar: N.Y. 1973, U.S. Dist. Ct. (ea. and so. dists.) N.Y. 1975. Ptnr. Forchelli & Forchelli, L.I., NY, 1973—. Recipient Am. Jurisprudence award, Bklyn. Law Sch., 1972. Mem.: Queens County Bar Assn., Shinnecock Anglers Club, L.I. City Lawyers Club (pres. 1986), Kappa Sigma. Methodist. State civil litigation, Landlord-tenant, Personal injury (including property damage). Office: Forchelli & Forchelli 32-02 30th Ave Long Island City NY 11102-1528

FORD, GEORGE BURT, lawyer; b. South Bend, Ind., Oct. 1, 1923; s. George W. and Florence (Burt) F.; m. Charlotte Ann Kupferer, June 12, 1948; children: John, Victoria, George, Charlotte. BS in Engring. Law, Purdue U., 1946; LLB, Ind. U., 1949. Bar: Ind. 1949, U.S. Dist. Ct. (no. dist.) Ind. 1949. Assoc. Jones, Obenchain & Butler, South Bend, Ind., 1949-52; ptnr. Jones, Obenchain, Ford, Pankow & Lewis, South Bend, 1953-93, of counsel, 1994—. Co-author: Forms for Indiana Corporations, 1967, 2nd edit. 1977. With U.S. Army, 1943-45, ETO. Fellow Am. Coll. of Trust and Estate Counsel; mem. ABA, Ind. Bar Assn., St. Joseph County Bar Assn. (pres. 1976-77), Phi Gamma Delta, Phi Delta Phi. Presbyterian (trustee 1966-68, elder 1967-70). Banking, Corporate, general, Probate (including wills, trusts). Office: Jones Obenchain LLP 600 Key Bank Bldg 202 S Michigan St Box 4577 South Bend IN 46634-4577

FORD, RICHARD EDMOND, lawyer; b. Ronceverte, W.Va., May 3, 1927; s. Grady Williams and Hazel Loraine (Fry) F.; m. Sally Frances Alexander, June 14, 1952; children: Richard Edmond Jr., Sally Anne, Melinda J. Student, U. N.C., 1950; BS in Bus. Adminstrn., W.Va. U., 1951, LL.B., 1954. Bar: W.Va. 1954. Assoc. Holt & Haynes, Lewisburg, W.Va., 1954-55; ptnr. Haynes & Ford, Lewisburg, 1955-74, Haynes, Ford & Rowe, Lewisburg, 1975-96, The Ford Law Firm, Lewisburg, 1997—. Dir. W.Va. Power Co., First Nat. Bank Ronceverte, Greenbrier Cable Corp. Bd. dirs. W.Va. U. Found., Daywood Found., v.p., 1986—; bd. dirs. Faculty Merit Found. W.Va., W.Va. Legal Svcs. Plan, 1973—79; trustee Greenbrier Coll. for Women, 1960—73; mem. exec. bd. Buckskin Coun. Boy Scouts Am.; mem. adv. bd. Greenbrier C.C. Ctr.; mem. vis. com. Coll. Law W.Va. U., 1972—74; mem. W.Va. Legislature, 1961—64. Served as ensign U.S. Maritime Svc., 1945—47. Recipient Outstanding Alumnus award W.Va. U. Law Sch., 1980, W.Va. U., 88. Fellow Am. Bar Found., Am. Judicature Soc.; mem. ABA (ho. of dels. 1977-80), W.Va. Bar Assn. (v.p. 1965-66, 75-76, pres. 1978-79), Greenbrier County Bar Assn. (pres. 1964-66, 81-82), W.Va. Law Sch. Assn. (pres. 1966-67), Nat. Conf. Commrs. Uniform State Laws, Am. Coll. Real Estate Lawyers, W.Va. U. Alumni Assn. (pres. 1971), Phi Beta Kappa, Sigma Chi, Phi Delta Phi, Order of Vandalia. Clubs: Masons, KT, Shriners, Lewisburg Elks. Democrat. Methodist. State civil litigation, Probate (including wills, trusts), Property, real (including real estate development, water). Office: The Ford Law Firm 203 W Randolph St Lewisburg WV 24901-1023

FORD, ROBERT DAVID, lawyer; b. New Orleans, Oct. 30, 1956; s. Thomas Paul and Inez Mary (Rodriguez) F.; m. Jean Ann Burg, May 5, 1979; children: Robert David Jr., Charlene Elizabeth, Timothy Michael. BA, U. New Orleans, 1978; JD, Loyola U., 1983. Bar: La. 1983, U.S. Dist. Ct. (ea. dist.) La. 1983, U.S. Dist. Ct. (mid. dist.) La. 1997, U.S. Ct. Appeals (5th cir.) 1985. Claims rep. State Farm Mut. Auto Ins. Co., Metairie, La., 1978-80; assoc. Hammett, Leake & Hammett, New Orleans, 1983-86; ptnr. Thomas, Hayes, Beahm & Buckley, New Orleans, 1986-95; mem. Chehardy, Sherman, Ellis, Breslin & Murray, Metairie, La., 1995-96; ptnr. Hailey, McNamara, Hall, Larmann & Papale, Metairie, 1996—. Mem. ABA (coms. on health law, profl. liability and products liability litigation 1992, subcoms. on hosp. and clinic med. devices and med. malpractice liability 1992), La. Bar Assn., La. Assn. Def. Counsel, Am. Soc. Law and Medicine, La. Soc. Hosp. Attys. of La. Hosp. Assn., Def. Rsch. Inst., Phi Kappa Theta, Pi Alpha Delta. Republican. Roman Catholic. Avocations: golf, softball. Health, Insurance, Product liability. Home: 8 Caney Ct Kenner LA 70065-3944 Office: Hailey McNamara Hall Larmann & Papale 1 Galleria Blvd Ste 1400 Metairie LA 70001-7543 E-mail: rford@hmhlp.com.

FORD, VICKIE LOUISE ARP, lawyer; b. Cartersville, Ga., Jan. 8, 1956; d. Perry H. and Marjorie Woods Arp; m. William Geary Ford, Apr. 16, 1947. JD, John Marshall Law Sch., Atlanta, 1998. Bar: Ga. 1999, U.S. Ct. Appeals Ga. 2001, U.S. Dist. Ct. Ga. 2001. Owner Ford Law Firm, Cartersville, Georgia 30120, Ga., 1999—. Active Rep. Party, Cartersville, Atlanta, Ga. Recipient Wall of Tolerance, Rosa Parks, Morris Dees, 2002. Mem.: Phi Alpha Theta. Republican. Baptist. Avocations: reading, gardening. General civil litigation, Property, real (including real estate development, water), Family and matrimonial. Office: Ford Law Firm 703 Joe Frank Harris Pkwy Cartersville GA 30120 Office Fax: 770-607-5759. E-mail: vickiefordlaw@aol.com.

FOREHAND, JON VINCENT, lawyer; b. Tallahassee, May 16, 1964; s. Cary C. and JoAnn (Jordan) F.; m. Christine Hopkins Forehand, Nov. 22, 1986; children: W. Chason, David Cary, Jordan Allyna. AA, Emmanuel Coll., Franklin Springs, Ga., 1984; BS, Lee Coll., Cleveland, Tenn., 1986; JD, U. Ga., 1990; cert. in risk mgmt. for chs. and schs., U. Cambridge, 2002. Bar: U.S. Ct. Appeals (11th cir.) 1990, Ga. Supreme Ct. 1990, U.S. Dist. Ct. 1990, Ga., U.S. Supreme Ct. 1996. Atty. Kirbo & McCalley, Moultrie, Ga., 1990-95, Kirbo, McCalley & Forehand, Moultrie, Ga., 1995-97, Allen & Forehand, Moultrie, Ga., 1998—. Dir. Extension Loan Fund, Inc., Oklahoma City, 1994—; nat. staff Royal Rangers, I.P.H.C., Oklahoma City, 1990-95. Dir. Am. Red Cross, Moultrie, Ga., 1993. Mem. Assn. Trial Lawyers Am., Christian Legal Soc. Criminal, Non-profit and tax-exempt organizations, Personal injury (including property damage). Office: Allen & Forehand PO Box 1687 Moultrie GA 31776-1687

FOREMAN, JAMES LOUIS, retired judge; b. Metropolis, Ill., May 12, 1927; s. James C. and Anna Elizabeth (Henne) F.; m. Mabel Inez Dunn, June 16, 1948; children: Beth Foreman Banks, Rhonda Foreman Wittig, Nanette Foreman Love. BS in Commerce and Law, U. Ill., 1950, JD, 1952. Bar: Ill. Ind. practice law, Metropolis, Ill.; ptnr. Chase and Foreman, Metropolis, until 1972; state's atty. State of Ill., Massac County, asst. atty. gen.; chief judge U.S. Dist. Ct. (so. dist.) Ill., Benton, 1979-92, sr. status, 1992—. Pres. Bd. of Edn., Metropolis. With USN, 1945-46. Mem. Ill. State Bar Assn., Metropolic C. of C. (past pres.). Republican. Home: 38 Hilanoa-East Dr Metropolis IL 62960-2533 Office: US Dist Ct 301 W Main St Benton IL 62812-1362

FORESTER, JOHN GORDON, JR., lawyer; b. Wilkesboro, N.C., Jan. 14, 1933; s. John Gordon and Mary Hope (Hendren) F.; m. Georgina Ramirez, June 26, 1957; children: John Gordon III, Robert Raoul, Georgina Yasué, Richard Alexander. BS; in Indsl. Relations, U. N.C., 1955; LL.B., George Washington U., 1962. Bar: D.C. 1962, Md. 1993. Internat. economist Dept. Commerce, 1958-62; confidential asst. to dep. asst. sec. commerce, 1962-63; law clk. to U.S. Dist. Judge L.P. Walsh, 1963-64; pvt. practice Washington, 1964-80; ptnr. Pohoryles & Greenstein, P.C., Washington, 1980-89, Greenstein Delorme & Luchs, P.C., Washington, 1989-95; pvt. practice, 1995—. Mem. Jud. Conf. D.C. Cir., 1981, 82, 92, adv. com. Civil Justice Reform Act, U.S. Dist. Ct., 1991-93; pres. Lawyers Mut. Ins. Co. of D.C., 1990-92. Contbr. articles to profl. jours. Pres. Friendly Citizens Assn., 1963, Gonzaga Fathers Club, 1974-76; chmn. bd. dirs. Henson Valley Montessori Sch.; bd. dirs. Sursum Corda Neighborhood Center, 1975-77. Lt. comdr. USNR, 1955-58. Mem. ABA (mem. ho. of dels. 2000-2002), D.C. Bar Assn. (pres. 2001-02), Md. Bar Assn., Coun. for Ct. Excellence (chmn. ct. improvement com.), George Washington U. Law Alumni Assn. (pres. D.C. chpt. 1988-89), Counsellors (pres. 1984-85), Barrister Inn (pres. 1976-77), Order Golden Fleece, Kappa Alpha Order, Phi Delta Phi. Roman Catholic. Home: 10701 Laurel Leaf Pl Potomac MD 20854-1770 Office: 1914 Sunderland Pl NW Washington DC 20036 E-mail: jgfcadence@aol.com.

FORESTER, KARL S. chief district court judge; b. 1940; BA, U. Ky., 1962, JD, 1966. With Eugene Goss Esp., 1966—68; mem. firm Goss & Forester, 1968—75, Forester, Forester, Buttermore & Turner, P.S.C., 1975—88; judge U.S. Dist. Ct. (ea. dist.) Ky., Lexington, 1988—. Mem. Ky. Bar Assn., Harlan County Bar Assn., Fayette County Bar Assn. Office: US Dist Ct PO Box 2165 Lexington KY 40588-2165

FORGER, ALEXANDER DARROW, lawyer; b. N.Y.C., Feb. 19, 1923; BA with honors, Princeton U., 1947; JD, Yale U., 1950. Bar: N.Y. 1951. Assoc. Milbank, Tweed, Hadley & McCloy, N.Y.C., 1950-57, ptnr., 1958—, chmn., 1984—92, spl. counsel, 1993—. Pres., Legal Svcs. Corp., 1994-97; bd. dirs. Oak Spring Farms, LLC Trustee Rockefeller U.; chmn. bd., Legal Aid Soc., 1984-92; v.p., Dorothea Leonhardt Found., Gerard B. Lambert Meml. Found., Inc. Fellow Am. Bar Found., N.Y. Bar Found., Am. Coll. Trust and Estate Counsel; mem. ABA (past state del. to ho. of dels.), N.Y. State Bar Assn. (past pres. ho. of dels.), Assn. Bar City of N.Y., Lawyers; Com. for Civil Rights Under Law. Estate planning, Family and matrimonial. Office: Milbank Tweed Hadley & McCloy 1 Chase Manhattan Plz Fl 47 New York NY 10005-1413 E-mail: aforger@milbank.com.

FORLANO, FREDERICK PETER, lawyer; b. N.Y.C., July 12, 1947; s. Pasquale Genaro and Theresa Susan (Hartmann) F.; children: Christopher S., Jason D., Jennifer R.; m. Sharon S. Guinnup, 1995. AS, Suffolk Community Coll., 1968; BA in Math., Adelphi U., 1969; JD, U. Houston, 1975. Bar: Tex. 1975, U.S. Dist. Ct. (so. dist.) Tex. 1976, U.S. Ct. Appeals (5th cir.) 1976, U.S. Ct. Appeals (11th cir.) 1981, U.S. Tax Ct. 1977. Commd. 2nd lt. USAF, 1970, advanced through grades to maj., 1984; ptnr. Finger, Small, Cohen & Forlano, Houston, 1975-88; pvt. practice law Houston, 1988—. Advisor, legal v.p. Meadows Civic Assn., Stafford, Tex., 1977, pres., 1978-79; advisor Parents Without Ptnrs., Houston, 1987—; trustee The Wilhelm Schole, 1977—. With USAFR (ret.), 1970-92. Mem. Tex. Bar Assn., Houston Bar Assn., Ft. Bend Bar Assn., Res. Officers Assn. Republican. Roman Catholic. Avocations: golf, horses. General civil litigation, Juvenile, Probate (including wills, trusts). Office: 3050 Post Oak Blvd Ste 1425 Houston TX 77056-6532 E-mail: fpforlano@aol.com.

FORMAN, JAMES DOUGLAS, lawyer; b. Mineola, N.Y., Nov. 12, 1932; s. Leo and Kathryn F.; m. Marcia Fore; children: Karli, Elizabeth. AB, Princeton U., 1954; LLB, Columbia U., 1957. Bar: N.Y. 1958. Pvt. practice, Mineola, 1957—. Author: Cry Havoc, 1988, The Big Bang, 1989, The Scottish Dirk: Reality and Romance, 1991, Prince Charlie's Year, 1991, Becca's Story, 1992, The Blunderbuss 1500-1900, 1994, about 40 others. Bd. mem. Landmarks com., Sands Point, N.Y., 1987—. Mem. Ky. Rifle Assn., Co. Mil. Historians. Avocations: portrait painting, woodworking. Landlord-tenant, Property, real (including real estate development, water). Home: 2 Glen Rd Port Washington NY 11050-1207 Office: 800 Port Washington Blvd Port Washington NY 11050 E-mail: jamesdforman@aol.com.

FORMELLER, DANIEL RICHARD, lawyer; b. Chgo., Aug. 15, 1949; s. Vernon Richard and Shirley Mae (Gruber) F.; m. Ann M. Paa, Aug. 17, 1974; children: Matthew Daniel, Kathryn Ann, Christina Marie. BA with honors, U. Ill., 1970; JD cum laude, DePaul U., 1976. Bar: (Ill.) 1976, (U.S. Dist. Ct. (no. and ctrl. dist.) Ill.) 1976, (U.S. Ct. Appeals (7th and 9th cirs.)) 1976, (U.S. Ct. Appeals (D.C. cir.)) 1995. Assoc. McKenna, Storer, Rowe, White & Farrug, Chgo., 1976-82, ptnr., 1982-86, Tressler, Soderstrom, Maloney & Priess, Chgo., 1986—. Editor: DePaul U. Law Rev., 1975—76. With USN, 1970—72, Vietnam. Mem. ABA, Ill. Bar Assn., Ill. Assn. Def. Trial Counsel (pres. 1994-95), Chgo. Bar Assn., Assn. Def. Trial Attys. (v.p. 2003). Federal civil litigation, General civil litigation, Product liability. Office: Tressler Soderstrom et al 233 S Wacker Dr Chicago IL 60606-6306 E-mail: dformeller@mail.tsmp.com.

FORNEA, ILENIA, lawyer, consultant; b. Jesolo, VE, Italy, Aug. 16, 1972; d. Albano Fornea and Nelina Zoccarato. Joint degree laurea, Univ. Bologna, Italy, 1996, MA in adminstrn. law, 2000; cert. attendance, Hague Acad. Internat. Law, Hague, Netherlands, 2001. Bar: Italy 2000. Legal trainee, legal asst. G. Bodo Law Office, Bologna, Italy, 1996—99; lawyer S.O.S. Il telefono Azzurro, Bologna, Italy, 2000—02, Morresi Law Office, Bologna, Italy, 2002—. Cons. Municipality Bologna, Bologna, Italy, 1999—2000, Finanza Imprese Progetti SAS, Bologna, Italy, 2001; rschr. joint project Unido CNA, Bologna, Padova, Italy, 2002. Author: Guida Agli Investimenti Egitto, Giordania, Marocco, Tunisia, 2002. Scholarship, Univ. Bologna, Italy, 1992, 1993, Erasmus Programme grantee, European Community, 1993. Avocations: travel, reading, jogging. Office: Morresi Law Office Dante 19 40125 Bologna Italy

FORNERIS, JEANNE M. lawyer; b. Duluth, Minn., May 23, 1953; d. John Domenic and Elva Lorraine (McDonald) F.; m. Michael Scott Margulies, Feb. 6, 1982. AB, Macalester Coll., 1975; JD, U. Minn., 1978. Bar: Minn. 1978. Assoc. Halverson, Watters, Bye, Downs & Maki, Ltd., Duluth, 1978-81, Briggs & Morgan, P.A., Mpls., St. Paul, 1981-83; ptnr. Hart & Bruner, P.A., Mpls., 1983-86; assoc. gen. counsel M.A. Mortenson Co., Mpls., 1986-90, v.p., gen. counsel, 1990-96; with Gen. Counsel, Ltd., Mpls., 1997-98; v.p., sr. counsel Medtronic, Inc., Mpls., 1999—. Instr. women's studies dept. U. Minn., Mpls., 1977-79. Author profl. edn. seminars; contbr. articles to profl. jours. Bd. dirs. Good Will Indusries Vocat. Enterprises, Inc., 1979-81; chmn. bd. trustees Duluth Bar Libr., 1981; mem. United Way Family and Individual Svcs. Task Force, Duluth, 1981. Nat. Merit Assn. scholar, 1971. Fellow Am. Coll. Constrn. Lawyers (bd. dirs.); mem. AMA, Am. Arbitration Assn. (mem. large complex case panel), Minn. State Bar Assn., Minn. Women Lawyers (bd. dirs.), U.S. Dist. Ct. Hist. Soc. (pres.). Democrat. Roman Catholic. Construction, Corporate, general, Government contracts and claims. Office: Medtronic Inc 7000 Central Ave NE Minneapolis MN 55432-3576

FORREST, HERBERT EMERSON, lawyer; b. N.Y.C., Sept. 20, 1923; s. Jacob K. and Rose (Fried) F.; m. Marilyn Lefsky, Jan. 12, 1952; children: Glenn Clifford, Andrew Matthew. Student, CCNY, 1941, Ohio U., 1943-44; BA with distinction, George Washington U., 1948, JD with highest honors, 1952. Bar: Va. 1952, D.C. 1952, U.S. Supreme Ct. 1956, Md. 1959, U.S. Ct. Appeals (D.C. cir.) 1953, U.S. Ct. Appeals (1st cir.) 1992, U.S. Ct. Appeals (2d cir.) 1971, U.S. Ct. Appeals (3d cir.) 1957, U.S. Ct. Appeals (4th cir.) 1956, U.S. Ct. Appels (5th cir.) 1981, U.S. Ct. Appeals (7th cir.) 1996, U.S. Ct. Appeals (8th cir.) 1991, U.S. Ct. Appeals (9th cir.) 1994, U.S. Ct. Appeals (11th cir.) 1981. Plate printer Bur. Engraving and Printing, Washington, 1942-43, 1946-52; law clk. to chief judge Bolitha J. Laws U.S. Dist. Ct., Washington, 1952-55; pvt. practice Washington, 1952-87; with Welch & Morgan, 1955-65, Steptoe & Johnson, 1965-85, of counsel, 1986-87; trial atty. fed. programs br. civil divsn. U.S. Dept. Justice, Washington, 1987—; chmn. adv. bd. D.C. Criminal Justice Act, 1971-74; sec. com. admissions and grievances U.S. Ct. Appeals, D.C., 1973-79; title-1 audit hearing bd. U.S. Office Edn. HEW, 1976-79; edn. appeals bd. U.S. Dept. Edn., 1979-82. Mem. Lawyer's Support Com. for Visitors Service Center, 1975-87 Contbr. articles to profl. jours.; mem. editl. bd. Duke Law Jour, 1969-75. Pres. Whittier Woods PTA, 1970-71. With F.A., Signal Corps U.S. Army, 1943-46. Recipient Walsh award in Irish history, 1952, Goddard award in commerce, 1952. Fellow Am. Bar Found. (life), ABA (council 1972-75, 1981-84, budget officer 1985-88, vice chmn. task force on sect. devel. 1987-89, chmn. com. on agy. rule making 1968-72, 1976-81, chmn. membership com. 1984-85, editor ann. reports 1973-88, adminstrv. law sect., fellow adminstrv. law and regulatory practice, mem. comm. com. public utilities law sect., vice chmn. industry regulation com. 1985-86, chmn. comm. subcom. 1983-85, antitrust law sect., internat. law sect., sect. judicial adminstrn., sect. sci. and tech., comm. forum); mem. George Washington Law Assn., Am. Judicature Soc., Va. State Bar Assn., Fed. Bar Assn. (chmn. jud. rev. com. 1981-85, vice chmn. adminstrv. law sect. 1985-87), Fed. Comm. Bar Assn. (del. to ABA Ho. Dels. 1979-81, exec. com. 1967-71, 76-84, v.p. 1981-82, pres. 1982-83, chmn. telecomm. com. 1983-87), D.C. Bar Assn. (past sec., exec. com.), NAM, Nat. Conf. Bar Pres., Washington Council Lawyers, Legal Aid and Pub. Defender Assn., Am. Arbitration Assn. (comml. panel 1976-87), D.C. Unified Bar (bd. govs. 1976-79, chmn. com. on employment discrimination complaint service 1973-79, chmn. task force on services to public 1974-78, chmn. com. on appointment counsel in criminal cases 1978-88, co-chmn. com. on participation govt. employees in pro bono activities 1977-79), Broadcast Pioneers, Order of Coif, B'nai Brith, Phi Beta Kappa, Pi Gamma Mu., Artus, Phi Eta Sigma, Phi Delta Phi. Democrat. Home: 8706 Bellwood Rd Bethesda MD 20817-3033 Office: US Dept Justice 22 Massachusetts Ave NW Rm 7112 Washington DC 20530 E-mail: herbert.forrest@usdoj.gov.

FORREST, ROBERT EDWIN, lawyer; b. Washington, July 31, 1949; s. Henry Smith and Jane (Witt) F.; m. Deirdre Loretto McGahey, Sept. 23, 1978; children: Matthew Henry, John Robert, Caitlin. BA, Northwestern U., 1971; JD, Georgetown U., 1974. Bar: D.C. 1975, Md. 1984, U.S. Ct. Appeals (D.C. cir.) 1976, U.S. Ct. Appeals (6th cir.) 1985, U.S. Ct. Appeals (11th cir.) 1991, U.S. Dist. Ct. D.C. 1976, U.S. Supreme Ct. 1980, U.S. Dist. Ct. (ea. and we. dists.) Mich. 1981. Law clk. to Hon. June L. Green U.S. Dist. Ct. D.C, Washington, 1974-75; tax div. trial atty. U.S. Dept. Justice, Washington, 1975-81; prin. ptnr. Raymond & Prokop, P.C., Southfield, 1981—. Adj. prof. U. Detroit/Mercy Sch. of Law, 1987—. Trustee Acad. of the Sacred Heart, 2002—. Fellow: Michigan Bar Furdhom; mem.: FBA (exec. bd. 1984—90, pres. 1989—90), Fed. Bar Found. (trustee 1995—), Oakland County Bar Assn. (tax com. 2001—02). Methodist. Federal civil litigation, Criminal, Taxation, general. Home: 4861 Malibu Dr Bloomfield Hills MI 48302-2252 Office: Raymond & Prokop PO Box 5058 Southfield MI 48086-5058 Fax: 248-357-2720. E-mail: rforrest@raypro.com.

FORRESTER, J. OWEN, federal judge; b. 1939; BS, Ga. Inst. Tech., 1961; LL.B., Emory U., 1966. Bar: Ga. 1966. Assoc. Fisher & Phillips, Atlanta, 1967-69; asst. U.S. Atty., Atlanta, 1969-76; magistrate U.S. Dist. Ct. (no. dist.) Ga., Atlanta, 1976-81, judge, 1981—. Office: US Dist Ct 1921 US Courthouse 75 Spring St SW Atlanta GA 30303-3309

FORRESTER, KEVIN KREG, lawyer; b. Beaver Dam, Wis., June 14, 1957; s. Roger Eugene and Gretchen Adeline (Yungclas) F.; m. Cheryl Kim Bahde, June 6, 1981; children: Courtney Kristine, Christopher Cody. BA, U. Calif., San Diego, 1980; JD, U. San Diego, 1986. Bar: U.S. Supreme Ct. Sales assoc. Century 21, Solana Beach, Calif., 1980-81; broker, assoc. Rand & Stewart Realtors, Rancho Santa Fe, Calif., 1981-83; law clk. Shernoff & Levine, San Diego, 1983-85; asst. to gen. counsel Pacific Scene, Inc., San Diego, 1985-87; atty. pvt. practice, Encinitas, Calif., 1987—. Ct. appointed mediator, bd. of arbitrators NASD Regulation, Inc.; San Diego County Superior Ct. pro tem judge. Pres. Colony of Olivenhain (Calif.) Town Coun., 1990, 91 Mem. Internat. Acad. Mediators, State Bar Calif., Calif. Assn. Realtors, San Diego County Bar Assn., North San Diego County Assn. Realtors, U. Calif. San Diego Alumni Assn. (gen. counsel 1992—, dir. 1985-92), William B. Enright Am. Inn of Ct. Republican. Avocation: running. Alternative dispute resolution, Property, real (including real estate development, water), Sports. Office: 4403 Manchester Ave Ste 205 Encinitas CA 92024-7903 E-mail: kforrester@psmkr.com.

FORROW, BRIAN DEREK, lawyer, corporation executive; b. N.Y.C., Feb. 6, 1927; s. Frederick George and Doris (Williams) F.; m. Eleanor Reid, Mar. 8, 1952; children: Lisa Coggins, Brian Lachlan, Catherine Frances, Derek Skylstead. AB, Princeton U., 1947; JD, Harvard U., 1950. Bar: N.Y. 1950, Conn. 1967, U.S. Supreme Ct. 1954. From assoc. to ptnr. Cahill, Gordon, Sonnett, Reindel & Ohl (and predecessors), 1950-68; v.p., gen. counsel Allied Chem. Corp., 1968-85, dir., 1969-85; sr. v.p., gen. counsel Allied-Signal Inc., 1985-92; pvt. practice, Greenwich, Conn., 1992—; of counsel Whitman Breed Abbott & Morgan, 1992-94. Bd. dirs. Union Tex. Petroleum, 1985-92. Contbr. articles to profl. publs. Mem. Greenwich Representative Town Meeting, 1993—; vestryman, former sr. warden, former diocesan rep., Episcopal Ch. Served to 1st lt. USAF, 1951-53. Mem. ABA, Am. Law Inst., Conn. Bar Assn., N.Y. State Bar Assn., Assn. Bar City of N.Y. (past chmn. com. corp. law depts.), Assn. Gen. Counsel, Am. Arbitration Assn. (bd. dirs. 1987-97), Corp. Bar Assn. Westchester-Fairfield (past pres., bd. dirs. 1986-91), Am. Corp. Counsel Assn. (bd. dirs. 1987-89), Assn. Corp. Counsel N.J. (past pres.), Indian Harbor Yacht Club (past bd. dirs.), Harvard Club N.Y., Ret. Men's Assn. Greenwich Conn. (officer, dir. 2003—). Republican. Corporate, general, General civil litigation. Home and Office: 704 Lake Ave Greenwich CT 06830-3361

FORRY, JOHN INGRAM, lawyer; b. Washington, Feb. 9, 1945; s. John Emerson and Marion Carlotta (MacArthur) F.; m. Carol Ann Micken, Jan. 12, 1980; children: Alicia Ann, Camilla Lorraine. BA, Amherst Coll., 1966; JD, Harvard U., 1969. Bar: Calif. 1970, D.C. 1998, N.Y. 1998, U.S. Tax Ct. 1977, U.S. Supreme Ct. 1975. Founding ptnr. Forry Golbert Singer & Gelles, L.A., 1973-80; sr. ptnr. Morgan, Lewis & Bockius, L.A., 1980-97, McDermott, Will & Emery, N.Y.C., 1997-98, Ernst & Young LLP, N.Y.C., 1999—. Co-author, editor: A Practical Guide to Foreign Investment in the United States, 1979, 3d edit., 1989, Joint Ventures in the United States, 1988, Differences in Tax Treatment of Foreign Investors, 1984, others; contbr. more than 40 articles to profl. jours. Co-founder Forry Fund in Philosophy and Sci., Amherst (Mass.) Coll., 1984—; mem. adv. group to U.S. Commr. of Internal Revenue, Washington, 1985-86. Mem. Internat. Bar Assn., Internat. Fiscal Assn., other bar assns. Republican. Roman Catholic. Avocations: philosophical implications of scientific developments, automobile racing, mountain climbing, scuba diving. Finance, Private international, Corporate taxation. Office: 444 E 82nd St Apt 27C New York NY 10028 Fax: 212-717-9545. E-mail: forryjo@aol.com.

FORSMAN, ALPHEUS EDWIN, lawyer; b. Montgomery, Ala., May 12, 1941; m. Greta Friedman, July 5, 1964; children: Ellen E., Jennifer Ann. BA with distinction, George Washington U., 1963, JD, 1967. Bar: Va. 1968, D.C. 1969, U.S. Supreme Ct. 1973, Mo. 1979; cert. trademark agt. Can. Trademark examiner U.S. Patent Office, Washington, 1967-69; atty. Marriott Corp., Washington, 1969-72; assoc. Roylance, Abrams, Berdo and Kaul, Washington, 1972-75, ptnr., 1975-78; trademark atty. Ralston Purina Co., St. Louis, 1978-81, trademark counsel, 1981-91, v.p., sr. trademark counsel, 1991-96; asst. v.p. Eveready Battery Co., Inc., St. Louis, 1986-98; asst. sec. Ralston Purina Co., St. Louis, 1999—2001, v.p., sr. counsel, 1996—2002; v.p. Eveready Battery Co., 1998-2000; v.p., sr. counsel Nestle Purina PetCare Co., 2001—02. Asst. sec. Continental Baking Co., 1990-95; adj. prof. law Washington U., 2000. Mem.: Bar Assn. Met. St. Louis. Republican. Episcopalian. Trademark and copyright. Home: 417 Glan Tai Dr Manchester MO 63011-4067

FORSSANDER, CHARLOTTE E. lawyer; b. Jönköping, Sweden, Nov. 17, 1969; Jur. kand., Lund (Sweden) U., 1993; M in Comparative Jurisprudence, NYU, 1998. Bar: N.Y. 1999. Law clk. Skovde (Sweden) Dist. Ct., 1993—95; counsel Stockholm Municipality, 1995—97; assoc. O'Melvery & Myers LLP, N.Y.C., 1998—2000, Vinge Law Firm, Stockholm, 2000—. Office: Vinge Law Firm Smalandsgatan 20 111 87 Stockholm Sweden

FORSTADT, JOSEPH LAWRENCE, lawyer; b. Bklyn., Feb. 21, 1940; BA, CCNY, 1961; LLB, NYU, 1964. Bar: N.Y. 1965, U.S. Supreme Ct. 1968. Spl. legal counsel to bd. justices Supreme Ct. N.Y. County, 1965-67; dep. commr. N.Y.C. Dept. Licenses, 1967-68, acting commr., 1968-69, N.Y.C. Dept. Consumer Affairs, 1969; asst. adminstr. Econ. Devel. Adminstrn., 1969; assoc. Stroock & Stroock & Lavan, N.Y.C., 1969-75, ptnr., 1976—. Lectr. trial practice N.Y. County Lawyers Assn., Practising Law Inst., 1993-94, Title Ins. Litig.; mem. N.Y.C. Rent Guidelines Bd., 1984-97; arbitrator U.S. Dist. Ct. (ea. dist.) N.Y.; spl. counsel Appellate Div. First Dept., Disciplinary Com.; mem. Housing Ct. Adv. Bd., 2001-02. Contbr. articles to profl. jours. Dist. campaign mgr. John V. Lindsay for Mayor of N.Y.C., 1965; campaign mgr. Congressman Theodore Kupferman, 1966; chmn. N.Y.C. Young People for Nixon, 1968, pres. N.Y. State Assn. Young Rep. Clubs, 1970-72; pres. N.Y. Young Rep. Club, 1969-71; vice-chmn. N.Y. Com. to Re-elect Pres. Nixon, 1972. Judge Jacob Markowitz scholar NYU Law Sch., N.Y.C., 1964; recipient Brotherhood award NCCJ, 1987. Mem. Fed. Bar Coun., Am. Judicature Soc., Phi Alpha Delta. Federal civil litigation, State civil litigation. Office: Stroock Stroock & Lavan 180 Maiden Ln Suite 32108 New York NY 10038-4937 E-mail: jforstadt@stroock.com.

FORSTER, JONATHAN SHAWN, lawyer; b. L.A., Nov. 28, 1970; s. Eric Gad Forster and Sally Forster Jones. BA, UCLA, 1992; JD, Loyola U., L.A., 1995. Bar: Calif. 1995, U.S. Dist. Ct. (ctrl. and so. dists.) Calif. 1995. Atty. Roquemore, Pringle & Moore, L.A., 1995-98, Jones, Kaufman & Ackerman LLP, L.A., 1998-2000, Xdrive Techs., Inc., L.A., 2000—02, Weinstock, Marion, Reisman, Shore & Neumann, LA, 2002—. Mem. ABA, L.A. County Bar Assn. Avocations: ice hockey, skiing. Commercial, contracts (including sales of goods; commercial financing), Corporate, general, Estate planning. Office: Weinstock Marion Resiman Shore & Neumann Ste 1500 1875 Century Pk E Los Angeles CA 90067 E-mail: jforster@weinstocklaw.com.

FORSTMOSER, PETER BRUNO, lawyer, educator; b. Zurich, Switzerland, Jan. 22, 1943; s. Alois and Ida (Locher) F.; divorced; children: Marco, Stefan. Lic. Juris, Zurich Law Sch., 1967, JD, 1970; LLM, Harvard U., 1972. Asst. prof. Zurich Law Sch., 1971-74, prof., 1974— ; assoc., Zurich, 1970-74; chief editor Swiss Lawyers Rev., 1973-2000; ptnr. Niederer Kraft & Frey, Zurich, 1974—; dir. Mikron Holding AG, Biel, Switzerland, 1976, Swiss Reins. Co., Zurich, 1990, chmn., 2000, Hesta AG, Zug, Switzerland, 1993; chmn. Commn. Inquiry on Misuse Inside Info., 1982-89, chmn. and mem. various legis. commns., 1976—; hon. prof. Beijing Normal U. Author: Schweiz. Genossenschaftsrecht, 1972-74, Schweiz. Aktienrecht, Aktienrechtliche Verantvortlikeit, 2d edit., 1987, Swiss Corporation Law, 1996, Swiss Company Law, 9th edit., 2003; contbr. articles to profl. jours. Pres. Liberales I nst., Zurich, 1979-2000. Maj. inf. Swiss Army, 1981-98. Mem. Zivilrechtslehrervereinigung, Schweiz. Anwaltsverband. Office: Niederer Kraft & Frey Bahnhofstrasse 13 8001 Zürich Switzerland

FORSYTHE, RANDALL NEWMAN, paralegal, educator; b. Hammond, Ind., Mar. 24, 1959; s. Perry Newman and Elwanda (Cox) F.; children: Kenneth Newman, Keith Randall. AA in Law Enforcement, Calumet Coll., Whiting, Ind., 1979, BA in Criminal Justice magna cum laude, BS in Mgmt. magna cum laude, Calumet Coll., Whiting, Ind., 1982; Lawyer's Asst. Cert., Roosevelt U., Chgo., 1986. Labor leader/painter Inland Steel Co., East Chicago, Ind., 1978-86; ins. and securities rep. Primerica, Portage, Ind., 1984-91; paralegal Katz, Brenman & Angel, Merrillville, Ind., 1987-91, Richard P. Komyatte & Assocs., P.C., Highland, Ind., 1991—; coord. paralegal divsn. Sawyer Coll., Merrillville, 1989-92, paralegal instr., 1989—95. Ct. apptd. spl. advocate Juvenile divsn. Lake County Superior Ct., Gary, Ind., 1987—97. Manuscript/book reviewer West Pub. Co., St. Paul, 1991—. Parliamentarian Orchard Dr. Bapt. Ch., Hammond, Ind., 1981-91. Mem. Assn. Trial Lawyers Am., Nat. Assn. Legal Assts., Ind. Legal Assts. (Ind. Legal Asst. of Yr. 1990, liaison to nat. orgn. 1989-92, 97). Avocations: coaching children's little league baseball, basketball, football teams, adult softball, hunting, fishing, camping. Office: Richard P Komyatte & Assocs PC 9650 Gordon Dr Highland IN 46322-2909

FORT, JAMES TOMLINSON, lawyer; b. Albany, N.Y., Apr. 12, 1928; s. Tomlinson and Beatrice (Lawson) F.; m. Judith Anne Davis, May 9, 1959; children: Edward Tomlinson, Madeline Annabelle. AB, Allegheny Coll.; LL.B., Yale U. Bar: Supreme Ct. Assoc. Reed Smith Shaw & McClay, Pitts., 1954-62, ptnr., 1962—. Trustee Allegheny Coll., Meadville, Pa., 1975—; dir. Pitts. Dance Council, 1977-83, Pitts. Ballet Theatre Inc. With USMC, 1953-54. Mem. Bar Supreme Ct. U.S., Am. Coll. Trial Lawyers. Clubs: Duquesne (Pitts.), Rivers. Democrat. Presbyterian. Federal civil litigation, General civil litigation, Education and schools. Home: 204 Woodcock Dr Pittsburgh PA 15215-1546 Office: Reed Smith LLP 435 6th Ave Pittsburgh PA 15219-1886

FORTENBAUGH, SAMUEL BYROD, III, lawyer; b. Phila., Nov. 6, 1933; s. Samuel Byrod Jr. and Katherine Francisca (Wall) F.; children: Samuel Byrod IV, Cristina Fortenbaugh Alemany, Katherine Fortenbaugh-Silliman, Francesca Cowden; m. Sharon A. Swartz, Nov. 17, 2001. BA, Williams Coll., 1955; LLB, Harvard U., 1960. Bar: N.Y. 1961, U.S. Dist. Ct. (so. dist.) N.Y. 1961. Assoc. Kelley Drye & Warren, N.Y.C., 1960—69, ptnr., 1970—79, Morgan, Lewis & Bockius, 1980—2001, sr. counsel, 2001—02; atty. pvt. practice, 2002—. Bd. dirs. Baldwin Tech. Co., Inc., Shelton, Conn., Security Capital Corp., Greenwich, Conn.; bd. dirs., sec. Furgueson Capital Mgmt. Inc., N.Y.C.; chmn. bd. dirs., sec. Wall Industries, Inc., Kannapolis, N.C.; chmn. bd. dirs. Knight Textile Corp, Saluda, S.C.; trustee Patroni Scholastici, New Brunswick, N.J., 1978—, sec. 1985—; lectr. profl. seminars. Contbr. articles to profl. jours. Mem. ABA, Assn. of Bar of City of N.Y. (mem. Young Lawyers com. 1962-65, corp. law com. 1976-79, com. on securities regulation 1982-85, chmn. com. on issue distbn. of securities 1984-85), Univ. Club (N.Y.C.), N.Y. Yacht Club, Indian Harbor Yacht Club (Greenwich, Conn.) (bd. dirs.), Phi Beta Kappa. Corporate, general, Mergers and acquisitions, Securities. Office: 1211 Ave of Ams 27th fl New York NY 10036

FORTUNE, LOWELL, lawyer; b. Colorado Springs, Colo., Dec. 12, 1941; s. Benjamin Acres and Wilma E. (Henry) F.; m. Beverly Jane Sanborn, June 30, 1963; children: Sabrina Fortune Allen, Christina Fortune Howery. BA, U. Denver, 1963, JD, 1966. Bar: U.S. Dist. Ct. Colo. 1966, U.S. Ct. Appeals (10th cir.) 1966, U.S. Supreme Ct. 1976. Assoc. White & Steele, Denver, 1966—71, ptnr., 1971—75; pres. Lowell Fortune, P.C., 1975—79, Fortune & Lawritson, P.C., 1979—95; with Fortune Law Firm, P.C., 1995—99, 2002—; spl. counsel Montgomery, Kolodny, Amatuzio, Dusbabek and Parker, L.L.P., 1999—2001. Author: The Year 2000 Problem and the Economic Loss Rule, 1999. Mem. Am. Bd. Trial Advocates. Product liability. Home: 5237 Bear Mountain Dr Evergreen CO 80439-5605 Office: 600 17th St Ste 2800 South Denver CO 80202-5402 E-mail: lowfort@mac.com.

FORTUNO, VICTOR M. lawyer; b. N.Y.C., Jan. 24, 1952; s. Victor M. Fortuno and Ceda Aguayo; m. Vicki Ann Clark; children: Adam R., Victor III, Scott, Erica, Bryce. AB in Econs., Columbia U., 1974, JD, 1977. Bar: Pa. 1977, U.S. Dist. Ct. (ea. dist.) Pa. 1977, U.S. Ct. Appeals (3d cir.) 1977, U.S. Supreme Ct. 1980, U.S. Ct. Appeals (D.C. cir.) 1987, D.C. 1988, U.S. Dist. Ct. D.C. 1988, U.S. Ct. Appeals (4th cir.) 1988, U.S. Dist. Ct. Ariz. 1991. Staff atty. Cmty. Legal Svcs., Inc., Phila., 1977-78; asst. dist. atty. Office Dist. Atty., Phila., 1978-83; staff atty. Legal Svcs. Corp., Washington, 1983-85, acting dir. compliance divsn., 1985-86, asst. gen. counsel, 1986, sr. litigation counsel, 1986-88, acting gen. counsel, 1987, 91, dep. gen. counsel, 1988-91, gen. counsel, 1991—, corp. sec., 1995—, v.p. legal affairs, 1999—. Adj. faculty Grantham Coll. Engring., 2001-02. Bd. dirs. Middleford HOA, 2002-, Friends of Legal Svcs. Corp., 2001—, Columbia Coll. Alumni Assn., 1981-83, Phila. Health Plan, 1980-83. Pulitzer Found. scholar, 1970-74, Assn. of Bar of City of N.Y. C. Bainbridge Smith scholar, 1974-77. Mem. ABA, D.C. Bar Assn., Fed. Small Agy. Coun. Home: 7479 Thorncliff Ln Springfield VA 22153-2153 Office: Legal Svcs Corp 3333 K St NW Washington DC 20007 Fax: 202-295-1620. E-mail: vfortuno@lsc.gov.

FOSCHIO, LESLIE GEORGE, judge; b. Oct. 29, 1940; s. Frank George and Sonia (Kaczynski) Foschio; m. Virginia Rose Kostur, June 27, 1964; children: John, Michael, Amy, Robert, Christa. BA cum laude, U. Buffalo, 1962; LLB cum laude, SUNY, Buffalo, 1965. Bar: N.Y. 1966, U.S. Ct. Appeals (7th cir.) 1973, U.S. Dist. Ct. (we. dist.) N.Y. 1975, U.S. Supreme Ct. 1975, U.S. Ct. Appeals (2d cir.) 1977, U.S. Ct. Appeals (DC cir.) 1977, U.S. Tax Ct. 1980. Law clk. to Hon. William B. Lawless, Jr. N.Y. State Supreme Ct., 1965; atty. Counsel's Office, SUNY, 1965-66; asst. dist. atty. Erie County, Buffalo, 1966-69; assoc. prof., asst. dean U. Notre Dame Law Sch., Ind., 1969-74; corp. counsel City of Buffalo, 1975-77; ptnr. Cohen Swados Wright Hanifin Bradford & Brett, Buffalo, 1978-80; commr. Dept. Motor Vehicles, State of N.Y., Albany, 1981-83; gen. counsel, sec., v.p. Barrister Info. Sys. Corp., Buffalo, 1983-91; U.S. magistrate judge U.S. Dist. Ct. (we. dist.) N.Y., 1991—. Lectr. law SUNY, Buffalo, 1966—68, Buffalo, 1978—80. Pres. Theodore Roosevelt Inaugural Nat. Hist. Site Found., Buffalo, 1978—87, trustee, 1978—; dist. chmn. Greater Niagara Frontier coun. Boy Scouts Am., Buffalo, 1980—82; dist. chmn. Eagle Scout; Dem. candidate Erie County N.Y. State Assembly, 1968; Dem. primary candidate for mayor Buffalo, 1977; trustee Theodore Roosevelt Assn., 1981—98. Recipient Character award, U. Buffalo, 1962, Disting.

Pub. Svc. award, N.Y. Jaycees, 1976, Outstanding Svc. Hwy Safety award, N.Y. State Assn. Traffic Safety, 1982, Alumnus of the Yr. award, H. C. Tech. HS, 1997, Outstanding Young Men of America, 1970, 1977; T. R. McConnell Leadership scholar, U. Buffalo, 1962. Fellow: Am. Bar Found. (life), N.Y. State Bar Found. (life; Action Unit 5 1980—83); mem.: Bar Assn. Erie County (dir. 1988—91), N.Y. State Bar Assn., Fed. Magistrate Judges Assn., U. Buffalo Alumni Assn. (dir. 1995—99, v.p. membership 1988—89, Disting. Alumnus award 1983), U. Buffalo Law Sch. Alumni Assn. (pres. 1980—81, Disting. Alumnus award for pub. svc. 1987), Phi Alpha Delta (hon.). Roman Catholic. Home: 46 Woodley Rd Buffalo NY 14215-1321 Office: 424 US Courthouse 68 Court St Buffalo NY 14202-3405 E-mail: lesliefoschio@nywd.uscourts.gov.

FOSTER, ARTHUR KEY, JR., retired lawyer; b. Birmingham, Ala., Nov. 22, 1933; s. Arthur Key and Vonceil (Oden) F.; m. Jean Lyles Foster, Jan. 7, 1967; children: Arthur Key III, Brooke Oden. BSE, Princeton U., 1955; JD, U. Va., 1960. Bar: Ala. 1960. Ptnr. Balch & Bingham, Birmingham, 1965-99. Trustee Episcopal Found. Jefferson County; bd. dirs. Met. YMCA, Downtown Club, Highlands Day Sch., Altamont Sch. Served to lt., USN, 1955-60. Mem. ABA, Ala. Bar Assn., Birmingham Bar Assn., Estate Planning Coun. of Birmingham, Nat. Assn. Bond Lawyers, Newcomen Soc. of U.S., Kiwanis (bd. dirs.). Republican. Episcopalian. Estate planning, Municipal (including bonds), Probate (including wills, trusts). Office: Balch & Bingham PO Box 306 Birmingham AL 35201-0306

FOSTER, C(HARLES) ALLEN, lawyer; b. Aug. 26, 1941; s. Charles Shearer and Bessie Lea (Long) F.; m. Susan Coomes; children: Charles Shearer Sanders II, Susan Elizabeth Coomes, Charles Henry Edward. BA summa cum laude, Princeton U., 1963; BA in Jurisprudence 1st class honors, Oxford (Eng.) U., 1965, MA in Jurisprudence, 1971; JD magna cum laude, Harvard U., 1967. Bar: N.C. 1967, D.C. 1994, U.S. Dist. Ct. (mid. dist.) N.C. 1968, U.S. Dist. Ct. (we. dist.) N.C. 1968, U.S. Dist. Ct. (ea. dist.) N.C. 1968, U.S. Tax Ct. 1970, U.S. Ct. Appeals (4th cir.), U.S. Ct. Appeals (5th cir.) 1970, U.S. Ct. Appeals (11th cir.) 1991, U.S. Ct. Appeals (10th cir.) 1993, U.S. Ct. Appeals (fed. cir.) 1995, U.S. Supreme Ct. 1971, U.S. Dist. Ct. D.C. 1985, U.S. Dist. Ct. (no. dist.) Tex. 1990, U.S. Dist. Ct. (so. dist.) Tex. 1991, U.S. Ct. Fed. Claims 1994. Assoc. McLendon, Brim, Brooks, Pierce & Daniels, Greensboro, N.C., 1967-72, ptnr., 1972-73; sec., dir., gen. counsel Spanco Industries, Inc., Greensboro and Sanford, N.C., 1973-75, Conestee, S.C., 1973-75; ptnr. Turner, Enochs, Foster, Sparrow & Burnley, Greensboro, 1975-81, Foster, Conner & Robson, 1983-88, Patton, Boggs LLP, 1988-99, Greenberg Traurig, Washington, 1999—. Sr. lectr. law Duke U., 1981-88; arbitrator Am. Arbitration Assn., mem. Nat. Acad. Arbitrators; pub. mem. N.C. Tax Rev. Bd., 1972-76; mem. N.C. Judicial Selection Study Comm., 1987-88; U.S. rep. Internat. Energy Agy. Dispute Resolution Ctr., Paris, 1984—; permanent panel arbitrator Martin Marietta and Atomic Trades and Labor Coun.; others. Author: Construction and Design Law, 1984—, Construction and Design Law Digest, 1981—, Law and Practice of Commercial Arbitration in North Carolina, 1984; contbr. articles to profl. jours. Co-founder, sec., bd. dirs. Greensboro Day Sch.; exec. com. Princeton U. Alumni Assn.; exec. com. Harvard Law Sch. Assn. N.C., 1970; Rep. candidate for atty.-gen. N.C., 1984; spl. counsel Rep. Nat. Com., 1989—; spl. litigation counsel N.C. Rep. Cen. Com., 1987—. Mem. ABA (litigation sect., labor and employment discrimination law sect., forum com. on constrn. industry), Am. Law Inst., Am. Arbitration Assn. (bd. dirs. 1980-83, nat. panels labor, constrn., internat. comml. arbitrators 1975—, chmn. N.C. regional adv. coun. 1979-83), Am. Coll. Constrn. Arbitrators (pres. 1983-84), Princeton U. Alumni Assn. (pres. alumni coun., exec. com. 1978-79, pres. mid. N.C. chpt. 1968-80), Phi Beta Kappa, Cap and Gown Club. Federal civil litigation, Labor (including EEOC, Fair Labor Standards Act, labor-management relations, NLRB, OSHA). Home: 3846 Cathedral Ave NW Washington DC 20016 E-mail: fostera@gtlaw.com.

FOSTER, CHARLES CRAWFORD, lawyer, educator; b. Galveston, Tex., Aug. 1, 1941; s. Louie Brown and Helen (Hall) F.; m. Marta Brito, Sept. 7, 1967 (div. Apr. 1986); children: John, Ruth; m. Lily Chen, Jan. 7, 1989; children: Zachary, Anthony. AA, Del Mar Jr. Coll., 1961; BA, U. Tex., 1963, JD, 1967. Bar: Tex. 1967, N.Y. 1969. Assoc. Reid & Priest, N.Y.C., 1967-69, Butler & Binion, Houston, 1969-73; ptnr. Tindall & Foster, Houston, 1973—. Hon. consul gen. Kingdom of Thailand, 1996—; adj. prof. immigration law U. Houston, 1985-89; bd. dirs. Greater Houston Partnership, 1997, chmn. econ. devel. adv. bd., 2000 World Trade Adv. Bd., 1997; chmn. Asia Soc.-Tex., bd. trustees, 1990—; bd. dirs. Houston World Affairs Coun., 1990; chmn. Inst. Internat. Edn., The Houston Club, 1999—, Houston Ballet Found., Assn. of Cmty. TV, Houston Holocaust Mus.; mem. Mayoral Adv. Bd. for Internat. Affairs and Devel./Asia, 1999—; pres. Houston Forum, 2002. Contbr. articles to profl. jours. Chmn. immigration reform Gov.'s Task Force of Tex., 1984—87; mem. Bush-Cheney Transition Adv. Com., 2000—01. Admiral Texan Navy, 2003. Decorated comdr. 3d class Order of the Crown (Thailand), comdr. Exalted Order of White Elephant (Thailand); Rotary Internat. fellow U. Concepción, Chile, 1964; recipient Houston Internat. Svc. award Houston Jaycees, 1996, Disting. Friend of China award U.S. China Friendship Found., 2000; honoree Am. Immigration Law Found., 1998' commd. adm. in Tex. Navy, Govt. of Tex., 2003. Mem. ABA (chmn. immigration com. internat. law and practice sect. 1982-90, chmn. coordinating com. on immigration and law 1987-89, fgn. rels. com. 2000—), Am. Immigration Lawyers Assn. (pres. 1981-82, Outstanding Svc. award 1985), Tex. Bar Assn. (chmn. com. law on immigration and nationality 1984-86), Tex. Bd. Legal Specialization (chmn. immigration adv. commn. 1979—), Houston Bar Assn., Asia Soc. (trustee 1992—, chmn. Houston Ctr. 1992—), Rotary, Houston Club (pres. 2001). Methodist. Avocations: mountain climbing, photography, travel. Immigration, naturalization, and customs. Home: 17 Courtlandt Pl Houston TX 77006-4013 Office: Tindall & Foster 2800 Chase Tower 600 Travis St Ste 2800 Houston TX 77002-3094

FOSTER, DAVID LEE, lawyer; b. Des Moines, Dec. 13, 1933; s. Carl Dewitt and Dorothy Jo (Bell) F.; m. Marilyn Lee Bokemeier, Aug. 12, 1957 (div. June 1978); children: Gwendolyn Foster Reed, Cynthia Foster Curry, David Lee Jr.; m. Kathleen Carol Walsh, Mar. 24, 1979; 1 child, John Wickersham. Student, Simpson Coll., 1951-52; BA, U. Iowa, 1954, JD, 1957. Bar: Iowa 1957, N.Y. 1958, Ohio 1964, U.S. Supreme Ct. 1975. Assoc. Cravath, Swaine & Moore, N.Y.C., 1957-63; from assoc. to ptnr. Jones, Day, Cockley & Reavis, Cleve., 1963-72; ptnr. Willkie Farr & Gallagher, N.Y.C., 1972—. Lectr. So. Meth. U., 1979-84, U. Pitts., 1984, Practicing Law Inst., N.Y.C., 1984-85; mem. adv. bd. Civil RICO Report LRP Publs., 1988—; bd. govs. N.Y. Ins. Exch., 1987-96. Contbr. chpts. to book, articles to legal jours. Mem., bd. trustees Cardigan Mountain Sch., 1995—, v.p., 2002—. Served with USNR, 1952-60. Fellow Am. Coll. Trial Lawyers, Internat. Acad. Trial Lawyers (bd. dirs. 1987-92); mem. Am. Counsel Assn. (pres. 1994-95, bd. dirs. 1992-98), River Club, Order of Coif, Phi Beta Kappa. Antitrust, Federal civil litigation, Insurance. Office: Willkie Farr & Gallagher 787 7th Ave New York NY 10019-6099 E-mail: dfoster@willkie.com.

FOSTER, DAVID SCOTT, lawyer; b. White Plains, N.Y., July 13, 1938; s. William James and Ruth Elizabeth (Seltzer) F.; m. Eleanore Stalker, Dec. 21, 1959; children: David Scott, Robert McEachron. BA, Amherst Coll., 1960; LLB, Harvard U., 1963. Bar: N.Y. 1963, D.C. 1977, Calif. 1978. Jud. law clk. U.S. Dist. Ct. (so. dist.) N.Y., 1963-64; assoc. Debevoise & Plimpton, N.Y.C., 1964-72; internat. tax counsel U.S. Treasury Dept., Washington, 1972-77; ptnr. Brobeck, Phleger & Harrison, San Francisco, 1978-90, Coudert Bros., San Francisco, 1990-91, Thelen, Reid & Priest LLP, San Francisco, 1991—. Mem. ABA, San Francisco Bar Assn., Internat. Fiscal Assn., Western Pension and Benefits Confs., St. Francis Yacht Club (San Francisco). Presbyterian. Pension, profit-sharing, and employee benefits, Taxation, general. Office: Thelen Reid & Priest LLP 101 2nd St Ste 1800 San Francisco CA 94105-3659

FOSTER, DENNIS JAMES, legal recruiting services executive; b. Cleve., Apr. 18, 1952; s. James Anthony and Anna Louise (Ritty) F.; m. Maureen Therese McGuire. BA magna cum laude, San Francisco State U., 1980. Paralegal Ruden, Barnett, McCloskey, Schuster & Schmerer, Ft. Lauderdale, Fla., 1973-75, Dorr, Cooper & Hays, San Francisco, 1976-78; paralegal adminstr. Sideman, Bancroft & Sutton, San Francisco, 1979-83; paralegal, video specialist Squire, Sanders & Dempsey, Cleve., 1983-84; mgr. litigation support svcs. Cefaratti, Renillo & Matthews, Cleve., 1984-88; specialist Legal Tech. Video, Cleve., 1984-88; pres. Major Legal Svcs. Ohio, 1988—. Cons., guest speaker, lectr. various law firms, Cleve., 1984—. Author: Legal Video Production Handbook, 1988. Mem. Nat. Assn. Legal Search Consultants, Cleve. Paralegal Assn. (trustee 1986-90, pres. 1989-90). Democrat. Roman Catholic. Office: 1111 Chester Ave Ste 510 Cleveland OH 44114-3516 E-mail: dennis@lawplacement.com.

FOSTER, JOHN ROBERT, lawyer; b. Long Beach, Calif., Feb. 13, 1940; s. Orlon c. and Catherine Rose Foster; m. Nancy Crandall, June 17, 1962; children: John Crandall, Christopher Peter, Blayney Robert, Courtland William. BA in History, San Jose State U., 1961; LLB, U. Calif., Berkeley, 1964. Bar: Calif. 1965, U.S. Dist. Ct. (no. dist.) Calif. 1965, U.S. Ct. Appeals (9th cir.) 1965; cert. specialist in probate, estate planning, and trust law. Dep. legis. counsel State of Calif., Sacramento, 1964-65; pres. Rusconi, Foster, Thomas & Wilson, APC, Morgan Hill, Calif., 1965—; asst. dist. atty. San Benito County, Hollister, Calif., 1967. Mem. Morgan Hill Unified Sch. Dist. Bd. Edn., 1967-74, 79-83, chmn. bd., 1969-71; councilman City of Morgan Hill, 1984-88, 97-98, mayor, 1984. Named Citizen of Yr., City of Morgan Hill. Mem. Calif. State Bar (past state bar exec. com. on estate planning, probate and trusts), Santa Clara County Bar Assn., Gilroy-Morgan Hill Bar Assn. (past pres.), Morgan Hill C. of C. (past pres.), Masons, Rotary (past pres. Morgan Hill). Republican. Methodist. Avocations: skiing, fly fishing, backpacking, camping. Corporate, general, Estate planning, Probate (including wills, trusts). Home: 17630 Black Oak Ct Morgan Hill CA 95037-9442 Office: Rusconi Foster Thomas & Wilson 30 Keystone Ave Morgan Hill CA 95037-4325 E-mail: bob@rftw.com.

FOSTER, JUDITH CHRISTINE, lawyer, writer; b. Columbus, Ohio, Nov. 25, 1952; d. Paul Marvel and Jean Harper (Uhland) F.; m. Sabah Amin Wali, Dec. 28, 1973; children: Samed Michel, Russeen Paul. BS in Natural Sci. and BA in Linguistics, Pa. State U., 1973; JD, Coll. William & Mary, 1979. Bar: Va. 1979, U.S. Ct. Appeals (4th cir.) 1979, U.S. Ct. Appeals (9th cir.) 1996, U.S. Supreme Ct. 1984. Pvt. practice, Fairfax, Va., 1980-90, Encino, Calif., 1991—. Mem. counsel U.S. Justice Found., Escondido, Calif., 1982-90; judge Internat. Moot Ct. Competition Assn. of Student Internat. Law Soc., 1984, 86. Author: (with Erich Pratt) Sanctuary: A People's Primer, 1986, monthly immigration newsletter, 1986-90. Del. Va. Reps., Fairfax, 1981, 85. Mem. Am. Immigration Lawyers Assn. (legis. com. 1985, D.C. chpt. 1980-90, L.A. chpt. 1992—). Immigration, naturalization, and customs, Private international. E-mail: jfoster_attorney_at_law@yahoo.com.

FOSTER, JULIE IRENE, lawyer; b. Billings, Mont., June 4, 1955; d. Robert Harrison and Sheila Irene (Dunstan) Asher; m. Craig Richard Foster, June 30, 1979; children: Cheryl Irene, Matthew Thomas, Mark Benjamin. BS magna cum laude, Cen. Conn. State U., 1977; JD, Western New Eng. Coll., 1981; MBA, U. Conn., 1988. Bar: Conn. 1982. Pvt. practice, Ridgefield, Conn., 1993—. Mem. Danbury Bar Assn., Danbury Med. Soc. Republican. Methodist. Criminal, Family and matrimonial, Probate (including wills, trusts). Home and Office: 805 N Salem Rd Ridgefield CT 06877-1714

FOSTER, M. SHANNON, lawyer, law enforcement educator; b. Ft. Smith, Ark., July 19, 1960; d. James Edward and Susan (Townley) F. BA, U. Calif., Irvine, 1992; JD, Loyola U., 1995. Bar: Ark. 1995, U.S. Dist. Ct. (we. dist.) Ark. 1998. Sales analyst, supr. Alcon Surg., Irvine, 1985-88; sr. fin. analyst Rockwell Internat., Newport Beach, Calif., 1988-92; dep. prosecuting atty. Office of Prosecutor, Little Rock, 1995-96; pvt. practice Ft. Smith, 1997—. Author: Domestic Violence Prosecution, 1996. Bd. dirs. Citizens Police Acad., Little Rock, 1996-97, Ft. Smith, 1998—; vol. Vol. Atty. Program, Ft. Smith, 1998-. Mem. AMA, Ark. Bar Assn., Sebastian County Bar Assn., Mensa, Golden Key Honor Soc. Democrat. Bankruptcy, Federal civil litigation, Family and matrimonial. Office: 703 Rogers Ave Fort Smith AR 72901-2409

FOSTER, MARK STEPHEN, lawyer; b. Edgerton, Mo., Feb. 6, 1948; s. George Elliott and Annabel Lee (Bradshaw) F.; m. Camille Pepper, June 27, 1970; children: Natalie Ashley, Stephanie Ann. BS, U. Mo., 1970; JD, Duke U., 1973. Bar: Mo. 1973, U.S. Ct. Mil. Appeals 1974, Hawaii 1975, U.S. Dist. Ct. Hawaii 1975, U.S. Dist. Ct. (we. dist.) Mo. 1977, U.S. Ct. Appeals (8th cir.) 1986, U.S. Supreme Ct. 1994. Assoc. Stinson, Mag & Fizzell, Kansas City, 1977-80, ptnr., 1980—2002, mng. ptnr., 1987-90, chmn. bd. dirs., 1998—2002; ptnr., co-mng. ptnr. Stinson Morrison Hecker, LLP, Kansas City, 2002—. Arbitration panelist Nat. Assn. Securities Dealers, N.Y.C., 1985—, Pvt. Adjudication Found., Durham, N.C., 1988—. Active Citizens Assn., Kansas City, 1982-92; pres. Spelman Med. Found., Smithville, Mo., 1984-88; bd. dirs. Alzheimers Assn. Metro. Kansas City, 1997—, 1st v.p., 1998, pres., 1999. Lt. comdr. USNR, ret. Mem. ABA, Hawaii Bar Assn., Mo. Bar Assn., Kansas City Met. Bar Assn., Am. Arbitration Assn. (panelist 1990—, large complex case adv. com. 1993—), Carriage Club (bd. dirs. 2000—, 2d v.p. 2001, 1st v.p. 2002, pres. 2003), Lawyers Edn. Assistance Program (bd. dirs. 2000—), Masons. Bankruptcy, General civil litigation, Labor (including EEOC, Fair Labor Standards Act, labor-management relations, NLRB, OSHA). Home: 1035 W 65th St Kansas City MO 64113-1813 Office: Stinson Morrison Hecker LLP PO Box 419251 1201 Walnut St Ste 2800 Kansas City MO 64106-2117

FOSTER, PHILIP CAREY, lawyer, state government official; b. Salisbury, Md., Jan. 5, 1947; s. Philip Kyle and Betty (Carey) F. BA, Coll. of Wooster, 1969; JD, Vanderbilt U., 1972. Bar: D.C. 1973, Md. 1973. Atty., advisor U.S. Dept. of Interior, Washington, 1972-73; assoc. Henry, Hairston & Price, Easton, Md., 1973-75; sole practice Easton, 1975—. Adj. instr. Chesapeake Coll., Wye Wills, Md., 1973-75; asst. state's atty. Talbot County, Easton, 1975-76; dep. state's atty. 1976-86, state's atty. Talbot County, 1986-89; mem. coordinating coun. State's Atty., 1989, Md. Ho. of Dels., 1989-91, mem. ways and means com., 1989-91. Chmn. Bd. of Zoning Appeals, Easton, 1978-81, Talbot County Dem. Cen. Com., Easton, 1974-78, 82-86; mem. State Bd. of Victim's Svcs., 1989; past pres., coach, referee Talbot County Youth Soccer League; mem. Talbot County Coun., 1998—. Mem. D.C. Bar Assn., Md. Bar Assn., Talbot County Bar Assn. (pres. 1987, chmn. pub. awareness com. 1978-89), Rotary, Elks. Democrat. Episcopalian. State civil litigation, Criminal, General practice. Office: 5 Fed St Ste 220 Easton MD 21601-2726

FOUDREE, BRUCE WILLIAM, lawyer; b. Des Moines, Mar. 27, 1947; s. Shie Wilbur and Dorothy Mable (Lynde) F.; m. Suzanne Joan Floss Reade, May 31, 1986; children: Andrew A., Grant R. BA, Drake U., 1969; student, U. Geneva, Switzerland, 1968, U. Vienna, Austria, 1968; JD, Drake U., 1972; LLM, U. Pa., 1975. Bar: Iowa 1972, U.S. Ct. Appeals (8th cir.) 1976, U.S. Supreme Ct. 1977, Ill. 1986. Asst. atty. gen. Iowa Dept. Justice, Des Moines, 1976-80; ins. commnr. Iowa Ins. Dept., Des Moines, 1980-86; of counsel Mitchell, Williams, Selig and Tucker, Little Rock, 1986-88; shareholder Keck, Mahin & Cate, Chgo., 1988-96; of counsel Lord, Bissell & Brook, Chgo., 1996—. Commr., chmn. Iowa Ins. Dept., 1980-86; commr. Iowa Health Data Commn., 1983-86, chmn. 1985. Assoc. editor Drake Law Rev., 1971-72; dir. Jour. Ins. Regulation, 1982-89. Mem. ABA (TIPS scope and correlation com. 1991-94, chmn. fin. svcs. com. 1990-91, professionalism com. 1994-96), Nat. Assn. Ins. Commrs. (chmn. 1984, pres. 1985), Ins. Regulatory Examiners Soc. Found. (bd. dirs. 1991—, chmn. 1999-2000), Iowa State Bar Assn., Union League Club of Chgo. (chmn. ins. group 1989-92), The Chicago Lighthouse (bd. dirs. 1995—, sec. 1998, chmn. 2002-). Avocations: travel, history, literature, music. Office: Lord Bissell & Brook 115 S La Salle St Fl 3600 Chicago IL 60603-3902 E-mail: bfoudree@lordbissell.com.

FOULKE, EDWIN GERHART, JR., lawyer; b. Perkasie, Pa., Oct. 30, 1952; s. Edwin G. and Mary Claire (Keller) F. BA, N.C. State U., 1974; JD, Loyola U., New Orleans, 1978; LLM, Georgetown U., 1993. Bar: S.C. 1979, U.S. Dist. Ct. S.C. 1979, U.S. Ct. Appeals (4th cir.) 1979, Ga. 1986, U.S. Ct. Appeals (11th cir.) 1986, D.C. 1989, U.S. Ct. Appeals (D.C. cir.) 1989, U.S. Supreme Ct. 1990, N.C. 1997. Assoc. Thompson, Mann & Hutson, Greenville, S.C., 1978-83, Rainey, Britton, Gibbes & Clarkson, Greenville, 1983-85; ptnr. Constangy, Brooks & Smith, Columbia, S.C., 1985-90; chmn. Occupational Safety and Health Rev. Commn., Washington, 1990-95; ptnr. Jackson Lewis, Greenville, S.C., 1995—. Instr. St. Mary's Dominican Coll., New Orleans, 1977-78. Field rep. Reagan/Bush Campaign, Columbia, 1980, S.C. state coord., 1984; sec., treas. Employment Labor Law Sect., Columbia, 1981-82. Mem. ABA, S.C. Bar Assn., Ga. Bar Assn., Greenville County Bar Assn. (chmn. pub. rels. com. 1984-85), SAR, Rotary. Roman Catholic. Avocations: swimming, tennis, skiing, golf. Office: Jackson Lewis & Krupman 301 N Main St Ste 2100 Greenville SC 29601-2122

FOUNTAIN, JOHN NICHOLAS, lawyer; b. High Point, N.C., Jan. 26, 1944; s. Robert Roy Fountain, Sr. and Hilda Burton Fountain; m. Doris Thomas Fountain (div. Feb. 1996); children: Laura Fountain Elms, Reed Nicholas; m. Julia Barkhurst Fountain, May 25, 1996. BA, Duke U., 1965; JD, Wake Forest U., 1968. Bar: N.C. 1968, 4th Cir. Ct. Appeals (ea. dist.) N.C., 4th Cir. Ct. Appeals (mid. dist.) N.C., U.S. Supreme Ct. Rsch. asst. N.C. Ct. Appeals, Raleigh, 1968—69; atty., ptnr. Bailey & Dixon, Raleigh, 1969—90; atty., shareholder, dir. Young, Moore & Henderson, Raleigh, 1990—. Elder, deacon, treas. White Meml. Presbyn. Ch., Raleigh; pres. Wake County and 10th Dist. Bar, Raleigh, 1988—89. Mem.: Wake County Bar Assn., N.C. Bar Assn. (chair, endowment, legis., adminstrn. law sect. 1979—, bd. govs. 1985—88), Raleigh Kiwanis (com. chair). Home: 2935 Rue Sans Famille Raleigh NC 27607-3046 Office: Young Moore & Henderson Box 31627 Raleigh NC 27622

FOWLER, DANIEL MCKAY, lawyer; b. Chgo., Mar. 25, 1950; m. Julia M. Duffy, Apr. 20, 1990; children: Douglas M., Peter M. BA, Monmouth Coll., 1972; JD, U. Denver, 1975. Bar: Colo. 1975, Wyo. 1994, U.S. Dist. Ct. Colo. 1975, U.S. Ct. Appeals (10th cir.) 1975. Shareholder Wood, Ris & Hames, P.C., Denver, 1975-87; pres. Fowler, Schimberg & Flanagan, P.C., Denver, 1987—. Mem. ABA, Colo. Bar Assn., Denver Bar Assn., Def. Rsch. Inst., Fedn. Ins. and Corp. Counsel, Colo. Def. Lawyers Assn., Denver Athletic Club, Lakewood Country Club. Avocations: motorcycle touring, skiing, boating, travel. General civil litigation, Insurance, Personal injury (including property damage). Office: Fowler Schimberg & Flanagan PC 1640 Grant St Ste 300 Denver CO 80203-1640 E-mail: d_fowler@fsf-law.com.

FOWLER, DAVID THOMAS, lawyer; b. Flushing, N.Y., June 16, 1955; s. David Thomas Jr. and Ellen (McGrath) F.; m. Margaret Anne Conway, Apr. 8, 1979; children: Matthew, Elizabeth, Timothy, Jacqueline. BA cum laude, St. John's U., 1977, JD, 1980. Bar: N.Y. 1981, U.S. Dist. Ct. (ea. and so. dists.) N.Y. 1981. Law clk. Richard J. Finamore, Great Neck, N.Y., 1979-80, assoc., 1981-83, Newman, Schlau, N.Y.C., 1983-86, ptnr., 1986-88; assoc. McCabe & Cozzens, Mineola, N.Y., 1988-92, ptnr., 1992-97, McCabe, Collins, McGeough & Fowler, LLP, Mineola, 1998—. Trustee Floral Park (N.Y.) Bellerose Sch. Dist., 1997—, v.p., 2000—; mem. bd. dirs. Brehon Law Soc. Nassau County, 2002-; co-v.p. L.I. chpt. Adoptive Parents Com., Bellmore, N.Y., 1996-98; treas., bd. dirs. Floral Park Little League, 1993-99, treas., 1994-97; mgr. baseball 1991-94, 2000—, softball, 1999-2000, 03-; coord. T-Ball program 1993-98. Recipient Disting. Svc. award L.I. chpt. Adoptive Parents Com., 1996, Ken Kramer award Floral Park Little League, 1998. Mem. Brehon Law Soc. of Nassau County (bd. dirs. 2002—), Nassau-Suffolk Trial Lawyers Assn., Nassau Bar Assn., Southside Civic Assn., Floral Park Indians Athletic Club (coord. basketball divsn. 1993—, coord. soccer divsn. 1995-97, basketball coach 1992—, soccer coach 1994—). Avocations: golf, softball, reading, basketball, travel. State civil litigation, Insurance, Personal injury (including property damage). Home: 43 Oak St Floral Park NY 11001-3409 Office: McCabe Collins McGeough Fowler LLP 114 Old Country Rd Mineola NY 11501-4400 E-mail: dfowler@mcmf4law@aol.com.

FOWLER, FLORA DAUN, retired lawyer; b. Washington , Aug. 11, 1923; d. Herman Hartwell and Flora Elizabeth (Adams) Sanford; m. Kenneth Leo Fowler, Aug. 22, 1941; children: Kenneth Jr., Michael, Kathleen, Daun, Jonathan, Colin, Kevin, James, Shawn, Maureen, Wendelyn, Liam, Tobias, Melanie. Student, Wilson Tchrs. Coll., 1940-41; AA, U. Md., 1973; JD, U. Balt., 1976. Bar: Fla. 1977, U.S. Dist. Ct. (mid. dist.) Fla. 1979, U.S. Ct. Appeals (5th and 11th cirs.) 1981. Staff atty. Cen. Fla. Legal Services Inc., Daytona Beach, 1978-80, mng. atty., 1980-81; pvt. practice, Daytona Beach, 1981-93; ret., 2001. Past editor Seabrook Acres Citizens' League Newsletter; columnist Bowie Express & Community Times; contbr. poems to New Voices in American Poetry, 1974. V.p. Seabrook (Md.) Acres Citizens League, 1970; past v.p. Prince Georges County Civic Fedn., Md.; past unit chmn. League of Women Voters, Prince Georges County; past pres., v.p., publicity chmn. Lanham-Bowie Dem. Club, Seabrook. Recipient Evening Star Trophy award Prince Georges County Civic Fedn., 1969. Mem. Fla. S. Ct. Hist. Soc. Democrat. Roman Catholic. Avocations: swimming, creative writing, cursillo. E-mail: daunfowler@msn.com.

FOWLER, PAUL RAYMOND, physician, lawyer; b. Washington, Apr. 30, 1958; s. Charles Raymond and Dora E. (Burger) Fowler; m. Mary Jane Weber, Oct. 4, 1986; children: Christina D., Laura M., Joshua P. BS, U. Md., 1980, postgrad., 1980-81; DO, U. Des Moines, Des Moines, Iowa, 1985; JD with honors, Drake U., 1994. Bar: U.S. Supreme Ct., Fla. 1995, Ill. 1996, D.C. 1996, Ky. 1998; diplomate Am. Bd. Forensic Examiners, Am. Osteo. Bd. Family Practice, Am. Osteo. Bd. Preventive Medicine, cert. Am. Bd. Disability Analysts, diplomate Am. Bd. Family Practice. Intern Des Moines Gen. Hosp., 1985-86; resident Ea. Va. Grad. Sch. Medicine, Norfolk, 1986-88; pvt. practice medicine Norfolk, 1988-90; staff Iowa Meth. Med. Ctr., Des Moines, 1990-95, Mercy Med. Ctr., Des Moines, 1992-94; med. dir. Occupational Health Svcs., Des Moines, 1990-95; chief physician Ford Motor Co., Hapeville, Ga., 1995-97; med. dir. Quorum Health Sys., Spartanburg, SC, 1997-2000; legal medicine officer to surgeon gen. U.S. Army, Washington, 2000—. Mem. mock trial team Med. Malpractice Rev. Bd., Commonwealth of Va., 1988—90, Drake U. Law Sch., 1992; assoc. clin. prof. U. Des Moines, 1990—; judge Nat. Mock Trial Coll. Comp., 1992; clin. prof. Pikevill Coll. Osteo. Medicine, 1997—; pvt. practice law, 1994—. Reviewer: Am. Forensic Examiner, 1997—, Fed. Practitioner; contbr. articles to profl. jours. Active Silver Spring Vol. Fire Dept., 1978—81; mem. bioethics com. Iowa Meth. Med. Ctr., Des Moines, 1992—95. Recipient Good Citizen award, Clifton Park Citizens Assn. Fellow: Am. Coll. Legal Medicine, Am. Acad. Family Physicians; mem.: Am. Osteo. Coll. Preventive and Occupl. Medicine (gen. counsel, trustee, v.p.), Am. Osteo. Assn. (tech. task force, ho. dels.), Md. Acad. Family Physicians (bylaws com., chmn. resolutions com.), Am. Bd. Med. Specialties, D.C. Bar Assn., Ill. Bar Assn., Ky. Bar Assn., Fla. Bar Assn., Phi Sigma (pres. 1984—85). Avocations: tennis, running, philately. Home: 18313 Leedstown Way Olney MD 20832 Office: Walter Reed Army Med Ctr Rm 2-65 Delano Hall Washington DC 20307-5001 E-mail: prfowler@pol.net.

FOX, DONALD THOMAS, lawyer; b. Council Bluffs, Iowa, June 12, 1929; s. Donald and Genevieve (Tinley) F.; m. Ana Clemencia Tercero-Graham; children: Mark, Matthew, Genevieve, Melissa. AB magna cum laude, Harvard U., 1951; LLB, N.Y. U., 1956; Brevet de Traduction et de Terminologie Juridiques, U. Paris, 1957, Diplôme de Droit Comparé, 1961. Bar: N.Y. 1957, U.S. Ct. Claims 1960, U.S. Dist. Ct. (so. and ea. dists.) N.Y. 1960, U.S. Ct. Appeals (2nd cir.) 1960, D.C. 1968, U.S. Tax Ct. 1973. Instr. Inst. Comparative Law, NYU, 1957-59; assoc. Davis, Polk, Wardwell, Sunderland & Kiendl, N.Y.C., 1958-67; ptnr. Fox Horan & Camerini, LLP and predecessor firms, N.Y.C., 1968—. Bd. dirs. Washington Sq. Legal Svcs., Inc., N.Y.C., 1974-85, Uniroyal Goodrich Tire Co., 1990-96, Michelin Licensing Svcs. Inc., Globalstar do Brazil, 1995-99; mem. adv. com. on history and theory Harvard U. Grad. Sch. Design, 1990—. Author: Conciliation of International Economic Disputes, 1964, Human Rights in Guatemala, 1979, Report on Contra Activity in Nicaragua, 1985, Violence in Colombia, 1989, Hungarian Constitutional Reform and the Rule of Law, 1993, Elections in Ethiopia, 1995, Elections in Nicaragua, 1996, 2000, Elections in Mexico, 1997, Lessons of the Colombian Constitutional Reform of 1991, 2002; editor: The Cambodian Incursion: Legal Issues, 1971; mem. panel advisors Jour. Internat. Law and Politics, 1968-99; contbr. articles to legal jours. Trustee Law Ctr. Found., N.Y.U., 1975-86, chmn. campaign fund, , 1980; mem. Am. Soc., 1975—; Coun. on Fgn. Rels., 1973—; Pres.'s assocs. Harvard U., 2000—. 1st lt. USAF, 1951-53. Named to Com. of Honor, Giulio Romano Exhbn., Mantova, Italy, 1989; Albert Gallatin fellow, 1978; Nat. scholar Harvard U., Root-Tilden scholar NYU, Fulbright scholar U. Paris. Fellow: Am. Bar Found. (life); mem.: The Century Assn. (chmn. wine com.), Humanitarian Found. for Nicaragua (exec. com. bd. dirs. 1991—96), NYU Alumni Fedn. (pres. 1983—85), NYU Law Alumni Assn. (pres. 1971—73), Assn. of Bar of City of N.Y. (chmn. com. lawyers role in search for peace 1969—71, chmn. com. profl. responsibility 1971—74, chmn. com. audit 1978—80, treas. 1982—84, chmn. fin. com. 1982—84), Am. Arbitration Assn. (panel arbitrators 1970—), Am. Assn. Internat. Commn. Jurists (exec. com., bd. dirs. 1970—, chmn. 1991—), Am. Law Inst. (sustaining life), Harvard Club of N.Y.C. Federal civil litigation, Corporate, general, Private international. Office: Fox Horan & Camerini LLP 825 3rd Ave New York NY 10022-7519 Fax: 212 269-2383. E-mail: dtfox@foxlex.com.

FOX, DOUGLAS LEE, lawyer; b. Exeter, N.H., June 7, 1951; s. Arthur G. and Theresa B. (Perry) F. BA, Northeastern U., Boston, 1973; JD, U. Miami, 1979. Bar: Mass. 1979, Fla. 1979, U.S. Dist. Ct. Mass. 1980, U.S. Ct. Appeals (1st cir.) 1981. Assoc. Shumway, Giguere, Byrne, Fox and Aloise, P.C., Worcester, Mass., 1980-85, ptnr., 1985—. Mem. faculty trial adv. seminar Harvard U. Law Sch., Cambridge, Mass., 1986; faculty workshops, seminars Mass. Continuing Legal Edn., 1989—. Contbng. author: Damages in Massachusetts Litigation 1993, Massachusetts Continuing Legal Education, 1998; mem. bd. editors Mass. Lawyers Weekly, 1993—. Trustee Mass. Assn. for Blind, Brookline, 1988-93, pres., 1991-92; chmn. Introducing Evidence at Trial Mass. Continuing Legal Edn., Worcester, 1999; mem. Holden Conservation Com., 1995—, chmn., 1996-2002. Fellow Mass. Bar Found.; mem. Mass. Bar Assn. (com.), Worcester County Bar Assn. (com., pres. award 1995), Fla. Bar, Am. Arbitration Assn. (panel arbitrators), Assn. Ski Def. Attys. General civil litigation, Personal injury (including property damage), Product liability. Office: Shumway Giguere & Fox PC 19 Cedar St Worcester MA 01609-2546 E-mail: lokifox@charter.net.

FOX, FRANCIS HANEY, lawyer; b. Attleboro, Mass., May 28, 1933; s. Francis Joseph and Mary Frances (Brady) F.; m. Cynthia Ann Blundell, Dec. 27, 1959; children: Cynthia, Martin, Matthew, Kalarn. BS in Econs., Coll. Holy Cross, 1955; LLB, Harvard U., 1963. Bar: Mass. 1963, U.S. Ct. Appeals (1st cir.) 1963, U.S. Supreme Ct. 1977. Assoc. Bingham, Dana & Gould, Boston, 1963-70; ptnr. Bingham McCutchen LLP and predecessor firms, Boston, 1970—. Mem. adv. com. on civil rules Jud. Conf. of U.S., 1992-98. Capt. USNR, 1955-78. Fellow Am. Coll. Trial Lawyers. Federal civil litigation, State civil litigation, Libel. Home: 77 Cottage St Sharon MA 02067-2132 Office: Bingham McCutchen LLP 150 Federal St Boston MA 02110-1726 E-mail: francis.fox@bingham.com.

FOX, GREGORY JOHN, lawyer; b. Phila., Sept. 27, 1954; s. Robert Joseph and Dora (De Lazzero) F. AB in Econs., Muhlenberg Coll., 1976; JD, Temple U., 1976, LLM in Taxation, 1984. Bar: Pa. 1979, U.S. Dist. Ct. (ea. dist.) Pa. 1979, U.S. Ct. Appeals (3d cir.) 1980. Assoc. Schnader, Harrison, Segal & Lewis, Phila., 1979-86, Montgomery, McCracken, Walker & Rhoads, Phila., 1986-88, ptnr., 1988—. Bd. dirs. Pa. Conv. Ctr. Authority. Pres.'s adv. bd. Archbishop Ryan H.S., Phila., 1996—; mem. Muhlenberg Coll. alumni bd., Allentown, Pa., 1997-2001; bd. trustees Muhlenberg Coll., 2002—; bd. dirs. St. Thomas More Soc., Phila., 1995—. Named one of top benefits lawyers in U.S., Nat. Law Jour., May, 1998. Republican. Roman Catholic. Avocations: biking, exercise, politics. Immigration, naturalization, and customs, Pension, profit-sharing, and employee benefits. Office: Montgomery McCracken Walker & Rhoads LLP 123 S Broad St Fl 24 Philadelphia PA 19109-1099

FOX, HAMILTON PHILLIPS, III, lawyer; b. Salisbury, Md., Sept. 18, 1945; s. Hamilton Phillips and Evelyn Louise (Jefferson) F.; m. Mary Shannon Lafans, Aug. 31, 1968 (dissolved); children: Gretchen Robinson, Hamilton Duke, Caleb Savage; m. Barbara Daniels Robinson, Dec. 13, 1986. BA with honors, U. Va., 1967; LLB, Yale U., 1970. Bar: Maine 1971, D.C. 1972, U.S. Dist. Ct. Md., U.S. Ct. Appeals (1st, 9th and D.C. cirs.), U.S. Supreme Ct. Law clk. to judge U.S. Ct. Appeals (1st cir.), Portland, Maine, 1970-71; law clk. to Hon. Stanley Reed and Lewis F. Powell Jr. U.S. Supreme Ct., Washington, 1971-72; asst. U.S. atty. U.S. Atty.'s Office, Washington, 1972-73, 74-77; asst. spl. prosecuter Watergate Prosecution Force, Washington, 1973-74; dep. chief organized crime sect. U.S. Dept. Justice, Washington, 1977-80; sole practice Washington, 1980-84; ptnr. Dewey, Ballantine, Bushby, Palmer & Wood, Washington, 1984-90; now ptnr. Sutherland, Asbill & Brennan, Washington. Lectr. law U. Va., Charlottesville, 1980-82; assoc. dep. counsel com. on standards of official conduct U.S. Ho. of Reps., 1983-84. Federal civil litigation, State civil litigation, Criminal. Home: 729 Massachusetts Ave NE Washington DC 20002-6007 Office: Sutherland Asbill Brennan 1275 Pennsylvania Ave NW Ste 1 Washington DC 20004-2415

FOX, JAMES CARROLL, federal judge; b. Atchison, Kans., Nov. 6, 1928; s. Jared Copeland and Ethel (Carroll) F.; m. Katharine deRosset Rhett, Dec. 30, 1950; children: James Carroll, Jr., Jane Fox Brown, Ruth Fox Jordan. BSBA, U. N.C., 1950, JD with honors, 1957. Bar: N.C. 1957. Law clk. U.S. Dist. Ct. (ea. dist.) N.C., Wilmington, 1957-58; assoc. Carter & Murchison, Wilmington, N.C., 1958-59; ptnr. Murchison, Fox & Newton, Wilmington, N.C., 1960-82; sr. fed. judge U.S. Dist. Ct. (ea. dist.) N.C., Wilmington, 1982—. Lectr. in field. Contbr. articles to profl. jours. Vestryman, St. James Episcopal Ch., 1973-75, 79-82. Mem. Hew Hanover County Bar Assn. (pres. 1967-68), Fifth Jud. Dist. Bar Assn. (sec. 1960-62). Office: US Dist Ct Alton Lennon Fed Bldg PO Box 2143 Wilmington NC 28402-2143

FOX, MARY ELLEN, lawyer; b. Upper Sandusky, Ohio, Aug. 8, 1956; d. Paul Eugene and Anne Marie (Walton) Fox; m. Thomas E. Osborn. BA in Acctg. and Polit. Sci., Ohio No. U., 1978, JD, 1981. Bar: Ohio 1981, U.S. Dist. Ct. (no. dist.) Ohio 1982. Assoc. Stansbery, Schoenberger and Scheck, Upper Sandusky, 1981-85; ptnr. Stansbery, Schoenberger, Scheck & Fox, Upper Sandusky, 1985-90; assoc. Osborn Co., LPA, Upper Sandusky, 1990-92; ptnr. Osborn & Fox Co., LPA, Upper Sandusky, 1993—. Bd. dirs. Community 1st Bank, N.A., Forest, Ohio, 1985—; solicitor Village of Nev., Ohio, 1982-99; libr. Wyandot County Law Libr., Upper Sandusky, 1983—; adj. prof.real estate law and fin., Ohio Northern U. Coll. of Law, 2001. Bd. dirs. Wyandot County Coun. on Alcoholism, Upper Sandusky, 1983-86, Pvt. Industry Coun., 1995-2000, Upper Sandusky C. of C., 1994—. Mem. ABA, Ohio Bar Assn. (family law com., banking law com., agrl. law com.), Wyandot County Bar Assn. (sec., treas. 1982, v.p. 1983, pres. 1984), Alpha Xi Delta (bldg. corp. bd. 1978-91, pledge advisor 1979-89, province sec. 1981-85, province pres. 1986-89, chpt. dir. 1986-91). Republican. Methodist. Avocations: walking, sewing, music, swimming. Banking, Family and matrimonial, General practice. Home: 14370 SH Route 2 # 37 Forest OH 45843 Office: Osborn & Fox Co LPA 116 E Wyandot Ave Upper Sandusky OH 43351-1430

FOX, MICHAEL DAVID, lawyer; b. N.Y.C., Aug. 14, 1940; s. Sol and Faye R. (Goor) F.; m. Geraldine Hill, Ag. 16, 1964; children— Thaddeus Hill, Amanda Curry. B.S., Carnegie Mellon U., 1962, M.S. in Indsl. Adminstrn., 1963; J.D., U. Pitts., 1969. Bar: Pa. 1970. Corp. market planning staff, field and divsn. sales engr. positions Westinghouse Electric, Pitts., Detroit and Youngwood, Pa., 1963-66, atty., gen. counsel staff, Pitts., 1969-74; assoc. Klett Rooney Lieber & Shorling (formerly Berkman Ruslander Pohl Lieber & Engel), Pitts., 1974-77, ptnr. 1978-90; shareholder, dir. Getsby and Lehman PC, 1990—; dir., vice chmn. MIT Enterprise Forum, Pitts.; adj. lectr. Grad. Sch. Bus., U. Pitts. Former mem. nat. alumni adv. counsel Grad. Sch. Indsl. Adminstrn., Carnegie Mellon U., chmn. Andrew Carnegie Soc.; pvt. investor forum Enterprise Corp. Mem. ABA, Pa. Bar Assn., Allegheny County Bar Assn. (chmn. antitrust and class action com. 1977-78, vice chmn. intellectual property sect., 1987), Pitts. Venture Capital Assn., Order of Coif, Pitts. Athletic Assn., Rivers Club. Corporate, general, Finance, Intellectual property. Home: 10 Dunmoyle Pl Pittsburgh PA 15217-1029

FOXHOVEN, JERRY RAY, lawyer; b. Yankton, S.D., July 24, 1952; s. Elmer William and Ida Elizabeth (Lubbers) F.; m. Julie Ann Greco, Apr. 6, 1985; children: Anthony Michael, Peter Joseph. BS summa cum laude, Morningside Coll., 1974; JD, Drake U., 1977. Bar: Iowa 1977, U.S. Dist. Ct. (so. and no. dists.) Iowa 1977, U.S. Ct. Appeals (8th cir.) 1977, U.S. Supreme Ct. 1981, Nebr. 1985, U.S. Dist. Ct. Nebr. 1985, Wis. 1986. Assoc. Critelli & Pille, Des Moines, 1977-79, ptnr., 1979-82, Foxhoven & McCann, Des Moines, 1982-88, Peddicord, Wharton, Thune, Foxhoven & Spencer, P.C., 1988-91; pvt. practice, 1991-2000; adminstr. Child Advocacy Bd., Des Moines, 2000—. Instr. criminaljustice dept. Des Moines Area Community Coll., Ankeny, Iowa, 197 8-81, Am. Inst. Banking, 1982-85. Mem. steering con. Culver for U.S. Senate, Des Moines, 1980; chmn. Iowa State Foster Care Rev. Bd., 1986-99; bd. dirs., nat. pres. Nat. Assn. Foster Care Reviewers, 1988-01; mem. parish coun. Sacred Heart Roman Cath. Ch., West Des Moines, 1982. Lodge: Masons (master 1990). Democrat. State civil litigation, Criminal, Personal injury (including property damage). Home: 1608 NW 101st St Clive IA 50325-6716 Office: Lucas Bldg 321 E 12th St 4th Fl Des Moines IA 50319-0083 E-mail: jfoxhoven@dia.state.ia.us.

FOXMAN, STEPHEN MARK, lawyer; b. Youngstown, Ohio, Aug. 10, 1946; s. Howard J. and Ruth R. (Zoritz) F.; m. Barbara Elaine Hirsch, July 4, 1982; children: Claire Rachel, Rebecca Jane. Gen. course cert., London Sch. Econs., 1967; BS in Econs., U. Pa., 1968; JD, Harvard U., 1971. Bar: Pa. 1971, D.C. 1973, U.S. Dist. Ct. (ea. dist.) Pa. 1975. Law clk. Superior Ct. Pa., Harrisburg, 1971-72; assoc. Ewing & Cohen, Phila., 1972-74, Goodman & Ewing, Phila., 1974-76, ptnr., 1976-83, Connolly, Epstein, Chicco, Foxman, Oxholm & Ewing, Phila., 1983-99, mem. exec. com., pres., 1994-99; ptnr., mem. exec. com. Eckert Seamans Cherin & Mellott, Phila., 1999—. Bd. dirs. Bread upon the Waters Scholarship Fund, Phila., 1986—, Hilary House Child Care, Inc., Phila., 1988-92, Chestnut Hill Commun. Assn., Phila., 1992-93; chmn. steering com. office automation program Phila. Sch. Dist., 1986-88. Mem. ABA, Phila. Bar Assn. (exec. com. real estate sect. 1989-92, founder, chmn. cyberspace and e-commerce law com. 1999-2000, exec. com. bus. sect. 2001—), Computer Law Assn. Republican. Commercial, contracts (including sales of goods; commercial financing), Property, real (including real estate development, water), Securities. Office: Eckert Seamans Cherin & Mellott 1515 Market St Fl 9 Philadelphia PA 19102-1933 E-mail: smf@escm.com.

FOY, HERBERT MILES, III, lawyer, educator; b. Statesville, N.C., Mar. 22, 1945; s. Herbert Miles Jr. and Perci Aileen (Lazenby) F.; m. Eleanor Jane Meschan, June 27, 1970; children: Anna Meschan, Sarah Aileen. AB, U. N.C., 1967; MA, Harvard U., 1968; JD, U. Va., 1972. Bar: N.C. 1973, U.S. Dist. Ct. (mid. and we. dists.) N.C., U.S. Ct. Appeals (4th cir.), U.S. Supreme Ct. Jud. clk. U.S. Ct. Appeals (5th cir.), Atlanta, 1972-73; assoc. Smith, Moore, Smith, Schell & Hunter, Greensboro, N.C., 1973-77, 81-83, ptnr., 1983-84; sr. atty. advisor office legal counsel U.S. Dept. Justice, Washington, 1977-81; assoc. prof. Sch. Law Wake Forest U., Winston-Salem, N.C., 1984-87, prof., 1987—, assoc. dean acad. affairs, 1990-95, Law Sch., Wake Forest U., Winston-Salem, 2000—. Contbr. articles to legal jours. Morehead scholar, 1963; Woodrow Wilson fellow, 1968. Mem. ABA, N.C. Bar Assn., N.C. State Bar Assn., Fosythe County Bar Assn., Order of Coif, Phi Beta Kappa. Democrat. Methodist. Avocations: banjo playing, gardening, athletics, poetry. Home: 2328 Oak Ridge Rd Oak Ridge NC 27310-9701 Office: Wake Forest U Sch Law PO Box 7206U Winston Salem NC 27109-7206

FOYE, THOMAS HAROLD, lawyer; b. Rapid City, S.D., Nov. 23, 1930; s. Harold Herbert and Jean Winifred (McCormick) F.; m. Laurene Fowler, Aug. 7, 1972; children: David Snyder, Stewart Snyder BS in Commerce, Creighton U., 1952; LLB, Georgetown U., 1955. Bar: S.D. 1955, D.C. 1955, U.S. Supreme Ct. 1968. Trial atty. tax div. U.S. Dept. Justice, Washington, 1955-58; assoc. Bangs, McCullen, Butler, Foye & Simmons, predecessor firms, Rapid City, 1958-60, ptnr., 1960—. Lectr. in field Fellow Am. Coll. Trust and Estate Counsel, Am. Bar Found.; mem. ABA, State Bar S.D. (pres. 1982-83), Pennington County Bar Assn. (pres. 1962), Am. Coll. Real Estate Lawyers, Internat. Acad. Estate and Trust Law., Am. Coll. Tax Counsel. Clubs: Arrowhead Country (Rapid City). Democrat. Roman Catholic. Avocations: snow skiing, water skiing, hiking. Corporate, general, Estate planning, Taxation, general. Office: Bangs McCullen Butler Foye & Simmons PO Box 2670 Rapid City SD 57709-2670

FOYLES, KIRSTEN ELLEFSON, lawyer; b. West Allis, Wis., June 11, 1973; d. Julian John and Karen Ann Ellefson; m. Jody Stuart Foyles; 1 child, Keegan Angelina. BA in Econ., U. Wis., Madison, 1991—95; JD, U. Louisville, 1995—98. Bar: N.C. Atty. Webb & Graves, PLLC, Aberdeen, NC, 1998—99; atty., owner Foyles Law Firm, PLLC, Southern Pines, NC, 1999—2000; atty., ptnr. Holshouser, Gamer, Foyles & Hayes, Pinehurst, NC, 2000—01; atty. Thigpen & Jenkins, LLP, Southern Pines, NC, 2001—. Adj. prof. Sandhills Cmty. Coll., Southern Pines, NC, 2000—02. Recipient Young Careerist, Bus. and Profl. Women's Assn., 2000. Mem.: Young Lawyer's Divsn. (dist. chair 2002—), Jr. League of Moore County (cmty. resource chair 2000—02), Moore County Bar Assn. (pres., v.p. 2001—03). Property, real (including real estate development, water), Criminal, General practice. Office: Thigpen & Jenkins LLP 300 PInehurst Ave Southern Pines NC 28387 Office Fax: 910-693-3746. E-mail: kirstenfoyles@earthlink.net.

FRAIDIN, STEPHEN, lawyer; b. Boston, July 29, 1939; s. Morris and Freda (Rozeff) F.; m. Lori Kramer, Oct. 27, 2001; children from previous marriage: Matthew, Sam, Sarah AB, Tufts U., 1961; JD, Yale U., 1964. Bar: N.Y. 1965. Ptnr. Fried, Frank, Harris, Shriver & Jacobson, N.Y.C., 1964—2003, Kirkland & Ellis, N.Y.C., 2003—. Vis. lectr. Yale U. Law Sch., 1988—, mem. exec. com.; bd. dirs. Children's Scholarship Fund. Contbr. numerous articles to profl. jours. Past chmn. UJA-Fedn., NY Lawyers Divsn. Recipient Judge Joseph M. Proskauer award, 2002. Mem. ABA, Assn. of Bar of City of N.Y. Corporate, general, Mergers and acquisitions.

FRANCE, BELINDA TAKACH, lawyer, business owner; b. Jacksonville, Fla., June 10, 1964; d. Bruce Albert and Bertha Loretta (Hawkins) Takach; m. Alden Whitney France, July 27, 1985. BS, U. Tampa, Fla., 1985; JD, Stetson U., 1987; LLM in Taxation, U. Fla., 1989. Bar: Fla. 1989, U.S. Dist. Ct. (mid. dist.) Fla. 1989, U.S. Ct. Claims 1989, U.S. Tax Ct. 1989, U.S. Ct. Appeals (11th cir.) 1989, U.S. Ct. Appeals (Fed. cir.) 1990. Tax preparer H&R Block, Tampa, 1983-84; acct. Robert Osborne & Assocs., Tampa, 1984-85; assoc. Thomas C. Little, P.A., Clearwater, Fla., 1987-88; co-counsel Bruce R. Young, P.A., Clearwater, 1988; prin. Belinda Takach France, P.A., Tallahassee, Fla., 1988—. Prof. Ft. Lauderdale Coll., Tallahassee, 1989; adj. instr. Tallahassee C.C., 1991—; vice chmn. bd. dirs. Someplace Else, Tallahassee; owner Catalyst Seminars; expert witness in taxation and pension matters. Mem. Tallahassee Rep. Women, 1989-90. Named Best Atty. Tallahassee mag., 2000. Mem. ABA (com. domestic rels. tax problems, com. attys. in small law firms), Fla. Bar Assn., Tallahassee Bar Assn., Tallahassee Women Lawyers Assn., Tallahassee C. of C. Estate planning, Probate (including wills, trusts), Taxation, general. Office: 703 E Tennessee St Tallahassee FL 32308-4984 E-mail: btf@francelawfirm.com.

FRANCESCHI, ERNEST JOSEPH, JR., lawyer; b. L.A., Feb. 1, 1957; s. Ernest Joseph and Doris Cecilia (Beluche) F. BS, U. So. Calif., 1978; JD, Southwestern U., L.A., 1980. Bar: Calif. 1984, U.S. Dist. Ct. (cen. dist.) Calif. 1984, U.S. Dist. Ct. (ea. dist.) Calif. 1986, U.S. Dist. Ct. (no. and so. dists.) Calif. 1987, U.S. Ct. Appeals (9th cir.) 1984, U.S. Supreme Ct. 1989. Pvt. practice law, L.A., 1984—; judge pro tem L.A. Superior Ct., 1999—. Mem. Assn. Trial Lawyers Am., Calif. Trial Lawyers Assn., L.A. Trial Lawyers Assn., Trial Lawyers for Pub. Justice, Fed. Bar Assn. Federal civil litigation, Personal injury (including property damage). Office: 445 S Figueroa St Ste 2600 Los Angeles CA 90071-1630

FRANCH, RICHARD THOMAS, lawyer; b. Melrose Park, Ill., Sept. 23, 1942; s. Robert and Julia (Martino) F.; m. Patricia Staufenberg, Apr. 18, 1971 (dec. Apr. 1994); children: Richard T. Jr., Katherine J.; m. Susan L. Rice, Sept. 1, 1995. BA cum laude, U. Notre Dame, 1964; JD, U. Chgo., 1967. Bar: Ill. 1967, U.S. Dist. Ct. (no. dist.) Ill. 1967, U.S. Supreme Ct. 1980, U.S. Ct. Appeals (2d cir.) 1984, U.S. Ct. Appeals (3d cir.) 1981, U.S. Ct. Appeals (6th cir.) 1991, U.S. Ct. Appeals (7th cir.) 1971, U.S. Ct. Appeals (8th cir.) 1981, U.S. Ct. Appeals (9th cir.) 1997, U.S. Dist. Ct. (no. dist.) Wis. 1989, U.S. Tax Ct. 1994. Assoc. Jenner & Block, Chgo., 1967-68, 70-74, ptnr., 1975—. Former mem. Ill. Supreme Ct. Rules Com. Served to capt. U.S. Army, 1968-70 Decorated Bronze star, Army Commendation medal. Fellow Am. Coll. Trial Lawyers; mem. Am. Law Inst. Antitrust, Federal civil litigation, State civil litigation. Office: Jenner & Block Ste 4600 One IBM Plz Chicago IL 60611 E-mail: dickfranch@aol.com., rfranch@jenner.com.

FRANCIS, JAMES CLARK, IV, judge; b. Tulsa, Okla., Oct. 3, 1952; s. James C. and F. Ruth Francis; m. Elizabeth Bradford, Aug. 19, 1978; children: Nathaniel, Jeremy. BA, Yale Coll., 1974, JD, 1978; M of Pub. Policy, Harvard U., 1978. Bar: N.Y. 1979, U.S. Dist. Ct. (so. dist.) N.Y. 1979, U.S. Dist. Ct. (ea. dist.) N.Y. 1980, U.S. Ct. Appeals (2nd cir.) 1980. Law clk. Hon. Robert L. Carter, N.Y.C., 1978-79; staff atty. Legal Aid Soc., N.Y.C., 1979-85; U.S. Magistrate judge U.S. Dist. Ct. (so. dist.) N.Y., N.Y.C., 1985-98, chief U.S. Magistrate judge, 1998—2000. Author: (chpts.) Moore's Federal Practice, 1997; curator exhibit Discreet Persons Learned in Law, 1995, Thou Shald Not Ration Justice, 2001. Mem. profl. adv. bd. Epilepsy Inst., N.Y.C.; bd. dirs. Port Washington (N.Y.) Soccer Club. Mem. N.Y. State Bar Assn. (jud. com. 1989—), Assn. Bar of City of N.Y. (fed. cts. com. 1995-98). Democrat. Avocations: travel, scuba, sports, coaching soccer. Office: US Court 500 Pearl St New York NY 10007-1316

FRANCIS, JEROME LESLIE, lawyer; b. Seattle, May 25, 1941; s. Leslie J. and Phyllis G. (Pike) F.; m. Jen H. Hough, Nov. 2, 1968; children: David S., Catherine E. BA in Bus. Adminstrn., U. WAsh., 1963; JD, San Francisco Law Sch., 1968. Bar: Mass. 1970. Sole practice, Sudbury, Mass., 1970-74; atty. legal dept. Texaco Inc., Boston, 1974-76, Cherry Hill, N.J., 1976-84, Denver, 1984-89; sr. atty. Star Enterprise (Texaco-SRI), Houston, 1989-98; atty. legal dept. Equiva Svcs. (Texaco-Shell-SRI), Houston, 1998—2002; ret. Mem. ABA, Mass. Bar Assn. Republican. Episcopalian. Corporate, general, Environmental, Property, real (including real estate development, water).

FRANCO, MARIA-LORINDA D. lawyer; s. Danilo Villareal and Zenaida Franco. BA, U. Calif., 1995; JD, U. Wash., 1999. Bar: Calif., U.S. Dist. Ct. (ctrl. dist.). Tutor physics and calculus U. (Irvine) Calif., 1993—95; rsch. atty. Orange County Superior Ct., Westminster, Calif., 2001—02; atty. Lim, Ruger and Kim, LLP, L.A., 2002—. Mem. bd. Praxis-UCI, Irvine, 1999—, Orange County Asian Am. Bar Assn., Orange, 2002—. Author: (poetry) Two Hands, 1996. Vol. Asian Pacific Am. Legal Ctr., L.A., 1996; co-chair outreach cmty. com. Asuan Pacific Am. Bar Assn., L.A., 2002—; mem. bd. Asian Pacific Islander Alumni Assn., Irvine, 1999—. Mem.: ABA, Philippine Am. Bar Assn. Avocations: yoga, tennis, creative writing, swimming, basketball. Labor (including EEOC, Fair Labor Standards Act, labor-management relations, NLRB, OSHA), Civil rights, Product liability. Office: Lim Ruger & Kim LLP 1055 W 7th St 2800 Los Angeles CA 90017

FRANCOIS, WILLIAM ARMAND, lawyer; b. Chgo., May 31, 1942; s. George Albert and Evelyn Marie (Smith) F.; m. Barbara Ann Sala, Aug. 21, 1965; children: Nicole Suzanne, Robert William. BA, DePaul U., 1964, JD, 1967. Bar: Ill. 1967. Pvt. practice, Lyons, Ill., 1967-68; with Am. Nat. Can Group, Inc., Chgo., 1970, sec., 1974, v.p., 1978, sr. v.p., gen. counsel, sec., 1999-2000; dep. gen. counsel N.Am. Pechiney Group, 1996-99; pvt. practice Lake Forest, Ill., 2000—. Served to capt. U.S. Army, 1968—70. Mem. ABA, Ill. Bar Assn., Chgo. Bar Assn., Am. Soc. Corp. Secs., Am. Corp. Counsel Assn. Commercial, contracts (including sales of goods; commercial financing), Corporate, general. Office: 642 Balmoral Ct Lake Forest IL 60045-4842 E-mail: chgowaf@aol.com.

FRANCOLINE, STACEY, lawyer; b. Manchester, Conn., Feb. 23, 1973; d. Rocco James and Joanne Francoline. BA, U. Conn., 1995; JD, Hamline U., 2001. Bar: Conn. 02, NY 02, U.S. Dist. Ct. Conn. 02. Assoc. Beebe and O'Neil, Norwich, Conn., 2002—. Mem.: ABA, Conn. Bar Assn., NY State Bar Assn. Avocations: scuba diving, cardio kickboxing. Personal injury (including property damage), Criminal. Office: Beebe and O'Neil 335 Washington St Norwich CT 06360

FRANK, ALIX, lawyer; b. Klagenfurt, Austria, Dec. 5, 1959; d. Otto Dkfm and Beatrix F.; m. Gunther Mag Thomasser. M, U. Salzburg, PhD, 1982. Ex ho. gen. counsel Wienerberger Baustoffindustrie, Vienna, 1989—. Mem. Austrian Bar Assn. (bd. dirs.), MacIntyre Straiter, EureseaU (v.p.). Computer, Mergers and acquisitions, Personal injury (including property damage). Office: Schottengasse 10 1010 Vienna Austria Fax: 0043 1 523 33 15. E-mail: austrolaw@alix-frank.co.at.

FRANK, BARRY H. lawyer; b. Nov. 19, 1938; s. David and Rose (Pearl) F.; married: Caryl Frank; children: Toby L., S. Kenneth, Gary A. BS, Pa. State U., 1960; LLB, Temple U., 1963. Bar: Pa. 1964. Staff atty. IRS, Phila., 1963-66; tax mgr. Ernst & Whinney, Phila., 1966-74; exec. v.p., gen. counsel N.F.I. Industries, Inc., Vineland, N.J., 1974-75; ptnr. Pechner, Dorman, Wolffe, Rounick & Cabot, Phila., 1975-87, Schnader, Harrison, Segal & Lewis, LLP, Phila., 1987—2003, Pelino & Lentz, PC, Phila.,

2003—. Instr. Temple U. Tax Inst., Phila., 1976—. Co-author: Alimony, Child Support and Counsel Fees; mem. editl. bd. The Practical Acct.; contbr. more than 60 articles to profl. jours. Mem. exec. com. Mayor's Small Bus. Adv. Coun., Phila., 1981-83. Mem. ABA, AICPA, Phila. Bar Assn., Pa. Inst. CPAs. Republican. Jewish. Corporate taxation, Estate taxation, Taxation, general. Office: Pelino & Lontz PC One Liberty Pl 1650 Market St Philadelphia PA 19103-7393 E-mail: bfrank@pelino.com.

FRANK, BEN WILLIAM, lawyer, administrator; b. Lampasas, Tex., Oct. 23, 1929; s. Hugo C. and Nadine G. (Machen) F.; m. Maymie A. Bowles, July 30, 1961 (dec. June 1994); children: Carl, Rick; m. Eleanor B. Bodenhamer, July 5, 1997. BA, U. Tex., 1956; LLB, Ark. U., 1964, JD, 1979. Bar: Ark. 1964. Claims mgr. CNA, Little Rock, 1958-64, Comml. Union, Little Rock, 1964-79; adminstr. Ark. Workers Compensation Commn., Little Rock, 1979-98. City judge, city atty. Traskwood, Ark., 1971-92; commr. Ark. Worker's Compensation Comm., Little Rock. Staff Sgt. USAF, 1948-54. Mem. Ark. Adjuster Assn. (pres. 1978), Claim Mgrs. Coun. (chmn. 1970), Ins. Arbitration Commn. (chmn. 1972), Ark. Spl. Arbitration Commn. (chmn. 1972-79), Little Rock Power Squadron. Republican. Lutheran. Avocation: boating. Home: 25 Shannon Dr Little Rock AR 72207-5144

FRANK, GEORGE ANDREW, lawyer; b. Budapest, Hungary, Apr. 6, 1938; came to U.S., 1957; s. Alex and Ilona (Weiss) F.; m. Carole Shames, Feb. 14, 1979; children: Cheryl, Charles. BS, Colo. State U., 1960; PhD in Organic Chemistry, MIT, 1965; JD, Temple U., 1977. Bar: Pa. 1977, U.S. Dist. Ct. (ea. dist.) Pa. 1977, D.C. 1980, U.S. Ct. Appeals (fed. cir.) 1982, U.S. Supreme Ct. 1984. Sr. chemist Rohm & Haas Co., Phila., 1965-69; lab. head Borden Chem., Phila., 1969-73; sr. scientist Thiokol Corp., Trenton, N.J., 1973-74; counsel Du Pont Corp., Wilmington, Del., 1974-85, sr. counsel, 1986-92, corp. counsel, 1992-2001, intellectual property law group leader, 2000-2001; of counsel, chair licensing and tech. transfer practice group Drinker Biddle & Reath LLP, Philadelphia, 2001—. External adv. com. Colo. State U. Coll. Natural Scis., 1996—; mem. intellectual property adv. com. Pa. Bar Inst., 2002--. Contbr. articles to profl. jours; patentee in field. Recipient Merck award Merck & Co., 1960; Sun Oil Co. grantee, 1964; fellow NIH. Mem. ABA (chair divsn. biotech. 1993-94, coun. 1994-98, chair chem. practice com. 1998-2000, chair divsn. biotech. and chem. practice 2000-02, chair divsn. profl. practice and sect. rels. 2002—), Phila. Patent Lawyers Assn. (chair bioscis. com. 1983-87, bd. govs. 1987-92, pres. 1992-93), Am. Intellectual Property Law Assn. (chair task force 1986), Benjamin Franklin Am. Inn of Cts. (v.p. 1996-97, pres. 1997-98). Republican. Avocations: tennis, squash, travel, books, opera. Intellectual property, Patent. Home: 520 Lindy Ln Bala Cynwyd PA 19004-1331 Office: Drinker Biddle & Reath LLP 1 Logan Square 18th & Cherry St Philadelphia PA 19103 E-mail: frankga@dbr.com.

FRANK, HARVEY, lawyer, author; b. N.Y.C., Aug. 24, 1930; s. Leon and Hannah (Lehr) F.; m. Judith Ellen Lewis, Nov. 29, 1959; 1 child, David . AB, NYU, 1951, LLM, 1961; JD, Harvard U., 1954. Bar: N.Y. 1954, Md. 1981, Ohio 1982. Ptnr. Hays Feuer Porter & Spanier, N.Y.C., 1963-69, Burns, Summit, Rovins & Feldesman, N.Y.C., 1970-74; prof. law Coll. William and Mary, Williamsburg, Va., 1974-80; adj. prof. Johns Hopkins U., Balt., 1981; ptnr. Benesch Friedlander, Coplan & Aronoff, Cleve., 1982-93; pvt. practice Law Offices Harvey Frank, Phila., 1993—. Sec. Banner Aerospace, 1990-93. Author: The ERC Closely Held Corporation Guide, 1981, 2d edit., 1984; contbr. articles to law jours. Mem. ABA, Am. Law Inst. Corporate, general, Securities. Home and Office: Law Offices of Harvey Frank 1215A Waverly Walk Philadelphia PA 19147

FRANK, JACOB, lawyer; b. Albany, Apr. 4, 1936; s. Isidore and Sara F.; m. Yoelith Frank, Aug. 26, 1936; children: Eytan, Michael, Adam, Orly. BEE, Rensselaer Poly. Inst., 1957; LLB, Am. U., 1963; postgrad., George Washington U. Coll. Law, 1964-67, NYU Law Sch., 1969-73. Bar: D.C. 1963, Mass. 1979, Va. 2001, U.S. Patent Office. Of counsel Alliance Law Group, Tysons Corner, Va., 2000—. Commercial, contracts (including sales of goods; commercial financing), Computer, Intellectual property. Home: 17040 Thousand Oaks Dr Haymarket VA 20169 E-mail: JYFRANK8@aol.com.

FRANK, JAMES STUART, lawyer; b. Milw., Aug. 22, 1945; s. Jerome M. and Sylvia (Segall) F.; m. Marjorie Slavick, July 16, 1967; children: Adam Robert, Benjamin Steven. B.S. in Econs., U. Wis., 1967, M.A. Indsl. Relations, 1971, J.D., 1971. Bar: Wis. 1971, D.C. 1971, N.Y. 1974. With NLRB, Washington, 1971-74, Simpson, Thacher & Bartlett, N.Y.C., 1974-83; mem. firm Vedder, Price, Kaufman, Kammholz & Day, N.Y.C., 1983-92; ptnr., exec. com. Phillips, Nizer LLP, 1992—. Bd. dirs. St. Ann's Sch., Bklyn. Served with USAR, 1968-74. Mem. ABA (labor law and EEO com.), N.Y. State Bar Assn. (labor law com.; practice and procedure before NLRB com.), Assn. of Bar of City of N.Y., Fed. Bar Council, Assn. Trial Lawyers Am., D.C. Bar Assn. Civil rights, Federal civil litigation, Labor (including EEOC, Fair Labor Standards Act, labor-management relations, NLRB, OSHA).

FRANK, JOHN LEROY, lawyer, government executive, educator; b. Eau Claire, Wis., Mar. 13, 1952; s. George LeRoy and Frances Elaine (Torgerson) F. BS summa cum laude, U. Wis., Eau Claire, 1974; JD cum laude, U. Wis., Madison, 1977. Bar: Wis. 1977, U.S. Dist. Ct. (we. dist.) Wis. 1977, U.S. Supreme Ct. 1982. Instr. law U. Wis., Madison, 1976-77; assoc. Garvey, Anderson, Kelly & Ryberg, S.C., Eau Claire, 1977-81; legis dir., counsel Congressman Steve Gunderson, Washington, 1981-85, chief of staff, counsel, 1985-89; staff coord. 92 Group, Washington, 1987-89; instr. Chippewa Valley Tech. Coll., 1989-93, 97—, paralegal program dir., 1992-93, 97-01, pvt. practice, 1990-93, 97—, chair dept. behavioral sci. & civic effectiveness, 2003—; counsel, minority cons. House Subcommittee on Livestock, Washington, Wis., 1993-95; counsel Congressman Steve Gunderson, Washington, 1993-97; dep. minority counsel House Com. on Agr., Washington, 1993-95, dep. chief counsel, 1995-97; commr. W. Ctrl. Wis. Regional Planning Commn., Eau Claire, 1998—; vis. prof. U. of Wis. - Eau Claire, Wis., 2002—03. Pol. analyst, commentator WEAU-TV, Eau Claire, Wis., 1998—; mem. Bush-Cheney Transition Adv. Com., 2001; vis. prof. U. Wis., Eau Claire, 2002-03. Mem.: FBA, ABA, Wis. Bar Assn., U. Wis. Alumni Assn. (outstanding sr. arts & scis. 1974, Disting. Achievement award 2001), The Presto Found. (v.p. 1992—93, bd. dirs. 1992—93, 2000—, v.p. 2000—), Wis. Assn. for Career and Tech. Edn. (legis. com. chair 2000—01, bd. dirs. 2000—, chmn. strategic planning com. 2001—02, pres. 2002—03), Phi Gamma Delta (Durrance award 1978), Phi Delta Phi. Republican. Lutheran. Address: 2113 Meadow Ln Eau Claire WI 54701-7965

FRANK, JOSEPH ELIHU, lawyer; b. Burlington, Vt., Jan. 28, 1934; s. Max and Sara Ruth (Bramson) F.; m. Catherine Hartman Layne, Aug. 28, 1971; children: Sara Rebecca, Cheryl Elizabeth. AB, Harvard U., 1956, JD, 1959. Bar: Vt. 1960, U.S. Dist. Ct. Vt. 1960, U.S. Ct. Appeals (2d cir.) 1961. U.S. Supreme Ct. 1965. Law clk. to judge U.S. Dist. Ct. Vt., 1960; asst. U.S. atty. Dist. of Vt., 1961; sole practice Burlington, 1961-68; mem. Paul, Frank & Collins P.C., Burlington, 1968-96, of counsel, 1996—. Spl. counsel to Vt. Hwy. Bd., 1962-75, to Pub. Service Bd., 1965-69; chmn. adv. com. civil rules Vt. Supreme Ct., 1983-89. Alderman, City of Burlington, 1971-73; trustee Med. Ctr. Hosp. of Vt., Burlington, 1977-86. Mem. ABA, Vt. Bar Assn. (pres. 1983-84), Chittenden County Bar Assn., Am. Judicature Soc. Alternative dispute resolution, General civil litigation, Condemnation (eminent domain). Home: 8 Bay Crest Dr South Burlington VT 05403-7713 Office: Paul Frank & Collins PC 1 Church St Burlington VT 05402-1307 E-mail: w1sov@earthlink.net.

FRANK, JULIE ANN, lawyer; b. Omaha, Aug. 5, 1953; d. Morton Stanley Frank and Elaine Edith (Meyerson) Potts; m. Howard Nathan Kaplan, Oct. 26, 1985; 1 child, Martin Kaplan. BA in Psychology, U. Tex., 1974; JD, Creighton U., 1979. Bar: Nebr. 1979, Tex. 1980. Clk. to Justice Nebr. Supreme Ct., Lincoln, 1979-80; assoc. Qualley, Larson & Jones, Omaha, 1980-81; sole practice Omaha, 1981-83; pntr. Pollak, Frank & Hicks, Omaha, 1983-90; ptnr. Frank & Gryva, Omaha, 1990—. Instr. Met. Community Coll., Omaha, 1982-84, Buena Vista Coll., Omaha, 1982-84, U. Nebr., 1983. Bd. dirs. Nebr. Civil Liberties Union, 1981-85, Omaha Jewish Family Svcs., 1989-97; sec. bd. Jewish Family Svcs., 1991-92, v.p., 1992-93, pres., 1993-96; adminstrv. coord. Douglas County Dems., 1982; del. Douglas County Conv., 1984, 86; mem. cen. com. Nebr. Dem. Com., 1984-86; mem. Nat. Coun. Jewish Women, Omaha; mem. community rels. com. Anti-defamation League, 1987-90, bd. dirs., 1992-94; chmn. Nebr. Women's Polit. Caucus; bd. dirs. Assn. of Jewish Family and Children's Agencies, 1996-2002—. Mem. ABA, Nebr. State Bar Assn. (co-chairperson Women and Law sect. 1987-88, bd. dirs. 1987-89), Omaha Bar Assn. (lawyers referral com., particpant in law day "Meet a Lawyer" program, 1986-88, 97). Bankruptcy, Criminal, Juvenile. Home: 661 N 57th St Omaha NE 68132-2031 Office: Frank & Gryva 1823 Harney St Ste 201 Omaha NE 68102-1913 E-mail: jfrank1@cox.net.

FRANK, LLOYD, lawyer, retired chemical company executive; b. N.Y.C., Aug. 9, 1925; s. Herman and Selma (Lowenstein) F.; m. Beatrice Silverstein, Dec. 26, 1954; children: Margaret Lois, Frederick. BA, Oberlin Coll., 1947; JD, Cornell U., 1950. Bar: N.Y. 1950, U.S. Supreme Ct. 1973. Lawyer, N.Y.C., 1950—64; sec., dir. Grow Group, Inc., N.Y.C., 1964-95; sr. ptnr., exec. com., chmn. corp. dept. Parker Chapin LLP, N.Y.C., 1985-99; sr. ptnr. Jenkens Gilchrist Parker Chapin, LLP, N.Y.C., 2000—. Bd. dirs. Volt Info. Scis. Inc., (NYSE) N.Y.C., Madison Industries, Inc., N.Y.C., Dryclean, USA, Inc., Miami, Fla., AMEX, Pub. Art Fund, Inc., N.Y.C., Park Electrochem. Corp., (NYSE) Lake Success, N.Y., Internat. Longevity Ctr. U.S.A. Ltd., N.Y.C., Kulite Semicondr., Inc., Leonia, N.J.; sec. Esquire Radio & Electronics, Inc., Bklyn.; lectr. Am. Mgmt. Assn., 1967-77, Probe Internat., Inc., 1975-77, Corp. Seminars, Inc., 1968-71. Mem. ABA (com. negotiated acquisitions), Assn. Bar City of N.Y. (com. on internat. environ. law com. on product liability, com. on lawyers in transition, com. on securities law), N.Y. County Lawyers Assn. (com. on corp. law depts.), Corporate, general, Public international, Securities. Home: 25 Central Park W Apt 17Q New York NY 10023-7211 Office: Jenkens & Gilchrist Parker Chapin LLP Chrysler Bldg 405 Lexington Ave New York NY 10174-0002 E-mail: lfrank@jenkens.com.

FRANK, RICHARD ASHER, lawyer, health products executive; b. Omaha, Nov. 4, 1936; s. Alexander David and Sarah R. (Katz) F.; m. Susan Marie Kling; children: Brian, Hilary, Alexander, Nicholas. AB, Harvard U., 1958, JD, 1962. Bar: D.C. 1962, U.S. Supreme Ct. Asst. legal advisor U.S. State Dept., Washington, 1962-69; dir. Ctr. Law and Social Policy, Washington, 1970-77; adminstr. NOAA, Washington, 1977-81; ptnr. Wald, Harkrader, Ross, Washington, 1981-87; pres. Population Svcs. Internat., Washington, 1987—. Adj. prof. Georgetown Law Sch., 1988—. Editor: The Constitution and the Conduct of Foreign Policy, 1976; contbr. articles to profl. jours. 1st lt. U.S. Army, 1959—66. Mem.: Coun. Fgn. Rels. Avocations: sailing, tennis. Home: 3405 Lowell St NW Washington DC 20016-5024 Office: Population Svcs Internat 1120 19th St NW Washington DC 20036-3605 E-mail: rfrank@psiwash.org.

FRANK, SAMUEL MERRITT, law educator; b. Cleveland, Ohio, Oct. 25, 1943; s. Merritt, Stanlae Azel and Merritt Helen Kettring. BA, Hiram Coll., 1966; JD, Case Western Res. U., 1968. Law clk. Hon. Don J. Young, US Dist. Ct., Toledo, 1968—70; staff atty. Advocates Basic Legal Equality, 1970—73; gen. counsel Prisoners Legal Svc. Project, Chgo., 1973—77; assoc. prof. criminal justice U. Ill., 1974—77; prof. law U. Toledo, Coll. Law, Toledo, 1977—. Chair, faculty governing com. Legal Inst. of Gt. Lakes, Toledo, 1998—. Ecology dir. Pioneer Scout Reservation, Erie Shores Coun., Boy Scouts of Am., Toledo, 1976—; bd. dirs. Black Swamp Bird Obs., Oak Harbor. Mem.: ABA (coun. sect. urban state and local govt. 1986—93, 2001—), Toledo Astron. Assn. (bd. dirs.). Avocations: hiking, reading, model railroading. Office: University of Toledo College of Law Toledo OH 43606 Office Fax: 419-530-7878. E-mail: fmerrit@utnet.utoledo.edu.

FRANKE, HARRY FREDERICK, lawyer; b. Milw., Oct. 13, 1922; s. Harry Frederick and Harriet Constance F.; m. Mary Louise Winkelman; children: Jay, John, Mary Ann, Mark. JD, U. Wis., 1949. Mem. Wis. State Legis., 1950-52, 52-56; ptnr. Cook & Franke. Served to capt. U.S. Army, 1943-46, lt. col. res. ret. Office: Cook & Franke 660 E Mason St Ste 401 Milwaukee WI 53202-3877

FRANKE, LINDA FREDERICK, lawyer; b. Mankato, Minn., Aug. 28, 1947; d. Cletus and Valeria (Haefner) Frederick; m. Willis L. Franke, Dec. 17, 1966; children: Paul W., Gregory J. BA, U. Mo., 1981, JD, 1984. Bar: Mo. 1985, U.S. Dist. Ct. (we. dist.) Mo. 1985. Rsch. assoc. Koenigsdorf, Kusnetzky and Wyrsch, Kansas City, Mo., 1984-85; asst. gen. counsel dept. revenue State of Mo., Independence, 1985-86; claims rep. workers' compensation Cigna Ins. Co., Overland Park, Kans., 1986-87; sr. claims rep. workers' compensation Gulf Ins. Co., Kansas City, Mo., 1987-88; worker's compensation atty. Fireman's Fund Ins. Co., Kansas City, 1988—2002; of counsel Fox Stretz & Quinn, Kansas City, Fox, Stretz & Quinn, Kansas City, 2002—. Mem. Mo. Worker's Compensation Com. U. Mo. scholar, 1980, 81. Mem. Platte County Bar Assn., Kansas City Met. Bar Assn. (adv. bd. workers' compensation com.). Workers' compensation. Home: 8117 NW Eastside Dr Weatherby Lake MO 64152-1666 Office: Fox Stretz & Quinn 2623 Holmes Kansas City MO 64108

FRANKE, PATRICK JOSEPH, lawyer; b. Dallas, July 7, 1968; s. Carl William and Dolores Ann Franke; m. Julie Lynn Pavelich, Aug. 14, 1993; children: Kathryn, Andrew, Matthew. BS in Polit. Sci., Santa Clara (Calif.) U., 1990; JD, U. Tex., 1993. Bar: Wash. 1993, U.S. Dist. Ct. (we. dist.) Wash. 1993. Atty. Smith & Leary P.L.L.C., Seattle, 1993-2000, Leary Franke Droppert P.L.L.C., Seattle, 2000—. Mem. Fed. Bar Assn. (ethics and practice com. 1997—), King County Bar Assn. (chmn. cmty. involvement com. 1997—), Phi Beta Kappa. Commercial, contracts (including sales of goods; commercial financing), Corporate, general, Mergers and acquisitions. Office: Leary Franke Droppert 1500 Forrth Ave Ste 600 Seattle WA 98101 E-mail: pfranke@lfdlaw.com.

FRANKEL, CRAIG M. lawyer; b. Atlanta, Aug. 16, 1961; s. Theodore Golden and Sidelle Simmons Frankel; m. Jana A. Eplan, Mar. 2, 1991; children: Gil Lev Eplan-Frankel, Tamir Eplan-Frankel, Meital Eplan-Frankel. BA, U. N.C., 1983. Bar: Ga. 1986, Ga. Supreme Ct. 1986, Ga. Ct. Appeals 1986, U.S. Dist. Ct. (no. dist.) Ga. 1987, U.S. Ct. Appeals (11th cir.) 1987. Jud. clk. John C. Godbold, Chief Judge, U.S. Ct. Appeals (11th cir.), Montgomery, Ala., 1986—87; assoc. Long, Aldridge & Norman, Atlanta, 1987—93; lawyer Meadows, Ichter & Trigg, Atlanta, 1993—99, Frankel & Assocs., LLC, Atlanta, 1999—. Exec. editor Ga. Law Rev., Athens, 1985—86. Mem. Am. Jewish Com., Atlanta, 1990—2003; bd. of trustees Hillside Hosp., Atlanta, 1998—2003; violinist Atlanta Cmty. Symphony Orch., Atlanta, 1987—2003, Montgomery Symphony Orch., Montgomery, Ala., 1986—87; founding vol. Hands On Atlanta, Atlanta, 1988—2003; mem. Morningside-Lenox Neighborhood Assn., Atlanta, 1990—2003; bd. of trustees; bd. of edn.; v.p. Temple Sinai, Atlanta, 1988—2001. Recipient Order of the Grail Honor Soc., U. of NC, 1983; Bryant T. Castellow scholar, U. Ga. Sch. Law, 1983—86. Mem.: ATLA, ABA, Atlanta Bar Assn., Ga. Bar Assn., Phi Beta Kappa. Avocation: violin. State civil litigation, Federal civil litigation, Appellate. Office: Frankel & Assocs LLC Ste 2840 75 Fourteenth St Atlanta GA 30309 Office Fax: 404-888-3731.

FRANKEL, JAMES BURTON, lawyer; b. Chgo., Feb. 25, 1924; s. Louis and Thelma (Cohn) F.; m. Louise Untermyer, Jan. 22, 1956; children: Nina, Sara, Simon. Student, U. Chgo., 1940-42; BS, U.S. Naval Acad., 1945; LLB, Yale U., 1952; MPA, Harvard U., 1990. Bar: Calif. 1953. Mem. Steinhart, Goldberg, Feigenbaum & Ladar, San Francisco, 1954-72; of counsel Cooper, White & Cooper, San Francisco, 1972-97. Sr. fellow, lectr. in law Yale U., 1971-72; lectr. Stanford U. Law Sch., 1973-75; vis. prof. U. Calif. Law Sch., 1975-76, lectr. 1992—; lectr. U. San Francisco Law Sch., 1994—; adj. asst. prof. Hastings Coll. Law, 1996—. Pres. Coun. Civic Unity of San Francisco Bay Area, 1964-66; chmn. San Francisco Citizens Charter Revision Com., 1968-70; mem. San Francisco Pub. Schs. Commn., 1975-76; trustee Natural Resources Def. Coun., 1972-77, 79-92, staff atty., 1977-79, hon. trustee, 1992—; chmn. San Francisco Citizens Energy Policy Adv. Com., 1981-82. Mem. ABA, Calif. Bar Assn.

FRANKEL, SANDOR, lawyer, author; b. N.Y.C., Nov. 16, 1943; s. David and Bessie (Edelson) F. BA, N.Y. U., 1964; LLB, Harvard U., 1967. Bar: N.Y. 1967, D.C. 1968, U.S. Supreme Ct. 1976. Staff mem. White House Task Force on Crime, 1967; counsel Nat. Commn. Reform Fed. Criminal Laws, 1968; asst. U.S. atty. for D.C., 1968-71; pvt. practice, 1971—. Lectr. N.Y. U. Inst. on Fed. Taxation, 1976, 77. Author: Beyond a Reasonable Doubt, 1972 (Edgar Allan Poe award), The Aleph Solution, 1978, How to Defend Yourself Against the IRS, 1985, 3d. edit. 1987; contbr. articles to profl. publs. Mem. Phi Beta Kappa. General civil litigation, State civil litigation, Criminal. Office: Frankel & Abrams 230 Park Ave New York NY 10169-0005

FRANKEL, WILLIAM HARRY, lawyer; b. Manhattan, N.Y., Dec. 11, 1955; s. George O. and Louise (Petchesky) Frankel; m. Zehava Hass, July 31, 1983. BSME cum laude, Tulane U., 1977, JD cum laude, 1980. Bar: Ill. 1980. Ptnr. Neuman, Williams, Anderson & Olson, Chgo., 1980-91; shareholder Brinks Hofer Gilson & Lione, Chgo., 1991—. Adj. prof. patent law DePaul U. Coll. Law, 1993-95. Author: A Student's Manual for Writing Formal Technical Reports, 1977; co-author: Designing an Effective Intellectual Property Compliance Program, 1993—; contbr. to profl. publs. Vol. Lawyers for Creative Arts, Chgo., 1981—, treas., 2000—03, v.p., 2003—. Mem. ABA, Intellectual Property Law Assn. Chgo. (sec. 2000-03), Chgo. Bar Assn., Am. Intellectual Property Law Assn., Decalogue Soc. Lawyers. Democrat. Jewish. Avocations: music, water sports, cycling, hiking. Office: Brinks Hofer Gilson & Lione NBC Tower 455 N Cityfront Plaza Dr Chicago IL 60611-5503

FRANKENHEIM, SAMUEL, retired lawyer; b. N.Y.C., Dec. 20, 1932; s. Samuel and Mary Emma (Ward) F.; m. Nina Barbara Mennerich, Sept. 2, 1960; children: Robert Mennerich, John Frederick. BA, Cornell U., 1954, LLB, 1959. Bar: N.Y. 1959, Mass. 1976. Law clk. N.Y. Ct. Appeals, 1959-61; assoc. Shearman & Sterling, attys., N.Y.C., 1961-68, ptnr., 1968-69; sr. v.p., dir. Damon Corp., Needham Heights, Mass., 1969-78; sr. v.p., gen. counsel mem. Office of Chmn. Gen. Cinema Corp., Chestnut Hill, Mass., 1979-92; counsel Ropes & Gray, Boston, 1992-2000. Mem. corp. Ptnrs. Healthcare Sys., Inc., 1999—. Bd. govs. Newell Health Care Sys., 1983—93; trustee Wang Ctr. for Performing Arts, Boston, 1987—97, Huntington Theatre Co., Boston, 1993—2002, overseer, 2002—; chmn. bd. Internat. Alliance of First Night Celebrations, 1994—99, treas., 1999—2000; overseer Newton-Wellesley Hosp., Newton, Mass., 1973—85, pres., 1980—82; overseer Wang Ctr. for Performing Arts, Boston, 1985—87; assoc. First Night, Inc., 1988, chmn. bd., 1991—93. 1st lt. USAF, 1955—57. Mem. ABA. Corporate, general. Home: 115 Shornecliffe Rd Newton MA 02458-2420

FRANKL, KENNETH RICHARD, retired lawyer; b. N.Y.C., May 23, 1924; s. Hugo Joseph and Sydney (Miller) F.; m. Jeanne Ritchie Silver, Aug. 6, 1972; 1 child, Kathryn; 1 son by previous marriage, Keith E. AB cum laude, Harvard U., 1945, LLB, 1950. Bar: N.Y. 1951, U.S. Ct. Appeals (2d cir.) 1956. Asst. dist. atty. N.Y. County, 1951-56; assoc. firm Liebman Eulau & Robinson, N.Y.C., 1959-60; asst. gen. atty. CBS, 1960-69; gen. counsel, asst. sec. Bishop Industries, Inc., 1969-70; v.p., gen. counsel, sec. RKO Gen., Inc. and Subs., 1970-84, cons.; ptnr. Law Offices of Ronald Kahn, N.Y.C., 1986; v.p. Charles H. Greenthal Comml. Co., N.Y.C., 1989-91. Dir. staff Spl. Com. to Study Defender Sys. of N.Y.C. Assn. of the Bar, 1957-58. Co-author: (report) Equal Justice for the Accused, 1959. Mem. Amagansett Citizen Adv. Com., East Hampton Jewish Ctr. Served Signal Corps U.S. Army, 1943—46, PTO. Decorated Okinawa Battle Star and Army Unit Commendation medal. Mem.: Harvard Club N.Y. Home: PO Box 955 67 Old Montauk Hwy Amagansett NY 11930

FRANKLAND, MATTHEW, lawyer; b. Margate, Eng., Jan. 11, 1964; s. Gordon Peter and Hazel Frankland. LLB, U. Wales, Aberystwyth, 1986. Bar: Wales 1988. Solicitor Garstangs, London, 1982—94, Simpson Curtis, London, Leeds, England, 1994—95; ptnr. Dechert, London, 1995—2003, Byrne & Ptnrs., 2003—. Advisor Advice Ctr. Pro Bono, Southwark, London, England, 2000—. Mem.: Serious Fraud Assn., London Criminal Cts. Solicitors' Assn., Criminal Appeal Lawyers Assn., Assn. Regulatory and Disciplinary Lawyers, Assn. Bus. Recovery Profls., Criminal Law Solicitors' Assn. Avocations: art, architecture, travel. Criminal, Administrative and regulatory. Home: 45 Arnold Estate Druid St London SE1 2DU England Office: Byrne & Ptnrs 1 Sekforde St London EC1R UBE England

FRANKLIN, BLAKE TIMOTHY, lawyer; b. San Mateo, Calif., Sept. 28, 1942; s. Harvey James and Marie Agnes (Leane) F. AB, Dartmouth Coll., 1963; JD, Harvard U., 1966. Bar: Calif. 1966, D.C. 1969, U.S. Supreme Ct. 1970, N.Y. 1976. AID contractor Peace Corps; vis. prof. comml. law U. Costa Rica, San Jose, 1966-68; assoc. Coudert Bros., Washington, 1969-74, ptnr. N.Y.C., 1975-83, Gibson Dunn & Crutcher, N.Y.C., 1983—. Bd. dirs. Union Theol. Sem., N.Y., Nat. Law Ctr. for Inter-Am. Free Trade, Tucson, Bolivian-Am. C. of C. Chancellor of vestry St. Michael's Ch., N.Y.C., 1987-93; trustee Aids Svc. Found. of Orange County, Calif., 1994-97; St. Hilda's and St. Hugh's Sch., N.Y.C., 1988-92; mem. bd. gov.'s USO, 1987-90. Mem. ABA, Inter-Am. Bar Assn., Am. Soc. Internat. Law, Assn. of Bar of City of N.Y. Episcopalian. Banking, Corporate, general, Private international. Office: Gibson Dunn & Crutcher 200 Park Ave Fl 47 New York NY 10166-0193

FRANKLIN, BRUCE WALTER, lawyer; b. Ellendale, N.D., Feb. 26, 1936; s. Wallace Henry and Frances (Webb) F.; m. Kristy Ann Jones, Feb. 7, 1944; children: Kevin, Monica, Taylor. Student, U. Mich., 1954-56; LLB, Detroit Coll. Law, 1962. Bar: Mich. 1963. Sole practice, Troy, Mich., 1962-90; mng. ptnr. Franklin, Bigler, Berry & Johnston, P.C., Troy, Mich., 1991-98, Franklin & Davis, Troy, 1998—. Bd. dirs. First Union-Newnan Bank; pres., CEO Landward III Devel. Corp. (Arbor Springs Plantation). Past chmn. Mich. Young Reps., United Meth. Retirement Cmtys.; bd. dirs. Peachtree Hosp., Wesley Woods. Served with U.S. Army. State civil litigation, Personal injury (including property damage), Product liability. Office: Landward III 250 Arbor Springs Plantation Dr Newnan GA 30265 E-mail: BFranklin@numail.org.

FRANKLIN, CHARLES SCOTHERN, lawyer; b. Knoxville, Tenn., Dec. 12, 1937; s. Samuel Leroy and Mildred (Gibson) F.; m. Lynn Kerr; children: Jill Parvin, Melissa Ann, Samuel Arthur. BS, U. Tenn., 1958, MS, 1960; LL.B., Vanderbilt U., 1966. Bar: Calif. 1967, Nev. 1971. Instr. econs. U. Tenn., Knoxville, 1960-61; Ford Found. fellow in econs. U. Calif.,

Berkeley, 1962; assoc. firm Kent Brookes & Anderson, San Francisco, 1966-70; gen. counsel, sec. Harrah's, Reno, 1970—79; pvt. practice Reno, 1980—85, Sacramento, 1985-94. Mem. Nev. State Bar, Calif. State Bar. Home: 2891 Greystone Cove N Atlanta GA 30341-5858

FRANKLIN, CHRISTINE CARROLL, lawyer; b. Glens Falls, N.Y., July 4, 1949; BA cum laude, Newton Coll., 1971; MA, U. Va., 1974; JD, UCLA, 1979. Bar: Calif. 1980, Ill. 1994, D.C. 1995, Colo. 1995, U.S. Dist. Ct. (ctrl. dist.) Calif. 1980, U.S. Dist. Ct. (so. dist.) Calif. 1987, U.S. Dist. Ct. (no. dist.) Calif. 1988, U.S. Dist. Ct. (no. dist.) Ill. 1995. Dep. atty. gen. Office of Calif. Atty. Gen., L.A., 1980-86; assoc. Weissburg & Aronson, L.A., 1987-89, Thelen, Marrin, Johnson & Bridges, L.A., 1989-94, ptnr., 1995-98; pvt. practice Chgo., 1998-2000; counsel Carr Futures Inc., Chgo., 2000—. Mem. ABA (adminstrv. law and regulatory practice sect. coun. 1996-99), Chgo. Bar Assn. Banking, General civil litigation, Insurance. Office: Carr Futures Inc Ste 1100 10 S Wacker Dr Chicago IL 60606 Fax: (312) 441-4359. E-mail: cfranklin@carrfutures.com.

FRANKLIN, FREDERICK RUSSELL, retired legal association executive; b. Mar. 20, 1929; s. Ernest James and Frances (Price) F.; m. Barbara Ann Donovan, Jan. 26, 1952; children: Katherine Elizabeth, Frederick Russell. AB, Ind. U., 1951, JD with high distinction, 1956. Bar: Ind. 1956. Trial atty. criminal div. and ct. of claims sect. civil div. U.S. Dept. Justice, Washington, 1956-60; gen. counsel Ind. State Bar Assn., Indpls., 1960-67; dir. continuing legal edn. for Ind., adj. prof. law Ind. U., Indpls., 1965-68; staff dir. profl. standards ABA, Chgo., 1968-70, legal edn. and admissions to the bar, 1972-92, sr. lawyers divsn., 1985-93; ret., 1993. Exec. v.p. Nat. Attys. Title Assurance Fund, Inc., Indpls., 1970-72. Trustee Olympia Fields (Ill.) United Meth. Ch., 1980-84; treas. bd. dirs. Olympia Fields Pub. Libr., 1984-91; mem. Olympia Fields Pub. Safety Bd., 1983-92. Capt. USAF, 1951-53. Named to Honorable Order Ky. Cols., 1967, 74, Adm. Tex. Navy, 1967, Adm. Nebr. Navy, 1972, 74, Sagamore of Wabash, 1972. Fellow Ind. Bar Found. (life); mem. ABA (coun. sr. lawyers divsn. 1993—, mem. com. bar admissions 1993-97, 99—, vice chair affiliate outreach com. divsn. sr. lawyers 1995—, vice-chmn. membership com. sr. lawyers divsn. 1995—, vice-chmn. pub. com. 1995—, vice-historian 1995-96, historian 1996—, long range planning com. 1995-2002, vice-chmn. social security com. 1998-2002, vice-chmn. real estate com. 1999-2002), Ind. State Bar Assn. (sec.-treas. sr. lawyers sect. 1998-2002, coun. sr. lawyers sect. 1996-2002, editor sr. lawyers sect. newsletter 1996-98, coun. profl. legal edn. sect. 2000-2002, vice-chmn. articles and bylaws com. 1994—, legal edn. and bar admissions com. 1990-2002, chmn. articles and bylaws com. 1999-2002, ho. of dels. 1999-2002, coun., profl. edn. sect.), Fed. Bar Assn. (officer, found. bd. dirs. 1974—, historian 1979—, life fellow 1976—, treas. sr. lawyers divsn. 1993-95, sec. 1995-97, dep. chmn. 1997-98, chmn. 1998-99, nat. coun. 1961-93, 97-2002, nat. v.p 1967-69, chpt. pres. 1965-66, chmn. admission to practice and recert. com. 1980-82, bd. dirs. Chgo. chpt. 1984-93), Nat. Orgn. Bar Counsel (pres. 1967), Ind. U. Air Force ROTC Alumni Assn. (pres. 1997-98), Lakeview Hills Homeowners Assn. (pres. 1997-99), Kiwanis, Elks, Order of Coif, Am. Legion (life), Phi Delta Phi. Home: 712 Romans Ct Bloomington IN 47401-8676

FRANKLIN, JAMES BURKE, lawyer; b. Statesboro, Ga., Mar. 11, 1938; s. Sam J. and Eva Claire (Burke) F.; m. Fay Foy Smith, Mar. 20, 1976; children— Julie Foy, Rebecca Claire. B.S., Ga. Inst. Tech.; J.D., U. Ga. Bar: Ga. U.S. Dist. Ct. (so. dist.) Ga. 1966. Assoc., Allen Edenfield, Brown & Franklin and predecessor Allen & Edenfield, 1966-69, ptnr., 1969-74; ptnr. Franklin, Taulbee, Rushing, Snipes, & Marsh P.C. and predecessor firms, Statesboro, Ga., 1974— ; magistrate U.S. Dist. Ct. (so. dist.) Ga., 1979-81. Chmn. Devel. Authority Bulloch County; pres. Bulloch County (Ga.) C. of C.; candidate for Republican nomination for Congress, 1st Dist. Ga., 1982. Served to 1st lt. U.S. Army, 1964-66. Mem. State Bar Ga. (bd. govs., pres. 2001-02), Ga. Trial Lawyers Assn. (v.p. 1986-1997). Methodist. Club: Rotary (pres.) (Statesboro). State civil litigation, General practice, Personal injury (including property damage). Office: 12 Siebald St PO Box 327 Statesboro GA 30458

FRANKLIN, JEANNE F. lawyer; b. N.Y.C., July 22, 1946; BA cum laude, Vassar Coll., 1968; JD, U. Va., 1971. Bar: Mich. 1971, U.S. Dist. Ct. Mich. (ea. dist.) 1975, U.S. Ct. Appeals (10th cir.) 1975, N.Mex. 1977, D.C. 1977, Va. 1981, U.S. Dist. Ct. Va. (ea. dist.) 1984. Sole practice, Alexandria, Va. Fellow: Am. Bar Found.; mem.: D.C. Bar (mem. health law sect.), Va. State Bar (mem. health law sect.), Am. Health Lawyers Assn., Alexandria Bar Assn., Va. Bar Assn. (mem. exec. com. 1997—, pres. 2000—01), ABA. Health, Labor (including EEOC, Fair Labor Standards Act, labor-management relations, NLRB, OSHA). Office: 604 Cameron St Alexandria VA 22314

FRANKLIN, JONATHAN ADLAI, law librarian; AM, Stanford U., JD, 1993; MLS, U. Wash., 1994. Sr. assoc. law libr. U. Mich. Law Libr., Ann Arbor, 1994—99; assoc. law libr. Gallagher Law Libr. - U.Wash., Seattle, 1999—2002. Office: Gallagher Law Library - U Wash 1100 NE Campus Pky Seattle WA 98105-6617 Office Fax: 206-685-2165. E-mail: jafrank@u.washington.edu.

FRANKLIN, SCOTT BRADLEY, accountant, lawyer; b. Milw., 1970; BBA in Acctg., U. Wis., 1992; JD, Marquette U., 1995. Bar: Wis. 1995, U.S. Dist. (ea. dist.) Wis. 1995, U.S. Tax Ct. Bar 1995; CPA, Wis. Intern Office U.S. Atty., Milw., 1993-94, Milwaukee County Circuit Ct., Milw., 1994; intern Office Dist. Counsel, IRS, Milw., 1994; tax mgr. Kohler and Franklin, CPA's, Milw., 1995—. Instr. Becker Conviser C.P.A. Rev. Course, Milw., 1996—; lectr. in field; media commentator; adj. prof. :Lakeland Coll. Online, 2001, 2002. Contbr. articles to profl. jours. Fellow Wis. Inst. CPA's (fed. taxation com. 1997—); mem. AICPA. Office: Kohler and Franklin CPA's 250 W Coventry Ct Ste 211 Milwaukee WI 53217-3966 E-mail: sbfcpa@execpc.com.

FRANKS, HERBERT HOOVER, lawyer; b. Joliet, Ill., Jan. 25, 1934; s. Carol and Lottie (Dermer) F.; m. Eileen Pepper, June 22, 1957; children: David, Jack, Eli. BS, Roosevelt U., 1954; postgrad., Am. U., 1960. Bar: Ill. 1961, U.S. Dist. Ct. (no. dist.) Ill. 1961, U.S. Supreme Ct. 1967. Ptnr. Franks, Gerkin & McKenna, 1985—. Chmn. Wonder Lake State Bank, Ill., 1979—, First Nat. Bank, Marengo, Ill., 1976-84, mem. exec. com., 1976—; vice-chmn. hotel mgmt. orgn. Bricton Group, Park Ridge, Ill., 1992-98. Bus. editor Am. U. Law Rev., 1959, 60. State pres. Young Dems. of Ill., 1970-72; trustee Hebrew Theol. Coll., Skokie, Ill., 1974—; trustee, sec. Forest Inst. Profl. Psychology, Springfield, Mo., 1979-91; chmn. Forest Hosp., Des Plaines, 1980-88. With U.S. Army, 1956-58. Mem.: Ill. Trial Lawyers (mng. bd. 1975—92, treas. 1985—87), Ill. State Bar Assn. (state pres. 2000—01), Shriners, Masons (33 deg.), Sigma Nu Phi (pres. 1980—82). Banking, Workers' compensation. Home: 19324 E Grant Hwy Marengo IL 60152-9438 Office: Franks Gerkin & McKenna 19333 E Grant Hwy Marengo IL 60152-8234 E-mail: franklaw@mc.net.

FRANKS, HERSCHEL PICKENS, judge; b. Savannah, Tenn., May 28, 1930; s. Herschel R. and Vada (Pickens) F.; m. Judy Black; 1 child, Ramona. Student U. Tenn.-Martin, U. Md.; JD, U. Tenn.-Knoxville; grad. Nat. Jud. Coll. of U. Nev. Bar: Tenn. 1959, U.S. Supreme Ct. 1968. Claims atty. U.S. Fidelity & Guaranty Co., Knoxville, 1958; ptnr. Harris, Moon, Meacham & Franks, Chattanooga, 1959-70; chancellor 3d Chancery div. of Hamilton County, 1970-78; judge Tenn. Ct. Appeals, Chattanooga, 1978—; spl. justice Tenn. Supreme Ct., 1979, 86, 87; presiding judge Hamilton County Trial Cts., 1977-78; spl. judge Tenn. Ct. of Criminal Appeals, 1990-92; mem. commn. to study appellate cts., 1990-92. Served with USNG, 1949-50, USAF, 1950-54. Mem. ABA (award of merit), Tenn. Bar Assn. (award of merit 1968-69), Tenn. Bar Found., Chattanooga Bar Found., Chattanooga Bar Assn. (pres. 1968-69, Founds. of Freedom award 1986), Am. Judicature Soc., Inst. Jud. Adminstrn., Optimists (pres. 1965-66), Community Service award 1971), Mountain City Club, City Farmers Club, Phi Alpha Delta. Mem. United Ch. of Christ. Address: 540 Mccallie Ave Ste 562 Chattanooga TN 37402-2039

FRANKS, STEPHEN F. retired judge; b. Biltmore, N.C., June 12, 1930; s. Thomas Hendricks and Margaret (Field) Franks; m. Mary Elizabeth Volbeda, Apr. 28, 1962; children: Stephen Bruce, Andrea Carol, Craig Thomas. BA, Duke U., 1952; LLB, JD, U. N.C., 1955. Bar: N.C. 1955, Calif. 1964, U.S. Supreme Ct. 1966. Dep. city atty. City Atty. Office, San Bernardino, Calif., 1964—66; counsel to mayor Mayor's Office, San Bernardino, 1966—69; legis. adv. County of San Bernardino, Sacramento, 1970—81; pvt. practice Hendersonville, NC, 1981—88; judge Dist. Ct. N.C., Hendersonville, 1988—2002; ret., 2002. Fed. aid coord. City of San Bernardino, 1966—69. Pres. County Bd. Edn., Sacramento, 1977—78, San Juan Unified Sch. Dist., Sacramento, 1979—80; mem. Child Fatality Prevention Team, Hendersonville, 2002; dir. Sacramento County Mental Health Assn. Comdr. JAG USN, 1955—60. Fellow: ATLA; mem.: N.C. Bar Assn., Univ. Club, Elks, Rotary (bd. dirs.). Republican. Episcopalian. Avocation: hiking. Office: 514 5th Ave W Hendersonville NC 28739 Office Fax: 828-697-6298. Business E-Mail: sffranks@mchsi.com.

FRANKS, WILLIAM J. judge; b. Uniontown, Pa., Jan. 6, 1932; m. Lena Franks; 1 child, Regina. BA in Pre-law, U. Pitts., 1953, LLB, 1956, JD, 1968; postgrad., U. Ga., 1958. Bar: Pa. 1956, U.S. Dist. Ct. (we. dist.) Pa. 1961. Pvt. practice, Uniontown, 1956-77; asst. dist. atty. Fayette County, Uniontown, 1960-69; judge Ct. Common Pleas Fayette County, Uniontown, 1978-96, presiding judge, 1996—2002, sr. judge, 2003—. Instr. bus. law U. Ga., 1958; instr. Am. Inst. Banking, 1960-65; solicitor Fayette County Contr., 1970; counsel Fayette County Child Welfare Svcs., Fayette County Cmty. Action Agy. With JAGC, U.S. Army, 1957-59. Mem. ABA, ATLA, Am. Judges Assn., Am. Arbitration Assn., Pa. Bar Assn., Fayette County Bar Assn., AMVETS, Cath. War Vets., Sons of Italy, KC (4th degree), Phi Beta Kappa, Phi Alpha Delta. Roman Catholic. Office: Fayette County Ct Common Pleas 61 E Main St Uniontown PA 15401-3514

FRANO, ANDREW JOSEPH, lawyer, civil engineer; b. Chgo., July 14, 1953; s. Joseph Neil Frano and Lorraine Rose (Jeczalik) Patchett-Keller; children: Alaina Marie, Jacqueline Elyse. BSCE, Bradley U., 1975, MSCE, 1976; JD, Chgo.-Kent Coll. Law, Ill. Inst. Tech., 1982. Registered profl. engr., Ill., Ind., Nebr., Wis., Minn., lic. gen. engring. constrn. contractor, Fla., Utah; bar: Ill. 1982, Nebr. 1986, U.S. Dist. Ct. (no. dist.) Ill. 1982, U.S. Dist. Ct. Nebr. 1992, Ariz. 1993, Tex. 1997. Soils lab. instr. and residence hall dir. Bradley U., Peoria, Ill., 1975-76; draftsman, engr. in tng. Harza Engring. Co., Chgo., 1973—76, civil engr., 1976—85; pvt. practice Chgo., 1982-85; pres. GEC Engring. Co. Inc., Chgo., 1985—86; corp. constrn. atty. Peter Kiewit Sons Inc., Omaha, 1986-92; asst. gen. counsel Harza Engring. Co., Chgo., 1992-95; owner The Law and Engring. Office of Andrew J. Frano, 1996—. Adj. asst. prof. dept. civil and architectural engring. Ill. Inst. Tech., Chgo., 1993—98; corp. atty., civil engr. T.J. Lambrecht Constrn., Inc., Joliet, Ill., 1996—98; prin. engr. Mirza-RSV Engring., Inc., Chgo. and Schaumburg, 1998—2000, Bloom Consultants, LLC, Schaumburg, 2001—. Chmn. San. Improvement Dist. 111, Sarpy County, Nebr., 1987-92; vol. atty. Chgo. Vol. Legal Svcs., 1983-85; bd. dirs., treas. Trails Assn. Inc., Roselle, Ill., 1983-86. Mem. ASCE, Tau Beta Pi, Chi Epsilon. Construction, General practice. Home: 2 N Dee Rd Unit 107 Park Ridge IL 60068-2871 Office: Bloom Consultants LLC 1870 N Roselle Rd Ste 101 Schaumburg IL 60195-3100 Fax: 847-843-3047. E-mail: afrano@bloomconsultants.com.

FRANTZ, ROBERT WESLEY, lawyer; b. Long Branch, N.J., Dec. 31, 1950; BS, Rutgers U., New Brunswick, N.J., 1973; JD, Rutgers U., Newark, 1977. Bar: N.J. 1977, U.S. Dist. Ct. N.J. 1977, U.S. Ct. Appeals (4th and 10th cirs.) 1978, U.S. Ct. Appeals (6th, 7th and 8th cirs.) 1979, D.C. 1980, U.S. Ct. Appeals (9th cir.) 1980, U.S. Dist. Ct. D.C. 1981. Trial atty. U.S. Dept. Justice, Washington, 1977-80; assoc. Hamel and Park, Washington, 1980-82; asst. gen. counsel Chem. Mfrs. Assn., Washington, 1982-85; counsel, environ. protection GE, Fairfield, Conn., 1985-88, Pittsfield, Mass., 1988-89; mgr. and counsel Environ. Remediation Program, Fairfield, Conn., 1989-95; mgr., sr. counsel Environ. Ops. Program, Fairfield, 1995-98; gen. mgr., counsel GE Engines Svcs., Cin., 1998—. Mem. sci. adv. bd. subcom. on risk reduction options U.S. EPA, 1996—. Contbr. articles to profl. publs.; editorial bd. Rutgers Law Rev., 1976. Mem. Newtown (Conn.) Charter Revision Commn., 1986-87, Glendale Planning Commn., 2000—. Mem. ABA (exec. editor Natural Resources and Environment 1986-93, coun. mem. sect. natural resources 1993-96). Avocations: sailing, golf, skiing, bicycling, woodworking. Federal civil litigation, General civil litigation, Environmental. Office: GE Engine Svcs 1 Neumann Way # Md-t164 Cincinnati OH 45215-1915

FRANTZ, THOMAS RICHARD, lawyer; b. Waynesboro, Pa., Sept. 10, 1947; s. John Richard and Janet (Donnelly) F.; m. Dianne Boffa June 22, 1985; children: Thomas Richard, Lindsey Amore, Elissa Noel. BA, Coll. William and Mary, 1970, JD, 1973, LLM, 1981. Bar: Va., U.S. Dist. Ct. (ea. dist.) Va. 1974, U.S. Ct. Appeals (4th cir.) 1974, U.S. Supreme Ct. 1978. Supr. tax dept. Peat Marwick, Mitchell & Co., 1973-74; officer, dir. Williams Mullen, Virginia Beach, Va., 1974—. Adj. prof. law Coll. William and Mary, 1981-82, trustee tax conf. 1984—; planning com. Old Dominion U. Tax Conf., 1977-81, chmn., 1981. Contbr. articles to profl. jours. King Neptune XXIII, Virginia Beach Neptune Festival, 1996; mem. exec. com. Va. Marine Sci. Mus., 1980—, pres., 2000-02, chmn., 2002--; bd. dirs. Cape Henry Collegiate Sch., 1986-98, chmn., 1991-92; bd. dirs. Virginia Beach Found., 1987—, chmn., 1995-97; bd. dirs. Virginia Beach Vision, 1993—, pres., 2002--; bd. dirs. Hampton Roads Partnership, 1997—. Capt. USAR, 1972-79. Mem. AICPA, ABA (tax, bus. and health law sects.), Am. Coll. Tax Counsel, Am. Coll. Trusts and Estates Counsel, Best Lawyers in Am. (tax, trusts and estates, corp. law), Am. Assn. Attys.-CPAs, Va. Bar Assn., Va. State Bar, Virginia Beach Bar Assn., Princess Anne Country Club, Cavalier Yacht and Country Club. Mem. Galilee Episcopal Ch. Corporate, general, Mergers and acquisitions. Address: 900 One Columbus Ctr Virginia Beach VA 23462 E-mail: frantzfam@aol.com., tfrantz@williamsmullen.com.

FRANZ, WILLIAM MANSUR, lawyer; b. Dayton, Ohio, Dec. 3, 1930; s. Robert and Muriel (Bisbee) F.; m. Jane Speers, May 26, 1962; children: David, Julie, Elizabeth, Susan. BA in Russian Studies, Syracuse U., 1953; LLB, Chgo.-Kent Coll. Law, 1959. Bar: Ill. 1959, U.S. Dist. Ct. (no. dist.) Ill. 1959. Assoc. Righeimer & Righeimer, Chgo., 1959, Corcoran & Corcoran, Evanston, Ill., 1959-61; ptnr. Franz & Franz, Crystal Lake, Ill., 1961-73, Franz, Naughton & Leahy, Crystal Lake, 1974-87, Franz & Kerrick, Crystal Lake, 1987-99, William Franz & Assocs., Crystal Lake, 1999—2003, Hinshaw & Culbertson, Crystal Lake, 2003—. Served to 1st lt. USAF, 1951-53. Mem. Ill. Bar Assn., McHenry County Bar Assn. Clubs: Crystal Lake Country. Lodges: Lions. Construction, General practice, Property, real (including real estate development, water). Home: 623 Leonard Pky Crystal Lake IL 60014-5209 Office: Hinshaw & Culbertson 453 Coventry Green Crystal Lake IL 60014-7504 E-mail: wfranz@hinshawlaw.com.

FRANZE, ANTHONY JAMES, pharmacist, lawyer; b. Albany, N.Y., Sept. 22, 1941; s. Vincent J. and Susie Franze; m. Kaoru Marie Nakamura, July 15, 1940; children: Vincent, Francis. BS in Pharmacy, St. John's Coll., 1963, JD, 1966. Bar: N.Y. 1966, U.S. Ct. Appeals (D.C. cir.) 1971, U.S. Patent Ct 1971; lic. pharmacist. Patent counsel Norwich (N.Y.) Eaton Pharms., 1970-84; assoc. city ct. judge City of Norwich, 1981-84; assoc. trademark and copyright coun. Bristol-Myers Squibb Co., N.Y.C., 1984-2000; ret., 2000. Mem. Emergency Svcs. Commn., Norwich, 1982-84; arbitrator N.Y.C. Small Claims Ct., N.Y.C., 1991—. Pres. PTO, Norwich, 1980-82; com. mem. Boy Scouts Troop 43, Princeton, N.Y., 1986-92. Col. U.S. Army, 1966-93 (active duty 1966-70). Mem. ABA, Am. Pharm. Assn., Am. Intellectual Property Assn., N.Y. State Bar Assn., Internat. Trademark Assn. Home: 387 Gallup Rd Princeton NJ 08540-7315

FRANZOI, JOSEPH FRANK, IV, lawyer; b. Neenah, Wis., May 31, 1955; s. Joseph F. and LaVerne L. (Reichow) F.; m. Patricia Ann Selingo, Aug. 2, 1980;children: Joseph F. V., Forest A. BSBA summa cum laude, Georgetown U., 1976; JD, U. Chgo., 1979. Bar: Wis. 1979, Fla. 1980. Pres. Franzoi and Franzoi SC, Menasha, Wis., 1980—. Bd. dirs. Faith Techs., Inc., AZCO, Inc.; corp. sec. Sch. Splty., Inc. Recipient Wall St. Jour. award, 1976, Dean's award, Georgetown U., 1976. Mem. ABA (taxation sect.), Wis. Bar Assn., Fla. Bar Assn., Milw. Athletic Club, Northshore Country Club (Appleton). Republican. Roman Catholic. Avocations: jogging, road rallying, hi-fi, office computerization. Corporate, general, Corporate taxation, Estate taxation. Home: 1650 Palisades Dr Appleton WI 54915-1029 Office: 514 Racine St Menasha WI 54952-2339

FRASIER, RALPH KENNEDY, lawyer, banker; b. Winston-Salem, N.C., Sept. 16, 1938; s. LeRoy Benjamin and Kathryn O. (Kennedy) F.; m. Jeannine Quick, Aug. 1981; children: Karen D. Frasier Alston, Gail S. Frasier Cox, Ralph Kennedy Jr., Keith Lowery, Marie Kennedy, Rochelle Doar. BS, N.C. Cen. U., Durham, 1963, JD, 1965. Bar: N.C. 1965, Ohio 1976. With Wachovia Bank and Trust Co., N.A., Winston-Salem, N.C., 1965-70, v.p., counsel, 1969-70; asst. counsel, v.p. parent co. Wachovia Corp., 1970-75; v.p., gen. counsel Huntington Nat. Bank, Columbus, Ohio, 1975-76, sr. v.p., 1976-83, sec., 1981-98, exec. v.p., 1983-98, cashier, 1983-98. V.p. Huntington Bancshares Inc., 1976-86, gen. counsel, 1976-98, sec., 1981-98; sec., dir. Huntington Mortgage Co., Huntington State Bank, Huntington Leasing Co., Huntington Bancshares Fin. Corp., Huntington Investment Mgmt. Co., Huntington Nat. Life Ins. Co., Huntington Co., 1976-88; v.p., asst. sec. Huntington Bank N.E. Ohio, 1982-84; asst. sec. Huntington Bancshares Ky., 1985-97; sec. Huntington Trust Co., N.A., 1987-97, Huntington Bancshares Ind., Inc., 1986-97, Huntington Fin. Services Co., 1987-98; dir. The Huntington Nat. Bank, Columbus, Ohio, 1998—; of counsel Porter Wright Morris & Arthur LLP, Columbus, 1998—; trustee OCLC Online Computer Libr. Ctr., Inc., Dublin, Ohio, 1999—, mem. fin. com., 2000—, mem. audit com., 2000-2002, chair 2002—, exec. com., 2002—, pers. and compensation com., 2002-03; dir. ADATOM.COM, Inc., Milpitas, Calif., 1999-2001, mem. compensation com., 1999-2001, chair audit com., 1999-2001. Bd. dirs. Family Svcs. Winston-Salem, 1966-74, sec., 1966-71, 74, v.p., 1974; chmn. Winston-Salem Transit Authority, 1974-75; bd. dirs. Rsch. for Advancement of Personalities, 1968-71, Winston-Salem Citizens for Fair Housing, 1970-74, N.C. United Community Svcs., 1970-74; treas. Forsyth County (N.C.) Citizens Com. Adequate Justice Bldg., 1968; trustee Appalachian State U., Boone, N.C., 1973-83, endowment fund, 1973-83, Columbus Drug Edn. and Prevention Fund, Inc., 1989-92; trustee, vice chmn. employment and Edn. Commn. Franklin County, 1982-85; mem. Winston-Salem Forsyth County Sch. Bd. Adv. Coun., 1973-74, Atty. Gen's Ohio Task Force Minorities in Bus., 1977-78; bd. dirs. Inroads Columbus, Inc., 1986-95, Greater Columbus Arts Coun., 1986-94, Columbus Urban League Inc., 1987-94, vice chmn., 1990-94; trustee Riverside Meth. Hosp. Found., 1989-90, Grant Med. Ctr., 1990-95, Grant/Riverside Meth. Hosps., 1995-97; trustee Ohio Health Corp., 1997—, treas., chair Fin./Audit Com., 2001—, exec. com., 2002—; dir. Cmty. Mutual Ins. Co., 1989-92, mem. audit com., 1989-92; trustee N.C. Ctrl. U., Durham, N.C., 1993-2001, vice-chmn., 1993-94, chmn. 1995, chair ednl. planning and acad. affairs com., 1995-98, audit, devel. and personnel coms., 1998-2001, chair audit com., 1999-2001; mem. Ohio Bd. Regents, 1987-96, vice-chmn., 1993-95, chmn., 1995-96; trustee Nat. Jud. Coll., Reno, Nevada, 1996-2002, fin. and audit com., 1997-2002 treas., chair, 1999-2002, Columbus Bar Found., 1998— (fellows com. 1998—, grants com., 1998—); AEFC Pension Adminstrn. Com. defined benefit plan of the ABA, Am. Bar Endowment, Am. Bar Found., and Nat. Jud. Coll., Chgo, Ill., 1998-2002. With AUS, 1958-64. Fellow Ohio Bar Found. (life); mem. ABA, Nat. Bar Assn., Ohio Bar Assn., Columbus Bar Assn. Banking, Health, Corporate, general. Office: Porter Wright Morris & Arthur LLP 41 S High St Ste 3100 Columbus OH 43215-6194 E-mail: rfrasier@porterwright.com., rfrasier@columbus.rr.com.

FRATTAROLI, CARMEN ANIELLO, lawyer; b. Stamford, Conn., May 5, 1948; s. Joseph and Carmella Rose (La Guardia) F.; m. Elizabeth Mary Dehn, Aug. 21, 1971; 1 child, Jaime Elizabeth. BA cum laude, U. N.H., 1970; JD cum laude, Suffolk U., 1973. Bar: Mass. 1973, U.S. Dist. Ct. Mass. 1974, U.S. Ct. Appeals (1st cir.) 1974. Law clk. to justices Mass. Superior Cts., Boston, 1973-74, chief law clk., 1974-75; ptnr. Costello, Frattaroli, Barrett, Gonthier & Goddard P.C., Salem, Mass., 1974-91; asst. dist. atty. Office Suffolk County Dist. Atty., Boston, 1975-76; atty. Law Offices of Carmen A. Frattaroli and Assocs., Salem, 1991—. Instr. Law North Shore Community Coll., Beverly, Mass., 1977-78; condr. legal malpractice seminars, bar assns., other orgns., 1985—. Editor: Suffolk Law Review, 1972-73. Mem., counsel Middleton (Mass.) Planning Bd., 1980-81, chmn., mem. local draft bd. No. 70 SSS, 1981—; mem. Beverly Planning Bd., 1986-88, Commn. for Social Justice, 1988-89. Recipient ofcl. citation Mass. Senate, 1988. Fellow Mass. Bar Found.; mem. Mass. Bar Assn. (bd. dels., form chmn., fee arbitration bd., election com., civil litigation coun.), Essex County Bar Assn. (bd. govs.), Salem Bar Assn., Assn. Trial Lawyers Am., Justinian Law Soc. Mass. (pres. 1988-89, Merit award 1983), North Shore C. of C., Salem Country Club, West Beach Corp. Avocations: skiing, racquetball. General civil litigation, Personal injury (including property damage). Office: Law Offices of Carmen A Frattaroli 76 Lafayette St Salem MA 01970-3674

FRAUEN, KURT HERMAN, lawyer; b. Chgo., Feb. 3, 1925; s. Herman Ernst Martin and Martha (Schranz) F.; m. Marion E. Green, July 20, 1954; children: Rodger, Leith, Keith, Kimberly, Susan, Eric. BS, Northwestern U., 1948; JD, Yale U., 1951. Bar: Wis. 1951, U.S. Dist. Ct. (ea. dist.) Wis. 1951, U.S. Dist. Ct. (we. dist.) Wis. 1955, U.S. Ct. Appeals (7th cir.) 1955, U.S. Supreme Ct. 1982. Assoc. Quarles, Spence & Quarles, Milw., 1951-55; ptnr. Wickham, Borgelt, Skogstad & Powell, Milw., 1955-70; sr. ptnr., shareholder Borgelt, Powell, Peterson & Frauen, Milw., 1970—. Presenter in field. Lt. (j.g.) USN, 1942-46, PTO. Fellow Am. Coll. Trial Lawyers (state chmn. 1979-81); mem. ABA, Fedn. Ins. and Corp. Counsel, Internat. Assn. Defense Counsel, Wis. Bar Assn., Civic Trial Counsel Wis. Republican. Congregationalist. Federal civil litigation, General civil litigation, Product liability. Home: 5635 N Shore Dr Milwaukee WI 53217-4860 Office: Borgelt Powell Peterson & Frauen 735 N Water St Ste 1500 Milwaukee WI 53202-4188

FRAUTSCHI, TIMOTHY CLARK, lawyer; b. Madison, Wis., Apr. 8, 1937; s. Lowell E. and Grace C. (Clark) F.; m. Pamela H. Hendricks, June 23, 1964; children: Schuyler, Jason; m. Susan B. Brumm, June 13, 1981; 1 child, Jacob. BA, U. Wis., 1959; LL.B., London Sch. Econs., U. Wis., 1963. Bar: Wis. 1963, U.S. Ct. Claims 1976, U.S. Tax Ct., 1976. Assoc. firm Foley & Lardner, Milw., 1963-70, ptnr., 1970—. Editor Wis. Law Rev. Co-founder Milw. Forum; pres. Lakeside Cmty. Coun., Present Music, Inc., 1991—98, Skylight Comic Opera, Ltd., 1980—85, Next Act Theatre, 2001—; bd. dirs. Am. Players Theater, Milw., Repertory Theater, Northcott Neighborhood House, United performing Arts Fund, Inc., Milw., Children's Svc. Soc., Wis. Theatre Tesseract; pres. Next Act Theatre, 1986—89, Watertower Landmark Trust, 1986—89; v.p. Frank Lloyd Wright Wis. Conservancy, 2001—; bd. dirs. St. Mary's Milw. Hosp. Found. Mem. Milw. Jr. Bar Assn. (pres. 1969-70), Milw. Bar Assn. (dir. 1971-74), Order of Coif,

Phi Beta Kappa (pres. Milw. chpt. 1968-70), Phi Kappa Phi, Phi Eta Sigma Taxation, general, Personal income taxation, State and local taxation. Office: Foley & Lardner US Bank Ctr 777 E Wisconsin Ave Ste 3800 Milwaukee WI 53202-5367

FRAZEN, MITCHELL HALE, lawyer; b. Great Lakes, Ill., Sept. 19, 1955; s. Sidney Joseph and Norma Ileane (Solomon) F.; m. Mary Elizabeth Huelsbusch, Sept. 14, 1974; children: Daniel Joseph, Christina Elizabeth. BA, U. Ill., 1977; JD, U. Mich., 1980. Bar: Ill. 1980, U.S. Dist. Ct. (no. dist.) Ill. 1980, U.S. Ct. Appeals (7th cir.) 1987, U.S. Dist. Ct. (ea. dist.) Wis. 1994, U.S. Ct. Appeals (8th cir.) 1995, U.S. Dist. Ct. (ea. dist.) Mich. 1995. Assoc. Phelan, Pope & John, Ltd., Chgo., 1980-87; shareholder Burditt & Radzius, Chartered, Chgo., 1987-98, dir., 1989-98; ptnr. Litchfield Cavo, Chgo., 1998—. Arbitrator, chairperson mandatory ct.-annexed arbitration program Cook County Cir. Ct., Chgo., 1990—, mediator vol. mediation program, 1992—. Bd. govs. Chgo. Coun. Lawyers, 1992-95; chair State Ct. Practices Com., 1995—. Mem. ABA, Chgo. Bar Assn., Phi Beta Kappa, Order of Coif. Democrat. Lutheran. General civil litigation, Insurance, Personal injury (including property damage). Home: 617 W Ruhl Rd Palatine IL 60074 Office: Litchfield Cavo 303 W Madison St Ste 200 Chicago IL 60606-3309 E-mail: frazen@litchfieldcavo.com.

FRAZIER, KENNETH C. pharmaceutical executive; BA in Polit. Sci., Pa. State U., 1975; JD, Harvard U., 1978. Bar: Pa. 1978, U.S. Dist. Ct. (ea. dist.) Pa. 1978, U.S. Supreme Ct. 2002. Ptnr. dept. litigation Drinker Biddle & Reath, 1978—92; v.p., gen. counsel, sec. Astra Merck, 1992—94; v.p. pub. affairs Merck & Co., Inc., 1994—96, v.p. pub. affairs, asst. gen. counsel, 1997—98, v.p., dep. gen. counsel, 1999, sr. v.p., gen. counsel, 1999—. Bd. dirs. Cornerstone Christian Acad., Legal Svcs. N.J.; chmn. Ethics Resource Ctr.; mem. adv. bd. Law and Econ. Ctr., U. Pa.; mem. adv. bd. Health Law and Policy Ctr., Seton Hall U.; mem. adv. bd. Rand Inst. for Civil Justice, CorporateProBono.Org; mem. Corp. Exec. Bd.'s Gen. Counsel Roundtable; mem. CLO Roundtable-U.S., Coun. on Fgn. Rels. Mem.: ABA, Am. Law Inst., Pa. Bar Assn. Office: Merck and Co Inc One Merck Dr Whitehouse Station NJ 08889-0100*

FREDERICI, C. CARLETON, lawyer; b. Jan. 17, 1938; s. Cecil Carleton and Lois Alida (Selzer) F.; m. Virginia A. Gregori, Oct. 14, 1961 (div.); m. Susan A. Low, Oct. 1, 1983; children: Gloria M., Carleton J., Charles W., Seth L. Student, Iowa State U., 1956; BA, U. Iowa, 1960, JD with high distinction, 1965. Bar: Iowa 1965, N.Y. 1966, U.S. Dist. Ct. (no. dist.) Iowa 1968, U.S. Dist. Ct. (so. dist.) Iowa 1969, U.S. Supreme Ct. 1970, U.S. Ct. Appeals (8th cir.) 1970, U.S. Ct. Appeals (3d cir.) 1973. Assoc. Willkie, Farr & Gallagher, N.Y.C., 1965-68, Shull, Marshall & Marks, Sioux City, Iowa, 1968-69, Davis, Brown, Koehn, Shors & Roberts, P.C., Des Moines, 1969-71, jr. ptnr., 1971-73, sr. ptnr., 1973-90, shareholder, 1990-95, counsel, 1996—. Spkr. Supreme Ct. Day, Law Sch. Drake U., 1973. Contbr. articles to legal publs. Vestryman St. Luke's Ch., bd. dirs., 1976-78, 82-85; mem. Polk County Rep. Cen. Com., 1969-71. 1st lt. U.S. Army, 1961-62. Mem. ABA (chmn. 8th cir. commn. on class actions and derivative suits), Iowa Bar Assn. (chmn. prison reform com., adv. mem. fed. practice commn., litigation sect. bench and bar com.), Polk County Bar Assn. (bench and bar com.), Assn. Bar City of N.Y., Am. Judicature Soc. (bd. dirs. Iowa 1990-96), Order of Coif, Wakonda Club. Federal civil litigation, State civil litigation. Office: Davis Brown Koehn Shors & Roberts PC 666 Walnut St Ste 2500 Des Moines IA 50309-3904 E-mail: ccf@lawiowa.com.

FREDERICKS, WESLEY CHARLES, JR., lawyer; b. N.Y.C., Mar. 31, 1948; s. Wesley Charles and Dionysia W. (Bitsanis) F.; m. Jeanne Maria Judson, May 19, 1973; children: Carolyn Anne, Wesley Charles III. BA, Johns Hopkins U., 1970; JD, Columbia U., 1973. Bar: N.Y. 1974, Conn. 1976, U.S. Supreme Ct. 1979. Assoc. Shearman & Sterling, N.Y.C., 1973-83, Cummings & Lockwood, Stamford, Conn., 1976; chmn. bd. Lotus Performance Cars, L.P., Norwood, N.J., 1983-87; group exec. cons. Group Lotus PLC, 1987; automotive industry cons., 1988-90; pres., CEO Mfrs. Products Co., 1990-94; counsel Gersten, Savage, Kaplowitz & Fredericks, LLP, N.Y.C., 1994, ptnr., 1995-98, Dorsey & Whitney LLP, N.Y.C., 1998—. Mem. Johns Hopkins U. Alumni Schs. Com. With USMC, 1968-69. Mem. ABA (vice-chmn. bus. law sect. com. on internat. bus. law, 2002—, co-chmn. subcom. multinat. mergers and acquisitions 1996—, mem. com. on negotiated acquisitions 1997—), Mashomack Fish and Game Preserve, Campfire Am. Club (N.Y.), Weston Gun Club (Conn.), Columbia Club of New York, Sigma Phi Epsilon. Republican. Congregationalist. Corporate, general, Private international, Mergers and acquisitions. Home: 221 Benedict Hill Rd New Canaan CT 06840-2913 Office: Dorsey & Whitney LLP 250 Park Ave New York NY 10177-0001

FREDMAN, HOWARD S. lawyer; b. St. Louis, Feb. 1, 1944; s. Manuel and Sydine Fredman; children: Jocelyn Bly, Amber Alexandra, Cameron Penn. BA, Princeton U., 1966; JD, Columbia U., 1969. Bar: Calif. 1970, U.S. Dist. Ct. (no. dist.) Calif. 1970, U.S. Ct. Appeals (9th cir.) 1970, U.S. Dist. Ct. (so. dist.) Calif. 1974, U.S. Dist. Ct. (ctrl. dist.) Calif. 1975, U.S. Dist. Ct. (ea. dist.) Calif. 1996, U.S. Dist. Ct. Colo. 2000. Law clk. to Hon. Milton Pollack U.S. Dist. Ct. (so. dist.) N.Y., N.Y.C., 1969-70; assoc. McCutchen, Doyle, Brown & Enersen, San Francisco, 1970-75; counsel, sr. atty., atty. legal divsn. Atlantic Richfield Co., L.A., 1975-87; assoc. Frandzel & Share, L.A., 1987-90, ptnr., 1990—99; pvt. practice L.A., 1999—2002; ptnr. Fredman/Lieberman LLP, L.A., 2002—. Mem. faculty Practicing Law Inst., 1982, 86-88; lectr., spkr. in field. Mem. editl. adv. bd. Calif. Causes of Action, 1998. Mem. com. to nominate alumni trustees Princeton Alumni Coun., 1998—2001, treas., exec. com., 2001—03, mem. strategic planning com., 1997—98; chair alumni schs. com. L.A. area Princeton, 1992—94. Recipient cert. of recognition, U.S. Dist. Ct. (ctrl. dist.) Calif., 2002. Mem. ABA, Assn. Bus. Trial Lawyers, Fed. Bar Assn., L.A. County Bar Assn. (chmn. antitrust sect. 1986-87, exec. com. antitrust sect. 1982—, nominating com. 1986-87, del. state bar conf. dels. 1987, 88), Princeton Club So. Calif. (pres. 1994-96). Democrat. Jewish. Antitrust, Intellectual property, General civil litigation. Office: Fredman/Lieberman LLP 1875 Century Park E Ste 2200 Los Angeles CA 90067-2523 E-mail: hsflawyer@aol.com.

FREDREGILL, ALAN, lawyer; b. Adel, Iowa, Mar. 19, 1948; BBA, U. Iowa, 1970; JD with honors, Drake U., 1974. Bar: Iowa 1975, Nebr. 1984. Atty. Heidman, Redmond, Fredregill, Patterson, Plaza, Dykstra & Prahl, LLP, Sioux City, Iowa. Mem.: Am. Mock Trial Assn. (Judges Hall of Fame 2002), Woodbury County Bar Assn., Internat. Assn. Arson Investigators, Iowa Acad. Trial Lawyers, Am. Coll. Trial Lawyers, Def. Rsch. Inst., Internat. Assn. Def. Counsel, Iowa Def. Counsel Assn. (bd. dirs. 1981—, pres. 1990—91), Iowa State Bar Assn. (unauthorized practice com. 1985—95, chmn. 1987—89, bd. govs. 1996—2003, pres. 2002—03), Nebr. State Bar Assn., Order of Coif, ABA (litigation sect.). Personal injury (including property damage), Insurance, Construction. Office: Heidman Redmond Fredregill et al PO Box 3086 701 Pierce St Ste 200 Sioux City IA 51102*

FREDRICKSON, BRYAN TIMOTHY, lawyer; b. Boulder, Colo., Jan. 4, 1956; s. Robert G. and Carol L. (Mentzer) F.; m. Jill R. Scroggs, June 6, 1981; children: Alexa Rae, Jenna Blanche, Hale Aaron. BA in Biology cum laude, U. Colo., 1979; JD, Cath. U. Am., 1984. Bar: Va. 1985, U.S. Ct. Appeals (4th cir.) 1985, Colo. 1990. U.S. Ct. Appeals (10th cir.) 1991, U.S. Dist. Ct. Colo. 1991. Legis. aide to Senator William Armstrong, U.S. Senate; assoc. Law offices L. Lawton Rogers, Alexandria, Va., 1984; legis. asst. to Rep. Ken Kramer U.S. Ho. of Reps., Washington, 1985-86; chief staff for Rep. Dan Schaefer, 1987-90; ptnr. Fredrickson & Johnson P.C., Canon City, Colo., 1990—. Dep. campaign mgr. Kramer for Senate, Denver, 1986; mem. 11th Jud. Dist. Jud. Performance Commn., 1994-98, 11th Jud. Dist. Nominating Commn., 1997-2001; city atty., Florence, Colo., 1999-; commr. Colo. Uniform State Laws Commn., 2003—; mem. state adv. com. Colo. Children's Campaign, 2000—. Del. Colo. Rep. Conv., 1978, 92, 98, 2002; pres. Fremont County/Valdai Russia Sister City Assn. Mem. ABA, Va. State Bar, Colo. Bar Assn., Rotary (pres.). Avocations: reading, golf. Home: 206 Cottage Ln Canon City CO 81212-2445 Office: Fredrickson & Johnson PC 831 Royal Gorge Blvd Ste 329 Canon City CO 81212-6706 E-mail: fredricksonjohnson@ris.net.

FREE, E. LEBRON, lawyer, mediator; b. Cleveland, Tenn., Jan. 27, 1940; s. James D. and Mary Kathleen (Hunt) F.; children: Jason LeBron, Ryan Edward. BA, Berea Coll., 1963; MTh, So. Meth. U., 1966; JD, Okla. City U., 1974. Bar: Ga. 1974, Fla. 1975, U.S. Dist. Ct. (mid. dist.) Fla. 1975, U.S. Supreme Ct. 1975; cert. cir. civil and family law mediator. Litigation atty. Jim Walter Corp., Tampa, Fla., 1975-79; prin. E. Lebron Free, P.A., Clearwater, Fla., 1980—. Editor Res. IPSA Loquitur, 1996—. Bd. dirs. Ye Mystice Krewe of Neptune, Pinellas County, Fla., 1980-90, capt., 1984; bd. dirs. Hospice of the Fla. Suncoast, 1981-91; chmn., 1984; mem. Met. Planning Orgn., Pinellas County, 1984, Zoning Bd., Clearwater, 1984; bd. dirs. Family Svc. Ctrs., 1993—. Mem. ABA, ATLA, Canakaris Inns of Ct. (bd. dirs. 1997—), Fla. Bar Assn. (family law sect., chmn. fee arbitration com. 1991), Fla. Acad. Trial Lawyers, Clearwater Bar Assn., Rotary (Paul Harris fellow 1992), Masons. Avocation: sailing. Family and matrimonial, Personal injury (including property damage), Probate (including wills, trusts). Office: 3005 State Rd 590 Ste 206 Clearwater FL 33759-2539 Fax: 727-726-4677.

FREED, DANIEL JOSEF, law educator; b. New York, May 12, 1927; s. Jules L. and Sara (Lobel) F.; m. Judith Darrow, June 30, 1967; children: Peter Jacob, Emily Sara;children from previous marriage: Jonathan Michael, Amy. BS, Yale U., 1948, LLB, 1951; LLD (hon.), New England Coll., 1994. Bar: N.Y. 1952, D.C. 1953, U.S. Supreme Ct. 1955. Atty.-investigator, preparedness subcom., com. on armed svcs., U.S. Senate, Washington, 1951-52; assoc. Ford, Bergson, Adams & Borkland, Washington, 1952-59; sr. trial atty. antitrust divsn. U.S. Dept. Justice, Washington, 1959-64, assoc. dir. office of criminal justice, 1964-66, acting dir., 1966-68, dir., 1968-69; prof. law and its adminstrn. Yale U., New Haven, 1969-75, clin. prof., 1975-94, clin. prof. emeritus, profl. lectr. in law, 1994—. Dir. clin. program law Yale U., 1969-72, dir. Daniel and Florence Guggenheim program in criminal justice, 1972-87, dir. criminal sentencing program, 1988-96. Co-author: (with Wald) Bail in the United States: 1964, publ.1964; editor (periodical) Fed. Sentencing Reporter, 1988—; contbr. articles to profl. jours. Trustee Vera Inst. Justice, NY, 1970—, Boston Grad. Sch. of Psychoanalysis, 2001—; pres. Yale Law Sch. Assn. Washington, 1968. With USN, 1945—46. Recipient Glenn R. Winters award Am. Judges Assn., 1992. Democrat. Jewish. Avocations: metal sculpture, swimming. Home: 53 Freed Rd Guilford VT 05301 Office: Yale Law Sch 127 Wall St PO Box 208215 New Haven CT 06520-8215 E-mail: daniel.freed@yale.edu.

FREED, DIANE SUSAN, lawyer; b. Buffalo, Jan. 16, 1957; d. Melvin Arnold and Marcia Joyce Freed; m. Thomas Coit Butler, Mar. 11, 1995. BA, U. Colo., 1979; JD, SUNY, 1982. Bar: Colo. 1982, U.S. Dist. Ct. 1985. Law clk. Goldstein & Freed, Buffalo, 1978—78; assoc. atty. Finke & Crane, Denver, 1982—86; pvt. practice Englewood, Colo., 1984—86; assoc. atty. Veto & Scott, PC, Lakewood, Colo., 1986—92; owner, pres. Diane S. Freed, PC, Lakewood, 1992—. Instr. ProSe Clinic, Golden, Colo., 1999—; pres. Le Tip of Lakewood, Colo., 1998—99. Bd. trustees Jefferson County Bar Assn., Golden, 1998—2000. Mem.: ABA, 1st Jud. Dist. Bar Assn., Colo. Bar Assn. Republican. Jewish. Avocations: jazzercise, golf, skiing, cooking, dogs. Family and matrimonial, Property, real (including real estate development, water). Office: Diane S Freed PC Ste 224 441 Wadsworth Blvd Lakewood CO 80226 Business E-Mail: dsfreedpc@qwest.net.

FREED, EVAN PHILLIP, lawyer; b. L.A., Sept. 11, 1946; s. Joseph Yale and Miriam Freed. BA, Calif. State U., L.A., 1970; JD, U. West L.A., 1978. Bar: Calif. 1979. Dep. pub. defender L.A. County Pub. Defender, 1982-87; criminal def. atty. Alt. Def. Counsel, L.A., 1987-95; criminal prosecutor City Atty., L.A., 1995-97; pvt. practice law Redondo Beach, Calif., 1997—. Mem. Calif. Pub. Defenders Assn., L.A. County Bar, Masons. Republican. Jewish. Avocation: computer internet. Criminal, Immigration, naturalization, and customs. Fax: 310-943-3111. E-mail: law@epfz.com.

FREED, KENNETH ALAN, lawyer; b. Buffalo, Apr. 28, 1957; s. Sherwood E. and Renee (Liebesman) F.; m. Odette Ashley Freed; children: David Benjamin, Daniel Lawrence, Lauren Allyssa. BA in Econs. magna cum laude, Boston U., 1979; JD, U. Chgo., 1982. Bar: Calif. 1982, U.S. Dist. Ct. (no. dist.) Calif., 1982. Prin., shareholder Feldman, Waldman & Kline, San Francisco, 1982-95; sr. v.p., gen. counsel Sydran Svcs., LLC, San Ramon, Calif., 1995—. Mem. ABA, Calif. Bar Assn. Commercial, contracts (including sales of goods; commercial financing), Franchising, Mergers and acquisitions. Office: 3000 Executive Pkwy Ste 515 San Ramon CA 94583-4254 E-mail: kfreed@sydran.com.

FREED, MICHAEL LEONARD, lawyer; b. San Diego, Dec. 5, 1942; s. Leonard T. and Violet Louise (French) F.; m. Pamela McDiarmid Prentice, Aug. 23, 1971; children: Christopher, Candice, Bryan. BS, San Jose State U., 1966; JD, Hastings Coll., 1974. Bar: Hawaii 1974, U.S. Dist. Ct. Hawaii 1974, U.S. Ct. Appeals (9th cir.) 1981. Assoc. Rush, Moore, Craven, Kim & Stricklin, Honolulu, 1974-80, ptnr., 1980-88, Rush, Moore, Craven & Stricklin, Honolulu, 1988-95, Freed & Webb, 1995—98, Michael L. Freed and Assocs., 1998—. Served to lt. USNR, 1966-71, Vietnam. Mem. Order of Coif. Roman Catholic. Avocation: big game fishing. State civil litigation, Construction, Labor (including EEOC, Fair Labor Standards Act, labor-management relations, NLRB, OSHA). Office: 737 Bishop St Ste 2350 Honolulu HI 96813-3296

FREEDMAN, BARBARA WIDMAN, lawyer; b. Phila., Sept. 1, 1947; d. Robert and Lillian (Kartoz) W.; m. Allan Perry Freedman, Dec. 22, 1968; children: Avraham T., Reena Z., Noam M. BA cum laude, Temple U., 1969, JD cum laude, 1977. Bar: Pa. 1977, D.C. 1980, U.S. Dist. Ct. (ea. dist.) Pa. 1980, U.S. Tax Ct., U.S. Ct. Appeals (3d cir.) 1981. Law clk. U.S Dist. Ct. (ea. dist.) Pa., Phila., 1977-78; assoc. Dechert Price & Rhoads, Phila., 1978-82; assoc., ptnr. Rawle & Henderson, Phila., 1983-85, 1985-86; ptnr. Saul, Ewing, Remick & Saul, Phila., 1987-92; owner Freedman & Assocs., 1992—96; ptnr. Duane Morris LLP, 1996—. Adj. prof. Temple U. Law Sch., Phila., 1981-98, mem. adminstrv. com. grad. tax program, 1987-89; lectr. planning forum Temple U., 1984-2001, mem. planning com. 1985-86; lectr. U. Pa. Tax Confs., Phila., 1986-98; mem. adv. bd. Phila. Tax Conf., 1989—, exec. com. 2000-2002, ch-chair, 2003-; mem. faculty Am. Law Inst., 1988. Contbg. editor Temple Law Quarterly, 1974-76; contbr. articles to profl. jours. Recipient Hornbook award West Publishing Co., 1975, 76, 77; Barenkopf scholar, 1976-77. Fellow Am. Coll. Tax Counsel; mem. ABA (tax sect., employee benefits com.), Pa. Bar Inst. (tax adv. bd. 2003-, lectr. 1995-2002), Phila. Bar Assn. (bd. govs. 1997-98, 2003-, nominating com. 1991, 92, 2003, sec.-treas. tax sect. 1994-95, vice- chmn. 2003-, exec. coun. 1985-88, 90-93, 96-99, chair fed. tax com. 1989, lectr. 1983-2002), Temple U. Law Sch. (mem. bd. visitors, chmn. planned group adv. coun.), Phila. Tax Supper Group (treas. 1985-86, pres. 1986-87), Sr. Tax Roundtable, Real Estate Tax Discussion Group (founding mem.). Pension, profit-sharing, and employee benefits, Corporate taxation, Taxation, general.

FREEDMAN, BART JOSEPH, lawyer; b. New Haven, Sept. 27, 1955; s. Lawrence Zelic and Dorothy (Robinson) F.; m. Esme Detweiler, Sept. 28, 1985; children: Luke Edward, Samuel Meade, Benjamin Zelic. BA, Carleton Coll., 1977; JD, U. Pa., 1982. Bar: Wash. 1984, U.S. Dist. Ct. (we. dist.) Wash. 1984, U.S. Ct. Appeals (9th cir.) 1985, U.S. Dist. Ct. (ea. dist.) Wash. 1988. Law clk. to chief justice Samuel Roberts Supreme Ct. Pa., Erie, 1982-83; asst. city solicitor City of Phila., 1984; assoc. Perkins Coie, Seattle, 1984-90; ptnr. Preston Gates & Ellis, Seattle, 1990—. Editor: Natural Resource Damages, 1993. Bd. dirs. Seattle Metrocenter YMCA, 1988-97, chmn. 1993-97, 2002—; bd. dirs. Leadership Tomorrow, 1996-97; chair Sierra Club Inner City Outings Program, Seattle, 1986-90; chmn. bd. advisors Earth Svc. Corps/YMCA, Seattle, 1990-97. Mem. ABA (com. on corp. counsel 1985-95), Wash. State Bar Assn., Seattle-King County Bar Assn. (participant neighborhood legal clinics 1985-94). Federal civil litigation, General civil litigation, Environmental. Office: Preston Gates & Ellis 701 5th Ave Ste 5000 Seattle WA 98104-7078 E-mail: bartf@prestongates.com.

FREEDMAN, FRANK HARLAN, federal judge; b. Springfield, Mass., Dec. 15, 1924; s. Alvin Samuel and Ida Hilda (Rosenberg) F.; m. Eleanor Labinger, July 26, 1953; children: Joan Robin Goodman, Wendy Beth Greedman Mackler, Barry Alan. LL.B., Boston U., 1949, LL.M., 1950; PhD (hon.), Western New Eng. Coll., Springfield, 1970. Pvt. practice law, 1950-68; mayor City of Springfield, 1968-72; judge U.S. Dist. Ct. Mass., Springfield, 1972-86, chief judge, 1986-92; now sr. judge, 1992—. Chmn. fund raising drs. Muscular Dystrophy, Leukemia Soc.; mem. Susan Auchter Kidney Fund Raising Com.; mem. Springfield City Council, 1960-67, pres., 1962; del. Republican Nat. Conv., 1964, 68; mem. Springfield Rep. Com., 1959-72. Served with USNR, 1943-46. Greenaway Drive Elem. Sch. rededicated as Frank H. Freedman Sch., 1974; recipient Silver Shingle award for disting. service Boston U., 1984. Mem. Hampden County (Mass.) Bar Assn., Lewis Marshall Club on Jurisprudence (pres.) Jewish. Office: US Dist Ct 1550 Main St Rm 525 Springfield MA 01103-1428

FREEDMAN, GERALD M. lawyer; b. Hampton, Va., July 26, 1943; s. Henry and Arlene L.; m. Kristin King; 1 child, Eliza King. BA, Columbia U., 1964, JD, 1967. Bar: N.Y. 1968, U.S. Dist. Ct. (so. and ea. dists.) N.Y. 1970, U.S. Ct. Appeals (2d cir.) 1976. Adminstr. Columbia U., N.Y.C., 1967-69; assoc. Kelley, Drye & Warren, N.Y.C., 1969-71, Trubin Sillcocks Edelman & Knapp, N.Y.C., 1971-76, ptnr., 1976-84, Morgan, Lewis & Bockius, N.Y.C., 1984—. Contbr. articles to profl. jours. Ptnr., N.Y.C. Partnership, 2001—. Mem. ABA, Assn. of Bar of City of N.Y., Am. Bankruptcy Inst., Univ. Club. Banking, Bankruptcy, Finance. Office: Morgan Lewis & Bockius 101 Park Ave Fl 44 New York NY 10178-0060 E-mail: gfreedman@morganlewis.com.

FREEDMAN, HELEN E. justice; b. N.Y.C., Dec. 15, 1942; d. David Simeon and Frances (Fisher) Edelstein; m. Henry A. Freedman, June 7, 1964; children: Katherine Eleanor, Elizabeth Sarah. BA, Smith Coll., 1963; JD, NYU, 1967. Bar: N.Y. 1970, U.S. Dist. Ct. (so. and ea. dists.), U.S. Supreme Ct. 1979. Staff atty. office of gen. counsel Am. Arbitration Assn., N.Y.C., 1967-69; assoc. Hubbel, Cohen & Stiefel, N.Y.C., 1970-71, Shaw, Bernstein, Scheuer, Boyden & Sarnoff, N.Y.C., 1971-74; law sec. Civil Ct., N.Y.C., 1974-76; sr. atty. housing litigation bur. N.Y.C. Dept. Housing Preservation and Devel., 1976; supervising atty. Dist. Coun. 37 Legal Svcs. Plan, N.Y.C., 1976-78; judge Civil Ct., N.Y.C., 1979-88; acting justice Supreme Ct., N.Y.C., 1984-88, justice, 1989-95; apptd. to appellate term 1st dept. NY Supreme Ct., N.Y.C., 1995-99, apptd. to comml. divsn., 2000—, pres. judge mass tort litigation panel, 2002—. Co-chair State Judges Mass Tort Litigation Com.; mem. pattern jury instrns. com., Supreme Ct. Justices; adj. prof. N.Y. Law Sch., 1999, 2000, 03; lectr. in field. Author: New York Objections, 1999, rev. edits., 2000, 01, 02; contbr. articles to profl. jours. Recipient Disting. Alumna award Smith Coll., 2000. Fellow Am. Bar Found., N.Y. State Bar Found.; mem. ABA (chair small claims ct. com. 1986-89, bioethics com. nat. conf. spl. ct. judges, N.Y. State Ct. del. to ann. meetings, nat. conf. spl. ct. judges, 1987, 88, Spl. Cts. Conf. award 1987, 88, 93, Jud. Excellence award 1998), Nat. Assn. Women Judges, N.Y. State Bar Assn. (del.), N.Y. Fed. State Jud. Coun., N.Y. Women's Bar Assn., N.Y. State Assn. Women Judges (pres. 1995-97), Assn. of Bar of City of N.Y. (mem. various coms., chair com. med. malpractice, v.p. 1994-95), Judges and Lawyers Breast Cancer Alert (pres.). Home: 150 W 96th St New York NY 10025-6469 Office: NY Supreme Ct 60 Centre New York NY 10007-1488

FREEDMAN, JAY WEIL, lawyer; b. Washington, May 19, 1942; s. Walter and Maxine (Weil) F.; m. Linda Newman, Aug. 7, 1966; children: Courteney, Spencer. BA, Williams Coll., 1964; JD, Yale U., 1967. Bar: D.C. 1968, U.S. Supreme Ct. 1973. Atty. office of gen. counsel FCC, 1967-68; assoc. Freedman, Levy, Kroll & Simonds, Washington, 1968-72, ptnr., 1972-2001, Foley & Lardner (formerly Freedman, Levy, Kroll & Simonds), Washington, 2001—. Pres. Am. Jewish Com., Washington, 1987—89; bd. dirs. Smithsonian Instn. Librs., 2001—, Georgetown Partnership, 2002—, Heifitz Internat. Music Inst., 2002—; pres. Washington Hebrew Congregation, 1982—84. Mem. ABA, D.C. Bar Assn., Woodmont Country Club (pres. 1997-99), Yale Law Sch. Alumni Assn. (exec. com. 1999—, sec. 2003—), Econ. Club. Washington, Phi Delta Phi. Corporate, general, Probate (including wills, trusts), Securities. Office: Foley & Lardner 3000 K Street NW Ste 500 Washington DC 20007 E-mail: jfreedman@foleylaw.com.

FREEDMAN, MONROE HENRY, lawyer, educator, columnist; b. Mt. Vernon, N.Y., Apr. 10, 1928; s. Chauncey and Dorothea (Kornblum) F.; m. Audrey Willock, Sept. 24, 1950 (dec. 1998); children: Alice Freedman Korngold, Sarah Freedman Izquierdo, Caleb (dec. 1998), Judah. AB cum laude, Harvard U., 1951, LLB, 1954, LLM, 1956. Bar: Mass. 1954, Pa. 1957, D.C. 1960, U.S. Dist. Ct. (ea. dist. N.Y.), U.S. Ct. Appeals (D.C. cir.) 1960, U.S. Supreme Ct. 1960, U.S. Ct. Appeals (2d cir.) 1968, N.Y. 1978, U.S. Ct. Appeals (9th cir.) 1982, U.S. Ct. Appeals (11th cir.) 1986, U.S. Ct. Appeals (Fed. cir.) 1987. Assoc. Wolf, Block, Schorr & Solis-Cohen, Phila., 1956-58; ptnr. Freedman & Temple, Washington, 1969-73; dir. Stern Community Law Firm, Washington, 1970-71; prof. law George Washington U., 1958-73; dean Hofstra Law Sch., Hempstead, N.Y., 1973-77, prof. law, 1973—, Howard Lichtenstein Disting. prof. legal ethics, 1989—2003; Drinko-Baker & Hostetler chair in law Cleve. State U., 1992; CFO Olive Tree Mktg. Internat., 1998—. Faculty asst. Harvard U. Law Sch., 1954-56, instr. trial advocacy and legal ethics, 1978—; lectr. on lawyers' ethics; exec. dir. U.S. Holocaust Meml. Coun., 1980-82, gen. counsel, 1982-83, sr. adviser to chmn., 1982-87; cons. U.S. Commn. on Civil Rights, 1960-64, Neighborhood Legal Services Program, 1970; legis. cons. to Senator John L. McClellan, 1959; spl. com. on courtroom conduct N.Y.C. Bar Assn., 1972; exec. dir. Criminal Trial Inst., 1965-66; expert witness on legal ethics state and fed. ct. proceedings, U.S. Senate and House Coms., U.S. Dept. Justice, FDIC; spl. investigator Rochester Inst. Tech., 1991; reporter Am. Lawyer's Code of Conduct, 1979-81; mem. Arbitration panel U.S. Dist. Ct. (ea. dist.) N.Y., 1986—; Inaugural Wickwire lectr. Dalhousie Law Sch., N.S., 1992; lectr. S.C. Bar Found., 1993, numerous profl. confs; adv. subgroup on ethics U.S. Dist. Ct. (ea. dist.) N.Y., 1994-96. Author: Contracts, 1973, Lawyers' Ethics in an Adversary System, 1975 (ABA gavel award, cert. of merit 1976), Teacher's Manual Contracts, 1978, American Lawyer's Code of Conduct, 1981, Understanding Lawyers' Ethics, 1990, (with Abbe Smith) 2d edit., 2002, Group Defamation and Freedom of Speech—The Relationship Between Language and Violence, 1995; co-editor; columnist Cases and Controversies, Am. Lawyer Media, 1990-96, (with Supreme Ct. Justice Ruth Bader Ginsburg) Freedom, Life, & Death: Materials on Comparative Constitutional Law, 1997; mem. panel acad. contbrs. Black's Law Dictionary, 2002—; television appearances include Donohue, CNN Money Line, CBS 60 Minutes, CNN Late Edition, Court TV, and others; contbr. articles to profl. jours. Recipient Martin Luther King Jr. Humanitarian award, 1987, The Lehman-LaGuardia Award for Civic Achievement, 1996. Fellow Am. Bar Found. (life); mem. ABA (ethics adv. to chair criminal justice sect. 1993-95, Michael Franck award 1998), ACLU (nat. bd. dirs. 1970-80, nat. adv. coun. 1980—, spl. litigation counsel 1971-73), Am. Law Inst. (consultative group on the law governing lawyers, 1990-99, consultative group on Uniform Comml. Code art. 2 1990-2002), Soc. Am. Law Tchrs. (mem. governing bd. 1974-79, exec. com. 1976-79, chmn. com. on profl. responsibility 1974-79, 87-90), ABA (vice chmn. ethical considerations com. criminal justice sect. 1989-90, ethics advisor to chmn. criminal justice sect., 1993-96), N.Y. State Bar Assn. (com. on legal edn. and admission to bar 1988-92, criminal justice sect. com. on profl. responsibility, 1990-92, award for Dedication to Scholarship and pub. svc. 1997), Assn. Bar City N.Y. (com. on profl. responsibility 1987-90, com. on profl. and jud. ethics 1991-92), Fed. Bar Assn. (chmn. com. on profl. disciplinary standards and procedures 1970-71), Am. Soc. Writers on Legal Subjects (mem. com. on constitution and bylaws 1999—), Am. Bd. Criminal Lawyers (hon. 2003-), Am. Jewish Congress (nat. governing coun. 1984-86), Am. Arbitration Assn. (arbitrator, nat. panel arbitrators 1964—, cert. svc. award 1986), Nat. Network on Right to Counsel (exec. bd., exec. com. 1986-90), Nat. Prison Project (steering com. 1970-90), Nat. Assn. Criminal Def. Lawyers (vice chmn. ethics adv. com. 1991-93, co-chmn., 1994). Democrat. Jewish.

FREEDMAN, ROBERT LOUIS, lawyer; b. Phila., Apr. 8, 1940; s. Abraham L. and Jane G. (Sunstein) F.; m. Diane Stoller, July 25, 1965; children: Elizabeth, Paul, Jonathan AB, Harvard U., 1962; MA in Econs., Columbia U., 1963, LLB, 1966. Bar: Pa. 1967. Law clk., 1966-68; assoc. Dechert Price & Rhoads, Phila., 1968-75, ptnr., 1975—; lectr. in law Temple U. Law Sch., 1969-74. Adj. prof. U. Pa. Law Sch., 1997—2001. Adv. com. on decedents' estates Pa. Joint State Govt. Commn.; trustee Fgn. Policy Rsch. Inst. Mem. Am. Law Inst., Am. Coll. Trust and Estate Counsel, Phila. Bar Assn. (chmn. sect. on probate and trust law 1983) Clubs: Germantown Cricket. Jewish. Estate planning, Probate (including wills, trusts), Estate taxation. Office: Dechert LLP 4000 Bell Atlantic Tower 1717 Arch St Philadelphia PA 19103-2793 E-mail: robert.freedman@dechert.com.

FREEDMAN, THEODORE LEVY, lawyer; b. Northampton, Mass., Dec. 28, 1947; s. David Asa and Charlotte (Levy) F.; m. Franceslynn Barile; children: Edward John, Moss. BA, Lawrence U., Appleton, Wis., 1969; JD, Northwestern U., 1972. Bar: D.C. 1973, N.Y. 1976, Ill. 1992. Counsel U.S. Securities & Exchange Com., Washington, 1972-75; assoc. Levy & Erens, Chgo., 1975-78, ptnr., 1978-85, Kirkland & Ellis, Chgo. and N.Y.C., 1985—. Bankruptcy, Commercial, contracts (including sales of goods; commercial financing), Corporate, general. Office: Kirkland & Ellis Citicorp Ctr 153 E 53rd St New York NY 10022-4611 Office Fax: 212-446-4900.

FREEHLING, DANIEL JOSEPH, law educator, law library director; b. Montgomery, Ala., Nov. 13, 1950; s. Saul Irving and Grace (Lieberman) L. BS, Huntingdon Coll., 1972, JD, U. Ala., 1975, MLS, 1977. Ref. libr., asst. to assoc. dean U. Ala. Sch. Law, Tuscaloosa, 1975-77; assoc. law libr. U. Md., Balt., 1977-79, Cornell U., Ithaca, N.Y., 1979-82; law libr. dir., assoc. prof. U. Maine, Portland, 1982-86; law libr. dir., assoc. prof. law Boston U., 1986-92, prof., 1992—, assoc. dean for adminstrn., 1993-97, assoc. dean for info. svcs., 1999—. Mem. steering com., law program com. Rsch. Librs. Group, 1989-91; treas. New Eng. Law Libr. Consortium, 1989-91; vice chair, chair-elect sect. on law librs. Assn. Am. Law Schs., 1990-91, chair, 1992. Mem.: ABA (accreditation com. 1995—2001, coun. sect. legal edn. and bar admission 2002—), Am. Assn. Law Librs. (chair acad. law librs. spl. interest sect. 1981—82, edn. com. 1982—83, membership com. 1983—84, program chair 1987—88, local arrangements co-chair 1992—93, chair mentoring and retention com. 1995—96). Home: 106 Washington St Topsfield MA 01983 Office: Boston U Law Sch Pappas Law Libr 765 Commonwealth Ave Boston MA 02215-1401

FREELAND, CHARLES, lawyer, accountant; b. Balt., July 18, 1940; s. Benjamin and Beatrice (Polakoff) F.; m. Beverly Klaff, July 15, 1965; children— Stephen Jason, Jennifer Jill, Gwen Nicole, Kimberly Suzanne. B.S., U. Md., 1962, LL.B., 1965; diploma U.S. Naval Justice Sch., 1966. Bar: Md. 1965, U.S. Dist. Ct. Md. 1965, U.S. Tax Ct. 1966, U.S. Ct. Mil. Apls. 1966, U.S. Ct. Claims 1968, U.S. Supreme Ct. 1969, U.S. Ct. Appeals (4th cir.) 1974. Fin. v.p. Collins Electronics Mfg. Co.; dir. fin. planning Cellu-Craft, Inc., Stevensville, Md., 1963-65; controller Braun-Crystal Mfg. Co., Inc., Middle Village, N.Y., 1969-70, BCN Design Products, Inc., Bayshore, N.Y., 1969-70; asst. city solicitor City of Balt., 1972-82; pvt. practice law and acctg., Balt., 1971-93; ptnr. Kaplan, Freeland & Schwartz, Balt., 1982-86; pres. Charles Freeland, PC, 1986—. Served to lt. USNR, 1965-68. Mem. Am. Judicature Soc., Am. Assn. Attys.-CPA's, ABA, Md. Bar Assn., Balt. County Bar Assn., Am. Assn. CPA's, Md. Assn. CPA's, Am. Arbitration Assn. (nat. panel 1970—). Democrat. Jewish. Club: Woodholme Country. Corporate, general, Corporate taxation, Personal income taxation. Home: PO Box 422 4 Timothys Green Ct Brooklandville MD 21022 Office: 1300 York Rd Ste 180 Lutherville MD 21093-6806

FREELS, JESSE SAUNDERS, JR., lawyer; b. Sherman, Tex., Feb. 8, 1943; s. Jesse Saunders Sr. and Margaret (Stout) F.; m. Valerie Wood, Jan. 16, 1971; children: J.S. "Trey" III, John Andrew. BA, BS, Howard Payne U., 1965; JD, St. Mary's U., San Antonio, 1969. Bar: Tex. 1969, U.S. Dist. Ct. (ea. and we. dists.) Tex. 1971. Asst. county atty. Grayson County, Sherman, 1969-71; ptnr. Doss, Thompson & Freels, Denison, Tex., 1971-78; judge Grayson County, Sherman, 1978-83; pres. Freels & Johnston, P.C., Sherman, 1983-2000; sole practice, 2000—. Bd. dirs. Am. Bank of Tex., Sherman, 1975—, Tex. Ctr. for the Judiciary, Austin, 1979-83. Mem. Tex. Bar Assn., Grayson County Bar Assn., Tex. Bar Found. (life), Masons (past master Lodge 403, Denison). Banking, Bankruptcy, General civil litigation. Home: 109 Spring Valley Dr Denison TX 75020-3724 Office: 114 S Crockett St Sherman TX 75090-5906

FREEMAN, ANTOINETTE ROSEFELDT, lawyer; b. Atlantic City, Oct. 7, 1937; d. Bernard Paul and Fannie (Levin) Rosefeldt; m. Alan Richard Freeman, June 22, 1958 (div. Apr. 1979); children: Barry David, Robin Lisa. BA, Rutgers U., 1972; JD, Ind. U., 1975; LLM, Temple U., 1979. Bar: Pa. 1975, Wash. 1992, U.S. Dist. Ct. (ea. dist.) Pa. 1976, U.S. Ct. Appeals (3d cir.) 1982. Substitute tchr. Washington Twp. Sch. Dist., Indpls., 1972; dep. prosecutor intern Marion County Prosecutor, Indpls., 1974-75; asst. dist. atty. City of Phila., 1975-76; mgr. EEO Wyeth Labs., Radnor, Pa., 1976-80, SmithKline & French Labs., Phila., 1980-82; sr. counsel SmithKline Beecham Corp., Phila., 1982-91; assoc. gen. counsel Amgen Inc. (formerly Immunex Corp.), 1991—; arbitrator Am. Arbitration Assn., 1976—. Counsel Regional Interests Developing Efficient Transp., 1983-85; adv. bd. Family Svc. Phila., 1980-81, Greater Phila. C. of C., 1983; pres. Croskey Ct. Condominium Assn., 1983-87; bd. dirs. Logan Sq. Neighborhood Assn., 1983-91, pres., 1985-87; v.p., sec. Friends of Logan Sq. Found., 1985-91; counsel Hapoel Games USA; chairperson Ctr. City Coalition for Quality of Life; atty. Vol. Lawyers for the Arts, Phila., 1985-91; bd. dirs. Sr. Employment and Ednl. Svc., BathHouse Theater, 1991-99, v.p. 1994-96; bd. dirs. Bellini preview group Seattle Opera Guild, 1994-96 ; mem. Assoc. Corp. Coun. for Arts., 1992-93; mem. adv. bd. regulatory affairs cert. program U. Wash.; bd. dirs. Music of Remberance, 2002—. Bd. dirs. Music of Remembrance, 2002—. Mem. ABA, Pa. Bar Assn., Phila. Bar Assn., Wash. State Bar Assn., Merit Employers Coun. (1st v.p. 1978-79), Phila. Women's Network, Phila. Lawyers Club, Phila. King County Med. Soc./King County Bar Assn. (med.-legal com.). Democrat. Jewish. Administrative and regulatory, Government contracts and claims, Labor (including EEOC, Fair Labor Standards Act, labor-management relations, NLRB, OSHA). Office: Amgen Inc 51 University St Seattle WA 98101-2936

FREEMAN, CHARLES E. state supreme court justice; b. Richmond, Va., Dec. 12, 1933; m. Marylee Voelker; 1 child, Kevin. BA in Liberal Arts, Va. Union U., 1954; JD, John Marshall Law Sch., 1962, LLD (hon.) , 1992. Bar: Ill. 1962. Pvt. practice, 1962—76; pvt. practice, Cook County, Chgo., 1962—76, asst. state's atty., 1964; asst. atty. Bd. Election Commrs., Chgo., 1964—65; mem. Ill. Indsl. Commn., Chgo., 1965—73, Ill. Commerce Commn., Chgo., 1973—76; judge law and chancery divsns. Cook County Cir. Ct., Chgo., 1976—86; judge Appellate Ct. Ill., 1986—90; justice Ill. Supreme Ct., 1990—, chief justice, 1997—2000. Recipient Cert. Achievement, Internat. Christian Fellowship Missions, Earl B. Dickerson award, Chgo. Bar Assn., Merit award, Habilitative Sys., Statesmanship award, Monarch Awards Found. of Alpha Kappa Alpha, Freedom award, John Marshall Law Sch. Mem.: ABA (task force opportunities minorities in jud. adminstrn. divsn., coms. opportunities minorities in profession, cert. Recognition), DuPage County Bar Assn., Cook County Bar Assn. (Kenneth E. Wilson award, Cert. Merit, Ida Platt award, Presdl. award, Jud. award), Ill. Judges' Assn., Ill. Jud. Coun. (Kenneth Wilson Meml. award, Meritorious Svc. award), Ill. State Bar Assn., Am. Judicature Soc., Am. Judges' Assn. Achievements include being first African-American to swear in a Mayor, City of Chicago, to serve on Illinois Supreme Court, 1990; being leader in case disposition by published opinion, 1988, 89.

FREEMAN, DAVID JOHN, lawyer; b. N.Y.C., Aug. 9, 1948; s. John L. and Josephine F. (Wilding) F.; m. Ellen Gogolick, Dec. 29, 1974; children: Matthew, Julie. BA, Harvard U., 1970; JD, 1975. Bar: Mass. 1975, D.C. 1977, N.Y. 1982, U.S. Dist. Ct. D.C. 1981, N.Y. 1982, U.S. Dist. Ct. D.C. 1981, U.S. Dist. Ct. (so. and ea. dists.) N.Y. 1982, U.S. Ct. Appeals (D.C. cir.) 1979, U.S. Ct. Appeals (2nd cir.) 1982, U.S. Supreme Ct. 1988. Spl. asst. to U.S. Senator Frank E. Moss, 1970-72; trial atty. FTC, Washington, 1975-77; assoc. Ginsburg, Feldman & Bress, Washington, 1977-81, Holtzmann, Wise & Shepard, N.Y.C., 1981-84; ptnr., 1984-94; ptnr., chmn. environ. dept. Battle Fowler, 1994-2000; head N.Y. environ. practice group Paul, Hastings, Janofsky & Walker, N.Y.C., 2000—. Spl. legal counsel N.Am. Environ. Affairs, UN Environ. Programme; co-chair emeritus ISO 14000 Legal Issues Forum, U.S. Tech. Com. to TC-207, Internat. Com. Standardization. Editor-in-chief: Jour. Environ Law Practice (West), 1998-2000. Mem. ABA (environment, energy and resources sect.), Assn. Bar City of N.Y., Harvard Law Sch. Assn., N.Y. State Bar Assn. (environ. law sect., co-chair hazardous waste com., co-chair task force on superfund reform). Federal civil litigation, Environmental. Office: Paul Hastings Janofsky & Walker LLP 75 E 55th St New York NY 10022-3205 E-mail: davidfreeman@paulhastings.com.

FREEMAN, FRANKLIN EDWARD, JR., state governmental assistant; b. Dobson, N.C., May 5, 1945; s. Franklin Edward and Clara E. (Smith) F.; m. Margaret Carson McKnight, 1966 (div. 1974); children: Margaret Elizabeth, Nancy Lorrin; m. Katherine Lynn Lloyd, Aug. 12, 1978; children: Katherine Ann, Franklin Edward III, Alexander Lloyd, Mary Clare. BA, U. N.C., 1967, JD, 1970. Bar: N.C. 1970. Rsch. asst. Assoc. Justice Dan K. Moore, Raleigh, N.C., 1970-71; asst. dist. atty. 17th jud. dist. N.C. Ct. System, 1971-73; exec. sec. Jud. Coun., 1973-78; asst. dir. Adminstrv. Office of Cts., Raleigh, 1973-78, dir., 1981-93; dist. atty. 17th jud. dist. N.C. Ct. System, 1979-81; sec. N.C. Dept. Correction, Raleigh, 1993-97; chief staff Gov. James B. Hunt, Jr., 1997-99; assoc. justice N.C. Supreme Ct., 1999-2001; sr. asst. for govt. affairs Gov. of N.C., 2001—. Contbr. articles to profl. jours. Tchr. Sunday sch. Main Street United Meth. Ch., Reidsville, 1974-81, chmn. every mem. canvas, 1980, chmn. adminstrv. bd., 1981; mem. Hayes Barton Meth. Ch., Raleigh; pres. Raleigh Host Lions Club, 1992—. Recipient Svc. award Conf. Superior Ct. Judges, Svc. award Conf. Dist. Ct. Judges, Svc. award N.C. Clks. Superior Ct. Assn., Svc. award N.C. Magistrates Assn. Mem. N.C. State Bar, N.C. Correctional Assn., Surry County Bar Assn., Rockingham County Bar Assn., 10th Dist. Bar Assn., 17th Dist. Bar Assn., State Correctional Adminstrs., Conf. State Ct. Adminstrs. (pres-elect 1992-93, bd. dirs. 1987-90, 94-95), Lions Club (pres. Raleigh Host club 1994), Delta Upsilon. Democrat. Avocations: horses, history, reading. Office: Gov's Office 20301 Mail Svc Ctr Raleigh NC 27699-0301*

FREEMAN, GEORGE CLEMON, JR., lawyer; b. Birmingham, Ala., Jan. 3, 1929; s. George Clemon and Annie Laura (Gill) F.; m. Anne Colston Hobson, Dec. 6, 1958; children: Anne Colston McEvoy, George Clemon III, Joseph Reid Anderson. BA magna cum laude, Vanderbilt U., 1950; LLB, Yale U., 1956. Bar: Ala. 1956, Va. 1958, D.C. 1974. Law clk. to Justice Hugo L. Black U.S. Supreme Ct., 1956; assoc. Hunton & Williams, Richmond, Va., 1957-63, ptnr., 1963-95, sr. counsel, 1995—. Contbr. articles to profl. jours. Pres. Va. chpt. Nature Conservancy, 1962—63; counsel Va. Outdoors Recreation Study Com. Va. Legis., 1963—65; mem. sect. 301 Superfund Act Study Group Congl. Adv. Com., 1981—82; mem. Falls James Com., 1973—89; chmn. adv. coun. Energy Policy Studies Ctr. U. Va., 1981—85; chmn. legal adv. com. to Va. Commn. on Transp. in the 21st Century, 1986—87; mem. Va. Gov.'s Commn. to Study Historic Preservation, 1987—88, Va. Coun. on the Environment, 1989—91; chmn. Va. Bd. Hist. Resources, 1989—91; mem. The Atlantic Coun., 1986—95; bd. dirs. Nat. Mus. Am. History, 1997—2002; chmn. Richmond City Dem. Com., 1969—71. Lt (j.g.) USN, 1951—54. Ctr. for Pub. Resources fellow, 1990—. Fellow Am. Bar Found. (Va. state chmn. 1986-90); mem. ABA (chmn. standing com. on facilities of Law Libr. of Congress 1967-73, coordinating group on regulatory reform 1981-85, nominating com. 1984-87, chmn. civil justice coordinating com. 1990-92, sect. bus. law, sect. coun. 1976-79, chmn. ad hoc com. on Fed. Criminal Code 1979-81, chmn. program com. 1981-82, chmn. ad hoc com. on tort law reform 1986-87, sect. del. to ho. of dels. 1983-87, sec. 1987-88, vice-chmn. and ed. The Business Lawyer 1988-89, chmn.-elect 1989-90, chmn. 1990-91), Richmond Bar Assn., Va. Bar Assn., Am. Law Inst. (coun. 1980—, advisor to coun. on project on compensation and liability for product and process injuries 1986-91, advisor restatement of law, THRD, torts apportionment 1993-97, advisor restatement law THRD torts gen. prins. 1997—), Am. Judicature Soc., Country Club of Va., Knickerbocker Club, Met. Club, Phi Beta Kappa, Phi Delta Phi, Omicron Delta Kappa, Alpha Tau Omega. Democrat. Episcopalian. Avocation: gardening. Administrative and regulatory, Environmental, Constitutional. Office: Hunton & Williams 951 E Byrd St Richmond VA 23219-0005 E-mail: gfreeman@hunton.com.

FREEMAN, GILL SHERRYL, judge; b. N.Y.C., June 24, 1949; d. Norman and Arlene (Vigdor) Jacovitz. Student, U. Wis., 1966-68; BS in Edn. cum laude, Temple U., 1970; MEd, U. Miami, Fla., 1973, JD cum laude, 1977. Bar: Fla. 1977, U.S. Dist. Ct. (so. dist.) Fla. 1977, U.S. Dist. Ct. (mid. dist.) Fla. 1984, U.S. Ct. Appeals (5th cir.) 1977. Tchr. Dade County Pub. Schs., Miami, 1970-76; assoc. Walton, Lantaff, Schroeder & Carson, Miami, 1977-82, Ruden, McClosky, Smith, Schuster & Russell, Miami, 1982—, ptnr., 1983-97; apptd. cir. ct. judge Dade County Fla., 1997—. Vice chair Fla. Supreme Ct. Gender Bias Commn., 1987—90; chair Fla. Supreme Ct. Gender Bias Study Implementation Commn., 1991—94; mem. Supreme Ct. Commn. Fairness, 1997, chair, 1999—; chmn. bd. distr. Journey Inst., 1997—2001. Trustee Dade County Law Libr., 1996—, chair, 2001—; bd. dirs. Family Counseling Svcs. of Greater Mami, 1995—, Spectrum Programs, 1993—, chair, 1996—98. Master: Family Law Inns Ct.; mem.: Cuban Am. Bar Assn., Fla. Assn. Women Lawyers (pres. 1984—85), Fla. Bar Assn. Avocations: alpine skiing, travel, tennis. Office: 73 W Flagler St Rm 303 Miami FL 33130

FREEMAN, LEE ALLEN, JR., lawyer; b. Chgo., July 31, 1940; s. Lee Allen and Brena (Dietz) F.; m. Glynna Gene Weger, June 8, 1968; children: Crispin McDougal, Clark Dietz, Cassidy Bree. AB magna cum laude, Harvard U., 1962, JD magna cum laude, 1965. Bar: Ill. 1966, D.C. 1966, Mont. 1986, U.S. Supreme Ct. 1969. Practiced in, Washington, 1965-68, Chgo., 1968—; law clk. to Justice Tom C. Clark, Washington, 1965-66; asst. U.S. atty., 1966-68; v.p. Freeman, Freeman & Salzman, P.C., 1970—; spl. asst. atty. gen. Ill., W.Va., 1969-82, 1973-79; spl. dep. atty. gen., 1971-82; spl. asst. corp. counsel, 1971-76. Pres. Chgo. Lyric Opera Guild; pres. Fine Arts Music Found.; dir. Chgo. Lyric Opera, 1995—; mem. Middlebury Coll. Arts Coun. Named Outstanding Young Citizen Chgo. Jaycees, 1976 Fellow: ABA Found.; mem.: ABA (coun. mem. antitrust sect. 1985—87), Am. Coll. Trial Lawyers, Chgo. Inn of Ct., Std. Club. Home: 232 E Walton St Chicago IL 60611-1507 also: 22 Bright Ln Wilsall MT 59086-9432 Office: 401 N Michigan Ave Chicago IL 60611-4255 E-mail: lfreemanjr@ffspc.com.

FREEMAN, LOUIS S. lawyer; b. Cin., Apr. 21, 1940; s. Emanuel and Sadye (Harris) F.; m. Diane Ruth Edson, Jan. 28, 1967; children: Matthew E., James H., Jill E. BBA, U. Cin., 1963; JD, Harvard U., 1966; LLM in Taxation, NYU, 1972. Bar: Ohio 1966, N.Y. 1968, Ill. 1975. CPA. Mem. staff Coopers & Lybrand, N.Y.C., 1966-68; assoc. Mudge, Rose, Guthrie & Alexander, N.Y.C., 1968-74, Sonnenschein Nath & Rosenthal, Chgo., 1974-76, ptnr., 1976-97, Skadden, Arps, Slate, Meagher & Flom, Chgo., 1997—. Adj. prof. of taxation Ill. Inst. Tech., Chgo.-Kent Coll. of Law Grads. Program in Taxation, 1985-89 Mem. bds. of contbg. editors Jour. Corp. Taxation, Jour. Real Estate Taxation, Jour. Taxation of Investments; bd. advisors the M&A Tax Report, Jour. Corp. Taxation; also author articles. Fellow Am. Coll. Tax Counsel; mem. ABA (tax sect. com. on corp. tax), Chgo. Bar Assn., (chmn. exec. com. of fed. tax com. 1986-87), N.Y. Sate Bar Assn. (tax sect. exec. com. 1990-92), Am. Law Inst. (tax adv. group subchpt. C. Fed. Income Tax Project), Met. Club of Chgo. Corporate taxation, Taxation, general, Personal income taxation. Office: Skadden Arps Slate Meagher & Flom 333 W Wacker Dr Chicago IL 60606-1220 E-mail: LFreeman@skadden.com.

FREEMAN, RICHARD MERRELL, lawyer, corporate director; b. Crawfordsville, Ind., July 2, 1921; s. F. Rider and Ruth (Merrell) F.; m. Joanne Spears, Nov. 26, 1943; children: Randy, Mark, Candy, Marcia. AB, Wabash (Ind.) Coll., 1943; LLB, Columbia U., 1948. Bar: Tenn. 1948, Ill. 1957. Atty. TVA, Knoxville, 1948-57, dir., 1978-86; partner firm Belnap, Spencer, Hardy & Freeman, Chgo., 1957-67; v.p. law Chgo. & Northwestern Transp. Co., Chgo., 1967-78, also dir., voting trustee. Exec. com. Fla. West Coast Symphony; bd. dirs. TVA, 1978-86. With USNR, 1943-46. Mem.: Phi Beta Kappa. Democrat. Mem. Community Ch. Home: 775 Longboat Club Rd #303 Longboat Key FL 34228

FREEMAN, TODD IRA, lawyer; b. Mpls., Nov. 24, 1953; s. Earl Stanley and Gretta Lois (Rudick) F.; m. Judy Lynn Sigel, June 15, 1975; children: Jennifer, Katie, Zachary. BS in Mktg., U. Colo., 1974; JD, U. Minn., 1978. Bar: Minn. 1978, U.S. Dist. Ct. Minn. 1978, U.S. Tax Ct. 1980; CPA, Minn. Acct. Coopers & Lybrand, Mpls., 1978-80; shareholder Larkin, Hoffman, Daly & Lindgren, Mpls., 1980—, treas., 1990—, also bd. dirs., 1990-93. Pres. The Group Inc. Mem. ABA (tax sect., past chmn. personal svc. orgns.), Minn. Soc. CPAs, Minn. State Bar Assn., Hennepin County Bar Assn. Avocations: tennis, golf. Corporate, general, Estate planning, Pension, profit-sharing, and employee benefits. Office: Larkin Hoffman Daly & Lindgren 7900 Xerxes Ave S Ste 1500 Minneapolis MN 55431-1128

FREER, ROBERT ELLIOTT, JR., retired lawyer; b. Washington, Jan. 19, 1941; s. Robert E. and Alice (Barry) F.; m. Roberta Stapleton Renchard, Dec. 31, 1972; children: Kimberly Dunlap, R. Elliott III, Ashleigh Hamilton, Daniel Renchard. AB, Princeton U., 1963; JD, U. Va., 1966. Bar: Va. 1966, D.C. 1968, U.S. Supreme Ct. 1973. Trial atty. FTC, 1966-69, atty. advisor to chmn., asst. to gen. counsel, 1970-71; exec. asst. to gen. counsel U.S. Dept. Transp., Washington, 1971-74; Washington counsel Kimberly Clark Corp., 1974-83; staff v.p., 1975-80; corp. v.p., 1980-84; gen. counsel, 1983-84; pvt. practice Washington, 1984-2000; ret., 2001; prin., owner Free Enterprise Found., 2002—. Mem. President's Commn. on White House Fellowships, 1985-93; pub. mem. Adminstrv. Conf. U.S., 1981-86; capt. land team President's Pvt. Sector Survey on Cost Control in Fedn. Govt., 1982-83; sec., gen. counsel U.S.-Cuba Bus. Coun., 1994-2000. Contbg. author, editor: Finding Our Roots/Facing Our Future: America in the 21st Century, 1997; contbr. articles to profl. jours. Founder, chmn. bd. trustees Washington Episc. Sch., 1986-94, chmn. emeritus, 1994—; chmn. bd. visitors Regent U. Sch. Law, 1995—; trustee Corcoran Gallery Art, 1986-93, asst. sec., chmn. bylaws com., 1990, sec., 1991; bd. trustees, pres. and CEO Free Enterprise Found., 2002—; chmn. Lawyers for the Republic, 1988—; asst. gen. counsel Rep. Nat. Conv., 1988, 92, 96; mem. Parents coun. Coll. Charleston, 1997, chmn., 2000-02. Mem. Rep. Nat. Lawyers Assn. (bd. govs. 1985-2000, gen. counsel 1985-89, vice chmn. 1988-89), Washington Met. Area Corp. Counsel Assn. (founder, pres. 1980-81, bd. dirs. 1980-84). Administrative and regulatory, Antitrust, Corporate, general. Home: PO Box 59604 Potomac MD 20859-9604 Office: Free Enterprise Found PO Box 21569 Charleston SC 29413

FREIER, ELLIOT G. lawyer; b. Huntington, N.Y., Apr. 2, 1961; s. Walter and Sondra J. Freier; children: Matthew V., Aaron M. BA in Econs., U. Va., 1983; JD, Yale U., 1986. Bar: Calif. 1986. Assoc. Irell & Manella LLP, L.A., 1986—92, ptnr., 1993—. Adv. bd. The M&A Tax Report, 1992—96. Mem. edtl. adv. bd.: Mergers and Acquisitions: The Monthly Tax Jour., 2000—03. Mem.: ABA (chmn. affiliated and related corps. com. 1996—97, tax sect.), Phi Beta Kappa. Avocations: tennis, alpine skiing. Corporate taxation, Taxation, general, Bankruptcy. Office: Irell & Manella LLP Ste 900 1800 Avenue of The Stars Los Angeles CA 90067 Office Fax: 310-203-7199. E-mail: efreier@irell.com.

FREIJE, PHILIP CHARLES, lawyer; b. Princeton, N.J., July 27, 1944; s. Brahim K. and Evelyn M. (Haddad) F.; m. Karen Mae Janovic, Oct. 18, 1969; children: Michael P., James C., Christine L. BA, U. Conn., 1966, JD, 1969; LLM, George Washington U., 1972. Bar: Conn. 1970, D.C. 1970, U.S. Supreme Ct. 1973. Assoc. Conway, Londregan, Leuba & McNamara, New London, Conn., 1969; atty.-advisor Office of Fgn. Direct Investment, U.S. Dept. Commerce, Washington, 1970-73, asst. dir. litigation, 1974; legal advisor Social & Econ. Statistics Adminstrn., U.S. Dept. Commerce, Washington, 1974-75; dep. asst. gen. counsel adminstrn./econ. affairs Office of Gen. Counsel, U.S. Dept. Commerce, Washington, 1975-81, dep. asst. gen. counsel econ. affairs/regulation, 1981-85, dep. chief counsel for econ. affairs, 1985-92, chief counsel for econ. affairs, 1992-98; bureau coun. U.S. Census Bureau U.S. Dept. Commerce, 1998—. Dir. Lake Barcroft Community Assn., Falls Church, Va., 1980-82. Mem. ABA, Fed. Bar Assn., Conn. Bar Assn., D.C. Bar Assn., Am. Judicature Soc. Home: 6212 Beachway Dr Falls Church VA 22041-1423 Office: US Dept Commerce 14th & Constitution Ave NW Washington DC 20230-0001

FREIS, JAMES HENRY, lawyer; b. New Brunswick, N.J., June 11, 1944; s. Peter Charles and Agnes (Clarkson) Freis; m. Maria Felicia Peters, Aug. 10, 1968; children: Jean Marie, James Henry Jr., Kathleen Marie. AB cum laude, St. Peters Coll., 1966; JD, Villanova U., 1969. Bar: N.J. 1969, N.Y. 1983. Law clk. to judge appellate divsn. Superior Ct. N.J., Newark, 1969—70; ptnr. Shanley & Fisher, PC, Morristown, Morristown, NJ, 1972—2002, Drinker, Biddle & Reath LLP, Florham Park, NJ, 2002—. Adv. com. pension commn. Newark Archdiocese Roman Cath. Ch; exec. com. banking law sect. N.J. State Bar Assn. Capt. U.S. Army, 1970—72. Mem.: ABA, Nat. Assn. Bond Lawyers. Banking, Commercial, contracts (including sales of goods; commercial financing), Municipal (including bonds). Office: Drinker Biddle & Reath LLP 500 Campus Dr Florham Park NJ 07932-1047

FRELS, KELLY, lawyer; b. Lolita, Tex., Dec. 28, 1943; s. Leon A. and Aileen K. Frels; m. Carmela Madden, Sept. 10, 1970; children: Jonathan, Catherine. BS in Edn., S.W. Tex. State U., San Marcos, 1966; JD, U. Tex., 1970. Bar: Tex., U.S. Dist. Ct. (so., no., we. and ea. dists.), U.S. Ct. Appeals (5th and 11th cirs.), U.S. Supreme Ct. Atty. Bracewell & Patterson, Houston, 1976-95, mng. ptnr., 1995-2001, mng. ptnr. Houston office, 2001—. Mem. bd. experts Lawyers Alert, 1984-88; mem. adv. bd. Edn. Law

Reporter, 1981-88; contbr. numerous articles to profl. jours. Bd. dirs., mem. exec. com. Greater Houston Partnership, 1998—, chair govt. rels. com., 1998-99, chair environ. adv. com., 2000, chair clean air task force, 2001—, chair quality of life com., 2001-02, chair flood task force, 2003. Mem. ABA (pub. edn. com. 1985-86), Houston Bar Assn. (bd. dirs. 1988-91, 95-96, treas. 1990, 2d v.p. 1991, 1st v.p. 1992, pres. 1994), State Bar Tex. (bd. dirs. 1995-98, chmn. sch. law sect. 1973-76, chair long range planning com. 1997-98, chair legal svcs. com. 1997-98, chair lawyer referral com. 1998-2001, vice chair nominating com. 1997-98, chair ann. meeting com. 2002-03, pres.-elect 2003-04), S.W. Tex. U. Alumni Assn. (pres. 1973), Houston Club (pres. 1999-2000). Roman Catholic. General civil litigation, Education and schools, Labor (including EEOC, Fair Labor Standards Act, labor-management relations, NLRB, OSHA). Home: 5607 Bordley Dr Houston TX 77056-2329 Office: Bracewell & Patterson LLP 711 Louisiana St Ste 2900 Houston TX 77002-2781 E-mail: kfrels@bracepatt.com.

FRENCH, JOHN, III, lawyer, director; b. Boston, July 12, 1932; s. John and Rhoda (Walker) F.; m. Leslie Ten Eyck, Jan. 11, 1957 (div. 1961); children: John B., Lawrence C.; m. Anne Hubbell, Jan. 9, 1965 (div. 1983); children: Daniel J., Susanna H.; m. Marina Kellen, Nov. 21, 1987. BA, Dartmouth Coll., 1955; JD, Harvard U., 1958. Bar: N.Y. 1959, D.C. 1988. Assoc. Milbank, Tweed, Hadley & McCloy, N.Y.C., 1961-68, Satterlee & Stephens, N.Y.C., 1968-73; asst. gen. counsel Continental Group, Inc., Stamford, Conn., 1973-81; v.p., gen. counsel, sec. Peabody Internat. Corp., Stamford, Conn., 1981-82; ptnr. Appleton, Rice & Perrin, N.Y.C., 1982-84, Beveridge and Diamond, N.Y.C., 1985-93, counsel, 1993-99; chmn. Tudor Assocs., LLC, N.Y.C., 1999—. Lectr. Practising Law Inst., 1979-83, Am. Law Inst., 1978; bd. dirs. Resorts Mgmt., Inc., Tudor Assocs., LLC, N.Y.C. Contbr. articles to profl. jours. Trustee Hudson River Found., YMCA-YWCA Camping Svcs. of Greater N.Y., Inc.; bd. dirs. Third St. Music Sch. Settlement House, Inc., N.Y.C., Internat. House, Inc., N.Y.C., Met. Opera Club, Young Concert Artists, Inc., 33 E. 70th St. Corp., Teatro alla Scala Found.; mem. Westchester County Planning Bd., 1974-85; mem. N.Y. State Environ. Bd., 1976-88. Capt. JAGC, USAF, 1958-61. Mem.: VFW, ABA, Am. Soc. Corp. Secs., Environ. Law Inst., Assn. of Bar of City of N.Y. (lectr.), N.Y. State Bar Assn. (lectr.), Mayflower Descs., Met. Opera Soc., Century Assn., Am. Legion, The Pilgrims, Knickerbocker Club, Harvard Club, River Club. Republican. Corporate, general, Environmental, Securities. Office: Tudor Assocs LLC 33 E 70th St New York NY 10021-4941 E-mail: tudor33@aol.com., tudorassoc@aol.com.

FRENCH, JOHN DWYER, lawyer; b. Berkeley, Calif., June 26, 1933; s. Horton Irving and Gertrude Margery (Ritzen) F.; m. Annette Richard, 1955; m. Berna Jo Mahling, 1986. BA summa cum laude, U. Minn., 1955; postgrad, Oxford U., Eng., 1955-56; LLB magna cum laude, Harvard U., 1960. Bar: D.C. 1960, Minn. 1963. Law clk. Justice Felix Frankfurter, U.S. Supreme Ct., 1960-61; legal asst. to commr. FTC, 1961-62; assoc. Ropes & Gray, Boston, 1962-63, Faegre & Benson, Mpls., 1963-66, ptnr., 1967-75, mng. ptnr., 1975-94, chmn. mgmt. com., 1989-94. Mem. adj. faculty Law Sch. U. Minn., 1965-70, mem. search com. for dean of Coll. of Liberal Arts, 1996; mem. exec. com. Lawyers Com. for Civil Rights Under Law, 1978—; co-chmn. U.S. Dist. Judge Nominating Commn., 1979; vice chmn. adv. com., mem. dir. search com., chmn. devel. office search com. Hubert Humphrey Inst., 1979-87. Contbr. numerous articles and revs. to legal jours. Chmn. or co-chmn. Minn. State Dem. Farm Labor Party Conv., 1970-90, 94, chmn. Mondale Vol. Com., 1972, treas., 1974; assoc. chmn. Minn. Dem.-Farmer-Labor Party, 1985-86; mem. Dem. Nat. Com., 1985-86; mem. Dem. Nat. Conv., 1976, 78, 80, 84, 88; trustee Twin Cities Public TV, Inc., 1980-86, mem. overseers com. to visit Harvard U. Law Sch., 1970-75, 77-82; chmn. Minn. steering com. Dukakis for Pres., 1987-88; mem. Sec. of State's Commn. on Electoral Reform, Minn., 1994; mem. Mayor's Commn. on Regulatory Reform, Mpls., 1995. With U.S. Army, 1955-56. Rotary Found. fellow, 1955-56 Mem. ABA (editorial bd. jour. 1976-79, commn. to study fed. trade 1969—), Minn. Bar Assn., Hennepin County Bar Assn., Jud. Coun. Minn., Lawyers Alliance for Nuclear Arms Control (nat. bd. dirs. 1982-84), U. Minn. Alumni Assn. (exec. com. 1985-87, v.p. 1989-91, pres. 1991-92, Vol. of Yr. award 1988), Phi Beta Kappa. Episcopalian. Administrative and regulatory, Antitrust, Federal civil litigation. Office: Faegre & Benson 2200 Wells Fargo Ctr 90 S 7th St Ste 2200 Minneapolis MN 55402-3901

FRENCH, TIMOTHY A. lawyer; b. New Britain, Conn., Aug. 22, 1959; s. George William and Joan (Stanley) F.; m. Jo Lynn Haley, Dec. 20, 1986; children: George William, Lindley Claire, Charles Stanley. AB, Harvard U., 1982; JD, Northwestern U., 1985. Bar: Ill. 1985, U.S. Dist. Ct. (no. dist.) Ill. 1985, U.S. Ct. Appeals (7th, 9th D.C. cirs.), U.S. Ct. Claims, U.S. Supreme Ct. Assoc. Gardner, Carton & Douglas, Chgo., 1986-89; ptnr. Neal, Gerber & Eisenberg, Chgo., 1989—. Contbr. articles to profl. jours. Mem. vestry St. Chrysostom's Ch., Chgo., 1996-97. Avocations: tennis, running, golf, skiing. Bankruptcy, General civil litigation, Commercial, contracts (including sales of goods; commercial financing). Office: Neal Gerber & Eisenberg 2 N Lasalle St Ste 2200 Chicago IL 60602-3801 E-mail: tfrench@ngelaw.com.

FRENKEL, DAVID ARIE, lawyer, educator; b. Tel Aviv, Feb. 2, 1940; s. Tsvi and Esther-Sarah (Berezovsky) F.; m. Naomi Davis, June 8, 1971; children: Esther, Tsvi, Dov, Dvora, Raya. MJurisprudence, Hebrew U., 1961, LLD, 1975. Bar: Israel. Pvt. practice, 1963-69, 81-89; asst., faculty of law Hebrew U., Jerusalem, 1969-72; instr., rschr. faculty of law and Inst. Legis. Rsch. & Comparative Law, Hebrew U., Jerusalem, 1972-75; dep. legal adviser Ministry of Edn. and Culture, Israel, 1974-76; dep., then legal advisor Ministry of Health, Israel, 1976-81; legal advisor Municipality of Beer-Sheva, Israel, 1990-97; assoc. prof. law, dept. bus. adminstrn. Ben-Gurion U. Sch. Mgmt., Beer-Sheva, Israel, 1997—. External tchr. Hebrew U. Jerusalem, Hadassah Med. Sch., Pub. Health Sch. and Faculty of Dental Medicine, 1978-2002; tutor Open U., 1993-2001; external tchr. Haifa U., Health Adminstrn. br., 1982-98, Bar-Ilan U., Ashkelon br., 1982-91; from tchr. to sr. lectr. Ben-Gurion U., Beer Sheva, 1981-97, with faculty of tech. dept. industry and adminstrn. engring., 1986-97; lectr. Hadassah Cmty. Coll., Jerusalem, 1974-87; mem. ethics com. for experiments on animals, Ben-Gurion U., Beer-Sheva, 1998—; chmn. ethics com. for Soroka U. Med. Ctr., Beer-Sheva, 1997—; judge local authorities disciplinary tribunal, 1996-2002. Author: Law of Cooperative Societies in Israel - Judicature and Legislation, 1966, Effect of Taxation on Registration of Rights in Land, 1972, Civil Judicature on Military and Security Matters, 1974, Law and Medicine - Military Aspects, 1985, Associations Law in Israel - The Law of not-for-profit Organizations in Israel, 2000, Partnership Law in Israel, 2002; co-author: (with G. Tedeschi) Law Citations, 1972, (with A. Kirschenbaum and N. Rakover) A Guide to the Sources of the Jewish Law, 1983, (with E. Davis) The Hebrew Amulet, 1995; co-editor Health Law in Can. Jour., 1980-87; contbr. chpts. to books and articles to profl. jour. Fellow, WHO, 1979. Fellow Royal Soc. Health, Royal Inst. Pub. Health and Hygiene; mem. Am. Soc. Law, Medicine and Ethics, Internat. Assn. Jewish Lawyers, Soc. for Medicine and Law in Israel, Internat. Dental, Ethics and Law Soc., World Assn. Med. Law, European Bus. and Ethic Network. Office: Ben Gurion U Dept Bus Admin Sch Mgmt Beer-Sheva Israel E-mail: dfrenkel@bgumail.bgu.ac.il.

FRENZEL, JAMES CHARLES, lawyer; b. Ft. Monmouth, N.J., Dec. 12, 1945; s. Charles H. and Virginia L. Frenzel; m. Susan B. Frenzel, Sept. 29, 1979; 1 child, Charles J. BA in History, Duke U., 1967, JD, 1970. Bar: Ga., N.C., U.S. Supreme Ct., U.S. Ct. Appeals (4th, 6th and 11th cirs.). Assoc. Womble, Carlyle, Sandridge & Rice, Winston-Salem, N.C., 1970-77, ptnr., 1977-90, Smith, Gambrell & Russell, Atlanta, 1990-91, Greene, Buckley, Jones & McQueen, Atlanta, 1991-95; prin. James C. Frenzel, P.C., Atlanta, 1995—. Vis. prof. Wake Forest U. Sch. Law, Winston-Salem, 1985-87; dir. Southeastern Bankruptcy Law Inst., Atlanta, 1980-2003. Author: Problem Loans in N.C., 1985, Secured Lending in Georgia, 1992; editor: How to Start a Pro Bono Bankruptcy Program, 1996. Bd. dirs. Continuing Legal Edn. in Ga., Athens, 1993; speaker Ctrl. Eastern European Initiative-U.S. Aid, Romania, 1996. Mem. ABA (mem. bus. sect. ethics com. 1996-2003), Ga. Bar Assn. (chmn. bankruptcy sect. 1994-95), N.C. Bar Assn. (chmn. bankruptcy sect. 1989-90). Bankruptcy. Home: 8985 Huntcliff Trace Atlanta GA 30350-1733 Office: Atlanta Financial Ctr Ste 155 3343 Peachtree Rd NE Atlanta GA 30326-1429 Personal E-mail: sbfrenzel@attbi.com. Business E-Mail: jcf-bklaw@mindspring.com.

FRERICKS, TIMOTHY MATTHEW, lawyer; b. Marion, Ohio, June 5, 1949; s. Theodore Paul and Dorothy Jane (Fetter) F. BA, Notre Dame U., 1971; JD, Ohio No. U., 1974. Bar: Ohio 1974. Ptnr. Frericks and Howard, Marion, 1974—. Contbr. articles to local newspaper. Bd. dirs. Marion Cath. H.S., 1982-85, Columbus Diocesan Schs., 1982-85, Marion Cadets Drum and Bugle Corps, 1978-88, sec., 1986—; trustee Marion H.A.N.D., Inc., 1989, Marion Shelter Program, Inc., 1988—; mem. tax adv. com. Columbus Diocesan Cath. Found., 1990—; rep. precinct capt., 1980—; pres. Marion County Rep. Club, 1982; founder Citizens for Responsible Govt., Marion, 1983—. Mem. Ohio Bar Assn., Marion County Bar Assn. (pres. 1993), Kiwanis (v.p. 1991, pres. 1992), Optimists (chmn. cmty. svc. 1975-82), KC. Family and matrimonial, Non-profit and tax-exempt organizations, Probate (including wills, trusts). Home: 2916 Neidhart Rd Marion OH 43302-8463 Office: Frericks & Howard 152 E Center St Marion OH 43302-3802

FREUD, NICHOLAS S. lawyer; b. N.Y.C., Feb. 6, 1942; s. Frederick and Fredericka (von Rothenburg) F.; m. Elsa Doskow, July 23, 1966; 1 child, Christopher. AB, Yale U., 1963, JD, 1966. Bar: N.Y. 1968, Calif. 1970, U.S. Tax Ct. 1973. Ptnr. Chickering & Gregory, San Francisco, 1978-85, Russin & Vecchi, San Francisco, 1986-93, Jeffer, Mangels, Butler & Marmaro, LLP, San Francisco, 1993—. Mem. joint adv. bd. Calif. Continuing Edn. of Bar, chair taxation subcom. 1987-87; mem. fgn. income adv. bd. Tax Management Internat. Jour., mem. bd. advs. The Jour. of Internat. Taxation; mem. adv. bd. NYU Inst. on Fed. Taxation; academician Internat. Acad. Estate and Tax Law; mem. tax commn., Union Internat. des Avocats. Author: (with Charles G. Stephenson and K. Bruce Friedman) International Estate Planning, rev. edit., 1997; contbr. articles to profl. jours. Fellow Am. Coll. of Tax Counsel; mem. ABA (tax sect. vice chair adminstrn. 2000-02, coun. dir. 1995-97, chair com. on U.S. activities of foreigners and tax treaties 1989-91, vice chair 1987-89, chair subcom. on tax treaties 1981-87), Calif. State Bar Assn. (taxation sect. exec. com. 1981-85, vice chair 1982-83, chair 1983-84, vice chair income tax com. 1981-82, chair 1982-83, vice chair personal income tax subcom. 1979-80, chair 1980-81, co-chair fgn. tax subcom. 1978-79, ert. specialist in taxation law), N.Y. State Bar Assn. (taxation sect., mem. com. on U.S. activities of fgn. taxpayers and fgn. activities of U.S. taxpayers), Bar Assn. of San Francisco, Bar Assn. of City of N.Y., San Francisco Tax Club (pres. 1988), San Francisco Internat. Tax Group. Private international, Taxation, general. Office: Jeffer Mangels Butler & Marmaro LLP 5th Fl Two Embarcedero Ctr San Francisco CA 94111-3824 E-mail: nsf@jmbm.com.

FREUDENTHAL, STEVEN FRANKLIN, lawyer, political organization chairman; b. Thermopolis, Wyo., June 8, 1949; s. Lewis Franklin and Lucille Iola (Love) F.; m. Janet Mae Mansfield, Aug. 30, 1969 (div. Sept. 1996); children: Lynn Marie, Kristen Lee; m. Barbara A. Crofts, Jan. 1, 1998; stepchildren: Shane C., Jeanne N. BA, Trinity Coll., Hartford, Conn., 1971; JD, Vanderbilt U., 1975. Bar: Wyo. 1975, U.S. Supreme Ct. 1981. Tax acct. Conn. Gen. Life Ins. Co., Hartford, Conn., 1971-72; asst. atty. gen. Wyo. Cheyenne, 1975-77; atty. gen. Wyo., 1981-82; state planning coordinator Office Gov. Wyo., Cheyenne, 1977-78; dep. under sec. Dept. Interior, Washington, 1978-79, exec. asst. to sec., 1979-80; ptnr Sherman & Howard, Cheyenne, Wyo., 1980-81; ptnr. Freudenthal, Salzburg & Bonds, Cheyenne, 1983—; mem. Wyo. Ho. Reps., 1987-91. Trustee United Med. Ctr., 1990-97, pres., 1993-96; bd. dirs. Cheyenne LEADS, 1990-93; chmn. Wyo. Dem. Party, 1999-2001. Office: 123 E 17th St Cheyenne WY 82003-0387 E-mail: steve@wyolaw.com.

FREUND, FRED A. retired lawyer; b. N.Y.C., June 18, 1928; s. Sidney J. and Cora (Strasser) F.; m. Rosalie Sampo, Nov. 18, 1975 (div. Apr. 1983); m. Patricia A. Gardner, Mar. 13, 1957 (div. Jan. 1967); children: Gregory G., K. Bailey AB, Columbia U., 1948, JD, 1949. Bar: N.Y. 1949, U.S. Supreme Ct. 1968. Law clk. to chief judge U.S. Dist. Ct. So. Dist. N.Y., N.Y.C., 1949-51; assoc. Kaye, Scholer, Fierman, Hays & Handler, N.Y.C., 1953-58, ptnr., 1959-93, ret., 1993. Served to 1st lt. USAF, 1951-53. Mem. ABA, Assn. Bar City N.Y., Phi Beta Kappa Home: 1085 Park Ave Apt 4C New York NY 10128-1179

FREUND, SAMUEL J. lawyer; b. Forenwald, Germany, Jan. 3, 1949; came to U.S., 1949; s. Abraham and Syma (Skop) F.;children: Alexandra, Stefanie. BSc in Acctg., Bklyn. Coll., 1971; JD, Bklyn. Law Sch., 1974; LLM in Taxation, NYU, 1980. Bar: N.Y. 1975, U.S. Dist. Ct. (so. and ea. dists.) N.Y. 1978, U.S. Tax Ct. 1981, Fla. 1981, N.J. 1988. Tax acct. Oppenheim, Appel and Dixon, N.Y.C., 1974-75, assoc., 1975; atty./advisor Bur. Hearing and Appeals, Dept. HEW, Johnstown, Pa., 1976-77; atty. Tax Dept. N.Y. State, N.Y.C., 1977-82; assoc. tax counsel CBS Inc., N.Y.C., 1982-84; sr. tax assoc. Am. Brands, Inc., N.Y.C., Friedman & Shaftan, P.C., 1986-89, Hugh Janow & Irwin Meyer, Pearl River, NY, 1990-96; pvt. practice Montclair, NJ, 1989-90, 96-97; v.p. taxation The Halpern Group, Springfield, NJ, 1998-99; of counsel Keenan Powers & Andrews, Hauppauge, NY, 2000—; adminstrv. law judge N.Y.C. Dept. Fin., 2001—. Mem.: ABA, Fla. Bar Assn. Avocations: computers, photography, music. Taxation, general, Personal income taxation, State and local taxation. E-mail: redbat@yahoo.com.

FREY, ANDREW LEWIS, lawyer; b. N.Y.C., Aug. 11, 1938; s. Daniel B. and Ruth J. Frey; children: Matthew S., Alexandra S. BA with high honors, Swarthmore Coll., 1959; LLB, Columbia U., 1962. Bar: N.Y. 1962, D.C. 1966, U.S. Supreme Ct. 1972. Law clk. to judge U.S. Ct. Appeals (D.C. cir.), 1963-64; spl. counsel to Gov. U.S. V.I., 1963-65; assoc. Koteen & Burt, Washington, 1965-70; ptnr. Dutton, Gwirtzman, Zumas, Wise & Frey, Washington, 1970-72; dep. solicitor gen. Office U.S. Solicitor Gen., Washington, 1972-86; ptnr. Mayer Brown Rowe & Maw, Washington, N.Y.C., 1986—. Notes editor Columbia Law Rev., 1961-62. Recipient John Marshall award Dept. Justice, 1975, Disting. Svc. award Atty. Gen., 1980, Presdl. award for Meritorious Svc., 1985. Mem. Am. Law Inst., Am. Acad. Appellate Lawyers, Phi Beta Kappa. Office: Mayer Brown Rowe & Maw 1675 Broadway Fl 19 New York NY 10019-5820 E-mail: afrey@mayerbrownrowe.com.

FREY, ERIC ALAN, lawyer; b. Terre Haute, Ind., Sept. 3, 1942; s. Harry E. and Dorothy G. (Castle) F.; m. Susan C., Sept. 7, 1963 (div. Apr. 1985); children: Jennifer, Eric II, Sarah, Jonathan; m. Ann L. Sackrider, June 15, 1985. AB, Ind. U., 1964, JD, 1967. Bar: Ind. 1967, U.S. Ct. Appeals (7th cir.) 1973, U.S. Supreme Ct. 1978. Law clk. to presiding justice U.S. Dist. Ct., Ft. Wayne, Ind., 1967-68; assoc. Rosenfeld & Wolfe, Terre Haute, 1968-70; ptnr. Rosenfeld, Wolfe & Frey, Terre Haute, 1970-79, Wolfe, Frey, Hunt & Olah, Terre Haute, 1979-86, Frey, Hunt, Hassler & Lorenz, Terre Haute, 1986—95; sole practitioner Fey Law Firm, 1995—. Mem. dem. precinct com. Vigo County, 1972-84; del. Ind. State Dem. Conv., Indpls., 1972—. Mem. Ind. Bar Assn. (counsel 1974-78), 7th Cir. Bar Assn., Ind. Trial Lawyers Assn., Terre Haute Bar Assn. (pres. 1974-75), Ind. Univ. Sch. of Law, Bloomington (pres., Law Sch. Alumni Assn. 2002—). Baptist. Avocations: running, tennis, bicycling. Federal civil litigation, State civil litigation, General practice. Home: 5231 Knightsbridge Ct Terre Haute IN 47803-9428 Office: Frey Law Firm 618 Wabash Ave Ste 200 Terre Haute IN 47807-1527 Office Fax: 812-235-2658. E-mail: eric.frey@freylaw.com.

FREY, HENRY CHARLES, lawyer; b. Flint, Mich., July 16, 1948; s. Frank Edgar and Anna Louise (Scholz) F.; m. Patricia Robinson, July 25, 1981 (div. Sept. 1993); children: Julia, Hillary; m. Susan Maree, July 29, 2000. BA cum laude, U. Mich., 1970; JD, Stetson U., 1973. Bar: Fla. 1973, Colo. 1974, U.S. Dist. Ct. Colo. 1974, U.S. Ct. Appeals (10th cir.) 1983. Staff atty. Colo. Rural Legal Svcs., Greeley, 1975-78, supervising atty., 1978-80; ptnr. Doyle, Otis, Frey & Hellerich, Greeley, 1980-98; pvt. practice Henry C. Frey, LLC, Greeley, 1998—. Colo. Supreme Ct. appointee to Bd. Law Examiners, Denver, 1982-92; mem. 19th Jud. Dist. Nominating Commn., 1982-87; grievance bd. hearing officer, 1999—; magistrate judge selection com. U.S. Ct. (Colo.), 1999—. Chmn. Patient Advocacy Team, Inc., Greeley, 1981-86. Mem. ATLA, Colo. Bar Assn. (bd. govs. 1982-84, Professionalism award 1996), Weld County Bar Assn. (chmn. litigation sect. 1988-90), Colo. Trial Lawyers Assn. Democrat. Avocations: mountain and rock climbing, skiing, cycling, tennis. General civil litigation, Personal injury (including property damage). Home: 1933 19th Ave Greeley CO 80631-5209 Office: Henry C Frey LLC 1035 37th Ave Ct Greeley CO 80634-4802 E-mail: hfrey1@mindspring.com.

FREYER, DANA HARTMAN, lawyer; b. Pitts., Apr. 17, 1944; m. Bruce M. Freyer, Dec. 21, 1969. Student, L' Institut De Hautes Etudes Internationales, Geneva, 1963-64; BA, Conn. Coll., 1965; postgrad., Columbia U., 1968, JD, 1971. Bar: N.Y. 1972, Ill. 1974, U.S. Dist. Ct. (no. dist.) Ill. 1974, U.S. Ct. Appeals (7th cir.) 1976, U.S. Supreme Ct. 1977, U.S. Dist. Ct. (so. dist.) N.Y. 1978, U.S. Dist. Ct. (ea. dist.) N.Y. 1981, U.S. Ct. Appeals (2d cir.) 1982. Staff atty. Legal Aid Soc. Westchester County, Mt. Vernon, N.Y., 1971-72; assoc. Friedman & Koven, Chgo., 1973-77, Skadden, Arps, Slate, Meagher & Flom, LLP, N.Y.C., 1977-88; spl. counsel Skadden, Arps, Slate, Meagher & Flom, N.Y.C., 1988-93, ptnr., 1994—. Pres. Westchester Legal Services, Inc., White Plains, N.Y., 1985-87, bd. dirs., 1978-98; U.S. Coun. for Internat. Bus. Arbitration Com.; London Ct. of Internat. Arbitration; adv. bd. World Arbitration and Mediation Report. Mem. ABA, Bar Assn. of City of N.Y., Internat. Bar Assn. Alternative dispute resolution, General civil litigation, Private international. Office: Skadden Arps Slate Meagher & Flom LLP 4 Times Sq Fl 48 New York NY 10036-6522

FREYTAG, SHARON NELSON, lawyer; b. May 11, 1943; d. John Seldon and Ruth Marie (Herbel) Nelson; children: Kurt David, Hillary Lee. BS with highest distinction, U. Kans., Lawrence, 1965; MA, U. Mich., 1966; JD cum laude, So. Meth. U., 1981. Bar: Tex. 1981, U.S. Dist. Ct. (no. dist.) Tex. 1981, U.S. Ct. Appeals (5th cir.) 1982, U.S. Supreme Ct. 1993, U.S. Dist. Ct. (so. dist.) Tex. 2001, U.S. Ct. Appeals (8th cir.) 2001, U.S. Ct. Appeals (fed. cir.) 2002. Tchr. English, Gaithersburg (Md.) H.S., 1966—70; instr. English, Eastfield Coll., 1974-78; law clk. U.S. Dist. Ct. (no. dist.) Tex., 1981-82, U.S. Ct. Appeals (5th cir.), 1982; ptnr., chmn. appellate practice sect. Haynes and Boone, Dallas, 1983—. Vis. prof. law So. Meth. U., 1985-86; faculty Appellate Adv. program NITA. Editor-in-chief Southwestern Law Jour., 1980-81; contbr. articles to profl. jours. Dir. Ctr. for Brain Health; dir. devel. bd. U. Tex. at Dallas. Woodrow Wilson fellow; recipient John Marshall Constl. Law award, Baird Cmty. Spirit award, 1995. Mem. ABA (litigation sect., co-chmn. subcom. on appellate rules), Fed. Bar Assn. (co-chmn. appellate practice and adv. sect. 1990-91), Tex. Bar Assn. (appellate coun. 1995-98), State Bar Tex. (bd. dirs., exec. com. 1997-2001), Dallas Bar Assn. (appellate coun.), Higginbotham Inn of Ct., Order of Coif, Phi Beta Kappa. Lutheran. Appellate, Federal civil litigation, State civil litigation. Office: Haynes & Boone 3100 Bank of America Plz Dallas TX 75202 E-mail: freytags@haynesboone.com.

FRICK, BENJAMIN CHARLES, lawyer; b. Overbrook, Pa., Feb. 23, 1960; s. Sidney Wanning and Marie Pauline Frick; m. Stephanie Ann Sears, June 1, 1991; children: Sarah Marie, Anna Elizabeth, Charles Andrew. BA, Cornell U., 1982; JD, U. Richmond, 1985; LLM in Taxation, Villanova U., 1994. Bar: Pa. 1985. Clk. to Hon. John B. Hannum US dist. ct., 1984; trust officer Provident Nat. Bank, Phila., 1985-89; sole practice Bryn Mawr, Pa., 1989—. Deacon, elder, Ardmore (Pa.) Presbyn. Ch. Mem.: S.R. (bd. dirs. Pa. Soc. 1987—, sec. 1991—95, treas. 1995—97, v.p. 1997—), ABA, Phila. Bar Assn., Pa. Bar Assn., Mil. Order Loyal Legion US (sec. 1993—95, v.p. 1995—97, comdr. 1997—99, judge adv.-in-chief 1997—2001, nat. v.p. 2001—), St. Andrew's Soc. Phila., Colonial Soc. Pa. (treas. 2000—03, v.p. 2003—), Soc. Mayflower Desc., Soc. Colonial Wars (bd. dirs. Pa. chpt. 1999—), The Phila. Club, Athenaeum Phila., Alpha Delta Phi, Phi Alpha Delta. Republican. Presbyterian. Estate planning, Probate (including wills, trusts), Estate taxation. Office: Bldg 1 Ste 303 919 Conestoga Rd Bryn Mawr PA 19010-1352

FRICK, ROBERT HATHAWAY, lawyer; b. Cleve., June 28, 1924; s. Claude Oates and Urshal May (Hathaway) F.; m. Lenore M. Maurin, Aug. 16, 1947 (dec. Sept. 1993); children: Elaine D. Frick , Barbara A. Frick Bundick, Catherine L. Frick Cayer. BBA, U. Mich., 1948, JD, 1950; postgrad. Harvard Bus. Sch., 1965. Bar: Mich. 1951, Ill. 1951, Ohio 1952, N.Y. 1962, U.S. Supreme Ct. 1981. Atty., Amoco Corp. (formerly Standard Oil Co. Ind.), Chgo., 1950, 52-60, Paris, 1960-62, N.Y.C., 1962-68, Chgo., 1968-71, assoc. gen. counsel, Chgo., 1972-87; pvt. practice, Cleve., 1951-52. Served with USAAF, 1943-46. Mem. ABA, Am. Soc. Internat. Law, Assn. of Bar of City of N.Y., Ill. Bar Assn., Chgo. Bar Assn., Order of Coif, Westmoreland Country Club, Meadows Country Club, Univ. Club Chgo., Mid Am. Club, Sigma Phi Epsilon. Republican. Administrative and regulatory, Corporate, general, Oil, gas, and mineral. Home: 921 Westerfield Dr Wilmette IL 60091-1810

FRICKE, RICHARD JOHN, lawyer; b. Ithaca, N.Y., Apr. 17, 1945; s. Richard I. and Jeanne L. (Hines) F.; m. Carol A. Borelli, June 17, 1967 (div. 1990); children: Laura, Richard, Amanda; m. Penny Yrizarry, Dec. 29, 1990 (div. 1999); children: Stephanie, Matthew, Tyler. BA, Cornell U., 1967, JD, 1970. Bar: Conn. 1970. Assoc. Gregory & Adams, Wilton, Conn., 1970-73; ptnr. Crehan & Fricke, Ridgefield, Conn., 1973-90; gen. counsel Connex Internat. Inc.; corp. counsel, pres. Safe Alternatives Corp. of Am., Inc.; pres., gen. counsel, dir. T.F.I. Industries, Inc.; gen. counsel, dir. Gold Mustache Pub. Corp., Inc.; sec., dir. DXTC.COM, Inc.; dir. Village Bank & Trust Co.; town atty. Town of Ridgefield, 1973-81. Bd. dirs. Gold Mustache Pub. Corp., Inc.; mem. Closing Mgmt. Svcs. LLC. Co-patentee low reactive pressure foam, polyurethane foam for cellulostic products. Bd. dirs. Ridgefield Community Ctr., Ridgefield Montessori, Ridgefield Community Kindergarten; founder, pres. Ridgefield Lacross League; constable Town of Wilton, Conn.; mem. Conn. Bar Commn. on Women, 1976. Mem. ABA, Conn. Bar Assn., Danbury Bar Assn. Democrat. Roman Catholic. Family and matrimonial, General practice, Property, real (including real estate development, water). Address: 440 Main St Ridgefield CT 06877-4525 E-mail: rickfricke@aol.com.

FRICKLAS, MICHAEL DAVID, lawyer; b. Somerville, N.J., Jan. 9, 1960; s. Richard L. and Anita (Alper) F.; children: Shanna E., Jaimee G., Gabriella S.; m. Donna J. Astion, Jan. 14, 1996. BSEE, U. Colo., 1981; JD magna cum laude, Boston U., 1984. Bar: Calif. 1987, Colo. 1990, N.Y. 1993. Assoc. Ware & Freidenrich, Palo Alto, Calif., 1984-87, Shearman & Sterling, N.Y., San Francisco, 1987-90; v.p., gen. counsel Minorco (U.S.A.) Inc., Denver, 1990-93; sr. v.p., dep. gen. counsel, mem. ops. com. Viacom, Inc., N.Y.C., 1993-98, sr. v.p., gen. counsel, sec., 1998-2000, exec. v.p., gen. counsel, sec., 2000—. Trustee Jazz at Lincoln Ctr., 1995—, Am. Jewish Com., N.Y. chpt., 1998—; mem. bd. vis. Boston U. Sch. Law, 1997—. Mem. ABA (gen. counsel com.), Am. Assn. Corp. Secs., Assn. Gen. Counsel. Computer, Mergers and acquisitions, Securities. Office: Viacom Inc 1515 Broadway New York NY 10036-8901

FRIED, CHARLES, law educator; b. Prague, Czechoslovakia, Apr. 15, 1935; came to U.S., 1941, naturalized, 1948; s. Anthony and Marta (Winterstein) F.; m. Anne Sumerscale, June 13, 1959; children: Gregory,

Antonia. AB, Princeton U., 1956; BA, Oxford (Eng.) U., 1958, MA, 1961; LLB, Columbia U., 1960; LLD (hon.), New Eng. Sch. of Law, 1987, Pepperdine U., 1994, Suffolk U., 1996. Bar: D.C. 1961, Mass. 1966. Law clk. to Hon. John M. Harlan U.S. Supreme Ct., 1960; from asst. prof. to prof. law Harvard U., Cambridge, 1961-85, Carter prof. gen. jurisprudence, 1981-85, 89-95, Carter prof. emeritus, disting. lectr. Law Sch., 1995-99, Beneficial prof. law, 1999—; assoc. justice Supreme Jud. Ct. Mass., Boston, 1995-99. Spl. cons. Treasury Dept. , 1961—62; cons. White House Office Policy Devel., Washington, 1982, Dept. Transp., Washington, 1981—82, Dept. Justice, 1983; solicitor gen. U.S. , 1985—89. Author: An Anatomy of Values, 1970, Medical Experimentation: Personal Integrity and Social Policy, 1974, Right and Wrong, 1978, Contract as Promise: A Theory of Contractual Obligation, 1981, Order and Law: Arguing the Reagan Revolution, 1991, (with David Rosenberg) Making Tort Law: What Should Be Done and Who Should Do It, 2003; contbr. legal and philos. jours. Guggenheim fellow, 1971-72 Fellow Am. Acad. Arts and Scis.; mem. Inst. Medicine, Am. Law Inst., Century Assn., Mass. Hist. Soc., Phi Beta Kappa. E-mail: fried@law.harvard.edu.

FRIED, DONALD DAVID, lawyer; b. N.Y.C., Feb. 28, 1936; s. Fred and Sylvia (Falk) F.; m. Joan Hilbert, Sept. 15, 1963; children: Neil, Derek. BA, CCNY, 1956; JD, Harvard U., 1959. Bar: N.Y. 1959. Assoc. Conboy, Hewitt, O'Brien & Boardman, N.Y.C., 1960-68, ptnr., 1968-86, Hunton & Williams, N.Y.C., 1986-88, 92-96; sr. counsel, 1996—; v.p., sec., assoc. gen. counsel Philip Morris Cos., Inc., N.Y.C., 1988-91. Corporate, general, Mergers and acquisitions, Securities. Home: 37 W 12th St New York NY 10011-8502 Office: Hunton & Williams 200 Park Ave Rm 4400 New York NY 10166-0091 E-mail: dfried@hunton.com.

FRIED, L. RICHARD, JR., lawyer; b. N.Y.C., Apr. 3, 1941; s. L. Richard and Jane (Kent) Wick F.; married Susan Fried; 1 child, Paula Suzanne. BS, U. Ariz., 1963, JD, 1966. Bar: Ariz. 1966, Hawaii 1968, U.S. Dist. Ct. No. Mariana Islands 1978, U.S. Ct. Claims 1978, U.S. Ct. Internat. Trade 1977, U.S. Tax Ct. 1977, U.S. Ct. Appeals (9th cir.) 1969, U.S. Supreme Ct. 1977. Assoc. Case, Kay & Lynch, Honolulu, 1967-72; ptnr., pres. Cronin, Fried, Sekiya, Kekina & Fairbanks, Honolulu, 1974—. Lawyer rep. 9th Cir. Jud. Conf., Hawaii, 1991-93, 2001. Mem. ABA, Assn. Trial Lawyers Am. (nat. committeeman 1980-82), Am. Bd. Trial Advocates (v.p. 1986-94), Hawaii Trial Lawyers Assn. (pres. 1981-82, 84—, Hawaii Trial Lawyer of Yr. 1994), Hawaii State Bar Assn. (bd. dirs. 1995-97), Ariz. State Bar Assn., Hawaii Acad. Plaintiffs Attys. (bd. dirs. 1994-96), Consumer Lawyers Hawaii (pres.-elect 2001, pres. 2002-), Exch. of Honolulu Club. Episcopalian. Aviation, Personal injury (including property damage), Product liability. Office: Cronin Fried Sekiya Kekina & Fairbanks 841 Bishop St Ste 1900 Honolulu HI 96813-3962 E-mail: rfried@croninfried.com.

FRIEDEN, CLIFFORD E. lawyer; b. L.A., Mar. 8, 1949; s. Sidney S. and Norma (Stern) F.; m. Dinah S. Baumring, June 20, 1971; children: Jamie, Kari, Curtis. BA, UCLA, 1971; JD, U. Calif., Berkeley, 1974. Bar: Calif. 1974, U.S. Dist. Ct. (so. dist.) Calif. 1974, U.S. Dist. Ct. (cen. dist.) Calif. 1977. Ptnr. Rutan & Tucker, Costa Mesa, Calif., 1974—. Mem. Orange County chpt. ARC, 1995-2001. Mem. Orange County Bar Assn. (del. state conv. 1983-95, chair judiciary com. 1987-88, bd. dirs. 1989-91), Order of Coif, Phi Beta Kappa. Avocations: sports, jogging. State civil litigation, Commercial, consumer (including collections, credit), Property, real (including real estate development, water). Office: Rutan & Tucker PO Box 1950 611 Anton Blvd Ste 1400 Costa Mesa CA 92626-1931

FRIEDL, BIRGIT E. lawyer; b. Vilsbiburg, Bavaria, Germany, Sept. 6, 1963; First state exam, Ludwigs Maximilians U., Munich, 1990, Dr. iur., 1993; second state exam, Oberlandesgericht, Munich, 1993. Bar: Munich Cts. 1995. Lectr. law King's Coll., London, 1993—96; lawyer BBLP Beiten Burkhardt, Munich, 1997—2001, Gibson, Dunn & Crutcher, Munich, 2002—. Author: Promissory Estoppel und vertragsänderungen im englischen Recht, 1993. Avocations: sailing, travel, tennis, skiing. Corporate, general, Mergers and acquisitions. Office: Gibson Dunn & Crutcher LLP Widenmayerstr 10 80538 Munich Germany

FRIEDL, RICK, lawyer, former academic administrator; b. Berwyn, Ill., Aug. 31, 1947; s. Raymond J. and Ione L. (Anderson) F.; m. Dawn Friedl; children: Richard, Angela, Ryan, Ariana. BA, Calif. State U., Northridge, 1969; MA, UCLA, 1976, postgrad., 1984; JD, Western State U., 1987. Bar: Calif. 1988, U.S. Dist. Ct. (ctrl. dist.) Calif. 1992. Dept. mgr. Calif. Dept. Indsl. Rels., 1973-78; mem. faculty dept. polit. sci. U. So. Calif., 1978-80; pres. Pacific Coll. Law, 1981-86; staff counsel state fund Calif., 1988-89; prin. Law Offices of Rick Friedl, 1989—. Author: The Political Economy of Cuban Dependency, 1982; tech. editor Glendale Law Rev., 1984; contbr. articles to profl. jours. Calif. State Grad. fellow, 1970-72. Mem. ABA, Calif. State Bar Assn., Los Angeles County Bar Assn., Am. Polit. Sci. Assn., Latin Am. Studies Assn., Acad. Polit. Sci., Pacific Coast Coun. Latin Am. Studies, Calif. Trial Lawyers Assn. Government contracts and claims, Property, real (including real estate development, water), Workers' compensation. Home: PO Box 2095 California City CA 93504-0095

FRIEDLAND, MICHAEL KEITH, lawyer, educator; b. Fontana, Calif., Nov. 11, 1966; s. Melvin L. and Carole J. F.; m. Jennifer M. Yuan, July 18, 1993; children: Robert, Steven. BA, U. Calif., Berkeley, 1988; JD, Harvard U., 1991. Bar: Calif. 1991, U.S. Supreme Ct. 1995, U.S. Ct. Appeals (fed. cir.) 1997. Assoc. Irell & Manella, LLP, Newport Beach, Calif., 1991-96; ptnr. Knobbe, Martens, Olson & Bear, LLP, Irvine, Calif., 1996—. Adj. prof. Whittier Law Sch., Costa Mesa, Calif., 1997—. Traffic commr. City of Redlands, Calif., 1984. Mem. Federalist Soc. Republican. Jewish. Avocations: tennis, theme parks. Federal civil litigation, Intellectual property. Office: Knobbe Martens Olson & Bear 2040 Main St 14th Fl Irvine CA 92614

FRIEDLANDER, D. GILBERT, lawyer; b. Hazleton, Pa., Sept. 10, 1946; BA, U. Tex., 1968, JD, 1971. Bar: Tex. 1972, N.Y. 1973. Sr. shareholder, bd. dirs. Johnson & Gibbs, 1973-91; gen. counsel Electronic Data Systems Corp., Plano, Tex., 1991—, sr. v.p., corp. sec., CSU for legal affairs, 1991—. Mem. ABA, N.Y. State Bar Assn., State Bar Tex. (corp. com., corp. banking and bus. law sect. 1980—, chmn. com. for rev. corp. tax law 1983-85), Dallas Bar Assn., Dallas Assn. Young Lawyers. Office: Electronic Data Systems Corp Mail Stop H3-3A-05 5400 Legacy Dr Plano TX 75024-3199*

FRIEDLANDER, JAMES STUART, lawyer; b. Chgo., Mar. 25, 1942; s. Earle E. and Sally J. (Meyer) F.; m. Sherfunissa Hassen, Sept. 27, 1969 (div. 2001); children: Samantha, Melissa, Natasha, Davina. BA, U. Wis., 1963; JD, Harvard U., 1966. Bar: Ill. 1966, D.C. 1979. Internat. legal advisor ministry external affairs Govt. of Malawi, Blantyre, 1968-71; counsel World Bank, Washington, 1972-75; mgr. Citibank, N.A., Nairobi, Kenya, 1975-78; assoc. Duncan, Allen and Mitchell, Nairobi, 1978-80, ptnr. Washington, 1980-88, Mitchell, Friedlander & Gittleman, Washington, 1988-91, Akin, Gump, Strauss, Hauer & Feld, LLP, Washington, 1991—2000, resident ptnr. Moscow, 1994-97. Bd. dirs. DAMconsult Ltd., Washington, Internat. Eye Found., Washington, 1990-94. Editor: Malawi Treaty Series, 1964-71, 1971. Vice chmn. Kenya Lawn Tennis Assn., Nairobi, 1981-83; vol. Peace Corps, Blantyre, 1966-68. Mem. ABA, Am. Soc. Internat. Law, Fed. Bar Assn. (chmn., sub-com. on internat. investment 1987-88), Westwood Country Club. Jewish. Avocations: tennis, piano, travel. Commercial, contracts (including sales of goods; commercial financing), Private international, International investment.

FRIEDLANDER, JEFFREY D. lawyer; b. 1947; BA, CUNY; JD, NYU. Bar: N.Y. 1971. Joined law dept. City of N.Y., 1970, first. asst. corp. counsel. Office: NYC Law Dept 100 Church St New York NY 10007-2601*

FRIEDMAN, ALVIN, lawyer; b. Bklyn., June 19, 1931; s. Isidor and Freda F.; m. Maryann Kallison, Mar. 27, 1955; children: Alan K., Margot N. BA with honors in Polit. Sci, Cornell U., 1952; LL.B. cum laude (editor Law Jour. 1956-57), Yale U., 1957. Bar: Tex. 1957, D.C. 1957. Asso. firm Covington & Burling, 1957-63; spl. asst. to gen. counsel Dept. Def., 1963-64, spl. asst. to asst. sec. def. for def. for internat. security affairs, 1964, dep. asst. sec. def. for internat. security affairs Far East and Latin Am., 1964-66; ptnr. Ginsburg & Feldman, Washington, 1966-67, Friedman and Medalie and predecessor firms, Washington, 1967-87; pvt. practice law Washington, 1988—. Served as 1st lt. USAF, 1952-54. Mem. Tex., D.C. bar assns. Office: 700 New Hampshire Ave NW Washington DC 20037-2406

FRIEDMAN, BARRY HOWARD, lawyer, physician; b. Joplin, Mo., Mar. 18, 1945; s. Marion and Esther (Lerner) Friedman; m. Marshal Lee Rosenthal, June 25, 1967; children: Heather Michelle, Jarrod David. BA, Western Md. Coll., 1965; MD, U. Md., 1969; JD, U. Balt., 1987, 1987; MBA, U. Balt., 1999. Bar: Md. 1987, Pa. 1987; diplomate Am. Bd. Radiology, Am. Bd. Nuc. Medicine, Am. Bd. Legal Medicine, Nat. Bd. Medicine Examiners. Intern Washington Hosp. Ctr., 1969-70; resident Sinai Hosp., Balt., 1970-73, fellow in diagnostic radiology, 1982-83; fellow in nuclear medicine Johns Hopkins Hosp., Balt., 1973-74, assoc. attending radiologist, 1983-88; pres. Chesapeake Imaging Specialists, Pikesville, Md., 1986-89; attending radiologist Northwest Hosp. Ctr., 1988-95, MRI Ctr. at Northwest Hosp. Ctr., 1990-98; physician adminstr. dept. health and mental hygiene State of Md., 1998—. Adj. prof. bus. law U. Balt., 1999—. Scholar France-Berrick Grad. Bus. scholar, 1997, 1998. Fellow: Am. Coll. Angiology, Am. Coll. Legal Medicine; mem.: ABA, Bar Assn. Balt. City, Baltimore County Med. Soc., Md. Soc. Radiology, Md. Trial Lawyers, Radiol. Soc. N.Am., Soc. Nuc. Medicine, Am. Coll. Radiology, Am. Coll. Physician Execs., Sigma Iota Epsilon. General civil litigation, Health, Personal injury (including property damage). Home: 6 Green Heather Ct Pikesville MD 21208-1516 Office: DHMH Rm 135 212 W Preston St Baltimore MD 21201-2323

FRIEDMAN, BART, lawyer; b. N.Y.C., Dec. 5, 1944; s. Philip and Florence (Beckerman) F.; m. Wendy Alpern Stein, Jan. 11, 1986; children: Benjamin Alpern, Jacob Stein. AB, L.I. U., 1966; JD, Harvard U., 1969. Bar: N.Y. 1970, Mass. 1972. Rsch. fellow Harvard U. Bus. Sch., Cambridge, Mass., 1969-70; assoc. Cahill, Gordon & Reindel, N.Y.C., 1970-72, 77-80, ptnr., 1980—; spl. counsel SEC, Washington, 1974-75, asst. dir., 1975-77. Bd. dirs. Calif. Inst. for the Arts. Mem. Ind. Task Force on Post-Conflict Iraq, 2003—; vis. com. Harvard U. Grad. Sch. Edn., 1995—2001, com. on univ. resources, 1996—; trustee Juilliard Sch., 1988—2001, vice chmn., 1994—2001; trustee Brookings Inst., 1997—, chmn. N.Y. adv. com., 1997—2001, mem. coun. fgn. rels., 1995—, joint task force on resources for fgn. affairs, ind. task force on non-lethal weapons; del. NATO Hdqrs. and Field, 1998; adv. bd. Remarque Inst. NYU, 1997—2002, Internat. Inst. for Strategic Studies, 2000; bd. dirs. Lincoln Ctr. for Performing Arts, 2002—, trustee, 2002—. Mem. Assn. Bar City of N.Y., Coun. Fgn. Rels., Explorers Club, The River Club, Links Club, The Tuxedo Club, Century Assn., The Met. Club (Washington). Corporate, general, Securities. Home: 1172 Park Ave Apt 5B New York NY 10128-1213 Office: Cahill Gordon & Reindel 80 Pine St Fl 17 New York NY 10005-1790

FRIEDMAN, BERNARD ALVIN, federal judge; b. Detroit, Sept. 23, 1943; s. David and Rae (Garber) F.; m. Rozanne Golston, Aug. 16, 1970; children: Matthew, Megan. Student, Detroit Inst. Tech., 1962-65; JD, Detroit Coll. Law, 1968. Bar: Mich. 1968, Fla. 1968, U.S. Dist. Ct. (ea. dist.) Mich. 1968, U.S. Ct. Mil. Appeals 1972. Asst. prosecutor Wayne County, Detroit, 1968-71; ptnr. Harrison & Friedman, Southfield, Mich., 1971-78, Lippitt, Harrison, Friedman & Whitefield, Southfield, 1978-82; judge Mich. Dist. Ct. 48th dist., Bloomfield Hills, 1982-88; U.S. dist. judge Ea. Dist. Mich., Detroit, 1988—. Lt. U.S. Army, 1967-74. Recipient Disting. Service award Oakland County Bar Assn., 1986. Avocation: running. Office: US Dist Ct US Courthouse Rm 238 231 W Lafayette Blvd Detroit MI 48226-2700

FRIEDMAN, DANIEL MORTIMER, federal judge; b. N.Y.C., Feb. 8, 1916; s. Henry Michael F. and Julia Freedman Friedman; m. Leah Lipson, Jan. 16, 1955 (dec. Dec. 1969); m. Elizabeth Ellis, Oct. 19, 1975 (dec. June 2002). AB, Columbia U., 1937, LLB, 1940. Bar: N.Y. 1941. Practice law, N.Y.C., 1940—42; with SEC, Washington, 1942—51, Justice Dept., Washington, 1951—59, asst. to solicitor gen., 1959—62, 2d asst. to solicitor gen., 1962—68, 1st dep. solicitor gen., 1968—78; chief judge Ct. Claims and U.S. Ct. Appeals, Washington, 1978—89, sr. judge, 1989—. With U.S. Army, 1942—46. Recipient Exceptional Svc. award, Atty. Gen., 1969. Office: US Ct Appeals Federal Circuit 717 Madison Pl NW Washington DC 20439-0002

FRIEDMAN, EDWARD DAVID, lawyer, arbitrator; b. Chgo. s. Jacob C. and Bessie (Levison) F.; m. Mary Louise Melia, Nov. 1, 1947 (dec. Feb. 1997); children: Michael, Daniel, Mary Eleanor, Elizabeth; m. Carol Green, Nov. 26, 1999. AB with honors, U. Chgo., 1935, JD cum laude, 1937. Bar: Ill. 1937, U.S. Ct. Appeals 1950, D.C. 1969, U.S. Supreme Ct. 1969. Law clk. to fed. master in chancery, Chgo., 1937-38; assoc. Rosenberg, Toomin & Stein, Chgo., 1938-39; gen. counsel staff SEC, 1939-42; chief counsel OPA, 1942-43; spl. asst. to dep. solicitor and solicitor Dept. Labor, Washington, 1943-48, dep. solicitor of labor, 1965-68, acting solicitor of labor, 1969; ptnr. Bernstein, Alper, Schoene & Friedman, Washington, 1969-75, Highsaw, Mahoney & Friedman, Washington, 1975-80, Friedman & Wirtz, 1980-90; chief law officer 5th regional office, also asst. gen. counsel NLRB, 1948-60; labor counsel to Senator John F. Kennedy, 1960-61, Senator Wayne Morse, 1961-65, U.S. Senate Labor and Pub. Welfare Com., 1961-65; counsel to majority and minority floor mgrs. Senators Clark and Case on Title VII of Civil Rights Bill, 1964; spl. asst. sec. labor fgn. farm labor program, 1965; counsel compaign conduct adminstrv. com. United Steelworkers Am., 1980-89. U.S. del. to OECD, Paris, 1968. Mem. editl. bd. U. Chgo. Law Rev, 1936-37. Mem. town coun., Garrett Park, Md., 1954-58, mayor, 1960-66; mem. Truro (Mass.)Zoning Bd. Appeals, 1999—. U. Chgo. James Nelson Raymond fellow, 1937. Mem. ABA, D.C. Bar Assn., Fed. Bar Assn., Order of Coif, U. Chgo. Alumni Club. Federal civil litigation, Appellate, Labor (including EEOC, Fair Labor Standards Act, labor-management relations, NLRB, OSHA). Home: 24 Gospel Path PO Box 1123 Truro MA 02666-1123 also: 1300 N Placita Parasol Green Valley AZ 85614-3643

FRIEDMAN, ELAINE FLORENCE, lawyer; b. N.Y.C., Aug. 22, 1924; d. Henry J. and Charlotte Leah (Youdelman) F.; m. Louis Schwartz, Apr. 10, 1949; 1 child, James Evan. BA, Hunter Coll., 1944; JD, Columbia U., 1946. Bar: N.Y. 1947, U.S. Dist. Ct. (so. and ea. dists.) N.Y., U.S. Ct. Appeals (2d cir.), U.S. Supreme Ct. 1954. Assoc. Oseas, Pepper & Siegel, N.Y.C., 1947-48, Bernstein & Benton, N.Y.C., 1948-51, Copeland & Elkins, N.Y.C., 1951-53; sole practice N.Y.C., 1953—. Bd. dirs. Health Ins. Plan of Greater N.Y. Mem. Fedn. Internat. des Femmes Juristes (v.p. U.S. chpt. 1993-95), N.Y. State Bar Assn., Hunter Coll. Alumni Assn., Columbia Law Sch. Assn. Jewish. Avocation: poetry. Family and matrimonial, General practice, Probate (including wills, trusts). Home: 2 Agnes Cir Ardsley NY 10502-1709 Office: 60 E 42nd St New York NY 10165-0006

FRIEDMAN, EUGENE STUART, lawyer; b. N.Y.C., Apr. 5, 1941; s. Abe and Etta (Fischer) F.; m. Karin L. Mehlem, Feb. 3, 1968; children: Gabrielle, Douglas, Jason. AB, NYU, 1961; LLB, Columbia U., 1964. Bar: N.Y. 1965, U.S. Supreme Ct. 1979. Atty. NLRB, San Francisco, 1965-67; assoc., ptnr. Cohen, Weiss & Simon, N.Y.C., 1968-86; sr. ptnr. Friedman & Wolf, N.Y.C., 1987—. Lectr. Ill. Inst. Continuing Legal Edn., Chgo., 1982-84, NYU Conf. Labor & Practicing Law Inst., N.Y.C., 1983-85; adv. bd. for labor and employment law ctr. NYU Law Sch. Contbr. articles to profl. jours. Active N.Y. State Task Force Plant Closings, N.Y.C., 1984. With USN, 1964-65. Mem. N.Y. State Bar Assn., Assn. of Bar of City of N.Y. (chmn. labor & employment law com. 1987-90), Am. Arbitration Assn. (law com.). Democrat. Jewish. Avocation: scuba diving. Labor (including EEOC, Fair Labor Standards Act, labor-management relations, NLRB, OSHA), Pension, profit-sharing, and employee benefits. Home: 277 W End Ave New York NY 10023-2604 Office: Friedman & Wolf 1500 Broadway Ste 2300 New York NY 10036-4056

FRIEDMAN, GREG STUART, lawyer, investment advisor; b. Washington, Oct. 3, 1951; s. Adolph Aaron and Florence (Haves) F.; m. Janis G. Friedman, Mar. 29, 1981 (div. Feb. 1996); children: Justin, Samantha, Brandon; m. Susan Hope Movshow, Feb. 9, 1996. Student, Emory U., 1969-71; BA in Urban Studies with honors, Washington U., St. Louis, 1972; JD, Boston U., 1976; postgrad., U. Md., 1981-84. Bar: Md. 1976, D.C. 1977, U.S. Dist. Ct. Md., U.S. Dist. Ct. D.C., U.S. Ct. Appeals (4th cir.), U.S. Supreme Ct. Assoc. Meisnere & Mika, P.C., Washington, 1976-79; counsel, asst. corp. sec. Nat. Corp. for Housing Partnerships, Washington, 1979-80; sr. assoc. Mahn Franklin & Goldenberg PC, Washington, 1982-85; prin. Deso & Greenberg, P.C., Washington, 1988-90; pvt. practice, Washington, 1980—82, 1985—88, Rockville, Md., 1990—; pres. Entity Mgmt. LLC, 1998—. Mem. D.C. LLC Legis. Adv. Panel, 1997. Trustee Hebrew Free Loan Assn. D.C., Rockville, 1993—; mem. alumni admission program Washington U., 1996—. Mem. Tax Mgmt. Real Estate Study Group. Democrat. Jewish. Avocations: skiing, watersports, investment matters. General civil litigation, Property, real (including real estate development, water), Taxation, general. Home: 6216 Mazwood Rd Rockville MD 20852-3528 Office: 109 N Adams St Rockville MD 20850 E-mail: gfriedman51@aol.com.

FRIEDMAN, HAROLD EDWARD, lawyer; b. Cleve., Apr. 7, 1934; s. Joseph and Mary (Schreibman) F.; m. Nancy Schweid, Aug. 20, 1961; children: Deborah, Jay, Susan. BS, Ohio State U., 1956; LL.B., Case Western Res U., 1959. Bar: Ohio 1960. Practiced in, Cleve., since 1960; ptnr. Simon, Haiman, Gutfeld, Friedman & Jacobs, 1967-80, Ulmer & Berne, 1981—; chair real property practice group. Sec., trustee Harry K. and Emma R. Fox Charitable Found.; pres. Jewish Vocat. Svcs., Cleve.; pres. Internat. Assn. Jewish Vocat. Svcs.; pres. Cleve. Hillel Found.; vice chmn. endowment fund Jewish Cmty. Fedn. Cleve., bd. dirs.; pres. Metro Health Found.; bd. dirs. Bur. Jewish Edn., Jewish Convalescence and Rehab. Ctr., Big Bros. Greater Cleve., Jewish Cmty. Fedn. Cleve., Jewish Family Svc. Assn., YES, Inc., Bellefaire/Jewish Children's Bur. Recipient Kane Leadership award Jewish Community Fedn. Cleve., 1974 Mem. ABA, Ohio Bar Assn., Cleve. Bar Assn., Oakwood Country Club. Corporate, general, Property, real (including real estate development, water), Taxation, general. Home: 23149 Laureldale Rd Cleveland OH 44122-2101 Office: 900 Bond Ct Bldg Cleveland OH 44114 E-mail: hfriedman@ulmer.com., hedwfried@aol.com.

FRIEDMAN, JAMES DENNIS, lawyer; b. Dubuque, Iowa, Jan. 11, 1947; s. Elmer J. and Rosemary Catherine (Stillmunks) F.; m. Kathleen Marie Maersch, Aug. 16, 1969; children: Scott, Ryan, Andrea, Sean. AB in Polit. Sci., Marquette U., 1969; JD, U. Notre Dame, 1972. Bar: Wis. 1972, U.S. Ct. Appeals (D.C. cir.) 1973, U.S. Ct. Appeals (7th cir.) 1976, U.S. Supreme Ct. 1978, U.S. Ct. Appeals (6th cir.) 1989, Ill. 1996, U.S. Tax Ct. 1997. Pvt. practice, Milw., 1972-81; ptnr. Quarles & Brady, Milw., 1981—. Presenter in field; mem. legis. coun. spl. study com. on regulation of fin. instns. State of Wis., 1986-87; bd. dirs. Concours Motors, Inc., Equal Justice Fund, Inc.; mem. dept. fin. instns. task force on fin. competitiveness 2005, State of Wis., 2000; mem., vice chair State of Wis. Supreme Ct., Office of Lawyer Regulation Preliminary Rev. Com., 2000—; mem. Gov.'s Adv. Coun. on Jud. Selection of the State of Wis., 2002. Mng. editor: Notre Dame Law Rev., 1971—72; contbr. articles to profl. jours. Alderman 4th and 7th dists. Mequon, Wis., 1979-85, pres. common coun., 1980-82, bd. ethics 1996-98, 2000—, chair blue ribbon visioning com. 1998-99; bd. dirs. Weyenrg, Pub. Libr. Found. Inc., 1983—, pres., 1984—; bd. dirs. Ptnrs. Advancing Values in Edn. Inc., 1987—, Wis. Law Found., 1998—; bd. visitors Marquette U. Ctr. for Study of Entrepreneurship, Milw., 1987-95; bd. dirs. Ozaukee Family Svcs., 1983-99, sec., 1993-98; bd. dirs. Notre Dame Club of Milw., 1984-88, sec., 1978, v.p., 1986-88; bd. dirs. Marquette Club of Milw., 1987-88; chair attys. unit United Way Fund Dr. Greater Milw., 1987; mem. St. James Ch., Mequon. Named Outstanding Sr., Coll. of Liberal Arts, Marquette U., 1969. Fellow Wis. Law Found., Am. Bar Found.; mem. ABA (banking law com. sect. bus. law); State Bar Wis. (chair bd. govs. 1999-2000, chair exec. com. 1999-2000, fin. com. 1997-98, strategic planning task force 1997-98, bd. govs. 1996-2000, exec. com. 1998-2000, internat. transactions sect. bd. dirs. 1984-99, sec. and chair-elect 1988-89, chair 1989-90, del. to ABA Ho. of Dels. 1980-82, standing com. on adminstrn. justice and judiciary 1979-81, legal edn. and bar admissions com. 1984-89, com. on minority lawyers 1992-99, chmn. 1997-1999, bd. dirs. young lawyers divsn. 1978-82, chmn. bar admission stds. and requirements com. 1979, So. Regional chair capital fund campaign 1998-99), Milw. Bar Assn., Wis. Acad. Trial Lawyers (bd. dirs. 1980-82), Wis. Bankers Assn., Milw. Country Club. Roman Catholic. Avocations: tennis, golf. Banking, Corporate, general, Health. Office: Quarles & Brady LLP 411 E Wisconsin Ave Ste 2040 Milwaukee WI 53202-4497 E-mail: jdf@quarles.com.

FRIEDMAN, JOEL WILLIAM, law educator; b. Mar. 16, 1951; s. Max Aaron and Muriel (Yudien) F.; m. Vivian Stoleru, Apr. 5, 1987; children: Alexa Erica, Chloe Gabriella, Max Aaron. BS, Cornell U., 1972; JD, Yale U., 1975. Bar: Calif. 1975, U.S. Dist. Ct. (cen. dist.) Calif. 1975. Asst. prof. Tulane U., New Orleans, 1976-79, assoc. prof., 1979-82, prof. law, 1982—, C.J. Morrow prof. law, 1985-86, Jack M. Gordon prof. procedural law and jurisdiction, 2002—, dir. tech., 1996—, dir. ITESM PhD program, 2000—. Vis. prof. law U. Tel Aviv, Israel, 1983, U. Tex. Law Sch., 1985-86, Chuo Law Sch., Tokyo, 1988, Hebrew U. of Jerusalem Law Sch., 1990; lectr. Fed. Jud. Ctr., Washington, 1987—; cons. La. Ho. of Reps., Baton Rouge, 1982-85, West Group, 1996—; bd. dirs. Ctr. for Computer-Assisted Legal Instrn., 1996-99; spl. master Pasadena Ind. Sch. Dist., Houston, 1987-93. Editor: Cases and Materials on Law of Employment Discrimination, 1983, 5th edit., 2001, The Law of Civil Procedure: Cases and Materials, 2002; contbr. articles to law revs. Pres., bd. dirs. Woldenberg Village, Inc., 1995-97; pres., bd. dirs., Jewish Fedn. Greater New Orleans, 2001—. Recipient Felix Frankfurter Faculty award for disting. tchg. Tulane Law Sch., 1989; Fulbright scholar, Israel, 1990. Mem. Am. Assn. Law Schs. (chair sect. on employment discrimination law 1987-88), Am. Law Inst., B'nai B'rith Hillel Found. (pres. New Orleans 1987-91), Internat. Assn. of Jewish Lawyers and Jurists La. Br. (pres. 1994-95). Democrat. Avocations: running, squash, scuba diving, skiing. Home: 1230 State St New Orleans LA 70118-6027 Office: Tulane Law Sch 6329 Freret St New Orleans LA 70118-6231 E-mail: jfriedman@law.tulane.edu.

FRIEDMAN, JOHN MAXWELL, JR., lawyer; b. N.Y.C., Oct. 31, 1944; s. John M. and Jane (Blum) F.; m. Laurie Suzanne Nevin, July 8, 1973 (div. 1988); children: David, Michael; m. Judith Zuckerman, Mar. 5, 1989; 1 child, Julia. AB, Princeton U., 1966; MA, U. Sussex, Brighton, Eng., 1967; JD, U. Chgo., 1970. Bar: N.Y. 1971, U.S. Ct. Appeals (2d cir.) 1971, U.S. Dist. Ct. (so. and ea. dist.) N.Y. 1972, U.S. Supreme Ct. 1974. Assoc.

Dewey Ballantine, N.Y.C., 1970-78, ptnr., 1978-96. Bankruptcy, Federal civil litigation, State civil litigation. Home: 80 Rocky Mountain Rd Roxbury CT 06783-1623 E-mail: johnmfriedman@earthlink.net.

FRIEDMAN, K. BRUCE, lawyer; b. Buffalo, Jan. 1, 1929; s. Bennett and Florence Ruth (Israel) F.; m. Lois G. Rosoff, June 15, 1986. AB, Harvard U., 1950; LL.B., Yale U., 1953. Bar: N.Y. 1955, D.C. 1956, Calif. 1958. Atty. CAB, Washington, 1955-57; practiced in San Francisco, 1958—; mem. firm Zang, Friedman & Damir, 1969-78, Cotton, Seligman & Ray, 1978-79, Friedman, McCubbin, Spalding, Bilter, & Roosevelt, Montgomery, San Francisco, 1980—. Lectr. law U. Calif. Law Sch., Berkeley, 1966-76; Pres. Econ. Roundtable San Francisco, 1964. Bd. dirs. San Francisco chpt. Am. Jewish Com., 1960-76; trustee World Affairs Council No. Calif., San Francisco, 1970-76; pres. San Francisco Estate Planning Council, 1973-74; regional dir. for No. Calif. Asso. Harvard Alumni, 1981-84; bd. dirs. Am. Coll. Trust and Estate Counsel Found., 2000—. Served with U.S. Army, 1953-55. Fellow Am. Coll. Trust and Estate Counsel, Am. Bar Found.; mem. ABA, State Bar Calif., San Francisco Bar Assn., Internat. Acad. Estate and Trust Law (treas. 1996—), Am. Law Inst., San Francisco Com. on Fgn. Rels., U. Calif. San Francisco Found., Univ. Club, Calif. Tennis Club, Commonwealth Club Calif., Harvard Club of San Francisco (pres. 1976-78), Rotary. Jewish. Estate planning, Probate (including wills, trusts), Estate taxation. Office: Friedman McCubbin Spalding Bilter Roosevelt & Montgomery 425 California St Ste 2500 San Francisco CA 94104-2207 E-mail: kbrucefriedman@fomlaw.com.

FRIEDMAN, LAWRENCE MILTON, lawyer; b. Chgo., Apr. 2, 1945; s. Armin C. and Mildred Friedman; m. Linda M. Friedman, June 25, 1967; children: Benjamin J., David K. BA, U. Ill., 1966; JD, Ohio State U., 1969. Bar: Ill. 1970, U.S. Tax Ct. 1970; CPA, Md., Ill. Ptnr. Coopers & Lybrand, Chgo., 1969-85, Lord, Bissell & Brook, Chgo., 1985—. Adj. prof. law IIT Chgo. Kent Coll. Law, Chgo., 1990—; mem. adv. bd. Hartford Inst. Ins. Tax, 1995-2000; spkr. on mergers, aquisitions and taxation. Mem. adv. bd. Ins. Tax Rev., 1987—; contbr. articles to law jours. Sec.-treas., dir. North Shore Performing Arts Ctr. Found. in Skokie, Ill., 1993-97; vice chmn., dir. Jewish Fedn. Met. Chgo., 1992-99. Mem. ABA, AICPA, Chgo. Fed. Tax Forum. Mergers and acquisitions, Corporate taxation, Insurance. Office: Lord Bissell & Brook 115 S La Salle St Ste 3200 Chicago IL 60603-3902

FRIEDMAN, MARVIN ROSS, lawyer; b. Mpls., July 13, 1941; s. H. W. and Katherine F.; widowed; children: Natasha E., Chloe J. BBA, U. Miami, 1966, JD, 1969. Bar: Fla. 1969. Pvt. practice, Coral Cables, Fla., 1970—. Founder Diabetes Rsch. Found.; hon. trustee Lowe Art Mus, Mus. Contemporary Art, Wolfsonian Mus., F.I.U. Art Mus.; Tri-county v.p. Miami City Ballet; hon. trustee Friends of the Libr., Met. Opera, N.Y.C., Mus. Modern Art, N.Y.C., Whitney Mus., N.Y.C., Guggenheim Mus., NY, Miami Art Mus. Mem.: ABA, ATLA, Am. Coll. Barristers, Million Dollar Advocates Forum, Dade County Trial Lawyers Assn., Fla. Acad. Trial Lawyers, Coral Gables Bar Assn., Dade County Bar Assn., Fla. Bar, English Speaking Union, Guild Hall Club, East Hampton (NY) Tennis Club, Fisher Island Club. Personal injury (including property damage), Product liability. Office: Friedman & Friedman 2600 S Douglas Rd Ste 1011 Coral Gables FL 33134-6142

FRIEDMAN, MORTON LEE, lawyer; b. Aberdeen, S.D., Aug. 4, 1932; s. Philip and Rebecca (Feinstein) F.; m. Marcine Lichter, Dec. 20, 1955; children— Mark, Philip, Jeffrey. Student, U. Mich., 1950-53; AB, Stanford U., 1954, LL.B., 1956. Bar: Calif. bar 1956. Mem. firm Kimble, Thomas, Snell, Jamison & Russell, Fresno, 1957, Busick & Busick, Sacramento, 1957-59; sr. ptnr. firm Friedman, Collard & Poswall (name now Friedman, Collard & Panneton), Sacramento, 1959—. Lectr. various law schs. and seminars; mem. Calif. Bd. Continuing Edn. Pres. Mosaic Law Congregation, 1977-80, 97-99; v.p. Sacramento Jewish Fedn., 1980-82; chmn. Sacramento campaign United Jewish Appeal, 1981; bd. dirs., former nat. v.p. Am. Israel Pub. Affairs Com.; mem. bd. Calif. State U. Inst., 1995-99; bd. dirs. Nat. Bd. AntiDefamation League. 1st lt. USAF, 1956. Recipient Sacramento Businessman of Yr. award Sacramento Met. C. of C., 1991, Best Lawyers in Am. award, Outstanding Philanthropists award Nat. Soc. Fund Raising Execs., 1999; Fulbright candidate Stanford Law Sch., 1956. Fellow Am. Coll. Trial Lawyers; mem. ABA, ATLA, Calif. Bar Assn., Sacramento County Bar Assn. (pres. 1976, Lawyer of Yr. 1999), Calif. Trial Lawyers Assn. (v.p. 1973-75), Capitol City Lawyers Club (past pres.), Am. Bd. Trial Advocates (adv., pres. 1977, Calif. Trial Lawyer of Yr. 1988, SCALE award 2002), West Sacramento C. of C. (dir.), Order of Coif. Democrat. Personal injury (including property damage). Home: 1620 McClaren Dr Carmichael CA 95608-5936 Office: Friedman Collard & Panneton 7750 College Town Dr Ste 300 Sacramento CA 95826-2386

FRIEDMAN, PENNY, lawyer; b. Cleve., Dec. 24, 1951; d. Harold Emanuel and Ruth (Resnick) F.; children: Rachel, Leah. AB in Econs. with high honors, U. Mich., 1973, JD cum laude, 1977. Bar: Ohio 1977. Atty. Taft, Stettinius & Hollister, Cin., 1977-80; v.p. property devel. Gt. Am. Broadcasting Co. (formerly Taft Broadcasting Co.), Cin., 1980-88; real estate portfolio mgr. Bartlett & Co., Cin., 1988-98; pres. Benefactors, LLC, 1998—. Mem. Cin. Downtown Progress Com., 1991-95, mem. exec. com., 1993-95; v.p. Cin. chpt. Am. Jewish Com., 1992-96, pres. 1996-98, mem. exec. com., 1990—; v.p. Leadership Cin. Alumni Assn., 1987-89; chmn. Family Svc. Cin. Area, 1991-92, pres., 1988-90, v.p., 1985-88, trustee, 1979-93, trustee emeritus, 1993—; vice-chmn. Cin. Devel. Fund, 1989-95; vice chmn. Devel. Corp. Cin., 1990-92, trustee, 1989-92; bd. dirs. Cin. Ctr. for Devel. Disorders, 1979-85, Seven Hills Neighborhood Houses, 1981-86; trustee Cin. Arts Assn., 1992—, mem. exec. com. 1994—; trustee Downtown Cin., Inc., 1998—, Cin. Psychoanalytic Inst., 1994-2002, The Wellness Cmty., 1999-2002; vice chair, trustee Knowledgeworks Found., 1999—; trustee Found. Family Svc., 2000— (v.p. 2002—), Greater Cin. Arts and Edn. Ctr., 1999—; trustee Project Grad. Cin., 2003—. Mem. Cin. Bar Assn., Phi Beta Kappa. Office: BeneFactors LLC 312 Walnut St Ste 3560 Cincinnati OH 45202-4026 E-mail: benefactors@fuse.net., psoul@aol.com.

FRIEDMAN, RALPH DAVID, lawyer; b. Phila., June 14, 1942; s. Albert H. and Reba (Goldstein) F.; m. Sandra Scott, July 11, 1965; children: Jennifer Amy, Susanne Jill. BSBA, Pa. State U., 1963; JD, Temple U., 1967. Bar: Pa. 1967, U.S. Dist. Ct. (ea. dist.) Pa. 1967, U.S. Tax Ct. 1978. Former jud. law clk. to presiding judge Ct. Common Pleas, Phila., 1968-70; ptnr. Friedman & Friedman, Jenkintown, Pa., 1970-98, 1998—. Bd. dirs., chmn. Chase Savs. and Loan Assn., Phila.; bd. dirs. Fred Waring Enterprises, Inc., Del. Water Gap. Author: (pamphlet) What You Should Know About Real Estate, 1978; contbr. articles to publs. Ward leader Cheltenham Twp. Regular Rep. Orgn., Glenside, Pa., 1987-92. Paul Harris fellow Rotary. Mem. Pa. Bar Assn., Rotary (pres. Elkins Park, Pa. club 1982-83, pres. 1989-90), Gundaker Found., Montgomery County Bar Assn., Rydal Country Club, Philmont Country Club. Republican. Jewish. Avocations: golf, fountain pen collecting, tennis, o gauge model trains. General practice, Personal injury (including property damage), Property, real (including real estate development, water). Office: Friedman & Friedman Ste 534 The Pavilion Jenkintown PA 19076 E-mail: rdf@rdflaw.com.

FRIEDMAN, RICHARD NATHAN, lawyer; b. Phila., June 13, 1941; s. Martin Harry Friedman and Caroline (Fruchtman) Shaines; 1 child, Melissa Danielle. BA, U. Miami, 1962, JD, 1965; LLM in Taxation, Georgetown U., 1967. Bar: Fla. 1965. Staff atty. SEC, Washington, 1965-66; pvt. practice Washington, 1966-67; individual practice law Miami, Fla., 1968—; CEO All-State Sports Agts., Inc., 1996—99; player agt. NBPA, 1996-99; spl. asst. village atty. Village of Pinecrest, 2001. Adj. prof. U. Miami, 1972-76; arbitrator N.Y. Stock Exch., 1973—, AAA, 1988-2000, AMEX, NASD, 1988—; founder, pres. All-Star Music Corp., 1996—. Columnist Cmty. Newspapers, Miami, 1989—; featured performer motion picture Lenny 1974, other TV and theatrical films; rec. artist, The Singing Attorney, For Love of Country, 1996, All My Love, 2001; author numerous pub. poems. Founder, pres. Am. Stockholders Assn., Inc., 1971-74, Stop Transit-Over People, Inc., 1975-87; chmn. Sales Taxes Oppressing People, Fla., 1987—; mem. endowment com. U. Miami, 1970—; mem. Soc. Univ. Founders, U. Miami, 1980; co-chmn. sports com. Fla. Bar, 1997-99. Recipient Merit cert. Dade County Bar Assn., 1972-73; numerous certs. of appreciation Rotary Internat., Kiwanis and other svc. orgns., 1970—; Richard N. Friedman Week held in his honor City of Homestead, Fla., Apr. 1978; named Hon. Citizen State of Tenn., 1970, Citizen of Day Dade County (Fla.), Radio Sta. WINZ, 1980; recipient Leaders award Sunrise Cmty., 1986. Mem. NARAS, Unified Bar D.C. Mergers and acquisitions, Securities, Corporate taxation. Office: 9655 S Dixie Hwy Ste 209 Miami FL 33156-2813 E-mail: busorgs@aol.com.

FRIEDMAN, ROBERT LAURENCE, investment professional; b. Mt. Vernon, NY, Mar. 19, 1943; s. Alvin S. and Frances (Feinsod) F.; m. Barbara Lander, Dec. 25, 1964; children: Lisa, Andrew. AB, Columbia Coll., 1964; JD, U. Pa., 1967. Bar: NY 1968. Assoc. Simpson, Thacher & Bartlett, NYC, 1967—74, ptnr., 1974—99; sr. mng. dir. The Blackstone Group LP, NYC, 1999—2002, sr. mng. dir., chief adminstrv. officer, chief legal officer, 2003—. Office: The Blackstone Group LP 345 Park Ave Fl 31 New York NY 10154-0004

FRIEDMAN, SAMUEL SELIG, lawyer; b. N.Y.C., July 25, 1935; s. Nathan and Anne M. (Sobel) F.; m. Maxine E. Goldfarb, Jan. 7, 1961; 1 child, Alison J. BS, MIT, 1956; MBA, U. Pa., 1959; LLB, Columbia U., 1965. Bar: N.Y. 1965, U.S. Dist. Ct. (so. and ea. dists.) N.Y. 1967, U.S. Supreme Ct. 1984. Assoc. Lord, Day & Lord, N.Y.C., 1965-72; ptnr., mem. exec. com. Lord Day & Lord, Barrett Smith and predecessor firm, N.Y.C., 1972-94; ptnr. Morgan, Lewis & Bockius LLP, N.Y.C., 1994—. Vice chmn., dir., mem. exec. com. Times Square Bus. Improvement Dist., 1992-95. 1st lt. U.S. Army, 1959-62. Mem. ABA, N.Y. State Bar Assn., Assn. of Bar of City of N.Y., MIT Club N.Y., The Penn Club, Phi Delta Phi. Avocations: travel, wine, sports. Corporate, general, Mergers and acquisitions, Securities. Office: Morgan Lewis & Bockius LLP 101 Park Ave New York NY 10178-0060

FRIEDMAN, STEPHEN J, lawyer; b. Mar. 19, 1938; s. A.E. Robert and Janice Clara (Miller) F.; m. Fredrica L. Schwab, June 25, 1961; children: Vanessa V., Alexander S. AB magna cum laude, Princeton U., 1959; LLB magna cum laude, Harvard U., 1962. Bar: N.Y. 1962, D.C. 1982. Law clk. to justice William J. Brennan Jr. U.S. Supreme Ct., 1963-64; spl. asst. to maritime adminstr. Maritime Adminstrn., Dept. Commerce, 1964-65; assoc. Debevoise & Plimpton, NYC, 1965-70, ptnr., 1970-77, 81-86, 93—; dep. asst. sec. for capital markets policy Dept. Treasury, Washington, 1977-79; commr. SEC, 1980-81; exec. v.p., gen. counsel E.F. Hutton Group Inc., NYC, 1986-88, Equitable Life Assurance Soc., NYC, 1988-93; ptnr. Debevoise & Plimpton, NYC, 1994—. Lectr. law Columbia U., N.Y.C., 1974—77, 1982—85. Author: An Affair With Freedom, the Opinions and Speeches of William J. Brennan, Jr., 1967; contbr. articles on legal and policy aspects of fin. inst. to profl. jours. Active Coun. on Fgn. Rels.; trustee, chmn. emeritus Am. Ballet Theatre, N.Y.C.; dir. United Way N.Y.C.; pres., trustee Practising Law Inst.; mem. bd. govs. NASD, 1991-94, Chgo. Bd. Options Exch., 1982-88; pres. Practicing Law Inst.; chmn. Asian U. for Women Support Found. With USAR, 1962-68. Mem. ABA, Assn. of Bar of the City of N.Y. (chmn. com. on securities regulation), Univ. Club. Office: Debevoise & Plimpton 919 3rd Ave 45th Fl New York NY 10022-6225

FRIEDMAN, VICTOR STANLEY, lawyer; b. N.Y.C., May 9, 1933; s. Harry and Rose (Cohen) F.; m. Sara Ann Riesner, June 21, 1958 (div.); children: Eric H., Diana B., Michael C.; m. Victoria Schonfeld, Mar. 7, 1984; children: Jared D., Rumyana L. AB, Harvard U., 1954; LLB, Yale U., 1957. Bar: N.Y. 1958, U.S. Dist. Ct. (so. dist.) N.Y. 1964, U.S. Dist. Ct. (ea. dist.) N.Y. 1966, U.S. Ct. Appeals (2nd cir.) 1966, U.S. Ct. Appeals (4th cir.) 1981, U.S. Ct. Appeals (3rd cir.) 1972, U.S. Ct. Appeals (8th cir.) 1970, U.S. Ct. Appeals (10th cir.) 1987, U.S. Supreme Ct. 1974. Asst. to dep. atty. gen. Dept. Justice, Washington, 1958-60; assoc. firm Fried, Frank, Harris, Shriver & Jacobson, N.Y.C., 1960-66, ptnr., 1967-99, of counsel, 1999—. Served with USAR, 1958-59 Mem. Assn. of Bar of City of N.Y., Am. Coll. Trial Lawyers. Antitrust, Federal civil litigation, Alternative dispute resolution. Office: Fried Frank Harris 1 New York Plz Fl 22 New York NY 10004-1980

FRIEDMAN, WILBUR HARVEY, lawyer; b. N.Y.C., May 2, 1907; s. Isador Peter and Zara (Sloat) F.; m. Frances Margolis, May 21, 1943. AB, Columbia U., 1927, LLB, 1930. Bar: N.Y. 1931. Law sec. U.S. Supreme Ct. Justice Harlan F. Stone, 1930-31; staff atty. Office of U.S. Solicitor Gen., 1931-32; mem. firm Proskauer Rose Goetz & Mendelsohn (now Proskauer Rose LLP), N.Y.C., 1932-40; ptnr. Proskauer, Rose, Goetz, & Mendelsohn, N.Y.C., 1940—. Lectr. Inst. on Fed. Taxation, NYU, 1943-65, lectr. Sch. Gen. Edn., 1955-60; bd. dirs., sec. Lawrence M. Gelb Found.; bd. dirs. Cancer Rsch. Inst., 1983-99; chmn. exec. com. bd. visitors Law Sch., Columbia U., 1977-91. Contbr. articles to profl. jours. Chmn. bd. overseers Edith C. Blum Art Inst. at Bard Coll., 1985-93; mem. Rockefeller U. Coun., 1986—; mem. med. ctr. adv. bd. N.Y. Hosp.-Cornell Med. Ctr., 1986—. Mem. ABA (mem. ho. dels. 1978-87), N.Y. State Bar Assn. (mem. exec. com. sect. taxation 1968-76), Assn. of Bar of City of N.Y. (chmn. com. on mgmt. and operation of profl. practice 1981-85), N.Y. County Lawyers Assn. (pres. 1975-77, mem. exec. com. 1977-79, chmn. com. on taxation 1948-54, chmn. com. on group ins. 1960-74, chmn. spl. com. on consumer agreements 1977-83), Lotos Club, Princeton U. Club, Phi Beta Kappa, Phi Beta Kappa Assocs., Tau Delta Phi. Home: 1016 5th Ave Apt 2D New York NY 10028-0132 Office: Proskauer Rose LLP 1585 Broadway Rm 2016 New York NY 10036-8299 E-mail: wfriedman@proskauer.com.

FRIEND, EDWARD MALCOLM, III, lawyer, educator; b. Birmingham, Ala., Oct. 12, 1946; s. Edward M. Jr. and Hermione Frances (Curjel) F. BA in History, U. Ala., 1968, JD, 1971. Bar: Ala. 1971. Shareholder Sirote and Permutt, P.C., Birmingham, 1971—, pres., 1991-93. Chmn. Birmingham Area C. of C., 1990-91; chmn. dist. bd. dirs. Colonial Bank Ala., Birmingham, 1985-2000; vice chair Colonial Bank Ctrl. Dist., 2000—; adj. prof. U. Ala., Birmingham, 1994—. Chmn. Birmingham Area chpt. ARC, 1987-88; chmn. bd. NCCJ, 1983, nat. bd., 1981-88; pres. coun. U. Ala., Birmingham, 1980-94, Birmingham Jewish Fedn., 1984-89, United Way Ctrl. Ala., 1984-99, chmn., 1993-94, gen. campaign chmn., 1989; bd. dirs. Childrens Hosp. Ala., 1986—; exec. com. Ala. Symphony Assn., 1980-82, bd. dirs., 1982-85, Birmingham Festival Arts, 1978-88, pres., 1984-85, chmn., 1985-86; mem. nat. leadership coun. United Way Am.; pres. Big Bros./Big Sisters Greater Birmingham, 1980, chmn., 1981-83; trustee St. Vincent's Hosp., 1982-86, v.p., 1984-86, Ala. Sch. Fine Arts Found., 1985-91; trustee Cmty. Foun. of Greater Birmingham, 2002–; chmn. Leadership Ala., 1993; bd. dirs. Boy Scouts Am., 1996—, Comty. Found. Greater Birmingham, 2002-. Recipient Brotherhood award Nat. Conf. Christians and Jews, 1987; named to Ala. Acad. of Honor; named Lawyer of Yr., Birmingham Legal Secretarial Assn., 1976, Outstanding Alumnus, U. Ala. Sch. Law, 1984. Mem. So. Inst. Health Law (chmn. 1985-87), Nat. Health Lawyers Assn. (bd. dirs. 1992-95), Farrah Law Soc. (chmn. 1982-84). General practice, Health, Property, real (including real estate development, water). Office: Sirote and Permutt PC 2311 Highland Ave South Birmingham AL 35205-4004 E-mail: efriend@Sirote.com.

FRIES, JOSEPH MICHAEL, lawyer; b. Bklyn., Aug. 21, 1937; s. Jerome E. and Sophia (Kabat) F.; m. Fredi Ann Lieberman, June 17, 1959; children— Charles, David. A.B. with high honors in Govt., Cornell U., 1958; LL.B. cum laude, Harvard U., 1961. Bar: D.C. 1961. Assoc. Arent Fox, Kintner, Plotkin & Kahn, Washington, 1961-68, ptnr., 1969— . Corporate, general, Property, real (including real estate development, water), Corporate taxation. Home: 6509 Tall Tree Ter Rockville MD 20852-3732 Office: Arent Fox Kintner Plotkin & Kahn Washington Sq 1050 Connecticut Ave NW Ste 500 Washington DC 20036-5303 E-mail: friesj@arentfox.com.

FRIESE, ROBERT CHARLES, lawyer; b. Chgo., Apr. 29, 1943; s. Earl Matthew and Laura Barbara (Mayer) F.; m. Chandra Ullom; children: Matthew Robert, Mark Earl, Laura Moore. AB in Internat. Rels., Stanford U., 1964; JD, Northwestern U., 1970. Bar: Calif. 1972. Dir. Tutor Applied Linguistics Ctr., Geneva, 1964-66; atty. Bronson, Bronson & McKinnon, San Francisco, 1970-71, SEC, San Francisco, 1971-75; ptnr. Shartsis, Friese & Ginsburg, San Francisco, 1975—. Pres., bd. dirs. Custom Diversification Fund Mgmt., Inc., 1993—; dir.-co-founder Internat. Plant Rsch. Inst., Inc., San Carlos, Calif., 1978-86. Chmn. bd. suprs. Task Force on Noise Control, 1972-78; chmn. San Franciscans for Cleaner City, 1977; exec. dir. Nob Hill Neighbors, 1972-81; bd. dirs. Nob Hill Assn., 1976-78, Palace Fine Arts, 1992-94, San Francisco Beautiful, 1986—, pres., 1988-2000; chmn. Citizens Adv. Com. for Embarcadero Project, 1991—; mem. major gifts com. Stanford U.; bd. dirs. Presidio Heights Neighborhood Assn., 1993—, pres., 1996-98; bd. dirs. Inst. of Range and the American Mustang, 1990—. Mem. ABA, Assn. Bus. Trial Lawyers (bd. dirs.), Calif. Bar Assn., Bar Assn. San Francisco (bd. dirs. 1982-85, chmn. bus. litigation com. 1978-79, chmn. state ct. civil litigation com. 1983-90, new courthouse com. 1993-95), Assn. SEC Alumni (bd. dirs. 1995—, 1st v.p. 2002—), Lawyers Club of San Francisco, Mensa, Calif. Hist. Soc., Commonwealth Club, Swiss-Am. Friendship League (chmn. 1971-79). Federal civil litigation, State civil litigation, Securities. Office: Shartsis Friese & Ginsburg 1 Maritime Plz Fl 18 San Francisco CA 94111-3404 E-mail: rcf@sfglaw.com.

FRIEZE, H(AROLD) DELBERT, lawyer; b. Tulsa, Feb. 15, 1943; s. Harold William and Violet Izenna (Schnelle) F.; m. Connie Dixon, Dec. 28, 1966; 1 child, Todd William. BBA, U. Okla., 1966; JD, U. Tulsa, 1975. Bar: Okla. 1975, U.S. Dist. Ct. (no. dist.) Okla. 1975, U.S. Dist. Ct. (ea. dist.) Okla. 1976. Ptnr. Petrik & Frieze, Broken Arrow, Okla., 1975—. Bd. dirs. 1st Nat. Bank & Trust Co., Broken Arrow. Bd. mem. Broken Arrow Bd. Adjustment, 1976-78; asst. city atty. City Broken Arrow, 1978-81; bd. dirs. Broken Arrow Community Found., 1999—, bd. dirs. Angel Flight of Oklahoma, 1997—, Broken Arrow Public Schs. Adv. Council, 2001—. Mem. Tulsa County Bar Assn. Lodges: Rotary (past pres. Broken Arrow club, Paul Harris fellow 1983). Republican. Methodist. State civil litigation, Commercial, contracts (including sales of goods; commercial financing), Property, real (including real estate development, water). Office: Petrik & Frieze 121 E College St Broken Arrow OK 74012-3910

FRIGERIO, CHARLES STRAITH, lawyer; b. Detroit, Mar. 8, 1957; s. Louie John and LaVern (Straith) F.; m. Annette Angela Russo, Oct. 18, 1985; 1 child, Charles Anthony. BA, St. Mary's U., 1979, JD, 1982. Bar: Tex. 1982, U.S. Ct. Appeals (5th cir.) 1987, U.S. Supreme Ct. 1987; cert. in personal injury trial law. Pros. atty. City Attys. Office, San Antonio, 1982-84; trial atty. City Atty's. Office, San Antonio, 1984—; litigation chief and chief prosecutor City Atty.'s Office, San Antonio, 1995; pvt. practice law enforcement litigation San Antonio, 1995—. Mem. Dem. Nat. Com., San Antonio, 1976; asst. mgr. local campaigns, San Antonio, 1976-84. Mem.: ABA, Cath. Lawyers Assn., Nat. Bd. Trial Advocacy, San Antono Bar Assn., Fed. Bar Assn., Tex. Bar Assn., Delta Epsilon Sigma. Democrat. Roman Catholic. Home: 317 Cleveland Ct San Antonio TX 78209-5862 Office: Riverview Towers 111 Soledad St Ste 840 San Antonio TX 78205-2219

FRIGNANI, ALDO, law educator; b. Modena, Italy, Nov. 23, 1937; s. Frignani Armando and Vaccari Adele; m. Grosso Patrizia; 1 child, Luca Andrea. Lic., Faculty Internat. Droit Guipparve, 1963; JD, U. Faculty Law, 1962. Asst. rschr. U. Ferrara, Italy, 1962—68; prof. in charge U. Padua, 1968—72, U. Turin, 1972—80; prof. U. Padua, 1980—81, U. Modena, 1982—86, U. Turin, 1985—. Author: Factoring, Learning, Franchising Venture Capital Managed Buy-Out, 1996; co-author: Italian Ordinary Law, 1992, (handbook) European Competition Law, 1999. Mem.: Assn.Coviuersazioli di Diritto Baucani (chmn. 1995—), Internat. Bar Assn., Internat. Acad. Comparative Law. Office: Frignani & Assocs Studio Legale Via Argonne 1 10133 Turino Italy Fax: 0034 011/8601886. E-mail: frizmani@innetc.it.

FRISBIE, CHARLES, lawyer; b. Kansas City, Mo., June 1, 1939; s. A.C. Jr. and Florence (Waddell) F.; m. Julia Louise Ross, June 28, 1969; children: Ross Waddell, Andrew James Louis. AB, Princeton U., 1961; JD, U. Mich., 1964. Bar: Mo. 1964, U.S. Supreme Ct. 1968. Assoc. Lathrop Righter Gordon & Parker, Kansas City, Mo., 1964-70; ptnr. Lathrop & Norquist, Kansas City, Mo., 1971-94; mem. Lathrop & Gage L.C., Kansas City, Mo., 1994—. Lt. USAFR, 1964-70. Mem. ABA, Mo. Bar Assn. (chmn. internat. law com. 1995-97), Kansas City Country Club (sec., bd. dirs. 1981-84). Republican. Episcopalian. Avocations: golf, reading. Banking, Commercial, contracts (including sales of goods; commercial financing), Property, real (including real estate development, water). Home: 808 Romany Rd Kansas City MO 64113-2013 Office: Lathrop & Gage LC 2345 Grand Blvd Ste 2600 Kansas City MO 64108-2617

FRISBIE, CURTIS LYNN, JR., lawyer; b. Greenville, Miss., Sept. 13, 1943; s. Curtis Lynn and Edith L. (Brantley) F.; m. Gena F. Johnson, May 30, 1965; children: Curtis L. III, Mark A. BSBA, U. Ala., 1966; JD, St. Mary's U., San Antonio, 1971. Bar: Tex. 1971; U.S. Dist. Ct. (no. dist.) Ga. 1974, U.S. Dist. Ct. (no. dist.) Tex. 1978, U.S. Dist. Ct. (we. dist.) Tex. 1985, U.S. Dist. Ct. (ea. and so. dists.) Tex. 1986, U.S. Dist. Ct. (ea. dist.) Wis. 1986; U.S. Tax Ct. 1986; U.S. Ct. Appeals (5th cir.) 1975, U.S. Ct. Appeals (10th cir.) 1982, U.S. Ct. Appeals (8th cir.) 1987; U.S. Supreme Ct. 1977. Trial atty. Antitrust divsn. U.S. Dept. Justice, Atlanta, 1971-73; assoc. King & Spalding, Atlanta, 1974-77; ptnr. Gardere Wynne Sewell LLP (formerly Gardere & Wynne LLP), Dallas, 1978—. Assoc. editor St. Mary's Law Jour., 1970-71. Capt. USMC, 1966-69, Vietnam. Fellow Tex. Bar Found. (life), Dallas Bar Assn. (life); mem. ABA (antitrust and bus. law sect.), Tex. Bar Assn. (antitrust sect., mem. coun. 1995—, vice chair, chair elect 2000-01, chair 2001-02), Dallas Bar Assn. (pres. antitrust and trade regulation sect. 1993), Coll. State Bar Tex., Phi Alpha Delta. Avocations: scuba diving, fishing, hunting. Antitrust, Trademark and copyright. Home: 5605 Palomar Ln Dallas TX 75229-6417 Office: Gardere Wynne Sewell LLP Thanksgiving Tower 1601 Elm St Ste 3000 Dallas TX 75201-4761 E-mail: cfrisbie@gardere.com.

FRISCH, HARRY DAVID, lawyer, consultant, investment company executive; b. N.Y.C., June 5, 1954; s. Isaac and Regina (Rottenberg) Frisch; m. Sherry Beth Bannerman, 1992; children: Rachel Michele, Michael Elliot. BS, CCNY, 1976; postgrad., Rutgers U., 1976-77; JD, Pace U., 1980. Bar: N.Y. 1981, U.S. Dist. Ct. (so. and ea. dists.) N.Y. 1981, U.S. Ct. Appeals (2d cir.) 1984, U.S. Supreme Ct. 1986, U.S. Ct. Appeals (5th cir.) 1987. Law clk. Shearson Hayden Stone, Inc., N.Y.C., 1977-80; assoc. gen. counsel Shearson Loeb Rhoades, Inc., N.Y.C., 1980-82; asst. v.p., asst. corp. sec., assoc. gen. counsel Shearson/Am. Express, Inc., N.Y.C., 1982-85; v.p., sr. litigator, assoc. gen. counsel Shearson Lehman Bros., Inc., N.Y.C., 1985-88; 1st v.p., sr. litigator, assoc. gen. counsel Shearson Lehman Hutton, Inc., N.Y.C., 1988-90, Shearson Lehman Bros., Inc., N.Y.C., 1990-93; 1st v.p., sr. litigator, asst. gen. counsel Smith Barney Shearson Inc., N.Y.C., 1993-94; asst. gen. counsel Gruntal & Co. Inc., N.Y.C., 1994-97, Gruntal & Co., L.L.C., N.Y.C., 1997-99; spl. counsel Lubiner & Schmidt, N.Y.C., 1999; sr. v.p., compliance mgr. Datek Online Holdings Corp., Jersey City, 1999—2002, Ameritrade Holding Corp., 2002—. Contbr. articles to profl. jours. Mem.: ABA, Fed. Bar Coun., N.Y. County Lawyers Assn., Assn. Bar

City of N.Y., N.Y. State Bar Assn. Democrat. Jewish. Federal civil litigation, Securities. Home: 2 Waterview Dr Ossining NY 10562-2442 Office: Datek Online Holdings Corp 70 Hudson St 10th Fl Jersey City NJ 07302 E-mail: hdfrisch@optonline.net.

FRITH, DOUGLAS KYLE, retired lawyer; b. Henry County, Va., Sept. 2, 1931; s. Jacob and Sally Ada (Nunn) F.; m. Ella Margaret Tuck, Sept. 10, 1960; children: Margaret Frith Ringers, Susan Elaine. AB, Roanoke Coll., 1952; JD, Washington and Lee U., 1957. Bar: Va. 1957. Pvt. practice, 1957-58; assoc. Taylor & Young, Martinsville, Va., 1957-58; ptnr. Young, Kiser & Frith, 1960-71, Frith, Gardner & Gardner, 1973-78; pres. Douglas K. Frith & Assocs., P.C., Martinsville, 1979-99; ret., 1999. Bd. dirs. Frith Constrn. Co., Inc., Frith Equipment Corp.; substitute judge 21st Gen. Dist. Ct., 21st Juvenile and Domestic Relations Dist. Ct., 1969-80. Chmn. March of Dimes, 1960, Brotherhood Week, 1960; capt. profl. div. United Fund, 1971. With U.S. Army, 1952-54. Mem. ABA, Am. Bd. Trial Advocates, Va. Bar Assn., Martinsville-Henry County Bar Assn. (pres. 1970-71), Va. Trial Lawyers Assn. (dis. v.p. 1970-71, del. at large 1971-77), Kiwanis. Republican. Baptist. Estate planning, Personal injury (including property damage), Property, real (including real estate development, water). Address: 1409 Whittle Rd Martinsville VA 24112

FRITZ, COLLIN MARTIN, lawyer; b. Des Moines, June 8, 1947; s. Collin Wilburn and Jeanne (Wills) F.; m. Susyn Miller; children: Courtney, Skylar, Collyn. BA, U. Iowa, 1969, JD, 1973. Bar: Iowa 1974, Hawaii, 1977, U.S. Dist. Ct. Hawaii 1976, U.S. Ct. Appeals (9th cir.) 1980. Ptnr. Trecker Rosenberg & Fritz, Kailua, Hawaii, 1976-79, Trecker & Fritz, Kailua, 1979-80, McKenzie, Trecker & Fritz, Honolulu, 1980-93, Trecker & Fritz, 1994—. Bd. dirs. ARC, Honolulu, 1979-82, ACLU, Honolulu, 1977-83; pres. Consumer Lawyers Hawaii. Fellow Hawaii Acad. Plaintiffs Attys.; mem. ABA (columnist), Am. Trial Lawyers Assn., Hawaii Bar Assn.(dir.), Honolulu Club. Product liability, Personal injury (including property damage), Professional liability. Office: Trecker and Fritz 820 Mililani St Ste 701 Honolulu HI 96813-2986

FRIX, PAIGE LANE, lawyer, accountant; b. Washington, Apr. 13, 1961; d. William Elza Smith Jr. and Janet Helen (Peoples) Davis; m. Kemmy Deane Frix, July 29, 1993; 1 child, Avery Karlin. BBA, U. Okla., 1984, JD, 1987. Bar: Okla. 1987; CPA, Okla. Pvt. practice, Muskogee, Okla., 1987—; sec. Frix Constrn. Co., Inc., Muskogee, 1999—. Instr. Becker CPA Rev. Course, Tulsa, 1988-97; cons. Frix & Foster Constrn. Co., Inc., Muskogee, 1990—. Sunday sch. tchr. Honor Heights Meth. Ch., Muskogee, 1996—; trustee Steve Yaffe Charitable Trust, Muskogee; bd. dirs. Promoting Animal Welfare Soc., Inc., Muskogee, 1992—, Kids Space, Muskogee County Child Advocacy Ctr., Muskogee, 1999—; mem. Five Civilized Tribes Mus. Aux., 1997—; Cub Scout den leader Boy Scouts Am. Mem. Okla. Bar Assn., Muskogee County Bar Assn., Muskogee Edn. Found., Cub Scout Den Leader. Democrat. Corporate, general, Taxation, general, Construction. Home and Office: PO Box 284 Muskogee OK 74402-0284

FRIZELL, SAMUEL, law educator; b. Buena Vista, Colo., Aug. 30, 1933; s. Franklin Guy and Ruth Wilma (Noel) F.; m. Donna Mae Knowlton, Dec. 26, 1955 (div. June 1973); children: Franklin Guy III, LaVerne Anne; m. Linda Moncure, Jul. 3, 1973 (div. June 1996); m. Jeannette Graham, Jan. 1997. AA cum laude, Ft. Lewis Coll., 1957; BA cum laude, Adams State Coll., 1959, EdM, 1960; JD, Hastings U. Calif., 1964. Bar: Calif. 1965. Assoc. atty. McCutcheon, Black, Verleger & Shea, Calif., L.A., 1964-67; atty. Law Offices Samuel Frizell, Santa Ana, Calif., 1967-82; adj. prof. Cerritos Coll., Norwalk, Calif., 1977-81, Western State U., Fullerton, Calif., 1982-84, assoc. prof., 1984-90, prof., 1990-98, prof. emeritus, 1998—; cons. Law Offices Samuel Frizell, Mira Loma, Calif., 1982-98. Author: Frizell's Torts Tips, 1992; contbr. articles to profl. jours.; editor law jour. Mem. Main St. Adv. Panel, Garden Grove, Calif., 1975-76; judge pro-tem Orange County Superior Ct., Santa Ana, 1979-80; chair, com. atty. advertising Orange County Bar Assn., 1975; bd. dirs. Orange County Trial Lawyers Assn., 1972-75; adv. panel to legal assts. Cerritos Coll., Norwalk, 1982-86. Fellow Soc. Antiquaries; mem. Order of the Coif. Avocations: history, reloading and target shooting, saddle making. Office: Western State U 1111 N State College Blvd Fullerton CA 92831-3000 E-mail: SJFrizell@Earthlink.net.

FRIZZELL, GREGORY KENT K. judge; b. Wichita, Kans., Dec. 13, 1956; s. D. Kent and Shirley Elaine (Piatt) F.; m. Kelly Susan Nash, Mar. 9, 1991; children: Benjamin Newcomb, Hannah Kirsten, Robert Nash, David Gregory, Elizabeth Piatt, Jubilee Kathryn. BA, U. Tulsa, 1981; JD, U. Mich., 1984. Bar: Okla. 1985, U.S. Dist. Ct. (no., ea. and we. dists.) Okla. 1985, U.S. Ct. Appeals (10th cir.) 1985, U.S. Supreme Ct. 1990. Jud. clk. to judge U.S. Dist. Ct. for No. Dist. Okla., Tulsa, 1984-86; pvt. practice Tulsa, 1986-95; gen. counsel Okla. Tax Commn., 1995-97; dist. judge Tulsa County, 1997—. Master of the bench Hudson, Hall, Wheaton Chpt. of Amer. Inns of Ct., Tulsa. Counsel bd. dirs. Tulsa Speech and Hearing Assn., 1987-95, pres., 1994-95. Mem. Okla. Bar Assn., Am. Inns of Ct. (past pres. local chpt.), Rotary, Federalist Soc. Office: Tulsa County Courthouse 500 S Denver Ave Tulsa OK 74103-3838

FROEBE, GERALD ALLEN, lawyer; b. The Dalles, Oreg., Feb. 16, 1935; s. Earl Wayne and Ethelene Alvina (Ogle) F.; m. Olivia Ann Tharaldson, Aug. 31, 1958; children: Dana Lynn, Heidi Ann. BBA, U. Oreg., 1956, LLB, 1961; LLM, NYU, 1962. Bar: N.Y. 1962, Oreg. 1962, U.S. Dist. Ct. Oreg. 1962. Auditor Arthur Andersen & Co., Seattle, 1956-58; lawyer, ptnr. Miller, Nash, Wiener, Hager & Carlsen, Portland, Oreg., 1962—99. Editor-in-chief Oreg. Law Rev., Eugene, 1960-61. Republican. Christian. Avocations: hiking, travel. Estate planning, Pension, profit-sharing, and employee benefits, Taxation, general. Home: 1109 SW Ardmore Ave Portland OR 97205-1004 Office: 1109 SW Ardmore Ave Portland OR 97205

FROHLICH, ANTHONY WILLIAM, lawyer, master commissioner; b. Covington, Ky., Dec. 8, 1954; s. Kenneth Raymond and Joan Jude (Laake) F.; m. Candace Powell Robbins, May 31, 1975; children: Kenneth Zane, Matthew Andrew. BS, No. Ky. U., 1976, JD, 1980. Bar: Ky. 1980, U.S. Dist. Ct. (ea. dist.) Ky. 1981. Staff atty. Boone County (Ky.) Child Support Program, 1980-97; city atty. City of Walton, 1980-89; master commr. Boone County Cir. Ct., Burlington, Ky., 1989—; asst. commonwealth atty. 54th Jud. Dist., Burlington, Ky., 1984-89; ptnr. Mathis, Dallas & Frohlich, Florence, Ky., 1980-96, Law Office of Anthony W. Frohlich, Florence, Ky., 1996—. Pres. Soccer Tech., Union, Ky., 1994. Bd. dirs. No. Ky. Soccer Club, Florence, 1994; state coach Ky. Youth Soccer, 1994-96; coaching dir. Ky. Olympic Devel. Program Dist. One, Florence, 1992-94; soccer coach DHL USA men's nat. team, 2000-2001; active Union Town Plan Steering Com., 1999; bd. dirs. Greater Cin. Consumer Credit Counseling, 1999-2002; nominating chmn. Boy Scout Am., 1999-2001; mem. steering com. Boone County Parks & Recreation, 2000—. Named Coach of Yr., No. Ky. Soccer Club, 1992. Mem. ATLA, Ky. Bar Assn., Boone County Bar Assn. (treas. 1980), Ky. Acad. Trial Lawyers. Roman Catholic. Avocations: coaching soccer, basketball. General practice, Personal injury (including property damage), Other. Home: 9253 Us Highway 42 Union KY 41091-9470 Office: Law Office Anthony Frohlich PO Box 396 Florence KY 41022-0396 E-mail: awfpsc42@fuse.net.

FROHNMAYER, DAVID BRADEN, academic administrator; b. Medford, Oreg., July 9, 1940; s. Otto J. and MarAbel (Braden) F.; m. Lynn Diane Johnson, Dec. 30, 1970; children: Kirsten (dec.), Mark, Kathryn (dec.), Jonathan, Amy. AB magna cum laude, Harvard U., 1962; BA, Oxford (Eng.) U., 1964, MA (Rhodes scholar), 1971; JD, U. Calif., Berkeley, 1967; LLD (hon.), Willamette U., 1988; D Pub. Svc. (hon.), U. Portland, 1989. Bar: Calif. 1967, U.S. Dist. Ct. (no. dist.) Calif. 1967, Oreg. 1971, U.S. Dist. Ct. Oreg. 1971, U.S. Supreme Ct. 1981. Assoc. Pillsbury, Madison & Sutro, San Francisco, 1967-69; asst. to sec. Dept. HEW, 1969-70; prof. law U. Oreg., 1971-81, spl. asst. to univ. pres., 1971-79; atty. gen. State of Oreg., 1981-91; dean Sch. Law U. Oreg., 1992-94, pres., 1994—. Chmn. Conf. Western Attys. Gen., 1985-86; chmn. Am. Coun. Edn. Govtl. Rels. commn, 1996-98; bd. dirs. Umpqua Holding Co. Mem. Oreg. Ho. of Reps, 1975-81; mem. coun. pub. reps. NIH, 1999-2000; bd. dirs. Fred Hutchinson Cancer Rsch. Ctr., 1994-2000, Nat. Marrow Donor Program, 1987-99, Fanconi Anemia Rsch. Fund, Inc., Tax Free Trust of Oreg. Fund; active Oreg. Progress Bd. Recipient awards Weaver Constl. Law Essay competition Am. Bar Found., 1972, 74, Advocacy award Research!Am., 1999, Albert B. Sabin Heroes of Sci. award Ams. for Med. Progress Ednl. Found., 2000; Rhodes scholar, 1962. Fellow Am. Acad. Arts and Scis.; mem. ABA (Ross essay winner 1980), Oreg. Bar Assn., Calif. Bar Assn., Nat. Assn. Attys. Gen. (pres. 1987, Wyman award 1987), Round Table Eugene, Order of Coif, Phi Beta Kappa, Rotary. Republican. Presbyterian. Home: 2315 McMorran St Eugene OR 97403-1750 Office: U Oreg Johnson Hall Office Pres Eugene OR 97403 E-mail: pres@oregon.uoregon.edu.

FROHNMAYER, JOHN EDWARD, lawyer, legal scholar, ethicist, writer; b. Medford, Oreg., June 1, 1942; s. Otto J. and Marabel (Braden) F.; m. Leah Thorpe, June 10, 1967; children: Jason Otto, Jonathan Aaron. BA in Am. History, Stanford U., 1964; MA in Christian Ethics, U. Chgo., 1969; JD, U. Oreg., 1972. Bar: Oreg. 1972, Mont. 1995. Assoc. Johnson, Harrang & Mercer, Eugene, Oreg., 1972-75; ptnr. Tonkon, Torp, Galen, Marmaduke & Booth, Portland, Oreg., 1975-89; 5th chmn. Nat. Endowment for the Arts, Washington, 1989-92; writer, lectr. on art, ethics and politics, 1992—; pvt. practice, 1972-89, 1995—. Mem. Oreg. Arts Commn., 1978-85, chmn., 1980-84; bd. dirs. Internat. Sculpture Symposium, eugene, 1974; chmn. screening com. Oreg. State Capitol Bldg., 1977. Author: Leaving Town Alive, 1993, Out of Tune: Listening to The First Amendment, 1994; editor-in-chief Oreg. Law Rev., 1971-72; singer; appeared in recital, oratorio, mus. comedy and various other mus. prodns. Trustee Holladay Park Pla.; founding mem. chamber choir Novum Cantorum; bd. dirs. Chamber Music Northwest, Western States Arts Found.; mem. Nat. Endowment for the Arts Opera-Mus. Theater, 1982, 83. With USN, 1966-69. Sr. fellow Freedom Forum, 1993; recipient People for the Am. Way Ann. 1st Amendment award, 1992, Oreg. Gov. Arts award, 1993, Intellectual Freedom award Mont. Libr. Assn., 1997, Citation of Merit, Mu Phi Epsilon, 1998. Fellow Am. Leadership Forum; mem. ABA (com. comml. transactions litigation), Oreg. State Bar Assn. (chmn. bar com. domestic law 1975-76, procedure and practice com. 1984-85), Multnomah County Bar Assn., City Club Portland (bd. dirs.), Sta. L. Rowing Club (sec.), Order of the Coif (legal hon. 1972). Home and Office: 14080 Lone Bear Rd Bozeman MT 59715-6620 E-mail: frohn@wtp.net.

FROLIK, LAWRENCE ANTON, law educator, lawyer, consultant; b. Lincoln, Nebr., Jan. 10, 1944; s. Elvin F. and Rita K. (Haley) F.; m. Ellen M. Doyle, Sept. 25, 1973; children: Winnefred, Cornelius. BA with distinction, U. Nebr., 1966; JD cum laude, Harvard U., 1969, LLM cum laude, 1972. Asst. prof. U. Pitts., 1975-78, assoc. prof., 1978-81, prof., 1981—; dir. Pitts. office programing Gruter Inst. for Law & Behavioral Rsch. Bd. dirs. Kendal Corp. Author: Federal Tax Aspects of Injury, 1993, Loss and Damage, 1987; co-author: Pennsylvania Elder Law Manual, 1988, Advising the Elderly and Disabled Client, 1991, 2d edit., 1999, The Elderly and the Law: Cases and Materials, 1991, 2d edit., 1999, Elder Law in a Nutshell, 1995, 3d edit., 2003, Residence Options for Older or Disabled Clients, 1997, Aging and the Law: An Interdisciplinary Reader, 1999. Mem. exec. com. Gruter Inst. Law and Behavioral Rsch., Penn. AARP exec. coun., 2002—. Capt. U.S. Army, 1969-71. Fellow Am. Bar Found., Am. Coll. Trust and Estate Counsel; mem. Phi Beta Kappa. Home: 4345 Schenley Farms Ter Pittsburgh PA 15213-1206 Office: U Pitts Sch Law 3900 Forbes Ave. Pittsburgh PA 15260 E-mail: frolik@law.pitt.edu.

FROMM, FREDERICK ANDREW, JR., lawyer; b. Grosse Pointe Farms, Mich., Aug. 2, 1951; s. Frederick Andrew and Jeanette (Sellars) F.; m. Kathleen Ann Lewis, Sept. 25, 1976; children: Andrew Blair, Jennifer Kathleen. BS, Mich. State U., 1973; JD, U. Detroit, 1976. Bar: Mich. 1976, U.S. Dist. Ct. (ea. dist.) Mich. 1976. Law clk. to M.J. Kelly Mich. Ct. Appeals, Detroit, 1976-77; atty. legal staff GM, Detroit, 1977-92, sr. counsel, atty., practice area mgr., 1997—. V.p., gen. counsel, sec. Delco Electronics Corp., 1992-96. Mem. Mich. Bar Assn., Ind. Bar Assn. Commercial, contracts (including sales of goods; commercial financing), Environmental. Home: 2887 Chestnut Run Dr Bloomfield Hills MI 48302-1105 Office: GM Corp MC 482-C23-D24 300 Renaissance Ctr Detroit MI 48265-3000 E-mail: fred.fromm@gm.com.

FROMM, JEFFERY BERNARD, lawyer; b. Washington, Oct. 9, 1947; s. Seymour Morris and Frances Sylvia (Goldstein) F.; m. Mary Ellen Sommer, Sept. 11, 1971; children: Aaron M., David P. BS in Elec. Engring., BA in Physics, U. Pa., 1970; JD magna cum laude, Widener U., 1981. Bar: Pa. 1982, Calif. 1982, U.S. Ct. Appeals (9th and fed. cirs.) 1982, Colo. 1988. Patent atty. Hewlett-Packard Co., Palo Alto, Calif., 1981-83, sr. patent atty., 1983-85, mng. patent counsel Andover, Mass., 1985-87, sr. mng. counsel intellectual property Ft. Collins, Colo., 1987—2002; pvt. intellectual property legal practice, 2002—. Asst. scout master Boy Scouts Am., Ft. Collins, 1988-96; asst. coach-umpire Little League, Andover and San Jose, Calif., 1983-87. Mem. IEEE, ABA, ATPLA, Pa. Bar Assn., Calif. Bar Assn., Colo. Bar Assn., Intellectual Property Owners Assn. (past chmn. discovery com.), Phi Delta Phi. Avocations: skiing, golf. Computer, Patent, Trademark and copyright. Office: PO Box 7399 PMB 332 Breckenridge CO 80424-7399 E-mail: jeff@fromms.ws.

FROMMER, WILLIAM S. lawyer; b. Bklyn., Sept. 27, 1942; s. Herbert S. and Molly B. Frommer; m. Karen Beagle, July 31, 1966; 1 child, Hillary. BEE, Cornell U., 1965; JD, Am. U., 1969. Bar: N.Y. 1970, U.S. Patent Office 1970, U.S. Ct. Customs and Patent Appeals 1975, U.S. Ct. Appeals (fed. cir.) 1982, U.S. Supreme Ct. 1985. Assoc. Marn & Jangarathis, NYC, 1969—73, Curtis, Morris & Safford, P.C., NYC, 1973—76, ptnr., 1976—97; founding ptnr. Frommer, Lawrence & Haug, NYC, 1997—. Mem. Am. U. Law Rev., 1967—69. Mem.: ABA, Internat. Bar Assn., Internat. Patent and Trade Assn., N.Y. State Bar Assn., N.Y. Patent Law Assn. Intellectual property, Patent, Trademark and copyright. Office: 745 5th Ave New York NY 10151-0099

FROSH, BRIAN ESTEN, lawyer, state senator; b. Washington, Oct. 8, 1946; s. Stanley Benjamin and Judith Lee (Wirkman) F.; m. Marcy Masters, Nov. 19, 1984; children: Elena, Alexandra. Student, U. Stockholm, 1966-67; BA, Wesleyan U., 1968; JD, Columbia U., 1971. Legis. asst. Sen. Harrison Williams U.S. Senate, Washington, 1972-76; ptnr. Kass, Skalet & Frosh, Washington, 1976-79, Bingaman, Davenport & Lovejoy, Santa Fe, 1979-81; pvt. practice Bethesda, Md., 1981—96; ptnr. Karp, Frosh, Lapidus, Wigodsky and Norwind, Washington, 1996—; del. Md. Gen. Assembly, Annapolis, 1987-95, chmn. Montgomery County House del., 1991-93; state senator Md. State Senate, 1995—, dep. majority leader, 2001—02, chmn. jud. procs. com., 2003—; mem. gov.'s task force on energy Md. Gen. Assembly, Annapolis, 1989-94; chmn. environ. subcom. Econ. and Environ. Affairs Com., 1995—2002; mem. Chesapeake Bay Commn., 1995—2002. Legis. acts include Md. Recycling Act, Newspaper Recycling Act, Oil Spills Bill, Bay Protection and Oil Exploration, also others; bd. dirs. State Nat. Bank Md. Bd. dirs. Hebrew Home Greater Washington, 1986-95, Jewish Cmty. Ctr. Greater Washington, 1983-89; mem. Montgomery County Charter Rev. Commn., 1983-86; nat. adv. commn. SBA, 1981-82. Recipient citation Chesapeake Bay Found., 1991, cert. of merit Montgomery County Common Cause Md., 1991; Clean Air award Sierra Club, 1991, Conservationist of Yr. award, 1989; Lawmaker of Yr. award Am. Lung Assn. Md., 1991, Outstanding Svc. award Am. Heart Assn. Md. Mem. Wesleyan U. Alumni Assn. (exec. com. 1986-89). General civil litigation, Commercial, contracts (including sales of goods; commercial financing). Address: Miller Senate Office Bldg 2E Annapolis MD 21401 Office: Ste 800W 7315 Wisconsin Ave Bethesda MD 20814-3217

FROSS, ROGER RAYMOND, lawyer; b. Rockford, Ill., Mar. 8, 1940; s. Hollis H. and Dorothy (George) F.; m. Madelon R. Rose, Feb. 14, 1970; 1 child, Oliver. AB, DePauw U., 1962; JD, U. Chgo., 1965. Bar: Ill. 1965. Assoc. Norman and Billick, Chgo., 1965-70; ptnr. Lord, Bissell & Brook, Chgo., 1970—, mng. pntr., 1982-87. Bd. dirs. Hyde Park Bank and Trust Co., Chgo., 1975—; pres. Hyde-Park-Kenwood Devel. Corp., 1998—. Bd. dirs. Hyde Park Neighborhood Club, Chgo., 1970—, pres. 1972-73; bd. dirs., mem. exec. com. South East Chgo. Commn., 1978—; mem. Community Conservation Council, Chgo., 1980-99; bd. dirs., sec. Chgo. Metro History Fair, 1991—; bd. dirs. The Joyce Found., 1991—, Lab. Sch. U. Chgo., 1991-94, Citizens Com. of the Juvenile Ct., 1973-96. Rector schlor DePauw U., Greencastle, Ind., 1958-62. Mem. ABA, Ill. Bar Assn., Chgo. Bar Assn. (chmn. com. juvenile delinquents 1972). Office: Lord Bissell & Brook Harris Bank Bldg 115 S La Salle St Ste 3500 Chicago IL 60603-3801

FROST, BARBARA SHERRY, lawyer; b. Montclair, N.J., Oct. 24, 1948; d. William Nathan and Margaret (Naperstick) F.; m. Melvyn Jay Simburg, Jan. 1, 1981; children: Suzanne Simburg, Stephen Simburg. BS, U. Ill., 1970; JD, U. Denver, 1975. Bar: Colo. 1975, Wash. 1976, U.S. Dist. Ct. (we. dist.) Wash. 1976; cert. yoga instr. Law clk. King County Superior Ct., Seattle, 1976; legal advisor Seattle-King County Ombudsman, 1976-79; assoc. Sindell, Levy & Frost, 1979-82; contract atty. in pvt. practice Seattle, 1982-89; asst. city atty. Seattle City Atty.'s Office, 1990—. Mem. com. Wash. Self-Insured Assn., 1991-2001. Mem. editorial bd. Alternate Dispute Resolution Deskbook, 1990; mem. Law Rev., U. Denver, 1974-75. Bd. dirs. Puget Sound Blood Ctr., Seattle, 1980-92, v.p., 1985-92; co-chair Faces for Life, 2000. Mem. Seattle-King County Bar Assn. (co-chair jud. screening com. 1992-95, jud. and cts. com. 1995—), Wash. Women Lawyers (bd. dirs. 1977-78). Office: Office Seattle City Atty 600 4th Ave 4th fl Seattle WA 98104 E-mail: Barbara.Frost@seattle.gov.

FROST, BARRY WARREN, lawyer; b. Glen Ridge, N.J., Aug. 17, 1947; m. Nancy Teich, Aug. 16, 1970; children: Benjamin, Alison. BS, Bradley U., 1969; JD, N.Y. Law Sch., 1976. Bar: N.J. 1976, U.S. Dist. Ct. N.J. 1976, U.S. Dist. Ct. (so. and ea. dists.) N.Y. 1977, N.Y. 1977. Assoc. Gladstein & Isaac, N.Y.C., 1972-77; ptnr. Teich, Groh & Frost, Trenton, N.J., 1977—. Banking, Bankruptcy, Commercial, contracts (including sales of goods; commercial financing). Office: Teich Groh & Frost 691 Highway 33 Trenton NJ 08619-4407 E-mail: teich1g2f3@aol.com.

FROST, EDMUND BOWEN, lawyer; b. Pueblo, Colo., Dec. 5, 1942; s. Hildreth and Doris (Bowen) F.; m. Molly Spitzer; children: Julia A., Elizabeth E., Edmund N., Luette S. BA, Dartmouth Coll., 1964; JD magna cum laude, U. Mich., 1967. Bar: Colo. 1967, D.C. 1970, U.S. Supreme Ct. 1980. Assoc. Steptoe & Johnson, Washington, 1969-75; chief legal advisor to commr. ICC, Washington, 1975-76; asst. dir. for gen. litigation Bur. Competition, FTC, Washington, 1976-77; v.p., gen. counsel Chem. Mfrs. Assn., Washington, 1978-82; ptnr. Kirland & Ellis, Washington, 1982-88, Davis, Graham & Stubbs, Washington, 1988-94; sr. v.p. and gen. counsel Clean Sites, Inc., Alexandria, Va., 1994-99. Contbr. articles to profl. jours. Participant pub. policy dialogs on environ. issues Keystone (Colo.) Ctr., 1980—; guest artisan Washington Nat. Cathedral, 1997—; pres., bd. dirs. Vincent Palumbo Ctr. for Stonecarving and Indsl. Arts, Inc., 2001—. Capt. U.S. Army, 1967-69. Mem. Cosmos Club Washington. Avocations: sculpture and stone carving, skiing, mountain climbing, tuba and euphonium. Federal civil litigation, Environmental, Non-profit and tax-exempt organizations. Home: 3309 35th St NW Washington DC 20016-3141 E-mail: ebfrost@leonardFrost.com.

FROST, JEROME KENNETH, lawyer; b. July 4, 1939; s. Carl Kenneth and Madeline May (Michel) F.; m. Carol Ann Brown, May 16, 1967; children: Arthur, Carl, Anya, Jonah, Jerome. BA, Siena Coll., 1962; JD, Boston Coll., 1965. Bar: N.Y. 1965, U.S. Dist. Ct. (no. dist.) N.Y. 1965, U.S. Ct. Appeals (2d cir.) 1982. Assoc. Wagar, Taylor, Howd & Brearton, Troy, N.Y., 1965-66; ptnr. Lee, LeForestier & Frost, Troy, N.Y., 1967-75; sole practice Troy, N.Y., 1976—. Asst. corp. counsel City of Troy, 1970-73, Rensselaer County Pub. Defender, 1995—. Editor Boston Coll. Law Rev., 1965. Player, agt. Lansingburgh Little League, 1982-87. Named one of Best Lawyers in Am., 2001—02, 2003—; Presdl. scholar, Boston Coll., 1965. Mem. Rensselaer County Bar Assn., Order of Coif, Alpha Sigma Nu, Delta Epsilon Sigma, Alpha Kappa Alpha, Alpha Mu Gamma. Roman Catholic. Avocation: French language. Criminal, Family and matrimonial, Personal injury (including property damage). Home: 20 Deepkill Ln Troy NY 12182-9738 Office: 105 Jordan Rd Troy NY 12180-8376 E-mail: jfrost@frostfirm.com.

FRUE, WILLIAM CALHOUN, lawyer; b. Pontiac, Mich., Dec. 29, 1934; s. William Calhoun and Evelyn Laura Frue; m. Eloise Saunders, June 22, 1956 (div. Dec. 1989); m. Jane Torres Fletcher, Dec. 30, 1989; children: William C. III, John C., Michael C., Victoria. BA, Washington & Lee U., 1956; LLB, U. N.C., 1960. Bar: N.C. 1960, U.S. Dist. Ct. (we. dist.) N.C. 1961, U.S. Tax Ct. 1968, U.S. Ct. Appeals (4th cir.) 1988. Rsch. asst. Inst. of Govt., Chapel Hill, N.C., 1958-60; assoc. Wright & Shuford, Asheville, N.C., 1961-69; ptnr. Shuford, Frue & Sluder, Asheville, 1969-72, Shuford, Frue & Best, Asheville, 1973-84, The Frue Law Firm, Asheville, 1984—. Editor Popular Govt. mag., 1958-60. Chmn. Asheville Police Retirement Fund, 1973-83, Morehead Scholarship Selectincom., 1965-90, Asheville Planning and Zoning Commn., 1982-92. Mem. N.C. Bar Assn., Buncombe County Bar Assn., (sec., v.p. 1978-92), Trout Unl d. (N.C. coun. 1965). Democrat. Episcopalian. Avocations: fishing, camping. State civil litigation, Probate (including wills, trusts), Property, real (including real estate development, water). Office: PO Box 7627 Asheville NC 28802-7627

FRUG, GERALD E. law educator; b. 1939; AB, U. Calif.-Berkeley, 1960; JD, Harvard U., 1963. Bar: Calif. 1964, N.Y. 1969. Frank Knox fellow London Sch. Econs., 1963-64; law clk. to chief justice Supreme Ct. Calif., 1964-65; assoc. Heller, Ehrman, White & McAuliffe, San Francisco, 1965-66; spl. asst. to chmn. EEOC, 1966-69; assoc. Cravath, Swaine & Moore, N.Y.C., 1969-70; gen. counsel Health Services Adminstrn., N.Y.C., 1970-72, 1st dep. adminstr., 1972-73, adminstr., 1973-74; assoc. prof. U. Pa. Law Sch., Phila., 1974-78, prof., 1978-81, Harvard U. Law Sch., 1981-94, Samuel R. Rosenthal prof. law, 1994-2000, Louis D. Brandeis prof., 2000—. Mem. Phi Beta Kappa. Office: Law Sch Harvard U Cambridge MA 02138

FRYBURGER, LAWRENCE BRUCE, lawyer, mediator, writer; b. Cin., Apr. 7, 1933; BA, U. Cin., 1956; LLB with nat. honors, U. Tex., 1958. Bar: Tex. 1959, U.S. Dist. Ct. (we. dist.) Tex. 1961, U.S. Ct. Appeals (5th cir.) 1962, U.S. Supreme Ct. 1963, U.S. Dist. Ct. (so. dist.) Tex. 1972, U.S. Dist. Ct. (no. dist.) Tex. 1981, U.S. Ct. Appeals (11th cir.) 1981; bd. cert. labor and employment law Tex. Bd. Legal Specialization. Pvt. practice, San Antonio, 1959—. Spl. prof. labor relations law San Antonio Coll., 1968; originator Tex. Young Lawyer's Inst. Author: Policies, Procedures and People: A Blueprint for Human Resources, 1997; contbr. articles to law jours.; mem. editorial bd. Tex. Lawyers Practice Guide, 1964. Mem. San Antonio Bd. Adjustment, 1969-72; chmn. lawyer's div. United Fund, San Antonio and Bexar County, 1967-68. Sutphin scholar U. Cin., 1956. Mem. ABA, Tex. Bar Assn. (program chmn. current devels. in labor law inst. 1978, mem. coun. labor law sect. 1978-80), San Antonio Bar Assn. (chmn.

lawyer reference plan 1970-73), Tex. Young Lawyers Assn. (bd. dirs. 1964-66), San Antonio Young Lawyers Assn. (pres. 1963-64, Outstanding Young Lawyer award 1967), Tex. Assn. of Residential Care Communities (spl. labor law counsel 1996—), Phi Delta Phi, Sigma Chi. Alternative dispute resolution, Civil rights, Labor (including EEOC, Fair Labor Standards Act, labor-management relations, NLRB, OSHA).

FRYDMAN, JAN ERIC, lawyer, executive, diplomat; b. Stockholm, Sept. 9, 1958; s. P. and M.J. Frydman. BBA in Fin. and Econs. with honors, U. Oreg., 1980; diploma in civil law, diploma in tax and fin. law, U. Stockholm Law Sch., 1982; cert., U. Paris-Sorbonne, 1984; LLM cum laude, U. Stockholm Law Sch., 1989; cert., U. Nice, 1991; PIL, Harvard Law Sch., 1998, Ecole National d'Administration, 2002. Group comdr. Royal Swedish Air Force, Stockholm, 1981-82; mktg. mgmt. The Procter & Gamble Co., Stockholm, 1982-84; corp. officer, head internat. fin. instns. The First Nat. Bank of Chgo., Stockholm, 1984-87; v.p., dep. CEO Am. Profls. Ins. Co., Indpls., 1987-88; atty. at law Carl Swartling Advokatbyra, Stockholm, 1989-91, Mannheimer Swartling, N.Y.C., 1991-92, Stockholm, 1992-95; head of info. Stockholm, 1995-96; legal advisor European Commn., Brussels, 1996-99, prin. adminstr., 1999—2003, deputy head, intl. div., 2003—. Dir. Interbrands HB, Stockholm, 1989-2000; country corr. Internat. Banking Law Jour., Oxford, Eng., 1990-94, Internat. Co. and Comml. Law Rev., Oxford, Eng. 1990-94. Author: Japanese Tort Law, 1989; contbr. articles to profl. jours. Recipient Superior Acad. Achievement award U. Oreg., 1979, Internat. Student of Yr. award U. Oreg., 1979; Sweden-Am. Found. scholar, 1978, Inst. Internat. Edn. scholar, 1978, U. Oreg. scholar, 1978-80. Mem. ABA, Swedish Bar Assn., Internat. Bar Assn., Sweden-Am. Found., Am. Club Sweden, Swedish Club of Brussels, Alpha Kappa Psi, Beta Gamma Sigma. Avocations: travel, photography, music, reading, swimming. Office: 200 Rue de la Loi 1049 Brussels Belgium

FRYE, HELEN JACKSON, federal judge; b. Klamath Falls, Oreg., Dec. 10, 1930; d. Earl and Elizabeth (Kirkpatrick) Jackson; m. William Frye, Sept. 7, 1952; children: Eric, Karen, Heidi; 1 adopted child, Hedy; m. Perry Holloman, July 10, 1980 (dec. Sept. 1991). BA in English with honors, U. Oreg., 1953, MA, 1960, JD, 1966. Bar: Oreg. 1966. Public sch. tchr., Oreg., 1956-63; with Riddlesberger, Pederson, Brownhill & Young, 1966-67, Husband & Johnson, Eugene, 1968-71; trial judge State of Oreg., 1971-80; U.S. dist judge Dist. Oreg. Portland, 1980-95; sr. judge U.S. Dist. Ct., Portland, 1995—. Mem. Phi Beta Kappa. Office: 1107 US Courthouse 1000 SW 3rd Ave Portland OR 97204-2930

FRYE, HENRY E. retired state supreme court chief justice; b. Ellerbe, N.C., Aug. 1, 1932; s. Walter A. and Pearl Alma (Motley) F.; m. Edith Shirley Taylor, Aug. 25, 1956; children: Henry Eric, Harlan Elbert. BS in Biol. Scis., A & T U., N.C., 1953; JD with honors, U. N.C., 1959. Bar: N.C. 1959. Asst. U.S. atty. (middle dist.), N.C., 1963-65; prof. law N.C. Central U., Durham, 1965-67; practice law Greensboro, N.C., 1967-83; rep. N.C. Gen. Assembly, 1969-80, N.C. Senate, 1980-82; assoc. justice N.C. Supreme Ct., Raleigh, 1983-99, chief justice, 1999—2001; of counsel Brooks, Pierce, McLendon, Humphrey & Leonard, LLP, Greensboro, NC, 2001—. Organizer, pres. Greensboro Nat. Bank, 1971-80. Deacon Providence Baptist Ch. Capt. USAF, 1953-55. Mem. ABA, N.C. Bar Assn., Greensboro Bar Assn., Nat. Bar Assn., Am. Judicature Soc. (chair bd. dirs. 1995-97), Kappa Alpha Psi. Office: Brooks Pierce McLendon humphrey & Leonard LLP 2000 Renaissance Plaza 230 N Elm St PO Box 26000 Greensboro NC 27420-1841 Fax: 336-378-1001. E-mail: hfrye@brookspierce.com.

FRYE, ROLAND MUSHAT, JR., lawyer; b. Princeton, N.J., Feb. 8, 1950; s. Roland Mushat and Jean (Steiner) F.; m. Susan Marie Pettey, Jan. 23, 1988. AB cum laude, Princeton U., 1972; JD, Cornell U., 1975. Bar: Pa. 1975, D.C. 1978, U.S. Ct. Appeals (D.C. cir.) 1991, U.S. Supreme Ct. 1991. Litigation assoc. White and Williams, Phila., 1975-77; litigation atty. U.S. Dept. Energy, Washington, 1977-79, asst. solicitor, 1979-80; presiding officer Fed. Energy Regulatory Commn., Washington, 1980-83, chief presiding officer, 1983-85, supervisory atty., 1985-88, adv. atty., 1988-91; energy atty. Pepper, Hamilton & Scheetz, Washington, 1991-92; sr. atty. Office Commn. Appellate Adjudication U.S. Nuclear Regulatory Commn., Washington, 1992—. Mediator Ctr. for Cmty. Justice, D.C. Superior Ct., 1984-86. Editor Cornell Law Rev., 1974-75; mem. editl. bd. Sidwell Friends Sch. Alumni Mag., 1994-2003; contbr. articles to profl. jours. Mem. schs. and ann. giving coms. Princeton U., Washington and Phila., 1978-91; arbitrator Better Bus. Bur. Greater Washington, 1983-86, Phila. Ct. Common Pleas, 1975-77; mem. Sidwell Friends Sch. Parents Assn., treas. 2001-03. Capt. USAR. Recipient Outstanding Young Man Am. award U.S. Jaycees, 1979. Mem. ABA, D.C. Bar Assn. (fee arbitration panel 1983-89, com. on alt. dispute resolution 1983-87), Fed. Bar Assn., Fed. Energy Bar Assn. (adminstrv. practice com. 1991-92), Sidwell Friends Sch. Alumni Assn. (exec. com. 1985-93, 94-2003, v.p. 1987-89, pres. 1989-93, Newmyer award), Soc. Cin., St. Andrews Soc., Prettyman-Leventhal Am. Inn of Ct. (barrister 1989-92, master 1992-99, exec. com. 1992-99, program chmn. 1993-95, counsellor 1995-96, pres.-elect 1996-97, pres. 1997-98, nat./emeritus mem. 1999—), Cosmos Club. Presbyterian. Avocations: trout fishing, singing, travel. Home: 220 N Royal St Alexandria VA 22314-3329 Office: US Nuclear Regulatory Commn 11555 Rockville Pike Rockville MD 20852-2739 E-mail: rmf@nrc.gov.

FRYMAN, VIRGIL THOMAS, JR., lawyer; b. Maysville, Ky., Apr. 9, 1940; s. Virgil Thomas and Elizabeth Louis (Marshall) F. AB cum laude, Harvard U., 1962, LLB, 1966. Bar: N.Y. 1967, U.S. Ct. Appeals (2d cir.) 1967, U.S. Dist. Ct. (so. and ea. dists.) N.Y. 1968, U.S. Supreme Ct. 1970, U.S. Ct. Appeals (6th cir.) 1988,U.S. Ct. Appeals (11th cir.) 2002, U.S. Dist. Ct. (ea. and we. dists.) Ky. 1988. Assoc. Cravath, Swaine & Moore, N.Y.C., 1966-73; asst. U.S. atty. U.S. Dist. Ct. (so. dist.) N.Y., N.Y.C., 1973-78; assoc. gen. counsel Price Waterhouse, N.Y.C., 1978-86; staff counsel select com. to investigate covert arms transactions with Iran, U.S. Ho. Reps., 1987; mem. Greenebaum, Doll & McDonald PLLC, Lexington, Ky., 1988—. Contbr. to Proving Federal Crimes, 6th edit., 1976. Mem. ABA, Assn. Bar City of N.Y., Ky. Bar Assn., Fayette County Bar Assn., Harvard Club, Idle hour Country Club. Democrat. Episcopalian. Federal civil litigation, State civil litigation, Criminal. Home: Fed Hill Washington KY 41096-0173 Office: Greenebaum Doll & McDonald PLLC 300 W Vine St Ste 1100 Lexington KY 40507-1665

FUDGE, EDWARD WILLIAM, lawyer; b. Lester, Ala., July 13, 1944; s. Benjamin Lee and Sybil Belle (Short) F.; m. Sara Faye Locke, June 23, 1967; children: Melanie, Jeremy. AA, Fla. Coll., Tampa, 1965; BA, Abilene Christian U., 1967, MA, 1968; JD, U. Houston, 1988. Bar: Tex. 1988, U.S. Ct. Appeals (5th cir.), U.S. Dist. Ct. (so. dist.) Tex. Minister Ch. of Christ, Kirkwood, Mo., 1968-72; editor-in-chief The C.E.I. Pub. Co., Athens, Ala., 1972-75; editor The Good Newspaper, Houston, 1982-85; propr. Providential Press, Houston, 1982—99; assoc. Jenkens & Gilchrist, Houston, 1988-91, Simmons, Fletcher & Fudge, Houston, 1991-97, Lanier Law Firm, Houston, 1997—. Author numerous books; contbr. articles to profl. jours. Elder Bering Dr. Ch. of Christ, Houston, 1983-90, 92-97; bd. dirs. Christian Conciliation Svc., Houston, 1983-85, Christ's Prison Fellowship, 1993-96. Mem. ABA, Houston Bar Assn., Tex. Bar Assn., Evang. Theol. Soc. (past regional officer). Avocations: writing, publishing, lecturing, teaching. Personal injury (including property damage). Office: Lanier Law Firm 6810 FM 1960 W Houston TX 77069

FUENTES-OSTOS, FRANCISCO, lawyer, consultant; s. Francisco Fuentes-Hungler and Adelina Fuentes; m. Alicia Perez-Helguera, July 6, 1991; children: Ana Fuentes, José María Fuentes, Francisco Fuentes Jr. J.D., Escuela Libre de Derecho, Mexico, 1990; LL.M., Cambridge U., England, 1991—92. Bar: Mex. 1990. Fgn. assoc. Clifford Chance Rogers & Wells, N.Y.C., 1992—93; ptnr. Mijares, Angoitia, Cortés y Fuentes, S.C., Mex. City, Mexico, 1994—. Scholar Internat. Scholarship, Brit. Coun., 1991. Mem.: ABA (assoc.), Mex. City Country Club (bd. dirs. 2002—). Finance, Mergers and acquisitions, Antitrust. Office: Mijares Angoitia Cortés y Fuentes SC Montes Urales No 505 3rd Fl Mexico City 11000 Mexico Office Fax: (52)(55) 5520-1065.

FUJIEDA, ATSUSHI, lawyer; b. Iyomishima City, Ehime, Japan, Nov. 20, 1955; s. Shizuka and Yachiyo Fujieda; m. Takako Fujieda, Nov. 3, 1984; children: Sayaka, Arisa. LLB, U. Tokyo, 1980; LLM, UCLA, 1987. With Nagashima & Ohno, Tokyo, 1982—87, Paul, Hastings, Janofsky & Walker, L.A., 1987—88, Covington & Burling, Washington, 1988, Nagashima Ohno & Tsunematsu, Tokyo, 1988—. Author: U.S. Transfer Pricing Regulations, 1995, Taxation of Transfer of Technology, 2002. Mergers and acquisitions, Taxation, general, Transfer pricing. Office: Nagashima Ohno & Tsunematsu 3-12 Kioi-cho Chiyoda-ku Tokyo 102-0094 Japan

FULLER, DAVID OTIS, JR., lawyer; b. Grand Rapids, Mich., May 28, 1939; s. David Otis and Virginia Chapin (Emery) F.; m. Isabelle Patrice Gigout, July 5, 1968; children: Thomas Andrew, Christian Scott, Pierre Emery, Margaret Isabelle. BA, Wheaton Coll., 1961; JD, Harvard U., 1964; postgrad., George Washington U., 1963, U. Paris, 1966. Bar: Mich., 1964, N.Y., 1967, U.S. Supreme Ct., 1968. Law clk. U.S. Ho. of Reps. Judiciary Com., 1963; assoc. Amberg, Law & Fallon, Grand Rapids, 1964-65; asst. dist. atty. N.Y. County, 1966-72, law sec. to justice, 1972-73; corp. atty. Pan Am. World Airways, Inc., 1973-74; dep. gen. counsel Reader's Digest Assn., Inc., 1974-84; pvt. practice N.Y.C., 1984-87; ptnr. Baker, Nelson & Williams, N.Y.C., 1987-94, Bosworth, Gray & Fuller, Bronxville, N.Y., 1994—; justice Tuckahoe Village, N.Y., 1986—. Lectr. Am. Bar Assn., Practicing Law Inst., Bronx C.C. Editor: Harvard Jour. on Legislation, 1962-64; contbr. articles to profl. jours. Warden Episc. Ch., 1991-97. Mem.: ABA, Fed. Bar Coun., Westchester County Magistrates Assn. (pres. 1993—94), Westchester County Bar Assn., NY State Magistrates Assn. (v.p. 2002—), Am. Arbitration Assn. (arbitrator 1983—96), Assn. Bar City NY (comms. law com. 1984—87), NY State Bar Assn. (chmn. privacy com. 1982—84), Internat. Bar Assn., Harvard Club (N.Y.C.). Republican. Avocations: fishing, skiing, coins, racquet sports, French. General civil litigation, General practice, Intellectual property. Office: Bosworth Gray & Fuller 116 Kraft Ave Bronxville NY 10708-3810 E-mail: dofjr@aol.com.

FULLER, DEBRA LYNN, lawyer, consultant; b. Fairbanks, Alaska, Nov. 30, 1959; d. Jerry Frank and Mary Alice Fuller; children: Dane Michael, Patric Luis. AA, U. Md., 1980, U. Maine, 1982; BA, U. Tex., San Antonio, 1987; JD, St. Mary's Sch. Law, 1994. Bar: Tex. 1995. Supr. Clarke Am., San Antonio, 1983—91; law clk. Duarte, Ramirez & Hegeman, San Antonio, 1995; atty. Duarte & Assoc., San Antonio, 1995—99; regional atty. Tex. Dept. of Protective & Regulatory Svcs., San Antonio, 1999—. Cons. St. Mary's Legal Clinic, San Antonio, 1993—. Bldr. Habitat for Humanity, San Antonio, 1993—96. Mem.: State Bar Tex. Roman Catholic. Avocations: reading, travel, walking. Home: 814 Thornedike Dr San Antonio TX 78245 Office: Tex Dept Protective & Regulatory Services 3635 SE Military San Antonio TX 78223

FULLER, JACK ARTHUR, lawyer; b. San Pedro, Calif., May 26, 1952; s. Donald E. and Jeanne W. F. BA, U. Calif., Santa Barbara, 1975; JD, McGeorge Sch. Law, Sacramento, 1978. Bar: Calif. 1978. Dep. dist. atty. L.A. County, L.A., 1979-83; pvt. practice Long Beach, Calif., 1983—. Mem. L.A. County Bar Assn., Long Beach Bar Assn. (spkr. domestic violence def. 1994, bd. govs. 1995-96), Calif. Attys. for Criminal Justice. Avocation: golf. Office: Law Offices of Jack A Fuller 301 E Ocean Blvd # 250 Long Beach CA 90802 E-mail: jackafuller@earthlink.net.

FULLER, PERRY LUCIAN, lawyer; b. Central City, Nebr., Oct. 26, 1922; s. Perry L. and Ruth (Howorth) F.; m. Alice Moorman, Mar. 6, 1948; 1 child, Leslie Ann Fuller. Student, U. Chgo. Law Sch., 1946-47; AB, U. Nebr., 1947, JD, 1949. Bar: Ill. 1950, U.S. Supreme Ct. Mem. staff Chgo. Crime Commn., 1949; sr. ptnr. Hinshaw & Culbertson and predeccessors, Chgo., 1956—. Lectr. in law U. Chgo., 1970-76, mem. vis. com., 1991-93. Vice chmn. exec. com. Law in Am. Soc. Found., 1966, chmn., 1967—69, pres., 1969—95; chmn. Cook County CSC, 1967—69; mem. Ill. Law Enforcement Commn., 1971—72; v.p. Fed. Defender, Inc., 1964; trustee Village of Winnetka, 1992—96; bd. dir. Winnetka Cmty. Chest, Ill., 1966—69, Ill. Humane Soc., 1978—, pres., 1986. 1st lt. USMC, 1942—46, Capt. USMC, 1952—53. Decorated Air medal. Fellow Am. Coll. Trial Lawyers (state chmn. 1972-74), Am. Bar Found., Ill. Bar Found.; mem. ABA (chmn. pub. relations com. 1968-69, gavel awards com. 1974-77, chmn. 1976-78), Ill, Fed., 7th Cir. Chgo. (bd. mgrs. 1967-69) bar assns., Am. Law Inst., Am. Judicature Soc., Internat. Assn. Def. Counsel (chmn. Continuing Legal Edn. bd. 1982-86, exec. com. 1983-86), Soc. Trial Lawyers Ill. (bd. dirs. 1967-68, 73-74, sec. 1975-76, pres. 1977-78), Def. Rsch. Inst. (chmn. insts. com. 1986-90), Scribes , Legal Club, Law Club (pres. 1987-88). Republican. General civil litigation, Product liability, Professional liability. Home: 1093 Fisher Ln Winnetka IL 60093-1503 Office: Hinshaw & Culbertson 222 N La Salle St Ste 300 Chicago IL 60601-1081

FULLER, SAMUEL ASHBY, lawyer, mining company executive; b. Indpls., Sept. 2, 1924; s. John L.H. and Mary (Ashby) F.; m. Betty Winn Hamilton, June 10, 1948; children— Mary Cheryl Fuller Hargrove, Karen E. Fuller Wolfe, Deborah R. BS in Gen. Engring, U. Cin., 1946, JD, 1947; cert. fin. planner, Coll. for Fin. Planning, 1989. Bar: Ohio 1948, Ind. 1951, Fla. 1984. Cleve. claims rep. Mfrs. and Mchts. Indemnity Co., 1947-48; claims supr. Indemnity Ins. Co. N.Am., 1948-50; with firm Stewart, Irwin, Gilliom, Fuller & Meyer (formerly Murray, Mannon, Fairchild & Stewart), Indpls., 1950-85, Lewis Kappes Fuller & Eads (name changed to Lewis & Kappes), Indpls., 1985-89, of counsel, 1990—2000; pres., dir. Irsugo Consol. Mines, Ltd., 1953-80. Dir. Ind. Pub. Health Found., Inc., 1972-84; staff instr. Purdue U. Life Ins. and Mktg. Inst., 1954-61; instr. Am. Coll. Life Underwriters, Indpls., 1964-74; mem. Ind. State Bd. Law Examiners, 1984-96, treas. 1987-88. Bd. dirs. Southwest Social Centre, Inc., 1965-70; pres., dir. Westminster Village North, Inc., 1981-89. Fellow: Indpls. Bar Found.; mem.: Fla. Bar, 7th Cir. Bar Assn., Ind. State Bar Assn. (bd. mgrs. 1986—88), Lincoln Hills Golf Club, Sun City Ctr. Golf and Racquet Club, Masons, Beta Theta Pi. Republican. Roman Catholic. Home: 306 Thornhill Pl Sun City Center FL 33573-5842 E-mail: samuel105@peoplepc.com.

FULLER, WILLIAM SIDNEY, lawyer; b. Auburn, Ala., Aug. 9, 1931; s. William Melton and Ernestine (Torbert) F.; m. Joyce Jeffrey, Nov. 5, 1953; children: Jeffrey Melton, Barbara Rush. BS, Auburn U., 1953; LLB, U. Ala., 1956, JD, 1969. Bar: Ala. 1956. Student asst. to dean U. Ala. Law Sch., 1954—55; law clk. to U.S. dist. judge, Montgomery, Ala., 1956—57; practice law Andalusia, 1957—; former city atty. City of Andalusia. Dir., sec. Covington County Bank; lectr. Southeastern Trial Inst.; mem. grievance com. Ala. State Bar, 1968-71, mem. bd. commrs., 1979-81; mem. law and contemporary affairs adv. council Auburn U. Author: Personal Injury Treatises. Mem. ABA, Ala., Covington County bar assns., Am. Trial Lawyers Assn., Am. Bd. Trial Advocates, Ala. Plaintiff Lawyers Assn., Ala. Trial Lawyers Assn. (pres. 1968), Phi Delta Phi, Kappa Alpha, Alpha Phi Omega. Presbyterian (elder, trustee, past chmn. bd. deacons Sunday sch. tchr.). Club: Andalusia (dir., pres. 1972), Topsl Beach and Racket (Destin, Fla.). Federal civil litigation, State civil litigation, Personal injury (including property damage). Home: 100 S Ridge Rd Andalusia AL 36420-4214 Office: 28 S Court Sq Andalusia AL 36420-3918

FULSHER, ALLAN ARTHUR, lawyer; b. Portland, Oreg., July 5, 1952; s. Rémy Walter and Barbara Lee (French) F.; m. Karen Louise Schmid, Dec. 28, 1974 (dec. Sept. 1990); children: Brian Rémy, Louise Katherine, Elizabeth Alane. BA in Biology, U. Oreg., 1974, BA in Econs., 1976; JD, U. of Pacific, 1979. Bar: Oreg. 1979, Calif. 1980, U.S. Dist. Ct. Oreg. 1980, U.S. Dist. Ct. (ea. dist.) Calif. 1981, U.S. Ct. Appeals (9th cir.) 1982, U.S. Dist. Ct. (no. dist.) Calif. 1985, U.S. Dist. Ct. (so. dist.) Calif. 1986. Assoc. Law Offices of Jacques B. Nichols PC, Portland, 1979-82, Ragen, Roberts, O'Scannlain, Robertson & Neill, Portland, 1982-83; shareholder Bauer, Hermann, Fountain & Rhoades PC, Portland, 1983-87, v.p., 1984-87; shareholder, v.p. Fulsher and Weatherhead PC, Portland, 1987-88, pres., 1988—2001; gen. counsel Peregrine Holdings, Ltd., Beaverton, Oreg., 1993-97, Peregrine Capital, Inc., Beaverton, 1993-2000; mgr. Stamford Bridge, LLC, 1995—; gen. counsel Redfire, Inc., 2000—02, Serra Pacific Acceptance, LLC, Portland, 2001—, Serra Capistrano Funding, LLC, Portland, 2002—. Pres., mgr. ProSoccer, LLC, Tigard, Oreg., 1998-2001; gen. counsel World Indoor Soccer League, LLC, Dallas, 1998-2000. Republican. Roman Catholic. Avocations: basketball, automobile racing and restoration, coaching youth and adult sports. Communications, Finance, Mergers and acquisitions. Home: 16399 SE Sager Rd Portland OR 97236-5509 Office: Serra Capistrano Funding LLC 8525 N Lombard St Ste 212 Portland OR 97203-3156

FUNDERBURK, RAYMOND, judge; b. Phila., Mar. 2, 1944; s. Walter and Inez (Prince) F. AA, Olive-Harvey Coll., 1972; BA, U. Ill., 1974; MPA, Roosevelt U., 1975; JD, U. Ill., 1978. Bar: Ill. 1979, U.S. Dist. Ct. (no. dist.) Ill. 1979, U.S. Ct. Appeals (7th and fed. cirs.) 1983, U.S. Supreme Ct. 1983. Staff atty. Cook County Legal Assistance, Harvey, Ill., 1978-80, mng. atty., 1980-82; assoc. O. Kenneth Thomas Ltd., Harvey, 1982-83, Jones, Ware & Grenard, Chgo., 1983-88, Earl L. Neal and Assocs., Chgo., 1988-93; judge Cir. Ct. of Cook County, Chgo., Ill., 1993—. Bd. dirs. Cook County Legal Assistance Found., Oak Park, Ill., chmn. 1985-87; active legal adv. bd. Thornton Community Coll., South Holland, Ill., 1982—, Aunt Martha's Service, Park Forest, Ill., 1981-83. Chmn. Zoning Bd. of Appeals, Park Forest, 1988-99, Housing Bd. of Appeals, Park Forest, 1988-99, Equal Employment Opportunity Bd., Park Forest, 1988-99, Housing Rev. Bd., Park Forest, 1988-99; bd. dirs. Park Forest Pub. Library, 1982. Served with U.S. Army, 1965-67. Recipient Cert. of Appreciation Aunt Martha's Youth Svc., 1980, Thornton C.C., 1985, Wendell Phillips H.S., 1985, South Suburban YMCA, 1986, 1987, City Ptnr. award U. Ill. Chgo., 1995; named Disting. Grad., U. Ill. Coll. of Law, 1998-99, Olive-Harvey Jr. Coll., 2001. Mem. ABA, Chgo. Bar Assn., Cook County Bar Assn., Ill. Jud. Coun., Ill. Judges Assn., Phi Alpha Delta, Alpha Phi Alpha. Democrat. Avocations: running, chess, tennis. Office: Cir Ct of Cook County Ill Rm 2600 Richard J Daley Ctr Dearborn & Randolph Sts Chicago IL 60602

FUNK, DAVID ALBERT, retired law educator; b. Wooster, Ohio, Apr. 22, 1927; s. Daniel Coyle and Elizabeth Mary (Reese) F.; children— Beverly Joan, Susan Elizabeth, John Ross, Carolyn Louise; m. Sandra Nadine Henselmeier, Oct. 2, 1976 Student, U. Mo., 1945-46, Harvard Coll., 1946; BA in Econs., Coll. of Wooster, 1949; MA, Ohio State U., 1968; JD, Case Western Res. U., 1951, LLM, 1972, Columbia U., 1973. Bar: Ohio 1951, U.S. Dist. Ct. (no. dist.) Ohio 1962, U.S. Tax Ct. 1963, U.S. Ct. Appeals (6th cir.) 1970, U.S. Supreme Ct. 1971. Ptnr. Funk, Funk & Eberhart, Wooster, Ohio, 1951-72; assoc. prof. law Ind. U. Sch. Law, Indpls., 1973-76, prof., 1976-97, prof. emeritus, 1997—. Vis. lectr. Coll. of Wooster, 1962-63; dir. Juridical Sci. Inst., Indpls., 1982—. Author: Oriental Jurisprudence, 1974, Group Dynamic Law, 1982; (with others) Rechtsgeschichte und Rechtssoziologie, 1985, Group Dynamic Law: Exposition and Practice, 1988; contbr. articles to profl. jours. Chmn. bd. trustees Wayne County Law Library Assn., 1956-71; mem. Permanent Jud. Commn., Synod of Ohio, United Presbyn. Ch. in the U.S., 1968. Served to seaman 1st class USNR, 1945-46 Harlan Fiske Stone fellow Columbia U., 1973; recipient Am. Jurisprudence award in Comparative Law, Case Western Res. U., 1970 Mem. Assn. Am. Law Schs. (sec. comparative law sect. 1977-79, chmn. law and religion sect. 1977-81, sec.-treas. law and social sci. sect. 1983-86), Am. Soc. for Legal History, Pi Sigma Alpha. Republican. Home: 6208 N Delaware St Indianapolis IN 46220-1824

FUNKHOUSER, ROBERT BRUCE, lawyer; b. Calgary, Alta., Can., Jan. 3, 1959; AB, Harvard U., 1981; JD, Fordham U., 1987. Bar: N.Y. 1988, D.C. 1993. Law clk. Hon. Lloyd F. MacMahon, N.Y.C., 1987-88; assoc. Hughes Hubbard & Reed, N.Y.C., 1988-92, Washington, 1992-97, counsel, 1997—. Editor Fordham Law Rev., 1986-87. Mem. ABA (antitrust and litigation sects.). Antitrust, General civil litigation, Insurance. Office: Hughes Hubbard & Reed LLP 1775 I St NW Washington DC 20006-2402 E-mail: funkhous@hugheshubbard.com.

FUOCO, PHILIP STEPHEN, lawyer; b. Riverside, N.J., Oct. 28, 1946; s. Francis and Mary Helen Fuoco; m. Carol Freeman, June 7, 1969; 1 child. BA in Philosophy, U. Notre Dame, 1968; JD, Villanova (Pa.) U., 1971. Bar: N.J. 1972, U.S. Dist. Ct. N.J. 1972, Pa. 1973, U.S. Dist. Ct. (ea. dist.) Pa. 1975, U.S. Ct. Appeals (3d cir.) 1977, U.S. Supreme Ct. 1980; cert. criminal trial atty. N.J. Supreme Ct. Trial atty. civil rights div. U.S. Dept. Justice, Washington, 1971-75; asst. U.S. atty. U.S. Dist. Ct. (ea. dist.) Pa., Phila., 1975; pvt. practice N.J., 1975—. Adj. prof. law Rutgers U., Camden, 1997-2000. Contbr. articles to profl. jours. and law revs. Mem. Haddonfield Environ. Commn., 1991—93; apptd. mem. com. on model jury charges-criminal N.J. Supreme Ct., 1996—2002, apptd. mem. dist. IV ethics com., 1997—2001, apptd. mem. com. on character, 2001; mem. steering com. First Night Haddonfield, 1999; bd. dirs. Steininger Ctr., 1990—92, Haddonfield Zoning Bd., 1984—88. Recipient Stivale d'Italia award for excellence Italian Tribune of Newark, N.J., 2003; NEH fellow, 1978. Mem. ABA, ACLU, Nat. Assn. Dist. Attys., Nat. Assn. Criminal Def. Lawyers, Camden County Bar Assn. (trustee 1986-89), N.J. Bar Assn., Camden County Inns of Ct., Lions (Haddonfield pres. 1986-87). Civil rights, Federal civil litigation, Criminal. Office: 24 Wilkins Place Haddonfield NJ 08033-2406

FUREY, JOHN J. lawyer; b. Coaldale, Pa., Nov. 3, 1949; s. James J. and Georgene C. (Young) F.; m. Jill A. Luscombe, Nov. 23, 1975; children: Matthew J., Andrew S. BS, Villanova U., 1971, JD, 1975, LLM, 1984. Bar: Pa. 1975, Fla. 1994; CPA, Pa. VISTA vol. Vols. in Service to Am., Rose Hill, N.C., 1971-72; staff atty. Legal Services N.E. Pa., Wilkes-Barre, 1975-77; atty. Legal Services Corp., Phila., 1977-80, dep. regional dir., 1980-81; assoc. corp. counsel Mrs. Paul's Kitchen's, Phila., 1981-82; asst. counsel, asst. sec. Campbell Soup Co., Camden, N.J., 1982-85, assoc. counsel, asst. sec., 1985-89, assoc. counsel, dep. corp. sec., 1989-90; corp. counsel, dep. corp. sec., 1990-92; corp. sec., corp. counsel Campbell Soup Co., Camden, N.J., 1992-97, corp. sec., 1997—. Corporate, general, Pension, profit-sharing, and employee benefits, Securities. Office: Campbell Soup Co Campbell Pl Camden NJ 08103*

FURGESON, WILLIAM ROYAL, federal judge; b. Lubbock, Tex., Dec. 9, 1941; s. W. Royal and Mary Alyene (Hardwick) F.; m. Marion McElroy, Aug. 15, 1964 (div.); m. Juli Ann Bernat, July 29, 1973; children— Kelly Lynn, Houston, Joshua, Seth, Jill BA in English, Tex. Tech Coll., 1964; JD with honors, U. Tex., 1967. Bar: Tex. 1969, U.S. Dist. Ct. (we. dist.) Tex. 1971, U.S. Ct. Appeals (5th cir.) 1974, U.S. Supreme Ct. 1976. Law clk. to presiding judge U.S. Dist. Ct. for No. Dist. Tex., 1969-70; ptnr. Kemp, Smith, Duncan & Hammond, El Paso, Tex., 1970-94; judge U.S. Dist. Ct. (we. dist.) Tex., Midland/Odessa, 1994—. Gen. campaign chmn. El Paso United Way, 1979, 1st v.p., 1980, pres., 1981; mem. Jewish Fedn., El Paso, 1980-86; trustee Baylor U. Coll. Dentistry, 1982-86; chmn. YWCA Capital Devel. Campaign, 1986-87. Served to capt. U.S. Army, 1967-69 Decorated Bronze Star; recipient Service award Social Workers of El Paso, 1982, Faculty award U. Tex. Law Sch., 1983, Dean Leon Green award Tex. Law

Review, 2001. Mem. El Paso Bar Assn. (pres. 1982-83, Outstanding Young Lawyer award 1972), Am. Law Inst., U. Tex. Law Sch. Assn. (pres. 1978), U. Tex. Law Rev. Assn. (pres. 1982-83), El Paso Legal Assistance Soc. (bd. dirs. 1972-78), NCCJ (chmn. El Paso region 1980), ABA, Fed. Bar Assn. (pres. West Tex. chpt. 1987), Am. Law Inst., Tex. Bar Assn. (sec., treas., chair anti-trust and trade regulation sect. 1985-86), Am. Bar Found., Tex. Bar Found. Democrat. Jewish. Office: US Dist Ct 200 E Wall St Ste 301 Midland TX 79701-5248

FURMAN, HOWARD, mediator, arbitrator, lawyer; b. Newark, Nov. 30, 1938; s. Emanuel and Lilyan (Feldman) F.; m. Elaine Sheitleman, June 12, 1960 (div. 1982); children: Deborah Toby, Naomi N'chama, David Seth; m. 2d Janice Wheeler, Jan. 14, 1984. BA in Econs., Rutgers U., 1966; JD cum laude, Birmingham Sch. Law, 1985. Bar: Ala. 1985, U.S. Dist. Ct. (no. dist.) Ala. 1986, U.S. Dist. Ct. (so. dist.) Ala. 1996. Designer/draftsman ITT, Nutley, N.J., 1957-61; pers. mgr. Computer Products Inc., Belmar, N.J., 1962-64, Arde Engring. Co., Newark, 1964-66; econs. instr. Rutgers U., New Brunswick, N.J., 1966-74; dir. indsl. rels. Harvard Ind. Frequency Engring. Labs. Divsn., Farmingdale, N.J., 1966-74; commr. Fed. Mediation and Conciliation Svc., Birmingham, 1974-96; pvt. practice Birmingham, 1985—. Instr. bus. law Jefferson State C.C., 1989-95; instr. human resources mgmt. Nova U., 1993; prof. personal property, adminstrv. law, sales and alternative dispute resolution Birmingham Sch. Law, 1993—. Pres. Ocean Twp. Police Res. (N.J.), 1968. Recipient ofcl. commendation Fed. Mediation and Conciliation Svc., 1979, 81-82, 88. Mem. ABA, Ala. Bar Assn., Birmingham Bar Assn., Soc. Profls. in Dispute Resolution, Fed. Soc. Labor Rels. Profls., Indsl. Rels. Rsch. Assn., Sigma Delta Kappa. Jewish. Home: 900 Kathryne Cir Birmingham AL 35235-1722 E-mail: hfesq@bellsouth.net.

FURNESS, PETER JOHN, lawyer; b. Providence, Jan. 30, 1956; s. Robert I. and Elsie R. (Mooradian) F.; m. Alison M. Furness; children: Lindsey Elizabeth, Jonathan Peter. BA, U. R.I., 1979; JD, U. Pitts., 1982. Bar: Pa. 1982, U.S. Dist. Ct. (we. dist.) Pa. 1982, R.I. 1987, Mass. 1989, U.S. Dist. Ct. Mass. 1989. Ptnr. Nixon Peabody LLP, Boston/Providence, 1991—. Lectr. Nat. Bus. Inst., Inc., 1986—. Author: (seminar books) NBI Foreclosure in Rhode Island, 1986, NBI Basic Bankruptcy in Rhode Island, 1988, NBI Protection of Secured Interests in Bankruptcy, 1989. Mem. ABA, Am. Bankruptcy Inst., Fed. Bar Assn., Pa. Bar Assn., R.I. Bar Assn., Mass. Bar Assn., Comml. Law League, Phi Beta Kappa, Phi Kappa Phi. Avocations: photography, golf, vol. work with nonprofit orgns. Banking, Bankruptcy, Commercial, contracts (including sales of goods; commercial financing). Office: Nixon Peabody LLP 1 Citizens Plz Providence RI 02903-1344 E-mail: pfurness@nixonpeabody.com.

FURTADO, DAVID JEFFREY, lawyer, consultant; b. Hampton, Va., Sept. 30, 1965; s. Richard John and Mary Louise Furtado; 1 child, Emily Kate. BS, U. R.I., 1988, MS, 1992; JD, U. Denver, 1996. Bar: Colo. 1997, Ala. 1997, Mass. 1997, U.S. Dist. Ct. Colo. 1997, U.S. Ct. Appeals (10th cir.) 1997. Jr. claims rep. Comml. Union Ins. Co., Boston, 1988—93; atty. Franklin D. Azard, Denver, 1997—99; pvt. practice Denver, 1999—. 1st lt. USAR, 1981—91. Mem.: ATLA, ABA, Colo. Bar Assn. Democrat. Avocations: softball, weightlifting. Personal injury (including property damage), Insurance, Criminal. Office: The Furtado Law Firm LLC 1115 Grant St G-1 Denver CO 80203

FURTH, FREDERICK PAUL, lawyer; b. West Harvey, Ill., Apr. 12, 1934; s. Fred P. and Mamie (Stelmach) F.; children: Darby, Ben Anthony, Megan Louise; m. Peggy Wollerman, July 19, 1986. Student, Drake U., 1952-53; BA, U. Mich., 1956, JD, 1959; postgrad., U. Berlin, 1959, U. Munich, Fed. Republic Germany, 1960. Bar: Mich. 1959, N.Y. 1961, D.C. 1965, U.S. Supreme Ct. 1965, Calif. 1966. Assoc. Cahill, Gordon, Reindel & Ohl, N.Y.C., 1960-64; with Kellogg Co., Battle Creek, Mich., 1964-65; assoc. Joseph L. Alioto, San Francisco, 1965-66; sr. ptnr. The Furth Firm LLP, San Francisco, 1966—. Bd. dirs. Robert Half Internat.; chmn., propr. Chalk Hill Winery. Trustee, chmn. bd. Furth Family Found., San Francisco; bd. dirs. Franklin and Eleanor Roosevelt Inst., 1996—, The Ctr. for Democracy, Washington; chmn. Internat. Jud. Conf., Strasbourg, France, 1992-. Mem. ABA, Internat. Bar Assn., N.Y. Bar Assn., San Francisco Bar Assn., State Bar Calif., Assn. of Bar of City of N.Y., St. Francis Yacht Club, Olympic Club. Office: The Furth Firm LLP 201 Sansome St San Francisco CA 94104-2303 E-mail: fpfurth@aol.com.

FUSCO, ANDREW G. lawyer; b. Punxsutawney, Pa., Jan. 11, 1948; s. Albert G. and Virginia N. (Whitesell) F.; m. Deborah K. Lucas; children: Matthew, Geoffrey, David. BS in Bus. Adminstrn. and Fin., W.Va. U., 1970, JD, 1973. Bar: W.Va. 1973, U.S. Ct. Appeals (4th cir.) 1974, U.S. Supreme Ct. 1977, U.S. Ct. Appeals (fed. cir.) 1985, U.S. Tax Ct. 1995. Pvt. practice, Morgantown, W.Va., 1973-85; prin. Fusco & Newbraugh, L.C., Morgantown, 1985-98, The Fusco Legal Group, L.C., Morgantown, 1998-2001; mem. Eckert Seamans Cherin & Mellott, LLC, 2001—. Pros. atty. Monongalia County, W.Va., 1977-81; instr. Coll. Bus. and Econs., Law Ctr., W.Va. U., 1975-76, instr. W.Va. U. Sch. Journalism, 1997—; dir. Pitts. Environ. Systems Inc., 1983-86. Author: Antitrust Law (West Virginia Practice Handbook), 1991; editor, contbg. author: Twenty Feet From Glory (John R. Goodwin), 1970, Business Law (John R. Goodwin), 1972, Beyond Baker Street (Michael Harrison), 1976. Bd. dirs. W.Va. Career Colls., 1971-76; mem. profl. adv. bd. Childbirth and Parent Edn. Assn., 1975-82, Rape and Domestic Violence Info. Ctr., 1977-81; mem. W.Va. Sec. State's Tribunal on Election Reform, 1977-81; chmn. Monongalia County Drug Edn. Task Force, 1978-80; mem. bd. advisors Nat. Smokers Alliance, 1998-99; mem. vis. com. W.Va. U. Coll. Law, 2000—. Recipient Am. Jurisprudence award Bancroft-Whitney Publ. Co., 1971; named Outstanding Young Man of Morgantown, 1979. Mem. ABA (civil RICO com., antitrust law sect.), Monongalia County Bar Assn., Am. Judicature Soc., W.Va. Bar Assn., Baker St. Irregulars of N.Y., Sherlock Holmes Soc. London, Bootmakers of Toronto, Nat. Dist. Attys. Assn., Sons of Italy, W.Va. Law Sch. Assn., Monongalia Arts Ctr. (pres., treas., vice-chmn., trustee). Democrat. Roman Catholic. Antitrust, General civil litigation, Corporate, general. Home: 332 Horseshoe Rd Morgantown WV 26508-5308 Office: Eckert Seamans Cherin & Mellott 2400 Cranberry Sq Morgantown WV 26508-9209 Fax: 304-594-1181. E-mail: agf@escm.com.

FUSTÉ, JOSÉ ANTONIO, federal judge; b. San Juan, Puerto Rico, Nov. 3, 1943; BBA, U. P.R., San Juan, 1965, LLB cum laude, 1968. Ptnr. Jimenez & Fuste, Hato Rey, P.R., 1968-85; judge U.S. Dist. Ct. P.R., San Juan, 1985—. Prof. U. P.R., 1972-85, 96-2002. Office: US Courthouse CH-133 150 Ave Carlos Chardon San Juan PR 00918-1758

FUSTER, JAIME B. supreme court justice; b. Guayama, P.R., Jan. 12, 1941; s. Jaime L. and Maria Luisa (Berlingeri) Fuster; m. Mary Jo Fuster, Dec. 19, 1966; children: Maria Luisa, Jaime. BA, Notre Dame U., 1962; JD, U. P.R., 1965; LLM, Columbia U., 1966; SJD, Harvard U., 1974; LLD (hon.), Temple U., 1985. Bar: P.R. 1966. Prof. law U. P.R., 1966—73, 1978—80; project dir. Study on Legal Profession of P.R. Ctr. Social Rsch., 1970—73; dean Law Sch. U. P.R., 1974—78; ednl. cons. Office of Cts. Adminstrn. Govt. of P.R., 1978—80; dep. asst. atty. gen. U.S. Dept. Justice, Washington, 1980—81; pres. Cath. U. P.R., 1981—84; mem. Congress from P.R., Washington, 1984—92; resident commr. Commonwealth of P.R., 1984—92; assoc. justice P.R. Supreme Ct., 1992—. Cons., lectr. in field. Author: Political and Civil Rights in Puerto Rico, 1968, The Duties of Citizens, 1973, The Lawyers of Puerto Rico: A Sociological Study, 1974, Law and Problems of Elderly People, 1978; editor-in-chief: U. P.R. Law Rev., 1964—65; contbr. chapters to books, articles to profl. jours. Named One of Outstanding Young Men of Am., U.S. Jr. C. of C., 1978. Mem.: Interam. Bar Found. (bd. dirs. 1975—79), Assn. Am. Colls. (adv. bd. 1980—84). Democrat. Roman Catholic. Avocation: tennis. Office: PO Box 2392 San Juan PR 00902-2392 E-mail: jaimefb@tribunales.prstar.net.

FUTCH, DOROTHY HELEN, librarian, paralegal; b. Alachua, Fla., Aug. 17, 1931; d. David Malcolm and Burdine (Slaughter) Futch. BA, Fla. State U., 1951; MS, Simmons Coll., 1960; cert. paralegal, City Coll. San Francisco, 1980. Cataloger Oakland (Calif.) Pub. Libr., 1961—76; file supr. Orrick, Herrington & Sutcliffe, San Francisco, 1977—80; probate paralegal R.E. Neuman Probate Referee, San Francisco, 1982—89; database mgr. Natkin, Weisbach, Higginbothan, San Francisco, 1990—93; adminstr. Cool Shades Internat., San Francisco, 1995—. Editor: (newsletter) Oak Leaves, 1969—76; translator: Astucia, 1995—2000. Pres. Oakland Pub. Libr. Staff Assn., 1973, Luis Inclan Soc., 2003—; mem. Rep. Nat. Com., 2003—. Lewis State Tchrs. scholar, State of Fla., Tallahassee, 1948—51. Mem.: Luis Inclan Soc. (pres. 2003—), Gamma Phi Beta. Republican. Baptist. Home: Apt 212 631 O'Farrell San Francisco CA 94109

FUTTER, VICTOR, lawyer; b. N.Y.C., Jan. 22, 1919; s. Leon Nathan and Merle Caroline (Allison) F.; m. Joan Babette Feinberg, Jan. 26, 1943; children: Jeffrey Leesam, Ellen Victoria Futter, Deborah Gail Futter Cohan. AB in Govt. and English with honors, Columbia U., 1939, JD, 1942. Bar: N.Y. 1942, U.S. Supreme Ct. 1948. Assoc. Sullivan & Cromwell, 1946-52; with Allied Corp. (now Honeywell Internat.), Morristown, N.J., 1952-84, assoc. gen. counsel, 1976-78, v.p., sec., 1978-84; dir. Allied Chem. Nuclear Products, 1977-84; gen. counsel, sec. to bd. trustees Fairleigh Dickinson U., 1984-85. Spl. prof. law Hofstra Law Sch., 1976-78, 88-89, 94—, spl. cons. to the dean, 1997—; lectr., seminar on corp. in modern soc. Columbia U. Law Sch., 1986-98; mem. consultative group Principles of the Law of Nonprofit Orgns., 2002—. Editor: Columbia Law Rev.; editor-in-chief: Nonprofit Governance and Management, 2002; contbr. articles to profl. jours. Trustee, dep. mayor Village of Flower Hill, N.Y., 1974-76; mem. senate Columbia U., 1969-75; chmn. bd. Columbia Coll. Fund, 1970-72; pres. parents and friends com. Mt. Holyoke Coll., 1978-80; pres. Flower Hill Assn., 1968-70; bd. dirs. N.Y. Young Dems., 1948-52, Nat. Exec. Svc. Corps, 1997-2003, Soc. Columbia Grads., 1998-2003; co-chmn. fund drive Port Washington Cmty. Chest, 1965-66, bd. dirs., 1965-75; mem. coun. overseers C.W. Post, 1984-85; bd. dirs. Acad. Polit. Sci., 1986-94; bd. dirs. Greenwich House, 1985—, vice chair, 1999—; bd. dirs. Nat. Assn. Local Arts Agys.-Arts for Am., 1989-91, Am. Soc. Corp. Secs., 1987-90, pres. N.Y. chpt., 1983-84; chmn. Com. on Nonprofits, 1992-97; bd. dirs. Justice Resource Ctr., 1992-97; chair ad hoc Lunch Group for Nonprofits, 1993—. Maj. AUS. Recipient Alumni medal Columbia U., 1970, Disting. Svc. award Am. Soc. Corp. Secs., 1994; James Kent scholar. Fellow Am. Bar Found.; mem. ABA (coun. sr. lawyers divsn. 1989-97, chair 1995-96, chair Editl. Bd. Experience, 1989-95, liaison to ABA CEELI program 1990-99, sec. on bus. law, corp. laws com., com. on non-profit corps., com. on corp. govs., sect. on internat. law and practice 1990—, bd. govs., program and planning com. 1999-2002), Assn. of Bar of City of N.Y. (com. on internat. human rights 1983-85, com. on 2d century 1985-89, sr. lawyers com. 1989-2002, chair 1992-95, nonprofit com. 1995-96, Disting. Svc. award Individual Mentor Program 1995), Am. Law Inst. (consultative group for restatement of law governing lawyers 1987-98, consultative group for prins. of non profit orgns.), Nat. Assn. Corp. Dirs. (pres. N.Y. chpt 1988-89), Nat. Assn. Coll. Univ. Attys. (sec. on personal rels., tenure and retirement programs 1984-86), Am. Judicature Soc., N.Y. Lawyers Alliance for World Security, Columbia Coll. Alumni Assn. (pres. 1972-74, Pres.'s Cup award 1999), The Supreme Ct. Hist. Soc., Playwrights First, U.S. Lawn Tennis Assn., Am. Philatelic Soc., Univ. Club (coun. 1996-99, chair spl. events com. 1993-2000, chair club activities com. 1996-99), Manhasset Bay Yacht Club, Cold Spring Harbor Beach Club, Village Club of Sands Point (golf com. 1999-2000), Phi Beta Kappa. E-mail: vandjfut@optonline.net.

FUTTERMAN, RONALD L. lawyer; b. Chgo., Mar. 5, 1943; s. Sol and Edythe (Greenberg) F.; m. Pamela Ann Hayes, June 5, 1966; children; Elizabeth, Samantha. BBA, U. Wis., Madison, 1964; JD, Northwestern U., 1967. Bar: Ill. 1967, U.S. Dist. Ct. (no. dist.) Ill. 1967, U.S. Ct. Appeals (7th cir.) 1975, U.S. Ct. Appeals (D.C. cir.) 1977, U.S. Supreme Ct. 1984. Atty. anti-trust divsn. U.S. Dept. Justice, Chgo., 1967-73; assoc. Pressman & Hartunian, Chgo., 1973-78, ptnr., 1978-82, Hartunian, Futterman & Howard, Chartered, Chgo., 1982-91, Futterman & Howard, Chartered, Chgo., 1991—. Instr. law and psychology Adler Sch. Profl. Psychology, Chgo., 1999—. Active Ill. Sch. Dist. 113 Polit. Caucus, Deerfield, 1976-78, chmn. publicity, 1977-78; pres. South Park Elem. Sch. PTO, Deerfield, 1980-81. Mem. ABA, Chgo. Bar Assn., Chgo. Coun. Lawyers (v.p. 1983-84, 88—, bd. govs. 1984-88). Federal civil litigation, State civil litigation, Civil rights. Office: Futterman & Howard Chartered 122 S Michigan Ave Ste 1850 Chicago IL 60603-6199 E-mail: rfutterman@futtermanhoward.com.

GAAL, JOHN, lawyer; b. Flushing, N.Y., Oct. 10, 1952; s. Stephen Alfred and Marjorie (Lappin) G.; m. Barbara Jeanne Zacher, Aug. 5, 1973; children: Bryan A., Adam C., Benjamin Z. BA cum laude, U. Notre Dame, 1974, JD magna cum laude, 1977. Bar: N.Y. 1978, U.S. Ct. Appeals (D.C. cir.) 1978, U.S. Dist. Ct. (no. dist.) N.Y. 1979, U.S. Supreme Ct. 1986. Law clk. to judge U.S. Ct. Appeals (D.C. cir.), Washington, 1977-78; assoc. Bond, Schoeneck & King, Syracuse, N.Y., 1978-85, ptnr., 1986—. Bd. dirs. Legal Svcs. of Ctrl. N.Y., Syracuse, 1981-87, 94-2000, pres. 1999-2000—; adj. prof. Sch. of Mgmt., Syracuse U., 1989-92, Coll. of Law, 2001. Editor: Senior Citizens Handbook, 1988; contbg. author: Public Sector Labor and Employment Law, 1988; co-chair editl. bd. Jour. Coll. and Univ. Law, 2000-02; columnist The Bus. Jour., 1998-2000; mem. bd. advs. N.Y. Employment Law Practice Newsletter, 2001-; contbr. articles to profl. publs. Bd. dirs. Transitional Living Svcs., 2001—. Fellow Am. Bar Found.; mem. ABA (labor and employment law sect.), N.Y. State Bar Assn. (exec. com. labor and employment law sect., chair young lawyer sect. 1989-90, spl. com. on AIDS and the law 1988, spl. com. on mandatory pro bono svc. 1989, ho. of dels. 1987-89, 90-91, co-chair adhoc com. ethics 1999—). Democrat. Roman Catholic. Labor (including EEOC, Fair Labor Standards Act, labor-management relations, NLRB, OSHA). Home: 8006 Austrian Pine Cir Manlius NY 13104- Office: Bond Schoeneck & King 1 Lincoln Ctr Fl 18 Syracuse NY 13202-1324 E-mail: jgaal@bsk.com.

GAAR, NORMAN EDWARD, lawyer, former state senator; b. Kansas City, Mo., Sept. 29, 1929; s. William Edward and Lola Eugene (McKain) G.; children: Anne, James, William, John; m. Marilyn A. Wiegraffe, Apr. 12, 1986. Student, Baker U., 1947-49; AB, U. Mich., 1955, JD, 1956. Bar: Mo. 1957, Kans. 1962, U.S. Supreme Ct. 1969. Assoc. Stinson, Mag, Thomson, McEvers & Fizzell, Kansas City, 1956-59; ptnr. Stinson, Mag & Fizzell, Kansas City, 1959-79; mng. ptnr. Gaar & Bell, Kansas City, St. Louis, Overland Park, Wichita, Kans., 1979-87; ptnr. Burke, Williams, Sorensen & Gaar, Overland Park, L.A., Camarillo, Fresno, Costa Mesa, Calif., 1987-96; shareholder McDowell, Rice, Smith & Gaar, Overland Park, 1996—. Mem. Kans. Senate, 1965-84, majority leader, 1976-80; faculty N.Y. Practising Law Inst., 1969-74; adv. dir. Panel Pubs., Inc., N.Y.C. Mcpl. judge City of Westwood, Kans., 1959-63, mayor, 1963-65. With USN, 1949-53. Decorated Air medal (2); named State of Kans. Disting. Citizen, 1962. Fellow Am. coll. Bd. Coun.; mem. ABA, Am. Radio Relay League, Nat. Assn. Bond Lawyers, Calif. Assn. Bond Lawyers (charter), Russian-Am. Internat. Studies Assn. (dir. 2000--), Flying Midshipmen Assn., Assn. Naval Aviators, Tailhook Assn., Antique Airplane Assn., Exptl. Aircraft Assn., People to People. Republican. Episcopalian. Municipal (including bonds), Securities. Office: 7101 College Blvd Ste 200 40 Executive Hills Shawnee Mission KS 66210-1891 E-mail: ngaar@earthlink.net., ng@mrsg.com.

GABAY, DONALD DAVID, lawyer; b. Bklyn., Apr. 1935; s. Harry I. and Rachel Gabay. BBA, CCNY, 1956; LLB, Bklyn. Law Sch., 1961. Bar: N.Y. 1962. Pvt. practice law, N.Y.C., 1962-75; chief counsel N.Y. State Assembly Com. on Ins., Albany, 1975-78; 1st dep. supt. N.Y. State Ins. Dept., N.Y.C., 1978-84; ptnr. Stroock & Stroock & Lavan, LLP, N.Y.C., 1984—. Pres. Ins. Fedn. N.Y., 1994-98, 99—, chmn. Served with U.S. Army, 1956-58. Named Ins. Man of Yr., Ind. Ins. Brokers Assn., 1973; recipient Pub. Service award Bklyn. Ins. Brokers Assn., 1977, ann. achievement award Council Ins. Brokers, 1981, Outstanding Achievement award CCNY Alumni Assn., 1981, Pub. Service award Ind. Ins. Agts. Assn., 1984, Torch of Liberty award ins. div. Anti-Defamation League, 1984. Insurance. Office: Stroock Stroock & Lavan LLP 180 Maiden Ln New York NY 10038-4925 E-mail: dgabay@stroock.com.

GABBARD, DOUGLAS, II, (JAMES GABBARD), judge; b. Lindsay, Okla., Mar. 27, 1952; s. James Douglas and Mona Dean (Dodd) G.; m. Connie Sue Mace, Dec. 30, 1977 (div. Feb. 1979); m. Robyn Marie Kohlhaas, June 18, 1981; children: Resa Marie, David Ryan, James Douglas III, Michael Drew. BS, Okla. U., 1974, JD, 1977; grad., Nat. Jud. Coll., 1987, U. Kans. Law Orgnl. Econs., 1997. Bar: Okla. 1978. Ptnr. Stubblefeild & Gabbard, Atoka, Okla., 1978; sole practice Atoka, 1979; asst. dist. atty. State of Okla., Atoka, 1979-82, 1st asst. dist. atty. Atoka, Durant and Coalgate, 1982-85; dist. judge 25th Jud. Dist. State of Okla., Atoka and Coalgate, 1985—; presiding judge South East Adminstrn. Dist., Okla., 1992—, State Ct. Tax Review, Okla., 1992—. Presiding judge of emergency panel of State Ct. Criminal Appeals, State Ct. on Judiciary Trial divsn., 1997—, vice-presiding judge 2003—; mem. Supreme Ct. Com. on Civil Jury Instructions, 2002—; dir. Okla. Trial Judges Assn., 1996-; mcpl. judge City of Atoka, 1978-79; chmn. Chickasaw Nation Ethics Commn., 2003—. Mem. Bryan County/Durant Arbitration Com., 1984; negotiator Bryan Meml. Hosp. Bd., Durant, 1984-85. Mem. Okla. Bar Assn. (legal ethics com. 1988-90, jud. adminstrv. com. 1988-90, resolutions com., 1998—, long range planning com. 1999—, bench and bar com. 1999—), Okla. Jud. Conf., Am. Judges Assn., Masons. Democrat. Methodist. Avocations: painting, carpentry, reading. Home: 1401 S Walker Dr Atoka OK 74525-3611 Office: County Ct House Atoka OK 74525

GABBERT, A(NTHONY) REX, judge, educator; b. Kansas City, Mo., Sept. 25, 1956; s. Harry V. Gabbert, Sr. and Dorothy A. Gabbert-Phillips; m. Melissa Pate, Jan. 1, 1993; children: Hannah, Samantha. BA, U. Mo., Kansas City, 1980; JD, Miss. Coll., 1985. Bar: Mo. 1986, U.S. Supreme Ct. 1990, Kans. 1991. Pvt. practice, 1986, 1991—94; asst. pros. atty. Clay County, Liberty, Mo., 1987—91; pros. atty. City of Gladstone, Mo., 1991—92; mcpl. judge City of North Kansas City, 1993—94; assoc. cir. judge 7th Jud. Cir. Mo., Liberty, 1994—. Adj. prof. Penn Valley Coll., Kansas City, 1996—, William Jewell Coll., Liberty, 1997—, Rockhurst U., Kansas City, 2002—. 6th congl. dist. rep. U.S. Atty. Selection Com., 1993; bd. dirs. Clay, Platte, Ray Mental Health Tax Commn., 1988—89. Mem.: ABA, Kansas City Met. Bar Assn., Clay County Bar Assn., Kans. Bar Assn., Mo. Bar Assn. Office: Cir Ct 11 S Water St Divsn 6 Liberty MO 64068-2330

GABEIRAS VAZQUEZ, PATRICIA, lawyer, law educator; b. Madrid; Degree in law, Complutense U., Madrid, 1993; LLM European Law, Carlos III U., Madrid, 1995. Specialist in intellectual property and comml. law; lectr. comml. law Carlos III U., Madrid. Office: Estudio Jurídico Legal and Fiscal SL Calle Moreto 5 Madrid 28014 Spain Office Fax: 0034 914298435.

GABEL, GEORGE DESAUSSURE, JR., lawyer; b. Jacksonville, Fla., Feb. 14, 1940; s. George DeSaussure and Juanita (Brittain) G.; m. Judith Kay Adams, July 21, 1962; children: Laura Gabel Hartman, Meredith Gabel Harris. AB, Davidson Coll., 1961; JD, U. Fla., 1964. Bar: Fla. 1964, D.C. 1972. With Toole, Taylor, Moseley, Gabel & Hair, Jacksonville, 1966-74, Gabel & Hair (formerly Wahl & Gabel), Jacksonville, 1974-98; ptnr., mem. dirs. com. Holland & Knight, Jacksonville, 1998—2001, exec. ptnr., 2002—. Mem. Fla. Jud. Nominating Commn., 4th cir., 1982-86. Pres. Willing Hands, Inc., 1971-72; chmn. N.E. Fla. March of Dimes, 1974-75; mem. budget com. United Way, 1972-74, chmn. rev. com., 1976; bd. dirs. Ctrl. and So. brs. YMCA, 1973-79, Camp Immokalee, 1982-86; elder Riverside Presbyn. Ch., 1970-77, 80-86, 90-92, 97—, clk. session, 1975-76, 85-86, trustee, 1988-91; pres. Riverside Presbyn. Day Sch., 1977-79; chmn. Nat. Eagle Scout Assn., 1974-75; pres. Boy Scouts Am., North fla. Coun. 1993-96, silver Beaver award, 1978; trustee Davidson Coll., 1984-95; Norwegian Consul, 1989—; pres. Jacksonville Consular Corps, 1992-93, 96—. Capt. U.S. Army, 1964-66. Named Internat. Person of Yr., Jacksonville Area C. of C., 2002. Fellow Am. Coll. Trial Lawyers, Am. Bar Found.; mem. ABA (chmn. admiralty and maritime law com., 1980-81. chmn. media law and defamation torts com. 1988-89. tort and ins. practice sect.), ATLA, Am. Counsel Assn. (bd. dirs. 1980-82, pres. 1992-93), Maritime Law Assn. U.S. (bd. dirs. 1994-97), Assn. Average Adjusters (overseas subscriber), Fla. Bar (chmn. grievance com. 1973-75, chmn. admiralty law com. 1978-89, chmn. media and comms. law com. 1990-91), Southeastern Admiralty law Inst. (bd. govs. 1973-75), Duval County Legal Aid Assn. (bd. dirs. 1971-74, 81-84), Am. Inn of Ct. (master of bench, sec.-treas. 1990-95), Rotary of Jacksonville (bd. mem. 1982-84, 88-89, pres. 87-88), World Affairs Coun. of Jacksonville (exec. com. 2001—). Democrat. Admiralty, Federal civil litigation, State civil litigation. Home: 1850 Shadowlawn St Jacksonville FL 32205-9430 Office: Holland & Knight 50 N Laura St Ste 3900 Jacksonville FL 32202-3622

GABERINO, JOHN ANTHONY, JR., lawyer; b. Tulsa, Aug. 6, 1941; s. John A Sr and Elizabeth (McCafferty) Gaberino; m. Marjory Ann Diamond, Aug. 21, 1965; children: Christina M, Megan E, Courtney L, John A III, Kathleen A. AB cum laude, Georgetown U., 1963, JD, 1966. Bar: Okla 1966, US Dist Ct (no & we dists) Okla, US Ct Appeals (10th cir) 1968, US Tax Ct 1968, US Supreme Ct 1994. Assoc. Huffman, Arrington & Kihle, Tulsa, 1968-75; ptnr. Arrington, Kihle, Gaberino & Dunn, Tulsa, 1975-87, also bd. dirs., 1987-97; sr. v.p., gen. counsel ONEOK, Inc., 1998—. Counsel, bd dirs St Francis Health Sys, Inc, Tulsa, Okla., 1989—97. Chmn. Law Ctr. Alumni Bd. Georgetown U., 1990—92, bd. govs., 1990—, chair, 2000—02, bd. dirs., 2000—02; pres. Georgetown U. Club Okla; past chmn. Georgetown U. AAP Okla.; bd. regents Georgetown U., 2002—; past chmn Christ the King Bd Educ; past pres. bd. trustees Monte Cassino Sch.; past chmn. bd. trustees Monte Cassino Sch. Endowment Fund; bd. dirs. W K Warren Found, Tulsa Area United Way, Tulsa Pub. Schs. Found.; chmn. bd. dirs. Operation Aware Inc, 1991; bd. dirs. The Salvation Army-Tulsa Region, 2002—. Capt U.S. Army, 1966—68. Recipient John Carroll Medal, Georgetown Univ, 1993. Fellow: Am. Bar Found. (life; chair 2000—01); mem.: NCCJ (bd dirs Tulsa chpt, pres 1993—95), Okla. Fellows of the Am. Bar Found. (chair 2000—01), Tulsa County Bar Found (bd dirs 1993—99, pres 1994), Tulsa Bar Asn (secy 1988, chmn construction and bylaws comt, bd dirs 1989, 1991—94, pres 1993), Okla Bar Asn (mem bd govs 1990—92, 1995, vpres 1995, mem bd govs 1997—99, pres 1998), Metropolitan Tulsa CofC (bd dirs 1996—, chair 2001), Southern Hills Country Club (mem bd govs 1990—95, 1st vpres 1991—93, pres 1994), Knights Holy Sepulchre (hon soc Cath ch), Phi Beta Kappa. Republican. Roman Catholic. Avocations: golf, tennis. Corporate, general, Health, Utilities, public. Office: ONEOK Inc 100 W 5th St Tulsa OK 74103-4240

GABOVITCH, STEVEN ALAN, lawyer, accountant; b. Newton, Mass., Feb. 7, 1953; s. William and Annette (Richman) G.; m. Rhonda Merle Kitover, Aug. 6, 1978; childre: Daniel J., Lindsey D. BS in Acctg., Boston Coll., 1975, JD, 1978; LLM in Taxation, Boston U., 1982. Bar: Mass. 1978, R.I. 1979, U.S. Dist. Ct. R.I. 1979, U.S. Tax Ct. 1980, U.S. Ct. Appeals (1st cir.) 1980, U.S. Dist. Ct. Mass. 1981, U.S. Ct. Appeals (fed. cir.) 1982, U.S. Supreme Ct. 1983; CPA, Mass. Tax specialist Peat, Marwick, Mitchell & Co., Providence, 1978-80; prin. William Gabovitch & Co., Boston, 1980-

97; pvt. practice Stoughton, Mass., 1998—. Lectr. on bankruptcy taxation. Contbr. articles to profl. jours. Mem.: Boston Bar Assn., Mass. Bar Assn., R.I. Bar Assn., Nat. Soc. Tax Profls., Beta Gamma Sigma. Bankruptcy, Taxation, general, Personal income taxation. Office: 378 Page St 3 Deerfield Corp Ctr Stoughton MA 02072 E-mail: steve@gabovitch.com.

GABOVITCH, WILLIAM, lawyer, accountant; b. June 18, 1922; s. Ezra and Lena Ruth (Elkins) Gabovitch; m. Annette Richman, Feb. 7, 1951; children: Steven A., Ellis. BSBA, Boston U., 1943; JD, Boston Coll., 1949; LLM in Taxation, NYU, 1950. CPA Mass.; bar: Mass. 49, U.S. Dist. Ct. Mass., U.S. Dist. Ct. R.I., U.S. Ct. Appeals (1st cir.), U.S. Tax Ct., U.S. Ct. Claims, U.S. Ct. Appeals (fed. cir.), U.S. Supreme Ct. Sr. ptnr. William Gabovitch & Co., CPAs, Boston, 1962—. Lectr. in legal acctg. and taxation Boston Coll. Law Sch., 1959—70; examiner and trustee in bankruptcy, state ct. receiver. Campaign treas. Congressman Robert F. Drinan, 1970—84. Lt. (s.g.) USNR, 1943—46. Mem.: ABA, Mass. Soc. CPAs, Boston Bar Assn., Mass. Bar Assn., Mensa, Masons. Home: 33 Old Nugent Farm Rd Gloucester MA 01930-3169 Office: 256 Hanover St Boston MA 02113-2337

GABRIEL, EBERHARD JOHN, lawyer; b. Bucharest, Romania, Mar. 22, 1942; arrived in U.S., 1952, naturalized, 1955; s. William and Margaret (Eberhart) Krzyzewski; m. Janice Josephine Jedrzejewski, Aug. 21, 1965; children: John, Stephanie, Christopher. BA in English, St. Joseph's Coll. of Ind., 1963; JD, Georgetown U., 1966. Bar: Md. 1966, Minn. 1993, U.S. Supreme Ct. 1972. Staff atty. Fgn. Claims Settlement Commn., Washington, 1966-68; sr. v.p., gen. counsel Govt. Employees Fin. Corp., Denver, 1968-87; pres., CEO MNC Am. Indsl. Banks, Denver, 1987-89; v.p., asst. gen. counsel and compliance officer ITT Consumer Fin. Corp., Mpls., 1989-94; pvt. practice Mpls., 1994-95; coun. Comml. Credit Co., Balt., 1995-99; sr. v.p., gen. counsel Citibank USA, Wilmington, Del., 1995—2002; assoc. gen. counsel Citi Fin., Balt., 2002—. Fellow St. Joseph's Coll.; pres. Indsl. Bankers Assn. Colo., 1985-89; sec., treas. Indsl. Bank Savs. Guaranty Corp. Colo., 1973-83, pres., 1983-87; lectr. advanced mgmt. program Am. Fin. Svcs. Assn., 1974-81, 85, 87, law com. 1978-89, bd. dirs., 1988-89. Bd. dirs. Jeffco/Lakewood (Colo.) C. of C., 1974-80, 82-86, chmn., 1984-85; mem. Jefferson County DA Adult Diversion Coun., 1985-89; mem. Jefferson Found., 1985-87; mem. adv. coun. Colo. Office Regulatory Reform, Colo. Dept. Regulatory Aggys., 1984-89; trustee Lakewood Polit. Action Com., 1978-89, chmn., 1986-87, Lakewood on Parade, 1980, chmn. bd. govs., 1982; vice chmn. fin. divsn. United Way Metro Denver, 1982. Mem. ABA, Am. Corp. Counsel Assn., Md. Bar Assn., Phi Alpha Delta. Roman Catholic. Banking, Commercial, consumer (including collections, credit), Corporate, general. Home: 6178 Mississippi Ln New Market MD 21774-6247 E-mail: gabelex@aol.com, gabrielg@citifinancial.com.

GADDIS, LARRY ROY, lawyer; b. Pratt, Kans., Nov. 8, 1941; s. Wade G. and Lorena (Pearce) G.; m. Barbara Ann Law, June 14, 1972; children: Jeffrey Wade, Aaron Paul. BA, U. Colo., Boulder, 1963; JD, U. Colo., 1969. Bar: Colo. 1969, U.S. Dist. Ct. Colo. 1969, U.S. Ct. Appeals (10th cir.) 1969. Staff atty. Pikes Peak Legal Services, Colorado Springs, Colo., 1969-71, dir., 1971-73; ptnr. Gaddis, Kin & Herd, P.C., Colorado Springs, 1973—. Vis. prof. U. Colo.-Colorado Springs, 1971-74; mem. Colorado Springs Estate Planning Coun., 1983—, pres., 1991. Bd. dirs. Colorado Springs Sch., 1973-96, pres., 1987-91, trustee emeritus, jud. performance commn., 1993-99; chmn. Colo. Springs Cmty. Trust, 1999—, Pikes Peak Cmty. Found., 1997—; chmn. profl. adv. coun. Cath. Diocese of Colorado Springs, 1996-99; mem. Colo. Legal Svcs. Bd., 1999—. Mem. El Paso County Bar Assn. (probate sect. 1982—, pres. 1988), Colo. Bar Assn. (exec. council 1978), ABA, Phi Kappa Alpha. Democrat. Episcopalian. Corporate, general, Probate (including wills, trusts), Property, real (including real estate development, water). Office: 118 S Wahsatch Ave Colorado Springs CO 80903-3677

GADSDEN, CHRISTOPHER HENRY, lawyer, educator; b. Bryn Mawr, Pa., Aug. 7, 1946; s. Henry White and Patricia (Parker) G.; m. Eleanore R.B. Hoeffel, July 27, 1968; children: William C., Eleanore P., Patricia C. BS, Yale U., 1968, JD, 1973. Bar: Pa. 1973, U.S. Dist. Ct. (ea. dist.) Pa. 1973. Assoc. Drinker Biddle & Reath, Phila., 1973-80, ptnr., 1980-98, mng. ptnr., 1998-2001; founding ptnr. Gadsden Schneider & Woodward LLP, King of Prussia, Pa., 2001—. Lectr. law U. Pa. Law Sch., Phila., 1986-89, 93. Author: Pennsylvania Estate Planning, 1996; contbg. author: Local Public Finance and the Fiscal Squeeze, 1977; co-editor: Administration of Estates, 1983. Mem. vestry St. Thomas Ch., Whitemarsh, Ft. Washington, Pa., 1980-82; trustee Abington (Pa.) Meml. Hosp., 1980—, chair bd. trustees, 1994-98; pres. bd. trustees Germantown Acad., Ft. Washington, 1987-90. With U.S. Army, 1968—70. Fellow Am. Coll. Trust and Estate Counsel; mem. Phila. Bar Assn. (probate and trust law sect., chair 1994), Phila. Cricket Club. Democrat. Avocations: squash, tennis, gardening. Estate planning, Non-profit and tax-exempt organizations, Probate (including wills, trusts). Home: 140 W Chestnut Hill Ave Philadelphia PA 19118-3702 Office: Gadsden Schneider & Woodward LLP 700 S Henderson Rd Ste 345 King Of Prussia PA 19406 E-mail: cgadsden@gsw-llp.com.

GADSDEN, JAMES, lawyer; b. Bryn Mawr, Pa., July 5, 1949; s. Charles C. and Marie Ella (Dittmann) G.; children: Hilary DuBois Nieukirk, Courtney Dittmann; m. Barbara Chase Howard, May 4, 1991. BA in Polit. Sci. with distinction, U. Rochester, 1971; JD, Columbia U., 1974. Bar: U.S. Dist. Ct. (ea. dist., so. dist.) N.Y. 1975, N.Y. 1975, U.S. Ct. Appeals (2d cir.) 1975, U.S. Ct. Appeals (3d cir.) 1999, U.S. Dist. Ct. (no. dist.) N.Y. 2001. Assoc. Carter, Ledyard & Milburn, N.Y.C., 1974-83, ptnr., 1984—. Fellow Am. Bar Found.; mem. ABA (bus. law sect., chmn. trust indentures and indenture trustees), Assn. of Bar of City of N.Y. (project fin. com. 1999—), Fed. Bar Coun., Down Town Assn. Democrat. Episcopalian. Bankruptcy, General civil litigation, Commercial, contracts (including sales of goods; commercial financing). Home: 315 Mills Rd North Salem NY 10560 Office: Carter Ledyard & Milburn 2 Wall St Fl 13 New York NY 10005-2072 E-mail: gadsden@clm.com.

GAERTNER, GARY M., SR., judge; b. St. Louis; m. Maureen Gaertner: children: Gary M., Lisa, Mark. Student, JD, St. Louis U.; grad., Nat. Jud. Coll., U. Nev., Mo. Trial Jedges Coll., Am. Acad. Jud. Edn., U. N.H., Sch. Law U. Va., Stanford U. Laaw Sch., Harvard U. Sch. Law. Bar: Mo., Ill., U.S. Dist. Ct., U.S. Ct. Appeals, U.S. Supreme Ct. After pvt. practice; served as asst. city counselor City of St. Louis, until 1964, assoc. city counsel, 1964-97, city counselor, 1967-69; judge 22d Jud. Cir. Mo., 1969-85, including presiding judge criminal divs., juvenile judge, asst. presiding judge, and presiding judge and chief adminstrv. officer; chief judge Ct. Appeals, Ea. Dist. Mo., 1985. Past pres. Mo. Council Juvenille Ct. Judges; former chmn. juvenile subcom. Mo. Council Criminal Justice, region 5; former mem. St. Louis Commn. on Crime and Law Enforcement. Bd. dirs. Boys Town Mo.; v.p. Khoury Internat. Leagues, Policeman and Fireman's Fund of St. Louis, Shared Resource Enterprises Inc.; former dist. chmn., now dist. vice-chmn. Tomahawk dist Boy Scouts Am.; past mem. exec. bd. St. Louis Area council Boy Scouts Am. Served with USCG. Recipient awards, including Judiciary award St. Louis Grand Jury Assn., Man of Yr. award George Khoury Internat. Assn., Spl. Act. award U.S. Assn. Fed. Investigators; named an Outstanding Young St. Lousiaian, St. Louis Jaycees; diploma Jud. Ksills Am. Acad. Jud. Edn. Mem. ABA, Mo. Bar Assn., Mo. Assn. Trial Attys., Bar Assn. Met. St. Louis, Lawyers Assn. Met. St Louis. Am. Judicature Soc., Phi Delta Phi. Office: 111 N 7th St Saint Louis MO 63101-2100

GAFFNEY, MARK WILLIAM, lawyer; b. Spokane, Wash., July 3, 1951; s. William Joseph and Anne Veronica (McGovern) G.; m. Jean Elizabeth O'Leary, Oct. 8, 1988. BA, U. Notre Dame, 1973; JD, George Washington U., 1976. Bar: Wash. 1976, N.Y. 1982, D.C. 1984, Conn. 1984. Law clk. antitrust divsn. U.S. Dept. Justice, Washington, 1974-76; trial atty. N.Y.C., 1976-81; assoc. Solin & Breindel, P.C., N.Y.C., 1982-83; ptnr. Chapman, Moran & Gaffney, Stamford, Conn., 1984-85; of counsel Kaplan & Kilsheimer, N.Y.C., 1985-93; corp. counsel Sta. WLNY-TV, Inc., Melville, N.Y., 1993-95. Recipient Spl. Achievement award U.S. Dept. Justice, 1978, 79. Mem. ABA, Assn. of Bar of City of N.Y., Conn. Bar Assn., N.Y. Athletic Club. Republican. Roman Catholic. Antitrust, Federal civil litigation, State civil litigation. Home: 1395 Roosevelt Ave Pelham NY 10803-3605 Office: 1328 Boston Post Rd Larchmont NY 10538 E-mail: mgaffney@concentric.net.

GAFFNEY, RICHARD COOK, lawyer; b. Sewickley, Pa., July 14, 1931; s. John Edward and Florence Loretta (Cook) G.; m. Virginia Brady, May 15, 1954; children: Richar dCook, Charles, Kathleen, Robert, Virginia, Eileen. BS in Chem. Engring., Carnegie-Mellon U., 1953; JD, Duquesne U., 1959; exec. MBA, U. Pitts., 1982. Bar: Pa. 1960, U.S. Dist. Ct. (we. dist.) Pa. 1960. Mng. patent atty. Chevron Corp., Moraga, Calif. Mem. Patent Law Assn. Pitts. (asst. program chmn. 1981, program chmn. 1982). Computer, Patent. Mailing: 2915 Crystal Falls Dr Humble TX 77345-1303 E-mail: txgaffney@aol.com.

GAGAN, JAMES EPHRIAM, lawyer; b. Pawtucket, R.I., Dec. 24, 1916; s. Walter Joseph and Eva (Audette) G.; m. Claire R. Mazerolle, 1939 (div. 1947); 1 child, Barbara Ann; m. Gertrude Durgin, July 18, 1950; children—Jamie, Brian, Patricia. J.D., U. Maine, 1952. Bar: Maine 1952, U.S. Dist. Ct. Maine 1953, U.S. Tax Ct. 1953. City solicitor, corp. counsel City of Westbrook, Maine, 1960-86; ptnr. Gagan & Desmond, Westbrook, 1976-86; of counsel Desmond & Rand, Westbrook, 1986—. Mem. Maine Gov.'s Exec. Council, 1965-66. Served with USN, 1943-45, ATO. Mem. Maine Bar Assn., Cumberland Bar Assn. (pres. 1980). Democrat. Roman Catholic. Lodge: Kiwanis (pres. Westbrook 1972). General practice, Probate (including wills, trusts). Home: 6600 Sunset Way Apt 204 St Petersburg Beach FL 33706-2171

GAGE, FRED KELTON, lawyer; b. Mpls., June 20, 1925; s. Fred K. and Vivian L. G.; m. Dorothy Ann, Sept. 7, 1974; children: Deborah, Penelope, Amy, Lawrence. BS, U. Minn., 1948, LLB, 1950. Bar: Minn. 1950. Assoc. Wilson, Blethen & Ogle, Mankato, 1950-55; ptnr. Blethen, Gage, Krause, Blethen, Corcoran, Berkland & Peterson and predecessor firms, Mankato, 1955-90, of counsel, 1991—. Mem. State Bd. Profl. Responsibility, Minn. Supreme Ct., 1974-82, mem. legal svcs. adv. com., 1996—. Mem. Mankato Sch. Bd., 1957-66, Minn. State Coll. Bd., 1960-64; mem. Minn. Senate from 11th Legis. Dist., 1966-72; Mem. Minn. Sports Facilities Commn., 1976-84. Served with USN, 1943-46. Named Mankato Outstanding Young Man of Yr., 1956, Outstanding Man of Minn., Mankato Jr. C. of C., 1958 Fellow Am. Bar Found.; mem. ABA (assembly del. 1980-86), Minn. Bar Assn. (chmn. tax sect. 1956-58, pres. 1977-78), Order of Coif. Methodist. Federal civil litigation, State civil litigation, Corporate, general. Office: Blethen Gage & Krause PO Box 3049 127 S 2nd St Mankato MN 56001-3658 E-mail: kgage@bglow.com.

GAGGINI, JOHN EDMUND, lawyer; b. Chgo., Dec. 17, 1949; BA cum laude, Knox Coll., 1971; MS, Ohio U., 1972, JD magna cum laude, 1975; LLM, NYU, 1976. Bar: Ill. 1975, D.C. 1977; CPA, Ill. Law clk. to Hon. Shiro Kashiwa U.S. Ct. Claims, 1976-77; ptnr. McDermott, Will & Emery, Chgo. Adj. prof. law Chgo.-Kent Coll. Law, 1987—. Mem. ABA, Ill. State Bar Assn., Chgo. Bar Assn. (chmn. state and local tax com. 1986-87), Phi Kappa Phi, Phi Beta Kappa, Beta Alpha Psi, Phi Gamma Mu, Phi Alpha Delta. Office: McDermott Will & Emery 227 W Monroe St Ste 4700 Chicago IL 60606-5096

GAGLIARDO, THOMAS JAMES, lawyer; b. Cleve., June 13, 1947; BA, John Carroll U., 1968; JD, Cath. U. Am., 1974. Bar: Md., D.C., U.S. Ct. Appeals (4th, D.C. and 6th cirs.), U.S. Supreme Ct. Pres. Md. Employment Lawyers Assn., 2000—. Named Lawyer of Yr., Met. Washington Employment Lawyers Assn., 2000. Mem.: Assn. Conflict Resolution, Md. State Bar (exec. coun. labor and employment sect.). Civil rights, Federal civil litigation, Labor (including EEOC, Fair Labor Standards Act, labor-management relations, NLRB, OSHA). Office: Ste 500 8701 Georgia Ave Silver Spring MD 20910-3723

GAGNARD, CANDYCE C. lawyer; b. Alexandria, La., Aug. 6, 1970; d. Donald James Sr. Gagnard and Karen Gaspard White; m. John W. II Houghtaling. BA in English, U. Denver, 1992; JD, Loyola U., New Orleans, 1997. Bar: La. Ptnr. Bennett Law Office, Marksville, La., 1997—2002; city prosecutor City of Marksville, 1998—2002; assoc. Gainsburgh, Benjamin, David, Meunier & Warshauer, New Orleans, 2002—. Mem.: ATLA, New Orleans Bar Assn., La. Trial Lawyers Assn. Personal injury (including property damage), General civil litigation. Office: Gainsburgh Benjamin David Meunier & Warshauer 2800 Energy Ctr 1100 Poydras St New Orleans LA 70163 Office Fax: 504-528-9973. E-mail: CGagnard@gainsben.com.

GAGNON, CRAIG WILLIAM, lawyer; b. St. Cloud, Minn., Dec. 19, 1940; s. Marvin Sylvester and Signa Gunhild (Johnson) G.; children: Nicole, Jeffrey, Camille; m. Pam Peglow, Nov. 8, 1980; children: Claire, Jillian, Jane. BA, U. Minn., 1964; JD magna cum laude, William Mitchell Coll. Law, 1968. Bar: Minn. 1968, U.S. Dist. Ct. Minn. 1968, U.S. Tax Ct. 1972, U.S. Supreme Ct. 1970. Ptnr. Oppenheimer, Wolff & Donnelly, Mpls., 1968—. Chmn. bd. Equity Bank; bd. dirs. XOX Corp., First Fla. Bank. Trustee William Mitchell Coll. Law, St. Paul. 1989—, chmn. bd., 1999-2000. Named Alumnus of Notable Achievement, U. Minn. Fellow Am. Coll. Trial Lawyers; mem. Metro Breakfast Club (pres. 1993), Am. Bd. Trial Advocates (assoc.), Am. Law Inst. Avocations: hunting, fishing, golf. Federal civil litigation, General civil litigation, Professional liability. Home: 4807 Sunnyside Rd Edina MN 55424-1109 Office: Oppenheimer Wolff & Donnelly 45 S 7th St Ste 3400 Minneapolis MN 55402-1609 E-mail: cgagnon@oppenheimer.com.

GAGRAT, RUSTAM JEHANGIR, lawyer; b. Bombay; s. Jehangir Rustam and Maneck (Jehangir) G.; m. Lia Gagrat, July 10, 1994; 1 child, Jeh. BA with honors in Politics, Bombay U., 1979; BA with honors in Law, Cambridge (Eng.) U., 1981, MA, 1985; Program Instrn. for Lawyers, Harvard U., 1993. Advocate, India; solicitor, Eng. and Wales & Bombay. Sr. ptnr. Gagrat & Co., Advocates and Solicitors, Bombay, 1981—, Gagrat & Co., Supreme Ct. Advocates, New Delhi, 1990—. Bd. dirs. Pub. and Pvt. Ltd. Cos.; mem. coms. of C. of C.; presenter papers at internat. and domestic law confs. Tata scholar Cambridge JN Tata Trust, Bombay, 1979-81; recipient Rustomji Mulla prize Bombay Law Soc., 1984. Mem. Supreme Ct. of India Bar Assn., Law Soc. Eng. and Wales, Internat. Bar Assn., Internat. Law Assn., Bombay Law Soc., Bombay Bar Assn., Delhi Bar Assn., Oxford and Cambridge Soc., Willingdon Club, Cricket Club India, Bombay Gymkhana, Royal Western India Turf Club. Avocations: literature, music, history, art. Home: 9 Om Ratan New Worli Bombay 400 025 India Office: Gagrat & Co Alli Chambers Nagindas Master Rd Fort Mumbai Bombay 400 001 India Fax: 022-2657876. E-mail: gagratbm@vsnl.com.

GAINES, IRVING DAVID, lawyer; b. Milw., Oct. 14, 1923; s. Harry and Anna (Finkelman) Ginsburg; m. Ruth Rudolph, May 22, 1947 (dec. Apr. 5, 1979); children: Jeffrey S., Howard R., Mindy S. Gaines Pearce; m. Lois Shier, Nov. 25, 1979. BA, U. Wis., Madison, 1943; JD, 1947; postgrad., U. Pa., 1943-44. Bar: Wis. 1947, Fla. 1971, U.S. Dist. Ct. (ea. dist.) Wis. 1947, U.S. Dist. Ct. (we. dist.) Wis. 1970, U.S. Dist. Ct. (so. dist.) Fla. 1972, U.S. Dist. Ct. (mid. dist.) Fla. 1976, U.S. Ct. Appeals (7th cir.) 1954, U.S. Ct. Appeals (11th cir.) 1981, U.S. Supreme Ct. 1954. Sole practice, Milw., 1947-72; ptnr. Gaines & Saichek, S.C. (and predecessor firm), Milw., 1972-78; sr. ptnr. Gaines Law Offices, S.C., Milw., 1979—. Arbitrator N.Y. Stock Exch., 1988—, Nat. Assn. Securities Dealers, 1988—, Am. Stock Exch., 1988—; mediator Wis. Ct. of Appeals, Dist. I; interpretor Hinustani Intelligence. Contbr. articles to profl. jours. Mem. bd. visitors U. Wis. Law Sch., 1987—96, Milw. County Cir. Ct. Commn., 1997—. Served with U.S. Army, 1943—46. Mem.: ATLA (state committeeman 1981—83, lectr.), ABA (com. on current lit. on real property law, com. on law and medicine negligence sect., various coms. on title ins. litig. and real estate), Bar Assn. U.S. Ea. Dist. of Wis., Am. Arbitration Assn. (arbitrator 1966—, nat. panel arbitrators), Milw. Bar Assn. (exec. com. 1974—77, cts. com., past chmn. unauthorized practice of law com., econs. of law com., past chmn. negligence sect., appellate bench bar com.-civil, bench-bar com., lectr. programs, seminars), Wis. Acad. Trial Lawyers (pres. 1958—59, 1970—71, lectr.), 7th Fed. Cir. Bar Assn., State Bar Assn. Wis. (bd. govs. 1982—85, publs. com. 1982—91, past mem. com. on ethics, rsch. planning and earlier settlement coms., lectr. CLE seminars, convs.), Fla. Bar Assn. (bd. editors Fla. Bar Jour. 1972—84). Personal injury (including property damage), Insurance, Property, real (including real estate development, water). Home: 7821 N Mohawk Rd Milwaukee WI 53217-3123 Office: 312 E Wisconsin Ave Ste 208 Milwaukee WI 53202-4305

GAINES, ROBERT PENDLETON, retired lawyer; b. Daytona Beach, Fla., Apr. 6, 1927; s. Marion Toulmin and Marion (Howie) G.; m. Doris Bolton, July 8, 1961; children: Jennifer, Amante, Edmund. BA, U. Fla., 1950, LLB, 1956. Bar: Fla. 1956, U.S. Dist. Ct. (no. dist.) Fla. 1956, U.S. Ct. Appeals (5th cir.) 1958, U.S. Ct. Appeals (11th cir.) 1982, U.S. Supreme Ct. 1988. From assoc. to ptnr. Beggs & Lane and predecessor firms, Pensacola, Fla., 1956—2002; ret., 2002. Mem. Fla. Commn. on Local Govt., Tallahassee, 1973-74. Lt. U.S. Army, 1945-47, 1950-53, Korea. Mem.: Pensacola Jaycees (bd. dirs.), Pensacola C. of C. (pres. 1969), Southeastern Admiralty Inst., Maritime Law Assn. U.S., Internat. Assn. Def. Counsel, Fla. Def. Lawyers Assn. (pres. 1974—75), Order of the Coif, Rotary, Phi Beta Kappa. Democrat. Episcopalian. Avocation: fishing. Admiralty, Federal civil litigation, State civil litigation. Home: 8839 Burning Tree Rd Pensacola FL 32514-5606

GAINES, WEAVER HENDERSON, lawyer; b. Ft. Meade, S.D., Aug. 31, 1943; s. Weaver Henderson and Bertha Louise (Harris) G. AB in Philosophy, Dartmouth Coll., 1965; LLB, U. Va., 1968. Bar: N.Y. 1969, Pa. 1979, U.S. Dist. Ct. (so. dist.) N.Y. 1973, U.S. Dist. Ct. (ea. dist.) N.Y. 1975, U.S. Ct. Appeals (2d cir.) 1975. Assoc. Dewey, Ballantine, Bushby, Palmer & Wood, N.Y.C., 1970-79; sr. staff counsel INA Corp., Phila., 1979; asst. gen. counsel, sec. Thyssen-Bornemisza Inc., N.Y.C., 1979-82, v.p. strategic projects, 1982-85; v.p., dep. gen. counsel Mut. of N.Y., N.Y.C., 1985-86, sr. v.p., gen. counsel, 1986-90, exec. v.p., gen. counsel, 1990-92; pres. Unified Mgmt. Corp., 1989-90; chmn. Ixion Biotechnology, Inc., Alachua, Fla., 1993—2002, chmn. bd., 2002—. Bd. dirs. Unified Fin. Svcs., Inc., Voyetra Turtle Beach, Inc., Ixion Biotechnology, Inc., BIO Fla. Inc., Fla. Rsch. Consortium, Inc., Dance Alive!. Bd. dirs. N.Y. Lawyers for Nixon, 1972; sr. advisor Bush/Quayle '92. Capt. U.S. Army, 1968-70, Vietnam. Decorated Bronze Star. Mem. ABA, Assn. Bar City N.Y., N.Y. Athletic Club, Haile Plantation Golf and Country Club. Republican. Episcopalian. Antitrust, Corporate, general, Insurance. Office: Ixion Biotechnology Inc 13709 Progress Blvd Alachua FL 32615-9495 E-mail: weaver.gaines@worldnet.att.net.

GAIR, ANTHONY HENRY, lawyer; b. N.Y.C., Dec. 24, 1948; s. Harry Archibald and Harriet Ella Gair; m. Ellen Alexis Linzanetz-Gair, July 1, 1968; 1 child, Daniel A. BA, L.I. U., 1971; JD, Thomas Cooley Law Sch., 1980; LLM, NYU, 1985. Bar: NY 80, U.S. Dist. Ct. (so. and ea. dists.) 80. Assoc. Gair, Gair, Conason, Steigman & Mackauf, N.Y.C. Lectr. CLE Fordham U. Sch. Law, 1986—97; mem. med. malpractice panel Supreme Ct. Kings County, 1985—, Supreme Ct. Bronx County, 1989—. Contbg. author: Controversies in Surgery, Vol. 4, 2001; contbr. articles to legal jours. Recipient Am. Jurisprudence award in criminal procedure and constl. law. Mem.: ATLA, ABA, Roscoe Pound Found., Am. Soc. Writers on Legal Subjects, Am. Bd. Trial Advocates, NY State Trial Lawyers Assn., NY County Lawyers Assn., Westchester County Bar Assn., Bronx County Bar Assn., NY State Bar Assn. (overall planning co-chmn. Doe or Die: The Vital Aspects of Your Case 2001, co-chmn. Sweating the Small Stuff - The Basics of Motions, Objections 2000), Assn. Bar City NY (mem. products liability com. 1994—96), Order of Barristers. Democrat. Avocations: motorcycling, gardening. Personal injury (including property damage), Civil rights, Product liability. Office: Gair Gair Conason, Steigman & Mackauf 80 Pine St New York NY 10005

GAITHER, JAMES C. lawyer; b. Oakland, Calif., Sept. 3, 1937; s. Horace Rowan Jr. and Charlotte Cameron (Castle) G.; m. Susan Good, Apr. 30, 1960; children: James Jr., Whitaker, Reed, Kendra. BA in Econs., Princeton U., 1959; JD, Stanford U., 1964. Bar: Calif. 1964, U.S. Dist. Ct. D.C. 1965, U.S. Dist. Ct. (no. dist.) Calif. 1965, U.S. Ct. Appeals (D.C. cir., 7th cir., 9th cir.), 1965, U.S. Supreme Ct. Law clk. to chief justice Earl Warren, Washington, 1964-65; spl. asst. to asst. atty. gen. John W. Douglas, Washington, 1965-66; staff asst. Pres. Lyndon B. Johnson, Washington, 1966-69; atty. Cooley Godward LLP, San Francisco, 1969-71, ptnr., 1971—, mng. ptnr., 1984-90, sr. counsel, 2000—; mng. dir. Sutter Hill Ventures, 2000. Cons. to sec. HEW, 1977, chmn. ethics adv. bd., 1977—80; bd. dirs. Levi Strauss & Co., San Francisco; bd. dir. Kineto, Milpitas, Calif.; bd. dirs. Siebel Sys., San Mateo, nVidia Corp., Santa Clara, Satmetrix, Mountain View, Calif., Hewlett Found.; with James Irvine Found.; former vice chair Carnegie Endowment for Internat. Peace; former trustee The RAND Corp. Editor: Stanford Law Rev., 1963—64. Former pres. bd. trustees, Stanford (Calif.) U.; mem. exec. com. bd. vis. Sch. Law Stanford U.; former chmn. bd. trustees Branson Sch., Ross, Calif., Ctr. for Biotech. Rsch. San Francisco; past trustee Family Svc. Agy. San Francisco, St. Stephens Parish Day Sch., Belvedere, Calif., The Scripps Rsch. Inst.; past trustee, chmn. protem Marin Cmty. Found, Marin County, Calif.; past pres. bd. trustees Marin County Day Sch., Corte Madera; past pres. bd. trustees Marin Ednl. Found., San Rafael; past treas., trustee Rosenberg Found.; past v.p., trustee, vice chmn. San Francisco Devel. Fund; past chmn. Dean's Adv. Coun. Stanford Law Sch., chmn. capital campaign; Inst. Capt. USMC, 1959-61. Recipient Disting. Pub. Svc. award HEW, 1977, Stanford Assocs. award Stanford U., 1989, 97; named Entrepreneur of Yr. Harvard Bus. Sch., 1979. Fellow Am. Acad. Arts and Scis.; mem. ABA, Calif. Bar Assn., San Francisco Bar Assn., Order of Coif, Phi Delta Phi (province 12). Democrat. Presbyterian. Avocations: tennis, hiking, camping, fishing, photography. Corporate, general, Mergers and acquisitions, Securities. Office: Sutter Hill Ventures 755 Page Mill Rd # A-200 Palo Alto CA 94304

GAITHER, JOHN FRANCIS, JR., lawyer; b. Evansville, Ind., Mar. 31, 1949; s. John F. and Marjilee G.; m. Christine Luby, Nov. 26, 1971; children: John F. III, Maria Theresa. BA in Acctg., U. Notre Dame, 1971, JD, 1974. Bar: Ind. 1974, Ill. 1975, U.S. Ct. Appeals (7th cir.) 1975, U.S. Ct. Mil. Appeals 1977. CPA, Ind. Law clk. to Hon. Wilbur F. Pell, Jr. Ct. of Appeals 7th Cir., Chgo., 1974-76; assoc. atty. Bell, Boyd & Lloyd, Chgo., 1979-82; sr. atty. Baxter Healthcare Corp., Deerfield, Ill., 1982-83, asst. sec., sr. atty., 1983-84, asst. sec., asst. gen. counsel, 1984-85; sec., asst. gen. counsel Baxter Internat. Inc., Deerfield, 1985-87, sec., dep. gen. counsel, 1987-91; v.p. law/devel. Baxter Diagnostics Inc., Deerfield, 1991-92; v.p. law, strategic planning Baxter Global Businesses, Deerfield, 1992-93; dep. gen. counsel, v.p. strategic planning Baxter Internat. Inc., Deerfield, 1993-94, corp. v.p., corp. devel., 1994-2001; v.p., sec., gen. counsel Global Healthcare Exch., LLC, Westminster, Colo., 2001—. Editor-in-chief Notre Dame Lawyer, 1973-74; contbr. articles to profl. jours. Lt. comdr. USNR, 1976-79. Mem. ABA, Ill. Bar Assn., Ind. Bar Assn.,

Chgo. Bar Assn., Ind. Assn. CPAs. Avocations: sailing, skiing. Corporate, general, Mergers and acquisitions, Securities. also: 11000 Westmoor Cir Ste 400 Westminster CO 80021 E-mail: jgaither@ghx.com.

GAJARSA, ARTHUR J. circuit court judge; b. Norcia, Italy, Mar. 1, 1941; arrived in U.S., 1949; m. Melanie E. Gajarsa. BSEE, Rensselaer Polytech. Inst, 1962; JD, Georgetown U., 1967; MA in Econs., Cath. U., 1968. Bar: U.S. Patent Office 1963, DC 1968, U.S. Dist. Ct. DC 1968, U.S. Ct. Appeals (DC cir.) 1968, Conn. 1969, U.S. Supreme Ct. 1971, DC Superior Ct. 1972, U.S. Ct. Appeals (DC cir.) 1972, U.S. Ct. Appeals (9th cir.) 1974, U.S. Dist. Ct. (no. dist.) N.Y. 1980. Patent examiner U.S. Patent Office, Dept. Commerce, 1962—63; patent adviser USAF, Dept. Def., 1963—64, Cushman, Darby & Cushman, 1964—67; law clk. to Judge Joseph C. McGarraghy U.S. Dist. Ct. (D.C.), Washington, 1967—68; atty. office gen. counsel Aetna Life and Casualty Co., 1968—69; spl. counsel, asst. to commr. Indian affairs Bur. Indian Affairs, Dept. Interior, 1969—71; assoc. Duncan and Brown, 1971—72; ptnr. Gajarsa, Liss & Sterenbuch, 1972—78, Gajarsa, Liss & Conroy, 1978—80, Wender, Murase & White, 1980—86; ptnr., officer Joseph, Gajarsa, McDermott & Reiner, P.C., 1987—97; judge U.S. Ct. Appeals Fed. Cir., Washington, 1997—. Contbr. articles to profl. jours. Trustee Rensselaer Neuman Found., 1973—, Found. Improving Understanding of Arts, 1982—96, Outward Bound, 1987—96, Rensselaer Polytech. Inst., 1994—; gov. John Carroll Soc., 1992—99; regent Georgetown U., 1995—2000, bd. dirs., 2000—. Recipient Sun and Balance medal, Rensselaer Polytech. Inst., 1990, Rensselaer Key Alumni award, 1992, Albert Demers Fox award, 1999, Gigi Pieri award, Camp Hale Assn., 1992, 125th Anniversary medal, Georgetown U. Law Ctr., 1995, Order of Commendatore, Republic of Italy, 1995, Alumni Fellows award, Rensselaer Alumni Assn., 1996, Paul Dean award, Georgetown U., 1999. Mem.: Am. Judicature Assn., DC Bar Assn., Nat. Italian Am. Found. (bd. dirs. 1976—99, gen. counsel 1976—89, pres. 1989—92, vice-chair 1993—96), Fed. Cir. Bar Assn. Office: US Ct Appeals Fed Cir 717 Madison Pl NW Washington DC 20439-0002

GALANIS, JOHN WILLIAM, lawyer; b. Milw., May 9, 1937; s. William and Angeline (Koroniou) G.; m. Patricia Caro, Nov. 29, 1969; children: Lia Galanis Economou, William, Charles, John. BBA cum laude, U. Wis., 1959; JD, U. Mich., 1963; postgrad. (Ford Found. grantee), London Sch. Econs., 1964. Bar: Wis. 1965; CPA, Wis. Assoc. firm Whyte & Hirschboeck S.C., Milw., 1964-68; sr. v.p., gen. counsel, sec. MGIC Investment Corp. and Mortgage Guaranty Ins. Corp., Milw., 1968-88; ptnr. Galanis, Pollack & Jacobs, S.C., Milw., 1988—. Assoc. editor: Mich. Law Rev, 1962-63. Bd. visitors Law Sch. U. Mich., Sch. Bus. U. Wis.; past chmn. Milw. Found.; bd. dirs., past pres. Milw. Boys' and Girls' Club; pres. Family Svc. Milw. Recipient Disting. Svc. award Internat. Inst., Hope Chest award Nat. MS Soc., Disting. Alumni award Milw. Boys' Club, Disting. Svc. award Milw. Civic Alliance Club, 1989. Mem. ABA, Wis. Bar Assn., Milw. Bar Assn., Am. Hellenic Ednl. Progessive Assn., Order of Coif, Milw. Athletic Club, Blue Mound Golf and Country Club. Greek Orthodox. Corporate, general, Finance, Insurance. Home: 1200 Woodlawn Cir Elm Grove WI 53122-1639 Office: MGIC Pl Milwaukee WI 53201

GALANT, HERBERT LEWIS, lawyer; b. N.Y.C., Oct. 16, 1928; s. Charles A. and Bertha (Rosenberg) G.; m. Fern Judith Laikin, Feb. 10, 1957; children: Peter B., John M., Amy E. BA cum laude, U. Wis., 1949; LLB magna cum laude, Harvard U., 1952; LLM, NYU, 1960. Bar: N.Y. 1955, U.S. Dist. Ct. (so. dist.) N.Y. 1956, U.S. Ct. Appeals (2d cir.) 1959. Assoc. Fried, Frank, Harris, Shriver & Jacobson, N.Y.C., 1955-61, ptnr., 1962-95, co-chair, 1992-95, of counsel, 1995—. Editor: Harvard U. Law Rev., 1950-52. Mem. Tenafly Twp. (N.J.) Bd. Ethics, 1978-88, Tenafly Twp. Planning Bd., 1997-2000. 1st lt. USAF, 1952-54. Mem. Assn. of Bar of City of N.Y., Harvard U. Club (N.Y.C.). Democrat. Jewish. Corporate, general, Finance, Securities. Home: 150 Tekening Dr Tenafly NJ 07670-1219 Office: Fried Frank Harris Shriver & Jacobson 1 New York Plz Fl 22 New York NY 10004-1980 E-mail: herbgala@aol.com.

GALATZ, HENRY FRANCIS, lawyer; b. N.Y.C., Feb. 5, 1947; s. Julius D. and Dorothy (Kirschen) G.; children: Benjamin Chase, Brandon Kyle. BA, U. Ariz., 1970, MEd, MA with honors, 1973; JD, U. the Pacific, 1979. Bar: Ill. 1981, U.S. Ct. Appeals (7th cir.) 1981, U.S. Dist. Ct. (no. dist.) Ill. 1982, U.S. Dist. Ct. (ea. dist.) Mich. 1982, U.S. Ct. Appeals (6th cir.) 1982, U.S. Dist. Ct. (ea. dist.) Mo. 1985, U.S. Supreme Ct. 1985, U.S. Dist. Ct. Mont. 1986, U.S. Dist. Ct. (we. dist.) Tex. 1987, U.S. Dist. Ct. (no. dist.) Calif. 1992, U.S. Dist. Ct. Nebr. 1993, U.S. Dist. Ct. (no. dist.) Ohio 1997, U.S. Ct. Appeals (11th cir.) 2000; cert. coach and referee U.S. Soccer Fedn. Cons. labor rels. Phoenix Closures, Chgo., 1974-75, Galatz Elec. Corp., Las Vegas, Nev., 1975-80; labor counsel W.W. Grainger, Inc., Skokie, Ill., 1980—; pvt. practice Olympia Fields, Ill., 1981—. Hearing officer Ill. State Bd. Edn., Chgo., 1982—: atty. Chgo. Legal Svcs. Found., 1983—, Ill. Inst. for Dispute Resolution, 1992—; mem. com. Employment Law Inst., Northwestern U., Evanston, Ill.; adv. coun. H-F Bus. Ptnr., 2000; mem. pres. counsel McGeorge Sch. Law, 2001-. Pres., coach Homewood-Flossmoor (Ill.) Soccer Club, 1985—, Intercollegiate Varsity Athletics (soccer and lacrosse); co-chair soccer Ill. Prairie State Games, 1992; pres. P.O.P.S. Homewood-Flossmoor H.S., 1996—; mem. bd. edn., pers. chairperson Homewood-Flossmoor H.S., 1998—, mem. improvement coun., 2001-. Recipient Judge Mason Rothwell Award, 1979, Cert. of Merit Chgo. Legal Svcs. Found., 1983. Mem. ABA, ATLA, Am. Corp. Counsel Assn. (labor and employment sect.), Ill. Bar Assn., Chgo. Bar Assn., Am. Arbitrators Assn. (arbitrator), Am. Judicature Soc., Ill. Trial Lawyers Assn., North Shore (Ill.) Labor Counsel Assn., Phi Delta Phi, Alpha Epsilon Pi. Democrat. Jewish. Avocations: soccer, lacrosse. Federal civil litigation, Education and schools, Labor (including EEOC, Fair Labor Standards Act, labor-management relations, NLRB, OSHA). Home: PO Box 374 Flossmoor IL 60422-0374 Office: W W Grainger Inc 100 Grainger Pkwy Lake Forest IL 60045-5201

GALATZ, NEIL GILBERT, lawyer; b. N.Y.C., Jan. 22, 1933; s. Julius D. and Dorothy (Kirschen) G.; m. Elaine Bricker, Aug. 20, 1961; children: Leesa, Lara. BA, Adelphi U., 1953; JD, Columbia U., 1956. Bar: N.Y. 1957, Nev. 1958, U.S. Dist. Ct. Nev. 1958, U.S. Ct. Appeals (9th cir.), U.S. Supreme Ct. 1976. Sr. trial dep., dist. atty. Clark County Dist. Attys. Office, Las Vegas, 1959-61; assoc. Langerman, Begam & Lewis, Phoenix, 1961-62; ptnr. Wiener, Goldwater & Galatz, Las Vegas, 1967-76; sr. ptnr. Neil G. Galatz & Assocs., Las Vegas, 1976—. Deans couns., Univ. Nev., 1995-97; spl. adv., Nev. Legis. Com., 1970-71; co-chmn., Plaintiff's Lead Counsel Cmte. MGM Multi-Dist. Fire Litigation, 1980-82, Hilton Fire Litigation, 1981-86; chmn. PEPCON Explosion Plaintiffs Com., 1988-92; lectr. in field. Mem. ATLA (gov. 1967-72, 76-77, 2001-03, chmn. midwinter convs. 1964, 68, 71, 73, 76, 85, student advocacy program 1973-74, legal inst. program 69, 71, citation for outstanding leadership, 1971), Internat. Acad. Trial Lawyers, Am. Bd. Trial Advocates, Western Trial Lawyers Assn. (pres. 1964-65). Internat. Soc. Barristers, Nat. Bd. Trial Advocacy, Nev. State Bar Assn. (bd. govs. 1990-00). Personal injury (including property damage), Product liability. Office: Neil G Galatz & Assocs 710 S 4th St Las Vegas NV 89101-6707 E-mail: neilgalatz@aol.com.

GALBRAITH, JAMES MARSHALL, lawyer, business executive; b. Iowa City, Oct. 4, 1942; s. John Semple and Laura (Huddleston) G.; m. Margaret Rodi, Aug. 19, 1966; children: Margaret Laura, Katherine Lou, Robert James. BA, Pomona Coll., 1964; JD, Stanford U., 1967. Bar: Calif. 1968. Assoc. Gibson, Dunn & Crutcher, Los Angeles, 1967-68; ptnr. Rodi, Pollock, Pettker, Galbraith & Cahill, Los Angeles, 1968-84, of counsel, 1984—2003; pres. Bell Helmets Internat., Inc., San Marino, Calif., 1980-84; ptnr. Palm Properties Co., San Marino, Calif., 1979—2001. Pres., dir. Van de Kamp's Bakers, Inc., San Marino, Calif., 1984—87; ptnr. Huntington Hotel Assocs., San Marino, 1986—95; pres. Crestmont Fin. Svcs., Inc., 1991—, Crestmont Industries, LLC, 1996—. Author: In the Name of the People, 1977, The Money Tree, 1982, Fear of Failure, 1993, Patient Power, 1995; mem. bd. editors Stanford Law Rev., 1965-67. Trustee Pomona Coll., 1987-89, hon. trustee, 1989—; trustee, mem. exec. com. Children's Hosp. L.A., 1986-91, hon. trustee, 1991—; mem. Soc. of Fellows, Huntington Libr. Art Gallery and Bot. Gardens, 1982—; mem. Young Pres. Orgn., 1979-93. Mem. State Bar Calif., Phi Beta Kappa. Clubs: California (L.A.), Valley Hunt (Pasadena). Episcopalian. Home: 1640 Oak Grove Ave San Marino CA 91108-1109 Office: 2600 Mission St San Marino CA 91108-1676

GALBRAITH, ROBERT LYELL, JR., lawyer; b. Rochester, N.Y., May 18, 1960; s. Robert Lyell and Barbara Williams Galbraith; m. Debra Lee Dastyck, June 25, 1985; children: Taylor, Mary. BA, Hamilton Coll., 1982; JD, U. Buffalo, 1986. Bar: N.Y. 1987, U.S. Dist. Ct. (we. dist.) N.Y. 1987. Assoc. Osborn, Reed, VandeVate & Burke, Rochester, N.Y., 1986-88, Saperston & Day, P.C., Rochester, 1989-92, ptnr., 1992-98, chmn. R.E. practice group, 1994-98; ptnr. Davidson, Fink, Cook, Kelly & Galbraith LLP., Rochester, 1998—, mng. ptnr., 2001—. Mem. nat. atty. adv. bd. Citifin. Mortgage Co.; adv. bd. mem. Ticor/Chgo. Title Ins. Co., Rochester, 1991—; assoc. mem. N.Y. State Econ. Devel. Coun., Rochester, 1991-2000; adv. bd. dirs. Rochester Binding and Finishing, Rochester, 1993-96. Bd. mem., pres. Mental Health Assn., Rochester, 1991-2000; coach Brighton (N.Y.) Town Soccer, 1996-2001. Named Vol. of the Yr., Mental Health Assn., Rochester, 1995, one of 40 under 40 Rochester Bus. Jour., 1996. Mem. N.Y. State Bar Assn. (exec. com. for young lawyers sect., liason to real property exec. 1992-97), Monroe County Bar Assn. (real estate sect., pres. 1992-2000). Avocations: skiing, reading, soccer, football. Banking, Commercial, contracts (including sales of goods; commercial financing), Property, real (including real estate development, water). Office: Davidson Fink Cook Kelly & Galbraith LLP 28 E Main St Ste 900 Rochester NY 14614-1916 E-mail: rgalbraith@dfckg.com.

GALBUT, MARTIN RICHARD, lawyer; b. Miami Beach, Fla., June 27, 1946; s. Paul A. and Ethel (Kolnick) G.; m. Cynthia Ann Slaughter, June 4, 1972; children: Keith Richard, Lindsay Anne. BS in Speech, Northwestern U., 1968, JD cum laude, 1971. Bar: Ariz. 1972, U.S. Dist. Ct. Ariz. 1972, U.S. Ct. Appeals (9th cir.) 1972. Assoc. Brown, Vlassis & Bain PA, Phoenix, 1971-75; founder, ptnr. McLoone, Theobald & Galbut PC, Phoenix, 1975-86; of counsel Furth, Fahrner, Bluemle & Mason, 1986-89; founder Galbut & Hunter, PC, Phoenix, 1989—. Presenter guest Law Talk cable TV; former judge pro tem Maricopa County Superior Ct.; lectr. comml. real estate litigation, arbitration, mediation and intellectual property law Lorman Bus. Seminars, others. Contbr. articles to profl. jours. Chmn., Ariz. State Air Pollution Control Hearing Bd., 1984-89; active Govs. Task Force on Urban Air Quality, 1986, City Phoenix Environ. Quality Commn., 1987-88; bd. dirs. Men's Art Council Phoenix Art Mus.; bd. dirs., founder Ariz. Asthma Found. Clarion de Witt Hardy scholar, Kosmerl scholar; Russel Sage grantee. Mem. ABA, Ariz. State Bar Assn. (lectr., securities law litigation com. and sect.), Am. Arbitration Assn. (arbitrator), Nat. Assn. Securities Dealers (arbitrator, trainer and lectr.). Democrat. Jewish. Avocations: painting, collecting antiques and fine art, international travel, golf. Antitrust, General civil litigation, Securities. Office: Galbut & Hunter PC 2425 E Camelback Rd Ste 1020 Phoenix AZ 85016-4216

GALE, FOURNIER JOSEPH, III, lawyer; b. Mobile, Ala., Aug. 3, 1944; s. Fournier J. Jr. and Clara (Beckham) G.; m. Louise Smith, Aug. 7, 1965; children: Carolyn, Jeanette. BA, U. Ala., 1966, JD, 1969; postgrad., Oxford U., summer 1968. Bar: Ala. 1969. From assoc. to ptnr. Cabaniss, Johnston, Gardner, Dumas & O'Neal, Birmingham, Ala., 1969-84; ptnr. Maynard, Cooper & Gale, PC, Birmingham, 1984—. Bd. dirs. McWane, Inc., Birmingham; gen. counsel, bd. dirs. Bus. Coun. Ala., Birmingham, 1977—; bd. dirs., So. Rsch. Inst.; mem. Ala. Permanent Study Commn. on Judiciary, 1977-83; mem. Jefferson County Jud. Nominating Commn., 1993-2000; chmn. Ala. Commn. on Higher Edn., 1998-2003; spl. counsel to Gov. Don Siegelman, 1999-2002. Mem. Leadership Birmingham, 1986-87; pres. U. Ala. Law Sch. Found., 1987-89. Mem. ABA (standing com. on environ. law, standing com. on fed. judiciary), Birmingham Bar Assn. (pres. 1989), Ala. Young Lawyers Assn. (pres. 1976-77), Am. Judicature Soc. (bd. dirs. 1980-85), Jud. Conf. Ala., Am. Bar Found., Kiwanis. Roman Catholic. Administrative and regulatory, General civil litigation, Environmental. Home: 2937 Southwood Rd Birmingham AL 35223-1232 Office: Maynard Cooper & Gale PC 2400 Amsouth Harbert Plz Birmingham AL 35203-2600

GALE, JOHN QUENTIN, lawyer; b. Hartford, Conn., June 16, 1951; s. John J. and Doris A. (Boissoneault) G.; m. Tracy Thompson, Sept. 23, 1978; children: Adrienne Hope, Calabria T., Aurelia D., Nathaniel J. BSEE, U. Pa., 1973; JD, U. Conn., 1977. Bar: Conn. 1977, U.S. Dist. Ct. 1978. Engr. GE, Valley Force, Pa., 1972-74; staff atty., corp. counsel City of Hartford, 1977; ptnr. Calvocoressi & Gale, Hartford, 1977—2000, Gale & Kowalyshyn, LLC, 2000—. Bd. dirs. New Horizons, Inc., pres., 1998-2000; bd. dirs. Farmington, Conn. Vision Svcs., Inc., Hartford, Immanuel House, Inc., Silver Svc., Inc. Founder, editor Professional Discipline Digest, 1991. Trustee Bloomfield (Conn.) United Meth. Ch., 1991—, Hartford Pub. H.S. Alumni Assn., 1998--; founder, trustee Noah Webster Sch. Alumni Assn., 1998--; treas. Hartford Dem. Town Com., 1994-2002. Recipient Salutation for Improving City award Hartford Courant Columnist-Tom Condon, 1993. Mem. Conn. Bar Assn. (mem. profl. discipline com. 1987—, chmn. profl. discipline com. 1994—), Greater Hartford C. of C. (govt. affairs com. 1988-93), Lions Club (dir. 1980—), Phi Delta Phi (hon.). Avocations: recreational sports, bluegrass mandolin, 1941 oldsmobile, golf, 1897 house. General practice, Personal injury (including property damage), Probate (including wills, trusts). Office: Gale & Kowalyshyn LLC 363 Main St Fl 4 Hartford CT 06106-1845 E-mail: jgale@lawlordsofhartford.com.

GALE, RANDALL GLENN, lawyer; b. Nanticoke, Pa., Apr. 20, 1952; s. Joseph John and Mary Elizabeth (Glenn) G.; m. Pamela Louise Pethick, Aug. 10, 1974; children: Randall Glenn Jr., Christopher Scott. BA summa cum laude, Wilkes Coll., 1974; JD, Dickinson Sch. of Law, 1977. Bar: Pa. 1977, U.S. Dist. Ct. (mid. dist.) Pa. 1977, U.S. Ct. Appeals (3d cir.) 1977. Law clk. to judge U.S. Dist. Ct., Harrisburg, Pa., 1977-79; dep. atty. gen. Pa. Dept. of Justice, Harrisburg, 1979-81; sr. dep. atty. gen. Pa. Office Atty. Gen., Harrisburg, 1982-85; assoc. Thomas & Thomas, Harrisburg, 1985-91; ptnr. Thomas, Thomas & Hafer, Harrisburg, 1991—. Mem. tort liabilities subcom. Pa. Transp. Adv. Com., Harrisburg, 1984-85; dir. Camp Hill Sch. Dist.; mem. bd. dels. Harrisburg Area C.C. Mem. Pa. Bar Assn., Dauphin County Bar Assn., Ctrl. Pa. Claims Assn., Pa. Def. Inst., West Shore Country Club. Republican. Avocations: gardening, golf. Insurance, Personal injury (including property damage), Workers' compensation. Home: 236 Willow Ave Camp Hill PA 17011-3652 Office: Thomas Thomas & Hafer 305 N Front St PO Box 999 Harrisburg PA 17108-0999

GALELLA, JOSEPH PETER, lawyer; b. N.Y.C., Oct. 19, 1956; s. Joseph Anthony and Stella Agnes (McKee) G.; m. Elaine Fowler, Aug. 15, 1981; 1 child, Joseph George. BA, Franklin & Marshall Coll., 1978; JD, U. Miami, 1981. Bar: Fla. 1981, N.Y. 1982, U.S. Dist. Ct. (so. dist.) Fla. 1982, U.S. Ct. Appeals (11th cir.) 1982. Assoc. Karsch & Meyer, N.Y.C., 1981—82; pvt. practice Peekskill, N.Y., 1983—; office counsel Kenneth Pregno Agy., Ltd., Peekskill, 1984—; of counsel Hersh & Hersh, Peekskill, 1994—. Rep. Franklin & Marshall Coll. Alumni Admissions Program, 1979-90; bd. dirs. Peekskill Field Library, 1985—, pres. 1998—. Mem. Fla. Bar, N.Y. State Bar Assn., Westchester County Bar Assn., Peekskill Bar Assn. (pres. 1993-94), Ossing Bar Assn., Yorktown Bar Assn. Democrat. Roman Catholic. Avocations: swimming, racquetball, tennis, reading. Probate (including wills, trusts), Property, real (including real estate development, water). Home: 110 Mountain View Rd Cortlandt Manor NY 10567-6238

GALINDO, MARIE ALSACE, art historian, lawyer; b. Mexico City, May 18, 1973; d. Alejandro Galindo and Margarita Roel; m. Hector Arvizu, Dec. 21, 2002. Degree in Law, Nat. Autonomous U. Mex., Mexico City, 1999; Degree in Art History, Iberoamerican U., Mexico City, 1999; LLM, U. London, 2000. Bar: Mexican Bar Assn. 2001. Assoc. Von Wobeser y Sierra, Mexico City, 2000—. Contbr. articles to profl. jours. Scholar, Ministry Edn., 1999, 2000. Mem.: ABA, Internat. Bar Assn. (chair Mexican sect. of art and cultural property com. 2002—), Mexican Bar Assn. Roman Catholic. Achievements include research in paleography from old Spanish to actual Spanish of a XVI century original manuscript. Avocations: reading, piano, scuba diving, bicycling, travel. Office: Von Wobeser y Sierra Guillermo Gonzalez Camarena 1100-7 floor 01210 Mexico City Mexico Office Fax: +52-55-52581098/99. Personal E-mail: mariealsace@hotmail.com. E-mail: mgalindo@vwys.com.mx.

GALL, JOHN R. lawyer; b. San Francisco, 1945; BA, Miami U., 1967; JD, Ohio State U., 1970. Bar: Ohio 1971. Ptnr. Squire, Sanders & Dempsey, Columbus, Ohio. General civil litigation, Intellectual property. Office: Squire Sanders & Dempsey 1300 Huntington Ctr 41 S High St Columbus OH 43215-6101 E-mail: jgall@ssd.com.

GALL, ROBERT JAY, lawyer; b. Athens, Ohio, Jan. 18, 1957; s. Homer B. Jr. and Jean Elliott Gall; m. Cherie Hill, Dec. 4, 1982; 1 child, Anna Claire. AB, Miami U., 1979; JD, Coll. of William and Mary, 1982. Bar: Ohio 1982, U.S. Ct. Appeals (6th cir.) 1982, U.S. Dist. Ct. (so. dist.) Ohio 1983, U.S. Supreme Ct. 1985. Atty. Mollica, Gall, Sloan & Sillery, Athens, 1982—. Bd. dirs. Hocking Valley Bank. Former bd. dirs., vice-chair Ohio U. Coll. Osteo. Medicine, Athens, chair Sheltering Arms Hosp. Found., Athens; vice chmn. Athens County Port Authority; bd. dirs. Ohio U. Inst. Local Govt. and Rural Devel.; bd. dirs., past chair Dairy Barn Cultural Arts Ctr. Fellow Am. Coll. Trust and Estates Counsel; mem. Ohio State Bar Assn. (bd. govs. sect. for estate planning probate and trust law), Athens County Bar Assn. (past pres.), Athens Area C. of C. (bd. dirs., past chair). Corporate, general, Estate planning, Probate (including wills, trusts). Office: Mollica Gall Sloan & Sillery Co LPA 35 N College St Athens OH 45701-2529 E-mail: rgall@mgss.com.

GALLAGHER, BYRON PATRICK, JR., lawyer; b. Bay City, Mich., Feb. 29, 1964; s. Byron Patrick and Ethel Jean (Gebowski) G.; m. Michelle Francis Burdick, May 21, 1994; children: Byron Patrick III, Grace Katherine. AB, Kenyon Coll., Gambier, Ohio, 1986; JD, Washington U., St. Louis, 1989. Bar: Mich. 1989, U.S. Dist. Ct. (we. dist.) Mich. 1990, U.S. Dist. Ct. (ea. dist.) Mich. 1995. Ptnr. Gallagher Duby, PLC, Lansing, 1998—. Bd. dirs., initial incorporator Summit Cmty. Bank. Bd. dirs. Ingham County Social Svc. Bd., Mason, Mich., 1991-92, Ingham County Commn., Mason, 1993-97, Mich. Underground Storage Tank Fin. Assurance Authority, 1996-2002; dir. State Bldg. Authority, 2002—; Rep. cand. Mich. State Senate, 1998. Mem. Ingham County Bar Assn. (bd. dirs. 1996-99, bench bar com. 2000—), County Club of Lansing, Mich. Athletic Club. Republican. Avocations: flying, golf. Corporate, general, Probate (including wills, trusts), Property, real (including real estate development, water). Home: 951 Walbridge Dr East Lansing MI 48823 Office: Gallagher Duby PLC 2510 Kerry St Ste 210 Lansing MI 48912-3671

GALLAGHER, GEORGE R. retired judge; Former sr. judge D.C. Ct. Appeals. Office: 500 Indiana Ave NW Ste 6000 Washington DC 20001-2131

GALLAGHER, JEROME FRANCIS, JR., lawyer; b. Passaic, N.J., Sept. 16, 1958; s. Jerome F. and Iris (Torres) G.; m. Deirdre O. Stewart, Sept. 27, 1992; children: Nicholas, Colin, Caroline. BS in Man and Tech. with distinction, N.J. Inst. Tech., Newark, 1980; JD, Rutgers U., Newark, 1983. Bar: N.J. 1983, U.S. Dist. Ct. N.J. 1983, U.S. Ct. Appeals (3d cir.) 1994. Assoc. Shanley & Fisher, P.C., Morristown, N.J., 1983-84, Dunn, Pashman, Sponzilli, Swick & Finnerty, Esq., Hackensack, N.J., 1984-90; ptnr. Baron, Gallagher & Perzley, Esq., Parsippany, N.J., 1990-99, Greiner Gallagher & Cavanaugh LLC, Parsippany, 1999—. Mem. adv. coun. civil and environ. engrng. dept. N.J. Inst. Tech., 1999—. Mem. adv. bd. dept. civil and environ. engrng. N.J. Inst. Tech.; panelist Lorman N.J. Collections Practice Seminar, 2000—02; pres. St. Mary's H.S. Assn., Wharton, NJ, 1993—95, 2000—01. Mem. N.J. State Bar Assn., Comml. Law League Am. Bankruptcy, State civil litigation, Commercial, consumer (including collections, credit). Office: Greiner Gallagher & Cavanaugh LLC 2001 Route 46 Ste 202 Parsippany NJ 07054-1315 E-mail: jerrygal@greinergallagherlaw.com.

GALLAGHER, R. LOUIS, II, lawyer; b. Trenton, NJ, Aug. 12, 1958; s. R. Louis and Evelyn Gallagher; m. Karen G. Gallagher, Jan. 2, 1982; children: R. Louis III, Laura Colleen, Ryan Patrick. BA, Coll. William and Mary, 1988; JD, Calif. We. Sch. Law, 1990. Bar: N.J. 1991, U.S. Dist. Ct. N.J. 1991, D.C. 1993, U.S. Ct. Appeals (3d cir.) 1999, U.S. Supreme Ct. 2000. Solo practitioner, Mt. Holly, NJ, 1995; ptnr. Kessler Tutek Gladreiter Satin & Gallagher, Bordentown, NJ, 1996—2002; solo practitioner R. Louis Gallagher, Hainesport, NJ, 2002—. Judge advocate Am. Legion State of N.J., Trenton, 1997—. V.p. N.J. Sch. Bds. Advocacy, 1998—2000, trustee, 2002—; chmn. Burlington County Dem. Com., 2000—02. E-9 USNR, 1979—2002. Roman Catholic. Criminal, Education and schools. Office: 1487 State Hwy 38 West Hainesport NJ 08036 E-mail: rlgallagherlaw@aol.com.

GALLAGHER, RICHARD SIDNEY, lawyer; b. Minot, N.D., May 10, 1942; s. J.W.S. and Esther T. (Tappon) G.; m. Ann Rylands Larson, June 24, 1972; children: Elizabeth, Catherine. BSBA, Northwestern U., 1964; JD, Harvard U., 1967. Ptnr., chmn. dept. tax and individual planning Foley & Lardner, Milw., 1967—. Bd. dirs. Badger Meter Found., Milw. Bd. chmn. Milw. Youth Symphony Orchs., Milw., 1980-82; bd. chmn. Milw. County Performing. Arts Ctr., Milw., 1986-91; dir. Curative Rehab. Ctr., Milw., 1988-93, United Performing Arts Fund, 1991-99; pres. Donors Forum of Wis., 1997-2000. Lt. comdr., USN, 1967-69, Vietnam. Fellow Am. Coll. Tax Counsel, Am. Coll. of Trust and Estate Coun., Am. Law Inst.; mem. ABA (chmn. exempt orgns. com., sect. of taxation 1989-91, chmn. com. on adminstrn. of trusts and estates, sect. probate and trust law 1996-98). Probate (including wills, trusts), Estate taxation, Taxation, general. Office: Foley & Lardner US Bank Ctr 777 E Wisconsin Ave Milwaukee WI 53202

GALLEGOS, LARRY DUAYNE, lawyer; b. Cheverly, Md., Mar. 23, 1951; s. Belarmino R. and Helen (Schlotthauer) G.; m. Claudia M. King, Oct. 1, 1994; 1 child, Will Adam. BS summa cum laude, U. Puget Sound, 1978; JD, Harvard U., 1981. Bar: Colo. 1981, U.S. Dist. Ct. Colo. 1981, U.S. Tax Ct. 1989. Assoc. Pendleton & Sabian, Denver, 1981-83, O'Connor & Hannan, Denver, 1983-86, ptnr., 1986-89, Rossi & Judd, P.C., Denver, 1989-92, Berliner Zisser Walter & Gallegos, P.C., Denver, 1992—2003, Gallegos & Assocs., P.C., 2003—. Served with U.S. Army (ARCOM), 1972-74. Mem. ABA (real property, probate and trust law sect.), Colo. Bar Assn., P.O.E.T.S., Colo. Trial Lawyers Assn., Denver Bar Assn., U.S. Golf Assn. Avocations: tennis, golf. General civil litigation, Commercial, contracts (including sales of goods; commercial financing), Finance. Office: Gallegos & Assocs PC 7720 E Belleview Ave Ste B-350 Greenwood Village CO 80111 Business E-Mail: lgallegos@revealmail.com.

GALLIAN, RUSSELL JOSEPH, lawyer; b. San Mateo, Calif., Apr. 24, 1948; m. Pauline G. Davis, Sept. 29, 2000; children: Lisa, Cherie, Joseph, Russell, Yvette, Jason, Ryan, Jennifer. BS, U. San Francisco, 1969, JD with honors, 1974. Bar: Calif. 1974, Utah 1975, U.S. Ct. Appeals (10th cir.) 1975, U.S. Supreme Ct. 1990; CPA, Calif. Staff acct. Arthur Andersen & Co., CPAs, San Francisco, 1969-71; treas., contr. N.Am. Reassurance Life Svc. Co., Palo Alto, Calif., 1972-74; assoc. VanCott Bagley Cornwell &

McCarthy, Salt Lake City, 1975-77; sr. ptnr. Gallian & Westfall, Wilcox & Welker, St. George, Utah, 1977—. Chmn. Tooele (Utah) Planning Commn., 1978—80; atty. City of Tooele, 1978—80, Town of Ivins, Utah, 1982—2000, Town of Sprindgdale, Utah, 1987—90, Town of Virgin, 1995—2000, 2003—, City of Santa Clara, 2001—; commr. Washington County, 1993—96; chmn. Washington County Econ. Devel. Coun., 1993—96; bd. dirs. Dixie Ctr., 1993—96; mem. Habitat Conservation Plan Steering Com., 1993—99; atty. Town of Rockville, 1987—, Town of Virgin, 2002—. Mem. ABA, Utah State Bar Assn., Tooele County Bar Assn. (pres. 1978-79), So. Utah Bar Assn. (pres. 1986-87). Republican. Mem. Lds Ch. Banking, Property, real (including real estate development, water). Office: Gallian & Westfall Wilcox & Welker LC 59 S 100 E Saint George UT 84770-3422 E-mail: carma@gwwwlaw.com.

GALLIGAN, MATTHEW G. lawyer; b. New Haven, Sept. 1, 1923; s. Matthew J. and Mary J. (Gordon) G.; m. Anne Elizabeth Reynolds, Apr. 10, 1950. BS, Fordham U., 1947; JD, Georgetown U., 1950. Bar: Conn. 1951. Sole practice , Wallingford, Conn., 1952. Asst. pros. atty. Town of Wallingford, 1953-55, town atty., 1956-57, 1960-69; counsel joint senate ho. judiciary com. Conn. Gen. Assembly, 1971; mem. adv. bd. Am. Nat. Bank, 1979. Corporator Meriden-Wallingford (Conn.) Hosp., 1975. Mem. Conn. Bar Assn., New Haven County Bar Assn., Meriden-Wallingford Bar Assn. Lodges: Elks, Rotary. Roman Catholic. General practice, Probate (including wills, trusts), Property, real (including real estate development, water). Office: 300 Long Hill Rd Wallingford CT 06492-4948 Fax: 203-269-8334. E-mail: m.galligan@snet.net.

GALLIGAN, THOMAS C., JR., dean, law educator; AB, Stanford U., 1977; JD, U. Puget Sound (now Seattle U.), 1981; LLM, Columbia U., 1986. With Lane Powell Moss & Miller, Seattle; prof. law Paul Hebert Law Ctr. La. State U., Dale E. Bennett prof. law, 1997, exec. dir. La. Jud. Coll., 1996-98; dean, prof. law U. Tenn., Knoxville, 1998—, Elvin E. Overton Disting. prof. law, 2003—. Spkr. on legal topics to various groups, 1987—. Co-author: Legislation and Jurisprudence on Maritime Personal Injury Law, 1997, Louisiana Tort Law, 1996, supplemented 1997, 2000, 01, 02, Personal Injury in Admiralty, 2000, Admiralty in a Nutshell, 4th edit., 2000, Tort Law: Cases, Materials, and Problems, 3d edit., 2002; contbr. articles to law revs. and acad. jours. Recipient John Minor Wisdom award for acad. excellence in legal scholarship Tulane Law Rev., 1996-97. Office: 1505 W Cumberland Ave Ste 278 Knoxville TN 37996-0001 Fax: 423-974-6595. E-mail: galligan@libra.law.uth.edu.

GALLOWAY, DIANE, lawyer; b. N.Y.C., Mar. 9, 1961; m. Christopher Hancock, Aug. 10, 1985; children: Philip Hancock, Oliver Hancock. BA in Law, Cambridge (Eng.) U., 1982; LLM, Harvard U., 1984. Cert.: Law Soc. Eng. (Solicitor) 1983. Ptnr. Richards Butler, London, 1995—. Alternative dispute resolution, General civil litigation, Private international, Shipping/Commodities. Office: Richards Butler Beaufort House15 St Botolph St London EC2A7EE England Office Fax: 0044 207247 5091. E-mail: dg@richardsbutler.com.

GALLOWAY, HUNTER HENDERSON, III, lawyer, small business owner; b. Abingdon, Va., Nov. 16, 1945; s. Hunter Henderson Jr. and Katherine Cosby (Hines) G.; m. Linda Sharlene Alley, June 20, 1971 (div. Feb. 1975); m. Deborah Lynn Brannon, Dec. 18, 1977; children: Andrew Michael, Hunter Henderson IV, Patrick B., Thomas J. BBA, U. N.C., 1968, JD, 1972. Bar: N.C. 1972, U.S. Dist. Ct. (mid. dist.) 1974, U.S. Tax Ct. 1976, U.S. Ct. Appeals (4th cir.) 1979, U.S. Supreme Ct. 1983. Assoc. Hoyle, Hoyle & Boone, Greensboro, 1972-78; sole practice Greensboro, 1978—. Tchr. U. N.C., Greensboro, 1974-82; dealer Galloway Buick Co., Greensboro, 1978—. Served with N.C. N.G., 1968-74. Recipient Wall Street Jour. award, U. N.C., 1968. Mem. ABA, N.C. Bar Assn., Greensboro Bar Assn., N.C. Acad. Trial Lawyers, Rotary, Bald Head Island Club, Greensboro Country Club. Democrat. Presbyterian. Avocations: trap shooting, hunting, camping. Commercial, consumer (including collections, credit), Property, real (including real estate development, water). Home: 1815 Nottingham Rd Greensboro NC 27408-5612 Office: Galloway Buick Co 401 N Murrow Blvd Greensboro NC 27401-3009 E-mail: ronclarkattrap@hotmail.com.

GALTON, STEPHEN HAROLD, lawyer; b. Tulare, Calif., Dec. 23, 1937; s. Harold Parker and Marie Rose (Tuck) G.; m. Grace Marilyn Shaw, Aug. 15, 1964; children: Mark (dec.), Bradley, Jeremy, Elisabeth. BS, U. So. Calif., 1966, JD, 1969. Bar: Calif. 1970, U.S. Ct. Appeals (9th cir.) 1973, U.S. Dist. Ct. (no. dist.) Calif. 1973, U.S. Dist. Ct. (cen. dist.) Calif. 1970, U.S. Dist. Ct. (ea. and so. dists.) Calif. 1973. Assoc. Martin & Flandrick, San Marino, Calif., 1970-71, ptnr., 1971-72; assoc. Booth, Mitchell, Strange & Smith, L.A., 1973-77, ptnr., 1978-85, Galton & Helm, L.A., 1986—. Contbr. articles to profl. jours. Mem. ABA (litigation, tort, ins. sects.), Am. Bd. Trial Advs., Calif. State Bar Assn. (del. 1974-81, chair fed. cts. com.), Wilshire Bar Assn. (pres. 1986-87), Los Angeles County Bar Assn. (trustee 1987-89). Presbyterian. Federal civil litigation, State civil litigation, Insurance. Office: Galton & Helm 500 S Grand Ave Ste 1200 Los Angeles CA 90071-2624 E-mail: sgalton@galtonhelm.com., shgalton@earthlingk.net.

GALVIN, CHARLES O'NEILL, law educator; b. Wilmington, N.C., Sept. 29, 1919; s. George Patrick and Marie (O'Neill) G.; m. Margaret Edna Gillespie, June 29, 1946; children: Katherine Marie, George Patrick, Paul Edward, Charles O'Neill, Elizabeth Genevieve. BSc, So. Meth. U., 1940; MBA, Northwestern U., 1941, JD, 1947; SJD, Harvard U., 1961; LLD, Capital, 1990. Bar: Ill. 1947, Tex. 1948, U.S. Dist. Ct. (no. dist.) Tex. 1948, U.S. Tax Ct. 1949; CPA, Tex. Pvt. practice, Dallas, 1947-52; from asst. to assoc. prof. So. Meth. U., Dallas, 1952-55, prof., 1955-82, dean Sch. Law, 1963-78; Centennial prof. law Vanderbilt U., Nashville, 1983-90, Centennial prof. emeritus, 1990—, exec. in residence, 1990-93; of counsel Haynes and Boone, LLP, Dallas, 1994—. Thayer tchg. fellow Harvard U., 1956-57; vis. prof. U. Mich., 1957, Duke U., 1979, Pepperdine U., 1980; Raymond Rice Disting. vis. prof. U. Kans., 1990; adj. prof. law U. Tex., 1995-97, So. Meth. U., 1996—; bd. dirs. State Farm Ins., Bloomington, Ill., 1980-95; trustee Am. Tax Policy Inst., 1992-97. Author: Estate Planning Manual, 1987; tax editor Oil and Gas Reporter; co-editor: Texas Will Manual, 1972—. Chmn. Dallas County Community Action, Dallas 1970-72; pres. Cath. Found., Dallas, 1963-67. Served to lt. comdr. USNR, 1942-46. Recipient Disting. Alumnus award So. Meth. U., 1984, Disting. Alumnus award Northwestern U., Chgo., 1993, John Rogers award Southwestern Legal Found., Dallas, 1997, McGill award Cath. Found., 1997. Fellow Am. Bar. Found., Tex. Bar Found., Dallas Bar Found.; mem. AICPA, ABA, Tex. Bar Assn., Dallas Bar Assn., Am. Law Inst. (life), Am. Judicature Soc., Tex. Soc. CPA's, Order of Coif, Am. Tax Policy Inst., U.S. Supreme Ct. Soc. (trustee), Tex. Supreme Ct. Soc. (trustee), Phi Delta Theta, Beta Gamma Sigma. Roman Catholic. Home: 4240 Twin Post Rd Dallas TX 75244-6741 Office: Haynes and Boone LLP 3200 Nations Bank Plz 901 Main St Dallas TX 75202-3789 E-mail: cogalvin@swbell.net.

GALVIN, MICHAEL JOHN, JR., lawyer; b. Winona, Minn., July 8, 1930; s. Michael John Sr. and Margaret Elizabeth (O'Donohue) G.; m. Frances Dennis Culligan, Sept. 7, 1957; children: Sean, Kevin, Kathleen, Nora, Mary, Margaret, Patricia. BA, U. St. Thomas, 1952; LLB, U. Minn., 1957. Bar: Minn. 1957, U.S. Dist. Ct. Minn. 1957, U.S. Supreme Ct. 1961. With sales and svc. Badger Machine Co., Winona, 1950-56; mgr. Oaks Hotel Inc., Winona, 1950-56; ptnr. Briggs & Morgan, P.A., St. Paul, 1957—. Pres. St. Paul Winter Carnival Assn., 1970; sec. St. Paul Area C. of C., 1968-71; trustee U. St. Thomas, 1978-85, Coll. St. Catherines, St. Paul, 1999—; nat. chmn. U. Minn. Law Sch. Ptnrs. in Excellence Program, 2000-01; chmn. Indianhead Coun. Boy Scouts Am., 2003—. Lt. USAF, 1952-54, USAFR, 1954-60. Named Oustanding Young Man, City St. Paul, 1964, Boss of Yr., St. Paul Jaycees, 1990; recipient Disting. Alumnus award, U. St. Thomas, 1983, Great Living St. Paulite award, St. Paul Area C. of C., 2000, Eugene and Mary Fry Cmty. award, Cretin-Derham Hall Schs., 2000, Disting. Alumnus award, U. Minn. Law Sch., 2001, Monsignor James Lavin award, U. St. Thomas, 2003. Mem. ABA (labor and employment law sect.), Minn. Bar Assn. (treas. 1991-93, pres.-elect 1993, pres. 1994-95, chair labor and employment law sect. 1984), Ramsey County Bar Assn. (exec. coun. 1965-68, 83-86, pres. 1984-85), Minn. Vol. Attys. Corp. (pres. 1993-94), Univ. Club (pres. 1962), Minn. Club (pres. 1971), St. Paul Athletic Club (pres. 1986), St. Paul Area C. of C. (bd. dirs. 1995—, chmn. 1997-98). Republican. Roman Catholic. Administrative and regulatory, General practice, Labor (including EEOC, Fair Labor Standards Act, labor-management relations, NLRB, OSHA). Office: Briggs & Morgan 2200 1st St N Saint Paul MN 55109-3210 E-mail: mgalvin@briggs.com.

GALVIN, ROBERT J. lawyer; b. New Haven, Dec. 10, 1938; s. Herman I. and Freda (Helfand) Galvin; m. Susan I. Goldstein, Oct. 15, 1960 (div.); children: David B., Peter J. AB, Union Coll., Schenectady, N.Y., 1961; JD, Suffolk U., Boston, 1967. Bar: Mass. 1967, U.S. Dist. Ct. Mass. 1967, U.S. Supreme Ct. 1988. Pvt. practice, Boston, 1967-78; ptnr. Lippman & Galvin, Boston, 1978-84; of counsel Gage, Tucker & Vom Baur, Boston, 1984-86; ptnr. Davis, Malm & D'Agostine, Boston, 1986—. Lectr. Boston Ctr. Adult Edn., 1972—89, bd. dirs., v.p., 1979—, chmn. fin. com., 1985—86, pres., 1987—91; lectr. Northeastern U., Boston, 1977—78. Real estate columnist: Boston Ledger, 1981, co-author, editor: Massachusetts Condominium Law, 1988, 1991, 1993, 1996, 1997, 1998, 2003; contbr. book; co-author: (book) Crocker's Notes on Common Forms, 1999, 2000, 2003; contbr. articles to profl. jours. Bd. dirs., v.p. Rental Housing Assn. divsn. Greater Boston Real Estate Bd., 1974; bd. dirs. Beech Hill Found., Inc., 1989—, Thoreau Soc., Inc., 1993—, chmn. fin. com., chmn. exec. com., 1999—2000, v.p., 2001—. Recipient Watler Harding Disting. Svc. award, 2001. Fellow: Mass. Bar Found. (life; mem. Greater Boston 3 grantmaking adv. com. 1997, 1998, 1999); mem.: Cmty. Assns. Inst. (mem. atty.'s com. New Eng. chpt.), Mass. Conveyancer's Assn., Am. Arbitration Assn. (mem. comml. arbitration panel), Mass. Continuing Legal Edn. (real estate curriculum adv. com. 1983—87), Mass. Bar Assn. (coun. mem. property law sect. 1977—80, chmn. condominium com. 1979—91), Soc. Censure, Reproof and Arraignment Pub. Error, Abstract Club. Property, real (including real estate development, water). Home: 344 Pond St Jamaica Plain MA 02130-2447 Office: Davis Malm & D'Agostine PC One Boston Pl Ste # 3700 Boston MA 02108 E-mail: rgalvin@davismalm.com.

GAMBLE, E. JAMES, lawyer, accountant; b. Duluth, Minn., June 1, 1929; s. Edward James and Modesta Caroline (Reichert) G.; m. Lois Kennedy, Apr. 3, 1954; children: John M., Martha M., Paul F. AB, U. Mich., 1950, JD, 1953. Bar: Mich. 1953, D.C. 1980; CPA, Mich. Tax acct. Ernst & Ernst, Detroit, 1957-59; assoc. Dykema, Gossett, Spencer, Goodnow & Trigg, Detroit, 1959-67; ptnr. Dykema Gossett, Detroit, 1967-94, Gamble, Rosenberger & Joswick LLP, Bloomfield Hills, 1994—. Adj. prof. law Wayne State U., Detroit, 1964-79; adj. lectr. law U. Mich., Ann Arbor, 1979-81, 93; co-reporter, prin. draftsman Uniform Principal and Income Act (1997); mem. adv. com. Restatement of the Law, 3rd, Property, Wills and Other Donative Transfers, Restatement of the Law, 3rd, Trusts; counsel Mich. State Bd. Accountancy, Lansing, 1973-77. Author: (handbook) The Revised Uniform Principal and Income Act, 1966; contbr. articles to profl. jours. Trustee Rehab. Inst., Inc., Detroit, 1961-84, chmn. bd. trustees, 1974-77; bd. dirs., sec. Jr. Achievement Southeastern Mich., 1973-86; trustee Walsh Coll. Accountancy and Bus. Adminstrn., Troy, Mich., 1975-87, Alma (Mich.) Coll., 1981-91; mem. Fin. and Estate Planning Coun. Detroit, bd. dirs., 1969-76, pres., 1975. Lt. USN, 1953-57. Recipient Bronze Leadership award Jr. Achievement, Inc., 1985 Fellow Am. Coll. Tax Counsel, Am. Coll. Trust and Estate Counsel (bd. regents 1988—, chmn. estate and gift tax com. 1989-92, pres. 1998-99), Academician, Internat. Acad. Estate and Trust Law (exec. coun. 2001—), Am. Bar Found. (life), Mich. State Bar Found.; mem. ABA (mem. spl. com. on profl. rels. with AICPA 1968-70), Mich. Bar Assn. (mem. various coms.), Detroit Bar Assn. (chmn. taxation com. 1968-74), Detroit Bar Assn. Found. (trustee, treas. 1973-79), Birmingham Athletic Club, Leland Country Club. Presbyterian. Estate planning, Probate (including wills, trusts), Estate taxation.

GAMBLE, JOSEPH GRAHAM, JR., lawyer; b. Des Moines, June 12, 1926; s. Joseph Graham and Ella Theolian (Hildreth) G.; m. Jane Elizabeth Wilkinson, Sept. 20, 1974. AB, U. Fla., 1948; LLB, U. Ala., 1950. Bar: Ala. 1950, U.S. Dist. Ct. (no. dist.) Ala. 1951, U.S. Ct. Appeals (5th cir.) 1955-81, U.S. Ct. Appeals (11th cir.) 1981, U.S. Supreme Ct. 1960. Assoc. Spain, Gillon & Young, Birmingham, Ala., 1950-60; with Liberty Nat. Life Ins. Co., Birmingham, Ala., 1960-83, asst. gen. counsel, 1973-83; sec. Torchmark Corp., Birmingham, Ala., 1980-86, asst. gen. counsel, sec., 1983-86; sole practice Birmingham, Ala., 1987—; ret., 1998. Bd. dirs. Travelers Aid Soc., Birmingham, 1976-95, Birmingham Hospitality Network, 1997—. Fellow Life Office Mgmt. Assn.; mem. ABA, Ala. Bar Assn., Birmingham Bar Assn., Phi Alpha Delta. Republican. Episcopalian. Corporate, general, Insurance, Probate (including wills, trusts). Home: 3333 Spring Valley Ct Birmingham AL 35223-2006 Office: 6 Office Park Cir Ste 318 Birmingham AL 35223-2542

GAMBONI, CIRO ANTHONY, lawyer; b. Bklyn., Aug. 16, 1940; m. Gail Pollack, Aug. 1, 1965; children: Dina, Lee. BBA cum laude, CCNY, 1963; LLB cum laude, NYU, 1965; LLM in Taxation, Georgetown U., 1969. Bar: N.Y., U.S. Dist. Ct. (so. dist.) N.Y., U.S. Tax Ct. Ptnr. Cahill, Gordon & Reindel, N.Y.C. Mem. patron com. Lincoln Ctr. Theatre, N.Y.C. Served to capt. JAGC, U.S. Amry, 1966-69. Mem. N.Y. State Bar Assn. (tax. sect.), NYU Law Review, Order of Coif, Beta Gamma Sigma, Beta Alpha Psi. Clubs: Downtown Assn., Lotos (N.Y.C.). Avocation: non-profit theater. Corporate taxation. Office: Cahill Gordon & Reindel 80 Pine St Fl 17 New York NY 10005-1790

GAMBRELL, DAVID HENRY, lawyer; b. Atlanta, Dec. 20, 1929; s. E. Smythe and Kathleen (Hagood) G.; m. Luck Coleman Flanders, Oct. 16, 1953; children: Luck Coleman, David Henry, Alice Kathleen Hagood, Mary Latimer. BS, Davidson Coll., 1949; JD cum laude, Harvard U., 1952. Bar: Ga. 1951. Pvt. practice, Atlanta, 1952-54, 56—; teaching fellow Harvard Law Sch., 1954-55; partner firm Gambrell & Stolz, LLP, 1963—. U.S. senator from Ga. to succeed Richard B. Russell Coms. on Banking and Space, 1971-72. Bd. editors: Am. Bar Assn. Jour, 1969-70. Chmn. Ga. Gov.'s Com. on Postsecondary Edn., 1978-79; bd. dirs. Nat. Legal Aid and Defender Assn., 1965-69; chmn. Dem. Party of Ga., 1970-71; trustee Ga. Legal History Found., 1996—, Lawyers Found. of Ga., 1997—; bd. dirs. Buckhead Coalition, Inc., 2003—. Mem. ABA (ho. of dels. 1975), Atlanta Bar Assn. (pres. 1965-66), State Bar Ga. (pres. 1967-68), Lawyers Club Atlanta, Ga. C. of C. (bd. dirs. 1989-92), N.C. Soc. Cin., Ga. Hist. Soc. (bd. curators 1999-2001), Met. Club (Washington), Piedmont Driving Club, Commerce Club, Capital City Club, Peachtree Golf Club, Sigma Alpha Epsilon, Omicron Delta Kappa. Democrat. Presbyterian. General civil litigation, Corporate, general, Property, real (including real estate development, water). Home: 3205 Arden Rd NW Atlanta GA 30305-1918 Office: Gambrell & Stolz 303 Peachtree St NE Ste 4300 Atlanta GA 30308-3254 E-mail: dgambrell@gambrell.com.

GAMBRELL, JAMES BRUTON, III, lawyer, educator; b. Rochester, Minn., Jan. 17, 1926; s. James Bruton Gambrell and Martha Judson Corley; m. Helen Jeanette Roddy, Aug. 12, 1950; children: Jamey, Gretchen, James Bruton IV. BS in Mech. Engring, U. Tex., 1949; MA in Econs, Columbia U., 1950; LL.B., N.Y. U., 1957. Bar: D.C. 1957, Okla. 1958, Calif. 1961, N.Y. 1967, Tex. 1976. Mem. staff Tex. Legis. Council, Austin, 1950; instr. econs. Baylor U., Waco, Tex., 1950-51; mem. tech. staff (engr.) Bell Telephone Labs., Murray Hill, N.J., 1951-53, mem. patent staff N.Y.C., 1953-57; admitted to practice before U.S. Patent Office, 1954; asst. patent atty. Well Surveys, Inc., Tulsa, 1957-59; assoc. Townsend & Townsend, San Francisco, 1959-61; spl. asst. to commr. patents, dir. office legis. planning U.S. Patent Office, Washington, 1961-63; ptnr. Fowler, Knobbe & Gambrell, Santa Ana, Calif., 1963-66; prof. law N.Y. U., N.Y.C., 1966-76, patent counsel, 1967-76; prof. law U. Houston, 1976-82; ptnr. Pravel, Gambrell, Hewitt, Kimball & Krieger, Houston, 1976-92, Gambrell, Wilson & Hamilton, Austin, Tex., 1993-95, Akin, Gump, Strauss, Hauer & Feld L.L.P., Austin, Tex., 1995-2000; vis. prof. law U. Tex., Austin, 2000—02. Cons. to Practicing Law Inst., N.Y.C., 1966-71, Commn. Revision Fed. Ct. Appellate System, 1974, Energy and Rsch. Adminstrn., 1976; commr. patents Patent Adv. Com., 1968-72. Author: Patent Law Perspectives, 2d edit., 6 vols., 1970-88; editor: Orange County Bar Bull., 1965-66; mem. adv. bd.: Patent, Trademark and Copyright Jour., 1972-86, 94—. Lt. (j.g.) USNR, 1943-46. Mem. ABA, Calif. Bar Assn., Tex. Bar Assn., Am. Intellectual Property Law Assn. (bd. mgrs. 1977-80), Licensing Execs. Soc., Internat. Trademark Assn., Copyright Soc., Intellectual Property Panel of Experts, Am. Arbitration Assn., Ctr. for Pub. Resources. Alternative dispute resolution, Federal civil litigation, Intellectual property. Home: 3801 Cima Serena Dr Austin TX 78759-8229 also: PO Box 584 Hunt TX 78024 E-mail: jim@gambrell.org., gambrell@classicnet.net.

GAMBRO, MICHAEL S. lawyer; b. N.Y.C., July 15, 1954; s. A. John and Rose A. (Grandinetti) G.; m. Joan L. Thurneyssen, Aug. 9, 1980; children: Dana E., Merrill R., Christopher J. BS summa cum laude, Tufts U., 1976; JD, Columbia U., 1980. Bar: N.Y. 1981, U.S. Dist. Ct. (so. dist.) N.Y. 1981, U.S. Dist. Ct. N.J. 1981, N.J. 1983, Calif. 1988. Assoc. Cadwalader, Wickersham & Taft, N.Y.C., 1980-86, ptnr., 1987-88, L.A., 1988-94, N.Y.C., 1994—. Harlan Fiske Stone scholar, 1978-79, 1979-80. Mem. ABA, Phi Beta Kappa, Psi Chi. Corporate, general, Securities. Office: Cadwalader Wickersham & Taft 100 Maiden Ln New York NY 10038-4818

GAMMON, JAMES ALAN, lawyer; b. Keokuk, Iowa, Jan. 30, 1934; s. Tench Temme and Helen Dolores Gammon; m. Joanne Mott, Aug. 31, 1957; children— Daniel, Thomas, Matthew, Kelly, Timothy. BS in Commerce cum laude, U. Notre Dame, 1956; JD, Georgetown U., 1959. Bar: D.C. 1959. Assoc. McGrath & McGrath, Washington, 1959-62; ptnr. Molnar & Gammon, Washington, 1962-72; sole practice Washington, 1972-76; ptnr. Gammon & Tierney, Washington, 1976, Gammon & Grange, Washington, 1977-89, of counsel, 1989—; pres. Gammon Media Brokers Inc., Washington, 1981-98; chmn. Gammon Media Brokers, LLC, Phoenix, 1998—; exec. v.p. Rodriguez Comm. Inc., Washington, 1999—2003, Momentum Media Capital, 2001—03. Mem. Fed. Communications Bar Assn., Christian Legal Soc., Nat. Assn. Media Brokers (pres. 1989-91). Republican. Roman Catholic. Avocation: body building. Office: 8280 Greensboro Dr Fl 7 Mc Lean VA 22102-3807 E-mail: jimg@rodcom.com.

GANDY, H. CONWAY, retired judge, state official; b. Washington, Nov. 3, 1934; s. Hoke and Anne B. (Conway) G.; m. Carol Anderson, Aug. 29, 1965; children: Jennifer, Constance, Margaret. BA, Colo. State U., 1962; JD, U. Denver, 1968. Bar: Colo. 1969, U.S. Dist. Ct. Colo. 1969. Pvt. practice, Ft. Collins, Colo., 1969-81; adminstrv. law judge divsn. adminstrv. hearings State of Colo., Denver, 1981-99. Bd. dirs. Foothills-Gateway Rehab. Ctr., 1970-80, Colo. State Bd. Dental Examiners, 1976-81; Dem. candidate for Colo. Senate, 1974, dist. atty., 1976; trustee Internat. Bluegrass Music Assn. Trust Fund, 1990—; pres. Colo. chpt. Nat. Assn. Adminstrv. Law Judges, 1985-86. With USN, 1954-58. Mem. Sertoma (Centurion award 1973, Tribune award 1975, Senator award 1977, 79, sec. Honor club 1977-78, pres. Ft. Collins club 1978-79, pres. Front Range club 1988-89). Home: 724 Winchester Dr Fort Collins CO 80526-2636 E-mail: hcgcag@attbi.com.

GANGLE, SANDRA SMITH, arbitrator, mediator; b. Brockton, Mass., Jan. 11, 1943; d. Milton and Irene M. (Powers) Smith; m. Eugene M. Gangle, Dec. 21, 1968; children: Melanie Jean, Jonathan Rocco. BA, Coll. New Rochelle, 1964; MA, U. Oreg.; JD, Willamette U., 1980. Bar: Oreg. 1980. Instr. French Oreg. State U., Corvallis, 1968-71, Willamette U., Salem, Oreg., 1971-74; instr. ESL Chemeketa C.C., Salem, 1975-79; labor arbitrator Salem, 1980—; pvt. practice, 1980-86, 96—; ptnr. Depenbrock, Gangle & Greer, 1986-96. Mem. Oreg., Idaho, Wash., Mont., Calif. and Alaska Arbitration Panels; mem. NASD securities arbitration and mediation panel, mediator employment bus. and disabilities disputes; clin. prof. Portland State U., 1981-84; cons. State Oreg., 1981; mem. mediation panel for disabilities issues Key Bridge Found.; mem. USPS Redress mediation panel. Contbr. articles to profl. jours. Land-use chmn. Faye Wright Neighborhood Assn., Salem, 1983-84; mem. Civil Svc. Commn., Marion County Fire Dist., Salem, 1983-89; mem. U.S. Postal Svc. Expedited Arbitration Panel, 1984-91; mem. Salem Neighbor-to-Neighbor Mediation Panel, 1986-91; mem. labor arbitrator panel Fed. Mediation & Conciliation Svc., 1986—; mem. panel Prudential APCOM reviewers, 1999-2000; ct. apptd. arbitrator, mediator Marion, Polk & Yamhill Counties, 1996—; mem. Marion County Cir. Ct. Dispute Resolution Commn., 1993-95; trustee Salem Peace Plaza, 1985-97; convenor Salem Peace Roundtable, 1995; bd. dirs. Salem YWCA, 1997-2002; bd. dirs. Salem City Club, pres., 2001; chair planning com. joint conf. between Oreg. Women Lawyers and Assn. Women Solicitors, 1998. NDEA fellow, 1967. Fellow Chartered Inst. Arbitrators (London); mem. Am. Arbitration Assn. (arbitrator/mediator), Assn. for Conflict Resolution (chpt. co-pres. 1993-94), Oreg. State Bar Assn. Alternative dispute resolution. Office: Sandra Smith Gangle PC PO Box 904 Salem OR 97308 E-mail: gangle@open.org.

GANGSTAD, JOHN ERIK, lawyer; b. New Brunswick, N.J., May 16, 1948; s. Edward Otis and Ruth Margaret (Fletcher) G.; m. Cynthia Diane Coffman, July 5, 1974; children: Allison, Erik, Amy. BA, U. Tex., 1970, JD, 1974. Bar: Tex. 1974, U.S. Dist. Ct. (no. dist.) Tex. 1974. Assoc. Turner, Hitchins, McInnery, Webb & Hartnett, Dallas, 1974-76, ptnr., 1977-81, Brown McCarroll & Oaks Hartline, L.L.P., Austin, Tex., 1982-2000, Bickerstaff, Heath et al., Austin, 2000—. Partnership com. State Bar Tex., 1981-98. Bd. dirs. Found. for the Homeless, Austin, 1988—. With USNG. Mem. ABA, Tex. Bar Assn., Order of Coif. Presbyterian. Avocations: golf, reading. Corporate, general, Mergers and acquisitions, Securities. Home: 3106 Eaneswood Dr Austin TX 78746-6717 Office: Bickerstaff Heath et al 1700 FrostBank Plz 816 Congress Ave Ste 1700 Austin TX 78701-2443 E-mail: jgangstad@bickerstaff.com.

GANN, PAMELA BROOKS, academic administrator; b. 1948; BA, U. N.C., 1970; JD, Duke U., 1973. Bar: Ga. 1973, N.C. 1974. Assoc. King & Spalding, Atlanta, 1973; 1975assoc. Robinson, Bradshaw & Hinson, P.A., Charlotte, 1974; asst. prof. Duke U. Sch. Law, Durham, 1975—78, assoc. prof., 1978—80, prof., 1980—99, dean, 1988—99; pres. Claremont McKenna Coll., Claremont, Calif., 1999—. Vis. asst. prof. U. Mich. Law Sch., 1977; vis. assoc. prof. U. Va., 1980 Author: (with D. Kahn) Corporate Taxation and Taxation of Partnerships and Partners, 1979, 83, 89; article editor Duke Law Jour. Mem. Am. Law Inst., Coun. Fgn. Rels., Order of Coif, Phi Beta Kappa Office: Claremont McKenna Coll Office Pres 500 E 9th St Claremont CA 91711-5903

GANNAM, MICHAEL JOSEPH, lawyer; b. Savannah, Ga., Nov. 10, 1922; s. Karam George and Annie (Abraham) G.; m. Marion Collins DeFrank, June 11, 1949; children: James, Ann, Elizabeth, Joseph. JD, U. Ga., 1948; MA, U. N.C., 1950. Bar: Ga. 1948, U.S. Dist. Ct. (so. dist.) Ga. 1950, U.S. Supreme Ct. 1971, U.S. Ct. Appeals (11th cir.) 1971. Assoc. Bouhan, Lawrence, Williams & Levy, Savannah, Ga., 1950-59; ptnr. Findley, Shea, Friedman, Gannam, Head & Buchsbaum, Savannah, Ga., 1959-70, atty. pvt. practice, 1970-81; sr. ptnr. Gannam and Gnann, Savannah, Ga., 1981—. Instr. bus. law polit. sci. and history Armstrong State Univ., 1951-62, mem. new campus planning and design com. Bd. dirs. Historic Savannah Found.; bd. dirs., legal counsel Telfair Acad. Arts &

Scis.; past pres. Legal Aid Soc. Savannah; mem. Savannah-Chatham Bd. Zoning Appeals, 1961-63, Savannah Arts Com., 1982-85; chmn. Gilmer Lectr. Series Fund, 1980—; bd. dirs. Savannah Coun. World Affairs, 1983-87; pres. Savannah Bar Assn.; bd. govs. State Bar Ga., 1968-99; mem. New Chatham County Courthouse Planning and Design Com.; mem. Ga. Bicentennial Commn., 1986, 87, 88. With USAAF, PTO, 1943-46. General civil litigation, General practice, Probate (including wills, trusts). Home: 235 E Gordon St Savannah GA 31401-5003 Office: Gannam & Gnann 130 W Bay St Savannah GA 31401-1109 E-mail: jgannam@gannam-gnann.com.

GANNON, JOHN SEXTON, lawyer, management consultant, arbitrator, mediator; b. East Orange, N.J., Apr. 7, 1927; s. John Joseph and Agnes (Sexton) G.; m. Diane Ditchy, Aug. 11, 1951; children: Mary Catherine, John, Lanie Elizabeth, James. BA, U. Mich., 1951; JD, Wayne State U., Detroit, 1961. Bar: Mich. 1962, Tenn. 1971, U.S. Ct. Appeals (6th cir.) 1977, U.S. Dist. Ct. (mid. dist.) Tenn. 1989; Rule 31 approved mediator Tenn. Supreme Ct. Labor negotiator, mgr. employee rels. Chrysler Corp., Highland Park, Mich., 1951-61; labor counsel, mgr. employee rels. Ex-Cell-O Corp., Highland Park, 1961-65; assoc. Constangy & Powell, Atlanta, 1966; v.p. employee rels., labor counsel Werthan Industries, Nashville, 1967-80; ptnr. Dearborn & Ewing, Nashville, 1980-90; pvt. practice Nashville, 1991—; chmn. bd. dirs. Elk Brand Mfg. Co., Inc., Nashville, 2002—. Mem. adj. faculty Owens Sch., Vanderbilt U., Nashville, 1975—85; instr. Soc. Human Resource Mgmt. Profl. cert. program Mid. Tenn. State U., 1993—2000; pres. Employee Rels. Svcs., Nashville, 1987—; chair bd. dirs. Elk Brand Mfg. Co. Inc., Nashville, 2002—. Contbr. articles to profl. jours. Mem. Birmingham (Mich.) Bd. Zoning Appeals, 1963-66; mem. Human Rels. Commn., Nashville, 1979-89; chmn. Tenn. Citizens for Ct. Modernization, Nashville, 1979-80; chmn. Pvt. Industry Coun., Nashville, 1986-95. With USN, 1945-47. Mem. ABA, FBA (former chmn. sr. lawyers divsn. mediation and arbitration com.), Tenn. Bar Assn., Nashville Bar Assn., Nat. Orgn. Social Security Claimants Reps., Am. Arbitration Assn. (panel employment mediators and arbitrators), Univ. Club, Hillwood Country Club, Kiwanis. Alternative dispute resolution, Labor (including EEOC, Fair Labor Standards Act, labor-management relations, NLRB, OSHA), Pension, profit-sharing, and employee benefits. Home: 216 Jackson Blvd Nashville TN 37205-3300 E-mail: jg216@msn.com.

GANNON, MARTIN C. lawyer; b. Buffalo, Dec. 26, 1932; AB, Va. Mil. Inst., 1955; JD, Washington Coll. Law, 1961. Bar: Va. 1962. Ptnr. Gannon & Cottrell, P.C., Alexandria, Va. Mem.: ATLA, ABA (mem. family law sect.), Fairfax Bar Assn., Alexandria Bar Assn. (co-chmn. family law sect.), Va. State Bar (bd. govs. family law sect. 1981—85, chmn. 1983—84), Delta Theta Phi. Family and matrimonial. Office: Gannon and Cottrell PC PO Box 1286 Alexandria VA 22313-1286 Office Fax: 703-836-9086.*

GANNON, MICHAEL JOHN, lawyer; b. Amityville, N.Y., Sept. 22, 1954; s. Woodrow John and Marjorie Elizabeth Gannon; m. Dorothy M. Gannon; children: Carey C. Rose, Miranda K. Carlson, Andrew M. BA, SUNY, Bimnhampton, 1977; JD, Ind. U., 1982. Bar: Ind. 1983, U.S. Ct. Appeals (7th cir.) 1983, Vt. 1985, U.S. Dist. Ct. Vt. 1985, U.S. Ct. Appeals (2d cir.) 1985, U.S. Supreme Ct. 1989. Law clk. to Hon. Robert L. Boyt U.S. Dist. Ct., Indpls., 1983—84; atty. Dowas, Rachlin & Martinez, Burlington, Vt., 1984—87; ptnr. Pierson, Affolter & Wadhaus, Burlington, 1987—95; mng. shareholder Affolter, Gannon & Rose, Ltd., Essex Junction, Vt., 1996—. State civil litigation. Office: Affolter Gannon and Rose Ltd 15 Brickyard Rd Ste 2 Essex Junction VT 05452 Office Fax: 802-878-6269. Business E-Mail: affelga@aol.com.

GANO, KENNETH REDMAN, JR., lawyer; b. Charleston, Ill., Mar. 11, 1952; s. Kenneth Redman Gano and Melba Maxine Gano Brown; m. Charlotte Amelia Carlet, May 21, 1983; children: Jacob Redman, James Alexander Greer, Benjamin Isaac. BA, Ea. Ill. U., 1977; JD, No. Ill. U., 1980. Bar: Ill. 1980, U.S. Dist. Ct. (ctrl. dist.) Ill. 1980, U.S. Dist. Ct. (so. dist.) Ill. 1989, U.S. Ct. Appeals (7th cir.) 1991. Assoc. Ron Tulin, Ltd., Charleston, 1980-82; ptnr. Newton & Gano, Charleston, 1982-84; office mgr. Gano Welding Supplies, Charleston, 1984-89; pvt. practice, 1989—. Instr. Lakeland Coll., Mattoon, Ill., 1980-82, Eastern Ill. U., Charleston, 1983. Mem.: Ill. Bar Assn. Office: 938 6th St Charleston IL 61920 Personal E-mail: triumphs@consolidated.net.

GANS, WALTER GIDEON, lawyer; b. Trutnov, Czechoslovakia, Jan. 11, 1936; s. Frederick and Erna (Mueller) G.; m. Harriet Arlene Goldhagen, Oct. 6, 1938 (dec.); children: David Ian, Erik Anthony; m. Katherine Elizabeth Halligan, Feb. 10, 1947. BA, Bowdoin Coll., 1957; JD, NYU, 1961, LLM in Comparative Law, 1967. Bar: N.Y. 1961. Assoc. Fried, Frank, harris, Shriver & Jacobson, N.Y.C., 1961-63; internat. atty. Latex Corp., N.Y.C., 1963-67; assoc. counsel Olin Corp., New Haven and Stamford, Conn., 1967-71, counsel, 1972-75, sr. counsel internat., 1975-79; v.p., gen. counsel and sec. Siemens Corp., N.Y.C., 1979-99; spl. counsel Kaye Scholer, 2001. Active CPR Inst. for Dispute Resolution, mem. exec. com. 1995—; active European Am. Gen. Counsel Group; dir. Food and Drug Law Inst.; mem. Conf. Bd. Coun. of Chief Legal Officers; mem. lawyers com. Human Rights' Internat. Rule Coun. Fellow Coll. Comml. Arbitrators; fem. ABA (mem. antitrust, bus. law, dispute resolution, litigation, internat. law and practice sects.), Am. Arbitration Assn. (internat. panel arbitrators, corp. counsel com.), Am. Fgn. Law Assn., Am. Corp. Counsel Assn. (N.Y.C. chpt. bd. dirs.), N.Y. State Bar Assn., Assn. Bar City of N.Y. (fgn. and comparative law com. 1973-75, 82-85, com. corp. law depts. 1986-89, fed. cts. com. 1992-95, adv. com. corp. lawyers 1992-95, 125th anniversary campaign com.), Internat. Bar Assn., The Corp. Bar. Alternative dispute resolution, Corporate, general, Private international. Office: 425 Park Ave Ste 1836 New York NY 10022

GANTT, CHARLES DAVID, lawyer; b. Winston-Salem, N.C., Oct. 2, 1956; s. Charles Heman and Augusta Pharr G.; m. Charise Lowery, Aug. 11, 1979; children: Brett Daniel, Carrie Michelle. BA in Econs., U. N.C., 1978; JD, Campbell U., 1981. Bar: N.C. 1981, U.S. Dist. Ct. (we. dist.) N.C. 1981, U.S. Ct. Appeals (4th cir.) 1984, U.S. Dist. Ct. (mid. dist.) N.C. 1985, U.S. Supreme Ct. 1985. Pvt. practice, Asheville, N.C., 1981—. Spkr. in field. Mem. Buncombe County Bd. Commrs., 1996—; chmn. Land of Sky Regional Coun., 2002—; mem. Met. Sewerage Dist. Bd., 1999—. Democrat. Methodist. Avocations: hiking, camping. Pension, profit-sharing, and employee benefits, Workers' compensation. Office: 82 Church St Asheville NC 28801-3622 E-mail: lawyer@davidgantt.com.

GANTZ, DAVID ALFRED, lawyer, university official; b. Columbus, Ohio, July 30, 1942; s. Harry Samuel and Edwina (Bookwalter) G.; m. Susan Beare, Aug. 26, 1967 (div. Feb. 1989); children: Stephen David, Julie Lorraine; m. Catherine Fagan, Mar. 28, 1992. AB, Harvard U., 1964; JD, Stanford U., 1967, M in Jud. Sci., 1970. Bar: Ohio 1967, D.C. 1971, U.S. Ct. Internat. Trade 1983, U.S. Ct. Appeals (9th cir.) 1972, U.S. Supreme Ct. 1972. Asst. prof. law U. Costa Rica, San Jose, 1967-69; law clk. U.S. Ct. Appeals, San Francisco, 1969-70; asst. legal advisor U.S. Dept. State, Washington, 1970-77; ptnr. Cole & Corrette, Washington, 1977-83, Oppenheimer Wolff & Donnelly, Washington, 1983-90, Reid & Priest, Washington, 1990-93, of counsel, 1993-97, Dorsey & Whitney, 1997-99; prof. law, dir. inter trade law program U. Ariz. Coll. Law, Tucson, 1993—; assoc. dir. Nat. Law Ctr. for Inter-Am. Free Trade, 1993—. Panelist U.S.-Can. Free Trade Agreement, 1989-92, Am. Arbitration Assn., 1996—, NAFTA, 1994—; judge OAS Adminstrv. Tribunal, 1987-95; adj. prof. Georgetown U. Law Ctr., 1982-93; vis. prof. law George Washington U., 2003—. Contbr. numerous articles on internat. law to profl. jours. Pres. Potomac River Sports Found., 1992-94. Mem. ABA, Am. Soc. Internat. Law, Potomac Boat Club (Washington, bd. dirs. 1986-93). Office: Ariz James E Rogers Coll Law 1201 E Speedway Blvd Tucson AZ 85721 E-mail: gantz@law.arizona.edu.

GANZ, CHARLES DAVID, lawyer; b. N.Y.C., Oct. 1, 1946; s. Harold Leonard and Mimi (Platzker) G.; m. Carol Susan Fisher, June 5, 1969; children: Jonathan, Adam, Melissa. AB, Franklin and Marshall Coll., 1968; JD, Duke U., 1972; LLM in Taxation, NYU, 1976. Bar: N.Y. 1973, U.S. Ct. Appeals (2d cir.) 1973, Ga. 1976, U.S. Dist. Ct. (so. and ea. dists.) N.Y. 1973, U.S. Ct. Appeals (11th cir) 1979, U.S. Dist. Ct. (no. dist.) Ga. 1979. Assoc. Cahill Gordon & Reindel, N.Y.C., 1972-76, Gambrell & Russell, Atlanta, 1976-77, ptnr., 1978-81, Branch, Pike & Ganz, Atlanta, 1982-95, Sutherland, Asbill & Brennan, Atlanta, 1998—. Trustee, pres. Ga. Fed. Tax Conf., 1985-87; trustee The Davis Acad., Japan Am. Soc. Ga., 1999—. Trustee Atlanta Ballet, 1980-82; trustee, pres. Am.-Israel Ednl. Inst. of the S.E., 1999—. Served to staff sgt. USAR, 1968-74. Mem. ABA, Ga. Bar Assn., N.Y. Bar Assn., Atlanta Bar Assn., Atlanta Tax Forum, The Standard Club (trustee 2003—). Jewish. Corporate, general, Securities, Corporate taxation. Home: 160 Hidden Falls Ln NW Atlanta GA 30328-1960

GANZ, DAVID L, lawyer; b. N.Y.C., July 28, 1951; s. Daniel M. and Beverlee (Kaufman) G.; m. Barbara Bondanza, Nov. 3, 1974 (div. 1978); m. Sharon Ruth Lamnin, Oct. 30, 1981 (div. 1996); children: Scott Harry, Elyse Toby, Pamela Rebecca; m. Kathleen Ann Gotsch, Dec. 28, 1996. BS in Fgn. Svc., Georgetown U., 1973; JD, St. John's U., 1976. Bar: N.Y. 1977, D.C. 1980, N.J. 1985; cert. mediator U.S. Dist. Ct. (N.J.). Assoc. Regan, Dorsey & De Riso, Flushing, N.Y., 1977-79; ptnr. Durst & Ganz, N.Y.C., 1979-80; mng. ptnr. Ganz, Hollinger & Towe, N.Y.C., 1981-98, Ganz & Hollinger, N.Y.C., 1999—. Exec. com. Industry Coun. Tangible Assets, Washington, 1983—, bd. dirs.; pres. World Mint Coun., 1993-95; cons. in field. Author: A Critical Guide to the Anthologies of African Literature, 1973, A Legal and Legislative History of 31 USC Sec 342d-324i, 1976, The World of Coin Collecting, 1980, 3d edit., 1998, The 90 Second Lawyer, 1996, The 90 Second Lawyer's Guide to Selling Real Estate, 1997, How to Get an Instant Mortgage, 1997, Planning Your Rare Coin Retirement, 1998, Guide Commemorative Coin Values, 1999, Official Guide to America's State Quarters, 2000, rev. edit., 2002; corr. Numis. News Weekly, 1969-73, 96—, asst. editor, 1973-74, spl. corr., 1974-75, columnist, 1969-76, 96—; contbg. editor, columnist COINage Mag., 1974—; columnist Coin World, 1974-96, COINS Mag., 1973-83; contbr. articles to profl. jours. Presdl. appointee Annual Assay Commn., 1974; bd. dirs. Georgetown Libr. Assocs., Washington, 1982—, Bialystoker Home & Infirmary for the Aged, N.Y.C., 2001—; mem. N.Y. County Draft Bd., 1984, Bergen County, N.J., 1985—, vice chair, 1996—; mem. Citizens Commemorative Coin Adv. Com. U.S. Treas., 1993-96; sec., mem. Zoning and Adjustment Bd., Fair Lawn, N.J., 1988-92, chmn., 1993-97; elected mem. Dem. County Com. Bergen County, 1988-96, borough coun. Borough of Fair Lawn, 1998—, mayor, 1999—, Bergen County freeholder, 2003—; atty. Zoning Bd. Adjustment, Paramus, 2002-2003. Decorated Order of St. Agatha (Republic of San Marino). Fellow Am. Numis. Soc. (life); mem. Am. Numis. Assn. (life, legis. coun. 1978-81, 83-95, elected bd. govs. 1985-95, v.p. 1991-93, pres. 1993-95), Assn. of Bar of City of N.Y. (com. on state legis. 1987-90), N.Y. State Bar Assn. (mem. civil practice com., chmn. subcom. 1978-84), Profl. Numis. Guild Inc. affiliated mem. 1989—, gen. coun. 1981-92), Am. Soc. Internat. Law, Nat. Assn. Coin and Precious Metals Dealers (asoc. mem., gen. coun. 1981-85), Flushing Lawyers Club (pres. 1982-83). Democrat. Jewish. Avocation: numismatics. Commercial, contracts (including sales of goods; commercial financing), Private international, Legislative. Office: Ganz & Hollinger PC 1394 3rd Ave New York NY 10021-0404 E-mail: davidlganz@aol.com.

GANZ, HOWARD LAURENCE, lawyer; b. N.Y.C., Apr. 3, 1942; s. Myron and Beatrice (W.) Ganz; children: Beth, David. BA, Colgate U., 1963; LLB, Columbia U., 1966. Bar: N.Y. 1966, U.S. Dist. Ct. (so. dist.) N.Y. 1968, U.S. Dist. Ct. (ea. dist.) N.Y. 1969, U.S. Dist. Ct. (no. dist.) Calif. 1984, U.S. Ct. Appeals (3rd cir.) 1974, U.S. Ct. Appeals (4th cir.) 1985, U.S. Dist. Ct. (9th cir.) 1984, U.S. Dist. Ct. (D.C. cir.) 1986, U.S. Supreme Ct. 1986. Law clk. to Hon. Marvin E. Frankel U.S. Dist. Ct., N.Y.C., 1966-68; assoc., ptnr., co-chair sports law group, mem. exec. com. Proskauer Rose LLP, N.Y.C., 1968—. Articles editor: Columbia Law Rev. Named One of 100 Best Lawyers in N.Y., N.Y. Mag., 1995, One of Best Lawyers in America, 1997. Fellow Coll. Labor and Employment Lawyers; mem. Fed. Bar Coun., N.Y. State Bar Assn., N.Y. County Lawyers Assn., Assn. of Bar of City of N.Y. (chair com. on sports law 2003--). General civil litigation, Labor (including EEOC, Fair Labor Standards Act, labor-management relations, NLRB, OSHA), Sports. Office: Proskauer Rose LLP 1585 Broadway New York NY 10036-8299 Fax: 212-969-2900. E-mail: hganz@proskauer.com.

GANZ, MARY KEOHAN, lawyer; b. Weymouth, Mass., Nov. 17, 1954; d. Francis and Margaret (Quinn) Keohan; m. Alan H. Ganz, Sept. 7, 1980. BA magna cum laude, Emmanuel Coll., 1976; JD, Suffolk U., 1979. Bar: Mass. 1979, U.S. Dist. Ct. Mass. 1979, N.H. 1981, U.S. Dist. Ct. N.H. 1981. Pvt. practice, Seabrook, N.H., 1981—. With Anna Jaques Hosp., 2002—. Bd. dirs. My Greatest Dream Inc., Seabrook, 1985—; corporator Anna Jaques Hosp., 2002—. Mem. ABA, N.H. Bar Assn., Rockingham County Bar Assn., Seabrook Bus. and Profl. Assn. (pres. 1986-87), Seacoast Vis. Nurses Assn. (bd. dirs. 1994-2001, sec. 1997-98, v.p. 1998-99, pres. 1999-2001), Phi Delta Phi, Kappa Gamma Pi. Roman Catholic. General practice. Office: 779 Lafayette Rd Seabrook NH 03874-4215

GARASIA, ANJANA, lawyer; b. Sisva, Gujarat, India, Dec. 11, 1927; d. Jashvant D. and Shakuntala Garasia; m. Paris B. Lee, June 1, 2002. BA, NYU, 1994; JD, Rutgers U., Newark, 1997. Bar: N.J. 1997. Assoc. Garces & Grabler, New Brunswick, NJ, 1997—98; ptnr. Lee & Garasia, LLC, Edison, NJ, 1998—. Mem.: ATLA, Am. Immigration Lawyers Assn. Immigration, naturalization, and customs, Criminal, General practice. Office: Lee and Garasia LLC 190 Lincoln Hwy 27 Edison NJ 08820 Office Fax: 732-625-0919. Business E-Mail: leeandgarasia@aol.com.

GARBAN, BLAISE JEAN-FRANCOIS, lawyer; b. Viry-chatillon, France, Jan. 30, 1968; s. Daniel Garban and Michel Neurrisse; m. Catherine Fabeck; 1 child, Anna. LLM, U. Pierre Mendes France, Grenoble, 1993. Bar: Cour Superieure de Justice Luxembourg 1996. Lawyer Clifford Chance, Luxembourg, 1995—98; legal counsel Ses Astra S.A., Luxembourg, 1998—2001; lawyer Le Goueff Avocats, Luxembourg, 2001—. Author: (newsletter) The Link. Communications, Corporate, general, Mergers and acquisitions. Office: Le Goueff Avocats 9 Avenue Guillaume L-1651 Luxembourg Luxembourg

GARBARINO, ROBERT PAUL, retired administrative dean, lawyer; b. Wanaque, N.J., Oct. 6, 1929; s. Attillio and Theresa (Napello) G.; m. Joyce A. Sullivan, June 29, 1957; children: Lynn, Lisa, Mark, Steven. BBA cum laude, St. Bonaventure U., 1951; JD with highest class honors, Villanova U., 1956. Bar: Pa. 1956, U.S. Dist. Ct. (ea. dist.) Pa. 1956, U.S. Ct. Appeals (3d cir.) 1962, U.S. Supreme Ct. 1962, U.S. Tax Ct. 1966, U.S. Ct. Internat. Trade 1966. Law clk. U.S. Dist. Ct. (ea. dist.) Pa., Phila., 1956-57; asst. counsel Phila. Electric Co., Phila., 1957-60, asst. gen. counsel, 1960-62; ptnr. Kania & Garbarino & predecessor firm, Phila. and Bala Cynwyd, Pa., 1962-81; assoc. dean adminstrn. Sch. Law Villanova (Pa.) U., 1981-96. Right-of-way cons. Edison Electric Inst., N.Y.C., 1960—62; trustee reorgn. Tele-Tronics Co., Phila., 1962—64; mem. bd. consultors Law Sch. Villanova U., 1967—81, mem. bd. consultors (life mem.), 1996—2003, chmn., vice chmn. bd. consultors, 1971—76; chmn. Profl. Sports Career Counseling Panel Villanova U.; mem. pres.'s adv. coun. St. Bonaventure U., NY, 1975—86, chmn., 1976—78. Contbr. articles to profl. jours.; 1st editor-in-chief Villanova U. Law Rev., 1954. Mem. community leadership seminar Fels Inst. Local and State Govt., 1961. Staff sgt. USMC, 1951-53. Mem. ABA, Phila. Bar Assn., Order of Coif. Home: 120 Ladderback Ln Devon PA 19333-1815

GARBER, PAUL WILLIAM, lawyer; b. Boston, Nov. 16, 1934; s. Rubin Elias and Sarah Rose Garber. AB in Medieval History magna cum laude, Harvard Coll., 1956, JD, 1961; diploma in Command and Staff, U.S. Naval War Coll., 1967, diploma in Naval Warfare, 1970. Registered Land Court Title Examiner, 1966. Atty. Garber and Garber, Esqs., Boston, 1961-76, pres., 1976—; consul. Consulate of Chile, Boston, 1974—. Author: (with Philip C. Garber) The Political Constitution of Chile-An English Translation, 1981; contbr. articles to profl. jours. Pres. constn. chpt. Naval Res. Assoc., 1973-75, Navy Chpt. 5 Res. Officers Assn., 1979, First Region Naval Res. Assn., 1980, exec. v.p. 1971-72, Club Chileno, hon. pres., 1974-80, dir. Alumni Assoc., West End House, 1963-99, Scholarship Com., 1976-99, bd. dirs. Eastern Mass. chpt. Navy League U.S., 1976-85; judge Adv. Mass. Bay Coun., NLUS, 1985-99, dir. emeritus, 1999—; trustee USS Constitution Mus., 2003—. Capt. USNR, 1956-86. Decorated Navy Commendation medal, USN; knight comdr. order Bernardo O'Higgins, Govt. Chile, 1979, grand officer, 1999. Mem.: Surface Warfare Assn., USS Constn. Mus., Navy League U.S., Medieval Acad. Am., USN Inst., Naval War Coll. Found. (life), Mil. Officers Assn. Am. (life), Boston Athenaeum (life), Caleuche Club Litoral Valparaiso, Wardroom Club, Harvard Club of Boston. Avocations: gardening, reading, antiquarian rsch. Office: Consulate of Chile 1 Bernardo O'Higgins Cir Brighton MA 02135 E-mail: conchile.org@attbi.com.

GARBIS, MARVIN JOSEPH, judge; b. Balt., June 14, 1936; s. Samuel and Adele E. (Warshaw) G.; m. Phyllis Lorraine Zaroff, Aug. 27, 1961; children: Kendall Rose, Jason Anders, Kerri Jill. BES., Johns Hopkins U., 1958; JD, Harvard U., 1961; LLM, Georgetown U., 1962. Bar: D.C. 1961, Md. 1962. Trial atty. Tax Div., Dept. Justice, Washington, 1962-67; sole practice Balt., 1967-71; ptnr. Garbis, Marvel & Junghans, Balt., 1971-86, Melnicove, Kaufman, Weiner, Smouse & Garbis, Balt., 1986-88, Johnson & Gibbs, Washington, 1988-89; judge U.S. Dist. Ct. Md., 1989—. Lectr. U. Md. Law Sch., 1970-85, NYU Fed. Tax Inst., 1970, 74, 79, 87-88; adj. prof. Georgetown U. Law Sch., 1978-80, U. Balt. Law Sch., 1982—; adviser on tax procedure study, jud. com. U.S. Senate, 1969-70; mem. adv. commr. to commr. IRS, 1982; mem. adv. coun. U.S. Claims Ct., 1982—; mem. Md. Inst. for Continuing Profl. Edn. for Lawyers, 1978-80, pres., 1980-82. Author: (with Frome) Procedures in Federal Tax Controversy, 1968, (with Schwait) Tax Refund Litigation, 1971, Tax Court Practice, 1974, (with Struntz) Cases and Materials on Federal Tax Procedure, Civil and Criminal, 1981, (with Junghans and Struntz) Federal Tax Litigation, 1985, (with Struntz and Rubin) Cases and Materials on Tax Procedure and Tax Fraud, 2d edit., 1987, (with Rubin and Morgan) Cases and Material on Tax Procedure and Tax Fraud, 3d edit., 1991; contbr. articles to profl. jours. Recipient Jules Ritholz Meml. Merit award, 1996; E. Barrett Prettyman fellow, Georgetown Law Sch., 1961—62. Mem. Fed. Bar Assn. (pres. Balt. chpt. 1972-73, nat. vice chmn. tax com. 1974-76), Md. Bar Assn. (chmn. tax sect. 1970-71, chmn. continuing legal edn. 1973-80), ABA (chmn. ct. procedure com., tax sect. 1975-77), Balt. Bar Assn. (bd. govs. 1974-79), Fed. Cir. Bar Assn. (bd. dirs. 1985—). Am. Law Inst., Md. Inst. Continuing Profl. Education Lawyers (pres. 1981-82) judge. Office: US Dist Ct 101 W Lombard St Ste 530 Baltimore MD 21201-2605 E-mail: judge_garbis@mdd.vscourts.gov.

GARBRECHT, LOUIS, lawyer; b. Tulsa, Jan. 21, 1949; s. Louis and Amy (Harris) G.; m. Susan Kay Adams, July 1982; children: Kenneth, Douglas, Steven, Ursala, Heidi. BA, U. Wash., 1971; JD, U. Denver, 1975. Bar: Idaho 1975, U.S. Dist. Ct. Idaho 1975, U.S. Supreme Ct. 1980. Mng. atty. Idaho Legal Aid Svcs., Twin Falls, 1975-80; pvt. practice Twin Falls, 1980-82, Coeur D'Alene, Idaho, 1982—. Mem. Idaho State Bar (comml. law bankruptcy sect.). Democrat. Avocations: snow skiing, raquetball. Bankruptcy, Workers' compensation. Home and Office: 1400 E Sherman Ave Coeur D Alene ID 83814-4044

GARCIA, CHARINA PALOMARES, lawyer; B in Econs., U. Calif., Berkeley, 1991; JD, U. Wash., 1997. Bar: Calif. 1998. Atty. Fallon, Bixby, Cheng & Lee, San Francisco, 1997—2003, Cornerstone Law Group, San Francisco, 2003—. Bd. dirs. English Lang. Inst. Bay Area/Asians Job Opportunities, Berkeley, Calif. Mem.: Calif. Svc. Ctr., Filipino Bar Assn. No. Calif. (bd. dirs. 2000—), Am. Immigration Lawyers Assn. (exec. bd. No. Calif. 1999—, CSC liaison 2002—). Immigration, naturalization, and customs. Office: Cornerstone Law Group Ste 2360 595 Market St San Francisco CA 94105

GARCIA, HUMBERTO SIGIFREDO, lawyer; b. Harlingen, Tex., July 6, 1944; s. Porfirio and Margarita (Herrera) G.; m. Lana Cheryl Caswell, Aug. 9, 1975. BA, Lamar U., 1974; JD, U. Tex., 1977. Bar: Tex. 1978, U.S. Dist. Ct. (ea. dist.) Tex. 1978, U.S. Dist. Ct. (so. dist.) Tex. 1979, U.S. Ct. Appeals (5th cir.) 1979, U.S. Supreme Ct. 1982. Ptnr. Mehaffy, Garcia & Bradford, Beaumont, Tex., 1977-83; asst. U.S. atty. east dist. State of Tex., Sherman, 1983—2002, U.S. atty. east dist., 2003—. Instr. Lamar U., Beaumont, 1980-83; bd. dirs. Western State Bank, Denton, Tex. Served to capt. USMC, 1968-71. Mem. ABA, Fed. Bar Assn., Tex. Bar Assn, Kappa Sigma. Democrat. Presbyterian. Avocations: long distance running, fishing, photography, cars. Office: Torre Chardon Ste 1201 350 Carlos Chardon Ave San Juan PR 00918*

GARCIA GIORGANA, RICARDO, lawyer, consultant; b. Mexico City, Sept. 9, 1975; s. Francisco Garcia and Rosa Maria Giorgana. Degree in Law, Escuela Libre de Derecho, Mexico City, 2001. Mexican Republic: Gen. Direction Professions 2003. Atty. Mexico City's City Hall, 1995—98, Natividad Abogados, Mexico City, 1998—2000; atty., jr. assoc. Sesma, Sesma & McNeese, S.C., Mexico City, 2000—. Alt. dir. Fondo Privado De Socorros Jose Maria Olloqui, Mexico City, 2002—. Contbr. articles to profl. jours. Mem.: Mexican Am. C. of C. Avocations: swimming, tennis, golf. Corporate, general, Bankruptcy, Transportation, Mexican. Office: Sesma Sesma & McNeese SC Idaho 14 03810 Mexico City Mexico Office Fax: 52 55 56 87 05 63. E-mail: rgarcia@sesmalaw.com.mx.

GARCIA-PERROTE, IGNACIO, lawyer, law educator; b. Madrid, Oct. 19, 1956; s. José María García-Perrote and María Angeles Escartín; m. Paloma Rodulfo, Apr. 14, 1982; children: Guillermo, Pablo. Lic. in Law, U. Autonoma, Madrid, 1979; PhD in Law, 1986. Prof. labor law U. Autonoma, Madrid, 1987-92; chaired prof. of labor law U. Cantabria, Santander, Spain, 1992-98, U. Castilla La Mancha, Cuenca, Spain, 1998—; ct. atty. Constitutional Ct., Madrid, 1989-92; ptnr. Uría & Menéndez Abogados, Madrid, 1999—. Arbitrator Interconferal Svc. Mediation and Arbitration, 1999—. Author: Ley y Autonomía Colectiva, 1987 (PhD award 1987), Instituciones y Derecho del Trabajo, 2nd edit., 1991, La Prueba en el Proceso de Trabajo, 1994, Derecho de Seguridad Social, 2nd rev. edit., 1999; chief editor: Labour Law Jour., 1999—. With Red Cross, Madrid, 1980—. Mem. Spanish assn. Labour and Social Security Law, Assn. Ct. Attys. of Constitutional Ct., DAR Assn. Avocations: travel, reading, sports, music. , Pension, profit-sharing, and employee benefits, Workers' compensation. Office: Uría Menéndez Abogados Jorge Juan 6 28001 Madrid Spain Fax: +34 915 860 330. E-mail: igp@uria.com.

GARCIA-RUIZ, FERNANDO, lawyer; b. Mexico, Jan. 15, 1964; MBA, Instituto Panamerica-no de Alta Direccion de Espresas, Mexico, 1994; JD, U. Panamericana, Mexico, 1987. Jr. atty. Perez, Chow and Assoc., Mexico, 1985—86; analyst Ministry of Fin., Mexico, 1986; jr. atty. Miranda & Estavillo, Mexico, 1986—88; sr. atty. Bufete, Garcia Ruiz & Assoc.,

Mexico, 1988—. Chmn. bd. Found. Jesus Garcia Figueroa, 1996—, Casade los Niños Palo Solo, 2002. Recipient Gran Cruz Merito Forense, Assn. Nat. de Abogados, Mexico, 1999. Mem.: Internat. Lawyers Group, Barra Mexicana de Abogados. Corporate, general, Communications. Office: Bufete Garcia Ruiz Fuente del Pescador 131 52780 Huixquilucan Mexico Home: Castillo de Winds Sayavedra Edo de Mexico Mexico

GARCIA SANTOS COY, LUIS GERARDO, lawyer; b. Mexico City, Fed. Dist., Mexico, Aug. 27, 1967; s. Luis Garcia and Angelina Santos Coy; m. Camila Muñoz, Sept. 15, 1995; children: Camila Garcia Muñoz, Lucia Garcia Muñoz, Maria Garcia Muñoz. LLB, Iberoamericana, Mex. City, 1990. Lic.: Sec. Pub. Edn. 1993. Asst. conciliator Sec. del Trabajo y Previsión Social, Mex. City, 1987—88; paralegal Creel, Garcia-Cuellar y Muggenburg, S.C., Mex.City, 1989—90, assoc. Mex. City, 1991—2000, ptnr. Mex.City, 2000—. Mergers and acquisitions, Corporate, general, Antitrust. Office: Creel Garcia-Cuellar y Muggenburg SC Paseo los Tamarindos 60 Fed Dist Mexico City 05120 Mexico Office Fax: (52-55) 11 05 06 10. E-mail: luis.garcia@creel.com.mx.

GARDE, JOHN CHARLES, lawyer; b. Lyndhurst, N.J., Aug. 17, 1961; s. John Charles and Jean (Shepherd) G.; m. L. Allison Ghenn, Aug. 9, 1986. BA, Drew U., 1983; JD, William and Mary, 1986. Bar: N.J. 1986, U.S. Ct. N.J. 1986, U.S. Ct. Appeals (2nd, 3rd and 7th cirs.) 1990. Law sec. to presiding judge Superior Ct Appellate div., Hackensack, N.J., 1986-87; assoc. McCarter & English, Newark, 1987-94, ptnr., 1995—. Contbr. William and Mary Law Rev. Warden St. Thomas Epis. Ch., 1987—; trustee St. Phillip's Acad., 1996-2000; trustee Diocese of Newark Episcopal Properties and Fin., 2001—, judge ecclesiastical ct., 1996-2000. Mem. ABA, N.J. State Bar Assn., Essex County Bar Assn., Order of the Coif, Phi Beta Kappa. Republican. Episcopalian. General civil litigation, Insurance, Product liability. Office: McCarter & English 100 Mulberry St Newark NJ 07102-4004

GARDELLA, ROBERT CHRISTOPHER, lawyer; b. Detroit, June 24, 1964; s. Robert Lawrence and Mary Ann (Burns) G.; m. Janet Marie Roney, Oct. 5, 1996. BA in Journalism, Mich. State U., 1986; JD, Thomas M. Cooley Law Sch., 1992. Ct. clk. to Hon. Judge Daniel A. Burress, Howell, Mich., 1990-92; law clk., 1992-93; assoc. atty. Burchfield, Park & Assoc., P.C., Brighton, Mich., 1993-94; pvt. practice Brighton, 1995—. Mem. ABA, State Bar Mich.(Rep. Assembly, 1999—), Livingston County Bar Assn. (sec., treas. 1996-97, v.p. 1997-98, pres. 1998-99). Republican. Roman Catholic. Avocations: golf, tennis, softball. General practice, Transportation. Office: 8163 W Grand River Ste 100 Brighton MI 48114-9482

GARDINER, LESTER RAYMOND, JR., lawyer; b. Salt Lake City, Aug. 20, 1931; s. Lester Raymond and Sarah Lucille (Kener) G.; m. Janet Ruth Thatcher, Apr. 11, 1955; children: Allison Gardiner Bigelow, John Alfred, Annette Gardiner Weed, Leslie Gardiner Crandall, Robert Thatcher, Lisa Gardiner West, James Raymond, Elizabeth Gardiner Smith, David William, Sarah Janet Boyden. BS with honors, U. Utah, 1954; JD, U. Mich., 1959. Bar: Utah 1959, U.S. Dist. Ct. Utah 1959, U.S. Ct. Appeals (10th cir.) 1960. Law clk. U.S. Dist. Ct., 1959; assoc. then ptnr. Van Cott, Bagley, Cornwall & McCarthy, Salt Lake City, 1960-67; ptnr. Gardiner & Johnson, Salt Lake City, 1967-72, Christensen, Gardiner, Jensen & Evans, 1972-78, Fox, Edwards, Gardiner & Brown, Salt Lake City, 1978-87, Chapman & Cutler, 1987-89, Gardiner & Hintze, 1990-92; CEO and pres. Snowbird Ski and Summer Resort, Snowbird Corp., 1993-97; prin., mgmt. cons. Ray Gardiner Assocs., 1998—. Reporter, mem. Utah Sup. Ct. Com. on Adoption of Uniform Rules of Evidence, 1970-73, mem. com. on revision of criminal code, 1975-78; master of the bench Am. Inn of Ct. I, 1980-90; mem. com. bar examiners Utah State Bar, 1973; instr. bus. law U. Utah, 1965-66; adj. prof. law Brigham Young U., 1984-85. Mem. Republican State Central Com. Utah, 1967-72, mem. exec. com. Utah Rep. Party, 1975-78, chmn. state convs., 1980, 81; mem. Salt Lake City Bd. Edn., 1971-72; bd. dirs. Salt Lake City Pub. Library, 1974-75; trustee Utah Sports Found., 1987-91; bd. dirs. and exec. com. Salt Lake City Visitors and Conv. Bur., 1988-91, 93-98. Served to 1st lt. USAF, 1954-56. Mem. Utah State Bar Assn. Mem. Lds Ch. Office: Ray Gardiner Assocs 93 Laurel St Salt Lake City UT 84103-4349

GARDNER, ANNE LANCASTER, judge; b. Corpus Christi, Tex., Aug. 19, 1942; d. Jack Quinn and DeWitte (Benton) Lancaster; m. Terry Gardner; 1 child, Travis Gregory. BA, U. Tex., 1964, LLB, 1966. Bar: Tex. 1966. Asst. dir. CLE State Bar Tex., 1966-67; law clk. to U.S. Dist. Ct. judge, 1967-71; ptnr. Simon, Peebles, Haskell, Gardner & Betty, Ft. Worth, 1971-85, McLean, Sanders, Price, Head & Ellis, P.C., Ft. Worth, 1985-88, Shannon, Gracey, Ratliff & Miller, Ft. Worth, 1988-2000, chair appeals sect.; justice Ct. of Appeals (2d dist.) Tex., 2000—. Mem. adv. commn. State Bd. Legal Specialization Appellate Civil Law, chair, 1993-94; mem. Tex. Supreme Ct. adv. com., 1993-98; chmn. merit selection Panel for U.S. Magistrate Judges, no. dist. Tex., 1995. Editor legal jours. Fellow Tex. Bar Found. (life); mem. ABA, Tarrant County Bar Assn. (dir., v.p., pres.-elect 1993, pres. 1994), Tex. Assn. Def. Counsel (bd. dirs.).

GARDNER, ARNOLD BURTON, lawyer; b. N.Y.C., Jan. 3, 1930; s. Harry P. and Ruth G. (Gutfreund) G.; m. Sue Shaffer, Aug. 24, 1952; children— Jonathan H., Diane R. BA summa cum laude, U. Buffalo, 1950; LL.B., Harvard U., 1953. Bar: N.Y. State bar 1954. Assoc. firm Kavinoky & Cook (and predecessor), Buffalo, 1953-58, ptnr., 1958—, sr. ptnr., 1977—. Mem. Buffalo Bd. Edn., 1969-74, pres., 1971-72; mem. nat. bd. govs. Am. Jewish Com., 1972-95, nat. v.p., 1986-89; chmn. N.Y. State Edn. Dept. Task Force on Tchr. Edn. and Certification, 1975-77; trustee SUNY, 1980-99, vice chmn., 1991-95; bd. govs. Hebrew Union Coll., Jewish Inst. Religion, Cin., 1981-87; trustee N.Y. State Archives, 1994—; mem. N.Y. State Bd. Regents, 1999—. With U.S. Army, 1954-56. Recipient Community Service award NCCJ, 1974, 88, Lawyer of Yr. U. Buffalo Sch. of Law, 1994. Mem. N.Y. State Bar Assn., Erie County Bar Assn., Am. Law Inst. Clubs: Buffalo. Corporate, general, Education and schools, Sports. Home: 89 Middlesex Rd Buffalo NY 14216-3617 Office: Kavinoky & Cook 120 Delaware Ave Rm 600 Buffalo NY 14202-2793 E-mail: agardner@kavinokycook.com.

GARDNER, BRIAN E. lawyer; b. Des Moines, July 13, 1952; s. Lawrence E. and Sarah I. (Hill) G.; m. Rondi L. Veland, Aug. 7, 1976; children: Meredith Anne, Stephanie Lynn, John Clinton. BS, Iowa State U., 1974; JD, U. Iowa, 1978. Bar: Iowa 1978, Mo. 1978, Kans. 1979, U.S. Ct. Appeals (10th cir.) 1980, U.S. Dist. Ct. Kans. 1979, U.S. Dist. Ct. (we. dist.) Mo. 1978. Assoc. Morrison, Hecker, Curtis, Kuder & Parrish, Kansas City, Mo., 1978-80, Parker & Handsaker, Nevada, Iowa, 1980-81, Morrison, Hecker, Curtis, Kuder & Parrish, Overland Park, Kans., 1981-83; ptnr. Morrison & Hecker, Kansas City, Mo., 1983—2002, mng. ptnr., 1990—93, 1996—2002; city atty. Mission Hills, Kans., 1992—; co-mng. ptnr. Stinson Morrison Hecker LLP, Kansas City, 2002—. Bd. dirs. Overland Park Conv. and Visitors Bur., 1985-97, chmn., 1988-90; dir., mem. exec. com. Johnson County C.C. Found., Overland Park, 1990—, pres., 1997-98; bd. dirs. KCPT, 1993-99, 2000—, chmn., 1997-98; active Kansas City Area Devel. Coun., 1992—, Civic Coun. Greater Kansas City, 1998—. Mem. Kans. Bar Assn., Kans. Assn. Def. Counsel, Kansas City Met. Bar Assn., Mo. Bar Assn., Johnson County Bar Assn., Blue Hills Country Club, Cardinal Key, Phi Beta Kappa. Lutheran. Avocation: golf. Environmental, Land use and zoning (including planning). Office: Stinson Morrison Hecker LLP 2600 Grand Blvd Kansas City MO 64108-4606

GARDNER, DALE RAY, lawyer; b. Broken Arrow, Okla., May 8, 1946; s. Edward Dale and Dahlia Faye (McKeen) G.; m. Phyllis Ann Weinschrott, Dec. 27, 1969. BA in History, So. Ill. U., 1968; MA in History, St. Mary's U., San Antonio, 1975; JD, Tulsa U., 1979. Bar: Okla. 1979, Colo. 1986, Tex. 1991, U.S. Ct. Mil. Appeals 1988, U.S. Ct. Claims 1989, U.S. Dist. Ct. (no. dist.) Okla. 1981, U.S. Dist. Ct. Colo. 1986, U.S. Dist. Ct. (so. dist.) Tex. 1992, U.S. Ct. Appeals (10th cir.) 1986. Pvt. practice, Sapulpa, Okla., 1979-80, 94—; asst. dist. atty. child support enforcement unit 24th Dist. Oklahoma, Sapulpa, 1980-86, 94-95; pvt. practice Aurora, Colo., 1986-91, Houston, 1991-94; mng. atty. Hyatt Legal Svcs., Aurora, 1988-89; city atty. City of Sapulpa, Okla., 1996-99. Author: Immigration Act of 1965: The Preliminary Results, 1974, Teapot Dome: Civil Legal Cases that Closed the Scandal, 1989. Mem. Child Support Enforcement, Sapulpa, 1980-86, 94-96; trustee United Way, Sapulpa, 1985, 95, subchair for attys. campaign, 2000, 2002; Domestic Violence Counsel, Sapulpa, 1985; chmn. bd. trustees, elder, deacon 1st Presbyn. Ch., Sapulpa, 1985. Capt. U.S. Army, 1969-75, Vietnam., lt. col Res., judge adv., ret. Mem. Okla. Bar Assn., Tex. Bar Assn., Creek County Bar (pres. 2003), Gold Coat Club (pres.), Sertoma (pres. Sapulpa 1985, pres. Collumbine 1988, 90, Sertoman of Yr. 1985), Rotary Internat. Democrat. Avocations: fishing, post card collecting. Home: 1533 Terrill Cir Sapulpa OK 74066-2567 Office: 7 S Park St Sapulpa OK 74066-4219 E-mail: ltcja@sbcglobal.net.

GARDNER, ERIC RAYMOND, lawyer; b. Derry, N.H., Nov. 13, 1946; s. William Rudolph and Lois Brooks (Wilson) G.; m. Kathleen Linda Chertok, June 14, 1969 (div. Mar. 1985); children: Matthew Eric, Thomas Martin; m. Melissa Rae Hastings, Oct. 21, 1988. BA in Polit. Sci., U. N.H., 1969; JD, Boston U., 1972. Bar: N.H. 1972, Mass. 1972, U.S. Dist. Ct. Vt., 1987, U.S. Supreme Ct. 1979. Law clk. N.H. Supreme Ct., Concord, 1972-73; assoc. Goodnow, Arwe, Ayer & Prigge, Keene, N.H., 1973-76; ptnr. Goodnow, Arwe, Ayer, Prigge & Gardner, Keene, N.H., 1977-81; pvt. practice Keene, N.H., 1981—. Appointee N.H. Supreme Ct. Profl. Conduct Com., Concord, 1984-93; sr. counsel Am. Coll. Barristers. Editor Boston U. Law Rev., 1971-72. Clk., dir. Monodnock United Way, Keene, 1975-80; dir. Keene Family YMCA, 1974-82; chair Cheshire County Crimestoppers, Inc., 1997-98. Fellow N.H. Bar Found.; mem. ABA, ATLA, Am. Bd. Trial Advocates, Nat. Bd. Trial Advocacy, N.H. Trial Lawyers Assn., Million Dollar Advocates Forum, Greater Keene C. of C. (clk., dir. 1975-80). Avocations: flying, golf, tennis, skiing, travel. Personal injury (including property damage), Product liability, Professional liability. Office: PO Box C 372 West St Keene NH 03431-2455

GARDNER, J. STEPHEN, lawyer; b. Dayton, Ohio, May 10, 1944; s. David L. and Mary (Webb) Gardner; m. Sandra Ellen Ott, Dec. 23, 1967; children: Stephen, Truett, P.J. BA in Math., U. Fla., 1966, JD, 1969. Bar: Fla. 1969, U.S. Dist Ct. (mid. dist.) Fla. 1971. Co-founder, ptnr. Ott & Gardner, Tampa, Fla., 1971-72, Bucklew, Ramsey, Ott & Gardner, Tampa, 1972-75; ptnr. Trinkle & Redman, Brandon, 1976-81; co-founder, shareholder Bush, Ross, Gardner, Warren & Rudy, P.A., Tampa, 1981—. Mem. adv. bd. SouthTrust Bank, 1986, South Hillsborough Cmty. Bank, 1988-92. Past chmn. Tampa Downtown Partnership; past pres. Davis Islands Civic Assn.; bd. dirs. Young Life Tampa, 1972, 88; bd. dirs. F.L.O.A.T., Inc., 1986-87, v.p. 1987; mem. Leadership Tampa Class of 1980; mem. bd. counelors U. Tampa, 1976-84; chmn. pastor-parish com. Hyde Park United Meth. Ch., 1982, chmn. ch. and society com., 1975, chmn. budget raisning com., 1984, lay leader, 1985, Sunday sch. supt., 1986-87, Sunday sch. tchr., 1973-86, mem. adminstrv. bd., 1974-87, chmn., 1976, co-chmn. capital campaign com., 1997, chmn. bd. trustees, 2000. 1st lt. U.S. Army, 1969-71, Vietnam; capt. USAR, 1972-75. Decorated Bronze star with oak leaf cluster. Mem. AMA, Fla. Bar Assn. (probate rules com. 1985-87), Hillsborough County Bar Assn., Tampa Tennis Assn. (past pres.), Ye Mystic Krewe Gasparilla, Tampa Yacht and Country Club (past commodore), Exch. Club (past pres. Tampa), Univ. Club Tampa (past pres.). Methodist. Banking, Probate (including wills, trusts), Property, real (including real estate development, water). Office: Bush Ross Gardner Warren & Rudy PA PO Box 3913 Tampa FL 33601-3913

GARDNER, RUSSELL MENESE, lawyer; b. High Point, N.C., July 14, 1920; s. Joseph Hayes and Clara Emma-Lee (Flynn) G.; m. Joyce Thresher, Mar. 7, 1946; children: Winthrop G., Page Stansbury, June Thresher. AB, Duke U., 1942, JD, 1948. Bar: Fla. 1948, U.S. Ct. Appeals (5th cir.) 1949, U.S. Tax Ct. 1949, U.S. Supreme Ct. 1985. Ptnr. McCune, Hiaasen, Crum, Gardner & Duke and predecessor firms, Ft. Lauderdale, Fla., 1948-90, Gunster, Yoakley, & Stewart, 1990—. Bd. govs. Shepard Broad Law Ctr. Nova S.E. U. Trustee Mus. of Art, Inc., Ft. Lauderdale, pres., 1964-67; bd. dirs. Stranahan House, Inc., 1981—, pres., 1983-85; bd. dirs. Ft. Lauderdale Hist. Soc., 1962—, pres. 1975-85, pres. emeritus, 1985—; mem. estate planning council Duke U. Sch. Law; bd. dirs., vice chmn. Broward Performing Arts Found., Inc., 1985—. Served to lt. USNR, 1943-49. Fellow Am. Coll. Trust and Estate Counsel; mem. ABA (real property, probate, trust sect.), Am. Judicature Soc., Fla. Bar Assn. (probate, guardianship rules com. 1978-2002, probate law com.), Broward County Bar Assn. (estate planning council), Coral Ridge Country Club, Lauderdale Yacht Club, Tower Club. Republican. Presbyterian. Probate (including wills, trusts), Property, real (including real estate development, water), Estate taxation. Office: PO Box 14636 Fort Lauderdale FL 33302-4636 E-mail: rgardner@gunster.com.

GARDNER, STEPHEN HENRY, lawyer; b. Dallas, Aug. 5, 1951; s. Willard Henry and Mary Frances (Brown) G.; m. Kathi Buchanan Child, Sept. 2, 1972 (div. Dec. 1977); m. Margaret Grace Bonner, Dec. 11, 1982; children: James Bonner, Mary Elizabeth. BA with honors, U. Tex., 1972, JD, 1975. Bar: Tex. 1976, N.Y. 1983, U.S. Supreme Ct. 1980, U.S. Ct. Appeals (2d cir.) 1984, U.S. Ct. Appeals (5th cir.) 1978, U.S. Ct. Appeals (7th cir.) 1999, U.S. Ct. Appeals (8th cir.) 1990, U.S. Ct. Appeals (9th cir.) 1993, U.S. Ct. Appeals (D.C. cir.) 1988, U.S. Dist. Ct., Ark. (ea. and we. dists.) 1986, U.S. Dist. Ct., Ill. (middle and no. dists.) 1999, U.S. Dist. Ct., N.Y. (ea. and so. dists.) 1983, U.S. Dist. Ct., Tex. (we. dist.) 1977, U.S. Dist. Ct., Tex. (no. dist.) 1984, U.S. Dist. Ct., Tex. (so. dist.) 1993, U.S. Dist. Ct., Tex. (ea. dist.) 2002. Staff atty. Legal Aid Soc. of Cen. Tex., Austin, 1975—81; students atty. U. Tex., Austin, 1982; asst. atty. gen. State of N.Y., N.Y.C., 1982—84, State of Tex., Dallas, 1984—91. Fellow Consumer Law Ctr., Boston, 1980-81; coun. mem. Consumer Adv. Coun. of the Fed. Res. Bd., Washington, 1986-89. Contbr. articles to profl. jours. Bd. dir. Legal Svcs. of North Tex., Dallas, 1987-89. Adm. Tex. Navy. Recipient Good Old Boy award Tex. Women's Polit. Caucus, 1987, Marvin award Nat. Assn. Attys. Gen., 1988, Hall of Fame award Ctr. for Sci. in the Pub. Interest, 1991. Mem. Tex. Bar Assn., Honorable Order of Ky. Cols., N.Y. State Bar Assn. Democrat. Home: 3230 Bryn Mawr Dr Dallas TX 75225-7645 Office: Law Office Stephen Gardner PC 6060 N Central Expy Ste 560 Dallas TX 75206

GARDNER, STEVEN LESLIE, lawyer; b. Cleve., Nov. 4, 1950. B.S., Ohio State U., 1972, J.D. cum laude, 1976; M.S.M., Case Western Res. U., 1973. Bar: Ohio 1976. Assoc., Zacks Luper & Wolinetz, Columbus, Ohio, 1976-77; asst. atty. gen. State of Ohio, Columbus, 1977-81; atty. Frost & Assocs., Columbus, 1981-84, McDonald, Hopkins Burke & Haber Co., LPA, Cleve., 1984— . Mem. Ohio State Bar Assn., Cleve. Bar Assn., Cuyahoga County Bar Assn. (trustee 1998—). General civil litigation, Commercial, contracts (including sales of goods; commercial financing), Personal injury (including property damage). Office: 2100 Bank One Center Cleveland OH 44114-2653 E-mail: sgardner@mhbh.com.

GARDNER, WOODFORD LLOYD, JR., lawyer; b. Pryor, Okla., Feb. 4, 1945; s. Woodford Lloyd Sr. and Capitola Overstreet (Arterburn) G.; m. Sandra Kaye Bishop, Aug. 7, 1966; children: Allison Wood, John Bishop. BS, Western Ky. U., 1967; JD, U. Ky., 1969. Bar: Ky. 1969, U.S. Dist. Ct. (ea. dist.) Ky. 1969, U.S. Dist. Ct. (we. dist.) Ky. 1979. Law clk. to presiding justice U.S. Dist. Ct. (ea. dist.) Ky., Lexington, 1969; ptnr. Redford, Redford & Gardner, Glasgow, Ky., 1971-91, Richardson, Gardner, Barrickman & Alexander, Glasgow, Ky., 1992—; commr. Glasgow Water Co., 2000—. Bd. dirs. South Ctrl. Bank of Barren County, Inc., Nat. Park Concessions, Inc., Mammoth Cave, Ky., chmn. bd, pres., 2001; judge, exec. Barren County, Glasgow, 1982-94; atty. Commonwealth of Ky., 1975-76. Mng. editor Ky. Law Jour., 1968-69; co-editor: Barren County Heritage; contbr. articles to profl. jours. With U.S. Army, 1969-71. Recipient Ernie award Glasgow-Barren County C. of C., 1988. Mem. Ky. Bar Assn. (ho. of dels. 1978-85), Barren County Bar Assn. (pres. 1978-79). Banking, General civil litigation, General practice. Office: Richardson Gardner Barrickman & Alexander 117 E Washington St Ste 1 Glasgow KY 42141-2696

GARFIELD, MARTIN RICHARD, lawyer; b. NYC, Feb. 19, 1935; s. Harry and Sarah (Spielman) G.; 1 child, Robin; m. Sophia Csala, Aug. 2001. BA, Hunter Coll., 1957; JD, Bklyn. Law Sch., 1964. Bar: N.Y. 1965, U.S. Dist. Ct. (ea. and so. dists.) N.Y. 1979, U.S. Supreme Ct. 1996. Assoc. Figueroa & Madow, N.Y.C., 1965-68, Schneider Kleinick & Weitz, N.Y.C., 1968-70; ptnr. Breadbar Garfield & Solomon, N.Y.C., 1970-86; sr. ptnr. Breadbar Garfield & Schmelkin, N.Y.C., 1986—. Arbitrator Civil Ct. N.Y. County, 1986—; mgr. N.Y. State Athletic Commn., 1996—. Mem. Am. Trial Lawyers Assn., N.Y. State Bar Assn. (torts, ins. sect.), N.Y. Trials Lawyers Assn. Avocations: tennis, basketball, boxing analysis, body building. Personal injury (including property damage), Product liability. Office: Breadbar Garfield & Schmelkin 11 Park Pl Fl 10 New York NY 10007-2895

GARFIELD, ROBERT EARL, lawyer; b. Cleve., Sept. 23, 1937; s. Irwin Charles Garfield and Mathilda Rose; m. Joan Susan Ross, Mar. 24, 1963; children: Mark Clayton, Steven Matthew, Patricia Faith. BA, Western Res. U., 1959; LLB, Cornell U., 1962; LLM, Georgetown U., 1969. Bar: Ohio 1962. Trial atty. Office Chief Counsel, IRS, Washington, 1963-68; assoc. Arter & Hadden, Cleve., 1968-69; ptnr. Hertz & Kates, Cleve., 1969-72, Chattman, Garfield, Friedlander & Paul, Cleve., 1973—92; of counsel Garfield and Lasko, Cleve., 1992-2002, Keevican and Weiss, 2003—. Bd. dirs., counsel Cleve. Childrens Mus., 1981; chmn. bd. of trustees The Singing Angels; bd. dirs., gen. counsel Commerce Exchange Bank, ATI, Inc. Served to capt. USAR, 1966-68. Mem. ABA, Ohio State Bar Assn., Cleve. Bar Assn., Oakwood Club, Sharon Golf Club. Jewish. Avocations: golf, music, travel, history of WWII. Home: 32450 Chestnut Ln Cleveland OH 44124-4330

GARFUNKEL, ALAN J. lawyer; b. Savannah, Ga., Oct. 26, 1947; s. Sylvan Adler Garfunkel and Eve D. (Darmstadter) Goldmann; m. Lori A. Corsun, June 27, 1993; children: S. Jonathan, Michael J., Danielle A., Joshua B. AB, NYU, 1968, LL.M. in Taxation, 1975; JD, Columbia U., 1972. Bar: N.Y. 1972, U.S. Dist. Ct. (so. and ea. dists.) N.Y. 1974, U.S. Ct. Appeals (2d cir.) 1975, U.S. Tax Ct. 1975. Sr. trial atty. Office of Chief Counsel, IRS, N.Y.C., 1972-77; assoc. firm Proskauer Rose Geotz & Mendelsohn, N.Y.C., 1977-80; atty. pvt. practice, N.Y.C., 1980—. Served with USAR, 1969-74. Mem. N.Y. State Bar Assn. (tax sect.), New York County Lawyers Assn., Bar Assn. of City of N.Y., Omicron Delta Epsilon. Corporate taxation, Personal income taxation, State and local taxation. Home: 63 Lincoln Rd Scarsdale NY 10583-7533 Office: 477 Madison Ave New York NY 10022-5802 E-mail: ajgnyclaw@aol.com.

GARGANO, FRANCINE ANN, lawyer; b. Plainfield, N.J., Feb. 10, 1957; d. Rosalie Janice Gargano. BA Seton Hall U., 1980; JD cum laude, Detroit Coll. of Law, 1983. Bar: N.J. 1983, U.S. Supreme Ct. 1986. Sole practice, North Plainfield, N.J., 1983—; dir. YWCA Legal Clinic, Plainfield, 1983—; Union County coordinator Haitian Pro Bono Projects, ABA, Plainfield, 1983—. Rsch. asst. prof. Detroit Coll. Law, Detroit, 1980-83. Author: Homosexual Marriages Are Not Possible. Trustee Plainfield Area YWCA, 1983-84; bd. dirs. Haitian Advancement Assn., Elizabeth, N.J., 1983-84; mem. N. Plainfield Bd. Adjustment; mem. Historic Preservation commn., Youth Svcs. commn., Mcpl. Alliance. Recipient Internat. Legal Scholar award Detroit Coll. Law Internat. Law Soc., 1980-82, Jessup Internat. Law Competition award, 1982, H. Rakol Scholarship award Detroit Bar Assn., 1982, Vol. of Yr. Congl. award, 1995. Mem. ABA, Union County Bar Assn., N.J. Bar Assn., Plainfield Bar Assn., Am. Immigration Lawyers Assn., Detroit Coll. Law Internat. Law Soc. (pres. 1980-82), Vicinage 13 Women's Bar Assn. (pres.), Somerset County Bar Assn. (chmn. ADR com.). Democrat. Roman Catholic.. General practice, Immigration, naturalization, and customs, Probate (including wills, trusts). Office: 55 Mountain Blvd Warren NJ 07059-5699 E-mail: garganof@webtv.net.

GARIBALDI, MARIE LOUISE, former state supreme court justice; b. Jersey City, Nov. 26, 1934; d. Louis J. and Marie (Serventi) G. BA, Conn. Coll., 1956; LLB, Columbia U., 1959; LLM in Tax. Law, NYU, 1963. Atty. Office of Regional Counsel, IRS, N.Y.C., 1960-66; assoc. McCarter & English, Newark, 1966-69; ptnr. Riker, Danzig, Scherer, Hyland & Pernutti, Newark, 1969-82; assoc. justice N.J. Supreme Court, Newark, 1982-2000. Contbr. articles to profl. jours. Trustee St. Peter's Coll.; co-chmn. Thomas Kean's campaign for Gov. of N.J., 1981, mem. transition team, 1981; mem. Gov. Byrne's Commn. on Dept. of Commerce, 1981. Recipient Disting. Alumni award NYU Law Alumni of N.J., 1982; recipient Disting. Alumni award Columbia U., 1982 Fellow Am. Bar Found.; mem. N.J. Bar Assn. (pres. 1982), Columbia U. Sch. Law Alumni Assn. (bd. dirs.) Roman Catholic.

GARLAND, MERRICK BRIAN, federal judge; b. Chgo., Nov. 13, 1952; AB summa cum laude, Harvard U., 1974, JD magna cum laude, 1977. Bar: D.C. 1979, U.S. Dist. Ct. D.C. 1980, U.S. Ct. Appeals (D.C. and 9th cirs.) 1980, U.S. Ct. Appeals (4th cir.) 1983, U.S. Ct. Appeals (10th cir.) 1996, U.S. Supreme Ct. 1983. Law clk. to judge U.S. Ct. Appeals (2d cir.), N.Y.C., 1977—78; law clk. to justice U.S. Supreme Ct., Washington, 1978—79; spl. asst. to atty. gen. U.S. Dept. Justice, Washington, 1979—81; from assoc. to ptnr. Arnold & Porter, Washington, 1981—89; assoc. ind. counsel U.S. Dept. Justice, Washington, 1987—88, asst. U.S. atty., 1989—92; ptnr. Arnold & Porter, Washington, 1992—93; dep. asst. atty. gen., criminal divsn. Dept. Justice, Washington, 1993—94, prin. assoc. dep. atty. gen., 1994—97; judge U.S. Ct. Appeals, Washington, 1997—. Lectr. Harvard U. Law Sch., 1985—86. Author: Deregulation and Jud. Rev., Harvard Law Rev., 1985, Antitrust and State Action, Yale Law Jour., 1987, Antitrust and Federalism, Yale Law Jour., 1987. Mem.: Phi Beta Kappa. Office: US Court of Appeals 333 Constitution Ave NW Washington DC 20001-2802

GARLAND, RICHARD ROGER, lawyer; b. Princeton, Ill., Aug. 20, 1958; s. Louis Roger and Irene Marie (Tonozzi) G. BA in Polit. Sci. summa cum laude, U. S. Fla., 1979; JD with honors, U. Fla., 1982. Bar: Fla. 1982, U.S. Dist. Ct. (mid. dist.) Fla. 1983, U.S. Ct. Appeals (11th cir.) 1987, U.S. Supreme Ct. 1988, U.S. Ct. Appeals (fed. cir.) 1995; Fla. Bar cert. in appellate practice, 1995. Instr., supr. appellate advocacy U. Fla., Gainesville, 1981-82; assoc. Dickinson, O'Riorden, Gibbons, Quale, Shields & Carlton, Venice, Fla., 1983-85, Sarasota, Fla., 1986-90; ptnr., sr. atty. Dickinson & Gibbons, Sarasota, Fla., 1991—. Pres. parish coun. San Pedro Cath. Ch., North Port, Fla., 1986-92; mem. Sarasota County Libr. Adv. Bd., 1999-2001. Mem. ABA, Fla. Bar Assn., Sarasota County Bar Assn. (editor newsletter 1991-93, bd. dirs. 1994-96, treas. 1996-97, sec. 1997-98, v.p. 1998-99, pres.-elect 1999-2000, pres. 2000-01), Judge John M. Scheb Am. Inn of Ct. (treas. 1998-99, counselor 1999-2000, pres.-elect 2000-01, pres. 2001-02, master), U. South Fla. Alumni Assn., Sarasota County Gator Club (bd. dirs. 2001-02, v.p. 2002-03), Phi Kappa Phi, Pi Sigma Alpha. Democrat. Roman Catholic. Appellate, General civil litigation, Health. Office: Dickinson & Gibbons PA 1750 Ringling Blvd Sarasota FL 34236-6836 E-mail: rgarland@dglawyers.com.

GARLAND, SYLVIA DILLOF, lawyer; b. N.Y.C., June 4, 1919; d. Morris and Frieda (Gassner) Dillof; m. Albert Garland, May 4, 1942; children: Margaret Garland, Paul B. BA, Bklyn. Coll., 1939; JD cum laude, N.Y. Law Sch., 1960. Bar: N.Y. 1960, U.S. Ct. Appeals (2d cir.) 1965, U.S. Ct. Claims 1965, U.S. Supreme Ct. 1967, U.S. Customs Ct. 1972, U.S. Ct. Appeals (5th cir.), 1979. Assoc. Borden, Skidell, Fleck and Steindler, Jamaica, N.Y., 1960-61, Fields, Zimmerman, Skodnick & Segall, Jamaica, 1961-65, Marshall, Brater, Greene, Allison & Tucker, N.Y.C., 1965-68; law sec. to N.Y. Supreme Ct. justice Suffolk County, 1968-70; ptnr. Hofheimer, Gartlir & Gross, N.Y.C., 1970—. Asst. adj. prof. N.Y. Law Sch., 1974-79; mem. com. on character and fitness N.Y. State Supreme Ct., 1st Jud. Dept., 1985—, vice chmn., 1991—. Author: Workman's Compensation, 1957, Labor Law, 1959, Wills, 1962; contbg. author: Guardians and Custodians, 1970; editor-in-chief Law Rev. Jour., N.Y. Law Forum, 1959-60 (svc. award 1960); contbr. articles to mag. Trustee N.Y. Law Sch., 1979-90, trustee emeritus, 1991—; pres. Oakland chpt. B'nai Brith, Bayside, N.Y., 1955-57. Recipient Disting. Alumnus award N.Y. Law Sch., 1978, Judge Charles W. Froessel award N.Y. Law Sch., 1997. Mem. ABA (litigation sect., family law sect.), N.Y. State Bar Assn. (family law sect.), Queen's County Bar Assn. (sec. civil practice 1960-79), N.Y. Law Sch. Alumni Assn. (pres. 1976-77), N.Y. Law Forum Alumni Assn. (pres. 1963-65). Jewish. General civil litigation, Family and matrimonial, Appellate. Home: 425 E 58th St New York NY 10022-2300

GARLICK, MICHAEL, lawyer, franchise consultant; b. N.Y.C., Oct. 20, 1944; s. Nathan S. and Gertrude (Finkel) G.; m. Judith Ann Schaufeld, May 12, 1977; children: Nathan S., Max Aaron, Jacob Abraham. B.A., Lehigh U., 1966; J.D., NYU, 1969. Bar: N.Y. 1970, Fla. 1971, Calif. 1973, D.C. 1974, Tex. 1995, Co. 1995, U.S. Dist. Ct. (so. dist.) Fla. Gen. counsel Internat. House of Pancakes Fla., Miami, 1970-74, cons., 1983— ; sr. ptnr. Garlick, Cohn, Darrow & Hollander, Miami, 1974-79; gen. counsel Internat. Adv. Group, Inc., Miami, 1980—; Editor Lawletter, 1981-83. Served with U.S. Army, 1969. Mem. Forum Com. on Franchising, ABA, Dade County Bar Assn. North Miami Beach Karate (pres. 1970-80), Tai Chi Chaun Assn. (pres. 1983—), Phi Beta Kappa, Beta Alpha Psi. Office: 1515 N Federal Hwy Boca Raton FL 33432-1911

GARMAN, RITA B. judge; b. Aurora, Ill., Nov. 19, 1943; m. Gill Garman; children: Sara Ellen, Andrew Gill. BS in econs., U. Ill., 1965; JD with distinction, U. Iowa, 1968. Asst. state atty. Vermilion County, 1969—73; pvt. practice Sebat, Swanson, Banks, Lessen & Garman, 1973; assoc. cir. judge, 1974—86; cir. judge Fifth Jud. Cir., 1986—95, presiding cir. judge, 1987—95; judge Fourth Dist. Appellate Ct., 1996—2001; Supreme Ct. justice Ill. State Supreme Ct., 2001—. Mem.: Ill. Judge's Assn., Vermilion County Bar Assn., Iowa Bar Assn., Ill. State Bar Assn. Office: 3607 N Vermilion Ste 1 Danville IL 61832

GARNER, MARY MARTIN, lawyer; b. Little Rock; d. Jared Owen and Mary Augusta (Conery) Martin; m. Meryl Everett Garner, Aug. 24, 1943 (dec.). JD, George Washington U., 1942. Bar: D.C. 1942, U.S. Supreme Ct. 1973. Atty. Office of Gen. counsel, Divsn. Natural Resources, USDA, Washington, 1944-72, dep. dir., 1972-74; sole practice Washington, 1975—. Legal counsel Nat. Assn. Soil Conservation Dists., Washington, 1975—; mem. adv. task force on pollution in Great Lakes, U.S.-Can. Joint Commn., Windsor, Ont., Can., 1976-79; bd. dirs. Inter-Am. Bar Found., Washington, 1976—, Fed. Bar Bldg. Corp., 1983—. Contbr. articles to profl. jours., chpts. to books, papers. Pres. Washington Club Preservation Fund, 1991—. Recipient Citation for Outstanding Contbn. to Advancement of Human Rights, Capital Area divsn. UN Assn. of U.S., Washington, 1983, Nat. Assn. Conservation Dists. Disting. Svc. award, 1972. Mem. ABA (vice chmn. com. on agr., adminstrv. law sect. 1979-81), Fed. Bar Assn. (chmn. internat. law sect. 1981-82, Outstanding Leadership award 1982), Internat. Bar Assn. (mem. governing coun. 1976-91), Washington Fgn. Law Soc., Inter-Am. Bar Assn. (asst. sec. 1978-85, mem. governing coun. 1985—), Bar Assn. D.C. (chmn. Inter-Am. relations com. 1976-77, Superior Svc. award 1977), Zonta Internat. Found. (bd. dirs. 1988-93), Women's Bar Assn. of D.C. (pres. 1957-58), Soil Conservation Soc. Am., George Washington U. Club (bd. dirs. 2000—), Phi Alpha Delta. Clubs: Nat. Lawyers (bd. govs.), The Washington Club Preservation Fund (dir.). Roman Catholic. Environmental, Private international, Property, real (including real estate development, water).

GARNER, ROBERT EDWARD LEE, lawyer; b. Bowling Green, Ky., Sept. 26, 1946; s. Alto Luther and Katie Mae (Sanders) G.; m. Suzanne Marie Searles, Aug. 22, 1981; children: Jessica Marie, Abigail Lee. BA, U. Ala., Tuscaloosa, 1968; JD, Harvard U., 1971. Bar: Ga. 1971, U.S. Dist. Ct. (no. dist.) Ga. 1974, U.S. Ct. Appeals (5th cir.) 1974, U.S. Ct. Appeals (11th cir.) 1981, Ala. 1982, U.S. Ct. Appeals (4th cir.) 1991, S.C. 1992. Assoc. Gambrell, Russell & Forbes, Atlanta, 1972-76, ptnr., 1976-80, Haskell, Slaughter & Young and predecessors, Birmingham, Ala., 1981-88, mng. ptnr., 1986-87, of counsel, 1988-90; gen. counsel, sec. Builders Transport, Inc., 1988-90; ptnr. Nelson, Mullins, Riley & Scarborough, Atlanta and Columbia, S.C., 1991-96; mem. Haskell Slaughter Young & Rediker, LLC, Birmingham, 1996—, mng. ptnr., 2000—02. 1st lt. JAGC, USAF, 1971-72. Mem. ABA (com. on fed. regulation of securities, subcom. on disclosure matters and continuous reporting, ad hoc com. on pub. co. info. practices), State Bar Ga., Ala. State Bar, Birmingham Bar, S.C. Bar, U. Ala. Alumni Assn., Harvard U. Alumni Assn., Am. Soc. Corp. Secs. (mem. tech. com.), Phi Alpha Theta, Pi Sigma Alpha. Republican. Corporate, general, Finance, Securities. Home: 284 Kings Crest Ln Pelham AL 35124-2846 Office: Haskell Slaughter Young & Rediker LLC 2001 Park Pl North Ste 1400 Birmingham AL 35203-2618 E-mail: relg@hsy.com.

GARNETT, STANLEY IREDALE, II, lawyer, utility company executive; b. Petersburg, Va., Aug. 11, 1943; s. Stanley Arthur and Edith (Keirstead) G.; m. Beverly Jackson; children: Matthew S.A., Andrew F.W., Christie, Alfred. BA, Colby Coll., 1965; MBA, U. Pa., 1967; JD, NYU, 1973. Bar: N.Y. 1974. Sr. fin. analyst Standard Oil Co. of N.J., N.Y.C., 1967-70; assoc. Milbank, Tweed, Hadley & McCloy, N.Y.C., 1973-81; v.p.-legal and regulatory Allegheny Power Sys., Inc., N.Y.C., 1981-90, v.p. fin., 1990-94, sr. v.p. fin., 1994-95; sr. advisor Putnam, Hayes & Bartlett, 1996-97, 98-00; exec. v.p. Fla. Progress Corp., St. Petersburg, 1997-98; ptnr. PA Consulting Group, 2000—. Bd. dirs. Bay Corp Holdings, Inc. Vice chmn. Episcopal Ch. Bldg. Fund; trustee, sec. ICB Internat. Ctr. for Disabled. Joseph P. Wharton scholar, 1965-67. Mem. ABA, N.Y. State Bar Assn. Republican. Episcopalian. Property, real (including real estate development, water). Home: 1000 Monterey Blvd NE Saint Petersburg FL 33704-2310 E-mail: stan.garnett@paconsulting.com.

GARRELS, SHERRY ANN, lawyer; b. Chgo., Feb. 5, 1956; d. William Henry and Jacqueline Ann G.; m. Timothy Anthony Marion, Aug. 1, 1987 (div. June 1988); 1 child, William Garrels-Marion; 1 child, Georgianna Garrels-Rogers. BA, Barat Coll., 1980; certificate, Trinity Coll., 1989; JD, Western State U., 1990. Bar: Calif. 1992, U.S. Dist. Ct. (ctrl. dist.) Calif. 1992, U.S. Dist. Ct. (no. dist.) Calif. 1993, U.S. Dist. Ct. (so. dist.) Calif. 1996, U.S. Ct. Appeals (9th cir.) 1994, U.S. Tax Ct. 1996. Pvt. practice, Huntington Beach, Calif., 1992—; judge pro tem West Justice Ctr., Westminster, Calif., 1998—. Arbitrator Nat. Panel Consumer Arbitrators, Huntington Beach, 1996, State Panel Consumer Arbitrators, Huntington Beach, 1996, Better Bus. Bureau, 1996—, U.S. C. of C., 1996, Huntington Beach C. of C., 1996. Editor The Dictum, 1989. Active 4th of July Exec. Bd., Huntington Beach, 1996—. Mem. Assn. Trial Lawyers, L.A. Trial Assn., Orange County Bar Assn., St. Bonny Golf Classic (dir. 1991-97), Delta Theta Phi. Republican. Presbyterian. Avocations: swimming, golf, scuba diving. State civil litigation, Criminal, Property, real (including real estate development, water). Office: 5942 Edinger Ave Ste 113-702 Huntington Beach CA 92649-1763 also: West Justice Ctr 8141 13th St Westminster CA 92683-4593 Fax: 714-374-0104.

GARRETSON, ROBERT H. lawyer; BA in Bus. Econs./Acctg., U. Calif.; JD, Georgetown U. CPA Va.; bar: Calif. 2001, D.C. 2002. Mgr. Hughes Elecs., L.A., 1994—95, KPMG LLP, Long Beach, 1995—96, sr. mgr. Washington, 1996—2000; atty. Gibson, Dunn & Crutcher, L.A., 2001—. Insurance, Professional liability, Commercial, contracts (including sales of goods; commercial financing). Office: Gibson Dunn & Crutcher 333 S Grand Ave Los Angeles CA 90071-3197 Fax: 213-229-7520. E-mail: rgarretson@gibsondunn.com.

GARRETT, BROOX GRAY, JR., lawyer; b. Brewton, Ala., Sept. 18, 1948; s. Broox Gray and Louise Liles (Harold) Garrett; m. Elizabeth Ann Kirkman, June 20, 1970; children: Broox Gray III, John Kirkman. BA in History, Washington and Lee U., 1970; JD, U. Ala., 1973. Bar: Ala. 1973, U.S. Dist. Ct. (so. dist.) Ala. 1975. Ptnr. Thompson , Garrett & Hines, Brewton, 1975—. Bd. dirs. BankTrust of Brewton, South Ala. Bancorp; bd. dirs., chmn. fund dir., pres. United Fund, Brewton, 1978; jud. compensation com. State of Ala.; commr. 21st Jud. Cir. Pres. Brewton Coun. Arts, 1982; bd. dirs., vice-chmn. Brewton Devel. Authority, 1982—; pres. Escambia County Young Dem., Ala., 1974—78; bd. dirs., pres. Escambia County Cattlemen's Assn., Brewton, 1981—82. Mem.: ABA, Escambia County Bar Assn. (pres.), Ala. Def. Lawyers Assn., Ala. Bar Assn. (sec. real property probate and trust sect. 1976—77), Rotary (sec. local chpt. 1976—77, pres.-elect 1984—85). Episcopalian. General practice, Insurance, Property, real (including real estate development, water). Office: Thompson Garrett & Hines LLP 218 Belleville Ave Brewton AL 36426-2010

GARRETT, CAREY EDWARD, judge; b. Knoxville, Tenn., Nov. 18, 1933; s. Albert Seaton and Mary Inez Garrett; m. Aggie Irene Calloway, June 2, 1956; children: Stephen C., Tim E. BS in Bus. Adminstrn., U. Tenn., 1958, JD, 1960. Pvt. practice, Knoxville, 1960—82; judge Knox County Juvenile Ct., Knoxville, 1982—. With USMC, 1952—54. Mem.: Tenn. Coun. Juvenile and Family Ct. Judges (pres. 1988—89, Elizabeth McCain Meml. award 1989), Nat. Coun. Juvenile and Family Ct. Judges. Presbyterian. Home: 7900 Seven Islands Rd Knoxville TN 37920 Office: Knox County Juvenile Ct 3323 Division St Knoxville TN 37919

GARRETT, DEBORRA ELIZABETH, lawyer; b. Cambridge, Mass., June 6, 1951; d. Joseph Francis and Joan Kathryn (Nauheimer) G.; children: Francis, Joan. BA in Polit. Sci., Pa. State U., 1972; JD, George Washington U., 1976. Bar: Pa. 1976, U.S. Dist. Ct. (ea. dist.) Pa. 1977, Wash. 1979, U.S. Dist. Ct. (we. dist.) Wash. 1979, U.S. Ct. Appeals (9th cir.) 1987, U.S. Supreme Ct. 1990. Staff atty. NLRB, Phila., 1976-79, Evergreen Legal Svcs., Bellingham, Wash., 1979-81; pvt. practice Bellingham, 1981-83; ptnr. Raas, Johnsen, Garrett & Stuen, Bellingham, 1983-93, Zender Thurston, P.S. (formerly Simonarson, Vissar, Zender and Thurston), Bellingham, 1993—. Mem. Bellingham Planning Commn., 1986-93. Mem. Wash. State Bar Assn. (hearing officer 1991—), Whatcom County Bar Assn., Wash. Women Lawyers, Nat. Employment Lawyers Assn. Democrat. Avocations: mountain hiking and climbing, textiles, llamas. Alternative dispute resolution, Labor (including EEOC, Fair Labor Standards Act, labor-management relations, NLRB, OSHA). Office: Zender Thurston PS 1700 D St Bellingham WA 98225-3101

GARRETT, HOWARD LEON, lawyer; b. Tampa, Fla., July 7, 1929; s. Herbert and Frances (Adams) G.; m. Marie Leonora Garcia, Dec. 10, 1950; children— Gloria Susan, Howardene Gay, Leslie Marie Garrett. A.A., U. Fla., 1947, LL.B., 1949, J.D. 1967. Bar: Fla. 1949, U.S. Dist. Ct. (so. dist.) Fla. 1950, U.S. Ct. Appeals (5th cir.) 1950, U.S. Supreme Ct. 1983; cert. cir. civil mediator. Ptnr. Sells & Garrett, 1949-53; ptnr. firm Garrett & Garrett, P.A., Tampa, Fla., 1953— ; assoc. city judge, Tampa, 1965; chmn. Code Enforcement Bd., 1980-84. Author essays on alcoholism (Fla. Bar Assn. award 1983). Served with USAR, 1948-52. Mem. Lawyer-Pilot Bar Assn., Hills County Criminal Def. Lawyers, Hills County Bar Assn., Palma Ceia Golf and Country Club. Democrat. Criminal, Personal injury (including property damage), Probate (including wills, trusts). Office: Garrett & Garrett PA 3314 Henderson Blvd Ste 208 Tampa FL 33609-2934

GARRETT, RICHARD G. lawyer; b. N.Y.C., Oct. 16, 1948; BA magna cum laude, Emory U., 1970, JD, 1973. Bar: Ga. 1973, Fla 1979; U.S. Dist. Ct. (no. dist.) Ga. 1973, (so. dist.) Fla. 1979, U.S. Dist. Ct. (so. dist. trial bar) Fla. 1979; U.S. Ct. Appeals (5th cir.) 1974; U.S. Ct. Appeals (9th. cir., 11 cir.) 1981; U.S. Supreme Ct. 1981. Program dir., instr. rsch., writing and advocacy Emory U. Sch. Law, 1972-73; gen. counsel Greenberg, Traurig, Miami, Fla. Past chmn. litigation dept., exec. com. bd. dirs. Greenberg, Traurig, Miami. Editor Emory Law Journal, 1972-73. Recipient 1st place and Best Brief award Region V Nat. Moot Ct. Competition, 1972. Mem. ABA, The Fla. Bar Assn., State Bar Ga., Omicron Delta Kappa, Order of the Barristers. Banking, Property, real (including real estate development, water), Securities. Office: Greenberg Traurig 1221 Brickell Ave Miami FL 33131-3224

GARRETT, THEODORE LOUIS, lawyer; b. New Britain, Conn., Sept. 4, 1943; s. Louis and Sylvia (Greenberg) G.; m. Bonnie Garrett, Nov. 27, 1968; children— Brandon, Natalie. BA, Yale U., 1965; JD, Columbia U., 1968. Bar: N.Y. 1968, D.C. 1971, U.S. Supreme Ct. 1973. Law clk. to Judge J. Joseph Smith U.S. Ct. Appeals for 2d Circuit, 1968-69; spl. asst. to asst. atty. gen. William H. Rehnquist Dept. Justice, Washington, 1969-70; law clk. to Chief Justice Warren E. Burger U.S. Supreme Ct., 1970-71; assoc. Covington & Burling, Washington, 1971-76, ptnr., 1976—. Editor, prin. author: Corporate Counsel Environmental Law Guide, 1993; author: Environmental Law and the Eleventh Amendment, 2000; co-author: Clean Air Act Desk Book, 1991; contbg. author: A Practical Guide to Environmental Law, 1987, Liability for Hazardous Waste Sites Under CERCLA, 1988, Practice Under the New Federal Sentencing Guidelines, 4th edit., 2001, Environmental Dispute Handbook, 1991, Environmental Litigation, 1991, 2d edit., 1999; editor, contbg. author: The Environmental Law Manual, 1992, RCRA Policy Documents, 1993, RCRA Practice Manual, 1994; contbr. articles to profl. jours. Named One of 100 Influential Lawyers in Nat. Law Jour., 1994. Mem. ABA (chair sect. environ., energy and resources, mem. exec. com. 1995-2001, exec. bd. Environ. Lawyer, adv. bd. ABA Jour., contbg. author Trends, mem. task force on superfund reform, liaison standing com. on environ.law, mem. exec. com. 1995-2002), D.C. Bar Assn. (steering com. environment, energy and natural resources sect., 1991-97, co-chair 1992-94, chair coun. on sects, 94-95). Administrative and regulatory, Federal civil litigation, Environmental. Home: 6604 Broxburn Dr Bethesda MD 20817-4710 Office: Covington & Burling 1201 Pennsylvania Ave NW PO Box 7566 Washington DC 20044-7566 E-mail: tgarrett@cov.com.

GARRETT, WILLIAM WALTON, retired law educator; b. Birmingham, Ala., Aug. 13, 1926; s. H. Bascom and Josephine (Pattillo) G.; m. Marion Huey, July 31, 1950; children: Susan Garrett Hodgson, William W. Garrett Jr. A.C.E., Oreg. State U., 1946; BBA, U. Ala., 1950; LLB, Birmingham Law Sch., 1954; JD, Cumberland Law Sch., 1961; LLM, Yale U., 1962. Merchant WW Garrett & Son, Birmingham, 1950-60; atty. in pvt. practice Birmingham, 1954-61; prof. law U. Memphis, Tenn., 1962-85, ret., 1985. Author: Tennessee Divorce Alimony and Child Custody, 2002; editor Tenn. Family Law Letter, 1985—. Sunday sch. tchr. First United Meth. Ch., Waynesville, N.C., 1987—; project dir. Haywood Habitat for Humanity, 1995—. With U.S. Army, 1943-46. Democrat. Avocations: librarian, swimming, volunteering. Home: PO Box 911 1873 Lakeshore Dr Lake Junaluska NC 28745-8700

GARRIGLE, WILLIAM ALOYSIUS, lawyer; b. Camden, N.J., Aug. 6, 1941; s. John Michael and Catherine Agnes (Ebeling) G.; m. Jeannette R. Regan, Aug. 15, 1965 (div.); children: Maeve Regan, Emily Way; m. Rosalind Chadwick, Feb. 17, 1984; 1 child, Susan Chadwick. BS, LaSalle U., 1963; LLB, Boston Coll., 1966. Bar: N.J. 1966, U.S. Dist. Ct. N.J., U.S. Ct. Appeals (3rd cir.) 1973, U.S. Supreme Ct., 1973; cert. civil trial atty., N.J.; cert. civil trial adv., Nat. Bd. Trial Advocacy; diplomate Am. Bd. Profl. Liability Attys. Assoc. Taylor, Bischoff, Neutze & Williams, Camden, 1966-67, Moss & Powell, Camden, 1967-70; ptnr. Garrigle and Palm, Cherry Hill, N.J., 1970—. Sr. counsel Am. Coll. Barristers. With USAR, 1959-67. Mem. ABA, N.J. State Bar Assn., Burlington County Bar Assn., Camden County Bar Assn., Internat. Assn. Def. Counsel, Def. Rsch. Inst., N.J. Def. Assn., Am. Bd. Trial Advs. (diplomate; pres. South Jersey chpt. 2001), Fedn. of Ins. and Corp. Counsel, Trial Attys. N.J., Camden County Inn of Ct. (master of the bench, chmn. 1989-96, treas. 1996—), Tavistock Country Club. Federal civil litigation, State civil litigation, Insurance. Home: 223 E Main St Moorestown NJ 08057-2905 Office: Garrigle and Palm 1415 Route 70 E Ste 204 Cherry Hill NJ 08034-2237 E-mail: garrigle@aol.com.

GARRISH, THEODORE JOHN, lawyer; b. Detroit, Jan. 6, 1943; s. Theodore and Adella Beatrice (Kimball) G.; m. Joy Ann Ziegler, Aug. 4, 1967 (div. 1979); children: Theodore John, Amelia Sutter. AB, U. Mich., 1964; JD cum laude, Wayne State U., 1968. Bar: Mich. 1969, D.C. 1972. Trial atty. U.S. Dept. Justice, Washington, 1969-72; pub. opinion analyst Com. for Reelection of Pres., Washington, 1972; chief advt. substantiation FTC, Washington, 1973-74; asst. spl. counsel to Pres. Washington, 1974; asst. to sec. U.S. Dept. Interior, Washington, 1976, legis. counsel, 1981-82; gen. counsel Consumer Product Safety Commn., Washington, 1976-78; ptnr. Deane, Snowdon, Shutler, Garrish & Gherardi, Washington, 1978-81; gen. counsel Dept. Energy, Washington, 1983-85, asst. sec., 1985-89; fed. inspector Alaska Natural Gas Transp. System, 1986-89; Wash. counsel The Flanagan Group, 1989-91; pres. Brewery Mgmt. Co., 1989-94, Kent Island Investment Co., 1989-91, chmn., 1991-94; mng. ptnr. Wild Gooose Brewery, 1989-91, dir., 1994-98. Mem. U.S. Adminstrv. Conf., Washington, 1976-78, 83-85, President's Commn. on Catastrophic Nuclear Accidents, 1988-90; sr. v.p. Am. Nuclear Energy Coun., 1991-94; v.p. Nuclear Energy Inst., 1994-2000; energy program mgr. Bechtel Nat., Inc., 2001—; instr. George Washington U., 1995-98; legis. coun. U. Calif., 2000-01. Del. Mich. Rep. Conv., 1966; asst. to group dir. Presdl. Inaugural Com., 1973, dep. exec. dir., 1981; mem. adv. com. on human concerns Rep. Nat. Com., 1979; adv. Nat. Policy Forum, 1994-96; dir. Nat. Energy Resources Orgn., 1987-2001, counsel, 2001—. Mem. FBA, Mich. Bar Assn., D.C. Bar Assn., Alpha Delta Phi Congregationalist. Legislative, Natural resources. Home: 103 Chesapeake Ave Annapolis MD 21403-3305 Office: 1015 15th St Ste 700 Washington DC 20005-2605 E-mail: tedco2000@hotmail.com.

GARRITY, VINCENT FRANCIS, JR., lawyer; b. Phila., July 26, 1937; s. Vincent Francis and Anne (Glenn) G.; m. Maryellen O'Brien, May 8, 1965; children: Vincent III, Ellen, Christopher, Elisa. AB cum laude, Coll. of Holy Cross, Worcester, Mass., 1959; LLB, Harvard U., 1962. Bar: Pa. 1963, U.S. Dist. Ct. (ea. dist.) Pa. 1963. Assoc. Duane, Morris & Heckscher, Phila., 1963-70; ptnr. Duane, Morris LLP, Phila., 1970—2002, co-chmn. bus. law dept., 1981—94, of counsel, 2003—. Lectr., U. Pa. Law Sch., 2000, 02, 03; disting. practitioner in residence Cornell Law Sch., 2001; adj. prof. Temple U. Sch. Law, 1996—; presenter, panelist in field. Contbr. numerous articles to profl. jours. With USAR, 1962—68. Fellow Am. Bar Found.; mem. ABA (com. on corp laws bus. law sect. 1983-89, participant in preparation Model Bus. Corp. Act, vice chmn. 1991-95, chmn. 1995-98, com. on negotiated acquisitions), Pa. Bar Assn. (chmn. sect. corp. banking and bus. law 1981-83, vice chmn. Title 15 task force on 1988 Pa. Bus. Corp. Law 1983—, Spl. Achievement award 1982), Am. Law Inst. (elected), Merion Golf Club (Ardmore, Pa.), Union League Phila. Roman Catholic. Corporate, general. Home: 118 Derwen Rd Bala Cynwyd PA 19004-2710 E-mail: garrity@duanemorris.com.

GARSON, ANDREW S. lawyer; b. N.Y.C., Nov. 12, 1952; m. Virginia Geiss, June 15, 1981; children: Danielle M, Sara A. BA with honors in Am. History, Clark U., Worcester, Mass., 1974; JD, Boston U., 1978. Bar: Mass. 1978, N.Y. 1979. Asst. dist. atty. Kings County Dist. Atty., Bklyn., 1978—82; assoc. trial atty. Martin Clearwater & Bell, N.Y.C., 1982—88; trial atty./ptnr. Belair & Evans, N.Y.C., 1988—99; sr. ptnr. Garson Gerspach DeCorato & Cohen, N.Y.C., 2000—. Lectr. in field. Contbr. Mem.: ATLA, N.Y. State Bar Assn., N.Y. State Trial Lawyers Assn. Avocation: triathlon competition. Personal injury (including property damage), Health, Professional liability. Office: Garson Gerspach DeCorato & Cohen LLP One Wall Street Ct 14 Fl New York NY 10005 Office Fax: 212-742-1471. Personal E-mail: garson@ggdclaw.com. E-mail: garson@ggdclaw.com.

GARTH, BRYANT GEOFFREY, law educator, foundation executive; b. San Diego, Dec. 9, 1949; s. William and Patricia (Feild) G.; m. Gwendolyn Sessions; children: Heather, Andrew, Daniela. BA magna cum laude, Yale U., 1972; JD, Stanford U., 1975; PhD, European U. Inst., Florence, Italy, 1979. Bar: Calif. 1975, Ind. 1988. Law clk. to judge U.S. Dist. Ct. (no. dist.) Calif., San Francisco, 1978-79; asst. prof. Ind. U., Bloomington, 1979-82, assoc. prof., 1982-85, prof., 1985-92, dean Law Sch., 1986-90; dir. Am. Bar Found., Chgo., 1990—. Cons. Ont. Law Reform Commn., 1984-85, 94, World Bank Argentina Project, 1993-94, World Bank Ecuador Project, 2003; vis. assoc. prof. U. Mich., Ann Arbor, 1983-84; bd. dirs. Internat. Human Rights Law Inst.; mem. bd. visitors Stanford U. Law Sch., 1993-2000. Author: Neighborhood Law Firms for the Poor, 1980; co-editor: Access to Justice: A World Survey, 1978, Access to Justice: Emerging Issues and Perspectives, 1979, Dealing in Virtue, 1996, Internationalization of Palace Wars, 2002; contbr. articles to profl. jours. V.p. H.G. & K.F. Montgomery Found. Rsch. grantee NSF, 1982, 91, 92, 95, 99, 2001, Nat. Inst. Dispute Resolution, 1985, Ind. Supreme Ct., 1989, Italian Coun. Rsch., 1989, Keck, 1995, MacArthur, 1997. Mem.: Law and Soc. Assn., Am. Law Inst. Democrat. Office: Am Bar Found 750 N Lake Shore Dr Chicago IL 60611-4403 E-mail: bggarth@abfn.org.

GARTH, LEONARD I. judge; b. Bklyn., Apr. 7, 1921; s. Frank A. and Anne F. Goldstein; m. Sarah Miriam Kaufman, Sept. 6, 1942; 1 child, Tobie Gail Garth Meisel. BA, Columbia U., 1942; postgrad., Nat. Inst. Pub. Affairs, 1942—43; LLB, Harvard U., 1952. Bar: N.J. 1952. Mem. firm Cole, Berman & Garth (and predecessors), Paterson, NJ, 1952—70; judge U.S. Dist. Ct. for Dist. N.J., Newark, 1970—73; U.S. cir. judge Ct. Appeals for 3d Cir., 1973—; lectr. Inst. Continuing Legal Edn.; lectr., coadj. mem. faculty Rutgers U. Law Sch., 1978—98, Seton Hall Law Sch., 1980—95. Mem. N.J. Bd. Bar Examiners, 1964—68; mem. com. on revision gen. and admiralty rules Fed. Dist. Ct. N.J.; former mem. com. on fin. disclosure Jud. Conf. U.S.; adv. bd. Fed. Cts. Study Com. Pres.; trustee Harvard Law Sch. Assn. N.J., 1958—63; adv. bd. Law and Soc. Major of Ramapo Coll. 1st lt. U.S. Army, 1943—46. Mem.: FBA, ABA (N.J. fellows, appellate judges conf.), Am. Law Inst., Passaic County (N.J.) Bar Assn. (pres. 1967—68). Office: Ct Appeals ML King Jr Fed Bldg 50 Walnut St Rm 5040 Newark NJ 07102-3506 also: 20613 US Courthouse Philadelphia PA 19106 E-mail: chambers_of_judge_leonard_garth@ca3.uscourts.gov.

GARTNER, HAROLD HENRY, III, lawyer; b. L.A., June 23, 1948; s. Harold Henry Jr. and Frances Mildred (Evans) G.; m. Denise Helene Young, June 7, 1975 (div. 2002); children: Patrick Christopher, Matthew Alexander. Student, Pasadena City Coll., 1966-67, George Williams Coll., 1967-68, Calif. State U., Los Angeles, 1969; JD cum laude, Loyola U., Los Angeles, 1972. Bar: Calif. 1972, U.S. Dist. Ct. (cen. dist.) Calif. 1973, U.S. Ct. Appeals (9th cir.) 1973. Assoc. Hitt, Murray & Caffray, Long Beach, Calif., 1972; dep. city atty. City of L.A., 1972-73; assoc. Patterson, Ritner & Lockwood, L.A., 1973-79; mng. ptnr. all offices Patterson, Ritner, Lockwood, Gartner & Jurich, L.A., Ventura, Bakersfield, and San Bernardino, Calif., 1991—. Instr. law Ventura Coll., 1981. Recipient Am. Jurisprudence award Trusts and Equity, 1971. Mem. ABA, Am. Bd. Trial Advocates, Calif. Bar Assn., Ventura County Bar Assn., Nat. Assn. Def. Counsel, Assn. Am. Bd. Trial Advocates, So. Calif. Def. Counsel, Ventura County Trial Lawyers Assn. Clubs: Pacific Corinthian Yacht. Republican. Avocations: sailing, scuba diving, flying. State civil litigation, Insurance, Personal injury (including property damage). Home: 272 Camino Toluca Camarillo CA 93010 Office: Patterson Ritner Lockwood Gartner & Jurich 260 Maple Ct Ste 231 Ventura CA 93003-3570 E-mail: hgartner@dock.net.

GARTON, THOMAS WILLIAM, lawyer; b. Ft. Dodge, Iowa, Jan. 19, 1947; s. H. Boyd and Ruth A. (Porter) G.; m. Marcia K. Hoover, June 21, 1969; children: Geoffrey, Matthew. BA, Carleton Coll., 1969; JD magna cum laude, U. Minn., 1974. Assoc. Fredrikson & Byron, PA, Mpls., 1974-80, shareholder, 1980—, chmn. corp. practice group. Adj. prof. William Mitchell Coll. Law, St. Paul, Minn., 1977-80, U. Minn. Law Sch., Mpls., 1980; bd. dirs. RS/Eden Programs; presenter continuing legal edn. seminars on tax, mergers and acquisitions, and bus. planning, 1977—. With U.S. Army, 1969-71. Mem. ABA (tax sect.), Minn. Bar Assn. (dir. tax coun. 1987-89). Corporate, general, Mergers and acquisitions, Corporate taxation. Office: Fredrikson & Byron PA 4000 Pillsbury Ctr 200 S Sixth St Minneapolis MN 55402-1425 E-mail: tgarton@fredlaw.com.

GARTS, JAMES RUFUS, JR., lawyer; b. Meadville, Pa., Mar. 22, 1949; s. James Rufus and Priscilla Jane (Greer) G.; m. Susan Damian Hord, June 3, 1971; children: Katherine Elizabeth, James Rufus III, Emily Alice. BA, Tulane U., 1971, JD, 1974. Bar: Tenn. 1974, U.S. Dist. Ct. (we. dist.) Tenn. 1983, U.S. Ct. Appeals (6th cir.) 1984. Assoc. Chandler, Manire, Harris and Shelton, Memphis, 1974-76; asst. dist. atty. gen. State of Tenn., Memphis, 1976-79; ptnr. Harris, Shelton, Dunlap, Cobb and Ryder, Memphis, 1979—; spl. judge Shelby County, 1984. Lectr. continuing edn. Memphis State U., 1988—. Pres. Lakewood Hills Property Owners Assn., 1989-93. Fellow Am. Coll. Trial Lawyers; mem. ABA, Tenn. Bar Assn., Memphis Bar Assn. (bd. dirs. 1989-90, 2000-01), Memphis Lawyers Jour. Club, Phi Beta Kappa. Republican. Federal civil litigation, State civil litigation, Criminal. Home: 3200 Homewood Dr Memphis TN 38128-4408 Office: Harris Shelton Dunlap Cobb & Ryder 1 Commerce Sq Ste 2700 Memphis TN 38103

GARVEY, JANE ROBERTS, lawyer; b. N.Y.C., Oct. 21, 1919; d. George Alexander and Helen Hickson (Hernon) Roberts; m. Francis Bernard Garvey, June 1, 1946; children: Ellen, Jane, Francis B. Jr. BA, Coll. New Rochelle (N.Y.), 1938; LLB, Columbia U., 1941. Bar: N.Y. 1942, U.S. Bd. Immigration Appeals 1957, U.S. Immigration and Naturalization Svc. 1957, U.S. Supreme Ct. 1958. Jr. assoc. Wikes, Riddel, Bloomer, Jacobi & Maguire, N.Y.C., 1942-44; assoc. Jackson, Nash, Brophy, Barringer & Brooks, N.Y.C., 1944-46; ptnr. Francis B. Garvey Esq., Babylon, N.Y., 1946—. Gov., internat. dir. Zonta Internat., Chgo., 1982-86; dir. planned giving Am. Heart Assn., 1984-87. Recipient spl. commendation USN, 1946, hon. commendation Suffolk County (N.Y.) Legislature, 1983, Angela Merici award for achievement in profl. and civic activities, Ursula Lauris citation for Disting. Svc. to Coll. of New Rochelle, 1978; named Hon. Big Sister of Yr., Big Sister/Big Bros., Washington, 1977, named to LAdy Comdr. Equestrian Order of the Holy Sepulchre granted by Pope John XXIII, named Woman of Yr., Zonta Internat., Suffolk County, 1991. Mem. ABA, N.Y. Bar Assn., Babylon Yacht Club, Southward Ho Golf Club (hon.), Zonta Internat. Found. (pres. 1998-2000). Republican. Roman Catholic. Avocations: sailing, travel. Probate (including wills, trusts), Estate taxation, Personal income taxation. Home: 64 W Islip Rd West Islip NY 11795-4536 Office: Francis B Garvey PO Box 788 Babylon NY 11702-0788

GARVEY, JOHN HUGH, dean, law educator; b. Sharon, Pa., Sept. 28, 1948; s. Cyril T. and Claudia C. (Evans) G.; m. Jeanne Barnes Walter, Aug. 30, 1975. AB, U. Notre Dame, 1970; JD, Harvard U., 1974. Bar: Ky. 1976, U.S. Supreme Ct. 1982. Law clk. to chief judge U.S. Ct. Appeals (2d cir.), N.Y.C., 1974-75; assoc. Morrison & Foerster, San Francisco, 1975-76; asst. prof. Coll. Law U. Ky., Lexington, 1976-79, assoc. prof. Coll. Law, 1979-80, prof. Coll. Law, 1981-94; Univ. Rsch. prof. Coll. Law, 1989-90, Ashland prof., 1990-94; prof. Notre Dame Law Sch., South Bend, Ind., 1994-99; dean Boston Coll. Law Sch., Chestnut Hill, 1999—. Asst. to Solicitor Gen., U.S. Dept. Justice, Washington, 1981-84; vis. prof. law sch. U. Mich., Ann Arbor, 1985-86; chmn. constl. law sect. Assn. Am. Law Schs., Washington, 1991-93, chmn. law and religion sect., 1998-99. Author: Modern Constitutional Theory, 1989, 4th edit., 1999, The First Amendment, 1992, 2d edit., 1995, What Are Freedoms For?, 1996. Fellow Danforth Found., 1970. Mem. Am. Law Inst. Office: Boston Coll Law Sch Stuart HseM307 885 Centre St Newton Center MA 02459

GARVEY, RICHARD ANTHONY, lawyer; b. N.Y.C., Jan. 10, 1950; s. James Joseph Garvey and Janet Mary (Mooney) Rowse. AB, Boston Coll., 1972; JD, Harvard U., 1975. Bar: N.Y. 1976. Assoc. Simpson Thacher & Bartlett, N.Y.C., 1975-82, ptnr., 1982-93, 97—. Mem. ABA, N.Y. State Bar Assn., Assn. Bar City N.Y., Phi Beta Kappa. Corporate, general, Mergers and acquisitions, Securities. Address: c/o Simpson Thacher & Bartlett 425 Lexington Ave New York NY 10017 E-mail: rgarvey@stblaw.com.

GARWOOD, WILLIAM LOCKHART, judge; b. Houston, Tex., Oct. 29, 1931; s. Wilmer St. John and Ellen Burdine (Clayton) Garwood; m. Merle Castlyn Haffler, Aug. 12, 1955; children: William Lockhart, Mary Elliott. BA, Princeton U., 1952; LLB with honors, U. Tex., 1955. Bar: Tex. 1955, U.S. Supreme Ct. 1959. Law clk. to judge U.S. Ct. Appeals (5th cir.), 1955—56; mem. Graves, Dougherty, Hearon, Moody & Garwood (and predecessor firms), Austin, Tex., 1959—79, 1981; justice Supreme Ct. Tex., Austin, 1979—80; judge U.S. Ct. Appeals (5th cir.), 1981—97, sr. judge, 1997—; dir. Anderson, Clayton & Co., 1976—79, 1981, exec. com., 1977—79, 1981. Mem. adv. com. on appellate rules U.S. Cts., 1994—2001, chair, 1997—2001. Pres. Child and Family Svc. of Austin, 1970—71, St. Andrew's Episcopal Sch., Austin, 1972; bd. dirs. Cmty. Coun. Austin and Travis County, 1968—72, Human Opportunities Corp. Austin and Travis County, 1966—70, Mental Health and Mental Retardation Ctr. Austin and Travis County, 1966—69, United Fund Austin and Travis County, 1971—73; mem. adv. bd. Salvation Army, Austin, 1972—. With U.S. Army, 1956—59. Fellow: Tex. Bar Found. (life); mem.: Tex. Law Rev. Assn. (pres. 1990—91, dir. 1986—96), Am. Law Inst. (life), Chancellors, Phi Delta Phi, Order of Coif. Episcopalian. Office: US Ct Appeals Homer Thornberry Jud Bldg 903 San Jacinto Blvd Austin TX 78701-2451

GARY, THOMAS, lawyer; b. Englewood, NJ, Apr. 29, 1950; s. Alfred and Gloria Gary; m. Deborahann Theresa Berko (div.); 1 child, Jordan Ian; m. Olga C. Puerto, Nov. 23, 1994. BA, Oberlin Coll., 1972; JD, Emory U., 1975; LLM in Taxation, U. Miami, 1984, MBA, 1997. Bar: Pa. 1975, Mo. 1980, US Supreme Ct. 1980, Fla. 1983, US Dist. Ct. (so. dist.) Fla. 1986, US Dist. Ct. (no. dist.) Fla. 2002, US Ct. Appeals (11th cir.) 1986. Law clk. to Hon. Caleb R. Layton III, Wilmington, Del., 1975-76; assoc. in contract litigation White and Williams, Phila., 1976-78; assoc. in comml. litigation Morgan, Lewis & Bockius, Phila., 1978-80; ptnr. in labor litig. Elliot, Kaiser & Freeman, Kans. City, Mo., 1980-82; assoc. in contract and comml. litig. Niewald, Waldeck, Norris & Brown, Kans. City, Mo., 1982-83; dir. tax practice Beasley, Olle & Downs, Miami, Fla., 1984-85; prin. Thomas Gary & Assoc., P.A., Coral Gables, Fla., 1985-99; sr. asst. atty. gen. antitrust sect. State of Fla., Tallahassee, 1999—. Bd. editors The Matrimonial Strategist, 1975—. Mem. oversight com. Put Something Back, 1996-99; mem. Coral Gables City/HS Rels. Com., 1995-99. Mem. ABA, Tallahassee Bar Assn. Federal civil litigation, State civil litigation, Family and matrimonial. Home: 1384 White Star Ln Tallahassee FL 32312-7520 Office: Office of Atty Gen PL-01 The Capitol Tallahassee FL 32399-1050 E-mail: tom_gary@oag.state.fl.us.

GARZA, REYNALDO G. federal judge; b. Brownsville, Tex., July 7, 1915; s. Ygnacio and Zoila (Guerra) Garza; m. Bertha Champion, June 9, 1943; children: Reynaldo G., David C., Ygnacio Daniel, Bertha Victoria, Monica Bernadette. AA, Brownsville Jr. Coll., 1935; BA, U. Tex., 1937; LLB, U. Tex. Sch. of Law, 1939; LLD (hon.), U. St. Edwards, Austin, Tex., 1965. Bar: Tex. 1939. Sole practice, 1939—42, 1946—50; ptnr. Sharpe, Cunningham & Garza, 1950—60, Cunningham, Garza & Yznaga, 1960—61; judge U.S. Dist. Ct. Tex., Brownsville, 1961—74, chief judge, 1974—79; circuit judge U.S. Ct. Appeals (5th cir.), Brownsville, Tex., 1979—82, sr. judge, 1982—. Treas. Cameron County Child Welfare Bd., 1950—52; mem. Tex. Good Neighbor Commn., 1957—61; commr. City of Brownsville, 1947—49; trustee Brownsville Ind. Sch. Dist., 1941—42. Served with USAF, 1942—45. Decorated knight Order St. Gregory the Great, Pius XII; recipient Pro Ecclesia et Pontifice medal, Pope Pius XII, 1952. Mem.: State Bar of Tex., Cameron County Bar Assn. Office: US Ct Appeals 600 E Harrison St Brownsville TX 78520-7114

GASAWAY, LAURA NELL, law librarian, legal educator; b. Searcy, Ark., Feb. 24, 1945; d. Merel Roger and Carnell (Miller) G. BA, Tex. Woman's U., 1967, MLS, 1968; JD, U. Houston, 1973. Bar: Tex. 1974. Catalog libr. U. Houston, 1968-70, cataloging-circulation libr., 1970-72, asst. law libr., 1972-73, law libr., asst. prof. law, 1973-75; dir. law libr., prof. law U. Okla., Norman, 1975-85; dir. law libr., prof. law U. N.C., 1985—; copyright cons. Recipient Calvert prize U. Okla., 1978, 81, Compton award Ark. Librs. Assn., 1986. Fellow Spl. Librs. Assn. (H.W. Wilson award 1983, John Cotton Dana award 1987, Fannie Simon award, 1992); mem. ABA, State Bar Tex., N.C. Bar Assn., Am. Assn. Law Librs. (pres. 1986-87). Democrat. Author: Growing Pains: Adapting Copyright for Libraries, Education and Society, 1997; co-author: (with Maureen Murphy) Legal Protection for Computer Programs, 1980, (with James Hoover and Dorothy Warden) American Indian Legal Materials, A Union List, 1981, (with Bruce S. Johnson and James M. Murray) Law Library Management during Fiscal Austerity, 1992, (with Sarah K. Wiant) Libraries and Copyright: A Guide to Copyright in the 1990s, 1994, (with Michael D. Chiorazzi) Law Librarianship: Historical Perspectives, 1996, Growling Pains: Adapting Copyright for Libraries, Education and Society, 1997. Office: U NC Law Libr Clb # 3385 Chapel Hill NC 27599-0001

GASBARRO, PASCO, JR., lawyer; b. Providence, Apr. 3, 1944; s. Pasco and Helen (Casali) G.; m. Mary Alyce McNamara, May 30, 1967; children: Pasco, John A., Christopher E. AB, Brown U., Providence, 1966; JD, Boston U., 1969. Bar: R.I. 1969, U.S. Dist. Ct. R.I. 1971, Mass. 1972, U.S. Dist. Ct. Mass. 1974. Law clk. R.I. Supreme Ct., Providence, 1969-70; atty. R.I. Legal Svcs., Providence, 1970-71, New Eng. Elec., Westborough, Mass., 1971-76; counsel Narragansett Elec. Co., Providence, 1976-79; asst. gen. counsel New Eng. Elec., Westborough, 1979-83; ptnr. Hinckley, Allen & Snyder LLP, Providence, Boston, Concord, NH, 1983—. Del. White House Conf. on Small Bus., 1995; mem. adv. Advanced Technol. Mfg. Ctr. Former chmn. adv. coun. R.I. Small Bus. Devel. Ctr.; mem. adv. bd. Advanced Tech. and Mfg. Ctr. Mem. ABA, R.I. Bar Assn., Brown Club of R.I. Corporate, general, General practice, Utilities, public. Office: Hinckley Allen & Snyder LLP 1500 Fleet Ctr Providence RI 02903-2319

GASIORKIEWICZ, EUGENE ANTHONY, lawyer; b. Milw., Jan. 7, 1950; s. Eugene Constantine and Loretta Ann (Kasprzak) G.; m. Jana Jamieson, Jan. 12, 1980; children: Suzanne A., Alexei E. AB, Regis Coll., 1971; JD, U. Miss., 1974. Bar: Wis. 1974, U.S. Supreme Ct. 1986. Law clk. to presiding justice Miss. Supreme Ct., Jackson, 1974-75; assoc. Schoone, McManus & Hanson SC, Racine, Wis., 1975-79; ptnr. Hanson & Gasiorkiewicz SC, Racine, Wis., 1979-90; pres., shareholder Hanson, Gasiorkiewicz & Weber, SC, Racine, 1990-96, Hanson & Gasiorkiewicz, SC, Racine, 1997—. Lectr. labor law U. Wis., Racine, 1975-76, worker's comp., State Bar Wis., 1984-86, med. malpractice, Wis. Acad. Trial Lawyers, 1986. Mcpl. judge Village of Wind Point, Wis., 1983-85; moot ct. instr., The Prairie Sch., Racine, 1986-87. Named one of Best Lawyers in Am., Consumer Guide, 2001. Mem. State Bar Wis. (spl. ethics com. regarding trust accts. 1988-89), Assn. Trial Lawyers Am., Am. Arbitration Assn., Wis. Acad. Trial Lawyers (bd. dirs. 1999—), Nat. Bd. Trial Advocacy (cert. civil trial advocate), Racine County Bar Assn. (liaison local physicians and attys. 1990—). Roman Catholic. Avocation: tennis. Federal civil litigation, Personal injury (including property damage). Home: 3929 S Brook Rd Franksville WI 53126-9303 Office: Hanson & Gasiorkiewicz SC 2932 Northwestern Ave Racine WI 53404-2249 E-mail: info@lawracine.com.

GASKELL, JUDITH ANN, law librarian; b. Littlefork, Minn., Oct. 22, 1945; d. Charles Thomas and Mabel Harriet (Armitage) G. BA, Carleton Coll., 1967; MA, U. Chgo., 1975; JD, DePaul U., 1980. Bar: Ill. 1980. Law firm libr. Sonnenschein, Carlin, Nath & Rosenthal, Chgo., 1974-76; reference libr. U. Chgo. Law Libr., Chgo., 1977-79, head pub. svcs., 1980-83; dir. law libr. DePaul U. Law Libr., Chgo., 1983—. Bd. dirs. Chgo. Libr. System, pres., 1999-2001. Bd. dirs. Shirley Heinze Environ. Fund, Michigan City, Ind., 1992—, chair Land Strategy Com. 1997-. Mem. Am. Assn. Law Librs., Assn. Am. Law Schs. (chair sect. on law librs. 2001-2002), Chgo. Assn. Law Librs. (pres. 1983-84, Agnes Harvey Reid award 1990-91). Avocations: environmental restoration, natural gardening. Office: DePaul Univ Law Libr 25 E Jackson Blvd Chicago IL 60604-2289

GASS, DAVID, lawyer; b. Appleton, Wis., May 21, 1956; s. Orville Eugene and Lois Helen (Bellin) G.; m. Cheryl Ann Schloss, Feb. 22, 1986. BA, U. Wis., 1978, JD, 1981. Bar: Wis. 1981, U.S. Dist. Ct. (ea. and we. dists.) Wis 1981. Assoc. Rohde, Dales, Melzer, TeWinkle & Gass, Sheboygan, Wis., 1981-85; ptnr. Rohde Dales LLP, Sheboygan, Wis., 1986—. Chair Sheboygan County Rep. Com., 1996—, chair, 2002—; mem. City of Sheboygan Planning Commn., 1985—, City of Sheboygan Park and Forestry Commn., 1983—; bd. dirs. Vis. Nurses Assn., pres., 1986-90; past v.p., bd. dirs. Big Bros.-Big Sisters Sheboygan County; pres. Calvary Evang. Luth. Ch., Sheboygan, 1984-86, mem. ch. coun., 1992—; bd. dirs. Ptnrs. for Community Devel., Inc., pres. 1989—; bd. dirs. Sheboygan Area United Way, 1990—, pres., 2000-01; bd. dirs. Sheboygan Meml. Hosp. Found., Inc., VNA Found., Inc., Insight, Inc., Rehab. Ctr. of Sheboygan County, 1999—; bd. dirs. U. Wis.-Sheboygan Found., 1997—, v.p., 2002—; mem. ethics com. Sheboygan Meml. Med. Ctr., 1990—. Mem. ABA, Wis. Bar Assn., Sheboygan County Bar Assn., Sheboygan Jaycees (pres. 1984-85, Outstanding Wis. Pres. award 1985), Sheboygan County C. of C. (bd. dirs. 1990—), Optimists (pres. Sheboygan 1988-89, Disting. Pres. award 1989), Sheboygan County C. of C. (bd. dirs.). Avocations: woodworking, reading, sports. Bankruptcy, Commercial, consumer (including collections, credit), General practice. Office: Rohde Dales LLP 607 Plaza 8 Ste 400 Sheboygan WI 53081-4513

GASS, RAYMOND WILLIAM, lawyer, consumer products company executive; b. Chgo., Apr. 6, 1937; s. William Frederick and Clara Gertrude (Grotman) G.; m. Patricia Ann Thomas, Apr. 20, 1968; children: Elizabeth Ann, Katharine Patricia, Christina Susanne. BS, Purdue U., 1959; LLB, U. Ill., 1962. Bar: Ill. Patent examiner U.S. Patent Office, Washington, 1962-63; atty. Armour and Co., Chgo., 1963-70; sr. atty. Greyhound Corp., Chgo., 1970-71; sr. v.p., gen. counsel, sec. John Morrell & Co., Chgo., 1971-89; v.p., gen. counsel Alberto-Culver Co., Melrose Park, Ill., 1989-98. Bd. dirs. Am. Chemet Corp., Columbia Paint and Coating Co. Mem. ABA, Chgo. Bar Assn. (chmn. corp. law depts. 1975-77) Antitrust, Corporate, general, Labor (including EEOC, Fair Labor Standards Act, labor-management relations, NLRB, OSHA).

GASSER, CHRISTOPH JOHANNES, lawyer; b. St. Gallen, Switzerland, Jan. 30, 1969; s. Hans Emil and Annemarie Madelaine Gasser. LLD summa cum laude, U. Berne, Switzerland, 1997; LLM, U. Mich., 1998. Bar: Switzerland 1994. Law clk. Krneta & Ptnrs., Berne, 1991—92, Dist. Ct. Burdgorf, Berne, 1992; acad. rsch. asst. U. Berne, 1994—97; rschr. Swiss Trademark Office, Berne, 1995; legal counsel Swatch Group, Bienne, Switzerland, 1996; fgn. atty. Pennie & Edmonds LLP, N.Y.C., 1998; atty. Lenz & Staehelin, Zurich, 1999—. Lectr. U. Zurich, Switzerland, 1999—, Swiss Fed. Inst. Tech., Zurich, 2000—. Author: (book) Information Highway, 1996, Fair Use in Copyright, 1997; contbr. articles to profl. jours. Mem.: Licensing Execs. Soc. Internat., Internat. Assn. Protection Intellectual Property, Internat. Trademark Assn. (mem. ADR com. 2002—). Trademark and copyright, Intellectual property, Sports. Office: Lenz & Staehelin Bleicherweg 58 8027 Zürich Switzerland

GASSERE, EUGENE ARTHUR, lawyer, business executive; b. Beaumont, Tex., Oct. 20, 1930; s. Victor Eugene and Althea June (Haight) G.; m. Mary Alice Engelhard, Aug. 4, 1956; children— Paul, John, Anne. BS, U. Wis., 1952, JD, 1956; postgrad., Oxford U., 1956-57. Bar: Wis. bar 1956. Asst. counsel Wurlitzer Co., Chgo., 1958-61, Campbell Soup Co., Camden, N.J., 1961-65; asst. to pres. Thilmany Pulp & Paper Co., Kaukauna, Wis., 1966-68; with Skyline Corp., Elkhart, Ind., 1968-92, v.p., gen. counsel, asst. sec., 1973-92, ret., 1992—. Pres., bd. dirs. Elkhart Urban League, 1972-73, Elkhart Symphony, 1975-76, Elkhart Concert Club, 1976-77. Served with U.S. Army, 1952-54. Mem. Wis. Bar Assn., Phi Mu Alpha. Home: PO Box 165 Mindoro WI 54644-0165 Office: Skyline Corp 2520 Bypass Rd Elkhart IN 46514-1584 E-mail: pelt2ridge@aol.com.

GAST, RICHARD SHAEFFER, lawyer; b. Pueblo, Colo., Aug. 1, 1956; s. Robert Shaeffer and Ann (Day) G.; m. Beverly Paterson, Aug. 22, 1981; children: Charles Edward, Robert Shaeffer. BA, Stanford U., 1978; JD, U. Colo., 1981. Bar: Colo. 1981, U.S. Dist. Ct. Colo. 1981. Assoc. March, Myatt, Korb, Carroll & Brandes, Ft. Collins, Colo., 1981-85; shareholder, officer, dir. March & Myatt, P.C., Ft. Collins, Colo., 1985-97, Myatt Brandes & Gast PC, Ft. Collins, 1998—. Bd. dirs. Elk Falls Ranch Co., Legacy Land Trust; mem. Jud. Performance Commn., 1992-94. Contbg. editor U. Colo. Law Rev., 1980-81. Organizer local fundraising Am. Cancer Soc., Ft. Collins, 1985-86; mem. Larimer County Land Use Plan Citizens' Rev. Com., Ft. Collins, 1986; mem. choices 95 com., Ft. Collins, 1988; dir. Colo. Lawyers Trust Account Found., 1990-96, chair, grants com., 1990-96, pres., 1995-96; bd. dirs. Ft. Collins Area United Way, 1991-98, pres., 1996-97; bd. dirs. Neighbor to Neighbor, Inc., 1988-91; hearing officer Poudre Sch. Dist., 1995-97. Mem. ABA (corps., bus. and banking law sect.), Colo. Bar Assn. (mem. exec. coun. young lawyers divsn. 1988-91, chmn. 1990-91, bd. govs. 1990-91, 97-98, v.p. 1997-98, exec. coun. 1997-98, budget com. 1997-2000, real estate sect. coun. 1998—, chair 2003—, bd. govs. 1990-91, 97-98, long-range planning com. 2000-01, joint mgmt. com. 2001—, chair 2003-, Outstanding Young Lawyer 1987), Larimer County Bar Assn. (chmn. legal aid program 1986, chmn.-elect young lawyers sect. 1986-87, chmn. 1987-88), Ft. Collins C. of C. (legis. affairs commn. 1988-92). Democrat. Episcopalian. Avocations: skiing, running, soccer, backpacking, mountain biking. Banking, Corporate, general, Property, real (including real estate development, water). Home: 1129 Oakmont Ct Fort Collins CO 80525-2865 Office: Myatt Brandes & Gast PC 323 S College Ave Ste 1 Fort Collins CO 80524-2845 E-mail: rgast@verinet.com.

GASTL, EUGENE FRANCIS, lawyer; b. Shawnee, Kans., Apr. 28, 1932; s. Bert J. and Bessie C. (Bell) G.; m. Deanna J. Cordon, June 7, 1959 (div. May 1978); children: Philip E., Catherine L., David B., Brenda M.; m. Arline Blackwood, June 15, 1979. BA, U. Kans., 1954, LLB, 1956, JD, 1968. Bar: Kans. 1956, U.S. Dist. Ct. Kans. 1956. Sole practice, Shawnee, 1959—. State rep. Kans. Legislature, Topeka, 1961-65, 71-79, senator, 1965-69. Served to specialist grade 3 U.S. Army, 1956-58. Mem. ABA, Kans. Bar Assn., Johnson County Bar Assn., Assn. Trial Lawyers Am., Shawnee C. of C. (v.p. 1965-67). Lodges: Optimist (bd. dirs. 1961-63). Democrat. Methodist. Avocation: reading. Family and matrimonial, Probate (including wills, trusts), Workers' compensation. Home: 5420 Bluejacket St Shawnee Mission KS 66203-1924 Office: 5811 Nieman Rd Shawnee Mission KS 66203-2855

GASTWIRTH, DONALD EDWARD, lawyer, literary agent; b. N.Y.C., Aug. 7, 1944; s. Paul and Tillie (Scheinert) G. BA, Yale U., 1966, JD, 1974. Bar: Conn. 1979, U.S. Dist. Ct. Conn. 1981. Mem. advt. staf New Yorker mag., N.Y.C., 1967-68; v.p. Reader's Press, New Haven, 1968-74, dir., 1968-75; exec. v.p. Mainstream TV Studio, New Haven, 1974-77, dir., 1974-79; pres. Quasar Assocs., New Haven, 1979-89; account exec. Bache Halsey Stuart Shields Inc., New Haven, 1977-79; ptnr. Gastwirth, McMillan & Still, New Haven, 1981-84; pres. Don Gastwirth & Assocs. Literary Agy., New Haven, 1984—. Adj. prof. law Thomas Jefferson Sch. Law, 1996-99; lectr. in field; advisor fund raising, mem. benefit com. John Steinbeck Lit. Project, 1986-94; assoc. fellow Trumbull Coll., Yale U. Assoc. prodr. Yankee Fishing (TV series, 1995-98); contbr. to Nat. Rev., Wall St. Jour., New Haven Register; mem. bd. advisors Yale Lit. Mag., 1987-94, Touchstone Mag., 1990-95, 98-99. Trustee Yale Ctr. for Parliamentary History, 1995-2002. Mem.: PEN Writers Assn., ABA, Writers Guild Am., Berzelius Soc., Lambs Club, Yale Club (N.Y.), Elizabethan Club. Entertainment, Intellectual property. Home and Office: 265 College St New Haven CT 06510-2420

GASTWIRTH, STUART LAWRENCE, lawyer; b. N.Y.C., Feb. 26, 1939; s. Jack Keith and Lillian (Gurchinsky) G.; m. Norma Blechman, June 13, 1965; children: Andrew Evan, David Eric, Jason Marc. BA, Hofstra U., 1959; JD, Cornell U., 1962. Bar: N.Y. 1963. Assoc. Cole & Deitz, N.Y.C., 1962-67; atty. Central State Bank, N.Y.C., 1967-69; ptnr. Semon & Gastwirth, Jericho, NY, 1969-75; sole practice Jericho, 1975-81; ptnr. Gastwirth, Mirsky & Stein LLP, Manhasset, Southampton, NY, 1997—. Chmn. Adult Edn. Adv. Com., Great Neck, 1982; mem. exec. com. PTA North H.S., Great Neck, 1983—85, pres., 1984—87, corr. sec., 1992, 1993, 2d v.p., 1994, 1st v.p., 1995, pres., 1998—2000; pres. bd. dirs. Kings Point Civic Assn., 1998—2000. Mem. Nassau County Bar Assn., N.Y. State Bar Assn., Bank Lawyers Conf. of N.Y., Exchange Club of North Shore (pres. 1972-73, L.I., N.Y.), Great Neck Cmty. Fund. Jewish. Corporate, general, Probate (including wills, trusts), Property, real (including real estate development, water). Home: 49 Fairway Dr Manhasset NY 11030-3906 E-mail: gaslaw@aol.com.

GATES, GREGORY ANSEL, lawyer; b. Cortland, N.Y., Sept. 25, 1953; s. Herbert Ansel and Mary (O'Connor) G.; m. Margaret Anne Schell, Aug. 9, 1975; children: Ryan Mary, Connor Ansel. BA, SUNY, Oswego, 1975; JD, Albany Law Sch. Union U., 1978. Bar: N.Y. 1979, U.S. Dist. Ct. (no. dist.) N.Y. 1979, U.S. Dist. Ct. (no. dist.) Calif. 1985, U.S. Ct. Appeals (2d cir.) 1993, U.S. Supreme Ct. 1994. Assoc. Levene Gouldin and Thompson, Binghamton, N.Y., 1979-84, ptnr., 1984-85, Hickey, Sheehan and Gates, Binghamton, N.Y., 1985--. Mem. Continuing Edn. Adv. Com., Binghamton, 1982-87. Commn. of Elections Broome County Gov., Binghamton, 1984-97, town justice, 1997—; pres. Broome County Magistrates Assn., 2002-; dir. Broome Sports Found., 1987--; counsel Broome County Democratic Com., 1984-87. Mem. ABA, N.Y. Bar Assn., Assn. Trial Lawyers Am., Broome County Bar Assn. (dir. 1988-91). Democrat. Roman Catholic. Avocations: hockey, golf, travel. General civil litigation, Criminal, Personal injury (including property damage). Office: Hickey Sheehan and Gates PO Box 2124 Binghamton NY 13902-2124

GATES, STEPHEN FRYE, lawyer, business executive; b. Clearwater, Florida, May 20, 1946; s. Orris Allison and Olga Betty (Frye) G.; m. Laura (Daignault), June 10, 1972. BA in econ., Yale U., 1968; JD, MBA, Harvard U., 1972. Bar: Fla., 1972; Mass., 1973; Ill., 1977; Colo. 1986. Assoc.

Choate, Hall, and Stewart, Boston, 1973-77; atty. Amoco Corp., Chgo., 1977-82, gen. atty., 1982-86; regional atty. Amoco Prodn. Co., Denver, 1987-88; asst. treas. Amoco Corp., Chgo., 1988-91, assoc. gen. counsel, corp. sec., 1991-92; v.p. Amoco Chem. Co., 1993-95; v.p., gen. counsel Amoco Corp., Chgo., 1995-98; exec. v.p., group chief of staff BP Amoco, London, 1999-2000; sr. v.p., gen. counsel, sec. FMC Corp., Chgo., 2000—01; ptnr. Mayer, Brown, Rowe,and Maw, Chgo., 2002—03; sr. v.p. and gen. counsel Conoco Phillips Corp., Houston, 2003—. Bd. dirs. Nat. Legal Ctr. Pub. Interest, Wash., 1999—. Trustee Newberry Libr., Chgo., 1998—; Appleseed Found., 2003-; mem. adv. coun. Chgo. Schweitzer Urban Fellows Program, 1996—; mem. adv. bd. Chgo. Vol. Legal Svcs. Found., 1996-98; mem. Chgo. Crime Commn., 2000—, bd.dirs. 2000-03. Knox fellow, 1972-73. Fellow: Am. Bar Found., Royal Soc. Arts (London); mem.: ABA, Yale Club, Chgo. Club, Univ. Club. Corporate, general, Securities. Office: Conoco-Phillips Corp 600 N Dairy Ashford Houston TX 77252

GAUGHAN, DENNIS CHARLES, lawyer; b. Buffalo, July 3, 1955; s. Charles Joseph Gaughan and Mary Lynn Rucker; m. Mary Rose DeBergalis, Sept. 22, 1989; children: Charles Joseph, Dennis Charles Jr., Joseph Rocco. BA, Syracuse U., 1978; JD, N.Y. Law Sch., 1982. Bar: N.Y. 1984, U.S. Dist. Ct. (we. dist.) N.Y. 1984, U.S. Ct. Appeals (2d cir.) 1984, U.S. Supreme Ct. 1988. Counsel Erie County Dept. Social Svcs., Buffalo, 1984-89; pvt. practice, Hamburg, N.Y., 1989—. Asst. town atty. Town of Hamburg, 1995—; prosecutor Village of Blasdell, N.Y. Chmn. Hamburg Rep. Ctrl. Com. 1988-90. Served with USAR, 1983-89. Mem. Erie County Bar Assn., KC, Am. Legion, Am. Vets. Roman Catholic. Bankruptcy, Criminal, Family and matrimonial. Home: 5516 Pebble Beach Dr Hamburg NY 14075-5860 Office: 6161 S Park Ave Hamburg NY 14075-3837

GAUGHAN, JOHN STEPHEN, lawyer; b. Chgo., Dec. 26, 1932; s. James Joseph and Margaret (Monaghan) G.; m. Barbara L. Jansen, Aug. 10, 1959; children: Brian, Dennis, Kevin. BS, DePaul U., 1954, JD, 1962. Bar: Ill. 1962, Calif. 1969. Supr. rules and regulations State of Ill. Dept. Revenue, Chgo., 1962-67; supr. charitable trust Ill. Atty. Gen., Chgo., 1967-68; sole practice Santa Ana, Calif., 1969—. Served with U.S. Army, 1954-56. Mem. ABA, Calif. Bar Assn., Ill. Bar Assn. Lodges: Elks. General civil litigation, Commercial, consumer (including collections, credit), Probate (including wills, trusts). Home: 4 Rue Chateau Royal Newport Beach CA 92660-5904 Office: 17291 Irvine Blvd Ste 411 Tustin CA 92780-2932

GAUJAL-JOSEPH, MARIE-FRANCE JEANNE, lawyer; b. Paris, Sept. 11, 1945; d. Bernard Marie-Francois and Marthe-Juliette (Cassan) Gaujal; m. Bernard-Etienne Joseph, Oct. 22, 1979; children: Alexandre, Charles-Edouard. Maitrise de Droit, Faculty de Droit, Paris, 1967; Cert. D'Aptitude Profession D'Avocat, Institut d'Etudes Politiques, Paris, 1968; postgrad., Institut de Droit des Affaires, Paris, 1978-79. Atty./avocat in pvt. practice, Pris, 1971—; avocat Gide-Loyrette-Nouel, Pris, 1975—; conseiller Cabinet Ministre Industrie, Pris, 1975-76. Home: 78 Ave de la Bourdonnais 75007 Paris France Office: Cabinet Gide-Loyrette-Nouel 26 cours Albert Ler 75008 Paris France

GAUNT, JANET LOIS, arbitrator, mediator; b. Lawrence, Mass., Aug. 23, 1947; d. Donald Walter and Lois (Neuhart) Bacon; children: Cory C., Andrew D. BA, Oberlin Coll., 1969; JD, Wash. U., St. Louis, 1974. Bar: Wash. 1974, U.S. Dist. Ct. (we. dist.) Wash. 1974, U.S. Ct. Appeals (9th cir.) 1978. Assoc. Davis, Wright, Todd, Riese & Jones, Seattle, 1974-80; arbitrator/mediator Seattle, 1981—. Dir. Seattle King County Labor Law Sect., 1976-77; mem. Pacific Coast Labor Law Planning Com., 1977-83; com. vice chmn. Wash. State Task Force on Gender and Justice on the Cts., 1987-89; chmn. Wash. Pub. Employment Rels. Commn., Olympia, 1989-96. Author, editor: Alternative Dispute Resolution, 1989; author: Public Sector Labor Mediation and Arbitration, Arbitration and Mediation in Washington, 2d edit., 1995. Recipient Pass the Torch award, Wash. Women Lawyers, 1999. Mem. Nat. Acad. Arbitrators (dir. rsch. and edn. found. 1991-96, bd. govs. 1998-2001, v.p. 2002—), Am. Arbitration Assn., Wash. State Bar Assn., Wash. Women Lawyers (state co-pres. 1986). E-mail: j.gaunt@attbi.com.

GAUTHIER, CELESTE ANNE, lawyer; b. New Orleans, Oct. 25, 1969; d. Wendell Haynes and Anne (Barrios) G.; 1 child, Trenton Michael; m. Michael F. Balluff, Jan. 1, 2000. BA in Sociology, U. New Orleans, 1992; JD, Loyola U., New Orleans, 1995. Bar: La. 1996, U.S. Dist. Ct. (ea. dist.) La. 1996, U.S. Ct. Appeals (5th cir.) 1996. Law clk. Gauthier & Murphy, Metairie, La., 1992-95; law clk. to Hon. Judge Burns 24th Jud. Dist. Ct., Gretna, La., 1996, law clk. to Hon. Judge Sullivan, 1997-98; assoc. Gauthier, Downing, LaBarre, Dean & Sulzer, Metairie, La., 1998—, The Gauthier Law Firm, Metairie. Advocate Jeff 25, Jefferson, La., 1997—. Mem. Young Dems. Am., 1995—, St. Catherine of Siena Parish, Metairie, 1994—. Mem.: ABA, ATLA, Young Leadership Coun., La. Trial Lawyers Assn. (chair People's Law Sch. spring 1999, coun. dirs. 2001—03, ho. of dels. 24th jud. dist. 2003—), New Orleans Bar Assn., Jefferson Bar Assn. (treas. young lawyers sect. 1998—99, chair 2000—01, ho. of dels. 24th jud. dist. 2003—), La. State Bar Assn. (young lawyers dist. 2 rep. 1998—2002), La. Bar Found., Fed. Bar Assn., Country Day Parents Assn. (young leadership coun. 1998—2002, Jefferson chamber 1998—, Jefferson young leaders 2001—). Democrat. Roman Catholic. Avocations: spending time with my son, skiing, reading, walking, culinary interests. General civil litigation, Personal injury (including property damage), Product liability. Office: The Gauthier Law Firm 3500 N Hullen St Metairie LA 70002-3420 E-mail: celeste@gauthier-downing.com.

GAY, CARL LLOYD, lawyer; b. Seattle, Nov. 11, 1950; s. James and Elizabeth Anne (Rogers) G.; m. Robin Ann Winston, Aug. 23, 1975; children: Patrick, Joel, Alexander, Samuel, Nora. Student, U. of Puget Sound, 1969-70; BS in Forestry cum laude, Wash. State U., 1974; JD, Willamette U., 1979. Bar: Wash. 1979, U.S. Dist. Ct. (we. dist.) Wash. 1979. With Taylor & Taylor, 1979-82, Taylor, Taylor & Gay, 1982-85; prin. Greenaway & Gay, Port Angeles, Wash., 1985-91, Greenaway, Gay & Tassie, Port Angeles, 1991-96, Greenaway, Gay & Angier, Port Angeles, 1996—2001, Greenaway, Gay & Tulloch, 2002—. Judge pro tem Clallam County, Port Angeles, 1981-85; commr. superior Ct., 1985-91; judge Juvenile Ct., 1985-87; instr. Guardian Ad Litem Program, Port Angeles, 1985—, Peoples Law Sch., 1989—. Bd. dirs. Cmty. Concert Assn., Port Angeles, 1982—85, 1994—, pres., 1984—85, 1988—89, 1999—2000; bd. dirs. Am. Heart Assn., 1987—, Clallam County YMCA, 1987—2002, exec. com., 1995—; adv. com. Salvation Army, Port Angeles, 1982—; subdivsn. chmn., bd. dirs. United Way Clallam County, 1987—; bd. dirs., pres. Friends of Libr., Port Angeles, 1983—91; trustee Fisher Cove, 1988—; advisor youth in govt. program YMCA, 1986—; chmn. long-range planning com. Port Angeles Sch. Dist.; bd. govs. Peninsula Coll. Found., 2000—; advisor United Meth. Youth Coun., 1987—, trustee, 1989—; pres. Holy Trinity Luth. Ch., 2001—. Named Clallam County Citizen of Yr., 1987; recipient Disting. Svc. award, Clallam County Pro Bono Lawyers, 1998, YMCA, 1992. Mem.: ATLA, ABA (real property, probate and trust and gen. practice sects.), Wash. State Trial Lawyers Assn., Superior Ct. Judges Assn. (com.), Nat. Coun. Juvenile and Family Ct. Judges, Clallam County Bar Assn. (pres. 1995), Wash. Bar Assn. (real property, probate, elder law and trust sects.), Kiwanis (local bd. dirs. 1982—84, pres. 1986—87, Kiwanian of Yr. 1983—84). Lutheran. Avocations: backpacking, cross country skiing, raquetball, sailing. Commercial, contracts (including sales of goods; commercial financing), Probate (including wills, trusts), Property, real (including real estate development, water). Home: 3220 Mcdougal St Port Angeles WA 98362-6738 Office: Greenaway Gay & Tulloch 829 E 8th St Ste A Port Angeles WA 98362-6452 E-mail: clgay@tenforward.com.

GAY, E(MIL) LAURENCE, lawyer; b. Bridgeport, Conn., Aug. 10, 1923; s. Emil Daniel and Helen Lillian (Mihalich) Gulyassy; m. Harriet A. Ripley, Aug. 2, 1952; children: Noel L., Peter C., Marguerite S., Georgette A. BA, Yale U., 1946; JD magna cum laude, Harvard U., 1949. Bar: N.Y. 1950, Conn. 1960, Calif. 1981, Hawaii 1988. Assoc. Root, Ballantine, Harlan, Bushby & Palmer, N.Y.C., 1949—52; mem. legal staff U.S. High Commr. Germany, Bad Godesberg, 1952—53; law sec., presiding justice appellate div. 1st dept. N.Y. Supreme Ct., N.Y.C., 1953—54; assoc. Debevoise, Plimpton & McLean, N.Y.C., 1954—58; v.p., sec.-treas., gen. counsel Hewitt-Robins, Inc., Stamford, Conn., 1958—65; pres. Litton Gt. Lakes Corp., N.Y.C., 1965—67; sr. v.p. fin. AMFAC, Inc., Honolulu, 1967—73, vice chmn., 1974—78; fin. cons. Burlingame, Calif., 1979-82; of counsel Pettit & Martin, San Francisco, 1982—88, Goodsill, Anderson, Quinn & Stifel, Honolulu, 1988—. Editor: Harvard Law Rev., 1948—49. Pres. Honolulu Symphony Soc., 1974—78; officer, dir. numerous arts and ednl. orgns.; bd. dirs. Loyola Marymount U., 1977—80, San Francisco Chamber Soloists, 1981—86, Honolulu Chamber Music Series, 1988—. 1st lt. U.S. Army, 1943—46. Mem.: ABA, Hawaii State Bar Assn. (vice chair bus. law soc. 1997—98), Phi Beta Kappa. Republican. Roman Catholic. Avocations: music, literature. Commercial, contracts (including sales of goods; commercial financing), Corporate, general, Securities. Home: 1159 Maunawili Rd Kailua HI 96734-4641 Office: Goodsill Anderson Quinn & Stifel 1099 Alakea St #1800 Honolulu HI 96814 Office Fax: 808-547-5880.

GAY, SARAH ELIZABETH, lawyer; b. Cambridge, Mass., May 24, 1950; d. Frank Smith and Jane (Spencer) Fussner; m. Kirk D. Gay; 1 child, John Russell. BA, Harvard/Radcliffe, 1972; JD, U. Oreg., 1975. Bar: Alaska 1976, U.S. Dist. Ct. Alaska 1976, U.S. Ct. Appeals (9th cir.) 1976, U.S. Supreme Ct. 1980. Assoc. Ely, Guess & Rudd, Anchorage, 1975-77; asst. atty. gen. natural resources sect. State of Alaska, Anchorage, 1977-88, asst. atty. gen. oil spill sect., 1989-91, sect. supr. natural resources sect., 1991-93; corp. counsel Alaska Safari, Inc., Alaska Valhalla Lodge, Inc., Anchorage, 1993—; pvt. practice Anchorage, 1993—. Workshop leader U. Oreg. Law Sch., Eugene, 1989; chmn. Anchorage Mcpl. Airports Adv. Com., 1990-93; food safety adv. com. Dept. Environ. Conservation, State Alaska, 2000—. Mng. bd. editor U. Oreg. Law Rev., Eugene, 1975. Citizens' adv. bd. Land Conservation & Devel. Bd., Salem, Oreg., 1975. Mem. Alaska Bar Assn. Law Examiners, Phi Delta Phi. Avocations: commercial pilot, sport fish lodge operator. Natural resources. Address: Valhalla Lodge Nondalton AK 99640 Fax: 907-243-6095. E-mail: sarah@valhallalodge.com.

GAYLE, GIBSON, JR., lawyer; b. Waco, Tex., Oct. 15, 1926; s. Gibson and Elsie (Little) G.; m. Martha Jane Wood, May 29, 1948; children: Sally Ann, Alice, Gibson III, Jane, Philip. AB, LLB, Baylor U., 1950; D Human Medicine (hon.), Baylor Coll. Medicine, 1991. Bar: Tex. 1950. Since practiced in, Houston; sr. ptnr., chmn. exec. com. Fulbright & Jaworski., 1979-92; adj. prof. U. Tex. Law Sch. Instr. U. Houston Law Sch., 1951-55. Bd. editors: Am. Bar Assn. Jour, 1967-72. Trustee M.D. Anderson Found.; bd. govs. Harris County Ctr. for Retarded, 1956-76; Tex. Med. Ctr. Inc., Leon Jaworski Found.; bd. dirs., pres. Am. Bar Endowment, 1970-80; chmn. Baylor Coll. Medicine, 1982-91, trustee, 1977—. 2d lt. F.A. AUS, 1945-47. Fellow Am. Bar Found. (dir. 1978-79), Tex. Bar Found. (chmn. 1968-69); mem. ABA (chmn. jr. bar conf. 1959-60, ho. of dels. 1960-62, 63—, sec. 1963-67), Houston Bar Assn., State Bar Tex. (dir. 1966-69, pres. 1976-77), Houston C. of C. (dir. 1979-87) Federal civil litigation, State civil litigation, General practice. Home: 11727 Broken Bough Cir Houston TX 77024-5115 Office: Fulbright & Jaworski LLP 1301 Mckinney St Ste 5100 Houston TX 77010-3031

GEAN, THOMAS C. prosecutor; BA, U. Ark.; JD, Vanderbilt U. Atty. Alston and Bird, Atlanta, 1988—92, Gean, Gean and Gean, Ft. Smith, Ark., 1992—96; prosecuting atty. Sebastian County Dist. Atty.'s Office, 1997—2001; U.S. atty. western dist. U.S. Dept. Justice, Ark., 2001—. Office: Rm 216 30 S 6th St Fort Smith AR 72901*

GEARHEART, MARK EDWIN, lawyer; b. Wichita, Kans., July 20, 1955; BS, U. No. Colo., 1977; JD, U. Calif., San Francisco, 1980. Bar: Calif. 1980, U.S. Dist. Ct. (no. dist.) Calif. 1980; cert. specialist in workers compensation, Calif. Assoc. Ury and Goldstein, Vallejo, Calif., 1980-83; mng. atty. Boxer, Ury & Gearheart, Pleasant Hill, Calif., 1983-92; pvt. practice, Pleasant Hill, 1992-93; ptnr. Gearheart & Otis, Pleasant Hill, 1993—. Mem. ATLA, ABA, Nat. Workplace Injury Litigation Group, Calif. Applicants Attys. Assn. (pres. Walnut Creek chpt. 1998—). Democrat. Workers' compensation. Office: Gearheart & Otis 367 Civic Dr Ste 17 Pleasant Hill CA 94523-1935

GEARHISER, CHARLES JOSEF, lawyer; b. Dyersburg, Tenn., Aug. 14, 1938; s. Charles Josef Gearhiser and Mary Josephine (Plant) Wickham; m. Joy Edwards; children: Charles J. III, Laura, Christy. BS, Austin Peay State U., 1960; LLB, U. Tenn., 1961. Bar: Tenn. Assoc. Strang, Fletcher, Carriger & Walker, Chattanooga, 1961-63; law clk. to presiding justice U.S. Dist. Ct. (ea. dist.) Tenn., Chattanooga, 1963-64; asst. U.S. atty. Dept. Justice, Chattanooga, 1964-66; ptnr. Stophel, Caldwell & Heggie, Chattanooga, 1966-74, Gearhiser, Peters, Lockaby & Tallant and predecessor firms, Chattanooga, 1974—. U.S. commnr., 1966-73; U.S. magistrate U.S. Dist. Ct. (ea. dist.) Tenn., 1973-78, Chattanooga. Chmn. bd. dirs. S.E. Tenn. Legal Services, Chattanooga, 1978-81. Fellow Am. Coll. Trial Lawyers, Tenn. Bar Found.; mem. ABA, Tenn. Bar Assn. (bd. govs. 1992, 1994, 1999), pres-elect, 1999-2001, pres. 2001-2002, Chattanooga Bar Assn. (sec., treas 1972-73, pres. 1973-74), Assn. Trial Lawyers Am., Tenn. Trial Lawyers Assn., Chattanooga Trial Lawyers Assn., Nat. Inst. Trial Advocacy (civil trial adv. 1981), Am. Bd. Trial Advs. (charter mem. Tenn. chpt.), Order of Coif. Democrat. Methodist. Federal civil litigation, General civil litigation, Personal injury (including property damage). Home: 12 N Crest Rd Chattanooga TN 37404-1827 Office: Gearhiser Peters Lockaby & Tallant 320 McCallie Ave Chattanooga TN 37402-2018

GEARY, JAMES H. lawyer; b. Midland, Mich., Nov. 8, 1946; s. James Edward and Ruth Alice (Cary) G.; m. Judith Ellery McHugh, Aug. 22, 1967; children: Patricia Jean, Christopher James. BA, U. Mich., 1968, JD, 1972. Bar: U.S. Dist. Ct. (we. dist.) Mich. 1972, U.S. Dist. Ct. (ea. dist.) Mich. 1974, U.S. Ct. Appeals (6th cir.) 1973, U.S. Ct. Appeals (5th cir.) 1978, U.S. Ct. Appeals (11th cir.) 1981, U.S. Supreme Ct. 1981, U.S. Ct. Appeals (7th cir.) 1994, U.S. Ct. Appeals (8th cir.) 1996, U.S. Ct. Appeals (3d cir.) 1997, U.S. Ct. Appeals (10th cir.) 2000; cert. trial advocate Nat. Bd. Trial Advocacy 1990. Law clk. to judge U.S. Ct. of Appeals 6th Cir., Mich., 1972-73; assoc. Howard & Howard, Kalamazoo, Mich., 1973-80; ptnr. Little & Geary, Kalamazoo, 1980-83, Howard & Howard, Kalamazoo, 1983—. Chmn. Ad-Hoc Sub-Com. on Examinations, Grand Rapids, Mich., 1980-82; faculty Western Mich. Univ. Trial Advocacy Inst., 1982; guest lectr. Western Mich. Univ.; lectr. and commentator Inst. of Continuing Legal Edn., 1980—; chmn. Civil Justice Adv. Group, 1991-95. Chmn. selective service Western Dist. of Mich. Appeal Bd., Grand Rapids, 1985. Served with U.S. Army, 1969-71. Mem. ABA, Kalamazoo County Trial Lawyers Assn. (pres. 1984-85), State Bar of Mich. (co-chmn. U.S. cts. com. 1985-86, 1998—), Western Mich. Fed. Bar Assn. (bd. dirs.), Kalamazoo Optimist Hockey Assn. Avocations: hockey, soccer officiating. Federal civil litigation, State civil litigation, Labor (including EEOC, Fair Labor Standards Act, labor-management relations, NLRB, OSHA). Address: Howard & Howard Atty 100 Portage St Ste 200 Kalamazoo MI 49007-4818

GEARY, WILLIAM LEE, lawyer; b. Portsmouth, Ohio, July 17, 1952; s. Eugene Jennings and Leona Winnefred (Philips) G.; children: Ian Anthony Stanley. BA in English, Ohio State U., 1974; JD, Ohio No. U., 1978. Bar: Ohio 1979, U.S. Dist. Ct. (so. dist.) Ohio 1979; lic. real estate salesperson, Ohio. Ptnr. Hamilton Kramer, Columbus, 1979-95; pvt. practice Columbus, 1995—; pres. Abby Lane/Dana Temporaries, Columbus, 1988—2002, Maclain Svcs., Columbus, 1993—2002, Geary Securities, Charleston, W.Va., 1995—, Geary Realty, Charleston, W.Va., 1995—, Ian Inc., Columbus, 1996—2002. Mem. Franklin County Domestic Rels. Mediator Accreditation Com., Columbus, 1994-96; cmty. faculty Marion (Ohio) Tech. Coll., 1994-1995. Bd. dirs. Cmty. Mediation Svcs. of Ctrl. Ohio, Columbus, 1993-97; pres. German Village Sertoma, Columbus, 1995-96, sec., 1996—97; vol. Christmas in April, AmeriFlora. Recipient Am. Jurisprudence Book award, 1977, 78. Mem. Ohio State Bar Assn., Columbus Bar Assn. Family and matrimonial. Office: Waterford Tower 155 W Main St Ste 101 Columbus OH 43215-5063 E-mail: wgeary5558@aol.com.

GEBHARDT, BRUCE J. federal agency administrator; b. Balt. BA in Sociology, Western Ill. U.; MA in Criminology, Sam Houston State U. Instr. law enforcement and criminal justice Sauk Valley Coll., Dixon, Ill., Western Ill. U., Macomb; spl. agt. FBI, Quantico, Va., 1974, Denver, San Francisco, 1978—81, supr. L.A., 1981—86, supr. drug sect. criminal investigative divsn. Washington, 1986—91, asst. insp. in inspection divsn., 1986—91, asst. spl. agt. in charge Newark, 1991—94, insp. inspection divsn. Washington, 1994—95, spl. agt. in charge Phoenix, 1995—98, San Francisco, 1998, exec. asst. dir. Washington. Office: FBI J Edgar Hoover FBI Bldg 935 Pennsylvania Ave NW Washington DC 20535*

GEBO, STEPHEN WALLACE, lawyer; b. Watertown, N.Y., Apr. 2, 1951; s. Wallace Anthony and Yolanda (Leana) G.; m. Kathleen Lenair Hunt, Aug. 7, 1976; children: Allison, Carolynn, Sarah. AB, Hamilton Coll., 1973; JD, Cornell U., 1976. Bar: N.Y. 1977, U.S. Dist. Ct. (no. dist.) N.Y. 1978, U.S. Ct. Appeals (2d cir.) 1980. Assoc. Proskauer, Rose, Goetz & Mendelson, N.Y.C., 1976-77, Pearis, Resseguie, Kline & Barber, Binghamton, N.Y., 1977-78, Conboy, McKay, Bachman & Kendall, Watertown, 1978-81, ptnr., 1981—. Assoc. editor Cornell U. Law Rev., 1974-75, editor, 1975-76. Bd. dirs. March of Dimes, Watertown, 1979-82, Jefferson County Women's Ctr., Watertown, 1980-89, St. Patrick's Sch., 1996-98. Mem. N.Y. State Bar Assn., Jefferson County Bar Assn., Ives Hill Country Club (bd. dirs. 1991-2001), Phi Beta Kappa. Clubs: Ives Hill Country (Watertown). Republican. Roman Catholic. Avocation: golf. General civil litigation, Insurance, Personal injury (including property damage). Home: 155 Paddock St Watertown NY 13601-3916 Office: Conboy McKay Bachman & Kendall 407 Sherman St Watertown NY 13601-3958

GEDDIE, ROWLAND HILL, III, lawyer; b. Tuscaloosa, Ala., Jan. 7, 1954; s. Rowland Hill Jr. and Mary Martha (McGaughy) G.; m. Peggy O'Neal Emmons, Aug. 13, 1977; children: Mary Catherine, Virginia Jane. BA, U. Miss., 1976, JD, 1978. Bar: Miss. 1978, U.S. Dist. Ct. (no. dist.) Miss. 1978, Tex. 1979, Mo. 1995. Assoc. Baker & Botts, Houston, 1978-87; assoc. gen. counsel Lower Colo. River Authority, Austin, Tex., 1987-88; sr. counsel Houston Industries Inc./Houston Lighting & Power Co., 1988-92; contract atty. Tandy Corp./TE Electronics Inc., Ft. Worth, 1993; v.p., gen. counsel, sec. O'Sullivan Industries Holdings Inc., Lamar, Mo., 1993—. Treas. Southgate Civic Club, Houston, 1991-92. Presdl. scholar U.S. Govt., Washington, 1972. Mem.: Am. Corp. Counsel Assn., Lamar Swim Team Assn., Inc. (pres. 2000—02), Lamar Rotary Club (v.p. 2001—02, pres. 2002—03). Methodist. Avocations: personal computers, cycling, scuba diving, swimming. Corporate, general, Securities. Home: 1503 Gulf St Lamar MO 64759-1830 Office: O'Sullivan Industries Inc 1900 Gulf St Lamar MO 64759-1899 E-mail: rowland.geddie@osullivan.com.

GEDDY, VERNON MEREDITH, JR., lawyer; b. Norfolk, Va., Apr. 12, 1926; s. Vernon Meredith and Carrie Cole (Lane) G.; m. Marie Lewis Sibley, Dec. 22, 1949; children: Anne Lewis Geddy Cross, Vernon M. Geddy III AB cum laude, Princeton U., 1949; LL.B., U. Va., 1952. Bar: Va. Ptnr. Geddy & Harris (and predecessor firms), Williamsburg, Va., 1952-80; ptnr. McGuire, Woods, Battle & Boothe (and predecessor firms), Williamsburg, Va., 1980-91, Geddy, Harris & Geddy (and predecessor firms), Williamsburg, 1991-99, Geddy, Harris, Franck & Hickman, L.L.P., Williamsburg, 1999—. Former dir. United Va. Bankshares, Nat. Ctr. for State Cts. Mem. Williamsburg City Coun., Va., 1968-80; trustee Colonial Williamsburg Found., 1981-95, Va. Hist. Soc., Richmond, 1981-88, 93-99, Va. Mus. Fine Arts, 1982-91; bd. dirs. Williamsburg Cmty. Hosp., 1969-85, WHRO, Pub. Telecoms. for Hampton Roads, Jamestown-Yorktown Found.; chmn. Williamsburg Cmty. Health Found. Sgt. USAAF, 1944-46, PTO. Named to Raven Soc. Fellow Am. Bar Found. (award 1976); mem. ABA, Va. Bar Assn. (pres. 1972-73), Va. State Bar, Williamsburg Bar Assn. (pres. 1975-93), Omicron Delta Kappa, Commonwealth Club. Episcopalian. Office: Geddy Harris Franck & Hickman LLP PO Box 379 1177 Jamestown Rd Williamsburg VA 23185

GEE, ROBERT NEIL, law librarian; b. Miami, Okla., June 22, 1956; s. Robert Sanford and Nancy Ann (Neil) G. AA, Tulsa Jr. Coll., 1976; BA, U. Okla., 1978, JD, 1981; LLM, George Washington U., 1984. Bar: Okla. 1981, U.S. Suprem Ct. 1986, D.C. 1989. Legal reference specialist Library of Congress, Washington, 1984-94; chief law libr. pub. svcs. Law Libr. of Congress, Washington, 1994—. Mem. ABA (recipient Silver Key cert. 1981), Fed. Bar Assn., Okla. Bar Assn., Am. Judicature Soc., D.C. Bar Assn., Phi Delta Phi. Avocations: reading, bowling, travel, current events.

GEEKER, NICHOLAS PETER, lawyer, judge; b. Pensacola, Fla., Dec. 15, 1944; BA in English, La. Poly. Inst., 1966; JD, Fla. State U., 1969. Bar: Fla. 1969, U.S. Dist. Ct. 1970, US. Supreme Ct., 1980. Assoc. firm Merritt & Jackson, Pensacola, 1969; law clk. U.S. Dist. Judge D.L. Middlebrooks, Tallahassee, 1970-73; asst. state atty. Fla. 1st Jud. Circuit, 1973; asst. U.S. atty. No. Dist. Fla., 1973-76, U.S. atty., 1976-82; sole practice Pensacola, Fla., 1982-85; circuit judge Fla. 1st Jud. Circuit, 1985—. Mem. Fed.-State Joint Com. on Law Enforcement. Mem. Fla. Bar Assn., Fla. Trial Lawyers Assn. (editor Newsletter 1975), Phi Delta Phi. Office: 190 Government St Pensacola FL 32501-5773

GEFKE, HENRY JEROME, lawyer; b. Milw., Aug. 4, 1930; s. Jerome Henry and Frances (Daley) G.; m. Caroline Ann Lawrence, June 25, 1955 (div. Jan. 1968); children: Brian Lawrence, David Jerome; m. Mary Clare Nuss, Aug. 28, 1976; children: Lynn Marie, James Scott. BS, Marquette U., 1952, LL.B., 1954; postgrad., Ohio State U., 1955-56. Bar: Wis. 1954, Tax Ct. U.S 1969; C.P.A., Wis. Accountant-auditor John G. Conley & Co. (C.P.A.s), Milw., 1956-59; with J.I. Case Co., Racine, Wis., 1959-68, corp. sec., asst. gen. counsel, 1965-68; assoc. Maier & Mulcahy, S.C., Milw., 1968-69; prin. Mulcahy, Gefke & Wherry, S.C., Milw., 1969-73; individual practice law Milw., 1973—. Corp. officer, dir. various bus. corps. Pres., bd. dirs. Big Bros., Greater Racine, 1965-67; trustee Racine County Instns., 1960-63; bd. dirs., sec., legal counsel Racine Transitional Care, Inc., 1973-76; bd. dirs., legal counsel Our Home Found., Milw., 1979-82; bd. dirs. Racine County Mental Health Assn., 1963-67, Alliance for Mentally Ill Milw. County, 1986-88; bd. dirs., sec., legal counsel Glendale Econ. Devel. Corp., 1996—; bd. dirs. Glendale Bus. Coun., 1996-97; bd. dirs. Glendale Assn. of Commerce, Inc., 1997—, treas., 1998-2000, pres. 2000-02. Mem. Wis. Bar Assn., Milw. Bar Assn., Wis. Inst. CPA's, Delta Sigma Pi, Delta Theta Phi. Home: 5521 N Lydell Ave Glendale WI 53217-5042 Office: 400 W Silver Spring Dr Milwaukee WI 53217-5053 E-mail: hjgjdcpa@aol.com.

GEFREH, PAUL THOMAS, lawyer; b. Scranton, Pa., Apr. 17, 1953; s. Adam and Florence (Ksiazek) G.; m. Nanette Neudeck, July 16, 1983; children: Mark, Tasha. BA, N.D. State U., 1974; JD, U. Neb., 1977. Bar: Colo. 1977, U.S. Dist. Ct. Colo. 1977, U.S. Ct. Appeals (10th cir.) 1987. Computer programmer U.S. Dept Transp., Washington, 1974-75; ptnr. Lebel & Gefreh, Colorado Springs, Colo., 1977-78; assoc. Murray, Baker & Wendelken, Colorado Springs, 1978-81, Hendricks & Hendricks P.C., Colorado Springs, 1981-84; sole practice Colorado Springs, 1984—; dir. Ent Fed. Credit Union, 1997—. Trustee U.S. Bankruptcy Ct., Denver,

1984—. Officer Pikes Peak Children's Advs., Colorado Springs, 1978-84. Mem. ABA, Colo. Bar Assn., El Paso Bar Assn., Colorado Springs Jaycees (officer 1978-84). Roman Catholic. Avocations: hiking, gardening. Bankruptcy, Commercial, consumer (including collections, credit), Construction. Office: 2125 N Academy Blvd Colorado Springs CO 80909-1507 Office Fax: 719-597-4534. E-mail: Paul.Gefreh@PSINET.com.

GEHAN, MARK WILLIAM, lawyer; b. St. Paul, Dec. 19, 1946; s. Mark William and Jean Elizabeth (McGee) G.; m. Lucy Lyman Harrison, Aug. 25, 1971; children: Hark Harrison, Alice McGee. BA, U. Notre Dame, 1968; JD, U. Minn., 1971. Bar: Minn. Asst. county atty. Ramsey County Atty.'s Office, St. Paul, 1972-76; prosecutor, Met. Area Dist. Urban County Attys. Bd., St. Paul, 1976-77; ptnr. Collins Buckley Sauntry & Haugh, St. Paul, 1978—. Bd. dirs. Minn. State Bd. Pub. Def., St. Paul, 1982-90. Pres. St. Paul Charter Commn., 1986-94. Mem. Minn. Bar Assn. (pres. 1998-99), Ramsey County Bar Assn. (pres. 1990-91). Avocations: scuba diving, tennis, guitar. State civil litigation. Office: Collins Buckley Sauntry & Haugh First Nat Bank Bldg 332 Minnesota St Ste W1100 Saint Paul MN 55101-1379 E-mail: mgehan@cbsh.net.

GEHRES, JAMES, retired lawyer; b. Akron, Ohio, July 19, 1932; s. Edwin Jacob and Cleora Mary (Yoakam) G.; m. Eleanor Agnew Mount, July 23, 1960. BS in Acctg., U. Utah, 1954; MBA, U. Calif.-Berkeley, 1959; JD, U. Denver, 1970, LLM in Taxation, 1977. Bar: Colo. 1970, U.S. Dist. Ct. Colo. 1970, U.S. Tax Ct. 1970, U.S. Supreme Ct. 1973, U.S. Ct. Appeals (10th cir.) 1978, U.S. Ct. Claims 1992. Atty. IRS, Denver, 1965-80, atty. chief counsel;s office, 1980—2002; ret., 2002. Contbr. articles to profl. jours. Treas., dir. Colo. Fourteeners Initiative. With USAF, 1955-58, capt. Res. ret. Mem. ABA, Colo. Bar Assn., AICPA, Colo. Soc. CPAs, Am. Assn. Atty.-CPAs, Am. Judicature Soc., Order of St. Ives, The Explorers Club, Am. Alpine Club, Colo. Mountain Club, Colo. Mountain Club Found. (bd. dirs., pres.), Beta Gamma Sigma, Beta Alpha Psi. Democrat. Office: 935 Pennsylvania St Denver CO 80203-3145

GEHRIG, MICHAEL FORD, lawyer; b. Cin., Jan. 25, 1947; s. John Richard and Mary Bonita (Ford) G.; m. Barbara Jane Rigg, June 16, 1973; children: Michael Ford, Caroline Cristina, Angela Victoria. BA, Ohio State U., 1970; JD, Chase Coll. Law, Cin., 1974. Bar: Ohio 1974, U.S. Dist. Ct. (so. dist.) Ohio 1974, U.S. Dist. Ct. (ea. dist.) Ky. 1983, U.S. Supreme Ct., 1985. Assoc. Beall, Hermanies & Bortz, Cin., 1974-76; mem. firm Gehrig & Gehrig, Cin., 1976-79, Gehrig, Parker & Baldwin, Cin., 1979-88, Fingerman, Guckenberger & Gehrig, 1988-96, Gehrig, Gelwicks & Eynon, 1996—; lectr. various legal seminars. Contbr. articles to jours., chpts. to books. Recipient book awards Chase Coll. Law, 1971, 73, 74. Mem. ABA, Ohio State Bar Assn., Cin. Bar Assn., Assn. Trial Lawyers Am. (sustaining), Am. Bd. Trial Advocates, Ohio Acad. Trial Lawyers (sustaining), Cin. Hist. Soc., English Speaking Union, Cin. Athletic Club, Univ. Club, Hyde Park Golf & Country Club, Phi Gamma Delta. Episcopalian. Personal injury (including property damage). Office: 1140 Bartlett Bldg 36 E 4th St Ste 1140 Cincinnati OH 45202-3809

GEHRING, RONALD KENT, lawyer; b. Ft. Wayne, Ind., Feb. 5, 1941; s. Ronald G. and Beverly M. (Failor) G.; m. Teresa L. Eyer, June 18, 1966; children: Gregory D., Douglas K., Suzanne C. AB, Ind. U., 1963, JD, 1967. Bar: Ind. 1967, U.S. Dist. Ct. (no. and so. dists.) Ind. 1967, U.S. Ct. Appeals (7th cir.) 1975. Assoc. Peters, McHie, Enslen & Hand, Hammond, Ind., 1967-70; ptnr. Tourkow, Danehy, Crell, Hood & Gehring, Ft. Wayne, 1971-79, Grossman, Boeglin & Gehring and predecessor, Ft. Wayne, 1980-84; pvt. practice, Ft. Wayne, 1984—. Panelist Ind. Collection Law Seminar, 1982-83; atty. Ind. Dist. Luth. Ch. Bd. dirs. Concordia Cemetery Assn., 1982-83, Luth. Assn. Broadcasting, Inc. Mem. ABA, Ind. Trial Lawyers, Comml. Law League, Ind. Bar Assn., Allen County Bar Assn., Phi Delta Phi. Commercial, consumer (including collections, credit), Probate (including wills, trusts), Property, real (including real estate development, water). Office: 202 W Berry St Ste 321 Fort Wayne IN 46802-2242

GEIGER, ALEXANDER, lawyer; b. Kosice, Czechoslovakia, May 21, 1950; came to U.S., 1965; s. Emil and Alice (Brickmann) G.; m. Helene R. Mortar, May 28, 1972; children: Theodore, Aviva. AB, Princeton U., 1972; JD, Cornell U., 1975. Bar: N.Y. 1976, U.S. Dist. Ct. (we. dist.) N.Y. 1976, U.S. Supreme Ct. 1980, U.S. Ct. Appeals (2d cir.) 1985, U.S. Tax Ct. 1986. Assoc. Nixon, Hargrave, Devans & Doyle, Rochester, N.Y., 1975-82; sr. ptnr. Geiger & Rothenberg, Rochester, 1982—. Adj. asst. prof. St. John Fisher Coll., Rochester, 1977-78. Mem. N.Y. State Bar Assn., Monroe County Bar Assn., Assn. Trial Lawyers Am., Rochester Inns of Ct. (master). Jewish. Federal civil litigation, State civil litigation, Personal injury (including property damage). Home: 227 Brittany Ln Pittsford NY 14534 also: 30 Newport Pkwy # 3009 Jersey City NJ 07310 Office: Geiger & Rothenberg 45 Exchange Blvd Ste 800 Rochester NY 14614-2093 also: Geiger and Rothenberg 83 Maiden Ln 13th Fl New York NY 10038 Business E-Mail: ageiger@geigroth.com.

GEIGER, JAMES NORMAN, lawyer; b. Mansfield, Ohio, Apr. 5, 1932; s. Ernest R. and Margaret L. (Bauman) G.; m. Paula Hunt, May 11, 1957; children: Nancy G., John W. Student Wabash Coll., Crawfordsville, Ind., 1950-51; BA, Ohio Wesleyan U., 1954; JD, Emory U., 1962, LLD, 1970. Bar: Ga. 1961, U.. Dist. Ct. (mid. dist.) Ga. 1966, U.S. Ct. Appeals (5th and 11th cirs.) 1980, U.S. Dist. Ct. (so. dist.) Ga. 1983. Ptnr. Henderson, Kaley, Geiger and Thurmond, Marietta, Ga., 1962-64, Nunn, Geiger and Hunt, Perry, Ga., 1964-72, Geiger & Geiger, P.C. and predecessors, 1972—. Trustee Westfield (Ga.) Schs., 1970-74, bd. vis., 2003—; mem. civilian adv. bd. Warner Robins AFB, 1976; chmn. coun. ministries Perry United Meth. Ch., 1970-71, mem. adminstrv. bd., 1968—. Capt. USAF, 1954-57. Mem. ABA, Ga. Bar Assn., Houston County Bar Assn., South Ga. C. of C. (bd. dirs.) Perry C. of C. (pres. 1976, 90), Perry Kiwanis (pres. 1968, Man of Yr. 1968), Perry Club Coun. (pres. 1967), Phi Delta Phi, Pi Sigma Alpha. Methodist. Commercial, contracts (including sales of goods; commercial financing), General practice, Property, real (including real estate development, water). Home: 1910 Northside Rd Perry GA 31069-2223 Office: Geiger & Geiger 1007 Jernigan St Perry GA 31069-3325

GEIS, JEROME ARTHUR, lawyer, legal educator; b. Shakopee, Minn., May 28, 1946; s. Arthur Adam and Emma Mary (Boegemann) G.; m. Beth Marie Bruger, Aug. 11, 1979; children: Jennifer, Jason, Joan, Janice. BA in History, Govt. magna cum laude, St. John's U., Collegeville, Minn., 1968; JD cum laude, U. Notre Dame, 1973; LLM in Taxation, NYU, 1975. Bar: Minn. 1973, U.S. Dist. Ct. Minn. 1973, U.S. Tax Ct. 1973, U.S. Ct. Appeals (8th cir.) 1973. Law clk. Minn. Supreme Ct., St. Paul, 1973-74; assoc. Dudley & Smith, St. Paul, 1975-76, Briggs & Morgan P.A., St. Paul, 1976-79, chief tax dept., 1983-95. Adj. prof. tax law William Mitchell Coll. of Law, St. Paul, 1976-83. Columnist Minn. Law Jour., 1986-89, Bench & Bar, 1990—; edit. cons.: Sales and Use Tax Alert; former reviewer Summary Reporter: Finance and Commerce, Minnesota State Bar Assn.; corr. State Tax Notes. Bd. dirs. Western Townhouse Assn., West St. Paul, 1979, St. Matthews Cath. Ch., West St. Paul, 1981; adv. bd. Minn. Inst. of Legal Edn., 1984—. Served to specialist 4th class U.S. Army, 1969-71. Fellow Am. Coll. Tax Counsel; mem. ABA, Am. Law Inst., Tax Inst. Am. (chmn. sales and use tax commn. 1988-90), Nat. Tax Assn., Am. Judicature Soc., Minn. Bar Assn. (bd. dirs. tax coun. sect. 1984-93, 94-97, 99—, chmn. 1990-91), Ramsey County Bar Assn., Minn. Taxpayers Assn. (bd. dirs. 1988—), Inst. Property Taxation, Supreme Ct. Hist. Soc., Nat. Assn. State Bar Tax Sects. (exec. com. 1993—), Citizens League, Minn. Club (bd. dirs. 1997-2000), KC, Kiwanis (bd. dirs. 2000-02). Corporate taxation, Personal income taxation, State and local taxation. Home: 1116 Dodd Rd Saint Paul MN 55118-1821 Office: Briggs & Morgan PA 2200 1st St N Saint Paul MN 55109-3210 E-mail: JGeis@Briggs.com.

GEISLER, SHERRY LYNN, magistrate; b. Durango, Colo., Aug. 18, 1956; d. George Walter and Evelyn Ruth (MacLean) Geisler; m. Harvey Lee Slade, June 6, 1981 (div. Aug. 11, 1993); 1 child, Sherry (Rachel) Orona. Grad. H.S., Springerville, Ariz., 1974; student, Northland Pioneer Coll., Springerville, Ariz., 1986-90, Res. Police Acad., 1986. Clk. Round Valley Justice Ct., Springerville, 1981-84, chief clk., 1984-88, office mgr., judge pro tem, 1988-93, justice of the peace, 1993—; city magistrate City of Springerville and Eagar, Ariz., 1993—. Mentor judge Ariz. Supreme Ct., 1994—; edn. chair Ariz. Justice Ct. Assn, 1994-96. Mem. Nat. Judges Assn. (dir. State of Ariz.), Am. Judges Assn., Ariz. Cts. Assn., State of Ariz. Justice of the Peace Assn. (pres. 1995-99). Ariz. Magistrates Assn. Democrat. Avocations: crafts, gardening, travel, scuba diving. Home: PO Box 1202 Springerville AZ 85938-1202 Office: Round Valley Justice Ct PO Box 1356 Springerville AZ 85938-1356

GEISLER, THOMAS MILTON, JR., lawyer; b. Orange, N.J., Jan. 16, 1943; s. Thomas M. and Helen K. (Thomas) G.; m. Sarah Ann Farrell Geisler, Aug. 6, 1977; children: Sarah C., Ann. C. AB in Math. (cum laude), Harvard Coll., Cambridge, Mass., 1965; JD, Harvard Law Sch., Cambridge, Mass., 1968. Bar: NJ, NY, Conn., U.S. Dist. Ct. (2d cir.), U.S. Supreme Ct. Asst., base legal officer U.S. Naval Submarine Base, New London, Conn., 1969-71; appellate def. counsel Naval Appellate Review Activity, Washington, 1971-72; assoc. Shearman & Sterling, N.Y.C., 1973-80, ptnr., 1980-91; pvt. practice N.Y.C., 1991-96, New Haven, Conn., 1994—. Dir., bd. dirs. Friends of Harvard Law Record, Cambridge, Mass., 1997—. Author: Am. Jur. Proof of Facts 3d, 1995, 1996, 1998, 1999, 2001; editor: Trial Practice Newsletter, 1986—2001. Lt., USNR, 1969-72. Recipient Litigation Star ABA Litigation Sect., 1997, Navy Achievement award USN, Washington, 1971. Mem. ABA (trial practice com.), Conn. Bar Assn., Harvard Club of So. Conn., Harvard Club of N.Y.C., Quinnipiack Club, Madison Beach Club. Presbyterian. Avocations: tennis, squash, theater , concerts. Appellate, Federal civil litigation, State civil litigation. Office: 205 Church St Ste 508 New Haven CT 06510 E-mail: T1827@aol.com.

GEISMER, ALAN STEARN, JR., lawyer; b. Cleve., June 23, 1948; s. Alan S. and Barbara (Peck) G.; m. Susan Dangel, Oct. 17, 1976; children: Lily, Sarah. AB magna cum laude, Harvard U., 1970, JD, 1975; cert., Cambridge U., 1972. Bar: Mass. 1975, U.S. Dist. Ct. Mass. 1975, U.S. Ct. Appeals (1st cir.) 1979. Assoc. Dangel & Smith, Boston, 1975-77, Mason & Martin, Boston, 1977-79, Goldstein & Manello, Boston, 1979-80; ptnr. Berlin, Clarey & Green, Boston, 1980-86, Kassler & Feuer P.C., Boston, 1986-99, Lane, Altman & Owens, LLP, Boston, 1999-2001, Sugarman, Rogers Barshak & Cohen P.C., Boston, 2001—. Bd. dirs. Concert Dance Co., Boston, 1981-91, pres., 1985-91; bd. dirs. Jewish Family and Children's Svc., Boston, 1986—, clk., 1989-90, v.p., 1990-93, pres. 1993-96; bd. dirs. Dance Umbrella, Boston, 1991-95; bd. dirs. World Music, Boston, 1995—; bd. dirs. Vol. Lawyers for the Arts, 1994—, clk., 1997-2002, pres., 2002—; bd. dirs. Assn. Jewish Family and Children's Agy., 1996-2002; bd. trustees Pro Arte Chamber Orch., 2001—. Knox fellowship Harvard Coll., 1970. Fellow Am. Acad. Matrimonial Lawyers (bd. mgrs. Mass. chpt. 1995-98, 2001—); mem. ABA, Boston Bar Assn., Longwood Cricket Club (Chestnut Hill, Mass.), Badminton & Tennis Club. Democrat. Avocations: skiing, bicycling, kayaking, tennis, hiking, biking. Entertainment, Family and matrimonial. Home: 61 Lexington Ave Cambridge MA 02138-3320 Office: Sugarman Rogers Barshak & Cohen PC 101 Merrimac St Boston MA 02114-4737 E-mail: geismer@srbc.com.

GELB, JOSEPH DONALD, lawyer; b. Wilkes-Barre, Pa., Dec. 13, 1923; s. Edward and Esther (Fierman) G. m. Anne Mirman, July 3, 1955; children: Adam, Roger. Student, Pa. State Coll., 1943; BS, U. Scranton, 1950; LLB, George Washington U., 1952. Bar: D.C. 1954, Md. 1963, U.S. Supreme Ct. 1972. Adjudicator War Claims Commn., 1952-54; pvt. practice Washington and Md., 1954-69; ptnr. Gelb & Pitsenberger, Washington, 1969-74; prin. Joseph D. Gelb Chartered, Washington, 1974-80, Gelb, Abelson & Siegel, P.C., Washington, 1980-82, Gelb & Siegel, P.C., Washington, 1982-85, Joseph D. Gelb, Chartered, Washington, 1985-93, Gelb & Gelb, P.C., Washington, 1994—. Served with USAAF, 1943-46 Mem. Md. Bar Assn., D.C. Bar Assn., Bethesda Country Club, B'nai B'rith, Masons. General civil litigation, Personal injury (including property damage), Product liability. Home: 9620 Annlee Ter Bethesda MD 20817-1410 also: 525 N Ocean Blvd Pompano Beach FL 33062-4640 Office: Gelb & Gelb PC 1120 Connecticut Ave NW Washington DC 20036-3902 E-mail: lawyers@gelbandgelb.com.

GELB, JUDITH ANNE, lawyer; b. N.Y.C., Apr. 5, 1935; d. Joseph and Sarah (Stein) G.; m. Howard S. Vogel, June 30, 1962; 1 child, Michael S. BA, Bklyn. Coll., 1955; JD, Columbia U., 1958. Bar: N.Y. 1959, U.S. Dist. Ct. (so. and ea. dists.) N.Y. 1960, U.S. Ct. Appeals (2d cir.) 1960, U.S. Ct. Mil. Appeals 1962. Asst. to editor N.Y. Law Jour., N.Y.C., 1958-59; confidential asst. to U.S. atty. ea dist. N.Y., Bklyn., 1959-61; assoc. Whitman & Ransom, N.Y.C., 1961-70, ptnr., 1971-93, Whitman Breed Abbott & Morgan LLP, N.Y.C., 1993-2000, Winston & Strawn, N.Y.C., 2000—. Mem.: ABA (individual rights sect., real property and trust law sect.), Assn. Bar City N.Y., N.Y. State Dist. Attys. Assn., N.Y. State Bar Assn. (trusts and estates com.), Fed. Bar Coun., Columbia Law Sch. Alumni Assn. (bd. dirs.), Princeton Club. Estate planning, Probate (including wills, trusts), Estate taxation. Home: 169 E 69th St New York NY 10021-5163 Office: Winston & Strawn 200 Park Ave New York NY 10166-0005 E-mail: jgelb@winston.com.

GELB, RICHARD MARK, lawyer; b. N.Y.C., June 12, 1947; s. Harold Seymour and Sylvia Mildred (Miller) G.; m. Gail Kleven, July 29, 1973; 1 child, Daniel Kleven. BA, NYU, 1969; JD, Boston Coll., 1973. Bar: Mass. 1973, N.Y. 1975, D.C. 1975, U.S. Dist. Ct. (so. and ea. dists.) N.Y. 1975, U.S. Ct. Appeals (2d cir.) 1975, U.S. Dist. Ct. Conn. 1977, U.S. Ct. Appeals (1st cir.) 1978, U.S. Dist. Ct. Mass. 1978, U.S. Supreme Ct. 1980. Assoc. Proskauer Rose, LLP, N.Y.C., 1975-77; ptnr. Gelb & Gelb LLP, Boston, 1987—. Contbr. articles to profl. publs. Mem. Mass. Bar Assn. (ethics com. 1991-96, civil litig. coun. 1994-96, chmn. bus. litig. com. 1992-94, assoc. editor Mass. Law Rev. 1982-87), Am. Inn of Ct. Found. (trustee 1994-98), Boston Inn of Ct. (co-pres. 1993-94), Boston Coll. Law Sch. Intellectual Property Am. Inns of Ct. (pres. 1998-2000, treas. 2001-02), Boston Coll. Law Sch. Alumni Coun. (v.p. comms. 2001-03), Suffolk U. Law Sch. Litig. Am. Inn Ct. (co-pres. 2002—), Pi Sigma Alpha. Democrat. Jewish. Federal civil litigation, State civil litigation. Home: 60 Pine Hill Rd Swampscott MA 01907-2240 Office: Gelb & Gelb LLP 20 Custom House St Ste 1030 Boston MA 02110-3559

GELBER, DON JEFFREY, lawyer; b. L.A., Mar. 10, 1940; s. Oscar and Betty Sheila (Chernitsky) G.; m. Jessica Jeasun Song, May 15, 1967; children: Victoria, Jonathan, Rebecca, Robert. Student UCLA, 1957-58, Reed Coll., 1958-59; AB, Stanford U., 1961, JD, 1963. Bar: Calif. 1964, Hawaii 1964, U.S. Dist. Ct. (cen. and no. dists. Calif.) 1964, U.S. Dist. Ct. Hawaii 1964, U.S. Ct. Appeals (9th cir.) 1964, U.S. Supreme Ct. 1991. Assoc. Greenstein, Yamane & Cowan, Honolulu, 1964-67; reporter Penal Law Revision Project, Hawaii Jud. Council, Honolulu, 1967-69; assoc. H. William Burgess, Honolulu, 1969-72; ptnr. Burgess & Gelber, Honolulu, 1972-73; prin. Law Offices of Don Jeffrey Gelber, Honolulu, 1974-77; pres. Gelber & Wagner, Honolulu, 1978-83, Gelber & Gelber, Honolulu, 1984-89, Gelber, Gelber, Ingersoll, Klevansky & Faris, Honolulu, 1990-2002, Gelber, Gelber, Ingersoll & Klevansky, 2002--; legal counsel Hawaii State Senate Judiciary Com., 1965; adminstrv. asst. to majority floor leader Hawaii State Senate, 1966, legal counsel Edn. Com., 1967, 68; majority counsel Hawaii Ho. of Reps., 1974; spl. counsel Hawaii State Senate, 1983. Contbr. articles to legal pubs. Mem. State Bar Calif., ABA (sect. bus. law), Am. Bankruptcy Inst., Hawaii State Bar Assn. (sect. bankruptcy law, bd. dirs. 1991-93, pres. 1993). Clubs: Pacific, Plaza (Honolulu). Bankruptcy, Federal civil litigation, Property, real (including real estate development, water). Office: Gelber Gelber Ingersoll & Klevansky 745 Fort Street Mall Ste 1400 Honolulu HI 96813-3877

GELBER, LOUISE C(ARP), lawyer; m. Milton Gelber (dec.); children: Jack, Bruce, Julie McCoy. BA, JD, U. Calif., 1944. Bar: Calif. 1945, U.S. Dist. Ct. (so. dist.) Calif. 1945, U.S. Supreme Ct. 1965. Pvt. practice; commr. Calif. Bd. Examiners for Nursing Home Adminstrs.; adminstr. Calif. Dept. Consumer Affairs. Speaker local drug rehab. hosp.; mem. Vis. Nurses Bd.; commr. Calif. Adv. Cost Control to State Govt.; mem. temporary judge panel L.A. County; settlement officer dispute resolution svc. Pasadena Superior Ct. Mem. editorial staff U. Calif. Law Rev. Calif. nominee for State Assembly, 1992; judge pro tem Rio Hondo Mcpl. Ct.; pro bono Bd. Legal Aid; v.p. local PTA; mem., invocator Arcadia Coord. Coun.; bd. dirs. Foothill Apt. Assn., People-For People; active ARC, Community Chest, United Way, Boy Scouts Am., Girl Scouts U.S. Mem. ABA, Calif. Bar Assn., Foothill Bar ASsn., L.A. County Bar ASsn., Pomona Valley Bar Assn., Citrus Bar Assn., Arcadia C. of C. (legis. com.), So. Calif. Women Lawyers (treas.), Pasadena C. of C., Bus. and Profl. Women Lawyers (past state legis. chmn., state legis. adv.), Order of Eastern Star, LWV, Sierra. General practice, Property, real (including real estate development, water). Home and Office: 1225 Rancho Rd Arcadia CA 91006-2241 E-mail: french.court@verizon.net.

GELFMAN, PETER TRUSTMAN, lawyer; b. New Rochelle, N.Y., Oct. 3, 1963; s. Robert William and Phyllis (Trustman) G.; m. Marguerite Gabrielle Dreifuss, Sept. 6, 1992; children: Justine Caroline, Max Sokoloff. AB magna cum laude, Harvard Coll., 1986; JD, Yale U., 1989. Bar: N.Y. 1989, D.C. 1990, U.S. Dist. Ct. (so. and ea. dists.) N.Y. 1990, U.S. Ct. Appeals (2d cir.) 1991. Assoc. Cravath, Swaine & Moore, N.Y.C., 1989-91; asst. U.S. Atty. U.S. Dist. Ct. (so. dist.), N.Y.C., 1992-96; sr. atty. Westvaco Corp., N.Y.C., 1996-99; sr. assoc. gen. counsel Sequa Corp., N.Y.C., 1999—. Mem. Town Village Civic Club, Scarsdale, N.Y., 1998—, co-chair edn. com., 1999-2001, 1st v.p., 2001-02, pres., 2002-03; bd. edn. Mt. Pleasant Cottage UFSD, Pleasantville, N.Y., 1999—; bd. ethics Scarsdale (N.Y.) Village, 1999—; mem. legis. adv. com. Scarsdale (N.Y.) Bd. Edn., 2000-02. Mem. ABA, Am. Corp. Counsel Assn., Assn. Bar City of N.Y., Harvard Club N.Y.C. Commercial, contracts (including sales of goods; commercial financing), Corporate, general. Office: Sequa Corp 200 Park Ave Fl 44 New York NY 10166-0005

GELHAUS, ROBERT JOSEPH, lawyer, publisher; b. Missoula, Mont., Oct. 17, 1941; s. Francis Joseph and Bonnie Una (Mundhenk) G. AB magna cum laude, Harvard Coll., 1963; LlB, Stanford U., 1968. Bar: Calif. 1970, U.S. Dist. Ct., U.S. Ct. Appeals 1970. Assoc. firm Howard, Prim, Rice, Nemerovski, Canady & Pollak, San Francisco, 1970-74; sole practice San Francisco, 1974—. Editor in chief Harcourt Brace Jovanovich Legal & Profl. Publs., Inc., 1974-78; pres. Robert J. Gelhaus, A Profl. Corp., 1978—; instr. econs. U. Wash., 1964-65; instr. law Stanford Law Sch., 1968-69; cons. FCC, 1968-69; asst. Calif. Law Revision Commn., 1967-68. Author (with James C. Oldham): Summary of Labor Law, 12th edit., 1972. Mem. Calif. Bar Assn., Harvard Club San Francisco, Order Coif, Omicron Delta Epsilon. Antitrust, Federal civil litigation, Labor (including EEOC, Fair Labor Standards Act, labor-management relations, NLRB, OSHA). Home: 1756 Broadway San Francisco CA 94109-2458

GELINAS, ROBERT ALBERT, lawyer; b. Springfield, Mass., May 28, 1930; s. Albert Edward and Alvena Loretta Gelinas; m. Judith Ann Marcure, Jan. 30, 1954; children: Lyn Ann, William, John, Michele. BS, St. Michael's Coll., 1951; LLB, Boston U., 1953. Bar: Mass. 1953, U.S. Dist. Ct. Mass. 1959, U.S. Ct. Appeals (1st cir.) 1965. Ptnr. Bulkley, Richardson and Gelinas LLP, Springfield, Mass., 1957—. Spl. asst. atty. gen., Mass., 1964-70; mem. faculty trial advocacy program Mass. CLE; trustee Holyoke C.C., 1992-2002, chmn. bd. trustees, 1999-2001. Mem. Mass. Rep. Com., 1964-72; chmn. profl. unit United Way, Springfield, 1996; mem. com. Nat. Conf. Chicopee Cmty. Ctr., past pres. Recipient Tree of Life award Jewish Nat. Fund, 1997. Mem. ATLA, Mass. Acad. Trial Attys., Mass. Bar Assn., Hampden County Bar Assn. (exec. com., medico-legal com. 1992—). Roman Catholic. Avocation: outdoor activities. Administrative and regulatory, Personal injury (including property damage), Corporate taxation. Office: Bulkley Richardson and Gelinas LLP 1500 Main St Ste 2700 Springfield MA 01115-0001 E-mail: rgelinas@bulkley.com.

GELLER, KENNETH STEVEN, lawyer; b. N.Y.C., Sept. 22, 1947; s. Edward and Sylvia R. (Tannenbaum) G.; m. Judith B. Ratner, Sept. 9, 1990; children: Eric Jonathan, Lisa Beth. BA magna cum laude, CCNY, 1968; JD magna cum laude, Harvard U., 1971. Bar: N.Y. 1972, U.S. Dist. Ct. (so. and ea. dists.) N.Y. 1972, U.S. Ct. Appeals (2d cir.) 1972, U.S. Ct. Appeals (D.C. cir.) 1974, U.S. Supreme Ct. 1975, U.S. Ct. Appeals (10th cir.) 1976, D.C. 1986, U.S. Ct. Appeals (6th cir.) 1987, U.S. Ct. Appeals (4th cir.) 1987, U.S. Ct. Appeals (9th cir.) 1988, U.S. Ct. Appeals (5th and 11th cirs.) 1990, U.S. Dist. Ct. D.C. 1991, U.S. Ct. Appeals (3rd and 7th cirs.) 1991, U.S. Ct. Appeals (Armed Forces) 1995, U.S. Ct. Appeals (8th cir.) 1996, U.S. Ct. Appeals (fed. cir.) 1999. Law clk. U.S. Ct. Appeals (2d cir.), 1971-72; assoc. Nickerson, Kramer, Lowenstein, Nessen & Kamin, N.Y.C., 1972-73; asst. spl. prosecutor Watergate Spl. Prosecution Force, Washington, 1973-75; asst. to solicitor gen. Dept. Justice, Washington, 1975-79, dep. solicitor gen., 1979-86; ptnr. Mayer, Brown, Rowe & Maw (formerlyMayer, Brown & Platt), Washington, 1986—, mng. ptnr., 1995—. Mem. adv. bd. State and Local Legal Ctrs., 1986-92; mem. adv. com. on rules U.S. Ct. Appeals for Armed Forces, 1994—; mem. adv. com. on procedures Ct. Appeals D.C. Cir., 2000—. Co-author: (Stern, Gressman, Shapiro & Geller) Supreme Court Practice, 8th edit., 2002; contbg. author: Business and Commercial Litigation in Federal Courts, 1998; contbr. articles to profl. jours. Mem. vis. com. Harvard U. Law Sch.; trustee, chmn. publs. com. Supreme Ct. Hist. Soc. Recipient Younger Fed. Lawyer award FBA, 1981, Presdl. Disting. Exec. award. Office: Mayer Brown Rowe & Maw 1909 K St NW Washington DC 20006-1152 E-mail: kgeller@mayerbrown.com.

GELLHORN, ERNEST ALBERT EUGENE, lawyer; b. Oak Park, Ill., Mar. 30, 1935; s. Ernst and Hilde Betty (Obermeier) G.; m. Jaquelin Ann Silker, Feb. 1, 1958; children: Thomas Ernest, Ann Lois. BA cum laude, U. Minn., 1956, LLB magna cum laude, 1962. Bar: Ohio 1962, Va. 1975, Ariz. 1976, D.C. 1986, Calif. 1990. Assoc. Jones, Day, Reavis & Pogue, Cleve., Washington, L.A., 1962-66; prof. law Duke U. Law Sch., 1966-70, U. Va. Law Sch., 1970-75; dean Coll. Law, Ariz. State U., Tempe, 1975-78, U. Wash. Law Sch., Seattle, 1978-79; T. Munford Boyd prof. U. Va. Law Sch., Charlottesville, 1979-82; dean, Galen J. Roush prof. Case Western Res. U. Sch. Law, Cleve., 1982-86; ptnr. Jones, Day, Reavis & Pogue, L.A., Washington, 1986-94; George Mason U. Found. prof. law, 1995—. Sr. counsel Commn. CIA Activities Within U.S., 1975. Co-author: Antitrust Law and Economics, 4th edit., 1994, Administrative Law and Process, 4th edit., 1997, The Administrative Process, 4th edit., 1993. Lt. USNR, 1956-59. Mem. ABA, Ariz. Bar Assn., Va. Bar Assn., Ohio Bar Assn., D.C. Bar Assn., Calif. Bar Assn., Phi Beta Kappa, Order of Coif. Administrative and regulatory, Antitrust, Appellate. Home: 2907 Normanstone Ln NW Washington DC 20008-2725 E-mail: gellhorn@pipeline.com.

GELTMAN, EDWARD ALAN, lawyer; b. Newark, Apr. 14, 1946; s. Donald and Muriel G.; m. Elizabeth Ann Glass, Jan. 2, 1989; children: Andrew, Jeffrey, Rachel. BA with honors, Franklin & Marshall Coll., 1968; JD with honors, George Washington U., 1971. Bar: D.C. 1971, U.S. Ct. Appeals (D.C. cir.) 1971, U.S. Supreme Ct. 1980. Trial atty. FTC, Washington, 1971-73; assoc., then ptnr. Nicholson & Carter, Washington,

1973-79; ptnr. Squire, Sanders & Dempsey, Washington, 1979—. Contbr. articles to profl. jours. Mem. ABA (antitrust sect.), Order of Coif. Office: Squire Sanders & Dempsey 1201 Pennsylvania Ave NW Washington DC 20004-2491

GEMELLO, MATTHEW ROBERT, lawyer; b. Palo Alto, Calif., Jan. 25, 1971; s. John Michael and Linda Marino Gemello; m. Tamara Moon Gemello, May 27, 2001. BA, U. Calif. San Diego, 1993; JD, Northwestern U., 1997. Corp. lawyer Brobeck, Phleger & Harrison LLp, San Francisco, 2000—, Crosby Heafey Roach & May, San Francisco, 1999—2000, Jackson Tufts Cole & Black LLP, San Francisco, 1996—99. Mem.: ABA. Office: Brobeck Phleger & Harrison LLP One Market Spear Tower San Francisco CA 94105 Office Fax: 415-442-1010. E-mail: mgemello@brobeck.com.

GENBERG, IRA, lawyer; b. Newark, July 27, 1947; s. Jack and Ann (Lerman) G.; m. Rosemary Lawlor, Jan. 15, 1981; children: Jack Michael, Anne Rebecca. AB magna cum laude, Rutgers U., 1969; JD, U. Pa., 1972. Bar: Ga. 1972, D.C. 1978. Assoc. Haas, Holland, Levison & Gibert, Atlanta, 1972-75; ptnr. Stokes, Shapiro, Fussell & Genberg, Atlanta, 1975-87; ptnr., head litigation sect. Smith, Gambrell & Russell LLP, Atlanta, 1987—. Spkr. Seminar on Constrn. Litigation, Atlanta, 1985, Seminar on Constrn. Law, Atlanta, 1986; co-chmn. Seminar on Trying A Complex Constrn. Case, 1994. Contbr. articles to Constrn. Bus. Review Mag. Mem. ABA, Ga. Bar Assn., Atlanta Bar Assn., D.C. Bar Assn. Antitrust, Construction. Office: Smith Gambrell & Russell LLP 1230 Peachtree St NE Atlanta GA 30309-3592

GENEGO, WILLIAM JOSEPH, lawyer; b. Albany, Mar. 27, 1950; s. William Joseph and Olga Alice (Sultan) G. BS in Bus. and Pub. Adminstrn. magna cum laude, NYU, 1972; JD, Yale U., 1975; LLM, Georgetown U., 1977. Bar: D.C. 1975, Calif. 1982, U.S. Supreme Ct. 1984, other dist. and appellate cts. Spl. asst. state's atty. Cir. and Dist. Cts. Montgomery County, Md., 1975-77; staff atty. legal intern program Georgetown U. Law Ctr., Washington, 1975-77, adj. prof., dep. dir. legal intern program, 1977-79; cons., vis. supervising atty. Yale Legal Svcs. Orgn., Law Sch. Yale U., New Haven, 1977; with Baker & Fine, Cambridge, Mass., 1980-81; asst. clin. prof. Law Ctr. U. So. Calif., L.A., 1981-83, assoc. clin. prof., 1983-86, clin. prof., 1986-89, adj. prof., 1990-92; vis. prof. law Boston U., 1990, UCLA, 1991-92; pvt. practice Law Offices of William J. Genego, Santa Monica, Calif., 1990-2000; ptnr. Nasatir, Hirsch, Podberesky & Genego, Santa Monica, 2000—. Mem. practitioners' adv. group U.S. Sentencing Commn., 1989—; presenter in field. Mem. adv. bd. Criminal Practice Manual, Bur. Nat. Affairs, 1987-2000; editor Yale Law Jour., 1974-75; contbr. articles to legal publs. Bd. dirs. Nat. Network for Right to Counsel, 1986-88. Recipient Ann. Humanitarian award inmate rep. com. Fed. Correctional Instn., Danbury, Conn., 1974. Mem. NACDL (chairperson com. on rules of practice and procedure 1991—, Pres.'s award 1988), ABA (mem. ad hoc com. on U.S. Sentencing Commn. 1986—, chairperson competency com. sect. criminal justice 1983-85), Nat. Legal Aid and Defender Assn. (chairperson def. counsel competency com. 1984-87), Calif. Pub. Defenders Assn., Calif. Attys. for Criminal Justice. Appellate, Criminal. Office: Main St Law Bldg 2115 Main St Santa Monica CA 90405-2215

GENEL, NOAH D. lawyer; b. N.Y.C., May 18, 1971; BA, Union Coll., Schenectady, N.Y., 1993; JD, Fordham U., 1998. Bar: N.Y. 1999, U.S. Dist. Ct. (so. and ea. dists.) N.Y. 1999. Assoc. Schulte Roth & Zabel LLP, N.Y.C., 1998—2001, Morvillo Abramowitz Grand Iason & Silberberg, PC, N.Y.C., 2001—. Mem.: ABA, The Assn. of the Bar of the City of N.Y., Nat. Assn. Criminal Def. Lawyers, N.Y. State Bar Assn. white collar criminal defense, General civil litigation. Office: Morvillo Abramowitz et al PC 565 Fifth Ave New York NY 10017 Office Fax: 212-856-9494. E-mail: ngenel@magislaw.com.

GENIA, JAMES MICHAEL, lawyer; b. Chgo., Sept. 16, 1964; s. Anthony Leo and Anne Louise (Hawley) G. BA, Augsburg Coll., 1987; JD, William Mitchell Coll. Law, 1990. Bar: Minn. 1990, U.S. Dist. Ct. Minn. 1992, U.S. Ct. Appeals (8th cir.) 1994, U.S. Supreme Ct. 1999. Judicial law clk. State Minn., Duluth, 1990-92; dep. solicitor gen. Mille Lacs Band of Ojibwe Indians, Onamia, Minn., 1992-93, solicitor gen., 1993-99; atty. Lockridge Grindal Nauen, Mpls., 1999—. Bd. dirs. Woodlands Nat. Bank, Onamia, 1996—, chmn., 1997—; vice-chmn. bd. dirs. Anishinabe O.I.C., Onamia, 1992-99; bd. dirs. Johnson Inst. Found., 1998—; bd. dirs. Minn. Am. Indian C. of C., 2001—; lectr. Am. Indian sovereignty and treaty rights various univs., cntinuing edn. seminars, civic groups, 1992—; adj. prof. St. Cloud State U., 1999—. Actor Mille Lacs Cmty. Theater, Onamia, 1996—. Bd. dirs. Johnson Inst. Found., 1998—. Named Atty. of Yr., Minn. Lawyer Newspaper, 1999, named One of Top 100 All-Time Grads., William Mitchell Coll. Law, 2000. Mem. ATLA, Fed. Bar Assn., Minn. Am. Indian Bar Assn., Minn. State Bar Assn., William Mitchell Coll. Law Alumni Assn. (bd. dirs. 1996-99). Avocations: softball, golf, jogging, reading, acting. Office: Lockridge Grindal Nauen 100 Washington Ave S Ste 2200 Minneapolis MN 55401-2179 E-mail: jmgenia@locklaw.com.

GENIESSE, ROBERT JOHN, lawyer; b. Appleton, Wis., Sept. 16, 1929; s. Arthur John and Rhoda (Miller) G.; m. Jane Elizabeth Fletcher, June 10, 1961; children: Julia Forrest, Thomas Guy. BA magna cum laude, Williams Coll., 1951; LLB cum laude, Harvard U., 1957. Bar: N.Y. 1958, D.C. 1982. Assoc. Debevoise and Plimpton, N.Y.C., 1957-61, 64-66, ptnr., 1966-94; asst. U.S. atty. So. Dist. N.Y., 1962-63, chief appellate atty., 1963-64. Editor Harvard Law Rev., 1955-57. Bd. dirs. Legal Action Ctr., N.Y., 1973-78, Environ. Def. Fund, 1974-82; trustee Williams Coll., 1974-87; trustee World Monuments Fund, 1993—, sec., gen. counsel, 1995—; trustee Nat. Bldg. Mus., 1994-2000; trustee Sterling and Francine Clark Art Inst., Williamstown, Mass., 1974-2001, pres., 1987-98; trustee Ringling Mus. Art, Sarasota, Fla., 2001—. 1st lt. Inf. U.S. Army, 1952-54. Mem. N.Y. State Bar Assn., D.C. Bar Assn., Soc. Alumni of Williams Coll. (pres. 1973-74), Phi Beta Kappa. Federal civil litigation, Corporate, Private international. Home: PO Box 516 Boca Grande FL 33921-0516 also: 2101 Connecticut Ave NW Apt 61 Washington DC 20008-1757 Office: Devevoise & Plimpton 555 13th St NW Ste 1100E Washington DC 20004-1163

GENKIN, BARRY HOWARD, lawyer; b. Philadelphia, Aug. 8, 1949; s. Paul and Pearl (Rosenfeld) G.; m. Marian (Block), Aug. 15, 1975; children: Matthew Todd, Kimberly Beth. BS(hon.) , Pa. State U., 1971; JD (hon.) , U. Md., Balt., 1974; LLM in taxation, Georgetown U., 1977. Bar: Pa., 1975; Wash., 1977; N.Y., 1995. Spl. counsel divsn. corp. fin. SEC, Washington, 1975-78; ptnr. Blank, and Rome , LLP, Phila., 1979-93; firm officer, fin. ptnr., exec. com., co-chmn. corp. dept., dist. com., mgmt. com. Blank, Rome, Comisky, and McCauly LLP, Phila., chmn. budget com. Pres. bd. dirs. Smeal Bus. Sch., Pa. State U., pres., 2003-2005; lectr. various orgn. Contbr. U. Balt. Law Rev., 1991—; lectr. various orgn. Mem. ABA; Pa. Bar Assn.; Savs. Insts.; Pa. Savs. League; N.J. Savs. League,; Meadowlands Country Club; Heuisler Honor Soc.; Omicron Delta Kappa. Banking, Mergers and acquisitions, Securities. Home: 544 Howe Rd Merion Station PA 19066-1129 Office: Blank & Rome LLP One Logan Sq Philadelphia PA 19103

GENOVA, DIANE MELISANO, lawyer; b. Aug. 8, 1948; d. Joseph Louis and Ines (Fiumana) Melisano; m. Joseph Steven Genova, Jan. 15, 1983; children: Anthony Robert, Matthew Edward. AB, Barnard Coll., 1970; postgrad., Harvard U., 1970-71; JD, Columbia U., 1975. Assoc. Milbank, Tweed, Hadley & McCloy, N.Y.C., 1975-80; v.p., asst. resident counsel Morgan Guaranty Trust Co. N.Y., N.Y.C., 1981-90, mng. dir., assoc. gen. counsel, 1990-2000, J.P. Morgan Chase & Co., N.Y.C., 2001—. Harlan Fiske Stone scholar, 1972-75. Mem. Assn. of Bar of City of N.Y., N.Y. State Bar Assn., Internat. Swaps and Derivatives Assn. (bd. dirs. 1999—). Roman Catholic. Banking, Finance. Office: J P Morgan Chase & Co 399 Park Ave New York NY 10022 E-mail: genova_diane@jpmorgan.com.

GENTILE, CARMEN JAMES, lawyer; b. Buffalo, N.Y., July 15, 1951; s. Vincent David and Frances Joan (Fichera) G. BA, Canisius Coll., 1973; JD, George Mason U., 1980. Asst. corp. counsel City of Buffalo, 1983—. Municipal (including bonds), Personal injury (including property damage). Office: 1126 City Hall 65 Niagara Sq Buffalo NY 14202-3331 E-mail: cgentile@ch.ci.buffalo.ny.us.

GENTILE, GARY, lawyer; b. Pitts., Oct. 7, 1946; s. Dominick and Jean Mary Gentile; m. Jean Malinic; children: Liza, Ben, Jordan. BS, Washington and Jefferson U., 1968; JD, U. Pitts., 1971. Bar: Pa. 71, U.S. Supreme Ct. 78. Exec. dir. Allegheny County Housing Authority, Pa., 1978—81; asst. pub. defender, dir. juvenile divsn., chief counsel homicide divsn. Pub. Defender's Office, Pa.; ptnr. Goldberg Gruener Gentile et al, Pitts. Former vice chmn. domestic rels. com. Supreme Ct. of Pa.; chmn. hearing com. Pa. Disciplinary Bd. Fellow: Am. Acad. Matriminial Lawyers; mem.: Pa. Trial Lawyers Assn., Allegheny County Bar Assn., Pa. Bar Assn., Allegheny County Bar Assn. (former mem. judiciary com.), Granfalloons. Office: Goldberg Gruener Gentile et al 310 Grant St Pittsburgh PA 15219-2202

GENTRY, GAVIN MILLER, lawyer; b. N.Y.C., Oct. 5, 1930; s. Curtis Gavin and Grace (Wattenbarger) Gentry, Curtis Gavin and Grace (Wattenbarger) Gentry; m. Mary Jane Coleman, Sept. 28, 1963; children: Janie Coleman, Grace Eleanor; m. Mary Jane Coleman, Sept. 28, 1963. BS, JD, U. Tenn., 1954. Bar: Tenn. 1954, U.S. Dist. Ct. (we. dist.) Tenn. 1956, U.S. Supreme Ct. 1978. Trial counsel U.S. Army, 1954—56; ptnr. Armstrong & Allen PLLC, Memphis, 1956—76, sr. ptnr., 1976—98; ret., 1998. Redrafting com. Tenn. Corp. Law; guest lectr. Memphis State U., U. Tenn. Ctr. Health Scis. Author: Great Destinations in the Smokies, 1995. Treas. Tenn. br. Maureen Connelly Brinker Tennis Found., 1972—79; pres. Les Passees Rehab. Ctr., 1977, Lausanne Sch., 1975—78; elder Idlewild Presbyn. Ch.; Pres.'s coun. Rhodes Coll., 1970—; bd. dirs. Girl Scouts U.S.A., 1973—75; pres. Memphis Tennis Assn., 1960—66, Tenn. Tennis Assn., 1960—61. 1st lt. U.S. Army, 1954—56. Recipient Faculty prize, U. Tenn., 1953, numerous awards for tennis. Mem.: ABA, Am. Soc. Law and Medicine, Nat. Health Lawyers Assn., Tenn. Hosp. Assn., Am. Soc. Hosp. Attys., Tenn. Bar Assn., Memphis and Shelby County Bar Assn. (bd. dirs. 1989—90), Univ. Club (Memphis). General civil litigation, Corporate, general, Health. Office: Armstrong & Allen PLLC Brinkley Plz 80 Monroe Ave Ste 700 Memphis TN 38103-2467

GENTRY, MACK A. lawyer; b. Knoxville, Tenn., July 18, 1944; s. Edgar C. and Elizabeth (Cates) G.; m. Cheryl T. Gentry; children: Tucker J., Carter L., Cates E. BSBA, U. Tenn., 1966, JD, 1968; LLM in Taxation, NYU, 1976. Bar: Tenn. 1969, U.S. Dist. Ct. (ea. dist.) Tenn. 1983, U.S. Tax Ct. 1972, U.S. Claims Ct. 1983, U.S. Ct. Appeals (6th cir.) 1985, U.S. Ctl. Appeals (fed. cir.) 1986, Colo. 2001. Assoc. Kramer, Johnson, Rayson, Greenwood & McVeigh, Knoxville, 1972—75; founder Gentry, Tipton, Kizer & McLemore, P.C., Knoxville, 1976, pres., 1976—2000; pvt. practice law Knoxville, 2000—. Trustee Tenn. Fed. Tax Inst.; bd. dirs. Met. YMCA, Knoxville Zoo, U. Tenn. Coll. Law Alumni Adv. Coun. Mem. Tenn. Bar Assn., Knoxville Bar Assn. (chmn. tax sect. 1978-79), Beta Alpha Psi, Phi Delta Phi (v.p. 1966). Estate planning, Taxation, general. Office: 900 S Gay St Ste 2300 Knoxville TN 37902

GEORGACOPULOS, DIMITRIS HARALAMBOS, lawyer; b. Athens, Attica, Greece, Sept. 10, 1968; s. Haralambos Dimitris Georgacopoulos and Alice Sophia Georgacopoulos - Doukas. Degree in Pvt. Law, U. Social Scis., Toulouse, France, 1991, postgrad. degree in comml. law, 1992. Cert.: Athens Bar Assn. (Athens Ct. Appeals) 1996. Assoc. M. & P. Bernitsas Law Offices, Athens, 1997—99; ptnr. M. & B. Bernitsas Law Offices, Athens, 1999—. Avocations: European medieval history, travel, basketball. Banking, Mergers and acquisitions, Construction, Finance. Office: M & P Bernitsas Law Offices 5 Lykavittou St 106 72 Athens Greece Office Fax: 210 36 40 805. E-mail: dg-bern@otenet.gr.

GEORGE, ALEXANDER ANDREW, lawyer; b. Missoula, Mont., Apr. 26, 1938; s. Andrew Miltiadin and Eleni (Efstathiou) G.; m. Penelope Mitchell, Sept. 29, 1968; children: Andrew A., Stephen A. BBA honors, U. Mont., 1960, JD, 1962; postgrad., John Marshall U., 1964-66. Bar: Mont. 1962, U.s. Ct. Mil. Appeals 1964, U.S. Tax Ct. 1970. Sole practice, Missoula, 1966—. Mem. adv. com. U. Mont. Tax Inst., 1973-76; adj. lectr. U. Montana Law Sch. Corp. Taxation. Pres. Missoula Civic Symphony, 1973; nat. dir. Assn. Urban and Cmty. Symphony Orch., 1974, Mont. Eye Endowment Found.; pres. Greek Orthodox Ch., 1978, 91. Served to capt. JAG U.S. Army, 1962-66. Recipient Jaycee Disting. Svc. award, 1973. Mem.: Mont. Soc. CPA, Mont. Law Found. (treas. 1986—92), Western Mont. Bar Assn. (pres. 1971, lifetime achievement award 1998), State Bar Mont. (pres. 1981), Glacier-Waterton Internat. Peace Pk. Assn. (bd. dirs. 1999—2002), Ahepa (pres. 1967, state gov. 1968), Rotary (pres. 1972, state chmn. found. 1977, membership com. chmn. 1978), Sigma Nu (alumni trustee 1966—71), Alpha Kappa Psi, Phi Delta Phi. Corporate, general, Probate (including wills, trusts), Corporate taxation. Home: 4 Greenbrier Ct Missoula MT 59802-3342 Office: 210 N Higgins Ave Ste 234 Missoula MT 59802-4497

GEORGE, JOHN MARTIN, JR., lawyer; b. Normal, Ill., Dec. 17, 1947; s. John and Ada George; m. Judy Ann Watts; children: Sarah, Michael. AB with high honors, U. Ill., 1970, AM, 1971; PhD, Columbia U., 1976; JD cum laude, Harvard U., 1982. Bar: Mass. 1982, U.S. Dist. Ct. Mass. 1983, Ill. 1984, U.S. Dist. Ct. (no. dist.) Ill. 1984, U.S. Ct. Appeals (11th cir.) 1987, U.S. Ct. Appeals (9th cir.) 1988, U.S. Ct. Appeals (7th cir.) 1992, U.S. Ct. Appeals (3d cir.) 2000. Assoc. Hill & Barlow, Boston, 1982-84, Sidley & Austin (now Sidley, Austin, Brown & Wood), Chgo., 1984-89, ptnr., 1989—. Editor Harvard U. Law Rev., 1980-82. Sr. warden Trinity Ch., 1998-2000. Mem. ABA, Chgo. Bar Assn., Mid-Day Club, Phi Beta Kappa. Democrat. Episcopalian. Federal civil litigation, Professional liability, Securities. Office: Sidley Austin Brown & Wood Bank One Plz Chicago IL 60603-2003 E-mail: jgeorge@sidley.com.

GEORGE, KATIE, lawyer; b. Chillicothe, Ohio, Sept. 4, 1953; d. Harry Paul and Tina Lillian George; m. Nov. 25, 1972 (div. Nov. 1983); 1 child, Alison; m. Timothy John Nusser, June 30, 1985. BBA, U. Toledo, 1983, JD, 1986, MBA, 1989. Bar: Ohio 1987, U.S. Dist. Ct. (no. dist.) Ohio 1993, Fla. 1994. Law clk. Allotta, Singer & Farley, Co., LPA, Toledo, 1985-86; mgmt. specialist Dept. Pub. Utilities City of Toledo, 1987-91, acting commr. Dept. Health, 1992-93, acting mgr. Dept. Pub. Safety, 1991-94; pvt. practice Toledo, 1987-96, Pensacola, Fla., 1996—; asst. dist. legal counsel State of Fla., 1996-97, chief legal counsel, 1997—. Part-time instr. U. Toledo, 1987-88, U. West Fla., 1997. Bd. dirs. Toledo BlockWatch, 1993, Ohio Pub. Employers Labor Rels. Assn., 1991-92; mem. Missing and Exploited Children Comprehensive Action Program, 1997-99. Mem. Fla. Bar Assn., Escambia Santa Rosa Bar Assn. Avocations: gardening, photography, scuba diving. Administrative and regulatory, Government contracts and claims, Labor (including EEOC, Fair Labor Standards Act, labor-management relations, NLRB, OSHA). Office: 160 Governmental Ctr Ste 601 Pensacola FL 32501

GEORGE, KIMBERLY ANN, lawyer; b. Worcester, Mass., Mar. 6, 1969; d. Robert Peter and Patricia Jane (Amster) George; m. Charles Andrew Hajdu; 1 child, Noah Robert Hajdu. BA, Purdue U., 1991; JD, Suffolk U., 1995. Bar: Hawaii 1995, U.S. Dist. Ct. Hawaii 1995, Mass. 1996, U.S. Dist. Ct. Mass. 1997. Immigration counsel NH Cath. Charities Inc., Windham, NH, 1996—. Mem.: ABA, Hawaii State Bar Assn., Am. Immigration Lawyers Assn., Phi Kappa Phi, Omicron Delta Kappa, Phi Beta Kappa. Office: NH Catholic Charities Inc 23 Searles Rd Windham NH 03087

GEORGE, NICHOLAS, lawyer, entrepreneur; b. Seattle, July 11, 1952; s. Harry and Mary (Courounes) G.; children: Harry Nicholas, James Michael. BA in Polit. Sci. cum laude, Whitman Coll., 1974; MBA in Mktg. and Corp. Planning, U. Chgo., 1979; JD, U. Puget Sound, 1989. Bar: Wash. 1991, U.S. Dist. Ct. (we. dist.) Wash. 1991, U.S. Ct. Appeals (9th cir.) 1991, U.S. Tax Ct. 1992, U.S. Dist. Ct. (ea. dist.) Wash. 1994, U.S. Supreme Ct. 1994. Fin. cons. Pacific Western Investment Co., Lynnwood, Wash., 1975-77; planning dir. Clinton Capital Ventures, Seattle, 1979-81; corp. planning mgr. Tacoma Boatbldg., 1981-83; pres. MegaProf Investors, Bellevue, Wash., 1983-89; practice trial-settlement law bus., Seattle, 1989—. Free-lance coll. counselor, Seattle, 1980—. Author: Legitimacy in Government: Ideal, Goal, or Myth? 1974. Bd. auditor St. Demetrios Greek Orthodox Ch., Seattle, 1982-83; bd. dirs. Hellenic Golfers Assn., Seattle, 1981-83. Mem. ABA, Assn. Trial Lawyers Am., Wash. State Bar Assn., Wash. Assn. Criminal Def. Lawyers, Wash. State Trial Lawyers Assn., Fed. Bar Assn., Nat. Assn. Criminal Def. Lawyers, Tacoma-Pierce County Bar Assn., Seattle-King County Bar Assn., Wash. Defender Assn., Wash. State Hist. Soc., Am. Inst. Archeol., Phi Alpha Delta. Greek Orthodox. Avocations: weightlifting, travel, family history, football coaching, writing. Home: 5007 80th St SW Lakewood WA 98499-4077 Office: Ste 102 2412 N 30th Tacoma WA 98407

GEORGE, PAUL M. law librarian, library director; Assoc. libr. rsch. svcs. Harvard Law Sch.; dir. Biddle Law Libr. U. Pa., Phila., 2002—. Office: U Pa Biddle Law Libr 3460 Chestnut St Philadelphia PA 19104-3406*

GEORGE, RICHARD NEILL, retired lawyer; b. Watertown, N.Y., Apr. 6, 1933; s. Wendell Dow and Frances Laura (Small) G.; m. Patricia Harman Jackson, June 21, 1958; children: Frances Harman, Richard Neill, Mary Elizabeth AB, Yale U., 1955; JD, Cornell U., 1962. Bar: N.Y. 1962. Assoc. Nixon Peabody, LLP (formerly Nixon, Hargave, Devans & Doyle), Rochester, N.Y., 1962-70, ptnr., 1970-2000, ret., 2000. Committeeman, Brighton Town Republican Com., Rochester, 1966-78; ruling elder Twelve Corners Presbyn. Ch., Rochester, 1977-79, 84-87; mem. permanent jud. commn. Presbytery of Genesee Valley, 1988-94, moderator. Capt. USAF, 1956-59. Mem. ABA, N.Y. State Bar Assn., Monroe County Bar Assn., Fed. Energy Bar Assn., Exeter Alumni Assn. of Rochester (pres. 1970—), Country Club of Rochester, Yale Club (N.Y.C.), Amelia Island Club. Republican. Avocations: golf, reading. Administrative and regulatory, FERC practice, Utilities, public. Home: 14 Oakfield Way Pittsford NY 14534-1888

GEORGE, RONALD M. state supreme court chief justice; b. L.A., Mar. 11, 1940; AB, Princeton U., 1961; JD, Stanford U., 1964. Bar: Calif. 1965. Dep. atty. gen. Calif. Dept. Justice, 1965-72; judge L.A. Mcpl. Ct., L.A. County, 1972-77, Superior Ct. Calif., L.A. County, 1977-87, supervising judge criminal divsn., 1983-84; assoc. justice 2d dist., divsn. 4 Calif. Ct. Appeal, L.A., 1987-91; assoc. justice Calif. Supreme Ct., San Francisco, 1991-96, chief justice, 1996—. Mem. Calif. Judges Assn. (pres. 1982-83), Conf. Chief Justices (pres.-elect). Avocations: hiking, skiing, running. Office: Calif Supreme Court 350 Mcallister St Fl 5 San Francisco CA 94102-4797

GEORGE, W. PEYTON, lawyer; b. Ada, Okla., Oct. 2, 1936; s. William Peyton and Jodie (Kite) G.; m. Nancy Whorton, Aug. 14, 1966; 1 child, Richard Peyton. BS, U. Ctrl. Okla., 1961; grad., FBI Acad., 1962; JD, Am. U., 1969; postgrad., Army War Coll., 1981. Bar: Va. 1969, D.C. 1970, Okla. 1986. Oil field worker, Okla. and Tex., 1954-59; officer Oklahoma City Police Dept., 1959-62; agt. FBI, Va., N.J., D.C., 1962-69; congl. liaison for sec. Agr. USDA, Washington, 1969-73; ptnr. W. Peyton George, P.C., Washington, 1973-81, Miles & Stockbridge, Washington, 1981-90, Lathrop & Gage, L.C., Washington, 1990—2001, New Capitol Solutions, Santa Fe, 2001—. Col. USAR, 1957-91. Decorated Legion of Merit, Meritorious Svc. medal with oak leaf cluster. Mem. Masons (32 deg.), Shriner. Republican. General practice. Office: New Capitol Solutions 907 Old Santa Fe Trail Santa Fe NM 87505 Business E-Mail: peyton@newcapitolsolutions.com.

GEORGES, PETER JOHN, lawyer; b. Wilmington, Del., Sept. 8, 1940; s. John Peter and Olga Demetrius (Kazitoris) G. BS in Chemistry, U. Del., 1962; JD, John Marshall Law Sch., 1970; LLM in Patent and Trade Regulations, George Washington U., 1973. Bar: Ill. 1970, U.S. Ct. Appeals (fed. cir.) 1972, D.C. 1973, U.S. Supreme Ct. 1973, Del. 1977. Chemist engring. labs Bell & Howell Co., Chgo., 1966; patent coordinator Armour & Co., Chgo., 1967; patent agt., atty. UOP Inc., Chgo., 1968-71, Washington counsel Arlington, Va., 1972-77; ptnr. Kile, Gholz, Bernstein & Georges, Arlington, 1977-78; assoc., then ptnr. Law Office Sidney W. Russell, Arlington, 1978-83; mng. officer Breneman & Georges (and predecessor law firms), Alexandria, 1983—; founding ptnr. Lenastri Properties and Joanastri Properties, Alexandria, Va. Served to 1st lt. USMC, 1963-65, Vietnam. Mem. ABA, Ill. Bar Assn., D.C. Bar Assn., Del. Bar Assn., Fed. Cir. Bar Assn., Assn. Trial Lawyers Am., Am. Intellectual Property Law Assn., Am. Hellenic Lawyers Soc. Federal civil litigation, Patent, Trademark and copyright. Home: 1637 13th St NW Washington DC 20009-4302 Office: Breneman & Georges 3150 Commonwealth Ave Alexandria VA 22305-2712

GEORGIEV, GEORGI VLADIMIROV, lawyer; b. Varna, Bulgaria, Jan. 22, 1968; s. Vladimir Georgiev and Shejina Vasileva Georgieva; m. Tracy Lynn Hailey Georgieva, July 16, 1997; 1 child, Sebastian Watson. LLB, Sofia U., 1991; MA, U. Hull, 1994. Bar: Varha. Sr. legal adv. Varha (Bulgaria) Shipyard, 1991—93, Bureau Veritas, Varha, 1994—97, KPMG Bulgaria, Sofia, 1997—2000, dep. mgr. tax and legal dept., 2000—02; mgr. and sr. lawyer Hayhurst Berlad Robinson, Sofia, Bulgaria, 2002—. Pres. youth orgn. Dem. Party, Sofia, 1990—93. Recipient Chiwning award, Fgn. Office U.K., 1993. Avocations: sports, travel. Commercial, contracts (including sales of goods; commercial financing), Corporate, general, Mergers and acquisitions. Home: 37 Primorska Street 9000 Varha Bulgaria Office: Hayhurst Bercad Robinson 24 Vasil Levski Blvd 1000 Sofia Bulgaria E-mail: ggeorgiev@harlaw.net.

GEPP, RANDY C. lawyer; b. Detroit, Dec. 31, 1951; s. Ramon and Alice Gepp; m. Alice Gepp; children: Ryan, Mason, Wes. BA, Kalamazoo Coll., 1974; JD with distinction, Emory U., 1977. Bar: Ga. 1977, Fla. 1978, Calif. 1978, U.S. Dist. Ct. (no. dist.) Ga. 1977, U.S. Dist. Ct. (so. dist.) Ga. 1978, U.S. Ct. Appeals (11th cir.), U.S. Ct. Appeals (4th cir.), U.S. Supreme Ct. Ptnr. Thompson, Mann & Hutson, Atlanta, 1977—89, Hollowell, Foster & Gepp, PC, Atlanta, 1989—. Mediator USA&M, Atlanta, 1985—95, Resolution Resources Corp., Atlanta, 1990—. Contbr. articles. Mem.: Atlanta Bar Assn. (pres. labor and employment sect. 1995—96, sec. 1994—95), Druid Hills Club, Lawyers Club of Atlanta, Order of Coif. Labor (including EEOC, Fair Labor Standards Act, labor-management relations, NLRB, OSHA), Civil rights. Office: Hollowell Foster & Gepp PC 1200 Harris Tower 233 Peachtree St NE Atlanta GA 30303 Office Fax: 404-880-3364. E-mail: rcg@ahlaw.com.

GEPPERT, JOHN GUSTAVE, JR., lawyer; b. DuBois, Pa., July 1, 1956; s. John Gustave and Patricia C. (Greenland) G.; m. Karen M. Platt, Jan. 30, 1988. BBA, U. Notre Dame, 1978; JD, Seton Hall U., 1983. Bar: N.J. 1983, U.S. Dist. Ct. N.J. 1983, U.S. Ct. Appeals (3d cir.) 1984. Law clk. to judge U.S. Ct. Appeals for 3d Cir., Newark, 1983-84; assoc. Pitney, Hardin, Kipp & Szuch, Morristown, N.J., 1984-86, Wiley, Malehorn & Sirota, Morristown, 1986-88, ptnr., 1988—. Editor-in-chief Seton Hall Law Rev., 1982-83. Active Rockaway Twp. (N.J.) City Coun., 1980-83, Rockaway Twp.

Planning Bd., 1982; trustee N.J. Tchrs. Pension and Annuity Fund, Trenton, 1981-83; pres., bd. dirs. Literacy Vols. Am., Morris County, 1997-99; bd. dirs. United Way Morris County, 1997—. Mem. ABA, N.J. Bar Assn., Morris County Bar Assn., Lions (bd. dirs. Rockaway 1983-88). Republican. Avocations: sports, travel, reading. General civil litigation, Education and schools. Office: Wiley Malehorn & Sirota 250 Madison Ave Morristown NJ 07960-6108 E-mail: jgeppert@wmands.com.

GERALDSON, RAYMOND I., JR., lawyer; b. Racine, Wis., Oct. 19, 1940; s. Raymond I. Sr. and Evelyn (Thorpe) G.; m. Melinda Paine, June 13, 1964; children: Amy Geraldson-Bhote, Raymond I. III. BA, DePauw U., 1962; JD, Northwestern U., 1965. Bar: Ill. 1965, D.C. 1966, U.S. Dist. Ct. (no. dist.) Ill. 1967. Ptnr. Pattishall, McAuliffe, Newbury, Hilliard & Geraldson, Washington, 1965-67, Chgo., 1967—. Adj. prof. John Marshall Law Sch. 1978—; lectr. in field. Contbr. articles on trademark law to profl. jours. Trustee Kendall Coll., 1985—, chmn., 1990-2000. Mem. ABA, Ill. State Bar Assn. (coun. sect. intellectual property law 1978-82, chmn. 1980-81), Chgo. Bar Assn., 7th Crct. Intellectual Property Law Assn. Chgo. (bd. dirs. 1984-86, 92-93, pres. 1991-92), Internat. Trademark Assn. (bd. dirs. 1985-87), Am. Intellectual Property Law Assn., Lawyers for Creative Arts (hons. coun. 1994—, bd. dirs. 1974-94, pres. 1976-78), Lawyers Club Chgo., Econ. Club Chgo., Sunset Ridge Country Club, Union League Club of Chgo., Sigma Chi. General civil litigation, Intellectual property, Trademark and copyright. Office: Pattishall McAuliffe Newbury Hilliard & Geraldson 311 S Wacker Dr Ste 5000 Chicago IL 60606-6631

GERARD, WHITNEY IAN, lawyer; b. N.Y.C., Oct. 31, 1934; s. Harold Todd and Beatrice Roma (Meyer) G.; m. Marion Lehane, Apr. 1, 1966; children: Ian Alexandre, Stefan Meredith. AB, Princeton U., 1956; JD, Harvard U., 1963. Bar: N.Y. 1964. Wine exporter Alexis Lichine et Cie, Bordeaux, France, 1956-58; wine cons. S.S. Pierce Co., Boston, 1960-75; assoc., then ptnr. Alexander and Green, N.Y.C., 1963-84; ptnr., chmn. internat. practice comm. Chadbourne and Parke LLP, N.Y.C., 1984—. Bd. dirs. U. Cape Town Fund, Inc., N.Y.C., Dreyfus Liquid Assets, Inc., The Dreyfus Fund, Inc., Dreyfus Worldwide Dollar Money Market Fund, Inc., Dreyfus Lifetime Portfolios, Inc., Dreyfus Short Intermediate Mcpl. Bond Fund, Dreyfus Short Intermediate Govt. Fund. and other Dreyfus funds. 1st lt. USAF, 1958-60. Mem. ABA, N.Y. State Bar Assn., Internat. Bar Assn., Univ. Club, Ancient Order of Beefeaters (Chief Warder 1965-90). Democrat. Avocations: classical music, ballet, theater, mountain hiking, literature. Home: 940 Park Ave New York NY 10028-0311 also: 102 W Center Rd West Stockbridge MA 01266-9378 Office: Chadbourne & Parke LLP 30 Rockefeller Plz New York NY 10112-0129 E-mail: wgerard@chadbourne.com.

GERBER, CLAUS, lawyer; b. Wiesbaden, Germany, Aug. 14, 1962; 1st state exam, Gutenberg U., Mainz, Germany, 1991; 2nd state exam, Ct. Appeals, Frankfurt, 1994; LLM, Fordham U., 1996. Bar: Frankfurt 1994, N.Y. 1997. Atty. Jones Day Reavis & Pogue, Frankfurt, 1996—98; assoc. Wessing, Frankfurt, 1998—2000, ptnr., 2000—02, Latham & Watkins, Frankfurt, 2002—. Mem.: ABA. Office: Latham & Watkins Platz der Einheit 2 60327 Frankfurt Germany

GERBER, DAVID A. lawyer; b. N.Y.C., Dec. 4, 1944; AB, U. Rochester, 1966; PhD, U. Tex., 1970; JD, UCLA, 1977. Bar: Calif. 1977, U.S. Dist. Ct. (ctrl. dist.) Calif. 1978, U.S. Dist. Ct. (no., ea. and so. dists.) Calif. 1982, U.S. Ct. Appeals (9th cir.) 1978, U.S. Ct. Appeals (1st cir.) 1981, U.S. Ct. Appeals (3d cir.) 1985, U.S. Ct. Appeals (7th cir.) 2001, U.S. Supreme Ct. 1986. Litig. atty. Loeb & Loeb, L.A., 1977-93, Nordman, Cormany, Hair & Compton, Oxnard, Calif., 1993-95, D. Gerber Law Offices, Channel Islands Harbor, Calif., 1995—. Contbr. articles to profl. jours. Trustee L.A. Copyrigt Soc., 1991-94. Mem. State Bar Calif. (exec. com. of intellectual property sect. 1988-91). Federal civil litigation, General civil litigation, Trademark and copyright. Office: 3600 Harbor Blvd Ste 226 Oxnard CA 93035-4184 E-mail: dgerberlaw@aol.com.

GERBER, JOEL, federal judge; b. Chgo., July 16, 1940; s. Peter H. and Marcia L. (Weber) G.; m. Judith R. Smilgoff, Aug. 18, 1963; children— Jay Lawrence, Jeffrey Mark, Jon Victor BSBA, Roosevelt U., Chgo., 1962; JD, DePaul U., Chgo., 1965; LL.M., Boston U., 1968. Bar: Ill. 1965, Ga. 1974. Trial atty. IRS, Boston, 1965-72, staff asst. to regional counsel Atlanta, 1972-76, dist. counsel Nashville, 1976-80, dep. chief counsel Washington, 1980-83, acting chief counsel, 1983-84; judge U.S. Tax Ct., Washington, 1984—; gen. counsel ATF Credit Union, Boston, 1968-70; lectr. Vanderbilt U. Sch. Law, Nashville, 1976-80. Lectr. U. Miami Grad. Law Sch., 1986-90. Recipient awards U.S. Treasury Dept., 1979, 81, 82; Presdl. Meritorious Exec. Rank award, 1983. Office: US Tax Ct 400 2nd St NW Rm 432 Washington DC 20217-0002

GERBER, LAWRENCE, lawyer; b. Chgo., Oct. 2, 1940; BBA, Loyola U. Chgo., 1962; JD, Northwestern U., 1965. CPA Ill.; bar: Ill. 1965. Ptnr. McDermott, Will & Emery, Chgo., mng. ptnr., 1991—. Author: Hospital Restructuring: Why, When and How, 1983. Mem.: Ill. Assn. Hosp. Attys., Am. Acad. Hosp. Attys. Office: McDermott Will & Emery 227 W Monroe St Ste 4400 Chicago IL 60606-5096

GERBER, ROBERT EVAN, judge; b. N.Y.C., Feb. 12, 1947; s. Milton M. and Miriam (Simon) G. BS with high honors, Rutgers U., 1967; JD magna cum laude, Columbia U., 1970. Bar: N.Y. 1971, U.S. Dist. Ct. (so. and ea. dists.) N.Y. 1972, U.S. Ct. Appeals (2d cir.) 1973, U.S. Ct. Appeals (9th cir.) 1974, U.S. Ct. Appeals (10th cir.) 1975, U.S. Ct. Appeals (11th cir.) 1983, U.S. Supreme Ct. 1983, U.S. Ct. Appeals (5th cir.) 1987, U.S. Ct. Appeals (6th cir.) 1989, U.S. Ct. Appeals (3d cir.) 1997. Assoc. Fried, Frank, Harris, Shriver & Jacobson, N.Y.C., 1970-71, 72-78, ptnr., 1978-2000; judge U.S. Bankruptcy Ct. (so. dist.) N.Y., N.Y.C., 2000—. Served to 1st lt. USAF, 1971-72. James Kent scholar, 1970, Harlan Fiske Stone scholar, 1969. Mem. ABA, Assn. Bar City N.Y. (sec. spl. com. on energy 1974-79), Fed. Bar Coun., Am. Bankruptcy Inst., Tau Beta Pi. Office: US Bankruptcy Ct US Custom House One Bowling Green New York NY 10004

GERBERDING COWART, GRETA ELAINE, lawyer; b. Ft. Wayne, Ind., Aug. 17, 1960; d.Ruth (Hostrup) G., stepmother Joanie Wyatt Gerberding; m. T. David Cowart, Aug. 12, 1995. BS with high distinction, Ind. U., 1982; JD cum laude, 1985. Bar: Ind. 1985, U.S. Dist. Ct. (so. dist.) Ind., CPA, Ind., CEBS. Sr. tax cons. Ernst & Whinney, Indpls., 1985-87; assoc. Klineman, Rose, Wolf and Wallack P.C., Indpls., 1987-89, Hall Render Killian Heath & Lyman P.C., Indpls., 1989-95; ptnr. Haynes and Boone, L.L.P., Dallas, 1996—. Presenter at seminars. Author: (with G.P. Gooch) Trust and Estate Income Tax Reporting and Planning, 1985; contbr. chpts. to books, articles to profl. jours. including Jour. Deferred Compensation, 403(b) Answer Book, Benefits Law Jour. Chmn. hospitality area Virginia Slims Tennis Tournament, Indpls., 1987-89; vol. Jello Tennis Classic Tennis Tournament, Indpls., 1990-91; coord. Hospitality and Ball Kids, 1990, Jr. Jamboree GTE Tennis Tournament, Indpls., 1990; vol. Ctr. for Exploration The Children's Mus., Indpls., 1991-94; com. on funding Vision 2002 Luth. Camp Assn., Inc., 1993-94, bd. dirs., 1997—, chmn., 2001—; com. mem. Arcadia Found.; women's retreat com. King of Glory Luth. Ch., 1997—, fin. com., 2000—; bd. dirs. Brianwood Retreat Ctr., 1998-2001. Glen Peters fellow Ind. U., 1984. Fellow Ind. Bar Found.; mem. ABA (com. marital deduction legis. real property and probate sect. 1986-87, tax section, gen. income tax com. 1987-89, employee benefits com. 1988—, subcom. health plan design and state regulation 1993—, health care task force 1994—, chmn. COBRA subcom. 1997-2002, vice chair employee benefits com. 2002—), Ind. Bar Assn. (acct.-lawyers com. 1986-89, co-chmn. com. on legis. 1988-92, coun. tax sect. 1988-96, sec.-treas. 1991-92, vice-chmn. tax sect. 1992-93, chair elect 1993-94, chair 1994-95), Indpls. Bar Assn., Indpls. Jaycees (treas. 4th Festival 1987 monthly dinner meetings 1988), West Indy Racquet Club (USTA Volvo Tennis Team 1986-87, RCA tounament credentials com. 1993-94), Indpls. Racquet Club (USTA Volvo tennis team 1988-91, 96). Avocations: tennis, golf, skiing, swimming, artwork. Health, Pension, profit-sharing, and employee benefits, Taxation, general. Office: Haynes and Boone LLP 901 Main St Ste 3100 Dallas TX 75202-3789

GERDE, CARLYLE NOYES (CY GERDE), lawyer; b. Long Beach, Calif., Oct. 22, 1946; m. Priscilla A. Murphy, July 4, 1976. BA in Am. Studies, Purdue U., 1967; JD, Ind. U., 1970. Bar: Ind. 1971, U.S. Supreme Ct. 1976, U.S. Tax Ct. 1980. Ptnr. Hanna Gerde & Russell, Lafayette, Ind., 1972-86; registered lobbyist Ind. Twp. Assn., 1975-86; spl. counsel Nat. Assn. Towns and Twps., Washington, 1976-86. Adj. prof. indsl. engring. Purdue U., 1972-96; participant White House Conf. Rural Policy, 1978, White House Conf. on Block Grants, 1981, White House Conf. on Liability Ins., 1986; mem. Ind. Gen. Assembly Study Commn. Bd. of govs. Tippecanoe County Hist. Assn., Lafayette, 1976-00, Ams. for Nuclear Energy, Washington (co-founder, v.p. 1977-00); pres. Battle Ground (Ind.) Hist. Corp., 1986; del. State of Ind. GOP Conventions. Mem. Ind. State Bar Assn., Tippecanoe County Bar Assn., Nat. Assn. Town and Twp. Attys. (co-founder, v.p. 1985-88), Am. Agrl. Lawyers Assn., Lafayette Country Club, Skyline Club, Columbia Club. Office: Hanna & Gerde PO Box 1098 Lafayette IN 47902-1098 E-mail: gerde@hannagerde.com.

GERDES, DAVID ALAN, lawyer; b. Aberdeen, S.D., Aug. 10, 1942; s. Cyril Fredrick and Lorraine Mary (Boyle) G.; m. Karen Ann Hassinger, Aug. 3, 1968; children: Amy Renee, James David. BS, No. State Coll., Aberdeen, 1965; JD cum laude, U. S.D., 1968. Bar: S.D. 1968, U.S. Dist. Ct. S.D., 1968, U.S. Ct. Appeals (8th cir.) 1973, U.S. Supreme Ct. 1973. Assoc. Martens, Goldsmith, May, Porter & Adam, Pierre, S.D., 1968-73; ptnr. successor firm May, Adam, Gerdes & Thompson, Pierre, 1973—. Chmn. disciplinary bd. S.D. Bar, 1980-81, mem. fed. practice com. U.S. Dist. Ct., S.D., 1986-91, 94—; mem. fed. adv. com. U.S. Ct. Appeals (8th cir.), 1989-93; bd. dirs. U.S.D. Law Sch. Found., 1973-84, pres., 1979-84. Mng. editor U. S.D. Law Rev., 1967—68; author: Physician's Guide to South Dakota Law, 1982. Chmn. Hughes County Rep. Ctrl. Com., 1979-81; del. Rep. State Conv., co-chair platform com., 1988, 90; state ctrl. committeeman, 1985-91. Served to lt. Signal Corps, AUS, 1965-68. Mem. ABA, Nat. Coun. Bar Pres., Internat. Assn. Def. Counsel, Assn. Def. Trial Attys., Am. Judicature Soc., Am. Bd. Trial Advocates, State Bar S.D. (chmn. professionalism com. 1989-90, pres. 1992-93), Pierre Area C. of C. (pres. 1980-81), S.D. C. of C. (bd. dirs. 1998—), Lawyer-Pilots Bar Assn., Def. Rsch. Inst., Am. Soc. Med. Assn. Counsel, Kiwanis, Elks. Republican. Methodist. Utilities, public, Health, Insurance. Office: May Adam Gerdes & Thompson PO Box 160 503 S Pierre St Pierre SD 57501-0160

GEREN, GERALD S. lawyer; b. Chgo., Nov. 10, 1939; s. Ben and Sara (Block) G.; m. Phyllis Freeman, Feb. 11, 1962; children: Suzanne, Gregory, Bradley. BSMetE, Ill. Inst. Tech., 1961; JD, DePaul U., 1966. Bar: Ill. Supreme Ct. 1966, U.S. Ct. Customs and Patent Appeals 1967, U.S. Patent and Trademark Office 1967, U.S. Dist Ct. (no. dist.) Ill. 1969, U.S. Supreme Ct. 1972, U.S. Ct. Appeals (7th cir.) 1972, U.S. Ct. Appeals (fed. cir.) 1982. Engr. Internat. Harvester, Chgo., 1961-64; atty. Corning Glass Works, Corning, N.Y., 1966-69; assoc. Silverman & Cass, Chgo., 1969-70, Siegal & Geren, Chgo., 1970-71; ptnr. Epton, Mullin & Druth, Chgo., 1971-84, Hill, Steadman & Simpson, Chgo., 1984-94, Gerald S. Geren Ltd., Chgo., 1994-96, Lee, Mann, Smith, McWilliams, Sweeney & Ohlson, 1997—2002, Barnes & Thornburg, 2003—. Contbr. articles to Indsl. Rsch. and Devel., Design News mags. Pres. Chgo. High Tech. Assn., 1981-86, v.p., 1986-87; mem. strategic planning com. Econ. Devel. Commn., Chgo., 1986-91; mem. Ill. Ctr. for Indsl. Tech., 1984-90, Ill. Mfg. Tech. Network, Chgo., 1986-91; mem. pres.' coun., rsch. coun., alumni bd. Ill. Inst. Tech., 1991—, The Leukemia Soc. Am. (Ill. chpt. bd. mem. 1988-90). Mem. ABA, Ill. Bar Assn., Chgo. Bar Assn., Patent Law Assn. Chgo., Am. Intellectual Property Law Assn., Execs. Club, Chgo. Econ. Club, Comml. Club Chgo. (small bus. com. 1985—), Met. Club Chgo. Federal civil litigation, Patent, Trademark and copyright. Office: Lee Mann Smith McWilliams Sweeney & Ohlson 209 S La Salle St Ste 410 Chicago IL 60604-1203

GERHART, EUGENE CLIFTON, lawyer; b. Bklyn., Apr. 7, 1912; s. Herman Eugene and Mary Elizabeth (Hamilton) G.; m. Mary Richardson Schreiber, Mar. 30, 1939; children: Catherine Gerhart Landon, Virginia Gerhart Mason. AB, Princeton U., 1934; LLB, Harvard U., 1937. Bar: N.J. 1938, N.Y. 1945. Practiced in, Newark, 1938-43, Binghamton, N.Y., 1946—; counsel firm Coughlin & Gerhart, Binghamton; sec. to Judge Manley O. Hudson, Secretariat/League of Nations, Geneva, 1934; lectr. bus. law U. Newark, 1942-43, Triple Cities Coll., 1946-48, Harpur Coll., Endicott, N.Y., 1953-55; lectr. indsl. and labor relations Cornell U., Ithaca, N.Y., 1946; dir., gen. counsel Columbian Mut. Life Ins. Co., 1949-83, acting pres., 1969-70, chmn. bd., 1970-82. Mem. coun. SUNY, Cortland, 1967-77, chmn., 1971-77; mem. Select Task Force on Ct. Reorgn. N.Y. State Senate; mem. jud. nominating com. 3d Jud. Dept., State of N.Y.; mem. N.Y. Unified Ct. Sys. Judicial Records Disposition and Archives Devel. Com. Author: American Liberty and Natural Law, America's Advocate: Robert H. Jackson, Robert H. Jackson: Lawyer's Judge, 2003, Arthur T. Vanderbilt: The Compleat Counsellor, Quote It!, Quote It II, The Lawyer's Treasury, Quote It Completely!, 1998, World Reference Guide to more than 5500 Memorable Quotations from Law and Literature, 1998; spl. contbg. author: Law Office Econs. and Mgmt, 1962— ; mem. editl. bd. Quar. Report of Conf. on Personal Fin. Law, 1965; contbr. articles to legal, other publs. Chmn. Harpur Forum SUNY, Binghamton, 1983-84. Lt. USNR, 1943-46. Fellow Am. Bar Found., Am. Coll. Probate Counsel, N.Y. State Bar Found.; mem. ABA (editor Jour. 1946-67, Ross Essay award 1946), Internat. Assn. Ins. Counsel, Assn. Life Ins. Counsel, Am. Judicature Soc., Am. Law Inst., N.Y. State Bar Assn. (editor-in-chief jour. 1961-97, editor-in-chief emeritus 1997—, Disting. Svc. award 1998), Assn. Bar City N.Y., Broome County Bar Assn. (pres. 1961-62, Lifetime Achievement award 1995), Selden Soc., Broome County Princeton Alumni Assn., Harvard Law Sch. Assn. Upstate N.Y. (pres. 1955-57), Scribes (pres., dir. 1966-67), St. Andrew's Soc. Clubs: Rotary (pres. 1969-70), Cosmos, Oteyokwa Lake (pres. 1971-73), Nassau, Harvard of N.Y., Princeton of N.Y. Republican. Corporate, general, Estate planning, Insurance. Home: 34 W End Ave Binghamton NY 13905-4026 Office: 20 Hawley St Binghamton NY 13901-3216

GERICKE, DIETER ANDREAS, lawyer; b. Zurich, Switzerland, Apr. 13, 1965; JD summa cum laude, U. Zurich, 1991, PhD summa cum laude, 1996; LLM, Harvard U., 1999. Bar: Zurich, Switzerland. Law clk. Dist. Ct., Meilen, Switzerland, 1991—93; rsch. asst. U. Zurich, 1994—95; lawyer Lenz & Staehelin, 1996—98; fgn. lawyer Hale and Dorr, Boston, 1999; lawyer Homburger, Zurich, 2000—. Bd. dirs. Gericke Holding AG, Regensdorf, Switzerland, 2000—, BIH S.A., Neuchatel, Switzerland, 2000—. Author: Authorized Capital, 1996, Capital Increase, 2002. Pres. Student Cir., U. Zurich, 1987—90; bd. mem. Theater an der Winkelwiese, Zurich, Switzerland, 1996—. 1st lt. Swiss Infantry, 1986—. Landon H. Gammon fellow, Harvard Law Sch., Cambridge, Mass., 1998. Mem.: Internat. Bar Assn., Swiss Bar Assn., Zurich Bar Assn. Avocation: music. Mergers and acquisitions, Securities, Finance. Office: Homburger Weinbergstrasse 56/58 8006 Zürich Switzerland

GERLACH, FRANKLIN THEODORE, lawyer; b. Portsmouth, Ohio, Apr. 11, 1935; s. Albert T. and Nora Alice (Hayes) G.; m. Cynthia Ann Koehler, Aug. 1, 1958; children: Valarie, Philipp. BBA, U. Cin., 1958; MPA, Syracuse U., 1959; JD, U. Cin., 1961. Bar: Ohio 1961, U.S. Dist. Ct. (so. dist.) Ohio 1969, U.S. Supreme Ct. 1971. Dir. purchasing, planning and renewal City of Portsmouth, 1961-62, city mgr., 1962-66, mayor, 1990-97; asst. dir. Ohio U., Portsmouth, 1966-68; sole practitioner law Portsmouth, 1968—. Solicitor Village New Boston, Ohio, 1968-70; trustee Ohio Acad. Trial Lawyers, Columbus, 1984-85. Recipient Outstanding Young Man of Ohio award Portsmouth Jaycees, 1968, Ohio Jaycees, 1969. Mem. Scioto County Bar Assn. (pres. 1986). Democrat. Avocation: antiques. Administrative and regulatory, Personal injury (including property damage), Workers' compensation. Home: 1221 20th St Portsmouth OH 45662-2924 Office: 814 7th St Portsmouth OH 45662-4128 E-mail: lawyergg@zoomnet.net.

GERLITS, FRANCIS JOSEPH, lawyer; b. Chgo., Mar. 29, 1931; s. John T. and May (Cameron) G.; m. Suzanne Long, June 20, 1953; children: Kathleen, Karen, Mary Cameron, Francis Jr. Ph.B., U. Notre Dame, 1953; JD, U. Chgo., 1958. Bar: Ill. 1958. Ptnr. Kirkland & Ellis, Chgo., 1964-95, of counsel, 1995; gen. counsel Internat. Harvester Co. (now Navistar Internat. Corp.), Chgo., 1985-90. Mem. ABA, Order of Coif, Tavern Club, Chicago Club Corporate, general, Mergers and acquisitions, Securities. Office: Kirkland & Ellis 200 E Randolph St Fl 54 Chicago IL 60601-6636

GERLT, WAYNE CHRISTOPHER, lawyer; b. Hartford, Conn., Mar. 7, 1948; m. Elaine Della Barnarda, Feb. 27, 1970; 3 children. BA, U. Conn., 1970; JD, Capital U., 1975. Bar: Ohio 1975, Conn. 1976, U.S. Dist. Ct. Conn. 1976, U.S. Supreme Ct. 1979. Sole practice, South Windsor, Conn., 1984—. Mem. ABA, Conn. Bar Assn., Order of Curia. Roman Catholic. Family and matrimonial, General practice, Property, real (including real estate development, water). Home: 2620 Ellington Rd South Windsor CT 06074-2207 Office: 435 Buckland Rd PO Box 1132 South Windsor CT 06074-1132

GERMAN, JUNE RESNICK, lawyer; b. N.Y.C., Feb. 24, 1946; d. Irving and Stella (Weintraub) Resnick; m. Harold Jacob German, May 31, 1974; children: Beth Melissa, Heather Alice, Bret. BA, U. Pa., 1965; JD, NYU, 1968. Bar: N.Y. 1968, U.S. Dist. Ct. (ea. and so. dists.) N.Y. 1974, U.S. Ct. Appeals (2d cir.) 1973, U.S. Supreme Ct. 1973. Atty., sr. atty., supervising atty. Mental Health Info. Svc., N.Y.C., 1968-77; atty., advisor Course in Human Behavior Mems. of N.Y. State Judiciary, Nassau and Suffolk County, 1980; pvt. practice Huntington, N.Y., 1985—. Contbg. author: Bioethics and Human Rights, 1978, Mental Illness, Due Process and the Acquitted Defendant, 1979; contbr. chpts. to books, articles to profl. jours. Chmn. Citizen's Ad Hoc Com. Constrn. of the Dix Hills Water Adminstrn. Bldg., Huntington, N.Y., 1985-90; mem. Citizens Adv. Com. for Dix Hills Water Dist., Huntington, 1992—; dir. House Beautiful Assn. at Dix Hills, 1986—, Citizens for a Livable Environment and Recycling, Huntington, 1989-93; active Suffolk County (N.Y.) Dem. Com., 1986—, Deer Park Avenue Task Force, Town of Huntington, 1997-98, Dix Hills Revitalization Com., 1999-2000. Mem. Suffolk County Bar Assn. Jewish. Avocations: tennis, hiking, travel. Civil rights, Federal civil litigation, General practice. Office: 150 Main St Huntington NY 11743-6908

GERMANY, GARVIN HOLT, JR., retired judge, lawyer; b. Dallas, May 16, 1926; s. Garvin Holt G. and Vera Emily Terry; m. Jerry Ann McSpodden, Aug. 13, 1950; (div. Oct., 1981); children: Cindy Lou Beswick, Terri Germany; m. Joyce ann Proske Welch, Feb. 20, 1982. Bar: Tex. 1955, U.S. Dist. Ct. (no. dist.), U.S. Dist. Ct. (ea. dist.), U.S. Dist. Ct. (so. dist.), U.S. Ct. Appeals (New Orleans), Mil. Ct. Appeals. Assoc. Perry & Wilson, Wichita Falls, Tex., 1955-56, Renfro & Johnson, Dallas, 1956-60; lawyer Joint Claims Com., Dallas, 1960-62; ptnr. Holder Kenyon Germany & Shaw, Freeport, Tex., 1962-90; judge CCL # 2 and probate Brazoria County, Tex., 1991-98; ret., 1998. Bd. dirs. Brazoria Cmty. Hist. Mus., Brazoria, 1986—, Brazoria County Hist. Mus., Angleton, Tex., 1991—. With USN, 1944-46; 1st lt. USAF, 1951-53. Mem. Dallas Jr. Bar Assn. (pres., lesser offices 1956-96), Masons (past master 1968-69, dist. dep. grand master 22/A grand lodge 1981-82, bd. dirs. 1986—), Rotary, Kiwanis (pres. 1968-69). Methodist. Avocations: flying, model building, restoring, airplanes, genealogy. Home: 614 McBride Pkwy Angleton TX 77515

GERNON, ROBERT L. judge; b. Sabetha, Kans., July 29, 1943; children: Rebecca Gernon Wilson, Kristin Gernon Olson. BSBA, U. Kans.; JD, Washburn U., 1969; LLM in Jud. Process, U. Va., 2001. Asst. atty. Shawnee County, presentence investigator; probation officer; pvt. practice, 1970—79; atty., county counselor Brown County, 1971—75; judge 22d Dist., 1979—88, adminstrv. judge, 1981—88; mem. Ct. Appeals, 1988—2002; justice Kans. State Supreme Ct., Topeka, 2003—. Trial advocacy instr. U. Kans. Sch. Law; chmn., program coord. ann. program Ann. Survey of Law Com.; faculty advisor Nat. Jud. Coll.; spkr. in field; mem. task force on permanency planning U.S. Supreme Ct. Fellow: Kans. Bar Found., Am. Bar Found.; mem.: Kans. Dist. Judges' Assn. (mem. legis. com.), Kans. Bar Assn. (continuing legal edn. com. 1986—, mem., past chair pub. info. com., mem. com. on professionalism, Outstanding Svc. award 1991, Professionalism award 2001). Office: Kans Jud Ctr 301 W 10th Topeka KS 66612

GERRARD, JOHN M. state supreme court justice; b. Schuyler, Nebr., Nov. 2, 1953; BS, Nebr. Wesleyan U., 1976; MPA, U. Ariz., 1977; JD, U. of Pacific, 1981. Pvt. practice, Norfolk, 1981-95; city atty. City of Battle Creek, Nebr., 1982-95; justice Nebr. Supreme Ct., Lincoln, 1995—. Office: Nebr Supreme Ct 2219 State Capitol Lincoln NE 68509-8000 also: PO Box 98910 Lincoln NE 68509

GERRINGER, ELIZABETH (THE MARCHIONESS DE ROE DEVON), writer, lawyer; b. Edmund, Wis., Jan. 7, 1934; d. Clyde Elroy and Matilda Evangeline Knapp; m. Roe (Don Davis) Devon Gerringer-Busenbark, Sept. 30, 1968 (dec. Dec. 1972). Student, Madison Bus. Coll., 1952, San Francisco State Coll., 1953-54, Vivian Rich Sch. Fashion Design, 1955, Dale Carnegie Sch., 1956, Arthur Murray Dance Studio, 1956, Biscayne Acad. Music, 1957, L.A. City Coll., 1960-62, Santa Monica (Calif.) Jr. Coll., 1963; JD, U. Calif., San Francisco, 1973; postgrad., Wharton Sch., U. Pa., 1977, London Art Coll., 1979; PhD, U. Cambridge, 1979; student, Goethe Inst., 1985. Bar: Calif., 1965. Ordained to ministry, 1978. Atty. Dometrik's JIT-MAP, San Francisco, 1973—. Cons., systems analyst for banks and pub. accounting agys.; pres., tchr. Environ Improvement, Originals by Elizabeth. Actress Actors Workshop San Francisco, 1959, 65, Theatre of Arts Beverly Hills, Calif., 1963, also radio; artist, poet, singer, songwriter, playwright, dress designer; author: The Cardinal, 1947, Explorations in Worship, 1965, The Magic of Scents, 1967, New Highways, 1967, The Grace of Romance, 1968, Happening-Impact-Mald, 1971, Seven Day Rainbow, 1972, The Day of the Lone Survivor, 1972, Zachary's Adversaries, 1974, Fifteen from Iowa, 1977, Bart's White Elephant, 1976, Skid Row Minister, 1978, Points in Time, 1979, Special Appointment-A Clown in Town, 1979, Happenings, 1980, Candles, 1980, The Stranger in the Train, 1983, Votes from the Closet, 1984, Wait for Me, 1984, The Stairway, 1984, The River is a Rock, 1985, Happenings Revisited, 1986, Comparative Religion in the United States, 1986, Lumber in the Skies, 1986, The Fifth Season, 1987, Summer Thoughts, 1987, Crimes of the Heart, 1987, Toast Thoughts, 1988, The Contrast of Russian Literature Through the Eyes of an American Artist, 1988, A Thousand Points of Light, 1989, The Face in The Mirror, 1989, Sea Gulls, 1990, Voices on the Hill, 1991, It's Tough to Get a Matched Set, 1991, Equality, 1991, Miss Geranium, 1991, Forest Voices, 1991, Golden Threads, 1991, Castles in the Air, 1991, The Cave, 1991, Angels, 1991, Real, 1991, An Appeal to Reason, 1992, We Knew, 1992, Like It Is, 1992, Politicians Anonymous, 1993, Wheels Within Wheels, 1994, A Tree for All Seasons, 1995, The Visitor, 1995, Time Frames, 1996, Save the Dance, 1998, Flowers For My Grandfather, 1999, Last Day at Mission Rock, 1999, Waiting for the Train, 1999, The Influence of Rural Life Upon Culture, 1999, The Crowd, 2001, Without Saying Goodbye, 2002, The Moon's Agreement, 2003. Steering com. Explorations in Worship. Address: 1008 10th St #275 Sacramento CA 95814-3502 Fax: 916-442-3735.

GERSCH, CHARLES FRANT, lawyer; b. N.Y.C., Oct. 30, 1942; BA, NYU, 1964; MA, New Sch. for Social Rsch., 1969; JD, U. Puget Sound, 1986. Bar: Wash. 1987, U.S. Dist. Ct. (we. dist.) Wash. 1988. Vol. VISTA Housing Code Enforcement, South Bronx, N.Y., 1967-68; editorial rsch. mgr. Fawcett Pubs., N.Y.C., 1969-71; instr. sociology William Woods Coll., 1972-74, Chapman Coll., 1974-81; vol. law clk. Thurston County Wash. Superior Ct., 1986; pvt. practice Tacoma, 1988—. Mem. Wash. State Bar Assn., Tacoma/Pierce County Bar Assn. Constitutional, Criminal.

GERSHEL, ALAN M. prosecutor; b. Nov. 19, 1951; s. Marvin and Francine G.; m. Linda, Aug. 3, 1975; children: Jessica Sara, Bradley Ross. BS, Northeastern U., 1974; MS, Ind. State U., 1975; JD, U. Detroit, 1978. Bar: Mich. 1978, U.S. Ct. Appeals (6th cir.) Mich. 1980. Asst. atty., criminal chief ea. dist. U.S. Dept Justice, Detroit, 1993—, interim U.S. atty., 2000—01; currently adjunct prof. U. of Detroit Mercy Sch. of Law, Mich. Office: Assist US Atty 211 W Fort St 2001 Detroit MI 48226-3211*

GERSKE, JANET FAY, lawyer; b. Nov. 14, 1950; d. Bernard G. Gerske and L. Fay (Knight) Capron. BS, Northwestern U., 1971; JD, U. Mich., 1978. Bar: Ill. 1978, U.S. Dist. Ct. (no. dist.) Ill. 1978. Pvt. practice, Chgo., 1978—80, 1984—; assoc. Jerome H. Torshen Ltd., Chgo., 1980—84. Chpt. chair Ind. Voters Ill./Ind. Precinct Orgn., Chgo., 1982—83; co-chmn. Ill. Women's Agenda Com., 1985—88, fin. officer, 1987—88; dir. Chgo. Abused Women Coalition, 1986—90, sec., treas., 1988—90; co-chair legal status of women com. Young Lawyers sect. Chgo. Bar Assn., 1984—85; co-chair rights of women com. Ill. Women's Bar Assn., 1985—86, dir., 1988—90. Democrat. General civil litigation, Pension, profit-sharing, and employee benefits. Home: 850 W Oakdale Ave Chicago IL 60657-5122

GERSON, MERVYN STUART, lawyer; b. Cleve., Nov. 1, 1936; s. Philip Gerson and Rena (Friedman) Davis; m. Linda Hanff, Feb. 14, 1965; children: Laurie Jean Powazek, Philip Stuart, Michael Craig. AB, U. Mich., 1957; JD, 1960. Atty. advisor U.S. Tax Ct., Washington, 1960-62; atty. Gerson, Grekin & Wynhoff, Honolulu, 1981—. Fellow Am. Coll. Trust and Estate Counsel (regent 1995—), Am. Coll. Tax Counsel. Estate planning, Probate (including wills, trusts), Estate taxation. Office: Gerson & Hieneman 1001 Bishop St Ste 780 Honolulu HI 96813-3410

GERSON, STUART MICHAEL, lawyer; b. N.Y.C., Jan. 16, 1944; s. James and Ethel (Cherney) G.; m. Pamela Somers, July 28, 1979; children: James Barker, Somers Elizabeth, Lindsey Dakota. BA in Polit. Sci., Pa. State U., 1964; JD, Georgetown U., 1967. Bar: D.C. 1968, N.Y. 1999, U.S. Supreme Ct. 1974, U.S. Ct. Appeals (DC cir.) 1972, U.S. Ct. Appeals (5th cir.) 1972, 81, U.S. Ct. Appeals (9th cir.) 1978, U.S. Ct. Appeals (2d cir.) 1979, U.S. Ct. Appeals (11th cir.) 1981, U.S. Ct. Appeals (6th cir.) 1982, U.S. Ct. Appeals (4th cir.) 1984, U.S. Ct. Appeals (3d cir.) 1985, U.S. Ct. Appeals (8th cir.) 1986, U.S. Ct. Appeals (1st, 7th, 10th, fed. cirs.) 1989. Asst. U.S. atty. City of Washington, 1972-75; assoc., then ptnr. Reed Smith Shaw & McClay, Washington, 1975-80; pvt. practice; ptnr. in charge litigation Epstein, Becker & Green, Washington, N.Y.C., 1980-89; adj. prof. of law Georgetown U., 1991; asst. atty. gen. in charge civil div. U.S. Dept. Justice, Washington, 1989-93; acting Atty. Gen. U.S., 1993; atty. and head of litigation Epstein, Becker & Green, P.C., Washington and N.Y.C. Bd. dirs. Counsel for Ct. Excellence; mem. bd. legal advisors Heritage Found, Washington Legal Found., Nat. Legal Ctr. for the Pub. Interest. Contbr. articles to profl. jours. Gen. counsel Nat. Rep. Senatorial Com., Washington, 1985-86; sr. advisor presdl. campaign George Bush, 1988; leader transition team Office Pres. Elect, 1988; advisor Transition Office Pres. Elect, 2000. Capt. USAF, 1967-72. Decorated Meritorious Svc. Medal. Fellow Am. Bar Found.; mem. ABA, D.C. Bar Assn. (steering com. litigation 1985-93), The Barristers (pres.), Am. Health Lawyers Assn., Am. Inns of Ct., Metro. Club, Lawyers Club. Episcopalian. Avocations: competitive running, national track and field official, sailing, reading history. Office: Epstein Becker & Green PC 1227 25th St NW Ste 700 Washington DC 20037-1175 also: 250 Park Ave New York NY 10177-0001

GERSOVITZ, JEREMY, lawyer; b. Montreal, Que., Can., July 28, 1956; came to U.S., 1984; s. Benjamin and Sarah Valerie Gersovitz; 1 child, Alexander Samuel. BA in Polit. Sci., Columbia Coll., 1980; MS in Journalism, Northwestern U., Chgo., 1985; JD, U. Mont., 1992. Bar: Mont. 1992, U.S. Dist. Ct. Mont. 1992. Law clk. to Judge T.C. Honzel, 1st Jud. Dist., Helena, Mont., 1992-94; pvt. practice Townsend, Mont., 1994-95; part-time pub. defender Broadwater County, Townsend, Mont., 1994-95; pvt. practice Helena, 1995-97; part-time pub. defender Lewis & Clark County, Helena, 1995-97, pub. defender, 1997—. Mem. bd. editors The Mont. Lawyer., 1996—. Mem. ABA, State Bar Mont., 1st Jud. Dist. Bar Assn. Jewish. Home and Office: 532 N Warren St Helena MT 59601-4014

GERSTEIN, JOE WILLIE, lawyer; b. Atlanta, July 29, 1927; s. Arthur and Tena (Hartman) G.; m. Doris Renate Florsheim, May 20, 1956 (dec. 2000); children: Ellen Claire Gerstein Crooke, Kim Carol Gerstein Wainer; m. Sheila Brooks Kamensky. Oct. 20, 2001. AB, Duke U., 1949, JD, 1952. Bar: Ga. 1953, U.S. Tax Ct., U.S. Ct. Appeals (fed. cir.) 1965, U.S. Supreme Ct. 1967. Sr. ptnr. Gerstein, Carter & Chestnut and predecessor firm Gerstein & Carter, Atlanta and Doraville, Ga., 1957-76; sole practice Doraville, 1976—. Former city atty, Doraville; lectr. on taxes, wills, trust and estates at various civic, profl. and ch. orgns.; bd. dirs. Atlanta Estate Planning Council. Contbg. editor Duke U. Law Rev. Past dir. Social Service Fedn. Atlanta. Served with USN, 1944-47. Fellow Am. Coll. Trust and Estate Counsel; mem. ABA, Ga. Bar Assn., Atlanta Bar Assn., Decatur-DeKalb Bar Assn., Met. Atlanta Council Rotary Club Pres. (past chmn.), Comml. Law League Am. (past nat. recording sec.), Atlanta Tax Forum, Big Canoe Men's Golf Assn. (golf com.), Zeta Beta Tau (v.p. AU chpt.), Phi Delta Phi. Clubs: Standard (Atlanta) (legal and golf coms.). Lodges: Rotary (North DeKalb past pres.), Masons (past offices), B'nai B'rith (Gate City past v.p.). Jewish. Estate planning, Probate (including wills, trusts), Taxation, general. Office: 6485 Peachtree Industrial Blvd Doraville GA 30360-2112 Home: 1073 Tennyson Pl NE Atlanta GA 30319-1924

GERSTEIN, MARK DOUGLAS, lawyer; b. Chgo., Nov. 16, 1959; s. Robert Henry and Helene Roberta Gerstein; m. Julia Sara Wolf, Apr. 13, 1986; children: Allison Ruth, Evan Benjamin. BA, U. Mich., 1981; JD, U. Chgo., 1984. Bar: Ill., U.S. Dist. Ct. (no. dist.) Ill. Ptnr., assoc. Katten Muchin & Zavis, Chgo., 1984-96; equity ptnr. Latham & Watkins, Chgo., 1996—, equity ptnr., global co-chair mergers and acquisitions group, 1999—. Dir. Assocs. Ravinia Festival, Chgo., 1996-2000, Youth Guidance, Chgo., 1995—. Mem. Chgo. Bar Assn. (chmn. com. on corp. control 1998-99), Standard Club. Avocations: sailing, cycling. Corporate, general, Mergers and acquisitions, Securities. Office: Latham & Watkins 233 S Wacker Dr Ste 5800 Chicago IL 60606-6362 E-mail: mark.gerstein@lw.com.

GERSTMAN, GEORGE HENRY, lawyer; b. N.Y.C., July 25, 1939; m. Rozanne Millman, Dec. 24, 1960; children: Heidi Ann, Gary Daniel. BSEE, U. Ill., 1960; JD with honors, George Washington U., 1963. Bar: Ill. 1964, U.S. Dist. Ct. (no. dist.) Ill. 1964, U.S. Patent Office 1964, U.S. Supreme Ct. 1971, U.S. Ct. Appeals (7th cir.) 1971, U.S. Ct. Appeals (2d cir.) 1980, U.S. Ct. Appeals (Fed. cir.) 1982. Patent examiner U.S. Patent Office, Washington, 1960-63; assoc. Dressler, Goldsmith et al, Chgo., 1963-70; ptnr. Lettvin & Gerstman, Chgo., 1970-75, Gerstman, Ellis & McMillin, Ltd., Chgo., 1976-99, Seyfarth Shaw, Chgo., 2000—. Asst. patent editor George Washington Law Rev., 1962-63. Govt. appeal agt. Selective Svc. System, Evanston, Ill., 1967-73; mem. Northbrook (Ill.) Bd. Zoning Appeals, 1971-90. Mem.: Standard Club (Chgo.), Order of Coif, Patent Law Assn. Chgo., Am. Intellectual Property Law Assn., Chgo. Bar Assn., ABA. Avocations: art, boating. Federal civil litigation, Patent, Trademark and copyright. Home: 219 Sheridan Rd Kenilworth IL 60043-1216 Office: Seyfarth Shaw 55 E Monroe St Ste 4200 Chicago IL 60603-5863

GERTLER, MEYER H. lawyer; b. New Orleans, Oct. 28, 1945; s. David and Sadie (Redman) G.; m. Marcia Raye Goldstein, Aug. 23, 1967; children— Louis, Danielle, Joshua. B.A., Tulane U., 1967, J.D. 1969. Bar: La. 1970, U.S. Dist. Ct. (ea. and mid. dists.) 1970, U.S. Ct. Apppeals (5th cir.) 1970, U.S. Supreme Ct. 1970. Ptnr. Uddo & Gertler, New Orleans, 1970-76, Gertler & Gertler, New Orleans, 1977-86, Gertler, Gertler & Vincent, New Orleans, 1986-95, Gertler, Gertler, Vincent & Plotkin, 1996—; mem. Asbestos Litigation Group. Mem. La. Trial Lawyers Assn., Am. Trial Lawyers Assn., ABA, Sup. Ct. Hist. Soc., Am. Judicature Soc. Democrat. Jewish. Clubs: B'nai B'rith, Masons. Federal civil litigation, State civil litigation, Product liability. Office: Gertler Gertler Vincent & Plotkin 127 Carondelet New Orleans LA 70130 Home: # 129 127 Carondelet St New Orleans LA 70130-2501

GERTZ, THEODORE GERSON, lawyer; b. Chgo., Sept. 8, 1936; s. Elmer and Ceretta (Samuels) G.; m. Suzanne C., June 19, 1960; children: Craig M., Candace C., Scott W. BA, U. Chgo., 1958; JD, Northwestern U., 1962. Bar: Ill. 1962, U.S. Dist. Ct. (no. dist.) Ill. 1962. Assoc. Marks, Marks & Kaplan, Chgo., 1962-64, Lowitz, Vihons & Stone, Chgo., 1964-66, ptnr., 1966-71, Pretzel & Stouffer, Chgo., 1971-94, Shefsky, Froelich, Chgo., 1995—. Gen. counsel Hull House Assn., Chgo., 1977—, Blind Svc. Assn., Chgo., 1987—, Lawyers for the Creative Arts, Citizens Against Suburban Sprawl, Mettawa, Ill., 1995—. Author: A Guide to Estate Planning, Illinois Advance Estate Planning. Dir., treas. Mettawa Open Lands, 1987—; former trustee Village of Mettawa, 1994—, Pub. Interest Law Initiative, Chgo; bd. mem., Lawyers for the Creative Arts, 2002—. With U.S. Army, 1962-64. Fellow Ill. Bar Found., Ill. Bar Assn., Chgo. Bar Assn., Law Club. Democrat. Jewish. Avocations: reading, nature, working out, dancing, traveling. Estate planning. Home: 950 Benson Ln Libertyville IL 60048-2406 Office: Shefsky and Froelich 444 N Michigan Ave Ste 2600B Chicago IL 60611-3998

GERVAIS-GRUEN, ELIZABETH, lawyer; b. Papa, Hungary, Feb. 04; arrived in U.S., 1921; d. Samuel Friedmann and Vilma Kohn; m. Ralph Gervais, Feb. 7, 1970; m. Rudolph Gruen, Aug. 2, 1934 (div.); children: Richard Gruen, Robert Gruen, S. Daniel Gruen, David Gruen. Student, St. John's U., 1929—31, LLB, 1934. Bar: N.Y. 1936, N.Y. Supreme Ct. 1936, U.S. Supreme Ct. 1969. Law clk. Law Office of Samuel Newfield, 1934—36; ptnr. Rudolf Gruen and Elizabeth Gruen, 1936—38; asst. to town atty. James Dowsey, Jr. Nassau County, NY, 1938—40, asst. to county atty. James Dowsey, 1940—43; pvt. practice, 1943—58; pvt. practice Immigration and Naturalization Law, 1958—. Pres. Nassau County Women's Assn., 1968—70; bd. trustees Blumenthal Jewish Home, 1989—93; pres. Durham-Chapel Hill Jewish Fedn., 1988—90; chair Am. Affairs com. Hadassah, 1960—64, 1972—74; founder, mem. Women's Ctr., Chapel Hill, NC; chair, advisor youth activity com. Temple Beth El, Great Neck L.I., NY, chair, advisor Temple Teens, chair, advisor Coll. Youth com., pres. Sisterhood; mem. long-term planning com. Temple Beth Zion, Buffalo; chair women's group Judea Reform Congregation, Durham, NC, 1976—78, mem. long-term planning com., hon. chmn. Capitol Campaign. Recipient Sara Mutt Evans award, Jewish Fedn. and Cmty. Svc., 1992. Mem.: Commn.-Status of Women Attys. (Status of Women Attys. in N.C. com. mem.), N.C. Bar Assn. (chair Immigration and Nationality com. 1981—99), Am. Immigration Lawyers Assn. (chair N.C. chpt. 1980—84, bd. govs., founder N.C. chpt., hon. fellow 2002, Sam Williamson Mentor award 2000, Carolinas chpt. Mentor award in honor Elizabeth Gervais-Gruen established 1999, Elizabeth F. Gervais-Gruen Mentor award 1999, Pres.'s Commendation 1992). Avocations: reading, analyzing law, collecting Judaic artifacts, collecting ancient glass, collecting minerals and fossils, philately. Office: 914 Crestwood Ln Chapel Hill NC 27517

GERWIN, LESLIE ELLEN, lawyer, public affairs and community relations executive; b. L.A., May 18, 1950; d. Nathan and Beverly Adele (Wilson) G.; m. Bruce Robert Leslie, July 3, 1978; 1 child, Jonathan Gerwin Leslie. BA, Prescott Coll., 1972; JD, Antioch Sch. Law, 1975; MPH, Tulane U., 1988. Bar: D.C. 1975, N.Y. 1981, U.S. Dist. Ct. D.C. 1977, U.S. Dist. Ct. (so. dist.) N.Y. 1980. Staff asst. U.S. Congress, Washington, 1970-72; cons. Congl. Subcom., Washington, 1972-73; instr. U. Miami Law Sch., Coral Gables, Fla., 1975-76; assoc. prof. law Yeshiva U., N.Y.C., 1976-86; vis. assoc. prof. law Tulane Law Sch., New Orleans, 1983-84; pub. policy cons. New Orleans, 1987—; pres. Ariadne Cons., New Orleans, 1994—; dir. devel. and community rels. Planned Parenthood La., Inc., New Orleans, 1989-90; legal advisor La. Coalition for Reproductive Freedom, 1990-92; exec. v.p. Met. Area Com., New Orleans, 1992-94; exec. dir. Met. Area Com. Edn. Fund, New Orleans, 1992-94. Bd. dirs. Inst. for Phys. Fitness Rsch., N.Y.C., 1982-86, Challenge/Discovery, Crested Butte, Colo., 1977-80; cons. FDA, Washington, 1977-78, U. Judaism, L.A., 1974-75; mem. Met. Area Com. Leadership Forum, New Orleans, 1988; adj. asst. prof. La. State U. Sch. Medicine, 1996—, La. State U. Med. Sch., Dept. of Public Health and Preventive Medicine. Contbr. articles to profl. jours. Mem. Ind. Dem. Jud. Screening Panel, N.Y.C., 1980; bd. dirs. New Orleans Food Bank for Emergencies, 1987-89; profl. adv. com. MAZON-A Jewish Response to Hunger, L.A., 1986-89; bd. dirs. Second Harvesters Food Bank Greater New Orleans, 1989-94, La. State LWV, 1990-91, Anti-Defamation League, New Orleans, 1989-95, Jewish Endowment Found., 1987-93; trustee Jewish Fedn. Greater New Orleans, 1989-95, 97-99, mem. exec. com., 1997-99; trustee Emergency Food and Shelter Program, S.E. La., 1988—; v.p. Tulane U. B'nai B'rith Hillel Found., 1987-90; steering com. Citizens for Pers. Freedom, 1989-91; steering com. Metro 2000, 1989-90; sec. New Orleans sect. Nat. Coun. Jewish Women, 1990-91, state pub. affairs chmn., 1992-96; bd. Contemporary Arts Ctr., 1993-97; chair, bd. advocates Planned Parenthood La., 1995—; v.p. Edn. Tikvat Shalom Conservative Congregation, 1995-97, chair New Orleans Israel Bonds, 1996-98; mem. Cmty. Rels. Com., 1986-99, vice chair, 1995-97, chair 1997-99; adminstr. Area Tng. Ctr., USTA, New Orleans, 1996-2001; v.p. ritual Shir Chadosh Conservative Congregation, 2002—. Fellow Inst. of Politics, 1990-91; scholar Xerox Found., 1972-75; Decorated Order of Barristers; named One of Ten Outstanding Young Women of Am., 1987; recipient Herbert J. Garon Young Leadership award Jewish Fedn. Greater New Orleans, 1990; named YWCA Role Model, 1992. Mem. ABA, N.Y. Bar Assn., N.Y. Acad. Scis., Am. Pub. Health Assn., D.C. Bar Assn., Nat. Moot Ct. Honor Soc., Pub. Health Honor Soc., Calif. State Dem. Club (Key Svc. award 1988), Delta Omega.

GESKE, ALVIN JAY, lawyer; b. Whitefish, Mont., Apr. 17, 1942; s. Alvin Emil and Ada Jay (Best) G.; m. Cheryl S. Glaze, Aug. 10, 1968; children: David, Daniel. BA in Econs. with high honors, So. Meth. U., 1964; JD with honors, U. Chgo., 1967; LLM in Taxation with high honors, George Washington U., 1974. Bar: Tex. 1967, D.C. 1972, U.S. Ct. Appeals (4th cir.) 1984, U.S. Tax Ct. 1982, U.S. Ct. Claims 1992. Atty. Jackson, Walker, Winstead, Cantwell & Miller, Dallas, 1967-68; from atty. to asst. br. chief legis. and regulation divsn. Office Chief Counsel IRS, Washington, 1970-74; atty. Childs, Fortenbach, Beck & Guyton, Houston, 1974-75; legis. atty. Joint Com. on Taxation U.S. Congress, Washington, 1975-78, asst. legis. counsel, 1978-81; atty. Davis & McLeod, Washington, 1981-83, Richard P. Sills PC, Washington, 1983-85, Stein, Sills & Brodsky PC, Washington, 1985-87, Wickham & Geske, Washington, 1987, Sills & Brodsky PC, Washington, 1988-93, Holland & Knight, Washington, 1993—. Contbr. articles to profl. jours. With U.S. Army, 1968-70. Mem. ABA (past chmn. com. on agr. sect. taxation), Order of Coif, Phi Beta Kappa, Phi Delta Phi. Estate taxation, Taxation, general. Office: Holland & Knight 2099 Pennsylvania Ave NW Washington DC 20006 E-mail: ageske@hklaw.com.

GESKE, JANINE PATRICIA, law educator, former state supreme court justice; b. Port Washington, Wis., May 12, 1949; d. Richard Braem and Georgette (Paulissen) Geske; m. Michael Julian Hogan, Jan. 2, 1982; children: Mia Geske Berman, Sarah Geske Hogan, Kevin Geske Hogan. Student, U. Grenoble, U. Rennes; BA, MA in Tchg., Beloit Coll., 1971; JD, Marquette U., 1975, LLD, 1998, LLD (hon.), 1994; DHL (hon.), Mt. Mary Coll., 1999. Bar: Wis. 1975, U.S. Dist. Ct. (ea. & we. dists.) Wis. 1975, U.S. Supreme Ct. 1978. Tchr. elem. sch., Lake Zurich, Ill., 1970-72; staff atty., chief staff atty. Legal Aid Soc., Milw., 1975-78; asst. prof. law, clin. dir. Law Sch. Marquette U., Milw., 1978-81; hearing examiner Milw. County CETA, Milw., 1980-81; judge Milw. County Circuit Ct., Milw., 1981-93; justice Supreme Ct. Wis., 1993-98; disting. prof. law Marquette U. Law Sch., Milw., 1998—. Dean Wis. Jud. Coll.; mem. faculty Nat. Jud. Coll.; instr. various jud. tng. programs, continuing legal edn. Fellow ABA, mem. Am. Law Inst., Am. Arbitration Assn., Soc. Profls. in Dispute Resolution, Wis. Bar Assn., Wis. Assn. Mediators, Milw. Bar Assn., Nat. Women Judges Assn., 7th Cir. Bar Assn., Alpha Sigma Nu. Roman Catholic. Office: Marquette U Law Sch PO Box 1881 Milwaukee WI 53201-1881

GESSEL KALINOWSKA VEL KALISZ, BEATA, lawyer, arbitrator; b. Warsaw, June 11, 1964; d. Mieczyslaw Skaryszewski and Wanda; m. Grzegorz Kalinowski vel Kalisz, June 18, 1999; children: Jozef, Klemens. MA in Internat. Comml. Law, U. Warsaw, 1989. Legal advisory apprentice Chamber Legal Advisors, Warsaw, 1990—92; advisor, mgr. legal dept. Pro-Invest Internat., Warsaw, 1990—91; head legal dept. Warsaw office Arthur Andersen, 1991; assoc. Weil, Gotshal & Manges, Nabarronathanson, Warsaw, 1991—92; mng. ptnr. Beata Gessel, Andrzey Chajec & Ptnrs., Warsaw, 1993—. V.p. Found. for the Contemporary Art Collection of the Nat. Mus., Warsaw, 1996—; arbitrator Arbitration Ct., Polish C. of C., Warsaw, 1999; bd. mem. Found. for Capital Market Stds. Devel., Warsaw. Contbr. chapters to books, articles to profl. jours. Mem.: Polish Bus. Roundtable, Internat. Bar Assn. Avocations: art, hiking. Mergers and acquisitions, Finance, Securities. Office: Beata Gessel Andrzej Chajec & Ptnrs Widok 8 00-023 Warsaw Poland

GEST, HOWARD DAVID, lawyer; b. Bergenfield, N.J., Jan. 24, 1952; m. Lucy Acevedo; 1 child, Aaron. AB in Econs., U. Calif., Berkeley, 1974; JD, Hastings Coll., 1977. Bar: Calif. 1977. Staff atty. U.S. Ct. Appeals (9th cir.), San Francisco, 1977-78; asst. U.S. atty. Cen. Dist. Calif., L.A., 1978-83; ptnr. Sidley & Austin, L.A., 1983-99, Burhenn & Gest, L.A., 2000—. General civil litigation, Environmental. Office: Burhenn & Gest LLP Ste 2200 624 S Grand Ave Los Angeles CA 90017 E-mail: hgest@burhenngest.com.

GETHING, HEATHER, solicitor; b. Sedgefield, England, May 1, 1958; d. George Albert Gething and Mary Belcher. BA in Law, Liverpool U., 1979. Trainee Kingsford Dorman, London, 1981—83; solicitor Herbert Smith, 1984—91, ptnr., 1991—, head tax, 2001—. Author: Demutualisation, 1996. Corporate taxation. Office: Herbert Smith Exch House Primrose St London EC2A 4HS England Fax: 0207 374 0888.

GETNICK, NEIL VICTOR, lawyer; b. Bklyn., Oct. 28, 1953; s. Irving Murray and Zita (Ellman) G.; m. Margaret Joan Finerty, May 21, 1978. BA in Govt. magna cum laude, Cornell U., 1975, JD, 1978. Bar: N.Y. 1979, U.S. Dist. Ct. (so. and ea. dists.) N.Y. 1983. Asst. dist. atty. trial divsn. N.Y. County, N.Y.C., 1978-81, asst. dist. atty. frauds bur., 1981-82; ptnr. Getnick & Getnick, N.Y., 1983—. Mem. Criminal Justice Act panel U.S. Dist. Ct. for So. Dist. N.Y., N.Y.C., 1984-89. Editor-in-chief: Civil Prosecution News, 1994-96. Recipient Pub. Citizenship award N.Y. Pub. Interest Rsch. Group, 1977. Mem. ABA (litigation and criminal law sects.), N.Y. State Bar Assn. (exec. com. comml. and fed. litigation sect., chair com. on civil prosecution), Assn. of Bar of City of N.Y., N.Y. County Lawyers Assn., Internat. Assn. Ind. Pvt. Sector Inspectors Gen. (pres. 1994—), Internat. Assn. of Ind. Pvt. Sector Inspectors Gen. (pres. 1994—). General civil litigation, Corporate, general, Criminal. Office: Getnick & Getnick Rockefeller Ctr 620 5th Ave 4th Flr New York NY 10020-2457

GETSCHOW, KEN, mediator, consultant; b. Erie, Pa., Feb. 23, 1943; s. Kenneth Edward and Rita Agnes Getschow; m. Sydney Ann Gruber, Mar. 17, 1988; m. Lois Ann Ferguson, Aug. 28, 1970 (div. May 12, 1983); children: Ryan Webb, Marianne Elizabeth Elliott, Scott Michael Webb, Christian Oliver, Kenneth Edward Getschow, III. BS, Penn State U., State College, Pa., 1965; MA, San Jose State U., San Jose, CA, 1971; EdD, U. of San Francisco, 1978. Mediator Supreme Ct. of Va., 2001. Media specialist Contra Costa County Schs., Pleasant Hill, Calif., 1968—73; dist. coord. Stockton Unified Sch. Dist., Calif., 1973—74; state edn. cons. Calif. Dept. of Edn., Sacramento, 1974—81; asst. county supt. Inyo County, Independence, Calif., 1981—83, county supt. schs., 1983—87; dist. supt. Needles Unified Sch. Dist., Needles, Calif., 1986—89; dir. of edn. PA Dept. of Corrections, Albion, Pa., 1994—98; asst. state supt. Commonwealth of Va., Richmond, Va., 1998—2001; sch. adminstr. State of Del., Wilmington, Del., 2001—; mediator ADR Alternatives, Wilmington, Del., 2001—. State del. Va. Correctional Assn., Richmond, 2000—01. Editor: (weekly newspaper) Suburban Gazette (Disting. Educator Award, 1984). Elections officer New Castle County, Wilmington, Del., 2002. With USAR, 1966—72. Mem.: Am. Arbitration Assn. Home: 22 Quindome Dr New Castle DE 19720 Office: ADR Alternatives PO Box 5467 Wilmington DE 19808 Home Fax: 302-328-0943; Office Fax: 302-995-8572. Personal E-mail: drkeg2@aol.com.

GETTEN, THOMAS FRANK, lawyer; b. Akron, Ohio, Oct. 11, 1947; s. Frederick Bush and Edna (Vandever) Getten; m. Nancy Hobson, Aug. 16, 1972; children: Elisabeth, Douglas, Ted. BS in Petroleum Enging., La. State U., 1970, JD, 1974. Bar: La. 1974. Petroleum engr. Standard Oil Calif., LA and New Orleans, 1970—71; shareholder Liskow & Lewis, New Orleans, 1974—95; ptnr. Nesser, King & LeBlanc, New Orleans, 1996; gen. counsel Forcenergy, Inc., Miami, 1997—2001; ptnr. King, LeBlanc & Bland, New Orleans, 2001—. Mem.: ABA, La. Bankers Assn. (coun. com.), New Orleans Bar Assn., La. Bar Assn., Order of Coif, Tau Beta Pi. Republican. Episcopalian. Banking, Commercial, contracts (including sales of goods; commercial financing), Property, real (including real estate development, water). Office: King LeBlanc & Bland LLP 201 St Charles Ave Ste 3800 New Orleans LA 70170 Business E-Mail: tgetten@klb-law.com.

GETTLER, BENJAMIN, lawyer, manufacturing company executive; b. Louisville, Ky., Sept. 16, 1925; s. Herbert and Gertrude (Cohen) G.; m. Deliaan Angel, Mar. 1972; children: Jorian, Thomas, Gail, John, Benjamin. BA in Econs. with high honors, U. Cin., 1945; JD (Frankfurter scholar), Harvard U., 1948. Bar: Ohio 1949, U.S. Supreme Ct. 1955. Ptnr. Brown & Gettler, Cin., 1951-73, Gettler, Katz & Buckley, Cin., 1973-87; chmn. bd. Am. Controlled Industries Inc., Cin., 1973-86; chmn. bd. dirs., pres. Colorpac Inc., Franklin, Ohio, 1973-86; chmn. bd., pres. Vulcan Internat. Corp., Wilmington, Del., 1988—, Vulcan Corp., Clarksville, Tenn., 1988—; chmn. exec. com. Valley Industries, Inc., Cin., 1973-86; vice chmn. bd. Cin. Southern R.R., 1987-91; chmn. bd. Trusthouse, Inc., Cin., 1987—. Chmn. bd. dirs. ACI Internat., Inc., Cin., 1990—; spl. counsel U. Cin., 1975-77, trustee, 1994-2003, vice chmn. bd., 1999-2000, chmn., 2000-2002; bd. dirs. PNC Bank, Ohio, 1988-96. Chmn. bd. Jewish Inst. Nat. Security Affairs, 1994-98, chmn. policy com., 1998—; chmn. Cin. Bonds for Israel, 1969; chmn. Nat. Israel Commn., Nat. Jewish Cmty. Rels. Adv. Coun., 1981-82; mem. Ohio, Ky. and Ind. Mass Transit Policy Com., 1970-75; pres. Cin. Jewish Cmty. Rels. Coun., 1978-80; trustee Jewish Hosp. Cin., 1978-92, chmn., 1991-92; chmn. Midwest Hosp. Sys., Inc., 1987-90, 92-93; pres. Jewish Found. Cin., 1995-99, chmn., 1999-2002; trustee Health Alliance Greater Cin., 1995-96, 2000-2001; chmn. Cin. Coalition for Reagan, 1980; co-chmn. Hamilton County Reagan Bush Campaign Ohio, 1984; chmn. Rep. Fin. Com., Hamilton County, 1991-92; mem. Hamilton County Rep.

Policy Com., 1990—; trustee Rockwern Found., 1998—, Southwest Ohio Regional Transit Authority, 2003—. Capt. U.S. Army, 1955-56. Mem. ABA, Cin. Bar Assn., Shoe Last Mfrs. Assn. (pres. 1984-85), Footwear Industries Am. (bd. dirs. 1989-2000), Phi Beta Kappa, Omicron Delta Kappa. Clubs: Coldstream Country, Harvard. Office: Vulcan Corp 30 Garfield Pl Ste 1040 Cincinnati OH 45202-4322

GETTNER, ALAN FREDERICK, lawyer; b. N.Y.C., Dec. 25, 1941; s. Victor Salomon and Henriette Seldner (Herrmann) G.; m. Monah Lawrence, Jan. 19, 1969. BA, Yale U., 1963; MA, U. Chgo., 1964; PhD, Columbia U., 1971, JD, 1979. Bar: N.Y. 1980. Assoc. Debevoise & Plimpton, N.Y.C. and Paris, 1979-84, Holtzmann, Wise & Shepard, N.Y.C., 1984-85, ptnr., 1986-95, mem. exec. com., 1992-94; ptnr. Patterson, Belknap, Webb & Tyler, LLP, N.Y.C., 1995—, chmn. bus. devel. com., 2000—02. Mem. ABA (sect. on bus. law, com. on opinions), Assn. Bar City N.Y., Internat. Bar Assn., Internat. Law Assn., The Lotos Club. Corporate, general, Private international, Mergers and acquisitions. Office: Patterson Belknap Webb & Tyler LLP 1133 Ave Americas New York NY 10036-6710 E-mail: agettner@pbwt.com.

GETTO, ERNEST JOHN, lawyer; b. Dubois, Pa., May 24, 1944; s. Ernest F. and Olga (Gagliardi) G.; m. Judith Payne, Aug. 19, 1967; children: Matthew Payne, Christopher Ernest, Sarah Elizabeth. BA, Cornell U., 1966; JD, Vanderbilt U., 1969. Bar: N.Y. 1970, Calif. 1973. Assoc. Simpson Thacher & Bartlett, N.Y.C., 1969-73; from assoc. to ptnr. Kadison, Pfaelzer, Woodard, Quinn & Rossi, Los Angeles, 1973-80; ptnr. Latham & Watkins, L.A., 1980—. Lectr. in field. Contbr. articles to profl. jours. Bd. dirs. Calif. Pediatric Ctr., Los Angeles, 1977—. Mem. ABA, Calif. Bar Assn., L.A. Bar Assn., N.Y. State Bar Assn., Jonathan Club, Wilshire Country Club. Republican. Roman Catholic. General civil litigation, Entertainment, Toxic tort. Office: Latham & Watkins 505 Montgomery St San Francisco CA 94111 Home: 1904 Broadway St San Francisco CA 94109

GETTY, CHARLES A. judge; b. Johnstown, Pa., July 3, 1939; s. Charles H. and Julia D. G.; m. Sally Hare, Apr. 16, 1998; children: Colleen, Thomas. Degree in bus., U. Pitts., 1961; JD, Duquesne Law Sch., 1972. Bar: Penn. 1972, U.S. Dist. Ct. (we. dist.) Penn. 1975, U.S. Supreme Ct. 1980. Pvt. practice Cambria County Bar Assn., Johnstown, Pa., 1972-95; worker compensation judge Commonwealth of Pa., Johnstown, 1995—. With USNR, 1962-82. Mem. VFW, Am. Legion, Elks. Republican. Avocation: british sport cars. Home: 325 Diamond Blvd Johnstown PA 15905-2713 Office: Commonwealth of Pa 609 Main St Johnstown PA 15901-2111

GETTY, GERALD WINKLER, lawyer; b. Chgo., June 17, 1911; s. Oliver and Pearl (Winkler) G.; m. Helen Brennan, Oct. 2, 1938 (dec. 1966); children: Michael, Muriel, Marie; m. Gracia Gibbs, June 3, 1967. JD, DePaul U., 1938, JD (hon.), 1972. Bar: Ill. 1938, Ind. 1938, U.S. Supreme Ct. 1960. Lawyer U.S. Govt., Chgo., 1938-42; pub. defender Cook County, Chgo., 1942-72; ptnr. Getty and Getty, Dolton, Ill., 1972-83; prin. Gerald W. Getty and Assocs., Dolton, 1983—. Author: Public Defender, 1972, Theory of Condominium and Cooperative Apartment Law, 1993. Mem. Elks. Criminal, Personal injury (including property damage), Property, real (including real estate development, water). Home and Office: 4033 Lake Getty Ln Irons MI 49644

GEWIRTZ, PAUL D. lawyer, legal educator; b. May 12, 1947. s. Herman and Matilda (Miller) G.; m. Zoë Baird, June 8, 1986, children: Julian, Alec. AB summa cum laude, Columbia U., 1967; JD, Yale U., 1970. Bar: D.C. 1973, U.S. Supreme Ct. 1976. Law clk. to Hon. Marvin E. Frankel U.S. Dist. Ct. So. Dist. N.Y., 1970-71, to Justice Thurgood Marshall, U.S. Supreme Ct., Washington, 1971-72; assoc. Wilmer, Cutler & Pickering, Washington, 1972-73; atty. Ctr. Law and Social Policy, Washington, 1973-76; assoc. prof., then prof. Yale Law Sch., New Haven, 1976—; Potter Stewart prof. of law, 1992—; director The China Law Ctr., Yale Law Sch., 1999—; dir. Global Constitutionalism Project, 1996-; Spl. Rep. the Presdl. Rule of Law Initiative, US Dept. of State, 1997-98; U.S. rep. European Commn. on Democracy through Law, 1996-2000. Author: Law's Stories, 1996; The Case Law System in America, 1989; contbr. numerous articles to profl. jours. Mem. Coun. on Fgn. Rels., Am. Law Inst. Office: Yale U Law Sch PO Box 208215 New Haven CT 06520-8215 E-mail: paul.gewirtz@yale.edu.

GHEZZI, SHERYL RAE, lawyer, real estate broker; b. Chgo., Nov. 12, 1955; d. Raymond Marion and Carol Jean (Sabell) G. BA, Lake Forest Coll., 1977; JD, John Marshall Sch. Law, 1984. Bar: Ill. 1984. Assoc. Hoffman, Burke & Bozick, Chgo., 1984-86; sole practice Chgo., 1986—. Mem. ABA, Ill. State Bar Assn., Chgo. Bar Assn., Women' Bar Assn. Ill., Assn. Trial Lawyers Am., ISBA Mil. Affairs Com. Roman Catholic. State civil litigation, Family and matrimonial, General practice. Office: 4433 Touhy Ste 333 Lincolnwood IL 60712 Home: 6440 N Kilbourn Lincolnwood IL 60712-3435

GHIARDI, JAMES DOMENIC, lawyer, educator; b. Gwinn, Mich., Nov. 10, 1918; s. John B. and Margaret M. (Troselio) G.; m. Phyllis A. Lindmeier, Sept. 5, 1945; children— Catherine, Jeanne, Mary. PhB, Marquette U., 1940, LLB, 1942, JD, 1968. Bar: Wis. bar 1942. Prof. law Marquette U. Law Sch., Milw., 1946-89, prof. law emeritus, 1990—; research dir. Def. Research Inst., Milw., 1962-72; of counsel firm Kluwin, Dunphy, Hankin & McNulty, Milw., 1972-87. Author: Personal Injury Damages, Wisconsin, 1964, Punitive Damages, Vol. I, 1981, Vol. II, 1985; contbr. articles to profl. jours. Served to capt. Med. Adminstrv. Br. U.S. Army, 1942-45. Recipient award for teaching excellence Marquette U. Faculty, 1971, Edward A. Uhrig Found., 1971, Alumni of Yr. award Marquette U. Law Sch., 1971, Charles L. Goldberg award for outstanding pub. svc. Wis. Law Found., 1986, Charles C. Pinckney award for legal scholarship and svc. to the legal profession N.Y. Def. Bar Assn., 1986. Fellow Am. Bar Found.; mem. ABA (mem. ho. of dels. 1967-80, Disting. Prof. Torts and Ins. Law award Torts and Ins. Practice sect. 1989), Milw. Bar Assn. (Lifetime Achievement award 1993), State Bar Wis. (gov., mem. exec. com. 1962-72, pres. 1970-71), Am. Law Ins., Wis. Bar Found., Am. Legion. Office: Sensenbrenner Hall Marquette U Law Sch PO Box 1881 Milwaukee WI 53201-1881

GIACCHETTA, ANDRE ZONARO, lawyer; b. Jundial, Brazil, July 1, 1974; s. Dalberto Mario Giacchetta Filho and Sonia Zonaro Giacchetta. Degree in law, U. State Sao Paulo, 1996. Bar: Sao Paulo, Brazil 1996. Trainee Pinheiro Heto Aduogados, Sao Paulo, 1994—96, jr. assoc. atty., 1996—98, assoc., 1999—2002, sr. assoc., 2002—. Mem.: ASPI, AIPPI, ABPI. Avocations: movies, theater , reading, volleyball, guitar. Intellectual property, Patent, Trademark and copyright. Office: Pinheiro Neto Advogados Rue Boa Visa 254 9th Fl 01014-907 São Paulo Brazil Fax: 55 11 3106-7632.

GIALLANZA, CHARLES PHILIP, lawyer; b. Hornell, N.Y., Nov. 18, 1950; s. Charles Joseph Jr. and Rena Eugena (Foster) G.; children: Charles Edward, Juleah Marie. AS in Aerospace Sci., U. Albuquerque, 1977; BA in Polit. Sci. and English, U. South Fla., 1979; JD, John Marshall Law Sch., 1982. Bar: Ga. 1983, U.S. Dist. Ct. (no. dist., Atlanta divsn.) Ga. 1983; cert. air traffic contr. FAA. With USAF, 1971-79; air traffic contr. USAF Res., McDill AFB, Tampa, Fla., 1977—79, Dobbins AFB, 1980-81, USN Res., Dobbins AFB; assoc. James B. Pilcher, P.C., Atlanta, 1982-83; pvt. practice Snellville, Ga., 1983—. Advocate assisting Cubans detained in Atlanta prison, 1985, 86; capt. Ga. Def. Force, 1985-86. Recipient photography awards USAF, 1975. Mem. Ga. Bar Assn., Atlanta Bar Assn., Gwinnet Bar Assn. (law day com. 1987-88, Pro Bono Project award for outstanding svc. to citizens of Gwinnett County and the legal cmty. 2000). Avocations: cross-training, running, weightlifting. State civil litigation, Family and matrimonial, Personal injury (including property damage). Office: 3881 Stone Mountain Hwy Ste 5 Snellville GA 30039-3978 Fax: 770-978-4450. E-mail: Charles@GiallanzaLaw.com.

GIAMPIETRO, WAYNE BRUCE, lawyer; b. Chgo., Jan. 20, 1942; s. Joseph Anthony and Jeannette Marie (Zeller) G.; m. Mary E. Fordeck, June 15, 1963; children: Joseph, Anthony, Marcus. BA, Purdue U., 1963; JD, Northwestern U., 1966. Bar: Ill. 1966, U.S. Dist. Ct. (no. dist.) Ill. 1966, U.S. Ct. Appeals (7th cir.) 1967, U.S. Tax Ct. 1977, U.S. Supreme Ct. 1971. Assoc. Elmer Gertz, Chgo., 1966-73; mem. firm Gertz & Giampietro, Chgo., 1974-75; pvt. practice, 1975-76; ptnr. Poltrock & Giampietro, 1976-87, Witwer, Burlage, Poltrock & Giampietro, 1987-94, Witwer, Poltrock & Giampietro, Chgo., 1995—2002, Stitt, Klein, Daday, Aretos & Giampietro LLC, Arlington Heights, Ill., 2003—. Former cons. atty. Looking Glass divsn. Traveler's Aid Soc. Contbr. articles to profl. jours. Pres. Chgo. 47th Ward Young Republicans, 1968; bd. dirs. Ravenswood Conservation Commn. Lutheran. Avocation: stamp collecting. General civil litigation, Constitutional, Labor (including EEOC, Fair Labor Standards Act, labor-management relations, NLRB, OSHA). Home: 23 Windsor Dr Lincolnshire IL 60069-3410 Office: Stitt Klein Daday Aretos & Giampietro LLC 121 S Wilke Ste 500 Arlington Heights IL 60005 Business E-Mail: wgiampietro@skdaglaw.com.

GIANFRANCESCO, PAUL RICHARD, lawyer; b. Phila., Aug. 14, 1967; s. Arnold and Rita (Gianfranceso) Hoffman. BS, John Jay Coll., 1989; JD, D.C. Sch. of Law, 1992. Bar: Pa., D.C. Asst. city solicitor City of Phila. Health and Human Svs. Unit, Phila., 1992—; pvt. practice Washington, 1995—. Mem. Phila. Bar Assn., Sons of Italy. Democrat. Roman Catholic. Avocations: running, sailing, motocycles. Criminal, Juvenile. Office: 16th Fl 1515 Arch St Philadelphia PA 19102

GIANNINI, MATTHEW CARLO, lawyer, educator; b. Youngstown, Ohio, July 12, 1950; s. Matthew and Graziella (Nistri) G. BS, Youngstown State U., 1973, postgrad., 1973-75; JD, U. Dayton, 1978. Bar: Ohio 1978, U.S. Dist. Ct. (no. dist.) Ohio 1978, U.S. Supreme Ct. 1982. Assoc. D'Apolito, Infante, Huberman and Gentile, Youngstown, 1978-84; ptnr. D'Apoloito, Infante and Giannini, Youngstown, 1984—; asst. prof. forensic psychiatry Northeastern Ohio U. Coll. Medicine, 1981-84, assoc. prof. forensic psychiatry, 1984—. Agt. Safeco Title Ins. Co., 1978—; sr. cons. forensic medicine Fair Oaks Psychiatry Hosp., Summit, N.J., 1979—; instr. Paralegal Inst. Ohio, 1980—; instr. comml. law Youngstown State U., 1980—. Author: (with A.J. Giannini and A.E. Slaby) Physicians Guide to Overdose and Detoxification, 1984; contbr. numerous articles to profl. jours., chpts. to books. Mem. ABA, Am. Inst. Biol. Scis., Ohio Bar Assn. Republican. Roman Catholic. Avocations: tennis, golf. Corporate, general, Family and matrimonial, Personal injury (including property damage). Home: 7284 Yellow Creek Dr Poland OH 44514-2647 Office: 1040 S Commons Pl Ste 200 Youngstown OH 44514

GIANOTTI, ERNEST F. lawyer; b. Price, Utah, Nov. 28, 1925; s. Ernest F. and Elizabeth (Crockett) G.; m. Alice Chambers, Oct. 31, 1960 (div. Apr. 1976); m. Rebecca Steinlicht, May 16, 1982; children: Stefani Knoeller, Christine Schadlich, Lisa Shalongo. JD, U. of Pacific, 1955. Bar: Mont. 1960, U.S. Dist. Ct. Mont. 1961, High Ct. Am. Samoa 1971, U.S. Ct. Appeals (9th cir.) 1972, High Ct. Trust Ter. 1977, U.S. Supreme Ct. 1977, Commonwealth, No. Marianas 1978, High Ct. Marshall Islands 1983, U.S. Dist. Ct. No. Marianas 1983, Hawaii 1985, U.S. Dist. Ct. Hawaii 1985. Sole practice, Great Falls, Mont., 1960-77; assoc. judge High Ct., Trust Territory, Pacific Islands, 1977-85; sole practice Kona, Hawaii, 1985—. Del. S. Pacific Judge's Conf., Australia, Saipan, 1982-84. Eastern chmn. State of Mont. Carter for Pres., 1976. Served with USN, 1943-46. Mem. AM. Trial Lawyers Assn., Mont. Bar Assn., Hawaii Bar Assn., VFW. Clubs: Marshall Island Yacht, Kona Billiken (bd. dirs. 1986). Lodges: Shriners, Elks. Democrat. Avocations: skiing, sailing, scuba diving. Criminal, Private international.

GIANOULAKIS, JOHN LOUIS, lawyer; b. St. Louis, Nov. 22, 1938; s. Louis John and Marie (Pappas) G.; m. Louise Marotta, Jan. 1961 (dec. 1970); children: Christopher Louis, Kia Louise, Candlin Hamilton Dobbs; m. Dora Rodliff Deady, Sept. 2, 1972. AB, Wash. U., 1960; JD, Harvard U., 1963. Bar: Mo. 1963, U.S. Dist. Ct. (ea. dist.) Mo. 1963, U.S. Ct. Appeals (8th cir.) 1974, U.S. Supreme Ct. 1975, U.S. Ct. Appeals (7th cir.) 1982, U.S. Ct. Appeals (6th cir.) 1987. From assoc. to ptnr. Thompson, Walther & Shewmaker, St. Louis, 1963-70; ptnr. Kohn, Shands & Gianoulakis, St. Louis, 1971-73, Kohn, Shands, Elbert, Gianoulakis & Giljum, LLP, St. Louis, 1973—. Mem., pres. bd. dirs. Legal Svcs. of Ea. Mo., Inc., St. Louis, 1972-81; mem. bar com. 22d Jud. Cir., St. Louis, 1977-85. V.p., pres. University City (Mo.) Sch. Bd., 1970-76; vice-chair Washington U. Alumni Bd. Govs., 2000-01, exec. vice-chair, 2001-2002, chair 2002-03; bd. trustees Washington U., 2001-03. Recipient Arts and Scis. Disting. Alumnus award Washington U., 2000. Fellow: Am. Coll. Trial Lawyers; mem.: ABA, Bar Assn. Met. St. Louis, Mo. Bar Assn., Spanish Lake Cmty. Assn. (dir. 1999—), Mo. Bluffs Assn. (pres. 1999—2001), Noon Day Club, Norwood Hills Country Club. Democrat. Federal civil litigation, Education and schools, Labor (including EEOC, Fair Labor Standards Act, labor-management relations, NLRB, OSHA). Home: 44 Clearview Park Saint Louis MO 63138-3302 Office: Kohn Shands Elbert Gianoulakis & Giljum LLP One US Bank Plz 24th Fl Saint Louis MO 63101 E-mail: jgianoulakis@ksegg.com.

GIARDA, RAFFAELE, lawyer; b. Rome, July 6, 1966; JD magna cum laude, U. Rome Sapienza Sch. Law; Dottore in Giurisprudenza, U. Rome, 1989; M in Comparative Jurisprudence, NYU, 1994. Bar: Italy 1992. Assoc. Baker & McKenzie, Rome, 1989—97, local ptnr., 1997—99, internat. ptnr., 1999—. Vice-statutory auditor Sodalia SpA, Rome, 1992—96. Author: Telecommunication Laws in Europe, 1998; contbr. articles to profl. jours. Active Italian Assn. for the Deaf and Blind, Rome, 1997. With Italian Mil., 1985—86. Scholar, Baker & McKenzie, 1993. Mem.: Nat. Assn. Italian Telecom. Users, Italian Assn. for Cancer Rsch., Assn. for the Convergence of Comm. Sys. (hon.). Avocations: art, music, travel, skiing, water-skiing. Mergers and acquisitions, Communications, Corporate, general. Office: Baker & McKenzie Viale di Villa Massimo 57 00161 Rome Italy

GIBBES, WILLIAM HOLMAN, lawyer; b. Hartsville, S.C., Feb. 25, 1930; s. Ernest Lawrence and Nancy (Watson) G.; m. Frances Hagood, May 1, 1954; children: Richard H., William H. Jr., Lynn. BS, U. S.C., 1952, LLB, 1953. Bar: S.C. 1953, U.S. Ct. Mil. Appeals 1954, U.S. Dist. Ct. S.C. 1956, U.S. Supreme Ct. 1959, U.S. Ct. Appeals (4th cir.) 1965. Asst. atty. gen., Columbia, S.C., 1957-62; ptnr. Berry & Gibbes, Columbia, 1962-68, Berry, Lightsey, Gibbes, Columbia, 1968-72; mem. Gibbes Law Firm, P.A., Columbia, 1972—; house of dels. S.C. Bar, 1994-96. Chief judge U.S. Army Legal Svcs. Agy., 1980-83. Author: Control of Highway Access - Its Prospects and Problems, Legal Dimensions of Community Health Planning, 1969, Manual for Fee Appraisors, 1960; contbr. articles to S.C. Law Review, Law Rev. Digest, 1960. Chmn. bd. dirs. U. S.C. YMCA, 1956-60. Brig. gen. JAGC, USAR 1980-83. Recipient Legion of Merit, U.S. Army, 1983. Mem. ABA (mil. laws com. 1984-90, meml. com.), S.C. Bar Assn. (exec. com. 1961-62), Am. Bd. Trial Advocates (sec.-treas. 1994-95, pres.-elect 1995-96, pres. 1996-97), Judge Advs. Assn. (pres. 1982-83), Richland County Bar Assn., S.C. Credit Ins. Assn. (gen. counsel 1963-94), Tarantella Club, Caprician Club, Summit Club, Doonbeg (Ireland) Golf Club, Forest Lake Country Club, Kiawah Island Club, Kappa Sigma Kappa, Omicron Delta Kappa, founding mem. Doonberg Golf Club, Cnty. Clare Ireland, 2002. Episcopalian. General civil litigation, Estate planning, Probate (including wills, trusts). Home: 35 Avian Tr Columbia SC 29206-4965 E-mail: gibbesbill@msn.com.

GIBBONS, JULIA SMITH, federal judge; d. John Floyd and Julia Jackson (Abernathy) Smith; m. William Lockhart Gibbons, Aug. 11, 1973; children: Rebecca Carey, William Lockhart Jr. BA, Vanderbilt U., 1972; JD, U. Va., 1975. Bar: Tenn. 1975. Law clk. to judge U.S. Ct. Appeals, 1975-76; assoc. Farris, Hancock, Gilman, Branan, Lanier & Hellen, Memphis, 1976-79; legal advisor Gov. Lamar Alexander, Nashville, 1979-81; judge 15th Jud. Cir., Memphis, 1981-83, U.S. Dist. Ct. (we. dist.) Tenn., Memphis, 1983—2002, chief judge, 1994-2000; judge U.S. Ct. Appeals (6th cir.), Memphis, 2002—. Fellow: Memphis and Shelby County Bar Found., Tenn. Bar Found., Am. Bar Found.; mem.: Memphis Bar Assn., Phi Beta Kappa, Order of Coif. Presbyterian. Office: US Ct Appeals 1157 Federal Bldg 167 N Main St Memphis TN 38103-1816

GIBBONS, MARK, judge; B, U. Calif., Irvine, 1972; JD, Loyola U., L.A., 1975. Pvt. practice, Las Vegas, Nev., 1975—96; judge Clark County Dist. Ct., Nev., 1996—98, presiding judge civil divsn., 1998—2001; chief judge 8th Jud. Dist. Ct., Nev., 2001—02; assoc. judge Nev. Supreme Ct., Carson City, 2002—. Office: Nev Supreme Ct 201 Carson St Carson City NV 89701-4702

GIBBONS, ROBERT JOHN, lawyer; b. Bklyn., Dec. 3, 1944; s. David Thomas and Virginia Marie G.; m. Judith Ann Borst, Nov. 23, 1968; children: Robert, Sharon, Suzanne. BA, St. John's U., Jamaica, N.Y., 1966; JD, Fordham U., 1969. Bar: N.Y. 1970. Assoc. Mudge, Rose, Guthrie, Alexander & Ferdon, N.Y.C., 1969-76; ptnr. Wood, Dawson et al, N.Y.C., 1976-77, Debevoise & Plimpton, N.Y.C., 1977—. Trustee New Canaan County Sch., Conn., 1983-91, pres. bd. trustees, 1988-91; bd. dirs. New Canaan Baseball Inc., 1982-88, New Canaan Field Club; mem. Utilities Commn. Town of New Canaan, 1986-90. Mem. ABA, N.Y. State Bar Assn., Assn. of Bar of City of N.Y. Corporate, general, Finance, Securities. Home: 221 Michigan Rd New Canaan CT 06840-2223 Office: Debevoise & Plimpton 919 3rd Ave Fl 23 New York NY 10022-6225

GIBBONS, WILLIAM JOHN, lawyer; b. Chgo., Jan. 22, 1947; s. Edward and Lottie (Gasiorek) G.; children: Maximilian Clay, Bartholomew David, Ariel Katherine. BA, Northwestern U., 1968, JD, 1972. Bar: Ill. 1972, U.S. Dist. Ct. (no. dist.) Ill. 1972, U.S. Ct. Appeals (9th cir.) 1980, U.S. Supreme Ct. 1982, U.S. Ct. Appeals (7th cir.) 1984, U.S. Ct. Appeals (3rd cir.) 2002. Assoc. Kirkland and Ellis, Chgo., 1972-76; ptnr. Hedlund, Hunter and Lynch, Chgo., 1976-82, Latham and Watkins, Chgo., 1982—, mng. ptnr. Chgo. office, 1995-2000. Served with USAR, 1968-74. Mem.: ABA, Chgo. Coun. Lawyers, Seventh Cir. Bar Assn., Chgo. Bar Assn. (chair class action com. 1994—95), Riverpark Club (Chgo.). Antitrust, Federal civil litigation, State civil litigation. Home: 4900 S Kimbark Ave Chicago IL 60615-2922 Office: Latham & Watkins Sears Tower Ste 5800 Chicago IL 60606-6306

GIBBS, FREDERICK WINFIELD, lawyer, communications company executive; b. Buffalo, Mar. 22, 1932; s. Walter L. M. and Elizabeth Mari (Georgi) G.; m. Josephine Janice Jarvis, Dec. 20, 1954; children: Michael, Mathew, Robyn. BA cum laude, Alfred U., 1954; JD with Tax honors, Rutgers U., 1989. Bar: Pa. 1989, N.J. 1989, U.S. Dist. Ct. N.J. 1989. With N.Y. Tel. Co., 1954-65, ITT, 1965-86; mng. dir. ITT Standard Electrica, S.A., 1971-75; chief exec. officer ITT Standard Electrica, Brazil, 1975-77; exec. dir. ops. ITT Communications Ops. Group ITT Communications Ops. Group, 1977; corp. v.p. ITT, 1977-80; pres. U.S. Tel. and Tel. Corp., 1977-79, exec. dir., sr. group exec., 1980-86; dir. System 12, ITT, 1979-80; exec. v.p. ITT, 1980-86, ITT Telecommunications Corp., 1983-86; pvt. practice law Pemberton, N.J., 1989-95; founding ptnr. Gibbs & Gregory Attys. at Law, Pemberton, 1995—. Cons. ITT, 1986-89, The World Bank/IFC, 1989—; pres. Mulberry Hill Enterprises, 1989—; bd. dirs. ACT Mfg.. Eion Mfg. Trustee Alfred U., 1981—; trustee Whitesbog Found., 1996—, pres. bd. trustees, 2000—; mem. planning bd. Barnegat Light, N.J., 1992-2002; elected Borough Coun., Barnegat Light, 1992, re-elected, 1995, 98; bd. dirs. Burlington County Red Cross, 1999—, Our Gang Players, Inc. Named Hon. Citizen of Rio de Janeiro, 1973; inducted to Alfred Univ. Athletic Hall of Fame, 1993. Mem. ABA, N.J. Bar Assn., Pa. Bar Assn., Burlington County Bar Assn., Barnegat Light Taxpayers Assn. (v.p. 1989-90, pres. 1990-92), Rotary Internat. (bd. dirs. Pemberton club 1996-97, v.p. 1997-98, pres. 1999-00, Pemberton Rotarian of Yr. 1996-97). Home: 12 E 17th Street Rd Barnegat Light NJ 08006

GIBBS, LAWRENCE BLAIR, lawyer; b. Hutchinson, Kans., Aug. 31, 1938; married; 2 children. BA, Yale U., 1960; JD, U. Tex., 1963. Assoc., then ptnr. Branscomb, Gary, Thomasson & Hall, Corpus Christi, Tex., 1963-72; dep. chief counsel IRS, Washington, 1972-73, acting chief counsel, 1973, asst. commr., 1973-75; ptnr. Johnson and Swanson, Dallas, 1976-86; commr. IRS, Washington, 1986-89; ptnr. Johnson & Gibbs, Washington and Dallas, 1989-94; mem. Miller & Chevalier, Washington, 1994—. Bd. advisors Taxation Mergers & Acquisitions. Trustee So. Fed. Tax Inst. Mem. ABA (vice chmn. adminstrn. sect. taxation 1991-92), FBA, State Bar Tex. (chmn. taxation sect. 1978-86), D.C. Bar Assn., Am. Law Inst., Communities Found. Tex. Adv. Bd., Am. Coll. Trust and Estate Counsel (bd. regents 1990-96). Office: Miller & Chevalier 655 15th St NW Ste 900 Washington DC 20005-5799 E-mail: lgibbs@milchev.com.

GIBLIN, LOUIS, lawyer; b. Omaha, Neb., Nov. 1, 1944; s. Richard and Mary (Mahoney) G.; m. Janis Schoblocher, May 20, 1977; 1 child, Marijo. AB, Creighton U., 1966; MBA, U. Chgo., 1968; cert. in investment mgmt., Princeton U., 1986; MS, Northwestern U., 1998; JD, Chgo.-Kent Coll. of Law; cert. in employment law, Chgo.-Kent Coll. Law. Cert.: (mediation law). Asst. v.p. No. Trust. Co., Chgo., 1968-73; v.p. MGIC Investment Corp., Milw., 1973-85; 1st v.p. Smith Barney Harris Upham and Co., Milw., 1985-93. Chmn. fin. analyst seminar Northwestern U., Evanston, Ill., 1990; adj. faculty U. Wis., Milw., 1985—; adviser Financiers U. Wis., Milw., 1986—; sr. exam. grader Inst. CFAs, 1986—; fin. svcs. vol., corp. cons. Skoda Koncern, Czech Republic, 1993—. Founder Joint Univ./Soc. Scholarship program, CFA exam, 1988; trustee St. Stephen's Ch., Milw., 1989-99; chmn. investment com., mem. fin. com. & ops. com. United Way, Milw., 1989-2002; mem. Oak Creek (Wis.) Housing Authority, City of Oak Creek Cost Reduction Com., Oak Creek Econ. Devel. Authority; mem. Creighton U. Alumni Senate, 1991-99; mem. adv. com. Creighton U.; bd. dirs. Creighton U. Alumni, 1993. Pulitzer Prize nominee, 1985. Mem. Internat. Soc. Fin. Analysts (charter), Internat. Inst. Forecasters, N.Y. Soc. Security Analysts, Nat. Assn. Bus. Economists, Nat. Options and Futures Soc. (bd. dirs. 1986-93), Deutsch-Amerikanischer Nat. Kongress, North Atlantic Cultural Exch. League, Internat. Inst. Am. Host, Milw. Investment Analysts Soc. (bd. dirs. 1988-99), Fin. Analysts Fedn. (bd. dirs.), Milw. Investment Analysts Soc. (pres. 1989-90), Mensa. Corporate, general, Estate planning, Finance. Home: 7468 S Logan Ave Oak Creek WI 53154-2234

GIBSON, BEVERLY CULLEN, lawyer; b. Charlottesville, Va., May 21, 1958; d. Joseph Edwin and Beverly Anne (Hartman) G. BA, U. Va., 1980; JD, U. Richmond, 1984. Bar: Va. 1984, U.S. Bankruptcy Ct. 1985, U.S. Dist. Ct. (ea. dist.) Va. 1986, U.S. Ct. Appeals (4th cir.) 1992. Pvt. practice, Norfolk, Va., 1985—. Bankruptcy, Criminal, Family and matrimonial. Office: 125 Saint Pauls Blvd Ste 504 Norfolk VA 23510-2734

GIBSON, CALVIN ROE, lawyer; b. Waukegan, Ill., June 13, 1962; s. Herman C. and Alma I. (Poyner) G.; m. Phyllis J. Thomas, June 13, 1995; children: Clayton Alexander, Benjamin Andrew. BA, U. Ark., Little Rock, 1985, BA, 1987, JD, 1989, MPA, 1997. Bar: Ark. 1989, U.S. Ct. Appeals (8th cir.) 1989, U.S. Supreme Ct. 1992. Staff atty. Ark. Hwy. Commn., Little Rock, 1992-2000; pvt. practice Little Rock, 1989-92; rschr. Carl Vinson Inst. Govt., U. Ga., 2000—02; with Office of Civil Rights, USDA, Washington, 2003—. Republican. Methodist. Avocation: flying. Administrative and regulatory, Labor (including EEOC, Fair Labor Standards Act, labor-management relations, NLRB, OSHA), Property, real (including real estate development, water). Office: Reporters Bldg 300 7th St SW Washington DC 20024 E-mail: calvin.gibson@usda.gov.

GIBSON, ERNEST WILLARD, III, retired state supreme court justice; b. Brattleboro, Vt., Sept. 23, 1927; s. Ernest William and Dorothy Pearl (Switzer) G.; m. Charlotte Elaine Hungerford, Sept. 10, 1960; children: Margaret, Mary, John. BA, Yale U., 1951; LLB, Harvard U., 1956. Bar: Vt. State's atty. Windham County, Vt., 1957-61; mem. Vt. Ho. of Reps., 1961-63, chmn. judiciary com., 1963; chmn. Vt. Pub. Svc. Bd., 1963-72; judge Vt. Superior Ct., 1972-83; assoc. justice Vt. Supreme Ct., 1983-97, ret., 1997. Chancellor Episcopal Diocese Vt., 1977-98, trustee, 1972-99, pres. bd. trustees, 1991-99, dep. to gen. conv., 1976-94. Served in U.S. Army, 1945-46, 51-53, Major Army Nat. Guard, 1956-71. Mem. Vt. Bar Assn. Avocations: bridge, tennis. Home: 11 Baldwin St Montpelier VT 05602-2110

GIBSON, JOHN ROBERT, federal judge; b. Springfield, Mo., Dec. 20, 1925; s. Harry B. and Edna (Kerr) G.; m. Mary Elizabeth Vaughn, Sept. 20, 1952 (dec. Aug. 1985); children: Jeanne, John Robert; m. Diane Allen Larrison, Oct. 1, 1986; stepchildren: Holly, Catherine. AB, U. Mo., 1949, JD, 1952. Bar: Mo. 1952. Assoc. Morrison, Hecker, Curtis, Kuder & Parrish, Kansas City, Mo., 1952-58, ptnr., 1958-81; judge U.S. Dist. Ct. (we. dist.) Mo., 1981-82, U.S. Ct. Appeals (8th cir.), Kansas City, 1982-94, sr. judge, 1994—. Mem. Mo. Press-Bar Commn., 1979-81; mem. com. on adminstrn. of magistrate sys. Jud. Conf. U.S., 1987-91, mem. security and facilities com., 1995-2001. Vice chmn. Jackson County Charter Transition Com., 1971-72; mem. Jackson County Charter Commn., 1970; v.p. Police Commrs. Bd., Kansas City, 1973-77. Served with AUS, 1944-46. With U.S. Army, 1944—46. Recipient Citation of Merit award U. Mo. at Columbia Sch. of Law, 1994. Fellow Am. Bar Found.; mem. ABA, Mo. State Bar (gov. 1972-79, pres. 1977-78; Pres.' award 1974, Smithson award 1984), Kansas City Bar Assn. (pres. 1970-71), Lawyers Assn. Kansas City (Charles Evan Whittaker award 1980), Fed. Judges Assn. (bd. dirs. 1991-97), Phi Beta Kappa, Omicron Delta Kappa. Presbyterian. Office: US Ct Appeals 8th Cir 400 E 9th St Ste 1040 Kansas City MO 64106-2695*

GIBSON, JOHN WHEAT, lawyer; b. Waco, Tex., June 27, 1946; s. John Wheat and Dorothy (Carpenter) G.; m. Melanie McGarrahan Gibson; children: Madeleine, Ruth, Abigail, Jack. BA, U. Tex., 1969, MA, 1976; cert., Casa Nicaraguense, 1986; JD, Baylor U., 1986. Bar: Tex. 1986, U.S. Dist. Ct. (no. dist.) Tex. 1987, U.S. Ct. Appeals (5th cir.) 1988, U.S. Supreme Ct., 2000. Copy editor Waco Tribune Herald, 1976-78; editor Clifton (Tex.) Record, 1978; instr. Temple (Tex.) Jr. Coll., 1978-82, Ea. Ill. U., Charleston, 1982-83; paralegal McLennan County Jail, Waco, 1985-86; staff atty. Proyecto Adelante, Dallas, 1986-87; assoc. Natkin & Flores-Saldivar, Ft. Worth, 1987; pvt. practice law Dallas, 1988—; ponente Primera Jornada Internacional de Juristas, San Salvador, El Salvador, 1990. Reporter Sta. KWTX, Waco, 1981-82. Cons. Com. in Solidarity with People El Salvador, 1986-88, adviser, 1988; cons. Cooperativo Refugiados Centroamericanos, 1986-88, Centro Social Hispanico, 1997-99; bd. dirs. Am.-Arab Anti-Defamation Com., 1998-2000. Recipient Friend of Youth award Optimist Club, Temple, 1980, Adviser of Yr. award Tex. Intercollegiate Press Assn., 1980. Mem. Tex. Bar Assn., Nat. Lawyers Guild (co-chair Tex.-Okla. region 2001-02), Tex. Trial Lawyers Assn. (pres. student chpt. spring 1985), Am. Immigration Lawyers Assn., ACLU. Green Party. Episcopalian. Avocations: bicycling, camping. General civil litigation, Constitutional, Immigration, naturalization, and customs. Office: 701 Commerce St Ste 110 Dallas TX 75202-4521

GIBSON, KEITH RUSSELL, lawyer, educator; b. Fulton, N.Y., Feb. 24, 1954; s. Keith Melvin and Retha (Thatcher) G.; children: Emily Michelle, Robin Bethany, Kyle Russell. BA, Lycoming Coll., 1976; paralegal cert., Adelphi U., 1977; JD, Oklahoma City U., 1984. Bar: Okla. 1984, U.S. Dist. Ct. (no., we., ea. dists.) Okla. 1984. Paralegal Thatcher & Miller, Lewistown, Pa., 1978-81; law clk. Chief Justice Don Barnes Okla. Supreme Ct., Oklahoma City, 1983-84; assoc. Pate & Payne, Oklahoma City, 1984-91; sr. atty. Williams, Box, Forshee & Bullard, P.C., Oklahoma City, 1991—. Instr. Oklahoma City U. Legal Asst. Program, 1990-98, officer Sch. of Law Alumni Assn., 1994-96; lectr. Okla. Foreclosure and Repossession Nat. Bus. Inst.; paralegal issues instr. Inst. for Paralegal Edn.; legal advisor Okla. Just Compensation Act. Originator and participant Met. Ch. Legal Clearinghouse, Oklahoma City, 1995. Mem. Oklahoma City U. Law Alumni Assn. (officer 1994-96, participant fundraising 1996), North Oklahoma City Rotary (bd. dirs. 1994-95, sec. 1995-96, Newcomer of Yr. 1991, Pres.'s award 1993-94, Benefactor award Rotary Found. 1993), Friends of the Oklahoma City Libr. Assn., Federalist Soc. (Okla. chpt.), Conf. Consumer Fin. Law. Republican. Bankruptcy, General civil litigation, Commercial, consumer (including collections, credit). Home: 2713 NW 158th St Edmond OK 73013-8819 Office: Williams Box Forshee & Bullard PC 522 Colcord Dr Oklahoma City OK 73102-2202

GIBSON, REGINALD WALKER, federal judge; b. Lynchburg, Va., July 31, 1927; s. McCoy and Julia Ann (Butler) G.; 1 child, Reginald S. BS, Va. Union U., 1952; postgrad., Wharton Grad. Sch. Bus. Adminstrn., U. Pa., 1952-53; LL.B., Howard U., 1956. Bar: D.C. 1957, Ill. 1972. Agt. IRS, Washington, 1957-61; trial atty. tax div. U.S. Dept. Justice, Washington, 1961-71; sr. tax atty. Internat. Harvester Co., Chgo., 1971-76, gen. tax atty., 1976-82; judge U.S. Ct. of Fed. Claims, Washington, 1982-95; sr. judge U.S. Ct. Fed. Claims, Washington, 1995—. Mem. bus. adbv. council Chgo. Urban League, 1974-82. Served with AUS, 1946-47. Recipient cert. award U.S. Dept. Justice Atty. Gen., 1969, recipient spl. commendation U.S. Dept. Justice Atty. Gen., 1970, Wall St. Jour. award, 1952, Am. Jurisprudence award, 1956; named Alumni of Yr. Howard U. Sch. Law, 1984. Mem. D.C. Bar Assn., Chgo. Bar Assn., Fed. Bar Assn., Nat. Bar Assn., Claims Ct. Bar Assn., J. Edgar Murdock Am. Inn of Ct. (taxation com.). Clubs: Nat. Lawyers (Washington). Baptist. Home: 6305 Chaucer View Cir Alexandria VA 22304-3548 Office: 717 Madison Pl NW Washington DC 20439-0002

GIBSON, REX HILTON, lawyer; b. Galveston, Tex., May 17, 1963; BBA, Southern Meth. U., 1985, JD, 1988. Bar: Tex. 1988, U.S. Tax Ct. 1989, U.S. Ct. Claims 1992. Tax assoc. Exxon Co., U.S.A., Houston, 1988, tax atty., 1988-92, sr. tax atty., 1992, Exxon Co., Internat., Florham Park, N.J., 1992-95, Exxon Ventures (CIS) Inc., Houston, 1995-99; tax counsel ExxonMobil Internat. Ltd., London, 2000—01, ExxonMobil Devel. Co., Houston, 2001—. Mem. ABA (taxation sect., natural resources com. 1995—, environ. taxes com. 1990—), State Bar Tex. (taxation sect., oil, gas & minerals law sect. 1989—), Houston Bar Assn. (taxation sect. 1995—), Houston Livestock Show and Rodeo Assn., Beta Alpha Psi. Avocations: snow skiing, hiking, fishing, golf. Oil, gas, and mineral, Private international, Corporate taxation. Office: ExxonMobil Devel Co Ste 1670 17001 Northchase Dr Houston TX 77060 E-mail: rex.h.gibson@exxonmobil.com.

GIBSON, RICK J. lawyer; b. Elmhurst, Ill., May 12, 1967; s. William George and Diane Gibson; m. Beth Ann Branscome, May 16, 1992; 1 child, Keegan William. BBA magna cum laude, Loyola U., Chgo., 1991, MBA, 1994; JD magna cum laude, U. Pitts., 1996. Bar: Ohio 96. Assoc. Jones Day, Columbus, Ohio, 1996—. Mem.: ABA (mem. legal opinion com. 1998—). Avocation: running. Mergers and acquisitions, Corporate, general. Office: Jones Day 41 S High St Ste 1900 Columbus OH 43215 Fax: 614-461-4198. E-mail: rjgibson@jonesday.com.

GIBSON, VIRGINIA LEE, lawyer; b. Independence, Mo., Mar. 5, 1946; BA, U. Calif., Berkeley, 1972; JD, U. Calif., San Francisco, 1977. Bar: Calif. 1981. Assoc. Pillsbury, Madison & Sutro, San Francisco, 1980-83; ptnr. Chickering & Gregory, San Francisco, 1983-85, Baker & McKenzie, San Francisco, 1985—2001, White & Case, LLP, Palo Alto and San Francisco, 2001—. Mem. ABA (tax sect.), Nat. Assn. Stock Plan Profls., Nat. Ctr. for Employee Ownership, Calif. Bar Assn. (exec. com. tax sect. 1985-88), San Francisco Bar Assn. (internat. taxation sect.), Western Pension and Benefits Conf. (pres. San Francisco chpt. 1989-91, program com. 1984-88). Pension, profit-sharing, and employee benefits, Environmental. Office: White & Case LLP 3 Embarcadero 22d Fl San Francisco CA 94111 also: White & Case LLP 5 Palo Alto Sq 3000 El Camino Real Palo Alto CA 94306 E-mail: vgibson@whitecage.com.

GIERBOLINI-ORTIZ, GILBERTO, federal judge; b. 1926; BA, U. P.R., 1951, LL.B., 1961. Asst. U.S. atty. Commonwealth P.R., 1961-66; judge Superior Ct. Bayamon, P.R., 1966-67, Superior Ct. Caguas, P.R., 1967-69; solicitor P.R., 1969-72, asst. atty. gen. for antitrust, 1970-72; pvt. practice Jose H. Pico, 1973-74, Arias Cestero, Gierbolini & Garcia Soto, 1974-75, Nido, Berrios, Menendez & Gierbolini, 1975-77, Dubon, Gonzalez & Berrios, 1977-80; judge U.S. Dist. Ct. P.R., San Juan, 1980—, chief judge, 1991-93; sr. judge, 1993—. Prof. U. P.R., Cath. U. Law Sch. Chmn. State Elections Bd., P.R., 1972. Capt. U.S. Army, 1951-57. Office: US Courthouse and PO Bldg 3d Fl Ste 342 300 Recinto Sur St Hato Rey San Juan PR 00901-1907 E-mail: Gierbolini@prd.uscourts.gov.*

GIERLACH, DAVID J. lawyer; b. Binghamton, N.Y., Apr. 8, 1957; s. Joseph J. and Jacquelyn T. Gierlach; m. Ida M. Teiti; children: Elaine, Alexandra, Joseph. BA, N.Y. State U., Binghamton, 1974—77; MA, Maryknoll Sch. Theology, 1977—81; JD, U. Hawaii, 1986—89. Bar: Hawaii 1989. Assoc. Cader Shutte, Honolulu, 1989—90; pvt. practice Honolulu, Hawaii, 1990—. Editor (in Chief): (jour.) U. Hawaii Law Rev., 1988—89. Regional chair Episcopal Ch., Honolulu, 2001—02. Mem.: Assn. of Trial Lawyers, Hawaii Bar Assn. Civil rights, Personal injury (including property damage), Professional liability. Office: 345 Queen St Fl 2 Honolulu HI 96813-4727

GIEVERS, KAREN A. lawyer; b. Culver City, Calif., Apr. 27, 1949; d. Ernest Conrad and Josephine Theresa (Passolt) Prevost; m. Joseph R. Gievers, Nov. 16, 1968 (dec. Feb. 1987); children: Daniel Steven, Donna Ann; m. Frank J. Bach, Nov. 23, 1997. AA, Miami Dade C.C., 1974; BA, Fla. Internat. U., 1975; JD cum laude, U. Miami, 1978. Bar: Fla. 1978, U.S. Dist. Ct. (so. dist.) Fla. 1978, U.S. Dist. Ct. (mid. and no. dist.) Fla. 1979, U.S. Ct. Appeals (5th cir.) 1979, U.S. Ct. Appeals (11th cir.) 1981, U.S. Ct. Claims 1980, U.S. Supreme Ct. 1982; cert. civil trial atty Fla. Bd. Legal Specialties, 1985, Nat. Bd. Trial Advocacy, 1992. Assoc. Sams, Anderson, Gerstein & Ward, P.A., Miami, 1978, Anderson, Moss, Russo & Gievers, P.A., Miami, 1979-83; ptnr., 1983—87; pvt. practice Karen A. Gievers, P.A., 1987—. Bd. editors: So. Dist. Digest, 1981-85. Lectr. FACT, Miami, 1984; pres. Operation SafeDrive, 1987—; mem. MADD, 1986; bd. trustees We Will Rebuild, 1992-93; candidate treas., ins. commr. State of Fla., 1994, candidate sec. state, 1998. Mem. Fla. Bar Assn. (mem. trial lawyers exec. coun. 1985-88, editor trial lawyers sect. 1984, vice-chmn. evidence com. 1985-88, chmn. 1988-89), Am. Bd. Trial Advocates (pres. elect Fla. 2002), Acad. Fla. Trial Lawyers (chmn. pub. com. 1984-86, bd. dirs. 1985-87, treas. 1988-89, sec. 1987-88, pres. elect 1989-90, pres. 1990-91, recipient Pres.'s award 1986, 90), Assn. Trial Lawyers Am., Dade County Bar Assn. (bd. dirs. 1981-84, 85-87, treas. 1987-88, sec. 1988-89, 2nd v.p. 1989-90, 1st v.p. 1990-91, pres.-elect 1991-92, pres. 1992-93), Dade County Trial Lawyers Assn. (sec. 1984, treas. 1985, pres. 1987), Fed. Bar Assn., Fla. Assn. Women Lawyers, Children's Advocacy Found. (pres., dir. 2000), Zool. Soc. Fla., Fla. Consumer Fedn. (bd. dirs. 1985-87), Lions Internat., Gray Panthers, Banker's, Gov.'s. Democrat. Federal civil litigation, State civil litigation, Personal injury (including property damage). Office: 524 E College Ave Tallahassee FL 32301-2529

GIFFEN, DANIEL HARRIS, lawyer, educator; b. Zanesville, Ohio, Feb. 11, 1938; s. Harris MacArtor and Anne Louise (Crawford) G.; m. Jane Louise Cayford, Nov. 23, 1963 (div. 1970); children: Sarah Louise, Thomas Harris; m. Linda Eastin, Aug. 19, 1972. AB, Coll. of William and Mary, 1960; MA, U. Pa., 1962, MA, 1967; testamur, U. Exeter, Eng., 1971; JD, Case Western Res. U., 1973. Bar: Ohio 1973. Corp. asst. U. Pa. Lippincott Libr., Phila., 1961-63; assoc. curator La. State Mus., New Orleans, 1963-64; sec. N.H. Hist. Soc., Concord, 1964-69; asst. dir. Syracuse (N.Y.) U. Arents Rsch. Libr., 1969-70; pvt. practice Cleve., 1973-99; asst. prof. law Cleve. State U., 1976-79; asst. prof. Kent (Ohio) State U., 1980-98, prof. emeritus, 1998—. Editor Walter Drane Co., Cleve., 1974-76; lectr. Monadnock C.C., Peterborough, N.H., 1968-69; vis. scholar London Libr., 1991-92. Author: Adventures in Vermont, 1969, Adventures in Maine, 1969, New Hampshire Colony, 1970; contbr. articles to profl. jours. Hon. life mem. Pres.'s Coun., Coll. William and Mary, 1980. Recipient Kenyon English Prize scholarship, 1956; fellow Heritage Found., 1959-60, Nat. Trust, 1959-61, 67, 73. Fellow Saltire Soc. (Scotland); mem. ABA, Ohio Bar Assn., Am. Soc. Interior Design, Am. Assn. Mus., Am. Assn. State and Local Historians, Nat. Trust, Soc. Archtl. Historians, Masons, Shriners. Episcopalian. Home: 6058 Mad River Rd Centerville OH 45459-1508

GIFFORD, WILLIAM C. lawyer, educator; b. Aurora, Ill., Sept. 18, 1941; AB, Dartmouth Coll., 1963; LLB, Harvard U., 1966. Bar: Ill. 1966, D.C. 1968, N.Y. 1976, Paris 1994. Assoc., ptnr. Ivins, Phillips & Barker, Washington, 1967-74; assoc. prof. Cornell Law Sch., 1974-78; counsel, ptnr. Wilmer, Cutler & Pickering, 1978-83; ptnr. Davis Polk & Wardwell, N.Y.C., 1983-98, sr. counsel, 1998—; prof. law Cornell U. Law Sch., 2001—. Vis. lectr. Yale Law Sch., 2003. Author: International Tax Planning, 1974, 2d edit., 1979; (with E.A. Owens) International Aspects of U.S. Income Taxation, 1982. Estate planning, Corporate taxation, Taxation, general. Office: Davis Polk & Wardwell 450 Lexington Ave New York NY 10017-3911 E-mail: gifford@dpw.com.

GIGUIERE, MICHELE LOUISE, lawyer; b. Spokane, Feb. 11, 1944; d. Karl Earl and Mildred Elaine (Phillips) G. BA, U. Pacific, 1965; MS, U. So. Calif., 1969; JD, Lincoln Law Sch., 1980. Bar: Calif. 1980. Exec. trainee J.W. Robinson Co., L.A., 1965-66; tchr. Novato (Calif.) Unified Sch. Dist., 1967-78; asst. dept. mgr. Emporium, San Rafael, Calif., 1970—74; atty. pvt. practice, Fair Oaks and Sacramento, Calif., 1980—. Mem. State Bar Calif., Sacramento County Bar Assn., Calif. Women Lawyers, Women Lawyers Sacramento. Democrat. Presbyterian. General practice, Landlord-tenant, Property, real (including real estate development, water). Office: 4811 Chippendale Dr Ste 702 Sacramento CA 95841-2554 E-mail: michelegiguiere@msn.com.

GIL, GUILLERMO, prosecutor; Acting U.S. atty. Dept. Justice, Hato Rey, PR, 1993—2002, asst. U.S. atty., 2002—. Office: US Attys Office Fed Bldg 350Carlos E Chardon Ave Hato Rey San Juan PR 00918*

GILBERG, KENNETH ROY, lawyer; b. Phila., Feb. 2, 1951; s. Leonard David and Roslyn (Tennis) G.; m. Nanci Jane Schwartz, Sept. 7, 1974. BA, Lebanon Valley Coll., 1973; JD, Widener U., 1976. Bar: Pa. 1976. Assoc. Pechner, Dorfman et. al., Phila., 1976-84, ptnr., 1984-87, Myerson & Kuhn, Phila., 1988-89; prin. Kenneth R. Gilberg and Assocs., Bala Cynwyd, Pa., 1989—99; ptnr. Mesirov Gelman Jaffe Cramer & Jamieson, LLP, Phila., 1990—2000, Schnader Harrison Segal & Lewis, LLP, Phila., 2000—02; shareholder Buchanan Ingersoll, Phila., 2002—. Contbr. articles to profl. jours. Past pres. Golden Slipper Camp; past pres., past chmn. Golden Slipper Club and Charities. Recipient Meritorious Achievement award Pa. Sports Hall of Fame, 1974; named Most Valuable Player Mid-Atlantic Conf., 1973. Mem. Phi Alpha Delta (charter). Republican. Avocations: lacrosse, racquetball, photography, golf, tennis. Labor (including EEOC, Fair Labor Standards Act, labor-management relations, NLRB, OSHA), Pension, profit-sharing, and employee benefits. Office: Buchanan Ingersol Eleven Penn Ctr 1835 Market St 14th Fl Philadelphia PA 19103-2985 E-mail: gilbergkr@bipc.com.

GILBERT, BLAINE LOUIS, lawyer; b. Phila., Aug. 26, 1940; s. Arthur I. and Marcia R. (Kaufman) G.; m. Sondra Gilbert; children: Beth M., Kimberly J. AA, Balt. Jr. Coll., 1961; postgrad., Am. U., 1962; JD, U. Balt., 1965. Bar: Md. 1966, U.S. Dist. Ct. Md. 1968, U.S. Supreme Ct. 1974. Exec. asst. ins. commr. State of Md., Balt., 1965-66; assoc. Polovoy & Polovoy, Balt., 1966-72; ptnr. Angeletti & Gilbert, Balt., 1972-79, Gilbert & Levin, Balt., 1979-92, Blaine L. Gilbert and Assocs. P.A., Balt., 1993—. Mem. ABA, Balt. Bar Assn., Am. Immigration Lawyers Assn., Am. Judicature Soc., Md. Trial Lawyers Assn. Avocations: music, screenwriting. State civil litigation, Entertainment, Immigration, naturalization, and customs. Home: 2B Dorsett Hills Ct Owings Mills MD 21117-1131 Office: Blaine L Gilbert & Assocs PA Lower Level 200 E Lexington St Baltimore MD 21202-3530 Fax: 410-539-6440. E-mail: blglaw@aol.com.

GILBERT, HOWARD N(ORMAN), lawyer, director; b. Chgo., Aug. 19, 1928; s. Norman Aaron and Fannie (Cohn) G.; m. Jacqueline Glasser, Feb. 16, 1957; children: Norman Abraham, Harlan Wayne, Joel Kenneth, Sharon. PhB, U. Chgo., 1947; JD, Yale U., 1951. Bar: Ill 1951, U.S. Dist. Ct. (no. dist.) Ill. 1955, U.S. Ct. Appeals (7th cir.) 1956. Ptnr. Rusnak, Deutsch & Gilbert, Chgo., 1962-79, Aaron, Schimberg, Hess & Gilbert, Chgo., 1980-84; sr. ptnr. Holleb & Coff, Chgo., 1984-2000, Wildman, Harrold, Chgo., 2000—. Bd. dirs. Jewish Fedn. Met. Chgo., 1977-83; chmn. bd. dirs., pres. Mt. Sinai Hosp. Med. Ctr., Chgo., 1968-69; trustee Chgo. Hosp. Coun., 1979-84; mem. Bd. Jewish Edn., 1972-77; mem. vis. com. Coll. of U. Chgo., 1997—. Mem. ABA, Chgo. Bar Assn., Chgo. Coun. Lawyers, Ill. Soc. Health Lawyers, Standard Club, Bryn Mawr Country Club. Democrat. Jewish. Health, Property, real (including real estate development, water). Office: Wildman Harrold Allen & Dixon 225 W Wacker Dr Ste 3000 Chicago IL 60606-1224 E-mail: gilbert@wildmanharrold.com.

GILBERT, J. PHIL, federal judge; b. 1949; BS, U. Ill., 1971; JD, Loyola U., Chgo., 1974. Ptnr. Gilbert & Gilbert, Carbondale, Ill., 1974-83, Gilbert, Kimmel, Huffman & Prosser, Carbondale, 1983-88; circuit judge First Jud. Circuit, Ill., 1988-92; fed. judge U.S. Dist. Ct. (so. dist.) Ill., Benton, 1992—, chief judge, 1993—. Spl. asst. atty. gen. Pub. Aid Enforcement Divsn., 1974-75; asst. city atty. City of Carbondale, 1975-78; active Nat. Coun. Govt. Ethics Laws, 1988—; mem. Ill. State Bd. Elections, 1982, vice chmn., chmn., 1983-85. Bd. dirs. Friends of Morris Libr., 1988—; active Edn. Coun. 100, 1989—, Boy Scouts Am. Mem. Ill. State Bar, Jackson County Bar Assn., Ill. Judges Assn. (mem. com. jud. retention), Phi Alpha Delta. Office: US Dist Ct 301 W Main St Benton IL 62812-1362

GILBERT, JAMES H. judge; b. Minneapolis, Mar. 11, 1947; three children. BA, U. Minn., 1969, JD, 1972. Bar: Minn., 1972; Wis., 1984; U.S. Dist. Ct. Minn., 1974; U.S. Tax Ct., 1978; U.S. Ct. Appeals (8th cir.), 1989; U.S. Supreme Ct., 1988. Lawyer, v.p., mng. ptnr. Meshbesher, Singer, and Spence Ltd., Mpls., 1971—; assoc. justice Minn. State Supreme Ct., Mpls., 1998—. Park Commr. City of Orono, Minn., 1988—; bd. dir. Minn. Drug Abuse Resistance Edn. Inc.,(D.A.R.E.) Mem. Minn. Bar Assn. Avocations: skiing, hunting, golf, tennis, snowmobiling. Office: 422 Minn Judicial Ctr 25 Rev Dr Martin Luther King Jr Blvd Saint Paul MN 55155

GILBERT, KEITH THOMAS, lawyer, consultant; b. Harlingen, Tex., Jan. 29, 1959; BBA, Baylor U., 1982; JD, South Tex. Coll. Law, Tex. A & M U., 1989. Bar: Tex. 1990, U.S. Dist. Ct. (so. dist.) Tex. 1992. Ptnr. Gilbert & Mestemaker, Houston, 1991-96; pvt. practice Houston, 1996-2000, Gilbert & Maxwell, Houston, 2000—. Legal rep. Tex. Editor: World Trade Policy, 1979. Avocations: chess, muscle cars, stamp collecting, wine. Appellate, State civil litigation, Election. Office: PO Box 1984 Houston TX 77251-1984

GILBERT, PENNY XENIA, lawyer; b. West Bromwich, U.K., Jan. 7, 1960; d. R. L. and M.K. Gilbert; m. John Whittaker, Aug. 3, 1991; children: Max, Emilia. BA, U. Oxford, U.K., 1982, DPhil, 1987. Tech. asst. Bristows, London, 1986-87, trainee solicitor, 1989-91, solicitor, 1991-98, ptnr., 1998—. Intellectual property, Patent. Office: Bristows 3 Lincoln's Inn Fields London WC2A 3AA England Fax: 011 44 207 400 8050. E-mail: penny.gilbert@bristows.com.

GILBERT, RONALD RHEA, lawyer; b. Sandusky, Ohio, Dec. 29, 1942; s. Corvin and Mildred (Millikin) G.; children: Elizabeth, Lynne, Lisa; m. Wendy Wawrzyniak, Apr. 2, 2002; 1 stepchild, Joshua Sisco. BA, Wittenberg U., 1964; JD, U. Mich., 1967, postgrad., 1967-68, Wayne State U., 1973-74. Bar: Mich. 1968, U.S. Dist. Ct. (ea. and we. dists.) Mich. 1968, U.S. Ct. Appeals (6th cir.) 1968, U.S. Ct. Appeals (9th cir.) 1977, U.S. Ct. Appeals (7th cir.) 1984, U.S. Ct. Appeals (3d cir.) 1988, U.S. Ct. Appeals (4th cir.) 1989, U.S. Ct. Appeals (8th cir.) 1990, U.S. Ct. Appeals (10th cir.) 1991, U.S. Ct. Appeals (11th cir.) 1992, U.S. Ct. Appeals (2nd cir.), 1992. Assoc. prosecutor Wayne County, Mich., 1969; assoc. Rouse, Selby, Dickinson, Shaw & Pike, Detroit, 1969-72; ptnr. Charfoos, Christensen, Gilbert & Archer, P.C., Detroit, 1972-84; sole practice, 1984—. Instr. Madonna Coll., Detroit, 1977-81; mem. faculty Inst. Continuing Legal Edn., 1977—; speaker symposium on social security law Detroit Coll. Law, 1984; state bar grievance investigator; vol. chmn. Aquatic Injury Safety Found; mgr. web sites Found. for Spinal Cord Injury Prevention, Care and Cure (fscip.org), Found. for Aquatic Injury Prevention (aquaticisf.org). Co-author: Social Security Disability Claims, 1983; contbr. articles to legal jours. Founder, chmn. Aquatic Injury Safety Group, 1982-89, Found. for Aquatic Injury Prevention, 1988, Found. for Spinal Cord Injury Prevention, 1988; chmn. aquatic safety com. Nat. Safety Coun., 1987; data collection subcom. of Nat. Swimming Safety Com. for Consumer Products Safety Commn.; bd. dirs. Nat. Coordinating Coun. on Spinal Cord Injuries; patron Detroit Art Inst., Detroit Zool. Soc.; mem. Pres.' Club U. Mich.; mem. Detroit Council on World Affairs, 1968-73, Council for Nat. Coop. in Aquatics; mem. combined fed. campaign Nat. Health Agy. Mich.; founder Spinal Cord Injury Traumatic Brain Injury Adv. Com. Mich. Pub. Health Chronic Adv. Com.; co-founder Safe Kids Coalition Southeastern Mich.; mem. Nat. Safe Kids Coalition. Mem. ATLA, Mich. Trial Lawyers Assn., System Safety Soc., ABA, Mich Bar Assn., Detroit Bar Assn., Am. Arbitration Assn., Am. Judicature Soc., Nat. Spinal Cord Injury Assn. (sec. 1988, bd. dirs., exec. com., chmn. prevention com.), Nat. Head Injury Assn., Mich. Head Injury Assn., Am. Standards and Testing Materials (com. F-24 on water parks and playgrounds, mem. com. F-8), World Water Parks Assn., Nat. Environ. Health Assn., Nat. Pub. Health Assn., Nat. Eagle Scout Assn. (alumni), Blue Key, Pi Kappa Alpha, Pi Sigma Alpha, Pi Delta Epsilon, Fenton Rotary, Fenton Village Theatre, U. Mich. Club, Spring Meadows Country Club. State civil litigation, Insurance, Personal injury (including property damage). Office Fax: 810-714-4782. E-mail: ron@fscip.org., ron@aquaticisf.org., rrgpc@aol.com.

GILBERTSON, DAVID, state supreme court justice; Former judge S.D. Cir. Ct. (5th jud. cir.), Pierre; assoc. justice S.D. Supreme Ct., Pierre, 1995—2001, chief justice, 2001—. Office: 500 E Capitol Ave Pierre SD 57501-5070

GILDAN, PHILLIP CLARKE, lawyer; b. West Palm Beach, Fla., July 17, 1959; s. Herbert Leonard and Kathleen (Yeager) G.; m. Laurie Beth Leinwand, Aug. 25,1985; children: Tyler Ross, Jacob Lee. AB magna cum laude, Dartmouth Coll., 1981; JD cum laude, Harvard U., 1984. Bar: Fla. 1984, U.S. Ct. Appeals (11th cir.) 1986, U.S. Supreme Ct. 1989. Assoc.

Nason, Gildan, Yeager, Gerson & White, P.A., West Palm Beach, 1984-89, shareholder, 1989-96, Greenberg Traurig PA, West Palm Beach, 1997—. Lectr. Reinventing Govt. Symposium, Hollywood, Fla., 1994, Risk Mgmt. State Conf., Deerfield Beach, Fla., 1995. Contbr. articles to profl. jours. Dir. Com. for Good Govt., Palm Beach, Fla., 1990-94. Mem. Fla. Bar Assn., Palm Beach County Bar Assn., Am. Inns of Ct. LIV (exec. com. 1991-94), Phi Beta Kappa. Corporate, general, Mergers and acquisitions, Utilities, public. Office: Greenberg Traurig PA 777 S Flagler Dr Ste 300 West Palm Beach FL 33401-6161

GILDEA, BRIAN MICHAEL, lawyer; b. New Haven, Nov. 1, 1939; s. Thomas Michael and Lillian Frances (Reilly) G.; children: Larysa Albina, Stefan Bohdan. AS, New Haven U., 1964; BA, Providence Coll., 1967; JD, Suffolk U., 1970. Bar: Conn. 1970, U.S. Dist. Ct. Conn. 1971, U.S. Ct. Appeals (2d cir.) 1975, U.S. Ct. Appeals (3d cir.) 1979, U.S. Ct. Appeals (5th cir.) 1984, U.S. Supreme Ct. 1975. Legal adviser City of Boston, 1969-70; assoc. Celentano, Ivey & Gery, New Haven, 1970-73; ptnr. Celentano & Gildea, New Haven, 1973-74; pvt. practice New Haven, 1974—. Bd. dirs. St. Mary's High Sch., New Haven, 1975-77; mem. Bethany (Conn.) Town Charter Commn., 1976; del. U.S./Japan Bilateral Session, 1988, U.S./China Joint Session on Trade and Econ. Law, 1987. With USAF, 1958-62. Recipient Svc. award Providence Coll., New Haven, 1979, Friar award St. Mary's Alumni Assn., 1980. Mem. ABA, Def. Rsch. Inst., Conn. Bar Assn., New Haven County Bar Assn., Am. Lawyers Assn. Democrat. Roman Catholic. Avocations: bicycling, tennis, skiing, photography. Federal civil litigation, Immigration, naturalization, and customs, Insurance. Office: 512 Blake St New Haven CT 06515-1287

GILDENHORN, JOSEPH BERNARD, lawyer, businessman, former diplomat; b. Washington, Sept. 17, 1929; s. Oscar and Celia (Koval) G.; m. Alma Lee Gross, June 28, 1953; children: Carol Winer, Michael Saul. BS, U. Md., 1951; LLB, JD, Yale U., 1954. Bar: D.C. 1954, U.S. Ct. Appeals (D.C. cir.) 1954, U.S. Supreme Ct. 1954. Ptnr. Brown, Gildenhorn & Jacobs, 1955—; vice chmn. D.C. Nat. Sovran Bank, Washington, 1979-89; amb. to Switzerland Dept. State, Bern, 1989-93; ptnr. The JBG Cos. Adj. prof. George Washington U., D.C. Bar Assn.; pres. JBG Properties, Inc., 1956-88; vice chmn. adv. bd. D.C. metro region BB&T Bank, 1985-2003; bd. dirs. The Mills Corp.; D.C. chmn. George W. Bush for Pres., 2000, trustee U. Md. College Park Found., Inc.; chmn. bd. trustees Woodrow Wilson Internat. Ctr. for Scholars, 2002—. Mem. editl. bd. Yale Law Jour., 1954. D.C. campaign chmn. Bush-Quayle, 1988; past pres., bd. dirs. Hebrew Home Greater Washington, 1975-77; treas. Coun. Am. Ambassadors, 2000; bd. dirs. Washington Jewish Cmty. Found., Inst. for Study of Diplomacy, Georgetown U., Ctr. for Strategic and Internat. Studies, UN Watch, Geneva, Internat. Inst. Strategic Studies; treas. Am. Joint Distbn. Com., 1999—; pres. bd. dirs. Jewish Fedn. Greater Washington, 1988-89; vice chmn. D.C. Sports Commn.; participant Nat. Prayer Breakfast, 2000. With AUS, 1954-56. Recipient David Ben Gurion award State of Israel, 1977, Hyman Goldman Humanitarian award, 1984, B'nai B'rith Humanitarian award, 1985, Ourisman Cmty. Svc. award, 1987, Ottenstein Cmty. Svc. award, 1991, B'nai B'rith Disting. Alumnus award, 1983, Jewish Inst. for Nat. Security Affairs Leadership award, 1993, U. Md. Disting. Alumnus award, 1996, Leadership award Washington Inst., 1999, Corp. Citizenship award Woodrow Wilson Internat. Ctr. for Scholars, 2000; named Philanthropist of the Yr., Nat. Soc. of Fundraising Execs., 2000; named Washingtonian of Yr. Washingtonian mag., 1996. Mem. Order of Coif, Team 100, Presdl. Trust. Property, real (including real estate development, water). Home: 2030 24th St NW Washington DC 20008-1608 Office: Ste 300 5301 Wisconsin Ave NW Washington DC 20015

GILES, ROBERT EDWARD, JR., lawyer; b. Bremerton, Wash., Dec. 17, 1949; s. Robert Edward Sr. and Alice Louise (Morton) G.; m. Barbara Susan Miller, Aug. 21, 1971; children: Steven, William, Thomas, James. BA in Fin., U. Washington, 1971, JD, 1974. Bar: Wash. 1974, U.S. Tax Ct. 1974. From assoc. to fin. ptnr. Perkins Coie, Seattle, 1974-86, mng. ptnr., 1986—. Bd. dirs. Jr. Achievement, Seattle, 1984—; bd. dirs., sec. Wash. Coun. for Econ. Edn., 1981-91; v.p., chief Seattle coun. Boy Scouts Am., 1996-2002. Capt. U.S. Army, 1974. Mem. ABA, Wash. State Bar Assn., Greater Seattle C. of C. (trustee 1994-97, 2000—). Avocations: hiking, climbing. Corporate, general, Corporate taxation, Personal income taxation. Home: 22018 NE 137th St Woodinville WA 98072-5802 Office: Perkins Coie 1201 3rd Ave 48th Fl Seattle WA 98101-3029

GILES, WILLIAM JEFFERSON, III, lawyer; b. Manila, Apr. 10, 1936; came to U.S., 1938; s. William Jefferson and Gardner (Anderson) G.; m. Nancy Gifford Seff, May 9, 1957; children: William Jefferson IV, Gregory Gifford. BS, U. Calif., Berkeley, 1957; postgrad., Golden Gate Coll., 1958-59, Stanford U., 1960; JD, U. S.D., 1961. Bar: Iowa 1961, U.S. Dist. Ct. Iowa 1961, U.S. Ct. Appeals (8th cir.) 1971, U.S. Supreme Ct. 1971, Nebr. 1982, U.S. Ct. Appeals (9th cir.) 1988. Pvt. practice, Sioux City, Iowa, 1961—. Of counsel Whicher & Whicher, Sioux City, 1966-75, Whicher & Hart, Sioux City, 1975-77; lectr. in field. Contbr. articles to profl. jours. Bd. dirs. Sioux City Mus. and Hist. Soc., 1976-79, Sioux City Cmty. Theatre, 1974-76. Capt. USAR, 1957-68. Recipient Gold Seal award Phi Beta Kappa, 1953. Fellow Am. Acad. Matrimonial Lawyers (chmn. bankruptcy com. 1992-99), Internat. Acad. Matrimonial Lawyers; mem. ABA, ATLA, Iowa Bar Assn., Iowa Assn. Trial Lawyers, Comml. Law League Am., Sioux City Country Club, Phi Delta Phi, Phi Phi. Republican. Bankruptcy, Family and matrimonial, Personal injury (including property damage). Home: 3827 Country Club Blvd Sioux City IA 51104-1327 Office: 322 Frances Bldg 505 5th St Sioux City IA 51101 also: 3940 Hideaway Acres Crofton NE 68730-0088 also: 3 Sloane Gardens London SW1 W8EA England

GILFORD, STEVEN ROSS, lawyer; b. Chgo., Dec. 2, 1952; s. Ronald M. and Adele (Miller) G.; m. Anne Christine Johnson, Jan. 2, 1974; children: Sarah Julia, Zachary Michael, Eliza Rebecca. BA, Dartmouth Coll., 1974; JD, M of Pub. Policy Scis., Duke U., 1978. Bar: Ill. 1978, U.S. Dist. Ct. (no. dist.) Ill. 1978, U.S. Ct. Appeals (7th cir.) 1981, U.S. Ct. Appeals (D.C. cir.) 1984, U.S. Ct. Appeals (5th cir.) 1988, U.S. Dist. Ct. (ea. dist.) Mich. 1995. Assoc. Isham, Lincoln & Beale, Chgo., 1978—85, ptnr., 1985—87, Mayer, Brown, Rowe & Maw, Chgo., 1987—. Adminstrv. law editor Duke Law Jour., 1976-77. Participating atty. ACLU, 1983—2000; sec. Evanston (Ill.) YMCA, 1985, vice chmn., 1986—92; v.p. ACLU, 1995—96; elected mem. bd. edn. dist. 202 Evanston Twp. H.S., 1993—, v.p., 1995—96, 2003—, pres., 1996—98, mem. joint task force on safety, 1995—96; mem. Met. Family Svcs., Evanston Skokie Valley Cmty. Adv. Bd., 1997; mem., bd. dirs. Met. Family Svcs., 1998—; mem. Legal Aid Soc., 2001—; chmn. fin. com. Evanston Twp. H.S., 2001—; mem. exec. com. ED-RED, 2002—; Bd. dirs. Evanston (Ill.) YMCA, 1982—92; bd. dirs. Ill. ACLU, 1991—96; bd. dirs. Roger Bawldwin Found., 1993—96. Mem. ABA, Ill. Bar Assn., Chgo. Bar Assn. General civil litigation, Insurance, Libel. Home: 2728 Harrison St Evanston IL 60201-1216 Office: Mayer Brown Rowe & Maw 190 S La Salle St Ste 3100 Chicago IL 60603-3441

GILFOYLE, NATHALIE FLOYD PRESTON, lawyer; b. Lynchburg, Va., May 4, 1949; d. Robert Edmund and Dorothea Henry (Ward) Gilfoyle; m. Christopher Y.W. Ma, Sept. 9, 1978; children: Olivia Otey. Rohan James. BA, Hollins Coll., 1971; JD, U. Va., 1974. Bar: Mass. 1974, D.C. 1977. Staff counsel Rate Setting Commn., Boston, 1974-76; ptnr. Peabody, Lambert & Meyers, Washington, 1976-84, McDermott, Will and Emery, 1984-96; gen. counsel Am. Psychol. Assn., 1996—. Bd. dirs. ACLU Nat. Capital Area, Washington, 1980-83, St. Columbia's Nursery Sch., 1992-99, D.C. Bar Atty. Client Arbitration bd., chmn., 1994-95. Mem. APA, ABA, D.C. Bar Assn. (legal ethics com. 1998-2001), Mass. Bar Assn., Women's Bar Assn. Mem.: ABA, Mass. Bar Assn., Women's Bar Assn., DC Bar Assn. (legal ethics com. 1999—2001, gen. counsel 2002—). Episcopalian. Office: APA 750 1st St NE Washington DC 20002-4241 E-mail: ngilfoyle@apa.org.

GILHOUSEN, BRENT JAMES, lawyer; b. Anacortes, Wash., Sept. 24, 1946; s. Darrell J. and Jean Sarah (Sabatine) G.; m. Sandra M. King, Aug. 13, 1983; 2 children: Lindsay Elizabeth, Shane Shroeder. BA, Wash. State U., 1968; JD, U. Oreg., 1973. Bar: Wash. 1973, U.S. Dist. Ct. (we. dist.) Wash. 1973, U.S. Ct. Appeals (9th cir.) 1973, U.S. Supreme Ct. 1980, Mo. 1981, U.S. Ct. Appeals (4th cir.) 1986. From atty.-advisor to sr. atty. U.S. EPA, Seattle, 1973-80; from environ. atty. to asst. gen. counsel-environ. Monsanto Co., St. Louis, 1980-97; asst. gen. counsel-environ. Solutia Inc., St. Louis, 1997—. Mem. Superfund Settlements Project, Washington, 1988-95, 2001—; legal com. Chem. Industry Inst. Toxicology, Rsch. Triangle Park, N.C., 1986-99; mem. environ. law adv. com. Nat. Chamber Litigation Ctr., Washington, 1992-97. Mem. editl. bd. Hazardous Waste Strategies Update, 1994-2001. With USAR, 1968-74. Mem. ABA (sect. environ., energy and resources, chair corp. counsel com. 1994-96, vice-chair hazardous waste com. 1991-99), Am. Chem. Coun. (mem. enforcement subgroup 1995—), Def. Rsch. Inst., Forest Hills Country Club, Indian Wells Country Club.. Republican. Avocations: skiing, golf, boating. Administrative and regulatory, Federal civil litigation, Environmental. Home: 1 Peakmont Ln Chesterfield MO 63005-6806 Office: Solutia Inc 575 Maryville Centre Dr Saint Louis MO 63141-5813 E-mail: bjgilh@solutia.com.

GILHULY, PETER MARTIN, lawyer; b. Stamford, Conn., Aug. 20, 1961; s. Robert T. and Anne (Kilby) G.; m. Namhee Han, Aug. 20, 1988; children: Emma, Thompson Young, John Daniel. BA with honors, Wesleyan U., Middletown, Conn., 1983; JD cum laude, Harvard U., 1990. Bar: Calif. 1990, U.S. Dist. Ct. (ctrl. dist.) Calif. 1990. Vol. U.S. Peace Corps, Argali, Nepal, 1983-86; assoc. Latham & Watkins, L.A., 1990-98, ptnr., 1998—, nat. chair pro bono com., 1998—2003. Mem. adv. bd. Pacific Gemini LLC, L.A., 1995-97. Contbr. articles to law jours. Bd. dirs. Pub. Counsel, L.A., 1995-96; bd. govs. Fin. Lawyers Conf., 1999-2002; chmn. bd. dirs. A Place Called Home, L.A., 2001—. Recipient President's award Los Angeles County Barristers, 1998. Avocations: skiing, running, tennis. Bankruptcy, Commercial, consumer (including collections, credit), Corporate, general. Office: Latham & Watkins 633 W 5th St Ste 4000 Los Angeles CA 90071-2005

GILL, AMBER MCLAUGHLIN, lawyer; b. Houston, Dec. 12, 1960; d. Donald Buford and Wanda Jo (Windham) McLaughlin; m. Raymond Penn Gill, Aug. 16, 1997. BSc cum laude, Sam Houston State U., 1982; JD, Tex. Tech. Sch. Law, 1986. Bar: Tex. 1986, Okla. 1987, U.S. Dist. Ct. (no. dist.) Okla. 1987, U.S. Dist. Ct. (western dist.) Tex. 1989, U.S. Ct. Appeals (5th cir.) 1989, U.S. Dist. Ct. (we. dist.) Okla. 1996, U.S. Ct. Appeals (10th cir.) 1996, U.S. Supreme Ct. 1998. Atty. Jones, Bryant & Nigh, Enid, Okla., 1986-88; trust dept. mgr. Travis Bank & Trust, Austin, Tex., 1988; atty. White & Allison, Austin, Tex., 1988-89; asst. county atty Travis County Atty's Office, Austin, Tex., 1989-91, asst. dist. attorney, 1992-95; pvt. practice Enid, Okla., 1995—. Contract labor attorney Jones & Wyatt, Enid, 1995-97. Bd. dirs. Garfield County Child Advocacy Coun., 1997—, treas. 1997-99, 2002-. Mem. Okla. Criminal Def. Lawyers Assn. Avocations: snow skiing, tennis, jogging, horse back riding. Criminal, Family and matrimonial, Juvenile. Office: PO Box 3802 Enid OK 73702-3802 E-mail: ambergill@coxinet.net.

GILL, E. ANN, lawyer; b. Elyria, Ohio, Aug. 31, 1951; d. Richard Henry and Laura (Beeler) G.; m. Robert William Hempel, Aug. 4, 1973; children: Richard, Peter, Mary. AB, Barnard Coll., 1972; JD, Columbia U., 1976. Bar: N.Y. 1977, U.S. Supreme Ct. 1982. Assoc. Mudge, Rose, Guthrie & Alexander, N.Y.C., 1976-77, Dewey Ballantine L.L.P., N.Y.C., 1977-84, ptnr., 1985—. Mem. ABA, Nat. Assn. Bond Lawyers. Corporate, general, Finance, Municipal (including bonds). Home: 255 W 90th St New York NY 10024-1109 Office: Dewey Ballantine 1301 Ave of the Americas New York NY 10019-6022 E-mail: agill@deweyballantine.com.

GILL, RICHARD LAWRENCE, lawyer; b. Chgo., Jan. 8, 1946; s. Joseph Richard and Dolores Ann (Powers) G.; m. Mary Helen Walker, July 14, 1990; children: Kyla Marie, Matthew Joseph. BA, Coll. of St. Thomas, St. Paul, 1968; JD, U. Minn., 1971. Bar: Minn. 1971, U.S. Dist. Ct. Minn. 1971, U.S. Supreme Ct. 1979, U.S. Ct. Appeals (8th cir.) 1983, U.S. Ct. Appeals (4th cir.) 1990, Ill. 1992. Spl. asst. atty. gen. State of Minn., St. Paul, 1971-73; assoc. Maun, Hazel, Green, Hayes, Simon & Aretz, St. Paul, 1974-77; ptnr. Gill & Brinkman, St. Paul, 1978-84, Robins, Kaplan, Miller & Ciresi, Mpls., 1984—2002, of counsel, 2002—. Vol. Courage Ctr., Golden Valley, Minn., 1981—; youth football coach Maplewood (Minn.) Athletic Assn., 1978-80; youth basketball coach Orono (Minn.) Athletic Assn., 1999—; mem. athletics adv. bd. U. St. Thomas, 2002—. Mem. ABA, Minn. Bar Assn., Hennepin County Bar Assn., Ramsey County Bar Assn., Assn. Trial Lawyers Am., Minn. Trial Lawyers Assn., Town and Country Club. Avocations: skiing, tennis, golf. General civil litigation, Patent, Product liability. Office: Robins Kaplan Miller & Ciresi 800 Lasalle Ave Ste 2800 Minneapolis MN 55402-2015 E-mail: rlgill@rkmc.com.

GILLEN, JAMES ROBERT, lawyer, insurance company executive; b. N.Y.C., Nov. 14, 1937; s. James Matthew and Katharine Isabel (Fritz) G.; m. Rita Marie Wahleithner, June 15, 1963 (div. 1992); children: Jennifer Elaine, Nancy Louise, Paula Anne; m. Edda Lya Pacheco, Dec. 10, 1994. AB magna cum laude, Harvard U., 1959, LLB cum laude, 1965. Bar: N.Y. 1966, N.J. 1975. Assoc. firm White & Case, N.Y.C., 1965-72; v.p., assoc. gen. counsel Prudential Ins. Co. Am., Newark, 1972-77, sr. v.p., assoc. gen. counsel, 1977-80, sr. v.p. pub. affairs, 1980-84, sr. v.p., gen. counsel, 1984-98. Mem. bd. trustees Columbia Inst. Investor Project, 1981—97; legal adv. com. N.Y. Stock Exch., 1986—89; mem. adv. bd. Ascertain Solutions, Inc., 2001—02. Trustee United Way Essex and West Hudson Counties, 1981-90, pres., 1986-88; mem. Mendham Twp. (N.J.) Bd. Edn., 1981-82; trustee N.J. Shakespeare Festival, 1991-99, Mendham Twp. Libr., 1979-82; dir., chmn. Neurol. Inst. N.J., 1998—. Lt. (j.g.) USN, 1959-62. Mem. ABA, N.J. Bar Assn., Assn. Life Ins. Counsel, Harvard Club (N.Y.C.), Morris Country Golf Club. Corporate, general, Finance, Insurance. Home: 72 Washington Valley Rd Morristown NJ 07960-3332

GILLESPIE, GEORGE JOSEPH, III, lawyer; b. NYC, May 18, 1930; s. George Joseph Jr. and Dorothy Elizabeth (McKenna) G.; m. Eileen Tracy Dealy, July 27, 1955; children: Gail Gillespie Garcia, John D., Myles D., Eileen G. Fahey. AB magna cum laude, Georgetown U., 1952; LL.B. magna cum laude, Harvard U., 1955. Bar: N.Y. 1957. Assoc. Cravath, Swaine & Moore, LLP, N.Y.C., 1956-62, ptnr., 1963—. Bd. dirs. Washington Post Co., White Mountains Holdings Inc. Trustee, pres. John M. Olin Found., Pinkerton Found., Arthur Ross Found., William S. Paley Found., Edward E. Ford Found., Edmond J. Safra Philanthropic Found.; bd. dirs., sec. Mus. TV and Radio; chmn. exec. com. Madison Square Boys and Girls Club; chmn. emeritus Nat. Multiple Sclerosis Soc.; trustee Jackson Lab., Convent of The Sacred Heart, Greenwich, Conn. Frederick Sheldon Travel fellow Harvard U., 1955-56. Mem. Century Assn., Winged Foot Golf Club, Prouts Neck Country Club, Falmouth Country Club, Double Eagle Club, Am. Yacht Club, Portland Country Club. Republican. Roman Catholic. Office: Cravath Swaine & Moore Worldwide Pla 825 8th Ave Fl 43 New York NY 10019-7475

GILLESPIE, JAMES DAVIS, lawyer; b. Elkin, N.C., Apr. 30, 1955; s. John Banner and Jerry Sue (Swaim) G.; m. Tommie Lee Johnson, Aug. 13, 1977 (div. Dec. 1995); 1 child, John Foster; m. Regina Lee Robinson, July 11, 1998. BA, U. N.C., 1977; JD, Samford U., 1980. Bar: N.C. 1980, U.S. Dist. Ct. (mid. dist.) 1982, U.S. Dist. Ct. (we. dist.) N.C. 1983, U.S. Ct. Appeals (4th cir.) 1984. Ptnr. Neaves & Gillespie, Elkin, 1980—. Mem. Surry-Yadkin Mental Health Authority, Mt. Airy, N.C., 1981-91, vice chmn., 1987-89, chmn. 1990-91. Bd. editors: Cumberland Law Rev., 1978-80. Commr. Town of Jonesville, N.C., 1983-85, mayor, 1985-93; mem. exec. com. N.W. Piedmont Coun. Govts., 1987, sec., 1988-89, chmn., 1990-91. Mem. ABA, Assn. Trial Lawyers Am., N.C. Bar Assn., N.C. Trial Lawyers Assn., Surry and Yadkin Counties Bar Assn., Elkin Jaycees (bd. dirs. 1981-83, v.p. 1983-84), N.C. Acad. Trial Lawyers, Greater Elkin-Jonesville C. of C. (charter, bd. dirs. 1987-90), Phi Alpha Delta, Soc. Curia Honoris. Democrat. Methodist. Avocations: tennis, basketball, reading, travel. Criminal, Family and matrimonial, Personal injury (including property damage). Home: 516 Westbrook St Jonesville NC 28642-2658 Office: Neaves & Gillespie 124 W Main St Ste A Elkin NC 28621-3433 E-mail: neavesgillespie@aol.com.

GILLESSEN, FREDERICK, lawyer; b. Bonn, Germany, Nov. 12, 1967; Degree in law, U. Bonn, 1993, JD, 1999, PhD, 1999. Bar: Regional Ct. Düsseldorf. Rsch. asst. U. Bonn., 1990-97; assoc. Bruckhaus Westrick Heller Löber, Düsseldorf, 1998-2000, Freshfields Bruckhaus Deringer, Düsseldorf, 2000—. Author: European Transnational Mergers and Company Migration in the U.K. and Ireland, 2000. With German Army, 1986-88. Banking, Corporate, general, Mergers and acquisitions. Office: Freshfields Bruckhaus Deringer Freiligrathstrasse 1 Düsseldorf D-40479 Germany Office Fax: 49 211 4979103.

GILLETTE, W. MICHAEL, state supreme court justice; b. Seattle, Dec. 29, 1941; s. Elton George and Hazel Irene (Hand) G.; m. Susan Dandy Marmaduke, 1989; children: Kevin, Saima, Ali, Quinton. AB cum laude in German, Polit. Sci., Whitman Coll., 1963; LLB, Harvard U., 1966. Bar: Oreg. 1966, U.S. Dist. Ct. Oreg. 1966, U.S. Ct. Appeals (9th cir.) 1966, Samoa 1969, U.S. Supreme Ct. 1970, U.S. Dist. Ct. Vt. 1973. Assoc. Rives & Rogers, Portland, Oreg., 1966-67; dep. dist. atty. Multnomah County, Portland, 1967-69; asst. atty. gen. Govt. of Am. Samoa, 1969-71, State of Oreg., Salem, 1971-77; judge Oreg. Ct. Appeals, Salem, 1977-86; justice Oreg. Supreme Ct., Salem, 1986—. Avocation: officiating basketball.

GILLEY, STEPHEN D. prosecutor; b. Morehead, Ky., Nov. 3, 1959; s. Charles R. and Barbara M. Gilley. BBA, Morehead State U., 1980; MBA, U. Ky., 1981, JD, 1996. Sr. atty. Ky. Ct. Appeals, Frankfort, 1997—. Office: Ky Ct Appeals 360 Democrat Dr Frankfort KY 40601-8209

GILLIG, JOHN STEPHENSON, lawyer; b. Lexington, Ky., May 27, 1951; Bar: Ky. 1976, U.S. Dist. Ct. (ea. and we. dist.) Ky. 1984, U.S. Ct. Appeals (6th cir.) 1984, U.S. Supreme Ct. 1984. Law clk. Ky. Supreme Ct., Frankfort, 1976-77; policy analyst Congl. Sunbelt Coun., U.S. Ho. of Reps., Washington, 1981-83; asst. atty. gen. Ky. Atty. Gen., Frankfort, 1984-95, environ. spl. coun., 1992-95; counsel to spkr. Spkr.'s Office Ky. Ho. of Reps., Frankfort, 1995—, chief of staff Spkr.'s Office, 1999—. Mem. criminal rules adv. com. Ky. Supreme Ct., Frankfort, Ky., 1988-92, task force on ethics, 1989-91; mem. legis. task force on sentencing Legis. Rsch. Commn., Frankfort, 1990-91; commr. Ky. Emergency Response Commn., Frankfort, 1995, Nat. Conf. of Commissioners on Uniform Senate Laws, 1997—. Author: Kentucky Post-Conviction Manual, 1990; contbr. articles to profl. jours. Officer, bd. dirs. Ky. YMCA Youth Assn., Frankfort, 1987-94, 96—. Paul Harris fellow Rotary Internat., 1990; recipient Disting. Svc. award Ky. Commonwealth Attys. Assn., 1992. Methodist. Avocations: state and local history, naval history. Office: Office Spkr of the House State Capitol 700 Capitol Ave Ste 309 Frankfort KY 40601-3415

GILLILAND, JOHN CAMPBELL, II, lawyer; b. Bellefonte, Pa., June 4, 1945; s. John Campbell and Miriam Ruth (Forsythe) G.; m. Karen Gardner, Nov. 2, 1997; children: Jennifer, John, David. BA, Pa. State U., 1967; JD, Georgetown U., 1971. Bar: Pa. 1971, Ind. 1979, Ky. 1991, Ohio 1992. Ptnr. McQuaide, Blasko & Brown, Inc., State College, Pa., 1974-79, DeFur, Voran, Hanley, Radcliff & Reed, Muncie, Ind., 1979-90; prin. Gilliland & Assocs., Covington, Ky., 1991-2000; sr. counsel Locke Reynolds LLP, Indpls., 2000—01; prin. Gilliland Law Office, Indpls., 2001—02; ptnr. Gilliland & Caudill LLP, 2002—. Lectr. econs. dept. Ball State U., Muncie. Bd. dirs. United Way Delaware County, v.p., 1983-85; bd. dirs. Vis. Nurses Assn.; v.p. Muncie chpt. ARC, 1983-85; bd. govs. Friends of Bracken Libr. Served to capt. U.S. Army, 1971-72. Fellow Rotary Found., Queens Coll., Belfast, Ireland, 1968-69. Mem. ABA, Ind. Bar Assn., Ky. Bar Assn., Ohio Bar Assn., Am. Health Lawyers Assn., Ind. Soc. Hosp. Attys. (chmn. 1989), Pa. Soc. Hosp. Attys. (pres. 1978-79), East Central Ind. Pers. Assn. (bd. dirs.). Republican. Presbyterian. Corporate, general, Health, Labor (including EEOC, Fair Labor Standards Act, labor-management relations, NLRB, OSHA). Home: 3446 Kenilworth Dr Indianapolis IN 46228- Office: 6650 Telecom Dr Ste 100 Indianapolis IN 46278 E-mail: jcg@gilliland.com

GILLINGHAM, STEPHEN THOMAS, financial planner; b. St. Paul, May 30, 1944; s. Thomas Elmwood and Barbara Alice (Sickles) G.; m. Carolyn Jean Alvey, June 5, 1976; children: Kenneth, Brett. BA, Juniata Coll., 1966; JD, The George Washington U., 1969. Bar: Va. 1971; CFP; ChFC. Tax specialist Price Waterhouse, Washington, 1969-71; tax law specialist IRS, Washington, 1971-77; sr. tax lawyer Internat. Paper Co., N.Y.C., 1977-83; dir. tax rsch. and planning The Singer Co., Stanford, Conn., 1983-88; tax counsel Am. Cyanamid Co., Wayne, N.J., 1988-95; fin. planner The Thompson Group, Inc., White Plains, N.Y., 1995—. Lectr. World Trade Inst., 1980-90. Contbg. editor Tax Lawyer, 1984-88. With U.S. Army, 1970—75. Named one of Outstanding Young Men in Am., Jaycees, 1979. Mem. Va. Bar Assn., N.J. Tax Group (chmn. 1991-95), Tax Execs. Inst., Fin.Planning Assn. Avocations: golf, swimming, hiking. Home: 4 Northway Hartsdale NY 10530-2109 Office: The Thompson Group Inc 244 Westchester Ave White Plains NY 10604-2907 E-mail: stgill@cyburban.com.

GILLIS, RICHARD, solicitor; b. Dundee, Scotland, Apr. 22, 1950; s. Harold and Anne Gillis; m. Anna Burland, 1982 (div. 1993). Student, Coll. of Law, Guildford, Eng., 1970-73, Kenya Sch. Law, Nairobi, 1977. Lic. solicitor, Eng., 1975; advocate, Kenya, 1978. Solicitor Greater London Coun., 1975—77; advocate Archer & Wilcock, Nairobi, Kenya, 1977—80; solicitor Shoosmiths, Northampton, England, 1980—81; asst. to sec. TI Group plc, Birmingham, England, 1981—85; co. sec. ABB Transp. Holdings Ltd., Derby, England, 1985—95; clk. to coun. and co. sec. U. Derby, 1995—2002, mng. dir. family cos., 2001—. Dir. Crewe (Eng.) Devel. Agy., 1992—95, vice chmn., 1993—95; mem. CBI East Midlands Reg. Coun., England, 1993—95; trustee ABB Transp. Pension Plan, Derby, 1991—95; mem. Stakeholders' Forum, Derby City Challenge, 1993—98. Chmn. property com. Coun. of Order of St. John for Derbyshire, 1994—, Officer of the Order, 1999; regional mem., coun. 1999-2003, chpt. chmn. audit com. and Priory Regulations Steering Group, Priory of England and Islands of the Order of St. John, 1999—; trustee St. John Ambulance, 1999-2003. Named an Honorary Life Member, Court of the U. of Derby. Fellow: Royal Soc. Arts (life); mem.: Worshipful Co. of Basketmakers (liveryman, steward 2000—01), Athenaeum, Maccabaeans, Nottingham Club, Guild of Freemen of City of London (life), City Livery Club (life), Nairobi Club (life). Avocations: music, historical films, watching tennis, freemasonry. Home: Thatched Cottage Shirley Ashbourne Derbyshire DE6 3AS England Office: 49 Meadowside Dundee DD1 1EQ Scotland

GILLMAN, MICHAEL JOSEPH, lawyer; b. Bay City, Mo., June 6, 1939; s. Robert E. and Betty J. (Lindebaum) G.; m. Betty Jean Gradowski, Jan. 27, 1962; children: Michael A., Stephen S., Jason R., Andrew B., Christian A. BA, U. Mich., 1961; JD, Cooley Law Sch., 1983. Bar: Mich.

1983. Compensation coord. Dow Chem. Co., Midland, Mich., 1966-71; chmn. Mich. Workmans Compensation Appeals Bd., Lansing, 1971-83; assoc. Conlin, Benham, Ducey, Listman & Chuhran, P.C., Traverse City, Mich., 1983-87, mng. shareholder, 1987—. Mem. Mich. Rep. Ctrl. Com., 1967-72; mem. Bay County (Mich.) Commn., 1967-71. Recipient Disting. Svc. award Bay City Jaycees, 1970; inducted Mich. Workers Compensation Hall of Fame, 2002. Mem. Internat. Assn. Indsl. Accident Bds. and Commns. (chmn. com. 1975-79, exec. com. 1979-83). Avocations: basketball, fishing, deer hunting, U. Mich. athletics. Workers' compensation. Home: 995 Pine Ridge Dr Traverse City MI 49686-2873

GILLMOR, JOHN EDWARD, lawyer; b. Phila., Oct. 26, 1937; s. John Edward and Louise Ann (Porter) G.; m. Allis Dale Brannon, Aug. 17, 1968; children: Sarah, Abigail, Susan, Eleanor, John, Matthew. BA, Swarthmore Coll., 1959; LL.B., U. Pa., 1962. Bar: D.C. 1962, N.Y. 1963, Tenn. 1972, Pa. 1980. Assoc. Dewey Ballantine Bushby Palmer & Wood, 1962-63, 66-71; v.p., corp. counsel Hosp. Affiliates Internat., Nashville, 1971-78, sr. v.p., gen. counsel, 1978-79; staff v.p., asst. gen. counsel INA Corp., Phila., 1980; sr. v.p., gen. counsel INA Health Care Group, 1981; partner Gillmor, Mills & Gillmor, 1981-83; dir., exec. v.p. Health Am. Corp., 1983-86; ptnr. Gillmor, Anderson & Gillmor, 1986-89, Dearborn & Ewing, 1989-92, Boult, Cummings, Conners & Berry, Nashville, 1992—. Trustee Univ. Sch. Nashville, 1990-2002; bd. dirs. Nashville Opera Assn., 1991-2002, pres.-elect; bd. dirs. Hoosier CARE, Inc. With USMC, 1963-66. Mem. ABA, Assn. of Bar of City of N.Y., Nashville Bar Found., Tenn. Bar Assn., Nashville Bar Assn. Republican. Finance, Health, Mergers and acquisitions. Home: 1700 Graybar Ln Nashville TN 37215-2106 Office: Boult Cummings Conners & Berry 414 Union St Ste 1600 Nashville TN 37219-1744 E-mail: jgillmor@bccb.com.

GILLS, JEANNE M. lawyer; b. New Orleans, Apr. 5, 1971; BSEE with honors, Mich. State U., 1991; JD, U. Chgo., 1994. With 3M, Minn., Mich., 1988—90, IBM, Ill., Minn., 1992—93, Keck, Mahin & Cate, Chgo., 1993—96, Foley & Lardner, Chgo., 1996—. Avocations: gourmet cooking, writing restaurant reviews, foreign travel, reading, collecting ethnic art. Intellectual property. Office: Foley & Lardner 333 N Wabash Ave Ste 3300 Chicago IL 60611

GILMAN, KAREN FRENZEL, legal assistant; b. Syracuse, N.Y., Jan. 11, 1947; d. Charles Henry and Cora Adell (Haith) Frenzel; m. Lawrence Sanford Gilman, June 5, 1970 (div. Feb. 9, 1977). AAS in Horticulture, SUNY, Morrisville, 1967; BS, Cornell U., 1969, MS in Floriculture and Ornamental Hort., 1971; attended, Syracuse Univ. Coll., 1983. Cert. legal asst. Floral designer Fortino of Fayetteville (N.Y.), 1965-69, 76-79, 81-84, Fallon's Florist, Raleigh, N.C., 1973-74; salesperson Finley Fine Jewelry, N.Y.C., 1979-80; legal asst. Agway, Inc., Dewitt, N.Y., 1984; legal asst. gen. legal Carrier Corp., Syracuse, N.Y., 1984-91, legal asst. intellectual property, 1992—. Mem. adv. bd. legal asst. program Syracuse U. Coll., 1986-90. Contbr. articles to profl. jours. Henry Strong Denison fellow, 1969. Mem. Pi Alpha Xi, Phi Theta Kappa. Avocations: gardening, biking. Office: Carrier Corp PO Box 4800 Carrier Pkwy Syracuse NY 13221

GILMAN, RONALD LEE, judge; b. Memphis, Oct. 16, 1942; s. Seymour and Rosalind (Kuzin) Gilman; m. Betsy Dunn, June 11, 1966; children: Laura M., Sherry I. BS, MIT, 1964; JD cum laude, Harvard U., 1967. Bar: Tenn. 1967, U.S. Supreme Ct. 1971. Mem. Farris, Mathews, Gilman, Branan & Hellen, Memphis, 1967—97; judge U.S. Ct. Appeals (6th cir.), 1997—. Judge Tenn. Ct. Judiciary, 1979—87; lectr. trial advocacy U. Memphis Law Sch., 1980—97. Contbr. articles to profl. jours. Regional chmn. ednl. coun. MIT, 1968—88; active Chickasaw coun. Boy Scouts Am., 1993—2000; mem. Leadership Memphis; bd. dirs Memphis Jewish Home, 1984—87. Recipient Sam A. Myar Jr. Meml. award for outstanding svc. to legal profession and cmty., 1981. Mem.: ABA (ho. of dels. 1990—97), Am. Arbitration Assn. (mem. large, complex case panel 1993—97), Tenn. Bar Assn. (spkr. ho. of dels. 1985—87, pres. 1990—91), Memphis Bar Assn. (pres. 1987), Am. Coll. Trust and Estate Counsel, Am. Judicature Soc., Am. Law Inst., 6th Cir. Jud. Conf. (life). Democrat. Jewish. Office: Fed Bldg 167 N Main St Ste 1176 Memphis TN 38103-1824

GILMAN, SHELDON GLENN, lawyer; b. Cleve., July 20, 1943; BBA, Ohio U., 1965; JD, Case Western Res. U., 1967. Bar: Ohio 1967, Ky. 1971, Ind. 1982, Fla. 1984, D.C. 1985, Tenn. 1985, U.S. Supreme Ct. 1987. Assoc./ptnr. Louisville law firms, 1972—; ptnr. Lynch, Cox, Gilman & Mahan, P.S.C., Louisville, 1987—. Gen. counsel Louisville Assn. Life Underwriters, 1977, 78, 90; adj. prof. law U. of Louisville Sch. of Law. Bd. dirs., chmn. Louisville Minority Bus. Resource Ctr., 1975-80; pres. Congregation Adath Jeshurun, 1986-88; bd. dirs., v.p., sec. Louisville Orch., 1982-85; bd. dirs. City of Devondale, Ky., 1976, United Synagogue of Cons. Judaism, N.Y., 1989-98, also pres. Ohio Valley region. With JAGC, AUS, 1968-71. Fellow Am. Coll. Trust and Estate Counsel, Am. Bar Found.; mem. ACLU (bd. dirs. 1998—), Ky. Bar Assn. (ethics com. 1982—, ethics hotline com. 1990), Louisville Employee Benefit Council (pres. 1980). Pension, profit-sharing, and employee benefits, Probate (including wills, trusts), Corporate taxation. Office: Lynch Cox Gilman & Mahan 400 W Market St Ste 2200 Louisville KY 40202-3354 E-mail: SGilman@lcgandm.com.

GILMORE, DAVID L. judge; b. Washington, Pa., Oct. 28, 1944; s. Charles Jean and Dorothy (Beck) Gilmore; m. Janice Lynn Kughn, June 21, 1969; children: Melissa K., Thomas J. BS, California U. of Pa., 1966; JD, Duquesne U., Pitts., 1970. Bar: Pa. 1971, U.S. Dist. Ct. (we. dist.) Pa. 1972. Pvt. practice, Washington, Pa., 1970—87; asst. dist. atty. Washington County, Washington, Pa., 1972—73, asst. county solicitor, 1973—74, county solocitor, 1974—75, county commr., 1976—83; judge Ct. of Common Pleas, Washington, 1984—, pres. judge, 2003—. Cpl. USMCR, 1966—72. Democrat. Presbyterian. Avocation: cooking. Office: Court of Common Please Courthouse Main St #2001 Washington PA 15301 Business E-Mail: gilmored@co.washington.pa.us.

GILMORE, JAMES STUART, III, lawyer, governor; b. Richmond, Va., Oct. 6, 1949; s. James Stuart, Jr. and Margaret Kandle G.; m. Roxane Gilmore; children: Jay, Ashton BA, U. Va., 1971, JD, 1977. Atty. Harris, Tuck, Freasier & Johnson, 1977-80, Benedetti, Gilmore, Warthen & Dalton, 1984-87; commonwealth's atty. Henrico County, Va., 1987-93; atty. gen. Commonwealth of Va., 1993-97; ptnr. LeClair Ryan, Richmond, Va., 1997; gov. Commonwealth of Va., 1998—2002; ptnr. Kelley Drye, Washington, 2002—. Alt. del. Rep. Nat. Conv., 1976; chmn. Henrico County Rep. Com., 1982-85. With U.S. Army, 1971-74. Mem. Nat. Dist. Atty. Assn., Va. Bar Assn., Va. Trial Lawyers Assn., Va. Commonwealt Attys. Assn. Methodist. Office: Kelley Drye 1200 19th St NW Ste 500 Washington DC 20036*

GILMORE, JERRY CARL, lawyer; b. Memphis, Tex., Dec. 29, 1933; s. Hugh Bailey and Gladys Herd (Jones) G.; m. Martha Niendorff, Dec. 1, 1956; children: Daniel, Susan, Charles. BA, U. Tex., 1955, JD, 1957. Bar: Tex. 1957. Practice law, Dallas, 1957—. Pres. North Ctrl. Tex. Coun. Govts., 1974-75, gen. counsel, 1986—, also exec. bd.; chmn. steering com. transp. Nat. League of Cities, 1974; mem. Dallas City Coun., 1971-75. Mem. City of Dallas Transit Bd., 1979-80; former bd. dirs., pres. Suicide Prevention of Dallas; former chmn. bd. trustees Dallas County Mental Health-Mental Retardation Ctr.; trustee Dallas C.C. Dist., 1976-92, chmn. 1981-82, 85-86; trustee Meth. Med. Ctr., Dallas, 1986—, vice chmn., 1990-96, chmn., 1996—; ; bd. dirs. Meth. Hosp. Dallas, 1996—; ; bd. dirs. home mission bd. So. Bapt. Conv., 1979-85, chmn. 1983-85; active Dallas Area Rapid Transit Bd., 1993-95; bd. trustees Tex. Scottish Rite Hosp. for Children, 1994—. Named Outstanding Young Lawyer, Dallas Jr. Bar Assn., 1971; recipient Outstanding Community Service award Oak Cliff Civitan Club, 1972, Justinian award Dallas Lawyers Auxiliary, 2001. Mem. ABA, Dallas Bar Assn., Tex. Bar Assn., High Noon Club of Dallas (pres. 1967-68), Dallas Assembly, Oak Cliff C. of C., Masons, Lions, Delta Theta Phi. Methodist. Home: 19 Turtle Creek Bnd Dallas TX 75204-1635 Office: 1700 Pacific Ste 2800 Dallas TX 75201-7357

GILMORE, JOHN ALLEN DEHN, lawyer; b. Boston, Mar. 18, 1947; s. Myron Piper and Sheila (Dehn) G.; children: Dehn, Thomas. BA, Harvard U., 1970, JD, 1974. Bar: Mass. 1974. Assoc. Hill & Barlow, Boston, 1974-81, ptnr., 1981—, hiring ptnr., 1982-87, mem. mgmt. com., 1988-92, chmn. litigatin dept., 1992—2002; ptnr. Pipert Rudnick, 2003—. Bd. dirs. Mass. Correctional Legal Svcs., Boston, 1982-86; mem. Mass. Jud. Nominating Coun., 1993-97. Fiske fellow, 1970-71. Mem. ABA, Mass. Bar Assn., Boston Bar Assn. Democrat. Federal civil litigation, General civil litigation. Home: 47 Reservoir St Cambridge MA 02138-3335 Office: Piper Rudnick One International Pl Boston MA 02110

GILMORE, MARJORIE HAVENS, civic worker, lawyer; b. N.Y.C., Aug. 16, 1918; d. William Westerfield and Elsie (Medl) Havens; m. Hugh Redland Gilmore, May 8, 1942; children: Douglas Hugh, Anne Charlotte Gilmore Decker, Joan Louise. AB, Hunter Coll., 1938; JD, Columbia U., 1941. Bar: N.Y. 1941, Va. 1968. Rsch. asst. N.Y. Law Revision Commn., 1941-42; assoc. Spence, Windels, Walser, Hotchkiss & Angell, N.Y.C., 1942, Chadbourne, Wallace, Parke & Whiteside, N.Y.C., 1942-43; atty. U.S. Army, Washington, 1948-53. Sec., Thomas Jefferson Jr. High Sch. PTA, 1956-58; chmn. by-laws rev. com., Long Point Corp., Ferrisburg, Vt., 1981-93; parliamentarian Wakefield High Sch. PTA, 1959-60, chmn. citizenship com., 1960-61; publicity chmn. Patrick Henry Sch. PTA, sec., 1964-65; parliamentarian Nottingham PTA, 1966-69; mem. extra-curricular activities com. Arlington County Sch. Bd.; area chmn. fund drive Cancer Soc., 1955-56; active Girl Scouts U.S.A., 1963-70; mem. '41 com. Columbia Law Sch. Fund. Recipient Constl. Law award Hunter Coll., 1938. Mem. Arlington Fedn. Women's Clubs (rec. sec. 1979-80), No. Dist. Va. Fedn. Women's Clubs (rec. sec. 1979-80), No. Dist. Va. Fedn. Women's Clubs (chmn. legis. com. 1986-88, chmn. pub. affairs no. dist. 1988-90), Williamsburg Woman's Club of Arlington (corr. sec. 1970-72, 97-98, 1st v.p. 1972-74, pres. 1974-76, 98-99, chmn. comms. 1981-82, chmn. legis. com. 1982-86, 90-98, pres. 1998-2000, pub. affairs chmn. 2000—), Columbia Law Sch. Alumni Assn., Alpha Sigma Rho. Presbyterian. Home: 3020 N Nottingham St Arlington VA 22207-1268

GILMOUR, RICHARD H. judge; b. Sacramento, Sept. 7, 1941; m. Janet Ann Walker, June 15, 1963; children: Dana, Donald. BA, U. Calif., Berkeley, 1963; JD, Hastings Coll. Law, San Francisco, 1968. Supervising dep. dist. atty. Dist. Atty.'s Office, Sacramento, 1970-92; mcpl. ct. judge Sacramento Cts., 1992-94, superior ct. judge, 1994—. Adj. prof. U. of the Pacific, Sacramento, 1986-91. Judge peer ct. Sacramento Juvenile Ct., 1998—. Lt. (j.g.) USNR, 1963-65. Named Pros. of the Yr. Calif. Dist. Atty.'s Assn., 1991. Mem. Anthony M. Kennedy Inn of Ct. (mem. emeritus 1995—). Office: Sacramento Cts 720 9th St Sacramento CA 95814-1302

GILROY, TRACY ANNE HUNSAKER, lawyer; b. St. Louis, Aug. 13, 1959; d. Raymond Thomas Hunsaker and Dorothy Jayne (Hickman) Hunsaker Reilly. BA, U. Dayton, 1981; JD, St. Louis U., 1984. Bar: Mo. 1984, Ill. 1985. Atty. Mo. State Hwy. and Transp. Dept., St. Louis, 1984-89; of counsel Draheim & Pranschke, St. Louis, 1989-94; pvt. practice The Gilroy Law Firm, St. Louis, 1994—. Mem. ABA (strategic comms. bar svcs. standing com., reporter The Affiliate, bd. dirs. LPM solo divsn., chair solo and small firm practitioners 2002--, chair, standing com. on Solo & Small Fines), Mo. Bar Assn. (chair eminent domain com., legis. com., bd. govs. 1998—), St. Louis Bar Found. (pres. 1998-99), St. Louis Met. Bar Assn. (pres. 1997-98, chair young lawyers sect. 1993, chair legis. com. 1985-87, chair, vice-chair, chair trial sect., chair social com., chair auction com., media com.), Woman Lawyers Assn. (mem.-at-large, chair legis. com. 1984-87, sec. 1987), Lawyers Assn., Assn. Trial Lawyers Am. Avocations: golf, skiing, running, writing, painting. Office: Gilroy Law Firm 1610 Des Peres Rd # 300 Saint Louis MO 63131-1813

GINDIN, WILLIAM HOWARD, judge; b. Perth Amboy, N.J., Sept. 1, 1931; s. Jac Paul and Belle Ruth (Steinberg) G.; m. Jane Hersh, June 24, 1954; children: Thomas L., Suzanne Hinsdale; m. Emily Shimkin, Dec. 25, 1965; children: Geoffrey A. Drucker, Janine Drucker Gordon. AB, Brown U., 1953; JD, Yale U., 1956. Bar: N.J. 1956, U.S. Supreme Ct. 1965, U.S. Ct. Appeals (3d cir.) 1980. Assoc. Gindin & Gindin, Plainfield, N.J., 1956-62, ptnr. Plainfield & Bridgwater, N.J., 1962-82; adminstrv. law judge Newark, 1982-85; U.S. bankruptcy judge Trenton, 1985-90, 90—; chief, 1990-98. Adj. prof. Rutgers Camden Law Sch., 1988-93; lectr. Inst. Continuing Legal Edn., Profl. Edn. Systems, Inc.; bd. govs. Nat. Conf. Bankruptcy Judges (3d cir.), 1989-92. Mem. editl. bd. N.J. Bar Assn. Jour., 1962-72. Mem. Plainfield Human Relations Commn., 1965-72, chmn., 1968-72; pres. Temple Sholom, Plainfield, 1979-81; regional v.p. Union Am. Hebrew Congregations, 1983-86; trustee Princeton Jewish Ctr.1994-96, Jewish Cmty. Found. of Mercer-Bucks 1998-2000; mem. Opera Festival of N.J. Fellow: Assn. Fed. Bar (adv. bd.), Bankruptcy Inn of Ct. (pres. 1995—99), Am. Bar Found., Am. Coll. Bankruptcy; mem.: ABA, Am. Judicature Soc., N.J. Bar Assn., Mercer County Bar Assn., Union County Bar Assn., Plainfield Bar Assn., Plainfield Rotary (Paul Harris fellow, pres. 1974—75). Home: 30 James Ct Princeton NJ 08540-2633 Office: US Bankruptcy Ct 402 E State St Trenton NJ 08608-1507

GINSBERG, ERNEST, lawyer, banker; b. Syracuse, N.Y., Feb. 14, 1931; s. Morris Henry and Mildred Florence (Slive) G.; m. Harriet Gay Scharf, Dec. 20, 1959; children: Alan Justin, Robert Daniel. BA, Syracuse U., 1953, JD, 1955; LLM, Georgetown U., 1963. Bar: N.Y. 1955, U.S. Supreme Ct. 1964. Pvt. practice law, Syracuse, 1957-61; mem. staff, office chief counsel IRS, Washington, 1961-63; tax counsel Comptr. of Currency, Washington, 1964-65, assoc. chief counsel, 1965-68; v.p. legal affairs, sec. Republic Nat. Bank N.Y., N.Y.C., 1968-74; sr. v.p. legal affairs, sec. Republic Nat. Bank, N.Y.C., 1975-86, exec. v.p., gen. counsel, sec., 1984-86, vice chmn. bd., gen. counsel, 1986-94, vice chmn. bd., 1990-99. Sr. v.p., sec. legal affairs Republic N.Y. Corp., N.Y.C., 1974-84, exec. v.p., gen. counsel, sec., 1984-86, vice chmn. bd., gen. counsel, sec., 1986-94, vice chmn. bd., 1986-99, also bd. dirs.; bd. visitors Syracuse U. Coll. Law; bd. dirs. Safra Nat. Bank of N.Y., N.Y.C. Chmn. emeritus Roundabout Theatre Co., N.Y.C. With U.S. Army, 1955-57. Mem. Am. Bankers Assn. (bd. dirs. 1995-97), Am. Bankers Coun. (co-chmn. 1992-94), N.Y. State Bankers Assn. (pres. 1993-94), Bankers Roundtable (bd. dirs. 1995-97), Phi Sigma Delta, Phi Delta Phi. Administrative and regulatory, Banking, Corporate, general.

GINSBURG, CHARLES DAVID, lawyer; b. N.Y.C., Apr. 20, 1912; s. Nathan and Rae (Lewis) G.; m. Marianne Laïs; children by previous marriage: Jonathan, Susan, Mark. AB, W.Va. U., 1932; LLB, Harvard U., 1935. Bar: W. Va. 1935, U.S. Supreme Ct. 1940, D.C. 1946, U.S. Ct. Appeals (2d, 3rd, 4th, 7th, and Fed. cirs.) 1946, U.S. Claims Ct. 1960, U.S. Tax Ct. 1961. Atty. for public utilities div. and office of gen. counsel SEC, 1935-39; law sec. to Justice William O. Douglas, 1939; asst. to commr. SEC, 1939-40; legal adviser Price Stblzn. Div., Nat. Def. Adv. Com., 1940-41; gen. counsel Office Price Adminstrn. and Civilian Supply, 1941-42, OPA, 1942-43; pvt. practice law Ginsburg, Feldman and Bress, Washington, 1946-98; founding ptnr. Ginsburg, Feldman & Bress, 1946-98; sr. counsel, firm Powell, Goldstein, Frazer & Murphy, LLP, 1998; adminstrv. asst. to Senator M.M. Neely, W.Va., 1950; adj. prof. internat. law Georgetown U. (Grad. Sch. Law), 1959-67. Dep. commr. U.S. del. Austrian Treaty Commn., Vienna, 1947; adviser U.S. del. Council Fgn. Ministers, London, 1947; Mem. Presdl. Emergency Bd. 166 (Airlines), 1966; mem. Pres.'s Commn. on Postal Orgn., 1967; chmn. Presdl. Emergency Bd. 169 (Railroads), 1969; exec. dir. Nat. Adv. Commn. Civil Disorders, 1967 Author: The Future of German Reparations; Contbr. to legal jours. Bd. mem., chmn. exec. com. Nat. Symphony Orch. Assn., 1960-69; bd. govs. Weizmann Inst., 1965 (hon. fellow 1972); mem. vis. com. Harvard-Mass. Inst. Tech. Joint Ctr. on Urban Studies, 1969; trustee St. John's Coll., 1969-76, chmn. bd., 1974-76; overseers com. Kennedy Sch. Govt. Harvard, 1971—; mem. coun. Nat. Harvard Law Sch. Assn., 1972—, gen. counsel Dem. Nat. Com., 1968-70. Served from pvt. to capt. AUS, 1942-46; dep. dir. econs. div. Office Mil. Govt., 1945-46, Germany. Decorated Bronze Star, Legion of Merit; recipient Presdl. Cert. of Merit. Mem. ABA, Fed. Bar Assn, Am. Law Inst., Coun. on Fgn. Rels., Met. Club, Army and Navy Club, Phi Beta Kappa. Democrat. Administrative and regulatory, Probate (including wills, trusts), Corporate, general. Home: 619 S Lee St Alexandria VA 22314-3819 Office: 1001 Pennsylvania Ave NW Washington DC 20004-2505 E-mail: DGinsbur@PGMF.com.

GINSBURG, MARTIN DAVID, lawyer, educator; b. N.Y.C., June 10, 1932; s. Morris and Evelyn (Bayer) Ginsburg; m. Ruth Bader, June 23, 1954; children: Jane, James. AB, Cornell U., 1953; JD, Harvard U., 1958; LLD (hon.), Lewis and Clark Coll., 1992, Wheaton Coll., 1997. Bar: N.Y. 1959, D.C. 1980. Practiced in N.Y.C., 1959-79; mem. firm Weil, Gotshal & Manges, N.Y.C., 1963-79; of counsel firm Fried, Frank, Harris, Shriver and Jacobson, Washington, 1980—; Charles Keller Beekman prof. law Columbia U. Law Sch., N.Y.C., 1979-80; prof. law Georgetown U. Law Center, Washington, 1980—; lectr. U. Leiden, The Netherlands, 1982; lectr. Salzburg Seminar Austria, 1984; mem. tax divsn adv. group Dept. Justice, 1980-81; mem. adv. group to Commr. Internal Revenue, 1978-80; mem. adv. bd. U. Calif. Securities Regulation Inst., 1973-91. Adj. prof. law NYU, 1967—79; vis. prof. law Stanford U., Calif., 1978, Harvard U., Cambridge, Mass., 1986, U. Chgo., 1990, NYU, 1993; cons. joint com. on taxation U.S. Congress, 1979—80, acad. advisor, 2000—01; chmn. tax adv. bd. Commerce Clearing House, 1982—94; mem. bd. advisors NYU/IRS Continuing Profl. Edn. Program, 1983—88, co-chmn., 1986—88; sub coun. on capital allocation, co-chmn. taxation expert group Competitiveness Policy Coun., 1993—95; chmn. tax adv. bd. Little, Brown, 1994—96; bd. dirs. Chgo. Classical Rec. Found.; lectr. various tax insts. Co-author: Mergers, Acquisitions, and Buyouts, 4 vols., 2003; contbr. Mem. vis. com. Harvard Law Sch., 1994—98. 1st lt. arty. U.S. Army, 1954—56. Recipient Chair named in his honor, Georgetown U. Law Ctr., 1986, Marshall-Wythe Medallion, Coll. of William and Mary Sch. Law, 1996, Outstanding Achievement award, Tax Soc. NYU, 1993, Viccenial medal, Georgetown U., 2000. Fellow: Am. Bar Found. (bd. dirs. 2000—03), Am. Coll. Tax Counsel; mem.: ABA (mem. com. corp. taxation, tax sect. 1973—, chmn. com. simplification 1979—81, mem. tax sect. coun. 1984—87, tax systems task force 1995—97), Assn. Bar City N.Y. (chmn. com. taxation 1977—79, mem. audit com. 1980—81), N.Y. State Bar Assn. (mem. tax sect. exec. com. 1969—, chmn. tax sect. 1975, ho. of dels. 1976—77), Am. Law Inst. (cons. Fed. Income Tax Project 1974—93). Office: 600 New Jersey Ave NW Washington DC 20001-2022 E-mail: ginsbma@ffhsj.com.

GIOFFRE, BRUNO JOSEPH, lawyer; b. June 27, 1934; s. Anthony B. and Louise (Giorno) G.; m. Kathleen M. Bartlik, Nov. 14, 1959; children: Kathleen, Lisa, Michael, Christopher, B. Scott, David, Kerry. BA, Cornell U., 1956, JD, 1958. Bar: N.Y. 1958, U.S. Dist. Ct. (so. dist.) N.Y. 1973. Of counsel Gioffre & Gioffre, P.C., Purchase, NY, 1958—99, counsel, 2000—. Justice Town of Rye, N.Y., 1965-99. Vice-chmn. bd. trustees United Hosp.; counsel Port Chester Pub. Libr.; chmn. bd. dirs. Sound Fed. Savs. Bank and Charitable Found. Mem. ABA, N.Y. Bar Assn., N.Y. Magistrate's Assn., Westchester County Magistrate's Assn., Westchester Bar Assn., Port Chester-Rye Bar Assn., Elks, KC. Probate (including wills, trusts), Property, real (including real estate development, water). Home and Office: 2900 Westchester Ave Purchase NY 10577-2552

GIOIA, DANIEL AUGUST, lawyer; b. Bellerose, N.Y., Dec. 23, 1950; s. Joseph Daniel and Concetta P. (Della Femina) Gioia; m. Helen Dumas, June 30, 1973; children: Martha Dumas Picarello, Thomas Joseph, David Albert, Carl Daniel. BA in Govt., Georgetown U., 1972; JD, Am. U., 1975. Bar: Ind. 1975, U.S. Dist. Ct. (no. and so. dist.) Ind. 1975. Ptnr. Spangler, Jennings & Dougherty, Merrillville, Ind., 1975—, mng. ptnr., 2002—. Adj. prof. med. malpractice Sch. of Law Valparaiso U., Ind., 1998—; mem. Commn. for C.L.E. Ind. Supreme Ct., 1992—98; mem. Conclave for Legal Edn., Ind. State Bar Assn., 1996, 2002. Mem.: Lake County Bar Assn. (bd. mgrs. 1987—91, pres. 1990), Valpo Soccer Club (pres. 1992—98), Am. Inn of Ct. (pres. Calumet chpt. 2003—). Roman Catholic. Avocations: soccer referee and coach, gourmet cooking, coin collecting. Alternative dispute resolution, Family and matrimonial, Personal injury (including property damage). Home: 4221 Oak Grove Cir Valparaiso IN 46383-2084 Office: 8396 Mississippi St Merrillville IN 46410 E-mail: dhgioia@attbi.com., dgioia@sjdlaw.com.

GIORDANO, LAWRENCE FRANCIS, lawyer; b. Buffalo, Feb. 17, 1953; s. Anthony Jerome and Martha Ann (Taylor) G.; m. Elaine Kristie Thomas, May 29, 1976; children: Bradley Thomas, Evan Taylor. BS with highest honors in Psychology, Denison U., 1975; JD, Georgetown U., 1978. Bar: Tenn. 1978, U.S. Dist. Ct. (ea. dist.) Tenn. 1979, U.S. Ct. Appeals (6th cir.) 1980, U.S. Supreme Ct. 1983. Assoc. Stone & Hinds, P.C., Knoxville, Tenn., 1978-81, ptnr., 1981-88, Thomforde & Giordano, P.C., Knoxville, 1988-90, McCampbell & Young, P.C., Knoxville, 1990-91, London, Amburn & Giordano, Knoxville, 1991-92, Susano, Sheppeard & Giordano, Knoxville, 1993-94; spl. counsel Lewis, King, Krieg & Waldrop, P.C., Knoxville, 1994-97, shareholder, 1997—. Spl. judge Knox County Gen. Sessions Ct., 1988—; adminstrv. law judge State of Tenn. Dept. Edn., 1994-96; adj. prof. U. Tenn. Coll. Law, 1993—; instr. Knoxville Police Acad., 1989. Mem. exec. bd. Knoxville Metro Soccer League, 1980-85; mem. community network Knox County Youth Alcohol Hwy. Safety Project, Knoxville, 1987-90. Nat. Merit scholar, 1971-75, Kenneth I. Brown scholar, 1974. Mem. ABA, Tenn. Bar Assn. (Law Through Liberty award, 2000), Knoxville Bar Assn. (bd. govs. 1986-92, treas. 1986-90, sec. 1991-92), Def. Rsch. Inst., Am. Inns of Ct. (master of the bench 1991—, pres. 1994-95), Sertoma (v.p. chpt. 1987-89, pres. 1989-90), Phi Beta Kappa, Omicron Delta Kappa. Democrat. Roman Catholic. Avocations: soccer, gardening, reading, theater. General civil litigation, Criminal, General practice. Home: 1822 Nantasket Rd Knoxville TN 37922-5769 Office: Lewis King Krieg & Waldrop 620 Market St Fl 5 Knoxville TN 37902-2231

GIORZA, JOHN C. lawyer; b. Lexington, Mo., May 25, 1950; s. Alphonso Ceno and Iris (Polla) G.; m. Jane Ray Dempsy, Sept. 5, 1981. BA, Westminster Coll., 1972; MBA, U. Mo. 1974, 1974; JD, U. Mo., 1978. Bar: U.S. Dist. Ct. (we. dist.) Mo. 1978. Assoc. Aull, Sherman & Worthington, Lexington, 1978-83; ptnr. Aull, Sherman, Worthington, Giorza & Hamilton, Lexington, 1983—. Bd. dirs. Bank Midwest Lexington, N.A. Mem. ABA, Mo. Bar Assn., Mo. Assn. Trial Attys., Kansas City Bar Assn., Lafayette County Bar Assn. (pres. 1979-80), U. Mo. Alumni Assn. (bd. dirs. Lafayette county chpt.). Clubs: Shirkey Golf (Richmond, Mo.) (pres. 1982-85); Lexington Investors. Lodges: Lions (v.p. local chpt. 1983, 88). Avocations: travel, golf, sporting events. Commercial, consumer (including collections, credit), General practice, Probate (including wills, trusts). Home: 66 Lakeview Dr Lexington MO 64067-2101 Office: Aull Sherman Worthington Giorza & Hamilton PO Box 280 Lexington MO 64067-0280

GIOVANNIELLO, JOSEPH, JR., lawyer; b. Bklyn., Aug. 4, 1958; s. Joseph and Margaret Montgomery (Torr) G.; m. Deborah Kesselman, June 25, 1988. BA, Yale U., 1980; JD, U. Va., 1983. Bar: N.Y. 1984, D.C. 1984, Hawaii 1984, U.S. Dist. Ct. (so. and ea. dists.) 1985, U.S. Ct. Appeals (2d and 3d cirs.) 1988. Law clk. U.S. Dist. Ct., Honolulu, 1983-84; assoc. Paul, Weiss, Rifkind, N.Y.C., 1984-86, Shereff, Friedman, Hoffman & Goodman, N.Y.C., 1986-91, Kornstein Veisz & Wexler, N.Y.C., 1991-96; asst. gen.

counsel Ladenburg Thalmann & Co. Inc., N.Y.C., 1996-98, gen. counsel, 1998—. Mem. Am. Corp. Counsel Assn., N.Y. State Bar Assn., Assn. of Bar of City of N.Y. General civil litigation, Corporate, general, Securities. E-mail: jgiovanniello@ladenburg.com.

GIPPIN, ROBERT MALCOLM, lawyer; b. Cleve., Feb. 3, 1948; s. Morris and Helena (Weil) G.; children: Sarah, Joshua, Rebecca, Alanna; m. Susan Smith. AB, Dartmouth Coll., 1969; JD, Harvard U., 1973. Bar: Ohio 1973. Asst. to dir. Ohio Dept. Commerce, Columbus, 1973; exec. sec. Ohio Real Estate Commn., Columbus, 1974-75; pros. Mcpl. Ct., Cuyahoga Falls, Ohio, 1975; ptnr. Thompson, Hine, Cleve. Active exec. com. Summit County Dem. Party, Akron, 1975, Planned Parenthood; pres. Summit County Coun., 1982-84, Project Learn, 1997—. Mem. Akron Bar Assn., Ohio Bar Assn., Phi Beta Kappa. Jewish. Avocations: reading, tennis, cooking. Administrative and regulatory, General civil litigation, Environmental. Home: 929 Eaton Ave Akron OH 44303-1311 Office: Thompson Hine 3900 Key Ctr Cleveland OH 44114 E-mail: robert.gippin@thompsonhine.com.

GIPSON, HARVEY LOFTON, lawyer; b. Memphis, Feb. 18, 1931; s. Raymond Turner and Frances Lenora (Boling) G.; m. Cara Evelyn Holland (dec. Feb, 1993); children: Gloria Ray Gipson Ingles, Harvey Lofton Jr. BBA, Memphis State U., 1959; LLB, So. Law U., 1962. Asst. controller City Products, Memphis, 1959-61; internal auditor Plough Inc., Memphis, 1961-62; atty., charge legal dept. W.R. Grace & Co., Memphis, 1963-65; pvt. practice Memphis, 1965—. Staff sgt. USAF, 1951-55. Recipient Nat. Def. Medal, USAF, Reno, 1953, Good Conduct Medal, 1953. Mem. ABA, Tenn. Trial Lawyers Assn., Alchymia Shrine. Methodist. Family and matrimonial, Personal injury (including property damage), Workers' compensation. Office: 156 Court Ave Memphis TN 38103-2212

GIPSTEIN, MILTON FIVENSON, lawyer, psychiatrist; b. Schenectady, N.Y., Aug. 31, 1951; s. Milton and Evelyn G.; m. Carol Grace Gipstein, July 21, 1974; children: Steven Mark, Richard Seth. BA, Columbia U., 1972; MD, SUNY, Syracuse, 1976; JD, U. N.C., 1981. Bar: Mass., 1982; Diplomate Am. Bd. Psychiatry and Neurology. Resident psychiat. U. N.C., Chapel Hill, 1976-79; pvt. practice of psychiat. Dept. Corrections N.C., Raleigh, 1979-81; med. dir. Brockton (Mass.) Dist. Ct. Clinic, 1981-86, Bridgewater (Mass.) St. Hosp., 1986-87, Charter Hosp. of Aurora, Colo., 1988—91; med. dir. of forensic svcs. Columbine Psychiatric Hosp., Littleton, Colo., 1991—96; med. dir. forensic psychiatry divsn. Marvin Foote Youth Detention Facility, Englewood, Colo., 1997-2000. Cons. med.-legal N.C. Legal Aid Soc., Raleigh, 1976-81, forensic Mass. Treatment Ctr. Sexually Dangerous, Bridgewater, 1981-88, psychiat. La. Gov.'s Task Force Mental Health, Baton Rouge, 1982, Jefferson Ctr. Mental Health, 1996-98; med.-legal cons. Med. Evaluators, Inc., Denver, 1991-2000; legal counsel indigent clients mental health Com. Pub. Counsel Svcs., Boston, 1982-88; lectr. mental health legal advisors com. Law and Mental Health for Mass. Supreme Ct., Boston, 1982-88. Cons. Pub. Health Adv. Com. Town of Sharon, Mass., 1983-88, Mental Health Legal Advisors Com. Mass. Supreme Ct., Boston, 1985-88; v.p. cmty. affairs Heights Elem. Sch. PTA, Sharon, 1983-88; adv. com. gifted and talented Cherry Creek H.S., 1992-97, Campus Middle Sch., 1993-96. Mem. ABA, Mass. Bar Assn., Am. Profl. Practice Assn. Avocations: boating, antique documents, swimming.

GIRARD, NETTABELL, lawyer; b. Pocatello, Idaho, Feb. 24, 1938; d. George and Arranetta (Bell) Girard Student, Idaho State U., 1957-58; BS, U. Wyo., 1959, JD, 1961. Bar: Wyo. 1961, D.C. 1969, U.S. Supreme Ct. 1969. Practiced in, Riverton, 1963-69; atty.-adviser on gen. counsel's staff HUD; assigned Office Interstate Land Sales Registration, Washington, 1969-70; sect. chief interstate land sales Office Gen. Counsel, 1970-73; ptnr. Larson & Larson, Riverton, 1973-85; pvt. practice Riverton, 1985—. Condr. course on women and law; lectr. in field. Editor Wyoming Clubwoman, 1966-68; bd. editors Wyo. Law Jour., 1959-61; writer Obiter Dictum column Women Lawyers Jour., Dear Legal Advisor column Solutions for Seniors, 1988-94; featured in Riverton Ranger, 1994; also articles in legal jours. Chmn. fund dr. Wind River chpt., ARC, 1965; chmn. Citizens Com. for Better Hosp. Improvement, 1965; chmn. subcom. on polit. legal rights and responsibilities Gov.'s Comm. on Status Women, 1965—69, mem. adv. com., 1973—93; local chmn. Law Day, 1966, 1967, county chmn., 1994—97; mem. state bd. Wyo Girl Scouts USA, sec., 1974—89, bd. dirs., 2001—; state vol. adv. Nat. Found. March of Dimes, 1967—69; legal counsel Wyo. Women's Conf., 1977; gov. apptd. State Wyo. Indsl. Siting Coun., 1995—2001; rep. Nat. Conf. Govs. Commn. , Washington, 1966. Recipient Spl. Achievement award HUD, 1972, Disting. Leadership award Girl Scouts USA, 1973, Franklin D. Roosevelt award Wyo. chpt. March of Dimes, 1985, Thanks Badge award Girl Scout Coun., 1987, Women Helping Women award Riverton Club Soroptimist Internat., 1990, Spl. award 27 yrs. svc. Wyo. Commn. for Women, 1964-92, Appreciation award Wyo. Sr. Citizens and Solutions for Srs., 1994, Arts in Action Pierrot award for outstanding musician, 1998, Disting. Svc. award Wyo. Music Edn. Assn., 2003. Mem. AAUW (br. pres., condr. seminar on law for layman Riverton br. 1965), Wyo. Bar Assn., Fremont County Bar Assn. (Spl. Recognition cert. 1997), DC Bar Assn., Women's Bar Assn. DC, Internat. Fedn. Women Lawyers, Am. Judicature Soc., Assn. Trial Lawyers Am., Wyo. Trial Lawyers Assn., Nat. Assn. Women Lawyers (del. Wyo., nat. sec. 1969-70, v.p. 1970-71, pres. 1972-73), Wyo. Fedn. Women's Clubs (state editor, pres.-elect 1968-69, treas. 1974-76), Prog. Women's Club (pres.-elect. 1994-95), Riverton Chautaqua Club (pres. 1965-67, 2000-01), Riverton Civic League (pres. 1987-89), Kappa Delta, Delta Kappa Gamma (state chpt. hon.). Bankruptcy, Commercial, contracts (including sales of goods; commercial financing), General practice. Home: PO Box 687 Riverton WY 82501-0687 Office: 513 E Main St Riverton WY 82501-4440

GIRARDS, JAMES EDWARD, lawyer; b. Manhasset, N.Y., Aug. 16, 1963; s. H.V. and Barbara (Davis) G.; m. Julie Ann Calame, June 27, 1987; children: Jessica Lauren, James Edward. BS, Baylor U., 1986; JD, St. Mary's Law Sch., 1989. Bar: Tex. 1989, U.S. Dist. Ct. (no., so. and ea. dists.) Tex. 1991, U.S. Ct. Appeals (5th cir.) 2000. Assoc. Law Offices Windle Turley, P.C., Dallas, 1989-94; prin. Tracy & Girards, Dallas, 1994-97, The Girards Law Firm, Dallas, 1997—. Contbr. articles to profl. jours. Recipient Am. Jurisprudence Contracts award AmJur Pub. Co., 1986. Mem. ATLA (pres.'s club 1999-), Tex. Trial Lawyers Assn. (dir. 1999—), Dallas Trial Lawyers Assn. (dir. 1998—), Dallas Bar Assn., Dallas Assn. Young Lawyers, State Bar Tex., Coll. of State Bar of Tex., Am. Mensa, Ltd., Million Dollar Advocates Forum. Personal injury (including property damage). Office: 10000 N Central Expy Ste 750 Dallas TX 75231

GIRBAU, RAMON, lawyer; b. Sabadell, Barcelona, Spain, Jan. 2, 1961; Licence in Law, U. AutÓnoma de Barcelona, 1984; LLM in European Law, U. Libre Bruxelles, Belgium, 1987. Lawyer Courtaulds Fibres, S.A., Barcelona, 1985—87, Estudio Legal, Barcelona, 1987—89; lawyer, ptnr. Garrigues Abogados y Asesores Tributarios, Barcelona, 1989—. Assoc. prof. corp. and bus. law U. Ramon Llull, Barcelona, 1997—. Co-author: Commercial Agency and Distribution Agreements in the European Union, 2000, E-Commerce Law in Europe & USA, 2002. Scholar, Patronat Català Pro Europa, Barcelona, 1986. Mem.: Internat. Assn. Young Lawyers, Barcelona Bar Assn. Mergers and acquisitions, Corporate, general, Antitrust. Office: Garrigues AbogadosyAsesores Tributarios Avinguda Diagonal 654 B 1 08034 Barcelona Spain Office Fax: +34 93 253 37 90. E-mail: ramon.girbau@garrigues.com.

GIRERD, CAROLE, lawyer; b. Lyon, France, Apr. 21, 1970; Maitrise Droit des Affaires, U. Lyon III; postgrad., McGill U., Montreal, Que., Can., 1992; degree de droit de la concurrence, U. Montpellier I, France, 1993. Bar: Paris Ct. Appeals 1999. Lawyer European Commn., Brussels, 1995—97, Sales, Vincent & Ptnrs., Paris, 1997—99, Bredin Prat & Ptnrs., Paris, 1999—2001, Lamy Ribeyre & Ptnrs., Lyon, 2001—. Recipient Direction Générale Concurence Consomnation répression fraudes award, French Competition Adminstrn., 1994. Antitrust, Commercial, contracts (including sales of goods; commercial financing), Commercial, consumer (including collections, credit), Franchising. Office: Lamy Ribeyre 40 rue de Bonnel 69003 Lyon France

GIROUX, EUGENE XAVIER, lawyer; b. Somerville, Mass., May 8, 1928; s. Eugene H. and Mary E. (Cotter) G.; married, May 9, 1953; children: Susan M., E. Mark, Jacqueline L. BA, Boston Coll., 1952, LLB, 1957. Bar: Mass. 1957. Safety engr. Merchants Mutual Ins., Boston, 1952-54; pvt. practice Boston, 1957-61, 64—; asst. U.S. atty. U.S. Dept. Justice, Boston, 1961-64. With U.S. Army, 1946-47, Korea. Mem. Mass. Bar Assn. Democrat. Roman Catholic. Avocations: grandchildren, boating, photography, travel, music. General civil litigation, Criminal, General practice. Home and Office: 8 Grant Ave Wellesley MA 02481-6002

GIRTH, MARJORIE LOUISA, lawyer, educator; b. Trenton, N.J., Apr. 21, 1939; d. Harold Brookman and Marjorie Mathilda (Simonson) G. AB, Mt. Holyoke Coll., 1959; LLB, Harvard U., 1962. Bar: N.J. 1963, U.S. Supreme Ct. 1969, N.Y. 1976. Pvt. practice, Trenton, 1963-65; rsch. assoc. Brookings Instn., 1965-70; assoc. prof. law SUNY Law Sch., Buffalo, 1971-79, prof., 1979-91, assoc. dean, 1986-87; dean Ga. State U. Coll. Law, Atlanta, 1992-96, prof., 1992—. Vis. prof. U. Va. Law Sch., 1979-80; Southeastern Bankruptcy Law Inst. vis. prof. Emory Law Sch., spring 1991, vis. scholar, 1996; vis. legal educator W.Va. U. Coll. of Law Vis. Com., 1994-95; chancellor's search adv. com. Bd. of Regents, 1993-94. Author: Poor People's Lawyers, 1976, Bankruptcy Options for the Consumer Debtor, 1981, (co-author) Bankruptcy: Problem, Process, Reform, 1971. Bd. dirs. Buffalo and Erie County YWCA, 1972-76, Buffalo Unitarian-Universalist Ch., 1981-84, Feminist Women's Health Ctr., 1993-94, ACLU, Ga., 1995-2001, Unitarian-Universalist Congregation of Atlanta, 1999—; mem. commn. on peace, justice and human rights Internat. Assn. Religious Freedom, 1976-79; chmn. Erie County Task Force on Status of Women, 1985-87. Recipient award for pioneering achievements N.Y. State 8th Jud. Dist. Splty. Bar Assn. and Com. on Women in the Cts., 2000. Fellow Lawyers Found. Ga.; mem. ABA (mem. coun. bus. law sect. 1985-89, chmn. consumer bankruptcy com. 1983-86), Am. Arbitration Assn. (comml. arbitration panel 1997—), Assn. Am. Law Schs. (profl. devel. com. 2002—, nominations com. 1996), Am. Law Inst., N.Y. State Bar Assn. (mem. exec. com. bus. law sect. 1980-91, chmn. bankruptcy law com. 1980-82, chmn. banking corp. bus. law sect. 1986-87, mem. ho. of dels. 1990-91), Ga. Supreme Ct. (commn. on racial and ethnic bias in ct. sys. 1993-95, commn. on equality 1995—, sec. 1998-2000), Ga. Assn. Women Lawyers, Law Sch. Admissions Coun. (audit com. 1995-97, 1999—, fin. and legal affairs com., 1997-99), Mt. Holyoke Alumnae Assn. (centennial award 1972). Office: Ga State U Coll Law PO Box 4037 Atlanta GA 30302-4037 E-mail: mgirth@gsu.edu.

GISLESON, SOREN ERIK, lawyer; b. New Orleans, June 4, 1970; s. K. Eric and Janet Walton Gisleson; m. Alyisen Jain Pickett, Aug. 3, 1995; children: Savannah, Dante, Ava. BA in Philosophy, U. Colo., 1993; JD, Loyola U., New Orleans, 1999. Law clk. Judge Carl Barbier U.S. Dist. Ct. (ea. dist.) La., New Orleans, 1999—2000; assoc. Herman, Herman, Katz & Cotlar, New Orleans, 2000—. Mem.: ATLA, ABA, New Orleans Bar Assn. Civil rights, Insurance, Personal injury (including property damage). Office: Herman Herman Katz & Cotlar 820 O Keefe Ave New Orleans LA 70113

GISSEL, L. HENRY, JR., lawyer; b. Houston, Oct. 20, 1936; BA, Rice U., 1958; LLB, So. Meth. U., 1961; postgrad., Georgetown U. Bar: Tex. 1961. Of counsel Fulbright & Jaworski, Houston. Fellow Am. Coll. Trust and Estate Counsel (pres. 1995-96, regent 1981-87, 91-97, regent emeritus 1997—), Am. Bar Found. (bd. cert. estate planning and probate lab, Tex. bd. legal specialization); mem. ABA (sect. real property probate and trust law, chair 1988-89, Internat. Acad. Estate Trust Law (academician 1986-87), coun. 1981-90, 94-97), Am. Bar Assn. (sect. del. 1994-97), Houston Bar Assn. (chmn. probate trust sect. 1982-83). Estate planning, Probate (including wills, trusts), Estate taxation. Office: Fulbright & Jaworski 1301 Mckinney St Ste 5100 Houston TX 77010-3031

GIST, HOWARD BATTLE, JR., lawyer; b. Alexandria, La., Sept. 17, 1919; s. Howard Battle and Marcie (Luckett) G.; m. Rosemary Flynn, Sept. 30, 1950; children: Howard Battle III, Marcie, Stephanie, Robert C., Ellen K., William M. Student, Washington and Lee U., 1936—38; BA, Tulane U., 1941, JD, 1943. Bar: La. 1943. Mem. firm Gist, Methvin, Alexandria, 1946—. Bd. dirs. Security First Nat. Bank, Alexandria, chmn. bd., 1983-93, dir. emeritus, 1993. Named 2000 Disting. Atty., La. Bar Found., 2000. Fellow Am. Coll. Trial Lawyers; mem. La. State Bar Assn. (pres. 1977-78), Alexandria Bar Assn. (pres. 1967), La. City Attys. Assn. (past pres.), La. Def. Attys. (pres. 1972-73), La. State Law Inst. (mem. coun. 1964—, past v.p.). General civil litigation, Insurance, Probate (including wills, trusts). Office: Gist Methvin 4615 Parliament Dr Ste 101 Alexandria LA 71309-1871

GITTER, ALLAN REINHOLD, lawyer; b. Yonkers, N.Y., Aug. 26, 1936; s. George Reinhold and Katherine (Allan) G.; divorced; children: Alison, Ryne, Kent; m. Sandra Case Gitter, Apr. 2, 1988. BA, Washington & Lee U., 1958; LLB, U. Mich., 1961. Bar: N.C. 1963, U.S. Dist. Ct. (mid., ea. and we. dists.) N.C. 1964, U.S. Ct. Appeals (4th cir.) 1964, U.S. Dist. Ct. (mid. dist.) Pa. 1998. From assoc. to ptnr. Womble, Carlyle, Sandridge & Rice, Winston-Salem, N.C., 1969—. Fellow Am. Coll. Trial Lawyers; mem. Am. Bd. Trial Advs. Federal civil litigation, State civil litigation, Insurance. Home: 1077 E Kent Rd Winston Salem NC 27104-1113 Office: Womble Carlyle Sandridge & Rice One W 4th St Winston Salem NC 27101 E-mail: agitter@wcsr.com.

GITTER, MAX, lawyer; b. Samarkand, Uzbekistan, Nov. 17, 1943; came to U.S., 1950; s. Wolf and Paula (Nissenbaum) G.; m. Elisabeth Karla Gesmer, June 22, 1969; children: Emily F., Michael A. AB, Harvard U., 1965; LLB, Yale U., 1968. Bar: N.Y., D.C., U.S. Dist. Ct. (so. and ea. dists.) N.Y., U.S. Ct. Appeals (2d, D.C., 4th and 9th cirs.), U.S. Supreme Ct. Instr. U. Chgo. Law Sch., 1968-69; assoc. Paul, Weiss, Rifkind, Wharton & Garrison, N.Y.C., 1969-76, ptnr., 1976-99, Cleary, Gottlieb, Steen & Hamilton, N.Y.C., 1999—. Vis. lectr. law Yale U., 1986-88; mem. Internat. Steering Com. on Free Trade with Israel; vice-chmn., Yivo Inst. for Jewish Rsch. Spl. counsel Mayor of N.Y.C. to Investigate Office of Chief Medical Examiner, 1985. Mem. Fed. Bar Coun., Assn. Bar City of N.Y. (vice chmn. com. on profl. and jud. ethics 1985-86), Am. Law Inst. (spkr., panelist 1985-89), Practicing Law Inst. (spkr., panelist 1983-92), N.Y. State Bar Assn. (exec. com. sect. on comml. and fed. litigation 1994-99), Internat. Arbitration Inst. Federal civil litigation, State civil litigation. Office: Cleary Gottlieb Steen & Hamilton Rm 200 One Liberty Plz Ste 4300 New York NY 10006-1470 E-mail: mgitter@cgsh.com.

GIUFFRA, ROBERT JOSEPH, JR., lawyer; b. Bklyn., Feb. 17, 1960; s. Robert Joseph and Mary Josephine (McAnena) G. AB summa cum laude, Princeton U., 1983; JD, Yale U., 1987. Bar: N.Y. 1989, U.S. Dist. Ct. (so. and ea. dists.) N.Y. 1989, D.C. 1990, Conn. 1991, U.S. Tax Ct., U.S. Ct. Appeals (2d, 5th, 6th, 9th, and 11 cirs.). Staff asst. Office Pub. Liaison, White House, Washington, 1981-82; rsch. asst. rsch. program in criminal justice Princeton (N.J.) U., 1983-84; law clk. to Judge Ralph K. Winter, Jr. U.S. Ct. Appeals (2d cir.), N.Y.C., 1987-88; law clk. to chief justice William H. Rehnquist U.S. Supreme Ct., Washington, 1988-89; assoc. Sullivan & Cromwell, N.Y.C., Washington, 1989—95, 1996—97, ptnr. Washington, 1998—; chief counsel U.S. Senate Com. Banking, Ho., and Urban Affairs, Wash., 1995—. Articles editor Yale Law Jour., 1986-87; contbr. articles to profl. publs. Mem. ABA, Fed. Bar Coun., Phi Beta Kappa. Roman Catholic. Home: Apt 5A 985 Fifth Ave New York NY 10021 Office: Sullivan & Cromwell 125 Broad St New York NY 10004-2489

GIUFFRÉ, JOHN JOSEPH, lawyer; b. Bklyn., Nov. 30, 1963; s. John B. and Marilyn N. G.; m. Lauren P. Dippel, Sept. 1, 1990; children: John Paul, Danielle Emily. BA, Columbia Coll., 1984; JD cum laude, U. Pa., 1987. Bar: N.J. 1987, N.Y. 1988, Conn. 1988, Pa. 1988, U.S. Dist. Ct. (so. and ea. dists.) N.Y. 1989. Assoc. labor and employment law sect. Morgan, Lewis & Bockius, N.Y.C., 1987-88; assoc. McLaughlin & McLaughlin, Bklyn., 1988-93; founding ptnr. Giuffré & Kaplan, PC, Hicksville, N.Y., 1994—. Editor: U. Pa. Jour. Comparative Bus. and Capital Market Law, 1985-86; sr. editor: U. Pa. Jour. Internat. Bus. Law, 1986-87. Vol. lawyer Bklyn. Bar Assn. Vol. Lawyer Project, 1992-93; trustee 1st Presbyn. Ch., Flushing, N.Y., 1991-92, pres. bd. trustees, 1993, elder, 1996—; bd. dirs. Flushing Christian Sch., 1994-2002. Mem. Nassau County Bar Assn., Phi Beta Kappa. Avocations: reading, studying history, teaching sunday school, raising Johnny and Daniella. General civil litigation, Personal injury (including property damage), Probate (including wills, trusts). Office: Giuffré & Kaplan PC 28 E Old Country Rd Hicksville NY 11801-4207

GIULITTO, PAULA CHRISTINE, lawyer; b. Ravenna, Ohio, June 20, 1967; d. Joseph and F. Jean G.; m. Lawrence A. Sutter III, Nov. 22, 1997. BS, Miami (Ohio) U., 1989; JD, U. Akron, 1992. Bar. Ohio 1992. Assoc. Giulitto & Berger Attys. at Law, Ravenna, 1992—. Bd. dirs. ARC, Ravenna, 1994-2000, chair bd. 1997-2000; bd. dirs. Boys and Girls Club, Ravenna, 1996-2000. Mem. ABA, ATLA, Ohio State Bar Assn., Portage County Bar Assn. (pres. 2003—). State civil litigation, Family and matrimonial, Personal injury (including property damage). Office: Giulitto & Berger 222 W Main St PO Box 350 Ravenna OH 44266-0350

GIUSTI, WILLIAM ROGER, lawyer; b. N.Y.C., Oct. 27, 1947; s. John Eletto and Rita Marie (Lucarini) G.; m. Ingrid Gerke, Dec. 12, 1980. AB, Columbia Coll., 1969; postgrad., Oxford U., 1969-71; JD, Yale U., 1974. Bar: N.Y. 1975. Law clk. to judge U.S. Ct. Appeals (2d cir.), N.Y.C., 1974-75; assoc. Cravath, Swaine & Moore, N.Y.C., 1975-80, Shearman & Sterling, N.Y.C., 1980-82, ptnr., 1983—. Mem.: Yale (N.Y.C.). Roman Catholic. Commercial, contracts (including sales of goods; commercial financing), Finance, Oil, gas, and mineral. E-mail: wgiusti@shearman.com.

GIVAN, RICHARD MARTIN, retired state supreme court justice; b. Indpls., June 7, 1921; s. Clinton Hodel and Glee (Bowen) G.; m. Pauline Marie Haggart, Feb. 28, 1945; children: Madalyn Givan Hesson, Sandra Givan Chenoweth, Patricia Givan Smith, Elizabeth Givan Whipple. LL.B., Ind. U., 1951. Bar: Ind. 1952. Ptnr. with Clinton H. Givan, 1952-59, Bowen, Myers, Northam & Givan, 1960-69; justice Ind. Supreme Ct., 1969-74, chief justice, 1974-87, assoc. justice, 1987-95; ret.; dep. pub. defender, 1952-53; dep. atty. gen., 1953—64; dep. pros. atty. Marion County, 1965-66; ret., 1995. Mem. Ind. Ho. Reps., 1967-68 Served to 2d lt. USAAF, 1942-45. Mem. Ind. Bar Assn., Indpls. Bar Assn., Ind. Soc. Chgo., Newcomen Soc. N.Am., Internat. Arabian Horse Assn. (past dir., chmn. ethical practices rev. bd.), Ind. Arabian Horse Club (pres. 1971-72), Indpls. 500 Oldtimers Club, Lions, Sigma Delta Kappa. Mem. Soc. Of Friends. Home: 6690 S County Road 1025 E Indianapolis IN 46231-2495

GIVENS, RICHARD AYRES, lawyer; b. N.Y.C., June 16, 1932; s. Meredith Bruner and Ruth Wheelock (Ayres) G.; m. Janet Eaton, Aug. 24, 1957; children: Susan Ruth, Jane Lucile. AB, Columbia U., 1953; MS in Econs., U. Wis., 1954; LLB, Columbia U., 1959. Bar: N.Y. 1959, U.S. Dist. Ctr. (so. and ea. dists.) N.Y. 1960, U.S. Ct. Appeals (2d cir.) 1962, U.S. Supreme Ct. 1966, U.S. Ct. Claims 1980, U.S. Ct. Appeals (4th cir.) 1981. Assoc. Hughes, Hubbard & Reed, N.Y.C., 1959-61; asst. U.S. atty. So. Dist. N.Y., 1961-71; regional dir. FTC, N.Y.C., 1971-77; counsel Botein, Hays & Sklar, N.Y.C., 1977-89; law clk. to Hon. Vincent L. Broderick U.S. Dist. Ct. (so. dist.) N.Y., White Plains, 1992-95; law sec. to Hon. Jay Gold acting Supreme Ct. Justice N.Y., 1995-96. Chmn. program on drafting documents in plain lang., 1981. Author: Manual of Federal Practice, 5th edit., 1998, Advocacy: The Art of Pleading a Cause, 1980, 3d rev. edit., 1992, Legal Strategies for Industrial Innovation (Best Law Book of 1982 award Assn. Am. Pubs.), 1982; Antitrust: An Economic Approach, 1983; contbr. articles to profl. jours. With U.S. Army, 1954-56. Mem. ABA, N.Y. State Bar Assn. (chmn. task force on simplification 1985-89, legis. com., antitrust sect. 1980-83), Assn. of Bar of City of N.Y. Democrat. Unitarian Universalist. Died Feb. 7, 2003.

GIVENS, STANN WILLIAM, lawyer; b. Appleton, Wis., Feb. 20, 1950; s. Paul Ronald and Leona (Janssen) G.; m. Bonnie MacGregor, Aug. 28, 1971; children: Christian MacGregor, Emily Kate. BS, Bucknell U., 1971; JD, Fla. State U., 1973. Bar: Fla. 1974, U.S. Ct. Appeals (5th cir.) 1974, U.S. Dist. Ct. (mid. dist.) Fla. 1974. Asst. state atty. Hillsborough State Atty.'s Office, Tampa, Fla., 1973-75; asst. city atty. City of Tampa, 1975-77; atty. Stann W. Givens, P.A., Tampa, 1977-93, Knox and Givens, P.A., 1993—. Race dir. Gasparilla Distance Classic, Tampa, 1980-81, dir., 1977-85; elder Temple Terrace (Fla.) Presbyn. Ch., 1976—; moderator permanent jud. commn. Synod of South Atlantic of Presbyn. Ch., 1977-88. Recipient Outstanding Young Men Am. award, 1980, 77, Outstanding Community Svc. award Boys Club Tampa, 1981, Professionalism award Family Law Inn of Tampa, 1999. Fellow: Am. Acad. Matrimonial Lawyers; mem.: Hillsborough County Bar Assn. (chair family law sect. 1988—89), Fla. Bar (cert. in marital and family law, past chair marital and family law bd. cert. com., chair 13th jud. cir. grievance com. 1999—2000). Presbyterian. Avocations: youth sports, golf. Criminal, Family and matrimonial, Personal injury (including property damage). Office: Knox and Givens PA 607 W Horatio St Tampa FL 33606-2272 E-mail: givens@tampafamilylaw.com.

GIVHAN, ROBERT MARCUS, lawyer; b. Mineral Wells, Tex., May 10, 1959; s. Walter Houston Givhan and Marion Blackwell Callen Stothart; m. Janet Lee Dothard, May 6, 1989; children: Vivian Lee, Charlotte Ann, Virginia Mae. BA, U. Ala., Tuscaloosa, 1981; JD, Cumberland Sch. Law, Birmingham, Ala., 1986. Bar: Ala. 1987, D.C. 1989, U.S. Supreme Ct. 1989, U.S. Ct. Appeals (D.C. and 11th cirs.), U.S. Dist. Ct. (so., mid. and no. dists.) Ala. 1987. Assoc. Perry and Russell, Montgomery, Ala., 1987-88; dep. dist. atty. 15th Jud. Cir. of Ala., Montgomery, 1988-91; dep. atty. gen. Office of Atty. Gen. of Ala., Montgomery, 1991-95; ptnr. Johnston Barton Proctor & Powell LLP, Birmingham, 1995—. Contbr. articles. Fellow: Am. Coll. Pros. Attys.; mem.: Am. Health Lawyers Assn., Birmingham Bar Assn. (co-chmn. econs. law practice com. 1998, chmn. 1999, co-chmn. jud. and legal reform com. 2002, chmn. 2003), Ala. State Bar Assn., ABA (vice chmn. antitrust competition and trade regulation com. adminstrv. 1994—2000). Episcopalian. Avocations: whitewater rafting, hiking, music collecting, book collecting. Antitrust, General civil litigation, Health. Office: 2900 AmSouth/Harbert Plz 1901 6th Ave N Birmingham AL 35203-2618 Home: 1601 Shades Park Cove Birmingham AL 35209 E-mail: rmg@jbpp.com.

GIVHAN, THOMAS BARTRAM, lawyer; b. Lexington, Ky., Sept. 24, 1926; s. Thomas Holman and Eva Mae (Beck) G.; m. Sharon Rose Richard, June 10, 1949 (dec.); children: Elisè Charles, Ellen Foster, Aaron Todd. JD, U. Ky., 1951. Bar: Ky. 1951, U.S. Dist. Ct. (ea. dist.) Ky. 1957, U.S. Dist. Ct. (we. dist.) Ky. 1957, U.S. Supreme Ct. 1972. City atty. City of Shepherdsville, Ky., 1953-57; county atty. Bullitt County, Shepherdsville, 1958-61, 66-73, 1982-89; mem. Ky. Ho. of Reps., Frankfort, 1974-78, chmn. judiciary com., 1976-78. Mem. Ky. Gov.'s Ad Hoc Com. on Jud. Reform, Frankfort, 1976. Chmn. Bullitt County Dem. Party, 1968-71; mem.

Bullitt County Planning Commn., 1995—. With USMC, 1945-46, PTO. Mem. ABA, Ky. Bar Assn. (ho. of dels. 1964-68, character and fitness com. 1968-74, CLE award 1981), Bullitt County Bar Assn. (sec./treas. 1956-61). General civil litigation, General practice, Personal injury (including property damage). Office: Givhan Spainhour & Stuart PSC Profl Bldg PO Box 65 Shepherdsville KY 40165-0065 E-mail: givspain@aol.cpm.

GIZA, DAVID ALAN, lawyer; b. Chgo., May 16, 1958; s. Bruno Frank and Marianne Theresa (Mozdren) G.; m. Karen Ann Van Maldegiam, Nov. 5, 1988. BS, DePaul U., 1981; JD, John Marshall U., 1984. Bar: Ill. 1985, U.S. Dist. Ct. (no. dist.) Ill. 1985. Atty. pvt. practice, Chgo., 1985-86; assoc. Larry Karchmar, Ltd., Chgo., 1986-87, Kovitz, Shifrin & Waitzman, Chgo., 1987; atty. W.W. Grainger, Inc., Skokie, Ill., 1987-91, Lincolnshire, Ill., 1991—, divsn. atty., 1993-96, sr. atty., 1996-98, asst. gen. counsel, 1998—2002; pvt. practice Corp. Law Assocs., Northfield, Ill., 2002—. Trustee Village of Libertyville, Ill., 1995—; chmn. Camp Lake (Wis.)/Ctr. Lake Rehab. Dist., 1990—. Mem. Am. Trial Lawyers Assn., Am. Corp. Counsel Assn., Ill. State Bar Assn., Chgo. Bar Assn., Lake County Bar Assn. Republican. Roman Catholic. Avocations: politics, water sports, reading, travel, cooking. General civil litigation, Commercial, contracts (including sales of goods; commercial financing), Corporate, general. Office: Corp Law Assocs 400 Central Ave #150 Northfield IL 60093 Fax: 847-816-1799. E-mail: dave@corplawassociates.com.

GJERTSEN, O. GERARD, lawyer; b. Bklyn., June 24, 1932; s. Ole Gerhard and Hilma (Jorgensen) G.; m. Carol Ann Jurkops, June 2, 1962; children: Gerard, Gary, Krista, Karen. BA, Columbia Coll., 1954; JD, NYU, 1958. Bar: N.Y. 1958, U.S. Dist. Ct. (so. dist.) N.Y. 1960. Ptnr., counsel Thacher Proffitt & Wood, N.Y.C., 1964—. Vice chmn. Tuckahoe (N.Y.) Urban Renewal Agy. With U.S. Army, 1954-55. Mem. ABA, N.Y. State Bar Assn., Assn. of Bar of City of N.Y., Westchester County Bar Assn., White Plains Bar Assn., Scarsdale Golf Club. Avocations: music, sports. Estate taxation, Property, real (including real estate development, water). Home: 262 Dante Ave Tuckahoe NY 10707-3015 Office: Thacher Proffitt & Wood 50 Main St White Plains NY 10606-1934

GLADDEN, JAMES WALTER, JR., lawyer; b. Pitts., Feb. 23, 1940; s. James Walter and Cynthia Unice (Hales) G.; m. Patricia T. Kuehn, Aug. 21, 1993; children: James, Thomas, Robert. AB, DePauw U., 1961; JD, Harvard U., 1964. Bar: Ill. 1964, U.S. Sup. Ct. 1978. Ptnr. Mayer, Brown, Rowe & Maw, Chgo., 1964—. Mem. ABA. Federal civil litigation, Labor (including EEOC, Fair Labor Standards Act, labor-management relations, NLRB, OSHA). Home: 1426 Chicago Ave Apt 5N Evanston IL 60201 Office: Mayer Brown Rowe & Mau 190 S La Salle St Ste 3900 Chicago IL 60603-3441 E-mail: jgladden@mayerbrownrowe.com.

GLADDEN, JOSEPH REAH, II, lawyer; b. Atlanta, Oct. 5, 1942; s. Joseph Rhea I and Frances (Baker) G.; m. Sarah Elizabeth (Bynum), Aug. 21, 1965; children: Joseph III, Elizabeth. BA, Emory U., 1964; LLB, U. Va., 1967. Bar: Ga., 1968; U.S. Dist. Ct. (no. dist.) Ga., 1968; U.S. Ct. Appeals (5th cir.), 1968; U.S. Ct. Appeals (11th cir.), 1985. Assoc. King and Spalding, Atlanta, 1967-73, ptnr., 1973-85; v.p., sr. staff counsel The Coca Cola Co., Atlanta, 1985-87, v.p., dep. gen. counsel, 1987-90, v.p., gen. counsel, 1990-91, sr. v.p., gen. counsel, 1991—99, exec. v.p., gen. counsel, 1999—2000; ret. Atlanta, 2001. Bd. dirs. Coca Cola Enterprises, Emory Healthcare; chmn. bd. dir. Wesley Woods Inc., Coca Cola Amatil. Chmn. bd. trustees Agnes Scott Coll.; bd. dir. Atlanta Ballet; trustee Lovett Sch.; Acad. Search Cons. Svc. Mem. ABA (com. corp. law, gen. counsel); Am. Corp. Counsel Assn.; Ga. Bar Assn.; State Bar Ga.; Assn. Gen. Counsel; Atlanta Bar Assn.; Commerce Club; Piedmont Driving Club. Antitrust, Federal civil litigation, Corporate, general. E-mail: sjgladden@mindspring.com.

GLADSTONE, ALAN, labor law and industrial relations consultant; b. N.Y.C., Dec. 7, 1930; s. Saul Joseph and Sally (Levine) G.; m. Gloria Gersht, Mar. 8, 1959; children: James Nathaniel, Elizabeth Anne. BA, CUNY, 1951; JD, Yale U., 1954. Bar: N.Y.; U.S. Dist. Ct. (so. dist.) N.Y. 1956. With Kay, Scholer, Fierman, Hays and Handler, 1956-58, ILO, 1958-90; dir. Internat. Inst. for Labor Studies, Geneva, 1976-84; dir. indsl. rels. and labor adminstrn. dept. ILO, Geneva, 1984-90; labor law and indsl. rels. cons., Geneva, 1991—. Author: Voluntary Arbitration, 1985; author, editor Employers Associations and Industrial Relations, 1984, Labour Relations in a Changing Environment, 1992; contbg. author: Comparative Labour Law and Industrial Relations, 1993; editor Internat. Labour Law Reports (ann.). Vice chmn. Am. Dems. Abroad/Switzerland, 1985—; bd. dirs. Am. Citizens Abroad, Geneva, 1991—. With U.S. Army, 1954-56. Mem. Internat. Indsl. Rels. Assn. (sec. 1984-93), Geneva Law Soc. (exec. com. 1985-95), Am. Internat. Club (exec. com. 1991-2002). Avocations: skiing, tennis. E-mail: glad@freesurf.ch.

GLANCY, WALTER JOHN, lawyer; b. L.A., Mar. 8, 1942; s. Walter Perry and Elva Thomasin (Douglass) Glancy; m. Jane Whetstone Schroeder, 1995; children from previous marriage: Jill Marie, Gregory Owens. AB, Princeton U., 1964; BA, Oxford U., Eng., 1966; LLB, Yale U., 1969. Bar: Tex. 1971. Law clk. to assoc. justice Byron R. White U.S. Supreme Ct., 1969-70; staff asst. Nat. Security Council, 1970-71; staff asst. to Peter M. Flanigan, The White House, 1971; assoc. then ptnr. Jackson, Walker, Winstead, Cantwell & Miller, Dallas, 1972-76; ptnr. Hughes & Luce and predecessor, Dallas, 1976-85, Baker & Botts, Dallas, 1985-88, Hughes & Luce, Dallas, 1988-90; pvt. practice Dallas, 1991-95, 97-99; cons. Meyer, Hendricks, Victor, Osborn & Maledon, Phoenix, 1991-95; ptnr. Weil, Gotshal & Manges LLP, Dallas, 1995-96. Sr. v.p., gen. counsel, dir. Holly Corp., 1999—; adj. lectr. corp. taxation So. Meth. U. Sch. Law, 1988. Note and comment editor Yale Law Jour., 1968-69. Bd. mgmt. Dallas YMCA Urban Svcs., 1975—84; bd. dirs. Dallas Family Guidance Ctr., 1982—96, pres. bd. dirs., 1985—86; bd. dirs. Child & Family Guidance Ctrs., Dallas, 1996—2003, pres. bd. dirs., 2001—02; bd. dirs. Dallas Opera, 1984—88, 1996—97; bd. trustees Hockaday Sch., Dallas, 1989—95; mem. adminstrv. bd. Lovers Ln. United Meth. Ch., Dallas, 1984—86, 1988—89; deacon Park Cities Bapt. Ch., Dallas, 1996—. Nat. Merit scholar, 1960-64, Marshall scholar, 1964-66. Mem.: ABA, State Bar Tex. (profl. ethics com. 1982—, chmn. tax sect. 1985—86, chmn. profl. ethics com. 1999—), Am. Law Inst., Dallas Bar Assn. (chmn. legal ethics com. 1980—81), Order of Coif, Park Cities Rotary Club (pres. 2003—), Phi Beta Kappa. Republican. Corporate, general, Corporate taxation, Taxation, general. Home: 9162 Clearlake Dr Dallas TX 75225-2001 Office: 100 Crescent Ct Ste 1600 Dallas TX 75201-6915

GLANCZ, RONALD ROBERT, lawyer; b. Bay City, Mich., Jan. 29, 1943; s. Alexander and Ella (Josehart) Glancz; m. Margie Joan Pensler, Dec. 28, 1969. BA in Pre-Legal Studies, U. Mich., 1964, JD cum laude, 1968. Bar: Mich. 1968, U.S. Ct. of Appeals (D.C. cir.) 1969, U.S. Supreme Ct. 1972, D.C. 1974. Atty. civil divsn. Appellate Sec. U.S. Dept. Justice, Washington, 1968-75, asst. dir. civil divsn., 1975-79; dir. litigation divsn. Office of the Comptr. of the Currency, Washington, 1979-84; asst. gen. counsel Fed. Deposit Ins. Corp., Washington, 1984-88; ptnr. Venable Baetjer Howard & Civiletti, LLP, Washington, 1991—. Contbr. Mem.: ABA (vice chair banking law com.), Jewish Found. for Group Homes (pres. 2001—02), The Exchequer Club Washington, Order of Coif. Banking, Federal civil litigation, Corporate, general. Office: Venable Baetjer Howard & Civiletti LLP 1201 New York Ave NW Ste 1000 Washington DC 20005-6197

GLANSTEIN, JOEL CHARLES, lawyer; b. Jersey City, May 16, 1940; s. Harry I. and Katherine G.; m. Eleanor Elovich, July 2, 1966; children: David Michael, Stacey Alison. BA with honors, Lehigh U., 1962; LLB, NYU, 1965, LLM in Labor Law, 1969. Bar: N.Y. 1967, D.C. 1975, U. S. Ct. Appeals (2d cir.) 1970, U.S. Supreme Ct. 1971, U.S. Ct. Appeals (1st cir.) 1972, U.S. Ct. Appeals (3d cir.) 1978, U.S. Ct. Appeals (11th and 9th cirs.) 1981, U.S. Ct. Appeals (5th cir.) 1982, U.S. Ct. Appeals (6th cir.) 1984, U.S. Ct. Appeals (7th cir.) 1999. Assoc. Pressman & Scribner, N.Y.C., 1968-69; ptnr. Scribner, Glanstein & Klein, N.Y.C., 1970-72, Markowitz & Glanstein, N.Y.C., 1972-79, O'Donnell & Schwartz, N.Y.C., 1980-90, O'Donnell, Schwartz, Glanstein & Rosen, N.Y.C., 1991-99, O'Donnell, Schwartz, Glanstein, Rosen et al, LLP, N.Y.C., 1999-2001, O'Donnell, Schwartz & Glanstein, N.Y.C., 2001, O'Donnell, Schwartz, Glanstein & Lilly, LLP, N.Y.C., 2002—. Adj. assoc. prof. N.Y. Law Sch., N.Y.C., 1980-95. Fellow Coll. of Labor and Employment Lawyers, Inc.; mem. ABA (labor and employment law sect., com. on internat. labor law 1976, com. on law of alternative dispute resolution 1976), N.Y. State Bar Assn. (labor and employment law sect., chmn. 1987-88), N.Y. County Lawyers Assn., D.C. Bar Assn., Maritime Law Assn. U.S., Cornell Club (N.Y.C.). Admiralty, Labor (including EEOC, Fair Labor Standards Act, labor-management relations, NLRB, OSHA), Pension, profit-sharing, and employee benefits. Office: O'Donnell Schwartz Glanstein & Lilly LLP 305 Madison Ave Rm 1022 New York NY 10165-0100

GLANTZ, WENDY NEWMAN, lawyer; b. L.I., N.Y., Dec. 16, 1956; d. Sidney and Sarah (Rudnitsky) Newman; m. Ronald Paul Glantz, Dec. 29, 1983. BS, SUNY, Stonybrook, 1978; JD, Nova Law Ctr., 1982. Bar: Fla., 1983. Assoc. Glazer & Glazer, Hallandale, Fla., 1983-85; ptnr. Pasin & Glantz, Lauderhill, Fla., 1985-86, Glantz & Glantz, Plantation and Miami, Fla., 1986—. Seminar leader Marital Strategies, Ft. Lauderdale, 1985—. Editor Pipeline, 1985-86; contbr. articles to profl. mags. Co-chairperson, editor Parents Anonymous, 1986—, mem. adv. bd.; chairperson Bus. Profl. Group of Sunrise Jewish Ctr., 1988—; sponsor Jewish Community Ctr., mem. fund raising com.; mem. South Fla. Symphony, Women of Fine Arts. Mem. ABA (family law sect.), NAFE (pres. S.E. chpt. 1985—), Fla. Bar Assn. (family law sect.), Assn. Trial Lawyers Am., Broward County Bar Assn. (program coord. continuing legal edn. family law sect.), West Broward Bar Assn. (pres. 1989-90), Fla. Assn. Women Lawyers (bd. dirs.), Broward County Women Lawyers Assn. (pres. 1988-90), Nat. Assn. Women Bus. Owners (Broward chpt.), Plantation C. of C. Family and matrimonial. Office: Glantz & Glantz 7951 SW 6th St Ste 200 Fort Lauderdale FL 33324-3223

GLANVILLE, ROBERT EDWARD, lawyer; b. Binghamton, N.Y., Aug. 1, 1950; s. Robert S. and Betty J. (Garlick) G.; m. Susan Anne Kime, Sept. 3, 1970. BA magna cum laude, SUNY, Binghamton, 1972; JD magna cum laude, Cornell U., 1976. Bar: N.Y. 1977, U.S. Dist. Ct. (we. dist.) N.Y. 1978, U.S. Supreme Ct. 1981, U.S. Ct. Appeals (2d cir.) 1985, U.S. Ct. Appeals (D.C. cir.) 1991. Law clk. Appellate Divsn., 4th Dept., Rochester, 1976-78; from assoc. to ptnr. Phillips, Lytle, Hitchcock, et. al., Buffalo, N.Y., 1978-85, 88—; ptnr. Prahl & Glanville, Buffalo, 1986-88. Mem. ABA, N.Y. State Bar Assn., Erie County Bar Assn., Am. Gas Assn. Avocations: whitewater kayaking, sailing, mountaineering, flying. Federal civil litigation, State civil litigation, Utilities, public. Home: 9385 S Hill Rd Boston NY 14025-9667 Office: Phillips Lytle Hitchcock 3400 HSBC Ctr Buffalo NY 14203-2887

GLANZER, MONA N. lawyer, arbitrator; b. N.Y.C., July 29, 1931; d. David and Henrietta (Schweitzer) Sorcher; m. Murray A. Glanzer, Sept. 20, 1953; children: Michael John, Marla Curtis, James S. LLB, Bklyn. Law Sch., 1953. Bar: N.Y. 1954, U.S. Dist. Ct. (so. and ea. dists.) N.Y. 1965, U.S. Supreme Ct. 1976, U.S. Ct. Appeals (2d cir.) 1981. Editor CCH Pension Plan Guide, Chgo., 1953—54; assoc. Harry H. Rains, Rains, Pogrebin & Scher, Mineola, NY, 1965—71; ptnr. Rains & Pogrebin, P.C., Mineola, 1971—2000. Arbitrator AAA Pension and Employee Benefits U.S. Dist. Ct., NY, 1985—, Nassau County Bar Employment Rels. Bd., CSEA Discipline Panel. Contbr. articles to profl. jours. Mem. adv. com. Recodification N.Y. State Workers' Compensation Law Project, 1985-87; bd. dirs. Suffolk County Coalition Against Domestic Violence, Project Literacy/Outreach Inc. Recipient Presdl. Pvt. Sector Initiative Commendation citation, Profl. Achievement award Nassau County Bar Assn. Fellow ABA Found.; mem. Am. Arbitration Assn. (panel 1987—, arbitrator), Coun. Lic. Physiotherapists N.Y. (hon.), N.Y. State Assn. Profl. Land Surveyors (hon.), N.Y. State Bar Assn. (chair labor and employment law sect. 1988-89, chair com. pension, welfare and related plans 1983-86, chair com. labor standards legis. 1986-87), Nassau-Suffolk Women's Bar Assn. (pres. 1986-87). Alternative dispute resolution, Labor (including EEOC, Fair Labor Standards Act, labor-management relations, NLRB, OSHA), Pension, profit-sharing, and employee benefits. E-mail: monanglanzer@aol.com.

GLASER, ARTHUR HENRY, lawyer, mediator; b. Jersey City, May 1, 1947; s. Ned C. and Lorraine I. (Neil) G.; m. Waynelia Potter, Mar. 19, 1994; children: Kimberly N., Kevin M., Daniel J. BS, Hampden-Sydney Coll., 1968; JD, U. Va., 1973. Bar: Ga. 1973, U.S. Dist. Ct. (no. and mid. dists.) Ga., U.S. Ct. Appeals (11th cir.). Assoc. Swift, Currie, McGhee & Hiers, Atlanta, 1973-78, ptnr., 1978-83, Drew, Eckl & Farnham, Atlanta, 1983-98, Self, Glaser & Davis, LLP, Atlanta, 1999—; with Henning Mediation, 1999—. Mem. ABA, Ga. Bar Assn., Atlanta Bar Assn. Presbyterian. Insurance, Libel, Personal injury (including property damage). Home: 1540 Burnt Hickory Rd NW Marietta GA 30064-1308 Office: Self Glaser & Davis LLP Ste 1650 400 Interstate North Pkwy SE Atlanta GA 30339-5029 E-mail: ahg@sgdlaw.com.

GLASER, LENORE MERYL, lawyer; b. Harvey, Ill., Aug. 4, 1950; BA, Reed Coll., 1973; JD, Northeastern U., 1980. Bar: Mass. 1980, U.S. Dist. Ct. Mass. 1980, U.S. Ct. Appeals (1st cir.) 1980. Housing atty. Western Mass. Legal Svcs., Holyoke, 1980-83; staff atty. Inquilinos Boriqus en Accion, Boston, 1983-85; assoc. Johnson & Somberg, Boston, 1985-87, ptnr., 1987-90; pvt. practice Boston, 1990-96; of counsel Stern, Shapiro, Weissberg & Garin, Boston, 1996—. Adj. prof. Suffolk U. Law Sch., Boston, 1985-87, U. Mass., Boston, 1985, 87, 90. Contbr. articles to profl. jours. Curi-clk. La Alianza Hispana, Boston, 1994—. Mem. Mass. Bar Assn., Mass. Criminal Def. Lawyers (bd. dirs.), Nat. Soc. Criminal Def. Lawyers. Office: 25 Kingston St 60 Boston MA 02110

GLASER, ROBERT EDWARD, lawyer; b. Cin., Jan. 12, 1935; s. Delbert Henry and Rita Elizabeth (Arlinghaus) G.; m. Kathleen Eileen Grannen, June 17, 1961; children— Petra M., Timothy X., Mark G., Bridget M., Christopher D., Jenny M., Michael F. BS in Bus. Adminstrn. cum laude, Xavier U., Cin., 1955; LLB, U. Cin., 1960; LLM, U. Chgo., 1962; postgrad., U. Tuebingen, Fed. Republic of Germany, 1961. Bar: Ohio 1960, U.S. Dist. Ct. (no. dist.) Ohio 1963, U.S. Ct. Appeals (6th cir.) 1964, U.S. Tax Ct. 1970, U.S. Ct. Internat. Trade 1971, U.S. Ct. Fed. Claims 1992, U.S. Ct. Appeals (fed. cir.) 2000. Assoc. Arter & Hadden, Cleve., 1963-69, ptnr., 1970-2001, chmn., 1983-92; ret., 2001. Arbitrator Cuyahoga County Ct. Common Pleas, Ohio, 1972—, Med. Malpractice Panel, 1985—, Mediator Settlement Week, 1990; lectr. Cleve. Tax Inst., 1966—2000, mem. exec. com., 1980—84, chmn., 1982; lectr. Can.-U.S. Law Inst., 1980, Res. Officers Assn., 1970—, Ret. Officers Assn., 1995—; mem. qualified list of neutrals IRS Rev. Proc., 2003—. Contbr. articles to legal jours. Sec. Bay View Hosp., 1972-81; trustee Mental Health Rehab. and Rsch., Inc., 1975-86, mem. exec. com., 1977-81, pres., 1979-81; mem. men's com. Cleve. Play House, 1965-2003; mem. joint mental health and corrections com. Fedn. Cmty. Planning, 1978-81; mem. Cleve. Coun. on Fgn. Affairs, 1987-2002; mem. vis. com. Coll. Law Cleve. State U., 1987-97; mem. Soc. of Benchers, Case Western Res. Univ. Coll. Law, 1988—; trustee Univ. Circle, Inc., 1989-99, mem. exec. com., 1989-99. Col. U.S. Army, ret. Ford Found. grantee, 1960. Fellow Am. Bar Found. (life); mem. Ohio Bar Assn. (gen. tax com. 1998—, lawyer assistance com. 1999—), Nat. Bar Assn., Cleve. Bar Assn. (trustee 1983-87, chmn. bd. of com. grievance and discipline trial com. 1993, gen. tax com. 1983—, lawyer assistance com. 1999—), Legal Aid Soc. Cleve., Am. Judicature Soc., 8th Jud. Conf. (life), Am. Arbitration Assn. (nat. and internat. panel arbitrators 1969—), Citizens League Greater Cleve., Order of Coif, Union Club, Pentagon Officers Athletic Club, Serra Internat., Cleve. Club (exec. com. 1987-88, 90-91, 93-98, 2000—, pres. 1994-96, 2002—), KC. Roman Catholic. Private international, Corporate taxation, Personal income taxation. Home: 22895 Mastick Rd Cleveland OH 44126-3145 Office: Arter & Hadden 1100 Huntington Bldg 925 Euclid Ave Cleveland OH 44115-1475

GLASGOW, NORMAN MILTON, lawyer; b. Washington, Aug. 14, 1922; children: Norman M., Heather Glasgow Harris, Glenn. BS, U. Md., 1943; LLB, JD, BA, George Washington U., 1949. Bar: D.C. 1949, U.S. Supreme Ct. 1956, Md. 1960. Assoc. Wilkes, McGarraghy & Artis, Washington, 1949-55; ptnr. Wilkes & Artis, Washington, 1955-82; pres. Wilkes, Artis, Hedrick & Lane, Washington, 1982-86, sr. prin., 1988-2000; ptnr. Holland & Knight, LLP, Washington, 2001—. Bd. dirs., gen. counsel Greater Washington Bd. Trade, 1966, 87, 88; mem., chmn. Md. PAC, 1981-93; bd. govs. Washington Bldg. Congress; mem. Citizens Tech. Adv. Com. for Drafting Bldg. Code and Zoning Regulations, Washington, Commrs. Citizens Adv. Com. on Zoning, Washington, Balt. conv. Ctr. Authority Transp. Revenue Com., Gov.'s Salary Commn., Gov.'s Spl. Com. Vehicle Emissions Inspection Program, Gov.'s Adv. Redistricting Com.; chmn. Gov.'s Task Force Statewide Bldg. Performance Stds., Md. Stadium Authority, 1993-97, Md. Econ. Growth, Resource Protection and Planning Commn., co-chair subcom. for updating state planning and zoning laws, 1993-97; chmn. Md. Econ. Growth Task Force; mem. Gov.'s Western Md. Econ. Devel. Strategies Task Force, 1998—, co-chair Updating Md. Zoning and Planning Regulations (Article 66B). 1st lt. U.S. Army, 1942-46, ETO. Recipient Outstanding Alumni award George Washington U., 1985, Outstanding Svc. award D.C. Real Estate, Greater Washington Bd. Trade, 1978. Mem. Supreme Ct. Bar Assn., D.C. Bar Assn., Md. Bar Assn., Urban Land Inst., Am. Soc. Planning Ofcls., Washington Bldg. Congress, Nat. Assn. Bus. Economists, Nat. Conf. States in Bldg. Codes and Stds., Lambda Alpha. Avocation: gardening. Land use and zoning (including planning), Property, real (including real estate development, water). Home: 9012 Brickyard Rd Potomac MD 20854-1634 Office: Holland & Knight 2099 Penn Ave NW Washington DC 20006-2803

GLASS, FRED STEPHEN, lawyer; b. Asheboro, N.C., Oct. 17, 1940; s. Emmett Frederick and Colene F. (Foust) G.; m. Gloria A. Grant, June 12, 1964; 1 child, Elizabeth Foust; m. Martha G. Daughtry, June 9, 1982. BA, Wake Forest U., 1963, JD, 1966. Bar: N.C. 1966, U.S. Dist. Ct. (ea. dist.) N.C. 1966, (mid. dist.) N.C., (we. dist.) N.C.; U.S. Ct. Appeals (4th cir.), U.S. Supreme Ct. Rsch. asst. presiding justice N.C. Supreme Ct., 1966-67; ptnr. Miller, Beck, O'Briant and Glass, Asheboro, N.C., 1971-77; exec. dir. and legal counsel N.C. Democratic Party, 1977-78; dep. commr. N.C. Indsl. Commn., 1978; spl. Congl. asst. 4th Congl. Dist., N.C., 1979; ptnr. Harris, Cheshire, Leager and Southern, Raleigh, N.C., 1979-86, Poyner and Spruill, Raleigh, 1987-94, Brooks, Stevens & Pope, P.A., Cary, 1994-98; mng. ptnr. Glass & Vining, LLC, Cary, 1998-2000, Johnson, hearn, Vinegar & Gee PLLC, 2001—. Prof. law and govt. Asheboro Jr. Coll. Bus., 1973-76; bd. dirs. Capital Bank; mem. Gov.'s commn. mil. affairs, N.C., commn. Battleship N.C. Author: The Legal Handboook for North Carolina Businesses, 2003, Your Estate Planning Handbook, Business Considerations for North Carolina Healthcare Providers; contbg. editor: N.C. Will Drafting and Probate Practice Handbook, 1983; contbr. articles to profl. jours. Pub. chmn., United Appeal; bd. dirs., Randolph County Emergency Med. Technician Bd., Capital Bank; chmn.-elect Cary C. of C., bd. dirs., vice-chair govt. relations com.; mem. adv. bd. Naval War Coll. ops. law; active Dem. campaigns, Boy Scouts Am., council commr. for Roundtables, 1980-89, asst. dist. commr. 1979-84, asst. scoutmaster; mem. nat. com. Boy Scouts of Am., council ex. bd., council commr., chancellor, council commrs. coll., 1980-83, Boy Scouts Am. Nat. Com., 1987-90, coun. pres. 1994-96; force judge adv. COMRNCF, 1985-89; v.p. Healthcare Bus. Mgmt., LLC. Rear adm. JAGC, USNR. Disting. Svc. Medal award, 1996. Meritorious Svc. medal with gold star, Meritorious Unit Commendation, Nat. Meritorious Svc. award USNR, 1995, Navy Commendation medal with Gold Star, Nat. Defense Svc. medal with Bronze Star, Seabee Combat Warfare Specialist Cert.; recipient numerous Scouters Tng. award Boy Scouts Am., Disting. Eagle Scout award, 1991, Young Man of Yr. award City Asheboro. Mem.: ABA (standing com. on armed forces law), N.C. Bar Found., N.C. Coun. Entrepreneurial Devel., N.C. Def. Lawyers Assn. (computers in litigation support 1989), N.C. Bar Assn. (chmn. young lawyer sect. Randolph County, computers in law office 1995), 19th Jud. Dist. Bar Assn. (pres. 1974—75), Randolph County Bar Assn. (pres. 1971—74), Cary C. of C. (bd. dirs., chmn. elect), Club, Sovereign Mil. Order Temple Jerusalem, Naval Order U.S. Democrat. Methodist. General civil litigation, Nuclear power, Health. Home: 243 Chimney Rise Drive Cary NC 27511-7216 Office: PO Box 1776 Raleigh NC 27602 Fax: 919-743-2201. E-mail: sglass@jhvglaw.com.

GLASS, ROY LEONARD, lawyer; b. Littleton, N.H., Jan. 27, 1947; s. Jack Irving and Noreen (Leiuthwait) Kline; m. Suzanne Schmidt Goldstein, May 20, 1967 (div. Oct. 1978); 1 child, Shannon Renee; m. Patricia Lee Wimbish, Dec. 9, 1978 (div. 1988); 1 child, Ashley Leigh; m. Lauren Rachel Adams, Aug. 8, 1998. AA with honors, St. Petersburg Jr. Coll., Fla., 1971; BA, U. South Fla., 1972; JD, Fla. State U., 1975. Bar: Fla. 1976, U.S. Dist. Ct. (mid. dist.) Fla. 1977, U.S. Dist. Ct. (no. dist.) Fla. 1978, U.S. Supreme Ct. 1979, U.S. Ct. Appeals (11th cir.) 1983. Assoc. Meyers, Mooney & Adler, Orlando, Fla., 1976-78, Barrett, Boyd & Bajoczky, Tallahassee, 1978-79; sole practice Tallahassee, 1979-81; ptnr. Deserio & Glass, St. Petersburg, Fla., 1981-82; assoc. Battaglia, Ross, Hastings, Dicus & Andrews, St. Petersburg, 1982-85; sole practice St. Petersburg, 1985—. Lectr. Floridians Against Constl. Tampering, Fla., 1984. Capt. U.S. Army, 1966-70, Vietnam. Mem. ABA, ATLA, Am. Arbitration Assn., Fla. Acad. Trial Lawyers (mem. spkrs. bur.), Fla. Bar Assn. (health law com. 1984-85, chmn. health care profls. subcom. 1984-85, mem. exec. coun. health care sect. 1986-94, mem. spkrs. bur., chair client security fund com. 2003—), St. Petersburg Bar Assn. (legis. com. 1983-85, liaison med. soc., med. rels. com. 1985—, trial lawyers 1987—, mem. spkrs. bur.), Pinellas County Trial Lawyers Assn., St. Petersburg C. of C. (urban solutions task force 1983-84), Phi Delta Phi, Phi Kappa Phi, Beta Gamma Sigma. Clubs: Suncoast Tiger Bay (St. Petersburg, Fang & Claw award 1983), Breakfast Sertoma (Cert. of Appreciation 1984), Westgate High Twelve (Cert. of Appreciation 1987), Fla. Bar Health Law Sect. (Meritorious Svc. award 1994), Am. Coll. Barristers (sr. counsel), Roscoe Pound Inst. State civil litigation, Insurance, Personal injury (including property damage). Office: 5501 Central Ave Saint Petersburg FL 33710-8050

GLASSEN, JAMES WARREN, lawyer; b. Moberly, Mo., Dec. 16, 1954; s. Benjamin Marshall and Geraldine (Butts) G.; m. Mary Anne Davis, Dec. 26, 1987; children: Benjamin Marshall II, Meghan Anne Shon. BSBA, Georgetown U., 1977; JD, U. Mo., Kansas City, 1982. Bar: U.S. Dist. Ct. D.C. 1983, N.Y. 1989, N.J. 1989, U.S. Dist. Ct. N.J., U.S. Ct. Appeals (D.C. cir.), U.S. Dist. Ct. (ea. and so. dists.) N.Y., U.S. Ct. Appeals (3d cir.). Legis. dir. to U.S. Congressman Harold L. Volkmer, Washington, 1976-83; assoc. Lipsen, Hamberger, Whitten & Hamberger, Washington, 1983-88, Postner & Rubin, N.Y.C., 1988-89; dep. atty. gen. N.J. Atty. Gen.'s Office, Trenton, 1989-94; ptnr. Roth & Glassen, Summit, N.J., 1994-97; of counsel Scarinci & Hollenbeck, Secaucus, N.J., 1997-99; dep. atty. gen. N.J. Divsn. of Criminal Justice, Trenton, 1999—2003, Office of Atty. Gen., 2003—. Chair Union County (N.J.) Commn. Human Rels., 1998; mem. N.J. DEP Task Force on County Environ. Health Act, Trenton, 1994-95. Revisor: New Jersey State Grand Jury Manual, 1993. Mem. D.C. Bar Assn., U.S. Tax Ct.,

N.J. Bar Assn. Democrat. Roman Catholic. Avocation: golf. General civil litigation, Criminal, Environmental. Office: Office of Atty Gen Hughes Justice Complex PO Box 080 Trenton NJ 08625-0085

GLASSER, IRA SAUL, civil liberties organization executive; b. Bklyn., Apr. 18, 1938; s. Sidney and Anne (Goldstein) Glasser; m. Trude Maria Robinson, June 28, 1959; children: David, Andrew, Peter, Sally. BS in Math., Queens Coll., 1959; MA in Math., Ohio State U., 1960; LLD (hon.) , N.Y. Law Sch., 2001. Instr. math. Queens Coll., N.Y.C., 1960—63; lectr. math. Sarah Lawrence Coll., Bronxville, NY, 1962—65; assoc. editor Current Mag., N.Y.C., 1962—64, editor, 1964—67; assoc. dir. N.Y. Civil Liberties Union, N.Y.C., 1967—70, exec. dir., 1970—78, ACLU, 1978—2001. Cons. U. Ill.-Champaign-Urbana, 1964—65; dir. Asian Am. Legal Def. and Edn. Fund, N.Y.C., 1974—; pres., bd. dirs. Drug Policy Alliance N.Y. (formerly Lindesmith Ctr./Drug Policy Found.), 1991—. Author: Visions of Liberty: The Bill of Rights for All Americans, 1991; co-author: Doing Good: The Limits of Benevolence, 1978; contbr. articles to profl. jours. Chmn. St. Vincents Hosp., N.Y.C., Cmty. Adv. Bd., N.Y.C., 1970—72. Recipient Martin Luther King, Jr. award, N.Y. Assn. Black Sch. Suprs., 1971, Gavel award, ABA, 1972, Allard K. Lowenstein award, Park River Ind. Dem., 1981, Malcolm, Martin, Mandela award, Greater Bapt. Trinity Ch., 1993, Justice in Action award, Asian Am. Legal Def. and Edn. Fund, 1999. Avocation: sports.

GLASSER, ISRAEL LEO, federal judge; b. N.Y.C., Apr. 6, 1924; s. David and Sadie (Krupp) G.; m. Grace Gribetz, Aug. 24, 1952; children—Dorothy, David, James, Marjorie. LL.B., Bklyn. Law Sch., 1948; BA, CUNY, 1976. Bar: N.Y. 1948. Fellow Bklyn. Law Sch., 1948-49, instr., 1950-52, asst. prof. law, 1952-53, asso. prof., 1953-55, prof., 1955-69, adj. prof., 1969-77, dean, 1977-81; judge U.S. Dist. Ct. N.Y., 1981—99, sr. judge, 1993—. Judge N.Y. State Family Ct., N.Y.C., 1969-77 Mem. ABA, Assn. of Bar of City of N.Y. Office: US Dist Ct 225 Cadman Plz E Brooklyn NY 11201-1818 E-mail: leo_glasser@nyed.uscourts.gov.

GLASSER, MICHAEL A. lawyer; b. Norfolk, Va., Nov. 17, 1953; BA with distinction, U. Va., 1975; JD, U. Richmond, 1978. Bar: (Va.) 1978, U.S. Dist. Ct. Va. (ea. dist.) 1978, U.S. Ct. Appeals (4th cir.) 1978, U.S. Supreme Ct. 1997. Ptnr. Glasser & Glasser, Norfolk. Mem.: Va. State Bar (pres. 2001—02). Office: Glasser & Glasser Crown Ctr Bldg 580 E Main St Ste 600 Norfolk VA 23510

GLASSMAN, CAROLINE DUBY, state supreme court justice; b. Baker, Oreg., Sept. 13, 1922; d. Charles Ferdinand and Caroline Marie (Colton) Duby; m. Harry Paul Glassman, May 21, 1953; 1 son, Max Avon. LLB summa cum laude, Williamette U., 1944. Bar: Oreg. 1944, Calif. 1952, Maine 1969. Atty. Title Ins. & Trust Co., Salem, Oreg., 1944-46; assoc. Belli, Ashe, Pinney & Melvin Belli, San Francisco, 1952-58; ptnr. Glassman & Potter, Portland, Maine, 1973-78, Glassman, Beagle & Ridge, Portland, 1978-83; justice Maine Supreme Judicial Ct., Portland, 1983-97. Lectr. Sch. Law, U. Maine, 1967-68, 80 Author: Legal Status of Homemakers in State of Maine, 1977. Mem.: ATLA, Russian Am. Rule of Law Consortium, Maine Trial Law Assn., Maine Bar Assn., Calif. Bar Assn., Oreg. Bar Assn., Am. Law Inst. Roman Catholic. Home: 56 Thomas St Portland ME 04102-3639

GLASSMAN, STEVEN J. lawyer; b. N.Y.C., 1944; BS, MIT, 1964; JD, Georgetown U., 1968. Bar: N.Y. 1970. Patent examiner U.S. Patent Office, 1964-65; asst. sect. chief, counsel tech. utilization Nat. Aeronautics and Space Adminstrn., 1966-71; asst. U.S. Atty. so. dist. N.Y. U.S. Atty's. Office, 1971-76, chief civil rights sect. so. dist. N.Y., 1974-75, chief civil appellate atty. so. dist. N.Y., 1975-76; ptnr. Kaye Scholer LLP, N.Y.C., 1979—. Editor Georgetown Law Jour., 1967-68. Mem. ABA, Assn. Bar City N.Y., Fed. Bar Coun., Phi Delta Phi. Office: Kaye Scholer LLP 425 Park Ave New York NY 10022-3506

GLAVIN, A. RITA CHANDELLIER (MRS. JAMES HENRY GLAVIN III), lawyer; b. Schenectady, N.Y., May 11, 1937; d, Pierre Charles and Helen C. (Fox) Chandellier; m. James H. Glavin, III, June 1, 1963; children: Helene, James, Rita, Henry. AB cum laude, Middlebury Coll., 1958; JD, Union U., 1961. Bar: N.Y. 1961, U.S. Dist. Ct. (no. dist.) N.Y. 1961, U.S. Tax Ct. 1965, U.S. Supreme Ct. 1978. Assoc. Eugene Steiner, Albany, N.Y., 1961-64, Helen Fox Chandellier, Schenectady, 1965-76; mem. Glavin and Glavin, Waterford, Schenectady, 1965-86, 87—, Albany, 1965-86, 87—. Del. 4th Jud. Dist. Nominating Conv., 1966—67; confidential law clk. presiding justices N.Y. State Ct. Claims, 1968—71; surrogate judge Saratoga County, 1986; dir. assn. coun. mems. and coll. trustees SUNY, 1991—2002, sec., 1996—2002. Mem. edit. bd. Albany Law Rev., 1960-61. Sec. Bellevue Women's Med. Ctr., 2001—02; bd. dirs., chmn. fin. com. Schenectady YWCA, 1979—81; bd. dirs. Schenectady Jr. League, 1974, 1976; del. pub. affairs com. N.Y. State Jr. League, 1976; sec. Bellevue Maternity Hosp., Inc., 1966—2001, bd. dirs., 1966—83, bd. advisors, 1984—2001; bd. dirs. Bellevue Women's Med. Ctr., 2001—02; trustee Middlebury Coll., 1978—88, chmn. law com., 1982—88, vice chmn. bd. dirs., 1986—87; trustee Waterford Hist. Mus. and Cultural Ctr., Inc., 2000—, sec., 2002—; mem. univ. coun. SUNY, Albany, 1985—2002; tech. advisor HSA Northeastern N.Y. Maternity and Pediat. Com., 1976. Mem. N.Y. State Bar Assn. (mem. ho. of dels. 1987-88, nominating com. 1988-90), Saratoga County Bar Assn. (exec. com. 1981—, v.p. 1985, pres. 1986), Schenectady County Bar Assn., Phi Beta Kappa, Kappa Kappa Gamma. General practice. Office: Glavin & Glavin PO Box 40 69 2nd St Waterford NY 12188-2422

GLAZE, THOMAS A. state supreme court justice; b. Jan. 14, 1938; s. Phyllis Laser; children: Steve, Mike, Julie, Amy, Ashley. BSBA, U. Ark., 1960, JD, 1964. Exec. dir. Election Research Council Inc., 1964-65; legal advisor Winthrop Rockefeller, 1965-66; staff atty. Pulaski County Legal Aid, 1966-67, asst. then dep. atty. gen., 1967-70; pvt. practice law, 1970-79; chancellor Ark. Chancery Ct., 6th Jud. Cir., 1979-80; judge Ark. Ct. Appeals, 1981-86; assoc. justice Ark. Supreme Ct., 1987—. Co-author Ark. Election Act, 1969, Ark. Consumer Act; lectr. U. Ark.; adj. faculty U. Ark., Little Rock. Past bd. dirs. Vis. Nurses Corp., Youth Home Inc. Office: Ark Supreme Ct Justice Bldg 625 Marshall St, 120 Justice Bldg Little Rock AR 72201-1054

GLAZER, BARRY DAVID, lawyer; b. Cleve., Oct. 10, 1948; s. Jacob J. and Constance (Schwartz) Glazer; m. Deborah Werbner, Sept. 28, 1984. AB, Miami U., Oxford, Ohio, 1970; JD, Mich. Law Sch., 1973. Bar: Minn. 1973, U.S. Dist. Ct. Minn. 1973, France Conseil Juridique 1981. Assoc. Dorsey & Whitney, Mpls., 1973—78, ptnr., 1979—80, resident ptnr. Paris, 1980—86, London, 1986—91, mng. ptnr. Brussels, 1991—2000, London, 2001—. Mem.: Union Internat. des Avocats, Internat. Bar Assn., ABA. Corporate, general, Private international. Office: Dorsey & Whitney LLP 21 Wilson St London EC2 England

GLAZER, DONALD WAYNE, lawyer, business executive, educator; b. Cleve., July 26, 1944; s. Julius and Ethel (Goldstein) G.; children: Elizabeth M., Mollie S. AB summa cum laude, Dartmouth Coll., 1966; JD magna cum laude, Harvard U., 1969; LLM, U. Pa., 1970. Bar: Mass. 1970. Assoc. Ropes & Gray, Boston, 1970-78, ptnr., 1978-92, counsel, 1992-96; ptnr. Am. Bus. Ptnrs. LLC, Boston, 1996-98; pres. Mugar/Glazer Holdings, Inc., Boston, 1992-95; vice chmn. fin. New Eng. TV Corp. and WHDH-TV, Inc., Boston, 1992-93; adv. counsel Goodwin Procter LLC, Boston, 1997—; co-founder, corp. sec. Provant, Inc., Boston, 1998—, vice-chmn., 2002. Instr. corp. fin. Boston U. Law Sch., 1975; lectr. law Harvard U., Cambridge, Mass., 1978-91; trustee GMO Trust, Boston, 2000—. Co-author: Massachusetts Corporation Law and Practice, 1991, Glazer and FitzGibbon on Legal Opinions, 1992, 2d edit., 2001; co-editor First Ann. Inst. on Securities Regulation, 1970; contbr. articles to legal jours. Past chmn., trustee Cowen Slavin Found.; past trustee Santa Fe Neuroscis. Inst.; past dir. Newton Girls Soccer League, past co-chmn. intramural com.; past trustee, past treas. Hillel Founds. of Greater Boston Inc.; past trustee Program for Young Negotiators. Fellow Salzburg Seminar in Am. Studies, 1975 Mem. ABA (past chmn. legal opinions com., co-reporter Legal Opinion Prins., past chmn. subcom. on employee benefits and exec. compensation, fed. securities law com., past co-chmn. task force on sec. 16 devels.), Boston Bar Assn. (past chmn., corp. sec., past chmn. securities law com., past co-chmn. legal opinions com.), Am. Law Inst., Tri-Bar Legal Opinions Com. (co-reporter Third-party Closing Opinions). Jewish. Corporate, general, Finance, Securities. Home: 225 Kenrick St Newton MA 02458-2731

GLAZER, JACK HENRY, lawyer; b. Paterson, N.J., Jan. 14, 1928; s. Samiel and Martha (Merkin) G.; m. Zelda d'Angleterre, 1979. BA, Duke U., 1950; JD, Georgetown U., 1956; postgrad., U. Frankfurt, Germany, 1956-57; SJD, U. Calif., Berkeley, 1977. Bar: D.C. 1957, Calif. 1968. Atty. GAO and NASA, 1958-60; mem. maritime divsn. UN Internat. Labour Office, Geneva, Switzerland, 1960, spl. legal adv., 1960-62; atty. NASA, Washington, 1963-66; chief counsel NASA-Ames Rsch. Ctr., Moffett Field, Calif., 1966-88; gov. Calif. Maritime Acad., 1975-78; asst. prof. Hastings Coll. Law, 1985-87; prof., assoc. dean bus. sch. San Francisco State U., 1988-92; dir. San Francisco Palace Fine Arts, 1995. Contbr. articles to profl. jours. Comdr. Calif. Naval Militia, ret. Capt. JAGC, USNR, ret. Mem. Calif. Bar Assn., D.C. Bar Assn., White's Inn (reader). Office: White's Inn 37 White St San Francisco CA 94109-2609 E-mail: whitesinn@aol.com.

GLAZER, RONALD BARRY, lawyer; b. Phila., Jan. 13, 1943; m. Adele J. Kay, June 12, 1965; children: Jodi M. Glazer, Jennifer G. Shorr. AB cum laude, Dickinson Coll., 1964; LLB cum laude, U. Pa., 1967. Bar: Pa. 1967, Fla. 1975. Sr. ptnr. Wolf, Block, Schorr & Solis-Cohen LLP, Phila., 1987—. Lectr. Pa. Bar Inst. Author: Pennsylvania Condominium Law and Practice, 1975, 3d edit., 1995. Mem. ABA, Pa. Bar Assn., Phila. Bar Assn. (chmn. real property law sect. 1987), Internat. Coun. Shopping Ctrs., Am. Coll. Real Estate Lawyers, Cmty. Assns. Inst., Coll. of Lawyers. Finance, Landlord-tenant, Property, real (including real estate development, water). Office: Wolf Block Schorr 1650 Arch St Ste 2100 Philadelphia PA 19103-2029

GLAZER, STEVEN DONALD, lawyer; b. Paterson, N.J., May 13, 1948; s. Morris B. and Shirley (Arbeit) G.; m. Christine Stupak, June 6, 1970; children: Daniel C., Joshua M., Thomas A. AB, BSEE, Rutgers U., 1971; MS, Fairleigh Dickinson U., 1975; JD with honors, Rutgers U., 1979. Bar: N.J. 1979, U.S. Dist. Ct. N.J. 1979, N.Y. 1980, U.S. Dist. Ct. (ea. and so. dists.) N.Y. 1980, U.S. Ct. Appeals (fed. cir.) 1982, U.S. Patent and Trademark Office 1979, U.S. Supreme Ct. 1992. Electronics engr. U.S. Army Signal Corps, Ft. Monmouth, N.J., 1971-76; assoc. Cooper & Dunham, N.Y.C., 1979-81, Davis Hoxie Faithfull & Hapgood, N.Y.C., 1981-85, ptnr., 1986-88, Weil, Gotshal & Manges, N.Y.C., 1988—. Co-editor-in-chief The Jour. of Proprietary Rights. With U.S. Army, 1971-74; lt. col. USAR. Avocation: amateur radio. Computer, Patent, Trademark and copyright. Home: 634 Riverside Dr Cranford NJ 07016-1951 Office: Weil Gotshal & Manges 767 5th Ave Conc Fl 1 New York NY 10153-0119

GLAZIER, SANDRA DEBORAH, lawyer; b. Detroit, Oct. 7, 1956; m. Manny David Glazier, June 18, 1978; children: Michael S., Zachary A. BA with high distinction, Wayne State U., 1978, JD, 1982. Bar: Mich., 1982, U.S. Dist. Ct. (ea. dist.) Mich., 1982, U.S. Dist. Ct. (we. dist.) Mich., 1984. Clk. Hon. Steven N. Andrews Oakland County Cir. Ct., Pontiac, Mich., 1979-82; prin., atty. Schlussel, Lifton, Simon, Rands, Kaufman, Galvin & Jackier, Southfield, Mich., 1982-90; pvt. practice, West Bloomfield, Mich., 1990—. Adj. prof. Walsh Coll., Troy, Mich., 1990; mem. adv. com. Friend of the Court Citizen's Study Group Oakland County Commn., 1999. Mem. projects com. Oakland Pratt Found.; bd. dirs. Detroit Friends of Jewish Theol. Sem., 1999—. Recipient Teen Yr. Nat. Coun. Jewish Women, Southfield, 1974. Mem. ABA, Mich. Bar Assn. (bench-bar com.), Oakland County Bar Assn. (chmn. alimony subcom. 1995, mem. family law sect., asst. chmn. family law sect. 1997-98, co-chmn. family law sect. 1997-98 Oakland County Bench-Bar Retreat, mem. pub. adv. com. on jud. candidates 1998—, chair family law sect. 1998-99, participant jud. retreat 1998), Phi Beta Kappa. Avocations: skiing, needlepoint. Estate planning, Family and matrimonial, Probate (including wills, trusts). Office: 7001 Orchard Lake Rd Ste 330B West Bloomfield MI 48322-3607

GLEASON, JAMES MULLANEY, lawyer, insurance executive; b. Sept. 27, 1948; s. Harry H. and Dorothy (Mullaney) Gleason; m. Margaret McGuire; children: Matthew, Katherine. BA, Briar Cliff Coll., 1973; JD, Creighton U., 1976. Bar: (Iowa) 1976, Nebr. 1976. From asst. counsel to asst. v.p. Woodmen of the World, Omaha, 1976—93, asst. v.p., 1993—. With U.S. Army, 1968—69. Fellow: Life Mgmt. Inst. (master), Life Office Mgmt. Assn.; mem.: Assn. Life and Health Claims, Nebr. Fraternal Congress (pres. 1993—94), Internat. Claim Assn. (pres. 2002—03, exec. com.), Assn. Fraternal Benefit Counsel. Democrat. Roman Catholic. Civil rights, Insurance, Personal injury (including property damage). Office: Woodmen of World Life Ins Soc 1700 Farnam St Ste 2200 Omaha NE 68102-2007 E-mail: jgleason2@cox.net.

GLEESON, PAUL FRANCIS, retired lawyer; b. Bronx, June 20, 1941; s. William Francis and Julia Anne (Dargis) G.; children: Kevin F., Sean W., Brendan J., Colleen J. AB in History, Fordham U., 1963; JD, U. Chgo., 1966. Assoc. Vedder, Price, Kaufman & Kammholz, Chgo., 1966-73, ptnr., 1973-2000; ret., 2000. Adj. prof. DePaul U. Sch. of Law, 1991. Co-author (with Day, Green & Cleveland) The Equal Employment Opportunity Compliance Manual, 1978; columnist: (with B. Alper) Gleeson and Alper on Employment Law, Merrill's Illinois Legal Times, 1988-90. Capt. U.S. Army, 1966-68, Vietnam. Decorated Bronze Star; Floyd Russell Mechem scholar, 1963-66. Mem. Order of Coif, Phi Beta Kappa. Roman Catholic.

GLEKEL, JEFFREY IVES, lawyer; b. N.Y.C., Apr. 8, 1947; s. Newton and Gertrude (Burr) G.; m. Cynthia R. Leder, June 18, 1988; 1 child, David L. AB, Columbia U., 1969; JD, Yale U., 1972. Bar: N.Y. 1973, U.S. Supreme Ct. 1981, U.S. Ct. Appeals (2d cir.) 1974, U.S. Dist. Ct. (so. dist.) N.Y. 1974. Law clk. to judge U.S. Dist. Ct. (so. dist.) N.Y., 1972-73; asst. U.S. atty. So. Dist. N.Y., 1973-77; law clk. to justice Byron R. White U.S. Supreme Ct., Washington, 1977-78; ptnr. Skadden, Arps, Slate, Meagher and Flom, N.Y.C., 1980—. Editor, contbr.: Civil Litigation Practice, 1990; Business Crimes, 1982; note and comment editor Yale Law Jour., 1971-72; contbr. articles to law jours. Mem. Assn. Bar City of N.Y. (chmn. com. fed. legislation 1984-87), ABA. Federal civil litigation, Constitutional, Criminal. Office: Skadden Arps Slate Meagher & Flom 4 Times Sq New York NY 10036-6522

GLENDENNING, DON MARK, lawyer; b. Dallas, Dec. 24, 1953; s. Don Thomas and Nancy (Malloy) G.; m. Carol Peterson, Dec. 30, 1979. BA, Rice U., 1976; JD, Stanford U., 1979. Bar: Tex. 1979. Assoc. Rain Harrell Emery Young & Doke, Dallas, 1979-85; ptnr. Rain, Harrell, Emery, Young & Doke, Dallas, 1985-87; shareholder Locke Liddell & Sapp (formerly Locke Purnell Rain Harrell, P.C.), Dallas, 1987-98; ptnr. Locke Liddell & Sapp LLP, Dallas, 1999—. Pres. Human Rights Initiative North Tex., Tex.; bd. dirs. Nat. Tree Trust, Dallas Trees and Park Found.; chmn. Thanks-Giving Found.; bd. dirs., pres. Scenic Dallas; bd. dirs. Scenic Tex., Dallas Zool. Soc. Republican. Presbyterian. Corporate, general, Securities. Office: Locke Liddell & Sapp LLP 2200 Ross Ave Ste 2200 Dallas TX 75201-6776

GLENDON, MARY ANN, law educator; b. 1938; BA, U. Chgo., 1959, JD, 1961, M Comparative Law, 1963. Bar: Ill. 1964, Mass. 1980. Legal intern. EEC, Brussels, Belgium, 1963; assoc. Mayer, Brown & Platt, Chgo., 1963-68; prof. Boston Coll., 1968-86; vis. prof. Harvard U., 1974-75, prof., 1986—. Vis. prof. U. Chgo., 1983, 84, 86. Author: Rights Talk, 1991, A Nation Under Lawyers, 1994, A World Made New: Eleanor Roosevelt and the Universal Declaration of Human Rights, 2001. Foreign Law fellow U. Libre de Bruxelles, 1962-63, Ford Found. fellow, 1975-76. Mem. Am. Acad. Arts & Scis., Pres.'s Coun. Bioethics. Office: Harvard U Law Sch Cambridge MA 02138

GLENN, ROBERT EASTWOOD, lawyer; b. Catlettsburg, Ky., Dec. 24, 1929; s. Albert Sidney and Pauline Elizabeth (Eastwood) G.; m. Clydenne Reinhard, Mar. 16, 1956; children: Pauline Glenn O'Brien, Robert Eastwood Jr. BS cum laude, Washington and Lee U., 1951, JD cum laude, 1953. Bar: Va. 1952, U.S. Dist. Ct. (we. dist.) Va. 1958, U.S. Ct. Appeals (4th cir.) 1974, U.S. Supreme Ct. 1975, U.S. Tax Ct. 1994. Assoc. Eggleston & Holton, Roanoke, Va., 1957-60; ptnr. Glenn, Feldmann, Darby & Goodlatte, Roanoke, 1960—2003, of counsel, 2003—. Mem. Va. Bd. Bar Examiners, Richmond, 1982—, pres., 1993—. Mem. State Coun. for Higher Edn. for Va., 1980-84; rector Radford (Va.) U., 1975-79, bd. visitors, 1972-79; chmn. Roanoke City Rep. Com., 1968-70, Roanoke Valley ARC, 1974-76; mem. Va. Found. for Humanities, 1995-01. Fellow: Va. Bar Found., ABA Found.; mem.: ABA, Roanoke Bar Assn. (pres. 1980—81), Va. Bar Assn., Roanoke Regional C. of C. (pres. 1988), Shenandoah Club (pres. 2001—03), Roanoke Country Club, Order of Coif, Beta Gamma Sigma. Roman Catholic. Communications, Corporate, general, Property, real (including real estate development, water). Home: 3101 Allendale St SW Roanoke VA 24014-3118 Office: Glenn Feldmann Darby & Goodlatte 210 1st St SW Ste 200 Roanoke VA 24011-1607 E-mail: rglenn@gfdg.com.

GLENNON, CHARLES EDWARD, retired judge, lawyer; b. Monticello, Ill., Apr. 5, 1942; s. William Edward and Beatrice Jane (Pierson) G.; m. Sylvia Ann McClintock, Aug. 24, 1965 (div. Aug. 1972); children: David, Caroline; m. Victoria Louise Pearre, Oct. 26, 1974 (div. May 2001); 1 child, Andrew. BA, U. Ill., 1964, JD, 1966. Bar: Ill. 1966, U.S. Supreme Ct. 1974. Assoc. Fellheimer & Fellheimer, Pontiac, Ill., 1968-73; ptnr. Gomien & Glennon Ltd., Dwight, Ill., 1973-75; cir. judge State of Ill., Pontiac, 1976-98; temporarily recalled to bench, 1999, 2003; chief judge 11th cir., 1991-95. Lectr., author criminal law Ill. Village atty., Dwight, 1973-75; chmn. Salvation Army Adv. Bd., Pontiac, 1976; chmn. criminal law com. Ill. Jud. Conf., 1989-99, del., mem. exec. com., 1993-98; former mem. Regional Youth Planning Commn., Livingston County Commn. on Children and Youth; mng. dir. Nat. Arts Found., 1998—. With U.S. Army, 1966-68. Fellow Ill. Bar Found.; mem. Livingston County Bar Assn. (pres. 1991-93), Ill. Bar Assn., Ill. Judges Assn., Am. Assn. Juvenile and Family Ct. Judges, Lions, Rotary, Elks. Republican. Episcopalian. Home: 402 Carol Ct Pontiac IL 61764 also: N1930 Beach Rd Lake Geneva WI 53147 E-mail: chasness@aol.com.

GLICK, CYNTHIA SUSAN, lawyer; b. Sturgis, Mich., Aug. 6, 1950; d. Elmer Joseph and Ruth Edna (McCally) G. AB, Ind. U., 1972; JD, Ind. U.-Indpls., 1978. Bar: Ind. 1978, U.S. Dist. Ct. (so. dist.) Ind. 1978, U.S. Dist. Ct. (no. dist.) Ind. 1981, U.S. Supreme Ct. 2000. Adminstrv. asst. Gov. Otis R. Bowen of Ind., 1973-76; dep. pros. atty. 35th Jud. Cir., LaGrange County, Ind., 1980-82, pros. atty., 1983—90; pvt. practice LaGrange, Ind., 1979—. Campaign aide Ind. Rep. State Ctr. Com., Indpls., 1972-73; chmn. La Grange County Rep. Ctrl. com. Named Hon. Spkr., Ind. Ho. of Reps., 1972, Sagamore of the Wabash, Gov. of Ind., 1974. Fellow Ind. Bar Found.; mem. ABA, Ind. State Bar Assn., LaGrange County Bar Assn. (pres. 1983-86), DAR, Order Eastern Star, Phi Delta Phi, Delta Zeta. Methodist. General practice. Home and Office: 113 W Spring St Lagrange IN 46761-1843

GLICK, LESLIE ALAN, lawyer; b. N.Y.C., May 22, 1946; s. Leo S. and Sylvia (Hall) G. BS, Cornell U., 1967, JD, 1970. Bar: N.Y. 1971, D.C. 1971, Md. 1974, U.S. Ct. Internat. Trade 1971, U.S. Supreme Ct. 1974. Ptnr. Porter Wright Morris & Arthur, Washington, 1987—. Author: Multilateral Trade Negotiations, 1984, Trading with Saudi Arabia, 1980, Guide to U.S. Customs and Trade Laws, 1991, 2d edit., 1996, Understanding the North American Free Trade Agreement, 1993, 2d edit., 1995; author, co-editor, contbr. Manual for the Practice of U.S. International Trade Law, 2001. Active Dem. State Cen. com., Md., 1982-84; chmn. adv. com. on Consumer Affairs, Montgomery County, Md., 1982-84. Mem. Fed. Bar Assn. (chmn. internat. law sect. 1986-88). Public international, Legislative, Trademark and copyright. Office: Porter Wright Morris & Arthur 1919 Pennsylvania Ave NW Washington DC 20006

GLICKMAN, FRED ELLIOTT, lawyer; b. N.Y.C., Sept. 1, 1946; s. Stanley and Anita (Lipow) G.; m. Margery Feinschreiber, Apr. 24, 1977; children— David, Michael, Laura. B.A., Dartmouth Coll., 1968; M.B.A., U. Chgo., 1971; J.D., Columbia U., 1974. Bar: Ill. 1974, Fla. 1982, U.S. Dist. Ct. (no. dist.) Ill. 1974, U.S. Dist. Ct. (so. dist.) Fla. 1983, U.S. Tax Ct. 1978. Assoc. Sonnenschein, Carlin, Nath & Rosenthal, Chgo., 1974-75; atty. Allied Van Lines, Broadview, Ill., 1975-76; assoc. Fishel and Kahn, Chgo., 1976-77, Laser Schostok, Kolman & Flank, Chgo., 1977-81; ptnr. Feinschreiber & Assocs., Key Biscayne and Miami, Fla., 1981-85; sole practice, Miami, 1985— . Contbr. articles to profl jours. Mem. S. Miami Kendall Bar Assn (bd. dirs. 1996—, pres. 2002—). State civil litigation, Corporate, general, Estate planning. Home: 13740 SW 78th Ct Miami FL 33158-1108 Office: Ste 508 9200 S Dadeland Blvd Miami FL 33156-2713

GLICKMAN, GLADYS, lawyer, writer; b. N.Y.C., Feb. 28, 1920; d. Reuben and Sadie (Levy) Glickman. BA, Bklyn. Coll., 1939; JD, DePaul U., 1959. Bar: Ill. 1959, N.Y. 1961. Editor Bur. Nat. Affairs, Inc., Washington, 1942-44, Research Inst. Am., N.Y.C., 1944-48; asst. dir., labor rels. rsch. Continental Can Co., N.Y.C., 1948-51; supr. Wage Stabilization Bd., N.Y.C., 1951-53; writer, editor Matthew Bender and Co., N.Y.C., 1959—; corp. counsel Parents Magazine Enterprises, Inc., N.Y.C., 1961-78; v.p. legal Gruner and Jahr, USA Pub., N.Y.C., 1978-93. Author: Franchising, 1969, (with others) Warrens Forms of Agreement, 1964. Mem. ABA, N.Y. County Lawyers Assn. (com. mem.), Ill. State Bar Assn. Jewish. E-mail: Glickfran@aol.com.

GLICKMAN, STEPHEN, state supreme court justice; Ptnr. Zuckerman, Spaeder, Goldstein, Taylor & Kolker, 1980-99; judge D.C. Ct. Appeals, 1999—. Office: DC Ct Appeals 6th Pl 500 Indiana Ave NW Ste 2 Washington DC 20001-2131

GLICKSTEIN, HOWARD ALAN, law educator; b. N.Y.C., Sept. 14, 1929; s. Samuel and Fannie (Greenblat) G. BA magna cum laude, Dartmouth Coll., 1951; LLB, Yale U., 1954; LLM, Georgetown U., 1962. Bar: N.Y. 1954, U.S. Supreme Ct. 1962, D.C. 1980. Assoc. Proskauer, Rose, Goetz & Mendelsohn, N.Y.C., 1956-60; staff atty. Civil Rights divsn. Dept. of Justice, 1960-65; gen. counsel U.S. Commn. on Civil Rights, Washington, 1965-68, staff dir., 1968-71. Cons. in law, 1971-73; adj. prof., dir. Ctr. for Civil Rights U. Notre Dame, 1973-75; prof., dir. equal employment litigation clinic Howard U. Sch. Law, Washington, 1976-80; dir. Task Force on Civil Rights Reorgn., Exec. Office of Pres., Washington, 1977-78; dean, prof. U. Bridgeport Sch. Law, Conn., 1980-85, Touro Coll. Law, 1986—. Contbr. articles to profl. jours. Bd. dirs. Fund for Modern Cts.; commr. Suffolk County Human Rights Commn.; chair Town Huntington Bd. Ethics and Fin. Disclosure, 1999—. With U.S. Army, 1954-56. Mem. ABA (former chmn. affirmative action com., sect. legal edn. and admissions to bar), Soc. Am. Law Tchrs. (bd. dirs., former pres.), N.Y. State Commn. on Fiduciary

Appointments, N.Y. State Bar Assn. (mem. spl. com. pub. trust and confidence in the legal sys.). Office: Touro Coll Sch Law Coll Law 300 Nassau Rd Huntington NY 11743-4346

GLIDDEN, JOHN REDMOND, lawyer; b. Sanford, Maine, July 24, 1936; s. Kenneth Eugene and Kathryn (Gilpatrick) G.; m. Jacqueline R. Scales, Aug. 6, 1964; children— Ian, Claire, Jason Student, U. Wis., 1954-55; BS, Coe Coll., 1958; LL.B., U. Iowa, 1961. Bar: Iowa 1961, Ill. 1965. Assoc. firm Williams & Hartzell, Carthage, Ill., 1965-67; ptnr. Hartzell, Glidden, Tucker & Hartzell and predecessor firms, Carthage, 1969—. City atty. City of Carthage, 1969— Capt., judge advocate USAF, 1961-65. Mem. ABA, Fed. Bar Assn., Ill. Bar Assn., Iowa Bar Assn., Hancock County Bar Assn., Am. Trial Lawyers Assn., Ill. Trial Lawyers Assn. (governing bd. 1973-80), Am. Legion, Carthage Golf Club (bd. dirs. 1967—), Phi Delta Phi, Sigma Nu. Home: PO Box 70 1625 N Highway 94 Carthage IL 62321-3435 Office: PO Box 70 Carthage IL 62321-0070

GLIEBERMAN, HERBERT ALLEN, lawyer; b. Chgo., Dec. 6, 1930; s. Elmer and Jean (Gerber) G.; m. Evelyn Eraci; children— Ronald, Gale, Joel Student, U. Ill., 1947, Roosevelt U., 1948-50; JD, Chgo. Kent Coll. Law, 1953. Bar: Ill. 1954, D.C. 1987. Pvt. practice, Chgo., 1954—; lectr. Chgo. Kent. Coll. Law, Ill. Inst. Continuing Legal Edn. Lectr. in field numerous instns. including ABA, ATLA, Am. Acad Matrimonial Lawyers, Inst. Law Inst., others. Author: Some Syndromes of Love, 1965, Know Your Legal Rights, 1974, Confessions of A Divorce Lawyer, 1975, Closed Marriage, 1978, Four Weekends to an Ideal Marriage, 1981; former host 2 radio shows for NBC Sta. WMAQ: Ask the Lawyer, Law and Controversy; contbr. articles to profl. jours. Former trustee Chgo. Kent. Coll. Law; former bd. dirs. Chgo. Coun. on Alcoholism. Mem. Am. Acad. Matrimonial Lawyers (cert. of appreciation 1967), Decologue Soc. Lawyers (cert. of appreciation 1965, 66, 68), Assn. Trial Lawyers Am. (cert. of appreciation 1973), Ill. Trial Lawyers Assn. (cert. of appreciation 1974), ABA, Ill. State Bar Assn., Chgo. Bar Assn. Jewish (bd. dirs., pres. Temple) Family and matrimonial. Office: 19 S La Salle St Chicago IL 60603-1401 Fax: (312) 236-3417. E-mail: hglieber@aol.com.

GLIEGE, JOHN GERHARDT, lawyer; b. Chgo., Aug. 3, 1948; s. Gerhardt John and Jane (Heidke) Gliege; children: Gerhardt, Stephanie, Kristine. BA, Ariz. State U., 1969, MPA, 1970, JD, 1974. Bar: Ariz. 1974. Pvt. practice, Scottsdale, Ariz., 1974-81, Flagstaff, Ariz., 1981-94, 98—, 1998—, Sedona, Ariz., 1994-97, Williams, Ariz., 1997-98. Prof. paralegal studies No. Ariz. U., Flagstaff, 1981—83, prof. urban planning and cmty. devel., 1984—99; prof. paralegal studies Yavapai C.C., Prescott, Ariz., 1995—97, Coconino C.C., 2001—. Administrative and regulatory, Environmental, Municipal (including bonds). Address: PO Box 1388 Flagstaff AZ 86002-1388 E-mail: jgliege@earthlink.net.

GLINIECKI, JUDITH YVONNE, lawyer; b. Mt. Gilead, Ohio, Feb. 2, 1966; d. August Conrad and Valerie (Bloom) Gliniecki; m. Sergiusz Szeremeta, June 17, 1995; 1 child, Natalia Teresa. BA, Wellesley (Mass-)Coll., 1988; JD, Harvard U., Cambridge, Mass., 1991. Bar: (Ohio) 1991. Assoc. Vorys, Sater, Seymour and Pease, Columbus, Ohio, 1991—94; counsel Hunton & Williams, Warsaw, 1994—2002; jr. ptnr. Law Office Piontek, Rymar, Slazak, Wisniewski & Assocs. L.P., Warsaw, 2002—. Contbr. articles to Warsaw Bus. Jour. Corporate, general, Private international, Intellectual property. Office: Piontek Rymar Slazak Wisniewski ul Swietojerska 5/7 Warsaw 00236 Poland Office Fax: +48226350617. E-mail: j.gliniecki@lawyer.com.pl.

GLINN, FRANKLYN BARRY, lawyer; b. Newark, Oct. 22, 1943; s. Dave and Gertrude (Weinstein) G.; m. Sandra Lee Scales, Nov. 3, 1943; children: MacAdam Jordan, Dara Elisabeth, Daniel Garrett. BAE, U. Fla., 1965, JD, 1968. Bar: Fla. 1969, U.S. Ct. Appeals (5th cir.) 1969, U.S. Dist. Ct. (so. dist.) Fla. 1970. Assoc. Ser, Greenspahn & Keyfetz, Miami, Fla., 1969-70, Ser & Keyfetz, 1970-72, Rabin, Sassoon & Ratiner, Miami, Fla., 1972-74; ptnr. Ratiner & Glinn, Miami, Fla., 1974—2000, Glinn & Somera, P.A., Miami, Fla., 2000—. Mem. ABA, Am. Judicature Soc., Am. Trial Lawyers Assn., Acad. Fla. Trial Lawyers, Am. Arbitration Assn. Democrat. Jewish. State civil litigation, Personal injury (including property damage), Workers' compensation. Office: Ste 401 2100 Coral Way Miami FL 33145-2657

GLINSEK, GERALD JOHN, lawyer; b. Akron, Ohio, Jan. 16, 1939; s. Rudolph Paul and Angela Louise (Stanger) G.; m. Karen Rosemary Mehen, Oct. 17, 1968 (div. Aug. 1990); children: Kelli, Daniel; m. Maureen Louise Nuosce, May 7, 1994 (dec. Aug. 1998); 1 child from previous marriage, Rebecca Ann; m. Debra K. Gable, Oct. 22, 2002. BA, U. Akron, 1963, JD, 1967. Bar: Ohio 1967, U.S. Dist. Ct. (no. dist.) Ohio 1969, U.S. Ct. Appeals (6th cir. 1986), U.S. Supreme Ct. 1986. Asst. pros. atty. Summit County Prosecutors Office, Akron, 1967-71; pvt. practice Akron, 1971—. With U.S. Army, 1957. Mem. ABA, Ohio Bar Assn., Akron Bar Assn. (treas. 1981), Summit County Legal Aid Soc. (pres. 1978-82), Phi Kappa Tau (advisor 1982—). Democrat. Roman Catholic. Avocations: travel, skiing. Criminal, Family and matrimonial, Personal injury (including property damage). Home: 1861 Wiltshire Rd Akron OH 44313-6101 Office: 88 S Portage Path Akron OH 44303-1023

GLITZENSTEIN, ERIC ROBERT, lawyer; b. N.Y.C., July 29, 1957; s. Irving and Gertrude (Weinstein) G. BA, Johns Hopkins U., 1978; JD magna cum laude, Georgetown U., 1981. Bar: D.C. 1982, U.S. Ct. Appeals (D.C. cir.) 1982, U.S. Supreme Ct. 1988. Law clk. to Judge Thomas Flannery, U.S. Dist. Ct. for D.C., Washington, 1981-82; dir. Freedom of Info. Clearinghouse, Washington, 1982-83; staff atty. Pub. Citizen Litigation Group, Washington, 1983-89; of counsel Harmon, Curran, Gallagher & Spielberg, Washington, 1989—; mng. ptnr. Meyer & Glitzenstein, Washington, 1993—; pres. Wildlife Adv. Project, Washington, 1999—. Adj. prof. Georgetown U. Law Ctr., 1993-99. Co-author: Judicial Record of Robert Bork, 1987, Litigation under FOIA and Privacy Act 1985-91; contbr. articles to profl. jours. Recipient First Amendment award Playboy Found., 1989. Mem. ABA (vice chmn. com. on govt. info. 1990-93), Fed. Bar Assn. (chmn. com. on govt. info. 1989—, mem. exec. com. on adminstrv. law 1989-90), D.C. Bar. Office: Meyer & Glitzenstein 1601 Connecticut Ave NW Washington DC 20009-1035

GLOSBAND, DANIEL MARTIN, lawyer; b. Salem, Mass., July 3, 1944; s. Leon Glosband and Ruth Pauline (Wentworth) Glosband School; m. Merrily Cotton, Dec. 23, 1967; children: Alexander, Gabriel, Oliver. BA, U. Mass., 1966; JD, Cornell, U., 1969. Bar: Mass. 1969, U.S. Dist. Ct. Mass. 1970, U.S. Ct. Appeals (1st cir.) 1971, U.S. Dist. Ct. Conn. 1971, U.S. Dist. Ct. Vt. 1974, U.S. Supreme Ct. 1982. Assoc., then ptnr. firm Widett & Widett, Boston, 1969-75; ptnr. Goldstein & Manello, Boston, 1976-87, Goodwin, Procter LLP, Boston, 1988—. Advisor Am. Law Inst. Transnat. Insolvency Project, 1994—2000. Contbr. numerous articles on bankruptcy to profl. jours. Fellow: Mass. Bar Found., Am. Bar Found., Am. Coll. Bankruptcy (sec. 2001—); mem.: ABA (sect. on corps., chmn. internat. bankruptcy com. 1990—95), Boston Bar Assn. (chmn. bankruptcy com. 1977—80), Mass. Bar Assn. (chmn. bankruptcy com. 1980—83), Internat. Bar Assn. (sect. bus. law, vice chmn. insolvency and creditors rights com. 1997—2000, del. UN Commn. Internat. Trade Law). Democrat. Jewish. Bankruptcy. Home: 34 Atlantic Ave Swampscott MA 01907-2404 Office: Goodwin Procter LLP Exchange Pl Boston MA 02109-2803 E-mail: dglosband@goodwinprocter.com.

GLOSE, HERBERT JAMES, lawyer, educator; b. Buffalo, N.Y., Nov. 17, 1957; s. Herbert John and Bernadine Margaret Glose; m. Anne Glose, Mar. 20, 1982; children: Herbie, Lauren, Patrick. Student, U. Rochester, 1975-76; BA magna cum laude, U. Notre Dame, 1979; JD cum laude, SUNY, Amherst, 1982. Bar: N.Y. 1983, U.S. Dist. Ct. (we. dist.) N.Y. 1983. Ptnr. Moot & Sprague, Buffalo, N.Y., 1983-90, Giardino & Schober, LLP, Buffalo, 1990-97, Harris Beach LLP, Hamburg, N.Y., 1997—. Counsel to bd. United Way Buffalo and Erie County, 1990—; mem. adv. bd. Kids Voting N.Y., Buffalo, 1996—. Bd. dirs. Taste of Buffalo, 1990—, chair, 1994; bd. dirs., v.p. Buffalo Jr. C. of C., 1985-90; bd. dirs. Amherst Meals on Wheels, 2001—. Named Torchbearer 1996 Olympic Torch Run, U.S. Olympic Com./United Way, Atlanta, 1996. Mem. N.Y. State Bar Assn., Bar Assn. Erie County (corp. law com. 1983—, chair 1996-99), St. Benadicts Golf League, Amherst (N.Y.) C. of C. Avocations: golf, coaching little league baseball, hockey dad. Corporate, general, Finance, Non-profit and tax-exempt organizations. Office: Harris Beach LLP One Grimsby Dr Hamburg NY 14075

GLOSSER, JEFFREY MARK, lawyer; b. 1936; married; 1 child. BS in Econs. with distinction, U. Pa., 1958; LLB, Harvard U., 1961. Bar: D.C. 1962. Law clk. U.S. Ct. Claims, 1963-64; assoc. Emery & Wood, Washington, 1965-69; ptnr. Jeffrey M. Glosser, P.C., Washington, 1969-86, Whiteford, Taylor & Preston, Washington, 1987-95. Instr. CLE courses sponsored by D.C. Bar, 1976-95. Mem. ABA (adminstrv. law sect., various coms.), D.C. Bar Assn. (numerous coms.), Fed. Bar Assn. (U.S. Claims Ct. com.), Fed. Cir. Bar Assn. (rules com. 1985-95). Administrative and regulatory, Federal civil litigation, Legislative. E-mail: glosser@mac.com.

GLOSSER, WILLIAM LOUIS, lawyer; b. Johnstown, Pa., Aug. 30, 1929; s. Saul I. and Eva (Hurwitz) G.; m. Patricia Freeman, Feb. 5, 1932; children: Alix Paul, Jill P., Jonathan. BS, Temple U., 1951; LLB, U. Pa., 1954. Bar: Pa. 1954, Fla. 1956, U.S. Dist. Ct. (we. dist.) Pa. 1956, U.S. Dist. Ct. (so. dist.) Fla. 1957. Assoc. Broad and Cassel, Miami Beach, Fla., 1956-57; sole practice Coral Gables, Fla., 1957-61, Johnstown, 1962—. Magistrate judge U.S. Dist. Ct. (we. dist.) Pa., 1972-93; corp. sec., dir. Glosser Bros., Inc., Johnstown, 1969-85; of counsel Smorto, Persio, Webb & McGill, Johnstown, 1988—. Bd. dirs. Lee Hosp., Johnstown, Greater Johnstown (Pa.) Cmty. Found., ret.; mem. Johnstown adv. coun. Pa. Human Rels. Commn.; pres. United Jewish Fedn. Johnstown, 1970-75, 2000—; chmn. fund drive United Way, 1985, pres., 1987-88; bd. dirs. Mt. Aloysius Coll., 1980-84, Cmty. Found. Greater Johnstown, Pa., 1990—. With U.S. Army, 1954-56. Mem. Pa. Bar Assn., Fla. Bar Assn., Cambria County Bar Assn., Greater Johnstown C. of C. (pres. 1985), Rotary (pres. 1990), B'nai B'rith (pres. lodge 1965-67, 83-84). Jewish. Personal injury (including property damage), Probate (including wills, trusts), Securities. Home: 521 Luzerne St Johnstown PA 15905-2324 Office: Smorto Persio Webb & McGill 430 Main St Johnstown PA 15901-1823

GLOTTA, RONALD DELON, lawyer; b. Lajunta, Colo., Mar. 18, 1941; s. John Wallace and Marian (Kisner) G.; m. Sharon S. Glotta, Aug. 27, 1961 (div. Mar. 1986); children: Holly Ann, Jeffrey Delon; m. Marietta Lynn Baba, June 23, 1990 (div. Oct. 1998). BA with honors, U. Kans., 1963; JD, U. Mich., 1966. Bar: Mich. 1966. Atty. Marcus, McCroskey, Libner, Reamon, Williams & Dilley, Muskegon, Mich., 1966-68; ptnr. Philo, Maki, Moore, Pitts, Ravitz, Glotta, Cockrel & Robb, Detroit, 1968-70; prin. Glotta & Adelman, Detroit, 1970-85, Glotta, Rawlings & Skutt, Detroit, 1985-96, Glotta, Skutt & Assts, Detroit, 1996—. Mem. Phi Beta Kappa. Labor (including EEOC, Fair Labor Standards Act, labor-management relations, NLRB, OSHA), Personal injury (including property damage), Workers' compensation. Home: 2065 Hyde Park Rd Detroit MI 48207-3885 E-mail: rglotta@winstarmail.com.

GLOVER, DURANT MURRELL, lawyer; b. Wilmington, N.C., Mar. 6, 1951; s. Murrell Kelso and Erma Elizabeth (Williams) G.; m. Carol Ann Marquett, Dec. 16, 1978. AB, Duke U., 1973; JD with honors, U. N.C., 1976. Bar: N.C. 1976, U.S. Dist. Ct. (mid. dist.) N.C. 1976, U.S. Ct. Appeals (4th cir.) 1977, U.S. Supreme Ct. 1980. Assoc. Frassineti & Shaw, Greensboro, N.C., 1976-77; ptnr. Frassineti & Glover, Greensboro, 1977—. Mem., counsel Tarheel Triad Girl Scout Council Inc., Colfax, N.C., 1980—. Mem. N.C. Bar Assn., Greensboro Bar Assn. (editor Greensboro Bar News 1983-87, bd. dirs. 1987-89), Order of Coif. Republican. Presbyterian. Commercial, consumer (including collections, credit), Probate (including wills, trusts), Property, real (including real estate development, water). Home: 405 Staunton Dr Greensboro NC 27410-6070 Office: Frassineti & Glover PO Box 1799 Greensboro NC 27402-1799 E-mail: dmglover@bellsouth.net.

GLOVER, HARRY ALLEN, JR., lawyer; b. Chgo., Mar. 9, 1949; s. Harry Allen and Charlotte (Ley) G.; m. Mary Kathryn Burnette, July 18, 1986; children: Bryan Timothy, Ashley Marie, Kyle Ley. BA, U. Va., 1971, JD, 1975. Bar: Va. 1975, U.S. Ct. Appeals (6th cir.) 1975, U.S. Ct. Appeals (4th cir.) 1978. Law clk. U.S. Ct. Appeals (6th cir.), Danville, Ky., 1975-76; assoc. Woods, Rogers & Hazlegrove, Roanoke, Va., 1976-81, ptnr., 1982—. Mem. editorial bd. Va. Law Rev., 1973-75. Mem. ABA, Va. Bar Assn., Va. State Bar (bd. govs. adminstrv. law sect. 1985-89, 99—), Order of Coif, Phi Beta Kappa. Corporate, general, Administrative and regulatory, Estate planning. Office: Woods Rogers & Hazlegrove PO Box 14125 Roanoke VA 24038-4125

GLOVSKY, SUSAN G. L. lawyer; b. Boston, Apr. 16, 1955; d. Leonard B. and Marilyn S. (Shapiro) Loitherstein; m. Steven M. Glovsky, May 25, 1980; 1 child, Lowell Elliott. BS in Chemistry, U. Vt., 1977; JD, Boston U., 1980. Bar: Mass. 1980, Mich. 1980, U.S. Dist. Ct. (ea. dist.) Mich. 1980, U.S. Patent Office 1981, N.Y. 1982, U.S. Dist. Ct. Mass. 1982, U.S. Ct. Appeals (1st cir.) 1982, U.S. Ct. Appeals (fed. cir.) 1991, U.S. Supreme Ct. 1995. Assoc. Levin, Levin, Garvett & Dill, Southfield, Mich., 1980-81, Ladas & Parry, N.Y.C., 1981-82, Dahlen & Gatewood, Boston, 1982-83; ptnr. Dahlen & Glovsky, Boston, 1983-85; pvt. practice Boston and Salem, Mass., 1985-93; of counsel Hamilton, Brook, Smith & Reynolds, Mass., 1993-97, prin., 1998—. Adj. prof. Suffolk U. Law Sch. Mem. ABA, Mass. Bar Assn., Boston Bar Assn., Boston Patent Law Assn. (past pres., chmn. litigation com. 1989-2001), Am. Arbitration Assn. (panel arbitrators 1985—, co-chmn. intellectual property adv. com. 1999—). Jewish. Avocations: swimming, skiing. Federal civil litigation, Patent, Trademark and copyright. Home: 36 Shaw Dr Wayland MA 01778-3214 Office: Hamilton Brook Smith & Reynolds 530 Virginia Rd PO Box 9133 Concord MA 01742 E-mail: susan.glovsky@hbsr.com.

GLYNN, GERARD FRANCIS, law educator; b. Richmond Heights, Mo., May 9, 1963; s. Lawrence Francis and Marie Margaret (Costello) G.; m. Angela Katherine Halladay, Aug. 20, 1988; children, Kevin Joseph, Jacob Francis, Grace Marion. BA, St. Louis U., 1985; JD, Am. U., 1989, MS, 1991; LLM, Georgetown U., 1993. Bar: D.C. 1989, Md. 1990, Fla. 1992, Ark. 1995. Asst. dir. devel. Habitat for Humanity, Americus, Ga., 1985-86; Prettyman fellow Georgetown U., Washington, 1989-91; clin. prof. Fla. State U., Tallahassee, 1991-94; dir. legal clinic U. Ark., Little Rock, 1994—99; dir. clin. programs Barry U., 2000—. Mem. ABA, NACC. Roman Catholic. Avocations: running, biking, swimming. Office: Barry U Sch Law 6441 E Colonial Dr Orlando FL 32807

GNICHTEL, WILLIAM VAN ORDEN, lawyer; b. Summit, N.J., Jan. 11, 1934; s. William Stone and Edith Parrot (Van Orden) G.; m. Emily Hopkins Martenet, July 11, 1959 (dec.); children: William Van Orden Jr., Edwin Martenet; m. Mary B. Gayley, June 7, 1996. BA, Trinity Coll., 1956; LLB, Columbia U., 1959. Bar: N.Y. 1961, Mass. 1997. Ptnr. Whitman & Ransom, N.Y.C., 1968-88, resident ptnr., 1980-85; ptnr. Chadbourne & Parke, N.Y.C., 1988-92; spl. counsel Law Firm of Salah Al-Hejailan, Riyadh, Saudi Arabia, 1986-95. Co-chmn. pub. policy com. bus. law sect. Boston Bar Assn.; lectr. in field. Contbr. articles to profl. jours. Mem. Assn. of Bar of City of N.Y. (co-chmn. subcom. Com. Internat. Security Affairs), Union Club, Knickerbocker Club (N.Y.C.), Onteora Club (Tannersville, N.Y.; exec. vp. 1974-75, pres. 1976-77, bd. dirs. 1970-77), Masons, Phi Delta Phi. Episcopalian. Banking, Finance, Private international. Address: PO Box 431 Lincoln MA 01773-0431 E-mail: WVOGLAW@mindspring.com.

GODBEY, ROBERT CARSON, lawyer; b. Houston, June 7, 1953; s. Charles Perry and Bobbye Lee Godbey; m. Ellen Carson, June 2, 1979. BS, BSEE magna cum laude, So. Meth. U., 1975; JD cum laude, Harvard U., 1980. Bar: U.S. Patent Office, 1981, Hawaii 1988. Telecommunications engr. Southwestern Bell, Dallas, 1975-76, Tex. Instruments, Dallas, 1976-77; assoc. Peabody, Lambert & Meyers, Washington, 1980-84; asst. U.S. atty. U.S. Dept. of Justice, Washington, 1984-87, Honolulu, 1987-91; ptnr. Godbey Griffiths Reiss, 1991—. Mem. ABA, IEEE, Hawaii State Bar Assn. (past chmn. intellectual property sect. 1994-96, past chmn. tech. com., 1995-97), Phi Beta Kappa, Tau Beta Pi. General civil litigation, Intellectual property. Office: 2300 Pauahi Tower 1001 Bishop St Honolulu HI 96813-3429

GODBOLD, GENE HAMILTON, lawyer; b. Mullins, S.C., June 14, 1936; s. John Dalton and Mildred (Stalvey) G.; m. Janice Louise McKay, June 24, 1960; children: Lori McKay, Scott Hamilton, Stephanie Louise. BA, Furman U., Greenville, S.C., 1958; LLB, Tulane U., 1963. Bar: Fla. 1963, U.S. Dist. Ct. (mid. dist.) Fla. 1964, U.S. Ct. Appeals (5th cir.) 1964. Assoc. Maguire, Voorhis & Wells, Winter Park, Fla., 1963-68, ptnr., 1968-84, pres., 1978-84, Godbold, Allen, Brown and Builder, P.A., Winter Park, 1984-88, Goldbold & Downing, P.A., 1988-94, Godbold, Downing, Sheahan & Bill, P.A., 1994—. Served to 1st lt. U.S. Army, 1958-60. Mem. Fla. Bar, Orange County Bar Assn. (mem. exec. com. 1968-72, pres. 1971-72), Interlachen Country Club. State civil litigation, Property, real (including real estate development, water). Address: 222 W Comstock Ave Ste 101 Winter Park FL 32789-4272 E-mail: ggodbold@gdsblaw.com.

GODBOLD, JOHN COOPER, judge; b. Coy, Ala., Mar. 24, 1920; s. Edwin Condie and Elsie (Williamson) Godbold; m. Elizabeth Showalter, July 18, 1942; children: Susan, Richard, John C., Cornelia. BS, Auburn U., 1940; JD, Harvard U., 1948; LLD (hon.) , Samford U., 1981, Auburn U., 1988, Stetson U., 1994. Bar: Ala. 1948. With firm Richard T. Rives, Montgomery, 1948-49; ptnr. Rives & Godbold, 1949-51, Godbold & Hobbs and successor firms, 1951-66; cir. judge U.S. Ct. Appeals (5th cir.), 1966-81, chief judge, 1981, U.S. Ct. Appeals (11th cir.), 1981-86, sr. judge, 1987—; dir. Fed. Jud. Ctr., Washington, 1987-90. Mem. Fed. Jud. Ctr. Bd., 1976—81. With field arty. U.S. Army, 1941—46. Mem.: FBA, ABA, Montgomery County Bar Assn., Ala. Bar Assn., Phi Kappa Phi, Omicron Delta Kappa, Alpha Tau Omega. Episcopalian. Office: US Ct Appeals 11th Circuit One Church Street Montgomery AL 36104

GODBOUT, ARTHUR RICHARD, JR., lawyer; b. Hartford, Conn., Oct. 7, 1957; s. Arthur Richard and Elizabeth Anne (Desmond); m. Elizabeth G. Godbout. BSBA, Georgetown U., 1979, JD, 1986. Bar: Conn. 1987. Pres. A.R. Godbout & Co., Avon, Conn., 1987—. Property, real (including real estate development, water). Home: 8 Cheltenham Way Avon CT 06001-2444 Office: PO Box 1175 Avon CT 06001-1175

GODDARD, CLAUDE PHILIP, JR., lawyer; b. Long Beach, Calif., Oct. 31, 1952; s. Claude Philip and Doris Marian (Dow) G.; m. Ellen Kohn, May 23, 1981; children: Marian Laura, Nora Margaret. BS with distinction, U.S. Naval Acad., 1974; JD cum laude, U. Pa., 1979. Bar: N.H. 1979, D.C. 1985, Va. 1999, U.S. Dist. Ct. D.C. 1989, U.S. Ct. Appeals (9th cir.) 1985, U.S. Ct. Appeals (fed. cir.) 1991. Ensign U.S. Navy, 1974, advanced through grades to lt. comdr., 1987, atty., 1979-87, resigned, 1987; assoc. Keck, Mahin & Cate, Washington, 1987-89, ptnr., 1990, Jenner & Block, Washington, 1990-95; shareholder Kilcullen, Wilson and Kilcullen, Chartered, Washington, 1995-99, Wickwire Gavin, P.C., Vienna, Va., 1999—. Federal civil litigation, General civil litigation, Government contracts and claims. E-mail: cgoddard@wickwire.com.

GODDARD, TERRY, state attorney general; BA, Harvard U., 1969; JD, Ariz. State U., 1976. Mayor City of Phoenix, 1983-90; of counsel Bryan Cave, Phoenix, 1990-94; atty. gen. State of Ariz., 2003—. Bd. dirs. Ariz. Theater Co., Ariz. Family and Child Devel. Ctr., Homeward Bound, Neighborhood Coalition of Phoenix; former pres. Nat. League of Cities, 1989; former chmn. Ariz. Mcpl. Water Users Assn., Maricopa Assn. Govts., govt. and non-profit group Valley of the Sun United Way, Regional Pub. Transp. Authority, Rebuild Am. Coalition; adv. bd. State and Local Legal Ctr. Comdr. USNR, 1970—. Mem. ABA, State Bar Ariz., Maricopa County Bar Assn. Democrat. Office: Atty Gen 1275 W Washington St Phoenix AZ 85007

GODFREY, CULLEN MICHAEL, lawyer; b. Ft. Worth, Apr. 8, 1945; s. Cullen Aubrey and Agnes (Eiland) G.; m. Melinda McDonald, Aug. 29, 1970. BA, U. Tex., 1968, JD, 1970. Bar: Tex. 1969, U.S. Dist. Ct. (we. dist.) Tex. 1971, U.S. Ct. appeals (5th cir.) 1979, U.S. Ct. Appeals (11th cir.) 1981. Ptnr. Sloan, Muller & Godfrey, Austin, Tex., 1969-72; staff atty. Hunt Oil Co., Dallas, 1972-74, Tesoro Petroleum Corp., San Antonio, 1974-75, sr. atty., 1975-78, asst. gen. counsel, 1978-82, FINA, Inc., Dallas, 1982-88, gen. counsel, 1988-90; v.p., sec., gen. counsel Am. Petrofina, Inc. (now FINA, Inc.), Dallas, 1990-95, sr. v.p., sec., gen. counsel, 1995-2000; vice chancellor, gen. counsel U. Tex. Sys., Austin, 2000—. Author: Legal Aspects of the Purchase and Sale of Oil and Gas Properties, 1992; contbr. articles to profl. jours. Bd. trustees Dallas Mus. Art, 1993-95, 98-2000; bd. dirs. United Way Met. Dallas, Inc., 1999-2000, gen. campaign chmn., 1999; bd. dirs. Dallas County Heritage Soc., 1998-2000; mem. exec. bd. dirs. Cir. 10, Boy Scouts Am., 1999-2000. Recipient Excellence in Corp. Practice award, Am. Corp. Counsel Assn., 1998, Anti-Defamation League Jurisprudence award, 1999. Fellow: Dallas Bar Found. (sustaining life fellow), Tex. Bar Found.(sustaining life fellow); mem.: Am. Laws Inst., Ctr. Am. and Internat. Law (rsch. fellow), Greater Dallas Crime Commn. (bd. dirs. 1991—2000, chmn. bd. dirs. 1997—99), Tex. Bus. Law Found. (bd. dirs. 1990—, chmn. bd. dirs. 1995—98), Tex. Bd. Legal Specialization (bd. cert. oil, gas and mineral law), State Bar Tex. (coll. mem. 1989—, coun. oil, gas and mineral law sect. 1992—95, coun. bus. law sect. 1998—, chmn. bus. law sect. 2002—03, Cert. Merit 1999—2003), ABA (chmn.subcom. on fgn. investment reporting, internat. law sect. 1984—87). Corporate, general, Oil, gas, and mineral, Private international. Office: U Tex Sys Office Gen Counsel 201 W 7th St Austin TX 78701 E-mail: mgodrey@utsystem.edu.

GODFREY, RICHARD CARTIER, lawyer; b. Harvey, Ill., Sept. 25, 1954; s. Richard L. and Rosemary (Cartier) G.; m. Alice Bacon Woolsey, Aug. 27, 1983; children: John Cartier, Polly Woolsey. BA magna cum laude, Augustana Coll., 1976; JD magna cum laude, Boston U., 1979. Bar: Ill. 1979, U.S. Dist.Ct. (no. dist.) Ill. 1979, U.S. Dist.Ct. (cen. dist.) Ill. 1988, U.S. Dist.Ct. (we. dist.) Mich. 1990, U.S. Dist.Ct. (no. dist.) Ind. 1999, U.S. Dist. Ct. Colo. 2002, U.S. Ct. Appeals (7th cir.) 1983, U.S. Ct. Appeals (6th cir.) 1988, U.S. Ct. Appeals (8th cir.) 1994, U.S. Ct. Appeals (10th cir.) 1996, U.S. Ct. Appeals (11th cir.) 1997, U.S. Ct. Appeals (5th & 9th cirs.) 1999, U.S. Ct. Appeals (2d. cir.) 2002, U.S. Ct. Appeals (1st cir.) 2003, U.S. Ct. Appeals (3d cir.) 2003, U.S. Claims Ct. 1990, U.S. Supreme Ct. 2000. Assoc. Kirkland & Ellis, Chgo., 1979-85, ptnr., 1985—. Mem. ABA, Ill. Bar Assn., Chgo. Bar Assn. Administrative and regulatory, Antitrust, Federal civil litigation. Home: 623 N Euclid Ave Oak Park IL 60302-1619 Office: Kirkland & Ellis Ste 6048 200 E Randolph Dr Chicago IL 60601

GODINER, DONALD LEONARD, lawyer; b. Bronx, N.Y., Feb. 21, 1933; s. Israel and Edith (Rubenstein) G.; m. Caryl Mignon Nussbaum, Sept. 7, 1958; children: Clifford, Kenneth. AB, NYU, 1953; JD, Columbia U., 1956. Bar: N.Y. 1956, Mo. 1972. Gen. counsel Stromberg-Carlson,

Rochester, N.Y., 1965-71; assoc. gen. counsel Gen. Dynamics Corp., St. Louis, 1971-73; v.p., gen. counsel Permaneer Corp., St. Louis, 1973-75; ptnr. Gallop, Johnson, Godiner, Morganstern & Crebs, St. Louis, 1975-80; sr. v.p., gen. counsel, sec. Laclede Gas Co., St. Louis, 1980-98; of counsel Stone, Leyton and Gershman, P.C., St. Louis, 1999—. Editor Columbia U. Law Rev., 1955-56. Served with U.S. Army, 1956-58. Mem.: ABA, Bar Assn. of Metropolitan St. Louis. Commercial, contracts (including sales of goods; commercial financing), Corporate, general, Utilities, public. Home: 157 Trails West Dr Chesterfield MO 63017-2553 Office: Stone Leyton & Gershman PC 7133 Forsyth Blvd Ste 500 Saint Louis MO 63105-2122

GODOFSKY, STANLEY, lawyer; b. N.Y.C., May 24, 1928; s. Eli and Lily (Deutsch) G.; m. Elaine Gloria Weiss, Dec. 15, 1951 (dec. Feb. 1994); m. Phyllis A. Schaevitz, Jan. 16, 2000. AB, Columbia U., 1949, JD, 1951. Bar: N.Y. 1951, U.S. Supreme Ct. 1961. Assoc. Rogers & Wells, and predecessors, N.Y.C., 1951-64, ptnr., 1965-89. Co-adj. lectr. Rutgers Law Sch., 1990-91, adj. prof., 1992-93; adj. prof. Nova U. Law Sch., 1991-93; spl. asst. counsel N.Y. State Crime Commn., 1952. Bd. editors Columbia Law Rev., 1950, bd. revising editors, 1951. Trustee Jewish Community Ctr. White Plains, N.Y., 1983-89; mem. commn. on law and social action Am. Jewish Congress, 1986-98. Mem. ABA, Am. Law Inst., N.Y. State Bar Assn., Assn. of Bar of City of N.Y., Internat. Assn. Jewish Lawyers and Jurists (bd. govs. Am. sect. 1990-98, exec. com. and coun. 1999—). Home: 17858 Deauville Ln Boca Raton FL 33496-2457 E-mail: jenice45@bellsouth.net.

GODONE-MARESCA, LILLIAN, lawyer; b. Buenos Aires, June 9, 1958; d. Armand C.E. Godone-Signanini and E. Nydia Soracco-Godone; m. Paul Alexander Maresca-Lowell (dec.); children: Catherine Victoria, Gerard Frank, Warren Paul. BA, Cath. U. Buenos Aires, 1975, MA, 1977, JD summa cum laude, 1979, advanced tchg. degree in jud. sci., 1981. Bar: Dist. Ct. Buenos Aires 1980, Calif. 1995, U.S. Dist. Ct. (ea. dist.) Calif. 1995, U.S. Dist. Ct. (so. dist.) Calif. 1998; lic. real estate broker, Calif. Advisor Sub-Sec. of State for Fgn. Trade, Buenos Aires, 1982; pvt. practice law Buenos Aires, 1982-86; therapist Ocean Pkwy. Developmental Ctr., N.Y., 1992; pvt. practice law Sacramento, 1995-96, San Diego, 1997—. Asst. instr. Cath. U., Buenos Aires, 1983-86; adj. instr. U.S. Internat. U., San Diego, spring 1998. Contbr. articles to profl. jours.; author of poetry. Vol. San Diego Vol. Lawyer Program, 1993-94, Legal Svcs. No. Calif., Sacramento, 1995-96; catechist St. Ignatius, Sacramento, 1995-96, St. Michael's, Poway, Calif., 1997-98. Mem. Internat. Soc. Poets (disting.), State Bar Calif., Mothers Twins Club. Republican. Roman Catholic. Avocations: spending time with her children, the right to life, writing. Bankruptcy, Family and matrimonial, Personal injury (including property damage). Home: 202 Calle Florecita Escondido CA 92029

GODOY, CESAR EDUARDO, lawyer, consultant; b. Guadalajara, Jalisco, Mexico, Dec. 28, 1963; s. Victor Manuel Godoy and Luz Maria Tejeda; m. Laura Lopez, Apr. 3, 1993; children: Cesar Eduardo, Andres Benjamin. Law degree, U. de Guadalajara, Guadalajara, Jalisco, Mexico, 1991—95, DDS, 1981—85. Cedula Profesional: Direccion de Profesiones 1995. Dir. penal issues and operational security department Ortega Abogados y Consultores, S.C., Guadalajara, Mexico, 1993—2003. Cons. Am. C. of C., Guadalajara, Mexico, 1994—2003. Securities, Personal injury (including property damage), Criminal. Office: Ortega Abogados y Consultores SC Avenida La Paz # 2530 Jalisco Guadalajara 44100 Mexico Office Fax: 01 52 33 36 15 27 96. E-mail: prosper@prodigy.net.mx.

GODWIN, KIMBERLY ANN, federal agency administrator, lawyer; b. Fargo, N.D., July 18, 1960; d. Robert Chandler and Kathryn Marie (Haney) G. BA in Polit. Sci., U. N.H., 1980; MS in Mass Comm., JD, Boston U., 1984. Bar: D.C. 1984, U.S. Supreme Ct. 1990. Legal intern Army Corps of Engrs., Waltham, Mass., 1983-84; assoc. Booz, Allen & Hamilton, Inc., Bethesda, Md., 1986-88; cons. Dept. State, Washington, 1984-86, asst. dir. comm. interagy. affairs, 1988-92, chief of policy diplomatic telecom. svc., 1992-96, dir. external affairs, 1997—. Cons. Elton Assocs., Inc., Arlington, Va., 1984—. Mem. ABA (vice chmn. internat. comm. com. 1989—), Phi Beta Kappa, Pi Sigma Alpha. Avocations: flying, tennis, skiing. Home: 6215 Walhonding Rd Bethesda MD 20816-2138 Office: Dept State IRM/EA Rm 4428 2201 C St NW Washington DC 20520-0001

GODWIN, ROBERT ANTHONY, lawyer; b. Phila., Apr. 24, 1938; s. Robert Anthony and Mary (MacElderry) G.; m. Isabel A. Tumelty; children: Cara G., Marisa A., Elise D. BS, Villanova U., 1960, JD, 1963. Bar: Pa. 1964, U.S. Dist. Ct. (ea. dist.) Pa. 1964, U.S. Ct. Appeals (3d cir.) 1964, U.S. Supreme Ct. 1980. Vol. defender, Phila., 1964; assoc. Eastburn & Gray, Doylestown, Pa., 1968-70; asst. pub. defender Bucks County, Pa., 1969-71; sole practice Newtown, Pa., 1971—73; ptnr. Timby and Godwin, 1973—75; atty. Robert A. Godwin & Assocs., 1975—. Served with JAG, USMC, 1964-68, JAG, USMCR, 1968-92, col. USMCR, ret. Mem. Pa. Bar Assn., Pa. Trial Lawyers Assn., Bucks County Bar Assn., Rotary. Federal civil litigation, State civil litigation, General practice. Office: Box 450 110 S State St Newtown PA 18940-3508

GOEBEL, HANS P. lawyer; Law Degree, ITAM, Mexico City, 1995; LLM (hon.) , Northwestern U., 1999. Lic.: atty. at law Inst. Tech. Autónomo Mex. Assoc. Jauregui, Navarrete, Nader Rojas, S., Mexico City, 1995—2002, ptnr., 2003—. Banking, Mergers and acquisitions, Corporate, general.

GOEBEL, JOHN J. lawyer, director; b. St. Charles, Mo., Feb. 3, 1930; s. Francis Joseph and Elizabeth (Lawler) G.; m. Margaret Mary Rooney, May 10, 1958; children— Laura, Margaret, John, Matthew BS, LL.B., St. Louis U., 1953. Bar: Mo. 1953, U.S. Dist. Ct. (ea. dist.) Mo. 1957. Jr. exec. Constrn. Escrow Service Inc., St. Louis, 1955-56; jr. ptnr. Bryan Cave LLP, St. Louis, 1956-66, ptnr., 1966-98, sr. counsel, 1998—. Served to 1st lt. USAF, 1953-55 Mem. ABA, St. Louis Bar Assn., Mo. Bar Assn., Bellerive Country Club, Noonday Club, Port Royal Club. Roman Catholic. Home: 245 Little Harbour Ln Naples FL 34102-7606 Office: Bryan Cave 1 Metropolitan Sq Ste 3600 Saint Louis MO 63102-2750 E-mail: jjgoebel@bryancavellp.com.

GOEBEL, WILLIAM HORN, lawyer; b. N.Y.C., Dec. 7, 1941; s. Harry H. and Maxine (Hamburger) G.; m. Barbara Golden, July 30, 1966; children: Jason, Pamela. AB, Columbia U., 1963; JD, NYU, 1966. Bar: N.Y. 1966. Assoc. Bernard Trencher, N.Y.C., 1966-69; real estate atty. J.C. Penney Co., Inc., N.Y.C., 1969-71; assoc. gen. counsel N.K. Winston Corp., N.Y.C., 1971-72, Teachers Ins. and Annuity Assn. Am./Coll. Retirement Equities Fund, N.Y.C., 1972-2000; bus. devel. and legal cons. Stewart Title Ins. Co., 2000—. Lectr. NYU Sch. Continuing Edn., 1985—; sr. coun. Team Leader, 1991-2000; mem. adv. bd. Commonwealth Land Title/Transamerica Title Ins. Co., 1992-2000; v.p. M.O.A. Enterprises, Inc./M.O.A Holdings, Inc., 1992-2000. Pres. Oyster Bay Jewish Ctr., 1976—78. Mem. Assn. of Bar of City of N.Y., N.Y. State Bar Assn. (fin. subcom. of real estate sect. 1998—, subcom. on zoning and land use planning), Barnard-Columbia Hillel Soc. (pres.'s coun. 2002—). Commercial, contracts (including sales of goods; commercial financing), Property, real (including real estate development, water). Office: Stewart Title Ins Co 4th Fl 300 E 42nd St New York NY 10017 E-mail: bgoebel@optonline.net., bgoebel@stewart.com.

GOECKELER, STEPHAN, lawyer; b. Wimbern, Germany, Aug. 10, 1965; s. Bruno Josef and Brigitte (Schubert) Goeckeler; m. Andrea Knocke, Nov. 10, 1989; children: Christoph Duncan, Nicholas Bruno, Lucas Connor. First state exam, U. Heidelberg, Germany, 1990, JD, 1992. Bar: Germany 1993, Calif. 1996. Assoc. Hengeler Mueller, Dusseldorf, Germany, N.Y.C., Morrison & Foerster, San Francisco, Palo Alto, Calif., 1995—97; ptnr. Flick Gocke Schaumburg, Bonn, Germany, 1997—. Mem. supervisory bd. Media! AG fuer innovative Medientechnologie, Munich, 2002—. Author: Die Gesellschaft buergerlichten Rechts, 1992, Die Virtuelle Hauptversammlung, 2002, Beck'sches Handbuch der AG, 2003. Commercial, contracts (including sales of goods; commercial financing), Corporate, general, Mergers and acquisitions. Office: Flick Gocke Schaumburg Johanna-Kinkel-Str 2-4 53175 Bonn Germany

GOELZER, DANIEL LEE, lawyer; b. Milw., Feb. 14, 1947; s. Gerald Howard and Roberta (Hart) G.; m. Angela C. Carcone, Jan. 9, 1988; children: Christina H., Mary E.; 1 child by previous marriage, Michael W. BBA, U. Wis., 1969, JD, 1973; LLM, George Washington U., 1979. Bar: Wis. 1973, D.C. 1979, U.S. Dist. Ct. (we. dist.) Wis. 1973, U.S. Ct. Appeals (7th cir.) 1974, U.S. Ct. Appeals (2d, 9th and D.C. cirs.) 1975, U.S. Supreme Ct. 1976. Auditor Touche, Ross & Co., Milw., 1969-70; law clk. to Hon. U.S. Ct. Appeals, Chgo., 1973-74; atty. SEC, Washington, 1974-78, exec. asst. to chmn., 1978-83, gen. counsel, 1983-90; ptnr. Baker and McKenzie, Washington, 1990—2002; bd. mem. Pub. Co. Acctg. Oversight Bd., Washington, 2003—. Adj. prof. Georgetown U. Law Ctr., Washington, 1986-92. Contbr. articles to profl. jours. With USAR, 1969-75. Mem. ABA, AICPA, Fed. Bar Assn. Republican. Congregationalist. Avocation: amateur radio. Administrative and regulatory, Corporate, general, Securities. Home: 5941 Searl Ter Bethesda MD 20816-2022 Office: Pub Co Acctg Oversight Bd 1666 K St NW Washington DC 20006 E-mail: dgoelzer@aol.com.

GOETTEL, GERARD LOUIS, federal judge; b. N.Y.C., Aug. 5, 1928; s. Louis and Agnes Beatrice (White) G.; m. Elinor Praeger, June 4, 1951; children: Sheryl, Glenn, James. Student, The Citadel, 1946-48; BA, Duke U., 1950; JD (Harlan Fiske Stone scholar), Columbia U., 1955. Bar: N.Y. 1955. Asst. U.S. atty. So. Dist. N.Y., N.Y.C., 1955-58; dep. chief atty. gen.'s spl. group on organized crime Dept. Justice, N.Y.C., 1958-59; assoc. firm Lowenstein, Pitcher, Hotchkiss, Amann & Parr, N.Y.C., 1959-62; counsel N.Y. Life Ins. Co., N.Y.C., 1962-68; with Natanson & Reich, N.Y.C., 1968-69; asso. gen. counsel Overmyer Co., N.Y.C., 1969-71; asst. counsel N.Y. Ct. on the Judiciary, 1971; U.S. magistrate U.S. Dist. Ct., So. Dist. N.Y., 1971-76; U.S. dist. judge U.S. Dist. Ct., Conn. Dist. Ct., Waterbury, 1976—, now sr. judge. Adj. prof. law Fordham U. Law Sch., 1978-87, Pace U. Law Sch., 1988-91; mem. com. on criminal justice act Jud. Conf. U.S., 1981-87, mem. cir. com. on pretrial phase of civil litigation, chmn. dist. coms. on discovery and criminal justice act 1982-85. Mem. council Fresh Air Fund, N.Y.C., 1961-64; bd. dirs. Community Action Program, Yonkers, N.Y., 1964-66. Served to lt. (j.g.) USCG, 1951-53. Mem.: Greenwoods Country (Winsted, Conn.), Boyne South Golf Club (Naples, Fla.), Greenwood Country Club (Winsted, Conn.). Office: 14 Cottage Pl Waterbury CT 06702-1904*

GOETZ, CLARENCE EDWARD, retired judge, retired chief magistrate judge; b. Balt., Feb. 4, 1932; AA, U. Balt., 1961, LLB, 1964. Bar: Md. 1964. Assoc. Hackney & Yourtee, Anne Arundel County, Md., 1965-66; asst. U.S. atty. for Md., 1966-70; U.S. magistrate judge for Md., 1970-97. Asst. prof. U. Balt., 1975, Towson State Coll., 1976; cons., arbitrator, mediator. Mem. Fed. Magistrate Judges Assn. E-mail: CKGoetz@comcast.net.

GOETZ, MAURICE HAROLD, lawyer; b. N.Y.C., Mar. 29, 1924; s. Morton M. and Elsie (Klein) G.; m. Pearl Goldberg, Sept. 12, 1948; children: Susan Goetz Zwirn, Janet L., Jill K. B Social Scis. in Econs. and History, CCNY, 1947; JD, Harvard U., 1950. Bar: N.Y. 1951. Assoc. Bandler Haas & Kass, N.Y.C., 1951-57; ptnr. Bandler Kass & Goetz, N.Y.C., 1957-66, Friedlander, Gaines, Ruttenberg & Goetz, N.Y.C., 1966-74, Rosenman & Colin, N.Y.C., 1974-92; of counsel KMZ Rosenman, N.Y.C., 1993—. Lectr. on labor law Contbr. articles to Nat. Law Jour., Fed. Publs., Inc., others. Office: KMZ Rosenman 575 Madison Ave New York NY 10022-2585

GOFF, COLLEEN MULLEN, lawyer; b. Galveston, Tex., Sept. 8, 1948; d. Brooks William and Frances Earle (White) M.; m. Darrell Lee Goff II, July 3, 1982. BA with high honors, U. Tex., 1974, MA, 1979; JD, St. Mary's U., 1984. Bar: Tex. 1984. Atty. Zachry Construction Corp., San Antonio, 1983—. Mem. ABA, Tex. Bar Assn., San Antonio Bar Assn., Bexar County Women's Bar Assn., San Antonio World Affairs Coun. (bd. dirs. 1993-98), Coll. of the State Bar Tex., San Antonio Free Trade Alliance (bd. mem.), Phi Beta Kappa, Phi Delta Phi. Episcopalian. Avocations: gardening, antiques. Construction, Government contracts and claims, Pension, profit-sharing, and employee benefits. Office: Zachry Construction Corp 2600 Tower Life Bldg San Antonio TX 78205-3118

GOFF, MICHAEL HARPER, retired lawyer; b. Hartford, Conn., Aug. 4, 1927; s. Charles Weer and Fern (Harper) G.; m. Katharine Lyman Bliss, Feb. 11, 1949 (div.); children— Carlin Weer, Peter Lyman; m. Patricia Darilyn King, Apr. 20, 1984 Student, Loomis Sch., Conn., 1942-45, Bethany Coll., 1945, Trinity Coll., Conn., 1949; BA, Swarthmore Coll., 1950; LL.B., Columbia U., 1953. Bar: N.Y. 1953. Assoc. Debevoise & Plimpton, 1953-60, ptnr., 1961-91; asst. to dir. Legis. Drafting Rsch. fund, 1951-53. Lectr. Banking Law Inst., 1966; cons. Atty. Gen. State of N.Y., 1977; spl. cons. Temp. Commn. to Study Orgnl. Structure City N.Y., 1953-54 Served with USNR, 1945-46; to 2d lt. F.A., AUS, 1946-48 Harlan Fiske Stone Scholar, Columbia U., 1951-52; Robert Noxon Toppan prize, Columbia U., 1952; E. B. Convers Prize, Columbia U., 1953 Mem. ABA, N.Y. State Bar Assn., Assn. Bar City N.Y., Moorings Club (Fla.), Phi Delta Phi, Kappa Sigma. Democrat. Episcopalian. Corporate, general, Finance, Securities. Home: 151 Anchor Dr Vero Beach FL 32963-2957

GOGLIA, CHARLES A., JR., lawyer; b. Phila., Aug. 26, 1931; s. Charles and Marie A. (Beckman) G.; m. Patricia A. Morrissey, July 26, 1958; children: Philip L., Catherine A. BS, St. Joseph's U., Phila., 1953; LLB, Boston Coll., 1958. Bar: Mass. 1958, U.S. Dist. Ct. Mass. 1959, U.S. Ct. Appeals (1st cir.) 1964, U.S. Tax Ct. 1977, U.S. Supreme Ct. 1993. Atty. Sheff & Gens, Boston, 1958-61, Foley, Hoag & Eliot, Boston, 1961-68, ptnr., 1968-74; pvt. practice Wellesley, Mass., 1974—. Corporator, trustee, mem. bd. investment, exec. com. Bank Five for Savs., Burlington, Mass., 1974-92; mem. hearing com. Bd. Bar Overseers, Boston, 1984-86; arbitrator Nat. Assn. Dispute Resolution, Inc., 2001—. Counsel Town of Nantucket, Mass., 1970-82, spl. counsel, 1982-85, Town of Weston, Mass., 1974-85, town counsel, 1986-92, spl. counsel, 1992—, mem. zoning bd. appeals, 1964-66, 74-85, mem. planning bd., 1973-74; spl. counsel Mass. Cable TV Commn., Boston, 1973-74. With USNAR, 1951-59. Mem. Wellesley Country Club (past pres.). Avocations: golf, travel. State civil litigation, Corporate, general, Property, real (including real estate development, water). Home: 1 Hopewell Farm Rd Natick MA 01760-5570 Office: Wellesley Office Pk 65 William St Wellesley MA 02481-3802

GOINS, FRANCES FLORIANO, lawyer; b. Buffalo, Jan. 30, 1950; d. William and Anita (Graziano) Floriano; m. Gary Mitchell Goins; children: Matthew W., Mark W. MusB, Cleve. Inst. Music, 1971; MusM, Case Western Res. U., 1973, JD, 1977. Bar: Ohio 1977, U.S. Dist. Ct. Ohio 1978, U.S. Ct. Appeals (6th cir.) 1979, N.Y. 1984, U.S. Dist. Ct. NY 1984, U.S. Supreme Ct. 2002. Law clk to Hon. Frank J. Battisti U.S. Dist. Ct. (no. dist.) Ohio, Cleve., 1977-78; ptnr. Squire, Sanders & Dempsey, Cleve., 1986—. Mem. vis. com. bd. overseers Case Western Res. U., Cleve., 1984-2000; faculty Nat. Inst. Trial Advocacy, Cleve.; faculty, lectr. trial advocacy seminar Cleve. State U. Sch. Law, 1989-90. Editor-in-chief law rev. Case Western Res. Sch. Law, 1976-77. Trustee, chairperson devel. com. Lyric Opera Cleve., 1985-92, 2003—; founding trustee Shoreby Club Cleve.; v.p. bd. trustees Bay Village Montessori Sch., 1994-96; trustee No. Ohio Breast Cancer Coalition, 2003—. Mem. ABA (bus. law sect., bus. lit. com., corporate governance com. 1995—, fed. regulation of securities com., subcom. on civil litigation and SEC enforcement 1992—), Ohio Women's Bar Assn. (founding mem.), Ohio State Bar Assn. (ad hoc com. on bus. cts. 1994-99), Cleve. Bar Assn. (com. on women and the law 1987-2000, ethics com. 1988-90, securities law inst., jud. selection com. 1996-2001). Democrat. Roman Catholic. Banking, General civil litigation, Securities. Office: Squire Sanders & Dempsey 4900 Key Tower 127 Public Sq Ste 4900 Cleveland OH 44114-1304

GOLAN, STEPHEN LEONARD, lawyer; b. Chgo., Oct. 22, 1951; s. Leonard Walter and Carol (Pepper) G.; m. Sharon D. Robson, Aug. 16, 1980; children: Brianna, Jenna, Melissa. BA, Claremont (Calif.) Men's Coll., 1974; MBA, JD, Northwestern U., 1978. Bar: Ill. 1978, U.S. Dist. Ct. (no. dist.) Ill. 1978, U.S. Ct. Appeals (7th cir.) 1993. Ptnr. Seyfarth, Shaw, Fairweather & Geraldson, Chgo., 1978-93; founding ptnr. Field & Golan, Chgo., 1993—. Mem. ABA, AICPA, Nat. Assn. JD-MBA Profls. (bd. dirs. 1984-86), Ill. Bar Assn., Chgo. Bar Assn., Tavern Club (mem. jr. com. 1984-86), Exmoor Country Club (Highland Park, Ill.), Lake Forest Caucus. Republican. Episcopalian. Commercial, contracts (including sales of goods; commercial financing), Computer, Corporate, general. Office: Field & Golan 15th Fl 3 First National Plz Chicago IL 60602 E-mail: slgolan@fieldgolan.com.

GOLD, EDWARD DAVID, lawyer; b. Detroit, Jan. 17, 1941; s. Morris and Hilda (Robinson) Gold; m. Francine Sheila Kamin, Jan. 8, 1967; children: Lorne Brian, Karen Beth. Student, Wayne State U., 1958-61; JD, Detroit Coll. Law, 1964. Bar: Mich. 1965, U.S. Dist. Ct. (ea. dist.) Mich. 1965, U.S. Ct. Appeals (6th cir.) 1965, D.C. 1966. Atty. gen. counsel FCC, Washington, 1965-66; ptnr. Conn, Conn & Gold, Detroit, 1966-67, May, Conn, Conn & Gold, Livonia, Mich., 1967-69, Hyman, Gurwin, Nachman, Gold & Alterman, Southfield, Mich., 1971-88, Butzel Long, Bloomfield Hills, Mich., 1988—. Mem. Oakland County Criminal Justice Coordinating Coun., 1976—77; chmn. Friend of the Ct. Adv. Com., Lansing, Mich., 1982—88; contbr. lectr. Inst. Continuing Legal Edn., Ann Arbor, Mich., 1981—, Mich. Trial Lawyers Assn.; adj. prof. U. Detroit Mercy Sch. Law, 2001—. Author: (book) Michigan Family Law, 1988; contbr. articles to legal jours. Mem. Southfield Transp. Commn., 1975—77; chairperson atty. disp. bd. Tri-County Hearin Panel 71, 1994—2002; chmn. attys.' divsn. Jewish Welfare Fedn., Detroit; mem. nat. young leadership cabinet United Jewish Appeal, N.Y.C., 1978—80; pres. Jewish Family Svc., Detroit, 1988—90; bd. dirs. Oakland County Legal Aid Soc., 1979—84. Scholar Tau Epsilon Rho, 1963. Fellow: Am. Acad. Matrimonial Lawyers (bd. dirs. 1988—93, pres. Mich. chpt. 1992—93, nat. bd. govs. 1988—2001, nat. v.p. 2001—), Am. Coll. Family Trial Lawyers; mem.: Am. Arbitration Assn., Bar Assn. D.C., Southfield Bar Assn. (pres. 1975—76), Oakland County Bar Assn. (bd. dirs. 1984—93, pres. 1992—93), Mich. Bar Assn. (coun. real property law sect. 1973—81, coun. family law sect. 1974—75, 1977—82, chmn. family law sect. 1981—82, rep. assembly 1978—82, Lifetime Achievement award), Alpha Epsilon Pi (nat. pres. 1976—77, Order of Lion award 1986). Avocation: golf. Corporate, general, Family and matrimonial, Property, real (including real estate development, water). Office: Butzel Long Ste 200 100 Bloomfield Hills Pkwy Bloomfield Hills MI 48304 E-mail: Gold@Butzel.com.

GOLD, GERALD SEYMOUR, lawyer; b. Cleve., Feb. 2, 1931; s. David N. and Geraldine (Bloch) G.; 1 child, Anne; m. Rosemary Grdina, 1994. AB, Case-Western Res. U., 1951, LLB, 1954. Bar: Ohio 1954, U.S. Supreme Ct. 1961. Practiced in, Cleve., 1954-60; chief asst. legal aid defender Cuyahoga County, Cleve., 1960-61, chief legal aid defender, 1961-65; assoc. Ulmer, Byrne, Laronge, Glickman & Curtis, Cleve., 1965-66; ptnr. Gold, Rotatori, Schwartz & Gibbons, Cleve., 1966—. Instr. in law Case-Western Res. U., 1965-66, Cleve. State Law Sch., 1968-69, Case-Western Res. Law-Medicine Center, 1961-77; lectr. to bar assns. commr. Cuyahoga County Pub. Defender, 1977-81. Contbg. author: American Jurisprudence Trials, 1966; Contbr. articles to law revs. Fellow Am. Coll. Trial Lawyers, Am. Bd. Criminal Lawyers, Ohio State Bar Found., Internat. Soc. Barristers; mem. ABA (criminal justice coun.), Cuyahoga County Criminal Ct. Bar Assn. (chmn., Lifetime Achievement award 1995), Ohio Bar Assn. (chmn. criminal law sect. 1974-78, ho. of dels. 1986—), Greater Cleve. Bar Assn. (Merit award 1974, trustee 1978—, pres. 1982-83), Nat. Assn. Criminal Def. Lawyers (pres. 1977, Merit award 1975), Ohio Acad. Trial Lawyers (chmn. criminal law sect. 1970-75), Ohio Assn. Criminal Def. Lawyers (bd. dirs. 1990), Case-Western Res. U. Law Alumni Assn. (pres. 1974-75, Outstanding Alumnus award 1991), Soc. Benchers, Court of Nisi Prius Club, Cleve. Skating Club. Federal civil litigation, State civil litigation, Criminal. Home: 33000 Pinetree Rd Pepper Pike OH 44124-5514 Office: 526 Superior Ave E Ste 1500 Cleveland OH 44114-1497

GOLD, I. RANDALL, lawyer; b. Chgo., Nov. 2, 1951; Albert Samuel and Lois (Rodrick) G.; m. Marcey Dale Miller, Nov. 18, 1978; children: Eric Matthew, Brian David. BS with high honors, U. Ill., 1973, JD, 1976. Bar: Ill. 1976, U.S. Dist. Ct. (no. dist.) Ill. 1976, Fla. 1979, U.S. Dist. Ct. (so. dist.) Fla. 1979, U.S. Ct. Appeals (5th and 7th cirs.) 1979, U.S. Tax Ct. 1979, U.S. Ct. Appeals (11th cir.) 1981, U.S. Supreme Ct. 1982, U.S. Dist. Ct. (mid. dist.) Fla. 1987; CPA, Ill., Fla. Tax staff Ernst & Ernst, Chgo., 1976-77; asst. state atty. Cook County, Ill., 1977-78, Dade County, Miami, Fla., 1978-82; spl. atty. Miami Strike Force U.S. Dept. Justice, Fla., 1982-87; pvt. practice Miami, 1987-92; asst. U.S. atty. U.S. Dist. Ct. (mid. dist.) Fla., 1992—, dep. chief Orlando div., 2002—. Lectr. Roosevelt U., Chgo., 1976-77; vice chmn. fed. practice com. on criminal sect. Fla. Bar, 1986-88, profl. ethics com., 1992-2001; instr. Rollins Coll. paralegal program, 1992-97; adj. prof. criminal justice program U. Ctrl. Fla., 1994—; adj. prof. law U. Orlando, 1998-99. Co-chmn. Greater Oviedo Cmty. Devel. Program, 1992-93; adviser Jr. Achievement, Chgo., 1976-78, Miami, 1982-84; coach, judge Nat. Trial Competition, U. Miami Law Sch., 1983-86, 88, 90; mentor Seminole County Sch., 1994—; coach mock trial program legal project Dade County Pub. Schs., 1985-89, 91-92, ptnr. program, 1989-92. Mem.: FBA, ATLA, ABA (govt. litigation counsel, complex crimes com.litigation sect.), AICPA, Am. Inns of Ct. (master), Am. Assn. Atty. CPAs, Seminole County Bar Assn., Orange County Bar Assn. (bankruptcy com.), Ctrl. Fla. Bankruptcy Lawyers Assn., Fla. Inst. CPAs (com. on rels. with Fla. Bar 1985—86, bd. dirs. South Dade chpt. 1987—92), Ill. Soc. CPAs, Ill. Bar Assn., Fla. Bar, U. Ill. Alumni Club (v.p.), Delta Sigma Pi. Jewish. Office: 80 N Hughey Ave Ste 201 Orlando FL 32801-2224

GOLD, MARTIN ELLIOTT, lawyer, educator; b. N.Y.C., Jan. 6, 1946; s. Herman and Rose (Zippin) G.; 1 stepchild, Ariane. BA, Cornell U., 1967; JD, Harvard U, 1970, MPA, 1971. Bar: N.Y. 1972, U.S. Dist. Ct. (so. and ea. dists.) N.Y. 1974, U.S. Ct. Appeals (2d cir.) 1974. With Operation Crossroads Africa, The Gambia, 1965; cons. U.S. Dept. Justice, 1968; assoc. Freshfields, London, 1969; rsch. fellow Ctr. Law and Devel. Sri Lanka, Cambridge, Mass., 1971-73; assoc. Debevoise & Plimpton, N.Y.C., 1973-78; chief econ. devel. divsn. N.Y.C. Law Dept., 1978-85, N.Y.C. dir. corp. law, 1980-85; ptnr. Sidley Austin Brown & Wood, N.Y.C., 1985—. Adj. prof. Columbia U., 1987—; guest lectr. Fordham U., Yale U., Cornell U., U.S. Conf. of Mayors, U.S. Justice Dept., others. Author: Law and Social Change: A Study of Land Reform in Sri Lanka, 1977; contbr. articles to profl. jours. Mem. Legal Aid Soc., 1975-81, Cornell Real Estate Coun., 1988—; bd. dirs. Environ. Action Coalition, 1988-2002, INFORM, 1989—, J.F. Kennedy Sch., Tri State Coun., 1991-97; chmn. Ridgefield Coun. Lake Assns. Recipient awards Rockefeller Bros. Fund, 1979, 80, Fund for City N.Y., 1981, Leadership award J.F. Kennedy Sch. Mem. ABA, Internat. Assn. Attys. and Execs. in Corp. Real Estate, Nat. Coun. for Pub. and Pvt. Partnerships, Natural Resources Def. Coun., Assn. Bar City N.Y. (environ, mcpl., energy and real poperty and housing law coms.), Common Cause, Cornell Club. Commercial, contracts (including sales of goods; commercial financing), Environmental, Property, real (including real estate development, water).

GOLD, PETER FREDERICK, lawyer; b. N.Y.C., Nov. 10, 1945; s. John and Dolores (Soyer) G.; m. Dee Crafferty, June 6, 1982; children: Joshua, Katharine. BA, Cornell U., 1967; MSc, London Sch. Econs., 1968; JD, NYU, 1971. Bar: D.C. 1988, N.Y. 1972, U.S. Dist. Ct. (so. dist.) N.Y. 1972, U.S. Dist. Ct. (ea. dist.) N.Y. 1972. Assoc. atty. Paul, Weiss, Rifkind, Wharton & Garrison, N.Y.C., 1971-75; legis. dir. Senator Gary Hart, Washington, 1975-81; ptnr. Wellford, Wegman, Krulwich, Gold & Hoff, Washington, 1981-84, Winthrop, Stimson, Putnam & Roberts, Washington, 1984-94; pres. The Gold Group, Chartered, Washington, 1994—, C.G. Sloan & Co., Inc., 1995-97. Editor in chief Review of Law and Social Change, 1970. Nat. policy dir. Hart for Pres. Campaign, Washington, 1984; chmn., founder First Book, Washington, 1992—; dir. Share Our Strength, Washington, 1990—; mem. Clinton-Gore Transition Team, Washington, 1992. Recipient Disting. Visitor Program European Econ. Community, Brussels, Belgium, 1982. Mem. D.C. Bar Assn., Fed. Bar Assn., N.Y.C. Bar Assn., Kenwood Golf & Country Club, Four Streams Golf Club. Democrat. Jewish. Avocations: tennis, golf. Antitrust, Private international, Legislative. Home: 13640 Glenhurst Rd North Potomac MD 20878-3921 Office: The Gold Group Chartered 1319 F St NW Ste 1000 Washington DC 20004-1106

GOLD, SIMEON, lawyer; b. Hartford, Conn., Jan. 3, 1949; s. Charles and Claire (Goldschein) G.; m. Heide Aline Turkel, Aug. 30, 1970; children: Jana, Craig. BS, Cornell U., 1970; JD, Harvard U., 1973. Bar: N.Y., U.S. Dist. Ct. (so. dist.) N.Y., U.S. Ct. Appeals (2d cir.). Assoc. Weil, Gotshal & Manges LLP, N.Y.C., 1973-81, ptnr., 1981—. Bd. dirs. Lawyers Alliance for N.Y. Contbr. articles to profl. jours. Mem. Coun. of Bus. Exec. Assn. for Help of Retarded Children, N.Y.C., Legal Aid Soc., N.Y.C.; bd. trustees Dalton Sch., 1997-2000. Mem. ABA, N.Y. State Bar Assn. (chair bus. law sect. 2000-01, chair corp. law com. 1993-97), Assn. of Bar of City of N.Y., N.Y. County Lawyers Assn., Harmonie Club, Old Oaks Country Club. Avocations: skiing, tennis, golf, travel. Corporate, general, Securities, Restructuring. Office: Weil Gotshal & Manges LLP 767 5th Ave Fl Concl New York NY 10153-0119 E-mail: simeon.gold@weil.com.

GOLD, STEVEN MICHAEL, lawyer; b. Bklyn., Sept. 19, 1953; s. Joseph and Gladys (Guss) G.; m. Susan Schwartz, Jan. 9, 1977; children: Rachel, David, Hannah. BA, Hobart Coll., 1975; JD, Cornell U., 1978. Bar: Conn. 1979, N.Y. 1979, U.S. Dist. Ct. Conn. 1979, U.S. Dist. Ct. (no. dist.) N.Y. 1979. Confidential law asst. 3d dept. appellate div. N.Y. Supreme Ct., Albany, 1978-79; assoc. Schatz & Schatz, Ribicoff & Kotkin, Hartford & Stamford, Conn., 1979-86, ptnr. Stamford, 1987-96, Shipman & Goodwin, LLP, Stamford, 1996—. Treas. Cmty. Coun. Westport/Weston, Conn., 1985, 1st v.p., 1987, bd. dirs., 1985-87; bd. dirs., counsel Urban League Greater Bridgeport, 1987-92; bd. dirs., v.p. Stamford Symphony Soc., 1990-95, counsel, 1994-95; bd. dirs. Nursing and Home Care, 1996-97, Women's Bus. Devel. Ctr., 2001-. Mem. ABA, N.Y. State Bar Assn., Conn. Bar Assn., Stamford/Norwalk Regional Bar Assn. (dir. 2002—), Assn. Comml. Fin. Attys., Assn. Corporate Growth, Nat. Assn. Transp. Practitioners (treas. Conn. chpt. 1983-85), Entrepreneurship Inst. (adv. bd. 1989-91), Phi Delta Phi, Pi Gamma Mu. Democrat. Jewish. Avocation: squash. Commercial, contracts (including sales of goods; commercial financing), Computer, Corporate, general. Office: Shipman & Goodwin LLP One Landmark Sq Stamford CT 06901 E-mail: sgold@goodwin.com.

GOLD, STUART WALTER, lawyer; b. N.Y.C., Mar. 3, 1949; s. Morris I. and Barbara (Walters) G.; m. Michele M. Cardella, June 26, 1983. BA in Polit. Sci., Bklyn. Coll., 1969; JD, NYU, 1972. Bar: N.Y. 1973, U.S. Supreme Ct. 1983, U.S. Ct. Appeals (2d, 3d, 7th, 8th, 9th and D.C. cirs.). Law clk. to judge U.S. Dist. Ct. (so. dist.) N.Y., 1972-73; assoc. Cravath, Swaine & Moore LLP, N.Y.C., 1973-80, ptnr., 1980—. Bd. dirs. N.Y. Lawyers for Pub. Interest, N.Y.C., 1982—. Mem. ABA, N.Y. State Bar Assn., Assn. of Bar City of N.Y. Democrat. Avocations: tennis, travel. Antitrust, Federal civil litigation, Libel. Office: Cravath Swaine & Moore 825 8th Ave Fl 39 New York NY 10019-7475

GOLDBERG, ALAN JOEL, lawyer; b. Bklyn., Jan. 22, 1943; s. Ralph and Dorothy (Rolnick) G.; 1 child, Cary Adam. BA, U. Miami, 1965, JD, 1968. Bar: Fla. 1968, U.S. Supreme Ct., U.S. Ct. Appeals (4th cir.). Ptnr. Goldberg, Young, Goldberg & Borkson, P.A., Ft. Lauderdale, Fla., 1968-82; atty. City of Margate, Fla., 1969-70, City of Tamarac, Fla., 1970-71; pvt. practice Ft. Lauderdale, 1982—. Pres. Diversified Realty Holdings Co., 1996—; exec. v.p. Holland Sheltair Aviation Group, 2002—. Mem. Citizen's Task Force on Transp., State of Fla.; mem. Broward County Planning Coun., 1984-92, chmn., 1988, 91; bd. dirs. Boys and Girls Clubs of Broward County, Inc., 1995—, pres., 1999-2000, chmn. bd. dirs., 2000-01 Mem. ABA, Fla. Bar Assn. Republican. Property, real (including real estate development, water). Office: 4860 NE 12th Ave Fort Lauderdale FL 33334

GOLDBERG, AUBREY, lawyer; b. Suffolk, Va., Dec. 2, 1940; s. Meyer R. and Miriam (Pear) G.; m. Joanne Holland, Aug. 25, 1963; children: Devon Jon, Jennifer Jonine. BA, Coll. William & Mary, 1963, JD, 1966. Bar: Va. 1966, Nev. 1968, U.S. Dist. Ct. Nev. 1968, U.S. Ct. Appeals (9th cir.) 1985. Ptnr. Greenman, Goldberg, Raby & Martinez, Las Vegas, 1970—; settlement judge Nev. Supreme Ct., 1997—. Served to capt. USAF, 1966-70 Vietnam; lt. col. USAFR. Mem. ABA, Nev. Bar Assn. (bd. govs. 1986-93, pres. 1992-93), Clark County Bar Assn. (pres. 1978, 1st annual pres. award 1985), Las Vegas C. of C., Assn. Trial Lawyers Am., Nev. Trial Lawyers Assn. Democrat. Jewish. Avocations: tennis, weight lifting, jogging. General practice, Personal injury (including property damage), Workers' compensation. Office: Greenman Goldberg Raby & Martinez 601 S 9th St Las Vegas NV 89101-7012

GOLDBERG, CHARLES L. lawyer; b. Los Angeles, June 7, 1940; . William M. and Mary S. (Schuster) G.; m. Diane Gail Walker, Dec. 18, 1966; children: Cori lynn, Julie Karen, Robert Yale. BA, UCLA, 1964, JD, 1967. Bar: Calif. 1968, U.S. Dist. Ct. (so., cen. and ea. dists.) Calif., U.S. Ct. Appeals (9th cir.), U.S. Supreme Ct. Ptnr. Goldberg & Frant, San Diego, 1968—88, Goldberg & Hall, San Diego, 1988—96, Seltzer Caplan McMahon Vitek, San Diego, 1996—. Instr. criminal law Grossmont Coll., San Diego, 1978-79. Fellow Am. Bd. Criminal Lawyers (bd. dirs., pres. 1995-96); mem. San Diego Trial Lawyers Assn. (bd. dirs. 1983-85), Calif. Trial Lawyers Assn. (lectr.),Calif. Attys. for Criminal Justice, Nat. Assn. Criminal Defense Lawyers, San Diego Criminal Lawyers Club (founding mem.). Criminal. Office: Seltzer Caplan McMahon Vitek 750 B St Ste 2100 San Diego CA 92101-8122

GOLDBERG, DAVID, lawyer, law educator; b. N.Y.C., Dec. 31, 1934; s. Philip and Esther (Dobbs) G.; m. Emily Ruth Messing, Aug. 17, 1958; children: Sara, Ari. BA, CUNY, 1956; LLB, Yale U., 1959. Bar: N.Y. 1960. Law clerk to judge U.S. Dist. Ct., N.Y.C., 1960-62; assoc. Kaye, Scholer, Fierman, Hays and Handler, N.Y.C., 1962-68, ptnr., 1969-83, Cowan, Liebowitz and Latman, N.Y.C., 1983—. Adj. prof. law NYU, 1976-96. Contbr. articles on copyright and trademark law to N.Y. Law Jour., other profl. jours. Pres. Hillcrest Jewish Ctr., Jamaica Estates, N.Y., 1987-89. Served as sgt. U.S. Army, 1959-60. Mem. ABA (fin. officer sect. intellectual property law 1986-89, spkr. on copyright devels. 1984, 85, 87, 90, 2000), Copright Soc. USA (pres. 1978-80, hon. trustee 1980—, spkr. on copyright devels. annually 1984—), U.S. Trademark Assn. (spkr. on trademarks and copyright overlap 1987). Democrat. Avocation: fishing. Entertainment, Trademark and copyright. Office: Cowan Liebowitz and Latman 1133 Avenue of the Americas New York NY 10036-6710 E-mail: dxg@cll.com.

GOLDBERG, GREGORY EBAN, lawyer; b. Denver, Oct. 9, 1967; BA, Dartmouth Coll., 1990; JD, Columbia Law Sch., 1995. Bar: Colo. 1995, U.S. Dist. Ct. Colo. 1995, U.S. Ct. Appeals (10th cir.) 1995. Law clk. to Judge Paul J. Kelly Jr. U.S. Ct. Appeals (10th cir.), Santa Fe, 1995-96; assoc. Arnold & Porter, Denver, 1996-99; asst. U.S. atty. Maj. Crimes & Appellate divsn., Denver, 1999—2003; assoc. Holland & Hart, Denver, 2003—. Bd. dirs. Anti-Defamation League, Denver, 1998—. Recipient U.S. Dept. of Justice Dirs. award, 2002. Mem. Colo. Bar Assn., Dartmouth Alumni Assn. (bd. dirs.), Graland Alumni Assn. (bd. dirs. 1995-2000). Avocations: snowshoeing, mountain biking, backpacking, home renovations. Administrative and regulatory, Corporate, general, Environmental. Office: Holland & Hart 555 17th St Ste 3200 Denver CO 80202 E-mail: ggoldberg@hollandhart.com.

GOLDBERG, HAROLD PHILIP, lawyer; b. N.Y.C., Apr. 23, 1939; s. Samuel and Naomi (Freedman) G.; m. Ann Benyes, Feb. 4, 1961 (div.); m. Mary Ciccone, Aug. 28, 1982 (div.); children: William, Michele. BA, U. Vt., 1960; JD, Syracuse U., 1963. Bar: N.Y. 1963, U.S. Dist. Ct. (no. and we. dists.) N.Y. Ptnr. Crystal, Manes & Rifken, Syracuse, 1965-74, Goldberg & Sanders, Syracuse, 1974-84; pres. Goldberg, Harding & Talev, Syracuse, 1984-90; trustee U.S. Bankruptcy Ct (no. dist.), Syracuse, 1973—; ptnr. Goldberg & Fabiano, Syracuse, 1993-98, Martin, Martin & Woodard, LLP, Syracuse, 1998—. Bd. dirs. Consumer Credit Counselling Services Cen. N.Y. Mem. N.Y. State Bar Assn. (com. bankruptcy law). Lodges: B'nai B'rith (pres. 1968-69). Bankruptcy, State civil litigation, Commercial, consumer (including collections, credit). Office: 1 Lincoln Ctr Syracuse NY 13202-1324

GOLDBERG, JOLANDE ELISABETH, law librarian, lawyer; b. Pforzheim, Germany, Aug. 11, 1931; came to U.S., 1967; d. Eugen and Luise Rosa (Thorwarth) Haas; m. Lawrence Spencer Goldberg, Sept. 7, 1969; children: Daniel Scott, Elisa Miriam, Clarissa Anna. Referendar, U. Heidelberg, 1957, PhD, 1963; postdoctoral, U. London, 1976-77. Bar: Germany 1961. Mem. rsch. staff Acad. Scis. and Humanities, Heidelberg, 1961-67; rsch. assoc. U. Heidelberg, 1964-67; cataloger, law specialist Libr. of Congress, Washington, 1967-72, asst. law classification specialist, 1972-80, law classification specialist, 1980—, sr. cataloging policy specialist, 1997—. Sculptor, potter Torpedo Factory Art Ctr., Alexandria, Va., 1974—; lectr. Smithsonian Inst., Washington, 1988—. Author: Probschlag & Meistersignatur, 1963; contbr. articles to profl. jours. Exec. bd. dirs. Friends Torpedo Factory Art Ctr., Alexandria, 1987—. Volkswagenwerk Found. rsch. fellow, Fed. Republic of Germany, 1964-65, German Rsch. Assn. fellow, 1966, German Libr. Inst. grantee, 1981, Robbins Collection sr. rsch. fellow U. Calif. Berkeley, 1995. Mem. ABA, ALA (Marta Lange award for disting. librarianship in law and polit. sci. 1999, Assn. Coll. and Rsch. Librs. divsn. Marta Lange Congl. Quarterly award 1999), Am. Soc. Internat. Law, Internat. Soc. for Knowledge Orgn., Am. Assn. Law Librs. (Tech. Svcs. Spl. Interest sect. exec. bd. dirs. 1987-91, 2003-, citation for exceptional contbn. 1992, Reneé Chapman Meml. award 1999, Joseph L. Andrews Bibliographie award 2002), Torpedo Factory Artist Assn., The Art League. Democrat. Jewish. Office: Libr Of Congress Washington DC 20540-4305 Fax: (202) 707-6629. E-mail: jgol@loc.gov.

GOLDBERG, JOSEPH, lawyer; b. Washington, Aug. 21, 1950; s. Morris and Rose (Levin) G.; m. Christine Marie Riggott, Mar. 29, 1980; children: Benjamin R., Louis E. BS, Ohio U., 1972; JD, U. Pa., 1975. Bar: Pa. 1975, N.J. 1981, D.C. 1980, U.S. Ct. Appeals (3d cir.) 1980, U.S. Dist.Ct. (mid. dist.) Pa. 1987, U.S. Supreme Ct. 1989. Assoc. Margolis, Edelstein & Scherlis, Phila., 1975-81; ptnr. Margolis Edelstein, Phila., 1982—. Author: State and Local Government Immunity to Tort Claims, 1992, 2d edit., 1997. Mem. ABA, Pa. Def. Rsch. Inst., Pa. Jud. Rules Com., Phila. Assn. Def. Counsel, Phila. Bar Assn. Avocation: scuba diving. Civil rights, General civil litigation, Personal injury (including property damage). Office: Margolis Edelstein The Curtis Ctr 4th Fl Independence Sq West Philadelphia PA 19106

GOLDBERG, MARK JOEL, lawyer; b. Pitts., June 2, 1941; s. Charles J. and Eleanore (Letwin) G.; m. Wendy Witt, Dec. 23, 1988; children: Michael, Wendy, Josh, Jamie. BA, Washington and Jefferson Coll., 1963; JD, Case Western Res. U., 1966. Bar: Pa. 1966, Ohio 1966, U.S. Tax Ct. 1969, U.S. Supreme Ct. 1972. Assoc. Jerome Silver, Cleve., 1966-67; pvt. practice, Pitts., 1967-69; ptnr. Goldberg & Wedner, Pitts., 1969-80; ptnr., shareholder Gillotti Goldberg & Capristo, Pitts., 1981-91, Goldberg Gentile & Voelker, Pitts., 1991-92, Goldberg, Gruener, Gentile, Horoho & Avalli, P.C., Pitts., 1992—. Mem. drafting com. Pa. Divorce Code, 1978-80, 88; frequent lectr. Pa. Bar Inst., Pa. Trial Lawyers Assn., Am. Acad. Matrimonial Lawyers. Contbr. articles to profl. jours. Committeeman Dem. Party, Pitts., 1970's; pres. bd. dirs. Parent and Child Guidance Ctr., Pitts., 1984-86. Fellow Am. Acad. Matrimonial Lawyers (pres. Pa. chpt. 1988-90, nat. bd. govs. 1991-95); mem. Am. Coll. Family Trial Lawyers (diplomate, officer), Allegheny County Bar Assn. (coun. mem. family law sect. 1972—, chmn. 1982-84), Pa. Bar Assn. (family law sect. chmn. 1986-88), Westmoreland Country Club, Rivers Club. Jewish. Avocations: golf, travel. Family and matrimonial. Home: 14 Carmel Ct Pittsburgh PA 15221-3618 Office: Goldberg Gruener Et Al 230 Grant Bldg Pittsburgh PA 15219-2200 E-mail: mgoldberg@gggha.com.

GOLDBERG, MARTIN STANFORD, retired lawyer; b. Youngstown, Ohio, July 11, 1924; s. George and Bee (Walker) G.; m. Donna Mae Lowry, Nov. 18, 1962; children: Jeffrey A., Jeralyn Goldberg Mercer. BA, JD, Ohio State U., 1952. Bar: Ohio 1952, Calif. 1981. Sole practice law, Youngstown, Ohio, 1952—2001. Served with USAF, 1942-45, PTO. Decorated D.F.C. Mem. ABA, Calif. Bar Assn., Ohio Bar Assn., Mahoning County Bar Assn., Am. Trial Lawyers Assn. Clubs: Lodges: Masons, Friars Club. Lodges: Masons, Friars. Republican. Jewish. Avocations: reading, writing, music. Home: 74513 Old Prospector Trl Palm Desert CA 92260-5624

GOLDBERG, MARVIN ALLEN, lawyer, business consultant; b. Phila., Jan. 9, 1943; s. Daniel and Elizabeth (Katz) G.; m. Kathryn Elizabeth Balotsky, Apr. 27, 1974; children: Robert Andrew, MaryBeth Anne. BS, Temple U., 1964, JD, 1967. Bar: Pa. 1968, U.S. Dist. Ct. (ea. dist.) Pa. 1980, U.S. Supreme Ct. 1976. Estate tax atty. IRS, Phila., 1967—68; staff atty. Legal Aid Soc. Northampton County, Easton, Pa., 1969-70, Northampton County Pub. Defender, Easton, Pa., 1969-70; pvt. practice law Phila., 1970-76; tchr. Inst. for Paralegal Tng., Phila., 1973; staff atty. Legal Aid Soc. Phila., 1974-76; CEO Goldberg & Assocs., P.C., Phila., 1976—. Cons. Butcher Trade Exchange, Ft. Washington, Pa., 1982-92. Mem. Chestnut St. Assn., Phila; dir. Sr. Citizen Judicare Project, Phila., 1977. With USAF, 1967-73. Fellow Roscoe Pound Inst.; mem. ABA, Phila. Bar Assn., Phila. Trial Lawyers Assn., Assn. Trial Lawyers Am., Pa. Trial Lawyers Assn., Attys. Across Am. (founding mem.), Jewish War Vets, Beta Gamma Sigma, Phi Alpha Delta. Avocations: running, flying, sailing, chess, algebra, 19th century physics. Aviation, Insurance, Personal injury (including property damage). Office: Goldberg & Assocs PC 1334 Walnut St Fl 5 Philadelphia PA 19107-5311

GOLDBERG, MAUREEN MCKENNA, state supreme court justice; b. Pawtucket, R.I., Feb. 11, 1951; m. Robert D. Goldberg. Grad., St. Mary's Acad., 1969; AB cum laude, Providence Coll., 1973; JD cum laude, Suffolk U., 1978. Bar: R.I. 1978, Mass. 1978, U.S. Ct. of Appeals (1st cir.) 1979. Asst. atty. gen. Adminstr. of the Criminal Divsn., 1978-84; town solicitor South Kingstown, 1985-87, Town of Westerly, 1987-90, acting town mgr., 1990; spl. legal counsel R.I. State Police; apptd. assoc. justice Superior Ct., 1990-96; assoc. justice R.I. Supreme Ct., 1997—. Mem. ABA, R.I. Bar Assn., R.I. Trial Judges Assn., Pawtucket Bar Assn. Office: Rhode Island Supreme Ct 250 Benefit St 7th Fl Providence RI 02903-2719

GOLDBERG, MICHAEL BRADLEY, lawyer; b. Chgo., Mar. 1, 1971; s. Sherman I. and Susan K. G.; m. Marnie R. Goldberg, June 21, 1997; children: Jacob Hunter, Shane Riley. Student, U. Vt., 1989-91; BS, Lake Forest Coll., 1993; JD, Washington U., St. Louis, 1996; grad. Squadron Officer Sch., Air U., Maxwell AFB, Ala., 1998. Bar: Ill., D.C., Tex. Commd. 2nd lt. USAF, advanced through grades to capt., 1996; JAG Air Intelligence Agy., San Antonio, 1996-2000; legal advisor Air Force Human Intelligence Team, 1997-2000; litigation assoc. Mayer, Brown and Platt, Chgo., 2000—02; litigation atty. Cox & Smith, Inc., San Antonio, 2002—. Legal advisor Air Force Human Intelligence Team, 1997—. Chmn. Cmty. Rels. Coun. Jewish Fedn. San Antonio, 1998; mem. advocacy and cmty. infrastructure coun. San Antonio C. of C., mil. affairs com.. Mem. ABA, ATLA, Ill. Bar Assn., Chgo. Bar Assn., D.C. Bar Assn., San Antonio Bar Assn., Tex. Bar Assn., Fed. Bar Assn. Jewish. Avocations: public speaking, golf, guitar, baseball. Federal civil litigation, General civil litigation, State civil litigation.

GOLDBERG, NEIL A. lawyer; b. N.Y.C., Dec. 24, 1947; s. Bernard G. Goldberg; children: Jane Hana, Robert Saul. BA cum laude, SUNY, Stony Brook, 1969; JD cum laude, SUNY, Buffalo, 1973. Bar: N.Y. 1974, U.S. Dist. Ct. (we. dist.) N.Y. 1974. Sr. ptnr. Saperston & Day P.C., Buffalo, 1974—2001, Goldberg Segalda, Buffalo, 2001—; pres. DRI, 2000—01. Editor Products Liaility in New York, 1997; co-editor in chief Preparing for and Trying the Civil Lawsuit. Mem.: ABA, Erie County Bar Assn., N.Y. State Bar Assn. (past chmn. product liability com. torts, ins. and compensation law sect. 1986—), Am. Arbitration Assn. (bd. dirs. 1985—, product liability adv. coun.), Def. Rsch. Inst. (past pres.), Internat. Assn. Def. Counsel. General civil litigation, Insurance, Product liability. Office: Goldberg Segalla 120 Delaware Ave Ste 500 Buffalo NY 14202 Office Fax: 716-566-5401. Business E-Mail: ngoldberg@goldbergsegalla.com.

GOLDBERG, RICHARD ROBERT, lawyer; b. New York, Apr. 27, 1941; s. Joseph and Anne (Blumfield) G.; m. Rita Ann Zieve, June 30, 1963; 1 child, Andrew Louis. BA, Pa. State U., 1961; LLB, U. Md., 1964. Bar: Md. 1964, U.S. Ct. Appeals (4th cir.) 1970, U.S. Supreme Ct. 1974, U.S. Ct. Appeals (5th cir.) 1978, U.S. Ct. Appeals (D.C. cir.) 1992, Pa. 1994, N.J. 1994. Asst. city solicitor to Mayor and City Coun. City of Balt., 1965-70; atty. The Rouse Co., Columbia, Md., 1970-78, v.p., assoc. gen. counsel, 1978-94; ptnr. Ballard, Spahr, Andrews & Ingersoll, Phila., 1994—. Author: Real Estate Development of Downtown Projects, 1981; author and editor: (handbooks) Commercial Real Estate Leasing, Commercial Real Estate Financing; contrbr. numerous articles to profl. publs. Chmn. Jewish Coun. of Howard County, Md., 1975-77, chmn. ann. campaign, 1978, 80, 87; pres. Temple Isaiah, Columbia, 1978-79; bd. trustees Jewish Fedn. Howard County, 1993-94. Mem. ABA (sec. real property, probate and trust law, chmn. prohibited transactions com. 1983-85, chmn. mgmt. property com. 1985-87, chmn. nat. insts. and satellite programs 1987-89, advisor UCC drafting com. article 1, article 3, article 9), Md. State Bar Assn., Pa. Bar Assn., Phila. Bar Assn., Am. Law Inst. (advisor restatement of the law of mortgages), Anglo-Am. Real Property Inst. (sec. 1990-92, chair-elect 1994, chair 1995), Am. Coll. Real Estate Lawyers (v.p. 1989-90, pres.-elect 1990-91, pres. 1991-92), Urban Land Inst., Am. Coll. of Mortgage Attys., Internat. Coun. Shopping Ctrs. (past chmn. law conf. com., mem. govtl. affairs com., econ. affairs subcom.). Property, real (including real estate development, water). Home: 325 S 2nd St Philadelphia PA 19106-4317 Office: Ballard Spahr Andrews & Ingersoll 1735 Market St Ste 5100 Philadelphia PA 19103-7599 E-mail: goldbergr@ballardspahr.com.

GOLDBERG, STANLEY JOSHUA, federal judge; b. Balt., Feb. 16, 1939; s. Isidore and Lillian Frances (Kravatz) G.; m. Susan Jane Coplin, July 1, 1962; Rachel Hilary, David Mark. BS, U. Md., 1960, LLB, 1964; postgrad., NYU, 1966-69. Bar: Md. 1964, U.S. Dist. Ct. Md. 1964, N.J. 1967, U.S. Dist. Ct. N.J. 1967, U.S. Tax Ct. 1968. Tax trial atty. office of chief counsel IRS, N.Y.C., 1965-69, 1971-76, spl. trial atty., 1976-84, asst. dist. counsel, 1984-85; assoc. Buckmaster, White, Mindel & Clarke, Balt., 1970; spl. trial judge U.S. Tax Ct., Washington, 1985—. Mem.: D.C. Bar Assn. (hon.), Am. Coll. Tax Counsel (hon.). Office: US Tax Ct 400 2nd St NW Washington DC 20217-0002

GOLDBERG, STEVEN SELIG, education law educator; b. Bklyn., Jan. 8, 1950; s. Harry Louis and Ruth (Bartnofsky) G. BA, SUNY, Binghamton, 1970; JD, Bklyn. Law Sch., 1973; MA, Columbia U., 1976; PhD, U. Pa., 1985. Bar: Pa. 1974, US Dist. Ct. (ea. dist.) Pa. 1976, US Ct. Appeals (3d cir.) 1976, Nebr. 1980. Atty. Camden Regional Legal Svc., NJ, 1976, Edn. Law Ctr., Phila., 1976-80; fellow law psychology grad. tng. program U. Nebr., Lincoln, Nebr., 1980-81; pvt. practice Phila., 1982-85; asst. prof. edn. law U. ND, Grand Forks, ND, 1986-88; assoc. prof. Arcadia U., Glenside, Pa., 1988-93, prof., 1993—; adj. prof. edn. sch. U. Pa. Law Sch., Phila., 1990—2002; adj. prof. edn. law Rutgers Law Sch., Camden, NJ, 1995—. Appellate officer Pa. Spl. Edn. Appeals Panel, 1995—; editl. adv. bd. West's Edn. Law Reporter, 1987—; mem. profl. adv. bd. Montgomery County (Pa.) Assn. for Children with Learning Disabilitis, Pa. Assn. Children with Learning Disabilities, 1976-80; cons. right to edn. assistance group Pa. Dept. Edn. Author: Special Education Law, 1982; editor: Readings on Equal Education, 1991; (with P. Zirkel) Digests of Supreme Court Cases in Education, 1995, 4th edit., 2001; co-host, prodr. show Sta. KFJM Pub. Radio U. ND, 1987; prodr. videotapes; contbr. articles to profl. jour. Mem. ABA (dispute resolution sect., co-chair edn. com. 1997), Phila. Bar Assn., Am. Ednl. Rsch. Assn (chmn. edn. law 1989-90), Edn. Law Assn. (bd. dir. 2000—), Soc. for Profl. Dispute Resolution (co-chmn. edn. sector). Jewish. Office: Arcadia U Church And Easton Rd Glenside PA 19038

GOLDBERGER, ALAN STEVEN, lawyer; b. Newark, Jan. 31, 1949; s. Milton Howard and Miriam (Kaplan) G.; m. Carole Selikowitz, Oct. 13, 1985. AB, Franklin and Marshall Coll., 1971; JD, Rutgers U., 1974. Bar: N.J. 1975, N.Y. 1985, Md. 1999, U.S. Dist. Ct. N.J. 1975, U.S. Dist. Ct. (so. dist.) N.Y. 1992, U.S. Dist. Ct. Md. 1999. Ptnr. Goldberger & Goldberger, Clifton, N.J., 1975—. Author: Sports Officiating: A Legal Guide, 1984; co-author: Sport, Physical Activity, and the Law, 1993, 2002. Mem.: ABA (vice chmn. nonprofit corps. com., bus. law sect., co-chmn. nonprofit athletic orgn. sub-com., chmn. trade assns. com.), Nat. Assn. Girls and Women in Sport (chmn. com. legal issues), Internat. Assn. Approved Basketball Ofcls. Jewish. Avocations: officiating basketball, baseball and football. State civil litigation, Non-profit and tax-exempt organizations, Sports. Home: 530 Valley Rd PO Box 43447 Montclair NJ 07043-0447 Office: Goldberger & Goldberger 1373 Broad St PO Box 447 Clifton NJ 07015-0447 E-mail: alan@refereelaw.com.

GOLD-BIKIN, LYNNE Z. lawyer; b. N.Y.C., Apr. 23, 1938; d. Herbert Benjamin Zapoleon and Muriel Claire (Wimpfheimer) Sarnoff; m. Roy E. Gold, Aug. 20, 1956 (div. July 1976); children: Russell, Sheryl, Lisa, Michael; m. Martin H. Feldman, June 28, 1987. BA summa cum laude, Albright Coll., 1973; JD, Villanova Law Sch., 1976; hon., 1996. Bar: Pa. 1976, U.S. Dist. Ct. (ea. dist.) Pa. 1976, U.S. Supreme Ct. 1979. Assoc. Pechner, Dorfman, Wolffe, Rounick & Cabot, Norristown, Pa., 1976-81; ptnr. Olin, Neil, Frock & Gold-Bikin, Norristown, 1981-82; pres. Gold-Bikin, Welsh & Assocs., Norristown, 1982-96, Wolf, Block, Schorr & Solis-Cohen, Norristown, 1996—. Course planner for 12 manuals on continuing legal edn., 1978—; pres. coun. Albright Coll., Reading, Pa., 1982-87. Author: Pennsylvania Marital Agreements, 1984, Divorce Practice Handbook, 1994; contbg. editor, Fairshare Mag., 1987—. Named to Pa. Honor Roll of Women, 1996. Fellow Am. Acad. Matrimonial Lawyers,

Internat. Acad. Matrimonial Lawyers, Am. Bar Found., Am. Law Inst., Pa. Bar Found.; mem. ABA (family law sect. chair 1994-95, ho. of dels. 1995, bd. govs. 1998-2001), Pa. Bar Assn. (family law sect. coun. mem. 1980-89), Montgomery County Bar Assn. (chmn. family law com. 1984-86), Pa. Trial Lawyers Assn. (chmn. family law sect. 1988-90). Family and matrimonial. Office: Wolf Block Schorr & Solis-Cohen PO Box 869 Norristown PA 19404-0869

GOLDBLATT, STANFORD JAY, lawyer; b. Chgo., Feb. 25, 1939; s. Maurice and Bernice (Mendelson) G.; m. Ann Dudley Cronkhite, June 17, 1968; children: Alexandra, Nathaniel, Jeremy. BA magna cum laude, Harvard U., 1960, LLB magna cum laude, 1963. Bar: Ill. 1963. Law clk. U.S. Ct. Appeals, 5th Jud. Circuit, New Orleans, 1963-64; mem. firm Winston & Strawn, Chgo., 1964-67; v.p. Goldblatt Bros., Inc., Chgo., 1967-76, pres., chief exec. officer, 1976-77, chmn. exec. com., 1977-78; ptnr. Hopkins & Sutter, 1978-97, Winston & Strawn, Chgo., 1997—. Dir. MacLean-Fogg Co. Trustee U. Chgo., Cancer Rsch. Found., U. Chgo. Hosps. Mem. Econ. Club, Racquet Club, Comml. Club. Office: Winston & Strawn 35 W Wacker Dr Ste 4200 Chicago IL 60601-9703

GOLDBLATT, STEVEN HARRIS, law educator; b. Bklyn., Apr. 30, 1947; s. J. Irving and Ethel (Epstein) G.; m. Irene P. Burns, June 12, 1981; children: Sarah P., Elizabeth G.B. BA, Franklin & Marshall Coll., 1967; JD, Georgetown U., 1970. Bar: Pa. 1970, D.C. 1981. With Phila. Dist. Atty.'s Office, 1970-81; dir. Appellate Litigation Program Georgetown U. Law Ctr., Washington, 1981-83, prof. law, dir. Appellate Litigation Progam, 1983—. Chair rules adv. com. U.S. Ct. Appeals for Armed Forces, 1998—. Co-author: Analysis and Commentary to the Pennsylvania Crime Code, 1973, Three Prosecutors Look at the Crimes Code, 1974, Ineffective Assistance of Counsel: Attempts to Establish Minimum Standards for Criminal Cases, 1983; reporter Criminal Justice in Crisis, 1988, Achieving Justice in a Diverse America, 1992, An Agenda for Justice: ABA Perspectives on Criminal and Civil Justice Issues, 1996. Mem. ABA (criminal justice sect. chmn. amicus curiae briefs com. 1981-99, crisis in criminal justice com. 1990-91, criminal justice standards com.). Office: Georgetown U Law Ctr 600 New Jersey Ave NW Washington DC 20001-2075 E-mail: goldblat@law.georgetown.edu.

GOLDEN, ARTHUR F. lawyer; b. Bklyn., Apr. 14, 1946; s. Isadore and Dorothy (Schisel) G.; m. Elisabeth Lee Smith, Aug. 28, 1971; children—Frederick Tucker, James Alexander, Eliza Emerson BS, Rensselaer Poly. Inst., 1966; JD, NYU, 1969. Bar: N.Y. 1970, U.S. Ct. Appeals (2d cir.) 1970, U.S. Dist. Ct. (so. dist.) N.Y. 1972, U.S. Supreme 1975, U.S. Ct. Appeals (D.C. cir.) 1979, D.C. 1980, U.S. Dist. Ct. D.C. 1980, U.S. Dist. Ct. (ea. dist.) N.Y. 1972, U.S. Dist. Ct. (no. dist.) Ohio 1985, U.S. Ct. Appeals (6th cir.) 1985, U.S. Ct. Appeals (7th cir.) 1996. With Davis Polk & Wardwell, N.Y.C., 1969—, ptnr., 1978—; mgmt. com., 1996—; co-founder Washington office Davis Polk, 1980-82, bd. dirs. Bd. dirs. Emerson Electric Co., 2000-, ESCO Electronics Corp., mem. exec. com., chmn. compensation com., 1990-96, Burns Internat. Svs. Corp., mem. exec. and audit and fin. coms., 1996-2000, Allegiance Corp., mem. audit and pub. policy com., 1996-99. With USAR, 1968—74. Mem. ABA, Assn. of Bar of City of N.Y., N.Y. State Bar Assn., N.Y. State Communities Aid Assn. (bd. mgrs. 1986-89), New Canaan Winter Club (pres. 1988-91, bd. govs. 1987-93), Country Club New Canaan, River Club N.Y.C. Antitrust, Federal civil litigation, Mergers and acquisitions. Home: 72 Saint George Ln New Canaan CT 06840-2032 Office: Davis Polk & Wardwell 450 Lexington Ave Fl 29 New York NY 10017-3911

GOLDEN, BRUCE PAUL, lawyer; b. Chgo., Dec. 4, 1943; s. Irving R. and Anne K. (Eisenberg) G. SB in Elec. Sci. and Engring., MIT, 1965, SM in Elec. Engring., 1966; JD, Harvard U., 1969. Bar: Ill. 1969, U.S. Dist. Ct. (no. dist.) Ill. 1970, U.S. Ct. Appeals (7th cir.) 1994, U.S. Supreme Ct. 1995, cert.: (arbitrator); lic. real estate broker. Assoc. McDermott, Will & Emery, Chgo., 1970-75, ptnr., 1976-91; of counsel Fishman & Merrick, P.C., Chgo., 1991-92, Coffield, Ungaretti & Harris, Chgo., 1992-96; Bruce P. Golden and Assocs., Chgo., 1996—; gen. counsel Piranha, Inc., 2000—02. Officer, dir. various corps.; speaker bank law, securities law, venture capital seminars Contbr. articles to Banking Law Jour., contbg. editor, 1979— Chmn. MIT Enterprise Forum Chgo.; bd. dirs. Entrepreneurship Inst. Chgo., Chgo. chpt. U.S. Entrepreneurs Network, Ill. Small Bus. Devel. Ctr., Kellogg Sch. Bus. community services com. Mem. MIT Alumni of Chgo. (dir. 1993—), Union League. Banking, General civil litigation, Securities. Home and Office: 4137 N Hermitage Ave Chicago IL 60613-1820

GOLDEN, DANIEL LEWIS, lawyer; b. N.Y.C., May 7, 1913; s. Louis and Rose (Rosen) G.; m. Evelyn Shayevitz, July 9, 1941 (dec.); children: Roger M., Leslie Rosemary; m. Eugenia Alice Norman, Feb. 14, 1997. BS, Lafayette Coll., 1934; LLD (hon.), 1993; JD, Rutgers U., 1938. Bar: N.J. 1939, D.C. 1976, U.S. Supreme Ct. 1957. Practice, South River, 1940—; now of counsel Greenbaum, Rowe, Smith, Ravin, Davis & Himmell LLP, Woodbridge, N.J. Active survey legal systems USSR, East Europe for State Dept. Exchanges Programs, also for ABA, N.J. Bar Assn., 1961-75. Chmn. ethics Com., 1967; mem. N.J. Gov.'s Commn. on Individual Liberty and Personal Privacy, 1977-84; bd. trustees Lafayette Coll., 1975-80. Lt. USAAF, 1942-45. Recipient Kidd hon. citation for law Lafayette Coll., 1970, Bell Disting. Svc. Alumni award, 1985; Rutgers Law award, 1971, Lawyer of Yr. N.J. Commn. on Professionalism, 1998. Fellow Am. Bar Found. (state chmn. 1985-90, nat. chmn. 1992-93), Am. Acad. Martimonial Lawyers; mem. ABA (ho. of dels. 1972-90, chmn. adv. commn. on election law), N.J. Bar Assn. (pres. 1970-71, editorial bd. N.J. Lawyer mag. 1969—), Middlesex County Bar Assn. (pres. 1960-61), Assn. Trial Lawyers Am., Trial Attys. N.J. (bd. trustees 1969—, Lifetime Achievement award 1986), N.J. Bar Found. (Medal of Honor award 1991), Pi Lambda Phi (honoree 1997). General civil litigation, Family and matrimonial, Private international. Office: Greenbaum Rowe Smith Ravin Davis & Himmel LLP PO Box 5600 Metro Corp Campus One Woodbridge NJ 07095

GOLDEN, E(DWARD) SCOTT, lawyer; b. Miami, Fla., Sept. 25, 1955; s. Alvan Leonard and Fay Betty (Gray) G.; m. Jane Eileen DeKlavon, June 9, 1979; children: Daniel Bryan, Kimberly Michelle. Student, So. Fla. Christian Coll., 1975-76; BS, MIT, 1978; JD, Harvard U., 1981. Bar: Fla. 1981, U.S. Dist. Ct. (so. dist.) Fla. 1982, U.S. Tax Ct. 1982, U.S. Supreme Ct. 1991, U.S. Dist. Ct. (mid. dist.) Fla. 1993. Assoc. Roberts and Holland, Miami, 1981-82, Valdes-Fauli, Richardson, Cobb & Petrey, P.A., Miami, 1982-83; v.p. Buck and Golden, P.A., Ft. Lauderdale, Fla., 1983-88; sole practice Ft. Lauderdale, Fla., 1988—. Judge negotiations competition Nova Southeastern U. Editor-in-chief Harvard Jour. of Law and Pub. Policy, 1980-81; contbr. articles to profl. jours. Mem. West Lauderdale Bapt. Ch., Broward County, Fla., 1982-98, chmn. deacons, 1984-86, 87-88, elder, 1994-98; mem. MIT Edni. Coun., 1995—; del. Fla. Rep. Conv., 1987, 90; mem. Rep. Exec. Com., Broward County, 1984-94. Named one of Outstanding Young Men of Am., 1986; nominee Order of Silver Knight; Western Electric grantee, 1972-74. Mem. Christian Legal Soc., Broward County Christian Legal Soc. (pres. 1985-86, 94-95, 2000), Zeta Beta Tau. Lodges: Optimists (treas. Dade County Carol City High Sch., 1971-72). Avocations: sports, politics, bible study. Corporate, general, Probate (including wills, trusts), Property, real (including real estate development, water). Home: 5410 Buchanan St Hollywood FL 33021-5708 Office: 644 SE 4th Ave Fort Lauderdale FL 33301-3102 E-mail: esglaw@bellsouth.net.

GOLDEN, ELLIOTT, judge; b. Bklyn., June 28, 1926; s. Barnet David and Rose (Fistel) G.; m. Ana Valbuena, July 8, 1990; children: Jeffrey Stephen, Marjorie Ruth, Peter Michael (dec.); stepchildren: Robert, Elizabeth, William, John. Student, Maritime Acad., 1944-46, NYU, 1947-48; LLB, Bklyn. Law Sch., 1951. Bar: N.Y. 1952, U.S. Dist. Ct. (ea. dist.) N.Y. 1953, U.S. Tax Ct., U.S. Dist. Ct. (so. dist.) N.Y. 1953, U.S. Supreme Ct. 1961. Assoc. Golden & Golden, 1952-64; asst. dist. atty. Kings County, N.Y., 1956-64, chief asst. dist. atty., 1964-76, acting dist. atty., 1968; judge Civil Ct. of City of N.Y., 1977-78; justice Supreme Ct. State of N.Y., 1979-98, jud. hearing officer, 1998-2000. Adj. assoc. prof. N.Y.C. Tech. Coll., 1987-93; arbitrator, mediator Nat. Arbitration & Mediation, 1998—; cons. in field. Contbr. articles to profl. jours. Bd. trustees Greater N.Y. coun. Boy Scouts Am.; hon. vice chmn. March of Dimes; bd. dirs. Bklyn. Philharmonia; mem. adv. bd. Bklyn. PAL; chmn. Bklyn. Lawyers div. Fedn. Jewish Philanthropies; co-chmn. Bklyn. Lawyers div. State of Israel Bonds; assoc. trustee Temple Beth Emeth of Flatbush; mem. exec. com. Lawyers div. United Jewish Appeal; past pres. counsel Hosp. Relief Assn.; bd. dirs. Kings Bay YM-YMHA of Bklyn.; bd. dirs. Bklyn. ARC, Archway Sch. for Spl. Children, Bklyn. Sch. for Spl. Children. Recipient Cert. of Merit, Hosp. Relief Assn., numerous plaques, awards and certs. of appreciation various civic orgns. Mem. Nat. Dist. Attys. Assn. (dir. 1976-77, Disting. Svc. award), Combined Coun. Law Enforcement Ofcls. State N.Y., N.Y. State Dist. Attys. Assn. (sec. 1965-77), K.P. (supreme coun.). Avocations: golf, fishing, computers. E-mail: egolden@hvc.rr.com.

GOLDEN, LOREN S. lawyer; b. 1943; State atty. Carroll County; pvt. practice West Dundee, Ill. Mem.: Ill. State Bar (3d v.p., bd. govs., treas. 1994—95). Office: Ste 201A 2400 Big Timber Rd Elgin IL 60123*

GOLDEN, T. MICHAEL, state supreme court justice; b. 1942; BA in History, U. Wyo., 1964, JD, 1967; LLM, U. Va., 1992. Bar: Wyo. 1967, U.S. Dist. Ct. 1967, U.S. Ct. Appeals (10th cir.) 1967, U.S. Supreme Ct. 1970. Mem. firm Brimmer, MacPherson & Golden, Rawlins, Wyo., 1971-83, Williams, Porter, Day & Neville, Casper, Wyo., 1983-88; chief justice Wyo. Supreme Ct., Cheyenne, 1994—96, justice, 1988—. Mem. Wyo. State Bd. Law Examiners, 1977-82, 86-88. Capt. U.S. Army 1967-71. Office: Wyo Supreme Ct Bldg 2301 Capitol Ave Cheyenne WY 82002

GOLDEN, THOMAS M. lawyer; b. Nov. 1947; Grad., Pa. State U., 1969, Dickinson U. Mng. ptnr. Golden Masano Bradley. Mem. adv. bd. Nat. Penn Bank. Mem. adv. bd. Jesuit Ctr. for Spirtual Growth. Fellow: Pa. Bar Found.; mem.: Pa. Bar Assn. (Ho. of Dels., zone 2 gov., vice chair editl. com., chair client and cmty. rels. com., task force for quality of life/balance, task force on entities and ops., pres.-elect, pres. 2003—, Spl. Achievement award 2000), Berks County Bar Assn. (dir. 1990—93, pres. 1992), Berks County Golf Assn. (past pres.). Office: Pa Bar Assn PO Box 186 100 South St Harrisburg PA 17108-0186*

GOLDEN, WILSON, lawyer; b. Holly Springs, Miss., Feb. 15, 1948; s. Woodrow Wilson and Constance Annette (Harris) G.; m. Krista Nix, July 10, 1999; children from previous marriage: Wilson Harris, Lewis Hamilton, Pamela Camille. BPA, U. Miss., 1970, JD, 1977. Bar: Miss. 1977, U.S. Dist. Ct. (no. and so. dists.) Miss. 1977, U.S. Ct. Appeals (5th cir.) 1977. Pub. affairs journalist PBS/Miss. Authority for Ednl. TV, Jackson, 1970-72; asst. sec. Miss. State Senate, Jackson, 1972-76; ptnr. Lane & Henderson, Greenville, Miss., 1977-80, Watkins Ludlam & Stennis, Jackson, 1980-89; pvt. practice Jackson, Washington, 1990-96; v.p. govt. rels. ICF Kaiser Internat., Inc., Fairfax, Va., 1996—99; sr. congl. liaison U.S. Dept. Transp., Washington, 1999-2001; v.p. Jefferson Govt. Rels., Washington, 2001—. Mem. Dem. State Exec. Com., 1976-84, 88-96; mem. Miss. Gov.'s Constl. Study Commn., 1986; mem. Dem. Nat. Com., 1990-92; charter mem. Dem. Leadership Coun. NETWORK, 1988; USDOT rep. Miss. Spl. Task Force for Econ. Devel. Planning, 2000—. Major USAR, 1970-90. Recipient Disting. Reporting award Am. Polit. Sci. Assn. 1971, U.S. Law Week award Bur. Nat. Affairs, Inc., Washington, 1978. Mem.: Miss. Bar Assn. Democrat. Presbyterian. Legislative. Home: 7037 E Haycock Rd Falls Church VA 22043-2319 E-mail: Wilsongolden@aol.com.

GOLDENBERG, PHILIP, lawyer; b. London, Apr. 26, 1946; s. Nathan and Edith Goldenberg; m. Lynda Anne Silver, Oct. 12, 1985; children: Jonathan, Philippa, Benjamin, Joshua. Student, St. Paul's Sch., London, 1959—63, Pembroke Coll., Oxford, 1964—68. Admitted as solicitor: Eng. 1972. Assoc. Linklaters & Paires, London, 1972—82, SJ, Berwin, 1982—83, ptnr., 1983—. Author: Fair Welfare, 1968, The Business Guide to Directors' Responsibilities, 2001; co-author: Sharing Profits, 1986; co-editor: New Outlook, 1977; mem. editl. adv. bd.: Bus. Law Rev., 1994—. Liberal Democrat. Jewish. Corporate, general, Mergers and acquisitions, Labor (including EEOC, Fair Labor Standards Act, labor-management relations, NLRB, OSHA). Office: SJ Berwin 222 Grays Inn Rd London WC1X 8XF England Fax: 44(0) 207 533 2533. E-mail: philipgoldenberg@sjberwin.com.

GOLDENBERG, STEPHEN BERNARD, lawyer; b. Cambridge, Mass., Feb. 10, 1943; s. Alexander M. and Gertrude (Perlmutter) G. AB, Kenyon Coll., 1964; postgrad., Georgetown U. Law Sch., 1964-65; JD, Boston Coll., 1967. Bar: Mass. 1967, Fla. 1990, U.S. Supreme Ct. 1994. Assoc. Myer Israel, Boston, 1968—74; ptnr. Israel & Goldenberg, 1974—91, Goldenberg, Walters & Lipson, Brookline, 1991—98, Goldenberg, Walters & Popkewitz, 1998—. Chmn. rent control bd., Brookline, 1972-75; mem. Brookline Bd. Selectmen, 1976-85, chmn., 1983-84. Mem. ABA, Mass. Bar Assn., Mass. Conveyancers Assn., Brookline C. of C. (pres.). Democrat. Corporate, general, Probate (including wills, trusts), Property, real (including real estate development, water). Office: Goldenberg Walters et al 7 Harvard St Brookline MA 02445-7970 E-mail: sbgat23@aol.com.

GOLDENHERSH, ROBERT STANLEY, lawyer; b. St. Louis, July 23, 1922; s. Boris and Sarah (Lapushin) G.; m. Jeanne Waldman, June 18, 1950; children: Lawrence E., Margaret J., Louise E. JD, Washington U., 1947; LLM in Taxation, NYU, 1948. Bar: Mo. 1947, U.S. Dist. Ct. (ea. dist.) Mo., U.S. Ct. Appeals (8th cir.), U.S. Supreme Ct. 1956. Sr. ptnr. Rosenblum, Goldenhersh, Silverstein & Zafft P.C., St. Louis, 1953—. Pres. Congregation Temple Israel, St. Louis, 1975-76; chmn. law sch. div. Elliot Soc. of Washington U., St. Louis, 1984; charter mem. Creve Couer Squires (Mo.), 1980—. Mem. ABA, Mo. Bar Assn., St. Louis Co. Bar Assn., Bar Assn. City of St. Louis, Order of the Coif. Clubs: Westwood Country. Democrat. Jewish. Avocations: tennis, golf, fishing. E-mail: rsg@rgs&z.com. Commercial, contracts (including sales of goods; commercial financing), Property, real (including real estate development, water), Taxation, general. Home: 211 Rondelay Ct Saint Louis MO 63141-7702 Office: Rosenblum Goldenhersh et al 4th Fl Pierre Laclede Ctr 7733 Forsyth Blvd Ste 400 Saint Louis MO 63105-1812

GOLDER, FREDERICK THOMAS, lawyer, educator; b. Brookline, Mass., July 5, 1943; s. Michael and Ida Shirley (Gropman) G.; Caron Sue Cohen, Oct. 8, 1966; children: Rachel Beth, David Ross, Naomi Lea. BA in English, U. Mass., 1965; JD, Suffolk Sch. Law, 1968; spl. student, Harvard U., 1968; LLM in Labor, NYU, 1969. Bar: Mass. 1968, U.S. Dist. Ct. Mass. 1969, U.S. Ct. Appeals (1st cir.) 1970, U.S. Supreme Ct. 1972. Formerly ptnr. Bernstein, Golder & Field, P.A., Boston. Adj. faculty Northeastern U., Boston, 1972—, Suffolk U. Law Sch.; faculty Mass. Sch. Law, 1988—; writer, Wilmette, Ill., 1982—; labor arbitrator and mediator. Author: Fair Employment Law, 1979, Wage and Hour Law, 1983, Health, Safety, etc., 1984, Legal Compliance Checkups: Business Clients, 1985, Labor and Employment Law: Compliance and Litigation, 1986, 2d edit., 1999, Uncivil Rights: Protecting and Preserving Your Job Rights, 1999, Federal Employment Rights, 2001, Employment Discrimination Law, 2002. Mem. gov.'s adv. bd. Mass. Commn. Against Discrimination. Fellow Mass. Bar Found.; mem. Fed. Bar Assn. (disting. service award 1984), Mass. Bar Assn., Assn. Trial Lawyers Am., Mass. Acad. Trial Attys. (disting. faculty award 1984, 86), Plaintiff Employment Lawyers Assn. (bd. dirs. 1986—). Civil rights, Federal civil litigation, Labor (including EEOC, Fair Labor Standards Act, labor-management relations, NLRB, OSHA).

GOLDER, LEONARD HOWARD, lawyer, writer; b. Boston, June 6, 1950; s. Hershel and Pauline (Glass) G.; 1 child, Robert. BA, Clark U., 1972; JD, New Eng. Sch. Law, 1980. Bar: Mass. 1981, U.S. Dist. Ct. Mass. 1981, U.S. Supreme Ct. 1984; lic. notary pub., Mass.; lic. real estate broker, Mass. Assoc. Law Offices Jacob Shair, West Roxbury, Mass., 1982-85; dir. collections unit Mass. Dept. Pub. Welfare, Boston, 1985-87; pvt. practice Stow, Mass., 1987—. Creator: (polit. game) Compromise, 1987; columnist to newspapers; contbr. articles to profl. jours. Social worker Tufts Mental Health, Boston, 1973-81; selectman Town of Stow, Mass., 1991-97, chmn. Stow Bd. Selectmen, 1994; chmn. Stow Dem. Com., 1994—; adv. mem. Stow Master Plan, 1994-97; mem. Middlesex County adv. bd., Cambridge, Mass., 1994-97, mem. Stow Cable TV Monitoring Com., 1999—, publicity dir. Middlesex-Worcester Area Dem. Coalition; bd. trustees Parker Charter Sch., Ayer, Mass., 2001-, mem. Glodis-Barrios Commn., Mass. Dem. Party, 2003 Avocations: collecting sports and polit. memorabilia, reading, travel. Alternative dispute resolution, Legislative, Personal injury (including property damage). Home and Office: 67 Old Bolton Rd Stow MA 01775-1212 E-mail: leonardhgolden@cs.com.

GOLDFARB, BERNARD SANFORD, lawyer; b. Cleve., Apr. 15, 1917; s. Harry and Esther (Lenson) Goldfarb; m. Barbara Brofman Goldfarb, Jan. 4, 1966; children: Merdeith Stacy, Lauren Beth. AB, Case Western Res. U., 1938, JD, 1940. Bar: Ohio 1940. Since practiced in, Cleve.; sr. ptnr. firm Goldfarb & Reznick, 1967-95; pvt. practice Cleve., 1997—. Spl. counsel to atty. gen. Ohio, 1950, 1971—74; mem. Ohio Commn. Uniform Traffic Rules, 1973—80. Contbr. legal jours. Served with USAAF, 1942-45. Mem.: ABA, Cuyahoga County Bar Assn., Greater Cleve. Bar Assn., Ohio Bar Assn. Federal civil litigation, General practice, Labor (including EEOC, Fair Labor Standards Act, labor-management relations, NLRB, OSHA). Home: 39 Pepper Creek Dr Pepper Pike OH 44124-5279 Office: 55 Public Sq Ste 1500 Cleveland OH 44113-1998

GOLDFARB, RONALD LAWRENCE, lawyer, writer; b. Jersey City, N.J., Oct. 16, 1933; s. Robert S. and Aida J. (Weintraub) G.; m. Joanne Jacob, June 9, 1957; children: Jody, Nicholas, Maximilian Goldfarb. AB, Syracuse U., 1954, LLB, 1956; LLM, Yale, 1960, JSD, 1962. Bar: N.Y. 1956, Calif. 1959, D.C. 1962, U.S. Supreme Ct. 1965. Spl. asst. to U.S. atty. gen. (organized crime sect.), 1961-64; ptnr. Goldfarb and Assocs. and predecessor law firms, 1966—. Dir. Brookings Instn. program on cts. and adminstrn. Justice, 1966-67; mem. staff counsel com. on law and social action Am. Jewish Congress, 1960-61; cons. Pres.'s Poverty Program, 1964, Riots Commn., 1967-68 Author: The Contempt Power, 1963, Ransom: A Critique of the American Bail System, 1965, (with Alfred Friendly) Crime and Publicity, 1967, (with Linda Singer) After Conviction--A Review of the American Correction System, 1973, Jails: The Ultimate Ghetto, 1975, Migrant Farm Workers: A Caste of Despair, 1981, (with James Raymond) Clear Understandings: A Guide to Legal Writing, 1983, (with Gail Ross) The Writer's Lawyer: Essential Legal Advice for Writers and Editors in All Media, 1989, Perfect Villains, Imperfect Heroes: Robert F. Kennedy's War Against Organized Crime, 1995, TV or Not TV: Television, Justice and Courts, 1998. Served to capt. JAG Corps USAF, 1957-60. Capt. JAG Corp. USAF, 1957—60. Arthur Garfield Hays fellow N.Y.U., 1960-61; Woodrow Wilson fellow. Mem. ACLU, D.C. Bar Assn., N.Y. Bar Assn., Calif. Bar Assn., Cosmos Club, Sigma Alpha Mu., Phi Delta Phi. General civil litigation, Criminal. Office: 1501 M St NW Washington DC 20005-1700

GOLDFEIN, SHEPARD, lawyer; b. Englewood, N.J., 1948; AB, Rutgers U., 1970, JD, 1975; MA, U. Chgo., 1977. Bar: N.Y. 1976, N.J. 1977. Ptnr. Skadden, Arps, Slate, Meagher & Flom LLP, N.Y.C. Editor: Rutgers Law Rev., 1974-75. Mem. Phi Beta Kappa, Pi Sigma Alpha. Office: Skadden Arps Slate Meagher & Flom LLP 4 Times Sq 34th Fl New York NY 10036-6595 E-mail: sgoldfei@skadden.com.

GOLDMAN, ALAN BARRY, lawyer, accountant; b. Bklyn., July 9, 1954; s. Lester and Sonya Goldman; m. June Marie Bohling, Sept. 15, 1979; children: Tanya, Zachary. BS, SUNY, Albany, 1976; JD, St. John's U., Jamaica, N.Y., 1983. Bar: N.Y. 1984, U.S. Dist. Ct. (ea. dist.) N.Y. 1984, U.S. Tax Ct. 1984, U.S. Ct. Mil. Appeals 1988, U.S. Supreme Ct. 1988; CPA, N.Y., Fla.; diplomate Am. Bd. Forensic Accts. Pvt. practice, Floral Park, N.Y.; ptnr. Kimmel Blau & Goldman, CPA's, Rockville Centre, N.Y. Mem. ABA, AICPA, Am. Assn. Attornies-CPAs, N.Y. State Bar Assn., N.Y. State Soc. CPA's, Fla. Inst. CPA's. Probate (including wills, trusts), Property, real (including real estate development, water), Taxation, general. Home: 31 Vanderbilt Way Valley Stream NY 11581-2333 Office: 16 Verbena Ave Floral Park NY 11001-2712

GOLDMAN, ALLAN BAILEY, lawyer; b. Auburn, N.Y., Jan. 1, 1937; s. Charles and Rose Hortense (Abrahams) G.; m. Eleanor Ruth Levy, May 26, 1963; children; Jennifer Brooke Horwitz, Andrea Allison Gellert. AB magna cum laude, Harvard U., 1958, JD, 1963; LHD (hon.), Hebrew Union Coll.-Jewish Inst. Religion, 1992. Bar: Calif. 1964, D.C. 1977, U.S. Supreme Ct. 1977. Assoc. Wyman, Bautzer, Kuchel & Silbert, Beverly Hills, Calif., 1963-67, ptnr. L.A., 1967-91, Katten, Muchin, Zavis & Rosenman, L.A., 1991—. Judge pro-tem Calif. Mcpl. and Small Claims Cts.; arbitrator Calif. Superior Ct. Contbr. articles to profl. jours. Chmn. Attys. for Brown for Gov., officer Brown for Pres., 1976; founder L.A. Com. for Civil Rights Under Law, Mus. Contemporary Art, L.A., Fraternity of Friends of L.A. Music Ctr.; trustee Calif. Mus. Sci. and Industry, 1981-89, St. John's Hosp. and Health Ctr. Found., 1978—, exec. com., 1979-89, bd. dirs., 1989-95, treas., 1990-94, chmn., 1994-95; chmn. nat. bd. trustees Union of Am. Hebrew Congregations, 1987-91; bd. govs. Hebrew Union Coll.-Jewish Inst. Religion, 1988—, bd. overseers L.A. campus, 1981-85, 88—; trustee SKirball Cultural Ctr., 1997—; pres. Leo Baeck Temple, L.A., 1975-77; mem. Conf. Pres.'s Major Jewish Orgns., 1987-91; mem. synagogue funding com. Jewish Fedn. Coun. of Greater L.A., 1979, chmn., 1985-88; Calif. Commn. Jud. Nominees Evaluation, 1999-2002. Lt. USNR, 1958-60. Mem. Calif. Bar Assn., D.C. Bar Assn., Regency Club. Democrat. Jewish. Avocations: trekking, running, tennis. Home: 347 Conway Ave Los Angeles CA 90024-2603 Office: Katten Muchin Zavis Rosenman 2029Century Park E Ste 2600 Los Angeles CA 90067 E-mail: allan.goldman@kmzr.com.

GOLDMAN, ARNOLD JOSEPH, lawyer; b. May 30, 1931; s. Reuben and Esther (Simon) G.; m. Lynn Kay Grundstein, June 15, 1958; children: Jonathan, Lisa, Ruth. AB, Cornell U., 1953; LLB, Harvard U., 1956. Bar: N.Y. 1956, U.S. Dist. Ct. (we. dist.) N.Y. 1956, U.S. Tax Ct. 1971, U.S. Ct. Appeals (4th cir.), 1976, Fla. 1988. Assoc. Nixon, Hargrave, Devans & Doyle, Rochester, 1958-62; ptnr. Goldman & Goldman, Rochester, 1962—. Co-author: Business Law-Principles and Practices, 1983, 2000. Served with U.S. Army, 1956-58. Decorated Commendation ribbon. Jewish. Corporate, general, General practice, Property, real (including real estate development, water). Office: Goldman & Goldman 3 Leeward Ln Rochester NY 14618

GOLDMAN, BRIAN ARTHUR, lawyer, accountant; b. Balt., June 30, 1946; s. Marvin L. and Edythe R. Goldman; m. Eileen G. Safro, Aug. 22, 1970; children: Jonathan S., Evan M. BS in Real Estate Planning, Am.U., 1968; JD, U. Md., 1971. Bar: Md. 1972, U.S. Dist. Ct. Md. 1972, U.S. Tax Ct. 1977, U.S. Supreme Ct. 1977. Acct., Balt., 1974—; mem. Burke, Gerber & Wilen, 1972-77, Sapero & Sapero, 1977-78; pvt. practice, 1978-83; ptnr. Goldman and Fedder, P.A., Balt., 1983-85, Fedder & Garten, P.A., 1986-88, Goldman & Vetter, P.A., 1989—. Asst. prof. income taxation U. Balt., 1974-75. Mem. ABA, Md. Bar Assn., Balt. City Bar Assn., Md. Assn. CPAs,

Ctr. Club, Woodholme. Commercial, consumer (including collections, credit), Corporate, general, Property, real (including real estate development, water). Office: Goldman & Vetter PA 36 S Charles St Ste 2401 Baltimore MD 21201-3108 E-mail: bgoldman@goldmanvetter.com.

GOLDMAN, ELISABETH PARIS, lawyer; b. Pitts., Jan. 11, 1939; d. Harold H. and Silvia F. (Koenigsberg) Paris; m. Alvin Lee Goldman, Nov. 23, 1956; children: Polly, Douglas. BA, Queens Coll., 1964; JD, U. Ky., 1975. Bar: Ky. 1975, Calif. 1977. Chief law clk. Supreme Ct. Ky., Frankfort, 1975-76; pvt. practice Elisabeth Goldman PSC, Lexington, Ky., 1977—. Bd. dirs. ACLU Louisville, Ky., 1987-90, Hadassah, Chamber Music Soc., Fayette County Health Care Bd.; pres. Ctrl. Ky. Jewish Fedn., 1993-95, Ctrl. Ky. Civil Liberties Union, 1988-90, James Lane Allen PTA, Lexington, Ky., 1971-72. Recipient Pro-Bono Svc. award Ky. Bar Assn., Frankfort, 1994-2001. Mem. Am. Acad. Adoption Attys., Order of Coif, Phi Beta Kappa. Democrat. Avocations: skiing, hiking, dog training. Family and matrimonial. Office: Elisabeth Goldman PSC 118 Old Lafayette Ave Lexington KY 40502-1704 E-mail: egoldman@adoptionattorneys.org.

GOLDMAN, ERIC SCOT, lawyer; b. Quincy, Mass., Mar. 5, 1957; s. Terry and Harriet (Goldstein) G.; m. Lora Anderson, June 18, 1983; children: William, Daniel, Leigh. BA, Boston Coll., 1979; MS in Criminal Justice, Northeastern U., 1980; JD, Suffolk U., 1987. Bar: Mass. 1987, U.S. Dist. Ct. Mass. 1987, U.S. Mil. Ct. Appeals. Adminstr. McLean Hosp., Belmont, Mass.; caseworker Norfolk County Dist. Atty.'s Office, Dedham, Mass.; atty. McDermott & Padis, Milton, Mass., 1983-93; assoc. Lynch & Lynch, South Easton, Mass., 1993-98, Lang & Morgera, Boston, 1998-99; ptnr. Finneran, Byrne & Drechsler, LLP, Boston, 1999—. Mediator Norfolk-Plymouth County; bd. dirs. Criminal Justice Scis. Inst., Washington. Recipient Cert. of Recognition, Norfolk County Dist. Atty., Commonwealth of Mass. Dist. Ct. Mem. Mass Acad. Trial Attys., Norfolk, Plymouth and Bristol County Bar Assn., Braintree Rifle and Pistol Club (pres. 1988—). Avocations: scuba diving, Karate, music, firearms training. General civil litigation, Criminal, Insurance. Home: 36 Forge Way Duxbury MA 02332-4743 Office: Finneran Byrne & Drechsler Eastern Harbor Office Pk 50 Redfield St Boston MA 02122-3630

GOLDMAN, GARY CRAIG, lawyer; b. Dec. 28, 1951; s. Ronald Walter and Connie Sylvia (Stein) G.; m. Diane Rose Lane, Oct. 1, 1977; children: Justin Edward, Gregory David. BA magna cum laude, Temple U., 1973; JD, Villanova U., 1976. Bar: Pa. 1976, U.S. Dist. Ct. (ea. dist.) Pa. 1981. Jud. law clk. Common Pleas Ct., Northampton County, Pa., 1976-77; asst. atty. gen. office of legal counsel Pa. Dept. Pub. Welfare, Phila., 1977-81, asst. counsel, 1981-84; staff counsel CDI Corp., Phila., 1984-86, v.p., assoc. gen. counsel, 1986—. Mem. faculty, planning chmn. Nationwide Comml. Real Estate Leasing Programs. Author: Drafting a Fair Office Lease, 1989, 2d edit., 2000; contbg. author: The Commercial Real Estate Tenant's Handbook, 1987, The Practical Real Estate Lawyer's Manual, 1987, Commercial Tenants' Leasing Transactions Guide, 1991, Office Planning and Design Desk Reference, 1992, Negotiating and Drafting Office Leases, 1995; assoc. editor: Villanova Law Rev., 1974-76; contbr. articles to legal jours. Mem. ABA, Am. Corp. Counsel Assn., Phila. Bar Assn. Republican. Jewish. Avocation: golf. Corporate, general, Labor (including EEOC, Fair Labor Standards Act, labor-management relations, NLRB, OSHA), Landlord-tenant. Home: 210 Fox Hollow Dr Langhorne PA 19053-2477 Office: CDI Corp 1717 Arch St Fl 35 Philadelphia PA 19103-2713

GOLDMAN, GLORIA A. lawyer; b. Bamberg, Germany, Oct. 7, 1948; d. Esther and Harry Praw(Stepfather); m. Michael V. Goldman, Dec. 11, 1945; children: Maurice H., Larissa A. BS, Wayne State U., 1970; JD, U. Ariz., 1990. Bar: Ariz. 1991, D.C. 2001. Pvt. practice, Tucson. Named one of Top 50 Pro Bono Attys. in Ariz., Ariz. Bar Found., 2002, Best Lawyers in Am., 2001—. Mem.: U. Ariz. Law Coll. Assn. (bd. mem. 1991—), Am. Immigration Lawyers Assn. (Ariz. state chairperson 1997—98, enforcement com. liaison 2001—, bd. govs. 2002—, Pro Bono award 1996). Avocation: travel. Immigration, naturalization, and customs. Home: 6919 Gleneagles Tucson AZ 85718 Office: Gloria A Goldman PC 1575 W Ina Rd Tucson AZ 85704 Home Fax: 520-797-1407; Office Fax: 520-797-1407. Personal E-mail: ggoldmansprint@earthlink.net. E-mail: ggoldmansprint@earthlink.net.

GOLDMAN, JASON BRIAN, lawyer; b. Phila., Mar. 23, 1970; s. Herbert Steven and Yvonne (Keller) Goldman; m. Andrea Grizzaffi, July 31, 1993; children: Jacob Joseph, Ben Stephen. AA, Edison CC, Ft. Myers, Fla., 1990; BS in Criminology, BS in Polit. Sci., Fla. State U., 1992; JD, Loyola U., New Orleans, 1995. Bar: Fla. 1995, U.S. Dist. Ct. (mid. dist.) Fla. 1995. Atty, shareholder, adminstrv. mng. ptnr. Wotitzky, Wotitzky, Ross et. al., Punta Gorda, Fla., 1995—. Adj. prof. Edison CC, Ft. Myers, 1998—. Atty. advisor Charlotte County Team Ct. Program, Port Charlotte, 1997—; hearing officer Charlotte County Sch. Bd., Port Charlotte, 2000—; HS basketball referee Coral Coast Basketball Ofcls. Assn., Port Charlotte, Fla., 1997—. Mem.: ABA, Charlotte County Bar Assn. (v.p. 1996—99), Acad. Fla. Trial Lawyers. Democrat. Avocation: sports. Personal injury (including property damage), Criminal, General practice. Office: Wotitzky Wotitzky Ross et al 223 Taylor St Punta Gorda FL 33950 Office Fax: 941-639-8617. Business E-Mail: jgoldman@wotitzkylaw.com.

GOLDMAN, JERRY STEPHEN, lawyer; b. Bklyn., Sept. 7, 1951; s. Bernard I. and Charlotte (Emerling) G.; children by previous marriage: Rachel Dawn, Samantha. BA with honors, NYU, 1973; JD, Boston U., 1976; LLM in Taxation, Temple U., 1983. Bar: Mass. 1977, N.Y. 1977, U.S. Dist. Ct. (ea. and so. dists.) N.Y. 1980, U.S. Supreme Ct. 1981, Pa. 1982, U.S. Tax Ct. 1983, U.S. Dist. Ct. (ea. dist.) Pa. 1983, U.S. Ct. Appeals (3d cir.) 1983, U.S. Dist. Ct. Mass. 1997, U.S. Ct. Appeals (1st cir.) 1997. Sr. asst. dist. atty. Kings County Dist. Atty.'s Office, Bklyn., 1976-82; pvt. practice N.Y.C., Phila., 1982—; mng. ptnr. Law Offices of Jerry S. Goldman. Dir., pres. Huntingdon Brook Cmty. Assn., Bucks Co, Pa., 1985-89. Chmn. Upper Southampton Planning Commn., 1984—90; bd. dirs., counsel Citizens Crime Commn., Phila., 1983—95; bd. dirs. NYU Alumni Assn.; v.p. Coll. Arts and Scis.; mem. Phila. Estate Planning Coun., N.Y. Estate Planning Coun., Delaware Valley Venture Group; atty. Phila. Vol. Lawyers for the Arts, 1983—. Mem. ABA, N.Y. State Bar Assn., Pa. Bar Assn., Phila. Bar Assn., Fed. Bar Assn., N.Y. New Media Assn. Avocations: cross-country skiing, music. Corporate, general, Estate planning, Taxation, general. Office: 1601 Market St Philadelphia PA 19103 also: 13th Fl 111 Broadway New York NY 10006 E-mail: jgoldman@goldmanlawyers.com.

GOLDMAN, MARVIN GERALD, lawyer; b. L.A., June 1, 1939; s. Harry Eli Goldman and Esther Cynthia Brodsky; m. Marilynn Sue Cohen, Oct. 11, 1964; children: Daniel, Sharon, Haviva. AB, UCLA, 1960, JD, 1963; LLM in Comparative Law, NYU, 1964. Bar: Calif. 1964, N.Y. 1966, D.C. 1981. Assoc. Reid & Priest, N.Y.C., 1965—73; ptnr. Thelen Reid & Priest, N.Y.C., 1974—. Author: El Al: Star in the Sky, 1990; editor Thelen Reid & Priest Internat. Bus. Transactions Newsletter, 1983-99. Ford Found. grantee NYU Sch. Law, 1963-64; Fulbright grantee U.S. Govt. Mexico, 1964-65; UCLA Law Rev. award 1963. Mem. ABA (sect. internat. law and practice, chmn. internat. coml. arbitration com. 1979-83), Internat. Bar Assn. (internat. constrn. projects com.), Am. Arbitration Assn. (internat. arbitration com.), U.S. Coun. for Internat. Bus. (arbitration com.), World Airline Hist. Soc. Avocations: civil aviation history, antique airline postcards, javanese gamelan, philately, fluorescent minerals. Office: Thelen Reid & Priest LLP 875 3d Ave New York NY 10022-6225 E-mail: mgoldman@thelenreid.com.

GOLDMAN, MICHAEL DAVID, lawyer; b. Jersey City, Oct. 16, 1942; s. Nathaniel J. and Ruth Goldman; m. Faith I. Frankel, June 5, 1966; children: Leigh S., Amy P. AB, Pa. State U., 1964; JD, Villanova (Pa.) U., 1967. Bar: Del. 1968. Law clk. to presiding judge Ct. Chancery, Wilmington, Del.; ptnr. Potter Anderson & Corroon, Wilmington, 1974—, chmn., 1999—. Chmn. bd. Bar Examiners State of Del., 1988-90, vice chmn., 1986-87; spkr., planning com. Tulane Corp. Law Inst., 1988—. Contbr. articles in field to profl. jours. Mem. state exec. bd. Muscular Dystrophy Assn., 1974-76; chmn. atty. div. United Way, Del., 1977, chmn. profl. div., 1978, 80-81; chmn. Am. Jewish Com., Del., 1981-82; chmn. Jewish Community Rels. Com., 1982; bd. dirs. Jewish Fedn. Del., 1982-85. Mem. ABA (bus. sect., corp. laws com. 1995—), Del. Bar Assn. (chmn. sect. on Del. corp. law 1990-92, chmn. subcom. bus. combination statute). General civil litigation, Corporate, general, Mergers and acquisitions. Office: Potter Anderson & Corroon Hercules Plz PO Box 951 Wilmington DE 19899-0951 E-mail: mgoldman@potteranderson.com.

GOLDMAN, NATHAN CARLINER, lawyer, educator; b. Charleston, S.C., Mar. 19, 1950; s. Reuben and Hilda Alta (Carliner) G.; m. Judith Tova Feigon, Oct. 28, 1984; children: Michael Reuben, Miriam Esther. BA, U. S.C., 1972; JD, Duke U., 1975; MA, Johns Hopkins U., 1978, PhD, 1980. Bar: N.C. 1975, Tex. 1985, U.S. Dist. Ct. (mid. dist.) N.C. 1975. Paralegal City Atty.'s Office, Durham, N.C., 1975-76; asst. prof. govt. dept. U. Tex., Austin, Tex., 1980-85; pvt. practice Houston, 1985-86; assoc. Liddell, Sapp, Zivley, Hill & LaBoon, Houston, 1986-88; pvt. practice Houston, 1988-2000; atty. Amour Law Office, 2000—. Adj. prof. space law U. Houston, 1985-88; rsch. assoc. Rice U. Inst. Policy Analysis, 1986—; lectr. bus. law, 1988-95; mem. coordinating bd. Space Architecture, U. Houston, 1985—; v.p. Internat. Design in Extreme Environments Assn., U. Houston, 1991—; vis. asst. prof. U. Houston-Clear Lake, 1989-91, 99—; adj. prof. South Tex. Coll. Law, 1994-95; gen. counsel Internat. Space Enterprises, 1993—, Globus Ltd. Co., 1994—; info. officer Israel Consulate, 1996-97, atty. Judith G. Cooper, P.C. Author: Space Commerce, 1985, American Space Law, 1988, 2d edit., 1996, Space Policy: A Primer, 1992; editor: Space and Society, 1984; assoc. editor Jour. Space Commerce, 1990-91; exec. editor Space Governance, 1996-99; also articles. Mem. com. on governance of space U.S. Bicentennial Commn., 1986-88, Clear Lake (Tex.) Area Econ. Devel. Found., 1987, Space Collegium, Houston Area Rsch. Ctr., 1987; pres. Windermere Civic Assn., 1990-92; bd. dirs. Hebrew Acad., 1994-96, Men's Club United Orthodox Synagogues, 1994—, pres., 1999-2002. U.S. Dept. Justice grantee, 1979-80, U. Tex. Inst. for Constructive Capitalism U. grantee, 1983; E.D. Walker Centennial fellow, 1984; NASA Summer fellow U. Calif., 1984. Fellow Internat. Inst. Space Law; mem. ABA, Tex. Bar Assn., Nat. Space Soc. (v.p. 1989-91), Inst. for Social Sci. Study Space (mem. adv. bd. 1990, editor Space Humanization Jour. 1993-2000), Am. Astronautical Soc., Inst. for Design in Extreme Environment Assn. (v.p. 1991-96), Space Bus. Roundtable. Avocations: reading, hiking, baseball, softball. Corporate, general, Immigration, naturalization, and customs, Private international. Home: 9406 Cliffwood Dr Houston TX 77096

GOLDMAN, RICHARD HARRIS, lawyer, director; b. Boston, June 17, 1936; s. Charles M. and Irene M. (Marks) Goldman; m. Patricia Grollman, June 21, 1959; children: Elaine, Stephen. BA, Wesleyan U., 1958; LLB, NYU, 1961. Bar: Mass. 1961, U.S. Dist. Ct. Mass. 1961. Mem. Slater & Goldman, Boston, 1961—76, Widett, Slater & Goldman, PC, Boston, 1976—93, Sullivan & Worcester LLP, Boston, 1993—. Past trustee, chmn. audit com. and clk. Grove Bank. Co-author: The Ritual Dance Between Lessee and Lender; contbr. articles to profl. jours. Former chmn. Newton (Mass.) Human Rights Commn.; hon. trustee, former v.p. Temple Israel. Mem.: ABA, Mass. Conveyancers Assn., Boston Bar Assn. (chmn. leasing com. 1996—97, lectr., chmn. seminar comml. real estate fin. 1997, real estate steering com. 1997—, co-chair real estate sect. 1999—2002), Mass. Bar Assn., Belmont Country Club (v.p., sec.). Corporate, general, Probate (including wills, trusts), Property, real (including real estate development, water). Home: 47 Vaughn Ave Newton MA 02461-1038 Office: Sullivan & Worcester LLP 1 Post Office Sq Ste 2300 Boston MA 02109-2129

GOLDMAN, RICHARD LURIE, lawyer; b. N.Y.C., May 3, 1925; s. Samuel and Harriet (Lurie) G.; m. Priscilla Dilks, Apr. 23, 1960; children: Robert Prescott, Sally Dilks. B.A., Bklyn. Coll., 1948; LL.B., Columbia U., 1951. Bar: N.Y. 1952, U.S. Tax Ct. 1952, D.C. 1961, U.S. Supreme Ct. 1961. Assoc. in Law Columbia Law Sch., N.Y.C., 1951-52; assoc. Cravath, Swaine & Moore, N.Y.C., 1952-57; atty.-advisor Chief Counsel's Office, IRS, Washington, 1957-61; ptnr. Valicenti Leighton Reid & Pine, N.Y.C., 1963-70, Goldman & Gladstone, N.Y.C., 1981—. U.S.A. nat. reporter to Internat. Fiscal Congress, 1975; chmn. Reporters to Congress, 1985. Contbr. articles to legal jours. Exec. bd. Westchester-Putnam Coun. Boy Scouts Am., White Plains, N.Y., 1980—. Served to capt. AUS, 1943-46, 61-62. Harlan Fiske Stone scholar, 1949-51. Mem. Internat. Fiscal Assn. (U.S.A. br., mem. nat. coun. 1978— , v.p. N.Y. region 1986-90, exec. v.p. 1990-92, pres. 1992-94, pres. emeritus 1994—), ABA (mem. tax sect., chmn. personal holding co. subcom. 1969-72, corp.-stockholder relationships com. 1955-77, 80—, com. on U.S. activities of foreigners and tax treaties 1976—, real property, probate and trust law sect. 1988—, internat. law and practice sect. 1988—), N.Y. State Bar Assn. (mem. tax sect., chmn. fgn. portfolio sales corp. subcom., com. on internat. fin. and investment 1973-75, coms. on tax policy 1974, 87, 89-91, reorgns. 1972, 89, 92-94, U.S. activities of fgn. taxpayers 1974—, fgn. activities of U.S. taxpayers 1976-84, 96—, com. on internat. investment 1993—, com. on internat. estates 1987—, internat. law and practice sect., real property, probate and trust law sect. 1988—, trusts and estates law sect. 1987—), Assn. Bar City N.Y. Republican. Fax: 914-725-6864. Private international, Probate (including wills, trusts), Corporate taxation. Home: 200 Old Army Rd Scarsdale NY 10583-2613 Office: Goldman & Gladstone 880 3rd Ave New York NY 10022-4730

GOLDMAN, WILLIAM LEWIS, lawyer; b. Phila., May 13, 1919; s. Samuel and Grace Sunderland (Rice) G.; m. Jean Beneski, July 5, 1947; children: William Lewis Jr., Robert Edward, Jan Grace, Lee Ann, Jeanne. BS, Temple U., 1947, JD, 1951. Bar: Pa. 1951, U.S. Dist. Ct. (ea. dist.) Pa. 1951, D.C. 1951. Prin. Law Offices William L. Goldman, Doylestown, Pa., 1951—. Lt. comdr. USN, 1943-47, CBI. Fellow Am. Acad. Matrimonial Lawyers, Internat. Acad. Matrimonial Lawyers; mem. Pa. Bar Assn. (chairperson family law sect. 1989-90), Pa. chpt. Am. Acad. Matrimonial Lawyers (bd. mgrs.). Republican. Roman Catholic. Avocation: travel. Commercial, consumer (including collections, credit), Family and matrimonial, General practice. Office: 90 E State St Doylestown PA 18901-4362 E-mail: lawyers@goldmanlawoffices.com.

GOLDROSEN, DONALD NORMAN, lawyer; b. Glen Ridge, N.J., Jan. 5, 1956; s. Leonard Martin and Joan Goldrosen; m. Suzanne Marie Bardgett, Aug. 2, 1986; children: Bruce, Melissa. BS in Acctg., U. Del., 1978; JD, Villanova U., 1982. Bar: Tex. 1982, Va. 1986. Staff acct. Mironov, Goldman & Wortzel, East Brunswick, N.J., 1979; assoc. Childs, Fortenbach, Beck and Guyton, Houston, 1982-85; assoc., ptnr. Reed, Smith LLP, Fairfax, Va., 1985—, real estate sect. chmn., 1996—. Mem. law sch. com. George Mason U. Century Club, Fairfax, 1994-97. Mem. staff Villanova Law Rev., 1981, lead articles editor, 1982. Coach youth soccer and basketball Annandale (Va.) Boys and Girls Club, 1994—. Mem. Beta Alpha Psi. Avocations: golf, skiing, tennis. Property, real (including real estate development, water). Office: Reed Smith LLP 3110 Fairview Park Dr Ste 1400 Falls Church VA 22042-4503

GOLDSCHMID, HARVEY JEROME, law educator; b. N.Y.C., May 6, 1940; s. Bernard and Rose (Braiker) G.; m. Mary Tait Seibert, Dec. 22, 1973; children: Charles Maxwell, Paul MacNeil, Joseph Tait. AB, Columbia U., 1962, JD, 1965. Bar: N.Y. 1965, U.S. Supreme Ct. 1970. Law clk. to judge 2d Circuit Ct. Appeals, N.Y.C., 1965-66; assoc. firm Debevoise & Plimpton, N.Y.C., 1966-70; asst. prof. law Columbia U., 1970-71, assoc. prof., 1971-73, prof., 1973-84, Dwight prof. law, 1984—, founding dir. Ctr. for Law and Econ. Studies, 1975-78; gen. counsel SEC, 1998-99, adv. to chmn., 2000, commr., 2002—; of counsel Weil, Gotshal & Manges, N.Y.C., 2000—02. Cons. in field to pub. and pvt. orgns.; mem. planning and program com. 2d Cir. Jud. Conf., 1982-85; reporter 2d Cir. Jud. Conf. Evaluation Com., 1980-82, 88-89; mem. legal adv. com. N.Y.S.E., 1997-98, chmn. subcom. on corp. governance. Author(with others) Cases and Materials on Trade Regulation, 1975, 4th edit., 1997; editor: (with others) Industrial Concentration: The New Learning, 1974, Business Disclosure: Government's Need to Know, 1979, The Impact of the Modern Corporation, 1984. Chmn. bd. advisors program on philanthropy and the law NYU Sch. Law, 1992-94; bd. dirs. Nat. Ctr. on Philanthropy and the Law, 1996—; nat. coun. Washington U. Sch. of Law, 1999—; bd. dirs. Greenwall Found., 1996—, vice chair, 1999-2002. Fellow Am. Bar Found.; mem. ABA (task force on lawyers polit. contbrns. 1997-98), Am. Law Inst. (reporter part IV, duty of care and the bus. judgment rule, corp. governance project 1980-93), N.Y. State Bar Assn., Assn. Bar City N.Y. (v.p. 1985-86, chmn. exec. com. 1984-85, chmn. com. on antitrust and trade regulation 1971-74, com. on the 2d century, chmn. com. on securities regulation 1992-95, chmn. audit com. 1988-96, chmn. com. on corp. takeover legislation 1985-86, 88-92, treas., mem. exec. com. 1996-98, chmn. nominating com. 2000-01), Assn. Am. Law Schs. (chmn. sect. antitrust and econ. regulation 1976-78), Am. Assn. Internat. Commn. Jurists (sec.-treas., bd. dirs. 1969-2002), Century Assn., Riverdale Yacht Club (bd. dirs. 1987-90), Phi Beta Kappa. Office: US SEC 450 Fifth St NW Washington DC 20549 E-mail: goldschmidh@sec.gov.

GOLDSCHMIDT, LYNN HARVEY, lawyer; b. Chgo., June 14, 1951; d. Arthur and Ida (Shirman) H.; m. Robert Allen Goldschmidt, Aug. 27, 1972; children: Elizabeth Anne, Carolyn Helene. BS with honors, U. Ill., 1973; JD magna cum laude, Northwestern U., 1976. Bar: Ill. 1976. Ptnr. Hopkins & Sutter, Chgo., 1976-2001, Foley & Lardner, Chgo., 2001—02; prin. D and G Cons. Group, 2002—. Articles editor Northwestern U. Law Rev. Mem. Airport Coun. Internat., N. Am., Order of Coif. Aviation, Municipal (including bonds). Office: D&G Cons Grp 120 S LaSalle St Chicago IL 60603 E-mail: lhg@dg-cg.com.

GOLDSMITH, HOWARD MICHAEL, lawyer; b. Atlantic City, Mar. 22, 1942; s. Leonard M. and Annette (Rothenberg) G.; m. Molly Hartman, Dec. 17, 1943; 1 child, Michael Stephen. BS in Bus., Rider Coll., 1965; JD, Dickinson Sch. Law, 1968. Bar: Pa. 1968, U.S. Dist. Ct. (ea. dist.) Pa. 1969, U.S. Supreme Ct. 1973, U.S. Ct. Claims 1980, U.S. Ct. Appeals (3d cir.) 1982, U.S. Ct. Appeals (fed. cir.) 1988. Prin. Howard M. Goldsmith, P.C., Phila., 1998—. Apptd. custody rules com., divorce code rev. com., support guidelines com. Phila. county Ct. Common Pleas, Phila.; procedural rules com. Pa. Supreme Ct., 1997-2003. Apptd. master pro tem to hear custody and support cases Phila. County; lectr. in family law. Bd. dirs. Jewish Cmty. Ctr., Klein Br., press., 1987-90. Fellow Am. Acad. Matrimonial Lawyers (pres. Pa. chpt. 2002-03), Internat. Acad. Matrimonial Lawyers; mem. ABA (family law sect.), Pa. Bar Assn. (family law sect., chair 1997-98), Phila. Bar Assn. (chmn. 1987, past chmn. adoption com., commr. jud. selection and retention commn. 1987), Vidocq Soc., B'nai B'rith. Jewish. Office: 7716 Castor Ave Philadelphia PA 19152-3602

GOLDSMITH, MICHAEL LAWRENCE, lawyer; b. N.Y.C., Dec. 10, 1962; s. Sheldon and Roslyn Goldsmith; m. Lorraine Bondi, Au. 31, 1986; children: Alexandra, Gavin. BA, NYU, 1983; JD, George Washington U., 1986. Bar: N.Y. 1987, U.S. Dist. Ct. (ea. and so. dists.) N.Y. 1992. Ptnr. Scheich Goldsmith & Drieshpoon, P.C., Richmond Hill, Hicksville, N.Y., 1989—. Arbitrator Civil Ct. Queens County, 1993—. Asst. editor Queens County Bar Bull., 1995—; prodr. (local TV show) Martial Arts/Self Def., 2001—; contbr. articles to profl. jours. Mem. Bethpage (N.Y.) State Park Trail Users Com., 1995—; tchr. martial arts Hicksville Sch. Dist., 1997—; student martial arts Twelve Towns YMCA, 1989—; tchr. martial arts Jita Kyoei Judo Club, 2002—; mem. vision 2020 com. Town of Oyster Bay, 2001—. Rudin scholar NYU, 1981-82. Mem. N.Y. Trial Lawyers Assn., Queens County Bar Assn., N.Y. State Trial Lawyers Assn., John Marshall Lawyers Assn. (bd. dirs. 1993—, sec. 1993-96), South Shore Audubon Soc. (bd. dirs. 1998-99, v.p. 1999-2002, contbr. Skimmer 1998-2002), Kiwanis Club. Avocations: martial arts, birding. General practice, Personal injury (including property damage), Probate (including wills, trusts). Office: Scheich Goldsmith et al 103-42 Lefferts Blvd South Richmond Hill NY 11419-2012 also: 109 Newbridge Rd Hicksville NY 11801-3908 E-mail: Michaelg@panix.com., mgoldsmith@sgdpclaw.com.

GOLDSMITH, WILLIS JAY, lawyer; b. Paris, Feb. 21, 1947; arrived in U.S., 1949; s. Irving and Alice (Rosenfeld) Goldsmith; m. Marilynn Jacobson, Aug. 12, 1973; children: Andrew Edward, Helene Sara. AB, Brown U., 1969; JD, NYU, 1972. Bar: N.Y. 1973, U.S. Ct. Appeals (2d cir.) 1975, D.C. 1978, U.S. Ct. Appeals (4th cir.) 1979, U.S. Ct. Appeals (D.C. cir.) 1979, U.S. Supreme Ct. 1980, U.S. Ct. Appeals (6th cir.) 1985, U.S. Ct. Appeals (7th cir.) 1989, U.S. Ct. Appeals (3d cir.) 1991, U.S. Ct. Appeals (5th cir.) 1998. Atty. Dept. Labor, Washington, 1972-74; assoc. Guggenheimer & Untermyer, NYC, 1974-77, Seyfarth, Shaw, Fairweather & Geraldson, Washington, 1977-79, ptnr., 1979-83, Jones Day, Washington, 1983—, chmn. labor and employment law practice, 1991—. Adj. prof. law Georgetown U., 1988—91; mem. Nat. Adv. Com. on Ergonomics, 2003—. Editor (contbg.): Employee Rels. Law Jour., 1983—91; editor: (assoc.) Occupl. Safety and Health Law; mem. editl. adv. bd. Benefits Law Jour., 1991—2002. Fellow, Coll. Labor and Employment Law, 1997—. Mem.: ABA (sec. labor and employment law com. on employee benefits, com. on occupl. safety and health), Nat. Adv. Com. on Ergonomics, D.C. Bar Assn., NYU Ctr. for Labor and Employment Law (bd. dirs.), Kenwood Golf and Country Club Bethesda, Met. Club Washington. Democrat. Jewish. Labor (including EEOC, Fair Labor Standards Act, labor-management relations, NLRB, OSHA), Pension, profit-sharing, and employee benefits. Home: 6409 Elmwood Rd Chevy Chase MD 20815-6621 Office: Jones Day Reavis & Pogue 51 Louisiana Ave NW Washington DC 20001-2113 E-mail: wgoldsmith@jonesday.com.

GOLDSTEIN, ABRAHAM SAMUEL, lawyer, educator; b. N.Y.C., July 27, 1925; s. Isidore and Yetta (Crystal) G.; m. Ruth Tessler, Aug. 31, 1947 (dec. Feb. 1989); children: William Ira, Marianne Susan; m. Sarah Feidelson, May 7, 1995. BBA, CCNY, 1946; LL.B., Yale U., 1949, MA (hon.), 1961, Cambridge (Eng.) U., 1964; LL.D. (hon.), N.Y. Law Sch., 1979, DePaul U., 1987. Bar: D.C. bar 1949. Law clk. to judge U.S. Ct. Appeals, 1949-51; partner firm Donohue & Kaufmann, Washington, 1951-56; mem. faculty Yale Law Sch., 1956—, prof. law, 1961—, dean, 1970-75, Sterling prof. law, 1975—. Vis. prof. law Stanford Law Sch., summer 1963; vis. fellow Inst. Criminology, fellow Christ's Coll. Cambridge U., 1964-65; faculty Salzburg Seminar in Am. Studies, 1969, Inst. on Social Sci. Methods on Legal Edn., U. Denver, 1970-72; vis. prof. Hebrew U., Jerusalem, 1976, UN Asia and Far East Inst. for Prevention Crime, Tokyo, 1983, Tel Aviv U., 1986; cons. Pres.'s Com. Law Enforcement, 1967; mem. Conn. Bd. of Parole, 1967-69, Conn. Commn. Revise Criminal Code, 1966-70; mem. of the Conn. Planning Com. on Criminal Adminstrn., 1967-71; sr. v.p. Am. Jewish Congress, 1977-84, mem. exec. com., 1977-89, gov. coun., 1989-94. Author: The Insanity Defense, 1967, The Passive Judiciary, 1981, (with L. Orland) Criminal Procedure, 1974, (with J. Goldstein) Crime, Law and Society, 1971; contbr. numerous articles and revs to profl. jours. Served with AUS, 1943- 46. Guggenheim fellow, 1964-65, 75-76, Am. Acad. Arts & Scis., 1975—. Office: Yale Law Sch PO Box 208215 New Haven CT 06520-8215

GOLDSTEIN, BENJAMIN, lawyer, law educator; b. Phila., Dec. 2, 1949; s. Harry and Bella (Hochman) G. BS in Education, Temple U., 1971; JD, John Marshall U., Chgo., 1975. Bar: Ill. 1975, N.J. 1976, U.S. Ct. Appeals (7th cir.) 1975, (3rd cir.) 1978; U.S. Supreme Ct. 1978. Law clerk Cir. Ct. Cook County, Chgo., 1973-75; pvt. practice Chgo., 1975-76, Voorhees, N.J., 1976-80; atty., shareholder Maressa, Goldstein, Birsner, Patterson, Drinkwater & Oddo, Berlin, N.J., 1980—; solicitor Zoning Bd., Waterford, N.J., 1987-90, Township Com., Winslow, N.J., 1987-90; solicitor for mayor and coun. City of Lavallette (N.J.), 1995—98. Adj. prof. law Camden County Coll., Blackwood, N.J., 1984-2000; arbitrator Superior Ct. N.J., Camden, 1990—; cons. Camden County Dem. Com., Runnemede, N.J., 1988-89; solicitor Kennedy Hosp. Sys., Stratford, N.J., 1994—. Author: (chpt.) Opening Statements, 1995, 2001; spkr. in field. Mem. ATLA, N.J. Trial Lawyers Assn., ABA, N.J. State Bar Assn. (mock trial judge 1994—). Avocations: flying, scuba diving, boating, horseback riding, piano. Health, Personal injury (including property damage), Professional liability. Office: Maressa Goldstein Birsner Patterson Drinkwater & Oddo 191 W White Horse Pike Berlin NJ 08009-2021 E-mail: Maressalaw@snip.net.

GOLDSTEIN, CHARLES ARTHUR, lawyer; b. N.Y.C., Nov. 20, 1936; s. Murray and Evelyn V. Goldstein; m. Judith Stein, Sept. 29, 1962 (div. 1982); 1 child, Deborah Ruth; m. Carol Sager, Nov. 10, 1990 (div. 1995). AB, Columbia U., 1958; JD cum laude, Harvard U., 1961. Bar: N.Y. 1962. Law clk. U.S. Ct. Appeals (2d cir.), 1961-62; assoc. Fried, Frank, Harris, Shriver & Jacobson, N.Y.C., 1962-69; ptnr. Schulte Roth & Zabel, N.Y.C., 1969-79, Weil, Gotshal & Manges, N.Y.C., 1979-83, counsel, 1983-85; ptnr. Shea & Gould, N.Y.C., 1985-94, Sutherland, Asbill & Brennan, N.Y.C., 1994-95; counsel Squire, Sanders & Dempsey, N.Y.C., 1996-01; counsel to amb. Ronald S. Lauder, 2001—. Lectr. Columbia U. Law Sch. Gen. counsel to Citizens Budget Commn., 1980-87; mem. Temp. Commn. on City Fins., 1975-77; mem. Gov.'s Task Force on World Trade Ctr. Mem. Am. Coll. Real Estate Lawyers. Republican. Property, real (including real estate development, water). Home: 220 E 65th St New York NY 10021-6620 Office: 767 Fifth Ave Ste 4200 New York NY 10153 E-mail: cgoldstein@rslmgmt.com.

GOLDSTEIN, DEBRA HOLLY, judge; b. Newark, Mar. 11, 1953; d. Aaron and Erica (Schreier) Green; m. Joel Ray Goldstein, Aug. 14, 1983; children: Stephen Michael, Jennifer Ann. BA, U. Mich., 1973; JD, Emory U., 1977. Bar: Ga. 1977, Mich. 1978, D.C. 1978, Ala. 1984. Tax analyst atty. Gen. Motors Corp., Detroit, 1977-78; trial atty. U.S. Dept. Labor, Birmingham, Ala., 1978-90; U.S. adminstrv. law judge office hearing and appeals Social Security Adminstrn., Birmingham, 1990—. New judge faculty U.S. adminstrv. law judges Social Security Adminstrn., 1991, 93—; co-chair Girl Scout Pluralism Think Tank, 1999. Mem. editl. bd. The Ala. Lawyer, 1994-99, The Addendum, 1995-99. Mem. United Way, Birmingham, mem. vis. allocation team, 1998—, mem. planning com., 2001—; mem. Birmingham Bus. and Profl. Women Fedn., mem. steering com., 1995—2000; leader Girl Scout Troop, 1992—; bd. dirs. Cahaba Girl Scout Coun., 1996—2002; mem. Leadership for Diversity Initative, 1995—96, Leadership Birmingham, 1997—98, Momentum, 2002—03; bd. dirs. Temple Emanu-El, 2000—03, YWCA, 2002—. Mem. ABA, Ga. Bar Assn., D.C. Bar Assn., Mich. Bar Assn., Birmingham Bar Assn. (bd. dirs. women's sect. 1999—), Ala. Bar Assn., Zonta (co-pres. 1996-98), B'nai B'rith Women (chair S.E. region 1984-86, Women's Humanitarian award 1981), Hadassah (social action v.p. 2000-01). Jewish. Office: Social Security Adminstrn 1910 3rd Ave N Birmingham AL 35203-3585

GOLDSTEIN, EDWARD DAVID, lawyer, former glass company executive; b. N.Y.C., July 12, 1927; s. Michael and Leah (Kirsh) G.; m. Rhoda Gordon, Apr. 18, 1950; children: Linda, Ellen, Ruth, Michael. BA, U. Mich., 1950, JD with distinction, 1952. Bar: Calif. 1952. Assoc. Orrick, Dahlquist, Herrington & Sutcliffe, San Francisco, 1952-54, Johnston & Johnston, San Francisco, 1954-56; with legal dept. Ohio Match Co., Hunt Foods & Industries, 1956-58; asst. gen. mgr., sales mgr. Glass Containers Corp., Fullerton, Calif., 1958-62, v.p., gen. mgr., 1962-68, pres., CEO, 1968-83. Chmn. bd. Knox Glass Co., Fairmount Glass Cos., 1967-68; gen. counsel FHP, Internat., FHP, Inc., 1985-87. Chmn. bd. trustees St. Jude Hosp., Fullerton, 1984-88. Served with USNR, 1945-46. Mem. ABA, State Bar Calif., Orange County Bar Assn., Nat. Health Lawyers Assn., Am. Arbitration Assn., Am. Coll. Legal Medicine (assoc.-in-law), Calif. Soc. Healthcare Attys. Home: 2230 Yucca Ave Fullerton CA 92835-3320 Office: 110 E Wilshire Ave STe 305 Fullerton CA 92832-1900 E-mail: edgatty@aol.com.

GOLDSTEIN, FRANK ROBERT, lawyer; b. July 31, 1943; s. Morris Herman and Maxine (Herzfeld) G.; m. Phyllis Ellen Levy, Jan. 26, 1967; children: Matthew Alexander, Andrew Stephen. AB, Duke U., 1964; LLB, U. Md., 1967. Bar: Md. 1967, D.C. 1981, Mass. 1985. Clk. to chief justice U.S. Dist. Ct. Md., Balt., 1967—68; assoc. Piper & Marbury, Balt. and Washington, 1968—74, ptnr. Washington, 1974—88, Morgan, Lewis & Bockius LLP, Washington, 1989—96, Sidley Austin Brown & Wood LLP, Washington, 1997—. Bd. govs. Reconstructionist Rabbincal Coll., Wyncote, Pa. 1992-94; bd. dirs. Washington-Balt. Regional Assn., 1984-93, Al Marah Neighborhood Assn., Bethesda, Md., 1982-85, Paine Webber Mortgage Fin. Inc., Columbia, Md., 1987-93 Author: Mournful Numbers, 1995; co-author: District of Columbia Limited Liability Company Forms and Practice Manual, 1995. Pres. Meadowbrook Neighborhood Assn., Potomac, Md., 1990—93, Tidesfall Neighborhood Assn., Columbia, Md., 1972; bd. visitors U. Md. Sch. Law, Balt., 1992—2001; pres. Adat Shalom Reconstructionist Congregation, Bethesda, Md., 1982—85. Fellow Am. Bar Found.; mem. ABA, D.C. Bar Assn. (chmn. ptnr. com. 1985-86, treas. 1988-89), Mass. Bar Assn., Md. State Bar Assn. (chmn. ptnr. com. 1980-82, chmn. sect. legal edn. and admission to bar com. 1975, chmn. D.C. corp. code rev. project 1989-93), Order of Coif. Jewish. Corporate, general, Finance, Securities. Home: 11516 Big Piney Way Potomac MD 20854-1365 Office: Sidley Austin Brown & Wood LLP 1501 K St NW Washington DC 20005 E-mail: fgoldstein@sidley.com.

GOLDSTEIN, HOWARD SHELDON, lawyer; b. Apr. 22, 1952; s. Jerome Harold and Goldie Goldstein; m. Amy Ruth, 1980. BA, CUNY, 1974; JD, Bklyn. Law Sch., 1977. Bar: N.Y. 1978, U.S. Dist. Ct. (so. and ea. dists.) N.Y. 1978. Assoc. Loew & Cohen, Esquires, N.Y.C., 1976-82, ptnr., 1982-87, Cohen & Goldstein, N.Y.C., 1988—. Contbr. articles to profl. jours. Mem. N.Y. State Bar Assn. (family law com., legis. com.), N.Y. County Lawyers Assn., Nassau County Bar Assn., N.Y.C. Bar Assn. (legal referral svcs.). Republican. Jewish. General practice, Corporate, general, Family and matrimonial. Office: Cohen & Goldstein Esqs LLP 32 Broadway Rm 1700 New York NY 10004-1670 E-mail: cohengolds@aol.com.

GOLDSTEIN, HOWARD WARREN, lawyer; b. N.Y.C., Mar. 29, 1949; s. Murray and Claire (Millrod) G.; m. Wendy Jo Zacharius, Sept. 9, 1973; children: Lindsay Rebecca, Amanda Mikael, Justin Zacharius. BA, Northwestern U., 1970; JD, NYU, 1973. Bar: N.Y. 1974, U.S. Dist. Ct. (so. and ea. dists.) N.Y. 1974, U.S. Ct. Appeals (2d cir.) 1975, U.S. Ct. Appeals (10th cir.) 1984, U.S. Ct. Appeals (6th cir.) 1985, U.S. Ct. Appeals (3d cir.) 1997, U.S. Supreme Ct. 1984, U.S. Claims Ct. 1988. Law clk. to judge U.S. Dist. Ct. (ea. dist.) N.Y., 1973-74; assoc. Cravath, Swaine & Moore, N.Y.C., 1974-76; asst. U.S. atty. Office of U.S. Atty. (so. dist.) N.Y., N.Y.C., 1976-80; assoc. Mudge, Rose, Guthrie, Alexander & Ferdon, N.Y.C., 1980-81, ptnr., 1982-90, Fried, Frank, Harris, Shriver & Jacobson, N.Y.C., 1990—. Author: Grand Jury Practice, 1998; co-author: The Rights of Crime Victims, 1985, RICO: Civil and Criminal, Law and Strategy, 1989, Corporate Sentencing Guidelines, 1993. Mem. Fed. Bar Coun., Assn. of Bar of City of N.Y., Nat. Assn. Criminal Def. Lawyers, N.Y. Coun. Def. Lawyers, Order of Coif, Phi Beta Kappa. Jewish. Federal civil litigation, Criminal. Office: Fried Frank Harris Shriver & Jacobson One New York Plz New York NY 10004

GOLDSTEIN, IRWIN MELVIN, lawyer; b. Bklyn., Oct. 17, 1944; s. Oscar D. Goldstein and Berdie (Grossman) Schames; m. Maxine B. Herzog, June 14, 1970; children: Oliver M., Evan D., Shawn M. BA, Bklyn. Coll., 1964; JD, St. John's U., Bklyn., 1967; LLM, NYU, 1968. Bar: N.Y. 1968, Fla. 1978. Ptnr. Reynolds, Richards, LaVenture, Hadley & Davis, N.Y.C., 1970-81; mgr. Ira Sarinsky & Co., P.C., N.Y.C., 1982-84, M. Sternlieb & Co., P.C., Hackensack, N.J., 1984-85; ptnr. McGladrey & Pullen, LLP (formerly Edward Issacs & Co.), N.Y.C., 1985—. Probate (including wills, trusts), Estate taxation, Personal income taxation. Home: 96 Margaret Ave Lawrence NY 11559-1826 E-mail: Irwin_Goldstein@rsmi.com.

GOLDSTEIN, KENNETH B. lawyer; b. Bklyn., Sept. 16, 1949; s. Nathan and Isabella (Solow) G. BA, Tulane U., 1973, JD, 1974; postdoctoral, Fordham U., 1979. Bar: N.Y. 1977, U.S. Dist. Ct. (so. and ea. dist.) N.Y. 1980, U.S. Ct. Appeals (D.C. cir.) 1981. Gen. mgr., v.p. Middletown (N.Y.) Window Cleaning Co., Inc., 1974; tchr. various schs., Middletown and Chester, N.Y., 1975-77; asst. sr. v.p., dir. mktg. Saks Fifth Ave, N.Y.C., 1977-79; sr. asst. dist. atty. Orange County, Goshen, N.Y., 1979-81; assoc. Zola & Zola, N.Y.C., 1981-83, Freedman, Weisbein & Samuelson P.C., Garden City, N.Y., 1983-85, Jaffe & Asher, N.Y.C., 1985-91, Raoul Lionel Felder P.C., N.Y.C., 1991—. Bd. dirs. Middletown Window Cleaning Co., Inc. Bd. dirs. New Orleans Jazz and Heritage Found., 1972-74, Jewish Family Svcs. Orange County, 2000—. Named one of Outstanding Young Men in Am., 1980. Mem. ABA, N.Y. State Bar Assn., Middletown Bar Assn., Orange County Bar Assn., Order of DeMolay. Republican. Jewish. Avocations: swimming, art, dance, opera. State civil litigation, Family and matrimonial, Landlord-tenant. Home: 145 E 35th St Apt 2me New York NY 10016-4121 also: PO Box 3 Middletown NY 10940-0003 Office: Raoul Lionel Felder PC 437 Madison Ave New York NY 10022-7001

GOLDSTEIN, MICHAEL B. lawyer; b. N.Y.C., Sept. 29, 1943; s. Isaac and Betty (Friedman) G.; m. Jinny M. Loewenthal, Dec. 18, 1966; 1 child, Eric Loren. BA in Govt., Cornell U., 1964; JD, NYU, 1967. Bar: N.Y. 1967, Ill. 1974, D.C 1978. Spl. asst., dep. mayor Office of Mayor, N.Y.C., 1965-66, asst. city adminstr., dir. univ. rels., 1969-72; dir. N.Y.C. Urban Corps, 1966-69; assoc. vice chancellor for urban and govtl. affairs, assoc. prof. urban scis. U. Ill., Chgo., 1972-78; mem. Dow, Lohnes & Albertson PLLC, Washington, 1978—. Practice leader Ednl. Inst. Rels.; chmn. task force on pub. policy Commn.on Higher Edn. and Adult Learner Am. Coun. on Edn.; mem. bd. advisors Stanford Forum for Coll. Financing. Contbr. articles to profl. texts and jours. Pres. Nat. Ctr. for Pub. Svc. Internship Programs, 1975-77; bd. dirs., officer Washington Ctr. Internships and Acad. Seminars, 1977—; bd. dirs. and gen. counsel Washington Ballet, 1978—; bd. dirs. Greater Washington Rsch. Ctr., 1982-96, Chgo. Urban Corps, 1972-75, Am. Assoc. Higher Edn., 1998—; trustee Fielding Inst., 1989-94, 98—; trustee, chmn. fin. com. Mt. Vernon Coll., 1991-96; dir. Am.-Russian Cultural Cooperation Found., 1995—; bd. visitors Mt. Vernon Coll., 1996-98; bd. dirs. Sta. WETA, 1997-99. Wall St. Jour. Newspaper Fund fellow, 1963, Loeb fellow Harvard U., 1972. Mem. ABA (chmn. edn. law com. 1991-92), D.C. Bar Assn. (vice chair edn. task force 1999—), FBA (co-chmn. edn. grants com. 1985-86, 91-92), Nat. Assn. Coll. and Univ. Attys. (mem. ctrl. office com. 1986-88, vice chmn. pvt. bar com. 1989-90, chair continuing legal edn. com. 2001—), Nat. Soc. Internships and Exptl. Edn. (pres. 1972), Am. Assn. Higher Edn. (dir. 1997-2003). Democrat. Jewish. Administrative and regulatory, Education and schools, Mergers and acquisitions. Office: Dow Lohnes & Albertson 1200 New Hampshire Ave NW Washington DC 20036-6802

GOLDSTEIN, MICHAEL GERALD, lawyer, director; b. St. Louis, Sept. 21, 1946; s. Joseph and Sara G. (Finkelstein) G.; m. Ilene Marcia Ballin, July 19, 1970; children: Stephen Eric, Rebecca Leigh. BA, Tulane U., 1968; JD, U. Mo., 1971; LLM in Taxation, Washington U., 1972. Bar: Mo. 1971, U.S. Dist. Ct. (ea. dist.) Mo. 1972, U.S. Tax Ct. 1972, U.S. Ct. Appeals (8th cir.) 1974, U.S. Supreme Ct. 1976. Atty. Morris A. Shenker, St. Louis, 1972-78; ptnr. Lashly, Caruthers, Baer & Hamel and predecessor, St. Louis, 1979-84, Suelthaus & Kaplan, P.C. and predecessors, St. Louis, 1974-91; ptnr., chmn. dept. tax & estate planning Husch & Eppenberger, 1991-99; pres., CEO 1st Fin. Resources, 1999—2001; sr. v.p. EPS Fin. Solutions Corp., 1999-2000; sr. v.p., gen. counsel The Benefits Group, Inc., 2001—; pres., COO Benefits Group Worldwide, 2003—. Adj. prof. tax law Washington U. Sch. Law, 1986-97; planning com. Mid-Am. Tax Confs., chmn. ALI/ABA Tax Seminar; lectr., author taxation field. Author: BNA Tax Mgmt. Portfolios, ABA The Insurance Counselor Books; contbr. articles to profl. jours. Bd. dirs. Jewish Family and Children's Svc. St. Louis, 1980—, pres., 1986-88; bd. dirs. Jewish Fedn. of St. Louis; trustee United Hebrew Temple, 1986-88; grad. Jwish Fedn. St. Louis Leadership Devel. Coun.; co-chmn. lawyers divsn. Jewish Fedn. St. Louis Campaign, 1981-82, Leadership St. Louis, 1988-89. Capt. USAR, 1970-78. Fellow Am. Coll. Tax Counsel, Am. Coll. Trust and Estate Counsel; mem. ABA (chmn. tax seminar, group editor newsletter for taxation sect.), Am. Law Inst., Mo. Bar Assn., Bar Assn. Met. St. Louis, St. Louis County Bar Assn. Corporate taxation, Estate taxation, State and local taxation. Home: 2011 Yacht Mischief Newport Beach CA 92660-6713 Office: 1875 Century Park East Ste 2100 Los Angeles CA 90067

GOLDSTEIN, SAMUEL S. judge; b. Hartford, Conn., July 4, 1925; s. Harry and Eva Rose Goldstein; m. Roberta I. Caplan, Oct. 9, 1957. BA, Trinity Coll., 1948; LLB, Yale U., 1951. Bar: Conn. 1951, U.S. Dist. Ct. (fed. dist.) Conn. 1952, U.S. Supreme Ct. 1963. Judge Conn. Superior Ct., 1983—. Corporation coun. Town of West Hartford, Conn., 1967—69, charter revision, 1971. With USAF, 1944—46. Mem.: ABA, Conn. Rose Soc. (pres. 1991).

GOLDSTEIN, STUART WOLF, lawyer; b. Buffalo, N.Y., Sept. 9, 1931; s. Joseph and Esther (Wolf) G.; m. Myra Saft Stuart, June 1960 (dec. Aug. 1981); children: Jeffrey, Jonathan, Meryl; m. Nancy Baynes Lux, 1993. Student, U. Buffalo, 1949-52, JD, 1955; postgrad., U. Va., 1956. Bar: N.Y. 1956, Fla. 1974, Ariz. 1977, U.S. Supreme Ct. 1960, U.S Dist. Ct. (we. dist.) N.Y. 1956, U.S. Ct. Mil. Appeals 1957, U.S. Ct. Appeals (2d cir.) N.Y., 1978, U.S. Dist. Ct. Ariz. 1981. Sole practice, Buffalo, 1960-79, 82-85, Phoenix, 1980-82, 85—. Pres., founder Cystic Fibrosis Found., Buffalo, 1960; fund-raiser United Fund, United Jewish Appeal; pres. Boys League; active Erie County Spl. Task Force on Energy, Buffalo, 1978. 1st lt. JAG, U.S. Army, 1956-60. Fellow Ariz. Bar Found.; mem. ATLA, Ariz. State Bar Assn., N.Y. Trial Lawyers Assn., Erie County Trial Lawyers, Ariz. Trial Lawyers Assn. (Ariz. real property sect.), N.Y. State Bar Assn., Fla. Bar Assn., Am. Arbitration Assn., Maricopa County Bar Assn., Buffalo Skating Club, Curling Skating Club (legal counsel). Avocations: astronomy, breeding boston terriers. General civil litigation, General practice, Personal injury (including property damage). Office: 2700 N 3rd St Ste 2010 Phoenix AZ 85004-4602 E-mail: stugoldstn@aol.com.

GOLDSTEIN, WILLIAM MARKS, lawyer; b. Phila., Aug. 28, 1935; s. David and Estelle (Marks) G.; m. Lilia E. Demchuk; 1 child, Laura; children by previous marriage: Adam, Benjamin, Daniel. AB, Princeton U., 1957; JD magna cum laude, Harvard U., 1960. Bar: Pa. 1961, D.C. 1977. Law clk. to judge U.S. Ct. Appeals, Phila., 1960-61; assoc. firm Morgan Lewis & Bockius, Phila., 1961-66, ptnr., 1967-75, 77-82, Drinker, Biddle & Reath LLP, Phila., 1982—; dep. asst. sec. for tax policy Dept. Treasury, Washington, 1975-76. Contbr. numerous articles on fed. taxation to legal publs. Mem. Democratic Party Com. Lower Merion, Pa., 1965-68; candidate for Sch. Bd. Lower Merion, 1965, for state legis., 1966. Mem. ABA, Pa. Bar Assn., Phila. Bar Assn., D.C. Bar Assn., Am. Law Inst., Am. Coll. Tax Counsel. Jewish. Home: 787 Trephanny Ln Wayne PA 19087-1931 Office: Drinker Biddle & Reath LLP 1 Logan Sq 18th & Cherry St Philadelphia PA 19103-6996 E-mail: Goldstwm@dbr.com.

GOLDSTEN, ROBERT EMANUEL, lawyer, investor; b. Charlottesville, Va., Oct. 8, 1916; s. Joseph and Rebecca S. (Shapero) B.; m. Janice F. Wasserman, Nov. 30, 1979; children by previous marriage: Douglas Kahn, Ina Lee. BS in Commerce, U. Va., 1937, LLB, 1940. Bar: Va. 1939, D.C. 1941. Ptnr. Goldsten Bros. Developers & Builders, Washington, 1941-72; pres. Gen. Mortgage Corp., Washington, 1948-66, Vero Beach (Fla.) Yacht Basin, Inc., 1957-71, Devel. Funding Corp., Washington, 1972-74; v.p. Allied Fin. Corp., Silver Spring, Md., 1950-58, World Wide Airlines, Burbank, Calif., 1960-62; pres., CEO McLean (Va.) Savs. & Loan Assn., 1977-80; dir. McLean Fin. Corp., 1981-87; chmn. U.S. Mortgage Credit Corp., 1983-87, Allied Protective Sys. Inc., 1981-88; pres. Gen. Funding Corp., Washington, 1998—. Vis. lectr. real estate mgmt. Am. U., 1950-57. Pres., Brotherhood, Washington Hebrew Congregation, 1955-56; treas., bd. dirs. Washington Area Coun. on Alcoholism and Drug Abuse, 1971-77, Carl G. Jung Fund of Washington, 1976-79; co-founder Washington Inst. Natural Medicine, 1998; mem. D.C. governing bd. Anti-Defamation League, 1997—. Recipient award for outstanding contbn. to success of Home Builders Met. Washington, 1966, Spl. Beautification award City of Alexandria, Va., Disting. Svc. award Washington Area Coun. Alcoholism and Drug Abuse, 1977. Mem. U. Va. Alumni Club Washington, Indian Spring Club, Woodmont Country Club, Tower Club, Boca Rio Golf Club, Univ. Club, B'nai B'rith, Georgetown Club. Democrat. Home and Office: #8 Harborage Isle Fort Lauderdale FL 33316-2303 also: 3134 Ellicott St NW Washington DC 20008-2025

GOLEMON, RONALD KINNAN, lawyer; b. Atlanta, Tex., Nov. 22, 1938; s. William Layton and Avis (Bogle) G.; m. Jacqueline Alice Burst, Sept. 2, 1966; children: Donald Brent, Jennifer Alice. BS in Indsl. Mgmt. Engring., U. Okla., 1961; LLB, U. Tex., 1967. Bar: Tex. 1967, U.S. Ct. Appeals (5th cir.) 1970, U.S. Dist. Ct. (so. dist.) Tex. 1968, U.S. Dist. Ct. (we. dist.) Tex. 1981, U.S. Dist. Ct. (no. dist.) 1986. Engr. asst. Tex. Water Pollution Control Bd., Austin, 1964-67; assoc. Keys, Russell, Watson & Seaman, Corpus Christi, Tex., 1967-71, ptnr., 1971-73, Brown McCarroll, LLP (formerly Brown McCarroll & Oaks Hartline), Austin, 1973—; mng. ptnr. Brown McCarroll & Oaks Hartline, 1989-94. Contbg. author The Southwestern Legal Foundation, 40th Annual Institute on Oil and Gas Law and Taxation, 1989, The Southwestern Legal Foundation, 43rd Annual Institute on Oil and Gas Law and Taxation, 1992; contbr articles to profl. jours. Alt. mem. RCRA permit adv. com. U.S. EPA, 1983; mem. Gov.'s Hazardous Waste Task Force, 1984-85; v.p. St. Stephen's Sch. PTA, 1985-86, pres., 1986-87; mem. cmty. adv. bd. Ronald McDonald House, Austin, 1990—. Mem. ABA (chmn. standing com. constnl. and by-laws 2001—, ho. dels. 2000—, mem. standing com. membership & liaison 1997-2000, mem. market rsch. task force 1995-96, chmn. sect. natural resources, energy and environ. law 1994-95, chmn.-elect 1993-94, vice-chmn. 1992-93, mem. coun. liaison environ. group 1989-91, chmn. air quality com. 1986-89, vice chmn. 1982-86), State Bar Tex. (chmn. environ. law sect. 1971-72), Tex. Mining and Reclamation Assn. (dir. 1988-2000), Travis County Bar Assn., U. Tex. Law Alumni Assn. (pres. 1984-85, mem. exec. bd. 1984-86), Tex. Corriente Cattle Assn. (bd. dirs. 2002). Avocations: ranching, hunting, skiing, golf. Administrative and regulatory, Environmental. Office: Brown McCarroll LLP 111 Congress Ave Ste 1400 Austin TX 78701-4043 E-mail: kgolemon@mailbmc.com.

GOLENBOCK, SUSAN A. lawyer, film producer; b. N.Y.C., Apr. 18, 1948; d. Justin M. Golenbock, Hazel B. Holub; m. Marc Weisenfreund. JD, Boston U., 1974. Bar: NY 1977. Resident counsel Cannon Films, N.Y.C.; atty. Bernstein & Obstfeldt, N.Y.C., 1976—79; counsel Brisun Entertainment Corp., Astoria, NY, 1979—94; pvt. practice entertainment atty. Pound Ridge, NY, 1994—. Prodr.: (documentaries) The Stolen Eye, 2002, The Angry Eye, 2001 (CINE Golden Eagle; The New York Festivals WorldMedal; Chris Award; Audience Favorite, Palm Springs International Film Festival, 2001, Telly award, Axiem award); (films) The Right Temptation, 2000, Brainscan, 1994, Bloodrush (aka Happy Hell Night), 1992. Mem.: N.Y. County Bar Assn., Westchester County Bar Assn., N.Y. Women in Film and TV. Entertainment. Home and Office: 28 Twin Fawn Lane Pound Ridge NY 10576 Fax: 914-764-8036.

GOLINO, ANTONIO, lawyer; b. Rome, Mar. 4, 1971; arrived in U.S., 00; s. Salvatore Golino and Marzi Adriana. JD with honors, U. Rome, 1995; LLM in Banking, and Corp. Fin. Law, Fordham U., 2001. Bar: Italy 01, NY 02. Legal advisor Assicurazioni Generali SpA, London, 1996—2000; assoc. Vinson & Elkins LLP, N.Y.C., 2001—. Mem. nat. coun. Alleanza Nazionale, Italy, 1991—95. Recipient Erasmus scholarship, European Union, 1996, award of merit, Nat. Ctr. Missing and Exploited Children, 2003. Mem.: ABA (mem. fed. securities law com. 2002—), Italy-Am. C. of C., Ordine Degli Avvocati di Roma, Assn. Bar City NY (mem. banking com. 2002—). Roman Catholic. Avocation: scuba diving. Mergers and acquisitions, Securities, Corporate, general. Office: Vinson & Elkins LLP 666 5th Ave 26th Fl New York NY 10103 Fax: 917-843-5307. E-mail: agolino@velaw.com.

GOLIS, PAUL ROBERT, lawyer; b. San Francisco, Sept. 25, 1954; BA with high distinction, Calif. State U., Long Beach, 1977; JD, Syracuse U., 1981. Bar: Fla. 1984, U.S. Dist. Ct. (so. dist.) Fla. 1985, U.S. Ct. Appeals (11th cir.) 2000. Assoc. Russell L. Forkey, P.A., Ft. Lauderdale, Fla., 1984-85, Josias & Goren, P.A., Ft. Lauderdale, 1985-88; sr. trial atty. State of Fla. Dept. Transp., Ft. Lauderdale, 1988-90; asst. county atty. Palm Beach County, West Palm Beach, Fla., 1990-91; assoc. Scott, Royce, Harris, Bryan & Hyland, Palm Beach Gardens, Fla., 1991-93, Watterson, Hyland & Klett, Palm Beach Gardens, 1993-98; pvt. practice, Boca Raton, Fla., 1998—. Featured spkr. on eminent domain issues Palm Beach County Bar Assn., West Palm Beach, 1993, West Palm Beach, 96, West Palm Beach, 99, West Palm Beach, 2001; on legal ethics Nat. Bus. Inst., West Palm Beach, 1999, West Palm Beach, 2001, on land use, 00; on eminent domain issues Fla. Bar, 2002; spl. master code enforcement issues Town of Hypoluxo, 2002—. Bd. dirs. Aid to Victims of Domestic Abuse, Inc., 1990-99, v.p., 1993-97, pres. 1997-99, mem. adv. bd., 1999-2001, aux. bd., 2002—; bd. dirs. Boca Raton Soc. for Disabled, Inc., 1999-2002, treas. 2001-02. Mem. ABA, Fla. Bar Assn. (eminent domain com. 1989—, vice chair 2002—), Palm Beach County Bar Assn. (vice chmn. environ., land use and eminent domain CLE com. 1993-95, chmn. 1995-99, mem. 2000—, jud. rels. com. 1996-99, professionalism com. 2001-). State civil litigation, Condemnation (eminent domain). Office: 2000 Glades Rd Ste 306 Boca Raton FL 33431-8504 E-mail: Parogo@adelphia.net.

GOLL, GEOFFREY STEVEN, lawyer; b. Columbus, Ohio, Feb. 2, 1944; s. Carl F. and Dru R. Goll; m. Kim Shauck; children: Megan E., Yvonne M. B.A., Denison U., 1966; J.D., Ohio State U., 1973. Bar: Ohio 1973, U.S. Dist. Ct. (no. dist.) Ohio 1974, U.S. Supreme Ct. 1980. Ptnr. Law Offices of Geoffrey S. Goll L.P.A., Salem, Ohio, 1982— . Mem. exec. bd. Columbiana coun. Boy Scouts Am., 1978, mem. nat. coun., 1981-92, pres., 1984-85; mem. exec. bd. Mobile Meals of Salem, Inc., 1976— ; mem. adv. bd. Salem Salvation Army, 1979-81, chmn., 1981; mem. exec. bd. Salem Area Indsl. Devel. Corp., 1980— , Columbiana County Port Authority, 1981-96, Columbiana Bd. Elections, 1984-91; vice chmn. Columbiana County Republican Central Com., 1977-84; elder Presbyn. Ch.; trustee Salem Cmty. Found., 1995—, Salem Rotary Club Found., 1995—, Saxon Scholarship Found., 1988—; mem. Salem Ohio Utilities Com., 1993—, chair, 1995—. Served to lt. col. USAFR, 1966-93. Recipient District Merit award Boy Scouts Am., 1980, Silver Beaver award, 1984. Mem. ABA, Columbiana County Bar Assn. (sec.-treas. 1979—), Ohio State Bar Assn. (local com. 1980—), Columbiana County Mental Health Assn., Ohio State U. Alumni Assn. (trustee Columbiana County 1979-81, pres. 1984-86), Salem C. of C. (bd. dirs. 1979, 81-85, pres. 1984-85). Clubs: Saxon. Lodges: Elks, Rotary (v.p. Salem club 1984, pres. 1985). Avocations: golf; travel. Home: 1989 Quaker Ln Salem OH 44460-1875 Office: PO Box 92 Salem OH 44460-0092

GOLOMB, DAVID BELA, lawyer; b. Bklyn., Apr. 19, 1949; s. Maurice and Rita (Pick) G.; m. Lisa Ann Cutler, June 17, 1984. BA, Cornell U., 1970; JD, St. John's U., 1974. Bar: N.Y. 1975, U.S. Dist. Ct. (so. dist.) N.Y. 1977, U.S. Dist. Ct. (ea. dist.) N.Y. 1978, U.S. Ct. Appeals (2d cir.) 1979, U.S. Supreme Ct. 1979. Trial atty. N.Y.C. Legal Aid Soc., 1974-77; adminstr. N.Y.C. Office of Dep. Mayor, 1977-78; spl. asst. atty. gen. N.Y. State Office of Medicaid Fraud Control, 1978-80; trial atty. Fuchsberg and Fuchsberg, N.Y.C., 1980-83, Paul D. Rheingold, PC, N.Y.C., 1983-84; ptnr. Rheingold & Golomb PC, N.Y.C., 1984-87; pvt. practice N.Y.C., 1987—. Lectr. ABA Nat. Inst. on Med. Malpractice, 1985, Ross Labs. Ann. Roundtable on Pediats., 1986. Mem. ABA, ATLA (N.Y. state del. 1992-94, gov. 1994—, exec. com. 2000—), Am. Bd. Trial Advs., Am. Inn of Ct., N.Y. State Bar Assn., Assn. of Bar of City of N.Y. (tort litigation com.), N.Y. State Trial Lawyers Assn. (bd. dirs. 1990-92, parliamentarian 1992-93, treas. 1993-95, sec. 1995-96, 2d v.p. 1996-97, 1st v.p. 1997-98, pres.-elect 1998-99, pres. 1999-2000, immediate past pres. 2000-01, chmn. jud. screening com., chmn. med. malpractice com., mem. com. on state legis., co-chmn. seminars on malpractice), N.Y. County Lawyers Assn. Federal civil litigation, State civil litigation, Personal injury (including property damage). Home: 40 Hampton Rd Scarsdale NY 10583-3025 Office: Law Office David B Golomb 230 Park Ave Ste 527 New York NY 10169-0005 E-mail: golomblaw@aol.com.

GOLOMB, GEORGE EDWIN, lawyer; b. Newark, Jan. 28, 1947; s. Max and Elizabeth G.; m. Cynthia Lifson, 1984. BA, Yale U., 1968; JD, U. Pa., 1972. Bar: N.Y. 1974, N.J. 1977, D.C. 1985, Md. 1985. Law clk. to judge U.S. Dist. Ct. (ea. dist.) N.Y., Bklyn., 1974-76; trial atty. civil div. U.S. Dept. Justice, Washington, 1980-84, 1980-84; pvt. practice Balt., 1986—. Contbr. articles to profl. jours.; co-author: Federal Trial Guide, Federal Evidence Practice Guide, 1989. Fellow, Hague Acad., 1971, Phelps Assn. fellow, 1967. Mem. Balt. City Bar Assn. (exec. com. mem. 1986-96, 1999-2000, 02—, sec. 2003—), Md. State Bar Assn. (bd. govs. 1995-97, 2000-02, labor and employment law, chmn. CLE com. 2002—, com. on professionalism 1997-2002), Md. Inst. for Continuing Profl. Edn. for Lawyers (trustee 2002—). Federal civil litigation, State civil litigation. Office: 111 S Calvert St Ste 2700 Baltimore MD 21202-6143 E-mail: goegle@erols.com.

GOLPER, JOHN BRUCE, lawyer; b. El Paso, Tex., Sept. 6, 1950; s. Marvin Norman and Jean Rose (Becker) G.; m. Leslie Ann Lawry, Mar. 21, 1981; children: Matthew Brent, Brian Yale, Todd Nicholas. BA with honors, Ind. U., 1972; JD, UCLA, 1975. Bar: Calif. 1975, U.S. Dist. Ct. (cen. dist.) Calif. 1975, U.S. Ct. Appeals (9th cir.) 1977, U.S. Dist. Ct. (no. and so. dists.) Calif. 1981, U.S. Supreme Ct. 1981, U.S. Ct. Appeals (3d cir.) 1982, U.S. Dist. Ct. (ea. dist.) Calif. 1986. Extern law clk. Calif. Ct. Appeal 1st Dist., San Francisco, 1974; assoc. Bodkin, McCarthy, Sargent & Smith, Los Angeles, 1975-78; ptnr. Parker Milliken, Clark, O'Hara & Samuelian, Los Angeles, 1978-86, Ballard, Rosenberg, Golper & Savitt, LP, University City, 1986-. Mem. Calif. Comparable Worth Task Force, Sacramento, 1984-86. Grable Meml. scholar Ind. U., 1968, Ind. State scholar, 1968, Honors Div. Merit scholar, 1971-72; recipient cert. of Recognition, Compensation Practices Assn. San Diego County, 1983, 84; named among Top 25 Attys. of San Fernando Valley, San Fernando Bus. Jour., 2002. Mem. ABA, Calif. Bar Assn., Los Angeles County Bar Assn., Fed. Bar ASsn., Assn. Bus. Trial Lawyers, Def. Rsch. and Trial Lawyers Assn., So. Calif. Def. Counsel, Indsl. Rels. Rsch. Assn., Jonathan Club. Republican. Jewish. Federal civil litigation, State civil litigation, Labor (including EEOC, Fair Labor Standards Act, labor-management relations, NLRB, OSHA). Office: Ballard Rosenberg Golper & Savitt LLP 10 Universal City Plz Universal City CA 91608-1097 E-mail: jgolper@BRGSlaw.com.

GOLTZ, SUSAN ACKERMAN, lawyer; b. Newark, N.J., Dec. 12, 1946; d. Morris and Ruth (Abend) Ackerman; 1 dau., Amanda Lauren. Student, Beaver Coll., Glenside, Pa., 1964-66, City of London Coll., Eng., 1966-67; BA, U. Mich., 1968, postgrad., 1968-69; JD, NYU, 1971. Bar: N.Y. 1971, D.C. 1978. Asst. dist. atty. Bronx County, N.Y., 1971-74; legal officer U.S. Supreme Ct., Washington, 1974-78; assoc. Chapman, Duff & Paul, Washington, 1978-79; ptnr. DiSalle & Staudinger, Washington, 1979-88, corp. dir., cons., 1988—. Mem. adv. bd. Bur. Prosecution and Def. Service, State of N.Y., 1979; conferee Nat. Conf. Causes of Popular Dissatisfaction with Adminstrn. of Justice, St. Paul, 1976. Mem. ABA, Nat. Women's Law Ctr. Network, NYU Law Alumni Assn. Federal civil litigation, Corporate, general, Private international. Home and Office: 435 E 79th St New York NY 10021-1034

GOLUB, ANDREY VLADIMIROVICH, lawyer; b. Ukraine, June 24, 1975; LLB, Kiev (Ukraine) State U., 1996; M in Internat. Law, Lund (Sweden) U., 1998. Bar: Ukraine 1996. Jr. legal adviser Cabinet Ministers Ukraine, Agy. for Coordination Internat. Tech. Assistance, Kiev, 1995—96; prin. legal adviser Cabinet Ministers Ukraine, Ministry Fgn. Econ. Rels. and Trade, Kiev, 1998—99; dep. chief legal dept. Joint-Stock Shipping Co. Ukrrichflot, Kiev, 1999—2000; intern-assoc. Flavell Cubrick LLP, Ottawa, Canada, 2001—02; assoc. Attys.-at-law Magister & Ptnrs., Kiev, 2000—02. Alternative dispute resolution, Corporate, general, Government contracts and claims, International trade law. Office: Attys-At-Law Magister & Ptnrs prov Muzeyny 10 01601 Kiev Ukraine Office Fax: 380 44 255 5687. Personal E-mail: pigeon_ag@mail.ru. E-mail: agolub@magisters.com.

GOMES, JOAO JOSE VEIGA, lawyer; b. Lisbon, Jan. 28, 1940; s. Jose Gabriel Dematos and Florinda Velga Gomes; m. Fernanda Maria Gouvea Da Veiga, Aug. 24, 1964; children: Maria Joao, Joao Gabriel, Fernando, Joana. Grad., Lisbon Classic U., 1962. Pub. atty. Min. Justice, Louvenco Marques, Portugal, 1963—66; atty. Lisbon, 1967—75; sr. ptnr. Veija Gomes Bena , 1975—99; ptnr. Smiafiertner Veiga Gomes & Uolmoneo, 2000—. Lt. Portuguese Mil., 1964—66. Trademark and copyright, Mergers and acquisitions, Corporate, general. Office: 66 - 5th Fl 1069-075 Lisbon Portugal

GOMEZ, DAVID FREDERICK, lawyer; b. Los Angeles, Nov. 19, 1940; s. Fred and Jennie (Fujier) G.; m. Kathleen Holt, Oct. 18, 1977. BA in Philosophy, St. Paul's Coll., Washington, 1965, MA in Theology, 1968; JD, U. So. Calif., 1974. Bar: Calif. 1975, U.S. Dist. Ct. (cen. dist.) Calif. 1975, U.S. Dist. Ct. (ea. dist.) Calif. 1977, Ariz. 1981, US. Dist. Ct. Ariz. 1981, U.S. Ct. Claims 1981, U.S. Ct. Appeals (9th cir.) 1981, U.S. Supreme Ct. 1981; ordained priest Roman Cath. Ch., 1969. Law clerk/staff atty. Nat. Labor Relations Bd., Los Angeles, 1974-75; ptnr. Gomez, Paz, Rodriguez & Sanora, Los Angeles, 1975-77, Garrett, Bourdette & Williams, San Francisco, 1977-80, Van O'Steen & Ptnrs., Phoenix, 1981-85; pres. Gomez & Petitti, PC, Phoenix, 1985—. Faculty Practicing Law Inst., 1989; instr. contracts law Nat. Lawyers Guild, Peoples Coll. Law, 1975-76; mem. Missionary Soc. St. Paul the Apostle (Paulist Fathers), 1963-75. Author: Somos Chicanos: Strangers in Our Own Land, 1973; co-author: Advanced Strategies in Employment Law, 1988, Arizona Employment Law Handbook, Vol. 2, 1995. Fellow: Ariz. Bar Found.; mem.: ABA, Ariz. State Bar Assn. (com. on rules of profl. conduct 1991—97, civil jury instrns. com. 1992—94, peer rev. com. 1992—2000, task force on future of the legal profession 1998—2001), Ariz. Employment Lawyers Assn. (bd. dirs. 1996—), Calif. State Bar Assn., Nat. Employment Lawyer's Assn., Los Abogados Hispanic Bar Assn., Maricopa County Bar Assn. Democrat. Federal civil litigation, State civil litigation, Labor (including EEOC, Fair Labor Standards Act, labor-management relations, NLRB, OSHA). Office: 2525 E Camelback Rd Ste 860 Phoenix AZ 85016-4279 E-mail: dfg@gomezlaw.net.

GOMEZ, JOHN HAMILTON, lawyer; b. Portsmouth, Va., May 10, 1965; s. John Ferdinand and Amanda Kathryn Gomez; m. Lisa Prange Gomez, Sept. 13, 1997. BBA, U. San Diego, 1989; JD, Yale U., 1993. Bar: Calif. 94, U.S. Dist. Ct. (so. dist.) Calif. 94, U.S. Dist. Ct. (cen. dist.) Calif. 95, U.S. Ct. Appeals (9th cir.) 97. Law clk. to Hon. Marilyn L. Huff U.S. Dist. Ct. (so. dist.) Calif., San Diego, 1993—94; assoc. Latham & Watkins, L.A., 1994—97, McClellan & Assocs., San Diego, 2000—; asst. U.S. states atty. Dept. Justice, So. Dist. Calif., San Diego, 1997—2000. Recipient Commr.'s Interagy. award, INS, Washington, 1999. Mem.: Am. Inns of Ct., Consumer Attys. San Diego. Democrat. Roman Catholic. Avocations: reading, surfing, martial arts, golf, running. Product liability, Personal injury (including property damage), Insurance. Office: McClellan & Assocs 1144 State St San Diego CA 92101 Fax: 619-544-0540. E-mail: john@mcclellanlaw.com.

GONG, GLORIA MARGARET, lawyer, pharmacist; b. Yreka, Calif., Oct. 12, 1953; d. Kenneth Wayne and Patricia Ann (Farley) McCain; m. Peter-Poon Ming Gong, Apr. 3, 1976; children: George-Wayne, Cynthia-May, Miranda-Lin. Pharmacist Degree, U. of the Pacific, Stockton, Calif., 1976; JD, Calif. Pacific Law Sch., Bakersfield, 1992. BAr: Calif. 1992, U.S. Dist. Ct. (ea., ctr. and so. dists.) Calif. 1992. Pharmacist Gong's Pharmacy, Tehachapi, Calif., 1978-93; atty. Gong & Hirsch, Bakersfield, 1994-97; pvt. practice, 1997—. Mem.: ATLA, ABA, Kern County Bar Assn., L.A. County Bar Assn., Lambda Kappa Sigma. Bankruptcy, Personal injury (including property damage), Immigration, naturalization, and customs. Office: 6840 District Blvd Bakersfield CA 93313 Office Fax: 661-397-0701. E-mail: ggong@legalemail.com.

GONICK, PETER B. lawyer; b. N.Y.C., Aug. 22, 1966; s. Paul and Angela Mary Gonick; m. Edie Anne Adams, Sept. 14, 1996; children, Elena Adams, Evan Adams. BS in Econ., U. Pa., 1988; JD, U. Wash., 1995. Bar: Wash. 1995, U.S. Dist. Ct. (we. dist.) Wash. 1998. Legal asst. Ballard Spahr Andrews & Ingersoll, Phila., 1988-89; law clk. justice Rosselle Pekelis Wash. State Supreme Ct., Olympia, 1995-96; staff atty. Pub. Defenders Assn., Seattle, 1996-97; assoc. McKay Chadwell, PLLC, Seattle, 1998—. Notes and comments editor Wash. Law Rev., 1995. Agrl. vol. U.S. Peace Corps, Mbeya II, Zaire, 1990-91; pro bono atty. N.W. Immigration Rights Project, Seattle, 1998. Recipient Judge Lawless Meml. award King County Judges, Seattle, 1993, Criminal Law and Contracts Law award Am. Jurisprudence, 1993. Mem. Wash. State Bar Assn., Wash. Assn. Criminal Def. Lawyers, King County Bar Assn., Delta Theta Phi. Avocations: hiking, running, literature. Criminal. Office: McKay Chadwell PLLC 1601 One Union Sw 600 University Ave Seattle WA 98101

GONSON, S. DONALD, lawyer; b. Buffalo, June 13, 1936; s. Samuel and Laura Rose (Greenspan) G.; m. Dorothy Rose, Aug. 28, 1960; children: Julia, Claudia AB, Columbia U., 1958; JD, Harvard U., 1961; postgrad., U. Bombay, India, 1961-62. Bar: Mass. 1962, N.Y. 1983. With Hale and Dorr, Boston, 1962—, sr. ptnr., 1972-2000, of counsel, 2000—. Co-chmn. Speech-Tech., N.Y.C., 1987; instr. in law Boston U., 1963-65, bd. trustees Boston Five Cents Savs. Bank, 1978-83, bd. advisors, 1983-88; adj. prof. internat. law Tufts U. Fletcher Sch. Law and Diplomacy, 1999—; lectr. Fin. Times (U.K.), Instnl. Investors, New Eng. Law Inst., Mass. Soc. CPA's. Chmn. Mass. Comty. Devel. Fin. Corp., 1976-82; pres. Cambridge Ctr. for Adult Edn., 1985-88; bd. dirs. Boston Psychoanalytic Soc. and Inst., 1994—. Fulbright scholar, 1961-62. Fellow Am. Bar Found.; mem. ABA, Internat. Bar Assn., Mass. Bar Assn., Boston Bar Assn. (chmn. internat. law sect. 1998-2001), Harvard Club. Private international, Mergers and acquisitions, Education and schools. Home: 32 Hubbard Park Rd Cambridge MA 02138-4731 Office: Hale & Dorr LLP 60 State St Boston MA 02109-1816 E-mail: donald.gonson@haledorr.com.

GONYNOR, FRANCIS JAMES, lawyer; b. Cambridge, Mass., Nov. 6, 1959; s. James Francis and Beverly Joan (Lintz) G.; m. Deborah Lynn Snyder, July 25, 1981; children: Brian Christopher, Caroline Jane, Madeline Marie. AA, U. Fla., 1978, BA, 1980; JD, U. Houston, 1983. Bar: Tex. 1983, U.S. Dist. Ct. (so. dist.) Tex. 1983, U.S. Ct. Appeals (5th cir.) 1983. Assoc. Eastham Watson Dale & Forney, Houston, 1983-88, ptnr., 1988—. Mediator Am. Arbitration Assn., 1992. Contbr. articles to profl. jours. Mem. Maritime Law Assn., Houston Bar Assn., Coll. of the State Bar of Tex. Admiralty, Federal civil litigation, Environmental. Home: 3327 Spring Trail Dr Sugar Land TX 77479-3050 Office: Eastham Watson Dale Forney 808 Travis St Fl 20 Houston TX 77002-5706 E-mail: gonynor@easthamlaw.com.

GONZALES, DANIEL S. lawyer; b. San Antonio, Nov. 10, 1959; s. Sam and Mary Louise (Stewart) G.; m. Mary David McCauley, May 16, 1980 (div. 1983); m. Devon Elaine Cattell, Jan. 1, 1988 (div. 2001). BA, U. Notre Dame, 1981; JD, Stanford U., 1984. Bar: Calif. 1986, U.S. Dist. Ct. (no. dist.) Calif. 1986, U.S. Tax Ct. 1987, U.S. Ct. Appeals (9th cir.) 1988, U.S. Dist. Ct. (ea. dist.) Calif. 1990. Trivia game writer Axlon Games, Sunnyvale, Calif., 1984; legal writer Matthew Bender & Co., San Francisco, 1984—86; assoc. Carey & Carey, Palo Alto, Calif., 1986—96, Ferrari, Olsen, Ottoboni & Bebb, San Jose, Calif., 1996—97, Bryant, Clohan, Eller, Maines & Baruh, San Jose, 1997—2001, Eller & Assocs., San Jose, 2002—. Mng. editor Stanford Jour. Internat. Law, 1983-84. Candidate Menlo Park (Calif.) City Coun., 1988; bd. dirs. Page Mill YMCA, Palo Alto, 1993-99, YMCA of the Midpeninsula, 1999—, Project Match, San Jose, 1997—, pres., 1998-99, 2002-03; pres. Menlo Park Dispute Resolution Svc., 1994-95; backup guitarist, keyboardist for Beau Brummels 35th Anniversary Summer of Love Concert, San Francisco, 2002. U. Notre Dame scholar, 1977, Nat. Merit scholar, 1977, scholar Nat. Hispanic Scholarship Bd., 1980. Mem. ABA, San Mateo County La Raza Lawyers (pres. 1994), Santa Clara County Bar Assn. (chmn. minority access com. 1994, chmn. judiciary com. 1995), San Mateo County Bar Assn., Palo Alto Area Bar Assn. Democrat. Avocations: guitar, college football. Corporate, general, Land use and zoning (including planning), Property, real (including real estate development, water). Office: Eller & Assocs 60 S Market St Ste 1201 San Jose CA 95113

GONZALES, PONCIANO JR. CONCEPCION, lawyer; b. Manila, Philippines, Nov. 16, 1948; s. Ponciano Sanchez and Beatriz Concepcion Gonzales; m. Mila Lelay Cervantes Gonzales, Sept. 14, 1974; children: Maida Cervantes, Mia Esther Cervantes, Aris Cervantes. LLB, U. Philippines, 1969—75, AB Polit. Sci., 1969. Philippines: Supreme Ct. 1974. Action officer Pub. Assistance Office - Depart of Nat. Def., Manila, Philippines, 1974—74; assoc. lawyer Norberto Gonzales Law Office, Manila, Philippines, 1974—76, Bengzon Law Office, Makati, Philippines, 1976—86; ptnr. Bengzon Law Office (Jimenez Gonzales Liwanag Bello Valdez Caluya & Fernandez (JGLaw), Makati, Philippines, 1986—. Pres. Integrated Bar Philippines, Makati City, Philippines, 2001—. Mem.: Integrated Bar Philippines, Legal Mgmt. Coun. Philippines. Avocations: golf, tennis, history, watching tv. Aviation, General practice, Personal injury (including property damage), Aerospace. Office: JGLaw SOL Bldg Amorsolo St Legaspi Vill Makati City 1229 Philippines Office Fax: (632) 817-3251. E-mail: pcgonzales@jglawph.com.

GONZALES, RICHARD JOSEPH, lawyer; b. Tucson, Mar. 5, 1950; s. Diego D. and Helen O. (Olivas) G.; children: Adrianne, Laura. BA, U. Ariz., 1972, JD, 1975. Bar: Ariz. 1976, U.S. Dist. Ct. Ariz. 1976, U.S. Ct. Appeals 1977, U.S. Supreme Ct. 1993. Asst. pub. defender Pima County Pub. Defenders Office, Tucson, 1976-77; dep. atty. criminal div. Pima County Atty.'s Office, Tucson, 1977-80; ptnr. Gonzales & Villarreal, P.C., Tucson, 1980-96, The Gonzales Law Firm, Tucson, 1997—. Assoc. instr. bus. law Pima Community Coll.,Tucson, 1977, criminal law, 1978-80; judge pro tem Pima County Superior Ct., 1983—; magistrate City of South Tucson, 1982-85; spl. magistrate City of Tucson, 1982-85; comn. appellate ct. appointments, 1991-95; sr. coun. Coll. Master Advocates and Barristers, 2002. Mem. Tucson Tomorrow, 1984-89, Citizen's adv. coun. Sunnyside Sch. Dist., 1986-88; chmn. com. Udall for Congress 2d Congl. Dist., United Way Hispanic Leadership Devel. Program, 1984-86, vice-chmn., 1983-84, chmn., 1984-85; bd. dirs. Girls Club of Tucson, Inc., 1980-81, Teatro Carmen, Inc., 1981-84, Sunnyside Devilaides, Inc., 1982-83, Alcoholism Coun. Tucson, 1982-83, Crime Resisters, 1984-85, La Frontera Ctr., Inc., 1985-96, Crime Prevention League, 1985-87; gen. counsel U. Ariz. Hispanic Alumni; bd. dirs. U. Ariz. Law Coll. Assn., 1984-95, Am.-Israel Friendship League, 1990—, Tucson Internat. Mariachi Conf., 1990—. Named one of Outstanding Young Men of Am. U.S. Jaycee's, 1980; recipient Vol. of Yr. award United Way Greater Tucson, 1985, Cmty. Svc. award Ariz. Minority Bar Assn., 1992, Citizen Svc. award U. Ariz. Hispanic Alumni, 1995, League United Latin Am. Citizen's F.B.I. Community Svcs. Award, 1996, human betterment award Roots & Wings, Inc., 1996, Centennial Achievement award U. Arizona Alumni Assn., 1998, Noche De Las Estrellas Award, Sunnyside High Sch., 2000; honoree State Bar Arizona One Hundred Women & Minority Lawyers, 2001. Fellow Ariz. Bar Found.; mem. ABA, Ariz. Bar Assn., Pima County Bar Assn., Assn. Trial Lawyers Am., Ariz. Trial Lawyers Assn. (bd. dirs.), Nat. Orgn. on Legal Problems of Edn., Supreme Ct. Hist. Soc., Univ. Ariz. Alumni Assn. (bd. dirs. 1988-91), Tucson 30, Phi Delta Phi. Lodges: Optimists (Optimist of Yr. 1981). Democrat. Roman Catholic. Criminal, General practice, Personal injury (including property damage). Office: The Gonzales Law Firm 3501 N Campbell Ave Ste 104 Tucson AZ 85719-2032

GONZALEZ, CARLOS A. lawyer; b. Havana, Cuba, July 24, 1960; s. Jorge A. and Ondina (Santos) G.; m. Marilyn Marvin, Aug. 22, 1988; children: Matthew M., Jordan R. BS, Fla. State U., 1983; MA in Religion, Yale U., 1986; JD, Vanderbilt U., 1989. Bar: Ga. 1989, U.S. Dist. Ct. (no. dist.) Ga. 1991, U.S. Ct. Appeals (11th cir.) 1992, U.S. Dist. Ct. (mid. dist.) Ga. 1993, U.S. Dist. Ct. (ctrl. dist.) Ala., 2002, Ga., 1992, Ga. Ct. Appeals, 1992; fed. ct. spl. master. Law clk. to Judge Harold L. Murphy U.S. Dist. Ct. (no. dist.) Ga., Rome, 1989-91; fed. ct. appointed mediator Geier U. Tenn., U.S. Dist. Ct. (mid. dist.), Tenn., 1999-2000, fed. ct. appointed monitor, 2001—; fed. ct. monitor, spl. master Knight v. Alabama, U.S. Dist. Ct. (no. dist.) Ala., Birmingham, Ala., 1993—; assoc. Rogers & Hardin, Atlanta, 1992-93; pvt. practice Atlanta, 1993—; ptnr. Evans & Gonzalez, Atlanta, 1997-99. Cons. in higher edn., 1994—, alternative dispute resolution; assoc. editor Vanderbilt Law Rev., 1988-89; bd. dirs. Network for Instrnl. TV, Inc., 2002; fed. ct. appointed mediator, 2000. Assoc. editor: Vanderbilt Law Rev., 1988—89. Fellow Inst. for Ministry, Law and Ethics, Salt Lake City. Mem. ABA, Am. Judicature Soc., Atlanta Bar Assn., Fed. Bar Assn., Hispanic Bar Assn., Phi Delta Phi. Methodist. Civil rights, Federal civil litigation, Education and schools. Home: 3087 Belingham Dr NE Atlanta GA 30345-1574 Office: PO Box 450888 Atlanta GA 31145-0888

GONZALEZ, ERVIN AMADO, lawyer; b. Miami, Fla., June 6, 1960; s. Amado Ervin and Esther Maria Gonzalez; m. Janice Barbara Milian, Aug. 22, 1987. BA summa cum laude, Biscayne Coll., 1982; JD cum laude, U. Miami, 1985. Bar: Fla. 1985, U.S. Dist. Ct. (so. and mid. dists.) Fla. 1986, D.C. 1988, Tex. 1991, Colo. 1991, U.S. Ct. Appeals (11th cir.) 1991, U.S. So. Dist. Tex. 1992; cert. specialist in civil trial law, Fla. 1991, Nat. Bd. Trial Advocacy, 1992; cert. specialist in bus. litigation law, Fla. 1998. Law clk. Anderson, Moss Russo & Gievers, P.A., Miami, 1983; assoc. Fine, Jacobson, et al, Miami, 1985-87; ptnr. Gievers & Gonzalez, P.A., Miami, 1987-89, Robles & Gonzalez, 1989-2000, Colson Hicks Eidson Colson Cooper Matthews Martinez Gonzalez Kalbac & Kane, Coral Gabes, Fla., 2000—. Adj. prof. trial skills U. Miami Sch. Law, 1992—; dir. continuing legal edn.; mem. Fla. bar rules of Civil Procedure Com.. Assoc. editor Inter Am. Law Rev., 1983-85; contbr. numerous articles to profl. jours. Mem. new generation com. United Way, Miami, 1985-86, legal com. Spanish Am. League Against Discrimination, Miami, 1986—. Mem. Acad. Fla. Trial Lawyers (chmn. environ. law sect., mem. continuing legal edn. com.), Dade County Bar Assn. (bd. dirs. young lawyers sect. 1987—, bd. dirs. 1990—, sec. 1997, v.p. 1998, pres.-elect 1999, pres. 2000-01), Dade County Trial Lawyers Assn. (bd. dirs., sec., pres. 1995-96), Miami C. of C. (trustee, chmn. environ. awareness com.,com. mem. 1985—, Leadership Miami award 1988). Democrat. Roman Catholic. General civil litigation, Insurance, Personal injury (including property damage). Office: Colson Hicks Eidson Colson Cooper Matthews Martinez Gonzalez Kalbach & Kane 255 Aragon Ave 2d Fl Coral Gables FL 33134 E-mail: ervin@colson.com.

GONZALEZ, JOE MANUEL, lawyer; b. N.Y.C., Aug. 18, 1950; s. Reinaldo Fabregas and Mary Louise (Cermeno) G.; m. Ruia Jane Whiteside, Dec. 30, 1977; children: Matthew Ray, Jane Marie, Jeffrey Joseph, Joseph Manuel. BA, U. South Fla., 1972; JD, Gonzaga U., 1980; LLM in Taxation, Georgetown U., 1981. Bar: Fla. 1981, U.S. Tax Ct. 1983, U.S. Dist. Ct. (mid. dist.) Fla. 1984, U.S. Ct. Appeals (11th cir.) 1984, U.S. Supreme Ct. 1985. Atty. Gonzaga U. Legal Services, Spokane, Wash., 1980; mng. ptnr. Cotterill, Gonzalez, Hayes & Grantham, Fla., 1981-88, Cotterill & Grantham, Pa., 1982-92, Cotterill, Gonzalez & Grantham, Pa., Pa., 1992-93; prin. Joe M. Gonzalez, P.A., 1993—; atty. Hispanic Def. League, Tampa, Fla., 1982-90. Assoc. editor Gonzaga Law Rev. Spl. Report: Pub. Sector Labor Law, 1980. Mem. Sheriff's Hispanic Adv. Coun., Hillsborough County, Fla., 1982-93, City of Tampa Hispanic Adv. Coun., 1983—, chmn. 1993—, U. So. Fla. Hispanic Adv. Bd., 1999-2001; chmn. citizens adv. com. Hillsborough County Planning Commn., 1988-90; pres. Tampa Hispanic Heritage, Inc., 1985-93; founder Carnavale En Tampa, Inc., 1986-90; master of ceremonies Gasparilla Sidewalk Art Festival, 1988; mem. police chief's adv. com., 1988-93; sec. Hispanic Bus. Inst. Fla., Inc., 1988-93; dir. Housing and Edn. Alliance, 2001— . Mem. ABA, Fla. Bar Assn. (jud. nominating prodedures com. 1988-89), Hillsborough County Bar Assn., Assn. Trial Lawyers Am., Nat. Inst. for Trial Advocacy, Complete Census Count Com., Rotary, Phi Delta Phi. Democrat. Presbyterian. Estate planning, Family and matrimonial, State civil litigation. Home: 5801 Mariner St Tampa FL 33609-3411 Office: 304 S Willow Ave Tampa FL 33606-2147

GONZALEZ, JOSE ALEJANDRO, JR., federal judge; b. Tampa, Fla., Nov. 26, 1931; s. Jose A. and Luisa Secundina (Collia) G.; m. Frances Frierson, Aug. 22, 1956 (dec. Aug. 1981); children— Margaret Ann, Mary Frances; m. Mary Sue Copeland, Sept. 24, 1983 BA, U. Fla., 1952, JD, 1957; LLD, Nova Southeastern U., 1998. Bar: Fla. 1958, U.S. Dist. Ct. (so. dist.) Fla. 1959, U.S. Ct. Appeals 1959, U.S. Supreme Ct. 1963. Practice in, Ft. Lauderdale, 1958-64; claim rep. State Farm Mut., Lakeland, Fla., 1957-58; assoc. firm Watson, Hubert and Sousley, 1958-61, ptnr., 1961-64; asst. state atty. 15th Cir. Fla., 1961-64; cir. judge 17th Cir. Ft. Lauderdale, 1964-78, chief judge, 1969-70; assoc. judge 4th Dist. Ct. Appeals, West Palm Beach; U.S. dist. judge So. Dist. Fla., 1978—, sr. judge, 1996—. Bd. dirs. Arthritis Found., 1962-72; bd. dirs. Henderson Clinic Broward County, 1964-68, v.p., 1967-68. Served to 1st lt. AUS, 1952-54. Recipient Kupferman award Laymen's Nat. Bible Assn., 1991; named Broward County Outstanding Young Man, 1967, one of Fla.'s Five Outstanding Young Men, Fla. Jaycees, 1967, Broward Legal Exec. of Yr., 1978. Mem.: ABA, Broward County Bar, Fla. Bar Assn., Fed. Bar Assn., Am. Judicature Soc., Pittsfield Country Club, Lauderdale Yacht Club, Fla. Blue Key, Kiwanian Club (pres. 1971—72), Greenock Country Club, Pittsfield Country Club, Ft. Lauderdale Jaycees (dir. 1960—61), Phi Alpha Delta, Sigma Chi (Significant Sig). Democrat. Office: US Dist Ct 205 US Courthouse 299 E Broward Blvd Fort Lauderdale FL 33301-1944 Home: Ste 205D 299 E Broward Blvd Fort Lauderdale FL 33301-1902

GONZALEZ, RAUL A. retired state supreme court justice, lawyer; b. Weslaco, Tex., Mar. 22, 1940; s. Raul G. and Paula (Hernandez) G.; m. Dora Blanca Champion, Dec. 22, 1963; children— Celeste, Jaime, Marco, Sonia BA in Govt., U. Tex., Austin, 1963; JD, U. Houston, 1966; LLM, U. Va., 1986. Bar: Tex. 1966. Asst. U.S. atty. U.S. Dist. Ct. (so. dist.) Tex., Brownsville, 1969-73; ptnr. Joe Walsh & Assocs., Brownsville, 1973, Gonzalez & Hamilton, Brownsville, 1974-78; judge 103d Dist. Ct. Tex., Brownsville, 1978-81, Ct. Appeals (13th cir.), Corpus Christi, Tex., 1981-84; justice Tex. Supreme Ct., Austin, 1984-98; ret., 1998; of counsel Locke Liddell & Sapp LLP, Austin, 1998—. Bd. dirs. Brownsville Boy's Club, Brownsville Community Devel. Corp., So. Tex. Rehab. Ind. Sch. Dist.; U.S. Recipient Outstanding Performance Rating award Dept. Justice, 1972, Toll fellow, 1987. Mem. Christian Legal Soc., Christian Conciliation Service, ABA, Tex. Bar Found. Avocations: jogging, racquetball. Home: 10511 River Plantation Dr Austin TX 78747-1125 Office: Locke Liddell & Sapp LLP 100 Congress Ave Ste 300 Austin TX 78701-2748 E-mail: rgonzalez@lockeliddell.com.*

GONZALEZ, RENEE E. lawyer; b. Pitts., Jan. 6, 1963; d. Raymond A. and Rue E. Gonzalez; m. Ernest M. Schirra Jr., Aug. 5, 1984; 1 child, Michaela Rue. BSBA, Duquesne U., 1984, JD, 1987. Bar: Pa. 1991, Tex. 1990, U.S. Claims Ct. 1990. Tax atty. Exxon Co. U.S.A., Houston, 1987—91; sr. tax atty. Exxon Corp., Dallas, 1991—94, Exxon Chem. Internat., Brussels, 1994—97; tax counsel Exxon Co. U.S.A., 1997—98, Exxon-Mobil Corp., 1998—2002; tax mgr. Exxon Mobil Inter-Am. Inc., Coral Gables, Fla., 2002—. Mem.: ABA. Avocations: travel, sports. Corporate taxation. Office: Exxon Mobil Inter-Am Inc 396 Alhambra Cir Coral Gables FL 33134

GONZALEZ LUNA, RODRIGO, lawyer; b. Guadalajara, Jalisco, Mexico, May 20, 1967; s. Carlos González Luna and Sofía Castellanos; m. Jenefer Anne Teague Hutchison, Feb. 15, 1997; children: Sabrina González Luna Teague, Emilio González Luna Teague. LLM, U. Kent, Canterburry, Eng., 1994. Bar: Mexican Bar Assn. 1991. Ptnr. White & Case LLP, Mexico City, 2000—00, Romo, Paillés, Gúzman y González Luna, S.C., Mexico City, 2000—02. Avocations: travel, reading, classical music, tennis. Corporate, general, Property, real (including real estate development, water), Mergers and acquisitions. Office: Rodrigo González Luna - Abogados Camino al Desierto de los Leones # 5696 01780 Mexico City Mexico Home Fax: (52 55) 54 25 42 67; Office Fax: (52 55) 54 25 42 67. Personal E-mail: rodrigoglezluna@prodigy.net.mx. E-mail: rodrigoglezluna@prodigy.net.mx.

GOOCH, ANTHONY CUSHING, lawyer; b. Amarillo, Tex., Dec. 3, 1937; s. Cornelius Skinner and Sidney Seale (Crawford) G.; m. Elizabeth Melissa Ivanoff, May 27, 1963 (div. Nov. 1983); children: Katherine C., Jennifer C. Gooch Avery, Melissa G., Andrew E.; m. Linda B. Klein, Nov. 7, 1987. BA, U. of South, 1959; diploma, Coll. of Europe, 1960; JD, NYU, 1963, M in Comparative Law, 1964. Bar: N.Y. 1963. Assoc. Cleary, Gottlieb, Steen & Hamilton, N.Y.C., Paris, Brussels, 1963-72, ptnr. Rio de Janeiro, 1973-78, N.Y.C., 1978-99, sr. counsel, 2000—; gen. counsel Internat. Inst. Rural Reconstruction, 2000—02, bd. trustees, 2002—. Co-author: Loan Agreement Documentation, 1982, 2d edit., 1991, Swap Apreement Documentation, 1987, 2d edit., 1988, Documentation for Derivatives, 1993, Credit Support Supplement, 1995, Cross-Product Risk Mgmt. Supplement, 2000, 4th edit., 2002, Documentation for Loans, Assignments and Participations, 1996; articles editor NYU Law Rev., 1962-63. Bd. trustees Internat. Inst. Rural Reconstrn., 2002—; v.p. planned giving Assoc. Alumni, U. of the South, Sewanee, Tenn. Mem. ABA, N.Y. State Bar Assn., Assn. Bar City N.Y., New York County Lawyers Assn. Episcopalian. Home: 7 Mine Hill Rd Redding CT 06896-2701 E-mail: agooch@cgsh.com., tonygooch@aol.com.

GOOD, DOUGLAS JAY, lawyer; b. Bklyn., Mar. 29, 1947; s. Sidney B. and Sophie (Mohel) G.; m. Lynda Edes, Feb. 25, 1979; 1 child, Sara. BA, Columbia U., 1967; JD, NYU, 1971. Bar: N.Y. 1972, U.S. Dist. Ct. (so. and ea. dists.) N.Y. 1973, U.S. Ct. Appeals (2d cir.) 1975, U.S. Supreme Ct. 1976, U.S. Ct. Appeals (11th cir.) 1989. Staff atty. Legal Aid Soc. Rockland County, Inc., New City, N.Y., 1972-73, dir., 1973-81; assoc. Ruskin, Moscou, Faltishchek, P.C., Mineola, NY, 1981-85, ptnr., 1985—, mng. ptnr., 1990-98. Adj. lectr. NYU Inst. for Paralegal Studies, N.Y.C., 1982-85; adj. asst. prof.; bd. dirs. Nassau/Suffolk Law Svcs. Com., Inc., 1986—, chairperson, 1987—; bd. dirs. Nassau Bar Tech. Ctr., Inc., 1995-2000, sec., 1995, vice chmn., 1996, pres. 1998. Mem.: ABA, Fed. Bar. Coun., Nassau County Bar Assn. (bd. dirs. 1996—99, adv. bd. We Care Fund 2000—, sec. 2001—02, treas. 2002—03, 2nd v.p. 2003—), N.Y. State Bar Assn. Jewish. General civil litigation, Commercial, contracts (including sales of goods; commercial financing). Office: Ruskin Moscou Faltischek PC 190 EAB Plaza 15th Fl E Tower Uniondale NY 11556-0190

GOODALE, JAMES CAMPBELL, lawyer, media executive, television producer/host; b. Cambridge, Mass., July 27, 1933; s. Robert Leonard and Eunice (Campbell) G.; m. Toni Krissel, May 3, 1964; children: Timothy Fuller, Ashley Krissel; foster child: Joseph Clayton Akiwenzie. Grad., Pomfret Sch., 1951; BA, Yale U., 1955; JD, U. Chgo., 1958. Bar: N.Y. 1960. Assoc. Lord, Day and Lord, N.Y.C., 1959-63; gen. atty. N.Y. Times Co., 1963-67, gen. counsel, 1967-72, sr. v.p., 1972-73, exec. v.p., 1973-79, vice-chmn., 1979-80; ptnr. Debevoise and Plimpton, 1980-93, founder, head media-comm. and intellectual property sect., 1980—96, mem. exec. com., 1981-84, of counsel, 1994-96; co-prodr., host Digital Age (formerly The Telecom. and Info. Revolution), 25 WYNE, N.Y.C., 1995—. With Cmty. Law Office, East Harlem, 1968-70; vis. lectr. Yale U. Law Sch., 1977-80; adj. prof. NYU Sch. Law, 1983-86, Fordham Law Sch., 1986—; affiliated scholar N.Y. Law Sch., 1995—; mem. N.Y. State Privacy and Security Com., 1976-79; 2nd cir. Commn. Reduction of Burdens and Costs in Civil Litigation, 1977-80; vice chmn. N.Y. State Jud. Commn. on Minorities, 1987-90, chmn., 1990-91, bd. dirs. com. to protect journalists, 1989—, chmn., 1989-94; mem. adv. bd. Comm. and the Law, 1980—; pres., owner Midtown Skating Corp., 1981-90; chmn. bd. Cable TV Law and Fin., 1981—; trustee N.Y.C. Citizens Budget Commn., 1990-98; advisor U.S. Supreme Ct. Jud. Conf. Com. on the Judiciary, 1980-89; chmn., founder PLI Comm. Law Seminar, 1972—; sec. N.Y. Observer, 1988-92, Paris Rev. Found., 2001-. Author: All About Cable, 1987; compilor, editor: The New York Times Company vs. U.S., 1971; bd. editors: Media Law Reporter (co-founder), Nat. Law Jour., 1983—; columnist nat. and N.Y. law jours.; contbr. articles on comms. law to profl. jours. Mem. rules com. Dem. Nat. Conv., 1988; chmn. N.Y. lawyer com. for Dukakis, 1988; former bd. dirs. N.Y. Times, N.Y. Times Neediest Cases Fund, N.Y. Times Found.; former trustee Pomfret Sch., Gunnery Sch., St. Bernard's Sch., Boys' Club N.Y., Salzburg Seminar, Fed. Bar Coun.; mem. vis. com. U. Chgo. Law Sch., 1977-80; bd. dirs. Human Rights Watch, 1994-96, Sky Rink Scholarship Fund, Inc., 1990-99, Citizens Pub. Utilities, 1996-99, Ice Theatre of N.Y., 1999—, Internat. Ctr. Journalists, 1998—. With AUS, 1958-59, Res., 1959-64. Named one of 200 Rising Leaders in U.S., Time mag., 1974, with 100 Most Influential Lawyers in U.S., Nat. Law Jour., 1991-97, one of Best Lawyers in Am., 1991-99; William Brinckerhoff Jackson scholar, 1954-55, Nat. Honor scholar U. Chgo. Law Sch., 1955-58. Fellow Inst. Judicial Adminstrn., N.Y. State Bar Assn. (chmn. spl. com. on pub. access to info. and proc. 1979-84, spl. com. on media law 1985-92); mem. N.Y.C. Bar Assn. (chmn. comm. law com. 1978-83, mem. corp. law com. 1977-81), ABA (governing bd. comm. law forum, commn. on pub. understanding about law 1979-82), Fed. Bar Coun. (trustee 1980-84), Columbia U. Seminars on Media and Society. Clubs: Yale (gov. 1964-67), Century Assn, Economic, St. Elmo, Elihu (gov. 1966-70), Washington Conn. (gov. 1972-78). Communications, Corporate, general, Libel. Office: Debevoise & Plimpton 919 3rd Ave Fl 30 New York NY 10022-6225

GOODE, BARRY PAUL, lawyer; b. N.Y.C., Apr. 11, 1948; s. Hy and Charlotte (Langer) G.; m. Erica Tucker, Sept. 1, 1974; children: Adam, Aaron. AB magna cum laude, Kenyon Coll., 1969; JD cum laude, Harvard U., 1972. Bar: Mass. 1972, Calif. 1975, Hawaii 1995, U.S. Dist. Ct. Mass. 1972, U.S. Dist. Ct. (no. dist.) Calif. 1975, U.S. Dist. Ct. (ctrl. dist.) Calif. 1983, U.S. Dist. Ct. Hawaii 1995, U.S. Ct. Appeals (9th cir.) 1976, U.S. Ct. Appeals (6th cir.) 1999, U.S. Supreme Ct. 1986. Spl. asst. Sen Adlai E. Stevenson III, Washington, 1972-74; assoc. McCutchen, Doyle, Brown & Enersen, San Francisco, 1974-80, ptnr., 1980-2001; legal affairs sec. Gov. Gray Davis, 2001—. Co-author: Federal Litigation Guide, 1985. Advisor Gov.'s Com. to Review Water Law, San Francisco, 1979; bd. dirs. Stanford Pub. Interest Law Found., 1979-82; bd. dirs. Coro No. Calif., 1997—. Mem. San Francisco Bar Assn. (exec. com. environ. law sect. 1989-91), Am. Law Inst. Federal civil litigation, State civil litigation, Environmental. Office: Gov Gray Davis State Capitol Sacramento CA 95814

GOODELL, ROBERT D. lawyer, educator; b. Deadwood, S.D., Oct. 29, 1947; s. Winn B. and Loretta Marie (Nikont) G.; m. Jane Liepold, Sept. 30, 1972 (div. 1992); m. Renee Marie Brown, Oct. 30, 1992; 1 child, Madeline Meredith. BMus magna cum laude, Yankton (S.D.) Coll., 1969; MMus, Northwestern U., 1972; JD cum laude, U. Minn., 1977. Bar: Minn. 1977, U.S. Dist. Ct. Minn. 1978, U.S. Ct. Appeals (8th cir.) 1981. Atty. Minn. County Attys. Coun., St. Paul, 1978, State Pub. Defender, Mpls., 1979-80, 82-84, Douglas W. Thomson Law Firm, St. Paul, 1981, Washington County Atty., Stillwater, Minn., 1984-86, Anoka County Atty., Anoka, Minn., 1986—. Adj. prof. Hamline U. Law Sch., St. Paul, 1990—, William Mitchell Coll. Law, St. Paul, 1982-84; instr. Minn. Bur. Criminal Apprehension, St. Paul, 1991—; mem. Minn. Crime Victims Adv. Coun., 1995—. Mem. Minn. Crime Victims Reparations Bd., St. Paul, 1995—. Named Pub. Sector Lawyer of Distinction, Minn. Jour. Law and Politics, 1996. Mem. Minn. State Bar Assn., Anoka County Bar Assn. Avocations: music, reading, long distance bicycling. Office: Anoka County Attys Office 2100 3rd Ave Anoka MN 55303-2265 E-mail: rdgoodel@co.anoka.mn.us.

GOODELL, SOL, retired lawyer; b. St. Louis, Aug. 24, 1906; s. Abram and Jennie (Silverberg) G.; m. Beatrice Cholden, Feb. 24, 1946 (dec. Mar. 1998); children: Thomas C., Susan Jean. LLB, U. Tex., 1929. Bar: Tex. 1929. Asso. prof. law U. Tex. Law Sch., 1929-30; asso., then mem. firm Thompson & Knight, and predecessors, Dallas, 1930-76, of counsel, 1976—. Former chmn. bd. Greenhill Sch., Dallas; former trustee bd. devel. U. Tex., Dallas; former trustee, v.p. Excellence in Edn. Found.; former sec., trustee Goals for Dallas; former trustee Dallas Grand Opera Assn.; former pres. Found. for Callier Ctr. and Communication Disorders. Served to capt. AUS, 1942-46. Mem. ABA, Dallas Bar Assn., State Bar Tex. Jewish (trustee, past pres. temple). Home: 5927 Joyce Way Dallas TX 75225-1626 Office: 1700 Pacific Ave Ste 3300 Dallas TX 75201-4656

GOODFRIEND, HERBERT JAY, lawyer; b. N.Y.C., Sept. 9, 1926; s. Sidney and Blanche (Prager) G.; m. Barbara Gottlieb, Oct. 12, 1952; children: Sandra, Beth Ann. AB, NYU, 1947, LLB, 1950, LLM in Taxation, 1953. Bar: N.Y. 1950, U.S. Dist. Ct. (so. dist.) N.Y. 1951, U.S. Dist. Ct. (ea. dist.) N.Y. 1982, U.S. Ct. Appeals (2nd cir.) 1953, U.S. Tax Ct. 1954. Assoc. Otterbourg, Steindler Houston & Rosen, N.Y.C., 1950—83, ptnr., 1983—86; counsel Summit, Solomon & Feldesman, 1986-93, Philips, Nizer, 1993—. Counsel N.Y. Bd. Trade, N.Y.C., 1981-87, bd. dirs., 1982-88; spl. master Supreme Ct. New York County, N.Y.C., 1977-79; vice chmn., bd. dirs. Jones Apparel Group, Inc., 1990-98., sec., 1990-2001. Columnist N.Y. Law Jour., 1977-79 Treas., dir. N.Y.C. Alliance Against Sexual Abuse, 2001—. With U.S. Army, 1945-46. Fellow Am. Bar Found., Coll. Law Practice Mgmt.; mem. ABA (chmn. econs. law practice sect. 1984-85, ho. of dels. 1994-97), N.Y. State Bar Assn. (chmn. com. on law office econ. and mgmt. 1983-85), N.Y. County Lawyers Assn. (com. on arbitration 1974-87), NYU Club (v.p. exec. com. 1976-80), Adelphi U. Inst. for Paralegal Tng. (adv. bd. 1976-96), Am. Apparel Mfg. Assn. (fin. mgmt. com. 1980-2001), Tau Delta Phi (nat. pres. 1952-57). Avocations: golf, computers. Home: 176 E 71st St New York NY 10021-5159 Office: Phillips Nizer 666 Fifth Ave New York NY 10103 E-mail: hgoodfriend@pillipsnizer.com.

GOODHARTZ, GERALD, law librarian; b. N.Y.C., Oct. 23, 1938; s. Jack and Anna (Sperling) G.; m. Carol Scialli, Aug. 18, 1969; children: Joanna, Allison. BSCE, CCNY, 1961; MLS, U. So. Calif., 1970. Night reference asst. Assn. Bar of City of N.Y., 1956-61; libr. asst. Cravath, Swaine & Moore, N.Y.C., 1961-65; head libr. Rosenman, Colin, Freund, Lewis & Cohen, N.Y.C., 1965-69, Keatinge & Sterling, L.A., 1969-70, Kaye, Scholer, Fierman, Hays & Handler, N.Y.C., 1970-98; mgr. info. svcs. Broad and Cassel, Orlando, 1998-99; dir. libr. svcs. Brown Raysman Millstein Felder & Steiner LLP, N.Y.C., 1999—. Libr. planning cons. Olympic Towers, N.Y.C., 1975; lectr. in field. Mem. ABA, ALA, Am. Assn. Law Librs. (cert.), Law Libr. Assn. Greater N.Y., Assn. Law Librs. of Upstate N.Y., Spl. Librs. Assn., Am. Soc. Info. Scientists, Am. Mgmt. Assn., Assn. Info. Mgrs., Nat. Micrographics Assn. Office: Brown Raysman Millstein Felder & Steiner LLP 900 3rd Ave New York NY 10022

GOODHINES, JAMES RICHARD, prosecutor, law educator; b. Syracuse, N.Y., Mar. 12, 1969; s. Richard Allen and Nancy Jean Goodhines; m. Lori Kristin Odierna, May 25, 1997; 1 child, Caroline Ann. BA in English Lit., LeMoyne Coll., 1992; JD, Western New Eng. Coll., 1995. Bar: Mass. 1995, U.S. Dist. Ct. Mass. 1996. Asst. dist. atty. Hampden County Dist. Attys. Office, Springfield, Mass., 1995—. Lectr. Mass. Criminal Justice Tng. Coun ., Agawam, Mass., 1997—, Western New Eng. Coll., Springfield, 1998—. Mem.: UNICO Nat. (chmn. scholarship com. 2001—, Longmeadow chpt.). Democrat. Roman Catholic. Avocations: sports, theater , music. Office: Hampden County Dist Atty Office Hall of Justice 50 State St Springfield MA 01103

GOODING, DAVID MICHAEL, judge; b. Jacksonville, Fla., June 10, 1952; s. Marion William and Eunice (Drawdy) Gooding; m. Cathy Rhoden, Aug. 3, 1974; children: Sara Lynn, John Thomas. BA, U. Fla., 1974; JD, U. Miami, 1988. Bar: Fla. 1988, U.S. Dist. Ct. (mid. dist.) Fla. 1988. Asst. state atty. Office of State Atty., Jacksonville, Fla., 1988—89; assoc. Penland & Penland, P.A., Jacksonville, 1989—92; shareholder Kent, Ridge & Crawford, Jacksonville, 1992—97, Kent, Crawford & Gooding, Jacksonville, 1997—2002; circuit ct. judge Jacksonville, 2002—. Adult tchr. Christ Ch., 1994—96, nursery vol., 1991—94; elder South Jacksonville Presbyn. Ch., 1991—94; bd. dirs. Samaritan Counseling Ctr., Jacksonville, 1990—94, Girls, Inc., Jacksonville, 1997—2001, pres., 1999—2000, endowment trustee, 2000—; bd. dirs. Southside United Meth. Presch., Jacksonville, 1995—97, Luth. Social Svcs., Jacksonville, 2001—, Family Farm of N.E. Fla., Jacksonville, 2001—. Mem.: ABA, Christian Legal Soc. (trustee 1997—2000), Fla. Bar, York Rite, Shriners (1998 imperial conv. com. 1997—98), Royal Order of Jesters, Scottish Rite, Masons. Presbyterian. Office: Duval County Courthouse 330 E Bay St Rm 356 Jacksonville FL 32202 E-mail: dgooding@coj.net.

GOODKIND, CONRAD GEORGE, lawyer; b. Arlington, Va., Aug. 8, 1944; s. Bernard Arthur and Sylvia (Lieber) G.; m. Sandra Timme, Aug. 27, 1966; children: Carley M., Adam B., Erica L., Anne G. BS, U. Wis., 1966, JD, 1969. Bar: Wis. 1969, U.S. Dist. Ct. (ea. and we. dists.) Wis. 1969. Assoc. Kivett & Kasdorf, Milw., 1969-71; counsel Citizens' Study Com. on Jud. Orgn., Madison, Wis., 1971-73; dep. commr. securities State of Wis., Madison, 1973-79; assoc. Quarles & Brady, Milw., 1979-81, ptnr., 1981—, mem. exec. com., 1983—. Adj. prof. securities law U. Wis. Law Sch., Madison, 1975-79, Marquette U. Law Sch., Milw., 1981-83; mem. Gov.'s Bus. Cts. Task Force, 1994-98, state regulation com. Nat. Assn. Securities Dealers, Inc., Washington, 1986-92; bd. dirs. Able Distbg. Corp.; bd. dirs., sec. Cade Industries, Inc., 1989-99; sec. Brady Corp., 1999—. Bd. dirs. Milw. Repertory Theatre, 1995-2001, exec. com. mem., 1997-2001. Mem. ABA (vice chmn. state regulation securities com. 1986-89, chmn. 1989-92, vice chmn. bus. law sect. com. on insts. and seminars 2001—), Wis. Bar Assn. (chmn. securities com., 1981-95, bd. dirs. sect. bus. law 1991-2001, vice chair sect. bus. law 1996-98, chair 1998-2000). Corporate, general, Mergers and acquisitions, Securities. Office: Quarles & Brady LLP 411 E Wisconsin Ave Ste 2550 Milwaukee WI 53202-4497 E-mail: cgg@quarles.com.

GOODMAN, ALFRED NELSON, lawyer; b. Jan. 21, 1945; s. Bernard R. and Mildred (Schlanger) Goodman. BS in Mech. and Aerospace Scis., U. Rochester, 1966; JD, Georgetown U., 1969. Bar: N.Y. 1970, D.C. 1971, U.S. Supreme Ct. 1974. Patent examiner U.S. Patent Office, Washington, 1969—71; assoc. Roylance, Abrams, Berdo & Goodman, LLP, Washington, 1971—74, ptnr., 1975—. Mem.: ABA, Bar Assn. D.C. (chmn. patent, trademark and copyright law sect. 1984—85, bd. dir. 1985—86), Am. Patent Law Assn. Antitrust, Patent, Trademark and copyright. Home: 4948 Sentinel Dr Bethesda MD 20816-3556 Office: Roylance Abrams Berdo & Goodman LLP 1300 19th St NW Ste 600 Washington DC 20036-1649

GOODMAN, BARRY JOEL, lawyer; b. N.Y.C., May 28, 1953; s. Walter Louis and Shirley (Lenzer) G.; m. Nicole Goodman; children: Aaron, Rebecca, Noah. BA, Bradley U., 1974; JD with honors, Stetson U., 1977. Bar: Fla. 1977, U.S. Ct. Appeals 1978, Mich. 1979, U.S. Dist. Ct. (we. dist.) Fla., U.S. Dist. Ct. (ea. dist.) Mich. With Diecidue, Ferlita & Prieto, Tampa, Fla., 1977-78; assoc. Provizer, Eisenberg et al, Southfield, Mich., 1979-82, Thurswell, Chayet & Weiner, Southfield, 1982-87, ptnr., 1987-93; owner Gordon, Goodman & Acker, Southfield, 1993-98, Goodman Acker, Southfield, 1998—. Lectr. Inst. Continuing Legal Edn., Ann Arbor, Mich., Mich. Trial Lawyer's Assn., State Bar of Mich. Officer-at-large Mich. Dem. Party; v.p. Anti-Defamation League, 1983—; bd. dirs. B'nai B'rith Youth Orgn., Mich., 1995—97, West Bloomfield (Mich.) Woods Homeowners Assn., 1980—83. Mem.: State Bar of Mich. (bd. mem. negligence sect.), Oakland County Trial Lawyers Assn., Oakland County Bar Assn., Mich. Trial Lawyers Assn. (bd. dirs. 1985—, treas. 1995, sec. 1996, v.p. 1997, pres.-elect 1998, pres. 1999—2000), ATLA. Democrat. Jewish. Avocations: tennis, golf, reading, theater. Personal injury (including property damage). Office: Goodman Acker PC 17000 W 10 Mile Rd 2nd flr Southfield MI 48075-2945 Business E-Mail: bgoodman@goodmanacker.com.

GOODMAN, BARRY S. lawyer; b. Jersey City, June 7, 1951; s. Milton and Margaret Goodman; m. Emily J. Reynolds, Dec. 5, 1982. BA cum laude, Rutgers Coll., 1973; JD, Rutgers U., Newark, 1977. Bar: N.J., U.S. Dist. Ct. N.J., U.S. Ct. Appeals (3rd cir.), U.S. Supreme Ct. Jud. law clk. hon. Eugene L. Lora Superior Ct. N.J. Appellate Divsn., Hackensack, 1977-78; atty. Essex-Newark Legal Svcs., Orange, N.J., 1978-79, Crummy, Del Deo, Dolan & Purcell, Newark, 1979-84, Greenbaum, Rowe, Smith, Ravin, Davis & Himmel LLP, Woodbridge, N.J., 1984—. Author: (manual) New Jersey Students' Rights, 1977; mem. editl. bd. Rutgers Law Rev., 1976-77; contbr. articles to profl. jours. Vol. atty. Essex-Newark Legal Svcs., 1979-81; mem. Kinoy Fellowship Adv. Com., Newark, 1991-96; mem. 20th reunion conf. com. Rutgers Constnl. Litigation Clinic, Newark, 1991; co-chairperson Hunterdon County Dems. for Clinton Com., Flemington, N.J., 1992; mem. Hunterdon County Dem. Com., Flemington, 1994—, mem. exec. com., 1996-2000, 2002-; mem. funds allocation com. United Way Hunterdon County, Clinton, 1995—, agy. admissions com., 1996, trustee, 1997—, treas. 1998-99, exec. com., 1998—, spl. gifts com., 1998—, cmty. rels. com., 1998—, v.p., 1999-2001, pres., 2001-2003; mem. Hunterdon County Health and Human Svcs. Adv. Coun., Flemington, 1998-2000. Mem. ABA (litigation sect., antitrust sect.), Fed. Bar Assn. N.J., N.J. State Bar Assn. (civil trial sect., antitrust sect., real property and probate sect.), Trial Attys. N.J. (trustee 1996—), Middlesex County Bar Assn., Hunterdon County Bar Assn., Rutgers-Newark Sch. Law Alumni Assn. (annual reunion dinner com. 1992, co-chair 1999, annual spring dinner com. 1995-98, treas. 1999-2000, sec. 2000-01, v.p. 2001-2002, pres. elect 2002-2003, pres. 2003), IOLTA fund of the bar assn. of N.J. (trustee, 2003-), Phi Beta Kappa, Phi Kappa Phi. Antitrust, General civil litigation, Professional liability. Office: Greenbaum Rowe Smith Ravin Davis & Himmel LLP 99 Wood Ave S Iselin NJ 08830-2715

GOODMAN, ELIZABETH ANN, lawyer; b. Marquette, Mich., Aug. 11, 1950; d. Paul William and Pearl Marie Goodman; m. Herbert Charles Gardner, Sept. 24, 1977. Student, U. Munich, 1970-71; BA cum laude, Alma (Mich.) Coll., 1972; JD cum laude, U. Mich., 1977. Bar: Minn. 1978, Mich. 1978, U.S. Dist. Ct. Minn. 1979. Cert. real property law specialist, real property sect. Minn. Bar Assn. High sch. tchr. Onaway (Mich.) High Sch., 1973-74; assoc. Dorsey & Whitney LLP, Mpls., 1978-82; ptnr. Dorsey & Whitney, Mpls., 1983-99; v .p., chief gen. counsel Ryan Cos. , 2000—. Mem. Am. Corp. Counsel Assn., Minn. Bar Assn., Hennepin County Bar Assn. Environmental, Land use and zoning (including planning), Property, real (including real estate development, water). Office: Ryan Cos 50 S 10th St Ste 300 Minneapolis MN 55403-2012

GOODMAN, GARY A. lawyer; b. N.Y.C., Mar. 8, 1948; s. Nathaniel and Edith (Rosen) G.; m. Susan Schachter, Aug. 13, 1972; children: Max, Jonah, William, Zachary, Holden. AB in History summa cum laude, Economics with honors, U. Rochester, 1970; JD, NYU, 1973. Bar: N.Y. 1974, U.S. Dist. Ct. (so. dist. and ea. dist.) N.Y. 1974, U.S. Dist. Ct. Guam, 1975, U.S. Ct. Appeals (2d cir.) 1975, Calif. 1996, Tex. 1996. Ptnr. Sonnenschein Nath & Rosenthal, N.Y.C., 2002—. Contbr. numerous articles to profl. jours.. Mem. bd. edn. Locust Valley (N.Y.) Ctrl. Sch. Dist., 1995-96, v.p., 1996-97, pres., 1997-98. Mem.: ABA (vice chmn. internat. investment in real estate com. 1983—90, chmn. Pacific Rim trans. subcom. real estate financing com. 1987—88), Comml. Mortgage Securities Assn., Assn. Fgn. Investors in Real Estate, Real Estate Bd., Internat. Coun. Shopping Ctrs. (task force environ. issues 1987—90, law com. 1991—94), Assn. Bar of City of N.Y. (uniform state laws com. 1978—80, real property law com. 1991—94, land use com. 1994—97, real property law com. 1997—2000), N.Y. State Bar Assn. (chmn. fgn. investment in U.S. real estate com. 1987—88). Office: Sonnenschein Nath & Rosenthal 1221 Ave of the Americas New York NY 10020 E-mail: ggoodman@sonnenschein.com.

GOODMAN, HAROLD S. lawyer; b. St. Louis, Aug. 17, 1937; s. David and Eva Katherine (Wasserman) G.; m. Karen K. Mauldin, Aug. 5, 1979; 1 child, James Richardson. AB, U. Mo., 1960; LLB, JD, Washington U., St. Louis, 1963. Bar: Mo. 1963. Assoc., ptnr. Bishop & Goodman, St. Louis, 1963—70; v.p., gen. counsel, sec. World Color Press, Inc., St. Louis, 1970-75; pvt. practice St. Louis, 1975-81; ptnr. Gallop, Johnson & Neuman, L.C., St. Louis, 1981—. Mem. St. Louis County CSC, 1976-80; trustee Cystic Fibrosis Found., 1971—2002, pres., 1975; mem. Mo.-St. Louis Met. Airport Authority, 1980-86; trustee-at-large Nat. Cystic Fibrosis Found., 1984-90; mem. Laumeier Sculpture Park, 1996—, chmn. bd. trustees, 2001—; mem. Cmty. in Partnership., 1986-88. Mem. ABA, Mo. Bar Assn., Bar Assn. St. Louis, Washington U. Law Alumni Assn. (pres. 1976-77), Zeta Beta Tau (pres. trustee corp. 1964-69), Phi Delta Phi. Home: 340 Falling Leaves Ct Saint Louis MO 63141-7405 Office: Gallop Johnson & Neuman LC 101 S Hanley Rd Ste 1600 Saint Louis MO 63105-3489 E-mail: hsgoodman@gjn.com.

GOODMAN, LEWIS ELTON, JR., lawyer; b. Lynchburg, Va., Jan. 27, 1936; s. Lewis Elton and Mary (Oliver) G.; m. Elizabeth Shumaker, July 10, 1960; children: William L., Lee E. JD, U. Richmond, 1973. Bar: Va. 1973, U.S. Dist. Ct. (we. dist.) Va. 1973, U.S. Ct. Appeals (4th cir.) 1979, U.S. Supreme Ct. 1986. Pvt. practice, Danville, Va., 1973—. Bankruptcy, Probate (including wills, trusts), Property, real (including real estate development, water). Office: 520 Piney Forest Rd Danville VA 24540-3352

GOODMAN, LOUIS J. lawyer; b. Newark, July 14, 1953; BA, U. Rochester, 1975; JD, U. Calif., San Francisco, 1980. Dep. dist. atty. Alameda County, Oakland, Calif., 1981-87. Mem. Hayward South Rotary (past pres.). Office: 1290 B St Ste 307 Hayward CA 94541-2996 E-mail: ljgoodman@yahoo.com.

GOODMAN, MARK N. lawyer; BA, Prescott Coll., 1973; JD summa cum laude, Calif. Western Sch. Law, 1977; LLM, U. Calif., Berkeley, 1978. Bar: Ariz. 1977, U.S. Dist. Ct. Ariz. 1978, U.S. Ct. Appeals (9th cir.) 1978, U.S. Supreme Ct. 1981. Practice Law Offices Mark N. Goodman, Prescott, Ariz., 1978-79, 81-82, Mark N. Goodman, Ltd., Prescott, 1983—88; ptnr. Alward and Goodman, Ltd., Prescott, 1979-81, Goodman Law Firm, P.C., Prescott, 1988—. Author: The Ninth Amendment, 1981; contbr. articles to profl. jours.; notes and comments editor Calif. Western Law Rev., 1976. Bd. dirs. Yavapai Symphony Assn., Prescott, 1981-84, N. Ariz. chpt. Alzheimer's Assn., 1995-97. Mem.: ATLA, ABA, Nat. Acad. Elder Law Attys., Yavapai County Bar Assn. (v.p. 1981—82), State Bar Ariz. (vice chmn. fee arbitration com. 1988—2002), Def. Rsch. Inst. State civil litigation, Commercial, consumer (including collections, credit), Property, real (including real estate development, water). Office: Goodman Law Firm PC PO Box 2489 Prescott AZ 86302-2489 E-mail: info@goodmanlaw.com.

GOODMAN, MAX A. lawyer, educator; b. Chgo., May 24, 1924; s. Sam and Nettie (Abramowitz) G.; m. Marlyene Monkarsh, June 2, 1946; children: Jan M., Lauren A. Packard, Melanie Murez. AA, Herzl Jr. Coll., 1943; student, Northwestern U., 1946-47; JD, Loyola U., 1948; LLD (hon.), Southwestern U. Sch. Law, 2000. Bar: Calif. 1948; cert. family law specialist, 1980, 85, 90. Pvt. practice, L.A., 1948-53; ptnr. Goodman, Hirschberg & King, L.A., 1953-81; prof. Southwestern U. Sch. Law, L.A., 1966—. Lectr. Calif. Continuing Edn. of the Bar, 1971—90. Contbr. articles to profl. jours. Served to cpl. U.S. Army, 1943-45. Mem. ABA (chmn. law sch. curriculum com. family law sect. 1987-88, family law sect. 1987-88, 97-98), State Bar Calif. (del. conf. dels. 1972, 80-87, 91, exec. com. family law sect. 1981-85), Los Angeles County Bar Assn. (chmn. family law sect. 1971-72, editor family law handbook 1974-89). Avocation: contract bridge. Office: Southwestern U Sch Law 675 S Westmoreland Ave Los Angeles CA 90005-3905 Business E-Mail: mgoodman@swlaw.edu.

GOODMAN, RICHARD SHALEM, lawyer, orthopedic surgeon; m. Jemi Horn; children: Lorraine, Carolyn Pianin, Deborah Lieb, Keith London, Evan London. BA, Alfred (N.Y.) U., 1955; MD, N.Y. U., 1960; JD, Touro Coll., 1987. Bar: N.Y. 1991, U.S. Ct. Claims 1995, U.S. Ct. Mil. Appeals 1995, U.S. Ct. Appeals 1995, U.S. Supreme Ct. 1995; lic. physician, N.Y., Calif.; diplomate Am. Bd. Orthopedic Surgery. Intern Ind. U. Med. Ctr., Indianapolis, 1960—61; asst. resident in gen. surgery Bronx Mcpl. Hosp. Ctr., 1961—62; resident in orthopedics N.Y.C. Med. Ctr. and various others, 1964—67; attending physician St. Catherine of Sienna Hosp. (formerly St. John's Episcopal Hosp.), Smithtown, NY, 1967—, pres. med. staff, 1978; attending physician Cmty. Hosp. Suffolk, Smithtown, 1967—96; cons. in orthop. LIJ Hosp., New Hyde Park, NY, 1996—; adjunct staff dept. Orthop. Surgery North Shore U. Med. Ctr., 2001—. Asst. prof. dept. anatomy SUNY, Stony Brook, 1971-88, Stonybrook Found. Pres. Marine Scis. Rsch. Ctr., 1984-87; pres. staff Community Hosp. of We. Suffolk, 1977-78; policy advisor Inst. Advancement Health Care Mgmt., U. Albany, SUNY, 1992—; cons. to numerous bus., govt. agys., and ins. cos.; presenter, speaker, and panelist in fields. Author: (with others) American Jurisprudence Proof of Facts, 3d Series, vol. 2 Pelvic Injuries, 1988, Handling Soft Tissue Injury Cases: Medical Aspects, 1988, 2d edit., 1993, Preparing & Winning Medical Negligence Cases, 1989, 2d edit., 1994, Legal Medicine: Legal Dynamics of Medical Encounters, 2d edit., 1990; contbr. articles to med. and legal jours.; contbr. chpts. to books; mem. editl. bd. Orthopedics and Orthopedics Today, 1984-87, Med. Malpractice Prevention; bd. editorial cons. Medical Malpractice Prevention. Trustee Alfred U., 1978-84; policy adv. Inst. Advancement Health Care Mgmt. U. Albany; nat. chmn. U. Albany Parents Fund, 1991-94; nat. chmn. U. Albany Parent's Fund, 1991-92; active Arthritis Found. Fellow: Am. Coll. Legal Med. (mem. policy and planning com., program chmn. annual meeting 1988—), Am. Acad. Orthoped. Surgeons; mem.: Pitts. Inst. Legal Med., Nat. Health Lawyers Assn., Assn. Bar City N.Y., Suffolk County Bar Assn., N.Y. Bar Assn., Am. Acad. Legal and Industrial Med. (bd. govs.), N.Y. State. Soc. Orthoped. Surgeons, Arthritis Found., PanAm. Med. Assn., Internat. Coll. Surgeons, N.Y. State Med. Soc., Suffolk County Med. Soc., Am. Rheumatism Assn., Am. Coll. Sports Med., Am. Soc. Law and Med., Ea. Orthoped. Assn., Am. Coll. Legal Medicine (chmn. exhibits com. ann. meeting 1989—90, mem. policy and planning com., mem. program com. ann. meeting 1989—90, co-chmn. exhibitor's com. 1993, mem. rsch. com. 1993, mem. com. to confer with com. Med. Soc. State N.Y. 1991—, mem. student awards com. 1993, chmn. computer bull. bd. sys. 1995, assoc. editor Communique and newsbriefs), Bach Aria Group (bd. dirs. 1970—88), NYU Bellevue Alumni Assn., Stony Brook Yacht Club, Mutton Town Golf Club, Univ. Club. Office: 285 E Main St Smithtown NY 11787 also: 70 Glen Cove Rd Roslyn Heights NY 11577 also: 743 Columbia Tpke East Greenbush NY 12061

GOODMAN, ROBERT UHLE, lawyer; b. Shreveport, La., Apr. 18, 1929; s. Uhle Slater and Edith (Caskey) Goodman; m. Martha Knox McGuffin, Mar. 22, 1957. BA, Washington and Lee U., 1950; LLB, La. State U., 1953. Bar: La. 1953. Ptnr. Naff, Goodman, and Johns and successor firms, Shreveport, 1956—89; pvt. practice Robert U. Goodman, P.C., Shreveport, 1989—. Former asst. city atty. City of Shreveport; former asst. atty. gen. State of La.; bd. dirs. Pioneer Bank, Aeropres Corp., Sound Fighter Sys., Inc. Gen. counsel Housing Authority City of Shreveport; bd. dirs., former pres. North La. Goodwill Industries Rehab. Ctr., Inc.; former bd. dirs. Salvation Army; chancellor, former vestry mem. St. Mark's Cathedral, 1965—; past pres. Holiday in Dixie. Capt. USAF, 1953—55. Recipient Runner-up Outstanding Man of Yr. Mem.: Housing and Devel. Law Inst., 5th Cir. Bar Assn., Garden of the Gods Club, Ambassadors Club (past chmn.), Cambridge Club, Shreveport Club. Republican. Episcopalian. Corporate, general, Banking, Probate (including wills, trusts). Office: 416 Travis Ste 1105 Shreveport LA 71101 Fax: 318-221-1749. E-mail: goodman@prysm.net.

GOODMAN, STANLEY, lawyer; b. Cin., June 16, 1931; s. Sol and Ethel (Barsman) G.; m. Diane Elaine Kassel, Apr. 15, 1956; children: Julie Lerner, Jeffrey Stephen, Richard Paul. BA, U. Cin., 1953, JD, 1955. Bar: Ohio 1955, Ky. 1976. Ptnr. Goodman & Goodman, Cin., 1955—. Dir. Winbco Tank Co., Ottumwa, Iowa; lectr. Ohio Bar Continuing Legal Edn. Series. Mem. ABA, Am. Health Lawyers Assn., Ohio State Bar Assn. (chair eminent domain com. 1997-2000), Ky. Bar Assn., Cin. Bar Assn., Bankers Club, Ridge Club. Jewish. Corporate, general, Estate planning, Property, real (including real estate development, water). Office: 123 E 4th St Cincinnati OH 45202-4003 E-mail: sgoodman@goodlaw.com.

GOODMAN, STANLEY LEWIS, lawyer; b. N.Y.C., Jan. 13, 1953; s. Irving and Sherry Goodman; m. Merryl Schazberg, Aug. 19, 1979; children: Sara, Shana. BA in History, Columbia Coll., 1974; JD, NYU, 1977. Bar: N.Y. 1978, U.S. Dist. Ct. (so. and ea. dists.) N.Y. 1980, U.S. Ct. Appeals (2d cir.) 1982, N.J. 1987, U.S. Dist. Ct. N.J. 1987. Atty. NLRB, Bklyn., 1978—81, Chaikin & Chaikin, N.Y.C., 1981—86; assoc. Grotta, Glassman & Hoffman, Roseland, NJ, 1980—. Co-author: (book) West N.J. Practice Employment Law, Vol. 18. Labor (including EEOC, Fair Labor Standards Act, labor-management relations, NLRB, OSHA). Office: Grotta Glassman and Hoffman PA 75 Livingston Ave Roseland NJ 07068 Office Fax: 973-942-9125. Business E-Mail: goodmans@ggrlaw.com.

GOODMAN, STEPHEN MURRY, lawyer; b. Phila., Oct. 8, 1940; s. Edward and Jean (Landau) G.; m. Janis Freeman, Jan. 8, 1983; children: Carl, Rachel. BS cum laude, U. Pa., 1962, LLB magna cum laude, 1965. Bar: D.C. 1967, Pa. 1969. Law clerk to Hon. David Bazelon U.S. Ct. Appeals (D.C. cir.), Washington, 1965-66; law clk. to Hon. William J. Brennan Jr. U.S. Supreme Ct., Washington, 1966-67; ptnr. Goodman & Ewing, Phila., 1970-83, Wolf, Block, Schorr & Solis-Cohen, Phila., 1983-94, Morgan, Lewis & Bockius LLP. Mem. Order of Coif. Democrat. Jewish. Avocation: profl. jazz pianist. Office: Morgan Lewis & Bockius LLP 1701 Market St Philadelphia PA 19103-2903

GOODPASTURE, PHILIP HENRY, lawyer; b. Lisbon, Portugal, Sept. 16, 1960; s. Henry McKennie and Ellen Ingabor (Moller) G.; m. Paige Everett Hargroves, June 25, 1994. BA with high distinction, U. Va., 1982, JD, 1985. Bar: Va. 1985, U.S. Dist. Ct. (ea. dist.) Va. 1985. Assoc. Christian & Barton and predecessor firm, Richmond, Va., 1985-92, ptnr., 1993—, vice-chmn. corp. team, 1994-97, mem. exec. com., 1998. Dir. Downtown Presents Inc., Richmond, 1993-2001, Va. League for Planned Parenthood, Richmond, 1989-95, Vol. Emergency Families for Children, Richmond, 1998-2000; dir. Parliament City of Richmond, 1997-98; mem. Leadership Metro Richmond, 1994; mem. Leadership Devel. Coun. ARC, 1995. Mem. Va. Bar Assn., Richmond Bar Assn. Corporate, general, Entertainment, Mergers and acquisitions. Office: Christian & Barton 909 E Main St Ste 1200 Richmond VA 23219-3013 E-mail: pgoodpasture@cblaw.com.

GOODRICH, JOHN BERNARD, lawyer, consultant; b. Spokane, Wash., Jan. 4, 1928; s. John Casey and Dorothy (Koll) G.; m. Therese H. Vollmer, June 14, 1952; children— Joseph B., Bernadette M., Andrew J., Philip M., Thomas A., Mary Elizabeth, Jennifer H., Rosanne M. JD, Gonzaga U., 1954. Bar: Wash. 1954, Ill. 1955. Indsl. traffic mgr. Pacific N.W. Alloys, Spokane, 1950-54; asst. to gen. counsel Cromium Mining & Smelting Corp., Chgo., 1954-56; with Monon R.R., 1956-69, atty., gen. solicitor, 1956-66, sec., 1957-69, treas., 1959-66, v.p. law, 1966-69; also dir.; sec.-treas. I.C.G.R.R., Chgo., 1970-79, sec., gen. atty., 1979-85; gen. counsel Ill. Devel. Fin. Authority, Chgo., 1985-92, spl. counsel, 1993; atty., cons. pvt. practice, Park Forest, Ill., 1994—. Mem. Park Forest Traffic and Safety Commn., 1963-66; mem. Park Forest Recreation Bd., 1966-77, chmn., 1969-70; trustee Village of Park Forest, 1977-80; mem. bd. Sch. Dist. 163, 1984-89; pres. South Cook Orgn. for Pub. Edn., 1988-89; conf. and meeting planner The Compassionate Friends, Inc., Oak Brook, Ill., 1991-94; bd. dirs. Park Forest Art Ctr., 1993-95, Ill. Philharm. Orch., 1994-98, treas., 1995-98; mem. adv. bd. Chgo. Self Help Ctr., 1993-94; bd. dirs. Ill Self Help Coalition, 1994-96; treas. Bereaved Parents of the U.S.A., 1995-2000, bd. dirs. 2000—, Tall Grass Arts Assn., 1999—; trustee Chgo. South Suburban Mass Transit Dist., 1996—, treas., 2000—. Inducted into Park Forest Hall of Fame, 1998. Mem. KC, The Parkforesters, Inc. (pres. 1998—, dir.), Kiwanis. Republican. Roman Catholic. Administrative and regulatory, Legislative, Non-profit and tax-exempt organizations. Home and Office: 35 Cunningham Ln Park Forest IL 60466-2094

GOODRICH, THOMAS MICHAEL, engineering and construction executive, lawyer; b. Milan, Tenn., Apr. 28, 1945; s. Henry Calvin and Billie Grace (Walker) Goodrich; m. Gillian Comer White, Dec. 28, 1968; children: Michael, Braxton, Charles, Grace. BSCE, Tulane U., 1968; JD, U. Ala., 1971. Bar: Ala. 1971. Adminstrv. asst. Supreme Ct. Ala., Montgomery, 1971—72; various mgmt. positions BE & K, Inc., Birmingham, Ala., 1989—95, pres., CEO, 1995—, also bd. dirs. Bd. dirs. First Comml. Bank, Energen Corp., Birmingham. Bd. dirs. Birmingham Civil Rights Inst., Constrn. Industry Inst., Birmingham Area coun. Boy Scouts Am., U. Ala. Health System; trustee Nat. Bldg. Mus., Elsenhowen Exchg. Fellow. Capt. U.S. Army, 1970—72. Mem.: Constrn. Industry Roundtable, Assn. Builders and Contractors (pres. 1990), Ala. State Bar Assn., ABA, TAPPI. Avocation: hunting, jogging.. Office: B E & K Inc 2000 Internat Park Dr Birmingham AL 35243

GOODRIDGE, ALLAN D. lawyer; b. Bucharest, Romania, June 12, 1936; s. Benjamin F. and Fanny M. (Weissman) G.; m. Lora, Sept. 12, 1965; children: Jeremy P., Andrew P. BA, Harvard U., 1957; JD, Columbia U., 1960. Bar: N.Y., U.S. Dist. Ct. (so. dist., ea. dist. N.Y.), U.S. Ct. Appeals (2d circuit). Assoc. Wickes, Riddell, Bloomer, Jacobi & McGuire, N.Y.C., 1960-64, Spitzer & Feldman, N.Y.C., 1965, Demov, Morris & Hammerling, N.Y.C., 1965-70, ptnr., 1970-85, Schnader, Harrison, Segal & Lewis, N.Y.C., 1985—. Mem. ABA, N.Y. Bar Assn. Clubs: Harvard (N.Y.C.). Home: 336 Central Park W New York NY 10025-7111 Office: Schnader Harrison Ste 3100 140 Broadway New York NY 10005 E-mail: agoodridge@shsl.com.

GOODSELL, G. VERNE, lawyer; b. Watertown, S.D., Jan. 22, 1943; AA, Miltonvale Wesleyan Coll., 1964; BS, No. State Coll., 1967, MS, 1970; JD, Washburn U. Topeka, 1973. Bar: S.D. 1974. Atty. Gunderson, Palmer, Goodsell & Nelson, LLP, Rapid City, SD. Mem.: ABA (vice chair litigation com. gen. practice sect. 1990), Black Hills Claims Assn. (pres. 1984—85), Pennington County Bar Assn. (pres. 1981), Am. Jurisprudence Assn., Assn. Trial Lawyers Am., S.D. Trial Lawyers Assn., State Bar S.D. (commr. 1984—87, professionalism com. 1989, mem. disciplinary bd. 1990—95, co-chair disciplinary bd. 1995—96, chair advt. com. 1999—2000, chair ethics com. 2000, pres.-elect 2002, mulit-jurisdictional/internet com.). Administrative and regulatory, Professional liability, Product liability. Office: Gunderson Palmer Goodsell and Nelson LLP 3d and 4th Fls PO box 8045 Rapid City SD 57709-8045*

GOODSTEIN, BARNETT MAURICE, lawyer; b. Dallas, Oct. 1, 1921; s. Arthur Louis and Viola Esther (Levy) G.; m. Mira Brodsky, Jan. 26, 1947; children— Pamela Renee, Heather Ann, Robin Leslie. Student, Rice Inst., 1938-40; BA, MA, U. Tex., Austin, 1942; postgrad., U. Wis., 1949-51; JD, So. Meth. U., 1957. Bar: Tex. 1957, U.S. Dist. Ct. (no. dist.) Tex. 1963, U.S. Supreme Ct. 1971. Acting dir. case analysis Wage Stblzn. Bd., Dallas, 1951-53; practice of law Dallas, 1957—; pres. Goodstein & Starr, P.C., 1977-91, Goodstein, Starr & Pascoe, P.C., 1991—95; adminstrv. law judge City of Dallas, 1994—95; atty. pvt. practice, 1995—. Lectr. econs. So. Meth. U., Dallas, 1946-48, 51-60; lectr. Massey Realty Coll., Real Estate Inst., Dallas; labor arbitrator, 1953—; former permanent arbitrator City of San Antonio, Police Officers' Assn.; mem. permanent arbitration panel Tinker AFB, Okla., 1984-88, Am. Fedn. Govt. Employees, 1984-90, SW Bell Telephone, AT&T, CWA, IBEW, 1988—, FAA, 1993—, Nat. Assn. Air Traffic Specialists, 1994—, Ga. Pacific, 1994—. UPIU, 1994—, U.S. Customs and INS, 2001--, also various VA Med. Facilities, paper and copper industries, others; mem. permanent panel Dallas Area Rapid Transit Sys., 1988-90, 94-96; adminstrv. law judge City of Dallas, 1994-96. Hearing officer work suspensions appeals bd. City of Dallas, 1981-83; trustee Dallas County Sch. Bd., 1980—, v.p., 1990-91, 2003—; past trustee Temple Emanu-El; mem. legal representation com. Nat. Acad. Arbitrators, 1992-96, chmn. legal affairs com. 1997-99. Served with USAAF, 1942-46, China, 1945-46. Mem.: ABA, Am. Arbitration Assn. (Southwestern adv. coun. 1985—92), Indsl. Rels. Rsch. Assn. (pres. North Tex. chpt. 1985—86, neutral mem. bd. dirs. North Tex. chpt. 1990—92), Nat. Acad. Arbitrators (chmn. S.W. region 1987—88), Tex. Bar Assn. Alternative dispute resolution, Probate (including wills, trusts), Property, real (including real estate development, water). Home: 6427 Forest Creek Dr Dallas TX 75230-2814 Office: Law Offices of Barnett M Goodstein Ste 215J 4230 Lyndon B Johnson Fwy Dallas TX 75244-5816 E-mail: bgoodsteinb@aol.com.

GOODSTEIN, ROBERT I. lawyer; b. Hollywood, Fla., Jan. 12, 1952; BS, U. Fla., 1973, JD, 1976; LLM, U. Wash., 1987. Asst. pub. defender Felony divsn. CHEIF, Jacksonville, Fla., 1976-80; pvt. practice Greenspan, Goodstein & Link, Jacksonville, 1980-86; asst. regional coun. U.S. EPA, Seattle, 1987-89; assoc. Short, Cressman & Burgess, Seattle, 1989-90; gen. counsel Port of Tacoma, Wash., 1991—; ptnr. Eisenhower & Carlson, Tacoma, 1995-99, Goodstein Law Group PLLC, Tacoma, 1999—. Environmental, Property, real (including real estate development, water). Office: Goodstein Law Group PLLC 625 Commerce St Ste 340 Tacoma WA 98402-4632

GOODWIN, ALFRED THEODORE, federal judge; b. Bellingham, Wash., June 29, 1923; s. Alonzo Theodore and Miriam Hazel (Williams) G.; m. Marjorie Elizabeth Major, Dec. 23, 1943 (div. 1948); 1 child, Michael Theodore; m. Mary Ellin Handelin, Dec. 23, 1949; children: Karl Alfred, Margaret Ellen, Sara Jane, James Paul. BA, U. Oreg., 1947; JD, 1951. Bar: Oreg. 1951. Newspaper reporter Eugene (Oreg.) Register-Guard, 1947—50; practiced in Eugene until, 1955; circuit judge Oreg. 2d. Jud. Dist., 1955—60; assoc. justice Oreg. Supreme Ct., 1960—69; judge U.S. Dist. Ct. Oreg., 1969—71, U.S. Ct. Appeals for (9th cir.), Pasadena, Calif., 1971—88, chief judge, 1988—91, sr. judge, 1991—. Editor: Oreg. Law Rev., 1950—51. Adv. bd. Eugene Salvation Army, 1956—60; chmn., 1959; Bd. dirs. Central Lane YMCA, Eugene, 1956—60, Salem (Oreg.) Art Assn., 1960—69. Capt., inf. AUS, 1942—46, ETO. Mem.: ABA (ho. of dels. 1986—87), Am. Law Inst., Am. Judicature Soc., Order of Coif, Alpha Tau Omega, Sigma Delta Chi, Phi Delta Phi. Republican. Office: US Ct Appeals 9th Cir PO Box 91510 125 S Grand Ave Pasadena CA 91105-1621

GOODWIN, JOHN ROBERT, lawyer, law educator, author; b. Morgantown, W.Va., Nov. 3, 1929; s. John Emory and Ruby Iona Goodwin; m. Betty Lou Wilson, June 2, 1952; children: John R., Elizabeth Ann Paugh, Mark Edward, Luke Jackson, Matthew Emory. BS, W.Va. U., 1952, LLB, 1964, JD, 1970. Bar: W.Va., U.S. Supreme Ct. Formerly city atty., county commr., spl. pros. atty.; then mayor City of Morgantown; prof. bus. law W.Va. U., Morgantown, 1964—80; prof. hotel and casino law U. Nev., Las Vegas, 1980—93, prof. emeritus, 1994—; pvt. practice, Morgantown, 1964—. Author: Legal Primer for Artists, Craftspersons, 1987, Hotel Law, Principles and Cases, 1987, Twenty Feet from Glory, 1970, Bus. Law, 3d edit., 1976, High Points of Legal History, 1982, Travel and Lodging Law, 1980, Desert Adventure, Gaming Control Law, 1985; editor Hotel and Casino Letter; past editor Bus. Law Rev., Bus. Law Letter. 1st lt. U.S. Army, Korean War. Named Outstanding West Virginian, State of W.Va.; named Hon. Gen. Gov. of W.Va., 1970. Democrat. Commercial, consumer (including collections, credit), Entertainment, Property, real (including real estate development, water). Home: Casa Linda 48 5250 E Lake Mead Blvd Las Vegas NV 89156-6751 also: Goodwin Bldg 2d Fl Morgantown WV 26505

GOODWIN, JOSEPH R. judge; b. 1942; BS, W.Va. U., 1965, JD, 1970. Ptnr. Goodwin & Goodwin, 1970-95; judge U.S. Dist. Ct. (so. dist.) W.Va., Charleston, 1995—. Editor W.Va. Law Rev. Mem. W.Va. U. Bd. Advisors, 1981-86; bd. visitors W.Va. U. Coll. Law, 1995-98, chmn., 1998. With USAR, 1965-67. Mem. ABA, W.Va. State Bar Assn., Jackson County Bar Assn., 4th Cir. Jud. Conf. Office: US Dist Ct So Dist WVa 300 Virginia St Charleston WV 25301*

GOODWIN, ROBERT CRONIN, lawyer; b. Cleve., Mar. 17, 1941; s. Robert Clifford and Marion (Schmadel) G.; m. Judith Mary Baxter, June 7, 1968; children: Anne, Helen, Sharon, Katherine. AB, Fordham U., 1963; JD, Georgetown U., 1969. Bar: D.C. 1970, Md. 1990. Vol. Peace Corps, Thailand, 1964-65; asst. cmty. devel. advisor AID, Thailand, 1965-66; atty. advisor Office Gen. Coun., Dept. Commerce, 1969-74; dep. asst. gen. coun. internat. & resouce devel. programs Fed. Energy Adminstrn., Washington, 1974-77, asst. gen. coun. internat. conservation & resource devel., 1977; asst. gen. coun. internat. trade & emergency preparedness Dept. Energy, Washington, 1977-79; ptnr. Thompson, Hine & Flory, 1979-82; v.p., gen. coun. China Energy Ventures, Washington, 1982-86; ptnr. Goodwin & Soble, 1986-90; pvt. practice, 1990-92; exec. v.p., gen. coun., dir. Chindex Internat., Inc., 1992—; dir. Med. Adv. Sys., Inc., 1999—2002. Guest lectr. internat. petroleum contracts East China Petroleum Inst. Beijing, 1985; frequent lectr. on internat. contracts and Chineses legal and bus. issues; adj. assoc. prof. internat. mgmt. progam, U. Md., 1990—. Editor-in-chief Law and Policy in International Business, 1968-69; co-editor Legal Environ. for Fgn. Direct Investment in U.S., 1994; contbr. articles to profl. jours. Mem. bd. sch. bd., 1980-83. Recipient cert. of Merit Fed. Energy Adminstrn., 1974, cert. Spl. Acheivement, 1974, 76. Mem. ABA, D.C. Bar Assn., Thai-Am. Assn. (chmn. bus. com. 1991, pres. 1995), Nat. Coun. U.S. China Trade (chmn. legal com. 1987), Am. Corp. Counsel Assn., Md.-China Bus. Coun. (bd. dirs., v.p. 1999—). Administrative and regulatory, Commercial, contracts (including sales of goods; commercial financing), Private international. Home: 3710 Bradley Ln Chevy Chase MD 20815-4257 Office: 7201 Wisconsin Ave Ste 703 Bethesda MD 20814-4850

GOODWIN, WALTER HENRY, lawyer, educator; b. Columbia, S.C., Dec. 14, 1954; s. Willie Belton and Margaree (Jackson) Goodwin. SB in Math., MIT, 1977; MA in Math., U. Nebr., Omaha, 1980; JD summa cum laude, Mich. State U., 1985. Bar: Nebr. 1985, Ohio 1987. Assoc. Baird, Holm Law Offices, Omaha, 1985—87, Vorys, Sater, Seymour & Pease, Columbus, Ohio, 1987—91; asst. gen. counsel Honda Am. Mfg., Inc., Marysville, Ohio, 1991—94; pvt. practice Charlotte, NC, 1995—. Cons. United Ho. Prayer All People, Washington, 1991—. Lt. col. USAF, 1978—. Mem.: Ohio Bar Assn., Nebr. Bar Assn. Avocations: piano, reading mysteries, crossword puzzles. Labor (including EEOC, Fair Labor Standards Act, labor-management relations, NLRB, OSHA), Commercial, contracts (including sales of goods; commercial financing), Personal injury (including property damage). Home and Office: 4607 Brownes Ferry Rd Charlotte NC 28269-8923 Personal E-mail: whgoodwi@usa.net.

GOOGASIAN, GEORGE ARA, lawyer; b. Pontiac, Mich., Feb. 22, 1936; s. Peter and Lucy (Chobanian) G.; m. Phyllis Elaine Law, June 27, 1959; children— Karen Ann, Steven George, Dean Michael BA, U. Mich., 1958; JD, Northwestern U., 1961. Bar: Mich. 1961. Assoc. Marentay, Rouse, Selby, Fischer & Webber, Detroit, 1961-62; asst. U.S. Atty. U.S. Dept. Justice, Detroit, 1962-64; assoc. Howlett, Hartman & Beier, Pontiac and Bloomfield Hills, Mich., 1964-81; ptnr. Googasian Hopkins Hohauser & Forhan, Bloomfield Hills, Mich., 1981-96, The Googasian Firm, Bloomfield Hills, 1996—. Mem. bd. law examiners State of Mich., 1997—2002, pres., 2001—02. Author: Trial Advocacy Manual, 1984, West Groups Michigan Practice Torts, vols. 14 and 15, 2001. Pres. Oakland Parks Found., Pontiac, 1984-89; chmn. Oakland County Dem. party, Pontiac, 1964-70; state campaign chmn. U.S. Senator Philip A. Hart, Detroit, 1970; bd. dirs. Big Bros. Oakland County. 1968-73 Fellow Am. Bar Found., Am. Coll. Trial Lawyers, Internat. Acad. Trial Lawyers; mem. ABA (del. 1992-93, exec. coun. nat. conf. bar pres. 1993-96), ATLA, Am. Bd. Trial Advocates, State Bar Mich. (pres. elect 1991-92, pres. 1992—), Oakland County Bar Assn. (pres. 1985-86), Oakland Bar Found. (pres. 1990-92). Clubs: U. Mich. Club Greater Detroit. Presbyterian. Federal civil litigation, State civil litigation, Personal injury (including property damage). Home: 3750 Orion Rd Oakland MI 48363-3029 Office: 6895 Telegraph Rd Bloomfield Hills MI 48301-3138

GOOLRICK, ROBERT MASON, lawyer; b. Fredericksburg, Va., Mar. 25, 1934; s. John T. and Olive E. (Jones) G.; m. Audrey J. Dippo (div.); children: Stephanie M., Meade A. BA with distinction, U. Va., 1956, JD, 1959. BAr: Va. 1959, D.C. 1959, U.S. Dist. Ct. D.C. 1961, U.S. Ct. Appeals (D.C. cir.) 1961. Assoc. Steptoe & Johnson, Washington, 1959-65, ptnr., 1965-79; sole practice Alexandria, Va., 1979-83; cons. bus., oil and gas fin. Instr. U. Va. Law Sch. Author: Public Policy Toward Corporate Growth, 1978, Corporate Mergers and Acquisitions under Federal Securities Laws, 1978. Mem. ABA (corps. sect.), Jefferson Soc., Raven Soc., Order of Coif, Phi Beta Kappa. Commercial, contracts (including sales of goods; commercial financing), Corporate, general. Home: 7462 Cross Gate Ln Alexandria VA 22315-4618 Office: PO Box 150672 Alexandria VA 22315-0672 E-mail: rmgoolrick@starpower.net.

GOOLSBY, ALLEN CUNNINGHAM, III, lawyer; b. Richmond, Va., Oct. 19, 1939; s. Allen C. Goolsby Jr. and Adelaide Rawles; m. Louanna Godwin. BA, Yale U., 1961; LLB, U. Va., 1968. Bar: Va., U.S. Dist. Ct. (ea. dist.) Va. Ptnr. Hunton & Williams, Richmond, Va., 1975—. Bd. dirs. Noland Co. Author: Virginia Corporation Law Practice, 1990, Goolsby on Virginia Corporations, 2002. Fellow Am. Bar Found., Va. Bar Found. Office: Hunton & Williams Riverfront Plz East Tower PO Box 1535 Richmond VA 23218-1535

GOOTEE, JANE MARIE, lawyer; b. Jasper, Ind., July 5, 1953; d. Thomas H. and Anne M. (Dreifke) G. BA, Ind. U., 1974; JD cum laude, St. Louis U., 1977. Bar: Ind. 1977, Mo. 1978, Mich. 1980, Ohio 1983, U.S. Dist. Ct. (so. dist.) Ind. 1977, U.S. Dist. Ct. (ea. dist.) Mich. 1980, U.S. Ct. Appeals (7th cir.) 1978, U.S. Supreme Ct. 1980, U.S. Ct. Appeals (6th cir.) 1982, U.S. Ct. Appeals (4th cir.) 1986. Dep. atty. gen. Ind., Indpls., 1977-79; corp. atty. Dow Chem. Co., Midland, Mich., 1979-81, ea. div. counsel, 1981-84, sr. atty., 1984-86, Mich. div. counsel, 1986-90, Dow Europe sr. staff counsel, 1990-94, asst. gen. counsel fin. law, 1994-99, asst. gen. counsel litigation, 1999-2002, dep. dir. global ethics and compliance, 2003—; adv. com. Nat. Chamber Litigation Ctr. Environ. Law, 1985-90; chair Dow Epidemiology Instl. Rev. Bd., 1984-90; pro-bono def. Midland Cir. Ct., 1980-81. Bd. dirs. Big Sisters Midland, 1979-81, 84-86, Big Bros./Big Sisters Midland, 1986-90, also pres., 1988-89; exec. bd. Lake Huron Area coun. Boy Scouts Am., 1988-90, N.Y.C. YWCA Acad. of Women Achievers, 1988. Fellow Mich. State Bar Found; mem. ABA, Mo. Bar, Mich. Bar Assn. Corporate, general, Product liability, Mergers and acquisitions. Home: 1303 Foxwood Dr Midland MI 48642 Office: Dow Legal Dept 2030 Dow Ctr Midland MI 48674 E-mail: jgootee@dow.com.

GOOTNICK, MARGERY FISCHBEIN, lawyer; b. Rochester, N.Y., Oct. 24, 1927; d. Morris R. and Regina (Kroll) Fischbein; m. Lester T. Gootnick, Mar. 1, 1952; children— Jonathon, David, Amy. B.A., Harvard U., 1949; J.D., Cornell U., 1952. Bar: N.Y. 1952. Assoc. Stone & Hoffenberg, Rochester, N.Y., 1952-55; sole practice, Rochester, 1968—; permanent arbitrator Am. Airlines and Assn. Profl. Flight Attendants, NW Airlines and Teamsters Local 2000, Presbyn. Hosp.-N.Y. State Nurses Assn., U. Rochester and U. Rochester Security Guards Union, numerous others; chmn. Fgn. Service Impasse Disputes Panel, Washington, 1983-97; apptd. fgn. svc. grievance bd. U.S. State Dept., 1997; mem. exec. com. N.Y. State Bar, 1998. Mem. Rep. Jud. Screening Com., Rochester, 1976—. Mem. ABA, Fed. Bar Assn., Nat. Acad. Arbitrators (v.p. 1992-94, chair membership com. 1988-91, exec. com. 1987, bd. govs. 1983-86), N.Y. State Bar Assn. (labor and employment sect. chair elect 1994—, exec. com. 1982—), Soc. Fed. Labor Rels. Profls. (1st v.p. 1993—), Am. Arbitration Assn. (upstate N.Y. labor adv. panel). Office e-mail: mornings@ix.netcom.com. Labor (including EEOC, Fair Labor Standards Act, labor-management relations, NLRB, OSHA). Home and Office: 46 Knollwood Dr Rochester NY 14618-3513

GOOTT, ALAN F(RANKLIN), lawyer; b. Washington, Aug. 6, 1947; BA, George Washington U., 1969; JD cum laude, Harvard U., 1973. Bar: N.Y., 1974, U.S. Dist. Ct. (so., ea. dists.) N.Y. 1974, U.S. Ct. Appeals (2d cir) 1974. Assoc. Kaye Scholer LLP, N.Y.C., 1973-82, ptnr., 1982—. Antitrust, Product liability, General civil litigation. Office: Kaye Scholer LLP 425 Park Ave New York NY 10022-3506 E-mail: agoott@kayescholer.com.

GOPMAN, HOWARD Z. lawyer; b. Kansas City, Mo., Oct. 29, 1940; s. Norman S. and Rose E. G.; m. Carol Ann, Mar. 25, 1979; children: James, William. BS, U. Wis., 1962, JD, 1965, MBA, 1967. Cert. Wis. 1965, Ill. 1969, U.S. Dist. Ct. (no. dist.) Ill. 1969. Trial atty. FTC, Washington, 1967-69; assoc. Quinn, Jacobs & Barry, Chgo., 1969-71, Katz, Karacic & Mansfield, Chgo., 1971-73, Michaelson & Marder, Chgo., 1973-74; prin. Howard Z. Gopman & Assocs. Ltd., Skokie, Ill., 1974—. Pres., dir. Am. Realty & Mgmt., Ltd., Skokie, 1977—; comml. arbitrator Am. Arbitration Assn., Chgo., 1977—; arbitrator Nat. Assn. Securities Dealers, Inc., N.Y. Stock Exch., Inc., Nat. Futures Assn., Cir. Cts. Cook and Lake Counties, Ill., Nat. Arbitration Forum. Contbr. articles to profl. jours. Hearing officer Ill. Office Edn., Chgo., 1977—. Mem. ABA, Ill. State Bar Assn., Wis. Bar Assn. Corporate, general, Property, real (including real estate development, water), Securities. Office: 5225 Old Orchard Rd Ste 24B Skokie IL 60077-1027

GORA, DANIEL MARTIN, lawyer; b. Chgo., Oct. 27, 1969; s. Martin O. and Jacqueline K. (Lancaster) G. BS, No. Ill. U., 1992; JD, Hamline U., 1995; MBA, U. St. Thomas, Mpls., 1996, MSS, 1999. Bar: Minn. 1995, Ill. 1996. Assoc. Spence, Ricke & Thurmer, St. Paul, 1992-96; ptnr. Weatherman, Wolters & Gora, Roseville, Minn., 1995-97; counsel Carlson Cos. Inc., Mpls., 1998-99; info. tech. specialist, sr. cons. Pillsbury Co., 1999-2000; legal mgr. Thomson Legal & Regulatory Svcs., 2000—. Mem. faculty Minn. Sch. Bus., Oakdale, 1996—, Met. State U., Mpls., 1997—. Judge Am. Mock Trial Assn., Minn., 1994-99. Dean's Law scholar Hamline U., 1992, Ill. Gen. Assembly scholar, 1988. Mem. ABA, Minn. Bar Assn., Ill. Bar Assn., Chgo. Bar Assn., Acad. Polit. Sci., Golden Key Nat. Honor Soc., Phi Sigma Alpha. Avocations: golf, basketball, reading, theater. Commercial, contracts (including sales of goods; commercial financing), Computer, Labor (including EEOC, Fair Labor Standards Act, labor-management relations, NLRB, OSHA). E-mail: goralaw@email.com., dan.gora@westgroup.com.

GORDON, ARNOLD MARK, lawyer; b. Norwich, Conn., Oct. 2, 1937; s. Barney and Rose (Bilsky) G.; m. Carolyn. BSBA, Wayne State U., Detroit, 1959, JD, 1962. Bar: Mich. 1962. With Gordon & Gordon P.C. and predecessor firms, Southfield, Mich.; arbitrator Am. Arbitration Assn., 1969—. Lectr. in field. Mem. Am. Coll. Trial Lawyers, State Bar Mich. (chmn. med.-legal com. 1976—, negligence sect. 1977-78, pub. negligence sect. bull.), Detroit Bar Assn. (co-chmn. trial advocacy program continuing legal edn. 1972—), Assn. Trial Lawyers Am. (exec. bd. Mich. 1967—), Mich., Detroit trial lawyers assns., Tau Epsilon Rho. Clubs: Masons. Office: Gordon & Gordon PC 17250 W 12 Mile Rd Ste 119 Southfield MI 48076-2663 E-mail: agordon404@aol.com.

GORDON, CAREY NATHANIEL, lawyer, federal agency administrator; b. Cleve., Mar. 11, 1950; s. Murray Byron and Pearl Miriam (Jackson) G.; m. Lois Elizabeth Bradshaw, Nov. 28, 1981. BA, Ohio State U., 1972; MA, U. London, 1973; postgrad., Cambridge (Eng.) U., 1973-74; JD, Cleve. State U., 1977. Bar: Ohio 1977, D.C. 1978, U.S. Supreme Ct. 1983. Assoc. Rippner Schwartz & Carlin, Cleve., 1977-80, ptnr., 1980-84; spl. advisor Atty. Gen.'s Chambers, Khartoum, Sudan, 1984-85; contract advisor U.S. Agy. for Internat. Devel., Khartoum, Cairo, Kinshasa, Islamabad, 1986-94, contracting officer Abidjan, Ivory Coast, 1995-97, Phnom Penh, Cambodia, 1997—. Vis. lectr. U. Khartoum, 1984-85. Bd. dirs., treas. Internat. Sch. of Phnom Penh, 2000—02. Mem. Fed. Bar Assn., Cleve. Bar Assn. Office: USAID Box 47 Am Embassy Bangkok Apo AR 96546

GORDON, DAVID ZEVI, retired lawyer; b. Bklyn., Mar. 2, 1943; s. Isidore and Yaffa S. (Stern) G.; m. Karen Baranker, Apr. 25, 1971; children: Ilana, Naomi. BA magna cum laude, Yeshiva U., 1964; JD cum laude, MBA, Columbia U., 1969. Bar: N.Y. 1970, U.S. Dist. Ct. (so. dist.) N.Y. 1973, U.S. Ct. Appeals (2d cir.) 1973. Assoc. Spear and Hill, N.Y.C., 1969-71; sr. assoc. LeBoeuf Lamb Leiby & McRae, N.Y.C., 1971-77; ptnr. Finley Kumble Heine & Underburg, N.Y.C., 1977-78, David Z. Gordon and Assocs., N.Y.C., 1978-81; mng. ptnr. Moroze Sherman Gordon & Gordon, P.C., N.Y.C., 1981-96. Trustee, exec. com. Stern Coll. for Women, 1990-96; co-chmn. United Jewish Appeal, Operation Exodus, 1991-96, Project Renewal, 1987-96, exec. com. Israel econ. devel.; chmn. Israel Bonds, Bronx, 1988-96; co-chmn. bd. dirs. Am. Com. for Shaare Zedek Med. Ctr., Jerusalem, 2000—. Recipient Heritage award Yeshiva U., 1988, Star of Peace and Hope award Israel Bonds, 2002, Cmty. Svc. award Shaare Zedek Med. Ctr. 2002. Mem. ABA, N.Y. State Bar Assn., N.Y.C. Bar Assn. (mem. com. condemnation and tax certiorari), Real Estate Tax Bar Assn. Democrat. Corporate, general, Property, real (including real estate development, water), Securities. E-mail: FLASHGORDON@peoplepc.com.

GORDON, EDGAR GEORGE, retired lawyer; b. Detroit, Feb. 27, 1924; s. Edgar George and Verna Florence (Hay) G.; m. Alice Irwin, Feb. 4, 1967; children: David A., J. Scott. AB, Princeton U., 1947; JD, Harvard U., 1950. Bar: Mich. 1951, U.S. Supreme Ct. 1953. Assoc. Poole, Warren & Littell, Detroit, 1950-54; ptnr. Poole, Warren, Littell & Gordon, Detroit, 1953-63; gen. counsel Hygrade Food Products Corp., Detroit, 1963-69, sec., 1966-69, v.p., 1968-69; v.p., sec. counsel City Nat. Bank of Detroit, 1969-81; v.p., sec., gen. counsel No. States Bancorp, 1970-81; v.p., sec., counsel First of Am. Bank Corp., Kalamazoo, 1981-84; also ptnr. Howard & Howard, Kalamazoo, 1981-2000; ret., 2000. Dir. First Citizens Bank, Troy, Mich., 1973-81, First Nat. Bank, Plymouth, Mich., 1974-81; pres., chmn. bd. First of Am. Mortgage Co., Kalamazoo, 1978-84. Commr. City of Kalamazoo, 1995-2001. Lt. (j.g.) USN, 1943-46. Mem. ABA, Mich. Bar Assn., Kalamazoo Bar Assn., Country Club of Detroit (Grosse Pointe, Mich.). Republican. Presbyterian. Banking, Corporate, general, Probate (including wills, trusts). Home: 4339 Lakeside Dr Kalamazoo MI 49008-2802

GORDON, EVAN L. lawyer; b. N.Y.C., July 10, 1941; s. Myron P. and Henrietta (Lediger) Gordon. AB, Columbia U., 1963, LLB, 1966. Bar: N.Y. 1966, U.S. Dist. Ct. (so. and ea. dists.) N.Y. 1968, U.S. Dist. Ct. (no. and we. dists.) N.Y. 1985, U.S. Ct. Appeals (2nd cir.) 1967, U.S. Ct. Appeals (8th cir.) 1988, U.S. Ct. Appeals (11th cir.) 1986, U.S. Supreme Ct. 1976. Ptnr. Delson & Gordon, N.Y.C., 1968-78, Wofsey, Certilman et al, N.Y.C., 1978-85, Bangser & Weiss, N.Y.C., 1986-89; pvt. practice N.Y.C., 1990—. Contbg. author: The Law of Gray and Counterfeit Goods, 1987. Mem. corp. and security del. to Ea. Europe through People to People Internat., 1990. Mem. ABA (securities litigation com. 1977—), N.Y. State Bar Assn., Assn. of Bar of City of N.Y., Fed. Bar Council. General civil litigation. Home: 400 E 56th St New York NY 10022-4147 Office: 230 Park Ave New York NY 10169-0005

GORDON, JACK ELLIOTT, JR., lawyer; b. Apr. 10, 1944; Tulsa; s. Jack Elliott and Janelle (Stallings) G.; m. Elise Murray, July 26, 1999; children— Casey Lee, Jacob Elliott. B.A., U. of South, Sewanee, Tenn., 1966; J.D., U. Ark., 1969. U.S. Dist. Ct. (10th cirs.). Assoc., Bassmann, Gordon, Mayberry & Scarth, Claremore, Okla., 1972-76; ptnr. Gordon & Gordon, Claremore, 1976-; head litig. Havis, Gordon, McMahan, Peter, and Thompson, 1998-. Mng. editor: U. Ark. Law Rev., 1968-69. Served to 1st lt. AUS, 1969-72. Mem. Assn. Trial Lawyers Am., Okla. Trial Lawyers Assn., Okla. Criminal Def. Lawyers Assn.; fellow Am. Coll. Trial Lawyers. Democrat. Episcopalian. State civil litigation, Criminal, General practice. Home: 24615 S 4150 Rd Claremore OK 74017 Office: Havis Gordon McMahon and Peters 111 S Muskogee Ave Claremore OK 74017 E-mail: lawyermn@aol.com.

GORDON, JAMES S. lawyer, director; b. N.Y.C., Feb. 15, 1941; s. George S. and Sylvia A. (Wolfson) Gordon; m. Marica G. Gordon, Dec. 22, 1968 (dec.); children: Daniel, Sarah; m. Debbie S. Pase, June 15, 1996. BA with high honors, U. Fla., 1962; LLB, Yale U., 1965. Bar: Ill. 1965, Fla. 1966, U.S. Supreme Ct. 1974. Asst. prof. Ind. U. Sch. Law, Bloomington, 1967-68, assoc. prof., 1969; ptnr. Feiwell, Galper & Gordon, Chgo., 1970-72; pvt. practice Chgo., 1972-80; pres. James S. Gordon, Ltd., Chgo., 1981-93; chmn. Gordon, Glickman, Flesch, Woody & Rosenwein, Chgo., 1994—. Editor: Yale Law Jour., 1963—65; contbr. articles to profl. jours. Ford Found. grantee, 1965—66. Mem.: Order Coif (exec. com.), Yale U. Law Alumni Assn., Fla. Blue Key, Birchwood Club (Highland Park, Ill.), Lawyers Club Chgo., Phi Beta Kappa, Phi Alpha Delta. Antitrust, Bankruptcy, Federal civil litigation. Office: 140 S Dearborn St Ste 404 Chicago IL 60603-5202 E-mail: jgordon@lawggf.com.

GORDON, JOHN BENNETT, lawyer; b. Des Moines, Nov. 21, 1947; s. Bennett and Mary (Adelman) G.; m. Joanne Dunbar Westgate, Jan. 17, 1976; children: Anne Dunbar, Bennett Westgate, Susan Julia. AB, Princeton U., 1969; JD, Harvard U., 1973. Bar: Minn. 1974, U.S. Dist. Ct. Minn. 1974, U.S. Ct. Appeals (8th cir.) 1974, U.S. Supreme Ct. 1985. Clerk U.S. Ct. Appeals (5th cir.), Newnan, Ga., 1973-74; assoc. law firm Faegre & Benson, Mpls., 1974-80, ptnr., 1981—. Mem. Minn. State Bar Assn., Hennepin County Bar Assn. (pres. 1985-86). Federal civil litigation, State civil litigation, Environmental. Office: Faegre & Benson 90 S 7th St Ste 2200 Minneapolis MN 55402-3901 E-mail: jgordon@faegre.com.

GORDON, KEVIN DELL, lawyer; b. Oklahoma City, June 23, 1958; s. James Dell and Mary Lurana (Tracewell) G.; m. Janice Linn Mathews, Aug. 4, 1979; children: Tracewell, Elise. BA cum laude, Westminster Coll., 1981; JD, Washington U., 1984. Bar: Okla. 1984, U.S. Dist. Ct. (we., no. and ea. dists.) Okla. 1984, U.S. Ct. Appeals (10th cir.) 1985, U.S. Supreme Ct. Shareholder, dir. Crowe & Dunlevy, Oklahoma City, 1984—. Adj. prof. health law U. Okla. Law Sch., 1997—. Editor Washington U. Law Quarterly, 1982-84. Trustee, past pres. Youth Svcs. Oklahoma County, 1986—; chair adv. com. Okla. Assn. Youth Svcs., 1994-98. Mem. ABA (ins. coverage com. 1990—), Health Law, Okla. Bar Assn. (uniform laws com. 1994-97, coord./moderator ann. ins. law update 1999—, mentorship com. 1999—, Outstanding CLE award 1999), Am. Health Lawyers Assn. (HMO and ins. coms. 1998—, HMO and health plans practice group-leadership team 2002-, vice chair 2002-), Oklahoma County Bar Assn. (professional com. 2000-02, legal aid com. 1990-98, cmty. svc. com. 1997-99), Ruth Bader Ginsberg Am. Inn of Ct. (chair mentoring com. 1996-99, chair membership com. 1999-2000, pres. 2002-, Master of Yr. 1998), U.S. C. of C. (employee benefits com. 2001-), Order of Coif. Avocations: sports, gardening, guitar, reading. General civil litigation, Health, Insurance. Home: 8309 Glenwood Ave Oklahoma City OK 73114-1111 Office: Crowe & Dunlevy 20 N Broadway Ave Ste 1800 Oklahoma City OK 73102-8273

GORDON, LOUIS, lawyer; b. Detroit, May 10, 1933; s. Isador and Esther (Kraizman) G.; m. Patricia Janis, Nov. 25, 1973 (div. Mar. 1986); children: Aaron, Marla; m. Johanna C. Gordon, Aug. 15, 1987 (dec.); children: Susan, Laurie. BSBA, Wayne State U ., 1955, JD, 1958. Sole practitioner, Detroit, 1959-75; owner Louis Gordon, P.C., Southfield, Mich., 1976—; spl. asst. atty. gen. State of Mich., Lansing, 1975—. Mem. ABA, Mich. Trial Lawyers Assn., Oakland Bar Assn. Avocations: tennis, golf, sailing, skiing, power boating. Insurance, Personal injury (including property damage), Product liability. Office: Gordon & Pont PC 21700 Northwestern Hwy Ste 1100 Southfield MI 48075-4923 Fax: 248 395 4101. E-mail: Lawmich@aol.com.

GORDON, MICHAEL, lawyer; b. Newark, Oct. 12, 1953; s. Carl and Rose (Katz) G.; m. Arlene Cahn, Oct. 16, 1988; children: Jeremy, Carmel, Sarah. BA, Columbia U., 1975; JD, Rutgers U., 1979. Bar: N.J. 1980, U.S. Dist. Ct. N.J. 1980, U.S. Ct. Appeals (3d cir.) 1984. Adj. prof. Montclair State U., Upper Montclair, N.J., 1978-79; atty. N.J. Dept. of Environ. Protection, Trenton, 1979-80; sole practice Montclair, 1980-83; ptnr. Gordon, Gordon P.C., West Orange, N.J., 1983—. Spl. environ. counsel State of N.J. cities of Newark, Ridgefield, Montclair and Lafayette, N.J.; vis.lectr. Rutgers U., Newark, 1985. Contbr. articles to profl. jours., chpt. to book. Vol. atty. Legal Services of Essex, Newark, 1984—, Essex County Dem. Com., 1987; dem. candidate U.S. House of Reps. 11th dist. of N.J., 1990; mem. Govs. Emergency Solid Waste Task Force, 1990; mem. Gov. James McGrevey Transition Team on Environ. Issues, 2002. Recipient Cert. of Achievement, Ironbound Com. Against Toxic Waste, Newark, 1985, Outstanding Vol. award Essex Newark Legal Services, 1985. Mem. ATLA (Gold Medal for Disting. Achievement 1997), N.J. Assn. Trial Lawyers (chmn. environ. law com. 1986-88). Federal civil litigation, State civil litigation, Environmental. Office: 80 Main St West Orange NJ 07052-5460

GORDON, ROBERT A. food products executive; b. 1952; Ptnr. Pillsbury Winthrop LLP; sr. v.p., gen. counsel Safeway, Inc., 2000—. Office: Safeway Inc 5918 Stoneridge Mall Rd Pleasanton CA 94588-3229*

GORDON, ROBERT EUGENE, lawyer; b. L.A., Sept. 20, 1932; s. Harry Maurice and Minnie (Shaffer); 1 child, Victor Marten. BA, UCLA, 1954; LLB, U. Calif., Berkeley, 1959, JD, 1960; cert., U. Hamburg, Fed. Republic Germany, 1960. Bar: Calif. 1960. Assoc. Lillick, Geary, McHose, Roethke & Myers, Los Angeles, 1960-64, Schoichet & Rifkind, Beverly Hills, Calif., 1964-67; ptnr. Baerwitz & Gordon, Beverly Hills, 1967-69, Ball, Hunt, Hart, Brown & Baerwitz, Beverly Hills, 1970-71; of counsel Jacobs, Sills & Coblentz, San Francisco, 1972-78; ptnr. Gordon & Hodge, San Francisco, 1978-81; pvt. practice San Francisco, 1981—89, Corte Madera, Calif., 1989—2002, Sausalito, Calif., 2002—. Adj. prof. entertainment law Hastings Coll. of Law, San Francisco, 1990-91, U. Calif., Berkeley, 1992. Served to 1st lt. U.S. Army, 1954-56. Mem. ABA (forum com. on entertainment and sports law), Los Angeles Copyright Soc. (bd. trustees 1970-71), Copyright Soc. of the USA. Avocations: cycling, skiing. Entertainment, Trademark and copyright. Home: 35 Elaine Ave Mill Valley CA 94941-1014 Office: One Harbor Dr Ste 106 Sausalito CA 94965

GORDON, STEPHEN LOUIS, lawyer; b. Syracuse, N.Y., Oct. 31, 1956; s. Richard E. and Carole (Silverstein) G.; m. Lorraine (Winheim) Gordon, Oct 24, 1999; children, Samantha and Dana; 2 stepchildren, Matthew Fenster and Emily Fenster. AB, Cornell U., 1978; JD, Harvard U., 1981. Bar: N.Y 1982. Ptnr. Cravath, Swaine & Moore, N.Y.C., 1981—. Mem. ABA (tax sect.), N.Y. State Bar Assn. (tax sect.), Assn. of Bar of City of N.Y. Corporate taxation, Taxation, general. Office: Cravath Swaine & Moore 825 8th Ave Fl 38 New York NY 10019-7475

GORDON, SYDNA H. lawyer; b. Decatur, Tex., Mar. 28, 1946; d. Albert Sidney Holbert and Lilliam Inez Jameson; m. Don G. Gordon, Feb. 16, 1964; 1 child, Jeannice. BA in Spanish & English, East Tex. St U. (know as Tex. A&M), Commerce, 1968; JD, So. Meth. U., Dallas, 1977. Bar: Tex. 1977. Sr. atty. Fed. Res. Bank Dallas, 1977—79; pvt. practice Garland, Tex., 1979—86; assoc. lawyer Law Offices of Earl Luna, Dallas, 1986—89, Heard, Goggan, Blair & Williams, Dallas, 1989—94; ptnr. Gay, McCall, Isaacks, Gordon & Roberts, P.C., Plano, Tex., 1994—. Bd. trustees Garland (Tex.) Indep. Sch. Dist., Tex., 1983—98, Tex. Assn. Sch. Bds., Austin, Tex., 1992—98, sec., 1997—98; bd. dirs. Garland Edn. Fund, 1997—2002. Fellow: State Bar Tex.; mem.: Tex. Bar Found., Kiwanis Garland. Avocations: reading, snow skiing, traveling. Office: Gay McCall Isaacks Gordon & Roberts PC 777 E 15th St Plano TX 75074

GORDON, WILLIAM STOUT, lawyer; b. Liberty Center, Ind., Apr. 12, 1913; s. James Orin and Pearl Elizabeth (Stout) G.; m. Laura Kenner, Sept. 17, 1935; children: James Kenner, William Sumner. BS in Bus., Ind. U., 1934; JD with distinction, U. Mich., 1937. BAr: Ind. 1937, U.S. Dist. Ct. (no. dist.) Ind. 1937. Assoc. Slaymaker, Merrell, Locke, Indpls., 1937-42; spl. agt. FBI, 1942-45; ptnr. Gordon, Glenn, Miller, Bendall & Branham, Huntington, Ind., 1945—. Dir. Garrett Industries, Inc., Weaver Popcorn Co., Inc., Shuttleworth, Inc. Bd. dirs. Huntington YMCA Found., Huntington Coll. Found.; trustee Huntington Coll., 1971-80. Fellow Am. Coll. Trial Lawyers, Am. Bar Found., Ind. Bar Found.; mem. ABA, Ind. Satte Bar Assn. (pres. 1973-74), Am. Judicature Soc., Ft. Wayne Country Club, Oak Arbor Club (Vero Beach, Fla.), Masons Republican. Presbyterian. Banking, Corporate, general, Probate (including wills, trusts). Home: 1510 Oak Harbor Blvd Apt 301 Vero Beach FL 32967-7360

GORE, GEORGE HENRY, lawyer, artist; b. Oak Park, Ill., June 22, 1923; s. Robert Hayes and Lorena Claire (Haury) G.; m. Leona M. O'Grady; children: Stephen H., Gregory J., Georgene M. Urbanek, Kathleen Gore Whitney. JD U. Notre Dame, 1948; LLM, NYU, 1950. Bar: Fla. 1948. Assoc. Saunders, Buckley & O'Connell, Fort Lauderdale, Fla., 1950; sole practice, Fort Lauderdale, 1951-54; ptnr. Saunders, Curtis, Ginestra & Gore, Ft. Lauderdale, 1954—2000, of counsel, 2000—; sec., dir. North Am. Co., Fort Lauderdale, 1950—. Mem. law adv. coun. U. Notre Dame, Ind., 1965—88; trustee Gore Family Meml. Found., 1973—; bd. dirs. Ralph J. Baudhuin Oral Sch. of Nova U., Ft. Lauderdale, 1956—88 pres., 1981—88; trustee Holy Cross Hosp., Inc., Fort Lauderdale, 1966—96, chmn. bd., 1984-87; mem. coun. Village of Sea Ranch Lakes, Ft. Lauderdale, 1959-63; bd. dirs. Hospice Care of Broward County, Inc., 1981-83; mem. Fla. Govs. Challenge program, Ft. Lauderdale, 1982. Artwork represented in permanent collections U. Notre Dame, Carlow Coll., Holy Cross Hosp. and Convent, Assumption Ch.; others. Served with U.S. Army, 1942-45, ETO. Decorated Purple Heart, Bronze Star. Mem. Fla Bar (exec. coun. tax sect. 1955-57), Knights of St. Gregory (knight comdr.), Coral Ridge Yacht Club, Tower Club, U. Notre Dame Club. Republican. Roman Catholic. Estate planning, Probate (including wills, trusts), Personal income taxation. Home: 23 Minnetonka Rd Fort Lauderdale FL 33308-2908

GORELICK, JAMIE SHONA, lawyer; b. N.Y.C., May 6, 1950; d. Leonard and Shirley (Fishman) G.; m. Richard E. Waldhorn, Sept. 28, 1975; children: Daniel H., Dana E. BA, Harvard U., 1972, JD, 1975. Bar: D.C. 1975, U.S. Dist. Ct. D.C. 1976, U.S. Tax Ct. 1976, U.S. Ct. Claims 1976, U.S. Ct. Appeals (D.C. cir.) 1976, U.S. Ct. Appeals (5th cir.) 1977, U.S. Supreme Ct. 1979, U.S. Ct. Appeals (Fed. cir.) 1982, U.S. Ct. Internat. Trade 1984, U.S. Dist. Ct. Md. 1985, U.S. Ct. Appeals (4th cir.) 1986, U.S. Ct. Appeals (3d. cir.) 1988. With Miller, Cassidy, Larroca & Lewin, Washington, 1975-79, 80-93; asst. to sec., counselor to dep. sec. U.S. Dept. Energy, 1979—80; gen. counsel Dept. Def., 1993—94; dep. atty. gen. Dept. Justice, Washington, 1994-97; vice chair Fannie Mae, Washington, 1997—2003; commr. Nat. Commn. on Terrorist Threats Upon the U.S., 2002. Mem. chmn.'s adv. coun. U.S. Senate Jud. Com., 1988-93; tchr. Trial Advocacy Workshop Harvard Law Sch., Cambridge, Mass., 1982, 84; vice chair task force evaluation of audit investigative inspection components Dept. Def., 1979-80; mem. sec.'s transition team Dept. Energy, 1979; bd. dirs. Fannie Mae, United Technologies Corp., Schlumberger Ltd., Fannie Mae Found., John D. & Catherine T. MacArthur Found., D.C. Coll. Access, Am.'s Promise-Alliance for Youth, Nat. Park Found., Carnegie Endowment, 1989-93, Nat. Women's Law Ctr., 1991-93, Bazelon Ctr. Mental Health Law, Washington Legal Clinic for Homeless, Local Initiatives Support Corp., Nat. Legal Ctr. for the Pub. Interest; bd. overseers Harvard Coll.; mem. nat. security adv. panel CIA; mem. Pres.'s Intelligence Rev. Panel, 2001-2002; mem. threat reduction adv. com. Dept. of Def.; coun. mem. Am. Law Inst., D.C. Bar Found.; co-chair adv. com. Presdl. Commn. on Critical Infrastructure Protection; mem. Nat. Commn. Support Law Enforcement, Washington, 1995—; mem. nat. security adv. panel CIA; mem. threat reduction adv. com. Dept. Def; mem. Supreme Ct. Judicial Fellow. Selection Com. Mem. editl. bd. Corp. Criminal Liability Reporter, 1986-93, Destruction of Evidence, 1989; contbr. articles to profl. jours. Mem. bd. overseers Harvard Coll., 1989-93. Fellow Am. Bar Found.; mem. ABA (chair complex crimes litigation com. litigation sect. 1984-87, vice-chair complex crimes litigation com. 1983-84, Nat. Commn. to Support Law Enforcement, 1995—, sec. litigation sect. 1988-90, coun. mem. 1990-93, com. on profl. discipline, ho. of dels. 1991-93, 97—), D.C. Bar (pres. 1992-93, bd. govs. 1982-88, sec. bd. govs. 1981-82, bar found. advisors 1985-93, legal ethics com.), Womens Bar Assn., Am. Law Inst. (coun.), Coun. on Fgn. Rels. Office: Fannie Mae 3900 Wisconsin Ave NW Washington DC 20016-2892

GOREN, STEVEN ELIOT, lawyer; b. Detroit, Apr. 9, 1960; s. Robert and Judith A. (Wise) G.; m. Eva Calmidis, Sept. 25, 1980; children: Robert C., Sophia J. BA with high distinction, U. Mich., 1981, JD cum laude, 1984. Bar: Mich. 1984, Ohio 2001, U.S. Dist. Ct. (ea. dist.) Mich. 1984. Atty. Dickinson, Wright, Moon, VanDusen & Freeman, Bloomfield Hills, Mich., 1984-86, pvt. practice, Birmingham, Mich., 1986—91. Adjunct prof. U. Detroit Law Sch., 1989-95; med. malpractice task force Mich. Trial lawyers, 1989; mem. litigation adv. com., Inst. Continuing Legal Edn. Contbr. articles to profl. jours. Precinct Del. Democratic Party, Beverly Hills, Mich., 1990-91. Mem.: Mich. Trial Lawyers Assn. (exec. bd. 2000—03). Personal injury (including property damage), Product liability. Office: 30400 Telegraph Rd Ste 470 Bingham Farms MI 48025-5818

GORES, CHRISTOPHER MERREL, lawyer; b. N.Y.C., Aug. 27, 1943; s. Guido James and Mary (Callaway) G.; children: Ellen, Eugenia. AB, Princeton U., 1965; LLB, Columbia U., 1968. Bar: N.Y. 1968, Tex. 1973, U.S. Dist. Ct (no. dist.) Tex. 1977. Assoc. Akin, Gump, Strauss, Hauer & Feld, LLP, Dallas, 1973-79, ptnr., 1979—. Bd. dirs. Shakespeare Festival of Dallas, 1982-88. Lt. USNR, 1969-72. Commercial, contracts (including sales of goods; commercial financing), Corporate, general, Mergers and acquisitions. Office: Akin Gump Strauss Hauer & Feld LLP 1700 Pacific Ave Ste 4100 Dallas TX 75201-4675 E-mail: cgores@akingump.com.

GORHAM, CHARLES, lawyer; b. Birmingham, Ala., Nov. 5, 1974; s. Charles William and Martha Janice (Lovell) Gorham. BA, Washington U., 1996; JD, U. Ala., Tuscaloosa, 1999; LLM, Georgetown U., 2000. Bar: Ala. 1999, Mo. 2001, D.C. 2002. Assoc. The Stolar Partnership, St. Louis, 2000—. Mem. adv. counsel St. Alexian Bros. Salus Place, St. Louis, 2002—. Estate taxation, Taxation, general, Corporate taxation. Office: The Stolar Partnership 911 Washington Ave 7th Fl Saint Louis MO 63101

GORINSON, STANLEY M. lawyer; b. Bklyn., May 30, 1945; s. Rubin and Lena (Shulman) G.; children: Ross Evan, Hunter Lloyd. BA cum laude, Bklyn. Coll., 1967; JD with honors, Rutgers U., 1973. Bar: N.Y. 1974, U.S. Dist. Ct. (so. dist.) N.Y. 1976, U.S. Ct. Appeals (2nd cir.) 1976, Md. 1984, D.C. 1984, U.S. Dist. Ct. D.C. 1984, U.S. Ct. Appeals (D.C. cir.) 1985, U.S. Dist. Ct. (ea. dist.) Mich. 1986, U.S. Ct. Appeals (6th cir.) 1988, U.S. Supreme Ct. 1979. Atty. judgments sect. U.S. Dept. Justice, Washington, 1973-76, asst. chief transp. sect., 1977-80, chief spl. regulated industries, 1980-84; assoc. Wachtell, Lipton, Rosen & Katz, N.Y.C., 1976-77; chief counsel Pres. Com. on Three Mile Island, Washington, 1979; ptnr. Pillsbury, Madison & Sutro, Washington, 1984-91, Winthrop, Stimson, Putnam & Roberts, Washington, 1991-93, Preston Gates Ellis & Rouvelas Meeds, Washington, 1993-2001, Kilpatrick Stockton LLP, Washington, 2001—. Contbg. author: Report on Regulatory Reform, 1985; also articles. Cons. NSF, Washington, 1982-83. Mem. ABA (bd. editors Antitrust Law Devels. 1984-87, chmn. comms. subcom. antitrust sect. 1985-88, chmn. criminal practice subcom. litigation sect. 1985-89, adminstrv. law sect., chmn. industry regulation com. antitrust sect. 1988-92, mem. edn. com. dispute resolution sect. 1994—), Fed. Comm. Bar Assn., N.Y. State Bar Assn. Administrative and regulatory, Antitrust, Federal civil litigation. Office: Kilpatrick Stockton LLP 607 14th St NW Ste 900 Washington DC 20005 E-mail: sgorinson@kilpatrickstockton.com.

GORMAN, CHRIS, lawyer; b. Frankfort, Ky., Jan. 22, 1943; m. Vicki Lynn Beekman; two sons. Grad., U. Ky. Bar: Ky., 1967. Former ptnr. Conliffe, Sandman, Gorman, and Sullivan, Louisville; former dir. civil divsn. Jefferson County Attys. Office; atty. gen. Ky., 1992-95; gen. counsel Taylor Bldg. Corp. Am., Louisville, 1996—; ptnr. Sheffer, Hutchinson, Kinney, Louisville, 1999—2002; atty. Conliffe, Sandman & Sullivan, 2002—. Office: Conliffe, Sandman & Sullivan 2000 Waterfront Plz 325 W Main St Louisville KY 40202 E-mail: cgorman999@aol.com.*

GORMAN, JAMES EDWARD, lawyer; b. Summit, Ill., Nov. 11, 1930; s. James Edward and Mae Catherine (Jiracek) G.; m. Beverly Ann Fink; children: Gregory, Stephen, Robert, William Mudge, Ann, James, Mary. BA, St. Ambrose Coll., 1952; JD, U. Ill., 1955. Bar: Ill. 1956, U.S. Dist. Ct. (so. dist.) Ill. 1958, U.S. Ct. Appeals 1979, U.S. Supreme Ct. 1980. Assoc. Heyl, Royster, Voelker and Allen, Peoria, Ill., 1957-59, Bernard, Gorman, Davidson, Edwardsville, Granite City, Ill., 1959-61; ptnr. Reed, Armstrong, Gorman, Mudge & Morrissey, Edwardsville, Ill., 1961—. With U.S. Army, 1955-57. Mem.: ATLA, ABA (Ill. atty. disciplinary panel 1974—94), Ill. Def. Coun., Madison County Bar Assn., Ill. Trial Lawyers Assn., Am. Coll. Trial Lawyers, Ill. Bar Assn., KC. Roman Catholic. Insurance, Personal injury (including property damage). Office: Reed Armstrong Gorman Mudge & Morrissey PC 115 N Buchanan St Edwardsville IL 62025-1771

GORMAN, JOSEPH GREGORY, JR., lawyer; b. Chgo., Sept. 27, 1939; s. Joseph Gregory Sr. and Genevieve C. (Smith) G.; m. Mary (Molly) O'Donovan, Mar. 23, 1968; children: Jennifer Ann Gorman Patton, Joseph Gregory III. BA, U. Calif., Berkeley, 1961; MBA, UCLA, 1963, JD, 1966. Bar: U.S. Dist. Ct. (cen. dist.) Calif. 1967, U.S. Ct. Appeals (9th cir.) 1967, U.S. Tax Ct. Assoc., ptnr. Sheppard, Mullin, Richter & Hampton LLP, L.A., 1966—. Chair death and gift tax com. Los Angeles County Bar Assn., chair probate & trust law sect., 1980-81; chair death and gift tax com. Calif. State Bar, 1976-77; co-founder U. So. Calif. Probate & Trust Conf., 1974—; mem. adv. bd. U. Miami Heckerling Inst. Estate Planning, 1978—. Contbr. articles to profl. jours. Served with USAR, Calif. NG, 1962-68. Fellow Am. Coll. Trust and Estate Counsel, Academician, The Internat. Acad. of Estate and Trust Law. Clubs: Annandale Golf (Pasadena); Jonathan (Los Angeles). Republican. Roman Catholic. Estate planning, Probate (including wills, trusts), Estate taxation. Office: Sheppard Mullin Richter & Hampton LLP 333 S Hope St Fl 48 Los Angeles CA 90071-1448 E-mail: jgorman@sheppardmullin.com.

GORMAN, ROBERT DENNIS, lawyer; b. Santa Fe, N.Mex., Nov. 3, 1955; s. Robert D. and Virginia M. Gorman; m. Cathy M. Sanchez, Sept. 9, 1978; children: Sarah, Lillian, Stephanie. BBA, U. N.Mex., 1977, JD, 1983. Bar: N.Mex. 1983, U.S. Dist. Ct. N.Mex. 1983, U.S. Tax Ct. 1983, U.S. Ct. Appeals (10th cir.) 1983, U.S. Ct. Claims 1993, U.S. Supreme Ct. 1993. CPA, N.Mex. Auditor, rsch. adminstr. N.Mex. State Auditor, Santa Fe, 1977-84; pvt. practice acctg., Santa Fe and Albuquerque, 1978-83; assoc. Eaves, Darling & Porter, Albuquerque, 1983-89; pvt. practice, Albuquerque, 1989—. Supervisory com. First Fin. Credit Union, Albuquerque, 1990-92; instr. bus. law U. Phoenix, 1991. Parish and fin. coun. mem. Holy Rosary Parish, Albuquerque, 1988—. Mem. ABA, AICPA, N.Mex. State Bar (dir. tax sect. 1984-95), N.Mex. Soc. CPAs (ethics com. 1998). Democrat. Roman Catholic. Avocations: skiing, running. Probate (including wills, trusts), Property, real (including real estate development, water), Taxation, general. Office: 1201 Lomas Blvd NW Albuquerque NM 87102-1893 E-mail: rgorman@nm.net.

GORNIG, GILBERT-HANNO MICHAEL, law educator; b. Deggendorf, Bavaria, Germany, Oct. 9, 1950; s. Fred-Helge and Lieselotte Maria-Theresia (Deimhard) G.; m. Doris Gabriele Putz, May 22, 1982; children: Christopher, Carolin. Dr.iur.utr., Julius Maximilians U., 1984, Dr.iur.utr.habil., 1986. Dir. Inst. for Pub. Internat. Law Georg August U., Goettingen, 1990-95, dean faculty of law, 1995-96; dir. Inst. for Pub. Law Philipps U., Marburg, 1996—, prof.'s chair, 1996—; judge Hessischer Verwaltungsgerichtshof, 1996—. Author: (book) The Subject Related Government Act, 1985, The Prohibition of Refoulement in Public International Law, 1987, Freedom of Opinion with Freedom of the Press in the Light of the Marxist-Leninist Conception of Fundamental Human Rights, vol. 10, 1987, Freedom of Expression and Information on Human Rights, 1988, The Hitler-Stalin Pact, 1990, The Memel Area, 1991, State Succession and Germany's Unification, Part II, 1992, The Law of Public Order and Police Law, 1992, The Northern East Prussia, 1999, The Legal Destiny of Danzig's Cultural Goods, 1999, Territorial Development and Extinction of the State of Prussia, 2000, Law of Demarcation in the Baltic Sea, 2002; editor: Studies in Public and Public International Law; contbr. articles to profl. jours. Mem.: Soc. Germany Related Rsch., Marburg Soc. Scholars, Kant Soc., Internat. Inst. Ethnic Groups Rights and Regionalism, Internat. Commn. Jurists, German Assn. Pub. Internat. Law, Danzig Soc. Sci. Rsch., Assn. German Lectrs. Pub. Law, Assn. Study World Refugee Problems, Assn. German, Italian and French Judges in Adminstrv. Cts. Office: Inst Oeffentliches Recht Savignyhaus Universitaetsstr 6 35037 Marburg Germany Office Fax: 06421/283853. E-mail: gornig@mailer.uni-marburg.de.

GORRELL, J. WARREN, JR., lawyer; b. Lexington, Ky., Feb. 7, 1954; s. John Warren and Geraldine (Standiford) G.; m. Catherine Rice, June 3, 1978; children: Sarah Elizabeth, Courtney Rice, Michael Warren. AB magna cum laude, Princeton U., 1976; JD, U. Va., 1979. Bar: D.C. 1979, N.Y. 1995. Assoc. Hogan & Hartson, Washington, 1979-85, ptnr., 1986—, mem. exec. com., 1991-94, 95-97, dir. corp. and securities group, 1997—. Mem. ABA (bus. sect. 1979—), Nat. Assn. Real Estate Investment Trusts, City Club Washington. Episcopalian. Avocations: tennis, golf, reading. Office: Hogan & Hartson LLP 555 13th St NW Ste 800E Washington DC 20004-1161 E-mail: jwg@dc1.hhlaw.com.*

GORRIN, EUGENE, lawyer; b. Irvington, N.J., Apr. 22, 1956; s. Harry and Ruth (Goldberg) G. BA, Rutgers U., 1978; JD, George Washington U., 1981; LLM in Taxation, NYU, 1982. Bar: N.J. 1981, U.S. Dist. Ct. N.J. 1981, U.S. Tax Ct. 1982, U.S. Supreme Ct. 1985. Assoc. Ozzard, Rizzolo, Klein, Mauro & Savo, Somerville, NJ, 1982-83; Assoc. Levine, Furman & Davis, East Brunswick, NJ, 1984-88; ptnr. Cole, Schotz, Meisel, Forman & Leonard, P.A., Hackensack, NJ, 1988-98; v.p., corp. adv. specialist Family Office Group Merrill Lynch Trust Co., Pennington, NJ, 1999—2000, sr. trust officer, mgr. spl. assets real estate fiduciary svcs. group, 2001—. Contbr. articles to profl. pubs. Mem. ABA (taxation sect.), N.J. Bar Assn. (taxation sect.), Phi Alpha Delta. Estate planning, Corporate taxation, Personal income taxation. Home: 2607 Frederick Ter Union NJ 07083-5603 Office: Merrill Lynch Trust Co 1300 Merrill Lynch Dr Pennington NJ 08534 E-mail: eugene_gorrin@ml.com.

GORSKE, ROBERT H. retired lawyer; b. Milw., June 8, 1932; s. Herman Albert and Lorraine (McDermott) G.; m. Antonette Dujick, Aug. 28, 1954; 1 child, Judith Mary (Mrs. Charles H. McMullen). Student, U. Wis., Milw., 1949-50; BA cum laude, Marquette U., 1953, JD magna cum laude, 1955, MS in Clin. Psychology, 1996; LLM (W.W. Cook fellow), U. Mich., 1959; student, Hague Acad. Internat. Law, The Netherlands, 1981. Bar: Wis. bar 1955, D.C. bar 1975, U.S. Supreme Ct. bar 1970; cert. Gerontology, Marquette U., 2002. Assoc. firm Quarles, Spence & Quarles, Milw., 1955-56; atty. Allis-Chalmers Mfg. Co., West Allis, Wis., 1956-62; instr. law U. Mich. Law Sch., Ann Arbor, 1958-59; lectr. law Marquette U. Law Sch., Milw., 1963; assoc. firm Quarles, Herriott & Clemons, Milw., 1962-64; atty. Wis. Electric Power Co., Milw., 1964-67, gen. counsel, 1967-94, v.p., 1970-72, 76-94, dir., 1991-94; mem. firm Quarles & Brady, Milw., 1972-76; gen. counsel Wis. Energy Corp., Milw., 1981-94. Tutor in psychiatry Med. Coll. Wis., 1995. Contbr. articles to profl. jours.; Editor-in-chief: Marquette Law Rev, 1954-55. Bd. dirs. Guadalupe Children's Med. Dental Clinic, Inc., Milw., 1976-86; bd. dirs. Milw. Urban League, 1991-94, treas., 1993-94; trustee Ronald McDonald House, Wauwatosa, Wis., 1987-94; trustee St. Mary's Parish, Elm Grove, Wis., 2003-. Mem. State Bar Wis., Edison Electric Inst. (vice chmn. legal com. 1975-77, chmn. 1977-79), Am. Arbitration Assn. (panelist comml. arbitrators 1985—), Ctr. for Pub. Resources (com. on alt. dispute resolution 1985-94, exec. com. 1991-94, panel disting. neutrals 1991-94). Alternative dispute resolution, Corporate, general, Utilities, public.

GORTON, NATHANIEL M. federal judge; b. 1938; m. Jodi Linnell; 3 children. AB, Dartmouth Coll., 1960; LLB, Columbia U., 1966. Bar: Mass. 1966, U.S. Dist. Ct. Mass. 1967, U.S. Ct. Appeals (5th cir.) 1975, U.S. Ct. Appeals (9th cir.) 1977, U.S. Ct. Appeals (1st cir.) 1979, U.S. Ct. Appeals (11th cir.) 1990. Assoc. Nutter, McClennen & Fish, Boston, 1966-69, Powers & Hall, P.C., Boston, 1970-74, ptnr., dir., 1975-92; judge U.S. Dist. Ct., Mass., 1992—. Trustee Buckingham Browne & Nichols Sch., Cambridge, Mass., 1984-93, chmn., 1989-93; mem. corp. New Eng. Home for Little Wanderers; mem. Wellesley Town Meeting, 1971-86; sr. warden All Saints Episcopal Ch., Brookline, Mass., 1975-80; apptd. Mass. Citizens Commn. on Gen. Ct., 1976; mem. com. Modern Legis., 1967-69; coach Wellesley Little League and Youth Hockey, 1983-87; bd. dirs. Rep. Club Mass., 1991-92; mem. fin. com. Citizens for Joe Malone, 1989-90; mem. Weld/Cellucci Com., 1989-90; program chmn. Boston chpt. Ripon Soc., 1967-68. (Lt. (j.g.) USNR, 1960-62. Mem. Boston Bar Assn. (law day classroom program, 1987-93, litigation, adminstrn. justice sect.). Avocations: hockey, tennis, skiing, sailing, mem. Boston Atoms Hockey N.Am.-(nat. finalist 1988, 91). Office: US Dist Ct 595 Main St Worcester MA 01608-2093

GOSS, JAMES WILLIAM, lawyer; b. London, Ont., Can., Mar. 10, 1941; s. Joseph Allen and Virginia Ruth (Farrah) G.; m. Rita Meyer, Aug. 2, 1969; children: Anne Candace, Jennette Courtney. BBA, West Mich. U., 1966; MS, U. Ill., 1972; JD, Georgetown U., 1974. Bar: Mich. 1974, U.S. Dist. Ct. (ea. dist.) Mich. 1974, U.S. Ct. Appeals (6th cir.) 1974. Sr. acct. Price Waterhouse & Co., Washington, 1969-71; assoc. Miller, Canfield, Paddock & Stone, Detroit, 1974-82, James W. Goss P.C., Southfield, Mich., 1982-88; ptnr. Dean & Fulkerson, Troy, Mich., 1988-95, James W. Goss P.C., Grosse Pointe Farms, Mich., 1995—. Adj. lectr. U. Mich. Law, Ann Arbor, 1978-82. Bd. dirs. Old Newsboys Goodfellow Fund of Detroit, 1990—96, Adrian Coll., 1991—96; bd. dirs., v.p. Svc. to Older Citizens Soc., Grosse Pointe, Mich., 1997—2001; assoc., bd. govs., mem. exec. com. William L. Clements Libr. U. Mich., 1998—. Named Outstanding Goodfellow, Old Newsboys Goodfellows of Detroit, 1991; recipient Disting. Alumni award Western Mich. U., 1995. Mem. Georgetown U. Law Alumni Assn., Grosse Pointe Yacht Club, Georgetown Club of Mich., Commanderie de Bordeaux, Hundred Club, Rotary (Grosse Pointe Rotarian of Yr. 2000-01), Masons. Presbyterian. Avocations: philately, wine collecting, cartographic collecting. General civil litigation, Estate planning, Taxation, general. Home: 398 Rivard Blvd Grosse Pointe MI 48230-1629 Office: 230 Punch and Judy Bldg 21 Kercheval Ave Grosse Pointe MI 48236-3698 E-mail: jameswgoss@earthlink.net.

GOSS, JEFFERY ALAN, lawyer; b. Sydney, N.S.W., Australia, July 31, 1953; s. Henry George and Marjorie Edna (Gaughan) G.; m. Christine Joan Tebb, Feb. 22, 1975; children: Mathew Alan, Adam Eric. LLB, Sydney U., 1975. Articled clk. Dunhill, Morgan & Macready, Sydney, Australia, 1974—76; solicitor, 1976-77, Middletons, Moore & Bevins, Sydney, 1977-80, assoc. ptnr., 1980-82, ptnr., 1982-99, resident ptnr. Hong Kong, 1982-83, chmn. Sydney partnership, 1996—98; mng. dir. Andelain Cons. Pty. Ltd., Sydney, 1999—2002; nat. mng. ptnr. KPMG Legal, Sydney, 2002—. Legal asst. Sydney U. Legal Aid Scheme, 1975; custodian State Libr. N.S.W. E-mail: jgoss@kpmg.com.au.

GOSS, RICHARD HENRY, lawyer; b. Worcester, Mass., Oct. 24, 1935; s. George Lee and Marion Bernadine (Henry) G.; children: Margaret Elizabeth, Richard Henry Eric, Emily Charlotte; m. Eleanor Kirsten Berg, Nov. 27, 1971. Student, Mich. State U., 1952-54; BA in Econs., Clark U., 1956; JD, Northwestern U., 1959. Bar: Ill. 1959, U.S. Supreme Ct. 1970. Asst. cashier Nat. Blvd. Bank of Chgo., 1959-61; v.p. Paul D. Speer & Assocs. Inc., Mcpl. Fin. Cons., Chgo., 1962-68; mng. ptnr. Chapman and Cutler, Attys. at Law, Chgo., 1968-95. Bd. dirs. Japan Am. Soc. Chgo., 1987-96, v.p., chmn. mem. com., 1988-90; chmn. bd. dirs. Brays Island Plantation Colony, Inc., 1995-97. Mem. Eastman (N.H.) Golf Club. Republican. Episcopalian. Avocations: hunting, skeet, sporting clays and trap shooting, travel, oriental studies. Finance, Municipal (including bonds), Securities. Home: 7 Par Brae Eastman Box 1316 Grantham NH 03753

GOSSAGE, ROZA, lawyer, educator; b. Landreis Celle Lohheide, Germany, Mar. 21, 1947; came to U.S., 1949; d. Abram and Lola (Strubel) Berlinski; m. David Jordan Gossage, Feb. 21, 1970; children: Brenda, Sara, Leah. BA, U. Ill., 1968; JD, DePaul Sch. Law, 1971. Bar: Ill. 1971, Fla. 1972, Mo. 1981, U.S. Dist. Ct. (no. dist.) Ill. 1971, U.S. Dist. Ct. (so. dist.) Ill. 1978, U.S. Ct. Appeals (7th cir.) 1972. Law clk. U.S. Dist. Ct. (no. dist.) Ill., Chgo., 1971-72; atty. State's Atty.'s Office of Cook County, Ill., 1972-74, State's Atty.'s Office of St. Clair County, Belleville, Ill., 1974-78, Hutnick & Gossage, Belleville, 1978—89; pvt. practice Belleville, 1990—. Atty. Commn. to Revise and Rewrite Pub. Aid Code of Ill., Springfield, 1978-80; atty. Village of Summerfield, Ill., 1983—89; arbitrator Better Bus. Bur., St. Louis, 1982—; lectr. in family law. Bd. dirs. YWCA, St. Clair County, Ill., 1981-89; co-chair continuing legal edn. Women's Lawyers of Greater St. Louis, 2001-2002. Mem. St. Clair County Bar Assn., Met. Women's Bar Assn. (bd. dirs. 1981—), Ill. Bar Assn., Mo. Bar Assn., Fla. Bar Assn., So. Ill. Network of Women, Ill. State Bar Assn. (family law sect., chair CLE, secual orientation and gender identity com.). Commercial, consumer (including collections, credit), Family and matrimonial, Personal injury (including property damage). Office: 521 W Main St Ste 110 Belleville IL 62220-1535

GOSSELS, CLAUS PETER ROLF, lawyer; b. Berlin, Aug. 11, 1930; came to U.S., 1941; s. Max and Charlotte (Lewy) G.; m. Nancy Lee Tuber, June 29, 1958; children: Lisa Rae, Amy Devra, Daniel Joshua. AB, Harvard U., 1951, LLB, 1954. Bar: Mass. 1955, U.S. Dist. Ct. Mass. 1957, U.S. Ct. Appeals (1st cir.) 1957, U.S. Supreme Ct. 1965. Assoc. Sullivan & Worcester, Boston, 1956-65; mem. Zelman, Gossels & Alexander, Boston, 1965-72, Weston, Patrick, Willard & Redding, Boston, 1972—. Master Superior Ct. Mass., 1984—; guardian ad litem, conservator Mass. Probate and Family Ct. Co-author, editor: Vetaher Libenu, 1980, Chadesh Yameynu, 1997. Moderator Town of Wayland, Mass., 1982—. With U.S. Army, 1954-56. Mem. Mass. Bar Assn., Boston Bar Assn., Mass. Moderators Assn., Mass. Acad. Trial Lawyers. Jewish. Avocations: reading, tennis, travel, gardening, theatre. General civil litigation, Education and schools, Family and matrimonial. Home: 32 Hampshire Rd Wayland MA 01778-1021 Office: Weston Patrick Willard & Redding 84 State St Boston MA 02109-2299

GOSTIN, IRWIN, retired lawyer; b. N.Y.C., July 22, 1927; s. Herman and Vera (Ostrinsky) G.; m. Ruth Gostin (div. 1963); children: Theodore David, Leslie Ann Gostin Sikes, Deborah Lynn Gostin; m. Margit Gostin (div. 1984); m. Mary L. Gostin, Jan. 27, 1990. AB, UCLA, 1948; JD, Harvard U., 1951. Bar: Calif. 1952, U.S. Dist. Ct. (cen. dist.) Calif. 1952, U.S. Ct. Appeals (9th cir.) 1952, U.S. Dist. Ct. (so. dist.) Calif. 1957. Pvt. practice, L.A., 1952-56; ptnr. Gostin & Katz, San Diego, 1957-70; pres. Gostin & Katz Inc., San Diego, 1971-78, Irwin Gostin, APL, San Diego, 1979-94; admin. sec. Nat. Lawyer's Guild, L.A., 1953—56. Mem. legal panel, chmn. ACLU, San Diego, 1958-67, pres., 1968; pres. San Diego Children's Home Soc., 1967; sec.-treas. Breeden-Schmidt Found., 1991—. With U.S. Army, 1945-46. Mem. San Diego County Bar Assn., Assn. Trial Lawyers Am., Calf. Trial Lawyers Assn., San Diego Trial Lawyers Assn. (pres. 1969). Avocation: thoroughbred horse racing. Personal injury (including property damage). Home: 11216 Pergola Point Ct Las Vegas NV 89144

GOSTIN, LAWRENCE O. lawyer, educator; b. Oct. 19, 1949; s. Joseph and Sylvia (Berkman) G.; m. Jean Catherine Allison, July 30, 1977; children: Bryn Gareth, Kieran Gavin. BA summa cum laude, SUNY, Brockport, 1971; LLD (hon.), SUNY; JD, Duke U., 1974. Bar: N.Y. 1981, Coun. Europe. Legal dir. Nat. Assn. Mental Health, London, 1975-82; vis. fellow U. Oxford Ctr. for Criminol. Rsch., 1982-83; gen. sec. Nat. Coun. Civil Liberties, London, 1983-85; sr. fellow in health law Harvard U. Sch. Pub. Health, 1985—. Vis. prof. social policy McMaster U., Hamilton, Ont., Can., 1978-79; exec. dir. Am. Soc. Law, Medicine, and Ethics, Boston, 1987-94; adj. assoc. prof. Sch. Pub. Health, Harvard U., 1988—, adj. prof., 1990—, lectr. Law Sch., 1990—; vis. prof. Georgetown U. Law Ctr., 1993-94, assoc. prof., 1994-95, prof., 1996—; prof. Johns Hopkins Sch. Hygiene and Pub. Health, 1994—; co-dir. Georgetown/Johns Hopkins Program on Law and Pub. Health; dir. CDC Collaborating Ctr. on Law and the Pub.'s Health; legis. coun. U.S. Senate Labor and Human Resources Com., Washington, 1987, 88; bd. dirs., nat. exec. com. Am. Civil Liberties Union, 1987—; assoc. dir. Harvard U. WHO Internat. Collaborating Ctr. on Health Legis., 1989— Western European editor Internat. Jour. Law and Psychiatry, London, 1978-81; editor in chief: Law Medicine & Health Care; exec. editor: Am. Jour. Law and Medicine; sect. editor Jour. AMA; editor: Secure Provision, 1985, AIDS and the Health Care System, 1990, Surrogate Motherhood: Politics and Privacy, 1990, Implementing the Americans with Disabilities Act, 1993; co-editor: Law, Science and Medicine, 2d edit., 1996; author: Human Rights and Public Health in the AIDS Pandemic, 1997, The Rights of Persons with HIV Disease, 1996, Mental Health Services: Law and Practice, 1986, Institutions Observed, 1986, Mental Health: Tribunal Procedure, 1984, 2d edit., 1992, A Human Condition, 1975, 2d vol., 1977, Civil Liberties in Conflict, 1988, Public Health Law: Power, Duty, Restraint, 2000, The AIDS Pandemic: Complacency, Injustice and Unfulfilled Expectations, 2003; editor Public Health law and Ethics: A Reader, 2002, The Human Rights of Persons with Intellectual Disabilities: Different But Equal, 2003. Legal affairs com. Internat. League Socs. for Mentally Handicapped, Brussels, 1980—; trustee Cobden Trust, London, 1983-85; chmn. Advocacy Alliance, London, 1981-84; sec. All Party Parliamentary Civil Liberties Group, London, 1984-85; bd. dirs. ACLU, 1986—, exec. com., 1988—; mem. com. experts drafting conventions on human experientation UN, Siracusa, Italy, 1980-82. Recipient Rosemary Deldridge Meml. award Nat. Consumer Coun. U.K., 1983; fellow Kennedy Inst. Ethics, 1994—, Fulbright fellow U. Oxford, 1974-75. Avocations: climbing, vegetable growing. Home: 10413 Masters Ter Potomac MD 20854-3862 Office: Georgetown U Law Ctr 600 New Jersey Ave NW Washington DC 20001-2075 E-mail: gostin@law.georgetown.edu.

GOTTESMAN, A(RTHUR) EDWARD, lawyer; b. Hillside, N.J., July 29, 1937; s. Joseph Jack Gottesman, Sadonia Herskowitz; m. Patricia Jo Matson; m. Allison Pierce Coudert (div.); children: Polly Moore, Catherine Coudert. BA, U.Chgo., 1954; LLB, Yale U., 1957. Bar: N.Y. 1959. Ptnr. Coudert Bros., London, 1963—70; sr. ptnr. Gottesman Jones & Partners, London, 1970—. Pres. Am. C. of C., London, 1981—83; chmn. Derby Internat. Corp., Luxembourg, 1986—98, Exeter Internat. Corp., Luxembourg, Prin. Healthcare Fin. Ltd., London. Dir. London Bach Orch., 1980—89; Member Yale University President's Council on International Activities, New Haven. Private US Army, 1960—61, Fort Dix, N.J. Mem.: Yale Club, Reform Club. Mergers and acquisitions, Corporate taxation, Corporate, general. Office: Centenary International Corporation 1120 Avenue of the Americas New York NY 10036 Personal E-mail: centenint@aol.com. Business E-Mail: gottesmanjones@aol.com.

GOTTHELF, BETH, lawyer; b. Detroit, Mar. 24, 1958; BS in Pub. Adminstrn., Oakland U., 1980; JD, U. Detroit, 1985. Bar: Mich. 1986, U.S. Dist. Ct. (ea. dist.) Mich. 1986. Claims rep. Social Security Adminstrn., Pontiac, Mich., 1979-82; law clk. U.S. Atty.'s Office, Detroit, 1984-85; asst. prof. law Clement-Ferrand U. de Droit, France, 1985-86; jud. law clk. Mich. Ct. Appeals, Detroit, 1986-87; assoc. Philip G. Tannian PC, Detroit, 1987—89, Honigman, Miller, Schwartz and Cohn, Detroit, 1989—91; from assoc. to shareholder Seyburn, Kahn, Ginn, Bess and Serlin PC, Southfield, Mich., 1991—2003; shareholder Butzel Long, Bloomfield Hills, Mich., 2003—. Bd. dirs. JVS, Inc. Bd. dirs., vice chair Nat. Multiple Sclerosis Soc., Detroit Area Comml. Bd. Realtors, S.E. Mich. Coun. Govts.

(environ. policy adv. coun.), Greater Detroit C. of C. (chair task force on water and sewer issues); bd. dirs. U. Cancer Found. Mem. ABA (solid and hazardous waste com., chmn. water and wetlands, natural resources, energy and environ. law sect., mem. fed. adv. com. on storm water),Internat. Women's Forum, Am. Electroplaters and Surface Finishers Assn., Oakland County Bar Assn. (past chair environ. law sec.), Mich. State Bar Assn. (environ. law sect., past chair, coun. mem., program com., solid waste/hazardous waste/ins. com., superfund com., past sec., treas.). Jewish. Environmental, Natural resources, Property, real (including real estate development, water). Office: Butzel Long Ste 200 100 Bloomfield Hills Pkwy Bloomfield Hills MI 48304 E-mail: gotthelf@butzel.com.

GOTTLIEB, DANIEL SETH, lawyer; b. Los Angeles, Sept. 19, 1954; s. Seymour and Blanche Joyce (Kaufman) G.; m. Marilynn Jeanne Payne, July 21, 1985; children: Gwendolyn Z., Rebecca Lucinda. BA summa cum laude, Columbia U., 1976; JD, Harvard U., 1980. Bar: Wash. 1980, U.S. Dist. Ct. (we. dist.) Wash. 1980. Assoc. Riddell, Williams, Bullitt & Walkinshaw, Seattle, 1980-86, ptnr., 1986-95; prin. Graham & James LLP/Riddell Williams P.S., Seattle, 1996-97; mem. Gottlieb, Fisher & Andrews, PLLC, Seattle, 1997—. Coord. S.E. Legal Clinic, Seattle, 1984-86. Mem. Seattle Fremont Adv. Com. Recipient Achievement award Seattle-King County Econ. Devel. Coun., 1990. Mem. ABA, Nat. Assn. Bond Lawyers, Wash. State Bar Assn., King County Bar Assn. (treas. 1993-95, 2d v.p. 1995-96, 1st v.p. 1996-97, pres. 1997-98, bd. dirs. young lawyers divsn. 1987-90, treas. 1987-88, vice-chmn. 1988-89, chmn. 1989-90, chmn. legal info. and referral clinics com. 1986-87, Helen Geisness award 2001), Wash. State Assn. Mcpl. Attys., Wash. Coun. Sch. Attys., Wash. State Soc. Hosp. Attys., Bainbridge Island-North Kitsap Jewish Chavurah (v.p. and sec. 1993-95). Jewish. Avocations: tuba, hiking, bicycling. Municipal (including bonds). Home: 4880 NE North Tolo Rd Bainbridge Island WA 98110-3461 Office: Gottlieb Fisher & Andrews PLLC 1325 Fourth Ave Ste 1200 Seattle WA 98101-2531 E-mail: dan@goandfish.com.

GOTTLIEB, IRA LEONARD, lawyer; b. N.Y.C., Sept. 3, 1938; s. Joseph S. and Jaye (Rice) G.; m. Jane Mallory Snyder Campbell, Aug. 24, 1965 (div. 1971); 1 child, Katherine; m. Julie Carol Keller, Oct. 11, 1974; children: Justin, Anne. BA, CCNY, 1960; JD, U. Wis., 1968. Bar: Oreg. 1969, U.S. Dist. Ct. Oreg. 1970, U.S. Supreme Ct. 1976. Sales Peter Pan Inc., Boston, 1963-65; clk. Oreg. Supreme Ct., Salem, 1968; atty. Multnomah County Legal Aid, Portland, Oreg., 1968-71; adj. prof. law Lewis & Clark Coll., Portland, 1971-81; pvt. practice Portland, 1971-81, 95—; ptnr. Keller, Gottlieb & Gorin, Portland, 1981-95. Contbr. articles to profl. jours. 1st lt. U.S. Army, 1960-62. Fellow: Am. Acad. Matrimonial Lawyers. Jewish. Appellate, Family and matrimonial. Office: 621 SW Morrison St Ste 350 Portland OR 97205-3806 E-mail: igottlaw@i-205net.com.

GOTTLIEB, JAMES RUBEL, federal agency administrator, lawyer; b. N.Y.C., July 2, 1947; s. Robert J. Gottlieb and Mildred C. Blaufox; m. Roberta James, 1974; children: Zoe, Zachary. BA, Mich. State U., 1969; MA, NYU, 1970; JD, N.Y. Law Sch., 1974. Bar: N.Y. 1974, D.C. 1983. Trial asst. Fuchsberg & Fuchsberg, 1971-74, assoc., 1974-77; adminstrv. asst., legis. dir., counsel for rep. Ted Weiss U.S. House of Reps., 1977-83, staff dir., chief counsel Human Resources & Intergovt. Rels. Subcom., 1983-93; chief counsel, staff dir. Senate Com. on Vets. Affairs, Washington, 1993-94; minority chief counsel, staff dir. Senate Com. Vets. Affairs, Washington, 1995—2000; chief of staff Senator John D. Rockefeller IV, 2000—. Democrat. Office: Office of Sen John D Rockefeller IV 531 Hart Senate Office Washington DC 20510-4802

GOTTLIEB, JONATHAN W. lawyer; b. Washington, June 24, 1959; s. Julius Judah and Charlotte (Papernick) G.; m. Deborah Jo Levine, June 28, 1987; children: Maya Lane, Seth Joseph. BA with honors, DePaul U., 1982; student, Am. U., 1984-85; JD, N.Y. Law Sch., 1985. Bar: Pa. 1986, D.C. 1989, U.S. Ct. Appeals (D.C. cir.) 1990. Trial atty. Fed. Energy Regulatory Commn., Washington, 1987-88; assoc. Wickwire, Gavin & Gibbs, Washington, 1988-89, Ballard Spahr Andrews & Ingersoll, Washington, 1990-92, Reid & Priest, Washington, 1992-94, ptnr., 1995-98, Thelen Reid & Priest, Washington, 1998-99, Baker & McKenzie, Washington, 1999—. Chmn. legal affairs task force Nat. Hydropower Assn., 1992-95; counsel Mid-Atlantic Ind. Power Producers; gen. counsel Power Markets Devel. Co. (PPL Global), 1995-96; adv. bd. Bradley Energy Internat., 1997—; acting gen. counsel Packard Bell NEC, Inc., 1998. Contbg. editor Project Fin. Monthly; editor Competitive Utility, 1993—. Donor mem. Corning Mus. Glass. Mem. Fed. Energy Bar Assn., Pa. Bar Assn., D.C. Bar Assn., Southeastern Energy Soc. Republican. Avocations: glass collecting, stained glass making, gardening. Finance, Utilities, public. Home: 9317 W Parkhill Dr Bethesda MD 20814-3966 E-mail: jonathan.w.gottlieb@bakernet.com.

GOTTLIEB, PAUL MITCHEL, lawyer; b. N.Y.C., Mar. 30, 1954; s. Henry Gottlieb and Thelma Ethel (Friedman) Miller; m. Helene Manya Roiter, Apr. 3, 1982; children: Jordan Seth, Zachary Michael. BA, Hobart Coll., 1976; JD, MBA, Washington U., St. Louis, 1980. Bar: Ill. 1980, U.S. Dist. Ct. (no. dist.) Ill. 1980, N.Y. 1988. Assoc. Rudnick & Wolfe, Chgo., 1980-81; ind. trader Chgo. Bd. of Trade, 1981—82; staff atty. Chgo. Merc. Exch., 1983-84, v.p. market regulation, 1984—87; commodity counsel Morgan Stanley and Co. Inc., N.Y.C., 1987-89; spl. counsel commodities, futures and derivative products Skadden, Arps, Slate, Meagher & Flom, N.Y.C., 1989-92; ptnr., chair derivative products practice group Seward & Kissel, N.Y.C., 1992-96; dir., sr. counsel structured products & commodities Union Bank of Switzerland, N.Y.C., 1996-98; sr. v.p., dep. gen. counsel PaineWebber Inc., N.Y.C., 1998—2000; exec. dir. UBS Warburg LLC, N.Y.C., 2000-01; mng. dir., COO RBC Dominion Securities Corp., N.Y.C., 2001—; sr. v.p. Royal Bank of Can., 2001—. Eisenhower fellow to New Zealand, 1992; adj. prof. Ctr. for Tech. & Fin. Svcs. Polytechnic U. Contbr. chpts. to books, articles to profl. jours. Mem.: Securities Industry Assn. (law and compliance divsn.), Chgo. Bd. Trade, Chgo. Mercantile Exch., N.Y. Stock Exch. Jewish. Avocations: coaching youth hockey and lacrosse, golf, skiing. Administrative and regulatory, Finance, Securities. Home: 11 Highpoint Pl West Windsor NJ 08550-5238 Office: RBC Dominion Securities Corp 1 Liberty Plz 165 Broadway New York NY 10006-1404

GOTTS, ILENE KNABLE, lawyer; b. Phila., Nov. 25, 1959; d. Harry Lee and Ethel Beatrice (Teitelman) Knable; m. Michael D. Gotts, May 25, 1986; children: Isaac, Samuel. BA magna cum laude with hon., U. Md., 1980; JD cum laude, Georgetown U., 1984. Bar: D.C. 1984, N.Y., 1997, U.S. Dist. Ct. D.C. 1986, U.S. Ct. Appeals (D.C. cir.) 1985, U.S. Dist. Ct. Md. 1987, U.S. Ct. Appeals (fed. cir.) 1989, U.S. Supreme Ct. 1988. Staff atty. FTC, 1984-86; assoc. Foley & Lardner, Washington, 1986-92, ptnr., head legis./adminstrv. group, antitrust practice group, 1992-96; ptnr. Wachtell, Lipton, Rosen & Katz, N.Y.C., 1996—. Adj. prof. George Washington U. Law Ctr., 1995-96. Mem. editl. bd. The Practical Lawyer, 1994—; mem. editl. adv. bd. The Antitrust Counselor, 1995—; mem. adv. bd. Antitrust Trade and Regulatory Report, 2003-; contbr. articles to profl. jours. Mem. legal adv. bd. NOW Legal and Edn. Fund., 2001—. Recipient Sklar award U. Md., 1980; Mary Elizabeth Robey scholar. Mem.: NOW (legal adv. bd. 2001—), FBA (chair health care com. of antitrust sect. 1991—95, chair antitrust and trade regulation sec. 1995—97), ABA (health care com. antitrust sect. 1988—, consumer protection com. 1994—96, vice chair intellectual property com. 1994—97, vice chair Clayton Act com. 1997—98, chair 1998—2001, coun. 2001—, chair merger rev. task force 1998—, editor The Merger Rev. Process, 2d edit.), Internat. Bar Assn., N.Y. Women's Bar Assn., N.Y. State Bar Assn. (exec. com. antitrust law sect. 2000—), Washington Coun. Lawyers (exec. com. and bd. dirs. 1988—97, pres. 1994—95), Am. Law Inst., D.C. Bar (steering com., antitrust and trade regulation com. 1994—95), Phi Beta Kappa, Mortar Board, Phi Alpha Theta, Pi Sigma Alpha, Phi Kappa Phi. Democrat. Jewish. Administrative and regulatory, Antitrust. Office: Wachtell Lipton Rosen & Katz 51 W 52d St New York NY 10019 E-mail: ikgotts@wlrk.com.

GOTTSCHALK, STEPHEN ELMER, lawyer; b. Rochester, Minn., Oct. 9, 1947; s. Elmer H. and Ruth F. (Thurley) G.; m. Lorilyn J. Dopp, Feb. 14, 1970; children: Andrew Stephen, Stephanie Beth, Lorissa Christine, Michael Donald. BS, Valparaiso U., 1969, JD, 1972. Bar: Minn. 1972, U.S. Dist. Ct. (Minn.) 1972. Jud. clk. Minn. Supreme Ct., St. Paul, 1972-73; assoc. Dorsey & Whitney, Minn., 1973-78, ptnr., 1979—, dept. head employee benefits dept., 1986-91, 98—. Adj. prof. employee benefits Sch. Law U. Minn. Mem. pres. adv. coun., Valparaiso U., 1983—; bd. dirs. Twin Cities Habitat for Humanity, Inc. Recipient Svc. award Valparaiso Alumni Assn., 1986. Mem. Midwest Pension Conf. Avocation: squash. Corporate, general, Education and schools, Pension, profit-sharing, and employee benefits. Home: 4339 Fremont Ave S Minneapolis MN 55409-1720 Office: Dorsey & Whitney 50 S 6th St Ste 1500 Minneapolis MN 55402-1498 E-mail: gottschalk.steve@dorseylaw.com.

GOTTSCHALK, THOMAS A. lawyer; b. Decatur, Ind., July 5, 1942; s. John Simson and Edith (Liechty) G.; m. Barbara J. Risen, Aug. 28, 1965; children: Deborah, Diane. AB, Earlham Coll., 1964; JD, U. Chgo., 1967. Bar: Ill. 1967, D.C. 1986, U.S. Supreme Ct. Assoc. Kirkland & Ellis, Chgo., 1967-73, ptnr., 1973-94; sr. v.p., gen. counsel Gen. Motors Corp., Detroit, 1994—2001, exec. v.p., 2001—. Trustee Earlham Coll., Richmond, Ind., 1972—, chmn., 1985-91. Mem. ABA (mem. litigation, antitrust and criminal law sects.), D.C. Bar Assn., Chgo. Coun. of Lawyers, Conf. Bd. Coun. of Chief Legal Officers; mem. bd. of trustees, Am. Univ., Wash., D.C. Administrative and regulatory, Antitrust, General civil litigation. Office: Gen Motors Corp 300 Renaissance Ctr Detroit MI 48265-0001*

GOTTSCHLICH, GARY WILLIAM, lawyer; b. Dayton, Ohio, Aug. 27, 1946; s. William Frederick and Rosemary Teresa Gottschlich; m. Sharon Melanie Plunkett, Oct. 7, 1978; children: David W., Andrew J., Thomas M. Bs, U. Dayton, 1968; cert., Univ. Coll., London, 1970; JD, U. NNotre Dame, 1971. Bar: Ohio 1971. Asst. pros. atty. Montgomery County, Dayton, 1971-73; assoc. Young, Pryor, Lynn & Jerardi, Dayton, 1973-80, ptnr., 1980-84, Louis & Froelich, Dayton, 1984-87, Porter, Wright, Morris & Arthur, Dayton, 1987-97, Gottschlich & Portune, Dayton, 1997—. Capt. USAR. Mem. ABA, ATLA, Ohio Bar Assn. (bd. govs. litigation sect.), Dayton Bar Assn. (treas. 1981-82), Miami Valley Trial Lawyers Assn. (founding), Rotary Club (pres. 2002—). Roman Catholic. Avocations: golf, sailing, squash. Home: 5260 Little Woods Ln Dayton OH 45429-2124 Office: Gottschlich & Portune LLP The Historic Armory 201 E Sixth St Dayton OH 45402-2836

GOTUZZO, GIANINA, lawyer, law educator; b. Lima, Peru, Aug. 15, 1975; d. Eduardo Gotuzzo and Mirtha Oliva. JD, Pontificia U. Catolica, Lima, 1999; LLM, Cornell U., 2000. Bar: Lima 1999, N.Y. 2002. Trainee Estudio Grau Abogados, Lima, 1995—99, assoc., 1999—2003. Prof. comml. law and corps. Pontificia Univ. Cath. del Peru Law Sch., Lima, 2001—. Dir., editor: Themis-Revista de Derecho, 1996—98. Corporate, general, Commercial, contracts (including sales of goods; commercial financing), Mergers and acquisitions. Office: Hernandez & Rossello Abogados Av Javier Prado Oeste 795 Magdalena Lima Peru

GOTWALS, CHARLES PLACE, JR., lawyer; b. Muskogee, Okla., May 19, 1917; s. Charles Place and Anna M. (Koehler) G.; m. Mary Frances Brownlee, Jan. 31, 1948 (dec. Mar. 1982); children: Charles William, James Robert, Frances Ann, Virginia Hunt; m. Marion Miller, Jan. 6, 1984. AB, U. Okla., 1938, JD, 1940. Bar: Okla. 1940. Pvt. practice, Tulsa, 1940—; ptnr. Gable & Gotwals, until 1990; of counsel, 1990—. Sr. warden Trinity Episcopal Ch., Tulsa, 1984-87, also former vestryman and jr. warden. Served to maj. AUS, 1942-46, ETO. Decorated Bronze Star Mem. ABA, Tulsa County Bar Assn. (sec. 1949), Okla. Bar Assn., Am. Judicature Soc., Order of Coif, Phi Beta Kappa, Phi Delta Phi, Beta Theta Pi. Clubs: Kiwanian (pres. 1961), Tulsa, Summit. Office: 1100 Oneok Plz 100 W 5th St Tulsa OK 74103-4240

GOUGH, JOHN FRANCIS, lawyer; b. Phila., Nov. 28, 1934; s. John Joseph and Honora Veronica (Garrity) G.; m. Natalie Smith, Mar. 8, 1984; children: David, Robert, J. Joseph II, Richard, Jonathan, Kristin. AB cum laude, St. Joseph's U., 1957; JD, Yale Law Sch., 1960. Bar: Pa. 1961, N.J. 1994, U.S. Dist. Ct. (ea. dist.) Pa. 1961, U.S. Ct. Appeals (3d cir.) 1966, U.S. Supreme Ct. 1967. Assoc. Erskine, Barbieri & Sheer, Phila., 1960-65, White and Williams, Phila., 1965-68, ptnr., 1968-80, Toll, Ebby & Gough, Phila., 1980-87; ptnr., chmn. corp. dept. Abrahams & Loewenstein, Phila., 1987-88; ptnr. Hoyle, Morris & Kerr, Phila., 1988-92, Montgomery, Mccracken, Walker & Rhoads, LLP, Phila., 1992-98, co-chair bus. bankruptcy sect., 1998; ptnr. Hoyle, Morris & Kerr LLP, Phila., 1998-2000; of counsel Montgomery, McCracken, Walker & Rhoads, LLP, Phila., 2000—. Exec. com. Ea. Dist Bankruptcy Conf., 1989—; faculty co-chmn. and lectr. Temple Grad. Sch. Law C.L.E. Program, 1989-92; lectr. U. Pa. Grad. Sch., Temple Law Sch., 1990—. Author course materials for profl. and ednl. orgns. Pres. Highfield Sch. PTA, Plymouth, Pa., 1966-68, Greene Towne Montessori Sch., Phila., 1979-80; mem. exec. com., sec. Schuylkill River Devel. Corp., 2000—; chmn. Tidal Schuylkill River Master Plan Task Force; treas. Rittenhouse Savoy Owners Assn. Mem. ABA, Am. Law Inst., Phila. Bar Assn. (pres. Jr. Bar Assn. 1964-65), Hosp. Attys. S.E. Pa. (pres. 1977-79), Am. Bankruptcy Inst. (bd. cert. in bus. bankruptcy), Yale Club Phila. Avocations: tennis, gardening, fitness. Bankruptcy, Corporate, general, Mergers and acquisitions. Office: Montgomery, McCracken, Walker & Rhoads, LLP 123 South Broad Street Philadelphia PA 19109 Fax: 215-772-7620. E-mail: jgough@mmwr.com.

GOUGINSKI, NIKOLAI TODOROV, lawyer, consultant; b. Sofia, Bulgaria, Feb. 11, 1971; s. Jodor Iliev Gouginski and Elena Anastasova Gouginska. LLB, U. Sofia, 1995; LLM with highest hons., George Washington U., 1999. Bar: Sofia. Law clk. to chief judge Sofia (Bulgaria) Dist. Ct., 1995—96; lawyer FRRC, Budapest, Hungary, 1996—98; sr. assoc. Djingov, Gouginski, Kutchukov & Velichkov, Sofia, 1999—. Avocations: mountain trekking, mountain biking. Antitrust, Private international, Commercial, contracts (including sales of goods; commercial financing). Office: Djingov Gouginski Kyutchukov & Velichkov 10 Tsar Osuoboditel Blvd 1000 Sofia Bulgaria Fax: 3592 920 3586. E-mail: nikolai.gouginski@dgkv.com.

GOULD, RODNEY ELLIOTT, lawyer, university dean, educator; b. Boston, June 3, 1943; s. Samuel H. and Sylvia (Gerrish) G.; m. Nancy Lund, Sept. 10, 1968; children: Jody R., Amy L. Student, London Sch. Econs., 1963-64; AB, Colby Coll., 1965; JD, Columbia U., 1968. Bar: D.C. 1969, N.Y. 1969, Mass. 1975, Pa. 2001, U.S. Dist. Ct. (so. dist.) N.Y. 1969, U.S. Dist. Ct. D.C. 1969, U.S. Ct. Appeals (2d cir.) 1969, U.S. Ct. Appeals (D.C. cir.) 1970, U.S. Dist. Ct. Mass. 1975, U.s. Ct. Appeals (3d and 8th cirs.) 1981, U.S. Ct. Appeals (1st cir.) 1989, U.S. Supreme Ct. 1989, U.S. Ct. Appeals (6th cir.) 1990, U.S. Ct. Appeals (4th cir.) 1998. Law clk. to judge U.S. Dist. Ct. for So. Dist. N.Y., 1968-69; assoc. Covington & Burling, Washington, 1969-75, Rosenman Colin Freund Lewis & Cohen, N.Y.C., 1979-82; assoc. dir. FTC, Boston, 1975-78; antitrust counsel Digital Equipment Co., Maynard, Mass., 1983-84; gen. counsel Internat. Weekends, Boston, 1985-86; ptnr. Rubin Hay & Gould, Framingham, Mass., 1986—. Adj. prof. Law Sch., Western New Eng. U., Springfield, Mass., 1980-82, Northeastern U., Boston, 1983—, Boston U., 1985—; lectr. in field. Editor Columbia Law Rev., 1967-68. Bd. dirs. Mass. Aububon Soc., 1996—. Mem. ABA, Mass. Bar Assn., N.Y. Bar Assn., D.C. Bar Assn., Phi Beta Kappa. Antitrust, Travel. Home: 84 Gordon Rd Newton MA 02468-1617 Office: Rubin Hay & Gould 205 Newbury St Framingham MA 01701-4581

GOULDIN, DAVID MILLEN, lawyer; b. Binghamton, N.Y., Mar. 8, 1941; s. Paul C. and Virginia M. Gouldin; m. Deborah A. Gouldin, Aug. 20, 1966; children: Robert, Michael, Lauryn, Derek. AB, Princeton U., 1963; JD, Cornell U., 1966. Bar: N.Y., U.S. Dist. Ct. N.Y. Ptnr. Levene, Gouldin & Thompson, LLP, Binghamton, 1966—. Mem. N.Y. State Bd. Law Examiners, 1999—. Author: (with others) Commercial Litigation in New York Courts, 1995. Chmn. Broome County (N.Y.) Arena, 1981; chmn. Broome County Health Fair, 1986-87; gen. chmn. ministry endowment campaign Broome County Coun. Chs., 1986-87; pres. United Way Broome County, 1982-84; mem. United Way N.Y. State, 1985-99, chmn., 1991-92; chancellor Wyo. conf. United Meth. Ch., 1987—; bd. dirs. Roberson Ctr. for Arts, 1983-89, United Health Svcs. Hosps., 1990-2002; bd. dirs. Broome County Urban League, 1994-2000, sec., 1995-2000; trustee Wyo. Sem., 1973-88, Miller S. Gaffney and Adelaide S. Gaffney Found., 1996—; trustee Edwin A. Link and Marion C. Link Found., 1989—, chmn., 1993—. Recipient Sertoma Svc. to Mankind Dist. award, 1988, Disting. Citizens award Baden-Powell coun. Boy Scouts Am., 1996; named to Sect. Four Hall of Fame, 1978, Outstanding Young Men of Am., 1974, Sect. IV Hall of Fame, 1978; named Man of Yr. Post 80 Am. Legion Hall of Fame, 1989. Mem. N.Y. State Bar Assn. (chmn. TICL sect. 1992, Root-Stimson award 1987, John Leach award 1999), Broome County Bar Assn. (pres. 1989), Fedn. Bar 6th Dist. (pres. 1974), Rotary. Republican. Federal civil litigation, State civil litigation, Personal injury (including property damage). Home: 85 Highland Ave Binghamton NY 13905-4039 Office: PO Box F1706 Binghamton NY 13902-0106 E-mail: dgouldin@binghamtonlaw.com.

GOUNLEY, DENNIS JOSEPH, lawyer; b. Jan. 29, 1950; s. George Gerard and Elizabeth Mary (Maggioncalda) G.; m. Martha Ann Zatezalo, Sept. 25, 1976. BA, St. Joseph's Coll., Phila., 1971; JD, Dickinson Sch. Law, 1974. Bar: Pa. 1974, U.S. Dist. Ct. (we. dist.) Pa. 1995, U.S. Ct. Appeals (3d cir.) 1976, U.S. Supreme Ct. 1977. Pvt. practice, Greensburg, Pa., 1974-83, 90—; ptnr. Gounley & O'Halloran, Greensburg, 1984-90. Westmoreland County mental health rev. officer, 1991—. Coun. mem. Franklin Towne Condominium Assn., Murrysville, Pa., 1976-79. Mem. Pa. Bar Assn., Westmoreland Bar Assn., Murrysville-Export Rotary Club (pres. 1999-00). Republican. Roman Catholic. General civil litigation, Probate (including wills, trusts), Property, real (including real estate development, water). Home: 3590 N Hills Rd Murrysville PA 15668-1438 Office: 15 E Otterman St Greensburg PA 15601-2543

GOURVITZ, ELLIOT HOWARD, lawyer; b. Lewiston, Pa., Sept. 21, 1945; s. Louis and Irene (Brass) Gourvitz; m. Bonnie S. Hirsch; children: Evan, Amy, Ross, Ari. BA, Rutgers U., 1966, JD, 1969. Bar: N.J. 1969, N.Y. 1985, U.S. Dist. Ct. N.J. 1969, U.S. Dist. Ct. (ea. dist.) Wis. 1985, U.S. Ct. Appeals 93d cir.) 1972, U.S. Ct. Appeals (2d, 4th, 5th, 7th, 8th, 9th, 10th, and fed. cirs.) 1982, U.S. Tax Ct. 1970, U.S. Ct. Claims 1970, U.S. Ct. Internat. Trade 1985, U.S. Supreme Ct. 1973, cert.: N.J. (matrimonial atty.). Pvt. practice, Springfield. Chmn., Early Settlement Panel of Union County, NJ; panelist Essex and Middlesex Counties. Contbr. articles to profl. jours. Named Man of Yr., United Cerebral Palsy League Union County, 1980. Fellow: Internat. Acad. Matrimonial Lawyers, Am. Acad. Matrimonial Attys. (pres. N.J.); mem.: N.Y. State Bar Assn., N.J. Bar Assn., Am. Coll. Trial Lawyers (diplomate). Family and matrimonial.

GOUTTIERE, JOHN P. lawyer; b. Toledo, Mar. 18, 1949; BA in Am. Studies, Bowling Green State U., 1971; JD, Ohio No. U., 1974. Bar: Ohio 1974, U.S. Dist. Ct. (no. dist.) Ohio 1975, U.S. Supreme Ct. 1997. Ptnr. Ferstle & Gouttiere, Toledo, 1975-85; pres. John P Gouttiere Co. LPA, Toledo, 1985—. Adj. prof. U. Toledo Coll. Law. Pres. Corp. for Legal Svcs. and Assistance to the Poor, 1996-99, Toledo Legal Aid Soc., bd. trustees, 1987-96, pres., 1994-96. Mem. Am. Bankruptcy Inst., Ohio State Bar Assn., Lucas County Bar Assn. (pres. 1986), Toledo Bar Assn., Comml. Law League Am. Commercial, contracts (including sales of goods; commercial financing), Probate (including wills, trusts), Property, real (including real estate development, water). Office: John P Gouttiere Co LPA 520 Madison Ave Ste 1026 Toledo OH 43604-1341 E-mail: JohnG@GouttiereLaw.com.

GOVER, ALAN SHORE, lawyer; b. Lyons, N.Y., Sept. 5, 1948; s. Norman Marvin and Beatrice L. (Shore) G.; m. Ellen Rae Ross, Dec. 4, 1976; children: Maxwell Ross, Mary Trace. AB, Tufts U., 1970; JD, Georgetown U., 1973. Bar: Tex. 1973, D.C. 1980, U.S. Dist. Ct. (so. dist.) Tex. 1974, U.S. Dist. Ct. (we. dist.) Tex. 1976, U.S Dist. Ct. (no. dist.) Tex. 1988, U.S. Dist. Ct. (ea. dist.) Tex. 1990, U.S. Ct. Appeals (5th cir.) 1974, U.S. Ct. Appeals (D.C. cir.) 1977, U.S. Dist. Ct. (we. dist.) 1979, U.S. Ct. Appeals (2d cir.) 1979, D.C. 1980, U.S. Ct. Appeals (9th and 11th cirs.) 1981, U.S. Ct. Appeals (8th cir.) 1981, U.S. Supreme Ct. 1976. Assoc. Baker & Botts, Houston, 1973-80, ptnr., 1981-85, Weil, Gotshal & Manges, Houston, 1985—2001; Houston ptnr. Dewey Ballantine LLP, 2001—. Co-author: The Texas Nonjudicial Foreclosure Process, 1990; editor, chmn. editorial bd. P.L.I. Oil and Gas and Bankruptcy Laws, 1985. V.p. Congregation Beth Israel, Houston, 1996-2001, pres., 2001—; trustee Houston Ballet, 1986—, v.p., 1993-96; chmn. ann. fund St. John's Sch., Houston, 1993-95, trustee 1996—; trustee Retina Rsch. Found., Houston, St. John's Sch., Houston, 1996—; chmn. East Downtown Mgmt. Dist., Houston, 2000—.. Fellow Tex. Bar Found.; mem. ABA, Coronado Club, N.Y. Athletic Club, The Argyle (San Antonio). Jewish. Finance, Mergers and acquisitions, Utilities, public. Office: Dewey Ballantine LLP 700 Louisiana St Ste 1900 Houston TX 77002

GOWA, ANDREW, real estate investor, lawyer; b. N.Y.C., Nov. 6, 1949; s. Everett M. and Louise (Friedman) G.; m. Robin P. Lincoln May 21, 1995; children: Catherine J., Jon T., Timothy M., Melissa Lincoln, Jennifer Lincoln. AB magna cum laude, Tufts U., 1971; JD, U. Pa., 1974. Bar: Pa. 1974, N.Y. 1982. From assoc. to ptnr. Blank, Rome, Comisky & McCauley, Phila., 1974-84; sr. v.p North Atlantic Investment Corp., Phila., 1984-85; pres., chief exec. officer First Equity Devel. Corp., West Chester, Pa., 1984-90; ptnr. Schnader Harrison Segal & Lewis LLP, Phila., 1990—2002; chmn. Gowa Lincoln, PC, Phila., 2002—. Bd. dirs. Equitrust Real Estate Corp., West Chester; developer Brampton Chase, Malvern, Pa., 1988-89; faculty Grad. Builders Inst. Pa. State U., State Coll., 1987-90; faculty Pa. Bar Inst., 1991—; chmn. Allegheny Cardiovascular Inst., 1997, Likoff Cardiovascular Inst., 1995-97. Mem. Tufts U. Alumni Coun., Medford, Mass., 1982—; bd. overseers Tufts U., Medford, 1988-93; bd. dirs. Kaiserman Ctr. Jewish Community Ctrs. Phila, 1982-88. Recipient Disting. Service medal Tufts U., 1982. Mem. Pa. Bar Assn. (ho. dels. 1983-87), Phila. Bar Assn. (bd. govs. 1985, chmn. real estate sect. 1985, exec. com. real estate sect. 1983-89), Am. Coll. Real Estate Laywers, Internat. Coun. Shopping Ctrs. Avocations: amateur radio, cooking. Office: Gowa Lincoln PC 1525 Locust St Ste 1000 Philadelphia PA 19102 Fax: 215-320-9006. E-mail: andy@gowalaw.com.

GOWDY, FRANKLIN BROCKWAY, lawyer; b. Burlington, Iowa, Dec. 27, 1945; s. Franklin Kamm and Dorothy Faye (Brockway) G.; m. Jennifer June McKenrick, Nov. 27, 1982; stepchildren: Jeffrey F. Hammond, Tracy Lawrence, Jonathan R. Hammond, Julie E. Rawls. BA in Polit. Sci., Stanford U., 1967; JD, U. Calif., Berkeley, 1970. Bar: U.S. Dist. Ct. (no. dist.) Calif. 1971, U.S. Ct. Appeals (9th cir.) 1971, U.S. Supreme Ct. 1979, U.S. Dist. Ct. (cen. dist.) Calif. 1984. Assoc. Brobeck, Phleger & Harrison, San Francisco, 1971-78, ptnr., 1978—. Fellow Am. Coll. Trial Lawyers; mem. ABA, Calif. Bar Assn., San Francisco Bar Assn., Assn. Bus. Trial Lawyers (bd. govs.). Antitrust, Federal civil litigation, State civil litigation.

Home: 3428 Shangrila Rd Lafayette CA 94549-2423 Office: Morgan Lewis Bockius LLP Spear St Tower 1 Market Plz San Francisco CA 94105-1420 E-mail: fgowdy@brobeck.com.

GOWIN, RICHARD BRYAN, lawyer; b. Louisville, Oct. 16, 1969; s. Charles R. and Sherrin M. Gowin; m. Lisa M. Gowin, Dec. 19, 1998. BS, U. Ky., 1992, JD, 1996. Bar: Ky. 1997. Law clk. U.S. Army Corps Engrs., Louisville, 1992, Ky. Local Governance Project, Lexington, Ky., 1993-96; atty. Hoge & Assocs., Louisville, 1997—2002; pvt. practice Louisville, 2002. Mem. ABA, Ky. Bar Assn., Louisville Bar Assn. (family law sect.). Family and matrimonial. Home: 3226 Eagle Pass Louisville KY 40213-1273 Office: Bryan Gowin Atty at Law Ste 506 Legal Arts Bldg 200 S 7th St Louisville KY 40202

GRAB, FREDERICK CHARLES, lawyer; b. N.Y.C., Aug. 1, 1946; s. Daniel Justin and Elizabeth (Kam) G. BS in Aerospace Engring., Polytech U. N.Y., 1967; JD, U. So. Calif., 1977. Bar: Calif. 1978, U.S. Dist. Ct. (cen. dist.) Calif. 1978, U.S. Supreme Ct. 1988, U.S. Ct. Appeals (9th cir.) 1989. Deputy atty. gen. Calif. Atty. Gen., L.A., 1977-2000. Polit. journalist: ; contbr. articles to profl. jours. Polit. activist. Avocations: playwright, author, composer, musican.

GRABOW, RAYMOND JOHN, mayor, lawyer; b. Cleve., Jan. 27, 1932; s. Joseph Stanley and Frances (Kalata) G.; m. Margaret Jean Knoll, Nov. 27, 1969; children: Rachel Jean, Ryan Joseph. BSBA, Kent State U., 1953; JD, Western Res. U., 1958. Bar: Ohio 1958. Counsel No. Ohio Petroleum Retailers Assn., Cleve., 1965-78; counsel, trustee Alliance of Poles Fed. Credit Union, 1972; also gen. counsel Alliance of Poles of Am., Parma Polish Am. League; councilman City of Warrensville Heights (Ohio), 1962-68, mayor, 1968-98. Sec. Space Comfort Co., S.S.K., Inc.; fed. panelist U.S. Dist. Ct.; active Dem. Exec. Com. Cuyahoga County, 1966—98, precinct com., 1966—80; trustee Brentwood Hosp., Nat. League Cities, Brentwood Found.; bd. govs. Meridia Southpoint Hosp., 1996—99. Mem. Ohio Jud. Conf. (life), Ohio State Bar Assn., Cuyahoga County Bar Assn., Cleve. Bar Assn., U.S. Conf. of Mayors, Am. Legion, PLAV Vets, Cleve. Soc., Warrensville Heights C. of C. (trustee 1989-98), Ohio Assn. Pub. Safety Dirs., Ohio Mcpl. League, Mcpl. Treas. Assn., Order of Alhambra, Fraternal Order of Eagles, West Harbor Lagoons Assn. (pres.). Home: 10545 Cambridge Cir Cleveland OH 44133- Office: 5005 Rockside Rd Cleveland OH 44131-2194 Business E-Mail: rjggf@juno.com.

GRACE, JAMES MARTIN, JR., lawyer; b. Columbus, Ohio, Sept. 6, 1967; s. James Martin and Letitia Jean (Stively) G.; m. Michèle Lee Sirna, June 22, 1991. BA, U. Notre Dame, 1989; JD cum laude, U. Houston, 1992. Bar: Tex. Law clk. to Hon. Samuel B. Kent U.S. Dist. Ct. (so. dist.) Tex., Galveston, 1992-93; assoc. Baker Botts, LLP, Houston, 1993-2000; sr. counsel Enron N.Am. Corp., Houston, 2000-2001; mgr. Enron Wholesale Svcs., Houston, 2001—02; dir. Tex. state affairs Ctr. Point Energy Inc., Houston, 2002—. Author tchr.'s guide: Copyright Law, 1992. Adv. coun. Local Initiatives Support Corp.; pres. R Club PAC, 1998-99; co-chair Young Profls. for Aspiring Youth, 2000-02. Mem.: Greater Heights Area C. of C. (bd. dirs. 2002—), Houston Law Rev. Alumni Assn. (dir.), Houston Bar Assn., State Bar Tex., U. Notre Dame Alumni Assn. (treas. Class of '89), Notre Dame Club Houston (bd. dirs.), Houston Jaycees (dir. edn. 1993—94, legal counsel 1994, Outstanding Leadership award 1993, Silver Key award 1994), Order of the Barons, Phi Delta Phi. Republican. Roman Catholic. Avocations: soccer, football, reading. Mergers and acquisitions, Securities. Office: Ctr Point Energy Inc 1111 Louisiana St Houston TX 77002 E-mail: jim.m.grace@centerpointenergy.com.

GRACE, WALTER CHARLES, retired prosecutor; b. Elmira, N.Y., Mar. 4, 1947; s. Claude Henry and Grace Anne (Richardson) G.; m. Barbbara Lynn Eaglen, Oct. 3, 1981; children: Katherine Anne, Charles Brigham. BA History, Duke U., 1969; JD, U. Tenn., 1972. Bar: Ill., 1972; U.S. Dist. Ct. (ea. and so. dists.) Ill., 1972. Asst. state's atty. Jackson County, Murphysboro, Ill., 1972-73; assoc. Donald R. Mitchell Law Office, Carbondale, Ill., 1973-74; atty. Jackson County Pub. Defender, Murphysboro, 1974-77; ptnr. Lockwood & Grace, Carbondale, 1977-78, pvt. practice, 1978-79; ptnr. Hendricks, Watt & Grace, Murphysboro, 1979-82; assoc. Feirich, Schone, Mager, Green & Assocs., Carbondale, 1982-83, Feirch, Schoen, Mager, Green & Assocs., Carbondale, 1983-88; state's atty. Jackson County State's Atty., Murphysboro, 1988-93; U.S. Atty. U.S. Atty.'s Office, Fairview Heights, Ill., 1993—2002. Chmn. Jackson County Child Advocacy Adv. Bd., 1988-93; adv. bd. Ill. State Violent Crime Victim's Adv. Bd., 1988-90; com. mem. Jackson County Juv. Justice Task Force, 1988-93; exec. com. Ill. State's Atty.'s Assn., 1991-93; legis. com. Ill. Sate's Atty.'s Assn., 1992-93; co-chmn. Jackson County SAFE Policy/Gang Policy Interagy. Steering Com. Adv. Bd., 1991-93; master So. Ill. Am. Inn. of Ct., 1992—; others. Active NAACP., Carbondale; mem. Jackson County Heart Fund Campaign, 1976-77; bd. dirs. Carbondale United Way, 1978-80, capt. campaign drive, profl. div., 1980; mem. planning com. John A. Logan Coll.-Jackson County Bar Assn. Continuing Edn. Programs; mem. adv. com. to Corrections and Law Enforcment Programs, So. Ill. U. Sch. of Tech. Careers, 1978-89; mem. Hill House Board, Inc., 1979-84; pres. 1980-82; lector St. Francis Xavier Ch., Carbondale. Mem. Jackson County Bar Assn. (sec. 1978-79, pres. 1980-81), Ill. State Bar Assn. (mem. criminal law sect., family law sect., tort law sect.), ABA (family law and criminal law sects.), Assn. Trial Lawyers of Am., Nat. Legal Aid and Defender Assn., Ill. Pub. Defenders Assn., So. Ill. Am. Inns of Ct. (barrister 1993-95). Democrat. Roman Catholic. Avocations: golf, swimming, cooking, enology.*

GRAD, FRANK PAUL, law educator, lawyer; b. Vienna, May 2, 1924; came to U.S., 1939, naturalized, 1943; s. Morris and Clara Sophie (Scher) G.; m. Lisa Szilagyi, Dec. 6, 1946; children: David Anthony, Catharine Ann. BA magna cum laude, Bklyn. Coll., 1947; LLB, Columbia U., 1949. Bar: N.Y. 1949. Assoc. in law Columbia U. Law Sch., N.Y.C., 1949-50, asst. dir. Legis. Drafting Research Fund, 1953-55, assoc. dir., 1956-68, dir., 1969-95, faculty, 1954-69, prof., 1969—, Joseph P. Chamberlain prof. legis., 1982-95, Joseph P. Chamberlain prof. emeritus legis. and spl. lectr., 1995—; legal adv. com. U.S. Council Environ. Quality, 1970-73; mem. N.Y. Deptl. Com. Ct. Adminstrn., Appellate Div., 1st Dept., 1970-74; counsel N.Y. State Spl. Adv. Panel Med. Malpractice, 1975; legal counsel Nat. Mcpl. League, 1967-88. Cons. in field; reporter U.S. Superfund Study group, 1981-82; dir. rsch. N.Y.C. Charter Revision Commn., 1982-83, N.Y. State-City Commn. on Integrity in Govt., 1986. Author: Public Health Law Manual, 1st edit., 1965, 2d rev. edit., 1990, The Drafting of State Constitutions, 1963, Environmental law: Sources and Problems, 3d edit., 1985, 4th edit. (with Joel Mintz), 2000, Treatise on Environmental Law, 8 vols., 1973—; co-author other legal reports; contbr. articles to profl. jours.; draftsman mcpl. codes and state legislation. With AUS, 1943-46. 10th Horace E. Read Meml. lectr. Dalhousie Law Sch., 1984. Mem. ABA, APHA, Assn. of Bar of City of N.Y., N.Y. Bar Assn., Am. Law Inst., Am. Soc. Law and Medicine, World Conservation Union (commn. on environ. law 1991—), Human Genome Orgn., Internat. Coun. Environ. Law, N.Y.. Soc. Med. Jurisprudence. Office: Columbia U Sch Law 435 W 116th St New York NY 10027-7297 E-mail: fgrad@law.columbia.edu.

GRADDICK, CHARLES ALLEN, lawyer; b. Mobile, Ala., Dec. 10, 1944; s. Julian and Elvera (Smith) G.; m. Corinne Whiting, Aug. 19, 1966; children: Charles Allen, Herndon Whiting, Corinne. JD, Cumberland Sch. Law, 1970. Bar: Ala. 1970. Clk. Ala. Supreme Ct., 1970; asst. dist. atty. County of Mobile, Ala., 1971-75, dist. atty., 1975-79; atty. gen. State of Ala., Montgomery, 1979-87; ptnr. Thorton, Farish and Gaunt, Montgomery, 1987-89, Anderson, Graddick and Nabors, P.C., Montgomery, 1989-90; dist. atty. Montgomery County, Montgomery County, Ala., 1991-93; ptnr. Graddick & Belser, P.C., Montgomery and Mobile, 1992-99, Sims, Graddick & Dodson, Mobile, 2000—. Served with USNG, 1969-96. Named Outstanding Young Man of Mobile, Mobile Jaycees, 1976, State Conservationist of Yr., Ala. Wildlife Fedn.; recipient cert. appreciation Ala. Peace Officers, 1978, Appreciation award Optimists, 1978. Mem. ABA, ATLA, Ala. Bar Assn., Mobile Bar Assn., Montgomery Bar Assn., Ala. Trial Lawyers Assn., Ala. Dist. Attys. Assn., Nat. Dist. Attys. Assn., Nat. Assn. Attys. Gen. Republican. Episcopalian. Office: Sims Graddick & Dodson 205 Saint Emanuel St Mobile AL 36602-3009 E-mail: cag@simsgraddick.com.

GRADER, SCOTT PAUL, lawyer; b. Bklyn., June 25, 1956; s. Jack and Bernice Grader; m. Patricia Lande, Feb. 11, 1995; one child, Louisa Frances Duo. BA with honors, CUNY, 1977; JD with honors, Rutgers U., 1980; LLM, U. London, 1983. Bar: N.Y. 1981. Asst. gen. counsel N.Y.C. Office of Econ. Devel., 1981-82; assoc. Cahill, Gordon & Reindel, N.Y.C., 1984-86, Paul, Weiss, Rifkind, Wharton & Garrison, N.Y.C., 1986-97, counsel, 1998—. Assoc. editor Rutgers-Camden Law Rev., 1978-80. Hague Acad. Internat. scholar, The Hague, The Netherlands, 1983. Mem. Assn. of Bar of City of N.Y. Corporate, general, Mergers and acquisitions, Securities. Home: 670 W End Ave Apt 14C New York NY 10025-7328 Office: Paul Weiss Rifkind Wharton & Garrison 1285 Ave of the Ams New York NY 10019 E-mail: sgrader@paulweiss.com.

GRADY, GREGORY, lawyer, banker; b. Takoma Park, Md., Oct. 10, 1945; s. Francis Joseph Grady and Deane (McGehee) Black; m. Carol Love Harrison, Feb. 25, 1978; children: Olivia Love, Blake McGregor, Harrison Edwards. Grad., Bullis Sch., Potomac, Md., 1964; BA in Econs., U. Va., 1969; JD, Tulane U., 1972. Bar: D.C. 1973, U.S. Ct. Appeals (D.C. cir.) 1973, U.S. Ct. Appeals (4th cir.) 1975, U.S. Supreme Ct. 1976, U.S. Ct. Appeals (5th cir.) 1977, U.S. Ct. Appeals (10th cir.) 1979, U.S. Ct. Appeals (11th cir.) 1981, U.S. Ct. Appeals (6th cir.) 1982, U.S. Dist. Ct. 1988. Staff atty., supervisory atty. FPC, Washington, 1972-74; assoc. Littman, Richter, Wright & Talisman, P.C., Washington, 1974-79; mem. Wright & Talisman, P.C., Washington, 1979—, pres., chmn. bd. dirs., chmn. exec. com., 1997-98, mng. mem., 1999—. Bd. dirs. Bank of Franklin, Miss., D.R. McGehee Ins. Agy., Inc., Miss. Mem. Energy Bar Assn., D.C. Bar Assn., The Federalist Soc., Congl. Country Club. Republican. Episcopalian. Administrative and regulatory, Federal civil litigation, FERC practice. Home: 666 Live Oak Dr Mc Lean VA 22101-1569 Office: Wright & Talisman PC 1200 G St NW Ste 600 Washington DC 20005-3838

GRADY, JOHN F. federal judge; b. Chgo., May 23, 1929; s. John F. and Lucille F. (Shroder) G.; m. Patsy Grady, Aug. 10, 1968; 1 child, John F. BS, Northwestern U., 1952, JD, 1954. Bar: Ill. 1955. Assoc. Sonnenschein, Berkson, Lautmann, Levinson & Morse, Chgo., 1954-56; asst. U.S. atty. No. Dist. Ill., 1956-61, chief criminal divsn., 1960-61; assoc. Snyder, Clarke, Dalziel, Holmquist & Johnson, Waukegan, Ill., 1961-63; practice law Waukegan, 1963-76; judge U.S. Dist. Ct. (no. dist.) Ill., Chgo., 1976-86, chief judge, 1986-90, sr. judge, 1994—. Mem. com. criminal law U.S. Jud. Conf., 1982-87, adv. com. civil rules, 1984-90, chair, 1987-90; mem. bench book com. Fed. Jud. Ctr., 1988-93; mem. Nat. State-Fed. Jud. Coun., 1990-92, Jud. Panel on Multidist. Litigation, 1992-2000. Assoc. editor: Northwestern U. Law Rev. Mem. Phi Beta Kappa Office: US Dist Ct Rm 2286 219 S Dearborn St Ste 2286 Chicago IL 60604-1802*

GRADY, JOSEPH HAROLD, lawyer, former judge; b. Williamsport, Pa., Feb. 27, 1917; s. Thomas Leo and Edythe (Grange) G.; m. May 26, 1942; children— Maureen Grady Callahan, Joseph Harold, Kathleen Grady Travers, Thomas L. B.A., Loyola U., Balt., 1938; LL.B., U. Md., 1942. Bar: Md. 1942. Spl. agt. FBI, Washington, 1942-46; asst. and dep. state's atty., Balt., 1947-56; state's atty. City of Balt. 1956-59; mayor City of Balt., 1959-62; assoc. judge Cir. Ct. for City of Balt., 1962-80, chief judge, 1980-84; ptnr. Siskind, Burch, Grady & Rosen, Balt., 1984— . Democrat. Roman Catholic. State civil litigation, General practice. Home: Lutherville Timonium, Md. Died Jan. 9, 2002.

GRADY, KEVIN E. lawyer; b. Charlotte, N.C., Jan. 19, 1948; s. Thomas F. and Rosemary (Loughran) G.; m. Mary Beth O'Brien, Dec. 27, 1975; children: Martin E., Donald F. BA, Vanderbilt U., 1969; JD, Harvard U., 1974. Bar: Ga. 1974, U.S. Dist. Ct. (no. dist.) Ga. 1975, U.S. Ct. Appeals (11th cir.) 1981, U.S. Supreme Ct. 1990. Assoc. Jones, Bird & Howell, Atlanta, 1974-76; trial atty. Antitrust divsn. U.S. Dept. Justice, Atlanta, 1976-77; ptnr. Alston & Bird, Atlanta, 1977—. Editor: Georgia Hospital Law Manual, 1997. Mem. bd. trust Vanderbilt U., 1995-97; hon. consul gen. of Sri Lanka to Georgia, 2000—. Recipient Top Hat award St. Vincent de Paul Soc., 1995. Mem. ABA (chair antitrust sect. 2003-), Ga. Acad. Healthcare Attys. (pres. 1997-98), Am. Health Lawyers Assn. (vice chair antitrust program 1992-99, chair 1999—), Am. Counsel Assn. (dir. 1991-2000, pres. 1995), State Bar Ga. (health law sect., chair 1999-2000). Democrat. Roman Catholic. Avocations: running, reading. Antitrust, Federal civil litigation, Health. Office: Alston & Bird 1201 W Peachtree St NW Ste 4200 Atlanta GA 30309-3449

GRADY, MARK F. dean, law educator; b. 1948; AB, UCLA, 1970, JD, 1973. Bar: Pa. 1975. Dir. office of policy planning & evaluation FTC, Washington, 1975-77; project mgr. Am. Mgmt. Systems, Inc., Arlington, Va., 1978-79; prof. Northwestern U., Chgo., 1985—92; John M. Olin vis. prof. law and econs. Duke U., 1992—93; prof. law UCLA; dean and prof. law George Mason U., Arlington, Va., 1997—. Minority Counsel Senate Jud. Com., Washington, 1979; mem. Cons. Dept of Energy, Washington, 1978. Fellow U. Chgo. 1977, Civil Liability Yale, 1982. Mem. Phi Beta Kappa. Office: George Mason U Sch Law Dean Office Rm 209 3301 N Fairfax Dr Arlington VA 22201-4498

GRADY, MAUREEN FRANCES, lawyer; b. N.Y.C., Oct. 6, 1960; d. Frank J. and Pauline (Laberge) G. BA, Manhattan Coll., 1982; JD, Georgetown U., 1985. Bar: N.Y. 1986, U.S. Dist. Ct. (so. and ea. dists.) N.Y. 1987, U.S. Ct. Appeals (2d cir.) 1990. Assoc. Griffin, Scully & Savona, N.Y.C., 1985-87, Morris & Duffy, N.Y.C., 1987-88, Summit, Rovins & Feldesman, N.Y.C., 1988-89; asst. gen. counsel N.Y.C. Transit Authority, 1989-92; trial atty. Fireman's Fund Ins. Co., N.Y.C., 1992-97; sr. assoc. DeCicco Gibbons & McNamara, P.C., N.Y.C., 1998-99; assoc. Kral Clerkin Redmond Ryan Perry & Girvan, N.Y.C., 1999-2000, Schwartzapfel Novick Truhowsky & Marcus, P.C., 2000-2001. Asst. vice pres. Am. Arbitration Assn., 2001—, N.Y. state EMT, 2000-. Recipient Bur. Nat. Affairs award, 1985. Mem. Assn. Bar City N.Y. (young lawyers com. 1987-90, constrn. law com. 1991-92, spl. com. on alcoholism and substance abuse 1994-97, sec. spl. com. on alcoholism and substance abuse 1995-97, product liability com. 1995-98, lesbian, gay, transgender rights com. 2001—, chair 2003—, mem. spl. task force on women in the cts., 2003-), Phi Beta Kappa, Epsilon Sigma Pi, Phi Alpha Theta. Insurance, Personal injury (including property damage), Product liability. E-mail: GradyM@adr.org.

GRADY, THOMAS MICHAEL, lawyer; b. Boston, Nov. 10, 1952; s. John C. and Jean M. (Harvey) G.; m. Jacquelyn Roberts, May 15, 1982; children: David R., Caroline M. AB, Harvard U., 1975; JD, Suffolk U., 1981. Bar: Ill. 1981, Pa. 1987. Atty. Container Corp. Am., Chgo., 1981-84, regional atty. Carol Stream, Ill., 1984-86, sr. regional atty. Valley Forge, Pa., 1986; sr. counsel Rohm & Haas Co., Phila., 1986—. Mem. Am. Corp. Counsel Assn., Nat. Agrl. Chems. Assn. (law com. 1990-93). Antitrust, Corporate, general, Mergers and acquisitions. Home: 537 Beaumont Cir West Chester PA 19380-6437 Office: Rohm and Haas Co Independence Mall Philadelphia PA 19105

GRAEBNER, CAROL F. lawyer; b. 1954; BA internat. rels., Dickinson Coll.; law degree, Am. Univ. Exec. v.p. and gen. coun. Dynegy Inc.; sr. v.p. and gen. coun. Duke Energy Internat., 1998; gen. coun. Conoco Global Power, Inc. Office: Office of Gen Coun 1000 Louisiana Ste 5800 Houston TX 77002*

GRAF, SHERYL SUSAN, lawyer; b. Auburn, Wash., Feb. 23, 1959; d. Lawrence S. and Joyce May Graf; widowed, 1983; m. Gerald Cox, Feb. 14, 1987. AA, Grossmont Coll., El Cajon, Calif., 1977; JD, Thomas Jefferson Sch. Law, San Diego, 1994. Bar: Calif. 1995, U.S. Dist. Ct. (so. dist.) Calif. 1995, U.S. Supreme Ct. 1999. Exec. adminstr. Anacomp, Inc., San Diego, 1980-91; lawyer Law Offices of Sheryl S. Graf, El Cajon, Calif., 1995—. Contbr. articles to law revs. Mem. San Diego County Bar Assn. (chair solo and small firm sect. 1996-97), Calif. Attys. for Criminal Justice, Foothills Bar Assn. (bd. dirs. 2000-03), Calif. Women Lawyers, Lawyers Club East County (bd. dirs. 1997—, pres. 1999-01), Delta Theta Phi. Avocation: skiing. Bankruptcy, Criminal, Family and matrimonial. Office: 275 E Douglas Ave Ste 115 El Cajon CA 92020-4548

GRAFF, DOUGLAS ERIC, lawyer; b. Cleve., Apr. 7, 1953; s. Richard Alison and Lois Marie (Boehmer) G.; m. Jean Stevens, Jan. 20, 1989; children: Jenna Leigh, Joel Douglas. BA, Capital U., 1974; MPA, Am. U., 1981; JD, Ohio State U., 1984. Bar: Ohio 1985, U.S. Dist. Ct. (so. dist.) Ohio 1986, U.S. Ct. Appeals (6th cir.) 1995, U.S. Supreme Ct. 1997. Program analyst Nat. Adv. Coun. Edn. Disadvantaged Children, Washington, 1975-76; v.p. ops. Royal Gen. Co., Cleve., 1976-80; pvt. practice law Columbus, OH, 1985—; assoc. counsel, dir. hosp. med. staff svcs. Ohio State Med. Assn., 1985-91; mng. ptnr. Graff & Assocs., L.P.A., 1991—; ptnr., mem. exec. com. Robins Preston Beckett Graff et al., Columbus, 1998-2000. Adj. faculty dept. health and human svcs. Columbus State U., 1993—; bd. dirs. Columbus Blue Cross/Blue Shield Fed. Credit Union, 1986-95, pres., 1988-94; speaker in field. Author: Physician's Guide to Ohio Law, 1989, Ohio Model Medical Staff By-laws, 1990, Law of Massage Therapy in Ohio, 1992, 96, 2000, Medical Records and the Law in Ohio, 1993, 98; contbr. articles to profl. jours. Mem. ABA, Am. Soc. Assn. Execs., Nat. Health Lawyers Assn., Ohio State Bar Assn., Ohio Soc. Assn. Execs., Columbus Bar Assn., Delta Sigma Rho, Tau Kappa Alpha, Phi Alpha Delta. Administrative and regulatory, Health, Property, real (including real estate development, water). Home: 13391 Havens Corners Rd SW Pataskala OH 43062-7784 Office: 604 E Rich St Columbus OH 43215-5341 Fax: 614-228-8811. E-mail: deg@grafflaw.com.

GRAFFEO, VICTORIA A. state supreme court judge; b. Rockville Centre, NY, Apr. 13, 1952; m. Edward E. Winders. BA, SUNY, Oneonta, 1974; JD Albany Law Sch., Union U., 1977. Pvt. practice, 1978—82; asst. counsel N.Y. State Div. Alcoholism and Alcohol Abuse, 1982—84; counsel to minority leader pro tempore Kemp Hannon N.Y. State Assembly, 1984—89, chief counsel to minority leader Clarence D. Rappleyea Jr., 1989—94; solicitor gen. State of NY, 1995—96; judge NY State Supreme Ct. (3d jud. dist.), 1996—98; assoc. justice Appellate div., 3d dept., 1998—2000; assoc. judge N.Y. Ct. Appeals, 2000—. Office: 20 Eagle St Albany NY 12207

GRAFFER, JACOPO, lawyer; b. Trento, Italy, Aug. 23, 1973; s. Filippo Graffer and Loredana Zampini. Law degree, U. Bologna, 1999. Jr. assoc. Franzosi, Dalmero & Ptnrs., Milan, 1999—2001; trainee Clifford Chance Rogers & Wells, N.Y.C., 2001; assoc. Notarbartolo and Gervasi, Milan, 2001—. Contbr. articles to profl. jours. Intellectual property, Commercial, contracts (including sales of goods; commercial financing), Patent. Home: V G Bruno 13 20154 Milan Italy Office: Franzosi, Dalnegro & Ptnrs Corso diPorta Vittoria 9 20122 Milan Italy Office Fax: 02 54179920.

GRAFSTEIN, JOEL M. lawyer; b. N.Y.C., May 27, 1948; s. Max G. and Elaine (Weisner) G.; m. Andree M. Clement, Aug. 4, 1974; 1 son, Michael Louis. BS, U. Bridgeport, 1970; JD, N.Y. Law Sch., 1973; LLM, NYU, 1974. Bar: N.Y. 1973, Conn. 1973, U.S. Dist. Ct. Conn. 1973, U.S. Tax Ct. 1973. Assoc. Rome & Case, Bloomfield, Conn., 1974-82, Albrecht, Zelman, Hartford, Conn., 1982-83; ptnr. Lublin, Wolfe, Kantor & Silver, East Hartford, Conn., 1984—1989. Author: Connecticut Collection Law 1982, 83; Connecticut Foreclosure Law, 1984, 87; Bankruptcy: A Primer, 1984, 2d edit., 1987; The Connecticut Unfair Trade Practices Act, 1986, Problem Loans in Connecticut, 1988, Connecticut Forclosure Law, 2001, Chmn. Republican Town Com., Barkhamstead, Conn., 1980-82; region chmn. Disaster Relief Com., Hartford, 1978-83. Mem. ABA, Conn. Bar Assn. (exec. com. 1978-83), Hartford County Bar Assn. Club: Lions (treas. 1976-80) (Bloomfield, Conn.). Bankruptcy, Corporate, general. Home: 20 Pond Rd Canton CT 06019-2623 Office: Grafstein & Assoc 10 Melrose Dr Farmington CT 06034

GRAGG, KARL LAWRENCE, lawyer; b. Watertown, N.Y., Sept. 25, 1946; s. Karl Lawrence and Pauline (Sykes) G.; m. Maureen Gilluly, Dec. 13, 1975; children: Meaghan Christina, Erika Lawrence, Jenny Camille. BS, Fla. State U., 1968; JD, U. Fla., 1974, LLM in Taxation, 1975. Bar: Fla. 1975, U.S Dist. Ct. (so. dist.) Fla., U.S. Tax Ct., U.S. Ct. Appeals (5th cir.). Assoc. Mershon, Sawyer, Johnson, Dunwoody & Cole, Miami, Fla., 1975-80, ptnr., 1980-82, Gunster, Yoakley, Criser & Stewart, Palm Beach, Fla., 1982-84, Walker Ellis Gragg & Deaktor, Miami, 1984-86, White & Case, LLP, Miami, 1987—. Adj. prof. law U. Miami, 1978-89; mem. tax com. Fla. Ho. of Reps., Tallahassee, 1983. Contbr. articles to U. Fla. Law Rev. Vol. Miami United Way, 1977-80. Mem. ABA (taxation sect.), Nat. Assn. State Bar (chmn. 1986), Am. Coll. Tax Counsel, Fla. Bar Assn. (tax sect., chmn. tax sect. 1991, chmn. coun. of sect.), Nat. Assn. Indsl. and Office Parks (bd. dirs. 1989-91), Ctr. for Health Techs., Inc. (bd. dirs. 1992-98), Japan Soc. South Fla. (bd. dirs. 1990-98). Corporate taxation, Taxation, general, State and local taxation. Office: White & Case LLP 200 S Biscayne Blvd Ste 4900 Miami FL 33131-2352

GRAHAM, DAVID, lawyer; b. Newcastle Upon Tyne, Eng., Sept. 14, 1958; s. Arthur and Audrey Graham; m. Janette Tuerese Flynn, July 4, 1990; children: Emma Jane, Samantha Frances. BA, Oxford U., 1981. Bar: Eng. and Wales 1984, Hong Kong 1998. Trainee solicitor Freshfields, London, 1982-84, solicitor, 1984-87, N.Y.C., 1987-90, ptnr. London, 1992-98, Hong Kong, 1998—2001; acting gen. counsel Asia Pacific Morgan Stanley Dean Witter, Hong Kong, 1999—2001; gen. counsel, mng. dir. Asia Pacific Morgan Stanley Dean Witter, 2001—. Joint sec. Panel on Takeovers adn Mergers, London, 1990-92. Author: (book) Practitioners Guide to U.K. Takeovers and Mergers, 3d. edit., 1997. Mem. City of London Solicitors Co., Law Soc. Eng. and Wales, Law Soc. Hong Kong. Avocations: golf, tennis. Corporate, general, Mergers and acquisitions. Home: House 41 Strawberry Hill 8 Plunketti Rd The Peak Hong Kong Hong Kong Office: Morgan Stanley Dean Witter Asia Limited 6F Tower II Exchange Sq Central Hong Kong Hong Kong

GRAHAM, DAVID ANTONY, lawyer; b. N.Y.C., Feb. 3, 1953; s. Lorenz Bell Jr. and Adele (Hersher) G.; children: Xochitl, Joaquin, Esmeralda, Erica, Julian, Miguel. AA, Community Coll., Denver, 1976; BA in Econs., U. Denver, 1978; JD, U. N.Mex., 1981. Bar: Colo. 1981, N.Mex. 1982, Alaska 1997, U.S. Dist. Ct. Colo. 1981, U.S. Ct. Appeals (10th cir.) 1981, U.S. Dist. Ct. N.Mex. 1982. Ptnr. Graham & Graham, Denver, 1981-82, San Luis, Colo., 1982-85, Lopez, Chavez & Graham, Taos, N.Mex., 1985-88; pvt. practice Taos, 1988—. City atty. Municipality of San Luis, 1983-94. Capt. CAP. Fellow HEW, 1978-81; grantee U. Denver, 1976-78. Mem. Assn. Trial Lawyers Am., N.Mex. Trial Lawyers Assn., Aircraft Owners and Pilots Assn. State civil litigation, Criminal, Personal injury (including property damage). Office: 408 Lake St Sitka AK 99835-7469 E-mail: dgsitka@att.net.

GRAHAM, DAVID BROWNING, lawyer; b. Wildwood, N.J., Dec. 20, 1942; s. William Browning and Mary Graham; m. Linda Lea Beasley, Feb. 20, 1971; children: Owen, Mary. BS, La. State U., 1966, JD, 1969. Bar: La. 1969, D.C. 1972, U.S. Ct. Appeals (D.C. cir.) 1974, Ill. 1980, Ohio 1999. Atty. U.S. EPA, Washington, 1972-73; corp. counsel Nat. Rural Elec. Coop. Assn., Washington, 1973-77; dir. office hearing and appeals U.S. Dept. Interior, Arlington, Va., 1977-79; dep. gen. counsel Velsicol Chem. Corp., Chgo., 1979-84; ptnr. Freedman, Levy, Kroll & Simonds, Washington, 1984-89, Kaye, Scholer, Fierman, Hays & Handler, Washington, 1989-92, Howrey & Simon, Washington, 1992-98, Baker & Hostetler, Cleve., 1998—2003, Kaufman & Canoles, Williamsburg, Va., 2003—. Mem. bd. advisors Toxics Law Reporter, Washington, 1987—, Chem. Waste Litigation Reporter, Washington, 1986—. Co-author: Emergency Response: Is Your Company Ready?, 2002, New Approaches to Environmental Law and Agency Regulation: The Daubert Litigation Approach, 2000; contbr. articles to profl. jours. Mem. ABA (former officer sect. environ., energy & environ. law), D.C. Bar Assn., Ohio Bar Assn., Cleve. Bar Assn. Presbyterian. Avocations: running, skiing. Environmental. Office: Kaufman & Canoles 1200 Old Colony Ln Williamsburg VA 23188

GRAHAM, DONALD LYNN, federal judge; b. Salisbury, N.C., Dec. 15, 1948; s. Ernest Jethro and Mildred (Donald) G.; m. Brenda Joyce Savage, Sept. 27, 1969; 1 child, Sherrian Lynne. BA magna cum laude, W.Va. State Coll., 1971; JD, Ohio State U., 1974. Bar: Ohio 1974, U.S. Ct. Mil. Appeals, 1974, Fla. 1980, U.S. Dist. Ct. (so. dist.) Fla. 1980, Supreme Ct. 1980, U.S. Ct. Appeals (5th and 11th cirs.) 1981. Asst. U.S. atty. U.S. Dist. Ct. (so. dist.) Fla., Miami, 1979-84; ptnr. Raskin & Graham, Miami, 1984-91; judge U.S. Dist. Ct. (so. dist.) Fla., Miami, 1991—. Instr. U. Md., Hanau, Fed. Republic Germany, 1977-78, Embry Riddle U., Homestead, Fla., 1978-79. Maj., asst. staff judge adv. U.S. Army, 1974-79. Recipient Arthur S. Fleming award Washington Jaycees, 1982, Superior Performance award U.S. Dept. Justice; named one of Outstanding Young Men of Am., 1984. Mem. Assn. Trial Lawyers Am., Nat. Bar Assn., Fed. Bar Assn. (so. Fla. pres. 1984-85, treas. 1982-83), Fla. Bar Assn., N.Y. Bar Assn., Ohio Bar Assn., NAACP, Alpha Phi Alpha. Democrat. Baptist. Avocations: fishing, reading. Office: US Courthouse 99 NE 4th St Rm 1155 Miami FL 33132-2138

GRAHAM, HAROLD STEVEN, lawyer; b. Kansas City, Mo., Feb. 1, 1950; s. Martie Sydney and Elsie Helen (Bradford) G.; m. Deborah Ruth Glick, Apr. 8, 1973; children: Elizabeth, Jonathan, Joshua, Lauren. BS, U. Wis., 1972; JD, U. Chgo., 1976. Bar: Mo. 1976. Assoc. Lathrop, Koontz & Norquist, Kansas City, 1976-81; mem. Lathrop & Norquist, L.C., Kansas City, 1982-95, Lathrop & Gage L.C., Kansas City, 1996—. Active Kansas City Tomorrow Alumni Assn. Year X; bd. dirs. Hyman Brand Hebrew Acad., Kansas City, 1985-99, Beth Shalom Synagogue, Kansas City, 1983-88, Jewish Cmty. Campus, 1992-98. Mem. ABA (sect. on real property and trust law, sect. on bus. law), Assn. for Corporate Growth, Mo. Bar Assn. (property law com.), Kansas City Met. Bar Assn., Assn. for Corp. Growth (Kansas City chpt.). Avocations: tennis, running. Banking, Corporate, general, Finance. Office: Lathrop & Gage LC 2345 Grand Blvd Ste 2600 Kansas City MO 64108-2617

GRAHAM, JAMES LOWELL, federal judge; b. 1939; BA, JD summa cum laude, Ohio State U., 1962. Pvt. practice Crabbe, Brown, Jones, Potts & Schmidt, Columbus, Ohio, 1962-69, Graham, Dutro, Nemeth, and predecessors, Columbus, 1969-86; judge U.S. Dist. Ct. (so. dist.) Ohio, Columbus, 1986—. Faculty Ohio Jud. Coll., Ohio Legal Inst. Chmn. Ohio Bar Examiners, 1974, Devel. Commn. City of Columbus, 1976-77; mem. legal svcs. Salvation Army of Columbus, 1967-77, legal sect. United Way Campaign, 1976-80. Fellow Am. Coll. Trial Lawyers; mem. Capital U. Coll. of Law Assn. (dean's coun.), Ohio State U. Alumni Assn. Office: US Dist Ct 169 US Courthouse 85 Marconi Blvd Columbus OH 43215-2823

GRAHAM, JOHN JOSEPH, lawyer, economics educator; b. New Haven, Sept. 12, 1920; s. Hugh Munson and Alice W. (Cummings) G. BA in Econs., Yale U., 1942, MA, 1943; JD, Boston Coll., 1946; MA, Boston U., 1949; DHL (hon.), Am. Coll. Greece, 1997. Bar: Mass. 1946, U.S. Dist. Ct. Mass. 1947, U.S. Dist. Ct. Conn. 1949, U.S. Cir. Ct. Appeals (1st cir.) 1947, U.S. Cir. Ct. Appeals (2d cir.) 1953, U.S. Supreme Ct. 1952. Pvt. practice, Boston, 1946—; asst. commerce counsel New Haven R.R., 1947-49; atty. Rwy. Express Agy., Northeastern U.S., 1949-53; arbitrator Fed. Med. and Conciliation Svc. Am. Arbitration Assn., N.Y.C. and Washington, 1953—. Lectr. in econs. Northeastern U. Grad. Sch. Bus. Adminstrn., Boston, 1953-68; vis. prof. econs. Am. Coll. of Greece, Athens, 1981—. Spl. asst. atty. gen. Commonwealth of Mass., 1961; pres. Mass. Consumer Assn., 1961; fin. trustee Met. Transit Authority, Boston, 1957-61; commr. State Dept. Pub. Utilities, Mass., 1957. Yale Labor-Mgmt. Inst. fellow, 1948. Mem. World Peace Through Law Ctr. (founding mem.), Nat. Economists Club (founding mem.), Acad. Polit. Sci. (life), Am. Econ. Assn., Mansfield Law Soc. U.K., Fed. Bar Assn., Yale Club. Roman Catholic. General civil litigation, General practice, Private international. Home and Office: PO Box 1962 Boston MA 02105-1962

GRAHAM, PHILIP L., JR., lawyer; b. N.Y.C., 1943; BA, Harvard U., 1965, JD, 1968. Bar: N.Y. 1971. Mem. Sullivan & Cromwell, N.Y.C. General civil litigation. Office: Sullivan & Cromwell 125 Broad St Fl 28 New York NY 10004-2489

GRAHAM, ROBERT CLARE, III, lawyer; b. Albuquerque, Mar. 24, 1955; s. Robert C. Jr. and Helen (Hoagland) G.; children: Jennifer, Jessica, Kourtney, Kate. BA, DePauw U., 1977; JD magna cum laude, Pepperdine U., 1980. Bar: Mo. 1980, Ill. 1981, U.S. Dist. Ct. (ea. dist.) Mo. 1981. Assoc. Shephard, Sandberg & Phoenix, St. Louis, 1980-82, Suelthaus & Kaplan, PC and predecessors, St. Louis, 1982-91, Armstrong Teasdale, LLP, St. Louis, 1991—. Chmn. Kirkwood (Mo.) Greentree Festival, 1985. Named one of Outstanding Young Men in Am. Jaycees, 1981; recipient Outstanding Service to the Community of Kirkwood award. Mem. ABA, Ill. Bar Assn., Mo. Bar Assn., Bar Assn. Met. St. Louis, St. Louis County Bar Assn. Republican. Presbyterian. Banking, Corporate, general, Property, real (including real estate development, water). Office: Armstrong Teasdale LLP 1 Metropolitan Sq Ste 2600 Saint Louis MO 63102-2740 E-mail: rgraham@armstrongteasdale.com.

GRAHAM, STEPHEN MICHAEL, lawyer; b. Houston, May 1, 1951; s. Frederick Mitchell and Lillian Louise (Miller) G.; m. Joanne Marie Sealock, Aug. 24, 1974; children: Aimee Elizabeth, Joseph Sealock, Jessica Anne. BS, Iowa State U., 1973; JD, Yale U., 1976. Bar: Wash. 1977. Assoc. Perkins Coie, Seattle, 1976-83, ptnr., 1983-2000, Orrick, Herrington & Sutcliffe LLP, Seattle, 2000—. Bd. dirs. Wash. Spl. Olympics, Seattle, 1979—83, pres., 1982—83; trustee Friends of the Children of King County, 2002—; mem. Seattle Fair Campaign Practices Commn., 1982—88; mem. exec. com. Cornish Coll. Arts, 1989—91, trustee, 1994—96, Seattle Repertory Theatre, 1993—95, Seattle Children's Theatre, 1996—98, mem. exec. com., 1997—98; trustee Fred Hutchinson Cancer Rsch. Ctr., 1999—2003; mem. bd. exec. com. Lawyers WSA, 2002—; trustee Arboretum Found., 1994—96; mem. Seattle Bd. Ethics, 1982—88, chmn., 1983—88; mem. exec. com. Sch. Law Yale U., 1988—92, 1993—97; bd. dirs. Wash. Biotech. and Biomed. Assn., 1996—, mem. exec. com., 1997—. Mem.: Wash. State Bar Assn., ABA, Rainier Club, Wash. Athletic Club. Episcopalian. Commercial, contracts (including sales of goods; commercial financing), Corporate, general, Securities. Office: Orrick Herrington & Sutcliffe Ste 900 719 Second Ave Seattle WA 98104-7063

GRAHAM, THOMAS RICHARD, lawyer; b. Shelbyville, Ind., Nov. 23, 1942; s. Kermit A. and Esther L. (Thompson) G.; m. Rosemond Eve Toner, June 12, 1965; children: Rachel Graham Cody, Thomas Ian. BA, Ind. U., 1965; JD, Harvard U., 1968. Bar: D.C. 1970, U.S. Supreme Ct. 1973. Exec. asst. to pres. Ford Motor de Venezuela, Caracas, 1968-70; vis. prof. law U. Catolica Andres Bello, Caracas, 1968-70; legal officer UN, Geneva, 1970-73; dep. gen. counsel Office U.S. Trade Rep., Washington, 1974-79; vis. prof. U. N.C., Chapel Hill, 1979-80; assoc. Patton, Boggs & Blow, Washington, 1980-81; counsel, ptnr. Kilpatrick & Cody, Washington, 1981-85; ptnr. Skadden, Arps, Slate, Meagher & Flom, Washington, 1985-2000, King & Spalding, Washington, 2000—. Adj. prof. law Georgetown U., Washington, 1977-85, 95-98; vis. fellow Brookings Instn., Washington, 1978-79; sr. assoc. Carnegie Endowment, Washington, 1979-80. Co-editor: Managing Trade Relations in the 1980's, 1983, Trade and Environment, 1982; contbr. articles to profl. jours. Chief advisor on internat. trade John Glenn Presdl. Campaign, 1984. Mem. ABA (chmn. subcom. exports 1985-89), Am. Soc. Internat. Law (chmn. internat. econ. law sect. 1981-83). Avocations: history, sports. Private international, Public international. Home: 6115 33rd St NW Washington DC 20015-2403 Office: King & Spalding Ste 1000 1730 Pennsylvania Ave NW Washington DC 20006-4706

GRAHAM, WILLIAM EDGAR, JR., lawyer, retired utility company executive; b. Jackson Springs, N.C., Dec. 31, 1929; s. William Edgar and Minnie Blanch (Autry) G.; children: William McLaurin, John McMillan, Sally Faircloth. AB, U. N.C., 1952, JD with honors, 1956. Bar: N.C. bar. Law clk. U.S. Ct. Appeals 4th Circuit, 1956-57; individual practice law Charlotte, N.C., 1957-69; judge N.C. Ct. Appeals, 1969-73; sr. v.p., gen. counsel Carolina Power & Light Co., Raleigh, N.C., 1973-81, exec. v.p., 1981-85, vice chmn., 1985-93; counsel Hunton & Williams, 1994—. Served with USAF, 1952-54. Mem. ABA, N.C. Bar Assn., Wake County Bar Assn. Presbyterian. Home: 510-508 Glenwood Ave Raleigh NC 27603 Office: Hunton & Williams PO Box 109 Raleigh NC 27602-0109 E-mail: dgraham@hunton.com.

GRAMLICH, CHARLES J. lawyer; b. Springfield, Ill., July 20, 1938; s. Harold J. and Caroline F. (Jallas) G.; children— Ann, Brant. B.S., Bradley U., 1963; J.D., John Marshall Law Sch., 1966. Bar: Ill. 1967. Asst. state's atty. Sangamon County, Ill., 1967-68; state's atty. Edgar County, Ill., 1968-70; assoc. Pefferle, Maddox and Gramlich, Springfield, Ill., 1970-78; sole practice, Charles J. Gramlich Law Offices, P.C., Springfield, 1978-80; ptnr. Gramlich and Morse, P.C., Springfield, 1980-85; pres. Gramlich Law Offices, P.C., 1985—99; assoc. cir. judge 7th Jud. Cir. Ct., Sangamon County, Ill., 1999—. Trustee Capital Twp., 1997-99. Trustee Springfield Park Dist., 1976-80; assoc. cir. judge Sanjamon County, Ill. 7th Jud. Cir., 1999--. Republican. Roman Catholic. Office: 200 S 9th Rm 532 Springfield IL 62701-1602

GRAMMIG, ROBERT JAMES, lawyer; b. Oceanside, Calif., June 15, 1956; s. Richard Adolf and Mary Elizabeth (Spisak) G.; m. Laurel Jean Lenfestey, Aug. 10, 1996; children: Clare Marie, James Richard. BA, MA, U. Pa., 1978; JD, Harvard U., 1981. Bar: Fla. 1982, D.C. 1986, U.S. Dist. Ct. (mid. dist.) Fla. 1982, U.S. Ct. Appeals (11th and 5th cirs.) 1982, U.S. Supreme Ct. 1985. Law clk. to Hon. Thomas A. Clark U.S. Ct. Appeals (5th and 11th cirs.), Atlanta, 1981-82; assoc. Holland & Knight, Tampa, Fla., 1982-88, ptnr., 1989—. Bd. dirs. Child Abuse Coun., Tampa, 1993-97; mem. Leadership Tampa, 1994-95; Sec. Tampa Bay Internat. Trade Coun., 1994, vice chmn., 1995. Mem. Tampa Bay Coun. on Fgn. Rels., German Am. C. of C., U.S.-Austrian C. of C., Phi Beta Kappa. Republican. Roman Catholic. Corporate, general, Private international, Securities. Home: 21 Bahama Cir Tampa FL 33606-3317 Office: 100 N Tampa St Ste 4102 Tampa FL 33602-4322

GRANADE, CALLIE VIRGINIA SMITH S. lawyer, federal district judge; b. Lexington, Va., Mar. 7, 1950; d. Milton Hannibal and Callie Dougherty (Rives) Smith; m. Fred King Granade, Oct. 9, 1976; children: Taylor Rives, Milton Smith, Joseph Kee. BA, Hollins Coll., 1972; JD, U. Tex., 1975. Bar: Tex. 1975, Ala. 1976, U.S. Ct. Appeals (5th cir.) 1976, U.S. Dist. Ct. (so. dist.) Ala. 1977, U.S. Supreme Ct. 1980, U.S. Ct. Appeals (11th cir.) 1981. Law clk. to chief judge U.S. Ct. Appeals (5th cir.), Montgomery, Ala., 1975-76; asst. U.S. atty. U.S. Dept. Justice, Mobile, 1977, sr. litigation counsel, 1987-90; chief criminal sect. U.S. Atty.'s Office, Mobile, 1990-97; 1st asst. U.S. Atty., 1997—2001; acting U.S. Atty., 2001; U.S. Dist. Judge Southern Dist. of Ala., 2002—, Chief Judge, 2003—. Mem. ABA, Fed. Bar Assn., Ala. State Bar Assn., Tex. State Bar Assn., Mobile Bar Assn., Am. Coll. Trial Lawyers. Presbyterian. Office: US Courthouse 113 St Joseph St Mobile AL 36602

GRANAT, RICHARD STUART, lawyer, educator; b. N.Y.C., Nov. 11, 1940; s. George and Judith G.; m. Nancy Ruth Wruble, Dec. 23, 1962; children: Lisa, Hilary, Peter, David. BA, Lehigh U., 1962; JD (Harlan Fiske Stone scholar), Columbia U., 1965. Bar: Md. 1966, D.C. 1977. Asst. counsel U.S. OEO, Washington, 1965-67, dir. housing programs, 1967-78; asst. dir. Model Cities Agy. Office of Mayor, Balt., 1968-69; dir. Cmty. Planning and Evaluation Inst., Balt., 1970-71; pres. Univ. Rsch. Corp. Mgmt. Svcs. Corp., Balt., 1970-77; pvt. practice Washington and Md., 1969—. Pres. Automated Lagal Systems, Inc., Phila., 1984—89; dir. MA in Legal Studies Program, Antioch Sch. Law, 1979—83; pres., chmn. bd. Ctr. for Legal Studies, Washington, 1979—89; chmn. bd. dirs. Ctr. Sch., Rockville, Md.; pres. Inst. Paralegal Tng., Inc., Phila., 1982—89, The Phila. Inst., 1987—89, Inst. for Employee Benefits Tng., 1986—89, The Inst. for Law and Tech., Phila., 1990—92, Interactive Legal Media, Inc., 1992—96; instr. Rutgers Sch. Law, Camden, NJ, 1992—94, Sch. Lang., U. Balt., 1995—; adj. prof. Sch. Law, U. Md., 1994—, dir. Ctr. for Law Practice Tech., 1994—, dir. Peoples Law Libr., 1996—2000, dir. Ctr. for On-Line Mediation, Inc., 1996—2000; pres. The Granat Group, LLC, Am. Law On Line, Inc., 2001—. Mem. ABA, Md. Bar Assn., D.C. Bar Assn. Civil rights. Home: 320 Morgause Pl N Baltimore MD 21208-1430 Office: 9141 Reisterstown Rd Owings Mills MD 21117 E-mail: richard@granat.com.

GRANATA, LINDA M. lawyer; b. Montreal, June 9, 1951; d. Albert Joseph and Marylka (Aksamit) G. BS in Broadcasting, U. Fla., 1974; JD, Nova U., 1988. Bar: Fla. 1988, U.S. Dist. Ct. (so. dist.) Fla. 1989, U.S. Ct. Appeals (11th cir.) 1990, U.S. Tax Ct. 1990. Pres. Mkt. Makers, Inc., Miami, Fla., 1978-88, Ethylene Eaters, Inc., North Miami, Fla., 1981-88, 92—; law clk. to Hon. Paul M. Marko III 17th Cir. Ct., Ft. Lauderdale, Fla., 1986-87; corp. counsel Quantum Assocs., Inc., Miami Beach, 1988-89; assoc. Richard C. Fox, P.A., Boca Raton, Fla., 1989-90; pvt. practice North Miami, 1990-93; corp. counsel World Trade Consortium, Inc., Miami, 1993-99; pvt. practice Miami, 2000—. Arbitrator Nat. Assn. Securities Dealers, 1990—, Nat. Futures Assn., 1990-95, N.Y. Stock Exch., 2003—; guardian ad litum 17th Cir. Ct. Broward County, 1996-99. Mem. Am. Arbitration Assn., Nat. Panel Consumer Arbitrators. Alternative dispute resolution, Corporate, general, Commercial, contracts (including sales of goods; commercial financing). Office: PO Box 246046 Pembroke Pines FL 33024-0117 E-mail: legal-1@earthlink.net.

GRANDE, THOMAS ROBERT, lawyer; b. Providence, Dec. 27, 1952; s. Albert and Gloria (Palmieri) G. Student, U. Copenhagen, 1975; BA in Govt., Bates Coll., Lewiston, Maine, 1976; JD, U. Hawaii, 1985. Bar: Hawaii, 1985, U.S. Dist. Ct. Hawaii 1985, U.S. Ct. Appeals (9th cir.) 1985. Exec. dir. Common Cause Hawaii, Honolulu, 1979-82; law clk. to chief justice Federated States Micronesia Supreme Ct., Pohnpei, Caroline Islands, 1985; ptnr. Davis Levin Livingston Grande, Honolulu, 1985—. Contbr. articles to profl. jours. Vista Vol. Waimanalo Coun. Community Orgns., 1978; candidate for nat. governing bd. Common Cause, Washington, 1983; vol. ACLU, Honolulu, 1983-84; organizer Com. to Keep Waimanalo Rural, 1984; bd. dirs. Hawaii's Thousand Friends, Honolulu, 1987, Hawaii Lawyers Care, 1988. Recipient Outstanding Contbn. to the Delivery of Legal Svcs. award Hawaii Lawyers Care, 1994. Mem. ABA (sec. litig., chair state law subcom. of com. on class actions, editor-in-chief ABA Survey of State Class Action Law), ATLA (co-chair Qui Tam Litigation Group), Hawaii Bar Assn. (chmn. lawyer referral com. 1991-94), Consumer Lawyers Hawaii (mem. bd. govs. 1993—, parliamentarian 1993-94, sec. 1994-95, v.p. 1995-96), Am. Inns of Ct. (barrister 1989-90). Avocations: hiking, reading, martial arts, gardening. General civil litigation, Health, Native American. Office: 400 Davis Levin Livingston Grande 851 Fort St Honolulu HI 96813 Fax: 808545-7802. E-mail: tgrande@davislevin.com.

GRANHOLM, JENNIFER MULHERN, governor; b. Vancouver, B.C., Can., Feb. 5, 1959; arrived in U.S., 1962; d. Civtor Ivar and Shirley Alfreda (Dowden) Granholm; m. Daniel Granholm Mulhern, May 23, 1986; children: Kathryn, Cecelia, Jack. BA, U. Calif., Berkeley, 1984; JD, Harvard U., 1987. Bar: Mich. 1987, U.S. Dist. Ct. (ea. dist.) Mich. 1987, U.S. Ct. Appeals (6th cir.) 1987. Jud. law clk. 6th Cir Ct. Appeals, Detroit, 1987—88; exec. asst. Wayne County Exec., Detroit, 1988—89; asst. U.S. atty. Dept. Justice, Detroit, 1990—94; corp. counsel Wayne County, Detroit, 1994—98; atty. gen. State of Mich., 1999—2002, gov., 2003—. Gen. counsel Detroit/Wayne County Stadium Authority, 1996—98. Contbr. articles to profl. jours. Commr. Great Lakes Commn.; mem. bd. Cyberstate-.org YWCA. Mem.: Inc. Soc. Irish Lawyers, Women's Law Assn., Detroit Bar Assn. Democrat. Roman Catholic. Avocations: running, family, laughing. Office: Gov Office PO Box 30013 Lansing MI 48909*

GRANOFF, GARY CHARLES, lawyer, investment company executive; b. N.Y.C., Feb. 2, 1948; s. N. Henry and Jeannette (Trum) G.; m. Leslie Barbara Resnick, Dec. 21, 1969; children: Stephen, Robert, Joshua. BBA in Acctg., George Washington U., 1970, JD with honors, 1973. Bar: N.Y. 1974, Fla. 1974, U.S. Dist. Ct. (so. dist.) N.Y. 1976. Assoc. Dreyer & Traub, N.Y.C., 1973-75; ptnr. Ezon, Langberg & Granoff, N.Y.C., 1975-78, Granoff & Walker, N.Y.C., 1982-92, Granoff, Walker & Forlenza PC, N.Y.C., 1993—; pvt. practice N.Y.C., 1978-81; pres., also bd. dirs. Elk Assocs. Funding Corp., N.Y.C., 1979—, GCG Assocs., Inc., N.Y.C., 1982—; pres., dir. Gemini Capital Corp., 1996—; pres., chmn. Ameritrans Capital Corp., 1999—. Atty. del. to U.S.-China Joint Session on Trade, Investment and Econ. Law, Beijing, 1987; dean's adv. bd. George Washington U. Law Sch., 1993—. Campaign vol. Mondale for Pres., N.Y.C., 1984; fundraiser Robert Garcia for Congress, Dem. Senatorial Campaign Com., N.Y.C., 1987—88; active N.Y. Lawyers for Dukakis Com., 1988; chmn. N.Y.C. chpt. George Washington U. Nat. Law Ctr. Leadership Gifts Com., 1998—; trustee George Washington U., 1998—, Parker Jewish Inst. for Health Care and Rehab., 2001—; chmn. fin. com. George Washington U., 2001—. Recipient Jacob Burns award George Washngton U. Law Sch., 1998. Mem. ABA, N.Y. State Bar Assn., Fla. Bar Assn., Assn. Bar City N.Y., People to People Internat., Nat. Assn. Investment Cos. (legis com.), George Washington U. Alumni Assn. (chmn. N.Y.C. chpt., bd. dirs. law sch. alumni assn., alumni com. 21 century, trustee), North Shore Country Club (chmn. legal com., bd. govs. 1994-96, 98-2001, chmn. admissions com. 1999-2001). Avocations: golf, tennis, skiing. Commercial, contracts (including sales of goods; commercial financing), Finance, Property, real (including real estate development, water). Office: Granoff Walker & Forlenza 747 3rd Ave Fl 4 New York NY 10017-2803

GRANT, ARTHUR GORDON, JR., lawyer, educator; b. New Orleans, May 16, 1945; s. Arthur Gordon and Martha (McCutchon) G.; children: Arthur Gordon III, Kathryn S., Douglas M. BA, U. N.C., 1967; JD, Tulane U., 1970. Bar: La. 1970, U.S. Ct. Appeals (5th cir.) 1970, U.S. Dist. Ct. (ea. and mid. dists.) La. 1970, U.S. Dist. Ct. (we. dist.) La. 1970, U.S. Ct. Appeals (11th cir.) 1981, U.S. Supreme Ct. 1990, U.S. Dist. Ct. (so. dist.) Tex. 1998. Assoc. Montgomery, Barnett, Brown, Read, Hammond & Mintz, New Orleans, 1970-73, ptnr., 1973—. Admiralty and maritime law instr. U. New Orleans Sch. Naval Architecture, 1990—; bd. dirs. Am. Boat and Yacht Coun., 1990-98, 2002-. Author: Recreational Craft, Jurisdiction, Claims and Coverage, 1989; contbg. author: Recreational Boating Law, 1992, Benedict on Admiralty, Vol. 8, 7th edit., 1995. Bd. govs. Propellor Club Port of New Orleans, 1989-90, 92-94. Fellow La. Bar Found.; mem. Fed. Bar Assn., Navy League of U.S., La. Bar Assn., Soc. Naval Architects and Marine Engrs., Maritime Law Assn. U.S. (vice chmn. recreational boating com. 1990-94, vice chmn. Hull and P&I ins. com.), Bar Assn. 5th Fed. Cir., Southeastern Admiralty Law Inst., So. Yacht Club. Episcopalian. Avocations: hunting, fishing, boating, civil war history. Admiralty, Product liability, Environmental. Office: Montgomery Barnett Brown Read Hammond & Mintz 3200 Energy Ctr New Orleans LA 70163 E-mail: ggrant@monbar.com.

GRANT, BURTON FRED, lawyer; b. Chgo., Mar. 16, 1938; s. Louis Z. and Ruth (Kaplan) G.; m. Joan Carolyn Friedman, July 11, 1965; children: Robin, Steven, Lauren. BA, De Paul U., 1959, JD, 1962; LLM, John Marshall U., 1965. Bar: Ill. 1963, U.S. Dist. Ct. (no. dist.) Ill. 1963. Sole practice, Chgo., 1963-73; ptnr. Grant, Kaplan & Grant, Chgo., 1973-76, Grant, Grant & Stein, Chgo., 1977-81; prin. Grant & Grant, Chgo., 1981—. Adj. prof. De Paul U. Sch. Law, Chgo., 1979-83. Contbr. articles to profl. jours. Named one of Leading Attorneys at Law in Family Law in State of Ill., (pub.) Law and Leading Attorneys, one of 20 Top Divorce Lawyers North Shore Mag., 1997. Fellow Am. Acad. Matrimonial Lawyers (cert.); mem. ABA, Ill. Bar Assn., Chgo. Bar Assn., N.W. Suburban Bar Assn. (cert. appreciation 1986), North Suburban Bar ASsn. (bd. mgrs. 1992—), Lake County Bar Assn., Phi Alpha Delta. Avocations: travel, photography. Family and matrimonial. Office: Grant & Grant 180 N La Salle St Ste 2400 Chicago IL 60601-2787 also: 707 Skokie Blvd Ste 600 Northbrook IL 60062-2841

GRANT, ISABELLA HORTON, retired judge; b. L.A., Sept. 24, 1924; d. John Daniel and Hannabelle (Horton) Grant. BA, Swarthmore Coll., 1944; MA, UCLA, 1946; JD, Columbia U., 1950; LLD (hon.), Molloy Coll., 1976. Jr. profl. asst. OSS, Washington, 1944-45; economist Inst. Indsl. Rels., UCLA, 1946-47, Office Price Stblzn., L.A., 1951-52; ptnr. Livingston, Grant, Stone & Kay, San Francisco, 1953-79; judge Mcpl. Ct., San Francisco, 1979-82, Superior Ct., San Francisco, 1982-97; ret., 1997. Bd. dirs. Kid's Turn, Pocket Opera. Fellow ABA; mem. Am. Arbitration Assn., San Francisco Ethics Commn. (chair 1999), San Francisco Bar Assn. (bd. dirs. 1978-79), Acad. Matrimonial Lawyers (pres. No. Calif. chpt. 1976), Assn. Family and Conciliation Cts. (pres. Calif. chpt. 1987-89), Nat. Coll. Probate Judges (William W. Treat award 2000), Queen's Bench (pres. 1964), Calif. Tennis Club, Phi Beta Kappa. E-mail: ihortongrant@cs.com.

GRANT, JOHN P. lawyer; b. Omaha, Nebr., June 24, 1951; BA, U. Nebr., 1973; JD, Creighton U., 1976. Bar: Nebr. 1976. Atty. Grant Law Offices, PC, Omaha. Mem.: Nebr. State Bar Assn. (Ho. Dels. 1990—, chair 1999). Personal injury (including property damage), Workers' compensation, General civil litigation. Office: Grant Law Offices PC 3717 Harney St Omaha NE 68131-3848*

GRANT, M. DUNCAN, lawyer; b. Madison, Wis., Apr. 22, 1950; s. David Evans and Margaret Jane (Bloomfield) G.; m. Marcia Joan Cox, Sept. 18, 1970 (div. Dec. 1975); 1 child, Thomas David; m. Margaret Ann MacDonald, Mar. 24, 1990 (div. Jan. 1995); m. Victoria Lynn Nichols, Oct. 14, 2000. AB, Princeton U., 1972; JD, U. Pa., 1975. Bar: Pa. 1975, Del. 1991, U.S. Dist. Ct. (ea. dist.) Pa. 1976, U.S. Ct. Appeals (3d cir.) 1977, U.S. Supreme Ct. 1980, U.S. Dist. Ct. (Del.) 1992, U.S. Ct. Appeals (10th cir.) 1986, U.S. Ct. Appeals (11th cir.) 1996, U.S. Ct. Appeals (fed. cir.) 2002. Law clk. to judge U.S. Ct. Appeals (3d cir.), Phila., 1975-76; assoc. Pepper Hamilton LLP, Phila., 1976-83, ptnr., 1983—. Ed. in chief U. Penn Law Review. Am. fellow Salzburg Seminar, 1986. Mem. ABA, Pa. Bar Assn., Phila. Bar Assn., Del. State Bar Assn. Democrat. Avocations: baseball, wine, golf. Federal civil litigation, General civil litigation, State civil litigation. Home: 415 Gate Ln Philadelphia PA 19119-2815 Office: Pepper Hamilton LLP 3000 Two Logan Sq 18th & Arch Sts Philadelphia PA 19103-1083 E-mail: grantm@pepperlaw.com.

GRANT, MERWIN DARWIN, lawyer; b. Safford, Ariz., May 7, 1944; s. Darwin Dewey and Erma (Whiting) G.; m. Charlotte Richey, June 27, 1969; children: Brandon, Taggart, Christian, Brittany. BA in Econs., Brigham Young U., 1968; JD, Duke U., 1971. Bar: Ariz. 1971, U.S. Dist. Ct. Ariz., U.S. Dist. Ct. (we. dist.) Tex., U.S. Ct. Appeals (5th, 7th, 8th, 9th and 10th cirs.), U.S. Tax Ct., U.S. Supreme Ct. Pres. Merwin D. Grant, P.C., Phoenix, 1977—; ptnr. Beus, Gilbert & Morrill, Phoenix, 1984—93; pres. Grant Williams P.C., Phoenix, 1994—. Guest condr. Phoenix Symphony Orch., 1989. Bd. dirs. Grand Canyon coun. Boy Scouts Am., Phoenix, 1974-76, Maricopa Hosp., Health Sys. Bd., 1997—, Ariz. Motorsports Charitable Found.; pres., bd. dirs. Golden Gate Settlement, Phoenix, 1975-80, 84-88, Phoenix Internat. Raceway Charities, Ariz. Acad. Decathalon Assn., exec. com., 1999-2002; charter mem. Rep. Presl. Task Force, Washington, 1984—; vice chmn. Ariz. Joint County Tobacco Revenue Use and Security Charitable Trust, 2000—; mem. Ariz. Joint House/Senate Ad Hoc Com. on Health Care Dists., 2001; chmn. Citizens' Task Force, Maricopa County Hosp., 2002—. Fellow Ariz. Bar Found.; mem. ABA (litigation sect.), Assn. Trial Lawyers Am., Kiwanis (bd. dirs. Phoenix chpt. 1972-79). Federal civil litigation, State civil litigation, Private international. Office: Grant Williams PC 3200 N Central Ave Ste 2400 Phoenix AZ 85012 E-mail: grant@phxlaw.com.

GRANT, PATRICK ALEXANDER, lawyer, association administrator; b. Denver, Nov. 14, 1945; s. Edwin Hendrie and Mary Belle (McIntyre) G.; m. Carla Clyde Yancey, Aug. 16, 1975; children: Mary Cameron, Sara Mansur, Alexis Hendrie. BA with honors, Colgate U., 1967; MBA, Denver U., 1973; JD, Drake U., 1976. Bar: Colo. 1977. Law clk. to Judge Donald P. Smith, Jr. Colo. Ct. Appeals, Denver, 1976-77; assoc. Grant, McHendrie, Haines & Crouse, PC, Denver, 1977-83, ptnr., v.p., 1984-91, also bd. dirs.; state rep. Colo. Gen. Assembly, Denver, 1984-92, vice-chmn. fin. com., 1987-88, chmn. audit com., 1989-90, chmn. judiciary com., 1988-92, chmn. legal svcs. com., 1988-89. Mem. Colo. Coun. Elected Ofcls. for Soviet Jewry, Denver, 1985-92, Colo. Spl. Task Force Tort Liability and Ins., Denver, 1985; bd. dirs. Colo. Sports Hall of Fame, 1992-98, Colo. State U. Livestock Leader Coun. Kent Denver Leadership Fund, 1996-97, upper sch. chmn. parents divsn.; mem. Denver Cmty. Mental Health Commn., 1985-86; mem. exec. coun., planning com. St. Joseph Hosp., Denver, 1985-88; mem. Denver Bd. for Developmentally Disabled, 1987-88; vestryman, jr. warden St. Barnabas Parish, Denver, 1979-84; adv. com. Nat. Ctr. Preventive Law, 1987-90; bd. dirs. Colo. Jud. Inst., 1990-96, bd. govs. Colo. State U. system, 2001—; exec. bd. Parents Assn., Gettysburg (Pa.) Coll., 1997-2001, chmn. parents fund, 2000-01, nat. campaign steering com. Gettysburg Coll., 2000-01, Colgate U. (N.Y.) Soc. of Families steering com.; exec. bd. Denver coun. Boy Scouts Am., scout show chmn., 1997—; Roundup Riders of Rockies, 1989—; mem. bd. govs. Colo. State U. Sys., 2001—. Bd. dirs. Assoc. Rodeo Coms., Gates Found. fellow John F. Kennedy Sch. Govt. Harvard U., 1985, Toll Fellow Coun. of State Govts., 1987; recipient Outstanding Alumni award Kent Denver Country Day Sch., 1986, Colo. Wildlife Fedn. Appreciation award, 1987, Disting. Svc. to Higher Edn. award U. Denver, 1988, Bus. Legis. of Yr., award Colo. Pub. Affairs Coun., 1989, Outstanding Achievement award EPA, 1989, award of honor Hist. Denver, 1989, Stephen H. Hart award Colo. Hist. Soc., 1990, Spl. Recognition award AIA; named one of Outstanding Young Men in Am., U.S. Jaycees, 1980, Legislator of Yr. Associated Builders and Contractors, 1991, Gen. Heritage award for Former Legislator, 1997, mem. Grant Family Recipient, Citizen of West, 2000. Mem. Colo. Med. Soc. Found. (bd. dirs., pres. 1997-99, pres. emeritus 1999—), Western Stock Show Assn. (exec. com., bd. dirs. 1984—, exec. v.p., CEO 1990-91, pres., CEO 1991—), Metro Denver C. of C. (chmn. econ. devel. coun. 1995-96, co-chmn. pub. affairs coun. 1999-2000, co-chmn. entrepeneurship coun. 2001-02), Assn. Rodeo Coms. (bd. dirs. 2000—). Republican. Episcopalian. Avocations: wood chopping, horseback riding. Environmental, Property, real (including real estate development, water), Transportation. Home: 3777 S Dahlia St Englewood CO 80110-4215 Office: 4655 Humboldt St Denver CO 80216-2818

GRANT, PAUL, chemical engineer, manufacturer's representative, real estate broker; b. Patuxent River, Md., May 19, 1949; s. Ralph F. and Elizabeth (Payne) G. BS in Chem. Engring., Auburn U., Ala., 1971; MS in Chem. Engring., U. Md., College Park, 1975; Cert. Hungarian linguist, U.S. Army, 1972. Lic. real estate broker. Sales engr. Mixing Equipment Co., Rochester, N.Y., 1976-78; precious metals salesman James U. Blanchard & Co., New Orleans, 1979; owner, operator PK Grant & Co., Lakewood, Colo., 1979—. Instr. Jr. Achievement Project Bus., Lakewood, Colo., 1984; state chmn. Libertarian Party, La., 1979, Libertarian Party candidate for gov. Colo., 1982, nat. chmn. Libertarian Party, 1983-85. Served with U.S. Army, 1971-74 Basketball scholar Pensacola Jr. Coll., Fla., 1967-69; named Nat. Merit scholar Auburn U., 1969-71; recipient Outstanding Translator award U.S. Army Def. Intelligence Agy., 1974 Office: Paul Grant 6426 S Quebec St Englewood CO 80111

GRANT, PAULA DIMEO, lawyer, nursing educator, mediator; b. Bridgeport, Conn., Aug. 3, 1943; d. Samuel Peter and Emilie Alyce (DiChiera) DiMeo; m. James Mullett Grant, Nov. 26, 1975. AS in Nursing, U. Bridgeport, 1973; BSN cum laude, Boston Coll., 1975; JD, No. Va. U., 1982; MA in Nursing, NYU, 1994. Bar: D.C. 1985, U.S. Ct. Appeals (D.C.) 1985, U.S. Dist. Ct. D.C. 1985, U.S. Supreme Ct. 1989, U.S. Dist. Ct. Md. 1995. RN, Conn. Coronary care nurse Cornell Med. Ctr., N.Y.C., 1969-70; with Trans World Airlines, Chgo. and N.Y.C., 1980—84; pvt. practice, Washington, 1986-98; of counsel Ross & Hardies, Washington, 1998—. Mediator Superior Ct. D.C., 1991—2003; clin. asst. prof. cmty. and preventive medicine N.Y. Med. Coll., 1992—96; adj. prof. dept. nursing Columbia U. Tchrs. Coll., N.Y.C., 1993, 94; adj. asst. prof. nursing Sacred Heart U., Fairfield, Conn., 1998—99, mem. adv. coun., 1998—2000; co-chair Annual TAANA Conf., Washington, 2003. Mem. task force for women Boston Coll., 2003. Mem. ABA, ATLA, D.C. Bar Assn., Am. Assn. Nurses Attys. (co-chmn. legis. affairs com. 1987-91, bd. dirs. N.Y. Met. chpt. 1986-88, sec. 1986-87, nat. bd. dirs. 1996-2000, pres. Found. 1998-99), Conn. Nurses Assn. (chmn. cabinet on econ. and gen. welfare 1985-88), Nurse Atty. Resource Group, Inc. (co-founder), Task Force for Women are Boston Coll., Sigma Theta Tau. Roman Catholic. Avocations: reading, theater, music. Office: Ross and Hardies 65 E 55th St 31st Fl New York NY 10022

GRANT, ROBERT NATHAN, lawyer; b. Newburgh, N.Y., Mar. 7, 1930; s. Henry and Helen (Berkowitz) Grusky; m. Barbara Weil, Feb. 10, 1952; children— Susan, Elizabeth Grant Ellerton, Nancy Grant Gray. BA, Yale U., 1951; LLB, Harvard U., 1956. Bar: Ill. 1956, N.Y. 1990; registered fgn. lawyer, U.K. Assoc. Sonnenschein Nath & Rosenthal, Chgo., 1956-65; ptnr. Sonnenschein, Nath & Rosenthal, Chgo., 1965—. Sec. UNR Industries, Inc., Chgo., 1979-90; sec. San Diego Padres Prof. Baseball Team, 1974-78. Contbr. articles to profl. jours. Trustee The Nature Conservancy-Ill., 1978—88; pres. Legal Aid Soc. Ill., 1988—94, Winnetka (Ill.) Pub. Schs. Found., 1995—98; bd. dirs. Winnetka Pub. Schs. Found.; pres. Winnetka Cmty. House, 2000—01, Winnetka Bd. Edn., 1980—81, mem., 1974—81, Winnetka Planning Commn., 1975—77, New Trier Twp. Caucus, 1974; bd. dirs. United Charities, 1984—94, mem. legal aid com., 1982—, vice chmn., 1986—87, chmn., 1987—94; bd. dirs. New Trier HS Ednl. Found., 2001—, chmn. 1st lt. USAF, 1951—53. Recipient William H. Avery award for 10 yrs. svc. as chmn. Legal Aid Soc., 1994. Mem. ABA (vice-chmn. commercial leasing com.), Scholarship and Guidance Assn. (bd. dirs. 1968-92, pres. 1979-83), Harvard Law Sch. Spl. Gifts, Yale Alumni Recruiting Com., Standard Club, Yale Club (N.Y.C.), Phi Beta Kappa. Avocations: tennis, jogging, travel, reading. Commercial, contracts (including sales of goods; commercial financing), Corporate, general, Property, real (including real estate development, water). Home: 1165 Hamptondale Ave Winnetka IL 60093-1811 Office: Sonnenschein Nath & Rosenthal 233 S Wacker Dr Ste 8000 Chicago IL 60606-6491 E-mail: rgrant@sonnenschein.com.

GRANT, RUSSELL PORTER, JR., lawyer, petroleum land man; b. Ft. Sill, Okla., Nov. 5, 1943; s. Russell Porter and Jimmie (Bell) G.; m. Janice Rae Lockley, Nov. 19, 1966; 1 child, Russell Porter III. BS, U.S. Mil. Acad., 1966; JD, U. Miss., 1974. Bar: Miss. 1974, U.S. Dist. Ct. (no. dist.) Miss. 1974, U.S. Ct. Appeals (5th cir.) 1980, U.S. Dist. Ct. (so. dist.) Miss. 1992. Ptnr. Patterson & Patterson, Aberdeen, Miss., 1974-80; petroleum landman Aberdeen, 1980-81; ops. landman Hughes & Hughes Oil and Gas, Jackson, Miss., 1981-84; mgr. gas contracts Hughes Ea. Petroleum, Ltd., Jackson, 1984-88; corp. counsel Hughes Ea. Petroleum, Inc., Jackson, 1988-89; pvt. practice Jackson, 1989-90, 91; assoc. Overstreet & Kuykendall, Jackson, 1990-91; ptnr. McKibben, Grant & Assocs., Jackson, 1991-95; pvt. practice Jackson, 1995-2000; petroleum landman, 2000—. Mem. legal com. Interstate Oil and Gas Compact Commn., Oklahoma City, 1992—; speaker Oil and Gas Inst., U. Ala., 1990, natural gas seminar Miss. Natural Gas Assn., 1986. Co-chair exec. com. Monroe County Rep. Party, Aberdeen, 1980; pres. Aberdeen Exch. Club, 1978-79; mem. Monroe County (Miss.) Port Authority, 1979-80. Capt. U.S. Army, 1966-72. Named Outstanding Com. Chair, Aberdeen C. of C., 1979. Mem. Miss. Oil and Gas Lawyers (pres. 1986-87), Miss. Assn. Petroleum Landmen (v.p. 1987-88, pres. 1994-95), Miss. Bar (chmn. natural resources sect. 1988-89), Am. Assn. Profl. Landmen (cert. profl. landman), The Federalist Soc., Nat. Lawyers Assn. Episcopalian. Avocations: art, architecture, gardening, music, history. Commercial, contracts (including sales of goods; commercial financing), Oil, gas, and mineral, Property, real (including real estate development, water). Home and Office: 1818 Aztec Dr Jackson MS 39211-6503 E-mail: grantjr@unidial.com.

GRANT, STEPHEN ALLEN, lawyer; b. N.Y.C., Nov. 4, 1938; s. Benton H. and Irene A. Grant; m. Anne. K. Bagley, Feb. 11, 1961 (div. Nov. 1975); children: Stephen, Katharine, Michael; m. Anne-Marie Laignel, Dec. 8, 1975; children: Natalie, Elizabeth, Alexandra. AB, Yale U., 1960; LLB, Columbia U., 1965. Bar: N.Y. 1965, U.S. Supreme Ct. 1969. Law clk. to judge U.S. Ct. Appeals (2d cir.), N.Y.C., 1965-66; assoc. Sullivan & Cromwell, N.Y.C., 1966-73, ptnr., 1973—2002. Mem. Japan-U.S. Friendship Commn., U.S.-Japan Conf. on Cultural and Ednl. Interchange, 1989-92. Lt. (j.g.) USNR, 1960-62. Mem. ABA, N.Y. State Bar Assn., Assn. of Bar of City of N.Y., Coun. Fgn. Rels. Clubs: Down Town, Links. Corporate, general, Private international, Securities. Office: 200 E 66th St Ste C2103 New York NY 10021-9187

GRANT, SUSAN IRENE, lawyer; b. N.Y.C., Apr. 27, 1953; d. Walter Arnold and Beatrice L. (Thalheimer) G.; m. Brian A. King, June 24, 1990; 1 child, Alexander Grant King. BA, NYU, 1974; JD, Columbia U., 1977. Bar: N.Y. 1978, U.S. Dist. Ct. (so. and ea. dists.) N.Y. 1978. Assoc. Law Offices of Rita Eredics, Esq., Flushing, NY, 1977-78; staff atty. The Dreyfus Corp., N.Y.C., 1978-85; asst. gen. counsel Prudential-Bache Securities Inc., N.Y.C., 1985-89, asst. v.p., 1986-89; asst. gen. counsel, assoc. v.p. Prudential Mut. Fund Mgmt., Inc., N.Y.C., 1987-89; asst. counsel First Investors Corp., N.Y.C., 1989-94; sr. counsel, chief compliance officer Royce & Assocs., N.Y.C., 1994-96; sr. atty. Van Eck Assocs. Corp., N.Y.C., 1996-98, Weil, Gotshal & Manges LLP, N.Y.C., 1998—2002; pvt. practice Forest Hills, NY, 2002—. Mem. ABA, N.Y. State Bar Assn., Bar Assn. City N.Y. Corporate, general, Securities. Home: 11045 Queens Blvd Forest Hills NY 11375-5501 Office: 11045 Queens Blvd Forest Hills NY 11375-5501 E-mail: bakfinguru@aol.com.

GRANT, WALTER MATTHEWS, lawyer, corporate executive; b. Winchester, Ky., Mar. 30, 1945; s. Raymond Russell and Mary Mitchell (Rees) G.; m. Ann Carol Straus, Aug. 5, 1967; children— Walter Matthews II, Jean Ann, Raymond Russell II. ABJ, U. Ky., Lexington, 1967; JD, Vanderbilt U., 1971. Bar: Ga. 1971, Tenn. 1992. Assoc. Alston & Bird, Atlanta, 1971-76, ptnr., 1976-83; v.p., gen. counsel, sec. Contel Corp., Atlanta, 1983-91; sr. v.p., gen. counsel Smith & Nephew N.Am., Memphis, 1991-93; sr. v.p., gen. counsel, sec. The Actava Group Inc., Atlanta, 1993-96, Bruno's Supermarkets, Inc., Birmingham, Ala., 1996—2002. Bd. dirs. SCB Computer Tech., Inc., Memphis, Hat Shack, Inc., Atlanta. Editor in chief Vanderbilt Law Rev., 1970-71, Ga. State Bar Jour., 1979-82 Baptist. Corporate, general, Mergers and acquisitions. Home: 23 Rose Gate Dr NE Atlanta GA 30342-4161

GRASECK, ARTHUR VINCENT, lawyer; b. Hollis, N.Y., Nov. 24, 1935; s. Arthur Vincent and Mabel Hazel (Farleigh) G. BA, Hobart Coll., 1957; LLB, Yale U., 1963; LLM, NYU, 1968. Atty. Nassau County Probation Dept., Westbury, N.Y., 1964; staff atty. N.Y. State Labor Rels. Bd., N.Y.C., 1965-68; staff coun. Nassau County Law Svcs., Hempstead, N.Y., 1969; dep. Nassau County Atty. Nassau County Attys. Office, Mineola, N.Y., 1969-70; asst. N.Y. State Assemblymen Landis, Albany, N.Y., 1970; staff atty. Legal Aid Soc. of Suffolk County, Hauppauge, N.Y., 1970-71; pvt. practice Port Washington, N.Y., 1971-98, Islip Terrace, N.Y., 1998—. Mem. L.I. Progressive Coalition, Messapequq, N.Y., 1990—; panelist Civil Rights Program, Practicing Law Inst., N.Y.C., 1996. Lt. (j.g.) USN, 1957-60. Mem. Fed. Bar Coun., Yale Club of N.Y.C., Phi Beta Kappa. Democrat. Methodist. Civil rights. Home and Office: 1870 Spur Dr S Islip Terrace NY 11752-1513

GRASLIE, THOMAS ERIC, lawyer; b. Rapid City, S.D., Oct. 28, 1950; s. Orville Thomas and Helen Maxine Graslie; m. Carol Marie Zielike, Sept. 7, 1985; children: Lydia Marie, Serri Ann, Emily Louise. Student, Schiller Coll., Germany, 1972; BA, S.D. State U., 1973; JD, U. S.D., 1976. Bar: S.D. 1976, U.S. Dist. Ct. (we. dist.) S.D. 1985, U.S. Supreme Ct. 1996. State's atty. Harding County, Buffalo, S.D., 1976-88; city atty. Town of Buffalo, 1976—; pvt. practice, Buffalo, 1976—, Rapid City, 1986—. Mem. Bd. Water and Natural Resources S.D., Pierre, 1977-80, Bd. Minerals and Environ. S.D., Pierre, 1980-86; pres. Harding County Reps., 1977-82. Mem. ABA, ATLA, S.D. Bar Assn., S.D. Trial Lawyers Assn., Am. Judicature Soc., S.D. Mcpl. Attys. Assn. (pres. 1986-88), Harding County C. of C. (pres. 1979-85), Pennington County Ambs. (prs. 1995), Lions (pres. 1979-80), Masons, Shriners. Avocations: reading, hunting, ranching. Oil, gas, and mineral, General practice, Probate (including wills, trusts). Office: 231 E St Joseph St Rapid City SD 57701-2916 also: 100 Main St Buffalo SD 57720

GRASMICK, JOSEPH CHRISTIAN, lawyer, anthropologist; b. Yankton, S.D., Nov. 6, 1949; s. Veldon and Ruth (Bahm) G.; children: Maria, Vanessa, Joshua. BA in Polit. Sci., SUNY, Fredonia, 1974; MA in Anthropology, JD cum laude, SUNY, Buffalo, 1978, postgrad., 1979—. Bar: N.Y. 1979, Fla. 1999, U.S. Dist. Ct. (we. dist.) N.Y. 1981. Rschr. Louis Harris and the Roper Ogrn., N.Y.C., 1970-72; vol. Peace Corps Senasa Nat. Health Agy., Paraguay, 1972-75; rsch. assoc. comparative Latin Am. Law SUNY, Buffalo, 1976; intern Application Standards br. Internat. Labor Orgn., Geneva, 1977; rep. UN Econs. Soc. Commn. Lawyers Com. for Internat. Human Rights, Geneva, 1978; owner Law Office of Joseph C. Grasmick, Buffalo, 1979—. Author: U.S. Immigration for Businesses, Investors and Workers, 1981, U.S. Immigration for Canadian Business INTERNET Web Site, 1995, Grasmick's TNHandbook for Canadians, 2000, 2d edit.; editor Buffalo Law Rev., 1977-78, Immigration Newsletter, 1979—; legal reporter Can.-U.S. Bus. Immigration Handbook, 1991-99; contbr. articles to profl. jours. Ford Found. rsch. fellow, London, 1977, Fulbright Found. rsch. fellow, Paraguay, 1979-80, Orgn. of Am. States rsch. fellow, Paraguay, 1979-80, Inter-Am. Found. rsch. fellow, 1979-81; grad. fellow SUNY, Buffalo, 1977, Baldy fellow, 1978. Mem. ABA, Am. Immigration Lawyers Assn. (chmn.), Law and Soc. Assn., Am. Anthrop. Assn., Soc. for Legal and Polit. Anthropology, Latin Am. Studies Assn., Can. Bar Assn., N.Y. State Bar Assn., Fla. Bar Assn., Erie County Bar Assn., Niagara Falls Bar Assn. Immigration, naturalization, and customs. Office: 300 Internat Dr Ste 100 Williamsville NY 14221 E-mail: jgrasmick@grasmick.com.

GRASSI, JOSEPH F. lawyer, mediator, arbitrator; b. N.Y.C., Dec. 6, 1949; BA, Queens Coll., 1970; JD, NYU, 1974. Bar: NY 1974, U.S. Dist. Ct. (so. and ea. dists.) NY 1977, U.S. Ct. Appeals (2d cir.) 1975, U.S. Claims Ct. 1996. Law asst. appellate divsn., 2d judicial dept. Supreme Ct. State of N.Y., 1975-76; assoc. Milbank, Tweed, Hadley & McCloy, N.Y.C., 1976-79; asst. corp. counsel Corp. Counsel of N.Y.C., 1979-83; pvt. practice N.Y.C., 1983—. Mem. ABA, N.Y. County Lawyers' Assn., N.Y. Bldg. Congress. General civil litigation, Construction, Government contracts and claims. Office: 275 Madison Ave Rm 900 New York NY 10016-0601

GRASSIA, THOMAS CHARLES, lawyer, writer; b. Westfield, Mass., Aug. 26, 1946; s. Thomas C. and Assunta (Abatiell) G.; m. Judith Chace Cranshaw, Aug. 15, 1970; children: Susan C., Joseph C. BA, Boston U., 1968; JD, Suffolk U., 1974. Bar: Mass. 1974, U.S. Dist. Ct. Mass. 1976, U.S. Supreme Ct. 1980. Asst. v.p. Plymouth Rubber Co., Canton, Mass., 1969-71; ptnr. P.T.S. Computer Svcs., Waltham, Mass., 1971-81, D'Angio & Grassia, Waltham, 1974-85, Grassia & Assocs., P.A., Natick, Mass., 1985—98, Grassia, Murphy & Whitney, P.A., Natick, 1998—2002, Grassia, Murphy & Lupan, P.A., Natick, 2002—. Agt. Lawyers Title Ins. Co., First Am. Title Ins. Co., Fidelity Nat. Title Ins. Co., Stewart Title Ins. Co.; bd. dirs. many regional corps; pres., treas., bd. dirs. Lender's Title & Abstract Co., Ltd., Natick. Author: Campfires, 2000; contbr. articles to profl. publs., lectr. on law, pub. interest subjects. Mem. Bd. Health, Sherborn, Mass., 1976-81, Bd. Selectmen, Sherborn, 1981-85; trustee Leonard Morse Hosp., Natick, 1981-84; mem. Met. Boston Hosp. Coun., Burlington, Mass., 1983-84; mem., team leader Sherborn Fire and Rescue Dept., 1974—; former mem. Sherborn Sch. Bd. Long Planning com., sherborn Police Chief Selection com., Sherborn Emergency Med. Com. Mem. ABA, Mass. Bar Assn., Mass. Conveyances Assn., Am. Arbitration Assn. (comml. arbitration bd.), New Eng. Helicopter Pilots Assn. (past pres., chmn. bd. dirs.). Corporate, general, Property, real (including real estate development, water), Sports. Home: PO Box 178 Sherborn MA 01770-0178 Office: Grassia Murphy & Lupan PA 5 Commonwealth Rd Natick MA 01760-1526 E-mail: tgrassia@gmllaw.com.

GRAU, VICENTE, lawyer; b. Mexico City, Mex., Feb. 4, 1969; s. Emilio Grau and Juana Alonso; m. Alejandra Francisco-Revilla, Oct. 12, 2002. LLB, Inst. Tech. (ITAM), Mexico City, 1994; LLM, Konstanz (Germany) U., 1997. Bar: Mex. Bar Assn. Law asst. Santamarina y Steta, Mexico City, 1990—94, assoc., 1994—95, 1997—2002, ptnr., 2003—. Exch. atty. CMS Hasche Sigle PS (formerly Sigle Loose Schmidt-Diemitz), 1997; prof. bus. law U. Ams., Mexico City, 1999. Avocations: books, travel, motorcycling. Corporate, general, Commercial, contracts (including sales of goods; commercial financing), Securities. Office: Santamarina y Steta SC Campos Eliseos 345 11560 Mexico City Mexico Office Fax: 52 55 52 80 62 14. E-mail: vgrau@s-s.com.mx.

GRAUBARD, SEYMOUR, lawyer; b. N.Y.C., Mar. 8, 1911; s. John and Edna (Kiesler) G.; m. Blanche Kazon, Aug. 24, 1941; 1 child, Katherine (Mrs. William Calvin). AB, Columbia U., 1931, LL.B., 1933. Bar: N.Y. 1933. Legislative asst. to bd. aldermen, N.Y.C., 1934-35; ptnr. Joseph D. McGoldrick, N.Y.C., 1936-37; law sec. to comptroller N.Y.C., 1937-41; sec. to justice Supreme Ct. N.Y. County, 1942, 45-46; practice in N.Y.C., 1949-75; counsel Graubard & Miller, 1975—. Lectr. municipal govt. N.Y. U., New Sch. Social Research, 1938-40 Co-author: Building Regulation in New York City, 1944. Mem. N.Y.C. Commn. Govtl. Operations, 1959-61, Coordinating Council Criminal Justice, 1967-70; Nat. chmn. Anti-Defamation League, B'nai B'rith, 1970-76; pres. ADL Found., 1976-80; chmn. bd. dirs. Fund for N.Y.C., to, 1978; bd. dirs. Palm Beach Civic Assn., 1996—. Served to maj. U.S. Army, 1942-45. Mem. Assn. Bar City N.Y. (past chmn. com. city cts.), N.Y. State Bar Assn., N.Y. County Lawyers Assn. Clubs: City (trustee past pres.), Harmonie (N.Y.C.). Home: 2784 S Ocean Blvd Palm Beach FL 33480-5506

GRAUMAN, NANCY, lawyer; b. Seattle, Nov. 4, 1968; d. David Willis and Joyce Marie Grauman. AB cum laude, Vassar Coll., Poughkeepsie, N.Y., 1991; JD cum laude, Loyola U., L.A., 1998. Bar: Calif. 1998. Summer assoc. White & Case, L.A., 1997; assoc. O'Melveny & Myers, L.A., 1998—2002, Gilchrist & Rutter Profl. Corp., Santa Monica, Calif., 2002—03, Piper Rudnick LLP, LA, 2003—. Recipient Am. Jurisprudence Bancroft-Whitney award for civil procedure and legal writing, Bancroft-Whitney, 1996. Mem.: Order of the Coif, Phi Alpha Delta. Avocations: cooking, travel, music. Office: Piper Rudnick LLP 1999 Ave of Stars Fl 4 Los Angeles CA 90067

GRAUPNER, HELMUT MANFRED LEOPOLD, lawyer; b. Tullnerbach, Austria, Jan. 26, 1965; s. Helmut Gustav Leopold Graupner and Edith Maria Zika. LLM, U. Vienna, 1989, JD, 1996. Bar: Austria 2000, Czech Republic 2000. Legal asst. Vienna Cts., 1993-94; legal asst. law firm Vienna, 1995-98, Prague, 1999; pvt. practice Vienna, 2000—. Staff dept. for protection of youths and apprentices Vienna Chamber of Labor, 1987-2000; expert com. for revision of law on sexual offences Ministry of Justice of Austria, Vienna, 1996—; expert group on sexual orientation discrimination European Union Commn., 2002—; rschr. on sexuality and the human rights law, child and youth sexuality, homosexuality, pornography and prostitution; sci. com. Ctr. Rsch. and Comparative Legal Studies on Sexual Orientation and Gender Identity, Turin, 2001--; lectr. U. Innsbruck, 2002--. Mem. editl. bd. Jour. Homosexuality; contbr. numerous articles to profl. jours. Mem. steering com. Internat. Lesbian and Gay Youth Assn. (IGLYO), 1989—90; pres. Rechtskomitee Lambda, Vienna, 1991—; spokesperson Platform Against Art 209, Vienna, 1991—; bd. dirs. Homosexuelle Initiative (HOSI), Wien, Vienna, 1985—91. Mem.: Europe Internat. Lesbian and Gay Law Assn. (v.p. for Europe 2000—), World Assn. for Sexology. Office: Helmut Graupner JD Maxingstr 22-24/4/9 A-1130 Vienna Austria E-mail: hg@graupner.at.

GRAVES, H. BRICE, retired lawyer; b. Charlottesville, Va., Sept. 1, 1912; BS, U. Va., 1932, MS, 1933, PhD, LL.B., 1938. Bar: N.Y. 1940, Va. 1949. Assoc. Cravath, Swaine & Moore, N.Y.C., 1938-42, 45-48; ptnr. Hunton & Williams, Richmond, Va., from 1949. Planning com. U. Va. Ann. Tax Conf., 1971-82, trustee emeritus, 1989—; lectr. in field Contbr. articles to profl. jours. Mem. Richmond Bar Assn., Va. Bar Assn. (chmn. taxation com. 1971-73), ABA (chmn. com. exempt orgns. tax sect. 1963-65, com. mem. 1975-77), Am. Law Inst., Richmond Estate Planning Council, Am. Coll. Tax Counsel Corporate taxation. Home: 10,000 Cedarfield Ct Cottage 20 Richmond VA 23233 Office: Hunton & Williams PO Box 1535 Richmond VA 23218-1535

GRAVES, JAMES E. state supreme court justice, educator; BA in Sociology, Millsaps Coll.; JD, MPA, Syracuse U. Pvt. practice; head Human Svcs. Dept. atty. gen.'s office, chief legal counsel Miss. Dept. Human Svcs.; spl. asst. atty. gen. Ctrl. Miss. Legal Svcs., staff atty.; dir. divsn. child support enforcement Miss. Dept. Human Svcs.; cir. ct. judge 7th Cir. Dist., 1991—2001; justice Miss. Supreme Ct., 2001—. Instr. trial advocacy Harvard Law Sch., 1998, 99, 2000; adj. prof. media and civil rights law Jackson State U. Advocate pub. sch. activities; coach student mock trial teams.

Named Parent of Yr., 2000—01; recipient Judge of Yr. award, Nat. Conf. Black Lawyers, 1992, Disting. Jurist award, Nat. Bar Assn., 1996, Innovation award, Hinds County Bar Assn., 2000. Office: PO Box 249 Jackson MS 39205*

GRAVES, JOHN WILLIAM, state supreme court justice; b. Paducah, Ky., Oct. 17, 1935; m. Mary Ann Breivo; children: James Anthony, Kevin Andrew. BS, U. Notre Dame, 1957; postgrad., U. Louisville, 1957-58; JD, U. Ky., 1963. Bar: Ky. 1963. Dist. judge, 1984-88; circuit ct. judge McCracken Cir., 1989-95; justice Ky. Supreme Ct., 1995—. Col. U.S. Army Res. Decorated Army Commendation medal, Army Meritorious Svc. medal. Office: Kentuky Supreme Court 222 Kentuky Avenue, PO Box 993 Paducah KY 42003

GRAVES, PATRICK LEE, lawyer; b. Pasadena, Calif., Sept. 16, 1945; s. James Edward and Virginia (Dudley) G.; children: Carrie Kathleen, Michael Patrick. AS, Citrus Jr. Coll., Glendora, Calif., 1969; BS, Calif. State Polytechnic U., 1973; BS in Law, Western State U., 1973, JD, 1975. Bar: Calif. 1975, U.S. Dist. Ct. (cen. dist.) Calif. 1976, U.S. Ct. Appeals (9th cir.) 1978, U.S. Supreme Ct. 1980. Assoc. Lynberg & Watkins, Los Angeles, 1975-80, ptnr., 1981-93, Graves & King, Irvine, Calif., 1993—. Settlement officer Los Angeles Superior Ct., 1988—, arbitrator, 1981—; arbitrator San Bernardino Superior Ct., 1990—; mediator L.A. Superior Ct., 1993—, Riverside Superior Ct., 1996—, AAA-Inland Empire, 1996—. Judge pro tem L.A. Superior Ct., 1992—. Sustaining mem. Rep. Nat. Com., Washington, 1979—; mem. Nat. Rep. Congl. Com., 1980—. Mem. ABA, San Bernardino County Bar Assn., Assn. So. Calif. Def. Counsel (chmn. 1988, bd. dirs. 1996—), Def. Rsch. Inst., Upland (Calif.) C. of C. Avocations: flyfishing, golf. Government contracts and claims, Personal injury (including property damage), Property, real (including real estate development, water). Home: 32302 Alipaz St 246 San Juan Capistrano CA 92672 Office: Graves & King 30448 Rancho Viejo Rd Ste 200 San Juan Capistrano CA 92675

GRAVES, RAY REYNOLDS, retired judge; b. Tuscumbia, Ala., Jan. 10, 1946; s. Isaac and Olga Ernestine (Wilder) Graves; children: Claire Elise, Reynolds Douglass. BA, Trinity Coll., Hartford, Conn., 1967; JD, Wayne State U., 1970. Bar: Mich. 1971, U.S. Dist. Ct. (ea. dist.) Mich. 1971, U.S. Ct. Appeals (6th cir.) 1972, U.S. Supreme Ct. 1976, D.C. 1977. Defender Legal Aid and Defender Assn., Detroit, 1970-71; assoc. Liberson, Fink, Feiler, Crystal & Burdick, 1971-72, Patmon, Young & Kirk, 1972-73; ptnr. Lewis, White, Clay & Graves, 1974-81; mem. legal dept. Detroit Edison Co., 1981; judge U.S. Bankruptcy Ct., Ea. Dist. Mich., Detroit, 1982-2002; chief judge U.S. Bankruptcy Ct., 1991-95; prin. BBK, Ltd., Southfield, Mich., 2002—. Mem. U.S. ct. com. State Bar Mich. Trustee Mich. Opera Theatre, 1986—88; vestry Christ Ch. Episcopal, Grosse Pointe, Mich., 1994—97; del Diocesan Conv. Episcopal Ch., Mich., 1997; bd. dirs. Mich. Cancer Found. Fellow: Am. Coll. Bankruptcy; mem.: D.C. Bar Assn., Detroit Bar Assn., Wolverine Bar Assn., Assn. Black Judges Mich., World Peace Through Law Conf., World Assn. Judges, Nat. Conf. Bakruptcy Jduges (bd. govs. 1984—88), Iota Boulè (Sire Archon 1999—2001), Sigma Pi Phi, Delta Kappa Epsilon. Episcopalian. Office: BBK Ltd 300 Galleria Officentre # 103 Southfield MI 48034 Office Fax: 248-603-8374. Business E-Mail: rgraves@e-bbk.com.

GRAVES, TODD PETERSON, prosecutor; BA, U. Mo., 1988; JD, U. Va. Assoc. Skadden Arps, N.Y.C.; with Bryan Cave, 1992—94; prosecutor Platte County, Mo.; U.S. atty. Mo. western dist. U.S. Dept. Justice, 2001—. Republican. Office: 400 E 9th St 5th Fl Kansas City MO 64106

GRAVING, RICHARD JOHN, law educator; b. Duluth, Minn., Aug. 24, 1929; s. Lawrence Richard and Laura Magdalene (Loucks) G.; m. Florence Sara Semel; children: Daniel, Sarah. BA, U. Minn., 1950; JD, Harvard U., 1953; postgrad., Nat. U. Mex., 1964-66. Bar: Minn. 1953, N.Y. 1956, U.S. Dist. Ct. (so. dist.) N.Y. 1956, Pa. 1968, U.S. Dist. Ct. (we. dist.) Pa. 1968, Tex. 1982, U.S. Dist. Ct. (so. dist.) Tex. 1982. Assoc. Reid & Priest, N.Y.C., 1955-61, Mexico City, 1961-66; v.p. Am. & Fgn. Power Co., Inc., Mexico City, 1966-68; atty. Gulf Oil Corp., Pitts., 1968-69, Madrid, 1969-73, London, 1973-80, Houston, 1980—82; pvt. practice London, 1982—84; prof. law South Tex. Coll., Houston, 1983—; prof. Bush Grad. Sch.. Tex. A&M U., Coll. Sta., 2001—. With U.S. Army, 1953-55. Mem. Am. Soc. Internat. Law. Home: 8515 Ariel St Houston TX 77074-2806 Office: 1303 San Jacinto St Houston TX 77002-7000

GRAY, CAROLYN DOPPELT, lawyer; b. Elmira, N.Y., Apr. 10, 1940; d. Frederic Amster and Lucille (Greenebaum) D.; m. Thomas Allen Gray, 1982; 1 child, Emilie Sara Gray. AA, Stephens Coll., 1959; BA in Journalism, U. Mo., 1961; JD, Ind. U., 1979. Dir. pub. rels. Ft. Wayne (Ind.) Fine Arts Found., 1962-65; pres., treas. The Toidey Co., Ft. Wayne, Ind., 1965-81; pvt. practice Ft. Wayne, Ind., 1979-81; dir. Office Women's Bus. Ownership, SBA, Washington, 1981-85; pres. Appalachian Found., Washington, 1985-86; dep. asst. sec. Office Human Devel. Svcs., HHS, Washington, 1986-88, commr. Adminstrn. Devel. Disabilities Office, 1988-89; spl. counsel Saul, Ewing, Remick & Saul, Washington, 1990-92; ptnr. Epstein Becker & Green, P.C., Washington, 1992—2003, Barnes & Thornburg, Washington, 2003—. Gen. counsel, sec., treas. Inst. Disability Resources, Washington, 1994-1997; pres. Gray Devel. Group, Inc., Rockville, Md., 1989— Author: (handbook) What You Absolutely Must Know About The Americans with Disabilities Act, 1992, (handbook) The ADA: Next Steps for Employers: How to Successfully Fit the ADA Into Your Workforce Picture, 1993; editl. adv. bd. Disability Law Reporter Svc., 1993; editl. bd. Nat. Disability Law Reporter, 1991—; contributing editor: Disability Compliance Bulletin, 1991—. Mem. task force on pediatric AIDS and HIV, HHS, 1988-89; exec. dir. President's Adv. Com. on Women's Bus. Ownership, 1983-84; mem. President's Task Force for Legal Equity for Women, 1983-86. Recipient Disting. Svc. award Ft. Wayne (Ind.) Jaycees, 1975. Mem. ABA, Ind. Bar Assn., D.C. Bar Assn., Jr. League of Washington, Univ. Club; bd. overseers Hebrew Union Coll. Jewish Inst. Religion, N.Y., 1990-. Republican. Jewish. Avocation: residential and commercial design. Office: Barnes & Thornburg Ste 900 750 17th St NW Washington DC 20006-4607

GRAY, CHARLES ROBERT, lawyer; b. Kirksville, Mo., Aug. 22, 1952; s. George Devon and Bettie Louise (McCormick) G.; m. Dana Elizabeth Kehr, June 1, 1974; children: Jennifer, Jessica, Marcus, Gregory, Victoria. BS, N.E. Mo. State U., 1974; JD, U. Mo., Kansas City, 1978. Bar: Mo. 1978, Va. 1993, U.S. Dist. Ct. (we. dist.) Mo. 1978, U.S. Ct. Appeals (fed. cir.) 1992, U.S. Ct. Appeals (4th cir.) 1995, U.S. Supreme Ct. 1981; cert. mediator; cert. hearing officer Va. Supereme Ct., 1997. Pvt. practice, Parkville, Mo., 1978-81; asst. pub. defender 5th Judicial Cir. Ct. Mo., St. Joseph, 1978-79; pub. defender 6th Judicial Cir. Ct. Mo., Platte City, 1981; asst. dist. counsel Army Corps of Engrs., Kansas City, 1981-82, Vicksburg, Miss., 1982-83; chief counsel space shuttle, MX missile U.S. Army, Vandenberg AFB, Calif., 1983-85, chief counsel troop support agy. Ft. Lee, Va., 1985-87; fraud counsel Def. Gen. Supply Ctr. Dept. of Def., Richmond, Va., 1987-93; pvt. practice, Chester, Va., 1993-99; asst. atty. gen. Atty. Gen.'s Office State of Va., 1999—; owner Pvt. Jud. Svcs., Inc., Chester, 1993—. Adj. prof. St. Leo Coll., Ft. Lee, 1986-91, John Tyler Coll., Chester, Va., 1994—; mem. dispute resolution coun. VA, 2002, mem. adv. oversite panel. Mem. Selective Svc. Draft Bd., Brookfield, Mo., 1972-74; pres. Old Towne Parkville Assn., 1979-81, Chester (Va.) Youth Sports Boosters, 1989-91; den leader Boy Scouts Am., Chester, 1991—. Victor Wilson honor scholar, 1977; recipient Am. Jurisprudence award Coop-Bancroft-Whitney, 1989. Mem. ATLA, Am. Arbitration Assn. (mem. nat. panel arbitrators 1994—, mem. govt. disputes panel 1995—, mem. constrn. panel 1995—, mem. comml. panel 1995—), Def. Rsch. Inst. (approved mem. panel on mediation and arbitration), Mo. Bar Assn., Va. Bar Assn., Va. Trial Lawyers Assn. Methodist. Avocations: coaching youth sports, cub scouts, softball, tennis, basketball. Construction, General practice, Personal injury (including property damage). Home: 3813 Terjo Ln Chester VA 23831-1839 Office: Pres Presiding Ofcl PO Box 34386 Chester VA 23834 E-mail: cgray@oag.state.va.us.

GRAY, ELISABETH SOMMERS, lawyer; b. Shreveport, La., Sept. 11, 1970; d. Gary Franklin and Ann Richardson Gray; m. John Bernard Von der Haar, Sept. 14, 2002. BA in Spanish, U. Oreg., 1993; JD, Vanderbilt U., 1998. Bar: Ky. 1998, U.S. Dist. Ct. (we. and ea. dists.) Ky. 1999, U.S. Dist. Ct. (ctrl. dist.) Tenn., U.S. Dist. Ct. Ind. 1999, U.S. Ct. Appeals (6th cir.) 1999. Assoc. Greenebaum Doll McDonald, Louisville, 1998—. Vol. Big Bros./Big Sisters, Louisville, 2000—; bd. dirs. Am. Cancer Soc., Louisville, 2002—. Mem.: Louisville Bar Assn., Women Lawyers Assn., Inn of Ct. (assoc.). Office: Greenebaum Doll & McDonald 3300 National City Tower Louisville KY 40202 E-mail: esg@gdm.com.

GRAY, ELIZABETH VAN DOREN, lawyer; b. Columbia, S.C., Jan. 3, 1949; d. Robert Lawson and Elizabeth Dacus (Gaines) Van Doren; m. James Cranston Gray, Jr., Apr. 30, 1982; children: James Cranston III, Elizabeth Gaines. BA in Internat. Studies, U. S.C., 1970, JD cum laude, 1976; student, St. Mary's Coll., Raleigh, N.C., 1966-67. Bar: S.C. 1977, U.S. Dist. Ct. S.C. 1977, U.S. Ct. Appeals (4th cir.) 1980, U.S. Ct. Appeals (6th cir.) 1989, U.S. Supreme Ct. 1998. Assoc. McNair Law Firm, PA, Columbia, 1977-82, shareholder, 1982-87; ptnr. Glenn Irvin Murphy Gray & Stepp, Columbia, 1987—2000; now ptnr. Sowell Gray Stepp & Lafitte, LLC, Columbia. Contbr. articles to profl. jours. Mem. ABA, Am. Coll. Trial Lawyers, John Belton O'Neal Inn of Ct., S.C. Bar (pres. 2001-02), S.C. Women Lawyers Assn. (bd. dirs. 1995-99, sec. 1997-98), Richland County Bar Assn. Episcopalian. Commercial, contracts (including sales of goods; commercial financing). Office: Sowell Gray Stepp & Lafitte LLC PO Box 11449 Columbia SC 29211 Home: 8 Mahalo Ln Columbia SC 29204-3380

GRAY, FRANK TRUAN, lawyer; b. Prince Frederick, Md., Oct. 22, 1920; s. John B. and Aimèe Atlee (Truan) Gray; m. Sally A. Jackson, Dec. 31, 1976; children: John W., Edward A., Philip L., Theodora R. AB, Princeton U., 1942; student, Cambridge (Eng.) U., 1945; LL.B., Harvard U., 1948. Bar: Md. 1949. Assoc. firm Piper & Marbury, Balt., 1948-56, ptnr., 1957-90. Asst. atty. gen. State of Md., 1955—56; pres. Balt. Estate Planning Coun., 1975—76. Editor: Harvard Law Rev., 1947—48. Pres. Citizen's Planning and Housing Assn., Balt., 1960—62; bd. dirs. Balt. Neighborhoods, Inc., 1959—85, Balt. Bar Found., 1985—93; trustee Provident Hosp., Inc., 1961—74, Leonard and Helen R. Stulman Charitable Found., 1991—. Fellow: Md. Bar Found., Am. Bar Found. (chmn. Md. 1993—98); mem.: ABA, Balt. Bar Assn., Md. Bar Assn., Am. Law Inst. Office: Piper Rudnick LLP 111 S Calvert St Ste 1950 Baltimore MD 21202-6193

GRAY, FRED DAVID, lawyer; b. Montgomery, Ala., Dec. 14, 1930; s. Abraham and Nancy G.; m. Bernice Hill, June 17, 1956; children: Deborah R., Vanessa, Fred D., Stanley F. BS, Ala. State U., 1951; JD, Case Western Res. U., 1954. Bar: Ala. 1954, Ohio 1954, U.S. Dist. Ct. (mid. dist.) Ala. 1955, U.S. Supreme Ct. 1956, U.S. Ct. Appeals (5th cir.) 1958, U.S. Dist. Ct. (no. dist.) Ala. 1963, U.S. Tax Ct. 1968, U.S. Ct. Appeals (11th cir.) 1982. Sr. ptnr. Gray, Langford, Sapp & McGowan and predecessor firm, Montgomery and Tuskegee, Ala., 1983—. Author: (book) Bus Ride to Justice, 1995, The Tuskegee Syphilis Study, 1998. City atty. City of Tuskegee, 1965—; cooperating atty. NAACP Legal Def. Fund, Inc.; local gen. counsel Tuskegee U.; spl. asst. to atty. gen. State of Ala., 1975; past mem. Ala. Adv. Com. U.S. Commn. on Civil Rights; mem. Tuskegee Civic Assn. (life, award 1981); elder Tuskegee Ch. of Christ; chmn., trustee Southwestern Christian Coll., Terrell, Tex. Recipient Constl. Law award Ala. Civil Liberties Union, 1968, Disting. Alumni award Ala. State U., 1974, Social Engr.'s citation, 1975, Martin Luther King, Jr. Meml. Drum Major award So. Christian Leadership Conf., 1980, Black Achievers award, Ala. chpt. SCLC 1981, Fletcher Reed Andrews Grad. Yr. award Case Western Res. U., 1985, Man Yr. award Southwestern Christian Coll., 1986, Charles Hamilton Medallion of Merit Washington Bar Assn., 1986; honored by Miller Brewing Co. Gallery of Greats: Black Attys. Counsels for the Cause, 1989. Mem. ABA, Assn. Trial Lawyers Am., Ala. Trial Lawyers Assn., Ala. State Bar Assn. (pres.-elect 2001-02, pres. 2002-03),Nat. Bar Assn. (pres. 1985-86, 1st Ann. Equal Justice award 1977), Macon County Bar Assn. (past pres.), Nat. Bar Inst., NAACP (life), Soc. Benchers, Omega Psi Phi, Sigma Pi Phi. Honored by Miller Brewing Co. Gallery of Greats: Black Attys. Counsels for the Cause, 1989. Civil rights, Commercial, consumer (including collections, credit), General practice. Office: Gray Langford et al PO Box 830239 Tuskegee AL 36083-0239 also: 400 S Union St Ste 205 Montgomery AL 36104-4316*

GRAY, J. CHARLES, lawyer, cattle rancher; b. Leesburg, Fla., Mar. 26, 1932; s. G. Wayne and Mary Evelyn (Albright) G.; m. Saundra Hagood, Aug. 18, 1955; children: Terese Ren. John Charles Jr., Lee Jerome. BA, U. Fla., 1955, JD, 1958. Bar: Fla. 1958. County atty. Orange County, Fla., 1978-85; chmn. Gray, Harris & Robinson, P.A. Chmn. Fla. Turnpike Authority, 1965-67; city solicitor City of Orlando (Fla.), 1960-61; pres. Santa Gertrudis Breeders Internat., 1981-83. Chmn. pres.'s coun. advisors U. Ctrl. Fla., 1978-84; pres. U. Ctrl. Fla. Found., 1990-91, dir. emeritus; past pres. Orange County U. Fla. Alumni Assn., Pi Kappa Alpha Alumni Assn.; past dist. v.p. U. Fla. Alumni Assn.; mem. U. Fla. Pres.'s Coun.; mem. Com. of 100; founding bd. dirs. Fla. Epilepsy Found.; chmn. Econ. Devel. Commn. Mid. Fla., 1987-89; mem. Fla. Econ. Devel. Adv. Coun; mem., bd.dirs. O-Force of Ctrl. Fla. Recipient J. Thomas Guerney Lifetime Svc. award, James B. Green award for Econ. Devel., Fla. Pub. Rels. award; inducted into U. Fla. Hall of Fame, Roast & Toast Fla. Pub. Relations Assn.. Mem. ABA, Fla. Bar Assn., Orange County Bar Assn., Citrus Club of Orlando (past dir.), Univ. Club of Orlando (past dir.), Seven Seas Cruising Assn. (commodore; World Circumnavigator award), bd. dir. O'Force: adv. bd. of "Seeds of Peace" Republican. Episcopalian. Property, real (including real estate development, water). Home: PO Box 3068 Orlando FL 32802-3068 Office: Ste 1400 301 E Pine St Orlando FL 32801-2725 Personal E-mail: cgray4@cfl.rr.com. Business E-Mail: cgray@GrayHarris.com.

GRAY, JAN CHARLES, lawyer, business owner; b. Des Moines, June 15, 1947; s. Charles Donald and Mary C. Gray; 1 child, Charles Jan. BA in Econs., U. Calif., Berkeley, 1969; MBA, Pepperdine U., 1986; JD, Harvard U., 1972. Bar: Calif. 1972, D.C. 1974, Wyo. 1992. Law clk. Kindel & Anderson, L.A., 1971-72; assoc. Halstead, Baker & Sterling, L.A., 1972-75; sr. v.p., gen. counsel and sec. Ralphs Grocery Co., L.A., 1975-97; pres. Am. Presidents Resorts, Custer, S.D., Casper/Glenrock, Wyo., 1983—; owner Big Bear (Calif.) Cabins-Lakeside, 1988—; pres. Mt. Rushmore Broadcasting, Inc., 1991—; owner Sta. KGOS/KERM, Torrington, Wyo., 1993—, Sta. KRAL/KIQZ, Rawlins, Wyo., 1993—, Sta. KZMX, Hot Springs, S.D., 1993—, Sta. KFCR, Custer, S.D., 1992—, Sta. KQLT-FM, Casper, Wyo., 1994—, Sta. KASS-FM, Casper, 1995—, Sta. KVOC-AM, Casper, 1997—, KAWK-FM, Rapid City, S.D., 1997—, KHOC, Casper, Wyo., 1998—, Mt. Rushmore Farm Horse Racing, 1999—. Judge pro tem L.A. Mcpl. Ct., 1977-85; instr. bus. UCLA, 1976-85, Pepperdine MBA Program, 1983-85; arbitrator Am. Arbitration Assn., 1977-97; media spokesman So. Calif. Grocers Assn., 1979-90, Calif. Grocers Assn., 1979-97, Calif. Retailers Assn., 1979-97; real estate broker, Calif., 1973—. Contbg. author: Life or Death, Who Controls?, 1976; contbr. articles to profl. jours. Trustee South Bay U. Coll. Law, 1978-79; mem. bd. visitors Southwestern U. Sch. Law, 1983—; mem. L.A. County Pvt. Industry Coun., 1982-96, exec. com. 1984-88, chmn. econ. devel. task force, 1986-89, chmn. mktg. com. 1991-93; mem. L.A. County Martin Luther King, Jr. Gen. Hosp. Authority, 1984—; mem. L.A. County Aviation Commn, 1986-92, chmn., 1990-91; L.A. Police Crime Prevention Adv. Coun., 1986—; Angelus Plaza Adv. Bd., 1983-85; bd. dirs. RecyCAL of So. Calif., 1983-89; trustee Santa Monica Hosp. Found., 1986-91, adv. bd., 1991—; mem. L.A. County Dem. Cen. Com., 1980-90, L.A. City Employees' Retirement System Commn., 1993—; del. Dem. Nat. Conv., 1980. Recipient So. Calif. Grocers Assn. award for outstanding contbns. to food industry, 1982, appreciation award for No on 11 Campaign, Calif./Nev. Soft Drink Assn., 1983; Tyler Price Meml. award Mex.-Am. Grocers Assn., 1995, Radio Affiliate of Yr.-Classic Rock ABC, 1998. Mem.: Casper Country Club, Petroleum Club, L.A. Athletic Club, Harvard Club of So. Calif., Ephebian Soc. L.A., U. Calif. Alumni Assn., Town Hall L.A., So. Calif. Bus. Assn. (bd. dirs. 1981—99, mem. exec. com. 1982—99, sec. 1986—91, chair 1991—98), Food Mktg. Inst. (govt. rels. com. 1977—97, chmn.lawyers, economists 1993—95, benefits coun. 1993—97), Calif. Retailers Assn. (supermarket com.), L.A. World Affairs Coun., L.A. Pub. Affairs Officers Assn., San Fernando Valley Bar Assn. (chmn. real property sect. 1975—77), L.A. County Bar Assn. (exec. com. corp. law depts. sect. 0179—, exec. com. barristers sect. 1974—75, exec. com. corp. law depts. sect. 1974—76, exec. com. barristers sect. 1979—81, chmn. 1989—90, trustee 1991—93, jud. evaluation com. 1993—, nominating com. 1994), Calif. Bar Assn., ABA, Phi Beta Kappa. Corporate, general. Home: 2793 Creston Dr Los Angeles CA 90068-2209 Office: PO Box 2515 Casper WY 82602-2515

GRAY, JOHN FISHER, lawyer; BA SCL, Ind. U., Bloomington, 1984; JD, Harvard U., Cambridge, Mass., 1987. Bar: Pa, 1987, U.S. Dist. Ct. (ea. dist.) Pa. 1988. Law clk. Hon. Marvin Katz, U.S. Dist. Ct. E. D. Pa., Phila.a, 1987—88; assoc. Pepper, Hamilton & Scheetz, Phila., 1988—91; atty. ICI Americas Inc. / ZENECA Inc., Wilmington, Del., 1991—95; sr. counsel Basell Polyolefins, Wilmington, 1995—. Pres. Autism Soc. of Del., Wilmington, Del., 2001—03, v.p., 1998—2001; vestry St. Mark's Ch., Phila., 2002—03; trustee and officer Episcopal Chapel at Harvard and Radcliffe, Cambridge, Mass., 1986—97. Mem.: ABA, Phila. Bar Assn. (assoc.), Phi Beta Kappa. Office: Basell Polyolefins 2801 Centerville Rd Wilmington DE 19808-1652

GRAY, JOHN LEONARD, retired lawyer; b. N.Y.C., Feb. 14, 1924; s. James E. and Edna M. Gray; m. Margaret S. Gray, Aug. 23, 1947 (div. Jan. 1976); children: Linda S., James S.; m. Elizabeth Z. Gray, Apr. 24, 1976. BChE, Pratt Inst., N.Y.C., 1943; JD, Albany Law Sch., 1948. Bar: N.Y. 1951, Ohio 1951. Patent counsel, gen. counsel Battelle Meml. Inst., Columbus, Ohio, 1949-72; ptnr. Kegler Brown Hill & Ritter, Columbus, 1972-89, of counsel, 1989—. V.p. Battelle Devel. Corp., Scientific Advances Inc. Lt. (j.g.) USN, 1943-46, PTO, ATO. Mem.: Navy League (bd. dirs. 1990—2002), Ohio C. of C. (bd. dirs., exec. com. 1994—), Rotary (pres. 1994—95). Intellectual property, Patent, Trademark and copyright. E-mail: grayjl@keglerbrown.com.

GRAY, JON R. judge; b. Little Rock; AB, Grinnell Coll., 1973; JD, U. Mo., Kansas City, 1976. Bar: Mo. 77. Judge Jackson County Cir. Ct., Kansas City, Mo., 1987—. Methodist. Office: Cir Ct Jackson County 415 E 12th St Kansas City MO 64106 Fax: 816-881-3950.

GRAY, KARLA MARIE, state supreme court chief justice; b. May 10, 1947; BA, MA in African History, Western Mich. U.; JD, Hastings Coll. of Law, San Francisco, 1976. Bar: Mont. 1976, Calif. 1977. Law clk. to Hon. W. D. Murray U.S. Dist. Ct., 1976-77; staff atty. Atlantic Richfield Co., 1977-81; pvt. practice law Butte, Mont., 1981-84; staff atty., legis. lobbyist Mont. Power Co., Butte, 1984-91; justice Supreme Ct. Mont., Helena, 1991-2000, chief justice, 2000—. Mem. Mont. Supreme Ct. Gender Fairness Task Force. Fellow Am. Bar Found., Am. Judicature Soc., Internat. Women's Forum; mem. State Bar Mont., Silver Bow County Bar Assn. (past pres.), Nat. Assn. Women Judges. Avocations: travel, reading, piano, family genealogy, cross-country sking. Office: Supreme Ct Mont PO Box 203001 Helena MT 59620-3001

GRAY, LILLIA ANN, lawyer; b. Miami, Fla., Aug. 18, 1955; d. Elbert Lewis and Lillia Irene (Aschiero) G. AA, Miami-Dade Community Coll., 1976; BA summa cum laude, Cen. Wesleyan Coll., 1979; JD, U. S.C., 1984. Bar: S.C., Ga. Shareholder Cooper, Coffas, Moore and Gray, P.A. Life mem. Girl Scouts of Am. Mem. Ga. State Bar Assn., Comml. Law League, S.C. Bar Assn., S.C. Bankruptcy Law Assn., S.C. Women Lawyers Assn., Fed. Bar Assn. Bankruptcy, Commercial, consumer (including collections, credit).

GRAY, MARVIN LEE, JR., lawyer; b. Pitts., May 9, 1945; s. Marvin L. and Frances (Stringfellow) G.; m. Jill Miller, Aug. 14, 1971; children: Elizabeth Ann, Carolyn Jill. AB, Princeton U., 1966; JD magna cum laude, Harvard U., 1969. Bar: Wash. 1973, U.S. Supreme Ct. 1977, Alaska 1984. Law clk. to judge U.S. Ct. Appeals, N.Y.C., 1969-70; law clk. to justice U.S. Supreme Ct., Washington, 1970-71; asst. U.S. atty. U.S. Dept. Justice, Seattle, 1973-76; ptnr. Davis Wright Tremaine, Seattle, 1976—, mng. ptnr., 1985-88. Staff counsel Rockefeller Commn. on CIA Activities in U.S., Washington, 1974; lectr. trial practice U. Wash. Law Sch., Seattle, 1979-80. Lay reader Episcopal Ch. of Ascension, Seattle, 1982-94. Capt. USAF, 1971-73. Fellow Am. Coll. Trial Lawyers; mem. ABA, Am. Law Inst. Antitrust, Federal civil litigation. Office: Davis Wright Tremaine 1501 4th Ave Ste 2600 Seattle WA 98101-1688

GRAY, OSCAR SHALOM, lawyer; b. N.Y.C., Oct. 18, 1926; BA, Yale U., 1948, JD, 1951. Bar: Md. 1951, D.C. 1952, U.S. Supreme Ct. 1952. Atty.-adviser legal adviser's office U.S. Dept. State, Washington, 1951-57; sec. Nuclear Materials and Equipment Corp., Apollo, Pa., 1957-64, treas., 1957-67, v.p., 1964-71, dir., 1964-67; spl. counsel Presdl. Task Force on Communications Policy, Washington, 1967-68; cons. U.S. Dept. Transp., Washington, 1967-68, acting dir. office environ. impact, 1968-70; sole practice Washington, 1970—, Balt., 1971—. Adj. prof., professorial lectr. Law Ctr. Georgetown U., Washington, 1970-71; lectr. Cath. U. Am., Washington, 1970-71; assoc. prof. U. Md., Balt., 1971-74, prof., 1974-93, Jacob A. France prof. of torts, 1993-96, prof. emeritus, 1996—; vis. prof. U. Tenn., 1977. Author: Cases and Materials on Environmental Law, 1970, 2d edit., 1973, supplements, 1974, 1975, 1977; author: (with F. Harper and F. James Jr.) The Law of Torts, 2d edit., 1986; author: 3d edit., vol. 1, 1996; author: (with H. Shulman and F. James Jr.) Cases and Materials on the Law of Torts(with D. Gifford) 4th edit., 2003; contbr. articles to profl. legal jours. Mem.: ABA, D.C. Fedn. of Civic Assns. (parliamentarian 1991—99, 2000—03), D.C. Bar Assn., Am. Law Inst. (adviser Restatement of the Law, Third, Torts: Products Liability), Selden Soc. (state correspondent Md.), Phi Beta Kappa, Order of Coif. State civil litigation, Insurance. Office: 500 W Baltimore St Baltimore MD 21201-1602

GRAY, PAULETTE MICHELLE, lawyer; b. Chgo., Sept. 15, 1969; m. Robert L. Gray, Oct. 31, 1998; 1 child, Liam B. BA, U. Minn., 1991; JD, John Marshall Law Sch., 1996. Bar: Ill. 1996, U.S. Dist. Ct. (no. dist.) Ill. 1996. Assoc. Lake, Toback and Yavitz, Chgo., 1996—98, Gitlin and Gitlin, Woodstock, Ill., 1998—2002, Gitlin Law Firm, Woodstock, 2002—. Contbr. . Mem.: McHenry County Bar Assn. (bd. govs. 2001—, pres. Family Law sect. 2000—01, sec./treas. Family Law sect. 1999—2000), Appellate Lawyers Assn. Ill., Ill. State Bar Assn. (Family Law sect. coun. 2000—). Avocations: gardening, reading. Family and matrimonial, Appellate. Office: Gitlin Law Firm 663 E Calhoun St Woodstock IL 60098

GRAY, RANDALL JOSHUA, law librarian; b. Santa Monica, Calif., Sept. 30, 1949; s. Joshua and Eunice M. (Serr) G.; BA in English, San Fernando Valley State Coll., 1972; MLS, UCLA, 1974, cert. of specialization in law librarianship, 1974; m. Roberta Christine Johnsen, June 15, 1973. Intern, L.A. County Law Libr., 1973-74; asst. libr. O'Melveny & Myers, L.A., 1974-76; law libr. Adams, Duque & Hazeltine, L.A., 1976-82, dir. info. svcs., 1982-84; sales rep. Callaghan & Co. Law and Tax Publs., 1984-85;

mgr. info. svcs. Haight, Brown & Bonesteel, L.A., 1986—; instr. Inst. Pvt. Law Librs., Biltmore Hotel, L.A., 1980, UCLA Extension, 1980, Practising Law Inst., 1981; participant Calif. State Colls. Internat. Studies Program, Uppsala, Sweden, 1971; chmn. 10th Ann. Inst. on Calif. Law, 1982. Mem. Am. Assn. Law Libr., So. Calif. Assn. Law Librs. (chmn. cons. com. 1980, v.p. 1981-82, pres. 1982-83), UCLA Grad. Sch. Libr. and Info. Sci. Students Assn. (pres. 1973-74). Author: Effective Administration: Better Decisions through Information, 1981. Home: 521 Ramona Ave Sierra Madre CA 91024-2230 Office: Haight Brown & Bonesteel 6080 Center Dr Ste 800 Los Angeles CA 90045-1574

GRAY, ROBERT JOSEPH, lawyer; b. Oak Park, Ill., Feb. 15, 1966; s. Donald Frank and Jane Gray; m. Danalee Jacobson, Sept. 2, 1995; 1 child, Parker Robert. BA, U. Ill., 1988; JD, Marquette U., 1991. Bar: Wis. 1991, U.S. Dist. Ct. (ea. and we. dists.) Wis. 1991. Assoc. Jerome A Maeder Law Office, Wausau, Wis., 1991—. Mem. ABA, ATLA, Wis. Bar Assn., Marathon County Bar Assn., Phi Alpha Delta. Pension, profit-sharing, and employee benefits, Personal injury (including property damage), Workers' compensation. Office: Jerome A Maeder Law Office 602 Jackson St Wausau WI 54403-5549 E-mail: gray@dwave.net.

GRAY, WILLIAM R. lawyer; b. Peoria, Ill., Aug. 25, 1941; s. John J. and Alverna K. (Kennedy) G.; m. Tiana M. Yeager, June 12, 1982; children: Ann Katherine, Thomas William. BA, U. Colo., 1963, JD, 1966. Bar: Colo. 1966; U.S. Dist. Ct. Colo. 1966; U.S. Ct. Appeals (10th cir.) 1976. Dep. dist. atty. Dist. Atty.'s Office/10th Jud. Dist., Pueblo, Colo., 1967-69, Dist. Atty.'s Office/20th Jud. Dist., Boulder, Colo., 1969-70; dep. state pub. defender Colo. State Pub. Defender, Boulder, 1970-72; ptnr. Miller & Gray, Boulder, 1973-85, Purvis Gray, LLP, Boulder, 1985—. Mem./vice chair, chmn., Colo. Supreme Ct. grievance com., 1983-88, mem. criminal rules com., 1982-84; adj. prof. law U. Colo. Sch. of Law, Boulder, 1984. Bd. dirs. Mental Health Ctr. of Boulder County, 1972-78. Fellow Am. Coll. Trial Lawyers (Courageous Advocacy award 1985), Internat. Soc. Barristers, Internat. Acad. Trial Lawyers, Am. Bar Found., Colo. Bar Foun., Colo. Bar Assn. (Professionalism award 1995), Am. Bd. Trial Advocates. Democrat. Environmental, Personal injury (including property damage), Product liability. Office: Purvis Gray LLP Ste 501 1050 Walnut St Boulder CO 80302-5144 E-mail: bgray@purvisgray.net.

GRAY-FUSON, JOAN LORRAINE, lawyer; b. Glendale, Calif., Mar. 25, 1938; d. Stanley Wayne Brune and Maxine Lorraine (Falconer) Talkin; m. Darrell Herbert Gray, June 26, 1959 (div. 1972); children: Michael Herbert Gray, Thomas Edward Gray; m. Arnold Max Fuson, Dec. 18, 1977; stepchildren: Marie Fuson Hudson, Karen Fuson, Gregory J. Fuson. BA in Edn., Calif. State U., 1960; JD, U. of the Pacific, 1978. Bar: Calif. 1978, U.S. Dist. Ct. (ea. dist.) Calif. 1978. Tchr. Rio Linda Union Sch. Dist., Sacramento, Calif., 1960-65; pvt. practice Sacramento, 1978-81; staff counsel State of Calif. Water Resources Control Bd., Sacramento, 1982-91; sr. staff counsel State of Calif. Dept. of Conservation, Sacramento, 1991—. Elder on session Fremont Presbyn. Ch., Sacramento, 1995-97. Avocations: gardening, folk dancing, fitness. Office: Dept of Conservation 801 K St # Ms24-3 Sacramento CA 95814-3500

GRAYSHAW, JAMES RAYMOND, judge; b. Cleve., Apr. 3, 1948; s. Thomas J. and Bettie Lee Grayshaw; m. Susan Hancher, Oct. 15, 1980; 1 child, John H. BA, L.I. U., Bklyn., 1970; JD, Bklyn. Law Sch., 1975. Legal asst. Cadwalader, Wickersham & Taft, N.Y.C., 1975-77; law asst. Civil Ct., City N.Y., 1977-80; sr. law asst. Supreme Ct., State N.Y., 1980-82; judge housing part Civil Ct., City N.Y., 1983—. Judge advocate Cmty. Advocacy Ctr., N.Y.C., 1996. Sgt. U.S. Army, 1970-72. Mem. Queens Bar Assn., Protestant Lawyers N.Y.C. (dir. 1980—), Vietnam Vets. Am., 16th Inf. Reg. Assn., Masons, Sovereign Mil. Order of Temple of Jerusalem. Democrat. Episcopalian. Home: 21107 28th Ave Bayside NY 11360-2508 Office: Civil Ct City NY 89-17 Sutphin Blvd Jamaica NY 11435 E-mail: jgrayshaw@aol.com., jgraysha@courts.state.ny.us.

GRAYSON, EDWARD DAVIS, lawyer, manufacturing company executive; b. Davenport, Iowa, June 20, 1938; s. Charles E. and Isabelle (Davis) G.; m. Alice Ann McLaughlin; children: Alice Anne, Maureen Isabelle, Edward Davis Jr. BA, U. Iowa, 1960, LLB, 1964. Bar: Iowa 1964, Mass. 1967. Atty. Goodwin, Procter & Hoar, Boston, 1967-74; sr. v.p., gen. counsel Wang Labs., Inc., Lowell, Mass., 1974-92; v.p., gen. counsel Honeywell, Inc., Mpls., 1992—99. Trustee U. Lowell, Mas., 1981-87, chmn. bd. trustees, 1982-85, 87; dir. Bus. Econs. Edn. Found., 1992—. Capt. USAF, 1964-67. Mem. ABA (com. corp. law depts.), Mass. Bar Assn. (bd. dels. 1977-80), Greater Mpls. C. of C. (dir. 1992—). Corporate, general.*

GRAYSON KURZWEIL, BETTE RITA, lawyer; b. Newark, July 10, 1947; d. Sidney and Joan (Rosenman) G.; m. Stanley Noah Kruzweil, Aug. 17, 1975; children: Jeremy, Cynthia. BA, NYU, 1969; JD, Bklyn. Law Sch., 1977. Bar: N.J. 1977. Pvt. practice, Union and Springfield, N.J., 1977—. Former real estate counsel City of Plainfield, N.J.; former spl. real estate counsel City of Orange; former rev. atty. for State Bank South Orange, N.J.; chairperson Fee Arbitration Com. Union County, N.J.; mem. adv. bd. Crown Bank, 1998—. V.p. Millburn (N.J.) Hadassah, 1985-87, mem. steering com. for planned gifts, 1996-99; trustee Internat. Youth Orgn., 1997—; treas. Millburn Hoopsters, 1997-99. Recipient Trust Bklyn. Law Sch., 1974, Woman of Excellence award Union County, 1998. Mem. Women Lawyers Union County (pres. 1990-92, v.p. 1988-90, sec. 1983-84, treas. 1986-88). Democrat. Family and matrimonial, Land use and zoning (including planning), Property, real (including real estate development, water). Office: 140 Mountain Ave Springfield NJ 07081-1725

GRAZIANO, CRAIG FRANK, lawyer; b. Des Moines, Dec. 7, 1950; s. Charles Dominic and Corrine Rose (Comito) G. BA summa cum laude, Macalester Coll., 1973; JD with honors, Drake U., 1975. Bar: Iowa 1976, U.S. Dist. Ct. (no. and so. dists.) Iowa 1978, U.S. Ct. Appeals (8th cir.) 1977, U.S. Supreme Ct. 1988. Law clk. to Hon. M. D. Van Oosterhout U.S. Ct. Appeals (8th cir.), Sioux City, Iowa, 1976-78; pvt. practice Dickinson, Mackaman, Tyler & Hagen, PC, Des Moines, 1978-98; with Office of Consumer Advocate, Iowa Dept. Justice, Des Moines, 1999—. Mem. Gov.'s Task Force on Quality and Efficiency in Govt., 1999—2000. Mem. Iowa Bar Assn. (chair specialization com. 1993-96, chair adminstrv. law sect. 1996-99), Order of Coif, Phi Beta Kappa. Administrative and regulatory, Appellate, Utilities, public. Home: 500 44th St Des Moines IA 50312-2408 Office: 310 Maple St Des Moines IA 50319-0063 E-mail: craig.graziano@mchsi.com., cgraziano@mail.oca.state.ia.us.

GREANEY, JOHN M. state supreme court justice; b. Westfield, Mass., Apr. 8, 1939; s. Patrick Joseph and Margaret Irene (Fitzgerald) G.; m. Susan H. Greaney, Nov. 23, 1967. 1 child, Jessica S. BA summa cum laude, Holly Cross Coll., 1960; JD, NYU, 1963; LLD (hon.), Westfield State Coll., 1967, Western New England Coll., 1969; LLD, New England Law Sch., 1991. Bar: Mass., Supreme Judicial Ct., U.S. Dist. Ct., U.S. Supreme Ct. Ptnr. Ely & King, Springfield, Mass., 1963-73; presiding judge Hampden County Housing Ct., Springfield, Mass., 1973-75; assoc. judge Mass. Superior Ct., Boston, 1975-76; assoc. justice Mass. Appeals Ct., Boston, 1976-84, 1976-84, chief justice, 1984-89; assoc. justice Mass. Supreme Judicial Ct., Boston, 1989—. Former faculty mem. Western New England Law Sch., Westfield State Coll.; co-chair. Supreme Judicial Ct's Gender Bias Study Commn; mem. bd. Tribunes WGBY-Channel #57. Former assoc. editor Mass. Law Review. Trustee, dir. Westfield Atheneum, participant Child and Family Svcs. Program. Fellow Am. Bar Found.; mem. ABA (litigation, judicial adminstrn. section), Hampden County Bar Assn.(former mem. exec. com., grievance com., treas.), Mass. Bar Assn.(former chmn. Young Lawyers section, bd. delegates, exec. com., grievance com., legal svc. to the poor com.,(current) civil litigation, criminal law sections), Am. Law Inst. Avocations: competitive running, reading. Office: Mass Supreme Jud Court Pemberton Sq 1300 New Courthouse Boston MA 02108-1701

GREASON, MURRAY CROSSLEY, JR., lawyer; b. Wake Forest, N.C., Dec. 12, 1936; s. Murray Crossley and Evelyn Elizabeth (Hackney) G.; m. Joan Millicent Wilder. BS magna cum laude, Wake Forest U., 1959, JD magna cum laude, 1962. Bar: N.C. 1962. Assoc. firm Womble Carlyle Sandridge & Rice, PLLC, Winston-Salem, N.C., 1965-70; mem. firm Womble Carlyle Sandridge & Rice, Winston-Salem, N.C., 1970—; mng. ptnr. firm Womble Carlyle Sandridge & Rice, PLLC, Winston-Salem, 1988-96. Vis. lectr. Wake Forest U., 1972-74. Pres. Winston-Salem Estate Planning Coun., 1973; trustee Denmark Loan Fund, scholarships to Wake Forest U.; bd. visitors Wake Forest Law Sch., 1983-2000, chmn. 1994-2000; trustee Wake Forest U., 1990, vice chmn., 1997-2002, chmn., 2003—; chmn. N.W. N.C. chpt. ARC, 1996; chmn. bd. United Way Forsyth County, 1995; mem. Commn. on Ministry Episcopalian Diocese N.C., 1983-93; bd. dirs. Winston-Salem Alliance, 2000—, Idealliance, 1998—, Wake Forest U. Health Scis., 2000—. Capt. JAG, AUS, 1962-65. Fellow Am. Coll. Tax Coun.; mem. ABA, N.C. Bar Assn., Forsyth County Bar Assn. (pres. 1986-87), Winston-Salem C. of C. (bd. dirs., vice chmn. 2001, chmn. 2002), Wake Forest U. Alumni Assn. (pres. 1973), Forsyth Country Club, Phi Beta Kappa, Omicron Delta Kappa. Episcopalian. Corporate, general, Mergers and acquisitions. Home: 745 Arbor Rd Winston Salem NC 27104-2209 Office: Womble Carlyle Sandridge PLLC PO Box 84 Winston Salem NC 27102-0084 E-mail: mgreason@wcsr.com.

GREAVES, JOHN ALLEN, lawyer; b. Kansas City, Mo., Feb. 18, 1948; s. John Allen Greaves and Nancy Lee (Farmer) Greaves-Meltzer; m. Sharon Louise Peace Ventura, Dec. 23, 1967 (div. Mar. 1971); 1 child, Karen Christine Greaves Calogne; m. Jerri Lynn Crawford, Sept. 5, 1981. BA in Polit. Sci., U. Mo., 1976; MPA, JD with honors, Drake U., 1992. Bar: Iowa 1992, U.S. Dist. Ct. (so. dist.) Iowa 1992, Calif. 1994, U.S. Dist. Ct. (no. and cen. dists.) Calif. 1994, U.S. Dist. Ct. (so. and ea. dists.) Calif. 1995, U.S. Dist. Ct. N.Mex. 1995, U.S. Ct. Appeals (9th cir.) 1995, U.S. Dist. Ct. (no. dist.) N.Y. 1996, U.S. Dist. Ct. S.C. 1995, U.S. Ct. Appeals (4th and 10th cirs.) 1996, U.S. Dist. Ct. (no. dist.) Ill. 2000, D.C. 2001, U.S. Dist. Ct. (so. and ea. dists.) N.Y. 2002; lic. airline transport pilot. Pres., CEO VIPilot Svcs., Inc., Kansas City, 1980-83; pilot Air Illinois, Carbondale, Ill., 1983-84, Wright Airlines, Cleve., 1983-84, ComAir Airlines, Cin., 1984-88; jud. law clk. to Hon. Arthur E. Gamble Iowa Dist. Ct., Des Moines, 1990-91; pvt. practice Des Moines, 1992-94; shareholder Baum, Hedlund, Aristei, Guilford & Schiavo, L.A., 1994—. Mem. plaintiffs' steering com. Atlantic S.E. Airlines crash, Carrollton, Ga., 1995, Singapore Airlines crash, Taipei, Taiwan, 2000, MDL-1448 Am. Airlines 587 crash, Belle Harbor (Queens), N.Y., 2001; mem. plaintiffs' exec. com. Sept. 11, 2001 Tort Litigation. Recipient Safety award, Nat. Air Disaster Found., 2002. Mem. ABA (mem. forum on air and space com.), ATLA, Air Line Pilots Assn. (coun. 37, chmn. contract adminstrn. com. 1985-87, Disting. Svc. award), Lawyer/Pilot Bar Assn., State Bar Calif., State Bar Iowa, Iowa Trial Lawyers Assn., Inn Ct., Delta Theta Phi. Avocations: aviation, snow and water skiing, boating and sailing, tennis, golf. Aviation, Personal injury (including property damage), Product liability. Home: 3664 May St Los Angeles CA 90066-3606 Office: Baum Hedlund Aristei Guilford & Schiavo 12100 Wilshire Blvd Ste 950 Los Angeles CA 90025-7107 E-mail: jgreaves@baumhedlundlaw.com.

GRECH, CHRISTOPHER ALAN, lawyer, consultant; b. Richmond, Va., Oct. 5, 1960; s. George Alfred and Stella Mary Grech. BS in Mktg. and Mgmt., Fordham U., 1982; JD, Calif. Western Sch. of Law, San Diego, 1985. Bar: N.J. 1987, U.S. Dist. Ct. N.J. 1987, Md. 1993, D.C. 1994, N.Y. 1995. Solo practitioner, Hackensack, N.J., 1988-94, Berlin, Md., 1994—. Mem. ABA, City of Balt. Bar Assn., Bergen County Bar Assn., Internat. Law Soc., Md. Trial Lawyers Assn., Worcester County Bar Assn., Ocean Pines Yacht Club, Ocean Pines Country Club, KC, Phi Alpha Delta. Avocations: fishing, tennis, boating, jogging, bicycling. General civil litigation, Criminal, General practice. Home: PO Box 236 Showell MD 21862-0236

GRECO, GUY BENJAMIN, lawyer; b. Glen Ridge, N.J., May 28, 1951; s. Benjamin Francis and Dorothy Ann (Smith) G.; m. Marietta Suzanne D'Oro, June 16, 1973 (div. 1984); m. Pamela Ann Beckham McGuire, Feb. 2, 1993. BA, Rutgers U., 1973, JD, 1976. Bar: N.J. 1976, Oreg. 1977, U.S. Dist. Ct. N.J. 1976, Oreg. 1977, U.S. Supreme Ct. 1984. Assoc. Litchfield, Macpherson & Carstens, Newport, Oreg., 1977—81; ptnr. Greco & Escobar, Newport, 1981—89; pvt. practice Newport, 1989—. Chmn. Lincoln County Red Cross, Newport, 1979; pres. Oreg. Coast Coun. for the Arts, 1988-89. Mem. ABA, Oreg. Bar Assn., Lincoln County Bar Assn., Oreg. State Bar (counsel 1985, spl. task force on legal technicians 1991-92, legal assts. com. 1989-92, unlawful practice of law com. 1992-95, disciplinary bd. 1993-99, legal ethics com. 1995-98, client security fund com., 1998-2002, uniform criminal jury instrn. com. 2003—, local profl. responsibility com. 1985-88, 2003—). Democrat. Criminal, Personal injury (including property damage), Workers' compensation. Office: PO Box 1070 Newport OR 97365-0081 E-mail: greco@pioneer.net.

GRECO, JOSEPH DOMINIC, JR., lawyer; b. Jersey City, Aug. 22, 1955; s. Joseph Dominic Sr. and Bernice Amelia (Tamburello) G.; m. Sharon K. Hayes, Apr. 17, 1982; children: Meghan Kathleen, Joseph Dominic III, Christine Anne. BS in Bus. Mgmt. cum laude, St. Peters Coll., Jersey City, 1977; JD, Fordham U., 1980. Bar: N.J. 1980, U.S. Dist. Ct. N.J. 1980. Law clk. to Hon. Frederick W. Kuechenmeister Bergen County Dist. Ct., Hackensack, N.J., 1980-81; assoc. Carluccio & Carluccio, Hoboken, N.J., 1981-83, ptnr., 1983—. Chmn. issues com. to elect Tom Hynes N.J. senator, Maywood, 1982. Benjamin Darling scholar. Mem. ABA, N.J. Bar Assn., Hudson County Bar Assn. (pro bono legal svcs. program). Democrat. Roman Catholic. State civil litigation, Property, real (including real estate development, water), Estate taxation. Office: Carluccio Greco & Machese PO Box 230 51 Newark St Ste 404 Hoboken NJ 07030-5617

GRECO, THOMAS JOSEPH, lawyer; b. Washington, Nov. 22, 1957; s. Daniel Rudolph and Patricia Ann (McKennedy) G.; m. Cynthia Kaye Zorn, Sept. 12, 1982; children: Max Andrew, James Brandon, Molly Elizabeth, Jordan Scott. BA magna cum laude, U. Md., 1979; JD, Cath. U. Am., 1983. Bar: D.C. 1983. Asst. counsel Am. Bankers Assn., Washington, 1983—87, asst. gen. counsel, 1987—88, assoc. gen. counsel, 1989—98; pres. ABAecom, 1999; v.p. legal and policy Digital Signature Trust, LLC, 1999—. Advisor drafting com. articles 3, 4, 4A, 5, 8, and 9 Nat. Conf. Commrs. Uniform State Laws, Chgo., 1987-98; mem. study group on internat. electronic funds transfer Dept. State, Washington, 1988; speaker numerous confs. Contbr. articles to legal jours.; editor: UCC 4A: A Practical Guide for Bankers and Bank Counsel, 1991. Mem. ABA (com. on cyberspace law and Uniform Comml. Code 1988). Democrat. Office: Digital Signature Trust LLC 15200 Shady Grove Rd Ste 350 Rockville MD 20850-3902 E-mail: tom.greco@digsigtrust.com., t.greco@mindspring.com.

GREEK, DAROLD I. lawyer; b. Kunkle, Ohio, Mar. 30, 1909; s. Albert F. and Iva (Shaffer) G.; m. Catherine Johnson, Oct. 12, 1935 (dec. 1962); 1 child, Darold I (dec.); m. Elizabeth Tracy Ridgley, Sept. 18, 1970 (dec. May 1972); stepchildren— Thomas B., David Ridgley; m. Nadine Berry Weisheimer Bivens, Dec. 23, 1976; stepchildren— Richard A. Weisheimer, Jon B. Weisheimer. Student, Bowling Green State U., 1926-28; LL.B., Ohio State U., 1932. Bar: Ohio 1932. Treas., Williams County, Ohio, 1932-33; atty. Ohio Dept. Taxation, 1934-36; practiced in Columbus, 1937-89; ptnr. George, Greek, King, McMahon & McConnaughey (and predecessors), 1937-79; of counsel Baker & Hostetler, 1979-89. Mem. Ohio Bar Assn., Columbus Bar Assn. (pres. 1966-67), The Golf Club, Naples Yacht Club, Hole in the Wall Golf Club. Presbyterian. Home: 6635 Lake of Woods Pt Galena OH 43021 also: 2901 Gulf Shore Blvd N Naples FL 34103-3937 Office: 65 E State St Columbus OH 43215-4213

GREEN, BARRY, lawyer; BA in Am. Studies cum laude, Brandeis U., 1979; JD, Tulane U., 1982. Bar: N.Mex. 1982, U.S. Dist. Ct. N.Mex. 1986. Asst. dist. atty. Dist. Atty.'s Office, Santa Fe, 1983; pvt. practice Santa Fe, 1983—92, 2002—. Active Ctr. for Auto Safety, 1985. Recipient Pro Bono award Lawyer Referral Project for Elderly, N.Mex., 1987. Mem. Assn. Trial Lawyers Am., N.Mex. Trial Lawyers Assn., N.Mex. Bar Assn. (mem. fee arbitration com.). Democrat. Administrative and regulatory, Commercial, consumer (including collections, credit), Commercial, contracts (including sales of goods; commercial financing). Office: 200 W DeVargas St Ste 7 Santa Fe NM 87501-2643

GREEN, CAROL H. lawyer, educator, journalist; b. Seattle, Feb. 18, 1944; BA in History/Journalism summa cum laude, La. Tech. U., 1965; MSL, Yale U., 1977; JD, U. Denver, 1979. Reporter Shreveport (La.) Times, 1965-66, Guam Daily News, 1966-67; city editor Pacific Jour., Agana, Guam, 1967-68, reporter, editl. writer, 1968-76, legal affairs reporter, 1977-79; asst. editor editl. page Denver Post, 1979-81, house counsel, 1980-83, labor rels. mgr., 1981-83; assoc. Holme Roberts & Owen, 1983-85; v.p. human resources and legal affairs Denver Post, 1985-87, mgr. circulation, 1988-90; gen. mgr. Distbn. Systems Am., Inc., 1990-92; dir. labor rels. Newsday, 1992-95, dir. comm. & labor rels., 1996-97; v.p. Weber Mgmt. Cons., 1997-98; v.p. human resources and labor rels. Denver Post, 1998—2000; v.p. human resources Denver Newspaper Agy., 2000—. 1985 speaker for USIA, India, Egypt; mem. Mailers Tech. Adv. Com. to Postmaster Gen., 1991-92. Recipient McWilliams award for juvenile justice, Denver, 1971, award for interpretive reporting Denver Newspaper Guild, 1979. Mem.: ABA, Soc. Human Resources Mgmt., Colo. and Internat. Women's Forum, Denver Bar Assn. (co-chair jud. selection and benefits com. 1982—85, 2nd v.p. 1986), Newspaper Assn. Am. (mem. human resources and labor rels. com.), Colo. Bar Assn. (bd. govs. 1985—87, chair BAR-press com. 1980), Leadership Denver. Episcopalian.

GREEN, DENNIS JOSEPH, lawyer; b. Milw., Sept. 28, 1941; m. Janet McQueen; children: Karla Pope, Cheryl Ashley, Deborah. BS in Mgmt., U. Ill., 1963, JD, 1968. Bar: Ill. 1968, Mo. 1968. Atty. Monsanto Co., St. Louis, 1968-75, asst. co. counsel, 1975-76, counsel, 1976-79; gen. counsel, sec. Fisher Controls Internat. Inc., Clayton, Mo., 1979-85, v.p., gen. counsel, sec., 1985-93; v.p., assoc. gen. counsel Emerson Electric Co., St. Louis, 1992—. 1st lt. U.S. Army, 1963-65. Commercial, contracts (including sales of goods; commercial financing), Product liability, Public international. Office: Emerson Electric Co PO Box 4100 8000 W Florissant Ave Saint Louis MO 63136-1494 E-mail: dennis.green@emrsn.com.

GREEN, DONALD HUGH, lawyer; b. Elizabeth, N.J., May 16, 1929; s. Mortimer Jordan and Edna (Reinherz) G. ;m. Carol Margaret Medsger, Sept. 20, 1960; children: Michael, Margaret, Matthew, Mark. AB, Syracuse U., 1951; LLB, Harvard U., 1954. Bar: Fla. 1956, N.Y. 1957, D.C. 1960. Atty. Office of Legal Counsel, U.S. Dept. Justice, Washington, 1958-60, atty. civil div., 1960-61; assoc. Bergson & Borkland, Washington, 1961-65; ptnr. Fisher, Sharlitt, Gelband & Green, Washington, 1965-66, Wald, Harkrader & Ross, Washington, 1966-87; vice chmn. exec. com. mng. ptnr. Pepper, Hamilton LLP, Washington, 1987—, mem. exec. com., mng. ptnr. DC office, 1995—2000. Mem. faculty curriculum com. Legal Edn. Inst., U.S. Dept. Justice, Washington, 1985-92; lectr. Georgetown Law Ctr., Washington, 1981—, various symposia D.C. Bar; adj. prof. Georgetown Law Ctr., 1992—; appointed defense adv. com. on women in the svcs. Sec. of Defense, 1999, exec. com. 1999-01. Contbr. articles to profl. jours. Mem., chmn. trustees Cedar Ln. Unitarian Ch., Bethesda, 1972-75. Col. USMCR, 1954-85. Decorated Legion of Merit. Mem. ABA, Fed. Bar Assn., Am. Arbitration Assn., Dev. Rsch. Inst., Joint Svcs. Com. on Profl. Ethics, Nat. Panel Arbitrators, Fed. Am. Inn of Ct. (pres. 1994-95). Democrat. Avocations: painting, sailing, tennis. Federal civil litigation, Private international. Home: 5610 Wisconsin Ave Apt 18A Chevy Chase MD 20815-4415 Office: Pepper Hamilton LLP Hamilton Sq 600 14th St NW Washington DC 20005-2008 E-mail: greendh@pepperlaw.com.

GREEN, HARLAND NORTON, lawyer, accountant; b. Los Angeles, Feb. 14, 1930; s. William and Lena (Schwimer) G.; m. Melva Nudelman, Dec. 20, 1953. BS in Acctg., UCLA, 1951, JD, 1953; LLM in Taxation, U. S.C., 1962. Bar: Calif. 1955, U.S. Supreme Ct. 1963. Accountant J. Arthur Greenfield & Co., CPA's, Los Angeles, 1956-58; assoc. atty. Rosenthal & Green and predecessors, Beverly Hills, Calif., 1958-61, ptnr., 1961-68; pvt. practice Beverly Hills, 1969-72; pres. Harland N. Green, P.C., Beverly Hills, 1972—. Contbr. articles to UCLA Law Rev. Vice chmn., bd. trustees So. Calif. chpt. Nat. Multiple Sclerosis Soc.; elder Ahavat Zion Messianic Synagogue. Named an Outstanding Trustee So. Calif. chpt. Multiple Sclerosis Soc., 1966, Most Valuable Trustee, 1976. Mem. ABA, Calif. Bar Assn., Beverly Hills Bar Assn., Assn. Attys.-CPA's Los Angeles Copyright Soc., Order of Coif, Phi Beta Kappa, Beta Gamma Sigma. Estate planning, Probate (including wills, trusts), Estate taxation.

GREEN, JAMES FRANCIS, lawyer, consultant; b. Pittsfield, Mass., Oct. 1, 1948; s. Earl Levi and Frances Eleanor (Walshi) G.; m. Eileen Mary Kelly, July 31, 1971; childen: Michael Walshe, Maura Kelly, Kelsey Kathryn. BA, St. Anselm Coll., 1970; JD, Suffolk U., 1973. Bar: Mass 1973, U.S. Dist. Ct. Mass. 1874, U.S. Ct. Appeals (D.C. cir.) 1975, U.S. Dist. Ct. D.C. 1975, U.S. Supreme Ct. 1977, U.S. Ct. Appeals (4th cir.) 1978. Rsch. counsel Joint Com. on Jud. Reform of Joint Jud. Com. of Gen. Ct. Commonwealth of Mass., Boston, 1973-74; ptnr. Drucas, Edgerton & Green, Salem, Mass., 1974; gen. ptnr. Ashcraft & Gerel, Washington, 1975—; mem. Herman, Mathis, Casey, Kitchens and Gerel. Presdl. appointment Nat. Ad Hoc Com. on Disability. Mem. Mass. Bar Assn., Boston Bar Assn., Fed. Bar Assn. (bd. dirs. Washington chpt. 1985-86, internat. law com.), Bar Assn. D.C., D.C. Bar Assn., ABA (torts and ins. practice law sects., vice chmn. nat. com. on liaison with the jud. adminstrn.), Assn. Trial Lawyers Am. (sect. chmn. nat. com. workers compensation 1989-90), Am. Soc. Law and Medicine. Democrat. Roman Catholic. Federal civil litigation, Personal injury (including property damage), Workers' compensation. Home: 6522 Heather Brook Ct Mc Lean VA 22101-1607 Office: Ashcraft & Gerel 2000 L St NW Ste 400 Washington DC 20036

GREEN, JAY NELSON, lawyer; b. Kilgore, Tex., Jan. 11, 1958; s. James Perry and Ouida Norris G.; m. Ellen Elizabeth Bradley, Aug. 16, 1980; children: Cullen, Mason, Weston. BBA, Baylor U., 1979, JD, 1982. Bar: Tex.; U.S. Dist. Ct. (ea. dist. Tex.) 1983; U.S. Ct. Appeals (5th cir.) 1983; cert. Tex. Bd. Legal Specialization, assoc. Am. Bd. Trial Advs., Tex. Bar Found. Mem. staff Potter, Minton, Roberts, Davis & Jones, Tyler, Tex., 1982—2002; pvt. practcie, 2002—. Pres. Tyler Teen Ct, Inc., 1990-91; v.p. Smith County Young Lawyers, Tyler, 1985; instr. Tyler Jr. Coll., 1987; adj. prof., assoc. Baylor Sch. Law. Mem. steering com. Bush Re-election for Smith County, Tyler, 1998; chmn. Smith County, Tom Phillips Campaign, Tyler, 1988. Named Smith County Outstanding Young Lawyer, 1991. Baptist. Avocations: golf, family. Municipal (including bonds), Personal injury (including property damage), Professional liability. Office: 3650 Old Bullard Rd Ste 230 Tyler TX 75701

GREEN, JEFFREY C. lawyer; b. Newark, July 6, 1941; s. Albert and Mildred (Rosenberg) G.; m. Iris Landow, Aug. 23, 1964; children: Michelle, Marlene. BA, Rutgers U., 1963, JD, 1966; postgrad., Nat. Coll. State Judiciary, Reno, 1974-75. Bar: N.J. 1966, U.S. Dist. Ct. N.J. 1966. Law clk. to judge N.J. Superior Ct., Middlesex County Ct., New Brunswick,

1966-67; assoc. Toolan, Romond & Burgess, Perth Amboy, N.J., 1967-68; ptnr. Green & Green and predecessors, Somerset, N.J., 1968—. Prosecutor Franklin Twp. Mcpl. Ct., Somerset, 1969-70, mcpl. judge, 1970-76, 97—; judge Millstone (N.J.) Mcpl. Ct., 1970-76, Manville (N.J.) Mcpl. Ct., 1972-73; atty. Cranbury (N.J.) Bd. Adjustment, 1978—. Legal counsel Temple Beth El, Somerset, 1974—; bd. dirs. Middlesex County Legal Svcs. Corp., New Brunswick, 1983—. Named Man of Yr., Temple Beth El, 1984; recipient Pro Bono Achievement award Middlesex County Legal Svcs. Corp., 1985, 87. Mem. N.J. State Bar Assn. (trustee 1997-2003, Gen. Practitioner of Yr. award 1997), Middlesex County Bar Assn. (pres. 1985-86), Middlesex County Bar Found. (trustee 1990—, pres. 1994-95), Franklin Twp. Jaycees (pres. 1970-71), Lions Club. Democrat. Commercial, contracts (including sales of goods; commercial financing), Corporate, general, General practice. Home: 3 Denise Ct Somerset NJ 08873-2834 Office: Green & Green PO Box 5321 Somerset NJ 08875-5321

GREEN, JERSEY MICHAEL-LEE, lawyer; b. Washington, Feb. 29, 1952; m. Jonelle Sue Burke, May 12, 1988. BA in criminology, U. Md., 1976; JD, Syracuse U., 1983. Bar: Colo. 1983, U.S. Dist. Ct. Colo. 1983, U.S. Ct. Appeals (10th cir.) 1983, U.S. Tax Ct. 1983, U.S. Ct. Appeals (9th cir.) 1987, U.S. Supreme Ct. 1988, U.S. Ct. Appeals (2d cir.) 1990, U.S. Dist. Ct. Ariz. 1994. Atty. Wagner & Waller, P.C., Denver, 1983-86, Waller, Mark & Allen, P.C., Denver, 1986-89, Orten & Hindman P.C., Denver, 1989-90, Elrod, Katz, Preeo, Look, Moison & Silverman, P.C., Denver, 1990-97, Preeo, Silverman & Green, P.C., Denver, 1998-99, Preeo, Silverman, Green & Egle, P.C., Denver, 1999—. Mem. exec. com. staff Lawyers for Romer, Denver, 1986; precinct committeeman, 1989-92. Recipient Syracuse (N.Y.) Def. Group scholarship, 1982. Mem. Assn. Trial Lawyers Am., Colo. Trial Lawyers Assn., Arapahoe County Bar Assn., Syracuse U. Alumni Assn. (pres. Colo. 1987-89). Democrat. Avocations: mountaineering, skiing, running. General civil litigation. Office: Preeo Silverman Green & Eagle PC 1401 17th St Ste 800 Denver CO 80202-1246 E-mail: Jersey@preeosilv.com.

GREEN, JESSE JOSEPH, lawyer; b. San Antonio, Sept. 4, 1961; s. Joseph Hughes Jr. and Mildred (Hardin) G.; m. Mary Margaret Pollard, June 23, 1989; children: Molly Jule, Hannah Katherine. BA, BBA, So. Meth. U., 1982; JD, U. Tex., 1986. Bar: Tex. 1986. Claims adjuster USAA Ins. Co., San Antonio, 1982-83; assoc. Locke Purnell Rain Harrell and predecessor firm, Dallas, 1986-90; pvt. practice Ray E. Green & Assocs., P.C., Dallas, 1990-98; gen. counsel Parker Coll. Chiropractic, Dallas, 1998—. Asst. prof. ethics Parker Coll. Chiropractic, Dallas, 1992—; tchg. quizmaster U. Tex. Law Sch., Austin, 1985-86. Mem. Tex. Law Rev., 1984-86. Mem. Coll. of State Bar Tex., Am. Health Lawyers Assn., Nat. Assn. Coll. and Univ. Attys. Roman Catholic. Education and schools, Health, Non-profit and tax-exempt organizations. Office: Parker Coll Chiropractic 2500 Walnut Hill Ln Dallas TX 75229-5668 E-mail: jgreen@parkercc.edu.

GREEN, JOHN CAWLEY, lawyer; b. Washington, Mar. 2, 1910; s. Kirt and Linda (Cawley) G.; m. June Lazenby, Sept. 5, 1936. BS, U.S. Naval Acad., 1934; JD, Georgetown U., 1940. Bar: D.C. bar 1939. Examiner U.S. Patent Office, 1936-40; chief engr. Nat. Inventors Council (examining and analyzing civilian inventions directed to def. effort in cooperation with Armed Services), 1940-56, exec. dir., 1956-63; exec. sec. Publ. Bd., 1945-63, dir. civilian investigations of German and Japanese sci. and tech., 1945-48; also in charge release of fed. research data; adviser Dept. State and ICA; dir. Office Tech. Services, U.S. Dept. Commerce, Washington, 1945-63; charge release fgn. sci. reports; dir. Research and Devel. div. Office Emergency Planning, 1963-66; dir. Office Analysis and Research, 1966-67; practice law Washington, 1967-77; pres. John C. Green Assos., 1968-77. Cons. tech. adviser Internat. Conf. on Alien Patents, London, 1946; mem. com to examine sci. programs Dept. Commerce, NAS, 1958, mem. panels on sci., tech. in econ. devel. Argentina, 1969, Indonesia, 1971. Recipient His Majesty's medal for services in cause of freedom U.K., 1948; award for sci. efforts U.S. Sec. Army and Navy; exceptional service medal Sec. Commerce; medal Royal Swedish Acad. Engring. Scis., 1963 Fellow AAAS; mem. D.C. Bar Assn., Nat. Fedn. Sci. Abstracting and Indexing Svcs. (pres. 1963-64), Cosmos Club. Home: 464 W Joyce Ln Arnold MD 21012-2207

GREEN, JOYCE HENS, federal judge; b. N.Y.C., Nov. 13, 1928; d. James S. and Hedy (Bucher) Hens; m. Samuel Green, Sept. 25, 1965 (dec.); children: Michael Timothy, June Heather, James Harry. BA, U. Md., 1949; JD, George Washington U., 1951, LLD, 1994. Practice law, Washington, 1951-68, Arlington, Va., 1956-68; ptnr. Green & Green, 1966-68; assoc. judge Superior Ct., D.C., 1968-79; judge U.S. Dist. Ct. for D.C., 1979—; judge presiding U.S. Fgn. Intelligence Surveillance Ct., 1988-95. Bd. advisors George Washington U. Law Sch., 1991-2001; jud. br. com. Jud. Conf. U.S., 1995-2001. Co-author: Dissolution of Marriage, 1986, supplements, 1987-89, Marriage and Family Law Agreements, 1985, supplements, 1986-89. Chair Task Force on Gender, Race and Ethnic Bias for the D.C. Cir. Recipient Alumni Achievement award George Washington U., 1975, Profl. Achievement award, 1978, Outstanding Contbn. to Equal Rights award Women's Legal Def. Fund, 1976, hon. doctor of Laws George Washington U., 1994, U.S. Dept. Justice Edmund J. Randolph award, 1995. Fellow Am. Bar Found.; ABA (jud. adminstrn. divsn., chair nat. conf. fed. trial judges 1997-98), Fed. Judges Assn., Nat. Assn. Women Judges, Va. Bar, Bar Assn. D.C. (jud. honoree of Yr. 1994), D.C. Bar, D.C. Women's Bar Assn., (pres. 1960-62, woman lawyer of yr. 1979), Exec. Women in Govt. (chmn. 1977), Woman's Forum of Washington D.C. Office: US Dist Ct E Barrett Prettyman US Courthouse 333 Constitution Ave NW Washington DC 20001-2802

GREEN, NATHANIEL KIMBALL, lawyer; b. Fitchburg, Mass., May 18, 1951; s. Walter Albert and Calista (Haskell) G.; m. Ann Marie Scalaro, June 11, 1971; children: Amy, Nathaniel Jr. BA, Ctrl. Conn. State U., 1976; JD, Western New Eng. Coll., 1985. Bar: Mass. 1985, U.S. Dist. Ct. Mass. 1989. Pvt. practice, Holyoke, Mass., 1986-88; atty.-in-charge Berkshire County office Com. for Pub. Counsel Svcs., Pub. Defender Divsn., Pittsfield, Mass., 1988—. With U.S. Army, 1976-79. Mem. Nat. Assn. Criminal Def. Attys., Mass. Assn. Criminal Def. Attys., Mass. Bar Assn., Hampden County Bar Assn., Berkshire County Bar Assn. Democrat. Episcopalian. Office: Com for Pub Counsel Svcs 139 North St Pittsfield MA 01201-5101

GREEN, PHILIP BURTON, lawyer; b. Chgo., Aug. 2, 1947; s. Floyd Burton and Helen Marie (Krick) G. B.A. in Econs., Duke U., 1969; J.D., U. Ill., 1973. Bar: Ill. 1973, Colo. 1973, U.S. Dist. Ct. Colo. 1973, U.S. Dist. Ct. (no. dist.) Ill. 1973, U.S. Ct. Appeals (9th cir.) 1982, U.S. Supreme Ct. 1980. Staff atty. VISTA, ACTION, Denver, 1973-74; sole practice, Denver, 1974-80; sr. ptnr. Green & Josefiak, Denver, 1981— ; counsel Catholic Community Services, Inc., Denver, 1974— . Mem. ABA, Am. Trial Lawyers Assn., Colo. Bar Assn., Colo. Trial Lawyers Assn. Federal civil litigation, State civil litigation, Juvenile. Office: Green & Josefiak 1660 S Albion St Ste 918 Denver CO 80222-4046

GREEN, RICHARD, lawyer, psychiatrist, educator; b. Bklyn., June 6, 1936; s. Leo Harry and Rose (Ingber) G.; m. Melissa Hines; 1 child, Adam Hines-Green. AB, Syracuse U., 1957; MD, Johns Hopkins U., 1961; JD, Yale U., 1987. Diplomate Am. Bd. Psychiatry and Neurology. Intern Kings County Hosp., Bklyn., 1962-64; resident in psychiatry UCLA Neuropsychiat. Inst., 1962-64, NIMH, Bethesda, Md., 1965-66; from asst. prof. to prof. dept. psychiatry UCLA, 1968-74; prof. psychiatry and psychology SUNY, Stony Brook, 1974-85; prof. psychiatry UCLA, 1986-94, prof. law, 1988-90, prof. emeritus psychiatry, 1994—; affiliated lectr., faculty of law Cambridge U., 1994-2001. Faculty mem. law sch. UCLA, 1991-92; head dir. of rsch., cons. psychiatrist Gender Identity Clinic Charing Cross Hosp., London; vis. fellow, sr. rsch. fellow Inst. Criminology, Cambridge U., 1994-2001. Author: Sexual Identity Conflict in Children and Adults, 1974, The Sissy Boy Syndrome and the Development of Homosexuality, 1987, Sexual Science and the Law, 1992; co-editor: Transsexualism and Sex Reassignment, 1969, Impotence, 1981, Sociolegal Control of Homosexuality: A Multination Comparison, 1997; editor: Human Sexuality: A Health Practitioner's Text, 1975, 2d edit., 1979, Jour. Archives of Sexual Behavior, 1971—2001. Vol. atty., ACLU, LA. Vis. scholar U. Cambridge, Eng., 1980-81, Fulbright scholar King's Coll., London, and Univ. Cambridge, 1992; fellow Ctr. Advanced Study in Behavioral Scis., Stanford, Calif., 1982-83. Fellow: Internat. Acad. Sex Rsch. (founding pres. 1973, elected pres. 1998—), Soc. Sci. Study of Sex (pres. 1974—77), Royal Coll. Psychiatrists; mem.: D.C. Bar Assn., Calif. Bar Assn. Avocations: photography, traveling, antiques. Office: Charing Cross Hosp Gender Identity Clinic Dept Psychiatry London W6 8RF England E-mail: richard.green@ic.ac.uk.

GREEN, RICHARD ALAN, lawyer; b. Springfield, Mass., Apr. 25, 1926; s. Herman and Emma (Rudnick) G.; m. Lorna H. Paul, Sept. 6, 1957; children: Charles C., Thomas F. AB cum laude, Harvard U., 1947, LL.B., 1952. Bar: N.Y. 1954, D.C. 1975, Md. 1987. Assoc. Steinberg & Patterson, N.Y.C., 1954-57; asst. U.S. atty. So. Dist. N.Y., 1957-59; 1st asst. counsel N.Y. State Commn. Investigation, 1960; individual practice law N.Y.C., 1961-64; dir. ABA Project on Standards for Criminal Justice, 1964-73; dep. dir. Nat. Commn. on Reform of Fed. Criminal Laws, 1967-71; lectr. U. Va. Sch. Law, 1971; dep. dir. Fed. Jud. Center, Washington, 1971-74; partner Rowley and Green, Washington, 1974-80, Stohlman, Beuchert, Egan & Smith, Washington, 1981-2000. Served with USN, 1944-46. Mem. ABA, Am. Law Inst., D.C. Bar Assn., Assn. of Bar of City of N.Y., Harvard (N.Y.C.) Club. Federal civil litigation, State civil litigation, Criminal. Home: 1050 N Stuart St Apt 714 Arlington VA 22201-5749

GREEN, ROBERT ALEXIS, JR., lawyer, judge; b. Gainesville, Fla., June 14, 1938; s. Robert Alexis and Lucile (Harris) G.; m. Saundra Marie Jones, June 6, 1959; children: Katherine Marie, Melanie Green Hancock, Robert Alexis III. AB, U. Fla., 1959, BA, 1960, LLB, JD, 1962. Bar: Fla. 1963, U.S. Dist. Ct. (all dists.) Fla. 1970-72, U.S. Supreme Ct. 1967; cert. sr. judge county, family, cir. civil mediator/arbitrator, Fla. Ptnr. Green & Pierce, Attys. at Law, Gainesville, 1965-69; pub. defender 8th jud. cir. State of Fla., Gainesville, 1963-72, circuit judge 8th jud. cir., 1973-86; ptnr. Green & Hobbs P.A., Starke, Fla., 1986-87; ptnr., pres. R.A. Green, P.A., Starke, 1988—; sr. judge, 1999—. Pres. Fla. Mediation Acad. Inc., Starke, 1995-98. Recipient L. Clayton Nance award Fla. State Pub. Defender Assn., 1973, Reginald Heber Smith award Nat. Legal Aid and Defender Assn., 1973; Ford Found. grantee, 1964-67. Mem. Fla. Acad. Profl. Mediators (diplomate; pres. 1995), Am. Arbitration Assn. (Whitney North Seymour medal 1991, comml., complex case & construction panelist 1997—). Methodist. Alternative dispute resolution. Office: RA Green PA 4317 Seminole St Starke FL 32091-9748 E-mail: buzzy@atlantic.net.

GREEN, ROBERT S. lawyer; b. Newark, Feb. 9, 1927; s. Mortimer J. and Edna Vera (Reinherz) G.; m. Estelle Rothenberg, Jan. 29, 1961; children—Peter, Sara AB, Cornell U., 1948; JD, Columbia U., 1953. Bars: N.Y. 1954, Fla. 1957, D.C. 1959. Law clk. Cir. Judge Harold R. Medina, 1953-54; ptnr. Brennan, Londan & Buttenweiser, N.Y.C., 1963-70, Green, Sharpless & Greenstein, N.Y.C., 1971-80, Nixon, Peabody LLP, N.Y.C., 1981-94; counsel Pepper Hamilton LLP, N.Y.C., 1995-99, Wollmuth Maher & Deutsch, 2000—. Contbr. articles to profl. jours. Founder, trustee Citizens for Clean Air, 1964-68; trustee William Alanson White Inst., N.Y.C., 1968-89 ; advisor U.S. Senator Robert F. Kennedy, 1966-68. Served with USNR, 1945-46, PTO Mem. Am. Law Inst. Democrat. Jewish. Avocations: sailing, travel. Home: 90 Riverside Dr New York NY 10024-5306 E-mail: rgreen@wmd-law.com.

GREEN, SAUL A. lawyer; BA, U. Mich., 1969; JD, U. Mich. Law, 1972. Asst. U.S. Atty., eastern dist. Mich U.S. Dept Justice, Mich., 1973—76; chief counsel U.S. Dept. of Housing and Urban Devel., Detroit, 1976—89; corp. counsel Wayne County, Mich., 1989—93; U.S. atty. Ea. Dist. Mich., Detroit, 1994—2001; ptnr. Miller, Canfield, Paddock and Stone, PLC, Detroit, 2001—, dir., Minority Bus Practice Group, Corp. Criminal Def. Group, 2001—. Office: Miller, Canfield, Paddock and Stone, PLC 150 West Jefferson, Suite 2500 Detroit MI 48226 Office Fax: 313-496-8453. E-mail: greens@millercanfield.com.

GREEN, SHELDON NEAL, lawyer; b. Memphis, May 7, 1952; s. Jake and Esther (Wagerman) G.; m. Julie Margolin Parker, Apr. 5, 1981 (div. Nov. 1981). BS in Econs., MBA, U. Pa., 1974; JD, U. Mich., 1977. Bar: Ill. 1977, Tenn. 1979. Assoc. McDermott Will & Emery, Chgo., 1977-79; pvt. practice Memphis, 1979—. Mem. ATLA, Memphis and Shelby County Bar Assn. Personal injury (including property damage). Home: 8388 Bergen Dr Cordova TN 38018-7314 Office: Green Kay and Green 2612 Poplar Ave Memphis TN 38112-3823

GREEN, THOMAS B. lawyer, computer company executive; b. Salt Lake City, Feb. 5, 1955; BA magna cum laude, U. Utah, 1977, JD, 1980. Bar: Utah 1981, Tex. 1988. Law clk. to Hon. Monroe G. McKay U.S. Ct. Appeals (10th cir.), 1980—81; law clk. to Hon. Warren E. Berger U.S. Supreme Ct., 1982—83; with Kimball, Parr, Crockett & Waddoups, Salt Lake City, 1983—87; ptnr. Jones, Day, Reavis & Pogue, Dallas, 1989—90; gen. counsel Trammwell Crow Co., Dallas, 1988—89, exec. v.p., gen. counsel, 1990—92, Chgo. Title Ins. Co., 1992—94; sr. v.p. law and adminstrn. Dell Computer Corp., Round Rock, Tex., 1994—. Exec. editor: Utah Law Rev., 1979—80. Mem.: ABA, Order of Coif, State Bar Tex. Office: Dell Computer Corp Legal Dept 1 Dell Way Round Rock TX 78682-2244 Office Fax: 512-728-8935.*

GREEN, WILLIAM PORTER, lawyer; b. Jacksonville, Ill., Mar. 19, 1920; s. Hugh Parker and Clara Belle (Hopper) G.; m. Rose Marie Hall, Oct. 1, 1944; children: Hugh Michael, Robert Alan, Richard William. BA, Ill. Coll., 1941; JD, Northwestern U., Evanston, Ill., 1947. Bar: Ill. 1947, Calif. 1948, U.S. Dist. Ct. (so. dist.) Tex. 1986, U.S. Ct. Customs and Patent Appeals, U.S. Patent and Trademark Office 1948, U.S. Ct. Appeals (fed. cir.) 1982, U.S. Ct. Appeals (5th and 9th cir.), U.S. Supreme Ct. 1948, U.S. Dist. Ct. (cen. dist.) Calif. 1949, (so. dist.) Tex.1986. Pvt. practice, L.A., 1947—; mem. Wills, Green & Mueth, L.A., 1974-83; of counsel Nilsson, Robbins, Dalgarn, Berliner, Carson & Wurst, L.A., 1984-91; of counsel Nilsson, Wurst & Green L.A., 1992—. Del. Calif. State Bar Conv., 1982—, chmn., 1986. Bd. editors Ill. Law Rev., 1946; patentee in field. Mem. L.A. world Affairs Coun., 1975—; deacon local Presbyn. Ch., 1961-63. Mem. ABA, Calif. State Bar, Am. Intellectual Property Law Assn., L.A. Patent Law Assn. (past. sec.-treas., mem. bd. govs.), Lawyers Club L.A. (past treas., past sec., mem. bd. govs., pres. 1985-86), Los Angeles County Bar Assn. (trustee 1986-87), Am. Legion (past post comdr.), Northwestern U. Alumni Club So. Calif., Big Ten Club So. Calif., Town Hall Calif. Club, PGA West Golf Club (La Quinta, Calif.), Phi Beta Kappa, Phi Delta Phi, Phi Alpha. Republican. Patent, Trademark and copyright. Home: 3570 Lombardy Rd Pasadena CA 91107-5627 Office: 707 Wilshire Blvd Ste 3200 Los Angeles CA 90017-3514 E-mail: wpgreen@aol.com.

GREENAWALT, ROBERT KENT, lawyer, law educator; b. Bklyn., June 25, 1936; s. Kenneth William and Martha (Sloan) G.; m. Sanja Milic, July 14, 1968 (dec. Nov. 1988); children: Robert Milic, Alexander Kent Anton, Andrei Milenko Kenneth; m. Elaine Pagels, June 1995; children: Sarah Pagels, David. AB with honors, Swarthmore Coll., 1958; Ph.B.; Keasbey fellow, Oxford (Eng.) U., 1960; LL.B.; Kent scholar, Columbia U., 1963. Bar: N.Y. 1963. Law clk. to Justice Harlan, U.S. Supreme Ct., 1963-64; spl. asst. AID, Washington, 1964-65; mem. faculty Columbia U. Law Sch., 1965—, prof. law, 1969—, Cardozo prof., 1979—, Univ. prof., 1990—. Dep. solicitor gen. U.S., 1971-72; assoc. dir. N.Y. Inst. Legal Edn., 1969; vis. prof. Stanford U. Law Sch., 1970, Northwestern U. Law Sch., 1983, Marshall-Wythe Sch. Law, 1985, N.Y.U. Law Sch., 1989-90; atty. Lawyers Com. Civil Rights, 1965, trustee, 1992; mem. staff Task Force Law Enforcement N.Y.C., 1965; vis. fellow All Souls Coll. Oxford (Eng.) U., 1979 Co-author: The Sectarian College and The Public Purse, 1970; author: Legal Protections of Privacy, 1976, Discrimination and Reverse Discrimination, 1983, Conflicts of Law and Morality, 1987, Religious Convictions and Political Choice, 1988, Speech, Crime and the Uses of Language, 1989, Law and Objectivity, 1992, Private Consciences and Public Reasons, 1995, Fighting Words, 1995, Statutory Interpretation: Twenty Questions, 1999; editor in chief Columbia U. Law Rev., 1962-63; contbr. articles to legal jours. Recipient Ivy award Swarthmore Coll., 1958; fellow Am. Council Learned Soc., 1972-73. Fellow Am. Acad. Arts and Scis.; mem. Am. Philos. Soc., Am. Law Inst., Am. Soc. Polit. and Legal Philosophy (pres. 1992-93). Office: Columbia U Law Sch 435 W 116th St New York NY 10027-7201

GREENAWALT, WILLIAM SLOAN, lawyer; b. Bklyn., Mar. 4, 1934; s. Kenneth William and Martha Frances (Sloan) G.; m. Jane DeLano Plunkett, Aug. 17, 1957 (div. May 1986); m. Peggy Ellen Freed Tomarkin, Oct. 31, 1987; children: John DeLano, David Sloan, Katherine Downs. AB, Cornell U., 1956; LLB, Yale U., 1961. Bar: N.Y. 1962, U.S. Dist. Ct. (so. and ea. dists.) N.Y. 1962, U.S. Ct. Apls. (2d cir.) 1962, U.S. Supreme Ct. 1966. Assoc. Sullivan & Cromwell, N.Y.C., 1961-65; N.E. regional legal svcs. dir. U.S. Office Econ. Opportunity, N.Y.C., 1965-68; assoc. Rogers & Wells, N.Y.C., 1968-69, ptnr., 1969-77, sr. ptnr., 1977-81, Halperin, Shivitz, Eisenberg, Schneider & Greenawalt, N.Y.C., 1981-86, Eisenberg Honig Fogler Greenawalt & Davis, N.Y.C., 1986-91, Bangser Klein Rocca & Blum, N.Y.C., 1991-93, Loselle Greenawalt Kaplan Blair & Adler, N.Y.C., 1993-97, Loselle Greenawalt Kaplan & Blair, N.Y.C., 1997-99, Meyer Greenawalt Taub & Wild, LLP, N.Y.C., 1999-2001; pvt. practice N.Y.C., 2001—. Lectr. in field. Bd. editors: Yale Law Jour., 1959-61; contbr. articles in field to profl. jours. Chmn. bd. dirs. Applied Resources, Inc., N.Y.C., 1968-70; chmn. Cmty. Aid Employment of Ex-Offenders, Westchester, N.Y., 1971; pres. Westchester Legal Svcs., 1971-74, bd. dirs., 1975-91; mem. N.Y. State Gov.'s Task Force on Elem. and Secondary Edn., 1974-75; mem. Pres. Carter's Task Force on Criminal Justice, 1976; adv. coun. N.Y. State Senate Dems., 1978—; asst. and acting treas. N.Y. State Dem. Party, 1990-96, vice chair, 1996-2000, 9th jud. dist. rep. 2002—, state com., 1974—, exec. com. 1990-2000, 02—; chair Greenburgh Dem. Party, 1997-2002; mem. Greenburgh Recreation Commn., 1976-83, Dem. Statewide Spl. Commn. on Polit. Ethics, 1986-87, Statewide Spl. Commn. on Election Law and Campaign Spending Reform, 1989-95; pres. Westchester Crime Victims Assistance Agy., 1981-82; commr. Taconic State Pks., Recreation and Hist. Preservation Commn., 1984-96, chmn., 1989-96; vice chmn. N.Y. State Coun. on Pks., Recreation and Hist. Preservation, 1989-94; moderator Scarsdale Congl. Ch., 1988-90; mem. Westchester County Parks, Recreation and Conservation Bd., 1998—, vice chmn., 1999—; mem. Westchester County Execs. Transition Team on Planning, 1997. Lt. comdr. USN, 1956-58, with Res., 1961-68. Fellow N.Y. Bar Found.; mem. ABA, Am. Arbitration Assn. (mem. panel comml. arbitrators 1977—), N.Y. State Bar Assn. (chmn. com. on availability of legal svcs. 1968-70, chmn. action unit 3 1979-81, chmn. spl. commn. on alternatives to jud. resolution of disputes 1981-85), Assn. of Bar of City of N.Y., Nat. Legal Aid and Defenders Assn., Sphinx Head, Aleph Samach, County Tennis Club Westchester (Scarsdale, N.Y., pres. 1979-80), Yale Club (Yale Law jour. 1959-61), Phi Alpha Delta, Chi Psi. Democrat. Congregationalist. Federal civil litigation, State civil litigation. Home: 24 Lewis Ave Hartsdale NY 10530 Office: Law Offices William S Greenawalt 230 Park Ave Rm 2525 New York NY 10169-0199 E-mail: wsgreenawalt@aol.com.

GREENBACKER, JOHN EVERETT, retired lawyer and naval officer; b. Meriden, Conn., Oct. 4, 1917; s. Charles and Isabel Alice Francis G.; m. Carolyn Robertson Perrow, July 25, 1942; children: Susan Oller, John E. Jr., Florence Arnold, Christopher F. Student, U. Conn., 1935-36; BS, U.S. Naval Acad., 1940; JD, Georgetown U., 1949, LLM, 1969; MA, U.S. Naval War Coll., George Washington U., 1964. Bar: D.C. 1949, Md. 1970, Va. 1976, U.S. Dist. Ct. (we. dist.) Va. 1979. Commd. ensign U.S. Navy, 1940, advanced through grades to capt., 1960, comdg. officer subchaser, 1942-43, comdg. officer destroyer escorts, 1943-46, comdg. officer destroyer, 1955-57, comdg. officer attack transport, 1962-63, comdr. destroyer div. 262, 1961-62, comdr. destroyer squadron 6, 1965-66, ret., 1969; sr. atty. legal dept. Balt. Gas & Electric Co., 1969-72, mem. finance dept., 1972-74, treas., 1974-76; practice law Halifax, Va., 1976-94; estate planning cons., 1994—. Home: 4185 Grubby Rd Halifax VA 24558-2425

GREENBAUM, JEFFREY ALAN, lawyer; b. Ft. Benning, Ga., Feb. 9, 1968; s. Thomas L. and Rosalie (Montag) Greenbaum. BA summa cum laude, Brandeis U., Waltham, Mass., 1990; JD, Columbia U., N.Y.C., 1993. Bar: NY 1994, U.S. Dist. Ct. (so. and ea. dists.) NY 1995. Assoc. Paul, Weiss, Rifkind, Wharton & Garrison, N.Y.C., 1993-97, Frankfurt, Kurnit, Klein & Selz, N.Y.C., 1997-2000, ptnr., 2001—. Harlan Fiske Stone scholar Columbia U., N.Y.C., 1991-93. Mem. ABA (consumer protection com.), Assn. Bar of City of N.Y. (chair com. on consumer affairs), Phi Beta Kappa. Entertainment, Intellectual property, Trademark and copyright. Office: Frankfurt Kurnit Klein & Selz 488 Madison Ave Fl 9 New York NY 10022-5754

GREENBAUM, MAURICE COLEMAN, lawyer; b. Detroit, Apr. 3, 1918; s. Henry and Eva (Kayman) G.; m. Beatrice Wiener, June 28, 1942. BA, Wayne State U., 1938; JD, U. Mich., 1941; LLM, NYU, 1947. Bar: Mich. 1941, N.Y. 1947, Conn. 1948. Assoc. Herman H. Copelon, New Haven, 1948—50, Greenbaum, Wolff & Ernst, N.Y.C., 1950—54, ptnr., 1955—82, Katten, Muchin, Zavis & Rosenman (formerly Rosenman & Colin, LLP), N.Y.C., 1982—91, counsel, 1991—. Mem. vis. com. U. Miami Sch. Marine and Atmospheric Sci.; mem. adv. com. Great Neck Sr. Citizen Ctr.; mem. adv. com. Helen Merrill Fund; bd. dirs. Humanity in Action, Rosenstiel Found., Mandeville Found., World Rehab. Fund. Co-author: Estate Tax Techniques; grad. editor Tax Law Rev., 1946-47. Village Justice, Kings Point, N.Y., 1985—; assoc. trustee North Shore U. Hosp., Manhasset, N.Y.; bd. trustees N.Y. Found., 1967-83. Served to maj. U.S. Army, 1941-45. Democrat. Jewish. Home: 24 Cow Ln Kings Point NY 11024-1517 Office: Katten Muchin Zavis & Rosenman 575 Madison Ave 11th Fl New York NY 10022-2585

GREENBERG, HAYLEY, lawyer; b. N.Y.C., NY; d. Jerry and Sheila Greenberg. BA in Acctg., CUNY, 1989; JD, Bklyn. Law Sch., 1993. Bar: NY 1995, U.S. Dist. Ct. (ea. and so. dists.) NY. Ptnr. Greenberg & Merola, N.Y.C., 1996—. Pres. Justice for Animals, Inc., 1995—. Mem.: ATLA, ABA, Bklyn. Bar Assn., Queens County Bar Assn., NY State Trial Lawyers Assn., NY State Bar Assn. Avocation: animal rights. Personal injury (including property damage), Entertainment, General practice. Office: Greenberg & Merola LLP 521 5th Ave Ste 1700 New York NY 10175 Fax: 516-887-1720. E-mail: hayley@bdvu.net.

GREENBERG, JACK, lawyer, law educator; b. N.Y.C., Dec. 22, 1924; s. Max and Bertha (Rosenberg) G.; m. Sema Ann Tanzer, 1950 (div. 1970); children: Josiah, David, Sarah, Ezra; m. Deborah M. Cole, 1970; children: Suzanne, William Cole. AB, Columbia U., 1945, LLB, 1948, LLD, 1984, Morgan State Coll., Central State Coll., 1965, Lincoln U., 1977, John Jay Coll. Criminal Justice, 1983, De Paul U., 1994. Bar: N.Y. 1949. Rsch. asst. N.Y. State Law Revision Commn., 1949; asst. counsel NAACP Legal Def. and Ednl. Fund, 1949-61, dir.-counsel, 1961-84; argued in sch. segregation, sit-in, employment discrimination, poverty, capital punishment, other cases before U.S. Supreme Ct.; adj. prof. Columbia U. Law Sch., 1970-84, prof., vice-dean, 1984-89; dean Columbia Coll., 1989-93; prof. Columbia U. Law Sch., 1993—. Cons. Ctr. Applied Legal Studies, U. Witwatersrand, 1978; vis. lectr. Yale U. Law Sch., 1971; vis. prof. CCNY, 1977, Tokyo U., 1993-94, 99, St. Louis U. Law Sch., 1994, Lewis and Clark Law Sch., 1994-98, Princeton U., 1995, U. Munich, 1998; lectr. Harvard U. Law Sch., 1983, Shikes fellow, 1981; disting. lectr. humanities Columbia Coll. Physicians and Surgeons, 1998, U. Nurenberg-Erlangen, 1999. Author: (with H. Hill) Citizens Guide to Desegregation, 1955, Race Relations and American Law, 1959, Judicial Process and Social Change, 1976, (with James Vorenberg) Dean Cuisine or the Liberated Man's Guide to Fine Cooking, 1990, Crusaders in the Courts, 1994; contbg. author: Race, Sex and Religious Discrimination in International Law, 1981; contbr. articles to profl. jours. Bd. dirs. N.Y.C. Legal Aid Soc., Internat. League for Human Rights, Mex.-Am. Legal Def. Fund, 1968-75, Asian Am. Legal Def. Fund, 1980—, Human Rights Watch, 1978-98, NAACP Legal Def. and Ednl. Fund. Co-recipient Grenville Clark prize, 1978; hon. fellow U. Pa. Law Sch., 1975. Fellow AAAS, Am. Coll. Trial Lawyers; mem. ABA (commn. to study FTC, adv. com. to spl. com. on crime prevention, sect. on individual rights and responsibilities, Silver Gavel award, Thurgood Marshall prize, Presdl. Citizens medal 2001), N.Y. State Bar Assn. (exec. dir. spl. com. study state antitrust laws 1956), Am. Law Inst., Bar Assn. City N.Y. (Cardozo lectr. 1973) Adminstrv. Conf. U.S. Home: 118 Riverside Dr New York NY 10024-3708 Office: Columbia Law Sch 435 W 116th St New York NY 10027-7297

GREENBERG, LAWRENCE ALLAN, lawyer; b. Bklyn., Nov. 1, 1946; s. Joseph David and Shirley Albert Greenberg; m. Diane Sonia Daniel, Mar. 28, 1976; children: Jason Scott, Michelle Wendy. BA, Duke U., 1968; JD, Columbia U., 1972. Bar: N.Y. 1973, Pa. 1980, N.J. 1980, Fla. 1981. Assoc. Schwartz, Mermelstein, Burns, Lesser & Jacoby, N.Y.C., 1973-76, Marshall, Bratter, Green, Allison & Tucker, N.Y.C., 1976-79, Liebman & Flaster, Cherry Hill, N.J., 1979-80; v.p. Chase Manhattan Pvt. Bank, Palm Beach, Fla., 1980-2001; dir., sr. banker Citigroup Pvt. Bank, Palm Beach, 2001—. V.p., treas. Jewish Arts Found., Palm Beach, 1987—. Mem. N.Y. State Bar Assn., Fla. Bar Assn., N.Y.C. Bar Assn., Palm Beach Bar Assn. Avocations: reading, jogging. Home: 1740 Grantham Dr West Palm Beach FL 33414-8974 Office: Citigroup Pvt Bank 241 Royal Palm Way Palm Beach FL 33480 E-mail: lawrence.a.greenberg@citigroup.com.

GREENBERG, MORTON IRA, federal judge; b. Philadelphia, Pa., Mar. 20, 1933; s. Harry Arnold and Pauline (Hofkin) Greenberg; m. Barbara-Ann Kissel, May 29, 1987; children from previous marriage: Elizabeth, Suzanne, Lawrence. AB, U. Pa., 1954; LLB, Yale U., 1957. Bar: N.J. 1958, U.S. Dist. Ct. N.J. 1958, U.S. Ct. Appeals (3d cir.) 1972, U.S. Supreme Ct. 1973. Law clk.office of atty. gen. State of N.J., Trenton, NJ, 1957—58, dep. atty. gen., 1958—60, asst. atty. gen., 1971—73; pvt. practice Cape May, 1960—71; judge law div. Superior Ct. N.J., New Brunswick, 1973—76, judge chancery and gen. equity divs. Trenton, 1976—80, judge appellate div., 1980—87; judge U.S. Ct. Appeals (3d cir.), Trenton and Phila., 1987—. Office: US Ct Appeals US Courthouse 402 E State St Ste 7050 Trenton NJ 08608-1507

GREENBERG, MORTON PAUL, lawyer, consultant, life settlement broker; b. Fall River, Mass., June 2, 1946; s. Harry and Sylvia Shirley (Davis) Greenberg; m. Louise Beryl Schindler, Jan. 24, 1970; 1 child, Alexis Lynn. BSBA, NYU, 1968; JD, Bklyn. Law Sch., 1971. Bar: N.Y. 1972; CLU Am. Coll., 1975. Atty. Hanner, Fitzmaurice & Onorato, N.Y.C., 1971—72; dir., counsel, cons. on advanced underwriting The Mfrs. Life Ins. Co., Toronto, 1972—98; mng. gen. agt. for life settlements Viaticus, Inc., Chgo., 1999—2001; prin. life settlement broker Parker, Co., 1998—. Mem. sales ideas com. Million Dollar Roundtable, Chgo., 1982—83, 4th ann. George M. Graves meml. lectr., 1991; mem. adv. bd. Keeping Current, 1999—; spkr. on law, tax, life settlements, and advanced underwriting various profl. groups. Contbr. articles to profl. jours.; author: (tech. jour.) ManuBriefs. Mem.: ABA, Soc. Fin. Svcs. Profls., Nat. Assn. Ins. and Fin. Advisors, Internat. Platform Assn., Assn. for Advanced Life Underwriting (mem. bus. ins. and estate planning steering com. 1989—93), N.Y. State Bar Assn., Stern Sch. Bus. Alumni Assn., NYU Alumni Assn. Estate planning, Corporate taxation, Personal income taxation. Office: PO Box 183 7617 E Sunrise Trail Parker CO 80134-6915

GREENBERG, MYRON SILVER, lawyer; b. L.A., Oct. 17, 1945; s. Earl W. and Geri (Silver) G.; m. Shlomit Gross; children: David, Amy, Sophie, Benjamin. BSBA, UCLA, 1967; JD, 1970. Bar: Calif., 1971, U.S. Dist. Ct. (middle dist.) Calif. 1971, U.S. Tax Ct. 1977; cert. splst. in taxation law bd. legal specialization State Bar Calif.; CPA, Calif. Staff acct. Touche Ross & Co., L.A., 1970-71; assoc. Kaplan, Livingston, Goodwin, Berkowitz, & Selvin, Beverly Hills, Calif., 1971-74; ptnr. Steefel, Levitt, & Weiss, 1975—82, Myron S. Greenberg, a Profl. Corp., Larkspur, Calif., 1982—. Professorial lectr. tax. Golden Gate U.; instr. U. Calif., Berkeley, 2002-. Author: California Attorney's Guide to Professional Corporations, 1977, 79; bd. editors UCLA Law Rev., 1969-70. Mem. San Anselmo Planning Commn., 1976-77; mem. adv. bd. cert. program personal fin. planning U. Calif., Berkeley, 1991—; bd. dirs. Marin County Estate Planning Coun., 2001—, v.p. 2003. Mem.: ABA, AHA (bd. dirs. Marin county chpt. 1984—90, pres. 1988—89), Calif. Bd. Legal Specialization (chair taxation law adv. commn. 1998—2001, chmn. 2001), Real Estate Tax Inst. Calif. Cont. Edn. Bar (planning com.), Marin County (Calif.) Bar Assn. (bd. dirs. 1994—2001, pres. 1999), L.A. County Bar Assn., Larkspur C. of C. (bd. dirs. 1985—87). Democrat. Jewish. Corporate taxation, Estate taxation, Personal income taxation. Office: # 205 700 Larkspur Landing Cir Larkspur CA 94939-1711 E-mail: msg@eplaw.com.

GREENBERG, PHILIP ALAN, lawyer; b. Bklyn., Aug. 2, 1948; s. Harry and Jeannette (Nataf) G. BA cum laude, Bklyn. Coll., 1970; JD, N.Y.U., 1973. Bar: N.Y. 1974, U.S. Dist. Ct. (ea. and so. dists.) N.Y. 1975, U.S. Ct. Appeals (2d cir.) 1975, U.S. Supreme Ct. 1977 N.J. 1988. Assoc. Kamerman & Kamerman, N.Y.C., 1973-78, ptnr., 1978-82, Segal, Liling, Erlitz & Greenberg, N.Y.C., 1982, Segal, Liling & Greenberg, N.Y.C., 1982-84, Segal & Greenberg, N.Y.C., 1984; mng. ptnr. Segal, Post, DeMott & Crow, N.Y.C., 1985, Segal, Greenberg, McDonald & Maher, N.Y.C., 1985-86, Segal, Greenberg & McDonald, N.Y.C., 1986-87, Segal & Greenberg, N.Y.C., 1987-93, Bizar & Martin, N.Y.C., 1993-95; ptnr. Wallman Greenberg Gasman & McKnight, N.Y.C., 1995-2000, Law Offices of Philip A. Greenberg, N.Y.C., 2000—. Mem. faculty para legal Sobelsohn Sch., 1988-2000. Trustee Congregation Emunath Israel, 1984-99, chmn. law and ins. com., 1987-99. Mem. ABA (com. mem., lit. mem.), N.Y. Bar Assn., Assn. of Bar of City of N.Y., Mason (Maimonides-Marshall #739, master), Masters & Wardens Assn. (past pres. 6th Manhattan 1990-91, sec. 200003, pres. 2003—), Internat. Assoc. Tribune, Phi Alpha Delta. Democrat. Jewish. General civil litigation, Corporate, general, Family and matrimonial. Home: 7 Francisco Ave Little Falls NJ 07424-2316 Office: Law Offices of Philip A Greenberg 350 5th Ave Ste 3000 New York NY 10118 E-mail: lawman802@aol.com.

GREENBERG, ROBERT JAY, law educator; b. N.Y.C., Nov. 22, 1959; s. Murray Louis and Jeanette (Adams) G.; m. Dafna Rena Fuerst, June 29, 1993; children: Ashira Esther, Aliza Gila, Leora Adina. BA, Yeshiva U., 1981, JD, 1984, LLM, 2000. Bar: N.Y. 1986, N.J. 2000, Conn. 2001, D.C. 2001, Wyo. 2003, U.S. Dist. Ct. N.Y. (ea. and so. dists.) 1986, U.S. Dist. Ct. N.Y. (no. and we. dists.) 2000, U.S. Dist. Ct. N.J. 2000, U.S. Ct. of Internat. Trade 2002, U.S. Ct. Appeals (2d cir.) 1998, U.S. Ct. Appeals (fed. cir.) 2001, U.S. Supreme Ct. 1989; lic. real estate broker N.Y., notary public N.Y., N.J. Asst. to judge N.Y.C. Civil Ct., Bklyn., 1982; assoc. Simon, Meyrowitz, Meyrowitz and Schlussel, N.Y.C., 1983-86; instr. Bruriah High Sch. for Girls, Elizabeth, N.J., 1985-87; lectr. Nat. Acad. for Paralegal Studies, Mahwah, N.J., 1987-88; sr. legal editor Matthew Bender and Co., Inc., N.Y.C., 1987-94. Adj. asst. prof. bus. law Yeshiva U., N.Y.C., 1994-98, asst. prof., 1998—; lectr. NYU Inst. Paralegal Studies, N.Y.C., 1994-2000, adj. assoc. prof., 2001—; instr. dept. paralegal studies Queens College CUNY, 1994—. Asst. to author: Judaism and Vegetarianism, Judaism and Global Survival. Lectr. in Jewish law, Young Israel of Staten Island, 1976-93, Congregation Beth Yehuda, Staten Island, 1980-93, Young Israel of Forest Hills, Queens, 1993-2003, Queens Jewish Ctr., 2000-2003, Congreg. Ohr Moshe, Queens, 2003-. Recipient Disting. Svc. award Congregation Beth Yehuda, 1988, Outstanding Svc. award, 1991. Mem.: ABA, Acad. of Legal Studies in Bus., N.Y. County Lawyers Assn., N.Y. State Bar Assn. Democrat. Office: 75-27 171st St Fresh Meadows NY 11366-1416

GREENBERG, STEPHEN MICHAEL, lawyer, business executive; b. Passaic, N.J., July 27, 1944; s. Joseph Louis and Bess S. (Stein) G.; m. Sandra Lafer, Sept. 1, 1967; children: Seth, Sindy, Scott. BA, Washington (Pa.) Jefferson Coll., 1965; JD with honors, George Washington U., 1968. Bar: U.S. Dist. Ct. N.J. 1968, U.S. Ct. Appeals (3d cir.) 1968, U.S. Dist. Ct. (no. dist.) Ind. 1972, N.Y. 1983. Exec. asst. U.S. atty. N.J. Justice Dept., Newark, 1970-71; ptnr. Robinson, Wayne & Greenberg, Newark, 1971-82; gen. ptnr. Lafer Mgmt. Corp., N.Y.C., 1989—; ptnr. Hellring, Lindeman, Goldstein, Siegel, Stern & Greenberg, Newark, 1983-90; chmn. bd. dirs., sec. Flex Holding Co., N.Y.C., 1985-88; chmn. bd. dirs., acting chief exec. officer Graphic Scanning Corp., Teaneck, N.J., 1986-88; ptnr. Stern & Greenberg, Roseland, N.J., 1990—; CEO, vice chmn. Netzphone, Inc., 2000—. Bd. dirs. Switchco, Inc., Teaneck, Israel Investors Corp., N.Y.C.; chmn. bd. dirs. Time and Space Processing Inc., Santa Clara, Calif., bd. dirs. Winstar. Nat. vice chmn. United Jewish Appeal, N.Y.C., 1986—; v.p. Am. Friends of Hebrew U., N.Y.C., 1986-89; apptd. to Op. Independence by Prime Minister of Israel, Jerusalem and N.Y., 1986—. Recipient Lehman Leadership award United Jewish Appeal, 1984. Mem. ABA, N.J. Bar Assn. (Outstanding Profl. Achievement award 1986). Democrat. Home: 616 S Orange Ave Maplewood NJ 07040-1047 Office: Net2Phone Inc 520 Broad St Newark NJ 07102

GREENBERG, STEVEN MOREY, lawyer; b. Jersey City, N.J., Apr. 9, 1949; s. Joseph and Rhoda (Weisenfeld) G. AB cum laude, Syracuse U., 1971; JD, U. Pa., 1974. Bar: N.J. 1974, U.S. Dist. Ct. N.J. 1974, N.Y. 1980, U.S. Dist. Ct. (so. dist.) N.Y. 1986, U.S. Dist. Ct. (ea. dist.) N.Y. 1986, U.S. Ct. Appeals (3d cir.) 1987, U.S. Ct. Fed. Claims 1989. Assoc. Carpenter, Bennett & Morrissey, Newark, 1974-77, Cole, Berman & Belsky, Rochelle Park, NJ, 1977-79; pvt. practice Hackensack, NJ, 1979-94; atty. Bergenfield (N.J.) Rent Leveling Bd., 1985-89, 92-93, 99, Bergenfield Planning Bd., 1993-96; ptnr. Greenberg & Marmorstein, Hackensack, NJ, 1994-97, Greenberg & Lanz, Hackensack, NJ, 1997—. Trustee Jewish Ctr. of Teaneck, NJ, 1978—, mem. exec. com., 1992—97, v.p., 1992—94, pres., 1994—97; trustee United Jewish Appeal Fedn., Bergen County and N. Hudson, 1997—, exec. com., 2000—, chmn. planning and allocations com., 2000—02, chmn. sub-com Jewish edn., 1997—, chmn. com. campus youth svcs., 1998—2000, assoc. campaign chmn., 2002—, v.p., 2001—03, treas., 2003—, trustee, Endowment Found., 2003—; pres. Jewish Inst. Bioethics, N.Y.C., 1998—; trustee Jewish Assn. for Devel. Disabilities, 1999—, Jewish Family Svc. Inc., Bergen County, 1986—96, mem. exec. com., 1990—96, treas., 1990—92, v.p., 1992—96; trustee Bergen County HS Jewish Studies, 2000—; mem. cmty. advocacy program United Jewish Appeal Fedn. of Bergen County and North Hudson Resource Coun., 1991—, dir., 1995—; mem. Jewish Cmty. Rels. Coun. Bergen County and North Hudson, 1986—93, 1999—; trustee Assn. Jewish Fedns., NJ, 2002—, mem. exec./ops. com., 2002—03; mem. adv. bd. dirs. Jewish Home and Rehab. Ctr., Jersey City and River Vale, NJ, 1982—90, chmn. pers. com., 1986—, exec. com., 1987—, v.p., 1990—; mem. gov. body, exec. com., chmn. pers. com. Jewish Home at Rockleigh, 1999—, v.p., 2003—; mem. gov. body Jewish Home Found. N.J., Inc., 2003—; mem. NJ regional adv. bd. Anti-Defamation League, 1989—, mem. exec. com., 1989—; mem. NJ Leadership Think Tank The Allen and Joan Bildner Ctr. Study of Jewish Life Rutgers U., 2001—; dir. Union for Traditional Judaism, 1993—97. Recipient Second Century award Jewish Theol. Sem. Am., 1988, Friends Lubavitch Cmty. Svc. award Jewish Ctr. Teaneck, 1997, Ma'ayanot Yeshiva H.S. Girls, 2001, Anti-Defamation League Americanism award, 2003. Mem. ABA, N.J. Bar Assn., Bergen County Bar Assn., N.Y. State Bar Assn., Assn. Transp. Practitioners, Phi Kappa Phi, Pi Sigma Alpha. State civil litigation, Commercial, contracts (including sales of goods; commercial financing), Corporate, general. Home: 96 Westminster Ave Bergenfield NJ 07621-3916 Office: 2 University Plz Hackensack NJ 07601-6202 E-mail: smg@greenberglanz.com.

GREENBERGER, HOWARD LEROY, lawyer, educator; b. Pitts., July 16, 1929; s. Abraham Harry and Alice (Levine) G.; m. Bette Jo Bergad, June 15, 1959. BS magna cum laude, U. Pitts., 1951; JD cum laude, NYU, 1954; diploma in law (Fulbright scholar), Oxford (Eng.) U., 1955. Bar: Pa. 1955, D.C. 1954, N.Y. 1969, U.S. Supreme Ct. 1964. Law clk. U.S. Ct. Appeals (3d cir.), 1958-60; assoc. Kaufman & Kaufman, Pitts., 1960-61; assoc. prof. law NYU, 1961-65, prof., 1965—2001, prof. emeritus, 2001—; assoc. dean NYU Sch. Law, 1968-72; dean and dir. Practising Law Inst., 1972-75; senator NYU, 1994—. Cons. in field.; v.p. Nat. Ctr. Para-Legal Tng.; pres. Early Am. Industries Assn., 1979-82; chmn. Commn. on Fgn. Grad. Study, AALS. Author: (with G. Cole) The Meriden Experiment, 1973; Study of the Quality of Continuing Legal Education in the U.S, 1980; contbr. articles to legal publs.; chmn. editorial bd. Jour. Legal Edn, 1974-77. Pres. N.Y.C. chpt. Am. Jewish Com., 1977-79, nat. bd. govs., 1979-85; vice chmn., gen. counsel Coalition to Free Soviet Jews, 1977—; trustee Law Ctr. Found., 1973-91, Am. Friends of Hebrew U. Jerusalem, 1986—; chair New Amsterdam dist. Boy Scouts Am., 1990—, Ctr. on Social Welfare Policy and Law, 1991—, Blaustein Inst. on Human Rights, 1992—. Capt. JAGC, U.S. Army, 1955-58. Recipient Alumni Meritorious Svc. award NYU, 1977, Stanley Isaacs award Am. Jewish Com., 1982, Gt. Tchr. award NYU, 1993, Friendship award Govt. of Germany, 1988, Robert B. McKay Disting. Svc. award N.Y.U. Sch. of Law, 1997, Great Tchr. award 1999; Root-Tilden grantee NYU, 1954. Fellow Am. Bar Found.; mem. ABA, Assn. of Bar of City of N.Y., N.Y. County Lawyers Assn. (bd. dirs. 1990—), Am. Law Inst., Assn. Am. Law Schs., NYU Club (pres. 1981-83, Masons, Sojourners, Order of Coif, Phi Epsilon Pi. Democrat. Jewish. Home: 4 Washington Square Vlg Apt 16 New York NY 10012-1936 Office: NYU Sch Law Vand Hall 40 Washington Sq S New York NY 10012-1005

GREENBERGER, I. MICHAEL, lawyer; b. Scranton, Pa., Oct. 30, 1945; s. David and Betty (Kabatchnick) G.; m. Marcia Devins, July 19, 1969; children: Sarah Devins, Anne Devins AB, Lafayette Coll., 1967; JD, U. Pa., 1970. Bar: D.C. 1971, U.S. Dist. Ct. D.C. 1971, U.S. Ct. Appeals (D.C. cir.) 1971, U.S. Supreme Ct. 1975. Law clk. to Judge Carl McGowan U.S. Ct. Appeals for D.C. Circuit, Washington, 1970-71; legis. asst. to U.S. Congresswoman Elizabeth Holtzman, 1972-73; atty., advisor Office of Criminal Justice, Office U.S. Atty. Gen., 1973; assoc. Shea & Gardner, Washington, 1973-77, ptnr., 1977-97; dir. divsn. of trading and markets U.S. Commodity Futures Trading Commn., 1997-99; counselor to U.S. Atty. Gen., 1999, prin. dep. assoc., atty. gen., 1999-2001; vis. prof. U. Md. Law Sch., 2001—02, prof., 2002—; dir. U. Md. Ctr. for Health and Homeland Security, Md., 2002—. Bd. govs. D.C. Bar, 1995—98, com. on legal ethics, 1993—95; mem. D.C. Cir. Adv. Com. on Procedures, 1983—89; mem. steering com. D.C. Pro Bono Partnership, 1994—97, Lafayette Coll. Leadership Coun., 1994—99; mediator office of cir. exec. U.S. Cts. for D.C., 1989—; mem. D.C. Cir. Jud. Conf., 1983—; legal cons. Software Engring. Inst. Carnegie-Mellon U., Pitts., 1986—87; mem. steering com. Pres.'s Working Group on Fin. Markets, 1997—99; mem. hedge fund task force Internat. Orgn. Secs. Commrs., 1999. Editor-in-chief U. Pa. Law Rev., 1969-70; contbr. articles to profl. jours. Bd. dirs. Washington Legal Clinic for the Homeless, 1993-98, Am. Rivers, 1993-98, sec., 1995-98; bd. dirs. MIT Enterprise Forum Washington, 1984-87, Advanced Tech. Assn. Md., 1985-87, D.C. Prisoners' Legal Svc. Project, 1997-98. Mem. Am. Law Inst., Phi Beta Kappa. Commercial, contracts (including sales of goods; commercial financing), Intellectual property, Securities. Address: 2757 Brandywine St NW Washington DC 20008-1041 E-mail: mgreenberger@law.umaryland.edu.

GREENBLATT, MORTON HAROLD, retired assistant attorney general; b. Waterbury, Conn., Oct. 31, 1916; s. Samuel F. and Dorothy K. (Katz) G.; m. Evelyn Lipman, Oct. 26, 1947; children: Sarah Beth, Ruth, David. BA, Yale U., 1937; LLB, Harvard U., 1940. Bar: Conn. 1941, U.S. Dist. Ct. Conn. 1947, U.S. Supreme Ct. 1961, U.S. Ct. Appeals (7th cir.) 1971. Pvt. practice, Waterbury, Conn., 1941, 46-47; v.p., of counsel Ellmore Silver Co., Meriden, Conn., 1946-61; pvt. practice Meriden, 1961-67; asst. pros. atty. 7th Cir. Ct., Meriden, 1962-66; asst. corp. counsel City of Meriden, 1966-81; asst. atty. gen. State of Conn., Hartford, 1982-86; of counsel Pomeranz, Drayton and Stolnich, Hartford, 1986-96; ret., 1996. Sec. Meriden Planning Commn., 1953-55; pres. Meriden Bd. Edn., 1959-61; active Temple B'nai Abraham, 1946-85, pres., 1977-79; chmn. Solid Waste Mgmt. Commn. Branford, 1986-92, rep. policy bd. South Cen. Conn. Regional Water Dist., 1988-92; bd. assessment appeals Branford, 1987-91, 97—. Maj. USAAF, 1942-46. Mem. Meriden-Wallingford Bar Assn., Conn. Bar Assn., Am. Arbitration Assn., Conn. Assn. Mcpl. Attys. (treas.), New Haven County Bar Assn. Jewish. Home: 55 Canterbury Rd Hamden CT 06514-2016

GREENBLATT, RAY HARRIS, lawyer; b. Milw., June 29, 1931; s. Charles and Ethel (Harris) G.; m. Betty Goldsmith, July 11, 1955 (dec. Mar. 1967); children: Walter, Robert, Edward; m. Helen Judith Pick, Mar. 29, 1969 (div. Dec. 1969). BS in Econs., U. Pa., 1953; JD magna cum laude, Harvard U., 1956. Bar: Ill. 1956. Assoc. Mayer, Brown, Rowe & Maw, 1956-64, ptnr., 1965-94. Arbitrator, mediator Am. Arbitration Assn., 1970-96; hearing officer Ill. State Banking Bd., 1989; lectr. Sch. for Bankers U. Wis., Madison, 1964, 73, Ill. Inst. Continuing Legal Edn., 1973. Contbr. articles to profl. jours. Pres. Winnetka (Ill.) Bd. Edn., 1974-75, mem. 1969-74; vol. tchr. economics, poetry and debate, Providence-St. Mel Sch., Chgo., 1994-98. Mem. ABA, Chgo. Literary Club (pres. 2000-2001), Cliff Dwellers Club, Lake Shore Country Club. Jewish. Banking, Commercial, contracts (including sales of goods; commercial financing), Corporate, general. Home: 1003 Westmoor Rd Winnetka IL 60093-1855 E-mail: rayofsunsh@aol.com.

GREENE, ADDISON KENT, lawyer, accountant; b. Cardston, Alta., Can., Dec. 23, 1941; s. Addison Allen and Amy (Shipley) G.; m. Janice Hanks, Aug. 30, 1967; children: Lisa, Tiffany, Tyler, Darin. BS in Acctg., Brigham Young U., 1968; JD, U. Utah, 1973. Bar: Utah 1973, Nev. 1974, U.S. Tax Ct. 1979. Staff acct. Seidman and Seidman, Las Vegas, Nev., 1968-69, Peat Marwick Mitchell, Los Angeles, 1969-70; atty. Clark Greene & Assocs., Ltd., Las Vegas, 1973—. Instr. Nev. Bar Rev., Las Vegas, 1975-78; bd. dirs. Cumorah Credit Union. Mem. Citizen's for Responsible Gov't, Las Vegas, 1979—; asst. dist. com. mem. Boy Scouts Am., Las Vegas, 1985—. Mem. ABA, Utah Bar Assn., Nev. Bar Assn., Nev. Soc. CPA's (assoc.), Am. Assn., Pension Actuaries (assoc.). Republican. Mem. Lds Ch. Avocations: golf, snow skiing. Estate planning, Pension, profit-sharing, and employee benefits, Probate (including wills, trusts). Office: Clark Greene & Assocs Ltd 3770 Howard Hughes Pkwy Ste 195 Las Vegas NV 89109-0976

GREENE, BERNARD HAROLD, lawyer; b. Bklyn., Sept. 21, 1925; s. Max and Clara (Pasweg) G.; m. Magda C. Schwartz, Sept. 19, 1948; children: Michael, Edith, Susan, Jonathan, David. BBA magna cum laude, CCNY, 1948; LLB cum laude, Yale U., 1951. Bar: N.Y. 1952. Assoc. Paul, Weiss, Rifkind, Wharton & Garrison, N.Y.C., 1951-60, ptnr., 1960-94, of counsel, 1995—. Vis. lectr. Yale Law Sch., New Haven, 1972-78, 81-83; adj. prof. N.Y. Law Sch., N.Y.C., 1985-88. Chmn. deferred giving and estate planning com. Community Svc. Soc., N.Y.C., 1975-82. 1st lt. U.S. Army, 1943-47. Mem. Assn. Bar City N.Y. (mem. surrogate's ct. com. 1958-61) State civil litigation, Probate (including wills, trusts), Estate taxation. Home: 153 Union St Montclair NJ 07042-2102 Office: Paul Weiss Rifkind Wharton & Garrison Rm 200 1285 Avenue of the Americas New York NY 10019-6065

GREENE, IRA S. lawyer; b. N.Y.C., Nov. 21, 1946; s. Melvin and Syd (Semmelman) G.; m. Robin Colin, Dec. 29, 1973; children: Jessica, Alexander. BA, Syracuse U., 1968; postgrad., U. Buffalo, 1968-69; JD, N.Y. U., 1971. Bar: N.Y. 1972, U.S. Dist. Ct. (so. and ea. dists.) N.Y. 1972, U.S. Ct. Appeals (2d cir.) 1974. Counsel Gainsburg, Gottlieb, Levitan & Cole, N.Y.C., 1982—84; ptnr. Gainsburg, Gottlieb, Levitan, Greene & Cole, N.Y.C., 1984—86, Gainsburg, Greene & Hirsch, Purchase, NY, 1986—91, Squadron, Ellenoff, Plesent & Sheinfeld, N.Y.C., 1991—2002, Hogan & Hartson, N.Y.C., 2002—. Lectr. in field. Mem. Assn. Comml. Fin. Attys., Bank Lawyers Conf., Bankruptcy Lawyers Bar Assn., Assn. of Bar of City of N.Y. Banking, Bankruptcy, Commercial, contracts (including sales of goods; commercial financing). Office: Hogan & Hartson LLP 875 Third Ave New York NY 10022

GREENE, JOHN JOSEPH, lawyer; b. Marshall, Tex., Mar. 19, 1946; s. William Henry and Camille Anne Greene. BA, U. Houston, 1969, MA, 1974; JD, South Tex. Coll., 1978. Bar: Tex. 1978, U.S. Supreme Ct. 1982. Asst. atty. City of Amarillo, Tex., 1978-79, Harris County, Tex., 1979-83; pvt. practice, 1983—; city atty. City of Conroe (Tex.), 1983-89; sr. asst. city atty. City of Austin (Tex.), 1990—. Capt. USAR, 1969-76. Decorated Bronze Star, Air Medal. Roman Catholic. Office: 114 W 7th St Ste 400 Austin TX 78701-3008

GREENE, JOHN THOMAS, judge; b. Salt Lake City, Nov. 28, 1929; s. John Thomas and Mary Agnes (Hindley) G.; m. Dorothy Kay Buchanan, Mar. 31, 1955; children: Thomas Buchanan Greene, John Buchanan Greene, Mary Kay Greene Platt. BA in Polit. Sci., U. Utah, 1952, JD, 1955. Bar: Utah 1955, U.S. Dist. Ct. (10th cir.) 1955, U.S. Supreme Ct. 1966. Pvt. practice, Salt Lake City, 1955-57; asst. U.S. atty., 1957-59; ptnr. Marr, Wilkins & Cannon (and successor firms), Salt Lake City, 1959-75; ptnr., pres., chmn. bd. dirs. Greene, Callister & Nebeker, Salt Lake City, 1975-85; judge U.S. Dist. Ct., Salt Lake City, 1985—. Author: (manual) American Mining Law, 1960; contbr. articles to profl. jours. Chmn. Salt Lake City Cmty. Coun., 1970-75, Utah State Bldg. Authority, Salt Lake City, 1980-85; Regent Utah State Bd. Higher Edn., Salt Lake City, 1982-86. Recipient Order of Coif U. Utah, 1955, Merit of Honor award, 1994, Utah Fed. Bar Disting. Svc. award, 1997. Fellow ABA Found. (life); ABA ho. of dels. 1972-92, bd. govs. 1987-91; mem. Dist. Judges Assn. (pres. 10th cir. 1998-2000), Utah Bar Assn. (pres. 1971-72, Judge of Yr. award 1995), Am. Law Inst. (life, panelist and lectr. 1980-85, advisor 1986-98); Phi Beta Kappa. Mem. Lds Ch. Avocations: travel, reading, tennis. Office: US Dist Ct 350 S Main St Ste 447 Salt Lake City UT 84101-2180 E-mail: JTGJR@hotmail.com, Thomas_Greene@utd.uscourts.gov.

GREENE, RICHARD LAWRENCE, lawyer; b. L.A., Oct. 16, 1938; s. Robert and Mildred (Dorfman) G.; m. Lorrie Lee Levin, Jan. 27, 1963; children: Dana Michele, Julie Alyson, Elisa Suzanne. AA, U. Calif., Berkeley, 1958, BS, 1960, LLB, 1963. Bar: Calif. 1964. Ptnr. Bronson, Bronson & McKinnon, San Francisco, 1971-84, Greene, Radovsky, Maloney & Share, San Francisco, 1984—. Adj. prof. law U. Calif., Berkeley, 1984; lectr. tax insts. Contbr. articles to profl. jours. Bd. dirs. Koret Found., San Francisco, 1981—, San Francisco Hearing and Speech Cen., 1982-86. Served with USAR, 1963-69. Mem. Calif. Bar Assn. (V. Judson Kelin award taxation sect. 1981), Order of Coif, Concordia Club, Phi Beta Kappa.

Jewish. Avocations: tennis, sports, kachina dolls, contemporary art. Estate planning, Corporate taxation, Personal income taxation. Office: Greene Radovsky Maloney & Share LLP 4 Embarcadero Ctr Ste 400 San Francisco CA 94111

GREENE, ROBERT MICHAEL, lawyer; b. Buffalo, Jan. 14, 1945; s. Gerald Henry and Dorothy Louise (Doll) G.; m. Catherine Ellen Ostanski, Sept. 28, 1974; children: Amy, Megan, Timothy, Daniel. BA, Canisius Coll., 1966; JD, U. Notre Dame, 1969; LLM, NYU, 1971. Bar: N.Y. 1970, U.S. Dist. Ct. (we. dist.) N.Y. 1970, U.S. Ct. Appeals (2d cir.) 1970. Atty. VISTA, N.Y.C., 1969-71; assoc. Phillips, Lytle, Hitchcock, Blaine & Huber, LLP, Buffalo, 1971-75, ptnr., 1976-81, mng. ptnr., 1982-95, CEO, 1982—2003. Del. White House Conf. on Small Bus., 1986; bd. dirs. Cello Pack Corp., Gioia Mgmt., Inc. Author: Managing Partner 101: A Primer on Law Firm Leadership, 1990, Making Partner, A Guide for Law Firm Associates, 1992; co-author: Summary of Land Use Regulation in the State of New York and State Land Use Programs, 1974; editor: The Quality Pursuit: Assuring Standards in the Practice of Law, 1989; bd. editors Law Practice Mgmt. mag., 1989-93, articles editor, 1992-93. Trustee Canisius Coll., 1971-77, 92-2000, chmn. 1993-97; chmn. Shea's Ctr. for Performing Arts, Buffalo, 1981-85; pres. Zool. Soc. of Buffalo, 1987-92; chmn. Buffalo Philharm. Orch., 1997-99; pres. bd. Cath. Edn. Diocese of Buffalo, 1987-97; trustee Western N.Y. Pub. Broadcasting Assn., 1984—, chmn. 1993-96; Greater Buffalo Devel. Found., 1992-93; bd. dirs. Greater Buffalo Partnership, 1993-2000, sec. 1996-2000; trustee Buffalo Philharm. Orch. Found., 2001—, chmn., 2003—; trustee Found. of Diocese of Buffalo, 2000—, Zool. Soc. Buffalo Found., 1999—, WNED Found., 2001—; bd. dirs. Albright-Knox Art Gallery, 2000—. Recipient LaSalle award Canisius Coll., 1980, Bd. Regents Dist. Citizens Achievement award, 1987, Disting. Alumni award 1991, Signum Fidei award St. Joseph's Collegiate Inst., 1990, Golden Marquee award Shea's Buffalo Theatre, 1984, Theodore Roosevelt Exemplary Citizen award, 1993, Person of Yr. award Notre Dame Club of Buffalo, 1994, Brotherhood award Nat. Conf., 1997, Chmn.'s award Buffalo Niagara Partnership, 1999, Humanitarian award Niagara Luth. Health Found., 2000, Caritas award St. Joseph Hosp. Found., 2003. Mem. N.Y. State Bar Assn., Erie County Bar Assn., U. Notre Dame Law Assn. (bd. dirs. 1988—), Buffalo Club (bd. dirs. 1997-2000), Cherry Hill Club. Democrat. Roman Catholic. Corporate, general, Health. Office: Phillips Lytle Hitchcock Blaine & Huber LLP 3400 HSBC Ctr Buffalo NY 14203-2887 Fax: 716-852-6100. E-mail: rgreene@phillipslytle.com.

GREENE, STEPHEN CRAIG, lawyer; b. Watertown, N.Y., Apr. 27, 1946; s. Harold Adelbert and Mildred Esther (Baker) G.; m. Nancy Jean Adams, Mar. 28, 1965; children: Kathryn, Stephen, Hilary. AB, Syracuse U., 1967, JD, 1970. Bar: N.Y. 1971, U.S. Tax Ct., 1977. Asst. to pres. SUNY, Oswego, 1970-73; assoc. firm Leyden E. Brown, Oswego, 1973-75; ptnr. Brown and Greene, 1976-81; pvt. practice law, 1981—. Bd. dirs. Found. Corp. Legal Studies, Inc., 1968-70, United Way of Oswego County, Inc., 1985-88, Campbell's Point Assn., 1994-96, Oswego Hosp., 1981-2000, mem. exec. com., 1985-2000, pres., 1996-98; pres. Oswego Health, Inc., 19972002; town atty. Oswego, 1972—; counsel Oswego County Bd. Realtors, 1978—; mem. Oswego County Rep. com., 1974-85, counsel, 1980-83; gen. counsel Express Abstract Co., 1992-95. Recipient Inst. Counsel, 1970. Mem. ABA, N.Y. Bar Assn., Oswego County Bar Assn., Greater Oswego C. of C. (bd. dir. 1980-87), Oswego Country Club (counsel 1977-81), Masons, Shriners, Phi Delta Phi. Corporate, general, Probate (including wills, trusts), Property, real (including real estate development, water). Home: PO Box 115 611 W 1st St Oswego NY 13126-4137 Office: PO Box 60 85 W Bridge St Oswego NY 13126-2011

GREENE, STEVEN KEVIN, lawyer; b. Englewood, N.J., Oct. 8, 1960; s. Martin S. G. and Claire McCormick; m. Colleen Patricia Nann, Sept. 5, 1956 (div. June 1998); 1 child, Blair Timothy; m. Tiffani Anne Cook, Sept. 22, 2001. BA, George Washington U., 1983; JD, Drake U., 1986. Bar: N.J. 1986, U.S. Dist. Ct. N.J. 1986. Atty. Psak & Parker, Middlesex, N.J., 1986-88, Leonard & Butler, Morristown, N.J., 1988-92, Bongiovanni, Collins & Warden, Denville, N.J., 1992-96; of counsel Indie & McNamara, P.C., Princeton, NJ, 1996—. Mem. N.J. Bar Assn. Democrat. Jewish. Avocations: road running, baseball, family. General civil litigation, Criminal, Personal injury (including property damage). Office: 31 Jefferson Plz Princeton NJ 08540

GREENEBAUM, LEONARD CHARLES, retired lawyer; b. Langgoens, Germany, Feb. 6, 1934; came to U.S. 1937, naturalized, 1952; s. Norbert and Henny Lisa (Greenbaum) G.; m. Barbara Rosendorf, Feb. 10, 1957; children: Beth Lynn, Cathy Sue, Steven I. BS cum laude in Commerce, Washington and Lee U., 1956, JD cum laude, 1959. Bar: D.C. 1959, Va. 1959., Md. 1965. Atty. Sachs, Greenebaum & Tayler and predecessor firms, Washington, 1959-64, ptnr., 1964-75, mng. ptnr., 1975-90; ptnr., D.C. coord. litigation Baker & Hostetler, Washington, 1990-95, firmwide litigation group chair, 1996-2000, ret., 2001. Arbitrator Am. Arbitration Assn., Washington, 1975-2000; mem. Washington and Lee U. Law Coun. Chmn. bd. Davis Meml. Goodwill Industries, Washington, 1979-82; bd. dirs. Coun. for Ct. Excellence. Capt. U.S. Army, 1957. Recipient Svc. to Handicapped People award Davis Meml. Goodwill Industries, 1982. Fellow: Am. Bar. Found. (life); mem.: Md. Bar Assn., D.C. Bar Assn., Isle of Palms, Wild Dunes Country Club, Country Club of Charleston, Bethesda (Md.) Country Club. Jewish. Federal civil litigation, Criminal, General practice. Fax: 843-406-8777. E-mail: curlyccc@comcast.net.

GREENER, RALPH BERTRAM, lawyer; b. Rahway, N.J., Sept. 23, 1940; s. Ralph Bertram and Mary Ellen (Esch) G.; m. Jean Elizabeth Wilson, Mar. 21, 1964; children: Eric Wilson, Erin Hope, Nicholas Christian. BA, Wheaton Coll., 1962; JD, Duke U., 1968. Bar: Minn. 1969, U.S. Dist. Ct. 1969, U.S. Tax Ct. 1988. With Fredrikson & Byron P.A., Mpls., 1969—. Chmn. Minn. Lawyers Mutual Ins. Co., Mpls. 1981—; pres. Nat. Assn. of Bar-Related Ins. Cos., 1989-90. 1st Lt. USMCR, 1962-65. Recipient award of profl. excellence Minn. State Bar Assn., 1993. Mem. Rotary Club (pres. Mpls. 2002-03). Corporate, general, Insurance, Nonprofit and tax-exempt organizations. Home: 1018 W Minnehaha Pky Minneapolis MN 55419-1161 Office: Fredrikson & Byron PA 4000 Pillsbury Ctr 200 S 6th St Minneapolis MN 55402-1425 E-mail: rgreener@fredlaw.com.

GREENER, RICHARD H. lawyer; b. Sept. 21, 1942; children: Heidi, Richard, Robert, Nicholas, Whitney, Natalie. BA, U. Wash., 1965; JD, U. Idaho, 1968. Bar: Wash. 1968, Idaho 1968, U.S. Supreme Ct. 1971. Ptnr. Kidwell and Greener, Boise, Idaho, 1968—72, Web, Johnson, Redford and Greener, Boise, 1973—77, Cosho, Humphrey, Greener and Welsh, Boise, 1977—. Judge justice ct. Latah County, Moscow, 1966—68. Mem. adv. bd. Boise Little Theater, 2000—; commr. Ada County Planning and Zoning, Ada, Idaho, 1973—74. Fellow: Am. Coll. Trial Lawyers; mem.: Am. Bd. Trial Advocates, Crane Creek Country Club, Arid Club. General civil litigation. Home: 1348 E Corniche Ct Boise ID 83706 Office: Cosho Humphrey Greener and Welsh 815 W Washington St Boise ID 83702

GREENFELD, ALEXANDER, lawyer; b. Wilmington, Del., Jan. 19, 1929; s. Abraham and Annie (Colton) G. BA, U. Del., 1949; LLB, U. Pa., 1953. Bar: D.C. 1953, Del. 1953, U.S. Ct. Appeals (D.C. cir.) 1953, U.S. Ct. Appeals (3d cir.). Assoc. Albert Simon, Wilmington, 1956; dep. atty. gen. Office Atty. Gen., Wilmington, 1957-58; pvt. practice, Wilmington, 1959-60, Washington, 1990-95; atty. FCC, Washington, 1960-61; U.S. atty. for Del., U.S. Dept. Justice, Wilmington, 1961-69; corp. counsel N.Y. Times Co., N.Y.C., 1972-79; prof. media law U. Calif., Berkeley, 1979-84, U. Md., College Park, 1984-89; legal rschr., Washington, 1992—. Sr. counsel Reporters Commn. for Freedom of Press, Washington, 1984—; corp. counsel U.S. News & World Report, Washington, 1985-88;counsel Am. Journalism Rev., College Park, Md., 1986 atty. U.S. Senate, Washington, 1992. Contbr. articles to legal jours. Pres. Del. Ednl. TV Assn., 1956, Del. chpt. Am. Assn. for UN, 1956; personal counsel to state chmn. Dem. Com. Del., 1970-71; gen. counsel and legislative dir. N.Y. State Consumer Protection Bd., N.Y.C. and Albany investigations 1971; spl. asst. Security of Investigations to Pres. N.Y.C. Off-track Betting Corp., 1971-72.. Recipient Outstanding Tchg. award, Panhellenic Assn. U. Md., 1986. Mem. Del. Bar Assn., D.C. Bar Assn. General civil litigation, Criminal, Libel. Home and Office: 4201 Butterworth Pl NW Apt 314 Washington DC 20016-4552

GREENFIELD, JAMES ROBERT, lawyer; b. Phila., Mar. 31, 1926; s. Milton and Katherine E. (Rosenberg) G.; m. Phyllis Chaplowe, Aug. 17, 1947 (dec. May 1978); m. Joyce MacDonald Koehler, Mar. 22, 1980. BS, Bates Coll., 1947; JD, Yale U., 1950. Bar: Conn. 1950, U.S. Dist. Ct. Conn. 1951, U.S. Ct. Appeals (2d cir.) 1966, U.S. Supreme Ct. 1959. Atty. Chaplowe & Greenfield, 1950-54, Markle & Greenfield, New Haven, 1954-58; sr. ptnr. Lander, Greenfield & Krick, New Haven, 1958-80, Greenfield, Krick & Jacobs, New Haven, 1980-90, Greenfield & Murphy, New Haven, 1990-98; of counsel Tyler Cooper & Alcorn, New Haven, 1998—. Lectr. U. Conn. Law Sch., 1966-67, 71-72, 75-76 Mem. editorial bd. Conn. Bar Jour, 1963-77. Pres. New Haven Symphony, 1976-78, Conn. Bar Found., 1976-77; bd. dirs. Nat. Jud. Coll., 1978-84. With USNR, 1944-46. Fellow Am. Bar Found. (state chmn. 1985-90); mem. ABA (state del. 1975-78, bd. govs. 1978-81, ho. of dels. 1972-83, spl. com. on goverance 1983-84, chmn. various coms.), Conn. Bar Assn. (pres. 1973-74, Disting. Profl. Svc. award 1989), Judicature Soc. (bd. dirs. 1983-87, 2002-), Am. Law Inst., Am. Acad. Matrimonial Lawyers (pres. Conn. chpt. 1993-94), Internat. Acad. Matrimonial Lawyers, New Haven County Bar Assn. (pres. 1969-70, Lifetime Achievment award 1993, Conn. Law Tribune Svc. to the Profn. award 2002), Yale Law Sch. Assn. (sec. 1977-80), Quinnipiack Club, Mory's. Family and matrimonial. Office: Tyler Cooper & Alcorn 205 Church St New Haven CT 06510-1805 E-mail: greenfield@tylercooper.com.

GREENFIELD, MICHAEL C. lawyer; b. Chgo., May 4, 1934; BA, U. Ill., 1955; JD, Northwestern U., 1957. Bar: Ill. 1957, Ind. 1982, U.S. Suprmee Ct. 1974. Asst. states atty. Cook County, Ill., 1957-58; ptnr. Asher, Gittler & Greenfield, Ltd., Chgo., 1959—, Asher, Gittler, Greenfield & D'Alba, Ltd., Chgo. Mem. inquiry bd. Ill. Supreme Ct. Disciplinary Commn., 1973-77, mem. hearing bd., 1978-94, 97—, vice chmn., 1984, chmn., 1985, mem. oversight comm., 1995-96. Mem. ABA, Ill. Bar Assn., Chgo. Bar Assn., Internat. Found. Employee Benefit Plans (bd. dirs. 1977-80, 85-88, 92-94). Labor (including EEOC, Fair Labor Standards Act, labor-management relations, NLRB, OSHA), Pension, profit-sharing, and employee benefits. Office: Asher Gittler Greenfield & D'Alba Ltd 200 W Jackson Blvd Ste 1900 Chicago IL 60606-4397 E-mail: mcg@ulaw.com.

GREENLAW, DAWN SHARON, lawyer; b. Lawton, Okla., Oct. 9, 1969; d. Douglas Warren and Linda Ann Greenlaw. BA in Polit. Sci., U. Vt., 1990, MPA, 1991; MA in Polit. Sci., Boston Coll., 1993; JD, U. Conn., Hartford, 1996, LLM, 2003, Boston U., 2000; postgrad., Dartmouth Coll., 2001—. Bar: Conn., 1996, Mass., 1997, U.S. Dist. Ct. Conn., 1997. Pvt. practice atty., West Hartford, Conn., 1996-97; sr. corp. atty. Exec. Risk, Inc., Simbury, Conn., 1997—99; asst. v.p., asst. counsel Chubb Group of Ins. Cos., 1999—. Adj. prof. criminology Cuny Coll., Mass., 1996. Notes and comments editor Conn. Ins. Law Jour., 1994-96; mem. staff Ann. Rev. Banking Law, 1998. Recipient Am. Jurisprudence award, 1994. Republican. Roman Catholic. Commercial, contracts (including sales of goods; commercial financing), Corporate, general, Insurance. Home: 45 Cobblestone Rd Glastonbury CT 06033-2505 Office: Chubb Splty Ins 82 Hopmeadow St Weatogue CT 06089-9694

GREENLEAF, WALTER FRANKLIN, lawyer; b. Griffin, Ga., Sept. 21, 1946; BA, Mich. State U., 1968; MA, U. N.C., 1970; JD, U. Ala., 1973. Law clk. U.S. Dist. Ct., Birmingham, Ala., 1973-74; assoc. Sirote, Permutt, et al., Birmingham, Ala., 1975-76; assoc., then ptnr. Welbaum Guernsey, Hingston, Greenleaf & Gregory, LLP, Miami, Fla., 1976—. Construction, Insurance, Probate (including wills, trusts). Home: 417 Madeira Ave Miami FL 33134-4234 Office: Welbaum Guernsey Hingston Greenleaf & Gregory LLP 901 Ponce De Leon Blvd Miami FL 33134-3073 Business E-Mail: fgreenleaf@welbaum.com.

GREENLEE, JIM MING, prosecutor; B in Engring., JD, U. Miss. Atty. Taylor and Whitwelll, 1981—85; ptnr. Taylor, Jones, Alexander, Greenlee, Seale and Ryan, 1985—87; asst. U.S. atty. No. Dist. Miss. U.S. Dept. Justice, 1987—2001, U.S. atty., 2001—. Office: 900 Jefferson Ave Oxford MS 38655

GREENLEY, BEVERLY JANE, lawyer, educator; b. Cleve., Sept. 24, 1947; d. Gaylord H. and Joan C. (Gurklis) G. BA, Principia Coll., 1969; JD, U. Mo., 1976; LLM, Washington U., 1981. Bar: Mo. 1976, Ill. 1977, U.S. Tax Ct. 1979. Ptnr. McCarter & Greenley, St. Louis, 1976-81, McCarter, Snyder & Greenley, St. Louis, 1981-85; assoc. prof. law Stetson U. Coll. Law, St. Petersburg, Fla., 1981-85; ptnr. Gage & Tucker, St. Louis, 1985-87, Husch, Eppenberger, Donohue, Cornfeld & Jenkins, St. Louis, 1987-90, McCarter & Greenley, St. Louis, 1990—. Estate planning lectr. for CLE programs, 1997—; estate planning expert witness, 2000—. Co-author: Missouri Lawyer's Guide, 1984. Mem. Mo. Bar Assn., Ill. Bar Assn. Estate planning, Probate (including wills, trusts), Taxation, general. Office: 1 Metropolitan Sq Ste 2100 Saint Louis MO 63102-2797 E-mail: bgreenley@mccartergreenley.com.

GREENMAN, FREDERICK F., JR., lawyer; b. N.Y.C., Feb. 22, 1933; s. Frederick F. and Mildred G.; m. Angela Lancieri; children: Paul Rudolph, Jodi La Bourene. BA, Harvard U., 1954, LLB, 1961, LLM, 1963. Bar: N.Y. 1962. Assoc. Hays, Sklar & Herzberg, N.Y.C., 1962-66; asst. U.S. atty. So. Dist. N.Y., N.Y.C., 1966-69; assoc. Linden and Deutsch, N.Y.C., 1969-70; ptnr. Deutsch Klagsbrun & Blasband (and predecessor firm), 1971-2001. Legal advisor Am. Adoption Congress. Mem. Assn. Bar City N.Y., N.Y. State Bar Assn. Jewish. General civil litigation, Trademark and copyright. Office: 641 Lexington Ave New York NY 10022-4503 E-mail: FFGreenman@aol.com.

GREENO, EDWARD PATRICK, lawyer; b. London, May 10, 1958; s. Edward and Brenda Greeno. LLB, U. London, 1980. Clk. Herbert Smith, London, 1981—83, asst. solicitor, 1983—89, ptnr., 1989—. Mem.: Chartered Inst. Arbitration. Office: Herbert Smith Exch Ho Primrose St London EC2A 2HS England Fax: +44 207 374 0888. E-mail: ted.greeno@herbertsmith.com.

GREENSPAN, JEFFREY DOV, lawyer; b. Chgo., July 19, 1954; s. Philip and Sylvia (Haberman) G.; m. Eleanor Helen Goldman, Aug. 28, 1983. BS in Econs., U. Ill., Urbana, 1976; JD, Ill. Inst. Tech., 1979. Bar: Ill. 1979, U.S. Dist. Ct. (no. dist.) Ill. 1979, U.S. Ct. Appeals (7th cir.) 1979. Atty. Govs. Office Consumer Services, Chgo., 1978-80; asst. pub. defender Cook County Pub. Defenders Office, Chgo., 1980-81; asst. corp. counsel Village of Skokie, Chgo., 1981-91; of counsel Fioretti & Des Jardins, Chgo., 1990-91; with Ancel, Glink, Diamond, Cope & Bush, P.C., Chgo., 1991-99, Fioretti & Des Jardins, Chgo., 1999-2001; gen. counsel, dir. land acquisition CorLands, Chgo., 2001—. Sec., treas. Polit. Cons., Inc., Skokie, 1984—. Author polit. computer software Master Campaigner, 1984. Mem. Niles (Ill.) Twp. Dem. Orgn., 1976—; chmn. Niles Twp. Com. on Youth, 1982-85, TRY-Citizens for Drug Awareness, Niles, 1983-84; mem. Centereast Bd. Authority, 1998—; bd. dirs. Niles Twp. H.S., 1999—. Mem. Chgo. Bar Assn. (chmn. devel. of law com. 1990-91, chmn. local govt. law com. 1992-93). Environmental, Land use and zoning (including planning), Property, real (including real estate development, water). Home: 9445 Keeler Ave Skokie IL 60076-1442 Office: 25 E Washington St Ste 1650 Chicago IL 60602-1805 E-mail: jgreenspan@corlands.org.

GREENSPAN, LEON JOSEPH, lawyer; b. Phila., Feb. 10, 1932; s. Joseph and Minerva (Podolsky) G.; m. Irene Gordon, Nov. 2, 1958; children: Marjorie, David, Michael, Lisa. AB, Temple U., 1955, JD, 1958. Bar: N.Y. 1959, N.J. 1985, Fla. 1985, Pa. 1986, Conn. 1991, U.S. Tax Ct. 1973, U.S. Supreme Ct. 1969. Pvt. practice law, White Plains, N.Y., 1959-64; ptnr. Greenspan and Aurnou, White Plains, 1964-77, Greenspan, Jaffe & Rosenblatt, White Plains, 1987-91, Greenspan & Greenspan, White Plains, 1992—. Counsel Brown, Boston; lectr. Fla. Bar CLER Program, 1991, 92, 99; atty. Tarrytown (N.Y.) Housing Authority. Pres. Hebrew Inst., White Plains; vice chmn. ann. dinner NCCJ. Recipient Pres.'s award Union Orthodox Synagogues, 1982, Owl Club award Temple Univ., 2001; honoree Hebrew Inst., White Plains, 1983. Mem. ABA, N.J. Bar Assn., Fla. Bar Assn., Westchester County Bar Assn., White Plains Bar Assn., N.Y. State Trial Lawyers Assn., Criminal Cts. Bar Assn. Westchester County, N.J. Bar Assn. General civil litigation, Criminal, Taxation, general. Home: 14 Pinebrook Dr White Plains NY 10605-4713 Office: Greenspan & Greenspan 150 Grand St 6th Fl White Plains NY 10601-4400

GREENSPAN, MICHAEL EVAN, lawyer; b. White Plains, N.Y., Jan. 18, 1967; s. Leon Joseph and Irene (Gordon) G.; m. Diane Gloria Blum, July 2, 1989; children: Daniel, Marc, Julia. BA magna cum laude, Temple U., 1988, JD, 1991. Bar: N.Y. 1992, U.S. Dist. Ct. (so. and ea. dists.) N.Y. 1992, U.S. Dist. Ct. Conn. 1992, U.S. Ct. Appeals (2d cir.) 1993, U.S. Ct. Appeals (11th cir.) 1996. Assoc. Greenspan, Jaffe & Rosenblatt, White Plains, 1991-92; ptnr. Greenspan & Greenspan, White Plains, 1992—. Mem. com. civil practice laws and rules State Bar N.Y.; Temple U. del. Symposium on the Presidency, Washington, 1987. Mem. exec. com. Loucks Track & Field Games, White Plains, 1991—. Recipient Lewis F. Powell Jr. medallion Am. Coll. Trial Lawyers Assn., 1991, James J. Manderino award Phila. Trial Lawyers Assn., 1991. Mem. ATLA, N.Y. Trial Lawyers Assn., Barristers Soc., N.Y. State Bar Assn., Westchester County Bar Assn., White Plains Bar Assn., Westchester Track and Field and Cross-Country Ofcls. Orgn., Golden Key, Order of Omega, Phi Beta Kappa, Pi Sigma Alpha, Phi Alpha Theta, Delta Tau Delta. Republican. Jewish. Avocations: officiating high school track and field, race walking, basketball. General civil litigation, Criminal, Personal injury (including property damage). Office: Greenspan & Greenspan 150 Grand St White Plains NY 10601-4821 E-mail: GandGEsqs@aol.com.

GREENSPON, ROBERT ALAN, lawyer; b. Hartford, Conn., Apr. 17, 1947; s. George Arthur and Shirley Jean (Shelton) G.; m. Claire Alice Stone, Aug. 21, 1971; children: Colin Haynes, Alison Shelton. AB, Franklin and Marshall, 1969; JD, Columbia U., 1972. Bar: Conn. 1973, N.Y. 1998, U.S. Dist. Conn. 1973, U.S. Ct. Appeals (2d cir.) 1983. Assoc. Robinson & Cole, Hartford, Conn., 1972-78, ptnr., 1978-81, Stamford, Conn., 1981-86; sr. v.p., gen. counsel Guinness Peat Aviation Corp., Stamford, N.Y.C., N.Y.C., Shannon, Ireland, 1985-92; ptnr. Latham & Watkins, N.Y.C., 1992—. Contbr. articles to profl. jours. Mem. ABA (comml. fin. services, aircraft fin.), Conn. Bar Assn., N.Y. State Bar Assn., Internat. Bar Assn., Southwestern Legal Found. (bd. advisors internat. and comparative law ctr.). Federal civil litigation, Commercial, contracts (including sales of goods; commercial financing), Private international. Home: 49 Old Farm Rd Darien CT 06820-6119 Office: Latham & Watkins 885 3rd Ave Fl 10 New York NY 10022-4834

GREENSTEIN, RICHARD HENRY, lawyer; b. Newark, June 29, 1946; s. Jacob Harold and Florence G.; m. Irene Beth Polishuk, July 4, 1973; children: Suzanne Beth, Jonathan Henry. AB, Rutgers Coll., 1968; JD, Boston U., 1971. Bar: N.J. 1971, U.S. Dist. Ct. N.J. 1971, U.S. Supreme Ct. 1985. Law clk. Superior Ct. N.J., Elizabeth, 1971-72; asst. county prosecutor Union County Prosecutor, Elizabeth, 1972-74; assoc. atty. Mandel, Wysoker, Sherman, et al, Perth Amboy, N.J., 1974-77, Fox and Fox, Newark, 1977-83; ptnr. Kein, Pollatschek & Greenstein, Union, N.J., 1983—. Atty. Young Astronauts N.J. Inc., 1989—; mem. ethics com. Supreme Ct. Dist. N.J., 1991-95. Lighting dir. Wash. Sch. PTA Show, Westfield, N.J., 1985-94. Mem. Exchange Club Union (pres.-elect, dir. 1983—). Jewish. Avocations: skiing, hiking, reading. Banking, Corporate, general, Land use and zoning (including planning). Home: 743 Saint Marks Ave Westfield NJ 07090-2035 Office: Kein Pollatschek & Greenstein 2042 Morris Ave Union NJ 07083-6028

GREENWALD, ANDREW ERIC, lawyer; b. N.Y.C., May 31, 1942; s. Harold and Lillian G.; m. Paula S., Aug. 20, 1967; children: Brooke Ellen, Karen Michelle. BS, U. Wis., 1964; JD, Georgetown U., 1967. Bar: D.C. 1968, Md. 1969, U.S. Ct. Appeals Md. 1969. Lawyer Nat. Labor Rels. Bd., Washington, 1967-68; asst. corp. counsel D.C. Govt., 1968-69; shareholder Joseph, Greenwald & Laake PA, Greenbelt, Md., 1969—. Past mem. dept. family and cmty. devel. U. Md. Contbr. articles to profl. jours. Active adv. com. Georgetown U. Continuing Legal Edn., 1991, Georgetown U. Law Ctr. Alumni Bd., 1995. Mem. ATLA (chmn. tort sect. 1985), ABA, Nat. Inst. Trial Advocacy, Am. Bd. Profl. Liability Attys., Am. Bd. Trial Advocates, William B. Bryant Inn, Am. Inns of Ct. General civil litigation, Personal injury (including property damage), Product liability. Office: Joseph Greenwald & Laake PA 6404 Ivy Ln Ste 400 Greenbelt MD 20770-1407

GREENWALD, THOMAS ALBERT, lawyer; b. Brookfield, Wis., Aug. 12, 1962; s. Albert Donald and Sharon Lee Greenwald; m. Deborah Lynn Hannon, June 25, 1963; children: Thomas Albert, Asher Hill. BBA in Fin., U. of Wis., Milw., 1987; JD, Tex. Tech Sch. of Law, Lubbock, Texas, 1989—92. Bar: Tex. 1992, cert.: Tex. Bd. of Legal Specialization (family law) 1997, bar: US. Dist. Ct. (no. dist.) Tex. 2000. Ptnr. McKnight, McKnight & Greenwald, L.L.P., Dallas, 1992—94, Goranson, Bain & Larsen, L.C., Dallas, 1994—. Mem. ct. rules com. State Bar Tex., Austin, 2001—. Contbr. Bd. of edn. Calvary Sch., Dallas. Recipient Named as a Best Lawyer in Dallas Under 40, D Mag. Fellow: Am. Acad. Matrimonial Lawyers, Collin County Bench Bar Found. (life; bd. dirs. family law sect.), Dallas Bar Found. (life; bd. dirs. family law sect., officer family law sect.); mem.: Collin County Bar Assn., Dallas Bar Assn. Family and matrimonial. Office: Goranson Bain & Larsen LC 8150 North Central Expy Ste 1850 Dallas TX 75206 Office Fax: 214-373-9959. E-mail: tgreenwald@gbl-law.com.

GREENWOOD, DANN E. lawyer; b. Dickinson, N.D., Sept. 21, 1952; s. Lawrence E. and Joyce E. (Henley) G.; m. Debra K. Ableidinger, June 15, 1975; children: Jay, Lindsey, Paige. BSBA magna cum laude, U. N.D., 1974, JD, 1977. Bar: N.D. 1977, U.S. Dist. Ct. N.D. 1980. Ptnr. Greenwood, Greenwood & Greenwood and predecessor firms, Dickinson, 1977-98, Greenwood & Ramsey PLLP, 1998—. Mem. N.D. Supreme Ct. Disciplinary Bd., 1983-89, Northern Lights Boy Scouts Council, Dickinson, 1985—; bd. dirs. Legal Assistance N.D., Bismarck, 1980-86. Mem. N.D. Bar Assn. (pres. 1998-99), Stark-Dunn County Bar Assn., N.D. Trial Lawyers Assn. (sec. 1983-84, treas. 1984-85, v.p. 1985-86, pres. 1987-88), Kiwanis, Masons, Shriners, Elks. Lutheran. General civil litigation, Family and matrimonial, Personal injury (including property damage). Home: PO Box 688 Dickinson ND 58602-0688 E-mail: shadyln@ndsupernet.com., grlawdg@ndsupernet.com.

GREER, ALAN GRAHAM, lawyer; b. El Dorado, Ark., May 31, 1939; s. Arthur W. and Marie (Ross) G.; m. Patricia A. Seitz, Aug. 14, 1981. BS, U.S. Naval Acad., 1961; JD, U. Fla., 1969. Ptnr. Richman, Greer Weil Brumbaugh, Miami, Fla., 1969—. Chmn. emeritus WLRN Pub. Radio and TV Sta.; bd. dirs. Camillus Ho. Past chmn. Dade County Coun. Arts and

Scis.; past mem. Fla. State Task Force on Water Issues, Gov.'s Bus. Adv. Coun. on Edn.; co-chmn. site selection com. Dem. Nat. Com., 1992, also trustee. With USN, 1961-67. Fellow Internat. Soc. Barristers, Am. Coll. Trial Lawyers; mem. ABA (standing com. on professionalism), Fla. Bar Assn. (cert., past chmn. internat. law com.). Federal civil litigation, State civil litigation, Professional liability. Home: 224 Ridgewood Rd Miami FL 33133-6614 Office: Richman Greer Weil Brumbaugh Miami Ctr 10th Fl 201 S Biscayne Blvd Miami FL 33131-4332 E-mail: agreen@richmangreer.com.

GREER, ALLEN CURTIS, II, lawyer, investment management executive; b. New Rochelle, N.Y., Dec. 6, 1951; s. Allen Wilkinson and Nancy (Carroll) G.; children: Katharine Burrage, Constance Carroll, Genevieve Forbes. AB, Harvard U., 1972, JD, 1975. Assoc. Cadwalader, Wickersham & Taft, N.Y.C., 1975-79, Palmer & Dodge, Boston, 1979-82; ptnr. Gaston & Snow, Boston and N.Y.C., 1982-91, Rogers & Wells, 1991-97, Cadwalader, Wickersham & Taft, N.Y.C., 1997-99, of counsel, 1999—; with Westbrook Real Estate Counsel, 1999—. Bd. dirs. various pvt. cos. Mem.: Urban Land Inst., Nat. Assn. Real Estate Investment Trusts. Mergers and acquisitions, Property, real (including real estate development, water), Securities. Office: Westbrook Ptnrs One Beacon St Ste 3400 Boston MA 02108 E-mail: cgreer@westbrookpartners.com.

GREER, BERNARD LEWIS, JR., lawyer; b. Knoxville, Tenn., Sept. 11, 1940; s. Bernard Lewis and Margaret Strickland (Vinsinger) G.; m. Lynda Lea Kidd, June 11, 1966; children: Andrew Scott, William Vinsinger. BA magna cum laude, U. Tenn., 1962, postgrad., 1964-65; JD, Emory U., 1968. Bar: N.Y. 1969, Ga. 1975; conseil juridique France, 1971. Assoc. Willkie Farr & Gallagher, N.Y.C., 1968-71, 73-74, Willke, Farr & Gallagher, Paris, 1971-73, Shoob, McLain, Merritt & Lyle, Atlanta, 1974-77, O'Callaghan, Saunders & Stumm, 1977-85; ptnr. Alston & Bird, Atlanta, 1985—. Mem. adv. bd. Internat. and Comparative Law Ctr., Southwestern Legal Found., 1978—; participant various seminars; lectr. on European bus. instns. and practice Emory U. Law Sch., Atlanta, 1975—, Ga. State U. Law Sch., 1975—. Mem. Emory U. Law Rev., 1967-68; mem. edit. bd. The European Lawyer; contbr. to legal publs. Counsel, trustee, mem. exec. com. Atlanta Bot. Garden, Inc.; mem. exec. com., bd. dirs. Ga. Coun. for Internat. Visitors, 1986-93, pres., 1989-90; bd. visitors U. Tenn. Coll. Liberal Arts, Knoxville, 1988-91. 1st lt. U.S. Army, 1962-64. Internat. bus. fellow S.E. region, 1988. Mem. ABA, Internat. Bar Assn. (coun. bus. law sect. 1990-94, sec. gen. 2000-02, chmn. WTO working group), State Bar Ga. (chmn. internat. law sect. 1982-83, chmn. com. on internationalization of practice of law 1989—), State Bar N.Y., Atlanta Bar Assn., Assn. Bar City N.Y., Soc. Internat. Bus. Fellows, Am. Arbitration Assn. (panel of arbitrators 1987—), Lex Mundi (chair-elect, treas., mem. exec. com.), Scabbard and Blade, Omicron Delta Kappa, Pi Sigma Alpha, Pi Delta Phi, Phi Eta Sigma. Corporate, general, Private international, Securities. Office: Alston & Bird 1 Atlantic Ctr Atlanta GA 30309-3400

GREER, CHARLES EUGENE, company executive, lawyer; b. Columbus, Ohio, Mar. 28, 1945; s. Earl E. Greer and Margaret I. Cavanass; 1 child, Erin Elizabeth. BS, Ind. U., 1972, JD, 1976. Bar: Ind. 1976. Pres. Willoughby Industries, Inc., Indpls., 1976-91, pres., CEO, 1991-93; ptnr. Ice Miller Donadio & Ryan, 1976-91; pres. ECM Corp., Indpls., 1993—, Loggins, Inc., Indpls., 1995—, bus. turnaround specialist, 1995—. Served to sgt. USAF, 1965-68, Vietnam. Mem. Ind. Bar Assn., Order of Coif, Phi Eta Sigma, Beta Gamma Sigma. Office: 5581 Sunset Ln Indianapolis IN 46228-1468

GREER, GORDON BRUCE, retired lawyer, writer; b. Butler, Pa., Feb. 17, 1932; s. Samuel Walker and Winifred (Fletcher) G.; m. Nancy Linda Hannaford, June 14, 1959; children: Gordon Bruce, Alison Clark. BA, Harvard U., 1953, JD cum laude, 1959. Bar: Wis. 1959, Mass. 1961. Assoc. Foley, Sammond & Lardner, Milw., 1959-61; assoc. Bingham Dana LLP, Boston, 1961-67, ptnr., 1967-97, of counsel, 1997—2002; ret., 2002. Lectr. Boston U. Sch. Law, 1998-2002; bd. dirs. Strong Mut. Funds., Menomonee Falls, Wis. Editor Harvard Law Rev. Vos. 71, 72; author: World in Conflict. Maj. USAFR (ret.) Mem. Mass. Bar Assn., Boston Bar Assn., Brae Burn Country Club, Harvard Club (Boston). Republican. Corporate, general, Private international. Home: 45 Fieldmont Rd Belmont MA 02478-2606

GREER, RAYMOND WHITE, lawyer; b. Port Arthur, Tex., July 20, 1954; s. Mervyn Hardy Greer and Eva Nadine (White) Swain; m. Pamela V. Brown; children: Emily Ann, Sarah Kelly, Jonathan Collin. BA magna cum laude, Sam Houston State, 1977; JD, U. Houston, 1981. Assoc. Hoover, Cox & Shearer, Houston, 1980-83, Hinton & Morris, Houston, 1983-85; pvt. practice Houston, 1985-86; prin. Morris & Greer, P.C., Houston, 1986-90, Raymond W. Greer & Assocs., P.C., Houston, 1990-98, Rigg & Greer, Houston, 1998—. Lectr. in field; mem. dist. 4 grievance com. State Bar Tex. Mem. adv. com. Enterprising Girls Scouts Beyond Bars, San Jacinto coun., 1996-98. Recipient Outstanding Alumnus award, Dept. English, Sam Houston U., 1986, Disting. Alumni, Tex. Omicron chpt., Alpha Chi, 1996. Mem.: ABA, Ft. Bend County Bar Assn., Houston Bar Assn., State Bar Tex., Sam Houston State U. Alumni Assn. (2d v.p., chmn. membership com., combined charter and membership com. 1995—96, 1st v.p. 1996—97, pres. 1997—98). Avocations: golf, reading. Federal civil litigation, State civil litigation, Family and matrimonial. Office: Rigg & Greer 13333 Southwest Fwy Ste 100 Sugar Land TX 77478-3545

GREFE, ROLLAND EUGENE, lawyer; b. Ida County, Iowa, June 27, 1920; s. Alfred William and Zoma Corrine (Lasher) G.; m. Mary Arlene Cruikshank, June 12, 1943; 1 son, Roger Frederick. BA, Morningside Coll., 1941; JD, State U. Iowa, 1946. Bar: Iowa 1946. Assoc. Schaetzle, Williams & Stewart, Des Moines, 1946-48, Schaetzle, Swift, Austin & Stewart, Des Moines, 1948-52; ptnr. Schaetzle, Austin & Grefe (and related firms), Des Moines, 1952-60, Austin, Grefe & Sidney, Des Moines, 1960-71; sr. ptnr. Grefe & Sidney, Des Moines, 1971-95; mem. Grefe & Sidney P.L.C., 1995—. Dir. Freeman Decorating Co., 1969— , Cowles Syndicate, Inc., 1982-86; mem. bd. mgrs. Lawyers Com. Network, L.L.C., 1997-2000, chair, 1998-2000. Bd. dirs. Des Moines Area C.C., 1966-76, pres., 1967-76; bd. dirs. Westminster Presbyn. Ch. Found., 1975-89, Iowa State Bar Found., 1979-91; trustee Des Moines Water Works, 1984-99, pres., 1987, 91, 96. Lt. USNR, 1942-45. Fellow Am. Bar Found., Am. Coll. Trust and Estate Counsel; mem. ABA (ho. of dels. 1982-96, Iowa state del. 1992-93, bd. govs. 1993-96, standing com. on tech. and info. systems 1998-2001, sr. lawyers divsn. chair internet and tech. com. 2000-02), Assn. Endowment Found. Coll. (mem. pension plan adminstrn. com. 1994-2000), Polk County Bar Assn. (pres. 1971-72), Iowa State Bar Assn. (bd. govs. 1972-76, pres. 1978-79, chmn. com. on long-range planning 1979-81, Award of Merit 1982), Des Moines Estate Planners, Lincoln Inne. Clubs: Sertoma (Des Moines), Des Moines Embassy (Des Moines), Wakonda (Des Moines). Republican. Presbyterian. Corporate, general, Probate (including wills, trusts), Taxation, general. Home: 3524 Grand Ave Apt 803 Des Moines IA 50312-4344 Office: PO Box 10434 2222 Grand Ave Des Moines IA 50312-5306 E-mail: Rgrefe@grefesidney.com.

GREGERSON, GARY LEROY, lawyer; b. Indio, Calif., May 26, 1936; s. Worthen Earl and Werdna Dale (Musgrave) G.; m. Sharon P. Porter, Apr. 18, 1955. Bar: Calif. 1972, U.S. Dist. Ct. (ea. dist.) Calif. 1976, Utah 1979, U.S. Dist. Ct. Utah 1979, U.S. Ct. Appeals (10th cir.) 1988. Ptnr. Leonard & Lyde, Oroville, Calif., 1972-78; pvt. practice Provo, Utah, 1979-86; city atty. Provo City Corp., 1986—. Author: Utah Roadside History, 1996. Mem. Utah Mcpl. Attys. (pres. 1992), Internat. Mcpl. Lawyers Assn. (rep. for State of Utah 2003—). Office: Provo City Corp 351 W Center St Provo UT 84601-4338

GREGG, JOHN PENNYPACKER, lawyer; b. Phila., May 25, 1947; s. William Pemberton and Sarah E. (High) G. AB, Trinity Coll., 1969; JD, Villanova U., 1974. Bar: Pa. 1974, U.S. Dist. Ct. (ea. dist.) Pa. 1974. Tchr., dir. student activities The Pennington (N.J.) Sch., 1969-71; atty. Pub. Defenders Office, Norristown, Pa., 1974—, High, Swartz, Roberts & Seidel, Norristown, 1975—. Bd. dirs. Rittenhouse Book Distbr. Inc., King of Prussia, Pa. Bd. dirs. Phila. Toboggan Co., Lansdale, 1987-91, Lower Merion Shared Housing Corp., Ardmore, Pa., 1991-95, Lower Merion Affordable Housing, Narberth, Pa., 1995—, The Episcopal Acad., Merion, Pa., 1986-89; ann. giving com. Inglis House, Phila., 1991-92. Recipient Legion of Honor Chapel of the Four Chaplains, Phila., 1980, Harry L. Green Svc. award, 1990, Disting. Svc. award Episcopal Acad., 1990. Mem. Pa. Bar Assn., Montgomery Bar Assn. (com. chmn. 1991-94). Criminal, Family and matrimonial. Home: 635 Walnut Ln Haverford PA 19041-1225 Office: High Swartz Roberts & Seidel 40 E Airy St Norristown PA 19401-4803

GREGG, JON MANN, lawyer; b. Louisville, Oct. 22, 1943; s. James Willard and Margaret Josephine (Mann) G.; m. Jeanette Ruth Brandner, June 18, 1966 (div. Oct. 1980); children: Heather Suzanne, Douglas Robert; m. Carol Ruth Slonneger, July 9, 1983; children: Catherine Marie, Emma Celeste. BS in Acctg., U. Ill., 1965; LLB, Harvard U., 1968. Bar: Ill. 1968. Assoc. Sidley & Austin, Chgo., 1968-74, ptnr., 1974—. Mem. ABA, Chgo. Bar Assn. Avocations: flying, aerobatics, tennis, sailing. Mergers and acquisitions, Corporate, general, Securities. Home: 344 W Wisconsin St Unit D Chicago IL 60614-5452 Office: Sidley Austin Brown & Wood 10 S Dearborn Bank One Plz Chicago IL 60603-2000 Business E-Mail: jgregg@sidley.com.

GREGOIRE, CHRISTINE O. state attorney general; b. Auburn, Wash. m. Michael Gregoire; 2 children. BA, U. Wash.; JD cum laude, Gonzaga U., 1977. Clerk, typist Wash. State Adult Probation/ Parole Office, Seattle, 1969; caseworker Wash. Dept. Social and Health Scis., Everett, 1974; asst. atty. gen. State of Wash., Spokane, 1977—81, sr. asst. atty. gen., 1981—82, dep. atty. gen. Olympia, 1982—88; dir. Wash. State Dept. Ecology, 1988—92; atty. gen. State of Wash., 1992—. Chair States/B.C. Oil Spill Task Force, 1989—92, Puget Sound Water Quality Authority, 1990—92, Nat. Com. State Environ. Dirs., 1991—92. Bd. dirs. Wash. State Dept. Ecology, 1988—92. Named Woman of Yr., Am. Legion Aux., 1999; named one of 25 Most Influential Working Mothers, Working Mother mag., 2000; recipient Conservationist of Yr. award, Trout Unlimited/N.W. Steelhead & Salmon Coun., 1994, Gov.'s Child Abuse Prevention award, 1996, Myra Bradwell award, 1997, Wyman award, 1997—98, Bd. of Gov.'s award for professionalism, WSBA, 1997, Kick Butt award, The Tobacco Free Coalition of Pierce County, 1997, Wash. State Hosp. Assn. award, 1997, Citizen Activist award, Gleitsman Found., 1998, Woman of Achievement award, Assn. for Women in Comm. Matrix Table, 1999, Pub. Justice award, WSTLA, 1999, Excellence in Pub. Health award, Wash. State Assn. Local Pub. Health Ofcls., 1999, Women in Govt. award, Good Housekeeping, 1999, Spl. Recognition award, Wash. State Nurses Assn., 2000. Mem.: Nat. Assn. Attys. Gen. (consumer protection and environment com., energy com., children and the law subcom.). Democrat. Office: Attorney Generals Office 1125 Washington St SE PO Box 40100 Olympia WA 98504-6200*

GREGORY, GEORGE G. retired lawyer; b. Whittier, Calif., Dec. 21, 1932; BA, Harvard U., 1954, LLB, 1957. Bar: Calif. 1957, U.S. Supreme Ct. 1962. Assoc. Gibson, Dunn & Crutcher, L.A., 1957-65, ptnr., 1966-69; v.p., sec. Cordura Corp. (formerly Computing & Software), L.A., 1969-74; ptnr. Collins, Gregory & Rutter, L.A., 1974-77, Hughes, Hubbard & Reed, L.A., 1977-83; exec. v.p. H.F. Ahmanson & Co., L.A., 1983-97; ret., 1997. Mem. State Bar Calif., Phi Beta Kappa. Banking, Corporate, general, Property, real (including real estate development, water).

GREGORY, GEORGE WILLIAM, lawyer; b. Midland, Mich., Sept. 15, 1948; s. Frederick W. Gregory and Tula (Bitzer) Seidenstucker; m. Lorraine F. New, Aug. 10, 1973; 1 child, Frederick W. II. BA, Mich. State U., 1972; MBA, Wayne State U., 1976, JD, 1980. Bar: Mich. 1980, U.S. Dist. Ct. (ea. dist.) Mich. 1980, U.S. Tax Ct. 1980. Claims examiner VA, Detroit, 1972-73; revenue agt. IRS, Detroit, 1973-80; assoc. Raymond, Rupp & Weinberg, Troy, Mich., 1980-82, Lee, Gregory, Sternberg, P.C., Birmingham, Mich., 1986-89, shareholder, 1989—; assoc. George W. Gregory PLLC, Birmingham, Mich., 2000—. Asst. prof. Wayne State U., Detroit, 1981-87. Contbr. articles to profl. publs. Reporter Mich. Estate Tax Act, 1993; bd. dirs. Common Ground, Royal Oak, Mich., 1985-90. With U.S. Army, 1969-70, Vietnam. Mem. ABA, AICPA (tax sect.), State Bar Mich. (mem. coun. tax sect. 1992—, vice chmn. 1996-97, chmn. 1997-98, sec.-treas. 1995-96, chmn. estates and trust com. 1991-92), Oakland County Bar Assn., Mich. Assn. CPAs. Estate planning, Estate taxation, Taxation, general. Office: George W Gregory 2476 Kingston Rd Troy MI 48084-2707

GREGORY, LEWIS DEAN, trust company executive; b. Wichita, Kans., May 13, 1953; s. Harry Samuel III and Virginia Dorothy (Womer) G.; m. Laura Lorraine Davis, March 4, 1978; children: Paul Lewis, Erin Elizabeth. BA in Communications, U. Kans., Lawrence, 1975; MS in Journalism, U. Kans., 1976; JD, Washburn U., 1983. Bar: Kans. 1984, U.S. Dist. Ct. Kans. 1984. Cons. Delta Upsilon Frat., Inc., Indpls., 1975-76; mktg. rep. IBM, Kansas City, Mo., 1976-80; assoc. Frazey, Wix & Vetter, Wichita, 1983-84; trust mktg. mgr. Bank IV Wichita, 1984-86; v.p., trust officer, sales mgr. BancOklahoma Trust Co., Tulsa, 1986-88, Boatmen's Trust Co., Kansas City, 1988-97; sr. v.p., dist. trust mgr. Merrill Lynch Trust Co., 1997—. Dir. Am. Heart Assn., Wichita, Kans., 1985-86; pres. YMCA Men's Club, Tulsa, 1987-88; del. Rep. Party, Tulsa, 1988; trustee Leukemia Soc., 1992-96. Mem. ABA, Kans. Bar Assn., Johnson County Bar Assn., Kansas City Met. Bar Assn., Estate Planning Soc. (bd. dirs. 1996-98), Kiwanis, Kans. Univ. Alumni Assn. (pres. Greater Kansas City chpt. 1994-96, nat. bd. dirs. 1997-2002), Delta Upsilon (Indpls. dir. 1987-90, dir. Kans. chpt. 1977-90). Republican. Methodist. Avocation: running. Home: 12205 Aberdeen Rd Leawood KS 66209-1208 E-mail: lewis_gregory@ml.com.

GREGORY, LEWIS J. judge, lawyer; b. Muncie, Ind., May 27, 1952; m. Katherine Gerber, Dec. 17, 1988; children: Adam, Alexander, Anne. BS, Ball State U., 1974; JD, Ind. U., 1988. Bar: Ind. 1988, U.S. Dist. Ct. (no. and so. dists.) Ind. 1988. Exec. asst. to gov. State of Ind., Indpls., 1981—85, chmn. Ind. Parole Bd., 1985—89; dep. prosecutor Marion County, Johnson County, Indpls., Franklin, Ind., 1989—94; pvt. practice Greenwood, Ind., 1994—; judge Greenwood City Ct., 1996—. Office: Greenwood City Ct 186 Surina Sq Greenwood IN 46143

GREGORY, WILLIAM STANLEY, lawyer; b. Greenwood, Miss., Mar. 12, 1949; s. Carlyle and Charlotte Ruby (Richardson) G.; m. Vicki Sue Lovelady, Aug. 15, 1970. BS in Commerce and Bus. Adminstrn., U. Ala., 1971, MBA, 1973, JD, 1974. Bar: Ala. 1974, U.S. Dist. Ct. (mid. dist.) Ala. 1979, U.S. Ct. Appeals (5th cir.) 1979, U.S. Ct. Appeals (11th cir.) 1980, U.S. Tax Ct. 1979, U.S. Dist. Ct. (no. dist.) Ala. 1991. Assoc. Johnson, Thorington, North, Haskell & Slaughter, Montgomery, Ala., 1974-78; jr. ptnr. Johnson & Thorington, Montgomery, Ala., 1979-90; sr. ptnr. Thorington & Gregory, Montgomery, Ala., 1990-2000; ptnr. Bradley, Arant, Rose & White LLP, Montgomery, Ala., 2000—. Spl. asst. atty. gen. State of Ala., Montgomery, 1978-82; mem. taxpayer bill of rights drafting com. tax sect. Ala. State Bar, Montgomery, 1990-91. Pres. Montgomery Symphony Assn., 1980, 92, Highland Ave. Adult & Sr. Citizens Ctr., Montgomery, 1986-99; mem. Montgomery Estate Planning Coun. Capt. USAR, 1971-75. Mem. SAR, Kiwanis (v.p. 1989-90). Presbyterian. Avocation: music. Corporate, general, Municipal (including bonds), State and local taxation. Home: 8218 Wynlakes Blvd Montgomery AL 36117-5101 Office: 401 Adams Ave Ste 780 Montgomery AL 36104 E-mail: sgregory@barw.com.

GREIF, JOSEPH, lawyer; b. N.Y.C., June 25, 1943; s. Jacob J. and Dorothy (Harrison) G.; m. Aline Bohm, Jan. 1, 1966; children: Jeffrey, Julie. BBA, U. Pitts., 1964; JD, NYU, 1967. Bar: N.Y. 1967, D.C. 1968, U.S. Tax Ct. 1986; CPA, Md., D.C. Instr. No. Va. C.C., Annandale, 1967-68; mgmt. cons. Computer Sci. Corp., Silver Spring, Md., 1967-70; tax mgr. Arthur Andersen & Co., Washington, 1970-75; sr. assoc. Ginsberg, Feldman & Bress, Washington, 1975-77; ptnr. Touche Ross & Co., Washington, 1977-84, McGuffie, Greif, Whitney & Handal, Washington, 1984-90; of counsel McNeily, Rosenfeld & Rubenstein, Washington, 1991-98, Neimark & Nadel, Ft. Lauderdale, Fla., 1998—, Washington, 1998—. Lectr. George Washington U. Grad. Sch. Bus., Washington, 1993-95. Co-author, editor: Managing Membership Societies, 1979; contbr. articles on taxation, comml. leasing, computer systems contracting, exec. compensation, exec. contracts to profl. jours. Bd. dirs. Nat. Assn. for Mental Health, Washington, 1973-75, Combined Health Appeal, Washington, 1980-81, Assn. Devel. Coun., Washington, 1987-89; task force mem. White House Task Force on Charitable Giving, Washington, 1979-80. Mem. AICPA (chmn. fed. tax divsn. task force on exempt orgns. 1983-86), ABA, D.C. Bar Assn., Am. Soc. Assn. Execs. (mem. govt. affairs and long range planning coms., Outstanding Svc. award, tech. sect. coun. 1996—), D.C. Inst. CPAs, Greater Washington Soc. Assn. Execs. (tech. task force 1994—), Computer Law Assn. Avocations: boating, squash. Office: Greif Legal Econs Svcs 1717 K St NW Ste 600 Washington DC 20036 Fax: 202-204-2235.

GREIG, BRIAN STROTHER, lawyer; b. Austin, Tex., Apr. 10, 1950; s. Ben Wayne Greig and Virginia Ann (Strother) Higgins; m. Jane Ann Sentilles, June 17, 1972; children: Travis Darden, Grace Hanna. BA, Washington and Lee U., 1972; JD, U. Tex., 1975. Bar: Tex. 1975, U.S. Dist. Ct. (ea. dist.) Tex. 1976, U.S. Ct. Appeals (5th cir.) 1976, U.S. Dist. Ct. (so. dist.) Tex. 1977, U.S. Dist. Ct. (we. dist.) Tex. 1980, U.S. Supreme Ct. 1980, U.S. DIst. Ct. (no. dist.) Tex. 1984, U.S. Ct. Appeals (11th cir.) 1984. Law clk. to chief judge U.S. Dist. Ct., Beaumont, Tex., 1975-76; sr. ptnr. Fulbright & Jaworski L.L.P., Austin, 1976—. Mem. Austin Tomorrow On-Going Goals Assembly Com., 1981; pres. Austin Mgmt. Lawyers Forum, 1987, 93. Editor-in-chief Tex. Assn. Bus. Employment Law Handbook; mem. editl. bd. Tex. Labor Letter, 1994-2001. Pres. Austin Lawyers and Accts. for Arts, 1981; trustee Laguna Gloria Art Mus., Austin, 1983-91, pres., 1989-90, chmn., 1990-91; bd. dirs. Zachary Scott Theater Ctr., Austin, 1981; mem. devel. bd. Inst. Texan Cultures, 1991-98; trustee Westminster Manor Health Facilities Corp. of Travis County, Tex., 1991-96, sec., 1995-96; trustee St. Stephen's Episcopal Sch., 1995-2001; pres. Austin Mus. Art, 1991-92, trustee, 1991-93; bd. dirs. The Capital of Tex. Pub. Telecomms. Coun., Inc. (KLRU-TV), 2001—. Fellow Tex. Bar Found. (life), Am. Coll. Labor and Employment Lawyers; mem. ABA, FBA, Am. Arbitration Assn. (employment adv. coun. 1995—), Tex. Bar Assn., Travis County Bar Assn., Tex. Commn. on Human Rights (chmn.'s task force), Tex. Assn. Bus. (bd. dirs. 2000—), Tarry House Club, Headliners Club (trustee 1998—), Austin Assembly. Methodist. Avocations: hunting, fishing. General civil litigation, Construction, Labor (including EEOC, Fair Labor Standards Act, labor-management relations, NLRB, OSHA). Office: Fulbright & Jaworski LLP 600 Congress Ave Ste 2400 Austin TX 78701-3271 E-mail: bgreig@fulbright.com.

GREIGG, RONALD EDWIN, lawyer; b. Washington, June 29, 1946; s. Edwin E. and Helen Marie (Marcy) G.; m. Patricia Anne Crowe, June 5, 1968; children: Elizabeth, Rebecca. BBA, Am. U., 1969, MBA in Fin., 1971; JD, Stetson U., 1976. Registered patent atty.; bar: Fla. 1976, D.C. 1978, Va. 1985, U.S. Dist. Ct. (mid. dist.) Fla. 1976, U.S. Dist. Ct. (ea. dist.) Va. 1988, U.S. Ct. Appeals (D.C. cir.) 1979, U.S. Ct. Appeals (fed. cir.) 1982, U.S. Supreme Ct. 1980. Assoc. David E. De Serio, St. Petersburg, Fla., 1977-78, Edwin E. Greigg, Washington, 1979-82, Harris, Barrett & Dew, St. Petersburg, Fla., 1982-84; ptnr. Greigg & Greigg, Arlington, Va., 1984-99; mng. dir. Greigg & Greigg PLLC, Alexandria, 1999—. Author: A Guide to the FTC Franchise Disclosure Rule, 1979, Patent Infringement Damages, 1988. Mem. D.C. Bar Assn., Fla. Bar Assn., Va. Bar Assn., Inst. of Trademark Attys. (London), Internat. Trademark Assn., Phi Alpha Delta. Republican. Episcopalian. Avocations: sailing, classic cars. Computer, Patent, Trademark and copyright. Office: Greigg & Greigg PLLC #1 1423 Powhatan St Ste 1 Alexandria VA 22314-1389 Fax: 703-838-5554. E-mail: rgreigg@greigg.com.

GREILSHEIMER, JAMES GANS, lawyer; b. N.Y.C., Oct. 14, 1937; s. Jerome J. and Lillian (Gans) G.; m. Louise B. Steiner, Aug. 11, 1974; children: Lauren, Julie, Michael, Jeremy. AB cum laude, Princeton U., 1959; LLB, Harvard U., 1962. Bar: N.Y. 1963, D.C. 1969. Asst. U.S. atty. So. Dist. N.Y., 1963-68; litigating asst. corp. counsel City of N.Y., 1974-77, 1st asst. corp. counsel, 1978-80; ptnr. Blank Rome LLP and predecessor firms, N.Y.C., 1993—. Mediator mediation program U.S. Dist. Ct. (so. dist.) N.Y., 1993—. Mem., sec. N.Y.C. Charter Rev. Commn., 1982-83; pres. N.Y. chpt. Am. Jewish Com., 1981-84; v.p. Jewish Cmty. Rels. Coun. N.Y., 1981-85, bd. dirs., 1995-2001; bd. dirs. Com. on Decent Unbiased Campaign Tactics, 1983-93, Non-profit Coordinating Com., N.Y., 1985—, Vol. Cons. Group, Inc., 1986—; v.p., bd. dirs. Fund for Pub. Schs., Inc., 1986-91, pres., 1992-2002; mem. Citizens Budget Commn., Inc., 1991-93. Mem.: Assn. Bar of City of N.Y. (mcpl. affairs com. 1979—81, govt. ethics com. 1990—98, com. on condemnation and tax certiorari 1993—95, 2001—), N.Y. County Lawyers Assn. (bd. dirs. 1981—87, chmn. fed. cts. com. 1977—80, spl. com. on condemnation 1990—), N.Y. State Bar Assn. (spl. com. on cts. and cmty. 1975—81). Administrative and regulatory, General civil litigation, Constitutional. Office: Blank Rome LLP 405 Lexington Ave New York NY 10174-0002 E-mail: jgreilsheimer@blankrome.com.

GREILSHEIMER, WILLIAM HENRY, lawyer; b. N.Y.C., Sept. 28, 1941; s. Jerome Jacob and Lillian (Gans) G.; m. Carol Leslie Horwitz, Sept. 6, 1970; children: Jeffrey Mark, Deborah Lynn. AB, Dartmouth Coll., 1963; JD, Yale U., 1966. Bar: N.Y. 1967, U.S. Ct. Appeals (2d cir.) 1968, U.S. Dist. Ct. (so. and ea. dists.) N.Y. 1968, U.S. Dist. Ct. Conn. 1997, U.S. Supreme Ct. 1970. Ptnr. Delson & Gordon, N.Y.C., 1967-73, Burns, Summit, Rovins & Feldeslman, N.Y.C., 1973-81, Ferber, Greilsheimer, Chan & Essner, N.Y.C., 1981-96, counsel, 1997-98. Lectr., co-author continuing legal edn. program, 1987. Trustee Stephen Wise Free Synagogue, N.Y.C., 1987-90. Mem. ABA, Assn. of Bar of City of N.Y. (com. on lectures and continuing edn. 1991-93, com. on corp. law 1993-95), N.Y. County Lawyers Assn. (corp. law com., securities and exchanges com.). Democrat. Jewish. Avocations: jogging, tennis, cross-country skiing. Corporate, general, Private international, Securities. Home: 91 Central Park W New York NY 10023-4600 Office: 420 Lexington Ave New York NY 10170-0002 E-mail: whg@greils.com.

GREINER, MARY LOUISE, lawyer, psychotherapist; b. St. Louis, Aug. 18, 1949; d. Theodore H. and Dorothy E. (Walters) G.; m. S. Charles Baber. BA, Hamline U., 1971; JD, U. Minn., 1974; MSSW, U. Tex., 1994. Bar: Minn. 1974, U.S. Dist. Ct. Minn. 1974, Hawaii 1976, U.S. Dist. Ct. Hawaii 1976, Tex. 1989. Staff atty. Fed. Res. Bank, Mpls., 1974-75; instr. L.A. Community Coll. Extension, Okinawa, Japan, 1975-76; assoc. Stubenberg Law Firm, Honolulu, 1976-77; spl. counsel State of Hawaii, Honolulu, 1977; counsel Control Data Corp., Mpls., 1978-87; pres. Greiner & Assoc., Bloomington, Minn., 1987-88; assoc. gen. counsel Electronic Data Systems Corp., Plano, Tex., 1989-92; clin. social worker, mediator Pastoral Counseling & Edn. Ctr., Dallas, 1994—. Mem. Internat. Inst. Bioenergetic Analysis, State Bar Tex., Tex. Lawyers Concerned for Lawyers (bd. dirs.). Unitarian Universalist. Avocations: travel, reading, needlepoint. Alternative dispute resolution, Health. Office: Pastoral Counseling and Edn Ctr 4525 Lemmon Ave Ste 200 Dallas TX 75219-2100 E-mail: mgreiner@flash.net.

GREINER, ROBERT PHILIP, lawyer, real estate broker; b. Herkimer, N.Y., July 3, 1930; s. Max Henry and Margaret Mary (O'Hara) G. BA, U. Rochester, 1951; MBA, Syracuse U., 1957; LLB, UCLA, 1964. Bar: Calif. 1965; CPA, Calif.; lic. real estate broker, Calif. Pvt. practice acct., CPA, 1962-64; lawyer L.A. Pub. Defenders Office, 1965-87; pvt. practice lawyer and real estate broker Calif., 1987—. Pres. Guide Dog Boosters, Los Alamitos, Calif., 1984. Staff sgt. USAF, 1951-55. Mem.: World Affairs Coun. Sonoma County. Property, real (including real estate development, water), Criminal. Home and Office: 730 Natalie Dr Windsor CA 95492-8870

GREINER, STEPHEN W. lawyer; b. N.Y.C., Dec. 14, 1944; BA, Syracuse U., 1965; JD, NYU, 1968. Bar: N.Y. 1969. Mem. Willkie Farr & Gallagher, N.Y.C. Mem. Assn. Bar City N.Y., Order of Coif. Office: Willkie Farr & Gallagher 787 7th Ave New York NY 10019-6018 E-mail: sgreiner@willkie.com.

GRENIER, EDWARD JOSEPH, JR., lawyer; b. N.Y.C., Nov. 26, 1933; s. Edward Joseph and Jane Veronica (Farrell) G.; m. Patricia J. Cederle, June 22, 1957; children: Victoria-Anne, Edward Joseph III, Peter C. BA summa cum laude, Manhattan Coll., N.Y.C., 1954; LLB magna cum laude, Harvard U., 1959. Bar: D.C. 1959, N.Y. 1983, U.S. Ct. Appeals (D.C. cir.) 1959, U.S. Ct. Mil. Appeals 1960, U.S. Ct. Appeals (3d cir.) 1966, U.S. Supreme Ct. 1966, U.S. Ct. Appeals (9th cir.) 1973, U.S. Ct. Appeals (10th cir.) 1977, U.S. Ct. Appeals (5th cir., 11th cir.) 1982. Law clk. U.S. Ct. Appeals (D.C. cir.), 1959-60; assoc. Covington & Burling, Wahsington, 1960-68; ptnr. Sutherland, Asbill & Brennan, Wahsington, 1968—. Speaker in field of energy related issues to profl. orgns. Contbr. articles in field to legal jours. Chmn. bd. trustees, mem. exec. com. Connelly Sch. Holy Child, Potomac, Md., 1976-85, trustee, 1976-88; bd. dirs. D.C. Recording for the Blind, Washington, 1977-89. 1st lt. USAF, 1954-56. Fellow: Am. Bar Found.; mem.: ABA (chmn. sec. adminstrv. law 1986—87, sec., del. Ho. of Dels. 1991—97), Am. Inns of Ct. (master of bench Prettyman-Leventhal Inn of Ct. 1988—2000, pres. 1991—92, counselor 1997—98), Energy Bar Assn. (bd. dirs. 1986—89, 1995—2001, v.p. 1995—96, pres.-elect 1996—97, pres. 1997—98, del. Ho. of Dels. 1999—2001), D.C. Bar Assn., Fed. Bar Assn., Congl. Country Club, Met. Club. FERC practice, Administrative and regulatory. Office: Sutherland Asbill & Brennan LLP 1275 Pennsylvania Ave NW Washington DC 20004-2415 E-mail: egrenier@sablaw.com.

GRENIG, JAY EDWARD, law educator; b. Salt Lake City, Apr. 18, 1943; s. Robert Edward and Betty (Gifford) G.; m. Sharon Flanigan, Dec. 22, 1967; children: Robert Jay, Alejandro Edward, Christian Michael. Student, U. Ariz., 1961-63; BA, Willamette U., Salem, Oreg., 1966; postgrad., Ariz. State U., 1968-69; JD, U. Calif.-Hastings Coll. Law, 1971. Bar: Calif. 1972, U.S. Dist. Ct. (no. dist.) Calif. 1973, U.S. Ct. Appeals (9th cir.) 1974, U.S. Ct. Claims 1974, Wis. 1980. Asst. dean Coll. of Law Willamette U., Salem, 1971-72; assoc. firm Johnson & Stanton, San Francisco, 1972-73; sole practice San Mateo, Calif., 1973-77; assoc. prof., dir. Employment Law Inst., Pepperdine U. Sch. Law, Malibu, Calif., 1977-79; prof. law Marquette U. Sch. Law, Milw., 1980—. Lectr. U. So. Calif. Grad. Sch. Pub. Adminstrn., L.A., 1978; reporter civil justice reform act adv. group U.S. Dist. Ct. (ea. dist.) Wis., 1991-97; pres., bd. dirs. Ctr. Pub. Representation, 1993-97; mem. Wis. Judicial Council, 2002—; reporter U.S. Dist. Ct. (ea. dist) Wis., 1991—. Author: (with others) Private Sector Labor Law, 1980, West's Federal Jury Practice and Instructions, 5th edit., 2001, West's California Education Code Forms, 1992, California Government Codes Forms with Practice Commentaries, 1998, Labor Arbitration Advocacy, 1989, West's Federal Forms, 1992, Wisconsin Civil Procedure, 1994, Wisconsin Civil Discovery, 1996, Alternative Dispute, 1997; editor Calif. Sch. Law Digest, 1973-84, Wisconsin Civil Discovery, 1996, West's Alternative Dispute Resolution, 1997, Illinois Civil Discover, 2000, West's Federal Jury Practice and Instructions (5th edit.), 2000; contbr. articles to legal publs. Bd. trustees Univ. Lake Sch., 1992-95. With U.S. Army, 1966-68. Mem. Am. Law Inst., Am. Arbitration Assn. (regional adv. bd. L.A. 1979), Assn. Am. Law Schs. (chmn. labor and employment law sect. 1991-92), State Bar Assn. Wis., Nat. Acad. Arbitrators (bd. govs.), Order of Coif, Thurston Soc. Home: 122 Birch Rd Delafield WI 53018-1305 Office: Marquette U Law Sch 1103 W Wisconsin Ave Milwaukee WI 53233-2313 E-mail: jgrenig@earthlink.net.

GRESHAM, ZANE OLIVER, lawyer; b. Mobile, Ala., Dec. 16, 1948; S. Charles Brandon and Lillian Ann (Oliver) G.; m. Marian Gan, Mar. 3, 1988. BA cum laude, Johns Hopkins U., 1970; JD magna cum laude, Northwestern U., 1973. Bar: Calif. 1973. Assoc. Morrison & Foerster, San Francisco, 1973-79, ptnr., 1980—, co-chair land use and environ. law group, 1987-97, co-chair airports and aviation law group, 1996—; chair Latin Am. Group, 1998—. Dir., v.p. (Latin Am.) Internat. Private Water Assn., 1999—; dir. Fromm Inst., 2000—. Cons. editor: Environ. Compliance and Litigation Strategy. Pres. San Francisco Forward, 1980-85; bd. dirs. Regional Inst. Bay Area, Richmond, Calif., 1989-95, Regional Parks Found., Oakland, Calif., 1992—, pres., 1995; spl. counsel Grace Cathedral, San Francisco, 1991—; dir., exec. v.p. Pan Am. Soc. Calif., 1995-97, pres. 1998—; vice chmn. Nat. Youth Sci. Found., 1997—. Mem. State Bar Calif., Urban Land Inst., Lambda Alpha. Avocations: opera, sketching. Private international, Land use and zoning (including planning). Office: Morrison & Foerster 425 Market St Ste 3100 San Francisco CA 94105-2482 E-mail: zgresham@mofo.com.

GRESSMAN, EUGENE, lawyer; b. Lansing, Mich., Apr. 18, 1917; s. William Albert and Bess Beulah (Nagle) G.; m. Nan Alice Kirby, Aug. 6, 1944; children: William, Margot and Nancy (twins), Eric. AB, U. Mich., 1938, JD with distinction, 1940; LLD, Seton Hall U., 1994. Bar: Mich. 1940, D.C. 1948, Md. 1959, U.S. Supreme Ct. 1945. Atty. SEC, Washington, 1940-43; law clk. to Justice Frank Murphy, U.S. Supreme Ct., 1943-48; ptnr. firm Van Arkel, Kaiser, Gressman, Rosenberg & Driesen, Washington, 1948-77, of counsel, 1977-81, Bredhoff & Kaiser, Washington, 1981-84, Brand & Frulla, Washington, 1984—. Spl. counsel U.S. Ho. of Reps., 1976-84; William Rand Kenan Jr. prof. law U. N.C., Chapel Hill, 1977-87, prof. emeritus, 1987—; disting. vis. prof. Fordham U. Law Sch., 1982-83, 1987-88; Disting. vis. prof. Seton Hall U. Law Sch., 1987-94; vis. prof. law Ohio State U., 1967, Mich. Law Sch., 1969, George Washington U., 1971-77, Ind. U., 1976, Cath. U. Am., 1977; judge Appeals Tax Ct. Montgomery County, Md., 1959-62; chmn. rules com. U.S. Ct. Appeals for 4th Cir., 1984-89. Author: (with Robert L. Stern and others) Supreme Court Practice, 1950, 8th edit., 2002; (with Charles A. Wright and others) Federal Practice and Procedure: Jurisdiction, vol. 16, 1977; (with David Crump and David Day) Cases and Materials on Constitutional Law, 1989, 4th edit., 2002; contbr. articles to profl. jours. Fellow Am. Acad. Appellate Lawyers (hon.); mem. ABA, Fed. Bar Assn., D.C. Bar, Am. Law Inst., Am. Judicature Soc., Order of the Coif, Order of Barristers, Phi Beta Kappa, Delta Theta Pi (lifetime achievement award). Home: 325 Glendale Dr Chapel Hill NC 27514-5915 Office: U NC Sch Law Chapel Hill NC 27599-3380 E-mail: egressma@email.unc.edu.

GREVE, GUY ROBERT, lawyer; b. Bay City, Mich., Oct. 25, 1947; m. Nancy Lisbeth Mueller, Sept. 21, 1991; 1 child, Tyler James. BA, U. Mich., 1970; postgrad., U. Kent, Canterbury, Eng., 1974; JD, Detroit Coll., 1975. Bar: Mich. 1975, U.S. Dist. Ct. (ea. dist.) Mich. 1975. Ptnr. Patterson & Greve, Bay City, 1975-78; asst. atty. City of Bay City, 1975-76, atty., 1976-78; pvt. practice Bay City, 1978—. One-man shows include; co-chair Day in Life of Bay Country Photo Project, 2000. Bd. dirs. Am. Cancer Soc., 1975—2001, pres., 1982—83, Muse-Hopper Mobile Mus., Mich., 1980—82; co-chair Delta Coll. Scholarship Fundraiser, 2001; mem. steering com. Friends State Theater, 2001—; bd. dirs. Bay Arts Coun., 1999—, Women's Crisis Ctr., Bay City, 1977—79. Named Disting. Alumnus, Handy HS, 1985; recipient Disting. Svc. award, Bay City Jaycees, 1981. Mem.: ATLA, ABA, Mich. Trial Lawyers Assn., Bay County Bar Assn. (Liberty Bell chmn. 1994—98, bd. dirs. 1994—2000, pres. 1998—99), Mich. Bar Assn. (rep. assembly 1999—2001), Bay Area C. of C., Studio 23 (hon.), Elks Club (Lodge #88), Saginaw Bay Yacht Club, U. Mich. Alumni Club (Bay City chpt. pres. 1994—97), Optimists (pres. Bay City 1979—80, lt. gov. Mich. 1985—86, chmn. new club bldg. 1986—87, chmn. club svcs. 1989—90, asst. gov. Mich. 1996—97, internat. conv. com. 1997, founder, chair travel series 1993—). State civil litigation, Family and matrimonial, Personal injury (including property damage). Home: 2300 Nurmi Dr Bay City MI 48708-6872 Office: PO Box 851 919 Washington Ave Bay City MI 48707 E-mail: ggreve@juno.com.

GREW, ROBERT RALPH, lawyer; b. Metamora, Ohio, Mar. 25, 1931; m. Anne Gano Bailey, Aug. 2, 1958. AB in Letters and Law, U. Mich., 1953, JD, 1955. Bar: Mich. 1955, N.Y. 1958. Assoc. Carter, Ledyard & Milburn, N.Y.C., 1957-68, ptnr., 1968-98, of counsel, 1999—. Lectr. legal problems in banking and in venture capital investments Practising Law Inst. Mem. Pilgrims of U.S., English Speaking Union (nat. v.p. 1989-93), Union Club, Lansdowne Club (London). Republican. Banking, Corporate, general, Property, real (including real estate development, water). Office: Carter Ledyard & Milburn 2 Wall St New York NY 10005-2001 also: 1401 Eye I St NW Washington DC 20005 E-mail: grew@clm.com.

GREY, SAMUEL T. lawyer; b. St. Croix, V.I., Aug. 1968; BS, U. V.I., 1991; JD, Creighton U., 1994. Bar: V.I. 1994. Atty. Legal Svcs. V.I., 1994—97; assoc. Nichols Newman Logan & D'Eramo, P.C., Christiansted. Probate (including wills, trusts), Banking. Office: Nichols Newman Logan & D'Eramo 1131 King St Ste 204 Christiansted VI 00820*

GRIBBON, DANIEL MCNAMARA, lawyer; b. Youngstown, Ohio, Jan. 27, 1917; s. James Edward and Loretta (Hogan) G.; m. Jane Retzler, Sept. 13, 1941; children: Diana Jane Gribbon Motz, Deborah Ann Gribbon Alt. AB, Case Western Res. U., 1938; JD, Harvard U., 1941. Bar: N.Y. 1942, D.C. 1946, U.S. Supreme Ct. 1950. Clk. Judge Learned Hand, N.Y.C., 1941-42; assoc. Covington & Burling, Washington, 1946-50, ptnr., 1950—. Chmn. adv. com. on procedures U.S. Ct. Appeals (D.C. cir.), 1983-88 Served with USNR, 1942-46. Fellow Am. Bar Found.; mem. Am. Coll. Trial Lawyers, D.C. Bar Assn. (chmn. bd. profl. responsibility 1976-79). Clubs: Met. (Washington) (pres. 1981-82); Chevy Chase (Md.). Roman Catholic. Antitrust, Federal civil litigation, Corporate, general. Office: Covington & Burling 1201 Pennsylvania Ave NW Washington DC 20004-2401 Fax: 202-778-5310. E-mail: dgribbon@cov.com.

GRIER, PHILLIP MICHAEL, lawyer, former association executive; b. Quitman, Ga., Aug. 31, 1941; s. Phillip Moore and Helen Dale Parrish (Cottingham) Grier. BA, Furman U., 1963; JD, U. S.C., 1969. Bar: S.C. 1969, U.S. Dist. Ct. S.C. 1969, U.S. Ct. Appeals (4th cir.) 1972, U.S. Supreme Ct. 1978, U.S. Ct. Appeals (fed. cir.) 1985. Assoc. Haynsworth, Perry, Bryant, Marion & Johnstone, Greenville, SC, 1969—70; asst. to pres. U. S.C., Columbia, 1969, staff counsel, 1970—74, gen. counsel, 1974—79; exec. dir., CEO Nat. Assn. Coll. and Univ. Attys., Washington, 1979—96; cons. Fulbright & Jaworski, Washington, 1996—2000. Bd. dirs. Am. Coun. Edn., 1992—94; mem. adv. bd. Ctr. for Constl. Studies, U. Notre Dame and Mercer U., 1981—92; mem. secretariat of nat. higher edn. orgns. Nat. Ctr. for Higher Edn., Washington, 1979—96. Author (with Joseph P. O'Neill): Financing in a Period of Retrenchment: A Primer for Small Private Colleges, 1984; editor: The Corporate Counsellors Deskbook (Non-Profit Organizations Supplement), 1983; editor, contbg. author: Legal Deskbook for Administrators of Independent Colleges and Universities, 1982, 1983, 1984; editor: Coll. Law Digest, 1980—96; mem. editl. adv. com.: West Pub. zco., 1980—96, editl. bd.: Jour. Coll. and Univ. Law, 1979—96. With U.S. Army, 1963—66, with USAR, 1966—74. Mem.: Ancient and Honorable Artillery Co., Mil. Order Fgn. Wars, St. Nicholas Soc. of N.Y., Soc. Colonial Wars, Order of St. John, Cosmos Club (legal affairs com. 1986—90, com. reciprocity 1988—90, house com. 1990—95, chmn. 1992—95), City Tavern Club (bd. govs. 1992—2000, sec. 1994, v.p. 1996—99). Administrative and regulatory, Federal civil litigation, Corporate, general.

GRIESA, THOMAS POOLE, federal judge; b. Kansas City, Mo., Oct. 11, 1930; s. Charles Henry and Stella Lusk (Bedell) G.; m. Christine Pollard Meyer, Jan. 5, 1963. AB cum laude, Harvard U., 1952; LL.B., Stanford U., 1958. Bar: Wash. 1958, N.Y. 1961. Atty. Justice Dept., 1958-60; with firm Symmers, Fish & Warner, N.Y.C., 1960-61, Davis Polk & Wardwell, N.Y.C., 1961-72, partner, 1970-72; judge U.S. Dist. Ct. So. Dist. N.Y., 1972—, chief judge, 1993-2000. Mem.: Stanford Law Rev., 1956-58. Bd. visitors Stanford Law Sch., 1982-84; bd. dir. Greater N.Y. Coun. Boy Scouts of Am. Served to lt. (j.g.) USCGR, 1952-54. Mem. Bar Assn. City N.Y., Union Club N.Y.C. Christian Scientist. Office: US Dist Ct US Courthouse 500 Pearl St New York NY 10007-1316

GRIFF, HARRY, lawyer; b. Worcester, Mass., May 27, 1952; s. Joseph J. and Dorothy J. (Goldsmith) Griff; m. Joan G. Garovoy, May 27, 1973; children: Joshua, Jordana. BA with high distinction, U. Mich., 1973, JD with distinction, 1977. Bar: Mich. 1977, Colo. 1982. Legal counsel Social Security Adminstrn., HHS, Balt., 1978—79; trial atty. U.S. Dept. Justice, Washington, 1979—81; assoc. Dufford, Waldeck, Ruland, Wise & Milburn, Grand Junction, Colo., 1981—83; atty. Harmon & Griff, P.C., Grand Junction, Colo., 1983—86; ptnr. Foster, Larson, Laiche & Griff, Grand Junction, Colo., 1986—99, Griff, Larson, Laiche & Volkmann, Grand Junction, Colo., 1999—2001, Griff, Larson & Laiche, Grand Junction, Colo., 2001—. Legal counsel Grand Junction br., NAACP, Colo., 1983—84, Walker Field, Colo. Pub. Airport Authority, Grand Junction, 1984—97; bd. dirs. Paradise Hills Homeowners Assn., Grand Junction, Colo., 1984—87, Ptnrs., Inc., 1988—94, KPRN Pub. Radio Sta., 1989—91. Bd. dirs. Grand Junction Jewish Cmty. Ctr., 1984—89, Colo. Lawyers Trust Acct. Found., 1986—92, Mus. Western Colo., 1997—2001, Vol. Ctrl., 1996—99, Downtown Devel. Authority, 2002—, Avalon Theatre, 2002—, Friends of Kulture and Entertainment for the Grand Valley, 2003—. Mem.: ABA, Mesa County Bar Assn. (bd. dirs. legal aid program 1984—89), Colo. Bar Assn., Assn. Trial Lawyers Am. Democrat. General civil litigation, Family and matrimonial, Personal injury (including property damage). Home: 2636 Chestnut Dr Grand Junction CO 81506-8390 Office: Griff Larson & Laiche 422 White Ave Fl 3 Grand Junction CO 81501-2555 Business E-Mail: harry@gllvlaw.com.

GRIFFIN, CAMPBELL ARTHUR, JR., retired lawyer; b. Joplin, Mo., July 17, 1929; s. Campbell Arthur and Clara M. (Smith) G.; m. Margaret Ann Adams, Oct. 19, 1958; children: Campbell A., Laura Ann. BA, U. Mo., 1951, MA in Acctg., 1952; JD, U. Tex., 1957. Bar: Tex. 1957. Assoc. Vinson & Elkins, LLP, Houston, 1957-67, ptnr., 1968-92, mgmt. com., 1981-90, mng. ptnr. Dallas, 1986-89. Adj. prof. adminstrv. sci. Jones Grad. Sch. Adminstrn., Rice U., 1992-94. Mem. ofcl. bd. Bethany Christian Ch., Houston, 1962-69, chmn. bd. elders, 1968; bd. dirs. Houston Pops Orch., 1982-87, Cornell Co. Inc. (NYSE), 1996-2000; councilman City of Hunters Creek Village, Tex., 1993-95; pres. Windcliff Property Owners Assn., Estes Park, Colo., 1995-96; bd. dirs. Cornell Cos., Inc. (NYSE), 1996-2000; active St. Martin's Epsicopal Ch., Houston. Mem. Houston Bar Assn., State Bar Tex. (bus. law sect. chmn. 1974-75), Tex. Bus Law Found. (chmn. 1988-89, dir. 1988-2000), Houston Racquet Club (dir. 1992-94). Corporate, general, Securities.

GRIFFIN, ROBERT PAUL, former United States senator, state supreme court justice; b. Detroit, Nov. 6, 1923; s. J.A. and Beulah M. G.; m. Marjorie J. Anderson, 1947; children— Paul Robert, Richard Allen, James Anderson, Martha Jill. AB, BS, Central Mich. U., 1947, LLD, 1963; JD, U. Mich., 1950, LLD, 1973; LL.D., Eastern Mich. U., 1969, Albion Coll., 1970, Western Mich. U., 1971, Grand Valley State Coll., 1971, Detroit Coll. Bus., 1972, Detroit Coll. Law, 1973; L.H.D., Hillsdale (Mich.) Coll., 1970; J.C.D., Rollins Coll., 1970; Ed.D., No. Mich. U., 1970; D. Pub. Service, Detroit Inst. Tech., 1971. Bar: Mich. 1950. Pvt. practice, Traverse City, Mich., 1950-56; mem. 85th-89th congresses from 9th Dist. Mich., Washington, 1957-66; mem. U.S. Senate from Mich., Washington, 1966-79; counsel Miller, Canfield, Paddock & Stone, Traverse City, 1979-86; assoc. justice Mich. Supreme Ct., Lansing, 1987-95. Trustee Gerald R. Ford Found. Served with inf. AUS, World War II, ETO. Named 1 of 10 Outstanding Young Men of Nation U.S. Jaycees, 1959 Mem. ABA, Mich. Bar Assn., D.C. Bar Assn., Kiwanis.

GRIFFIN, WILLIAM MELL, III, lawyer; b. Tallahassee, Feb. 1, 1957; s. William Mell Jr. and June Winona (Cooper) G.; m. Kathryn Elizabeth Lawson, Dec. 11, 1993; children: William Mell IV, George Lawson, James Porter. BA, U. Va., 1979; JD, So. Meth. U., 1982. Bar: Ark. 1982, U.S. Dist. Ct. (ea. and we. dists.) Ark. 1982, U.S. Ct. Appeals (8th cir.) 1983. Assoc. Friday, Eldredge & Clark, Little Rock, 1982-87, ptnr., 1987—. Mem. ABA (torts and ins. practice sect.), Am. Bd. Trial Advocates (advocate), Ark. Bar Assn., Pulaski County Bar Assn., William R. Overton Inn of Ct., Ark. Def. Counsel, Def. Rsch. Inst., Fedn. Ins. and Corp. Counsel, Leadership Greater Little Rock, Phi Delta Phi. Avocations: running, hunting. Federal civil litigation, State civil litigation, Insurance. Home: 420 Midland St Little Rock AR 72205-4177 Office: Friday Eldredge & Clark 2000 1st Commercial Bldg Little Rock AR 72201

GRIFFITH, EDWARD, lawyer; b. Wilkes-Barre, Pa., Feb. 9, 1948; s. Edward Meredith Griffith and Jane (Randall) Griffith Jones; m. Linda Christine Scribner, Aug. 9, 1969 (div. July 1982); children: Trevor Scribner, Stewart Randall; m. Katherine Greybill, Oct. 24, 1987. BA, Lehigh U., 1970; JD, Dickinson Sch. Law, 1973. Bar: Pa. 1973, U.S. Dist. Ct. (ea. dist.) Pa. 1973, U.S. Ct. Appeal (3rd cir.) 1973, U.S. Supreme Ct. 1978. Ptnr. Duane, Morris LLP, Phila., 1973—. Cons. Pa. State Bd. Law Examiners, Phila, 1974-77. Master John E. Stively Inn of Ct.; mem. ABA, Pa. Bar Assn., Chester County Bar Assn. Republican. Presbyterian. Avocations: hunting, fishing, gardening. General civil litigation, Insurance, Personal injury (including property damage). Office: Duane Morris LLP Station Square Three Ste 105 Paoli PA 19301 E-mail: griffith@duanemorris.com.

GRIFFITH, EMLYN IRVING, lawyer; b. Utica, N.Y., May 13, 1923; s. William A. and Maud A. (Charles) G.; m. Mary L. Kilpatrick, Aug. 13, 1946; children: William L., James R. AB, Colgate U., 1942; JD, Cornell U., 1950; 10 hon. doctorates. Bar: N.Y. 1950, U.S. Supreme Ct. 1954. Pvt. practice law, Lockport, NY, 1950—52, Rome, 1952—. Bd. dirs. various corps. and founds.; chmn. N.Y. Photonics Devel. Corp., 2001—. Contbr. articles to profl. jours. in U.S. and U.K. Mem. N.Y. State Bd. Regents, 1973-96, Gov.'s Com. on Librs., 1976-80; co-chmn. State Conf. Professions, 1974-77, 85-90; mem. U.S. Forum Edn. Orgn. Leaders, 1978-80, Intergovtl. Adv. Coun. on Edn., 1982-86; del. to China-U.S. Joint Session on Trade and Law, Beijing, 1987, Soviet-Am. Conf. on Comparative Edn., Moscow, 1988, N.Y. State-USSR Lawyers Conf., Moscow, 1990; pres. Nat. Assn. State Bds. Edn., 1979-80, Nat. Assn. State Bds. Edn. Found., 1997-99; pres. Nat. Welsh-Am. Found., 1981-83; v.p. Hon. Soc. Cymmrodorion, London, 1988—; trustee, bd. pensions United Presbyn. Ch., 1966-72, Aerospace Edn. Found., 1979-96, Erie Canal Mus., 1996-2003, Cazenovia Coll., 1996—. Maj. USAAC, 1942-46. Recipient Disting. Svc. to Am. Edn. award Nat. Assn. State Bds. Edn., 1995, Conspicuous Svc. award State of N.Y., 1992, Exceptional Svc. citation Air Force Assn., 1980; Doolittle fellow Aerospace Edn. Found., 1988, Welsh Heritage award Nat. Welsh Am. Found., 1997. Fellow Am. Bar Found. (life), N.Y. Bar Found. (life, recipient Root-Stimson award for pub. svc. 1986, bd. dirs. 1989—); mem. ABA (com. pub. edn. 1974—), N.Y. State Bar assn. (ho. dels. 1974-76, co-chmn. com. atty. professionalism, 1989-92, mem. bd. editors Bar Jour. 1986-97), Oneida County Bar Assn. (pres. 1974-75), State Conf. County Bar Officers (chmn. 1974-76), Osgoode Soc. Can., Selden Soc., Eng., Phi Gamma Delta Internat. (pres. bd. trustees 1982-86, pres. edn. found. 1992-94). General practice, Probate (including wills, trusts), Property, real (including real estate development, water). Office: 225 N Washington St Rome NY 13440-5742

GRIFFITH, H(OWARD) MORGAN, lawyer; b. Phila., Mar. 15, 1958; s. A. Hundley and Charlotte Virginia (Burford) G. BA, Emory and Henry Coll., 1980; JD, Washington and Lee U., 1983. Bar: Va. 1983, U.S. Dist. Ct. Va. 1985. Assoc. Lutins & Shapiro, Roanoke, Va., 1983-84; pvt. practice Salem, Va., 1984-87; ptnr. Griffith & Varney, Salem, 1987-89; pvt. practice Salem, 1989—; house majority leader, 2000—. Del. Va. Gen. Assembly, 1994—; dir. Salem Bank & Trust; bd. vis. Emory and Henry Coll. Vice-chmn. Salem Rep. Com., 1984-86, chmn., 1986-88, 91-93; bd. dirs. Legal Aid Soc. of Roanoke Valley, 1991-92; advisor, sponsor Legal Explorers Post Boy Scouts of Am., Salem, 1988-89; chmn. Catawba dist. Blue Ridge Mountains coun., Boy Scouts Am., 1984-86, vice chmn., 1987-88, dist. chmn., 1988-91, v.p. rels. and membership, 1991-93; com. mem. Stonegate Swim Club, Salem, 1984-88, bd. dirs., 1991—; mem. state bd. dirs. Easter Seals Va. Recipient Dist. Award of Merit, Boy Scouts Am., 1990-91, Silver Beaver award, 1994. Mem. Va. State Bar Assn., Roanoke County-Salem Bar Assn. (pres. 1995-96), Lions (bd. dirs. 1988-90). Episcopalian. Avocations: swimming, ornithology, ichthyology. Criminal, General practice, Personal injury (including property damage). Office: 113 E Main St Salem VA 24153-3804

GRIFFITH, JAMES D. retired lawyer; b. Evanston, Ill., Aug. 28, 1929; s. Wendell Crabtree and Mary Griffith; m. Elizabeth Meyer, Sept. 21, 1957 (div. July 1987); children: Ian Hunt, Alison Gail Griffith; m. Phyllis A. Zaruba Oct. 22, 1994. BA, DePauw U., 1951; MA in Modern European History, U. Ill.; JD, Northwestern U., Chgo., 1953. Bar: Ill. 1953, Mich. 1973, Ind. 1980. Assoc. Campbell, Clithero & Fischer, Chgo., 1956-63; ptnr. Graham, Stevenson & Griffith, Chgo., 1963-67; prin. Pauker & Griffith, Ltd., Chgo., 1969-79; pvt. practice, Chgo., 1967-69, 80-95; ret., 1995. Magistrate Village of Glenview, Ill., 1961-65. Contbr. articles to profl. jours. Founder, pres. Com. on Lake Michigan Pollution, Wilmette, Ill., 1967-69, Fifty Percent, Chgo., 1991—; active Chgo. Crime Commn., 1967-72; mem. exec. com. New Trier Dem. Orgn.; pres. Lake Michigan Fedn., Chgo., 1973-74, 92-94; pres. Glenview Civic Party, 1981; dir. Family Svc. Ctr., Wilmette, 1997-2000. With U.S. Army, 1954-56; trustee Village of Wilmette, 2003-. Mem. Chgo. Coun. on Fgn. Rels., Sheridan Shore Yacht Club (Wilmette, commodore 1970), Wilmette Harbor Rotary (sec. 2002-03). Avocations: sailing, tennis, hiking, canoeing, bridge. General civil litigation, Estate planning, General practice. Home: 1210 Glendenning Rd Wilmette IL 60091-1547

GRIFFITH, STEVEN FRANKLIN, SR., lawyer, real estate title insurance agent and investor; b. New Orleans, July 14, 1948; s. Hugh Franklin and Rose Marie (Teutone) G.; m. Mary Elizabeth McMillan Frank, Dec. 9, 1972; children: Steven Franklin Jr., Jason Franklin. BBA, Loyola U., New Orleans, 1970, JD, 1972. Bar: La. 1972, U.S. Dist. Ct. (ea. dist.) La. 1975, U.S. Ct. Appeals (5th cir.) 1975, U.S. Supreme Ct. 1976. With Law Offices of Senator George T. Oubre, Norco, La., 1971-75; sole practice Destrehan, La., 1975—. Pres. 29th Jud. Dist. Bar Assn., 1999-2002. Fellow: La. Bar Found.; mem.: ATLA, ABA, St. Charles Parish Bar Assn. (pres. 1999—2002), Fed. Bar Assn., New Orleans Trial Lawyers Assn., La. Trial Lawyers Assn., La. State Bar Assn. (ho. of dels. 1987—). Democrat. Insurance, Personal injury (including property damage), Property, real (including real estate development, water).

GRILLER, GORDON MOORE, court administrator; b. Sioux City, Iowa, Feb. 3, 1944; s. Joseph Edward and Arlene (Searles) G. m. Helen Mary Friederichs, aug. 20, 1966; children: Heather, Chad. BA in Political Sci., U. Minn., 1966, MA in Pub. Affairs, 1969. Mgnt. analyst Hennepin County Adminstr., Mpls., 1968-72; asst. court adminstr. Hennepin County Municipal Ct., Mpls., 1972-77, ct. adminstr., 1977-78; judicial dist. adminstr. 2nd Dist. Ct. Minn., St. Paul, 1978-87; ct. adminstr. Superior Ct. Ariz., Phoenix, 1987—2002, Trial Cts. in Maricopa County Ariz., Phoenix, 2002—. Bd. dirs. Nat. Ctr. State Cts., 1997—, Nat. Conf. Metro Cts., 1999—. Vice-chmn. Bloomington Sch. Bd., Minn., 1981-87. Sgt. USAAF, 1968-74 Res. Recipient Warren E. Burger award Inst. Ct. Mgnt.,1988, Leadership Fellows award Bush Leadership Program, 1974. Mem. Nat. Assn. Trial Ct. Adminstrs.(pres. 1983-84), Ariz. Ct. Assn., Nat. Assn Ct. Mgmt. (award of merit), Am. Judicature Soc., (bd. dirs. 1997—). Lutheran. Avocations: running, kyaking, racquetball, scuba diving. Home: 8507 E San Jacinto Dr Scottsdale AZ 85258-2576 Office: Superior Ct Ariz 201 W Jefferson St Fl 4 Phoenix AZ 85003-2205

GRIMALDI, NEIL VINCENT, lawyer; b. N.Y.C., Jan. 27, 1947; s. Vincent and Frances Grimaldi. B in Fgn. Svc., Georgetown U., 1968; JD, St. John's U., 1973. Bar: N.Y.; ordained min. Interfaith Sem., 1999. Prosecutor Bronx Dist. Atty. Office, N.Y.C., 1974—77; pvt. practice N.Y.C., 1979—. Pres. Grimaldi Corp., N.Y.C., 1999—. Author: The Grand Journey, 1999. Mem.: Masonic Order Free Masons. Democrat. Criminal, Appellate, Civil rights. Home: 2860 Butree Ave New York NY 10461 Office: Grimaldi Corp 67 Wall St 22d Fl New York NY 10005

GRIMES, STEPHEN HENRY, retired state supreme court justice; b. Peoria, Ill., Nov. 17, 1927; s. Henry Holbrook and June (Kellar) G.; m. Mary Fay Fulghum, Dec. 29, 1951; children: Gay Diane, Mary June, Sue Anne, Sheri Lynn. Student, Fla. So. Coll., 1946-47; BS in Bus. Adminstrn. with honors, U. Fla., 1951, LLB with honors, 1954; LLD (hon.), Stetson U., 1980. Bar: Fla. 1954, U.S. Dist. Ct. (no. and so. dists.) 1954, U.S. Ct. Appeals (5th cir.) 1965, U.S. Supreme Ct. 1972. Since practiced in, Bartow, Fla.; ptnr. Holland and Knight and predecessor firm, Tallahassee, 1954-73, 98—; judge Ct. Appeal 2d Dist. Fla., Lakeland, Fla., 1973-87, chief judge, 1978-80; chmn. Conf. Fla. Dist. Cts. Appeal, 1978-80; justice Fla. Supreme Ct., Tallahassee, 1987-97, chief justice, 1994-96; chair Article V Task Force, 1994-96, Supreme Ct. Workload Study Commn., 2000-2001. Mem. Fla. Jud. Qualification Commn., 1982-86, vice chmn., 1985-86; chmn. Fla. Jud. Coun., 1989-94. Contbr. articles U. Fla. Law Rev., 1951, 54. Bd. dirs. Bartow Meml. Hosp., 1958-61, Bartow Library, 1968-78; trustee Polk Community Coll., Winter Haven, Fla., 1967-70, chmn., 1969-70; bd. govs. Polk Pub. Mus., 1976-97; bd. dirs., chmn. Elder Care. Lt. (j.g.) USN, 1951-53. Fellow Am. Coll. Trial Lawyers; mem. ABA, Fla. Bar Assn. (bd. govs. jr. bar 1956-58, bd. dirs. trial lawyers sect. 1967-69, sec. 1969, vice chmn. appellate rules com. 1976-77, vice chmn. tort litigation rev. commn. 1985-86), 10th Cir. Bar Assn. (pres. 1966), Am. Judicature Soc., Bartow C. of C. (pres. 1964), Rotary (dist. gov. 1960-61). Episcopalian (sr. warden 1964-65, 77). Office: Holland & Knight LLP 315 S Calhoun St Tallahassee FL 32301-1856 E-mail: sgrimes@hklaw.com.

GRIMM, PATRICIA LEE, lawyer; b. Cleve., Aug. 15, 1949; d. William Albert and Mary Julie (Ziska) Schumann. BS in Edn., Ohio State U., 1971, M.Counseling, 1973; JD, Capital U., Columbus, 1983. Bar: Ohio 1983. Tchr. Columbus City Schs., 1973-79; supr. Night Pros., Newark, Ohio, 1980-83; law clk. Ohio State Med. Bd., Columbus, 1981-83; pvt. practice law Columbus, 1983—. Vol. mediator Franklin Cts., Columbus, 1987. Bd. trustes Fathers & Children for Equal Justice, 1988. Delta Theta Phi. Office: 6245 Evans Rd New Albany OH 43054-9540

GRIMSHAW, THOMAS TOLLIN, lawyer; b. Mpls., Oct. 31, 1932; s. U.L. and Judith (Austrid) G.; children: Scott, Lynn, Steve, Lisa, Shane. Student, Hamline U., 1951; BA, U. Minn., 1953; JD, Northwestern U., 1956. Bar: Ill., Colo. 1956. Assoc. Calkins, Rodden & Kramer, Denver, 1956-62; pvt. practice Denver, 1963-64; ptnr. Calkins, Kramer, Grimshaw & Harring, Denver, 1965-84, of counsel, 1984-94; ptnr. Grimshaw & Harring, 1994—. Bd. dirs. Colo. Housing Fin. Authority, Denver, 1987-98; mem. Nat. Conf. Commrs. on Uniform State Laws, 1987—, Colo. Coun. on Econ. Edn., 1987-2000; bd. dirs. Sturm Financial Group Inc., Exempla, Inc., LMC Found., Inc., Cmty. Found., Exempla Healthcare, The Edn. Found. State rep. Colo. Gen. Assembly, Denver, 1967-70; mem., chmn. Colo. Housing Bd., Denver, 1970-74; bd. dirs., chmn. State Bd. for Comm. Colls. and Occupl. Edn., Denver, 1979-86; bd. dirs. Cen. Bapt. Theol. Sem., Kansas City, Kans., 1978-88, 94—. Mem. Denver Bar Assn. (chmn. pub. relations com. 1969-70), Colo. Bar Assn. (bd. govs. 1969-70, chmn. pub. relations com. 1970-71, sr. v.p. 1971-72, chmn. legis. com. 1972-77), ABA, Denver Athletic Club (past bd. dirs.), Jacques DeMolay, Colo. Consistory. Republican. Baptist. Land use and zoning (including planning), Municipal (including bonds), Property, real (including real estate development, water). Office: Grimshaw & Harring 1700 Lincoln St Ste 3800 Denver CO 80203-4538 E-mail: tomg@grimshawharring.com.

GRIMWADE, RICHARD LLEWELLYN, lawyer; b. Chgo., Apr. 26, 1945; s. Eric Illingworth and Pauline J. (Crandall) G.; m. Alexandra M. Galbraith, Feb. 22, 1981; children: Eric Montgomery, Sara Elizabeth. BA, Lawrence U., 1967; JD cum laude, U. Wis., 1971. Bar: Wis. 1971, N.Y. 1971, Ill. 1978, Calif. 1981, U.S. Dist. Ct. (so. and ea. dists.) N.Y., 1971, U.S. Dist. Ct. (no. dist.) Wis., 1971, U.S. Dist. Ct. (no. dist.) Ill., 1978, U.S. Dist. Ct. (ctrl. dist.) Calif., 1981, U.S. Ct. Appeals (2d cir.) 1971, U.S. Ct. Appeals (7th cir.) 1978, U.S. Ct. Appeals (9th cir.) 1981. Atty. Davis Polk, N.Y.C., 1971—76; ptnr. Barton Klugman, L.A., 1983-93; pvt. practice L.A., 1993—. Mem. U. Wis. Law Rev., 1969-71. Bd. mgrs. Ketchum Downtown YMCA, L.A., 1991-97; trustee Reform L.A. Pub. Schs. (LEARN), 1993-97. Recipient 3 Am. Jurisprudence awards for evidence, legis., and acctg. and law Bancroft-Whitney, 1970. Mem.: State Bar Calif., Toastmasters (Best Performer award 1996, Best Table Topics award 1997, Best Spkr. award), Order of Coif. Avocations: gardening, poetry, running, public speaking, history. General civil litigation, Insurance, Professional liability. Home: 22372 Dardenne St Calabasas CA 91302

GRINNELL, JOSEPH FOX, lawyer; b. July 4, 1923; s. Robert L. and Mary King G.; m. Marjorie Volwiler, Aug. 24, 1946; children: Stephen F., Christine K. Burcham, James W. BA, Yale U., 1945; JD, Northwestern U., 1949. Bar: Ill. 1949, U.S. Dist. Ct. (no. dist.) Ill. 1949, Minn. 1954. Assoc. Winston-Strawn, Chgo., 1949-54; sr. v.p. law Investors Diversified Svcs., Mpls., 1954-83; of counsel Pepin Dayton Herman Graham & Getts, Mpls., 1983-87. Bd. dirs. Guthrie Theater, Mpls., 1970-71, Minn. Orch. Assn., Mpls., 1976-78; bd. dirs., chmn. Minn. Pollution Control Agy., Mpls., 1973-81. Served to lt. (j.g.) USN, 1942-46, PTO. Democrat. Presbyterian. Home: 8155 Parkview Ln Bloomington MN 55438

GRISCHKE, ALAN EDWARD, lawyer; b. Milw., Mar. 2, 1945; s. Rupert Edward and Velma Pearl (Springer) G.; m. Christine A. Bremer, July 4, 1981 (div.). BS, U. Wis., Stevens Point, 1968; postgrad., U. Miami, Fla., 1969; JD, Loyola U., Chgo., 1971. Bar: Ill. 1971, Wis. 1982, U.S. Dist. Ct. (no. dist.) Ill. 1971, U.S. Dist. Ct. (we. and ea. dist.) Wis. 1982, U.S. Ct. Appeals (7th cir.) 1979, U.S. Supreme Ct. 1979; cert. civil trial specialist. Asst. atty. gen. Ill. Atty. Gens. Office, Chgo., 1971-73; regional counsel Ill. Dept. Mental Health, Chgo., 1973-75, gen. counsel, 1975-80; ptnr. Grischke & Assocs., Ltd., Chgo., 1980-82; assoc. Trembath, Hess, Miller & Seidl, Wausau, Wis., 1982; ptnr. Mallery Law Offices SC, Wausau, Wis., 1983-85; pvt. practice Wausau, Wis., 1985-89; pres. Grischhke & Bremer LLSC, Wausau, Wis., 1989—2003, Grischke, Molinaro & Laughlin, LLSC, Wausau, 2003—. Adj. prof. John Marshall Law Sch., Chgo., 1975-81; faculty U. Ill., Abraham Lincoln Sch. Medicine, Chgo., 1976-80, Loyola U., Stritch Sch. Medicine, Chgo., 1980-82; chmn. Midwest Consortium Mental Health Attys., 1975-76, Nat. Assn. State Mental Health Attys., 1976-80; bd. dirs. Dept. Natural Resources, Wis., 2003—. Mem. ABA (sustaining), Am. Trial Lawyers Assn., Wis. State Bar Assn. (bd. profl. responsibility dist. 16 1990-98), Marathon County Bar Assn., Wis. Acad. Trial Lawyers (sustaining, bd. dirs. 1986-88). State civil litigation, Personal injury (including property damage), Product liability. Home: 608 Excel Dr Wausau WI 54401-2165 Office: PO Box 847 1400 Merrill Ave Wausau WI 54402-0847 E-mail: aeg@alangrischke.com.

GRISSOM, GARTH CLYDE, lawyer, director; b. Syracuse, Kans., Jan. 24, 1930; s. Clyde and Bernice Minnie (Eddy) G.; m. Elena Joyce Kerst, Aug. 17, 1958; children: Colin, Grady, Cole, Kent. BS, Kans. State U., 1951; LL.B., Harvard U., 1957. Bar: Colo. 1957, U.S. Dist. Ct. (fed. dist.) Colo., 1957, U.S. Ct. Appeals (10th crct.) 1957, U.S. Supreme Ct. 1989. Ptnr., mem., counsel Sherman & Howard, L.L.C., Denver, 1963—. Sec., counsel, trustee Mile High United Way, Denver, 1985-88; trustee Kans. State U. Found., Manhattan, 1962-89; mem. Colo. Gov.'s Commn. on Life and the Law, 1990-99, chmn., 1996-99. Mem. ABA, Colo. Bar Assn., Denver Bar Assn. (pres. 1985-86, award of merit 1994), Rotary (sec. Denver 1983-84, bd. dirs. 1983-86, pres. 1989-90), Pi Kappa Alpha (pres. 1968-70). Corporate, general, Mergers and acquisitions, Securities. Home: 1777 Larimer St Apt 1610 Denver CO 80202-1548 Office: Sherman & Howard LLC 633 17th St Ste 3000 Denver CO 80202-3665

GRISWOLD, THOMAS L. lawyer; b. Kansas City, Mo., Sept. 23, 1949; s. Thomas L. and Betty L. Griswold; m. Noreen M. Puhala, Apr. 23, 1988; children: Alisha Beth, Shannon Blake. BA cum laude, Washburn U., Topeka, Kans., 1973; MPA, U. of Kans., 1976, JD, 1980. Bar: Kans. 1981, Mo. 1990, U.S. Dist. Ct. (we. dist.) Mo. 1990. Staff planner Topeka-Shawnee County Met. Planning Agencies, Topeka, 1968—74; chief planner City of Topeka Dept. of Labor Svcs., Topeka, 1974—75; audit supr. State of Kans. Legis. Divsn. of Post Audit, Topeka, 1975—78; mem. firm Payne & Jones, Chartered, Overland Park, Kans., 1981—. Editor in chief Kans. Law Rev., 1980. Contbr. Bd. mem. City of Topeka Legal Aid Soc., Topeka, Kans., 1973—74. With USMCR, 1969. Recipient Burdick Prize, U. of Kans. Sch. of Law, 1979, various awards, Am. Jurisprudence, 1978—80, Am. Judicature Soc. award, 1980. Mem.: ABA, The Mo. Bar, Kans. Bar Assn., Order of the Coif. Family and matrimonial, General civil litigation. Office: Payne & Jones Chartered 11000 King St Overland Park KS 66210 Office Fax: 913-469-0132.

GRMELA, ZOLTAN, lawyer; b. Karcag, Hungary, June 18, 1966; s. Jozsef Grmela and Aniko Koos; m. Krisztina Vogl, July 6, 1991; children: Mate, Bence, Zsofia. JD, Miskolc (Hungary) U., 1990; LLM, NYU, 1992. Bar: Hungary 1995. Prof. Miskolc U., 1990—92; fgn. assoc. Arnold & Porter, Budapest, Hungary, 1992—95; ptnr. Gardos, Benke, Mosonyi, Tomori, Budapest, 1995—2000, Weil, Gotshal & Manges, Budapest, 2000—. Mergers and acquisitions, Corporate, general, Finance. Office: Weil Gotshal & Manges Szabadsag Ter 7 1054 Budapest Hungary

GROBE, CHARLES STEPHEN, lawyer, accountant; b. Columbus, Ohio, May 5, 1935; s. Harry A. and Bertha S. (Swartz) G.; m. Ila Silverman, Aug. 30, 1964; children— Eileen, Kenneth. BS, U. Calif. at Los Angeles, 1957; JD, Stanford, 1961. Bar: Calif. 1962; CPA, Calif. Tax accountant, Beverly Hills, Calif., 1961-63; tax atty. Los Angeles, 1963—. Author: Guide to Investing Pension and Profit-Sharing Trust Funds, 1973, Guardianship, Conservatorship and Trusts on Behalf of Persons Who Are Mentally Retarded— An Assessment of Current Applicable Laws in the State of California, 1974, Using an Individual Retirement Savings Plan and the Related Rollover Provisions of the Pension Reform Act of 1974, 1975, Guide to Setting Up a Group Term Life Insurance Program Under IRC Section 79, 1976, Practical Estate Planning, 1988, Planning for Incapacity, 1989, Planning to Reduce the Generation Skipping Tax, 1989, Estate Planning Considerations for Community Property Interests, 1990, Legal and Tax Problems of Joint Tennancy as a Form of Ownership, 1990, The Tax Economics of Using the Generating Skipping Tax Exemptions, 1992, The Tax Economics of Gifting Property, 1992, Saving Estate Taxes with Life Insurance and a Life Insurance Trust, 1992, Family Wealth Transfer Planning, The Tax Economics of a Qualified Personal Residence Trust, also articles. Capt. AUS, 1957-64. Mem. ABA, State Bar Calif., L.A. County Bar Assn., Beverly Hills Bar Assn., Calif. Soc. CPAs. Estate planning, Estate taxation, Taxation, general. Home: 11959 Foxboro Dr Los Angeles CA 90049 Office: 12110 Wilshire Blvd Los Angeles CA 90025-1104

GROCE, STEVEN FRED, lawyer; b. Springfield, Mo., Aug. 6, 1956; s. Robert V. and Celeste Groce. BA in Psychology, S.W. Mo. State U., 1980; JD, U. Mo., Kansas City, 1984. Bar: Mo. 1984, U.S. Dist. Ct. (we. dist.) Mo. 1984, U.S. Supreme Ct., 1990. Ptnr. Groce & DeArmon, P.C., Springfield, 1984—. Mem. U.S. Supreme Ct. Bar, Mo. Bar Assn., Tex. Bar Assn., Internat. Bar Assn., Nat. Assn. Criminal Def. Lawyers (life). Criminal, Personal injury (including property damage), Property, real (including real estate development, water). Office: Ste B-100 1200 E Woodhurst Dr Springfield MO 65804-4261

GROETZINGER, JON, JR., lawyer, consumer products executive; b. N.Y.C., Feb. 12, 1949; s. Jon M. and Elinor Groetzinger; m. Carol Marie O'Connor, Jan. 24, 1981; 3 children. AB magna cum laude, Middlebury Coll., 1971; JD in Internat. Legal Affairs, Cornell U., 1974. Bar: N.H. 1974, N.Y. 1980, Mass. 1980, Fla. 1982, Md. 1985, Ohio 1991, U.S. Supreme Ct. 1980. Assoc. McLane, Graf, Greene, Raulerson and Middleton, P.A., Manchester, N.H., 1974-76; atty. John A. Gray Law Offices, Boston, 1978-81; pvt. practice N.H., Boston, 1977-81; chief internat. counsel Martin Marietta Corp., Bethesda, Md., 1981-88; pres., exec. v.p. Martin Marietta Overseas Corp., Bethesda, 1984-88; sr. v.p., gen. counsel, corp. sec. Am. Greetings Corp., Cleve., 1988—. Chmn. internat. adv. bd. Case Western Res. U. Law Sch., 1995—, disting. adj. prof., 1992—. Trustee Middlebury (Vt.) Coll., 1974—76, mem. bd. overseers, 1977—; vice chmn. Cleve. Coun. on World Affairs, 2002—, chmn. strategic planning com., 2000—02, mem. exec. com., 2000—03, trustee, 1992—96, 1998—, Can.-U.S. Law Inst.; mem. exec. com. The Conf. Bds. Coun. Chief Legal Officers, 1996—, membership chmn., 1997—98, program chair, 1999—2000, coun. chmn., 2000—02; chmn. Greater Cleve. Gen. Counsel Assn., 2001—, pres., 2001—; bd. dirs. Lake Erie Coll., 2002—. Mem. ABA, N.H. Bar Assn., Fla. Bar Assn., Ohio Bar Assn., Cleve. Bar Assn., Md. Bar Assn., Am. Soc. Corp. Secs. (sec. Ohio chpt. 1995—, v.p. 1996-97, pres. 1997-98, adv. com. 1998—), Soc. of Benchers, Phi Beta Kappa. Commercial, contracts (including sales of goods; commercial financing), Corporate, general, Private international. Office: Am Greetings Corp 1 American Rd Cleveland OH 44144-2301 E-mail: jgroetzi@yahoo.com.

GROH, JENNIFER CALFA, law librarian; b. Patchogue, N.Y., Mar. 28, 1970; d. Anthony Bernard and Mary (Fogerty) C.; m. William Matthew Groh, May 10, 1997. BA in Social Sci., St. Joseph's Coll., 1992; MA in Internat. Edn., NYU, 1993; MSLS, Pratt Inst., Bklyn., 1996. Reference page Patchogue (N.Y.)-Medford Libr., 1986-93; from libr. asst. to sr. libr. Morgan & Finnegan, N.Y.C., 1994—. NYU grad. scholar, 1992, Law Libr. Assn. scholar, N.Y. 1995, Am. Assn. Law Librs. scholar, 1996. Mem. ALA, Spl. Librs. Assn., Law Libr. Assn. Greater N.Y. Home: 21 Mohawk Dr North Babylon NY 11703-3303 Office: Morgan & Finnegan 345 Park Ave New York NY 10154-0053

GROISS, FRED GEORGE, lawyer; b. Glen Cove, N.Y., Mar. 12, 1936; s. Frederick F.W. and Dorothy C. (Roberts) G.; m. Jacqueline C. Grosse; children— Frederick C., Katherine E., Jennifer L. AB, Cornell U., 1958, LL.B., 1961. Bar: N.Y. 1961, Wis. 1963, U.S. Dist. Ct. (ea. dist.) Wis., 1963, U.S. Ct. Appeals (7th cir.) 1965. Assoc. Sage, Gray, Todd & Sims, N.Y.C., 1961-63; assoc. Porter, Quale, Porter & Zirbel, Milw., 1963-65, Brady, Tyrrell, Cotter & Cutler, Milw., 1965-70; ptnr. Quarles & Brady, Milw., 1970-2000; ret. Lectr. various labor law confs. Mem. Gov.'s Commn. on Civil Service Reform, Madison, Wis., 1977-78 Mem.: Wis. Bar Assn. (bd. dirs. labor law sect. 1975—77), Greencroft ACAC Club. Republican. Avocation: sports. Labor (including EEOC, Fair Labor Standards Act, labor-management relations, NLRB, OSHA). Home: 2460 Dunmore Rd Charlottesville VA 22901-9447 E-mail: fgroiss@cstone.net.

GRONDINE, ROBERT FRANCIS, lawyer; b. Milford, Mass., Jan. 29, 1952; s. Albert Francis and Mary Roselma (Credit) G.; m. Aiko Morii, June 28, 1979; 1 child, Michelle Morii. AB, Dartmouth Coll., 1974; postgrad., Cornell U., 1974-75, Harvard U., 1979-80; JD, Boston U., 1980. Bar: N.Y. 1981, Mass. 1981, U.S. Dist. Ct. (ea. and so. dists.) N.Y. 1981, Calif. 1990, D.C. 1991. Assoc. Baker & McKenzie, N.Y.C., 1980-82, Tokyo, 1982-86, ptnr., 1986-92, White & Case, L.L.P., Tokyo, 1992—. Mem.: Coun. on Fgn. Rels. (U.S.), Am. C. of C. in Japan (bd. govs. 1994—95, v.p. 1996, bd. govs. 1998, v.p. 1999, pres. 2000—01, chmn. 2002, bd. govs. 2002—). Aviation, Commercial, contracts (including sales of goods; commercial financing), Private international. Office: White & Case LLP 1-19-1 Kanda-nishikicho Chiyoda-ku Tokyo 101-0054 Japan E-mail: rgrondine@tokyo.whitecase.com.

GROPPER, ALLAN LOUIS, bankruptcy judge; BA, Yale U., 1965; JD, Harvard U., 1969. Bar: N.Y. 1969, U.S. Dist. Ct. (so. and ea. dists.) N.Y. 1971, U.S. Ct. Appeals (2d cir.) 1971, U.S. Supreme Ct. 1974. Atty. Civil Appeals Bur., Legal Aid Soc., N.Y.C., 1969-71; assoc. White & Case, N.Y.C., 1972-77, ptnr., 1978-2000; bankruptcy judge U.S. Bankruptcy Ct., N.Y.C., 2000—. Adj. prof. Fordham Law Sch., 2003—. Bd. dirs. Browning Sch., 1990—, pres., 1997-2000; bd. dirs. Legal Aid Soc., 1990-2000, v.p., 1996-2000; bd. dirs. N.Y. Lawyers for Pub. Interest, 1990-2000. Mem. ABA, Assn. of Bar of City of N.Y. (v.p. 1995-96, mem. exec. com. 1991-96, chmn. 1994-95), N.Y. State Bar Assn. Office: US Bankruptcy Ct Alexander Hamilton Custom House 1 Bowling Green New York NY 10004

GROSECLOSE, LYNN HUNTER, lawyer; b. Marion, Va., Apr. 22, 1943; s. Byron Glen and Wilma Comer G.; m. Sharon L. Pair; children: Seth, Zachery, Meredith. BA, Emory & Henry Coll., 1964; postgrad., Emory U., 1964-65; JD, U. Va., 1970. Bar: Fla. 1971, U.S. Dist. Ct. (mid. dist.) Fla. 1972, U.S. Ct. Appeals (5th cir.) 1980, U.S. Ct. Appeals (11th cir.) 1981, Colo. 1993. Prof. Orlando Jr. Coll., Fla., 1965-67; atty. Langston & Massey, Attys., Lakeland, Fla., 1971-75; ptnr. Sprott & Groseclose, Attys., Lakeland, 1975-80, Jacobs, Valentine, Groseclose, Lakeland, 1980-84, Lane, Trohn, Bradenton, Fla., 1984-96, Brown, Clark, Sarasota, Fla., 1996-99, Thompson, Goodis, Thompson, Groseclose & Richardson, Sarasota, 1999—. Sr., jr. warden St. Davids Episcopal Ch.; pres., bd. dirs. Vols. in Svc. to Elderly, Gulfcoast Legal Svcs., Sarasota Manatee Legal Aid. Mem. Sarasota County Bar Assn., Manatee County Bar Assn., Colo. Bar Assn., Fla. Def. Lawyers Assn., Fedn. Def. and Corp. Counsel, Fla. Bar Found. (legal assistance to poor com. 1997-2002). Democrat. Avocations: history, remodeling, golf. Insurance, Personal injury (including property damage), Professional liability. Office: Thompson Goodis Thompson Groseclose & Richardson PO Box 730 Bradenton FL 34206 Home: 7102 Bluebell Ct Bradenton FL 34202-4195

GROSMAN, ALAN M. lawyer; b. Mar. 13, 1935; s. Charles M. and Grace (Fishman) G.; m. Bette Bloomenthal, Dec. 27, 1967; children, Ellen, Carol. BA, Wesleyan U., 1956; MA, Yale U., 1957; JD, N.Y. Law Sch., 1965. Bar: N.J. 1965, U.S. Dist. Ct. N.J. 1965, U.S. Supreme Ct. 1969. Ptnr. Grosman & Grosman and predecessors, Millburn, N.J., 1965—; asst. prosecutor Essex County, N.J., 1968-69; prosecutor Millburn, 1981—. Mem. family practice com. NJ Supreme Ct., 1984—88, mem. dispute resolution task force, 1987—88, mem. com. on women in the cts., 1991—93; chmn. NJ Trade Coun., 1975—77, dir., 1978—; adj. prof. family law Rutgers U. Sch. Law, 2002—; lectr. in field. Author: New Jersey Family Law, 1999, with supplement, 2003; reporter: New Haven Jour., 1959—60, Newark Evening News, 1961—62; contbr. articles to profl. jours. Mem. ABA (chmn. alimony, maintenance and support com. family law sect. 1983-87, editor ABA Family Law Quar. 1993—), N.J. State Bar Assn. (exec. editor N.J. Family Lawyer 1980-91, mem. exec. com. family law sect. 1980—, chmn. sect. 1987-88, appellate practice com. 1995—), Am. Acad. Matrimonial Lawyers (pres. N.J. chpt. 1983-85, nat. bd. govs. 1984-88, editor Jour. AAML 1980-90), Essex County Bar Assn. (chmn. family law com. 1970-72), N.Y. Law Sch. Alumni Assn. (bd. dirs. 1988-98), Millburn-Short Hills Rep. Club, Inc. (counsel 1988—), Phi Beta Kappa. Family and matrimonial. Address: 75 Main St Ste 205 Millburn NJ 07041-1322

GROSS, ALLEN JEFFREY, lawyer; b. Wheeling, W.Va., May 2, 1948; s. Arthur and Bertyl (Kahn) G.; m. Carolyn McGuire, May 2, 1982; children: Alexander, Lindsay. BS, Ohio State U., 1970; JD, Georgetown U., 1974. Bar: Pa. 1974, U.S. Dist. Ct. (ctrl. and we. dists.) Pa., Calif. 1989, U.S. Dist. Ct. (no., so. and ctrl. dists.) Calif. 1989, U.S. Ct. Appeals (3d and 6th cirs.). Ptnr. Morgan, Lewis & Bockius, Phila., 1974-89, Orrick, Harrington & Sutcliffe, L.A., 1989-93; now with Mitchell, Silberberg & Knupp, L.A. Mem. Corp. Counsel Inst. adv. bd. Georgetown U. Law Ctr. Author: Survey of Wrongful Discharge Cases in the United States, 1979, Employee Dismissal Laws, Forms, Procedures, 1986, 2d edit. 1992. Fellow Coll. Labor and Employment Lawyers Inc.; mem. ABA (chair trial advocacy supcom. 1989-93, employee rights and responsibilities com. 1991—, co-chair Nat. Advocacy Inst. 1992), Calif. Bar Assn., Pa. Bar Assn. (mgmt. chair Employee Rights Responsibilities com., Sect. Insts. Spl. Programs sub-com.), L.A. County Bar Assn. Labor (including EEOC, Fair Labor Standards Act, labor-management relations, NLRB, OSHA). Office: Mitchell Silberberg & Knupp 11377 W Olympic Blvd Los Angeles CA 90064-1625

GROSS, BRYON WILLIAM, lawyer; b. Rochester, N.Y., Jan. 28, 1964; s. William E. Gross and Diana L. Peets; m. Pamela J. Murray, Feb. 28, 1993; children: Adam M., Matthew W., Sarah H. BA, St. Lawrence U., 1986; JD, We. New Eng. Coll., 1990. Pvt. practice, Springfield, Mass., 1993-98; assoc. Gallo & Iacovangelo, Rochester, N.Y., 1998—. Vol. VITA, 1989-98. Mem. N.Y. State Bar Assn., Mass. Trial Lawyers Assn., Monroe County Bar Assn. (guardian and ct. evaluations com. 1998). General civil litigation, Estate planning, Workers' compensation. Office: Gallo and Iacovangelo 39 State St Rochester NY 14614

GROSS, EDWARD JORDAN, lawyer; b. Nashville, May 25, 1939; s. Leslie Cordell and Irma Gross; m. Barbara Page Gross, June 30, 1961; children: Jay, Jamie, Jonathan, Jeremy, Jennie. LLB, Nashville U., 1986, JD, 1969. Bar: Tenn. 1966, U.S. Dist. Ct. Tenn. 1968, U.S. Ct. Appeals (6th cir.) 1969. Law clk. Pub. Def., Nashville, 1965—66; asst. dist. atty. Dist. Attys. Office, 1966—70; atty. pvt. practice, 1971—. Mem.: ABA. Democrat. Mem. Ch. Of Christ. Criminal, Family and matrimonial, Personal injury (including property damage). Office: Pky Towers Ste 1814 404 James Robertson Pky Nashville TN 37219

GROSS, MARVIN SAMUEL, lawyer; b. Pasadena, Calif., Dec. 24, 1951; s. Leonard Edward and Ruth (Nadler) G.; m. Rhonda Cavin, Sept. 30, 1989. BA, U. Calif., Irvine, 1974; JD, U. San Diego, 1977. Bar: Calif. 1977, Nev. 1978. Atty. Ashleman, Sabbath & Rohay, Las Vegas, Nev., 1977-79, State Indsl. Atty., Las Vegas, Nev., 1979-82, King, Clark, Gross & Sutcliffe, Las Vegas, Nev., 1982-94, King, Gross & Sutcliffe, Las Vegas, Nev., 1994—. Mem. ABA, Am. Trial Lawyers, Nev. Trial Lawyers (pres. 1993-94), Clark County Bar Assn. Workers' compensation. Office: King Gross & Sutcliffe 3017 W Charleston Blvd Ste 50 Las Vegas NV 89102-1987

GROSS, RICHARD BENJAMIN, lawyer; b. Santa Monica, Calif., Sept. 26, 1947; s. Edward L. and Adele P. Gross; m. Pamela McGovern, June 1, 1985; 1 child, Hannah McGovern. Student, UCLA, 1965-68; BA, U. Calif., Berkeley, 1970; JD, Harvard U., 1973; postgrad., Cambridge (Eng.) U., 1973-74. Bar: N.Y. 1975, U.S. Dist. Ct. (so. dist.) N.Y. 1975, U.S. Ct. Appeals (2d cir.) 1975, Ill. 1987. Assoc. White & Case, N.Y.C., 1974-77; assoc. counsel Am. Express Co., N.Y.C., 1977-82; sr. v.p., gen. counsel and sec. Citicorp Diners Club, Inc., Chgo., 1982-90; sr. v.p., gen. counsel Citicorp Ins. Group, Inc., N.Y.C., 1990-91; sr. v.p., gen. counsel, sec. Ambac Fin. Group, Inc., N.Y.C., 1991-98; mng. dir., gen. counsel U.S. Trust Corp., N.Y.C., 1998—2001. Bd. dirs. Randall's Island Sports Found., 1999—, sec., treas., 2000—. Mem. ABA (com. of corp. gen. counsel, com. on fed. regulation of securities, com. on banking), N.Y. State Bar Assn., Assn. of the Bar of the City of N.Y., Am. Soc. Internat. Law, Am. Soc. Corp. Secs., Am. Corp. Counsel Assn. Banking, Corporate, general, Securities. E-mail: richardbgross@aol.com.

GROSS, WOLFGANG, lawyer; b. Ulm, Germany, July 27, 1962; s. Guenther and Gunda Gross; m. Anne-Kathrin Kesnath; 1 child, Christopher Maximilian. Dr.jur., U. Kontanz, 1989. Bar: Frankfurt, Germany 1994. Asst. tchr. U. Konstanz, Germany, 1987—89; with legal dept. DG Bank Deutsche Genossenschaftsbank, Frankfurt, 1989—90; sr. counsel Deutsche Bank AG, 1991—2000; ptnr. Hengeler Mueller, 2001—. Author: Capital Markets Law, 2d edit., 2003; co-author: Underwriting Business, 2d edit., 2003, Stock-Corproation Law, 2003. Mem.: German Corp. Law Assn., Internat. Bar Assn., Assn. German Jurists. Corporate, general, Mergers and acquisitions, Securities. Office: Hengeler Mueller Bockenheimer Landstr 60325 Frankfurt Germany E-mail: wolfgang.gross@hengeler.com.

GROSSBERG, DAVID, lawyer; b. N.Y.C., Sept. 14, 1925; s. Meyer and Ethel Grossberg; m. Miriam Weissner, Mar. 22, 1959; children: Amy, Robert. BS, CCNY, 1947; LLB, Harvard U., 1950. Bar: N.Y. 1951. With Berlack, Israels & Liberman, N.Y.C., 1951-54, Cohen & Grossberg, N.Y.C., 1954—. Served with U.S. Army, 1943-45, ETO. Mem.: Assn. Bar of City of N.Y. Entertainment, General practice, Trademark and copyright. Office: Cohen & Grossberg 770 Lexington Ave New York NY 10021-8165

GROSSBERG, MARC ELIAS, lawyer; b. Houston, Dec. 26, 1940; s. Sylvester and Leah (Hochman) G.; m. Eva M. Wolski, Jan. 3, 1981; 1 child, Nicole; children from previous marriage: Lee Ann Krishnan, Toni Oreck. BS in Polit. Sci., U. Houston, 1961; JD with honors, U. Tex., 1965. Bar: Tex. 1965, Calif. 1966, Fla. 1980, U.S. Supreme Ct. 1980; bd. cert. fed. income taxation, Tex. Acct. Brochstein Toomim & Co CPAs (now Deloitte Touche), Houston, 1961-62; law clk. hon. Walter Ely U.S. Ct. Appeals (9th cir.), L.A., 1965-66; assoc. Fulbright & Jaworski, Houston, 1966-71; ptnr. Schlanger Mills Mayer & Grossberg, LLP, Houston, 1974-99, Thompson & Knight LLP, Houston, 1999—. Pres. Imprint, Inc., 2000—02, chmn. bd. dirs., 2002—. Articles editor: Tex. Law Rev. Advanceman, speech writer 1968 Hubert Humphry Presdl. Campaign; pres. Tex. Bill of Rights Found., Houston, 1971-72, Jewish Family Svc., Houston, 1986-87, U. Tex. Law Rev. Assn., Inprint, Inc., 2000-2002; commr. Housing Authority City of Houston, 1974-78. Mem. ABA (tax sect. and litig. sects.), Order of Coif. Democrat. Jewish. Avocations: family, writing, reading, exercise. Nonprofit and tax-exempt organizations, Corporate taxation, Taxation, general. Office: Thompson & Knight LLP Ste 3300 333 Clay St Houston TX 77002 E-mail: marc.grossberg@tklaw.com.

GROSSI, FRANCIS XAVIER, JR., lawyer, educator; b. Somerville, Mass., May 8, 1943; s. Francis Xavier and Angela Mary (LoGiudice) G.; m. Betty Morene Ballenger, May 12, 1962 (div. 1987); children: Francis Xavier III, Gina Maria, Andrea Mary, Cynthia Marie; m. Milada Dvorak, Dec. 31, 1987; children: Lukas Paolo, Anna Milada. BS, U. Mo., 1964; JD magna cum laude, U. Mich., 1967. Bar: D.C. 1968, U.S. Ct. Appeals (7th and 9th crcts.) 1969, U.S. Tax Ct. 1970, U.S. Ct. Appeals (4th crct.) 1972, U.S. Ct. Appeals (2d crct.) 1973, Ill. 1977. Appellate atty. U.S. Dept. Justice, Washington, 1967-69; assoc. Williams & Connolly, Washington, 1970-76; ptnr., chmn. litigation dept. Katten Muchin & Zavis, Chgo., 1977-95; ptnr. Bates, Meckler, Bulger & Tilson, Chgo., 1995—98; of counsel Studio Associato LCA, Padua, Italy, 1999—. Adj. prof. Loyola U. Law Sch., Chgo., 1979-81, DePaul Law Sch., Chgo., 1981-94; lectr. Grad. Sch., U. Padua, 2000—, Masaryk U. Law Sch., Brno, Czech Republic, 2001—; faculty Nat. Inst. Trial Advocacy, Chgo., 1989—; chmn. com. Chgo. Coun. Lawyers, 1991-92. Contbg. author: Survey Bankruptcy Law, 1981; author, editor (legal publ.) Evidence Practice Guide. Mem. Joint Civic com. Italian Ams., 1988; bd. dirs. Italian Am. Polit. Coalition, 1995-96; pres. Univ. Village Assn., Chgo., 1992-95. With USMCR, 1960. Fellow Am. Coll. Trial Lawyers; mem. Austrian Arbitration Soc., Order of Coif. Democrat. Roman Catholic. Avocations: writing, camping, workshop. General civil litigation. Home: Piazza del Sole 1/10 35031 Abano Terme PD Italy Office: Studio Associato LCA Galleria Borromeo 3 35137 Padova Italy E-mail: f.grossi@lca-studio.com.

GROSSMAN, CLAUDIO M. lawyer; b. Valparaiso, Chile, Nov. 26, 1947; came to U.S., 1982; s. David and Berta (Guiloff) G.; m. Irene Klinger, Aug. 14, 1971; children: Sandra, Nienke. DSc in Law, U. Amsterdam, The Netherlands, 1980; JD, U. Chile, 1971. Dean Washington Coll. Law. Mem. Inter-Am. Commn. on Human Rights, Washington, 1994—. Mem. Inter-Am. Bar Assn. (coun. 1989—). Home: 5011 Warren St NW Washington DC 20016-4371 Office: Stanford University Law School Dean's Office, Rm 200 Stanford CA 94305-8610*

GROSSMAN, DEBRA A. lawyer, real estate manager, radio talk show host; b. Cleve., July 29, 1951; d. Morris M. and Idelle R. (Bialosky) G. BA, Syracuse U., 1973; JD, Suffolk U., 1976. Bar: Mass. 1977, U.S. Dist. Ct. Mass. 1977. Sole practice, Lexington, Mass., 1977-79; ptnr. Kurland & Grossman, P.C., Lowell, Mass., 1979-94; property mgr. KD Mgmt. Co., Lowell, 1983—94, Chelmsford, Mass., 1994—; talk show host "Legal Briefs" WCCM Radio, Lawrence, Mass., 1989-97. Lectr. Greater Lowell Alzheimers Assn., 1987; vice chair Lowell Hist. Bd., 1995—97, chair, 1997—2001; mem. corp. adv. bd. Suitability, Inc., 2001—; Bd. dirs. Downtown Lowell Bus. Assn., 1987. Mem. Mass. Assn. Women Lawyers (asst. treas. 1981-82, bd. dirs. 1979-81), Mass. Bar Assn. (mem. family law sect.), Mass. Acad. Trial Lawyers, Greater Lowel Bar Assn. (bd. dirs. 1993-96, Lawyer for the Day program dir. 1990-92), Syracuse U. Alumni Club, Greater Boston Club, Assn. Trial Lawyers Am., Mass. Family and Probate Am. Inn Ct. General civil litigation, Family and matrimonial, Personal injury (including property damage). Office: Kurland & Grossman PC 139 Billerica Rd Chelmsford MA 01824-3619 E-mail: dgrossman@nrmail.com.

GROSSMAN, JEROME KENT, lawyer, accountant; b. St. Louis, Apr. 15, 1953; s. Marvin and Myra Lee (Barnholtz) G.; m. Debbie Ada Kogan, Aug. 7, 1977; children: Hannah Felicia, Marni Celeste. AB cum laude, Georgetown U., 1974, JD, 1977. Bar: Mo. 1977, D.C. 1978, U.S. Ct. Claims 1979, U.S. Tax Ct. 1979, Del. 1980, U.S. Dist. Ct. Del. 1982; CPA, Mo. Acct., controller U.S. Dept. State, Washington, 1974-77; acct. Arthur Andersen & Co., St. Louis, 1977-79; mem. firm Bayard, Handelman and Murdoch, P.A., Wilmington, Del., 1979-88; ptnr. Young Conaway Stargatt & Taylor LLP, Wilmington, 1988—. Co-author: ALI-ABA Course of Study on the Reform Act of 1984, 86. V.p. Jewish Cmty. Ctr., Wilmington, 1986—88, 1989—90, treas., 1989—90; trustee Milton & Hattie Kutz Found., 2001—, Harry Cohen Found., 2002—; bd. dirs. Congregation Beth Shalom, Wilmington, 1985—, pres., 1990—92; treas. Jewish Fedn. Del., 1989—90; pres. Del. Gratz Hebrew H.S., 1997—2000, trustee, 1995—, Jewish. Com. of Del. Endowment Fund., 1988—95; co-chmn. Del. State Com. State of Israel Bonds, 1992—95, chmn., 1995—2000; bd. dirs., trustee Del. Symphony Assn., 1998—, vice chmn., 1999—2001. Fellow: Am. Coll. Tax Counsel; mem.: AICPA (mem. coun. 2000—01), ABA (chmn. inventories subcom. 1982—86, vice chmn. 1986—88, chmn. 1988—90, tax sect., com. on tax acctg.), Del. Soc. CPAs (chmn. tax com. 1980—85, coun. 1985—87, ethics com. 1989—92, coun. 1993—2002, pres. 2000—01), Del. Tax Inst. (planning com. 1985—86, 1994—), Del. Bar Assn. (chair sect. of taxation 1996—97), Alpha Sigma Nu. Democrat. Avocations: choir, opera, bridge. Estate planning, Corporate taxation, Taxation, general. Home: 803 Westover Rd Wilmington DE 19807-2978 Office: Young Conaway Stargatt & Taylor LLP PO Box 391 Wilmington DE 19899-0391 E-mail: jgrossman@ycst.com.

GROSSMAN, ROBERT LOUIS, lawyer; b. Cleve., Dec. 20, 1954; s. Sidney and Lillian Belle (Davis) G.; m. Rochelle Carol Shear, Nov. 7, 1987; children: Zachary, Jonathan, David, Andrew. BA with honors, Ohio State U., 1975, JD with Honors, 1978, MA with honors, 1979. Bar: Ohio 1978, U.S. Ct. Appeals (5th cir.) 1979, Fla. 1982. Law clk. U.S. Dist. Ct. (so. dist.) Ohio, Columbus, 1977-78; sr. atty. U.S. Govt. EEOC, Houston, 1979-82; shareholder Greenberg, Traurig, P.A., Miami, 1982—. Editor: Florida Corporate Practice, 2d edit., 1991. Chmn. South Dade Jewish Leadership Coun., 1997-99; bd. dirs. Greater Miami Jewish Fedn. South Dade, Miami, 1987—, campaign chmn., 1995-97; bd. dirs. Greater Miami Jewish Fedn., 1995—, exec. com., 1997-99, Alper Jewish Comm. Ctr., 1997-2000, exec. com., 1998-2000; bd. dirs. Children's Bereavement Ctr., 2000—, Orgn. Leadership Advancement Miami, 2001-; chmn. Exec. Inst. OLAM, 2001-; Beacon coun., 2000—; chmn. Exec. Inst. for Orgn. for Leadership Advancement in Miami, 2001-03; chmn. Fedn. Agy., Day Sch. and Synagogue Campaign, 2003—; bd. dirs. Temple Beth Am., 2003—. Donald Becker Meml. scholar Ohio State U., 1975, 76, fellow, 1978; Robert Russell fellow Greater Miami Jewish Fedn., 1998; recipient Stanley C. Myers Young Leadership award Greater Miami Jewish Fedn., 1999, Put Something Back Cmty. award, 2003. Mem. ABA (corp. securities sect.), Fla. Bar Assn., Dade County Bar Assn., Order of Coif. Avocations: sports, reading, travel. Corporate, general, Mergers and acquisitions, Securities. Office: Greenberg Traurig 1221 Brickell Ave Miami FL 33131-3224

GROSSMAN, THEODORE MARTIN, lawyer; b. N.Y.C., Dec. 31, 1949; s. Albert and Sylvia Pia (Greenstein) G.; m. Linda Gail Steinbook, Dec. 5, 1976; children: Andrew Scott, Michael Steven. AB, Cornell U., 1971, JD, 1974. Bar: N.Y. 1975, U.S. Ct. Appeals (D.C. cir.) 1981, U.S. Ct. Appeals (2nd cir.) 1982, U.S. Ct. Appeals (5th cir.) 1984, U.S. Dist. Ct. (no. dist.) Ohio 1986, Ohio 1987, U.S. Dist. Ct. (so. dist.) N.Y. 1988, U.S. Dist. Ct. (ea. dist.) N.Y. 1988, U.S. Ct. Appeals (6th cir.) 1988. Assoc. Debevoise, Plimpton, Lyons & Gates, N.Y.C., 1974-77, Rosenman Colin Freund Lewis & Cohen, N.Y.C., 1977-80; trial and appellate counsel fed. programs br. of civil div. U.S. Dept. Justice, Washington, 1980-84; assoc. Jones Day, Cleve., 1984-86, ptnr., 1987—. Editor Cornell U. Law Rev., 1974. Trustee Cleve. Ctr. for Contemporary Art, 1992-96, treas., 1992-94. Fellow Am. Coll. Trial Lawyers; mem. ABA. General civil litigation. Home: 2979 Broxton Rd Cleveland OH 44120-1819 Office: Jones Day 901 Lakeside Ave E Cleveland OH 44114-1190 E-mail: tgrossman@jonesday.com.

GROSSMAN, VICTOR G. lawyer; b. N.Y.C., Nov. 21, 1951; s. Jacob and Frances (Gaezer) Grossman; m. Jamie Williams, Apr. 8, 1984; children: Robert William, Sarah Frances. BA in Am. Studies with honors, Brandeis U., 1973; JD, Hofstra U., 1978. Bar: NY 1979, US Dist Ct (so and ea dists) NY 1980, US Supreme Ct 1984. Pvt. practice, White Plains, N.Y., 1979-82; atty. Aurnou Kurzman Midler & Friedman, White Plains, 1982-87; pvt. practice Carmel, N.Y., 1987—. Mem zoning bd appeals Town of Southeast , Brewster, NY, 1989—91, dep supr, 1994—96; legislator Putnam County Legis, Carmel, 1990—92. State civil litigation, Criminal, Family and matrimonial. Home: 40 Seven Oaks Ln Brewster NY 10509-1610 Office: Nine Fair St Carmel NY 10512-1213

GROSSMANN, RONALD STANYER, lawyer; b. Chgo., Nov. 9, 1944; s. Andrew Eugene and Gladys M. Grossmann; m. Jo Ellen Hanson, May 11, 1968; children: Kenneth Frederick, Emilie Beth. BA, Northwestern U., 1966; JD, U. Mich., 1969. Bar: Oreg., 1969. Law clk. Oreg. Supreme Ct., Salem, 1969-70; assoc. Stoel Rives LLP, Portland, Oreg., 1970-76, ptnr., 1976—. Mem.: Am. Coll. Employee Benefits Counsel, Oreg. Bar Assn., ABA. Corporate, general, Pension, profit-sharing, and employee benefits, Personal income taxation. Office: Stoel Rives LLP 900 SW 5th Ave Ste 2600 Portland OR 97204-1268 E-mail: rsgrossmann@stoel.com.

GROVE, JACK FREDERICK, lawyer, educator; b. Hamilton, Ohio, Aug. 31, 1953; s. James Edward and Eleanor Katherine (Schlichter) G.; m. Susan Kathleen Flick, July 24, 1976; 1 child, Adam Nathaniel. B.S. in Agr., Ohio State U., 1975; J.D., U. Dayton, 1979. Bar: Ohio 1979, U.S. Dist. Ct. (so. dist.) Ohio 1979, U.S. Supreme Ct. 1984. Law clk. to Judge Fred B. Cramer, Hamilton, Ohio, 1979-80; asst. pros. atty. Butler County, Hamilton, 1980-87 ; instr. fin. Miami U., Oxford, Ohio, 1981-84; ptnr. Grove & Marre, Fairfield, Ohio, 1979-87; sole practice, Fairfield, 1988—; bd. dir. adv. council Hamilton Tool Co., 1982-86. Mem. exec. com. Butler County Reps., Hamilton, Ohio, 1980-81; propr. Copper Fox Stables, Silverwood Farm. Mem. ABA, OhioState Bar Assn., Butler County Bar Assn., Cin. Bar Assn., Sierra Club, Nat. Snaffle Bit Assn. (area dir. 1989), Am. Quarter Horse Assn. (Decade Svc. recognition), Ohio Quarter Horse Assn. (sec. 1997-98), Ky. Cols., Gamma Sigma Delta. Republican. State civil litigation, Land use and zoning (including planning), Property, real (including real estate development, water). Home: 7006 Fairfield Rd Oxford OH 45056-8817 Office: 1251 Nilles Rd Ste 10 Fairfield OH 45014-7205

GROVER, DOUGLAS E. lawyer; b. Bklyn., May 11, 1950; s. Perry and Harriet (Steinberg) G.; m. Emily Jackness, Aug. 25, 1984; children: Sarah, Jenny. BA, Colgate U., 1972; JD, Bklyn. Law Sch., 1975. Bar: N.Y. 1976, U.S. Dist. Ct. (ea. and so. dists.) N.Y. 1976, U.S. Ct. Appeals (2d cir.) 1976, U.S. Supreme Ct. 1978. Asst. Kings County Dist. Atty., Bklyn., 1980-90; spl. atty. Organized Crime Strike Force, U.S. Dept. Justice, Bklyn., 1990—2003; ptnr. Thompson Hine LLP, 2003—. Mem. City Island Yacht Club. Commercial, contracts (including sales of goods; commercial financing), Criminal. Office: Thompson Hine LLP One Chase Manhattan Plz 58th Fl New York NY 10005-1401

GROVES, STEPHEN PETERSON, SR., lawyer; b. Charleston, SC, June 4, 1956; s. George Francis Jr. and Helen (Peterson) G.; m. Amy B. Rothschild; children: Danel, Joshua, Stephen Jr., Sumter. BA, Coll. Charleston, 1979; JD, U. S.C., 1986. Bar: S.C. 1986, U.S. Dist. Ct. S.C. 1987, U.S. Ct. Appeals (4th cir.) 1987, U.S. Supreme Ct. 1990, U.S. Ct. Appeals (7th, 11th, Fed. cirs.) 1991, U.S. Ct. Appeals (5th, 6th and 9th cirs.) 1993, U.S. Ct. Appeals (10th cir.) 1996. Asst. to city planner Charleston Dept. Planning and Urban Devel., 1976-77; asst. to legal coordinator Neighborhood Legal Asst. Program, Charleston, 1978; police officer, detective Charleston County Police Dept., 1980-83; law clk. to dean U. S.C. Law Sch., 1983-86; assoc. Young, Clement, Rivers & Tisdale, Charleston, 1986-91, ptnr., 1991—2003; spl. coun. Nexsen, Pruett, Jacobs, Pollard & Robinson, LLC. Contbg. editor S.C. Civil Procedure, 1985, Domestic Relations in South Carolina, 1986, ABA Tips Property Insurance Law Subcommittee-Annotations Standard, Fire and Extended Coverage, 1994, Coverage Litigation Insurance, 1998, others. Mem. ATLA, ABA (co-editor ABA-YLD Arson Reporter 1988-90, ABA TIPS Comml. Torts Newsletter 1991—, chair ABA TIPS bus. torts com. 1997—, vice chair ABA TIPS appellate adv. com. 1994—, vice chair ABA TIPS civil procedure and evidence com. 1994—), Internat. Bar Assn., S.C. Bar (ethics adv. com. 1995—, profl. responsibility com. 1995—), Charleston County Bar Assn., Am. Judicature Soc., S.C. Def. Trial Lawyers Assn. (amicus curaie brief com. 1990—), Libel Def. Resource Ctr. (contbg. editor 50-state ann. survey), Def. Rsch. Inst., Christian Legal Soc., Sigma Nu, Pi Sigma Alpha, Omicron Delta Kappa. Republican. Roman Catholic. Avocations: sports, coaching. General civil litigation, Insurance, Utilities, public. Office: Nexsen Pruett Jacobs Pollard & Robinson LLC 205 King St Ste 400 Charleston SC 29401 E-mail: sgroves@npjp.com.

GRUBE, KARL BERTRAM, judge; b. Elmhurst, Ill., Jan. 13, 1946; s. Karl Ludwig and Gerturde (Bertram) G.; m. Mary B. Harr, May 4, 1974 (div. Aug. 1991); m. Julia Ross, Dec. 28, 1998. BSBA, Elmhurst Coll., 1967; JD, Stetson U., 1970; M in Judicial Studies, U. Nev., 1992. Asst. pub. defender State of Fla., Clearwater, 1970-73, county ct. judge St. Petersburg, 1977—; pvt. practice Seminole, Fla., 1973-76; city atty. City of Redington Beach, Fla., 1975-76. Asst. dean Fla. Jud. Coll., Tallahassee, 1984-85; faculty mem., course coord., mem. faculty coun. Nat. Jud. Coll., chair faculty coun., 2000—; mem. Nat. Hwy. Traffic Safety Jud. Tng. Implementation Bd. Contbr. articles to profl. jours. Dir. Pinellas Comprehensive Addiction Svcs., Clearwater, 1982-88. Jud. fellow U.S. Dept. Transp., 1998, Nat. Hwy. Traffic Safety Adminstn., 1999. Mem. ABA (conf. chmn. divsn. jud. adminstrn. 1992, del. to jud. divsn. coun. 1997—, Dedicated Svc. award 1991), Fla. Bar Assn. (civil rule com.), Colo. Bar Assn., Fla. Conf. County Ct. Judges (pers. com. 1984-85), Rolls Royce Owner's Club (editor 1982-84). Lutheran. Avocations: collecting fountain pens, collecting antique watches, auto restoration. Office: Pinellas County Ct 501 1st Ave N Ste A212 Saint Petersburg FL 33701-3732

GRUEN, MICHAEL STEPHAN, lawyer; b. L.A., Mar. 25, 1942; s. Victor and Elsie Caroline (Krummeck) G.; m. Susanna Lloyd, July 18, 1964; m. Vanessa Elisabeth Ahlfors, Jan. 3, 1976; children: Madeleine Gruen, Alexis Cutchins, Viveca Gruen; stepchildren: Stefan Keneas, Sebastian Keneas. BA cum laude, Harvard U., 1963; LLB, UCLA, 1966. Bar: Calif. 1966, N.Y. 1967, U.S. Ct. Appeals (2d cir.) 1976, U.S. Supreme Ct. 1975, U.S. Dist. Ct. (so. and ea. dists.) N.Y. 1986. Assoc. Paul, Weiss, Rifkind, Wharton & Garrison, N.Y.C., 1966-69, Gilinsky, Stillman & Mishkin, N.Y.C., 1969-70, Wolf, Popper, Ross, Wolf & Jones, N.Y.C., 1970-74; gen. counsel Bio-Med. Scis., Inc., Fairfield, N.J., 1974-75; pvt. practice N.Y.C., 1975-80; mem. Gruen & Muskin, N.Y.C., 1980, Gruen, Muskin & Thau, N.Y.C., 1981-88, Gruen, Gilliatt & Livingston, N.Y.C., 1989-90, Gruen & Livingston, N.Y.C., 1990-97, Gruen & Farrelly LLP, N.Y.C., 1998—2001; counsel Vandenberg & Feliu, LLP, 2002—. Contbr. articles to legal and gen. publs. Chmn. Historic Dists. Coun., 1974—79; dir. Learning Through an Expanded Arts Program, 2001—; mem. bd. advisors Prep divsn. Bklyn. Coll. Ctr. for Performing Arts, 1980—83; mem. law com. Mcpl. Art Soc., 1987—; pres. Riverside Dems., N.Y.C., 1971—72; bd. dirs. Columbia Land Conservancy, 1986—2002, pres., 1988—91; bd. dirs. N.Y. Landmarks Conservancy, 1972—94, mem. adv. coun., 1994—97; dir. Abingdon Theatre Co. N.Y., 2001—; bd. dirs. Boys' Athletic League, 1966—82. Mem. ABA (litig. sect.), N.Y. State Bar Assn., Assn. of Bar of City of N.Y. General civil litigation, Constitutional, Corporate, general. Office: Ste 1502 110 E 42nd St New York NY 10017-8521 E-mail: mgruen@vanfeliu.com.

GRUENBERG, MAX F., JR., lawyer; b. San Francisco, Sept. 25, 1943; m. Kayla Epstein; children: Bruce Leonard, Daniel Suchanan. BA, Stanford U., 1965; JD, UCLA, 1970. Bar: Alaska 1970, U.S. Supreme Ct. 1980. Pvt. practice, Anchorage, 1974—; ptnr. Gruenberg & Clover, Anchorage, 1984—. Mem. Alaska Ho. of Reps., 1985-92, 2003-, Ho. Majority Leader, 1987-88, 91-92. Fellow Am. Acad. Matrimonial Lawyers. Appellate, Family and matrimonial, Legislative. Office: Gruenberg Clover & Holland 880 H St Ste 201 Anchorage AK 99501-3450

GRUENBERGER, PETER, lawyer; b. Czechoslovakia, May 19, 1937; came to U.S., 1941; s. Leslie and Olga (Zollman) G.; m. Carin Lamm; children: Karen, Richard, Lauren. AB, Columbia U., 1958, LLB, 1961. Bar: N.Y. 1962, U.S. Dist. Ct. (so., ea. and no. dists.) N.Y. 1962, U.S. Ct. Appeals (1st and 2d cirs.) 1963, U.S. Supreme Ct. 1964. Assoc. Hughes, Hubbard & Reed, N.Y.C., 1962-69; ptnr. Weil, Gotshal & Manges, N.Y.C., 1970—, mng. ptnr. Tex. office Houston, 1988-90. Contbr. articles on litigation to profl. jours. Served as 1st lt. U.S. Army, 1961-62. Harlan Fiske Stone scholar, 1959-61. Mem. ABA (chmn. various coms. 1973-75, 79-86, spl. com. on class actions and discovery 1977-86, governing council 1975-78, litigation sect.), Assn. of Bar of City of N.Y. (grievance com. 1975-77). Property, real (including real estate development, water). Office: Weil Gotshal & Manges 767 5th Ave Fl Concl New York NY 10153-0119

GRUENDER, RAYMOND W. prosecutor; BA, MBA, JD, Washington U. Assoc. Lewis, Rice and Fingersh, 1987—90; asst. US atty. Eastern Dist. , Mo., 1990—94, Eastern Dist., Mo., 2000; ptnr. Thompson Coburn, 1994—2000; US Atty. Eastern Dist., Mo. Office: Thomas F Eagelton US Courthouse 111 S St Rm 20 Saint Louis MO 63102 Office Fax: 314-539-2309.

GRUND, JAMES ARTHUR, lawyer; b. Logansport, Ind., Jan. 8, 1919; s. Arthur Mack Grund and Charlotte Lillian (Crismond) Grund Guthrie; m. Constance Hurst, June 27, 1942; children: James H, Jeffrey A., Jane Anne. LLB, Ind. U., 1949. Bar: Ind. 1949, U.S. Supreme Ct. 1973. Ptnr. Fern Grund & Grund, Peru, Ind.; judge City of Peru, 1960-68; dep. prosecutor Miami County (Ind.), Peru, 1968-70, 79-82, pros. atty., 1970-79. Chmn. fund drive Miami County United Fund, Peru, 1963; mem. adv. bd. Salvation Army, Peru, 1955-85. Served as sgt. USAAF, 1941-45, CBI. Mem. Miami County Bar Assn. (past pres.), Am. Legion, Elks, Sigma Alpha Epsilon. Republican. Commercial, contracts (including sales of goods; commercial financing), Criminal, Probate (including wills, trusts). Home: 126 E Main St Peru IN 46970-2338 Office: Fern Grund & Grund 2 1/2 N Broadway Ste 200 Peru IN 46970-0670

GRUNFELD, DAVID I. lawyer; b. Phila., June 23, 1943; s. Joseph and Beatrice R. (Shoenfeld) G.; m. Sandra S. Grunfeld, June 26, 1966; children: Eric, Ken. BS, Lehigh U., 1965; JD, U. Pa., 1968. Bar: Pa. 1968, U.S. Dist. Ct. (ea. dist.) Pa. 1968, U.S. Supreme Ct. 1972. Assoc. Steinberg, Greenstein, Richman & Price, Phila., 1968-72; ptnr. Steinberg, Greenstein, Gorelick & Price, Phila., 1972-82, Bluestein, Rutstein & Mirarchi (also predecessor firms), Phila., 1982-86, Rosenwald, Pollack & Grunfeld, Phila., 1986-89; of counsel Gratz, Tate, Spiegel, Ervin & Ruthrauff, Phila., 1989-92; sole pratitioner, 1992—. Bd. dirs. Jewish Family & Children's Agy., Phila., 1986—, Family Svcs. of Montgomery County, 1997—, Meth. Svcs. for Children and Famlies, 1997—. Mem. ABA (family law sect.), Phila. Bar Assn. (family law sect. exec. com. 1982-88, editor-in-chief newsletter 1988-90, sec. 1990, treas. 1991, vice chair 1992, chair 1993), Pa. Bar Assn. (family law sect.), Comml. Law League Am., Ea. Dist. Bankruptcy Conf., NOW, Phila. Jaycees (pres. 1975-76), Tau Epsilon Rho. Democrat. Jewish. Bankruptcy, Commercial, consumer (including collections, credit), Family and matrimonial. Office: 21 S 12th St 9th Fl Philadelphia PA 19107-4114 Office Fax: 215-665-8063. E-mail: dgrunfeld@rcn.com.

GRUSH, JULIUS SIDNEY, lawyer; b. Los Angeles, Dec. 4, 1937; children: Robin, Randi, Ronna, Rodney. BS, UCLA, 1960; postgrad., U. Calif., San Francisco, 1960-62; LLB, Southwestern U., 1964. Bar: Calif. 1965. Dep. city atty. City of Los Angeles, 1965-67; sole practice Los Angeles, 1967—. Prof. Bar-Bri Harcourt Brace Pubs. Bar Course, Los Angeles, 1986—. Pres. Lockhurst Booster Club; mem. City of Hope (past pres.). Mem. ABA, Los Angeles Bar Assn., Beverly Hills Bar Assn., Century City Bar Assn., Phi Alpha Delta. Republican. State civil litigation, Corporate, general, Property, real (including real estate development, water). Office: 1900 Avenue of the Stars Fl 25 Los Angeles CA 90067-4301

GRUTMAN, JEWEL HUMPHREY, lawyer, writer; b. N.Y.C., Mar. 13, 1931; d. Robert and Gladys Humphrey; m. Robert W. Bjork, June 26, 1954 (div. Apr. 22, 1975); 1 child, Bruce Bjork; m. Roy Grutman, Oct. 30, 1975 (wid. 1994); m. Fredrick Yonkman, July 4, 1998. BA magna cum laude, Mt. Holyoke Coll., 1952; LLB, Columbia U., 1955. Bar: N.Y., U.S. Dist. Ct. (So. Dist.) N.Y. 1971, U.S. Dist. Ct. (ea. dist.) N.Y. 1974, U.S. Dist. Ct. Conn. 1984, U.S. Supreme Ct. 1984. Atty. Debevoise & Plimpton, N.Y.C., 1954-60; ptnr. Eaton Van Winkle, N.Y.C., 1976-79, Grutman Greene & Humphrey, N.Y.C., 1979—. Co-author: (with CD-ROM) The Ledgerbook of Thomas Blue Eagle, 1994 (Christopher award 1995, Internat. Reading Assn. award), The Sketchbook of Thomas Blue Eagle, 2001, (CD-ROM) The Journey of Thomas Blue Eagle, 1995 (Best Project award Intermedia, Asia, 1995, Creative NGee ANN Disting. award 1995, EMMA award best visual content 1996); asst. prodr., editor (ednl. film on art) Where Time is a River (1st prize Women's Film Festival); contbr. photograph illustrations: The Reforming Power of the Scriptures, 1996; developer series of designs based on Native Am. art; contbr. articles to mags. and newspapers. Dir. Inwood Ho., N.Y.C., 1970-80; past mem. various coms. Mt. Holyoke Coll.; mem. com. sr. advisors N.Y. Commn. for Internat. Bus. and UN, 1997; past chmn. com. to establish Barbara Black Fellowship at Columbia U. Law Sch.; past pres. 85th St. Playground Assn., N.Y.C.; active supporter The Children's Storefront, Harlem, N.Y.C., N.Y. Jr. League. Mem. Assn. Bar City N.Y., The Stanwich Club (Greenwich, Conn.). Avocations: opera, golf, tennis, poetry. Federal civil litigation, Constitutional, Libel. E-mail: bijou203@optonline.net.

GRZEZINSKI, DENNIS MICHAEL, lawyer; b. Sheboygan, Wis., Jan. 4, 1950; s. Donald Joseph and Elfrieda Elizabeth (Walz) G.; m. Jane Porath, May 14, 1988. AB, Princeton U., 1972; JD, Yale U., 1975. Bar: Wis. 1975. Law clk. to judge U.S. Dist. Ct., Milw., 1975-77; assoc. Frisch Dudek Ltd., Milw., 1977-81, also bd. dirs., 1981-91; pvt. practice law Milw., 1991—. Bd. dirs. Midwest Environ. Advocates INc., 2000—. Commr. Milw. Met. Sewage Dist., 1989-98, 99—, chmn., 1991-92, 2003—, vice chair, 1993-94; sec., treas. Vocat. Edn. Alternative Milw., Inc., 1985-90; pres. bd. dirs. Wis. Civil Liberties Union, Milw., 1983-85, sec., 1985-89; bd. dirs. Legal Action Wis., Inc., Milw., 1982-90; pres. bd. dirs. Urban Ecology Ctr., Milw., 2000—. Named Mem. of Yr., Wis. Civil Liberties Union, 1986. Mem. ABA, State Bar Wis. (bd. dirs. environ. law sect. 1991—), Milw. Bar Assn. (co-chair environ. law sect. 1992-93), Assn. Trial Lawyers Am., Wis. Acad. Trial Lawyers. Avocations: photography, hiking, camping, reading, gardening. Federal civil litigation, State civil litigation, Environmental. Home: 3025 N Farwell Ave Milwaukee WI 53211-3307 Office: 312 E Wisconsin Ave Ste 210 Milwaukee WI 53202-4305 E-mail: dennisglaw@execpc.com.

GUARINI, FRANK JOSEPH, lawyer, real estate developer; b. Jersey City, N.J., Aug. 20, 1924; s. Frank J. G., Sr. and Caroline Loretta Critelli. BA, Dartmouth Coll., 1946; JD, NYU, 1950, LLM, 1955; LHD (hon.), St. Peter's Coll., 1994; DLitt (hon.), N.J. City U., 1993. Bar: N.J. 1951, D.C. 1994, N.Y. 1995. Sr. ptnr. Guarini & Guarini, Jersey City, N.J., 1951—; senator State of N.J., Trenton, 1966-73; mem. Ho. of Reps., Washington, 1979-93; U.S. rep. UN Gen. Assembly, 1995—96. Bd. dirs. John Cabot U., Rome, 1994—; founder Guarini Ctr. for Govtl. Affairs St. Peter's Coll., Jersey City, N.J., 1994—; bd. dirs. Washington Ctr. for Interns, 1993-96, The New Cmty. Found., Newark, 1993-94; pres., chmn. Nat. Italian Am. Found., 1999—; rep. U.S. UN, N.Y.C., 1997-98; alumni trustee Hague (The Netherlands) Acad. Internat. Law, 1956-60. Fellow ABA; mem. Am. Trial Lawyers Assn. (nat. bd. govs. 1975-78), N.J. State Bar Assn. (mem. gen. coun. 1960-63), N.Y. Athletic Club. Democrat. Roman Catholic. Avocations: skiing, tennis, archeology, travel. Property, real (including real estate development, water), Taxation, general, Trademark and copyright. Office: Guarini & Guarini 30 Montgomery St Ste 15 Jersey City NJ 07302-3821 Fax: 201-938-1503. E-mail: gsdinc@msn.com.

GUBITS, DAVID BARRY, lawyer; b. New Brighton, Pa., July 12, 1941; s. Harry William and Florence Leonore (Weiner) G.; m. Ruth Miriam Farkas, Apr. 11, 1965; children: Jonathan, Daniel. AB, Brown U., 1963; JD, NYU, 1966. Bar: N.Y. 1967, U.S. Dist. Ct. (no. dist.) N.Y. 1967, U.S. Ct. Appeals (2nd cir.) 1969, U.S. Dist. Ct. (so. and ea. dists.) N.Y. 1977, U.S. Supreme Ct. 1978. Assoc. Appellate Div. 3rd Dept., Albany, N.Y., 1966-68, Gerald N. Jacobowitz, Walden, N.Y., 1967-72; ptnr. Jacobowitz & Gubits, LLP., Walden, 1973—. Dep. atty. Village of Washingtonville (N.Y.), 1973—, Village of Highland Falls (N.Y.), 1976—, Village of Maybrook (N.Y.), 1983—; mem. adv. coun. Stewart Airport Land Authority, New Windsor, N.Y., 1972-81; pres. UJA/Fedn. Rockland County, 1991-92, exec. bd., 1988—. Mem. N.Y. State Bar Assn. (land use control com. 1979-81, real estate devel. com. 1982-84, real estate fin. com. 2000--, atty. opinion letters com. 2000--), ABA (fed. grants com. 1979-84, banking law com. 2000--), Orange County Bar Assn. (chmn. continuing legal edn. com. 1979-80), Mohonk Preserve (land protection com., 2001—), John Burroughs Soc., Maverick Concerts (trustee, 2002—). Avocations: wilderness canoeing, history. Commercial, contracts (including sales of goods; commercial financing), General practice, Property, real (including real estate development, water). Home: PO Box 162 Stone Ridge NY 12484 Office: Jacobowitz & Gubits LLP 158 Orange Ave PO Box 367 Walden NY 12586-0367 E-mail: dbg@jacobowitz.com.

GUBLER, JOHN GRAY, lawyer; b. Las Vegas, June 16, 1942; s. V. Gray and Loreta N. (Newton) G.; m. Mollie Boyle, Jan. 10, 1987; 1 child, J. Gray; children from previous marriage: Laura, Matthew. BA, U. Calif.-Berkeley, 1964; JD, U. Utah, 1971; LLM in Taxation, NYU, 1973. Bar: Nev. 1971, U.S. Dist. Ct. Nev. 1973, U.S. Tax Ct. 1974, U.S. Ct. Appeals (9th cir.) 1978. Dep. pub. defender Clark County, Nev., 1973-74; ptnr. Gubler & Gubler, Las Vegas, 1974-88, ptnr. Gubler and Peters, Las Vegas, 1989—; instr. continuing edn. community coll. Served with U.S. Army, 1966-68. Mem. Clark County Bar Assn., ABA, State Bar of Nev. (disciplinary com. 1979-88), Las Vegas-Paradise Rotary (pres. 1981-82), Knife & Fork Club (pres. 1978-80). Ch of Jesus Christ of Latter Day Saints. Estate planning, Probate (including wills, trusts). Office: Gubler & Peters 302 E Carson Ave Ste 601 Las Vegas NV 89101-5989

GUDAITIS, CHRISTY MYERS, lawyer; b. Louisville, Ky., Sept. 27, 1959; d. Frank R. and Mary (Helm) Myers; m. James Victor Gudaitis. AB, Duke U., 1981, JD, 1986. Bar: N.C. 1986. Assoc. Hureton & Williams, Raleigh, NC, 1986—87; assoc., ptnr. Smith Helm Mulliss & Moore, Charlotte, NC, 1987—94; sr. corp. counsel Carolinas Healthcare Sys., Charlotte, 1994—99; asst. couns. Duke U., Durham, NC, 1999—. Health, Corporate, general, Mergers and acquisitions. Office: Duke University 2400 Pratt St Ste 4000 Durham NC 27710

GUDE, NANCY CARLSON, lawyer; b. Kane, Pa., Aug. 5, 1948; d. Edward Walter and Theo Alberta (Herzog) Carlson. BA in History, Pa. State U., 1969; MS in Computer Sci., U. Central Fla., 1981; JD, Thomas M. Cooley Law Sch., 2001. Bar: Fla. 2001. Programmer Group Hospitalization, Inc., Washington, 1969-70; programmer analyst Space Age Computer Sys., Washington, 1970-73, Ky. Fried Chicken, Louisville, 1973-75; sys. analyst Sentinel Comm. Co., Orlando, Fla., 1975-77, programming supr., 1977-78, sys. and programming mgr., 1978-80, asst. dir. data processing, 1980-81, mgr. staff devel., 1981-82; mgmt. info. svcs. mgr. Sun-Sentinel Co., Ft. Lauderdale, Fla., 1982-83, v.p., dir. info. sys., 1983-94, sys. cons., 1994-98; assoc. atty. Walton Lantaff Schroeder & Carson, Ft. Lauderdale, 2002—. Adj. instr. U. Ctrl. Fla., Orlando, 1981—82. Participant Leadership Broward X; chair LBX Artserve Intervention Group. Recipient Thomas M. Cooley Leadership Achievement award, 2001. Mem.: Pa. State U. (Ft. Lauderdale chpt., treas. 1990—92, v.p. 1992—93, pres. 1993—95). Presbyterian. Home: 1101 River Reach Dr Apt 216 Fort Lauderdale FL 33315-1177

GUDEMAN, LEROY DENNIS, lawyer; b. Francesville, Ind., May 25, 1926; s. Joseph Benjamin and Hulda (Getz) G.; children: Jay, Jerry, Mary Ann, Thomas, Andrew, Susan; m. Kay Crecelius, July 21, 1990. AB, Ind. U., 1950, JD, 1954. Bar: Ind. 1954, U.S. Dist. Ct. (no. and so. dists.) Ind. 1954. Pvt. practice, Knox, Ind., 1957--. Pres. Starke County Fine Arts Commn., Knox, 1986--. Cpl. U.S. Army, 1955-57. Mem. ABA, Ind. State Bar Assn., Starke-Pulaski Bar Assn. (pres. 1982-84), Kiwanis (pres. Knox chpt. 1967-68). Republican. Avocations: golf, fishing. Probate (including wills, trusts), Property, real (including real estate development, water). Home: 1021 W 50 S Knox IN 46534-9467 Office: 14 E Washington St Knox IN 46534-1147

GUDINO PELAYO, JOSE DE JESUS, judge; b. Mexico, June 6, 1943; Grad., U. Iberoamericana de Mexico, 1972. Magistrate Collegiate Cir. Ct., 1984—95; min. Supreme Ct. Justice, Mexico City, 1995—. Office: Suprema Corte de Justicia de la Nacion Pino Suarez No 2 Door 403 3rd Fl Col Centro 06065 Mexico City Mexico

GUEHL, ROBERT LEE, lawyer; b. Troy, Ohio, Dec. 2, 1946; s. John Joseph and Lucille (Spires) G.; m. Martha T. Thierwechter, Sept. 25, 1971 (div. Aug. 1981); children: Heidi, Jason; m. Susan G. Cope, June 4, 1987. BA in History, Ohio State U., 1970, JD, 1973; LLM, George Washington U., 1979. Bar: Ohio 1973, Colo. 1974, U.S. Supreme Ct. 1979, U.S. Dist. Ct. (no. dist.) 1980. Staff atty. USAF, Washington, 1979-80; asst. pub. defender County of Columbiana (Ohio), Lisbon, 1980—; ptnr. Goll & Guehl, Salem, Ohio, 1980-87; pvt. practice Salem, 1987—; law dir. City of Salem, 1992—99. Trustee Forensic Ctr., Salem, 1984-87; pres. Salem Community Theatre Group, 1984; trustee Salem Hist. Soc., 1992—; trustee Salem Cmty. Found., 1998—; dir. Leadership Columbiana County, 2002—; trustee Leadership Columbiana County, 2002—. Served to capt. U.S. Army, 1973-82, with USAF Res., 1982-93. Named one of Outstanding Young Men of Am. U.S. Jaycees, 1981, 83, named YWCA Man of Yr., 2000; fellow Forensic Medicine Armed Forces Inst. Pathology, 1976-77. Mem. ABA, Ohio Bar Assn., Ohio Acad. Trial Lawyers, Columbiana County Bar Assn., Forensic Fellows Soc., Assn. Trial Lawyers Am., Ohio State U. Alumni Assn. (life). Lodges: Kiwanis (pres. Salem chpt. 1986—). Republican. State civil litigation, General practice, Personal injury (including property damage).

GUERRA, LUIS P. lawyer; m. Lisa Brewer. M.C.L, U. of San Diego, San Diego; Juris Doctorate, Universidade Catholica Portuguesa, Portugual, 1989. Atty. Charles M. Brewer, ltd., Phoenix, Ariz., 1997—. Mem. Los Abagados- Maricopa County Hispanic Bar Assn., Phoenix; memeber Hispanic Nat. Bar Assn., Washington; mem. Attorney's Info. Exch. Group, Birmingham, Ala., Trial Lawyers for Pub. Justice, Washington. Active mem. Los Abagados- Maricopa County Hispanic bar Assn., Phoenix, Ariz. Mem.: Hispanic Nat. Bar Assn. (wash.). Office: Charles M Brewer Ltd 5500 N 24th Street Phoenix AZ 85016 Office Fax: 602-381-1152.

GUERRI, WILLIAM GRANT, lawyer; b. Higbee, Mo., Mar. 30, 1921; s. Grant and Pearl (Zambelli) G.; m. Millicent K. Branding; children: Paula Ann Guerri Baker, Glenda Kay, William Grant. AB, Central Meth. Coll., 1943; LLB, Columbia, 1946. Bar: NY 1946, Mo. 1947. Ptnr. Thompson Coburn LLP, St. Louis, 1956—. Mem. bd. editors: Columbia Law Rev, 1945-46. Hon. mem. bd. dirs. St. Louis Heart Assn., chmn., 1972-73; bd. dirs. United Way Greater St. Louis, 1976-94; curator Ctrl. Meth. Coll., 1981-97. Fellow The Fellows of Am. Bar; mem. ABA, Mo. Bar Assn. (trustee 1984-92), Bar Assn. Met. St. Louis, Assn. of Bar of City of N.Y., Am. Law Inst., Am. Judicature Soc., Noonday Club, Round Table Club, Phi Delta Phi. Federal civil litigation, State civil litigation, Corporate, general. Home: Apt 308 14300 Conway Meadows Ct E Chesterfield MO 63017-9612 Office: Thompson Coburn LLP Ste 3000 1 US Bank Plz Saint Louis MO 63101-1643 E-mail: wguerri@thompsoncoburn.com.

GUERRIERI, JOSEPH, JR., lawyer; b. Detroit, June 11, 1947; s. Joseph Guerrieri; m. Ursula Annemarie Koch, Aug. 30, 1969; children: Joseph III, Justin Matthew. BA, U. Mich., 1969; JD with honors, George Washington U., 1972. Bar: D.C. 1973, U.S. Ct. Appeals (2d, 3d, 4th, 5th, 6th, 7th, 8th, 9th and D.C. cirs.), U.S. Supreme Ct. Law clk. to Hon. Nicholas S. Nunzio, 1972-73; asst. U.S. atty. D.C., 1973-77; ptnr. Guerrieri Edmond & Clayman, Washington, 1985—. Fellow ABA (co-chmn. railway and airline labor com. 1982-85, union adminstrn. and procedure com. 1988-91, law and employment sect.), Coll. Labor and Employment Law, Laborers Int. Union N. Am. (spl. elections officer), Assn. Am. Trial Lawyers. Federal civil litigation, Labor (including EEOC, Fair Labor Standards Act, labor-management relations, NLRB, OSHA). Office: Guerrieri Edmond & Clayman Ste 700 1625 Massachusetts Ave NW Washington DC 20036-2243

GUESS, JAMES DAVID, lawyer; b. Lampasas, Tex., Jan. 21, 1941; s. David Ira and Lila Blanch (Reagan) G.; m. Susan Lawyer, Dec. 19, 1981; children: Corey, Stephanie, Casey, Chris. BS in Edn., Southwestern U., 1963; JD, St. Mary's U., 1968. Bar: Tex. 1968, U.S. Dist. Ct. (we. dist.) Tex. 1974, U.S. Ct. Appeals (5th cir.) 1974, U.S. Dist. Ct. (so. dist.) Tex. 1978, U.S. Dist. Ct. (no. dist.) Tex. 1982. Assoc. Groce Locke & Hebdon, San Antonio, 1968-74, ptnr., 1975-86; shareholder Groce Locke & Hebdon P.C., San Antonio, 1986-96, Jenkens & Gilchrist, San Antonio, 1996-99, Law Offices of James D. Guess, San Antonio, 1999—. Sustaining mem. Products Liability Adv. Coun.; mem. Am. Bd. Trial Advs. With USN, 1961—67, Vietnam. Mem.: Internat. Assn. Def. Counsel, Def. Rsch. Inst. (bd. dirs. 1998—2001), Tex. Assn. Def. Counsel (past pres.). Avocations: sports, golf, hunting. Aviation, Product liability. Home: 13318 Southwalk St San Antonio TX 78232-4843 E-mail: jamesdguess@sbcglobal.net.

GUEVARA, ROGELIO E. federal agency administrator; BS in Polit. Sci. and Adminstr., Calif. State U., 1972. With Bur. Narcotics and Dangerous Drugs (now Drug Enforcement Adminstrn.), L.A., 1972, Drug Enforcement Adminstrn., Monterrey, Mexico, 1978—82, Riverside, Calif., 1982—85, with pub. affairs office L.A., 1985—87, supr. in charge S.E. Asian Heroin Enforcement Group, 1987—92, with Office Congl. and Pub. Affairs Arlington, Va., 1992—94, insp. Office Profl. Responsibility, 1994—97, asst. spl. agt. in charge, 1997—2000, spl. agt. in charge Caribbean field divsn. San Juan, PR, 2000—02, chief ops. Alexandria, Va., 2002—. Office: Drug Enforcement Adminstrn 2401 Jefferson Davis Hwy Alexandria VA 22301*

GUGGENHEIM, MARTIN FRANKLIN, law educator, lawyer; b. N.Y.C., May 29, 1946; s. Werner and Fanny (Monatt) G.; m. Denise Silverman, May 29, 1969; children: Jamie, Courtney, Lesley. BA, SUNY, Buffalo, 1968; JD, NYU, 1971. Bar: N.Y. 1972, U.S. Dist. Ct. (so. dist. and ea. dist.) N.Y. 1973, U.S. Ct. Appeals (2d cir.) 1974, U.S. Ct. Appeals (3d cir.) 1979, U.S. Ct. Appeals (6th cir.) 1977, U.S. Supreme Ct. 1976. Staff atty. Legal Aid Soc., N.Y.C., 1971-72, dir. spl. litig. unit, juvenile rights divsn., 1972-73; clin. instr. NYU Sch. Law, N.Y.C., 1973-75; staff atty. juvnile rights project ACLU, N.Y.C., 1975-79, acting dir., 1976-77; asst. prof. clin. law NYU, N.Y.C., 1975-77, assoc. prof. clin. law, 1977-79, prof. clin. law, 1980—; of counsel Mayerson & Stutman LLP, N.Y.C., 2001—. Exec. dir. Washington Sq. Legal Svcs., Inc., N.Y.C., 1986-2000; pres. Nat. Coalition for Child Protection Reform, 2000—; pres., founding dir. Family Def. Law Project, Inc., N.Y.C., 1992-2000; advisor program for children Edna McConnell Clark Found., 1993-2001; dir. clin. and advocacy programs NYU, 1989-2002; founding dir. Ctr. for Family Representation, N.Y.C., 2002--; cons. juvenile justice stds. project ABA/Inst. Jud. Adminstrn., 1979-81; acting dir. Clin. Advocacy Programs, Sch. of Law NYU, 1988-89. Author: (with Alan Sussman) The Rights of Parents, 1980, Abuse and Neglect Volume, 1982, The Rights of Young People, 2d edit., 1985, (with Anthony G. Amsterdam and Randy Hertz) Trial Manual for Defense Attorneys in Juvenile Court, 1991, (with Alexandra Lowe and Diane Curtis) The Rights of Families, 1996. Dir. William J. Brennan Ctr., NYU, 1995-2000; mem. adv. bd. N.Y.C. Adminstrn. Children, 1997—; pres. Nat. Coalition for Child Protection Reform, 2000—. Arthur Garfield Hays Civil Liberties fellow, 1970-71, Criminal Law Edn. and Rsch. fellow, 1969-70; Kathryn A. McDonald award Assn. of the Bar of the City of N.Y., 2000. Mem. ABA, Am. Assn. Law Schs., Assn. of Bar of City of N.Y. Office: NYU Sch Law 161 Ave of the Americas New York NY 10013 E-mail: martin.guggenheim@nyu.edu.

GUGGENHEIMER, JOAN, law administrator; BA, Binghamton Univ.; JD, Columbia Univ. Gen. coun. Citigroup's Global Corp. and Invest. Bank, Chgo.; head of diversity Smith Barney; Co-head of Anti-Money Laundering Citigroup, co-Gen. Coussel; assoc. Smith Barney, 1985; dep. gen. coun. for litig. Citigroup's Global Corp. and Investment Bank, Chgo., gen. counsel of the Inst. Bus., gen. coun.; clk. US Court of Appeals for the Second Circuit; litig. Davis Polk and Wardwell, 1980; chief legal officer Bank One - Former Gen. Coun. of Globil Corp. and Invest. Bank at Citigroup, Chgo. Editor: (tabloid) Law Rev./Columbia Univ. Ater joining Bank One in 2000, Christine Edwards successfully built Law, Compliance, and Gov. Rels. into a single dept.; helped establish strong working rels with regulators; significantly cut expenses and reduced reliance on outside coun.; established Bank Ones's Fed. Gov. Rels. Office in Wash. DC; and helped establish Bank One as a leader in corp. governance. Office: Office of Gen Coun Bank One Corp 1 Bank One Plz Chicago IL 60670*

GUGGENHIME, RICHARD JOHNSON, lawyer; b. San Francisco, Mar. 6, 1940; s. Richard E. and Charlotte G.; m. Emlen Hall, June 5, 1965 (div.); children: Andrew, Lisa, Molly; m. Judith Perry Swift, Oct. 3, 1992. AB in Polit. Sci. with distinction, Stanford U., 1961; JD, Harvard U., 1964. Bar: Calif. 1965, U.S. Dist. Ct. (no. dist.) Calif. 1965, U.S. Ct. Appeals (9th cir.) 1965. Assoc. Heller, Ehrman, White & McAuliffe , 1965-71; ptnr. Heller, Ehrman, White & McAuliffe, 1972—. Spl. asst. to U.S. Senator Hugh Scott, 1964; bd. dirs. Comml. Bank of San Francisco, 1980-81, Global Savs. Bank, San Francisco, 1984-86, North Am. Trust Co., 1996-99. Mem. San Francisco Bd. Permit Appeals, 1978—86; bd. dirs. Marine World Africa USA, 1980—86; mem. San Francisco Fire Commn., 1986—88, Recreation and Parks Commn., 1989—92; chmn. bd. trustees San Francisco Univ. H.S., 1987—90; trustee St. Ignatius Prep. Sch., 1987—96; dir. Olympic Club, 2000—02, pres., 2002. Mem.: Am. Coll. Probate Counsel, Mayacama Golf Club, Olympic Club (bd. dirs. 1999—2002, pres. 2002), Thunderbird Country Club (Rancho Mirage, Calif.), Chevaliers du Tastevin (San Francisco), Wine and Food Soc., Bohemian Club. Estate planning, Probate (including wills, trusts), Estate taxation. Home: 2621 Larkin St San Francisco CA 94109-1512 Office: Heller Ehrman White & McAuliffe 333 Bush St San Francisco CA 94104-2806

GUIDRY, SUSAN GAIL, lawyer; b. New Orleans, Nov. 18, 1954; d. Laurence Young and Gail (Groetsch) Compagno. BA cum laude, U. Southwestern La., 1975; JD cum laude, Loyola U. Sch. Law, 1986. Bar: La. 1986, all La. fed. and state cts. Assoc. Barham & Churchill, New Orleans, 1986-88, Naquin & Ourso, New Orleans, 1988-91, Barham & Assocs., New Orleans, 1991-92; in-house counsel Agy. Rent-A-Car, Inc., New Orleans, 1992-93; sole practice New Orleans, 1993—. Mem. ABA, Assn. Women Attys., La. State Bar Assn., New Orleans Bar Assn., La. Assn. Def. Counsel. General civil litigation, Insurance, Personal injury (including property damage). Office: 125 S Genois St New Orleans LA 70119 Office Fax: 504-482-3302. E-mail: sgguidry@bellsouth.net.

GUILD, ALDEN, retired lawyer; b. Boston, July 3, 1929; s. Howard Redwood and Frances Allen (Warren) G.; m. Ruth Ineta Creighton, Sept. 14, 1957; 1 child, Heather Louise. BA, Dartmouth Coll., 1952; JD, U. Chgo., 1957; LLD (hon.), Norwich/Vt. Coll., 1977. Bar: Vt. 1958, U.S. Dist. Ct. Vt. 1958. With law dept. Nat. Life Ins. Co., Montpelier, Vt., 1957-90, asst. v.p., counsel, corp. sec., 1974-83, v.p., gen. counsel, 1983-89, sr. v.p., gen. counsel, 1989-90; ret. McKee, Giuliani & Cleveland, Montpelier, of counsel, 1990-97. Author: Stock-Purchase Agreements, 1960, Professional-Partnership Purchase Agreements, 1961, Business-Partnership Purchase Agreements, 1962; contbr. articles to legal jours. Trustee Norwich U., 1972-96, Vt. Coll., 1967-72, Kimball U. Acad., 1972-74, Wood Art Gallery, 1961-72; mem. Dartmouth Coll. Alumni Council, 1975-78. Served with USAF, 1950-53, Korea. Recipient Disting. Service award Montpelier Jr. C. of C., 1962 Mem. Vt. Bar Assn., Assn. Life Ins. Counsel, Am. Coun. Life Ins., VFW, Am. Legion, Order of Coif, Lake Mansfield Trout Club (Stowe, Vt.), Masons, Elks, Phi Beta Kappa, Theta Chi. Republican. Home: 63 Murray Rd Montpelier VT 05602-8514

GUILFORD, ANDREW JOHN, lawyer; b. Santa Monica, Calif., Nov. 28, 1950; s. Howard Owens and Elsie Jennette (Hargreaves) G.; m. Loreen Mary Gogain, Dec. 22, 1973; children: Colleen Catherine, Amanda Joy. AB summa cum laude, UCLA, 1972, JD, 1975. Bar: Calif. 1975, U.S. Dist. Ct. (cen. dist.) Calif. 1976, U.S. Ct. Appeals (9th cir.) 1976, U.S. Supreme Ct. 1979, U.S. Dist. Ct. (so. dist.) Calif. 1981, U.S. Dist. Ct. (no. and ea. dists.) Calif. 1990. Assoc. Sheppard, Mullin, Richter & Hampton, L.A. and Orange County, Calif., 1975-82, ptnr. Orange County, 1983—. Lectr. The Rutter Group, Encino, Calif., 1983—, Continuing Edn. of the Bar, Berkeley, 1978—, Hastings Ctr. for Advocacy, San Francisco, 1988; judge pro tem, arbitrator Calif. Superior Ct., 1983—; mem. commn. future legal profession and state bar; mem. adv. task force on multi-juristictional practice, task force on self-represented litigants. Author UCLA Law Review, 1975. Mem. Amicus Publico, Santa Ana, Calif., 1986; bd. dirs. Constl. Rights Found., 1990, Pub. Law Ctr. Orange County, 1990—, Baroque Music Festival, 1992-96, NCCJ, 1995-99, UCLA Law Alumni Assn., 1992-95; subdeacon, warden, del. Episcopal Ch. Recipient resolution of commendation Calif. State Senate and Assembly, Outstanding Svc. award Poverty Law Ctr., 1991, Bernard E. Witkin Amicus Curiae award Calif. Jud. Coun., Jurisprudence award Anti-Defamation League, J. Reuben Clark award, cert. of recognition U.S. Congress, others; co-recipient President's Pro Bono award State Bar; Regents scholar U. Calif., Berkeley, 1968-72; named one of Calif.'s 100 Most Influential Attys., The Daily Jour., Bus. Litigation Trial Lawyer of Yr., Orange County Trial Lawyers Assn Fellow Am. Coll. Trial Lawyers; mem. ABA, FBA (bd. dirs. 2001—), Assn. Bus. Trial Lawyers (founding officer Orange County chpt., pres. 2000-2001), Am. Arbitration Assn. (arbitrator large complex case program 1993-95), Calif. Bar Assn. (pres. 1999-2000, bd. govs. 1996-2000), Orange County Bar Assn. (bd. dirs. 1985-87, officer 1988-90, pres. 1991, chmn. bus. litigation sect. 1983, state bar conv. 1986, 87, law-motion com. 1982, standing com. trial ct. delay reduction 1987-93), 9th Cir. Jud. Conf. (rep. 1990-93, 99—), Phi Beta Kappa (sec.-treas. 1978-80, v.p. 1980-84), Pi Gamma Mu, Sigma Pi. Republican. Avocations: theater, photography, sports, gardening, poetry. Alternative dispute resolution, Federal civil litigation, State civil litigation. Office: Sheppard Mullin Richter & Hampton 650 Town Center Dr Fl 4 Costa Mesa CA 92626-1993 Home: 31852 Camino del Cielo Trabuco Canyon CA 92679-3400 E-mail: aguilford@sheppardmullin.com.

GUILFORD, ROBERT E. lawyer; b. Cleve., Apr. 14, 1933; s. Isadore H. and Malvene G.; m. Edel Singer, 1960 (div. 1963); 1 child, Steven; m. Judith Cagen, May 5, 1990. BA in Philosophy with honors, U. Va., 1955; JD, Harvard U., 1958. Bar: Calif. 1959, U.S. Dist. Ct. (cen. dist.) Calif. 1959, U.S. Dist. Ct. (no. dist.) Calif. 1964, U.S. Dist. Ct. (no. dist.) N.Y. 1996, U.S. Ct. Appeals (9th cir.) 1959. Asst. U.S. atty. Dept. Justice, L.A., 1958-59; legal staff MCA Universal, Universal City, Calif., 1959-65; gen. counsel World Horizons Inst., Newport Beach, Calif., 1965-70; ptnr. Bryant, Maxwell, Guilford & Sheahan, 1970-75; outside counsel Home Savings & Loan Assn., Beverly Hills, Calif., 1975-80; pvt. practice Santa Monica, Calif., 1980-85; gen. counsel Mus. of Flying, Santa Monica, Calif., 1985-90; assoc. counsel Am. Golf Corp., Santa Monica, Calif., 1987-90; pvt. practice, 1990—93; shareholder Baum, Hedlund, Aristei, Guilford & Schiavo, 1993—. V.p., chief pilot, trustee Mus. Flying, Santa Monica; v.p. Supermarine Aviation Ltd., Liberty Aero Corp., NATO Aviation. Mem. State Bar Calif., Lawyer-Pilot's Bar Assn., Aircraft Owners and Pilots

Assn., Exptl. Aircraft Assn., Classic Jet Aircraft Assn. (chmn. bd. dirs.), Warbirds Am. (co-founder), Hunter Flight Test Ltd. (v.p.), Nat. Air Disaster Forum (Safety award 2002), Mustang Pilots Club (founder, pres.), Phi Eta Sigma. Avocation: pilot. Aviation, Personal injury (including property damage), Product liability. Office: Baum Hedlund Aristei Guilford & Schiavo 12100 Wilshire Blvd Ste 950 Los Angeles CA 90025-7107 E-mail: rguilford@baumhedlundlaw.com.

GUIN, DON LESTER, insurance company executive; b. Shreveport, La., Nov. 5, 1940; s. Lester and Ethelyn (Dumas) G.; m. Mary Ann Guin, Feb. 3, 1979. BBA in Ins., U. Ga., 1962; BS in Law, Kensington U., Glendale, Calif., 1987, JD, 1989. Bar: Calif. 1990, U.S. Ct. Appeals (5th and 9th cirs.) 1990, U.S. Dist. Ct. (no. dist.) Calif. 1990, U.S. Ct. Appeals (fed. cir.) 1991, U.S. Dist. Ct. (ea. dist.) Tex. 1991, U.S. Ct. Internat. Trade 1991, U.S. Ct. Fed. Claims 1992, U.S. Supreme Ct. 1994. Adjuster, supr. Lindsey & Newsom, Beaumont, Tex., 1963-71, mgr. Port Arthur, Tex., 1968-71, asst. to pres. Tyler, Tex., 1971-74, v.p. ops., 1977-84, sr. v.p., 1984—; sr. v.p. adminstrn. and legal Lindsey Morden, 1990—; sr. v.p., corp. sec. Lindsey Morden Claims Svc. Inc., Lindsey Morden Claims Mgmt., 1992-93, sr. v.p., treas. U.S. Ops., 1993—, sr. v.p., corp. treas., chief legal officer, 1995—; sr. v.p., corp. treas. and sec. Vale Nat. Training Ctrs, Inc., 1993—; exec. v.p., corp. treas, corp. sec., chief legal officer, 1995—; exec. v.p. Cunningham Lindsey U.S., Inc., 2000—, Vale Nat. Tng. Ctr., 2001—. Bd. dirs. Lindsey Morden Claims Svc., Inc., Lindsey Morden Claims Mgmt., Inc., exec. com., mgmt. com., compensation com., incentive com., Vale Nat. Tng. Ctrs., Lindsey & Newsom Inc.; trustee Lindsey and Newsom Benefit Trusts, 1990-91, plan adminstr. Lindsey Morden Profit Sharing Retirement Trust, 1994, Lindsey & Newsom Retirement Funds, 1990—; sr. v.p., corp. sec., CLO Lindsey Morden Group, Inc., 1996—; mem. adv. bd. Kemper Ins. Group; sr. v.p., corp. sec. Lindsey & Newsom, Vale Nat; bd. dirs. Tyler Mus. Art, chmn. pers. policy com., chair fin. com., 1999; exec. v.p. Cunningham Lindsey, U.S., Inc., 2000. Author: Analysis of Garage Liability, 1972, Dishonesty Claims Handling, 1973, Casualty Reporting Manual, 1975, Sexual Harassment in the Workplace, 1986, (audio cassette) Beating the Bears of Bad Faith, 1991, (video cassette) Bad Faith and Preventing Errors and Omissions Claims, 1987. Trustee Lindsey Morden Benefit Trusts, Lindsey Morden Retirement Trusts, 1992—; dir. assoc. U. Tex Health Ctr., 1995; budget allocation panelist United Way Tyler/Smith County, Tex., 1995; bd. dirs. Tyler Mus. of Art, 1996. Mem. ABA (internat. law sect., corp. law sect.), Can. Bar Assn., Nat. Assn. Def. Counsel, Nat. Assn. Ind. Ins. Adjusters (data processing com. 1976, legis. com. 1990), Bar Assn. D.C., Bar Assn. U.S. Fed. Cir., Defense Inst. Trial Lawyers Assn. (ins. law com.), State Bar Calif. (internat. law sect., tort sect., litigation sect., labor and employment law sect.), Nat. Employee Benefit Found., Def. Rsch. Inst., Alameda County Bar Assn., Inter-Pacific Bar Assn., Italian-Am. Bar Assn., Bar Assn. 5th Fed. Cir., Optimist Club, Kiwanis Club, Sabre Club, Lawyers Club San Francisco, Ins. Soc. U. Ga. (charter mem.), Circle K-Kiwanis. Home: 17389 Hidden Valley Ln Flint TX 75762-9611 Office: Lindsey Morden Claims Svcs Inc 211 Brookside Dr Tyler TX 75711

GUIN, JUNIUS FOY, JR., federal judge; b. Russellville, Ala., Feb. 2, 1924; s. Junius Foy and Ruby (Pace) G.; m. Dorace Jean Caldwell, July 18, 1945; children: Janet Elizabeth Smith, Judith Ann Mullican, Junius Foy III, David Jonathan. Student, Ga. Inst. Tech., 1940-41; AB magna cum laude, U. Ala., JD with honors, 1947; LLD, Magic Valley Christian Coll., 1963. Bar: Ala. 1948. Pvt. practice law, Russellville; sr. ptnr. Guin, Guin, Bouldin & Porch, 1948-73; fed. dist. judge U.S. Dist. Ct. (no. dist.) Ala., Birmingham, from 1973, now sr. judge; commr. Ala. Bar, 1965-73, 2d v.p., 1969-70. Pres. Abstract Trust Co., Inc., 1958-73; sec. Iuka TV Cable Co., Inc., Haleyville TV Cable Co., Inc., 1963-73; former dir., gen. counsel First Nat. Bank of Russellville, Franklin Fed. Savs. & Loan Assn. of Russellville.; Lectr. Cumberland-Samford Sch. Law, 1974— , U. Ala. Sch. Law, 1977— Chmn. Russellville City Planning Com., 1954-57; 1st chmn. Jud. Commn. Ala., 1972-73; mem. Ala. Supreme Ct. Adv. Com. (rules civil procedure), 1971-73; mem. adv. com. on standards of conduct U.S. Jud. Conf., 1980-87, mem. com. on Fed.-State Jurisdiction, 1982-88, mem. ad hoc com. on cameras in the courtroom, 1982-83; Rep. county chmn., 1954-58, 71-72, Rep. state fin. chmn., 1972-73; candidate for U.S. Senator from, Ala., 1954; Ala. Lawyers' Finance chmn. Com. to Re-elect Pres., 1972; former trustee Ala. Christian Coll., Faulkner U., Magic Valley Christian Coll., Childhaven Children's Home; elder Ch. of Christ. Served to 1st lt., inf. AUS, 1943-46. Named Russellville Citizen of Year, 1973; recipient Dean's award U. Ala. Law Sch., 1977 Mem. ABA (mem. spl. com. on resdl. real estate transactions 917-73), Am. Radio Relay League, Ala. Bar Assn. (com. chmn. 1965-73, Award of Merit 1973), Jefferson County Bar Assn., Fed. Bar Assn., Am. Law Inst., Ala. Law Inst. (dir. 1969-73, 76—), Am. Judicature Soc., Farrah Law Soc., Farrah Order Jurisprudence (now Order of Coif), Phi Beta Kappa, Omicron Delta Kappa, Delta Chi. Office: US Dist Ct 619 US Courthouse 1729 5th Ave N Birmingham AL 35203-2000

GUINN, STANLEY WILLIS, lawyer; b. Detroit, June 9, 1953; s. Willis Hampton and Virginia Mae (Pierson) G.; m. Patricia Shirley Newgord, June 13, 1981; children: Terri Lanae, Scott Stanley. BBA with high distinction, U. Mich., 1979, MBA with distinction, 1981; MS in Taxation with distinction, Walsh Coll., 1987; JD cum laude, U. Mich., 1992. CPA Mich., cert. mgmt. acct., Mich.; bar: Calif., U.S. Dist. Ct. (so. dist.) Calif., U.S. Tax Ct. Tax mgr. Coopers & Lybrand, Detroit, 1981-87; tax cons. Upjohn Co., Kalamazoo, 1987-89; litigation atty. Brobeck, Phleger & Harrison, 1992-94, Coughlan, Semmer & Lipman, San Diego, 1994-95; consumer fin. atty. Bank Am. NT & SA, San Francisco, 1995-98, GreenPoint Credit, LLC, San Diego, 1998—. Served with USN, 1974-77. Mem.: ABA, AICPA, Conf. on Consumer Fin. Law, Inst. Cert. Mgmt. Accts., Atty.-CPA, Inc., San Diego County Bar, Calif. State Bar Assn., Delta Mu Delta, Beta Alpha Psi, Beta Gamma Sigma, Phi Kappa Phi. Republican. Mem. Christian Ch. Avocations: tennis, racquetball, hiking. General civil litigation, Commercial, consumer (including collections, credit), Taxation, general. Home: 3125 Crystal Ct Escondido CA 92025-7763 Office: GreenPoint Credit 10089 Willow Creek Rd San Diego CA 92131-1603 E-mail: stan.guinn@greenpoint.com.

GULBENKIAN, PAUL BASIL, solicitor; b. London, Mar. 23, 1940; s. Krikor Parsegh and Vergine Gulbenkian; children from previous marriage: Vergine, Sylvia; m. Jacqueline Chamlian, Dec. 15, 1990. LLB, London U., 1961. Solicitor Supreme Ct. Eng., Wales. Asst. solicitor Isadore Goldman Solicitors, London, 1966-70, ptnr., 1970-89, sr. ptnr., 1989—, Gulbenkian Harris Andonian Solicitors, London, 1989—. Chmn. Camden C.A.B. Svc. Com., London, 1978—83, Monitoring of Articles Panel, 1986—89; asst. recorder Crown Ct., 1992—98, recorder, 1998—; asst. commr. Boundry Commn. England and Wales, 2000—; part-time immigration adj., 1989—; hon. cons. Am. Embassy Ct. St. James and to the Vatican. Contbr. articles to profl. jours. Trustee Am. Charitable Orgns. Found., Found. Internat. Health, Holiday Care Charity, the Rudolf Kempe Meml. Trust. Recipient 3 Encyclicals His Holiness Vasken I, 1978-80, St. Mesrob medal, 1978; admitted as Freeman, City of London, 2001. Fellow Royal Soc. Arts; mem. The Law Soc. (hon. auditor 1987-89), Solicitors Family Law Assn. (founder), Immigration Law Practitioners Assn. (founder), European Immigration Lawyers Group (founder), Coun. Immigration Judges (founder), Holborn Law Soc. (pres. 1984-85). Armenian. Avocations: music, tennis, squash, walking. Immigration, naturalization, and customs. Office: Gulbenkian Harris Andonian 125 High Holborn London WC1V 6QA England

GULINO, FRANK, lawyer, educator; b. Bklyn., Aug. 14, 1954; s. Frank C. and Frances (Cataldo) G.; m. Donna Regina Cramer, June 30, 1984; children: Frank Regis, Mary Elise. BA, NYU, 1976; JD, Fordham U., 1979. Bar: N.Y. 1980, U.S. Dist. Ct. (no., so. ea. and we. dists.) N.Y. 1980, U.S. Tax Ct. 1980, U.S. Ct. Mil. Appeals 1980, U.S. Ct. Appeals (2d cir.) 1980, U.S. Ct. Internat. Trade 1982, U.S. Supreme Ct. 1983, U.S. Ct. Claims 1985, U.S. Ct. Appeals (8th and fed. cirs.) 1985, D.C. 1986, U.S. Dist. Ct. Nebr. 1986, U.S. Dist. Ct. Hawaii 1986, U.S. Ct. Appeals (3d, 5th, 6th, 7th, 9th, 10th and 11th cirs.) 1986, U.S. Ct. Appeals (D.C. cir.) 1988. Law clk. to U.S. magistrate U.S. Dist. Ct. (so. dist.) N.Y., N.Y.C., 1979-80; assoc. Donovan, Leisure, Newton & Irvine, N.Y.C., 1980-83, Carro, Spanbock, Fass, Geller, Kaster & Cuiffo, N.Y.C., 1984-86; dep. gen. counsel N.Y.C. Housing Authority, 1986-88; assoc. Summit Rovins & Feldesman, N.Y.C., 1988; of counsel Stockfield & Fixler, N.Y.C., 1988-89, ptnr., 1989-91, Stockfield, Fixler & Gulino, N.Y.C., 1991-94, Fixler & Gulino, L.L.P., N.Y.C., 1995—98, Fixler & Assocs., LLP, N.Y.C., 1998—2001; counsel Brecher, Fishman, Pasternack, Popish, Heller, Rubin & Reiff, P.C., N.Y.C., 2001—03, ptnr., 2003—. Adj. assoc. prof. Fordham U. Sch. Law, N.Y.C., 1983-88. Author: Judgments in Federal Civil Practice, 1989, supplement, 1993, 97, 2000. Mem. ABA (mem. coun. appellate lawyers), Fed. Bar Coun., N.Y. State Bar Assn. (atty. advisor high sch. mock trial program 1980-87), N.Y. State Trial Lawyers Assn., Assn. Trial Lawyers of Am. Appellate, General civil litigation, Personal injury (including property damage). Office: 222 Broadway New York NY 10038-2510

GULLAND, EUGENE D. lawyer; b. Endicott, N.Y., Aug. 27, 1947; s. George Raymond and Virginia (Fisher) G.; m. Kristin Spearing, Aug. 29, 1970; children: Michael Spearing, Molly Spearing, Samuel Spearing. AB, Princeton U., 1969; JD, Yale U., 1972. Bar: D.C., Va., U.S. Supreme Ct., U.S. Ct. Appeals (1st, 2d, 3d, 4th, 6th, 7th, 9th, D.C., Fed. cirs.), U.S. Dist. Ct. D.C., (ea. dist.) Va., Md., Ariz., Ind. Assoc. Covington & Burling, Washington, 1973-80, ptnr., 1980—. Practitioner before London Ct. Internat. Arbitration, Internat. C. of C., Am. Arbitration Assn., also other arbitral tribunals; mem. faculty Nat. Inst. for Trial Advocacy, Am. Judicature Soc. Trustee Loudoun Day Sch., Leesburg, Va., 1986-98; vestryman, treas. Our Redeemer Ch., 1987-97; mem. alumni schs. com. Princeton U. Capt. U.S. Army, 1972-73. Woodrow Wilson scholar Princeton U., Princeton U. scholar. Mem. Nat. Assn. Coll. and Univ. Attys., Phi Beta Kappa. Am. Judicature Soc., Henlopen Acres Beach Club Administrative and regulatory, Federal civil litigation, Private international. Home: Little River Farm Aldie VA 20105 Office: Covington & Burling 1201 Pennsylvania Ave NW Washington DC 20004-2401 E-mail: egulland@cov.com.

GULLBORG, PETER WILLIAM, lawyer; b. Evanston, Ill., Dec. 28, 1960; s. Allan Peter and Ruth Mcelhaney Gullborg. BS, MS, U. Mo., 1984; MS, MBA, Tex. A&M U., 1990; JD, U. Md., 1994. Bar: Mo. 1995, Ill. 1998. Asst. pub. defender Mo. Pub. Defender Sys., Statewide, Mo., 1995—98; atty. Kortenhof & Ely, 1998—99, Sandberg, Phoenix & von Gontard, 1999—2001, Herzog, Crebs & McGhee, St. Louis, 2001—02, Law Offices Thomas Noonan, St. Louis, 2002—; engr. Dept. of Def., 1989—94. V.p. & gen. counsel Riverside Group, Inc., 2000—; gen. counsel St. Louis DAV, 2001—03, spl. litigation counsel, 2003—; atty. St. Louis Volunteers Lawyer Program, 2000—. Contbr. articles to profl. jours. Mem.: ABA, Mo. Bar Assn., Ill. Bar Assn., Bar Assn. Met. St. Louis, Mo. Athletic Club. Product liability, Corporate, general, General civil litigation. Office: Law Offices Thomas Noonan 701 Market St Ste 1100 Saint Louis MO 63101

GULLEN, CHRISTOPHER ROY, lawyer; b. Detroit, Feb. 17, 1950; s. George Edgar and Mary Ruth Gullen; m. Sheila Rae Collins, Aug. 25, 1973; children: Brian Christopher, Katelyn Elizabeth. BA, U. Mich., 1972; JD, Ohio Northern U., 1975. Bar: Mich. 1975, U.S. Dist. Ct. (ea. dist.) Mich. 1975, U.S. Ct. Appeals (6th cir.) 1978. Law clk. Mich. Ct. Appeals, Lansing, 1975-77; ptnr. Gullen & Fitzsimmons, Rochester, Mich., 1977-82, Sarvis, Gullen & Herrmann, Birmingham, Mich., 1982-86; pub. liability atty. Kmart Corp., Troy, Mich., 1986-90, pub. liability counsel, 1990-99, dir. risk mgmt. and pub. liability, 2000—02. Mediator Oakland County Cir. Ct., 1986—. Author: Rules and Regulations of the Science Court, 1980. Mem. ABA, Mich. Bar Assn. General civil litigation. Office: James E Logan & Assocs Ltd 7011 Orchard Lake Rd West Bloomfield MI 48322 E-mail: cgullen@jeloganltd.com.

GULLY, RUSSELL GEORGE, lawyer; b. San Angelo, Tex., Feb. 18, 1955; s. Frank Arthur and Dolores Ann (Dierschke) G.; m. Patricia Prost, Aug. 4, 1984; children: Monica, Teresa, Rachel. BA in Math., U. Tex., 1976, MA in Math., 1978, JD, 1984. Bar: Tex. 1984. Computer software instr. Tex. Instruments, Austin, 1978-81; atty. Thompson & Knight L.L.P., Dallas, 1984—. State advocate KC, 1996-98. Mem. ABA, S.W. Benefits Assn., Dallas Benefits Soc., Tex. Bar Assn., Dallas Bar Assn. Avocations: audiobooks, gardening. Pension, profit-sharing, and employee benefits. Office: Thompson & Knight LLP 1700 Pacific Ave Ste 3300 Dallas TX 75201-4693 E-mail: russell.gully@tklaw.com.

GUNDERSON, BRENT MERRILL, lawyer; b. Vernal, Utah, Apr. 16, 1960; s. Merrill Ray and Betty Velate (Norton) G.; m. Julie Phillips, Oct. 28, 1983; children: Adam Brent, Jeremy Phillip, Matthew Norton, Hannah, Rachel, Mariah, Kayla, Jacob Elden. BA, Brigham Young U., 1984; JD, Columbia U., 1987. Bar: Ariz. 1987, U.S. Dist. Ct. Ariz. 1987, U.S. Tax Ct. 1994. Ptnr. Brown & Bain, Phoenix, 1987—96; pvt. practice Gunderson Denton & Profitt, P.C., Mesa, Ariz., 1996—. Pres. Ariz. Mgmt. Soc., Phoenix, 1996-97. Asst. dist. commr. Boy Scouts Am., Mesa, Ariz., 1994-97, scoutmaster troop 611, Mesa, 1991-94, troop 761, Mesa, 1999-2002, mem. varsity scout com., 2002--, chair, 1997-98; precinct capt. Mesa Rep. Precincts 47 & 17, 1988-94; cubmaster pack 761, Boy Scouts Am., 1998-99; mem. Ariz. Cmty. Found. Breakfast Series com., 2001—; mem. profl. advisors. com. Leave a Legacy, Ariz. Recipient Mesa Dist. award of Merit, 1997, Scoutmaster award of Merit Boy Scouts Am., 1992, named to Scout Leader Hall of Fame, 1993, Scouting Family Hall of Fame, 1999. Mem. Am. Immigration Lawyers Assn. (v.p. Ariz. chpt. 1992-93, Maricopa County Bar Found. (bd. dirs. 1991-95), East Valley Estate Planning Coun. (bd. dirs. 1997-2001, pres. 1999-2000), Am. Immigration Lawyers Assn., Ariz. Mgmt. Soc. (bd. dirs. 1997—). Mem. Lds Ch. Avocations: backpacking, fishing, China. Estate planning, Immigration, naturalization, and customs, Probate (including wills, trusts). Office: Gunderson Denton & Profitt PC 123 N Centennial Way Ste 150 Mesa AZ 85201-6747

GUNDERSON, ROBERT VERNON, JR., lawyer; b. Memphis, Dec. 4, 1951; s. Robert V. and Suzanne (McCarthy) G.; m. Anne Durkheimer, May 15, 1982; children: Katherine Paige, Robert Graham. BA with distinction, U. Kans., 1973; MBA, U. Pa., 1974; MA, Stanford U., 1976; JD, U. Chgo., 1979. Bar: Calif. 1979, U.S. Dist. Ct. (no. dist.) Calif. 1979. Assoc. Cooley, Godward, Castro, Huddleson & Tatum, San Francisco and Palo Alto, Calif., 1979-84, ptnr., 1984-88, Brobeck, Phleger & Harrison, Palo Alto, 1988-95, mem. exec. com., 1991-95, chmn. bus. and tech. practice, 1992-95; founder, ptnr. Gunderson Dettmer Stough Villeneuve Franklin & Hachigian, Menlo Park, Calif., 1995—. Panelist Venture Capital and Pub. Offering Negotiation, San Francisco and N.Y.C., 1981, 83, 85, 92, Practicing Law Inst., N.Y.C. and San Francisco, 1986; moderator, panelist Third Ann. Securities Law Inst., 1985; dir. Heartport, Inc., Redwood City, Calif., Biospect, Inc., South San Francisco, Calif., Concurrent Pharms., Ft. Washington, Pa., Seabiscuit Inc., Palo Alto, Calif., Theranance, Inc., South San Francisco, Inc.; sec. Dionex Corp., Sunnyvale, Calif., 1983-88, Southwall Techs., Inc., Palo Alto, 1985-88, Conductus, Inc., Sunnyvale, 1992-2001, Remedy Corp., Mountain View, Calif., 1995-97; vis. lectr. U. Santa Clara Law Sch., 1985, 89. Exec. editor U. Chgo. Law Rev., 1978-79; contbr. articles to profl. jours. Mem. ABA (bus. law sect., various coms.), State Bar Calif. (panelist continuing legal edn. 1984), San Francisco Bar Assn., Am. Fin. Assn., Wharton Club (San Francisco Bay area). Avocations: contemporary art, music, travel. Corporate, general, Securities. Home: 243 Polhemus Ave Menlo Park CA 94027-5442 Office: Gunderson Dettmer Stough Villeneuve 155 Constitution Dr Menlo Park CA 94025-1106

GUNEWARDENE, ROSHANI MALA, lawyer; b. London, July 30, 1961; d. Swarna L. Gunewardene. BA, Sweet Briar Coll., 1985; JD, U. Conn., 1988; LLM, Columbia U., 1990. Bar: Fla. 1988, U.S. Ct. Appeals (llth cir.) 1988, U.S. Dist. Ct. (mid. and so. dists.) Fla. 1989, U.S. Supreme Ct. 1992. Cert. legal intern Office of Pub. Defender, West Palm Beach, Fla., summer 1987; assoc. Blackwell & Walker, PA, Miami, Fla., 1988-89, George T. Ramani, PA, Coral Gables, Fla., 1990-91, 92-93, Melton & Assocs., PA, Orlando, Fla., 1992; on-call assoc. Leon B. Cheek, III, Esquire, Fern Park, Fla., 1995-98; pvt. practice Altamonte Springs, Fla., 1993—. Mem. arbitrator panel U.S. Dist. Ct. for Mid. Dist. Fla., 1996—; cons., assoc. Orange County Bar Assn., Orlando, 1998-99, 2000-02. Contbr. articles to law jours. Mem. Human Rels. Bd., Orlando, Fla., 1993-99, vice chmn., 1995-97, chmn., 1997-98; mem. Seminole County Sheriff's Civilian Rev. Bd., Sanford, Fla., 1998-01; vol. pub. interest law grant chpt. U. Conn. Sch. Law, 1986-87; vol. Ryan's Nursing Home, Amherst, Va., 1983-84; vol. worker braille transl. project Blind Coun., Colombo, Sri Lanka, 1976-78. Scholar Sweet Briar Coll., 1984-85. Mem.: Better Bus. Bureaus Inc. (arbitrator 1996—99, 2002—05), Fla. Bar (student edn. and admissions to the bar com. 1993—94, profl. ethics com. 1996—99, 2002—), Am. Immigration Lawyers Assn., Nat. Assn. Securities Dealers (arbitrator 1997—2002). Avocations: stamp collecting, music, movies. Construction, Criminal, Immigration, naturalization, and customs. Office: San Sebastian Sq PO Box 162032 Altamonte Springs FL 32716-2032 E-mail: roshanigunewardene@hotmail.com.

GUNGER, RICHARD WILLIAM, lawyer; b. Auburn, N.Y., Aug. 7, 1963; s. William Bruce and Lita Patricia G.; m. Barbara Jean Taber, Nov. 24, 1984; children: William Robinson, James Taber. BA magna cum laude, Alfred U., 1985; JD cum laude, Syracuse U., 1988. Bar: N.Y. 1989, U.S. Dist. Ct. (no. dist.) N.Y. 1991, U.S. Dist. Ct. (we. dist.) N.Y. 1993, U.S. Supreme Ct. 1993. Assoc. Albert D. DiGiacomo, Syracuse, N.Y., 1988-89, Cuddy, Durgala & Timian, Auburn, N.Y., 1989-90; atty. pvt. practice, Auburn, N.Y., 1990—. Bd. dirs. Cayuga Counseling, Auburn. Alan L. Ponyman scholar, 1985. Mem. ABA, N.Y. State Bar Assn. Cayuga County Bar Assn., KC. Bankruptcy, Family and matrimonial, General practice. Office: 5 Court St Auburn NY 13021-3713

GUNN, ALAN, law educator; b. Syracuse, N.Y., Apr. 8, 1940; s. Albert Dale and Helen Sherwood (Whitnall) G.; m. Bertha Ann Buchwald, 1975; 1 child, William BS, Rensselaer Poly. Inst., 1961; JD, Cornell U., 1970. Bar: D.C. 1970. Assoc. Hogan & Hartson, Washington, 1970-72; asst. prof. law Washington U., St. Louis, 1972-75, assoc. prof., 1975-76; assoc. prof. law Cornell U., Ithaca, N.Y., 1977-79, prof., 1979-84, J. duPratt White prof., 1984-89; prof. law U. Notre Dame, Ind., 1989-96, John N. Matthews prof., 1996—. Apptd. spl. advocate St. Joseph County Probate Ct., 2001—. Author: Partnership Income Taxation, 1991, 3d edit., 1999; (with Larry D. Ward) Cases, Text and Problems on Federal Income Taxation, 5th edit., 2002; (with Vincent R. Johnson) Studies in American Tort Law, 1994, 2d edit., 1999. Methodist. Office: U Notre Dame Law Sch Notre Dame IN 46556

GUNN, ALBERT EDWARD, JR., internist, educator, lawyer, administrator; b. Port Washington, N.Y., Oct. 31, 1933; s. Albert Edward and Esther Frances (Williams) G.; m. Joan Marie Jacoby, May 18, 1968; children: Albert Edward III, Emily Williams Gunn Hebert, Andrew Robert, Clare Margaret Gunn Berchelmann, Catherine Ann, Philip David. BS, Fordham Coll., 1955, LLB, 1958; MB BCh BAO, Nat. U. Ireland, Galway, 1967. Bar: NY 1958, U.S. Ct. Mil. Appeals 1959, D.C. 1972, U.S. Supreme Ct. 1972, U.S. Ct. Appeals (D.C. cir.) 1972; diplomate Am. Bd Internal Medicine, lic. physician Pa., NY, Fla., Va., Ga., Tex., Eng., Wales. Owner, agt. Albert E. Gunn Ins. Agy., Port Washington, 1953-65; intern Montefiore Hosp., N.Y.C., 1967-68; resident in medicine Roosevelt Hosp., N.Y.C., 1968-70; USPHS trainee in neurology U. Rochester, NY, 1970-72; asst. dir. govtl. rels. AMA, Washington, 1972-74; med. dir. Geriat. Svcs. Suffolk County, Hauppauge, NY, 1974-75, Rehab. Ctr., U. Tex./M.D. Anderson Cancer Ctr., 1975-88, chief rehab. sect., 1988-93, chief geriat. sect., 1993-2000, dep. chmn. dept. internal med. spltys., 1998-2000; prof. mgmt. and policy scis. U. Tex. Houston Sch. Pub. Health, 2001—. Asst. prof. medicine U. Tex. Med. Sch., Houston, 1976-80, assoc. prof., 1980-2000, prof., 2000—, also assoc. dean for admissions; med. dir. Region IV, Tex. Med. Found., 1986-93; del.-at-large White House conf. on Handicapped Individuals, 1977; pres. Mus. Med. Sci., 1990; cons. CDC, Legal Svcs. Corp., Nat. Libr. Medicine. Co-author: Rehabilitation of the Cancer Patient, 1976, AIDS in Africa, 1988; editor, contbg. author: Cancer Rehabilitation, 1984; mem. editl. bd. Cancer Bull., 1977-90, Gerontology and Geriatrics Edn., 1984-2003, Linacre Quar.; contbr. articles to profl. jours. Mem. nat. adv. health coun. HEW, 1974-75; mem. adv. com. Nat. Inst. Law Enforcement and Criminal Justice, Law Enforcement Assistance Adminstrn., U.S. Dept. Justice, 1974-76; mem. bd. regents Nat. Libr. Medicine, NIH, 1983-87, chmn., 1986-87, chmn. lit. selection tech. adv. com., 1988-91; bd. dirs. Right to Life Advs., 1977-78, Tex. Med. Ctr. Libr., 1990. With USAF Strategic Air Command, 1958-61, capt. Res., 1961-75. Fellow ACP; mem. Tex. Med. Assn. (trustee ins. trust, chmn. bd. trustees 1997-2000), Harris County Med. Soc. (exec. bd. 1986-90, v.p. 1998), Royal Coll. Physicians London (licentiate), Royal Coll. Surgeons Eng., Houston Acad. Medicine (bd. dirs. 1986-90, pres. 1990), Houston Bar Assn., D.C. Bar, Cath. Med. Assn. (regional bd. dirs. 1992—, Thomas Linacre award 1997), Sons of Union Vets. of Civil War, Am. Legion, KC, Army and Navy Club, Cosmos Club, Petroleum Club (Houston), Giraud (San Antonio). Roman Catholic. Home: 2329 Watts Rd Houston TX 77030-1139 Office: U Tex MD Anderson Cancer Ctr 1515 Holcombe Blvd Box 515 Houston TX 77030-4009

GUNN, MICHAEL PETER, lawyer; b. St. Louis, Oct. 18, 1944; s. Donald and Loretto Agnes (Hennelly) G.; m. Carolyn Ormsby Ritter, Nov. 27, 1969; children: Mark Thomas, Christopher Michael, John Ritter, Elizabeth Jane. JD, St. Louis U., 1968. Bar: Mo. 1968, U.S. Dist. Ct. (ea and we. dists.) Mo. 1968, U.S. Tax Ct. 1972. Assoc. Gunn & Gunn, St. Louis, 1968-81; ptnr. Gunn & Lane, St. Louis, 1981-86; pvt. practice Ballwin, Mo., 1986—. Rep. ea. dist. Mo. Ct. Appeals. Sgt. U.S. Army, 1969-75. Mem. ABA (ho. of dels. 1988—), St. Louis Bar Assn., The Mo. Bar (bd. govs. 1990-2001, exec. com. 1993-94, pres.-elect 1998-99, pres. 1999-2000), Lawyers Assn. St. Louis (pres. 1981-82), St. Louis Bar Found. (pres. 1988-89), Bar Assn. Met. St. Louis (pres. 1987-88), Nat. Conf. Bar Founds. (trustee 1990-95, pres. 1993-94). Roman Catholic. State civil litigation, Estate planning, Probate (including wills, trusts). Home: 2232 Centeroyal Dr Saint Louis MO 63131-1910 Office: The Gunn Law Firm PC Ste 240 1714 Deer Tracks Trail Saint Louis MO 63131

GUNNING, FRANCIS PATRICK, lawyer, insurance association executive; b. Scranton, Pa., Dec. 10, 1923; s. Frank Peter and Mary Loretta (Kelly) G.; m. Nancy C. Hill, Aug. 10, 1951; 1 son, Brian F. Student, City Coll. N.Y., 1941-43; LLB, St. John's U., 1950. Bar: N.Y. 1950. Legal editor Prentice Hall Pub. Co., N.Y.C., 1950-51; legal specialist Tchrs. Ins. & Annuity Assn. Am., Coll. Retirement Equities Fund, N.Y.C., 1951-53, asst. counsel, 1953-57, assoc. counsel, 1957-60, counsel, 1960-65, asst. gen. counsel, 1965-67, assoc. gen. counsel, 1967, v.p., assoc. gen. counsel, 1967-73, sr. v.p., gen. counsel, 1973-74, exec. v.p., gen. counsel, 1974-88, ret., 1988. Trustee, mem. exec. and audit coms. Mortgage Growth Investors (now MGI Properties). Contbr. articles on mortgage financing to profl. jours. With USAAF, 1943-46. Mem. ABA, N.Y. State Bar Assn., Am. Land Title Assn., Am. Law Inst., Assn. of Bar of City of N.Y., Assn. Life Ins. Counsel, Nat. Assn. Coll. Univ. Attys., Am. Coll. Real Estate Lawyers. Republican. Roman Catholic. Home and Office: 32 Kewanee Rd New Rochelle NY 10804-1324

GUNNING, TIMOTHY MICHAEL, lawyer; b. Subic Bay, The Philippines, Aug. 2, 1964; s. Jean-Jacques and Irene Marie Gunning. BA in English, Boston Coll., 1986; JD, U. Md., Balt., 1990. Bar: Md. 1990, U.S. Dist. Ct. Md. 1990. Law clk. to Hon. James B. Dudley Cir. Ct. Howard County, Md., 1990—91; asst. state atty. Baltimore County, Towson, Md., 1991—96; assoc. Howell, Gately, Whitney & Carter LLP, Towson, 1996—97; pvt. practice Towson, 1997—. Mem.: Fed. Bar Assn., Md. State Bar Assn., Md. Criminal Def. Attys. Assn., Nat. Assn. Criminal Def. Attys. Avocations: fly fishing, hunting, skiing, exercise. Criminal, Professional liability, Personal injury (including property damage). Office: 305 Washington Ave Ste 301 Towson MD 21204 Office Fax: 410-296-3443. Business E-Mail: tgunning@radicus.net.

GUNTER, JOSEPH CLIFFORD, III, lawyer; b. Ft. Worth, Apr. 26, 1943; s. Joseph Cliford Jr. and Helen (Wright) G.; children: Joseph Clifford IV, Grant Norwood. BA, U. Tex., 1965, JD, 1967. Bar: Tex. 1967. Assoc. McDonald Sanders Ginsberg New Kirk Gibson & Webb, Ft. Worth, 1967-68; ptnr. Bracewell & Patterson, Houston, 1968—. Adv. Am. Bd. Trial Advocates. Lt. USNR, 1967-73. Fellow Am. Coll. Trial Lawyers, Tex. Bar Found., Houston Bar Found.; mem. ABA, State Bar Tex., State Bar Colo. Episcopalian. Avocations: golf, tennis. skiing, sailing. Office: Bracewell & Patterson 711 Louisiana St Ste 2900 Houston TX 77002-2781

GUNTER, MICHAEL DONWELL, lawyer; b. Gastonia, N.C., Mar. 26, 1947; s. Daniel Cornelius and DeNorma Joyce (Smith) G.; m. Barbara Jo Benson, June 19, 1970; children: Kimberly Elizabeth, Daniel Cornelius III. BA in History with honors, Wake Forest U., 1969; JD with honors, U. N.C., 1972; MBA with honors, U. Pa., 1973. Bar: N.C. 1972, U.S. Dist. Ct. (mid. dist.) N.C. 1974, U.S. Tax Ct. 1975, U.S. Supreme Ct. 1979, U.S. Claims Ct. 1982, U.S. Ct. Appeals (D.C. cir.) 1985, U.S. Ct. Appeals (4th cir.) 1992. Ptnr. Womble Carlyle Sandridge & Rice PLLC, Winston-Salem, N.C., 1974—; chmn. employee benefits practice group. Bd. dirs. G & J Enterprises Inc., Gastonia, Indsl. Belting Inc., Gastonia. Contbr. articles to profl. jours. Coach youth basketball Winston-Salem YMCA, 1981-90; advisor Winston-Salem United Way Christmas Cheer Toy Shop, 1975; fundraiser Deacon Club Wake Forest U., also mem. exec. com., strategic planning com., athletic coun., 1987—, v.p., pres., 1990-92; bd. dirs. Goodwill Industries, Winston-Salem, 1987—, chmn. bd., sec., chmn. fin. com.; bd. dirs. Centenary Meth. Ch., 1980; mem. cmty. problem solving com. United Way, 1988-99; mem. Leadership Winston-Salem, former mem. Alumni Coun. Wake Forest U., Cert. Com. NCAA, long range planning com. athletic dept. William E. Newcombe scholar U. Pa., 1972-73; selected One of Best Employee Benefits and Corp. Lawyers in Am., Nat. Law Jour. Fellow Am. Coll. Employee Benefits Counsel (charter); mem. ABA, So. Pension Conf., N.C. Bar Assn. (former chmn. tax sect., mem. continuing legal edn. com., sports and entertainment law com.), Forsyth County Bar Assn., Forsyth County Employee Benefit Coun., Winston-Salem Estate Planning Coun. (past bd. dirs.), Profit Sharing Coun. Am., ESOP Assn., Profit Sharing Coun., Assn. of Pvt. Pension and Welfare, Forsyth Country Club (former pres., bd. dirs.) Order of Coif, Rotary (former bd. dirs. Reynolda club). Democrat. Avocations: golf, fishing. Mergers and acquisitions, Pension, profit-sharing, and employee benefits, Corporate taxation. Home: 128 Ballyhoo Dr Lewisville NC 27023-9633 Office: Womble Carlyle Sandridge & Rice PLLC One West Fourth St Winston Salem NC 27101 E-mail: mgunter@wcsr.com.

GUNTER, RUSSELL ALLEN, lawyer; b. Amarillo, Tex., Feb. 21, 1950; s. J.B. and Shirley Ann (Russell) G.; children: Kim, Sarah, Laura, Rachel, Lindsay. BS in Polit. Sci., So. Ark U., 1972; JD, Tex. Tech U., 1975. Bar: Ark., 1975, Tex, 1975, U.S. Dist. Ct. (ea. and we dists.) Ark. 1975, U.S. Supreme Ct. (8th cir.) 1975, U.S. Dist. Ct. (no. dist.) Tex. 1976, U.S. Ct. Appeals (5th cir.), 1980, U.S. Supreme Ct. 1986. Assoc. Gaines N. Houston, Little Rock, 1975-79, Wallace, Dover & Dixon, P.A., Little Rock, 1979-90, McGlinchey Stafford Lang P.L.L.C., Little Rock, 1990-97; Cross, Gunter, Witherspoon & Galchus P.C., Little Rock, 1997—. Mem. ABA (com. on practice and procedure before NLRB labor sect.), Soc. for Human Resource Mgmt. (cert. sr. profl. in human resources), Ark. Bar Assn., Tex. Bar Assn. Labor (including EEOC, Fair Labor Standards Act, labor-management relations, NLRB, OSHA). Office: 500 E Markham St Ste 200 Little Rock AR 72201-1747

GUPTA, RAJAT KUMAR, lawyer, accountant; b. New Delhi, Apr. 22, 1960; arrived in U.S., 1970; s. Ravindra Kumar and Rama G. BBA, Rutgers Coll., New Brunswick, N.J., 1978-82; JD, Rutgers U., Newark, 1985-88. Bar: N.J. and Pa. 1989, U.S. Tax Ct. 1992; lic. CPA. Staff acct. Borrelli & Assocs., Highland Park, NJ, 1983-84, S. Kirschenbaum & Co., CPA, East Brunswick, N.J., 1984-85; tax assoc. Coopers & Lybrand, Princeton, N.J., 1988-89; pvt. practice atty. New Brunswick, 1989-98; sr. assoc. Spevack & Cannan, P.A., Iselin, NJ, 1998—2000; fin. specialist N.J. Supreme Ct. - Office Atty. Ethics, Trenton, 2000—03; gen. counsel Premier Abstract and Title Agy., Inc., Cranbury, NJ, 2003—. Mentor Rutgers Law Sch., Seton Hall Law Sch., Asian and Pacific Law Students Assn. Prodn. editor Rutgers Computer & Technology Law Jour., 1987-88, Cannonball-One Lap of America, 1988; contbr. articles to profl. jours. Arbitrator Better Bus. Bur., Newark, 1986—87; vol. atty. Rutgers U. Off Campus Housing Ctr., 1996—2000; mem. com. on character N.J. Supreme Ct., 1997—2000. Mem.: AICPA, ABA, Accts. for Pub. Interest, Mercer County Bar Assn., Asian and Pacific Lawyers Assn. Hindu. Avocations: tennis, travel, photography, art. Commercial, consumer (including collections, credit), Property, real (including real estate development, water). Office: 1006 Eastpark Blvd Cranbury NJ 08512

GURFEIN, RICHARD ALAN, lawyer; b. N.Y.C., Nov. 4, 1946; s. Jack and Ruth (Kronowitz) G.; m. Erica P. Temchin, Oct. 20, 1978; children: Jared L., Amanda, Jessica M., Sarah R. BE, NYU, 1967; JD, Bklyn. Law Sch., 1971. Bar: N.Y. 1972, U.S. Dist. Ct. (so. and ea. dists.) N.Y. 1973, U.S. Supreme Ct. 1976, U.S. Ct. Appeals (2d cir.) 1990. Assoc. Mark B. Wiesen, PC, N.Y.C., 1972-78; ptnr. Wiesen & Gurfein, N.Y.C., 1978-82, Wiesen, Gurfein & Jenkins, N.Y.C., 1982-2001; pres. Triall.com, Inc., 1997—; prin. Richard A. Gurfein & Assocs., PLLC, 2001—02; founder and ptnr. Gurfein Douglas LLP, 2002—. Moderator, lectr. Nassau Acad. Law, 1984—, N.Y. State Trial Lawyers Inst., 1985—, treas., 1989-91, pres. 1995-96. Recipient Crown of Good Name award Inst. Jewish Humanities, 1996. Mem. Assn. Trial Lawyers Am., N.Y. State Trial Lawyers Assn. (lectr. continuing legal edn. 1985—, bd. dirs. 1986—, chmn. com. on coms. 1987-88, exec. com. 1987—, dep. treas. 1988-89, treas. 1989-91, sec. 1991-92, v.p. 1992-94, pres. elect 1994-95, pres. 1995-96, past pres. 1996—), N.Y. County Lawyers Assn., Nassau County Bar Assn. (chmn. com. on med. jurisprudence 1983-86), Million Dollar Advocates Forum, N.Y. State Bar Assn., Bklyn. Bar Assn. Avocations: astronomy, amateur radio, photography, golf, computing. State civil litigation, Personal injury (including property damage), Product liability. Office: Gurfein Douglas LLP 11 Park Pl Rm 1100 New York NY 10007-2889 E-mail: rgurfein@trial1.com.

GURLEY, RICHARD T. lawyer; b. Aurora, Ill., June 1, 1961; Student, Creighton U.; BSBA, Ind. U., 1983; JD, Drake U., 1986. Bar: Fla. 1987, U.S. Dist. Ct. (mid. dist.) Fla. 1988, U.S. Ct. Appeals (11th cir.) 1988, Ill. 1993, Colo. 1993, U.S. Dist. Ct. Colo. 1998. Asst. state atty. 6th Jud. Cir., Clearwater, Fla., 1986—91, lead trial atty., 1987—89, divsn. dir., 1989—91; atty. Fox & Grove, Chartered, St. Petersburg, Fla., 1991—94; ptnr. Kidder, Gurley & Bennett, St. Petersburg, Fla., 1994—97; atty. Carlson & Meissner, Clearwater, 1997—98; ptnr. Carlson, Meissner & Gurley, Clearwater, 1999—. Sponsor ski team Buddy Werner Ski Club, Powderhorn Resort, Mesa, Colo., 2000—; bd. dirs. Performing Arts Conservatory, Grand Junction, 1999—, pres., 2001. Mem.: ATLA, Pinellas County (Fla.) Trial Lawyers Assn. (pres. 1995), Colo. Trial Lawyers Assn. (eagle mem.), Colo. Workers Compensation Edn. Assn. Avocation: downhill skiing. Personal injury (including property damage), Workers' compensation, Criminal. Office: Carlson Meissner & Gurley 851 Grand Ave Grand Junction CO 81501 Office Fax: 970-255-6660.

GURRIERI, MARIO CHARLES, lawyer; b. Plainfield, N.J., July 12, 1947; s. Mario James and Lillian I. (Casabona) G. BA, Rutgers U., 1969; JD, Columbia U., 1972. Bar: N.J. 1972, U.S. Dist. Ct. N.J. 1972, U.S. Ct. Appeals (3d cir.) 1972. Assoc. Shanley & Fisher, Newark, 1972-73; ptnr. Snevily, Ely, Williams & Gurrieri Westfield, N.J., 1973—2000; sr. ptnr. Dughi, Hewit & Palatucci, Cranford, N.J., 2000—. Planning bd. atty. Borough of Garwood (N.J.), 1980—87; arbitrator Matrimonial Settlement Panel, Union County, N.J., 1977— . Mem. Colonia Country Club (bd. dirs. 1982—97, pres. 1996-97), Phi Beta Kappa. Roman Catholic. State civil litigation, Family and matrimonial, Personal injury (including property damage). Home: 210 Lynn Ln Westfield NJ 07090-1811 Office: Dughi Hewit & Palatucci 340 North Ave Cranford NJ 07016 E-mail: mgurrieri@dhplaw.net.

GURSTEL, NORMAN KEITH, lawyer; b. Mpls., Mar. 24, 1939; s. Jules and Etta (Abramowitz) G.; m. Jane Evelyn Golden, Nov. 24, 1984; children: Todd, Dana, Marc. BA, U. Minn., 1960, JD, 1962. Bar: Minn. 1962, U.S. Dist. Ct. Minn. 1963, U.S. Supreme Ct. 1980. Assoc. Robins, Davis & Lyons, Mpls., 1962-67; prin. Gurstel & Gurstel, Mpls., 1967-97. Arbitrator Hennepin County Dist. Ct., 1988-91; parttime referee family ct. Hennepin County Dist.; lectr. U. Minn. Family Law Seminar. Mem. ABA (corp. banking and bus. law and family law sects.), Minn. Bar Assn. (co-chmn. family ct. com. bankruptcy law sect. 1966-67, family law and bankruptcy law), Hennepin County Bar Assn. (chmn. family law com. 1964-65, vice chmn. 1981-91, fee arbitration bd., creditors remedy com.), Fed. Bar Assn., Assn. Trial Lawyers Am., Minn. Trial Lawyers Assn., Am. Acad. Matrimonial Lawyers, Nat. Council Juvenile and Family Ct. Judges, Comml. Law League Am. (recording sec. 1980-81, bd. govs. 1983-89, pres. 1987-88), Comml. Law League Fund for Pub. Edn. (sec. 1981-83, pres. 1989-92, bd. dirs. 1989-94), Phi Delta Phi. Clubs: Oak Ridge Country (Mpls.). Lodges: Shriners, Masons. Jewish. Bankruptcy, Commercial, contracts (including sales of goods; commercial financing), Family and matrimonial. Office: Marc Shawn Inc 3330 Galleria Edina MN 55435 E-mail: marcshawmen@att.com.

GURULI, ZVIAD VLADIMIR, law administrator, consultant; b. Tbilisi, Georgia, Feb. 1, 1975; s. Vladimir Vasili Guruli and Leila Philimon Sigua; m. Erin Lee Mills, May 16, 2002. Law degree with honors, Ivane Javakhishvili Tbilisi State U., Georgia, 1996; JD, Loyola U., 2000; LLM with distinction, Georgetown U., 2002. Bar: La. 2000. Head of dept. for bus. cooperation with fgn. countries Internat. Assn. GII, Tbilisi, Georgia, 1991—92; trainee Ministry of Fgn. Affairs of Ga., 1992—94; dir. of internat. ops. Musa Ltd., 1994—97; dep. dir. American-Georgian Acad. of Medicine and Surgery, 1996—97; asst. to the pres. Eduard Shevardnadze Found. Democracy and Revival, 1996—97; personal interpreter Ministry of Fgn. Affairs of Ga., 1997—97; rsch. asst. immigration law Loyola U. Sch. Law, New Orleans, 1998—99, tchg. asst. appellate advocacy class, 1999—99; law clk. (pro bono) Cath. Charities, 2000. Named Nat. Champion, Tulane Mardi Gras Nat. Sports Law Competition, Tulane U. Law Sch., 1999; recipient CALI Excellence for Future award in Internat. Project Fin., Georgetown U. Law Ctr., 2002, Second Pl., Stetson Internat. Moot Ct. Competition, Stetson Law Sch., 1999; scholar Dean's Law scholar, Loyola U. Sch. Law, 1997—2000. Mem.: ABA, La. Bar Assn. Personal E-mail: zguruli@hotmail.com.

GUSHEE, RICHARD BORDLEY, lawyer; b. Detroit, Aug. 25, 1926; s. Edward Tisdale and Norine Amelia (Bordley) G.; m. Marilyn Lucy Flynn, June 9, 1951; children: Jacqueline Lowe (dec. 1977), Peter Hale. BA, Williams Coll., 1947; JD, U. Mich., 1950. Bar: Mich. 1951, U.S. Supreme Ct. 1961. Assoc. Miller, Canfield, Paddock and Stone, Detroit, 1950-58, ptnr., 1959-93, of counsel, 1994—. Chmn. Tri-county Hearing Panel #18 of Atty. Discipline Bd. Former trustee United Community Svcs.; former chancellor Episc. Diocese Mich. With USAF, 1945. Mem. ABA. Office: Miller Canfield Paddock & Stone 150 W Jefferson Ave Ste 2500 Detroit MI 48226-4416 E-mail: gushee@millercanfield.com.

GUST, GERALD NORMAN, lawyer; b. Amery, Wis., Dec. 26, 1946; s. Orville Edward and Lucille Clarice (Warner) G.; m. Susan Jean Dudding, Oct. 3, 1970; children: Shayne, Thomas, Betsy, Megan. BS, U. Wis., River Falls, 1969; JD, U. Wis., 1972. Bar: Wis. 1972, U.S. Dist. Ct. (we. dist.) Wis. 1972. Ptnr. Cwayna, Novitzke, Byrnes, Gust, Williams & Erspamer Ltd., Amery, 1972-87, Novitzke & Gust, Amery, 1987—. Instr. U. Wis. Law Sch., Madison, 1983, 85, 87. Atty. City of Amery, 1975-80, Village of Deer Park, Wis., 1975-80; chmn. Polk County Dem. Party, Amery, 1973-79, DNR Appeal Panel, Amery, 1977; mem. Minn.-Wis. Boundary Area Commn., Amery, 1978-80; mem. Dist. Atty.'s Bd. Profl. Responsibility, 1982-94. Mem. ABA, Wis. Bar Assn., St. Croix Valley Bar Assn., Assn. Trial Lawyers Am., Wis. Acad. Trial Lawyers (bd. dirs. 1982-2001). Democrat. Lutheran. State civil litigation, Personal injury (including property damage), Workers' compensation. Office: # 399 314 Keller Ave N Amery WI 54001-1055

GUSTAFSON, ALBERT KATSUAKI, lawyer, engineer; b. Tokyo, Dec. 5, 1949; arrived in U.S., 1951; s. William A. and Akiko (Osada) Gustafson; m. Helen Melissa Laird, July 31, 1971 (div. 1975); m. Karen Jane Ekblad, Dec. 31, 1978 (div. 1987). BA with distinction, Stanford U., 1972; JD, U. Wash., 1980. Bar: Wash. 1981, U.S. Dist. Ct. (we. dist.) Wash. 1981, U.S. Ct. Appeals (9th cir.) 1984, NY 1993. Acoustics analyst Boeing Co., Seattle, 1973—74, material buyer, 1974; legal editor Book Pub. Co., Seattle, 1975—76; rsch. analyst Batelle Inst., Seattle, 1975—76; legal intern Office of U.S. Atty., Seattle, 1976; engr. U.P.R.R., 1977—85; corp. counsel Dorden, Inc., Centralia, Wash., 1984—87, Ansette Fin. Corp., Inc., Seattle, 1987—89, Precision Forms, Inc., 1988, Endo and Mamba, 1989—93; of counsel Barkats and Assocs., 1991—98; prin. Albert K. Gustafson, P.S., Seattle, 1981—93; pres. Shomei Corp., 1990—95, Shomei, Kokusai, Kabushki, Kaisha, 1991—95; v.p. Sierra Capital Mgmt., Inc., 1992—93; prof. internat. bus. law Sch. Internat. Studies Nichibei Kaiwa Gakuen, Tokyo, 1989—90, Nippon Tel. & Tel., 1989—90. Bd. dirs. Daiki, Inc.; v.p. ops. BND Sea and Airlines Corp., 1997—98; dir., counsel Zinza K.K., 1998—, pres., rep. dir., 2002—; rep. dir. Multipro K.K., 1998—2002. Mem. nat. bd. editors Prentice-Hall Rigos CPA Review, 1991—93. Sec. local 117-E United Transp. Union, 1984, local vice-chmn., 1984; Dem. precinct chmn., 1984. Named Kraft scholar, 1968, Calif. State scholar, 1968—72. Mem.: ABA, Japan-Am. Soc., Roppongi Bar Assn., Seattle-King County Bar Assn., Inter-Pacific Bar Assn., Asian Bar Assn., Internat. Bar Assn., Imperial Club, Century Ct. Club, City Club, College Club, Rotary, Order of DeMolay (master councilor 1968), Shriners, Masons. Presbyterian. Commercial, contracts (including sales of goods; commercial financing), Private international, Corporate, general. Address: #404 Asahi Iidabashi Mansion 1-9-6 Iidabashi Chiyoda-ku Tokyo 102-0072 Japan also: 75 Shoe Ln London England EC4 BQ also: 3917 Interlake Ave N Seattle WA 98103 also: 5 Krasnoznamenny By-str 690000 Vladivostok Russia also: PO Box 12 600 Main St Cobleskill NY 12043 also: 67 Wall St 22nd Fl New York NY 10005 Business E-Mail: ananda@gol.com.

GUSTMAN, DAVID CHARLES, lawyer; b. Yokuska, Japan, Mar. 16, 1954; s. David C. and Marilyn N. Gustman; m. Lisa S. Seyferth, Mar. 7, 1987; children: Hunter, David, Corrie. BA in Econs., U. Mich., 1975; JD, George Washington U., 1979. Bar: Ill. 1979, U.S. Dist. Ct. (no. dist.) Ill. 1979, U.S. Dist. Ct. (ea. dist.) Wis. 1988, U.S. Dist. Ct. (ctrl. dist.) Ill. 1990, U.S. Dist. Ct. (so. dist.) Ill. 1991, U.S. Ct. Appeals (fed. cir.) 1988, U.S. Ct. Appeals (7th cir.) 1990, U.S. Supreme Ct. 1994, U.S. Ct. Appeals (8th cir.) 1997, U.S. Dist. Ct. (ea. dist.) Mich. 1997. Clk. Arter & Hadden, Washington, 1977-78; assoc. Rooks, Pitts & Poust, Chgo., 1979-84, Freeborn & Peters, Chgo., 1984-86, ptnr., 1986—, chmn., mng. ptnr., 1996-2000, chmn., 2000—02. Mem. exec. com. Freeborn & Peters, 2000—; mem. BNA Antitrust and Trade Regulation Adv. Bd., 2002—. Articles editor: Jour. Internat. Law & Econs., 1978-79. Bd. dirs. Constitutional Rights Found., Chgo., 1982-88. Mem. ABA, Ill. State Bar Assn., Mich. Shores Club, Met. Club, Sheridan Shores Yacht Club. Avocations: skiing, sailing, running. Antitrust, General civil litigation. Office: Freeborn & Peters 311 S Wacker Dr Ste 3000 Chicago IL 60606-6679 Fax: 312-360-6571. E-mail: dgustman@freebornpeters.com.

GUTERMANN, ARNE K.E. lawyer; b. Antwerp, Belgium, Nov. 7, 1964; m. Caroline M.M. Boutry, Mar. 15, 1997; children: Elise S.M., Kilian J.P. Candidate in Law, U. Antwerp, Belgium, 1984; JD, Cath. U. Leuven, Belgium, 1987; LLM, U. Va., 1988; German Eignungspruefung, Grannemann & von Fuerstenberg, Baden-Baden, Germany, 1996. Bar: Brussels 1988, Frankfurt 1996. Internat. ptnr. Baker & McKenzie, Brussels, 1998—. Voting mem. Nat. Recruitment and Exam Commn. for Belgian Magistrates, Brussels, 1997—2000; part-time judge Comml. Ct. Brussels, Brussels, 1998—. Scholar Fulbright award, Fulbright Found., 1988. Mergers and acquisitions, Commercial, consumer (including collections, credit), Communications. Office: Baker & McKenzie Louizalaan 149 Brussels 1050 Belgium Office Fax: 02 639 36 99. E-mail: arne.gutermann@bakernet.com.

GUTFELD, NORMAN E. lawyer; b. Pitts., Dec. 8, 1911; s. Adolph and Fannie (Haupt) G.; m. Evelyn Kirtz, Aug. 9, 1938 (dec. Jan. 1989); children: Nancy Gutfeld Brown, Howard, Charles, Joan Gutfeld Miller, Rose Gutfeld Edwards, Steven. BA, Case-Western Res. U., 1933, LL.B., 1935. Bar: Ohio 1935. Individual practice law, Cleve., 1935-43; atty. U.S. Regional War Labor Bd., Cleve., 1944; assoc. firm Benesch, Friedlander & Morris, Cleve., 1944-53; treas. Builders Structural Steel Corp., Cleve., 1953-59; partner Garber, Gutfeld & Jaffe, Cleve., 1959-73, Simon, Haiman, Gutfeld, Friedman and Jacobs, Cleve., 1973-80; of counsel Hertz Kates Friedman & Kammer, Cleve., 1981-93; pvt. practice Cleve., 1993-95; retired, 1995. Mem. Cleveland Heights-University Heights Bd. Edn., 1956-63, pres., 1958-59; treas. Bur. Jewish Edn. Cleve., 1974-79; trustee Cleve. Jewish Community Fedn., 1976-77. Mem. Bar Assn. Greater Cleve., Ohio State Bar Assn., Citizen's League Cleve. Clubs: Cleve. City. Home: 3151 Mayfield Rd Cleveland Heights OH 44118

GUTHEINZ, JOSEPH RICHARD, JR., lawyer, former politician, investigative consultant, retired army officer and NASA official, educator, author; b. Camp Lejune, N.C., Aug. 13, 1955; s. Joseph R. Sr. and Rita C. (O'Leary) G.; m. Lori Ann Bentley, Jan. 16, 1976; children: Joseph, Christopher, Michael, Jim, Bill, Dave. AS, AA, Monterey Peninsula Coll., Calif., 1975; BA, Calif. State U., Sacramento, 1978, MA, 1979; postgrad., U. Calif., Davis, 1979-80; grad. U.S. Army Mil. Intelligence Officer Basic Course, U.S. Army Tactical Intelligence Sch., 1980; grad., U.S. Army Flight Sch., 1984; MS in Sys. Mgmt., U. So. Calif., 1985; JD, S. Tex. Coll. Law, 1996; grad. Criminal Investigators Basic Course (hon.), Fed. Law Enforcement Tng. Ctrs., 1988; grad. (disting.), Fed. Law Enforcement Tng. Ctrs. Office Inspector Gen., 1989. Bar: Tex. Supreme Ct. 1997, U.S. Dist. Ct. (so. dist.) Tex. 1997, U.S. Vets. Ct. Appeals 1998, U.S. Armed Forces Ct. Appeals 1998, U.S. Ct. Appeals (5th, 10th, 11th and fed. cirs.) 1998, U.S. Tax Ct. 1998, U.S. Supreme Ct. 2001; lic. FAA comml. pilot, cert. fraud examiner, tchr. credentials in aeronautics, mil. sci., bus. and indsl. mgmt., pub. svcs. and adminstrn., sociology and police sci. Calif. Officer U.S. Army, Kitzigen, Fed. Rep. Germany, 1980-82, capt., mil. intelligence officer Stuttgart, Fed. Rep. Germany, 1982-84, capt., aviator Ft. Polk, La., 1984-86; spl. agt. civil aviation security FAA, Oklahoma City, 1986-87; spl. agt. U.S. Dept. Transp., Denver, 1987-90; sr. spl. agt., acting sr. resident agent in charge Office Insp. Gen. NASA, Houston, 1990-2000; pvt. practice atty. Houston, 1996—; mentor, instr. organized crime U. Phoenix, 2002—. Police sci. instr. Ctrl. Tex. Coll., Nelligan, 1983; case agt. in pilot match investigation FBI/FAA Pilot Match Investigation, 1989—90; case agt. in charge of investigating space shuttle temperature transducers Grounded Shuttle Fleet, 1991; task force leader Nine Agy. Fed. Omniplan, 1992—96; guest spkr. Internat. Bus. Forum, 1995, Assn. Govt. Accts., 1996, NASA OIG Auditor Conf., 2000; chief NASA OIG investigator Russian Mir Space Stas. fire and collision, 1997; task force leader Bid and Proposal Investigation Rockwell Space and Ops. Co., 1996—2000; criminal def. atty., expert witness, 1997—; chief investigator and arresting agt. Jerry Whittridge the astronaut and CIA assassin impersonator, 1998, Op. Lunar Eclipse, 1998—2000; investigator Civilian Astronaut Corps., 1999—2002; task force leader Fed. Agy. Investigation Rockwell Internat./Boeing N.Am. and U.S. Alliance, 2000; task force leader Fed. Agy. Investigation; extensively quoted on Columbia disaster, 2003. Pres. Calif. State U. United Students for Life, 1976—79; chairperson Calif. Rally for Life, 1980; atty./activist against San Jacinto C.C. spl. election to annex parts of Clear Lake Texas; proponent Calif. Pro-Life Initiative, 1977; organizer Morton Downey Dem. Presdl. Campaign, 1979; bd. dirs. Sea Isle Property Owners, 2001—02; briefed Pres. Yeltsin's econ. advisors, 1995. Decorated U.S. Army Meritorious Svc. medal, Army Commendation medal; recipient letter of commendation FBI Dir. Louis Freeh, 1995, Tex. Spl. Commendation U.S. Atty. Office So. Dist., 1996, NASA Exceptional Svc. medal, 2000, Pres.'s Coun. for Integrity and Efficiency Career Achievement award, 2000; named Hon. Lt. Gov. Okla., 1987; Merit scholar South Tex. Coll. Law. Mem. Cert. Fraud Examiners, Tex. Bar Assn., Tex. Criminal Def. Lawyers Assn. Republican. Roman Catholic. Avocations: reading, teaching, public speaking, political activism, helping the poor. General practice. Office: 205 Woodcombe Houston TX 77062 E-mail: jguteinz@sbcglobal.net.

GUTHERY, JOHN M. lawyer; b. Broken Bow, Nebr., Nov. 22, 1946; s. John M. and Kay G.; m. Diane Messineo, May 26, 1972; 1 child, Lisa. BS, U. Nebr., 1969, JD, 1972. Bar: Nebr. 1972. Pres. Perry, Guthery, Haase & Gessford, P.C., L.L.O., Lincoln, Nebr., 1972—. Bd. govs. Nebr. Wesleyan U. Mem. ATLA, ABA (mem. litigation section), Nebr. Bank Attys. Assn. (past pres., 1985-86), Nebr. Assn. Trial Attys., Nebr. State Bar Assn. (pres. 1998-99, mem. Nebr.State Bar Found. mem. ho. dels. 1979-83, 87-95, exec. coun. 1988-94 pres. elect. 1997-98, chair Nebr. bankruptcy sect.), Lincoln Bar Assn. (bd. trustees, 1985-88, pres. 1990-91). Banking, General civil litigation, Personal injury (including property damage). Office: Perry Guthery Haase & Gessford PC LLO 233 S 13th St Ste 1400 Lincoln NE 68508-2003 E-mail: jguthery@perrylawfirm.com.

GUTHMAN, JACK, lawyer; b. Cologne, Germany, Apr. 19, 1938; came to U.S., 1939, naturalized, 1945; s. Albert and Selma (Cahn) G.; m. Sandra Polk, Nov. 26, 1967. BA, Northwestern U., 1960; LL.B., Yale U., 1963. Bar: Ill. bar 1963. Law clk. to dist. judge U.S. Dist. Ct. No. Ill., 1963-65; since practiced in Chgo.; ptnr. Sidley & Austin, 1970-94, Shefsky & Froelich Ltd., Chgo., 1995—. Mem. City Chgo. Zoning Bd. Appeals, 1970-75, chmn., 1975-87. Democrat. Jewish. Administrative and regulatory, Legislative, Property, real (including real estate development, water). Office: Shefsky & Froelich Ltd 444 N Michigan Ave Ste 2500B Chicago IL 60611-3998

GUTHRIE, JUDITH K. federal judge; b. Chgo., July 13, 1948; d. David Curtis and Kathleen McAfee G.; m. John H. Hannah, Jr., May 9, 1992. Student, Ariz. State U., 1966-68; BA, St. Mary's U., 1971; JD cum laude, U. Houston, 1980. Bar: Tex. 1981, U.S. Dist. Ct. (ea. dist.) Tex. 1982, U.S. Ct. Appeals (5th cir.) 1982, U.S. Dist. Ct. (no. dist.) Tex. 1983, U.S. Dist. Ct. (we. dist.) Tex. 1984. Editor Am. Coun. Edn., Washington, 1972-73; exec. asst. Tex. Ho. Reps., Austin, 1973-75; lobbyist Bracewell & Patterson, Austin, 1975-80, assoc. Houston, 1980-81; briefing atty. Tex. Ct. Appeals, Tyler, 1981-82; ptnr. Hannah & Guthrie, Tyler, Tex., 1982-86; magistrate judge U.S. Dist. Ct. (ea. dist.) Tex., Tyler, 1986—. Instr. legal asst. program,

Tyler Jr. Coll., 1986-87; apptd. Tex. Judicial Coun., 1991-97, gender bias task force, 1991-92; lectr. in field. Contbr. articles to profl. jours. Adv. bd. Main St. Project; legal asst. adv. bd. Tyler Jr. Coll., 1986—, chmn. adv. bd., 1996—; mem. Citizens Commn. Tex. Jud. Sys., 1992—93; bd. dirs. Habitat for Humanity, 2003—; former Dme. chmn. Smith County; former bd. dirs. Found. Women's Resources, Leadership Am., Leadership Tex. Mem.: ABA ((Fed. trial judges legis. com. 1991-93)), Smith County Bar Assn. ((chmn. law libr. com. 1985-2001)), State Bar Tex. ((various coms., including dist. 2A grievance com. 1990-96/chmn. 95-96)), 5th Cir. Bar Assn., Fed. magistrate Judges Assn., Am. Judges Assn., Habitit for Humanity (bd. dirs. 2003—). Office: US District Court 300 Federal Bldg & US Ct House 211 W Ferguson St Tyler TX 75702-7212

GUTHRIE, LAWRENCE SIMPSON, II, law librarian, journalist; b. Thomas, Okla., Dec. 2, 1953; s. Lawrence Simpson and Helen Marie (Janning) G. BS, Georgetown U., 1976, Anna Freud Ctr., London, 1979; MA, U. Okla., 1980; MS in Libr. Sci., Cath. U. Am., 1988. Asst. prof. psychology Tulsa Cmty. Coll., 1982-86; grad. libr. nursing/biology Cath. U. Am., Washington, 1986-89; law libr. interlibr. loan George Washington U. Law Libr., Washington, 1989-95, Covington & Burling, Washington, 1995—. Author: Sports Libraries, 1995, Medieval Library Taxonomies, 2003; contbr. articles to profl. jours. including History of Cataloging, 2003; start-up cons., D.C. corr. Urban Tulsa newspaper, 1990-93; founder Today's Events col. Tulsa World Newspaper, 1978-79; columnist Copyright Corner, Information Outlook, 1997—. Bd. dirs. Cath. U. Sch. Libr. and Info. Sci. Alumni Assn., Washington, 1990-92; moderator White House Conf. on Librs., Washington, 1991; donated Okla. flag to John F. Kennedy Ctr. Hall of States, Washington, 1988. Recipient commendation as educator of all levels Okla. Gov. & Legislature, 1989. Mem. Am. Assn. Law Librs., Spl. Librs. Assn. (copyright com. 1992-95, govt. rels. com. 1995—, chmn. 1996—, chmn. legal divsn. 1999-2000, Liverpool del. 2002), Nat. Press Club. Democrat. Roman Catholic. Avocations: ice skating, baseball, walking. Home: 2450 Virginia Ave NW Apt E317 Washington DC 20037-2654 Office: Covington & Burling 1201 Pennsylvania Ave NW Washington DC 20004-2401

GUTIERREZ, ALFONSO, lawyer; b. La Coruna, Spain, Aug. 30, 1968; Degree in law, Salamanca, 1991; LLM, Coll. Europe, 1993. Bar: Madrid 1999. Assoc. Gomez-Acebo & Pombo, Brussels, 1994—96, Forrester Norall & Sutton White & Case, 1996—98; sr. assoc. Uria & Menendez, Madrid, 1999—. Antitrust. Office: Uria & Menendez Jorge Joan 6 28001 Madrid Spain Fax: 0034 915860753. E-mail: agh@uria.com.

GUTIÉRREZ CHAMLATI, JORGE, lawyer; b. Mexico City, Mex., Apr. 4, 1970; arrived in Brazil, 1997; s. Jorge Gutiérrez Cruz and Salua Chamlati Rodea. Lawyer, Instituto Tecnologico de Estudios Superiores de Occidente (ITESO), Guadalajara, Mex., 1992; postdegree, Escuela Libre de Derecho, 1997. Lawyer Bayata and Assocs., S.C., Mexico City, 1995—96, Hardin, Hess & Hanhausen S.C., Mexico City, 1996—97, Trench, Rossi and Watanabe, Sao Paulo, Brazil, 1998—. Avocations: tennis, travel, reading. Corporate, general. Office: Trench Rossi and Watanabe Attys at Law Assoc Baker & McKenzie Ave Dr Chucri Zaidan 920 13th Fl 04583 904 São Paulo Brazil Office Fax: 55 11 5506 3455.

GUTIS, MARK PHILIP, lawyer; b. Mt. Vernon, N.Y., July 12, 1952; s. David Maxwell Gutis and Shirley (Morris) Queen; m. M. Joyal Guertin, June 2, 1974; 1 child, Sara Helene. BA, Syracuse U., 1974; MS, MLS, So. Conn. State Coll., 1978; JD (with honors), U. Conn., 1987. Bar: Conn. 1987, U.S. Dist. Ct. Conn. 1988. 2nd lt. USAF, 1974-77; staff libr. W.Va. U. Med. Ctr., Charleston, W.Va., 1979-80; libr., instr. We. Conn. State Coll., Danbury, Conn., 1980-83; libr. Whiting Forensic Inst., Middletown, Conn., 1983-87; legal asst. Gersten & Gersten, Hartford, Conn., 1987; atty. Brown & Welsh, Meriden, Conn., 1987-88, Green & Kleinman, Hartford, 1988-89; adminstrv. hearing officer Conn. Dept. Motor Vehicles, Wethersfield, Conn., 1989—; atty. Mark P. Gutis, Wethersfield, Conn., 1989—. Administrative and regulatory, General practice.

GUTKNECHT, TIMOTHY ARTHUR, lawyer; b. Detroit, Apr. 5, 1968; s. Bruce Arthur and Anita Jane (Thomas) G.; m. Heather Wall, June 9, 1990; 1 child, Andrew Michael. BA, Amherst Coll., 1990; JD, Washington U., St. Louis, 1993. Bar: Ill. 1993, Mo. 1994, U.S. Dist. Ct. (so. dist.) Ill. 1996, U.S. Ct. Appeals (7th cir.) 1997, U.S. Supreme Ct. 1998. Assoc. Crowder & Scoggins, Columbia, Ill., 1993—. Mem. ABA, Ill. State Bar Assn., St. Clair County Bar Assn., Monroe County Bar Assn. (pres. 1998-99). Appellate, General civil litigation, General practice. Office: Crowder & Scoggins Ltd 121 W Legion Ave Columbia IL 62236-2341 E-mail: tgutknecht@csowderscoggins.com.

GUTMAN, RICHARD EDWARD, lawyer; b. New Haven, Apr. 9, 1944; s. Samuel and Marjorie (Leo) G.; m. Jill Leslie Senft, June 8, 1969 (dec.); 1 child, Paul Senft; m. Rosann Seasonwein, Dec. 10, 1987. AB, Harvard U., 1965; JD, Columbia U., 1968. Bar: N.Y. 1969, U.S. Ct. Appeals (2d cir.) 1969, U.S. Dist. Ct. (so. and ea. dists.) N.Y. 1975, U.S. Supreme Ct. 1982, Tex. 1991. Counsel Exxon Corp., N.Y.C., 1978-90, Dallas, 1990-91, asst. gen. counsel, 1992-99, Exxon Mobil Corp., Dallas, 1999—. Pres. 570 Park Ave Apts., Inc., N.Y.C., 1984-89, past bd. dirs. Fellow Am. Bar Found. (life); mem. ABA (fed. regulation securities com., vice-chmn. 1995-98), Am. Law Inst., N.Y. State Bar Assn. (exec. com. 1983-86, 93—, securities regulation com. 1980—, chmn. 1993-97, chmn. bus. law sect. 2001-02), Assn. of Bar of City of N.Y. (securities regulation com. 1980-81, 83-86), Dallas Bar Assn., Coll. of the State Bar of Tex., N.A.M. (corp. fin. and mgmt. com.), Harvard Club (N.Y.C., admissions com. 1983-86, chmn. 1985-86, nominating com. 1986-87, bd. dirs. 1988-91, v.p. 1990-91), Harvard Club (Dallas bd. dirs. 1998-2001). Corporate, general, Finance, Securities.

GUTMAN, RICHARD MARTIN, lawyer; b. Chgo., Mar. 12, 1946; s. Raymond Tobias and Frieda (Garber) G.; m. Linda Ellen Fisher, June 14, 1987; children: Miriam, Eve. BA cum laude, Harvard U., 1967; JD, U. Chgo., 1973. Bar: Oreg. 1973, Ill. 1974, U.S. Dist. Ct. (no. dist.) Ill. 1974, U.S. Ct. Appeals (7th cir.) 1977, Pa. 1990, U.S. Dist. Ct. (mid. dist.) Pa. 1991, U.S. Supreme Ct. 1991, U.S. Ct. Appeals (3d cir.) 1993, N.J. 1996, U.S. Dist. Ct. N.J. 1996. Vol. Peace Corps, 1967-69; staff atty. ACLU Police Project, Chgo., 1973-74; pvt. practice, Chgo., 1975-90, Carlisle, Pa., 1990-95, Montclair, N.J., 1995—; dir. Polit. Surveillance Litigation Project, Chgo., 1975-90; investigator, writer Ralph Nader Congress project, Washington, 1972. Author: (with others) The Environment Committees, 1975; contbr. articles to prof. jours. Recipient 5th Anniversary award Alliance to End Repression, Chgo., 1975, Legal Eagle award Ind. Voters Ill.-Ind. Precinct Orgn., Chgo., 1981, Award of Distinction, 1st Unitarian Ch., Chgo., 1982, 1st Amendment award Citizens Alert, chgo., 1997. Mem. ACLU (pres. South Cen. Pa. chpt. 1992-95). Constitutional, Freedom of Information. Office: 55 Warfield St Montclair NJ 07043-1116

GUTTENTAG, JOSEPH HARRIS, lawyer, educator; b. Boston, Feb. 8, 1929; s. Samuel Alexander and Sara (Hurwitz) G.; m. Merna Fay Cohn, June 18, 1961; children: Steven, Adam, Alice AB, U. Mich., 1950; LLB, Harvard U., 1953. Bar: D.C. 1953, Mich. 1954. Internat. tax counsel U.S. Treasury, Washington, 1967-68; ptnr. Surrey & Morse, Washington, 1965-67, 68-79, Arnold & Porter, Washington, 1979-94, 1991-94; dep. asst. sec. internat. tax affairs U.S. Treasury, Washington, 1994-99, sr. advisor Office of Tax Policy, 1999-2000. Adj. prof. Howard Law Sch., Washington, 1964-67; professorial lectr. George Washington U. Sch. Law, 1968-75 Chmn. com. fiscal affairs Orgn. Econ. Coop. and Devel., Paris; mem. adv. commn. Elec. Commerce, 1999-2000; v.p. Levine Sch. Music. Capt. USAF, 1954-57. Mem. D.C. Bar Assn. (treas.), Am. Soc. Internat. Law. Democrat. Jewish. Private international, Corporate taxation.

GUTTERMAN, ALAN J. lawyer; b. Bklyn., Nov. 21, 1942; s. Hyman and Madeline (Wolfe) G.; m. Emily Scharer, June 23, 1966; children: David, Andrew, Glenn, Jamie. BA with honors, U. Rochester, 1964; JD, Rutgers U., 1967. Bar: N.J. 1967, U.S. Ct. Claims 1970, U.S. Ct. Appeals (3rd cir.) N.J. 1967, U.S. Supreme Ct. 1977. Law clk. U.S. Ct. Appeals 3rd Cir., 1967-68; assoc. Sills, Beck, Cummis, Radin & Tischman, Newark, 1968-71; sole practice Union, N.J., 1972-75; ptnr. Gutterman, Wolkstein & Klinger, LLP and predecessor firms, Westfield, N.J., 1975—. Editor: Rutgers Law Rev., 1966-67; contbr. N.J. Law Jour. Councilman, Westfield, N.J., 1979-83. Mem.: Union County Bar Assn., N.J. State Bar Assn. Republican. Jewish. Corporate, general, Probate (including wills, trusts), Property, real (including real estate development, water). Office: Gutterman Wolkstein & Klinger LLP PO Box 2850 240 E Grove St Westfield NJ 07091-2850 E-mail: ajgesq@verizon.net.

GUTTMAN, EGON, law educator; b. Neuruppin, Germany, Jan. 27, 1927; came to U.S., 1958, naturalized, 1968; s. Isaac and Blima (Liss) G.; m. Inge Weinberg, June 12, 1966; children: Geoffrey David, Leonard Jay. Student, U. Cambridge, 1945-48; LLB, U. London, London, England, 1950, LLM, 1952; post grad., Northwestern U. Sch. Law, 1958-59. Barrister: Eng. 1952. Sole practice, England, 1952-53; faculty Univ. Coll. and U. Khartoum, 1953-58; legal advisor to chief justice, 1953-58; founder, editor Sudan Law Jour. & Reports, Sudan, 1956-57; researcher, lectr. Rutgers U. Sch. Law, Newark, 1959-60; asst. prof. U. Alta., Edmonton, Canada, 1960-62; prof. Howard U. Law Sch., Washington, 1962-68, vis. adj. prof., 1968-96; adj. prof. law Washington Coll. Law, Am. U., Wash., 1964-68, Levitt Meml. Trust scholar-prof., 1968—, dir. JD-MBA joint degree program, 1990-2000; lectr. Practicing Law Inst., 1964—. Adj. prof. law Georgetown U. Law Ctr., 1972-74, Johns Hopkins U., Balt., 1973-81; vis. prof. Faculty of Law, U. Cambridge, Wolfson Coll., Eng., 1984, U. Haifa, Israel, 2000; atty.-fellow SEC, 1976-79; cons. to various U.S. agys. and spl. commns.; U.S. rep. to UNCITRAL working groups; mem. various ALI-ABA working groups on the revision of the uniform comml. code; mem. Sec. of State's Adv. Com. on Pvt. Internat. Law; arbitrator NY Stock Exch. and NASD, 1997—. Author: Crime, Cause and Treatment, 1956; author: (with A. Smith) Cases and Materials on Domestic Rels., 1962; author: Modern Securities Transfers; author: (with R.G. Vaughn) Cases and Materials on Policy and the Legal Environment, 1973, rev., 1978, 3d edit., 1980; author: Problems and Materials on Sales Under the Uniform Comm. Code and the Conventional on Internat. Sale of Goods, Comm. Transactions, vol. 2, 1990; author: (with L.F. Del Duca and A.M. Squilante) Problems and Materials on Secured Transactions Under the Uniform Comm. Code, Comm. Transactions, vol. 1, 1992; author: Problems and Materials on Negotiable Instruments Under the Uniform Comm. Code and the UN Conv. on Internat. Bills of Exch. and Internat. Promissory Notes, Comm. Transactions, vol. 3, 1993; author: (with F. Miller) supplement, 1996—98; author: (with R.B. Lubic) Secured Transactions-A Simplified Guide, 1996; author: Securities Laws in the United States-A Primer for Fgn. Lawyers, 1996—99; contbr. numerous articles, revs., briefs to profl. lit.; : supplement, 1997; author: 4th edit., 2002; author: (with L.F. Del Duca, F.H. Miller, P. Winship, W.H. Henning) Secured Transactions Under the Uniform Comm. Code and Internat. Commerce, 2002. Howard U. rep. Fund for Edn. in World Order, 1966-68; trustee Silver Spring Jewish Ctr., Md., 1976-79; mem. exec. com. Sha'are Tzedek Hosp., Washington, 1971-72, 97—. Leverhulme scholar, 1948-51; U. London studentship, 1951-52; Ford Found. grad. fellow, 1958-59, NYU summer workshop fellow, 1960, 61, 64; Levitt Meml. Trust scholar-professor 1982—; recipient Outstanding Svc. award Student Bar Assn., Am. U., 1970, Law Rev. Outstanding Svc. award, 1981, Washington Coll. of Law Outstanding Contbn. to Acad. Program Devel. award, 1981. Mem. Am. Law Inst., ABA, Fed. Bar Assn. Assn. Trial Lawyers Am., Brit. Inst. Internat. and Comparative Law, Soc. Pub. Tchrs. Law (Eng.), Hon. Soc. Middle Temple, Hardwick Soc. of Inns of Ct., Sudan Philos. Soc., Assn. Can. Law Tchrs., Am. Soc. Internat. Law, Can. Assn. Comparative Law, B'nai Brith, Argo Lodge, Phi Alpha Delta (John Sherman Myers award 1972). Home: 14801 Pennfield Cir Silver Spring MD 20906-1580 Office: Am U Washington Coll Law 4801 Massachusetts Ave NW Washington DC 20016-8196 Fax: (202) 274-4130. E-mail: guttman@wcl.american.edu.

GUY, RALPH B., JR., federal judge; b. Detroit, Mich., Aug. 30, 1929; s. Ralph B. and Shirley (Skladd) G.. AB, U. Mich., 1951, JD, 1953. Bar: Mich. 1953. Sole practice, Dearborn, Mich., 1954—55; asst. corp. counsel City of Dearborn, 1955—58, corp. counsel, 1958—69; chief asst. U.S. Atty.'s Office (ea. dist.), Detroit and Mich., 1968—70, U.S. Atty., 1970—76; judge U.S. Dist. Ct. (ea. dist.) Mich., Ann Arbor, 1976—85, U.S. Ct. Appeals (6th cir.), Ann Arbor, 1985—94, sr. judge, 1994—. Treas. Detroit-Wayne County Bldg. Authority, 1966—73; chmn. sch. study com. Dearborn Bd. Edn., 1973; mem. Fed. Exec. Bd., 1970—, bd. dirs., 1971—73. Recipient Civic Achievement award, Dearborn Rotary, 1971, Distinguished Alumni award, U. Mich., 1972. Mem.: FBA (pres. 1974—75), ABA (state chmn. sect. local govt. 1965—70), Out-County Suprs. Assn. (pres. 1965), Mich. Municipal League, Mich. Assn. Municipal Attys. (pres. 1962—64), Nat. Inst. Municipal Law Officers (chmn. Mich. chpt. 1964—69), Am. Judicature Soc., Dearborn Bar Assn. (pres. 1959—60), Detroit Bar Assn., State Bar Mich. (commr. 1975—), U. Mich. Alumni Club (local pres. Dearborn 1961—62), Rotary (local pres. 1973—74), Lambda Chi Alpha, Phi Alpha Delta. Office: US Ct Appeals PO Box 7910 200 E Liberty St Rm 226 Ann Arbor MI 48107 also: Potter Stewart US Courthouse 100 E 5th St Cincinnati OH 45202-3988

HAAKH, GILBERT EDWARD, lawyer; b. Rotterdam, Netherlands, July 25, 1923; came to U.S., 1946; s. Otto and Rose C. (Holder) H. BA, U. Calif., Berkeley, 1947; LLB, Harvard U., 1950. Bar: Calif. 1952, Mass. 1952, U.S. Dist. Ct. (ctrl. dist.) Calif. 1953, U.S. Dist. ct. (so. dist.) Calif. 1972, U.S. Supreme Ct. 1971. Assoc. O'Melveny & Myers, L.A., 1951-61; ptnr. Donnelley, Clark, Chase & Haakh, L.A., 1962-73, MacDonald, Halsted & Laybourne, L.A., 1974-86, Baker & McKenzie, L.A., 1987-93; of counsel Kindel & Anderson, L.A., 1994-96, McKenna Long & Aldridge, L.A., 1997—. Bd. dirs. various corps. Mem. ABA, Los Angeles County Bar Assn., Am. Soc. Corp. Secs. Corporate, general, Mergers and acquisitions, Securities. Office: McKenna Long & Aldridge 444 S Flower St Los Angeles CA 90071-2901 E-mail: ghaakh@mckennalong.com.

HAAS, GEORGE AARON, lawyer; b. N.Y.C., July 6, 1919; s. Herman Joseph and Violet (Cowen) H.; m. Miriam Durkin, Aug. 1942; children—Thomas Leonard, Karen Ann (Mrs. Michael Davenport), James G.D. AB, Princeton U., 1940; LL.B., Yale U., 1947. Bar: Ga. 1947. Since practiced in, Atlanta; partner Haas, Bridges & Kane (and predecessor firms), 1947—. Sec., dir. Lucerne Corp., East Freeway Corp., Crescent View Corp., Mountain View Corp., Lake Placid Corp. Mem. hosp. and health div. Atlanta Community Council, 1962-68; mem. tech. assistance com., del. White House Conf. on Children and Youth, 1970; state trustee from Ga. Nat. Easter Seal Soc. for Crippled Children and Adults, 1959-65, mem. exec. com., 1961-65, v.p., 1963-65, 1st v.p., 1965-66, mem. ho. of dels., 1965-73, pres. 1971-73; bd. dirs. 1965-73, chmn. formula rev. bd., mem. relations and standards rev. com., 1967-69, pres., 1969-71; trustee Ga. Easter Seal Soc. for Crippled Children and Adults, 1955-65, 78— , sec., 1957-58, pres., 1959-61, chmn. ho. of dels., 1967-69; Bd. dirs. Fulton-DeKalb chpt. Nat. Found.; mem. med. adv. bd. Ga. chpt. Am. Phys. Therapy Assn. Served to capt. F.A. AUS, World War II. Mem. ABA, Ga. Bar Assn., Atlanta Bar Assn. Clubs: Standard (Atlanta) (past sec., dir.). Lodges: Kiwanis. Home: 2575 Peachtree Rd NE Atlanta GA 30305-3694 Office: 2964 Peachtree Rd NW Atlanta GA 30305-2153

HAAS, JOSEPH ALAN, court administrator, lawyer; b. Riverside, Calif., June 30, 1950; s. Garland August and Pauline (Anderson) H.; m. Barbara Roberts, May 27, 1978; children: Natalie C., Christina R. BA in Econs., U. Wash., 1972, MA in Econs., 1974; JD, Seattle U., 1983. Bar: Wash. 1984, U.S. Dist. Ct. (we. dist.) Wash. 1984, Md. 1986, U.S. Ct. Appeals (4th cir.) 1986. Regional coord. Adminstrv. Office U.S. Cts., Washington, 1975-80; chief dep. clk. U.S. Dist. Ct. for Western Wash., Seattle, 1981-84; clk. U.S. Dist. Ct. Md., Balt., 1984-96, U.S. Dist. Ct. for S.D., Sioux Falls, 1996—. Mem. Nat. Assn. for Ct. Mgmt., Fed. Ct. Clks. Assn. (pres. 1987-88, pres. elect 2000-01, pres. 2001-03), Wash. State Bar Assn. Office: US Dist Ct 400 S Phillips Ave Rm 128 Sioux Falls SD 57104-6851

HABECK, JAMES ROY, lawyer; b. Berlin, Wis., Aug. 11, 1954; s. Roy J. and Phyllis J. (Hazelwood) H.; m. Penny Ann Gillman. BS, U. Wis., Stevens Point, 1976; JD, Marquette U., 1979. Bar. Wis. 1979, U.S. Dist. Ct. (ea. and we. dists.) Wis. 1979, U.S. Supreme Ct. 1990. Atty. Rutgers Law Office, Sheboygan Falls, Wis., 1979-80; pvt. practice Shawano, Wis., 1980—2002; judge Shawano County Courthouse, Shawano, Wis., 2002—. Family ct. commr. Shawano, Menominee County, 1983-2002; corp. counsel Shawano County, 1984-87, 90, 93; legal counsel Wis. Towns Assn., Shawano, 1987-2002. Pres. Big Brothers/Big Sisters, Shawano, 1984-88; v.p. Rep. Ctrl. Com., Shawano County, 1993-99, chmn. 1999-2002; atty. St. James Lutheran Ch., Shawano, 1983-2001. Named Friend of 4-H Shawano County 4-H, 1990. Mem.: Wis. Family Ct. Commrs. Assn. (sec.-treas, pres. 1992—96, bd. dirs. 1998—2002), Shawano County Bar Assn. (sec-treas, pres. 1987—93), Wild Turkey Fedn., White Tails Unltd., Shawano Area C. of C. (bd. dirs. 2000—03), Rotary (bd. dirs. 2001—), Shawano County Agrl. Soc. Lutheran. Avocations: scoring high sch. basketball games. Family and matrimonial, Municipal (including bonds), Probate (including wills, trusts).

HABERMANN, TED RICHARD, lawyer; b. Waupaca, Wis., Nov. 1, 1957; s. Richard Dale and Laura Aleen (Defrates) H. BS, U. Wis., 1980; JD, Valparaiso U., 1983. Bar: Ind. 1983, Tenn. 1989, U.S. Dist. Ct. (no and so. dists.) Ind. 1983, U.S. Dist. Ct. (mid. dist.) Tenn. 1990, U.S. Tax Ct. 1984, U.S. Supreme Ct., 1989. Mng. atty. Davisson & Davisson, P.C., Anderson, Ind., 1984-89; corp. counsel Spectra Distbn./Sound Stage Cos., Nashville, 1989-91; gen. counsel, sec. Servpro Industries, Inc., Gallatin, Tenn., 1991-98; asst. gen. counsel, asst. sec. Shoney's Inc., Nashville, 1998-2000; gen. counsel, sec. Servpro Industries, Inc., Gallatin, Tenn., 2000—02; v.p., gen. counsel, sec. Shoney's, Inc., Nashville, 2002—. Contbr. Valparaiso U. Law Rev. Mem. ABA, Ind. Bar Assn. (mem. forum on franchising), Tenn. Bar Assn., Jaycees (v.p. 1987), Exchange Club (dir. 1987), Sigma Phi Epsilon, Delta Theta Phi. Republican. Methodist. Franchising, Corporate, general. Home: 4724 Aaron Dr Antioch TN 37013-4218 Office: Shoney's Inc 1717 Elm Hill Pike Nashville TN 37210 E-mail: tedhabermann@msn.com., ted_habermann@shoneys.com.

HABIAN, BRUCE GEORGE, lawyer; b. Nov. 23, 1947; s. George and Doris Marie (Cipollina) H.. AB, Boston Coll., 1969; JD, Villanova U., 1972. Bar: N.Y. 1973, N.J. 1974, U.S. Dist. Ct. (so. and ea. dists.) N.Y. 1975, U.S. Ct. Appeals (2nd cir.) 1975, U.S. Supreme Ct. 1976. Asst. corp. counsel Office Corp. Counsel, N.Y.C., 1972—73; assoc. Martin, Clearwater & Bell, N.Y.C., 1973—79, ptnr., 1979—, sr. ptnr., 1983—. Lectr. Law Jour. Seminars Press; cons. N.Y. State Commr. Health, N.Y.C., NY, 1983. Mem.: ABA (litigation sect.), Internat. Assn. Def. Coun., Def. Rsch. Coun., Assn. Bar City N.Y., University (N.Y.C.). Republican. Roman Catholic. Federal civil litigation, State civil litigation, Personal injury (including property damage). Home: 993 Park Ave Apt 1B New York NY 10028-0809 Office: Martin Clearwater and Bell 220 E 42nd St New York NY 10017-5806

HABUSH, ROBERT LEE, lawyer; b. Milw., Mar. 22, 1936; s. Jesse James and Beatrice (Liebenberg) H.; m. Miriam Lee Friedman, Aug. 25, 1957; children: Sherri Ellen, William Scott, Jodi Lynn. BBA, U. Wis., 1959, JD, 1961. Bar: Wis. 1961, U.S. Dist. Ct. (ea. and we. dists.) Wis. 1961, U.S. Ct. Appeals (7th cir.) 1965, U.S. Supreme Ct. 1986. Pres. Habush, Habush & Rottier, S.C., Milw., 1961—. Lectr. U. Wis. Law Sch., Marquette U. Law Sch., State Bar Wis., other legal orgns. Author: Cross Examination of Non Medical Experts, 1981; contbr. articles to legal jours. Capt. U.S. Army, 1959-75. Recipient Evan P. Helfaer Donor award Nat. Assn. Fundraising Execs., 2000; named in his honor The Wis. Acad. of Trial Lawyers Robert L. Habush Trial Lawyer of Yr. Award, 2000. Mem. ATLA (bd. govs. 1983-86, pres. 1986-87, Harry Philo award 1999, Leonard Ring champion of Justice award 2002), ABA, Internat. Acad. Trial Lawyers (bd. dirs. 1983-87, 91-92), Internat. Soc. Barristers, Nat. Coll. Advocacy, Nat. Bd. Trial Advs., Am. Bd. Trial Advs., Am. Soc. Writers on Legal Subjects, Wis. Bar Assn., Wis. Acad. Trial Lawyers (pres. 1968-69), Inner Circle Advs., Trial Lawyers for Pub. Justice, Roscoe Pound Found. Federal civil litigation, State civil litigation, Personal injury (including property damage). Office: Habush Habush & Rottier 777 E Wisconsin Ave Ste 2300 Milwaukee WI 53202-5381

HACKEL-SIMS, STELLA BLOOMBERG, lawyer, former government official; b. Burlington, Vt., Dec. 27, 1926; d. Hyman and Esther (Pocher) Bloomberg; m. Donald Herman Hackel, Aug. 14, 1949; children: Susan Jane, Cynthia Anne; m. Arthur Sims, Aug. 28, 1980. Student, U. Vt., 1943-45; JD cum laude, Boston U., 1948. Bar: Vt. 1948, Mass. 1948, D.C. 1979, Va. 1982. Individual practice law, Burlington, 1948-49, Rutland, Vt., 1949-59, 73—; city prosecutor City of Rutland, 1957-63; commr. Vt. Dept. Employment Security, 1963-73; treas. State of Vt., 1975-77; dir. U.S. Mint, Dept. Treasury, Washington, 1977-81. Chmn. Vt. Municipal Bond Bank, 1975-77 Mem. Vt. Adv. Com. on Mental Retardation, Interdept. Council on Aging, Commn. on Status Women, Human Resource Inter-Agency Com., Emergency Resource Priorities Bd., Info. Planning Council, Legis. Council Equal Opportunity Com., Vt. Indsl. Devel. Authority, Vt. Housing Fin. Agy., Vt. Claims Commn., Vt. Tchrs. Retirement Fund. Bd., Vt. Home Mortgage Guaranty Bd.; chmn. Vt. State Employees Retirement Fund; ex-officio mem. Nat. Manpower Adv. Com., 1971-72, Fed. Adv. Council on Unemployment Ins., 1971-72; Pres. Rutland Girl Scouts Leaders Assn., 1949-50, Rutland League Women Voters, 1951-52, Rutland Council Jewish Women, 1955-56; chmn. womens div. Rutland Community Chest Dr., 1952, Rutland County-Vt. Assn. for Blind, 1953-56; pres. Rutland County Democratic Women's Assn., 1956-63; treas. Rutland City Dem. Com., 1957-63; former rep. office women's activities Dem. Nat. Com., Regional Council I., Women's CD Councils; mem. Vt. bd. Girl Scouts U.S.A.; chmn. Arlington County Tenant-Landlord Commn., Va., 1986— . Mem.: LWV, AAUW (pres. Rutland County br. 1961—62), Interstate Conf. Employment Security Agys. (v.p. region I 1966—68, legis. com. 1969, sr. v.p. 1970—71, pres. 1971—72), Am. Soc. Pub. Adminstrn., Vt. Coun. Social Agys., Bus. and Profl. Women's Club, Rutland County Bar Assn. (pres. 1973), Vt. Bar Assn., Emblem (dir. 1960-63), Woodmont Country; Internat. (Washington), Moorings Country Club (Naples, Fla.), Emblem Club (dir. 1960—63), Delta Phi Epsilon.

HACKENBERG, DAVID ALAN, lawyer, city official; b. Phila., June 28, 1939; s. Melvin Bert and Ruth Lenore (Good) H.; m. Marilyn Adella Jones, Aug. 10, 1963; children— Alan David, Jill Marie. B.A., Heidelberg Coll., 1962; J.D., Ohio No. U., 1968. Bar: Ohio 1968, U.S. Dist. Ct. 1969. Ptnr. Hackenberg, Beutler, Rasmussen, Findlay, Ohio, 1968— ; dir. law City of Findlay, 1972—, atty. for Village of McComb, Village of Mt. Blanchard . Pres. Parent Tchr. Orgn., Central Jr. High Sch., Findlay, 1984-85. Mem. Ohio State Bar Assn., Findlay Hancock Bar Assn. (pres. 1982), N.W. Ohio Bar Assn., Ohio Mcpl. Attys. Assn., Ohio Land Title Assn. Republican. Methodist. Lodges: Elks, Masons, Moose. Avocations: golf, tennis, photography, boating. Land use and zoning (including planning), Municipal (including bonds), Property, real (including real estate development, water). Home: 2030 Rush Creek Ct Findlay OH 45840-7448 Office: Hackenberg Beutler Rasmussen 314 W Crawford St Findlay OH 45840-3206

HACKETT, KEVIN R. lawyer; b. Atlantic City, N.J., Apr. 16, 1949; BA summa cum laude, Boston Coll., 1971; JD, Harvard U., 1974. Bar: N.Y. 1975. Ptnr. Shearman & Sterling, N.Y.C. Fellow Am. Coll. Real Estate Lawyers; mem. ABA, N.Y. State Bar Assn., Assn. Bar City of N.Y., Phi Beta Kappa. Commercial, contracts (including sales of goods; commercial financing), Landlord-tenant, Property, real (including real estate development, water). Office: 599 Lexington Ave Fl 1448 New York NY 10022-6030

HACKETT, ROBERT JOHN, lawyer; b. N.Y.C., Feb. 6, 1943; s. John P. and Marie S. (Starace) Hackett; m. Anita Carlile, Apr. 19, 1969; children: Robert John Hackett Jr., John Peter, Kathryn Marie. AB, Rutgers U., 1964; JD, Duke U., 1967. Bar: N.Y. 1967, Ariz. 1972. Assoc. Milbank, Tweed, Hadley, McCloy, N.Y.C., 1967—71; ptnr. Evans, Kitchel & Jenckes, Phoenix, 1971—89; dir. Fennemore Craig, Phoenix, 1989—, course dir. seminar on mergers and acquisitions, 1996, 1999. Mem. editl. bd. Duke Law Jour., 1966—67. Former bd. dirs. Xavier Coll. Prep., mem. steering com. for Fine Arts Ctr. capital campaign. Mem.: ABA (com. on fed. securities regulation), Maricopa County Bar Assn., State Bar Ariz. (past chmn. securities regulation sect.), Assn. Corp. Growth (past bd. dirs., past pres. Ariz. chpt.), Phoenix Duke U. Law Alumni Club (past pres.), Pi Sigma Alpha. Republican. Roman Catholic. Banking, Corporate, general, Securities. E-mail: rhackett@fclaw.com.

HACKETT, WESLEY PHELPS, JR., lawyer; b. Detroit, Jan. 3, 1939; s. Wesley P. and Helen (Decker) H.; children: Kelly D. Hackett Pell, Robin C. BA, Mich. State U., 1960; JD, Wayne State U., 1968. Bar: Mich. 1968, U.S. Dist. Ct. (we. dist.) Mich. 1971, U.S. Ct. Appeals (6th cir.) 1972, U.S. Dist. Ct. (ea. dist.) Mich. 1972, U.S. Supreme Ct. 1972, U.S. Ct. Mil. Appeals 1991. Law clk. Mich. Supreme Ct., Lansing, 1968-70; ptnr. Brown & Hackett, Lansing, 1971-73; pvt. practice Lansing, 1973-84; ptnr. Starr, Bissell & Hackett, Lansing, 1984-87; pvt. practice East Lansing, Mich., 1987-98, Saranac, Mich., 1998—. Adj. prof. Thomas M. Cooley Law Sch., Lansing, 1973—; instr. Lansing C.C., 1981-99. Author: Evidence: A Trial Manual for Michigan Lawyers, 1981, Hackett's Evidence: Michigan and Federal, 2d edit., 1995, Michigan Lawyers Manual Part L, 1994, revised, 2002; co-author: Hiring Legal Staff, 1990. Mem. City of East Lansing Planning Commn., 1969-72; mem. Village of Saranac Planning Commn., 2000—; bd. dirs. St. Vincent Home for Children, Lansing, 1974-82. 1st lt. USAF, 1961-65. Fellow Coll. Law Practice Mgmt.; mem. ABA (sec. gen. practice sect. 1990-91, vice-chair 1991-92, chair 1993-94, standing com. on lawyer referral and info. svcs. 1997-2000, sole practitioner of yr. 1994, founders award 1997), State Bar Mich. (chair legal econs. sect. 1990-91). Corporate, general, Estate planning, Property, real (including real estate development, water).

HACKMAN, MARVIN LAWRENCE, lawyer; b. Jasper, Ind., Jan. 29, 1934; s. Theodore Peter and Sarah Rose (Bellner) H.; m. Jane Marie Sermersheim, Aug. 23, 1958; children: Stephen J., Anne M., Michael A., Daniel T. AB summa cum laude, St. Joseph Coll., 1956; JD magna cum laude, Ind. U., 1959. Bar: Ind. 1959, U.S. Dist. Ct. (so. dist.) Ind. 1959, U.S. Ct. Appeals (7th cir.) 1960. Law clk. to chief judge U.S. Dist. Ct., Indpls., 1959-61; mem. Hackman Hulett & Cracraft LLP, Indpls., 1961—. Mem. ABA, Ind. State Bar Assn., Indpls. Bar Assn., Phi Delta Phi, Order of Coif. Corporate, general, Finance, Property, real (including real estate development, water). Home: 4021 Royal Pine Blvd Indianapolis IN 46250-2272

HACKNEY, H(IRAM) HAMILTON, III, lawyer; b. Balt., Feb. 9, 1962; s. H. Hamilton Jr. and Anne King (Bailey) H.; m. Susan Paardecamp, Sept. 14, 1996. BA, Middlebury Coll., 1984; JD, U. Utah, 1990. Bar: Colo. 1990, U.S. Dist. Ct. Colo. 1991, Mass. 1995, U.S. Dist. Ct. Mass. 1995. Assoc. Sherman & Howard, Denver, 1990-91, Holme, Roberts & Owen, Denver, 1991-94, Choate, Hall & Stewart, Boston, 1994—. Clk., dir. WasteCap Mass., Boston, 1995—; mem. steering com. environ. law sect. Boston Bar Assn., 1997-99, chair hazardous and solid waste com., 1997-99. Contbr. chpt. to book. Avocations: golf, tennis, skiing. Environmental. Office: Exchange Pl 53 State St Boston MA 02109-2804

HACKNEY, HUGH EDWARD, lawyer; b. McGregor, Tex., July 17, 1944; BA, So. Meth. U., 1966, JD, 1969. Bar: Tex. 1970. Mem. Fulbright & Jaworski, LLP, Dallas, 1970-97; lawyer Locke Purnell Rain Harrell, Dallas, 1998-99, Locke Liddell & Sapp LLP, Dallas, 1999—. Fellow: Coll. of Labor and Employment Lawyers; mem. ABA, London Ct. Internat. Arbitration, Chartered Inst. Arbitrators (London), State Bar Tex., Dallas Bar Assn., Houston Bar Assn., Phi Alpha Delta, Soc. Internat. Bus. Fellows, Internat. Bar Assn. General civil litigation, Private international, Labor (including EEOC, Fair Labor Standards Act, labor-management relations, NLRB, OSHA). Office: Locke Liddell and Sapp LLP 2200 Ross Ave Dallas TX 75201-6776

HADDAD, ERNEST MUDARRI, lawyer; b. Boston, Oct. 30, 1938; s. Abraham and Elaine (Mudarri) H.; m. Kathleen L. Tracy; 1 child, Barton Edward; children from previous marriage: Scott Cochrane, Mark Mudarri. BA, Trinity Coll., Hartford, Conn., 1960; LLB, Boston U., 1964. Bar: Mass. 1964, U.S. Dist. Ct. Mass. 1966, U.S. Supreme Ct., 1981. Asst. dean sch. law Boston U., 1966-71; asst. sec., gen. counsel Commonwealth of Mass. Exec. Office Human Svcs., Boston, 1971-76; gen. counsel Blue Cross and Blue Shield Mass. Inc., Boston, 1976-80; sec., gen. counsel The Mass. Gen. Hosp., Boston, 1981—2002, Ptnrs. HealthCare Sys., Inc., Boston, 1995—2002; assoc. dean , prof. law Boston U. Sch. Law, 2002—. Bd. dirs. Internat. Inst. Boston, 2002—. Program chmn., mem. exec. com. Boston Study Group, 1979—; Bd. dirs. New Eng. Legal Found., 2001—. Recipient Trinity Coll. Alumni medal for Excellence, 1990. Mem. ABA, Am. Health Lawyers Assn., Boston Bar Assn. (mem. coun. 1998-2002, exec. com. 1999-2002, fin. com. 1999-2002, treas. 2001-02), Boston Bar Found. (trustee, 1998—), Boston U. Law Sch. Alumni Assn. (pres. 1998-99). Corporate, general, Health, Non-profit and tax-exempt organizations. Home: 144 Mount Vernon St Boston MA 02108-1128 Office: 765 Commonwealth Ave Boston MA 02215 E-mail: ehaddad@bu.edu.

HADDEN, ARTHUR ROBY, lawyer; b. San Antonio, Feb. 13, 1929; s. Will Alexander and Kathleen (Westerman) H.; m. Marellyn Frances Denton, June 23, 1956; children: Neilson, Lynne, Wesley, Arthur. BBA, U. Tex., 1952, LLB, 1957. Bar: Tex. 1957, U.S. Dist. Ct. (ea. dist.) Tex. 1959, U.S. Ct. Appeals (5th cir.) 1961, U.S. Supreme Ct. 1970, U.S. Dist. Ct. (no. dist.) Tex. 1975. Lawyer Ramey, Brelsford, Hull and Flock, Tyler, Tex., 1957-70; U.S. atty. Ea. Dist. Tex., Tyler, 1970-77; lawyer, sole practice Law Offices Roby Hadden, Tyler, 1977-94; justice 12th Ct. Appeals, Tex., 1995-2000, 5th Ct. Appeals, Tex., 2001—. Mem. Fed. State Law Enforcement Commn. Tex., Austin, 1976-77. Mem. Human Subjects Investigation Commn. U. Tex. Hosp., Tyler, 1980-90, Mayor's Anti-Crime Task Force, Criminal Justice Div., Tyler, 1986-88. Capt. USAF, 1952-54. Fellow Tex. Bar Found.; mem. Smith County Bar Assn., Nat. Assn. Former U.S. Attys., Coll. of State Bar of Tex., Downtown Rotary Tyler, Rotary Internat. Republican. Avocations: jogging, mountaineering, snow skiing, tennis, swimming. Oil, gas, and mineral, Probate (including wills, trusts), Property, real (including real estate development, water). Home and Office: 3335 Heines Dr Tyler TX 75701-9034

HADDLETON, RUSSELL EDGECOMB, lawyer; b. Boston, Sept. 11, 1932; s. Frank Charles and Doris Elizabeth (Russell) H.; m. Constance Flanders Walker, June 11, 1959 (div. May 1972); children: Russell Flanders, Frank Burgess. AA in Bus. Adminstrn., Boston U., 1951, LLB, 1956, LLM in Taxation, 1962. Bar: Mass. 1957, U.S. Dist. Ct. Mass. 1959, U.S. Tax Ct. 1971, Fla. 1981. Asst. v.p. Avis, Inc., Boston, 1956-60; asst. counsel John Hancock Mut. Life Ins. Co., Boston, 1960-66; pres. Haddleton & Assocs. PC, Hyannis, Mass., 1966—. Contbr. articles to profl. jours. Mem. ABA (estate planning and drafting, adminstrv. provisions and estate planning and life ins. coms.), Internat. Bar Assn., Mass. Bar Assn. (chmn. edn. com., chmn. probate sect.), Barnstable County Bar Assn., Delta Sigma Rho, Phi Delta Phi. Republican. Unitarian Universalist. Probate (including wills, trusts), Estate taxation, Estate planning. Home: 65 Morris Island Rd Chatham MA 02633-2525 Office: 251 South St Hyannis MA 02601-3926

HADEN, CHARLES HAROLD, II, federal judge; b. Morgantown, W.Va., Apr. 16, 1937; s. Charles H. and Beatrice L. (Costolo) H.; m. Priscilla Ann Miller, June 2, 1956; children: Charles H., Timothy M., Amy Sue. BS, W.Va. U., 1958, JD, 1961. Ptnr. Haden & Haden, Morgantown, W.Va., 1961-69; state tax commr. W.Va., 1969-72; justice Supreme Ct. Appeals W.Va., 1972-75, chief justice, 1975; judge U.S. Dist. Ct. No. and So. Dists. W.Va., Parkersburg, 1975-82; chief judge U.S. Dist. Ct. (so. dist.) W.Va., 1982—2002. Mem. W.Va. Ho. of Dels., 1963-64; asst. prof. Coll. Law, W.Va. U., 1967-68; mem. com. adminstrn. probation system Jud. Conf., 1979-86; mem. 4th Cir. Jud. Coun., 1986-91, 96-2000, U.S. Jud. Conf., 1997—, chair exec. com., 2000-02. Mem. Bd. Edn., Monongalia County, W.Va., 1967-68; bd. dirs. W.Va. U. Found., 1986—; past. mem. vis. coms. W.Va. U. Coll. Law & Sch. Medicine. Recipient Outstanding Alumnus award W.Va. U., 1986; named Outstanding Appellate Judge in W.Va., W.Va. Trial Lawyers Assn., 1975, Outstanding Trial Judge in W.Va., 1982. Fellow Am. Bar Found., W.Va. State Bar Found.; mem. ABA, W.Va. Bar Assn., W.Va. State Bar Assn., Am. Judicature Soc., 4th Cir. Dist. Judges Assn. (pres. 1993-95), W.Va. U. Alumni Assn. (pres. 1982-83), W.Va. U. Order of Vandalia. Office: US Dist Ct PO Box 351 Charleston WV 25322-0351 E-mail: judge_haden@wvsd.uscourts.gov.

HADLEY, RALPH VINCENT, III, lawyer; b. Jacksonville, Fla., Aug. 20, 1942; s. Ralph V. and Clare (Cason) H.; m. Carol Fox Hadley, Sept. 18, 1993; children: Graham Kimball, Christopher Bedell, Blair Vincent. BS, U. Fla., 1965, JD, 1968. Bar: Fla. 1968, Calif. 1972. Assoc. Kurz, Toole, Taylor & Moseley, Jacksonville, 1968-69; asst. atty. gen. State of Fla., Orlando, 1972-73; ptnr. Davids, Henson & Hadley, Winter Garden, Fla., 1973-80; sr. ptnr. Hadley & Asma, Winter Garden, 1980-89, Parker, Johnson, Owen, McGuire, Michaud, & Hadley, Orlando, 1989-91, Owen & Hadley, Orlando, 1991-94, Hadley, Gardner & Ornstein, P.A., Winter Park, Fla., 1994-95; Swann, Hadley & Alvarez, P.A., Winter Park, 1995-2000; with Swann & Hadley, 2000—. Vice chmn. bd. dirs. Tucker State Bank, Winter Garden, 1981-88; vice chmn. bd. dirs., sec. Tucker Holding Co., Jacksonville, 1984-88; bd. dirs. BankFIRST, All Sign Products. Bd. dirs. Orange County Dem. Exec. Com., Orlando, 1974-81, Spouse Abuse, Inc., Orlando, 1975-81. Lt. comdr. USN, 1969-72, Vietnam. Recipient Navy Achievement medal, Award of Merit, Orange County Legal Aid Soc., 1987, Disting. Svc. award Judge J.C. Jake Stone Legal Aid Soc., 1989, Pres. Pro Bono Svc. award Fla. Bar, 1992. Mem. ABA, Fla. Bar Assn., Calif. Bar Assn., Orange County Bar Assn. (legis. chmn. 1979, 82), Am. Inn of Ct. (master), Winter Park C. of C. (bd. dirs. 1979-80), West Orange C. of C. (bd. dirs. 1979-82), Rotary. Presbyterian. Banking, Commercial, contracts (including sales of goods; commercial financing), Property, real (including real estate development, water). Office: 1031 W Morse Blvd Winter Park FL 32789-3715 E-mail: ralphh@swannhadley.com.

HADLEY, ROBERT JAMES, lawyer; b. Wilmington, Ohio, Oct. 27, 1938; s. Robert Edwin and Ethel Edith (Slade) H.; m. Judith Ellen Gilbert, Aug. 11, 1962; children: Scott, Laura, Stephen. BA in History cum laude, Ohio State U., 1960; LLB, Harvard U., 1963. Bar: Ohio 1963. Assoc. Smith & Schnacke, Dayton, 1963-69, ptnr., 1970-89, Thompson Hine LLP, Dayton, 1989—. Pres. Man-to-Man Assocs., 1978-84, Dayton Habitat for Humanity, 1988; v.p. COPE Halfway House, Dayton, 1982-85; dir., sec. Friendship Village of Dayton, 1985—; bd. dirs. Cmty. Blood Ctr., Dayton, 1987—; loaned exec. United Way, 1980-82, cabinet 2001-02; mem. Kettering Civic Band, 1968—, v.p. Parish Resource Ctr., 1996-99, pres., 1999-2000; bd. dirs. South Cmty. YMCA, 1996-98, Greater Dayton Youth for Christ, 1980-86, Dayton Area Peace Accords Project; mem., treas. Ministry of Money bd., 1992—. Named Kettering Man of the Yr., 1986; Rotary Found. grantee, Israel, 1974. Mem. ABA, Ohio Bar Assn., Dayton Bar Assn., Dayton Racquet Club, Rotary (pres. Kettering 1986-87, dist. gov., group rep. Dist. 667 1989-90, dist. gov. 1993-94), Phi Beta Kappa. Republican. Methodist. Avocations: music, travel, sports. Construction, Health, Property, real (including real estate development, water). Home: 4848 Glenmina Dr Dayton OH 45440-2002 Office: Thompson Hine LLP PO Box 8801 2000 Courthouse Plz NE Dayton OH 45401-8801 E-mail: bob.hadley@thompsonhine.com.

HADLOW, RICHARD B. lawyer; b. Jacksonville, Fla., Feb. 4, 1952; s. Earl Bryce and Jean Hutchinson Hadlow; m. Cynthia Ervin, July 6, 1974; children: Charles Bryce, Lee Mansfield, Michael Ervin. BA in Econs., Duke U., 1974; JD, Fla. State U., 1977; LLM in Taxation, U. Fla., 1978. Bar: Fla. Assoc. Holland & Knight LLP, Tampa, Fla., 1978—82; shareholder Bush Ross Gardner Warren & Rudy, P.A., Tampa, 1982—2002; assoc. Holland & Knight LLP, 2002—. Mem. bd. visitors Fla. State U. Coll., Tallahassee, 2002—; mem. Leadership Tampa, 1981; former bd. dirs. Leadership Tampa Alumni, Young Life Tampa; chmn. bd. counselors U. Tampa, 1988—89, bd. trustees, 1988—89; chmn. bd. trustees Berkeley Prep. Sch., 2001—03; pres. bd. dirs. Met. Ministries, 1993—95; jr. warden vestry St. John's Episcopal Ch., 1992. Mem.: ABA, Hillsborough County Bar Assn., Fla. Bar Assn., Fla. State U. Coll. Law Alumni Assn. (pres. 2001—02), Ye Mystic Krewe of Gasparilla, Palma Ceia Golf and Country Club, Univ. Club Tampa. Republican. Episcopalian. Corporate, general, Commercial, contracts (including sales of goods; commercial financing), Securities. Home: 2610 Sunset Dr Tampa FL 33629 Office: Holland & Knight LLP 400 N Ashley Dr Ste 2300 Tampa FL 33602

HAFER, JOSEPH PAGE, lawyer; b. Harrisburg, Pa., June 28, 1941; s. George Horace and Betty (Page) H.; m. Margaret B. Cady; children: Bradford G., Susan P., David E. AB, Lafayette Coll., 1963; JD with distinction, U. Mich., 1966. Bar: Pa. 1966, U.S. Dist. Ct. (mid. dist.) Pa. 1966, U.S. Supreme Ct. 1969, U.S. Ct. Appeals (3d cir.) 1976. Assoc. Metzger, Hafer, Keefer, Thomas & Wood, Harrisburg, 1966-77; mng. ptnr. Thomas, Thomas & Hafer, Harrisburg, 1977—. Adj. prof. law Dickinson Law Sch., Carlisle, Pa. Pres. Cumberland Valley Sch. Bd., Mechanicsburg, Pa., 1976-85; pres. Hampden Twp. Rep. Assn., Camp Hill, Pa. Fellow Am. Coll. Trial Lawyers; mem. ABA, Pa. Bar Assn., Assn. Trial Lawyers Am., Pa. Trial Lawyers Assn., Dauphin County Bar Assn. (ct. rels. com.). Methodist. Insurance, Personal injury (including property damage), Professional liability. Home: 1530 Waterford Camp Hill PA 17011-9000 Office: Thomas Thomas & Hafer PO Box 999 Harrisburg PA 17108-0999 E-mail: jph@tthlaw.com.

HAFETS, RICHARD JAY, lawyer; b. N.Y.C., Apr. 23, 1951; s. Meyer Hafets and Marilyn (Glanzrock) Bell; m. Claire Margolis, June 18, 1972; children: Brooke, Amy. BS in Bus. summa cum laude, Am. U., Washington, 1973, JD magna cum laude, 1976. Bar: Md. 1976, U.S. Dist. Ct. Md. 1976, U.S. Ct. Appeals (4th cir.) 1976, U.S. Supreme Ct. 1981, D.C. 1997, U.S. Dist. Ct. (D.C.) 1997. Assoc. Piper & Marbury, Balt., 1976-84, ptnr., 1984—, chmn. labor and employment practice, 1990—, chmn. hiring and assoc. coms., 1988-91. Labor atty. Balt. Symphony Orch., 1986-93; bd. dirs., gen. counsel Am. Cancer Soc., Balt., 1983-89; bd. dirs. Md. Ballet, Balt., 1978-80. Mem. ABA, Md. Bar Assn., Balt. City Bar Assn., Order of Coif. Avocations: horses, skiing. General civil litigation, Labor (including EEOC, Fair Labor Standards Act, labor-management relations, NLRB, OSHA). Home: 7346 Narrow Wind Way Columbia MD 21046-1262 Office: Piper Marbury Rudnick & Wolfe 6225 Smith Ave Baltimore MD 21209-3600 E-mail: richard.hafets@piperrudnick.com.

HAFIF, GREGORY KEITH, lawyer; b. Pomona, Calif., June 6, 1964; s. Herbert and Kay Hafif; m. Cynthia D. Hafif; children: Carter, Brooke. BS in Polit. Sci., BS in Bus., U. LaVerne, 1987; JD, Pepperdine U., 1990. Bar: Calif. 1990, U.S. Ct. Appeals (9th cir.) 1990, U.S. Supreme Ct. 1990. Atty. Law Offices Herbert Hafif, Claremont, Calif., 1982—90, trial lawyer, head bus. litig. dept., 1990—. Fundraiser Hafif Family Found., Claremont, 1990—; bd. visitors U. LaVerne Law Sch., Ontario, Calif., 2001—; assn. mem. L.A. County Fair, Pomona, Calif., 2001—. Mem.: Calif. Orgn. Consumer Advs. Avocation: golf. Office: Law Offices Herbert Hafif 269 W Bonita Ave Claremont CA 91711

HAFTER, JEROME CHARLES, lawyer; b. Orlando, Fla., May 16, 1945; s. Jerome Sidney and Mary Margaret (Fugler) H.; m. Jo Cille Dawkins, July 18, 1976; 1 child, Jerome Bryan. BA summa cum laude, Rice U., 1967; BA with first class honours, Oxford U., Eng., 1969, MA, 1976; JD, Yale U., 1972. Bar: Miss. 1974, U.S. Ct. Appeals (5th cir.) 1974, U.S. Dist. Ct. (no. and so. dists.) Miss. 1974. Law clk. to presiding judge U.S. Ct. Appeals (5th cir.), Jackson, Miss., 1972-73; assoc. Lake, Tindall, Hunger & Thackston (now Lake Tindall LLP), Greenville, Miss., 1973-76, ptnr., 1976—2001, Phelps Dunbar LLP, Jackson, Miss., 2001—. Chmn. Miss. Bd. Bar Admissions, Jackson, 1979-2002; sec., treas. Hafter Realty Inc., Greenville, 1969-92, pres., 1992—; mem. gov.'s constn. commn., Jackson, 1985-87; sec., gen. counsel Delta and Pine Land Co., Scott, Miss., 1993— Author: Family History of Peter Quin, 1964, 2d. rev. edit., 1970. Pres. Downtown Improvement Assn. Greenville, 1980—, Common Cause/Miss., 1976-78; mem. Greenville City Election Commn., 1978—, Greenville Mcpl. Sch. Bd., 1988—, pres., 1995-96, 99-2000, 02-03; chmn. com. on tax Miss. Econ. Council, Jackson, 1985, 87, 96-98, pres., Greenville Area C. of C., 1992. Served to 1st lt., C.E., U.S. Army, 1972, maj., USAR, 1972-92, ret. Marshall scholar, 1967-69; Leadership Miss. Program fellow, 1976-77; Best Lawyers in Am., 2001-02, 2003-04 Fellow Miss. Bar Found.; mem. ABA (vice chmn. com. on issues affecting legal profession, young lawyers div., 1980-82, law sch. accreditation com. 1998-2002, mem. coun. sect. legal edn. and admissions to bar 2000—), Miss. Bar Assn. (bd. dirs. young lawyers divsn. 1976-79, pres. fellows young lawyers divsn., 2000-01, chmn. sect. corp. fin. bus. law 1989-90), Fed. Bar Assn. (v.p. no. Miss. 1977-78, 81-82), Nat. Conf. Bar Examiners (MBE com. 1986-88, trustee 1989-2000, chmn. 1998-99), Am. Judicature Soc., Am. Law Inst., Greenville C. of C. (bd. dirs. 1976-79, pres. 1992-93), Washington County Hist. Soc. (pres. Greenville chpt. 1981), Miss. Bankruptcy Conf. (chmn. com. on bankruptcy rules 1988), Phi Beta Kappa. Clubs: Greenville Golf and Country (v.p. 1977-79); Huntercombe Golf (Nuffield, Eng.), Annandale Golf (Madison, Miss.); Vincents (Oxford, Eng.). Lodges: Kiwanis (Greenville pres. 1978-79, lt. gov. 1982-83). Episcopalian. Federal civil litigation, Commercial, contracts (including sales of goods; commercial financing), Corporate, general. Home: 315 Wetherbee St Greenville MS 38701 Office: Phelps Dunhar LLP PO Box 23066 Skytel Ctr 200 S Lamar St Jackson MS 39201 E-mail: hafterj@phelps.com., hafter@tecinfo.com.

HAGA, DAVID L. lawyer; BS, W.Va. U., 1958; LLB with high distinction, U. Ariz., 1965; LLM in Tax, NYU, 1967. Bar: Ariz. 1965, U.S. Dist. Ct. Ariz. 1965, U.S. Tax Ct. 1965, U.S. Ct. Appeals (9th cir.) 1965, U.S. Supreme Ct. 1965, cert.: Ariz. Bd. Legal Specialization (tax specialist). Law clk. to Hon. Jesse H. Udall Supreme Ct. State of Ariz., 1965—66; shareholder, atty. Gallagher & Kennedy, P.A., Phoenix, 1999—. Mem. com. exams. Ariz. Supreme Ct., 1987—94, chmn., 1993—94. Asst. editor: Ariz. Law Rev. Bd. dirs. Ariz. Found. Legal Svcs. and Edn., sec., 2002, treas., 2003; bd. visitors U. Ariz. Law Sch., 1998—2003. Mem.: ABA, Order of Coif, Ariz. Bar Assn. (mem. specialization com. 1983—87), Maricopa County Bar Assn., Ctrl. Ariz. Estate Planning Coun., State Bar Ariz. (mem. com. preparid and group legal svcs. 1974—76, mem. tax sect. 1974—, pres. 1981—82), Phoenix Country Club, Phi Delta Phi. Taxation, general, Probate (including wills, trusts), Commercial, contracts (including sales of goods; commercial financing). Office: Gallagher and Kennedy PA 2575 E Camelback Rd Phoenix AZ 85016-9225 Office Fax: 602-530-8500. Business E-Mail: dlh@gknet.com.*

HAGAN, MARY ANN, lawyer; b. Phila., Feb. 18, 1935; d. Harry A. and Marie (Farrell) H. BA, Immaculata (Pa.) U., 1956; MA in History, U. Pa., 1958; LLB, Temple U., 1963. Bar: Pa. 1964, U.S. Dist. Ct. Pa. 1972, U.S. Ct. Appeals (3d cir.) 1980, U.S. Tax Ct. 1965, U.S. Ct. Appeals for Federal Cir., 1996. Historian U.S. Dept. Interior, Phila., 1958-60; atty. Urban Renewal Adminstrn., Phila., 1963-65; trial atty. IRS, Office of Chief Counsel, Washington & Phila., 1965-73; supervisory trial atty. U.S. Equal Employment Opportunity Commn., Phila., 1973-77; pvt. practice Phila., 1978—. Arbitrator U.S. Dist. Ct., Phila., 1975—, mem. employment panel, 1989—, fed. mediator, 1991—; lectr., Phila. Bar Edn. Ctr., 1997. Author: Working With the Federal Sector Equal Employment Opportunity Regulations, 29 CFR 1614, 1997. Mem. Nat. Employment Lawyers Assn., Phila. Bar Assn. General civil litigation, Labor (including EEOC, Fair Labor Standards Act, labor-management relations, NLRB, OSHA), Probate (including wills, trusts). Office: 1700 Sansom St 4th Fl Philadelphia PA 19103

HAGBERG, CHRIS ERIC, lawyer; b. Steubenville, Ohio, Dec. 19, 1949; s. Rudolf Eric and Sara (Smith) H.; m. Viola Louise Wilgus, Feb. 19, 1978. BS, Duke U., 1975; JD, U. Tulsa, 1978; postgrad., Nat. Law Ctr., George Washington U. Bar: Okla. 1978, Va. 1979, U.S. Ct. Appeals (4th cir.) Calif. 1986. Law clk. to presiding justice U.S. Dist. Ct. (no. dist.) Okla.; asst. counsel ADP Selection Office Dept. Navy, Navy Regional Contracting Ctr., Washington; counsel Naval Supply Ctr., Pearl Harbor, Hawaii; Pacific area counsel Naval Supply Sys. Command, Dept. Navy, Makakilo, Hawaii; assoc. counsel Navy Supply Sys. Command, Washington; atty. Pettit & Martin, L.A., 1985-87, Seyfarth, Shaw, Fairweather and Geraldson, Washington, 1988-91, U.S. Coast Guard HQ, Washington, 1992-93, USN, 1993-95, Dept. Navy OGC/NSWC Carderock, West Bethesda, Md., 1995—. Contbr. articles to legal jours. Lt. USN, 1970-74. Recipient David I. Milsten award, 1978, 7 Am. Jurisprudence awards, 1976-78, First prize Dept. Navy Legal Writing Contest, 1981. Mem. ABA, FBA, Nat. Contract Mgmt. Assn., Order of Coif. Presbyterian. Administrative and regulatory, Government contracts and claims, Labor (including EEOC, Fair Labor Standards Act, labor-management relations, NLRB, OSHA). Home: 9810 Meadow Valley Dr Vienna VA 22181-3215

HAGBERG, VIOLA WILGUS, lawyer; b. Salisbury, Md., July 3, 1952; d. William E. and Jean Shelton (Barlow) Wilgus; m. Chris Eric Hagberg, Feb. 19, 1978. BA, Furman U., Greenville, S.C., 1974; JD, U. S.C., 1978, U. Tulsa, 1978; DOD Army Logistics Sch. honor grad. basic mgmt. def. acquisition, def. small purchase, advanced fed. acquisition regulation, Fort Lee, Va., 1981-82. Bar: Okla. 1978, Va. 1979, U.S. Ct. Appeals (4th cir.) 1979. With Lawyers Com. for Civil Rights, Washington, 1979; pub. utility specialist Fed. Energy Regulatory Commn., Washington, 1979-80; contract specialist U.S. Army, C.E., Ft. Shafter, Hawaii, 1980-81; contract officer/supervisory contract specialist Tripler Army Med. Ctr., Hawaii 1981-83; supervisory procurement analyst and chief policy Procurement Div. USCG, Washington, 1983; contracts officer and chief Avionics Engring Contracting Br., 1984; procurement analyst office of sec. Dept. Transp., 1984-85; contracting officer Naval Regional Contracting Ctr., Long Beach, Calif., 1985-87; chief acquisition rev. and policy, Hdqrs. Def. Mapping Agy., Washington, 1987-92, dir. acquisitions, Fairfax, Va., 1992-93, dir. acquisition policy, 1994-96; dir. acquisition polity, tech., and legis. programs Nat. Mapping and Imagery Agy., 1996-97, Office of Gen. Counsel. Mem. ABA (law student div. liaison 1977-78), Nat. Contract Mgmt. Assn., Va. State Bar Assn., Okla. Bar Assn., Phi Alpha Delta, Kappa Delta Epsilon.

Corporate, general, Environmental, Government contracts and claims. Home: 9810 Meadow Valley Dr Vienna VA 22181-3215 Office: Nat Imagery and Mapping Agy Office Gen Counsel 4600 Sangamore (MS-D-10) Bethesda MD 20816

HAGEFSTRATION, JOHN E., JR., lawyer; b. Huntsville, Ala., Apr. 29, 1961; s. John E. and Doris A. (Sherrill) H. BS, U. Ala., 1983; JD, U. Va., 1986. Bar: Ala. 1986. Ptnr. Bradley Arant Rose & White LLP, Birmingham, Ala., 1986—. Mem.: ABA, Birmingham Bar Assn., Ala. Bar Assn., Am. Coll. Real Estate Lawyers, Omicron Delta Kappa, Beta Gamma Sigma. Republican. Methodist. Banking, Corporate, general, Property, real (including real estate development, water). Office: Bradley Arant Rose & White LLP One Federal Pl/1819 Fifth Ave N Birmingham AL 35203-2736 Home: 2929 Westmoreland Dr Birmingham AL 35223-2725

HAGELIEN, PER, lawyer; b. Bergen, Norway, Sept. 16, 1943; s. Sverre and Gurly Hagelien; m. Henriette Galtung Døsvig, Sept. 4, 1964; 1 child, Even. JD law, U. Oslo, 1968; postgrad., U. Aix-en-Provence, France. Bar: (advokat, internat. law) 1970, (hoyesterettsadvokat) 1976. Ptnr. Martens (now Schjødt), Bergen, Norway, 1973—. Mem. referral com. internat. law European Union Law, Competition Law, Oslo, 1979—; mem. nat. bd. Den Norske Advokatforening, Oslo, 1981—84; presidency mem. Union Internat. des Avocats, Paris, 1983—94; mem. coun. of bars and law socs. European Union, Brussels, 1984—94; chmn. bd. Advokatfirmaet Schjødt AS, Oslo, 1993—95; judge arbitration ct., Bergen. Author: The Norwegian Legal System, 1994. Lt.-col. Mil. Law, 1980—86, Bergen. Avocation: skiing. Commercial, contracts (including sales of goods; commercial financing), Corporate, general, General civil litigation.

HAGEN, DAVID WARNER, judge; b. 1931; BBA, U. Wis., 1956; LLB, U. San Francisco, 1959. Bar: Washoe County 1981, Nev. 1992. With Berkley, Randall & Harvey, Berkeley, Calif., 1960-62; pvt. practice Loyalton, Calif., 1962-63; with Guild, Busey & Guild (later Guild, Hagen and Clark Ltd. and Guild & Hagen Ltd.), Reno, 1963-93; judge U.S. Dist. Ct. Nev., Reno, 1993—, chmn. 9th Cir. Art. III, Judge's Edn. Com., 1998—2000. Lectr U. Nev., 1968-72; acting dean Nev. Sch. of Law, 1981-83, adj. prof., 1981-87; mem. Nev. Bd. Bar Examiners, 1972-91, chmn., 1989-91; chmn. Nev. Continuing Legal Edn. Com., 1967-75; mem. Nev. Uniform Comml. Code Com. Sgt. USAF, 1949—52. Fellow Am. Coll. Trial Lawyers (state chmn. 1983-85); mem. Nev. Bar Assn., Calif. Bar Assn., Washoe County Bar Assn., Am. Bd. Trial Advocates (advocate), Nat. Maritime Hist. Soc., VFW, U.S. Sailing Assn. Office: US Dist Ct Fed Bldg & US Courthouse 400 S Virginia St Reno NV 89501-2193

HAGEN, GLENN W. lawyer; b. Detroit, July 8, 1948; s. William A. and Lilian (Abrolat) H.; m. Cynthia Winn, July 21, 1984. BS in Chemistry, U. Ala., 1970; JD, Valparaiso U., 1973. Bar: Mich. 1973, U.S. Dist. Ct. (we. dist.) Mich. 1974, Colo. 1981, U.S. Dist. Ct. Colo. 1982. Ptnr. Peters, Seyburn & Hagen, Kalamazoo, 1973-76; dep. city atty. City of Battle Creek, Mich., 1976-79; staff and regulatory counsel CF&I Steel Corp., Pueblo, Colo., 1979-81; gen. counsel Commonwealth Investment Properties Corp., Littleton, Colo., 1981-82; assoc. Berkowitz & Brady, Denver, 1982-83, Zarlengo, Mott, Zarlengo & Winbourn, Denver, 1983-87; pvt. practice Glenn W. Hagen, P.C., Denver, 1987—. Lectr. law office mgmt., constrn. law, small and mid-size bus. issues, corp. entity and formation issues Colo. Bar Assn. and Nat. Bus. Inst. Referee property tax appeals Douglas and Jefferson Counties; del. Colo. Rep. Com., 1986, 1990—2002; chmn. 18th Jud. Dist., 1999—; small bus. cons. South Met. Denver C. of C., 1994—2000. Mem.: ABA (young lawyers exec. coun. 1978—81, chmn. small bus. enterprises 1986, regional dir. constabars 1992—94, nat. editors conf. 1995, mem. constrn. forum 1996—), Highlands Ranch C. of C. (founder, bd. dirs., chmn. elect, treas. 2000—), Colo. Lawyers for Arts, Am. Arbitration Assn., Douglas-Elbert County Bar Assn., Denver Bar Assn, Colo. Bar Assn. (chmn. long range planning com. 1983—86, gen. practice exec. coun. 1985, bus. law sect. 1986—91, mem. exec. bd. chmn. budget com. 1987—89, mem. svcs. com. 1987—89, alt. dispute resolutions com. 1990—94, chmn.small firm section 1991—96, law office mgmt. com. 1995—, constrn. law sect. 1996—, chmn. 2001—), Mich. Bar Assn. (young lawyers exec. coun. 1978—80). Lutheran. Avocations: travel, photography, golf. General civil litigation, Construction, Corporate, general. Home: 2303 E Lansdowne Pl Highlands Ranch CO 80126-4936 Office: Highlands Ranch Bus Pk Ste 108 8925 S Ridgeline Blvd Highlands Ranch CO 80129-2354 Fax: 303-683-3521. E-mail: hagenlaw4biz@earthlink.net.

HAGERMAN, JOHN DAVID, lawyer; b. Houston, Aug. 1, 1941; s. David Angle and Noima L. (Clay) H.; m. Linda J. Lambright, June 25, 1975; children: Clayton Robert, Holly Elizabeth. BBA, So. Meth. U., 1963; JD, U. Tex., Austin, 1966. Bar: Tex. 1966, U.S. Ct. Appeals (5th cir.) 1967, U.S. Supreme Ct. 1969; cert. civil trial law, 1980-95; real estate broker Tex. Pres., owner Hagerman & Sereau, Inc., The Woodlands, Tex., 1966—. Condr. bank creditor rights seminars; mem. adv. bd. Klein Bank. Contbr. articles to profl. jours. Res. dep. sheriff Montgomery County, Tex.; former bd. dirs. Montgomery County Fair Assn., 1978—, Montgomery County Hosp. Dist. Found., Seven Coves Homeowners Assn. Mem. ABA, Tex. Bar Assn., Houston Bar Assn., Houston Outdoor Advtsg. Assn., Tex. Assn. Civil Trial Splsts., Tex. Assn. Bank Counsel, Comml. Real Estate Assn. Montgomery County, Houston Philosoph. Soc., Petroleum Club (Houston), Woodlands Country Club, Beta Theta Pi. Republican. Avocations: swimming, tennis, jogging, shooting. Banking, State civil litigation, Commercial, contracts (including sales of goods; commercial financing). Office: Hagerman & Seureau Inc 24800 Interstate 45 Ste 100 The Woodlands TX 77386-1987

HAGERMAN, MICHAEL CHARLES, lawyer, arbitrator, mediator; b. Webster City, Iowa, Aug. 20, 1951; s. Charles Arnold and Jill Hamilton (Son de Regger) H.; m. Birgit A. Hagerman; children: Kelly, Douglas, Alexander, Christine, Jacqueline. BA with honors, U. Iowa, 1973; MBA, U. Utah, 1978; JD, Drake U., 1981; Grad., U.S. Army Command/Gen. Staff, Coll., Ft. Leavenworth, Kans., 1988. Bar: Iowa 1981, Mass. 1995. Clk. Iowa Resources, Legal Aid of Polk County, and State of Iowa, Des Moines, 1978-81; contract atty. Fisher Controls Internat., Inc., Marshalltown, Iowa, 1981-84; contracts mgr. Emerson & Cuming, Inc., Canton, Mass., 1984-85; contract atty. GTE Govt. Sys., Taunton, Mass., 1986-90; v.p., gen. counsel, sec. ISI Sys., Inc., Andover, Mass., 1990-94; legal counsel Swan Tech. Inc., Marlboro, Mass., 1994-95; pvt. practice Franklin, Mass., 1995—; counsel Fleet Boston Fin., 1998—. Contbr. articles to profl. jours. Capt. U.S. Army, 1973-78, Germany; lt. col. U.S. Army Res. ret. Mem. Sigma Chi (chpt. Balfour award 1973), Phi Alpha Delta (chpt. pres. 1980-81). Avocations: sailing, writing, travel. Commercial, contracts (including sales of goods; commercial financing), Computer, Labor (including EEOC, Fair Labor Standards Act, labor-management relations, NLRB, OSHA). E-mail: mchagermanesq@msn.com.

HAGERTY, PATRICK JOHN, lawyer; s. Richard Gerard and Rosemary Hagerty; m. Marianne Louise Dietzen, May 9, 1987; children: Terese Marie, John Patrick, Ann-Marie Elizabeth, Luke Richard, Margaret Mary, Elizabeth Louise. BS in Bus. Mgmt., Quincy (Ill.) Coll., 1981; JD, St. Louis U., 1985. Bar: Mo. 1985, U.S. Dist. Ct. (ea. dist.) Mo. 1985, Ill. 1986, U.S. Ct. Appeals (8th cir.) 1986, U.S. Ct. Appeals (7th cir.) 1987, U.S. Ct. Appeals (6th cir.) 1994. Law clk. to Hon. Carl Gaertner Mo. Ct. of Appeals, Ea. Dist., St. Louis, 1985—86; assoc. Thompson Coburn, LLC, St. Louis, 1986—92; prin. Gray, Ritter & Graham, P.C., St. Louis, 1992—. Contbr. articles to profl. jours.; mng. editor St. Louis U. Law Jour., 1984—85. Vol. lawyer Trial Lawyers Care, N.Y.C., 2001—02, Legal Svcs. of Ea. Mo., Inc., St. Louis, 2000—02. Mem.: ATLA, ABA (tort and ins. practice sect.), Ill. State Bar Assn., Bar Assn. Met. St. Louis, Am. Bd. Trial Advocates, Acad. Rail Labor Attys., St. Louis U. Law Jour., St. Louis County Bar Assn., St. Clair County Bar Assn., Mo. Assn. Trial Attorneys, Mo. Bar Young Lawyers Divsn., Internat. Soc. Barristers, Internat. Soc. Primerus Law Firms (bd. dirs. 2001—02). Personal injury (including property damage), Product liability. Office: Gray Ritter & Graham PC 701 Market St Ste 800 Saint Louis MO 63101-1830 E-mail: phagerty@grgpc.com.

HAGGARD, WILLIAM ANDREW, lawyer; b. Miami, Feb. 20, 1942; s. Curtis Andrew and Marjorie (Tumlin) H.; m. Carole Ann Erali; children: Michael Andrew, Rebecca M. BA, Fla. State U., 1964; JD, Mercer U., 1967. Bar: Fla. 1967, U.S. Dist. Ct. (5th cir.) 1972, U.S. Supreme Ct. 1972, U.S. Ct. Appeals 1981. Clk. Fla. State Atty.'s Office, 1967; asst. state atty. Eleventh Jud. Cir., 1967-68; chief prosecutor, mil. judge, trial counsel USAF, 1968-71; assoc. Frates, Floyd, Pearson & Stewart, 1971-72; ptnr. Rentz, McClellan & Haggard, 1972-79, Rentz & Haggard, 1979-82; sr. ptnr. Haggard & Kirkland, 1982-89, Wm. Andrew Haggard & Assoc., 1989-93, Haggard & Stone, Coral Gables, Fla., 1993-95, Haggard Parks & Stone, P.A., 1995—, Haggard & Parks, P.A., 1999—2001, Haggard Parks Haggard & Bologna, P.A., 2001—. Instr. Fla. bar continuing legal edn., 1977-82; vis. lectr. U. Fla. Law Sch., 1977-82 Commr. Fla. Commn. on Ethics, 1990-91; mem. Mercer U. Alumni Bd.; bd. dirs. Fla. State U. Found.; chmn. Fla. State U. Coll. of Arts and Scis. Leadership Counsel; Gov. Bush appointee Fla. State Bd. Trustees. Fellow Internat. Acad. Trial Lawyers (state chair); mem. ATLA, ABA, Am. Bd. Trial Advocates, Dade County Bar Assn., Acad. Fla. Trial Lawyers (bd. dirs. 1995-96), Internat. Soc. Barristers, Million Dollars Advocates Club, Phi Delta Phi, Sigma Chi. Office: 330 Alhambra Cir Coral Gables FL 33134-5004 E-mail: mail@haggardparks.com.

HAGGERTY, JAMES JOSEPH, lawyer; b. Scranton, Pa., June 12, 1936; s. James J. Haggerty and Margaret W. Cummings; m. Cecelia Ellen Lynett; children: Jean Margaret McGrath, Mauri Elizabeth Collins, James Joseph Jr., Matthew Edward, Cecelia Ellen, Daniel Patrick, Kathleen Mary. BA in Econs., Holy Cross Coll., Worcester, Mass., 1957; JD, Georgetown U., 1960; LLD (hon.), U. Scranton, 1987; LHD (hon.), Villanova U., 1995. Bar: Pa. 1961, Ct. Common Pleas Lackawanna County 1961, U.S. Dist. Ct. (mid. dist.) Pa. 1961, U.S. Ct. Appeals (3d cir.) 1962, U.S. Ct. Claims 1985. Assoc. Farrell Butler Kearney & Parker, Scranton, 1961-62; law clk. to Hon. William J. Nealon U.S. Dist. Ct. (mid. dist.), Scranton, 1963-64; ptnr. Casey Haggerty and McDonnell, Scranton, 1965-70, Haggerty McDonnell O'Brien, Scranton, 1970-87; former sec. of commonwealth State of Pa., Harrisburg, 1987-89; gen. counsel to gov. Commonwealth of Pa., Harrisburg, 1989-93; ptnr. Haggerty, McDonnell & O'Brien, Scranton, 1993—. Apptd. by U.S. Dist. Ct. trustee in bankruptcy of Blue Coal Corp., 1976-86; mem. hearing com. 3.03 Disciplinary Bd. Pa. Supreme Ct.; permanent mem. Jud. Conf. U.S. 3d Jud. Cir.; mem. Fed. Jud. Screening Com., 1996-2001; chmn. bd. dirs. Shamrock Comm. Corp.; past bd. dirs. Specialty Plastics Products Inc.; past. bd. dirs., solicitor 1st Nat. Community Bank Dunmore. Trustee U. Scranton, 1979—86, chmn. bd., 1982—86, mem. Pres.'s Cir., mem. Pres.'s Club; chmn. Real Bob Casey Com., 1985—86; trustee Scranton Prep. Sch., 1995—2000, chmn. bd., 1999—2000; former bd. dirs. Lackawanna United Way, former chmn. profl. and geog. divsn.; bd. dirs. assocs. Scranton Area Found. With U.S. Army, with Pa. N.G. Mem. ABA, ATLA, Am. Bankers Assn., Pa. Bar Assn. (Spl. Achievement award 1988-89), Pa. Trial Lawyers Assn., Pa. Bankers Assn., Lackawanna Bar Assn. (past pres., bd. dirs.), Greater Scranton C. of C. (bd. dirs., former v.p.), Holy Cross Coll. Alumni Assn. N.E. Pa. (past pres., Outstanding Alumnus award 1982), Scranton Prep. Sch. Alumni Assn. (past mem. bd. govs., T. Donald Reinfret S.J. award Outstanding Alumnus of Yr. 1985), Friendly Sons of St. Patrick Lackawanna County (mem. exec. com., past pres.), Country Club Scranton (bd. dirs.). Roman Catholic. Office: Haggerty McDonnell & O'Brien 203 Franklin Ave Ste 1 Scranton PA 18503-1989 E-mail: hmolaw@epix.net.

HAGGERTY, ROBERT HENRY, lawyer; b. N.Y.C., Feb. 25, 1919; s. Daniel A. and Helen Marie (Henry) H.; m. Mary Rita O'Neil, Aug. 28, 1945 (dec. 1990); children: Robert Jr., Daniel J., Nancy D., Thomas H; m. Nadia Ismail, 1991. BBA, Manhattan Coll., 1940; LLB, Harvard U., 1953. Bar: N.Y. 1954, Fla. 1977. Assoc. Root, Ballantine, Harlan, Bushby & Palmer (now Dewey, Ballantine), N.Y.C., 1953—56, 1962—95, ptnr., 1965—; atty. Gen. Electric Co., N.Y.C. and Schenectady, N.Y., 1956-62. Bd. dirs. Ticor Title Guarantee Co., N.Y.C. Editor: PLI Real Estate Construction Current Problems, 1973; editor (vols. 8, 29, 58) PLI Real Estate Construction, 1969-72. Bd. dirs. Plandome (N.Y.) Property Assocs., 1965-76, pres., 1970-76; pres. Plandome Mills Property Owners, 1980-82; village justice of Plandome Manor, 1983-89, mayor, 1989-93. Served to maj. USMC, 1941-45, PTO. Decorated Silver Star, Purple Heart. Mem. Plandome Country Club, Grand Harbor Golf and Country Club. Roman Catholic. Address: Dewey Ballantine 1301 Avenue of the Americas New York NY 10019-6092 Home: 1870 Paseo del Lago Vero Beach FL 32967-7260

HAGGLUND, CLARANCE EDWARD, lawyer, publishing company owner; b. Omaha, Feb. 17, 1927; s. Clarance Andrew and Esther May (Kelle) H.; m. Dorothy Souser, Mar. 27, 1953 (div. Aug. 1972); children: Laura, Bret, Katherine; m. Merle Patricia Hagglund, Oct. 28, 1972. BA, U. S.D., 1949; JD, William Mitchell Coll. Law, 1953. Bar: Minn. 1955, U.S. Ct. Appeals (8th cir.) 1974, U.S. Supreme Ct. 1963; diplomate Am. Bd. Profl. Liability Attys. Ptnr. Hagglund & Johnson and predecessor firms, Mpls., 1973—; mem. Hagglund, Weimer and Speidel, PA; publ., pres. Common Law Publishing Inc., Golden Valley, Minn., 1991—. Pres. Internat. Control Sys., Inc., Mpls., 1979—, Hill River Corp., Mpls., 1976—; gen. counsel Minn. Assn. Profl. Ins. Agts., Inc., Mpls., 1965-86; CFO, Pro-Trac, software for profl. liability ins. industry. Contbr. articles to profl. jours. Served to lt. comdr. USNR, 1945-46, 50-69. Fellow Internat. Soc. Barristers; mem. Lawyers Pilots Bar Assn., U.S. Maritime Law Assn. (proctor), Acad. Cert. Trial Lawyers Minn. (dean 1983-85), Nat. Bd. Trial Advocacy (cert. in civil trial law, bd. dirs.), Douglas Amdahl Inns of Ct. (pres.), Ill. Athletic Club (Chgo.), Edina Country Club (Minn.), Calhoun Beach Club (Mpls.). Roman Catholic. Avocation: flying. Federal civil litigation, State civil litigation, Insurance. Home: 3168 Dean Ct Minneapolis MN 55416-4386 Office: Common Law Publishing Inc 5101 Olson Memorial Hwy Golden Valley MN 55422-5149 E-mail: hagglund@pro-ns.net.

HAGIN, T. RICHARD, lawyer; b. Thomasville, Ga., Sept. 13, 1941; s. Wesley R. and Elizabeth (Skinner) H.; m. Deborah Hayes, June 19, 1981; children: Jennifer Bridges, Lori Mikula; children from previous marriage: John Wesley Hagin, Grace Elizabeth Hagin. AA, North Fla. C.C., Madison, 1961; student, Fla. State U., 1961-62; JD, Stetson U., 1964. Fla. 1964, Oreg. 1992, U.S. Dist. Ct. (mid. dist.) Fla. 1965, U.S. Ct. Appeals (5th cir.) 1965, U.S. Ct. Appeals (11th cir.) 1981, U.S. Ct. Mil. Appeals 1991, U.S. Supreme Ct. 1971. Atty. Law Offices of David A. Davis, Bushnell, Fla., 1964; ptnr. Davis and Hagin, Bushnell, 1965; atty. in pvt. practice Bushnell, 1966-67; ptnr. Hagin, Hughes, Rardon & Rodriguez, Bushnell, 1989-1996, Getzen and Hagin, Bushnell, 1967-71; pres. Getzen & Hagin, P.A., Bushnell, 1971—. Local counsel CSX R.R., Bushnell, 1967-87, gen. counsel Tax Collector of Sumter County, Bushnell, 1976-95; forfeiture atty. Sumter County Sheriff Dept., Bushnell, 1983-89; county atty. Sumter County, Fla., 1969-76; city atty. City of Webster, Fla., 1966-87, City of Coleman, Fla., 1969-73; gen. counsel Sumter County Indsl. Authority, Bushnell, 1979-89, Sumter County Hosp. Authority, Bushnell, 1969-85. Mem. City Coun., Bushnell, 1967-69; pros. atty. Sumter County, 1969-73; chmn. Withlacoochee Regional Planning Coun., Ocala, Fla., 1973-75; chmn. 5th Jud. Cir. Grievance Com., 1973-76. Mem. ABA, Assn. Trial Lawyers Am., Fla. Bar, Oreg. Bar Assn., Acad. Fla. Trial Lawyers. Democrat. Personal injury (including property damage), Product liability, Workers' compensation. Office: Getzen and Hagin PO Box 248 Bushnell FL 33513-0019

HAGOOD, LEWIS RUSSELL, lawyer; b. Persia, Tenn., July 13, 1930; s. Hobart Verlin and Stella Rose (Carter) Hagood; m. Mary Evelyn Morrisette, Mar. 15, 1952; children: Lewis Russell Jr., Mary Victoria, Paul Gregory. Student, Lincoln Meml. U., Harrogate, Tenn., 1947-49; BS, E. Tenn. State U., 1952; JD, U. Tenn., 1963. Bar: Tenn. 1964, U.S. Dist. Ct. (ea. dist.) Tenn. 1964, U.S. Dist. Ct. (ea. dist.) Ky. 1975, U.S. Tax Ct. 1984, U.S. Ct. Appeals (6th cir.) 1968, U.S. Supreme Ct., cert.: Ea. Dist. Tenn. (fed. mediator), approved mediator: Tenn. Supreme Ct. Ptnr. McLellan, Wright, Hagood, Attys., Kingsport, Tenn., 1964-65; assoc. Arnett & Draper, Attys., Knoxville, Tenn., 1965-67; ptnr. Arnett, Draper & Hagood, Knoxville, 1967—. Mem., pres. Tenn. Bd. Law Examiners, 1994—2002; spkr., lectr. in field. Editor-in-chief: Tenn. Law Rev., 1963—64; contbr. articles to profl. jours. Mem. E. Tenn. chpt. March of Dimes, 1981—84; bd. dirs. Knoxville Symphony, 1977—, Knoxville Teen Ctr., Inc., 1975—97. With U.S. Army, 1954—56. Fellow: Tenn. Bar Found.; mem.: ABA, Knoxville Bar Assn., Tenn. Bar Assn. (past chmn. labor law sect.). Republican. Presbyterian. Avocations: golf, fishing, antique autos. Federal civil litigation, State civil litigation, Labor (including EEOC, Fair Labor Standards Act, labor-management relations, NLRB, OSHA). Office: Arnett Draper & Hagood Plz Towers Ste 2300 Knoxville TN 37929

HAGOORT, THOMAS HENRY, lawyer; b. Paterson, N.J., May 30, 1932; s. Nicholas Hugh and Rae (Sytsma) H.; m. Lois Ann Bennett, Sept. 6, 1954; children: Nancy Hagoort Treuhold, Susan Audrey. AB cum laude, Harvard U., 1954, LL.B. magna cum laude, 1957. Bar: N.Y. 1959. Assoc. firm Cleary, Gottlieb, Steen & Hamilton, N.Y.C., 1957-67, ptnr., 1968-90; gen. counsel Albany Internat. Corp., 1991—2002, Sr. V.P., 2002—. Note editor, Harvard Law Rev., 1956-57. Pres. Mountainside Hosp., Montclair, N.J., 1983-85, chmn. bd. trustees, 1985-88; pres. Internat. Baccalaureate of N.Am., N.Y.C., 1980-91, Montclair Bd. Edn. 1966-70; mem., Coun. of Found. Internat. Baccalaureate Orgn., Geneva, 1982-96, pres. and chair exec. com., 1990-96. Mem.: ABA, N.Y. State Bar Assn., Sea Pines Country Club, S.C. Yacht Club, Harvard Club of N.J. (pres. 1977—78). Democrat. Corporate, general, Finance, Mergers and acquisitions. Home: PO Box 3229 Hilton Head Island SC 29928-0229

HAGOPIAN, JACOB, federal judge; b. Providence; s. Bedros and Varvar (Leylegian) H.; m. Mary L. Pomoranski; children: Mark Jay, Dana Aquinas, Mary Lou, Jan Christian, Jon Gregory. AB, George Washington U., 1957; JD, Am. U., 1960; grad. thesis in internat. law, Judge Advocate Gen.'s Sch., 1964; postgrad., Indsl. Coll. Armed Forces, 1967. Bar: Va. 1961, R.I. 1964, U.S. Supreme Ct. 1964, U.S. Dist. Ct. R.I., U.S. Dist. Ct. (ea. dist.) Va., U.S. Ct. Appeals (D.C. cir.), U.S. Ct. Customs and Patent Appeals, U.S. Ct. Claims, U.S. Tax Ct. Enlisted U.S. Army, 1944, advanced through grades to 1st sgt. 11th Airborne Divsn., 2d lt. to 1st lt. 82d Airborne Divsn., parachutist, glider pathfinder, & jumpmaster qualified, 1948-50; capt. U.S. Army Security Agency, Washington, 1950-53, 56-60, with 501st Recon group, 1953, 1954-56; advanced through grades to col. U.S. Army, 1953-68; appellate judge U.S. Ct. Mil. Rev. U.S. Army Ct. Criminal Appeals, Washington, 1968-70; ret. colonel U.S. Army, 1970; appellate judge U.S. Army Judiciary, Washington, 1968-70; dir. law ctr. Roger Williams Coll., Providence, 1970-71; U.S. magistrate judge U.S. Dist. Ct., Providence, 1971—. Legal adv. to intelligence cmty. Spl. Ops., Berlin, 1960-63; group supv. def. appellate divsn. USA Judiciary, Washington, 1964-66; dep. and chief criminal law divsn. OTJAG dept. of army The Pentagon, Washington, 1966-68 mem. U.S. Army and U.S. Air Force Clemency and Parole Bd.; lectr. Fed. Judicial Ctr., Washington; adj. prof. Am. U., 1971—, Suffolk U. Law Sch.; vis. prof. Naval War Coll.; mem. hon. faculty fellow AV, 1997—, hon. program U. R.I.; mem. code com. Uniform Code of Mil. Justice, Sec. of Def., 2000—; U.S. magistrate judge Jud. Coun., 1st Cir. Ct. of Appeals. Contbr. articles to profl. jours. Decorated Legion of Merit (2) with first oak leaf cluster; recipient Army Commendation medal with oak leaf cluster. Mem. ABA (former cons. sect. criminal justice, vice chmn. com. on adequate def. and incentives in mil., former sec.-reporter com. mil. law, Houston Justice Assist award 1987, mem. code com. uniform code mil. justice 2000—), Fed. Bar Assn. (past pres. R.I. chpt., mem. nat. coun., mem. nat. chmn. com. criminal law, chmn. U.S. magistrate judge's com.), Inst. Jud. Adminstrn., U.S. Naval War Coll. Found., Nat. Def. U. Found. Office: US Dist Ct Two Exchange Ter Providence RI 02903 Fax: 401-752-7006.

HAHN, ELLIOTT JULIUS, lawyer; b. San Francisco, Dec. 9, 1949; s. Leo Wolf and Sherry Marion (Portnoy) H.; m. Toby Rose Mallen; children: Kara Rebecca, Brittany Atira Mallen, Michael Mallen, Adam Mallen. BA cum laude, U. Pa., 1971, JD, 1974; LLM, Columbia U., 1980. Bar: N.J. 1974, Calif. 1976, D.C. 1978, U.S. Dist. Ct. N.J. 1974, U.S. Dist. Ct. (cen. dist.) Calif. 1976, U.S. Supreme Ct. 1980. Assoc. von Malitz, Derenberg, Kunin & Janssen, N.Y.C., 1974-75; law clk. L.A. County Superior Ct., 1975-76; atty. Atlantic Richfield Co., L.A., 1976-79; prof. Summer in Tokyo program Santa Clara Law Sch., 1981-83; assoc. prof. law Calif. Western Sch. Law, San Diego, 1980-85; atty. Morgan, Lewis & Bockius, L.A., 1985-87; assoc. Whitman & Ransom, L.A., 1987-88, ptnr., 1989-93, Sonnenschein Nath & Rosenthal, L.A., 1993-97, Hahn & Bolson, LLP, 1997—. Vis. scholar Nihon U., Tokyo, 1982; vis. lectr. Internat. Christian U., Tokyo, 1982; adj. prof. law Southwestern U. Sch. Law, 1986-93, Pepperdine U. law Sch., 1986-93, U. So. Calif. Law Sch., 1997-98; lectr. U. Calif., Davis, Law Sch. Orientation in U.S.A. Law Program, 1994-97. Author: Japanese Business Law and the Legal System, 1984; contbr. chpt. on Japan to The World Legal Ency.; internat. law editor Calif. Bus. Law Reporter. Vice-chmn. San Diego Internat. Affairs Bd., 1981-85; bd. dirs. San Diego-Yokohama Sister City Soc., 1983-85, L.A.-Nagoya Sister City Soc., 1986-1996; mem. master planning com. City of Rancho Palos Verdes, Calif., 1989-91; advisor, exec. com. Calif. Internat. Law Sect., 1990-91, 95, appointee exec. com., 1991-94, vice-chmn., 1992-93, chair, 1993-94; appointee, trustee Palos Verdes Libr. Dist., 1993-94; bd. dirs. Internat. Student Ctr. UCLA, 1996—, pres., 2000-01. Mem. ABA, State Bar Calif., LA County Bar Assn. (bd. dirs. internat. sect., exec. com. Internat. Legal Sec. 1987—, sec. 1995-96, 2d v.p. 1996-97, 1st v.p. 1997-98, chmn. 1998-99, appointee Pacific rim com. 1990-98, chmn. 1991-92, 95-98, trustee 1997-98), Assn. Asian Studies, U. Pa. Alumni Club (pres. San Diego chpt. 1982, pres. coun. Phila. 1983), Anti Defamation League, Japanese-Am. Soc. (book rev. editor Seattle 1983-85). Jewish. Corporate, general, Private international, Labor (including EEOC, Fair Labor Standards Act, labor-management relations, NLRB, OSHA). Office: Hahn & Bolson LLP 1000 Wilshire Blvd # 1600 Los Angeles CA 90017-2457 E-mail: ehahn@hahnbolsonllp.com.

HAHN, FREDERIC LOUIS, lawyer; b. Chgo., Apr. 28, 1941; s. Max and Margery Ruth (Goodman) H.; m. Susan Firestone, Mar. 26, 1967; 1 child, Frederic Firestone. AB with highest distinction, Cornell U., 1962, MBA with highest distinction, 1963; JD magna cum laude, Harvard U., 1966. Bar: Ill. 1966; CPA, Ill. Assoc. Hopkins & Sutter, Chgo., 1966-72, ptnr., 1973-94, Mayer, Brown & Platt (now Mayer, Brown, Rowe & Maw), Chgo., 1994—. Bd. dirs. Lyric Opera of Chgo., 1988—. Recipient Gold medal (CPA exam) State of Ill., 1963. Mem. Phi Beta Kappa. Federal civil litigation, Non-profit and tax-exempt organizations, Corporate taxation. Home: 1377 Scott Ave Winnetka IL 60093-1444 Office: Mayer Brown Rowe & Maw 190 S La Salle St Ste 3100 Chicago IL 60603-3441 E-mail: fhahn@mayerbrownrowe.com.

HAHN, GARY LYNN, lawyer; b. Mishawaka, Ind., Feb. 18, 1949; s. Frederick and Joyce (Heningsmith) H.; m. Deborah Lynne King, June 26, 1971; children: Marla, Andrea. BA, Kalamazoo Coll., 1971; JD, U. Mich., 1976. Bar: Mich. 1976, U.S. Dist. Ct. (ea. dist.) Mich. 1976. Atty. Forsythe, Campbell et al, Ann Arbor, Mich., 1976-80; v.p., gen. counsel Data Scan Svc., Inc., Ann Arbor, 1980-86; atty., sole practitioner Ann Arbor, 1987—. Bd. dirs., sec. Xela Pack, Inc., Bridgewater, Mich., 1987—. City coun. mem. City of Saline, Mich., 1988-94, econ. devel. bd., 1990-97, planning commn., 1984-88. Recipient Svc. award City of Saline, 1994; Fulbright scholar Albert-Ludwigs-U., Freiburg, Germany, 1971-72. Mem. Washtenaw County Bar Assn., Kiwanis Club of Saline (pres. 1984-85), Phi Beta Kappa. Methodist. Avocations: travel, swimming, german language. Commercial, contracts (including sales of goods; commercial financing), Corporate, general, Property, real (including real estate development, water). Office: Pierce & Hahn 709 W Huron St Ste 200 Ann Arbor MI 48103-6705

HAHN, H. BLAIR, lawyer; b. Chapel Hill, N.C., Nov. 26, 1958; s. Herbert Ransom and Mary Anna Blair; m. Nancy Elizabeth Walker, May 18, 1985. BA in Bus. Mgmt., BA in Econs., N.C. State U., Raleigh, 1980; JD, U. S.C., 1992. Bar: S.C. 1992, U.S. Dist. Ct. S.C. 1992, U.S. Ct. Appeals (8th cir.) 1995, U.S. Dist. Ct. Ariz. 1997. Mem. Ness, Motley, Loadholt, Richardson & Poole, Charleston, SC, 1992—2002; ptnr. Richardson Patrick Westbrook & Brickman LLC, Charleston, 2002—. Bd. dirs. Atlantic Publ. Group, Charleston, 1985-2002. Editor: S.C. Bar Young Lawyers Newsletter, 1992-93. Personal injury (including property damage), Product liability. Office: Richardson Patrick Westbrook and Brickman LLC PO Box 1007 Mount Pleasant SC 29465 E-mail: bhahn@rpwb.com.

HAHN, STANLEY ROBERT, JR., lawyer, financial executive; b. Louisville, Dec. 8, 1946; s. Stanley Robert and Dorothy Dodd (Moseley) H.; children from previous marriage: Laura, Valerie, Kathy; (div.); m. LaDonna Marie Dees, Nov. 9, 1996. BBA in Fin., MBA, Ga. State U.; LLM in Litigation, JD, Atlanta Law Sch. Bar: Ga. 1983, U.S. Dist. Ct. (no. dist.) Ga. 1983, U.S. Ct. Appeals (11th cir.) 1983, U.S. Ct. Apppeals (4th cir.) 1985, U.S. Supreme Ct. 1986. Mgr. credit White-Westinghouse Corp., Atlanta, 1975-77; mgr. fin. Am. Can Co., Greenwich, Conn., 1977—; pvt. practice Atlanta, 1983—. Bd. dirs. HDC Investments Inc., Atlanta, Interest Unltd. Inc., Atlanta. Mem.: ABA, Nat. Assn. Credit Mgmt., Assn. Trial Lawyers Am., Assn. MBA Execs. Baptist. Avocations: golf, tennis, chess, billiards. General civil litigation, Family and matrimonial, Personal injury (including property damage). Office: Bldg E Ste 600 6185 S Buford Hwy Norcross GA 30071 Fax: 770-416-0195. E-mail: Robert@atlantalawyersonline.com.

HAIG, ROBERT LEIGHTON, lawyer; b. Plainfield, N.J., July 30, 1947; s. Richard Randall and Edith (Remington) H. AB, Yale U., 1967; JD, Harvard U., 1970. Bar: N.Y. 1971, U.S. Dist. Ct. (so. and ea. dists.) N.Y., U.S. Ct. Appeals (2d cir.). Assoc. Kelley Drye & Warren, N.Y.C., 1970-79, ptnr., 1980—. Mem. bd. advisers Law Dept. Mgmt. Adviser, 1995—. Co-author: Preparing for and Trying the Civil Lawsuit, 1987, 91, 94, 97, 2000, Federal Civil Practice, 1989, 93, 97, 2000, Federal Litigation Guide, 1992, 93, 94, Corporate Counsel's Guide, 1996, 97, Products Liability in New York, 1997, 2002; also contbr. chpts. to books, articles to profl. jours.; mem. bd. editors Fed. Litigation Guide Reporter, 1989—, In-House Law Practice Management, 1997—; editor-in-chief Comml. Litigation in N.Y. State Cts., 1995, Bus. and Comml. Litigation in Fed. Cts., 1998, Successful Partnering Between Inside and Outside Counsel, 2000. Co-chair Comml. Cts. Task Force, 1995—; mem. legis. com. Com. for Modern Cts., N.Y.C., 1986—, bd. dirs., 1994—, exec. com., 2001—; mem. Am. Law Inst., 1998—; mem. Nat. Ctr. State Cts., Lawyers Com., 2002-; mem. N.Y. State Conf. Bar Leaders, exec. coun., 1988-90, mem. dept. disciplinary com. appellate divsn., 1996-2001, 2003—, hearing panel chair, 1999-2001, policy com., 2003—; mem. N.Y. State Jud. Salary Commn., 1997—. Recipient award for excellence in continuing legal edn. Assn. Continuing Legal Edn. Adminstrs., 1991. Fellow Am. Bar Found. (life), N.Y. Bar Found. (life, bd. dirs. 2001—, v.p. 2002-03, pres. 2003—); mem. ABA (del. 1991—, standing com. on jud. selection, tenure and compensation 1995-96, com. on bus. cts. 1996—, chair subcom. on rels. between inside and outside counsel 1997—, spl. advisor standing com. fed. judiciary 2002), Assn. of Bar of City of N.Y. (mem. jud. com. 1985-88, chmn., 1989-92, mem. coun. on jud. adminstrn. 1989-92, chmn. 1996-99), N.Y. County Lawyers Assn. (exec. com. 1986-95, v.p. 1986-92, pres. 1992-94, dir. 1985—, chmn. com. on supreme ct. 1984-86, chmn. fin. com. 1988-90, lectr. 1984—, pres. Found. 1992-94), N.Y. State Bar Assn. (chmn. com. on fed. cts. 1986-88, del. 1988—, chmn. comml. and fed. litig. sect. 1988-90, lectr. 1985—, exec. com. 1991-94, mem. steering com. on commerce and industry 1997—, chair com. on multi-disciplinary practice and the legal profn. 1998-99, 1st Ann. award for Disting. Pub. Svc. comml. and fed. litig. sect. 1995). Federal civil litigation, General civil litigation, State civil litigation. Office: Kelley Drye & Warren LLP 101 Park Ave Fl 30 New York NY 10178-0062 E-mail: rhaig@kelleydrye.com.

HAIGHT, CAROL BARBARA, lawyer; b. Buffalo, May 3, 1945; d. Robert H. Johnson and Betty R. (Walker) Hawkes; m. H. Granville Haight, May 28, 1978 (dec. Nov. 1983); m. Dennis M. Nagel PE, Oct. 19, 1996; children: David Michael, Kathleen Marie. BSW summa cum laude, BA in Psychology summa cum laude, Widener U., Chester, Pa., 1980; JD cum laude, Widener U., Wilmington, Del., 1984. Assoc. Pepper, Hamilton & Scheetz, Phila., 1985-88, Hodgson, Russ, Andrews, Woods & Goodyear, Buffalo, 1988-90; pvt. practice Boca Raton, Fla., 1990—; corp. counsel Eilink Corp, Fremont, Calif., 2000. Arbitrator Am. Arbitration Assn., mediator, 1989—, mediation instr.; founding dir. Mediation Ednl. Svc., Fla. Supreme Ct. Cert. mediator and arbitrator, 1999-; vol. spkr. and coun. Hospice. Contbr. articles to profl. jours. Mem. Pa. Bar, Fla. Bar, Phi Kappa Phi Hon. Soc., Phi Alpha Delta, Phi Gamma Mu. Republican. Episcopalian. Avocations: scuba diving, skiing, tennis, sailing, ballroom dancing, flying. Commercial, contracts (including sales of goods; commercial financing), Corporate, general. Home: Braemar Isle Townhouse 9 4744 S Ocean Blvd Highland Beach FL 33487-5321 Fax: 561-368-1582. E-mail: cbhaight@yahoo.com.

HAIGHT, CHARLES SHERMAN, JR., federal judge; b. N.Y.C., Sept. 23, 1930; s. Charles Sherman and Margaret (Edwards) H.; m. Mary Jane Peightal, June 30, 1953; children: Nina E., Susan P. BA, Yale U., 1952, LL.B., 1955. Bar: N.Y. State 1955. Trial atty., admiralty and shipping dept. Dept. Justice, Washington, 1955-57; assoc. firm Haight, Gardner, Poor & Havens, N.Y.C., 1957-68, ptnr., 1968-76; judge U.S. Dist. Ct. for So. Dist. N.Y., 1976—. Bd. dirs. Kennedy Child Study Ctr.; adv. trustee Am.-Scandinavian Found., chmn., 1970-76; bd. mgrs. Havens Fund. Mem. Maritime Law Assn., U.S., N.Y. State Bar Assn., Bar Assn. City N.Y., Fed. Bar Council. Episcopalian. Office: US Dist Ct US Courthouse 500 Pearl St New York NY 10007-1316

HAILE, LAWRENCE BARCLAY, lawyer; b. Atlanta, Feb. 19, 1938; children: Gretchen Vanderhoof, Eric McKenzie (dec.), Scott McAllister. BA in Econs, U. Tex., 1958, LLB, 1961. Bar: Tex. 1961, Calif. 1962. Law clk. to U.S. Judge Joseph M. Ingraham, Houston, 1961-62; pvt. practice San Francisco, 1962-67, LA, 1967—. Instr. UCLA Civil Trial Clinics, 1974, 76; lectr. law Calif. Continuing Edn. of Bar, 1973-74, 80-89; nat. panel arbitrators Am. Arbitration Assn., 1965—. Mem. editl. bd. Tex. Law Rev, 1960-61; contbr. articles profl. jours. Mem. State Bar Calif., Tex., U.S. Supreme Ct. Bar Assn., Internat. Assn. Property Ins. Counsel (founding mem., pres. 1980), Vintage Motorsports Coun. (past pres.), Phi Delta Phi, Delta Sigma Rho. Federal civil litigation, State civil litigation, Insurance. Office: 425 E Ocean Blvd Unit 340 Long Beach CA 90802-4951 E-mail: lhaile1938@aol.com.

HAIMAN, IRWIN SANFORD, lawyer; b. Cleve., Mar. 19, 1916; s. Alfred W. and Stella H. (Weiss) H.; m. Jeanne D. Jaffee, Mar. 8, 1942; children: Karen H. Schenkel, Susan L. BA, Western Res. U., 1937; LL.B., Cleve. Marshall Law Sch., 1941; JD, Cleve. State U., 1969. Bar: Ohio 1941, U.S. Ct. Appeals (6th cir.) 1961, U.S. Supreme Ct. 1961. Asst. to pres. Tremco Mfg. Co., Cleve., 1936-42; house counsel William Edwards Co., Cleve., 1947-48; pvt. practice Cleve., 1948-68; ptnr. firm Garber, Simon, Haiman, Gutfeld, Friedman & Jacobs, 1968-80; ptnr. McCarthy, Lebit, Crystal & Haiman, 1981—. Lectr. in speech Western Res. U., 1948-70; dir. Washington Fed. Savs. and Loan Assn.; asst. law dir., prosecutor City of Lyndhurst, Ohio, 1965-79, law dir., 1979-84. Trustee Montefiore Home, Cleve., 1974-88 (life trustee 1988—)—, East End Neighborhood House, 1962-68; councilman City of South Euclid, 1948-54, pres., 1952-54; pres. Young People's Congregation, Fairmount Temple, 1951-52; sec., trustee Suburban Temple, 1962-65, trustee, 1983— , pres., 1984-87; chmn. speakers div., bd. dirs. Cleve. chpt. ARC, 1959-62; chmn. speaker and film div. Cleve. United Appeal, 1961-62; chmn. speakers div. Jewish Welfare Fund Cleve., 1973-79. Served as 1st lt. AUS, 1943-47. Mem. Ohio, Cleve. bar assns., Assn. Trial Lawyers Am., Zeta Beta Tau. Clubs: Oakwood Country, Lake Forest Country (pres. 1971-72, 75-79). Home: 20201 N Park Blvd Cleveland OH 44118-5000

HAIMS, BRUCE DAVID, lawyer; b. N.Y.C., Nov. 25, 1940; s. Samuel Harold and Judith (Feller) H.; m. Judith Jackson; children: Carolyn, Daniel, Nolan. BS in Econs., U. Pa., 1962; LLB magna cum laude, Harvard U., 1965; LLM in Taxation, NYU, 1972. Bar: Conn. 1965, N.Y. 1967, U.S. Ct. Appeals (2d cir.) 1968, U.S. Tax Ct. 1972. Assoc. Debevoise & Plimpton, N.Y.C., 1967-72, ptnr., 1973—. Bd. dirs. Axe Houghton Found., Brookfield Craft Ctr. Capt. U.S. Army, 1965-67. Mem. N.Y. State Bar Assn., Assn. of Bar of City of N.Y., Internat. Fiscal Assn. Corporate taxation, Non-profit and tax-exempt organizations, Taxation, general. Home: 470 W End Ave Apt 14A New York NY 10024-4933 Office: Debevoise & Plimpton 919 3rd Ave Fl 2 New York NY 10022-3904

HAINES, JOHN ALDEN, retired lawyer; b. Merrill, Mich., July 26, 1934; s. John Alden and Pearl Ann (Bader) H.; m. Esther Catherine Mueller, Aug. 25, 1956; children— Kimberly Ann, Kathryn Sue, John Alden III. A.A., Bay City Jr. Coll., 1953; B.A., U. Mich., 1955; J.D., Detroit Coll., 1958. Bar: Mich., 1959. Sole practice law, Bridgeport, Mich., 1959-67; sr. ptnr. Haines & Marti, 1968—99, Haines & Oeming, Bridgeport, 1992-99, ret. 1999; justice of peace Bridgeport Twp., 1961-68. Pres., bd. dirs. Bridgeport Civic Assn., 1963, 1966; dist. chmn. Boy Scouts Am., Saginaw. 1969; county del. Saginaw Republican Party, 1964, 84. Mem. Saginaw Bar Assn. (sec. 1980-82, dir. 1983-85, v.p. 1985-86, pres. 1986-87, Meritorious Service award, 1979, cert. commendation 1985), Mich. Bar Assn., Am. Judicature Soc., Bridgeport C. of C., (pres., dir. 1962-63), Delta Theta Phi. Lutheran. Clubs: Bridgeport Country, Bridgeport Gun. Avocations: golf, skiing. Personal injury (including property damage), Probate (including wills, trusts), Property, real (including real estate development, water). Home: 621 Churchgrove Rd Frankenmuth MI 48734-9791 Office: Haines & Oeming 6221 Dixie Hwy Bridgeport MI 48722-9513

HAINES, TERRY L. lawyer, consultant; b. Washington, Pa., Oct. 2, 1957; s. John A. and Ann C. Haines. BA, Oberlin Coll., 1979; JD, Vt. U., 1982. Bar: Pa. 1983, U.S. Dist. Ct. (we. dist.) Pa. 1983. Legis. asst. com. on judiciary Pa. Assembly, Harrisburg, 1983; sr. staff atty. FCC, Washington, 1983-87; rep. counsel com. on energy and commerce U.S. Ho. of Reps., Washington, 1987-91; chief of staff FCC, Washington, 1991-93; divsn. gen. counsel TCI East, Inc., Bethesda, Md., 1993-94; chief oper. officer, gen. counsel Boland & Madigan, Inc., Washington, 1995-2001; chief counsel, staff dir. U.S. Ho. of Reps. Com. on Fin. Svcs., Washington, 2001—03; ptnr. Alexander Strategy Group, Washington, 2003—. Avocations: golf, history. Legislative, Banking, Securities. Office: Alexander Strategy Group 3000 K St NW Ste 101 Washington DC 20007

HAINES, THOMAS DAVID, JR., lawyer; b. Dallas, Oct. 30, 1956; s. Thomas David Sr. and Carol V. (Mullins) H.; m. Nanette Cluck, Mar. 1, 1986; children: Bennett Ann, Maison Cluck. BS in Polit. Sci., Okla. State U., 1979; JD, U. Okla., 1982. Bar: Okla. 1982, N.Mex. 1983, U.S. Ct. Appeals (10th cir.) 1983, U.S. Dist. Ct. N.Mex. 1983. Assoc. Hinkle, Cox, Eaton, Coffield & Hensley, Roswell, N.Mex., 1982-87, ptnr., 1988—. Contbg. editor N.Mex. Tort and Worker's Compensation Reporter, 1987-90, Employment Law Deskbook for New Mexico Employers, 1997, 99. Coach Roswell Youth Soccer Assn., 1995—98, 2001; youth sponsor First United Meth. Ch., Roswell, 1986—88, chmn. stewardship com., 1990—91, chmn. adminstrv. coun., 1998—99, trustee, 1996—98. Mem. State Bar Assn. N.Mex. (com. on continuing legal edn., young lawyers divsn. 1989—, mem. med.-legal rev. commn. 1988—), Chaves County Bar Assn., N.Mex. Def. Lawyer's Assn., N.Mex. Trial Lawyer's Assn., Kiwanis (Roswell club, Outstanding Club Sec. award 1993-95, pres. 1998-99, named one Outstanding Young Men in Am. 1990), George L. Reese Am. Inn of Ct. (barrister), Phi Delta Phi, Phi Kappa Phi. Republican. Avocations: golf, basketball, music, politics. Insurance, Personal injury (including property damage), Workers' compensation. Office: Hinkle Cox Eaton Coffield & Hensley 400 N Pennsylvania Ave Ste 700 Roswell NM 88201-4777 E-mail: thaines@hinklelawfirm.com.

HAINES, THOMAS W. W. lawyer; b. Balt., Oct. 10, 1941; s. John Summer and Clara Elizabeth (Ward) H.; m. Vivienne Wilson, Jan. 3, 1981; children: Robert S., Elizabeth E., John M. BA, Cornell U., 1963; LLB, U. Md., 1967. Bar: Md. 1967, U.S. Dist. Ct. Md. 1968, U.S. Ct. Appeals (4th cir.) 1972, U.S. Tax Ct. 1973, U.S. Supreme Ct. 1975. Assoc. Semmes, Bowen & Semmes, Balt., 1968-75, ptnr., 1975-95, Venable, Baetjer & Howard, LLP, Balt., 1995—. Fellow Am. Coll. Trust and Estate (counsel); mem. ABA, Md. Bar Assn., Bar Assn. Balt. City, Gibson Island Club, Maryland Club. Banking, Corporate, general, Intellectual property. Office: Venable Baetjer & Howard LLP 1800 Mercantile Bank Trust 2 Hopkins Plz Ste 2100 Baltimore MD 21201-2982 E-mail: twhaines@venable.com.

HAIRE, SUSAN LEIGH, lawyer; b. Morganton, N.C., Aug. 19, 1970; d. Robert Walter and Faye (Carswell) Peeler; m. David Robert Haire, May 21, 1994; 1 child, Alexander Robert. BS in Psychology, U. N.C., 1992; JD in Law, N.C. Ctrl. U., 1995. Bar: N.C. 1996. Assoc., clk. Simpson, Kuehnert & Vinay (formerly Kuehnert & Ayers), Morganton, 1993—97; ptnr. Starnes, Teele, Aycock, et. al., Morganton, 1998—. Mem. adv. com. 1st Bapt. Ch., Hickory, NC; sec. Sterling St. Assn., Morganton, 2001—; pres. Keller Com., Morganton. Baptist. Avocations: piano, walking, reading, fishing. Office: Starnes Teele Aycock et al 118 N Sterling St Morganton NC 28655

HAJE, PETER ROBERT, lawyer; b. N.Y.C., July 31, 1934; s. Arnold John and Edna Marie (Bossert) H.; m. Helen Heineman, Aug. 13, 1943; children: Michael James, Katherine Joy, Lily Elizabeth. BA, Cornell U., 1955; LLB, Harvard U., 1960. Bar: N.Y. 1961, U.S. Dist. Ct. (so. dist.) N.Y. 1965, U.S. Ct. Appeals (2d cir.) 1965, D.C. 1970, U.S. Ct. Appeals (D.C. cir.) 1981. Assoc. Paul, Weiss, Rifkind, Wharton & Garrison, N.Y.C., 1960-68, ptnr., 1969-90; exec. v.p., gen. counsel Time Warner Inc., N.Y.C., 1990-99, gen. counsel emeritus, 2000—; counselor AOL Time Warner, 2000—02; bus. and legal cons., 2000—. Corporate, general, Mergers and acquisitions, Securities. Office: 1285 Ave of the Americas Ste 3021 New York NY 10019

HAJEK, FRANCIS PAUL, lawyer; b. Hobart, Tasmania, Australia, Oct. 21, 1958; came to U.S., 1966; s. Frank Joseph and Kathleen Beatrice (Blake) H. BA, Yale U., 1980; JD, U. Richmond, 1984. Bar: Va. 1984, U.S. Dist. Ct. (ea. dist.) Va. 1984, U.S. Ct. Appeals (4th cir.) 1986. Law clk. to presiding magistrate U.S. Dist Ct., Norfolk, Va., 1984-85; assoc. Seawell, Dalton, Hughes & Timms, Norfolk, 1985-87, Weinberg & Stein, Norfolk, 1987-89, I'Anson-Hoffman Am. Inn of Ct., 1991-97; ptnr. Wilson, Hajek & Shapiro, P.C., Virginia Beach, Va., 1989—. Legal counsel United Transp. Union, 1999—. Mem. ABA, ATLA, Am. Rail Labor Acad., Va. Bar Assn., Norfolk-Portsmouth Bar Assn. (chmn. exec. com. young lawyer's sect. 1990-91). Roman Catholic. Avocations: squash, tennis. Federal civil litigation, State civil litigation, Personal injury (including property damage). Home: 1001 Caton Dr Virginia Beach VA 23454 Office: Hajek & Shapiro PO Box 5369 Virginia Beach VA 23471-0369 E-mail: fhajek@whslaw.com.

HAJEK, ROBERT J., SR., lawyer, real estate broker, commodities broker, nursing home owner; b. May 17, 1943; s. James J. Sr. and Rita C. (Kalka) H.; m. Maris Ann Enright, June 19, 1965 (div. Oct. 1991); children: Maris Ann, Robert J., David, Mandie. BA, Loras Coll., 1965; JD, U. Ill., 1968. Bar: Ill. 1968, U.S. Tax Ct. 1970, U.S. Dist. Ct. (no. dist.) Ill. 1971, U.S. Ct. Appeals (7th cir.) 1972, U.S. Supreme Ct. 1972; lic. real estate broker, Ill., Nat. Assn. Securities Dealers; registered U.S. Commodities Futures Trading Commn. Ptnr. Hajek & Hajek, Berwyn, Ill., 1968-76; pres., bd. chmn. Hajek, Hajek, Koykar & Heying, Ltd., Westchester, Ill., 1976-85; pres., CEO Land of Lincoln Real Estate, Ltd., Glendale Heights, Ill., 1985-89, also bd. dirs.; ptnr., owner Camelot Manor Nursing Home, Streator, Ill., 1978—, Ottawa (Ill.) Care Ctr., 1981—, Glenwood House Nursing Home, Streator, 1988—, Sullivan House Nursing Home, Ottawa, 1991—, Law Ctr. Bldg., Westchester, 1976-91. Exec. v.p., gen. counsel Ottawa Long Term Care, Inc.; owner Garfield Ridge Real Estate, Chgo, 1973-78, Centre Realty, Westchester, 1976-85; ptnr. Westbrook Commodities, Chgo., 1983; v.p., bd. mem., gen. counsel DeHart Gas and Oil Devel., Ltd., 1970-73; prin. Northeastern Okla. Oil and Gas Prodn. Venture, Tulsa, 1982—; exec. v.p., gen. counsel Garrett Plante Corp., 1978—; bd. dirs. Land of Lincoln Savs. and Loan, 1981-89, Home Title Svcs. of Am., Inc., 1981-89, Land of Lincoln Ins. Agy., Inc., 1981-89, Medema Builders, Inc., 1983-88, Ptnrs. of Ill., Inc., 1984-89, The Ill. Co., 1984-88, Ill. Co. Properties, Inc., subs. of Ill. Co., 1984-87, Ottawa Long Term Care, Inc., 1982—, Garrett Plante Corp., 1978—, St. Mary's Living Square, Chgo., 1985-92. Sr. boys' basketball coach Roselle Recreation Assn., Ill., 1981-83. Mem. ABA, Ill. Bar Assn., Nat. Assn. Realtors, Ill. Assn. Realtors, N.W. Suburban Bd. Realtors, Ill. Health Care Assn., Amateur Radio Club, No. Ill. DX Assn., Phi Alpha Delta. Republican. Episcopalian. Banking, Construction, Property, real (including real estate development, water). Address: 9001 SW 122nd Ave Miami FL 33186

HAJKOVA, GABRIELA, lawyer; b. Celadna, Czech Republic, Dec. 4, 1970; d. Ferdinand Hajek and Ludmila Hajkova; m. Zbynek Hajek, Sept. 2, 2000; 1 child, Tomas Hajek. ML, Charles U, Prague, Czech Republic, 1995; DESS, Toulouse U, Toulouse, France, 1996. Bar: Czech Republic 2000. Jr. attny. law Ondrej Peterka, Prague, Czech Republic, 1997—2000; assoc. Peterka & Leuchterova vos, Prague, Czech Republic, 2000—01; ptnr. Peterka, Leuchterova & partners v.o.s., Prague, Czech Republic, 2001—. Avocations: music, sports. Corporate, general, Labor (including EEOC, Fair Labor Standards Act, labor-management relations, NLRB, OSHA), Commercial, contracts (including sales of goods; commercial financing). Office: Peterka, Leuchterova & ptnrs vos Na Prikope 15 11000 Prague Czech Republic

HALAGAO, AVELINO GARABILES, lawyer; b. Santa Lucia, Ilocos Sur, The Philippines, Nov. 4, 1938; came to U.S., 1972; s. Manuel Habon and Marciana Garabiles H.; m. Concepcion Lorenzana Jimeno, aug. 1, 1962; children: Jesus Michael, Arleen Bernadette, Avelino Jr., Anna Maria, Amanda Marie. LLB, San Beda Coll. Law, Manila, 1962; M in Comparative Law, George Washington U., 1986. Bar: Va. 1987, D.C. 1992, The Philippines 1963. Ptnr. Bello, Halagao & Pimentel, Manila, 1963-65; atty. Commn. on Elections, Manila, 1965-70; judge Republic of The Philippines, Manila, 1970-72; trust officer Nat. Bank Washington, 1973-87; assoc. Coates & Davenport, McLean, Va., 1987-88; mng. ptnr. Avelino G. Halagao & Assocs., Tysons Corner, Va., 1989—. Pres., chmn. bd. dirs. Manuel H. Halagao & Sons Transp. Co., Manila, 1968-72; chmn. bd. dirs. QX, Inc., Washington, 1995-97. Mem. Philippine-Am. Bar Assn. (founder, treas. 1976-78, pres. 1984-85, Leadership and Disting. Membership award 1990), Ilocano Soc. Am. (co-founder, pres. 1983-84). Roman Catholic. Avocations: basketball, golfing, fishing, dancing, singing. Corporate, general, Immigration, naturalization, and customs, Personal injury (including property damage). Home: 3311 Cullers Ct Woodbridge VA 22192-1086 Office: Avelino G Halagao & Assocs 2010 Corporate Ridge Ste 700 Mc Lean VA 22102

HALBERSTAM, MALVINA, law educator, lawyer; b. Kempno, Poland, May 2, 1937; came to U.S., 1947; d. Marcus and Pearl (Halberstam) H.; m. Wolf Z. Guggenheim (dec. 2002); children: Arye, Achiezer. BA cum laude, Bklyn. Coll., 1957; JD, Columbia U., 1961, MIA, 1964. Bar: N.Y. 1962, U.S. Dist. Ct. (so. dist.) N.Y. 1963, U.S. Ct. Appeals (2d cir.) 1965, U.S. Supreme Ct. 1966, Calif. 1968. Law clk. Judge Edmund L. Palmieri Fed. Dist. Ct. (so. dist.) N.Y., 1961-62; rsch. assoc. Columbia Project on Internat. Procedure, 1962-63; asst. dist. atty. N.Y. County, 1963-67; with Rifkind & Sterling, L.A., 1967-68; sr. atty. Nat. Legal Program on Health Problems of the Poor, L.A., 1969-70; prof. Sch. Law Loyola U., L.A., 1970-76; prof. Benjamin N. Cardozo Sch. Law Yeshiva U., N.Y.C., 1976—. Vis. prof. Gould Law Ctr., U. So. Calif., L.A., 1972-73, U. Va. Sch. Law, 1975-76, U. Tex. Sch. Law, summer 1974, Hebrew U., Jerusalem, 1984-85; counselor on internat. law U.S. State Dept. Office of Legal Adviser, 1985-86; cons., 1986-92. Author: (with De Feis) Women's Legal Rights: International Agreements An Alternative to ERA?, 1987; articles and rev. editor Columbia Law Rev., 1960-61; reporter Am. Law Inst. Model Penal Code Commentaries, 1977-81; contbr. articles, commentary, book revs. to profl. jours. Mem. Bklyn. Coll. Alumni Adv. Bd. on Women's Career Devel. and Leadership Program.; adv. com. to standing com. on law and nat. security, ABA; study group on shape Arab-Israeli settlement, humanitarian, and demographic issues Coun. on Fgn. Rels. Kent scholar (2x); Stone scholar; recipient Jane Marks Murphy prize. Mem.: Assn. Am. Law Schs. (chair sect. internat. law 2002—03), Am. Assn. Jewish Lawyers and Jurists (bd. govs.), Internat. Law Assn. (Am. br. exec. com., human rights com.), Assn. Bar City of N.Y. (coun. on internat. affairs), Am. Soc. Internat. Law, Am. Law Inst., Columbia Law Sch. Alumni Assn., Phi Beta Kappa. Home: 160 Riverside Dr New York NY 10024-2106 Office: Yeshiva U Benjamin N Cardozo Sch Law 55 Fifth Ave New York NY 10003-4391 E-mail: halbrstm@ymail.yu.edu.

HALE, GRAYSON S. lawyer; b. Ark., 1969; BS, Ark. Tech. U., 1991; MBA, U. Ctrl. Ark., 1992; JD cum laude, U. Ark., 1998; postgrad., So. Meth. U., 1998—2000. CPA; bar: Tex. 1998, N.C. 2002, Ark. 2003. Atty. Jenkens & Gilrhirst, Dallas, 1998—2000, Brobeck, Phleger & Harrison, 2000—02, Poyner & Sprvill LLP, Relaigh, NC, 2002—. Mem. Leadership Raleigh C. of C., 2002. Mem.: Tex. Bar Assn., N.C. Bar Assn., Tex. Soc. CPA's. Mergers and acquisitions, Securities, Corporate, general. Office: Poyner & Sprvill LLP 3600 Glenwood Ave Raleigh NC 27612 Fax: 919-783-1075. E-mail: ghale@poyners.com.

HALE, JAMES THOMAS, retail company executive, lawyer; b. Mpls., May 14, 1940; s. Thomas Taylor and Alice Louise (Mc Connon) H.; m. Sharon Sue Johnson, Aug. 27, 1960; children: David Scott, Eric James, Kristin Lynn. BA, Dartmouth Coll., 1962; LLB, U. Minn., 1965. Bar: Minn. Law clk. Chief Justice Earl Warren, U.S. Supreme Ct., 1965-66; asso. firm Faegre & Benson, Mpls., 1966-73, ptnr., 1973-79; v.p., dir. corp. growth Gen. Mills, Inc., 1979-80, v.p. fin. and control consumer non-foods, 1981; sr. v.p., gen. counsel, corp. sec. Dayton-Hudson Corp., Mpls., 1981-2000; exec. v.p., gen. counsel, corp. sec. Target Corp., 2000—. Adj. prof. U. Minn., 1967-73. Mem. exec. com. Fund Legal Aid Soc., others. Mem. Order of Coif, Phi Beta Kappa. Office: Target Corp 1000 Nicollet Mall Minneapolis MN 55403-2467

HALE, JANET, federal agency administrator; b. Buffalo, Apr. 2, 1949; d. Herman Haltom and Rachel (Townes) H. BS, Miami U., Oxford, Ohio, 1971; M.P.A., Harvard U., 1980. Adminstrv. asst. State Rep. Tom Gallagher of Fla., Washington, 1974-76; research asst. House Republican Com., Washington, 1976-77; spl. asst. Senator Edward Brooke, Boston, 1977-79; spl. asst. to sec., dir. exec. secretariat HUD, Washington, 1981-82, dep. asst. sec. for policy, fin. mgmt. and adminstrn., 1982-86; asst. sec. Dept. of Transportation, Washington, 1986—89; Asst. Sec. Budget, Tech., and

Finance Dept HHS, Washington, 2002—03; Under Sec. Mgmt. Dept. Homeland Security, 2003—. Bd. dirs. Big Sisters Boston, 1978-80 Avocation: tennis. Office: Navel Security Station Nebraska & Massachusetts Ave NW Washington DC 20393*

HALE, KATHRYN SCHOLLE, lawyer; b. Pitts., Dec. 17, 1953; d. Robert Anthony and Audrey T. (Turlick) Scholle; m. Jonathan Bradford Hale, Oct. 5, 1985; children: Jessica Katherine, Benjamin Robert. BA cum laude, Wesleyan U., 1974; JD, NYU, 1977, LLM (Taxation), 1980. Bar: Conn. 1977, N.Y. 1980. Assoc. Tyler, Cooper, Grant, New Haven, Conn., 1977-78, Schoeman Marsh Updike & Welt, N.Y.C., 1980-82, Bergman Horowitz Reynolds & DeSarbo, New Haven, 1982-84; pvt. practice South Windsor, Conn., 1984-91, 97—. Adj. prof. Western New Eng. Coll. Sch. Law, 1984-86; cons. mcpl. revenue, 1996; bd. dirs., chair legal com. Citizens Opposed to Radioactive Environment, South Windsor, 1991-96. Grad. editor: (legal periodical) Tax Law Rev., 1979-80; assoc. editor: (legal periodical) Jour. of Internat. Law and Politics, 1976-77. Trustee Adelphic Lit. Soc., Middletown, Conn., 1986-91; mem. Town Coun., Town of South Windsor, 1993-97; environ. orgn. rep. Conn. Low Level Radioactive Waste Adv. Com., Hartford, 1991-93; mem. South Windsor Agrl. Land Preservation Adv. Com., 1993; alt. mem. South Windsor Econ. Devel. Commn., 1993; mem. South Windsor Dem. Town Com., 1993—. Mem. People's Action for Clean Energy, Clean Water Action, Alpha Delta Phi Soc. (founding). Democrat. General practice, Property, real (including real estate development, water). Home and Office: 54 Orchard Hill Dr South Windsor CT 06074-3021 E-mail: Kathaleesq@aol.com.

HALE, LOUIS DEWITT, lawyer; b. Caddo Mills, Tex., June 10, 1917; s. Ernest Louis and Ethel M. (Massay) H.; m. Carol Gene Moore, June 8, 1947; children: Janet Sue Hale Wilde, Nancy Carol Hale (dec.). BA, U. Tex., 1937, MA, 1940. Bar: Tex. 1940, U.S. Dist. Ct. (so. dist.) Tex. 1947, U.S. Ct. Appeals (5th cir.) 1974, U.S. Supreme Ct. 1946. Classification analyst Office Emergency Mgmt., Washington, 1941-42; classification officer Office Def. Transp., Washington, 1942-43; pvt. practice Corpus Christi, Tex., 1946—81, Austin, Tex., 1981—. State rep. Tex. Legislature, 1939-40, 53-62, 65-78, spkr. pro tempore, 1961-62, chmn. jud. com., 1961-62, 69-74; gen. counsel House Gen. Investigating Com., Austin, 1989-92, Tex. Assn. Builders, Austin, 1978-81. Author: Streamlining Texas Judiciary, 1972; contbr. articles to profl. jours. Mem. Tex. Jud. Coun., Austin, 1961-65, 69-81; chmn. jud. com. Tex. Constnl. Conv., Austin, 1974. Active duty USAF, 1947-73, res., ret. lt. col. Recipient Disting. Svc. award Jr. C. of C., 1952. Mem. ABA, State Bar Tex. (Disting. Svc. award 1971, 73, 75), Tex. Assn. Builders (hon. life), Tex. State Tchrs. Assn. (hon. life, Disting. Svc. award 1961). Democrat. Baptist. Avocations: public speaking, historical research, coin collecting. Administrative and regulatory, Education and schools, General practice. Home: 7106 Montana Norte Austin TX 78731-2124 Office: 5808 Balcones Dr Ste 101 Austin TX 78731-4276

HALES, DANIEL B. lawyer; b. Oak Park, Ill., Sept. 29, 1941; s. Burton W. and Marion (Jones) H.; m. Deborah J. Dorr, June 4, 1966; children, Daniel R.J., Marion P., George B. BA in Econs., U. Mich., 1963; Juris Doctorate, Northwestern U., 1966. Bar: Ill.1966, U.S. Dist. Ct. (no. dist.) Ill. 1967, U.S. Ct. Appeals (7th cir.) 1968, U.S. Supreme Ct. 1977. Ptnr. Peterson, Ross, Schloerb & Seidel, Chgo. Gen. counsel The Philadelphia Soc., Chgo.; dir. Chgo. Crime Commn. Pres., dir. Americans for Effective Law Enforcement Inc., Chgo.; bd. dirs. Duncan YMCA, Chgo.; chmn. Ill. Lawyers for Reagan and Bush, 1980; gen. counsel New Trier Twp., Winnetka, Ill. Republican Orgn.; mem. bd. govs. United Rep. Fund of Ill. Mem. Chgo. Bar Assn. (trust law com. 1975—), Ill. State Bar Assn., The Law Club, N.E. Commonwealth Club, N.E. Federalist Soc. (advisor). Office: 711 Oak St # 102 Winnetka IL 60093

HALEY, GEORGE BROCK, JR., retired lawyer; b. Atlanta, Feb. 9, 1926; s. George Brock and Naomi Esther (Alverson) H.; m. Marjorie Elizabeth Griffiths, June 24, 1950; children: Susan Haley Brumfield, Katherine Haley Herman, George Brock III, Victor Pearse. AB, Harvard U., 1948, LLB, 1951. Bar: Ga. 1951, D.C. 1976. Assoc. Kilpatrick & Cody (name changed to Kilpatrick Stockton), Atlanta, 1951-60, ptnr., 1960-93, of counsel, 1994—. Mem. Ga. Gov.'s Jud. Process Rev. Commn., Atlanta, 1988-89; v.p., trustee Frances Wood Wilson Found. Staff sgt. AUS, 1944-46, MTO. Mem. ABA, State Bar Ga., Atlanta Bar Assn., Atlanta Lawyers Club, Capital City Club. Methodist. Avocations: boating, hiking. General civil litigation, Utilities, public, State and local taxation. E-mail: ghaley@kilpatrickstockton.com.

HALEY, GEORGE PATRICK, lawyer; b. Bad Axe, Mich., Sept. 23, 1948; s. Glen Kirk and Bernice (Cooper) H.; m. Theresa L. Thomas, Dec. 24, 1975. BS, U. Mich., 1970; MS, U. Calif., Berkeley, 1971; JD, Harvard U., 1974. Bar: Calif. 1974, U.S. Dist. Ct. (no. dist.) Calif. 1974, U.S. Dist. Ct. (ea. dist.) Calif. 1980. Assoc. Pillsbury Winthrop LLP, San Francisco, 1974-81, ptnr., 1982—. Prof. U. Shanghai, Shanghai-San Francisco Sister City Program, 1986-1989. Author numerous articles uniform commercial code, project fin. Dir. Calif. Shakespeare Festival, Berkeley, 1986-93; dir. Nat. Writing Project, 1996—. Mem. ABA (chmn. com. 1976-93), Am. Coll. Comml. Fin. Lawyers, State Bar Calif. (chmn. fin. instns. com. 1980, commercial code com. 1988). Republican. Methodist. Avocations: tai chi chuan, golf, cooking. Home: 1825 Marin Ave Berkeley CA 94707-2414 E-mail: ghaley@pillsburywinthrop.com.

HALEY, JOHN HARVEY, lawyer; b. Hot Springs, Ark., May 29, 1931; s. Harvey H. and Anne (Tanner) H.; m. Cynthia Martin, Sept. 7, 1997. AB, Emory U., 1952; LLB, U. Ark., 1955. Bar: Ark. 1955, U.S. Dist. Ct. (we. dist.) Ark. 1955, U.S. Ct. Appeals (8th cir.) 1955, U.S. Supreme Ct. 1971. Clk. Ark. Supreme Ct., Little Rock, 1955-56; ptnr. Rose Law Firm, Little Rock, 1956-71, Haley, Young, Bogard & Gitchell, Little Rock, 1971-73, Laser, Sharp, Haley, Young & Boswell, Little Rock, 1973-82, Haley, Polk & Heister, Little Rock, 1982—86, Arnold, Grobmyer & Haley, Little Rock, 1986—96; owner Haley Law Firm, Little Rock, 1996—2002; of counsel Eichenbaum, Liles & Heister, Little Rock, 2002—. Bd. dirs. North Ark. Telephone Co., Flippin, Ark.; Munro and Co., Hot Springs, Ark., Rose Creek Industries, Plaza Partnership, Talweg, LLC, Memphis; lectr. U. Ark. Law Sch., Little Rock, 1956-60, CLU instr., 1961-65; spl. counsel liquidation and rehab. Ark. Ins. Dept., 1967-71; pres. Combustion Technologies LLC, Little Rock, 1996—. Editor Ark. Law Rev., 1954-55. Chmn. Ark. State Bd. Correction, 1967-72, Ark. State Bd. Law Examiners, 1960-63, Election Rsch. Coun., Little Rock, 1961-64; dir. Wildwood Ctr. Performing Arts, Little Rock, 1994-99, Florence Crittenden Home, Little Rock, 1994-99; scoutmaster Second Presbyn. Ch. Troop, Little Rock, 1962-65. Methodist. Avocations: piloting, sailing, bicycling, underwater photography, skiing. Property, real (including real estate development, water), Estate taxation, Corporate taxation. Home: 3614 Doral Dr Little Rock AR 72212-2920 Office: Haley Companies PO Box 3730 Little Rock AR 72203-3730 Fax: 501-227-5628. E-mail: enginery@aol.com.

HALEY, PAUL RICHARD, lawyer, state legislator; b. Boston, June 9, 1953; s. Robert Edward and Mary Louise (Hogan) H.; m. Jacqueline Suzanne Holmes, Oct. 11, 1986. BA in Econs., Harvard U., 1976; JD, Suffolk U., 1986. Bar: Mass., 1986; U.S. Dist. Ct. Mass., 1987; U.S. Supreme Ct., 1993. Asst. dist. atty. Norfolk County, Dedham, Mass., 1986-90; mem. Mass. Ho. of Reps., Boston, 1990—. Overseer South Shore Hosp., Weymouth, Mass. Comdr. USNR, 1977—. Mem. Mass. Bar Assn., Norfolk County Bar Assn., VFW, Elks. Democrat. Roman Catholic. Avocations: flying, athletics. Office: Mass Ho of Reps State House Rm 243 Boston MA 02133

HALEY, VINCENT PETER, lawyer; b. Phila., Oct. 6, 1931; s. Vincent Paul and Madeline R. (McCrystal) H.; m. Mary Ann Harron, Apr. 14, 1956; children— Paul V., Kevin G., Maureen T., Patricia Ann M., Kathleen A., Brian M., Regina E., Christopher P., Megan A. BS, Villanova, 1953, JD cum laude, 1959. Bar: Pa. 1960, Fla. 1979. Acct. Arthur Young & Co., CPAs, Phila., 1955-56; assoc. Schnader, Harrison, Segal & Lewis, Phila., 1959-67, ptnr., 1968-99, mem. exec. com., 1985-88, 89-94, sr. counsel, 2000—. Mem. bd. consultors Law Sch. Villanova U., 1985— ; lectr. in field. Sec. Mercy Health Sys., Bala Cynwyd, Pa., 1969—; mem. Archdiocese of Phila. Bd. Edn., 1973-79, pres., 1977-79; mem., bd. dirs. Police Athletic League of Phila., 1994-2001. With USNR, 1953-55. Mem. Pa. Bar Assn. (chmn. corp., banking and bus. law sect. 1979-81), Phila. Bar Assn., Villanova U. Law Alumni Assn. (pres. 1962-63), Huntingdon Valley Country Club, Roosevelt Racquet Club (Huntingdon Valley, Pa., bd. dirs. 1969-80, 91-94, 97-2000, treas. 1972-80), Order of Coif (chpt. v.p. 1962-63). Banking, Commercial, contracts (including sales of goods; commercial financing), Health. Home: 305 Madison Rd Huntingdon Valley PA 19006-6713 Office: Schnader Harrison Segal et al 1600 Market St Ste 3600 Philadelphia PA 19103-7287

HALL, ALBERT L. retired lawyer; b. Chgo., June 17, 1926; s. Albert L. and Orpah (Starratt) H.; m. Catherine Ann Comstock, Sept. 27, 1947; children: Terry Lee, David M., Margaret Ruth, Diane Marie. Grad., Lake Forest Acad., 1944; BS, U. Ill., 1949, MS, 1950; JD, Northwestern U., 1955. Bar: Ill. 1955, U.S. Dist. Ct. (no. dist.) Ill. 1955. Tchr. Washington Park High Sch., Racine, Wis., 1950-52; ptnr. Hall, Roach, Johnston et al, Waukegan, Ill., 1958-91, of counsel, 1991-95, Bollman & Lesser, Lake Forest, Ill., 1996—. Arbitrator Am. Arbitration Assn., 1975-90, 19th Jud. Cir. Ct. Ill., 1990-98. Bd. dirs. Lake County Children's Orthopedic Clinic, Inc., 1966—, pres., 1979-81. With USNR, 1944-46. Mem. Lake County Bar Assn., Waukegan-Lake County C. of C. (pres. 1968-69), Delta Tau Delta, Phi Alpha Delta. Clubs: City Club of Waukegan (pres. 1970). Home: 2048 Hickory St Waukegan IL 60087-5019

HALL, ANTHONY W., JR., lawyer; BA in Econs., Howard U.; JD cum laude, Tex. So. U. State rep. Tex. Legislature, 1973—79; mem. Houston City Coun., 1979—89; city atty. City of Houston, 1998—. Chmn. bd. dirs. Met. Transit Authority Harris County, 1990—92. Capt. U.S. Army, 1967—71. Decorated Puprle Heart, 3 Bronze Stars. Mem.: ABA, Houston Lawyers Assn., Houston Bar Assn., State Bar Tex., Nat. Bar Assn. Office: City Hall Annex 900 Bagby St 4th Fl Houston TX 77002-2527 Office Fax: 713-247-1195. Business E-Mail: susah.taylor@cityofhouston.net.*

HALL, CHARLES WASHINGTON, lawyer; b. Dallas, June 30, 1930; s. Albert Brown and Eleanor Pauline (Hopkins) H.; m. Mary Louise Watkins, Aug. 3, 1957; children: Katherine Louise, Allison Ash, Charles Washington III. BA, U. of South, 1951; JD, So. Meth. U., 1954, LLM in Taxation, 1959. Bar: Tex. 1954. Ptnr. Storey, Armstrong & Steger, Dallas, 1954-57; sr. ptnr. Fulbright & Jaworski, Houston, 1957—. Mem. adv. com. on tax litigation Dept. Justice, 1979-80; dir. Friedman Ind., Inc., Tex. Med. Ctr., Inc. Houston; mem. Commr. Internal Revenue Adv. Group, 1990-91; mem. adv. coun. U.S. Claims Ct., 1988—. Pres., trustee Sarah Campbell Blaffer Found., Houston; dir. Goodwill Industry, Houston, 1977-84; trustee Inst. Religion, Houston, 1990-2000, Killson Found., Houston, M.D. Anderson Found., Houston, Allbritton Found., Houston, Allbritton Art Inst., Houston, John S. Dunn Rsch. Found., Houston, Houston Child Guidance Ctr., 1984-86, The Howell Family Found., Houston; trustee, treas. Ctr Am. Intrnat. Law (formerly Southwestern Legal Found.), Dallas; S.W. Rsch. Inst., San Antonio; gov. Houston Forum, 1992-95. Recipient Disting. Alumni award, So. Meth. U., 1989. Fellow Am. Bar Found.; mem. ABA (chmn. sect. taxation 1987-88, ho. dels. 1991-95, nat. conf. lawyers and CPAs chmn. 1988-2000), Houston Bar Assn., Dallas Bar Assn., State Bar Tex. (chmn. sect. taxation 1970-71), Internat. Bar Assn., Am. Coll. Tax Counsel (regent 1982-91), Am. Law Inst., River Oaks Country Club, Petroleum Club, Coronado (pres. 1982-83), Houston City Club, Met. Club (Washington), Old Baldy Club, Order of St. Lazarus. Episcopalian. Office: Fulbright & Jaworski LLP 1301 Mckinney St Ste 5100 Houston TX 77010-3031

HALL, CYNTHIA HOLCOMB, federal judge; b. Los Angeles, Feb. 19, 1929; d. Harold Romeyn and Mildred Gould (Kuck) Holcomb; m. John Harris Hall, June 6, 1970 (dec. Oct. 1980). AB, Stanford U., 1951, JD, 1954; LL.M., NYU, 1960. Bar: Ariz. 1954, Calif. 1956. Law clk. to judge U.S. Ct. Appeals 9th Circuit, 1954—55; trial atty. tax div. Dept. Justice, 1960—64; atty.-adviser Office Tax Legis. Counsel, Treasury Dept., 1964—66; mem. firm Brawerman & Holcomb, Beverly Hills, Calif., 1966—72; judge U.S. Tax Ct., Washington, 1972—81, U.S. Dist. Ct. for central dist. Calif., Los Angeles, 1981—84; cir. judge U.S. Ct. Appeals (9th cir.), Pasadena, Calif., 1984—, sr. judge, 1997—. Lt. (j.g.) USNR, 1951—53. Office: US Ct Appeals 9th Cir 125 S Grand Ave Pasadena CA 91105-1621

HALL, DAVID, law educator, dean, law educator, department chairman; b. Savannah, May 26, 1950; s. Levi and Ethel Hall; m. Marilyn Braithwaite-Hall; children: Sakile, Kiamsha, Rahsaan. BS in Polit. Sci., Kans. State U., 1972; MA in Human Rels., U. Okla., 1975, postgrad., 1975—78, JD, 1978; LLM, Harvard U., 1985, Doctor Juridical Scis., 1988. Bar: Ill. 1978, Mass. 1978, Okla. 1978. Profl. basketball player Spaidero Pallacanestro, Inc., Udine, Italy, 1972—74; grad. asst. human rels. dept. U. Okla., Norman, 1974—75; lawyer Chgo. regional office Fed. Trade Commn., 1978—80; assoc. prof. law Sch. Law U. Okla., Norman, 1983—85; asst. prof. law Sch. Law U. Miss., 1980—83; assoc. dean academic affairs Sch. Law Northeastern U., Boston, 1988—92, prof. law, 1985—, dean Sch. Law, 1993—99, provost, 1999—. Instr. ethnic studies dept. and law ctr. U. Okla., Norman, 1975—79; Robert D. Klien U. lectr. Northeasteern U.; co-chair legal edn. forum Law Sch. Harvard U., Cambridge, Mass., 1984—85, co-coord. Nat. Symposium on the Constitution and Race, 1987; coord. law student outreach program Barron Assessment Ctr., Boston. Contbr. articles to profl. jours. Mem. bd. Mass. Civil Liberties Union, 1987—88, Inst. Affirmative action, Boston, TransAfrica Forum Scholars Adv. Coun., Washington, commn. on equal justice Mass. Legal Assistance Corp., 1995—, Nat. Consumer Law Ctr., 1993—; pres. African Cultural Soc. St. Paul A.M.E. Ch., Cambridge, Mass.; bd. dirs. Gang Peace Inc., 1995—. Named Professor of the Yr., NAACP, Outstanding Dean of Yr., Nat. Assn. Pub. Interset Lawyers, 1997; named to Savannah Athletic Hall of Fame; recipient African Am. 1st Oratory Competition, Black Rose award, Sigma Gamma Rho, Humanitarian award, Nat. Conf. Cmty. and Justice. Fellow: Am. Sociol. Assn.; mem.: ABA (standing com. lawyers' pub. svc. responsibility 1995—), Nat. Black Wholistic Soc. (pres. 1993, mem. bd. 1984—), Black Faculty and Staff Orgn., Nat. Conf. Black Lawyers (pres. Mass. chpt. 1986—), Okla. Bar Assn. (Outstanding Sr. award), Mass. Bar Assn. (mem. bd. minorities in the profession 1995—96), Boston Bar Assn., Assn. Law Sch. (diversity in legal edn. 1995—96), Order of the Coif. Office: Northeastern U Office of Provost 112 Hayden Hall 360 Huntington Ave Boston MA 02115-5005 E-mail: d.hall@nunet.neu.edu.

HALL, DONALD ORELL, lawyer, rancher; b. Waco, Tex., Nov. 11, 1926; s. Ernest Orell and Thelma (Day) H.; m. Mary Ann Morgan, Sept. 1, 1951; children: Lisa Don, Brett Clayton. LLB, Baylor U., 1951, JD, 1969. Bar: Tex. 1951, U.S. Dist. Ct. (we. dist.) Tex. 1955, U.S. Ct. Appeals (5th cir.) 1983, U.S. Supreme Ct. 1983. Assoc. Koehne & Fulbright, Waco, 1951-54; judge Waco, 1954-56; dist. atty. Office of Prosecutor, Waco, 1956-67; ptnr. Hall & Kettler, Waco, 1968-87; pvt. practice Waco, 1988—. Guest columnist, newspapers, 1955—. With USNR, 1943-46, PTO. Mem. ABA, Waco Bar Assn. (pres. 1955-56), Delta Theta Phi, Masons, Scottish Rite, York Rite. Republican. Baptist. Avocations: outdoors, sports, pilot, hunting, dog and horse breeding. Family and matrimonial, General practice, Personal injury (including property damage). Home and Office: 8208 Whippoorwill Dr Waco TX 76712-3412

HALL, FRED WILLIAM, JR., lawyer; b. Franklin, N.H., Sept. 22, 1920; s. Fred William and Grace Rachel (Canney) Hall; m. Jane Fell Coe, Sept. 23, 1950; children: Marcella, Susan, John. BS, U. N.H., 1941; JD, U. Mich., 1948; LLD (hon.), U. N.H., 1974. Mem. Govs. Judicial Selection Commn., 2000—. Bd. dirs. Jarvis Co., Inc., Rochester. Trustee U. N.H., 1966-73, chmn. bd., 1968-72; mem. N.H. Gov.'s Council, 1963-64, 2000-02, Gov.'s Judicial Selction Commn. Lt. col. U.S. Army, 1941-45, ETO. Decorated Silver Star with oak leaf cluster, Bronze Star with 2 oak leaf cluster; recipient Outstanding Civilian Service medal, Dept. Army, 1979, Civilian Aide to Sec. of the Army, 1970-78, U. N.H. Alumni Meritorious Service award, 1974, Charles Holmes Pettee medal, 1996; Paul Harris fellow, Rotary Found., 1984. Mem. ABA, N.H. Bar Assn. (pres. 1965-66), Rotary. Republican. Episcopalian. Home: 18 Eastern Ave Rochester NH 03867-1400 Office: Law Office Fred Hall Jr 59 S Main St PO Box 780 Rochester NH 03866-0780 Fax: 603-335-0946.

HALL, GLENN ALLEN, lawyer, state representative; b. Pekin, Ill., Oct. 22, 1955; s. Gerald Eugene and Vinetta Bell Hall; m. Mary Melodie Hall, Dec. 30, 1978; children: Kimberly, Jaired, Ellie, Chava, Justice. BS in Edn., U. Mo., 1980; JD, Regent U., 1989. Bar: Mo. 1989. Atty. Glenn Allen Hall, Atty. at law, Kansas City, Mo., 1989—2001; state rep. State of Mo., 1993-99; owner The Almond Branch, Salem, Mo., 2001—; atty. Glenn Allen Hall, Atty. at Law, Salem, Mo., 2001—. Author: No Justice in the Land, 1993, The Separation, 1999, When We Awake, 2003. Family and matrimonial, Estate planning, General practice. Office: 115 W 4th St Salem MO 65560 Fax: 573-729-2344. E-mail: salemjustice@earthlink.net.

HALL, HENRY LYON, JR., lawyer; b. Boston, July 23, 1931; s. Henry Lyon and Edith Page (Blanchard) H.; m. Jean Elizabeth Haring, Sept. 13, 1958; children: Henry Lyon, George B. AB, U. Mass., 1953; JD, George Washington U., 1962. Bar: Va. 1963, Mass. 1963. Assoc. Ropes & Gray, Boston, 1963-73, ptnr., 1973-97, of counsel, 1998—. Lectr., panelist seminars Mem. Mass. Gov.'s Commn. Sch. Dist. Orgn., 1971-73; mem. sch. com. Minuteman Reg. Vocat. Sch. Dist., 1971-83, chmn. 1971-75; mem. permanent audit com. town of Belmont, Mass., 1979—, chmn. 1982-92; chmn. by law rev. com. 1979-83, bylaw rev. com., 1983-91; town moderator, Belmont, 1991—; corporator, trustee Belmont Savs. Bank. Served in U.S. Army, 1953-56. Mem. ABA, Mass. Bar Assn., Mass. Moderators Assn. (bd. dirs. 1995—, 1st v.p. 1997-98, pres. 1998-99), Nat. Assn. Bond Lawyers, Va. State Bar, Boston Bar Assn., Mass. Taxpayers Found., Govt. Fin. Officers Assn., Mass. Charitable Soc., Mass. Mcpl. Assn., Order of Coif, Phi Delta Phi. Education and schools, Finance. Home: 22 Randolph St Belmont MA 02478-3540 Office: Ropes & Gray One International Place Boston MA 02110-2624 E-mail: hhall@ropesgray.com.

HALL, HOWARD HARRY, lawyer; b. Syracuse, N.Y., Jan. 9, 1933; s. Harold Gibner and Mildred E. (Way) H. AB, Syracuse U., 1953, JD, 1959. Bar: N.Y. 1960, U.S. Ct. Appeals (2d cir.) 1960, U.S. Dist. Ct. (we., no., so.dists.) N.Y. 1960, U.S. Supreme Ct. 1963, Calif. 1978, U.S. Ct. Appeals (9th cir.) 1978, U.S. Dist. Ct. (we. dist.) N.Y., U.S. Dist. Ct. (cen. and so. dist.) Calif., 1978. Assoc. Hiscock, Cowie, Bruce, Lee and Mawhinney, Syracuse, N.Y., 1959-61; pvt. practice Syracuse, N.Y., 1961-74, Long Beach, Calif., 1978-82, Paramount, Calif., 1982—. Commr. of edn. Syracuse, N.Y., 1968-72. Capt. USMC, 1953-56. Mem. State Bar of Calif., Calif. Trial Lawyers Assn. Criminal, Insurance, Personal injury (including property damage). Office: 15559 Paramount Blvd Paramount CA 90723-4330

HALL, JOHN HENRY, lawyer, historian, educator; b. Mound Bayou, Miss., Nov. 7, 1932; s. John and Icey M. (Roundtree) H.; m. Katie B. Green, Aug. 15, 1957. BS in Social Studies, Ind. U., 1970, MEd, 1971, MS in Secondary Sch. Adminstrn., 1972; JD, Southland U., 1981; EdD, Loyola U., Chgo., 1995; LLM comml. real estate, John Marshall Law Sch., Chgo., 2002. Bar: Ind. 1983, U.S. Supreme Ct. 1987. Foreman U.S. Reduction Co., East Chicago, Ind., 1957-62, shift supt., 1962-68; tchr. Gary (Ind.) Cmty. Schs., 1969-74, asst. prin., 1975—92; sole practice law Gary, 1983—; prof. law, racism and social change Ind. U., Gary, 1984. Legal resource Gary Community Sch. Corp., 1983-84; judge pro tem Lake County (Ind.) Superior Ct., East Chicago and Gary. Article writer Blacks in World History Information Newspaper (edn. and Cmty. Svc. awrd 1983), 1979—. Campaign mgr. Katie Hall State Rep., Indpls., 1976, Katie Hall Congress, Gary, 1984; Sunday sch., BTU tchr., served as chmn. deacon Van Buren (Miss.) Bapt. Ch., Served with USAF, 1952-57. Mem. ABA, Gary Secondary Prins. Assn. (sec./treas., v.p., pres., Outstanding Leadership award 1982), Lake County Bar Assn., Assn. Trial Lawyers Am., Phi Delta Kappa, Phi Alpha Delta. Democrat. Avocations: travel, creative writing, reading, walking, jogging. General civil litigation, General practice, Landlord-tenant, Civil rights. Office: PO Box 1498 Gary IN 46407-0498

HALL, JOHN HERBERT, lawyer; b. Orange, N.J., Dec. 5, 1942; s. Embert Brown Hall and Elizabeth (Sullivan) Carnahan; m. Suzanne Steeger, Aug. 21, 1965 (div. Apr. 1988); children: Christopher Evan, Jeremy Randall; m. Lisa Gersh, June 19, 1988; children: Samantha Gersh, Madeleine Gersh. BA, Wesleyan U., 1965; MBA, NYU, 1966; JD, Columbia U., 1969. Bar: N.Y. 1970, U.S. Dist. Ct. (so. dist.) N.Y. 1972, (ea. dist.) N.Y. 1981, U.S. Ct. Appeals (2d cir.) 1974, (10th cir.) 1977, (5th cir.) 1980, (11th cir.) 1981, (4th cir.) 1989, (D.C. cir.) 1982, U.S. Supreme Ct. 1981. Assoc. Debevoise, Plimpton, Lyons & Gates, N.Y.C., 1969-72, 73-78; grad. bus. Cmty. Law Offices, N.Y.C., 1972-73; ptnr. Debevoise & Plimpton, N.Y.C., 1979—, chair litigation dept., 1993—2002. Bd. dirs. Community Law Offices, 1974-2000, Legal Aid Soc. N.Y., 1980-88. Co-author: Takeovers-Attack and Survival, 1987, 2d edit., 1993. Bd. dirs. Vols. Legal Svcs., 1990-96, Welfare Law Ctr. Mem. ABA (criminal, bus. law, litigation sects.), N.Y. Lawyers for Pub. Interest (bd. dirs. 1987-00), Am. Judicature Soc., Supreme Ct. Hist. Soc., Assn. of Bar of City of N.Y. (fed. cts. com. 1981-84), Prep for Prep Inc. (dir. 1974), U.S. Cycling Fedn., Nat. Legal Aid/Defenders Assn., Law Soc. Eng. and Wales. Avocations: bicycle racing, tennis. Federal civil litigation, State civil litigation, Mergers and acquisitions. Home: 300 Central Park W Apt 19C New York NY 10024-1513 Office: Debevoise & Plimpton 919 3rd Ave 43rd Floor New York NY 10022-6225 E-mail: Jhhall@debevoise.com.

HALL, JOHN HOPKINS, retired lawyer; b. Dallas, May 10, 1925; s. Albert Brown and Eleanor Pauline (Hopkins) H.; m. Marion Martin, Nov. 23, 1957; children: Ellen Martin, John Hopkins II. Student, U. Tex., 1942, U. of South, Sewanee, Tenn., 1942-43; LL.B., So. Meth. U., 1949. Bar: Tex. bar 1949. Ptnr. Strasburger & Price, Dallas, 1957-93, ret., 1993. Served with U.S. Army, 1943-45. Fellow Tex. Bar Found., Am. Bar Found., Internat. Acad. Trial Lawyers, Am. Coll. Trial Lawyers; mem. Tex. Bar Assn., Tex. Assn. Def. Counsel, Internat. Assn. Def. Counsel, Fin and Feather Club. Episcopalian. Federal civil litigation, General civil litigation, State civil litigation.

HALL, JOHN THOMAS, lawyer, educator; b. Phila., May 14, 1938; s. John Thomas and Florence Sara (Robinson) H.; m. Carolyn Park Currie, May 26, 1968; children: Daniel Currie, Kathleen Currie. AB, Dickinson Coll., 1960; MA, U. Md., 1963; JD, U. N.C., 1972. Bar: N.C. 1972. Chmn. dept. speech Mercersburg (Pa.) Acad., 1960-63, U. Balt., 1963-69; research asst. N.C. Ct. Appeals, Raleigh, 1972-73, dir. pre-hearing research staff, 1974-75, asst. clk., marshall, librarian, 1980-81; counsel Dorothea Dix Hosp., Raleigh, 1974; asst. dist. atty. State of N.C., Raleigh, 1975-80,

81-83; pvt. practice Raleigh, 1973-74, 83—. Mem. faculty King's Bus. Coll., Raleigh, 1973-75, N.C. Bar Assn., 1987—; undercover inmate Cen. Prison Duke Ctr. on Law and Poverty, Durham, N.C., 1970; vis. lectr. dept. comm. N.C. State U., 2000—; faculty U. Phoenix Online, 2003—. Mem. Raleigh Little Theatre, Theatre in the Park, Raleigh; charter mem. Wake County Dem. Men's Club, 1977—. Named Best Actor, Raleigh Little Theatre, 1975, 77, 80, 82, 85, 86, 93, 98. Mem. ABA, N.C. Bar Assn., Wake County Bar Assn. (bd. dirs. 1986-89, vice chmn. exec. com. 1986-87), 10th Jud. Dist. Bar Assn. (bd. dirs. 1986-89, chmn. grievance com. 1987-90), Wake County Acad. Criminal Trial Lawyers (v.p. 1986-87), Scottish Clan Gunn Soc., Neuse River Valley Model R.R. (Raleigh). Avocations: model railroading, reading. Appellate, Criminal. Office: PO Box 1207 Raleigh NC 27602-1207

HALL, LEONARD ALLEN, lawyer; b. Kansas City, Kans., May 28, 1953; s. Richard Allen and Nancy (Meyer) H. BS in Bus., Emporia State U., 1976; JD, Washburn U., 1979. Bar: Kans. 1979. Sole practice, Olathe, Kans., 1979-80; asst. mcpl. counselor City of Olathe, 1980—. Columnist for Olathe Daily News, 1993—; writer Johnson County Barr Assn. Newsletter, 1995—. Bd. dirs. Nat. Deaf Volleyball Tournament, 1986—; pres. Legal Network for Deaf and Hard of Hearing, 1992—; bd. dirs. Kans. Commn. Deaf and Hard of Hearing, 1995-; v.p. Kans. Assn. Deaf, 1999-. Named All-Am., U.S. Track and Field Fedn., 1976, Outstanding Male Athlete for Deaf, World Game for Deaf Tryouts, Washington, 1976. Mem. Johnson County Bar Assn., Kans. Bar Assn., Emporia State Alumni Assn., Am. Deaf Volleyball Assn. (founder, pres. 1984-85), Midwest Athletic Assn. for Deaf (chmn. volleyball, 1984-86), Assn. for the Deaf, Masons, Olathe Club for Deaf (v.p. 1981-83, Kansas City Racquetball for Deaf (chmn. 1982-94), Kansas Com. for Deaf and Hard of Hearing, 1995-2001. Republican. Methodist. E-mail: hall@olatheks.org.

HALL, MICHAEL, disability processing specialist; b. N.Y.C., Sept. 20, 1947; s. Mark and Eva Hall; m. Karen Jane Klein; children: Ian D., Mitchell L. BA, CCNY, 1968; MA in Fgn. Affairs, U. Va., 1970; JD, Fordham U., 1975. Bar: N.Y. 1976, D.C. 1980. Disability processing specialist Social Security, Jamaica, NY. Home: 57 Florida Ave Commack NY 11725-5115 Office: NEPSC Proc Br 1 Jamaica Center Plz Jamaica NY 11432

HALL, MILES LEWIS, JR., lawyer; b. Fort Lauderdale, Fla., Aug. 14, 1924; s. Miles Lewis and Mary Frances (Dawson) H.; m. Muriel M. Fisher, Nov. 4, 1950; children: Miles Lewis III, Don Thomas. AB, Princeton U., 1947; JD, Harvard U., 1950. Bar: Fla. 1951, U.S. Supreme Ct., 1972, U.S. Ct. Appeals (11th cir.), U.S. Dist. Ct. (so. and mid. dist.) Fla. Since practiced in, Miami; ptnr. Hall & Hedrick, Miami, 1953—. Dir. Gen. Portland, Inc., 1974-81. Author: Election of Remedies, Vol. VIII, Fla. Law and Practice, 1958. Pres. Orange Bowl Com., 1964-65, dir., 1950—, sec., treas. 1984-86; vice-chmn., dir. Dade County (Fla.) ARC, 1961-62, chmn., 1963-64, dir., 1967-73; nat. fund cons. ARC, 1963, 66-68, trustee, 1985—; pres. Ransom Sch. Parents Assn., 1966; chmn. South Fla. Gov.'s Scholarship Ball, 1966; mem. exec. bd. South Fla. council Boy Scouts Am., 1966-67; citizens bd. U. Miami, 1961-66; mem. Fla. Council of 100, 1961-97, vice chmn., 1961-62; mem. Coral Gables (Fla.) Biltmore Devel. Com., 1972-73; mem. bd. visitors Coll. Law, Fla. State U., 1974-77; bd. dirs. Coral Gables War Meml. Youth Ctr. Assn. Inc., 1967—, pres., 1969-72; bd. dirs. Salvation Army, Miami, 1968-83, Fla. Citizens Against Crime 1984-89; bd. dirs. Bok Tower Gardens Found. Inc., 1987—, sec., 1991—; trustee St. Thomas U., 1990-96, vice chmn., 1993-96; trustee Fla. Supreme Ct. Hist. Soc., 1988—, v.p., 1991-92, pres., 1993-95. 2d lt. USAAF, 1943-45. Fellow Am. Bar Found. (life), Fla. Bar Found. (life); mem. ABA (Fla. co-chmn. membership com. sect. corp. banking and bus. law 1968-72), Dade County Bar Assn. (dir. 1964-65, pres. 1967-68), Fla. Bar Assn., Am. Judicature Soc., Miami-Dade County C. of C. (v.p. 1962-64, dir. 1966-68), Harvard Law Sch. Assn. Fla. (dir. 1964-66), Cottage Club, The Miami Club (v.p., dir. 1989-91, pres. 1990-91), Princeton Club So. Fla. (past pres.), Miami Found. for Cancer Rsch., Inc. (pres. 1998—), Alpha Tau Omega. Methodist. State civil litigation, Corporate, general, Estate planning. Home: 2707 Alhambra Cir Coral Gables FL 33134 Office: Hall & Hedrick 25 SE 2nd Ave Ste 1105 Miami FL 33131-1605

HALL, PETER W. prosecutor; BA, MA, U. N.C.; JD, Cornell U. From asst. U.S. atty to 1st asst. U.S. Atty. Dist. Vt. U.S. Dept. Justice, 1978—86; ptnr. Reiber, Kenlan, Schwiebert, Hall and Facey, Rutland, Vt., 1986—2001; U.S. atty. ea. dist. U.S. Dept. Justice, Vt., 2001—. Office: 11 Elmwood Ave PO Box 570 Burlington VT 05402*

HALL, RALPH CARR, retired lawyer, real estate consultant; b. Chgo., Mar. 28, 1928; s. Rupert Irving and Pauline Martha (Prime) H.; m. Barbara Fordyce, Jan. 21, 1950; children: Brett C., Brian C., Judson P., Trudy A. JD, Tulsa U., 1952. Bar: Okla. 1952, Tex. 1974. V.P. Hall Investment Co., Tulsa, 1948-58; pres. Realty Constrn. Co., Tulsa, 1958-61; real estate investment rep. Am. Oil Co., Birmingham, Ala., 1961-63; div. real estate mgr. Kroger Co., Nashville and Charlotte, N.C., 1963-66; v.p., real estate counsel H.E.B. Properties, Corpus Christi, Tex., 1966-85; pvt. practice, Corpus Chirsti, 1985-97. Real estate cons., 1985-2000; mediator Nueces County Dispute Resolution Ctr., 1994-97. Pres., bd. dirs. Goodwill Ind. South Tex., Corpus Christi, 1969-88; planning commr. City of Corpus Christi, 1990-95. Mem. SCORE, Tex. Bar Assn., Nueces County Bar Assn., Corpus Christi Pistol and Rifle Club (pres. bd. dirs. 1980). Republican. Episcopalian. Condemnation (eminent domain), Property, real (including real estate development, water).

HALL, STEPHEN CHARLES, lawyer; b. Carmel, Calif., Sept. 14, 1948; s. Melvin Wiley and Dorothy Louise (Hoyt) H.; m. Kristi Lee Roberts, Feb. 23, 1983; children: Spencer Stephen Rodrigo, Rachel Genevieve Cristina, Trevor Charles. AB, Dickinson Coll., 1971; JD, Vt. Law Sch., 1977. Bar: Pa. 1978, Va. 1979, U.S. Dist. Ct. (ea. dist.) Va. 1982, U.S. Dist. Ct. (we. dist.) Va. 1990, U.S. Ct. Appeals (4th cir.) 1982. Title atty. Chgo. Title Inst. Co., Richmond, 1978-79; assoc. Edward E. Willey Jr., P.C., Richmond, 1979-82; ptnr. Willey & Hall, P.C., Richmond, 1983-88; assoc. Hazel & Thomas, P.C., Richmond, 1988-90, ptnr., 1990-94, Keith & Hall, Richmond, 1994—. Contbr. articles to profl. jours. Past chmn. bd. trustees St. Michael's Episcopal Sch. Mem. Richmond Bar Assn. (past chmn. publs. com.), Chesterfield-Colonial Heights Bar Assn. (pres.-elect 2002-03, Bon Air Bus. and Profl. Assn. (past pres.), Salisbury Country Club. Episcopalian. Avocations: golf, photography. Federal civil litigation, General civil litigation, State civil litigation. Office: Hairfield Morton Watson & Adams PLC 2800 Buford Rd Ste 201 Richmond VA 23235

HALL, TERRENCE LYON, lawyer; b. Jackson, Mich., Oct. 24, 1949; s. Kenneth F. and Jean (Lyon) H. B.A., Stanford U., 1972; J.D., Detroit Coll. Law, 1978. Bar: Mich. 1978, U.S. Dist. Ct. (ea. dist.) Mich. 1978, U.S. Ct. Appeals (6th cir.) 1982. Ptnr., Terrence L. Hall & John W. Isgrigg, P.C., Pontiac, Mich., 1978—98; mem. Hall & Doran, P.L.C., Waterford, Mich., 1998- . Sec., Oakland County Br. ACLU Mich., 1982-87, now mem. exec. com.. Mem. ATLA, Mich. Bar Assn., Mich. Trial Lawyers Assn., Nat. Orgn. Social Security Claimants' Reps., Oakland County Bar Assn. Unitarian. Probate (including wills, trusts), Personal injury (including property damage), Family and matrimonial. Office: 4519 Highland Rd Waterford MI 48328-1132

HALL, THOMAS WAYNE, lawyer; b. Lancaster, Pa., Jan. 12, 1951; s. Denton F. Jr. and Eleanor Lingard H.; m. Peggy Donnelly, Oct. 6, 1984; children: Shane, Jamie, Trevor. BA, Pa. State U., 1972; JD, Villanova U., 1980. Bar: Pa. 1980, U.S. Dist. Ct. (ea. dist.) Pa. 1981. Assoc. Pepper Hamilton & Scheetz, Phila., 1980-85, Law Office William A. Atlee, Lancaster, Pa., 1985-90; ptnr. Atlee & Hall, Lancaster, Pa., 1990-98, Atlee, Hall & Brookhart, Lancaster, Pa., 1998—. William Goldman scholar, Phila., 1977-80. Personal injury (including property damage), Product liability, Professional liability. Office: Atlee Hall & Brookhart 8 N Queen St Lancaster PA 17603-3878

HALL, WILLIAM DARLINGTON, lawyer; b. Elkins, W.Va., Jan. 12, 1914; s. Nathan I. and Grace (Darlington) H.; m. Louise Brown, Aug. 3, 1949; children— Carolyn L., Dorothy K., Beverly G. B.E.E., W.Va. U., 1934, M.E.E., 1935, E.E., 1940; JD, George Washington U., 1946. Bar: D.C. 1945. Engr. Gen. Electric Co., Lynn, Mass., 1936-39; radio engr., patent adviser Signal Corps U.S. Army, Washington, 1939-47; chief patent sect., 1946-47; practiced in, 1947-74; partner firm Hall, Myers and Rose, 1974-89; of counsel Shlesinger & Myers, Bethesda, Md., 1989, Myers, Rose & Liniak, Bethesda, 1990-92, Myers, Liniak and Berenato, Bethesda, 1992-98, Hall, Priddy, Myers and Vande Sande, Potomac, Md., 1998—. Mem. Army-Navy Patent Adv. Bd., 1946-47 Patent. Home: 10850 Stanmore Dr Potomac MD 20854-1522 Office: Hall Priddy & Myers 10220 River Rd Potomac MD 20854-4916

HALLANAN, ELIZABETH VIRGINIA, federal judge; b. Charleston, W.Va., Jan. 10, 1925; d. Walter Simms and Imogene (Burns) H. , U. Charleston, 1946; JD, W.Va. U., 1951; postgrad, U. Mich., 1964. Atty. Crichton & Hallanan, Charleston, 1952-59; mem. W.Va. State Bd. Edn., Charleston, 1955-57, Ho. of Dels., W.Va. Legis., Charleston, 1957-58; asst. commr. pub. instns. Charleston, 1958-59; mem., chmn. W.Va. Pub. Service Commn., Charleston, 1969-75; atty. Lopinsky, Bland, Hallanan, Dodson, Deutsch & Hallanan, Charleston, 1975-83; sr. judge U.S. Dist. Ct. for So. Dist. W.Va., Charleston, 1983—. Recipient Hannah G. Solomon award Nat. Coun. Jewish Women, 1997, Justitia Officium award W.Va. U. Coll. Law, 1997; named Woman of Achievement, YWCA, 1997, West Virginian of Yr., Charleston Gazette, 1997. Mem. W.Va. Bar Assn. Office: US Dist Ct PO Box 2546 Charleston WV 25329-2546 E-mail: Judge_Hallanan@wvsd.uscourts.gov.

HALL-BARRON, DEBORAH, lawyer; b. Oakland, Calif., Oct. 7, 1949; d. John Standish Hall and Mary (Swinson) H.; m. Eric Levin Meadow, Feb. 1973 (div. June 1982); 1 child, Jesse Standish Meadow Hall; m. Richie Barron, 1997. Paralegal cert., Sonoma State U., Rohnert Park, Calif., 1984; JD, John F. Kennedy U., Walnut Creek, Calif., 1990. Bar: Calif. 1991. Paralegal Law Offices Marc Libarle/Quentin Kopp, Cotati, Calif., 1983-84, MacGregor & Buckley, Larkspur, Calif., 1984-86, Law Offices Melvin Belli, San Francisco, 1987-88, Steinhart & Falconer, San Francisco, 1988; mgr. Computerized Litigation Assocs., San Francisco, 1986; law clk. Morton & Lacy, San Francisco, 1989-91, assoc., 1991-96; atty. Law Offices of Charlotte Venner, San Francisco, 1996-97, Plastiras & Terrizzi, San Francisco, San Rafael, Calif., 1998, Bishop, Barry, Howe, Haney & Ryder, San Francisco, 1998-99, McLemore, Collins and Toschi, Oakland, Calif., 1999-2000, Nevin Levy, LLP, Walnut Creek, 2000—01, Curtis & Arata, Modesto, Calif., 2001—. Atty. Vol. Legal Svcs., San Francisco, 1991-96; judge San Francisco Youth Ct., 1995-97; com. chmn. Point Richmond (Calif.) coun., 1994-96. Recipient Whiley Manuel Pro Bono award State Bar Calif., 1993. Mem. Nat. Assn. Ins. Women, Def. Rsch. Inst., Bar Assn. San Francisco (del. 4th world conf. on women 1995, chair product liability com.), Internat. Com. Lawyers for Tibet (litigation com. 1991-97, co-chair women's com.), Ins. Claims Assn. (chmn. membership com. 1994-96), Hon. Order of Blue Goose Internat., Queen's Bench (chmn. employment com. 1994-97, bd. dirs. 1996—, newsletter editor and webmaster 1999), BASF intellectual property/entertainment law). Democrat. Avocations: sailing, playing guitar and saxaphone, home brewing, mountain biking, human rights advocate. Construction, Personal injury (including property damage), Property, real (including real estate development, water). E-mail: deborahhallbarron@msn.com.

HALLECK, CHARLES WHITE, lawyer, photographer, former judge; b. Rensselaer, Ind., July 6, 1929; s. Charles Abraham and Blanche (White) H.; m. Carolyn L. Wood, Dec. 23, 1950 (div. Oct. 1969); children: Holly Louise, Charles White, Todd Alexander, Heather Leigh, Heidi Lynne, William Hemsley, Hope Leslie; m. Jeanne Wahl, May 16, 1970. AB, Williams Coll., 1951; JD, George Washington U., 1957; LL.D. (hon.), St. Joseph's Coll., 1971; AA in Photography, Foothill Coll., Los Altos Hills, Calif., 1996. Asst. U.S. atty. for D.C., 1957-59; assoc. Hogan and Hartson, Washington, 1959-65; judge Superior Ct. D.C., 1965-77; mem. firm Lamb, Halleck & Keats, Washington, 1977-80; sole practice, 1980-86; photojournalist, 1986-99; fine art photographer, 1999—. Served with USNR, 1951-55; to lt. Res. (ret.). Mem. Beta Theta Pi, Phi Delta Phi.

HALLENBERG, ROBERT LEWIS, lawyer; b. Oct. 21, 1948; s. Daniel Ward and Anna Mae (Lewis) H.; m. Susan Annette Shaffer, Nov. 29, 1980; children: Shea F., Jonathan E.R., Robert Lewis Jr. BA, U. Ky., 1970, JD, 1973; LLM in Taxation, U. Miami, Fla., 1974. Bar: U. Ky. 1970, U.S. Dist. Ct. (we. dist.) Ky. 1975, U.S. Tax Ct. 1986. Ptnr. Woodward, Hobson & Fulton, Louisville, 1974—. Adj. prof. U. Louisville Sch. Law, 1974-80. Bd. dirs. Louisville Theatrical Assocs., 1980-90, v.p., sec., 1985-90; bd. dirs. Goodwill Industries Ky., 1987-93, sec., 1988-91; pres. Louisville Estate Planning Coun., 1979-80; bd. dirs. Louisville Estate Planning Forum, 1986-93, sec., 1992-93; mem. Estate Planning Coun. of Louisville, bd. dirs., 1989-95, pres., 1993-94; Besy Lawyers in Am., Trust Estate. Named one of Best Lawyers in Am. Fellow Am. Coll. Trust and Estate Counsel, Best Lawyers in Am. (trusts and estates); mem. ABA (subchpt. com. 1974-77, real property, probate and trust com. 1985—), Ky. Bar Assn. (sec. tax com. 1984-85), Owl Creek Country Club (bd. dirs. 1988-91, pres. 1989-90, treas. 1990-91). Republican. Episcopalian. Estate planning, Pension, profit-sharing, and employee benefits, Probate (including wills, trusts). Office: Woodward Hobson & Fulton 2500 Nat City Tower Louisville KY 40202 E-mail: bhallenberg@WHF-law.com.

HALLETT, JAMES M. lawyer; b. San Francisco, Sept. 10, 1947; s. Harold E. and Helen E. Hallett; m. Mary Ellen Hall, May 25, 1988; children (by previous marriage) Karen P., Joshua P. BA, Yale U., 1969; JD, U. Calif., Berkeley, 1972. Bar: Calif. 1972, U.S. Dist. Ct. (ctrl. dist.) Calif., U.S. Supreme Ct.; cert. specialist in criminal law, family law. Atty. L.A. County Pub. Defender, L.A., 1973-81; pvt. practice Manhattan Beach, Calif., 1981—. Mem. South Bay Bar Assn. (pres. 1993), Manhattan Beach Rotary (pres. 1987-88). Democrat. Roman Catholic. Avocations: swimming, tennis, golf. Criminal, Family and matrimonial, Juvenile. Office: 1001 6th St Ste 120 Manhattan Beach CA 90266-6750

HALLINAN, TERENCE, prosecutor; b. Dec. 4, 1936; s. Vincent and Vivian Hallinan; m. Lisa Streeter; 5 children. Grad., U. Calif., Berkeley. Mem. San Francisco Bd. Suprs.; dist. atty. City and County San Francisco, 1995—. Mem. Bay Area Air Quality Mgmt. Dist., Golden Gate Bridge Dist. Bd. Office: 850 Bryant St San Francisco CA 94103*

HALLMAN, WILLIAM H., III, lawyer; b. Lakeland, Fla., Aug. 19, 1953; s. William Henry Hallman II and Helen Hallman; m. Catherine Barbara Manson, Nov. 11, 1978; children: Amanda, Rebecca. BS, Nova Southeastern U., 1987, JD, 1991. Bar: Fla. 1992, U.S. Dist. Ct. (ctrl. dist.) Fla. 1993, U.S. Ct. Appeals (11th cir.). Of counsel Keeley, Hayes, et al, Boca Raton, Fla., 1992; atty. State Atty.'s Office, 5th Cir., Brooksville, Fla., 1992—95, William H. Hallman III P.A., Brooksville, Fla., 1995—. Bd. dirs. Withlacoochee Area Legal Svcs., Ocala, Fla.; mem. profl. ethics com. Fla. Bar, Tallahassee, 2001—; owner, pres. Circle H Ranch, 1980—92. V.p. Nature Coast Estate Planning Coun., 2001. Mem.: Hernando County Bar Assn. (pres. 1998—99), Sons of the Am. Revolution, Rotary Club of Brooksville (dir. 1995—99, Paul Harris fellow 1995). Republican. Presbyterian. Avocations: running, history, southeast U.S. travel. Probate (including wills, trusts), Criminal, General practice. Home: 9461 Walliien Dr Brooksville FL 34601 Office: William H Hallman III PA 503 E Jefferson St Brooksville FL 34601 Office Fax: 352-799-4491. E-mail: whh@bellsouth.net.

HALLORAN, MICHAEL JAMES, lawyer; b. Berkeley, Calif., May 20, 1941; s. James Joseph and Fern (Ogden) H.; m. Virginia Smedberg, Sept. 6, 1964; children: Pamela, Peter, Shelley. BS, U. Calif., Berkeley, 1962, LLB, 1965. Bar: Calif. 1966, D.C. 1979, Wyo. 1996. Assoc. Keatinge & Sterling, L.A., 1965-67, Pillsbury, Madison & Sutro, San Francisco, 1967-72, ptnr., 1973-90, 97—, mng. ptnr. Washington, 1979-82; exec. v.p., gen. counsel BankAm. Corp. and Bank of Am., San Francisco, 1990-96. Mem. legal adv. com. N.Y. Stock Exch., 1993-96; bd. overseers Inst. Civil Justice, 1994-98; chair sect. corp. securities banking and emerging cos. Pillsbury Madison & Sutro, 1997-2000. Editor: Venture Capital and Public Offering Negotiation, 1982—. Mem. corp. governance, shareholder rights and securities transactions com. Calif. Senate Commn., 1986-98; bd. dirs. Am. Conservatory Theater, 1994-2000. Mem. ABA (chmn. state regulation of securities com. 1981-84, mem. coun. of sect. of bus. law 1986-90, chmn. banking law com. 1992-96, mem. corp. laws com. 1997—), Bar Assn. San Francisco (bd. dirs. 1993-96). Avocations: skiing, golf, fishing, hiking. E-mail: halloran. Banking, Corporate, general, Securities. Office: Pillsbury Madison & Sutro LLP 50 Fremont St Fl 10 San Francisco CA 94105-2233 also: 2550 Hanover St Palo Alto CA 94304-1115 E-mail: mj@pillsgurylaw.com.

HALLORAN, MICHAEL JOHN, lawyer; b. St. Louis, June 4, 1951; s. Edward Anthony Halloran and Helen M. (Kickham) Phillips. BS in Commerce, St. Louis U., 1972, JD, 1975. Bar: Ill. 1975, U.S. Dist. Ct. (no. dist.) Ill. 1975, U.S. Ct. Appeals (7th cir.) 1975. Assoc. Seyfarth, Shaw, Fairweather & Geraldson, Chgo., Washington, 1975-78; atty. Beinhauer & Rouhana, N.Y.C., 1978-79; assoc. William B. Hanley & Assocs., Chgo., 1979-81, Bell, Boyd & Lloyd, Chgo., 1981-83, ptnr., 1983-86; pvt. practice, Chgo., 1987—. Federal civil litigation, General civil litigation, State civil litigation. Home: 800 S Wells St Apt 552 Chicago IL 60607-4531 Office: 53 W Jackson Blvd Ste 319 Chicago IL 60604-3695

HALLWEGER, MATTHIAS, lawyer; b. Traunstein, Bavaria, Germany, June 7, 1968; 1st state examination, U. Augsburg, Germany, 1993; PhD, U. Augsburg, 1999; 2nd state examination, High Ct. Munich, 1996. Bar: Regional Ct. Munich I, II. Jr. prof. U. Augsburg Sch. Law, 1996—99; ptnr. Kaufmann Lutz & Ptnrs., Munich, 1999—. Guest lectr. German law U. Buckingham, England, 1994; rechtsreferendar Law Firm Stranda Freeman, San Francisco, 1994, Barrister John C. Kelly, Sydney, Australia, 1996; mng. dir. Bibielle GmbH, Munich, 2001; pres. Eius a.V., Munich, 2001, Dr. Scherer Found., Vaduz, Fla., 2002. Author: Law Firms in the USA and Germany, 1999; contbr. articles to profl. jours. DAAD scholar, U. Pitts., 1996. Mem.: German-Am. Lawyers Assn. Corporate, general, Private international, Commercial, contracts (including sales of goods; commercial financing). Office: Kaufmann Lutz Stuck Abel v Lojewski Brienner Str 27 80333 Munich Germany

HALPER, EMANUEL B(ARRY), real estate lawyer, developer, consultant, author; b. Bronx, N.Y., June 24, 1933; s. Nathan N. and Molly (Rabinowitz) H.; m. Ilona Rubinstein, Mar. 5, 1961; children: Eve Brook, Dan Reed. AB, CCNY, 1954; JD, Columbia U., 1957. Bar: N.Y. 1958, Minn. 1982; real estate broker, N.Y. House counsel Howard Stores Corp., Bklyn., 1960; ptnr. Zissu, Berman, Halper & Gumbinger, N.Y.C., 1965-87, of counsel, 1987-97; ptnr. Can. Pacific Realty Co., Fairfield, N.J., 1970—; v.p. devel. Chase Enterprises, Hartford, Conn., 1987-89; pres. Texam. Horizon Ventures, 1989-93, Am. Devel. and Cons. Corp., Greenvale, N.Y., 1989—. Adj. prof. real estate NYU, 1973-83; spl. prof. law Hofstra U., 1998—. Author: Wonderful World of Real Estate, 1975 (republished as Conversations in Real Estate, 1990), Shopping Center and Store Leases, 1979, Ground Leases and Land Acqusition Contracts, 1988; columnist N.Y. Law Jour., 1982-1992; contbg. editor Real Estate Review, N.Y.C., 1973-99; chmn. editorial policy com. Internat. Property Investment Jour., Hempstead, N.Y., 1982-87. With USAR, 1957-63. Recipient Disting. Teaching award NYU, 1978, Dean's award Hofstra U. Law Sch., 1987. Mem. ABA (chmn. comml. leasing com. 1986-93, chmn. comml. and indsl. leasing group 1993-94, mem. supervisory coun. of real property, probate and trust law sect. 1994-2000, mem. standing com. on CLE, 1994-96, mem. standing com. pubs. 1997-98, Gavel award 1977, mem. standing com. on diversity 1999—), World Assn. Lawyers (chmn. internat. real estate com. 1982-90), Internat. Inst. for Real Estate Studies (chmn. bd. 1980-87), Am. Coll. Real Estate Lawyers. Jewish. Avocations: writing, painting, gardening, yoga, running. Construction, Property, real (including real estate development, water). Office: PO Box 261 Greenvale NY 11548-0261 E-mail: elh@aol.com.

HALPERIN, KYLE MALLARY, lawyer; b. New Hyde Park, N.Y., Nov. 2, 1965; d. Jerome Roger Halperin and Marleen Wynne Schuss; m. Jeffrey Travis Hellerman, May 30, 1993; 1 child, Cameron P. BA, Haverford Coll., 1987; JD, Yeshiva U., 1990. Bar: N.Y. 1991, D.C., U.S. Dist. Ct. (so. and ea. dists.) N.Y. 1991, U.S. Supreme Ct. Atty. Halperin Klein & Halperin, N.Y.C., 1990-95; ptnr. The Halperin Law Firm, LLP, N.Y.C., 1996—. Federal civil litigation, State civil litigation, Insurance. Office: The Halperin Law Firm LLP 964 3rd Ave New York NY 10155-0003 E-mail: kmhalperin@aol.com.

HALPERN, BARRY DAVID, lawyer; b. Champaign, Ill., Feb. 25, 1949; s. I.L. and Trula M. H.; m. Cynthia Ann Zedler, Aug. 4, 1972; children: Amanda M., Trevor H. BA, U. Kans., 1971, JD, 1973. Bar: Kans. 1973, Fla. 1975, Ariz. 1978, Colo. 1991, U.S. Dist. Ct. Kans. 1973, U.S. Dist. Ct. Ariz. 1978, U.S. Supreme Ct. 1976. Ptnr. Snell & Wilmer, Phoenix, 1978—. Mem. Gov.'s Task Force Edn. Reform, 1991, judge pro tem Maricopal County Superior Ct.; bd. dirs. Crisis Nursery, Phoenix, 1987, Friends of Foster Children, Phoenix, 1987, Phoenix Symphony, Combined Orgn. Met. Phoenix Arts and Scis., 1994—98, pres., 1996—97, mem. exec. com., 1998—2002. Mem. ABA, State Bar Ariz., State Bar, Fla., State Bar Kans., State Bar Colo., Maricopa County Bar Assn. (chmn. med.-legal com. 1995-96), Phoenix C. of C. (health care coun. 1993-96). General civil litigation, Health, Legislative. Office: Snell & Wilmer 1 Arizona Ctr Phoenix AZ 85004-2202

HALPERN, JAMES BLADEN, lawyer; b. Buffalo, Apr. 20, 1936; s. Philip and Goldene P. (Friedman) H.; m. Jessie Malkoff, July 6, 1958 (div.); 1 child, Jennifer; m. Niesa N. Brateman, Aug. 26, 1979; 1 child, Sheri. BA, Harvard U., 1958, JD, 1961. Bar: NY 1961, D.C. 1970. Atty. corp. fin. div. SEC, Washington, 1961-64; chief counsel-instns., instl. investor study, 1969-70; assoc. firm Proskauer Rose Goetz & Mendelsohn, N.Y.C., 1964-69; assoc. Arent Fox Kintner Plotkin & Kahn, PLLC, Washington, 1971-73, mem., 1974—. Mem. ABA, D.C. Bar Assn., Am. Law Inst. Democrat. Jewish. Corporate, general, Securities. Office: Arent Fox Kintner Et Al 1050 Connecticut Ave NW Washington DC 20036-5393

HALPERN, PHILIP MORGAN, lawyer; b. Derby, Conn., Apr. 17, 1956; s. Edwin Vincent and Carol Veronica (Gallagher) H.; m. Carolyn G. McElwreath, Mar. 11, 1989. BS magna cum laude, Fordham U., 1977; JD, Pace U., 1980. Bar: N.Y. 1981, U.S. Dist. Ct. (so. and ea. dists.) N.Y. 1981, U.S. Ct. Appeals (2d cir.) 1982, U.S. Tax Ct. 1984, U.S. Supreme Ct. 1985, U.S. Dist. Ct. Conn. 1989, Conn. 1989, U.S. Ct. Appeals (3d cir.) 1991; cert. trial adv. Nat. Bd. Trial Advocacy, 2002. Law clk. to sr. judge U.S. Dist. Ct. (so. dist.) N.Y., N.Y.C., 1980-82; assoc. litigation dept. Kimmelman, Sexter & Sobel, N.Y.C., 1982-83; ptnr. Collier, Halpern, Newberg, Nolletti & Bock, N.Y.C., 1983—; mng. ptnr. Collier, Haplern, Newberg, Nolletti & Bock LLP, White Plains, N.Y., 1996—. Arbitrator Civil Ct. City N.Y. and Am. Arbitration Assn., 1987-96; adv. coun. Bd. of Judges, So. Dist. of N.Y.,

1995—; mediator U.S. Dist. (so. dist.) N.Y., 1998—, mem. adv. com. on civil practice, 1999—. Author: Age Discrimination in Employment Act: Employers Can Enforce Releases Too!, 1997, Fair Value Proceedings: Fixing Fair Value in New York, 1996; author, editor: Civil Pretrial Proceedings in New York, 2 vols., 1999, updated annually. Chmn. Young Reps., Tuckahoe, N.Y., 1975-77; chmn. taxi commn. Village of Mamaroneck, N.Y., 1986-87, mem. planning bd., 1987-89. Fellow Am. Bar Found.; mem. N.Y. State Bar Assn. (com. on lawyer competency, com. on fed. judiciary), Assn. of Bar of City of N.Y., ATLA, N.Y. Trial Lawyers Assn., N.Y. County Lawyers Assn., Fed. Bar Coun., Profl. Golfers Assn. (adv. coun. metro. sect. 1992—), Westchester Country Club. Roman Catholic. Federal civil litigation, General civil litigation, State civil litigation. Office: Collier Halpern Newberg Nolletti & Bock LLP One N Lexington Ave White Plains NY 10601 also: 99 Park Ave New York NY 10016-1601

HALPERN, RALPH LAWRENCE, lawyer; b. Buffalo, May 12, 1929; s. Julius and Mary C. (Kaminker) H.; m. Harriet Chasin, June 29, 1958; children: Eric B., Steven R., Julie B. LL.B. cum laude, U. Buffalo, 1953. Bar: N.Y. 1953. Teaching assoc. Northwestern U. Law Sch., 1953-54; assoc. firm Jaeckle, Fleischmann, Kelly, Swart & Augspurger, Buffalo, 1957-58; asso. firm Raichle, Banning, Weiss & Halpern (and predecessors), 1958-59, ptnr., 1959-86, Jaeckle Fleischmann & Mugel LLP, Buffalo, 1986—. Pres. Buffalo Coun. World Affairs, 1972-74, Temple Beth Zion, Buffalo, 1981-83, Bur. Jewish Edn., 2000-02; chmn. Buffalo chpt. Am. Jewish Com., 1975-77; bd. govs. United Jewish Fedn., Buffalo, 1972-78, 91-97, 99—, v.p., 1992-95. Served to capt. JAGC U.S. Army, 1954-57. Mem. ABA (ho. dels. 1989-95, 97-99), N.Y. State Bar Assn. (chmn. com. profl. ethics 1971-76, chmn. com. jud. election monitoring 1983-86, chmn. spl. com. to consider adoption of ABA model rules of profl. conduct 1983-85, sec. internat. law and practice sect. 1992-93, vice chmn. 1993-95), Erie County Bar Assn., Am. Judicature Soc., Am. Law Inst. Antitrust, Federal civil litigation, Corporate, general. Home: 88 Middlesex Rd Buffalo NY 14216-3618 Office: Jaeckle Fleischmann & Mugel LLP 800 Fleet Bank Bldg Buffalo NY 14202-2292 E-mail: rlhalpern@compuserve.com., rhalpern@jaeckle.com.

HALPERT, DOUGLAS JOSHUA, lawyer; b. Bklyn., Nov. 9, 1962; s. Eugene and Miriam (Feigenbaum) H.; m. Yee-Wen Chen, July 22, 1989. BA in English Lit., U. Chgo., 1984; JD, Fordham Law Sch., 1988. Bar: N.Y. 1989, Ohio 1994. Immigration atty. Cohen, Swados, Wright, Hanifin, Bradford & Brett, Buffalo, 1988-94, Frost & Jacobs LLP, Cin., 1994-2000, Frost Brown Todd LLC, Cin., 2000—. Recipient Vol. Lawyer of Yr. award Cin. Bar Assn., 1998. Mem. Am. Immigration Lawyers Assn., Cin. Bar Assn., Alumni Schs. Com. of U. Chgo. Avocations: lit., writing, movies, sports. Office: Frost Brown Todd LLC 2200 PNC Ctr 201 E 5th St Cincinnati OH 45202-4182

HALPHEN-PEREZ, JORGE ENRIQUE, ambassador, lawyer; b. Panama, Mar. 8, 1930; s. Enrique Halphen-Rivera and Eva Perez de Halphen; m. Carmen Cecilia Perurena-Saa, Febr. 25, 1964 (div. Febr. 1981); children: Juan Carlos, Jose Antonio; m. Antonia Kovarick, July 8, 1988. AS, Menlo Coll., Calif., 1950; JD, Tulane U. Sch. Law, New Orleans, 1953. Bar: U.S. Dist. Ct., Ancon Divsn., Panama Canal Zone. Sole practitioner, Panama, 1953-60, 73-80; trust adminstr. Union Bank Los Angeles, 1960-64; mng. dir., Internat. Banking Divsn. Banco Nacional de Panama, 1964-73; first officer, Divsn. Budget & Finance IAEA, Vienna, 1980-83; ptnr. Morgan & Morgan, Panama, 1984-93; Panama's amb. to Austria, 1995—; concurrently amb. to Czech Republich, 1995—; dean of Latin Am. Ambs. to Austria. Spl. adv. to the gen. mgr. Banco Nacional de Panama at Convention Central Banks, Vina del Mar, Chile, 1970; rep. at numerous internat. conventions Banco Nacional de Panama, 1970-73. Co-author: (books) Panama Ship Registries, Naval Mortgage-Panama. Mem. Lions Club Internat. Panama, Union Club. Judge Tulane Moot Ct., Tulane U. Law Sch., 1953. Mem. Phi Alpha Delta. Roman Catholic. Avocations: flying, reading, classical music, concerts, opera. Office: Embassy of Panama Elisabethstrasse 4/5/4/10 A-1010 Vienna Austria E-mail: mail@empanvienna.co.at.

HALSEY, DOUGLAS MARTIN, lawyer; b. Warwick, R.I., 1953; s. Donald Post Jr. and Marita H.; m. Amy Klinow, Sept. 5, 1976; children: Mark, Meredith. BA, Columbia U., 1976; JD cum laude, U. Miami, 1979. Bar: Fla. 1979, U.S. Ct. Appeals (11th cir.), U.S. Dist. Ct. (so. dist.) Fla. Assoc. Paul & Thomson, Miami, Fla., 1979-85; ptnr. Thomson, Bohrer, Werth & Razook, Miami, 1985-88, Douglas M. Halsey, P.A., Miami, 1989-97, Halsey & Burns, P.A., Miami, 1997-2000, White & Case LLP, Miami, 2000—. Rsch. editor U. Miami Law Review, 1978-79. Mem. Alexis de Tocqueville Soc., United Way of Miami-Dade County, 1995—; chmn-.Children's Home Soc. Fla., 2000-2002; chmn. Foster Care Rev., Inc., Miami, Fla., 1998-2000. Mem. Fla. Bar (chmn. environ. and land use law sect. 1993-94, President's Pro Bono Svc. award 1991). Environmental. Office: First Union Fin Ctr 200 S Biscayne Blvd Ste 4900 Miami FL 33131-2352

HALTOM, B(ILLY) REID, lawyer; b. Artesia, N. Mex., Sept. 9, 1945; s. Felix Tucker and Shirley Mae (Lucado) H.; m. Elizabeth Ann Berger, Dec. 25, 1964; 1 child, Robb Reid. BA in Philosophy, U. N.Mex, 1969; JD, Tex. Tech U., 1972. Bar: N.Mex. 1973, U.S. Dist. Ct. N.Mex. 1977, U.S. Ct. Appeals (10th cir.) 1980, U.S. Ct. Claims 1980, U.S. Supreme Ct. 1992, U.S. Dist. Ct. Ariz. 1992. Ptnr. Nordhaus, Haltom, Taylor, Taradash & Bladh, Albuquerque, 1980—. Fellow ABA, N.Mex. State BAr Assn., Albuquerque Bar Assn., Albuquerque Lawyers Club. Avocations: snow and water skiing, tennis, gourmet cooking. Corporate, general, Oil, gas, and mineral, Finance. Office: Nordhaus Haltom Taylor Taradash & Bladh 405 MLK Jr Ave NE Albuquerque NM 87102-5310

HALVORSON, NEWMAN THORBUS, JR., lawyer; b. Detroit, Dec. 17, 1936; s. Newman Thorbus and Virginia Westbrook (Markle) H.; m. Sally Clark Stone, May 3, 1969; children: Christina English, Charles Burgess Westbrook. AB, Princeton U., 1958; LLB, Harvard U., 1961. Bar: Ohio 1962, D.C. 1963, U.S. Supreme Ct. 1965. Assoc. Covington & Burling, Washington, 1962-70; asst. U.S. atty. Office of U.S. Atty., Washington, 1983-85; assoc. ind. counsel (spl. prosecutor under Ethics in Govt. Act), 1987-90; ptnr. Covington & Burling, Washington, 1970-83, 85—. Editor, Harvard Law Rev., 1960-61; author: Intermediate Sanctions Regs: Many Questions Remain, Tax Notes, 1998. Sr. warden, Jr. warden, vestryman Christ Ch. Georgetown, Washington, 1983-86, 89-92, chmn. fin. com., 1992-96; bd. dirs. Lupus Found. D.C., 1974-85; mem., bd. dirs. Eugene and Agnes E. Meyer Found., Washington, 1976-91, chmn., 1989-90, asst. sec./treas., 1990—; bd. mgrs. Hist. Soc. Washington, 1995—, chmn. investment com., 1999—, chmn. audit comm., 2001-; bd. dirs. Coun. for Ct. Excellence, Washington, 1995—; trustee Potomac Sch., McLean, Va., 1980-86, chmn., 1981-83; mem. com. of 100 on Federal City, 1970—, trustee, treas., 1975-79; bd. trustees, mem. exec. com. Greater Washington Rsch. Ctr., 1997-2001; trustee Cleveland Park Hist. Soc., 1997—, pres. 2002—; dir. Rosedale Conservancy, 2002-03. With USMCR, 1961-67. Mem. ABA, D.C. Bar. Clubs: Met. (Washington), Chevy Chase (Md.). Republican. Episcopalian. Corporate, general, Corporate taxation, State and local taxation. Home: 3500 Lowell St NW Washington DC 20016-5025 Office: Covington & Burling 1201 Pennsylvania Ave NW Washington DC 20004-2401

HAMANN, DERYL FREDERICK, lawyer, bank executive; b. Lehigh, Iowa, Dec. 8, 1932; s. Frederick Carl Hamann and Ada Ellen (Hollingsworth) Hamann Geis; m. Carrie Svea Rosen, Aug. 23, 1954 (dec. 1985); children: Karl E., Daniel A., Esther Hamann Brabec, Julie Hamann Bunderson; m. Eleanor Ramona Nelson Curtis, June 20, 1987. AA, Ft. Dodge Jr. Coll., Iowa, 1953; BS in Law, U. Nebr., 1956, JD cum laude, 1958. Bar: Nebr. 1958, U.S. Dist. Ct. Nebr. 1958, U.S. Ct. Appeals (8th cir.) 1958. Law clk. U.S. Dist. Ct. for Nebr., Lincoln, 1958-59; ptnr. Baird, Holm, McEachen, Pedersen, Hamann & Strasheim, Omaha, 1959—2003, sr. counsel, 2003—. Chmn. adv. com. Supreme Ct. Nebr., Omaha, 1986-95; chmn. bd. Midwestern Cmty. Banks. Past pres. Omaha Estate Planning Coun. Mem. Nebr. Bar Found. (pres. 1981-86), Nebr. Assn. Bank Attys. (pres. 1985-86). Republican. Lutheran. Avocations: boating, reading. Banking, Corporate, general, Estate planning. Office: Baird Holm McEachen Pedersen Hamann & Strasheim 1500 Woodmen Tower Omaha NE 68102

HAMAR, MICHAEL BRUCE, lawyer; b. Syracuse, N.Y., Aug. 12, 1952; s. George D. and Marion Hibben (Phelps) H.; m. Linda Louise Ciavarella, Nov. 26, 1977; children: Lauren Alexandra, Peter Michael, Victoria Louise. BA with high distinction, U. Va., 1974, JD, 1977. Bar: Ala. 1977, Va. 1977, Tex. 1982, U.S. Dist. Ct. (so. dist.) Ala. 1979, U.S. Ct. Appeals (5th cir.) 1979, U.S. Ct. Appeals (11th cir.) 1981, U.S. Ct. Appeals (4th cir.) 1984, U.S. Dist. Ct. (ea. dist.) Va. 1985. Assoc. Armbrecht, Jackson, DeMouy et al., Mobile, Ala., 1977—81; staff atty. Allied Corp., Houston, 1981—83; assoc. Clark & Stant, P.C., Virginia Beach, Va., 1983—86, ptnr., 1986—91, Faggert & Frieden, P.C., Chesapeake, Va., 1991—95, Tavss, Fletcher, Earley & King, P.C., Norfolk, Va., 1995—2002, Payne, Gates, Farthing & Radd, P.C., Norfolk, Va., 2002—. Mem. Nat. Assn. Bond Lawyers, Ala. State Bar Assn., Va. State Bar Assn., Tex. State Bar Assn., Norfolk-Portsmouth Bar Assn., Athelstan Club, Phi Delta Phi (exchequer minor inn 1976-77). Lutheran. Avocations: surfing, sailing, snow skiing, reading. Corporate, general, Finance, Mergers and acquisitions. Home: 1597 Bay Point Dr Virginia Beach VA 23454-1431 Office: Payne Gates Farthing & Radd PC Ste 1515 999 Waterside Dr Norfolk VA 23501

HAMBLEN, LAPSLEY WALKER, JR., judge; b. Chattanooga, Tenn., Dec. 25, 1926; s. Lapsley Walker Sr. and Libby (Shipley) H.; m. Claudia Royster Terrell, Mar. 20, 1971; children by previous marriage: Lapsley Walker III, Allen M., William Shipley. BA, U. Va., 1949, LLB, 1953. Bar: W.Va. 1954, Ohio 1955, Va. 1957. Trial atty. IRS, Atlanta, 1955; atty. advisor U.S. Tax Ct., 1956; ptnr. Caskie Frost Hobbs & Hamblen and predecessor firms, Lynchburg, Va., 1957-82; dep. asst. atty. gen. tax divsn. U.S. Dept. Justice, 1982; judge U.S. Tax Ct., Washington, 1982-92, chief judge, 1992-94, 94-96, sr. judge, 1996-2000, ret., 2000. Former trustee So. Fed. Tax Inst.; former co-dir. ann. conf. on fed. taxation U. Va. Served with USN, 1945-46. Fellow: Am. Bar Found., Am. Coll. Trust and Estate Counsel, Am. Coll. Tax Counsel; mem.: Raven Soc., Phi Alpha Delta, Omicron Delta Kappa, Order of the Coif. Presbyterian.

HAMBURG, CHARLES BRUCE, lawyer; b. Bklyn., June 30, 1939; s. Albert Hamburg and Goldie (Blume) H.; m. Stephanie Barbara Steingesser, June 23, 1962; children: Jeanne M., Louise E. B.Chem. Engring., Poly. Inst. Bklyn., 1960; JD, Geroge Washington U., 1964. Bar: N.Y. 1964. Patent examiner U.S. Patent Office, 1960-63; patent atty. Celanese Corp. Am., N.Y.C., 1963-65, Burns, Lobato & Zelnick, N.Y.C., 1965-67, Nolte & Nolte, N.Y.C., 1967-75; prin. C. Bruce Hamburg, N.Y.C., 1976-79; ptnr. Jordan & Hamburg, L.L.P., N.Y.C., 1979—. U.S. corr. Patents and Licensing, Japan, 1986—. Author: Patent Fraud and Inequitable Conduct, 1972, 78, Patent Law Handbook, 1983-84, 84-85, 85-86, (in Japanese) Doctrine of Equivalents in U.S., 1995, 2nd edit. (in Korean), 1998; monthly columnist Patent and Trademark Rev., 1976-85; contbr. chpt. on U.S. patents: Patents Throughout the World, 1976—. Mem.: ABA, Internat. Fedn. Intellectual Property Attys., Licensing Execs. Soc., Internat. Assn. Protection Intellectual Property, NY Patent Trademark Copyright Law Assn., Am. Intellectual Property Assn., Masons. Intellectual property, Patent, Trademark and copyright. Office: 122 E 42nd St New York NY 10168-0002 E-mail: jandh@ipattorneys.com.

HAMBURGER, BRIAN S. lawyer, consultant; b. Charlotte, N.C., 1972; s. Jeffrey A. and Linda Hamburger; m. KariAnn Hamburger. BS in Econs. and Fin. Mgmt., Quinnipiac U., 1994; JD, U. Miami, 1998. Bar: (NY), (NJ), (DC). Chief compliance officer New Century Fin. Group, Princeton, NJ, 1995—2000; jud. intern to Judge Linnea R. Johnson U.S. Dist. Ct. So. Dist. Fla., Miami, 1996; jud. intern to Judge David M. Gersten State Fla. 3rd Dist. Ct. Appeal, Miami, 1996-97; law clk. enforcement divsn. U.S. Securities and Exch. Commn., Miami, 1997; atty. securities practice group Stark & Stark, Princeton, N.J., 1998-2000; mng. dir. MarketCounsel, Princeton, 2000—; mng. mem. Hamburger Law Firm, Princeton, 2000—. Mem. arbitrators NASD Dispute Resolution; arbitrator N.Y. Stock Exch. Contbr. articles to profl. jours. Recipient Pres.'s Pinnacle award, 1998; scholar Dean's Svc. scholar, U. Miami, 1997—98. Mem.: ABA, Securities Industry Assn. (compliance and legal divsn.), NY County Lawyers Assn. (com. securities and exchs.), DC Bar Assn., NY State Bar Assn., Nat. Soc. Compliance Profls., Soc. Fin. Svc. Profls., Fin. Planning Assn. NJ (Gold Key mem.), NJ State Bar Assn. Securities, Corporate, general.

HAMBY, GENE MALCOLM, JR., lawyer; b. Florence, Ala., Mar. 23, 1943; s. Gene Malcolm Sr. and Katherine (Koonce) H.; m. Judy Priscilla Brown, Apr. 10, 1971; children: Mark Clifton, Anne Tyler. BS with great honor, U. North Ala., 1965; JD, U. Ala., Tuscaloosa, 1968. Bar: Ala. 1968, U.S. Dist. Ct. (no. dist.) Ala. 1972, U.S. Ct. Appeals (11th cir.) 1981. Assoc. Heflin & Rosser, Attys., Tuscambia, Ala., 1968-70; ptnr. Pitts & Hamby, Sheffield, Ala., 1970-80; pvt. practice Sheffield, 1981-84; ptnr. Hamby & Baker, Attys., Sheffield, 1984-87, Jones, Hamby & Baker, Attys., Sheffield, 1987-89; pvt. practice, Sheffield, 1989—. Bd. dirs. Shoals Indsl. Devel. Authority, Sheffield, 1985-91, Law Sch. Found., U. Ala. Sch. Law, 1985—; past dist. v.p. U. Ala. Alumni, Tuscaloosa; past pres. U. North Ala. Alumni, Florence, Colbert County United Way, Sheffield; chmn. Sheffield Indsl. Devel. Bd., Sheffield, Sheffield Edn. Found., 1992-96; past bd. dirs. United Cerebral Palsy NW Ala., Sheffield, Shoals Indsl. Devel. Authority. With USAR, 1968-74. Recipient Kiwanis Citizen of Yr. award City of Sheffield, 1991, 2001. Mem. ATLA, ABA, Colbert County Bar Assn (past pres.), Ala. State Bar Assn., Ala. Trial Lawyers Assn. (past mem. exec. com.), Sheffield Bus. and Profl. Assn. (pres. 1999-2001), Kiwanis Club (past pres. Sheffield chpt.), Colbert County C. of C. (past pres.), Phi Kappa Phi. Democrat. Avocation: indian artifacts. State civil litigation, Personal injury (including property damage), Property, real (including real estate development, water). Home: PO Box 328 Sheffield AL 35660-0328 Office: 406 N Nashville Ave Sheffield AL 35660-2938

HAMBY, LEE ELLEN, lawyer; b. Moultrie, Ga., Jan. 22, 1957; d. Thomas L. and Rena (Bonner) H.; m. Paul E. Hopkins, May 3, 1980; children: William Douglas, Brennan Kathleen Hamby-Hopkins. BA, U. Va., 1979; JD with distinction, Emory U., 1987. Law clk. Superior Ct., Gainesville, Ga., 1987-89; staff atty. Legal Aid, Gainesville, 1990-91; rsch. asst. death penalty Superior Ct., Dawsonville, Ga., 1991-95; pvt. practice Sugar Hill, Ga., 1995—. Vol. McGovern campaign, Southern Ga., 1972, Atlanta, 1984, various animal protection groups, 1985—. Mem. ACLU, Ga. Trial Lawyers Assn., So. Poverty Law Ctr. (supporting mem.), People for the Ethical Treatment of Animals. Democrat. Buddhist. Avocations: reading, animals, sleeping, dreaming. Criminal, Pension, profit-sharing, and employee benefits, Elder. Home and Office: 4511 Old Suwanee Rd Sugar Hill GA 30518-4889

HAMEL, FRED MEADE, lawyer; b. Sheridan, Wyo., Nov. 26, 1943; s. Fred Herman and Marie (Kruger) H.; m. Michelle O'Bryan, Dec. 29, 1967; 1 child, Marc Steven. BSBA, U. Denver, 1965; JD, U. Colo., 1968. Bar: Colo. 1968, U.S. Dist. Ct. Colo. 1974, U.S. Ct. Appeals (10th cir.) 1977. Asst. sec. Union Investment Corp., Detroit, 1970—74; v.p. 1st Comml. Corp., Denver, 1970—74; prin. Fred M. Hamel Atty. At Law, Denver, 1974—. Pres. South Cen. Improvment Assn., 1978. Staff sgt. U.S. Army, 1968-70, Vietnam. Mem. Colo. Bar Assn., Denver Bar Assn. Avocation: golf. General civil litigation, Commercial, contracts (including sales of goods; commercial financing), Property, real (including real estate development, water). Office: 155 S Madison St Ste 206 Denver CO 80209-3013

HAMEL, LOUIS H., JR., lawyer; b. Haverhill, Mass., June 30, 1934; s. Louis H. and Dorothy A. (Berry) H.; m. Geraldine T. Griffin, Dec. 28, 1959 (div. 1977); children: Juliana, Louis III, Lucy, Paul, Mark J. BA, St. Paul's Coll., 1956; MA, Fordham U., 1959; JD, Harvard U., 1969. Bar: Mass. 1969, U.S. Dist. Ct. Mass. Instr. Manhattanville Coll., Purchase, N.Y., 1959-60; pres. Hamel Realty, Haverhill, Mass., 1961-69; assoc. Hale and Dorr, Boston, 1969-72, jr. ptnr., 1972-76, sr. ptnr., 1976-97, of counsel, 1998—. Contbr. articles to profl. jours. Bd. trustees Boston Chamber Music Soc., 1987—, pres., 1996-00. Office: Hale and Dorr LLP 60 State St Ste 25 Boston MA 02109-1816 also: 955 Main St Ste 202 Winchester MA 01890-4302 E-mail: louis.hamel@haledorr.com.

HAMEL, RODOLPHE, pharmaceutical company executive, retired lawyer; b. Lewiston, Maine, June 3, 1929; s. Rodolphe and Alvina Melanie (Bilodeau) H.; m. Marilyn Vivian Johnsen, June 10, 1957; children: Matthew Edward, Anne Melanie. BA, Yale U., 1950; LLB, Harvard U., 1953. Bar: Maine 1953, D.C. 1953, N.Y. 1957. Assoc. firm Shearman & Sterling, N.Y.C., 1956-66; v.p., corp. sec., gen. counsel Macmillan Inc., N.Y.C., 1972-73; internat. counsel Bristol-Myers Squibb Co. (formerly Bristol-Myers Co.), N.Y.C., 1966-72, 73, v.p., counsel internat. div., 1974-81, assoc. gen. counsel, 1978-89, v.p., 1983-92, gen. counsel, 1989-94, sr. v.p., 1992-94, cons., 1995—. 1st lt. AUS, 1953-56. Mem. ABA, N.Y. State Bar Assn., Assn. of Bar of City of N.Y., Yale Club. Corporate, general, Private international. Office: Bristol-Myers Squibb Co 345 Park Ave New York NY 10154-0004

HAMES, WILLIAM LESTER, lawyer; b. Pasco, Wash., June 21, 1947; s. Arlie Franklin and Nina Lee (Ryals) H.; m. Pamella Kay Rust, June 3, 1967; children: Robert Alan, Michael Jonathan. BS in Psychology, U. Wash., 1974; JD, Willamette U., 1981. Bar: Wash. 1981, U.S. Dist. Ct. (ea. dist.) Wash. 1982, U.S. Ct. Appeals (9th cir.) 1985, U.S. Dist. Ct. (we. dist.) Wash. 1985. Counselor Wash. Juvenile Ct., Walla Walla, Wash., 1974-76; reactor operator control rm. United Nuclear Inc., Richland, Wash., 1976-77; assoc. Sonderman, Egan & Hames, Kennewick, Wash., 1981-84, Timmons & Hames, Kennewick, 1984-86, Sonderman, Timmons & Hames, Kennewick, 1987-88; ptnr. Hames, Anderson & Whitlow, Kennewick, 1988—. Mem. Wash. State Bar Assn. (mem. exec. com. creditor, debtor sect.), Benton-Franklin County Bar Assn., Bankruptcy Bar Assn. (bd. dirs.), Fed. Bar Assn. (bd. dirs.), Am. Bankruptcy Inst. Democrat. Methodist. Bankruptcy, Commercial, consumer (including collections, credit), Personal injury (including property damage). Home: 410 W 21st St Kennewick WA 99337 Office: Hames Anderson & Whitlow PO Box 5498 Kennewick WA 99336-0498 E-mail: billh@hawlaw.com.

HAMILTON, CLYDE HENRY, judge; b. Edgefield, S.C., Feb. 8, 1934; s. Clyde H. and Edwina (Odom) Hamilton; children: John C., James W. BS, Wofford Coll., 1956; JD with honors, George Washington U., 1961. Bar: S.C. 1961. Reference asst. U.S. Senate Libr., Washington, 1958—61; Assoc. J.R. Folk, Edgefield, 1961—63; assoc., gen. ptnr. Butler, Means, Evins & Browne, Spartanburg, SC, 1963—81; judge U.S. Dist. Ct. S.C., Columbia, 1981—91, U.S. Ct. Appeals (4th cir.), Richmond, Va., 1991—. Gen. counsel Synalloy Corp., Spartanburg, 1969—80. Mem. editl. staff: Cumulative Index of Congl. Com. Hearings, 1935—58, bd. editors: George Washington Law Rev., 1959—60. Pres. Spartanburg County Arts Coun., 1971—73, Spartanburg Day Sch., 1972—74, sustaining trustee, 1975—81; past mem. steering com. undergrad. merit fellowship program and estate planning coun. Converse Coll., Spartanburg; trustee Spartanburg Meth. Coll., 1979—84; mem. S.C. Supreme Ct. Bd. Commrs. on Grievances and Discipline, 1980—81; del. Spartanburg County, 4th Congl. Dist. and S.C. Rep. Convs., 1976, 1980; mem., past chmn. fin. com. and adminstrv. bd. Trinity United Meth. Ch., Spartanburg, trustee, 1980—83. Capt. USAR, 1956—62. Recipient Alumni Disting. Svc. award, Wofford Coll., 1991, The Order of The Palmetto, Gov. Beasley, S.C., 1999. Mem.: S.C. Bar Assn., Piedmont Club (bd. govs. 1979—81). Office: US Ct Appeals 4th Cir 1901 Main St Columbia SC 29201-2443

HAMILTON, DAGMAR STRANDBERG, lawyer, educator; b. Phila., Jan. 10, 1932; d. Eric Wilhelm and Anna Elizabeth (Sjöström) Strandberg; m. Robert W. Hamilton, June 26, 1953; children: Eric Clark, Robert Andrew Hale, Meredith Hope. AB, Swarthmore Coll., 1953; JD, U. Chgo. Law Sch., 1956, Am. U., 1961. Bar: Tex. 1972. Atty. civil rights divsn. U.S. Dept Justice, Washington, 1965-66; asst. instr. govt. U. Tex., Austin, 1966-71; lectr. Law Sch. U. Ariz., Tucson, 1971-72; editor, rschr. Assoc. William O. Douglas U.S. Supreme Ct., Washington, 1962-73, 75-76; editor, rschr. Douglas autobiography Random House Co., 1972-73; staff counsel Judiciary Com. U.S. Ho. of Reps., 1973-74; asst. prof. L.B. Johnson Sch. Pub. Affairs U. Tex., Austin, 1974-77, assoc. prof., 1977-83, prof., 1983—, assoc. dean., 1983-87. Interdisciplinary prof. U. Tex. Law Sch., 1983—; vis. prof. Washington U. Law Sch., St. Louis, 1982, U. Maine, Portland, 1992; Godfrey Disting. vis. prof. U. Maine Law Sch., 2002; vis. fellow U. London, QMW Sch. Law, 1987—88; vis. prof. U. Maine, Portland, 2002; vis. fellow U. Oxford Inst. European & Comparative Law, 1998. Contbr. to various publs. Mem. Tex. State Bar Assn., Am. Law Inst., Assn. Pub. Policy Analysis and Mgmt., Swarthmore Coll. Alumni Coun. (rep.), Kappa Beta Phi (hon.), Phi Kappa Phi (hon.). Democrat. Mem. Soc. Of Friends. Civil rights, Constitutional, Education and schools. Home: 403 Allegro Ln Austin TX 78746-4301 Office: U Tex LBJ Sch Pub Affairs Austin TX 78713 E-mail: dagmar.hamilton@mail.utexas.edu.

HAMILTON, DAVID F. judge; b. 1957; BA magna cum laude, Haverford Coll., 1979; JD, Yale U., 1983. Law clk. to Hon. Richard D. Cudahy U.S. Ct. Appeals (7th cir.), 1983-84; atty. Barnes & Thornburg, Indpls., 1984-88, 91-94; judge U.S. Dist. Ct. (so. dist.) Ind., Indpls., 1994—. Counsel to Gov. of Ind., 1989-91; chair Ind. State Ethics Commn., 1991-94. V.p. for litigation, bd. dirs. Ind. Civil Liberties Union, 1987-88. Fulbright scholar, 1979-80; recipient Sagamore of the Wabash, Gov. Evan Bayh, 1991. Mem.: Am. Inns. of Ct. (Sagamore chpt., pres. 2001—, criminal law com. jud. conf. 2000—). Office: US Dist Ct So Dist Ind 46 E Ohio St Rm 330 Indianapolis IN 46204-1921

HAMILTON, JACKSON DOUGLAS, lawyer; b. Cleve., Feb. 5, 1949; m. Margaret Lawrence Williams, Dec. 19, 1971; children: Jackson Douglas Jr., William Schuyler Lawrence. BA, Colgate U., 1971; JD, U. Pa., 1974. Bar: Calif. 1974, U.S. Dist. Ct. (cen. dist.) Calif. 1974, U.S. Tax Ct. 1978, U.S. Ct. Claims 1984, U.S. Ct. Appeals (6th and 11th cirs.) 1988, N.C. 1991, U.S. Supreme Ct. 1991. Ptnr. Kadison, Pfaelzer, Woodard, Quinn & Rossi, L.A., 1986-87, Spensley, Horn, Jubas & Lubitz, L.A., 1987-91, Roberts & Stevens, Asheville, N.C., 1991—. Adj. prof. law U. San Diego, 1981, Golden Gate U., San Francisco, 1981-85, U. N.C., Asheville, 1994; cons. Calif. Continuing Edn. Bar, 1983-84, select com. on sports Calif. Senate, 1983-85. Editor Entertainment Law Reporter, 1979—; contbr. articles to profl. jours. Mem. ABA (tax sect., internat. law sect.), N.C. Bar Assn. (tax. sect. coun.). Republican. Episcopalian. Corporate, general, Corporate taxation, Taxation, general. Office: Roberts & Stevens BB & T Bldg Asheville NC 28802

HAMILTON, JEAN CONSTANCE, judge; b. St. Louis, Nov. 12, 1945; AB, Wellesley Coll., 1968; JD, Washington U., St. Louis, 1971; LLM, Yale U., 1982. Atty. Dept. of Justice, Washington, 1971-73, asst. U.S. atty. St. Louis, 1973-78; atty. Southwestern Bell Telephone Co., St. Louis,

1978—81; judge 22d Jud. Circuit State of Mo., St. Louis, 1982-88; judge Mo. Ct. Appeals (ea. dist.), 1988-90, U.S. Dist. Ct. (ea. dist.) Mo., 1990—, chief judge, 1995—2002. Office: US Courthouse 111 S 10th St Saint Louis MO 63102

HAMILTON, JOHN RICHARD, lawyer; b. El Dorado, Kans., Jan. 8, 1940; s. Silas H. and Ora B. (Barker) H.; m. Shirley A. Tekamp, June 16, 1960 (div. July 1976); children: Michele L., Brian J.; m. Louise Brock, Dec. 22, 1984. BS, Union U., 1962; JD, Washburn Law Sch., 1965. Bar: Kans 1965, U.S. Dist. Ct. Kans. 1965, U.S. Ct. Appeals (10th cir.) 1969. Ptnr. Crane, Martin, Claussen, Hamilton & Forbes, Topeka, 1965—84, Hamilton & Hannah, Topeka, 1985—87, Hamilton, Gregg, Barker & Johnson, Topeka, 1988—. Mem. ATLA, ABA, Kans. Bar Assn., Topeka Bar Assn., Kans. Trial Lawyers Assn. (bd. dirs., v.p. 1982-83), Am. Bd. Trial Advs., Topeka Country Club. Democrat. Federal civil litigation, State civil litigation, Condemnation (eminent domain). Home: 2334 SW Mayfair Pl Topeka KS 66611-2054 E-mail: jhamilton@hamiltongregg.com.

HAMILTON, ROBERT OTTE, lawyer; b. Marysville, Ohio, July 27, 1927; s. George Robinson and Annette (Otte) H.; m. Phyllis Eileen Clark, Dec. 16, 1962; children: Nathan Clark, Scott Robert. AB, Miami U., Oxford, Ohio, 1950; JD, U. Mich., 1953. Bar: Ohio 1953, U.S. Supreme Ct. 1960. Sole practice, Marysville, 1953—; pros. atty. Union County, Ohio, 1957-65; city atty. City of Marysville, 1956-81. Mem. Union, Morrow and Del. Mental Health Bd.,d 1957-72; pres. Marysville Jaycees, 1954; mem. Union County Rep. Exec. Com., 1955-65, sec., 1955-60. Served with USN, 1945-46, to lt. (j.g.) USNR, 1946-66. Mem. ABA, Ohio State Bar Assn. (chmn. jr. bar sect. 1961, ho. of dels. 1976-86, exec. com. 1983-86), Ohio State Bar Found. (pres. 1996), Union County Bar Assn. (pres. 1960), Ohio Acad. Trial Lawyers, Masons. Criminal, General practice, Probate (including wills, trusts). Home: 432 W 6th St Marysville OH 43040-1464 Office: 116 S Court St Marysville OH 43040-1545

HAMILTON, SCOTT, lawyer; b. Russell, Kans., Sept. 20, 1953; s. Richard Samuel and Dona May (Hogue) H.; l child, Wesley Arthur. BA, U. Tulsa, 1975; JD, Washington and Lee U., 1978. Bar: Va. 1978, Okla. 1981, U.S. Dist. Ct. (no. and we. dists.) Okla. 1981, U.S. Ct. Appeals (10th cir.) 1981. Law clk. Supreme Ct. Va., Richmond, 1978-80; staff atty. Legal Svcs. Ea. Okla., Muskogee, 1980-82, Legal Aid Western Okla., Oklahoma City, 1982-83, Legal Svcs. Ea. Okla., Tulsa, 1983-93, mng. atty., 1993—. Mem. Okla. Bar Assn., Tulsa County Bar Assn. Democrat. Home: 265 E 45th Ct Tulsa OK 74105-4401 Office: Legal Aid Svcs Okla Inc Ste 700 115 W 3rd St Tulsa OK 74103-3417 E-mail: scott.hamilton@legalaidok.org.

HAMLAR, PORTIA YVONNE TRENHOLM, lawyer, writer, educator; b. Montgomery, Ala. d. Harper Councill Sr. and Portia Lee (Evans) Trenholm; 1 child, Eric Lafayette. AB, Ala. State U., Montgomery, 1951; MA, Mich. State U., 1953; JD, U. Detroit, 1972; MPA, U. Mich., 2000. Bar: Mich. 1974, Ill. 1988. Atty. Chrysler Corp., Highland Park, Mich., 1973—80; asst. prof. law Widener U., Wilmington, Del., 1980—82; pvt. practice Southfield, 1982—2000; asst. to chancellor and dir. equity and affirmative action U. Wis., Stevens Point, 2001—. Editor DEOC Pub. Co., Rochester, Mich., 1977-81; mem. Orgn. Resources Counselors, Washington, 1974-80; exch. prof. Nat. Urban League, 1976-79. Author: Defending the Employer in OSHA Contests, 1977—82; mem. U. Detroit Law Rev., 1970—73; editor: Mich. Environ. Law Case Digest, 1990—2001. V.p. bd. dirs. Rochester Symphony Orch., 1983-86. Mem. ABA (chair subcom. labor law sect. 1975-80, spkr.), Mich. Women's Econ. Club (speaker), Alpha Kappa Mu, Mu Phi Epsilon, Kappa Beta Pi. Avocation: classical piano. Alternative dispute resolution, Education and schools. Home: 3602 Yvonne Dr Stevens Point WI 54481 Office: U Wis-Stevens Point Rm 210 Old Main Stevens Point WI 54481 E-mail: phamlar@charter.net.

HAMMER, DAVID LINDLEY, lawyer, writer; b. Newton, Iowa, June 6, 1929; s. Neal Paul and Agnes Marilyn (Reece) H.; m. Audrey Lowe, June 20, 1953; children: Julie, Lisa, David. BA, Grinnell Coll., 1951; JD, U. Iowa, 1956. Bar: Iowa 1956, U.S. Dist. Ct. (no. dist.) Iowa 1959, U.S. Dist. Ct. (so. dist.) Iowa 1969, U.S. Ct. Appeals (8th cir.) 1996, U.S. Supreme Ct. 1977. Ptnr. Hammer Simon & Jensen, Dubuque, Iowa, Galena, Ill.; mem. grievance commn. Iowa Supreme Ct., 1973-85, mem. adv. rules com., 1986-92. Author: Poems from the Ledge, 1980, The Game is Afoot, 1983, For the Sake of the Game, 1986, To Play the Game, 1986, The 22nd Man, 1989, The Quest, 1993, My Dear Watson, 1994, The Before Breakfast Pipe, 1995, A Dangerous Game, 1997, The Vital Essence, 1999, A Talent for Murder, 2000, Yonder in the Gaslight, 2000, Straight Up with a Twist, 2001, A Deep Game, 2001, The Game is Underfoot, 2002, You Heard What Jesse Said, 2003, My Dear Holmes, 2003. Bd. dirs. Linwood Cemetery Assn., 1973—, pres., 1983-84; bd. dirs. Dubuque Mus. Art, 1998-2001, hon. dir.; bd. dirs., past pres. Finley Hosp., hon. dir.; bd. dirs. Finley Found., 1988-95; past campaign chmn., past pres. United Way; past bd. dirs. Carnegie Stout Pub. Libr. With U.S. Army, 1951-53. Fellow Am. Coll. Trial Lawyers; mem. ABA, Young Lawyers Iowa (past pres.), Iowa Def. Counsel Assn. (pres. 1991-92, del. to Def. Rsch. Inst. 1992-93), Assn. Def. Trial Attys. (exec. coun. 1983-86, past chmn. Iowa chpt.), Iowa State Bar Assn. (past chmn. continuing legal edn. com.), Iowa Acad. Trial Lawyers, Dubuque County Bar Assn. (past pres.), Baker St. Irregulars. Republican. Congregationalist. General civil litigation, Insurance. Office: 770 Main St Dubuque IA 52001

HAMMERLE, KURT GEORG, lawyer; b. Rockford, Ill., May 29, 1965; s. Walter and Charlotte Josefa H. BSME, Va. Poly. Inst. and State U., 1988; JD, Coll. William and Mary, 1991. Bar: Va. 1991, U.S. Dist. Ct. (ea. dist.) Va. 1992, U.S. Ct. Appeals (4th cir.) 1991, U.S. Patent and Trade Office 1993, Ct. Appeals Fed. Cir. 1992. Assoc. Greene & Assocs., Mathews, Va., 1992-94; asst. commonwealth atty. Newport News (Va.) Commonwealth Atty., 1994-98; patent atty. NASA/Langley Rsch. Ctr., Hampton, Va., 1998—. Advisor Law Explorer Post, Newport News, Va., 1998. Mem. ABA, Am. Intellectual Property Lawyers Assn., Assn. Trial Lawyers Am., James Square Home Owner's Assn. (pres. 1996-99). Roman Catholic. Avocations: tennis, weightlifting, golf, skiing, rollerblading. Intellectual property, Patent. Office: NASA/Langley Rsch Ctr Mail Stop 212 3 Langley Blvd Stop 212 Hampton VA 23681-2143 E-mail: k.g.hammerle@larc.nasa.gov.

HAMMERMAN, EDWARD SCOTT, lawyer; b. Washington, Mar. 21, 1969; s. Murray Frederic and Marilyn (Hochberg) H. BA in English, Emory U., 1991; JD, Cath. U. Am., 1994. Bar: Pa. 1994, Fla. 1998, D.C. 1998. Staff atty. Venable, Washington, 1994-96; assoc. Leibowitz & Assocs., P.A., Miami, Fla., 1996-98, Collier Shannon & Scott, PLLC, Washington, 1998-99, Dickstein Shapiro Morin & Oshinsky, Washington, 1999—2002; founder Intermediary Copyright Royalty Svcs., 2002—; mng. mem. Hammerman, PLLC, Washington, 2002—. Editor newsletters Broadcasting and the Law, 1996-98, Ask the Expert, Office.com.; mng. editor newsletter Telecom Real Estate Advisor, 2002—. Bd. dirs. Am. Jewish Com., Miami, 1996-98. Mem. Fed. Comms. Bar Assn. (founder, co-chair 1992-94, law student com.), Assn. Emory Alumni (exec. com. 1998—), Masons. Democrat. Jewish. Administrative and regulatory, Communications, Intellectual property. Office: Hammerman PLLC 5335 Wisconsin Ave NW Ste 440 Washington DC 20015-2052 E-mail: ted@copyrightroyalties.com.

HAMMESFAHR, ROBERT WINTER, lawyer; b. Pittsfield, Mass., May 17, 1954; s. Frederick W. and Patricia Lue (Winter) H.; widowed; 1 child, Scott Gardner. BA, Colgate U., 1975; JD, Northwestern U., Chgo., 1978. Bar: Ill. 1978, U.S. Dist. Ct. (no. dist.) Ill. 1978, N.Y. 1991, U.S. Supreme Ct. 1989. Ptnr. Blatt, Hammesfahr & Eaton, Chgo., 1994-97, mng. ptnr., 1997-2000, chmn., 2000; mem. Cozen O'Connor, 2001—. Author: (with others) Punitive Damages: A Guide to the Insurability of Punitive Damages in the United States and Its Territories, 1988, Punitive Damages: A State-By-State Guide to Law and Practice, 1991, (pocket parts 1993, 96, Japanese edits., 1995, 99, 2000, 2001), 2d edit., 2002, The Law of Reinsurance Claims, 1994, Supplement 1997; editor, author: (with others) @Risk—Internet and E-commerce Insurance and Reinsurance, 2000, 2.0 version, 2002; contbr. articles to profl. jours. Mem. ABA, Chgo. Bar Assn. Avocations: tennis, skiing. State civil litigation, Environmental, Insurance. Office: Cozen O'Connor 222 S Riverside Plz Ste 1500 Chicago IL 60606-6000 E-mail: rhammesfahr@cozen.com.

HAMMOND, FRANK JEFFERSON, III, lawyer; b. Moss Point, Miss., Sept. 18, 1953; s. Frank Jefferson Jr. and Jane (Laird) H.; m. Gale Ray, May 30, 1975; children: Katharine Blakeney, Benjamin Laird. BBA, U. Mis., 1974, JD, 1976; LLM, U. Fla., 1978. Bar: Miss. 1977, U.S. Dist. Ct. (no. dist.) Miss. 1977, U.S. Dist. Ct. (so. dist.) Miss. 1977, U.S. Ct. Appeals (5th cir.) 1977, U.S. Tax Ct. 1978, U.S. Ct. Appeals (11th cir.) 1980, U.S. Supreme Ct. 1989. Mem. Corlew, Krebs & Hammond, P.A., Pascagoula, Miss., 1978-84, Watkins & Eager, PLLC, Jackson, Miss., 1984—. Adj. prof. U. Ala. Sch. Law, Mobile, 1983; adj. faculty U. So. Miss., Gautier, 1983-84; bd. dirs. Merchants and Marine Bank, Pascagoula, Miss. Bd. trustees Dantzler Meml. Meth. Ch., Moss Point, 1981-84. U. Fla. Grad. Council fellow, 1977; Richard B. Stephens scholar, 1978. Mem. ABA, Miss. State Bar (chmn. sect. estates and trusts 1988-89), Phi Kappa Phi, Beta Alpha Psi, Beta Gamma Sigma, Omicron Delta Kappa. Banking, Property, real (including real estate development, water), Taxation, general. Home: PO Box 650 Jackson MS 39205-0650 Office: Watkins & Eager PLLC 400 E Capitol St Ste 300 Jackson MS 39201-2610

HAMMOND, GLENN BARRY, SR., lawyer, electrical engineer; b. Roanoke, Va., Sept. 3, 1947; s. Howard Reichard and Billie (Cromer) H.; m. Vickie McComb, Dec. 29, 1973 (div.); 1 child, Glenn Barry II. BA, Va. Mil. Inst., 1969; MBA, So. Ill. U., 1974; JD, U. Richmond, 1978; BSEE, Nova Coll., 1995. Bar: Va. 1979, U.S. Dist. Ct. (we. dist.) Va. 1979, U.S. Ct. Appeals (4th cir.) 1981, U.S. Ct. Mil. Appeals 1989, Air Force Ct. Mil. Rev. 1989, U.S. Supreme Ct., 1992. Assoc. Wilson, Hawthorne & Vogel, Roanoke, 1978-79; pvt. practice Roanoke, 1979-80, 86—; atty., advisor to chief adminstrv. law judge Social Security Adminstrn., HHS, Roanoke, 1980-86; ptnr. Wooten & Hart P.C., 1995-98; pres. R.F. Cons., Inc., Roanoke, Va., 1998—. Pres., bd. dirs. LCH Broadcasting Group, Inc. Roanoke. Editor: Psychiatry in Military Law, 1988. Sr. vice-comdr. Mil. Order World Wars, Roanoke, 1981. Col. JAGC, USAF, 1969-75, Res. 1975—. Mem. Air Commando Assn. (life), DAV (life), VFW (life), AFA (life), Nat. Mil. Intelligence Assn. (life), Armed Forces Comms. Electronics Assn., Nat. Orgn. Social Security Claimants Reps., Masons. Pension, profit-sharing, and employee benefits. E-mail: bluetig@earthlink.net.

HAMMOND, JANE LAURA, retired law librarian, lawyer; b. nr. Nashua, Iowa; d. Frank D. and Pauline Hammond. BA, U. Dubuque, 1950; MS, Columbia U., 1952; JD, Villanova U., 1965, LHD, 1993. Bar: Pa. 1965. Cataloguer Harvard Law Libr., 1952-54; asst. libr. Sch. Law Villanova (Pa.) U., 1954-62; libr. Sch. Law, Villanova (Pa.) U., 1962-76; prof. law Sch. Law Villanova (Pa.) U., 1965-76; law libr., prof. law Cornell U., Ithaca, N.Y., 1976-93. Adj. prof. Drexel U., 1971-74; mem. depository libr. coun. to pub. printer U.S. Govt. Printing Office, 1975-78; cons. Nat. Law Libr., Monrovia, Liberia, 1989. Fellow ALA; mem. ABA (coun. sect. legal edn. 1984-90, mem. com. on accreditation 1982-87, mem. com. on stds. rev. 1987-95), PEO, Coun. Nat. Libr. Assn. (sec.-treas. 1971-72, chmn. 1979-80), Am. Assn. Law Librs. (sec. 1965-70, pres. 1975-76). Episcopalian. Office: Cornell U Sch Law Myron Taylor Hall Ithaca NY 14853

HAMMONS, TERRENCE GORDON, JR., lawyer; b. Pitts., Feb. 3, 1973; s. Terrence Gordon and Anita Loraine Hammons; m. Tara Patterson, Sept. 7, 2002. BA in English, Coll. William & Mary, 1996; JD, Georgetown U., 1999. Bar: Va. 1999, DC 2001. Assoc. Hunton & Williams, Richmond, Va., 1999—2000, McLean, Va., 2000—01, Arnold & Porter, McLean, 2001—. Spkr. Nat. Youth Leadership Forum, Washington, 2001—02; tchr. Marshal Brennan Program, Washington, 2001—02. Mentor Thurgood Marshall Acad., Washington, 2001—02. Mem.: ABA (mem. bus. law sect.), Kappa Alpha Psi. Democrat. Baptist. Avocation: football. Corporate, general, Mergers and acquisitions, Finance. Home: 1313 Delafield Pl NW Washington DC 20011 Office: Arnold and Porter 1600 Tysons Blvd Mc Lean VA 22102 Business E-Mail: terrence_hammons@aproter.com.

HAMNER, LANCE DALTON, prosecutor; b. Fukuoka, Japan, Sept. 18, 1955; parents Am. citizens; s. Louie D. and Mary Louise (Sloan) H.; m. Karla Jean Cleverly, Sept. 22, 1980; children: Lance Dalton Jr., Nicholas James, Louie Alexander, Samuel Sean, Victoria Jean. BS summa cum laude, Weber State Coll., 1984; JD magna cum laude, Ind. U., 1987. Bar: Ind., US Dist. Ct. (no., so. dist.) Ind. 1988. Atty. Barnes & Thornburg, Indpls., 1988-89; dep. prosecuting atty. Marion County Prosecutor's Office, Indpls., 1989-90; pros. atty. Johnson County, Franklin, Ind., 1990—. Legal corr. WGGR Radio News, Indpls., 1995; adj. prof. law Sch. Law Ind. U., Indpls., 1995—96, Bloomington, 1996—98; frequent spkr. on legal topics including search and seizure and interrogation law; lectr. Ind. Continuing Legal Edn. Forum, Indpls., 1992; mem. faculty Newly-Elected Pros. Sch. Ind. Pros. Attys. Coun., 1999; mem. faculty Indpls. Police Acad., 1999, Ind. Police Corps, 2000—. Author: Indiana Search & Seizure Courtroom Manual, 2001, 2002; editor: Ind. Law Jour., 1987. Asst. scoutmaster Boy Scouts Am., Franklin, Ind., 1995-99, scoutmaster, 1999—. Mem. Nat. Dist. Attys. Assn., Assn. Govt. Attys. in Capital Litigation, Ind. Prosecuting Atty.'s Coun., Nat. Eagle Scout Assn., Order of the Coif. Republican. Mem. Lds Ch. Avocations: family, fitness, writing. Office: Prosecutor's Office Courthouse Annex N 80 S Jackson St Franklin IN 46131-2353

HAMNER, REGINALD TURNER, lawyer; b. Tuscaloosa, Ala., June 4, 1939; s. Raiford Samuel and Ellie Wells (Turner) H.; m. Anne Ellen Young, Nov. 8, 1969; children: Patrick Turner, William Christian. BS, U. Ala., 1961, JD, 1965. Bar: Ala. 1965, U.S. Dist. Ct. (mid. dist.) Ala. 1966, U.S. Ct. Appeals (5th cir.) 1966, U.S. Ct. Mil. Appeals 1968, U.S. Supreme Ct. 1968, U.S. Ct. Appeals (11th and 5th cirs.) 1981. Law clk. Supreme Ct. Ala., Montgomery, 1965; dir. legal-legis. affairs Med. Assn., State of Ala., 1968-69; sec., exec. dir. Ala. State Bar, Montgomery, 1969-94; ct. project coord. U.S. Dist. Ct. for Mid. Dist.) Ala., Montgomery, 1995—. Bd. dirs. S.E. br., YMCA, Montgomery, 1978-81; former legal counsel govtl. adv. panels investigating Ala. Prison System; vice chmn. State Child Welfare Com.; dir. Attys. Ins. Mut. of Ala., Inc.; sec., treas. Ala. Law Found., 1987-93; chmn. Ala. Rhodes Scholarship Com., 1989-94. With JAG, USAF, 1965-68, col. USAFR, ret. Fellow Am. Bar Found. (life, state chmn. 1994-95); mem. ABA (com. mem., mem. ho. of dels. 1972-76, 85-89, 93, 96—), Am. Judicature Soc., Nat. Assn. Bar Execs. (pres. 1978-79), Am. Soc. Assn. Execs. (commr. certification com. 1991-94), Ala. Coun. Assn. Execs. (pres. 1984), Ala. Law Inst. (council), Jud. Conf. U.S. Ct. Appeals (11th cir. 1981-95), U. Ala. Nat. Alumni Assn. (pres. 1989-90), Montgomery Country Club, Omicron Delta Kappa, Alpha Epsilon Delta, Phi Alpha Delta, Delta Tau Delta. Episcopalian. Home: 7518 Wynford Cir Montgomery AL 36117-7498 Office: US Courthouse One Church St Ste C-563 Montgomery AL 36104

HAMPSON, THOMAS MEREDITH, lawyer; b. Ann Arbor, Mich., Feb. 18, 1929; s. Harold Snover and Louise Susan (Goetchius) H.; m. Margaret H. Clark, Nov. 24, 1951 (div. Dec. 1969); children: Melissa Clark, Douglas Meredith; m. Zena Collier, Dec. 30, 1969. BA, Cornell U., 1951, LLB with distinction, 1955. Bar: N.Y. 1955, U.S. Dist. Ct. (we. dist.) N.Y. 1955, U.S. Supreme Ct. 1964. Assoc. Harris, Beach, Wilcox, Rubin & Levey, Rochester, N.Y., 1955-62; ptnr. Harris Beach, LLP, Rochester, 1962—. Vis. instr. Cornell Law Sch., Ithaca, N.Y., 1969-75. Radio broadcaster The Jazz Scene, 1960-80, Jazz Notes, 1979-81, Mostly Jazz, 1985--; newspaper columnist, 1985-88. Chmn. Monroe County Fair Campaign Practices Com., Rochester, 1977-91; trustee Rochester Pub. Libr., 1976-98; dir. Cornell Lab. Ornithology, Ithaca, N.Y., 1984-90, Hawk Mountain Sanctuary Assn., 1990-98, Rundel Libr. Found., 1995—; bd. dirs. N.Y. State Civil Liberties Union, N.Y.C., 1963-69; commr. Rochester Civil Svc. Commn., 1997—, chmn. 2000—. 1st lt. USAF, 1951-53. Recipient Civil Liberties award N.Y. Civil Liberties Union, Genesee Valley chpt., 1987. Mem. ABA, N.Y. State Bar Assn., Monroe County Bar Assn., City Club (pres. 1965-66), Philosophers' Club (pres. 1985-88). Democrat. Unitarian Universalist. Avocations: birding, jazz. Commercial, contracts (including sales of goods; commercial financing), Corporate, general, Mergers and acquisitions. Home: 83 Berkeley St Rochester NY 14607-2207 Office: Harris Beach LLP 99 Garnsey Rd Pittsford NY 14534

HAMPTON, VERNE CHURCHILL, II, lawyer; b. Pontiac, Mich., Jan. 5, 1934; s. Verne Churchill and Mildred (Peck) H.; m. Stephanie Hall, Oct. 5, 1973; children: J. Howard, Timothy H., Julia C. Thibodeau. BA, Mich. State U., 1955; LLB, U. Va., 1958. Bar: Mich. 1958. Since practiced in, Detroit; ptnr. firm Dickinson Wright, 1967—. Bd. dirs., sec. Carhartt, Inc., R & R Radio Corp. Mem. Mich. Rep. Fin. Com.; bd. dirs. Detroit Bus./Edn. Alliance; corp. mem. Boys' Clubs Met. Detroit. Mem. ABA, State Bar Mich. (chmn. bus. law sect. 1980-84), Detroit Athletic Club, Country Club Detroit, Yondotega Club, Sigma Alpha Epsilon, Phi Alpha Delta. Republican. Episcopalian. Corporate, general, Securities. Home: 360 Provencal Rd Grosse Pointe Farms MI 48236-2959 Office: Dickinson Wright PLLC 500 Woodward Ave Ste 4000 Detroit MI 48226-3416 E-mail: vhampton@dickinson-wright.com.

HANAMI, TADASHI, legal educator emeritus; b. Tokyo, Feb. 15, 1930; s. Katsujiro and Sizuko (Sugiura) H.; 1 child, Tadaaki; m. Yasuko Sakukawa, June 1, 1990. B.L., Tokyo U., 1953, S.JD, 1960; Hon. doctor, Cath. U. of Lueven, Belgium, 1985, U. St. Martin de Porres, Peru, 1999. Prof. law Sophia U., Tokyo, 1965-99, prof. emeritus, 1999—; dean Sophia Law Sch., Tokyo, 1979-82; pub. commr. Labor Rels. Commn., Tokyo, 1967-79, chmn. ctrl. labor stds. coun., 1989-99, chmn., 1998—, Japan Inst. Labor, 2001—. Vis. prof. Cath. U. Leuven, 1977-78, Harvard Law Sch., Cambridge, Mass., 1984-85, 91. Author: Labor Relations in Japan Today, 1979, Labor Law and Industrial Relations in Japan, 1979; editor: Industrial Conflict Resolution in Market Economy. Rsch. grantee Humboldt Stupendiate, 1959-60; rsch. fellow Tokyo U., 1953-58, Japan Inst. Labor, Tokyo, 1958-65, Fulbright fellow, 1964-65, Ford Found., 1981-82. Mem. Internat. Assn. Indsl. Rels. (pres.), Internat. Assn. Labor Law and Social Security, Japan Labor Law Assn. (exec.). Avocation: tennis. Office: Japan Inst Labor Shinjuku Monolith 2-3-1 Tokyo Nishishinjuku 163-0926 Japan E-mail: thanami@jil.go.jp.

HANAU, PETER WOLFGANG, law educator; b. Berlin, July 13, 1935; s. Arthur Ferdinand and Hilde (Moll) H.; m. Eva Charlotte; children: Paul, Katharina, Max. Referendar, U. Göttingen, Fed. Republic of Germany, 1958; Dr. of Law, U. Göttinger, Fed. Republic of Germany, 1963, habilitation, 1968; Dr. of Law (hon.), Uppsala U., Sweden, 1989; LLD (hon.), Ritsumeikau U., Kyoto, Japan, 1990. Asst. prof. U. Göttingen, 1960-68; prof. pvt. law Free U., Berlin, 1968-71; prof. labor and civil law U. Cologne, Fed. Republic of Germany, 1971—. Rector U. Cologne, 1986-89. Co-author: Labour Law (9 edits.); contbr. articles to profl. jours. Mem. Deutscher Juristentag (bd. dirs.), Deutscher Arbeits Gerichtsverband (pres.), Rotary. Evangelican. Office: U Cologne Albertus-Magnus-Platz D-5000 Cologne 41 Germany

HANCOCK, JONATHAN CROMWELL, lawyer; b. Paducah, Ky., Apr. 19, 1971; s. William Rowland and Susan Cromwell Hancock. BS, Millsaps Coll., 1993; JD, U. Miss., Oxford, 1996. Bar: Tenn. 1996, U.S. Dist. Ct. Ark. 1998. Law clk. Cir. Ct. Judge John Daughaday, Mayfield, Ky., summer 1994; assoc. McKnight, Hudson, Lewis, Ford & Harrison, Memphis, 1996-97, Glankler Brown PLLC, Memphis, 1998—. Co-editor: Bur. of Nat. Affairs Employment Discrimination Law Chapter 42 Attorneys Fees, 1997. Republican. Methodist. Federal civil litigation, General civil litigation, Labor (including EEOC, Fair Labor Standards Act, labor-management relations, NLRB, OSHA). Office: Glankler Brown PLLC 1700 One Commerce Sq Memphis TN 38103

HANCOCK, S. LEE, business executive; b. Knoxville, Tenn., Aug. 11, 1955; s. Melton Donald and Alma Helen (McDaniel) Hancock; m. Kathleen Ann Koll, July 26, 1986. BS summa cum laude, Southwest Mo. State U., 1975; JD cum laude, So. Meth. U., 1979. CPA Mo.; bar: Mo. 1979, U.S. Dist. Ct. (we. dist.) Mo. 1979, U.S. tax Ct. 1982, U.S. Ct. Claims Calif. 1983, Calif. 1988, U.S. Supreme Ct. 1992. Assoc. Blackwell, Sanders, Matheny, Weary & Lombardi, Kansas City, Mo., 1979-83, ptnr., 1984-88, Allen, Matkins, Leck, Gamble & Mallory, Newport Beach, Calif., 1988-98, of counsel, 1998-99; pres., chmn., CEO, Go2 Systems, Inc., Newport Beach, Calif., 1998—2001, CEO, 1998—2002, Go2 Directory Sys., 2002—. Bd. dirs. Calif./Orange County Venture Forum, Orange County Cmty. Found., sec., 1994—95, pres., 1995—97; mem. Young Pres. Orgn., 2000—. Mem.: ABA, Lawyers Assn. Kansas City (pres. young lawyers sect. 1986—87, bd. dirs. 1986—87), Orange County Bar Assn., Mo. Bar Assn., Calif. Bar Assn., Young Execs. Am. (bd. dirs. Orange County chpt. 1992—96, pres. Orange County chpt. 1994—95), Order of Coif. Republican. Avocations: flying, sailing, skiing, photography. Home: 4 Hampshire Ct Newport Beach CA 92660-4933 Office: Go2 Systems Inc Ste 300 18400 Von Karman Ave Irvine CA 92612-1514

HAND, BRUCE GEORGE, lawyer; b. Oak Park, Ill., Apr. 11, 1942; s. Robert David and Dorothy Marie (Riedel) H.; m. Carolyn Jeanne Coleman, July 9, 1966; children: Keith John, Tracey Ellen, Katherine Anne. BA in Liberal Arts & Scis., U. Ill., 1964; JD, U. Oreg., 1969. Bar: Wash. 1969, U.S. Dist. Ct. (we. dist.) Wash. 1970. Assoc. Brumbach & Lamb, Seattle, 1969-74; pvt. practice Bellevue, Wash., 1974—. Trustee St. Thomas Sch., Medina, Wash., 1975-85, pres., 1985; trustee, pres. Hamlin Robinson Sch., Seattle, 1986-87. 1st lt. U.S. Army, 1964-66. Mem. Washington State Bar Assn., King County Bar Assn., East King County Bar Assn., Estate Planning Coun. Seattle. Republican. Episcopalian. Avocations: securities investment, reading. Estate planning, Family and matrimonial, Probate (including wills, trusts). Home: 2639 82nd Ave NE Medina WA 98039-1507 Office: 845 106th Ave NE Ste 200 Bellevue WA 98004-4308 E-mail: bhand52@aol.com.

HAND, JAMES STANLEY, lawyer; b. Mt. Kisco, N.Y., Mar. 14, 1949; m. Gail Stewart; children: Jordan, Alison. BA, UCLA, 1971; JD, U. N.D., 1980. Bar: N.D. 1980, U.S. Dist. Ct. N.D. 1980, U.S. Ct. Appeals (8th cir.) 1983. Assoc. Anderson and Assocs., Grand Forks, N.D., 1980-82; pvt. practice law Grand Forks, 1982-84; ptnr. Hand & Triplett, Grand Forks, 1984-87; state rep. for U.S. Senator Kent Conrad, 1987—. Adj. grad. faculty Embry-Riddle Aeronautical U., Grand Forks AFB, 1983; lectr. U. N.D., 1985-86. Pub. mem. N.D. Bd. Nursing, Bismarck, 1986-87; mem. Grand Forks County Child Care Resource and Referral Adv. Bd., 1991-96, Grand Forks Fed. Exec. Assn. Bd., 1996—. Recipient Hammer award Nat. Partnership for Reinventing Govt., 1998. Mem.: N.D. Bar Assn. Government contracts and claims, Immigration, naturalization, and customs, Legislative. Office: 102 N 4th St Grand Forks ND 58203-3738

HANDEL, RICHARD CRAIG, lawyer; b. Hamilton, Ohio, Aug. 11, 1945; s. Alexander F. and Marguerite (Wilks) H.; m. Katharine Jean Carter, Jan. 10, 1970. AB, U. Mich., 1967; MA, Mich. State U., 1968; JD summa cum laude, Ohio State U., 1974; LLM in Taxation, NYU, 1978. Bar: Ohio 1974, S.C. 1983, U.S. Dist. Ct. (so. dist.) Ohio 1975, U.S. Dist. Ct. S.C. 1979, U.S. Tax Ct. 1977, U.S. Ct. Appeals (4th cir.) 1979, U.S. Supreme Ct. 1979; cert. tax specialist. Assoc. Smith & Schnacke, Dayton, Ohio,

1974-77; asst. prof. U. S.C. Sch. Law, Columbia, 1978-83; ptnr. Nexsen, Pruet, Jacobs & Pollard, Columbia, 1983-87, Moore & Van Allen, Columbia, 1987-88, Nexsen Pruet Jacobs & Pollard, Columbia, 1988-89; chief tax policy and appeals S.C. Tax Commn., Columbia, 1989-95; chief coun. Policy S.C. Dept. of Revenue, Columbia, 1995—2003, gen. counsel, 2003—. Adj. prof. U. S.C. Sch. Law, 1990—2001. Contbr. articles to legal jours. Bd. dirs. Friends of Richland County Pub. Libr., 1993-99. With U.S. Army, 1969-70, Vietnam. Recipient Outstanding Law Prof. award, 1980-81; Gerald L. Wallace scholar, 1977-78. Mem. ABA (com. state and local taxes, chmn. membership com. 1997—, vice-chmn. com. tax procedures 1993-94, com. stds. tax practice, sec. 2003—), S.C. Bar Assn., Order of Coif. Office: SC Dept Revenue PO Box 125 301 Gervais St Columbia SC 29214-0702 E-mail: rickch@aol.com., handelr@sctax.org.

HANDELSMAN, LAWRENCE MARC, lawyer; b. N.Y.C., Jan. 17, 1945; s. David and Ruth (Litner) H.; m. Sara Pruzan, June 10, 1967; children: Sharon, Carolyn. BBA, CCNY, 1965; JD, NYU, 1968. Bar: N.Y. 1968, U.S. Ct. Mil. Appeals 1969, U.S. Dist. Ct. (so. and ea. dists.) N.Y. 1973, U.S. Ct. Appeals (2d cir.) 1973, Fla. 1978. Assoc. Stroock & Stroock & Lavan, N.Y.C., 1973-78, ptnr., 1979—. Served to capt. JAGC, U.S. Army, 1969-73. Mem. ABA (bus. bankruptcy com. 1969—), Assn. of Bar of City of N.Y. (bankruptcy com. 1974-77, 1985—). Bankruptcy, Federal civil litigation. Home: 22 Scarsdale Farm Rd Scarsdale NY 10583-1919 Office: Stroock & Stroock & Lavan 180 Maiden Ln Fl 36 New York NY 10038-4937 E-mail: lhandelsman@stroock.com.

HANDFORD, LEE A. lawyer; b. Iowa City, Iowa, Dec. 14, 1956; m. Mary Jackson; 1 child, Rylander. BS, Excelsior Coll., Albany, N.Y., 1989; JD, Tulane U., New Orleans, 1991. Bar: Pa. 1991, U.S. Ct. Mil. Appeals 1991, Va. 1998, U.S. Ct. Appeals (4th cir.) 1998, U.S. Dist. Ct. (ea. dist.) Va. 1998, U.S. Dist. Ct. (we. dist.) Va. 1998. Staff atty. U.S. Coast Guard, Office of Chief Counsel, Washington, 1991—94; asst. U.S. del. Internat. Maritime Orgn., Legal Com., Washington, 1992—94; staff atty. U.S. Coast Guard, Atlantic Area, Portsmouth, Va., 1994—98; spl. asst. U.S. atty. U.S. Atty.'s Office, Norfolk, Va., 1996—98; assoc. McGuireWoods LLP, Norfolk, Va., 1998—. Port dir. Southeastern Admiralty Law Inst., Norfolk, 2000—01. Contbr. Comdr. (sel.) U.S. Coast Guard, 2001—02, NY, NY and Guantanamo Bay, Cuba. Decorated Coast Guard Commendation Medal w/Gold Star USCG Atlantic Area, Coast Guard Achievement Medal w/Gold Star and O Device USCG Port Security Unit 305, Meritorious Svc. Medal U.S. Army 3rd Bn, 7th Spl. Forces Gp, Armed Forces Expeditionary Medal w/Bronze Star USCG Port Security Unit 305; recipient Best Comment award, Tulane Maritime Law Jour., 1991, Elliot B. Nixon prize, Maritime Law Assn. of U.S., 1996. Mem.: Norfolk and Portsmouth Bar Assn., Maritime Law Assn. of the U.S., Southeastern Admiralty Law Inst., Hampton Rds. Maritime Assn., Pi Kappa Phi. Corporate, general, Mergers and acquisitions, Admiralty. Office: McGuireWoods LLP 101 W Main St Ste 9000 Norfolk VA 23510-1655 E-mail: lhandford@mcguirewoods.com.

HANDLEMAN, AARON L. lawyer; b. Bridgeport, Conn., Mar. 31, 1946; s. Howard W. and Beatrice (Kaplan) H.; m. Sandra R. Landow, Aug. 31, 1969; children: Michelle, Jessica. BA, Marietta Coll., 1968; JD, George Washington U., 1971. Bar: D.C. 1971, U.S. Dist. Ct. D.C. 1971, Md. 1972, U.S. Supreme Ct. 1978. Ptnr. Danzansky, Dickey, Tydings et al, Washington, 1971-81, Finley, Kumble, Wagner, Heine, Underberg, Manley & Casey, Washington, 1981-87, Laxalt, Washington, Perito & Dubuc, 1988-90, Eccleston & Wolf, Washington, 1990—. Gen. counsel, bd. dirs. Cultural Alliance Greater Washington, 1981-89; trustee Marietta Coll., Ohio, 1985-90, 92—. Named Outstanding Young Alumni Marietta Coll., 1981. Mem. Marietta Coll. Alumni Assn. (pres. 1990-92). Democrat. Jewish. Federal civil litigation, Insurance, Professional liability. Home: 11713 Le Havre Dr Potomac MD 20854-3175 Office: Eccleston & Wolf 2001 S St NW Washington DC 20009

HANDLER, ARTHUR M. lawyer; b. N.Y.C., Feb. 16, 1937; BS, Queens Coll., 1957; LLB, Columbia U., 1960. Bar: N.Y. 1960, U.S. Dist. Ct. (ea. dist.) N.Y. 1960, U.S. Dist. Ct. (so. dist.) N.Y. 1963, U.S. Tax Ct. 1971, U.S. Ct. Appeals (2d cir.) 1971, U.S. Supreme Ct. 1965. Staff counsel SEC, Washington, 1960-61; law clk. to Judge Richard H. Levet, U.S. Dist. Ct. for So. Dist.N.Y., N.Y.C., 1961-62; asst. U.S. atty. So. Dist. N.Y., N.Y.C., 1962-65; assoc. Proskauer, Rose, Goetz & Mendelsohn, N.Y.C., 1965-67, Golenbock and Barell, N.Y.C., 1967-70, ptnr., 1970-89, Whitman & Ransom, N.Y.C., 1990-93, Burns Handler & Burns, N.Y.C., 1993-99, Handler & Goodman, N.Y.C., 1999—. Arbitrator Am. Stock Exchange, N.Y.C., 1986—. Vol. atty. Pres.'s Com. for Civil Rights under Law, Jackson, Miss., 1966. Mem. ABA, N.Y. State Bar Assn., Bar Assn. of City of N.Y., Fed. Bar Council, Am. Arbitration Assn. (arbitrator 1969—). Clubs: University (N.Y.C.); Lords Valley Country (Hawley, Pa.) (bd. govs. 1977-80). Avocations: golf, skiing, theatre, travel. Federal civil litigation, General civil litigation, State civil litigation. Office: Handler & Goodman LLP 805 3d Ave New York NY 10022

HANDLER, HAROLD ROBERT, lawyer; b. Jersey City, Aug. 24, 1935; s. Morris Sidney and Fan (Krieger) Handler; m. Lynne Tishman Handler; children from previous marriage: Maren, Jeremy, Jolyon. BS, Lehigh U., 1957; LLM, Columbia U., 1961. Bar: N.Y. 1961, U.S. Tax Ct. 1963, U.S. Ct. Appeals (2d cir.) 1980. Attys., advisor U.S. Tax Ct., Washington, 1961-63; assoc. Simpson Thacher & Bartlett, N.Y.C., 1963-69, ptnr., 1970-97, of counsel, 1998—. Adj. assoc. prof. law NYU, 1978-80. Chmn. fin. com., citizens adv. com. Met. Transp. Authority, N.Y.C., 1975—79; trustee Citizens Budget Commn.; chmn. bd., chmn. exec. com. Jewish Cmty. Ctr. in Manhattan, N.Y.C., 1992—2001; trustee Jewish Communal Fund, 1997—. Fellow Am. Coll. Tax Counsel; mem. ABA, N.Y. State Bar Assn. (chmn. subcom. tax sect. 1979-83, mem. exec. com. tax sect. 1990—, officer 1996-2000, chair 1999-20000), Assn. of Bar of City of N.Y. (chmn. tax com. 1983-86, mem. tax coun. 1990-98), Am. Law Inst., Inst. Fed. Taxation (panelist), Inst. Securities Regulation (panelist). Corporate taxation, Personal income taxation.

HANDLEY, GERALD MATTHEW, lawyer, educator; b. Phila., Dec. 7, 1942; s. John F. and Helen E. (Gerdelman) H.; m. Sandra I. Martin, June 13, 1970; children: Christopher, Elizabeth. BS, La Salle Coll., Phila., 1965; JD, U. Mo., Kansas City, 1972. Bar: Mo. 1972, U.S. Dist. Ct. (we. dist.) Mo. 1972, U.S.Supreme Ct., 1976, U.S. Ct. Appeals (8th and 10th cirs.) 1980, U.S Dist. Ct. Kans. 1998. Asst. pub. defender Office Pub. Defender, Kansas City, Mo., 1972-73, 1st asst. pub. defender, 1973-75, interim pub. defender, 1975-76; ptnr. Speck & Handley, Kansas City, 1980-90; pvt. practice Law Offices of G. Handley, Kansas City, 1991-92, 93—; ptnr. Handley Larsen, Kansas City, 1992-93. Lectr. Rockhurst Coll., Kansas City, 1976-78; instr. U. Mo. Sch. Law. Contbr. chpts. to law books. Pres., Home Owners Assn., Kansas City, 1980. Served with U.S. Army, 1966-67, Vietnam. Fellow Am. Bd. Criminal Lawyers; mem. ABA, NACDL, Fed. Bar Assn., Mo. Bar Assn., (Lon Hocker Trial Lawyer award 1977), Mo. Assn. Criminal Def. Lawyers (pres. 1980, hon. bd. dirs.), U.S. Supreme Ct. Bar Assn., 8th Cir. Bar Assn., Kansas City Met. Bar Assn. Roman Catholic. Avocations: golf, gardening. Criminal. Home: 22 W 54th St Kansas City MO 64112-2816 Office: 1100 Main Ste 2800 Kansas City MO 64105 E-mail: ghandley@swbell.net.

HANDLEY, LEON HUNTER, lawyer; b. Lakeland, Fla., Sept. 9, 1927; s. Driskle Hubert and Mamie (Denmark) H.; m. Mary Virginia Wolfe, May 2, 1953; children: Leon Hunter, Mary Ellen, Laura Catherine, Leann Virginia. BSBA with honors, U. Fla., 1949, JD, 1951. Bar: Fla. 1951, U.S. Dist. Ct. (so. dist.) Fla. 1952, U.S. Dist. Ct. (mid. dist.) Fla. 1962, U.S. Supreme Ct. 1956, U.S. Ct. Appeals (5th cir.) 1960, U.S. Ct. Appeals (11th cir.) 1981. Pres. Gurney & Handley, Orlando, Fla., 1951—. Bd. dirs. Orlando/Tampa Cracker Groves, Inc., Orlando, 1964—; v.p., bd. dirs. So. Indsl. Savs. Bank, Orlando, Claude H. Wolfe, Inc., Orlando, 1969—; pres., chmn. bd. dirs. Mine & Mill Supply Co., Lakeland, 1966—; gen. counsel, life dir., past pres. Cen. Fla. Fair; chmn. bd. trustees Sta. WMFE-TV. Pres. Chesley Magruder Charitable Trust; elder Presbyn. Ch.; trustee Lake Highland Prep. Sch., Orlando. Warrant officer U.S. Maritime Svc., 1945-46, ETO; sgt. U.S. Army, 1946-48, Korea; capt. USAFR, 1949-59. Named one of Best Lawyers in Am.; named to U. Fla. Hall of Fame. Fellow Am. Coll. Trial Lawyers; mem. ABA, Am. Bd. Trial Advocates (Fla. Trial Lawyer of Yr. 1966, advocate), Orange County Bar Assn. (past pres.), Fla. Bar Assn. (past pres. sta. jr. bar sect., bd. govs. 1959-60), Fedn. Ins. and Corp. Counsel, Internat. Assn. Def. Counsel, Assn. Def. Trial Attys., Trial Attys. Am., Am. Judicature Soc., Pres.'s Coun. (founder U. Fla. chpt.), Citrus Club, Orlando Country Club, Univ. Club, Masons (grand orator Fla. 1982, 86), K.T., Shriners, Scottish Rite (33d degree, insp. gen. hon. 1979), Rotary (pres. Orlando chpt. 1984, Paul Harris fellow), Travelers' Century Club, Fla. Blue Key (pres. 1951), Phi Delta Phi, Alpha Tau Omega (pres. U. of Fla. chpt. 1951), Phi Kappa Phi, Alpha Kappa Psi, Beta Gamma Sigma. Republican. Avocations: jogging, handball. General civil litigation, Personal injury (including property damage). Home: 1800 Turnberry Ter Orlando FL 32804-6015 Office: Gurney & Handley 225 E Robinson St Ste 450 Orlando FL 32801-1905

HANDLIN, DANITA L. lawyer; b. Ft. Ord, Calif., Oct. 25, 1963; d. Harry G. Jones Jr. and Joanne M. Jones; m. Dale L. Handlin Jr., May 11, 1997; 1 child, Alexandra Dayle. BBA, U. Houston, 1991, JD, 1998. Bar: Tex. 1999. Assoc. Allison Jones & Assocs., Houston, 1999—2000; atty. pvt. practice, 2000—. Mem.: ABA (mem. family sect.), Coll. of State Bar Tex., Assn. Women Attys., Houston Bar Assn. (mem. family sect.). Avocations: travel, scuba diving, reading. Family and matrimonial. Office: 11511 Katy Fwy Ste 540 Houston TX 77079 Fax: 281-752-8160. E-mail: dlhandlin@hotmail.com.

HANDLIN, JOSEPH JASON, lawyer; b. N.Y.C., Feb. 21, 1952; s. Nathan and Beatrice (Greenberg) H.; m. Laura Sara Ellin, Aug. 18, 1985. AB magna cum laude, Harvard U., 1973; JD, NYU, 1976. Bar: N.Y. 1977, U.S. Dist. Ct. (so. and ea. dists.) N.Y. 1977. Gen. counsel Muzak Corp., N.Y.C., 1977-78; assoc. Estroff, Frankel & Waldman, N.Y.C., 1978-80, Guggenheimer & Untermyer, N.Y.C., 1980-84, Dahan & Nowick, N.Y.C., 1984-86, Epstein, Becker, Borsody & Green P.C., N.Y.C., 1986-87; ptnr. Surkin & Handlin, N.Y.C., 1987-98; prin. Law Offices of Joseph J. Handlin, N.Y.C., 1998—. Adj. instr. Cardozo Law Sch., N.Y.C., 1983—88; asst. prof. NYU, 1988—2002, assoc. prof., 2002—. Recipient Lewis F. Powell, Jr. Medal for Excellence in Adv. Am. Coll. Trial Lawyers, 1975. Mem.: ABA, N.Y. County Lawyers Assn., Assn. of Bar of City of NY (sec. com. on small law firm mgmt. 1993—96, chair 1996—99, com. on real property law 1999—2002, com. on land use planning and zoning 2002—), N.Y. State Bar Assn. (ho. of dels. 1999—2003), Harvard Club (sec. admissions com. 1986—87, chmn. admissions com. 1990—92, bd. mgrs. 1992—95, sec. club 1996—2000, v.p. 2000—02, pres. 2002—). Property, real (including real estate development, water). Home: 345 S End Ave Apt 4N New York NY 10280-1064 Office: Law Offices of Joseph J Handlin 75 Maiden Ln Fl 3 New York NY 10038-4810 E-mail: jhandlin@ksi.com.

HANDZLIK, JAN LAWRENCE, lawyer; b. N.Y.C., Sept. 21, 1945; s. Felix Munso and Anna Jean Handzlik; children: Grant, Craig, Anna. BA, U. So. Calif., 1967; JD, UCLA, 1970. Bar: Calif. 1971, U.S. Dist. Ct. (cen. dist.) Calif. 1971, U.S. Ct. Appeals (9th cir.) 1971, U.S. Supreme Ct. 1975, U.S. Tax Ct. 1979, U.S. Dist. Ct. (no. dist.) Calif. 1979, U.S. Dist. Ct. (ea. dist.) Calif. 1981, U.S. Dist. Ct. (so. dist.) Calif. 1982, U.S. Ct. Appeals (2d cir.) 1984, U.S. Ct. Internat. Trade 1984. Law clk. to Hon. Francis C. Whelan, U.S. Dist. Ct. (cen. dist.) Calif., L.A., 1970-71; asst. U.S. atty. fraud and spl. prosecutions section criminal div. U.S. Dept. Justice, L.A., 1971-76; assoc. Greenberg & Glusker, L.A., 1976-78; ptnr., prin. Stilz, Boyd, Levine & Handzlik, P.C., L.A., 1978-84; prin. Jan Lawrence Handzlik, P.C., L.A., 1984-91; ptnr. Kirkland & Ellis, L.A., 1991—. Del. U.S. Ct. Appeals for 9th cir. Jud. Conf., L.A., 1983-85; counsel to ind. Christopher Commn. Study of the L.A. Police Dept., 1991; dep. gen. counsel to Hon. William H. Webster, spl. advisor to L.A. Police Commn. for Investigation of Response to Urban Disorders, 1992; mem. adv. com. for Office of L.A. County Dist. Atty., 1994-96; mem. standing com. on discipline U.S. Dist. Ct. Ctrl. Dist. Calif., 1997—2001, blue ribbon Rampart rev. panel for investigation of L.A.P.D. handling of Rampart corruption incident, 2003; deputy gen. counsel Rampart ind. rev. panel for investigation of police corruption L.A. Police Commn., 2000; mem. bd. adv. Money Laundering, Terrorism, and Financial Institutions, 2002. Mem. editl. adv. bd. DOJ Alert, 1994-95. Bd. dirs. Friends of Child Advs., L.A., 1987-91, Inner City Law Ctr., L.A., 1993-2000; mem. bd. judges Nat. and Calif. Moot Ct. Competition Teams, UCLA Moot Ct. honors program. Mem.: ABA (sect. criminal justice nat. com. on white collar crime 1991—, co-chair securities fraud subcom. 1994—98, west coast white collar crime com. 1996—98, vice chair 1998—2000, criminal justice sect. nominating com. 2000—01, chair 2000—02, gov. coun. 2002—, mem. sect. litig., chair 2000—02, vice chair 1998—2000), L.A. County Bar Assn. (coms. on fed. cts. 1988—2001, chair criminal practice subcom. 1989—90, fed. appts. evaluation 1989—93, white collar crime com. 1991—97, exec. com. criminal justice sect. 1997—2002, fed. cts. coord. com. 2001—), State Bar Calif. (sects. on criminal law and litigation), Fed. Bar Assn. (exec. com. 1997—), Chancery Club. Federal civil litigation, State civil litigation, Criminal. Office: Kirkland & Ellis 777 S Figueroa St Ste 3700 Los Angeles CA 90017-5835 E-mail: jan_handzlik@la.kirkland.com.

HANE, JEFFREY W. lawyer; b. Brainerd, Minn., Jan. 31, 1963; s. Thomas Loren and Donna Jean Hane; m. Linda Rae Bradseth, Aug. 14, 1993. BA in Polit. Sci., Bemidji State U., 1986; MA in Religion, So. Calif. Coll., 1992; JD, U. N.D., 1993. Bar: Minn. 1993, N.D. 1993, U.S. Dist. Ct. (no. dist.) Minn. 1993, U.S. Dist. Ct. N.D. 2001, U.S. Ct. Appeals (8th cir.) 1994. Atty. Brink, Sobolik, Severson, Malm, Hallock, Minn., 1992—; asst. county atty. Kittson County, Minn., Hallock, Minn., 1994—. Mem. Minn. State Bar Assn., N.D. State Bar Assn., Minn. Trial Lawyers Assn., Nat. Lawyers Assn., Christian Legal Soc., Order of the Coif, Order of Barristers. Avocations: carpenter, cross-country skiing. Office: Brink Sobolik Severson Malm 217 S Birch Ave Hallock MN 56728

HANES, JOHN GRIER, lawyer, state legislator; b. Cheyenne, Wyo., 1936; s. Harold H. and Mary Elizabeth H.; m. Liv Paul; children: Greg, Clint. BS in Bus. Adminstrn., U. Wyo., 1958, JD, 1960. Bar: Wyo. 1960, U.S. Ct. Appeals (10th cir.) 1960, U.S. Ct. Mil. Appeals, 1960, U.S. Supreme Ct. 1964. Dep. sec. of state State of Wyo., 1963-65; prin. Burke Woodard & Bishop, Cheyenne, 1965-90, of counsel, 1990—; atty. Wyo. Senate, 1967-71; mcpl. judge City of Cheyenne, 1970-73; mem. Burke, Woodard & O'Donnell, Cheyenne, Wyo., until 1990; of counsel Woodard & O'Donnell, P.C. and predecessor firms, Cheyenne, Wyo., 1990—; mem. Wyo. Ho. of Reps., 1993-99, Wyo. Senate, 1999—. Chmn. Senate Jud. Com. Vol. Cheyenne Frontier Days; mem. Heels; Rep. precinct committeeman, 1976-94. With U.S. Army JAGC. Mem. C. of C., Rotary (pres. 1982-83, dist. gov. 1990-91), Sigma Nu. Avocations: outdoor sports, travelling. Home: 848 Creighton St Cheyenne WY 82009-3231 Office: 1720 Carey Ave 600 Boyd Bldg Cheyenne WY 82001-4429

HANFORD, M. SHAE, lawyer; b. Rochester, N.Y., Jan. 15, 1948; d. Henry S. and Eleanor (McNamara) H.; m. William Lindenfelser; 1 child, Luis. BA, U. Toronto, Ont., Can., 1969; MA, Boston Coll., 1971; JD magna cum laude, SUNY, Buffalo, 1980. Bar: N.Y. 1981. Instr. St. John Fisher Coll., Rochester, 1971-73; counselor Monroe County Family Ct., Rochester, 1973-75; rsch. analyst Ctr. for Govtl. Rsch., Rochester, 1976-77; assoc. Mousaw Vigdor Reeves Heilbronner & Kroll, Rochester, 1980-87; asst. prof. bus. law Rochester Inst. Tech., 1987-88; sr. dep. county atty. Monroe County, Rochester, 1988—. Bd. dirs. Linkages, Rochester, 1996—. Avocations: mountain climbing, travel. Home: 68 Crosman Ter Rochester NY 14620-1828 Office: Monroe County 39 W Main St Ste 407 Rochester NY 14614-1476

HANGLEY, WILLIAM THOMAS, lawyer; b. Long Beach, N.Y., Mar. 11, 1941; s. Charles Augustus and Faustine Charmillot H.; m. Mary Dupree Hangley, July 24, 1965; children: Michele Dupree, William Thomas, Katherine Charmillot. BS in Music, SUNY-Coll. at Fredonia, 1963; LLB cum laude, U. Pa., 1966. Bar: Pa. 1966, U.S. Ct. Appeals (3d cir.) 1966, U.S. Dist. Ct. (ea. dist.) Pa. 1966. Assoc. Schnader, Harrison, Segal & Lewis, Phila., 1966-69; mem., CEO, Hangley Connolly Epstein Chicco Foxman & Ewing, Phila, 1969-94, CEO Hangley Aronchick Segal & Pudlin, 1994—; judge protem Phila. Ct. of Common Pleas, 1991—; mem. adv. bd. Pub. Interest Law Ctr. Phila. Contbr. articles to profl. publs. Bd. dirs. Ams. for Dem. Action, 1972-81. Fellow Am. Coll. Trial Lawyers (chmn. Com. on Fed. Rules of Evidence, 2001-, mem. Pa. State Com.), Am. Bar Found.; mem. ABA (co-chmn. litigation sect. com. on fed. procedure 1990-95—, co-chair task force on merit selection of judges 1995-97, mem. task force on discovery 1997-98, task force on judiciary 1998—), Pa. Bar Assn. (corp. and litigation coms., securities and antitrust subcoms., ho. dels. 1989-92), ACLU, Am. Law Inst., Phila. Bar Assn., Legal Club (v.p. 2001--), Jr. Legal Club, Order of Coif, U. Pa. Inns of Ct. (master of the bench). Roman Catholic. Federal civil litigation, Securities. Office: Hangley Aronchick Segal & Pudlin 1 Logan Sq Fl 27 Philadelphia PA 19103-6995

HANKIN, MITCHELL ROBERT, lawyer; b. Phila., May 16, 1949; s. Samuel and Harriet (Cohen) H. BA, Trinity Coll., Hartford, Conn., 1971; JD, Columbia U., 1974. Bar: Pa. 1974, U.S. Dist. Ct. (ea. dist.) Pa. 1975, U.S. Ct. Appeals (3d cir.) 1975. Assoc. Blank, Romeklaus, Comisky, Phila., 1974-75; asst. U.S. atty. U.S. Atty.'s Office, Phila., 1975-76; ptnr. Hankin Enterprises, Willow Grove, Pa., 1976—. Bd. dirs. Bank of Old York, Bank of King of Prussia (Pa.), Royal Bank of Pa. Mem. ABA, Pa. Bar Assn., Montgomery County Bar Assn., Phila. Bar Assn., Phi Beta Kappa. State civil litigation, Commercial, contracts (including sales of goods; commercial financing), Property, real (including real estate development, water). Home: 1115 Barberry Rd Bryn Mawr PA 19010-1907

HANKS, GEORGE CAROL, JR., state judge; b. Breaux Bridge, La., Sept. 25, 1964; s. George Carol and Quenola Reese Hanks; m. Stacey L. Hanks, Apr. 29, 1995. JD, Harvard U., 1989; BA summa cum laude, La. State U., 1986. Bar: Tex. 1989, U.S. Dist. Ct. (so. dist.) Tex. 1992, U.S. Ct. Appeals (5th cir.) 1993, U.S. Dist. Ct. Ariz. 1994. Jud. law clk., Houston, 1989-91; assoc. atty. Fulbright & Jaworski, Houston, 1991-96; shareholder Wickliff & Hall PC, Houston, 1996-2001; judge 157th Dist. Ct., State of Tex., 2001—02; justice Tex. Ct. Appeals (1st cir.), Houston, 2003—. Panel chmn. grievance com., spl. disciplinary counsel State Bar Tex., Houston, 1993-99. Contbr. articles to profl. jours. Bd. dirs. Big Bros. and Big Sisters, Houston, 1995-97, Houston chpt. ARC, 2001—. Fellow Houston Bar Assn.; mem. Fed. Bar Assn., Nat. Bar Assn., Am. Judges Assn., Houston Bar Assn. Avocations: aviation, scuba diving. Home: 12035 Circle Dr E Houston TX 77071 Office: 1037 San Jacinto Fl 10 Houston TX 77002 E-mail: ghanks@prodigy.net., george.hanks@1stcoa.courts.state.tx.us.

HANLON, MICHAEL GREGORY, lawyer; b. Palo Alto, Calif., May 7, 1953; s. Paul David and Carol Clair (Crowley) H. BA, U. Oreg., 1975; JD, Lewis & Clark Coll., Portland, 1979. Bar: Oreg. 1979, U.S. Dist. Ct. Oreg. 1979, U.S. Ct. Appeals (9th cir.) 1979, U.S. Supreme Ct. 1995. Assoc. Law Offices Henry A. Carey, Portland, 1979, 81-83; asst. atty. gen. Antitrust div. State of Oreg. Dept. Justice, Salem, 1980; pvt. practice Portland, 1983—. Mem. ABA, Oreg. State Bar Assn. (chair antitrust sect. 1999-2000), Multnomah County Bar Assn. (mem. MBA legis. com., chair professionalism com. 2000-01, Award of Merit 2001), U.S. Dist. Ct. (Oreg.) Hist. Soc., Univ. Club, Multnomah Athletic Club, Columbia-Edgewater Country Club. Democrat. Roman Catholic. Antitrust, Federal civil litigation, Securities. Office: Law Offices Michael G Hanlon 1300 Congress Ctr 1001 SW 5th Ave Portland OR 97204-1020

HANNA, HARRY MITCHELL, lawyer; b. Portland, Oreg., Jan. 13, 1936; s. Joseph John and Amelia Cecelia (Rask) H.; m. Patricia Ann Shelly, Feb. 4, 1967; 1 child, Harry M. Jr. BS, U. Oreg., 1958; JD, Lewis and Clark Coll., 1966. Bar: Oreg. 1966, U.S. Tax Ct. 1967, U.S. Dist. Ct. Oreg. 1970, U.S. Supreme Ct. 1971, U.S. Ct. Appeals (9th cir.) 1973, U.S. Ct. Claims 1973. Airport mgr. Port of Portland, 1964-66; mng. ptnr. Hanna & Purcella, Portland, 1966-80, Niehaus, Hanna, Murphy, Green, Holloway & Connolly, Portland, 1980-88; shareholder, v.p. Hanna Strader, P.C., Portland, 1988—. Judge pro-tempore U.S. Dist. Ct. Oreg., 1973-78; adj. prof. N.W. Sch. Law, Lewis and Clark Coll., Portland, 1976-77. Trustee Emanuel Med. Ctr. Found., 1989-94; pres. Ctrl. Cath. H.S. Bd., 1992-95; vice chair Life Flight Devel. Bd., 1994-97, chair, 1997—. Mem. ABA, Fed. Bar Assn., Oreg. State Bar Assn., Multnomah Bar Assn., Rotary (pres. East Portland club 1989-90). Avocations: tennis, hunting, fishing, coaching youth athletics. Corporate, general, Property, real (including real estate development, water), Taxation, general. Office: Hanna Strader PC 1300 SW 6th Ave Ste 300 Portland OR 97201-3461

HANNA, JOHN, JR., lawyer, educator, arbitrator, mediator; b. Dec. 19, 1934; m. Jane Merchant, Dec. 27, 1958; children: Elizabeth Hanna Morss, Katharine Hanna Morgan, John M. AB, Princeton U., 1956; LLB, Harvard U., 1959. Bar: N.Y. 1960, Mass. 1964, U.S. Dist. Ct. Mass. 1965, U.S. Dist. Ct. (ea. and so. dists.) N.Y. 1963, U.S. Dist. Ct. (no. dist.) N.Y. 1976, U.S. Dist. Ct. (we. dist.) N.Y. 1983, U.S. Ct. Appeals (1st and 2d cirs.) 1963. Assoc. Root, Barrett, Cohen, Knapp & Smith, N.Y.C., 1959-61; asst. U.S. atty. So. Dist. N.Y., 1961-63; assoc. Ropes & Gray, Boston, 1963-69; counsel N.Y. State Office Employee Rels. Govs. Office, Albany, 1969-73; dep. commr., gen. counsel N.Y. State Dept. Environ. Conservation, Albany, 1973-75; ptnr. Whiteman, Osterman & Hanna, Albany, 1975—. Adj. prof. Rensselaer Poly. Inst., Troy, NY, 1988—98; adj. prof. internat. environ. law The John Marshall Law Sch., 2001—. Co-author: New York State Bar Association Environmental Handbook, 1987, New York Treatise on Environmental Law, 1992. Mem. adv. bd. Inst. for Transnat. Arbitration; mem. Town of Chatham Planning Bd., NY, 1976—; co-chmn. Princeton U. Alumni Schs. Commn. No. N.Y., 1982—92; mem. N.Y. panel disting. neutrals CPR Inst. for Alt. Dispute Resolution; treas., trustee Shaker Mus. Found., Old Chatham, NY, 1978—96; trustee ea. N.Y. chpt. The Nature Conservancy, 1994—2002, chair conservation com., 1996—2002; trustee N.Y. State Archives Partnership Trust, 1995—, chair, 1996—; trustee The Olana Partnership, 2002—; mem. Princeton U. Alumni Schs. Commn. No. N.Y., 1982—95; mem. commn. on environ. law Internat. Union for Conservation of Nature, 1999—; vol. arbitrator VIS Internat. Comml. Moot, Pace U. Law Sch., 1998—2000; mem. adv. coun. Ctr. for Internat. Bus. and Trade Law, John Marshall Law Sch. Mem.: ABA (internat. comparative law sect.), N.Y. State Bar Assn. (1st vice chmn. 1981—83, chmn. 1983—84, ho. of dels. 2003—), Inst. of Arbitrators (London). Administrative and regulatory, Environmental, Private international. Office: Whiteman Osterman & Hanna One Commerce Plz Albany NY 12260 E-mail: jhanna@woh.com.

HANNA, JULIET MARIE, lawyer; b. Englewood, Colo., May 28, 1970; d. Bruce Edward and Kanchana Kosiyasthit Hanna; m. Michael James Reilly, Sept. 18, 1999. BA in Linguistics and Anthropology, UCLA, 1992; JD, Columbia U., 1998. Bar: Colo. 1998, U.S. Dist. Ct. Colo. 1998. Assoc. Gibson Dunn & Crutcher, LLP, Denver, 1998—. Author: (screenplay) Off Center, 2001 (film festival finalist, 2002); contbr. articles to profl. jours. Vol. Denver Pub. Schs., 1998—. Fulbright scholar, Inst. Internat. Edn., Cologne, Germany, 1993—94, European law fellow, Columbia U., 1996—97. Mem.:

ABA, Denver Bar Assn., Colo. Bar Assn., Internat. Bar Assn. Avocations: reading, writing, skiing, scuba diving, travel. Securities. Office: Gibson Dunn & Crutcher LLP 1801 California St Ste 4100 Denver CO 80202 Office Fax: 303-296-5310.

HANNA, KATHERINE MERRITT, lawyer; b. Keene, N.H., Sept. 5, 1953; d. George R. and Shirley (Garfield) H.; m. R. Shep Melnick, Jan. 24, 1981. BA, Mt. Holyoke Coll., 1975; JD, Boston Coll., 1979. Bar: N.H. 1979, U.S. Dist. Ct. N.H. 1979, U.S. Ct. Appeals (1st cir.) 1982. Legis. asst. U.S. Senate, Washington, 1975-77; law clk. to presiding justice U.S. Dist. Ct. of N.H., Concord, 1979-81; assoc. Wadleigh Law Firm, Manchester, N.H., 1981-85; ptnr. Castaldo, Hanna & Malmberg, Concord, 1985—. Incorporator N.H. Charitable Fund, Concord, 1982—; trustee Robert Frost Farm, Derry, N.H., 1982—. Del. Dem. Nat. Conv., 1972, 76, 84, N.H. Constituition Conv., 1974; rep. N.H. House Reps., 1975-77; legal counsel N.H. Dems., 1984-86. Mem. N.H. Bar Assn. (chair com. on cooperation with cts. 1989-90). General civil litigation, Construction, Health. Office: Castaldo Hanna & Malmberg PO Box 3701 Manchester NH 03105-3701

HANNAH, JIM, judge; b. Dec. 26, 1944; BSBA in Acctg., JD, U. Ark. Pvt. practice Lightle, Tedder, Hannah & Beebe; city atty. City of Searcy, Ark., 1969—78; juvenile judge White County, 1976—78; chancery,probate judge 17th Jud. Dist., 1979—99; justice Supreme Ct. Ark., 2000—. Faculty adv. Nat. Jud. Coll. Mem.: Arkansas Bar Assoc., Arkansas Jud. Coun., Arkansas Bd. of Pardons and Paroles (sec. 1972—79), White County Bar Assoc. (past pres., Treas., and Sec.), Am. Judges Assoc. Office: Justice Bldg Rm 230 625 Marshall St Little Rock AR 72201*

HANNAH, LAWRENCE BURLISON, lawyer; b. Urbana, Ill., Aug. 5, 1943; s. Lawrence Hugh and Margaret Alene (Burlison) H.; m. Kathleen O'Hara, Nov. 8, 1969; 1 child, Scott David. BA, Dartmouth Coll., 1965; JD cum laude, U. Pa., 1968. Bar: Wash. 1971, U.S. Dist. Ct. (we. dist.) Wash. 1971, Ct. of Appeals (9th cir.) 1971, U.S. Supreme Ct. 1990. Analyst U.S. Central Intelligence Agency, Langley, Va., 1969-71; ptnr. Perkins Coie, Bellevue, Wash., 1971—. Contbr. articles to profl. jours. Mem. King County Personnel Bd., Wash., 1984-90; mem. fin. com. Mcpl. Gov. Candidates, King County, 1972—. 1st lt. USAF, 1968-69. Mem. ABA, Wash. State Bar Assn., Seattle-King County Bar Assn. Methodist. Avocations: jogging, boating, tennis. Labor (including EEOC, Fair Labor Standards Act, labor-management relations, NLRB, OSHA), Municipal (including bonds). Home: 1610 W Lake Sammamish Pky SE Bellevue WA 98008-5229 Office: Perkins Coie 411 108th Ave NE Ste 1800 Bellevue WA 98004-5584

HANNAH, WAYNE ROBERTSON, JR., lawyer; b. Freeport, Ill., Aug. 18, 1931; s. Wayne Robertson and Edith (Biene) H.; m. Patricia Anne Matthews, June 1, 1957; children— Tamara Lee, Wendy, Wayne Robertson III BA, Ill. Coll., 1953; JD, NYU, 1957. Bar: Ill. 1957, U.S. Dist. Ct. (no. dist.) Ill., U.S. Supreme Ct. Ptnr. Sonnenschein, Nath & Rosenthal, Chgo., 1965—. Dir. Checker Motors Corp., N.Y.C. and Kalamazoo, 1982-86; lectr. Ill. Inst. Continuing Edn. Sec. 7th cir. Root-Tilden Scholarship Program NYU, 1967-94; chmn. Root-Tilden-Kern scholarship com., 1981-86, trustee law ctr., 1985—; pres. bd. Firman Cmty. Svcs, Chgo., 1972-75; trustee, pres., chmn. bd. Chgo. City Ballet, 1982-86. 2d lt. USMC, 1951-54. Root-Tilden scholar NYU, 1954-57; Fulbright scholar, 1953-54 Mem. ABA (real estate com.), Chgo. Bar Assn. (chmn. condominium subcom. real estate com. 1977-78, sec., dir. condominium assn. 1991—), Ill. Bar Assn. (real estate com.), Econ. Club (Chgo.), Skokie Country Club (Glencoe, Ill.). Presbyterian. Avocations: tennis, golf. Estate planning, Corporate, general, Property, real (including real estate development, water). Office: Sonnenschein Nath and Rosenthal 233 S Wacker Dr Ste 8000 Chicago IL 60606-6491 E-mail: wrh@sonnenschein.com.

HANNAN, MYLES, lawyer, banker; b. Rye, N.Y., Oct. 14, 1936; s. Joseph A. and Rosemary (Edwards) H.; m. Phyllis Wiley, Oct. 12, 2002; children from previous marriages: Myles Jr., Paul F., Thomas J., Kerry E. BA, Holy Cross Coll., 1958; LLB, Harvard U., 1964. Bar: N.Y. 1964, Mass. 1970, Md. 1994, D.C. 1996, U.S. Dist. Ct. (so. and ea. dists.) N.Y. 1966, U.S. Dist. Ct. Md. 1995. Assoc. Cadwalader, Wickersham & Taft, N.Y.C., 1964-69; v.p., gen. counsel, sec. High Voltage Engring. Corp., Burlington, Mass., 1969-73; v.p., sec. Stop & Shop Cos., Inc., Boston, 1973-79; group v.p. law and adminstrn. Del. North Cos., Inc., Buffalo, 1979-81; v.p., fin., gen. counsel, sec. Anacomp, Inc., Indpls., 1981-84; exec. v.p. Empire of Am. FSB, Buffalo, 1984-89; adminstrv. v.p. Berkeley Group Inc., Buffalo, 1990-91; ptnr. Linowes and Blocher LLP, Washington, 1992—. Trustee Studio Arena Theatre, Buffalo, 1986-89; bd. dirs. Buffalo Philharm. Orch., 1987-89. Lt. USNR, 1958-61. Finance, Landlord-tenant, Property, real (including real estate development, water). Home: 12108 Whippoorwill Ln North Bethesda MD 20852 Office: Linowes and Blocher LLP 1010 Wayne Ave Ste 1000 Silver Spring MD 20910-5615 E-mail: mh@linowes-law.com.

HANNIGAN, PATRICIA C. prosecutor; b. July 1949; BA, U. Mass.; JD, Rutgers U. Bar: Del. 1982. With U.S. Atty. Office, Wilmington, Del. Mem.: Del. State Bar Assn. (pres. 2002). Office: US Attys Office Ste 1100 1201 Market St PO Box 2046 Wilmington DE 19899-2046*

HANNON, TIMOTHY PATRICK, lawyer, educator, judge; b. Culver City, Calif., Nov. 29, 1948; s. Justin Aloysius and Ann Elizabeth (Ford) H.; m. Patricia Ann Hanson, May 1, 1976; children: Sean Patrick, James Patrick. Student, U. Vienna, 1968-69, Naval War Coll., 1988; BA, U. Santa Clara, 1970, JD cum laude, 1974. Bar: Calif. 1974, U.S. Dist. Ct. (no. dist.) Calif. 1974, U.S. Dist. Ct. (so. and ea. dists.) Calif. 1978, U.S. Ct. Appeals (9th cir.) 1978, Ct. Appeals Armed Forces 1979, D.C. 1981, U.S. Tax Ct. 1983, U.S. Ct. Claims 1983; cert. trial and def. lawyer Univorm Code Mil. Justice; cert. pilot with tailwheel endorsement, FAA. Assoc. N. Perry Moerdyke, Jr., Palo Alto, Calif., 1975-81; ptnr. Myerdyke & Hannon, Palo Alto, 1982-84, Attwood, Hurst, Knox & Anderson, 1984-86; pvt. practice Campbell, Calif., 1986-97; U.S. Adminstrv. law judge Social Security Adminstrn., 1997—. Instr. San Jose State U., 1985-89, De Anza Jr. Coll., Cupertino, Calif., 1987-97; instr. extension courses U. Calif., Santa Cruz, 1982-83; lectr. Lincoln Law Sch., San Jose, Calif., 1988-97, 2001—; arbitrator Santa Clara County Superior Ct., Santa Clara County Mcpl. Ct.; sr. mil. mem. Internat. Mil. Edn. Tng., Uganda, 1995; judge pro temp Santa Clara County Mcpl. Ct. Chmn., Menlo Park Housing Commn., 1979-81; allocations com. vol. United Way Clara County, 1987-90; mem. San Jose Vets. Meml. Com., 1993-99, treas., 1996-99; commr. Navy & Marine Corps Ct. Criminal Appeals, 2001-. Admiral Tex. Navy, 1998. With Calif. Army NG, 1970-76, capt., USNR, 1979—, commdg. officer, 1999-2001. Mem. Santa Clara County Bar Assn. (exec. com.), Santa Clara U. Nat. Alumni, U. Santa Clara Law Alumni Assn. (bd. dirs. 1980-81, sec. 1981-83, v.p. 1983-85, pres. 1985-87), Kiwanis. Roman Catholic. Avocation: flying. State civil litigation, Commercial, consumer (including collections, credit), General practice. Home: 806 Buckwood Ct San Jose CA 95120-3306 Office: Social Security Adminstrn 280 S 1st St # 300 San Jose CA 95113-3002 E-mail: tpatrick.hannon@ssa.gov.

HANOVER, RICHARD, lawyer, consultant, physician; b. N.Y.C. Student, NYU, 1968-71; AB in Psychology, Vassar Coll., 1973; MD, U. Autonoma de Guadalajara, Mexico, 1977; postgrad., N.Y. Med. Coll. Fifth Pathway, 1977-78; JD, Nova U., 1987. Bar: Fla. 1988, N.Y. 1989, U.S. Dist. Ct. (so. and ea. dists.) N.Y. 1990; diplomate Am. Bd. Internal Medicine, Am. Bd. Legal Medicine. Intern internal medicine Met. Hosp., N.Y.C., 1978-79; resident psychiatry CMDNJ-Rutgers, New Brunswick, N.J., 1979-80; pvt. practice medicine with Bernard Hanover M.D., N.Y.C., 1980-92; physician Group/Clinic Med. Practice, Ft. Lauderdale/Miami, Fla., 1984-88; resident in internal medicine N.Y. Downtown Hosp., N.Y.C., 1992-94; attending physician The Mount Sinai Hosp. Employee Health Svc., N.Y.C., 1994-95, Western Queens Cmty. Hosp., L.I., 1995—, Boro Med., P.C., N.Y.C., 1997—; law assoc. Kopff, Nardelli & Dopf, N.Y.C., 1989-90; litigation practice N.Y.C., 1990-92; pvt. cons. legal medicine, 1992—. Adj. asst. prof. cmty. and preventive medicine N.Y. Med. Coll., Valhalla, N.Y., 1991-94; clin. instr., preceptor, third yr. internal medicine clerkship/house staff The Mount Sinai Sch. Medicine, N.Y.C., 1994-95; alliance physician The Mount Sinai Hosp., N.Y.C., 1996—; assoc. physician The Mount Sinai Sch. Medicine, 1996—; spkr. in field. Contbr. articles to profl. jours. Fellow Am. Coll. Legal Medicine; mem. AMA, ABA, N.Y. State Bar Assn., Assn. of the Bar of the City of N.Y., N.Y. County Lawyers' Assn., Phi Alpha Delta. Health, Personal injury (including property damage). Office: 320 W 86th St New York NY 10024-3139

HANSBURY, STEPHAN CHARLES, judge; b. Mt. Holly, N.J., Nov. 3, 1946; s. Charles Clark and Kathryn Irene (Meyer) H.; m. Sharon Buckley; children: Elizabeth Kathryn, Jillian Judith, Stephanie Clark. BA, Allegheny Coll., 1968; MBA, Fairleigh Dickinson U., 1973; JD, Seton Hall U., 1977; cert. civil trial atty., Supreme Ct. N.J., 1989. Bar: N.J. 1977, U.S. Dist. Ct. (no. dist.) N.J. 1977, U.S. Supreme Ct. 1982. Dir. spl. programs Bloomfield (N.J.) Coll., 1968-71; dir. fin. aid Monmouth Coll., West Long Branch, N.J., 1971-72; asst. adminstr. Morris View, Morris Plains, N.J., 1972-78; assoc. Hansbury, Martin & Knapp, Morris Plains, 1978-87, pres., 1987-92; ptnr. Kummer Knox, Naughton & Hansbury, Parsippany, N.J., 1992-99, pres., 1996-97; ptnr. Cooper, Rose & English, LLP, 2000-2001; judge Superior Ct. of N.J., 2001—. Mem., gen. counsel Cheshire Home, Florham Park, N.J., 1978-2000, Ciba-Geigy Corp., Summit, N.J., 1980-92. Legis. aide Assemblyman Arthur Albohn, Morristown, N.J., 1980-83; mem. Morris County Bd. of Social Svcs., 1989-96, chmn. 1992-94; bd. dirs. Colonial Symhony. Mem. ABA, N.J. Bar Assn., Morris County Bar Assn. (trustee 1987-90), Rotary (pres. 1998-99), Morristown Club. Republican. Episcopalian. Avocations: tennis, golf, reading. Office: Courthouse PO Box 910 Morristown NJ 07963-0910

HANSELL, EDGAR FRANK, lawyer; b. Leon, Iowa, Oct. 12, 1937; s. Edgar Noble and Celestia Delphine (Skinner) H.; m. Phyllis Wray Silvey, June 24, 1961; children— John Joseph, Jordan Burke AA, Graceland Coll., 1957; BBA, U. Iowa, 1959, JD, 1961. Bar: Iowa 1961. Assoc. Nyemaster, Goode, McLaughlin, Voigts, West, Hansell & O'Brien, P.C., Des Moines, 1964-68, ptnr., shareholder, 1968—. Bd. dirs. The Vernon Co., Greater Des Moines Partnership, Downtown Cmty. Alliance, Inc., Des Moines Internat. Airport; mem. adv. com. to bd. dirs. The Lauridson Group, Inc.; adj. prof. law Drake U., Des Moines, 1990—98. Mem. editorial adv. bd. Jour. Corp. Law, 1985—. Bd. dirs. Des Moines Child Guidance Ctr., 1972-78, 81-87, pres., 1977-78; trustee Iowa Law Sch. Found., 1975-90, pres., 1983-87; bd. dirs. Iowa Natural Heritage Found., 1988-93, Iowa Sports Found., 1986-97; bd. dirs. Iowa State Bar Found., 1991-2000, pres., 1996-98. With USAF, 1961-64. Mem. ABA, Iowa Bar Assn. (pres. young lawyers sect. 1971-72, bd. govs. 1971-72, 85-87, mem. grievance commn. 1973-78, Merit award young lawyers sect. 1977, 98, chmn. corp. and bus. law com. 1979-85, pres. 1989-90), Polk County Bar Assn., Des Moines Club (pres. 1979-80). Corporate, general. Home: 139-37th Des Moines IA 50312-4303 Office: Nyemaster Goode Voigts West Hansell & O'Brien PC 700 Walnut St Ste 1600 Des Moines IA 50309-3800 E-mail: efh@nyemaster.com.

HANSELL, RONALD STEPHEN, lawyer, construction arbitrator; b. Lafayette, Ind., Aug. 20, 1948; s. Richard Grant and Regina Agnes (Minnicus) H.; m. Carolyn Stevens, Jan. 27, 2002; 1 child Sarah Neimeyer. BSCE, Purdue U., 1972, MSCE, 1974; JD, Ind. U., Indpls., 1979. Bar: Ind. 1979, U.S. Dist. Ct. (so. dist) Ind. 1979, U.S. Patent Office 1981, U.S. Supreme Ct. 1983, Ky. 1990, Mont. 2002, U.S. Dist. Ct. Mont. 2002, U.S. Ct. Appeals (7th cir.) Mont.; registered profl. engr. Ind., Ohio, Ky., land surveyor, Ind., Ohio. Engr. transp. regional planning commn. Allen County, Lima, Ohio, 1974-75; sr. project engr. RQAW & Assocs., Inc., Indpls., 1975-80; counsel regulatory affairs AMAX Coal Co., Indpls., 1980-83; assoc. Rocap, Rocap, Reese & Young, Indpls., 1984, Burris, Burris & Margerum, Indpls., 1985-87; pvt. practice law Indpls., 1987—. Chmn. infiltration-inflow and drainage subcom. Combined Sewer Overflow, citizens adv. com. Indpls. Dept. Pub. Works, 1980—. Served with USMC, 1968-70, Vietnam. 1st Marine Divsn. Mem. ASCE, ABA, ATLA. Ind. Bar Assn., Indpls. Bar Assn.,, Ky. Bar Assn., Ky.Acad. Trial Attys., Mont. Bar Assn., Western Mont. Bar Assn., Mont. Acad. Trial Attys., Am. Arbitration Assn., Natl. Arbitration Forum, Indianapolis Computer Soc., St. Thomas More Soc., Assn. of Former Intelligence Officers., 1st Marine Divsn. Assn., Viet Nam Vets. Chpt 1/5, Mil. Order Purple Heart, Elks. Republican. Roman Catholic. Avocations: tae kwon do karate, guitar, choral music. State civil litigation, Commercial, consumer (including collections, credit), Patent. Office: PO Box 999 Lolo MT 59847-0999 Home: 19560 Leo Hanson Rd Florence MT 59833-6144 Office Fax: 406-273-6626. E-mail: 2by4law@montana.com.

HANSELMANN, FREDRICK CHARLES, lawyer; b. Phila., Sept. 1, 1955; s. Helmuth Fredrick and Maria Elizabeth (Dougherty) H.; m. Mary Nina Johnson, May 7, 1983; children: Elizabeth Ryan, Peter Cornelius, Kevin Andrew, Charlotte Mary. BA magna cum laude, La Salle Coll., 1977; JD, U. Notre Dame, 1980. Bar: Pa. 1980, U.S. Dist. Ct. (ea. dist.) Pa. 1981, U.S. Dist. Ct. (mid. dist.) Pa. 1987, U.S. Ct. Appeals (3d cir.) 1981. Assoc. German, Gallagher & Murtagh, P.C., Phila., 1981-85, Wilson, Elser, Moskowitz, Edelman & Dicker, Phila., 1985-90; ptnr. Mylotte David & Fitzpatrick, Phila., 1990-99; of counsel McBreen, McBreen and Kopko, Phila., Pa., 1999—. Mem. ABA, Pa. Bar Assn., Phila. Bar Assn., Def. Rsch. Inst., Profl. Liability Underwriting Soc., Lawyers Club Phila., Notre Dame Club Phila., Avalon Yacht Club, Glen Lake (Mich.) Assn. Republican. Roman Catholic. General civil litigation, Insurance, Personal injury (including property damage). Home: 118 Azalea Way Flourtown PA 19031-2008 Office: McBreen McBreen & Kopko 8 Penn Ctr 1628 John F Kennedy Blvd Ste 1400 Philadelphia PA 19103 Fax: 215 864-2610. E-mail: fchlaw2@aol.com.

HANSEN, CHRISTOPHER AGNEW, lawyer; b. Yakima, Wash., Dec. 10, 1934; s. Raymond Walter and Christine F.M. (Agnew) H.; m. Sandra Ridgely Pindell, Aug. 4, 1959; Anne Ridgely, Christopher Agnew Jr., Eric Bruce. BS, Cornell U., 1957; JD, U. Md., 1963. Bar: Md. 1963, U.S. Supreme Ct. 1973, U.S. Ct. Appeals (4th cir.) D.C. 1978. Law clk. Cir. Ct. for Balt. County, Towson, Md., 1960-63; assoc. Piper & Marbury, Balt., 1963-74; of counsel Casey, Scott, Canfield & Heggestad PC, Washington, 1982-93; ptnr. Constable, Alexander & Skeen, Towson, 1984-86, Parks, Hansen & Ditch, Towson, 1986-94; of counsel Heggestad & Weiss, PC, Washington, 1993—2001; pvt. practice Towson, 1974-83, 95—. With U.S. Army, 1957-60. Mem. ABA, D.C. Bar, Md. State Bar Assn., Bar Assn. Balt. County, Balt. City Bar Assn., Phi Alpha Delta. Episcopalian. Federal civil litigation, State civil litigation, Insurance. Home: 800 Hatherleigh Rd Baltimore MD 21212-1614

HANSEN, CURTIS LEROY, federal judge; b. 1933; BS, U. Iowa, 1956; JD, U. N.Mex., 1961. Bar: N.Mex. Law clk. to Hon. Irwin S. Moise N.Mex. Supreme Ct., 1961-62; ptnr. Snead & Hansen, Albuquerque, 1962-64, Civerolo, Hansen & Wolf, P.A., 1964—92; dist. judge U.S. Dist. Ct., N.Mex., 1992—2003, sr. dist. judge, 2003—. Mem. State Bar N.Mex., Albuquerque Bar Assn., Am. Coll. Trial Lawyers, Am. Bd. Trial Advocates, Albuquerque Country Club. Office: US Courthouse Chambers Ste 660 333 Lomas Blvd NW Albuquerque NM 87102-2272

HANSEN, DAVID RASMUSSEN, federal judge; b. Exira, Iowa, 1938; BA, N.W. Mo. State U., 1960; JD, George Washington U., 1963. Asst. clk. to minority House Appropriations Com. Ho. of Reps., 1960—61; adminstrv. aide 7th Dist. Iowa, 1962—63; pvt. practice Jones, Cambridge & Carl, Atlantic, Iowa, 1963—64; capt., judge advocate General's Corps U.S. Army, 1964—68; pvt. practice Barker, Hansen & McNeal, Iowa Falls, Iowa, 1968—76; ptnr. Win-Gin Farms, Iowa Falls, 1971—; judge Police Ct., Iowa, 1969—73, 2d Jud. Dist. Ct., Iowa, 1976—86, U.S. Dist. Ct. (no. dist.), Cedar Rapids, Iowa, 1986—91, U.S. Ct. Appeals (8th cir.), Cedar Rapids, 1991—2002, chief judge, 2002—03, sr. judge, 2003—. Office: US Courthouse Rm 304 101 1st St SE Cedar Rapids IA 52401-1202*

HANSEN, H. REESE, dean, educator; b. Logan, Utah, Apr. 8, 1942; s. Howard F. and Loila Gayle (Reese) H.; m. Kathryn Traveller, June 8, 1962; children: Brian T., Mark T., Dale T., Curtis T. BS, Utah State U., 1964; JD, U. Utah, 1972. Bar: Utah, 1974. Atty. Strong, Poelman & Fox, Salt Lake City, 1972-74; from asst. prof. to assoc. prof. Brigham Young U., Provo, Utah, 1974-79, prof., 1979—, from asst. dean to assoc. dean, 1974-89, dean, 1989—. Commr. ex officio Utah State Bar, Salt Lake City, 1989—; commr. Nat. Conf. Commrs. on Uniform State Laws, 1988-95. Co-author: Idaho Probate System, 1977, Utah Probate System, 1977, Cases and Text on Laws of Trusts, 7th edit., 2001; editor: Manual for Justices of Peace--Utah, 1978; contbr. articles to profl. jours. Mem. Lds Ch. Office: Brigham Young U 348A Jrcb Provo UT 84602-1029

HANSEN, JOHANNUS EGHOLM, lawyer, law educator; b. Vestmanna, Denmark, Feb. 17, 1959; s. Sigfred Elias and Jastrid Alice Hansen; m. Vivi Sønderskov Møller, July 24, 1993; children: Janna, Daniel Egholm, Jastrid Egholm. Ships officer, Svendborg Navigationsskole (Denmark), 1984; ships master, Svendborg (Denmark) Navigationsskole, 1985; LLM, U. Copenhagen, 1991. Bar: Denmark and Faroe Islands 1994, (High Ct.) 1997. Apprentice officer D/S Norden A/S, Copenhagen, 1981—83, ships officer, 1985—86; assoc. Advokaterne Kindhestegade 14, Naestved, Denmark, 1991—92, Andreasse & Ptnrs., Copenhagen, 1992—94, lawyer, 1994—97; ptnr. Dania Law Firm, Copenhagen, 1997—, also bd. dirs.; asst. prof. Copenhagen U., 1997—. Chmn. bd. dirs. T.F. Holdings P/F, Torshavn, Faeroe Islands, 1999—2003; bd. dirs. DEF. Author: Faroese Business Law, 1998, Mergers & Acquisitions, 2000, 2002, European Restructuring Guide, 2002. Scholar, Dutch Govt., Internat. Ct. Justice, 1989. Mem.: Danish Cooperation for Constrn. Law, Danish Lawyers Assn., Internat. Bar Assn. Avocations: travel, sailing, sports, skiing, walking. Mergers and acquisitions, Property, real (including real estate development, water), Construction. Home: Trondhjemsgade 10 St Th DK-2100 Copenhagen Denmark Office: FLS Industries A/S Vigerslev Alle 77 DK 2500 Valby Denmark

HANSEN, JOHN ALTON, lawyer; b. La Junta, Colo., May 7, 1933; s. Alton Schow and Ora (Packer) H.; m. Mary C. Williamson, Nov. 9, 1957; children: James P., Julia R., Kathryn M., Steven J. LLB cum laude, Marquette U., 1957. Bar: Wis. 1957, U.S. Dist. Ct. (ea. dist.) Wis. 1957, U.S. Dist. Ct. (we. dist.) Wis. 1961, U.S. Ct. Appeals (7th cir.) 1960. Assoc. Rieser, Stafford, Rosenbaum & Rieser, Madison, Wis., 1960-64; ptnr. Stafford, Rosenbaum, Rieser & Hansen, Madison, Wis., 1964—2000. Contbr. articles to profl. jours. Bd. dirs. Woolsack Soc., Milw., 1983-89. Lt. USN, 1957-60. Mem. ABA, State Bar Wis., Am. Coll. Trial Lawyers, Dane County Bar Assn., Marquette U. Law Alumni Assn. (bd. dirs. 1975-79). Administrative and regulatory, General civil litigation, Product liability.

HANSEN, KENNETH D. lawyer, ophthalmologist; b. Seattle, Mar. 26, 1947; s. George R. and Elaine D. (Jacobsen) H.; m. Barbara Caleen, Oct. 8, 1976; 1 son, David Scott. BS in Psychology, U. Wash., 1969, JD, 1972, MD with honors, 1976. Bar: Wash. 1972, Mich. 1977, Ill. 1984, D.C. 1986, U.S. Supreme Ct. 1981; diplomate Am. Bd. Ophthalmology. Legal counsel Assn. Wash. Bus., Olympia, 1972-73; asst. atty. gen. State of Wash., Seattle, 1973-74; v.p., gen. counsel N.W. Med. Rsch. Found., Seattle, 1976-86; pres. Internat. Health Found., 1986—; intern medicine U. Mich. Hosp., Ann Arbor, 1977, resident in ophthalmology, 1978-80; sr. med. staff Henry Ford Hosp., Detroit, 1981-82; dir. ophthalmology Carbondale (Ill.) Clinic, 1983-86, chmn. dept. surgery, gen. counsel, 1984-86; clin. asst. prof. ophthalmology and med. humanities So. Ill. U., Carbondale, 1983-86; clin. asst. prof. ophthalmology U. Md., Balt., 1986—; gen. counsel Internat. Inst. for Biomed. Rsch., 2002—. Med.-legal adv. com. U. Mich. Hosp. System; cons. Nat. Def. Med. Coll., China; charter coun. mem. practicing physicians adv. coun. to Sec. of U.S. Dept. Health and Human Svcs., 1992-97; internat. med.-legal lectr. Assoc. editor Trauma, 1995—, Wash. Law Rev., 1971-72; contbr. articles to legal and med. profl. jours., publs. Recipient U. Wash. Med. Thesis Award, Gold Medal Egyptian Med. Syndicate, 1986; William Wallice Wilshire Meml. scholar; Anna C. Dunlap Meml. scholar; Grad. Rsch. fellow, 1975—; recipient Red Rose award Soc. Rsch. Adminstrs., 1989. Fellow Am. Coll. Legal Medicine (jud. coun., model statutes com., Pres.'s award 1989), Internat. Coll. Surgeons; mem. ABA, AMA, Wash. State Bar Assn., Mich. Bar Assn., Ill. Med. Soc. (med.-legal coun.), Ill. Bar Assn., Mich. Med. Schs. Coun. Deans (med.-legal adv. com.), Mich. Ophthalmology Soc. (Rsch. award 1981), Am. Acad. Ophthalmology, D.C. Bar Assn., Phi Delta Pi, Phi Eta Sigma, Pi Sigma Epsilon. Baptist. Home: 6501 Bright Mountain Rd Mc Lean VA 22101-1701 Office: 901 N Stuart St Ste 210 Arlington VA 22203

HANSEN, MICHELLE ANN, lawyer; b. St. Marys, Pa., Jan. 2, 1971; d. Frederick John and Constance Krug Mildrew; m. Curtis Ronald Hansen, Aug. 8, 1992. A Supervisory Leadership, Hawaii Pacific U., 1992; BA, St. Leo Coll., 1994; JD, Regent U., 1997. Bar: Va. 97. Commd. U.S. Army, 1998, advanced through grades to capt.; legal assistance atty. Ft. Eustis (Va.) Office Staff Judge Advocate, 1998—99, spl. asst. U.S. atty., trial counsel, 1999—2000, chief mil. justice, 2000—01, chief internat. and operational law, 2001—. Field screening officer, recruiter U.S. Army Judge Advocate Gen. Corps, Ft. Stewart, Ga., 2002—. Mem.: ABA, Judge Advocates Assn. Office: Ft Stewart Office Staff Judge Advocate Bldg T-53 60 McNeely Rd Fort Stewart GA 31314

HANSEN, SCOTT WILLIAM, lawyer, consultant; b. Salt Lake City, May 27, 1953; s. Jerome Reid and Berta Margaret (Lowe) H.; m. Peggy Anne Norton, May 25, 1997; 1 child, Madeleine Elizabeth Hansen. BS, U. Utah, 1975, MS, 1977; JD, Pepperdine U., 1980. Bar: Utah 1980, Idaho 1982, Tex. 1986. Assoc. Prince, Yeates & Geldzhler, Salt Lake City, 1980-81; ptnr. Kennedy, Crabtree & Hansen, 1981-86; cons. Wallace Assocs, Salt Lake City, 1986-88, Ketchum, Inc., Salt Lake City, 1990-92; pres. Fund Raising Counsel, Inc., Salt Lake City, 1982—; of counsel Richards, Brandt, Miller & Nelson, 1997—2000; ptnr. Buckland, Orton, Larger, Hansen, Waldo & Barton. Nat. trustee Sun Valley (Idaho) Ctr. for Arts and Humanities; mem., bd. trustees Nat. Adv. Coun. Western Folklife Ctr.; chair Utah Repertory Dance Co.; Tanner Planned Giving Commn. Utah Symphony; bd. dirs. Ronald McDonald House Charities. Mem. ABA (estate planning and drafting charitable giving com.), Utah Soc. Fund Raisers. Democrat. Estate planning, Probate (including wills, trusts), Estate taxation.

HANSEN, TORBEN INGEMANN, lawyer; b. Frederiksberg, Denmark, Dec. 7, 1936; s. Carl Johannes and Inger (Ingemann) H.; m. Randi Andersen. Candidatus Juris, U. Copenhagen, Denmark, 1961. Bar: Denmark 1967, High Ct. 1971, Supreme Ct. 1976. Officer of the crown Ministry of Edn. and Ministry of Fin., Denmark, 1961-67; pvt. practice Copenhagen, 1967—. Corr. Euromoney Internat. Fid. Law File, 1990. Legal asst. Chief. Mil. Prosecutor, 1962-63; mem. Pub. Rent Control Bd., Frederiksberg, 1974; lay jdge Housing Tribunal, Copenhagen, 1978-92; city counsellor City of Frederiksberg, 1985-89. Decorated knight of Dannebrog, 1999. Mem. Internat. Bar Assn., Danish Bar Assn., Lloyd's of London (underwriter 1986-92)), Rotary Internat., Frederiksberg Rotary (pres. 1988-89, Paul Harris fellow 1995). Conservative. Avocations: sailing, skiing, tennis. Home: Emanuel Olsens Vej 9 2000 Frederiksberg Denmark Office: Advokaterne Amaliegade 42 1256 Copenhagen Denmark also: 26 bd Raspail F75007 Paris France E-mail: kn@amalex.com.

HANSMANN, HENRY BAETHKE, law educator; b. Highland Park, Ill., Oct. 5, 1945; s. Elwood Hansmann and Louise Frances (Baethke) Moore; m. Marina Santilli, 1992; 1 child, Lisa Santilli. BA, Brown U., 1967; JD, Yale U., 1974, PhD, 1978. Asst. prof. law U. Pa. Law Sch., Phila., 1975-81, assoc. prof. law, econs. and pub. policy, 1981-83; prof. law Yale U., New Haven, 1983-88, Harris prof., 1988—. Author: The Ownership of Enterprise, 1996. John Simon Guggenheim Found. fellow, 1985-86. Mem. Am. Econs. Assn., Am. Law and Econ. Assn. Home: 240 Mercer St # 1603 New York NY 10012-1507 Office: Yale U Law Sch PO Box 208215 New Haven CT 06520-8215 E-mail: henry.hansmann@yale.edu.

HANSON, ARNOLD PHILIP, retired lawyer; b. Berlin, N.H., July 11, 1924; s. Arnold H. and Evelyn (Renaud) H.; m. Della Ann Lavernoich, June 26, 1948; children: Arnold Philip, Caryl Hanson Brensinger, Julie E. Hanson Mook. BA, U. N.H., 1948; JD, Boston, 1951. Bar: N.H. 1951. Pvt. practice, Berlin, N.H., 1951-60; ptnr. Bergeron & Hanson, Berlin, 1960-80, Bergeron & Hanson, P.A., Berlin, 1980-87, Bergeron, Hanson & Bornstein, P.A., Berlin, 1988-91; county atty. Coos County, N.H., 1952-56; ret. Mem. ct. accreditation com. State of N.H., 1970-77, Regional Criminal Justice Planning Coun., 1978-88; ptnr. North Country TV Cable Co., Groveton, N.H., 1962-89; chmn. bd., chmn. exec. com. Berlin City Bank, 1975-87. Chmn. city Republican Conv., Berlin, 1952-54; bd. dirs. Rep. State Com., 1958-60; del. Rep. Nat Com., 1964; trustee A.V. Hosp., 1976-85, mem. coms., 1976-86; area chmn. fundraising campaigns including ARC, U. N.H. Centennial Fund, Crippled Children, N.H. Children's Aid Soc., Boy Scouts Am., Boston U. Law Sch. Centennial Fund, St. Paul's Sch. Advanced Studies Program, A.V. Hosp. Bldg. Fund maj. gifts program, Frank Kenison Fund Boston U. Law Sch.; mem. U. N.H. 50th Reunion Fund Raising Class of 1948, 1996-98. Served with USN, 1943-46. Recipient Silver Shingle award Boston U. Sch. Law, 1977, Alumni Meritorius award U. N.H., 1986. Fellow Am. Bar Found.; mem. N.H. Bar Assn. (pres. 1974-75, bd. govs. 1973-76), Coos County Bar Assn. (pres. various yrs.), Tri-Legal County Svcs., N.H. Alumni Assn. (bd. dirs. 1974-77), Boston U. Alumni Assn., Am. Legion (post judge adv. 1952-64), VFW (post judge adv. 1952-93), Nashua Country Club (Nashua, N.H.), Seven Lakes Country Club (Ft. Myers, Fla.), Kiwanis (pres. 1966). Lutheran. General practice, Personal injury (including property damage), Probate (including wills, trusts). Home: 55 Hawthorne Village Rd Nashua NH 03062-2271 also: 13190 Oakmont Drive #8 Fort Myers FL 33907-8020 E-mail: dahanson@aol.com.

HANSON, AVARITA LAUREL, lawyer; b. N.Y.C., July 21, 1953; d. Earle L. and Gloria (Troupe) H.; m. William A. Alexander, June 14, 1975; children: Justin, Colin. AB, Radcliffe Coll., 1975; JD, U. Pa., 1978. Bar: Tex. 1979, U.S. Ct. Appeals (5th cir.) 1980, U.S. Dist. Ct. (so. dist.) Tex. 1980, U.S. Dist. Ct. (no. dist.) Ga. 1981, U.S. Ct. Appeals (11th cir.) 1981, Ga. 1983. Assoc. Fulbright & Jaworski, Houston, 1978-82; pvt. practice Houston and Atlanta, 1982—; judge Fulton County Juvenile Ct., 1995-97; exec. dir. examining bds. divsn. Ga. Sec. of State, 1997-99; prof. John Marshall Law Sch., 2000—, acad. dean, 2001—. Ptnr. Secret & Assocs., Atlanta, 1983-84; dir. pro bono project Ga. Bar Assn. and Ga. Legal Svcs. Program, 1985-89; clk. Fulton County Commn., 1990-95; bd. dirs. Atlanta Legal Aid Soc., 1986—, Ga. Legal Svcs. Program, 1995—. Exec. producer TV show Legally Speaking, 1983-90. Candidate coun. City of College Park, Ga., 1985; trustee Ben Hill United Meth. Ch., 1985-88; bd. dirs. YWCA Greater Atlanta, 1989-92. Mem. Ga. Assn. Black Women Attys. (pres. 1985), Atlanta Bar Assn. (adv. bd. 1989—), Gate City Bar Assn. (pres. 1991), Leadership Atlanta, Leadership Ga. (bd. trustees), Radcliffe Coll. Alumnae Assn. (bd. dirs.), Atlanta Women's Network, Ga. Women's Polit Caucus, Harvard Club Ga. (pres. 1994, v.p. 1987-90), Harvard Alumni Assn. (bd. dirs. 1990-93, 95—), Leadership Am. Democrat. Avocation: gourmet cooking. General practice. Office: John Marshall Law Sch 1422 W Peachtree St Atlanta GA 30309 E-mail: avarita@aol.com.

HANSON, BRUCE EUGENE, lawyer; b. Lincoln, Nebr., Aug. 25, 1942; s. Lester E. and Gladys (Diessner) H.; m. Peggy Pardun, Dec. 25, 1972 (dec. Nov. 1989). BA, U. Minn., 1965, JD, 1966. Bar: Minn. 1966, U.S. Dist. Ct. Minn. 1966, U.S. Tax Ct. 1973, U.S. Ct. Appeals (8th cir.) 1973, U.S. Ct. Appeals (fed. cir.) 1983, U.S. Supreme Ct. 1970. Shareholder Doherty, Rumble & Butler, P.A., St. Paul, 1966-99; ptnr. Oppenheimer, Wolff & Donnelly, LLP, Mpls., 1999—. Dir., sec. Am. Saddlebred Horse Assn.; bd. trustees, chair United Hosp., 1996-98. Mem. ATLA, Hennepin County Bar Assn., Minn. State Bar Assn., Am. Health Lawyers Assn., Minn. Soc. Hosp. Attys., North Oaks Golf Club, Order of Coif, Phi Delta Phi. Federal civil litigation, State civil litigation, Health. Home: 23 Evergreen Rd Saint Paul MN 55127-2077 Office: Oppenheimer Wolff & Donnelly LLP 45 S 7th St Ste 3300 Minneapolis MN 55402-1614 E-mail: BHanson@Oppenheimer.com.

HANSON, DAVID JAMES, lawyer; b. Neenah, Wis., July 20, 1943; s. Vernon James and Dorothy O. Hanson; m. Diana G. Severson, Aug. 25, 1965 (div. Sept. 1982); children: Matthew Vernon, Maja Kirsten, Brian Edward; m. Linda Hughes Bochert, May 28, 1983; children: Scott Charles, Sarah Katherine. BS, U. Wis., 1965, JD, 1968. Bar: Wis. 1968, U.S. Dist. Ct. (we. dist.) Wis. 1968, U.S. Dist. Ct. (ea. dist.) Wis. 1969, U.S. Ct. Appeals (7th cir.) 1970, U.S. Supreme Ct. 1971. Asst. atty. gen. State of Wis. Dept. of Justice, Madison, 1968-71, dep. atty. gen., 1976-81; asst. chancellor, chief legal counsel U. Wis., Madison, 1971-76; ptnr. Michael, Best & Friedrich LLP, Madison, 1981—. Lectr. Law Sch., U. Wis., Madison, 1972-75; chair govt. law sect. State Bar Wis., Madison, 1979-88. Contbr. articles to profl. jours. Bd. dirs. Sand County Found., Madison, 1988—, Wis. Ctr. for Academically Talented Youth, Madison, 1991-94, trustee Edgewood Coll., Madison, 1997—. Mem. ABA, Madison Club, Blackhawk Country Club. Democrat. Unitarian Universalist. Avocations: canoeing, skiing, golf, biking, hunting. Corporate, general, Health, Utilities, public. Office: Michael Best & Friedrich PO Box 1806 Madison WI 53701-1806 E-mail: djhanson@mbf-law.com.

HANSON, GARY A. lawyer, legal educator, university administrator; b. Santa Fe, Sept. 30, 1954; s. Norman A. Hanson and Mary Gene (Moore) Garrison; m. Tracey J. Tannen, Mar. 11, 1982; children: Paul, Carly, Sean. BS magna cum laude, U. Utah, 1976; JD, Pepperdine U., 1980. Bar: Calif. 1980, U.S. Dist. Ct. (cen. dist.) Calif. 1980, U.S. Ct. Appeals (9th cir.) 1980. Pvt. practice, Westlake Village, Calif., 1980-82; assoc. gen. counsel Pepperdine U., Malibu, Calif., 1982-83, acting gen. counsel, 1983-84, univ. gen. counsel, 1984—2000, v.p., gen. counsel, 2000—. Adj. prof. law Pepperdine U., Malibu, 1982—, lectr. bus. law, 1986—; pro bono atty. San Fernando Valley Christian Sch., L.A., 1982-83; mem. Pro Bono Estate Adv. Svc., San Diego, 1983-86; cons. West Ednl. Pub. Co., 1988. Contbr. articles to profl. jours.; pres. Ind. Colls. and Univs. jour., 1989. Recipient Pres.'s award San Diego Christian Found., 1984. Mem. ABA, L.A. County Bar Assn., Nat. Assn. Coll. and Univ. Attys. Republican. Corporate, general, Education and schools. Office: Pepperdine U 24255 Pacific Coast Hwy Malibu CA 90263-4607

HANSON, HEIDI ELIZABETH, lawyer; b. Portsmouth, Ohio, Nov. 13, 1954; BS, U. Ill., 1975, JD, 1978. Bar: Ill. 1978, U.S. Dist. Ct. (no. dist.) Ill., U.S. Ct. Appeals (7th cir.). Atty. water, air and land pollution divs. Ill. EPA, Springfield, Ill., 1978-85, atty. water pollution div. Maywood, Ill., 1985-86; assoc. Ross & Hardies, Chgo., 1987-89, ptnr., 1990-94; founder H.E. Hanson Law Offices, Western Springs, Ill., 1994—. Named hon. Ky. Col., 2000. Mem.: Indsl. Water, Waste and Sewer Group, Air and Waste Mgmt. Assn., Chgo. Bar Assn., Chicagoland C. of C. Avocation: gardening. Administrative and regulatory, Environmental. Office: 4721 Franklin Ave Ste 1500 Western Springs IL 60558-1720

HANSON, JOHN J. lawyer; b. Aurora, Nebr., Oct. 22, 1922; s. Peter E. and Hazel Marion (Lounsbury) H.; m. Elizabeth Anne Moss, July 1, 1973; children from their previous marriages— Mark, Eric, Gregory. AB, U. Denver, 1948; LL.B. cum laude, Harvard U., 1951. Bar: N.Y. bar 1952, Calif. bar 1955. Asso. firm Dewey, Ballantine, Bushby, Palmer & Wood, N.Y.C., 1951-54; ptnr. firm Gibson, Dunn & Crutcher, L.A, 1954—, mem. exec. com., 1978-87, adv. ptnr., 1991—. Contbr. articles to profl. jours. Trustee Palos Verdes (Calif.) Sch. Dist., 1969-73. Served with U.S. Navy, 1942-45. Fellow Am. Coll. Trial Lawyers; mem. Am. Bar Assn., Los Angeles County Bar Assn. (chmn. antitrust sect. 1979-80), Bel Air Country Club. Antitrust. Home: 953 Linda Flora Dr Los Angeles CA 90049-1630 Office: Gibson Dunn & Crutcher 333 S Grand Ave Ste 4400 Los Angeles CA 90071-3197

HANSON, KENT BRYAN, lawyer; b. Litchfield, Minn., Sept. 17, 1954; s. Calvin Bryan and Muriel (Wessman) H.; m. Barbara Jane Elenbaas, Aug. 24, 1974; children: Lindsay Michal, Taylor Jordan, Chase Philip. AA with high honors, Trinity Western Coll., 1974; BA, U. B.C., Vancouver, 1976; JD magna cum laude, U. Minn., 1979. Bar: Minn. 1979, U.S. Dist. Ct. Minn. 1980, U.S. Ct. Appeals (8th cir.) 1980, U.S. Dist. Ct. (we. dist.) Wis. 1983, Wis. 1985, U.S. Ct. Appeals (9th cir.) 1989, U.S. Dist. Ct. Ariz. 1992, Ohio 1993, Calif. 1994. Assoc. Grossman, Karlins, Siegel & Brill, Mpls., 1979-81, Gray, Plant, Mooty, Mooty & Bennett, Mpls., 1981-85; ptnr. Bowman & Brooke, Mpls., 1986-95; CEO Hanson, Marek, Bolkcom & Greene, Ltd., Mpls., 1996—. Bd. dirs. Inner City Boys Club, Ctrl. Free Ch., Mpls., 1979-81; 12th ward del. Mpls. Dem. Farmer Labor Com. Conv., 1982; mem. exec. bd. Ctrl. Free Ch., Mpls., 1986; chair exec. bd. Ctrl. Community Ch., 1993-96. Mem. ABA, State Bar Assn. Wis., Minn. Def. Lawyers Assn., Minn. State Bar Assn., Hennepin County Bar Assn., Calif. State Bar Assn., State Bar of Ohio, Def. Rsch. Inst. Avocations: classical music, golf, tennis, computers, motorcycles. Federal civil litigation, State civil litigation, Product liability. Office: Hanson Marek Bolkcom & Greene Ltd 2200 Rand Tower 527 Marquette Ave Minneapolis MN 55402-1302

HANSON, SAMUEL LEE, judge; b. Mankato, Minn., Aug. 26, 1939; s. Lester Kenneth and Margaret Dorothy (Brockmeyer) H.; m. Beret Elizabeth Brown, July 28, 1962 (div. Apr. 1976); children: Greta E., Chrystina E., Benjamin D.; m. Mirja Pirkko Karikosky, Sept. 23, 1977; children: Leif O., Luke A., Jai N. BA, St. Olaf Coll., 1961; LLB, William Mitchell Coll. Law, 1965. Bar: Minn. 1966, U.S. Dist. Ct. Minn. 1966, U.S. Ct. Appeals (8th cir.) 1966, U.S. Supreme Ct. 1971. Law clk. to hon. Douglas K. Amdahl Hennepin County Dist. Ct., Mpls., 1965; law clk. to hon. Robert J. Sheran Minn. Supreme Ct., St. Paul, 1966; assoc. Briggs and Morgan, St. Paul, Minn., 1966—2000, pres., 1988-93; appt. Ct. of Appeals, Minn., 2000—02; Supreme Ct. Justice Minn. Supreme Ct., Minn., 2002. Mem. adv. com. Minn. Supreme Ct., St. Paul, 1984-86; adj. prof. William Mitchell Coll. Law, St. Paul, 1966-71. Contbr. articles to profl. jours. Bd. dirs. Rural Ventures Inc., Mpls., 1981-87, Rural Tech. Partnership, St. Paul, 1987—, Global Vols., St. Paul, 1984—. Fellow Am. Coll. Trial Lawyers (chair Minn. chpt. 1991), Am. Bd. Trial Advocates, Crossroads, Inc. Avocations: rural development, organizational development. Home: 5510 Edgewater Blvd Minneapolis MN 55417-2605 Office: Minn. Supreme Ct 305 Minn Jud Ctr 25 Rev Martin Luther King Jr Blvd Saint Paul MN 55155*

HANSON, VICTOR G. lawyer; b. Detroit, Oct. 26, 1923; s. Ernest A. and Laura Marie (Palmer) H.; m. Laura Ella Udell, Dec. 31, 1971 (dec. Sept. 2002). LLB, Wayne State U., 1949. Bar: Mich. 1949, U.S. Dist. Ct. (ea. dist.) Mich. 1951, U.S. Dist. Ct. (we. dist.) N.Y. 1952, U.S. Supreme Ct. 1952, U.S. Ct. Appeals (7th cir.) 1952, U.S. Ct. Appeals (2d, 6th and 8th cirs.) 1954, U.S. Dist. Ct. (no. and ea. dists.) Ohio 1954, U.S. Dist. Ct. Hawaii, 1957; U.S. Dist. Ct. (so. dist.) N.Y., U.S. Dist. Ct. Minn., U.S. Dist. Ct. (ea. dist.) Wis. Pvt. practice, Detroit, 1949—. Atty. AFL-CIO, Seafarers Internat. Union, Maritime Trades Dept., Tugmen's Union, Dredgemen's Union, Riggers' Union, Sailors Union Pacific, Marine Engrs. Beneficial Assn. Mem. Mich. Port Commn., Bd. Immigration Appeals, 1954, Immigration and Naturalization Svc., 1954, Gov.'s Spl. Fgn. Trade Expansion Commn., 1962. With USMC, 1945 Mem. ABA (V.P. Labor's Internat. Hall of Fame, com. Am. and maritime law), Am. Arbitration Assn. Labor (including EEOC, Fair Labor Standards Act, labor-management relations, NLRB, OSHA), Maritime. Office: 19268 Grand River Ave Detroit MI 48223-1798

HANSOTTE, LOUIS BERNARD, retired lawyer; b. Atlantic City, Oct. 3, 1927; s. Marcel Alfred and Bertha (Goldsmith) H.; m. Wilma Sleeper, Dec. 29, 1955; children: Beth Marcelle, Jeffrey Ronal. BS in Engring., U.S. Mil. Acad., 1950; LLB, LaSalle Extension U., 1961. Bar: Calif. 1962, U.S. Dist. Ct. (so. dist.) Calif. 1962. CLU. Commd. 2d lt. U.S. Army, 1950, advanced through grades to capt., 1953; served in Korea; resigned, 1955; agt., supr., then mgr. Pacific Mut. Life and Union Central Life, 1956-64; sr. ptnr. Hansotte, Nostrand & Lange, San Diego, 1964-94, ret., 1994—. Instr. bus. law, coord. real estate program and paralegal studies program Grossmont C.C., El Cajon, Calif., 1964-94. Author: Legal Aspects of California Real Estate, 1983; California Probate Real Estate Sales, 1983; A Whistleblower's Handbook, 2000, The Medi-Cal Enigma, 2001, Stop "It"-Identity Theft, 2002; contbr. articles to profl. jours. Mem. Calif. State Bar Assn., San Diego County Bar Assn., Nat. Assn. Life Underwriters, Am. Coll. of Life Underwriters, Calif. Assn. of Real Estate Tchrs., West Point Alumni Assn., Army Athletic Assn., West Point Soc. of San Diego (co-founder, past pres.). Probate (including wills, trusts), Property, real (including real estate development, water). Home: PO Box 19324 San Diego CA 92159-0324 E-mail: lhansotte@earthlink.net., medcal@earthlink.net., whistleblower@earthlink.net., mygoodname@earthlink.net.

HANTEL, PHILIP EDWARD, lawyer; b. Los Alamos, N.Mex., Aug. 4, 1972; s. Lawrence W. and Elizabeth G. Hantel. BA in Polit. Sci., U. Wash., 1994; JD, South Tex. Coll. Law, 1997. Bar: La. 1997, U.S. Dist. Ct. (we., mid. and ea. dists.) La. 1997, U.S. Ct. Appeals (5th cir.) 1997. Staff atty. La. Indigent Defender Bd., New Orleans, 1997, juvenile atty. Harvey, La., 1998; assoc. Beevers & Beevers LLP, Gretna, La., 1998-2000; pvt. practice New Orleans, 2000—. Mem. La. Criminal Def. Lawyers Assn., La. Pub. Defenders Assn., 5th Cir. Bar Assn., Fed. Bar Assn. Appellate, Criminal, Juvenile. Home: 2606 Royal St New Orleans LA 70117 Office: Philip Hantel Atty at Law 1050 S Jefferson Davis Pkwy Ste 314 New Orleans LA 70125 Fax: 504-304-3304.

HANZLIK, RAYBURN DEMARA, lawyer; b. L.A., June 7, 1938; s. Rayburn Otto and Ethel Winifred (Membery) H.; children: Kristina, Rayburn N., Alexander, Geoffrey. BS, Principia Coll., 1960; MA, Woodrow Wilson Sch. Fgn. Affairs, U. Va., 1968; JD, U. Va., 1974. Bar: Va. 1975, D.C. 1977. Staff asst. to Pres. U.S., Washington, 1971-73; assoc. dir. White House Domestic Council, 1975-77; atty. Danzansky Dickey Tydings Quint & Gordon, Washington, 1977-78, Akin Gump Strauss Hauer & Feld, Washington, 1978-79, Darling, Rae & Gute, L.A., 1979-81; adminstr. Econ. Regulatory Adminstrn., Dept. Energy, Washington, 1981-85; ptnr. Heidrick and Struggles, Inc., 1985-91, McKenna & Hanzlik, Irvine, Calif., 1991-92; chmn. Lanxide Sports Internat., Inc., San Diego, 1992-95, Stealth Propulsion Internat., Ltd., San Diego, Calif. and, Melbourne, Australia, 1994-97; exec. v.p. Commodore Corp., N.Y.C. and McLean, Va., 1997-98; atty. Trainum, Snowdon & Deane, Washington, 1999—; mng. dir. Washington Technology Strategies, 2002—. Contbg. author: Global Politics and Nuclear Energy, 1971, Soviet Foreign Relations and World Communism, 1965. Alt. del. Republican Nat. Conv., 1980; dir. Calif. Rep. Victory Fund, 1980; candidate U.S. Senate, 1980. Served to lt. USN, 1963-68, Vietnam. Republican. Christian Scientist. Administrative and regulatory, Corporate, general. E-mail: rayburn.hanzlik@verizon.net.

HARADA, HAJIME, lawyer; b. Tokyo, Sept. 10, 1947; s. Jiro and Yukiko (Takahashi) H.; m. Akiko Kawada, Apr. 1981; 1 child. LLB, Tokyo U., 1970; student, Legal Rsch. Ctr. Supreme Ct., Tokyo, 1974. With Export-Import Bank Japan, Tokyo, 1970-72; assoc. Iwata Law Firm, Tokyo, 1974-82, Kido & Ikeda Law Firm, Tokyo, 1982-93; ptnr. Kido, Ikeda & Harada Law Firm, Tokyo, 1993-99, Kido & Harada Law Firm, Tokyo, 1999—. Statutory auditor Koken Co., Ltd., Tokyo, 1997—, Fuji Xerox Learning Inst. Inc., 2000—. Contbr. articles to profl. jours., including Jurist, Jour. Japanese Inst. Internat. Bus. law, Copyright. Mem. Japan Fedn. Bar Assns., Japan Patent Attys. Assn., Licensing Execs. Soc. Japan. Avocation: driving. Office: Rm 828, New Kokusai Bldg 4-1 3 chome Marunouchi Chioduku Tokyo 100-0005 Japan E-mail: fwga9596@mb.infoweb.ne.jp.

HARAZIN, WILLIAM DENNIS, lawyer; b. Berwyn, Ill., Aug. 24, 1953; s. Robert John and Mary Ann H.; m. Becky R. French, Mar. 13, 1981. BS, Ill. State U., 1974, postgrad., 1975, JD, 1978. Bar: Ill. 1978, U.S. Dist. Ct. (no. dist.) Ill. 1978, N.C. 1981, U.S. Dist. Ct. (ea. and mid. dists.) N.C. 1981, U.S. Ct. Appeals (4th cir.) 1982. Lectr. So. Ill. U., Carbondale, 1977-78; assoc. Abramson & Fox, Chgo., 1978-79; instr. Durham (N.C.) Tech. Inst., 1979; atty. Ind. Legal Svcs., Raleigh, N.C., 1980-81; ptnr. Barringer, Allen & Pinnix, Raleigh, 1981-88; ptnr. property co. Harazin, French & Pinnix, Raleigh, 1982-95; instr. N.C. State U., Raleigh, 1982-95, vis. asst. prof., 1995—; owner Law Office of William D. Harazin, Raleigh, 1988—. Mem. legal adv. group. World Trade Ctr. N.C., RTP, N.C., 1990-95; vis. asst. prof. N.C. State U., 1995—. Mem. Raleigh Housing Appeals Bd., 1983-86, chmn., 1986-89; mem. Carbondale Fair Housing Bd., 1977-78; exch. mem. to Japan, Rotary Internat., Raleigh, 1986. Mem.: ABA (mem. com. internat. bus. law), N.C. Dist. Export Coun., N.C. Bd. Sci. and Tech. (internat. com. 1995—2000), World Trade Ctr. N.C. (bd. dirs. 1992—, chmn. 2001—), Wake County Bar Assn., N.C. Dist. Export Coun., N.C. World Trade Assn. (treas. 1985—90, Triangle chpt. pres. 1990—92, statewide pres. 1992—94), Ill. Bar Assn., N.C. Bar Assn. internat. law sect. (coun. mem. 1992—, treas. 1994—95, sec. 1995—96, vice-chair 1996—98, chair 1998—99, mem. bus. law sect.), Internat. Visitors Ctr. (bd. dirs. 1999—), N.C. Ctr. for World Langs. and Culture (bd. dirs. 1994—96), Nat. Assn. Eagle Scouts. Commercial, contracts (including sales of goods; commercial financing), Corporate, general, Private international. Office: 434 Fayetteville Street Mall Raleigh NC 27601-1701

HARBAUGH, DANIEL PAUL, lawyer; b. Wendell, Idaho, May 18, 1948; s. Myron and Manuelita (Garcia) Harbaugh. BA, Gonzaga U., 1970, JD, 1974. Bar: Wash. 1974, U.S. Dist. Ct. (ea. dist.) Wash. 1977, U.S. Ct. Appeals (9th cir.) 1978. Asst. atty. gen. State of Wash., Spokane, 1974-77; ptnr. Richter, Wimberley & Ericson, Spokane, 1977-83, Harbaugh & Bloom, P.S., Spokane, 1983—. Bd. dirs. Spokane Legal Svcs., 1982—86; bd. govs. LAWPAC, Seattle, 1980—92. Bd. dirs. Spokane Ballet, 1983-88; chpt. dir. Les Amis du Vin, Spokane, 1985-88; mem. Spokane County Civil Svc. Commn., 1991-2003, chmn., 1999-2003, Gonzaga U. Pres'. Coun., 1991-2000. Mem. ATLA, Wash. State Bar Assn. (spl. dist. counsel 1982-95, mem. com. rules for profl. conduct 1989-92, mem. legis. com. 1995-96), Spokane County Bar Assn. (chair med.-legal com. 1991), Wash. State Trial Lawyers Assn. (v.p. 1988-89, co-chair worker's compensation sect. 1992, 93, spl. select. com. on workers' corp. 1990—, forum 1994—, vice-chmn. 1994-97, mem. legis. com. 1995-98), Nat. Orgn. Social Security Claimants Reps., Internat. Wine and Food Soc. (pres. local chpt. 1989-91, cellar master 1994-96, cellar com. 2001—), Spokane Club, Spokane Country Club (adminstrv. com. 1995-98, chmn. 1991-98, trustee 1996-99, sec.-treas. 1997-98, pres. 1998-99, ex-officio 1999-2000, long range planning com. 1999-2001), Alpha Sigma Nu, Phi Alpha Delta. Roman Catholic. Alternative dispute resolution, Personal injury (including property damage), Workers' compensation. Office: Harbaugh & Bloom PS PO Box 1461 Spokane WA 99210-1461 E-mail: dan@hblaw2.com.

HARBISON, JAMES WESLEY, JR., lawyer; b. Mooresville, N.C., Aug. 30, 1934; s. James Wesley and Ola Mae (Bonney) H.; m. Margaret Geddes Morgan, Apr. 15, 1961; children: Anne, James. AB, Duke U., 1956; LLB, Yale U., 1959. Bar: N.C. 1959, N.Y. 1960, U.S. Dist. Ct. (so. and ea. dists.) N.Y. 1961, U.S. Ct. Appeals (2d cir.) 1962, U.S. Supreme Ct. 1968, U.S. Ct. Appeals (7th cir.) 1970, U.S. Ct. Appeals (5th cir.) 1975. Assoc. Simpson, Thacher & Bartlett, N.Y.C., 1960-73; ptnr. Wickes, Riddell, Bloomer, Jacobi & McGuire, N.Y.C., 1973-78, Morgan, Lewis & Bockius LLP, N.Y.C., 1979—. Served to capt. USAF, 1959-60, N.Y. A.N.G., 1960-68. Mem. ABA, N.C. Bar Assn., N.Y. State Bar Assn., Assn. of Bar of City of N.Y., Fed. Bar Council, Am. Judicature Soc. Clubs: Met., Yale (N.Y.C.). Democrat. Methodist. Antitrust, Federal civil litigation, State civil litigation. Home: 30 E End Ave New York NY 10028-7053 Office: Morgan Lewis & Bockius LLP 101 Park Ave Fl 44 New York NY 10178-0060

HARCHA, HOWARD H., III, judge; b. Portsmouth, Ohio, Mar. 23, 1957; s. Howard H., Jr. and Mary Lee Harcha; m. Peggy Lynn Harcha, Aug. 22, 1981; children: Heather Lynn, Howard IV, John, Matt. BS in Mktg., Ohio State U., 1979; JD, Ohio No. U., 1982. Bar: Ohio, U.S. Dist. Ct. (no. and so. dists.) Ohio. Prosecutor City of Portsmouth, 1982—91; lawyer Harcha and Harcha, Portsmouth, 1982—91; judge Portsmouth Mcpl. Ct., 1991—97, Scioto County Common Pleas, Portsmouth, 1997—. Mem.: Ohio State Bar Assn. (chmn. criminal law com. 1996—97), Ohio Acad. Trial Lawyers (bd. govs. 1985—89), Am. Judges Assn. (bd. govs. 2002). Methodist. Avocations: hunting, fishing, coaching youth. Home: 1933 Franklin Blvd Portsmouth OH 45662 Office: Scioto County Common Pleas Ct 602 7th St Portsmouth OH 45662 Office Fax: 740-355-8230. Business E-Mail: hharcha@zoomnet.net.

HARDCASTLE, GERALD WAYNE, judge; b. Ogden, Utah, June 1, 1946; s. Burnes and Mary Olive (Camden) Hardcastle; m. Kathy Ann Teague, Jan. 11, 1991; children: Gerri Lynn, Erik, Courtney, Whitney. BS, Weber State Coll., 1970; JD, U. Utah, 1973. Bar: Utah 1973, U.S. Dist. Ct. Utah 1973, Nev. 1974, U.S. Dist. Ct. Nev. 1974. Assoc. Steffen & Simmons, Las Vegas, Nev., 1974—75; dep. dist. atty. Clark County Dist. Atty. Office, Las Vegas, 1975—76, Esmeralda County Dist. Atty. Office, Goldfield, Nev., 1976; pvt. practice Las Vegas, 1976—92; judge U.S. Dist. Ct. Nev., Las Vegas, 1993—. With USNR, 1967—68. Recipient Commr.'s award, U.S. HHS, 1996. Office: Divsn Dept D 601 N Pecos Rd Las Vegas NV 89101-2408

HARDEE-THOMAS, MARVA A. lawyer; b. Manhattan, N.Y., Mar. 29, 1964; d. Nathaniel Pinckney and Betty (Seabrook) Hardee; m. Michael A. Thomas, July 6, 1996. BA in Polit. Sci., N.C. State U., 1986; JD, Seton Hall U., 1993. Bar: U.S. Dist. Ct. (so. dist.) S.C. 1997. Legal asst. Prudential Securities Inc., Manhattan, 1991-93; law clk. Jersey City Cir. Ct., 1993-94; legal asst. George Sink Attys., Charleston, S.C., 1994; asst. solicitor First Cir. Solicitor's Office, Orangeburg, S.C., 1994-95; pvt. practice Summerville, S.C., 1995—. Republican. Methodist. Criminal, Family and matrimonial, Personal injury (including property damage). Office: 130 E Richardson Ave Summerville SC 29483

HARDEN, RICHARD RUSSELL, lawyer; b. Oak Park, Ill., Apr. 22, 1958; s. James Edward Harden and Patricia Gilkison Murphy; m. Kathryn Diane Knosher, June 21, 1980; childen: Jeffrey Joseph, Colleen Elizabeth. BA, Knox Coll., 1980; JD, U. Ill., 1983. Bar: Ill. 1983. Assoc. Robert P. Moore & Assocs., Champaign, Ill., 1983-86, Thomas, Mamer & Haughey, Champaign, 1986-90, ptnr., 1990—. Spkr., mem. faculty Ill. Inst. for CLE, Champaign, 1997—, Carle Found., Champaign, 1998, Ill. Primary Healthcare Assn., 2001. Contbg. author: Medical Evidence, 1997, (supplement) 2000, Carle Selected Papers, 2000. Various positions, including scoutmaster, cubmaster, asst. scoutmaster, advisor, commr. Boy Scouts Am., Champaign, 1992—, advisor law exploring, learning for life divsn.; elder Westminster Presbyn. Ch., Champaign, 1989-92, 1998-2001. Mem. Ill. Bar Assn., Ill. Assn. Def. Trial Counsel, Champaign County Bar Assn., Def. Rsch. Inst., Phi Beta Kappa. Avocations: camping, hiking, canoeing, golf, climbing. General civil litigation, Personal injury (including property damage), Product liability. Office: Thomas Mamer & Haughey PO Box 560 30 E Main St Champaign IL 61824-0560 E-mail: Riharden@tmh-law.com.

HARDGROVE, JAMES ALAN, lawyer; b. Chgo., Feb. 20, 1945; s. Albert John and Ruth (Noonen) H.; m. Kathleen M. Peterson, June 15, 1968; children: Jennifer Anne, Amy Kristine, Michael Sheridan. BA, U. Notre Dame, 1967; cert. English law, U. Coll. Law, 1969; JD, U. Notre Dame, 1970. Bar: Ill. 1970, U.S. Ct. Appeals (7th cir.) 1970, U.S. Dist. Ct. (no. dist.) Ill. 1970, U.S. Dist. Ct. (cen. dist.) Ill. 1978, U.S. Supreme Ct. 1980. Law clk. to presiding justice U.S. Ct. Appeals (7th cir.), Chgo., 1970-71; assoc. Sidley & Austin, Chgo., 1971-76, ptnr., 1977—. Mem. ABA, Ill. Bar Assn., Chgo. Bar Assn., Legal Club. Antitrust, Federal civil litigation, State civil litigation. Home: 948 Ridge Ave Evanston IL 60202-1720 Office: Sidley Austin Brown & Word Bank One Plz 10 S Dearborn St Chicago IL 60603-2000 E-mail: jhardgro@sidley.com.

HARDIE, JAMES HILLER, lawyer; b. Pitts., Dec. 1, 1929; s. James H. and Elizabeth Gillespie (Alcorn) H.; m. Frances P. Curtis, Dec. 5, 1953; children: J. Hiller, Janet Hardie Harvey, Andrew G., Michael C., Rachel Hardie Share. AB, Princeton U., 1951; LL.B., Harvard U., 1954. Bar: Pa. 1955. Assoc. Reed Smith LLP, Pitts., 1954-62, ptnr., 1962-99, of counsel, 1999—. Mem. ABA, Am. Law Inst., Pa. Bar Assn. Corporate, general, Mergers and acquisitions, Securities. Office: Reed Smith LLP PO Box 2009 Pittsburgh PA 15230-2009 E-mail: jhardie@reedsmith.com.

HARDIN, ADLAI STEVENSON, JR., judge; b. Norwalk, Conn., Sept. 20, 1937; s. Adlai S. and Carol H. BA, Princeton U., 1959; LLB, Columbia U., 1962. Bar: N.Y. 1963, U.S. Dist. Ct. (so. and ea. dists.) N.Y. 1965, U.S. Supreme Ct. 1967, U.S. Ct. Appeals (2d cir.) 1965, U.S. Ct. Appeals (5th cir.) 1974, U.S. Ct. Appeals (3d cir.) 1977, U.S. Ct. Appeals (9th cir.) 1982, U.S. Ct. Appeals (4th and D.C. cirs.) 1985, U.S. Ct. Appeals (7th cir.) 1988. Assoc. Milbank, Tweed, Hadley & McCloy, N.Y.C., 1963, ptnr., 1971; judge U.S. Bankruptcy Ct., 1995—. Judge Bankruptcy Appellate Panel for 2d Circuit, 1996-2000. Trustee Spence Sch., 1981-87; former elder, trustee Madison Ave. Presbyn. Ch. With USAR, 1962-68. Mem. ABA (past chmn. N.Y. State membership com., antitrust sect., litigation sect.), Fed. Bar Coun. (trustee 1983-92, v.p. 1986-88, chmn. bd. dirs. 1990-92), Fed. Bar Found. (pres. 1992-94), N.Y. State Bar Assn. (mem. com. on profl. ethics, mem. jud. election monitoring com., mem. internat. litigation com.), Assn. of Bar of City of N.Y. (sec. 1979-82, chmn. com. on profl. and jud. ethics 1970-73, mem. spl. com. on lawyers role in securities transactions, mem. spl. com. to cooperate with ABA in revision of Canons of Ethics, mem. nominating com., mem. com. on membership, mem. com. on profl. discipline), Nat. Conf. Bankruptcy Judges, Am. Bankruptcy Inst., Westchester County Bar Assn. Office: US Bankruptcy Ct US Courthouse 300 Quarropas St White Plains NY 10601-4150

HARDIN, DALE WAYNE, retired lawyer, federal official; b. Peoria, Ill., Sept. 9, 1922; s. James P. and Lucille Maureen (Elgin) H.; m. Sandra L. Gorzen, July 3, 1939; children: Bradley J., Stacy Keaton, Rebecca M., J. Scott Keaton. AB in Polit. Sci., George Washington U., 1949, JD, 1951. Bar: Va. 1951, D.C. 1951, U.S. Dist. D.C. 1951, U.S. Ct. Appeals (D.C. cir.) 1951. Assoc. Mills & Partridge, Washington, 1951; spl. agent FBI, Washington, 1951-54; fin. counsel ICC, Washington, 1954-55, legis. counsel, 1955-64, presdl. appointee as commr., 1967-77, vice chmn., acting chmn. agy., 1971-73, chmn. rates divsn., 1975-77; Presdl. appointee, mem. Adminstrv. Conf. U.S., 1969-72; dir. dept. transp. and comm. U.S. C. of C., Washington, 1964-66; v.p. govt. affairs Overmeyer Co., Washington, 1966-67; spl. counsel Am. Trucking Assn., Washington, 1967; assoc. prof. polit sci. S.W. Tex. State U., San Marcos, Tex., 1977—, assoc. prof. emeritus, 1989-00, acting dean sch. liberal arts., 1986-87, chmn. dept. home econs., 1990-92; ret. law educator, 2000. Gen. counsel Transp. Assn. Am., Washington, 1959; moderator 14th Ann. Seminar, State Bar Tex., 1982, moderator profl. devel. program gen. paralegal skills, 1988, standing com. on legal assts., 1988-00; chmn. Tex. forum IV Conf. Legal Asst. Educators, 1985, chair forum VII, 1988; presenter papers in field. Bus. sec. George Washington U. Sch. Law Rev., 1951. With USMC, 1942—46, PTO. Mem. Soc. Former Spl. Agents FBI. Fed. Bar Assn., Va. State Bar., D.C. Bar, Phi Delta Phi. Avocation: golf. Home: 10829 River Plantation Dr Austin TX 78747-1490

HARDIN, HAL D. lawyer, former state attorney, judge, federal official; BS, Middle Tenn. State U. (MTSY); JD, Vanderbilt U., 1968; postgrad., State Jud. Coll., Reno. Bar: Tenn., U.S. Supreme Ct., D.C., U.S. Ct. Claims, U.S. Tax. Ct., U.S. Ct. Mil. Appeals, Tex., Ky. Fingerprint technician FBI; dir. St. Louis Job Corps Ctr.; vol. Peace Corps; asst. dist. atty.; pvt. practice; presiding judge Nashville Trial Cts., 1976-77; spl. judge Ct. of Appeals, 1977; U.S. atty. Middle Dist. Tenn., 1977-81; practice law Nashville, 1981—. Adj. prof. Aquinas Coll., Tenn. State Coll., 1975—76; adj. instr. fed. sentencing, criminal practice and procedure Nashville Sch. Law, 1994—. Bd. dirs. Nat. Assn. Former U.S. Attys., 1993—96, Leadership Nashville, 1983, Capital Case Resource Ctr., 1988—95, Leadership Alumni Assn., 1985. Master: Inns of Ct.; fellow: Tenn. Bar Found.; mem.: Nat. Peace Corps Assn. (bd. dirs. 2001—), Am. Bd. Trial Advs. (sec. Tenn. chpt. 1987, nat. bd. dirs. 1988—89, pres. Tenn. chpt. 1990), Tenn. Criminal Def. Attys. Assn., 6th Cir. Jud. Coun. (life), Nat. Criminal Def. Attys. Assn., Tex. Bar Assn., Tenn. Bar Assn. (gen. counsel 1982—90), Nashville Bar Assn. (bd. dirs. 1983—85, v.p. 1985). Federal civil litigation, State civil litigation, Criminal. Office: 218 3d Ave N Nashville TN 37201

HARDIN, WILLIAM DOWNER, retired lawyer; b. Newark, Sept. 27, 1926; s. Charles R. and Emma (Downer) H.; m. Rosemarie Koellhoffer, Jan. 19, 1952 (dec. Mar. 1996); m. Ruth M. Johnson, May 29, 1999; children: William Downer, David Gerth, Peter Roe. AB, Princeton, 1948; LL.B., Columbia, 1951. Bar: N.J. 1951. Law clk. N.J. Superior Ct., 1951-52; mem. firm Pitney, Hardin, Kipp & Szuch, Morristown, 1957-96; practiced in Newark and Morristown, 1952—. Mem. N.J. Bd. Bar Examiners, 1964-68, chmn., 1968; mem. local draft bd. SSS, 1953-74, chmn., 1970-74; mem. Family Svc. Bur., Newark, 1953-75, pres., 1960-66; mem. Family Svc. Morris County, 1976-85, 87-98, pres., 1979-82, 95-97, v.p., 1992-95; mem. membership com. Family Svc. Assn. Am., 1965-78, dir., 1971-79, 89-95; mem. Nat. Budget and Consultation Com., 1966-71, Coun. on Accreditation Svcs. for Families and Children, 1978-80. Trustee Newark Acad., 1952-85, pres., 1969-72, chmn., 1976-78; mem. Legal Svcs. of N.J., 1983-2002, chmn., 1990-96; mem. Legal Aid Soc. of Morris County, N.J., 1984-93, pres., 1989-90. With USNR, 1944-46. Mem. ABA, Fed. Bar Assn., N.J. Bar Assn., Essex County Bar Assn., Morris County Bar Assn., Morristown Club, Nassau Club, Coral Beach and Tennis Club, Short Hills Club, Princeton Club of N.Y., Morris County Golf Club. Episcopalian. Commercial, contracts (including sales of goods; commercial financing), Corporate, general, Securities. Home: 15 Gapview Rd Short Hills NJ 07078-2077 Office: 200 Campus Dr Florham Park NJ 07932-1007

HARDING, DON L. judge; b. St. Anthony, Idaho, Sept. 13, 1937; s. Ralph W. and Kathryn O. Harding; m. Janet Rigglee Harding, Sept. 12, 1964; children: Suzanne, Don. C., Stephen, Katie, Jennifer, Joseph, Michael, Hayley, Cody. BA in Acctg., George Washington U., 1964, JD, 1970. Pvt. practice, Malad, Idaho, 1972—77; magistrate judge 6th jud. dist. State of Idaho, 1977—83, adminstrv. judge 6th jud. dist., 1994—; pvt. practice Soda Springs, Idaho, 1983—94. Campaign and office worker Sen. Frank Church, 1960—64; campaign worker Congressman Ralph Harding, 1960—64. Served with U.S. Army, 1956, served with USAR, 1957—58. Mem. Lds Ch. Avocations: volunteer work for Boy Scouts of America, golf, travel. Home: PO Box 752 Soda Springs ID 83276 Office: 159 S Main St Soda Springs ID 83276

HARDING, MAJOR BEST, former state supreme court chief justice; b. Charlotte, N.C., Oct. 13, 1935; m. Jane Lewis, Dec., 1958; children: Major B. Jr., David L., Alice Harding Sanderson. BS, Wake Forest U., 1957, also LLD; LLM in Jud. Process, U. Va., 1995; LLD, Stetson U., 1991, Fla. Coastal Sch. Law, 1999. Bar: N.C. 1959, Fla. 1960. Staff judge adv. hdqrs., Ft. Gordon, Ga., 1960-62; asst. county solicitor Criminal Ct. of Record, Duval County, Fla., 1962-63; pvt. practice law, 1964-68; judge Juvenile Ct., Duval County, 1968-70, 4th Jud. Cir. of Fla., 1970-74, chief judge, 1974-77; justice Supreme Ct. of Fla., Tallahassee, 1991—2002, chief justice, 1998-2000. Supervisory judge Family Mediation Unit, 1984-90; mem. Matrimonial Law Commn. and Gender Bias Study Commn.; chair Fla. Ct. Edn. Coun., past mem. Jud. Conf.; 1st dean New Judges Coll., 1975, faculty mem. in probate and juvenile areas, until 1979; dean Fla. Jud. Coll., 1984-92, faculty mem., 1984—, mem. bench-bar commn.; chmn. Supreme Ct. com. on law-related edn., 1997—. Bd. dirs. Legal Aid Assn., Family Consultation Svc., Daniel Meml. Home; mem. bd. visitors Wake Forest Sch. Law, Winston-Salem, N.C., Reformed Theol. Sem., Orlando, Fla.; past pres. Rotary Club of Riverside, Jacksonville, Fla., Rotary Club of Tallahasee; chmn. U.S. Constn. Bicentennial Commn., Jacksonville; past mem., deacon, elder St. John's Presbyn. Ch.; commr. Gen. Assembly Presbyn. Ch. U.S., 1971. Recipient Award for Outstanding Contbn. to Field of Matrimonial Law Am. Acad. Matrimonial Lawyers, 1986, Disting. Svc. award Nat. Ctr. State Cts., 2001, William A. Dugger Profl. Integrity award Capital Rotary Club. Mem. ABA (mem. bar admission com., Commn. Lawyer Assistance Programs Jud. Recognition award), Am. Bd. Trial Advocates (Jurist of Yr. Jacksonville chpt. 2000), The Fla. Bar, N.C. State Bar Assn., Chester Bedell Inn of Ct. (past pres., ex-officio bd. mem., master emeritus Chester Bedell), Dade County Trial Lawyers Assn. (Justice Harry Lee Anstead professionalism award 1998), Scabbard and Blade, Tallahassee Am. Inn of Ct. (ex officio trustee), Tallahassee Bar Assn., Econ. Club of Fla. (treas.), Sigma Chi (Significant Sig award 1997), Phi Delta Phi. Episcopalian.*

HARDING, RAY MURRAY, JR., judge; b. Logan, Utah, Nov. 23, 1953; s. Ray M. Sr. and Martha (Rasmussen) H.; m. Anne Harding; children: Michelle, Nicole, Justin. BS, Brigham Young U., 1975; JD, J. Reuben Clark Law Sch., 1978. Bar: Utah 1978. Ptnr. Harding & Harding, American Fork and Pleasant Grove, Utah, 1978-85; owner Harding & Assoc., American Fork and Pleasant Grove, 1986-95; judge Utah County 4th Jud. Dist. Ct., 1995—. Atty. Lindon City and Pleasant Grove City, Utah, 1983-95, Alpine City, 1985-94, American Fork, Utah, 1985-95. Bd. trustees Utah Valley State Coll., 1986-95, chmn., 1991-93. Named Businessman of Yr., Future Bus. Leaders of Am., 1983. Mem. ABA, Utah State Bar Assn. Avocations: skiing, scuba diving, hiking, hunting, travel. Home: 11165 Yarrow Cir Highland UT 84003-9598 Office: Utah County 4th Judicial Dist Ct 125 N 100 W Provo UT 84601-2849

HARDTNER, QUINTIN THEODORE, III, lawyer; b. Shreveport, La., Mar. 5, 1936; s. Quintin Theodore and Jane (Owen) H.; m. Susan Mayer, June 30, 1962; children: Susan Owen, Quintin Theodore IV, George Jonathan. BBA, Tulane U., 1957, JD, 1961. Bar: La. 1961; cert. tax atty., estate planning and adminstrv. specialist. Assoc. Jones, Walker, Waechter, Poitevent, Carrere & Denegre, New Orleans, 1961-62; ptnr. Hargrove, Guyton, Ramey and Barlow, Shreveport, 1962-94; pres. Barlow & Hardtner L.C., Shreveport, 1994-2000; ptnr. Lemle & Kelleher, LLP, Shreveport, 2000—. Past dir. and chmn. Community Found. Shreveport-Bossier; past dir. Sci-Port Discovery Ctr.; mem., past pres. Com. of 100; past dir. Biomed. Rsch. Found. N.W. La. Past mem. adv. bd. Salvation Army; past trustee, past chmn. bd. All Sts. Episcopal Sch., Vicksburg, Miss.; past trustee, past chmn. St. Mark's Day Sch.; past trustee Southfield Sch.; past vestryman St. Mark's Episcopal Ch.; past bd. dirs., v.p. Shreveport Assn. for Blind; past bd. dirs. Family and Children's Svcs.; past co-chmn. Centenary Coll. Fund. Served to lt. USMC, 1957-59. Fellow Am. Coll. Trust and Estate Counsel, Am. Bar Found., La. Bar Found.; mem. ABA, La. State Bar Assn. (past mem ho. of dels., cert. tax atty., cert. estate planning and adminstrn. specialist), Ark.-La.-Tex. Tax Inst. (past bd. dirs.), Shreveport Bar Assn. (past pres.), Estate Planning Coun. Shreveport (past dir., past pres.), Shreveport Club, Cambridge Club, Rotary (past pres., bd. dirs.). Corporate, general, Estate planning, Probate (including wills, trusts). Home: 525 Southfield Rd Shreveport LA 71106 Office: 10th Fl Louisiana Tower 501 Edwards St Shreveport LA 71101-3537 E-mail: qhardtner@lemle.com.

HARDY, ASHTON RICHARD, lawyer; b. Gulfport, Miss., Aug. 31, 1935; s. Ashton Maurice and Alice (Baumbach) H.; m. Katherine Ketelsen, Sept. 4, 1959; children: Karin H. Wood, Katherine H. Foster. BBA, Tulane U., 1958, JD, 1962. Bar: La. 1962, FCC, 1976. Ptnr. Jones, Walker, Waechter, Poitevent, Carrere & Denegre, New Orleans, 1962-74, 76-82; gen. counsel FCC, Washington, 1974-76; ptnr. Fawer, Brian, Hardy, Zatzkis, New Orleans, 1982-86, Hardy & Popham, 1986-88, Walker, Bordelon, Hamlin, Theriot & Hardy, New Orleans, 1988-92, Hardy, Carey & Chautin, New Orleans, 1992—. Gen. counsel La. Assn. Broadcasters, 1976-86, Greater New Orleans Assn. Broadcasters, 1976—, La. Assn. Advt. Agys., 1982-86; lectr. in field; advance rep. to Pres. U.S., 1971-74. Bd. dirs. New Orleans Mission, 1989—, Met. Crime Commn. New Orleans, 1993—, vice-chmn., 1997-2002, United Christian Charities, 1993-99, Prison Fellowship/La., 1976—. Lt. USN, 1958-60. Named to Hall of Fame, Greater New Orleans Broadcasters Assn., 2001. Mem. La. Bar Assn. (del. ho. of dels. 1987-92), FCC Bar Assn., Nat. Religious Broadcasters (nat. bd. dirs. 2003— bd. dirs. S.W. chpt. 2003—), Christian Legal Soc., Metairie Country Club (pres. 1986), Comm Club. Administrative and regulatory, Commercial, contracts (including sales of goods; commercial financing), Communications. Home: 306 Cedar Dr Metairie LA 70005-3902 Office: Hardy Carey & Chautin LLP Ste 300 110 Veterans Memorial Blvd Metairie LA 70005-4960 E-mail: arhardy@bellsouth.net.

HARDY, HARVEY LOUCHARD, retired lawyer; b. Dallas, Dec. 2, 1914; s. Nat L. and Winifred F. (Fouraker) H.; m. Edna Vivian Bedell, Feb. 14, 1948; children: Victoria Elizabeth Hardy Pursch, Alice Anne Hardy Gannon. Bar: Tex. 1936, U.S. Dist. Ct. (so. and we. dists.) Tex. 1946, U.S. Ct. Appeals (5th cir.) 1946, U.S. Supreme Ct. 1949. First asst. dist. atty. Bexar County, San Antonio, 1947-50, acting dist. atty., 1950-51; city atty. San Antonio, 1952—53, Castle Hills, Tex., 1967—96, Helotes, Tex., 1984-96, Fair Oaks Ranch, Tex., 1973-96; legal adviser bd. trustees Fireman and Policemen's Pension Fund of San Antonio, 1956-96; ret. Legal advisor Grey Forest Utilities, 1986-96. Author: A Lifetime at the Bar: A Lawyer's Memoir, 1999. 1st lt. inf. U.S. Army, 1941-45. Decorated Bronze Star with cluster. Fellow Tex. Bar Found.; mem. Tex. Bar Assn., San Antonio Bar Found., Tex. Assn. City Atts., San Antonio Bar Assn. Methodist. Home: 215 Atwater Dr San Antonio TX 78213

HARDY, MICHAEL LYNN, lawyer; b. St. Louis, Aug. 28, 1947; s. William Frost and Ruth (Shea) H.; m. Martha Bond, Sept. 2, 1972; children: Brian M., Kevin S. AB, John Carroll U., 1969; JD, U. Mich., 1972. Bar: Ohio 1972. Assoc. Guren, Merritt, et al, Cleve., 1972-77, ptnr., 1977-84, Thompson Hine LLP and predecessor, Cleve., 1984—, ptnr.-in-charge Cleve. office, 2003—. Editor-in-chief Ohio Environ. Monthly, 1989-94, Ohio Environ. Law, 1992; bd. advisors Harvard Environ. Law Rev., 1976-78, The Environ. Counselor, 1988—. Trustee Nature Ctr. at Shaker Lakes. Capt. U.S. Army, 1969—74. Mem. ABA (nat. resources sect.), Ohio State Bar Assn. (sec. environ. law com. 1983-84, vice-chmn. 1984-86, chmn. 1987-91), Def. Rsch. Inst. (chmn. industrywide litig. com. 1989-91), Canterbury Golf Club; trustee Nature Ctr. Shaker Lakes 2001-; dir. Nat. Club Assn. 2002-. Administrative and regulatory, Federal civil litigation, Environmental. Home: 30649 Summit Ln Cleveland OH 44124-5836 Office: Thompson Hine LLP 3900 Key Ctr 127 Public Sq Cleveland OH 44114-1216 E-mail: mike.hardy@thompsonhine.com.

HARDY, WILLIAM ROBINSON, lawyer; b. Cin., June 14, 1934; s. William B. and Chastine M. (Sprague) H.; m. Leslie Warrington Bailey, Apr. 16, 1999; children from previous marriage: Anita Christina, William Robinson Jr. AB magna cum laude, Princeton U., 1956; JD, Harvard U., 1963. Bar: Ohio 1963, U.S. Supreme Ct. 1975. Life underwriter New Eng. Mut. Life Ins. Co., 1956-63; assoc. Graydon, Head & Ritchey, Cin., 1963-68, ptnr., 1968-98. Mem. panel comml. arbitrators Am. Arbitration Assn., 1972—, mem. panel large complex case program, 1993—, panel of mediators, 1993—, comml. arbitrator tng. faculty, 1998—; reporter joint com. for revision of rules of U.S. Dist. Ct. for So. Dist. Ohio, 1975, 80, 83, mem., 1990—. Bd. dirs. Cin. Union Bethel, 1968-82, pres., 1977-82, emeritus, 1982—; bd. dirs. Ohio Valley Goodwill Industries Rehab. Ctr., Cin., 1970—, pres., 1981-92; mem. Cin. Bd. Bldg. Appeals, 1976-2001, vice chmn., 1983, chmn., 1983-2001; pres. Hamilton County (Ohio) Alcohol and Drug Addiction Svcs. Bd., 1990-92; trustee Substance Abuse Mgmt. and Devel. Inc., 1998-99. Capt. USAR, 1956-68; maj. gen. Ohio Mil. Res., comdr., 1996-2001. Recipient award of merit Ohio Legal Ctr. Inst., 1975, 76, Ohio Commendation medal, 1999. Mem. ABA, AAAS, Ohio Bar Assn., Cin. Bar Assn., Ohio Acad. Trial Lawyers, Am. Arbitration Assn., Assn. for Conflict Resolution, 6th Cir. Jud. Conf. (life), Ohio Soc. Colonial Wars (gov. 1979), Princeton (N.Y.C.) Club, Interlachen Country Club (Winter Park, Fla.), Phi Beta Kappa. Mem. Ch. Of Redeemer. Alternative dispute resolution, Appellate, General civil litigation. Office: 432 Walnut St Ste 206 Cincinnati OH 45202-3909

HARDYMON, DAVID WAYNE, lawyer; b. Columbus, Ohio, Aug. 22, 1949; s. Philip Barbour and Margaret Evelyn (Bowers) H.; m. Monica Ella Sleep, Mar. 13, 1982; children: Philip Garnet, Teresa Jeanette. BA in History, Bowling Green State U., 1971; JD, Capital U., Columbus, Ohio, 1976. Bar: Ohio 1976, U.S. Dist. Ct. (so. dist.) Ohio 1976; U.S. Supreme Ct. 1980, U.S. Ct. Appeals (6th cir.) 1982, Ky. 1999, U.S. Dist. Ct. (no. dist.) Ohio 1999, W.Va. 2000, U.S. Dist. Ct. (so. dist.) W.Va. 2000. Asst. prosecuting atty. Franklin County Prosecuter's Office, Columbus, Ohio, 1976-81; assoc. Vorys, Sater, Seymour & Pease, Columbus, 1981-86, ptnr., 1987—. Mem. Chmn's. Club Franklin Country Rep. Orgn., 1983. Fellow Columbus Bar Found.; mem. Ohio State Bar Assn., Columbus Bar Assn. Avocations: sailing, archery. General civil litigation, Environmental, Product liability. Office: Vorys Sater Seymour & Pease PO Box 1008 52 E Gay St Columbus OH 43215-3161

HARFF, CHARLES HENRY, lawyer, retired diversified industrial company executive; b. Wesel, Germany, Sept. 27, 1929; s. Philip and Stephanie (Dreyfuss) H.; m. Marion Haines MacAfee, July 19, 1958; children—Pamela Haines, John Blair, Todd Philip BA, Colgate U., 1951; LL.B., Harvard U., 1954; postgrad., U. Bonn, Fed. Republic Germany, 1955. Bar: N.Y. 1955. Assoc. Chadbourne & Parke, N.Y.C., 1955-64, ptnr., 1964-84; sr. v.p., gen. counsel, sec. Rockwell Internat. Corp., Pitts., 1984-94, sr. v.p., spl. counsel, 1994-96, ret., 1996. Cons., 1996—2001; bd. dirs. Arvin Meritor, Inc. Trustee Christian A. Johnson Endeavor Found., N.Y.C., 1984-2001; bd. dirs. Atlantic Legal Found., 1989-98, Fulbright Assn., 1995-2002, pres., 2001. Fulbright scholar U. Bonn, Germany, 1955. Mem. ABA, N.Y. State Bar Assn., The Assn. Gen. Counsel, Harvard Club, Duquesne Club, Allegheny Country Club, Farm Neck Golf Club (Martha's Vineyard, Mass.). Corporate, general, Securities.

HARGESHEIMER, ELBERT, III, lawyer; b. Cleve., Jan. 4, 1944; s. Elbert and Agnes Mary (Heckman) H.; children: Heather Leigh, Elbert IV, Jon-Erik, Piper Elizabeth, Kevin R. Cross, Mark R. Dziob. AB, Cornell U., 1966; JD, SUNY, Buffalo, 1969. Bar: N.Y. 1970, U.S. Dist. Ct. (we. dist.) N.Y. 1971. Assoc. Miller, Bouvier, O'Connor & Cegielski, Buffalo, 1970-73, ptnr., 1973-74, Godinho & Hargesheimer, Hamburg, N.Y., 1974-84; pvt. practice law Hamburg, 1984—. Chief counsel Joint Legis. Commn. to Revise Bus. and Corp. Law, N.Y. State Assembly and Senate, 1974-75; prosecutor Village of Blasdell (N.Y.), 1978-80, 83-87, village atty. 1980-82; fund chmn. South Towns Hosp. Found., Inc., 1973-76, fin. chmn., bd. dirs., 1976-77, v.p., 1978-82; chmn. Hamburg Town Rep. Com., 1978-88; coord. Erie County Pretrial Svcs. Program, 1987-88; counsel Erie County Rep. Com., 1980-92; mem. Erie County Bd. Ethics, 1979-89, chmn. 1983.; charter mem., counsel S.W. Hamburg Taxpayers Assn. Named Mr. Rep., Town of Hamburg Rep. Club, 1982, Rep. of Yr., Hamburg Town Rep. Com., 1988. Mem. Western N.Y. Trial Lawyer's Assn., Theta Chi. Methodist. Corporate, general, Family and matrimonial, General practice. Home and Office: 22 Buffalo St Hamburg NY 14075-5002

HARGRAVE, RUDOLPH, state supreme court chief justice; b. Shawnee, Okla., Feb. 15, 1925; s. John Hubert and Daisy (Holmes) H.; m. Madeline Hargrave, May 29, 1949; children: Cindy Lu, John Robert, Jana Sue. LLB, U. Okla., 1949. Bar: Okla. 1949. Pvt. practice, Wewoka, Okla., 1949; asst. county atty. Seminole County, 1951-55; judge Seminole County Ct., 1964-67, Seminole County Superior Ct., 1967-69; dist. judge Okla. Dist. Ct., Dist. 22, 1969-79; justice Okla. Supreme Ct., Oklahoma City, 1978—, former vice chief justice, currently chief justice. Mem. Seminole County Bar Assn., Okla. Bar Assn., ABA Lodges: Lions; Masons. Democrat. Methodist. Office: Okla Supreme Ct State Capitol Bldg Room 202 Oklahoma City OK 73105

HARGROVE, WADE HAMPTON, lawyer; b. Clinton, N.C., Mar. 6, 1940; s. Wade Hampton and Susan (Baker) H.; m. Sandra Dunaway, June 7, 1969; children: Wade Hampton III, Andrew D. AB with honors, U. N.C., 1962, JD, 1965. Bar: N.C. 1965, D.C. 1967. Ptnr. Brooks, Pierce, McLendon, Humphrey, Leonard, Raleigh, NC, 1995—; gen. counsel, exec. dir. N.C. Assn. Broadcasters, 1970—, N.C. CATV Assn., 1980—; chmn. bd. dirs. 1st Union Nat. Bank, Raleigh, 1989-93. Mem. N.C. Gov.'s Coun. on State Policy , 1974—79; chmn. N.C. News Media Adminstrn. Justice Coun. , 1976; commr. N.C. Milk Commn. , 1976—78, chmn., 1988—2000; commr. N.C. Agy. Pub. Telecom. ; spl. advisor to U.S. at Internat. Conf. on Direct Satellite Broadcasts , Geneva, 1983; mem. legis. study Commn. on Open Govt. , 1993; chair N.C. Ctr. Pub. Policy Rsch., 1994—; bd. visitors U. N.C. , 1991—, U. N.C. Sch. Journalism , 1993—. Named to N.C. Assn. Broadcasters Hall of Fame, 1998; recipient Disting. Svc., N.C. Assn. Broadcasters, 1973, N.C. CATV Assn., 1985. Mem. ABA, N.C. State Bar, D.C. Bar, Fed. Comms. Bar Assn., U. N.C. Law Alumni Assn. (pres. 1991-94), Capital City Club (bd. govs. 1983-91), Figure Eight Yacht Club, Cardinal Club (bd. govs. 1992—), Order of the Long Leaf Pine. Presbyterian. Corporate, general, Utilities, public, Media. Home: 1005 Marlowe Rd Raleigh NC 27609-6971 Office: Brooks Pierce McLendon Humphrey Leonard 1600 First Union Bank Capitol Ctr Raleigh NC 27601-1309

HARING, EUGENE MILLER, lawyer; b. Washington, May 16, 1927; s. Horace E. and Edith (Miller) H.; m. Janet K. Marshall, Apr. 10, 1971. AB summa cum laude, Princeton U., 1949, A.M. (Woodrow Wilson fellow), 1951; LL.B., Harvard U., 1955. Bar: N.J. 1955, N.Y. 1983, U.S. Dist. Ct. N.J. 1955, U.S. Dist. Ct. (so. and ea. dists.) N.Y. 1992, U.S. Ct. Appeals (3d cir.) 1962, U.S. Supreme Ct. 1969. Asst. in instrn. Princeton U., 1950-52; assoc. McCarter & English, Newark, 1955-61, ptnr., 1961-97, chmn. exec. com., 1982-97, of counsel, 1997—. Cert. mediator U.S. Dist. Ct., 1994—; mediator CPR Inst. for Dispute Resolution, N.J. Panel, 1994—; mem. roster of mediators Judiciary of State of N.J.; mem. civil justice reform act adv. com. U.S. Dist. Ct. N.J., 1997-2000. Contbr. articles to profl. jours. Chmn. Princeton Twp. Zoning Bd. Adjustment, 1979-80, mem. bd., 1975-79; vestryman Trinity Episc. Ch., Princeton, 1975-79, 97-2000, warden, 1980-84; mem. com. on constn. and canons Episc. Diocese of N.J., 1980-87, chancellor, 1983-94, 99—, hon. canon, 2001—; trustee Gen. Theol. Sem., N.Y., 1987-90; mem. vis. com. Rutgers U. Law Sch., 1994-2000; trustee N.J. Jersey Shore Found., 1988-92. Served with USNR, 1945-46. Fellow Am. Bar Found. (life), Lawyers Adv. Com. (U.S. Ct. Appeals 3d cir. 1990-93, U.S. Dist. Ct. N.J. 1997—); mem. ABA, N.J. State Bar Assn.

(emeritus), N.J. State Bar Found. (trustee 1986-87, v.p. 1987-88, chmn. 1988-90), Essex County Bar Assn. (Spl. Merit award 1998), Mercer County Bar Assn., Am. Law Inst. (life), Harvard Law Sch. Assn. N.J. (pres. 1971-72, nat. v.p. 1972-73), Hist. Soc. U.S. Dist. Ct. for Dist. N.J. (trustee 1987-90, 97—), Hist. Soc. 3d Cir. Ct. Appeals (bd., dirs. 1993-2000), Nassau Club, Princeton, Springdale Golf Club, Princeton, Monmouth Hunt Club, Phi Beta Kappa. Republican. Avocation: golf. Federal civil litigation, State civil litigation, Insurance. Home: 75 Rosedale Ln Princeton NJ 08540-2417 Office: McCarter & English Gateway 4 100 Mulberry St Newark NJ 07102-4004 E-mail: eharing@mccarter.com.

HARIRI, V. M. arbitrator, mediator, lawyer, educator; BS, Wayne State U.; JD, Detroit Coll. Law; LLM, London Sch. Econs. and Polit.Sci.; diploma arbitration, Reading (Eng.) U. Pvt. practice internat. and U.S. bus. law, Detroit. Drafting com. Republic of Kazakhstan Code on Arbitration Procedure, Free Econ. Zone Legislation, Republic of Belarus; instr. internat. comml. arbitration Chartered Inst. Arbitrators, Am. Arbitration Assn. Fellow Chartered Inst. Arbitrators (exec. com. N.Am. br., founding com. and expert advisor); mem. ABA, Internat. Bar Assn., Am. Soc. Internat. Law, Am. Arbitration Assn., London Ct. Internat. Arbitration, World Jurist Assn., Mich. Trial Lawyers Assn. Office: 325 N Center St Ste E3 Northville MI 48167-1244

HARKEY, JOHN NORMAN, judge; b. Russellville, Ark., Feb. 25, 1933; s. Olga John and Margaret (Fleming) H.; m. Willa Moreau Charlton, May 24, 1959; children— John Adam, Sarah Leigh. AS, Marion (Ala.) Inst., 1952; LLB, BS, BSL, U. Ark., 1959, JD, 1969. Bar: Ark. 1959. Since practiced in, Batesville; pros. atty. 3d Jud. Dist. Ark., 1961-65; ins. commr. Ark., 1967-68; chmn. Ark. Commerce Commn., 1968-69; spl. justice Ark. Supreme Ct., 1988; judge juvenile divsn. Ark. 16th Dist., 1989-90; sr. ptnr. Harkey, Walmsley and related firms, Batesville, 1970-92; chancery and probate judge 16th Jud. Dist., Batesville, Ark., 1993-98, circuit and chancery judge, 1999-2001, circuit judge, 2001—. 1st lt. USMCR, Korea. Mem. Ark. Bar Assn., Am. Bar Register, U.S. Marine Corps League. Home: 490 Harkey Rd Batesville AR 72501-9294 Office: PO Box 2656 Batesville AR 72503-2656

HARKEY, ROBERT SHELTON, lawyer; b. Charlotte, N.C., Dec. 22, 1940; s. Charles Nathan and Josephine Lenora (McKenzie) H.; m. Barbara Carole Payne, Apr. 2, 1983; 1 child, Elizabeth McKenzie. BA, Emory U., 1963, LLB, 1965. Bar: Ga. 1964, U.S. Dist. Ct. (no. dist.) Ga. 1964, U.S. Ct. Appeals (1st, 5th, 7th, 9th and 11th cirs.) 1964-86, U.S. Supreme Ct. Assoc. Swift, Currie, McGhee & Hiers, Atlanta, 1965-68; atty. Delta Air Lines, Atlanta, 1968-74, gen. atty., 1974-79, asst. v.p. law, 1979-85, assoc. gen. counsel, v.p., 1985-88; gen counsel, v.p., 1988-90; gen. counsel, sr. v.p. Delta Air Lines, Atlanta, 1990-94, gen. counsel, sr. v.p., sec., 1994—. Mem. coun. Emory U. Law Sch., 1997—. Unit chmn. United Way, Atlanta, 1985; trustee Woodruff Arts Ctr., 1995—; bd. visitors Emory U., 1996-99. Mem. ABA (com. gen. counsels), Air Transport Assn. (chmn. law coun. 1996-98), State Bar Ga. (chmn. corp. counsel sect. 1992-93), Atlanta Bar Assn., Corp. Counsel Assn. Greater Atlanta (bd. dirs. 1990), Commerce Club, Lawyers Club of Atlanta, Cherokee Town and Country Club. Presbyterian. Avocations: tennis, reading. Aviation, Corporate, general, Labor (including EEOC, Fair Labor Standards Act, labor-management relations, NLRB, OSHA). Office: Delta Air Lines Hartsfield Atlanta Internat Airport Atlanta GA 30320

HARKINS, PATRICK NICHOLAS, III, lawyer; b. Jackson, Miss., Apr. 27, 1941; s. Patrick Nicholas and Mary Ruth (Gammon) H.; m. Mary Elizabeth Wilson, Apr. 12, 1969; children: Elizabeth Glenn, DeMatt Henderson. BBA, U. Notre Dame, 1963; JD, U. Miss., 1965. Bar: Miss. 1965, U.S. Dist. Ct. (no. and so. dists.) Miss. 1965, U.S. Ct. Appeals (5th cir.) 1965, U.S. Supreme Ct. 1968. Legis. asst. U.S. Congressman G.V. Montgomery, 1967-68; assoc. atty. Watkins, Pyle, Ludlam, Winter & Stennis, Jackson, 1969; atty. Watkins & Eager PLLC, Jackson, 1970—, ptnr., 1973—. Served to capt. U.S. Army, 1965-67. Fellow Am. Coll. Trial Lawyers, Miss. Bar Found. (pres. 1992-93); mem. ABA, DRI (pres.2001-2002), Miss. Bar Assn., Miss. Def. Lawyers Assn. (bd. dirs. 2003—), Internat. Assn. Def. Counsel (chair products liability 1995-97, dir. def. counsel trial acad. 1998), Hinds County Bar Assn., Jackson Country Club. Roman Catholic. General civil litigation, Personal injury (including property damage), Product liability. Home: 2060 Sheffield Dr Jackson MS 39211-5848

HARKINS, THAD, lawyer; b. San Antonio, Tex., Apr. 13, 1955; s. James Phillip and Nancy (Dougherty) Harkins. BS magna cum laude, So. U., 1976; JD, U. Tex. Austin, 1981. Cert.: Tex. Bd. Legal Specialization 1998. Asst. dir. Staff Counsel for Inmates Tex. Detention , Huntsville, 1981—83; counsel Legal Aid Soc. Ctrl. Tex., Belton, 1983—85, Law Office of Cecil Bain, San Antonio, 1986—87; shareholder Green, McReynolds & Harkins, San Antonio, 1988—97, Harkins, Latimer & Dahl, San Antonio, 1997—. Pres. Nat. Employment Lawyers Assn., San Antonio, 1999; chair negotiation com., fed. ct. San Antonio Bar, 1998—2001. Editor (treatise chpt.): Employment Discrimination Law, 2000—02. Treas. Musical Offering Chamber Orch., San Antonio, 1996—; bd. dirs. Tobin Hill Neighborhood Assn., San Antonio, 1998—2000; com. mem. San Antonio River Oversight Com., 1999—2001. Mem.: ABA (labor and employment sect.), State Bar Tex. (labor and employment sect.), Tex. Bar Found. Methodist. Avocation: golf. Labor (including EEOC, Fair Labor Standards Act, labor-management relations, NLRB, OSHA), Corporate, general. Office: Harkins Latimer & Dahl PC 405 N Saint Mary Ste 242 San Antonio TX 78205

HARLEY, COLIN EMILE, lawyer; b. Columbia, S.C., Mar. 27, 1940; s. William Hummel and Caroline (Monteith) H.; m. Emilia Saint Amand, June 5, 1965; children: Emile, Gray; m. Anita H. Laudone, May 20, 1978; children: Clayton, Victoria. AB, Dartmouth Coll., 1962; LLB, U. S.C., 1965; LLM, NYU, 1967. Bar: S.C. 1965, N.Y. 1968. Sole practice, Laurens, S.C., 1965; assoc. Davis Polk & Wardwell, N.Y.C., 1967-72, ptnr., 1973—; adj. asst. prof. taxation NYU Sch Law, 1970-75. Trustee Greenwich (Conn.) Country Day Sch., 1987-96, pres., 1994-96. With USMCR, 1961-67. Oil, gas, and mineral, Corporate taxation, Equipment leasing. Office: Davis Polk & Wardwell 450 Lexington Ave Fl 31 New York NY 10017-3982 E-mail: colin.harley@dpw.com.

HARLEY, HALVOR LARSON, banker, lawyer; b. Atlantic City, N.J., Oct. 7, 1948; s. Robison Dooling and Loyde Hazel (Gochnauer) Harley. BSc, U. S.C., 1971, MA, 1973; JD, Widener U., 1981. Bar: Pa. 1982, D.C. 1989, U.S. Ct. Appeals (3d cir.) 1987, U.S. Dist. Ct. (ea. dist.) Pa. 1987, U.S. Supreme Ct. 1988, U.S. Ct. Appeals D.C. 1989. Staff psychologist Columbia Area Mental Health Ctr., S.C., 1971-73; dir. Motivational Rsch. Cons., Columbia, 1973-79; psychologist Family Ct. Del., Wilmington, 1979; pvt. practice law Phila., 1982; v.p. investment banking Union Bank, L.A., 1982-88; v.p., mgr. Tokai Bank, Newport Beach., Calif., 1988-94; first v.p., regional mgr. Mellon Pvt. Asset Mgmt., Newport Beach, 1994-97, first v.p., 1994—; regional sales mgr. So. Calif. Pvt. Asset Mgmt., 1994—. Contbr. ; author: Help for Herpes, 1982; cinematographer:. Fundraiser Orange County Performing Art Ctr., 1983—84; trustee, exec. com. Orange County Mus. Arts; vol. Hosp. Ship HOPE, Sri Lanka, 1968—69; bd. dirs., v.p. exec. com. Alzheimers Assn. Orange County; bd. dirs. Lido Sands Homeowners Assn., Newport Beach, 1984—85, So. Calif. Entrepreneurship Acad., pres./bd. dirs.; bd. dirs. United Cerebral Palsy of Orange County; chmn. Bastile Day Com. Mem.: ATLA, World Trade Ctr. Assocs. Orange County (directing com. 1983—85), Indsl. League Orange County (membership com. 1983—84), Calif. Bankers Assn., Am. Bankers Assn., Am. Judicature Soc., Orange County Performing Arts Fraternity (trustee), Psi Chi (chpt. pres. 1971—73). Home: 5015 Lido Sands Dr Newport Beach CA 92663-2403 Office: Mellon Pvt Wealth Mgmt 4695 Macarthur Ct Ste 240 Newport Beach CA 92660-8851

HARLEY, ROBISON DOOLING, JR., lawyer, educator; b. Ancon, Panama, July 6, 1946; s. Robison Dooling and Loyde Hazel (Goehenauer) Harley; m. Suzanne Purviance Bendel, Aug. 9, 1975; children: Arianne Erin, Lauren Loyde. BA, Brown U., 1968; JD, Temple U., 1971; LLM, U. San Diego, 1985. Cert.: Calif. Bd. Legal Specialization (criminal law specialist since 1981) 1981, Nat. Bd. Trial Advocacy (criminal trial adv. since 1981) 1982, bar: Pa. 1971, Calif. 1976, NJ 1977, DC 1981, US Dist. Ct. (cen. and so. dists.) Calif. 1976, US Dist. Ct. NJ 1977, US Dist. Ct. (ea. dist.) Pa. 1987, US Ct. Appeals (9th cir.) 1982, US Ct. Appeals (3rd cir.) 1986, US Supreme Ct. 1980, US Ct. Mil. Appeals 1972. Asst. agy. dir. Safeco Title Ins. Co., LA, 1975—77; ptnr. Cohen, Stokke & Davis, Santa Ana, Calif., 1977—85; prin. prin. Harley Law Offices, Santa Ana, 1985—. Adj. prof. Orange County Coll. Trial Advocacy; adj. prof. paralegal program U. Calif.; instr. trial adv. programs US Army, USN, USAF, USMC; judge pro-tem Orange County Cts. Author: Orange County Trial Lawyers Drunk Driving Syllabus; contbr. articles to profl. jours. Trial counsel, def. counsel, mil. judge, asst. staff judge adv. USMC, 1971—75, regional def. counsel Western Region, 1986—90; bd. dirs. Orange County Legal Aid Soc. Lt. col. JAGC USMCR. Decorated Nat. Def. Svc. medal, Res. medal. Mem.: ATLA, ABA, Orange County Criminal Lawyers Assn. (found. com.), Orange County Trial Lawyers Assn., Orange County Bar Assn. (judiciary com., criminal law sect., adminstrn. of justice com.), Assn. Specialized Criminal Def. Advs., Nat. Assn. for Criminal Def. Attys., Calif. Pub. Defenders Assn., Calif. Attys. for Criminal Justice, Calif. Trial Lawyers Assn., Marine Corps Assn., Marine Corps Res. Officers Assn., Res. Officers Assn. Republican. Avocations: sports, physical fitness, reading. Criminal, Military. Home: 31211 Paseo Miraloma San Juan Capistrano CA 92675-5505 Office: Harley Law Offices 825 N Ross St Santa Ana CA 92701-3419

HARMAN, WALLACE PATRICK, lawyer; b. El Paso, Tex., Jan. 22, 1949; s. Wallace Irvin and Dorothy Louise (Pearson) H.; m. Gina Marie Ries, Dec. 31, 1988; children: Loren Patrick, Claire Marie. BA, Stanford U., 1972; JD, U. Calif., 1977. Bar: Calif. 1977, U.S. Ct. Appeals (9th cir.) 1977, N.Mex. 1978, U.S. Dist. Ct. N.Mex. 1978, U.S. Ct. Appeals (10th cir.) 1978. Zone adminstrn. mgr. Am. Motors Corp., Burlingame, Calif., 1972-74; atty., shareholder Sutin, Thayer & Browne, APC, Albuquerque, N.Mex., 1977-87, group leader comml. group, 1985-87; atty., shareholder, mng. ptnr., leader bus. group The Payne Law Firm, P.C., Albuquerque, 1987-91; atty., ptnr. Hisey & Wainwright, P.A., Albuquerque, 1991-92; atty., pres., chief exec. officer The Harman Law Firm, P.C., Littleton, CO, 1992—. Mem. N.Mex. Supreme Ct. Med.-Legal Panel, Albuquerque, 1978-80, 91—; mem. N.Mex. Supreme Ct. Lawyers Assistance Com., Albuquerque, 1991—; area rep. The Taft Sch., Watertown, Conn., 1992—; mem. mentorship program Hatings Coll. Law. Co-author: Recent Developments in Commerical Law, University of New Mexico Law Review, 1989. Bd. advisors Lovelace Med. Ctr., Albuquerque, 1980-89; mem. state bd. trustees The Nature Conservancy, N.Mex., 1984-88; adv. bd. Assistance League Albuquerque, 1982-89, Jr. League Albuquerque, 1984-87, Make-a-Wish Found. of N.Mex., Inc., 1996-97. Recipient AV Rating award Martindale-Hubbell, 1990. Mem. ABA, Albuquerque Bar Assn. Democrat. Avocations: photography, sports, computers, landscaping, writing. Banking, General civil litigation, Property, real (including real estate development, water). E-mail: harman@sandia.net.

HARMON, GAIL MCGREEVY, lawyer; b. Kansas City, Kans., Mar. 15, 1943; d. Milton and Barbara (James) McGreevy; m. John W. Harmon, June 11, 1966; children: James, Eve. BA cum laude, Radcliffe Coll., 1965; JD cum laude, Columbia U., 1969. Bar: Mass. 1970, D.C. 1976, U.S. Dist. Ct. D.C. Assoc. Gaston Snow & Ely Bartlett, Boston, 1970-75, Steptoe & Johnson, Washington, 1975-76, Roisman, Kessler & Cashdan, Washington, 1976-77; ptnr. Harmon, Curran & Tousley, Washington, 1977-90, Harmon, Curran, Spielberg & Eisenberg, Washington, 1990—. Pres. Women's Legal Def. Fund, 1982-84; steering com. Emily's List, 1985—; bd. dirs. Population Svcs. Internat., 1998—. Mem. Population Svcs. Internat. (bd. dirs.) Democrat. Episcopalian. Corporate, general, Taxation, general. E-mail: gharmon@harmoncurran.com.

HARMS, ALLAN L. patent lawyer; b. Auburn, Nebr., Feb. 14, 1945; m. Sally L. Lucas, Aug. 31, 1968; 2 children. BSEE, U. Nebr., 1968; MBA, U. Iowa, 1973, JD, 1974. Bar: Iowa 1974, U.S. Patent Office 1975. Lawyer White & Wenzel, Cedar Rapids, Iowa, 1974-75; patent lawyer Eells, Blackstock, Affeldt & Harms, Cedar Rapids, 1975-87, Wenzel, Piersall & Harms, P.C., Cedar Rapids, 1987-95, Wenzel & Harms, P.C., Cedar Rapids, 1995—. Asst. Linn County Atty., Cedar Rapids, 1975-83. Treas. Kennedy H.S. Choral League, 1992—93; bd. dirs. Invent Iowa, Iowa City, 1998—. Mem. ABA, Iowa State Bar Assn., Linn County Bar Assn. (tech. comm. 2000—), Iowa Intellectual Property Law Assn. (pres. 1990), SPEBSQSA Internat. (Harmony Hawks Chorus chpt. 1980—, treas. 1986-96, pres. Cedar Rapids chpt. 1997-98), Cedar Rapids Noon Lions Club (pres. 1992-93, Lion of the Yr. 1993). Avocations: barbershop quartet singing, band membership, volunteering. Patent. Office: Wenzel & Harms PC 2750 1st Ave NE Cedar Rapids IA 52402-4831 Fax: 319-363-8906. E-mail: wenzelharms@aol.com.

HARMS, DONALD C. lawyer; b. Detroit, May 27, 1941; s. Herbert R. and Elsa J. (McClelend) H.; m. Sue J. Kingsley, June 15, 1963; children: Kristin, Sharon, Melissa. BA, U. Mich., 1963; JD cum laude, Wayne State U., 1967. Bar: Mich. 1967, U.S. Dist. Ct. (ea. dist.) Mich. 1967. Ptnr. Larson & Harms, P.C., Farmington Hills, Mich., 1968—. Arbitrator Am. Arbitration Assn., Detroit, 1975—; bd. dirs. McKenzie Bay Internat., Ltd. Clk., Ward Evangel. Presbyn. Ch., Livonia, Mich., 1979-80, moderator Evang. Presbyn. Ch., 1984-85. Mem. State Bar of Mich. (pres. gen. practice sect. 1975-77), Farmington Hills C. of C. (pres. 1979), Kiwanis. Corporate, general, Estate planning, Property, real (including real estate development, water). Office: Larson & Harms PC 37899 W 12 Mile Rd Ste 300 Farmington MI 48331-3026 Business E-Mail: dharms@larsonharms.com.

HARMS, JOHN KEVIN, lawyer; b. Bittburg Air Base, Germany, Oct. 19, 1960; s. William Robert and Catherine Dorothy (Heslin) H.; m. Panela Tinkham, 1988; children: William Cameron Harms, Wade Devlin Harms. Student Wash. Seminar in Econ. Policy, Am. U., 1981; BPA magna cum laude, Loyola U., New Orleans, 1982; JD, Northwestern U., 1985; MBA, Western New Eng. Coll., 1989, U.S. Army Command & Gen. Staff Coll., 1997, U.S. Air War Coll., 1997; postgrad., Am. U., Washington, 1981, U.S. Army Command and Gen. Staff Coll., 1997, USAF Air War Coll., 1997, U.S. Navy Coll. Continuing Edn. Bar: Ill. 1985, U.S. Army Ct. Mil. Rev. 1986, U.S. Ct. Mil. Appeals 1991, Mass. 1994. Commd. 2d lt. USAR, 1982, advance through grades to lt. col., 2001; aide-de-camp to comdg. gen. 33d Inf. Brigade, Ill. Army Nat. Guard, 1983-85; rsch. asst. Am. Bar Found., Chgo., 1985; legal assistance atty. Office of Staff Judge Advocate, Ft. Devens, Mass., 1986; trial def. counsel U.S. Army Trial Def. Svc., Ft. Devens, Mass., 1986-87, sr. def. counsel, 1987-90; deputy staff judge adv. Office of Staff Judge Adv. Mil. Traffic Mgmt. Command Ea. Area, Bayonne, N.J., 1990-92; internat. ops. law atty. Third Mil. Law Ctr., U.S. Army Res., Boston, 1992-95; adv., environ. law specialist Office of the Staff Judge Adv., 1992-95; chief counsel Devens Res. Forces Tng. Area, Ft. Devens, Mass., 1995-96; atty., advisor govt. contracts and environ. law Electronic Sys. Ctr., Hanscom AFB, Mass., 1996—; adminstrv. and contract law atty. 94th Regional Support Command, Ft. Devens, 1996—2000, dep. staff judge adv., 2000—. Mem. North Western Law Rev., 1984-85; mem. 1st del. of Am. criminal lawyers to the Peoples Rep. of China as part of Citizen Amb. Program, People to People Internat., 1987. Cubmaster Cub Scout Pack 50, 1999—2001, Boy Scouts Am.; leader den Weblos, 2001—03; bd. trustee North Ctrl. Charter Essential Sch., Fitchburg, Mass., 2002—, sec., 2003—. Named Outstanding Young Man Am., 1988. Mem. ABA (spl. com. environ. crimes), Mass. Bar Assn. (mem. environ. law sect.), Boston Bar Assn. (mem. environ. law sect.), Bluekey Nat. Honor Fraternity, Alpha Sigma Nu, Delta Sigma Pi, Beta Gamma Sigma. Avocations: racewalking, novel writing, Kindai Insauma Ryu karate (green belt). Office: Office Staff Judge Advocate Attn ESC/JAS 35 Hamilton St Hanscom AFB MA 01731-2010

HARMS, STEVEN ALAN, lawyer; b. Detroit, Feb. 15, 1949; s. Herbert Rudolph and Elsa Jane (McClelland) H.; m. Nancy Gayle Banta, June 26, 1971; children: Jennifer Elizabeth, Heather Lynn, Robin Ann. BA, Hope Coll., 1970; JD, Detroit Coll. Law, 1975. Bar: Mich. 1975, U.S. Dist. Ct. (so. dist.) Mich. 1975, U.S. Ct. Appeals (6th cir.) 1982; bd. cert. creditors rights specialist. Ptnr. Muller, Muller, Richmond, Harms, Myers & Sgroi, P.C., Birmingham, Mich.; sec. gen. practice session State Bar Mich., 1982-83; mediator Oakland County Cir. Ct., 1990—. Lectr. in field; adj. prof. Bus. Law Walsh Coll., Troy, Mich., 1990—. Author: Successful Collection of a Judgement, 1981, Post Judgement Collection, 1988, Handling the Collection Case in Michigan, 1989, rev. edit., 2003, Collection Law, 2003, A Credit Manager's Guide to Collection Law, 2003; co-author: Attorney Fee Agreements, 1995; contbg. editor: Michigan Civil Procedure, 1997, rev. edit., 2002. Bd. dirs. fin. com. YMCA, North Oakland County, Mich., 1987—, chmn. bd., 1990-91. Mem.: Pearson Yacht Owners Assn. (commodore 1988-90), Hunter Sailing Assn. (vice commodore 1985-86, commodore 1987-88). Republican. Commercial, consumer (including collections, credit), Commercial, contracts (including sales of goods; commercial financing). Office: Muller Muller Richmond Harms Myers & Sgroi PC 33233 Woodward Ave Birmingham MI 48009-0903 E-mail: steve@mullerfirm.com.

HARNACK, DON STEGER, retired lawyer; b. Milw., June 19, 1928; s. Benjamin John and Katherine (Steger) H.; m. Rose Marie Ball, Oct. 17, 1959; children: Christopher Wallen, Gretchen Marie, Pamela Ann. BS, U. Wis., 1950; LLB, Harvard U., 1953. Bar: Wis. 1953, U.S. Dist. Ct. (ea. dist.) Wis. 1955, U.S. Tax Ct. 1957, Ill. 1959, U.S. Dist. Ct. (no. dist.) Ill. 1962, U.S. Ct. Appeals (6th and 7th cirs.) 1963, U.S. Ct. Claims 1966, U.S. Ct. Appeals (8th cir.) 1971, U.S. Supreme Ct. 1972. Assoc. Quarles, Spence & Quarles, Milw., 1955-57; trial atty. regional counsel IRS, Chgo., 1957-61; assoc. Dixon, Todhunter, Knouf & Holmes, Chgo., 1961-65; ptnr. McDermott, Will & Emery, Chgo., 1965-96, of counsel, 1997-98; ret., 2001. Contbr. articles to profl. jours. Active Winnetka (Ill.) Zoning Bd., 1971-75; park bd. atty. Winnetka Park Dist., 1978-83; pres. N.E. Ill. coun. Boy Scouts Am., 1982-83; life trustee ULC Boys and Girls Club, Chgo., UL Civic and Arts Found.; trustee Village of Winnetka, 1984-88. Served with U.S. Army, 1953-55, USNR, 1959-69. Recipient Silver Beaver award Boy Scouts Am., 1984, named distinguished Eagle Scout, 1996. Mem. ABA, Ill. Bar Assn., Wis. Bar Assn., Union League Club (bd. dirs., officer, v.p. 1981-87, pres. 1987-88). Republican. Avocations: fishing, golf, reading, flying. Federal civil litigation, Corporate taxation, State and local taxation. E-mail: bigcoho2@aol.com.

HARNDEN, EDWIN A. lawyer; BA Columbia U., 1969, JD Columbia U., 1972. Mng. ptnr. Barran Liebman LLP, Portland, Oreg.; pres. Oreg. State Bar, 2001—02. Past pres. Profl. Liability Fund. Fellow: Am. Bar Found. (life). Labor (including EEOC, Fair Labor Standards Act, labor-management relations, NLRB, OSHA). Office: ODS Tower 601 SW 2d Ave Ste 2300 Portland OR 97204-3159 Office Fax: 503-274-1212. E-mail: eharnden@barran.com.

HARNESS, WILLIAM WALTER, lawyer; b. Ottumwa, Iowa, Apr. 14, 1945; s. Walter W. and Mary E. (Bukowski) H.; m. Carolyn Margaret Barnes, Jan 4, 1969; children: Matthew William, Michael Andrew. BA, U. Iowa, 1967; JD, Cleve. State U., 1974. Bar: Ohio 1975, U.S. Dist. Ct. (no. dist.) Ohio 1975, D.C. 1976, U.S. Dist. Ct. D.C. 1976, U.S. Ct. Appeals (D.C. cir.) 1976, U.S. Ct. Appeals (5th cir.) 1981, U.S. Dist. Ct. (we. dist.) N.C. 1979, U.S. Ct. Appeals (1st cir.) 1980, U.S. Ct. Appeals (4th cir.) 1981, U.S. Ct. Appeals (11th cir.) 1981. Mem. labor rels. staff Monogram Industries, Cleve., 1970-75; asst. counsel Nat. Treasury Employees Union, Washington, 1975-77, nat. counsel, Atlanta, 1977—; lectr. Emory U., Atlanta, 1978—; participant various seminars Ga. State U. Pres. Spring Mill-Kingsborough Ct. Corp., Atlanta. Served to 1st lt. U.S. Army, 1967-70. Mem. ABA (com. on fed. labor-mgmt. 1981-84), D.C. Bar Assn. (bd. dirs.), Soc. Fed. Labor Relations Profls., Indsl. Relations Research Assn. Civil rights, Federal civil litigation, Labor (including EEOC, Fair Labor Standards Act, labor-management relations, NLRB, OSHA). Home: 1285 Mile Post Dr Atlanta GA 30338-4756 Office: Nat Treasury Employees Union 2801 Buford Hwy NE Ste 430 Atlanta GA 30329-2137

HARON, DAVID LAWRENCE, lawyer; b. Detroit, Sept. 24, 1944; s. Percy Hyman and Bess (Holland) H.; m. Pamela Kay Colburn, May 25, 1969; children: Eric, Andrea. BA, U. Mich., 1966, JD, 1969. Bar: Mich. 1969, U.S. Dist. Ct. (ea. dist.) Mich., 1969, U.S. Supreme Ct. 1974, U.S. Ct. of Appeals (6th cir.) 1996. Law clk. to chief judge Mich. Ct. Appeals, Detroit, 1969-70; assoc. Barris, Sott, Denn & Driker, Detroit, 1970-74; sr. ptnr. Josephson, Tennen, Haron and Bennett, Southfield, Mich., 1974-90; prin., shareholder, sr. v.p. Frank, Stefani, Haron and Weiner, Troy, Mich., 1990—; arbitrator Mich. Prudential Securities, Inc. Expedited Arbitrations, 1994-96. Cons. Universe Computer Software, 1985; pres., bd. dirs. S&H Licensing Corp., Southfield; panelist Ct. TV Law Ctr. Bar Assn. Mem. editorial bd. Prospectus Jour. Law Reform, 1969, (newsletter) Atty.'s Mktg. Report, 1986-88; contbr. articles to profl. jours. Mem. Farmington Hills Planning Commn., 1996—, vice-chair, 2000-01, chair, 2001-02, 03—; vol. handicap parking enforcement officer Farmington Hills Police Dept., 1990-93; bd. dirs. Forest Elem. Sch. PTO, 1983, 87-88; v.p. North Farmington Baseball for Youth, 1984; mem. Sta. WTVS Auction, Detroit, 1985-88; trustee C.A.T.C.H., 1996—, Temple Israel, West Bloomfield, Mich., 1987-93, tchr. Sunday Sch., 1986-88, chmn. Ritual com., 1988-93, advisor youth group, 1987-90; chmn. Farmington Hills Com. to Increase Voter Participation, 1987-89; bd. dirs. Met. Detroit chpt. Zionist Orgn. Am., 1987-90; pres. North Farmington H.S. Parent Club, 1989-95; mem. bd. advisors Farmington Hills Corps.-Salvation Army, 1997-2000; mem. site selection com. South Oakland County Habitat for Humanity; chair Cardozo Law Soc. of the Jewish Fedn. Met. Detroit, 1999-2002. Recipient Outstanding Alumnus award Mumford H.S., Detroit, 1985, Cert. recognition City of Farmington Hills, 1986. Fellow The Roscoe Pound Found., Mich. State Bar Found.; mem. ABA (mem. com. on comml. leasing 1987-94, real property, probate and trust law sect., mem. bus. law sect. com. on fed. regulation of securities, mem. subcom. on alternative dispute resolution, SEC enforcement matters), ASTM (mem. com. on environ. assessment 1992—), ATLA, Nat. Arbitration Forum (arbitrator), Assn. Health Lawyers Am. (co-chmn. fraud & abuse SISLC false claims/qui tam working group), Mich. Trial Lawyers Assn., Am. Soc. Writers on Legal Subjects, Internat. Assn. Jewish Lawyers and Jurists, Million Dollar Advocates Forum, State Bar Mich. (mem. pro bono com. real property sect. 1996-98, mem. professionalism com. 1994-2002, chmn. professionalism com. 1996-98, chmn. unauthorized practice of law com. 1990-92, mem. unauthorized practice of law com. 1999-2002, chmn. Ct. Appeals com. 1977-78, mem. rep. assembly 1999—), Nat. Assn. Securities Dealers (mediator, arbitrator), Am. Arbitration Assn. (arbitrator, mediator, spkr.), Comml. Law League Am., Detroit Bar Assn., Jewish Fedn., Oakland County Bar Assn. (participant Mich. law-related edn. project 1988-89, real estate com. 1990—, environ. law com. 1992-95, lawyer dispute conciliator, spkr. 1993, chmn. professionalism com. 1995-97, Cir. Ct. facilitator, master Inn of Ct. 1997—; recipient Professionalism award, 2003), Oakland County Bar Found. (trustee, treas. 2003-), U. Mich. Alumni Assn., U. Mich. Victor's Club, Zionist Orgn. (bd. dirs. Detroit 1987-90), Tau Epsilon Rho, Tau Delta Phi. Jewish. Corporate, general,

Property, real (including real estate development, water). Home: 34685 Old Timber Rd Farmington Hills MI 48331-1436 Office: Frank Stefani Haron and Weiner 5435 Corporate Dr Ste 225 Troy MI 48098-2624 Fax: 248-952-0890. E-mail: dharon@fsh-law.com.

HARP, CHADWICK ALLEN, lawyer, author, educator; b. Norristown, Pa., Mar. 24, 1969; s. Leroy Allen Jr. and Judith Ann (Beck) H. BA cum laude, George Washington U., 1991; JD, Dickinson Sch. Law, Carlisle, Pa., 1996. Bar: Pa. 1996. Various positions George Washington U. Med. Ctr., 1988-93, asst. to dean, 1990-93; law clk. Breidenbach, Breidenbach & Troncellitti, Norristown, Pa., 1994-96; atty. Fox, Differ, Callahan, Sheridan & McDevitt, Norristown, Pa., 1999-2000, Fox, Rothschild, O'Brien & Frankel, LLP, 2000; pvt. practice East Norriton, Pa., 2000—. Adj. prof. Montgomery County C.C., 1996—; facilitator U. Phoenix, 2001—; mem. faculty bus. edn. dept. Reading H.S., Pa., 2001—; pub. affairs intern Sec. Def., 1987—88. Author: Estate Planning For Individuals With Disabilities, 2002, Young Warriors, 2002, Return to the Lake, First Who You Are, Second What You Know: The Ten Habits of the Effective Teacher, 2002; contbr. articles to profl. jours. Bd. dirs. Pa. Children's Aid Soc., 1995—. Mem. ABA, Pa. Bar Assn., Montgomery Bar Assn., Nat. Acad. Elder Law Attys., Inc., Sigma Nu. Alternative dispute resolution, Constitutional, Probate (including wills, trusts). E-mail: chadwickharp@aol.com.

HARP, JOHN ANDERSON, lawyer; b. Helena, Ark., Nov. 30, 1950; s. Bert Seth and Mary Eleanor (Jolley) H.; m. Jane Van Cleave, Apr. 26, 1980; children: Anderson, Elizabeth, William, Hamilton. BA, Am. U., Washington, 1973; JD, Mercer U., Macon, Ga., 1980. Bar: Ga., Ala. Ptnr. Taylor, Harp & Callier, Columbus, Ga., 1985—. Co-author: Litigating Head Trauma Cases, 1991; bd. editors Neurolaw Letter, 1991—, Topics in Spinal Cord Injury Rehab., 1994—; issues editor Topics in Spinal Cord Injury Rehabilitation, vol. 6, no. 4, 2001; contbr. articles to profl. jours. Reservist USMCR with Office of Asst. Sec. of Def., The Pentagon, 1996-2000. Col., USMCR, 1995-2000, Marine Forces Pacific G-3, 2000-02. Mem. ABA, ATLA, Ga. Bar Assn., Ala. Bar Assn., Nat. Spinal Cord Assn. (bd. dirs. 1987-95), Marine Corps Res. Officers Assn. (bd. dirs. 1995-98, nat. pres. 1997-98, vice-chmn. bd. dirs. 1998-99, Non Sibi Sed Patriae award), Mercer U. Law Sch. Alumni Assn. (nat. v.p. 1997-98, nat. pres.-elect 1998-99, nat. pres. 1999—). Avocations: running, skiing. General civil litigation, Personal injury (including property damage), Product liability. Office: Taylor Harp & Callier 233 12th St Ste 900 Columbus GA 31901-2449

HARPER, ALFRED JOHN, II, lawyer; b. El Paso, Tex., Aug. 11, 1942; s. Mosely Lloyd and Marion M. (McClintock) H.; m. Cynthia Newkam; children— A. John, Leslie J. BA, North Tex. State U., 1964; LLB cum laude, So. Meth. U., 1967. Bar: Tex. 1967, U.S. Dist. Ct. (so. dist.) Tex. 1967, U.S. Dist. Ct. (no. dist.) Tex. 1975, U.S. Dist. Ct. (we. dist.) Tex. 1976, U.S. Dist. Ct. (ea. dist.) Tex. 1995, U.S. Ct. Appeals (5th cir.) 1968, U.S. Ct. Appeals (9th cir.) 1976, U.S. Ct. Appeals (11th cir.) 1982, U.S. Ct. Appeals (10th cir.) 1984, U.S. Ct. Appeals (6th cir.) 1990, U.S. Ct. Appeals (1st cir.) 1991, U.S. Ct. Appeals (2d cir.) 1995, U.S. Ct. Appeals (8th cir.) 2002, U.S. Supreme Ct. 1971. Assoc. Fulbright & Jaworski, L.L.P., Houston, 1967-74, ptnr., 1974—. Cert. labor and employment law specialist State Bar Tex. bd. legal specialization. Editor Jour. Air Law and Commerce, 1966-67; contbr. articles to profl. jours. With USMCR, 1960-66. Fellow Coll. Labor and Employment Lawyers; mem. ABA (past coun., labor and employment law sect., past mgmt. co-chmn. com. on devel. law under Nat. Labor Rels. Act, past mgmt. co-chmn. meetings and insts. com., labor law sect.), Tex. Bar Assn., Order of Coif, Houston Country Club. Republican. Methodist. Civil rights, Labor (including EEOC, Fair Labor Standards Act, labor-management relations, NLRB, OSHA), Pension, profit-sharing, and employee benefits. Office: Fulbright & Jaworski 1301 Mckinney St Houston TX 77010-3031 E-mail: ajharper@fulbright.com.

HARPER, CONRAD KENNETH, lawyer, former government official; b. Detroit, Dec. 2, 1940; s. Archibald Leonard and Georgia Florence (Hall) H.; m. Marsha Louise Wilson, July 17, 1965; children: Warren Wilson, Adam Woodburn. BA, Howard U., 1962; LLB, Harvard U., 1965; LLD (hon.), CUNY, 1990, Vt. Law Sch., 1994. Bar: N.Y. 1966. Law clk. NAACP Legal Def. and Ednl. Fund, N.Y.C., 1965-66, staff lawyer, 1966-70; assoc. Simpson Thacher & Bartlett, N.Y.C., 1971-74, ptnr., 1974—93, 1996—2002, of counsel, 2003—; legal adviser U.S. Dept. of State, Washington, 1993-96. Lectr. law Rutgers U., 1969-70; vis. lectr. law Yale U., 1977-81; cons. HEW, 1977; chmn. admissions and grievances com. U.S. Ct. Appeals, 2d cir., 1987-93; co-chmn. Lawyers' Com. for Civil Rights Under Law, 1987-89; mem. Permanent Ct. of Arbitration, The Hague, 1993-96, 98—, Adminstrv. Conf. U.S., 1993-95, Harvard Corp., 2000—; bd. dirs. N.Y. Life Ins. Co., Pub. Svc. Enterprise Group. Trustee Inst. Internat. Edn., 1992-93, N.Y. Pub. Libr., chmn. exec. com., 1990-93, vice-chmn. bd. trustees, 1991-93; trustee William Nelson Cromwell Found., 1990—, Met. Mus. of Art, 1996—; bd. mgrs. Lewis Walpole Libr., 1989-93; bd. visitors Fordham Law Sch., 1990-93, CUNY, 1989-93; vestryman Ch. of St. Barnabas, Irvington, N.Y., 1982-85; bd. dirs. Phi Beta Kappa Assocs., 1992-93; chancellor The Episc. Diocese of N.Y., 1987-92; bd. legal advisors Martindale-Hubbell, 1990-93. Fellow Am. Bar Found., N.Y. Bar Found., Am. Coll. Trial Lawyers, Am. Acad. Arts and Scis.; mem. Am Philos. Soc., ABA (bd. editors jour. 1980-86), Nat. Bar Assn., N.Y. State Bar Assn., Assn. of Bar of City of N.Y. (chmn. exec. com. 1979-80, pres. 1990-92), Am. Law Inst. (mem. coun. 1985—, 2nd v.p. 1998-2000, 1st v.p. 2000—), Am. Assn. for Internat. Commn. Jurists (bd. dirs. 1988-93), Am. Soc. Internat. Law (mem. exec. coun. 1997-2000, exec. com. 1998-2000, counselor 2000—), Met. Black Bar Assn., Acad. Polit. Sci. (bd. dirs. 1998—), Coun. Fgn. Rels., Grolier Club (coun. mem. 1993, 97—), Century Assn., Harvard Club (mem. bd. mgrs. 1993), Phi Beta Kappa. Democrat. Episcopalian.

HARPER, DAVID ALEXANDER, lawyer; b. Newport, R.I., Apr. 4, 1953; s. Luby Alexander and Westlake Addams H.; m. Linda Gilbert, June 6, 1975 (div. Oct. 1995); children: Mark, Beth, John; m. Deborah Brown, Feb. 10, 1996. AB, Cornell U., 1975; JD, Union U., 1982. Bar: N.Y. 1983, U.S. Dist. Ct. (no. dist.) N.Y. 1983. Assoc. Carusone Toomey & Carusone, Saratoga Springs, N.Y., 1983-86; pvt. practice Saratoga Springs, 1987-90, 1999—; ptnr. Harper & Pozefsky, Saratoga Springs, 1991—98. 1st. asst. dist. atty. Saratoga County, Ballston Spa, N.Y., 1987—. Chmn. Zoning Bd. Appeals, Saratoga Springs, N.Y., 1989-2001. With U.S. Army, 1975-79. Recipient Disting. Svc. award Legal Aid Soc. N.E. N.Y., 1996. Mem. N.Y. State Bar Assn., N.Y. State Dist. Attys. Assn., Saratoga County Bar Assn. (pres. 2000-01), Elks Club. Republican. Episcopalian. Avocation: sailing. State civil litigation, Criminal, Property, real (including real estate development, water). Office: 480 Broadway Saratoga Springs NY 12866-2051

HARPER, EMERY WALTER, lawyer; b. Hackensack, NJ, Feb. 25, 1936; s. Walter Van Saun and Dorothy Charlotte (Schmidt) H.; m. Judith Van Nest Hover, Sept. 9, 1961 (div. 1991); 1 child, Caroline Curry BA cum laude, Amherst Coll., 1958; LLB, Yale U., 1961. Bar: N.Y. 1962. Assoc. Lord Day & Lord, Barrett Smith, N.Y.C., 1961-69, ptnr., 1970-93, Schnader, Harrison, Segal & Lewis, N.Y.C., 1993-96, chmn. internat. maritime group, 1993-95; pres. Harper Cons., Inc., N.Y.C., 1997—; of counsel Inman Deming LLP, 1998—. Bd. dirs. The Shipping Network, Inc.; bd. dirs., founding mem. The Admiralty/Fin. Forum, Inc.; lectr. on maritime law Dalian, PRC, 1984; advisor U.S. del. to joint working group on liens and mortgages Internat. Maritime Orgn., 1st, 2d, 5th and 6th sessions UN Conf. on Trade and Devel., 1986-89; lectr. on admiralty and maritime financing; lectr. on ship fin. topics, Mex., Panama, Chile, Thailand, 1993-95; course dir. practice and techniques Financing Marine Assets and Ops., N.Y., 1995; organizer, pres. Am. Corps. in Coastwise Trade; participant U.S. Delegation to IMO/UNCTAD Joint Diplomatic Conf. on Maritime Liens and Mortgages, Geneva, 1993; cons. Inman Deming Internat., LLC, Washington, 1998—; del. to diplomatic conf. arrest of ships Internat. C. of C., 1999. Co-author: Essays on Maritime Liens and Mortgages and on Arrest of Ships, 1985; contbr. articles to profl. publs. Trustee The Gateway Sch., N.Y., 1975-83; deacon Brick Presbyn. Ch., 1970-76, elder, 1976-82, trustee, corp. sec., 1982-88; mem. legal adv. com. Liberian Shipowners Coun., 1988-2000; chmn. Subcom. on Liberian Maritime Law Revision, 1993-99; chmn. Marshall Islands Roundtable, 1999-2001; mem. Seatransport com. U.S. Coun. for Internat. Bus., 1987-91; dir. Cmty. Living Corp. Found., Inc., 2002—; bd. dirs. CLC Found., Inc., 2002—. With USAFR, 1961-67. Mem. ABA (chmn. admiralty and maritime law com., sect. internat. law and practice), Assn. of Bar of City of N.Y. (mem. admiralty com. 1974-80, 90-93, 98-2000, chmn. 1977-80), Maritime Law Assn. (founding chmn. com. on Marine financing 1978—), Com. Maritime Internat. (internat. subcom. on maritime liens and mortgages), N.Y. Amherst Alumni Assn. (pres. 1975-77), Pilgrims Soc., Union Club, Down Town Club. Admiralty, Banking, Private international. Office: 18 E 48th St Fl 10 New York NY 10017 also: East Tower 1301 K St NW Ste 800 Washington DC 20005-3373 E-mail: eharper974@aol.com.

HARPER, HARLAN, JR., lawyer; b. San Antonio, Sept. 15, 1928; s. Harlan and Julia Viola (Kelley) H.; m. Linda A. Steere, July 16, 1960; children: Anne Elizabeth, David Harlan. BA, So. Methodist U., Dallas, 1953, JD, 1957. Bar: Tex. 1957, U.S Dist. Ct. (no., ea. and we. dists.) Tex. 1957. Assoc. McNees & McNees, 1957, John Harrison, 1958-61; sr. ptnr. Fanning, Harper, Martinson, P.C. and predecessors, Dallas, 1961-97; semi-ret., 1997—. Served with USAF, 1953-55. Mem. Tex. Bar Assn., Pi Kappa Alpha. Baptist. State civil litigation, Insurance, Personal injury (including property damage).

HARPER, STEVEN JAMES, lawyer; b. Mpls., Apr. 25, 1954; s. James Henry and Mary Margaret H.; m. Kathy Joseph Loeb, Aug. 21, 1976; children: Benjamin James, Peter William, Emma Suzanne. BA with distinction, MA in Econs., Northwestern U., 1976; JD magna cum laude, Harvard U., 1979. Bar: Ill. 1979, U.S. Dist. Ct. (MNo. Dist.) Ill. 1979, U.S. Dist. Ct. (W.D.) Wisc. 1988, U.S. Ct. Appeals (10td Cir.) 1989, U.S. Dist. Ct. (E.D.) Mich. 1997, U.S. Ct. Appeals (5th Cir.) 2001, U.S. Ct. Appeals (3rd Cir.) 2002, U.S. Ct. Appeals (7th Cir.) 2002. Assoc. Kirkland & Ellis, Chgo., 1979-85, ptnr., 1985—; adj. prof. of law Northwestern U., Evanston, Ill., 1997—. Mem. ABA, Bd. of Visitors Northwestern U. 1999-; fellow Am. Coll. of Trial Lawyers 1999-. Federal civil litigation, State civil litigation, General civil litigation. Office: Kirkland & Ellis 200 E Randolph Dr Fl 54 Chicago IL 60601-6636

HARRAL, JOHN MENTEITH, lawyer; b. Ancon, Panama Canal Zone, June 25, 1948; s. Brooks Jared and Sara (Mumma) H.; m. Marjorie Van Fosson, Aug. 15, 1970; children: Alyse, Jessica. BBA, U. Miss., 1971, JD, 1974. Bar: Miss. 1974, U.S. Dist. Ct. (so. dist.) Miss. 1974, U.S. Ct. Appeals (5th cir.) 1977. Law clk. to Judge J.P. Coleman, U.S. Ct. Appeals (5th cir.), New Orleans, 1978-79; ptnr. White & Morse, Gulfport, Miss., 1979-92, Eaton & Cottrell, P.A., Gulfport, Miss., 1993-97; sole practitioner Gulfport, 1997—2002; mem. Butler, Snow, O'Mara, Stevens & Cannada, PLLC, Gulfport, 2002—. Mem. Miss. Gov.'s Jud. Nominating Com., 1990-93; instr. bus. law William Carey Coll.; mem. adv. bd. dirs. Whitney Nat. Bank. Chmn. Episc. Svcs. for Aging, Mississippi Gulf Coast, 1981-85, also bd. dirs.; bd. dirs. Make-A-Wish Found. Miss.; founder, pres. Gulfport Excellence, 1991—; bd. dirs. Christmas in April, Harrison County, 1994-2000, pres., 1995-96; bd. dirs. Lynn Meadows Discovery Ctr., 1996—, sec., exec. com., 1997-2000; lay eucharistic min. St. Mark's Episcopal Ch., Gulfport, 1980, vestryman, sr. and jr. warden, Sunday sch. tchr.; pres. Gulfport Downtown Assn., Inc., 1997-98, dir., 1998-2001; mentor Gulfport Schs., 1991—; Miss. commr. Nat. Conf. Commrs. on Uniform State Laws, 2000—; mem. Miss. Gulf Coast Econ. Devel. Coun. Lt. JAGC, USNR, 1974-78. Named to South Miss. Leadership Hall of Fame, 2002. Fellow: Miss. Bar Found.; mem.: ABA, Gulf Coast Law Inst. (bd. dirs. 1988—93), Harrison County Bar Assn. (pres. young lawyers sect. 1982, pres. 1987—88), Miss. Bar Assn. (bd. dirs. young lawyers divsn. 1982—84, commr. 1991—94), Miss. Coast C. of C. (bd. dirs. 1994—), Gulfport C. of C. (bd. dirs. 1995—97, pres. 1997), Gulfport Bus. Club (founder, v.p. 1999, pres. 2001—02), Bayou Bluff Tennis Club, Rotary (pres. 2002—03). Republican. Banking, General civil litigation, Insurance. Home: 12 Old Oak Ln Gulfport MS 39503-6210 Office: 1300 25th Ave Gulfport MS 39501- E-mail: john.harral@butlersnow.com.

HARRELL, CHARLES LYDON, JR., lawyer; b. Norfolk, Va., Oct. 22, 1916; s. Charles Lydon Sr. and Ethel Theresa (Toone) H.; m. Martha de Weese Guild, Feb. 5, 1943 (dec. March 1991); children: Charles Lydon III, John Morgan, Marshall Guild, deWeese Toone; m. Lynn Aikens Johnson, July 13, 1993. BA, Randolph-Macon Coll., 1938; LLB, U. Richmond, 1941. Bar: Va. 1940, U.S. Dist. Ct. (ea. dist.) Va. 1946, U.S. Bankruptcy Ct. (ea. and we. dist.) Va. 1946, U.S. Ct. Appeals (4th cir.) 1947, U.S. Ct. Internat. Trade 1950, U.S. Supreme Ct. 1952. Ptnr. Harrell & Landrum, Norfolk, 1947-76; pvt. practice, Norfolk, 1987—. Commr. in chancery Cir. Ct. Princess Anne County, 1950-76, City of Norfolk, 1955-77; spl. justice Princess Anne County, 1952-65. Mem. health care consumer coun. Naval Hosp., Portsmouth, 1980-90; mem. coun. of ch. Ghent United Meth. Ch., 1950—, tchr. Bible class, 1966—, master, mem. com. Boy Scouts of Am., Sea Scouts; mem. Coun. of Ministries, 1955-88, chmn. commn. on Christian concerns Meth. Ch., 1971-76; co-founder, chmn., pres. bd. dirs. Ghent Venture, Inc.; v.p. Norfolk Seaman's Soc., 1970-80, bd. dirs., 1990—, v.p.; bd. dirs. Handicaps Unltd. of Va., legis. chmn., legal advisor; vol. prayer counsellor Christian Broadcast Network, 1977-93; co-founder, bd. dirs. Va. Assn. of Blind, 1981—; dir. Norfolk Interfaith Coalition for the Elderly, Tidewater Christian Outreach Project; pres. Mobility on Wheels, Inc., 1980-83, bd. dirs., 1977—, v.p. 2000—; mem. com. for therapeutic recreation of handicapped people City of Norfolk, 1991-98; co-founder, v.p., dir. New Life Devel.; pro bono counsel Tidewater Legal Aid Soc., 1989—. Comdr. USN, to 1962. Decorated 9 campaign medals, 4 combat stars; recipient Cross Mil. Svc., UDC. Mem. ABA, Norfolk-Portsmouth Bar Assn., Va. State Bar Assn. (Lawyers Helping Lawyers), Va. Bar Assn., Jud. Soc., Christian Legal Soc., Am. Legion, VFW (past comdr.), Jr. C. of C., Jesus to the World Evangelistic Assn. (co-founder, bd. dirs., v.p., chmn. bd.), Christian Legal Soc., Gideons, Masons, Shriners, Kiwanis, Ret. Officers Assn., The Fleet Res., Tin Can Sailors Assn., Mine Warfare Assn., The Caine Mutineers, McNeil Law Soc., Phi Beta Kappa, Omicron Delta Kappa (sec. Tidewater Alumni chpt.), Tau Kappa Alpha. Avocations: swimming, scuba diving, spear fishing. Bankruptcy, General civil litigation, Property, real (including real estate development, water). Home and Office: 4464 Ocean View Ave Virginia Beach VA 23455

HARRELL, GARY PAUL, lawyer; b. Texas City, Tex., July 8, 1952; s. James Eugene Jr. and Mary Alice Harrell; m. Leigh Evans, May 27, 1978. BS, U. Tex., 1977, MA, 1979; cert. mgmt. healthcare facilities, UCLA, 1984; JD cum laude, Lewis & Clark Coll., 1991. Bar: Oreg. 1991, U.S. Dist. Ct. (fed. dist.) Oreg. 1991; diplomate Am. Coll. Healthcare Execs. Staff/charge nurse Healthcare Facilties, Austin, Tex., 1972-78; gen. mgr. Nursing Support Svcs., Austin, 1978-80; dir. edn. Downey (Calif.) Cmty. Hosp., 1980-84; v.p. patient care Grande Ronde Hosp., La Grande, Oreg., 1984-88; assoc. Lane Powell Spears Lubersky, Portland, Oreg., 1990-94; ptnr. Harrell & Nester, LLP, Portland, 1994—. Adj. prof., asst. prof. Calif. State U., Long Beach, 1980-84; pres. Oreg. State Bd. Nursing, Portland, 1987-90. Contbr. chpts. in books. With USNR, 1970-74. Recipient Am. Jurisprudence award, 1989. Fellow: Am. Coll. Health Care Adminstrs. (past pres. Oreg. chpt.), Healthcare Fin. Mgmt. Assn. (past pres. Oreg. chpt.); mem.: Oreg. Health Care Assn., Oreg. Health Lawyers Assn. (sec.), Am. Health Lawyers Assn., Oreg. Assn. Nurse Attys. (treas., past pres.), Oreg. State Bar (sec. exec. com. health law sect.). Avocations: flying, sailing, motorcycling. Administrative and regulatory, Corporate, general, Health. Office: Harrell & Nester LLP 1515 SW 5th Ave Ste 1022 Portland OR 97201-5445 E-mail: gharrell@health-law.net.

HARRELL, GLENN TRUSSELL, JR., judge; BA, U. Md., 1967, JD, 1970. Bar: Md. 1970. Assoc. O'Malley, Miles & Harrell, 1973-76, ptnr., 1977-91; assoc. county atty. Prince George's County, 1971-73; judge at large Ct. Spl. Appeals, 1991-99; judge Ct. Appeals (4th cir.), Prince George's County, Md., 1999—. Chair Commn. on Jud. Disabilities, 1996-98; mem. exec. com. Md. Jud. Conf., 1997-99; adj. prof. legal writing Sch. Law U. Balt., 1997—; lectr. in field. Mem. Md. Bar Found., Prince George's County Bar Found. Mem. Md. Bar Assn., Prince George's County Bar Assn. Office: Ct Appeals PO Box 209 Upper Marlboro MD 20773-0209

HARRELL, KYLE ALEXANDER, lawyer; b. Durham, N.C., Jan. 18, 1960; s. Robert Lewis and Alice Jamison Harrell; m. Shirley Ruth Skyers, May 30, 1998; children: Skye Alexandra, Vanessa Faith, Kyle Alexander II. BSCE, N.C. State U., 1984; JD, N.C. Ctrl. U., 1997. Bar: N.C. 1997, Conn. 2000, U.S. Dist. Ct. Conn. 2002. Design engr. Charlotte-Mecklenburg Utility Dept., Charlotte, NC, 1984—94; assoc. Micheaux and Micheaux, Durham, 1997; asst. pub. defender N.C. Dist. 26 Pub. Defender, Charlotte, 1997—99; ptnr. Skyers and Skyers, Bridgeport, 2000—02; mng. ptnr. The Barrister Law Group, 2002—. Bd. dirs., treas. Brooklawn Acad., Fairfield, Conn., 2001—; mem. Bd. Tax Assessment Appeals, Bridgeport, 2001, chmn., 2002. Mem.: ABA, Conn. Bar Assn., N.C. Bar Assn. (Pro Bono Student Year 1997). Criminal, Taxation, general, Personal injury (including property damage). Office: The Barrister Law Group 211 State 2d Fl Bridgeport CT 06604 Fax: 203-333-7178. E-mail: kaharrell@barristerlawgroup.com.

HARRELL, ROY G., JR., lawyer; b. Norfolk, Va., Sept. 14, 1944; s. Roy G. and Winifred B. H. BS with honors, The Citadel; LLB cum laude, Washington & Lee. Bar: Fla.; cert. in real property. Assoc. Jennings, Watts, Clarke & Hamilton, Jacksonville, Fla., 1971-75, Greene, Mann, Rowe, Stanton, Mastry & Burton, St. Petersburg, Fla., 1975-76, ptnr., 1976-83; founding ptnr. Baynard, Harrell, Ostow & Ulrich (formerly Baynard, Harrell, Mascara & Ostow), St. Petersburg, 1983-94; of counsel Carlton, Fields, Ward, Emmanuel, Smith & Cutler, P.A., St. Petersburg, 1994-98; ptnr. Holland & Knight LLP, St. Petersburg, 1998—. Coun. Am. Lawyer's Auxiliary, 1992-93. Notes editor Washington & Lee Law Review. Past chmn. governing bd. S.W. Fla. Water Mgmt. Dist., 1985-98; past co-chair Pinellas Anclote River Basin Bd.; former mem. policy com. Tampa Bay Nat. Estuary Program; former mem. Tampa Bay Water Coordinating Coun.; pres. United Way, Pinella County, 1986; grad. leadership St. Petersburg, 1976, Leadership Tampa Bay; past chmn. campus adv. bd. U. South Fla. Bayboro Campus; former bd. dirs. Bayfront Ctr. Found.; mem. Citizens Vision 2000; former bd. dirs. 1000 Friends of Fla.; immediate past chmn. bd. dirs. St. Anthony's Devel. Found.; former mem. bd. dirs. ARC, Tampa. Capt. U.S. Army, 1969-71. Recipient Leadership award Leadership St. Pete, 1986, Leadership award Nat. Assn. Leadership Orgn., 1986, PACE award Pinellas Emergency Mental Health Svcs. 1986, Human Svcs. award, 1987. Mem. ABA (mem. various coms.), Am. Coll. Mortgage Attys., Va. Bar Assn., Fla. Bar, St. Petersburg Bar Assn., Greater St. Petersburg C. of C. (Mem. of Yr. award 1981, pres. 1986-87), Leadership St. Pete Alumni Assn. (former chair bd. dirs.), Dragon Club, St. Petersburg Yacht Club, Suncoasters, Suncoast Tiger Bay Club, Anthonians (former pres.), Phi Sigma Alpha, Phi Alpha Delta. Office: Holland & Knight LLP 200 Central Ave Ste 1600 Saint Petersburg FL 33701-3326

HARRELL, WALTER HUGH, lawyer; b. Waco, Tex., May 29, 1924; s. Thomas Walter and Eula Lucille H.; m. Dorothy Marie Harrell, May 27, 1955; children: Gary D. Harrell, Stephen R. Harrell, Deborah K. Wasson. BBA, LLB, Baylor U., JD, 1950. Bar: Tex., U.S. Dist. Ct. (no. dist.) Tex., U.S. Ct. Appeals (5th cir.), U.S. Supreme Ct. Pvt. practice, Lubbock, Tex., 1951—. With U.S. Army. Republican. Baptist. Avocation: golf. General civil litigation, Personal injury (including property damage), Probate (including wills, trusts). Office: 1708 Metro Tower 1220 Broadway St Lubbock TX 79401-3201

HARRIMAN, JOHN HOWLAND, retired lawyer; b. Buffalo, Apr. 14, 1920; s. Lewis Gildersleeve and Grace (Bastine) H.; m. Barbara Ann Brunmark, June 12, 1943; children— Walter Brunmark, Constance Bastine, John Howland. AB summa cum laude, Dartmouth, 1942; JD, Stanford U., 1949. Bar: Calif. 1949. Assoc. firm Lawler, Felix & Hall, Los Angeles, 1949-55; asst. v.p., then v.p. Security Pacific Nat. Bank, Los Angeles, 1955-72, sr. v.p., 1972-85. Sec. Security Pacific Corp., 1971-85; dir. Master Metal Works; mem. nat. adv. coun. The Pub. Svc., 1992-93. Mem. L.A. adv. coun. Episcopal Ch. Found., 1977-79; mem. Republican Assocs., 1951-72 , trustee, 1962-72; mem. Calif. Rep. Central Com., 1956-69, 81— , exec. com., 1960-62, 81-84; mem. L.A. County Rep. Central Com., 1958-70, exec. com., 1960-62, vice chmn., 1962; chmn. Calif. 15th Congl. Dist. Rep. Central Com., 1960-62, Calif. 30th Congl. Dist. Rep. Central Com., 1962; treas. United Rep. Fin. Com. L.A. County, 1969-70; chmn. L.A. County Reagan-Bush campaign, 1980, co-chmn., 1984; exec. dir. Calif. Rep. Party, 1985-86. With USAAF, 1943-46. Mem. Am. Bar Assn., State Bar Calif., Phi Beta Kappa, Theta Delta Chi, Phi Alpha Delta. Clubs: California (Los Angeles); Lincoln, Breakfast Panel (pres. 1970-71).

HARRINGTON, CAROL A. lawyer; b. Geneva, Ill., Feb. 13, 1953; d. Eugene P. and M. Ruth (Bowersox) Kloubec; m. Warren J. Harrington, Aug. 19, 1972; children: Jennifer Ruth, Carrie Anne. BS summa cum laude, U. Ill., 1974, JD magna cum laude, 1977. Bar: Ill. 1977, U.S. Dist. Ct. (no. dist.) Ill. 1977, U.S. Tax Ct. 1979. Assoc. Winston & Strawn, Chgo., 1977-84, ptnr., 1984-88, McDermott, Will & Emery, 1988—. Speaker in field. Co-author: Generation-Skipping Tax , 1996, Generation-Skipping Transfer Tax, Warren, Gorham & Lamont, 2000. Fellow Am. Coll. Trusts and Estate Coun. (bd. regents 1999—); mem. ABA (chmn. B-1 generation skipping transfer com. 1987-92, coun. real property, probate and trust law sect. 1992-98), Ill. State Bar Assn., Chgo. Bar Assn. (trust law com. divsn. 1), Chgo. Estate Planning Coun. Estate planning, Probate (including wills, trusts), Estate taxation. Office: McDermott Will & Emery 227 W Monroe St Ste 3100 Chicago IL 60606-5096

HARRINGTON, JAMES TIMOTHY, lawyer; b. Chgo., Sept. 4, 1942; s. John Paul and Margaret Rita (Cunneen) H.; m. Roseanne Strupeck, Sept. 4, 1965; children: James Timothy, Roseanne, Maris Zajdela. BA, U. Notre Dame, 1964, JD, 1967. Bar: Ill. 1967, Ind. 1968, U.S. Dist. Ct. (no. dist.) Ill. 1967, U.S. Dist. Ct. (no. and so. dists.) Ind. 1968, U.S. Ct. Appeals (7th cir.) 1969, U.S. Ct. Appeals (4th cir.) 1977, U.S. Ct. Appeals (8th cir.) 1979, U.S. Ct. Appeals (3d cir.) 1981, U.S. Supreme Ct. 1979, U.S. Ct. Appeals (D.C. cir.) 1993. Law clk. U.S. Dist. Ct. (no. dist.) Ind., 1967-69; assoc. Rooks, Pitts & Poust, Chgo., 1969-75, ptnr., 1976-87, Ross & Hardies, Chgo., 1987—2003, McGuiness, Woods, Ross & Hardies LLP, 2003—. Lectr. environ. law, fed. procedures, adminstrv. law, 1960—. Vice chmn. Mid Am. Legal Found.; chmn., bd. dirs. Ill. Safety Coun. Fellow Am. Bar Found.; mem. Ill. Bar Assn., Ind. Bar Assn., Chgo. Bar Assn. (environ. law com., real estate com.), Indsl. Water Waste and Sewer Group (past chmn.), Air and Waste Mgmt. Assn. (bd. dirs. Lake Mich. sect.), Assn. Environ. Law Inst., Lawyers Club Chgo., Exec. Club Chgo., Union League Club Chgo. Roman Catholic. Federal civil litigation, State civil litigation, Environmental. Home: 746 Foxdale Ave Winnetka IL 60093-1908 Office: Ross & Hardies 150 N Michigan Ave Ste 2500 Chicago IL 60601-7567 E-mail: james.harrington@rosshardies.com.

HARRINGTON, JOHN MICHAEL, JR., lawyer; b. Boston, July 5, 1921; s. John Michael and Marie Bernadine (Ratchford) H.; m. Ellen Patricia White, May 12, 1951; children— John Michael III, Marc W., Francis X. B., Ellen M., Matthew J., Patrick W. AB, Harvard U., 1943, LL.B., 1949. Bar: Mass. 1949, U.S. Dist. Ct. (Mass.) 1950, U.S. Ct. Appeals (1st cir.) 1956, U.S. Supreme Ct. 1968. Law clk. Supreme Jud. Ct. Mass., Boston, 1949-50; assoc. Ropes & Gray, Boston, 1950-55, 57-61, ptnr., 1961-93, counsel, 1994—; asst. U.S. atty. Dist. of Mass., Boston, 1955-57. Trustee Winchester Sav. Bank, Mass., 1966-91; mem. Mass. Jud. Conduct Commn., Boston, 1978-81. Trustee Roxbury Latin Sch., Boston, 1962-67, St. Sebastian's County Day Sch., Needham, Mass., 1973-86; mem. fin. com. Town of Winchester, 1959-62. Served to capt. field arty. U.S. Army, 1943-46, ETO Fellow Am. Coll. Trial Lawyers, Am. Bar Found.; mem. ABA (standing com. on fed. judiciary 1st cir. 1978-84), Boston Bar Assn. Clubs: Union (v.p. 1982-86, pres. 1986-88), Curtis, Harvard (Boston). Democrat. Roman Catholic. Home: 19 Cabot St Winchester MA 01890-3501 Office: Ropes & Gray LLP One International Pl Boston MA 02110-2624

HARRINGTON, JOHN TIMOTHY, retired lawyer; b. Madison, Wis., May 26, 1921; s. Cornelius Louis and Emily (Chisholm) H.; m. Deborah Reynolds, May 23, 1948; children— Elizabeth Chisholm, Samuel Parker, Hannah Quincy, Jane McRae BS, Harvard U., 1942, LL.B., 1948. Bar: Wis. 1949. Assoc. Quarles & Brady and predecessor firms, Milw., 1948-58, ptnr., 1958-91; ret., 1991—. Served to lt. comdr. USNR, 1942-46, PTO Estate planning, Probate (including wills, trusts), Estate taxation. Home: 924 E Juneau Ave Milwaukee WI 53202-2748 Office: Quarles & Brady 411 E Wisconsin Ave Ste 2550 Milwaukee WI 53202-4497 E-mail: jtharrington@webtv.net.

HARRINGTON, KEVIN PAUL, lawyer; b. Paterson, N.J., Jan. 1, 1951; s. James John and Theresa Elizabeth (Giblin) H. BA, Niagara U., 1973; JD, N. E. Sch. Law, Boston, 1978. Bar: N.J. 1978, U.S. Dist. Ct. N.J. 1978, U.S. Supreme Ct. 1983. Judicial clerkship to hon. Thomas R. Rumana, Paterson, N.J., 1978-79; asst. prosecutor Passaic County Prosecutor's Office, Paterson, N.J., 1979-80; assoc. DeYoe & Guiney, Paterson, N.J., 1980-87; ptnr. Catania & Harrington, N. Haledon, N.J., 1987-99, Harrington and Lombardi, LLP, N. Haledon, 2000—. Pres., bd. trustees Clinic for Mental Health Svc., Paterson, N.J., 1990—. Recipient Civil Trial Atty. cert., Supreme Ct. N.J., 1986—. Master Am. Inns of Ct.; mem. ATLA, N.J. Def. Assn., N.J. Bar Assn., Passaic County Bar Assn. (trustee), Def. Rsch. Inst. Avocations: sports, golf, scuba diving. General civil litigation, Insurance, Personal injury (including property damage). Office: Harrington and Lombardi LLP 909 Belmont Ave Ste 3 North Haledon NJ 07508-2568

HARRIS, BAYARD EASTER, lawyer; b. Washington, July 22, 1944; s. Edward Bledsoe and Grace (Childrey) H.; m. Rebecca Bond Jeffress, June 10, 1967; children: Nicholas Bayard, Nathan Bedford (dec. 1989), Ellen Coley. AB in History, U. N.C., 1966; JD cum laude, U. S.C., 1973. Bar: Va. 1974, U.S. Dist. Ct. (we. dist.) Va. 1974, U.S. Ct. Appeals (4th cir.) 1974, U.S. Supreme Ct. 1982. Assoc. Woods, Rogers, Muse, Walker & Thornton, Roanoke, Va., 1973-79, ptnr., 1979-85, Woods, Rogers & Hazlegrove, Roanoke, 1985-90; pres. Ctr. for Employment Law, Roanoke, 1991-98; of counsel Woods, Rogers and Hazlegrove, PLC, 1998—; tchg. assoc. Roanoke Coll., Salem, Va., 2003—. Mem. Transp. Safety Bd., 1992-96. Comments and rsch. editor U. S.C. Law Rev., 1972-73. Chpt. chmn. ARC, Roanoke Valley, 1985-87, chmn. ea. ops. hdqrs., 1988-91; pres. Nathan's Gift Found. Lt. USNR, 1966-70. Recipient Clara Barton award ARC Roanoke Valley chpt., 1986. Mem. ABA (labor and employment sect. 1974—), Va. Bar Assn. (labor and employment com. and sect. 1974. Republican. Episcopalian. Avocations: golf, gardening. Civil rights, Federal civil litigation, Labor (including EEOC, Fair Labor Standards Act, labor-management relations, NLRB, OSHA). Office: Woods Rogers & Hazlegrove 10 S Jefferson St Ste 1400 Roanoke VA 24011-1331 E-mail: bharris@woodsrogers.com.

HARRIS, BENJAMIN HARTE, JR., lawyer; b. Sept. 12, 1937; s. Ben H. and Mary Cade (Aldridge) H.; m. Martha Elliott Lambeth, Aug. 26, 1961; children: Benjamin Harte, Wayt. AB, Davidson Coll., 1959; JD, U. Ala., 1962. Bar: Ala. 1964, U.S. Dist. Ct. (so. dist.) Ala. 1965, U.S. Ct. Appeals (5th cir.) 1981, U.S. Supreme Ct. 1971, U.S. Ct. Appeals (11th cir.) 1981. Assoc. Johnstone, Adams, Bailey, Gordon & Harris (formerly Johnstone, Adams, May, Howard & Hill, LLC), Mobile, Ala., 1964-70; mem. Johnstone, Adams, Bailey, Gordon & Harris, Mobile, 1971. Chmn. Atty's Ins. Mut. Ala., bd. dirs. Past bd. dirs., past pres. Boys' Club, 1989-95; past chmn., past trustee UMS Prep Sch.; v.p., bd. dirs. Gordon Smith Ctr.; mem. stds. com. United Way. Fellow: Ala. Bar Found. (past. pres., past trustee, past pres.), Am. Bar Found. (life); mem.: Nat. Conf. Bar Pres. (past exec. coun.), 11th Cir. Ct. Appeals Hist. Soc. (trustee, v.p.), Ala. Jud. Commn., Am. Arbitration Assn., Am. Judicature Soc., Ala. Def. Lawyers Assn., Ala. Law Sch. Found. (past pres., trustee, Pipes Disting. Alumnus award 2003), Ala. Law Inst., Ala. State Bar (bd. commrs. 1978—87, mem. exec. com., trustee bar found., past chmn. disciplinary commn., past pres.), Mobile County Bar Assn. (exec. com. 1980—87), ABA (past ho. of dels., past bd. govs.), Athelstan Club, Murray House (pres. 2003—, dir.), Mobile Rotary Club (Paul Harris fellow), Brock Inn of Ct. (pres. 1996—98). Episcopalian. General civil litigation, Oil, gas, and mineral, Workers' compensation. Office: PO Box 1988 Mobile AL 36633-1988

HARRIS, BRETT ROSENBERG, lawyer; b. Livingston, NJ, Nov. 24, 1966; s. Paul Irwin and Edith Rosenberg; m. Mitchell Paul Harris, Nov. 16, 1996; children: Alicia Rose, Cooper James. BA cum laude, Washington & Jefferson Coll., 1988; JD, NYU, 1991. Summer intern Ctr. for Law and Social Policy, Washington, 1989; summer assoc. Winthrop Stimson Putnam & Roberts, NYC, 1990; assoc. Fox & Fox, Newark, 1991-95, Wilentz, Goldman & Spitzer, P.A., Woodbridge, NJ, 1995—2000, ptnr., 2000—. Exec. editor NYU Rev. Law and Social Change, 1990-91. Mem. NJ State Bar Assn. (chair Internet and computer law com., dir. corp. and bus. law sect.), trustee of Temple Emanu-el of Westfield "I have a Dream" Foundation, Inc.; mem. of Medical and profl. advisory Coujn. of the Arnold P. Gold Found. Avocation: baseball scorer. Computer, Corporate, general. Home: 423 Everson Pl Westfield NJ 07090-3229 Office: Wilentz Goldman & Spitzer PA 90 Woodbridge Ctr Dr Ste 901 Woodbridge NJ 07095-1146 E-mail: bharris@wilentz.com.

HARRIS, CASPA, JR., lawyer, educator, association administrator; b. Washington, May 20, 1928; BS in Acctg., Am. U., 1958, JD, 1967. CPA Va.; bar: Va. 1967, D.C. 1968, U.S. Supreme Ct. Staff pub. rels. NIH, Bethesda, Md., 1955-58; sr. auditor KPMG Peat Marwick, Washington, 1958-62; chief internal auditor Howard U., Washington, 962-65, comptroller, 1965-71, v.p. bus. and fiscal affairs, treas., 1971-87; pres. Nat. Assn. Coll. and Univ. Bus. Officers, Washington, 1987-95; lawyer, cons. pvt. practice, Waterford, Va., 1995—. Prof. sch. of law Howard U., Washington, 1968-87, Kaufman-Cades CPA Rev. Sch., 1978-87, U. Ky., 1976—, U. Calif. Santa Barbara, 1984—.; chmn., bd. dirs. Coll. Constrn. Loan Assn., Coll. Constrn. Loan Ins. Co.; bd. dirs. Nat. Harmony Meml. Park, The Common Fund; adv. coun. Met. Life Pension dept., Systems & Computer Tech. Corp.; treas. bd. State of Va., 1982-86, mem. Civil Rights Appellate Rev. Divsn. U.S. Dept. Edn., 1988-90; adv. bd. on colls. and univs. IRS, 1984-95; Presdl. adv. bd. on Historically Black Colls. and Univs., 1990-93; cons. Cassidy & Assocs., Washington, Nat. Heart Inst. Past chmn. of bd. Nat. Assn. Coll. & Univ. Bus. Officers Assns., also other offices; past pres. Ea. Assn. Coll. and Univ. Bus. Officers; bd. dirs. Salvation Army Met. Washington, 1970-76; mem. USO Fin. Com., 1970-71, Health Welfare Coun. and United Givers Fund D.C., 1970-72, nat. scholarship com. Lone Star Industries, Inc., 1983-90; treas. and dir. Nat. Capital Area Health Care Coalition, 1983-84; bd. dirs., vice chmn. D.C. chpt. ARC, 1981-86; chmn. fin. com., dir., The College Bd., 1983-88; bd. visitors Norfolk State U., 2000—. Recipient Am. Univ. Disting. Alumni award 1968, Ea. Assn. Coll. & Univ. Bus. Officers, KPMG Peat Marwick award 1995, Nat. Assn. Coll. Stores, Earl Kintner award, 1995, Disting. Bus. Officers award Nat. Assn. Coll. and Univ. Bus. Officers, 1996. Mem. AICPA (minority recruitment com. 1969-72), Va. Soc. CPAs, Va. State Bar Assn., Bar Assn. D.C., Reston Lions Club (pres. 1978-79). Home: 39109 John Wolford Rd Waterford VA 20197-1616

HARRIS, CATHERINE KIRK, law librarian; b. Houston, Tex., Oct. 9, 1941; d. Joe and Mary Kirk; m. James L. Harris, Aug. 9, 1969; 1 child. BA in English, Sam Houston State U., 1962; MA in English, U. Tex. Austin, 1965, MLS, 1971; MA in Legal Studies, Southwest Tex. State U., 2000. Tchr. Spring Br. Ind. Sch. Dist., Houston, 1964—69; libr. Tex. A&M U. Libr., College Station, 1971—72; ref. libr. U. Ga., Athens, 1972—74; libr. Tex. Adv. Commn. on Intergovtl. Rels., Austin, 1981—89; law libr. Tex. State Law Libr., Austin, 1992—. Adj. prof. Grad. Sch. Libr. and Info. Sci. U. Tex. Austin, 1987—94; assisted pro se com. mem. Tex. Access to Justice Commn., Austin, 2002. Author (annotated biblio.): Conrad Aiken, Critical Recognition 1914-1971, 1983; contbr. Mem.: Southwestern Assn. Law Librs., Am. Assn. Law Librs., State Bar Tex. (legal assts. divsn.), State Agy Librs. Tex. (pres. 1987, 1996), Alpha Chi. Office: Tex State Law Libr 205 W 14th St Austin TX 78701

HARRIS, CHARLES ELMER, lawyer; b. Williamsburg, Iowa, Nov. 26, 1922; s. Charles Elmer and Loretto (Judge) H.; m. Marjorie Clark, Jul. 9, 1949 (div. June. 1969); m. Linda Rae Slaymaker, Nov. 25, 1992; children: Martha Ann, Julie Ann, Charles Elmer III. Student, St. Ambrose Coll., 1940-42; BSC., U. Iowa, 1946, JD, 1949. Bar: Iowa 1949. Mem. firm Brody, Parker, Roberts, Thoma & Harris, Des Moines, 1949-66, Herrick, Langdon, Belin Harris, Langdon & Helmick, Des Moines, 1966-78, Belin Harris Helmick, P.C., Des Moines, 1978-91, Belin, Harris, Lamson , McCormick, P.C., Des Moines, 1991-96; pvt. practice, Des Moines, 1997-99; ret., 1999. Lectr. tax schs., meetings, 1951, 55, 67, 69, 77-84, 90, 91. Comments editor: Iowa Law Rev., 1948-49. Bd. dirs. NCCJ, 1964-67, Iowa Bar Found., 1977-92, Iowa Law Sch. Found., 1977-90, United Way Found., 1981-89. Lt. (j.g.) USNR, 1943-46. Fellow Am. Coll. Trust and Estate Counsel; mem. ABA, Iowa Bar Assn. (bd. govs. 1973-80, Merit award 1980), Polk County Bar Assn. (pres. 1972-73), Polk County Jr. Bar Assn. (pres. 1952-53), Order of Coif, Sigma Chi, Delta Theta Phi. Roman Catholic. Corporate, general, Probate (including wills, trusts), Corporate taxation. Home: 5141 Robertson Dr Des Moines IA 50312-2170 E-mail: Harris5141@aol.com.

HARRIS, CHRISTY FRANKLIN, lawyer; b. Greensboro, N.C., Dec. 8, 1945; s. Luther Franklin and Rebecca Ann (Bluster) H.; children: Stacey Lynn, Aubrey Leigh. AA, Oxford Coll., Emory U.; BA, U. Fla., 1967, JD with honors, 1970. Bar: Fla. 1970, U.S. Dist. Ct. (mid. dist.) Fla. 1970, U.S. Ct. Mil. Appeals 1971, U.S. Ct. Appeals (11th cir.) 1984. Assoc. Holland & Knight, Lakeland, Fla., 1970, 1973-74; pres. Canan & Harris P.A., Lakeland, Fla., 1974-76; pres., sr. atty. Harris, Midyette & Clements P.A., Lakeland, Fla., 1976-89, Harris & Midyette, P.A., Lakeland, Fla., 1989-91, Harris, Midyette, Geary, Darby & Morrell, P.A., Lakeland, Fla., 1991-98, Harris, Midyette & Darby, P.A., Lakeland, Fla., 1998-2000; shareholder Peterson & Myers, P.A., Lakeland, Fla., 2000—. Mem. 10th cir. Grievance Com., Lakeland, 1976-79, 83-86, chmn. 1979, vice chmn., 1986; mem. Unauthorized Practice of Law Com., 1983-86; bd. dirs. Internat. Speedway Corp., 1984—. Bd. dirs. Program to Aid Drug Abusers, Lakeland, 1975-76, Campfire, 1979-85. Served to capt. USMCR, 1968-73, mil. judge, 1972-73. Named to Hon. Order of Ky. Cols., 1974. Mem. Lakeland Bar Assn., Attys. Title Ins. Fund, Grand Am. Rd. Racing Assn., LLC (founding mem.), Order of Coif, Phi Beta Kappa, Phi Kappa Phi. Republican. Avocations: motor sports, sport fishing. Commercial, contracts (including sales of goods; commercial financing), Corporate, general, Estate planning. Home: 1335 Longoak Dr N Lakeland FL 33811-2146 Office: Peterson & Myers PA 225 E Lemon St Ste 300 PO Box 24628 Lakeland FL 33802-4628 E-mail: charris@petersonmyers.com.

HARRIS, DALE RAY, lawyer; b. Crab Orchard, Ill., May 11, 1937; s. Ray B. and Aurelia M. (Davis) H.; m. Toni K. Shapkoff, June 26, 1960; children: Kristen Dee, Julie Diane. BA in Math., U. Colo., 1959; LLB, Harvard U., 1962. Bar: Colo. 1962, U.S. Dist. Ct. Colo. 1962, U.S. Ct. Appeals (10th cir.) 1962, U.S. Supreme Ct. 1981. Assoc. Davis, Graham & Stubbs, Denver, 1962-67, ptnr., 1967—, chmn. mgmt. com., 1982-85. Spkr., instr. various antitrust and comml. litig. seminars; bd. dirs. Lend-A-Lawyer, Inc., 1989-94. Mem. campaign cabinet Mile High United Way, 1986—87, chmn., atty. adv. com., 1988, sec., legal counsel, trustee, 1989—94, 1996—2001, mem. exec. com., 1989—2001, chmn. bd. trustees, 1996, 1997; trustee The Spaceship Earth Fund, 1986—89, Legal Aid Found. Colo., 1989—95, 2000—01; mem. devel. coun. U. Colo. Arts and Scis. dept., 1985—93; area chmn. law sch. fund Harvard U., 1978—81; bd. dirs. Colo. Jud. Inst., 1994—2003, vice chair, 1998; bd. dir. Colo. Lawyers Trust Account Found., 1996—2001; steering com. Youth-At-Work, 1994, School-To-Work, 1995; mem. jud. adv. coun. Colo. Supreme Ct., 2001—; bd. dirs. Rocky Mountain Arthritis Found., 2002—, Qualife Wellness Cmty., 2002—. With reserves USAR, 1962—68. Recipient Williams award, Rocky Mountain Arthritis Found., 1999. Fellow: Am. Bar Found. (Colo. state chmn. 1998—); mem.: Colo. Assn. Corp. Counsel (pres. 1973—74), Denver Bar Assn. (chmn. centennial com. 1990—91, bd. trustees 1992—95, pres. 1993—94, Merit award 1997), Colo. Bar Assn. (coun. corp. banking and bus. law sect. 1978—83, chmn. antitrust com. 1980—84, bd. govs. 1991—95, chmn. family violence task force 1996—2000, pres.-elect 1999—2000, co-chair multi-disciplinary practice task force 1999—2000, bd. govs. 1999—2002, pres. 2000—01, chmn. profl. reform initiative task force 2001—, chmn. transitions com. 2002—03), Colo. Bar Found. (award of merit 2002), ABA (antitrust and litigation sects.), Rotary (Denver), Denver Law Club (pres. 1976—77, Lifetime Achievement award 1997), Univ. Club, Colo. Forum, The Two Percent Club (exec. com. 1994—), Citizens Against Amendment 12 Com. (exec. com. 1994), Phi Beta Kappa. Antitrust, General civil litigation. Home: 2032 Bellaire St Denver CO 80207-3722 Office: Davis Graham & Stubbs 1550 17th St Ste 500 Denver CO 80202-1202 E-mail: dale.harris@dgslaw.com.

HARRIS, DON VICTOR, JR., lawyer; b. Nottingham Twp., Ind., Jan. 16, 1921; s. Don Victor and Nellie Florence (Dukes) H.; m. Joan Elliott Haffler, Aug. 15, 1959; children: Leigh Elliott (Mrs. John A. Hay), Meghan St. Clair (Mrs. Michel P. Zeisser). AB, DePauw U., 1943; JD, Harvard U., 1945. Bar: D.C. 1947. Law clk. to judge U.S. Ct. Appeals 2d Circuit, 1945-46; assoc. firm Covington & Burling, Washington, 1946-57, ptnr., 1957—. Lectr. in law George Washington U., 1963-64; lectr. tax insts.; mem. IRS Commr.'s Adv. Group, 1976 Contbr. articles to law jours.; Case editor: Harvard Law Rev. Bd. dirs. Oak Hill Cemetery Co.; bd. dirs. Found. for Preservation Historic Georgetown. Fellow Am. Coll. Tax Counsel, Am. Bar Found. (life); mem. Am. Law Inst. (life), ABA (chmn. sect. taxation 1976-77), D.C. Bar Assn., Fed. Bar Assn., Phi Beta Kappa, Beta Theta Pi, Am. Camellia Soc. (judge), Met Club, Chevy Chase Club, John's Island Club (Fla.). Episcopalian. Corporate taxation, Estate taxation, Personal income taxation. Home: 2803 P St NW Washington DC 20007-3067 also: John's Island 777 Sea Oak Dr No 715 Vero Beach FL 32963-3541 Office: Covington & Burling 1043-C 1201 Pennsylvania Ave NW Washington DC 20004-2401 E-mail: dharris@cov.com., ursa1921@aol.com.

HARRIS, DONALD RAY, lawyer; b. Lake Preston, S.D., Apr. 21, 1938; s. Raymond H. and Nona (Trousdale) H.; children: Beverly, Scott, Bradley, Lindi; m. Sharon K. Brown, Sept. 4, 1982. BA, State U. Iowa, 1959; JD, U. Iowa, 1961. Bar: Ill. 1963, U.S. Dist. Ct. (no. dist.) Ill. 1963, U.S. Ct. Appeals (3d, 4th, 6th, 7th, 9th and fed. cirs.) 1966-95, U.S. Dist. Ct. (we. dist.) Tex. 1989, U.S. Supreme Ct. 1977, U.S. Ct. Fed. Claims 1995, U.S. Dist. Ct. (ea. dist.) Wis. 1997. Assoc. Jenner & Block, Chgo., 1963-70, ptnr., 1970—. Lt. inf. U.S. Army, 1961-63. Mem. ABA, Ill. Bar Assn., Chgo. Bar Assn., Bar Assn. 7th Cir., Chgo. Coun. Lawyers, Am. Coll. Trial Lawyers, ITC Trail Lawyers Assn., Lawyers Club of Chgo. Federal civil litigation, State civil litigation, Criminal. Office: Jenner & Block One IBM Plz Chicago IL 60611-3586 E-mail: dharris@jenner.com.

HARRIS, EDWARD MONROE, JR., former office equipment company executive; b. Phila., June 5, 1923; s. Edward Monroe and Grace Ida (Wilson) H.; m. Marion Hoyt Stevens, Sept. 16, 1950; children: Edward Monroe, Marion Olney, Peter Duncan. BA, Yale U., 1943; LLB, U. Pa., 1949. Bar: N.Y. 1949. Assoc. Sullivan & Cromwell, N.Y.C., 1949-57; assoc. counsel Kennecott Copper Corp., N.Y.C., 1957-62; corp. counsel, sec. MacMillan Inc., N.Y.C., 1963-67; sec., gen. counsel Pitney Bowes Inc., Stamford, Ct., 1967-88, v.p., 1969-88. Dir. Conn. Joint Council on Econ. Edn., 1974-88; trustee Conn. Pub. Expenditure Council, 1979-85, exec. com., 1983-85; dir. Stamford Mus. and Nature Ctr. Inc., 1980-90, treas., 1982-84, first v.p., 1984-86, pres., 1986-88; trustee Edward W. Hazen Found., 1981-91; mem. adv. com. Conn. Comprehensive Plan for Secondary, Vocat. Career and Adult Edn., 1985; mem. bd. edn., Darien, Conn., 1966-90, chmn., 1967-90. Served to 1st lt. USMCR, 1943-46. Mem. C. of C. U.S. (edn., employment tng. com. 1976-86, environ. com. 1987-88), Conn. Bus. and Industry Assn. (bd. dirs. 1974-77). Republican. Presbyterian. Club: Wee Burn Country (Darien). Avocations: travel, gardening. Corporate, general.

HARRIS, GEORGE BRYAN, lawyer; b. Columbia, S.C., July 8, 1964; s. A. Bryan and Beverly Gaye (Bennett) H. BA, U. Ala., 1986; JD, U. Va., 1989. Bar: Ala. 1989, U.S. Dist. Ct. (no., mid., and so. dists.) Ala. 1990, U.S. Ct. Appeals (11th cir.) 1990, D.C. 1991, U.S. Ct. Appeals (5th cir.) 1992, U.S. Supreme Ct. 1993, London Ct. Internat. Arbitration 1995, U.S. Dist. Ct. (no. dist.) Tex. 1996, U.S. Ct. Appeals (4th cir.) 2000, U.S. Ct. Appeals (fed. cir.) 2000. Ptnr. Bradley Arant Rose & White LLP, Montgomery, Ala., 1996—. Spl. asst. atty. gen. for environment State of Ala., Montgomery, 1990-92. Mem. ABA (co-chairperson Y2K com. 2000—), Birmingham Bar Assn., Montgomery Bar Assn., U. Va. Law Alumni Assn., U. Ala. Alumni Assn., Bus. Coun. Ala. (charter mem., young exec. com.), Birmingham Mon. Morning Quarterback Club, Birmingham Area C. of C. (chair govt. affairs com.), Econ. Devel. Assn. Ala., So. Econ. Devel. Coun., Pub. Affairs Rsch. Coun. Ala. Roundtable, Monmouth Area C. of C. (bd. dirs. 2003—), Delta Tau Delta (v.p., bd. dirs. chpt. 1991-94). Methodist. General civil litigation, Legislative, Utilities, public. Office: Bradley Arant Rose & White LLP 401 Adams Ave Ste 780 Montgomery AL 36104 E-mail: gbharris@bradleyarant.com.

HARRIS, GORDON H. lawyer; b. Atlanta, May 7, 1938; s. Huie H. Harris and Elizabeth (McBrayer) Stroud; m. Dorothy Laing, Dec. 6, 1960; children: Sarah Overmeyer, Bruce McBrayer. BA in Math., U. Fla., 1961, JD with honors, 1965. Bar: Fla. 1966, U.S. Dist. Ct. (mid. dist.) Fla., U.S. Ct. Appeals (5th and 11th cirs.), U.S. Supreme Ct. 1966. Instr. legal writing and research U. Fla. Law Sch., Gainesville, 1965-66; assoc. Holland and Knight, Bartow, Fla., 1966-69; ptnr. Gray, Harris & Robinson, Orlando, Fla., 1969—; asst. atty. Orange County, 1978-84. Guest instr. Valencia Community Coll., 1978-80; atty. Tourist Devel. Council, 1977-84; asst. prosecutor Orange County, 1969-71. Exec. editor U. Fla. Law Rev., 1964-65. Mem. East Ctl. Fla. Regional Planning Council, Orlando, 1976-77; sr. warden St. Michael's Episc. Ch., 1980, lay reader 1966—; chmn. bd. trustees Trinity Prep. Sch., 1984—; exec. com. Fla. Citrus Bowl, 1982-85, bd. dirs. 1980-85; bd. dirs. March of Dimes 1977-82, Parents Anonymous of Fla., Inc., 1982-92, Valencia Community Coll. Found., 1978-90. Mem. ABA, Fla. Bar Assn., Orange County Bar Assn., Assn. Trial Lawyers Am., Acad. Fla. Trial Lawyers, U. Fla. Alumni Assn. (nat. pres. 1981, chmn. bd. 1982, dir. Gator boosters 1973-83, province comdr. 1993—, life), Am. Judicature Soc., Fla. Shrine Assn. (pres. 1982-83), Order of Coif, Fla. Blue Key, Phi Kappa Phi, Phi Delta Pi, Kappa Alpha, Kappa Alpha Order Found. (bd. trustees 1999). Clubs: Touchdown, Country, University (Orlando); Citrus. Lodges: Shriners (potentate 1983), Masons. Republican. Condemnation (eminent domain), Construction, General practice. Office: Gray Harris & Robinson PA PO Box 3068 Orlando FL 32802-3068

HARRIS, HARVEY ALAN, lawyer; b. St. Louis, Nov. 5, 1936; s. Irvin S. and Sylvia Zelda (Goodman) H.; m. Gloria Goldman, Aug. 14, 1960; children: Stephen J., David A., Linda A.; m. Linda Ruth Everett, Mar. 17, 1977; m. Judith A. Stackhouse, Dec. 19, 1992. AB magna cum laude, Harvard U., 1958, JD, 1961. Bar: Mo. 1961, U.S. Dist. Ct. (ea. dist.) Mo. 1963, U.S. Ct. Appeals (8th cir.) 1979, U.S. Supreme Ct. 1979. Ptnr. and chmn. The Stolar Partnership and predecessors, St. Louis, 1961—. Cons. Office Policy Devel. and Rsch., HUD; owner, ptnr. Fox Assocs., Inc., Metrotix. Author: Schumpeter's Theory of Innovation, 1958. Commr., treas., trustee St. Louis Sci. Ctr.; former chmn. St. Louis bi-state chpt. ARC; chmn. emeritus Sta. KETC-TV, St. Louis; commr., chmn. Bi-State Transit Authority Met. St. Louis; pres. St. Louis Jewish Fedn.; bd. dirs. Jewish Fedn. St. Louis, Barnes Jewish Hosp., St. Louis, St. Louis Symphony. Mem.: ABA, St. Louis Bar Assn., Mo. Bar Assn., Harvard of St. Louis (v.p. 1983), Noonday, Westwood (treas.), St. Louis Racquet, Phi Beta Kappa. Democrat. Corporate, general, Estate planning, Property, real (including real estate development, water). Home: 31 Westmoreland Pl Saint Louis MO 63108-1227 Office: 911 Washington Ave 7th Floor Saint Louis MO 63101 E-mail: harveystl@aol.com., hah@stolarlaw.com.

HARRIS, IRVING, lawyer; b. Cin., May 23, 1927; s. Albert and Sadye H.; m. Selma Schottenstein, June 18, 1950; children: Jeffrey Philip, Jonathan Lindley (dec.), Lisa Ann Hollister. Undergrad. degree, U. Cin., 1948, LLB, 1951. Ptnr. Cors, Hair & Hartsock, 1954-81, Hartsock, Harris & Schneider, Cin., 1981-82, Porter, Wright, Morris & Arthur, Cin., 1982-89; ptnr. firm Harris, Harris, Field Schacter & Bardach Ltd., Cin., 1989-2000. Mem. Ohio Trade Mission to Orient, 1973, to Eng. and Germany, 1974; spl. counsel to Atty. Gen. Ohio, 1963-71; life mem. 6th Cir. Jud. Conf.; lectr. Advising, Oper. and Rebuilding the Financially Distressed Co., 1991; bd. dirs. Bank One, Cin., 1993-2000, HRC Ltd. Partnership (Hyatt Regency (Cin.) Cin. Mem. Ohio Devel. Financing Commn., 1974—84, vice-chmn., 1978—79; spl. counsel Ohio Atty. Gen.'s Office for the Police and Firemen's Disability and Pension Fund, 1994—97; trustee Skidmore Coll., 1976—90, trustee emeritus, 1991—, Big Bros.; trustee Cin. Symphony Orch., 1989—96; bd. overseers U. Cin. Law Sch., 1998—; arbitrator Ct. of Common Pleas of Hamilton County, 2001—; mediator U.S. Dist. Ct. (so. dist.) Ohio Western divsn., 1999—. Mem. ABA (Sherman Act com., sect. on antitrust and bus. law 1969—, subcoms. on derivative actions, bankruptcy, litigation of bus. and corp. litigation 1992—), Ohio Bar Assn., Cin. Bar Assn., Am. Judicature Soc., Potter Stewart Inn of Ct. (master of the bench), Queen City Club, Univ. Club, Camargo Hunt Club, Cin. Tennis Club, Snowmass Country Club, Ocean Reef Club. Home: 18 Grandin Ln Cincinnati OH 45208-3365 Office: Harris Interests 3801 Carew Tower 441 Vine St Cincinnati OH 45202-2806

HARRIS, JANINE DIANE, lawyer; b. Akron, Jan. 12, 1948; d. Russell Burton and Ethel Harriett (Smith) H.; m. Robert I. Coward, Sept. 14, 1968 (div. 1977); m. John Richard Ferguson, Feb. 1, 1980; children: Brigit Grace, Rachel Anna. AB, Bryn Mawr Coll., 1970; JD, Georgetown U., 1975. Bar: Va. Supreme Ct. 1975, U.S. Dist. Ct. D.C. 1976, U.S. Ct. Appeals (D.C. cir.) 1976, D.C. Ct. Appeals 1976, U.S. Supreme Ct. 1978, U.S. Ct. Appeals (6th cir.) 1981, U.S. Ct. Appeals (8th cir.) 1981. Assoc. Baker & Hostetler, Washington, 1975-78, Pettit & Martin, Washington, 1978-79, Peabody, Lambert & Meyers, Washington, 1979-82, ptnr., 1983-84; sole practice, Washington, 1984—. pres. bd. trustees Burgundy Farm Country Day Sch., 1993-96; mediator and mentor/evaluator D.C. Superior Ct. Multi-Door Dispute Resolution Prog. Contbr. articles to legal jours. Mem. Nat. Conf.

Women's Bar Assns. (bd. dirs. 1984-87, pres.-elect 1987-88, v.p. 1986-87, pres. 1988-89), Nat. Found. for Womens' Bar Assn. (pres. 1985-88, dir. 1988-2001), Women's Bar Assn. D.C. (pres. 1984-85), D.C. Bar (bd. govs. 1984-88), ABA (com. on specialization), Va. Women Attys. Assn. Club: Bryn Mawr. Alternative dispute resolution, Federal civil litigation, Corporate, general.

HARRIS, JEFFREY, lawyer; b. Bklyn., Mar. 20, 1944; s. Herman and Pearl (Herman) H.; m. Joyce Rosa Meckler, June 22, 1975; 1 child, Daniela Rose. BS, NYU, 1965; JD, Syracuse U., 1968. Bar: N.Y. 1969, U.S. Supreme Ct. 1976, D.C. 1977, Va., 1990. Asst. U.S. atty. So. Dist. N.Y., U.S. Dept. Justice, N.Y.C., 1972-76; chief investigation rev. unit. U.S. Dept. Justice, Washington, 1976-77; dep. chief counsel U.S. Ho. of Reps., Korean Investigation, Washington, 1977-79; asst. dir. FTC, Washington, 1979-81; exec. dir. Atty. Gen.'s Task Force on Violent Crime, U.S. Dept. Justice, Washington, 1981; dep. assoc. atty. gen. U.S., Washington, 1981-83; sr. v.p. Capital Bank N.A., Washington, 1983-85; sr. v.p., counsel Capital Bancorp, Miami, Fla., 1983-85; ptnr. Sachs, Greenebaum & Tayler, Washington, 1985-90, Rubin, Winston, Diercks, Harris & Cooke, LLP, Washington, 1990—. Instr. Advocacy Inst., U. Calif. Hastings Coll. Law, San Francisco, 1979-83; adj. asst. prof. George Washington U., Washington, 1980 Lt. (j.g.) USN, 1968-71. Named Meritorious Exec. Pres. of U.S.; recipient Spl. Commendation, Att. Gen. of U.S.; decorated Navy Commendation medal, Vietnam Cross of Gallantry. Mem. ABA Office: Rubin Winston Diercks Harris & Cooke LLP 6th Fl 1155 Connecticut Ave NW Washington DC 20036-4306 E-mail: jharris@rwdhc.com.

HARRIS, JEFFREY MARK, lawyer, educator; b. Chgo., Mar. 11, 1946; s. Al J. and Sylvia (Ruskin) H.; m. Laura Elizabeth Fitzgerald, July 13, 1975; children: Michael, Brian, Andrea. BA, So. Ill. U., 1967; JD, DePaul U., 1971. Bar: Ill. 1972, Fla. 1975, U.S. Dist. Ct. (no. dist.) Ill. 1975, U.S. Dist. Ct. (so. dist.) Fla. 1976, U.S. Supreme Ct. Asst. state atty. State Atty.'s Office, Chgo., 1974-76, Ft. Lauderdale, Fla., 1976-78; pvt. practice, Ft. Lauderdale, 1978—. Adj. prof. Nova U. Law Ctr., Ft. Lauderdale, 1982-97. Mem. ABA, Fla. Bar Assn. (cert. in criminal law, chmn. grievance com. 1990, mem. law cert. com. 1990-93, evidence com. 1999), Nat. Assn. Criminal Def. Attys., Broward County Criminal Def. Bar Assn. (bd. dirs. 1989—, treas. 1991, v.p. 1992, pres. 1994), Broward County Bar Assn. (vice-chmn. 1998, chmn. bar/bench com. 1999), Fla. Criminal Def. Bar Assn. (bd. dirs. 1992—, sec. 2002), B'nai B'rith. Criminal. Office: One E Broward Blvd Fort Lauderdale FL 33301

HARRIS, JERALD DAVID, lawyer; b. July 14, 1947; s. Donald W. and Dorothy (Botwin) H.; m. Carol Sue Fohlen, Mar. 25, 1972; children: Alyse, Jeffrey, Danielle. BA, Miami U., Oxford, Ohio, 1969; JD, U. Cin., 1972. Bar: Ohio 1972, U.,S. Dist. Ct. (so. dist.) Ohio 1972, U.S. Ct. Appeals (6th cir.) 1977, U.S. Dist. Ct. (ea. dist.) Ky. 1978, U.S. Supreme Ct. 1978. Assoc. Kondritzer, Gold & Frank, Cin., 1972-75; ptnr., 1975-79; sole practice, 1979-81; sr. ptnr. Harris and Katz Co. LPA, Cin., 1982-88, Harris, Bella & Burgin A Legal Profl. Assn., 1988—. Lectr. U. Cin. Coll. Law, 1986—, adj. prof., 2002-03. Author: Ohio Workers' Compensation Act. 1986; editor Workers' Compensation Jour. Ohio. Co-chmn. young profl. div. Jewish Welfare fund; bd. dirs. Hillel; vice chmn. Isaac M. Wise Temple Bldg. Fund campaign; mem. Young Leadership Coun. of Jewish Fedn. of Cin.; v.p., bd. dirs. Bonds for Israel; mem. Jewish Cmty. Rels. Coun.-WCET; active Jerry Springer for Gov. campaign; county chmn. Supreme Ct. campaign; bd. dirs. ARC, 1975-79; founding sponsor Civil Justice Found.; adv. Atty. General's Workers' Compensation Coun.; mem. Indsl. Commn. Ohio. Mem. Cin. bar Assn. (past chmn. workers compensation com. 1983-86, other coms.), Ohio Bar Assn. (workers compensation com.), Assn. Trial Lawyers Am., Ohio Acad. TrialLawyers (chmn. social security and adminstrv. law sect. 1981-85, chmn. workers compensation edn., com., 1985, vice chmn., regional coord. workers compensation com., chmn. workers compensation sect. 1992-93, legis. coord. com. 1993, Service to legal Profession award 1981, Cert. of Appreciation 1983, Disting. Svc. award, 1985, 87, Hall of Fame award, 1998, trustee), Nat. Orgn. Social Security Claimants Reps. (Ohio chmn. 1981-83), Am. Soc. Law and Medicine, Ohio State Bar Assn. Coll. Cuyahoga bar Assn.) worker's compensation com.), Phi Alpha Theta. Personal injury (including property damage), Workers' compensation. Home: 10592 Cinderella Dr Cincinnati OH 45242-4909 Office: Harris & Burgin A Legal Profl Assn 9545 Kenwood Rd Ste 301 Cincinnati OH 45242-6100

HARRIS, JOEL B(RUCE), lawyer; b. N.Y.C., Oct. 15, 1941; s. Raymond S. and Laura (Greene) H.; m. Barbara J. Rous, June 13, 1965 (div.); 1 child, Clifford S.; m. Deborah Sherman, Apr. 1, 1986 (div.); children: Sydney Anne, Cassidy Raye. AB, Columbia U., 1963; LLB, Harvard U., 1966; LLM, U. London, 1967. Bar: N.Y. 1968, U.S. Dist. Ct. (so. dist.) N.Y. 1970, U.S. Ct. Appeals (2d cir.) 1970, U.S. Dist. Ct. (ea. dist.) N.Y. 1975, U.S. Supreme Ct. 1976, U.S. Ct. Appeals (3d cir.) 1980, U.S. Dist. Ct. (we. dist.) N.Y. 1981. Assoc. Simpson, Thacher & Bartlett, N.Y.C., 1967-70; asst. U.S. atty. So. Dist. N.Y., 1970-74, chief civil rights unit, 1973-74; assoc. Weil, Gotshal & Manges, N.Y.C., 1974-76, ptnr., 1976-86, Thacher, Proffitt & Wood, N.Y.C., 1986—; chmn. litigation dept., Latin Am. practice group. Speaker, panelist, moderator confs. Contbr. articles to profl. jours. Knox Meml. fellow, 1966-67. Fellow Am. Bar Found.; mem. ABA (chmn. com. internat. litigation 1981-84, chmn. com. personal rights litigation 1984-87), N.Y. State Bar Assn. (mem. internat. law and practice sect., sect. chair 1997-98, mem. exec. com. 1990—, chmn. internat. dispute resolution com. 1990-93, chmn. seasonal meeting 1993, 2001), Assn. Bar City N.Y., Inter-Am. Bar Assn., Fed. Bar Coun., Am. Soc. Internat. Law, Internat. Law Assn., Am. Judicature Soc. Federal civil litigation, State civil litigation, Private international. Home: 40 Prince St New York NY 10012-3426 Office: Thacher Proffitt & Wood 11 West 42nd St New York NY 10036 E-mail: jharris@tpwlaw.com.

HARRIS, K. DAVID, senior state supreme court justice; b. Jefferson, Iowa, July 29, 1927; s. Orville William and Jessie Heloise (Smart) H.; m. Madonna Theresa Coyne, Sept. 4, 1948; children: Jane, Julia, Frederick. BA, U. Iowa, 1949, JD, 1951. Bar: Iowa 1951, U.S. Dist. Ct (so. dist.) Iowa, 1958. Sole practice Harris & Harris, Jefferson, 1951-62; dist. judge 16th Judicial Dist., Iowa, 1962-72; justice Iowa Supreme Ct., Des Moines, 1972-99, sr. justice, 1999—. Served with U.S. Army, 1944-46, PTO. Mem. VFW, Am. Legion, Rotary. Roman Catholic. Avocation: writing poetry. Office: Iowa Supreme Ct State Capitol Bldg Des Moines IA 50319-0001

HARRIS, MICALYN SHAFER, lawyer, educator, arbitrator, mediator; b. Chgo., Oct. 31, 1941; d. Erwin and Dorothy (Sampson) Shafer. AB, Wellesley Coll., 1963; JD, U. Chgo., 1966. Bar: Ill. 1966, Mo. 1967, U.S. Dist. Ct. (ea. dist.) Mo. 1967, U.S. Supreme Ct. 1972, U.S. Ct. Appeals (8th cir.), 1974, N.Y. 1981, N.J. 1988, U.S. Dist. Ct. N.J., U.S. Ct. Appeals (3d cir.) 1993. Law clk. U.S. Dist. Ct., Mo., 1967-68; atty. The May Dept. Stores, St. Louis, 1968-70, Ralston-Purina Co., St. Louis, 1970-72; atty., asst. sec. Chromalloy Am. Corp., St. Louis, 1972-76; pvt. practice St. Louis, 1976-78; atty. CPC Internat., Inc., 1978-80; divsn. counsel CPC N.Am., 1980-84, asst. sec., 1981-88; gen. counsel S.B. Thomas, Inc., 1983-87; corp. counsel CPC Internat., Englewood Cliffs, NJ, 1984-88; assoc. counsel Weil, Gotshal & Manges, N.Y.C., 1988-90; pvt. practice, 1991; v.p., sec., gen. counsel Winpro, Inc., 1991—. Arbitrator Am., Arbitration Assn., NYSE, NASD; adj. prof. Lubin Sch. Bus. Pace U.; mediator. Mem.: ABA (Ctr. Profl. Responsibility, bus. law sect., past chair corp. counsel com., past chair subcom. counseling the mktg. function, mem. securities law com., tender offers and proxy statements subcom., chair task force on e-mail privacy, task force on electronic contracting, task force on conflicts of interest, ad hoc com. on tech., profl. responsibility com.), Am. Law Inst. (mem. consultative groups, restatement of agy. 3d, UCC Arts. 1 & 2, fgn. jurisdiction and judgments project, internat. jurisdiction & judgements projects), Computer Law Assn., N.J. Gen. Coun., Am. Corp. Counsel Assn. N.Y. (mergers and acquisitions com., corp. law com.), Mo. Bar Assn. (past chmn. internat. law com.), Bar Assn. Metro St. Louis (past chair TV com.), Assn. Bar City N.Y., N.J. Bar Assn. (computer law com.), N.Y. State Bar Assn. (exec. com. bus. law sect., securities regulation com., chair internet and technology law com., past chair subcom. on licensing, task force on shrink-wrap licensing, electronic comm. task force). Computer, Corporate, general, Finance. Address: 625 N Monroe St Ridgewood NJ 07450-1206

HARRIS, MICHAEL GENE, optometrist, educator, lawyer; b. San Francisco, Sept. 20, 1942; s. Morry and Gertrude Alice (Epstein) H.; m. Dawn Block; children: Matthew Benjamin, Daniel Evan, Ashley Beth, Lindsay Meredith. BS, U. Calif., 1964, M in Optometry, 1965, D in Optometry, 1966, MS, 1968; JD, John F. Kennedy U., 1985. Bar: Calif., U.S. Dist. Ct. (no. dist.) Calif. Assoc. practice optometry, Oakland, Calif., 1965-66, San Francisco, 1966-68; instr., coord. contact lens clinic Ohio State U., 1968-69; asst. clin. prof. optometry U. Calif., Berkeley, 1969-73, dir. contact lens extended care clinic, 1969-83, chief contact lens clinic, 1983—, assoc. clin. prof., 1973-76, asst. chief, then assoc. chief contact lens svc., 1970—, lectr., then sr. lectr., 1978—, vice chmn. faculty Sch. Optometry, 1983-85, 95—, prof. clin. optometry, 1984-86, clin. prof., 1986—, dir. residency program, 1993-95, asst. dean, 1994-95, assoc. dean, 1995—, acting dean, 2000; lectr. Peter's Meml. U. Calif. Sch. Optometry, 2000. Peter's Meml. lectr. U. Calif. Sch. Optometry, 2000; vis. prof. City U., London, 1984; vis. rsch. fellow U. NSW, Sydney, Australia, 1989; sr. vis. rsch. scholar U. Melbourne, Victoria, Australia, 1989, Victoria, 92; mem. ophthalmic devices panel med. device adv. com. FDA, 1990—, interim chmn., 1994; lectr., cons. in field; mem. regulation rev. com. Calif. Bd. Optometry; cons. hypnosis Calif. Optometric Assn., Am. Optometric Assn.; cons. Nat. Bd. Examiners in Optometry, Soflens divsn. Bausch & Lomb, 1973—, Barnes-Hind Hydrocurve Soft Lenses, Inc., 1974—87, Pilkinton-Barnes Hind, 1987—94, Contact Lens Co., 1977—2001, Palo Alto, Va., 1980, Primarius Corp., Cooper Vision Optics, 1979—, Alcon, 1980—, CIBA, 1976—, Vistakon, 1980—2000; co-founder Morton D. Sarver Rsch. Lab., 1986. Editor current comments sect. Am. Jour. Optometry, 1974-77; editor Eye Contact, 1984-86; assoc. editor The Video Jour. Clin. Optometry, 1988-92; cons. editor Contact Lens Spectrum, 1988—; author: Contact Lenses: Treatment Options for Ocular Disease, Contact Lenses for Pre & Post-Surgery; editor: Problems in Optometry, Special Contact Lens Procedures; Contact Lenses in Ocular Disease, 1990; mem. editl. bd. Contact Lens and Anterior Eye Jour.; contbr. chpts. to books, articles to profl. jours. Planning commnr. Town of Moraga, Calif., 1986, vice-chmn., 1987—88, chmn., 1988—90; mem. Town Coun., Moraga, 1992—96; mem. adv. planning commn. Medi-Cal., 1993—95, chmn., 1994—96, with managed care commn., 1995—, chmn. managed care commn., 1996—98; life mem. Bay Area Coun. for Rescue & Recovery, 1976—; grantor Michael G. Harris Family Endowment Fund U. Calif., Dr. Michael G. Harris Tchg. award U. Calif.; commr. Sunday Football League Contra Costa County, 1974—78; planner, fin. advisor College Pk. HS Track Project; mem. Pleasant Hill C. of C., Friends of Rodgers Ranch, Friends of Libr.; vice-mayor Town Coun., Moraga, 1994—95; city county rels. com. Contra Costa County, Calif.; planning commr. City of Pleasant Hill, Calif., 1999—2002, acting chmn. gen. plan task force, 2002, coun. mem., 2002—; vice chair Redevelopment Agy., Pleasant Hill, 2002—; founding mem. Young Adults divsn. Jewish Welfare Fedn., 1965—69, chmn., 1967—68; charter mem. Jewish Cmty. Ctr. Contra Costa County; founding mem. Jewish Cmty. Mus. San Francisco, 1984; para-rabinnic Temple Isaiah, Lafayette, Calif., 1987, bd. dirs., 1990, Jewish Cmty. Rels. Coun. Greater East Bay, 1979—83, Campolindo Homeowners Assn., 1981—85. Named Alumnus of Yr., U. Calif. Sch. Optometry, 1999; U. Calif. fellow, 1971; Calif. Optometric Assn. scholar, 1965, George Schneider meml. scholar, 1964. Fellow: AAAS, Prentice Soc. (pres.-elect 1994—96, pres. 1996—98), Assn. Schs. and Colls. Optometry (coun. on acad. affairs), British Contact Lens Assn., Am. Acad. Optometry (diplomate cornea and contact lens sect., chmn. contact lens papers, mem. contact lens com. 1974—, vice-chmn. contact lens sect. 1980—82, chmn. sect. 1982—84, immediate past chmn. 1984—86, chmn.jud. com. 1989—2001, chmn. bylaws com. 1989—, ethics taskforce 1999—); mem.: ABA, Contra Costa Bar Assn., Calif. Acad. Sci., Calif. State Bd. Optometry (regulation rev. com.), Internat. Soc. Contact Lens Rsch., Mex. Soc. Contactology (hon.), Nat. Coun. on Contact Lens Compliance, Am. Optometric Found., Internat. Assn. Contact Lens Educators, Assn. Optometric Contact Lens Educators, Calif. Optometric Assn., Am. Optometric Assn. (proctor 1969—79, cons. on hypnosis, mem. contact lens sect., position papers com., mem. com. on opthalmic stds., subcom. on testing and certification, cons. editor Jour.), Internat. Assn. Contact Lens Educators, Robert Gordon Sproul Assn. U. Calif., Mensa, Benjamin Ide Wheeler Soc. U. Calif., JFK U. Sch. Law Alumni Assn., U. Calif. Optometry Alumni Assn. (life), Pleasant Hill C. of C. Democrat. Office: U Calif Sch Optometry Berkeley CA 94720-0001 E-mail: mharris@uclink.berkeley.edu.

HARRIS, MICHAEL ROBERT, lawyer; b. Phila., Nov. 7, 1940; s. Philip and Charlotte (Karpf) H.; m. Deborah Bleshman, Sept. 18, 1942; children: Pamela, Suzanne. BS, U. Pa., 1962; JD, Harvard U., 1965; MA, Villanova U., 1967; LLM, NYU, 1971. Bar: Pa. 1965, Fla. 1973, U.S. Supreme Ct. 1977. Assoc. Mesirov, Gelman, Jaffe & Levin, 1965-67, Goodis, Greenfield, Narin & Mann, 1967-70; ptnr. Krekstein, Yohlin, Wolfson & Harris, Phila., 1970-76, Spencer, Sherr & Moses, Norristown, Pa., 1976-78, Michael R. Harris Assocs., Norristown, 1978-80, Boroff, Harris & Heller, Plymouth Meeting, Pa., 1980—. Lectr. law Villanova U. Law Sch., 1981-87. Mem. ABA, Pa. Bar Assn., Fla. Bar Assn., Phila. Bar Assn., Montgomery Bar Assn. Republican. Jewish. Probate (including wills, trusts), Estate taxation, Personal income taxation. Address: PO Box 1479 Lansdale PA 19446-0773 Office: Blank Rome Comisky & McCauley LLP 1200 N Fed Hwy Ste 417 Boca Raton FL 33432

HARRIS, MORTON ALLEN, lawyer; b. Columbus, Ga., Mar. 13, 1934; s. Alvin L. Harris and Harriett (Berman) Wolpin; m. Judye Rose Spielberger, Aug. 11, 1957; children: Alvin L., Wendy H., Tracy A., S. Beth. BBA, Emory U., 1956; JD, Harvard U., 1959. Bar: Ga. 1959, U.S. Ct. Appeals (5th and 11th cirs.) 1981, U.S. Tax Ct. 1981, U.S. Supreme Ct. 1981. With Page, Scrantom, Harris & Chapman, Columbus, 1959-93, Hatcher, Stubbs, Land, Hollis & Rothschild, Columbus, 1993—. V.p., bd. dirs. Small Bus. Coun. Am., pres., 1980—86; trustee Ga. Fed. Tax Conf., pres., 1988—89; trustee City of Columbus Pension Bd., 1993—2001, 2002—, vice-chair, 1996—2001. Contbg. author: Journal of Taxation, 1976, Business Organizations, 1976; dept. editor: The Tax Times, 1986-87; mem. editorial adv. bd. Practical Tax Lawyer, 1986—, Estate Planners Quarterly. Mem. Columbus Estate Planning Coun., 1964--, pres., 1973, Temple Israel, Inc., 1997-99, 2002--; trustee Inst. for Study Am. Cultures, 1983—, pres. 1997—; spl. advisor Muscogee County Sch. Dist. Health Improvement Program, Columbus, 1983—; trustee Resource One Found.; trustee Columbus State U. Found. Recipient Ann. Vol. award State of Ga., 1985. Fellow Am. Coll. Tax Counsel, Am. Coll. Employee Benefits Counsel, Am. Coll. Trust and Estate Counsel; mem. ABA (chmn. tax sect. personal svc. orgn. com. 1978-80, chmn. tax sect. membership com. 1983-86, mem. counsel tax sect. 1989-96, asst. sec. 1989-91, sec. 1991-93, task force on alt. tax sys. 1996-98, task force tax code simplification 2000-02, divsn. coord. liaison to IRS divsn. samll bus./self employed 2000-02), Jaycees (pres. Columbus chpt. 1966), Kiwanis (pres. Columbus chpt. 1971-72). Pension, profit-sharing, and employee benefits, Probate (including wills, trusts), Corporate taxation. Fax: 706-322-7747. E-mail: mah@hatcherstubbs.com.

HARRIS, RAY KENDALL, lawyer; b. Tucson, July 9, 1957; s. Ray Fisher and Mary Jane (Lewis) H.; m. Patricia Ellen Gallogly, Oct. 10, 1986; children: Ellen Rose, Austin William. BSBA, U. Ariz., 1979, JD, 1982. Bar: Ariz. 1982, U.S. Dist. Ct. Ariz. 1982, U.S. Ct. Appeals (9th cir.) 1985, U.S. Ct. Appeals (10th cir.) 1988, U.S. Ct. Appeals (fed. cir.) 2000. Assoc. Fennemore Craig PC, Phoenix, 1982-88, dir., 1988—. Bd. dirs. Ariz. Innovation Network, Phoenix, 1996-98, High Tech. Industry Cluster, Phoenix, 1998—, Ariz. Tech. Incubator, Scottsdale, 1998-2002; mem. Ariz. Tech. Coun., 2002—. Exec. editor Ariz. Law Rev., 1981-82. Mem. Friends of Sci. and Tech./Ariz. Sci. Ctr., Phoenix, 1994—. Mem. State Bar Ariz. (chair intellectual property sect. 1995-97), Computer Law Assn., Am. Intellectual Property Law Assn., Ariz. Software Assn. (bd. dirs. 1995-2001), Ariz. Technology Coun. (bd. dirs. 2001—). General civil litigation, Computer, Intellectual property. Home: 1410 W Ruth Ave Phoenix AZ 85021-4449 Office: Fennemore Craig PC 3003 N Central Ave Ste 2600 Phoenix AZ 85012-2913 E-mail: rharris@fclaw.com.

HARRIS, RICHARD EUGENE VASSAU, lawyer; b. Detroit, Mar. 16, 1945; s. Joseph S. and Helen Harris; m. Milagros A. Brito; children: Catherine, Byron. AB, Albion Coll., 1967; JD, Harvard U., 1970; postdoctoral, Inst. Advanced Legal Studies, London, 1970-71. Bar: Calif. 1972. Assoc. Orrick, Herrington, Rowley & Sutcliffe, San Francisco, 1972-77; ptnr. Orrick, Herrington & Sutcliffe, San Francisco, 1978-98; pvt. practice Richard E. V. Harris Law Office, Oakland, Calif., 1998—. Faculty Calif. Tax Policy Conf., 1987, 95; spkr. univ., govtl. and profl. groups. Knox fellow, Harvard U., 1970—71. Mem.: ABA (litigation sect. corp. counsel com., subcom. chmn. 1980—82, antitrust law sect. state action com. 1981—, vice chmn. 1982—83, vice chmn. govt. liability com. 1982—84, co-chmn. Nat. Insts. Antitrust Liability 1983, BOULDER task force 1983—84, coun. urban state and local govt. sect. 1983—88, litigation sect. corp. counsel com., subcom. chmn. 1983—, co-chmn. Nat. Insts. Antitrust Liability 1985, bus. law sect., SEC investigation atty.-client privilege waiver task f 1988, profl. conduct com., tax sect., state and local taxes com. 1989—, tax litigation com. 1992—, conflicts of interest task force 1993—96, internat. com. 1994—, corp. counsel com. 1995—, conflicts of interest com. 1996—, ad hoc com. on ethics 2000, com. on profl. conduct 2001—, Ctr. for Profl. Responsibility, ABA Ethics 2000 adv. group), Bar Assn. San Francisco (ethics com. 1980—), Am. Law Inst. (cons. restatements of law unfair competition 1991—94, governing lawyers com. 1991—2000, torts com. 1993—, agy. com. 1996—, trusts com. 1996—). Antitrust, Professional liability, State and local taxation.

HARRIS, ROBERT L(EE), judge; b. Spokane, Wash., Oct. 3, 1934; s. Roy L Harris, Celia A Reed; m. Mary Jo Bourke; children: Joanna, Marie, Robert. BA, Wash. State U., 1954; JD, U. Wash., 1958. Bar: Wash. 1958. Judge Superior Ct. of Wash., Vancouver, 1979—. Mem. Project 2001, Supreme Ct. Task Force, Bd. Jud. Adminstrn., trial ct. funding Supreme Ct. Task Force 2003, chmn. Pres. St. Joseph Cmty. Hosp., Vancouver, 1967—74. Mem.: Superior Ct. Judges Assn. (pres. 2001—02). Achievements include one of first judges to use therapists to debrief jurors following their trial to help provide psychological assistance in gruesome trials. Avocation: youth sports. Office: Superior Court PO Box 5000 Vancouver WA 98666 Office Fax: 360-397-6078.

HARRIS, RUTH JENSEN, lawyer; b. Mpls., Mar. 8, 1920; d. Anton and Edith Cecilia (Axtell) J.; m. Reginald Albright Harris, Nov. 25, 1966 (dec. Oct. 1995). BS, U. Minn., 1941, JD, 1943. Bar: Minn. 1944. Democrat. Unitarian Universalist. Home: 400 Selby Ave Apt 327 Saint Paul MN 55102-4511

HARRIS, SCOTT BLAKE, lawyer; b. N.Y.C., June 18, 1951; s. Stanley Robert and Adele Jean (Ganger) Harris; m. Barbara Straughn, Aug. 5, 1978. AB magna cum laude, Brown U., 1973; JD magna cum laude, Harvard U., 1976. Bar: DC 1977, U.S. Ct. Appeals (DC cir.) 1978, U.S. Supreme Ct. 1983. Law clk. to presiding justice U.S. Dist. Ct., Washington, 1976-77; assoc. Williams & Connolly, Washington, 1977-84, ptnr., 1984-93; chief counsel Bur. Export Adminstrn., U.S. Dept. Commerce, Washington, 1993-94; chief internat. bur. FCC, 1994-96; ptnr. Gibson, Dunn & Crutcher, Washington, 1996-98; mng. ptnr. Harris, Wiltshire & Grannis LLP, Washington, 1998—. Mem. adv. bd. Ctr. Wireless Tech., Va. Tech. U., 1996—, Satellite Comm. Mag., 1996—2000, Critical Infrastructure Fund, LLP, 1999—2000, Telecom. Reports Internat., 2000—02, Morphics Tech., Inc., 2000—02; adj. prof. Georgetown U. Law Ctr., 1996, 2001—02. Columnist: Aviation Week, 2000—01, Space News, 2001—. Trustee Fed. Comm. Bar Assn. Found., 1997—2000. Mem.: ABA (co-chair telecom. com., sect. internat. law 1999—2002), Fed. Comm. Bar Assn. (co-chair online comm. com. 2000—02), Phi Beta Kappa. Federal civil litigation, Communications, Private international. Home: 3409 Fulton St NW Washington DC 20007-1436 Office: Harris Wiltshire & Grannis LLP 1200 18th St NW Washington DC 20036-2506 E-mail: sharris@harriswiltshire.com.

HARRIS, STANLEY S. retired judge, arbitrator, mediator; b. Washington, Oct. 19, 1927; s. Stanley Raymond and Elizabeth (Sutherland) H.; m. Rebecca Ashley, Aug. 1, 1964; children: Scott Sutherland, Todd Ashley, Mark Ashley. BS, U. Va., 1951, JD, 1953. Bar: D.C. 1953, U.S. Supreme Ct. 1964. Assoc., then ptnr. Hogan & Hartson, Washington, 1953-70; judge Superior Ct. D.C., 1971-72, D.C. Ct. Appeals, 1972-82; U.S. atty. for D.C. Dept. Justice, 1982-83; judge U.S. Dist. Ct. D.C., 1983—, sr. judge, 1996—2001; ret., 2001; arbitrator, mediator. Mem. com. on criminal law Jud. Conf. U.S., 1988-94, chmn. com. intercircuit assignments, 1994-2000. Served with U.S. Army, 1945-47. Recipient Judiciary award Assn. Fed. Investigators, 1982. Mem. Bar Assn. D.C. (bd. dirs. 1970-72, Lawyer of Yr. award 1982, Disting. Career award 1996), Lawyers' Club of Washington (pres. 1998-99). Republican. Home: 4982 Sentinel Dr Apt 406 Bethesda MD 20816-3579

HARRIS, TERRELL LEE, prosecutor; BA, Rhodes Coll.; JD, U. Miss. Assoc. Kirkpatrick, Kirkpatrick and Efird, Memphis, 1986—87; asst. dist. atty. gen. Shelby County Dist. Atty.'s Office, 1987—2001; U.S. atty. we. dist. U.S. Dept. Justice, Tenn., 2001—. Office: 800 Clifford Davis Fed Office Bldg 167 N Main St Memphis TN 38103-1898*

HARRIS, TERRILL JOHNSON, lawyer; b. Greensboro, N.C., Aug. 15, 1965; d. Wilbur Everette Johnson Jr. and Ann Terrill Appenzeller; m. George Mitchell Harris III, Oct. 10, 1992; children: George Mitchell IV, Spencer Terrill. BA, Wake Forest U., 1987; JD, Duke U., 1990. Bar: N.C. 1990, D.C. 1991, U.S. Dist. Ct. (mid. dist.) N.C. 1990, U.S. Dist. Ct. (ea. dist.) N.C. 1992, U.S. Dist. Ct. (we. dist.) N.C. 1995, U.S. Ct. Appeals (4th cir.) 1994. Assoc. Smith Helms Mulliss & Moore, LLP, Greensboro, 1990-97, ptnr., 1998—. Mem. Am. Health Lawyers Assn., N.C. Bar Assn., N.C. Soc. Health Care Attys., Women's Profl. Forum. Avocations: reading, travel. General civil litigation, Health. Office: Smith Moore LLP 300 N Greene St Greensboro NC 27401-2167

HARRIS, THORNE D., III, lawyer; b. New Orleans, Nov. 5, 1950; s. Thorne D. and Myra (Banister) H. Jr.; m. Mary Margaret Hattier, June 18, 1971. BA in English, U. New Orleans, 1972; JD, La. State U., 1974. Bar: La. 1974, U.S. Dist. Ct. (ea. dist.) La. 1974, U.S. Dist. Ct. (mid. and we. dists.) La. 1976, U.S. Ct. Appeals (5th cir.) 1974, U.S. Ct. Appeals (11th cir.) 1981. With Sessions, Fishman, et al, New Orleans, 1974-81, Monroe & Lemann, New Orleans, 1981-82, McNulty, O'Conner, et al, New Orleans, 1982-84; pvt. practice New Orleans, 1984—. Pres. Micro Esq. divsn. Superior Software Inc.; cons. computer law and law office computer systems. Author: Legal Guide to Computer Software Protection: A Practical Handbook on Copyrights, Trademarks, Publishing and Trade Secrets, 1984, The Software Developer's Complete Legal Companion, 1994; contbr. articles to profl. jours. Mem. La. State U. Law Rev.; chmn. U. New Orleans Awards and Scholarship Com., 1980-88; mem. Civitan, New Orleans, 1977-78. Named One of Outstanding Young Men of Am., Jaycees, 1984, 86. Mem. ABA (sects. on sci. and tech., patent, copyrights and trademarks, corps. 1975-2000, chmn. software subcom. of copyright and new tech. com. 1984-86, chmn. subcom. piracy 1986-87, chmn. database com. 1987-89), La. State Bar Assn. (sects. on litigation, mineral law, ins. bus. and antitrust 1974—, founder, dir., head Tech. Resource Ctr., founder, 1st chair sole practitioners and small firms sect. 1991-95), New Orleans Bar Assn., Vol. Lawyers for Arts, Order of Coif, Phi Eta Sigma. Republican. Federal civil litigation, Computer, General practice. Office: 3350 Ridgelake Dr Ste 101 Metairie LA 70002 Fax: 603-462-3807. E-mail: Thorne@ThorneDHarrisIII.com.

HARRIS, WARREN WAYNE, lawyer; b. Houston, Nov. 5, 1962; BBA, U. Houston, 1985, JD, 1988. Bar: Tex. 1988, U.S. Ct. Appeals (5th cir.) 1989, U.S. Ct. Appeals (fed. cir.) 1995, U.S. Ct. Appeals (8th, 10th and 11th cirs.) 1996, U.S. Dist. Ct. (so., no., ea. and we. dists.) Tex. 1990, U.S. Supreme Ct. 1991; bd. cert. civil appellate law Tex. Bd. Legal Specialization. Briefing atty. Tex. Supreme Ct., Austin, 1988-89; assoc. Porter & Hedges, L.L.P., Houston, 1989-95, ptnr., 1996, Bracewell & Patterson, L.L.P., Houston, 1996—. Editor-in-chief: Houston Lawyer mag., 1991-92; assoc. editor: The Appellate Advocate, 1992-97; editor: Pocket Parts, 1993-95, The Appellate Lawyer, 1994-96; chair editl. bd. Tex. Bar Jour., 2002—. Fellow: Houston Young Lawyers Found. (vice-chair 1996—98), Houston Bar Found., Tex. Bar Found. (co-chair dist. 4 nominating com. 1994—2000); mem.: ABA (litigation sect. appellate practice com. 1990—, tort and ins. practice sect. appellate advocacy com. 1990—, chair 2000—01), Houston Lawyer Referral Svc. (trustee 1994—95), Houston Young Lawyers Assn. (pres. 1999—2000), Houston Bar Assn. (coun. appellate practice sect. 1993—, chair appellate practice sect. 1998—99, Pres.'s award 1993—94), Tex. Young Lawyers Assn. (bd. dirs. 1994—98, outstanding dir. 1995—96, Pres.'s award 1996—97), State Bar Pro Bono Coll., State Bar Coll. (bd. dirs. 1994—95), State Bar Tex. (appellate sect. 1988—, coun. 1997—2000, sec. 2002—), Stages Repertory Theatre (pres. 1994—95, chair 1994—95, bd. dirs. 1994—96, WineFest com. chair 1994—96), Order of Barons, Order of Barristers, Phi Delta Phi. Republican. Appellate, Commercial, contracts (including sales of goods; commercial financing), Personal injury (including property damage). Office: Bracewell & Patterson LLP 711 Louisiana St Ste 2900 Houston TX 77002-2781 E-mail: warren.harris@bracepatt.com.

HARRISON, CHARLES MAURICE, lawyer, former communications company executive; b. Anderson, S.C., Aug. 30, 1927; s. Emmitte Smallwood and Jessie Maysel (Hawkins) H.; m. Lorna Jean Tomalty, June 27, 1970; children: Suzanne Elizabeth, Linda Jean. AB, Marshall U., 1949; JD, W.Va. U., 1952. Bar: W.Va. 1952, D.C. 1958, N.Y. 1965, N.J. 1972. Legal asst. W.Va. Dept. Ins., Charleston, 1952-54; hearing examiner Pub. Svc. Commn., Charleston, 1954-57; atty. Chesapeake and Potomac Tel. Co., Washington and Charleston, 1957-64, Western Electric Co., N.Y.C., 1964-69; gen. atty., sec., treas. Bellcomm, Inc., Washington, 1969-71; asst. gen. counsel, asst. sec. Bell Tel. Labs., Murray Hill, N.J., 1971-75, gen. atty., sec., 1975-76, sec., gen. counsel corp. matters, 1976-84; asst. sec., asst. gen. counsel AT&T Bell Labs, 1985-87; gen. atty. AT&T, Berkeley Heights, N.J., 1987-89; of counsel Ventantonio & Wildenhain, Warren, N.J., 1993—. Bd. dirs. Somerset County C. of C. (chmn. 1990-92). Trustee Family Counseling Svcs. Somerset County, N.J., 1976-94, pres., 1978-81; chmn. R&D Coun. N.J., 1985-87, Bridgewater (N.J.) Commn. Substance Abuse, 1986-89, Bridgewater Mcpl. Facilities Commn., 1988-89, Bridgewater Twp. Alliance Com. on Alcoholism, 1989-99; bd. dirs. Martin Luther King Youth Ctr., 1984-90, Somerset Alliance for Future, 1992, N.J. affiliate Am. Heart Assn., 1991-94, Somerset County Coalition on Affordable Housing, 1995—; bd. dirs., pres. Somerset Treatment Svcs., 1992-99, bd. dirs., 2002--; mem. Bridgewater-Raritan Youth Svcs. Commn., chmn., 1989-90; mem. Bridgewater Planning Bd., 1989-94, chmn., 1992-94; mgmt. com. Ridewise Traffic Mgmt. Assn., 1992-96; mem. Somerset County Local Adv. Com. on Alcohol and Drug Abuse, 1992-99, Bridgewater Twp. Operation (police-pub.) Cooperation, 1992—, 200 Club of Somerset County, 1990—; trustee Henderson Meml. Scholarship Fund, 1993-99; mem. Twp. Coun., 1994-2001, coun. pres., 1996, 2000; mem. Bridgewater Zoning Bd. of Adjustment, 2002--. With AC, U.S. Army, 1945-46, W.Va. Air N.G., 1955-57, UsAFR, 1955-62. Named Somerset County Citizen of Yr., 1996. Mem. Rotary (pres. Somerville 2000—), Somerville Elks, Am. Legion. Republican.

HARRISON, DONALD, lawyer; b. N.Y.C., Mar. 2, 1946; s. David and Arlene Beverly (Johnson) H. BA magna cum laude, Harvard U., 1967, JD magna cum laude, 1971. Bar: D.C. 1973, U.S. Ct. Internat. Trade 1975, U.S. Ct. Appeals (Fed. cir.) 1982, U.S. Supreme Ct. 1979. Law clk. to judge Francis L. Van Dusen U.S. Ct. Appeals 3d circuit, Phila., 1972-73; ptnr. Gibson, Dunn & Crutcher, 1988—. Editor Harvard Law Rev., 1969-71. Private international. Office: Gibson Dunn & Crutcher Washington Sq 1050 Connecticut Ave NW Ste 900 Washington DC 20036-5306 E-mail: dharrison@gibsondunn.com.

HARRISON, EARL DAVID, lawyer, real estate executive; b. Bryn Mawr, Pa., Aug. 25, 1932; divorced; 1 child, H. Jason. BA, Harvard U., 1954; JD, U. Pa., 1960. Bar: D.C. 1960. Pvt. practice, Washington; exec. v.p. Washington Real Estate Corp., Washington, 1986-94; pres. EDH Assocs., Inc., 1994—. Capt. U.S. Army, 1954-57. Decorated Order of Rio Branco (Brazil); Order of Merit (Italy). Mem.: ABA, Coun. Internat. Restaurant Real Estate Brokers Ltd. (v.p., gen. coun.), Met. Washington Restaurant Assn., Nat. Restaurant Assn., Nat. Assn. Realtors, Greater Washington Comml. Assn. Realtors, Washington Assn. Realtors, D.C. Bar Assn., Internat. Coun. Shopping Ctrs., U. Pa. Club, Nat. Press Club, Harvard Club. Commercial, contracts (including sales of goods; commercial financing), Private international, Property, real (including real estate development, water). Office: 1077 30th St NW Ste 706 Washington DC 20007-3834 E-mail: david@edhlaw.com.

HARRISON, GUY NEWELL, lawyer; b. Longview, Tex., Dec. 14, 1946; s. Guy Franklin and Margaret Louise (Newell) H.; m. Lucinda Dodson, July 5, 1969; children: Parker Trigg Harrison, Worth McKinley Harrison. BBA, So. Meth. U., 1968, JD, 1974. Bar: Tex., U.S. Dist. Ct. Tex., U.S. Supreme Ct. Ptnr. Green & Harrison, Longview, Tex., 1974—. Pres. Longview YMCA, 1976-78; bd. dirs. YMCA of the USA, 1990-91, Good Shepherd Hosp. Found., Longview, 1989-91. Sgt. U.S. Army, 1968-70, Vietnam. Recipient Lowell Linnes award YMCA of the Midwest, 1979; named Atty. of Yr. Longview Legal Secs. Mem. Gregg Bar Assn., Tex. Trial Lawyers Assn., Tex. State Bar Assn. (bd. dirs. 1995-, chmn. 1997-98, pres.-elect 2001-02, pres. 2002-03); fellow (life) Tex. Bar Found. (trustee 1998-). Family and matrimonial, General practice, Personal injury (including property damage). Home: 1901 Warwick Cir E Longview TX 75601-3134 Office: 217 Center Longview TX 75601*

HARRISON, JOHN CONWAY, state supreme court justice; b. Grand Rapids, Minn., Apr. 28, 1913; s. Francis Randall and Ethlyn (Conway) H.; m. Ethel M. Strict; children: Nina Lyn, Robert Charles, Molly M., Frank R., Virginia Lee LLD, George Washington U., 1940. Bar: Mont. 1947, U.S. Dist. Ct. 1947. County atty. Lewis and Clark County, Helena, Mont., 1934-60; justice Mont. Supreme Ct., Helena, 1961-98, ret., 1998. Pres. Mont. TB Assn., Helena, 1951-54, Am. Lung Assn., N.Y.C., 1972-73, Mont. coun. Boy Scouts Am., Great Falls, Mont., 1976-78. Col. U.S. Army Mem. ABA, Mont. Bar Assn., Kiwanis (pres. 1953), Sigma Chi. Home: 215 S Cooke St Helena MT 59601-5143

HARRISON, JOSEPH HEAVRIN, lawyer; b. Evansville, Ind., July 23, 1929; s. Homer William and Lillie Isabelle (Heavrin) H.; m. Sharon Jeanene Miller, June 30, 1957 (div. 1976); children: Joseph Heavrin, Sara Ann; m. Julie Anne Gerard, Dec. 10, 1976; 1 child, Meghann. BA in Econs., U. Notre Dame, Ind., 1952; JD cum laude, U. Notre Dame, 1953. Bar: Ind. 1953, U.S. Dist. Ct. D.C. 1953, U.S. Dist. Ct. (so. dist.) Ind. 1953, U.S. Ct. Appeals (7th cir.) 1968, U.S. Tax Ct. 1984. Mng. ptnr. Bowers Harrison and predecessors, Evansville, Ind., 1955. Pres. Sandy's Assocs., Inc. (18 Hardee's franchised restaurants). Dir. Vanderburgh County Legal Aid Soc., Evansville, 1958—68, pres., 1964—65; Ind. counsel Bush Presdl. campaign, 1988; co-chair Ind. Lawyers for G.W. Bush, 2000—; chmn. Vanderburgh County Election Bd., 1979—90, Vanderburgh Rep. Fin. Com., 1982—89; mem. Evansville Econ. Devel. Commn., 1991—, pres., 1995—2001; Ind. commr. Ohio River Valley Water Sanitation Commn., 1982—, chmn., 1987; commr. Vanderburgh County Conv. & Vis. Bur., 1997—2001; bd. dirs. Arbor Hosp., 1991—94. With U.S. Army, 1953—55. Fellow Ind. Bar Found.; mem. ABA, Evansville Bar Assn., Ind. Bar Assn., Am. Judicature Soc., Evansville Country Club (pres. 1976), Oak Meadow Country Club. Republican. Roman Catholic. Avocations: golf, flying. Commercial, contracts (including sales of goods; commercial financing), Corporate, general, Property, real (including real estate development, water). Office: Bowers Harrison LLP PO Box 1287 25 NW Riverside Dr Evansville IN 47708-1255

HARRISON, MARION EDWYN, lawyer; b. Phila., Sept. 17, 1931; s. Marion Edwyn and Jessye Beatrice (Cilles) H.; m. Carmelita Ruth Deimel, Sept. 6, 1952; children: Angelique Marie (Mrs. Kevin B. Bounds), Marion Edwyn III, Henry Deimel. BA, U. Va., 1951; LLB, George Washington U., 1954, LLM, 1959. Bar: Va. 1954, D.C. 1958, Supreme Ct. 1958. Spl. asst. to gen. counsel Post Office Dept., 1958-60, assoc. gen. counsel, 1960-61, mem. bd. contract appeals, 1958-61; ptnr. firm Harrison, Lucey & Sagle (and predecessors), Washington, 1961-78, Barnett & Alagia, 1978-84; ptnr. Scott, Harrison & McLeod, 1984-86, Law Offices Marion Edwyn Harrison, Washington, 1986—; pres. Free Congress Rsch. and Edn. Found., Inc., 2002—. Mem. coun. Adminstrv. Conf. U.S., 1971—78, sr. conf. fellow, 1984—88; mem. D.C. Law Revision Commn., 1975—92; lectr. Nat. Jud. Coll., Reno, 1979, La. State U. Law Sch., Aix-en-Provence, 1987, 89, Tulane U. Law Sch., Crete, 1997, Hofstra U. Law Sch., Nice, 1999, Pa. State U. Dickinson Law Sch., Vienna, 2000, Tulane U. Law Sch., Thessalonika, 2001, St. Mary's U. Law Sch., Innsbruck, 2002; adv. dir. NationsBank, N.A., 1987—93. Contbr. articles to profl. publs.; editor-in-chief Fed. Bar News, 1960-63; mem. editorial bd. Adminstrv. Law Rev., 1976-89. Trustee AEFC Pension Fund, Chgo., 1986-92; pres. Young Rep. Fedn. Va., 1954-55; mem. Va. Rep. Cen. Com., 1954-55; bd. visitors Judge Adv. Gen. Sch., Charlottesville, Va., 1976-78; chmn. Wolf Trap Assn., 1984-87; bd. dirs. Wolf Trap Found., 1984-88; pub. mem. USIA Mission, Argentina, 1971. Officer AUS, 1955-58. Decorated Commendation medal. Fellow: Am. Bar Found. (life); mem.: FBA (nat. coun. 1966—82), ABA (chmn. sect. adminstrv. and reg. law 1974—75, ho. of dels. 1978—88, chmn. lawyers in govt. com. 1980—82, bd. govs. 1982—86, chmn. com. on fgn. and internat. orgns. 1986—87), Bar Assn. D.C. (chmn. adminstrv. law sect. 1970—71, bd. dirs. 1971—72), Inter-Am. Bar Assn., Soc. Mayflower Desc., Smithsonian Instn. (nat. bd. dirs. 1991—97), George Washington U. Law Assn. (pres. 1974—77), Federalist Soc., Gainey Ranch Golf Club (Scottsdale, Ariz.), Met. Club, Washington Golf and Country Club, Knight of Malta. Republican. Roman Catholic. Administrative and regulatory, General practice, Private international. Home: 4111 N Ridgeview Rd Arlington VA 22207-4617 Address: 7222 E Gainey Ranch Rd Scottsdale AZ 85258-1529 Office: 717 Second St NE Washington DC 20002 Address: Dufourstrasse 32 8008 Zurich Switzerland

HARRISON, MARK ISAAC, lawyer; b. Pitts., Oct. 17, 1934; s. Coleman and Myrtle (Seidenman) H.; m. Ellen R. Gier, June 15, 1958; children: Lisa, Jill. AB, Antioch Coll., 1957; LLB, Harvard U., 1960. Bar: Ariz. 1961, Colo. 1991. Law clk. to justices Ariz. Supreme Ct., 1960-61; ptnr. Harrison, Harper, Christian & Dichter, Phoenix, 1966-93, Bryan Cave, LLP, Phoenix, 1993—. Adj. prof. U. Ariz. Coll. Law, 1995-97, Ariz. State Coll. Law, 2001—; nat. bd. visitors, 1996—. Co-author: Arizona Appellate Practice, 1966; editorial bd. ABA/BNA Lawyers Manual on Profl. Conduct, 1983-86; contbr. articles to profl. jours. Chmn. Phoenix City bond Adv. Commn., 1976—79; pres. Valley Commerce Assn., 1978, Ariz. Friend of Talking Books, Inc., 2000—01; vice chmn. Maricopa County Dem. Cen. Com., 1967—68, Ariz. Dem. Com, 1969—70, legal counsel, 1970—72; del. Dem. Nat. Conv., 1968; bd. dir. Careers for Youth, 1963—67, pres., 1966—67; bd. dir. Planned Parenthood of Cen. and No. Ariz., 1992—98, pres., 1995; bd. dir. Ariz. Policy Forum, 2000—. Recipient Peggy Goldwater award, Planned Parenthood, 2003, Planned Parenthood of Ctrl. and No. Ariz., 2003. Fellow: Am. Acad. Appellate Lawyers (pres. 1993—94), Am. Bar Found.; mem.: ABA (standing com. profl. discipline 1976—84, chmn. 1982—84, chmn. commn. pub. understanding law 1984—87, chmn. coord. com. on professionalism 1987—89, com. on women in the profession, ethics com. 1999—2002, Michael Franck Profl. Responsibility award 1996, Peggy Goldwater award 2003, Disting. Hon. Alumnus award), Lawyers Com. for Civil Rights Under Law (bd. dirs.), Law Coll. Assn. U. Ariz. (bd. dir. 1999—, pres. 2002—), Am. Law Inst. (nat. coun., lawyers com. for human rights), Harvard Law Sch. Assn. (nat. exec. coun. 1980—84), Ariz. Civil Liberties Union, Am. Judicature Soc. (exec. com. 1983—86, bd. dir. 1983—87), Western States Bar Conf. (pres. 1978—79), Nat. Conf. Bar Pres., Am. Inns of Ct. (master, pres. Sandra Day O'Connor chpt. 1993—94), Ariz. Bar Found. (pres. 1991, Walter E. Craig Disting. Svc. award 2002), State Bar Ariz. (bd. govs. 1971—77, pres. 1975—76), Am. Bd. Trial Advocates, Maricopa County Bar Assn. (pres. 1970), Assn. Profl. Responsibility Lawyers (pres. 1992—93). General civil litigation, Professional liability. Office: Bryan Cave 2 N Central Ave Ste 2200 Phoenix AZ 85004-4406 E-mail: ellenmark@aol.com., mharrison@bryancave.com.

HARRISON, MICHAEL GREGORY, judge; b. Lansing, Mich., Aug. 4, 1941; s. Gus and Jean D. (Fuller) H.; m. Deborah L. Dunn, June 17, 1972; children: Abigail Ann, Adam Christopher, Andrew Stephen. AB, Albion (Mich.) Coll., 1963; JD, U. Mich., 1966; postgrad., Hague Acad. of Internat. Law, George Washington U. Bar: Mich. 1966, U.S. Dist. Ct. (ea. and we. dists.) Mich. 1967, U.S. Ct. Appeals (6th cir.). Asst. pros. atty. County of Ingham, Lansing, 1968-70, corp. counsel, 1970-76; judge 30th Jud. Cir. State of Mich., Lansing, 1976-2000; chief judge 30th Jud. Cir. State of Mich., Lansing, 1980-91; judge Ct. of Claims, 1979-2000; of counsel Foster, Swift, Collins and Smith, Lansing, 2000—. Counsel Capital Region Airport Authority, Lansing, 1970-76, Ingham Med. Ctr., Lansing, 1970-76; chmn. Ingham County Bldg. Authority, Mason, Mich., 1971-76; adj. prof. Thomas M. Cooley Law Sch., Lansing, 1976—. Editor Litigation Control, 1996; contbr. chpt. to Michigan Municipal Law, Actions of Governing Bodies, 1980; contbr. articles to profl. jours. Mem. shared vision steering com. United Way-C. of C.; mem. adv. bd. Hospice of Lansing, 1989—; pres. Greater Lansing Urban League, 1974-76, Lansing Symphony Assn., 1974-76; chmn. Mid. Mich. chpt. ARC, Lansing, 1984-86; bd. dirs., sec. St. Lawrence Hosp., Lansing, 1980-88; bd. dirs. ARC Gt. Lakes Regional Blood Svcs., 1991-95, Lansing 2000, 1987—, Greater Lansing Symphony, 2002—; mem. exec. bd. Chief Okemos coun. Boy Scouts Am., pres., 2003—; mem. criminal justice adv. com. Olivet Coll.; hon. bd. dirs. Lansing Area Safety Coun.; mem. State Bar Bd. Commrs., 1993-96; chair State Bar Rep. Assembly; mem. felony sentencing guidelines steering com., chmn. caseflow mgmt. coordinating com., mem. juror use and mgmt. task force Mich. Supreme Ct. Recipient Disting. Citizens award Boy Scouts Am., Disting. Vol. award Ingham County Bar Assn., award of judicial excellence ABA, Disting. Alumni award Albion Coll. Fellow: Mich. Bar Found., Am. Bar Found.; mem.: ABA (coun. mem. judicial divsn., coun. mem. tort and ins. practice sect., award of jud. excellence), Mich. State Bar Found. (pres. 1991—2000), Nat. Conf. State Trial Judges (exec. com. 1991—94, vice chmn. 1995—96, chmn. 1997—98), Mich. Judges Assn. (treas. 1991, sec. 1992, 2d v.p. 1993, 1st v.p. 1994, pres. 1995), Mich. State U. Am. Inn of Ct. (pres. 2001—, master), Am. Judicature Soc. (bd. dirs. 1996—2002), Rotary Club, Lansing (pres. 2001—02), Country Club, Lansing. Republican. Congregationalist. Avocations: skiing, golf, tennis, travel, photography. Office: 313 S Washington Sq Lansing MI 48933-2193 E-mail: mharrison@fosterswift.com.

HARRISON, ORRIN LEA, III, lawyer; b. Dallas, July 1, 1949; s. Orrin Lea Jr. and Annie Bell (Lassig) H.; m. Paula Diane Wagnon, May 29, 1971; children: Orrin IV, Erin, Lindsey. BA cum laude, U. of South; JD with honors, So. Meth. U. Bar: Tex. 1974, U.S. Dist. Ct. (no., so., ea. and we. dists.) Tex., U.S. Ct. Appeals (5th and 11th cirs.), U.S. Supreme Ct. From assoc. to ptnr. Locke, Purnell, Boren, Laney & Neely, Dallas, 1974-87; shareholder Locke, Purnell, Rain & Harrell, Dallas, 1987-92; ptnr. Vinson & Elkins, Dallas, 1992—2003, Akin Gump Strauss Hauer & Feld, Dallas, 2003—. Sec. 500 Inc., 1981, treas., 1982; chancellor Ch. of Incarnation, Dallas, 1985-97; bd. dirs. Dallas Econ. Devel. Coun., 1986-92, Medisend Internat., 1997-2000; mem. Leadership Dallas, 19881 mem. Dallas Bus. Com. for the Arts, 2001—; mem. Dallas Country Heritage Soc., 2001—. Lt. JAGC, USN, 1971-75. Fellow Am. Bar Found., Tex. Bar Found. (life); mem. ABA, State Bar of Tex. (bd. dirs. 1993-96), Dallas Bar Found. (trustee 1993-01), Am. Bd. of Trial Advocates (Dallas pres., 1989), Internat. Soc. of Barristers, Dallas Bar Assn. (bd. dirs. 1983-97, pres. 1992), Tex. Young Lawyers Assn. (bd. dirs. 1981-83), Dallas Young Lawyers Assn. (pres. 1980-81), Tower Club, Univ. Club, Jeremy Golf and Country Club, Lakewood Country Club. Republican. Episcopalian. Avocations: skiing, swimming, mountain biking. Antitrust, Federal civil litigation, State civil litigation. Home: 3624 Normandy Ave Dallas TX 75205-2103 Office: Akin Gump Strauss Hauer & Feld 1700 Main St Ste 4100 Dallas TX 75201-2975 E-mail: oharrison@akingump.com.

HARRISON, PATRICK WOODS, lawyer; b. St. Louis, July 14, 1946; s. Charles William and Carolyn (Woods) H.; m. Rebecca Tout, Dec. 23, 1967; children: Heather Ann, Heath Aaron. BS, Ind. U., 1968, JD, 1972. Bar: Ind. 1973, U.S. Dist. Ct. (so. dist.) Ind. 1973, U.S. Dist. Ct. Nebr. 1982, U.S. Supreme Ct. 1977. Assoc. Goltra, Cline, King & Beck, Columbus, Ind., 1972-73; ptnr. Goltra & Harrison, Columbus, 1973-78; pvt. practice Columbus, 1979-80; ptnr. Cline, King, Beck and Harrison, Columbus, 1980-85, Beck, Harrison & Dalmbert, Columbus, 1985—. Ind. Jud. Nominating Commn. nominee Ind. Supreme Ct., 1984. With U.S. Army, 1968-70. Fellow Ind. Trial Lawyers Assn. (bd. dirs. 1984, emeritus dir. 1999, Co-Trial Lawyer of Yr. 1999); mem. Am. Trial Lawyers Assn. Republican. Baptist. Avocation: golf. State civil litigation, Personal injury (including property damage). Home: 14250 W Mount Healthy Rd Columbus IN 47201-9309 Office: Beck Harrison & Dalmbert 320 Franklin St Columbus IN 47201-6732 E-mail: pharrison@direcway.com., woodyh@bhdatty.com.

HARRISON, RICHARD WAYNE, lawyer; b. Marfa, Tex., June 23, 1944; AA, Schreiner U., 1964; BBA, U. Tex. Austin, 1966; JD, U. Tex. Sch. Law, 1968. Ptnr. Florence & Harrison, Hughes Springs, Tex., 1968-69; pvt. practice Hughes Springs, Tex., 1969-73; asst. atty. gen. Atty. Gen.'s Office of Tex., Austin, 1973-74, chief tax divsn., 1974-76, spl. asst. atty. gen., 1976-78; ptnr. McGinnis, Lochridge & Kilgore, Austin, 1978-87, Jones, Day, Reavis & Pogue, Austin, 1987-94; mng. ptnr. Harrison & Rial LLP, Austin, 1994—2000; owner Rick Harrison & Assocs., Austin, 2000—02; ptnr. Fritz, Byrne, Head & Harrison LLP, Austin, 2002—. Trustee, treas. St. Andrew's Episcopal Sch., Austin; precinct chmn. Cass County Dem. Com., 1969-73; pres. Hughes Springs Indsl. Found., 1970; Cass County chmn. Salvation Army, 1970-72; area coord. Lloyd Bentsen for Senate Com., 1970; chmn. Hughes Springs United Fund Drive, 1972; mem. Austin Convocation Cursillo Steering Com., 1983-86, chmn., 1985-86; sr. warden St. Luke's-on-the-Lake Episcopal Ch., 1984. Fellow: Tex. Bar Found.; mem.: Schreiner Coll. Former Student Assn. (bd. dirs. 1984—88), Cass County Bar Assn. (past pres.), Travis County Bar Assn., State Bar of Tex. (fed. jud. com. 1980—83, bar jour. com. 1980—83), Barton Creek Country Club, Horseshoe Bay Country Club, Masons. Democrat. Federal civil litigation, State civil litigation, State and local taxation. Home: 1730 Camp Craft Rd Austin TX 78746-7317 Office: Fritz Byrne Head & Harrison LLP 98 San Jacinto Blvd Ste 2000 Austin TX 78701

HARRISON, ROSLYN SIMAN, lawyer; b. Phila., Mar. 6, 1935; d. Max and Stella (Shapiro) Siman; m. Saul E. Harrison, June 12, 1955 (div. Mar. 1990); children: Dana Lynn, Julia Anne, Michael E. BA summa cum laude, Bryn Mawr Coll., 1956; LLB with honors, Rutgers U., Newark, 1977. Bar: N.J. 1977, U.S. Dist. Ct. N.J. 1977, U.S. Ct. Appeals (3rd cir.) 1981, N.Y. 1985, U.S. Dist. Ct. (ea. dist.) N.Y. 1985, U.S. Dist. Ct. (so. dist.) N.Y. 1987, U.S. Supreme Ct. 1987, U.S. Dist. Ct. (ea. dist.) Pa. 1988, U.S. Ct. Appeals (fed. cir.) 1994. Tchr. history Longmeadow (Mass.) High Sch., 1957-59; instr. polit. sci. Webster Coll., Webster Groves, Mo., 1964-66; assoc. McCarter & English, LLP, Newark, 1977-85, ptnr., 1986-2000, of counsel, 2000—. Social Sci. Rsch. Coun. grantee, 1955. Mem. ABA, N.Y. State Bar Assn., Assn. Fed. Bar State of N.J., N.J. Bar Assn. (mem. curriculum adv. com. Inst. for Continuing Legal Edn. 1990-96, chmn. N.J. bar intellectual property law sect. 1993-95), N.J. Intellectual Property Law Assn. (chmn. copyright com. 1993, chmn. trademark com. 1994-95), Internat. Trademark Assn. (internat. com., meetings com., ADR com. panel of neutrals), Am. Arbitration Assn., John J. Gibbons Am. Inn. of Ct. (mem. com. 1993—). Office: 4 Gateway Ctr 100 Mulberry St Newark NJ 07102-4056 E-mail: rharrison@mccarter.com.

HARRISON, TOMASITA L. lawyer; b. N.Y.C., Apr. 30, 1970; d. Frank and Tomasita Harrison. BA, NYU, 1992; JD, Fordham U., 1999. Bar: N.Y. 2000, U.S. Dist. Ct. (so. and ea. dists.) N.Y. 2000. Assoc. McDermott Will & Emery, N.Y.C., 1999—2001, Edwards & Angell, N.Y.C., 2002—. Adv. bd. The Artists Forum, N.Y.C., 2001—. Mem.: ABA, P.R. Bar Assn., N.Y. State Bar Assn. Democrat. Avocations: art appreciation, fitness, travel. General civil litigation, Product liability, Toxic tort. Home: 573 Grand St #D1603 New York NY 10002 Office: Edwards & Angell LLP 750 Lexington Ave New York NY 10022

HARRISON, WILLIAM A. lawyer; b. Beppu, Japan, Oct. 13, 1953; arrived in U.S., 1955; s. Henry and Machiko Levy; m. Erika Pang Harrison, Aug. 6, 1985; children: Jamaal, Jordan, Kiira. BA, U. Hawaii, 1976, MA, 1981; JD, William Richardson, 1981. Bar: Hawaii 1981, N.J. 1982, U.S. Ct. Appeals (9th cir.) 1982, U.S. Supreme Ct. 1985, U.S. Ct. Appeals (fed. cir.) 1993. Ptnr. Harrison & Matsuoka, Attys. at Law, Honolulu. Chairperson litigation com. ACLU of Hawaii, Honolulu, 1982—84; lawyer select State Jud. Conf., Honolulu, 1991—94; pres. bd. Domestic Violence Clearing House, Honolulu, 1991—92; chairperson Jud. Selection Com., Honolulu, 1995—97. Del. Hawaii Dem. Party State Conv., Honolulu, 1988, 1990, 1992, 1994, 1996, 1998, 2000, 2002. Named Outstanding Young Man of Am., 1979, Newsmaker, Star Bull. Newspaper, Honolulu, 1990, Coach of Yr., Interscholastic League Honolulu, 1990. Mem.: Nat. Assn. Criminal Def. Lawyers (life). Lutheran. Avocations: surfing, golf. Criminal, Personal injury (including property damage), Professional liability. Office: Harrison & Matsuoka Ste 800 841 Bishop St Honolulu HI 96813

HARROLD, BERNARD, lawyer; b. Wells County, Ind., Feb. 5, 1925; s. James Delmer and Marie (Mounsey) H.; m. Kathleen Walker, Nov. 26, 1952; children— Bernard James, Camilla Ruth, Renata Jane. Student, Biarritz Am. U., 1945; AB, Ind. U., 1949, LLB, 1951. Bar: Ill. 1951. Since practiced in, Chgo.; assoc., then mem. firm Kirkland, Ellis, Hodson, Chaffetz & Masters, 1951-67; sr. ptnr. Wildman, Harrold, Allen & Dixon, 1967—. Note editor: Ind. Law Jour, 1950-51; contbr. articles to profl. jours. Served with AUS, 1944-46, ETO. Fellow Am. Coll. Trial Lawyers, Acad. Law Alumni Fellows Ind. U. Sch. Law; mem. ABA, Ill. Bar Assn. (chmn. evidence program 1970), Chgo. Bar Assn., Lawyers Club, Univ. Club, Order of Coif, Phi Beta Kappa, Phi Eta Sigma. Antitrust, General civil litigation,

Environmental. Home: 809 Locust St Winnetka IL 60093-1821 Office: Wildman Harrold Allen & Dixon 225 W Wacker Dr Fl 28 Chicago IL 60606-1229

HARROLD, DENNIS EDWARD, lawyer; b. Los Angeles, Nov. 7, 1947; s. Edward Adron and Helen Lucille (Morrison) H.; m. Mary Ann Padgett, Oct. 21, 1972; children: Teresa Lauren, Derek Christopher. BS, Ind. U., 1969; JD, 1972. Bar: Ind. 1972, U.S. Dist. Ct. (so. dist.) Ind. 1972, U.S. Ct. Mil. Appeals 1972, U.S. Ct. Appeals (7th cir.) 1982, U.S. Supreme Ct. 1986. Pub. defender Shelby Superior Ct., Shelbyville, Ind., 1976-77; assoc. Adams & Cramer, Shelbyville, 1976-78; sec. Soshnick, Bate and Harrold, P.C., 1979-85; sec. Bate, Harrold & Bate, P.C., Shelbyville, 1985-96, McNeely, Stephenson Thopy and Harrold, 1996—; sch. bd. atty. Shelbyville Central Schs., Ind., 1978—; atty. Shelby County office of family and children 1987-96; sch. bd. atty. Blue River Career Programs, 1994—. Mem. adv. bd. Salvation Army. Shelbyville, 1982-92. Served to capt. U.S. Army, 1972-76, Korea. Named Hon. Mem. Bar Republic of Korea, Ministry of Justice, Seoul, 1975. Fellow Ind. Bar Found.; mem. ABA, Ind. State Bar Assn. (ho. of dels. 1982-85), Shelby County Bar Assn. (pres. 1990-91), Indpls. Bar Assn., Assn. Trial Lawyers Am., Nat. Sch. Bds. Assn. Council Sch. Attys., Internat. Legal Soc. Korea, Ind. Trial Lawyers Assn., Ind. Pub. Defender Council, dir. Shelby County C. of C., pres. 1996-97, trustee Shelby Rural Elec. Cmty. Fund, Inc. Lions, Elks. Republican. Roman Catholic. General practice, Insurance, Personal injury (including property damage). Home: 2481 N Richard Dr Shelbyville IN 46176-9487 Office: 30 E Washington St Ste 400 Shelbyville IN 46176-1351

HARROLD, THOMAS J., JR., lawyer; b. Athens, Ga., July 22, 1944; s. Thomas J. and Virginia Harris Harrold; m. Constance P. Harrold, May 1, 1971; 1 child, Elizabeth Virginia. BA in History, Columbia U., 1966; JD, U. Ga., 1969. Bar: Ga. 1969, U.S. Dist. Ct. (no. dist.) Ga. 1969. From assoc. to ptnr. Fortson, Bentley, Griffin, Athens, Ga., 1969—76; dep. commr. Ga. Dept. Revenue, Atlanta, 1976—78; ptnr. Cofer, Beauchamp, Hanes & Harris, Atlanta, 1978—85, Glass, McCullough, Sherrill & Harrold, Atlanta, 1985—97, Miller & Martin, LLP, Atlanta, 1997—. Author: Starting and Operating a Business in Georgia, 1986. Pres. World Law Group, 1995—97; bd. trustees Ga. Econ. Devel. Found., Atlanta, 1988—; bd. dirs. German Am. C. of C., Atlanta, 1995—, Japan Am. Soc., Atlanta, 1992—. Capt. Ga. Air NG, 1969—75. Democrat. Methodist. Avocations: reading, jogging, travel. Private international, State and local taxation, Corporate, general. Office: Miller & Martin LLP 1275 Peachtree St Atlanta GA 30309 E-mail: tharrold@millermartin.com.

HARSHMAN, RAYMOND BRENT, lawyer; b. Athens, Ala., Feb. 16, 1948; s. L. Raymond and B. Katherine (Laubenthal) H.; m. Letha Lee, Nov. 30, 1974; 3 children. BSBA, U. Tenn., 1969; JD, So. Meth. U., 1973. Bar: Tex. 1973, U.S. Ct. Appeals (D.C. and 5th cirs.) 1986, U.S. Ct. Appeals (6th cir.) 1989, Colo. 1992, U.S. Ct. Appeals (11th cir.) 1992. Instr., atty. Abilene (Tex.) Christian U., 1973-74; tax acct./tax atty. Exxon Co., USA, Houston, 1974-76; gas contract rep. Tex. Gas Transmission Corp., Houston, 1976-78; atty. Diamond Shamrock Corp., Amarillo, Tex., 1978-81; sr. atty. Diamond Shamrock Exploration Co., Amarillo, Tex., f1981-86; assoc. counsel Maxus Energy Corp., Dallas, 1986-90, sr. counsel, 1991-99; ind. atty. Dallas, 2000; asst. city atty. Austin Energy, 2001—. Mem. State Bar Tex., Fed. Energy Bar Assn. Mem. Ch. of Christ. FERC practice, Commercial, contracts (including sales of goods; commercial financing), Utilities, public.

HART, BUSTER CLARENCE, lawyer; b. Promise City, Iowa, Mar. 19, 1923; s. Harry H. and Alfreda (DeBolt) H.; m. Jean E. Hart, July 7, 1933; children: Nannette, Kyle, Charles, Charlotte. AB, U. Iowa, 1947; JD, Harvard U., 1950. Bar: Minn. 1951, U.S. Ct. Mil. Appeals 1956, U.S. Supreme Ct. 1956. Ptnr. Briggs and Morgan, P.C., St. Paul, 1951-76, pres., 1976-83, Hart, Bruner, O'Brien & Thornton and predecessors, Mpls., 1983—. V.p. Downtown St. Paul, 1956—59; bd. dirs. Lakewood Coll. Found., 1974—76; mem. Minn. Citizens Com. for Voyageurs Nat. Park, 1975—; co. chmn. United Fund, bd. dirs., 1958—61, 1981—; mem. midwest regional adv. com. Nat. Park Svc. Lt. col. USAR. Fellow: Am. Bar Found.; mem.: Harvard Law Sch. Assn. (state pres. Minn., nat. v.p.), Am. Coll. Constr. Lawyers (past pres.), Am. Coll. Constrn. Arbitrators, Am. Bd. Trial Advocates (state pres. 1973), Am. Coll. Trial Lawyers, Internat. Assn. Ins. Counsel, Ramsey County Bar Assn., Fed. Bar Assn., Minn. Bar Assn. (chmn.ct. rules com. 1973—77), ABA (chmn. tort and ins. practice sect. 1980—81, Martin J. Andrew Lifetime Achievement award, Tips Andrew Hecker Lifetime Achievement award), ATLA, Minn. Club (bd. dirs. 1980—86), St. Paul Athletic Club, Phi Beta Kappa. Federal civil litigation, State civil litigation, Construction. Office: Fabyanske Westra & Hart 920 2d Ave S Ste 1100 Minneapolis MN 55402 E-mail: bchart@minnlaw.com.

HART, CLIFFORD HARVEY, lawyer; b. Flint, Mich., Nov. 12, 1935; s. Max S. and Dorothy H. (Fineberg) H.; m. Alice Rosenberg, June 17, 1962; children: Michael F., David E., Steven A. AB, U. Mich., 1957, JD, 1960. Bar: Mich. 1960, U.S. Dist. Ct. (ea. and we. dists.) Mich. 1962; cert. civil trial advocate. Assoc. Stevens & Nelson, Flint, 1960-62; ptnr. White, Newblatt, Nelson & Hart, Flint, 1962-64, Dean, Dean, Segar & Hart, P.C. and predecessor firms, Flint, 1965-97; pvt. practice Law Offices Clifford H. Hart, 1997—. Adj. assoc. prof. Flint Sch. Mgmt., U. Mich., 1972—; lectr. Inst. Continuing Legal Edn., Mich.; lectr. Mich. Jud. Inst. Pres. Vis. Nurse Assn., Flint, 1967; pres. Temple Beth El, 1973-75; trustee United Way Genesee County, 1981—, chmn. bd., 1990-91, sec., 1988-89, chmn. bd. dirs. Genesee County and Lapeer County, 1990-91; chair corp. adv. bd. U. Mich., Flint, 1988-93; mem. faculty Inst. Continuing Legal Edn., Ann Arbor, Mich., 1984—. Fellow: Roscoe Pound Found., Mich. Bar Found., Mich. Bar Found. (life); mem.: ATLA (bd. govs. 1979—, chmn. elections com. 1984—87, lectr., budget com. 1987—89, chair 1989—91, nat. parliamentarian 1990—91, exec. com. 1990—93, nat. treas. 1991—92, chair 1998—2004, exec. com. 1998—,), ABA, Nat. Bd. Trial Advocacy (cert.), Am. Judicature Soc., Genesee County Bar Assn. (pres. 1975—76), Mich. Trial Lawyers Assn. (pres. 1977—78, lectr.), Mich. State Bar Assn. (rep. assembly 1975—81, chmn. negligence law sect. 1981—82), B'nai B'rith (past pres.). Democrat. Federal civil litigation, General civil litigation, State civil litigation. Office: 1410 Mott Found Bldg 503 S Saginaw St Flint MI 48502-1807 E-mail: clhart@umich.edu.

HART, JEREMY MICHAEL, lawyer; b. Yuma, Ariz., Aug. 29, 1975; s. George Robert and Catherine Claire Moore; m. Shawna Melia Hart, Feb. 17, 2001; 1 child, Andrew Joseph. BA in Criminal Justice, Washburn U.; JD, U. Mo., Kansas City, 2001. Bar: Mo. 01, U.S. Dist. Ct. (we. dist.) Mo. 01, Kans. 02, U.S. Dist. Ct. Kans. 02. Assoc. Wonder Law Offices, Kansas City, Mo., 1998—. Mem.: ATLA, ABA, Kansas City Met. Bar Assn. (mem. mcpl. ct. com. 2001—), Kans. bar Assn., Mo. Bar Assn., KC (4th degree mem., advocate). Republican. Roman Catholic. Avocations: golf, reading, writing music. Office: Wonder Law Office 7447 Holmes Ste 201 Kansas City MO 64131 E-mail: jeremyhart@kc.rr.com.

HART, JOHN EDWARD, lawyer; b. Portland, Oreg., Nov. 21, 1946; s. Wilbur Elmore and Daisy Elizabeth (Bowen) H.; m. Bianca Mannheimer, Mar. 29, 1968 (div. 1985); children: Ashley Rebecca, Rachel Bianca, Eli Jacob; m. Serena Callahan, Nov. 9, 1991; 1 child, Katelyn Elizabeth. Student, Oreg. State U., 1965-66; BS, Portland State U., 1971; JD, Lewis and Clark Coll., 1974. Bar: Oreg. 1974, U.S. Dist. Ct. Oreg. 1974, U.S. Ct. Appeals (9th cir.) 1975. Ptnr. Schwabe, Williamson and Wyatt, Portland, 1973-92, Hoffman, Hart & Wagner, Portland, 1992—. Adj. faculty U. Oreg. Dental Sch., 1987—; legal cons. Oreg. Chpt. Obstetricians, Gynecologists, Portland, 1985—, Am. Cancer Soc. Mammography Project, 1987—. Contbr. articles to profl. jours. Co-chmn. Alameda Sch. Fair, Portland, 1983. With U.S. Army, 1967-68. Mem. ABA, Am. Coll. Trial Lawyers, Am. Bd. Trial Advocates (pres. 1995) Am., Inns of Ct., Oreg. State Bar Assn., Oreg. Assn. Def. Counsel (pres. 1989), Multnomah Athletic Club. Democrat. Presbyterian. Avocations: jogging, weight lifting, outdoor activities. General civil litigation, Health, Personal injury (including property damage). Office: Hoffman Hart & Wagner 1000 SW Broadway Ste 2000 Portland OR 97205-3072

HART, KENNETH NELSON, lawyer; b. Providence, Jan. 13, 1930; s. Gerald Ellerbeck and Dorothy Naomi (Nelson) H.; m. Carol Lee Hourula, Oct. 1, 1957; children: Lindsey, Lowell, Allison, Stephanie, Abigail, Jessica, Kevin, Rebecca. AB, Colby Coll., 1951; LLB, Boston U., 1957. Bar: Mass. 1957, N.Y. 1961, U.S. Ct. Appeals (2d cir.) 1963, U.S. Ct. Appeals (6th cir.) 1965, U.S. Supreme Ct. 1969, U.S. Ct. Appeals (3d. cir., D.C. cir.) 1981, U.S. Ct. Appeals (8th cir.) 1981. Trial atty. antitrust divsn. Dept. Justice, 1957-61; ptnr. Donovan Leisure Newton & Irvine, N.Y.C., 1961-97, chmn. exec. com., 1986-89, chmn. litigation dept., 1995-97; ptnr. Orrick Herrington & Sutcliffe, N.Y.C., 1998. Mem. bd. overseers Colby Coll., 1991-98. Served with USMC, 1951-53. Fellow Am. Coll. Trial Lawyers. Antitrust, Federal civil litigation, Appellate. Office: 187 Westcote Dr Wakefield RI 02879-5337 E-mail: knhart@yahoo.com.

HART, ROBERT M. lawyer; b. N.Y.C., Nov. 7, 1944; s. Charles John and Helen Ann (Hammond) H.; m. Dale Elizabeth McConaughy, Nov. 21, 1970; 3 children. BA, Marist Coll., 1966; JD, Duke U., 1969. Bar: N.Y. 1969, U.S. Ct. Appeals (2d cir.) 1970, U.S. Dist. Ct. (so. dist.) N.Y. 1979. Assoc. Donovan Leisure Newton & Irvine, N.Y.C., 1969-71, 74-77, London, 1972-73, ptnr. N.Y.C., 1977-84, 88-94, Dorsey & Whitney, N.Y.C., 1984-88; sr. v.p., gen. counsel, sec. Alleghany Corp., N.Y.C., 1994—; dir., chmn. comp.com. Chgo. Title Corp., 1998-2000. Sr. lectr. law Duke U., Durham, N.C., 1986—. Contbr. articles to profl. jours. Sr. Fellow Duke U., 1983—. Mem. ABA (securities regulation com. 1981—), N.Y. State Bar Assn., Assn. Bar City N.Y. (securities regulation com. 1979-82), Am. Law Inst. Corporate, general, Securities. Office: Alleghany Corp 375 Park Ave Ste 3201 New York NY 10152-3297

HART, RUSSELL HOLIDAY, retired lawyer; b. Chgo., May 1, 1928; s. Russell Holiday and Allegra (Prince) H.; m. Mary Gehres, June 16, 1951; children: Holiday Hart McKiernan, Robert Russell, Andrew Richard. AB, DePauw U., 1950; JD, Ind. U., 1956. Bar: Ind. 1956, U.S. Dist. Ct. (no. and so. dists.) Ind. 1956, U.S. Ct. Appeals (7th cir.) 1965, U.S. Supreme Ct. 1973. Assoc. Stuart & Branigin, Lafayette, Ind., 1956-61, ptnr., 1961-99; ret., 1999. Lectr. Ind. Continuing Legal Edn. Forum; tchr. trial lawyers Nat. Inst. for Trial Advocacy. Served with U.S. Army, 1951-53. Fellow: Acad. Law Alumni Ind. U. Sch. Law;, Ind. Bar Found. (sec., v.p. 1985), Internat. Acad. Trial Lawyers, Am. Coll. Trial Lawyers, Am. Bar Found., Internat. Soc. Barristers; mem.: ABA (del.), Nat. Assn. Railroad Trial Counsel (past pres.), Ind. Def. Lawyers Assn. (past pres.), Ind. Def. Trial Counsel (diplomate), Tippecanoe County Bar Assn. (past pres.), Ind. Bar Assn. (pres.-elect 1986—87, pres. 1987—88, bd. mgrs., former treas., chmn. trial lawyers sect.). General civil litigation, Environmental, Insurance. Office: Stuart & Branigin PO Box 1010 Lafayette IN 47902-1010

HART, STEPHEN STRONG, lawyer; b. Salt Lake City, June 25, 1952; s. William Glenn Napier and Ethel Cleone (Strong) H.; m. Kathleen Ann Pickens, June 15, 1971; children: Ryan Jay Strong, Brandon Lee, Justin William, Trenton Joseph. BS in Polit. Sci. magna cum laude, U. Utah, 1973, JD, 1976. Bar: Idaho 1976. Dep. pros. atty. Bonneville County, Idaho Falls, Idaho, 1976-78; sole practice Idaho Falls, 1979-81; ptnr. Law Offices of Hart & Hart, Idaho Falls, 1981-86, Hart & Kohler, Idaho Falls, 1986—2000, Hart Law Offices PLLC, Idaho Falls, 2000—. Pub. defender Bonneville County, 1980-94. Editor Jour. of Contemporary Law, 1973-74. Candidate, pros. atty. Idaho Falls Reps., 1978; committeeman precinct, Bonneville County, 1980; coach youth soccer and basketball, Idaho Falls, 1980-85; coach, officer East Bonneville Little League, 1981-90; scoutmaster Boy Scouts Am., Idaho Falls, 1982; coach Westside Little League, 1990-93, scout and youth leader, 1995—. Mem. ABA, Idaho Bar Assn., Assn. Trial Lawyers Am., Idaho Trial Lawyers Assn., 7th Dist. Bar Assn., Soc. Bar and Gavel, Phi Beta Kappa, Phi Kappa Phi, Pi Sigma Alpha. Mormon. Mem. Lds Ch. Avocations: hunting, fishing, collecting stamps, reading. Commercial, consumer (including collections, credit), Criminal, Family and matrimonial. Home: 1154 Caysie Cir Idaho Falls ID 83402-5188 Office: Hart Law Offices 482 Constitution Way Ste 313 Idaho Falls ID 83402-3543

HART, TIMOTHY RAY, lawyer, dean; b. Portland, Jan. 5, 1942; s. Eldon V. and Wanda J. (Hillyer) H.; m. Mary F. Barlow, Aug. 31, 1964 (div. Dec. 1975); children: Mark, Matthew, Marisa, Martin; m. Annette Bryant, Aug. 8, 1981. AA, San Jose City Coll., 1968; BA, San Jose State U., 1970; MA, Wash. State U., 1973; JD, San Joaquin Coll. Law, Fresno, Calif., 1983. Bar: Calif. 1983, U.S. Dist. Ct. (ea. dist.) Calif. 1983. Police officer City of Santa Clara, Calif., 1965-71; chief of police U. Idaho, Moscow, 1971-73; crime prevention officer City of Albany, Oreg., 1973-75; instr. criminal justice Coll. of Sequoias, Visalia, Calif., 1975-81, dir. paralegal dept., 1982-83, chmn., dir. adminstrn. justice divsn., 1983-88, assoc. dean instrn., 1988—; sole practice law Visalia, 1983—. Apptd. dep. chief police City of Sanger (Calif.), 1995, apptd. chief of police, 2001-02. Parliamentarian Interagy. Youth and Cmty. Svcs., Inc. With USAF, 1960-63. Mem. ABA, ATLA, Calif. Bar Assn., Assn. Criminal Justice Educators, Am. Criminal Justice Assn., Delta Phi. Mennonite. Family and matrimonial, Personal injury (including property damage). Home: 1012 W Hemlock Ave Visalia CA 93277-7435 Office: Coll Sequoias 915 S Mooney Blvd Visalia CA 93277-2214 E-mail: timothyh@cos.edu., tim95law@juno.com.

HART, TRIP, lawyer; BS, U. Pa., 1975; JD, U. Miami, 1978. Bar: Wash. 1979, U.S. Dist. Ct. (we. dist.) Wash. 1979. Family and matrimonial, Alternative dispute resolution, Probate (including wills, trusts). Office: 1224 Griffin Enumclaw WA 98022 E-mail: trip@tx3.net.

HART, WILLIAM THOMAS, federal judge; b. Joliet, Ill., Feb. 4, 1929; s. William Michael and Geraldine (Archambeault) H.; m. Catherine Motta, Nov. 27, 1954; children: Catherine Hart Fornero, Susan Hart DaMario, Julie Hart Boesen, Sally Hart Collins, Nancy Hart McLaughlin. JD, Loyola U., Chgo., 1951. Bar: Ill. 1951, U.S. Dist. Ct. 1951, U.S. Ct. Appeals (7th cir.) 1954, U.S. Ct. Appeals (D.C. cir.) 1977. Asst. U.S. atty. U.S. Dist. Ct. (no. dist.) Ill., Chgo., 1954-56; assoc. Defrees & Fiske, 1956-59; spl. asst. atty. gen. State of Ill., 1957-58; assoc. then ptnr. Schiff, Hardin & Waite, 1959-82; spl. asst. state's atty. Cook County, Ill., 1960; judge U.S. Dist. Ct. Ill., 1982—; now sr. judge. Mem. exec. com. U.S. Dist. Ct. (no. dist.) Ill., 1988-92; mem. com. on adminstrn. fed. magistrates sys., Jud. Conf. U.S., 1987-92, 7th cir. Jud. Coun., 1990-92; mem. edn. com. Fed. Jud. Ctr., 1994-99; chair No. Dist. Ill. Ct. Hist. Assoc., 1998—. Pres. adv. bd. Mercy Med. Ctr., Aurora, Ill., 1980-81; v.p. Aurora Blood Bank, 1972-77; trustee Rosary H.S., 1981-82, 93-98; bd. dirs. Chgo. Legal Asst. Found., 1974-76. Served with U.S. Army, 1951-53. Decorated Bronze Starl named to Joliet/Will County Hall of Pride, 1992. Mem. 7th Cir. Bar Assn., Law Club, Legal Club, Soc. Trial Lawyers, Union League Club of Aurora, Ill. (hon.), Inn of Ct., Serra Club of Aurora (v.p. 2000). Office: US Dist Ct No Dist Ill US Courthouse Rm 2246 219 S Dearborn St Chicago IL 60604-1702

HARTER, PHILIP J. lawyer, educator; b. Columbus, Ohio, Apr. 14, 1942; s. Joseph M and Edith R. Harter; m. Nancy G. Gammel; 1 child, Alexa. AB, Kenyon Coll., 1960—64; MA in Math., U. Mich., Ann Arbor, 1965—66, JD, 1966—69. Bar: D.C. 1971, Supreme Ct. U.S. 1979. Vis. prof. of law Vt. Law Sch., South Royalton, Vt., 1999—2003; dir. program on democracy and governance; mediator The Mediation Inst., Washington, 1998—2003; Earl F. Nelson prof. law U. Mo., Columbia, 2003—. Recipient Gellhorn award, Federal Bar Assn., 1998, award for Outstanding Contribution to the Pub. Policy of fostering the use of ADR, Soc. of Profls. in Dispute Resolution, 1992, award for Outstanding Achievement for Excellence and Innovation in Alternative Dispute Resolution, Ctr. for Pub. Resources, 1992. Mem.: ABA (chmn. sect. adminstrv. law and regulatory practice 1995—96, chmn. working group on regulatory reform 1995—98). Avocation: bicycling. Administrative and regulatory, Alternative dispute resolution. Address: 201 S Glenwood Ave Columbia MO 65211 Office: U Missouri Hulston Hall Columbia MO 65211 E-mail: harterpj@missouri.edu.

HARTLEY, CARL WILLIAM, JR., lawyer; b. Carthage, Mo., Aug. 12, 1946; s. Carl William and Doris Eillene (Wilcox) H.; m. Martha Anderson Gouch (div. 1991); children: Zach, Jordan. BS, U. Fla., 1968, JD with High Honors, 1976. Bar: Fla. 1976, U.S. Dist. Ct. (so. dist.) Fla. 1976, U.S. Dist. Ct. (mid. dist.) Fla. 1980. Sales rep. Scott Paper Co., Miami, Fla., 1971-73; assoc. Grenbherg, Traurig et al., Miami, 1976-80; ptnr. Thomas Thomas Hartley & Spraker, Orlando, Fla., 1980-83, Holland & Knight, Orlando, 1983-85, Hartley & Wall, Orlando, 1985—. Editor U. Fla. Law Rev., 1976. Democrat. Methodist. Avocations: fishing, hunting, camping. General civil litigation, Commercial, contracts (including sales of goods; commercial financing), Property, real (including real estate development, water). Office: Hartley & Wall PO Box 2168 Orlando FL 32802-2168 E-mail: cwhsec@hartleywall.com.

HARTLEY, KAREN JEANETTE, lawyer, mediator, consultant; b. Oakland, Calif., Aug. 2, 1950; d. Samuel Louis and Jean Iris (Beven) Ostrow; m. Terry Van Hook, Aug. 29, 1970 (div. Mar. 1976); m. William Headley, Jan. 22, 1977 (div. Mar. 1988). BA in Psychology with highest honors, UCLA, 1972; DMin, Sch. of Theology, Claremont, Calif., 1976; JD cum laude, U. San Diego, 1982. Bar: Calif. 1982, U.S. Dist. Ct. (9th cir.), 1983, Hawaii 1991, Oreg. 1996; ordained to ministry, Meth. Ch., 1973. Intern to asst. United Meth. Ch., 1969-71; asst. minister St. Paul's United Meth. Ch., San Bernardino, Calif., 1973-74; assoc. minister Claremont United Meth. Ch., 1974-76; sr. minister Santee (Calif.) United Meth. Ch., 1977-79; clk. Calif. Supreme Ct., San Francisco, 1981; cons. Regional Dept. Edn., San Diego, 1979-81; assoc. atty. Duke, Gerstel, Shearer & Bregante, San Diego, 1983-84, Finley, Kumble, Wagner et al, San Diego, 1984-87; prin. atty., mediator Hartley & Assocs., San Diego, 1987-95, Eugene, Oreg., 1996—99; coord. pub. policy dispute resolution for human svc. agys. Oreg. Dept. Human Svcs., Salem, 1999-2001; prin. atty. Hartley & Assocs., Eugene, 2001—. Mediator San Diego Mediation Ctr., 1990-95; prof. negotiation and mediation, instr. Mediation Clinic U. Oreg. Sch. Law, Eugene, 1996-97; instr. constrn. law Lane C.C., Eugene, 1996-99. Mem. Oreg. Bar Assn., Lan County Bar Assn. Avocations: art, travel. Construction, General practice. E-mail: karenhartley7@aol.com.

HARTMAN, JAMES MATTHEW, lawyer; b. Bklyn., May 28, 1928; s. Irving I. and Esther (Kramer) H.; m. Alys Florence Moses, Sept. 18, 1949 (div. Aug. 1963); children— Victoria I., Elizabeth A., Sarah M.; m. 2d Frances June Ouweleen, Feb. 29, 1964. B.A., NYU, 1950; LL.B., Columbia U., 1953. Bar: N.Y. 1954, U.S. Dist. Ct. (so. and ea. dists.) N.Y. 1957, U.S. Dist. Ct. (we. dist.) N.Y. 1964, U.S. Supreme Ct. 1964, U.S. Ct. Claims 1964, U.S. Ct. Appeals (2d cir.) 1969, U.S. Dist. Ct. (no. dist.) N.Y. 1976, D.C. 1980, Fla. 1982, U.S. Ct. Appeals (6th and 11th cirs.) 1982. Assoc. firm Swain & Moore, N.Y.C., 1954-55; sole practice N.Y.C., 1955-60; assoc. Fellner & Rovins, N.Y.C., 1960-61; ptnr. Harris Beach, Wilcox, Rochester, N.Y., 1962— ; adj. assoc. prof. Cornell U. Law Sch., 1973-77; instr. trial advocacy N.E. Region, Nat. Inst. Trial Advocacy, 1976— , nat. instr., 1981; instr. Hofstra Law Sch., 1978-81, Harvard Law Sch., 1979, Emory Law Sch., 1983, also various bar assns.; mem. Monroe County Med. Malpractice Arbitration Panels. Chmn. com. on health care for elderly Monroe County Health Planning Council, 1971-73; mem. health services and legal services coms. Human Resource Task Force; mem. pres.'s adv. bd., bd. regents McQuaid Jesuit High Sch., 1973-75; mem. Rochester Meml. Art Gallery, Rochester Mus. and Sci. Ctr.; bd. dirs. Rochester Eye Inst.; bd. dirs., mem. fin. com., mem. planning and coordinating com. St. Ann's Home for Aged; nat. bd. dirs. Abota Found. Served with AUS, 1946-48. Mem. ABA, Am. Bd. Trial Advocates (past pres. Rochester chpt., mem. nat. bd. dirs.), N.Y. State Bar Assn. (mem. ho. dels. 1973-76, chmn. trial lawyers sect. 1973-74, various other coms.), Monroe County Bar Assn. (past pres.), Am. Bd. Trial Advocates (Rochester chpt. past pres.), N.Y. Bar Found., Am. Bar Found. Clubs: Oak Hill Country, Hunt Hollow Ski. Federal civil litigation, State civil litigation. Home: 15 Oakfield Way Pittsford NY 14534-1886

HARTMAN, RONALD G. lawyer; b. Harrisburg, Pa., Aug. 13, 1950; s. Manny and Helene (Levine) H.; m. Leslie Ann Golomb, May 31, 1980; children: Molly, Samuel. BA, U. Pitts., 1972, JD, 1975. Bar: Pa. 1975, U.S. Dist. Ct. (we. dist.) Pa. 1975. Assoc. Baskin & Sears, Pitts., 1975-84; ptnr. Reed Smith LLP, Pitts., 1985—. Bd. dirs. Citizens League Southwestern Pa., Pitts., 1988, Am. Cancer Soc.-Allegheny County chpt., Pitts., exec. com., 1990—; bd. dirs. Jewish Family and Children's Svc. of Pitts., pres. 1995-97; bd. dirs. United Jewish Fedn. Greater Pitts., 1995-97, 98-2000, co-chmn. bus. and profl. divsn., 1989-91, mem. steering com. atty. divsn., 1992—; chair Cardoza Soc., 1999-2001; bd. dirs. Jewish Chronicle, 1997-2000. Mem. ABA, Pa. Bar Assn., Allegheny County Bar Assn. Jewish. Avocations: jogging, reading. Commercial, contracts (including sales of goods; commercial financing), Landlord-tenant, Property, real (including real estate development, water). Home: 500 Glen Arden Dr Pittsburgh PA 15208-2809 Office: Reed Smith LLP 435 6th Ave Pittsburgh PA 15219-1886

HARTMANN, CARL JOSEPH, lawyer, consultant; b. Rochester, N.Y., Apr. 21, 1954; s. Carl Joseph and Mary (Ercel) H.; m. Kimberly Lynn Japinga, Feb. 15, 1998. JD, Antioch Coll., 1979. Bar: N.Mex. 1980, V.I. 1993, D.C. 1994, U.S. Dist. Ct. N.Mex. 1981, U.S. Ct. Appeals (10th cir.) 1982, U.S. Ct. Appeals (3d cir.) 1988, U.S. Ct. Appeals (fed. cir.) 1993, U.S. Supreme Ct. 1985. Jud. intern U.S. Supreme Ct., Washington, 1979; jud. clk. N.Mex. Ct. Appeals, Santa Fe, 1980-81; asst. prof. law Antioch Coll. Sch. Law, Washington, 1982-85; ptnr. Law Offices of Carl Hartmann, Albuquerque, 1985-87; assoc. Campbell, Arellano & Rich, St. Thomas, V.I., 1988-89; special counsel Merrill Lynch Pvt. Capital, N.Y.C., 1989-91; ptnr. Law Offices of Carl Hartmann, N.Y.C., 1991—; of counsel Law Offices of Lawrence H. Schoenbach, N.Y.C., 1991—. Gen. counsel Emerging Comms., Inc., St. Croix, V.I., 1997-98, Innovative Comms., Corp., St. Croix, 1998—; spl. counsel U.S. Park Svc., Santa Fe, 1987. Author: Legal Analysis for Clinical Students, 1981; co-author: Private Law: An Introduction to Torts, 1980, Clinical Perspectives on Fair Employment, 1979; co-editor-in-chief Antioch Sch. of Law--Law Rev., 1979. Adv. bd. Our Lady of Czestochowa Sch., Paulus Hook, N.J., 1998-2001. Mem. Assn. of the Bar of the City of N.Y., V.I. Bar Assn. Roman Catholic. Avocations: fencing, flying, scuba, skiing, golf. Federal civil litigation, Corporate, general, Labor (including EEOC, Fair Labor Standards Act, labor-management relations, NLRB, OSHA). Home: 126 Sussex St Jersey City NJ 07302-6405 Office: Trinity Bldg 111 Broadway 13th Fl New York NY 10006 E-mail: hartmann@federal-litigation.com.

HARTMANN, MARKUS UWE, lawyer; b. Fairfax, Va., Feb. 3, 1964; s. Sonja Doris and Alfred Richard Hartmann; m. Colleen Marie Cavanaugh, Dec. 1, 1966; children: Olivia Marie, Markus Alfred. JD, Harvard Law Sch., Cambridge, MA, 1993—96; BA, The Colo. Coll., Colorado Springs, CO, 1984—86. Bar: Mass. 1997. Officer USMC, Quantico, Va., 1983—; student Harvard Law Sch., Cambridge, Mass., 1993—96; assoc./legal clk. Hale & Dorr LLP, Boston, Mass., 1995—98; counsel/asst. brand mgr. Te Procter & Gamble Co., Cincinnati, Ohio, 1998—2000; v.p. GE Info. Tech. Solutions, Newport, Ky., 2000—. Judge adv. USMC Reserves, Cincinnati. Maj. U.S. Marine Corps Res., 1998. Recipient Latimer Award, GE, 2001.

Corporate, general, Labor (including EEOC, Fair Labor Standards Act, labor-management relations, NLRB, OSHA), Computer. Office: GE Information Technology Solutions One Riverfront Place Newport KY 41071 Office Fax: 859-815-7300. E-mail: markus.hartmann@gecits.ge.com.

HARTMANN, UWE, lawyer; b. Zell/Mosel, Germany, Aug. 25, 1963; m. Uta Friedlein; children, Michael, Paul. JD, U. Wuerzburg, Germany, 1992, PhD, 1994. Cert. dist. ct. Frankfurt, Germany; advocat in Czech Republic. Assoc. BBLP Beiten Burkhardt Mittl & Wegener, Frankfurt, 1995-96, Prague, Czech Republic, 1997-98, ptnr. Duesseldorf, Germany, 1998-99, Frankfurt, 1999—2001, Weil Gotshal & Manges, 2001—. Bank clk. Deutsche Bank AG, Paris, 1990, Wuerzburg, Germany, 1988, Mainz, 1983-85; spkr. Inst. for Internat. Rsch. Diverse, Germany, 1997, Gustav Stresemann Inst., Bonn, Germany, 1995-96. Contbr. articles to profl. jours. Lt. German Fed. Armed Forces, 1985-87. Scholarship Konrad-Adenauer-Stiftung, 1989-92. Mem. German-Am. Lawyers Assn., Assn. Internat. étudiants des anciens étudiants en droit comparé. Corporate, general, Finance, Mergers and acquisitions. Office: Weil Gotshal & Manges Main Tower Neue Mainzer Str 52-58 60311 Frankfurt Germany Home Fax: 49-6192-309765; Office Fax: 49-69-21659-699. E-mail: uwe.hartmann@weil.com.

HARTNETT, WILL FORD, lawyer; b. Austin, Tex., June 3, 1956; s. James Joseph and Emily (High) Hartnett; m. Tammy Lynn Cotton, Dec. 7, 1996; children: Will, Winston. BA, Harvard U., 1978; JD, U. Tex., 1981. Bar: Tex. 1981, U.S. Ct. Appeals (5th cir.) 1985, U.S. Supreme Ct. 1985; cert. in Estate Planning and Probate Law Tex. Bd. Legal Specialization. Assoc. Turner & Hitchins, Dallas, 1981-82; ptnr. The Hartnett Law Firm, Dallas, 1982—. Bd. dirs. Tex. Guaranteed Student Loan Corp., Austin, 1987-90. Co-author: Annual Survey of Wills and Trusts, 1986. Mem. Tex. Ho. of Reps., 1991—; v. chmn. House Jud. Affairs Com., 1995-02, chmn., 2003—. Fellow: Tex. Bar Found., Am. Coll. Trust and Estate Coun.; mem.: SAR, Tex. Jud. Coun., Dallas Bar Assn., Mensa, St. Nicholas Soc., Harvard Club Dallas (bd. dirs., treas. 1983—95). Republican. Roman Catholic. State civil litigation, Probate (including wills, trusts). Home: 4722 Walnut Hill Ln Dallas TX 75229-6354 Office: The Hartnett Law Firm 4900 Thanksgiving Tower Dallas TX 75201 E-mail: will@hartnettlawfirm.com.

HARTRICK, JANICE KAY, lawyer; b. Baytown, Tex., Oct. 15, 1952; BA, Rice U., 1974; JD, U. Houston, 1976. Bar: Tex. 1977, La. 1980. With contracts sect. Texaco Corp., Houston, 1977-78; asst. gen. counsel Cities Exploration Co., Watson Oil Corp., Houston, 1978-79; sr. atty. Coastal Corp., Houston, 1979-87; chief counsel, v.p. Seagull Energy Corp., Houston, 1987-97; gen. counsel, sr. v.p. EEX Corp., Houston, 1997-2000; asst. gen. counsel Apache Corp., 2000—. Coun. Thompson and Knight, LLP, Houston. Contbg. editor Regulation of the Natural Gas Industry, 1980-84. Vice chair adv. bd. Internat. Oil and Gas Ednl. Ctr., Southwestern Legal Found.; trustee Rocky Mountain Mineral Law Found. Mem. ABA (chair oil and gas exploration and prodn.), Tex. Bar Assn., State Bar of Tex. (oil, gas and mineral law sect. chair 1999), La. Bar Assn. Avocation: track. Corporate, general, FERC practice, Utilities, public. Office: Apache Corp 2000 Post Oak Blvd Ste 100 Houston TX 77056-4400

HARTSOE, MARK CHARLES, lawyer; b. Phila., June 12, 1958; s. Charles Edwin and Joyce Wright Hartsoe; m. Amelia Mahood, Aug. 21, 1986; children: Watson, Henry, Theodore. Student, Wake Forest U., 1976—78; BS, Va. Commonwealth U., 1981; JD, U. Tenn., 1985. Bar: Va. 1985, Tenn. 1991, U.S. Ct. Appeals (6th cir.), cert.: U.S. Supreme Ct. Spl. asst. to U.S. atty. U.S. Dept. Interior, Knoxville, 1987—94; asst. atty. gen. State of Tenn., Knoxville, 1994—97; dep. city law dir. City of Knoxville Law Dept., 1997—2000; ptnr. Butler, Vines & Babb, PLLC, Knoxville, 2001—. Master gardener, vol. Knox Co. Agrl. Ext. Svc., Knoxville, 1994—2002; elder, mem. session Eastminster Presbyn. Ch., Knoxville, 1998—2000; v.p., bd. dirs. Town Hall East, Knoxville, 1999—2001; bd. dirs. Blount United Soccer Club. Mem.: Tenn. Bar Assn., Knoxville Bar Assn. Republican. Avocations: fly fishing, gardening, soccer. Personal injury (including property damage), General civil litigation, Condemnation (eminent domain). Home: 1609 Scenic Dr Maryville TN 37803 Office: Butler Vines & Babb PO Box 2649 Knoxville TN 37901 Office Fax: 865-637-3385. E-mail: mhartsoe@bvblaw.com.

HARTT, GROVER, III, lawyer; b. Dallas, Apr. 12, 1948; s. Grover Jr. and Dorothy June (Wilkins) H. BA with high honors, So. Meth. U., 1970, LLM in Tax, 1986; JD with high honors, Tex. Tech U., 1973. Bar: Tex. 1973, U.S. Dist. Ct. (no. dist.) Tex. 1974, U.S. Dist. Ct. (we. dist.) Tex. 1975, U.S. Ct. Appeals (5th cir.) 1975, U.S. Supreme Ct. 1976, U.S. Dist. Ct. (ea. dist.) Tex. 1999. Law clk. to presiding justice Ct. Criminal Appeals Tex., Austin, 1973-75; atty. Hartt and Hartt, Dallas, 1975-79; atty., advisor Office Spl. Counsel U.S. Dept. Energy, Dallas, 1979-80, dep. chief counsel, 1981-83; trial atty. tax divsn. U.S. Dept. Justice, Dallas, 1983-86, dep. atty.-in-charge tax divsn., 1986-95, asst. chief southwestern region civil trial sect. tax divsn., 1995—. Nat. spkr. on taxation, bankruptcy and litigation. Contbg. author: Collier on Bankruptcy; contbr. articles to profl. jours. Recipient Atty. Gen's award for disting. svc., 1996. Fellow Am. Coll. Bankruptcy; mem. ABA (mem. ct. procedure com. tax sect., chmn. bankruptcy litigation subcom. 1995—, mem. bus. bankruptcy com. bus. law sect., vice chmn. tax and fed. claims subcom. 1996-2000, chmn. 2000—), Tex. Bar Assn., Dallas Bar Assn., Am. Bankruptcy Inst., Coll. of State Bar of Tex., John C. Ford Am. Inn of Ct. (master of the bench 2000—). Office: US Dept Justice Tax Div 717 N Harwood St Ste 400 Dallas TX 75201-6506 E-mail: grover.hartt@usdoj.gov.

HARTWEGER, GORDON GRAVIUS, lawyer; b. Litchfield, Ill., July 14, 1939; s. Frank and Marjory (Smith) H.; m. Ethel K. Kovol, June 23, 1962; children: Gordon, Katherine, Kristina, Peter, Amy, John. BSEE, St. Louis U., 1961, JD, 1964. Bar: Mo. 1964, U.S. Dist. Ct. Mo. 1964, U.S. Tax Ct. 1988. Ptnr. Guilfoil, Symington & Petzall, St. Louis, 1964-77; pvt. practice St. Louis, 1977—. Gen. counsel Met. Collegiate Athletic Conf., St. Louis, 1976-85. Pres. Desmet Jesuit High Sch. Mens Club, St. Louis, 1991-92, St. Louis U. Tipoff Club, 1977. Mem. Mo. Athletic Club, Bar Assn. Met. St. Louis, ABA, Mo. Bar Assn., St. Louis County Bar Assn., Lawyers Assn. Republican. Roman Catholic. Avocations: reading, coaching athletics, swimming, camping, tennis. General civil litigation, Corporate, general, Franchising. Home: 11911 Greenwalk Dr Saint Louis MO 63146-4717 Office: Ste 420 120 S Central Ave Saint Louis MO 63105-3917

HARTY, JAMES QUINN, lawyer; b. Phila., Dec. 10, 1925; s. William Lawrence and Marie Sarita (Quinn) H.; m. Ann Elizabeth McGeeney, July 23, 1955; children: Michael, Martha Harty Scheines, Christopher, Patrick, Mark, Paul. AB, LaSalle Coll., 1949; MBA, U. Pa., Phila., 1952, LLB, 1959. Bar: Pa. 1961. Personnel mgr. Corning (N.Y.) Glass Works, 1952-56; lectr. Wharton Sch. U. Pa., Phila., 1956-59; assoc. Reed, Smith, Shaw & McClay, Pitts., 1961-70, ptnr., 1971-95, Plummer DeWalt & Linn, Pitts., 1995—. Research editor: Office Management Handbook, 1958. Mem. Thornburg Zoning Rev. Bd., Thornburg Borough Coun., Pitts., 1968-76. With USN, 1943-46, PTO, CBI. Fulbright lectr. U. Kanazawa, Japan, 1959-60. Mem. Pa. Bar Assn. (chmn. labor sect. 1982), Allegheny Bar Assn., Pitts. Athletic Assn. Clubs: Pitts. (gov. 1986-87), Chartiers Country (Pitts.). Roman Catholic. Avocation: golf. Civil rights, Labor (including EEOC, Fair Labor Standards Act, labor-management relations, NLRB, OSHA), Workers' compensation. Office: Plummer Harty Owsiany & Archer LLP 57th fl US Steel Tower 600 Grant St Pittsburgh PA 15219-1912 E-mail: jharty@p2law.com.

HARTZ, HARRIS L. lawyer; b. Balt., Jan. 20, 1947; s. Alvin Sidney and Muriel (Abrams) H.; m. Deborah Dillingham, July 23, 1977; children—Jacob Cameron, Andrew Samuel. A.B. summa cum laude, Harvard U., 1967, J.D. magna cum laude, 1972. Bar: N. Mex. 1972, U.S. Dist. Ct. N.Mex. 1972, U.S. Ct. Appeals (10th cir.) 1973. Asst. U.S. atty. Dept. Justice, Albuquerque, 1972-75; asst. prof. Coll. Law, U. Ill., Champaign, 1976; atty., exec. dir. Gov.'s Organized Crime Prevention Commn., Albuquerque, 1977-79; assoc. Poole, Tinnin & Martin, P.A., Albuquerque, 1979-82; assoc. Miller, Stratvert, Torgerson & Brandt, Albuquerque, 1982-83, ptnr., dir., 1983-88; judge N. Mex. Ct. Appeals, 1988-99; judge U.S. Court Appeals (10th cir.) Albuquerque, N. Mex., 2001-. Case and devels. editor Harvard Law Rev., 1971-72, editor 1970-71; bd. editors Litigation Mag., 1983-86. Mem. exec. com. Bernalillo County Republican Party, Albuquerque, 1982-83; Rep. nominee for N.Mex. Supreme Ct. elections, 1986, 92, 96; chmn. N.Mex. Racing Commn., 1987-88. Recipient Founders' award Nat. Kidney Found., N.Mex., 1997; nominee Joan Pew award Nat. Assn. State Racing Commrs., 1988. Mem. ABA (mem. adv. com. standing com. law & nat. security 1995-97), Am. Law Inst. (advisor restatement law agy. 1996—), Albuquerque Com. on Fgn. Relations (chmn. 1981-82), Am. Judicature Soc., Rotary Club of Albuquerque (pres. 1996-97), Phi Beta Kappa. Office: 710 US Courthouse 333 Lomas Blvd NW Albuquerque NM 87102*

HARTZ, STEVEN EDWARD MARSHALL, lawyer, educator; b. Cambridge, Mass., July 11, 1948; s. Louis and Stella (Feinberg) H.; m. Janice Lindsay, June 12, 1976. AB magna cum laude, Harvard Coll., 1970; JD, U. Chgo., 1974. Bar: N.Y. 1975, U.S. Dist. Ct. (so. and ea. dists.) N.Y. 1975, U.S. Ct. Appeals (2d cir.) 1975, Fla. 1979, U.S. Dist. Ct. (so. dist.) Fla. 1979, U.S. Tax Ct. 1979, U.S. Ct. Appeals (5th cir.) 1979, U.S. Supreme Ct. 1979, U.S. Ct. Appeals (11th cir.) 1981, U.S. Dist. Ct. (mid. dist.) Fla. 1984. Assoc. Cleary, Gottlieb, Steen & Hamilton, N.Y.C., 1974-79; asst. U.S. atty. U.S. Dept. Justice, Miami, Fla., 1979-82, dep. chief criminal divsn., chief fraud and pub. corruption sect., 1981-82; sole practice Miami, Fla., 1982-90; of counsel Akerman, Senterfitt & Eidson, P.A., Miami, 1980, ptnr., shareholder, 1991—. Lectr. dept. English, U. English, U. Miami, 1984, adj. assoc. prof., 1985-86. Co-author: Housing, A Community Handbook, 1973. Vol. atty. Mobilization for Youth Legal Svcs., N.Y.C., 1978. Recipient Dirs.' award U.S. Dept. Justice, 1981; Fulbright Hays scholar, 1970. Mem. ABA, FBA, Fla. Bar Assn., N.Y. State Bar Assn., Dade County Bar Assn., Assn. Bar City N.Y., Phi Beta Kappa. General civil litigation, Commercial, consumer (including collections, credit), Criminal. Office: One Southeast 3rd Ave 28th Fl Miami FL 33131-4943

HARTZELL, ANDREW CORNELIUS, JR., retired lawyer; b. Balt., Nov. 5, 1927; s. Andrew Cornelius and Mary Frances (Milholland) H.; m. Mary Leontine McPhillips, July 31, 1954; children: Andrew Cornelius III, Stephen Carroll, Mary Leontine, James Francis, John Michael, Peter Milholland. BA, Yale U., 1950, LL.B., 1953. Bar: N.Y. 1953, Ohio 1955, U.S. Supreme Ct. Law clk. Fed. Judge Irving R. Kaufman, N.Y.C., 1953-54; assoc. Thompson, Hine & Flory, Cleve., 1954-63, Debevoise, Plimpton, Lyons & Gates, N.Y.C., 1963-65; ptnr. Debevoise Plimpton and predecessor firms, 1966-96, chmn. litigation dept., 1989-92, of counsel, 1996-98. Author: The Treacherous Snows, 1993; contbr. articles to legal jours. and to Antitrust Advisor, McGraw-Hill Pub. Co., 1971, 78; Note and Comment editor Yale Law Jour, 1952-53. Mem. bd. archtl. rev. Village of Scarsdale, N.Y., 1965-67; mem. Adv. Coun. on Environ. Conservation, 1986-90, chmn., 1987-89; mem. Sch. Facilities Adv. Com., 1988-90; bd. dirs. Friends of Scarsdale Parks, 1991-2000; mem. Scarsdale Bowl com., 2001-02; Bd. Assessment Review, 1998-2003; Rep. candidate for Congress 18th dist. N.Y., 1994. With U.S. Army, 1946-48. Fellow Am. Coll. Trial Lawyers; mem. ABA, Union Internat. des Avocats, Scarsdale Golf Club, Yale Club N.Y., Town and Village Club (Scarsdale), Am. Alpine Club. Roman Catholic. Antitrust, Federal civil litigation, State civil litigation. Home: 7 Eastwoods Ln Scarsdale NY 10583-6401 Office: Debevoise & Plimpton 919 Third Ave New York NY 10022-3904

HARUTUNIAN, ALBERT T(HEODORE), III, judge; b. San Diego, May 15, 1955; s. Albert Theodore Jr. and Elsie Ruth H.; m. Rebecca Blair, 1999. BA, Claremont McKenna Coll., 1977; JD, U. Calif., Berkeley, 1980. Bar: Calif. 1980, U.S. Dist. Ct. (so. dist.) Calif. 1980, U.S. Ct. Apppeals (9th cir.) 1982, U.S. Supreme Ct. 1984. Law clk. to Hon. Howard B. Turrentine U.S. Dist. Ct., San Diego, 1980-81; assoc. Luce, Forward, Hamilton & Scripps, San Diego, 1982-87, ptnr., 1988-95; judge San Diego Mcpl. Ct., 1995-98, San Diego Superior Ct., 1998—. Spl. counsel standing com. on discipline U.S. Dist. Ct. Calif., San Diego, 1983-85; chmn. San Diego Bar Labor and Employment Sect., 1988-89; chmn. fed. cts. com. Calif. State Bar, 1989-90. Bd. dirs. ARC San Diego chpt., 1992-2002, Crime Victims Fund, 1995-97; bd. govs. Muscular Dystrophy Assn., San Diego, 1985; grad. LEAD Inc., San Diego, 1986; planning com. San Diego United Way, 1986-92. Named one of Outstanding Young Men of Am., 1983; recipient Outstanding Service award 9th Cir. Jud. Conf., 1986. Mem. ABA, Calif. State Bar Ct. (referee 1985-88), Am. Arbitration Assn. (arbitrator 1986-95), Calif. Judges Assn. (mem. criminal law and procedure com. 1997-2000), Boalt Hall Alumni Assn. (bd. dirs. 1994-97), Claremont McKenna Coll. Alumni Assn. (founding dir. San Diego chpt. 1984-2000), Rotary (bd. dirs. San Diego club 1995—). Republican. Avocations: music, golf. Office: San Diego Superior Ct PO Box 122724 San Diego CA 92112-2724

HARVELL, MICHAEL CLELAND, lawyer; b. Fairborne, Ohio, Aug. 6, 1946; s. John Cleland and Catherine (Kenefick) H.; m. Cynthia Howard, Sept. 26, 1970; children: Rebecca, Richard, Samuel BA, Yale U., 1968; JD cum laude, Boston U., 1975. Bar: N.H. 1975, U.S. Dist. Ct. N.H. 1975, U.S. Supreme Ct. 1986. Assoc. Sheehan, Phinney, Bass & Green, Manchester/Portsmouth, N.H., 1975-79, stockholder, 1980—. Bd. dirs., pres. Child and Family Svcs. N.H., Manchester, 1977-87; trustee, pres. Strawbery Banke Mus., Portsmouth, 1987-94; trustee Soc. Protection N.H. Forests, Concord, 1990-95; bd. advisors Nat. Trust for Hist. Preservation, 1995—; dir. Portsmouth Music Hall, 2001—. Lt. USN, 1968-72. Fellow N.H. Bar Found., N.H. Bar Assn. Independent. Avocations: tennis, sailing, travel. General civil litigation, Corporate, general. Home: 19 Water St Kittery ME 03904-1630 Office: Sheehan Phinney Bass & Green 1000 Elm St Ste 1801 Manchester NH 03101-1792 E-mail: mharvell@sheehan.com.

HARVEY, ALBERT C. lawyer; m. Nancy Rutherford; children: Anne, Elizabeth. BS, U. Tenn., 1961, JD, 1967. Law clk. Tenn. Supreme Ct.; asst. to pub. defender Shelby County, 1969-71; ptnr. Thomason, Hendrix, Harvey, Johnson & Mitchell, Memphis. Instr. med. and dental jurisprudence U. Tenn., Memphis. Bd. editors Tennessee Law Review. Pres. Goodwill Boys Club, 1983-85; active YMCA, Arthritis Found., Citizens Assn. Memphis and Shelby County, Shelby County War Memls.; sr. warden of vestry Calvary Episcopal Ch. Maj. gen. USMCR, comdg. gen. 4th Marine divsn. Recipient Sam A. Myar, Jr. award Tenn. Bd. Law Examiners, 1978. Fellow: Tenn. Bar Found. (pres. 2002—03), Am. Bar Found. (life); mem.: Memphis Area C. of C. (pres. mil. affairs coun.), Am. Inns. of Ct., Memphis Bar Assn. (v.p. 1989, pres. elect 1990, pres. 1991, pres. young lawyers divsn.), Tenn. Bar Assn. (bd. govs., pres. young lawyers conf. 2000—), Am. Bd. Trial Advocates (adv.), Am. Judicature Soc. (nat. bd. dirs.), ABA (bd. govs., ho. dels. charter mem. and coun. sect. litigation, young lawyers sect., fellow young lawyers divsn., com. on ethics and profl. responsibility, ethics 2000 spl. com.), Ctrl. Garden Area Assn. (pres.), Univ. Club Memphis (pres.), Kiwanis, Phoenix Club (1st v.p.), Navy League, U. Tenn. Nat. Alumni Assn. (pres. Memphis chpt., nat. bd. govs.). Construction, Personal injury (including property damage), Product liability. Office: 1 Commerce Sq 29th Fl Memphis TN 38103

HARVEY, ALEXANDER, II, federal judge; b. Balt., May 3, 1923; s. Fred B. and Rose (Hopkins) H.; m. Mary E. Williams, Feb. 24, 1951; children: Elizabeth H., Alexander IV. BA, Yale U., 1947; LLB, Columbia U., 1950. Bar: Md. 1950. Assoc. Ober, William, Grimes & Stinson, Balt., 1950-66, ptnr., 1953-66; asst. atty. gen. Md., 1957-58; judge U.S. Dist. Ct. Md., 1966-86, chief judge, 1986-91, sr. judge, 1991—. Mem. Gov.'s Com. To Study Blue Sky Law of Md., 1961; mem. character com. Ct. Appeals Md. for 8th Jud. Cir. Bd. dirs. Balt. Symphony Assn., 1966-68; pres., dir. Balt. Opera Guild, 1960; bd. dirs. Balt. Coun. Social Agys., 1957-63; trustee Ch. Home and Hosp., Balt., 1952-71. 1st lt. AUS, World War II, ETO. Mem. Am., Md., Balt. bar assns., Phi Beta Kappa. Episcopalian (vestry 1967-70). Home: 7300 Brightside Rd Baltimore MD 21212-1011 Office: US Dist Ct 101 W Lombard St Ste 404 Baltimore MD 21201-2605

HARVEY, CHARLES ALBERT, JR., lawyer; b. Beverly, Mass., Sept. 28, 1949; s. Charles A. and Phyllis B. (O'Rourke) H.; m. Whitney Ann Neville, Sept. 21, 1985; children: John Whitney, Charlotte Baird. AB, Assumption Coll., 1971; JD, U. Maine, 1974. Bar: Maine 1974, Mass. 1974, U.S. Supreme Ct. 1979. Assoc. Verrill & Dana, Portland, Maine, 1974-79, ptnr., 1979-95, Harvey & Frank, Portland, 1995—. Assoc. chief counsel President's Commn. on Accident at Three Mile Island, Washington, 1979; mem. adv. com. on civil rules Maine Supreme Jud. Ct., 1978-91, chmn. adv. com. on cameras in trial cts., 1991-93, cons. on civil rules, 1996—, chmn. adv. com. on civil rules, 1987-91; chmn. adv. com. on local rules U.S. Dist. Ct. Maine, 1985—, mem. civil justice adv. com., 1992-97; chmn. Maine Gov.'s Select Com. on Jud. Appointments, 1987-91; mem. Senator Olympia J. Snowe's adv. com. on appointment of U.S. Dist. Judge, U.S. Atty. and U.S. Marshal, 2001-02; chmn. grievance commn. Maine Bd. Overseers of the Bar, 1996-97. Contbr. articles to profl. jours. Trustee Portland Sympnony Orch., 1980-89, pres., 1987-89, adv. trustee, 1989—; trustee Portland Stage Co., 1984-87, adv. trustee, 1987—; trustee Waynflete Sch., 1990-96; adv. trustee Maine Childrens Mus., 1992-1999, Maine Vol. Lawyers for the Arts, 1994-1999. Fellow Portland Mus. of Art, 1993—. Fellow Am. Coll. Trial Lawyers, Maine Bar Found.; mem. Am. Law Inst. Republican. Federal civil litigation, General civil litigation. Office: 2 City Ctr Portland ME 04101-4010

HARVEY, GREGORY MERRILL, lawyer; b. Morris Twp., N.J., Jan. 6, 1937; s. Merrill Piercy and Dorothy Ceola (Gregory) H.; m. Emily Mitchell Wallace, June 14, 1969. AB, Harvard U., 1959; JD, Harvard Law Sch., 1962. Bar: Pa. 1963. Assoc. Morgan, Lewis & Bockius, Phila., 1962-69, ptnr., 1969-99, Montgomery, McCracken, Walker & Rhoads, Phila., 1999—. Chmn. City of Phila. Bd. Ethics, 1984-91; trustee Fairmount Park Art Assn., Phila., 1981—; co-chmn. 8th Ward Dem. Exec. Com., Phila., 1984—; bd. dirs. Ams. for Dem. Action Southeastern Pa. chpt., 1966-, bd. dirs. Conservation Ctr. Art and Historic Artifacts, Phila., 1995-. Recipient James Madison award Soc. Profl. Journalists, 1986, Judge Learned Hand Human Rels. award Am. Jewish Com., 1991. Fellow Am. Coll. Trial Lawyers; mem. ABA, Pa. Bar Assn., Phila. Bar Assn., Phila. Club, Franklin Inn (Phila.), Merion Cricket Club (Haverford, Pa.), Racquet Club (Phila.), Phi Beta Kappa. Appellate, General civil litigation, Libel. Home: 1939 Panama St Philadelphia PA 19103-6609 Office: Montgomery McCracken et al 123 S Broad St Philadelphia PA 19109-1099 E-mail: gharvey@mmwr.com.

HARVEY, JONATHAN MATTHEW, lawyer; b. Worcester, Mass., July 6, 1955; s. Irwin and Hannah H.; m. Lyssa Lynn Kligman, Dec. 17, 1977; children: Laurel Eden, Jordane Mills, Kyle Michael. BA cum laude, U. Ga., 1977; JD, U. S.C., 1981. Bar: S.C. 1981, U.S. Dist. Ct. S.C. 1982, U.S. Ct. Appeals (4th cir.) 1992. Asst. solicitor Fifth Judicial Circuit Solicitor's Office, Columbia, S.C., 1982-83; asst. atty. gen. Office of the Atty. Gen., Columbia, S.C., 1983-86; lawyer pvt. practice, Columbia, 1986—. Vice chair Richland Sch. Dist. Ednl. Found., 2001—02; fin. dir. Richland County Dems., Columbia, SC, 1987—88, mem. exec. com., 1987—90, 1998—2000; commr. East Richland County Pub. Svc. Dist., 1990—99, chmn., 1999—2000. Mem.: ATLA, S.C. Trial Lawyers Assn., S.C. Assn. Criminal Def. Lawyers (bd. dirs. 5th jud. cir. 1998—2001, treas. 2002—), S.C. Bar Assn., Richland County Bar Assn. Democrat. Avocations: tennis, outdoor activities. Administrative and regulatory, Criminal, Personal injury (including property damage). Office: 1804 Bull St Columbia SC 29201-2506

HARVEY, MARC S(EAN), lawyer, historian, law educator; b. N.Y.C., May 4, 1960; s. M. Eugene and Coleen (Jones) H. BA with highest honors, So. Ill. U., 1980; Pre-Law, Wash. U., 1980; JD, Southwestern U., 1983; MBA, Loyola Marymount U., L.A., 1984-86; postgrad., Oxford U. Christ Church Coll., 1994—97. Bar: Calif., U.S. Supreme Ct. Counsel U.S. SBA, L.A., 1982-83; counsel enforcement div. U.S. SEC, L.A., 1983-84; counsel State Farm Ins. Co., L.A., 1984-85, 20th Century Ins. Co., Woodland Hills, Calif., 1985-86; pvt. practice Encino, Calif., 1986—. Lectr. in field. Contbr. articles to profl. jours. Judge pro tem Culver Mcpl. Ct.; charter mem., trustee Rep. Presdl. Task Force, Washington, 1981—; mem. Nat. Rep. Senatorial Com., Washington, 1983—, Rep. Congl. Leadership Coun., Washington, 1987—, Rep. Senatorial Inner Cir., Washington, 1988—. Recipient 1st pl. essay award, VFW, 1976. Mem.: SAG, AFTRA, ATLA, ABA, L.A. Trial Lawyers Assn., Calif. Trial Lawyers Assn., Nat. Thespian Soc., Themis Soc., U.S. Supreme Ct. Hist. Soc. General civil litigation, Entertainment. Fax: 818-990-5812.

HARVEY, MORRIS LANE, lawyer; b. Madisonville, Ky., Apr. 22, 1950; s. Morris Lee and Margie Lou (Wallace) H.; m. Mary Topel; children: Morris Lane Jr., John French, Laura Kathleen. BS, Murray State U., 1972; JD, U. Ky., 1974. Bar: Ill. 1975, U.S. Dist. Ct. (so. dist.) 1979. Assoc. Hanagan & Dousman, Mt. Vernon, Ill., 1975-77; ptnr. Feiger, Quindry, Molt & Harvey and successor firms, Fairfield, Ill., 1977-85; sole practice Fairfield, 1986-97, Mt. Vernon, 1997—. Instr. Frontier C.C., Fairfield, 1977-79; spl. asst. atty. gen. State of Ill., Fairfield, 1977-82; Ill. pres. Woodman of World Life Inst. Soc., 1985-87; mem. nat. fraternal com., 1987-89, nat. legis. com., 1989-93, nat. jud. com., 1993-97. Recipient Outstanding Young Man Am. U.S. Jaycees, 1978, 81, 89. Mem. ABA, Ill. Bar Assn., Assn. Trial Lawyers Am., Ill. Trial Lawyers Assn., Am. Judicature Soc. State civil litigation, Family and matrimonial, Personal injury (including property damage). Home: 5 Webster Hill Est Mount Vernon IL 62864-2346 Office: 2029 Broadway St Mount Vernon IL 62864-2910

HARVEY, PETER C. state attorney general; BA in Polit. Sci., Morgan State U., 1979; JD, Columbia U., 1982. Bar: N.Y. 1984, D.C. 1985, N.J. 1989. Asst. U.S. atty. Dist. N.J., 1986—89; spl. asst. to N.J. Atty. Gen., 1989—90; law clk. for Hon. Dickinson R. Debevoise, Dist. Judge; ptnr. Riker, Danzig, Scherer, Hyland and Perretti LLP, Morristown, NJ; 1st asst. atty. gen., dir. divsn. criminal justice State of N.J., 2002—03, atty. gen., 2003—. Mediator U.S. Dist. Ct., NJ, N.J. Supreme Ct.; mem. lawyers' adv. com. U.S. Dist. Ct. for the Dist. N.J., U.S. Ct. of Appeals (3d cir.). Office: Richard J Hughes Justice Complex PO Box 080 Trenton NJ 08625*

HARVEY, TIMOTHY ROBERT, lawyer; b. Buffalo, N.Y., Feb. 14, 1951; s. Robert Clayton and Eloyce Lacey Harvey; m. Susan Elizabeth Richards, July 12, 1975 (div. 1986); 1 child, Colby M.; m. Deidre L. Mitchell, June 4, 1989. BS, St. Lawrence U., 1974; JD, Ohio No. U., 1979. Bar: N.Y. 1979, U.S. Dist. (we. dist.) N.Y. 1982, Eng. and Wales 2002. Asst. dist. atty. Erie County Dist. Attys. Office, Buffalo, 1979—81; assoc. atty. Moot & Sprague, Buffalo, 1981—88, ptnr., 1988—89; sr. v.p., gen. counsel, sec. Empire of Am. Fed. Savs. Bank, Buffalo, 1989—92; atty. Casey, Sanchez, Amigone & Kelleher, Buffalo, 1992—94; assoc. Watson, Bennett, Colligan, Johnson & Schechter, Buffalo, 1994—96; mgr. legal affairs Columbus McKinnon Corp., Amherst, NY, 1996—. Mem.: Law Soc. Eng. and Wales, Am. Corp.

Counsel Assn. Avocations: hiking, canoeing. Corporate, general, Labor (including EEOC, Fair Labor Standards Act, labor-management relations, NLRB, OSHA), Trademark and copyright. Office: Columbus McKinnon Corp 140 Audubon Pkwy Amherst NY 14228

HARVEY, WILLIAM BRANTLEY, JR., lawyer, former lieutenant governor; b. Walterboro, S.C., Aug. 14, 1930; s. William Brantley and Thelma (Lightsey) H.; m. Helen Coggeshall, Dec. 30, 1952; children: Eileen L., William Brantley, III, Helen C., Margaret D., Warren C. AB in Polit. Sci., The Citadel, 1951, LLD (hon.), 1978; JD magna cum laude, U. S.C., 1955. Bar: S.C. 1955. Since practiced in, Beaufort, S.C.; sr. ptnr. Harvey & Battey; mem. S.C. Ho. of Reps. from Beaufort County, 1958-74, chmn. rules com., mem. constl. revision com.; lt. gov. State of S.C., 1974-78. Bd. dirs., past chmn. Carolina Motor Club (AAA); mem. exec. com. Assoc. Marine Inst., past chmn.; bd. dirs., sec. Beaufort Marine Inst.; past chmn. Beaufort County Transp. Com.; pres. S.C. Bar, 1986—87; mem. S.C. State Bd. for Tech. and Comprehensive Edn.; chmn. AMI Found. Former commr. S.C. Dept. Hwys. and Pub. transp.; former commr., vice chmn. S.C. Parks, Recreation and Tourism Commn.; mem. Coastal Caroline coun. Boy Scouts Am.; pres. Beaufort Indsl. Park, Beaufort County Devel. Corp.; bd. dirs. The Citadel Found., Boys and Girls club of Beaufort; Lowcountry Habitat for Humanity, Mustard Seed Found. Mem. ABA, S.C. Bar Assn., Beaufort County Bar Assn., Rotary, Phi Beta Kappa, Kappa Alpha, Phi Delta Phi, Omicron Delta Kappa. Presbyterian (elder). Administrative and regulatory, Corporate, general, General practice. Home: 501 Pinckney St Beaufort SC 29902-4739 Office: Harvey & Battey Attys PO Box 1107 1001 Craven St Beaufort SC 29902-5577 E-mail: wbharvey@islc.net.

HARVIE, CRAWFORD THOMAS, lawyer; b. N.Y.C., Mar. 28, 1943; s. William Mead and Barbara Adele (Johnson) H.; m. Iris Ruth Alofsin, June 10, 1972; children: Katherine, Edward. AB, Stanford U., 1965; LLB, Yale U., 1968; cert. advanced mgmt. program, Harvard U., 1992. Bar: N.Y. 1969. Assoc. Debevoise & Plimpton, N.Y.C., 1971-75; counsel TRW, Inc., Cleve., 1976-77, sr. counsel, 1978-79, asst. gen. counsel, v.p., 1980-83; v.p. law TRW Automotive, Cleve., 1983-90; v.p., assoc. gen. counsel TRW Inc., 1990-95; sr. v.p., gen. counsel, sec. Goodyear Tire and Rubber Co., Akron, Ohio, 1995—. Trustee Cleve. Inst. of Music, 1989—, Akron Art Mus.; bd. overseers Blossom Music Ctr. Mem. Am. Corp. Counsel Assn., Assn. of Gen. Counsel, Chief Legal Officer Roundtable-U.S. Corporate, general. Home: 6537 Thornbrook Cir Hudson OH 44236-3552 Office: Goodyear Tire and Rubber Co 1144 E Market St Akron OH 44316-0001

HARVIN, DAVID TARLETON, lawyer; b. Houston, Feb. 15, 1945; s. William Charles and Ruth Helen (Beck) H.; m. Sarah Ann Hartman, Apr. 21, 1973; children: Kimberly Kate, William Hartman, John Andrew. BA, Yale U., 1967; JD, U. Tex., 1970. Bar: Tex. 1970, U.S. Dist. Ct. (so. dist.) Tex. 1972, U.S. Dist. Ct. (ea. dist.) Tex. 1977, U.S. Dist. Ct. (no. dist.) Tex. 1979, U.S. Dist. Ct. (we. dist.) Tex. 1988, U.S. Ct. Appeals (5th cir.) 1971, U.S. Supreme Ct. 1977. Law clk. U.S. Ct. Appeals (5th cir.), 1970-71; assoc. Vinson & Elkins L.L.P, Houston, 1971-77, ptnr., 1977—, mgmt. com., 2000—. Trustee Episcopal Theol. Sem. of S.W., 1995-2002, Stehlin Found. for Cancer Rsch., 1986-96, Kinkaid Sch., 1997-2003; vice-chancellor Episcopal Diocese of Tex. Fellow Am. Coll. Trial Lawyers, Tex. Bar Found., Houston Bar Found.; mem. ABA, Houston Country Club, The Downtown Club. Antitrust, Federal civil litigation, State civil litigation. Home: 111 Maple Valley Rd Houston TX 77056-1007 Office: Vinson & Elkins LLP 1001 Fannin St Ste 2300 Houston TX 77002-6706

HARWELL, DAVID WALKER, retired state supreme court chief justice; b. Florence, S.C., Jan. 8, 1932; s. Baxter Hicks and Lacy (Rankin) H.; married; children: Robert Bryan, William Baxter. LL.B., JD, U. S.C., 1958; HHD (hon.), Francis Marion U., 1987. Bar: S.C. 1958, U.S. Dist. Ct. S.C. 1958, U.S. Ct. Appeals 1964, U.S. Supreme Ct. 1961. Circuit judge 12th Jud. Ct. S.C., 1973-80; justice S.C. Supreme Ct., 1980-91, chief justice, 1991-94; ret., 1994; spl. counsel Nelson, Mullins, Riley and Scarborough. Mem. S.C. Ho. of Reps., 1962-73. Served with USNR, 1952-54. Mem. Am. Bar Assn., Am. Trial Lawyers Assn., S.C. Bar Assn., S.C. Trial Lawyers Assn. (Portrait and Scholarship award 1986). Presbyterian. Office: PO Box 2459 Myrtle Beach SC 29578-2459

HARWOOD, ROBERT BERNARD, JR., state supreme court justice; b. Oct. 17, 1939; Student, U. of the South, 1958—59; BS in Commerce and Bus. Adminstrn., U. Ala., 1962, JD, 1963. Spl. asst. atty. gen. State of Ala., 1969—75; dep. city judge City of Tuscaloosa, Ala., 1975—80; cir. judge Tuscaloosa County, 1991—2001; assoc. justice Ala. Supreme Ct., 2001. Lectr. law and trial advocacy U. Ala., 1979—83, 1989—99. Mem. exec. bd. Black Warrior coun. Boy Scouts Am., 1976—, pres., 1993; mem. leadership assn. United Way Tuscaloosa County; mem. Carroll Creek Vol. Fire Dept.; bd. dirs. FOCUS on Sr. Citizens of Tuscaloosa County. Recipient Silver Beaver award, Black Warrior Coun. Boy Scouts Am., 1994. Mem.: Am. Judges Assn., Tuscaloosa County Bar Assn. (pres. 1978—79), Tuscaloosa Inn of Ct. (pres. 1991—92), Ala. Bar Assn., ABA, Tuscaloosa County Cattlemen's Assn., Ala. Cattlemen's Assn., Order of the Coif. Republican. Episcopalian. Office: Ala Supreme Ct 300 Dexter Ave Montgomery AL 36104-3741

HASE, DAVID JOHN, lawyer; b. Milw., Feb. 27, 1940; s. John Henry and Catherine Charlotte (Leekley) H.; m. Penelope Sue Pritchard, Sept. 2, 1964; children: Jeffrey David, Jennifer Anne, John Paul. AB, Dartmouth Coll., 1962; LLB, U. Wis., 1965. Bar: Wis. 1965, U.S. Dist. Ct. (ea. dist.) Wis. 1965, U.S. Ct. Appeals (7th cir.) 1971, U.S. Ct. Appeals (D.C. cir.) 1975, U.S. Ct. Appeals (9th cir.) 1989, U.S. Supreme Ct. 1975. Assoc. Grootemaat, Cook & Franke, Milw., 1965-67, ptnr., shareholder, 1968-70; shareholder Cook & Franke S.C., Milw., 1970-73; legal counsel to gov. Wis., Madison, 1973-74; dep. atty. gen. State of Wis., Madison, 1974-76; assoc. Foley & Lardner, Milw., 1976-77, ptnr., 1977-94; shareholder Cook & Franke S.C., Milw., 1994—. Mem. Sch. Bd., Mequon, Wis., 1971-94, treas., 1973-75, pres., 1975-94. Mem. ABA. Democrat. Administrative and regulatory, General civil litigation, Securities. Home: 2108 W Raleigh Ct Mequon WI 53092-5416 Office: Cook & Franke SC 660 E Mason St Ste 401 Milwaukee WI 53202-3877 E-mail: hase@cf-law.com.

HASELTON, RICK THOMAS, lawyer; b. Albany, Oreg., Nov. 5, 1953; s. Shirley (Schantz) H. AB, Stanford U., 1976; JD, Yale U., 1979. Chair Oreg. State Bd. Bar Examiners, 1988-89, bd. dirs., 1986-88; mem. adv. com. on rules of practice 9th Cir. Ct., 1991-93. Law clk. U.S. Ct. Appeals (9th cir.) Oreg., Portland, 1979-80; from assoc. to ptnr. Lindsay, Hart, Neil & Weigler, Portland, 1979-93; sole practice Portland, 1993-94; assoc. judge Oreg. Ct. Appeals, Salem, 1994—. Chair Multnomah County Legal Aid, Portland, 1985-86, bd. dirs., 1982-87. Mem. ABA, Oreg. Bar Assn., ACLU (cooperating atty. 1982-94), Phi Beta Kappa. Jewish. Federal civil litigation, State civil litigation. Office: 300 Justice Blvd Salem OR 97310-0001

HASENAUER, JUDITH ANNE, lawyer; b. Rochester, N.Y., Sept. 28, 1946; d. William F. and Arline (Burns) H. AA, Monroe C.C., 1966; AB, U. Rochester, 1969; JD, Golden Gate U., 1973; CLU, Am. Coll., 1974. Bar: Calif. 1974, Conn. 1974, U.S. Dist. Ct. Conn. 1975, N.Y. 1983, D.C. 1983, Fla. 1993. Ptnr. Blazzard, Grodd & Hasenauer P.C., Westport, Conn., 1974—. Chmn. regulatory affairs com. Nat. Assn. for Variable Annuities, 1997—. Contbr. articles to profl. jours. Bd. dirs. Friends of Norwalk C.C., Conn., 1977-83; sec. Fairfield County CLUs, Conn., 1983-85. Insurance, Securities. Office: Blazzard Grodd & Hasenauer PC 1600 S Federal Hwy Ste 500 Pompano Beach FL 33062 E-mail: judith.hasenauer@BGHPC.com.

HASHIDATE, KENJI, lawyer; b. Chiba, Japan, June 22, 1947; BA, Waseda U., Tokyo, 1971; LLM, U. Wash., 1975; postgrad., Columbia U., 1975—76. Bar: Japan 1973. Assoc. Deveboise Plimpton Lyons & Gates, N.Y.C., 1976, Sullivan & Cromwell, N.Y.C., 1976—77, Coward Chance, London, 1977; mng. ptnr. Hashidate Law Office, Tokyo, 1980—. Author: Financing Corporations with Convertible Debentures in U.S.A., 1976, Regulation of Foreign Banking in the U.S.A., 1978; contbr. articles to profl. jours. Mem.: ABA (assoc.), First Tokyo Bar Assn. (exec. v.p.), Japan Fedn. Bar Assn. Avocations: golf, opera, playing bamboo flute. Finance, Intellectual property, Mergers and acquisitions. Office: Hashidate Law Office Imperila Hotel Tower 7th Fl 1-1 Uchisaiwaicho 1 chome Chiyoda-ku Tokyo 100-0011 Japan

HASHIZUME, KEVIN, lawyer; b. Van Nuys, Calif., July 21, 1971; s. John and Jacque Hashizume. BA, UCLA, 1994; JD, U. Iowa, 1999. Bar: Oreg. Atty. Morris & Olson, The Dalles, Oreg., 1999—2000, Van Valkenburgh & Hashizume, 2000—. V.p. The Dalles Art Ctr., 2002—03. Mem.: ABA, Oreg. Minority Lawyers, Oreg. State Bar Assn., Kiwanis. Republican. Criminal, Family and matrimonial, Juvenile. Home: 1411 15th St Hood River OR 97031 Office: 204 E 4th St The Dalles OR 97058 Fax: 541-296-4654. E-mail: hashizume@gorge.net.

HASKEL, JULES J. lawyer; b. Bklyn., Sept. 9, 1929; s. Manny and Sadie Haskel; m. Arlene Teitelbaum, Apr. 19, 1957; children: Lynn S. Haskel Lancaster, Barbara I. Haskel Weiner, Carol Haskel Solomon. BS in Journalism, Medill Sch. Journalism, Northwestern U., 1951; JD, NYU, 1954. Bar: N.Y. 1955, U.S. Dist. Ct. (so. and ea. dists.) N.Y. 1957, U.S. Tax Ct. 1958, U.S. Ct. Appeals (2d cir.) 1981, U.S. Supreme Ct. 1962. Assoc. Grossman & Grossman, N.Y.C., 1954-55; exec. dir. membership campaign ABA, N.Y.C., 1955-56; assoc. Otterbourg, Steindler, Houston & Rosen, N.Y.C., 1956-57, Newman & Bisco, N.Y.C., 1957-59; ptnr. Koopersmith & Haskel, Jamaica, N.Y., 1960-77, Durben & Haskel, Garden City, N.Y., 1977-87, Haskel, Hand & Lancaster, 1988-96, Jaspan Schlessinger Hoffman LLP, 1996—. Mem. surrogate's ct. adv. com. N.Y. State Office of Ct. Adminstrn., 1995—. Mem. law com. UJA-Fedn. Jewish Philanthropies of N.Y., 1978—; bd. dirs. Queens Legal Svcs. Corp., 1970-73. Fellow Am. Coll. Trust and Estates Counsel (fiduciary litig. com. 1994-2002); mem. ABA, N.Y. State Bar Assn. (ho. of dels. 1975-92, chmn. trusts and estates law sect. 1982, v.p. 1984-86, exec. com. 1986-89, chair action unit 4 jud. selection and ct. merger 1990-93), N.Y. State Bar Found. (bd. dirs. 1986-2002), Queens County Bar Assn. (pres. 1973-74, chmn. jud. com. 1978-79, editor bar bull. 1964-66), Jamaica Lawyers Club (pres. 1968-69), Nassau County Bar Assn., NYU Law Alumni Assn. (v.p. 1970-73, 77-81). Jewish. Estate planning, Probate (including wills, trusts), Estate taxation. Office: Jaspan Schlessinger Hoffman LLP 300 Garden City Plz Garden City NY 11530-3302

HASKELL, DONALD MCMILLAN, lawyer; b. Toledo, July 2, 1932; s. Irwin Wales and Grace (Lee) H.; m. Carol Jean Ross, June 19, 1954; children: Deborah Lee, Catherine Jean, David Ross. BA, Coll. of Wooster, 1954; JD, U. Mich., 1957. Bar: Ill. 1957, U.S. Dist. Ct. (no. dist.) Ill. 1958, U.S. Ct. Appeals (7th cir.) 1960, U.S. Supreme Ct. 1963, U.S. Ct. Appeals (10th cir.) 1974, Oreg. 1990. Ptnr. McKenna, Storer, Rowe, White & Haskell and predecessors, Chgo., 1957-75; sr. ptnr. Haskell & Perrin, Chgo., 1975-89, of counsel, 1989-2000. Commr. Clatsop County, Oreg., 1991-94; bd. dirs. N.W. Oreg. Econ. Alliance, 1993-98. Trustee Columbia River Maritime Mus., 1991—; chmn. Clatsop County Rep. Com., 1994-95; mem. Astoria Planning Commn., 1999-2002, chmn., 2001-02. Fellow Am. Bar Found., Ill. Bar Found.; mem. ABA (ho. of dels. 1982-92, bd. govs. 1987-90), Lawyers Club Chgo., Astoria Country Club. Lutheran. Home: 600 W Lexington Ave Astoria OR 97103-5726 Office: Wecoma Ptnrs Ltd PO Box 777 100 16th St Astoria OR 97103-3634

HASKELL, WYATT RUSHTON, lawyer; b. Birmingham, Ala., May 15, 1940; s. Preston Hampton and Mary Wyatt (Rushton) H.; m. Susan Porter Nabers, June 1, 1968; children: John Howze, Henry Devereux, Samuel Drayton. AB, Amherst Coll., 1961; LLB, Yale U., 1965. Bar: Ala. 1965. Assoc. Bradley, Arant, Rose & White, Birmingham, 1966-71; staff atty. So. Natural Gas Co., Birmingham, 1971-73; ptnr. Haskell, Slaughter, Young & Rediken, LLC, Birmingham, 1973—. Vis. rsch. asst. U. Muenster, Germany, 1965—66; vis. prof. U. Ala. Law Sch., 1970—73; bd. dirs. Bio Horizons Implant Systems, Inc. Contbr. articles to profl. jours. Bd. dirs. Ala. Shakespeare Fest, Montgomery, Folger Shakespeare Libr., Washington. Thomas Pope fellow Trinity Coll., Oxford. Mem. ABA, Ala. Bar Assn., Birmingham Bar Assn., Mountain Brook Club. Presbyterian. Municipal (including bonds). Home: 2964 Cherokee Rd Birmingham AL 35223-2609 Office: Haskell Slaughter et al 1400 Park Place Tower 2001 Park Place North Birmingham AL 35203 E-mail: wrh@hsy.com.

HASKIN, J. MICHAEL, lawyer; b. Kansas City, Mo., Sept. 25, 1949; s. Harley V. and Geraldine E. (Porterfield) H.; m. Pamela J. Lutz, May 22, 1999. BA, Baker U., 1971; JD, U. Mo., 1976. Bar: Kans. 1976, Mo. 1987, U.S. Fed. Tax Ct., U.S. Supreme Ct. Ptnr., atty. Haskin, Hinkle, Slater & Snowbarger, Olathe, Kans., 1976-83, Dietrich, Davis, Dicus, Rowlands, Schmitt & Gorman, Kansas City, Mo., 1984-88; pres., atty. J. Michael Haskin, PA, Olathe, 1989—. Bd. dirs., exec. com., The Assn. K-10 Corridor Devel., Inc., Lawrence, 1993-95. City councilman-at-large City of Olathe, 1989-93, mayor, 1993-95; mem., vice chmn., chmn. Stormwater Mgmt. Adv. Coun., Johnson County, Kans., 1989-95; bd. dirs. Olathe Pub. Libr., 1989-90, 93-95; bd. dirs. Hidden Glen Arts Festival, vice chmn., chmn., 1990—); mem. Mid-Am. Regional Coun. Perimeter Transp. Com., 1995—. Recipient Boss of Yr. award Johnson County Legal Secs. Assn., 1991-92, Cmty. Leadership award Olathe Area C. of C., 1992. Mem. Kans. Bar Assn., Mo. Bar Assn., Olathe Rotary Club (bd. dirs., pres. 1981—, Paul Harris award 1992, Olathe Rotarian of Yr. 1995), Olathe Arts Alliance (pres. 1988), Kaw Valley Philological Soc. Republican. Methodist. Avocations: golfing, sailing. Estate planning, Probate (including wills, trusts), Property, real (including real estate development, water). Office: PO Box 413 100 E Park St Ste 203 Olathe KS 66061-3463 E-mail: haskinlawoffice@aol.com.

HASKINS, CHARLES GREGORY, JR., lawyer; b. Chgo., Jan. 27, 1951; s. Charles G. and Ellen Barbara (Essman) H.; m. Gail Beaubien Ferbend, June 14, 1987; 1 child, Charles Robert. BA, U. Ill., 1972; JD, John Marshall Law Sch., 1976. Bar: Ill. 1976, U.S. Dist. Ct. (no. dist.) Ill. 1976. Assoc. George J. Cullen, Ltd., Chgo., 1976-82; shareholder George J. Cullen & Assoc., Ltd., Chgo., 1982-89, Cullen, Haskins, Nicholson & Menchetti, Chgo., 1989—. Mem.: ATLA, Workplace Injury Litigation Group (bd. dirs. 1997—2001, sec. 2001—02), Chgo. Bar Assn. (chmn. indsl. commn. com. 1987—88), Ill. Trial Lawyers Assn. (bd. mgrs. 1989—, co-chmn. workers compensation com. 1991—2001, co-editor Case Notebook 1992—, treas. 1997), Ill. Bar Assn., Workers Compensation Lawyers Assn. (bd. dirs. 1986—96, pres. 1989). Democrat. Roman Catholic. Avocations: golf, water skiing, snow skiing. Workers' compensation. Office: Cullen Haskins Nicholson & Menchetti 35 E Wacker Dr Ste 1760 Chicago IL 60601-2271

HASSELL, LEROY ROUNTREE, SR., state supreme court chief justice; b. Aug. 17, 1955; BA in Govt. and Fgn. Affairs, U. Va., 1977; JD, Harvard U., 1980. Bar: Va. Former ptnr. McGuire, Woods, Battle and Boothe; now justice Supreme Ct. of Va. Former mem. Va. gen. assembly task force to study violence on sch. property. Former mem. adv. bd. Massey Cancer Ctr.; mem. policy com., former chmn. Richmond Sch. Bd., ; former bd. dirs. Richmond Renaissance, Inc., Richmond chpt. ARC, Garfield childs Fund, Carpenter Ctr. for Performing Arts, St. John's Hosp., Legal Aid Ctrl. Va.; vol. Richmond Pub. Schs., Hospice vol.; elected sch. bd. chmn. 4 terms. Recipient Liberty Bell award 1985, 86, Black Achievers award, 1985-86, Outstanding Young Citizen award Richmond Jaycees, 1987, Outstanding Young Virginian award Va. Jaycees, 1987; one of youngest persons to both serve on the Richmond Sch. Bd. and to serve as bd. chmn. Mem. Va. Trial Lawyers Assn., Assn. Trial Lawyers Am., Va. Assn. Def. Attys., Old Dominion Bar Assn., Va. Bar Assn. Office: Supreme Ct of Virginia PO Box 1315 Richmond VA 23218-1315

HASSELMAN, ALLEN JOSEPH, lawyer; b. Ridgway, Pa., Mar. 8, 1934; s. Joseph John Hasselman and Florence Ann Pfingstler. BA, St. Bonaventure U., 1955; JD, Gerogetown U., 1961; MA, Cath. U. Am., 1978. Bar: Pa. 91, D.C. 92, Colo. 95. Rsch. asst. SIPC, Washington, 1972—79; fin. staff asst. NRCC, Washington, 1979—85; libr. Libr. of Congress, Washington, 1987—90, D.C. Office Health Plan, Washington, 1993—94; law libr. U.S. Dept. HUD, Washington, 1990—91, USEC, Bethesda, Md., 1995—97; law specialist Dept. Justice/FBI, Washington, 1999—. With U.S. Army, 1955—57. Scholar, Cath. U. Am., 1977. Mem.: ABA, Am. Assn. Law Librs., Pa. Bar Assn. Democrat. Roman Catholic. Avocations: travel, music, photography. Home: 1630 R St NW Apt 729 Washington DC 20009-6429 Office: Dept Justice 1325 G St NW Washington DC 20005

HASSETT, JOSEPH MARK, lawyer; b. Buffalo, May 1, 1943; m. Carol A. Melton, June 23, 1984; children: Matthew, Meredith. BA summa cum laude, Canisius Coll., 1964; LL.B. cum laude, Harvard U., 1967; MA with 1st class honors, Univ. Coll. Dublin, 1981, PhD, 1985. Bar: N.Y. 1967, D.C. 1970, U.S. Supreme Ct. 1976. Assoc. Hogan & Hartson, Washington, 1970-74, ptnr., 1974—. Bd. trustees Canisius Coll. Author: Yeats and the Poetics of Hate, 1986; contbr. articles to profl. publs. Mem. ABA, D.C. Bar Assn. Federal civil litigation, General civil litigation, State civil litigation. Home: 6035 Crimson Ct Mc Lean VA 22101-1818 Office: 555 13th St NW Washington DC 20004-1109

HASSETT, TIMOTHY JOHN, lawyer; b. Fairmont, Minn., Jan. 26, 1954; BA cum laude, Coll. St. Thomas (name now U. St. Thomas), St. Paul, 1976; JD cum laude, William Mitchell Coll. Law, 1981. Bar: Minn. 1981, U.S. Dist. Ct. Minn. 1982, U.S. Ct. Appeals (8th cir.) 1984, U.S. Tax Ct. 1985. Atty., shareholder Peterson, Fram & Bergmann, P.A., St. Paul, 1981-96, Felhaber, Larson, Fenlon & Vogt, P.A., St. Paul, 1996—. Instr. Minn. CLE, Builders Assn. Twin Cities, 1991—. Contbr. articles to profl. jours. Mem. Minn. State Bar Assn. (mem. legis. com. 1990-94, mem. real property coun. 1994—, bus. law sect., probate and estate law sect., instr. 1990—, sec. 2002-03), Ramsey County Bar Assn. (chmn. real property sect. 1988, co-chmn. 2002). Avocations: coaching, sports. Construction, Corporate, general, Property, real (including real estate development, water). Office: Felhaber Larson Fenlon and Vogt 2100 Minn World Trade Ctr 30 7th St E Saint Paul MN 55101-4901 E-mail: thassett@felhaber.com.

HASTIE, JOHN DOUGLAS, lawyer; b. Guthrie, Okla., Dec. 9, 1939; BA, U. Okla., 1961, LLB, 1964. Bar: Okla. 1964. Atty. Hastie and Kirschner, Oklahoma City, 1974-96, Andrews Davis Legg Bixler Milsten and Price, Oklahoma City, 1996-2001, Phillips McFall McCaffrey McVay & Murrah, P.C., Oklahoma City, 2001—. Adj. prof. U. Okla. Coll. Law, 1982—90, 2000—02; cons., lectr. in field. Contbr. articles to profl. jours. Capt. U.S. Army, 1964-66. Mem. ABA, Okla. Bar Assn., Cleve. County Bar Assn., Assn. of Bar of City of N.Y., Am. Coll. Real Estate Lawyers (gov. 1990-2000, exec. com. 1992-2000, pres. 1999, Frederick S. Lane award 2002), Anglo-Am. Real Property Inst., Am. Law Inst., Am. Coll. Mortgage Attys., Internat. Bar Assn. Banking, Commercial, contracts (including sales of goods; commercial financing), Property, real (including real estate development, water). Home: 914 Living Springs Trail Washington OK 73093 Office: Phillips McFall McCaffrey McVay & Murrah 401 W Main St Ste 444 Norman OK 73069-1319 E-mail: jdhastie@hastielaw.com.

HASTINGS, DOUGLAS ALFRED, lawyer; b. Oak Park, Ill., July 28, 1949; s. Douglas A. and Elaine M. (Schramm) H.; m. Virginia Joslin, May 28, 1982; children: Corey, Douglas. BA, Duke U., 1971; MPA, Memphis State U., 1977; JD, U. Va., 1981. Bar: D.C. 1981. Assoc. dir. Inst. for Govt. Studies, Memphis State U., 1976-77; adminstrv. intern Fed. Exec. Inst., Charlottesville, Va., 1977-78; project coord. Assn. Acad. Health Ctrs., Charlottesville, 1978-80; cons. Shenandoah PSRO, Charlottesville, 1980-81; ptnr. Epstein Becker & Green, Washington, 1981—. Vis. lectr. dept. health adminstrn. Duke U., Durham, N.C., 1985-90. Contbr. articles to profl. jours. Mem. ABA, Washington Coun. Lawyers, Am. Health Lawyers Assn. (bd. dirs. 1991—, pres. 2001-02), Inst. of Med. (bd. health svs. 2001—), Order of Coif, Phi Beta Kappa. Democrat. Unitarian Universalist. Avocations: baseball, tennis, basketball. Administrative and regulatory, Corporate, general, Health. Home: 5301 Burke Dr Alexandria VA 22309-3310 Office: Epstein Becker & Green 1227 25th St NW Fl 7 Washington DC 20037-1156

HASTINGS, EDWIN H(AMILTON), lawyer; b. Yonkers, N.Y., Jan. 2, 1917; s. Edwin H. Jr. and Emily (Clark) H.; m. Mabel Hurst, July 12, 1941 (div. June 1957); children: Judy H. Hastings Johnson, Jill S. Hastings Cane; m. Suzanne Saul, July 1, 1957; 1 child, Andrew C. AB, Amherst Coll., 1938; LLB, Columbia U., 1941. Bar: N.Y. 1941, R.I. 1946, U.S. Dist. Ct. R.I. 1947, U.S. Ct. Appeals (1st cir.) 1950, Mass. 1951. Assoc. Larkin, Rathbone & Perry, N.Y.C., 1941-42, Tillinghast, Collins & Tanner, Providence, 1946-53; ptnr. Tillinghast Collins & Graham, Providence, 1953-96, Tillinghast Licht Perkins Smith & Cohen, Providence, 1996—, cons. ptnr. estate planning and adminstrn. Bar examiner State of R.I., 1968-74, chmn. of bd., 1972-74; chmn. com. on future of criminal law R.I. Supreme Ct., 1973-75; bar examiner U.S. Dist. Ct. R.I., 1981-84. 1st lt. U.S. Army, 1942-46, 51-52, Korea. Mem. ABA, R.I. Bar Assn., Lawyers Alliance World Security. Baptist. Avocation: bird watching. Estate planning, Probate (including wills, trusts). Home: 210 Payton Ave Warwick RI 02889-5133 Office: Tillinghast Licht Perkins Smith & Cohen 10 Weybosset St Providence RI 02903-2818 E-mail: ehastings@tlslaw.com.

HASTINGS, WILLIAM CHARLES, retired state supreme court chief justice; b. Newman Grove, Nebr., Jan. 31, 1921; s. William C. and Margaret (Hansen) H.; m. Julie Ann Simonson, Dec. 29, 1946; children— Pamela, Charles, Steven. B.Sc., U. Nebr., 1942, JD, 1948; LHD (hon.), Hastings Coll., 1991. Bar: Nebr. 1948. With FBI, 1942-43; mem. firm Chambers, Holland, Dudgeon & Hastings, Lincoln, 1948-65; judge 3d jud. dist. Nebr., Lincoln, 1965-79, Supreme Ct. Nebr., Lincoln, 1979-88, chief justice, 1988-95; ret., 1995. Bd. dirs. Nat. Conf. Chief Justices, 1989-91. Pres. Child Guidance Ctr., Lincoln, 1962, 63; v.p. Lincoln Community Coun., 1968, 69; vice chmn. Antelope Valley coun. Boy Scouts Am., 1968, 69; pres. 1st Presbyn. Ch. Found., 1968—; mem. Lincoln Parks and Recreation Adv. Bd., Govs. task force correctional dept. medical svcs., 2000; mem. Nebr. Pub. Employees Retirement Bd. Served with AUS, 1943-46. Named to Nebr. Jaycee Hall of Fame, 1998. Mem. ABA, Nebr. Bar Assn. (George H. Turner award 1991, Pioneer award 1992), Am. Jud. Soc., Lincoln Bar Assn., Nebr. Dist. Judges Assn. (past pres.), Nat. Conf. Chief Justices (past bd. dirs.), Am. Judicature Soc. (Herbert Harley award 1997), Phi Delta Phi. Republican. Presbyterian (deacon, elder, trustee). Club: East Hills Country (pres. 1959-60). Home: 1544 S 58th St Lincoln NE 68506-1407

HASTINGS, WILMOT REED, lawyer, writer; b. Salem, Mass., May 29, 1935; s. Abner Horace and Florence (Hylan) H.; m. Joan Amory Loomis, Aug. 30, 1958; children: W. Reed, Jr., Melissa H., Claire A. AB magna cum laude, Harvard U., 1957, LL.B. magna cum laude, 1961; postgrad., U. Paris, 1957-58. Bar: Mass. 1961. Law clk. Chief Justice Raymond S. Wilkins, Boston, 1961-62; assoc. firm Bingham, Dana & Gould, Boston, 1962-68; 1st asst. and dep. atty. gen. Mass., 1968-69; spl. asst. and exec. asst. to undersec. state, 1969-70; gen. counsel HEW, 1970-73; ptnr. Bingham, Dana & Gould (now Bingham McCutchen), Boston and London, 1973-90; writer, 1990—. Home and Office: 45 Ward Ave Northampton MA 01060

HATCH, HAZEN VAN DEN BERG, lawyer; b. Battle Creek, Mich., Jan. 18, 1932; s. Hazen Jesse and Clare Janet (van den Berg) H.; m. Mary Lou Holmes, Dec. 27, 1955; children: Mary, David. BA, Dartmouth Coll., 1953; JD, U. Mich., 1956. Bar: Mich. 1956, U.S. Supreme Ct. 1959. Ptnr. various firms, Marshall, Mich., 1960-81, Hatch & Smith, Kalamazoo, Mich., 1981-93, Butler Durham & Toweson, Kalamazoo, Mich., 1993—. Contbr. articles to profl. jours. Del. Mich. Constitutional Conv., Lansing, 1961-62; trustee Marshall Sch. Bd., 1971-72. Lt. USAR, 1957-60. Recipient citation Mich. State Bar Assn., 1962. Fellow Mich. State Bar Found., Am. Coll. Trial Lawyers; mem. ABA, Kalamazoo County Bar Assn. Republican. Episcopalian. Avocation: golf. General civil litigation, Estate planning, Personal injury (including property damage). Office: Butler Durham & Toweson 202 N Riverview Dr Kalamazoo MI 49004-1310

HATCH, JOHN D. lawyer; b. Atlanta, Aug. 26, 1942; s. Ernest Healey and Charlotte Blanchard (Chazal) H.; m. Pamela Faye Carr, June 13, 1964; children: Wendy H. Duncan, A. Candice Hatch, Teresa H. Caraker. AA, Ctrl. Fla. Jr. Coll., Ocala, 1962; BS, Fla. State U., 1964; JD, Georgetown U., 1971. Bar: Fla. 1971, Conn. 1972, Tex. 1992, U.S. Dist. Ct. Conn. 1973, U.S. Dist. Ct. (no. dist.) Tex. 1992, U.S. Tax Ct. 1979, U.S. Supreme Ct. 1979; gen. securities lic., gen. prin. lic. Lt. USNR, 1964-71; atty. AEtna Life & Casualty, Hartford, Conn., 1971-74, counsel, 1974-83; v.p. and gen. counsel Continental Corp., N.Y.C., 1983-85; v.p. spl. ops. Comml. Life Ins. Co., Piscataway, N.J., 1985-87; v.p. and gen. counsel Associated Madison Cos., Inc., N.Y.C., 1987-88; sr. v.p. Resource Deployment, Inc., N.Y.C. and Ft. Worth, 1988-91; pres. Ins. Horizons, Inc., Ocala, Fla., 1992—, John D. Hatch, P.C., Ocala, 1992—. Gen. counsel Am. Health & Life Ins. Co., Ft. Worth, 1995—; bd. dirs. Pub. Svc. Mut. Ins. Co., N.Y.C., London and Midland Gen. Ins. Co., London, Ont. Mem. ABA (chmn. TIPS employee benefits com. 1983-84, TIPS fin. svcs. com. 1992-93), Assn. Life Ins. Counsel, Fed. Bar Assn., Internat. Assn. Ins. Law. Republican. Roman Catholic. Avocations: reading, boating, tennis. Commercial, consumer (including collections, credit), Corporate, general, Insurance. Home and Office: 840 SE 5th St Ocala FL 34471-2306

HATCH, MIKE, state attorney general; m. Patti Hatch; 3 children. BS in Polit. Sci. with honors, U. Minn., Duluth, 1970; JD, U. Minn., 1973. Commr. of commerce State of. Minn., 1983—89; pvt. practice law; atty. gen. State of Minn., 1999—. Democrat. Office: Minn Atty Gen's Office 1400 NCL Tower 445 Minnesota St Saint Paul MN 55101*

HATCHER, MICHAEL ROBERT, lawyer; b. Gloucester, Mass., July 3, 1962; s. Robert Arthur and Maureen (Conant) H.; m. Elizabeth Roche, Aug. 26, 1989. AB, Dartmouth Coll., Hanover, N.H., 1984; JD, Georgetown U., Washington, 1987. Bar: Mass. 1987, D.C. 1989, U.S. Dist Ct. D.C. 1989, U.S. Ct. Appeals (fed. cir.) 1990, U.S. Ct. Appeals (D.C. cir.) 1991, Md. 1994. Assoc. Israel & Raley Chartered, Washington, 1987-93; gen. counsel Koba Assocs., Inc./Koba Inst., Inc., 1994; assoc. Shaw, Pittman, Potts & Trowbridge, Washington, 1994-98, counsel, 1998—99, ptnr., 2000, Holland & Knight LLP, Washington, 2000—. Dep. gen. counsel Nat. Coalition Minority Bus., 1994—. Mem. ABA (vice-chair small bus. com. pub. contract law sect. 1996—), D.C. Bar Assn. Corporate, general, Government contracts and claims, Legislative. Office: Holland & Knight LLP 2099 Pennsylvania Ave NW Washington DC 20006

HATFIELD, JACK KENTON, lawyer, accountant; b. Medford, Okla., Jan. 26, 1922; s. Loate L. and Cora (Walsh) H.; m. D. Ann Keltner, Dec. 5, 1943 (dec. Sept. 1988); children: Susan Kathryn Hatfield Bechtold, Sally Ann Hatfield Clark; m. K. Dean Walker, Aug. 7, 1997; m. Dores Hamaker, Aug. 9, 2000. BS in BA, Phillips U., Enid, Okla., 1947; BA, Phillips U., 1953; LLB, Oklahoma City U., 1954, JD, 1967. Bar: U.S. Dist. Ct. (we. dist.) Okla. 1954, U.S. Supreme Ct. 1961, U.S. Dist. Ct. (no. dist.) Okla. 1967, U.S. Ct. Appeals (10th cir.) 1968; CPA 1954. Pvt. practice, Enid, Okla., 1954-58; with Dept. Interior, Tulsa, 1958-77; pvt. practice, Tulsa, 1977—. Mem. ABA, Okla. Bar Assn., Tulsa Co. Bar Assn., Am. Inst. CPA's, Okla. Soc. CPA's. Clubs: Petroleum. Avocations: photography, tennis. Estate planning, Probate (including wills, trusts), Personal income taxation. Home: 4013 E 86th St Tulsa OK 74137-2609 Office: 7060 S Yale Ave Ste 601 Tulsa OK 74136-5739

HATHAWAY, GARY RAY, lawyer; b. Liberal, Kans., July 5, 1942; s. Addison E. And Helen M. (Nix) H.; m. Sonja J. Brewer, Aug. 6, 1977. BA, Southwestern Coll., Winfield, Kans., 1964; JD, Washburn U., 1969. Bar: Kans. 1969, U.S. Dist. Ct. Kans. 1969, U.S. Ct. Appeals (10th cir.) 1979, U.S. Supreme Ct. 1978. County atty. Grant County, Ulysses, Kans., 1971-72, 80-84; ptnr. Hathaway, Kimball and Campbell, Ulysses, Kans., 1984-2000; pvt. practice Ulysses, Kans., 2000—. City atty. City of Ulysses, 1972-76. Mem. N.Am. Elk Breeders Assn., Am. Legion, Elks, Kiwanis, Phi Alpha Delta. Republican. Oil, gas, and mineral, General practice, Probate (including wills, trusts). Home: 218 N Wilson St Ulysses KS 67880-1950 Office: Law Office PO Box 27 Ulysses KS 67880-0527

HATHCOCK, J. ANDREW, judge; b. Syracuse, N.Y., Jan. 19, 1959; s. James S. and Margaret B. Hathcock; m. Valinda Bolton, Oct. 18, 2001; 1 child, Marshall Stewart. JD, U. Tex. Austin, 1984; BA magna cum laude, Rice U., 1981. Cert.: Tex. Supreme Ct. 1985, Cert. Spl. Competence in Family Law: Tex. Bd. of Legal Specialization 1990. Assoc. judge Child Protection Ct. of Ctrl. Tex., New Braunfels, Tex., 2000—; lectr., dir. U. of Tex. Sch. of Law, Austin, Tex., 1989—2000. Office: Child Protection Court of Central Texas 150 N Seguin Ave Ste 317 New Braunfels TX 78130

HATTERVIG, KAREN ANN, lawyer; b. Mitchell, S.D., Oct. 13, 1948; d. Gordon E. and Emma Sophia Larson; m. Jack A. Hattervig, Dec. 20, 1967 (div. Aug. 1973); children: Kimberly A., Thorpe-Jeffrey M. AA, BS, U. S.D., 1977, JD, 1981. Bar: S.D. 1981, U.S. Dist. Ct. (so. dist.) 1981, U.S. Ct. Appeals (8th cir.) 1981. Assoc. Strange, Strange & Palmer, Sioux Falls, S.D., 1981-82; supervising atty. East River Legal Svcs., Sioux Falls, S.D., 1982—. Active Minnehaha County Family Violence Task Force, Sioux Falls, 1982—, chair, 1994-99; chair S.D. Advocacy Network for Women, Sioux Falls, 1995—; active Wheels to Work Com., Sioux Falls, 1997—; treas. S.D. Coalition for Children, Sioux Falls, 1992-2001; chair Cmty. Outreach, Inc., Sioux Falls, 1994-2001. Named Friend of Social Work NASW. Mem.: So. Bar Assn. (chair family law com.). Democrat. Lutheran. Civil rights, Family and matrimonial, Government contracts and claims. Office: East River Legal Svcs 335 N Main Ave Ste 300 Sioux Falls SD 57104-6038 E-mail: e02@erlservices.com.

HAUBOLD, SAMUEL ALLEN, lawyer; b. Watertown, S.D., July 29, 1938; s. Gustuv Herman and Leone Marjorie (York) H.; m. Caroline V. Thompson. Sept. 27, 1969; 1 child, Caroline A. BS in Engring., Northwestern U.; JD, Harvard U. Bar: Ill. 1966, N.Y. 1990, U.S. Dist. Ct. (no. dist.) Ill. 1966, U.S. Ct. Appeals (7th cir.) 1970, U.S. Ct. Appeals (9th cir.) 1979, U.S. Supreme Ct. 1974. Assoc. Kirkland & Ellis, Chgo., 1966, ptnr., 1972—; resident ptnr. Kirkland & Ellis Internat., London, 1994—. Served to lt. USN, 1960-63. Mem. ABA, Ill. Bar Assn., Internat. Bar Assn., Mid-Am. Club, Saddle and Cycle Club (Chgo.), The Hurlingham Club (London), City of London Club. Presbyterian. Antitrust, Federal civil litigation, Nuclear power. Home: 40 S Eaton Pl London SW1W 9JJ England Office: Kirkland & Ellis Internat Old Broad St London EC2N 1HQ England

HAUCH, JEANNE MARIE, prosecutor; b. Camden, N.J., May 10, 1963; d. John P. and Elizabeth J. Hauch; m. R. Emmett Tyrell, Jr.. BA, Princeton U., 1985; JD, Yale U., 1988. Bar: N.Y. 1989, D.C. 1991. Law clk., Hon. Ralph Winter U.S. Ct. Appeals, 2d cir., 1988—89; law clk., Hon. Anthony M. Kennedy U.S. Supreme Ct., Washington, 1989—90; assoc. Gibson Dunn & Crutcher, Brussels and Washington, 1990—93; Fulbright scholar U. Paris, Sorbonne, 1992—93; assoc. Kellogg Huber & Hansen, Washington, 1993—95; asst. U.S. atty. U.S. Atty.'s Office, Washington, 1995—. Contbr. articles to law jours. and revs. Avocations: travel, cooking, sailing, skiing. Office: US Attys Office 555 Fourth St NW Washington DC 20530

HAUER, JAMES ALBERT, lawyer; b. Fond du Lac, Wis., Apr. 3, 1924; s. Albert A. and Hazel M. (Corcoran) H.; children: Stephen, John, Paul, Christopher, Patrick. BCE, Marquette U., 1948, LLB, 1949; bank mgmt. cert., Columbia U., 1957, U. Wis., 1959. Bar: Wis., U.S. Dist. Ct. (ea. dist.), U.S. Ct. Appeals (9th cir.), U.S. Dist. Ct. (fed. dist.) 1958. Patent counsel Ira Milton Jones, Milw., 1949; chief counsel Wauwatosa Realty, Milw., 1950-57; v.p. Wauwatosa (Wis.) State Bank, 1957-67; pres. Milw. We. Bank, 1967-69, Prem Constrn. Co., Milw., 1969-73; pvt. practice Elm Grove, Wis., 1973-86, Sun City, Ariz., 1986—. Pres., bd. dirs. Sunshine Svc., Sun City, Meals on Wheels, Sun City. With USMCR, 1942-45. Mem. Wis. Bar Assn., Ariz. Patent Law Assn. (charter). Land use and zoning (including planning), Patent, Property, real (including real estate development, water). Office: 9915 W Royal Oak Rd #1098 Sun City AZ 85351-3161

HAUGHT, JACK GREGG, lawyer; b. Indpls., Dec. 18, 1958; s. Jack Laidley and Marilyn Louise (Richardson) H.; m. Sarah Edith Lynn, Sept. 28, 1991; children: Elizabeth, Jack. AB, Ind. U., 1980; JD, U. Mich., 1983. Bar: Ohio 1983, D.C. 1986, U.S. Dist. Ct. (so. dist.) Ohio 1984, U.S. Ct. Appeals (6th cir.) 1983. Assoc. Topper, Alloway, Goodman, DeLeone & Duffey, Columbus, Ohio, 1983-85, Benesch, Friedlander, Coplan & Aronoff, Columbus, 1986-89, ptnr., 1993—; assoc. Dickstein, Shapiro & Morin, Washington, 1989-90; dep. atty. gen. Atty. Gen. Office, Columbus, Ohio, 1991-93. Contbg. editor The Developing Labor Law, 2d edit., 1987. Sr. advisor to Ohio campaign Clinton/Gore 1992 Campaign, Columbus, 1992; polit. dir. Ohio primary election Dukakis for Pres., Boston, 1988; chair Ohio Elections Commn., Columbus, 1993-94; mem. Presdl. Rank Rev. Bd., Washington, 1993; del. Dem. Nat. Conv., Atlanta, 1988, N.Y. 1980. Democrat. Government contracts and claims, Labor (including EEOC, Fair Labor Standards Act, labor-management relations, NLRB, OSHA), Legislative. Office: Benesch Friedlander Coplan & Aronoff 88 E Broad St Ste 900 Columbus OH 43215-3553 Home: 2436 Bexley Park Rd Columbus OH 43209-2120 Fax: 614-223-9330. E-mail: jghaught@bfca.com.

HAUGHT, SHARON KAY, lawyer; b. East Chicago, Ind., Jan. 31, 1959; d. Edwin Frank and Shirlee Mae Lebryk; m. Jeffrey Paul Haught, Aug. 17, 1991; children: Don Roger, Stephanie Marie. BS, Ball State U., 1981; JD, U. Dayton, 1984. Bar: Ohio 1984. Assoc. atty. Bank One Dayton (Ohio) NA, 1983-85; assoc. counsel Rubbermaid Inc., Wooster, Ohio, 1985-2000. Sec. St. Mary of the Immaculate Conception Sch.-Sch. Support Orgn., 2001-02; den leader Boy Scouts Am., 1999-2003, cubmaster, 2001-02, asst. cubmaster, 2002-03; girl scout leader Girl Scouts USA, 2001-03. Mem. ABA, Ohio Bar Assn. Republican. Roman Catholic. Avocations: music, art, photography, writing, computers. Commercial, contracts (including sales of goods; commercial financing), Environmental, Property, real (including real estate development, water). Home: 1589 Brentwood Dr Wooster OH 44691

HAUGHT, WILLIAM DIXON, lawyer, writer; b. Kansas City, Kans., June 12, 1939; s. Walter Dixon and Florence Louise (Rhoads) H.; m. Julia Jane Headstream, July 22, 1967; 1 dau., Stephanie Jane. BS, U. Kans., 1961; LL.B., U Kans., 1964; LL.M., Georgetown U., 1968. Bar: Kans. 1964, Ark. 1971. Assoc. Stanley, Schroeder, Weeks, Thomas & Lysaught, Kansas City, Kans., 1968-70; ptnr. Wright, Lindsey & Jennings, Little Rock, 1970-91; pvt. practice Little Rock, 1991-95; ptnr. Haught & Wade, 1996—. Author: Arkansas Probate System, 1977, 6th ed. 1999, (with others) Probate and Estate Administration: The Law in Arkansas, 1983. Served to capt. USAR, 1964-68, Korea, Washington. Mem. ABA (coun. chmn. coms.), Am. Coll. Trust and Estate Counsel (regent, editor studies program, chmn. editl. bd., state chair), Internat. Acad. Estate and Trust Law, Am. Law Inst., Am. Counsel Assn., Ark. Bar Assn. (chmn. probate law sect., chmn. econs. of law practice com., chmn. agrl. law com., chmn. juris law reform com.), Ctrl. Ark. Estate Coun., Pulaski County Bar Assn., Ark. Bar Found., Country Club of Little Rock. Presbyterian. Estate planning, Probate (including wills, trusts), Estate taxation. Office: Haught & Wade 111 Center St Ste 1320 Little Rock AR 72201-4405 E-mail: wdh@haughtwade.com.

HAUSELT, DENISE ANN, lawyer; BS, Cornell U., 1979, JD, 1983. Bar: N.Y. 1984, Ill. 1984, U.S. Dist. Ct. (we. dist.) N.Y. 1984, U.S. Bankruptcy Ct. 1984. Summer assoc. Wildman, Harrold, Allen & Dixon, Chgo., 1982; assoc. Nixon Peabody LLP, Rochester, N.Y., 1983-86; asst. counsel Corning (N.Y.) Inc., 1986-93, divsn. counsel, 1993-99, asst. gen. counsel, 1999-2000, asst. gen. counsel, asst. sec., 2000—01, corp. sec., 2001—. Bd. dirs. 171 Cedar Arts Ctr., The Rockwell Mus. Mem. adv. coun. Cornell Law Sch.; sec. Rockwell Mus., and Corning Inc. Found. Recipient Am. Jurisprudence Constl. Law prize, Cornell U., 1981. Mem.: ABA, Cornell Law Assn., Am. Corp. Counsel Assn. Republican. Avocations: sailing, skiing. Antitrust, Commercial, contracts (including sales of goods; commercial financing), Corporate, general. Office: Corning Inc Riverfront Plz Mp Hq E2 Corning NY 14831-0001

HAUSER, CHRISTOPHER GEORGE, lawyer; b. Syracuse, N.Y., May 15, 1954; s. W. Dieter and Nancy (Keating) H. BA, Washington & Jefferson Coll., 1976; JD, Dickinson Sch. Law, 1979. Bar: Pa. 1979, U.S. Dist. Ct. (we. dist.) Pa. 1981, N.Y. 1987, U.S. Supreme Ct. 1992. Legal asst. Pa. Dept. of Justice, Harrisburg, 1978-79; assoc. McDowell, McDowell, Wick & Daly, Bradford, 1979-83; ptnr. McDowell, Wick, Daly, Gallup, & Hauser, and predecessor firm McDowell, McDowell, Wick & Daly, Bradford, 1983—; broker, owner Re/Max Alpine Sales, Ellicottville, N.Y., 1991-93. Pres./owner Alpine Sales and Rental Mgmt., Inc., Ellicottville, N.Y., 1987-94; chmn. adv. bd. Office Econ. Cmty. Devel., Bradford, 1988—. Chmn. campaign Bradford Area United Way, 1984, v.p., 1987—89, pres., 1990—92; chmn. Downtown Bradford Revitalization Corp., 1986—, Bradford Parking Authority, 1986—94, 1999—; pres. Allegheny Highlands coun. Boy Scouts Am., Falconer, NY, 1986—88; dir. Bradford Econ. Devel. Corp., 1987—, Exch. Club, 1989—91; sec., treas. Bradford Redevel. Authority, 1992—96, chmn., 1992—96, 1996—; active Bradford Area Citizens Adv. Com., 1992; dir. N.W. divsn. Pa. Economy League, 1997—2003; dir., sec. Bradford Area Alliance, 1997—98, solicitor, 1998—; bd. dirs. Rt. 219 Assn., 1996—98; v.p. Continental One, 1998—, pres., 2000—; dist. justice McKean County, Pa., 2000—; dir. Bradford Regional Med. Ctr., 2000—. Recipient Outstanding Svc. award Bradford Area United Way, 1985, Silver Beaver award Allehany Highlands coun. Boy Scouts Am., 1990, Founder's award Order Arrow Boy Scouts Am., 1991, Cmty. Svc. award City of Bradford Office Econ. and Cmty. Devel., 1995; named Bus. Person of Yr. Bradford C. of C., 1986, One of Outstanding Young Men Am. U.S. Jaycees, 1983. Mem. N.Y. Bar Assn., Pa. Bar Assn., McKean County Bar Assn. (v.p. 1992-93, pres. 1994-96), Bradford Area Jaycees (pres. 1983-85), Pennhills Club (sec. 1985-90, 99-2000, pres. 1990-92, 2000—02, chmn. exec. com. 2002—), Bradford Club. Republican. Episcopalian. Corporate, general, Finance, Property, real (including real estate development, water). Home: 110 Congress St Bradford PA 16701-2228 Office: McDowell Wick Daly Gallup & Hauser PO Box 361 78 Main St Bradford PA 16701-2026 E-mail: cghauser@charter.net., mwdlaw@charter.net.

HAUSER, HELEN ANN, lawyer, consultant; b. Miami, Fla., July 23, 1948; d. Philip Jay and Ruth (Saltman) Fruitstone; m. Mark Jay Hauser; children: Robert Jeffrey, Cheryl Elaine, Lauren Yvonne. BA in English, Duke U., 1970; MA in English, U. Fla., 1972, PhD, 1975; JD, U. Miami, 1982. Bar: Fla. 1982, U.S. Dist. Ct. (so. dist.) Fla. 1982, U.S. Ct. Appeals (11th cir.) 1986, U.S. Supreme Ct. 1987, U.S. Dist. Ct. (mid. dist.) Fla. 1994. Instr. various colls., 1973-79; clk. to presiding justice Fla. 3d Ct. of Appeals, 1982-84; ptnr. Pines & Hauser, Miami, 1984-89; assoc. Law Offices of David P. Dittmar, Miami, 1989-91; ptnr. Dittmar & Hauser, P.A., Miami, 1991—. Vol. Guardian ad Litem Program, Juvenile Ct., Miami, 1985—; bd. dirs. Alhambra Orch. Angier B. Duke scholar Duke U., 1966-70; Harvey T. Reid fellow U. Miami Law Sch., 1979-82. Mem. Dade County Bar Assn., South Miami-Kendall Bar Assn., Fla. Assn. Women Lawyers. Avocations: playing violin, viola. Appellate, General civil litigation, Insurance. Office: Dittmar & Hauser 3250 Mary St Ste 400 Miami FL 33133-5232 E-mail: hhauserjd@aol.com.

HAUSER, RITA ELEANORE ABRAMS, lawyer; b. N.Y.C., July 12, 1934; d. Nathan and Frieda (Litt) Abrams; m. Gustave M. Hauser, June 10, 1956; children: Glenvil Aubrey, Ana Patricia. AB magna cum laude, CUNY Hunter Coll., 1954; D in Polit. Economy with highest honors, U. Strasbourg, France, 1955; Licence en Droit, U. Paris, 1958; student, Harvard U., 1955-56; LLB with honors, NYU, 1959; LLD (hon.), Seton Hall U., 1969, Finch Coll., 1969, U. Miami, Fla., 1971, Colgate U., 1995. Bar: D.C. 1959, N.Y. 1961, U.S. Supreme Ct. 1967. Atty. U.S. Dept. Justice, 1959-61; pvt. practice N.Y.C., 1961-67; ptnr. Moldover, Hauser, Strauss & Volin, 1968-72; sr. ptnr. Stroock & Stroock & Lavan, N.Y.C., 1972-92, of counsel, 1992—; pres. The Hauser Found., N.Y.C., 1990—; presdl. apptd. mem. Pres.'s Fgn. Intelligence Bd. and Intelligence Oversight Bd., 2001. Handmaker lectr., Louis Brandeis Lecture Series, U. Ky. Law Sch.; lectr. internat. law Naval War Coll. and Army War Coll.; lectr. St. Anthony's Coll., Oxford (England) U., 2002; Mitchell lectr. in law SUNY, Buffalo; USIA lectr. constl. law Egypt, India, Australia, New Zealand; bd. dirs. The Eisenhower World Affairs Inst.; U.S. chmn. Internat. Ctr. for Peace in Middle East, 1984-92; bd. dirs. Internat. Peace Acad., chair 1993—; U.S. pub. del. to Vienna follow-up meeting of Conf. on Security and Cooperation in Europe, 1986-88; mem. adv. panel in internat. law U.S. Dept. State, 1986-92, Am. Soc. Internat. Law Award to honor Women in Internat. Law; mem. Pacific Coun. on Internat. Policy, 1998-2000; bd. dirs. The Rand Corp. Contbr. articles to profl. jours. U.S. rep. to UN commn. on Human Rights, 1969-72; mem. U.S. del. to Gen. Assembly UN, 1969; vice chmn. U.S. Adv. Com. on Internat. and Cultural Affairs, 1973-77; mem. N.Y.C. Bd. Higher Edn., 1974-76, Stanton Panel on internat. info., edn., cultural rels. to reorganize USIA and Voice of Am., 1974-75, Mid. East Study Gruop Brookings Inst., 1975, 87-88, U.S. del. World Conf. Internat. Women's Yr., Mexico City, 1975; co-chair Com. for Re-election Pres., 1972, Presdl. Debates project LVW, 1976, Coalition for Regan/Bush; adv. bd. Nat. News Coun., 1977-79; bd. dirs. Bd for Internat. Broadcasting, 1977-80, Catalyst, Internat. Peace Acad., The Aspen Inst., The RAND Corp., U.S. Coun. Germany; trustee, exec com. N.Y. Philharm. Soc.; trustee Lincoln Ctr. Performing Arts; adv. bd. Ctr. For Law and Nat. Security, U. Va. Law Sch., 1978-84; vis. com. Ctr. Internat. Affairs Harvard U., 1975-81, John F. Kennedy Sch. Govt., Harvard U., 1992—, chair adv. bd. Hauser Ctr. for Non-Profit Orgns. at Harvard U.; dean's bd. advisor's Harvard Law Sch., 1996—, vice-chair, nat. co-chair univ. fund-raising campaign, 1997-2000, vice chmn. com. on univ. resources, 2002-; bd. advisors Mid. East Inst., Harvard U.; bd of visitors Georgetown Sch. Fgn. Svc., 1989-94; chmn. adv. panel Internat. Parlimentatry Group for Human Rights in Soviet Union, 1984-86; mem. Lawyers Com. for Human Rights, 1995—; mem. spl. refugee adv. panel Dept. State, 1981; bd. fellows Claremont U. Ctr. & Grad. Sch., 1990-94; former trustee Internat. Legal Ctr., Legal Aid Soc. N.Y., Freedom House; mem. Lawyer's Comm. Human Rights, 1996—. Fulbright grant U. Strasbourg, 1955; Intellectual Exch. fellow Japan Soc.; recipient Jane Addams Internat. Women's Leadership award, 1996, Women in Internat. Law award Am. Soc. Internat. Law, 1995, Fulbright award for Fulbright Alumni, 1997, Servant of Justice award, Legal Aid Soc. N.Y., 2000. Fellow ABA (life, mem. standing coms. on law and nat. security 1979-85, standing com. on world order under law 1969-78, standing com. on jud. selection, tenure, compensation 1977-79, coun. sect. on ind. rights and responsibilities 1970-73, advisor bd. jour. 1973-78); mem. Am. Soc. Internat. Law (v.p. 1988—, mem. exec. com. 1971-76), Am. Fgn. Law Assn. (bd. dirs.), Am. Arbitration Assn. (past bd. dirs.), Ams. Soc. (bd. dirs. 1988—), Coun. Fgn. Rels. (bd. dirs.), Internat. Inst. for Strategic Studies (London, bd. dirs. 1994—), Internat. Adv. Bd., Jaffee Ctr. for Strategic Studies, Tel Aviv Univ. (1999—), Am. Coun. on Germany, The Atlantic Coun. U.S., Friends of the Hauge Acad. Internat. Law (bd. dirs.), Assn. of Bar of City of N.Y., Catalyst (bd. dirs. 1989-96). Republican. Banking, Private international, Public international. Office: Stroock & Stroock & Lavan 180 Maiden Ln Fl 17 New York NY 10038-4937 also: The Hauser Found Office of Pres 712 5th Ave New York NY 10019-4108

HAUSHALTER, HARRY, lawyer; b. Tel Aviv, July 7, 1945; s. Leo and Ruth H.; m. Theresa Ann Lukowicz. BA magna cum laude, Rutgers U., 1967, JD, 1970. Bar: N.J. 1970, U.S. Dist. Ct. 1970, U.S. Ct. Appeals (3rd cir.) 1982, U.S. Supreme Ct. 1982. Tax atty. Arthur Anderson & Co., Newark, 1970-71; dep. atty. gen. N.J. Atty. Gen.'s Office, Trenton, 1972-90; atty. Conley & Haushalter, Princeton, N.J., 1990-98; pvt. practice Hamilton, N.J., 1998—. Author: Matthew Bender/N.J. Taxes, 1982. Trustee Rutgers Ctr. for Govt. Svcs., 1994—; mem. Supreme Ct. Com. on N.J. Jud. Tax Ct., 1982-2002. Mem. Phi Beta Kappa. State and local taxation. Office: Harry Haushalter Atty-at-Law 2119 Route 33 Ste A Hamilton NJ 08690-1740

HAUSMAN, BRUCE, retired lawyer; b. N.Y.C., Mar. 4, 1930; s. Samuel and Vera (Kuttler) H.; m. Jeanne Epstein, June 8, 1952 (div. Oct. 1992); children: Robert Lloyd, Arlene; m. Amy Kadin, Dec. 12, 1992. BA, Brown U., 1951; MS, Columbia U., 1952; postgrad., N.Y. Law Sch., 1979. Bar: N.Y. 1980. Dir. Belding Real Estate Corp., Corticelli Real Estate Corp., 1960-63; pres., dir. Va. Dyeing Corp., 1962-64, div. mgr., 1952-64; ptnr. Kastex Corp., L.A., 1964; regional sales mgr. Belding Heminway Co., Inc., 1965; pres., dir. contract knitting divsn. Mozzil Knits Inc., 1969-73; exec., adminstrv. officer apparel fabric divsn. Belding Heminway Co., Inc., N.Y.C., 1966-73, exec. asst. to chmn. bd., 1973-74, group pres. home furnishings divsn., 1975-79, corp. v.p., 1979, corp. counsel, 1987—92, sr. vice chmn., 1980-86, chmn. exec. com., 1981-86, cons., 1987-88, sr. v.p., 1988-92; ret., 1993; exec. adminstrv. head Belding Hausman Fabrics Inc., 1975-79. Adminstrv. officer Va. Dyeing Corp., Belding Corticelli Fiberglass Fabrics Inc.; pres. M.K. Leasing Corp., 1974; mem. exec. com. iiGroup, Inc., 1993, pres., CEO, 1995-99. Bd. overseers Parsons Sch. Design, 1975-91; trustee, mem. exec. com. Beth Israel Med. Ctr., N.Y.C., 1976-93, hon. trustee, 1993—; trustee, mem. exec. com. Beth Israel Nursing Home, 1991-93, hon. trustee, 1994—. Named Man of Yr., Fabric Salesmens Guild, Inc., 1972. Mem. Textile Salesmen's Assn. (bd. govs., Man of Yr. award 1987), Textile Distbrs. Assn. (gov. 1979, v.p. 1982, sec. 1983-87), Am. Arbitration Assn., NCCJ (bd. dirs. 1974-88).

HAUSMAN, C. MICHAEL, lawyer, judge; b. Chgo., Oct. 4, 1940; s. Charles Martin and Evelyn (Partridge) H.; children: Laura, Sarah, Craig, Karen, Richard, Ronald, Charles, Ashley, Courtney Megan. BS, Marquette U., 1962, JD, 1967. Bar: Wis. 1967, U.S. Dist. Ct. (ea. dist.) Wis. 1967, U.S. Supreme Ct. 1972. Ptnr. Frisch, Dudek & Slattery, Ltd., Milw., 1967-88; mcpl. judge City of Delafield, Wis., 1983—; ptnr. Slattery & Hausman, Ltd., Waukesha, Wis., 1988—2001, C. Michael Hausman and Assocs. Ltd., Delafield, Wis., 2001—. Lectr. State Bar of Wis. Family Law Seminars, Am. Acad. Matrimonial Lawyers; bd. dirs. Collaborative Family Law Coun. Wis., Inc., 2001—. Named Outstanding Young Man Brookfield (Wis.) Jaycees, 1975. Fellow: Am. Acad. Matrimonial Lawyers (pres. Wis. chpt. 1988—89), Internat. Acad. Matrimonial Lawyers; mem.: ATLA, Brookfield C.of C. (pres. 1977—78), Milw. Jr. Bar Assn. (bd. dirs. 1969—71), State Bar Wis., Wis. Acad. Trial Lawyers, Am. Arbitration Assn., Brookfield

Rotary (pres. 1980—81). Avocations: fishing, hiking, stamp and coin collecting. Family and matrimonial, Personal injury (including property damage), Workers' compensation. Home and Office: 329 GeneseeSt Delafield WI 53018

HAUSNER, JOHN HERMAN, judge; b. Detroit, Oct. 31, 1932; s. John E. and Anna (Mudrak) H.; m. Alice R. Kieltyka, Aug. 22, 1959. Ph.B. cum laude, U. Detroit, 1954, MA, 1957, JD summa cum laude, 1966. Bar: Mich. 1967, U.S. Ct. Appeals (6th cir.) 1968, U.S. Supreme Ct. 1971, U.S. Tax Ct. 1976, U.S. Ct. Claims 1976, U.S. Ct. Mil. Appeals 1976. Tchr. Detroit Pub. Schs., 1954, 56-59; tchg. fellow U. Cin., 1959-61; instr. U. Detroit, 1961-74, sole practice, 1967-69; asst. U.S. atty. Detroit, 1969-73; chief asst. U.S. atty. ea. dist. Mich., 1973-76; judge 3rd Jud. Cir. Mich., Wayne County, 1976-94; ret. 3d Jud. Cir. Mich., Wayne County, 1994, 1994. Lectr. Law Sch.; faculty adviser Nat. Jud. Coll., 1978-79. Author: Sebastian, The Essence of My Soul, 1982; contbr. articles to Detroit Advertiser. Served with U.S. Army, 1954—56. Mem. Fed. Bar Assn. (mem. exec. bd. Detroit chpt. 1976-82), State Bar Mich., Mich. Retired Judges Assn., Blue Key, Alpha Sigma Mu. Republican. Home: 22433 Louise St Saint Clair Shores MI 48081-2034 also: 8420 E Desert Palm Tucson AZ 85730-4723

HAUSRATH, LES A. lawyer; b. Cleve., June 8, 1947; m. Linda, June 26, 1971; 1 child, Daniel. BA, U. Calif., Berkeley, 1969, JD, 1973. Bar: Calif. 1973, U.S. Dist. Ct. (no. dist.) Calif. 1973, U.S. Ct. Appeals (9th cir.) 1975. Atty. Legal Aid Soc. Alameda County, Oakland, Calif., 1973-77, Sullivan, Jones & Archer, San Francisco, 1977-79, Armour, St. John, Wilcox & Goodin, San Francisco, 1979-81; ptnr. Wendel, Rosen, Black & Dean, Oakland, 1981—. Lectr. Contbr. articles to profl. jours. Commr., chair City Planning Commn., Oakland, 1997-2001; commr., chair Landmarks Adv. Bd., Oakland, 1991-96; mem. Gen. Plan Congress, Oakland, 1993-97. Mem. Internat. Right of Way Assn. (exec. bd. 1998—), Phi Beta Kappa. Condemnation (eminent domain), Land use and zoning (including planning), Property, real (including real estate development, water). Office: Wendel Rosen Black & Dean LLP 1111 Broadway Fl 24 Oakland CA 94607-4036

HAUVER, CONSTANCE LONGSHORE, lawyer; b. Abington, Pa., Oct. 9, 1938; d. Malcolm Rettew and Margaret Evans (Lyon) L.; m. Arthur R. Hauver, 1962 (div. Mar. 1979); 1 child, Sian; m. Giles Toll, 1990. BA with high honors, Swarthmore Coll., 1960; MA, UCLA, 1962; JD magna cum laude, U. Denver, 1967. Bar: Colo. 1968, U.S. Dist. Ct. Colo. 1968, U.S. Tax Ct. 1970. Libr. Friends Com. on Nat. Legis., Washington, 1960-61; lectr. U. Hawaii, Honolulu, 1963-64; assoc. Sherman & Howard, Denver, 1968-73, ptnr., 1973-91; vol. naturalist Lookout Mountain Nature Ctr., 1998—. Mem. grievance com. Colo. Supreme Ct., 1981-86. Co-contbr. legal articles. Trustee Rocky Mountain Women's Inst., Denver, 1987-90, Swedish Med. Ctr. Found., Denver, 1978-85; bd. dirs. Women's Forum Colo. Inc., Denver, 1988-89, Girls Count, Denver, 1995-2000, pres., 1996-97. Named New Vol. Naturalist of Yr., Lookout Mountain Nature Ctr., 1998, Vol. Naturalist of Yr., 2001; recipient Athena award, Alliance Profl. Women, 1987. Fellow Am. Coll. Probate Counsel; mem. Colo. Bar Assn. (chair probate and trust law sect. 1982-83), Denver Bar Assn. (del. to ABA Ho. of Dels. 1986-88), Rocky Mountain Estate Planning Coun. (pres. 1980-81). Democrat. Mem. Soc. Of Friends. Avocations: mountain climbing, kayaking, skiing, reading. Estate planning, Probate (including wills, trusts), Estate taxation.

HAVEL, RICHARD W. lawyer; b. Fairmont, Minn., Sept. 20, 1946; s. Thomas Earl and Elizabeth (Shiltz) H.; m. Arlene Havel, July 6, 1968; children: Stephanie, Derek. BA, Notre Dame U., 1968; JD, UCLA, 1971. Bar: Calif., U.S. Dist. Ct. (no., ea., cen. and so. dists.) Calif., U.S. Ct. Appeals (9th cir.). Atty. Shutan & Trost, L.A., 1971-80, Sidley & Austin, L.A., 1980—. Instr. law U. Loyola, 1975-80; bd. govs. Fin. Lawyers Conf., 1991-94, 95-98, officer, 1998-2001; spkr., panelist Bankruptcy Litigation Inst., 1989-95, ALI-ABA, 1989, 90, 91; chmn. L.A. City Indsl. Devel. Authority, 1993-98, bd. dirs., 1998-2000. Contbr. articles to profl. jours. Trustee Jonsson/UCLA Cancer Ctr., 1998—. Fellow Am. Coll. Bankruptcy, 1997; mem. ABA, Calif. Bar Assn., L.A. County Bar Assn. (comml. law & bankruptcy sect. bankruptcy subcom. 1986-89, exec. com. 1987-90, lawyer assistance com. 1985—), UCLA Law Alumni Assn. (trustee 1996—). Bankruptcy, Mergers and acquisitions. Office: Sidley & Austin 555 W 5th St 40th Fl Los Angeles CA 90013-1010 E-mail: RHavel@Sidley.com.

HAVENS, CHARLES W., III, retired lawyer; b. Balt., Mar. 22, 1936; m. Lucille Bowman; children— Charles W. IV, Jessica Madaline AB, Franklin and Marshall Coll., 1958; LL.B., U. Va., 1961. Bar: D.C. 1961, Va. 1961, U.S. Supreme Ct. Assoc. Covington & Burling, Washington, 1961-66; spl. asst. to gen. counsel Dept. Def., Washington, 1966-67, spl. asst. to asst. sec. def., 1967-70; gen. counsel then pres. Reins. Assn. Am., Washington, 1970-81; ptnr. LeBoeuf, Lamb, Leiby & MacRae, Washington, 1981—2000; ret., 2000. Contbr. articles to profl. jours. Mem. AIDA Reins. and Ins. Arbitration Soc. (founding, bd. dirs.), Met. Club, John's Island Club. Clubs: Metropolitan (Washington). Avocation: golf. Insurance. Home: # 396 1000 Beach Rd Vero Beach FL 32963 Office: LeBoeuf Lamb Greene MacRae 1875 Connecticut Ave NW Washington DC 20009-5728 Home (Summer): 4045 Mansion Dr NW Washington DC 20007

HAVENS, HUNTER SCOTT, lawyer; b. Cleve., Dec. 6, 1954; s. George Noble and Virginia Councell Havens; m. Gale Ann Havens, Oct. 18, 1996. BA, Case Western Res. U., 1980; JD, Cleve.-Marshall Coll. Law, 1984. Bar: Ohio 1984, U.S. Dist. Ct. (no. dist.) Ohio 1984. Ptnr. Quandt, Giffels & Buck, Cleve., 1984-2000, Mazanec, Raskin & Ryder Co., L.P.A., Cleve., 2000—02, Hermann, Cahn & Schneider Co., LLP, Cleve., 2002—. General civil litigation, Personal injury (including property damage), Product liability. Office: Hermann Cahn & Schneider Co LLP Ste 500 1301 E Ninth St Cleveland OH 44114

HAVIGHURST, CLARK CANFIELD, law educator; b. Evanston, Ill., May 25, 1933; s. Harold Canfield and Marion Clay (Perryman) H.; m. Karen Waldron, Aug. 28, 1965; children: Craig Perryman, Marjorie Clark. BA, Princeton U., 1955; JD, Northwestern U., 1958. Bar: Ill. 1958, N.Y. 1961. Assoc. Debevoise Plimpton Lyons & Gates, N.Y.C., 1958, 61-64; assoc. prof. law Duke U., Durham, NC, 1964-68, prof., 1968-86, 2002—, William Neal Reynolds prof., 1986—2002, emeritus, 2002—; interim dean Duke U. Sch. Law, 1999. Dir. Program on Legal Issues in Health Care Duke U., 1969-88; adj. scholar Am Enterprise Inst. Pub. Policy Rsch., 1976—; resident cons. FTC, Washington, 1978, Epstein, Becker & Green, Washington, 1989-90; scholar in residence Inst. Medicine of NAS, Washington, 1972-73, RAND Corp., Santa Monica, 1999. Author: Deferred Compensation for Key Employees, 1964, Regulating Health Facilities Construction, 1974, Deregulating the Health Care Industry, 1982, Health Care Law and Policy, 1988, 2d edit., 1998, Health Care Choices: Private Contracts as Instruments of Health Reform, 1995; editor Law and Contemporary Problems jour., 1965-70. With U.S. Army, 1958-60. Mem. Inst. Medicine of Nat. Acad. Sci., Order of Coif Office: Duke U Sch Law PO Box 90360 Durham NC 27708-0360 E-mail: hav@law.duke.edu.

HAVILAND, BANCROFT DAWLEY, lawyer; b. Yonkers, N.Y., May 13, 1925; s. Harold Bancroft and Dorothy (Dawley) H.; m. Dorothy MacFarland, Oct. 30, 1945; children: Lucy, William, Thomas, Amy. BA in Polit. Sci., U. Pa., 1947, LLB, 1949. Bar: N.Y. 1951, Pa. 1952. Gowen teaching fellow U. Pa. Law Sch., Phila., 1949-50; assoc. Donovan, Leisure, Newton & Irvine, Phila., 1950-51, Schnader, Harrison, Segal & Lewis, Phila., 1951-61, ptnr., 1961-90, ret., 1991. Trustee Westtown (Pa.) Friends' Sch., 1960-94, Media-Providence (Pa.) Friends' Sch., 1960-95; chmn. Westtown Sch. Com., 1988-93; commr. Rose Tree Soccer Club, Media, 1971-98, Aston Twp., Pa., 1954-61; justice of peace Middletown Twp., Pa., 1963-65. Lt. (j.g.) USN, 1943-45, PTO. Mem. ABA, Pa. Bar Assn., Phila. Bar Assn., Am. Judicature Soc., Order of Coif Lodges: Lions. Democrat. Mem. Soc. Of Friends. Avocations: woodworking, reading, gardening. Antitrust, Federal civil litigation, Family and matrimonial. Home: 21 Kendal Dr Kennett Square PA 19348 Office: Schnader Harrison Segal & Lewis 1600 Market St Ste 3600 Philadelphia PA 19103-7287

HAWASH, MICHAEL ANDREW, lawyer; b. Middlesbrough, Eng., Mar. 30, 1966; came to U.S., 1981; s. Ralph Hawash and Linda (Burnip) Kuschel. BA in History, U. Tex., 1990, BA in Govt., 1991; JD, U. Houston, 1994. Bar: Tex. 1994, U.S. Dist. Ct. (so., no., ea., and we. dists.) Tex. 1995, U.S. Ct. Appeals (5th cir.) 1996, U.S. Dist. Ct. (ea. dist.) La. 1996. Assoc. Meyer Orlando & Evans PC, Houston, 1993-2000, Verner Liipfert Bernhard McPherson and Hand, Chartered, Houston, 2000-01; spl. counsel Adams & Reese, Houston, 2001—. Mem. ABA, Fed. Bar Assn., Maritime Law Assn., State Bar Tex., Houston Young Lawyers Assn., Houston Bar Assn., Computer Game Developers Assn., Phi Delta Phi, Phi Kappa Psi. Admiralty, Insurance, Personal injury (including property damage). Home: 705 Main Ste 209 Houston TX 77002 Office: Adams & Reese LLP 4400 One Houston Ctr 1221 McKinney Houston TX 77010 E-mail: hawashma@arlaw.com.

HAWKE, ROGER JEWETT, lawyer; b. N.Y.C., July 2, 1935; s. John Daniel and Olga (Buchbinder) H.; m. Rose Marie Ferri, Aug. 15, 1964; children— Christopher, Allison, John BA cum laude, Amherst Coll., 1956; LL.B., Columbia U., 1959. Bar: N.Y. 1960, U.S. Supreme Ct. 1976. Assoc. Donovan, Leisure, Newton & Irvine, N.Y.C., 1960, 62-65; asst. U.S. atty. U.S. Atty.'s Office, So. Dist. N.Y., N.Y.C., 1965-69; assoc. Brown, Wood, Ivey, Mitchell & Petty LLP, N.Y.C., 1969-71, ptnr., 1971—2001, Sidley Austin Brown & Wood LLP, N.Y.C., 2001—. Arbitrator Nat. Assn. Securities Dealers. Acting village justice Village of Lloyd Harbor, N.Y., 1977-83, trustee, 1983-99; police commr., 1983-99, dep. mayor, 1983-99. With U.S. Army, 1961-62. Fellow: Am. Coll. Trial Lawyers; mem.: ABA, Am. Law Inst., N.Y. Law Inst. (exec. com.), Assn. of Bar of City of N.Y., Lloyd Neck Bath (pres. 1981). Office: Sidley Austin Brown & Wood LLP 787 Seventh Ave New York NY 10019

HAWKEY, G. MICHAEL, lawyer, real estate developer; b. Apr. 17, 1941; m. Frances Tripp, Feb. 27, 1971; children: Samuel, Eliza, MacKenzie. AB, Princeton U., 1963; postgrad., Columbia Bus. Sch., 1964; LLB, Cornell U., 1967. Bar: Mass. 1967. With Sullivan & Worcester LLP, Boston. Founder Sun Valley Properties, Pocatello, Idaho, Mettowee Valley Properties, Pawlet, Vt.; lectr. Mass. Restaurant Assn. Author: The Union-Management Controversy Over Subcontracting and Plant Relocation, 1963. Bd. dirs. Pacific. Internat. Inst., Lewiston, Idaho, 1992—97, St. Lukes Cancer Rsch. Found., Cork, Ireland, 1994—97; N.Am. bd. Michael Smurfit Grad. Sch. Bus., Univ. Coll., Dublin, 1994—98; trustee Maruzen Hawthorne Coll., Antrim, NH, 1991—92; bd. govs. Wianno Club, 1982—98. Mem. Internat. Coun. Shopping Ctrs., Mass. Real Estate Fin. Assn. (bd. dirs. 1989-92), Sr. Execs. Club of Mass. Real Estate Fin. Assn., Mass. Conveyancers Assn., The Country Club (Brookline, Mass.), Greyhawk Village Assn., Wianno Club Land use and zoning (including planning), Landlord-tenant, Property, real (including real estate development, water). Home: 26 Arlington Rd Wellesley MA 02481-6129 Office: Sullivan & Worcester LLP 1 Post Office Sq Ste 2300 Boston MA 02109-2129

HAWKINS, EDWARD J. retired lawyer; b. Fall River, Mass., June 24, 1927; s. Edward Jackson and Harriet (Sherman) H.; m. Janet Schwerdt; children: Daniel, George, Robert, Harriet. Grad., Phillips Acad., Andover, Mass., 1945; AB summa cum laude, Princeton U., 1950; LLB magna cum laude, Harvard U., 1953. Bar: Ohio 1954, D.C. 1990. Assoc., ptnr. Squire, Sanders & Dempsey, Cleve., 1953-78, ptnr. Cleve. and Washington, 1982-96, counsel, 1997-99; ret., 2000. Chief tax counsel U.S. Senate Fin. Com., Washington, 1979-80, minority tax counsel, 1981; gen. chmn. Cleve. Tax Inst., 1969. Contbr. articles to profl. jours. With U.S. Army, 1945-46. Mem. ABA (vice chmn. govt. rels. tax sect. 1987-89), D.C. Bar Assn., Phillips Acad. Alumni Assn. (alumni coun. 1967-70), Quadrangle Club. Democrat. Home: 7404 Park Terrace Dr Alexandria VA 22307-2039 E-mail: ejhawkins2@aol.com.

HAWKINS, FALCON BLACK, JR., federal judge; b. Charleston, S.C., Mar. 16, 1927; s. Falcon Black Sr. and Mae Elizabeth (Infinger) H.; m. Jean Elizabeth Timmerman, May 28, 1949; children: Richard Keith, Daryl Gene, Mary Elizabeth Hawkins Eddy, Steely Odell II. BS, The Citadel, 1958; LLB, U. S.C., 1963, JD, 1970. Bar: S.C. bar 1963. Leadingman electronics Charleston (S.C.) Naval Shipyard, 1948-60; salesman ACH Brokers, Columbia, S.C., 1960-63; from assoc. to sr. ptnr. firm Hollings & Hawkins and successor firms, Charleston, 1963-79; U.S. dist. judge Dist. of S.C., Charleston, 1979—, chief judge, 1990-93, sr. status, 1993—. Served with Mcht. Marines, 1944-45, with AUS, 1945-46. Mem. Jud. Conf. 4th Jud. Circuit, ABA, S.C. Bar Assn., Charleston County Bar Assn., Am. Trial Lawyers Assn., S.C. Trial Lawyers Assn., Carolina Yacht Club, Hibernian Soc. Charleston, Masons. Democrat. Presbyterian. Office: Hollings Jud Ctr PO Box 835 Charleston SC 29402-0835 Fax: 843-579-1499.

HAWKINS, MICHAEL DALY, federal judge; b. Winslow, Ariz., Feb. 12, 1945; s. William Bert and Patricia Agnes (Daly) H.; m. Phyllis A. Lewis, June 4, 1966; children: Aaron, Adam. BA, Ariz. State U., 1967, JD cum laude, 1970; LLM, U. Va., 1998. Bar: Ariz. 1970, U.S. Ct. Mil. Appeals 1971, U.S. Supreme Ct. 1974. Pvt. practice law, 1973—77; U.S. atty. Dept. Justice, Phoenix, 1977—80; pvt. practice law, 1980—84; judge U.S. Ct. Appeals (9th cir.), Phoenix, 1994—. Mem. Appellate Cts. Jud. Nominating Commn., 1985—89. Staff editor: Ariz. State U. Law Jour., 1968—70. Mem. Ariz. Lottery Commn., 1980—83, Commn. on Uniform State Laws, 1988—93. Capt. USMC, 1970—73. Recipient Alumni Achievement award, Ariz. State U., 1995. Mem.: ABA, Nat. Assn. Former U.S. Attys. (pres. 1989—90), Adminstrv. Conf. U.S. (pub. mem. 1985—94), Phoenix Trial Lawyers Assn., Ariz. Trial Lawyers Assn. (bd. dirs. 1976—77, state sec. 1976—77), State Bar of Ariz. (James Walsh Outstanding Jurist Award 2003), Maricopa County Bar Assn. (bd. dirs. 1975—77, 1981—89, pres. 1987—88).

HAWKINS, RICHARD MICHAEL, lawyer; b. Nevada City, Calif., July 23, 1949; s. Robert Augustus and Virginia June (Hawke) H.; m. Linda Lee Chapman, Sept. 27, 1975; child, Alexandra Michelle. BS in Math., U. Calif., Davis, 1971; JD, U. Calif., San Francisco, 1974; LLM in Taxation, U. Pacific, 1983. Bar: Calif. 1974, U.S. Dist. Ct. (ea. dist.) Calif. 1974, U.S. Dist. Ct. (no. dist.) Calif. 1982, U.S. Ct. Claims 1982, U.S. Tax Ct. 1982, U.S. Ct. Appeals (9th cir.) 1982, U.S. Supreme Ct. 1982. From assoc. to ptnr. Larue & Francis, Nevada City, 1974-76; ptnr. Larue, Roach & Hawkins, Nevada City, 1977-78; of counsel Berliner & Ellers, Nevada City; ptnr. Berliner, Spiller & Hawkins, Nevada City, 1981; sole practice Grass Valley, Calif., 1981—. Bd. dirs. 49er Fire Dist., Nevada City, 1977-81, 89-98, asst. fire chief, 1981-83, fire chief, 1983-89. Mem. ABA, Calif. State Bar (cert. specialist in estate planning, trust and probate law 1990), Nevada County Bar Assn. (v.p. 1976), Order of Coif, Phi Kappa Phi. Republican. Roman Catholic. Avocations: running, showing Morgan horses. Estate planning, Probate (including wills, trusts), Estate taxation. Home: 14762 Banner Quaker Hill Rd Nevada City CA 95959-8813 Office: 10563 Brunswick Rd Ste 2 Grass Valley CA 95945-7801 Fax: (530) 272-7861. E-mail: rhawk53@aol.com.

HAWKS, BARRETT KINGSBURY, lawyer; b. Barnesville, Ga., July 13, 1938; s. Paul K. and Nettie Glenn (Barrett) H.; m. S. Kathleen Pafford, Apr. 3, 1965 BBA, Emory U., 1960, LL.B., 1963; LL.M., Harvard U., 1964. Bar: Ga. Clk. Supreme Ct. Ga., 1963; Assoc. Gambrell, Russell, Moye & Richardson (now Smith, Gambrell & Russell), Atlanta, 1961-65; assoc. Sutherland, Asbill & Brennan, Atlanta, 1965-70, ptnr., 1970-82, 93—, Paul, Hastings, Janofsky & Walker, 1982-93. Served to lt. comdr. USNR. Mem. ABA (mem. coun. group pub. utility, transp. and comms. law sect.), State Bar Ga. (bd. govs. 1981-88), Atlanta Bar Assn., D.C. Bar Assn., Emory Law Sch. Alumni Assn. (pres. 1996-97), Emory Law Sch. Coun. (chmn., 1997-98), Capital City Club, Highlands Country Club. Presbyterian. Corporate, general, Utilities, public. Home: 3835 Club Dr Atlanta GA 30319-1109 Office: Sutherland Asbill & Brennan 999 Peachtree St NE Ste 2300 Atlanta GA 30309-3996

HAWKS, TIMOTHY EDWARD, lawyer; b. San Antonio, May 9, 1952; s. James E. and Charlene (Vorwald) H.; m. Mary Lewis McCormick, Aug. 8, 1980; children: Colleen, Laura, Tyler, Charlie. BA, Georgetown U., 1974; JD, U. Iowa, 1977. Bar: Iowa 1978, Wis. 1981. Staff atty. Wis. Employment Rels. Commn., Madison, Wis., 1978-81; ptnr. Shneidman, Hawks & Ehlke, S.C. and predecessor, Milw., 1981—. Mem. ABA, Wis. Bar Assn. (dir. labor law sect. 1983-84, officer 1990-92). Democrat. Roman Catholic. Labor (including EEOC, Fair Labor Standards Act, labor-management relations, NLRB, OSHA). Office: Shneidman Hawks & Ehlke 700 W Michigan St Milwaukee WI 53233-2415

HAWLEY, ROBERT CROSS, lawyer; b. Douglas, Wyo., Aug. 7, 1920; s. Robert Daniel and Elsie Corienne (Cross) H.; m. Mary Elizabeth Hawley McClellan, Mar. 3, 1944; children— Robert Cross, Mary Virginia, Laurie McClellan. BA with honors, U. Colo., 1943; LLB, Harvard U., 1949, JD, 1989. Bar: Wyo. 1950, Colo. 1950, U.S. Dist. Ct. Colo. 1950, U.S. Dist. Ct. Wyo. 1954, U.S. Ct. Appeals (10th cir.) 1955, Tex. 1960, U.S. Ct. Appeals (5th cir.) 1960, U.S. Supreme Ct. 1960, U.S. Dist. Ct. (so. dist.) Tex. 1961, U.S. Ct. Appeals (D.C. cir.) 1961, U.S. Ct. Appeals (8th cir.) 1979, U.S. Ct. Appeals (11th cir.) 1981, U.S. Dist. Ct. (we. dist.) Tex. 1987. Assoc. Bannister Weller & Friedrich, Denver, 1949-50; sr. atty. Continental Oil Co., Denver, 1952-58, counsel, Houston, 1959-62; ptnr., v.p. Ireland, Stapleton & Pryor, Denver, 1962-81; ptnr. Dechert Price & Rhoads, Denver, 1981-83, Hawley & VanderWerf, Denver, 1983-94; sole practice, Denver, 1994—; pres. Highland Minerals, Denver; bd. dirs. Bank of Denver; speaker oil and gas insts. Contbr. articles to Oil & Gas Pubs. Bd. dirs. Am. Cancer Soc., Denver, 1967-87, treas., 1981-82; chmn. U. Colo. Devel. Found., 1960-61; bd. dirs. Rocky Mountain Arthritis Found., 1987—, sec., 1993-94, vice chmn. Colo., 1994—; mem. adv. bd. ARC, 1988—; chmn. 1st Annual Retarded Children Campaign, 1963; dir. East Seal Chpt., 1966-68; bd. dirs. Craig Hosp., 1964-68. Lt. col. U.S. Army, Korean War. Recipient Alumni Recognition award U. Colo., Boulder, 1958, Meritorious Service award Monticello Coll., Godfrey, Ill., 1967, Humanitarian award Arthritis Found., 1992, Honored Lawyer award Law Club, 1993; Sigma Alpha Epsilon scholar, 1941-43. Mem. Denver Assn. Oil and Gas Title Lawyers (pres. 1983-84), Denver Petroleum Club (pres. 1978-79), Harvard Law Sch. Assn. Colo. (pres. 1980-81), Associated Alumni U. Colo. (pres. and bd. dirs. 1956-57), Law Club, Denver (pres. 1958-59), ABA, Colo. Bar Assn. (bd. govs. 2001—), Denver Bar Assn., Tex. Bar Assn., Wyo. Bar Assn., Fed. Energy Bar Assn. (legal and lands com.), Interstate Oil and Gas Compact Commn., Harvard Alumni Assn., Rocky Mountain Oil and Gas Assn., Rocky Mountain Petroleum Pioneers (pres. 1991-92), Wyo. Pioneer Assn., Chevaliers du Tastevin, Denver Country Club, Petroleum Club, Gyro Club, Univ. Club Denver, Garden of the Gods Club (Colo. Springs), Colo. Arlberg Club, Mile High Club, U. Colo. Alumni Club (Living Legend award). Republican. Episcopalian. Author, co-author: Landman's Handbook, Law of Federal Oil and Gas Leases, Problems of Surface Damages, Federal Oil and Gas Leases--The Sole Party in Interest Debacle. Banking, General civil litigation, Oil, gas, and mineral. Address: Unit 71 2552 E Alameda Ave Denver CO 80209-3322

HAWORTH, CHARLES RAY, lawyer; b. Little Rock, June 23, 1943; s. Clarence Frederick and Vinita Leona (Bowers) H.; m. Nancy Anne Patterson, Aug. 16, 1970; 1 child, Alan. BA, U. Tex., 1965, JD, 1967. Bar: Tex. 1967, U.S. Dist. Ct. (no. dist.) Tex. 1968, U.S. Dist. Ct. (we. and so. dists.) Tex. 1988, U.S. Dist. Ct. (ea. dist.) Tex. 1989, U.S. Ct. Appeals (5th cir.) 1968, U.S. Ct. Appeals (11th cir.) 1982, U.S. Supreme Ct. 1971; bd. cert. civil trial law Tex. Bd. Legal Specialization. Law clk. U.S. Ct. Appeals (5th cir.), Houston, 1967-68; assoc. Coke & Coke, Dallas, 1968-71; prof. law Washington U. Sch. Law, St. Louis, 1971-79; ptnr. Johnson & Gibbs, Dallas, 1979-85, Andrews & Kurth, Dallas, 1985-92; mng. ptnr. Scott, Douglass, Luton & McConnico, L.L.P., Dallas, 1992-95; ptnr. Owens, Clary & Aiken, L.L.P., Dallas, 1995—. Vis. prof. U. Va. Sch. Law, Charlottesville, 1975-76, U. Tex. Sch. Law, Austin, 1977; cons. Dept. Justice, Washington, 1978. Editor: Congress and the Courts, 1977; contbr. numerous articles to profl. jours. Bd. dirs. Dallas Opera, 1991-2000. Grantee Dept. of Justice, 1978. Mem.: Dallas Bar Assn. (chair bus. litigation sect. 2002), Tex. Bar Assn., Tower Club. Republican. Avocation: fishing. Federal civil litigation, General civil litigation, State civil litigation. Office: Owens Clary & Aiken LLP 700 N Pearl St Ste 1600 Dallas TX 75201

HAY, CEDRIC PETER, lawyer; b. Ann Arbor, Mich., July 16, 1961; s. Peter H. and Norma M. (Gossman) H.; m. Laura Stuckey, July 24, 1994; children: Heather M., Brittainie N. BA in Polit. Sci., U. Ill., 1985, JD, 1987. Bar: Fla. 1987, U.S. Dist. Ct. (mid. dist.) Fla. 1988. Shareholder Beil & Hay, P.A., Hudson, Fla., 1988—. Pres. Dist. Sch. Bd. Pasco County, Fla., Reading Assistance Program Adv. Coun. (Pasco Literacy Coun.), 1995-2000. Mem. ABA, West Pasco Bar Assn., Allgood-Altman Inn of Ct. (charter), Rotary Hudson (pres., bd. dirs. svc. chmn. 1989—, Paul Harris fellow, benefactor). Avocations: british darts, golf. Bankruptcy, Property, real (including real estate development, water). Office: 12312 US Highway 19 Hudson FL 34667-1948

HAY, DENNIS LEE, lawyer; b. L.A., Feb. 18, 1958; s. Frank Henry, Jr. and Kyoko (Sukuya) H.; m. Kerry Lynne Hatfield, Aug. 11, 1984; children: Michelle, Jason, Katheryne. BS in Fin., San Jose State U., 1984; JD, U. Honolulu, 1988. Bar: Calif. 1989. Law clk. Legal Aid Soc. of Alameda Co., Hayward, Calif., 1985-87, Cohn, Becker & Jacquint, Hayward, Calif., 1987, Souza, Coats, McInnis, Mehlhaff & Hay, Tracy, Calif., 1987-89, assoc. counsel atty., 1989-92; ptnr. Mehlhaff & Hay, Tracy, Calif., 1992—; judge pro tem San Joaquin Superior Cts. Prof. law U. Honolulu Law Sch., Modesto, Calif. Mem. Calif. Bar Assn., San Joaquin County Bar Assn. (chairperson bus. litig. sect. com. 1997-98, judicial liaison com. 2002-2003). Republican. Presbyterian. Avocations: drag racing, horse back riding, raquetball. General civil litigation, Commercial, consumer (including collections, credit), Commercial, contracts (including sales of goods; commercial financing). Office: Mehlhaff & Hay PO Box 1129 23950 S Chrisman Rd Tracy CA 95378-1129

HAY, JOHN LEONARD, lawyer; b. Lawrence, Mass., Oct. 6, 1940; s. Charles Cable and Henrietta Dudley (Wise) H.; m. Ruth Murphy, Mar. 16, 1997; 1 child, Ian. AB with distinction, Stanford U., 1961; JD, U. Colo., 1964. Bar: Colo. 1964, Ariz. 1965, D.C. 1971. Assoc. Lewis and Roca, Phoenix, 1964-69, ptnr., 1969-82, Fannin, Terry & Hay, Phoenix, 1982-87, Allen, Kimerer & LaVelle, Phoenix, 1987-94, Gust Rosenfeld, Phoenix, 1994—; judge pro tem Ariz. Ct. Appeals, 1999—. Bd. dirs. Ariz. Life and Disability Ins. Guaranty Fund, 1984-95, chmn., 1993-95. Co-author: Arizona Corporate Practice, 1996, Representing Franchisees, 1996. Mem. Dem. Precinct Com., 1966-78, Ariz. State Dem. Com., 1968-78; chmn. Dem. Legis. Dist., 1971-74; mem. Maricopa County Dem. Cen. Com., 1971-74; bd. dirs. ACLU, 1973-78; bd. dirs. Community Legal Svcs., 1983-89, pres., 1987-88; bd. dirs. Ariz. Club, 1994-96. Mem. ABA, Ariz. Bar Assn., Maricopa County Bar Assn. (bd. dirs. 1972-85), Assn. Life Ins. Counsel, Ariz. Licensors and Franchisors Assn. (bd. dirs. 1985—, pres. 1988-89), Ariz. Civil Liberties Union (bd. dirs. 1967-84, 95-2002, pres.

1973-77, 97-2000, Disting. Citizen award 1979), Phoenix C. of C. (chmn. arts and culture task force 1997-99). Corporate, general, Franchising, Commercial, contracts (including sales of goods; commercial financing). Home: 201 E Hayward Ave Phoenix AZ 85020-4037 Office: Gust Rosenfeld 201 E Washington St Ste 800 Phoenix AZ 85004- E-mail: jhay@gustlaw.com., johnlhay@cox.net.

HAY, PETER ALGERNON FRANC, lawyer; b. Melbourne, Australia, June 28, 1950; s. Peter Henry Hay and Marie Louis Henry; m. Sarah Catherine Robbins, Jan. 25, 2002; m. Robyn Patricia Vickers-Willis, Feb. 7, 1976 (div. Apr. 19, 1996); children: Patricia Marie Louise, Thomas Peter, William Charles Franc. LLB, U. of Melbourne, 1973. Solicitor Freehills, Melbourne, Australia, 1974—76, ptnr., 1977—, CEO/mng. ptnr., 2000—. Dir. Pacifica Group Ltd., Melbourne, Australia, 1989—, Alumina Ltd., Australia, 2002—. Home: 59 Cromwell Rd South Yarra 3141 Australia Office: Freehills 101 Collins St Melbourne 3000 Australia Office Fax: 61 3 9288 1567. Business E-Mail: peter_hay@freehills.com.

HAY, PETER HEINRICH, law educator; b. Berlin, Sept. 17, 1935; s. Edward and Margot (Tull) H.; 1 child, Cedric. BA, JD, U. Mich., 1958. Prof. law U. Ill., Champaign, 1963-91; dean Coll. Law U. Ill., Champaign, 1979-89; L.Q.C. Lamar prof. law Emory U., Atlanta, 1991—, interim dean, chief exec. and acad. officer, 2001—02. Hon. prof. U. Freiburg, Germany, 1976—; prof. U. Dresden, Germany, 1994-2000. Author: Law of the United States, 2002; co-author: Conflict of Laws, 3d edit., 2000; contbr. over 50 articles to profl. jours. Recipient Rsch. prize von Humboldt Found., Germany, 1990; Fulbright rsch. prof., 1992; Jean-Monnet prof., Bonn, Germany, 1994. Mem. Am. Law Inst., Am. Acad. Fgn. Law, Internat. Acad. Comparative Law. Office: Emory U Sch Law G523 Gambrell Hall 1301 Clifton Rd Atlanta GA 30322-2770

HAYDEN, JAMES FRANCIS, lawyer; b. Seattle, Nov. 4, 1954; s. Francis Eugene and Cathryn Cecelia (Smith) Yonaka H.; m. Mary Louise Fager, June 14, 1980; children: Elizabeth, Margaret, Catherine. AB, Harvard Coll., 1977, JD, 1980. Bar: D.C. 1981, N.Y. 1985. Cons. Boston Cons. Group, 1980-83; assoc. White & Case, N.Y.C., 1983-89, ptnr., 1990—. Mem. ABA, N.Y. State Bar Assn., D.C. Bar Assn., Bar Assn. of City N.Y. Corporate, general, Corporate taxation. Office: White & Case Bldg Ll 1155 Avenue Of The Americas New York NY 10036-2787

HAYDEN, JOSEPH A., JR., lawyer; b. Newark, Apr. 2, 1944; s. Joseph A. and Mary (Giblin) H.; m. Donna Heinrich, Aug. 26, 1967; children: Kathryn Elizabeth, Patrick Joseph; m. Katharine Jackson Sweeney, July 19, 1987. Student, Boston Coll., 1966; JD magna cum laude, Rutgers U., 1969. Bar: N.J. 1969, U.S. Dist. Ct. N.J. 1969, N.Y. 1981. Law sec. to chief justice N.J. Supreme Ct., Trenton, 1969-70; dep. atty. gen. organized crime and spl. prosecution sect. Div. Criminal Justice, Atty. Gen.'s Office, Trenton, 1970-73; pvt. practice DeCotis, Fitzpatrick, Glack, Hayden & Cole, Newark, Hoboken and Weehawken, N.J., 1973—. Mem. editl bd. N.J. Law Jour., 1998—. Counsel to Essex County Dems., 1976-80; mem. adv. com. U.S. Dist. Ct. N.J. Recipient outstanding contbn. to trial work award N.J. Criminal Def. Attys., 2000, Trial Attys. of N.J., 2001; named Top Lawyer N.J. Monthly mag., 1997-2000. Fellow Am. Coll. Trial Lawyers, Am. Bar Found.; mem. FBA (trustee 1996-99), N.J. State Bar Assn. (prosecutorial and jud. appointment com. 1992-97, trustee 1998-99), Assn. Criminal Def. Lawyers N.J. (trustee 1985—, founder, 1st pres.), Ct. of Appeal Lawyers 3rd cir. (adv. com.), Fed. Bar Assn. (program chair 1998-99, treas. 2000-2001). Democrat. Avocations: running, recreational basketball, skiing. General civil litigation, Criminal, Environmental. Home: 811 Hudson St Hoboken NJ 07030-5003 Office: Walder Hayden & Brogan PA 5 Becker Farm Rd Roseland NJ 07068

HAYDEN, RAYMOND PAUL, lawyer; b. Rochester, N.Y., Jan. 15, 1939; s. John Joseph and Orpha (Lindsay) H.; m. Suzanne Saloy, Sept. 1, 1962; children: Thomas Gerard, Christopher Matthew. BS in Marine Transit, SUNY Maritime Coll., 1960; LLB, Syracuse U., 1963. Bar: N.Y. 1963, U.S. Ct. Appeals (2d cir.) 1963, U.S. Dist. Ct. (ea. and so. dists.) N.Y. 1964, U.S. Supreme Ct. 1967. Assoc. Haight Gardner Poor & Havens, N.Y.C., 1963-70; asst. gen. counsel Commonwealth Oil Co., N.Y.C., 1970-71; ptnr. Hill Rivkins & Hayden LLP, N.Y.C., 1971—. Mem. Coll. Coun., SUNY Maritime Coll., 1977-98, chmn., 1983-98; mem. adv. coun. Tulane U. Admiralty Law Inst. Served as lt. (j.g.) USNR, 1960-70. Mem. ABA (chmn. standing com. on admiralty and maritime law 1982-86), Maritime Law Assn. U.S. (chmn. com. on admissions 1974-82, exec. com. 1988-91, membership sec. 1996-98, 2nd v.p. 1998-2000, 1st v.p. 2000-02, pres. 2002—), India House Club (bd. dirs. 2002—), Brookville Country Club (N.Y.). Admiralty, Insurance, Private international. Office: Hill Rivkins & Hayden LLP 45 Broadway New York NY 10006-3739 E-mail: rhayden@hillrivkins.com.

HAYEK, CAROLYN JEAN, retired judge; b. Portland, Oreg., Aug. 17, 1948; d. Robert A. and Marion L. (DeKoning) H.; m. Steven M. Rosen, July 21, 1974; children: Jonathan David, Laura Elizabeth. BA in Psychology, Carleton Coll., 1970; JD, U. Chgo., 1973; webmaster cert., Lake Washington Tech. Coll., 2000. Bar: Wash. 1973. Assoc. Jones, Grey & Bayley, Seattle, 1973-77; pvt. practice Federal Way, Wash., 1977-82; judge Federal Way Dist. Ct., 1982-95; ret., 1995. Task force Alternatives for Wash., 1973-75; mem. Wash. State Ecol. Commn., 1975-77; columnist Tacoma News Tribune Hometown Sect., 1995-96; bus. law instr. Lake Washington Tech. Coll., 2000-2001; exec. dir. People's Meml. Assn., Seattle, 2002—. Bd. dirs. 1st Unitarian Ch., Seattle, 1986-89, vice-chair 1987-88, pres. 1988-89; ch. adminstr. Northlake Unitarian Universalist Ch.; treas. Eastshore Unitarian Universalist Ch. Women's Perspective, 2001-2002; den leader Mt. Rainier coun. Boy Scouts Am., 1987-88, scouting coord., 1988-89; bd. dirs. Twin Lakes Elem. Sch. PTA; v.p. Friends of the Libr. Kirkland, 2000—; mem. Kirkland Planning Commn., 2002—. Recipient Women Helping Women award Federal Way Soroptimist, 1991, Martin Luther King Day Humanitarian award King County, 1993, Recognition cert. City of Federal Way Diversity Commn., 1995. Mem. AAUW (co-pres. Kirkland-Redmond br. 1999-2000, co-v.p. Lake Washington br. 2001-2003, pres. Federal Way br. 1978-80, 90-92, chair state level conf. com. 1986-87, diversity com. 1991-98, state bd. mem. 1995-97, dir. ESL project), ABA, Wash. Women Lawyers, Wash. State Bar Assn., King County Dist. Ct. Judges Assn. (treas., exec. com. 1990-93, com. chair, chair and rules com. 1990-94), Elected Wash. Women (dir. 1983-87), Nat. Assn. Women Judges (nat. bd. dirs., dist. bd. dirs. 1984-86, chmn. rules com. 1988-89, chmn. bylaws com. 1990-91), Fed. Way Women's Network (bd. dirs. 1984-91, 95-97, pres. 1985, program co-chair 1989-91, co-editor newsletter), Greater Fed. Way C. of C. (dir. 1978-82, sec. 1980-81, v.p. 1981-82), Sunrise Rotary (com. svc. chair, bd. dirs., membership com., Federal Way chpt. 1991-96, youth exch. officer 1994-95), Washington Women United (bd. dirs. 1995-97), Unitarian Universalist Women's Assn. (chair bylaws com. 1996), Eliot Inst. (bd. dirs. 1996-2000, vice-chair 1998-99, bd. chair 1999-2000, webmaster 1999-2002), Plaza on State Owners Assn. (bd. dirs. 1997-2000, pres. 1997-99, sec. 1999-2000, webmaster 2000—). E-mail: cjh@kirklandplaza.com.

HAYEK, JOHN WILLIAM, lawyer; b. Iowa City, Jan. 25, 1941; s. Will J. and Marjorie B. (Kurtz) H.; m. Patricia M. Hess, Dec. 21, 1968; children: Grace, Matthew, Andrew. BA, Harvard U., 1963, JD, 1966. Bar: Iowa 1966, U.S. Dist. Ct. (so. dist.) Iowa 1967, U.S. Dist. Ct. (no. dist.) Iowa 1968, U.S. Ct. Appeals (8th cir.) 1973. Ptnr. Hayek, Hayek, Brown & Moreland, L.L.P., Iowa City, 1966—. 1st asst. county atty. Johnson County, Iowa City, 1967-70; spl. counsel City of Iowa City, 1970-90, city atty., 1974-81; mem. 6th Jud. Dist. Nominating Commn., 1978-83. Fellow Iowa Acad. Trial Lawyers; mem. Iowa Bar Assn. (chair law practice mgmt. sect.), Johnson County Bar Assn. (pres. 1982-83), Assn. Trial Lawyers Iowa, Nat. Bd. Trial Advocacy, Iowa Def. Counsel Assn. Mason Ladd Inn of Ct. (emeritus master of the bench). Unitarian Universalist. General civil litigation, General practice, Property, real (including real estate development, water). Home: 531 Kimball Rd Iowa City IA 52245-5830 Office: Hayek Hayek Brown & Moreland LLP 120 1/2 E Washington St Iowa City IA 52240-3924

HAYES, BYRON JACKSON, JR., retired lawyer; b. L.A., July 9, 1934; s. Byron Jackson and Caroline Violet (Scott) H.; m. DeAnne Saliba, June 30, 1962; children: Kenneth Byron, Patricia DeAnne. Student, Pomona Coll., 1952-56; BA magna cum laude, Harvard U., LLB cum laude, 1959. Bar: Calif. 1960, U.S. Supreme Ct. 1963. Assoc. McCutchen, Black, Verleger & Shea, L.A., 1960-68, ptnr., 1968-89, Baker & Hostetler, 1990-97; ret., 1998. Trustee L.A. Urban Found., 1996—, CFO, 1998-2000, v.p., CFO, 2000—; trustee L.A. Ch. Ext. Soc. United Meth. Ch., 1967-77, pres., 1974-77, chancellor ann. conf. Pacific and S.W., 1979-86, dir. 1010 devel. corp., 1993—, v.p., 1995—; dir., pres. Pacific and S.W. United Meth. Found., 1978-84; dir., v.p. Padua Hills, Inc., 1999—. Named Layperson of yr. Pacific and S.W. Ann. Conf., United Meth. Ch., 1981; recipient Bishop's award, 1992, 2000. Mem. ABA, Am. Coll. Mortgage Attys. (regent 1984-93, pres. 1993-94), Calif. Bar Assn., Los Angeles County Bar Assn. (chmn. real property sect. 1982-83), Toluca Lake Property Owners Assn. (sec. 1990-94), Toluca Lake C. of C. (dir. 2001—), Pomona Coll. Alumni Assn. (pres. 1984-85), Pomona Coll. Torchbearers (pres. 2001-2003), Lakeside Golf Club.

HAYES, DAVID MICHAEL, lawyer; b. Syracuse, N.Y., Dec. 2, 1943; s. James P. and Lillie Anna (Wood) H.; m. Elizabeth S. Tracy, Aug. 26, 1972; children: Timothy T., AnnElizabeth S. AB, Syracuse U., 1965; LLB, U. Va., 1968. Bar: Va. 1968, N.Y. 1969. Assoc. Hiscock & Barclay, Syracuse, 1968-72; asst. gen. counsel Agway Inc., Syracuse, 1972-81, gen. counsel, sec., 1981-87, v.p., gen. counsel, sec., 1987-92, sr. v.p., gen. counsel, sec., 1992-2001; of counsel Bond, Schoeneck & King, Syracuse, 2001—. Adj. prof. law Syracuse U. Coll. Law, 1995—; former chmn. Nat. Coun. of Farmer Coops. Legal Tax and Acctg. Com. Bd. dirs., former pres. Boys and Girls Club of Syracuse. With Army N.G., 1968-74. Mem.: ABA, Va. State Bar, N.Y. State Bar Assn. (ho. of dels. 1995—99, 2002—, exec. com. of antitrust sect. 2001—), Onondaga County Bar Assn. (pres. 1998), N.Y. Bar Found., Skaneateles Country Club, Century Club. Democrat. Office: BS&K One Lincoln Ctr Syracuse NY 13202-1355 Fax: 315-281-8100. E-mail: dhayes@bsk.com.

HAYES, DAVID JOHN ARTHUR, JR., legal association executive; b. Chgo., July 30, 1929; s. David J.A. and Lucille (Johnson) H.; m. Anne Huston, Feb. 20, 1963; children— David J.A. III, Cary AB, Harvard U., 1952, JD, 1961. Bar: Ill. Trust officer, asst. sec. First Nat. Bank of Evanston, Ill., 1961-63; gen. counsel Ill. State Bar Assn., Chgo., 1963-66; asst. dir. ABA, Chgo., 1966-68, div. dir., 1968-69, asst. exec. dir., 1969-87, v.p., 1987-88, assoc. exec. v.p., 1989-90, sr. assoc. exec. v.p., 1990, exec. dir., 1990-94, exec. dir. emeritus, 1994—; exec. dir. Naval Res. Lawyers Assn., 1971-75; asst. sec. gen. Internat. Bar Assn., 1978-80, 90—, Inter-ABA, 1984—. Contbr. articles to profl. jours. Capt. JAGC, USNR Fellow Am. Bar Found. (life); mem. Ill. State Bar Assn. (ho. of dels. 1972-76), Nat. Orgn. Bar Counsel (pres. 1967), Chgo. Bar Assn., Michigan Shores Club. Home: 908 Pontiac Rd Wilmette IL 60091-1349 Office: ABA 750 N Lake Shore Dr Chicago IL 60611-4403 E-mail: djahayes@aol.com.

HAYES, DAVID RALPH, lawyer; b. Rochester, N.Y., Nov. 25, 1963; s. Ralph and Jeanette Arlene (Quintyne) H. BA, Howard U., 1985; JD, Yale U., 1988. Bar: N.Y. 1989, U.S. Ct. Appeals (2d cir.) 1995, U.S. Dist. Ct. (we. dist.) N.Y. 1991. Assoc. Paul, Weiss, Rifkind, N.Y.C., 1988-89; law clk. U.S. Ct. Appeals (2d cir.), N.Y.C., 1989-90; assoc. Phillips, Lytle, Buffalo, 1991-95; asst. corp. counsel City of Buffalo, 1995—. Bd. dirs. New Refuge House, Inc., Buffalo, 1992—2002. Mem. N.Y. State Bar Assn., Bar Assn. Erie County, Minority Bar Assn. (v.p., 1996-97), Phi Beta Kappa. Dem. Baptist. Avocations: stamp collecting, bicycling. Office: City of Buffalo Law Dept 1100 City Hall Buffalo NY 14202-3311

HAYES, DEWEY, lawyer; b. Ga., July 27, 1923; s. J.C. and Mary (Walsh) H.; m. Margaret Haley, June 16, 1951; children: Dewey Jr., Franklin, Candy. AB, Mercer U., JD, 1949. Bar: Ga. 1949, U.S. Supreme Ct. 1966. Mem. Ga. Ho. of Reps., 1953-56; dist. atty. Waycross Jud. Cir., Ga., 1957-80; sole practice Douglas, Ga., 1980—. Instr. law South Ga. Coll., 1973. Author: You and the Law, 1970, Georgia Warrants, 1972; Miranda, 1973; Search and Seizure, 1973. Mem. Ga. State Crime Commn., 1973-74. Served with U.S. Army, 1942-46, ETO, PTO. Mem. Nat. Dist. Atty.'s Assn., Dist. Attys. Assn. Ga. (pres. 1972), Am. Legion, V.F.W., Douglas Bar Assn. (pres. 1962—), Delta Theta Phi (pres. 1949), Kappa Sigma. Lodges: Elk, Lion, Woodman of World. Methodist. Insurance, Personal injury (including property damage), Workers' compensation. Office: 107 Madison Ave S Douglas GA 31533-5321

HAYES, DEWEY NORMAN, JR., lawyer; b. Douglas, Ga., May 7, 1955; s. Dewey N. and Margaret Harrell (Haley) H.; m. Clara June Carver, Mar. 10, 1984. AB, U. Ga., 1976; JD, Mercer U., 1979. Bar: U.S. Dist. Ct. (so. and mid. dists.) Ga. 1979, U.S. Ct. Appeals (5th and 11th cirs.) 1979. Sole practice, Douglas, 1979—; city atty. Ambrose, Ga., 1980—90; soliciter State Ct., Coffee County, Ga., 1985—89. V.p. Coffee County ARC, Douglas, 1980-85, Ga. Assn. Dem. County Chmn., 1985; mem. Dem. Exec. Com., Atlanta, 1985—. Mem. Ga. Assn. Dems. (v.p., co-chmn. 1985—), Nat. Coll. Advocacy (civil trial advocate 2002). Lodges: Lions (v.p. Douglas 1983—, pres. 1987, past pres. 1988, solicitor 1985-88). Democrat. Methodist. Home: 503 Dogwood Ave Douglas GA 31533-4714 Office: 105 S Madison Ave PO Box 37 Douglas GA 31534-0037

HAYES, GEORGE NICHOLAS, lawyer; b. Alliance, Ohio, Sept. 30, 1928; s. Nicholas John and Mary Irene (Fanady) H. BA, U. Akron, 1950; MA, Western Res. U., 1953, LLB, 1955. Bar: Ohio 1955, U.S. Dist. Ct. Alaska 1957, U.S. Ct. Appeals (9th cir.) 1958, Alaska 1959, U.S. Supreme Ct. 1964, Wash. 1972. Mcpl. ct. prosecutor, asst. county prosecutor Portage County, Ravenna, Ohio, 1955-57; asst. U.S. atty. Fairbanks and Anchorage, Alaska, 1957-59; dep. atty gen. State of Alaska, Anchorage, 1959-62; dist. atty. 3d Jud. Dist., Anchorage, 1960-62; atty gen. Juneau, Alaska, 1962-64; spl. counsel to Gov. on earthquake recovery program State of Alaska, Washington, 1964; stockholder Delaney, Wiles, Hayes, Gerety & Ellis, Inc. and predecessor, Anchorage, 1964-92, of counsel, 1992. Mem. ABA, Alaska Bar Assn, Anchorage Bar Assn. Democrat. Office: Delaney Wiles Hayes 1007 W 3rd Ave Anchorage AK 99501-1936

HAYES, GERALD JOSEPH, lawyer; b. Bronx, N.Y., July 24, 1950; s. James Joseph and Gladys (Guest) H.; m. Diane Elizabeth Willoughby, July 21, 1984; children: Erin Jane, Thomas Joseph, Cara Elizabeth. BA, U. Mass., 1972; JD, U. Miami, 1978. Bar: N.Y. 1979, U.S. Dist. Ct. (so. dist.) N.Y. 1979. Assoc. Baker & McKenzie, N.Y.C., 1978-85, ptnr., 1985—, mng. ptnr., 1995, 97, 99—, mem. policy com., 1997—, nominating com., 2002—. Mem. Bus. Coun. for UN, 1990-95. Nat. alumni adv. bd. U. Miami Sch. Law, 1992—. Mem. ABA (atomic energy com. pub. utility law sect. 1983, vice chair internat. tort and ins. law com., tort and ins. practice sect. 1997—), Assn. Bar City N.Y. (com. on nuclear tech. and law 1979-82, 85-88, com. on ins. law 1983-84), Nat. Assn. Ins. Commrs. (adv. com. on internat. law 1989-90), Nat. Risk Retention Assn. Nuclear power, Insurance, Private international. Office: Baker & McKenzie 805 3rd Ave New York NY 10022-7513

HAYES, J. MICHAEL, lawyer; b. St. Louis, Dec. 10, 1946; s. Frank J. and Louise J. (Lough) H.; m. Vicky J. Verbocy, May 27, 1972; children: Thomas K., James M. BS summa cum laude, SUNY, Brockport, 1973; JD, SUNY, Buffalo, 1976. Bar: N.Y. 1977, U.S. Dist. Ct. (we. dist.) N.Y. 1977. Assoc. Smith, Murphy & Schoepperle, Buffalo, 1977-79, Tenney, Smith & Scott, Buffalo, 1979-82, Terry D. Smith, Buffalo, 1982-86; ptnr. Smith, Keller, Hayes & Miner, Buffalo, 1986-94; pvt. practice, Buffalo, 1994—. General civil litigation, Personal injury (including property damage), Product liability. Office: 69 Delaware Ave Rm 1111 Buffalo NY 14202-3805 E-mail: jmh@jmichaelhayes.com.

HAYES, JOHN CHARLES, lawyer; b. Fairbanks, Alaska, Oct. 18, 1962; s. Charles Arthur and Barbara Ellen (Knott) H. BA, Boston U., 1984; MA, U. Mass., 1987; JD, Boston Coll., Newton, Mass., 1990. Bar: Mass. 1990, U.S. Dist. Ct. Mass., 1992. Trial atty. Com. for Pub. Counsel Svcs., Salem and Worcester, Mass., 1990—. Trainer Continuing Legal Edn., Boston, 1992—. Mem. Nat. Assn. Criminal Def. Lawyers, Mass. Assn. Criminal Def. Lawyers. Democrat. Office: Com Pub Counsel Svcs 1 Salem Grn Ste 408 Salem MA 01970-3790

HAYES, JOHN FRANCIS, lawyer; b. Salina, Kans., Dec. 11, 1919; s. John Francis and Helen (Dye) H.; m. Elizabeth Ann Ireton, Aug. 10, 1950; children: Carl Ireton, Ann Chandler. AB, Washburn Coll., 1941; LL.B., 1946. Bar: Kans. 1946, Mo. 1987. Pvt. practice, Hutchinson, Kans., 1946—; dir. Gilliland & Hayes, P.A. (and predecessors), 1946—. Mem. Commn. Uniform State Laws, 1975—; bd. dirs. Cen. Bank and Trust Co., Hutchinson, Cen. Fin. Corp., Waddell & Reed Funds. Mem. Kans. Ho. of Reps., 1953-55, 67-79, majority leader, 1975-77. Served as capt. AUS, 1942-46. Fellow Am. Bar Found., Am. Coll. Trial Lawyers; mem. Hutchinson C. of C. (pres. 1961), Kans. Assn. Def. Counsel (pres. 1972-73), Internat. Assn. Def. Counsel. Republican. Insurance, Probate (including wills, trusts). Home: 31 Pawnee Dr Hutchinson KS 67502 Office: 20 W 2nd Ave Fl 2 Hutchinson KS 67501 also: 1211 Penntower Bldg 3100 Broadway St Kansas City MO 64111-2406 also: Epic Ctr 301 N Main Ste 1300 Wichita KS 67202

HAYES, LARRY B. lawyer; b. Atlanta, Oct. 4, 1939; s. Luther F. and Ruby (Thomas) H.; m. Rebecca Thomason, Feb. 7, 1959; children: Laura Alison, Lawrence Bruce. BS in Pharmacy, U. Fla., 1962; JD, St. Mary's U., 1977. Bar: Tex. 1978, U.S. Dist. Ct. (no. dist.) Tex. 1979, U.S. Ct. Appeals (5th cir.) 1979; cert. personal injury trial law, Tex. Trial counsel Windle Turley PC, Dallas, 1978-82; ptnr. Ware & Hayes, Dallas, 1982-83; sr. trial atty. Green, Hayes & Ryan, Dallas, 1983-86; ptnr. Cantey & Hanger, Ft. Worth, 1986—. Mem. Tex. Bar Assn., Tex. Assn. Def. Counsel, Def. Rsch. Inst., Tarrant County Bar Assn., Tarrant County Civil Trial Lawyers Assn., Ridglea Country Club, Phi Delta Phi. Health, Personal injury (including property damage), Product liability. Home: 910 Houston St Apt 802 Fort Worth TX 76102-6228 Office: Cantey & Hanger Burnett Plaza 801 Cherry St Ste 2100 Fort Worth TX 76102-6898

HAYES, MARGARET MARY, lawyer; b. Southington, Conn., Oct. 26, 1957; BA magna cum laude, Tufts U., 1979; JD, U. Conn., 1982. Bar: Conn. 1982, U.S. Dist. Ct. Conn. 1982. Assoc. Anderson & Alden, Bristol, Conn., 1982-86, ptnr., 1986-87, Anderson, Alden & Hayes, Bristol, 1987—. 1st v.p. Bristol Girls' Club Family Ctr., 1986-88, pres., 1988-90; co-chair Bristol United Way Campaign, 1993, bd. dirs., 1993-94; v.p. Am. Heart Assn. (local), 1993-94; housing commr. City of Bristol, 1999-2002; chmn. Housing Authority, 2003—; bd. dirs. Bristol Boys & Girls Club, 1998—, Bristol Hosp. and Health Care, 2000—. Mem. ABA, Conn. Bar Assn., Hartford County Bar Assn., Bristol Bar Assn. (treas. 1986-88, v.p. 1988-89, pres. 1989-90), Assn. Trial Lawyers Am., Conn. Trial Lawyers Assn., Bristol C. of C., Rotary. Democrat. Roman Catholic. State civil litigation, Family and matrimonial, Personal injury (including property damage). Office: Anderson Alden Hayes Ziogas PO Box 1197 Bristol CT 06011-1197 E-mail: mhayes@aahzs.com.

HAYES, MARY DIANNE WIXTED, lawyer; b. Danbury, Conn., Jan. 4, 1942; d. Francis Joseph and Mary (Zwyner) Wixted; m. Paul P. Hayes, Jr., June 18, 1966. BA in Economics, Regis Coll., Weston, MA, 1961—64; JD, Suffolk U. Law Sch., Boston, 1968, LLM, 1968—70; MEd in Religious Edn., Boston Coll., Chestnut Hill, MA, 1989, MA in Theology, 1990—97; STL, Weston SJ Sch. of Theology, Cambridge, MA, 1997—2002. Bar: Mass. 1970, U.S. Dist. Ct. (Mass.) 1971, U. S. Supreme Ct. 1973, U.S. Ct. Appeals (1st cir.) 1979. Ptnr. Hayes and Hayes, Quincy, Mass., 1970—; volunteer atty. Irish Pastoral Centre, 1998—. Town meeting mem. Town of Milton, Milton, Mass., 1977—93; mem. Secular Franciscan Order, Boston, 1985—. Mem.: Am. Immigration Lawyers Assn., Mass. Conveyancers Assn. Inc., Mass. Assn. Women Lawyers (pres. 1993—94), Mass. Bar Assn. (chair probate law sect. coun. 1995—97), S. Shore Regis Club, Weston, Mass. (pres. 1973—75). Roman Catholic. Public international, Labor (including EEOC, Fair Labor Standards Act, labor-management relations, NLRB, OSHA). Office: Hayes and Hayes 31 Newcomb Street Quincy MA 02169-4507 Office Fax: 617-770-0191. Business E-Mail: Wixtedhaye@aol.com.

HAYES, NORMAN ROBERT, JR., lawyer; b. Schenectady, N.Y., Apr. 12, 1948; s. Norman Robert Sr. and Ethel May (Blair) H.; m. Alice S. Margitan, Oct. 14, 1972; children: Robert, Charles. BS, Clarkson U., 1970; JD, Union U., 1973. Bar: N.Y. 1974, U.S. Dist. Ct. (no. dist.) N.Y. 1974, U.S. Supreme Ct. 1978. Ptnr. Wemple, Daly, Casey, Hayes, Watkins & Harter, Schenectady, 1973-86; pvt. practice Clifton Park, N.Y., 1986-96; ptnr. Gordon, Siegel, Mastro, Mullaney, Gordon & Galvin, Clifton Park, N.Y., 1996—. Pres. Hayes Indsl. Inc., 1998—; chmn. Saratoga Econ. Devel. Corp., Saratoga Springs, NY; bd. dirs. Provantage Funding Corp., Ebeling Assocs.; adv. bd. dirs. Chase Manhattan Bank. Pres. County Knolls South Civic Assn., Clifton Park, 1975-76, Saratoga Closing Svcs., 2002. Served to capt. U.S. Army, 1973-74. Mem. ABA, N.Y. State Bar Assn., Schenectady County Bar Assn., Lake George Club (dir., treas. 2002). Republican. Banking, Commercial, contracts (including sales of goods; commercial financing), Corporate, general. Office: 3380 State Route 9L Lake George NY 12845-5511 E-mail: bob6@capital.net.

HAYES, PHILIP HAROLD, lawyer; b. Battle Creek, Mich., Sept. 1, 1940; s. Robert Harold and Maurine (Page) H.; m. Robin Hayes, May 20, 1995; 1 child, Rian; children from previous marriage: Elizabeth, Courtney. AB, Ind. U., 1963, JD, 1967. Bar: Ind. 1967, U.S. Dist. Ct. (so. dist.) Ind. 1967, D.C. 1977, U.S. Ct. Appeals (7th cir.) 1992. Dep. prosecutor Vanderburgh County, Evansville, Ind., 1967-68; ptnr. Cox & Hayes, Evansville, 1969-72; senator State of Ind., Evansville, 1971-74; pvt. practice Evansville, 1973-74, 77-79, 1980—; U.S. congressman U.S. Ho. of Reps., Washington, 1975-77; ptnr. Hayes & Young, Evansville, 1980-90, Hayes & Tornatta, Evansville, 1990-92. Legal counsel Airport Authority Dist., Evansville, 1980-84, Redevel. Commn., Evansville, 1984-88, Health and Hosp. Corp., Evansville, 1984-88, Vanderburgh County Atty., 2001-02. Editor, moderator pub. affairs TV program, 1977-78. Mem. ATLA, Evansville Bar Assn., D.C. Bar Assn., Ind. Bar Assn. Administrative and regulatory, General civil litigation, Property, real (including real estate development, water). Home: 218 Glenview Dr Evansville IN 47710-3737 Office: 400 Court St Evansville IN 47708 E-mail: phaylaw@aol.com.

HAYES, ROBERT E. lawyer; b. Denver, Nov. 12, 1950; BA, U. S.D., 1973, JD with honors, 1976. Bar: S.D. 1976, U.S.Ct. Appeals (8th cir.), 1977, U.S. Supreme Ct. 1980, U.S. Ct. Claims 1988, U.S. Ct. Appeals (D.C. cir.) 1989. Law clk. to Hon. Fred J. Nichol U.S. Dist. Ct. S.D., 1976-77; assoc. Davenport, Evans, Hurwitz & Smith, Sioux Falls, SD, 1977—79, ptnr., 1980—. Editor-in-chief U. S.D. Law Rev., 1975-76. Mem. ABA, State

Bar S.D. (chmn. debtor-creditor com. 1983-86, 1991-94, 1996-99, pres. 2002-03, Minnehaha County Bar Assn., Phi Beta Kappa. Bankruptcy, Commercial, consumer (including collections, credit), Property, real (including real estate development, water). Address: Davenport Evans Hurwitz & Smith LLP 206 W 14th St PO Box 1030 Sioux Falls SD 57101-1030*

HAYES, TIMOTHY GEORGE, lawyer, consultant; b. New London, Conn., June 27, 1954; s. George Melen and Lauretta C. (Bresnahan) Hayes; m. Barbara Joan White, Jan. 27, 1983; children: Laura Katherine, Kevin Michael. BS, Fla. State U., 1976, MS, 1977; JD, Stetson Coll. Law, 1982. Bar: Fla. 1982, U.S. Dist. Ct. (mid. dist.) Fla. 1983. Legis. aide Fla. State Rep. George H. Sheldon, Tallahassee, 1978-79; assoc. Alice K. Nelson, P.A., Tampa, Fla., 1982-83; ptnr. Cotterill, Gonzalez & Hayes, Lutz, Fla., 1983-84, Cotterill, Gonzalez, Hayes & Grantham, Lutz, 1984-88; sr. ptnr. Hayes & McClelland, Lutz, 1988-90, Hayes, Winick & Albrechta, Lutz, 1990-91, Hayes & Albrechta, P.A., Lutz, 1991-93, Hayes & Assocs., Lutz, 1993—. Bd. dirs. Tampa Bay Commuter Rail Authority, Tampa, 1990—97, Pasco County Econ. Devel. Coun., New Port Richey, Fla., 1990—92, Pasco Food Bank, chmn. bd., 2003; bd. dirs. Sunshine Youth Soccer Assn., 1997—99; bd. dirs., coach Ctrl. Pasco United Soccer Assn., 1995—2003, pres., 1996—98; mem. Tampa-Orlando High-Speed Transp. Study Task Force, 1992—94; mem. adv. bd. Pasco-Hernando C.C., 1994—95; bd. dirs., v.p. Heritage Park Found.; citizens adv. com. Pasco County Parks and Recreation, 1999—, Pasco County Natural Gas Pipeline, 2000; pres. United Soccer Assn., 2000—02; v.p. Hillsborough County Young Dems., Tampa, 1978, pres., 1979. Named Outstanding Young Man in Am., Jaycees, 1980, Citizen of Yr., Ctrl. Pasco C. of C., 2002; recipient Sam Walton Bus. Leader award, 1998. Mem.: ABA (real property, probate and trust law sect.), Fla. Bar Assn. (environ. and land use law sect., real property, probate and trust law sect.), Land O' Lakes C. of C. (v.p. 1988—89, pres. 1991—92, chmn. bd. 1992—93, bd. dirs.). Roman Catholic. Avocations: soccer, bicycling, camping, gardening. Land use and zoning (including planning), Probate (including wills, trusts), Property, real (including real estate development, water). Office: Hayes & Assocs 21859 State Road 54 Ste 200 Lutz FL 33549-6986

HAYNER, HERMAN HENRY, lawyer; b. Fairfield, Wash., Sept. 25, 1916; s. Charles H. and Lillie (Reifenberger) H.; m. Jeannette Hafner, Oct. 24, 1942; children: Stephen, James K., Judith A. BA, Wash. State U., 1938; JD with honors, U. Oreg., 1946. Bar: Wash. 1946, Oreg. 1946, U.S. Dist. Ct. Wash. 1947, U.S. Ct. Appeals (9th cir.) 1947. Asst. U.S. atty. U.S. Dept. Justice, Portland, Oreg., 1946-47; atty. City of Walla Walla, Wash., 1949-53; ptnr. Minnick-Hayner, Walla Walla, 1949—. Mem. Wash. State exec. bd. U.S. West, Seattle, 1988-95. Regent Wash. State U., Pullman, 1965-78; dir. YMCA, Walla Walla, 1956-67. Lt. col. Infantry, 1942-46. Decorated Bronze Star medal and four Battle Stars; recipient Disting. Svc. award Jr. C. of C., 1951, Wash. State U. Alumni award, 1988. Fellow ABA, Am. Coll. Trust & Estate Counsel; mem. Wash. State Bar Assn., Walla Walla County Bar Assn. (pres. 1954-55), Walla Walla C. of C. (merit award 1977, dir. 1973-88), Rotary (pres. 1956-57), Walla Walla Country Club (pres. 1956-57). Republican. Presbyterian. Avocations: golf, photography. Corporate, general, Probate (including wills, trusts). Home: PO Box 454 Walla Walla WA 99362 Office: Minnick-Hayner PO Box 1757 Walla Walla WA 99362 E-mail: jchayner@aol.com.

HAYNES, RICHARD, lawyer; b. Houston, Apr. 3, 1927; BBA, U. Houston, 1951, JD, 1956. Bar: Tex. 1956. Pvt. practice, 1956—. Adj. prof. law U. Houston, 1972—73; mem. permanent tchg. faculty Nat. Coll. for Criminal Def. Charter mem. Coll. Edn., Challenge Club, U. Houston; chmn. bd. regents Nat. Coll. for Criminal Def., 1980—81; mem. Nat. Neurofibromatosis Found.-Tex. Chpt.; bd. mem. Coll. Edn. Found. Bd., U. Houston. Fellow: Tex. Bar Found.; mem.: ABA, Houston Law Found. (bd. dirs.), Houston Bar Assn. (bd. dirs.), Harris County Criminal Lawyers Assn. (bd. dirs.), Tex. Trial Lawyers Assn., Tex. Criminal Def. Lawyers Assn. (bd. dirs.), Tex. Bar Assn. (bd. dirs.), Nat. Assn. Criminal Def. Lawyers, Am. Judicature Soc., Am. Bd. Trial Advs., Internat. Soc. Barristers, Phi Alpha Delta (alumni advisor 1979—80). Office: Richard Hayens & Assocs PC 4300 Scotland Houston TX 77007-7394*

HAYNES, WILLIAM J(AMES), II, lawyer; b. Waco, Tex., Mar. 30, 1958; s. William James and Caroline H.; m. Margaret Frances Campbell, 1982; 3 children. BA, Davidson Coll., 1980; JD, Harvard U., 1983; LLD (hon.), Stetson U., 1999. Bar: N.C. 1983, Ga. 1989, D.C. 1990. Law clk. to Hon. James B. McMillan U.S. Dist. Ct. N.C., Charlotte, 1983-84; assoc. Sutherland, Asbill & Brennan, Washington, 1989; spl. asst. to gen. counsel Dept. Def., Washington, 1989-90; gen. counsel Dept. Army, Washington, 1990-93; ptnr. Jenner & Block, Washington, 1993-96; v.p., assoc. gen. counsel Gen. Dynamics Corp., Falls Church, Va., 1996-98; gen. counsel Gen. Dynamics Marine Group, 1997-98; ptnr. Jenner & Block, Washington, 1999—2001; gen. counsel Dept. of Defense, 2001—. Capt. U.S. Army, 1984-88. Mem. ABA, N.C. Bar Assn., D.C. Bar Assn., Ga. Bar Assn. Presbyterian. Avocation: tennis. Federal civil litigation, Environmental, Government contracts and claims. Office: General Counsel of Dept Def 1600 Defense Pentagon Washington DC 20301

HAYNIE, TONY WAYNE, lawyer; b. Houston, Sept. 26, 1955; BA, U. Okla., 1978; postgrad., Boston U., Heidelberg Br., Fed. Republic Germany, 1980-81; JD, U. Tulsa, 1984; MBA, Okla. State U., 1993. Bar: Okla. 1985, U.S. Dist. Okla. 1985, U.S. Ct. Appeals (10th cir.) 1987, U.S. Ct. Appeals (5th cir.) 1992, U.S. Ct. Appeals (7th and D.C. cirs.) 1998, U.S. Supreme Ct. 1990. Assoc. Conner & Winters, Tulsa, 1984-90, ptnr., 1991-92, shareholder, dir., 1992—; pres., CEO The Colonneh Co., Tulsa, 1991—. Arbitrator N.Y. Stock Exch., 1991—93; trustee Transvoc, Inc., 1995—2000, pres. bd. trustees, 1998—99; adj. prof. Coll. Law U. Tulsa, 2002—. Adv. bd. mem. Tulsa Area United Way, 1998-99. 1st lt. U.S. Army, 1978—82. Mem. ABA (sect. bus. law and litig., chair subcom. on expert witness on trial evidence com. of litig. sect. 1991-94), Am. Inns of Ct. (barrister Hudson-Hall-Wheaton chpt. 1996—), Okla. Bar Assn., Okla. Bar Found., Tulsa County Bar Assn., Tulsa County Bar Found., Phi Delta Phi. Democrat. Methodist. Bankruptcy, Federal civil litigation, General civil litigation. Office: Conner & Winters 3700 1st Place Tower 15 E 5th St Tulsa OK 74103-4391 E-mail: thaynie@cwlaw.com.

HAYS, MELISSA PADGETT, lawyer; b. West Islip, NY, June 18, 1968; d. Olin Wright Jr. and Ellen (Medlin) Padgett; m. Robert Bond Hays, III, Mar. 21, 1998. BA, Emory U., 1990; JD, U. Ga., 1994. Bar: Ga. 1994, U.S. Dist. Ct. (so. dist.) Ga. 1994, Supreme Ct. of Ga., 1994, Tenn. 1998, Supreme Ct. of Tenn. 1998. Assoc. Harrison & Shapiro, Augusta, Ga., 1994-95, Garrett & Gilliard, P.C., Augusta, 1995-97; pvt. practice, Augusta, 1997-98; atty., litigation counsel Unum Provident Corp., Chattanooga, 1998—2002, asst. v.p., counsel, 2003—. Alumni mem. Leadership Augusta, 1997—; mem. Jr. League Chattanooga, 2000—. Mem. ABA, State Bar Ga., Tenn. Bar Assn., Southeastern Tenn. Lawyers Assn. for Women (pres. 2003). Insurance. Office: Unum Provident Corp Law Dept 1 Fountain Sq Chattanooga TN 37402-1307

HAYS, SARA L. lawyer, hotel executive; BA cum laude, Carleton Coll., 1984; JD, Northwestern U., 1989, MBA, 2000. Assoc. Coffield Ungaretti & Harris, Chgo., 1989—94; devel. counsel Hyatt Hotels Corp., 1994—97, gen. counsel, 1997—2000, v.p., gen. counsel, 2000—01, sr. v.p., gen. counsel, 2001—. Mem.: ABA, Am. Corp. Counsel Assn., Carleton Coll. Alumni Coun. Home: 2131 W Shakespeare Ave Chicago IL 60647 Office: Hyatt Hotels Corp 200 W Madison St Chicago IL 60606-3414

HAYSLIP, MICHAEL WARREN, lawyer, civil engineer; b. Cleveland, Ohio, Apr. 14, 1962; s. JoAnn (Romano) and Ronald E. Hayslip; m. Christa E. Chandler, July 16, 1988. JD, U.Dayton, Ohio, 1993. Registered Civil Engr., State of Ohio, 1998. Pres./owner NESTI, Dayton, Ohio, 2000—. Construction. Office: Nesti 8951 Treeland Ln Dayton OH 45458 Office Fax: 937-434-7233. Personal E-mail: hayslip@aol.com. E-mail: hayslip@aol.com.

HAYTHE, WINSTON MCDONALD, lawyer, educator, consultant, real estate investor; b. Reidsville, NC, Oct. 10, 1940; s. McDonald Swann and Henrietta Elizabeth (East) H.; m. Glenann Leigh Rogers, Aug. 17, 1963 (div. 1977); children: Sheila Elaine, Kevin McDonald, Rhonda Leigh. BS, S.W. Mo. State U., 1963; JD, Coll. William and Mary, 1967; postgrad., U. Va., 1968—69; grad., Command and Gen. Staff Sch., Ft. Leavenworth, Kans., 1982, U.S. Def. U., 1984; LLM, U.S. Army JAG Sch., 1976. Bar: Va. 1967, D.C. 1969. Assoc. Rhyne & Rhyne, Washington, 1969-72; sr. trial atty. AEC, Washington, 1972-73; asst. gen counsel, sr. atty. Consumer Produce Safety Commn., Washington, 1973-82; staff dir. legal office EPA, Washington, 1982-83, sr. atty. for enforcement policy, 1985-91, sr. atty. Nat. Enforcement Tng. Inst., 1991-94, asst. dir., 1994-96, sr. legal counsel, 1996-2001; sr. counsel Office of Criminal Enforcement, Forensics and Tng., 2001—. Legis. fellow U.S. Senate, Washington, 1983-85; adv. com. paralegal studies U. Md., 1980-95, chmn., 1992-95; adj. prof. law, 1978-94; law faculty U.S. Army Judge Adv. Gen.'s Sch., Charlottesville, Va., 1969-94, Nat. Advocacy Ctr. U.S. Dept. Justice, Columbia, S.C., 1999—; cons. Barrister Ent., Washington, 1978—; elected mem. undergrad. programs adv. coun. U. Md., 1993-95; guest lectr. George Washington U. Sch. Law, 1999-2002, adj. prof. law, 2002-. Trustee Georgetown Presbyn. Ch., 1995-98, v.p. trustees, 1996, pres. trustees, 1997-98, elder, mem. session, 2000-03, clk. of session, 2003—. Col. JAGC, USAR, 1967-94, ret. Fellow: Found. Fed. Bar Assn. (life); mem.: The Social List of Washington, Fed. Bar Assn. (mem. fed. career svcs. divsn. 1974—90, appt. mem. nat. coun. 1998—), DC Bar Assn., Va. State Bar Assn., Coll. William and Mary Law Sch. Assn. (bd. dirs. 1988—95), Cosmos Club, Knights Templar, Kappa Mu Epsilon. Presbyterian. Avocations: playing organ, piano, theater, concerts, reading. Home: 2141 P St NW Apt 402 Washington DC 20037-1031 Office: EPA (MC-2235A) 1200 Pennsylvania Ave NW Washington DC 20460-0001 E-mail: whaythe@hotmail.com.

HAYUTIN, DAVID LIONEL, lawyer; b. Phoenix, Apr. 19, 1930; s. Henry and Eva (Gaines) H.; m. Lee June Rodgers, June 15, 1951 AB, U. So. Calif., Los Angeles, 1952, JD, 1958. Bar: Calif. 1958. Assoc. Pillsbury Winthrop LLP and predecessor firms, Los Angeles, 1958-67, ptnr., 1967—. Author: Distributing Foreign Products in the United States, 1988, revised edit., 2000; assoc. editor So. Calif. Law Rev.; contbr. legal articles to profl. jours. Served to lt. (j.g.) USN, 1952-55. Mem. ABA, Internat. Bar Assn., Calif. Bar Assn., Maritime Law Assn., Mountaingate Country Club. Republican. Avocations: opera, golf. Antitrust, Commercial, contracts (including sales of goods; commercial financing), Private international. Office: Pillsbury Winthrop LLP 725 S Figueroa St Los Angeles CA 90017-5524 E-mail: dhayutin@pillsburywinthrop.com.

HAYWARD, EDWARD JOSEPH, lawyer; b. Springfield, Mo., Dec. 4, 1943; s. Joseph Hunter and Rosemary Hayward; m. Ellinor Duffey, Aug. 30, 1968; children: Jeffrey, Stephen, Susan. Student, U. d'Aix Marseille, Aix-en-Provence, France, 1963-64; AB, Stanford U., 1965; JD magna cum laude, Harvard U., 1971. Bar: N.Y. 1972, Minn. 1980. Assoc. Cleary, Gottlieb, Steen & Hamilton, N.Y.C. and Brussels, 1971-74, Oppenheimer Wolff & Donnelly, LLP, Brussels, 1975-79, ptnr. Mpls., 1978—. Pres. Twin Cities Fgn. Trade Zone Inc., Mpls., 1983-84. Chmn. legis. com. Minn. World Trade Assn., Mpls., 1984-87. Served to capt. U.S. Army, 1965-68. Mem.: ABA, Minn. Bar Assn. (councillor internat. law sect. 1983—, sec. 1986—88, vice chmn. 1988—89, chmn. 1989—90), Dist. Export Coun. (chmn. 1996—), German-Am. C. of C. (bd. dirs. 1994—99, 2000—), French-Am. C. of C. (bd. dirs. 1983—, pres. 1985—87, 1996—2001, nat. sec. 1988—). Republican. Presbyterian. Avocations: languages, sports. Corporate, general, Immigration, naturalization, and customs, Private international. Home: 6625 W Shore Dr Minneapolis MN 55435-1528 Office: Oppenheimer Wolff & Donnelly LLP 45 S 7th St Ste 3300 Minneapolis MN 55402-1609 E-mail: ehayward@oppenheimer.com.

HAYWARD, SAMUEL GEORGE, SR., lawyer; b. Hanover, N.H., Feb. 17, 1946; s. Frederick Reynolds and Lucy Eleanor Hayward; m. Barbara Baumann, Dec. 13, 1969; children: Samuel George Jr., Elizabeth Dalton. BA in History, Norwich U., 1968; JD, U. Louisville, 1973. Bar: Ky. 1974, U.S. Ct. Appeals (6th cir.) 1974. Pres., pvt. practice, Louisville, 1980-98; ptnr. Nicolas, Welsh & Hayward, Louisville, 1993—. Soccer coach Assumption H.S., Louisville, 1991-2000; pres. Ky. Youth Soccer, Lexington, 1992-93. 1st lt. U.S. Army, 1968-71, Korea. Mem. ABA, Ky. Bar Assn., Ky. Trial Lawyers Assn. Home: 5512 Apache Rd Louisville KY 40207-1614 Office: Adams Hayward & Welsh 4036 Preston Hwy Louisville KY 40213

HAZAN, SCOTT L. lawyer; b. N.Y.C., Sept. 13, 1948; s. Jacob and Mildred Hazan; m. Lorraine Hazan, June 25, 1972; children: Jeremy, Alissa. BA, Queens Coll., 1970; JD cum laude, Bklyn. Law Sch., 1973. Assoc., ptnr. Otterbourg, Steindler, Houston & Rosen, P.C., N.Y.C., 1973—. With U.S. Army, 1969—75. Mem.: ABA (bus. bankruptcy com., chpt. 11 subcom., claims trade subcom., task force on profl. compensation subcom.), Turnaround Mgmt. Assn., Am. Bankruptcy Inst., Bankruptcy Bar Assn. City of N.Y., N.Y. State Bar Assn. (subcom. on bankruptcy, former chmn. subcom. on revisions to the Debtor and Creditor Law State). Bankruptcy. Office: Otterbourg Steindler Houston & Rosen PC 230 Park Ave New York NY 10169

HAZARD, GEOFFREY CORNELL, JR., law educator; b. Cleve., Sept. 18, 1929; s. Geoffrey Cornell and Virginia (Perry) H.; m. Elizabeth O'Hara; children: James G., Katherine W., Robin P., Geoffrey Cornell III. BA, Swarthmore Coll., 1953, LLD (hon.), 1988; LLB, Columbia U., 1954; LLD (hon.), Gonzaga U., 1985, U. San Diego, 1985, Ill. Inst. Tech., 1990, Republica Italiana, 1998. Bar: Oreg. 1954, Calif. 1960, Conn. 1982, Pa. 1994. Assoc. Hart, Spencer, McCulloch, Rockwood & Davies, Portland, Oreg., 1954-57; exec. sec. Oreg. Legis. Interim Com. Jud. Adminstrn., 1957-58; assoc. prof. law, then prof. U. Calif., Berkeley, 1958-64; prof. law U. Chgo., 1964-71, Yale U., 1971-94, prof. mgmt., 1979-83, acting dean Sch. Orgn. and Mgmt., 1980-81, Sterling prof. law, 1986-94; trustee prof. U. Pa., Phila., 1994—. Mem. Adminstrv. Conf. U.S., 1971-78; jud. conf. U.S. com. on rules practice and procedure, 1994-2000. Author: (Law text) Research in Civil Procedure, 1963, Ethics in the Practice of Law, 1978; author: (with D.W. Louisell, C. Tait, W. Fletcher) Pleading and Procedure, 1972; author: 8th rev. edit., 1999; author: (with M. Taruffo) (Law text) American Civil Procedure, 1994; author: (with S. Koniak and R. Cramton) Law and Ethics of Lawyering 3d edit., 1999; author: (with W.W. Hodes) Law of Lawyering 3d edit., 2000; author: (with F. James and J. Leubsdorf) Civil Procedure 5th rev.edit., 2001; editor: Law in a Changing America, 1968; editor: (with D. Rhode) Legal Profession: Responsibility and Regulation, 1985; co-editor (with D. Rhode): Professional Responsibility and Regulation, 2002; contbr. Served with USAF, 1948-49. Fellow Am. Bar Found. (exec. dir. 1964-70, rsch. award 1986), Am. Acad. Arts and Scis.; mem. ABA (cons. code jud. conduct 1970-72, reporter stds. jud. adminstrn. 1971-77, reporter model rules of profl. conduct 1978-83), Am. Law Inst. (reporter restatement of judgments 1973-81, dir. 1984-99), Nat. Legal Aid and Defender Assn., Am. Judicature Soc., Selden Soc., Pa. Bar Assn., Calif. State Bar, Phi Beta Kappa. Episcopalian. Avocations: tennis, history, golf. E-mail: ghazard@law.upenn.edu.

HAZELTON, PENNY ANN, law librarian, educator; b. Yakima, Wash., Sept. 24, 1947; d. Fred Robert and Margaret (McLeod) Pease; m. Norris J. Hazelton, Sept. 12, 1971; 1 child, Victoria MacLeod. BA cum laude, Linfield Coll., 1969; JD, Lewis and Clark Law Sch., 1975; M in Law Librarianship, U. Wash., 1976. Bar: Wash. 1976, U.S. Supreme Ct. 1982. Assoc. law libr., assoc. prof. U. Maine, 1976-78, law libr., assoc. prof., 1978-81; asst. libr. for rsch. svcs. U.S. Supreme Ct., Washington, 1981-85, law libr., 1985, U. Wash., Seattle, 1985—, prof. law, assoc. dean libr. and computing svcs., 1985—. Tchr. legal rsch., law librarianship, Indian law; cons. Maine Adv. Com. on County Law Librs., Nat. U. Sch. Law, San Diego, 1985-88, Lawyers Cooperative Pub., 1993-94, Marquette u. Sch. Law, 2002. Author: Computer Assisted Legal Research: The Basics, 1993; author: (with others) Washington Legal Researcher's Deskbook, 3d edit., 2002; contbr. articles; gen. editor Specialized Legal Rsch. (Aspen). Recipient Disting. Alumni award U. Wash., 1992. Mem. ABA (sect. legal edn. and admissions to bar, chair com. on librs. 1993-94, vice chair 1992-93, 94-95, com. on law sch. facilities 1998—), Am. Assn. Law Schs. (com. law librs. 1991-94), Law Librs. New Eng. (sec. 1977-79, pres. 1979-81), Am. Assn. Law Librs. (program chmn. ann. meeting 1984, exec. bd. 1984-87, v.p. 1989-90, pres. 1990-91, program co-chair Insts. 1983, 95), Law Librs. Soc. Washington (exec. bd. 1983-84, v.p., pres. elect 1984-85), Law Librs. Puget Sound, Wash. State Bar Assn. (chair editl. adv. bd.), Wash. Adv. Coun. on Librs., Westpac. Office: U Wash Marian Gould Gallagher Law Libr 1100 NE Campus Pkwy Seattle WA 98105-6605

HAZLEHURST, ROBERT PURVIANCE, JR., lawyer; b. Spartanburg, S.C., Jan. 7, 1919; s. Robert Purviance and Lottie Lee (Nicholls) H.; m. Mary Kierulff, Feb. 20, 1947 (dec. July 1971); children: Ellen Hazlehurst Courtney, Charlotte Hazlehurst Leonesio, Anne Hazlehurst Goldberg; m. Dorothy Wilson Deemer, Jan. 7, 1972. AB, Princeton U., 1940; LL.B., Yale U., 1947. Bar: N.J. 1947. Since practiced in Newark and Morristown; ptnr. Pitney, Hardin, Kipp & Szuch, 1952-89. Bd. dirs. Princeton Fund, 1966-71, chmn. ann. giving campaign, 1967-68 Sec., trustee Greater Newark Hosp. Devel. Fund; trustee Kent Pl. Sch., Summit, N.J., 1960-70; trustee, v.p. Silver Hill Found., New Canaan, Conn., 1973-85; trustee United Hosps. Newark, 1958-73, pres., 1970-73. Served to capt. USAAF, 1942-45. Mem.: Short Hills (N.J.), Nassau (N.J.). Home: 38 Sinclair Ter Short Hills NJ 07078-1714

HEAD, BEN THOMAS, lawyer; b. Oklahoma City, Nov. 1, 1920; s. Ben Thomas Head and Virginia (Broados) Pine; m. Mary C. Johnston, June 17, 1949 (div. June 1983); children: Marcy, Paul, Eric; m. June Leftwich, Mar. 22, 1986. BBA, U. Okla., 1942, LLB, 1948, JD, 1970. Bar: Okla., Tex. Pres., chmn., chief exec. officer RepublicBank, Austin, Tex., 1978-84; sr. lectr. banking U. Tex., Austin, 1984-88; U.S. trustee U.S. Dist. Ct. (so. and we. dists.) Tex., Houston, 1988-93. Pres., CEO United Va. Bank (now SunTrust), Newport News, Va., 1975-78; chmn. City Savs., San Angelo, Tex., 1986-87. V.p. Oklahoma City C. of C., 1973, chmn. Austin C. of C., 1983; pres. progress com. Newport News., Va., 1978; bd. dirs., chmn. fin. com. Austin Presbyn. Sem., 1982-90; bd. dirs. fin. com. Tex. Presbyn. Found., 1988—; trustee, vice chmn. bd., Hampton U., 1980—. Col. U.S. Army, 1942-46, India. Named Exec. of Yr. Austin C. of C., 1983. Mem. Rotary. Avocations: golf, walking. Home: 3234 Tarryhollow Dr Austin TX 78703-1639 Office: 816 Congress Ave Ste 1200 Austin TX 78701-2442

HEAD, ELIZABETH, lawyer; b. Rochester, Minn., Dec. 17, 1930; d. Walter Elias and Ruth Winnogene (Evesmith) Bonner; m. C.J. Head, Dec. 30, 1950; 1 child, Alison Elizabeth. BA, U. Chgo., 1949, JD, 1952. Bar: Ill. 1952, Calif. 1955, N.Y. 1958, U.S. Supreme Ct. 1963, D.C. 1978. Atty. Nat. Labor Rels. Bd., Washington, 1953-54; assoc. Johnston & Johnston, San Francisco, 1954-56; atty. Aminoil Inc., San Francisco, 1956-57; teaching assoc. Law Sch. Columbia U., N.Y., 1957-58; assoc. Skadden Arps, N.Y., 1958-60; atty. The Coca-Cola Corp., N.Y., 1961-65; assoc. Kaye Scholer, N.Y., 1965-72, ptnr., 1973-82; mem. Hall & Estill, Tulsa, 1983-87; vis. fellow antitrust analysis Fed. Energy Regulatory Commn., Washington, 1987-89; gen. counsel Columbia U., N.Y.C., 1989-97. Arbitrator, mediator, 1998—. Trustee Mary Baldwin Coll., Staunton, Va., 1983-87. Mem. ABA (standing com. on dispute resolution 1983-90), Assn. of Bar of City of N.Y. (non-profit orgns. com. 1989-90, chair 1992-95, health law com. 1997-2000), Century Assn., Order of Coif, Phi Beta Kappa. Avocations: travel, music, art, theatre. Office: 303 E 57th St # 47F New York NY 10022-2947

HEAD, IVAN LEIGH, law educator; b. Calgary, Alta., Can., July 28, 1930; s. Arthur Cecil and Birdie Hazel (Crockett) H.; m. Barbara Spence Eagle, June 23, 1952; children: Laurence Allan, Bryan Cameron, Catherine Spence, Cynthia Leigh; m. Ann Marie Price, Dec. 1, 1979. BA, U. Alta., 1951, LLB, 1952; LLM, Harvard U., 1960; LLD (hon.), U. Alta., 1987, U. West Indies, 1987, U. Western Ont., 1988, U. Ottawa, 1988, U. Calgary, 1989, Beijing U., 1990, St. Francis Xavier U., 1990, U. Man., 1991, U. Notre Dame, 1991, Carleton U., 1996. Bar: Alta. 1953; Queen's Counsel, Can. Practiced in, Calgary, 1953-59; partner Helman, Barron & Head, 1955-59; fgn. service officer Dept. External Affairs, Ottawa, Kuala Lumpur, 1960-63; prof. law U. Alta., 1963-67; assoc. counsel to Minister of Justice, Govt. of Can., 1967-68, spl. asst. to prime minister of Can., 1968-78; pres. Internat. Devel. Rsch. Centre, Ottawa, 1978-91; prof. law, dir. Liu Centre for the study of global issues U. B.C., Vancouver, Canada, 1991—99, prof. emeritus, 2000—. Sr. fellow Salzburg Seminar; bd. dirs. Acad. Ednl. Devel., Can. World Youth. Author: International Law, National Tribunals and the Rights of Aliens, 1971, On a Hinge of History, 1991, The Canadian Way, 1995; editor: This Fire Proof House, 1967, Conversation with Canadians, 1972; contbr. articles to profl. jours. Trustee Internat. Food Policy Rsch. Inst., 1979-88; mem. Ind. Commn. on Internat. Humanitarian Issues, 1983-87. Decorated officer Order of Can.; officer Grand Cross, Order of The Sun (Peru); Chief Justice's medallist U. Alta. Law Sch.; Frank Knox Meml. fellow Harvard Law Sch., 1959-60; named to Sports Wall of Fame U. Alta. Mem. Internat. Law Assn., Can. Council Internat. Law, Can. Inst. Internat. Affairs, Am. Soc. Internat. Law, Law Soc. Alta., Inter-Am. Dialogue. Anglican. Home: 2343 Bellevue Ave West Vancouver BC Canada V7V 1C9 Office: U BC Faculty of Law Vancouver BC Canada V6T 1Z1 E-mail: ivanhead@shaw.ca.

HEAD, PATRICK JAMES, lawyer; b. Randolph, Nebr., July 13, 1932; s. Clarence Martin and Ellen Cecelia (Magirl) H.; m. Eleanor Hickey, Nov. 24, 1960; children: Adrienne, Ellen, Damian, Maria, Brendan, Martin, Sarah, Daniel, Brian. AB summa cum laude, Georgetown U., 1953, LL.B., 1956, LL.M. in Internat. Law, 1957. Bar: D.C. 1956, Ill. 1966. Assoc. John L. Ingolsby (and predecessor firm), Washington, 1956-64; gen. counsel internat. ops. Sears, Roebuck & Co., Oakbrook, Ill., 1964-70, counsel midwest ter. Skokie, Ill., 1970-72; v.p. Montgomery Ward & Co., Inc., Washington, 1972-76, v.p., gen. counsel, sec. Chgo., 1976-81; v.p., gen. counsel FMC Corp., Chgo., 1981-96; ptnr. Altheimer E. Gray, Chgo., 1997—2001, Williams Montgomery and John, Chgo., 2001—. Bd. visitors Northwestern Law, 1988-91. Mem. Chgo. Crime Commn.; bd. regents Georgetown U., Washington, 1981-87; bd. visitors Georgetown Law Sch., 1992—. Mem. ABA, D.C. Bar Assn., Chgo. Bar Assn., Am. Law Inst. Clubs: Met. (Washington); Chgo, Internat. Democrat. Roman Catholic. Administrative and regulatory, Federal civil litigation, Corporate, general. Office: Williams Montgomery & John Ltd 20 N Wacker Dr 21st Fl Chicago IL 60606-7407

HEALY, GEORGE WILLIAM, III, lawyer, mediator; b. New Orleans, Mar. 8, 1930; s. George William and Margaret Alford H.; m. Sharon Saunders, Oct. 26, 1974; children: George W. IV, John Carmichael, Floyd Alford, Hyde Dunbar, Mary Margaret. BA, Tulane U., 1950, JD, 1955. Bar: La. 1955, U.S. Supreme Ct. 1969. Assoc. Phelps, Dunbar, Marks, Claverie & Sims, New Orleans, 1955-58; ptnr. Phelps Dunbar LLP, 1958-95; of counsel Phelps Dunbar, 1996—. Mem. U.S. del. Comité Maritime Internat., Tokyo, 1969, Lisbon, 1985, Paris, 1990, Sydney, 1994, titulary mem. Mem. planning com. Tulane U. Admiralty Law Inst., dir. World Trade Ctr., 1993—; dir. New Orleans Pro Bono Project, 1995-97, La. Orgn. for Jud.

Excellence, 1997—. Fellow Am. Bar Found., Am. Coll. Trial Lawyers, Maritime Law Assn. U.S. (mem. exec. com. 1984-87, 2d v.p. 1988-90, 1st v.p. 1990-92, pres. 1992-94), La. Bar Found.; mem. ABA (ho. dels. 1993-95, 97-2000), New Orleans Bar Assn. (pres. 1992), Def. Rsch. Inst., La. Assn. Def. Counsel, New Orleans Assn. Def. Counsel, Com. Maritime Internat. Am. Found. (dir. 1990—), New Orleans Bar Assn. Inn of Ct. (master), Boston Club., La. Club, Stratford Club, Plimsoll Club, Recess Club (pres. 1978), Pinfeathers Hunting Club, New Orleans Lawn Tennis Club, Propeller Club, Mariners Club. Republican. Episcopalian. Admiralty. Home: 6020 Camp St New Orleans LA 70118-5902 Office: Canal Place 365 Canal St Ste 2000 New Orleans LA 70130-6534 Fax: 504-568-9130. E-mail: healyg@phelps.com.

HEALY, HAROLD HARRIS, JR., lawyer; b. Denver, Colo., Aug. 27, 1921; s. Harold Harris and Lorena (Isom) H.; m. Elizabeth A. Debevoise, May 24, 1952; 1 son, Harold Harris III. AB, Yale U., 1943, LL.B., 1949. Bar: N.Y. 1949, U.S. Supreme Ct 1957. Exec. asst. to U.S. atty. gen., Washington, 1957-59; mem. Debevoise & Plimpton, NYC, 1959-89, resident ptnr. Paris, 1964-67, of counsel NYC, 1989-92. Mem. Am. adv. council Ditchley Found., 1972-99; bd. dirs. Legal Aid Soc., 1968-89 , chmn., 1975-79, pres.'s coun., 1989—. Bd. dirs. Met. Opera Guild, 1975-2000, Acad. Am. Poets, 1993-94; nat. coun. Glimmerglass Opera, 1992—; adv. dir. Met. Opera Assn., 1986-95; trustee Vassar Coll., 1977-86. Capt. F.A., AUS, 1943-46, ETO. Decorated Bronze Star medal. Mem. ABA (mem. coun. sect. of internat. law and practice 1987-90), N.Y. State Bar Assn., Assn. Bar City of N.Y. (sec. 1959-61), Am. Law Inst., Order of Coif, Am. Soc. Internat. Law (mem. exec. coun. 1977-80), Internat. Law Assn., Internat. Bar Assn., Union Internationale des Avocats (pres. 1979-81), Am. Coll. Investment Counsel, Coun. Fgn. Rels., Pilgrims U.S., Yale Law Sch. Assn. (exec. com. 1974-82, v.p. 1980-82), Century Assn., Univ. Club, Met. Club, Phi Beta Kappa, Zeta Psi, Phi Delta Phi, Chevalier de la Legion d'Honneur. Republican. Episcopalian. Corporate, general, Private international, Securities. Home: 1170 5th Ave New York NY 10029-6527 Office: Debevoise & Plimpton 919 3rd Ave Fl 31 New York NY 10022-6225

HEALY, JAMES CASEY, lawyer; b. Washington, Feb. 19, 1956; s. Joseph Francis Jr. and Patricia Ann (Casey) H.; m. Kelly Anne Quinn, Nov. 4, 1995; 1 child, Caitlin Quinn. BS, Spring Hill Coll., 1978; JD, Emory U., 1982. Bar: Ga. 1983, Conn. 1983, U.S. Dist. Ct. Conn. 1984, U.S. Tax Ct. 1984, U.S. Supreme Ct. 1987. Assoc. Gregory and Adams PC, Wilton, Conn., 1982-87, ptnr., 1988-89, mng. ptnr., 1990-94, v.p., 1995—. Spl. counsel Wilton Police Commn., 1986-98; mem. Parks and Recreation Commn., 1991-2002, sec., 1991-93, chmn., 1997-2002; corporator Ridgefield Bank, 1997—; sec. Fire Commn., 2002—. Bd. dirs. Mark Lavin Meml. Offshore Med. and Safety Found., Empire, Mich., 1987—97; bd. dirs. Village Market, Inc. , 1988—90; chmn. leadership giving program United Way, 1991; bd. mgrs. Wilton Children's Ctr., 1996—98; athletic fields subcom.of building com. Wilton H.S., 1998—99; steering com. Wilton Family Recreation and Activity Ctr., 2000; bd. trustees Wilton Hist. Soc., 2001—; bd. dirs. Wilton Teen Ctr., 2001—. Mem. State Bar Ga., State Bar Conn. (exec. com., planning and zoning sect. 1992-94, 98—), Am. Planning Assn., Stamford/Norwalk Regional Bar Assn. (law office mgmt. com. 1994-96, co-chmn. land use com. 1996—, real estate broker's contract com. 1997-98), Real Estate Fin. Assn., Wilton C. of C. (bd. dirs. 1994-96). Republican. Roman Catholic. Land use and zoning (including planning), Property, real (including real estate development, water). Office: Gregory and Adams 190 Old Ridgefield Rd Wilton CT 06897-4023 E-mail: jhealy@gregoryandadams.com.

HEALY, JOSEPH FRANCIS, JR., lawyer, retired air transportation executive; b. NYC, Aug. 11, 1930; s. Joseph Francis and Agnes (Kett) H.; m. Patricia A. Casey, Apr. 23, 1955; children: James C., Timothy, Kevin, Cathleen M., Mary, Terence. BS, Fordham U., 1952; JD, Georgetown U., 1959. Bar: D.C. 1959. With gen. traffic dept. Eastman-Kodak Co., Rochester, N.Y., 1954-55; air transp. examiner CAB, Washington, 1955-59; practiced in Washington, 1959-70, 80-81; asst. gen. counsel Air Transport Assn. Am., 1966-70; v.p. legal Eastern Air Lines, Inc., N.Y.C. and Miami, Fla., 1970-80; ptnr. Ford, Farquhar, Kornblut & O'Neill, Washington, 1980-81; v.p. legal affairs Piedmont Aviation, Inc., Winston Salem, N.C., 1981-84, sr. v.p., gen counsel, 1984-89, ret., 1989; sr. v.p., gen. counsel Trans World Airlines Inc., Mt. Kisco, N.Y., 1993-94. Mem. bd. visitors Sch. Law Wake Forest U., 1988-96. 1st lt. USAF, 1952-54. Mem.: Nat. Aero. Assn., Fed. Bar Assn., Internat. Aviation Club (Washington), Phi Delta Phi, Beta Gamma Sigma. Aviation, Corporate, general. Home: 104 Overlink Ct Lynchburg VA 24503-3200

HEALY, JOSEPH ROBERT, lawyer; b. Troy, N.Y., Apr. 15, 1939; s. Thomas Francis and Isabel Kathryn (Eagle) H.; m. Sylvia Anne Tuccillo, May 14, 1976; 1 child, Daniel Joseph. BA in Sociology, Siena Coll., 1961; JD, Albany Law Sch., 1965. Bar: N.Y. 1973, U.S. Dist. Ct. (no. dist.) N.Y. 1973. Claims examiner Social Security Adminstrn., Glens Falls, N.Y., 1961-62; personnel examiner N.Y. State Dept. Civil Svc., Albany, 1962-69, sr. legal examiner, 1969-71, atty., 1971-75, sr. atty., 1975-82; assoc. atty., 1982-87; dir. civil svc. security ops., 1987-88; adminstrv. counsel internal controls, 1988-92; dir. investigations, 1992—. Author newsletter N.Y. State Orgn. Mgmt. Confidential Employees News Network. Active Woodland Hills Homeowners Assn., Clifton Park, N.Y. Republican. Roman Catholic. Home: 5 George Dr Clifton Park NY 12065-1811 E-mail: JHealy71@Hotmail.com.

HEALY, NICHOLAS JOSEPH, lawyer, educator; b. N.Y.C., Jan. 4, 1910; s. Nicholas Joseph and Frances Cecilia (McCarthy) H.; m. Margaret Marie Ferry, Mar. 29, 1937; children: Nicholas, Margaret Healy Parker, Rosemary Healy Bell, Mary Louise Healy White, Donall, Kathleen Healy Hamon. AB, Holy Cross Coll., 1931; JD, Harvard U., 1934. Bar: N.Y. 1935, U.S. Supreme Ct. 1949. Pvt. practice, N.Y.C., 1935—42; mem. Healy & Baillie (and predecessor firms), 1948—. Spl. asst. to atty. gen. U.S., 1945-48; tchr. admiralty law NYU Sch. Law, 1947-86, adj. prof., 1960—; Niels F. Johnsen vis. prof. maritime law Tulane Maritime Law Ctr., 1986; vis. prof. maritime law Shanghai Maritime Inst. (now Shanghai Maritime U.), 1981, 86, 88. Contbr. chpts. to Ann. Survey Am. Law, 1948-87; author: (with Sprague) Cases on Admiralty, 1950; (with Currie) Cases and Materials on Admiralty, 1965; (with Sharpe) Cases and Materials on Admiralty, 1974, 3rd edit., 1998; (with Sweeney) The Law of Marine Collision, 1998; editor: Jour. Maritime Law and Commerce, 1980-90, mem. editl. bd., 1969-79, 91—; assoc. editor: American Maritime Cases; mem. scientific bd. Il Dirittimo Marittimo; contbr. to Ency. Brit. Chmn. USCG Adv. Panel on Rules of the Road, 1966-72; mem. permanent adv. bd. Tulane Admiralty Law Inst. Lt. (s.g.) USNR, 1942-45. Fellow Am. Coll. Trial Lawyers; mem. ABA (ho. of dels. 1964-66), N.Y. State Bar Assn., Assn. of Bar of City of N.Y., N.Y. County Lawyers Assn., Maritime Law Assn. U.S. (pres. 1964-66), Assn. Average Adjusters U.S. (chmn. 1959-60), Com. Maritime Internat. (exec. coun. 1972-79, v.p. 1985-91, hon. v.p. 1991—), Ibero-Am. Inst. Maritime Law (hon.). Admiralty. Home: 132 Tullamore Rd Garden City NY 11530-1139 Office: Healy & Baillie 29 Broadway Fl 27 New York NY 10006-3201 Fax: 212-425-0131. E-mail: nhealy@healy.com.

HEAPHY, JOHN MERRILL, lawyer; b. Escanaba, Mich., Apr. 27, 1927; s. John Merrill and Catherine R. (Feeney) H.; m. Martha Jean Knowles, Nov. 16, 1951; children— John Merrill III, Catherine Jean Heaphy DeThorne, Barbara H. Murphy. BA, U. Mich., 1950; JD, Wayne State U., 1953. Bar: Mich. 1954. Atty. office of gen. counsel HEW, Washington, 1954-57; ptnr. Vandeveer & Garzia, P.C. and predecessor firms, Detroit, 1958-86, pres. firm, 1986-92; ret. Served with USNR, 1945-46. Fellow Am. Coll. Trial Lawyers; mem. ABA, Internat. Assn. Def. Counsel, Mich. Bar Assn., Delta Theta Phi, Alpha Sigma Phi. Republican. Aviation, General civil litigation, Personal injury (including property damage). Home: 14650 N Desert Rock Dr Tucson AZ 85737-7135 E-mail: JHHeaphy@aol.com.

HEARD, WYATT H. retired judge; b. Big Spring, Tex., Oct. 19, 1926; s. Dow Hubbard and Minerva (Gulley) Heard; m. Teddy Lewis, Aug. 24, 1956 (dec. Mar. 1974); children: Lawrence Pike, Teddy Heard Orr, Susanna Heard Kane, Denman Hilton; m. Heidi Frost, June 5, 1976; 1 child, Benjamin Frost. BBA, Baylor U., 1950, JD, 1952. Bar: Tex. 1952, U.S. Dist. Ct. (so. dist.) Tex. 1952, U.S. Ct. Appeals (5th cir.) 1952. Spl. agt. FBI, Washington, 1952—54; trial lawyer Baker Botts, Houston, 1954—66; trial lawyer, ptnr. Urban Coolidge Pennington & Heard, Houston, 1966—69; judge State of Tex., 190th Dist. Ct., Houston, 1969—92; of counsel Looper Reed Mark & McGraw, Houston, 1991—96, Taichert & Wiggins, Albuquerque, 1996—98, Hinckle Hensley Shanor & Martin, Albuquerque, 1998—2002; arbitrator, mediator Branch Law Firm, Albuquerque, 2002—. Author: How to Overcome Stress and Tension in Your Life, 1976. Founder Cmty. in Schs., Inc., Houston, 1979—; Sunday Sch. tchr. South Main Baptist Ch. and St. John's Episc. Ch.; bd. dirs. Cities in Schs., Inc., Washington, Crime Prevention Inst., 1994—. Cpl. Air Corps U.S. Army, 1945—46, France, commd. 2d lt. USAF, 1951. Recipient Leon Jaworski award, Houston Bar Assn., 1995, Disting. Alumni award, Waco (Tex.) H.S., 2001. Mem.: ABA, Houston Bar Assn., Tex. Bar Assn., Ex-Agts. FBI, Delta Sigma Phi, Phi Alpha Delta. Office Fax: 505-843-8319. E-mail: judgewyattheard@yahoo.com.

HEARIN, ROBERT MATLOCK, JR., lawyer; b. Tuscaloosa, Ala., Jan. 15, 1946; s. Robert M. Hearin and Annie Laurie Swaim; m. Zetta M. Bryant, Mar. 25, 1972; children: Andrew, Timothy. BA, U. Miss., 1968; JD, Tulane U., 1971. Bar: La. 1971, Calif. 1976, Tex. 1993. Mng. atty. New Orleans Legal Assistance Corp., 1972-75; sole practice law New Orleans, 1976-95; mng. atty. Hearin & Warriner, LLC, New Orleans, 1995—. Baseball coach Carrollton Booster Club, Inc., New Orleans, 1991, 92, 95, 97. 1st lt. U.S. Army, 1971-72. Mem.: L.A. Bar Found. (charter mem.). Presbyterian. Avocations: travel, sports, cooking. Admiralty, General civil litigation, Personal injury (including property damage). Office: Hearin & Warriner LLC 830 Union St Ste 400 New Orleans LA 70112-1405 E-mail: rmhjr@norleanslaw.com.

HEATH, CHARLES DICKINSON, lawyer, telephone company executive; b. Waterloo, Iowa, June 28, 1941; s. George Clinton and Dorothy (Dickinson) H.; m. Carilyn Frances Cain, June 3, 1972. BBA, U. Iowa, 1962, JD, 1966; MBA, U. Ariz., 1963. Bar: Iowa 1966, Pa. 1969, Ind. 1970, U.S. Supreme Ct. 1971, Wis. 1973, Ariz. 1975, Mich. 1979, Fla. 1979, Calif. 1989. Asst. gen. counsel Kohler Co., Wis., 1973-79; securities and tax counsel Kellogg Co., Battle Creek, Mich., 1979-81; assoc. gen. counsel Universal Telephone Inc., Milw., 1981-89, also corp. sec., 1987-89; atty. CenturyTel, Inc., LaCrosse, Wis., 1989—. Utilities, public, Securities, Corporate taxation.

HEATH, CLAUDE ROBERT, lawyer; b. Commerce, Tex., May 4, 1947; s. H. Harold and Laura (Hammond) H.; m. Jean L. Manning, May 18, 1974; children: John Hammond, William Hunter. BA, U. Tex., 1969, JD, 1972. Bar: Tex. 1972, U.S. Dist. Ct. (we. dist.) Tex. 1977, U.S. Ct. Appeals (5th cir.) 1981, U.S. Dist. Ct. (no. and so. dists.) Tex. 1991. Law clk. U.S. Dist. Ct. (we. dist.) Tex., Austin, 1972-73; asst. atty. gen., chmn. opinion com. Atty. Gen.'s Office, Austin, 1973-80; ptnr. Bickerstaff, Heath, Smiley, Pollan, Kever & McDaniel, Austin, 1980—. Mem. ABA, Tex. Bar Found., State Bar of Tex., Travis County Bar Assn. Democrat. Administrative and regulatory, Appellate, Civil rights. Home: 7605 Rustling Cv Austin TX 78731-1332 Office: Bickerstaff Heath Pollan Kever & McDaniel 816 Congress Ave Ste 1700 Austin TX 78701-2643

HEATON, JON C. lawyer; b. Brigham City, Utah, Aug. 31, 1942; s. Harley Lowry and Anne Jane (Lundburg) H.; m. Penny Bourquin, Dec. 30, 1961; children: John Patrick, Timothy A., J. Scott, Jennifer, L., Annelise. BS in Bus. with honors, U. Colo., 1964; JD, Vanderbilt U., 1972. Bar: Utah 1972, U.S. Dist. Ct. Utah 1972. Assoc. Butler, McHugh, Butler, Tune & Watts, Nashville, 1972, Prince, Yeates & Geldzahler, Salt Lake City, 1972-76, ptnr., 1976-80, sr. ptnr., 1980—. Bd. dirs., officer Koflach USA, Salt Lake City, 1988-92, Marker Bindings, Salt Lake City, 1983-96; atty. Park City (Utah) Ski Resort, 1975—, U.S. Ski Team, Park City, 1978-84, Whitmores Inc., Pentalon Corp.; judge pro tem 3d Cir. Cts., Salt Lake City, 1980—; mem. archtl. bd. State Utah. With USAF, 1964-69; brig. gen. Utah Air N.G. Mem. ABA, Utah State Bar, Salt Lake County Bar Assn., N.G. Assn. U.S., Order of Coif, Pi Kappa Alpha. Republican. Avocations: tennis, boating, wilderness areas, skiing, flying. Administrative and regulatory, Corporate, general, Property, real (including real estate development, water). Office: 175 E 4th S Ste 900 Salt Lake City UT 84111-2357 E-mail: jch@pyglaw.com.

HEATWOLE, MARK M. lawyer; b. Pitts., Jan. 28, 1948; s. Marion Grove and Phyllis Adelle (Leiter) H.; m. Sarah Ann Collier, Dec. 30, 1970; children: Mary Phyllis, Elizabeth Collier, Anna Bell. BA, Washington and Lee U., 1969, JD, 1972. Bar: Ill. 1972, U.S. Dist. Ct. (no. dist.) Ill. 1972, U.S. Ct. Appeals (7th cir.) 1977, U.S. Supreme Ct. 1980, U.S. Tax Ct. 1987. Assoc. Chadwell & Kayser, Ltd., Chgo., 1972-79, ptnr., v.p., 1979-89; ptnr. Winston & Strawn, Chgo., 1990—. Treas. Lyric Opera Chgo. Guild, 1980—81, v.p., 1980—81, chmn. fundraising, 1986; vice-chmn. Gorton Cmty. Ctr., 1986; chmn. bd. Gorton Cmty. Ctr. Found., 1986—89; trustee Barat Coll., 1982—85, The Admiral, Chgo., 1988—2001, Allendale Assn., 1991—2000; mem. Art Inst. of Chgo. Old Masters Soc., 1999—; Mem. 1st ward Rep. com. on candidates Lake Forest (Ill.) Caucus, 1985—88, chmn., 1987—88, vice-chmn., 1989—90, chmn., 1990—91; mem. session Lake Forest Presbyn. Ch., 1978—84, chmn. ch. and society com., 1980; bd. dirs. Lyric Opera Chgo. Guild, 1976—, Lake Forest Symphony, 1987—91, Rehab. Inst. Chgo. Enterprises, 1991—2001, Gorton Community Ctr., 1982—88. Mem.: ABA (continuing legal edn. com. 1978—79, mem. antitrust com. young lawyers sect. 1978—81, com. on civil practice and procedure antitrust sect. 1980, bus. law sect. 1986—, patent trademark and copyright sect. 1990—), Chgo. Bar Assn. (chmn. profl. responsibility com. young lawyers sect. 1977—78, mem. exec. com. 1978—79, bd. dirs.), Lawyers Club, Winter Club, Econ. Club Chgo., Shoreacres Club (bd. govs. 1996—, pres. 2002—). Republican. Corporate, general, Finance, Mergers and acquisitions. Office: Winston & Strawn 35 W Wacker Dr Ste 4200 Chicago IL 60601-1695 E-mail: mheatwol@winston.com.

HEAVICAN, MICHAEL G. prosecutor; BA, JD, U. Nebr. From dep. county atty. yo chief dep. county atty. Lancaster County, Nebr., 1975—81, county atty., 1981—91; chief of criminal div. U.S. Atty.'s Office Nebr., 1991—2001; U.S. atty. U.S. Dept. Justice, Nebr., 2001—. Office: 1620 Dodge St Ste 1400 Omaha NE 68102-1506*

HEBERT, JAY HOWELL, lawyer; b. Lake Charles, La., Jan. 31, 1961; s. John Roland and Cynthia Hope (Johnson) H.; m. Camille Renee Comeau, June 8, 1986; 1 child, Isabel Suzanne. BA summa cum laude, Rice U., 1983; JD magna cum laude, Harvard U., 1986. Bar: Tex. 1986, U.S. C. Appeals (5th cir.) 1987, U.S. Supreme Ct. 1990, D.C. 2001. Law clk. to presiding judge U.S. Ct. Appeals (5th cir.), Dallas, 1986-87; with Hughes & Luce LLP, Dallas, 1987—96, Vinson & Elkins LLP, Dallas, 1996—, Wash., DC, 1996—. Mem. Tex. Bar Assn., DC Bar Assn. Corporate, general, Mergers and acquisitions, Securities. Office: Vinson & Elkins LLP 1455 Pennsylvania Ave NW #500 Washington DC 20004

HECHT, DONALD STUART, lawyer; b. N.Y.C., Mar. 20, 1941; s. Murray Hecht and Jeanne (Morris) Friedman; m. Laura Ruth Dodes, Sept. 9, 1967; children: Brian, Daniel. BA, Hofstra Coll., 1962; JD, Bklyn. Law Sch., 1969. Bar: N.Y. 1970, U.S. Dist. Ct. (so. and ea. dists.) N.Y. 1975. Assoc. Sitomer, Sitomer & Porges, N.Y.C., 1970-73, Silver, Saperstein, Barnet & Soloman, N.Y.C., 1973-81; ptnr. Weber & Scharf, Massapequa, N.Y., 1981-82; sole practice Port Washington, N.Y., 1982-90; pvt. practice Manhasset, N.Y., 1991-96; small claims arbitrator Dist. Ct. Nassau County, 1988—; pvt. practice Garden City, N.Y., 1996-98; pvt. prac. Jericho, NY, 1998—. Cons., lectr. Bd. Cooperative Ednl. Svcs., Nassau County, N.Y. 1985—. Contbg. author, editor: Guardianship Practice in New York State, 1997; law columnist: Able Newspaper for the Disabled. Bd. dirs. United Cerebral Palsy Assn. Nassau County, 1982-87, 2002—, Epilepsy Found. of Long Island, 1983-99, v.p. 1987-96; bd. appeals Village of Port Washington North, 1984-85, trustee, 1985-87, dep. mayor, 1986-87; mem. Nassau County Dem. Com., 1984-87. 1st lt. USAF 1962-66. Mem. ABA, New York State Bar Assn., Bar Assn. Nassau County, Nat. Acad. Elder Law Attys., Am. Judges Assn., Lions (bd. dirs. 1982-83, asst. sec. 1983-84, Disting. Svc. award 1983, Lion of Yr. 1984), Iota Theta. Avocations: hiking, cooking, gardening. Estate planning, Probate (including wills, trusts), Elder. Home: 37 Seaview Ln Port Washington NY 11050-1737 Office: 350 Jericho Tpke Jericho NY 11753-1317 E-mail: dschecht@ix.netcom.com.

HECHT, NATHAN LINCOLN, state supreme court justice; b. Clovis, N.Mex., Aug. 15, 1949; s. Harold Lee and Mary Loretta (Byerly) H. BA, Yale U., 1971; JD cum laude, So. Meth. U., 1974. Bar: Tex. 1974, D.C. 1975, U.S. Dist. Ct. D.C. 1975, U.S. Dist. Ct. (no. and we. dists.) Tex. 1976, U.S. Ct. Appeals (D.C. cir.) 1975, U.S. Ct. Appeals (5th cir.) 1976, U.S. Supreme Ct. 1979. Law clk. to judge U.S. Ct. Appeals (D.C. cir.), 1974-75; assoc. Locke, Purnell, Boren, Laney & Neely, Dallas, 1976-80, ptnr., 1981; dist. judge 95th Dist. Ct., Dallas, 1981-86; justice Tex. 5th Dist. Ct. Appeals, 1986-89, Texas Supreme Ct., Austin, 1989—. Contbr. articles to profl. jours. Bd. visitors So. Meth. U., Dallas, 1984-87; trustee Children's Med. Found., Dallas, 1983-89; bd. dirs. Children's Med. Ctr. North, Dallas, 1985-89; elder Valley View Christian Ch., Dallas, 1981—. Lt. USNR, 1971-79. Named Outstanding Young Lawyer of Dallas, Dallas Assn. of Young Lawyers, 1984. Fellow Tex. Bar Found., Am. Bar Found.; mem. ABA, Dallas Bar Assn., D.C. Bar Assn., Am. Law Inst. Republican. Avocations: piano, organ, jogging, bicycling. Office: Tex Supreme Ct PO Box 12248 201 West 14th Room 104 Austin TX 78711

HECKMAN, JEROME HAROLD, lawyer; b. Washington, June 7, 1927; s. Morris and Pauline (German) H.; m. Margot Resh, June 16, 1948 (div. Oct. 1977); children: Eric Stephen, Carey Eugene; m. Ilona Ely Grenadier, Jan. 2, 1986. BSS, Georgetown U., 1948, LLB, 1953, JD, 1967. Bar: D.C. 1953, U.S. Supreme Ct. 1965. Assoc. Dow, Lohnes & Albertson, Washington, 1954-59, ptnr., 1959-62; sr. ptnr. Keller and Heckman, Washington, 1962—. Gen. counsel Soc. of Plastics Industry Inc., N.Y.C., Washington, 1954—, Broadcasting Publs. Inc. Mag., Washington (co. sold to L.A. Times), 1968-87, Disposables Assn. Inc. (now named Internat. Nonwovens and Disposables Assn.), 1958-67. Contbr. articles to profl. jours. Chmn. regional Rep. com., Md., 1966-72; pres. Plastics Acad., 1995-97. Named to Hall of Fame of Plastics Industry, 1987; recipient Spes Hominum award, Nat. Sanitation Found., 1987, William Bradbury award, Soc. Plastics, 2000, Paul R. Dean Disting. Alumni award Georgetown U. Law Ctr., 2001; Dirs. Citation, Ctr. Food Safety and Applied Nutrition, 2000. Mem. ABA, Bar Assn. D.C., George Town Club, Woodmont Country Club, Phi Delta Phi. Avocations: golf, tennis. Administrative and regulatory, Antitrust, Communications. Office: Keller & Heckman 1001 G St NW Ste 500 Washington DC 20001-4545

HECKT, MELVIN DEAN, lawyer; b. Dysart, Iowa, Apr. 21, 1924; s. Wesley T. and Ada Marie (Lawyer) H.; m. Dorothy M. Simons, Sept. 4, 1948; children— Janice, Paul, Mary, Barbara, William, Thomas. B.A. in Econs., State U. Iowa, 1948, J.D., 1950. Bar: Minn., 1950, Iowa 1950, U.S. Dist. Ct. (Minn.), U.S. Supreme Ct. Assoc. Snyder, Gale, Hoke, Richards, Janes (name changed to Bassford, Heckt, Lockhart & Mullin), Mpls., 1950-55, ptnr., 1955—94, ptnr. Luther, Heckt & Cameron, 1994-. Served with USMC, 1943-45. Decorated Bronze Star. Mem. Iowa Bar Assn., Minn. Bar Assn., Am. Legion, VKW, dir. Marine Corps Heritage Found. Republican. Lutheran. Contbr. articles to profl. jours. Probate (including wills, trusts), Estate planning. Address: 601 Carlson Pkwy Ste 750 Minnetonka MN 55305-5241

HEDGES, RICHARD HOUSTON, lawyer, epidemiologist; b. Louisville, July 16, 1952; s. Houston and Frances Ruth (Zemo) H.; m. Donna Jean Hough. BA, U. Ky., 1974; MA, Ea. Ky. U., 1975, MPA, 1983; PhD, U. Ky., 1986; JD, Capital U. Law, 1994. Bar: Ohio 1995. Rehab. specialist Commonwealth of Ky., Somerset, 1976-81, chief health planner Frankfort, 1981-82; asst. prof. U. Ky., Lexington, 1985-87; rsch. assoc. dept. med. behavioral sci. U. Ky. Coll. Medicine, Lexington, 1982-85; program adminstr. Rollman Psychiat. Inst., Cin., 1987-88; asst. prof. Ohio U., 1988-92, assoc. prof., 1992—; assoc. Garry Hunter, LPA, Athens, Ohio, 1997-98; ptnr. Thomas & Hedges LLC, 1998-99; pvt. practice, Athens, 1999—; magistrate Village of Coolville, Ohio, 2001—, Village of Chauncey. Asst. city atty. City of Nelsonville, Ohio, 1997—2001, city pros., 1997—2001; dir. divsn. on aging Ohio U. Health Promotion and Rsch., 1990—92, MHA grad. program coord., 1995—96; bd. dirs. Washington County Mental Health and Addiction Recovery Svcs., 1998—99; exec. dir. pro tem Health Recovery Svcs., 1998; solicitor Village of Chauncey, 2000. Author: Bioethics, Healthcare and the Law, 1999; contbr. articles to profl. jours. Mem. Athens County Domestic Violence Task Force, Athens County Victim's Assistance Adv. Fellow NIMH, 1984-86. Mem.: ATLA, ABA, Athens County Bar Assn., Washington County Bar Assn. (trustee at large 2000—02), Ohio Bar Assn., Am. Health Lawyers Assn., Healthcare Fin. Mgmt. Assn., Soc. Ohio Healthcare Attys., Ohio Acad. Trial Lawyers, Phi Delta Phi, Pi Sigma Alpha. Episcopalian. Avocations: backpacking, volleyball, bicycling, sailing. Family and matrimonial, Health, Labor (including EEOC, Fair Labor Standards Act, labor-management relations, NLRB, OSHA). Home: 275 Mooreland Rd Belpre OH 45714-9702 Office: 8 N Court St Ste 507 Athens OH 45701-2450 also: Ohio U Sch Health Sci E346 Grover Ctr Athens OH 45701 Fax: 740-592-3724.

HEDIEN, COLETTE JOHNSTON, lawyer; b. Chgo., 1939; d. George A. and Catherine (Bugan) Johnston; m. Wayne E. Hedien; 3 children. BS with honors, U. Wis., 1960; JD, DePaul U., 1981. Bar: Ill. 1981. Tchr. Sch. Dist. 39, Wilmette, Ill., 1960-63, Tustin (Calif.) Pub. Schs., 1964-66; extern law clk. to judge Chgo., 1980, U.S. Atty.'s Office, Chgo., 1980; pvt. practice Northbrook, Ill., 1981—. Atty. Chgo. Vol. Legal Svcs.; mem. Chgo. Appellate Law Com., 1982-83, chmn., 1987-88; chmn. Northbrook Planning Commn., 1984-89; founder Am. Women of Surrey (Eng.), 1975-77; founding dir. U. Irvine Friends of Libr., 1965-66; guidance vol. Glenbrook High Sch., 1984-89; trustee Village of Northbrook, 1989—; mem. Women's Bd. Field Mus. Bd. dirs. Ill. Project for Spl. Needs Children, 1998—. NSF scholar, 1962. Mem. ABA (com. on real property), Ill. Bar Assn., Chgo. Bar Assn., North Shore Panhellenic Assn. (rep. 1989—), Phi Kappa Phi, Kappa Alpha Theta (bd. dirs.).

HEDLUND, PAUL JAMES, lawyer; b. Abington, Pa., June 26, 1946; s. Frank Xavier and Eva Ruth (Hoffman) H.; m. Marta Louise Brewer, Dec. 7, 1985; children: Annemarie Kirsten, Brooke Ashley, Tess Kara. BSME, U. Mich., 1968; JD, UCLA, 1973. Bar: Calif. 1973, D.C. 1994, U.S. Dist. Ct. (ctrl. dist.) Calif. 1977, U.S. Dist. Ct. (ea. dist.) Calif. 1991, U.S. Dist. Ct. (no. dist.) N.Y. 1994, U.S. Patent and Trademark Office 1978, U.S. Ct. Appeals (9th cir.) 1994, U.S. Supreme Ct. 1997. Staff engr. So. Calif. Edison, L.A., 1968-70; ptnr. Hedlund & Samuels, L.A., 1974-88, Kananack, Murgatroyd Baum & Hedlund (and predecessor firms), L.A., 1988-92;

shareholder Baum, Hedlund, Aristei, Guilford & Schiavo, L.A., 1993—. Mem. discovery and trial teams MDL 817 aircrash at Sioux City Iowa United Airlines, Chgo., 1989; mem. plaintiffs' steering com. Alaska Airlines crash off Pt. Mugu, Calif., 2000; mem. plaintiffs' exec. com. Sept. 11, 2001 Tort Litigation; lectr. in field. Recipient Safety award, Nat. Air Disaster Found., 2002. Mem.: LA County Bar Assn., Consumer Attys. of LA, DC Bar Assn., State Bar Calif. Aviation, Personal injury (including property damage), Product liability. Office: Baum Hedlund Aristei Guilford & Schiavo 12100 Wilshire Blvd Ste 950 Los Angeles CA 90025-7107 E-mail: phedlund@baumhedlundlaw.com.

HEDMAN, GEORGE WILLIAM, lawyer; b. Chgo., Sept. 29, 1923; s. George Edward and Susan Welde (Dent) H.; m. Louisa Wetherbee, Apr. 26, 1947 (div. 1973); children: Mark, C. William, Jason; m. Evelyn L. Ramey, Jan. 1, 1987; children: David, Rebecca, Richard. JD, Ill. Tech., 1950; PhD in Psychology, Fla. Inst. Tech., 1981. Bar: Hawaii 1950, Am. Samoa 1953, Fla. 1956. Pvt. practice, Honolulu, 1950-53, Melbourne, Fla., 1962—; attorney gen. Govt. Am. Samoa, Pago Pago, 1953-55; exec. Edison Electric Inst., N.Y.C., 1956-62. Author: Florida's New No-Fault Divorce Law, 1973, Divorce Without (Much) Agony, 1978, Jesus Didn't Tell Us Everything, 1996, The Secret Life of Jesus Christ, 1999. Mem. Brevard County Sch. Bd., Titusville, Fla., 1968-72. Sgt. U.S. Army, 1943-46. Mem. Fla. Bar Assn., Hawaii State Bar Assn. Commercial, contracts (including sales of goods; commercial financing), Corporate, general, Probate (including wills, trusts). Home: 877 N Miramar Ave Apt 1106 Indialantic FL 32903-3028 Office: 108 W New Haven Ave Melbourne FL 32901 E-mail: fineprintbill@hotmail.com.

HEDSPETH, DAVID JOE, judge; b. Poplar Bluff, Mo., Feb. 10, 1947; s. Lennis Carrol and Easter Hulda Hedspeth; m. Mary Lou Troutman, Dec. 31, 1972. AA, So. Bapt. Coll., 1966; BS in Agr., U. Mo., 1969. Bar: Mo. 1975. Pvt. practice, Van Buren, Mo., 1975—76; probate judge Carter County, Van Buren, 1977—78; assoc. cir. judge 37th Jud. Cir., Van Buren, 1979—. With U.S. Army, 1969—71, West Germany. Democrat. Southern Baptist. Avocations: reading, short wave listening. Office: Cir Ct Divsn II Box 388 Courthouse Van Buren MO 63965

HEED, PETER W. state attorney general; b. West Chester, Pa., Apr. 2, 1950; s. Walter R. and Elizabeth Allen Heed; m. Patricia Longo, Oct. 3, 1983; children: Travis, Ethan. BA, Dartmouth Coll., 1972; JD, Cornell U., 1975. Bar: N.H. 1975, U.S. Dist. Ct. N.H. 1975, U.S. Ct. Appeals (1st cir.) 1976. Asst. atty. gen. State of NH, Concord, 1975-80; assoc. Cristiano and Krumphold, Keene, NH, 1980-82; sr. ptnr. Green, McMahon & Heed, Keene, NH, 1982—2001; county atty. Cheshire County, NH, 2001—03; atty. gen. State of NH, 2003—. Instr., paralegal studies, Keene State Coll., 1980-84; bd. govs. N.H. Health & Welfare Coun., Keene, 1985-90. Co-author: Canoe Racing: The Competitor's Guide, 1992; dir./prodr. (video) The General Clinton Regatta, 1989. Moderator, Town of Westmoreland, N.H., 1998—; mem. zoning bd. adjustment, Town of Roxbury, N.H., 1989-90; bd. govs., v.p. Norris Cotton Cancer Ctr., Dartmouth-Hitchand Hosp., Lebanon, N.H., 1993—; mem. U.S. Marathon Canoe and Kayak Team, 1982-83. Mem. ATLA (sustaining mem. 1987-2000), N.H. Trial Lawyers Assn. (bd. dirs. 1987-93). Republican. Avocations: canoe and kayak racing (7 times Nat. Marathon and Downriver Canoe Champion, World Masters Marathon Canoe Champion, Nike World Masters Games, 1998), nordic ski racing, marathon running, U.S. history. Office: PO Box 612 Keene NH 03431-0612 also: Atty Gen 33 Capitol St Concord NH 03301*

HEEG, PEGGY A. lawyer, gas industry executive; b. Louisville, June 25, 1959; BA with honors, U. Louisville, 1983, JD, 1986. Bar: Ky. 1986, DC 1987, Tex. 1987. Various Tenneco Energy, El Paso Corp., Houston, 1996—97, v.p., assoc. gen. counsel regulated pipelines, 1997—2001, sr. v.p., dep. gen. counsel, 2001, exec. v.p., gen. counsel, 2002—. Legal advisor to commr. Charles Stalon Fed. Energy Regulatory Commn., 1988; bd. dirs. El Paso Tenn. Pipeline Co. Mem.: ABA, Interstate Natural Gas Assn. Am., DC Bar, State Bar Tex., Ky. Bar Assn., Energy Bar Assn. Office: El Paso Corp Legal Dept 1001 Louisiana St Houston TX 77002 Office Fax: 713-420-2340. E-mail: peggy.heeg@elpaso.com.

HEENAN, MICHAEL TERENCE, lawyer; b. Pitts., Jan. 28, 1942; s. Paul Joseph and Helen (Chemas) H.; m. Maryte Victoria Narkevicius, Feb. 12, 1970 (dec. Dec., 1999); children: Garrett, Leslie, Suzanne. BS, Mount St. Mary's Coll., Emmitsburg, Md., 1964; JD, U. Pitts., 1967. Bar: Pa. 1967, D.C. 1972, U.S. Supreme Ct. 1974, U.S. Ct. Appeals (D.C. Cir), U.S. Ct. Appeals for Armed Forces, 1974, U.S. Ct. Fed. Claims 1975, U.S. Customs Ct. 1975, U.S. Ct. Appeals (3rd cir.) 1979, U.S. Ct. Appeals (Fed. Cir.) 1982, U.S. Ct. Appeals (4th cir.) 1987. Atty. adviser Bd. Vets. Appeals, Washington, 1971-73; trial atty. divsn. mine safety and health Office of Solicitor Dept. of Interior, 1973-74; assoc. Webster, Kilcullen & Chamberlain, 1974-76; ptnr. Kilcullen, Smith & Heenan, 1976-80, Heenan, Althen, & Roles, Washington, 1980-2003, Ogletree Deakins, 2003-; instr. internat. law U.S. Navy Res. Officers Sch., 1971-72. Author: Understanding MSHA, 1981, Enforcement, Administrative and Judicial Review, Coal Law and Regulation, 1983, Inspections and Investigations, Workplace Safety and Health, 1995, Employer Liability Related to Workplace Safety and Health Obligations at Cement Operations, 1996; co-author: (with Ronald E. Meisburg) Federal Regulation of Mine Safety and Health, Administration, Practice and Procedure, 1986, (with C. Gregory Ruffennach) National Institute of Occupational Safety and Health: Limits of Authority in Rulemaking Under the Federal Mine Safety and Health Act of 1977, 1992, (with Lynn M. Rausch) Vicarious Liability for Contract Mine Operations: Expanding Liability for Mineral Owners and Lessees, 1994, (with William K. Doran) Employee Protections, 1995, (with Lynn M. Rausch) NIOSH Investigations, Workplace Safety and Health, 1995, Safety and Health at Mines: A Manual for Operators and Contractors, 1999, Federal Regulation of Mine Safety and Health, Mine Health and Safety Mgmt., 2001, (with Margaret S. Lopez) Self Audits, Occupational Safety and Health Handbook, 2001; legal editor Pit & Quarry. Served to lt. USNR, 1968-71. Trustee Ea. Mineral Law Found., 1996—. Mem. ABA, Nat. Stone Assn. (coun. of counsel), Pa. Bar Assn., D.C. Bar Assn. Administrative and regulatory, Federal civil litigation, Labor (including EEOC, Fair Labor Standards Act, labor-management relations, NLRB, OSHA), Natural resources. Office: 2400 N St NW 5th Fl Washington DC 20037

HEFFELFINGER, THOMAS BACKER, lawyer; b. Mpls., Feb. 13, 1948; BA in History, Stanford U., 1970; JD, U. Minn., 1975. Bar: Minn. 1976, U.S. Dist. Ct. Minn. 1977, U.S. Ct. Appeals (8th cir.) 1983. Law clk. Office of the Hennepin County Atty., 1974-76, asst. atty. juvenile divsn., 1976, asst. atty. criminal divsn. trial sect., 1977-82, asst. atty. major offender unit, 1978-81, supr. burglary unit, 1981-82; asst. U.S. atty. criminal divsn. Dist. Minn., U.S. Dept. Justice, 1982-88, atty. white collar crime sect., 1982-85, supr. narcotics and firemans sect., 1985-86; ptnr. Opperman Heins & Paquin, 1988-91; U.S. atty. Dist. Minn., U.S. Dept. Justice, 1991-93; ptnr. Bowman and Brooke, 1993—2000, Best & Flanagan, 2000—01; U.S. atty. U.S. Dept. Justice, Minn., 2001—. Contbr. articles to profl. jours. Candidate Hennepin County Atty., 1986; bd. dirs. Mpls. Chpt. ARC, 1987—; mem. Hennepin County Task Force on Youth and Drugs, 1987-88, Minn. Ho. of Reps. Rep. Caucus Drug Task Force, 1989-90, Minn. Commn. on Violent Crime, 1991; chmn. Minn. Commn. on Jud. Selection, 1990-91; lectr. in field. Mem. Fed. Bar Assn., Minn. Bar Assn., Hennepin County Bar Assn. General civil litigation, Criminal, Native American. Office: 600 US Courthouse 300 S 4th St Minneapolis MN 55415*

HEFFERNAN, JAMES VINCENT, lawyer; b. Washington, Oct. 6, 1926; s. Vincent Jerome and Hazel Belle (Wiltfong) Heffernan; m. Virginia May Adams, June 26, 1954; children: David V., Douglas J., Alan P., Margaret L., Thomas A. AB, Cornell U., 1949, JD with distinction, 1952. Bar: D.C. 1953, Md. 1959, U.S. Ct. Claims 1955, U.S. Tax Ct. 1953, U.S. Supreme Ct. 1958. Assoc. Sutherland, Asbill & Brennan, Washington, 1952-59, ptnr., 1959—. Adj. prof. Georgetown U., Washington, 1978—79. Contbr. articles to profl. jours. With USN, 1945—46. Mem.: ABA, Bar Assn. D.C., Fed. Bar Assn., Kenwood Golf and Country Club, Met. Club (Washington), KC, Order Coif, Phi Alpha Delta. Democrat. Roman Catholic. Corporate taxation, Estate taxation, Personal income taxation. Home: 5216 Falmouth Rd Bethesda MD 20816-2913 Office: Sutherland Asbill & Brennan LLP 1275 Pennsylvania Ave NW Washington DC 20004-2415 E-mail: james.heffernan@sablaw.com., jvh3@cornell.edu.

HEFFERNAN, NATHAN STEWART, retired state supreme court chief justice; b. Frederic, Wis., Aug. 6, 1920; s. Jesse Eugene and Pearl Eva (Kaump) H.; m. Dorothy Hillemann, Apr. 27, 1946; children: Katie (Mrs. Howard Thomas), Michael, Thomas. BA, U. Wis., 1942, LLB, 1948; postgrad. in bus., Harvard U. Sch. Bus. Adminstrn., 1943-44; LLD (hon.), Lakeland Coll., 1995; LLD, U. Wis., 1999. Bar: Wis. 1948, U.S. Dist. Ct. (we. dist.) Wis. 1948, U.S. Dist. Ct. (ea. dist.) Wis. 1950, U.S. Ct. Appeals (7th cir.) 1960, U.S. Supreme Ct. 1960. Assoc. firm Schubring, Ryan, Peterson & Sutherland, Madison, Wis., 1948-49; practice in Sheboygan, Wis., 1949-59; partner firm Buchen & Heffernan, 1951-59; counsel Wis. League Municipalities, 1949; research asst. to gov. Wis., 1949; asst. dist. atty. Sheboygan County, 1951-53; city atty. City of Sheboygan, 1953-59; dep. atty. gen. State of Wis., 1959-62; U.S. atty. Western Dist. Wis., 1962-64; justice Wis. Supreme Ct., 1964—, chief justice, 1983-95. Lectr. mcpl. corps., 1961-64, appellate procedure and practice U. Wis. Law Sch., 1971-83; faculty Appellate Judges Seminar, Inst. Jud. Adminstrn., NYU, 1972-87; former mem. Nat. Council State Ct. Reps., chmn., 1976-77; ex-officio dir. Nat. Ctr. State Cts., 1976-77, mem. adv. bd. appellate justice project; former mem. Wis. Jud. Planning Com.; chmn. Wis. Appellate Practice and Procedure Com., 1975-76; mem. exec. com. Wis. Jud. Conf., 1978—, chmn., 1983; pres. City Attys. Assn., 1958-59; chair Citizens Panel on Election Reform; co-chair Equal Justice Coalition. Wis. chmn. NCCJ, 1966-67; past exec. bd. Four Lakes Coun., Boy Scouts Am.; gen. chmn. Wis. Dem. Conv., 1960, 61; mem. Wis. Found.; bd. dirs. Inst. Jud. Adminstrn.; visitors U. Wis. Law Sch., 1970-83, chmn., 1973-76; past mem. corp. bd. Meth. Hosp.; former curator Wis. Hist. Soc., curator emeritus, 1990; trustee Wis. Meml. Union, Wis. State Libr., William Freeman Vilas Trust Estate; v.p. U. Wis. Meml. Union Bldg. Assn.; former deacon Conglist. Ch. Lt. (s.g.) USNR, 1942-46, ETO, PTO. Recipient Disting. Svc. award NCCJ, 1968, Ann. Disting. Svc. award Wis. Mediation Assn., 1995, Lifetime Achievement award Milw. Bar Assn., 1995, Disting. Svc. award Dem. Party Sheboygan County, 1995; Disting. Jud. fellow Marquette U. Law Sch., 1996. Fellow Am. Bar Found. (life), Inst. for Jud. Adminstrn. (hon., bd. dirs., mem. faculty seminar), Wis. Bar Assn. (chmn. Wis. bar com. study on legal edn. 1995-96, hon. chmn. Equal Justice Coalition 1997—, Goldberg award for disting. svc.), Wis. Bar Found.; mem. ABA (past mem. spl. com. on adminstrn. criminal justice, mem. com. fed.-state delineation of jurisdiction, jud. adminstrn. com. on appellate ct., com. appellate time standards), Am. Law Inst. (life, adv. com. on complex litigation), Dane County Bar Assn., Sheboygan County Bar Assn., Am. Judicature Soc. (dir. 1977-80, chmn. program com. 1979-81), Wis. Law Alumni Assn. (bd. dirs., Disting. Alumni Svc. award 1989), Nat. Conf. Chief Justices (bd. dirs.), Nat. Assn. Ct. Mgmt., Wis. Rivers Alliance (bd. dirs.), Order of Coif, Iron Cross, U. Club (Madison, Wis.), Phi Kappa Phi, Phi Delta Phi. Clubs: Madison Lit. (pres. 1979-80); Harvard (Milw.); Harvard Bus. Sch. (Wis.). Home: 17 Thorstein Veblen Pl Madison WI 53705

HEFFINGTON, JACK GRISHAM, lawyer, banker, insurance company executive, horse breeder; b. Lawrenceburg, Tenn., Mar. 8, 1944; s. Charles Alexander and Kathlyn (Grisham) H.; m. Nancy Caroline Heffington, Sept. 29, 1979; children: Jacquelyn Elliott, Caroline Sutherland. B.S., Memphis State U., 1967; J.D., U. Ark., 1971. Bar: Tenn. 1971, Ala., 1972. Ptnr., Heffington & Thomas, Murfreesboro, Tenn., 1972— ; pres., chmn. Middle Tenn. Mortgage Co., Murfreesboro, 1973— ; pres., chmn. Keg Life Ins. Co. of S.C., Columbia, 1977— ; pres. South Tex. Bankers Life Ins. Co., Birmingham, Ala., 1993—; vice chmn. World Svc. Life Ins. Co. of Am., Winchester, Tenn., 1993—; owner Tan Oak Farms, Murfreesboro; dir. 1st Nat. Bank of Rutherford County, Murfreesboro. Mem. ABA, Ala. Bar Assn., Tenn. Bar Assn., Sigma Delta Chi. Mem. Ch. of Christ. Corporate, general. Home: PO Box 64 Christiana TN 37037-0064 Office: Heffington & Thomas 520 S Church St Murfreesboro TN 37130-4922

HEFFRON, HOWARD A. lawyer; b. N.Y.C., Oct. 3, 1927; s. Jack and Sophie (Malkin) H.; m. Stella Meller, July 4, 1946; children: James, Robert, Nancy. AB, Columbia U., 1948; LL.B., Harvard U., 1951. Bar: N.Y. State 1953, D.C. 1953. Practiced in, N.Y.C. and Washington, 1953-58, 61-66, 69-77, 79—; asst. U.S. atty. So. Dist. N.Y., 1953-57; 1st asst. tax div. and asst. dep. atty. gen. Dept. Justice, Washington, 1958-61; chief counsel Fed. Hwy. Adminstrn., Dept. Transp., Washington, 1967-69; apptd. by Pres. and confirmed by Senate as dir. Office Rail Pub. Counsel, Washington, 1977-79; prof. law U. Wash., Seattle, 1965-67. Cons. Pres.'s Commn. on Law Enforcement and Adminstrn. of Justice, Washington, 1965-66, Nat. Commn. on Product Safety, Washington, 1969-70 Author: Federal Consumer Safety Legislation, 1970. With U.S. Army, 1946-47. Appellate.

HEFTER, LAURENCE ROY, lawyer; b. N.Y.C., Oct. 13, 1935; s. Charles S. and Rose (Postal) H.; m. Jacquelyn Maureen Miller, June 13, 1957; children: Jeffrey Scott, Sue-Anne. B.M.E., Rensselaer Poly. Inst., 1957, MS in Mech. Engring., 1960; JD with honors, George Washington U., 1964. Bar: Va. 1964, N.Y. 1967, D.C. 1973. Instr. Rensselaer Poly. Inst., Troy, N.Y., 1957-59; patent engr. Gen. Electric Co., Washington, 1959-63; sr. patent atty. Atlantic Research Corp., Alexandria, Va., 1963-66; assoc. firm Davis, Hoxie, Faithfull & Hapgood, N.Y.C., 1966-69; mem. firm Ryder, McAulay & Hefter, N.Y.C., 1970-73, Finnegan, Henderson, Farabow, Garrett & Dunner, LLP, Washington, 1973—. Professorial lectr. trademark law George Washington U., 1981-90; mem. adv. com. U.S. Patent and Trademark Office, 1988-92, Trademark Rev. Commn., 1986-89. Bd. govs. Brand Names Ednl. Found., 2001—. Named in Best Lawyers in Am., Best Lawyers in Washington. Mem. ABA (chmn. patent office affairs com. patent, trademark and copyright sect. 1976-80, unfair competition com. 1980-81, governing com. franchise forum 1994-97), N.Y. State Bar Assn., D.C. Bar Assn., Va. Bar Assn. (dir. patent, trademark and copyright sect. 1976-78), Internat. Bar Assn. (chmn. trademark com. 1986-90), Am. Patent Law Assn. (chmn. trademark com. 1979-81, dir. 1981-84), U.S. Trademark Assn. (dir. 1982-84), Order of Coif, Alpha Epsilon Pi. Federal civil litigation, Patent, Trademark and copyright. Home: 6904 Loch Lomond Dr Bethesda MD 20817-4756 Office: 1300 I St NW Washington DC 20005-3314

HEFTLER, THOMAS E. lawyer; b. Jersey City, 1943; AB, Princeton U., 1965; JD cum laude, NYU, 1968. Bar: N.Y. 1968. Mem. Stroock & Stroock & Lavan LLP, N.Y.C. Corporate, general, Securities, Commodities. Office: Stroock & Stroock & Lavan LLP 180 Maiden Ln New York NY 10038-4925

HEGARTY, MARY FRANCES, lawyer; b. Chgo., Dec. 19, 1950; d. James E. and Frances M. (King) H. BA, DePaul U., 1972, JD, 1975. Bar: Ill. 1975, U.S. Dist. Ct. (no. dist.) Ill. 1976, U.S. Supreme Ct. 1980. Ptnr. Lannon & Hegarty, Park Ridge, Ill., 1975-80; pvt. practice Park Ridge, 1980—. Dir. Legal Assistance Found. Chgo., 1983—. Mem. revenue study com. Chgo. City Coun. Fin. Com., 1983; mem. Sole Source Rev. Panel, City of Chgo., 1984; pres. Hist. Pullman Found., Inc., 1984-85; apptd. Park Ridge Zoning Bd., 1993-94; pres. Park Ridge C. of C., 2002--. Mem. Ill. State Bar Assn. (real estate coun. 1980-84), Chgo. Bar Assn., Women's Bar Assn. Ill. (pres. 1983-84), NW Suburban Bar Assn., Park Ridge Women Entrepreneurs, Chgo. Athletic Assn. (pres. 1992-93), Park Ridge C. of C. (pres. 2002--). Democrat. Roman Catholic. Corporate, general, Probate (including wills, trusts), Property, real (including real estate development, water). Office: 301 W Touhy Ave Park Ridge IL 60068-4204

HEGGENESS, JULIE FAY, foundation administrator, lawyer; b. Long Beach, Calif., Nov. 9, 1959; d. Clark Richard Heggeness, June Lorraine Heggeness; 1 child, Thaddeus. BFA, U. So. Calif., 1982; JD, Western State U., 1998. Cert. specialist planned giving. Dir. Long Beach Meml. Med. Ctr., Long Beach, 1995—99, Meml. Med. Ctr. Found., Long Beach, 1999—. 1st v.p. Camp Fire U.S., Long Beach, 1999—2001; Leadership Long Beach Class of 2003 estate planning and trust coun., bd. mem. at large; mem. Nat. Coun. Planned Giving. Mem.: Long Beach (Calif.) Bar Assn., Assistance League Long Beach, Cameo Profl. Aux. Republican. Roman Catholic. Avocations: golf, gardening, skiing. Office: Meml Med Ctr Found 2801 Atlantic Ave Long Beach CA 90806 Office Fax: 562-933-3652. Personal E-mail: jheggeness@memorialcare.org.

HEIBERG, ROBERT ALAN, lawyer; b. St. Cloud, Minn., June 29, 1943; s. Rasmus Adolph and Irene (Shaffer) H.; m. Sharon Ann Olson, Aug. 2, 1969; children— Eric Robert, Mark Alan, Maren Ann BA summa cum laude, U. Minn., 1965, JD summa cum laude, 1968. Bar: Minn. 1968. Law clk. to assoc. justice Minn. Supreme Ct., 1968-69; assoc. Dorsey & Whitney, Mpls., 1969-73, ptnr., 1974—; instr. Law Sch., U. Minn., 1968-72, instr. legal assts. program, 1972-77. Articles editor Minn. Law Rev., 1967-68 Mem. adv. com. U. Minn. Legal Assts. Program, 1977-84, bd. visitors Law Sch., 1991-96. Mem. ABA (sect. real property, probate and trust law), Minn. Bar Assn. (chmn. com. on legal assts. 1979), Hennepin County Bar Assn., Am. Rose Soc. (accredited judge 1996), Order of Coif, Phi Beta Kappa Republican. Lutheran. Landlord-tenant, Property, real (including real estate development, water). Home: 4510 Wooddale Ave Minneapolis MN 55424-1137 Office: Dorsey & Whitney 50 S 6th St Ste 1500 Minneapolis MN 55402-1498 E-mail: heiberg.robert@dorseylaw.com.

HEIDER, JON VINTON, retired lawyer, corporate executive; b. Moline, Ill., Mar. 1, 1934; s. Raymond and Doris (Hinch) H.; m. Barbara L. Bond, Dec. 27, 1960 (div.); children: Loren P., John C., Lindsay L.; m. Mary R. Murray, Jan. 27, 1984. AB, U. Wis., 1956; JD, Harvard U., 1961; grad., Advanced Mgmt. Program, 1974. Bar: Pa. 1962, U.S. Dist. Ct. (ea. dist.) Pa. 1962, U.S. Ct. Appeals (3d cir.) 1962, U.S. Supreme Ct. 1991. Assoc. Morgan Lewis & Bockius, Phila., 1961-66; counsel Catalytic, Inc., Phila., 1966-68, Houdry Process & Chem. Co., Phila., 1968-70; counsel chems. group Air Products & Chems., Inc., Valley Forge, Pa., 1970-75, asst. gen. counsel, 1975-76, assoc. gen. counsel, 1976-78, gen. counsel Allentown, Pa., 1978-80; v.p. corp. affairs, sr. adminstrv. officer-Europe, Air Products Europe, Inc., London, 1980-83; v.p. corp. devel. Air Products & Chems., Inc., 1983-84; v.p., gen. counsel BF Goodrich Co., Akron, Ohio, 1984-88, sr. v.p., gen. counsel, 1988-94, exec. v.p., gen. counsel, 1994-98; ret., 1998. Trustee U. Akron, Bluecoats, Inc.; mem. distbn. com. Charles E. and Mabel M. Ritchie Meml. Found. Lt. USNR, 1956-58. Mem. ABA, Am. Law Inst., Assn. Gen. Counsel, Blossom Music Ctr. Bd. Overseers, Sisler McFawn Found. (chmn. distbn. com.), U. Wis. Found., Portage Country Club, Rolling Rock Club, Key Biscayne Yacht Club. Corporate, general. E-mail: JHeider-Fl@msn.com.

HEIDRICH, ROBERT WESLEY, lawyer; b. Chgo., Aug. 1, 1927; s. Carl G. and Harriet B. (Butzlaff) H.; m. Lennice L. Hubenbecker, June 19, 1948; children: John G., Robert G., Kimberly L. Student, U. Wis., 1944-45, 47-48; JD, DePaul U., 1951. Bar: Ill. 1951, Calif. 1974, Tenn. 1980. Atty. Brunswick Corp., Chgo., 1953-60, 65-69; v.p. Brunswick AG (Switzerland), 1960-61; dir. Brunswick Internat. Fin. AG (Switzerland), 1962-65; sec., corp. counsel Nat. Can Corp., Chgo., 1969-73; v.p., sec., gen. counsel, dir. Rohr Industries, Inc., Chula Vista, Calif., 1973-79; corp. v.p., gen. counsel Holiday Inn Hotels, Memphis, 1979-85; counsel Kaiser Steel Corp., LaVerne, Calif., 1985-87, San Diego Real Estate Devel., 1987—. Chmn. Riverside-Brookfield CMty. Caucus, 1972; bd. dirs., Am. Internat. Sch. Zurich, 1964-65; chmn. Jr. Achievement, Chgo., 1970-75. Served with U.S. Army, 1945-47. Mem. Frederick Law Olmstead Soc. (founding pres. 1967-69). Corporate, general, Property, real (including real estate development, water). Home: 5157 Long Branch Ave Apt 4 San Diego CA 92107-2032 Office: San Diego Devel PO Box 70075 San Diego CA 92167

HEIGHAM, JAMES CRICHTON, lawyer; b. Sheffield, Eng., Feb. 9, 1930; came to U.S., 1940; s. Clement and Vida (Crichton) H.; m. Katherine Little, Feb. 24, 1962; children: Thomas K. Blake, Susan Blake, Christopher J. AB, Harvard U., 1951, LLB, 1954. Bar: Mass. 1954, U.S. Supreme Ct. 1970. Assoc. Choate, Hall & Stewart, Boston, 1957-59, 62-65, ptnr., 1966-97; asst. U.S. atty. Dept. of Justice, Boston, 1960-61; ret. ptnr. Choate, Hall & Stewart, Boston, 1997—. Spl. asst. atty. gen. Commonwealth of Mass., Boston, 1968. Chmn. Planning Bd., Belmont, Mass., 1980-94, Capital Budget Com., 1980-94, chmn. fin. com., 1997—. 1st lt. USMC, 1954-57, lt. col. USMC ret. Mem. ABA, Mass. Bar Assn., Boston Bar Assn. Home: 62 Orchard St Belmont MA 02478-3510 Office: Choate Hall & Stewart 53 State St Exchange Pl Boston MA 02109 Fax: 617 248-4000.

HEILBRON, DAVID M(ICHAEL), lawyer; b. San Francisco, Nov. 25, 1936; s. Louis H. and Delphine A. (Rosenblatt) H.; m. Nancy Ann Olsen, June 21, 1960; children: Lauren Ada, Sarah Ann, Ellen Selma. BS summa cum laude, U. Calif., Berkeley, 1958; AB first class, Oxford U., Eng., 1960; LL.B. magna cum laude, Harvard U., 1962. Bar: Calif. 1962, U.S. Dist. Ct. (no. dist.) Calif. 1963, U.S Ct. Appeals (9th cir.) 1963, U.S. Ct. Appeals (D.C. cir.) 1972, U.S. Ct. Appeals (8th cir.), 1985, U.S. Ct. Appeals (1st cir.) 1987, U.S. Ct. Appeals (10th cir.) 1988, U.S. Ct. Appeals (7th cir.) 1988, U.S. Ct. appeals (11th cir.) 1988, U.S. Dist. Ct. Nev. 1982, U.S. Dist. Ct. (cen. dist.) Calif. 1983, U.S. Supreme Ct. 1988, U.S. Ct. Appeals (3rd cir.) 1992, (6th cir.), 1995, U.S. Ct. Appeals (2d cir.) 1998, U.S. Ct. Appeals (5th cir.) 1998. Assoc. McCutchen, Doyle, Brown & Enersen, San Francisco, 1962-69, ptnr., 1969—, mng. ptnr., 1985-88. Vis. lectr. appellate advocacy U. Calif., Berkeley, 1981-82, 82-83. Bd. trustees Golden Gate U., 1993-97, vice chair, 1995-97; bd. dirs. San Francisco Jewish Cmty. Ctr., 1974—, Legal Aid Soc., 1974-78, Legal Assistance to Elderly, San Francisco, 1980, San Francisco Renaissance, 1982—; pres. San Francisco Sr. Ctr., 1972-75; co-chmn. San Francisco Lawyers' Com. for Urban Affairs, 1976. Rhodes scholar. Fellow Am. Bar Found.; mem. ABA, Am. Coll. Trial Lawyers, Am. Arbitration Assn. (bd. dirs. 1986-98, 2002--, adv. coun. No. Calif. chpt. 1982—, chmn. 1987, jud. coun. 1986-88, exec. bd. 1994-98, instr. and panelist arbitrator tng. programs), Am. Acad. Appellate Lawyers, State Bar Calif. (chmn. com. cts. 1982-83. bd. govs. 1983-85, mem. commn. on discovery 1984-86, pres. 1985-86), Calif. Acad. Appellate Lawyers, Coll. Comml. Arbitrators, Bar Assn. San Francisco (chmn. conf. dels. 1975-76, pres. 1980). Clubs: Calif. Tennis. Democrat. Federal civil litigation, State civil litigation, Construction. Office: McCutchen Doyle Brown & Enersen 3 Embarcadero Ctr San Francisco CA 94111-4003

HEILIGENSTEIN, CHRISTIAN E. lawyer; b. St. Louis, Dec. 7, 1929; s. Christian A. and Louisa M. (Dixon) H.; children: Christie; m. Liselotte Warbanoff, Feb. 6, 1981. BS in Law, U.Ill., 1953, JD, 1955. Bar: Ill. 1956, U.S. Dist. Ct. (so. dist.) Ill. 1956, U.S. Ct. Appeals (7th cir.) 1956, U.S. Dist. Ct. (cen. dist.) Ill. 1960, U.S. Supreme Ct. 1978. Assoc. Listeman & Bandy, East St. Louis, Ill., 1955-61; sole practice Belleville, Ill., 1962-84; ptnr., pres. Heiligenstein & Badgley, Belleville, 1984-98; pres. C.E. Heiligenstein, P.C., Belleville, 1998—. Bd. dirs. Union Planters Corp., Union Planters Bank NA, 1998-2000, audit com. 1999-2000, Magna Bank and Magna Group, Inc., 1984-98; chair audit com. Magna Group, Inc., 1994-98. Bd. visitors U. Ill. Coll. of Law, 2000. Recipient Alumni of Month award U.

Ill. Law Sch., 1982; C.E. Heiligenstein Chair in Law named in his honor U. Ill., 1999. Mem. Ill. State Bar Assn., Internat. Acad. Trial Lawyers (bd. dirs. 1991-97), St. Clair County Bar Assn., St. Louis Bar Assn., Inner Circle Advs., Am. Bd. Trial Advs. (nat. bd. dirs. 1992, pres. St. Louis, So. Ill. region 1993), Am. Acad. Profl. Liabilities Attys. (Nat. bd. dirs., 1990-99), ATLA (bd. govs. 1985-87), Ill. Trial Lawyers Assn. (bd. mgrs. 1975-88, pres. 1989), Beach Club (bd. dirs. 1996, v.p. 1998), Old Guard Soc. of Palm Beach. Democrat. Personal injury (including property damage), Product liability, Workers' compensation. Home: 5200 Turner Hall Rd Belleville IL 62220-5628 E-mail: l.warbanoj@aol.com.

HEILMAN, PAMELA DAVIS, lawyer; b. Buffalo, July 2, 1948; d. George Henry and Natalie (Maier) Davis; m. Robert D. Heilman, June 27, 1970. AB, Vassar Coll., 1970; JD, SUNY, Buffalo, 1975. Bar: N.Y. 1976, Fla. 1980. Assoc. Hodgson, Russ, Andrews, Woods & Goodyear, Buffalo, 1975-84, ptnr., 1984—. Bd. dirs. United Way Buffalo, 1985-97, vice chmn., 1989-92, chair, 1993-97, gen. campaign chair, 1992; bd. dirs. D'Youville Coll., Buffalo, 2001—, WNY Internat. Trade Coun., Inc., Buffalo, 2001—, Fin. Instns., Inc., Warsaw, 2002—. Mem. ABA, N.Y. State Bar Assn. (vice chmn., exec. com., sect. on internat. law and practice 1988-90), Fla. Bar Assn., Erie County Bar Assn. Corporate, general, Private international, Non-profit and tax-exempt organizations. Office: Hodgson Russ Andrews Woods & Goodyear LLP One M&T Plz Buffalo NY 14211-1638 E-mail: pheilman@hodgsonruss.com.

HEINDL, PHARES MATTHEWS, lawyer; b. Meridian, Miss., Dec. 14, 1949; s. Paul A. and Leila (Matthews) H.; m. Linda Ann Williamson, Sept. 21, 1985; children: Lori Elizabeth, Jesse Phares, Jared Matthews. BSChemE, Miss. State U., 1972; JD, U. Fla., 1981. Bar: Fla. 1981, Calif. 1982, U.S. Dist. Ct. (cen. dist.) Calif. 1983, U.S. Dist. Ct. (mid. dist.) Fla. 1983; cert. civil trial lawyer Fla. Bar. Assoc. Lafollette, Johnson et al, L.A., 1982-83, Sam E. Murrell & Sons, Orlando, Fla., 1983-84; pvt. practice Orlando, Fla., 1984-93, Altamonte Springs, Fla., 1993—. Bd. cert. civil trial lawyer. Precinct coord. Freedom Coun., Orlando, 1986; pres. Friends of the Wekiva River, 1999-2001. Mem. Fla. Bar Assn., Calif. Bar Assn., Seminole County Bar Assn. (pres. civil trial sect. 1998), ATLA, Christian Legal Soc. (past pres. Ctrl. Fla.), Fla. Acad. Trial Lawyers, Workers Compensation Rules Com. Republican. Avocation: kayak racing. State civil litigation, Personal injury (including property damage), Workers' compensation. Home: 2415 River Tree Cir Sanford FL 32771-8334 Office: 222 S Westmonte Dr Ste 208 Altamonte Springs FL 32714-4269

HEINEMAN, ANDREW DAVID, retired lawyer; b. N.Y.C., Nov. 5, 1928; s. Bernard and Lucy (Morgenthau) H. BA, Williams Coll., 1950; LLB, Yale U., 1953. Bar: N.Y. 1953. Assoc. Proskauer Rose Goetz & Mendelsohn, N.Y.C., 1953—63; ptnr. Proskauer Rose LLP, N.Y.C., 1963—2002; ret., 2002. Pres., chmn. bd. dirs. Ernest and Mary Hayward Weir Found., N.Y.C., 1969-87, trustee Mt. Sinai Hosp. Med. Sch. and Med. Ctr., 1976—, Williams Coll., 1980-95, Abelard Found., 1976-96; Asphalt Green, 1992-96; bd. dirs. Jewish Home and Hosp. for Aged, 1967—, vice chmn. bd. dirs., 1992, chmn. bd. dirs. 1993-97; exec. asst. Citizens for Kennedy and Johnson, N.Y.C., 1960; mem. N.Y. Gov.'s Commn. on Minorities in Med. Schs., 1982. Mem. Yale Law Sch. Assn. N.Y. (pres. 1970-73), Yale Law Sch. Alumni Assn. (v.p. 1973-76, exec. com.), Audubon Soc., North Country Bird Club, Linnaean Soc. (life), Fedn. N.Y. State Bird Clubs, Brit. Naval Photog. Club. Estate planning. Office: Proskauer Rose LLP 1585 Broadway New York NY 10036-8299

HEINKE, REX S. lawyer; b. Harrisburg, Ill., June 9, 1950; s. William Richard and Versa Lee Heinke; m. Margaret Ann Nagle, May 6, 1978; children: William Rex, Meghan Bradley. BA, U. Witwatersrand, Johannesburg, Republic of South Africa, 1971; JD, U. Columbia, 1975. Bar: Calif. 1975. Ptnr. Gibson, Dunn & Crutcher, L.A., 1983-99, Greines, Martin, Stein & Richland, Beverly Hills, Calif., 1999—2001, Akin, Gump, Strauss, Hauer & Feld , L.A., 2001—. Appellate, Libel, Trademark and copyright. Office: 2029 Century Park E Ste 2400 Los Angeles CA 90067 E-mail: rheinke@akingump.com.

HEINLE, RICHARD ALAN, lawyer; b. New Kensington, Pa., May 13, 1959; s. Robert Alan and Barbara Jane (Klimeck) H.; m. Sharon Eileen Farrell, Oct. 20, 1990; children: Kelly, Kyra, Casey. AB with highest honors, U. Chgo., 1981; JD cum laude, Georgetown U., 1984. Bar: Ill. 1984, Fla. 1994. Assoc. Arnstein & Lehr, Chgo., 1984-89, Foley & Lardner, Chgo., 1989-93, ptnr. Orlando, Fla., 1994—2003; with Pohl & Short, P.A., Winter Park, Fla., 2003—. Counsel Better Bus. Bur. Ctrl. Fla., Orlando, 1996-2003. Bd. dirs. Better Bus. Bur. Ctrl. Fla., 2003—. Mem.: Fla. C. of C. (bd. dirs. 1999—2000), Mfrs. Assn. Ctrl. Fla. (bd. dirs. 1995—), Phi Beta Kappa. Roman Catholic. Avocations: golf, running. Mergers and acquisitions, Securities. Home: 8100 Vineland Oaks Blvd Orlando FL 32835-8215 Office: Pohl & Short PA 280 W Corton Ste 410 Winter Park FL 32789 E-mail: rheinle@alumni.uchicago.edu.

HEINRICH, RANDALL WAYNE, lawyer; b. Houston, Nov. 29, 1958; s. Albert Joseph Sr. and Beverly June Earles; m. Linda Carol Cheek, June 6, 1993; children: Angela Leigh, Conrad Randall. BA, Baylor U., 1980, postgrad., 1981, Rice U., 1981-82; JD, U. Tex., 1985. Bar: Tex. 1985. Assoc. Baker & Botts, Houston, 1985-87, Chamberlain, Hrdlicka, White, Williams & Martin, Houston, 1987-91, Norton & Blair, Houston, 1991-92; mem. Gillis Paris & Heinrich, Houston, 1992—; mng. dir. Baytree Investors, Houston, 1993-97. Mem. dirs.' circle Houston Grand Opera, 1991, The Arts Symposium, 1991, Center Stage, Alley Theater, Houston, 1992-93, Houston Entrepreneurs' Forum, 1990-91; bd. dirs. The Cadre, 1991-92; pres. Exchange Club of Bayou City, 1992-93. Mem. ABA (YLD securities law com. 1993-95, vice chmn. 1994-95), NASD Pool Securities Arbitrators, Am. Arbitration Assn. (mem. nat. panel neutrals), Houston Bar Assn., Forum Club Houston, Phi Delta Theta. Baptist. Home: 4318 Saint Michaels Ct Sugar Land TX 77479-2986 Office: Gillis Paris & Heinrich 8 Greenway Plz Ste 818 Houston TX 77046

HEINRICH, STEVEN ALLAN, lawyer; b. Missoula, Mont., Mar. 1, 1962; s. Albert Carl and Mary Morlan H. BA, U. Calgary, Alberta, Can., 1984; MA, U. Ill., 1989, PhD, 1991; postgrad., U. B.C., Vancouver, Can., 1991-92; JD, U. Wash., 1994. Bar: Oreg. 1994, U.S. Dist. Ct. Oreg. 1995, U.S. Ct. Appeals (9th cir.) 1995. Law clk. Mortimer & Rose, Vancouver, B.C., Can., 1992; jud. intern, clk. Benton County Cir. Ct., Corvallis, Oreg., 1993; assoc. Morley, Thomas & McHill, Lebanon, Oreg., 1994-98; atty. pvt. practice, Corvallis, 1998—. Contbr. articles to profl. jours. Rsch. travel grantee U. Ill., 1989; U. Ill. fellow, 1985, 89, 90; Arms Control Disarmament and Internat. Security scholarship MacArthur Found., U. Ill., 1989, Panvini scholar, 1992, Philip J. Weiss scholar, U. Wash., 1993, Law Found. B.C. scholar, 1992, entrance scholar, 1991, Sir James Lougheed award of distinction, 1990, 91, FLAS fellow, 1986, Louise McKinney scholar, 1982, 83, W. Vernie Reed scholar, 1980, 81, 82, U. Calgary Merit award, 1980, cert. Merit Province of Alta., 1980. Mem. Oreg. Bar Assn., Nat. Acad. Elder Law Attys., Oreg. State Bar (elder law sect. exec. com. 2001—, elder law sect. CLE planning com. 2000-, task force on lawyer competency 1995-96), Benton County Bar Assn., Rotary (Paul Harris fellow), Order of Coif, Phi Kappa Phi. Avocations: flying, scuba diving, canoeing, hiking. General civil litigation, Family and matrimonial, General practice.

HEINRICH, TIMOTHY JOHN, lawyer; b. Houston, Nov. 30, 1961; s. Albert J. and Beverly J. Heinrich; m. Tammy K. Morgan, Aug. 10, 1985; children: John, Allison, Michelle, Philip. BA, Washington U., St. Louis, 1984; JD, U. Tex., 1987. Bar: Tex. 1987. Assoc. Hiller Kornfeld Axelrad & Falik, Houston, 1987-90; assoc., shareholder Boyar & Miller, Houston, 1990—. Lay leader Terrace United Meth. Ch., Houston, 1994-97. Mem. Kiwanis (lt. gov. Houston 1997-98). Commercial, contracts (including sales of goods; commercial financing), Mergers and acquisitions, Property, real (including real estate development, water). Office: Boyar & Miller 4265 San Felipe St Ste 1200 Houston TX 77027-2917

HEINS, SAMUEL DAVID, lawyer; b. Providence, May 31, 1947; s. Maurice Haskell and Hadassah (Wagman) H.; children: Madeleine Sarah, Nora Anne. BA, U. Minn., 1968, JD, 1972. Bar: Minn. 1973, U.S. Dist. Ct. Minn., U.S. Ct. Appeals (8th cir.). Law clk. U.S. Dist. Ct. Minn., Mpls., 1972-73; assoc. Firestone Law Firm, St. Paul, 1973-76; ptnr. Tanick & Heins, Mpls., 1976-89, Opperman & Heins, Mpls., 1989-94, Heins, Mills & Olson, Mpls., 1994—. Vis. asst. prof. Sch. Architecture, U. Minn.-Mpls., 1974-89. Mem. Mpls. Charter Commn., 1983-84; pres. Minn. Lawyers Internat. Human Rights Com., Mpls., 1983-85, Minn. Ctr. for Torture Victims, Mpls., 1985-87, chmn., pres. Mem. ABA, Minn. State Bar Assn. (bd. govs. 1978-84). Federal civil litigation, State civil litigation.

HEINTZMAN, THOMAS G. lawyer; BA in Econs. cum laude, Harvard U.; grad., U. London, Osgoode Hall Law Sch. Bar: Ont. 1968, Nfld. 1977, Alta. 1990, cert.: Law Soc. Upper Can. (specialist in civil litigation). Ptnr. McCarthy Tretrault, Toronto, Canada, 1968—. Lectr. in field. Fellow: Internat. Acad. Trial Lawyers; mem.: Am. Coll. Trial Lawyers (past chair Can. jud. com.), Internat. Bar Assn. (past Can. mem. coun.), Can. Bar Assn. (past pres. 1994—95), Order of Can. (officer). General civil litigation, Appellate, Construction. Office: Ste 4700 Toronto Dominion Tower Toronto ON M5K 1E6 Canada

HEINY, JAMES RAY, lawyer; b. Albert Lea, Minn., Oct. 7, 1928; s. Albin James and Lola Marguerite (Keig) H.; m. Wava Jeanine Isaacson, Sept. 2, 1951 (dec. 1980); children: Jon Carl, Jane Ellen Heiny Smith, Ann Elizabeth Heiny Hohenshell, Thomas James; m. Norma Lou West, July 24, 1982. BA, Grinnell Coll., 1950; JD, U. Iowa, 1953. Bar: Iowa 1953. Assoc. Westfall, Laird & Burington, Mason City, Iowa, 1955-58; ptnr. Laird, Heiny, McManigal, Winga, Duffy & Stambaugh, Mason City, 1958—. Pres. Luth. Social Svcs. Iowa FODN, 1987—2001; bd. dirs. YMCA, Mason City, 1972—75; pres. Good Shepherd Geriatric Ctr., Inc., Mason City, 1960—72. With U.S. Army, 1953—55. Mem. ABA, Iowa State Bar Assn. (bd. govs. 1986-91), Cerro Gordo County Bar Assn. (pres. 1976). Republican. Avocations: amateur radio, bird watching, sports. Probate (including wills, trusts), Property, real (including real estate development, water), Personal income taxation. Home: 2040 Hunters Ridge Dr Mason City IA 50401-7500 Office: Laird Heiny McManigal Winga Duffy & Stambaugh 300 Wells Fargo Bank Bldg Mason City IA 50401 E-mail: jamesrh4@MCHSI.com., laird@netconx.net.

HEISE, JOHN IRVIN, JR., lawyer; b. Balt., Dec. 13, 1924; s. John Irvin and Ruby Belle (Carpenter) H.; m. Jacqueline Mosey Morley, Sept. 3, 1949; children: John Irvin III, Liane Des Roches, Jeff Howard, Suzanne Wolfrom. AB, U. Md., 1947; JD, U. Va., 1950. Bar: Md. 1950, D.C. 1953, U.S. Supreme Ct. 1962. Trial atty. civil divsn. Dept. Justice, Washington, 1950-52; assoc. Shea Greenman Gardner & McConnaughey, Washington, 1952-57; ptnr. Heise Jorgensen & Stefanelli, P.A., Silver Spring, Md., Gaithersburg, Md., 1957. Committeeman, merit badge counselor, dist. chmn. sustaining mem. dr. Boy Scouts Am.; chmn. Md. Ednl. Found., Inc., 1972-92. Maj. USAF, 1942-45. Recipient Gottwals award U. Md., 1978. Mem. ABA, Fed. Bar Assn., Md. Bar Assn., D.C. Bar Assn., Montgomery County Bar Assn., Md. Alumni Assn. (pres. 1966-67), Terrapin (pres. 1961-62), Omicron Delta Kappa, Phi Kappa Phi. Republican. Episcopalian. Administrative and regulatory, Federal civil litigation, Corporate, general. E-mail: heisejacks@aol.com.

HEISERMAN, ROBERT GIFFORD, lawyer; b. El Paso, July 5, 1946; s. Robert Gifford and Nancy Mildred (Wardlow) H.; m. Nancy Fay Price, Oct. 20, 1973; 1 child, Laura. BA, U. Oreg., 1968; JD, U. Denver, 1971. Bar: Ct. Colo. 1972, U.S. Dist. Ct. Colo. 1972, U.S. Dist. Ct. N.Mex. 1972, U.S. Dist. Ct. D.C. 1972, U.S. Dist. Ct. (so. dist.) Ala. 1974, U.S. Ct. Appeals (10th cir.) 1975, U.S. Supreme Ct. 1976. Legis. draftsman N.Mex. Legislature, Santa Fe, 1972-73; pvt. practice Santa Fe, 1973, Denver, 1974—. Adj. prof. immigration and nationality law and profl. responsibility courses U. Denver, 1981—. Active Emergency Med. Svcs. Coun., Denver, 1981—84. Mem. Am. Immigration Lawyers Assn. (nat. bd. govs., chmn. profl. ethics and grievances com. 1982-89, 98-2000, founder Colo. chpt., treas. Colo. chpt. 1978-81), ABA, Colo. Bar Assn., Denver Bar Assn., D.C. Bar Assn. Democrat. Methodist. Immigration, naturalization, and customs. Office: 1675 Broadway Ste 2280 Denver CO 80202-4675 Home: Ste 2280 1675 Broadway Denver CO 80202-4675 E-mail: info@heiserman.com.

HEISLER, QUENTIN GEORGE, JR., lawyer; b. Jefferson City, Mo., June 30, 1943; s. Quentin George and Helen (Reynolds) H.; m. Susan Davis, Jan. 24, 1970; children: Sarah, Thomas, Margaret. AB magna cum laude, Harvard U., 1965, JD, 1968. Bar: Ill. 1968, U.S. Dist. Ct. (no. dist.) Ill. 1969, Fla. 1977. Assoc. McDermott, Will & Emery, Chgo., 1968-69, 70-75, ptnr., 1975—; legal counsel Office Minority Bus. Enterprise, Dept. Commerce, Washington, 1969-70. Co-author: Working With Family Businesses, 1995; gen. editor: Trust Administration in Illinois, 1979. Chmn. Winnetka Caucus, Ill., 1983; mem. Winnetka Bd. Edn., 1985-89; trustee Shedd Aquarium, Hadley Sch. for the Blind, Winnetka; bd govs. Winnetka Cmty. House, 1998-99. Fellow Am. Coll. Trust and Estates Counsel; mem. Chgo. Coun. Estate Planning, Univ. Club, Harvard Club (bd. dirs. Chgo. chpt. 1984-95, pres. bd. 1989-91), Skokie Country Club (Glencoe, Ill.), Racquet Club (Chgo.). Estate planning, Probate (including wills, trusts), Estate taxation. Office: McDermott Will & Emery 227 W Monroe St Ste 3100 Chicago IL 60606-5096

HEISLER, STANLEY DEAN, lawyer; b. The Dalles, Oreg., Jan. 11, 1946; s. Donald Eugene and Roberta (Van Valkenburgh) Heisler. BA, Willamette U., 1968, JD, 1972. Bar: Oreg. 1972, U.S. Ct. Claims 1972, U.S. Tax Ct. 1972, U.S. Ct. Appeals (9th cir.) 1972, D.C. 1973, U.S. Ct. Appeals (fed. cir.) 1973, U.S. Ct. Mil. Appeals 1973, N.Y. 1985, U.S. Supreme Ct. 1985. Assoc. Heisler & Van Valkenburgh, The Dalles, 1973-74; ptnr. Heisler, Van Valkenburgh & Coats, The Dalles, 1975-81, Heisler & Heisler, The Dalles, 1982-84, Cohen & Shalleck, N.Y.C., 1985-88, Phillips, Nizer, Benjamin, Krim & Ballon, N.Y.C., 1988-91, Squadron, Ellenoff, Plesent, Sheinfeld & Sorkin, N.Y.C., 1991-94; mng. ptnr. Shays & Kemper, LLP, N.Y.C., 1994-98, Shays, Rothman, & Heisler, LLP, N.Y.C., 1999-2000, Shays, Heisler & Rosenthal, LLP, N.Y.C., 2000-01; pvt. practice Stanley D. Heisler, PC, N.Y.C., 2001—. Speechwriter Sec. of State Tom McCall, Salem, 1965, Gov. Tom McCall, Salem, 1966—68; speechwriter, legis. asst. U.S. Senator Bob Packwood, Washington, 1969—73; vice chmn. Pres.'s Air Quality Adv. Bd., Washington, 1973—76. Mem.: ABA, Assn. of Bar of City of N.Y., N.Y. State Bar Assn., Soc. Colonial Wars (mem. coun. N.Y. State chpt. 2003—), Sons of the Revolution, New Eng. Soc. in City of N.Y., Soc. for the Promotion of Hellenic Studies, Soc. Mayflower Descs. (bd. dirs. N.Y. chpt. 2001—), Soc. of the Descs. Washington's Army at Valley Forge, Edmund Rice (1638) Assn., Sons of the Am. Revolution, Princeton Club, Univ. Club (N.Y.C. and Portland, Oreg.), Arlington Club. Republican. Episcopalian. State civil litigation, Family and matrimonial. Home: 400 E 77th St Apt 8J New York NY 10021-2342 Office: Stanley D Heisler PC 276 5th Ave New York NY 10001-4509 E-mail: s.heisler@worldnet.att.net.

HEIST, ROBERT CONNOR, lawyer; b. Greenville, Miss., Oct. 8, 1964; s. Daniel Stuart Heist and Barbara Jean Breand. BS, U. Ill., 1986; JD, John Marshall Law Sch., 1985; MBA, Lake Forest U., 2003. Bar: Ill. 1990, U.S. Dist. Ct. (no. dist.) Ill. 1990, U.S. Ct. Appeals (7th cir.) 1992, U.S. Surpeme Ct. 1995. Assoc. Hinshaw & Gilbertson, Chgo., 1989—94; ptnr. Bates Meckler Bulges & Tilson, 1994—98, Bates & Carey, 1998—2000; atty. pvt. practice, 2000—. Mem.: ABA, Chgo. Bar Assn., Ill. State Bar Assn., Fed. Bar Assn., Def. Rsch. Inst., Assn. Def. Trial Counsel, Profl. Liability Underwriting Soc., Assn. Trial Lawyers Am. Professional liability, Commercial, contracts (including sales of goods; commercial financing), Corporate, general. Office: R Connor & Assocs 120 S Riverside Plz Ste 1605 Chicago IL 60602 Fax: 312-780-1973. E-mail: rconnor@aol.com.

HEITLER, GEORGE, lawyer; b. N.Y.C., Sept. 3, 1915; s. John J. and Celia (Zeichner) H.; m. Florence A. Posner, Apr. 21, 1940; children: James B., Richard S. BS, Columbia U., 1936, JD, 1938. Bar: N.Y. 1938, Ill. 1962. Asso. firm Cutler, Wilson & McMahon, N.Y.C., 1938-40; spl. asst. to David L. Podell; counsel to Hays, Podell & Schulman, N.Y.C., 1940; asso. atty. firm Coughlan & Russell; also mng. agt. and asst. sec. Central Manhattan Properties, Inc., N.Y.C., 1940-43; chief clk., legal adviser rents and claims bd. 4th Service Command, U.S. Army, 1943-45; engaged as bus. exec., also house counsel various comml. orgns., 1946-57; asst. sec., staff counsel Blue Cross Assn., N.Y.C., 1957-60, corporate sec., staff counsel, 1960-61; v.p., sec. Chgo., 1961-71; sr. v.p., corporate sec., gen. counsel, 1971-81; sr. v.p., legal counsel Nat. Blue Shield Assn., 1978-81; counsel to Kaye, Scholer, Fierman, Hays & Handler, N.Y.C., 1981-85. Spl. adviser Dept. Labor, also speaker and panelist. Author articles. Mem. Am., Chgo. bar assns., Assn. Bar City N.Y. Home: 700 John Ringling Blvd Sarasota FL 34236-1555 E-mail: fgheitfl@aol.com.

HEITNER, KENNETH HOWARD, lawyer; b. Jersey City, Apr. 1, 1948; s. Charles Fred and Molly (Vogelman) H.; m. Anne Barbara Siegel, June 14, 1970; children: Douglas, Andrew, Elizabeth. BA, Rutgers U., 1969; JD, NYU, 1973, LLM, 1977. Bar: N.Y. 1974, U.S. Dist. Ct. (so. and ea. dists.) N.Y. 1975, U.S. Tax Ct. 1976. Assoc. Weil, Gotshal & Manges, N.Y.C., 1973-81, ptnr., 1981—. With U.S. Army, 1969-75. Mem. ABA, N.Y. State Bar Assn. (exec. com. on bankruptcy , corps., net oper. losses, reorgns.), Tax Club, Assn. Bar City N.Y., Fairview Country Club (Greenwich, Conn., bd. govs. 1983-90). Corporate taxation, Personal income taxation. Office: Weil Gotshal & Manges LLP 767 5th Ave Fl Concl New York NY 10153-0119 E-mail: Kenneth.Heitner@Weil.com.

HEJTMANEK, DANTON CHARLES, lawyer; b. Topeka, July 22, 1951; s. Robert Keith and Bernice Louise (Krause) H.; m. Julie Hejtmanek; 1 child, Brian J. BBA in Acctg., Washburn U., 1973, JD, 1975. Bar: Kans. 1976, U.S. Dist. Ct. Kans. 1976, U.S. Tax Ct. 1976. Ptnr. Schroer, Rice, Bryan & Lykins, P.A., Topeka, 1975-86, Bryan, Lykins, Hejtmanek & Fincher P.A., Topeka, 1986—. Mem. ABA (rep. young lawyers Kans. and Nebr.), ATLA, Kans. Bar Assn. (pres. young lawyers 1985), Kans. Trial Lawyers Assn., Sertoma (pres. 1983, internat. pres. 1998-99). Republican. Presbyterian. Avocations: snow skiing, travel. Family and matrimonial, Personal injury (including property damage), Probate (including wills, trusts). Home: 2800 SW Burlingame Rd Topeka KS 66611-1316 Office: Bryan Lykins Hejtmanek & Fincher PA 222 SW 7th St Topeka KS 66603-3734

HEKTNER, CANDICE ELAINE, lawyer; b. Fargo, N.D., Apr. 22, 1948; d. Alfred G. and Hope E. Hektner; children: Nicole A, Brittany T. BA, Concordia Coll., Moorhead, Minn., 1970; JD, Valparaiso U., 1975. Bar: Minn. 1975, N.D. 1975, U.S. Dist. Ct. Minn. 1975, U.S. Dist. Ct. N.D. 1975. Assoc. Ochs Larsen Law Firm, Mpls., 1975-80; ptnr. Chadwick, Johnson & Condon, P.A., Mpls., 1980-91, Peterson & Hektner Ltd., Mpls., 1991—. Mem. ABA, Minn. Bar Assn., Minn. Def. Lawyers Assn. Lutheran. Family and matrimonial, Insurance, Workers' compensation. Office: Peterson & Hektner Ltd 7831 Glenroy Rd Minneapolis MN 55439-3132

HELANDER, ROBERT CHARLES, lawyer; b. Chgo., Oct. 30, 1932; s. William Eugene and Grace Pauline H.; m. Betty Jane Vinson, Apr. 8, 1961; children— Diana Chaffin, Alexander Christian, Nicholas Charles. BA, Amherst Coll., 1953; JD, Harvard U., 1956, P.MD, 1971. Bar: D.C. 1956, Ill. 1956, N.Y. 1979, U.S. Supreme Ct. 1960. Practice law, Chgo., 1956-62; Amherst fellow in Middle East, 1960-61; mem. firm Helander, Farmanfarmaian & Ghany, Tehran, Iran, 1962-65; assoc. gen. counsel Internat. Basic Economy Corp., Lima, Peru, 1965-68, v.p., 1968-71; v.p. devel. and adminstrn., gen. counsel IBEC, N.Y.C., 1971-73, group v.p. and pres., 1973-76; ptnr. firm Jones, Day, Reavis & Pogue (Surrey & Morse), N.Y.C., 1976-93; ptnr. Kaye, Scholer, Fierman, Hays & Handler, LLP, N.Y.C., 1993—2001; mng. ptnr. InterConsult., LLP, 2002—. Pres. Accion Internat., 1978-88; chmn. Pan Am. Soc., 1979-88, Am. Fund for Ind. Univs., 1987—, Fund for Multinat. Mgmt. Edn., 1981-91; bd. dirs. Internat. Law Inst., 1975, Ams. Soc., 1982—, Univ. Andes Found., 1983—, Near East Found., 1977—, Bolivarian Soc., 1980—, IESA Found., 1991—, chmn. Internat. Coun. Escuela Superior Adminstrn. de Negocios, 1999—, pres. Am. Foreign Law Assn., 2001-. Named Comendador, Orden del Sol (Peru). Fellow Am. Bar Found. (life); mem. ABA (chmn. inter-Am. law com. sect. internat. law and practice 1978-83, editor-in-chief Inter-Am. Legal Materials 1983-91, del to Inter Am. Bar Assn.), Assn. of Bar of City of N.Y. (inter-Am. affairs com.), Inter-Am. Bar Assn. (pres.), Am. Fgn. Law Assn. (pres. 2001—), Coun. Fgn. Rels., Carnegie Coun., Century Club. Republican. Episcopalian. Alternative dispute resolution, Insurance, Private international. Home: 3 Mountainview Dr Mountainside NJ 07092-2510 Office: PO Box 1337 Mountainside NJ 07092 E-mail: rch@interconsultllp.com.

HELBERT, MICHAEL CLINTON, lawyer; b. Wichita, Kans., Dec. 30, 1950; s. Robert Lee and Carrollyn Jean (Stull) H.; m. Sandra Sue Ziegler, Aug. 26, 1978; 1 son, Michael Ryan. BA, U. Kans.-Lawrence, 1972, J.D., 1975. Bar: Kans. 1975, U.S. Dist. Ct. Kans. 1975, U.S. Supreme Ct. 1980, U.S. Ct. Appeals (10th cir.) 1984. Intern, Douglas County Legal Aid, Lawrence, 1974-75; assoc. law firm Atherton, Hurt & Sanderson, Emporia, Kans., 1975-77; ptnr. firm Helbert & Bell, and predecessor firms, Emporia, 1978-81, prin., 1981-97; pvt. practice, 1998—; mem. Kans. Justice Iniative Commn., 1997—. Treas. Lyon County Rep. Ctrl. Com., 1986-94; mem. adv. bd. Kans. U. Endowment Assn., 1977-81; chmn. profl. divsn. United Way of Emporia, 1978. Mem. ATLA, Kans. Trial Lawyers Assn. (bd. govs. 1988—, state parliamentarian 1988-89, sec. 1989-90, v.p., 1997-99, pres. 2000-01), Kans. Bar Assn., Lyon-Chase County Bar Assn. (treas. 1982, v.p. 1983, pres. 1984), Emporia C. of C. (past dir., past vice-chmn.), Emporia Jaycees (past dir.), Kans. Jaycees (past dir.). Republican. Presbyn. State civil litigation, Personal injury (including property damage), Workers' compensation. Home: 2816 Lakeridge Rd Emporia KS 66801-5936 Office: 519 Commercial St Emporia KS 66801-4005 E-mail: mhelbert@helbertlawoffices.com.

HELDER, JAN PLEASANT, JR., lawyer; b. Marysville, Calif., Jan. 18, 1963; s. Jan Pleasant Sr. and Roleane Phylis (Harrison) H.; m. Barbara Irene Loring, July 14, 1990; children: Russell Wright, Zachary Allen, David Grant. BA in Econs., Calif. State U., Sacramento, 1986; JD, Georgetown U., 1989. Bar: Mo. 1989, U.S. Dist. Ct. (we. dist.) Mo. 1989, Kans. 1990, U.S. Dist. Ct. Kans. 1990, U.S. Ct. Appeals (10th cir.) 1994, U.S. Tax Ct. 1994. Exec. asst. to pres. Sacramento Trade Exch., 1983-84; legis. asst. Calif. Postsecondary Edn. Commn., Sacramento, 1985-86; assoc. Spencer, Fane, Britt & Browne, Kansas City, Mo., 1989-94, Sonnenschein Nath & Rosenthal, Kansas City, Mo., 1994-96, ptnr., 1996-2000, Stueve Helder Siegel LLP, 2001—. Judge pro tem City of Prairie Village (Kans.) Mcpl. Ct.; bd. dirs. Edn., Inc., bd. sec., 1994-95; bd. dirs. Young Audiences, vice pres., 1997-98, vice chmn., 1999-2001, sec., 2001-02. Bd. editor Bus. Torts Reporter, 1996—. Chair Calif. State Student Assn., Sacramento and Long Beach, 1984-85; mem. Leadership Mo., Jefferson City, 1992; mem. Centurions Leadership Program, 1993-95, mem. steering com., 1994-95; bd. dirs. Ivanhoe Neighborhood Coun., 2003—. Pursuit of Worthwhile Endeavors scholar Calif. State U., Sacramento, 1982. Mem. ABA (vice-chair bus. torts subcom., bus. and corp. litigation com., bus. sect. 1993-95, task force on Litigation Reform, chair bus. torts subcom. 1995—, co-chair,

Task Force on Year 2000 Legislation, 1999—), co-chair, Task Force on Litigation Reform and Rule Revision, 1999—, Am. Assn. Trial Lawyers; Nat. Inst. Trial Advocacy (western regional 1993), Kans. Assn. Trial Lawyers, Mo. Bar Assn., Kans. Bar Assn., Kansas City Met. Bar Assn., Johnson County Bar Assn., Greater Kansas City C. of C. (chair subcom. on labor and jud. 1990-91, fed. affairs com. 1989—), Ross T. Roberts Inn Ct. (barrister 1991-92), Am. Law Inst. Republican. Presbyterian. Avocations: jazz and classical and choral music, golf, tennis, running, politics. Federal civil litigation, General civil litigation, State civil litigation. Home: 2216 W 63rd St Shawnee Mission KS 66208-1903 E-mail: helder@shslitigation.com.

HELDMAN, JAMES GARDNER, lawyer; b. Cin., Mar. 7, 1949; s. James Norvin and Jane Marie (Gardner) H.; m. Wendy Maureen Saunders, Sept. 3, 1978; children: Dustin A., Courtney B. AB cum laude, Harvard U., 1971; JD with honors, George Washington U., 1974. Bar: D.C. 1975, U.S. Dist. Ct. (D.C. dist.) 1975, U.S. Ct. Appeals (D.C. cir.) 1975, U.S. Supreme Ct. 1980, Ohio 1981. Assoc. Perazich & Kolker, Washington, 1974-79, Wyman, Bautzer, Kuchel & Silbert, Washington, 1979-81, Strauss & Troy, Cin., 1981-83, ptnr., 1984—. Mem. ABA, Ohio State Bar Assn., Cin. Bar Assn. Avocations: tennis, platform tennis, biking. Finance, Property, real (including real estate development, water), Securities. Office: Strauss & Troy The Fed Res Bldg 150 E Fourth St Cincinnati OH 45202-4018

HELDMAN, PAUL W. lawyer, grocery store company executive; BS, Boston U., 1973; JD, U. Cin., 1977. Bar: Ohio 1977. Assoc. Beckman, Lavercombe & Well, 1977-82; atty. The Kroger Co., Cin., 1982-86; sr. atty. Kroger Co., Cin., 1986-87, sr. counsel, 1987-89, v.p., gen. counsel, 1989-92; v.p., sec., gen. counsel The Kroger Co., 1992-97, sr. v.p., sec., gen. counsel, 1997—. Corporate, general, Securities. Office: The Kroger Co 1014 Vine St Ste 1000 Cincinnati OH 45202-1100*

HELFAND, MARCY CAREN CAREN, lawyer; b. Chgo., Sept. 2, 1954; d. Irwin and Pauline H.; children: Eric and Alexis Weisbrod. BS with high hons., So. Meth. U., 1976, JD cum laude, 1979. Bar: Tex. 1979, U.S. Dist. Ct. (no. dist.) Tex.; cert. comml. real estate law, Tex. Bd. of Legal Specialization. Assoc. Freytag, Marshall, et al, Dallas, 1979-83, Jones, Day, Reavis & Pogue, Dallas, 1983-84; Of Counsel Morgan & Weisbrod, Dallas, 1984-94; pvt. practice Dallas, 1994—. Precinct chair Dallas Dem. Orgn., 1979—. Mem. ABA (chair remedies, miscellaneous clauses real property, probate and trust section 1993-95, chair lit. com. 2001--), Dallas Assn. Young Lawyers (chair continuing legal edn. com. 1983), Dallas Bar Assn., Coll. State Bar of Tex., Order of Coif. Commercial, contracts (including sales of goods; commercial financing), Finance, Property, real (including real estate development, water). Home: 7191 Kendallwood Dr Dallas TX 75240-5510 Office: 5580 Lbj Fwy Ste 270 Dallas TX 75240-6293 E-mail: mhelfand@swbell.net.

HELFER, MICHAEL STEVENS, lawyer, business executive; b. N.Y.C., Aug. 2, 1945; s. Robert Stevens and Teresa (Kahan) H.; m. Ricki Rhodarmer Helfer; children: Lisa, David, Matthew. BA summa cum laude, Claremont Men's Coll., 1967; JD magna cum laude, Harvard U., 1970. Bar: D.C. 1971. Law clk. to chief judge U.S. Ct. Appeals D.C., 1970-71; asst. counsel subcom. on constl. amendments Senate Judiciary Com., 1971-73; assoc. Wilmer, Cutler & Pickering, Washington, 1973-78, ptnr., 1978-2000, mgmt. com., 1990-98, chmn., 1995-98; exec. v.p. for corp. strategy Nationwide Ins./Fin. Svcs., Columbus, Ohio, 2000—03; pres. Nationwide Strategic Investments, 2002—03; gen. counsel Citigroup, Inc., N.Y.C., 2003—. Bd. dirs. Lawyers for Children Am., 1997-, Wexner Ctr. for Arts, 2002. Mem. Am. Law Inst. Democrat. Administrative and regulatory, Banking, Federal civil litigation. Home: 1049 Park Ave Apt 6C New York NY 10128 E-mail: helferm@citigroup.com.

HELGERSON, JOHN WALTER, lawyer; b. Cleve., Aug. 27, 1938; s. Floyd G. and Evelyn Ann (Wilder) H.; m. Dorothy Elizabeth Hart, Dec. 5, 1984, children from previous marriage: Heidi Wilder, Holly Ward. A.B., Wittenberg U., 1960; J.D., Yale U., 1963. Bar: Ohio 1963. Assoc., Porter Wright Morris & Arthur, Columbus, Ohio, 1963-93, ret. 1993, ptnr., 1968— ; ret. 1993; bd. dirs. Bry-Air, Inc., Sunbury, Ohio; mng. dir. Windsong Ltd., Grenada; chmn. lawyers div. United Way, 1979. Served to capt. USAR, 1963-70. Mem. Blue Key, Phi Gamma Delta, Pi Sigma Alpha, Pi Delta Epsilon, Tau Pi Phi, Capital Club, Grenada Yacht Club. Republican. Unitarian. Avocations: sailing, scuba diving, travel, deep sea fishing. Corporate, general, Mergers and acquisitions, Property, real (including real estate development, water). Home: PO Box 26 Saint George's Grenada

HELLER, ANNETTE PATSY SEIGEL, lawyer; b. St. Louis, Dec. 5, 1944; d. Alexander and Bernadine Seigel; m. Jack L. Heller, Aug. 6, 1972; children: Mark, Rebecca. BSBA, S.E. Mo. State U., 1967; JD, St. Louis U., 1976. Bar: Mo. 1976, U.S. Dist. Ct. (ea. dist.) Mo. 1984. Atty. Ralston Purina Co., St. Louis, 1976-83; pvt. practice St. Louis, 1983—; ptnr. Heller & Kepler, 1988—2002. Contbr. articles to profl. jours. Mem. Leadership St. Louis, 1986—. Mem. Mo. Bar Assn. (chmn. patent and trademark com. 1987-90, mem. bd. govs. 1993-99), Bar Assn. Met. St. Louis (treas. 1985-86, v.p. 1986-87), Women Lawyers Assn. (v.p. 1980-81, pres. 1981-82). Trademark and copyright. Home: 484 Whitree Ln Chesterfield MO 63017-2423 Office: 14323 S Outer Forty Ste 512 S Town And Country MO 63017

HELLER, PHILIP, lawyer; b. N.Y.C., Aug. 12, 1952; s. Irving and Dolores (Soloff) Heller; married; children: Howard Philip, John Philip, Madison Irene. Attended, Harvard Coll.; BA summa cum laude, Boston U., 1976, JD, 1979. Bar: Mass 1979, NY 1980, US Ct Appeals (1st, 2d & 9th cirs) 1980, US Supreme Ct 1983, Calif 1984, US Dist Ct (all dists) Calif, US Dist Ct (ea & so dists) NY, US Dist Ct Mass. Law clk. to judge Cooper U.S. Dist. Ct. (so. dist.) N.Y., N.Y.C., 1979; ptnr. Fagelbaum & Heller LLP, L.A. Mem.: ABA (litigation sect), Los Angeles County Bar Asn, Calif Bar Asn. Federal civil litigation, General civil litigation, State civil litigation. Office: Fagelbaum & Heller LLP 2049 Century Park E Ste 2050 Los Angeles CA 90067-3168 Fax: 310-286-7086. E-mail: ph@philipheller.com.

HELLER, ROBERT MARTIN, lawyer; b. N.Y.C., Feb. 12, 1942; s. Philip B. and Mildred S. (Friedman) H.; m. Amy S. Wexler, July 11, 1965; children: David B., Pamela L. BA, Columbia U., 1963, LLB, 1966. Bar: N.Y. 1967, D.C. 1992, U.S. Dist. Ct. (so. and ea. dists.) N.Y. 1970, U.S. Ct. Appeals (2d cir.) 1967, U.S. Supreme Ct. 1976. Law clk. to judge U.S. Ct. Appeals (2d cir.), N.Y.C., 1966-67; atty. adviser to commr. FTC, Washington, 1967-69; asst. to mayor for housing, city planning, transp. and model cities, sec. to cabinet City of N.Y., 1971-73; ptnr. Kramer Levin Naftalis & Frankel LLP, N.Y.C., 1974—, mng. ptnr., 1991-94. Adj. prof. architecture Columbia U., 1975—77; bd. visitors Columbia Law Sch., 1992—2000. Bd. govs. Hebrew Union Coll./Jewish Inst. Religion, 1996—; pres. bd. dirs. 1056 Fifth Ave. Corp., 1994-96; vice chair Union Am. Hebrew Congregations, 1999—; trustee Rabbi Marc H. Tanenbaum Found. James Kent scholar; Harlan Fiske Stone scholar. Mem. ABA, N.Y. State Bar Assn., Assn. of Bar of City of N.Y. (com. on antitrust and trade regulation 1996-99), Phi Beta Kappa. Avocations: aerobic walking, photography. Antitrust, Federal civil litigation, Mergers and acquisitions. Home: 1056 5th Ave New York NY 10028-0112 Office: Kramer Levin Naftalis & Frankel LLP 919 3rd Ave New York NY 10022-3902

HELLER, RONALD IAN, lawyer; b. Cleve., Sept. 4, 1956; s. Grant L. and Audrey P. (Lecht) Heller; m. Shirley Ann Stringer, Mar. 23, 1986 (dec. 2001); 1 child, David Grant. AB with high honors, U. Mich., 1976, MBA, 1979, JD, 1980. Bar: Hawaii 1980, U.S. Ct. Claims 1982, U.S. Tax Ct. 1981, U.S. Ct. Appeals (9th cir.) 1981, U.S. Supreme Ct. 1992; Trust Ter. Pacific Islands 1982, Rep. Marshall Islands 1982; CPA, Hawaii. Assoc. Hoddick, Reinwald, O'Connor & Marrack, Honolulu, 1980-84; ptnr. Reinwald, O'Connor & Marrack, Honolulu, 1984-87; stockholder, bd. dirs. Torkildson, Katz, Fonseca, Moore & Hetherington, Honolulu, 1988—. Adj. prof. U. Hawaii Sch. Law, 1981; arbitrator ct.-annexed arbitration program First Cir. Ct., State of Hawaii; author, instr. Hawaii Taxes. Bd. dirs. Hawaii Women Lawyers Found., Honolulu, 1984-86, Hawaii Performing Arts Co., Honolulu, 1984-93; panel of arbitrators Am. Arbitration Assn., 1987-99; actor, stage mgr. Honolulu Cmty. Theatre, 1983-87, Hawaii Performing Arts Co., Honolulu, 1982-87. Named NFIB Hawaii outstanding sm. bus. vol. 1998. Fellow Am. Coll. Tax Counsel; mem. AICPAs (coun. 1994-96, 2002-2003), ABA, Hawaii State Bar Assn. (chair tax sect. 1997-98, chair state and local tax com. 1994-95), Hawaii Soc. CPAs (chmn. tax com. 1985-86, legis. com. 1987-88, bd. dirs. 1988-2003, pres. 1994-95), Hawaii Women Lawyers. General civil litigation, Taxation, general, State and local taxation. Office: Torkildson Katz Fonseca Moore & Hetherington 700 Bishop St Ste 1500 Honolulu HI 96813-4187 E-mail: rheller@torkildson.com.

HELLER, STEPHEN REID, lawyer; b. Norfolk, Va., Jan. 25, 1956; s. Selwyn Bernard and Dorothy Leah H.; m. Karen Heller, June 13, 1982; children: Ilana Ruth, Naomi Ann. Degree in psychology, U. South Fla., 1978; JD, So. Meth. U., 1982. Bar: Tex. 1983, U.S. Ct. Appeals (5th cir.) 1983, U.S. Supreme Ct. 1988. Assoc., pvt. firm, Dallas, 1982-84; assoc. gen. counsel Safeco Title Co., Dallas, 1984-86; from assoc. to shareholder Stigall and Maxfield, Dallas, 1986-89; shareholder Hutchison, Boyle, Brooks and Fisher, Dallas, 1989-93; pvt. practice Dallas, 1993—. Bd. dirs. various internat. cos. Co-founder Dallas Virtual Jewish Cmty. web-page, 1994—, Bridwell Judaica lectr. series, 1994—; dir., v.p. Am. Jewish Com., 1990—2000; pres. Dallas Jewish Hist. Soc., 1992—96; founder Classic Jewish Text Seminars, 1989—; founding dir. Tex. Zionist Movement, Dallas, 1999—, Three Stars Cinema, 2000—, Beyt & Midrash of North Tex., 1999—; trustee So. Meth. U. Libr. Sys., 1999—. Mem. Dallas Bar Assn., Internat. Law Soc. Avocations: weight lifting, hiking. Office: 2651 N Harwood St Ste 200 Dallas TX 75201-1583

HELLMAN, ARTHUR DAVID, law educator, consultant; b. N.Y.C., Dec. 9, 1942; s. Charles and Florence (Cohen) H. BA magna cum laude, Harvard U., 1963; JD, Yale U., 1966. Bar: Minn. 1967, U.S. Ct. Appeals (3d cir.) 1976, U.S. Ct. Appeals (9th cir.) 1979, U.S. Supreme Ct. 1980, Pa., 1985. Law clk. to assoc. justice Minn. Supreme Ct., 1966-67; asst. prof. William Mitchell Coll. Law, St. Paul, 1967-70, U. Conn. Sch. Law, West Hartford, 1970-72; vis. asst. prof. U. Ill. Coll. Law, Champaign, 1972-73; dep. exec. dir. Commn. on Revision Fed. Ct. Appellate System, Washington, 1973-75; assoc. prof. U. Pitts. Sch. Law, 1975-80, prof., 1980—. Supervising staff atty. U.S. Ct. Appeals 9th cir., San Francisco, 1977-79, evaluation com., 1999-2001; vis. assoc. prof. U. Pa. Sch. Law, Phila., 1979; faculty Practicing Law Inst. Program on Fed. Appellate Practice, N.Y.C., 1984, Fed. Jud. Ctr. Nat. Workshop for Judges of U.S. Cts. of Appeals, 1993; planner Nat. Conf. Empirical Rsch. in Judicial Adminstrn., Tempe, Ariz., 1988; gen. editor U.S. Ct. Appeals 9th Cir. Project Improvements in Judicial Adminstrn., 1987-91; prin. investigator intercir. conflicts study Fed. Jud. Ctr., 1990; lectr., cons. and expert witness in field. Author: Laws Against Marijuana-The Price We Pay, 1975, Restructuring Justice-The Innovations of the Ninth Circuit and the Future of the Federal Courts, 1990; editor: Major Cases in First Amendment Law: Freedom of Speech, the Press, and Assembly, 1984; bus. editor: Yale U. Law Jour. Mem. liaison task panel on psychoactive drug use/misuse Pres.'s Commn. on Mental Health, 1977-78; conferee Pound Conf., 1976, The Future and the Courts Conf., 1990; conferee Nat. Conf. on State-Fed. Jud. Relationships, 1992; adv. bd. Western Legal History, 2001—. Recipient Chancellor's Disting. Rsch. award, U. Pitts., 2002; U. Pitts. Sch. Law disting. faculty scholar, 2001—. Fellow Am. Bar Found.; mem. ABA (subcom. on stds. of com. appellate staff attys., jud. adminstrn. divsn., future of cts. com. 1992—, conferee Nat. Conf. on State-Fed. Jud. Rels. 1992, conferee summit on civil justice improvements 1990), Pa. Bar Assn. (discovery rules com. 1995—), Am. Law Inst., Supreme Ct. Hist. Soc., Am. Judicature Soc. (drafting com. project on jud. election campaigns, bd. dirs. 1985-89, justice reform com. 1992-95, chair civil justice reform subcom. 1993-95, chair civil justice reform com. 1995-97, invited witness, hearings of Subcommitte on Courts, the Internet and Intellectual Property of the House Judiciary Com. 1999-2002. Office: U Pitts Law Sch Pittsburgh PA 15260

HELLRUNG, STEPHEN ANDREW, lawyer; b. St. Louis, July 7, 1947; s. J. W. and Alice T. Hellrung; m. Margaret M. Frailey; children: Margaret, Carolyn, Joseph, Leigh. AB, U. Notre Dame, 1969, JD, 1972. Bar: Mo. 1972, U.S. Dist. Ct. (ea. dist.) Mo. 1972, Ill. 1978, N.Y. 1983, Minn. 1998, N.C. 2000. Assoc. Rassieur, Long, Yawitz & Schneider, 1972—78; asst. gen. counsel A.E. Staley, Decatur, Ill., 1978—82; sr. v.p., sec., gen. counsel Bausch & Lomb, Inc., Rochester, NY, 1983—97; sr. v.p., gen. counsel, sec. Pillsbury Co., Mpls., 1997—98, Lowe's Cos., Inc., Mpls., 1999—. Corporate, general. Office: Lowes Companies Inc 1605 Curtis Bridge Rd Wilkesboro NC 28697

HELM, JOHN R. lawyer; b. Wabash, IN, Jan. 21, 1959; s. Donald and Martha Helm; m. Tamara Helm, July 25, 1998; 1 child, Jessica. BA, Wabash Coll., Crawfordsville, Ind., 1981; JD, I.U. Bloomington, 1984. Bar: IN 1984. Assoc. Free, Brand, Tosick & Allen, Greenfield, Ind., 1985—87, Hyatt Legal, Indianapolis, Ind., 1987—88, Schreckengast & Lovern, Indianapolis, Ind., 1988—90; ptnr. Schreckengast, Lovern & Helm, Indianapolis, Ind., 1990—2000; owner Schreckengast, Helm & Cueller, Indianapolis, Ind., 2000—03. Insurance, Personal injury (including property damage). Home: 3688 Saddle Club Rd Greenwood IN 46143 Office: Schreckengast Helm & Cueller 8007 S Meridian St Indianapolis IN 46217

HELM, T. KENNEDY, III, lawyer; b. Louisville, July 2, 1946; s. T. Kennedy Helm Jr. and Nell Hoge Helm; m. Elizabeth Jennifer Schmick, May 30, 1970; children: T. Kennedy IV, Mary Emily Mitchell. BA, Yale U., 1968; MA, Ind. U., 1970; JD, U. Va., 1974. Assoc. Stites & Harbison, Louisville, 1974—79, ptnr., 1979—, chmn., 1997—. Contbr. articles to profl. jours. Mem. Louisville and Jefferson County Urban Renewal Commn., 1975—76; bd. dirs. Louisville Mus. Natural History and Sci., 1979—82; bd. trustees Ky. Country Day Sch., 1988—94, 1995—98; bd. dirs. Louisville Zoo Found., 1993—97; mem. adv. bd. Summerbridge of Ky., 1992—96; mem. bd. advisors Presentation Acad., 1995—97; bd. dirs. Greater Louisville, Inc.; bd. overseers U. Louisville, 2000—; bd. dirs. Nat. Cuty BAnk Ky., 2002—. Mem.: Japan Am. Soc. Ky. (bd. dirs.), Tri-State Golf Assn. (bd. dirs. 1996—, pres. 1998). Aviation, Banking, Corporate, general. Office: Stites & Harbison 400 W Market St Ste 400 Louisville KY 40202

HELMAN, ROBERT ALAN, lawyer; b. Chgo., Jan. 27, 1934; s. Nathan W. and Esther (Weiss) H.; m. Janet R. Williams, Sept. 13, 1958; children: Marcus E., Adam J., Sarah E. Student, U. Ill., 1951-53; BSL, Northwestern U., 1954, LLB, 1956. Bar: Ill. 1956. Asso. firm Isham, Lincoln & Beale, Chgo., 1956-64, ptnr., 1965-66; ptnr. firm Mayer, Brown, Rowe & Maw, Chgo., 1967—. Bd. dirs. No. Trust Corp., The No. Trust Co., Dreyer's Grand Ice Cream Co., TCPL GP Inc. Co-author: Commentaries on 1970 Illinois Constitution, 1971; assoc. editor Northwestern U. Law Rev., 1955-56; contbr. articles to legal jours. Chmn. Citizens' Com. on Juvenile Ct., Cook County, 1969-81; pres. Legal Assistance Found., Chgo., 1973-76; chmn. vis. com. Northwestern U. Law Sch., 1989-92; bd. dirs. United Charities Chgo., 1967-73; hon. trustee Brookings Instn., Aspen Inst., 1986-92, Mus. of Contemporary Art. Mem. ABA, Chgo. Bar Assn., Am. Law Inst., Chgo. Coun. Lawyers, Legal Club Chgo., Law Club Chgo., Comml. Club, Chgo. Club, Mid-Day Club, Econs. Club, Order of Coif. Corporate, general, Utilities, public, Securities. Home: 4950 S Chicago Beach Dr Chicago IL 60615-3207 Office: Mayer Brown Rowe & Maur 190 S La Salle St Ste 3100 Chicago IL 60603-3441

HELMAN, STEPHEN JODY, lawyer; b. Houston, Dec. 14, 1949; m. Gail Stevenson, 1974; children: Kimberley Brooke, Courtney Elizabeth, Caitlin Rebecca. BA in Spanish and Religion, So. Meth. U., 1971; postgrad., Perkins Sch. Theology, 1971-73; JD with honors, U. Tex., 1978. Bar: Tex., 1978; cert. estate planning and probate law, 1987. Assoc. Graves, Dougherty, Hearon & Moody, Austin, Tex., 1978-85, ptnr., shareholder, 1985-93; ptnr. Osborne, Lowe, Helman & Smith, L.L.P., Austin, Tex., 1993-2000, Osborne & Helman, L.L.P., Austin, Tex., 2001—. Exam commr. in estate planning and probate law, Tex. Bd. Legal Specialization, 1990-94. Contbr. articles to profl. jours. Fellow Am. Coll. Trust and Estate Counsel (mem. profl. standards com. 1990-93); mem. ABA (mem. real property, probate, and trust law sects.), Coll. of the State Bar of Tex., State Bar Tex. (mem. real property, probate and trust law sects.), Travis County Bar Assn. (mem. probate and estate planning sect., pres. 1991-92, dir. 1989-92, ex-officio dir. 1992-93), Order of Coif. Avocations: nature photography, hiking. Estate planning, Probate (including wills, trusts), Estate taxation. Office: Osborne & Helman LLP 301 Congress Ave Ste 1910 Austin TX 78701-4041 E-mail: sjhelman@osbornehelman.com.

HELMER, DAVID ALAN, lawyer; b. Colorado Springs, May 19, 1946; s. Horton James and Alice Ruth (Cooley) H.; m. Jean Marie Lamping, May 23, 1987. BA, U. Colo., 1968, JD, 1973. Bar: Colo. 1973, U.S. Dist. Ct. Colo. 1973, U.S. Ct. Appeals (10th cir.) 1993, U.S. Ct. Claims 1990, U.S. Supreme Ct. 1991. Assoc. Neil C. King, Boulder, Colo., 1973-76; mgr. labor rels., mine regulations Climax Molybdenum Co., Inc. divsn. AMAX, Inc., Climax, Colo., 1976-83; prin. Law Offices David A. Helmer, Frisco, Colo., 1983—. Sec., bd. dirs. Z Comm. Corp., Frisco, 1983-90; cmty. bd. dirs. Wells Fargo Bank, N.A., Frisco, 1996—. Editor U. Colo. Law Rev., 1972-73; contbr. articles to legal jours. Bd. dirs. Summit County Coun. Arts and Humanities, Dillon, Colo., 1980-85; advisor Advocates for Victims of Assault, Frisco, 1984—; legal counsel Summit County United Way, 1983-95, v.p., bd. dirs., 1983-88; bd. dirs., legal counsel Summit county Alcohol and Drug Task Force, Inc., Summit Prevention Alliance, 1984—, Pumpkin Bowl Inc./Chldren's Hosp. Burn Ctr., 1989—; chmn. Summit County Reps., 1982-89; chmn. 5th Jud. Dist. (Colo.) Rep. Com., 1982-89; chmn. resolutions com. Colo. Rep. Conv., 1984, del. Rep. Nat. Com., 1984; chmn. reaccreditation com. Colo. Mountain Coll., Breckenridge, 1983, mem. steering com., 1997-99; founder, bd. dirs. Dillon Bus. Assn., 1983-87, Frisco Arts Coun., 1989—; atty. N.W. Colo. Legal Svcs. Project, Summit County, 1983—; mcpl. judge Town of Dillon, 1982—, Town of Silverthorne, Colo., 1982—; bd. dirs. Snake River Water Dist., 1998—, chmn., 2002—. Master Sgt. USAR, 1968-74. Mem. ABA, Colo. Bar Assn., (bd. govs. 1991-93, mem. exec. com. 1995-97), Continental Divide Bar Assn. (prs. 1991-95, v.p. 1995-97), Summit County Bar Assn. (pres. 1990-99), Dillon Corinthian Yacht Club (commodore local club 1987-88, 95-97, vice commodore 1994, club champion 1989-91, 94, 95, 97, 98, 2002, winner Colo. Cup, Colo. State Sailing Championships 1991, Dist. Champion 2000, Champion Dillon Open Regatta 2001), Phi Gamma Delta. Lutheran. State civil litigation, General practice, Property, real (including real estate development, water). Home: PO Box 300 352 Snake River Dr Dillon CO 80435-0300 Office: PO Box 868 611 Main St Frisco CO 80443-0868 E-mail: dave@helmerlaw.com.

HELMHOLZ, R(ICHARD) H(ENRY), law educator; b. Pasadena, Calif., July 1, 1940; s. Lindsay and Alice (Bean) H.; m. Marilyn P. Helmholz. AB, Princeton U., 1962; JD, Harvard U., 1965; PhD, U. Calif., Berkeley, 1970; LLD, Trinity Coll., Dublin, 1992. Bar: Mo. 1965. Prof. law and hist. Washington U., St. Louis, 1970-81; prof. law U. Chgo., 1981—. Maitland lectr. Cambridge U., 1987; Goodhart prof. Cambridge U., 2000-01. Author: Marriage Litigation, 1975, Select Cases on Defamation, 1985, Canon Law and the Law of England, 1987, Roman Canon Law in Reformation England, 1990, Spirit of Classical Canon Law, 1996, The Ius Commune in England: Four Studies, 2001. Guggenheim fellow, 1986; recipient Von Humboldt rsch. prize, 1992. Fellow Brit. Acad. (corr.), Am. Acad. Arts and Scis., Am. Law Inst., Medieval Acad. Am.; mem. ABA, Am. Soc. Legal History (pres. 1992-94), Selden Soc. (v.p. 1984-87), Univ. Club, Reform Club. Home: 5757 S Kimbark Ave Chicago IL 60637-1614 Office: U Chgo Law Sch 1111 E 60th St Chicago IL 60637-2776 E-mail: dick_helmholz@law.uchicago.edu.

HELMRICH, JOEL MARC, lawyer; b. Bklyn., Apr. 15, 1953; s. William and Edna (Steigman) H.; m. Barbara Ellen Richter, Sept. 2, 1984; children: Joshua David, Rachel Marysa. BS, Cornell U., 1975, MBA, 1976; JD, Syracuse U., 1979. Bar: Pa. 1979, U.S. Dist. Ct. (we. dist.) Pa. 1979, U.S. Ct. Appeals (3d cir.) 1997. Assoc. Tucker Arensberg, PC, Pitts., 1979-86; shareholder Tucker Arensberg, Pitts., 1986-99; ptnr. Meyer, Unkovic & Scott, LLP, Pitts., 1999—. Mem. Pa. Bar Assn., Allegheny County Bar Assn., Comml. Law League Am., Am. Bankruptcy Inst., Cornell Club. Avocations: golf, tennis. Bankruptcy, Commercial, consumer (including collections, credit), Corporate, general. Office: Meyer Unkovic & Scott LLP 1300 Oliver Bldg Pittsburgh PA 15222-2304 E-mail: jmh@muslaw.com.

HELMS, ROGER D. lawyer; b. Orlando, June 11, 1953; s. V.S. and Eunice Helms. BS magna cum laude, U. Ctrl. Fla., 1980; JD, U. Fla. Sch. Law, 1982. Bar: Fla., Cert. Civil Trial Law, Personal Injury. From assoc. to ptnr. Troutman, Williams, Irvin & Green, Winter Park, Fla., 1983—. Mem. ABA, Acad. Fla. Trial Lawyers. Avocations: offshore fishing, boating. Personal injury (including property damage), State civil litigation. Home: 2840 Bear Island Pointe Winter Park FL 32792-9426 Office: Troutman Williams Irvin Green & Helms 311 W Fairbanks Ave Winter Park FL 32789-5094

HELMSING, FREDERICK GEORGE, lawyer; b. Mobile, Ala., Dec. 30, 1940; s. Joseph Herman and Mary Gertrude (Zimlich) H.; m. Margaret Sue Oswalt, Mar. 22, 1969; children: Frederick George, Joseph Guy, Margaret Sue. BS in Acctg., Spring Hill Coll., 1963; JD, U. Ala., 1965; LLM in Taxation, NYU, 1967. Bar: Ala. 1965, Fla. 1989. Assoc. Gallalee, Denniston & Edington, Mobile, 1966-76; ptnr. Helmsing, Leach, Herlong, Newman & Rouse, Mobile, 1976—. Instr. U. South Ala., Mobile, 1969-78; instr. law U. Ala., Mobile, 1982 Dem. chmn. 1st Congl. Dist. Campaign, 1976. Fellow: Am. Coll. Trial Lawyers; mem.: ABA (mem. civil and criminal tax penalties com.), Mobile Area C. of C. (mem. taxation and world trade coms.), Mobile Bar Assn., Mobile County Bar Assn. (treas. 1969), Ala. State Bar Assn. (chmn. tax sect. 1979—80), Athelstan Country Club, Mobile County Club. Roman Catholic. General civil litigation, Criminal. Home: 240 Ridgelawn Dr E Mobile AL 36608-2417 Office: Helmsing Leach Herlong Newman & Rouse 200 LaClede Bldg 150 Government St Mobile AL 36602-3114

HELSTAD, ORRIN L. lawyer, legal educator; b. Ettrick, Wis., Feb. 9, 1922; s. Albert J. and Martha H. (Gimse) H.; m. Charlotte Dart Ankeney, June 26, 1954. Student, U. Wis., La Crosse, 1940-42; BS, U. Wis., Madison, 1948, LL.B., 1950. Bar: Wis. 1950. Research assoc. Wis. Legis. Council, 1950-61; assoc. prof. law U. Wis., Madison, 1961-65, prof., 1965-85; assoc. dean U. Wis. (Sch. Law), 1972-75, acting dean, 1975-76, dean, 1976-83, dean emeritus, 1985—, prof. emeritus, 1985—. Mem. consumer advisory council Wis. Dept. Agr., 1970-72; vice chmn. Wis. Supreme Ct. com. on the State bar, 1977; mem. Fed. Jud. Nominating Commn. Western Dist. Wis., 1979-83 Contbr. articles to law revs.; co-author, editor: Wisconsin Uniform Comml. Code Handbook, 1965, 1971. Recipient Disting. Svc. award Wis. Law Alumni Assn., 1991. Fellow Am. Bar Found.; mem. State Bar Wis., ABA (council sect. on local govt. law 1975-79), Wis. Bar Assn., Dane County Bar Assn., Am. Judicature Soc. Unitarian Universalist. Home: 8 Sebring Ct Madison WI 53719-3521

HELTON, ARTHUR CLEVELAND, advocate, lawyer, scholar, writer; b. St. Louis, Jan. 24, 1949; s. Arthur Cleveland Sr. and Marjorie Jane (Russell) H.; m. Jacqueline Dean Gilbert, May 14, 1982. AB, Columbia Coll., 1971; JD, NYU, 1976. Bar: N.Y. 1977, U.S. Dist. Ct. (so. and ea. dists.) N.Y. 1977, U.S. Ct. Appeals (2d cir.) 1978, U.S. Ct. Appeals (1st cir.) 1980, U.S. Ct. Appeals (4th and 9th cir.) 1988, U.S. Ct. Appeals (5th, 7th and 11th cir.) 1989, U.S. Ct. Appeals (3d cir.) 1994, U.S. Supreme Ct. 1980. Assoc. appellate counsel Legal Aid Soc., N.Y.C., 1976-79; assoc. Mailman & Rutheizer, N.Y.C., 1979-82; dir. refugee project Lawyers Com. Human Rights, N.Y.C., 1982-94; dir. migration programs, forced migration projects Open Soc. Inst., N.Y.C., 1994-99; vis. prof. internat. rels. Ctrl. European U., 1997-2000; course co-dir. Summer U. Ctrl. European U., 1999-2000. Adj. prof. law NYU, 1986-99; sr. fellow Coun. Fgn. Rels., 1999—; dir. Peace and Conflict Studies, Coun. Fgn. Rels., 2001—; chair U.S.A. br. Internat. Social Svcs., 2000—; adj. faculty Columbia Law Sch., 2001—. Author: The Price of Indifference: Refugees and Humanitarian Action in the New Century, 2002; (with others) Forced Displacement and Human Security in the Former Soviet Union: Law and Policy, 2000; The Rights of Aliens and Refugees: The Basic ACLU Guide to Alien and Refugees Rights, 1990; editor: Transnational Pubs., Inc.; series editor Free Movement, Forced Displacement and Human Security; contbr. articles to profl. jours. Recipient Pub. Svc. award Law Alumni Assn. NYU, 1987, Immigration and Refugee Policy award, Ctr. for Migration Studies, 2000, award for Distinction in Internat. Law and Affairs N.Y. State Bar Assn., 2002; individual grantee The German Marshall Fund, The Ford Found. Fellow Am. Bar Found.; mem. Coun. Fgn. Rels., ABA (co-chmn. immigration and nationality law com. sect. internat. law and practice 1997-2002, coord. com. on immigration law 1997-2000, adv. com. immigration pro bono devel. and bar activation project 2000-02, counselor 2002-2003, commn. on immigration policy, practice and pro bono 2002-2003, goal VIII officer 2003-), Internat. Bar Assn., Assn. Bar N.Y.C. (chmn. com. on immigration and nationality law 1982-85, legal assistance com. 1985-88, civil rights com. 1988-91, internat. human rights com. 1991-94, internat. law com. 1995-98, adminstrv. law com. 1999-2002), Pub. internatl. imm., naturalization, and customs. Home: 245 7th Ave Apt 10B New York NY 10001-7301 Office: Coun Fgn Rels 58 E 68th St New York NY 10021-5953 E-mail: ArthurHelton@msn.com., ahelton@cfr.org.

HEMINGWAY, RICHARD WILLIAM, law educator; b. Detroit, Nov. 24, 1927; s. William Oswald and Iva Catherine (Wildfang) H.; m. Vera Cecilia Eck, Sept. 12, 1947; children: Margaret Catherine, Carol Elizabeth, Richard Albert. BS in Bus, U. Colo., 1950; JD magna cum laude (J. Woodall Rogers Sr. Gold medal 1955), So. Meth. U., 1955; LL.M. (William S. Cook fellow 1968), U. Mich., 1969. Bar: Tex. 1955, Okla. 1981. Assoc. Fulbright, Crooker, Freeman, Bates & Jaworski, Houston, 1955-60; lectr. Bates Sch. Law, U. Houston, 1960; assoc. prof. law Baylor U. Law Sch., Waco, Tex., 1960-65; vis. assoc. prof. So. Meth. U. Law Sch., 1965-68; prof. law Tex. Tech U. Law Sch., Lubbock, 1968-71, Paul W. Horn prof., 1972-81, acting dean, 1974-75, dean ad interim, 1980-81; prof. law U. Okla., Norman, 1981-83, Eugene Kuntz prof. oil, gas and natural resources law, 1983-92, Eugne Kuntz prof. emeritus oil, gas & natural resources law, 1992—. Author: The Law of Oil and Gas, 1971, 2d edit., 1983, lawyer's edit., 1983, 3d edit., 1991, West's Texas Forms (Mines and Minerals), 1977, 2d edit., 1991, 85; contbg. editor various law reports, cases and materials. Served with USAAF, 1945-47. Mem. Tex. Bar Assn., Scribes, Order of Coif (faculty), Beta Gamma Sigma. Lutheran. Home: 600 W Arapaho Rd Apt 229 Richardson TX 75080

HEMINGWAY, WHITLEY MAYNARD, retired lawyer; b. Webster City, Iowa, Oct. 21, 1915; s. Max Maynard and Grace B. (Whitley) Hemingway; m. Elsie Mae O'Connor, Feb. 12, 1994; children from previous marriage: John, Susan, Frances(dec.) , Sarah(dec.). BA, U. Iowa, 1936, JD, 1938. Bar: Iowa 1938. Ptnr. Burnstedt & Hemingway, Webster City, 1938—42, Hemingway and successor firms, Webster City, 1946—2002. Atty. City of Webster City, 1946-57; jud. commr. 2d Jud. Dist. Iowa, 1965-71. Trustee Morrison Charitable Trust, 1953-2001; trustee, treas. Kendall Young Libr., Webster City, 1958-79. Lt. USN, 1942-46, ETO. Mem. ABA, Iowa Bar Assn., Hamilton County Bar Assn., Rotary, Elks, Webster City Country Club. Republican. Avocation: motorcycles. Probate (including wills, trusts), Property, real (including real estate development, water), Personal income taxation. Fax: 515-832-2071.

HEMLEBEN, SCOTT P. lawyer; b. Floral Park, N.Y., Nov. 18, 1943; s. Sylvester John and Mary Ruth (Bingham) H.; m. Suzanne Whatley, Aug. 4, 1973; children: Sarah Elizabeth, Mark Elliott, John Parker, Joseph Scott. BAE, U. Miss., 1964, JD, 1967. Bar: Miss. 1967, U.S. Dist. Ct. (so. dist.) Miss. 1969, U.S. Dist. Ct. (no. dist.) Miss. 1999, U.S. Ct. Appeals (5th cir.) 1985, U.S. Supreme Ct. 1971. Law clk. to chief justice Miss. Supreme Ct., Jackson, 1967-68; from assoc. to ptnr. Wells, Gerald, Brand, Watters & Cox, Jackson, 1968-77; ptnr. Gerald, Brand, Watters, Cox & Hemleben, 1977-90, Gerald & Brand, 1990-99, Gerald, Brand, Hemleben & Gourlay, LLC, 1999—. Bd. dirs. U.S. Oil and Gas Assn.; gov.'s rep. to Interstate Oil and Gas Compact Commn., 1992-2000. Fellow Miss. Bar Found.; mem. Hinds County Bar Assn. (pres. 1987-88), Miss. Bar Assn. (chmn. natural resources sect. 1989-90), Miss. Oil and Gas Lawyers Assn. (pres. 1973-74). Avocation: saltwater fishing. Administrative and regulatory, Federal civil litigation, Environmental. Home: 43 Avery Cir Jackson MS 39211-2403 E-mail: gbojp@netdoor.com.

HEMPE, A. HENRY, lawyer, state agency official; b. Milw., Mar. 16, 1938; s. Arnold Herman and Marcia Fleer Hempe; m. Cornelia Macy Gordon, June 26, 1965; children: Andrew, Amy. BS, U. Wis., 1962, JD, 1965. Bar: Wis. 1965, U.S. Dist. Ct. (we. dist.) Wis. 1966. Asst. dist. atty. Rock County, Janesville, Wis., 1965-67, county corp. counsel, 1967-72; ptnr. Hempe & Daniel, Janesville, 1972-76; shareholder, pres. Hempe, Hunsader & Schulz, S.C., Janesville, 1975-86; dep. sec. Wis. Dept. Employment Rels., Madison, 1987-88; commr. Wis. Employment Rels. Commn., Madison, 1987—, chair, commr., 1989-97. Author: Labor-Management Relations in the Public Sector, 2000. Mem., pres., v.p. Beloit (Wis.) Sch. Bd., 1980-86. bd. dirs. Sinnissipi Coun. Boy Scouts Am., Janesville, 1985-90, Rock County Humane Soc., Janesville, 1978-83, Assn. Labor Rels Agys. USA and Can., Washington, 1991-94; chair Human Rels. Commn., Beloit, 1972-76, Bd. Rev., Beloit. With USMCR, 1960-66, also res. Mem.: Wis. Bar Assn. Republican. Avocations: fishing, hunting, softball, jogging, dog training. Home: 5413 Trempealeau Trail Madison WI 53705 Office: Wis Employment Rels Commn 18 S Thornton Madison WI 53703

HEMRY, JEROME ELDON, lawyer; b. Kirksville, Mo., July 22, 1905; s. U.S.G. and Rose M. (Plumb) H.; m. Martha L. Langston, Aug. 1, 1934; children: Jerome Louis, Kenneth Marshall. AB, Oklahoma City U., 1926; JD, U. Okla., 1928; LL.M., Harvard U., 1929. Bar: Okla. 1928. Partner Hemry & Hemry, Oklahoma City, 1931-82, of counsel, 1983—; prof. law Central Okla. Sch. Law, 1931-41; dean, prof. law Langston U., 1948-49; dir., counsel Am. Gen. Life Ins. Co. Okla., 1959-79. Pres., gen. counsel Gen. Constrn. Corp., 1941-45; legislative counsel Okla. Chain Store Assn., 1941-44; Mem. Bd. Conf. Claimant's Okla. Ann. Conf.; treas. Oklahoma City S. Dist. Contbr. articles legal jours. Bd. dirs. Family and Children's Service, 1939-56. Mem. Okla. Assn. Mcpl. Attys. (pres. 1956-57), Am., Okla. bar assns., Order of Coif, Phi Delta Phi, Lambda Chi Alpha. Methodist (pres., counsel trustees). Clubs: Lions (Oklahoma City), Men's Dinner (Oklahoma City). Home: 2255 NW 55th St Oklahoma City OK 73112-7716 Office: 531 Couch Dr Oklahoma City OK 73102-2251

HENDERSON, DONALD BERNARD, JR., lawyer; b. Birmingham, Ala., June 27, 1949; s. Donald B. and Pauline V. (Szulinski) H.; m. Ruth Ann Jeffers, Sept. 12, 1981. BS, U. Ala., 1971, JD, 1974; LLM in Taxation, NYU, 1976. Bar: Ala. 1974, N.Y. 1983. Ptnr. Sirote & Permutt, Birmingham, 1976—83; sr. assoc. Mound, Cotton, Wollan and Greengrass, NYC, 1983—85; ptnr. Kroll & Tract, N.Y.C., 1985-88, LeBoeuf, Lamb, Greene & MacRae, L.L.P., N.Y.C., 1988—. Lectr. Birmingham chpt. Am. Coll., Bryn Mawr, Pa., 1977-82; bd. dirs. Jackson Nat. Life Ins. Co. N.Y., SunLife Assurance Co. N.Y., Zurich Life Ins. Co. N.Y.; counsel Bronxville Planning Bd., 1994-2001. Contbr. articles to profl. jours. Pres. Lenox Hill Dem. Club, N.Y.C., 1989-90; mem. Ala. State Dem. Com., 1978-83, N.Y.C. Cmty. Bd. Number 8, 1987-88, Republican Club of Bronxville; mem., vice-chair Bronxville Planning Bd., 2001—. Mem. ABA, N.Y. Bar Assn., Ala. Bar Assn. (sec. tax sect. 1982-83). Corporate, general, Insurance, Corporate taxation. Home: 108 Midland Ave Bronxville NY 10708-3206 Office: LeBouf Lamb Greene & MacRae LLP 125 E 55th St New York NY 10022-3502 E-mail: dhenderson@llgm.com.

HENDERSON, DOUGLAS BOYD, lawyer; b. Pitts., Sept. 21, 1935; s. Arthur G. and Mildred E. (Rickenbach) H.; m. Olivia Lauer, July 6, 1957; children: Scotland Weaver, Keith Arthur, Heather Alice Atkinson BS in Indsl. Engring., Pa. State U., 1957; JD with honors, George Washington U., 1963. Bar: Va. 1962, D.C. 1963. Mfs. agt. firm Arthur G. Henderson & Assos., Pitts., 1957-59; patent agt. Swift & Co., Washington, 1959-62; law clk. to Hon. Donald E. Lane U.S. Ct. Claims, Washington, 1962-63; assoc. Irons, Birch, Swindler & McKie, 1963—65; founding ptnr. Finnegan, Henderson, Farabow, Garrett and Dunner LLP, 1965—. Adv. coun. U.S. Ct. Fed. Claims, 1982—; legal adv. bd. Martindale-Hubbell/LEXIS, 1996—. Author: Third Party Practice in the United States Court of Claims or Two's Company, Three's A Crowd, 1976; contbr. articles to profl. jours. Bd. advisors George Washington U. Law Sch., 1991-97. Fellow: Am. Bar Found. (life); mem.: ABA (ho. of dels. 1999—), U.S. Ct. Fed. Claims Bar Assn. (bd. dirs. 1987—90, founder), Supreme Ct. Hist. Soc., Capital Soc., Intellectual Property Owners Assn., Internat. Trademark Assn., Am. Intellectual Property Law Assn., U.S. C. of C. (chmn. patent, trademark and copyright coun. 1980—82), ITC Trial Lawyers Assn. (founder), Bar Assn. D.C. (chmn. Ct. Claims com. 1973—74, chmn. patent, trademark and copyright law sect. 1974—75, bd. dirs. 1975—76, trustee rsch. found. 1980—81, chmn. Ct. Appeals for Fed. Cir. Com. 1982—83), Fed. Cir. Bar Assn. (bd. dirs. 1985—86, mem. jud. selection com. 1990—, bd. dirs. 1996—99, founder 1985), D.C. Bar Assn., Va. State Bar, Va. Bar Assn., Internat. Bar Assn., Tournament Players Club at Avenel, Congl. Country Club, Univ. Club, Burning Tree Club, Club at Franklin Sq. (bd. govs. 1990—95), Delta Theta Phi, Phi Gamma Delta. Patent, Trademark and copyright. Home: 10 Beman Woods Ct Potomac MD 20854-5481 Office: Finnegan Henderson Farabow Garrett & Dunner LLP 1300 I St NW Washington DC 20005-3315

HENDERSON, JANICE ELIZABETH, law librarian; b. N.Y.C., Dec. 22, 1952; d. James and Adeline M. (Fitzgerald) H. BA in Psychology, Hunter Coll., 1974; MS in Spl. Edn., CUNY, 1979; MS in Library Sci., Pratt Inst., 1980; JD, Bklyn. Law Sch., 1986. Law librarian Morgan, Lewis & Bockius, N.Y.C., 1977-83; reference librarian Weil, Gotshal & Manges, N.Y.C., 1983-85; law librarian Tenzer, Greenblatt et al, N.Y.C., 1985-86, Robinson, Silverman et al, N.Y.C., 1986-88, Kirkland & Ellis, N.Y.C., 1991-93; assoc. law libr. prof. CUNY Law Sch., N.Y.C., 1989-91; dir. libr. svcs. Epstein, Becker & Green, PC, 1993-98; dir. profl. devel. and libr. svcs. Baker & McKenzie, N.Y.C., 1998—2002; cons. N.Y.C., 2003—. Assoc. adj. prof. Sch. Libr. and Info. Sci., St. John's U., N.Y.C., 1990-93; spkr. in field. Book reviewer Legal Info. Alert newsletter, 1984-86. Mem. Am. Assn. Law Librs., Law Libr. Assn. Greater N.Y. (advt. mgr. 1986-89, bd. dirs. 1989-90, mem. continuing legal edn. com. 1990-92, co-chair 1992-94, v.p. 1995-96, pres. 1996-97, past pres. 1997-98), Practicing Law Inst. (mng. the law libr. 1997-98, program chair 1999-2000, program co-chair 2001—). Democrat. Roman Catholic. Home: PO Box 23060 Brooklyn NY 11202-3060 E-mail: janiceehenderson@att.net.

HENDERSON, KENNETH LEE, lawyer; b. Atlanta, Nov. 2, 1954; s. Hugh T. and Norma (Zollars) H.; m. Kathryn Graves, Aug. 14, 1976; children: Christine Mary, Jack Kenneth. BA with high honors, Auburn U., 1976; JD cum laude, NYU, 1979. Bar: N.Y. 1980, U.S. Dist. Ct. (so. and ea. dists.) N.Y. 1980. Assoc. Webster & Sheffield, N.Y.C., 1979-84, Finley, Kumble, Wagner, Heine, Underberg, Manley, Myerson, & Casey, N.Y.C., 1984-87; ptnr. Robinson Silverman Pearce Aronsohn & Berman, N.Y.C., 1987—2003, Bryan Cave LLP. Editor (with others): State Ltd. Partnership Law, 1987; articles editor Annual Survey Am. Law, 1978-79. Elder, trustee Fifth Ave. Presbyterian Ch., N.Y.C., 1987—; bd. dirs. Population Communications Internat., Inc., 1985—, chmn., 1999—; bd. dirs. Activisiion, Inc., 2001—. Root-Tilden scholar, 1976-79. Mem. ABA, N.Y. State Bar Assn., Assn. of Bar of City of N.Y., Order of Coif, Omicron Delta Kappa (leadership hon.), Phi Kappa Phi (scholastic hon.), Phi Gamma Delta. Democrat. Corporate, general, Securities, Mergers and acquisitions. Office: Bryan Cave LLP 1290 Avenue Of The Americas Fl 33 New York NY 10104-3300

HENDERSON, SUSAN ELLEN FORTUNE, lawyer, educator; b. Bluefield, W.Va., Dec. 21, 1957; d. William Edward and Gladys Ellen (Scott) Fortune. Student, Randolph-Macon Woman's Coll., 1976-78; BS summa cum laude, Bluefield State Coll., 1986; JD cum laude, Washington & Lee U., 1994. Bar: Va. 1994, W.Va. 1995. Legal sec., paralegal, office mgr. Katz, Kantor & Perkins, Bluefield, 1979-86; paralegal, office mgr. David Burton, Atty. at Law, Princeton, W.Va., 1986-91; assoc. Burton & Kilgore, Princeton, W.Va., 1994-95; sole practice Bluefield, 1995-97; instr. Bluefield State Coll., 1996-98; ptnr. Henderson & Fuda, 1997—. Tchr. Legal Learning Inst., Manassas, Va., 1995-96. Trustee Glenwood Park, Inc., chmn., 2002. Nat. Merit scholar, 1976, Disting. scholar Randolph-Macon Woman's Coll., 1976, Law scholar Washington & Lee U., 1991. Mem. ABA, ATLA, W.Va. Trial Lawyers Assn., Va. Trial Lawyers Assn., Main St. Bluefield Bd. of Dirs. Avocations: tennis, skiing, music, reading, landscaping. General civil litigation, Criminal, General practice. Home: 6 Oak Ln Bluefield WV 24701-4741 Office: Henderson & Fuda 3107 E Cumberland Rd Bluefield WV 24701-4960

HENDERSON, THOMAS HENRY, JR., lawyer, legal association executive; b. Birmingham, Ala., Feb. 4, 1939; s. Thomas Henry and Edna (Green) H.; m. Elaine Dauphin (div. 1983); children: Ashley, Michelle; m. Paulette Maehara, June 1988. BSBA, Auburn U., 1961; JD, U. Ala., 1966; LLM, Nat. Law Ctr., George Washington U., 1987. Bar: D.C. 1970, Ala. 1966. Trial atty. organized crime and racketeering sect. U.S. Dept. Justice, Washington, 1966-70, dep. sect. chief mgmt. labor sect., 1970-73; dep. chief counsel, subcom. on adminstrn. practice and procedure U.S. Senate, Washington, 1973-74; dep. sect. chief mgmt. and labor sect. Dept. Justice, Washington, 1974-76, chief pub. integrity sect., 1976-80, sr. counsel criminal div., 1980-83; bar counsel D.C. Ct. Appeals, Washington, 1983-87; CEO, ATLA, Washington, 1988—. Columnist Bar Counsels Page, Washington Lawyer mag., bi-monthly, 1983-87. Pres. Christmas in April, Washington, 1986-87. Mem. Am. Soc. Assn. Execs. (bd. dirs. 1994-97, vice chair 1997-98), Omicron Delta Kappa. Avocations: golf, skiing, fitness, outdoor adventure. Home: 6698 Glenbrook Rd Chevy Chase MD 20815-6515 Office: ATLA 1050 31st St NW Washington DC 20007-4409

HENDREN, JIMM LARRY, federal judge; b. 1940; BA, U. Ark., 1964, LLB, 1965. With Little & Enfield, 1968-69; pvt. practice Bentonville, Ark., 1970-77, 79-92; chancellor, probate judge Ark. 16th Chancery Dist., 1977-78; U.S. dist. judge We. Dist. Ark., 1992-96, chief judge, 1997—. Served to lt. comdr. JAGC, USN, 1965-70, USNR, 1970-83. Mem. ABA, Ark. Bar Assn. Office: US Dist Ct PO Box 3487 Fayetteville AR 72702-3487

HENDRICK, BENARD CALVIN, VII, lawyer; b. Odessa, Tex., Oct. 7, 1964; s. Benard Calvin VI and Marita Hendrick; m. Amy Camille Weatherby, Nov. 17, 1990; children: Benard Calvin VIII, Kaitlin Camille. BBA summa cum laude, Angelo State U., San Angelo, Tex., 1987; JD, U. Tex., 1990. Bar: Tex. 1990, U.S. Dist. Ct. (ea., we. and no. dists.) Tex. 1991, U.S. Ct. Appeals (5th cir.) 1995. Assoc. Shafer, Davis, Ashley, O'Leary & Stoker, Odessa, 1990-92, ptnr., 1992—. Bd. dirs. Permian Basin Rehab. Ctr., Odessa, 1992-97, Crystal Ball Found., Odessa, 1993-96, Parker House Ranching Mus., 2002—, Black River-A Ctr. for Learning, 1998—, Jim Parker Little League Baseball, 2000—; elder First Christian Ch., Odessa, 1995-98, 2000—. Fellow Tex. Bar Found.; mem. Tex. Assn. Def. Counsel (young lawyers com. 1998-2000), State Bar Tex., Ector County Bar Assn. (pres. 1998-99), Ector County Young Lawyers Assn. (pres. 1995), Def. Rsch. Inst. Republican. Mem. Christian Ch. Avocations: hunting, fishing, tae kwon do (1st degree). General civil litigation, Insurance, Personal injury (including property damage). Home: 2301 La Due Ln Odessa TX 79762 Office: Shafer Davis Ashley O'Leary & Stoker 700 N Grant Ave Ste 201 Odessa TX 79761-4576

HENDRICKS, JOHN CHARLES, lawyer; b. Sellersville, Pa., Oct. 26, 1941; m. Linda Ann Sauerland, Aug. 28, 1965; children— Karl Erik, Kirstin Ann. B.A. in Polit. Sci. cum laude, Dickinson Coll., Carlisle, Pa., 1963; J.D., George Washington U., 1966, LL.M. in Taxation, 1973. Bar: U.S. Dist. Ct. D.C. 1967, U.S. Ct. Appeals (D.C. cir.) 1970, U.S. Tax Ct. 1970, U.S. Supreme Ct. 1973, U.S. Ct. Claims 1974, Md. 1978. Assoc., Ash, Bauersfeld, Burton & Mooers, Washington, 1969-74, ptnr., 1975-77; ptnr. Bauersfeld, Burton, Hendricks & Vanderhoof, LLC, and predecessor firms, Md., 1977— ; speaker in field; Bd. dirs. Lutheran Social Services of Met. Washington, 1975-78, 80-86, pres. 1976, 84-86, chmn. fin. com., 1977-78, 80-83. Capt. U.S. Army, 1967-69. Mem. ABA, Md. Bar Assn., D.C. Bar Assn., Contbr. articles to profl. jours. Corporate, general, Estate planning, Personal income taxation. Home: 21414 Davis Mill Rd Germantown MD 20876-4422 Office: 7101 Wisconsin Ave Ste 1011 Bethesda MD 20814-4805 E-mail: jhendricks@bbhv.net.

HENDRICKS, KATHERINE, lawyer; b. Logan, Utah, Apr. 12, 1949; d. Charles Durrell and Leah Grace (Funk) H.; m. O. Yale Lewis, Jr., Sept. 7, 1985. BS, MS, MIT, 1972; JD, Boston U., 1975. Bar: Mass. 1976, Colo. 1982, Wash. 1984, U.S. Dist. Ct. Mass. 1979, U.S. Dist. Ct. (no. dist.) N.Y., U.S. Dist. Ct. Colo., U.S. Dist. Ct. Wash., U.S. Ct. Appeals (1st cir.), 1978, U.S. Ct. Appeals (9th cir.), 1984. Assoc. Palmer & Dodge, Boston, 1975-81, Garfield & Hecht, Aspen, Colo., 1981-84, Wickwire, Lewis, Goldmark & Schorr, Seattle, 1984-86; ptnr. Hendricks & Lewis, Seattle, 1986—. Mem. ABA, Wash. State Bar Assn. (chmn. intellectual property sect. 1991-92), Wash. Vol. Lawyers of Arts (bd. dirs. 1988-92, pres. 1991-92), Internat. Trademark Assn. MIT Enterprise Forum of N.W. (bd. dirs. 1988—, chmn. 1993-94), MIT Enterprise Forum (nat. bd. 1997—); Seattle-King County Bar Assn. Federal civil litigation, State civil litigation, Trademark and copyright. Office: Hendricks & Lewis 2675 1st Ave Seattle WA 98121-1304

HENDRICKS, RANDAL ARLAN, lawyer; b. Nov. 18, 1945; s. Clinton H. and Edith T. (Anderson) H.; m. Suann Rose, June 1, 1965 (div. 1976); children: Kristin Lee, Daehne Lynn; m. Jill Edith Duke, Mar. 22, 1982; 1 child, Bret Larson-Hendricks. Student, U. Mo., Kansas City, 1963-65; BS with honors, U. Houston, 1968, JD with honors, 1970. Bar: Tex. 1970, U.S. Dist. Ct. (so. dist.) Tex. 1970, U.S. Tax Ct. 1985. Assoc. Baker & Botts, Houston, 1970-71; pvt. practice Houston, 1971—; sr. v.p., mng. dir. Baseball, SFX Sports Group, Inc., 1999-2001, chmn., pres., CEO, 2001—, SFX Baseball Group LLC. Ptnr. Hendricks Sports Mgmt., Houston, 1977-81; pres. Hendricks Mgmt. Co., Inc., Houston, 1981-99; expert witness U.S. Senate Subcom. on Antitrust and Monopoly, 1972; mem. pub. adv. com. Houston/Harris County Sports Facility, 1995-96. Author: Inside the Strike Zone, 1994. Dir. profl. div. Excellence Campaign, U. Houston, 1971; bd. dirs. Cypress Creek Christian Ch., Spring, Tex., 1979-85. Mem. Houston Bar Assn., Assn. Reps. Profl. Athletes (bd. dirs. 1978-88, mem. at large 1978-79, treas. 1979-80, v.p. 1980-81, pres. 1981-82, chmn. ethics com. 1978-80, chmn. baseball com. 1981-88), Sports Lawyers Assn. (bd. dirs. 1992-2000), Order of Barons (chancellor 1969-70), Phi Kappa Phi, Phi Delta Phi. Property, real (including real estate development, water), Sports, Personal income taxation. Home: 20802 Highet Pl Tomball TX 77375-7042 Office: 400 Randal Way Ste 106 Spring TX 77388-8908 E-mail: randy.hendricks@SFX.com.

HENDRICKSON, GEORGE M. prosecutor; b. 1952; BA, U. Calif., Berkeley, 1974; JD, U. of the Pacific, 1977. Bar: Calif. 1977. Dep. dist. atty. Sacramento County Dist. Atty.'s Office, 1978-84; dep. atty. gen. Calif. Atty. Gen.'s Office, Sacramento, 1984—. Author: (manual) People's Remedies, 1986. Office: Attys Gens Office PO Box 944255 Sacramento CA 94244-2550

HENDRICKSON, THOMAS ATHERTON, lawyer; b. Indpls., May 12, 1927; s. Robert Augustus and Eleanor Riggs (Atherton) H.; m. Sandra Bly Shepard, Feb. 6, 1960; children: Thomas Shepard, Heidi Bly, Melanie Parke. BA, Yale U., 1949; LLB, Ind. U., 1952. Bar: Ind. 1952; cert. level II tax assessor-appraiser Ind. Former ptnr. Hendrickson, Travis, Pantzer & Miller. Mem. Indpls. Hist. Preservation Commn., 1982-83; mem. Marion County/Indpls. Hist. Soc., pres., 1984-85; mem. adv. bd. Fund for Landmark Indpls. Properties, 1984-85, Cath. Sem. Found. Indpls., Inc., 1985-94; former Marion County lay rep. planning com. Central Ind. Library Services Authority, recipient Outstanding Service award; former council pres. Indpls. Great Books. Served to lt. (s.g.) USNR, 1945-56. Fellow Ind. Bar Found.; mem. ABA (sec. on taxation, com. on state and local taxation), Ind. State Bar Assn. (taxation sect., ho. of dels. 1971-75, 79-89, asst. editor ABA Property Tax Deskbook 1995-98, author How to Challenge an Indiana Realty Assessment in Interstate Tax Insights 1992), Indpls. Bar Assn. (taxation sect.), Inst. Profls. in Taxation, Nat. Bus. Ins. (spkr. 2001—), Lawyers' Club. State and local taxation. Office: 7979 Lantern Rd Indianapolis IN 46256-1827 E-mail: thendrickson6@comcast.net.

HENDRIX, LYNN PARKER, lawyer; b. McCook, Nebr., Apr. 24, 1951; s. Jack Hall and Betty Lee (Parker) H.; m. Theresa Louise Zabawa, June 19, 1976; children: Paige Ashley, Parker Jerome, Pierce Reid. BSEE, U. Nebr., 1973, JD with distinction, 1978. Bar: Nebr. 1978, U.S. Dist. Ct. Nebr. 1978, Colo. 1979, U.S. Dist. Ct. Colo. 1979, U.S. Ct. Appeals (10th cir.) 1993, Wyo. 1993, Mont. 1995, N.Y., 2000, U.S. Patent Office, 1994. Surveyor Nebr. Dept. Roads, McCook, 1973; constrn. adminstr. Commonwealth Electric Co., Lincoln, Nebr., 1974, cons. engr., 1975; instr. U. Nebr., Lincoln, 1974-75; law clk. Nebr. Atty.-Gen., Lincoln, 1976-77; assoc. Holme Robert & Owen, LLP, Denver, 1978-83; ptnr. Holme Robert & Owen, Denver, 1984—. Editor-in-chief Nebr. Law Rev., 1977-78, exec. editor, 1976-77; contbr. articles to profl. jours. Sec., bd. dirs. Girls Club Denver, 1984-90, Girls Inc. of Metro Denver, 1992-94; trustee Rocky Mountain Minn. Law Found. Named Adm., Nebr. Navy. Mem. ABA, Colo. Bar Assn., Mont. Bar Assn., Nebr. Bar Assn., Wyo. Bar Assn., N.Y. Bar Assn., S.E. Law Club (pres. 1990-91), Meridian Golf Club, Tau Beta Pi, Sigma Tau (pres.), Eta Kappa Nu. Oil, gas, and mineral, Intellectual property, Computer. Home: 8125 S Glencoe Ct Littleton CO 80122-3876 Office: Holme Roberts & Owen LLP 1700 Lincoln St Ste 4100 Denver CO 80203-4541

HENDRIX, STEVEN EDWARD, lawyer; b. West Allis, Wis., Apr. 12, 1962; s. Val Edward Hendrix and Beverly V. Allard; m. Julia Wedgwood Roane, June 6, 1987; children: Daniel, Susana, John. BA, Carroll Coll., 1984; MA, U. Wis., 1986, JD, 1987; LLD, U. Mayor San Andres, Bolivia, 1995; SJD, San Carlos U., 2000. Bar: Wis. 87, U.S. Dist. Ct. (we. dist.) Wis. 87, DC 89, Pa. 89, U.S. Ct. Appeals (fed. cir.) 89, Ct. Internat. Trade 93, Bolivia 95, Guatemala 00. Counsel Export-Import Bank U.S., Washington,

1987—89; ptnr. Salas, Toro & Hendrix Law Offices, Caracas, Venezuela, 1989—91; legal and policy adviser U. Wis. Land Tenure Ctr., Madison, 1991—97; rule of law coord. U.S. AID, Washington, 1997—. Sr. rsch. fellow DePaul U. Sch. Law, Chgo., 2000—. Contbr. more than 50 articles to profl. jours. Relief coord. Hurricane Mitch Episcopal Ch., Guatemala, 1998—99. Recipient Human Rights award, Human Rights Ombudsman, Guatemala, 1999, Commendation, Pub. Def. Inst., 2001. Mem.: ABA, Woodrow Wilson Internat. Ctr. Scholars, Inter-Am. Bar Assn. Presbyterian. Avocation: Spanish language literature. Office: US AID Rm 5-9 RRB 1300 Pennsylvania Ave Washington DC 20523 Fax: 202-216-3262. E-mail: shendrix@usiad.gov.

HENDRY, ANDREW DELANEY, lawyer, consumer products company executive; b. N.Y.C., Aug. 9, 1947; s. Andrew Joseph and Virginia (Delaney) H.; 1 child, Robert. AB in Econs., Georgetown U., 1969; JD, NYU, 1972. Bar: N.Y. 1973. Va. 1981, Mich. 1984, Pa. 1987. Assoc. Battle and Fowler, N.Y.C., 1972-79; sr. corp. and fin. atty. Reynolds Metals Co., Richmond, Va., 1979-82; sr. staff counsel Burroughs Corp., Detroit, 1982-83, assoc. gen. coun., 1983-86, dep. gen. counsel, 1986-87; v.p. legal affairs Unisys Corp, Blue Bell, Pa., 1987-88, v.p., gen. counsel, 1988-91; sr. v.p., gen. counsel, sec. Colgate-Palmolive Co., N.Y.C., 1991—. Mem. adv. bd. Georgetown U. Law Ctr. Corp. Counsel Inst., 1999—; bd. editors The M&A Lawyer, 1996—, The Met. Corp. Counsel, 1993—. Dir., chmn., corp. adv. bd. Nat. Legal Aid and Def., Washington, 1992—99; dir. Lawyers Alliance for N.Y., 2000—; trustee The O'Neal School, 2001—; mem. Georgetown Coll. Adv. Bd., 2002—. With JAGC USAF, 1973. Fellow: Am. Bar Found.; mem.: ABA (corp. gen. counsel com. chmn. 1996—98, com. on corp. laws, standing com. on substance abuse), Georgetown Coll. Adv. Bd. (mem. 2002), Ctrl. European and Eurasian Law Inst. (dir. 2002, 2002), N.Y. State Bar Assn. (steering com. on commerce and industry 1997—), Am. Corp. Counsel Assn. (pres. Mich. chpt. 1985, chmn. nat. pro bono com. 1985—88, bd. dirs. emeritus N.Y. chpt.), Am. Law Inst., N.Y. Athletic Club. Corporate, general, Mergers and acquisitions, Securities. Office: Colgate-Palmolive Co 300 Park Ave New York NY 10022-7499

HENDRY, JOHN, state supreme court justice; b. Omaha, Aug. 23, 1948; BS, U. Nebr., 1970, JD, 1974. Pvt. practice, Licoln, 1974-1995; county ct. judge 3d Jud. Dist., 1995-98; chief justice Nebr. Supreme Ct., 1998—. Office: Rm 2214 State Capitol Lincoln NE 68509

HENDRY, ROBERT RYON, lawyer; b. Jacksonville, Fla., Apr. 23, 1936; s. Warren Candler and Evalyn Marguerite (Ryon) H.; children by previous marriage: Lorraine Evalyn, Lynette Comstock, Krista Ryon; m. Janet LaCoste. BA in Polit. Sci., U. Fla., 1958, JD, 1963. Bar: Fla. 1963; bd. cert. in internat. law. Assoc. Harrell, Caro, Middlebrooks & Whiltshire, Pensacola, Fla., 1963-66, Hewlliwell, Melrose & DeWolf, Orlando, Fla., 1966-67, ptnr., 1967-69; ptnr., pres. Hoffman, Hendry, Parker & Smith and predecessor Hoffman, Hendry & Parker, Orlando, 1969-77, Hoffman, Hendry & Stoner and predecessor, Orlando, 1977-82, Hendry, Stoner, Sims & Sawicki, Orlando, 1982-88, Hendry, Stoner, Townsend Sawicki & Brown, 1988-92, Hendry, Stoner, Sawicki & Brown, 1992—, Hendry, Stoner, DeLancett & Brown, 2002. Author: U.S. Real Estate and the Foreign Investor, 1983; contbr. articles to profl. jours. Mem. Dist. Export Coun., 1977-91, vice chmn., 1981, chair, 1995—, mem. nat. steering com., 1997—; bd. dirs. World Trade Ctr. and predecessor, Orlando, 1979-89, pres., 1980-82, 84; chmn. Fla. Gov.'s Conf. on World Trade, 1983; chmn. Fla. coun. on internat. edn., 1993-96; mem. internat. fin. and mktg. adv. bd. U. Miami Sch. Bus., Fla., 1979-90, Commn. on Internat. Edn., 1986-88; bd. dirs. Econ. Devel. Commn. of Mid-Fla., 2001—, Metro Orlando Econ. Devel. Commn., 2000—; mem. Metro Orlando Internat. Bus. Coun., 1994-96, Metro Orlando Internat. Affairs Commn., 1995—, Fla. Econ. Summit, 1996—; mem. internat. trade and econ. devel. bd. and audit com. Enterprise, Fla., 1997-2000; chmn. Fla. Trade Grant Review Panel, 1998—; mem. adv. com. Enterprise Fla. Internat. Bus. Devel., 2000—; mem. Free Trade Area of Ams. Com., 2001—; bd. dirs. Gulf of Mexico States Partnership, Inc., 2001, Golden Rule Found., 2000—, Gulf of Mex. Partnership, Inc., 2000—; co-chair Gulf of Mex. Accord Com. on Legal Infrastructure, 2002—; bd. advisors Fla. Free Trade Area of the Ams., 2001; founding mem. Scottish Exec., 2002—, Orlando Area Com. on Fgn. Affairs, 2002; mem. internat. programs adv. com. U. Fla. Levin Coll., 2000—. Lt. U.S. Army, 1958-60, capt. Army N.G., 1960-70. Mem. Fla. Coun. Internat. Devel. (bd. dirs. 1972-85, chmn. 1977-79, adv. bd. 1985-95, chmn. emeritus, 1991—, vice chair 1995-96, chair 1996-98), Fla. Bar (bd. cert. internat. lawyer 1999—, vice chmn. internat. law com. 1974-75, chmn. com. 1976-77, mem. exec. coun. internat. law sect. 1982—, original internat. law certification com. 1998—, chmn. 2001—), Fla. Assn. Voluntary Agys. for Caribbean Action (bd. dirs. 1987—, pres. 1989-91, past pres. 1991—), Orange County Bar Assn. (treas. 1971-74), Soc. Internat. Bus. Fellows, Brit.-Am. C. of C. (bd. dirs. 2000—, sec. 1984-85), Swiss Am. C. of C. (sec. Fla. chpt. 1996—), German Am. Bus. Chamber of Fla., Univ. Club. Corporate, general, Private international, Property, real (including real estate development, water). Office: Hendry Stoner DeLancett Et Al 200 E Robinson St Ste 500 Orlando FL 32801-1956

HENEGAN, JOHN C(LARK), lawyer; b. Mobile, Ala., Oct. 14, 1950; s. Virgil Baker and Marie (Fife) Gunter; m. Morella Lloyd Kuykendall, Aug. 5, 1972; children: Clark, Jim. BA in English and Philosophy, U. Miss., 1972, JD with honors, 1976. Bar: Miss. 1976, U.S. Dist. Ct. (no. dist.) Miss. 1976, N.Y. 1978, U.S. Dist. Ct. (so. dist.) N.Y. 1979, U.S. Ct. Appeals (5th and 11th cirs.) 1982, U.S. Ct. Appeals (2nd cir.) 1984, U.S. Dist. Ct. (so. dist.) Miss. 1984, U.S. Ct. Appeals (fed. cir.) 1995, U.S. Supreme Ct. 1995. Law clk. to judge U.S. Ct. Appeals (5th cir.), 1976-77; atty. Dewey, Ballantine, Bushby, Palmer & Wood, N.Y.C. and Washington, 1977-81; exec. asst., chief of staff to Gov. William Winter Jackson, Miss., 1981-84; atty. Butler, Snow, O'Mara, Stevens & Cannada, PLLC, Jackson, 1984—. Lectr. U. Miss. Ctr. for Continuing Legal Edn., 1985, 87, Miss. Jud. Coll., Oxford, 1982; mem. lawyers adv. com. U.S. Ct. Appeals for 5th Cir. Jud. Conf., 1991-93. Editor-in-chief Miss. Law Jour., 1976; editor Miss. Lawyer, 1985; contbr. articles to legal jours. Bd. dirs. Mississippians for Ednl. Broadcasting, Jackson, 1983-90, North Jackson Youth Baseball, Inc., 1991-97, Ctr. and Ctrl. S.W. Miss. Legal Svcs., 1997—, Hinds Co. Bar Assn., 2002—; co-pres. Chastain Mid. Sch. Parent Tchrs. Students Assn., 1995-96; mem. Miss. Ethics Commn., Jackson, 1984-87; del. Hinds County Dem. Conv., 1988; mem. Miss. Dem. Fin. Coun., 1988, Hinds County Dem. Exec. Com., 1989-92; Sunday sch. supt. Covenant Presbyn. Ch., 1989-90, elder, 1996-2002, deacon, 1991-96, moderator of diaconate, 1993-94. Recipient Cmty. Svc. award Hinds County Bar Assn., 1998. Mem. ABA, FBA, Miss. Bar Assn. (chmn. Law Day U.S.A. 1983), Miss. Def. Lawyers Assn., Miss. Law Jour. Alumni Assn. (bd. dirs. 1985—), 5th Cir. Bar Assn., Jackson C. of C., Am. Inns of Ct. (barrister Charles Clark chpt. 1991-93), Phi Kappa Phi, Phi Delta Phi, Omicron Delta Kappa. Avocations: reading, running. Antitrust, Federal civil litigation, Libel. Home: 2441 Eastover Dr Jackson MS 39211-6727 Office: 210 E Capitol St Fl 17 Jackson MS 39201-2306 E-mail: john.henegan@butlersnow.com.

HENG, GERALD C. W. lawyer; b. London, Mar. 6, 1941; arrived in U.S., 1964; s. Chong-Kwai and York-Choo (Eng); m. Eileen B-Y Tang; 1 child, Sharmaine. BS with honors, Harvard U., 1967; LLM in Taxation, Boston U., 1985; LLB, London U., 1973; JD, Suffolk U., 1983. Tchr. Malay and English langs. Ministry of Edn., Malaysia and Singapore, 1959-60; adminstr. hosp. and health Ministry of Health, Malaysia and Singapore, 1960-64; Fulbright fellow, scholar Inst. Internat. Edn., N.Y.C., 1964-69; atty. Heng Assocs., London, 1973-83, ptnr. Brookline, Mass., 1983—. Contbr. articles to newspapers including Boston Globe, Singapore Mirror, Boston Mag. and community newspapers. Mem. ABA, ATLA, Asian-Am. Lawyers Assn., Internat. Assn. Asian Ams. (pres. Boston chpt. 1981—), Boston Bar Assn. (specialist on internat. trade and human rights 1987—, gen. law practice and coms.), Mass. Acad. Trial Attys. Communications, General practice, Taxation, general. Home and Office: 19 Lillian Rd Framingham MA 01701-4820 E-mail: gcwebheng@gis.net.

HENGSTLER, GARY ARDELL, publisher, editor, lawyer; b. Wapakoneta, Ohio, Mar. 23, 1947; s. Luther C. and N. Delphine (Sims) H.; m. Linda K. Spreen, Mar. 8, 1969 (div. Aug. 1986); children: Dylan A., Joel S.; m. Laura M. Williams, Dec. 15, 1986. BS, Ball State U., 1969; JD, Cleve. State U., 1983. Bar: Ohio 1984, U.S. Dist. Ct. (no. dist.) Ohio 1984. Assoc. Blaszak, Schilling, Coey & Bennett, Elyria, Ohio, 1984-85; editor The Tex. Lawyer, Austin, 1985-86; news editor ABA Jour., Chgo., 1986-89, editor, pub., 1989-2000; dir. Donald W. Reynolds Nat. Ctr. Cts. & Media, Reno, 2000—. Home: 5055 Carnoustie Dr Reno NV 89502-9724 Office: Donald W Reynolds Nat Ctr Cts & Media U Nev Jud Coll Bldg 358 Reno NV 89557-0001 Fax: 775 327 2160. E-mail: hengstler@judges.org.

HENKE, MICHAEL JOHN, lawyer, educator; b. Evansville, Ind., Aug. 3, 1940; s. Emerson Overbeck and Beatrice (Arney) H.; m. Leni Edith Anderson, Mar. 20, 1966; children: Blake, Paige, Britt. BA summa cum laude, Baylor U., 1962, LLB, 1965; LLM, NYU, 1966. Bar: Tex. 1965, D.C. 1967. Assoc. Covington & Burling, Washington, 1966-73, Vinson & Elkins, Washington, 1974-76, ptnr., 1976—. Adj. prof. U. Va. Law Sch., 1988-94, 96—; chmn. pro bono adv. com. Legal Aid Soc., D.C., 1990-96, trustee, 1992—, chmn. ways & means com., 1997-2000, v.p., 2000—02, pres., 2002—; Washington adv. coun. Baylor Washington Program, 1989-92; sesquicentennial coun. of 150 Baylor U., 1993-95. Author: (with others) Petroleum Regulation Handbook, 1980, Natural Gas Yearbook, 1995; mem. editl. bd. Nat. Gas Mag., 1992-97, Best Lawyers in America, 1989—, Best Lawyers in Washington, 1997, Worlds Leading Competition and Antitrust Lawyers, 1997—, World's Leading Litigation Lawyers, 1997—; contbr. articles to profl. jours. Founder, chmn. Old Presbyn. Meeting House Day Care Ctr., Alexandria, Va., 1970-74; trustee Alexandria Country Day Sch., 2000—. Kenneson fellow. Mem. ABA (chmn. energy antitrust subcom. litigation sect. 1987-88, vice chmn. energy litigation com. 1988-89, chmn. 1989-92, chmn. ann. fall meeting 1993, divsn. dir. 1993-95, co-chmn. audiotaping and videotaping com. 1995-96, co-chmn. ins. coverage litigation com. 1996-98, coun. mem. 1998-2001, co-chair task force on judiciary 2001—, mem. Pres.'s Commn. on the 21st Century Judiciary 2002—), D.C. Bar Assn., Tex. Bar Assn., Coll. State Bar Tex., Baylor U. Alumni Assn. (bd. dirs. 1994-98), Am. Civil Trial Bar Roundtable, Met. Club, Belle Haven Country Club, Farmington Country Club (Charlottesville). Democrat. Avocations: skiing, flyfishing, tennis, backpacking. Administrative and regulatory, Antitrust, FERC practice. Home: 310 Charles Alexander Ct Alexandria VA 22301-1500 Office: Vinson & Elkins 1455 Pennsylvania Ave NW Fl 7 Washington DC 20004-1013 E-mail: mhenke@velaw.com.

HENKE, ROBERT JOHN, lawyer, mediator, consultant, engineer; b. Chgo., Oct. 13, 1934; s. Raymond Anthony and May Dorothy (Driscoll) H.; m. Mary Gabrielle Handrigan, June 18, 1960; children: Robert Joseph, Ann Marie. BSEE, U. Ill., 1956; MBA, U. Chgo., 1964; JD, No. Ill. U., 1979; postgrad., John Marshall Law Sch. Bar: Ill. 1980, Wis. 1980, U.S. Dist. Ct. (no. dist.) Ill. 1980, U.S. Dist. Ct. (we. and ea. dists.) Wis. 1980, U.S. Supreme Ct. 1984; registered profl. engr., Ill, Wis. Sr. elec. engr. Commonwealth Edison Co., Chgo., 1956-80; elec. engr. Peterson Builders, Sturgeon Bay, Wis., 1982-83; sr. elec., cost estimating engr. Sargent & Lundy Engrs., Chgo., 1985-94; instr. econs. and criminal law NE Wis. Tech. Inst., 1981-82; asst. dist. atty. Door County, Wis., 1981, ct. commr., 1981-82, sole practice, 1981-84, Lake County, Ill., 1984-94; pvt. practice cons., mediator Fish Creek, Wis., 1995-99; cons. Pittsboro, N.C., 1999—. Dir. Scand, Door County, 1981-82. Vice chmn. Door County Bd. Adjustment, 1983-84; atty. coach Wis. Bar Found. H.S. Moot Ct. Competition, Door County, 1984; vol. lawyers program, Lake County, Ill., 1985-95; sec., counsel, bd. dirs. Woodland Hills Condominium Assn., Gurnee, Ill., 1993-94. Served with USAR, 1958-63. Recipient award for pro bono work, 1994. Mem. ABA, IEEE, Wis. Bar Assn., Door Kewaunee Bar Assn. (pres. 1983-84), Chgo. Bar Assn., Am. Assn. Cost Engrs. Roman Catholic.

HENKIN, LOUIS, lawyer, law educator; b. Russia, Nov. 11, 1917; came to U.S., 1923, naturalized, 1930; s. Yoseph Elia and Frieda Rebecca (Kreindel) H.; m. Alice Barbara Hartman, June 19, 1960; children: Joshua, David, Daniel. AB, Yeshiva Coll., 1937; DHL, Yeshiva U., 1963; LLB, Harvard U., 1940; LLD, Columbia U., 1995; JD (hon.), Bklyn. Law Sch., 1997. Bar: N.Y. 1941, U.S. Supreme Ct. 1947. Law clk. to Judge Learned Hand, 1940-41; law clk. to Justice Frankfurter, 1946-47; cons. legal dept. UN, 1947-48; with State Dept., 1945-46, 48-57; U.S. rep. UN Com. Refugees and Stateless Persons, 1950; adviser U.S. del. UN Econ. and Social Coun., 1950, UN Gen. Assembly, 1950-53, Geneva Conf. on Korea, 1954; assoc. dir. Legis. Drafting Rsch. Fund, lectr. law Columbia U., 1956-57; prof. law U. Pa., 1958-62; prof. internat. law and diplomacy, prof. law Columbia U., 1962, mem. Inst. War and Peace Studies, 1962—, Hamilton Fish prof. internat. law and diplomacy, 1963-78, Harlan Fiske Stone prof. constl. law, 1978-79, univ. prof., 1979-88, univ. prof. emeritus and spl. svc. prof., 1988—; co-dir. Ctr. for Study of Human Rights, 1978-86, chmn. of directorate, 1986—. U.S. mem. Permanent Ct. Arbitration, 1963-69; adviser U.S. Del. UN Conf. on Law of the Sea, 1972-80; adv. panel on internat. law Dept. State, 1975-80, 93—; human rights com. U.S. Commn. for UNESCO, 1977-80, Internat. Covenant Civil and Polit. Rights, 1999-2002; Carnegie lectr. Hague Acad. Internat. Law, 1965; Frankel lectr. U. Houston, 1969; Gottesman lectr. Yeshiva U., 1975; Lockhart lectr. U. Minn. Law Sch., 1976; Francis Biddle lectr. Harvard Law Sch., 1978; lectr. Columbia U., 1979; Sherrill lectr. Yale U. Law Sch., 1981; Jefferson lectr. U. Pa. Law Sch., 1983; Irvine lectr. Cornell U., 1986; disting. lectr. Coll. Physicians and Surgeons, Columbia U., 1988; Solf lectr. Judge Adv. Gen.'s Sch., 1988; Cooley lectr. U. Mich. Law Sch., 1988; White lectr. La. State U., 1989; prin. lectr. The Hague Acad. Internat. Law, 1989; Blaine Sloane lectr. Pace U. Law Sch., 1991; Gerber lectr. U. Md. Law Sch., 1991; Nathanson lectr. law sch. U. San Diego, 1994; Sibley lectr. U. Ga. Law Sch., 1994; Brandeis lectr. Israel Acad. Scis. and Humanities, 1994; Phi Kappa Phi lectr., James Madison U., 1996, Doris and A. Leo Levin lectr. Bar Ilan U., Israel, 1996; cons. to govt., pres. U.S. Inst. Human Rights, 1970-93, Robert L. Levine lectr. Fordham Law Sch.; chief reporter Am. Law Inst., Restatement of the Law (3d), Fgn. Rels. Law of the U.S., 1979-87; bd. dirs. Lawyers Com. Human Rights, Immigration and Refugee Svcs. Am., v.p., 1994—; pres. Am. Soc. Internat. Law, 1992-94; vis. prof. law U. Pa., 1957-58; mem. human rights com. UN, 2000-02. Author: Arms Control and Inspection in American Law, 1958, The Berlin Crisis and the United Nations, 1959, Disarmament: The Lawyer's Interests, 1964, Law for the Sea's Mineral Resources, 1968, Foreign Affairs and the Constitution, 1972, 2nd edit., 1996, The Rights of Man Today, 1978, How Nations Behave: Law and Foreign Policy, 2nd edit., 1979; (with others) Human Rights in Contemporary China, 1986, Right v. Might: International Law and the Use of Force, 1989, 2nd edit., 1991, The Age of Rights, 1990, Constitutionalism, Democracy and Foreign Affairs, 1990, International Law: Politics and Values, 1995; editor: Arms Control: Issues for the Public, 1961, (with others) Transnational Law in a Changing Society, 1972, World Politics and the Jewish Condition, 1972, The International Bill of Rights: The International Covenant of Civil and Political Rights, 1981; (with others) International Law: Cases and Materials, 3d edit., 1993, 4th edit., 2001, Constitutionalism and Rights: The Influence of the United States Constitution Abroad, 1989, Foreign Affairs and the U.S. Constitution, 1990, Human Rights: Cases and Materials, 1999; bd. editors: Am. Jour. Internat. Law, 1967—, co-editor-in-chief, 1978-84; bd editors Ocean Devel. and Internat. Law Jour., 1973—, Jerusalem Jour. Internat. Relations, 1976—; contbr. articles to profl. jours. Served with AUS, 1941-45. Decorated Silver Star; recipient Law Alumni medal of excellence Columbia U. Sch. Law, 1982, Friedmann Meml. award Columbia Soc. Internat. law, 1986, Hudson medal Am. Soc. Internat. Law, 1995, Leadership in Human Rights award Columbia Human Rights Law Rev., 1995, Human Rights award Lawyers Com. for Human Rights, 1995, Outstanding Rsch. in Law and Govt. award Fellows of Am. Bar Found., 1997; Guggenheim fellow, 1979-80; Festschrift (Liber Amicorum): Politics, Values and Functions, Internat. Law in the 21st Century, Essays on Internat. Law in his honor, 1997, Louis Henkin Professorship in Human and Constitutional Rights established in his honor Columbia Law Sch., 1999. Fellow Am. Acad. Arts and Scis.; mem. Coun. Fgn. Rels., Am. Soc. Internat. Law (v.p. 1975-76, 88-90, pres. 1992-94, hon. v.p. 1994—, Goler T. Butcher medal for outstanding contbn. to internat. human rights law 2001), Internat. Law Assn. (v.p. Am. br., 1973—), Am. Soc. Polit. and Legal Philosophy (pres. 1985-87), Inst. de Droit Internat., Am. Polit. Sci. Assn., Internat. Assn. Constl. Law (v.p. 1982-95, hon. pres. 1995—), U.S. Assn. Constl. Law (hon. pres. 1997—), Am. Philos. Soc. (Henry M. Phillips prize in jurisprudence 2000). Home: 460 Riverside Dr New York NY 10027-6801 E-mail: henkin@law.columbia.edu.

HENNEKE, EDWARD GEORGE, lawyer; b. Flint, Mich., Jan. 28, 1940; s. Edward G. and Anna I. (Kielhorn) H.; m. Donna M. Wardosky, Jan. 24, 1970; children: Dawn, Shelley, Charlene; stepchildren: Scott, Tracy, Kurt Fraim. AA, Flint Jr. Coll., 1960; BS, U. Mich., Flint, 1962; JD, U. Mich., Ann Arbor, 1965. Bar: Mich. 1965, U.S. Dist. Ct. (ea. dist.) Mich. 1967, U.S. Ct. Appeals (6th cir.) 1974, U.S. Supreme Ct. 1971. Asst. pros. atty. Genesee County Pros. Atty., Flint, 1965-67; assoc. Ransom, Fazenbaker & Ransom, Flint, 1967-74; prin. ptnr. Keil, Ransom & Henneke, Flint, 1975-88, Henneke, McKone Fraim & Dawes, P.C. (and predecessor firm), Flint, 1988—. Flushing city atty., 1999—. Mem. planning com. Flushing Twp., 1986-92; bd. appeals, 1993—. Named Outstanding Alumnus, Flint U. Mich., 1971. Mem. ABA, Genesee County Bar Assn. (dir. 1978-81, pres. 1981-82). Avocations: hunting, golf, skiing. General civil litigation, Insurance, Probate (including wills, trusts). Office: Henneke McKone Fraim & Dawes PC 2222 S Linden Rd Ste G Flint MI 48532-5413 E-mail: ehenneke@hmfdlaw.com.

HENNELLY, EDMUND PAUL, lawyer, oil company executive; b. N.Y.C., Apr. 2, 1923; s. Edmund Patrick and Alice (Laccorn) H.; m. Josephine Kline; children: Patricia A. Anglin, Pamela J. Farley. BCE, Manhattan Coll., 1944; JD, Fordham U., 1950. Bar: N.Y. 1950. Instr. Manhattan Coll., 1947-50; litigation assoc. Cravath, Swaine & Moore, 1950-51, sr. litigation assoc., 1953-54; asst. gen. counsel CIA, Washington, 1951-52; assoc. counsel Time, Inc., N.Y.C., 1954-56; asst. legis. cons. Mobil Oil Corp., N.Y.C., 1956-60, legis. cons., 1960-61, mgr. domestic govt. rels. dept., 1961-67, mgr. govt. rels. dept., 1967-73, gen. mgr. govt. rels. dept., 1974-78, gen. mgr. pub. affairs dept., 1978-86; pres., CEO C. Remainder Corp., N.Y.C., 1986—. Bd. dirs. South Cay Trust. Contbr. articles on engring. and law to profl. jours. Trustee, vice chmn. Daytop Village Found.; mem. adv. com. N.Y. State Legis. Com. on Higher Edn., Nassau County (N.Y.) Energy Commn., L.I. Citizens' Com. for Mass Transit, N.Y. State Def. Coun.; mem. White House Conf. on Natural Beauty, 1963; bd. dirs. Nat. Coun. on Aging; exec. com. Pub. Affairs Rsch. Coun. of Conf. Bd.; mem. Nassau County Econ. Devel. Planning Coun.; commr. nat. com. Commn. for UNESCO, 1982-85, head U.S. del. with personal rank of amb. 22d Gen. Conf., 1983, mem. internat. adv. panel, 1989—; mem. Pres.' Intelligence Transition Team, 1980-81; cons. Pres.'s Intelligence Oversight Bd.; trustee Austen Riggs Ctr., Pub. Affairs Found. Lt., USNR, 1943-46, PTO, ETO. Decorated Knight of Malta, Knight of Holy Sepulchre. Mem. ABA, Fed. Bar Assn., Assn. Bar City of N.Y., Acad. Polit. and Social Scis., Am. Good Govt. Soc. (trustee), Tax Coun. (bd. dirs.), Pub. Affairs Coun. (bd. dirs.), Freedom House (trustee), Am. Mgmt. Assn., Pi Sigma Epsilon, Delta Theta Phi, Army-Navy Club, Meadows Country Club, Sarasota Yacht Club, Island Hills Country Club, Explorers Club, Knights of Malta, Knights Holy Sepulchre. Clubs: Army-Navy, Explorers. Lodges: K.M., Knights Holy Sepulcher. Oil, gas, and mineral. Home: 84 Sequams Ln E West Islip NY 11795-4508 also: 3941 Hamilton Club Cir Sarasota FL 34242-1109 Office: C Remainder Corp 21 Argyle Sq Babylon NY 11702-2712

HENNESSY, DANIEL KRAFT, lawyer; b. Summit, N.J., Jan. 4, 1941; s. Robert Emmett and Agnes Lyons (Lindle) H.; m. Susan Elizabeth (Bettina) Ware, June 17, 1972; children— Mary Elise, Daniel Joseph, Michael Ware, Catherine Anne. BS with highest honors, U.S. Naval Acad., 1963; JD cum laude, Harvard U., 1970. Bar: Tex. 1970. Commd. ensign U.S. Navy, 1963, advanced through grades to lt., 1966; service in Vietnam; resigned, 1967; ptnr. Hughes & Luce (formerly Hughes & Hill), 1973—. Editor: Harvard Law Rev, 1969-70. Mem. bd. advisers Jesuit Coll. Prep. Sch., Dallas, 1975-88; bd. dirs. Dallas-North Tex. region NCCJ, 1976-83, Catholics United for Faith, Inc., 1982-99 , Greater Dallas Right to Life Ednl. Found., 1974-86, Cath. Pro-life Com. of North Tex., 2001—, The Highlands Sch., 1986—. Decorated knight grand cross Equestrian Order of Holy Sepulchre of Jerusalem, Knight of Malta. Mem. Dallas Bar Assn., State Bar of Tex. Roman Catholic. Corporate, general, Finance, Property, real (including real estate development, water). Home: 4405 Beverly Dr Dallas TX 75205-3001 E-mail: hennesd@hughesluce.com.

HENNESSY, DEAN MCDONALD, lawyer, multinational corporation executive; b. McPherson, Kans., June 13, 1923; s. Ernest Weston and Beulah A. (Dunn) H.; m. Marguerite Sundheim, Sept. 6, 1946 (div. Sept. 1979); children: Joan Hennessy Wright, John D., Robert D. (dec.), Scott D. (dec.); m. Darlene MacLean, Apr. 4, 1981. AB cum laude, Harvard U., 1947, LLB, 1950; MBA, U. Chgo., 1959. Bar: Ill. 1951. Assoc. Carney, Crowell & Leibman, Chgo., 1950-53; atty. Borg-Warner Corp., Chgo., 1953-62; with Emhart Corp., Farmington, Conn., 1962-88, asst. sec., 1964-67, sec., gen. counsel, 1967-74, v.p., sec., gen. counsel, 1974-76, v.p., gen. counsel, 1976-86, sr. v.p., gen. counsel, 1986-88, ret., 1988. Incorporator Ill. Citizens for Eisenhower, 1952; chmn. Citizens Activities, Ill. Citizens for Eisenhower, 1952, 56; Justice of the peace, mem. bd. suprs. Proviso Twp., Ill., 1952-56; vice chmn. Jr. Achievement Chgo., 1959; program chmn. trade and industries divsn. United Rep. Fund Ill., 1961; trustee West Hartford Bicentennial Trust, Inc., 1976-77, Friends and Trustees of Bushnell Meml., Hartford, 1978-84; bd. dirs. Royal Homestead Condominium Assn., Juno Beach, Fla., 1990-93. Served to lt. (j.g.) USNR, 1943-46. Sheldon fellow Harvard U., 1947. Mem. ABA, Mfrs. Alliance for Productivity and Innovation (vice chmn. law coun. 1984-87, chmn. 1987, 88), John Harvard Soc. Republican. Presbyterian. Corporate, general.

HENNIGER, DAVID THOMAS, lawyer; b. Cuyahoga Falls, Ohio, Dec. 12, 1936; s. Herman Harrison and Wilma (Weeks) H.; m. LaRayne Virginia Kerlin, Apr. 9, 1965; children: Mark, Jill, Matthew, Michael. AA, St. Petersburg Jr. Coll., 1957; BS summa cum laude, Fla. So. Coll., 1959; JD cum laude, Stetson U., 1965. Bar: Fla. 1965, U.S. Dist. Ct. (mid. dist.) Fla. 1965, U.S. Ct. Appeals (5th cir.) 1966, U.S. Supreme Ct. 1971, U.S. Ct. Appeals (11th cir.) 1981. Diplomate Nat. Bd. Trial Advocacy. Assoc. Masterson, Lloyd, Sundberg & Rogers, St. Petersburg, Fla., 1965-75; ptnr. Lloyd and Henniger, P.A., St. Petersburg, 1975-84; assoc. Greene and Mastry, P.A., St. Petersburg, 1984-91; coll. atty. St. Petersburg Jr. Coll. Instr. Stetson Coll. Law, Gulfport, Fla., 1972-73; St. Petersburg Jr. Coll., 1968-73; pres. St. Petersburg Legal Aid Soc., 1976. Pres. Christian Arbitration Ctr., St. Petersburg, 1987—; v.p. Christian Businessmen's Com., 1981-82; chmn. sch. adv. com. Dixie Hollins High Sch., Kenneth City, Fla., 1985-86, pres. Parent Tchrs. Student Assn., 1987-88. Mem. ABA, Fed. Bar Assn., Am. Judicare Soc., Assn. Trial Lawyers Am., Fla. Trial Lawyers Soc., Am. Arbitration Assn. (panel arbitrators 1977-88), Christian Legal Soc. (treas. St. Petersburg 1984—). Avocations: basketball, photography. General civil litigation. Home: 5862 32nd Ave N Saint Petersburg FL 33710-1837 Office: St Petersburg Jr Coll PO Box 13489 Saint Petersburg FL 33733-3489

HENNING, JOEL FRANK, lawyer, author, publisher, consultant; b. Chgo., Sept. 15, 1939; s. Alexander M. and Henrietta (Frank) H.; m. Grace Weiner, May 24, 1964 (div. July 1987); children: Justine, Sarah-Anne, Dara; m. Rosemary Nadolsky, June 21, 1992; 1 child, Alexandra. AB, Harvard U., 1961, JD, 1964. Bar: Ill. 1965. Assoc. Sonnenschein, Levinson, Carlin, Nath & Rosenthal, Chgo., 1965-70; fellow, dir. program Adlai Stevenson Inst. Internat. Affairs, Chgo., 1970-73; nat. dir. Youth Edn. for Citizenship, 1972-75; dir. profl. edn. Am. Bar Assn., Chgo., 1975-78; asst. exec. dir. comm. and edn. ABA, 1978-80; ptnr. Joel Henning & Assocs., 1980-87; sr. v.p., gen. counsel, mem. exec. com. Hildebrandt, Internat., Inc., 1987—; pres., pub. LawLetters, Inc., 1980-89; pub. Lawyer Hiring and Tng. Report, 1980-89; Chgo. theater critic Wall St. Jour., 1989—; pub. Almanac of Fed. Judiciary, 1984-89; editor Bus. Lawyer Update, 1980-87. Mem. faculty Inst. on Law and Ethics, Council Philos. Studies; chmn. Fund for Justice, Chgo., 1979-85 Author: Law-Related Education in America: Guidelines for the Future, 1975, Holistic Running: Beyond the Threshhold of Fitness, 1978, Mandate for Change: The Impact of Law on Educational Innovation, 1979, Improving Lawyer Productivity: How to Train, Manage and Supervise Your Lawyers, 1985, Law Practice and Management Desk Book, 1987, Lawyers Guide to Managing and Training Lawyers, 1988, Maximizing Law Firm Profitability: Hiring, Training and Developing Productive Lawyers, 1991-98, also articles. Chmn. Gov.'s Commn. on Financing Arts in Ill., 1970-71; bd. dirs. Ill. Arts Council, 1971-81, Columbia Coll., Chgo.; bd. dirs., v.p., pub. edn. exec. com. ACLU of Ill.; trustee S.E. Chgo. Commn.; mem. Joseph Jefferson Theatrical Awards Com. Fellow Am. Bar Found. (life); mem. Am. Law Inst., ABA (ho. of dels.), Chgo. Bar Assn., Chgo. Council Lawyers (co-founder), Social Sci. Edn. Consortium. Corporate, general, General practice. Office: 150 N Michigan Ave Ste 3600 Chicago IL 60601-7572

HENRICK, MICHAEL FRANCIS, lawyer; b. Chgo., Feb. 29, 1948; s. John L. and A. Madeline (Hafner) H.; m. Cissi F. Henrick, Aug. 9, 1980; children: Michael Francis Jr., Derry Patricia. BA, Loyola U., 1971; JD with honors, John Marshall Law Sch., 1974. Bar: Ill. 1974, U.S. Dist. Ct. (no. dist.) Ill. 1974, U.S. Supreme Ct. 1979, Wis. 1985, U.S. Dist. Ct. (ea. dist.) Wis. 1985. Ptnr. Hinshaw & Culbertson, Chgo., Waukegan, Ill., 1974—. Recipient Corpus Juris Secundum award West Publ. Co., 1974. Mem. ABA, Def. Rsch. Inst., Ill. Bar Assn., Lake County Bar Assn., Ill. Hosp. Attys. Assn., Internat. Assn. of Def. Counsel, Ill. Def. Attys. Assn., Soc. Trial Lawyers Def. Rsch. Inst., Am. Inns of Ct. Personal injury (including property damage), Health. Office: Hinshaw & Culbertson 110 N West St Waukegan IL 60085-4330 E-mail: m.henrick@hinshawlaw.com.

HENRY, BRIAN THOMAS, lawyer; b. Chgo., Dec. 25, 1954; s. Thomas Joseph and Shirley Grace (Pfaff) H.; m. Mary Elizabeth Collins, Sept. 17, 1983; children: Kyle Justin, Erin Maureen, Colin Thomas. BA Honors in History magna cum laude, Loyola U., Chgo., 1977; JD, U. Ill., 1980. Bar: Ill. 1980, U.S. Dist. Ct. (no. dist.) Ill. 1980. Ptnr. Pretzel & Stouffe Chtd., Chgo., 1980—; fellow Am. Coll. of Trial Lawyers. Faculty instr. Ill. Assn. of Def. Trial Counsel Trial Acads., 1990-2003; seminar speaker Chgo. Bar Assn. Comparative Negligence Seminar, 1990, '91; cons. health care com. Inst. of Medicine of Chgo.; frequent lectr. med. groups. Editor-in-chief Recent Decisions Sect. of Ill. Bar Jour., 1979-80 Fellow Am. Coll. Trial Lawyers; mem. ASTL, ABA, Ill. Assn. Hosp. Attys., Ill. Assn. Def. Trial Counsel, Internat. Assn. Def. Counsel (faculty instr. trial acad. 2001), Ill. Bar Assn., Phi Alpha Theta, Phi Alpha Delta. General civil litigation, Personal injury (including property damage), Professional liability. Office: Pretzel & Stouffer Chtd 1 S Wacker Dr Ste 2500 Chicago IL 60606-4614

HENRY, DOUGLAS, lawyer, state legislator; b. May 18, 1926; married; six children. BA, LLB, Vanderbilt U. Mem. Tenn. Ho. of Reps. 79th Gen. Assembly, Tenn. Senate 87th-103rd Gen. Assemblies, chmn. fin., ways and means com., mem. fiscal rev. com., mem. ethics com., mem. rules com., Tenn. adv. com. on intergovtl. rels., mem. gen. welfare com., mem. pensions and ins. com., others. Past chgmn. So. Legis. Conf.; coun. mem. World Regions of the Coun. of State Govts. Bd. mem. YMCA; active Florence Crittenden Home, Family and Children's Svcs., Agape, Vanderbilt Cancer Ctr., Nashville Symphony, Opera Guild. Mem. Kiwanis Club, Tenn. Hist. Soc., Post 5 Am. Legion. Democrat. Office: 11 Legislative Plaza Nashville TN 37243-0021 E-mail: sen.douglas.henry@legislature.state.tn.us.*

HENRY, FREDERICK EDWARD, lawyer; b. St. Louis, Aug. 28, 1947; s. Frederick E. and Dorothy Jean (McCulley) H.; m. Vallie Catherine Jones, June 7, 1969; children: Christine Roberta, Charles Frederick. AB, Duke U., 1969, JD with honors, 1972. Bar: Ill. 1972, U.S. Dist. Ct. (no. dist.) Ill. 1972, Calif. 1982. Assoc. Baker & McKenzie, Chgo., 1972-79, ptnr., 1979—. Elder, session mem. Fourth Presbyn. Ch., Chgo., 2000—02; bd. dirs. Lincoln Park Conservation Assn., 1983—85, Old Town Triangle Assn., Chgo., 1980—83, pres., 1984. Recipient Willis Smith award, Duke U. Law Sch., 1972. Mem.: ABA, Calif. State Bar, Chgo. Bar Assn., Order of Coif. Private international, Corporate taxation. Home: 164 W Eugenie St Chicago IL 60614-5809 Office: Baker & McKenzie 1 Prudential Plz 130 E Randolph St Ste 3700 Chicago IL 60601-6342 E-mail: frederick.e.henry@bakernet.com.

HENRY, JAMES FRED, lawyer; b. Russell, Kans., Sept. 22, 1957; s. William Robert and Dorothea Katherine H.; m. Kelly Jo Morrison, June 17, 1993; children: Camille Marie, Natalie Suzanne, Karla Marie. BS, U. North Ala., 1978; MBA, Samford U., 1982; JD, Cumberland U., 1997. Bar: Ala. 1997, U.S. Dist. Ct. (no. dist.) Ala. 1997. Sales rep. AT&T, Birmingham, 1979-82, mgr. tech. support Mobile, 1983-86; br. mgr. Bell South, Louisville, 1987-88, regional mgr. Nashville, 1988-89, dir. mktg. Birmingham, 1989-94; atty. Johnston, Barton, Proctor & Powell, LLP, Birmingham, 1997—. Bd. trustees Highlands United Meth. Ch., Birmingham, 1998—, Found. Ileitis and Colitis, Birmingham, 1982-87. Mem. ABA, Am. Mgmt. Assn., Birmingham Bar Assn., Phi Gamma Delta. Methodist. Administrative and regulatory, General civil litigation, Health. Home: 543 Bristol Ln Birmingham AL 35226-1986 Office: Johnston Barton Proctor & Powell LLP 2900 S Harbert Plz Birmingham AL 35203

HENRY, JAMES RICHARD, lawyer; BA, SUNY, Potsdam, 1976; JD, Yale U., 1979. Bar: N.Y. 1980. Assoc. White & Case, N.Y.C. and Washington, 1979-81, Luster & Salk, Groton, N.Y., 1982-84; ptnr. Luster, Salk & Henry, Groton, 1984-87, Luster, Salk, Henry & Tischler, Groton, 1987-88; pvt. practice, Groton, 1989—. Mem. ABA, N.Y. State Bar Assn., Tompkins County Bar Assn., Groton Bus. Assn. General practice, Probate (including wills, trusts), Property, real (including real estate development, water). Office: PO Box 95 201 E Cortland St Groton NY 13073-0095

HENRY, PETER YORK, lawyer, mediator; b. Washington, Apr. 28, 1951; s. David Howe II and Margaret (Beard) H.; children: Ryan York, Zachary Price, Chance Hagdorn; m. Deidra B. Hagdorn, May 1995; 1 child, Chance Hagdorn Henry; stepchildren: Nathan Hebert, Christopher Hebert. B.B.A., Ohio U., 1973; J.D. St. Mary's U., San Antonio, 1976. Bar: Tex. 1976. Sole practice, San Antonio, 1976—. Mem. ATLA, Tex. Bar Assn., Tex Trial Lawyers Assn., San Antonio Trial Lawyers Assn. (bd. dirs. 1989-90), San Antonio Bar Assn., Phi Delta Phi. Insurance, Personal injury (including property damage), Workers' compensation. Home: 7642 Bluesage Cove San Antonio TX 78249-2541 E-mail: lawofpyh@aol.com.

HENRY, RAGAN AUGUSTUS, lawyer, communications executive; b. Sadiesville, Ky., Feb. 02; s. Augustus Wilson and Ruby Helen H.; m. Regina Amanda Goodwin, Mar. 20, 1980. BA, Harvard U., 1956, LLM, 1961. Bar: Pa. 1961. Assoc. Narin, Garfinkel & Mann, Phila., 1961-64; ptnr. Goodis, Greenfield, Henry, Edelstein, Phila., 1964-77, Wolf, Block, Schorr & Solis-Cohen, Phila., 1977-94; chmn. US Radio, Inc., Phila., 1980-96, MediaComm Nat., Inc., Phila., 1988—. Cons. Clear Channel Comm. Inc., San Antonio, 1996-97; tchr. S.I. Newhouse Sch., Syracuse, N.Y., 1979-83; lectr. Law Sch. Temple U., Phila., 1971-73, La Salle U., Phila., 1971-73. Bd. dirs. Phila. Mus. Art, 1986—; bd. dirs., treas. United Way Am., Washington, 1993-95, Elderhostel, Boston, 1984—. Pvt. U.S. Army, 1957-59. Recipient Outstanding Bus. award Urban Bankers Del. Valley, 1978, Human Rels. award Nat. Conf. Christians and Jews, 1981; named Broadcaster of Yr. Nat. Assn. Black Broadcasters, 1981. Methodist. Communications, Corporate, general. Office: 505 Waldron Ter Merion Station PA 19066-1325

HENRY, ROBERT HARLAN, federal judge, former attorney general; b. Shawnee, Okla., Apr. 3, 1953; BA, U. Okla., 1974, JD, 1976. Bar: Okla. 1976. Atty. Henry, West, Still & Combs, Shawnee, Okla., 1977—83, Henry, Henry & Henry, Shawnee, 1983—87; mem. Okla. Ho. of Reps., 1976—86; atty. gen. State of Okla., Oklahoma City, 1987—91; dean, prof. Okla. City U. Law Sch., 1993—94; judge U.S. Ct. Appeals (10th cir.), Oklahoma City, 1994—. Mem. Nat. Conf. Commrs. on Uniform State Law. Fellow: Am. Bar Found.; mem.: Nat. Assn. Attys. Gen. (chmn. state constl. law adv. com., vice-chmn. civil rights com.), Am. Coun. Young Polit. Leaders, Okla. Bar Assn. Office: US Ct Appeals 10th Cir 200 NW 4th St Rm 2021 Oklahoma City OK 73102-3026 also: Byron White US Cthse 1823 Stout St Denver CO 80257

HENRY, ROBERT JOHN, lawyer; b. Chgo., Aug. 1, 1950; s. John P. and Margaret P. (Froelich) Henry; m. Sara Mikuta; children: Cherylyn, Deanna, Laurin, Joseph Mikuta, Nicholas Mikuta. BA cum laude, Loyola U., Chgo., 1973, JD cum laude, 1975. Bar: Ill 1975, U.S. Dist. Ct. (no. dist.) Ill. 1975. Atty. Continental Ill. Nat. Bank, Chgo., 1975-77, Allied Van Lines, Inc., Chgo., 1977-81, assoc. gen. counsel, 1981-88, gen. counsel, 1988-90, v.p. adminstrn., gen. counsel, 1990-93, v.p. gen. counsel, 1993-99; v.p., assoc. gen. counsel SIRVA, Inc., Chgo., 1999—. Gen. counsel NFC N.Am., 1996-99. Alt. scholar Weymouth Kirkland Found., 1971. Mem. Chgo. Bar Assn., Am. Corp. Counsel Assn. Commercial, contracts (including sales of goods; commercial financing), Corporate, general, Securities. Office: SIRVA Inc PO Box 4403 Chicago IL 60680-4403 E-mail: robert.henry@sirva.com.

HENRY, THORNTON MONTAGU, lawyer; b. Bermuda, May 8, 1943; s. Otis R. and Barbara M. Henry; m. Ann Portlock, Aug. 28, 1971; children: Ruth Montagu, Thornton Bradshaw, John Gordon. BA, Washington and Lee U., 1966, LLB, 1969; LLM, Georgetown U. Bar: Fla. 1972, U.S. Dist. Ct. (so. dist.) Fla., U.S. Ct. Appeals (11th cir.), U.S. Tax Ct., U.S. Ct. Claims; cert. in taxation, Fla. Tax law specialist IRS, Washington, 1972-74; chmn., pvt. client svcs. group Jones, Foster, Johnston & Stubbs, PA, West Palm Beach, Fla., 1974—. Counsel, bd. profl. adv. Cmty. Found. for Palm Beach and Martin Counties; bd. dirs., 1st v.p., counsel Internat. Children's Mus. Pres., elder Meml. Presbyn. Ch.; chmn. scholarship fund Benjamin Sch.; bd. dirs., past pres. Rehab. Ctr. Children and Adults, Inc., Palm Beach; past pres. Planned Giving Coun., Palm Beach County; mem. adv. com. Habitat for Humanity; mem. planned giving com. Norton Mus. Art. Capt. C.E., U.S. Army, 1970-72. Mem. ABA (tax com.), Fla. Bar Assn., Fla. Bar (tax sect.), East Coast Estate Planning Coun. (past pres.), Palm Beach Tax Inst., Kiwanis (past pres.). Order St. John of Jerusalem (chmn.-elect., knight). Republican. Avocations: jogging, furniture restoration, reading, photography, missionary work. Estate planning, Probate (including wills, trusts), Estate taxation. Office: Jones Foster Johnston & Stubbs 505 S Flagler Dr Ste 1100 West Palm Beach FL 33401-5923 E-mail: thenry@jones-foster.com.

HENRY, WILLIAM OSCAR EUGENE, lawyer; b. Ocala, Fla., Mar. 30, 1927; s. Jesse Dawson and Alice M. (Johnson) H.; m. Bobbie Moorhead, May 9, 1952 (div.); children: Carol Ann, Robert Dawson, Jean Elizabeth; m. Mary Goode Croft, Dec. 1, 2000. BS in Journalism, U. Fla., 1950, JD, 1952. Bar: Fla. 1952, U.S. Dist. Ct. (mid. dist.) Fla., 1954; cert. cir. mediator Supreme Ct. Fla., tax lawyer Fla. Bd. Legal Specialization. Newspaperman The Marion Sun, Ocala, 1952-53; assoc. Holland, Bevis, McRae & Smith, Bartow, Fla., 1953-55; ptnr. Holland & Knight LLP (and predecessor firms), Bartow, Lakeland and Orlando, Fla., 1955—. Bd. dirs. Consol.-Tomoka Land Co., Daytona Beach, Fla.; arbitrator, mem. panel Am. Arbitration Assn. Contbr. articles to profl. jour. Legis counsel Office of Gov. of Fla., Tallahassee, 1963; bd. dirs. U. Fla. Found., Inc., 1977-87, Holland and Knight Found., Lakeland, 1982-97; v.p. Ctrl. Fla. coun. Boy Scouts Am., 1990-95; trustee Fla. Bar Found. Endowment Trust, 1991-99. Recipient Disting. Eagle Scout award, 1990, Silver Beaver award, 1992; named Outstanding Past Pres. Vol. Bar Assn. award Fla. Coun. Bar Assn. Pres., 1991-92. Fellow Am. Bar Found., Am. Coll. Trusts and Estates Coun., Am. Coll. Tax Coun., Am. Judicature Soc., Nat. Health Lawyers Assn., Fla. Bar Found. (bd. dirs. 1983-89, pres. 1988-89, Medal of Honor 1996); mem. ABA (ho. of dels. 1984-89, 93-99, exec. com. sect. officers conf. 1997-98), Fla. Bar (pres. 1983-84, Fla. Outstanding Tax Atty. award 1986), U. Fla. Nat. Alumni Assn. (bd. dirs., pres. 1968, Disting Alumnus award 1972, Alligator Hall of Fame 2000), Univ. Club, Citrus Club, Elks, Sigma Alpha Epsilon (pres. Fla. Upsilon alumni 1993—). Methodist. Corporate, general, Health, Corporate taxation. Home: 2150 Huron Trl Maitland FL 32751-3929 Office: Holland & Knight LLP 200 S Orange Ave Ste 2600 Orlando FL 32801-3453 E-mail: whenry@hklaw.com.

HENSCHEL, JOHN JAMES, lawyer; b. Mineola, NY, Aug. 11, 1954; s. John Jr. and Lilyan Marie (Dodge) H.; m. Yasmin Islami, May 26, 1980; children: John Christopher, Theodore Martin, Jessamyn Susanna. BA in Psychology, Fairfield U., 1976; JD, Seton Hall U., 1984. Bar: N.J. 1984, U.S. Dist. Ct. N.J. 1984, U.S. Dist. Ct. (so. and ea. dists.) N.Y. 1985, U.S. Ct. Appeals (3d cir.) 1996. Law sec. Hon. Marshall Selikoff, J.S.C., Freehold, NJ, 1984-85; assoc. McElroy, Deutsch & Mulvaney, Morristown, NY, 1985-88, Bumgardner, Hardin & Ellis, Springfield, NJ, 1988-90; ptnr. Tompkins McGuire & Wachenfeld, Newark, 1990-97; trial counsel Caron McCormick Constants & Wilson, Rutherford, NJ, 1997—2003; mediator Superior Ct. N.J., 1999—; corp. counsel Atlas Copco North Am. Inc., 2003—. Trustee Abdol H. Islami M.D. Found. for Med. Edn. Mem. ABA, N.J. Bar Assn., N.J. Bar Found. (trustee 1995-99, treas. 1999-2001, second v.p. 2001-2003, 1st v.p. 2003-), Am. Inns of Ct. (Justice William Brennan Jr. chpt.; master Seton Hall Law Alumni chpt., Marie L. Garibaldi chpt.), Essex County Bar Assn. Avocations: reading, sports. General civil litigation, Corporate, general, Product liability. Home: 3 Birchmont Ln Warren NJ 07059-5437 Office: 34 Maple Ave Pine Brook NJ 07058

HENSLEIGH, HOWARD EDGAR, lawyer; b. Blanchard, Iowa, Oct. 29, 1920; s. Albert Dales and Eula Fern (Bair) H.; m. Janice Lee Pedersen, Aug. 15, 1948; children: Susan Lee Hensleigh Harvey, Nancy Ann Hensleigh-Quinn, Jonathan Blair. BA, Iowa U., 1943, JD, 1947; postgrad., Columbia U., 1954-55. Bar: Iowa 1947, N.Y. 1955, Mass. 1968. Commd. U.S. Army, 1943, advanced through grades to col., 1965, ret., 1973; legal adviser U.S. Mission to NATO, Paris, 1958-60; dep. asst. gen. counsel office of Sec. Def. U.S. Govt., Washington, 1960-67, dep. asst. to sec. treas., 1967-68; asst. gen. counsel Raytheon Co., Bedford, Mass., 1968-91, ret., 1991; pvt. practice Carlisle, Mass., 1991—. Participated in U.S. Italy Internat. Ct. Justice, The Hague, 1989. Chmn. town com. Carlisle Reps., 1972-80, sch. com. Carlisle, 1973-75, bd. selectmen, 1977-80, Pres. 517th Parachute Regimental Combat Team Assn. Inc. (2003-). Mem. ABA (chmn. region I), Fed. Bar Assn., Am. Soc. Internat. Law. Government contracts and claims, Private international, Public international. Home and Office: 479 West St Carlisle MA 01741-1439 E-mail: hhensleigh@earthlink.net.

HENSLEY, WILLIAM MICHAEL, lawyer; b. Fresno, Calif., Apr. 25, 1954; s. Goldie Reeves and Allene (Watson) H.; m. Mari Bordona Calabrese, May 1981 (div. Jan. 1984); 1 child, Gilliann Mar; m. Anne Fields, Nov. 20, 1988. BA in Speech Comm., U. So. Calif., 1976; JD, Rutgers U., Camden, N.J., 1979. Bar: Calif. 1979, U.S. Dist. Ct. (no., ea., ctrl. and so. dists.) Calif., U.S. Ct. Appeals (9th cir.), U.S. Supreme Ct. Law clk. to Hon. Zenovich Calif. Ct. Appeals, 5th Appellate Dist., Fresno, 1979-81; assoc. Kadison, Pfaelzer, Woodard, Quinn & Rossi, L.A., 1981-87, Irell & Manella, L.A., 1987-92, Menke, Fahrney & Carroll, Costa Mesa, Calif., 1992-95; atty. Jackson, DeMarco & Peckenpaugh, Irvine, Calif., 1995—. Mem. editl. bd. Matthew Bender Calif. Real Estate Reporter, 1993—; contbr. articles to profl. jours. Mem. Orange County Bar Assn. Democrat. Mem. Ch. of Christ. Achievements include arguing more than 80 appellate cases in Calif. state and federal courts. Appellate, General civil litigation, Securities. Home: 25 Pacific Crst Laguna Niguel CA 92677-5314 Office: Jackson DeMarco & Peckenpaugh 2030 Main St Ste 1200 Irvine CA 92614 E-mail: mhensley@jdplaw.com.

HENSON, ROBERT FRANK, lawyer; b. Jenny Lind, Ark., Apr. 10, 1925; s. Newton and Nell Edith (Kessinger) H.; m. Jean Peterson Henson, Sept. 14, 1946; children: Robert F., Sandra Henson Curfman, Laura, Thomas, David, Steven. BS, U. Minn., 1948, JD, 1950. Bar: Minn. 1950, U.S. Supreme Ct. 1972. Atty. Soo Line R.R., 1950-52; ptnr. Cant, Haverstock, Beardsley, Gray & Plant, Mpls., 1952-66; sr. ptnr. Henson & Efron, Mpls., 1966-94, of counsel, 1995—; !. Chmn. Minn. Lawyers Profl. Responsibility Bd., 1981-86; co-chmn. Supreme Ct. Study Com. on Lawyer Discipline, 1992-94. Trustee Mpls. Found., 1974-85, Emma Howe Found, 1986-90; chmn. Hennepin County Mental Health and Mental Retardation Bd., 1968-70. Served with USN, 1943-46. Fellow Am. Bar Found.; mem. ABA, Hennepin County Bar Assn. (pres. 1968-69), Minn. Bar Assn., Order of Coif. Unitarian Universalist. Office: 220 S Sixth St Ste 1800 Minneapolis MN 55402-4503 Personal E-mail: rhenson@mn.rr.com. Business E-Mail: rhenson@hensonefron.com.

HENVEY, JOHN WILLIAM, lawyer; b. Washington, Aug. 18, 1945; s. John and Thelma Edna (Swaffar) H.; children: Kate, Scott. BA in Econs., Hardin-Simmons U., 1968; JD, U. Tex., 1973. Bar: Tex. 1973; cert. personal injury and civil trial specialist. Pvt. practice, Dallas, 1973—76, 1986—2001; assoc. Timothy E. Kelley, Dallas, 1976-86; atty. Mauerhen & Assocs., Azle, Tex., 2001—. 1st lt. U.S. Army, 1969-71, Vietnam. Decorated Bronze star. Mem. Coll. State Bar of Tex. Democrat. Methodist. General civil litigation, Personal injury (including property damage), Product liability. Office: 1501 Southeast Pkwy Azle TX 76020

HENWOOD, WILLIAM SCOTT, lawyer; b. Toronto, Ont., Can., May 24, 1949; s. William John and Muriel Mae (Scott) H.; m. Carol Elizabeth Nichols, Nov. 17, 1973; children: William Scott Jr., Cameron Nichols. BBA, Ga. State U., 1976; JD, Woodrow Wilson Coll. Law, 1978. Bar: Ga. 1979. Law clk. to reporter of decisions Supreme Ct. Ga., Atlanta, 1974-80, asst. reporter of decisions, 1980-84, reporter of decisions, 1984—. Co-author: Georgia's Appellate Judiciary: Profiles and History, 1987. Pres. Leafmore-Creek Park Civic Assn., Decatur, Ga., 1982-83, Briarcliff Cmty. Sports, Decatur, 1986-87; mem. Sesquicentennial Com., Supreme Ct. of Ga. With Army N.G., 1968-74. Fellow Ga. Bar Found.; mem. Assn. of Reporters of Jud. Decisions (pres. 1988-89), Ga. Legal History Found. (treas. 1984-96), Gridiron Secret Soc., Lawyers Club Atlanta (mem. exec. com. 1998-2003, pres. 2003—), Advocates Club (exec. bd. 1996-98), Burns Club (sec. 1992-93), Old War Horse Lawyers Club. Democrat. Presbyterian. Avocations: travel, hunting, sports car racing. Home: 2247 Springwood Dr Decatur GA 30033-2722 Office: Supreme Ct Ga Judicial Bldg Atlanta GA 30334 E-mail: henwoods@supreme.courts.state.ga.us.

HENZE, TOM, lawyer; BA, U. Ariz., 1968, JD, 1973. Bar: Ariz. 1973, U.S. Dist. Ct. Ariz. 1978. Shareholder Gallagher & Kennedy, P.A., Phoenix. Instr. Maricopa County CC Sys.; mem. com. criminal procedure and criminal delay reduction, mem. com. recommended ARiz. jury instrns., mem. criminal study com. Maricopa County Superior Ct.; past. lawyer del. 9th Cir. Jud. Conf. Mem. adv. bd. Liberty Wildlife Found. Fellow: ABA, Am. Bar Found., Am. Coll. Trial Lawyers; mem.: Calif. Attys. Criminal Justice, Ariz. Attys. Criminal Justice (bd. govs., John J. Flynn award), Nat. Assn. Criminal Def. Lawyers, State Bar Ariz. Assn. (mem. com. profl. responsibility, mem. bench and bar com.). Criminal, Environmental, Intellectual property. Office: Gallagher and Kennedy PA 2575 E Camelback Rd Phoenix AZ 85016-9225 Office Fax: 602-530-8500. Business E-Mail: teh@gknet.com.*

HENZE, WILLIAM F., II, lawyer; b. Cleve., Apr. 20, 1949; BA, Ohio Wesleyan U., 1971; JD, U. Ariz., 1974; LLM, NYU, 1976. Bar: Ariz. 1974, N.Y. 1977, Tex. 1984. Ptnr. Jones, Day, Reavis & Pogue, N.Y.C. Instr. in law NYU, 1974-76. Mem. Phi Beta Kappa. Banking, Corporate, general, Finance. Office: Jones Day Reavis & Pogue 599 Lexington Ave Fl C1A New York NY 10022-6030

HERALD, J. PATRICK, lawyer; b. Latrobe, Pa., Sept. 27, 1947; s. John P. and Doris Faye (Galvin) H.; m. Bridget Grace Tobin, Aug. 17, 1973; children: Brian Michael, Matthew Patrick, Molly Bridget, John Francis. AB in History, John Carroll U., 1969; JD, U. Notre Dame, 1972. Bar: Ill. 1972, U.S. Dist. Ct. (no. dist.) Ill. 1972, U.S. Ct. Appeals (7th cir.) 1975, U.S. Supreme Ct. 1978. Assoc. Baker & McKenzie, Chgo., 1972-79, ptnr., 1979—. Fellow Am. Coll. Trial Lawyers, Internat. Acad. Trial Lawyers; mem. ABA, Ill. Bar Assn., Chgo. Bar Assn., 7th Cir. Bar Assn., Soc. Trial Lawyers (bd. dirs. 1987-89), Internat. Assn. Def. Counsel, Chgo. Trial Lawyers Club (pres. 1982-83). Roman Catholic. Federal civil litigation, General civil litigation, State civil litigation. Home: 1721 N Normandy Ave Chicago IL 60707-3925 Office: Baker & McKenzie 1 Prudential Plz 130 E Randolph St Fl 3500 Chicago IL 60601-6213 E-mail: j.patrick.herald@bakernet.com.

HERB, F(RANK) STEVEN, lawyer; b. Cin., Nov. 9, 1949; s. Frank X. and Jean M. (Zurcher) H.; m. Jean L. Jeffers, June 21, 1971; children: Tracy Lynn, Jacquelyn Anne. BS, Bowling Green U., 1971; JD, U. Cin., 1974. Bar: Ohio 1974, Fla. 1978, U.S. Dist. Ct. (no., mid., and so. dists.) Fla., U.S. Ct. Appeals (11th cir.); cert. county and cir. ct. mediator, Fla. Supreme Ct. Assoc. Connaughton Law Offices, Hamilton, Ohio, 1974; jud. advocate gen., chief of civil law USAF, Tyndall AFB, Fla., 1975—78; ptnr. Nelson Hesse, Sarasota, Fla., 1979—. Author: (with others) Bennedicts on Admiralty, 1996, 97, 98; contbr. chpts. to books. Bd. dirs. Brock Wilson Found., Sarasota, 1983-92; pres. Riegels Landing Assn., Sarasota, 1986-90, 98-2000; dir., chmn. Siesta Key Utilities Assn., 1994—; mem. govt. rels. com. Nat. Marine Mfrs. Assn. Capt. JAGC USAF, 1975-78. Decorated USAF Meritorious Svc. medal. Mem. Ohio Bar Assn., Fla. Bar Assn. (chmn. 12th Jud. cir. unauthorized practice of law com. 1986-93, fee arbitration com. 12th jud. cir. 1996—), Sarasota Bar Assn., Def. Rsch. Inst., Maritime Law Assn., Am. Boat and Yacht Counsel, Nat. Marine Mfrs. Assn. (govt. rels. com.), The Field Club (commodore, dir. exec. com.). Republican. Roman Catholic. Avocations: boating, woodworking, skiing, tennis, golfing. Admiralty, Corporate, general, Product liability. Office: Nelson Hesse 2070 Ringling Blvd Sarasota FL 34237-7002 E-mail: Falcon71@aol.com.

HERBST, ABBE ILENE, lawyer; b. NYC, June 19, 1955; d. Seymour and Charlotte (Wolper) H. BA summa cum laude, Fordham U., 1976, JD, 1979. Bar: N.Y. 1980, N.J. 1980, U.S. Dist. Ct. (so. dist.) N.Y. 2002, U.S. Supreme Ct. 1986. Law clk. Keenan, Powers & Andrews, N.Y.C., 1978-79, assoc., 1980-83, DeForest & Duer, N.Y.C., 1983-90, ptnr., 1991—2001; shareholder Anderson Kill & Olick, PC, N.Y.C., 2002—. Editor: Fordham Urban Law Jour., 1978—79, AKO Estate Planning & Tax Advisor, 2002—. Recipient Outstanding Presentation award Cmty. Svc. Soc., N.Y.C., 1986. Mem. ABA, N.Y. State Bar Assn., N.J. State Bar Assn., N.Y. County Lawyers Assn., Fin. Women's Assn. N.Y., Riverdale Mental Health Assn.,

Phi Beta Kappa. Avocations: travel, collecting miniature cat figurines. Estate planning, Probate (including wills, trusts), Estate taxation. Office: Anderson Kill & Olick PC 1251 Ave of the Americas New York NY 10020

HERBST, TODD L. lawyer; b. N.Y.C., July 15, 1952; s. Seymour and Charlotte (Wolper) H.; m. Robyn Beth Kellman, June 3, 1979; children: Scott Marshall, Carly Nicole. BA, CUNY, 1974; JD, John Marshall Law Sch., 1977. Bar: NY 1978. Assoc. Max E. Greenberg, Cantor & Reiss, N.Y.C., 1977-83, mng. ptnr., 1984-87; sr. ptnr. Greenberg, Trager & Herbst LLP, N.Y.C., 1988—. Bus. cons. Gottlieb Skanska, Inc., N.Y.C., 1980—, Shimizu Corp., U.S., 1983—, Dillingham Constrn. Holdings, Inc., San Francisco, 1987—2001, Jolly Hotels, Italy, 1993—, NTT Internat. Corp., Japan and U.S., 1996—, Legal Commentary UPN News, N.Y.; lectr. Nat. Assn. Corp. Real Estate Execs. Exec. editor: John Marshall Law Rev. Mem. ABA (A/V rated), Am. Inst. Archs., N.Y. State Bar Assn., Am. Corp. Counsel Assn., N.Y. County Lawyers Assn. Avocations: poetry, automobiles. Commercial, contracts (including sales of goods; commercial financing), Construction, Property, real (including real estate development, water). Home: 7 Brookwood Ln New City NY 10956-2203 Office: Greenberg Trager & Herbst LLP 12th Fl 767 Third Ave New York NY 10017-2023 E-mail: therbst@ghtny.com.

HERCH, FRANK ALAN, law librarian, lawyer; b. Chgo., May 5, 1949; s. Robert Gilbert and Shirley (Berman) H.; m. Ruth Blackwell, Dec. 29, 1971; children: Nathaniel, Rachmiel. BA in Sociology and History, U. Calif., Davis, 1971; MLS, U. Calif., Berkeley, 1972; JD, U. Calif., Davis, 1975. Bar: Calif. 1981, U.S. Dist. Ct. (no. dist.) Calif. 1981. Reference libr. Alameda County Law Libr., Oakland, Calif., 1975-78; asst. law libr. Georgetown U. Law Ctr., Washington, 1978-81; atty. Blackwell, Herch & Herch, Oakland, 1981-87; libr. Cityline Info. Svc. Oakland Pub. Libr., 1984-87; dir. Clark County Law Libr., Las Vegas, Nev., 1987—97; assoc. dir. pub svc. San Diego County Pub. Law Libr., San Diego, 1998—99; project mgr. and law libr. U.S. Dept. Interior Libr., Wash., 2000—02; dep. project mgr. collection bldg. and tech. svs. NASA Goddard Space Flight Ctr. Libr. , Greenbelt, Md., 2002—. Lectr. John F. Kennedy U. Sch. of Law, 1977-78, St. Mary's Coll. Paralegal Program, Moraga, Calif., 1981-87; law libr. and rsch. cons. Nev. Civil Jury Instructions Com. Monterey Coll. of Law, Alameda County Bar Assn., Oakland, 1981-87; lectr. Legal Method and Process criminal justice dept. U. Nevada, Las Vegas, 1997, computer apllications parallel program U. San Diego, 1999, govt. info. sources San Jose State U. M.L.S. program Govt. Info. Sources, 2000. Editor U. Calif. Davis Law Rev., 1974-75, writer, 1973-74; editor Jazz Rag mag., 1975-85, book revs. Legal Pub. Rev., Legal Information Alert, Business Information Alert, 1989—. Steering com. Second Start: Adult Literacy Program, Oakland, 1984-87; mem. exec. bd. East Bay Info. and Referral Network, Berkeley, 1984-87; mem. Clark County Merit Ins. Task Force, 1992. Recipient Cert. of Leadership Nat. U., Oakland, 1987, Leadership award City of Oakland, 1987, Pro Bono Svc. award Nev. State Bar Assn., 1997. Mem. Am. Assn. Law Librs. (cert. 1978, v.p. West Pacific chpt. 1991-92, pres. 1992-93, sec. and treas. state, city and county law librs. spl. interest sect. 1989-92, chmn. regional meeting com., key issues forums, gov.'s conf. on future of librs. 1990, v.p., pres. elect, 1994—, legal info to the pub. special interest sect.), Nev. Libr. Assn. (chmn., bd. rep. so. dist. 1989). Avocations: writing fiction, playing guitar and keyboards, tennis, videotaping jazz performances, acting.

HERDZIK, ARTHUR ALAN, lawyer; b. Buffalo, June 6, 1950; s. Arthur Chester and Lottie Marie (Kowalczyk) H.; m. Jean Marie Rozler, Aug. 3, 1973; children: Julie, Karen, Lisa, Molly. BA magna cum laude, SUNY-Buffalo, 1972, JD, 1975. Bar: N.Y. 1976, U.S. Dist. Ct. (we. dist.) N.Y. 1976. Assoc. Miles, Cochrane, Grosse, Rossetti & Chelus, P.C., Buffalo, 1976-84; mem. Chelus, Herdzik & Speyer, P.C., Buffalo, 1985—. Acting judge Village of Lancaster, N.Y., 1980-82, village prosecutor, 1982-92, village atty., 1988—. Sr. editor Buffalo Law Rev., 1975. Committeeman Erie County Dem. Com., 1978-80, 82—, Lancaster chpt. chmn., 1998-2000, mem. exec. com., 1998-2000. Mem. ABA, N.Y. State Bar Assn., Erie County Bar Assn. (negligence com. 1990-93), Trial Lawyers Assn. Erie County, Am. Bd. Trial Advocates, Lions (pres. 1998-99, treas. 2000--), Phi Beta Kappa Democrat. Federal civil litigation, State civil litigation, General civil litigation. Home: 68 Church St Lancaster NY 14086-2638 Office: Chelus Herdzik Speyer Monte & Pajak PC 1000 Main Court Bldg 438 Main St Buffalo NY 14202-3208

HERGE, J. CURTIS, lawyer; b. Flushing, N.Y., June 14, 1938; s. Henry Curtis and Josephine E. (Breen) H.; m. Joyce Dorean Humbert, Aug. 20, 1960 (div. 1988); children: Cynthia Lynda, Christopher Curtis; m. Shirley Brooks Labonte, Dec. 22, 1989. Student, Cornell U., 1956-58; BA, Rutgers U., 1961, JD, 1963. Bar: N.Y. 1964, U.S. Supreme Ct. 1970, U.S. Ct. Claims 1974, D.C. 1974, Va. 1976. Assoc. Mudge Rose Guthrie & Alexander, N.Y.C., 1963-71; spl. asst. to atty. gen. U.S. Dept. Justice, Washington, 1973; assoc. solicitor conservation and wildlife U.S. Dept. Interior, Washington, 1973-74, asst. to sec. and chief staff, 1974-76; ptnr. Sedam & Herge, McLean, Va., 1976-85, Herge, Sparks & Christopher LLP, McLean, Va., 1985—. Bd. dirs. Diversified Labs., Inc., Ann E.W. Stone & Assocs., Inc., Palmer Tech. Svcs., Inc., Eaton Design Group, Inc., George Washington Banking Corp., Eaton Purchase Mgmt., Inc., George Washington Nat. Bank, Congl. Inst. Inc., Citizens United for Am., Am. Def. Lobby, Coun. Nat. Def., Renascence Found., The Am. Lobby Econ. Recovery Taskforce, Nat. Bank No. Va., Am. Freedom Found., Creative Response Concepts Inc., Congl. Inst., Inc.; spkr. in field. Adv. bd. Washington Legal Found., Nat. Taxpayers Legal Fund; Va. Commonwealth escheator Loudoun County and City of Fairfax, 1979-83; co-dir. spokesmen resources Com. for Re-election of Pres., 1971-72; mem. No. Va. Estate Planning Council; mem. natural resources coun. Rep. Nat. Com.; mem. Fairfax County Rep. Com., Conservative Rep. Com.; mem. Office Pres.-Elect Fed. Election Commn. Transition Team, 1980; co-chmn. N.Y. Honor Am. Day, 1970; expert witness, charitable fund-raising, U.S. Tax Ct. Sebastian Gaeta scholar Rutgers U., 1963. Mem. ABA, N.Y. State Bar Assn., Va. Bar Assn., D.C. Bar Assn., Capital Hill Club, Phi Kappa Sigma. Clubs: Capitol Hill. Administrative and regulatory, Non-profit and tax-exempt organizations, Probate (including wills, trusts). Home: 35 Rutherford Cir Potomac Falls VA 20165-6221 Office: Herge Sparks & Christopher LLP 6862 Elm St Ste 360 Mc Lean VA 22101-3867

HERLONG, HENRY MICHAEL, JR., federal judge; b. Washington, June 1, 1944; s. Henry Michael Sr. and Josie Payne (Blocker) H.; m. Frances Elizabeth Thompson, Dec. 30, 1983; children: Faris Elizabeth, Henry Michael III. BA, Clemson U., 1967; JD, U. S.C., 1970. Bar: S.C. 1970, U.S. Ct. Appeals (4th cir.) 1972, U.S. Dist. Ct. S.C. 1972. Legis. asst. U.S. Senator Strom Thurmond, Washington, 1970-72; asst. U.S. atty. Dept. Justice, Greenville, S.C., 1972-76, Columbia, S.C., 1983-86; U.S. Magistrate judge U.S. Dist. Ct., Columbia, S.C., 1986-91, U.S. Dist. judge Greenville, S.C., 1991—; prin. Coleman & Herlong, Edgefield, S.C., 1976-83. Dir. Edgefield (S.C.) Devel. Bd., 1978-83, S.C. Assn. of Counties, 1980-83; active S.C. Rural Devel. Bd., 1980-83, Edgefield County Coun., 1979-83. Capt. USAR, 1970-75. Mem. S.C. Bar, Edgefield County Bar, Lions Club, Sertoma Club. Republican. United Methodist. Avocations: hunting, fishing, gardening. Office: US Dist Courts PO Box 10469 300 E Washington St Greenville SC 29603-1000

HERMAN, FRED L. lawyer; b. New Orleans, Mar. 25, 1950; s. Harry and Reba (Hoffman) H.; m. Amanda Luria, Mar. 4, 1975. BA, Tulane U., 1972; JD, Loyola U.-New Orleans, 1975. Bar: La. 1975, U.S. Dist Ct. (ea. dist.) La. 1975, U.S. Ct. Appeals (5th cir.) 1978, U.S. Dist. Ct. (we. and mid. dists.) La. 1981, U.S. Ct. Appeals (11th cir.) 1981. Assoc. Herman & Herman, New Orleans, 1975-80; ptnr. Herman, Herman, Katz & Cotlar, New Orleans, 1980-87; pvt. practice New Orleans, 1987—. Ltd. ptnr. New Orleans Saints, 1985, legis. counsel, chief negotiator for mng. ptnr., 1987; adj. faculty Tulane U.; lectr. Loyola Sch. Law, New Orleans, La.; spl. minister Civil Dist. Ct. Parish of Orleans. Trial Lawyers Assn. Commr. New Orleans Pub. Belt R.R. Commn., 1983-93; mem. Jefferson Parish Child Abuse Advocacy Program, 1980-81; spl. counsel litigation, State of La.; spl. counsel City of New Orleans; judge pro tem., First City Ct., New Orleans, 1998; mem. adv. coun. Adult Rehab. Ctr. Salvation Army, 1991—. Mem. ATLA, Am. Arbitration Assn. (mediator, arbitrator), Nat. Health Lawyer Assn. (panel of mediators and arbitrators), La. Bankers' Assn. (bank counsel sect.), La. State Bar Assn. General civil litigation, General practice, Personal injury (including property damage). Office: 1010 Common St Ste 3000 New Orleans LA 70112-2421

HERMAN, JAMES EDWARD, lawyer; b. Kansas City, July 14, 1945; s. Everton Paul and Virginia May (Hutchinson); m. Denise deBellefeuille. H. B.A., U. Calif.-Santa Barbara, 1971; J.D., Calif. Western Law Sch., San Diego, 1975; LL.M., NYU, 1976. Bar: Calif. 1976. Sr. fellow Criminal Law Edn. and Research Center, NYU, 1975-76; atty. Pub. Defender's Office, Riverside County, Calif., 1976-80, Defenders Inc., San Diego, 1979-80, Santa Barbara County Public Defenders Office, 1980-84; assoc. Cappello and Foley, Santa Barbara, 1984—, ptnr. Reicker, Prau, Pyle, McRoy & Herman LLP, Santa Barbara, Calif.; lectr. voir dire and dramatic arts techniques applied to trials to various profl. orgns. Bd. dirs. Ensemble Theatre Project. Robert Marshall fellow, 1975-76. Mem. Assn. Trial Lawyers Am., Calif. Attys. for Criminal Justice, Calif. State Bar Assn. (2002-03). Federal civil litigation, State civil litigation, Criminal. Home: 215 E Mission St Santa Barbara CA 93101-1044 Office: Reicker Pfau Pyle McRoy & Herman LLP 1421 State St Ste B PO Box 1470 Santa Barbara CA 93102-1470*

HERMAN, KENNETH BEAUMONT, lawyer; b. Medford, Mass., Jan. 23, 1944; s. Beaumont Alexander and Winifred (Small) H.; m. Agnes Anne Burch, Sept. 18, 1976; children: Alexander Beaumont, Juliana Burch. AB, Harvard U., 1966; JD, Harvard Law Sch., 1969. Bar: N.Y. 1971. Tchr. St. Dominic Savio High Sch., East Boston, Mass., 1969-70; assoc., then ptnr. Fish & Neave, N.Y.C., 1970—. Mem. Larchmont (N.Y.) Recreation Com., 1983-94, trustee Larchmont Hist. Soc., 1987-88. Mem. ABA, N.Y. State Bar Assn., N.Y. Intellectual Property Law Assn. (chmn. com. on incentives for innovation 1987-88), Licensing Execs. Soc., Internat. Trade Commn. Trial Lawyers Assn., Fed. Cir. Bar Assn., Am. Intellectual Property Law Assn., Assn. Bar of City of N.Y., Am. Arbitration Assn. (panel arbitrators). Avocations: sailing, skiing, kayaking, reading. General civil litigation, Patent, Trademark and copyright. Home: 810 Pirates Cv Mamaroneck NY 10543-4717 Office: Fish & Neave 1251 Sixth Ave Avenue of the Americas New York NY 10020-1105

HERMAN, RICHARD BRUCE, lawyer; b. White Plains, N.Y., 1957; children: Sabrina Lynn, Jordyn Bari, Noah Ross BA, Lehigh U., 1979; JD, Temple U., 1982; student, Yale U., 1993. Bar: N.Y. 1984, Pa. 1989, D.C. 1989, U.S. Ct. Appeals (2d cir.) 1984, U.S. Supreme Ct. 1987. Pvt. practice, N.Y.C. and White Plains, 1984—. Arbitrator Civil Ct., N.Y.C., 1991-92, N.Y. Supreme Ct., Westchester, White Plains, 1987-92. Recipient Pro Bono Svc. award N.Y. County Lawyers Assn., N.Y.C., 1992. Mem. ABA, N.Y. State Bar Assn., N.Y. State Trial Lawyers Assn., Am. Judges Assn., Westchester County Bar Assn. Avocations: football, baseball, golf. General civil litigation, General practice.

HERMAN, ROBERT STEPHEN, lawyer; b. Pitts., Aug. 1, 1954; s. Earl and Lena Herman; children: Kelsey, Brian, Kaley. Student, Tulane U., 1972-74; BA, U. Fla., 1976; JD, Loyola U., 1981. Bar: La. 1982, Tex. 1984, Mo. 1987. Assoc. Newman Drolla, New Orleans, 1982-84, Howard Abramson, Dallas, 1984-86, McDowell Rice, Kansas City, Mo., 1987-92; of counsel Kurlbaum Stoll, Kansas City, 1992-98; atty. Norris Keplinger & Herman LLC, Overland Park, Kans., 1998—2002; shareholder King Hershey, P.C., Kansas City, Mo., 2003—. Approved agt. The Bar Plan Title Ins. Co., Kansas City, 1997—; spkr. Paine Webber Fin. Planning Seminars, Overland Park, Kans., 1998—; spkr. in field. Coach Blue Valley Soccer Club, Overland Park, 1993-98; scout leader Boy Scouts Am., Leawood, Kans., 1998. Mem. ABA, Nat. Network Estate and Fin. Planning Attys., The Midwest Estate Planning Inst., Kansas City Metro. Bar Assn. Avocations: tennis, golf, scuba, travel. Commercial, contracts (including sales of goods; commercial financing), Estate planning, Property, real (including real estate development, water). Office: King Hershey PC 2345 Grand Blvd Ste 2100 Kansas City MO 64108

HERMAN, RUSS MICHEL, lawyer; b. New Orleans, Apr. 26, 1942; s. Harry and Reba Nell (Hoffman) Herman; m. Barbara Ann Kline, July 5, 1965; children: Stephen Jay, Penny Lynn, Elizabeth Rose. BA, Tulane U., 1963; LLB, Tulane U., 1966. Bar: La. 1966, U.S. Dist. Ct. La. 1966, U.S. Ct. Appeals (5th cir. and 11th cir) 1970, U.S. Supreme Ct. 1972, diplomate: Am. Bd. Profl. Liability Attys., Nat. Coll. Advocacy. Law clk. La. Ct. Appeals, 4th Cir., New Orleans, 1965—66; with Herman, Hermann, Katz & Cotlar (formerly Herman & Herman), New Orleans, 1966—, ptnr., sr. ptnr.; ptnr. Herman Mathis Casey Kitchens and Gerel. Lectr. in field; faculty Practicing Law Inst., Nat. Coll. Trial Advocacy; lectr. Tulane U., La. State U., Loyola U., New Orleans, Georgetown U.; guest TV programs including Good Morning Am., Today Show, CNN Newsline, others; mem. ethics panel U.ist. Ct., Ea. Dist. of La. Contbr. ; contbg. editor: Expert Witness Reporter, Trial Diplomacy Jour.; author (performer): (video) Trial Practice series, Courtroom Persuasion: Art, Drama and Science; author: Louisiana Personal Injury, 2 vols.; contbr. Pres. Civil Justice Found., 1987—88, Roscoe Pound Found., 1991—93; adv. coun. Nat. Jud. Coll. With USAF. Named one of Louisiana's Top Ten Litigators, Nat. Law Jour. Fellow: Internat. . Barristers, Internat. Acad. Trial Lawyers (dir.); mem.: ATLA (pres. 1989—90, chair r.r. hwy. crossing accident litigation group, co-chair Rezulin litigation group, Lifetime Achievement award 1999, Leonard M. hampion of Justice award 2001, Joe Tonahill award 1998), Am. Coll. Barristers (barrister), La. Trial Lawyers Assn. (pres. 1980—81, Outstanding Trial Lawyer 1977). Federal civil litigation, State civil litigation, Personal injury (including property damage). Home: 5346 Chestnut St New Orleans LA 70115-3053 Office: Herman Herman Katz & Cotlar 820 Okeefe Ave New Orleans LA 70113-1116

HERMAN, STEPHEN CHARLES, lawyer; b. Johnson City, N.Y., Apr. 28, 1951; s. William Herman and Myrtle Stella (Clark) Keithline; m. Jeanne Ellen Nelson, Sept. 9, 1972; children: Neelie Kristine, Stefanie Anne, Christopher William. Student, Cedarville Coll., 1969-72; BA, Wright State U., 1973; JD, Ohio No. U., 1976. Bar: Mo. 1977, Ill. 1977; U.S. Dist. Ct. (ea. dist.) Mo. 1978, U.S. Dist. Ct. (no. dist.) Ill. 1979, U.S. Dist. Ct. (ea. dist) Mich. 1988, U.S. Dist. Ct. (so. dist.) Tex. 1997; U.S. Ct. Appeals (D.C. cir.) 1979, U.S. Ct. Appeals (7th cir.) 1979, U.S. Ct. Appeals (5th cir.) 1980, U.S. Ct. Appeals (10th cir.) 1992; U.S. Supreme Ct. 1986, U.S. Ct. Internat. Trade, 1998. Atty. Mo. Pacific Railroad Co., St. Louis, 1977-78; assoc. Belnap, McCarthy, Spencer, Sweeney & Harkaway, Chgo., 1978-82; ptnr. Belnap, Spencer & McFarland, Chgo., 1982-83, Belnap, Spencer, McFarland & Emrich, Chgo., 1983-84, Belnap, Spencer, McFarland, Emrich & Herman, Chgo., 1984-89, Belnap, Spencer, McFarland, Herman, 1990-96, McFarland & Herman, 1996-01; atty. Stephen C. Herman, P.C., Chgo., 2001—. Mem. ABA, Mo. Bar Assn., Met. Bar Assn. St. Louis, Ill. State Bar Assn., Chgo. Bar Assn., Assn. Transp. Law, Logistics and Policy, Tower Club, Univ. Club (Chgo.). General civil litigation, Transportation, General practice. Home: 795 N McKinley Rd Lake Forest IL 60045-1836 Office: 20 N Wacker Dr Ste 1828 Chicago IL 60606-2905 E-mail: schrmn@aol.com.

HERMAN-GIDDENS, GREGORY, lawyer; b. Birmingham, Ala., Aug. 8, 1961; BA, U. N.C., 1984; JD, Tulane U., 1988; LLM in Estate Planning, U. Miami, 1993. Bar: N.C. 1988, U.S. Dist. Ct. (mid. dist.) N.C. 1988, Fla. 1992, U.S. Tax Ct. 2001, U.S. Supreme Ct. 1998, U.S. Tax Ct. 2001; cert. specialist in estate planning and probate law, N.C. State Bar Bd. Legal Specialization; grad. leadership triangle program 1996. Assoc. N. Joanne Foil, Atty. at Law, Durham, N.C., 1988-92, Catalano, Fisher, Gregory & Crown, Chartered, Naples, Fla., 1993, Northen, Blue, Rooks, Thibaut, Anderson & Woods, L.L.P., Chapel Hill, N.C., 1994-96; pvt. practice Chapel Hill, 1996—. Profl. adv. com. Triangle Cmty. Found., 1999—. Mem. Chapel Hill Bd. Adjustment, 1989—92; bd. dirs. Friends of Chapel Hill Sr.Ctr., 1994—97; mem. Orange County Adv. Bd. on Aging, 1994—97, vice chair, 1996—97; treas., bd. dirs. Orange County Literacy Coun., Carrboro, NC, 1994—98. Mem.: Durham/Orange Estate Planning Coun., Nat. Acad. Elder Law Attys., N.C. Bar Assn. (career devel. com. young lawyers divsn. 1990—91, law and aging com. young lawyers divsn. 1994—98, dir. young lawyers divsn. 1997—98, endowment com. 1997—, elder law sect. coun. 1998—2001, newsletter editor 2001—), ABA (probate and trust sect. 1996—, coms. on stds. of tax practice and tax practice mgmt. of tax sect., coms. on lifetime and testamentary charitable gift planning, com. on planning for execs. and profls. of real property), Psi Chi, Phi Beta Kappa. Estate planning, Probate (including wills, trusts), Estate taxation. Office: 1829 E Franklin St Ste 700D Chapel Hill NC 27514-5867 E-mail: ghgiddens@trust-specialist.com.

HERMANIES, JOHN HANS, retired lawyer; b. Aug. 19, 1922; s. John and Lucia (Eckstein) H.; m. Dorothy Jean Steinbrecher, Jan. 3, 1953 AB, Pa. State U., 1944; JD, U. Cin., 1948, D of Law (hon.), 1992. Bar: Ohio 1948. Atty. Indsl. Commn. Ohio, 1948-50; asst. atty. gen. State of Ohio, 1951-57, asst. to gov., 1957-59; ptnr. Hermanies & Major (formerly Beall, Hermanies, Bortz & Major), Cin., 1958-99; mem. bd. grievances and discipline Supreme Ct. Ohio, 1976-82; ret., 1999. Mem. Ohio Bd. Bar Examiners, 1963-68. Mem. Southwest Ohio Regional Transit Authority, 1973-76; trustee U. Cin, 1977-92, Found. Bd., 1992-99, trustee emeritus, 1999—; mem. bd. elections Hamilton County, Ohio, 1984-88; chmn. exec. com. Hamilton County Rep. Party, 1974-88. With USMC, WWII. Mem. ABA, Ohio Bar Assn., Cin. Bar Assn., Queen City Club, Highland Country Club, Hyde Park Golf and Country Club. Labor (including EEOC, Fair Labor Standards Act, labor-management relations, NLRB, OSHA), Workers' compensation. Home: 1201 Edgecliff Pl Cincinnati OH 45206-2847

HERMANN, DONALD HAROLD JAMES, lawyer, educator; b. Southgate, Ky., Apr. 6, 1943; s. Albert Joseph and Helen Marie (Snow) H. AB (George E. Gamble Honors scholar), Stanford U., 1965; JD, Columbia U., 1968; LLM, Harvard U., 1974; MA, Northwestern U., 1979, PhD, 1981; MA in Art History, Sch. Art Inst. Chgo., 1993; MLA, U. Chgo., 2001. Bar: Ariz. 1968, Wash. 1969, Ky. 1971, Ill. 1972, U.S. Supreme Ct. 1974. Mem. staff, directorate devel. plans U.S. Dept. Def., 1964-65; With Legis. Drafting Research Fund, Columbia U., 1966-68; asst. dean Columbia Coll., 1967-68; mem. faculty U. Wash., Seattle, 1968-71, U. Ky., Lexington, 1971-72, DePaul U., 1972—, prof. law and philosophy, 1978—, dir. acad. programs and interdisciplinary study, 1975-76, assoc. dean, 1975-78, dir. Health Law Inst., 1985—2000; lectr. dept. philosophy Northwestern U., 1979-81; counsel DeWolfe, Poynton & Stevens, 1984-89. Vis. prof. Washington U., St. Louis, 1974, U. Brazilia, 1976, U. P.R. Sch. Law, 1993; lectr. law Am. Soc. Found., 1975-78, Sch. Edn. Northwestern U., 1974-76, Christ Coll. Cambridge (Eng.) U., 1977, U. Athens, 1980; vis. scholar U. N.D., 1983; mem. NEH seminar on property and rights Stanford U., 1981; participant law and econs. program U. Rochester, 1974; mem. faculty summer seminar in law and humanities UCLA, 1978; Bicentennial Fellow of U.S. Constitution Claremont Coll., 1986; Law and Medicine fellow Cleve. Clinic., 1990; bd. dirs. Coun. Legal Edn. Opportunity, Ohio Valley Consortium, 1972, Ill. Bar Automated Rsch. Corp., 1975-81, Criminal Law Consortium Cook County, Ill., 1977-80; cons. Adminstrv. Office Ill. Cts., 1975-90; reporter cons. Ill. Jud. Conf., 1972-90; mem. Ctr. for Law Focused Edn., Chgo., 1977-81; faculty Instituto Superiore Internazionale Di Science Criminali, Siracusa, Italy, 1978-82; cons. Commerce Fedn., State of São Paulo, Brazil, 1975; residential scholar Christ Ch., Oxford, 1999. Editor: Jour. of Health and Hosp. Law, 1986-96, DePaul Jour. Healthcare Law, 1996—, AIDS Monograph Series, 1987—. Mem. Cook County States Atty. Task Force on Gay and Lesbian Issues, 1990—, Contemporary Arts Coun. Chgo., 1999—; bd. dirs. Ctr. Ch.-State Studies, 1982—, Horizons Cmty. Svcs., 1985—88, Chgo. Area AIDS Task Force, 1987—90, Howard Brown Health Ctr., 1994—; v.p. Inst. Genetics, Law and Ethics, Ill. Masonic Hosp., 1993—2000; trustee 860 N. Lakeshore Trust, Chgo., 1993—95; bd. visitors Oriental Inst. U. Chgo., 1995—; co-chair parity and inclusion com. Ill. HIV Prevention Cmty. Group Ill. Dept. Pub. Health; dir. Inst. Genetics, Law and Ethics, Ill. Masonic Hosp., 1993—2000; bd. dirs. Gerber-Hart Libr. and Archives, Mostly Music of Chgo., 1998—2001; mem. scholars' group ethics and med. rsch. NIH/U. Ill. Med. Sch. John Noble fellow Columbia U., 1968, Internat. fellow, NEH fellow, Law and Humanities fellow U. Chgo, 1975-76, Law and Humanities fellow Harvard U., 1973-74, Northwestern U., 1978-82, Criticism and Theory fellow Stanford U. 1981, NEH fellow Cornell U., 1982, Judicial fellow U.S. Supreme Ct., 1983-84, U. Ill. fellow med. ethids rsch. group; Dean's scholar Columbia U., 1968, Univ. scholar Northwestern U., 1979. Mem.: ABA, Am. Inn of Ct. (Abraham Lincolm Marowitz chpt.), Chgo. Coun. Fgn. Rels., Ill. Assn. Hosp. Attys., Am. Acad. Healthcare Attys., Am. Assn. Law Schs. (del., sect. chmn., chmn. sect. on jurisprudence), Soc. Am. Law Tchrs., Internat. Penal Law Soc., Soc. Writers on Legal Subjects, Soc. Phenomenology and Existential Philosophy, Soc. Bus. Ethics, Am. Philos. Assn., Am. Judicature Soc., Nat. Health Lawyers Assn., Internat. Assn. Philosophy of Law and Soc., Am. Soc. Polit. and Legal Philosophy, Am. Soc. Law, Medicine and Ethics, Am. Law Inst., Am. Acad. Polit. and Social Sic., Chgo. Bar Assn., Ill. Bar Assn., Soc. Contemporary Art Art Inst. Chgo., Evanston Hist. Soc., Northwestern U. Alumni Assn., Chgo. Literary Soc., Quadrangle Players, Renaissance Soc. (bd. dirs. 1995—), Lawyers Club Chgo., Arts Club Chgo., Cliff Dwellers Club, Tavern Club, Quadrangle Club, University Club, Hasty Pudding Club, Signet Club Harvard. Episcopalian.

HERMANN, PHILIP J. lawyer; b. Cleve., Sept. 17, 1916; s. Isadore and Gazella (Gross) H.; m. Cecilia Alexander, Dec. 28, 1945; children: Gary, Ann. Student, Hiram Coll., 1935-37; BA, Ohio State U., 1939; JD, Western Res. U., 1942. Bar: Ohio 1942. With Hermann Cahn & Schneider and predecessors, Cleve., 1946-86. Founder, former chmn. bd. Jury Verdict Rsch., Cleve.; pres. Legal Info. Pubs. Author: 1956, Better Settlements Through Leverage, 1965, Do You Need a Lawyer?, 1980, Better, Earlier Settlements through Economic Leverage, 1989, Injured? How to Get All the Money You Deserve, 1990, The 96 Billion Dollar Game: You are Losing, 1993, How to Select Competent Cost-effective Legal Counsel, 1993, Profit With the Right Lawyer, I Was Raised by a St. Bernard, 2003; contbr. articles to profl. jours. Served to lt. comdr. USNR, 1942-46, PTO. Mem. ABA (past vice chmn. casualty law com., past chmn. use of modern tech. com.), Ohio Bar Assn. (past chmn. ins. com., past chmn. fed. ct. com., past mem. ho. of dels.), Cleve. Bar Assn. (past chmn. membership com.), Am. Law Firm Assn. (past chmn. bd.), Fedn. Ins. Counsel. Clubs: Walden Golf and Tennis. Insurance, Personal injury (including property damage), Product liability. Home: Hunters Run Golf & Tennis Club 34F Southport Ln Boynton Beach FL 33436-6429

HERNANDEZ, ANTONIA, lawyer; b. Torreon, Coahuila, Mexico, May 30, 1948; came to U.S., 1956; d. Manuel and Nicolasa (Martinez) H.; m. Michael Stern, Oct. 8, 1977; children: Benjamin, Marisa, Michael. BA, UCLA, 1971, JD, 1974. Bar: Calif. 1974, D.C. 1979. Staff atty. Los Angeles Ctr. Law and Justice, 1974-77; directing atty. Legal Aid Found., Lincoln Heights, Calif., 1977-78; staff counsel U.S. Senate Com. on the Judiciary, Washington, 1979-80; assoc. counsel Mexican Am. Legal Def. Ednl. Fund, Washington, 1981-83, employment program dir., 1983-84, exec. v.p., dep. gen. counsel Los Angeles, 1984-85, pres., gen. counsel, 1985—. Bd. dirs. Golden West Financial Corp., Automobile Club of So. Calif., Am. Charities.

Contbr. articles to profl. jours. Active Inter-Am. Dialogue Aspen Inst., Nat. Com. Innovations in State and Local Govt., Nat. Endowment for Democracy, Pres.'s Commn. White House Fellowships. AAUW fellow, 1973-74. Mem. ABA, State Bar Calif., Washington D.C. Bar Assn., Mexican-Am. Roman Catholic. Avocations: gardening, outdoor sports. Office: Mexican Am Legal Def Ednl Fund 634 S Spring 11th Fl Los Angeles CA 90014-3921

HERNANDEZ, DAVID N(ICHOLAS), lawyer; b. Albuquerque, Nov. 5, 1954; s. B.C. and Evangeline (C De Baca) H.; m. Alice A. McLish, June 7, 1975. BA, U. N.Mex., 1975, MBA, 1978, JD, 1979. Bar: N.Mex. 1979, U.S. Dist. Ct. N.Mex. 1979. Law clk. to presiding justice N.Mex. Supreme Ct., Santa Fe, 1979-80; assoc. Knight, Custer & Duncan, Albuquerque, 1980-82; sole practice David N. Hernandez & Assoc., Albuquerque, 1982—; of counsel Western Glass & Panels, Albuquerque. Mem. com. rules appellate ct. procedure N.Mex. Supreme Ct., 1984—; bd. dirs. Delta Dental N.Mex., Albuquerque. Mem. Environ. Planning Commn., Albuquerque, 1984-86, PHS assocs. Presbyn. Healthcare Found., 1985—. Named one of Outstanding Young Men Am., 1980. Mem. ABA, N.Mex. Bar Assn. (pres. 2000-01), Albuquerque Bar Assn., Am. Judicatur Soc., Greater Albuquerque C. of C. (bd. dirs. 1982-86, polit. action com. 1983-85). Avocations: tennis, golf, reading, fishing, politics. Commercial, contracts (including sales of goods; commercial financing), Probate (including wills, trusts), Property, real (including real estate development, water).*

HERNANDEZ, FERNANDO VARGAS, lawyer; b. Irapuato, Mex., Sept. 8, 1939; came to U.S., 1942, naturalized, 1957; s. José Espinosa and Ana Maria (Vargas) H.; m. Bonnie Corrie, Jan. 8, 1966 (div. Feb. 1991); children: Michael David, Alexandra Rae, Marcel Paul. BS, U. Santa Clara, 1961; MBA, 1962; JD, U. Calif., Berkeley, 1966. Bar: Calif. 1967, U.S. Dist. Ct. (no. dist.) Calif. 1967. Sole practice law, San Jose, Calif., 1967—. Lectr. law Lincoln U.; lectr. bus. U. Santa Clara. Mem. San Jose Housing Bd., 1970-73; arbitrator Santa Clara County Superior Cts., 1979-2002, judge pro tem, 1979—. Contbg. editor to legal pleadings books. Mem. San Jose Civic Light Opera, 1981-83; founder Greater San Jose Hispanic C. of C.; bd. dirs. Tapestry in Talent, 2001—. Served with AUS, 1962-63. Mem. Calif. State Bar Assn., Santa Clara County Bar Assn. (chmn. torts sect. 1977-78, features editor In Brief mag. 1990-93), Calif. Trial Lawyers Assn. (bd. govs. 1979-82), Santa Clara County Trial Lawyers Assn., La Raza Lawyers Assn., Tapestry in Talent (bd. dirs. 2000—), Greater San Jose Hispanic C. of C. (founder, corp. counsel, bd. dirs. 2003—), Silicon Valley Capital Club, Silicon Valley Capital Club. Democrat. Roman Catholic. General civil litigation, Intellectual property, Personal injury (including property damage). Office: 46 S 1st St San Jose CA 95113-2406 E-mail: fvhlaw@pacbell.net.

HERNANDEZ, H(ERMES) MANUEL, lawyer; b. Bronx, N.Y., Mar. 16, 1955; s. Manuel and Aurora O'Neill H.; m. Hortensia Beatriz Carrasquillo, Aug. 28, 1980; children: Antonio, Victoria, Stephanie. BS in Criminal Justice magna cum laude, Met. State Coll. of Denver, 1976; JD, U. Denver, Denver, 1979. Bar: Colo. 1979, N.Y. 1986, D.C. 1986, Fla. 1988; cert. trial adv Nat. Bd. Trial Advocacy; cert. criminal trial specialist and criminal appellate specialist Fla. Bar 1993. Trial atty. criminal div. U.S. Dept. Justice, Washington, 1979-80; asst. U.S. atty. criminal and civil div. U.S. Dept. Justice (Colo., Puerto Rico, Fla. mid. dist.), 1980-89; pvt. practice Orlando, Fla., 1989—. Chmn. civilian rev. bd. Seminole County Sheriff's Office, Orlando, 1992-93. Mem. Nat. Criminal Def. Lawyers Assn., Fla. Fed. Bar Assn. (Orlando chpt., v.p. 1988-89, pres. 1989-90, 90-91, 1999-2001, nat. del. 1991, 92, 93, 2001), Fla. Bar, Fla. Assn.(chair criminal law sect., 2002-2003) Criminal Def. Lawyers, Hispanic Bar Assn. (charter mem. Orlando chpt.), Ctrl. Fla. Criminal Trial Lawyers Assn.. Republican. Roman Catholic. Avocations: music, history. Appellate, Federal civil litigation, Criminal. Office: PO Box 916692 Longwood FL 32791

HERNANDEZ, JUAN IGNACIO, lawyer; b. Torreon, Mex., May 13, 1954; s. Pascual Hernandez and Juana Guerra; m. Carolina Zambrano; children: Carolina, Ana Gabriela, Elizabeth. M. of Comparative Law, Escuela Libre de Derecho, Mex. City. Mem. Assn. Nacional Abogados de Empreza, Barra de Abogadis, Anade Seccion Comarca Lagunera (pres. 1996-98). Avocations: tennis, fishing. General civil litigation, Commercial, consumer (including collections, credit), Corporate, general. Office: Corp Juridico Ocampo 601 Oriente Coahuila CP 27000 Mexico Fax: (1) 7-17-75-44. E-mail: lic_hernandezguerra@hotmail.com.

HERNANDEZ, MACK RAY, lawyer; b. Austin, Tex., Sept. 8, 1944; s. Mack and Mary (Prado) Hernandez; 1 child, John Christopher; m. Jayne Webb Barrett, Aug. 2, 2001. BA, U. Tex., 1967, JD, 1970. Bar: Tex. 1970, U.S. Dist. Ct. (we. dist.) Tex. 1972. Staff atty. Travis County Legal Aid Soc, Austin, 1970-71; pvt. practice Austin, 1971—. Bd. dirs. Austin C. of C., 1983-86, Meals on Wheels, Austin, 1972-76; trustee Austin C.C., 1988—; vice-chair, 1990-92, chair, 1992-94; chmn. bd. dirs. Am. Cancer Soc., Austin, 1988-95; trustee Austin Mus. Art, 2000—. Mem. Tex. Bar Assn., Travis County Bar Assn., Coll. of State Bar, Tex. Bar Found. Avocations: travel, jogging, hiking, backpacking. State civil litigation, Commercial, contracts (including sales of goods; commercial financing), Probate (including wills, trusts). Office: 524 N Lamar Blvd Ste 202 Austin TX 78703-5422 E-mail: mrhernandez@hernandezlaw.com.

HERNANDEZ-DENTON, FEDERICO, supreme court justice; b. Santurce, P.R., Apr. 12, 1944; s. Federico and Teresa (Denton) Hernandez-Morales; m. Isabel Pico, 1966. BA, Harvard U., 1966, JD, 1969. Bar: P.R. 1971. Dir. Consumer Rsch. Ctr. and Bus. Adminstrn. Rsch. Ctr. U. P.R., 1970-72; dir. P.R. Consumer Svc. Adminstrn., 1973; sec. P.R. Dept. Consumer Affairs, 1973-76; asst. prof. Law Sch. Interam. U., P.R., 1977-84, dean, 1984-85; now justice Supreme Ct. P.R, San Juan. Chair Bd. Bar Examiners. Mem. ABA, Am. Law Inst., P.R. Bar Assn. Office: Supreme Ct of PR PO Box 9022392 San Juan PR 00902-2392

HERNDON, ROBERT D. judge; b. Mesa, Ariz., June 17, 1944; s. Robert William and Dora Elizabeth Herndon; m. Linda K. Herndon, Aug. 24, 1968; children: Melissa, Michelle, Michael. BS in Law, U. Oreg., 1966, JD, 1968. Bar: Oreg. 1968, U.S. Dist. Ct. Oreg. 1969. Ptnr. Ringle & Henderson, P.C., Gladstone, Oreg., 1968—86, Hutchison, Hammond, et. al., West Linn, Oreg., 1986—97; cir. ct. judge Clackamas County State of Oreg., Oregon City, 1997—. Pres. Willamette Falls Hosp. Found., Oreg., 1999—. Office: Clackamas County Courthouse 807 Main St Rm 304 Oregon City OR 97045 Office Fax: 503-655-8280.

HEROLD, KARL GUENTER, lawyer; b. Munich, Feb. 3, 1947; came to U.S., 1963; s. Guenter K.B. and Eleonore E.E. H.; children: Deanna, Donna, Nicole, Jessica, Christine, Karl-Matthäus. BS, Bowling Green State U., 1969; JD, Case Western Res. U., 1972. Bar: Ohio 1972, N.Y. 1985; avocat, France, 1992; mem. Anwaltskamer, Frankfurt, Germany. Ptnr.-in-charge, European bus. practice coord. Jones Day, Frankfurt, Germany, 1972—; coord. bus. practice Europe and Ctrl. and Ea. Europe Jones, Day. Trustee Internat. and Comparative Law Ctr. Southwest Legal Found., Dallas, 1983; bd. dirs. Didier Taylor Refractories Corp., Cin., Redland Corp., San Antonio, v.p., Redland Credit Corp., San Antonio, v.p., Redland Fin. Inc., San Antonio, v.p., 1979-86, Zircoa Inc., Solon, Ohio, 1988-92. Contbr. numerous articles to legal jours. Trustee Cleve. Internat. Program, 1982-88; chmn. bd. dirs. Frankfurt Internat. Sch., 1991-93; Am. councilor Germany-Am. adv. com., 1995-, Atlantik Bricke, Berlin, 1992-. Mem. ABA, Internat. Bar Assn., Order of Coif, Omicron Delta Kappa. Corporate, general, Private international. Office: Jones Day 222 E 41st St New York NY 10017 also: Jones Day Hochhaus am Park Grueneburg Weg 60323 Frankfurt Germany E-mail: KGHerold@JonesDay.com.

HERON, JULIAN BRISCOE, JR., lawyer; b. Washington, Dec. 17, 1939; s. Julian B. Sr. and Doris S. (Strange) H.; m. Kathleen Ann Sweeney, Aug. 13, 1983; children: Kimberle, Melissa, Julian III, Kevin, Kathleen. BS, U. Ky., 1962, LLB, 1965. Bar: Ky. 1965, D.C. 1966, U.S. Dist. Ct. D.C. 1966, Md. 1968, U.S. Ct. Appeals (D.C. cir.) 1968, U.S. Supreme Ct. 1968. Ptnr. Pope, Ballard & Loos, Washington, 1968-81, Heron, Burchette, Ruckert & Rothwell, Washington, 1981-90, Tuttle, Taylor & Heron, Washington, 1990—. Chmn. U.S. Agrl. Export Devel. Coun., 1983-85. Pres. Washington Internat. Horse Show, 1984, 85, Nat. Horse Show, 1994-96; mem. Dominican 3d Order Preachers. Capt. USAF, 1965-68. Fellow: ABA (chmn. agr. com. of adminstrv. law sect.); mem.: Bar Assn. D.C., Md. Bar Assn., Ky. Bar Assn., D.C. Bar Assn. (chmn. ethics com.), Va. Angus Assn. (bd. dirs., treas. 2000—), Barristers, Legatus, Knight of the Equestrian Order of the Holy Sepulchre of Jerusalem Legatus, KC, The Golf Club Va. Republican. Roman Catholic. Administrative and regulatory, Private international, Legislative. Office: Tuttle Taylor & Heron Ste 502 1025 Thomas Jefferson St NW Washington DC 20007-5201

HERPE, DAVID A. lawyer; b. Chgo., May 2, 1953; s. Richard S. and Beverly H.; m. Tina Demsetz, Aug. 21, 1977; children: Lauren E., Stacy P. BA in Econs., U. Ill., 1975; JD, U. Chgo., 1978. Bar: Ill. 1978, U.S. Dist. Ct. (no. dist.) Ill. 1979, U.S. Tax Ct. 1991. Assoc. then ptnr. Schiff, Hardin & Waite, Chgo., 1978-1996; ptnr. McDermott, Will & Emery, Chgo., 1996—. Co-author: Illinois Estate Planning, Will Drafting and Estate Administration Forms-Practice, 2nd edit., 1994; contbr. articles to legal jours. Mem. and dir. Chgo. Estate Planning Coun. (pres. 2000-01). Fellow Am. Coll. of Trust and Estate Counsel; mem. ABA. Estate planning, Probate (including wills, trusts), Estate taxation. Office: McDermott Will & Emery 227 W Monroe St Ste 3100 Chicago IL 60606-5096

HERPST, ROBERT DIX, lawyer, optics and materials technology executive; b. Teaneck, N.J., Jan. 23, 1947; s. Harold Dix and Anita Augusta (Adams) H.; children: Katherine Elizabeth, Lauren Gabrielle, Sarah Elizabeth; m. Theresa M. Jacobini, Oct. 24, 1987. BS, NYU, 1969; JD, Rutgers U., 1972. Bar: N.J., U.S. Supreme Ct. Assoc. Pitney, Hardin & Kipp, Morristown, N.J., 1972-77, BOC Group, Inc., Montvale, N.J., 1977-89, div. counsel, 1978-82, corp. counsel, asst. sec., 1982-88. Pres. Internat. Crystal Labs., Garfield, N.J., 1982-88, mng. dir., chmn. bd. dirs., 1988—. Patentee in field. Avocations: golf, politics, stock market, graphic arts. Corporate, general, Private international, Mergers and acquisitions. Office: Internat Crystal Labs 11 Erie St Garfield NJ 07026-2307

HERR, BRUCE, lawyer; b. Chgo., Aug. 12, 1943; s. Ross and Emilie (Robert) H.; m. Ellen Epstein, Feb. 22, 1968; children: Sarah, Rachel. BA cum laude, Harvard U., 1965, JD, 1968. Bar: N. Mex. 1969, Ill. 1970, U.S. Dist. Ct. N. Mex. 1969, U.S. Ct. Appeals (10th cir.) 1969, U.S. Supreme Ct. 1973. Staff atty. DNA Legal Svcs., Shiprock, N. Mex., 1969-70, Appellate Defender Project, Springfield, Ill., 1970-73; legal dir. Office of Ill. Appellate Defender, Springfield, 1973; appellate defender N. Mex. Pub. Defender Dept., Santa Fe, 1973-76; assoc., shareholder Montgomery & Andrews, PA, Santa Fe, 1976-99, of counsel, 1999-2000; with Office Lab. Counsel, Los Alamos Nat. Lab., 2000—. Mem. N. Mex. Supreme Ct. Com. on Civil Procedure Rules, 1983-98, chair, 1996-98, chair task force on electronic filing, 1994-96, mem. disciplinary bd., 2003—; mem. ethics adv. com. N. Mex. State Bar, 1985-88, 96-2002, chair employment and labor law sect., 1994-95; mem. legal com. Santa Fe Cmty. Fdn., 2002—. Pres. Friends of Santa Fe Pub. Libr., 1997-98; tutor Literacy Vols. Santa Fe, 1996-2001; bd. dirs. Santa Fe Bus. Incubator, Inc., 1995-96; v.p. Santa Fe Econ. Devel., Inc., 1999-2000. Lifetime hon. bd. mem. Santa Fe Bus. Incubator, Inc., 1996. Mem. ABA, First Jud. Dist. Bar Assn., Oliver Seth Am. Inn of Ct., Santa Fe County C. of C. (dir. 1992-96, chair 1995-96, Bd. Mem. of Yr. 1993-94). Avocations: running, hiking, reading, community activities. Civil rights, General civil litigation, Labor (including EEOC, Fair Labor Standards Act, labor-management relations, NLRB, OSHA). Home: 148 Elena St # A Santa Fe NM 87501-6528 Office: Los Alamos Nat Lab PO Box 1663 MS A-187 Los Alamos NM 87545-0001 E-mail: herr@lanl.gov.

HERR, PHILIP MICHAEL, lawyer, accountant; b. N.Y.C., June 22, 1955; s. Norman and Grace (Sporn) H.; m. Lorrie Wiener, Nov. 23, 1978; children: Gabrielle, Nicole, Adam. BS, BA magna cum laude, L.I. U., 1977; JD, Ohio No. U., 1980. Bar: N.Y. 1981, U.S. Tax Ct. 1982; CPA, N.Y. 1995; registered rep. 1998. Tax staff Ernst & Young, N.Y.C., 1980-83; tax supr. Wiss & Co., Livingston, N.J., 1983-88; tax mgr. Goldstein Golub Kessler & Co., N.Y.C., 1988-93; cons. N.Y.C., 1992-95; cons. estate bus. and fin. planning Guardian Life Ins. Co. of Am., N.Y.C., 1995-98; dir. advanced planning Kingsbridge Fin. Group, Inc., Pt. Pleasant Beach, NJ, 1998—; registered rep. AXA Advisors, LLC, 1998—. Adj. prof. bus. Ohio No. U., Ada, 1978-80, Fairleigh Dickinson U., Teaneck, N.J., 1983—, NYU Sch. Continuing Edn., N.Y.C., 1992-95. Contbr. articles to profl. jours., chpt. to book. Mem.: N.Y. State Soc. CPAs, N.Y. State Bar Assn., Assn. Advanced Life Underwriting. Jewish. Avocations: racquetball, tennis, power walking. Estate planning, Pension, profit-sharing, and employee benefits, Taxation, general. Office: Kingsbridge Financial Group Inc 501 Broadway Point Pleasant Beach NJ 08742

HERRERA, DENNIS J. lawyer; b. 1962; m. Anne Herrera; 1 child, Declan. BA, Villanova U.; JD, George Washington U. Bar: Calif. 1989. Dep. city. atty. City of San Francisco, city atty., 2002—; ptnr. Kelly, Gill, Sherburne & Herrera, San Francisco; chief staff U.S. Maritime Adminstrn., Washington; pres. San Francisco Police Commn.; with San Francisco Pub. Transp. Commn. Office: City Hall Rm 234 1 Doctor Carlton B Goodlett Pl San Francisco CA 94102 Office Fax: 415-554-4715. Business E-Mail: cityattorney@ci.sf.ca.us.*

HERRERO RODRIGUEZ DE MIÑON, MIGUEL, former Spanish member of parliament, lawyer, international legal consultant; b. Madrid, June 18, 1940; s. Miguel Herrero and Carmen Rodriguez de Miñon; m. Cristina de Jauregui Segurola, Nov. 6, 1975; children: Miguel, Cristina, Amaya. Student, U. Oxford, England, 1958, U. Luxembourg, 1962, U. Geneva, 1964; LLD, U. Madrid, 1965; BA, Licentiate Philosphy, U. Louvain, Belgium, 1966, 68; Licentiate Literature, U. Madrid, 1969. Sr. legal advisor Spanish Adminstrn. (Conejo de Estado), Madrid, 1966—; gen. sec. Ministry of Justice, Madrid, 1976-77; mem. parliament, 1977—93; leader parliamentary majority, 1980-81; leader opposition parliamentary group, 1982-87; spokesman fgn. affairs opposition parliamentary group, 1987—91. Drafter Spanish Constitution, 1977—78; mem. Trilateral Commn., 1982—, Real Acad. Ciencias Morales y Politicas, 1991—; pres. Constitutional Ct. (Andorra). Author: numerous books on constitutional law; contbr. articles to profl. jours. Decorated Encomienda Merito Civil, Gran Cruz San Raimundo de Peñafort, Gran Cruz Isabel La Catolica, Orden del Merito Constitucional (Spain); Order of Merit (Italy). Mem. Bar Assn. Madrid, Nuevo Club, Gran Peña, Casino de Madrid Club de Campo. Mem. Popular Party. Roman Catholic. Avocations: hunting, collecting antique books. Office: Mayor 70, bajo izq 28013 Madrid Spain

HERRING, CHARLES DAVID, lawyer, educator; b. Muncie, Ind., Mar. 18, 1943; s. Morris and Margaret Helen Herring; children: David, Margaret, Christopher. BA, Ind. U., 1965, JD cum laude, 1968. Bar: Ind. 1968, U.S. Dist. Ct. (so. dist.) Ind. 1971, Calif. 1971, U.S. Dist. Ct. (so. dist.) Calif. 1971. Rsch. assoc. Ind. U., 1965-68; intern Office of Pros. Atty., Monroe County, Ind., 1967-68; ptnr. Herring, Stubel & Lehr and predecessor Hering and Stabel, San Diego, 1972—92; pvt. practice San Diego, 1972—. Prof. law Western State U., 1972—91. Author: (with Jim Wade) California Cases on Professional Responsibility, 1976. Vice chmn. Valle de Oro Planning Com., Spring Valley, Calif., 1972-75; chmn. Valle de Oro Citizens Exec. Com. for Community Planning, Spring Valley, 1975-78. Served with JAGC, U.S. Army, 1968-72. Mem.: ABA (Best Brief award 1968), Calif. Trial Lawyers Assn., Conf. Spl. Ct. Judges, San Diego County Bar Assn., Calif. Bar Assn., Ind. Bar Assn., San Diego Lions Club (dir., bd. trustees, past pres.), Order of Coif. Republican. Avocations: computers, gardening, swimming, golf. General civil litigation, Insurance, Property, real (including real estate development, water). Home: 284 Sunnybrook Ln El Cajon CA 92021-7801 Office: Herring & Herring 755 Broadway Cir 2d Fl San Diego CA 92101-6160 E-mail: herringd@pacbell.net.

HERRING, JERONE CARSON, lawyer, bank executive; b. Kinston, N.C., Sept. 27, 1938; s. James and Isabel (Knight) H.; m. Patricia Ann Hardy, Aug. 6, 1961; children— Bradley Jerone, Ansley Carole. AB, Davidson Coll., 1960; LL.B., Duke U., 1963. Bar: N.C. 1963. Assoc. McElwee & Hall, North Wilkesboro, N.C., 1965-69; ptnr. McElwee, Hall & Herring, North Wilkesboro, 1969-71; exec. v.p., sec., gen. counsel Br. Banking & Trust Co., Winston-Salem, N.C., 1971—, BB&T Corp., Winston-Salem, 1995—. Served to capt. U.S. Army, 1963-65. Mem. ABA, N.C. Bar Assn., Am. Soc. Corp. Secs., Am. Corp. Counsel Assn. Presbyterian. Banking, Corporate, general. Office: 200 W 2d St Winston Salem NC 27101 E-mail: jherring@bbandt.com.

HERRINGER, MARYELLEN CATTANI, lawyer; b. Bakersfield, Calif., Dec. 1, 1943; d. Arnold Theodore and Corinne Marilyn (Kovacevich) C.; m. Frank C. Herringer; children: Sarah, Julia. AB, Vassar Coll., Poughkeepsie, N.Y., 1965; JD, U. Calif. (Boalt Hall), 1968; Exec. Program, Stanford Grad. Sch. Bus., 1994. Assoc. Davis Polk & Wardwell, N.Y.C., 1968-69, Orrick, Herrington & Sutcliffe, San Francisco, 1970-74, ptnr., 1975-81; v.p., gen. counsel Transamerica Corp., San Francisco, 1981-83, sr. v.p., gen. counsel, 1983-89; ptnr. Morrison & Foerster, San Francisco, 1989-91; sr. v.p. gen. counsel APL Ltd., Oakland, Calif., 1991-95, exec. v.p., gen. counsel, 1995-97; gen. counsel allied bus. Littler & Mendelson, San Francisco, 2000. Bd. dirs. Golden West Fin. Corp., World Savs. Bank, ABM Industries Inc. Author: Calif. Corp. Practice Guide, 1977, Corp. Counselors, 1982. Regent St. Mary's Coll., Moraga, Calif., 1986—, pres., 1990-92, trustee, 1990-99, chmn., 1993-95; trustee Vassar Coll., 1985-93, The Head-Royce Sch., 1993-2002, Mills Coll., 1999—, The Benilde Religious & Charitable Trust, 1999—, Alameda County Med. Ctr. Hosp. Authority, 1998-2002, Univ. Calif. Berkeley Art Mus., 2001—; bd. dirs. The Exploratorium, 1988-93. Mem. ABA, State Bar Calif. (chmn. bus. law sect. 1980-81), Bar Assn. San Francisco (co-chair com. on women 1989-91), Calif. Women Lawyers, San Francisco C. of C. (bd. dirs. 1987-91, gen. counsel 1990-91), Am. Corp. Counsel Assn. (bd. dirs. 1982-87), Women's Forum West (bd. dirs. 1984-87). Democrat. Roman Catholic. Corporate, general. E-mail: mherringer@aol.com.

HERRINGTON, JOHN DAVID, III, lawyer, director; b. Warren, Ohio, Nov. 19, 1934; s. John David Jr and Gertrude Francis (Herlinger) Herrington; m. Phoebe Jane Henderson, Mar. 16, 1957; children: Gay Annette, Joy Ann, Jennifer John. BSBA, Ohio State U., 1956. CPA Pa. With Price Waterhouse & Co., Pitts., 1956-63; asst. to sec.-treas. Fisher Sci. Co., Pitts., 1963-65, controller, 1965-71, v.p. fin., treas., 1971-78, sr. v.p. fin., treas., 1979-82; exec. dir. Reed Smith Shaw & McClay, Pitts., 1982-86; ret., 1986. Dir Hi Pure, Inc, Rochester Sci, Pfeiffer Glass, E & A Bldg Corp, F S de Mex, Conco Inc. Bd dirs Family and Children Serv Pittsburgh. With AUS, 1957—58. Mem.: Asn Legal Adminrs, Pa Soc CPAs, Am Inst CPAs, Planning Execs Inst, Tax Execs Inst, Fin Execs Inst. Home: 9402 Babcock Blvd Allison Park PA 15101-2011 also: 9721 S Old Oregon Inlet Rd Nags Head NC 27959-9376

HERROLD, DAVID HENRY, lawyer; b. Corpus Christi, Tex., Sept. 4, 1969; s. Donald Erwin and Mary Louise Herrold; m. Amy Lynn Fisher, Aug. 14, 1993. BA in Liberal Arts, U. Tex., 1992; JD, U. Tulsa, 1996. Bar: Okla. 1996, U.S. Dist. Ct. (no., and ea. dists.) Okla. 1996, U.S. Dist. Ct. (we. dist.) Okla. 1997, U.S. Ct. Appeals (10th cir.) 1997, U.S. Ct. Appeals (11th cir.) 1999, U.S. Supreme Ct. 2000. Law clk. Herrold, Herrold & Davis, Tulsa, 1992-94, Huffman Arrington et al, Tulsa, 1994-95; law clk., summer assoc. Conner & Winters, P.C., Tulsa, 1995-96, assoc., 1996—2001; shareholder Herrold, Herrold & Co., 2002—. Mem. ct. ops. com. Tulsa Bar, 1997-98, 2001-02, profl. responsibility com., 2002-03; mem. bankruptcy sect. Okla. Bar, 1997-98, mem. civil procedure sect. Okla. Bar, 1999—. Articles editor Tulsa Jour. of Comparative & Internat. Law, 1993-95; staff mem. Tulsa Law Jour., 1993-94. Participant Tulsa Bus. Forum, 1996-2000. Recipient Am.Jurisprudence award Contracts I, Tulsa, 1992, First Pl. award St. Francis Corp. Challenge, Tulsa, 1997-98. Mem. ABA, Okla. Bar Assn. (mem. litigation sect. 2001—), Tulsa County Bar Assn., The Summit, Tulsa Tex. Exes. (pres. 1996-98), The Res. Homeowners assn. (dir. and officer), Villages of Highland Park Homeowners' Assn., Am. Inns Ct., Phi Delta Phi. Republican. Presbyterian. Avocations: swimming, water sports, running, racquetball. Federal civil litigation, General civil litigation, Commercial, consumer (including collections, credit). Office: Herrold Herrold & Co Penthouse Ste II 5310 E 31st St Tulsa OK 74135-4304 Office Fax: 918-621-1141. E-mail: davidherrold@h2law.net.

HERSHATTER, RICHARD LAWRENCE, lawyer, writer; b. New Haven, Sept. 20, 1923; s. Alexander Charles and Belle (Blenner) Hershatter; m. Mary Jane McNulty, Aug. 16, 1980; 1 stepchild, Kimberly Ann Matlock Kleiman;children from previous marriage: Gail Brook, Nancy Jill, Bruce Warren. BA, Yale U., 1948; JD, U. Mich., 1951. Bar: Conn 1951, Mich 1951, US Supreme Ct 1959. Pvt. practice, New Haven, 1951-85, Clinton, Conn., 1985—99; state trial referee, 1984—. Author: The Spy Who Hated Licorice, 1966, The Spy Who Hated Caramel, 1968, The Spy Who Hated Fudge, 1970; ; 2d edit., 2001, Hung Jury, 2001, The Spy Who Hated Taffy, 2001. Mem. Branford Bd. Edn., Conn., 1963—71; mem. Clinton Rep. Town Com., Conn., 1982—2000, chmn., 1984—88. With Air Corps U.S. Army, 1942—44, With U.S. Inf., 1944—46. Mem.: Mystery Writers Am, Middlesex County Bar Asn, Conn. Sch. Attys. Coun. (pres. 1977), Banyan Bay Club (v.p., bd dirs 1988—), Masons. Alternative dispute resolution, Labor (including EEOC, Fair Labor Standards Act, labor-management relations, NLRB, OSHA), Probate (including wills, trusts). E-mail: hershatter@aol.com.

HERSHCOPF, GERALD THEA, lawyer; b. Feb. 8, 1922; s. Paul and Rose (Thea) Hershcopf; m. Elaine Yeckes, June 10, 1950; 1 child, Jane. AB, Columbia U., 1943; cert. in French Civilization, U. Paris, 1945; JD, Harvard U., 1949. Bar: N.Y. 1949, U.S. Dist. Ct. (so. dist.) N.Y. 1960, U.S. Supreme Ct. 1981. Assoc. Marshall, Bratter, Greene, Allison & Tucker, N.Y.C., NY, 1949—54; ptnr. Starr & Hershcopf, N.Y.C., 1954—56, Hershcopf, Stevenson, Tannenbaum, San Filippo, Donovan & Korn, 1956—91, Eisen, Hershcopf & Schulman, 1991—. Gen. ptnr. Norfolk Realty Corp., N.Y.C., 1961—86; chmn. bd. N.Am. Planning Corp., N.Y.C., 1968—71; pres. Consortium Met. Law Schs., N.Y.C., 1983—. B. dirs. N.Y. divsn. Am. Cancer Soc., 1997—98. Served with U.S. Army, 1943—46, ETO. Mem.: Real Estate Bd. N.Y., Judge Advs. Assn., N.Y. State Bar Assn. (gen. practice sect.), Assn. Bar City N.Y., Doubles Club (N.Y.C.), French-Am. C. of C., Harvard Club, N.Y. Athletic Club, Columbia U. Tennis Club, Beta Sigma Rho. Bankruptcy, Property, real (including real estate development, water), Estate taxation. Home: 737 Park Ave New York NY 10021-4256 Office: 609 5th Ave Fl 6 New York NY 10017-1021

HERSHEY, DALE, lawyer, educator; b. Pitts., Mar. 24, 1941; s. Henry E. and Elizabeth (Loeffler) H.; m. Susanne Jarrett Wilson, July 8, 1967; children: Lauren Dixon, Justin Alexander. BA, Yale U., 1963; LLB, Harvard U., 1966. Bar: Pa. 1966, U.S. Dist. Ct. (we. dist.) Pa. 1966, U.S. Ct. Appeals (3d cir.) 1971, U.S. Tax Ct. 1978, U.S. Supreme Ct. 1979, Ct. Internat. Trade 1999. Assoc. Eckert Seamans Cherin & Mellott, LLC, Pitts., 1966-75, mem., 1975—. Sr. lectr. law Grad. Sch. Indsl. Adminstrn. Carnegie Mellon U.; pres. Charleston Trust/U.S.A. Bd. dirs. Legal Aid Soc. Pitts., pres., 1983-89; hon. pres. Gateway to the Arts, Inc.; bd. dirs. Friends of Carnegie Libr., Pitts. Chamber Music Soc., pres., 1992-94; active Leadership Pitts., 1989-90. Mem. ABA, Internat. Bar Assn., Pa. Bar Assn. (Pro Bono award 1988), Allegheny County Bar Assn. (bd. dirs. Bar Found., mem. judiciary com. 1997-2000), Am. Law Inst., Harvard Law Sch. Assn. Western Pa. (pres. 1985-86), Harvard-Yale-Princeton Club, Yale Club (N.Y.C.), Yale Club (Pitts.) (pres. 1987-89). Unitarian Universalist. Antitrust, Federal civil litigation, Private international. Home: 311 Dorseyville Rd Pittsburgh PA 15215-1022 Office: Eckert Seamans Cherin & Mellott LLC 600 Grant St Ste 4400 Pittsburgh PA 15219-2702

HERSHNER, ROBERT FRANKLIN, JR., judge; b. Sumter, S.C., Jan. 21, 1944; s. Robert Franklin and Druie (Goodman) H.; m. Sally Sinclair, May 19, 1990; children: Bryan, Andrew. AB, Mercer U., 1966, JD, 1969. Bar: Ga. 1971, U.S. Dist. Ct. (mid. dist.) Ga. 1971, U.S. Dist. Ct. (so. dist.) Ga. 1979, U.S. Ct. Appeals (11th cir.) 1981, U.S. Supreme Ct. 1978. Atty. Ga. Legal Svcs. Corp., Macon, 1972; assoc. Adams, O'Neal, Hemingway & Kaplan, Macon, 1972-76; ptnr. Kaplan & Hershner, P.A., Macon, 1976-80; judge U.S. Bankruptcy Ct. for Mid. Dist. Ga., Macon, 1980—, chief bankruptcy judge, 1986—. Active Fed. Jud. Ctr. Com. on Bankruptcy Edn., 1990—99, chmn., 1994—99; elected mem. bd. Fed. Jud. Ctr., 2001—. Contbr. Georgia Lawyers Basic Practice Handbook, 2d edit., Post-Judgment Procedures, 1979; cons. Norton Bankruptcy Law and Practice. V.p. Macon Heritage Found., 1977-78. Capt. U.S. Army, 1970-75. Mem. Ga. Bar Assn., Macon Bar Assn., Nat. Conf. Bankruptcy Judges (gov., v.p. 1996-97, pres. 1997-98), Blue Key, Phi Eta Sigma. Methodist. Office: US Bankruptcy Ct PO Box 86 Macon GA 31202-0086

HERSKOVITZ, S(AM) MARC, lawyer; b. Munich, Jan. 1, 1949; came to U.S., 1949; s. Max and Bella Herskovitz; 1 child from previous marriage, David Michael; m. Barbara Hobbs, Nov. 28, 1990; 1 child, Daniel Max. BA, Pa. State U., 1970; MS in Edn. with highest honors, So. Ill. U., 1974; JD with honors, Fla. State U., 1987. Bar: Fla. 1987, U.S. Dist. Ct. (mid. dist.) Fla. 1988, U.S. Ct. Appeals (11th cir) 1988. Agy. mgr. Sun Personnel Svcs., Inc., Sarasota, Fla., 1978-80; claims adjuster Allstate Inc. Co., Lake Worth, Fla., 1980-84; sr. litigation atty. Fla. Dept. Fin. Svcs., Office of Ins. Reg., Tallahassee, 1987—. Mem. ABA, Assn. Trial Lawyers Am., Phi Kappa Phi. Democrat. Avocations: softball, reading. Home: 707 Lothian Dr Tallahassee FL 32312-2858 Office: Fla Dept Fin Svcs Office of Ins Reg 612 Larson Bldg Tallahassee FL 32399-0333

HERTZ, HOWARD, lawyer; b. Barrie, Ont., Can., Sept. 25, 1949; came to U.S., 1953; s. Percy B. and Sandra (Pushkoff) H.; m. Wendy Bennett, June 24, 1973; children: Ryan, Adam. BA, Wayne State U., 1972, JD, 1976. Bar: Mich. 1976. Atty. Legal Aid and Defenders Assn. of Detroit, 1976-78; pvt. practice Detroit, 1978-79; shareholder, v.p. Hertz, Schram and Saretsky, P.C., Bloomfield Hills, Mich., 1979—. Exec. bd., pres. Motor City Music Found. Fellow Mich. State Bar Found.; mem. ABA, NARAS, Mich. State Bar Assn. (chmn. arts, comm., entertainment and sports com. 1988-89), Internat. Assn. Entertainment Lawyers, ArtServe Mich., Inc. (bd. dirs.). Avocations: music, photography, travel. General civil litigation, Entertainment, Family and matrimonial. Office: Hertz Schram & Saretsky PC 1760 S Telegraph Rd Ste 300 Bloomfield Hills MI 48302-0183 E-mail: hhertz@hsspc.com.

HERTZ, STEPHEN G. lawyer; b. Brooklyn, Jan. 27, 1941; s. Hal R. and Ethel C. Hertz; m. Jacqueline S. Hertz; children: Scott J., Howard S. Goldberg, Bradley L. Goldberg. BA, U. Fla., 1962; JD, U. Miami, 1965. Bar: Fla. 1965, U.S. Dist. Ct. (so. dist.) Fla. 1966. Trial atty. Law offices of Stephen G. Hertz, Miami Beach, Fla., 1965—. Bd. dirs. Miami Beach Vis. & Conv. Authority, 2002—; chmn., bd. dirs. City of Miami Beach Nuisance Abatement Bd., 1998—2002; bd. dirs. City of Miami Beach Planning Bd. Mem.: ATLA, Miami Dade County Trial Lawyers Assn., Fla. State Guardianship Assn., South Fla. Guardianship Assn. (sec. 2002—), Miami Beach Bar Assn. (pres. 2002—), KP (chancellor comdr.), Phi Alpha Delta. Avocations: snow skiing, swimming, travel, tennis. Personal injury (including property damage), Probate (including wills, trusts), Property, real (including real estate development, water). Home: 565 North Shore Dr Miami Beach FL 33141 Office: Law Offices Stephen G Hertz 767 Arthur Godfrey Rd Miami Beach FL 33140 Office Fax: 305-538-0419. Business E-Mail: sgh@senatorlaw.com.

HERTZBERG, DAVID GORDON, retired lawyer; b. Detroit, Feb. 21, 1918; s. Harry Aaron and Sarah Silk Hertzberg; m. Millicent Brower, Aug. 28, 1942 (dec. Oct. 2000); children: Richard York, Jane Elyse Litin. BBA, U. Mich., 1939; LB, Harvard Law Sch., 1942, JD (hon.) , 1969. Bar: Mich. 1946, U.S. Supreme Ct. 1958. Estate tax agt. U.S. IRS, Detroit, 1946; tax atty. Hertzberg & Noveck, Detroit, 1947—88; ret., 1989. Trustee, v.p. Sigmund and Sophie Rohlik Found., Southfield, Mich., 1990—2003. Sr. lt. USN, 1942—46. Mem.: Masons (32 degree), Phi Beta Kappa. Avocations: sailing, skiing, running. Home: 22855 Shagbark Beverly Hills MI 48025-4771

HERZ, ANDREW LEE, lawyer; b. N.Y.C., Nov. 12, 1946; s. John W. and Elise J. H.; m. Jill K. Herz; children: Adam, Matthew, Daniel, Michael. BA, Columbia U., 1968, JD, 1971. Bar: N.Y. 1972. Assoc. Milbank, Tweed, Hadley & McCloy, N.Y.C., 1971-75, Nickerson, Kramer, Lowenstein, Nessen, Kamin & Soll, N.Y.C., 1975-76, Marshall, Bratter, Greene, Allison & Tucker, N.Y.C., 1977-80; gen. counsel N.Y. State Mortgage Loan Enforcement and Adminstrn. Corp., N.Y.C., 1980-81; ptnr. Richards & O'Neil, LLP, N.Y.C., 1981-2001, Bingham McCutchen LLP, N.Y.C., 2001—. Lectr. Real Estate Inst., NYU, 1988-93; cons. N.Y. Real Property Svcs., 1987. Author: Office Lease Operating Expense Clauses-Definitional Problems, 1986, Renegotiating Commercial Leases, 1993, Liability Risks for Ducking Loan Commitments, 1995; co-author: Japanese Yen Financing of U.S. Real Estate, 1989, Real Estate Management Agreements, 1990, Subleases: The Same Thing as Leases, Only Different, 2000; contbr. articles to profl. jours. Chmn. zoning bd. appeals Village of Ossining, N.Y., 1980-88; bd. dirs. Planned Parenthood N.Y.C., 1987-94, AIDS Resource Ctr., 1991-94, Commercial Real Estate Law Advisor, Realcomm, 2001-02. Harlan Fiske Stone Scholar, 1971. Mem.: ABA (vice chmn. 1988—90, chair real estate mgmt. com. 1990—91, co-chair real estate asset mgmt. com. 1992—94, chair real estate asset mgmt. com. 1994—95, lending and financing subcom. 1997—99, comml. office leasing com. 1999—2001, co-chair comml. leasing com. 1999—2001, real property divsn.), Urban Land Inst. (dir.), Real Estate Bd. N.Y., Assn. Bar City N.Y., N.Y. State Bar Assn. (co-chmn. comml. leasing com. 1991—96, exec. com. 1991—96, editor N.Y. Real Property Jour. 1996—97, real property sect.), Am. Coll. Real Estate Lawyers (vice chair office leasing com. 1997—98, chair office leasing com. 1999—2001), Columbia Law Sch. Alumni Assn. (dir.). Democrat. Commercial, contracts (including sales of goods; commercial financing), Property, real (including real estate development, water). Home: 31 Flint Ave Larchmont NY 10538-3807 Office: Bingham McCutchen LLP 399 Park Ave New York NY 10022-4689 E-mail: andrew.herz@bingham.com.

HERZ, ARNOLD D. lawyer; b. L.I., Mar. 8, 1962; BA in Polit. Sci., U. Mich., 1984; JD, Fordham U., 1991. Bar: N.Y. 1992, U.S. Dist. Ct. (ea. and so. dists.) N.Y. 1992. Assoc. Weil, Gotshal & Manges, LLP, N.Y.C., 1991—94, Leader & Berkon, LLP, N.Y.C., 1994—95, Kupfer, Rosen, N.Y.C., 1995; ptnr. Kupfer, Rosen & Herz, LLP, N.Y.C., 1996—2000; pvt. practice Port Washington, NY, 2000—. Mem. legal/bus. adv. bd. Prasad Project, N.Y.C., 2002—; mem. panel mediators U.S. Dist. Ct. (ea. dist.) and comml. divsn. Supreme Ctr State of N.Y., 2000—. Mem. legal adv. bd. Syda Found., South Fallsburg, NY, 2000—. Mem.: ABA, Fed. Bar Assn., Internat. Soc. Primerus Law Firms, Assn. Bar City of N.Y., N.Y. State Bar Assn. Alternative dispute resolution, Trademark and copyright, General practice. Office: 14 Vanderventer Ave Ste 255 Port Washington NY 11050 also: 40 Wall St 32d Fl New York NY 10005

HERZBERG, SYDELLE SHULMAN, lawyer, accountant; b. N.Y.C., July 24, 1933; d. Hyman and Rose (Green) S.; m. Norman Joseph Herzberg, June 23, 1962; 1 child, Gilbert. BS, NYU, 1955; JD, Bklyn. Law Sch., 1957. Bar: N.Y. 1958; CPA, N.Y. Pub. acct. M. Sharlach & Co, N.Y.C., 1955-62; pvt. practice acctg. and law New Rochelle, N.Y., 1962—. Mem. bd. edn. Solomon Schechter Sch. of Westchester, White Plains, N.Y., 1975-78, bd. dirs. PTA, 1975-78; pres. PTA bd. Westchester Hebrew High Sch., Mamaroneck, N.Y., 1980-82; mem. budget adv. bd. City of New Rochelle, N.Y., 1975. Mem. ABA, AICPA, N.Y. State Soc. CPA, N.Y. State Bar Assn., Huguenot-Thomas Paine Hist. Assn. (treas. 1987—, trustee 1987—), LWV (pres. New Rochelle chpt. 1983-85, treas. Westchester chpt. 1989—, budget chair N.Y. 1989-91, treas. N.Y. state 1991-99). Jewish. Probate (including wills, trusts), Property, real (including real estate development, water), Taxation, general. Home: 46 Longvue Ave New Rochelle NY 10804-4119 Office: 519 Main St New Rochelle NY 10801-6365

HERZECA, LOIS FRIEDMAN, lawyer; b. July 7, 1954; d. Martin and Elaine Shirley (Rapoport) Friedman; m. Christian S. Herzeca, Aug. 15, 1980; children: Jane Leslie, Nicholas Cameron. BA, SUNY-Binghamton, 1976; JD, Boston U., 1979. Bar: N.Y. 1980, U.S. Dist. Ct. (so. and ea. dist.) N.Y. 1980. Atty. antitrust div. U.S. Dept. Justice, Washington, 1979-80; assoc. Fried, Frank, Harris, Shriver & Jacobson, N.Y.C., 1980-86, ptnr., 1986—. Editor: Am. Jour. Law and Medicine, 1978-79. Mem. ABA, N.Y.C. Bar Assn. Corporate, general, Securities. Office: Fried Frank Harris Shriver & Jacobson 1 New York Plz Fl 22 New York NY 10004-1980

HERZOG, BRIGITTE, lawyer; b. St. Sauveur, France, Jan. 11, 1943; came to the U.S., 1970, naturalized, 1976; d. Roger and Berthe (Niobey) Ecolivet; m. Peter E. Herzog, June 29, 1970; children: Paul Roger, Elizabeth Ann. Licence en Droit, Law Sch. Pantheon, Paris, 1967; diploma d'Etudes Superieures in internat. and criminal law, Law Sch. Pantheon, 1968; diploma, Acad. Internat. Law, The Hague, The Netherlands, 1969; JD, Syracuse Coll. Law, 1975. Bar: Paris 1968, N.Y. 1976. Assoc. Chardenon Law Firm, Paris, 1968-70, Cleary, Gottlieb et al, Paris, 1976-77; staff atty. Carrier Corp., Syracuse, N.Y., 1977-83, sr. atty., 1983-84, asst. gen. counsel, 1984-86, counsel European and Transcontinental Ops. Surrey, Eng., 1986-89, assoc. gen. counsel Syracuse, 1990; dir. legal affairs Otis, Paris, 1990-92; v.p. legal affairs European and Transcontinental Ops. Otis Internat., Inc., 1992-97; dep. gen. counsel Otis Elevator Co.-Europe; v.p. legal affairs Otis Elevator North European Area, 1998—2001; dep. gen. counsel Otis WHP, Farmington, Conn., 2002—. Contbr. to Harmonization of Laws in EEC Fifth Sokol Colloquium, 1983; contbr. articles on French and internat. law to profl. jours. Bd. dirs. Syracuse Stage Guild, 1974-77; chair legal com. European Elevator Assn. Mem. ABA, Am. Fgn. Law Assn. Roman Catholic. Corporate, general, Private international. Home: 112 Erregger Rd Syracuse NY 13224-2220 Office: Otis 10 Farm Springs Farmington CT 06032

HERZOG, LESTER BARRY, lawyer, educator; b. Presov, Slovakia, July 3, 1953; came to U.S., 1965; s. Alexander and Flora (Braun) H.; m. Terry Lynn Hochhauser, Feb. 6, 1979; children: Simcha, Sarah, Chaim, Judah, Leah. BA, Rabbinical Sem. Belz, Bklyn., 1974; MBA with distinction, L.I. U., 1977; JD cum laude, Bklyn. Law Sch., 1983. Bar: N.Y. 1984, U.S. Dist. Ct. (ea. and so. dists.) N.Y. 1984; CPA, N.Y. Sr. auditor Seidman & Seidman, N.Y.C., 1977-83; sr. trial atty. Office Corp. Counsel N.Y.C. Law Dept., Bklyn., 1983-89; pvt. practice N.Y.C., 1989—. Adj. assoc. prof. law and acctg. L.I. U., Bklyn., 1985—. Contbr. articles to profl. jours. Mem. ABA, AICPA (exam grader 1981-83), N.Y. State Bar Assn. Democrat. Jewish. Avocations: chess, fishing, gardening. Home and Office: 1729 E 15th St Brooklyn NY 11229-2084

HESS, CHAD BRANDON, lawyer; b. Melbourne, Fla., July 18, 1974; JD, Stetson U., 1999. Bar: S.C. 2000. Assoc. Speiser Krause, PC, Washington, 1999—2002, Hood Law Firm, LLC, Charleston, SC, 2002—. Lector Grace Episc. Ch., Charleston, SC. Mem.: ATLA. Avocations: hunting, travel. General civil litigation, Personal injury (including property damage), Property, real (including real estate development, water). Personal E-mail: cbhess@hotmail.com.

HESS, EMERSON GARFIELD, lawyer; b. Pitts., Nov. 13, 1914; AB, Bethany Coll., 1936; JD, U. Pitts., 1939. Bar: Pa. 1940. Sr. ptnr. Hess, Reich, Georgiades, Wile & Homyak and predecessor firm Emerson G. Hess & Assocs., Pitts., 1940-92; of counsel DeMarco & Assocs., Pitts., 1992—. Solicitor Scott Twp. Sch. Bd., 1958-65; legal counsel Judiciary com. Pa. Ho. of Reps., 1967-69; solicitor Scott Twp., 1968-69, Crafton Borough, 1974-78, Authority for Improvements in Municipalities of Allegheny County, 1977-80. Bd. dirs. Golden Triangle YMCA, Pitts., 1945—, WQED Ednl. TV, Pitts., 1952-68; pres., dir. Civil Light Opera Assn., Pitts., 1967-68; mem. internat. com. YMCA World Svc., N.Y.C., 1968-78; trustee, chmn. Cen. Christian Ch., Pitts., 1962-63; pres. Anesthesia and Resuscitation Found., Pitts., 1964-88, Pa. Med. Rsch. Found., 1960-88. Mem. ABA, Pa. Bar Assn., Allegheny County Bar Assn. Corporate, general, Condemnation (eminent domain), Estate planning. Home: 43 Robin Hill Dr Mc Kees Rocks PA 15136-1238 Office: DeMarco & Assocs 946 Gulf Tower 707 Grant St Pittsburgh PA 15219-1908

HESS, GEORGE FRANKLIN, II, lawyer; b. Oak Park, Ill., May 13, 1939; s. Franklin Edward and Carol (Hackman) H.; m. Diane Ricci, Aug. 9, 1974; 1 child, Franklin Edward. BS in Bus., Colo. State U., 1962; JD, Suffolk U., 1970; LLM, Boston U., 1973. Bar: Pa. 1971, Fla. 1973, U.S. Tax Ct. 1974, U.S. Dist. Ct. (so. dist.) Fla. 1975. Assoc. Hart, Childs, Hepburn, Ross & Putnam, Phila., 1970-72; instr. Suffolk U. Law Sch., Boston, 1973-74; ptnr. Henry, Hess & Hoines, Ft. Lauderdale, Fla., 1974-79, Mousaw, Vigdor, Reeves & Hess, Ft. Lauderdale, Fla., 1979-94; pvt. practice Ft. Lauderdale, Fla., 1995—. Bd. dirs. Childrens Home Soc., Ft. Lauderdale, 1985-89, Nadeau Charitable Found., 1985-2000; trustee endowment fund All Sts. Ch., 1995—. Lt. USNR, 1963-66. Mem. ABA, SAR, Fla. Bar Assn., Broward County Bar Assn., Lauderdale Yacht Club, USN League, Phi Alpha Delta. Episcopalian. Estate planning, Probate (including wills, trusts). Home: 2524 Castilla Is Fort Lauderdale FL 33301-1505 Office: 333 N New River Dr E Fort Lauderdale FL 33301-2241

HESS, H. OBER, lawyer, director; b. Royersford, Pa., Nov. 8, 1912; s. Samuel Harley and Annamae (Wenger) H.; m. Dolores Groke, May 18, 1940; children: Antonine (Mrs. Joseph J. Gal), Roberta (Mrs. Edward S. Trippe), Liesa (Mrs. Arleigh P. Helfer, Jr.), Kristina (Mrs. Charles H. Bonner). AB, Ursinus Coll., 1933, LL.D. (hon.), 1979; LL.B., Harvard U., 1936; LL.D. (hon.), Muhlenberg Coll., 1964; D.F.A. (hon.), Phila. Coll. Art, 1981. Of counsel to Ballard, Spahr, Andrews & Ingersoll, Phila. Editor: Fiduciary Rev, monthly, The Nature of a Humane Society, 1976. Former mem. exec. com. Luth. Ch. in Am.; trustee Lankenau Hosp., Phila. U. of the Arts; former chmn. Mary J. Drexel Home, Lankenau Med. Rsch. Ctr.; former bd. dirs., sec. Phila. Orch. Assn., Acad. Music Phila.; former mem. Harvard Overseers Com. to Visit Law Sch.; former nat. chmn. Harvard Law Sch. Fund. Mem. ABA, Pa., Phila., Montgomery County bar assns., Harvard Law Sch. Assn. Clubs: Philadelphia, Union League, Philadelphia Country (Phila.). Home: 1400 Waverly Rd Muirfield 244 Gladwyne PA 19035-1254 Office: 1735 Market St Fl 51 Philadelphia PA 19103-7501

HESS, P. GREGORY, lawyer; b. Wheeling, W.Va., Sept. 15, 1946; s. Philip Tilman and Virginia Lamberton (Jackson) H.; m. Susan Marion Kyff, Aug. 16, 1969; children: Philip Andrew, Peter Gregory, Michael Trevor, Aimee Suzanne. AB, Princeton U., 1968; JD, Yale U., 1971; LLM in Taxation, NYU, 1976. Bar: N.Y. 1972, Fla. 1976. Assoc. Breed, Abbott and Morgan, N.Y.C., 1971-73; ptnr. Williamson and Green, N.Y.C., 1973-76, Williamson and Hess, N.Y.C., 1976-80; of counsel Christy & Viener, N.Y.C., 1980, ptnr., 1980-98, Salans, N.Y.C., 1999—2002, Schiff Hardin & Waite, N.Y.C., 2002—. Bd. dirs. Barr and Barr, Inc., N.Y.C. Trustee N.Y. Sch. for Deaf, White Plains, 1982—, pres., 1990-93, chmn., 1993-2002; bd. dirs. Ruby Bridges Found., Inc., 2001—, treas., 2001—; bd. dirs. Pro Mujer, Inc., 2001—, sec., 2002—; trustee Princeton (N.J.) Campus Club, 1972-97, NTID Found., Rochester, N.Y., 1999—; bd. dirs. Greater Westchester Youth Orchs. Assn., Inc., Millwood, N.Y., 1986-91, chmn., 1988-91; bd. dirs., v.p. Westchester Found. for the Deaf, Inc., Hawthorne, N.Y., 1997-2003. Mem. Princeton Club N.Y. Estate planning, Probate (including wills, trusts), Estate taxation. Home: 47 Quaker Bridge Rd Ossining NY 10562-1624 Office: Schiff Hardin & Waite 623 5th Ave NW New York NY 10022 Business E-Mail: ghess@schiffhardin.com.

HESS, SIDNEY J., JR., lawyer; b. Chgo., June 26, 1910; s. Sidney J. and Alma (Katz) Hess; m. Jacqueline Engelhardt, Aug. 28, 1948; children: Karen E. Hess Freeman, Lori Hess Pleiss. PhB, U. Chgo., 1930, JD, 1932. Bar: Ill. 1932. Practiced in, Chgo., 1932—; mem. firm Aaron, Schimberg & Hess, 1933—84, D'Ancona & Pflaum, 1985—. Bd. dirs., legal counsel Jewish Fedn. of Met. Chgo., 1968-95, v.p., 1972-74, pres., 1974-76; dir., legal counsel Jewish United Fund Met. Chgo., 1971-95, pres., 1974-76; legal counsel Jewish Welfare Fund Met. Chgo., 1969-73; bd. dirs. S. Silberman & Sons, Chgo. Metallic Products, Inc., Vienna Sausage Mfg. Co. Mem. exec. com. Anti-Defamation League, 1954-57, HIAS, 1974-90; mem. nat. devel. coun., aims com., citizens bd. U. Chgo.; bd. dirs. Schwab Rehab. Hosp., 1954-65, pres., 1959-64; trustee Michael Reese Founds., 1991—. Recipient Judge Learned Hand Human Rels. award Am. Jewish Com., 1979, Julius Rosenwald Meml. award Jewish Fedn. Met. Chgo., 1994, Army Commendation Medal (USAF); elected to Jewish Cmty. Ctrs. Hall of Fame, 1985, City of Chgo. Sr. Citizens Hall of Fame, 1987. Mem. ABA, Ill. State Bar Assn., Chgo. Bar Assn., Am. Judicature Soc., U. Chgo. Law Sch. Assn. (dir.), Std. Club (past pres., dir.), Mid-Day Club (Chgo.), Northmoor Country Club (Highland Park, Ill.), Tamarisk Country Club (Rancho Mirage, Calif.), Phi Beta Kappa, Pi Lambda Phi. Estate taxation, Corporate, general, Estate planning. Home: 1040 N Lake Shore Dr Chicago IL 60611-1165 Office: 111 E Wacker Dr Chicago IL 60601-3713 Fax: 312-602-3162. E-mail: shess@dancona.com.

HESS-MAHAN, THEODORE MICHAEL, lawyer; b. Boston, Oct. 29, 1959; s. John Mahan and Judith Dutra Mitchell; m. Anne Hess, Aug. 23, 1986; children: Bridget Leigh, Corey Michael, Maura Rose. BA Psychology, Tufts U., Medford, Mass., 1981; JD, Suffolk U., Boston, 1990. Bar: Mass. 1990, U.S. Dist. Ct. Mass. 1991, U.S. Ct. of Appeals (1st cir.) 1995, US Supreme Ct. 1996. Direct care W.E. Fernald State Sch., Waltham, Mass., 1981—82, occupl. therapy asst., 1982—83, adult edn. tchr., 1983—85, adult edn. program dir., 1985—86; ind. profl. rev. team leader Seaside Edn. Associates, Inc., Lincoln, Mass., 1986—87; legal intern Mass. Mental Health Legal Advisers Com., Boston, 1988; law clk. Mass. Supreme Jud. Ct., Boston, 1990—91; lawyer Ropes & Gray, Boston, 1991—97; assoc. Shapiro Haber & Urmy LLP, Boston, 1997—. Lead articles editor Suffolk U. Law Sch. Law Rev., Boston, 1989—90, law rev. staff, 1988—89; donahue lecture series dir. Suffolk U. Law Sch., Boston, 1989—90; faculty Boston Bar Found. Class Action Com., Mass., 2002—02, Mass. Bar Assn., Boston, 2002; voluntary student defender, Boston mcpl. ct., criminal divsn. Suffolk U. Law Sch., Boston, 1989—90; pre-trial conferencer Boston Mcpl. Ct-Boston Bar Assn. Pre-Trial Conf. Program, Boston, 1996—. Contbr. Commr. Newton Human Rights Commn., Newton, Mass., 2002—; mem. Uniting Citizens for Affordable Housing In Newton, Newton, Mass., 2001—02; co-chair/parent rep. Horace Mann Sch. Coun., Newton, Mass., 1998—2001; pres. Citizens for Affordable Housing in Newton Devel. Orgn., Inc., Newton, Mass., 2001—02; mem. Newton PTO Coun., Newton, Mass., 2002—. Recipient Outstanding Sr. award, Suffolk U. Law Sch., 1990. Mem.: ABA, ACLU, Mass. Bar Assn., Boston Bar Assn. General civil litigation, Civil rights, Securities, Class Actions. Office: Shapiro Haber & Urmy LLP 75 State St Boston MA 02109 Office Fax: 617-439-0134. E-mail: ted@shulaw.com.

HESTER, FRANCIS BARTOW, III, (FRANK HESTER), lawyer; b. Interlachen, Fla., Oct. 13, 1920; s. Francis Bartow Jr. and Flora McRae H.; m. Joyce Slate, Dec. 21, 1946; children: Susan Hester Elmore, Blanche Hester Wolfson, F. Bartow Hester Jr. Student, Ga. Inst. Tech., 1938-42, U. Ga., 1946; LLB, Emory U., 1948. Bar: Ga. 1952, U.S. Dist. Ct. (no. dist.) Ga. 1952, U.S. Ct. Appeals (4th cir.) 1990, U.S. Ct. Appeals (5th cir.) 1955, U.S. Ct. Appeals (6th cir.) 1967, U.S. Ct. Appeals (7th cir.) 1994, U.S. Ct. Appeals (11th cir.) 1981, Ga. Supreme Ct. 1952, Ga. Ct. Appeals 1952, U.S. Bd. Immigration Appeals 1985, U.S. Supreme Ct. 1960. Spl. agt. FBI, Cleve., Phila., Atlanta, 1948-51; criminal case trial lawyer Hester & Hester, 1952-99. Spl. investigator of fraud in Ga. State Govt., 1958-59. With Air Corp., U.S. Army, 1942-45. Commendation Ga. Ho. of Reps., 1997. Mem. Ga. Bar Assn., Ga. Assn. Criminal Def. Lawyers, Former Spl. Agts. of FBI Assn., Inc., Atlanta Bar Assn., Mason (32d degree), 6th Bomb Group Assn. (Tinian 1945), Cherokee Town & Country Club, Shriner (Yaarab temple), Sigma Alpha Epsilon. Democrat. Avocation: boating. Criminal. Home and Office: 5350 Larch Ln Gainesville GA 30506-6282

HESTER, PATRICK JOSEPH, lawyer; b. Worcester, Mass., Aug. 14, 1951; s. Joseph P. and Anne T. (O'Brien) H.; m. Ann E. Riley, July 11, 1987; children: Maureen M., Colleen A., Margaret R., Molly E. BS in Civil Engr., W.P.I., Worcester, Mass., 1973; MS in Civil Engr., Northeastern U., Boston, 1979; JD, Suffolk Law Sch., Boston, 1983. Bar: Mass. 1983, U.S. Dist. Ct. Mass. 1984, 1st Cir. Ct. Appeals, 1999, U.S. Supreme Ct. 2000. Civil engr. Stone & Webster, Boston, 1973; dist. engr. Algonquin Gas Transmission Co., Boston, 1973-75, engr., 1975-78, sr. engr., 1978-79, supr.,engr., 1979-82, project mgr., 1982-83, asst. mgr. gas supply, 1983-84, corp. atty., 1984-92, v.p., gen. counsel, 1992-97; asst. gen. counsel Duke Energy Corp., Boston, 1998—; gen. counsel M & N Mgmt. Co., 1998-99, sr. v.p., gen. counsel, 1999—. Profl. engr., Mass. Mem. ABA, Mass. Bar Assn., Fed. Energy Bar Assn., Boston Bar Assn., New England Corp. Counsel Assn., Guild Gas Mgrs., Soc. Gas Lighters, Chi Epsilon, Phi Delta Phi. Democrat. Roman Catholic. Avocation: sports. Commercial, contracts (including sales of goods; commercial financing), Corporate, general, FERC practice. Office: Duke Energy Corp 1284 Soldiers Field Rd Boston MA 02135-1003

HETHERINGTON, JOHN JOSEPH, lawyer; b. Phila., Jan. 22, 1947; s. Jack Joseph and Josephine J. (Krawiec) H.; children: Wendy Lynn, John Joseph, Patrick John. BA, U. Pa., 1974; JD, Gonzaga U., 1977. Bar: Pa. 1977, U.S. Dist. Ct. (ea. dist.) Pa. 1979, U.S. Ct. Appeals (3d cir.) 1983; cert. elder lawyer Nat. Elder Law Found., 1993, cert. 2000. Staff atty. Legal Services Northeast Pa., Wilkes-Barre, 1977-79; sole practice Chalfont, Pa., 1979-82, Hilltown, Pa., 1986—2000; assoc. Toll, Hetherington & Ghen, Doylestown, Pa., 1982-86; ptnr. Corr, Stevens & Fenningham, 2000—. Cons., lectr. pre-retirement workshops, Devon, Pa., 1984—; lectr. programs on elder law and social security claims CLE, 1981-99; mem. adj. faculty Bucks County C.C., 2002—. With USAF, 1966-69. Mem. Pa. Bar Assn. (chmn. com. legal affairs elderly and social security law 1987), Bucks County Bar Assn. (bd. dirs. 1987-90, com. legal problems of elderly, panelist), Nat. Acad. Elder Law Attys. Republican. Roman Catholic. Avocations: horticulture, collecting contemporary music, sailing. General civil litigation, General practice, Elder. Office: Corr Stevens & Fenningham 1035 W Bristol Rd PO Box 2911 Warminster PA 18974-0229

HETHERWICK, GILBERT LEWIS, lawyer; b. Winnsboro, La., Oct. 30, 1920; s. Septimus and Addie Louise (Gilbert) H.; m. Joan Friend Gibbons, May 31, 1946 (dec. Aug. 1964); children: Janet Hetherwick Pumphrey, Ann Hetherwock Lyons Winegeart, Gilbert, Carol Hetherwick Sutton, Katherine Hetherwick Hummell; m. Mertis Elizabeth Cook, June 7, 1967 (dec. May 2003). BA summa cum laude, Centenary Coll., 1942; JD, Tulane U., 1949. Bar: La. 1949. With legal dept. NorAm Energy Corp., Shreveport, La., 1949-53; dir. Blanchard, Walker, O'Quin and Roberts, PLC, Shreveport, 1953-99, of counsel, 2000—. Mem. Shreveport City Charter Revision Com., 1955; mem. Shreveport Mcpl. Fire and Police Civil Svc. Bd., 1956-92, vice chmn., 1957-78, chmn., 1978-88. Served with AUS, 1942-46. Recipient Tulane U. Law Faculty medal, 1949. Mem. ABA, La. Bar Assn., Shreveport Bar Assn. (pres. 1987), Energy Bar Assn., Order of Coif, Phi Delta Phi, Omicron Delta Kappa. Episcopalian. Home: 4604 Fairfield Ave Shreveport LA 71106-1432 Office: Bank One Tower Shreveport LA 71101

HETKE, RICHARD LOUIS, lawyer; b. Monrovia, Calif., June 1, 1952; s. Richard Louis and Susan (Botschner) H.; m. Holly Susan Hansen, June 3, 1983. AB, Dartmouth Coll., 1973; JD, Harvard U., 1978. Bar: Calif. 1978, Ill. 1980. Assoc. Thelen, Marrin, Johnson, San Francisco, 1978-80, Mayer, Brown & Platt, Chgo., 1980-82; counsel Household Internat., Northbrook, Ill., 1982-84; sr. counsel Kraft, Inc., Glenview, Ill., 1984—88; v.p., divsn. counsel Ameritech Corp., Chgo., 1988—2001; v.p., gen. coun. Hansen Tech., 1983—2000; CEO Am. Law Firm Assn., 2001—. Owner Halcyon Days Coll. Counseling, 1995—. Mem. ABA, Ill. Bar Assn., Phi Beta Kappa. Clubs: Dartmouth (Chgo.) (v.p. 1980—), Tuscumbia (Green Lake, Wis.). Avocations: sports memorabilia, golf, tennis. Antitrust, Corporate, general, Private international. Home: 310 N County Line Rd Hinsdale IL 60521

HETLAGE, ROBERT OWEN, lawyer; b. St. Louis, Jan. 9, 1931; s. George C. and Doris M. (Talbot) H.; m. Anne R. Willis, Sept. 24, 1960; children: Mary T., James C., Thomas K. AB, Washington U., St. Louis, 1952, LLB, 1954; LLM, George Washington U., 1957. Bar: Mo. 1954, U.S. Dist. Ct. (ea. dist.) Mo. 1954, U.S. Supreme Ct. 1957. Ptnr. Hetlage & Hetlage, 1958-65, Peper, Martin, Jensen, Maichel & Hetlage, St. Louis, 1966-97, chmn., 1994-97; of counsel Blackwell Sanders Peper Martin LLP, St. Louis, 1998—. 1st lt. U.S. Army, 1954-58. Fellow Am. Bar Found. (life, v.p. 2002—); mem. ABA (chmn. real property, probate and trust law sect. 1981-82), Bar Assn. Met. St. Louis (pres. 1967-68), Mo. Bar (pres. 1976-77), Am. Coll. Real Estate Lawyers (pres. 1985-86), Am. Judicature Soc., Anglo-Am. Real Property Inst. (chmn. 1991). Commercial, contracts (including sales of goods; commercial financing), Construction, Property, real (including real estate development, water). Office: Blackwell Sanders Peper Martin LLP 720 Olive St Saint Louis MO 63101-2338 E-mail: rohetlage@blackwellsanders.com.

HETLAND, JOHN ROBERT, lawyer, educator; b. Mpls., Mar. 12, 1930; s. James L. and Evelyn (Lundgren) H.; m. Mildred Woodruff, Dec. 1951 (div.); children: Lynda Lee Catlin, Robert John, Debra Ann Allen; m. Anne Kneeland, Dec. 1972; children: Robin T. Willcox, Elizabeth J. Pickett. BSL., U. Minn., 1952, JD, 1956. Bar: Minn. 1956, Calif. 1962, U.S. Supreme Ct, 1981. Practice law, Mpls., 1956-59; prof. law U. Calif., Berkeley, 1959-91; prof. emeritus, 1991—; prin. Hetland & Kneeland, PC, Berkeley, 1959—. Vis. prof. law Stanford U., 1971, 80, U. Singapore, 1972, U. Cologne, Fed. Republic Germany, 1988. Author: California Real Property Secured Transactions, 1970, Commercial Real Estate Transactions, 1972, Secured Real Estate Transactions, 1974, 1977; co-author: California Cases on Security Transactions in Land, 2d edit., 1975, 3d edit., 1984, 4th edit., 1992; contbr. articles to legal, real estate and fin. jours. Served to lt. comdr. USNR, 1953-55. Fellow Am. Coll. Real Estate Lawyers, Am. Coll. Mortgage Attys., Am. Bar Found.; mem. ABA, State Bar Calif., State Bar Minn., Order of Coif, Phi Delta Phi. Home and Office: 20 Red Coach Ln Orinda CA 94563-1112 E-mail: hetlandj@law.berkeley.edu.

HETTRICK, GEORGE HARRISON, lawyer; b. Piney River, Va., Aug. 15, 1940; s. Ames Bartlett and Frances Caryl (O'Brian) H.; children: Heather White Hettrick Brugh, Edward Lord. BA, Cornell U., 1962; JD, Harvard U., 1965. Bar: Va. 1965. Assoc. Hunton & Williams, Richmond, Va., 1965-73, ptnr., 1973—. Ptnr. in charge Church Hill Neighborhood Law Office Hunton & Williams, 1990—, chmn. Community Svc. com.; dir. Richmond Community Hosp., 1992—. Contbr. articles to profl. jours. Pres. bd. trustees Va. Episcopal Sch., Lynchburg, 1978—81; spl. counsel Gov. of Va., Richmond, 1971—72; vice-chmn. bd. dirs. Va. Port Authority, Norfolk, 1970—75, former commr., vice-chmn.; Va. State adv. com. Neighborhood Assistance Program; past dir., chmn. Peter Paul Devel. Ctr., Inc.; bd. dirs. Lawyers Helping Lawyers, St. Mary's Hosp., Stuart Circle Hosp., Richmond Cmty. Hosp., 1995—, Regional Meml. Med. Ctr; bd. dirs., v.p. Greater Richmond Bar Found.; active Henrico County (Va.) Cmty. Svcs. Bd., 1997—, chmn., 2002—; bd. dirs. Chesterfield/Colonial Heights Drug Ct. Found., 2002—. Capt. U.S. Army, 1966—68. Fellow Va. Law Found.; mem. ABA, Va. Bar Assn. (chmn. substance abuse com. 1995-96), Va. State Bar, Richmond Bar Assn. (chmn. pro bono com. 1998—). Republican. Episcopalian. Home: 6350 Memorial Dr Sandston VA 23150-6307 Office: Hunton & Williams PO Box 1535 Richmond VA 23218-1535 E-mail: ghettrick@hunton.com.

HEUBAUM, WILLIAM LINCOLN, retired lawyer; b. Chgo., Jan., 1938; s. Lincoln William and Hazel Lillian Heubaum; m. Mary Lynn Gilbert, June 19, 1965; children: Karl Franz, Joy Ann. BS (Forrestel scholar), Northwestern U., 1959, JD (Kosmerl scholar), 1965. Bar: Ill. 1965, Iowa 1973, Nebr. 1982. Atty. Hopkins & Sutter, Chgo., 1965-72; v.p., sec., gen. counsel IBP (formerly Iowa Beef Processors, Inc.), Dakota City, Nebr., 1972-82; ptnr. Bikakis, Heubaum, Vohs & Storm, Sioux City, Iowa, 1983-85; founder, mem. Crime Stoppers, 1982-98. Lectr. Chgo. Bar Assn. Continuing Legal Edn. Com. Mem. Local Bd. 12; asso. govt. appeal agt. Local Bd. 30, Ill. Selective Service System, 1967-72. Served to lt. Supply Corps USNR, 1959-62. Mem. Acacia, Masons, Moose, Rotary, Phi Alpha Delta. Republican. Methodist. Home: 204 Calumet Dr Yankton SD 57078-6751

HEUISLER, CHARLES WILLIAM, lawyer; b. Phila., May 24, 1941; s. Isaac Kilner and Mary Gertrude (Smith) H.; m. Judith Ann Hargadon, June 26, 1965; children: Karen L. Heuisler Murphy, Susan M. Heuisler McCabe, Charles W. Jr. BA in Modern Lang., Coll. of Holy Cross, 1963; JD, Villanova U., 1966. Bar: N.J. 1966, U.S. Dist. Ct. N.J. 1966, U.S. Ct. Appeals (3d cir.) 1970, U.S. Supreme Ct. 1972; cert. civil trial atty. Am. Bd. Trial Advs. Law clk. to Hon. John B. Wick, Superior Ct. of N.J., Chancery Divsn., Camden, 1966-67; shareholder Archer & Greiner, Haddonfield, N.J., 1972—. Counsel, mem. adv. bd. Haddonfield Symphony Soc., 1980—; chmn. South Jersey Performing Arts Ctr., 1992-98. Mem. FBA, N.J. Bar Assn. (trustee from Camden County 1989-93), Camden County Bar Assn. (pres. 1985-86, trustee, Peter J. Devine award 1991), Rotary (pres. Camden 1987-88). Avocations: tennis, sailing. General civil litigation, Intellectual property, Professional liability. Home: 1236 Folkestone Way Cherry Hill NJ 08034-3021 Office: Archer & Greiner PC One Centennial Sq Haddonfield NJ 08033 E-mail: cheuisler@archerlaw.com.

HEUMAN, DONNA, lawyer; b. Seattle, May 27, 1949; d. Russell George and Edna Inez (Armstrong) H. BA in Psychology, UCLA, 1972; JD, U. Calif., San Francisco, 1985. Cert. shorthand reporter, Calif. Owner Heuman & Assocs., San Francisco, 1978-86; lic. real estate broker Calif., 1990—; co-founder, chair, CFO Atherton Park Foods, Inc., Menlo Park, Calif., 1996—. Mem. Hastings Internat. and Comparative Law Rev., 1984-85; bd. dirs. Saddleback, 1987-89. Jessup Internat. Moot Ct. Competition, 1985; mem. North Fair Oaks Adv. Coun., vice chair, sec. 1993-95. Mem. ABA, NAFE, ATLA, AOPA, Nat. Shorthand Reporters Assn., Women Entrepreneurs, Mensa, Calif. State Bar Assn., Nat. Mus. of Women in the Arts, Calif. Lawyers for the Arts, San Francisco Bar Assn., Commonwealth Club, World Affairs Coun., Zonta (bd. dirs.). Office: 530 University Ave Palo Alto CA 94301-1901 E-mail: athpark@aol.com.

HEWES, GEORGE POINDEXTER, III, lawyer; b. Jackson, Miss., Oct. 25, 1928; s. George P. Jr. and Gertrude (Turner) H.; m. Helen Elizabeth Morrison, Nov. 19, 1954 (dec. July 1997); children: George P. IV, Laura L. Hewes Bell, Robert Russelll m. Joan Dean, Dec. 27, 1998. BBA, U. Miss., 1950, JD, 1954. Bar: Miss. 1954, U.S. Dist. Ct. (so. and no. dists.) Miss. 1954, U.S. Ct. Appeals (5th cir.) 1954, U.S. Supreme Ct. 1970. Enlisted U.S. Marine Corps, 1950, advanced through grades to lt. col., ret., 1975; sr. ptnr. Brunini, Grantham, Grower & Hewes, Jackson, 1955—2002. Bd. dirs. Trustmark Nat. Bank, Jackson. Chmn. United Way Campaign, 1985; chmn. bd. dirs. Magnolia Speech Sch. Deaf, 1986-87; chancellor Episc. Diocese Miss., 1984-2002. Fellow Am. Coll. Trial Lawyers (regent 1984-88); mem. ABA, Miss. State Bar Assn. (pres. young lawyers sect. 1963-64), Hinds County Bar Assn., Nat. Conf. Commrs. Uniform State Laws, Jackson Symphony Orch. Assn. (past pres.), Met. YMCA (past pres.), Jackson Jr. C. of C. (Young Man Yr. local and state 1962), Jackson Country Club, One Hundred Club Jackson (sec. 1984—, past pres.). Republican. Federal civil litigation, State civil litigation, Product liability. Home: 4 Rivers Creek Dr Jackson MS 39211-5900 Office: Brunini Grantham Grower & Hewes PO Box 119 Jackson MS 39205-0119 E-mail: ghewes@brunini.com.

HEWES, LAURENCE ILSLEY, III, lawyer, management, development, legal consultant; b. Palo Alto, Calif., Sept. 18, 1933; s. Laurence Ilsley, Jr. and Patricia Esther (Jackson) H.; m. Mary Clarke Darling, Oct. 1, 1960; children: Laurence Ilsley IV, Henry Patrick Darling, Mary Clarke Danforth. AB, Yale U., 1956, LLB, 1959. Bar: D.C. 1961, U.S. Dist. Ct. D.C., 1961, U.S. Ct. Appeals (D.C. cir.) 1961, U.S. Supreme Ct. 1966. Assoc. counsel U.S. Senate Comm. Labor and Human Resources, Washington, 1961; assoc. counsel Econ. Devel. Adminstrn. U.S. Dept. Commerce, Washington, 1961-62; staff dir., counsel Pres.'s Com. on Equal Opportunity in Armed Forces, Washington, 1962-63; assoc. then ptnr. Hydeman & Mason and successor firms, Washington, 1963-72; ptnr. Boasberg & Hewes (and successor firms), Washington, 1972-80, Wald Harkader & Ross, Washington, 1980-85; exec. dir., gen. counsel The Support Ctr., 1985-88; pres., chief exec. officer, gen. counsel Corp. Against Drug Abuse, 1989-93; legal, devel. and mgmt. cons. Washington, 1994—. Bd. dirs., Officer Taft Corp., Washington and N.Y.C., 1967-72; bd. dirs., mgr. Grants Mgmt. Adv. Svc., Inc., 1975-80; lectr. non-profit orgn. field. Contbr. articles to profl. jours., chpts. to books. Bd. trustees, Wooster Sch., Danbury Conn., 1981-89, Friends of Superior Ct. of D.C., 1973-87. Served with USAFR, 1959-66. Mem. ABA, D.C. Bar Assn., Cosmos Club, Yale Club (N.Y.C.), Mountain View Country Club. Democrat. Avocations: music, reading, bicycling, fly fishing, tennis.

HEWITT, PAUL BUCK, lawyer; b. St. Louis, July 27, 1949; s. John York and Kathryn Louise (Buck) H.; m. Marla Ivy Zimmers, Feb. 17, 1985; children: Anna Ruth, Rachel Elizabeth. BA in Econs., Northwestern U., 1971; JD cum laude, U. Wis., 1974. Bar: D.C. 1979, Wis. 1974. Law clk. to chief justice Wis. Supreme Ct., Madison, 1974-75; atty. Bureau of Competition FTC, Washington, 1975-78; assoc. Akin Gump Strauss Hauer and Feld, Washington, 1978-82, ptnr., 1983—. Articles editor Wis. Law Rev., Madison, 1973-74. Mem. ABA, D.C. Bar, Wis. Bar Assn. Administrative and regulatory, Antitrust, Federal civil litigation. Office: Akin Gump Strauss Hauer and Feld LLP Ste 400 1333 New Hampshire Ave NW Washington DC 20036-1564

HEYBURN, JOHN GILPIN, II, federal judge; b. 1948; m. Martha Keeney, 1976. BA, Harvard U., 1970; JD, U. Ky., 1976. Ptnr. Brown, Todd & Heyburn, Louisville, 1976-92; fed. judge U.S. Dist. Ct. (we. dist.), Louisville, 1992—. Bd. dirs. Kentuckians for Jud. Improvement, 1975-76; mem. Budget Com. Jud. Conf.of U.S., 1994—, chmn. 1997—; chair Jefferson County Crime Commn.; mem. vis. com. U. Ky., 1980; active Leadership Louisville Found. With USAR, 1970-76. Mem. ABA, Ky. Bar Assn., Louisville Bar Assn., U. Ky. Coll. Law Alumni Assn., Louisville Com. Fgn. Rels. Office: US Dist Ct 601 W Broadway Ste 239 Louisville KY 40202-2227

HEYCK, THEODORE DALY, lawyer; b. Houston, Apr. 17, 1941; s. Theodore and Richard and Gertrude Paine (Daly) H. BA, Brown U., 1963; postgrad., Georgetown U., 1963-65, 71-72; JD, N.Y. Law Sch., 1979. Bar: N.Y. 1980, Calif. 1984, U.S. Ct. Appeals (2d cir.) 1984, U.S. Supreme Ct. 1984, U.S. Dist. Ct. (so. and ea. dists.) N.Y. 1980, U.S. Dist. Ct. (we. and no. dists.) N.Y. 1984, U.S. Dist. Ct. (cen. and so. dists.) Calif. 1984, U.S. Ct. Appeals (9th cir.) 1986. Paralegal dist. atty., Bklyn., 1975-79; asst. dist. atty. Bklyn. dist., Kings County, N.Y., 1979-85; dep. city atty. L.A., 1985—. Bd. dirs. Screen Actors Guild, N.Y.C., 1977-78. Mem. ABA, ATLA, AFTRA, NATAS, SAG, Bklyn. Bar Assn., N.Y. Trial Lawyers Assn., N.Y. State Bar Assn., Calif. Bar Assn., Fed. Bar Coun., L.A. Coun. Bar Assn., Actors Equity Assn. Home: 2106 E Live Oak Dr Los Angeles CA 90068-3639 Office: Office City Atty City Hall E 200 N Main St Los Angeles CA 90012-4110

HEYER, JOHN HENRY, II, lawyer; b. Rochester, N.Y., May 4, 1946; s. Joseph Lester and Margaret Mary (Darcy) H.; m. Charla Ann Prewitt (dec.); children: Thomas, William, John III, Richard, Mary. BA, U. Colo., 1969; JD, U. Denver, 1972. Bar: Colo. 1973, U.S. Dist. Ct. Colo. 1973, N.Y. 1976, Pa. 1979, U.S. Dist. Ct. (we. dist.) N.Y. 1980, U.S. Supreme Ct. 1982. Atty. Texaco, Inc., Denver, 1973-75; sole practice Olean, N.Y., 1975—. Pres. Northeastern Land Svcs., Inc., Olean, N.Y., 1982—; v.p. Vector Capital Corp., Rochester, N.Y., 1985-87; chpt. 7 trustee U.S. Bankruptcy Ct., we. dist. N.Y., 1986—. Editor: New York Oil and Gas Statutes, 1985. Asst. dist. atty. Cattaraugus County, Olean, 1978-81; bd. dirs. Olean YMCA, 1989—, v.p. 1993-94, pres., 1994-99, pres. bd. trustees, 1999—; bd. dirs. Buffalo Philharm. Symphony Cir., v.p., 1993, pres., 1994-95; bd. dirs. Friends of Good Music, pres. 1994-95. Mem. N.Y. State Bar Assn. (real property sect., real property devel. com.), Erie County Bar Assn., Cattaraugus County Bar Assn. (sec.-treas. 1997, v.p. 1998, pres. 1999), Eastern Mineral Law Found. (trustee 1984—, exec. com. 1994-95), Ind. Oil and Gas Assn. N.Y. (bd. dirs. 1986—, sec. 1986-87, v.p. 1988—), SAR, Selden Soc. Roman Catholic. Bankruptcy, Oil, gas, and mineral, Property, real (including real estate development, water). Office: PO Box 588 201 N Union St Olean NY 14760-2738

HEYLER, GROVER ROSS, retired lawyer; b. Manila, June 24, 1926; s. Grover Edwin and Esther Viola (Ross) H.; m. Caroline Yarbrough, Aug. 10, 1949; children: Richard Ross, Sue Louise, Randall Arthur BA, UCLA, 1949; LLB, U. Calif., Berkeley, 1952. Bar: Calif. 1953. Assoc. Latham & Watkins, L.A., 1952-60, ptnr., 1960-93, chmn., corp. securities dept., 1967-89. Chmn. Nat. Alliance for Rsch. into Schizophrenia and Depression, NYC. Mem. Calif. Bar Assn. (com. on drafting Calif. corps. code 1971-75), Order of Coif, UCLA ALumni Assn. (bd. dirs. 1966-70, 1988-90), L.A. Country Club. Corporate, general, Mergers and acquisitions, Securities. Home: 491 Homewood Rd Los Angeles CA 90049-2713

HEYMAN, RALPH EDMOND, lawyer; b. Cin., Mar. 14, 1931; s. Ralph and Florence (Kahn) H.; m. Sylvia Lee Schottenstein, Jan. 2, 1984; children: Michael Cary, Cynthia Ann Heyman Eeg, Ginger Florence. AB magna cum laude (Rufus Choat scholar), Dartmouth Coll., 1953; LLB cum laude, Harvard U., 1956; LLM, U. Cin., 1957. Bar: Ohio 1956, Ill. 1957. Pvt. practice, Cin., 1956-58, Dayton, 1958—; assoc. Freiden & Wolf, 1956-58; from assoc. to ptnr. Smith & Schnacke, 1958-88; ptnr. Chernesky, Heyman & Kress, Dayton, Ohio, 1988—. Lectr. estate planning U. Cin., 1958-61; lectr. participant Southwestern Ohio Tax Inst., 1957-65; lectr., moderator Dayton Bar Assn. Tax Insts., 1975-79, 94; lectr. continuing edn. program U. Dayton, 1989; lectr. estate planning Dayton Area Tax Profls., 1993; lectr. on venture capital Miami Valley Venture Assn., 1998; dir., gen. counsel Towne Properties, Ltd., Sachs Mgmt. Corp., Inc., Aristocrat Products, Inc., K.k. Motorcycle Supply, Inc., The Sportsman's Guide. Recipient Robert A. Shapiro Vol. award 1998. Commr. Bd. Rural Zoning Commn. Montgomery County, 1969-71; bd. dirs., pres. Jewish Fedn. Dayton, 1993-97; nat. trustee NCCJ; past pres. Temple Israel; pres. Temple Israel Found., 1999-2001; dir. United Way Greater Dayton Area, 1999. Recipient Humanitarian award NCCJ, 1997, Robert A. Shapiro Vol. award, 1998. Mem. ABA, Ohio Bar Assn., Dayton Bar Assn. (chmn. tax com.), Cin. Bar Assn., Lawyers Club, Bicycle Club, Meadowbrook Club, Dayton City Club (past pres.), B'nai Brith, Phi Beta Kappa. Jewish. Office: Chernesky Heyman & Kress PLL PO Box 3808 1100 Courthouse Plz SW Dayton OH 45401-3808

HEYMAN, SIDNEY, lawyer, educator; b. Riga, Latvia, Feb. 1, 1925; came to U.S., 1927; s. Seymour and Paula H.; m. Doris A. Groudine, Sept. 9, 1-51; children: Susan Cohn, Sharon McDermott. BS, L.I. U., 1949; LLB, Bklyn. Law Sch., 1953, JD, 1967. Trial atty. Great Am. Ins., N.Y.C., 1953-59, Julius Diamond, N.Y.C., 1959-68, Chikovsky, Snyder & Heyman, Rochester, N.Y., 1969-82; ptnr. Cory & Heyman, Staten Island, 1969; pvt. practice Rochester, 1983—. Tchr. polit. sci. SUNY, Geneseo, 1989, 95. Staff sgt. U.S. Army, 1943-46, PTO. Avocation: competitive swimming. Insurance, Personal injury (including property damage). Office: 36 W Main St Ste 604 Rochester NY 14614-1701

HEYMANN, PHILIP BENJAMIN, law educator, academic director; b. Pitts., Oct. 30, 1932; BA, Yale U., 1954; LL.B., Harvard U., 1960. Bar: D.C. 1960, Mass. 1969. Trial atty. gen. Dept. Justice, Washington, 1961-65, asst. atty. gen. criminal div., 1978-81, dep. atty. gen., 1993-94; dep. adminstr. Bur. Security and Consular Affairs, Dept. State, Washington, 1965, acting adminstr., to 1967; dep. asst. sec. of state for Bur. Internat. Orgns., 1967, exec. asst. to under sec. of state, 1967-69; with Legal Aid Agy. of D.C., 1969; faculty law Harvard U., 1969—, James Barr Ames prof. law, dir. Harvard Law Sch. Ctr. for Criminal Justice. Assoc. prosecutor and cons. to Watergate Spl. Prosecution Force, summers 1973-75 Served with USAF, 1955-57.

HEYMANN, S. RICHARD, lawyer; b. Chgo., Sept. 18, 1944; s. Samuel R. and Ann (Menning) H.; m. Jane Ann Gebhart, June 14, 1980; children: Elizabeth Jane, Catherine Claire. BS, U. Wis., 1966; JD, U. Mich., 1969. Bar: Mo. 1969, Wis. 1988. Law clk. Minn. Supreme Ct., St. Paul, 1970-72; assoc. Bryan, Cave, McPheeters & McRoberts, St. Louis, 1972-79, ptnr., 1980-87, Foley & Lardner, Madison, Wis., 1987-99; dir. Inst. for Environ. Studies U. Wis., Madison, 1996—. Adj. prof. U. Wis. Law Sch.; fellow U. Wis. Bus. Ctr.Urban Land Econs. Rsch. Fellow, Ctr. for Urban Land Econs. Mem. U. Wis. Found., Wis. Alumni Assn. (bd. dirs. 1985-87), Madison Club, Maple Bluff Country Club. Corporate, general, Environmental, Labor (including EEOC, Fair Labor Standards Act, labor-management relations, NLRB, OSHA). Office: Univ Wis Inst Environ Studies 550 N Park St Rm 70 Madison WI 53706-1404 E-mail: srheymann@facstaff.wisc.edu.

HIATT, JOHNATHAN P. lawyer, labor union administrator; b. 1949; BA, Harvard U.; JD, U. Calif., Berkeley. Bar: Calif. 1975. Ptnr. Angoff, Goldman, et al, Boston, 1974—87; gen. counsel Svc. Employees Internat. Union, 1987—95, AFL-CIO, Washington, 1995—. Exec. dir. lawyers coordinating com. AFL-CIO, Washington. Bd. dir. Nat. Employment Law Project, NYU Ctr. Labor and Employment Law. Mem.: Peggy Browning Adv. Bd., DC Employment Justice Ctr., Appleseed Found., Am. Arbitration Assoc. Office: AFL CIO 815 Sixteenth St NW Washington DC 20006 Business E-Mail: jhiatt@aflcio.org.

HIBBS, LOYAL ROBERT, lawyer; b. Des Moines, Dec. 24, 1925; s. Loyal B. and Catharine (McClymond) H.; children: Timothy, Theodore, Howard, Dean. BA, U. Iowa, 1950, LLB, JD, 1952. Bar: Iowa 1952, Nev. 1958, U.S. Supreme Ct. 1971. Ptnr. Hibbs Law Offices, Reno, 1972—. Moderator radio, TV Town Hall Coffee Breaks, 1970-72; mem. Nev. State Bicycle Adv. Bd., 1996-2000, Reno Bicycle Coun., 1995-99; mem. Reno Parks, Restoration and Cmty. Svc. Commn., 1998--, chmn., 2001--. Fellow Am. Bar Found. (Nev. chmn. 1989-94); mem. ABA (standing com. Lawyer Referral Svc. 1978-79, steering com. state dels. 1979-82, consortium on legal svcs. and the pub. 1979-82, Nev. State Bar del. to Ho. of Dels. 1978-82, 89-90, bd. govs. 1982-85, mem. legal tech. adv. coun. 1985-86, standing com. on nat. conf. groups 1985-91, chmn. sr. lawyers divsn. Nev. 1988—), Nat. Conf. Bar Pres.'s Iowa Bar Assn., Nev. Bar Assn. (bd. govs. 1968-78, pres. 1977-78), Washoe County Bar Assn. (pres. 1966-67), Nat. Jud. Coll. (bd. dirs. 1986-92, sec. 1988-92), Assn. Def. Counsel No. Calif., Assn. Def. Counsel Nev., Assn. Ski Def. Attys., Aircraft Owners and Pilots Assn. (legal svcs. plan 1991—), Washoe County Legal Aid Soc. (co-founder), Lawyer-Pilots Bar Assn. (chmn. Nev.), Greater Reno C. of C. (bd. dirs. 1968-72), Phi Alpha Delta. Aviation, General civil litigation, Probate (including wills, trusts). Home: 2300 Salerno Dr Reno NV 89509 Office: 290 S Arlington Ave Ste 100 Reno NV 89501-1793 E-mail: loyalhibbs@aol.com.

HICKEN, JEFFREY PRICE, lawyer; b. Macomb, Ill., Oct. 25, 1947; s. Victor and Mary Patricia (O'Connell) H.; m. Mary Sarah Schmidt, Aug. 23, 1969; children: Andrew, Molly, Elizabeth. BA, Cornell Coll., 1969; JD, U. Ill., 1972. Bar: Minn. 1972, U.S. Dist. Ct. Minn. 1980, U.S. Ct. Appeals (8th cir.). Assoc. Weaver, Talle & Herrick, Anoka, Minn., 1972-77; sr. ptnr. Hicken, Scott & Howard, P.A., Anoka, 1977-00, 1998—. Mem. Minn. Family Law Certification Commn., 1999. Bd. dirs. Anoka Lyric Arts; precinct chair Dem. Farmer-Labor Party, Anoka, 1976—. Capt. U.S. Army, 1969-77. Recipient J. Franklin Littel scholarship Cornell Coll., Mt. Vernon, Iowa, 1969 Fellow Am. Acad. Matrimonial Lawyers (cert. arbitrator, bd. mgrs.); mem. Minn. State Bar Assn., Anoka County Bar Assn. (pres. 1990-91), City of Anoka Charter Commn. (chmn. 1978—). Democrat. Avocations: running, violin. Family and matrimonial. Home: 1700 West Ln Anoka MN 55303-1923 Office: Hicken Scott & Howard PA 2150 3rd Ave Ste 300 Anoka MN 55303-2200

HICKEY, JOHN HEYWARD (JACK HICKEY), lawyer; b. Miami, Fla., Dec. 18, 1954; s. Weyman Park Hickey and Alice Joan (Heyward) Brown. BA magna cum laude, Fla. State U., 1976; JD, Duke U., 1980. Bars: Fla. 1980, U.S. Dist. Ct. (so. dist) Fla. 1980, U.S. Dist. Ct. (mid. dist.) Fla. 1982, U.S. Ct. Appeals (5th cir.) 1982, U.S. Ct. Appeals (11th cir.) 1983, U.S. Supreme Ct. 1985. Trial lawyer Smathers & Thompson, Miami, 1980-85, Hornsby & Whisenand P.A., Miami, 1985—, ptnr., 1988, Hickey & Jones, Miami, 1988—99, Hickey Law Firm, PA, Miami, 1999—. Lectr. securities litigation Internat. Assn. Fin. Planners, 1989, 90, Fla. Inst. CPAs, 1990, Flood Ins. Conf., Columbus, Ohio, 1991, Scottsdale, Ariz., 1992, Orlando, Fla., 1993; lectr. admiralty law, Fla. Bar, 1994, 2000; lectr. slip and fall litigation ATLA, Montreal, Can., 2001-02. Contbg. author: Fla. Bar Jour., 1990, Trial mag., 2000, P&I Internat., 1998. Interviewer of prospective undergrads. Duke U. Alumni Adv. Com., 1984—; arbitrator Miami Marine Arbitration Coun. Mem. ABA (litigation mgmt./econs. com. 1986—, comml. transactions and banking com. 1986—), Fla. Bar (chmn. admiralty law com. 2000-01, chmn. grievance com. 1986-89, vice chmn. 1999—, lectr. Bridge the Gap seminars 1984-85, jud. evaluation com. 1985, chmn. 11th cir. fee arbitration com. 1991—, cert. civil trial lawyer 1990, lectr. admiralty law 1994, chair admiralty law com. 1997—), Dade County Bar Assn. (pres.-elect 2002-03, bd. dirs. 1998—, chmn. membership com. 1982-83, chmn. cir. ct. com. 1983-84, dir. 1984-86, chmn. young lawyers sect. meetings and programs com. 1985-86, chmn. young lawyers sect. sports com. 1984-85, exec. com. 1985—, chmn. profl. arbitration subcom. 1986—, cert. of merit 1985, 88, 89, 91, 921, 93, bd. dirs. 1990-93, 97—, chmn. banking and corp. litigation com. 1990, 91, 92, chmn. civil litigation com. 1992-93, exec. com. 1992-93, treas. 1999—, sec. 2000—, v.p. 2001—), Greater Miami C. of C., Coral Gables C. of C., Propellor Club of U.S. (Miami divsn.), Southeastern Admiralty Law Inst. (proctor), Maritime Law Assn., Miami Marine Arbitration Coun., Phi Beta Kappa. Admiralty, Product liability, Personal injury (including property damage). Office: Hickey Law Firm PA 1401 Brickell Ave Ste 510 Miami FL 33131-3501 Business E-Mail: hickey@hickeylawfirm.com.

HICKEY, JOHN KING, lawyer, career officer; b. Mt. Sterling, Ky. s. John Andrew and Anna Christine H.; m. Elizabeth Jane Pattavina, Nov. 23, 1944; children: Roger Dennis, John King, Patricia Elizabeth Corsini. JD, U. Ky., 1948; M in Internat. Affairs, George Washington U., 1974. Bar: Ky. 1949, Colo. 1958, U.S. Ct. Military Appeals 1959, U.S. Supreme Ct. 1959. Commd. 2d. lt. U.S. Army Air Forces, 1942; advanced through grades to col. USAF, 1964, ret., 1970; dir. legal judicial adminstrn. Council State Govts., Lexington, Ky., 1971-73; dir. continuing legal edn. U. Ky. Coll. Law, Lexington, Ky., 1973-86; pvt. practice Lexington, Ky., 1986—. Mem. Nat. Assn. Attorneys Gen. (outstanding contributions award 1973, sec.), U. Ky. Law Alumni Assn. (sec., treas. 1973-76, appreciation award 1976), Ctrl. Ky. Knife Club (plaque 1997). Democrat. Roman Catholic. Avocations: machairologist, reading, walking, swimming. General practice, Public international, Military. Office: 3340 Nantucket Dr Lexington KY 40502-3205

HICKEY, JOHN MILLER, lawyer; b. Cleve., June 4, 1955; s. Lawrence Thomas and Margaret (Miller) H.; m. Sharon Salazar, Aug. 4, 1984; children: Theodore James, John Salazar, Margaret Maureen. Student, U. Wales, U.K., 1975-76; BA, Tulane U., 1977; JD cum laude, Calif. We. Sch. Law, 1981; LLM in tax, NYU, 1982. Bar: Calif. 1981, N.Mex. 1983, U.S. Dist. Ct. N.Mex. 1983, U.S. Tax Ct. 1983, U.S. Ct. Appeals (10th cir.) 1983. Prodn. control mgr. Randall-Textron, Inc., Wilmington, Ohio, 1977-78; assoc. Montgomery & Andrews, Santa Fe, 1983-88; shareholder, dir. Compton, Coryell, Hickey & Ives, Santa Fe, 1988-93, Hickey & Ives, Santa Fe, 1993-97, Hickey & Johnson PA, Santa Fe, 1998-99, White, Koch, Kelly & McCarthy, P.A., Santa Fe, 1999—. Mem. legal com. Santa Fe Cmty. Found., 2000—; mem. adv. bd. Presbyn. Med. Svcs. Found. Mem.: State Bar N.Mex. (bd. dirs. taxation sect. 2002—). Republican. Roman Catholic. Avocations: bicycling, squash, reading. Estate planning, Probate (including wills, trusts), Taxation, general. Home: 806 Camino Zozobra Santa Fe NM 87505-6101 Office: White Koch Kelly & McCarthy PA 433 Paseo De Peralta Santa Fe NM 87501-1958

HICKEY, JOHN THOMAS, JR., lawyer; b. Evanston, Ill., July 9, 1952; s. John Thomas and Joanne (Keating) H.; m. Candis Bailey, July 7, 1979; children: Alison, Jack, Patrick, Claire, Matthew. AB, Georgetown U., 1974; JD, U. Chgo., 1977. Bar: Ill. 1977, U.S. Dist. Ct. (no. dist.) Ill. 1977, U.S. Ct. Appeals (7th cir.) 1977, U.S. Ct. Appeals (10th cir.) 1987. Assoc. Kirkland & Ellis, Chgo., 1977-83, ptnr., 1983—. Mem. adv. bd. Leading Lawyers Network. Fellow Am. Coll. Trial Lawyers. General civil litigation. Office: Kirkland & Ellis 200 E Randolph St Fl 59 Chicago IL 60601-6609

HICKEY, TIMOTHY ANDREW, lawyer; b. Cin., Feb. 24, 1945; s. Clifford Michael and Ellen Margaret (Hart) H.; m. Debra Dessart, June 30, 1973; children: Erin, Meghan, T. Andrew Jr., Kristin. BA, Georgetown U., 1967; JD, Chase Coll. Law, 1971. Bar: Ohio 1971, U.S. Ct. Appeals (6th cir.) 1971. Coord. Hamilton County Juvenile Ct., Cin., 1967-71, chief pub. defender, 1971-72; pvt. practice Cin., 1971—. Lectr. U. Cin., 1983—. Capt. USAR, 1967-75. Mem. ABA, Ohio State Bar Assn., Cin. Bar Assn. (chmn. various coms.)., Georgetown Club, Kenwood Country Club. Republican. Roman Catholic. Avocations: tennis, golf, coaching youth baseball. Criminal, Family and matrimonial, Juvenile.

HICKLE, WILLIAM EARL, lawyer, judge; b. Ft. Worth, Aug. 23, 1957; s. John Edward Sr. and Jean Gore Hickle; m. Debra Kruse, Jan. 27, 1982; children: David John, Mark Daniel, Nathan William, Sarah Elaine, Rachel Diane. BA in Chemistry, Baylor U., 1979; JD, U. Mo., 1982. Bar: Mo. 1983. Ptnr. Carnahan, Hickle & Calvert, L.L.C., Rolla, Mo., 1983—. Part-time mcpl. judge City of Rolla, 1996—; chmn. Mo. Head Injury Adv. Coun. to Gov., Jefferson City, 1996-98. Mem. Phelps County Bar Assn. (pres. 1988), Rolla Rotary Club (pres. 1992-93). Avocations: basketball, hunting, piano. Estate planning, Personal injury (including property damage), Product liability. Home: 1100 Ironhorse Rd Rolla MO 65401-4719 Office: Carnahan Hickle & Calvert LLC PO Box 698 406 N Main St Rolla MO 65401-3016 E-mail: hickle@rollanet.org.

HICKLIN, EDWIN ANDERSON, lawyer; b. Wapello, Iowa, June 13, 1922; s. Edwin Reichley and Leona Irene (Anderson) H.; m. Carolyn Woods, June 21, 1947 (dec. Aug. 1990); children: Kathryn Hicklin Gerst, Martha Hicklin Remley, Elizabeth Hicklin Barber; m. Margaret H. Weaver, Nov. 23, 1995. BA, U. Iowa, 1946, JD, 1948. Bar: Iowa 1948, U.S. Dist. Ct. (so. dist.) Iowa 1953, U.S. Ct. Appeals (8th cir.) 1964. Ptnr. Hicklin & Hicklin, Wapello, 1948-57, Hicklin & Matthews, Wapello, 1962-90. County atty. Louisa County, Wapello, 1952-56. Active Iowa Ho. of Reps., Des Moines, 1967-68, Iowa State Bd. Tax Rev., Des Moines, 1969-74, chmn., 1969-70. 1st lt. USAF, 1943-45 (B-24 pilot 13th AF); PTO. Mem. ABA, Iowa State Bar Assn. (com. on jud. adminstrn. 1969-73, chmn. 1972-73), Masons, Phi Delta Phi. Republican. Episcopalian. General practice. Office: Hicklin & Matthews 326 Van Buren St Wapello IA 52653-1223

HICKMAN, FREDERIC W. lawyer; b. Sioux City, Iowa, June 30, 1927; s. Simeon M. and Esther (Nixon) H.; m. Katherine Heald, July 15, 1964; children: Mary Sanders, Sara Ridder. AB, Harvard U., 1948, LLB magna cum laude, 1951. Bar: Ill. 1951. Asso. firm Sidley & Austin, Chgo., 1951-55; partner firm Hopkins & Sutter, Chgo., 1956-71, 75-92, sr. counsel, 1993-2001. Asst. sec. for tax policy Dept. Treasury, Washington, 1972-75; draftsman Ill. Income Tax, 1969; author and lectr. on taxation. Mem. Ill. Humanities Council, 1977-82; mem. Citizens Commn. on Public Sch. Fin., 1977-78; chmn. bd. trustees Am. Conservatory Music, 1980-90; pres. Nat. Tax Assn., 1989-90. Served with USN, 1945-46. Mem. ABA (chmn. com. on depreciation 1966-68, com. on capital formation 1976-78, coun. 1980-83, chmn. com. on tax structure and simplification 1991-92, Internat. Fiscal Assn. (dr. 1973-77), Am. Coll. Tax Counsel (regent 1989-92), Comm. Club (Chgo.), Union League (Chgo.), Mid-Day (Chgo.), Cliff Dwellers (Chgo.), Legal (Chgo., pres. 1980-81), Chikaming Country (Lakeside, Mich.) Club. Republican. Methodist. Home: 360 Green Bay Rd # 4E Winnetka IL 60093-4032 Office: Foley & Lardner 321 N Clark St Chicago IL 60610

HICKMAN, S. BARRETT, judge; b. Danbury, Conn., Oct. 3, 1929; s. Samual John and Bernice (Mosgrove) Hickman; m. Valerie Cook, Aug. 24, 1992; m. Ruth Hewitt, Sept. 7, 1952 (dec. Mar. 1987); children: Diane, John, Deborah, Bruce. BA, Hamilton Coll., 1951; LLB, Cornell U., 1959. Assoc, then ptnr. Kent, Hazzard, Jaeger, Wilson, Freeman & Greer, White Plains, NY, 1958—78; town justice Town of Carmel, 1966—76; dist. atty. Putnam County Dist. Attys. Office, 1977—79; judge Putnam County Ct., 1979—85; justice Supreme Ct. Putnam County, NY, 1986—. Staff sgt. USAF, 1952—56. Mem.: ABA, Surrogate's Assn. and Family Ct. Judges, N.Y. State County Judges Assn., Putnam County Bar Assn., Westchester County Bar Assn., N.Y. State Bar Assn. Office: Supreme Ct Putnam County 9th Jud Dist Chambers 40 Gleneida Ave Carmel NY 10512

HICKS, BETHANY GRIBBEN, judge, commissioner, lawyer; b. N.Y., Sept. 8, 1951; d. Robert and DeSales Gribben; m. William A. Hicks III, May 21, 1982; children: Alexandra Elizabeth, Samantha Katherine. AB, Vassar Coll., 1973; MEd, Boston U., 1975; JD, Ariz. State U., 1984. Bar: Ariz. 1984. Pvt. practice, Scottsdale and Paradise Valley, Ariz., 1984-91; law clk. to Hon. Kenneth L. Fields Maricopa County Superior Ct. S.E. dist., Mesa, 1991-93; commr., judge pro tem domestic rels. and juvenile depts. Maricopa County Superior Ct. Ctrl. and S.E. Dists., Phoenix and Mesa, Ariz., 1993-99; magistrate Town of Paradise Valley, Ariz., 1993-94; judge ctrl. dist. domestic rels. dept. Maricopa County Superior Ct., Phoenix, 1999-2000, presiding judge family ct. dept., 2000—02, judge S.E. dist. civil dept., 2002—. Mem. Jr. League of Phoenix, 1984-91; bd. dirs. Phoenix Children's Theatre, 1988-90; parliamentarian Girls Club of Scottsdale, Ariz., 1985-87, 89-90, bd. dirs., 1988-91; exec. bd., sec. All Saints' Episcopal Day Sch. Parents Assn., 1991-92, pres., 1993-94; active Nat. Charity League, 1995-99, Valley Leadership Class XIX, 1997-98; vol., Teach for Am., 1997—. Mem.: ABA, Nat. Assn. of Women Judges, Assn. Family Ct. Conciliators (bd. dirs. 2001—), Ariz. Women Lawyers' Assn. (steering com. 1998—), Maricopa County Bar Assn., State Bar Ariz. Republican. Episcopalian. Office: 222 E Javelina Ave Mesa AZ 85210- E-mail: bhicks@superiorcourt.maricopa.gov.

HICKS, C. FLIPPO, lawyer; b. Fredericksburg, Va., Feb. 24, 1929; s. Robert A. and Nell (Jones) Hicks; m. Patricia DeHardit (dec. 1983); children: Robert, Patricia Shull, J. Flippo(dec.) , Paula Mooradian; m. Martha Kent. BS in Commerce, U. Va., 1950, LLB, 1952. Bar: Va. 1952, U.S. Supreme Ct. 1955. Asst. atty. gen. Commonwealth of Va., Richmond, 1953-59; ptnr. Martin, Hicks, Ingles, Ltd., Gloucester, Va., 1959-91; gen. counsel Va. Assn. Counties, Richmond, 1991—2003; pvt. practice Gloucester, 2003—. Presdl. elector, 1968, 1976, 1980; pres. exec. coun. Episcopal Diocese of Va., 1970—71, mem. standing com., 1971—74. Fellow: Am. Bar Found.; mem.: ABA (Leader of the Yr. award gen. practice sect., Constbar Leader of the Yr. 1992), Defenders Commn. Va., Nat. Assn. Counties Civil Attys. (pres. 1999—, bd. dirs.), Va. State Bar (pres. 1990—91). Democrat. Episcopalian. Avocations: gardening, college sports. General civil litigation. Office: PO Box 1300 6517 Main St Gloucester VA 23061 E-mail: counsel@vaco.org.

HICKS, C. THOMAS, III, lawyer; b. NYC, Sept. 14, 1945; s. Charles Thomas and Jeane (Merritt) H.; m. Susan Massie, Dec. 30, 1967 (div. Dec. 1997); children: Melissa, Merritt. BSCE, Va. Tech. U., 1967; JD, U. Ga., 1970; LLM in Tax, Georgetown U., 1975. Bar: Ga. 1970, Va. 1972, D.C. 1981. Assoc. Boothe, Prichard & Dudley, Fairfax, Va., 1975—78; ptnr. Wickwire, Gavin & Gibbs, P.C., Vienna, Va., 1978—83, Shaw, Pittman, Potts & Trowbridge, McLean, Va., 1983—98; shareholder Greenberg Traurig, McLean, Va., 1998—2001; ptnr. Wilmer, Cutler & Pickering, McLean, Va., 2001—03, sr. counsel, 2003—. Gen. counsel Wolf Trap Found. Performing Arts, 1998-2001. Judge advocate USMC, Washington, 1971-75; co-founder, dir. No. Va. Transp. Alliance, McLean, Va., 1987-2001, gen. counsel, 1987-2001. Mem. Va. Bar Assn. (chair bus. law coun.), Va. State Bar (bus. law sec. bd. governors, chmn. 1997-99), Fairfax Bar Assn., Nat. Assn. Bond Lawyers, Va. Assn. Comml. Real Estate (co-founder, pres., dir. 1990-92), Nat Assn. Indsl. and Office Properties (dir. Va. chpt. 1985-91, pres. 1990), No. Va. Tech. Coun. (dir. 2000—, gen. counsel 1996-2000), Greater Washington Bd. Trade, Fairfax County C. of C. (dir. 1998—). Avocations: singing, sailing, tennis, golf. Home: 6643 Madison McLean Dr Mc Lean VA 22101 Office: Wilmer Cutler & Pickering 1600 Tysons Blvd 10th Fl Mc Lean VA 22102-4856 Business E-Mail: thomas.hicks@wilmer.com.

HICKS, DEWITT T., JR., lawyer; b. Memphis, June 1, 1933; s. Dewitt T. and Bertie Oakley Hicks; m. Grayce Harkey Hicks, May 26, 1956; 3 children. BS, Miss. State U., 1954; JD, U. Miss., 1959. Bar: Miss. Ptnr. Gholson, Hicks & Nichols, Columbus, Miss., 1959—. Part time city judge City of Columbus, city atty. Editor: Miss. Law Jour., 1959—60. Capt. USAF, 1954—57. Mem.: ABA, Lowndes County Bar Assn., Miss. State Bar Assn. (pres.), C. of C. (pres. 1980), Kiwanis (pres. 1966). Methodist. Avocations: hunting, fishing. Insurance, Product liability, Property, real (including real estate development, water). Home: PO Box 1111 Columbus MS 39703-1111 Office: Gholson Hicks & Nichols 710 Main St 3d Fl Columbus MS 39701 Fax: 662-327-6217. E-mail: dhicks@ghnlaw.com.

HICKS, J. PORTIS, lawyer; b. Detroit, May 16, 1938; s. Livingstone Porter and Mildred (Portis) H.; m. Julie A. Gildersleeve, June 1, 1963 (div. Apr. 1977); children: Darcy A., Tyler P; m. Laura J. Corwin, Oct. 25, 1995. BA in History, U. Mich., 1962, JD, 1964; cert., London Sch. Econs.-Polit. Sci., 1965. Bar: N.Y. 1966, U.S. Dist. Ct. (so. and ea. dists.) N.Y. 1971, U.S. Ct. Appeals (2d cir.) 1972, U.S. Supreme Ct. 1981. Assoc. Kelley Drye & Warren, N.Y.C., 1965-69, Pinheiro Neto, Barros & Freire, Sao Paulo, Brazil, 1969-71; assoc., then ptnr. Wender, Murase & White, N.Y.C., 1971-82; ptnr. Boulanger, Finley & Hicks, N.Y.C., 1982-84, 89-91, Drinker, Biddle, & Reath, N.Y.C., 1984-89, of counsel, 1989-91; ptnr. Boulanger, Hicks, & Churchill, N.Y.C., 1989—96, Winthrop Stimson Putnam & Roberts (now Pillsbury Winthrop), N.Y.C., 1996-2000, sr. counsel, 2000—. Mem.: Assn. Bar City N.Y. Office: Pillsbury Winthrop LLP 54 Lombard St London EC3V 9DH England E-mail: phicks@pillsburywinthrop.com.

HICKS, MARION LAWRENCE, JR., (LARRY HICKS), lawyer; b. Bethlehem, Pa., Sept. 5, 1945; s. Marion Lawrence and Martha (McCracken) H.; m. Beverly Brickman, Nov. 28, 1970; children: Yale McCracken, Hadley Brook, Kelley Hayden. BA History, Duke U., 1967; JD with honors, U. Tex., 1970. Bar: Tex. 1970. Law clerk 9th cir. U.S. Ct. Appeals, L.A., 1970-71; assoc. Thompson, Knight, Simmons & Bullion, Dallas, 1971-77; ptnr. Thompson & Knight, Dallas, 1977—. Dir. The Real Estate Coun.; spkr. in field. Editor Tex. Law Review; contbr. articles to profl. jours. Mem. ABA (real property, trust and probate sect.), Am. Coll. Mortgage Attys. (regent), State Bar Tex., Dallas Bar Assn. (past chmn. real property sect., legal aid and legal svcs. com.), Coll. State Bar Tex., Order of Coif, Tower Club (bd. govs.), Phi Delta Phi. Avocations: sports, hunting, fishing. Property, real (including real estate development, water), Finance, Banking. Home: 4310 Throckmorton St Dallas TX 75219-2240 Office: Thompson & Knight LLP 1700 Pacific Ave Ste 3300 Dallas TX 75201-4693 E-mail: larry.hicks@tklaw.com.

HIDEN, ROBERT BATTAILE, JR., lawyer; b. Boston, May 8, 1933; s. Robert Battaile Sr. and Clotilda (Waddell) H.; m. Ann Eliza McCracken, Mar. 27, 1956; children: Robert B. III, Elizabeth Patterson, John Hughes. BA, Princeton U., 1955; LLB, U. Va., 1960. Bar: N.Y. 1961, U.S. Ct. Appeals (2d cir.) 1974, U.S. Dist. Ct. (so. dist.) N.Y. 1975. Assoc. Sullivan & Cromwell, N.Y.C., 1960-67, ptnr., 1968-98, of counsel, 1999-2000, sr. counsel, 2001—. Articles editor and contbr. U. Va. Law Rev., 1959-60; contbr., mem. bd. editors Futures Internat. Law Letter, 1987-92. Trustee Hampton (Va.) U. and Hampton Inst., 1984-2003; mem. Dillard scholarship com. U. Va. Law Sch., 1984-98, 2001-02; gov. Ramapo (NJ) Coll. Found., 2002-; commr. Larchmont Little League, N.Y., 1964-68; chmn. Larchmont Jr. Sailing Program, 1977-78; vestry, jr. warden St. John's Episc. Ch., Larchmont, 1982-86, 99-2002. Served to lt. (j.g.) USNR, 1955-57. Mem. ABA, N.Y. State Bar Assn., Assn. of Bar of City of N.Y., N.Y. County Bar Assn., Am. Judicature Soc., Larchmont U. Club (pres. 1976-77), Larchmont Yacht Club (trustee 1979-85, sec. 1990—), Yale Club (N.Y.C.), Coral Beach Club (Bermuda), Raven Soc., Order of Coif, Omicron Delta Kappa. Democrat. Avocations: skiing, golf, sailing, tennis. Corporate, general, Mergers and acquisitions, Securities. Home: 2 Walnut Ave Larchmont NY 10538-4232 Office: Sullivan & Cromwell 125 Broad St Fl 28 New York NY 10004-2489

HIEKEN, CHARLES, lawyer; b. Granite City, Ill., Aug. 15, 1928; s. Samuel and Margaret (Isaacs) H.; m. Donna Jane Clanin, Jan. 6, 1961; children: Tina Jane, Seth Paul. SBEE, SMEE, MIT, 1952; LLB, Harvard U., 1957. Bar: Ill. 1957, Mass. 1958, U.S. Supreme Ct. 1960, U.S. Ct. Customs and Patent Appeals 1961, U.S. Ct. Claims 1963, U.S. Ct. Appeals (fed. cir.) 1982. Patent asst. Lab. Electronics, Boston, 1954-56, Fish, Richardson & Neave, Boston, 1956-57; assoc. Hill, Sherman, Meroni & Simpson, Chgo., 1957, Joseph Weingarten, Boston, 1957-58, Wolf, Greenfield & Hieken, Boston, 1958-61, ptnr., 1961-70; prin. Charles Hieken Law Offices, Waltham, Mass., 1970-87; ptnr. Fish & Richardson, Boston, 1987-94, prin., 1995—. Mem. Pres. Carter's adv. com. on indsl. innovation, 1979. Mem. pres.'s adv. coun. Bentley Coll., 1993—; mem. coun. Harvard Law Sch. Assn., 1998-02. Served with U.S. Merchant Marine, 1944-47, U.S. Army, 1952-54. Mem.: IEEE (sr.; life), Boston Patent Law Assn. (chmn. pub. rels. com. 1965—66, chmn. antitrust law com. 1966—70, 1978—80, treas. 1970—71, v.p. 1971—72, pres.-elect 1972—73, pres. 1973—74), Ill. State Bar Assn. (privileged mem.), Mass. Bar Assn. (chmn. intellectual property com. 1977—80), Boston Bar Assn. (civil procedure com. 1959—), Down Town Club (bd. govs., v.p. gen counsel), Tau Beta Pi, Eta Kappa Nu. Federal civil litigation, Patent, Trademark and copyright. Home: 193 Wilshire Dr Sharon MA 02067-1561 Office: Fish & Richardson PC 225 Franklin St 31st Fl Boston MA 02110-2804 E-mail: hieken@fr.com.

HIENTON, JAMES ROBERT, lawyer; b. Phoenix, July 25, 1951; s. Clarence J. Jr. and Lola Jean (Paxton) H.; m. Diane Marie DeBrosse, July 22, 1977. BA, U. Ariz., 1972; MBA, JD, Ariz. State U., 1975; LLM, Washington U., St. Louis, 1977. Bar: Ariz. 1975, U.S. Dist. Ct. (Ariz.) 1975. Corp. atty. Ariz. Pub. Service, Phoenix, 1975-76; asst. prof. Ariz. State U., Tempe, 1977; assoc. then ptnr. Gust, Rosenfeld, Divelbess et al, Phoenix, 1978-85; sr. tax ptnr. Evans, Kitchel and Jenckes, Phoenix, 1985-89; ptnr. Jennings, Strouss and Salmon, Phoenix, 1989-93; sr. shareholder Bonnett, Fairbourne, Friedman, Hienton, Miner & Fry, P.C., Phoenix, 1993-95, Ridenour, Hienton, Harper and Kelhoffer, P.C., Phoenix, 1995—. Officer, bd. dirs. Charter Govt., Phoenix, 1978-82; mem. Phoenix Citizens Charter Rev. Com., 1982; participant Phoenix Together; participant lst Phoenix Town Hall, 1981, 2d, 1982, 3d, 1983, recorder, 1983, 85; mem. Balanced Govt. Com., 1983; mem Phoenix Police and Fire Pension Bds., 1982-89; bd. dirs. Ariz. Theater Co., 1979-89; mem. class V, Valley Leadership, 1983-84; founding life mem. Ariz. Mus. Sci. and Industry. Mem. ABA, Ariz. Bar Assn., Maricopa County Bar Assn., Phi Kappa Phi. Clubs: Phoenix City. Republican. Corporate, general, Mergers and acquisitions, Corporate taxation. Home: 441 W Mclellan Blvd Phoenix AZ 85013-1141 Office: Ridenour Hienton Harper & Kelhoffer PC Ste 3300 201 N Central Ave Phoenix AZ 85004

HIER, MARSHALL DAVID, lawyer; b. Bay City, Mich., Aug. 24, 1945; s. Marshall George and Helen May (Copeland) H.; m. Nancy Speed Brown, June 26, 1970; children: John, Susan, Ann. BA, Mich. State U., 1966; JD, U. Mich., 1969. Bar: Mo. 1969. Assoc. Peper, Martin, Jensen, Maichel and Hetlage, St. Louis, 1969-76, ptnr., 1976-95; prin. Bertram, Peper and Hier, P.C., St. Louis, 1996—. Bd. dirs. Gateway Ctr. Met. St. Louis, Mercantile Libr. Assn., St. Louis Soc. Blind and Visually Impaired. Contbr. articles to profl. jours. Mem. St. Louis Bar Assn. (editor jour. 1988—), St. Louis Civil Round Table (former pres.). Baptist. Corporate, general, Private international, Securities. Home: 17141 Chaise Ridge Rd Chesterfield MO 63005-4457

HIERONYMUS, EDWARD WHITTLESEY, lawyer; b. Davenport, Iowa, June 13, 1943; BA cum laude, Knox Coll., 1965; JD with distinction, Duke U., 1968. Bar: Calif. 1969, Iowa 1968. Ptnr. O'Melveny & Myers, LA, 1974—96, of counsel, 1996—99. Contbr. articles on law to profl. jours. Exec. sec. Los Angeles Com. Fgn. Relations, 1975-86. Served with Judge Adv. Gen. U.S. Army, 1965-74. Mem. ABA (award for profl. merit 1968), Calif. Bar Assn. (founding co-chair natural resources subsect., real property sect. 1986-88), Los Angeles County Bar Assn., Iowa Bar Assn. Commercial, contracts (including sales of goods; commercial financing), Environmental, Property, real (including real estate development, water). Office: O'Melveny & Myers 400 S Hope St Los Angeles CA 90071-2899

HIGDON, FREDERICK ALONZO, lawyer, accountant; b. Lebanon, Ky., Aug. 30, 1950; s. William Joseph and Mary Rita Higdon; m. Nancy Lawrence Brents, Aug. 4, 1972; children: Ashley, Matthew, Scott. BS cum laude, Western Ky. U., 1972; JD, U. Louisville, 1975. Bar: Ky. 1975. Staff acct. Coopers & Lybrand, Louisville, 1972-74; tax acct. Peat, Marwick & Mitchell, Louisville, 1974-76; lawyer Spragens, Smith & Higdon, P.S.C., Lebanon, Ky., 1976—. Bd. dirs., vice chair Peoples Bank, Lebanon; asst. county atty. Marion County, Ky., 1992-96. Past pres. Lebanon/Marion County C. of C., Lebanon/Marion County Leadership Alumni Assn., Marion County Jr. Miss, Inc., 2001; past pres., dir. Marion County Pub. Libr., Lebanon, 1993-2001, Marion County Indsl. Found., Lebanon, 1997—. Mem. Ky. Bar Assn., Ky. Soc. CPAs, Marion County Bar Assn. (treas. 1978—). Avocations: snow skiing, hunting, fishing. General practice, Probate (including wills, trusts), Taxation, general. Office: Spragens Smith and Higdon PSC 15 Court Sq Lebanon KY 40033-1257

HIGGINBOTHAM, PATRICK ERROL, federal judge; b. Ala., Dec. 16, 1938; Student, U. Ala., 1956, Arlington State Coll., 1957, North Tex. State U., 1958, U. Tex., 1958; BA, U. Ala., 1960, LLB, 1961; LLD (hon.) , So. Meth. U., 1989. Bar: Ala. 1961, Tex. 1962, U.S. Supreme Ct. 1962. Assoc. to ptnr. Coke & Coke, Dallas, 1964—75; judge U.S. Dist. Ct. (no. dist.) Tex., Dallas, 1976—82, U.S. Ct. Appeals (5th cir.), Dallas, 1982—. Adj. prof. So. Meth. U. Law Sch., 1971—, adj. prof. constl. law, 1981—, U. Tex. Sch. Law, 1998; M.D. Anderson pub. svc. prof. in residence Tex. Tech. U. Sch. Law, 1999; John Sparkman jurist-in-residence U. Ala. Sch. Law, 1995, 97, 99; conferee Am. Assembly, 1975, Pound Conf., 1976; bd. suprs. Inst. Civil Justice Rand. Contbr. With JAG USAF, 1961—64. Named Outstanding Alumnus, U. Tex., Arlington, 1978, One of Nation's 100 Most Powerful Persons for the 80's, Next Mag.; recipient Dan Meador award, U. Ala., Samuel E. Gates Litigation award, Am. Coll. Trial Lawyers, 1997, A. Sherman Christensen award, 2002. Fellow: Am. Bar Found.; mem.: ABA, Ctr. for Am. and Internat. Law (bd. dirs. 1998—, chmn.), Am. Inns. of Ct. Found. (pres. 1996—2000), Farrah Law Soc., Dallas Inn of Ct., Nat. Jud. Coun. State and Fed. Cts., Am. Judicature Soc., Am. Law Inst., Dallas Bar Found., Dallas Bar Assn., Bench and Bar, Order of Coif (hon.), Omicron Delta Kappa. Office: US Ct Appeals 1302 US Courthouse 1100 Commerce St Dallas TX 75242-1027

HIGGINS, JOHN PATRICK, lawyer, mediator, educator, lobbyist; b. Beloit, Wis., Feb. 13, 1952; s. John Eugene and Catherine Marie (Beaudry) H. BA cum laude, St. Norbert Coll., 1973; postgrad., DePaul U. Law Sch., 1974-76; JD, U. Wis., Madison, 1977; MBA, Keller Grad. Sch. Mgmt., Milw., 1986; postgrad., U. Wis., Milw. Bar: Wis. 1977, U.S. Dist. Ct. (ea. and we. dists) Wis., 1977, U.S. Ct. Appeals (7th cir.), 1977, U.S. Supreme Ct., 1983. Assessment technician Kenosha County Assessor, Wis., 1973-75; law clk. various firms, Madison, Wis., 1976-77; claims atty. Employers Ins. of Wausau (Wis.), 1977-80, trial counsel, 1980-99; ptnr. Guttormsen, Hartley, Guttormsen, Wilk & Higgins, Kenosha, 2000—; mng. ptnr. Higgins Investment Properties, LLC, 2002—. Part time instr. North Ctrl. Tech. Inst., Wausau, 1980; adj. prof. Marian Coll., Fond du Lac, Wis., 1990-2000, Carthage Coll., Kenosha, Wis., 2000-01; dir. , v.p. legal John E. Higgins Appraisal Co., Kenosha, 1977-97; lectr., spkr. various profl. and fraternal groups; mem. dist. 1 investigative com. Office of Lawyer Regulation Wis. Supreme Ct., 2001—. Author articles and monographs. Bd. dirs., arbitrator Roman Cath. Archdiocese of Milw., 1983-85; mem. human rels commn. City of Kenosha, 1997—, vice chair, 1999-2001; mem. City of Kenosha Zoning Appeals Bd., 2001—, vice chmn., 2002—; bd. dirs. Michael Naidicz Found. Fellow Young Lawyers Assn.; mem. State Bar Wis. (bd. govs. 1990-91, bd. dirs. young lawyers divsn. 1978-87, sec. 1979-82, chmn. law reform com. 1984-87, chmn. planning conf. young lawyers divsn. 1986, chmn. gavel awards com. 1985-87, chmn. comm. com. 1984-87, interprofl. com. 1987-89, conv. & entertainment com. 1988-1992, 94-97, chmn., mem. various coms.), Thomas More Soc., State Bar Assn. Wis., Civil Trial Coun. Wis., Kenosha Bar Assn., St. Norbert Coll. Alumni

Assn. (exec. bd. dirs. 1979-87, chpt. liaison, editor chpt. newsletter, class devel. agt. 1998-99), Nat. Assn. State Bar Jours. (bd. trustee 1986-89), Am. Corp. Coun. Assn. (bd. dirs. 1989-98, pres. Wis. chpt. 1997-98), Am. Acad. ADR Attorneys, Phi Alpha Delta. State civil litigation, Insurance, Probate (including wills, trusts). Office: Guttormsen Hartley Guttormsen Wilk & Higgins 600 52d St Ste 200 Kenosha WI 53140 E-mail: JPH@kenoshalawyers.com.

HIGGINS, MARY CELESTE, lawyer, researcher; b. Chgo., Feb. 9, 1943; d. Maurice James and Helen Marie (Egan) H. AB, St. Mary-of-the-Woods Coll., Ind., 1965; JD, DePaul U., 1970; LLM, John Marshall Law Sch., Chgo., 1976; postgrad., Harvard U., 1981—82, MPA, 1982; MPhil, U. Cambridge (Eng.), 1983. Bar: Ill., 1970, U.S. Dist. Ct. (no. dist.) Ill. 1970. Pvt. practice, Chgo., 1970—72, 1979—80; atty. corp. counsel dept. Continental Bank, Chgo., 1972-76; asst. sec., asst. counsel Marshall Field & Co., Chgo., 1976-79; sr. atty. Mattel, Inc., Hawthorne, Calif., 1980-81; rsch. in revitalization and adjustment of U.S. Industries in U.S. and world markets, 1981-83; legal cons., 1983-85; Midwest regional officer Legal Svcs. Corp., 1985-87, assoc. dir., 1986, acting dir. office of field svcs., 1986-87, dir., 1987-89, Meridian One Corp., Alexandria, Va., 1990—. Recipient Am. Jurisprudence awards for acad. excellence, 1966-70. Mem. Ill. Bar Assn. Corporate, general, Private international, Public international. Home: 203 Yoakum Pkwy Apt 508 Alexandria VA 22304-3711

HIGHSMITH, SHELBY, federal judge; b. Jacksonville, Fla., Jan. 31, 1929; s. Isaac Shelby and Edna Mae (Phillips) H.; m. Mary Jane Zimmerman, Nov. 25, 1972; children— Holly Law, Shelby. AA, Ga. Mil. Coll., 1948; BA, JD, U. Kansas City, 1958. Bar: Fla. 1958. Trial atty., Kansas City, Mo., 1958-59, Miami, Fla., 1959-70; circuit judge Dade County, Fla., 1970-75; sr. ptnr. Highsmith, Strauss, Glatzer & Deutsch, P.A., Miami, 1975-91; judge U.S. Dist. Ct. (so. dist.) Fla., Miami, 1991—. Chief legal adviser Gov.'s War on Crime Program, 1967-68; spl. counsel Fla. Racing Commn., 1969-70; mem. Inter-Agy. Law Enforcement Planning Counsel of Fla., 1969-70. Served to capt. AUS, 1949-55. Decorated Bronze Star; recipient Outstanding Alumni Achievement Law award, U. Mo., 1998, Korean War Svc. medal, Pres. South Korea on 50th Anniversary of Korean War, Disting. Alumnus award, Ga. Mil. Coll., 2002. Fellow Internat. Soc. Barristers; mem. ABA, Dade County Bar Assn., Bench and Robe, Torch and Scroll, Miami Nat. Golf Club, Wildcat Cliffs Country Club, (Highlands, N.C.), Omicron Delta, Phi Alpha Delta. Republican. Roman Catholic. Office: Fed Justice Bldg 99 NE 4th St Rm 1027 Miami FL 33132-2138

HIGHT, B. BOYD, lawyer; b. Lumberton, N.C., Feb. 15, 1939; s. B. Boyd and Mary Lou (Lennon) H.; m. Mary Kay Sweeney, Mar. 31, 1962; children: Kathryn, Kevin. BA, Duke U., 1960; LLB, Yale U., 1966; diploma in comparative law, U. Stockholm, 1967. Assoc. O'Melveny & Myers, Los Angeles, 1967-74, ptnr., 1974-79, 81-84, 89—; dep. asst. sec. trans. and telecommunications U.S. Dept. State, Washington, 1979-81; exec. v.p., gen. counsel Sante Fe Internat. Corp., Alhambra, Calif., also bd. dirs. Bd. dirs. Planned Parenthood L.A., 1986-95, pres., 1992-94; mem. bd. overseers Rand Ctr. Russian and Eurasian Studies, 1987-2000, chair, 1994-2000; trustee Am. U. Cairo, 1987—, Autry Western Heritage Mus., 2002—; bd. dirs. Calif. Supreme Ct. Hist. Soc., 1993-2001; bd. overseers The Huntington, 1996—. Mem. Coun. Fgn. Rels., Pacific Coun. on Internat. Policy, Calif. Club, Los Angeles Country Club. Democrat. Federal civil litigation, General civil litigation, State civil litigation. Office: O'Melveny & Myers 400 S Hope St Los Angeles CA 90071-2899 E-mail: bhight@omm.com.

HIGHTOWER, JACK ENGLISH, former state supreme court justice, congressman; b. Memphis, Tex., Sept. 6, 1926; s. Walter Thomas and Floy Edna (English) H.; m. Colleen Ward, Aug. 26, 1950; children— Ann, Amy, Alison. BA, Baylor U., 1949; JD, 1951; LLM, Univ. Va., 1992. Bar: Tex. 1951. Since practiced in, Vernon; mem. Tex. Ho. of Reps., 1953-54; dist. atty. 46th Jud. Dist. Tex., 1955-61; mem. Tex. Senate, 1965-75, pro tempore, 1971; mem. 94th-98th Congresses from 13th Tex. Dist., 1975-85; 1st asst. atty. gen. State of Tex., 1985-87; justice Texas Supreme Ct., Austin, 1988-95; ret., 1996. Mem. Tex. Law Enforcement Study Commn., 1957; del. White House Conf. Children and Youth, 1970; alt. del. Dem. Nat. Conv., 1968; bd. regents Midwestern U., Wichita Falls, Tex., 1962-65; trustee Baylor U., 1972-81, acting gov., 1971; trustee Wayland Bapt. Univ., Plainview, Tex., 1991-2001, Bapt. Children's Home, 1959-62, Tex. Scottish Rite Hosp. Children, 1991—, Human Welfare Commn.; bd. dirs. Bapt. Standard, 1959-68; mem. Nat. Commn. on Librs. and Info. Sci., 1999—. With USNR, 1944-46. Named Outstanding Dist. Atty, Tex., Tex. Law Enforcement Found., 1959, Disting. Alumnus, Baylor U., 1978; recipient Knapp-Porter award Tex. A&M Univ., 1980. Mem. Tex. Dist. and County Attys. Assn. (pres. 1958-59), Scottish Rite Ednl. Assn. Tex. (exec. com. 1990—), Tex. Supreme Ct. Hist. Soc. (pres. 1991-98), Tex. Bar. Found. (fellow 1992), SAR, U.S. Supreme Ct. Hist. Soc., Tex. State Hist. Assn. (exec. coun. 1998-2002), Masons (grand master Tex. 1972), Lions (pres. Vernon 1961).

HIGUCHI, SHIRLEY A. lawyer; Grad., Georgetown U., 1984. Atty. Epstein, Becker & Green, PC; asst. exec. dir. legal and regulatory affairs APA, Washington. Mem.: Asian Pacific Am. Bar Assn. (bd. dirs.), D.C. Bar Assn. (treas. 1993, bd. govs. 1994—2000, pres.-elect, pub. svc. activities com., co-chair health law sect.'s steering com.). Office: Am Psychol Assn 750 First St NW Washington DC 20002*

HILBERT, JOHN WARREN, II, lawyer; b. Columbus, Ohio, Aug. 3, 1946; s. John Warren and Viola (Schatz) H.; m. Elaine Kay Baver, June 28, 1969; children: John Warren III, Scott Michael, Robert Louis. BA, Ohio State U., 1968, JD cum laude, 1971. Bar: Ohio 1971, U.S. Dist. Ct. (no. dist.) Ohio 1972, U.S. Ct. Appeals (6th cir.) 1983. Legal asst. Franklin County Prosecutors Office, Columbus, 1969-71; assoc. Fuller, Henry, Hodge & Snyder, Toledo, 1971-76; ptnr. Fuller & Henry, Toledo, 1976—98, mng. ptnr., 1989-94; ptnr. Shumaker, Loop & Kendrick, LLP, 1998—. Instr. real estate law U. Toledo, 1973-90. Contbr. law rev. Capt. USAR, 1968-79. Mem. ABA (mem. antitrust sect., Sherman act com., banking and bus. law sect.), Ohio Bar Assn. (banking and comml. law com.), Toledo Bar Assn., Order of Coif, Catawba Island Club (trustee 1982-87), Disting. Clown Corps., Kappa Sigma. Republican. Lutheran. Avocations: boating, skiing, fishing. Banking, Corporate, general, Property, real (including real estate development, water). Office: Fuller & Henry PO Box 2088 Toledo OH 43603-2088

HILBRECHT, NORMAN TY, lawyer; b. San Diego, Feb. 11, 1933; s. Norman Titus and Elizabeth (Lair) H.; m. Mercedes L. Sharratt, Oct. 24, 1980. BA, Northwestern U., 1956; JD, Yale U., 1959. Bar: Nev. 1959, U.S. Supreme Ct. 1963. Assoc. counsel Union Pacific R.R., Las Vegas, 1962; ptnr. Hilbrecht & Jones, Las Vegas, 1962-69; pres. Hilbrecht, Jones, Schreck & Bernhard, 1969-83, Hilbrecht & Assocs, 1983—, Mobil Transport Corp., 1970-72; gen. counsel Bell United Ins. Co., 1986-94; mem. Nev. Assembly, 1966-72, minority leader, 1971-72; mem. Nev. Senate, 1974-78; legis. commn., 1977-78; oper. mem. Corp. Svcs. Group, 1998—; pres. Corp. Svcs. Co., 1998—, Nev. Incorporating Co., 1998—; mng. mem. Amcorp LLC., 1999—. Asst. lectr. bus. law U. Nev., Las Vegas. Author: Nevada Motor Carrier Compendium, 1990, Nevada Corporation Handbook, 1999. Labor mgmt. com. NCCJ, 1963; mem. Clark County (Nev.) Dem. Ctrl. Com., 1959-80, 1st vice chmn., 1965-66; del. Western Regional Assembly on Ombudsman; chmn. Clark County Dem. Conv., 1966, Nev. Dem. Conv., 1966; pres. Clark County Legal Aid Soc., 1964, Nev. Legal Aid and Defender Assn., 1965-83; assoc. for justice Nat. Jud. Coll., 1993-96. Capt. AUS, 1952-67. Named Outstanding State Legislator Eagleton Inst. Politics, Rutgers U., 1969. Mem. ABA, ATLA, Am. Judicature Soc., Am. Acad. Polit. and Social Sci., State Bar Nev. (chmn. adminstrv. law com. 1991-94, chmn. sect. on adminstrv. law 1996), Nev. Trial Lawyers (state v.p. 1966), Am. Assn. Ret. Persons (state legis. com. 1991-94), Rotary, Las Vegas Rotary Found. (trustee 2002—), Elks, Phi Beta Kappa, Delta Phi Epsilon, Theta Chi, Phi Delta Phi. Lutheran. Administrative and regulatory, Utilities, public, Transportation. Office: 723 S Casino Center Blvd Las Vegas NV 89101-6716 E-mail: hilbrecht@lvcm.com.

HILDEBRAND, DANIEL WALTER, lawyer; b. Oshkosh, Wis., May 1, 1940; s. Dan M. and Rose Marie (Baranowski) H.; m. Dawn E. Erickson; children: Daniel G., Douglas P., Elizabeth A., Rachel E., Jacob E., Catherine E. BS, U. Wis., 1962, LLB, 1964. Bar: Wis. 1964, U.S. Dist. Ct. (we. dist.) Wis. 1964, N.Y. 1965, U.S. Dist. Ct. (so. and ea. dists.) N.Y. 1967, U.S. Ct. Appeals (2d cir.) 1968, U.S. Dist. Ct. (ea. dist.) Wis. 1970, U.S. Ct. Appeals (7th cir.) 1970, U.S. Supreme Ct. 1970, U.S. Tax Ct. 1986, U.S. Ct. Appeals (8th cir.) 1988, U.S. Ct. Appeals (D.C. cir.) 1991. Assoc. Willkie, Farr & Gallagher, N.Y.C., 1964-68; from assoc. to ptnr. DeWitt Ross & Stevens S.C., Madison, Wis., 1968—. Lectr. U. Wis. Law Sch., Madison, 1972—; mem. Joint Survey Com. on Tax Ememptions Wis. Editor: U. Wis. Law Rev., 1963-64. Pres. Wis. Law Foun., 1993-95, Wis. Jud. Commn., 1992-98, chmn., 1997-98. Fellow Am. Bar Found. (life), Wis. Bar Found.; mem. ABA (com. pub. fin. judicial campaigns 2001—, mem. trial practice com. litigation sect., ho. of dels. 1992—, standing com. on ethics 1997-2003, bd. govs. 2003—, Wis. state del. 1995-2003, bd. govs. 2003—), Wis. Bar Assn. (bd. govs. 1981-85, 86-93, mem. exec. com. 1987-93, chmn. 1988-89, pres. 1991-92), N.Y. State Bar Assn., Dane County Bar Assn. (pres. 1980-81), 7th Cir. Bar Assn., Am. Law Inst., Am. Acad. Appellate Lawyers, James E. Doyle Inn of Ct. Roman Catholic. Federal civil litigation, State civil litigation. Office: 2 E Mifflin St Ste 600 Madison WI 53703-2890 E-mail: dwh@dewittross.com.

HILDEBRANDT, GEORGE FREDERICK, lawyer; b. Claverack, N.Y., Mar. 28, 1959; s. Harry K. and Sophie Evelyn (Reutenauer) H. BA, Syracuse U., 1981, JD, 1984. Bar: N.Y. 1985, U.S. Dist. Ct. (no. dist.) N.Y. 1986, U.S. Supreme Ct. 1997, U.S. Ct. Appeals (2d cir.) 1998. Atty. Frank H. Hiscock Legal Aid Soc., Syracuse, N.Y., 1985-88; pvt. practice Syracuse, 1988—. Mem. Nat. Assn. Criminal Def. Lawyers, N.Y. State Trial Lawyers Assn. Criminal, Personal injury (including property damage). Office: 300 Crown Bldg 304 S Franklin St Syracuse NY 13202-1233

HILDER, PHILIP H. lawyer; b. Highland Park, Ill., July 2, 1955; BA, U. Iowa, 1977; JD, Boston Coll., 1981. Bar: Tex. 1985, Ill. 1981, U.S. Supreme Ct., U.S. Dist. Ct. (so., no., ea., and we. dists.) Tex., U.S. Dist. Ct. (no. dist.) Ill., Ariz., U.S. Ct. Appeals (5th cir.). Asst. U.S. atty. U.S. Dist. Ct. (so. dist.) Tex., 1984-87, 90; atty. in charge organized crime strike force U.S. Dept. Justice, Houston, 1987-90; pvt. practice Houston, 1991-97; ptnr. Hilder and Assocs., Houston, 1997—. Mem. FBA (v.p. 1994-95, pres. 1995-96), Inns of Ct. (Master of Bench), Wong Sun Soc. San Francisco. Avocation: traveling. Federal civil litigation, Criminal. Office: 819 Lovett Blvd Houston TX 77006-3905

HILDNER, PHILLIPS BROOKS, II, lawyer; b. Battle Creek, Mich., June 26, 1944; s. Phillips Brooks and Eva Marie (Burek) H.; divorced; 1 child, Phillips Brooks III. BS, Western Mich. U., 1967; JD, Detroit Coll. Law, 1971. Bar: Mich. 1971. Asst. prosecuting atty. Genesee County, Flint, Mich., 1971-73; ptnr. Conover, Hildner & Zielinski, Fenton, Mich., 1973-79; sole practice Fenton, 1980—. Sponsoring atty. Law Day Fenton H.S., 1973—. Mem. State Bar Mich., Genesee County Bar Assn., Fenton C. of C., 2d Century Club Detroit Coll. Law, Delta Theta Phi. Episcopalian. Avocations: fly fishing, hunting, running, exercise. General practice, Probate (including wills, trusts). Office: PO Box 87 115 W Shiawassee Ave Fenton MI 48430-2005

HILE, RICHARD C. lawyer; b. Silsbee, Tex., May 19, 1949; s. Hubert Hile and Johnnye Lou Epperson Hile; m. Susan Tonahill, Feb. 19, 1977; children: Jennifer Kuczaj, Lesley Collins Hile. BS in Govt., Lamar U., 1971; JD, Tex. Tech U., 1974. Bar: Tex. 1974, U.S. Dist. Ct. (ea. dist.) Tex. 1974, U.S. Ct. Appeals (5th cir.) 1975, U.S. Supreme Ct. 1981, U.S. Ct. Appeals (3d cir.) 1983, U.S. Dist. Ct. (so. dist.) Tex. 1993, U.S. Dist. Ct. (we. dist.) Tex. 1994. Law clk. to Hon. Joe Fisher U.S. Dist. Ct. (ea. dist.) Tex., Beaumont, 1974—75; ptnr. Tonahill, Hile, Lester & Jacobelli, Jasper, Tex., 1975—92, Dies & Hile, LLP, Austin, 1992—. Adv. bd. Entergy Corp., Beaumont, 1998—. Bd. regents Stephen F. Austin U., Nacogdoches, Tex., 1982—88; bd. dirs. Tex. Dept. Homing and Cmty. Affairs, Austin, 1991—95, Tex. Ctr. Legal Ethics, Austin, 1995—. Named Outstanding Alumni, Tex. Tex. U. Sch. Law, 1999. Fellow: Am. Bd. Trial Advs., Internat. Soc. Barristers, Internat. Acad. Trial Lawyers Assn. Construction, Product liability, Personal injury (including property damage). Home: 1508 Marshall Ln Austin TX 78703 Office: Dies and Hile LLP 1601 Rio Grande Ste 330 Austin TX 78701 Office Fax: 512-476-4397. Personal E-mail: rhile@swbell.net.

HILES, BRADLEY STEPHEN, lawyer; b. Granite City, Ill., Nov. 11, 1955; s. Joseph J. and Betty Lou (Goodman) H.; m. Toni Jonine Failoni, Aug. 12, 1977; children: Eric Stephen, Nina Catherine, Emily Christine. BA cum laude, Furman U., 1977; JD cum laude, St. Louis U., 1980. Bar: Mo. 1980, U.S. Dist. Ct. (ea. dist.) Mo., 1980, Ill. 1981. From assoc. to ptnr. Blackwell Sanders Peper Martin, St. Louis, 1980—. V.p., sec., gen. counsel Miss. Lime Co., 1992. Editor-in-chief St. Louis Univ. Law Jour., 1979-80; contbr. articles to profl. jours. Mem. Bar Assn. of Met. St. Louis (chmn. environ. and conservation law com. 1993-94). Republican. Baptist. Avocations: gospel singing, cycling. Environmental, Labor (including EEOC, Fair Labor Standards Act, labor-management relations, NLRB, OSHA). Home: 34 Meditation Way Ct Florissant MO 63031-6535 Office: Blackwell Sanders Peper Martin 720 Olive St Fl 24 Saint Louis MO 63101-2338

HILKER, WALTER ROBERT, JR., lawyer; b. L.A., Apr. 18, 1921; s. Walter Robert and Alice (Cox) H.; m. Ruth H. Hibbard, Sept. 7, 1943; children: Anne Katherine, Walter Robert III. BS, U. So. Calif., 1942, LLB, 1948. Bar: Calif. 1949. Sole practice, Los Angeles, 1949-55; ptnr. Parker, Milliken, Kohlmeier, Clark & O'Hara, 1955-75; of counsel Pacht, Ross, Warne, Bernhard & Sears, Newport Beach, Calif., 1980-84. Trustee Bella Mabury Trust; bd. dirs. Houchin Found. Served to lt. USNR, 1942-45. Decorated Bronze Star with V. Mem. ABA, Calif. Bar Assn., Orange County Bar Assn. Clubs: Spring Valley Lake Country (Apple Valley, Calif.); Balboa Bay (Newport Beach, Calif.). Republican. Home and Office: 143 Stonecliffe Aisle Irvine CA 92612-3778

HILL, ALFRED, lawyer, educator; b. N.Y.C., Nov. 7, 1917; m. Dorothy Turck, Aug. 12, 1960; 1 dau., Amelia. BS, Coll. City N.Y., 1937; LL.B., Bklyn. Law Sch., 1941, LL.D., 1986; S.J. D., Harvard U., 1957. Bar: N.Y. State bar 1943, Ill 1958. With SEC, 1943-52; prof. law So. Meth. U., 1953-56, Northwestern U., 1956-62, Columbia U., 1962-75, Simon H. Rifkind prof. law, 1975-87, Simon H. Rifkind prof. law emeritus, 1988—. Contbr. articles on torts, conflict of laws, fed. cts. constl. law to legal jours. Mem. Am. Law Inst. Home: 79 Sherwood Rd Tenafly NJ 07670-2734 Office: Columbia Law Sch New York NY 10027

HILL, BARRY MORTON, lawyer; b. Wheeling, W.Va., Sept. 13, 1946; m. Jacqueline Sue Jackson, Aug. 12, 1967 (div. Mar. 1988); children: Jackson Duff, Brandy; m. Lisa C. Wien, Jan. 7, 1989; 1 child, Gabriel Hunter. BS in Journalism, W.Va. U., 1968, JD, 1977. Bar: W.Va. 1977, U.S Dist. Ct. (no. and so. dists.) W.Va. 1977, Ohio 1978, U.S. Dist. Ct. (no. dist.) Ohio 1978, U.S. Ct. Appeals (3d, 4th, 6th and D.C. cirs.) 1984, U.S. Supreme Ct. 1984, U.S. Ct. Appeals (2d and 11th cirs.) 1986, Pa. 1986, U.S. Ct. Appeals (5th, 7th and 10th cirs.) 1988; cert. civil trial specialist Nat. Bd. Trial Adv., med. profl. liability trial splst. Am. Bd. Profl. Liability Attys. Ptnr. Hill Toriseva & Williams, Wheeling, W.Va. Mem. W.Va. Pattern Jury Instrn. Panel, 1986; mem. exec. com. for rev. jury selection U.S. Dist. Ct. (no. dist.) W.Va.; mem. W.Va. Bar Civil Procedure Rules Rev. com., 1987; chmn. W.Va. std. med. malpractice jury instrn. com., 2000; draftsman Interprofl. Code for Attys. and Physicians W.Va., 1987-88; adj. prof. Saba U. Sch. of Medicine, 1994—. Founding sponsor Civil Justice Found. Served to 1st lt. U.S. Army, 1969-71. Mem.: ATLA (sec. pres.' coun. 1987—88, key person com. 1987—88, pres.' coun. study com. 1988—, ins. practice com. 1988—, chmn. propulsid litigation group 2000—), So. Trial Lawyers Assn. (bd. govs. 1988—), W.Va. Trial Lawyers Assn. (pres. 1987—88, Outstanding mem. 1984), Pa. Trial Lawyers Assn., Ohio Acad. Trial Lawyers, Am. Bd. Profl. Liability Attys. (diplomate). Democrat. Avocations: scuba, tennis, travel, writing, golf. Federal civil litigation, State civil litigation, Product liability. Office: Hill Torisev & Williams& Hill 89 12th St Wheeling WV

HILL, BILL, prosecutor; b. Denison, Tex., Aug. 11, 1942; m. Candy Hill; 3 children. Bachelors Degree, So. Meth. U., 1964, Law Degree, 1967. Asst. dist. atty. Dallas County, 1967—73, dist. atty., 1999—; pvt. practice, 1973—99; spl. pros. Hopkins County, 1977. Mem. Criminal Justice Adv. Coun. for Victims Outreach, Joint Fed. and State Hate Crimes Task Force; founding mem., elder Park Cities Presbyn. Ch.; bd. dirs. Family Violence Prevention Coun., Dallas Children's Advocacy Ctr. Adv. Coun.; adv. bd. Southwestern Law Enforcement Inst. Fellow: Am. Coll. Trial Lawyers; mem.: So. Meth. U. Alumni Assn., Ctton Bowl Athletic Assn., Salesmanship Club Dallas. Office: Frank Crowley Cts Bldg LB 19 133 N Industrial Blvd Dallas TX 75207-4399*

HILL, CLYDE VERNON, JR., prosecutor; b. Oxford, Miss., May 30, 1952; s. Clyde Vernon and Doris Elizabeth Hill; m. Lisa K. Proctor, Aug. 18, 1984; children: Tara C., Ami E. (dec.), Christina K., Amanda G., Lisa Michelle. BS, Miss. State U., 1978; JD, U. Miss., 1983. Bar: Miss. 1983, U.S. Dist. Ct. (no. dist.) Miss. 1983. Asst. dist. atty. 11th Cir. Miss., Clarksdale, 1983-94, 5th Cir. Miss., Grenada, 1995—. Sunday sch. tchr. adult bible study. Mem. Miss. Prosecutors Assn. (bd. dirs. 1995—, v.p. 1999-2000, pres. 2001-02). Baptist. Avocation: farming. Home: 14 Northwoods Dr Grenada MS 38901-9274 Office: Dist Attys office 234 1st St Grenada MS 38901-2602 E-mail: cvhilljr@dixie-net.com.

HILL, DEBRA S. lawyer; b. Dennison, Ohio, Apr. 21, 1957; d. Richard A. and Shirley L. (Delcoma) Hill. BA, Kent State U., 1983, MA, 1986; JD, Case Western Reserve U., 1991. Bar: Ohio 1991, Fla. 1998. Gen. counsel Arthur Treachers, Inc., Jacksonville, 1994—97; vis. asst. prof. Fla. Costal Sch. of Law, Jacksonville, 1997—2001; shareholder Debra S. Hill, PA, Jacksonville, 2000; pres. Saculla Hill & Co., Inc., Jacksonville, 2001—02; mng. ptnr. Smith Hill Law Firm, Jacksonville, 2002—. Commercial, contracts (including sales of goods; commercial financing), Corporate, general, Trademark and copyright. Office: Smith Hill Law Firm 8810 Goodby's Executive Dr Ste C Jacksonville FL 32217

HILL, EARL MCCOLL, lawyer; b. Bisbee, Ariz., June 12, 1926; s. Earl George and Jeanette (McColl) H.; m. Bea Dolan, Nov. 22, 1968 (dec. Aug. 1998); children: Arthur Charles, John Earl, Darlene Stern, Tamara Fegert. BA, U. Wash., 1960, JD, 1961. Bar: Nev. 1962, U.S. Ct. Claims 1978, U.S. Ct. Appeals (9th cir.) 1971, U.S. Supreme Ct. 1978. Law clk. Nev. Supreme Ct., Carson City, 1962; assoc. Gray, Horton & Hill, Reno, Nev., 1962-65, ptnr., 1965-73, Marshall Hill Cassas & de Lipkau (and predecessors), Reno, 1974—, Sherman & Howard, Denver, 1982-91. Judge pro tem Reno mcpl. ct., 1964-70; lectr. continuing legal edn.; mem. Nev. Commn. on Jud. Selection 1977-84; trustee Rocky Mountain Mineral Law Found. 1976-95, sec. 1987-88. Contbr. articles to profl. jours. Mem. ABA, ATLA, State Bar Nev. (chmn. com on jud. adminstrn. 1971-77), Washoe County Bar Assn., Am. Judicature Soc., Lawyer Pilots Bar Assn., Soc. Mining Law Antiquarians (sec.-treas. 1975—), Prospectors Club. Natural resources, Oil, gas, and mineral, Administrative and regulatory. Office: Holcomb Profl Ctr 333 Holcomb Ave Ste 300 Reno NV 89502-1665 E-mail: ehill1@mhcl-law.com.

HILL, EDWARD HAYNES, lawyer; b. Dallas, Mar. 28, 1931; s. Clodius H. and Blanche (Haynes) H.; m. Ann Lynn Sadler, June 3, 1956; children— Ann, Amy. B.S., Tex. A&M U., 1953; J.D., U. Tex.-Austin, 1957. Bar: Tex. 1957. Staff atty. Phillips Petroleum Co., Midland, Tex., 1957-63; assoc. Underwood, Wilson, Berry, Stein & Johnson, Amarillo, Tex., 1963-66, ptnr., 1966-96, of counsel, 1996—; dir. Argonaut Energy Corp., Medallion Equipment Corp., Argonaut Internat. Corp. Served to col. JAG Corps, U.S. Army Res., 1978-83. Fellow Tex. Bar Found. (sustaining life); mem. ABA, State Bar Tex. (chmn. oil, gas and mineral law sect. 1979-80, dir. Tex. Methodist Found. 1996—, trustee McMurry U. 1997—, exec. editor Tex. Title Exam. Stds. editl. bd. 1992—), Amarillo Bar (pres.), Phi Delta Phi. Methodist. Clubs: Amarillo Country, Amarillo, Masons, Shriners. Corporate, general, Oil, gas, and mineral, Securities. Home: 3909 Doris Dr Amarillo TX 79109-5506

HILL, HAROLD NELSON, JR., lawyer; b. Houston, Apr. 26, 1930; s. Harold Nelson and Emolyn Eloise (Geeslin) H.; m. Betty Jane Fell, Aug. 16, 1952; children: Douglas, Nancy. BS in Commerce, Washington and Lee U., Lexington, Va., 1952; PhD, Washington & Lee U., 1981; LL.B., Emory U., 1957, PhD, 1986. Bar: Ga. 1957. Assoc., then partner firm Gambrell, Harlan, Russell, Moye & Richardson, 1957-66; asst. atty. gen. Ga., 1966-68; exec. asst. atty. gen., 1968-72; partner firm Jones, Bird & Howell, 1972-74; assoc. justice Supreme Ct. Ga., 1975-82, chief justice, 1982-86; ptnr. Hurt, Richardson, Garner, Todd & Cadenhead, Atlanta, 1986-92, Judicial Resolutions Inc., Atlanta, 1993-94; of counsel Long, Aldridge & Norman, Atlanta, 1994-95. Served with AUS, 1952-54. Fellow Am. Bar Found.; Mem. Am. Law Inst., State Bar Ga., Lawyers Club Atlanta, Old War Horse Lawyers Club. Methodist.

HILL, JAMES SCOTT, lawyer; b. Boston, Mar. 21, 1924; s. Benjamin B. and Dorothy (Scott) H.; m. Sally C. Foss, June 28, 1945; children: Richard B., Chessye F., Cynthia C., Michael O. BA magna cum laude, Williams Coll., 1947; JD, Columbia U., 1949. Bar: N.Y. 1949, N.J. 1958. Assoc. Baldwin, Todd & Lefferts, N.Y.C., 1949-50; corp. sec., atty. Johnson & Johnson, N.J., 1950-66; v.p., sec., gen. counsel Celanese Corp., N.Y.C., 1966-74; v.p., gen. counsel, dir. Liggett & Myers, Durham, N.C., 1974-76; v.p. law and govt. affairs CBS Inc., N.Y.C., 1976-78; group pres. law and regulatory affairs Am. Hosp. Supply Corp., Evanston, Ill., 1978-81; of counsel Shanley & Fisher, 1981-88, Smith, Stratton, Wise, Heher & Brennan, Princeton, N.J., 1988—. Judge Princeton (N.J.) Twp., 1959-65 Treas. N.J. Republican Fin. com., 1965-70; trustee John Seward Johnson Sr. Charitable Trusts, Princeton Med. Ctr., N.J. State Aquarium, Trinity Counselling Svc., Princeton, N.J.; chmn. Williams Coll. Devel. Coun.; chmn. Boyden Soc.-Deerfield Acad.; bd. dirs. Friends of Channel 13; mem. exec. com. Friends of the Inst. for Advanced Study, Princeton. Served to 1st lt. USAAF, 1943-46. Fellow Am. Coll. Trust and Estate Counsel (mem. charitable planning and exempt orgn. com.); mem. Assn. Gen. Counsel, Met. Club (Washington), Princeton Club (N.Y.C.), Mid-Ocean Club (Bermuda), Bedens Brook Club (bd. govs. 1995—), Springdale Club, Nassau Club (trustee 1993-96), Jasna Polana Golf Club (Princeton), Gasparilla Club (Boca Grande, Fla.), Chi Psi. Republican. Episcopalian (warden). Home: 155 Lambert Dr Princeton NJ 08540-2306 also: PO Box 1767 Boca Grande FL 33921-1767 Office: 600 College Rd E Princeton NJ 08540-6636

HILL, JOHN HOWARD, lawyer; b. Pitts., Aug. 12, 1940; s. David Garrett and Eleanor Campbell (Musser) H. BA, Yale U., 1962, JD, 1965. Bar: Pa. 1965, U.S. Dist. Ct. (we dist.) Pa. 1965, U.S. Ct. Appeals (3d cir.) 1965, U.S. Supreme Ct. 1982. Assoc. Reed, Smith, Shaw & McClay, Pitts., 1965-75, ptnr., 1975-90; of counsel Jackson Lewis LLP, Pitts., 1991—. Bd.

dirs. Travelers Aid Soc., Pitts., 1972-99, treas., 1982-87, pres., 1987-90; bd. dirs. Pitts. Opera, Pitts. Symphony Soc. Mem.: ABA, Allegheny County Bar Assn., Pa. Bar Assn., Pa. Soc., Hosp. Assn. Pa., Rolling Rock Club, Duquesne Club, Fox Chapel Golf Club, Phi Gamma Delta. Republican. Presbyterian. Home: 4722 Bayard St Pittsburgh PA 15213-1708 Office: Jackson Lewis LLP One PPG Pl 28th Fl Pittsburgh PA 15222-5414 E-mail: hillj@jacksonlewis.com.

HILL, JOSEPH C. lawyer; b. Kingston, N.Y., Sept. 23, 1964; BA, Fordham U., 1986; JD, Columbia U., 1989. Bar: N.Y., Spain. With Uria & Menendez, Madrid, Mayer, Brown & Platt, N.Y.C.; mng. dir., assoc. gen. counsel J.P. Morgan Chase & Co., N.Y.C., 1994—. Mem. Assn. Bar City N.Y. (chair inter-Am. affairs com.), Coun. on Fgn. Rels., Phi Beta Kappa. Banking, Private international, Mergers and acquisitions. Office: JP Morgan Chase & Co 270 Park Ave Fl 40 New York NY 10017-2014 E-mail: joe.hill@chase.com.

HILL, JUDITH DEEGAN, lawyer; b. Chgo., Dec. 13, 1939; d. William James and Ida May (Scott) Deegan; children: Colette M., Cristina M. BA, Western Mich. U., 1960; cert., U. Paris, Sorbonne, 1962; JD, Marquette U., 1971; postgrad., Harvard U., 1984. Bar: Wis. 1971, Ill. 1973, Nev. 1976, D.C. 1979. Tchr. Kalamazoo (Mich.) Bd. Edn., 1960-62, Maple Heights (Ohio) Bd. Edn., 1963-64, Shorewood (Wis.) Bd. Edn., 1964-68; corp. atty. Fort Howard Paper Co., Green Bay, Wis., 1971-72; sr. trust adminstr. Continental Ill. Nat. Bank & Trust, Chgo., 1972-76; atty. Morse, Foley & Wadsworth Law Firm, Las Vegas, 1976-77; dep. dist. atty., criminal prosecutor Clark County Atty., Las Vegas, 1977-83; atty. civil and criminal law Edward S. Coleman Profl. Law Corp., Las Vegas, 1983-84; pvt. practice law, 1989-99; ret., 1999. Bd. dirs. YMCA, Highland Park, 1973-75, Planned Parenthood of So. Nev., 1977-78, Nev. Legal Svcs., Carson City, 1980-87, state chmn., 1984-87; bd. dirs. Clark County Legal Svcs., Las Vegas, 1980-87, St. Jude's Ranch for Children, 1999-2001; mem. Star Aux. for Handicapped Children, Las Vegas, 1986-96, Greater Las Vegas Women's League, 1987-88; jud. candidate Las Vegas Mcpl. Ct., 1987, New Symphony Guild, Variety Club Internat., 1992-93; mem. Nat. Conf. for Cmty. and Justice, So. Nev., 1998-2000; mentor in Clark County Sch., 1999-2002. Auto Splties. scholar, St. Joseph, Mich., 1957-60, St. Thomas More scholar Marquette U. Law Sch., Milw., 1968-69; juvenile law internship grantee Marquette U. Law Sch., 1970; honored as one of first 100 Women Attys. in the State of Nev., Oct. 1999. Mem. Nev. Bar Assn., So. Nev. Assn. Women Attys., Children's Village Club (pres. 1980). Bankruptcy, Criminal, Family and matrimonial. Home: 521 Sweeney Ave Las Vegas NV 89104-1436 Fax: 702-384-4167.

HILL, KATHLEEN BLICKENSTAFF, lawyer, mental health nurse, nursing educator; b. Greenville, Ohio, Oct. 24, 1950; d. Donald Edward and Mary Ann (Subler) Berger; children: Benjamin Arin, Amanda Marie, Kathryn Megan; m. David M. Hill, Sr., Sept. 27, 2002. BS, Ohio State U., 1972, MS, 1973, sch. nurse cert., 1990; JD, Capitol U. Law Sch., 1998. Cert. sch. nurse grades K-12. Cons. cmty. educator S.W. Cmty. Mental Health Ctr., Columbus, 1973-77; patient and cmty. educator Daniel E. Blickenstaff, DDS, Inc., Columbus, 1977-86; staff nurse Riverside Meth. Hosp., Columbus, 1986-90; clin. instr. Columbus (Ohio) State C.C., 1989; from asst. to assoc. prof. Capitol U., Columbus, 1989-2000, prof., 2000—01, adj. prof., 2001—; assoc. Porter, Wright, Morris & Arthur LLP, Columbus, 2000—. Mem. cmty. svcs. com. Mid Ohio Dist. Nurses Assn., Columbus, 1990—2001, bd. dirs., 1991—94, mem. legis. com., 2002—. Leader Girl Scouts, Grandview Heights, Ohio, 1989-93; bd. dirs. H.S. PTO, Grandview Heights (Ohio) City Schs., 1990-93, treas. H.S. PTO, 1990-92, co-chair oper. levy, 1991. Mem.: ANA, ABA, Columbus Bar Assn. (health law com.), Ohio State Bar Assn. (health and disability law com.), Ohio Nurses Assn., Am. Health Lawyers Assn., Sigma Theta Tau. Avocations: quilting, sewing, gardening. Home: 1935 Marblecliff Crossing Ct Columbus OH 43204-4968 Office: Porter Wright Morris & Arthur LLP 41 S High St Ste 2900 Columbus OH 43215-6194 E-mail: kblicken@columbus.rr.com., khill@porterwright.com.

HILL, LUTHER LYONS, JR., lawyer; b. Des Moines, Aug. 21, 1922; s. Luther Lyons and Mary (Hippee) H.; m. Sara S. Carpenter, Aug. 12, 1950; children— Luther Lyons III, Mark Lyons. BA, Williams Coll., 1947; LLB, Harvard U., 1950; LLD (hon.), Simpson Coll., 1979. Bar: Iowa 1951. Law clk. to Justice Hugo L. Black U.S. Supreme Ct., 1950-51; assoc., ptnr. Henry & Henry, Des Moines, 1951-69; mem. legal staff Equitable Life Ins. Co. of Iowa, 1952-87, exec. v.p., 1969-87, gen. counsel, 1970-87; of counsel Nyemaster, Goode, McLaughlin, Voigts, Wiest, Hansell O'Brien, Des Moines, 1992—. Counsel, adminstr. Iowa Life and Health Ins. Guaranty Assn. Bd. dirs., past pres. United Comty. Svcs. Greater Des Moines; past trustee, past chmn. Simpson Coll., Indianola, Iowa. Capt. M.I., AUS, WWII, ETO. Mem. ABA, Iowa Bar Assn., Polk County Bar Assn., Assn. Life Ins. Counsel, Des Moines Club, Wakonda Club. Republican. Avocation: walking in the swiss mountains. Insurance, Probate (including wills, trusts). Home: 2801 Park Ave Des Moines IA 50321-1515 Office: Ste 1600 700 Walnut St Des Moines IA 50309-3929

HILL, MILTON KING, JR., retired lawyer; b. Balt., Nov. 29, 1926; s. Milton King and Mary Fusselbaugh (Hall) H.; m. Agnes Ciotti, June 11, 1949; children: Thomas Michael, Milton King, III, Susan Hill. BS in Bus. and Pub. Adminstrn., U. Md., 1950, JD, 1952. Bar: Md. 1952, U.S. Dist. Ct. Md. 1952, U.S. Ct. Appeals (4th cir.) 1952. Assoc. Smith, Somerville & Case, Balt., 1952-55, ptnr., 1955-90; ret. Mem. faculty Md. Hosp. Ednl. Inst. Served with USAF, 1944-46. Fellow Am. Coll. Trial Lawyers, Internat. Soc. Barristers; mem. Md. State Bar Assn., Md. Bar Assn., Nat. Conf. Commrs. Uniform State Laws (pres. 1981-83, chmn. model punitive damages act drafting com.), Assn. Def. Trial Counsel (pres. 1964-65), Internat. Assn. Ins. Counsel, ABA (ho. of dels. 1981-83), Md. Bar Found., Am. Acad. Hosp. Attys. Clubs: Potapskut Sailing Assn., Wednesday Law. Federal civil litigation, State civil litigation, Insurance. Home: 8810 Walther Blvd Apt 2329 Parkville MD 21234-5762 E-mail: khill2329@comcast.net.

HILL, PHILIP, retired lawyer; b. East Saint Louis, Ill., Mar. 13, 1917; s. Nehemiah William and Lulu Myrtle (Johnson) H.; m. Betty Jean Stone, July 4, 1942; children: William Stone, Thomas Chapman, Nancy Layton, Mary Anne. AB in Chemistry, U. Ill., 1937; PhD in Chemistry, Ohio State U., 1941; JD, John Marshall Law Sch., Chgo., 1968. Bar: Ill. 1968, U.S. Patent Office 1969, U.S. Ct. Appeals (fed. cir.) 1982. With Standard Oil Co. Ind., 1941-78, patent atty., 1969-73, dir. petroleum and corp. patents and licensing, 1973-78; ptnr. Hill & Hill, Lansing, Ill., 1978-86; pvt. practice law Philip Hill, P.C., 1987-96; ret., 1996. Cons. Univ. Patents, Inc., Norwalk, Conn., 1980-89; treas. Am. Waste Reduction Corp., 1992-96. Contbr. articles to profl. jours.; patentee in field. Mem.: Am. Chem. Soc., Am. Intellectual Property Law Assn., Ill. State Bar Assn., ABA, Kiwanis (Lansing, pres. 1959, 84), Sigma Xi, Phi Beta Kappa. Methodist. Patent. Home: 17946 Chicago Ave Lansing IL 60438-2261 Office: PO Box 187 Lansing IL 60438-0187

HILL, PHILIP BONNER, lawyer; b. Charleston, W.Va., May 1, 1931; AB, Princeton U., 1952; LLB, W.Va. U., 1957. Bar: W.Va. 1957, Iowa 1965. Assoc. Dayton, Campbell & Love, Charleston, W.Va., 1957-61; ptnr. Porter, Hill, Thomas, Williams & Hubbard, Charleston, 1961-65; v.p. Thomas & Hill, Charleston, 1961-65; assoc. counsel Equitable Life Ins. Co. of Iowa, Des Moines, 1965-68, counsel, 1968-75; ptnr. Riemenschneider, Hanes & Hill, Des Moines, 1975-79, Austin & Gaudineer, Des Moines, 1979-82, Snyder & Hassig, Sistersville and New Martinsville, W.Va., 1982-96, of counsel, 1997-99, Bowles Rice McDavid Graff & Love, PLLC, Martinsburg, W.Va., 2000—. Mem. staff W.Va. Law Rev., 1955-57; contbr. articles to profl. jours. Lt. USNR, 1952-54. Fellow W.Va. Bar Found.; mem. ABA (exec. coun. young lawyers sect. 1966-67), W.Va. State Bar (chmn. jr. bar sect. 1961-62, bd. govs. 1989-92), W.Va. Bar Assn. (pres. 1998-99), Iowa State Bar Assn., Assn. Life Ins. Counsel, Am. Land Title Assn., Am. Judicature Soc., Phi Delta Phi. Office: Bowles Rice McDavid Graff & Love PLLC PO Drawer 1419 101 S Queen St Martinsburg WV 25402-1419

HILL, RICHARD LEE, lawyer; b. Spanish Fork, Utah, May 17, 1951; s. Von and Maxine (Chambers) H.; m. Kathryn Smith, July 10, 1980; children: Natalie Kathryn, Nicole Charlene, Kristina Michelle, Kara Alexandra, Alexis Marie. BS cum laude, Brigham Young U., Hawaii, 1976; JD, Brigham Young U., 1979. Bar: Utah 1979, U.S. Dist. Ct. (cen. dist.) Utah 1979, U.S. Supreme Ct. 1979. Ptnr. Parker, McKeown, McConkie, Salt Lake City, 1979-82, Hill, Johnson, Schmutz, & P.C., Provo, Utah, 1982—. Gen. counsel Marie Osmond Inc., Provo, 1984—. Mem. Utah Arts Coun., 1994—; bd. dirs. Provo Theatre Co., 1987—. Mem. Utah Bar Assn., Riverside Country Club. Mem. Lds Ch. Avocation: acting. Bankruptcy, General civil litigation, Corporate, general. Office: Hill Johnson & Schmutz Ste 200 3319 N University Ave Provo UT 84604-4484

HILL, THOMAS ALLEN, lawyer; b. Salem, Ohio, Mar. 29, 1958; s. Charles Spencer and Dorothy Jane (Allen) H. BA magna cum laude, Hiram Coll., 1980; JD, George Washington U., 1984. Bar: Ohio 1984, Pa. 1987, D.C. 1988, U.S. Supreme Ct. 1989, Tex. 1990, Okla. 1991. Legis. intern Office of Hon. John Conyers, Jr., Washington, 1979; asst. to dean campus Life for Housing, conf. dir. Hiram (Ohio) Coll., 1980-81; corp. counsel Capital Oil & Gas Inc., Austintown, Ohio, 1984-93; gen. counsel, sec. North Coast Energy, Inc., Cleve., 1987-2001, Trinity Oil & Gas, Inc. subs. North Coast Energy Inc., Warren, Ohio, 1990-93; gen. counsel Eric Petroleum Corp., Canfield, Ohio, 2001—. Mem. mini-task force on notices of violation Ohio Div. Oil and Gas, Columbus, 1988-90; part-time fin. analyst Primerica Fin. Svcs., Inc., 1997-2000; corp. sec. Peake Energy, Inc., Ravenswood, W.Va., 2000-01. Mem. ABA, Ohio Bar Assn., Mahoning County Bar Assn., Pa. Bar Assn., Okla. Bar Assn., D.C. Bar Assn., State Bar Tex., Trumbull County Bar Assn., Ohio Oil and Gas Assn., Christian Legal Soc., Energy Bar Assn., Ohio Land Title Assn., Ohio Geneal. Soc., Mahoning Valley Hist. Soc., Austintown Hist. Soc., Gen. Soc., War of 1812, SAR, Order of Arrow, Kappa Delta Pi, Pi Gamma Mu. Republican. Avocations: local history, study of amaranth. Corporate, general, Oil, gas, and mineral, Property, real (including real estate development, water). Home: 4841 Westchester Dr Apt 102 Youngstown OH 44515-2548 Office: Eric Petroleum Corp 4206 1/2 Boardman-Canfield Canfield OH 44406

HILL, THOMAS CLARK, lawyer; b. Prestonsburg, Ky., July 17, 1946; s. Lon Clay and Corinne (Allen) H.; m. Barbarie Friedly, June 13, 1968; children: Jason L., Duncan L. BA, Case Western Reserve U., 1968; JD, U. Chgo., 1973. Bar: Ohio 1973, U.S. Supreme Ct. 1976. Assoc. atty. Taft, Stettinius & Hollister LLP, Cin., 1973-81, ptnr., 1981—. Author: Monthly Meetings in North America: A Quaker Index, 4th edit., 1998. Trustee, treas. Wilmington (Ohio) Coll., 1982-94, 99—, sec., 2002—; treas. Ams. sect. Friends World Commn. for Consultation, 1990-95, presiding clk., 1995-99, interim com., presiding clk., London, 2000—; trustee Wilmington Yearly Meeting of Friends (Quakers), 1986-98, Friends United Meeting, 1999—, presiding clk. trustees, 2002—. Mem. ABA, Ohio State Bar Assn., Cin. Bar Assn., Friends Hist. Assn. (bd. dirs. 1994-95). Republican. Mem. Soc. Of Friends. Avocation: Quaker history. Antitrust, Environmental, Insurance. Office: 425 Walnut St Ste 1800 Cincinnati OH 45202-3923 E-mail: hill@taftlaw.com.

HILL, TINA, prosecutor; d. Tommy and Toni Hill. BA in English, U. of Miss., Oxford, Mississippi, 1991—95; JD, U. of Miss. , Oxford, 1998. Bar: Miss. 1998, U.S. Dist. Ct. (no. and so.. dists.) Miss. 1998, U.S. Ct. of Appeals (5th cir.) 1998. Jud. law clk. Miss. Ct. of Appeals, Jackson, Miss., 1998—2000; spl. asst. atty. gen. Miss. Atty. General's Office, Jackson, Miss., 2000—. Vol. Blair E. Batson Children's Hosp., Jackson, Miss., Stewpot Cmty. Ctr., Jackson; tutor Boys and Girls Club, Jackson. Mem.: ABA, Miss. Women Lawyers Assn., Jackson Young Lawyers, Miss. Bar Assn. Office: Miss Atty Gens Office 301 N Lamar Jackson MS 39201

HILL, WILLIAM U. state supreme court chief justice; Atty. gen., Cheyenne, Wyo., 1995—98; justice Wyo. Supreme Ct., Cheyenne, 1998—2002, chief justice, 2002—. Office: Wyoming Supreme Court 2301 Capitol Ave Cheyenne WY 82001-3656

HILLBERG, MARYLOU ELIN, lawyer; b. Chgo., Nov. 6, 1950; d. Harold Andrew Hillberg and Eunice Elin (Anderson) Peterson; m. Andrew Charles Lennox, Aug. 6, 1983; children: Elin Elizabeth Lennox, David Andrew Lennox. BFA, San Francisco Art Inst., 1973; JD, U. Calif., San Francisco, 1979. Bar: Calif. 1979, U.S. Dist. Ct. (no. dist.) Calif. 1979. Dep. dist. atty. Sonoma County, Santa Rosa, Calif., 1980; sole practice Santa Rosa, 1981—. Asst. prof. Sonoma State U., Rohnert Park, Calif., 1982—; mem. United Christian Ch., mem. cmty. adv. coun., 1992—, chair, 1994-95; co-founder Redwood Empire Appellate Lawyers, 1998—. Chmn. bd. dirs. Sonoma County Drug Abuse Alternatives Ctr., Santa Rosa, 1983-84; bd. dirs. ACLU, Santa Rosa, 1982-84; mem. adv. coun. Sonoma County Cmty., 1992—. Mem. Sonoma County Women in Law (chairperson 1983-84), Calif. Pub. Defenders Assn., Criminal Appellate Def. Counsel, Calif. Atty. Criminal Justice. Democrat. Appellate, Criminal, Juvenile. Office: PO Box 1879 Sebastopol CA 95473 E-mail: hillberg@sonic.net.

HILLER, ALEECE, lawyer, mediator; b. Memphis; BA, Ind. U., 1985; JD, Memphis State U., 1991. Bar: Tenn 92, NC 00. Pvt. practice Law Office of Aleece M. Hiller, Memphis, 1992—98, Asheville, NC, 2000—; dir. cmty. mediation program Mediation Ctr., Asheville, 2000—. Mem. com. endowment fund Urban League, Memphis, 1994—98; bd. dirs. Hands On Memphis, 1996—98; treas., bd. dirs. Guardian ad Litem Assn., Asheville, 1999—2002. Mem.: Memphis Bar Assn., Tenn. Bar Assn., 28th Jud. Dist. Bar Assn., NC Bar Assn. Alternative dispute resolution, Probate (including wills, trusts). Office: Mediation Ctr 189 College St Asheville NC 28801

HILLESTAD, CHARLES ANDREW, lawyer; b. McCurtain, Okla., Aug. 30, 1945; s. Carl Oliver and Aileen Hanna (Sweeney) H.; m. Ann Ramsey Robertson, Oct. 13, 1973. BS, U. Oreg., 1967; JD, U. Mich., 1972. Bar: Colo. 1972, U.S. Dist. Ct. Colo. 1972, U.S. Ct. Appeals (10th cir.) 1972, Oreg. 1993; lic. real estate broker, Colo. Law clk. to presiding justice Colo. Supreme Ct., Denver, 1972-73; ptnr. DeMuth & Kemp, Denver, 1973-83, Cornwell & Blakey, Denver, 1983-90, Scheid & Horlbeck, Denver, 1990-93, Gablehouse & Epel, Denver, 1993-94; pvt. practice Cannon Beach, Oreg., 1994—. Co-developer award winning Queen Anne Inn, Capitol Hill Mansion and Cheyenne Canyon Inn Hotels (4-diamond award AAA); mem. ad hoc com. Denver Real Estate Atty. Specialists. Author: Preventive Law for Innkeepers, co-author: Annual Surveys of Real Estate Law for Colorado Bar Association; contbr. articles to profl. jours.; assoc. editor Inn Times. Past coun. mem. Denver Art Mus.; past chmn. Rocky Mountain chpt. Sierra Club; past v.p., bd. dirs. Seaside C. of C.; past bd. dirs. Hist. Denver, Inc. Staff sgt. U.S. Army, 1968-70. Recipient Colo. C. of Yr. award Colo. Bus. Mag., Award of Honor Denver Ptnrship., Newsmaker of Yr. and Outstanding Achievement awards Am. Assn. Hist. Inns, Tourism Person of Yr. award Denver Conv. and Visitor's Bur., Rocky Mountain Spectacular Inn award B&B Rocky Mountains Assn., Best Inns of Yr. awards County Inns Mag. and Adventure Rd. Mag., Best of Denver award Westward newspaper. Mem. ABA, Colo. Bar Assn., Oreg. Bar Assn., Denver Bar Assn., Colo. Lawyers for the Arts, POETS, Astoria C. of C., Seaside C. of C., Cannon Beach C. of C. Avocations: photography, art collecting, historic and environmental preservation, history and architecture reading, rafting. Commercial, contracts (including sales of goods; commercial financing), Landlord-tenant, Property, real (including real estate development, water). Office: PO Box 1065 1347 S Hemlock Cannon Beach OR 97110

HILLIARD, DAVID CRAIG, lawyer, educator; b. Framingham, Mass., May 22, 1937; s. Walter David and Dorothy (Shortiss) H.; m. Celia Schmid, Feb. 16, 1974. BS, Tufts U., 1959; JD, U. Chgo., 1962. Bar: Ill. 1962, U.S. Supreme Ct. 1966. Mng. ptnr. Pattishall, McAuliffe, Newbury, Hilliard & Geraldson, Chgo., 1983—2002, sr. ptnr., 2003—. Adj. prof. law Northwestern U., 1971—, chmn. Symposium Intellectual Property Law and the Corp. Client, 1987—; lectr. in advanced trademark law and info. regulation U. Chgo. Law Sch., 1999—. Author: Unfair Competition and Unfair Trade Practices, 1985, Trademarks, 1987, Trademarks and Unfair Competition, 1994, 5th edit., 2002, Trademarks and Unfair Competition Deskbook, 2001, 2d edit., 2003; editor-in-chief Chgo. Bar Record, 1978-81. Trustee Art Inst. Chgo., 1980—, vice-chmn., 1998-2000, exec. com., 1994-2000, chmn. sustaining fellows, 1981-85, chmn. adv. com. dept. architecture, 1981—, pres. aux. bd., 1977-79, chmn. exhbns. com., 1993—, chmn. bd. govs. of the sch., 1997-2000; trustee Newberry Libr., 1983—, exec. com., 1987—; trustee Robert Allerton Trust, 2002—; pres. Lawyers Trust Fund Ill., 1985-88; vis. com. DePaul U. Law Sch., U. Chgo. Sch. of Law, chmn., 1987-88, Northwestern U. Assocs., 1985—; profl. adv. bd. Atty. Gen. Ill., 1982-84; mem. Ill. Commn. on Rights of Women, 1983-85; bd. dirs. Ill. Inst. Continuing Legal Edn., 1980-82; pres. Planned Parenthood Assn. Chgo., 1975-77. Lt. JAGC, USN, 1962-66. Recipient Maurice Weigle award, 1974, Chgo. Coun. Lawyers award for jud. reform, 1983. Fellow Am. Coll. Trial Lawyers (chmn. courageous adv. com. 1995-97); mem. ABA (chmn. trademark divsn. 1986-87, mem. coun. 1991-95, intellectual property law sect.), Ill. Bar Assn., Chgo. Bar Assn. (pres. 1982-83, founding chmn. young lawyers sect. 1971-72), Internat. Trademark Assn. (bd. dirs. 1989-91, ADR panel of neutrals 1994—), Arts Club, Chgo. Club, Econ. Club, Grolier Club, Lawyers Club, Legal Club (pres. 1989-90), Univ. Club, Casino, Wayfarers Club (pres. 1994-95). Federal civil litigation, Intellectual property, Trademark and copyright. Home: 1320 N State Pkwy Chicago IL 60610-2118 Office: Pattishall McAuliffe Newbury Hilliard & Geraldson 311 S Wacker Dr Ste 5000 Chicago IL 60606-6631 E-mail: dhilliard@pattishall.com.

HILLIARD, RUSSELL F. lawyer; BS, Rensselaer Poly. Inst., 1973; JD, Cornell U., 1976; ML in Taxation, Boston U., 1985. Bar: N.H. 1976. Ptnr. Upton & Hatfield, LLP, Concord, NH. Mem. N.H. Bd. Bar Examiners, 1981—90, N.H. Legis. Ethics Commn., 1991—97. Fellow: Am. Coll. Tiral Lawyers; mem.: Merrimack County Bar Assn., Am. Arbitration Assn. (panel of arbitrators), N.H. Bar Assn. (pres.-elect 2001—02), ABA. Commercial, consumer (including collections, credit), Insurance. Office: Upton and Hatfield LLP PO Box 1090 10 Centre St Concord NH 03302-1090

HILLJE, BARBARA BROWN, lawyer; b. Carlisle, Pa., Dec. 18, 1942; d. R. Morrison and Gladys M. (Lauver) Brown; m. John W. Hillje, Mar. 23, 1968. AB, Vassar Coll., 1964; BS in Edn., Ind. U. Pa., 1965; MA, Temple U., 1971, ABD, 1977; JD, Villanova U., 1984. Bar: Pa. 1984, U.S. Dist. Ct. (ea. dist.) Pa. 1984, N.J. 1985, U.S. Dist. Ct. N.J. 1985, U.S. Supreme Ct. 1990. English tchr. Council Rock Sr. High Sch., Newtown, Pa., 1965-68; assoc. Harry J. Agzigian and Assocs., Levittown, Pa., 1985-87; pvt. practice Langhorne, Pa., 1987—. Contbr. articles to profl. journals. Bd. dirs., pres. bd. Children of Aging Parents, Levittown, Pa., 1985-93; mem. facility ethics com. Statesman Health & Rehab. Ctr., Levittown, Pa., 1996—; bd. dirs. D'Youville Manor, 2001—. Recipient Women Helping Women award Soroptimists of Indian Rock, Inc., 1995; named Woman of Yr., Lower Bucks AAUW, 1985, Neshaminy BPW, 1987, Legal Humanitarian of Yr., Bucks County United Way, 1994, Consumer Connection award, 1996. Mem. AAUW (bd. dirs. 1978—, legis. cons. Pa. divsn. 1990-92), Middletown-Newtown LWV (bd. dirs. 1983-89, citizen campaign watch adv. panel 1992, 94, 96), Pa. Bar Assn., Nat. Acad. Elder Law Attys., Older Women's League (legis. chair 1984-94, Women of Worth award 1993). Family and matrimonial, Probate (including wills, trusts), Elder. Office: 506 Corporate Dr W Langhorne PA 19047-8011

HILLMAN, DOUGLAS WOODRUFF, retired judge; b. Grand Rapids, Mich., Feb. 15, 1922; s. Lemuel Serrell and Dorothy (Woodruff) H.; m. Sally Jones, Sept. 13, 1944; children: Drusilla W., Clayton D. (dec.). Student, Phillips Exeter Acad., 1941; AB, U. Mich., 1946, LL.B., 1948. Bar: Mich. 1948, U.S. Supreme Ct. 1967. Assoc. Lilly, Luyendyk & Snyder, Grand Rapids, 1948-53; partner Luyendyk, Hainer, Hillman, Karr & Dutcher, Grand Rapids, 1953-65, Hillman, Baxter & Hammond, 1965-79; U.S. dist. judge Western Dist. Mich., Grand Rapids, 1979—, chief judge, 1986-91, sr. judge, 1991—2002; ret., 2002. Instr. Nat. Inst. Trial Adv., Boulder, Colo; dir. Fed. Judges Assn.; mem. jud. conf. com. on Adminstrn. of Magistrate Judges Sys., 1993-99; chair 6th Circuit Standing Com. on Jud. Conf. Planning; mem. exec. com. ABA jud. adminstrn. divsn. Nat. Conf. Fed. Trial Judges, 1995-98. Co-author articles in legal publs. Chmn. Grand Rapids Human Relations Commn., 1963-66; chmn. bd. trustees Fountain St. Ch., 1970-72; pres. Family Service Assn., 1967. Served as pilot USAAF, 1943-45. Decorated Air medal DFC; named One of 25 Most Respected Judges, Mich. Laywers Weekly, Grand Rapids Med. Hall Fame, 2001; recipient Ann. Civil Liberties award, ACLU, 1970, Disting. ALumni award, Ctrl. High Sch., 1986, Raymond Fox Advocacy award, 1989, Champion of Justice award, State Bar Mich., 1990, Profl. & Cmty. Svc. award, Young Lawyers Sect., 1996, Svc. to Profession award, Fed. Bar Assn., 1991; grantee Paul Harris fellow, Rotary Internat. Fellow Am. Bar Found.; mem. ABA, Mich. Bar Assn. (chmn. client security fund), Grand Rapids Bar Assn. (pres. 1963), Am. Coll. Trial Lawyers (Mich. chmn. 1979, com. on teaching trial and appellate adv.), 6th Circuit Jud. Conf. (life), Internat. Acad. Trial Lawyers, Fedn. Ins. Counsel, Internat. Assn. Ins. Counsel, Internat. Soc. Barristers (pres 1977-78, chair annual Hillman Trial Adv. Seminar 1982—), M Club of U. Mich. (com. visitors U. Mich. Law Sch.), Univ. Club (Grand Rapids), Torch Club. Home: 10743 Lost Valley Rd Montague MI 49437

HILLMAN, ROBERT ANDREW, law educator, former academic dean; b. N.Y.C., Dec. 23, 1946; s. Herman D. and Edith N. (Geilich) H.; m. Elizabeth Hall Kafka, Aug. 24, 1969; children: Jessica H., Heather D. BA, U. Rochester, 1969; JD, Cornell U., 1972. Bar: N.Y. 1973, Iowa 1976. Law clk. to judge U.S. Dist. Ct., N.Y.C., 1972-73; assoc. Debevoise & Plimpton, N.Y.C., 1973-74; prof. law U. Iowa, Iowa City, 1975-82, Cornell U., Ithaca, N.Y., 1982—, acad. dean, 1990-97, Edwin Woodruff prof. law. Author or co-author: Common Law and Equity Under the UCC, 1985, Law: Its Nature, Functions, and Limits, 1986, Contract and Related Obligation: Theory, Doctrine, and Practice, 1987, 2d edit., 1992, 3d edit., 1997, The Richness of Contract Law, 1997, Modern American Contract Law, 2000; contbr. articles to profl. jours. Mem. Am. Law Inst. Avocations: tennis, bicycling. Office: Cornell U Law Sch Myron Taylor Hall Ithaca NY 14853 E-mail: rah16@cornell.edu.

HILLS, CARLA ANDERSON, lawyer, former federal official; b. Los Angeles, Jan. 3, 1934; d. Carl H. and Edith (Hume) Anderson; m. Roderick Maltman Hills, Sept. 27, 1958; children: Laura Hume, Roderick Maltman, Megan Elizabeth, Alison Macbeth. AB cum laude, Stanford U., 1955; student, St. Hilda's Coll., Oxford (Eng.) U., 1954; LLB, Yale U., 1958; hon. degrees, Pepperdine U., 1975, Washington U., 1977, Mills Coll., 1977, Lake Forest Coll., 1978, Williams Coll., 1981, Notre Dame U., 1993, Wabash Coll., 1997. Bar: Calif. 1959, DC 1974, U.S. Supreme Ct. 1965. Asst. U.S. atty. civil divsn., L.A., 1958-61; ptnr. Munger, Tolles, Hills & Rickershauser, L.A., 1962-74; asst. atty. gen. civil divsn. Justice Dept., Washington, 1974-75; sec. HUD, 1975-77; ptnr. Latham, Watkins & Hills, Washington, 1978-86, Weil, Gotshal & Manges, Washington, 1986-88; U.S. trade rep. Exec. Office of the Pres., 1989-93; chmn., CEO Hills & Co. Internat. Cons., 1993—. Chair Nat. Com. for U.S.-China Rels.; bd. dirs. Inst. for Internat. Econs., CSIS, Asia Soc., Am. Internat. Group, AOL-Time Warner, Lucent Techs., Inc., Chevron Texaco Corp., TCW Group, Inc.; adj. prof.

Sch. Law UCLA, 1972; mem. Trilateral Commn., 1977—82, 1993—, Am. Com. on East-West Accord, 1977—79, Internat. Found. for Cultural Cooperation and Devel., 1977—89, Fed. Acctg. Stds. Adv. Coun., 1978—80; mem. corrections task force L.A. County Sub-Regional; mem. adv. bd. Calif. Coun. on Criminal Justice, 1969—71; mem. standing com. discipline U.S. Dist. Ct. for Ctrl. Calif., 1970—73; mem. Adminstrv. Conf. U.S., 1972—74; mem. exec. com. law and free soc. State Bar Calif., 1973; bd. councillors U. So. Calif. Law Ctr., 1972—74; trustee Pomona Coll., 1974—79, Brookings Instn., 1985; mem. at large exec. com. Yale Law Sch., 1973—78; mem. com. on Law Sch. Yale U. Coun.; Gordon Grand fellow Yale U., 1978; mem. Sloan Commn. on Govt. and Higher Edn., 1977—79; mem. adv. com. Princeton U., Woodrow Wilson Sch. of Pub. and Internat. Affairs, 1977—80; trustee Am. Productivity and Quality Ctr., 1988; coun. mem. Calif. Gov. Coun. Econ. Policy Adv., 1993—98, Coun. Fgn. Rels., 1993—, vice chair, 2001—; vice-chair bd. dirs. Inter-Am. Dialogue, 1999—. Co-author: Federal Civil Practice, 1961; co-author, editor: Antitrust Adviser, 1971, 3d edit., 1985; contbg. editor: Legal Times, 1978-88; mem. editorial bd. Nat. Law Jour., 1978-88. Trustee U. So. Calif., 1977-79, Norton Simon Mus. Art, Pasadena, Calif., 1976-80; trustee Urban Inst., 1978-89, chmn., 1983-89; co-chmn. Alliance to Save Energy, 1977-89; vice chmn. adv. coun. on legal policy Am. Enterprise Inst., 1977-84; bd. visitors, exec. com. Stanford U. Law Sch., 1978-81; bd. dirs. Am. Coun. for Capital Formation, 1978-82; mem. exec. com. Inst. for Internat. Econs., 1993—; mem. adv. com. MIT-Harvard U. Joint Ctr. for Urban Studies, 1978-82. Fellow Am. Bar Found.; mem. Am.'s Soc. (bd. dirs.), L.A. Women Lawyers Assn. (pres. 1964), ABA (chair publs. com. antitrust sect. 1972-74, council 1974, 77-84, chair 1982-83), Fed. Bar Assn. (pres. L.A. chpt. 1963), L.A. County Bar Assn. (fed. rules and practice com. 1963-72, chair issues and survey 1963-72, chair sub-com. revision local rules for fed. cts. 1966-72, jud. qualifications com. 1971-72), Am. Law Inst., Am.-China Soc. (bd. dirs. 1995—), Am. Soc. (bd. trustees), Asia Soc. (bd. trustees), Yale of So. Calif. Club (bd. dirs. 1972-74), Yale Club. Clubs: Yale of So. Calif. (dir. 1972-74); Yale (Washington). Antitrust. Office: Hills & Co 1200 19th St NW Ste 201 Washington DC 20036-2429

HILPERT, EDWARD THEODORE, JR., lawyer; b. Frazee, Minn., Apr. 29, 1928; s. Edward Theodore Sr. and Hulda Gertrude (Wilder) H.; m. Susan Hazelton, May 5, 1973. AB, U. Wash., 1954, JD, 1956. Bar: Wash. 1956, U.S. Dist. Ct. (we. dist.) Wash. 1956, U.S. Tax Ct. 1959, U.S. Ct. Appeals (9th cir.) 1959, U.S. Supreme Ct. 1970. Law clk. to Hon. George H. Boldt U.S. Dist. Ct. (we. dist.) Wash., Tacoma, 1956-58; assoc. Ferguson & Burdell, Seattle, 1958-63, ptnr., 1963-91; sr. ptnr. Schwabe, Williamson, Ferguson & Burdell, Seattle, 1992—. Exec. com. 9th cir. Jud. Conf., San Francisco, 1987-90. Judge pro tem Seattle Mcpl. Ct., 1971-80. Capt. USAR, 1946-49, 50-52, Korea. Mem. ABA, Mensa, The Rainer Club, Seattle Tennis Club, Broadmoor Golf Club, Sea Pines Country Club. Republican. Lutheran. Corporate, general, Estate planning, State and local taxation. Home: 10405 - 192nd Ave NE Redmond WA 98053 Office: Schwabe Williamson Ferguson & Burdell US Bank Ctr 1420 5th Ave Ste 3010 Seattle WA 98101-2393

HILTON, STANLEY GOUMAS, lawyer, educator, writer; b. San Francisco, June 16, 1949; s. Loucas Stylianos and Effie (Glafkides) Goumas; m. Raquel Estrella Villalba, Feb. 25, 1996; children: Loucas, Angelika, Karmen (triplets). BA with honors, U. Chgo., 1971; JD, Duke U., 1975; MBA, Harvard U., 1979. Bar: Calif. 1975, U.S. Dist. Ct. Calif. 1975, U.S. Ct. Appeals (9th cir.) 1983, U.S. Supreme Ct. 1985. Libr. asst. Duke U. Libr., Durham, N.C., 1972-75, Harvard U. Libr., Cambridge, Mass., 1977-79; minority counsel U.S. Senator Bob Dole, Washington, 1979-80; adminstrv. asst. Calif. State Senate, Sacramento, 1980-81; pvt. practice San Francisco, 1981—; CEO Froggg, Inc., 1999—, San Francisco Landlords Union, 1999—. Adj. assoc. prof. Golden Gate U., San Francisco, 1991—; profl. spkr.; polit. writer; pres. Fair Play In the Middle East Com., 2002—; tutor Harvard U., 1978—79. Author: Bob Dole: American Political Phoenix, 1988, Senator for Sale, 1995, Glass Houses, 1998 (Best writer 1998), To Pay or Not to Pay, 2003. Pres. Com. to Stick With Candlestick Park, San Francisco, 1992-96, Value Added Tax Now, San Francisco, 1994—, Save the 4th Amendment, San Francisco, 1995—; pres., CEO Animalism, Inc., San Francisco Landlord's Union, 2001—; CEO Fountain of Youth; alt. mem. San Mateo County Dem. Ctrl. Com., 2002--. Mem. Calif. State Bar, Abolish the Fed. Res. Bank Assn. (pres. 1999—), Hellenic Law Soc., Bechtel Toastmasters Club (pres.), Rhinoceros Toastmasters Club. Democrat. Avocations: philately, photography, classical music, ancient greek and roman history. Constitutional, Labor (including EEOC, Fair Labor Standards Act, labor-management relations, NLRB, OSHA). Office: 580 California St Ste 500 San Francisco CA 94104-1000

HILTS, EARL T. lawyer, government official, educator; b. Ilion, N.Y., Mar. 31, 1946; stepson Leon Thomas and Gertrude Annette (Daly) Butler; m. Mae Hwa Kim, Apr. 13, 1973; children: Troy Alan, Kimberly Michelle. BS, St. Lawrence U., 1967; JD, Albany Law Sch., 1970. Bar: N.Y. 1972. Gen. atty.-advisor Dept. Army Watervliet Arsenal, N.Y., 1978-80, supervisory atty.-advisor, 1980-99; ret., 1999; pvt. practice, 1999—. Adj. prof. Schnectady C.C., 1985—, St. Rose Coll., 1999—. Catechism instr. St. Mary's Ch., 1990-92; pee wee football coach, wrestling coach Shenendehowa Sch., 1983-87; little league coach West Crescent Halfmoon Baseball League, 1980-90. Capt. JAGC, U.S. Army, 1972-76. Scholar St. Lawrence U., 1963-67, Albany Law Sch., 1967-70. Mem. N.Y. State Bar Assn., Am. Legion, Pi Mu Epsilon. Republican. Roman Catholic. Home and Office: 28 Oakwood Blvd Clifton Park NY 12065-7413

HIMELES, MARTIN STANLEY, JR., lawyer; b. Balt., Mar. 13, 1956; s. Martin Stanley and Betty Jean (Applebaum) H.; m. Paula Kilimnik, Aug. 26, 1984. BA summa cum laude, Yale U., 1978; JD magna cum laude, Harvard U., 1981. Bar: N.Y. 1982, U.S. Dist. Ct. (so. and ea. dists.) N.Y. 1982, U.S. Ct. Appeals (4th cir.) 1982, U.S. Dist. Ct. Md. 1986, Md. 1989, U.S. Ct. Appeals (8th cir.) 1999, U.S. Supreme Ct. 2003. Law clk. to judge U.S. Ct. Appeals (4th cir.), Balt., 1981-82; assoc. Parker, Auspitz, Neesemann & Delehanty P.C., N.Y.C., 1982-86; asst. U.S. atty. U.S. Atty's. Office, Balt., 1986-90; ptnr. Zuckerman Spaeder LLP, Balt., 1990—. Fellow: Am. Coll. Trial Lawyers; mem.: Balt. Jewish Coun. (mem. bd. govs.), Levindale Hebrew Geriatric Ctr. and Hosp. (mem. bd. govs.), Fed. Bar Assn. (past pres. Md. chpt.), The Associated Jewish Cmty. Fedn. of Balt. (bd. dirs., mem. investment com.), Am. Jewish Com. (1st v.p. Md. chpt.), Phi Beta Kappa. Democrat. Federal civil litigation, General civil litigation, Criminal. Office: 100 E Pratt St Ste 2440 Baltimore MD 21202-1031 E-mail: mhimeles@zuckerman.com.

HIMELFARB, STEPHEN ROY, lawyer; b. Washington, Feb. 19, 1954; s. Jordan Sheldon and Marion (Soloman) H.; m. Anne Patricia Spille, June 26, 1983; children: Kara Michelle, Bradley Richard. BSBA, Am. U., 1976; JD, George Mason U., 1980. Bar: D.C. 1982, Md. 1982, Va. 1988, U.S. Dist. Ct. D.C. 1982, U.S. Dist. Ct. Md. 1982, U.S. Ct. Appeals (D.C. and 4th cirs.) 1982, U.S. Dist. Ct. (ea. dist.) Va. 1988, U.S. Tax Ct. 1990, U.S. Bankruptcy Ct. (ea. div.) Va. 1988, U.S. Supreme Ct. 1985. From v.p. to pres. ECA Bus. Comm. Network, Washington, 1982-85; ptnr. Himelfarb & Podryhula, Washington, 1984-93, Speights & Micheel, Washington, 1986-88, Sheeskin, Hillman & Lazar, PC, Rockville, Md., 1989-90, Ahmad & Himelfarb, PC, Rockville, Md., 1993-95; pvt. practice Bethesda, Md., 1995—. V.p. Video Shack Inc., Woodbridge, Va., 1984-95. Mem. ABA, Md. State Bar Assn., Va. Bar Assn., Assn. Trial Lawyers Am., Phi Delta Phi. Democrat. Jewish. Avocations: electronics, coin-op/americana collecting, model trains, radio control models. Commercial, contracts (including sales of goods; commercial financing), Corporate, general, Personal injury (including property damage). Home: 1214 Winter Hunt Rd Mc Lean VA 22102-2434 Office: 4701 Sangamore Rd Ste S-225 Bethesda MD 20816-2508

HIMELRICK, RICHARD G. lawyer; b. Detroit, Nov. 6, 1949; s. Richard G. and Mildred R. Himelrick; m. Shirley A. Himelrick, June 4, 1975; 1 child, Richard Todd. BA, Oakland U., 1971; JD, Wayne State U., 1974. Bar: Ariz. 76, U.S. Dist. Ct. Ariz. 76, U.S. Ct. Appeals (9th cir.) 77. Ptnr. Byrnes, Rosier & Himelrick, P.C., Scottsdale, Ariz., 1990—96, Tiffany & Bosco, P.A., Phoenix, 1997—. Contbr. articles to profl. jours. Mem.: ATLA, Pub. Investors Arbitration Bar Assn. Democrat. Avocations: reading, running, skiing. Securities, General civil litigation. Office: Tiffany & Bosco PA 1850 N Central Ave # 500 Phoenix AZ 85004 Fax: 602-255-0103. E-mail: rgh@tblaw.com.

HINCHEY, EDWARD THOMAS, lawyer; b. Boston, May 29, 1954; s. Thomas P. R. and Elizabeth W. Hinchey; m. Diane F. Hinchey, July 9, 1999; children: Margaret, Elizabeth, Susan. BA with honors, Occidental Coll., 1977; JD cum laude, Boston Coll., 1981. Bar: Mass. 1981, U.S. Dist. Ct. Mass. 1982, U.S. Ct. Appeals (1st cir.) 1983, U.S. Supreme Ct. 1990. Sr. ptnr. Sloane and Walsh, Boston, 1981—. Instr. Mass. Continuing Legal Edn., 1998, 2000—02. Bd. dirs. Caritas Cmtys. Mem.: ABA (mem. lit. sect., judge Nat. Trial Competition), Mass. Acad. Trial Attys. (instr.), Mass. Def. Lawyers Assn., Mass. Trial Lawyers Assn. (officer), Mass. Bar Assn. (instr. health law sect.), Def. Rsch. Inst., Am. Acad. Trial Lawyers (assoc.), Am. Bd. Trial Advs. (assoc.). Professional liability. Office: Sloane and Walsh Three Center Plz Boston MA 02108

HINCHEY, JOHN WILLIAM, lawyer; b. Knoxville, Tenn., June 18, 1941; s. Roy William and Ruth (Owenby) H.; m. Sherie Paulette Archer, May 12, 1968; children: Paul William, Meredith Marie, John Oliver. AB, Emory U., 1964, LLB, 1965; LLM, Harvard U., 1966; MLitt., Oxford U., 1980. Bar: Ga. 1965, U.S. Dist. Ct. (no., mid. and so. dists.) Ga. 1968, U.S. Ct. Appeals (11th cir.) 1968, U.S. Supreme Ct. 1969. Asst. atty. gen. State of Ga., Atlanta, 1968-72; ptnr. McConaughey & Hinchey, Decatur, Ga., 1972-76, Phillips & Mozley, Atlanta, 1976-84, Phillips, Hinchey & Reid, Atlanta, 1984-92, King and Spalding, Atlanta, 1992—. Contbr. to profl. jours. Mem.: ABA (chair Forum on Constrn. Industry), Nat. Constrn.Dispute Resolution Com., CPR Inst., Alternative Dispute Resolution Counsel, Chartered Inst. Arbitrators, London Ct. Internat. Arbitration, Atlanta Bar Assn. (chair constrn. law sect. 1999—2000), Ga. Bar Assn., Am. Arbitration Assn., Am. Coll. Constitution Lawyers (bd. govs. 2001—), Druid Hills Golf Club. Republican. Methodist. Alternative dispute resolution, Commercial, contracts (including sales of goods; commercial financing), Construction. Office: King & Spalding LLP 191 Peachtree St SW Atlanta GA 30303-1763 E-mail: jhinchey@kslaw.com.

HINDIN, SEYMOUR, lawyer; b. N.Y.C. s. Joseph S. and Sara L. (Altman) H.; m. Vera (dec. Mar. 1987); children: Steven D., Joel S. BA, NYU, 1939, JD, 1941. Bar: U.S. Dist. Ct. (so. dist.) N.Y. 1947, U.S. Dist. Ct. (ea. dist.) N.Y. 1959, U.S. Supreme Ct. 1961, U.S. Ct. Appeals (2d dist.) 1980. Atty. pvt. practice, N.Y.C., 1943—. Mem. Environ. Conservation Adv. Bd., Port Jefferson, NY, 1975—90; arbitrator U.S. Dist. Ct. Ea. Dist. N.Y., 1985, Dist. Ct. Suffolk County, 1985, Nassau County, 1985—90; adult edn. instr. Earl L. Vandermeulen H.S., Port Jefferson, 1975—86, Miller Place, 1983—85. Mem. Score-Counselor to Am. Small Bus., 1988. Recipient Ten Yr. award for Svc. Small Bus. Cmty., 1998, Gold Mem. award SCORE, 1999. Mem. Suffolk County Bar Assn. (Golden Anniversary Award of Practice of Law 1993), Knights of Pythias (Cosmopolitan Lodge chancellor comdr. 1946). General practice, Property, real (including real estate development, water), Estate taxation. Home: 105 E Gate Rd Port Jefferson NY 11777

HINDMAN, LARRIE C. lawyer; b. Meservey, Iowa, Mar. 30, 1937; s. Marvin C. and Fredona E. (Lemke) H.; m. Jeannie Carol Richey, June 18, 1961; children: Bryant C., Derek Cory. BS, Iowa State U., 1959; JD, U. Iowa, 1962. Bar: Mo. 1963, Kans. 1975. Ptnr. Stinson Morrison & Hecker LLP, Kansas City, Mo., 1962-2000. Contbr. legal articles to profl. jours. Mem.: Am. Land Title Assn. (lender counsel), Am. Coll. Real Estate Lawyers, Club at Porto Cima. Finance, Property, real (including real estate development, water), Native American. Home: 67 Grand Cove Dr Sunrise Beach MO 65079-9217 Office: Stinson Morrison & Hecker LLP 2600 Grand Blvd Ste 1200 Kansas City MO 64108-4606

HINE, JOHN CHARLES, lawyer; b. Winston-Salem, N.C., Dec. 30, 1948; s. George H. and Laura L. H.; m. Ann Moore, Aug. 14, 1971; childre: Neil, Laura. BS, U. N.C., 1971; JD, U. Tenn., 1974; LLM in Taxation, NYU, 1977. Bar: N.C., U.S. Surpeme Ct., U.S. Tax Ct., Ct. Mil. Appeals. Atty. IRS, Raleigh, N.C., 1974-76, Baddour, Parker, Hine & Orander, Goldsboro, NC, 1977—. Treas. Goldsboro-Wayne Airport Authority, 1982-87, N.C.; dir. Econ. Deve. Comm., Goldsboro, 1992-96. Lt. col. USAF, 1975-99. Mem. Rotary. Republican. Episcopalian. Avocations: hunting, camping, sports, flying. Estate planning, Probate (including wills, trusts), Corporate taxation. Home: 2507 Peachtree St Goldsboro NC 27534-4311 Office: PO Box 916 Goldsboro NC 27533-0916

HINER, LESLIE DAVIS, lawyer, consultant; b. Canton, Ohio, Sept. 30, 1957; d. Wendell Hughes and Margaret Alvina (Klebaum) Davis; m. Ward Christopher Hiner, July 23, 1983; children: Elaine Margaret, Travis Davis. BA, Coll. Wooster, 1980; JD, U. Akron, 1985. Bar: Ind. 1985. Intern Legis. Svcs. Agy., Indpls., 1984; assoc. Ecklund, Frutkin & Grant, Indpls., 1985-87; co-owner, v.p., gen. counsel Hiner Van & Storage, Kokomo, Ind., 1987-91; assoc. Russell McIntrye Jessup Hilligoss & Raquet, Kokomo, Ind., 1991-91; Ind. senate majority atty., 1993-94; pvt. practice, 1994-95; gen. counsel, elections dep. Ind. Sec. of State, 1995-97; pvt. practice, session atty. Rep. caucus Ind. Ho. of Reps., Indpls., 1997-2000, policy dir., caucus atty. Rep. caucus, 2000—. Mem. adj. faculty U. Indpls., 1986—87, 1992—. Bd. dirs. Montessori Children's Home, 1989—90, cmty. affairs com. chmn., 1990; mem. Altrusa Cmty. Affairs Com., 1989—91; schl. . bd. mem. Irving Community Schl. (Pub. Charter Schl.), 2002—; campaign chair Johnson for State Senate Re-election Com., 1990; campaign mgr. Kenley for State Senate, 1992; mem. fin. com. Howard County Reps., 1991; mem. bd. dirs. Irvington Cmty. Charter Sch., 2002—; mem. devel. adv. com. Ctr. on Philanrophy I.U. Charter Sch. Bd., 2003—; chair Irvington Cmty. Charter Sch., 2003—; bd. dirs. United Way, Howard County, 1990, exec. com., 1990, allocations coun., 1987—91, vice chmn., 1989, chmn., 1990, past chmn., 1991, campaign vol., 1988, 1989; atty. Legal Aid, Kokomo, 1987—91; vol. Bona Vista Rehab. Ctr., Capital Campaign Col., 1991; mem. Indpls. Symphonic Choir. Named Howard County Woman of the Yr. in Bus. Industry, 1991. Mem.: Indpls. Bar Assn. (women in law divsn., govt. practice divsn.), Federalist Soc. (bd. dirs. lawyers divsn. Indpls. chpt. 1994—), Ind. State Bar Assn. (women in law com. 2003—, improvements in the judicial system com. 2003—), Brebeuf Jesuit Mother's Assn., U. Akron Sch. Law Alumni Assn. (life), Richard D. Lugar Excellence Pub. Svc. Series Alumna, Greater Indpls. Rep. Women's Club (life). Lutheran. Avocations: piano, reading, needlepoint, tennis, singing. Administrative and regulatory, Education and schools, Legislative. Office: Ind Ho of Reps Statehouse 200 W Washington St Indianapolis IN 46204 E-mail: lhiner@iga.state.in.us.

HINERFELD, ROBERT ELLIOT, lawyer; b. N.Y.C., May 29, 1934; s. Benjamin B. and Anne (Blitz) H.; m. Susan Hope Slocum, June 27, 1957; children: Daniel Slocum, Matthew Ben. AB, Harvard U., 1956, JD, 1959. Bar: Calif. 1960. Asst. U.S. atty So. Dist. Calif., 1960-62; assoc. Leonard Horwin, Beverly Hills, Calif., 1962-66; mem. Simon, Sheridan, Murphy, Thornton & Hinerfeld, Los Angeles, 1967-74, Murphy, Thornton, Hinerfeld & Cahill, 1975-83, Murphy, Thornton, Hinerfeld & Elson, 1983-85, Manatt, Phelps & Phillips LLP, 1985-2000, sr. of counsel, 2000—; arbitrator bus. panel Los Angeles Superior Ct., 1979-82; assoc. ind. counsel (diGenova), 1993-95. Judge pro tempore Beverly Hills Municipal Court, 1967-74; clin. lectr. U. So. Calif. Law Center, 1980-81, guest lectr., 1993-96; expert witness, 1987—, legal affairs on-air guest spkr. sta. KCRW-FM, Santa Monica, Calif., 1998-99. Contbr. articles to profl. jours. Trustee Westland Sch., Los Angeles, 1970-75, Pacific Hills Sch., 1971-72. Fellow Am. Bar Found. (life); mem. ABA, Fed. Bar Assn., Assn. Profl. Responsibility Lawyers, Ctr. for Profl. Responsibility, Los Angeles County Bar Assn. (spl. com. jud. evaluation 1978-82, arbitration com. 1981-83, settlement officer 2d appellate dist. appellate case settlement project 1996—, spl. com. on appellate evaluation 1996-1999), Beverly Hills Bar Assn., State Bar Calif. (mem. com. on criminal law and procedure, chmn. spl. com. revision fed. criminal code, mem. disciplinary investigation panel dist. 7 1977-80, hearing referee State Bar Ct. 1981-83, referee rev. dept. 1984-87, exec. com. litigation sect. 1983-85, civil litigation adv. group 1985-88, mem. Jud. Nominees Evaluation Commn. 2000—), Am. Arbitration Assn. (arbitrator comml. panel 1966—), Calif. Acad. Appellate Lawyers (membership com. 1983-88, 2d v.p. 1985-87, 1st v.p. 1987-88, pres. 1988-89), Harvard Club So. Calif. (dir. 1974-83, sec. 1978-80, mem. prize book com. 1992-94), Harvard Club N.Y.C. Appellate, Alternative dispute resolution, Professional liability. Home and Office: 371 24th St Santa Monica CA 90402-2517

HINES, EDWARD FRANCIS, JR., lawyer; b. Norfolk, Va., Sept. 5, 1945; s. Edward Francis and Jeanne Miriam (Caulfield) H.; m. Elaine Geneva Carroll, Aug. 21, 1971; children: Jonathan Edward, Carolyn Adele. AB, Boston Coll., 1966; JD, Harvard U., 1969. Bar: Mass. 1969. Assoc. Choate Hall & Stewart, Boston, 1969-77, ptnr., 1977-2001, Hines & Corley LLC, Lexington, Mass., 2001—. Bd. dirs. Boston Med. Ctr., 1996—, Boston Med. Ctr. Ins. Co., Cayman Islands, 2003—; trustee Merrimac Fund Complex, 1996—. Trustee, treas. World Heart Fedn., Geneva, 2003—; trustee Social Law Libr., 1993—98; bd. dirs. Cath. Charities, 2002—, Assoc. Industries Mass., 1990—, chmn., 1996—98; bd. dirs. Am. Heart Assn., Dallas, 1984—86, 1991—2000, chmn., 1998—99; bd. dirs. Mass. Taxpayers Found., 1987—, Carroll Ctr. for the Blind, 1983—89, 1990—96, chmn., 1994—96. With USAR, 1969—75. Recipient Boston Coll. High Sch. St. Ignatius award, 1998, Gold Heart award, Am. Heart Assn., 2003. Fellow: Am. Coll. Trust and Estate Counsel; mem.: Mass. CLE (pres. 1985—87), Accion Internat. (bd. dirs. 1999—), Supreme Jud. Ct. Hist. Soc. (trustee 1989—96), Am. Coll. Greece (Athens bd. dirs., vice chmn. 1988—97), Boston Bar Found. (pres. 1995—97), Boston Bar Assn. (pres. 1988—89), Boston Coll. Club, North Andover Country Club. Estate planning, Taxation, general, State and local taxation. Office: Hines & Corley LLC Ste 3200 55 Hayden Ave Lexington MA 02421 E-mail: efh@hinesandcorley.com.

HINES, N. WILLIAM, dean, law educator, administrator; b. 1936; AB, Baker U., 1958; LLB, U. Kans., 1961; LLD, Baker U., 1999. Bar: Kans. 1961, Iowa 1965. Law clk. U.S. Ct. Appeals 10th cir., 1961-62; tchg. fellow Harvard U., 1961-62; asst. prof. law U. Iowa, 1962-65, assoc. prof., 1965-67, prof., 1967-73, disting. prof., 1973—, dean, 1976—. Vis. prof. Stanford U., 1974—75. Editor (notes and comments): Kans. Law Rev. Fellow, Harvard U., 1961—62. Fellow: Iowa State Bar Found., ABA Found.; mem.: Assn. Am. Law Schs. (exec. com. 2002—), Environ. Law Inst. (assoc.), Order of Coif, Jo. Co. Her. Trust (founder, pres.). Office: U Iowa Coll Law Iowa City IA 52242-0001

HINES, PRESTON HARRIS, state supreme court justice; b. Atlanta, Sept. 6, 1943; AB in Polit. Sci., Emory U., 1965, JD, 1968. Bar: Ga. 1968, U.S. Dist. Ct. Ga. 1973. Law clk. Civil Ct. Fulton County, 1968-69; pvt. practice Marietta, Ga., 1969-74; judge State Ct. of Cobb County, 1974-82, Superior Ct. of Ga., 1982—95; justice Ga. Supreme Ct., 1995—. Chmn. attys. divsn. Cobb County United Appeal, 1972; participant Leadership Ga., 1975, Leadership Atlanta, 1978-79; pres. YMCA Cobb County, 1976; co-treas. Cobb Landmarks Soc., 1976-77; former bd. dirs. Cobb County Emergency Aid Assn., Cobb-Marietta Girls Club, Ga. chpt. Leukemia Soc. Am., Cobb County Children's Ctr., Met. Atlanta Red Cross, First Presbyn. Day Kindergarten; mem. cmty. adv. com. Marietta-Cobb County LWV; bd. dirs. Kennesaw Coll. Found.; trustee Cobb Cmty. Symphony. Named Outstanding Young Man of Yr., Ga. Jaycees, 1975, Boss of Yr., Cobb County Legal Secs. Assn., 1975-76, 83-84. Mem. ABA, State Bar Ga. (chmn. Law Day com. 1975, mem. exec. com. younger lawyers sec. 1974-76), Cobb Jud. Cir. (sec. 1972-73, chmn. Law Day com. 1972), Joseph Henry Lumpkin Inn of Ct. Ga., Atlanta Lawyers Club, Kiwanis (bd. dirs. Marietta chpt., chmn. Key Club com., past chmn. spiritual aims com., past pres.), Cobb County C. of C., Sigma Alpha Epsilon (Atlanta and Marietta chpts.). Office: Supreme Court 244 Washington St Atlanta GA 30334

HINKLE, CHARLES FREDERICK, lawyer, clergyman, educator; b. Oregon City, Oreg., July 6, 1942; s. William Ralph and Ruth Barbara (Holcomb) H. BA, Stanford U., 1964; MDiv, Union Theol. Sem., N.Y.C., 1968; JD, Yale U., 1971. Bar: Oreg. 1971; ordained to ministry United Ch. of Christ, 1974. Instr. English, Morehouse Coll., Atlanta, 1966-67; assoc. Stoel Rives LLP (formerly Stoel, Rives, Boley, Jones & Grey), Portland, Oreg., 1971-77, ptnr., 1977—. Adj. prof. Lewis and Clark Law Sch., Portland, 1978-2001; bd. govs. Oreg. State Bar, 1992-95. Oreg. pres. ACLU, Portland, 1976-80, nat. bd. dirs., 1979-85; bd. dirs. Kendall Cmty. Ctr., 1987-93, Youth Progress Assn., 1994-98, Portland Baroque Orch., 1999-2000; mem. pub. affairs com. Am. Cancer Soc., 1994-99; mem. Oreg. Gov.'s Task Force on Youth Suicide, 1996. Recipient Elliott Human Rights award Oreg. Edn. Assn., 1984, E.B. MacNaughton award ACLU Oreg., 1987, Wayne Morse award Dem. Com. Oreg., 1994, Tom McCall Freedom of Info. award Women in Comm., 1996, Civil Rights award Met. Human Rights Commn., 1996, Pub. Svc. award Oreg. State Bar, 1997. Fellow Am. Bar Found.; mem. ABA (ho. of dels. 1998-2000), FBA, Multnomah County Bar Assn., City Club Portland (pres. 1987-88). Democrat. Communications, Constitutional, Libel. Home: 14079 SE Fairoaks Way Milwaukie OR 97267-1017 Office: Stoel Rives 900 SW 5th Ave Ste 2600 Portland OR 97204-1268 E-mail: cfhinkle@stoel.com.

HINMAN, HARVEY DEFOREST, lawyer; b. May 7, 1940; s. George Lyon and Barbara H.; m. Margaret (Snyder), June 23, 1962; children: George, Sarah, Marguerite. BA, Brown U., 1962; JD, Cornell U., 1965. Bar: Calif., 1966. Assoc. Pillsbury, Madison, and Sutro, San Francisco, 1965—72, ptnr., 1973—93; v.p., gen. counsel Chevron Texaco Corp., San Francisco, 1993—2002. Bd. dir. Legal Aid Soc., San Francisco. Bd. dir., sec. Holbrook Palmer Park Found., 1977—86; trustee Castillija Sch., 1988—89; bd. gov. Filoli Ctr., 1988—, pres., 1994—95; bd. dir. Phillips Brooks Sch., 1978—84, pres., 1983—84. Fellow: Am. Bar Found.; mem.: ABA, San Francisco Bar Assn. Commercial, contracts (including sales of goods; commercial financing), Oil, gas, and mineral, Private international. Office: 50 Fremont St San Francisco CA 94105

HINOJOSA, FEDERICO GUSTAVO, JR., judge; b. Edinburg, Tex., Apr. 16, 1947; s. Federico Gustavo and Zulema (Trevino) H.; m. Yolanda Silva, 1970 (div. 1977); children: Cynthia, Zelda Cassandra; m. Magdalena Garza, Oct. 30, 1992. BA, Pan Am. U., 1969; JD, U. Houston, 1977. Bar: Tex. 1977, U.S. Dist. Ct. (so. dist.) Tex. 1977, U.S. Ct. Appeals (5th cir.) 1980, U.S. Supreme Ct. 1980. Assoc. Clark, Lowes & Carrithers, Houston, 1977-79; ptnr. Clark & Hinojosa, Houston, 1979-81; child support atty. Tex. Dept. Human Resources, McAllen, 1981-83; asst. dist. atty. Hidalgo County, Edinburg, 1983-84; assoc. Atlas & Hall, McAllen, 1984-87; ptnr. Lewis, Pettitt & Hinojosa, McAllen, 1987-91; justice Tex. Ct. Appeals for 13th Dist., Corpus Christi, 1991—. Sgt. USAF, 1970-74. Mem. State Bar Tex., Mexican-Am. Bar Tex., Mexican-Am. Bar Assn. Coastal Bend (dir. 1993-94), Hidalgo County Bar Assn. (dir. 1986-90). Democrat. Office: 13th Ct Appeals 100 E Cano St Edinburg TX 78539-4548 E-mail: fghinojosa@courts.state.tx.us.

HINOJOSA, RICARDO H. federal judge; b. 1950; BA, U. Tex., 1972; JD, Harvard U., 1975. Judge U.S. Dist. Ct. (so. dist.) Tex.; law clk. Tex. Supreme Ct., 1975-76; assoc. Ewers & Toothaker, McAllen, Tex., 1976-79, ptnr., 1979-83; judge U.S. Dist. Ct. (so. dist.) Tex., McAllen, 1983—. Office: US Dist Ct So Dist Tex 1701 W Bus Hwy 83 Ste 1028 Mcallen TX 78501

HINSHAW, CHESTER JOHN, lawyer; b. Sacramento, Mar. 10, 1941; s. Chester Edward and Gertrude Lorraine (Miller) H.; m. Karen Forbes Breakey, Feb. 19, 1977. AB, Stanford U., 1963; JD, U. Calif., Berkeley, 1966. Bar: Calif. 1966, U.S. Dist. Ct. (no. dist.) Calif. 1967, U.S. Ct. Appeals (9th cir.) 1967, N.Y. 1968, U.S. Dist. Ct. (so. dist.) N.Y. 1972, U.S. Dist. Ct. (ea. dist.) N.Y. 1974, U.S. Ct. Appeals (2d cir.) 1974, U.S. Dist. Ct. (no. dist.) N.Y. 1980, U.S. Dist. Ct. (ea. dist.) Mich. 1982, U.S. Dist. Ct. (no. dist.) Tex. 1983, Tex. 1984, U.S. Ct. Appeals (5th cir.) 1984, U.S Supreme Ct. 1991. Assoc. Chadbourne & Parke, N.Y.C., 1967-74, ptnr., 1974-83, Jones, Day, Reavis & Pogue, Dallas, 1983-99. Lectr. U. Calif. Berkeley, 1966. Mem. ABA, Tex. Bar Assn., Calif. Bar Assn. Antitrust, Federal civil litigation, Private international. Home: 5510 Park Ln Dallas TX 75220-2158

HINTON, FLOYD, lawyer; b. Olympia, Wash., Sept. 11, 1923; s. Irma (Yost) Ness.; married; children: Denise C. Hinton Maaranen, Stefan V., Bradford R. BS, U. Org., 1948; LLB, Northwestern Law Sch., Portland, Oreg., 1958. Bar: Oreg. 1958, U.S. Dist. Ct. Oreg. 1959, U.S. Ct. Appeals (ith cir.) 1980. Sole practitioner, Portland, 1958-61; ptnr. Deich Hinton & Meece and predecessors, Portland, 1961-88; in house counsel Oreg. Ctrl. Credit Union, 1988—. Chmn. supervisory com. Oreg. Cen. Credit Union. Active in fin. devel. Oreg. Lung Assn., Portland, 1982-85; bd. dirs. N.W. Native Am. Arts Coun., 1985—. SErved with U.S. Army, 1943. Mem. Oreg. State Bar (author ins. and creditor rights for continuing legal edn. com.), Multnomah County Bar Assn., Oreg. Trial Lawyers Assn., Am. Arbitration Assn., Portland Art Assn., Portland City Club (mem. study groups), Viking Athletic Assn. (bd. dirs. 1985), Elks (trustee). State civil litigation, Commercial, consumer (including collections, credit), Family and matrimonial. Home: 17744 Highway 101 N # E 214 Brookings OR 97415-8135

HINTON, JAMES FORREST, JR., lawyer; b. Gadsden, Ala., Nov. 19, 1951; s. James Forrest Sr. and Juanita Grey (Weems) H. BA, Vanderbilt U., 1974; JD, U. Ala., 1977. Bar: Ala. 1977, D.C. 1979, U.S. Dist. Ct. (so. dist.) Ala. 1979, U.S. Ct. Appeals (5th cir.) 1980, U.S. Ct. Appeals (11th cir.) 1981, La. 1982, U.S. Dist. Ct. (ea. and mid. dists.) La. 1982, U.S. Dist. Ct. (no. dist.) Ala 1982, U.S. Supreme Ct. 1982, U.S. Dist. Ct. (we. dist.) La. 1983, U.S. Dist. Ct. (no. dist.) Ohio 1983, U.S. Ct. Appeals (D.C. cir.) 1984, U.S. Ct. Appeals (fed. cir.) 1985, U.S. Dist. Ct. (so. dist.) Tex. 1987, U.S. Dist. Ct. (no. dist.) Tex. 1991, Tex. 1992, Tenn. 1992, U.S. Dist. Ct. (ea. and we. dists.) Ark. 1992, U.S. Ct. Appeals (6th and 8th cirs.) 1992, U.S. Dist. Ct. (ea. and we. dists.) Tex. 1993, U.S. Dist. Ct. (mid. dist.) Ala. 1993, U.S. Dist. Ct. (ea. and mid. dist.) Tenn. 1994, U.S. Dist. Ct., Colo. 2000. Law clk. to chief judge U.S. Dist. Ct. (so. dist.) Ala., Mobile, 1977-79; ptnr. Darby, Myrick & Hinton, Mobile, 1979-82; dir. McGlinchey Stafford Lang, New Orleans, 1982-93; ptnr. Adams & Reese, New Orleans, 1993-97; shareholder Berkowitz, Lefkovits, Isom & Kushner, Birmingham, 1997—2003, Baker, Donelson, Bezman, Caldwell & Berkowitz, 2003—. Contbr. articles to profl. jours. Mem. ABA (antitrust, intellectual property, litigation sects.), FBA, La. Assn. Def. Counsel, Order of Coif, Phi Beta Kappa. Antitrust, General civil litigation, Intellectual property. Office: Baker Donelson Bearman Caldwell & Berkowitz PC 420 20th St N Ste 1600 Birmingham AL 35203-5200 E-mail: fhinton@blik.com.

HINTON, PAULA WEEMS, lawyer; b. Gadsden, Ala., Dec. 5, 1954; d. James Forrest and Juanita (Weems) H.; m. Steven D. Lawrence, Mar. 31, 1984; 1 child, David Hinton Lawrence. BA, U. Ala., 1976, MPA, JD, U. Ala., 1979. Bar: Ala. 1979, Tex. 1982, U.S. Dist. Ct. (so. dist.) Ala. 1980, U.S. Dist. Ct. (so. dist.) Tex. 1981, U.S. Dist. Ct. (no. dist.) Tex. 1988, U.S. Dist. Ct. (ea. and we. dists.) Tex. 1989, U.S. Dist. Ct. (no. and mid. dists.) Ala. 1993, U.S. Ct. Appeals (5th and 11th cirs.) 1981, U.S. Supreme Ct. Law clk. to magistrate U.S. Dist. Ct. Ala., Mobile, 1979-80; assoc. Vinson & Elkins, LLP, Houston, 1981-88; ptnr. Akin Gump Strauss Hauer & Feld, L.L.P., Houston, 1989—2001, Vinson & Elkins, Houston, 2001—. Mem. Supreme Ct. Gender Bias Reform Implementation Com., 1998—, co-chair, 2000—, chmn., 2002-. Bd. dirs. Planned Parenthood Houston and S.E. Tex., Inc., 2000—. Rotary fellow U. Sevilla, Spain, 1980-81. Mem.: ABA (mem. ligation sect., internat. law sect., antitrust and bus. litigation sect., women andthe law sect., alternate dispute resolution sect.), ATLA, Tex. Bar Found. (nominating co-chair 2002, co-chmn. nominating com. 2002), London Ct. of Internat. Arbitration, Internat. Bar Assn., Houston Bar Assn., Greater Houston Partnerships, Exec. Women's Partnership (steering com. 2002, Ma'at Justice award 2001), U. Houston Law Found. (adv. bd,), Houston Bar Found. (bd. dirs. 1994—96, chmn. 1996—97, bd. dirs. 2002—), State Bar Tex. (chair women in the profession com. 1996—98, mem. disciplinary rules of profl. conduct com. 2000—01, bd. dir. 2002—, mem. litigation sect., internat. law sect., antitrust and bus. litigation sect., alternative dispute resolution sect., women and law sect.). General civil litigation, Franchising. Office: Vinson and Elkins LLP 2300 First City Tower 1001 Fannin St Houston TX 77002-6760 Office Fax: 713-615-5543. Business E-Mail: phinton@velaw.com.

HINTON, QUINCY THOMAS, JR., lawyer; b. Lake Charles, La., July 1, 1941; s. Quincy Thomas and Maxine Elaine (Brooks) H.; m. Glynda Guthrey, Aug. 24, 1963; children— Christopher, Benjamin, Catherine. B.A., McNeese State U., 1964; J.D., Loyola U., New Orleans, 1967. Bar: La. 1967, U.S. Dist. Ct. (ea. dist.) La. 1967, U.S. Ct. Appeals (5th cir.) 1967, U.S. Supreme Ct. 1979, Tex. 1984, U.S. Dist. Ct. (so. dist.) Tex. 1984. Landman, Shell Oil Co., New Orleans, 1969-76; land mgr.-onshore Aminoil USA Inc., Houston, 1976-77; sr. profl. landman Gen. Crude Oil Co., Houston, 1977-78; mgr. land and legal dept. Jones Exploration, Houston, 1978-83; ptnr. Broadhurst, Brook, Mangham & Hardy Houston, 1983—86; pvt. law practice, 1986-88; sr. counsel Enron Oil & Gas Co., 1988-92; ind. landman atty., 1992-96; assoc. title atty. Rosie & Flanagan, P.C., 1996-98; pvt. law practice, ind. landman, Kingwood, Tex., 1998—p. Contbr. articles to profl. jours. Recipient Outstanding Service award Nat. Assn. Royalty Owners, 1984. Mem. Am. Assn. Petroleum Landmen, Tex. Bar Assn., La. Bar Assn., Houston Bar Assn., Houston Assn. Petroleum Landmen, Delta Theta Phi. Republican. Am. Baptist. Oil, gas, and mineral. Home: 3311 Riverlawn Dr Humble TX 77339-2532

HINTZEN, ERICH HEINZ, lawyer; b. Grosse Pointe, Mich., June 9, 1960; s. Heinz and Hanna Hintzen; m. Valerie L. Parker; children: Andrew P., Emma L. AB, U. Mich., 1983; JD, U. Minn., 1989. Bar: Tex. 1989, Mich. 1990, U.S. Dist. Ct. (we. dist.) Mich. 1991, U.S. Ct. Appeals (6th cir.) 1991, U.S. Dist. Ct. (ea. dist.) Mich. 1992, U.S. Dist. Ct. (ea. dist.) Tex. 1995, U.S. Dist. Ct. (we. dist.) Tex. 1995, U.S. Ct. Appeals (5th cir.) 1995, U.S. Supreme Ct. 1996, U.S. Dist. Ct. (no. dist.) Tex. 1997, U.S. Dist. Ct. (so. dist.) Tex. 1998. Briefing atty. to Justice C.L. Ray Tex. Supreme Ct., Austin, 1989-90; assoc. Miller, Canfield, Paddock & Stone, PLC, Detroit, 1990-95, 96-98, Parkers Parks & Rosenthal, LLP, Austin, 1995-96; prin. Miller Canfield Paddock & Stone, PLC, Troy, Mich., 1998—. Appellate, Product liability. Office: Miller Canfield Paddock & Stone PLC 840 W Long Lake Rd Ste 200 Troy MI 48098-6358

HIRAMATSU, TSUYOSHI, law educator; b. Changchun, Manchuria, China, Feb. 25, 1938; arrived in Japan, 1943; s. Kiyoshi and Takako (Obata) H.; m. Kyoko Hiramatsu, May 1, 1970; children: Asako, Utako, Takashi. LLD, Kyoto (Japan) U., 1985. Assoc. prof. Nara (Japan) Nat. Women's U., 1973-83, prof., 1983-88; prof. Law Sch. Kwansei-Gakuin U., Nishinomiya, Japan, 1988—. Rschr. Inst. of Pub. Law, U. Freiburg, Germany, 1975-76; vis. prof. Internat. Ombudsman Inst., U. Alta., Edmonton, Can., 1987; vis. prof. dept. polit. sci. Carleton U., Ottawa, Can., 1987, Jilin U. Sch. Law, Changchun, China, 1990. Author: Constitutional Law, 1979, Freedom of Information, 1983, Ombudsman, 1988, Privacy, 1991. Mem. deliberative coun. Mgmt. & Coordination Agy., Japan, 1991; bd. dirs. Japan Assn. Legal and Polit. Scis., Japanese Assn. Comparative Constitutional Law, v.p. Japan Pub. Law Assn. Recipient Mainichi Rsching. Japan award Mainichi Newspaper Pub. Co. Ltd., 1972. Avocation: bamboo flute. Home: 3-902-275 Sahodai Nara 630-8105 Japan Office: Kwansei Gakuin U Law Sch 1-1-155 Uegahara Nishinomia Hyogo 662-8501 Japan E-mail: tsuyoshi0857@yahoo.co.jp.

HIRSCH, BARRY, lawyer; b. N.Y.C., Mar. 19, 1933; s. Emanuel M. and Minnie (Levenson) H.; m. Myra Seiden, June 13, 1963; children: Victor Terry II, Neil Charles Seiden, Nancy Elizabeth. BSBA, U. Mo., 1954; JD, U. Mich., 1959; LL.M., N.Y. U., 1964. Bar: N.Y. bar 1960. Assoc., then partner firm Seligson & Morris, N.Y.C., 1960-69; v.p., sec., gen. counsel dir. B.T.B. Corp., 1969-71; v.p., sec., gen. counsel Loews Corp. (and subsidiaries), 1971-86, sr. v.p., sec., gen. counsel, 1986—. Bds. dirs. Neuberger and Berman Funds. Served to 1st lt. AUS, 1954-56. Mem. ABA, Assn. of Bar of City of N.Y., N.Y. State Bar Assn., Zeta Beta Tau, Phi Delta Phi. Corporate, general, Finance, Securities. Home: 1010 5th Ave New York NY 10028-0130 Office: Loews Corp 667 Madison Ave Fl 8 New York NY 10021-8087 E-mail: bhirsch@loews.com.

HIRSCH, DANIEL, lawyer; b. Bklyn., Feb. 26, 1940; s. Burton and Lee (Roller) H.; m. Trina Lutter, July 15, 1965 (div.); children: Jessica Elyse, Jeremy Bram. BS, U. Pa., 1960; JD, Columbia U., 1963. Bar: N.Y. 1964. Assoc. Carter Ledyard & Milburn, N.Y.C., 1964-68, counsel, 2001—; pvt. practice N.Y.C., 1968-74; prin. Jones, Hirsch, Connors & Bull, P.C., N.Y.C., 1974—2000; dir. Loral-Orion, Inc. Lt. USNR, 1965-75. Mem. N.Y. State Bar Assn., Assn. of Bar of City of N.Y., Fedn. Ins. and Corp. Counsel, Univ. Club. Corporate, general, Insurance, Private international. Office: Carter Ledyard & Milburn 2 Wall St New York NY 10005

HIRSCH, JEFFREY ALLAN, lawyer; b. Chgo., June 14, 1950; s. Leo Paul And Dorthy (Seidman) H.; m. Lennie Sue Henderson, June 16, 1979; children: Lea, Ashley. BSBA, U. Fla., 1972, JD with honors, 1975. Bar: Fla. 1975, U.S. Dist. Ct. (so. and mid. dists.) Fla. 1975. Assoc. Swann & Glass, Coral Gables, Fla., 1975-76, Glass, Schultz, Weinstein & Moss, Coral Gables, 1976-80; ptnr. Holland & Knight, Ft. Lauderdale, Fla., 1980-93; prin. shareholder Greenberg, Traurig, P.A., Ft. Lauderdale, Fla., 1993—. Exec. dir. Govtl. Research Ctr., Gainesville, Fla., 1975. Active Leadership Broward, Ft. Lauderdale, 1986—, Leadership Fla., 1994—. Mem. ABA, Fla. Bar Assn., Broward County Bar Assn. Avocations: reading, travel. Federal civil litigation, State civil litigation, Commercial, consumer (including collections, credit). Office: Greenberg Traurig PA 401 E Las Olas Blvd Ste 1500 Fort Lauderdale FL 33301-2278 E-mail: hirschj@gtlaw.com.

HIRSCH, JEROME S. lawyer; BA in Econs., SUNY, Binghamton, 1970; JD, Fordham U., 1974. Bar: N.Y. Assoc. Skadden, Arps, Slate, Meagher & Flom, N.Y.C., 1974-81, ptnr., 1982—. Mem. ABA, N.Y. State Bar Assn., Assn. of Bar of City of N.Y. Federal civil litigation, State civil litigation, Securities. Office: Skadden Arps Slate Meagher & Flom 4 Times Sq New York NY 10036-6595

HIRSCH, LARRY JOSEPH, retired retail executive, lawyer; b. Boston, July 1, 1938; s. Samuel and Anne (Rossman) H.; m. Kay Pollock, Mar. 16, 1974. BA, Syracuse U., 1962; JD, Suffolk U., Boston, 1968; grad. gemologist, Gem Inst. Am., Los Angeles, 1981. Bar: Mass. 1968, R.I. 1968, Fla. 1970. Mgr. Vality Dept. Store, Groton, Conn., 1962—63; asst. area dir. Am. Jewish Com., Miami, Fla., 1968—69; asst. city atty. City of Miami, Fla., 1969—71; atty Feuer & Feuer, Miami, Fla., 1971—74, Turano & Turano, Westerly, RI, 1974—78; asst. town solicitor Town of Westerly, RI, 1975—76; pres. Westerly Jewelry Co. Inc., Westerly, RI, 1978—2000; ret., 2000—; atty., 1974—. Mem. adv. bd. Fleet Bank, Westerly, 1984-90; chmn. adv. group Westerly Edn. Endowment Fund, 2000-01, dir., 2001—; bd. dirs. Washington Trust Bancorp, Inc., 1994—. Pres. Chariho-Westerly Animal Rescue League, 1976—2001; incorporator Cmty. Hosp. of Westerly, 1985—, bd. govs., 1995—2002, v.p., 1999—2002, trustee, 1984—94, mem. fin. com., 1984—2001, mem. human resources com., 1998—2000; trustee Ctr. for the Arts, Westerly, 1984; v.p. Westerly Heart Assn., 1986; incorporator Westerly Pub. Libr., 1997—; mem. site planning group West H.S., 1998—2000, mem. student handbook com., 1999—2000; mem. Dante Italian Heritage Soc., 1999—; pres. Local Devel. Corp., 1998—; v.p. Stand Up for Animals, 2002—; dir. Chariho-Westerly Animal Rescue League, 2001—; v.p. Congregation Sharon Zedek, 1993—; bd. dirs. Am. Heart Assn., Westerly, 1986—93; mem. Charter Revision Com. Westerly, 1985—89; bd. dirs., v.p. Joint Devel. Task Force, Westerly, 1988—, v.p., 1994—99, dir., 2001—, pres., 1999—2000; bd. dirs. Animal Rescue League of So. R.I., 1988—94; mem. adv. coun. Westerly Integrated Social Svcs. Program, 1996, chmn., 1997—2000; mem.salary rev. and benefits coms. Westerly Fire Dist., 1996—2002. With U.S. Army, 1958—60. Larry Hirsch Day named in his honor, Town of Westerly, 1980; recipient Someone Spl. award, Channel 26 WTWS TV, New London, Conn., 1987, Sam Walton Bus. Leadership award Westerly-Pawcatuck C. of C., 2000; named Columbus Citizen of Yr., Golden Key Club, Westerly, 1989, Citizen of Yr., Westerly-Pawcatuck C. of C., 2000. Mem.: Gemological Inst. Am., Am. Gem Soc. (cert. gemologist, L.A. 1986), New Eng. Appraisers Assn., Nat. Assn. Jewelry Appraisers, Westerly Track Club (pres. 1976, bd. dirs. 1976—95), Elks (Larry Hirsch Run 1980—), Fraternal Order of Police (assoc.; scholar com.). Avocations: long distance running, humane treatment of animals. E-mail: hirsch@riconnect.com.

HIRSCH, MILTON, lawyer; b. Chgo., Sept. 10, 1952; s. Charles Ira and Beverly Ruth (Kelner) H.; m. Ilene Lonnie Schreer, Feb. 16, 1986. BA, U. Calif., San Diego, 1974; MS, DePaul U., 1979; JD, Georgetown U., 1982. Bar: Fla. 1982, U.S. Dist. Ct. (so., mid. dists.) Fla. 1983, U.S. Dist. Ct. (no. dist.) Fla. 1985, U.S. Ct. Appeals (5th and 11th cirs.) 1983, U.S. Tax Ct. 1983, U.S. Ct. Claims 1983, U.S. Supreme Ct. 1988. Acct. Arthur Young & Co., CPAs, Chgo., 1977-79; asst. state atty. Office State Atty., Miami, Fla., 1982-84; assoc. Finley, Kumble, Wagner, Heine, Underberg, Manley et al, Miami, 1985-87; pvt. practice, Miami, 1987—. Adj. prof. Nova U. Law Sch., Ft. Lauderdale, Fla., 1988, 94, 95. Author: Florida Criminal Trial Procedure; contbg. editor Jour. Nat. Assn. Criminal Def. Attys., 1987—; contbr. articles to profl. jours. Mem. ABA (litigation sect.), Nat. Assn. Criminal Def. Lawyers, Fla. Bar Assn.), Fla. Criminal Def. Attys. Assn. (former pres., Presdl. award for Disting. Svc. 1987-88). Criminal, General practice. Office: Ste 1200 9130 S Dadeland Blvd Miami FL 33156-7848

HIRSCH, RICHARD GARY, lawyer; b. L.A., June 15, 1940; s. Charles and Sylvia (Leopold) H.; m. Claire Renee Recsei, Mar. 25, 1967; 1 child, Nicole Denise. BA, UCLA, 1961; JD, U. Calif., Berkeley, 1965. Bar: Calif. 1967, U.S. Dist. Ct. (ctrl. dist.) Calif. 1967, U.S. Supreme Ct. 1972, U.S. Ct. Appeals (9th cir.) 1989, U.S. Dist. Ct. (ea. dist.) Calif. 1991. Dep. dist. atty. L.A. Dist. Atty.'s Office, 1967-71; ptnr. Nasatir, Hirsch & Podberesky, Santa Monica, Calif., 1971—. Commr. Calif. Coun. Criminal Justice, 1977-81; mem. Spl. Com. on Cts. in the Media/Judicial Coun. Calif., 1979. Co-author: California Criminal Law Proceedings/Practice, 5 edits. Pres. bd. trustees Santa Monica Mus. Art, 1984-91; chmn. Greek Theatre Adv. Com., L.A., 1976-79; mem. L.A. Olympic Organizing Com., 1981-84; bd. dirs. Ocean Park Cmty. Ctr., 1995—, bd. chair, 1997-2001. Recipient Spl. Merit Resolution, L.A. City Coun., 1984, Criminal Def. Atty. of Yr. award Century City Bar Assn., 1996. Lifetime achievement and crim. courts bar assoc., 2003. Fellow Am. Bd. Criminal Lawyers (bd. dirs., v.p. 1998-2000, pres.-elect 2001, pres. 2002); mem. Calif. Attys. Criminal Justice (pres. 1987, bd. trustees), Criminal Cts. Bar Assn. (pres. 1981, Spl. Merit award 1988), L.A. County Bar Assn. (Criminal Def. Atty. of Yr. 1999), Santa Monica C. of C. (bd. dirs. 1995-97). Avocations: cooking, reading, community service. Criminal. Office: Nasatir Hirsch Podberesky & Genego 2115 Main St Santa Monica CA 90405-2215

HIRSCHFELD, MICHAEL, lawyer; b. Bronx, N.Y., July 4, 1950; s. Lawrence John and Ida (Miller) H.; m. Heidi P. Greenspan, June 17, 1973; children: Adam Lawrence, Philip Richard. BEE summa cum laude, CCNY, 1972; JD cum laude, U. Pa., 1975; LLM in Taxation, NYU, 1980. Bar: N.Y. 1976, U.S. Dist. Ct. (so. and ea. dists.) N.Y. 1976, U.S. Tax Ct. 1978. Assoc. Shearman and Sterling, N.Y.C., 1975-80, Roberts and Holland, N.Y.C., 1980-83, Carro, Spanbock, Kaster and Cuiffo, N.Y.C., 1983-85, ptnr., 1985-88, Winstown & Strawn, N.Y.C., 1988-98, Dechert, N.Y.C., 1998—. Lectr. NYU, Assn. of Bar of City of New York, ABA, ALI-ABA, PLI, Syracuse U., U. Tex., Tulane U., Georgetown U.; chmn. NYU Inst. Real Estate Taxation; co-chmn. 49th, 50th, 52d, 53d and 54th ann. Fed. Income Taxation Confs.; 11th-23d ann. NYU Confs. on Fed. Taxation of Real Estate Taxations: mem. nat. edn. bd., Business Entities (RIA publ.) Real Estate Tax Digest, Jour. of Internat. Tax, Tax. Mgmt. Real Estate Jour.; mem. adv. bd. Tax Mgmt. Real Estate, Inst. Fed. Tax. Co-author: Real Estate Limited Partnerships, 3rd edit., 1991; bd. editors Real Estate Tax Digest, BNA Tax Mgmt.; editl. adv. bd. NYU Real Estate Adv. Bd. Mem.: Am. Coll. Tax Counsel, Internat. Tax Assn., Assn. of Bar of City of N.Y. (mem. com. on taxation of bus. entities), N.Y. State Bar Assn. (exec. com. 1987—97, lectr., co-chmn. coms. on income from real property tax sect. 1988—91, co-chmn. com. on preferences and minimum tax 1991—92, co-chmn. com. on individuals 1992—93, co-chmn. com. U.S. activities of fgn. taxpayers 1993—96, co-chmn. com. on real property 1996—98, co-chmn. tax accts. 1997—98, com. on internat. mems.), Am. Law Inst. (lectr.), ABA (tax sect. vice chmn. ACRS depreciation recapture subcom. 1983—85, task force pres.'s tax reform proposals minimum tax subcom. 1985—86, chmn. syndications subcom. 1985—87, chmn. real estate tax problems com. 1989—91, co-chmn. govt. subcom. 1992—94, vice chmn. gov. submission com. 1992—95, chmn. govt. subcom. 1994—97, coun. 1997—2000, coun. dir. tax sect. internat. com. 1997—2000, vice chmn. individual income taxpayers com. 2000—02, vice chair com. ops. 2001—, lectr. taxaction sect., chair 911 task force). Avocation: music (drum). Corporate taxation, Taxation, general, Personal income taxation. Office: Dechert LLP 30 Rockefeller Plz Fl 22 New York NY 10112-2200 Fax: (212) 698-3599. E-mail: michael.hirschfeld@dechert.com.

HIRSCHHORN, ERIC LEONARD, lawyer; b. N.Y.C., Apr. 28, 1946; m. Leah Wortham, Oct. 31, 1981; children: Alexander, Elizabeth, Anne. BA, U. Chgo., 1965; JD, Columbia U., 1968. Bar: N.Y. 1968, U.S. Supreme Ct. 1972, D.C. 1973. Reginald Heber Smith Community Lawyer fellow MFY Legal Svcs., N.Y.C., 1968-71; counsel Dem. Study Group N.Y. State Assembly, Albany, 1971; legis asst. to Rep. Bella Abzug, U.S. Ho. of Reps., Washington, 1971-73; assoc. Cadwalader, Wickersham & Taft, N.Y.C., 1973-75; chief counsel subcom. on govt. info. and individual rights U.S. Ho. of Reps., Washington, 1975-77; dep. assoc. dir. internat. affairs & trade U.S. Office Mgmt. & Budget, Washington, 1977-80; dep. asst. sec. for export adminstrn. U.S. Dept. Commerce, Washington, 1980-81; ptnr. Winston & Strawn (formerly Bishop, Cook, Purcell & Reynolds), Washington, 1981—. Exec. sec. Industry Coalition on Tech. Transfer, Washington, 1986—. Author: The Export Control and Embargo Handbook, 2000; contbr. articles to profl. jours. Mem. Assn. Bar City N.Y., Computer Law Assn., Thurgood Marshall Am. Inn of Ct., ABA Ctr. on Profl. Responsibility, D.C. Bar (legal ethics com. 1997-98, 99—; vice-chmn. 2001—). Administrative and regulatory, Federal civil litigation, Private international. Office: Winston & Strawn 1400 L St NW Washington DC 20005-3508

HIRSCHKOP, PHILIP JAY, lawyer, educator; b. Bklyn., May 14, 1936; s. Abraham and Frances H.; children: Jacqueline, Jon David, Adam Abraham. AB, Columbia Coll., 1960; BS in Engring., Columbia U., 1961; JD, Georgetown U., 1964. Bar: Va. 1964, D.C. 1964, U.S. Dist. Ct. (ea. and we. dists.) Va. 1964, U.S. Dist. Ct. D.C. 1964, U.S. Ct. Mil. Appeals 1964, U.S. Ct. Appeals (4th and D.C. cirs.) 1965, U.S. Supreme 1967, U.S. Ct. Claims 1969, U.S. Dist. Ct. (no. dist.) Tex. 1973, U.S. Ct. Appeals (5th cir.) 1973, U.S. Tax Ct. 1974, U.S Ct. Appeals (11th cir.), 1981, N.Y., 1982, U.S. Dist. Ct. (ea. dist.) N.C., U.S. Dist. Ct. D.C. Patent examiner U.S. Patent Office, Washington, 1961-63; legis. asst. congressman Richard Ichord, Washington, 1964; pvt. practice Alexandria, Va., 1964—. Adj. prof. law Georgetown U., Washington, 1969-75; profl. law lectr. George Washington U., 2001; chair steering com. Nat. Prison Project, Washington, 1975—; spkr. in field. Contbr. articles to profl. jours. Nat. bd. dirs. ACLU, N.Y.C., 1966-86. With Spl. Forces, U.S. Army, 1954-56. Recipient Disting. Svc. award, Va. Trial Lawyers Assn., 1999, War Horse award, So. Trial Lawyers Assn., 2000. Fellow Va. Law Found.; mem. ATLA (state committeeman), PETA (gen. counsel), NCIA (dir., counsel), Va. Bar Assn., Alexandria Bar Assn., Trial Lawyers for Pub. Justice (bd dirs., founder 1986-96), Law Students Civil Rights Rsch. Coun. General civil litigation, Constitutional, Personal injury (including property damage). Office: Hirschkop & Assocs PC 108 N Columbus St Alexandria VA 22314-3013

HIRSH, ROBERT JOEL, lawyer; b. Shamokin, Pa., May 18, 1935; s. David and Rose (Coplansky) H.; children: Christine, Jonathan, Thomas. BS, U. Ariz., 1960, LLB, 1964. Bar: Ariz. 1964, U.S. Dist. Ct. Ariz. 1964, U.S. Ct. Appeals (9th cir.) 1968, U.S. Supreme Ct. 1971; cert. criminal specialist, State Bar of Ariz. Ptnr. firm Messing Hirsh & Franklin, Tucson, 1969-72, Hirsh & Hooker, Tucson, 1972-73, Hirsh, Shiner & Walker, Tucson, 1973-77, Hirsh & Bayles, Tucson, 1977-82, Hirsh & Fines, P.C., Tucson, 1982-84, Hirsh, Sherick & Murphy, P.C., 1985-90, Hirsh & Sherick, P.C., 1990-91, Hirsh, Davis, Walker & Piccarreta, P.C., 1991-95, Hirsh, Davis & Piccarreta, P.C., 1995-97, Hirsh, Bjorgaard & Rogers, PLC, 1998—2003, Hirsh & Rogers PLC, 2003—. Mem. ABA, State Bar Ariz, Ariz. Attys. for Criminal Justice (founder, pres. 1990), 9th Cir. Jud. Conf. (del. 1986-88), Ariz. Supreme Ct. Commn. on Cts. (task force mem.), Pima County Bar Assn., Ariz. State Bar Assn., Nat. Assn. Criminal Def. Lawyers, Calif. Attys. for Criminal Justice, Am. Bd. Criminal Lawyers, Am. Coll. Trial Lawyers. Criminal. Office: 177 N Church Ave Ste 700 Tucson AZ 85701-1119 E-mail: rhirsh@hbrlaw.com.

HIRSH, THEODORE WILLIAM, lawyer; b. Gary, Ind., Nov. 16, 1934; s. Phillip and Libby (Krieger) H.; m. Beatrice Elaine Given, Aug. 28, 1955; children: Robert, Margo, Elizabeth, Irwin. AB, Ind. U., 1954, JD, 1957. Bar: Ind. 1957, Ill. 1958, Md. 1965. Atty. Montgomery Ward & Co., Chgo., 1958; pvt. practice Gary, 1958-60; trial lawyer, chief counsel IRS, Chgo., 1960-65; ptnr. Venable, Baetjer & Howard, Balt., 1965-76, Miles & Stockbridge, Balt., 1978-86; prin. Sussman & Hirsh, P.A., Balt., 1976-78; ptnr. Melnicove, Kaufman, Weiner, Smouse & Garbis, P.A., Balt., 1986-89, Miles & Stockbridge, Balt., 1989-96; with Law Offices of Peter G. Angelos, P.C., Balt., 1996-99, Ballard, Spahr, Andrews & Ingersoll, LLP, Balt., 1999—. Taxation, general. Office: Ballard Spahr Andrews & Ingersoll LLP 300 E Lombard St Ste 1800 Baltimore MD 21202-6739 E-mail: hirsht@ballardspahr.com., twhirsh@aol.com.

HIRSHFIELD, STUART, lawyer; b. N.Y.C., Dec. 31, 1941; s. William Louis and Anne (Frank) H.; m. Susanne Drucker, Jan. 22, 1967; children: Matthew S., Edward R. BA, Syracuse U., 1963, JD, 1966. Bar: N.Y. 1966, U.S. Dist. Ct. (so. and ea. dists.) N.Y. 1968, U.S. Ct. Appeals (2nd cir.) 1968. Assoc. Krauss & Krauss, N.Y.C., 1966-67; atty. N.Y. Cen. RR, N.Y.C., 1967-69; assoc. Blum, Haimoff, Gersen, Lipson & Szabad, N.Y.C., 1969; atty. CIT Fin., N.Y.C., 1970-72; assoc. Shea & Gould, N.Y.C., 1972-77, ptnr., 1977-88; ptnr., chmn. bankruptcy practice group Dewey Ballantine, N.Y.C., 1988—2003; ptnr., head NY bankruptcy practice group Ropes & Gray LLP, NYC, 2003—. Bd. dirs. 565 Tenants Corp. Contbr. Asset Based Financing--A Transactional Guide, 1985. Assn. atty. Allenwood Civic Assn., Great Neck, N.Y., 1984; bd. visitors Syracuse U. Coll.

Law, 1990—, exec. com., 1991-96. With USAR, 1966-72. Fellow Am. Coll. Bankruptcy (2d cir. admissions coun. 1994-2001, chair 1998-2001, bd. regents 1998-2001, bd. dirs. 2001—), Am. Bar Found.; mem. ABA (com. on bankruptcy 1983—), N.Y. Bar Assn., Assn. Bar City N.Y. (corp. reogn. com. 1975-78, 82-85), Assn. Comml. Fin. Attys. (dir. 1980-93), Am. Coll. Bankruptcy Found. (bd. dirs. 2002—), Rockefeller Ctr. Club. Bankruptcy, Commercial, contracts (including sales of goods; commercial financing). Office: Ropes & Gray LLP 45 Rockefeller Plaza New York NY 10111

HIRSHON, JACK THOMAS, lawyer; b. L.A., July 25, 1931; s. Jack W. Hirshon and Dorothy Sanborn; m. Patricia Lee Boldt, Mar. 30, 1957; children: David, Susan, Lori, Thomas. BS, UCLA, 1955; LLB, Golden Gate Coll., 1962. Bar: Calif. 1963. Ins. adjuster, claim mgr. United Pacific Ins. Co., San Francisco, 1962-63; pvt. practice law Santa Clara County, 1963—2000, Tahoe City, Calif., 2000—. Planning commr. City of Cupertino, Calif., 1964-72. 1st lt. U.S. Army, 1955-57. Mem. Consumer Attys. Calif., Tahoe Truckee Bar Assn., Sunnyvale Bar Assn. (pres.), Kiwanis. Democrat. Roman Catholic. Avocations: golf, skiing, running, football, gemology. Insurance, Personal injury (including property damage). Office: 210 Grove St PO Box 5126 Tahoe City CA 96145 E-mail: jhirshon@aol.com.

HIRSHON, ROBERT EDWARD, lawyer; b. Portland, Maine, Apr. 2, 1948; s. Selvin and Gladys (Wein) H.; m. Roberta Lynn Miller, Aug. 16, 1969; children: Todd, Sara, Jason, Miriam. BA, U. Mich., 1970, JD, 1973. Bar: Maine 1973, U.S. Dist. Ct. Maine 1973, U.S. Ct. Appeals (1st cir.) 1977, U.S. Supreme Ct. 2000. Shareholder Drummond, Woodsum & MacMahon P.A., Portland, 1973—. Adj. prof. law U. Maine Law Sch. Contbr. articles to profl. jours. Chairperson Breakwater Sch Bd., Portland, 1978-85; mem. Zoning Bd. Appeals, Cape Elizabeth, Maine, 1983-90. Mem. ABA (mem. Ho. of Dels. 1992—, chair standing com. lawyers pub. svc. responsibility 1990-93, chair steering com. pro bono ctr. 1991-96, chair torts and ins. practice sect. 1996-97, chair standing com. on membership 1997-2000, pres. 2001-02), Maine Bar Assn. (pres. 1986, chair continuing legal edn. com. 1975-83), Cumberland County Bar Assn., Maine Bar Found. (pres. 1990). Avocations: reading, tennis, skiing. Banking, General civil litigation, Insurance. Home: 3 Oakhurst Rd Cape Elizabeth ME 04107 Office: Drummond Woodsum & MacMahon 245 Comml St Portland ME 04101 E-mail: rhirshon@dwm.law.com.

HIRSHON, SHELDON IRA, lawyer; b. Bklyn., Mar. 27, 1947; s. Jay and Jeanne (Benk) H.; m. Claudia Glenn Barasch; children: Ariel, Yaniv, Jessica. BS, NYU, 1968, JD, 1972, LLM, 1978. Bar: N.Y. 1972. Assoc. Graubard, Moskovitz, McGoldrick, Dannett & Horowitz, N.Y.C., 1972-76, Windels, Marx, Davies & Ives, N.Y.C., 1976-78, Krause, Hirsch & Gross, N.Y.C., 1978-80; assoc., ptnr. Stroock & Stroock & Lavan, N.Y.C., 1980-87; ptnr. Proskauer, Rose, Goetz & Mendelsohn, N.Y.C., 1987—. Mem. ABA, N.Y. Bar Assn., Assn. Bar City N.Y. Bankruptcy, Corporate, general. Office: Proskauer Rose LLP 1585 Broadway Fl 27 New York NY 10036-8299

HIRSHOWITZ, MELVIN STEPHEN, lawyer; b. N.Y.C., Dec. 11, 1938; s. Samuel Albert and Lillian Rose (Minkow) H.; m. Susan Bonnie Brezel, June 19, 1983; children: Lauren Allison, Emily Sara. BA with hons., Cornell U., 1960; LLB cum laude, Harvard U., 1963; MA in Biology, CUNY, 1977. Bar: N.Y. 1963, N.J. 1987, U.S. Dist. Ct. (so. dist.) N.Y. 1969, (ea. dist.) N.Y. 1977, N.J. 1993, U.S. Ct. Appeals (2d cir.) 1978, U.S. Supreme Ct. 1994. Assoc. atty. SEC, N.Y.C., 1963-65; sole practitioner Melvin Hirshowitz Law Office, N.Y.C., 1968-76, 87--; of counsel Hyman Bravin Law Offices, N.Y.C., 1976-87. Author: (manual) Proof of an Over the Counter Manipulation, 1964. Vice chmn. N.Y. Libertarian Party, 1970-72, candidate for surrogate ct. judge and ct. of appeals judge. Mem. N.Y. County Lawyers Assn. (com. on profl. ethics 1986-92, com. fed. legislation 1986-88), Assn. of Bar of City of N.Y. (com. on the civil ct. 1986-89), N.Y. State Bar Assn., Harvard Club of N.Y.C., Phi Beta Kappa, Pi Delta Epsilon. Republican. Jewish. Avocations: bird watching, art, tennis. General civil litigation, State civil litigation, Probate (including wills, trusts). Office: 630 3rd Ave New York NY 10017-6705 E-mail: mshlawoffices@aol.com.

HITCHCOCK, BION EARL, lawyer; b. Muscatine, Iowa, Oct. 9, 1942; s. Stewart Edward and Arlene Ruth (Eichelberger) H. BSEE, Iowa State U., 1965; JD, U. Iowa, 1968. Bar: Iowa 1968, Okla. 1968, U.S. Ct. Customs and Patent Appeals 1973, U.S. Ct. Appeals (fed. cir.) 1982. Atty. Phillips Petroleum Co., Bartlesville, Okla., 1968-69, 73-76; mgr. licensing Phillips Petroleum Co. Europe-Africa, Brussels, 1977-80; sr. patent counsel Phillips Petroleum Co., Bartlesville, 1980-84, assoc. gen. patent counsel, 1984-2000; asst. gen. counsel intellectual property Chevron Phillips Chem. Co., LP, Houston, 2000—02; pvt. practice Sugar Land, Tex., 2002—. Bd. dirs. Bartlesville Symphony Orch., 1973-77, 80-91, pres., 1975-77, 82-84; bd. dirs. Bartlesville Allied Arts and Humanities Coun., 1976-77, 80-86, 1st v.p., 1982-83; mem. Govt. and Fin. Goals for Bartlesville Com., 1974-75; bd. dirs. Bartlesville Cmty. Concert Assn., 1982-90, Okla. Assn. Symphony Orchs., 1983-88. Lt. JAGC, USN, 1969-73. Mem. ABA, Okla. Bar Assn. (dir. patent trademark and copyright sect. 1980-86, sec. 1982-83, vice chmn. 1983-84, chmn. 1984-85), Iowa Bar Assn., Washington County Bar Assn. (pres. 1981-82), Am. Intellectual Property Law Assn., Am. Judicature Soc., Fed. Cir. Bar Assn., Licensing Execs. Soc., Eta Kappa Nu. Private international, Patent, Trademark and copyright. Home: 1227 Misty Lake Ct Sugar Land TX 77478-5613 Office: 1227 Misty Lake Ct Sugar Land TX 77478-5613

HITCHING, HARRY JAMES, retired lawyer; b. N.Y.C., Nov. 20, 1909; s. Harry and Sara (James) H.; m. Virginia Wyber, June 1933 (dec. Feb. 12, 1972); children: Virginia B. (Mrs. Daniel Andrews), James F.; m. Jeanne Austin Buckner, Aug. 25, 1972. AB, Columbia, 1929, LL.B. (Kent scholar), 1931, JD, 1969. Bar: N.Y. 1932, Tenn. 1938, Ga. 1969. Pvt. practice, N.Y.C., 1931-37; prin. atty. TVA, 1937-40, asst., gen. counsel, 1940-44; mem. firm Miller and Martin, Chattanooga, 1944-46; partner Miller & Martin and predecessor firm Miller, Martin and Hitching, 1946-92. Gen. counsel Skyland Internat. Corp., Benwood Found., Chattanooga Area Regional Transp. Authority; div. counsel Vulcan Materials Co.; dir. Krystal Co. Mem. Miller Park Bd.; Chmn. bd. Tonya Meml. Found., Estate Planning Council Chattanooga; chmn. advisory bd. Chattanooga Salvation Army; bd. dirs. Chattanooga Opthalmol. Found., Community Found. Greater Chattanooga. Served to ensign USCGR, 1943-45. Mem. ABA, Tenn. Bar Assn., Ga. Bar Assn., Chattanooga Bar Assn. (v.p.), Chattanooga Bar Found., Chattanooga C. of C. (treas., dir., Newcomen Soc. N.Am. Clubs: Lookout Mountain Fairyland, Mountain City (Chattanooga), Lookout Mountain Golf (Chattanooga), Geology (Chattanooga), Torch (Chattanooga) (pres.). Episcopalian. Home: 1701 Wood Nymph Trl Lookout Mountain GA 30750-2640

HITE, DAVID L. lawyer; b. Thornville, Ohio, Apr. 30, 1916; s. Frank C. Hite and Mary Pannabaker; m. Maxine Witherbee, July 15, 1943; 1 child, Diane. BS, Kent Sate U., 1938; JD, Capital U., 1946. Neuropsychiat. fellow Psychology Ct. Neuropsychiat. Inst., Hartford, Conn., 1939; pvt. practice Utica and Newark, Ohio, 1946—. Capt. OSS, 1942-46. Mem. ABA (pub. utilities sect., small trusts and estate com., adminstrn. and distbrn. of estates com.), Ohio Bar Ass., Cleve. Bar Assn., Licking Bar Assn. Probate (including wills, trusts), Utilities, public. Office: Hite & Hite 964 N 21st St Ste D Newark OH 43055-7230 E-mail: hite@nextek.net.

HITT, LEO N. lawyer, educator; b. Pitts., Oct. 20, 1955; s. Joe Stephen and Laurene (Lally) H.; m. Mary Elizabeth Wolf, Jan. 26, 1985; children: Nancy Anne, Elizabeth Lea. BA summa cum laude, U. Pitts., 1977, JD cum laude, 1980; LLM in Taxation, N.Y.U., 1983. Bar: Pa. 1980, U.S. Dist. Ct. (we. dist.) Pa. 1983, U.S. Tax Ct. 1981, U.S. Ct. Fed. Claims, 1997. Atty., tax sr. Kenneth Leventhal & Co., N.Y.C., 1980-81; atty., tax counsel Touche Ross & Co., Pitts., 1981-83; assoc. Reed Smith LLP, Pitts., 1983-88, ptnr., 1989—. Adj. prof. tax grad. sch. Robert Morris Coll., Pitts., 1983—, tax grad. sch., law sch. Duquesne U., Pitts., 1987—, sch. law U. Pitts., 1988—; seminar speaker various profl. orgns., Pitts., 1983—. Comments editor: U. Pitts. Law Review, 1979-80. Mem. Allegheny County Bar Assn., Pitts. Internat. Tax Soc., Allegheny Tax Soc., Pitts. Tax Club. Democrat. Roman Catholic. Avocations: alpine skiing, opera, gourmet cooking. Corporate taxation, Taxation, general. Home: 4209 Summervale Dr Murrysville PA 15668-3515 Office: Reed Smith LLP 435 6th Ave Pittsburgh PA 15219-1886 E-mail: LHitt@ReedSmith.com.

HITTER, JOSEPH IRA, lawyer; b. Bklyn., Nov. 1, 1944; s. Harry H. and Annette (Fidler) H.; m. Ann Lois Jaffe, May 28, 1966; children: Jonathan C., Evan R. BS in Acctg., L.I. U., 1966; JD, St. John's U., 1969; LLM in Taxation, NYU, 1973. Bar: N.Y. 1970, U.S. Tax Ct. 1971, U.S. Supreme Ct. 1974. Tax specialist Arthur Young & Co., N.Y.C., 1969-72; tax atty. Pfizer, Inc., N.Y.C., 1972-73, supr. tax planning, 1973-74; sr. tax. specialist Mead Corp., Dayton, Ohio, 1974-76, mgr. fed. and internat. taxes, 1976-77, mgr. tax affairs, 1977-82, dir. taxation, 1982-98, v.p., 1999—. Bd. dirs. Dayton-Montgomery County Port Authority; chmn. tax policy com. Am. Paper Inst., 1987—. Advisor YWCA, Dayton, 1985-87; dir. Hillel Acad., Dayton, 1981-83. Mem. ABA Tax Execs. Inst. (chpt. pres. 1984-85), N.Y. State Bar Assn., Dayton Bar Assn. Clubs: Meadowbrook Country, Dayton Racquet. Republican. Avocations: golf, tennis. Corporate taxation, Taxation, general, State and local taxation. Office: The Mead Corp Courthouse Plz NE Dayton OH 45402

HITTNER, DAVID, federal judge; b. Schenectady, N.Y., July 10, 1939; s. George and Sophie (Moskowitz) H.; children: Miriam, Susan, George. BS, NYU, 1961, JD, 1964. Bar: N.Y. 1964, Tex. 1967. Pvt. practice, Houston, 1967-78; judge Tex. 133d Dist. Ct., Houston, 1978-86, U.S. Dist. Ct. (so. dist.) Tex., Houston, 1986—. Author 2 books; contbr. articles to profl. jours. Mem. nat. coun. boy Scouts Am. Capt. inf., paratrooper U.S. Army, 1965-66. Recipient Silver Beaver award Boy Scouts Am., 1974, Silver Antelope award Boy Scouts Am., 1988, Samuel E. Gates award Am. Coll. Trial Lawyers. Mem. ABA (Merit award), State Bar Tex. (Outstanding Lawyer in Tex. award), Houston Bar Assn. (Pres.'s and Dirs.' award), Am. Law Inst., Masons (33d degree), Order of Coif (hon.). Office: US Courthouse 515 Rusk St Ste 8509 Houston TX 77002-2603

HIXSON, WENDELL MARK, lawyer; b. Oklahoma City, Dec. 6, 1966; s. Wendell Dee and Mary Theresa (Landgraf) H.; m. Shaa Marie Green, June 22, 1996. BA, Conception Sem. Coll., 1989; JD, U. Okla., 1992. Bar: Okla. 1992, U.S. Dist. Ct. (we. dist.) Okla. 1992, U.S. Dist. Ct. (ea. and no. dists.) 1993, U.S. Ct. Appeals (10th cir.) 1993, U.S. Supreme Ct. 1995. Assoc. Stan Chatman, P.C., Yukon, Okla., 1992-94, Bill James, Yukon and Oklahoma City, 1994-96; pvt. practice Yukon, 1996—. Spl. mcpl. judge, Oklahoma City, 1997—2002; juvenile defender, City of Yukon, 1994—; indigent defender Okla. Indigent Def. Sys., Norman, 1994—. Mem. troop com. Boy Scouts Am., Oklahoma, 1992-97. Fellow Okla. Bar Found.; mem. U.S. Supreme Ct. Hist. Soc., Okla. Criminal Def. Lawyers Assn., Cath. Lawyers Guild of Archdiocese of Oklahoma City, Okla. Bar Assn. (chmn. 2003, litigation sect., sec. 1998-99, 2001, treas. 2000-01, family law sect., mem., vice-chmn. 2002, , criminal law com., mem. rules of profl. conduct com., del. ho. of dels. 1996, 97, 98, alternate del. 1999-2002, mem. strategic planning com., mem. legal ethics com. 2003--, Outstanding Young Lawyer 1998), Canadian County Bar Assn. (pres. 1997-98), mem. Legal Ethics Com. Republican. Roman Catholic. Criminal, Family and matrimonial, General practice. Office: 800 W Main Yukon OK 73099-1040 E-mail: ykn66law@prodigy.net.

HJELMFELT, DAVID CHARLES, lawyer; b. Chgo., Nov. 25, 1940; s. Allen T. and Doris (Hauber) H.; m. Kendall L. Lawrence, Aug. 17, 1969; children: Trevor Christian, Rebecca Kirstan. AB cum laude, Kans. State U., Manhattan, 1962; LLB, Duke U., 1965; MTh, Christian Life Sch. Theology, 2003. Bar: Kans. 1965, Colo. 1965, D.C. 1973, U.S. Supreme Ct. 1978, U.S. Ct. Appeals (D.C. cir.) 1973, U.S. Ct. Appeals (5th and 11th cirs.) 1981, U.S. Ct. Appeals (10th cir.) 1982. Vis. prof. Sch. Law U. Okla., Norman, 1970-71; staff atty. U.S. AEC, Albuquerque, 1971-73; ptnr. Goldberg, Fieldman & Hjelmfelt, Washington, Colo., 1973-78; sole practice Fort Collins, Colo., 1978-81; ptnr. Hjelmfelt & Larson, Fort Collins, Colo., 1981-90; sole practice Fort Collins, Denver, Colo., 1990-95, Denver, 1995—. Author: Antitrust and Regulated Industries, 1985, Executive's Guide to Marketing, Sales & Advertising Law, 1990; contbr. articles to profl. jours. Mem. coun. liberal edn. Kans. State U.; bd. dirs. Heritage Christian Sch., 1988; bd. dirs. Christian Conciliation Svc., Fort Collins. Lt. JAGC USNR, 1965-68. Mem. ABA (essential facilities monograph com. antitrust sect.), Colo. Bar Assn., Rep. Sen. Inside Circle Club. Antitrust, Federal civil litigation, Utilities, public. Office: 1212 Raintree Dr G-137 Fort Collins CO 80526

HLAVAC, DANA PAUL, lawyer, consultant; b. Bayshore, N.Y., Jan. 24, 1960; s. Raymond Zetterberg and Violet Hlavac; m. Rosanne M. Swinnich, May 29, 1982 (div. June 1995); children: Matthew, Nicole, Kelsey; m. Patty S. Herrman, Oct. 11, 1998. BA, Syracuse U., 1981; JD, U. Denver, 1988. Bar: Colo. 1988, Ariz. 1996. Pres., CEO Credit Systems Design, Inc., Colorado Springs, Colo., 1989-90; dep. dist. atty. 4th Jud. Dist. Atty. Office, Colorado Springs, 1990-92; owner, pres. Creative Strategies, Ltd., Colorado Springs, 1989—; pvt. practice, Colorado Springs, 1992-99; asst. dist. atty. 3d Jud. Dist., 1999-2001; pub. defender Mohave County, Kingman, Ariz., 2001—. Bd. dir. Cerebral Palsey Assn., Colorado Springs, 1989-95, pres. 1994-95; treas. Citizens to Elect David Stiver, Colorado Springs, 1996; pres. bd. dirs. Spl. Kids-Spl. Families, Inc. Capt. U.S. Army, 1981-85. Mem. ABA, Ariz. Bar Assn., Colo. Bar Assn., Ariz. Pub. Defender Assn. (dir., treas, 2001—), Nat. Assn. Criminal Def. Lawyers, Nat. Legal and Defender Assn., Am. Coun. Chief Defenders. Commercial, contracts (including sales of goods; commercial financing), Criminal. Office: Law Offices of Mohave County Pub Defender PO Box 7000 Kingman AZ 86402-7000 E-mail: dana.hlavac@co.mohave.az.us.

HOAGLAND, DONALD WRIGHT, lawyer; b. NYC, Aug. 16, 1921; s. Webster Comley and Irene (Wright) H.; m. Mary Tiedeman, May 14, 1949; children— Peter M., Mary C., Sara H., Ann W. BA, Yale U., 1942; LLB, Columbia U., 1948. Bar: N.Y. 1948, Colo. 1951. Assoc. firm Winthrop, Stimson, Putnam & Roberts, N.Y.C., 1948-51; ptnr. Davis, Graham & Stubbs, Denver, 1951-63, 66-87, of counsel, 1987—; with AID, 1964-66, asst. adminstr. devel. finance and pvt. enterprise, 1965-66, cons., 1967-75. Lectr. U. Denver Sch. Law, 1971-75; chmn. bd. Bi-Nat. Devel. Corp., 1968-70; dir. Centennial Fund, Inc., 2d Centennial Fund, Inc., Gryphon Fund, Inc., 1959-63; mem. Colo. Supreme Ct. Grievance Com., 1992-98. Active Denver Planning Bd., 1955-61, 67-70, chmn., 1959-61; bd. dirs., v.p. Denver Art Mus., 1959-63, 72-76, 79-82; bd. dirs. Colo. Urban League, 1960-63, 66-72, chmn. bd., 1968-72; adv. bd. Vols. Tech. Assistance vice-chmn. bd. Denver chpt. ARC, 1959-61; bd. dirs. Legal Aid Soc. Colo., 1972-84, pres., 1975-79; trustee Phillips Exeter Acad., 1960-67, Colo. Rocky Mountain Sch., 1981-84, Am. U., Washington, 1982-85; chmn. bd. dirs. Legal Aid Found., Colo., 1983-87; bd. dirs. Colo. Bus. Coalition for Health, 1988-89, Colo. Found. for Ednl. Excellence, 1998—; exec. dir. Ctr. for Health Ethics and Policy U. Colo., Denver, 1987-91; chmn. Colo. Health Data Commn., 1986-88, Gov. Romer's panel health advisors, 1992-94, Social Sci. Found. Denver U., 1995-97, Caring for Colo. Found., 1999-2002, Colo. Pub. Health and Edn. Rsch. Adv. Com., 2002—; pres. Colo. Found. Pub. Health and Environ., 1995-98; ethics com. Nat. Jewish Med. and Rsch. Ctr., 1993-2002. With USNR, 1943-45. Decorated Air medal with oak leaf cluster. Mem. ABA, Colo. Bar Assn., Denver Bar Assn. Home: 355 Garfield St Denver CO 80206-4509 Office: Davis Graham & Stubbs 1550 17th St Ste 500 Denver CO 80202 E-mail: donald.hoagland@dgslaw.com.

HOAGLAND, KARL KING, JR., lawyer; b. St. Louis, Aug. 21, 1933; s. Karl King and Mary Edna (Parsons) H.; m. Sylvia Anne Naranick, July 13, 1957; children: Elisabeth Parsons, Sarah Stewart, Karl King III, Alison T. BS in Econs., U. Pa., 1955; LLB, U. Ill., 1958. Bar: Ill. 1958, U.S. Dist. Ct. (so. dist.) Ill. 1958. V.p., gen. counsel, sec. Jefferson Smurfit Corp., St. Louis, 1960-92, Container Corp. Am., St. Louis, 1986-92; of counsel Hoagland, Fitzgerald, Smith & Pranaitis, Alton, Ill., 1987—. Chmn. bd. dirs. Millers' Mut. Ins. Assn. Ill., 1989-92. Asst. editor: U. Ill. Law Forum, 1957-58. Trustee, treas. Monticello Coll. Found., 1965—. 1st lt. USAF, 1958-60. Mem. Ill. Bar Assn., Madison County Bar Assn., Alton-Wood River Bar Assn., Lockhaven Country Club, Mo. Athletic Club, Crystal Lake Club, Orcas Tennis Club, Order of the Coif, Beta Gamma Sigma. Episcopalian. Avocations: tennis, skiing, hunting, fishing, golf. Corporate, general. Home (Winter): PO Box 1454 Eastsound WA 98245 Home (Summer): PO Box 130 Alton IL 62002 Mailing: 91 Hawthorne Dr Alton IL 62002

HOAGLAND, SAMUEL ALBERT, lawyer, pharmacist; b. Mt. Home, Idaho, Aug. 19, 1953; s. Charles Leroy and Glenna Lorraine (Gridley) H.; m. Karen Ann Mengel, Nov. 20, 1976; children: Hiliary Anne, Heidi Lynne, Holly Kaye. BS in Pharmacy, Idaho State U., 1976; JD, U. Idaho, 1982. Bar: Idaho 1982, U.S. Dist. Ct. Idaho 1982, U.S. CT. Appeals (9th cir.) 1984. Lectr. clin. pharmacy Idaho State U., Pocatello, 1976-78, lectr. pharmacy law, 1985-86, dean's adv. council Coll. Pharmacy, 1987-92; hosp. pharmacist Mercy Med. Ctr., Nampa, Idaho, 1978-79; retail pharmacist Thrifty Corp., Moscow, Idaho, 1980-82; assoc. Dial, Looze & May, Pocatello, 1982-89, Prescott & Foster, Boise, Idaho, 1989-90; gen. counsel Design Innovations and Rsch. Corp., 1991-95; pvt. practice, 1990—2001; assoc. Hoagland, Dominick & Hicks, PLLC, 2001. Chmn. malpractice panel Idaho Bd. Medicine, Boise, 1983-92, adminstrv. hearing officer, 1989-92; adj. assoc. prof. pharmacy law Idaho State U., 2002--. Contbr. to law publs. Bd. dirs. Cathedral Pines Camp, Ketchum, Idaho. Mem. Idaho State Bar Assn., Idaho Pharm. Assn., Idaho Trial Lawyers Assn., Boise Bar Assn., Capital Pharm. Assn., Am. Pharm. Assn., Idaho Soc. Hosp. Pharmacists (bd. dirs.), Am. Soc. Pharmacy Law, Flying Doctors Am. (Atlanta) (bd. dirs.). Administrative and regulatory, General civil litigation, General practice. Home: 11901 W Mesquite Dr Boise ID 83713-0813 Office: 1471 Shoreline Dr Ste 100 Boise ID 83702-9104

HOBBINS, ROBERT LEO, lawyer; b. Des Moines, June 5, 1948; s. Leo Michael and Margaret Ellen Hobbins; m. Carmela Theresa Tursi, Dec. 27, 1974; children: Brian, Patrick, Edward. BA magna cum laude, Creighton U., 1970; JD, NYU, 1973. Bar: Minn. 1973. Assoc. Dorsey & Whitney, Mpls., 1973-78, ptnr., 1979. Adj. faculty U. St. Thomas Sch. Law, 2002—. Root-Tilden scholar. Mem. ABA (labor sect., EEO law com.), Minn. State Bar Assn., Hennepin County Bar Assn., Creighton U. Alumni Assn. (v.p. 1994). Office: Dorsey & Whitney 50 S 6th St Ste 1500 Minneapolis MN 55402-4502 E-mail: hobbins.robert@dorseylaw.com.

HOBBS, CASWELL O., III, lawyer; b. Sherman, Tex., Aug. 25, 1941; s. Caswell Owen II and Marie Elizabeth (Bloomfield) H.; m. Anne Louise Simpson, June 7, 1968; children: Elizabeth Ellen, Emily Jane. BS, U. Kans., 1963; LLB, U. Pa., 1966. Bar: D.C. 1967, U.S. Ct. Appeals (4th cir.) 1975, U.S. Supreme Ct. 1972. Asst. to chmn., dir. Office of Policy Planning and Evaluation, FTC, Washington, 1970-73; assoc. Morgan Lewis & Bockius, Washington, 1973-76, ptnr., 1976—, chmn. Washington office mgmt. com., 1987-89, mem. governing bd., 1989-92, 95-99; lectr. Conf. Bd., ABA. Author: Antitrust Strategies for Mergers, Acquisitions, Joint Ventures and Strategic Alliances, 2000; contbr. articles to profl. jours. Trustee Legal Aid Soc. D.C., 1982-92, pres., 1989-91, pres. coun., 1991—. Served to capt. JAGC, USAR, 1966-72. Fellow ABA (chair antitrust sect. 1994-95, officer 1991-96, co-chair task force on competition policy 1993, mem. commn. to study the FTC, 1988); mem. Am. Law Inst. E-mail: cohobbs@morganlewis.com. Administrative and regulatory, Antitrust, Corporate, general. Office: Morgan Lewis & Bockius 1800 M St NW Lbby 6 Washington DC 20036-5828

HOBBS, GREGORY JAMES, JR., state supreme court justice; b. Gainesville, Fla., Dec. 15, 1944; s. Gregory J. Hobbs and Mary Ann (Rhodes) Frakes; m. Barbara Louise Hay, June 17, 1967; children: Daniel Gregory, Emily Mary Hobbs Wright. BA, U. Notre Dame, 1966; JD, U. Calif., Berkeley, 1971. Bar: Colo. 1971, Calif. 1972. Law clk. to Judge William E. Doyle 10th U.S. Cir. Ct. Appeals, Denver, 1971-72; assoc. Cooper, White & Cooper, San Francisco, 1972-73; enforcement atty. U.S. EPA, Denver, 1973-75; asst. atty. gen. State of Colo. Atty. Gen.'s Office, Denver, 1975-79; ptnr. Davis, Graham & Stubbs, Denver, 1979-92; shareholder Hobbs, Trout & Raley, P.C., Denver, 1992-96; justice Colo. Supreme Ct., Denver, 1996—. Counsel No. Colo. Water Conservancy, Loveland, Colo., 1979-96. Contbr. articles to profl. jours. Vol. Peace Corps-S.Am., Colombia, 1967-68; vice chair Colo. Air Quality Control Com., Denver, 1982-87; mem. ranch com. Philmont Scout Ranch, Boy Scouts Am., Cimarron, N.Mex., 1988-98; co-chair Eating Disorder Family Support Group, Denver, 1992—. Recipient award of merit Denver Area Coun. Boy Scouts, 1993, Pres. award Nat. Water Resources Assn., Washington, 1995. Fellow Am. Bar Found.; mem. ABA, Colo. Bar Assn., Denver Bar Assn. Avocations: backpacking, fishing, writing poetry. Office: Colo Supreme Ct 2 E 14th Ave Denver CO 80203-2115

HOBBS, J. TIMOTHY, SR., lawyer; b. Yakima, Wash., Sept. 23, 1941; s. Leonard M. and Virginia (Snider) H.; m. Barbara J. Hatfield, June 14, 1964; children: Amy Elizabeth, J. Timothy Jr. BA in Polit. Sci., U. Wash., 1964; JD, Am. U., 1968. Bar: D.C. 1969, U.S. Ct. Supreme Ct. 1973, U.S. Ct. Appeals Fed. Crct. 1982, U.S. Ct. Appeals (11th cir.) 1986, U.S. Ct. Appeals (5th cir.) 1989, U.S. Ct. Appeals (6th cir.) 1996. Assoc. Mason Fenwick & Lawrence, Washington, 1969-76, ptnr., 1977-82, sr. ptnr., 1982-91; ptnr., head intellectual property dept. Dykema Gossett, 1991-99; ptnr. Wiley, Rein & Fielding, Washington, 1999—. Author chpt. on copyright law, West's Federal Practice Manual, 1983. Pres. Arlington Outdoor Edn. Assn., 1990-92. Mem. D.C. Bar (chmn. trademark com. 1982-84), U.S. Trademark Assn. Forums (speaker 1988), Washington Golf and Country Club. Trademark and copyright. Home: 6135 Lee Hwy Arlington VA 22205-2134 Office: Wiley Rein & Fielding 1776 K St NW Washington DC 20006-2304

HOBBS, TRUMAN MCGILL, federal judge; b. Selma, Ala., Feb. 8, 1921; s. Sam F. and Sarah Ellen (Greene) H.; m. Joyce Cummings, July 9, 1949; children— Emilie C. Reid, Frances John Rose, Dexter Cummings, Truman McGill. AB, U. N.C., 1942; LL.B., Yale U., 1948. Bar: Ala. 1948. Practiced in, Montgomery, 1951-80; law clk. U.S. Supreme Ct., 1948-49; ptnr. Hobbs, Copeland, Franco & Screws, 1951-80; U.S. dist. judge Montgomery, 1980—; now sr. judge. Chmn. Ala. Unemployment Appeal Bd., 1952-58 Pres. United Appeal Montgomery; pres. Montgomery County Tb Assn.; v.p. Ala. Com. for Better Schs.; Chmn. Montgomery County Exec. Democratic Com., 1970. Served to It. USNR, 1942-46, ETO, PTO. Decorated Bronze Star medal. Fellow Am. Coll. Trial Lawyers; mem. Internat. Acad. Trial Lawyers, Ala. Plaintiffs Lawyers Assn. (past pres.), Ala. Bar Assn. (pres. 1970-71), Montgomery County Bar Assn. (past pres.) Home: 2301 Fernway Dr Montgomery AL 36111-1603

HOBERMAN, STUART A. lawyer; b. New York, Nov. 21, 1946; BBA, Baruch Coll., N.Y., 1969; JD, Bklyn. Law Sch., 1972; LLM, N.Y. Univ., 1973. Bar: N.Y., 1973, N.J., 1977, Pa., 1979, U.S. Supreme Ct., 1976. Assoc. Windels and Marx, N.Y.C., 1973-77, Wilentz, Goldman, and Spitzer, Woodbridge, NJ, 1977-80, ptnr., 1980—. Trustee, Emmanuel Cancer

Found., Kenilworth, N.J., 1983-90; trustee, Cancer Care of NJ, 1999—. Mem.: N.J. State Bar Assn. (bank law sect. chmn. 1986—87, corp. and bus. law sect. chmn. 1988—90, chmn. exec. com. of gen. coun. 1990—92, trustee 1990—94, trustee N.J. State Bar Found. 1992—, treas. 1995—96, trustee 1997—2001, pres. 1999—2001, first v.p. 2003—). Banking, Corporate, general, Finance. Office: Wilentz Goldman & Spitzer PO Box 10 90 Woodbridge Ctr Dr Ste 900 Woodbridge NJ 07095-1142

HOBLIN, PHILIP J., JR., securities lawyer; b. S.I., N.Y., July 31, 1929; s. Philip J. and Mary A. (Brown) H.; m. Eileen P. Killilea, Jan. 10, 1959; children: Philip, Monica, Michael. BS, Fordham U., 1951, LLD, 1957. Bar: N.Y. 1957. Regional atty. Bache & Co., N.Y.C., 1958-63; exec. v.p. Shearson Lehman Hutton, Inc., 1963-89; co-chmn. Inst. Fin. Law Ctr., N.Y.C., 1972-92; chief exec. officer Buttonwood Securities, 1989-90; of counsel Jenkens Gilchrist Parker Chapin, N.Y.C., 1990—. Adj. prof. law Fordham U., 1986-96; mem. Joint Industry Com. Securities Protection, 1969; mem. bd. arbitration N.Y. Stock Exch., 1977-89; chmn. arbitration com. Chgo. Bd. Options Exchange, 1977-78, mem. conduct com., 1979-80; mem. exec. and nat. arbitration coms. Nat. Assn. Securities Dealers, 1984-85, also mem. bus. conduct com. dist. 12, 1974-77; mem. Securities Industry Conf. on Arbitration, 1977—. Author: Securities Arbitration: Procedures, Strategies and Cases, 1988, 2d edit., 1991, Compliance and Business Procedures Manual, also law rev. articles. Served as spl. agt. USAF, 1951-53; col. (ret.). Mem. ABA, Security Industry Assn. (pres. compliance divsn. 1970-72, compliance divsn. award 1995), Am. Legion Res. Officers Assn. (v.p. air N.Y. state chpt. 1973-74, 87-88, pub. rels. sec. judge adv. gen. N.Y.C. chpt., pres. N.Y. state chpt. 1988-89), VFW, Mil. Order World Wars, Air Force Assn., Assn. Former OSI Agts., Respect for Law Alliance (former dir.), Ret. Officers Assn., Cornsch. Island Assn. (treas.), KC, Elks. Home: 499 N Broadway White Plains NY 10603-3235 Office: Jennings Gilchrist Parker Chapin 405 Lexington Ave New York NY 10174-0002

HOCH, RAND, lawyer, mediator; b. Everett, Wash., Apr. 2, 1955; s. Harold S. and Thelma (Frisch) H. AB in Am. Govt., Georgetown U., 1977; JD, Stetson U., 1985. Bar: Fla. 1985, U.S. Dist. Ct. (mid., so. dists.) Fla. 1986, U.S. Ct. Appeals (11th cir.) 1986, D.C. 1989. Adminstrv. aide Henry M. Jackson for Pres. Com., Washington, 1974-76; rsch. dir. Coun. Active Ind. Oil and Gas Producers, Washington, 1977; polit. cons. New South Communications, Washington and Fla., 1977-82; asst. to regional coord. North Shore Coun. on Alcoholism, Mass., 1978; exec. dir. Fund for A New Direction, Washington and West Palm Beach, Fla., 1979-91; real estate salesman Adams Cameron/Realty World, Ormond Beach, Fla., 1980-81; real estate broker South 1st Realty Inc., Ormond Beach, 1981-82; rsch. asst. Stetson U. Coll. of Law, St. Petersburg, Fla., 1983—85; law clk. real estate and constrn. De Santis, Cook, Gaskill & Silverman, North Palm Beach, Fla., 1984; labor, election and ERISA atty. Kaplan, Sicking & Bloom P.A., West Palm Beach, 1985-88; workers' compensation atty. Law Offices of Gerald Rosenthal P.A., West Palm Beach, 1989-91; gen. master div. worker's compensation Fla. Dept. Labor & Employment Security, 1991-92; judge compensation claims State of Fla., Daytona Beach, 1992-96; pvt. practice The Law & Mediation Offices of Rand Hoch, West Palm Beach, Fla., 1996—. Cons. in field. Contbr. articles to profl. jours. Mem. Dem. Exec. Com., Volusia County Fla., 1980-82, Pinellas County, Fla., 1983, Palm Beach County, 1989-92, 96—, chair, 1990, vice-chair, 1989-90; del. Fla. Dem. Conv., 1981, 83, 85, 87, 89, 91, 97, 99, 2001; alt. del. Dem. Nat. Conv., 1988, 2000; bd. dirs. ACLU, Palm Beach and Martin Counties, 1985-87, Fla. Consumer Fedn., 1987-89, Fla. Task Force, 1987-89, Nat. Gay & Lesbian Task Force, 1989-92, Palm Beach County Human Rights Coun., Inc., 1990-92, 2002—, Compass, Inc., 2002-03, Ctrl. Fla. Friends of 440, 1995-96; mem. exec. com. Lesbian and Gay Dems. of Am., 1988-92; regional coord. Dukakis for Pres., Fla., 1987-88; pres. Palm Beach County Human Rights Coun., 1987-92; chmn. pro tem employment practices rev. com. City West Palm Beach, 1990-91; mem. ethics ordinance adv. com. Palm Beach County, 1991-92; mem. Young Friends of Bob Graham, 1989-92, Leadership 2000, 1990-92, Young Friends of the Kravis Ctr., 1996—, Young Friends of the Norton Mus., 2001-03; mem. adv. bd. Volusia County Elections, 1993-94; bus. com. for culture Palm Beach County Cultural Coun., 1998—; trustee Fla. Stage, 2002—, sec., 2002—. Recipient Am. Jurisprudence Book awards, 1983, 84, Fred C. Fantz award, 1985, Hank Godley Meml. award Met. Bus. Orgn. of South Fla., 1992, Spectrum Lifetime Achievement award Greater Orlando Gay & Lesbian Cmty. Ctr., 1994, Compass Pub. Svc. award, 2003; named Charles A. Dana scholar, 1983-85. Mem. ABA (young lawyers divsn. 1985-91, labor and employment law sect. 1986-92, mem. sect. on individual rights and responsibilities 1990-92, 2002-2003, campaign ethics com. 1987-92), Fla. Bar Assn. (labor and employment law sect. 1989-93, workers compensation law sect. 1988--, equal opportunities law sect. 1999--, mem. editl. bd. Fla. Bar News and Fla. Bar Jour. 1995-01), D.C. Bar Assn., Acad. Trial Lawyers Am., Assn. Bipartisan Cons., Fla. Acad. Trial Lawyers, Am. Mediation Assn. (nat. bd. accredited mediators 1993—), Internat. Assn. Lesbian and Gay Judges (bd. dirs. 1993-95, v.p. 1995-97), Nat. Gay and Lesbian Lawyers Assn., Nat. Lesbian and Gay Bar Assn., Fla. Conf. Judges of Compensation Claims (pres. 1994-95, mem. exec. com. 1995-96), Volusia County Bar Assn. (mem. jud. evaluation rev. com. 1994), Palm Beach County Bar Assn. (alt. dispute resolution com. 1997—, workers compensation com. 1997—), Internat. Wine and Food Soc. (Boca Raton chpt.), Phi Alpha Delta, Lambda Legal Def. and Edn. Fund. Jewish. Avocation: political button collecting. Civil rights, Labor (including EEOC, Fair Labor Standards Act, labor-management relations, NLRB, OSHA), Workers' compensation. Office: 400 N Flagler Dr Apt 1402 West Palm Beach FL 33401-4315 E-mail: randhoch@usa.net.

HOCHBERG, BAYARD ZABDIAL, lawyer; b. N.Y.C., May 16, 1932; s. Abraham and Sonia (Pincus) H.; m. Arlene Beethoven, Feb. 15, 1953; children: Ronny Mark, Randy Jean, Elizabeth Joyce. BA, CCNY, 1953; LLB, JD, U. Va., 1958. Bar: Md. 1958, Va. 1958. Law bailiff to Hon. Joseph Allen, Supreme Bench of Balt., 1958-59; asso. law office Paul Berman, Esq., Balt., 1959-68; ptnr. Levin, Hochberg & Chiarello, Balt., 1968-82; sr. ptnr. Hochberg, Chiarello & Costello, Balt., 1983-2000, Hochberg, Costello & Baron, Balt., 2001—02, of counsel, 2002—. Mem. editl. bd.: Va. Law Rev, 1956-58. Served to maj. U.S. Army Res., 1953-75. Fellow Am. Coll. Trial Lawyers, Md. Bar Found.; mem. ABA (Md. del. standing com. on state legis. 1970-73, tort and ins. practice sect. 1979—2002), Md. Bar Assn. (chmn. ins., negligence and workmens compensation sect. 1973, exec. bd., state-city medicolegal com. 1979-91, chmn. 1983-86, ct. of appeals rules com. 1993-2002), ATLA, Balt. Bar Assn. (chmn. legis. com. 1968-69, bd. govs. 1969-70, jud. adminstrn. com. 1980-86, family law com. 1985-88), Balt. County Bar Assn. (family law com.), Md. Trial Lawyers Assn. (bd. govs. 1970-76, co-chmn. com. on legis. 1970-72, v.p. Balt. 1975, Amicus brief com. 1979-81), Order of Coif (bd. dirs. 1993-2001), Cavalier King Charles Spaniel Club (v.p. 1998-2001). Home: 1978 Shadybrook Trail Charlottesville VA 22911 Office: 528 E Joppa Rd Baltimore MD 21286-5403

HOCHBERG, FAITH S. U.S. district court judge; BA summa cum laude, Tufts U., 1972; JD magna cum laude, Harvard U., 1975. Law clk. to Hon. Spottswood W. Robinson III U.S. Ct. Appeals (D.C. cir.), 1975-76; pvt. practice Washington, Boston, Roseland, N.J., 1977-83; asst. U.S. atty. Dist. N.J., Newark, 1983-87; ptnr. Cole, Schotz, Bernstein, Meisel & Forman, Hackensack, NJ, 1987-90; sr. dep. chief counsel Office Thrift Supervision, U.S. Treasury Dept., Jersey City; dep. asst. sec. law enforcement U.S. Treasury Dept., Washington; U.S. Atty. Dist. of N.J., 1994-99; judge U.S. Dist. Ct., 1999—. Office: US Courthouse and PO Bldg Newark NJ 07102

HOCHBERG, RONALD MARK, lawyer; b. Bklyn., Apr. 3, 1955; s. Fred S. and Adele (Gunsberg) H.; m. Sharon A. Berg, Aug. 11, 1985; children: Rachel, Sarah. BA, Rutgers U., 1977; JD, Bklyn. Law Sch., 1980; LLM, U. Miami, 1982. Assoc. Klatsky & Klatsky, Red Bank, N.J., 1980-81, Fuerst, Singer & Yusem, Somerville, N.J., 1982-83, Law Offices of Steven Schanker, Melville, N.Y., 1983-86; ptnr. Schanker & Hochberg, Attys., Huntington, N.Y., 1986—. Frequent lectr. on estate planning; instr. Adelphi U., 1984-93. Columnist Financial World Mag., 1993-97; contbr. articles to profl. publs. Mem. ABA, N.Y. State Bar Assn., Estate and Tax Planning Coun. Avocations: skiing, sailing. Estate planning, Pension, profit-sharing, and employee benefits, Estate taxation. Office: Schanker & Hochberg 27 W Neck Rd PO Box 1905 Huntington NY 11743-2618 E-mail: mark@schankerhochberg.com.

HOCHMAN, KENNETH GEORGE, lawyer; b. Mt. Vernon, N.Y., Nov. 12, 1947; s. Benjamin S. and Lillian (Gilbert) H.; m. Carol K. Hochman, Apr. 8, 1979; children: Brian Paul, Lisa Erin. BA, SUNY, Buffalo, 1969; JD, Columbia U., 1972. Bar: Ohio 1973, Fla. 1977, N.Y. 1979. Assoc. Jones, Day, Reavis & Pogue, Cleve., 1972-79, ptnr., 1980—. Trustee Katharine Kenyon Lippitt Found., Cleve., 1988, Kenridge Fund, Cleve., 1989, Bolton Found., Cleve., 1990, Elisha-Bolton Found., Cleve., 1993. Trustee United Way of Cleve., 2002—. Harlan Fiske Stone scholar Columbia U., 1971, 72. Fellow Am. Coll. Trusts and Estate Counsel; mem. Phi Beta Kappa, Oakwood Club (Cleve.) (trustee 1997, officer 2000). Estate planning, Probate (including wills, trusts), Estate taxation. Office: Jones Day Reavis & Pogue 901 Lakeside Ave E Cleveland OH 44114-1190

HOCHMAN, STEPHEN ALLEN, lawyer; b. N.Y.C., June 25, 1935; s. Henry and Ida Hochman; m. Judith Cole, June 16, 1957; children: Glen, Susan, Lisa. BA, Cornell U., 1957, JD with distinction, 1959. Bar: N.Y. 1960, U.S. Supreme Ct. 1963, U.S. Dist. Ct. (so. dist.) N.Y. 1963. Assoc. Proskauer Rose Goetz & Mendelsohn, N.Y.C., 1960-64; ptnr. Feldman, Kramer, Bam & Nessen, N.Y.C., 1964-66, Kramer, Nessen & Hochman, 1966-68, Kramer, Levin, Nessen, Kamin & Frankel, N.Y.C., 1968-86, Friedman, Wittenstein & Hochman, N.Y.C., 1986—. Chmn. ALI/ABA Ann. Program on Corp. Acquisitions, 1985—, Program on Arbitration, Mediation and ADR, 1993—; mediator U.S. Dist. Ct. (so. and eas. dists.) N.Y., U.S. Bankrptcy Ct. (so. dist.) N.Y., N.Y. State Supreme Ct., N.Y. Stock Exch., NASD mediator, arbitrator; mediator trainer of mediators in N.Y. State Supreme Ct., also Spl. Master Appellate divsn., 1st dept. Contbr. articles to profl. jours. Trustee, sec. Beth Israel Med. Ctr., N.Y.C., 1982—, Jewish Communal Fund N.Y., N.Y.C., 1982—; mem. N.Y. State Adv. Commn. on Substance Abuse, 1977-83; trustee State Communities Aid Assn., N.Y. State, 1976—. 1st lt. USAR, 1959-60. Mem. ABA (former chair arbitration com. sect. dispute resolution, co-chair large/complex case sub-com.), Assn. of Bar of City of N.Y., Am. Arbitration Assn., Am. Law Inst., Order of Coif, Phi Kappa Phi. Alternative dispute resolution, Corporate, general, Mergers and acquisitions. Home: 303 West St White Plains NY 10605-5304 Office: Friedman Wittenstein & Hochman 101 E 52nd St New York NY 10022-6018 E-mail: shochman@prodigy.net.

HOCK, FREDERICK WYETH, lawyer; b. Newark, July 10, 1924; s. Herbert Hummel and Carol (Wyeth) H.; m. Alfheld Catherine Larsen, Mar. 4, 1945; children: Carolyn, Sandra, Rhonda; m. Ellen Barbara Weidner, June 28, 1975. AA, Princeton U., 1944; BA, Rutgers U., 1948, LLB, 1950, JD, 1968. Bar: N.J. 1949. Assoc. Stevenson, Willette & McDermott, 1949-51; pvt. practice, 1951-65; ptnr. Hock & Sharkey, East Orange, N.J., 1965-79; sr. ptnr. Hock Silverlieb & Kramer, Livingston, N.J., 1979-93, Gulkin, Hock & Lehr, 1994-2000, Hock Graziano & Koprowski, 2000—. Acting judge East Orange Mcpl. Ct., 1954-57; mem. adv. bd. Maplewood Bank and Trust Co., Livingston, 1987-91, Summit Trust Co., 1991-98. Chmn. Juvenile Conf. Com., 1958-62; trustee Cmty. Day Nursery of the Oranges & Maplewood, 1962-75, pres. 1973-75; trustee Founders Endowment Fund, 1954-87, House of Good Shepherd, 1970-90, Nu Beta Found., 1970-91; bd. dirs. Essex County chpt. ARC, 1987-91; post adv. VFW post 5445, 1955-90. With USMC, 1942-46. Mem. ABA, N.J. Bar Assn., Northwestern N.J. Estate Planning Coun. (dir. 1988-90), No. N.J. Estate Planning Coun., Marina Bay Club (trustee 2000—). Estate planning, Probate (including wills, trusts). Office: 155 Pompton Ave Ste 206 Verona NJ 07044

HOCKENBERG, HARLAN DAVID, lawyer; b. Des Moines, July 1, 1927; s. Leonard C. and Estyre M. (Zalk) H.; m. Dorothy A. Arkin, June 3, 1953; children: Marni Lynn, Thomas Leonard, Edward Arkin. BA, U. Iowa, 1949, JD, 1952. Bar: Iowa 1952. Assoc. Abramson & Myers, Des Moines, 1952-58, Abramson, Myers & Hockenberg, Des Moines, 1958-64; sr. ptnr. Davis, Hockenberg, Wine, Brown, Koehn & Shors, Des Moines, 1964-95; shareholder, dir. Sullivan & Ward, P.C., Des Moines, 1995—. Bd. dirs. West Des Moines State Bank, Rep. Jewish Coalition, Smoother Sailing Found. Mem. bd. editors U. Iowa Law Review. Mem. Citizens for Ind. Cts., Internat. Rels. and Nat. Security Adv. Coun., Rep. Nat. Com., 1978; chmn. Coun. Jewish Fedns., Small Cities Com., 1970-71; mem. exec. com. Am. Israel Pub. Affairs Com.; pres. Wilkie House, Inc., Des Moines, 1965-66, Des Moines Jewish Welfare Fedn., 1973-74; mem. Presdl. Commn. on White House Fellowships, 1988-92; mem. Holocaust Meml. Coun., 2003—; mem. ins. devel. bd. Iowa Dept. Econ. Devel. With USNR, 1945-46. Mem. Iowa State Bar Assn. (past chair professionalism com.), Des Moines C. of C. (pres. 1986, chmn. bur. econ. devel. 1979, 80, bd. dirs. 1986, chmn. Metro Forum), Des Moines Club, Pioneer Club, Delta Sigma Rho, Omicron Delta Kappa, Phi Epsilon Pi. Home: 2880 Grand Ave Des Moines IA 50312-4274 Office: Sullivan & Ward PC 801 Grand Ave Ste 3500 Des Moines IA 50309-8005 E-mail: bhockenberg@sullivan-ward.com.

HOCKLEY, STEPHEN JOHN, lawyer; b. Sydney, Australia, May 21, 1952; arrived in Japan, 1992; s. Allan Raymond and Ivy Margaret (Shaw) H.; m. Stephanie Winifred McGrath, Sept. 21, 1979 (div. 1985); children: Joseph Allen, Catherine Mary, William. BA, U. Sydney, 1975; B Laws, U. NSW, Sydney, 1981. Solicitor McKenzie, Cox, McAlary & Morton, Lismore, NSW, Australia, 1981-83; founding ptnr. S.J. Hockley & Co., Lismore, 1983-91; atty. New Tokyo Law Office, 1998—, Maruyama Internat. Law and Patent Office, Tokyo, 1998—. Cons. Kuze Cons., Tokyo, 1992—; rep. dir. NRC Japan, Ltd.; lectr. Temple U., Japan. Mem. NSW Law Soc., Roppongi Bar Assn. Avocations: surfing, military history. Home: Nakano 5-35-8 #201 Shin Tokyo Apts Nakanoku Tokyo 164-0001 Japan Office: Maruyana Internat Law 1-14 Akasaka 1-Chome Tameike Tokyo 107-0052 Japan also: 9th Fl Prudential Tower 13-10 Nagata-cho 2-chome Chiyoda-ku Tokyo 100-0014 Japan

HOCKSTAD, KAREN SUE, lawyer; b. Traverse City, Mich., June 4, 1965; d. Howard Jerry and Mary Agnes (Poore) H. BA in Polit. Sci., U. Mich., 1987; student, Northwestern Mich. Coll., 1982-83. Pvt. practice. Pres. Children's Hosp. Devel. Bd.; trustee Safety Coun. of Ctrl. Ohio; chmn. Woody Hayes Celebrity Golf Classic. Recipient 40 Under 40 award, Bu. First. Fellow Columbus Bar Found.; mem. Fed. Bar Assn., Mich. Bar Assn., Ohio Bar Assn., U. Mich. Alumni Assn., Kiwanis (social chmn., trustee). Corporate, general, Taxation, general, General civil litigation. Office: Chester Wilcox & Saxbe LLP 65 E State St Ste 1000 Columbus OH 43215-3441

HODES, PAUL WILLIAM, lawyer, record company executive; b. N.Y.C., Mar. 21, 1951; s. Robert Bernard and Florence (Rosenberg) H.; m. Margaret Ann Horstmann; children: Maxwell, Ariana. BA, Dartmouth Coll., 1972; JD, Boston Coll., 1978. Bar: N.H. 1978, Mass. 1980. Asst. atty. gen. Office of N.H. Atty. Gen., Concord, 1978-82; pres. Big Round Records, Inc., Concord, N.H., 1986—. Co-owner Big Round Music, LLC, 1986—. Bd. dirs. Capital Ctr. for Arts, 1990-97, 2002--, chair 1990-96; bd. dirs. Children's Entertainment Assn., 1995-99, Concord Cmty. Music Sch., 1997-99, N.H. Children's Alliance, 1997-2000, Tricinium Ltd., 2001—; mem. N.H. State Coun. on the Arts, 2001--. Recipient hon. award Parents Choice Found., 1987, 96. Mem. Am. Bd. Trial Advocates, NARAS, ASCAP, ATLA, Nat. Assn. Criminal Def. Lawyers, N.H. Assn. Criminal Def. Lawyers, N.H. Trial Lawyers. Federal civil litigation, Criminal, Entertainment. Office: Shaheen & Gordon PA PO Box 2703 Concord NH 03302-2703 also: Big Round Records Inc 70 Fisk Rd Concord NH 03301 E-mail: gtrpaul@aol.com., phodes@shaheengordon.com.

HODES, ROBERT BERNARD, lawyer; b. Bklyn., Aug. 25, 1925; s. James and Florence (Cohen) H.; m. Florence R. Rosenberg, Dec. 22, 1946 (div. Nov. 1984); 1 child, Paul; m. Cecilia Mendez, Dec. 18, 1984; children: James, Maria Paz. AB, Dartmouth Coll., 1946; LLB, Harvard U., 1949. Bar: N.Y. Supreme Ct. 1950, U.S. Dist. Ct. (so. dist.) N.Y. 1951, U.S. Tax Ct. 1955, U.S. Claims Ct. 1957, U.S. Ct. Appeals (2d cir.) 1959. Assoc. Willkie Farr & Gallagher, N.Y.C., 1949-56, ptnr., 1956-95, co-chmn., 1982-95, counsel, 1995—. Bd. dirs. K&F Industries, Inc., LCH Investments N.V., Loral Space & Telecomm., Ltd., Mueller Industries, Inc., Space Systems/Loral Inc., RV1 Guaranty Co., Ltd., Restructured Capital Holdings, Ltd. Active Cremer Found., Beaver Dam Sanctuary, Inc., Nat. Philanthropic Trust. Corporate, general, General practice, Corporate taxation. Home: 860 United Nations Plz New York NY 10017-1810 Office: Willkie Farr & Gallagher Equitable Ctr 787 7th Ave New York NY 10019-6099

HODES, SCOTT, lawyer; b. Chgo., Aug. 14, 1937; s. Barnet and Eleanor (Cramer) H.; m. Maria Bechily, 1982; children— Brian Kenneth, Valery Jane, Anthony Scott. AB, U. Chgo., 1956; JD, U. Mich., 1959; LLM, Northwestern U., 1962. Bar: Ill. 1959, D.C. 1962, N.Y. 1981. Assoc. Arvey, Hodes, Costello & Burman, Chgo., 1959-61, ptnr., 1965-91, Ross & Hardies, Chgo., 1992—. Bd. dirs. First Investors Life Ins. Co. NY, Richardson Electronics, Ltd., State Ill. Savs. and Loan Bd., Expressions of Culture, Inc. Author: The Law of Art and Antiques, 1966, What Every Artist and Collector Should Know About the Law, 1974; Assoc. news editor: Fed. Bar News, 1963-70; co-editor: Conf. Mut. Funds, 1966, Legal Rights in the Art and Collectors' World, 1986; Contbr. articles to profl. jours. Chmn. Philippine Exch. Nurses award com., 1966; nat. chmn. Lawbooks U.S.A., 1962-73; chmn. Mut. Funds and Investment Mgmt. Conf., 1966-75; co-chmn. Chgo. World Friendship Day, 1967; mem. Ill. Arts Coun., 1973-75; Committeeman Ill. 9th Dist. Dem. Com., 1970-82; bd. dirs. Michael Reese Hosp. Rsch. Inst., 1965-73, Found. of Fed. Bar Assn., 1970—, United Cerebral Palsy Chgo., 1976-84; governing bd. Chgo. Symphony Soc., 1978-1999; governing mem. Art Inst. Chgo., 1980—; com. on internat. investment and tech. Dept. State, 1980-83; bd. dirs. Chgo. Neighborhood Theatre Found., 1980-92, Harold Washington Found., 1988-2000; exec. com. Anti Defamation League, 1990-98; chmn. Mayor's Task Force on Neighborhood Land Use, 1986-88; chmn. Navy Pier Devel. Authority, 1988-89; mem. Ill. Atty. Gen. adv. com., 1991-95; spl. counsel Art in Embassies Program, Dept. State, 1992-94; co-chmn. Private Enterprise Rev. and Adv. Bd., Ill., 1992-94; pres. Lawyers Creative Arts, 2000—. Capt. JAGC, AUS, 1962-64. Decorated Army Commendation medal; named one of Chicago's ten outstanding young men Jr. Assn. Commerce and Industry, 1968, Chgo. Artist's award for Support of Visual Arts, 1996, Disting. Svc. award Lawyer's for the Creative Arts, 1997. 02169408, Fed. Bar Assn. (chmn. council financing 1966-71, chmn. younger lawyers div. 1963-64, nat. council 1965— , Distinguished Service award 1971, 75, 86, Earl Kintner award for Outstanding Service, 1998), Ill. Bar Assn., Chgo. Bar Assn., Chgo. Art Inst. (life), Chgo. Hist. Soc. (life), Judge Adv. Gens. Assn. (life), Zeta Beta Tau, Tau Epsilon Rho. Clubs: Standard, Econ. (Chgo.), Mid-Day. Lodges: Masons (32 degree). Jewish. Corporate, general, Intellectual property, Securities. Home: 1540 N Lake Shore Dr Chicago IL 60610-6684 Office: Ross & Hardies 150 N Michigan Ave Ste 2500 Chicago IL 60601-7567 E-mail: scott.hodes@rosshardies.com.

HODGE, JAMES EDWARD, lawyer; b. Alexander City, Ala., Sept. 24, 1936; s. William H. and Nellie (Greene) H.; m. Nancy Bates, Aug. 24, 1963; children: Stephanie Lynne, Christopher Murray, Timothy James, Michael Bates. BA, Stetson U., 1958; JD, U. Fla., 1963. Bar: Fla. 1963, U.S. Dist. Ct. (mid. dist.) Fla. 1963, U.S. Ct. Appeals (5th cir.) 1963, U.S. Supreme Ct. 1972, U.S. Ct. Appeals (11th cir.) 1981. Ptnr. Jones, Foerster & Hodge, Jacksonville, Fla., 1966-74, Foerster & Hodge, Jacksonville, 1974-82, Milne, Hodge & Milne, Jacksonville, 1982-85; pvt. practice Jacksonville, 1985-86; ptnr. Blackwell, Walker, Fascell & Hoehl, Jacksonville, 1986-87; chmn. Bus. Acquisitions, Inc., Jacksonville, 1988-91; pvt. practice Jacksonville, Fla., 1991—. Gen. counsel Gov. Fla. 1981-82. Pres. Cerebral Palsy Jacksonville, 1972; bd. dirs. Little League Baseball, Jacksonville, 1976-81, The Bolles Sch. Dads Assn., Jacksonville, 1978-82; bd. dirs. Jacksonville Port Authority, 1980-86, chmn., 1986-88; bd. dirs. The Bolles Sch. Dads Assn. Named one of Outstanding Young Men Am., 1968. Mem. ABA, Fla. Bar, Jacksonville Bar Assn. (bd. govs. 1972-73), Stetson U. Alumni Assn. (pres. 1968), Rotary (pres. West Jacksonville club 1979-80, The Robert T. Shircliff Svc. award 1988), Phi Delta Phi, Omicron Delta Kappa. Episcopalian. Avocations: tennis, reading biographies, spectator sports, walking, travel. Banking, Commercial, contracts (including sales of goods; commercial financing), Property, real (including real estate development, water). Office: PO Box 27055 Jacksonville FL 32205-0055

HODGE, RAY, lawyer; b. Jonesboro, Ark., Oct. 18, 1930; s. Charles R. and Neva Hodge; m. Betty M. Hodge, Nov. 25, 1959; children: Ryan, Raylene, Ronnie, Renee, Ricky, Roxann. BA, Wichita State U., 1964; JD, Oklahoma City U., 1967; postgrad., U. Nev., 1978. Bar: Kans. 1967, U.S. Dist. Ct. Kans. 1967, U.S. Ct. Appeals (10th cir.) 1969, U.S. Supreme Ct. 1970, U.S. Dist. Ct. (we. dist.) Mo. 1998, D.C. 1999. Capt. Sedgwick County Sheriff, Wichita, Kans., 1962—68; commd. officer/pilot USAR/Kans. N.G., 1965—86, col., 1986—91, ret., 1991; pvt. practice Wichita, Kans., 1967—77; spl. agt. Kans. Atty. Gen., Topeka, 1971—75; dist. judge State of Kans., Wichita, 1977—89; atty. Ray Hodge & Assocs., Wichita, 1989—. Bd. governours Kans. Trial Lawyers, Topeka; mcpl. ct. judge pro tem City of Wichita, United States. Decorated Legion of Merit, Meritorious Svc. medal. Mem.: Wichita Bar Assn. (life; mem. ethics com.), Reserve Officers Assn. (life). Professional liability, Insurance, Aviation. Home: 105 S Breezy Pointe Cir Wichita KS 67235

HODGE, VICTOR A(NTHONY), lawyer; b. Louisville, Apr. 4, 1947; s. Lester D. and Bridget T. H.; m. Barbara A., June 24, 1967; children: James Eric, Jill Marie. BA in Chemistry, Bellarmine Coll.; JD cum laude, U. Dayton. Bar: Ohio 1981, Fla. 1982. Forensic chemist Sanford Crime Lab, Fla., 1974-75, Miami Valley Regional Crime Lab, Dayton, Ohio, 1973-74, 75-80; assoc. Brannon & Cox Law Offices, Dayton, 1981-83; sole practice Dayton, 1983—. Served to sgt. U.S. Army, 1969—71. Mem. Ohio State Bar Assn., Dayton Bar Assn., Fla. Bar Assn., Ohio State Trial Lawyers Am., Am. Legion. Roman Catholic. Office: 130 W 2nd St Ste 810 Dayton OH 45402-1501 E-mail: attyhodge@aol.com.

HODGES, JOT HOLIVER, JR., retired lawyer, business executive; b. Archer City, Tex., Nov. 16, 1932; s. Jot Holiver and Lola Mae (Hurd) H.; m. Virginia Cordray Pardue, June 11, 1955; children: Deborah, Jot, Darlene. BS, BBA, Sam Houston State U., 1954; JD, U. Tex., 1957. Bar: Tex. 1958, U.S. Dist. Ct. (so. dist.) Tex. 1958, U.S. Ct. Appeals (5th cir.) 1958. Asst. atty. gen. State of Tex., Austin, 1958-60; chmn. bd. Presidio Devel. Corp., Missouri City, Tex., 1971. Organizer, founder 3 banks, several corps. and ltd. partnerships; residential and comml. real estate developer. Contbr. articles to legal, med., pharm., and hosp. jours. Capt. U.S. Army. Mem.

Houston Club, Quail Valley Country Club. Property, real (including real estate development, water), Banking. Home: 3527 Thunderbird St Missouri City TX 77459-2445 Office: 3660 Hampton Dr Ste 200 Missouri City TX 77459-3044

HODGES, RALPH B. state supreme court justice; b. Anadarko, Okla., Aug. 4, 1930; s. Dewey E. and Pearl R. (Hodges) H.; m. Janelle H.; children: Shari, Mark, Randy. BA, Okla. Baptist U.; LL.B., U. Okla. Atty. Bryan County, Okla., 1956-58; judge Okla. Dist. Ct., 1959-65; justice Okla. Supreme Ct., Oklahoma City, 1965—. Office: Okla Supreme Ct State Capital Bldg Rm 244 Oklahoma City OK 73105

HODINAR, MICHAEL, lawyer, publishing company executive; b. Prague, Czechoslovakia, Dec. 25, 1954; came to U.S., 1969; s. Adolf and Dagmar H.; m. Bernadette Callerame, Nov. 10, 1979. BA, Columbia U., 1977, MIA, 1981; JD, N.Y. Law Sch., 1983. Bar: N.J. 1984, N.Y. 1985, Conn. 1985, U.S. Dist. Ct. N.J. 1984, U.S. Dist. Ct. (ea. dist.) N.Y. 1985, U.S. Dist. Ct. (so. dist.) N.Y. 1986. Pvt. practice, Paramus, N.J., 1984-92, Pelham Bay, N.Y., 1985—, 1985—; pres., pub. VonPalisaden Publs., Inc., Paramus, 1986-92; pvt. practice Hillsdale, N.J., 1992—. Fin. cons. N.Y., N.J., Conn. Bus. editor Jour. Internat. Affairs, 1979-80. John Jay Nat. scholar, 1973, Solomon scholar, 1981. Mem. ABA, N.J. Bar Assn., N.Y. State Bar Assn., Columbia U. Sailing Club, Blue Key Soc., Phi Gamma Delta. Democrat. Roman Catholic. Avocations: tennis, sailing, skiing, travel. General practice, Personal injury (including property damage), Probate (including wills, trusts). Home and Office: 60 Saddlewood Dr Hillsdale NJ 07642-1336

HODOUS, ROBERT POWER, lawyer; b. Zanesville, Ohio, July 29, 1945; s. Robert Frank and Nancy Aurelia (Power) H.; m. Susan Cottrell Birkhead, Feb. 1, 1969; children: Robert Everett, Shannon Alycia. BA, Miami U., Oxford, Ohio, 1967; JD, U. Va., Charlottesville, 1970. Bar: Va. 1970. Assoc. firm McGuire, Woods & Battle, Charlottesville, 1970-71; asst. trust officer Nat. Bank & Trust Co., Charlottesville, 1971-72, trust officer, 1972-75, sec., 1975-79, Jefferson Bankshares, Inc. (formerly NB Corp.), Charlottesville, 1979-91, v.p., sec., 1985-91, sr. v.p., sec., 1987-91; asst. to pres. Jefferson Nat. Bank, Charlottesville, 1987-91; pvt. practice law Charlottesville, 1991-92; mem. firm Payne & Hodous, L.L.P., Charlottesville, 1992—. Author: Let's Really Change Taxes, 1998. Chmn. profl. div. Thomas Jefferson Area United Way, 1973, vice-chmn., 1978-79, campaign chmn., 1979-80, v.p. planning, 1981, pres., 1983; bd. dirs. Central Va. chpt. ARC, 1972-78, treas., 1972-75, chmn., 1975-77; commr. Charlottesville Redevel. and Housing Authority, 1974-78; mem. Region X Community Mental Health and Retardation Services Bd., 1973-79, chmn., 1974-76, mem. exec. com., 1976-78; v.p. Soccer Orgn. of Charlottesville-Albemarle, 1985-86, pres., 1986-88; co-pres. Greenbier Sch. PTA, 1985-86; chmn. recreation precinct Charlottesville City Dem. Com., 1971, Rep. com., 1992—; chmn. City Rep. Com., 2000—; bd. dirs. Charlottesville-Albemarle Community Found., 1987-2000, chmn. devel. com., 1991-93, mem. exec. and fin. coms., 1991-2000, chmn. fin. com., 1997-2000; mem. governing bd. Charlottesville Area Legis. Action Coalition, 2002--. Mem.: Charlottesville C. of C. (govt. affairs com. 1996—, co-chair 2002—), Computer Law Assn., Va. Bankers Assn. (com. drafted Va. Trust Subs. Act 1973, trust com. 1974—77, legal affairs com. 1986—91, large bank legis. coord. 1987—91), Va. State Bar, Charlottesville-Albemarle Bar Assn., Va. Bar Assn., Fairview Club (Charlottesville) (pres. 1974—75). Roman Catholic. Banking, Corporate, general, Pension, profit-sharing, and employee benefits. Home: 1309 Lester Dr Charlottesville VA 22901-3143 Office: 412 E Jefferson St Charlottesville VA 22902-5109

HOECKER, THOMAS RALPH, lawyer; b. Chicago Heights, Ill., Dec. 14, 1950; s. William H. and Norma M. (Wynkoop) H.; m. V. Sue Thornton, Aug. 28, 1971; children: Elizabeth T., Ellen T. BS, No. Ill. U., 1972; JD, U. Ill., 1975. Bar: Ill. 1975, Ariz. 1985. Assoc. Davis and Morgan, Peoria, Ill., 1975-80, ptnr., 1980-84; assoc. Snell and Wilmer, Phoenix, 1984-86, ptnr., 1987—. Mem. steering com. Western Pension Conf., Phoenix, 1986-92, pres., 1991-92. Fellow Am. Coll. Employee Benefits Coun. (charter), Ariz. Bar Found.; mem. ABA (chair tax sect. employee benefits com. 2002-03, co-chair legis. and adminstrv. subcom. of labor sect. employee benefits com. 1994-96), Ariz. Bar Assn., Ill. Bar Assn., Marciopa County Bar Assn., (mem. investment com. 1988-94). Avocation: fly fishing. Pension, profit-sharing, and employee benefits. Office: Snell Wilmer 1 Arizona Ctr Phoenix AZ 85004

HOEFFLIN, RICHARD MICHAEL, lawyer, judicial administrator, contractor; b. L.A., Oct. 20, 1949; s. David Greenfield and Gloria (Harrison) H.; m. Susan J. Amoroso, Mar. 29, 1969; children: Alyssa, Jennifer, Richard, II. BS in Acctg. cum laude, Calif. State U.-Northridge, 1971; JD, Loyola U., Los Angeles, 1974. Bar: Calif. 1974, U.S. Dist. Ct. (cen. dist.) Calif. 1974, U.S. Tax Ct. 1976, U.S. Dist. Ct. (no. and so. dists.) Calif. 1976, U.S. Supreme Ct. 1982. With Lewitt, Hackman, Hoefflin, Shapiro, Marshall & Harlan, 1974-2000, ptnr., 1977-2000; pvt. practice, 2000-; judge pro tem L.A. Superior Ct., 1982—I; cert. mediator, 1982-; judge pro tem, Ventura County, Superior Ct., 1991—, Fee Dispute Resolution Svcs. For L.A. County Bar. Co-founder Ventura County Homeowners For Equal Taxation, Westlake Village, Calif., 1978-79; pres., gen. counsel Westlake Hills Homeowners Assn., 1975-77; chmn. celebrity Love Match Tennis Tour. for John McEnroe United Cerebral Palsy/Spastic Children Found., 1990-96; bd. mem. Michael Hoefflin Found., 1996-, No. Ranch Country Club, 2000-2003, Alliance for Arts, 2000-. Mem. ABA, L.A. Bar Assn., Ventura County Bar Assn., San Fernando Valley Bar Assn. (co-chair bus. and real estate sect. 1995-97), Westlake Hills Owners Assn. (pres. 1977-78), North Ranch Country Club (pres. tennis assn. 1984-85). Republican. Roman Catholic. State civil litigation, Entertainment, Property, real (including real estate development, water). Office: 2659 Townsgate Rd #232 Westlake Village CA 91361 E-mail: rmhoefflin@hoefflinlaw.com.

HOEFLE, PAUL RYAN, lawyer; b. Aurora, Ill., July 25, 1956; s. Ronald Anthony and Shirley Ann Hoefle; m. Mary Beth Wredling, June 25, 1983; children: Mary Elyse, Mitchell, Matthew. BS in Fin. summa cum laude, U. Ill., 1978; JD, U. Mich., 1981. Bar: Wis., U.S. Dist. Ct. (ea. and we. dists.) Wis. Assoc. Frisch, Dudek & Slattery, Milw., 1981-86, shareholder, 1986-88, Slattery, Hausman & Hoefle, Waukesha, Wis., 1988-98; shareholder, mng. ptnr. Bode, Carroll, McCoy, Hoefle & Mihal, Waukesha, 1998—2001; ptnr. Laufenberg & Hoefle, SC, Milw., 2002—. Bd. dirs. Wildlife in Need, Oconomowoc, Wis., 1998-2000. Mem. State Bar Wis., Milw. Bar Assn., Waukesha Bar Assn., Wis. Acad. Trial Lawyers (bd. dirs. 1988—, exec. com. 1997—), Waukesha Rotary Club. Avocations: outdoor activities, children's activities. Personal injury (including property damage), Product liability, Professional liability. Office: Laufenberg & Hoefle SC 115 S 84th St Ste 330 Milwaukee WI 53214 Office Fax: 414-778-1770. E-mail: prh@lauflaw.com.

HOEHN, ELMER LOUIS, lawyer, state and federal agency administrator, educator, consultant; b. Memphis, Ind., Dec. 19, 1915; s. Louis and Agnes (Goss) H.; m. Frances Cory, June 10, 1943; children: Kathleen Gillmore, G. Patrick. BS, Canterbury Coll., 1936, Northwestern U., 1937; JD, U. Louisville, 1940. Bar: Ky. 1940, D.C. 1969, U.S. Supreme Ct. 1969, U.S. Ct. Appeals 1970, Ind. 1981. Prof. bus. and law Jeffersonville High Sch., Ind., 1937-41, Ind. U., 1940-41; with legal and personnel div. Am. Barge Lines, 1942-44; realtor Ind., 1949—; apptd. dir. by Gov. Ind. Oil and Gas, 1949-53; apptd. adminstr. by Pres. U.S. Oil Import Adminstrn., 1965-69; sec.-treas. Am. Assn. Oil Well Drilling Contractors, 1956-60; exec. sec. Ind. Oil Producers and Land Owners Assn., 1953-64; pvt. practice law Washington, 1969-91, Indiana, 1981—. ADR civil mediator, Ind., 1993; gov.'s rep. Interstate Oil & Gas Compact Commn., 1949—53, 1961—65; apptd. commr. by gov. Ohio River Greenway Devel. Commn., 1994; cons. petroleum, natural resources, energy and environment; chmn. Clark County Redevel. Commn., 1996—, Charlestown Ammo INAAP Reuse Authority, 1997—. Mem. Ind. Gen. Assembly, 1945- 49, minority floor leader, 1947, chief clk., 1949, Democratic chmn., Clark County, Ind., 1945-52; Ind. del. Dem. Nat. Conv., 1964, chmn. 8th Congl. Dist., 1952-58; mem. Ind. Dem. Exec. Com., 1952-58, Ind. and Midwest campaign mgr., LBJ campaign for president, 1960. Named Hon. Citizen, Ind. and Ky., Citoyen Honneur, Soufflenheim, France, Ambassador, Clark County, Ind., Disting. Benefactor, Clark Meml. Hosp. Interfaith Ctr.; recipient Humanitarian award, ARC, 2003, Chancellor's Medallion award, IUS, 2003, Helping Hand award, Haven House Svcs., Lewis & Clark Bicentennial Commemoration, Falls of the Ohio, 2003—. Mem. ABA, Fed. Bar Assn., Ky. Bar Assn. (Disting. sr. counselor 1990), D.C. Bar Assn., Ind. Bar Assn. (Disting. Sr. Counselor 1990), Coop. Oil and Gas Assns. (liason com. Washington 1969-91), Am. Inn of Ct., Univ. Club, Sigma Delta Kappa. Clubs: Nat. Lawyers, Nat. Press (Washington); Ind. Legislators (Indpls.); Filson (Louisville), Elks Country (Jeffersonville). Roman Catholic. Administrative and regulatory. Home: 2105 Utica Pike Jeffersonville IN 47130-5005

HOFELDT, JOHN W. lawyer; b. Elkhart Lake, Wis., Sept. 6, 1920; s. Johann Heinrich and Matilda A. (Kuester) H.; m. Marion Ruth Meyer, Nov. 27, 1943; children: Nancy R. Hofeldt Werley, William A., Mark R. Ph.B., U. Wis.-Madison, 1943, LL.B. (editor Law Rev. 1946-47), 1947. Bar: Wis. 1947, Ill. 1948. Since practiced in, Chgo.; ptnr. Haight & Hofeldt (and predecessors), 1955—89; ret., 1989. Lectr. John Marshall Grad. Sch., Chgo., 1971-91. Mem. Ill. Sch. Dist. 194 Bd. Edn., 1964-72. Served with USN, 1943-46. Mem. Am., Wis., Ill. bar assns., Patent Law Assn. Chgo. Clubs: Masons (Chgo.), Shriners (Chgo.), Union League (Chgo.). Republican. Home: 5555 Tancho Dr Madison WI 53718-1920

HOFER, ROY ELLIS, lawyer; b. Cin., Oct. 10, 1935; s. Eric Walter and Elsie Katherine (Ellis) H.; m. Suzanne Elizabeth Sturtz, June 6, 1956 (div. 1974); m. Cynthia Ann Corson, June 5, 1981; children: Kimberly, Tracy, Eric. BChemE, Purdue U., 1957; JD, Georgetown U., 1961. Patent examiner U.S. Patent & Trademark Office, Washington, 1957-59; patent agt. Exxon Corp., Washington, 1959-61; ptnr. Brinks Hofer Gilson & Lione, Chgo., 1961—, pres., 1995-99. Adv. com. No. Dist. Ill., 1991-95. Contbr. articles to profl. jours. Bd. dirs. Chgo. Lung Assn., 1982-83, Ctr. for Conflict Resolution, 1983-88, 90-91, pres., 1991-97; bd. dirs. Union League Club Chgo., 1984-88, Boys and Girls Club, Chgo., 1985-89, Ill. Inst. CLE, Chgo., 1986-88. Mem. ABA (dir. litigation sect. 1982-87), Fed. Cir. Bar Assn. (pres. 1993-94), Chgo. Bar Assn. (pres. 1988-89), Intellectual Property Law Assn. Chgo., Am. Intellectual Property Law Assn., Legal Club Chgo., Phi Eta Sigma, Tau Beta Pi, Omega Chi Epsilon. Republican. Alternative dispute resolution, Patent, Trademark and copyright. Office: Brinks Hofer Gilson & Lione Ste 3600 455 N Cityfront Plaza Dr Chicago IL 60611-5599

HOFER, STEPHEN ROBERT, lawyer; b. Anderson, Ind., July 25, 1950; s. Robert E. and Maxine (Hert) H.; m. Cheryl A. Stiles, Aug. 27, 1994; children: Victoria Sloane, Morgan BrynRose. AB, Ind. U., 1976; JD, Northwestern U., 1980. Bar: Calif. 1980, U.S. Dist. Ct. (ctrl. dist.) Calif. 1980, U.S. Ct. Appeals (9th cir.) 1980, U.S. Dist. Ct. (ea., no., and so. dists.) Calif. 1982, U.S. Supreme Ct. 1995. Mng. editor Daily Herald-Tel., Bloomington, Ind., 1972-74; asst. city editor Miami Herald, Ft. Lauderdale, Fla., 1976-77; atty. Gibson Dunn & Crutcher, L.A., 1980-84; venue press chief L.A. Olympic Organizing Com., 1983-84; v.p., gen. counsel Am. Golf Corp., Santa Monica, Calif., 1984-92; of counsel Bailey & Marzano, Santa Monica, 1992-98; ptnr., chair corp. and transactional dept. Bailey & Ptnrs., Santa Monica, 1998—. Instr. law U. So. Calif., L.A., 1983-84, lectr. aviation law Calif. State U., L.A. Sec., bd. dirs. Mus. of Flying, Santa Monica, 1986-89; bd. dirs. L.A. Philharmonic Assn., 1992-95, Santa Monica Symphony Assn., 1999-2000; pres. L.A. Philharmonic Bus. and Profl. Assn., 1992-95. Mem.: SAR, Sons of Union Vets. of Civil War, Jamestowne Soc. Democrat. Avocations: symphonic music and jazz, mountain climbing, travel, genealogy, photography. Aviation, Corporate, general, Property, real (including real estate development, water). Office: Bailey & Ptnrs 2d Fl 2828 Don Douglas Loop N Santa Monica CA 90405-2959 E-mail: SHofer@baileypartners.com.

HOFF, TIMOTHY, law educator, priest; b. Freeport, Ill., Feb. 27, 1941; s. Howard Vincent and Zillah (Morgan) H.; m. Virginia Nevill; children: Brian Charles, Morgan Witherspoon; stepchildren: Guy Baker, Katherine Baker. Student, U. London, 1961—62; AB, Tulane U., 1963, JD, 1966; LLM, Harvard U., 1970. Bar: Fla. 1967, Ala. 1973, U.S. Dist. Ct. (mid. dist.) Fla. 1967; ordained priest Episcopal Ch. Assoc. Williams, Parker, Harrison, Dietz & Getzen, Sarasota, Fla., 1968-69; asst. legal editor The Fla. Bar, 1969; asst. prof. U. Ala., 1970-73, assoc. prof., 1973-75, prof. law, 1975-93, Gordon Rosen prof., 1993—2002, prof. emeritus, 2002—. Cons. Ala. Law Inst.; reporter Ala. Adminstrv. Procedure Act, 1977—. Author: Alabama Limitations of Actions, 1984, 2d edit., 1992, Forms for Civil Trial Practice, 1991; contbr. articles to profl. jours. V.p., founding dir. Hospice of West Ala.; founding dir. Cmty. Soup Bowl, Inc.; Episc. priest assoc. Canterbury Chapel U. Ala.; rector St. Michael's Episc. Ch., Fayette, Ala., 1988-96, 2003—. Recipient Hist. Preservation Svc. award, 1976. Mem. ACLU, AAUP, Maritime Law Assn. U.S., Coun. on Religion and Law, Episc. Soc. for Ministry in Higher Edn., Univ. Club, Phi Beta Kappa, Order of Coif, Omicron Delta Kappa, Eta Sigma Phi. Democrat. Home: 2601 Lakewood Cir Tuscaloosa AL 35405-2727 Office: U Ala Law Sch 101 Paul W Bryant Dr E PO Box 870382 Tuscaloosa AL 35487-0382 E-mail: thoff@law.ua.edu.

HOFFA, THOMAS EDWARD, lawyer; b. Marshalltown, Iowa, Sept. 20, 1935; s. Harvey Edward and Janette (Nason) H. BS, Iowa State U., 1958; JD, John Marshall Law Sch., 1972. Bar: Ill. 1972, U.S. Dist. Ct. (no. dist.) Ill. 1972 (Gen. Bar), U.S. Tax Ct. 1976, U.S. Dist. Ct. (no. dist.) Ill. 1983 (Trial Bar), U.S. Ct. Appeals (7th cir.) 1987. Sole practice, Chgo., 1972—. With USAF, 1958-60. Mem. ABA, Assn. Trial Lawyers Am., Ill. State Bar Assn., Chgo. Bar Assn. Republican. Presbyterian. Appellate, General civil litigation, Criminal. Office: 30 W Chicago Ave Ste 1320 Chicago IL 60610-4339

HOFFER, MARK DAVID, lawyer; b. Bklyn., Sept. 7, 1951; s. Herbert and Ruth (Weitzner) H.; m. Ann Wax, May 30, 1976; children: William, Gail Beth, Alison Lynn. BA, Queens Coll., Flushing, 1973; JD, Yale U., 1976. Bar: N.Y. 1977, D.C. 1979, U.S. Ct. Appeals (4th cir.) 1977, U.S. Dist. Ct. Md. 1977, U.S. Dist. Ct. (so. and ea. dists.) N.Y. 1979. Law clk. to Judge Harrison L. Winter U.S. Ct. Appeals (4th cir.), 1976-77; assoc. Debevoise Plimpton Lyons & Gates, N.Y.C., 1977-80; asst. gen. counsel Grumman Corp., Bethpage, N.Y., 1993-94, corp. counsel, 1980-85; sr. v.p., gen. counsel Fin. Svcs. Corp. N.Y.C., 1986-89, N.Y. State Environ. Facilities Corp., Albany, 1990-92; exec. dir., counsel N.Y.C. Conflicts of Interest Bd., 1992-93; gen. counsel N.Y.C. Dept. Environ. Protection, Corona, N.Y., 1994—. Mem. ABA, Assn. Bar of N.Y.C. Home: 47-51 244th St Douglaston NY 11362 Office: NYC Dept Environ Protection 59-17 Junction Blvd 19th Fl Corona NY 11368

HOFFHEIMER, DANIEL JOSEPH, lawyer; b. Cin., Dec. 28, 1950; s. Harry Max and Charlotte (O'Brien) Hoffheimer; m. Elizabeth Lee Hoffheimer; children: Rebecca, Rachel, Leah. Grad., Phillips Exeter Acad., 1969; AB cum laude, Harvard Coll., 1973; JD, U. Va., 1976. Bar: Ohio 1976, U.S. Dist. Ct. (so. dist.) Ohio 1976, U.S. Ct. Appeals (6th cir.) 1977, U.S. Ct. Appeals (D.C. and fed. cir.) 1986, U.S. Ct. Internat. Trade 1986, U.S. Tax Ct. 1992, U.S. Supreme Ct. 1980, cert.: (Specialist Estate Planning Trust and Probate Law). Assoc. Taft, Stettinius & Hollister, Cin., 1976-84, ptnr., 1984—. Lectr. law Coll. Law, U. Cin., 1981-83; trustee Judges Hogan & Porter Meml. Trust; mem. adv. bd. Ohio Dist. Ct. Rev. Editor-in-chief U. Va. Jour. Internat. Law, 1975-76; co-author: Practitioners' Handbook Ohio First District Court Appeals, 1984, 2d edit., 1991, Federal Practice Manual, U.S. 6th Circuit Court of Appeals, 1999, Manual on Labor Law, 1988; mem. editl. bd. Probate Law Jour. Ohio, 2000—; contbr. articles to profl. jours. Mem. Cin. Symphony Bus. Rels. Com., 1977-86, Cin. Composers Guild, 1988-93, Ohio Supreme Ct. Com. Racial Fairness, 1993-2000; trustee Underground R.R. Freedom Mus., 1995—; mem. adv. bd. Consumer Protection, Cin., 1978-80, Hoxworth Blood Ctr. Univ. Cin. Hosp., 1994-99; mem. bd. Hebrew Union Coll. Jewish Inst. Religion, 1994—, WGUC-FM Pub. Radio, 1988—, vice chmn., 1993-96, chmn., 1996-98; trustee Cin. Chamber Orch., 1977-80, Seven Hills Sch., Cin., 1980-86, Internat. Visitors Ctr., Cin., 1980-84, Friends Coll. Conservatory of Music, Cin., 1985-86, Cin. Symphony Orch., 1988-94, 96—, sec., 1996-99, vice chair 1999-2000, chair, 2001—, Children's Psychiat. Ctr., Cin., 1986-89, treas., 1987-89; vice chmn. Jewish Hosp., Cin., 1989-92; Leadership Cin., 1989-90; sec., trustee Cin. Symphony Musicians Pension Fund, 1989-99, Jewish Cmty. Rels. Coun., 1990-98, v.p., 1996-98; sec. Nat. Conf. Commn. Justice, 1992-99, treas. 1999-2000, trustee emeritus, 2000—; counsel Cin. AIDS Commn., 1991—, Cin. Inst. Fine Arts Govt. Affairs Com., 1993-94, B'nai B'rith Nat. Coun. Legacy Devel., 1996-97; trustee Nat. Underground R.R. Freedom Ctr., 1995-. Named Outstanding Young Man, U.S. Jaycees, 1984, 98. Life fellow Am. Bar Found., Ohio Bar Found.; fellow Am. Coll. Trust and Estate Counsel; mem. ABA, Internat. Bar Assn., Internat. Trade Bar Assn., Internat. Arbitration Assn. (comml. arbitrator 1991-95), Fed. Bar Assn. (treas. 1984, sec. 1985, v.p. 1986-87, pres. 1987-88), Ohio State Bar Assn. (bd. govs. Est. Pl. Trust and Probate Law sect. 1996—), Cin. Bar Assn. (trustee 1988-93, v.p. 1990-91, pres. 1992-93, chair Cin. Acad. Leadership for Lawyers 1998-2000), Harvard Club of Cin. (bd. dirs. 1980-88, v.p. 1983-86, pres. 1986-87). Democrat. Avocations: music, tennis, chinese and japanese art. Estate planning, General practice, Probate (including wills, trusts). Home: 1 Forest Hill Dr Cincinnati OH 45208-1953 Office: 425 Walnut St Ste 1800 Cincinnati OH 45202-3923 E-mail: hoffheimer@taftlaw.com.

HOFFLUND, PAUL, lawyer; b. San Diego, Mar. 27, 1928; s. John Leslie and Ethel Frances (Cline) H.; m. Anne Marie Thalman, Feb. 15, 1958; children: Mark, Sylvia. BA, Princeton (N.J.) U., 1950; JD, George Washington U., 1956. Bar: D.C. 1956, U.S. Dist. Ct. D.C. 1956, U.S. Ct. Appeals (D.C. cir.) 1956, Calif. 1957, U.S. Dist. Ct. (so. dist.) Calif. 1957, U.S. Ct. Mil. Appeals 1957, U.S. Ct. Claims 1958, U.S. Ct. Appeals (9th cir.) 1960, U.S. Supreme Ct. 1964, U.S. Tax Ct. 1989. Assoc. Wencke, Carlson & Kuykendall, San Diego, 1961-62; ptnr. Carlson, Kuykendall & Hofflund, San Diego, 1963-65, Carlson & Hofflund, San Diego, 1965-72; Christian Sci. practitioner San Diego, 1972-84; arbitrator Mcpl. Cts. and Superior Ct. of Calif., San Diego, 1984-99; pvt. practice San Diego, 1985—. Adj. prof. law Nat. U. Sch. Law, San Diego, 1985-94; judge pro tem Mcpl. Ct. South Bay Jud. Dist., 1990-99; disciplinary counsel to U.S. Tax Ct., 1989—; asst. U.S. atty. U.S. Dept. of Justice, L.A., 1959-60, asst. U.S. atty. in charge, San Diego, 1960-61, spl. hearing officer, San Diego, 1962-68; asst. corp. counsel Govt. of D.C., 1957-59. Author: (chpt. in book) Handbook on Criminal Procedure in the U.S. District Court, 1967; contbr. articles to profl. jours. Treas. Princeton Club of San Diego; v.p. Community Concert Assn., San Diego; pres. Sunland Home Found., San Diego, Trust for Christian Sci. Orgn., San Diego; chmn. bd. 8th Ch. of Christ, Scientist, San Diego. With USN, 1950-53, comdr. JAGC, USNR, 1953-72, ret. Mem. ABA, San Diego County Bar Assn., World Affairs Coun., Phi Delta Phi. Democrat. Avocations: theater, classical music, bridge, fine art, biblical study. Estate planning, General practice, Probate (including wills, trusts). Home and Office: 6146 Syracuse Ln San Diego CA 92122-3301

HOFFMAN, ALAN CRAIG, lawyer, consultant; b. Chgo., Oct. 1, 1944; s. Morris Joseph and Marie E. Hoffman; m. Pamela Hoffman. BA, Carthage Coll., 1968; JD, John Marshall Law Sch., 1973. Bar: Fla. 1973, Ill. 1973, U.S. Dist. Ct. (no. dist.) Ill. 1974, U.S. Dist. Ct. (mid. dist.) Fla. 1981, U.S. Ct. Appeals (7th cir.) 1975, U.S. Ct. Appeals (5th and 11th cirs.) 1981, U.S. Supreme Ct. 1977. Staff atty. Cook County Legal Assistance Found., Brookfield, Ill., 1973-74, Patient Legal Svcs., Chgo., 1974; pvt. practice law Chgo., 1973—, River Grove, Ill., 1973-86, Oak Brook, Ill., 1980-87, Hinsdale, Ill., 1987-93; with assocs., 1980—. Spl. asst. atty. gen. Ill. Criminal Justice Divsn., Chgo., 1977—79, Ill. Condemnation Divsn., Chgo., 1980—87; pres. Almar, Ltd., 1986—91; v.p. Marach, Ltd., 1986—89, Hoffman Realty, 1978—; pres., dir. North Shore Greenview Bldg. Corp., 1978—2002; asst. prof. Lewis U., 1974—79; vis. prof. Coll. Law Paraprofl. Ctr., 1974—76, adj. prof., 1979—80; adj. prof. law Health Law Inst. Loyola U., Chgo., 2000—; assoc. prof. No. Ill. U., 1979—80; v.p. Adv. Svc., Inc.; cons. Med-Legal Cases, 1982—. Author (with F. Lane and D. Birnbaum): Lane's Medical Litigation Guide, 1981; contbr. Mem. Oak Park Twp. (Ill.) Mental Health Bd., 1975—80, v.p., 1975, chmn. program com., 1975—77, pres., 1978; mem. governing bd. Women In Need Growing Stronger, 1993—96; bd. govs. Jewish Fedn. Chgo., Coun. for Elderly, 1995—98; co-chair Rainbow House Bread and Roses Ann. Fundraiser, 1997—98. Fellow: Am. Coll. Legal Medicine (editl. bd. med. and legal textbook com. 1987—, textbook update com. 1988, program com. 1988—, legal com. 1988—, profl. devel. com. 1990—98, student awards com. 1992—, moot ct. competition com. 1992—98, co-chair com. violence and abuse in the family 1993); mem.: ATLA, ABA (civil procedure and evidence com. 1993—, comml. tort com. 1993—), Chgo. Acad. Law and Medicine, West Suburban Bar Assn., DuPage Bar Assn., Chgo. Bar Assn., Ill. State Bar Assn. (vice chmn. standing com. on mentally disabled 1975—77, chmn. 1977—78), Fla. Bar Assn. (health law com. 1983—84, out-of-state practitioner com. 1988—91), Ill. Trial Lawyers Assn. (profl. negligence com. 1982), Am. Soc. Law and Medicine, Mensa, Phi Alpha Delta. State civil litigation, Personal injury (including property damage), Workers' compensation.

HOFFMAN, ALAN JAY, lawyer; b. Phila., Aug. 31, 1948; s. Heinz Julius and Sylvia (Wise) H.; children: Jennifer, Lauren, Allison. BBA, Temple U., 1970; JD, Villanova U., 1973. Bar: Pa. 1973, U.S. Dist. Ct. (ea. dist.) Pa. 1973, U.S. Dist. Ct. Del. 1973, U.S. Ct. Appeals (3rd cir.) 1973, Del. 1977, U.S. Supreme Ct. 1984, D.C. 1990. Asst. U.S. atty. U.S. Dept. Justice, Wilmington, Del., 1973-78; ptnr. Dilworth, Paxson, Kalish & Kauffman, Phila., 1979-92, mem. exec. mgmt. com., 1989-90, chmn. new bus. com., 1990-91; ptnr. Blank, Rome, Comisky and McCauley, Phila., 1992—, mem. exec. mgmt. com., 1998—, co-chmn. atty. recruiting com., adminstrv. ptnr. in charge Wilmington, Del., chmn. litigation and dispute resolution dept., 1996—. Lectr. Widener Del. Law Sch., Wilmington, 1974, Mealy's Conf. on Toxic Torts, 1999—, Mealy's Conf. on MTBE pollution, 2000. Contbg. co-editor Villanova Law Rev., 1972-73; contbr. articles to profl. jours. Bd. dirs. Men's Club Temple Adath Israel, Merion, Pa., 1993-94; pres. Villanova Law Sch. Inn of Ct., 1999—. Recipient Atty. Gen.'s Spl. Commendation U.S. Dept. Justice, Washington, 1977. Fellow Am. Bar Found.; mem. ATLA, ABA, Pa. Bar Assn., Fed. Bar Assn., Phila. Bar Assn., Del. Bar Assn., Del. Trial Lawyers Assn., Pa. Trial Lawyers Assn., White Manor Country Club (pres. 1993—, 1st v.p. 1990-93, bd. dirs. 1988-90, admissions chmn. 1989—), J. Willard O'Brien Villanova Law Sch. Inn of Ct. (pres. 1999—). Avocation: golf. General civil litigation, Criminal, General practice. Office: Blank Rome Comisky & McCauley One Logan Sq Philadelphia PA 19103-6998

HOFFMAN, BARRY PAUL, lawyer; b. Phila., May 29, 1941; s. Samuel and Hilda (Cohn) H.; m. Mary Ann Schrock, May 18, 1978; children: Elizabeth Barron, Hayley Rebecca. BA, Pa. State U., 1963; JD, George Washington U., 1968. Bar: Pa. 1972, Mich. 1983. Asst. U.S. Senator Wayne Morse, Oreg., Washington; spl. agt. FBI, Washington; asst. dist. atty. Phila. Dist. Atty.'s Office; exec. v.p., gen. counsel Valassis Communications, Inc.,

Livonia, Mich., also bd. dirs. 1st lt. U.S. Army, 1963-65, Korea. Corporate, general. Home: 49933 Standish Ct Plymouth MI 48170-2882 Office: Valassis Communications Inc 19975 Victor Pkwy Livonia MI 48152-7001 E-mail: hoffmanb@valassis.com.

HOFFMAN, BONNIE HOPE, lawyer; b. Forest Hills, N.Y., May 24, 1969; BA, U. Va., 1991; JD, George Mason U. Sch. Law, 1994. Bar: Va. 1994, Md. 1995. Law clk. Hon James E. Bradberry, Newport News, Va., 1994—2000; asst. pub. defender Loudon County, Va., 1995—2000; dep. pub. defender, 2000—. Office: Public Defenders Office 3 East Market St Leesburg VA 20176

HOFFMAN, CARL H. lawyer; b. St. Louis, May 28, 1936; s. Carl Henry and Anna Marie (Remlinger) H.; m. Pamela L. Polk, May 8, 1971 (div. Novl 1982); children: Kurt M., Jennifer K. BS, St. Louis U., 1958; postgrad., U. Mex., Mexico City, 1958, U. Nev., 1960—61, Tex. Technol. Coll., 1961—62; JD, Washington U., St. Louis, 1966. Bar: Mo. 1966, Fla. 1969, U.S. Supreme Ct. 1970; cert. civil trial adv. Nat. Bd. Trial Advocacy. Pilot Eastern Airlines, Inc., Miami, Fla.; assoc. Spencer & Taylor, Miami, Fla., 1969—70; pvt. practice atty. Miami, 1970—80; ptnr. Hoffman & Hertzig, P.A., Coral Gables, Fla., 1980—. Capt. USAF, 1958-63. Mem. AIAA, ABA, ATLA, SAE Internat., Fla. Bar (cert. civil trial lawyer, cert. bus. litigation lawyer, chmn. aviation law com. 1997-98), Fla. Acad. Trial Lawyers, Am. Jurisprudence Soc., Greater Miami C. of C. (trustee). Aviation, General civil litigation, Personal injury (including property damage). Office: Hoffman & Hertzig PA 901 Ponce De Leon Blvd Ste 500 Coral Gables FL 33134-3073 E-mail: hoffhertz@att.net.

HOFFMAN, DANIEL STEVEN, lawyer, law educator; b. N.Y.C., May 4, 1931; s. Lawrence Hoffman and Juliette (Marbes) Ostrov; m. Beverly Mae Swenson, Dec. 4, 1954; children: Lisa Hoffman Ciancio, Tracy Hoffman Cockriel, Robin Hoffman Black. BA, U. Colo., 1951; LLB, U. Denver, 1958. Bar: Colo. 1958. Assoc., then ptnr. Fugate, Mitchem, Hoffman, Denver, 1951—55; mgr. of safety City and County of Denver, 1963—65; ptnr. Kripke, Hoffman, Carrigan, Denver, 1965—70, Hoffman, McDermott, Hoffman, Denver, 1970—78; of counsel Hoffman & McDermott, Denver, 1978—84; mem. Holme Roberts & Owen, LLC, Denver, 1984—94; dean Coll. Law, U. Denver, 1978—84, dean emeritus, prof. emeritus, 1984—; ptnr. McKenna & Cuneo LLP, Denver, 1994—2000, Hoffman Reilly Pozner & Williamson LLP, 2000—. Chmn., mem. Merit Screening Com. for Bankruptcy Judges, Denver, 1979—84; chmn. subcom. Dist. Atty.'s Crime Adv. Commn., Denver, 1984—; chmn. Senator Wirth's jud. nomination rev. com., Cong. DeGette's jud. nomination rev. com. Contbr. chpts. to books Mem. Rocky Mountain region Anti-Defamation League, Denver, 1985; bd. dirs. Colo. chpt. Am. Jewish Com., 1985, Legal Ctr., Denver, 1985—; mem. adv. com. Samaritan Shelter, Denver, 1985; chmn. Rocky Flats Blue Ribbon Citizens Com., Denver, 1980-83; mem. bd. visitors J. Reuben Clark Law Sch. Brigham Young U., 1986-88. With USAF, 1951-55. Recipient Am. Jewish Com. Nat. Judge Learned Hand award, 1993, Humanitarian award Rocky Mountain chpt. Anti-Defamation League, 1984, Alumni of Yr. award U. Denver Coll. Law, 1997, Lifetime Achievement award Colo. Trial Lawyers Assn., 2001. Fellow: Am. Bar Found., Colo. Bar Found., Am. Coll. Trial Lawyers (state chmn. 1975—76), Internat. Soc. Barristers; mem.: Am. Judicature Soc. (bd. dirs. 1977—81), Assn. Trial Lawyers Am. (nat. com. mem. 1962—63), Colo. Trial Lawyers Assn. (pres. 1961—62, Lifetime Achievement award 2001), Colo. Bar. Assn. (pres. 1976—77, Young Lawyer of Yr. award 1965), Order of Coif (hon.). Democrat. Jewish. Avocation: platform tennis. Federal civil litigation, State civil litigation, Personal injury (including property damage). Office: Hoffman Reilly Pozner & Williamson LLP Kittredge Bldg 511 16th St Ste 700 Denver CO 80202-4248 E-mail: dhoffman@hrpwlaw.com.

HOFFMAN, DARNAY ROBERT, management consultant; b. N.Y.C., Nov. 25, 1947; s. Bill and Toni (Darnay) H.; m. Jennifer Lea Sheppard, Aug. 20, 1984; children by previous marriage: Brandon, Brett; m. Sydney Biddle Barrows, May 14, 1994. BA, SUNY, 1977; MBA, CUNY, 1980; JD, Yeshiva U., 1982. Bar: N.Y. 1995, U.S. Dist. Ct. (so., ea., we. and no. dists.) N.Y. 1995, U.S. Ct. Appeals (fed. cir.) 1995, U.S. Tax Ct. 1995, U.S. Ct. Internat. Trade 1995, U.S. Dist. Ct. Colo. 2000, U.S. Dist. Ct. (no. dist.) Ga. 2000, U.S. Ct. Appeals (fed. cir.). Pres., mgmt. cons. Darnay Hoffman Assocs., Inc., 1969—; mgmt. cons. Hoffman Rsch. Group Inc., N.Y.C., 1977—; rsch. assoc. Baruch Coll., 1977-79. Bd. dirs. Hobton Realty Corp.; dir. Nat. Conf. Law Historians Am., 1987—. Author: Murder in the Wilderness, 1989, Allen Contact, 1989, (pamphlet) Products in Decline, 1980. Mem. ABA, ATLA, Am. Mgmt. Assn., Am. Mktg. Assn., Acad. Mgmt. Scis., Nat. Assn. Criminal Def. Attys., N.Y. State Bar Assn., N.Y. County Lawyers Assn., Assn. Bar of City of N.Y., N.Y. State Trial Lawyers Assn., Player's, Beta Gamma Sigma, Alpha Delta Sigma.

HOFFMAN, DAVID ALAN, lawyer; b. Balt., Jan. 3, 1947; s. Edward Joseph H. and Pauline (Narva) Jacobs; m. Marjorie Fox, Sept. 7, 1968 (div. 1978); m. Elisabeth Lawson Andrews, Sept. 27, 1980; children: Jessica, Jacob, Lily. AB summa cum laude, Princeton U., 1970; MA, Cornell U., 1974; JD magna cum laude, Harvard U., 1984. Bar: Mass. 1985, U.S. Dist. Ct. Mas. 1985, U.S. Ct. Appeals (1st cir.) 1985, U.S. Ct. Appeals (5th cir.) 1990, U.S. Supreme Ct. 1989. Instr. legal methods Harvard Law Sch., Cambridge, Mass., 1982-83, research asst., 1984; clk. 1st Cir. Ct. of Appeals, Boston, 1984-85; assoc. Hill & Barlow, Boston, 1985-92, mem., 1992—2002; with The New Law Ctr., Boston, 2002—. Adj. prof. law Harvard Law Sch., 1997-99, Northeastern U., 1994-96; staff atty. Civil Liberties Union Mass., 1988-89; mem. Supreme Judicial Ct. Standing Com. on Dispute Resolution, 1994-2002; mediator and arbitrator Mass. Office Dispute Resolution, Am. Arbitration Assn., Ctr. for Pub. Resources, Pvt. Adjudication Ctr. Co-author: Massachusetts Alternative Dispute Resolution, 1994; mem. editl. bd. Mass. Law Rev., 1987-89; contbr. articles to profl. jours. Bd. dirs. Walden Ctr. for Peace and Justice, Concord, Mass., 1987-89. Recipient Kennedy Prize for Best Thesis in English Dept., Princeton U., 1970. Mem. ABA (coun. mem. sect. individual rights and responsibilities, 1991-94, vice chair sect. dispute resolution), ACLU, Mass. Bar Assn. (commn. on the bicentennial the constitution 1986-88, chmn. individual rights and responsibilities sect. 1988-90), Boston Bar Assn. (chmn. ADR com. 1993-95), Nat. Lawyers Guild, Soc. Profls. in Dispute Rsolution (pres. N.E. chpt. 1998-2000) Alternative dispute resolution, General civil litigation, Family and matrimonial. Office: The New Law Ctr 99 Summer St Ste 1720 Boston MA 02110-2606

HOFFMAN, DONALD ALFRED, lawyer; b. Milw., May 4, 1936; s. Harry Gustav and Emily Frances (Schwartz) H.; m. Louise Hardie Chapman, June 8, 1963; children: Donald Hardie, Richard Rainey. BBA, U. Wis., 1958, JD, 1968. Bar: La. 1969, U.S. Supreme Ct. 1972, U.S. Ct. Appeals (5th cir.) 1973, U.S. Dist. Ct. (ea., mid. and we. dists.) La. Assoc. Lemle & Kelleher, New Orleans, 1968-73; ptnr. Lemle, Kelleher, Kohlmeyer, Matthews & Schumacher, New Orleans, 1973-75, McGlinchey, Stafford, Mintz & Hoffman, New Orleans, 1975-78; city atty. City of New Orleans, 1978-79; dir. Carmouche, Gray & Hoffman, New Orleans, 1979-82; sr. dir. Hoffman, Siegel, Seydel, Bienvenu & Centola, New Orleans, 1982—. Fellow Am. Bar Found., La. Bar Found.; mem. Am. Bd. Trial Advocates (sec.-treas. La. chpt.), French-Am. C. of C. (chmn. La. chpt.). Presbyterian. General civil litigation, Personal injury (including property damage), Product liability, Toxic tort. Home: 1524 4th St New Orleans LA 70130-5918 Office: Hoffman Siegel Seydel Bienvenu & Centola & Cordes 650 Poydras St New Orleans LA 70130-6101

HOFFMAN, DONALD M. lawyer; b. Los Angeles, Aug. 27, 1935; s. Henry Maurice and Viola Gertrude (Rothe) H. BS, UCLA, 1957, LL.B., 1960. Bar: Calif. 1961. Pvt. practice, L.A. County, 1961—; ptnr. firm Greenwald, Hoffman, Meyer & Montes, 1964—. Pres. L.A. Estate Planning Council. Served to 2d lt. U.S. Army. Mem. Am., Los Angeles County bar assns., Phi Alpha Delta, Beta Gamma Sigma. Clubs: Jonathan. Home: 3520 St Elizabeth Rd Glendale CA 91206-1226 Office: 500 N Brand Blvd Ste 920 Glendale CA 91203-1923

HOFFMAN, IRA ELIOT, lawyer; b. Highland Park, Mich., Jan. 3, 1952; s. Maxwell Mordecai and Leah (Silverman) Hoffman; m. Ruth Felsen, Aug. 19, 1975 (div. 1981); 1 child, Daniel Gideon; m. Meredith Lippman, Dec. 17, 1988; 1 child, Lauren Samantha. BA, U. Mich., 1973; MSc in Econs., London Sch. Econs., 1975; JD cum laude, U. Miami, 1983. Bar: Fla. 1983, U.S. Ct. Appeals (D.C. cir.) 1984, D.C. 1985, Md. 1991, U.S. Ct. Appeals (10th and 4th cirs.) 1992, U.S. Dist. Ct. D.C. 1992, U.S. Dist. Ct. Md. 1992, U.S. Ct. Appeals (fed. cir.) 1994, U.S. Ct. Fed. Claims 1998, U.S. Ct. Appeals (11th cir.) 2001, U.S. Dist. Ct. (so. dist.) Fla. 2001. Tchr. London Sch. Econs., 1975-77; rsch. assoc. Shiloah Ctr. Mid. East Studies, Tel Aviv U., 1978-80; staff atty. FTC, Washington, 1983; law clk. U.S. Ct. Appeals (D.C. cir.), Washington, 1983-84; assoc. Fried, Frank, Harris, Shriver & Jacobson, Washington, 1984-86, 87-88; counsel Ministry of Def. Mission to the U.S., Govt. of Israel, N.Y.C., 1986-87; counsel to vice chmn. U.S. Internat. Trade Commn., Washington, 1988-89; assoc. Howrey & Simon, Washington, 1989-91; pres. Israel Housing Investors, Inc., Rockville, Md., 1990-92; v.p. H.P.F. Prefab Constrn., Ltd., Givatayim, Israel, 1991-92; of counsel Savage & Schwartzman, Balt., 1992-94, McAleese & Assocs., P.C., McLean, Va., 1995-98, Grayson & Kubli, P.C., McLean, 1998—2001; pres. Smart Planet, LLC, Rockville, Md., 1998—2000; v.p. Grayson, Kubli & Hoffman, P.C., McLean, 2002—. Translator: (book) The Emergency of Pan-Arabism in Egypt, 1980; contbr. articles to profl. jours. Spl. counsel Nat. Sudden Infant Death Syndrome Found., Landover, Md., 1984—86; hon. counsel to chmn. Nat. Holocaust Meml. Coun., Washington, 1985. Mem.: ABA. Jewish. Avocations: travel, sports, history. Government contracts and claims, Private international, Public international. E-mail: hoffman@graysonlaw.net.

HOFFMAN, JAMES PAUL, lawyer, hypnotist; b. Waterloo, Iowa, Sept. 7, 1943; s. James A. and Luella M. (Prokosch) H.; 1 child, Tiffany K. B.A., U. No. Iowa, 1965, J.D. U. Iowa, 1967. Bar: Iowa 1967, U.S. Dist. Ct. (no. dist.) Iowa 1981, U.S. Dist. Ct. (so. dist.) Iowa 1968, U.S. Dist. Ct. (so. dist.) Ill, U.S. Tax Ct. 1971, U.S. Ct. Appeals (8th cir.) 1970, U.S. Supreme Ct. 1974. Sr. mem. James P. Hoffman, Law Offices, Keokuk, Iowa, 1967—; chmn. bd. Iowa Inst. Hypnosis. Fellow Am. Inst. Hypnosis; mem. ABA, Iowa Bar Assn., Lee County Bar Assn., Assn. Trial Lawyers Am., Ill. Trial Lawyers Assn., Iowa Trial Lawyers Assn. Democrat. Roman Catholic. Author: The Iowa Trial Lawyers and the Use of Hypnosis, 1980. State civil litigation, Personal injury (including property damage), Workers' compensation. Home and Office: PO Box 1087 Middle Rd Keokuk IA 52632-1087

HOFFMAN, JOEL ELIHU, lawyer; b. N.Y.C., Sept. 23, 1937; s. Samuel S. and Flora (Pasachoff) H.; m. Sandra Joyce Stone, June 3, 1962 (div. June 1985); children: Susanna Beth, Alexander Laurence, Jeremy Andrew; m. Katherine Louise Joss, Feb. 15, 1986. BA, NYU, 1957; LLB, Yale U., 1960. Bar: N.Y. 1960, D.C. 1963. Trial atty. antitrust div. U.S. Dept. Justice, Washington, 1960-63; assoc. Wald, Harkrader and Ross, Washington, 1963-68, ptnr., 1968-85, Sutherland, Asbill and Brennan, Washington, 1985-99, of counsel, 1999—. Adj. prof. law Franklin Pierce Law Sch., 1997—, Law Sch. George Mason U., 1998—. Mem. editorial adv. bd. Food Drug and Cosmetic Law Jour., 1981-89; contbr. articles to profl. jours. Mem. ABA (chmn. food and drug com. adminstrv. law sect. 1976-82, 95-99, vice chmn. consumer product regulation com. 1976—, coun. mem. 1973-76). Administrative and regulatory, Antitrust, Health. Office: Sutherland Asbill & Brennan 1275 Pennsylvania Ave NW Washington DC 20004-2415

HOFFMAN, JOHN FLETCHER, lawyer; b. N.Y.C., May 22, 1946; s. George Fletcher and Helen (Gilbert) H.; m. Coralie Tallman, June 29, 1969; children: Julie Gilbert, William Delano. BS, St. Lawrence U., 1969; JD, Washington and Lee U., 1975. Bar: N.Y. 1976, U.S. Dist. Ct. (so. dist.) N.Y. 1976, U.S. Dist. Ct. (ea. dist.) N.Y. 1978, U.S. Supreme Ct. 1980, U.S. Ct. Appeals (2d cir.) 1982, U.S. Dist. Ct. (no. dist.) Tex. 1988, U.S. Ct. Appeals (11th cir.) 1991, U.S. Ct. Appeals (fed. cir.) 1999. Assoc. Cadwalader, Wickersham & Taft, N.Y.C., 1975-83, ptnr., 1983-94; v.p., assoc. gen. counsel Schering-Plough Corp., Kenilworth, N.J., 1995—. Trustee First Unitarian Congl. Soc. Bklyn., 1980-83; v.p. fin. Unitarian Universalist Congregation of Monmouth County, 2002—; trustee, treas. Bklyn. Children's Mus., 1985-95. Mem. ABA, Order of Coif, Omicron Delta Kappa. Antitrust, Federal civil litigation, State civil litigation. Office: Schering Plough Corp 2000 Galloping Hill Rd Kenilworth NJ 07033-1328

HOFFMAN, JOHN FREDERICK, lawyer; b. Rochester, Ind., Apr. 2, 1922; s. George Edgar and Ethel Lucille (Yoder) H.; m. Patricia Helen Bennett, July 1, 1950. B.A., U. Mich., 1941; LL.B., Harvard U., 1947, LL.D., 1947. Bar: Ill. 1948, U.S. Dist. Ct. (no. dist.) Ill. 1948, U.S. Ct. Mil. Appeals 1954; Ind. 1957, U.S. Dist. Ct. (no. and so. dists.) Ind. 1958, U.S. Supreme Ct. 1962. Assoc. Bohrer, Blackman & Loman, Chgo., 1947-49, Edward Blackman, Chgo., 1949-56; sole practice, Lafayette, Ind., 1957-68; mem. Hoffman & Melichar, Lafayette, 1969-79; ptnr. Hoffman, Melichar & Luhman, Lafayette, 1979-85, Hoffman & Luhman, 1985-88; Hoffman, Luhman & Busch, 1989-2002; county atty. Tippecanoe County, 1971-82; drainage bd. atty., 1972-2002; drainage atty. Benton County, Fouler, Ind., 1985-2002, of counsel Hoffman, Luhman & Masson, 2003—. dir. Farmers & Mchts. Bank, Rochester, Ind., 1958-85. Fellow Ind. State Bar Assn., Ill. Bar Assn., Tippecanoe County Bar Assn., Am. Judicature Soc., Ct. of Appeals of 7th Cir. Assn. Republican. Bankruptcy, General civil litigation. Office: Hoffman & Luhmin 201 Main St Lafayette IN 47902-0099

HOFFMAN, JOHN RAYMOND, lawyer; b. Rochester, N.Y., July 24, 1945; s. Raymond Edward and Ruth Emily (Karnes) H.; m. Linda Lee Moore, Aug. 22, 1970; 1 child, Heather Anne. BA, Washburn U., 1967; JD, U. Mo.-Kansas City, 1971. Bar: Mo. 1972, Tenn. 1976, Kans. 1980, U.S. Supreme Ct. 1975. Law clk. United Telecom, Kansas City, Mo., 1967-70, gen. atty., 1970-75; gen. counsel, sec. United Telephone Sys.-S.E. Group, Bristol, Tenn., 1975-80; v.p., gen. counsel United Telephone Sys. Inc., Kansas City, Mo., 1980-84; sr. v.p. legal, dir. US Telecom, Inc., Kansas City, Mo., 1984-86; sr. v.p. external affairs Sprint Corp., Kansas City, Mo., 1986-99, ret., 2000; chmn. FCC N.Am. Numbering Coun., 1999—2000. Bd. dirs. United Telephone Co. of N.W., 1990-98. Bd. dirs. Ctr. Pub. Utilities, N.Mex. State U., 1989—90, Kansas City Area Econ. Devel. Coun., 1988—89, Trinity Luth. Hosp., Kansas City, 1984—89, Bishop Miege H.S. Found., 1990—92, 1999—2001, Health Initiatives, Inc., Kansas City, 1985—89, pres., 1986—89; bd. dirs. Kansas City Young Audiences, 1981—85, Johnson County Fire Dist., Prairie Village, Kans., 1982—86, Kansas City/Coro Found., 1983—84, Friends of the Zoo, Kansas City, 2000—01. Mem. ABA, Mo. Bar Assn., Tenn. Bar Assn., Kans. Bar Assn., Kansas City Bar Assn., Competitive Telecommunications Assn. (chmn. 1986-88), Ind. Telephone Pioneers Assn., Phi Delta Phi. Club: Optimist. Administrative and regulatory, Corporate, general, Utilities, public. Home: 17960 S Bond Ave Bucyrus KS 66013 Fax: 913-851-2628. E-mail: john_r_hoffman@yahoo.com.

HOFFMAN, LARRY J. lawyer; b. N.Y.C., Aug. 20, 1930; s. Max and Pauline (Epstein) H.; m. Deborah E. Alexander, Oct. 2, 1954; children: Lisa, Ken, Heidi, Mark. AA, U. Fla.; JD, U. Miami. Bar: Fla. 1954. Chmn. Greenberg, Traurig, PA, Miami, 1968—; also bd. dirs. Greenberg, Traurig, Hoffman, Lipoff, Rosen & Quentel, PA, Miami. Mem. ABA, Fla. Bar Assn., Dade County Bar Assn. Avocations: music, art, tennis, computers, photography. Commercial, contracts (including sales of goods; commercial financing), Corporate, general, Securities. Office: Greenberg Traurig 1221 Brickell Ave Miami FL 33131-3224 E-mail: hoffmanl@gtlaw.com.

HOFFMAN, MARK FREDERICK, lawyer; b. Bellevue, Wash., Mar. 30, 1971; s. Frederick Joseph and Molly K. Hoffman; m. Elizabeth Briggs, Aug. 17, 1996. AB summa cum laude, Princeton U., 1993; JD cum laude, U. Mich., 1996. Bar: Wash. 1996. Assoc. Graham & James LLP, Seattle, 1996—. Mem. ABA, Order of the Coif. Avocations: running, skiing, hiking, biking, reading. Corporate, general, Finance, Securities. Office: Gray Cary Ware & Freidenrich LLP 701 Fifth Ave Ste 7000 Seattle WA 98104

HOFFMAN, MATHEW, lawyer; b. Bklyn., Mar. 9, 1954; s. S. David and Naomi B. (Brosterman) H.; m. Bracha Hoffman; children: Ari, Gavriel, Shelhevet, Miri, Shira, Tova, Elisheva. BA, U. Mich., 1974; JD, Columbia U., 1977. Bar: N.Y. 1978, U.S. Dist. Ct. (so. and ea. dists.) N.Y. 1978, U.S. Ct. Appeals (2d and 7th cirs.) 1980, U.S. Dist. Ct. (we. dist.) Mich., 2003; ordained rabbi, 1988. Atty. Proskauer, Rose, N.Y.C., 1978-80, Gordon, Hurwitz, N.Y.C., 1980-85; ptnr. Koether, Harris & Hoffman, N.Y.C., 1985-89, Keck Mahin & Cate, N.Y.C., 1989-94, Rosen & Reade, N.Y.C., 1994-96; ptnr., head of litigation Todtman, Nachamie, Spizz & Johns, P.C., N.Y.C., 1997—. Contbr. articles to profl. jours. Mem. Jewish Flame (trustee 1979—). Federal civil litigation, State civil litigation, Securities. Home: 62 Rosehill Ave New Rochelle NY 10804-3615 Office: Todtman Nachamie Spizz & Johns PC 425 Park Ave New York NY 10022-3506 E-mail: mhoffman@tnsj-law.com.

HOFFMAN, MICHAEL WILLIAM, lawyer, accountant; b. Bowling Green, Ohio, Feb. 5, 1955; s. Oscar William and Marie Louise Hoffman; m. Lynne Ellen Steele, Aug. 31, 1975; children: Megan, Jessica, Kristine, Robert. BA in Acctg. summa cum laude, Bowling Green State U., 1976; JD, U. Toledo, 1981. Bar: Ohio 1981, Ga. 1983; CPA, Ga., Ohio. Acct. Ernst & Whinney, Toledo, 1976—81; acct., ptnr. Touche Ross & Co., Atlanta, 1981—86; v.p. Profl. Svcs. Network Inc., Atlanta, 1986; assoc. Chamberlain, Hrdlicka, White, Johnson & Williams, Atlanta, 1986—89; ptnr. Somers & Altenbach, Atlanta, 1989—91; chmn., CEO Hoffman & Assocs., Attys. at Law, LLC, Atlanta, 1991—. Organizing dir. Paces Bank & Trust Co., Atlanta; spkr. in field. Author: RIA's U.S.A. News for the Inbound Investor, 1983. Treas. Friendship Force Internat., 1984; mem. troop com. Boy Scouts Am. Recipient Leadership award Boy Scouts Am., Eagle Scout, 1986. Mem.: AICPA, ABA, Estate Planning Coun. of North Ga., Ga. Soc. CPAs (chmn. Tax Forum Com. 1990—92, chmn. Estate Gift & Trust Sect. 1997—2000, v.p. mgmt. com. 2000—01, bd. dirs. 2000—01, Disting. Chair award 1998—99), Am. Assn. Atty.-CPA, State Bar Ga. (fiduciary law sect., tax sect.), Bowling Green State U.-Atlanta Alumni Atty. CPA Assn. (parents adv. coun. 1999—), Atlanta Country Club (bd. dirs. 1998—2001). Republican. Roman Catholic. Avocations: golf, tennis, hiking, camping, reading, fishing. Estate planning, Taxation, general, Corporate, general. Home: 535 Willow Knoll Dr Marietta GA 30067-4647 Office: 6075 Lake Forrest Dr NW Ste 200 Atlanta GA 30328-3845 E-mail: hoff_law@bellsouth.net.

HOFFMAN, NATHANIEL A. lawyer; b. Cin., Mar. 4, 1949; s. Ralph H. and Betty (Goldfarb) H.; m. Sara Naomi Fishman, Aug. 3, 1980; children: Joshua, Rebecca, Esther, David. BA, Yale U., 1971; JD, U. Mich., 1975. Bar: Calif. 1975, Wis. 1983. Assoc. McDonough, Holland & Allen, Sacramento, 1975-78, Herz, Levin, Teper, Sumner & Croysdale, Milw., 1982-85; ptnr. Michael, Best & Friedrich, Milw., 1985—. Atty. N.Y.C. Pub. Devel. Corp., 1980-82. Mem. ABA, State Bar Wis., Milw. Bar Assn., State Bar Calif. Landlord-tenant, Property, real (including real estate development, water). Home: 3258 N 51st Blvd Milwaukee WI 53216-3236 Office: Michael Best & Friedrich 100 E Wisconsin Ave Ste 3300 Milwaukee WI 53202-4108 E-mail: nahoffman@mbf-law.com.

HOFFMAN, PAUL SHAFER, lawyer; b. Harrisburg, Pa., Dec. 12, 1933; s. Paul and Lucy Rose (Shafer) H.; m. Patricia Ann Rudisill, 1958; children: Eric, Kathryn, Julia, Margot. AB in Physics, Gettysburg Coll., 1957; JD, Harvard U., 1962. Bar: N.Y. 1963, U.S. Patent Office 1963, U.S. Dist. Ct. (so. dist.) N.Y. 1977, U.S. Ct. Appeals (2d cir.) 1977, U.S. Supreme Ct. 1977. Assoc. Kenyon & Kenyon, N.Y.C., 1962-63; application analyst IBM-ASDD, Yorktown, N.Y., 1963-66; dir. tech. research Matthew Bender Co., N.Y.C., 1966-68; v.p. Bowne and Co., Inc., N.Y.C., 1968-77; sole practice Croton-on-Hudson, N.Y., 1977—. Mem. Croton Sch. Bd., 1972-75, pres., 1974-75; trustee Village Croton-on-Hudson, 1977-81, acting village justice, 1991—; bd. dirs. Croton Caring Com., Inc., 1982—. Served to cpl. U.S. Army, 1952-54. Mem. N.Y. State Bar Assn. (assoc. editor-in-chief N.Y. State Bar jour. 1991-98), Westchester County Bar Assn., Computer Law Assn. (bd. dirs. 1984-94, 96-2001). Clubs: Harvard (N.Y.C.). Lodges: Masons. Republican. Lutheran. Commercial, contracts (including sales of goods; commercial financing), Computer, Trademark and copyright. Office: 139 Grand St Croton On Hudson NY 10520-2306

HOFFMAN, RICHARD BRUCE, lawyer; b. Columbus, Ohio, June 8, 1947; s. Marion Keith and Ruth Eileen (McLear) Hoffman; m. Sandra Kay Schenkel, July 26, 1975; children: Kipp Hunter, Tyler Blake. BS in Gen. Engring., U. Ill., 1970; JD, DePaul U., 1973; LLM, John Marshall Sch. of Law, 1981. Bar: Ill. 1973, U.S. Dist. Ct. (no. dist.) Ill. 1973, U.S. Patent and Trademark Office 1973, U.S. Ct. Appeals (7th cir.) 1979, U.S. Ct. Appeals (fed. and 9th cirs.) 1982. Assoc. McCaleb, Lucas & Brugman, Chgo., 1973-76, ptnr., 1976-84, Tilton, Fallon, Lungmus & Chestnut, Chgo., 1984-2001, Marshall, Gerstein & Borun LLP, Chgo., 2001—. Mem.: ABA, Intellectual Property Law Assn. Chgo., Internat. Trademark Assn., Am. Intellectual Property Law Assn., Chgo. Bar Assn., Ill. Bar Assn., Union League-Chgo., Lawyers Club Chgo. Federal civil litigation, Patent, Trademark and copyright. Office: Marshall Gerstein & Borun 6300 Sears Tower 233 S Wacker Dr Chicago IL 60606-6402 E-mail: rhoffman@marshallip.com.

HOFFMAN, VALERIE JANE, lawyer; b. Lowville, N.Y., Oct. 27, 1953; d. Russell Francis and Jane Marie (Fowler) H.; m. Michael J. Grillo, Apr. 4, 1996. Student, U. Edinburgh, Scotland, 1973-74; BA summa cum laude, Union Coll., 1975; JD, Boston Coll., 1978. Bar: Ill. 1978, U.S. Dist. Ct. (no. dist.) Ill. 1978, U.S. Ct. Appeals (3rd cir.) 1981, U.S. Ct. Appeals (7th cir.) 1983. Assoc. Seyfarth Shaw, Chgo., 1978—87, ptnr., 1987—. Adj. prof. Columbia Coll., 1985. Contbr. articles to legal publs. Dir. Remains Theatre, Chgo., 1981-95, pres., 1991-93, v.p., 1991-95; dir. The Nat. Conf. for Cmty. and Justice, Chgo. Region, 1993—, nat. trustee, 1995—; trustee bd. advisors Union Coll., 1996-99, trustee, 1999—, trustee, Grad. Coll. Union U., 2003—; dir. AIDS Found. of Chgo., 1997—, sec., 1999—; trustee Union Coll., 1999—, trustee Grad. Sch. of Union Univ., 2003-. Mem. ABA, Chgo. Bar Assn., Law Club Chgo., Univ. Club Chgo. (bd. dirs. 1984-87), Phi Beta Kappa. Administrative and regulatory, Entertainment, Labor (including EEOC, Fair Labor Standards Act, labor-management relations, NLRB, OSHA). Office: Seyfarth Shaw 55 E Monroe St Ste 4400 Chicago IL 60603-5713

HOFFMANN, BRIAN, lawyer; b. N.Y., Apr. 24, 1958; s. Charles and Shirley (Meretsky) H. AB, Colby Coll., 1979; JD, Georgetown U. Law Ctr., 1982. Bar: Wash. 1982, N.Y. 1990, Colo. (inactive) 1992. Assoc. Becker Gurman, Washington, D.C., 1982-84, Skadden Arps., Washington, D.C., 1984-92; shareholder Brownstein Hyatt, Denver, 1992-94; ptnr. McDermott, Will & Emery, N.Y., 1995—99, Cadwalader, Wickersham, & Taft, N.Y.C., 1999—2002, Clifford Chance US LLP, 2002—. Corporate, general, Mergers and acquisitions, Securities. Office: Clifford Chance US LLP 200 Park Ave New York NY 10166 E-mail: brian.hoffmann@cliffordchance.com.

HOFFMANN, CHRISTOPH LUDWIG, lawyer; b. Elsterwerda, Germany, Oct. 9, 1944; came to U.S., 1965; s. Gunther and Ruth (Hornschuh) H.; m. Susan Magnuson, June 18, 1983. Student, Freie U. Berlin, 1964-65; BA, U. Wis., 1966; JD, Harvard U., 1969. Bar: Mass. 1969, R.I. 1977.

Assoc. Bingham, Dana & Gould, Boston, 1969-76; asst. gen. counsel Textron Inc., Providence, 1976-83; v.p., gen. counsel, sec. Pneumo Corp., Boston, 1983-85; sr. v.p., gen. counsel, sec. Pneumo Abex Corp., Boston, 1985-91; v.p., sec., gen. counsel Raytheon Co., Lexington, Mass., 1991-94, sr. v.p. law, human resources and corp. adminstrn., sec., 1994-95, exec. v.p. law and corp. adminstrn., sec., 1995-98; ltd. ptnr. Carlisle 1999, L.P., 1998—. Bd. dirs. Assoc. Industries Mass., 1994, Med. Web Techs., Inc., 2001—; chmn., trustee Deaconess Glover Hosp., 1994—; mem. adv. bd. eLaw Forum Corp., 1999—. Mem. ABA, New Eng. Legal Found. (bd. dirs. 1991-98), Mass. Bar Assn., R.I. Bar Assn., Assn. Gen. Counsel.

HOFFMANN, MARTIN RICHARD, lawyer; b. Stockbridge, Mass., Apr. 20, 1932; m. Margaret Ann McCabe; children: Heidi H. Slye, William, Bern. AB, Princeton U., 1954; LLB, U. Va., 1961. Bar: D.C. 1961. Law clk. U.S. Ct. Appeals (4th cir.), 1961-62; asst. U.S. atty. Washington, 1962-65; minority counsel com. on judiciary Ho. of Reps., Washington, 1965-67; legal counsel to Senator C. Percy, U.S. Senate, Washington, 1967-69; asst. gen. counsel Univ. Computing Co., Dallas, 1969-71; gen. counsel AEC, Washington, 1971-73; spl. asst. to sec. and dep. sec. def. Washington, 1973-74; gen. counsel Dept. Def., Washington, 1974-75; sec. Dept. Army, Washington, 1975-77; mng. ptnr. Gardner, Carton & Douglas, Washington, 1977—89; v.p., gen. counsel, sec. Digital Equipment Corp., Maynard, Mass., 1989-93; of counsel Skadden, Arps, Slate, Meagher & Flom, Washington, 1996-2000. Sr. vis. fellow Ctr. for Policy, Tech. and Indsl. Devel., MIT, Cambridge, 1993-95; bd. dirs. Castle Energy, Phila., Sea Change Corp., Maynard, Mass., Mitretek Systems, Inc., Falls ch., Va.; chmn. Beamhit LLC, Columbia, Md. Maj. USAR, 1954-73. Mem. Met. Club. Home: 1546 Hampton Hill Cir Mc Lean VA 22101

HOFFMANN, MICHAEL RICHARD, lawyer; b. Des Moines, Apr. 26, 1947; s. Robert Wyman and Margaret Inez Wagner (stepmother) H. and Patricia Hilliard; m. Amy Marie Gales; children: Kurt Michael, Kristen Elaine, Kevin Richard. BS in Chemistry and Zoology, U. Iowa, 1969; JD, Drake U., 1972; LLM in Patent and Trade Regulation, George Washington U., 1973. Bar: Iowa 1972, U.S. Ct. Customs and Patent Appeals 1972, U.S. Patent and Trademark Office 1973, U.S. Dist. Ct. (so. and no. dists.) Iowa 1974, U.S. Ct. Appeals (8th cir.) 1976, U.S. Supreme Ct. 1977. Clerk Jones, Hoffmann & Davison, Des Moines, 1970-73; assoc. Bacon and Thomas, Arlington, Va., 1973-74; assoc. Jones, Hoffmann & Davison, Des Moines, 1974-79, ptnr., 1979-83; pres. Michael R. Hoffmann, P.C., Des Moines, 1983-95; pvt. practice, 1995-2002; atty. Hoffmann Law Firm, P.C., 2002—; del. U.S./Japan Bilateral Session: A New Era in Legal and Econ. Relations, Tokyo, 1988; mem. Iowa Def. Counsel, Def. Research Inst., Inc. Recipient Am. Jurisprudence award Bancroft-Whitney Co. and Lawyers Coop. Pub. Co., 1970-72. Mem. Iowa State Bar Assn., ABA (sci. and tech. sect.), Iowa Patent Bar Assn. (charter mem.), Am. Patent Law Assn., Am. Judicature Soc., Polk County Bar Assn., Iowa Assn. Workers' Compensation Lawyers, Internat. Assn. Indsl. Accident Bds. and Commns., Prairie Club (pres. Des Moines chpt. 1993-94), Nat. Rifle Club (Washington). Office: 3708 75th St Des Moines IA 50322-3002 E-mail: robolaw@aol.com.

HOFFMEYER, WILLIAM FREDERICK, lawyer, educator; b. York, Pa., Dec. 20, 1936; s. Frederick W. and Mary B. (Stremmel) H.; m. Betty J. Hoffmeyer, Feb. 6, 1960 (div.); 1 child, Louise C.; m. Karen L. Semmelman, 1985. AB, Franklin and Marshall Coll., 1958; JD, Dickinson Sch. Law, 1961. Bar: Pa. 1962, U.S. Dist Ct. (mid. dist.) Pa. 1981, U.S. Supreme Ct. 1983. Pvt. practice law, 1962-81; sr. ptnr. Hoffmeyer & Semmelman, 1982—. Adj. prof. real estate law York Coll. Pa., 1980-92, real estate law, paral legal program Pa. State U., 1978—. Autor: Abstractor's Bible, 1981, Pennsylvania Real Estate Installment Sales Contrct Manual, 1981, Real Estate Settlement Procedures, 1982, Contracts of Sale, 1984, How to Plot a Deed Description, 1985; author, lectr., moderator and course planner numerous Pa. Bar Inst. CLE Programs. Recipient Disting. Svc. award Gen. Alumni Assn. Dickinson Sch. Law, 1993, Pa. Bar medal, 1997. Mem. ABA, Pa. Bar Assn. (co-chmn. unauthorized practice of law com.), York County Bar Assn. (chmn. continuing legal edn. com. 1992-96), Am. Coll. Real Estate Lawyers, Lions (past pres. East York club), York Area C. of C. (chair small bus. support network 1997-99), Masons, Shriners (past pres. York County). General practice, Probate (including wills, trusts), Property, real (including real estate development, water). Address: 30 N George St York PA 17401-1214

HOFMANN, JOHN RICHARD, JR., retired lawyer; b. Oakland, Calif., June 24, 1922; s. John Richard and Esther (Starkweather) H.; m. Mary Macdonough, Feb. 6, 1954; children: John Richard III, Gretchen Hofmann, Sarah Worthington Hack, John Macdonough Alexander. AB, U. Calif., Berkeley, 1943; JD, Harvard U., 1949. Bar: Calif. 1950. Assoc. Pillsbury, Madison & Sutro, San Francisco, 1949-58, ptnr., 1959-92, of counsel, 1992-96, ret., 1996—; exec. v.p. MPC Ins., Ltd., 1988-96. City atty. City of Belvedere (Calif.), 1957-58. Mem. Calif. Bar Assn. Corporate, general, Insurance, Securities. Office: Pillsbury Winthrop LLP PO Box 7880 San Francisco CA 94120-7880

HOFMEISTER, KENT S. lawyer; BFA in Journalism, JD, So. Meth. U. Founding ptnr. Brown & Hofmeister, 1986—; asst. city atty. Dallas City Attys. Office, 1977—86, chief fed. litigation divsn. Bd. dirs. Dallas Summer Musicals. Mem.: FBA (pres., mem. exec. com. 1994—, pres. Dallas chpt., fifth cir. officer, chair fed. litigation sect., sect. coord.). Avocations: guitar, singing. General civil litigation. Office: Brown & Hofmeister 1717 Main St Dallas TX 75201*

HOFSTEAD, JAMES WARNER, laundry machinery company executive, lawyer; b. Jackson, Tenn., Feb. 3, 1913; s. Harry Oliver and Agnes Lucile (Blackard) H.; m. Ellen Frances Bowers, Dec. 27, 1940 (dec.); 1 child, Eda Lucile. AB, Vanderbilt U., 1935, LLB, 1938. Bar: Tenn. Pvt. practice law; v.p., bd. dirs. United Tel. Co., Nashville, 1969—, emeritus; ret.; pres., bd. dirs. Wishy Washy, Inc., Nashville, 1946—, Wishy Sales Inc., Nashville, 1959—, pres. emeritus. Capt. USMC, 1942-45. Mem. SAR (nat. committeeman, state pres. emeritus, nat. trustee), SCV, Vanderbilt Bar Assn. (pres. emeritus), So. Srs. Golf Assn., Soc. of Cincinnati, English Spkg. Union (chmn.), Soc. Colonial Wars (past gov. Tenn., past dep. gov. gen.), Nashville C. of C., Belle Meade Country Club, 200 Club, Exch. Club, Eccentric Club (London), Gasparilla 48 Club, Cumberland Club (charter), Sigma Chi. Home: 504 Elmington # 406 Nashville TN 37205 Office: 3729 Charlotte Pike Nashville TN 37209-3734

HOGAN, ILONA MODLY, lawyer; b. Erlangen, Fed. Republic of Germany, Nov. 23, 1947; arrived in U.S., 1951, naturalized, 1960; d. Stephen Bela and Gunda Pauline (Gastiger) Modly; m. Lawrence J. Hogan, Mar. 16, 1974; children: Matthew Lawrence, Michael Alexander, Patrick Nicholas, Timothy Stefan. Student, Marymount Coll., 1965-67; AB in Internat. Affairs, George Washington U., 1969; JD, Georgetown U., 1974. Bar: D.C. 1975, Md. 1975. Intern and clk. AID, 1965-69; adminstrv. and legis. asst. to mem. Ho. of Reps., 1969-72; editor Legis. Digest, Ho. of Reps., Washington, 1972-73; asso. and law clk. firm Trammell, Rand, Nathan and Lincoln, Washington, 1972-74; mng. ptnr. firm Hogan and Hogan, Washington and Md., 1974-93; of counsel Venable, Baetjer, Howard & Civiletti, Washington, 1989-91; pres. Amcom Inc., 1978—; of counsel Salisbury & McLister, Frederick, Md., 1993-2001; global mgr. Bechtel Telecom., 2001—. Mem. Prince George's Bd. Libr. Trustees, Md., 1976—78, Prince George's County Econ. Devel. Adv. Com., 1979—82; v.p. St. John's Sch. Bd., 1987—88, pres., 1989; treas. U. Md. Bd. Regents, 1988—95; trustee St. James Sch., 1989—90; mem. Lawyers Steering com. for Reagan-Bush, 1980; nat. vice-chmn. Assn. Execs. for Reagan-Bush, 1984; mem. bus. and industry adv. com. 50th Am. Presdl. Inaugural, 1985; mem. Md. steering com. Bush for Pres., 1988; mem. Presdl. Personnel Adv. Com., 1989, Gov.'s Higher Edn. Transition Team, 1988; elected mem. County Commrs. Frederick County, 1994—2001; Frederick County co-chair Bush-Cheney Campaign, 2000; bd. advisors Frostburg State U., 2001—03; trustee Frederick C.C. Found., 2001—03, Md. Higher Edn. Commn., 2003—. Mem.: ABA, D.C. Bar, Md. Bar Assn. Republican. Roman Catholic. Home: 5614 New Design Rd Frederick MD 21703-8306 Office: 5275 Westview Dr Frederick MD 21703-8306 E-mail: ilonahogan@aol.com., imhogan@bechtel.com.

HOGAN, JOHN W., JR., lawyer; b. Feb. 1939; BA, Coll. Holy Cross, 1961; JD, Conn. U., 1964. Bar: Conn. 1964. Sr. prin. Hogan & Rini, PC, New Haven. Mem. Nahley Mediation Panel, 1989—90; mng. trustee The David T. Langrock Found. Class gifts and bequests chair Coll. of the Holy Cross; chair New Haven Devel. Commn.; dir. The New Haven Regional Leadership Coun.; trustee Hosp. St. Raphael; dir., sec. and counsel The Found. of the Greater New Haven C. of C. and The Greater New Haven C. of C.; dir. Friends of Legal Svcs., New Haven; dir., sec. Shubert Performing Arts Ctr.; dir. The New Haven Land Trust; pres., dir. Vis. Nurse Assn. Greater New Haven. Recipient Citizen of Yr. award, Conn. Cts. of Probate, 1989. Mem.: Conn. Bar Assn (pres.-elect 2002—03, v.p. 2001—02, clients' security fund 1973—91, chair clients' security fund 1985—91, ho. dels. 1978—83, exec. com. banking law sect. 1981—98, chair awards com. 1996—2000, John Eldred Shields Meml. Disting. Profl. Svc. award). Estate planning, Insurance, Securities. Office: Conn Bar Assn PO Box 350 30 Bank St New Britain CT 06050-0350 also: Hogan & Rini PC 234 Church St New Haven CT*

HOGAN, MICHAEL R(OBERT), judge; b. Oregon City, Oreg., Sept. 24, 1946; married; 3 children. AB, U. Oreg. Honors Coll., 1968; JD, Georgetown U., 1971. Bar: Oreg. 1971, U.S. Ct. Appeals (9th cir.) 1971. Law clk. to chief judge U.S. Dist. Ct. Oreg., Portland, 1971-72; assoc. Miller, Anderson, Nash, Yerke and Wiener, Portland, 1972-73; magistrate judge U.S. Dist. Ct. Oreg., Eugene, 1973-91, dist. judge, 1991—, chief judge, 1995—; bankduptcy judge U.S. Dist. Oreg., Eugene, 1973-80. Mem. ABA, Oreg. State Bar Assn. Office: US Courthouse 211 E 7th Ave Eugene OR 97401-2773

HOGAN, THOMAS PATRICK, lawyer; b. Binghamton, N.Y., Mar. 30, 1948; s. Edward P. and Elizabeth Hogan; m. Linda S. Scheffler, Aug. 18, 1973; children: Edward, Michael, Kathleen. BBA, U. Notre Dame, 1970, JD, 1974. Atty. Rhoades, McKee, Boer, Goodrich & Titta, Grand Rapids, Mich., 1974—. Adj. faculty Grand Rapids C.C., 1980-97; chmn. exec. com. Rhoades, McKee, Boer, Goodrich and Titta, 1996—. Dir. Kent County Am. Cancer Soc., Grand Rapids, 1995-01, Grand Rapids Dental Found., 1996-01. Mem. State Bar Mich., Grand Rapids Bar Assn. Corporate, general, Estate planning, Property, real (including real estate development, water). Office: Rhoades McKee Boer Goodrich and Titta 600 Waters Bldg 161 Ottawa Ave NW Grand Rapids MI 49503-2701

HOGG, JESSE STEPHEN, lawyer; b. Whitesburg, Ky., Dec. 24, 1931; s. Doyle and Crystal (Eversole) H.; m. Lorella Joyce Graham, Jan. 26, 1957 (div. 1978); children: Laura Ellen, Stephen Graham. BSBA, Morehead State U., 1953; JD, U. Ky., 1958. Bar: Ky. 1958, Fla. 1962, U.S. Dist. Ct. (no., middle and so. dists.) Fla., U.S. Ct. Appeals (2d, 4th, 5th, 6th, 11th cirs.), U.S. Supreme Ct. Pvt. practice, Winchester, Ky., 1958-62; assoc. Fowler, White, Collins, Gillan, Humkey and Trenam, Tampa, Fla., 1962-65, ptnr., 1965-68, head dept. labor law, 1968-69; sr. ptnr. Hogg, Allen, Ryce, Norton and Blue P.A., various locations, Fla., 1969—2000, Hogg, Ryce & Sspencer, Coral Gables, Fla., 2000—. Served with U.S. Army, 1954-55. Mem. ABA (lab law sect. 1962—), Fla. Bar Assn. (labor law com. 1962—), Ky. Bar Assn. Clubs: Ocean Reef. Republican. Avocations: golf, boating, sport fishing. Construction, Labor (including EEOC, Fair Labor Standards Act, labor-management relations, NLRB, OSHA). Home: 7701 Erwin Rd Miami FL 33143-6249 Office: Hogg et al 7701 Erwin Rd Miami FL 33143

HOGLUND, JOHN ANDREW, lawyer; b. Cleve., July 19, 1945; s. Paul Franklin and Louise (Anderson) H.; m. Patricia Olwell, May 27, 1972; children: Britt Hannah, Maeve Olwell, Marc Paul-Joseph. BA, Augustana Coll., 1967; JD, George Washington U., 1972. Bar: Wash. 1973, U.S. Dist. Ct. (we. dist.) Wash. 1973, U.S. Ct. Appeals (9th cir.) 1973. Law clk. Wash. State Supreme Ct., 1973-74; assoc. Mooney, Cullen & Holm, Olympia, 1973-75; ptnr. Cullen, Holm, Hoglund & Foster, Olympia, 1975-81; pvt. practice, Olympia, 1981—; pres. Hoglund Group Internat., 1987—. Adj. prof. law sch. U. Puget Sound, Tacoma, Wash., 1989-90, trustee, 1984-92. Co-author: SKYCYL Practicing Law Manual, 1986-95, WSBA Book Automobile Negligence Law, 1988. Vice chmn. Group Health Coop., Olympia, 1978, Thurston County Dem. Cen. Com., Olympia, 1980; chmn. bd. dirs. S.W. Wash. Health Sys. Agy., 1979; alumni bd. dirs. George Washington U. Nat. Law Ctr., 1994-97, emeritus mem., 1997—. With U.S. Army, 1967-69. Named Boss of Yr. Thurston County Legal Secs. Assn., 1985. Mem. ABA, Thurston County Bar Assn. (trustee 1988-90, Svc. awards 1987, 90), ATLA, Wash. State Trial Lawyers Assn. (pres. 1983-84, Brandeis award 1980), Wash. State Trial Lawyers Found. (pres. 1985-87), Wash. State Bar Assn. (chmn. UPL com. 1979, CPR com., pub. rels. com., chmn. Lawyer Protection Fund com. 1999), Nat. Law Ctr. George Washington U. (alumni bd. 1994-2000), Kiwanis (Disting. Pres. award 1980). Insurance, Personal injury (including property damage).

HOGUE, TERRY GLYNN, lawyer; b. Merced, Calif., Sept. 23, 1944; s. Glynn Dale and Lillian LaVonne (Carter) H.; m. Joanne Laura Sharples, Oct. 3, 1969; children: Morgan Taylor, Whitney Shannon. BA, U. Calif., Fresno, 1966, postgrad., 1967; JD, U. Calif., San Francisco, 1972. Bar: Calif. 1972, Idaho 1975, U.S. Dist. Ct. (cen. dist.) Calif. 1973, U.S. Dist. Ct. Idaho 1975, U.S. Supreme Ct. 1976. Assoc. Reid, Babbage & Coil, Riverside, Calif., 1972-75; pvt. practice, Hailey, Idaho, 1975-77; ptnr. Campion & Hogue, Hailey, 1977-80, Hogue & Speck, Hailey and Ketchum, Idaho, 1980-82, Hogue, Speck & Aanestad, Hailey and Ketchum, 1982-97, Hogue & Dunlap, L.L.P., Hailey and Ketchum, 1998—. Bd. dirs. Blaine County Med. Ctr., Hailey, 1975-91. Sgt. U.S. Army, 1969-71. Mem. ABA, Calif. Bar Assn., Idaho Bar Assn. (hearing panel of profl. conduct bd. 1991-97, chmn. profl. conduct bd. 1994-95), 5th Jud. Dist. Bar Assn. (magistrate com. 1991-93, ethics com. 1991-93), Idaho Trial Lawyers Assn. (bd. dirs. 1982-93, treas. 1985-86, sec. 1986-87, v.p. 1988-89, pres. 1989-90), Assn. Trial Lawyers Am. (sec. coun. of pres. 1989-90, Atla Weideman Wisocki award 1990), Am. Inns. of Ct. (charter Master Bench chpt.), Hailey C. of C. (bd. dirs. 1975-83), Rotary. General civil litigation, Family and matrimonial, General practice. Home: PO Box 1259 500 Onyx Dr Ketchum ID 83340-1259 Office: Hogue & Dunlap LLP PO Box 460 Hailey ID 83333-0460 also: PO Box 538 Ketchum ID 83340-0538

HOHMAN, A. J., JR., lawyer; b. San Antonio, Dec. 19, 1934; s. A.J. and Helen (Stehling) H.; m. Mary C. Leonard, Aug. 30, 1958; children: Kristin Marie, Jonathan David. BA in Econs., LLB, St Mary's U., San Antonio, 1959. Bar: Tex. 1961, U.S. Dist. Ct. (we. and so. dists.) Tex. 1970, U.S. Ct. Appeals (5th cir.) 1971; U.S. Supreme Ct. 1974. Asst. dist. atty. Bexar County, San Antonio, 1961-64; ptnr. Hohman, Georges & Gehring, San Antonio, 1964-93. Editor: Barrister News, 1958-59. Bd. dirs. St. Peter's and St. Joseph's Ch.'s Home, San Antonio, 1974-2003, 92-96, pres., 1980-81, 86-87; pres. Ursuline Acad., San Antonio, 1982-84, bd. dirs., 1984-87. 1st lt. U.S. Army, 1959-61. Fellow Am. Bd. Trial Advocates (pres. San Antonio chpt. 1983-84); mem. Tex. Trial Lawyers Assn. (assoc. dir. 1981-88), San Antonio Trial Lawyers Assn. (pres. 1980), Am. Trial Lawyers Assn. (1975-93). Democrat. Roman Catholic. Avocations: travel, all outdoor activities, reading. General civil litigation, State civil litigation, Personal injury (including property damage). Office: Hohman Georges & Gehring 4940 Broadway Ste 101 San Antonio TX 78209 Fax: 210-223-1496.

HOHNHORST, JOHN CHARLES, judge; b. Jerome, Idaho, Dec. 25, 1952; m. Raelene Casper; children: Jennifer, Rachel, John. BS in Polit. Sci./Pub. Adminstrn., U. Idaho, 1975, JD cum laude, 1978. Bar: Idaho 1978, U.S. Dist. Ct. Idaho 1978, U.S. Ct. Appeals (9th cir.) 1980, U.S. Ct. Claims 1983, U.S. Supreme Ct. 1987. Adminstrv. asst. to Sen. John M. Barker Idaho State Senate, 1975; ptnr. Hepworth, Lezamiz & Hohnhorst, Twin Falls, Idaho, 1978—2001; dist. judge 5th Jud. Dist. Ct., Twin Falls County, Idaho, 2001—. Contbr. articles to profl. jours. Mem. planning & zoning commn. City of Twin Falls, 1987-90. Mem. ABA, ATLA, Idaho State Bar (commr. 1990-93, pres. 1993), Am. Coll. Trial Lawyers, Idaho Trial Lawyers Assn. (regional dir. 1985-86), 5th Dist. Bar Assn. (treas. 1987-88, v.p. 1988-89, pres. 1989-90), Am. Acad. Appellate Lawyers, Greater Twin Falls C. of C. (chmn. magic valley leadership program 1988-89, bd. dirs. 1989-92), Phi Kappa Tau (Beta Gamma chpt., Phi award 1988). Office: Theron Ward Jud Bldg 427 Shoshoe St N PO Box 126 427 Twin Falls ID 83303-0126

HOINES, DAVID ALAN, lawyer; b. St. Paul, Oct. 18, 1946; s. Arnold H. and Patricia (Olson) H.; m. Bonnie K. Smith, June 4, 1983. BA, Calif. State U., San Jose, 1969; JD, Santa Clara U., 1972; LLM in Taxation, Boston U., 1973. Bar: Fla. 1975, Calif. 1975, N.Y. 1999, U.S. Dist. Ct. (so. dist.) Fla. 1975, U.S. Dist. Ct. (no. dist.) Calif. 1980, U.S. Dist. Ct. (mid. dist.) Fla. 1984, U.S. Dist. Ct. (ctrl. dist.) Calif. 1990, U.S. Ct. Claims 1980, U.S. Tax Ct. 1975, U.S. Ct. Appeals (fed. cir.) 1990, U.S. Ct. Appeals (4th cir.) 1985, U.S. Ct. Appeals (5th cir.) 1978, U.S. Ct. Appeals (9th cir.) 1980, U.S. Ct. Appeals (11th cir.) 1981, U.S. Supreme Ct. 1980; cert. civil trial lawyer. Pvt. practice, Ft. Lauderdale, Fla., 1975—. Adj. instr. Nova U. Ctr. for Study of Law, 1977. Author: Taxman and the Textbook, The Ripon Forum, 1972. Mem. ABA, ATLA., Broward County Bar Assn., Fla. Bar Assn., Calif. Bar Assn., State Bar of N.Y., Hundred Club of Broward County, Tau Delta Phi. Avocations: ocean diving (free and scuba), snowskiing, running, boating, reading. General civil litigation, Probate (including wills, trusts), Taxation, general. Office: 1290 E Oakland Park Blvd Fort Lauderdale FL 33334-4443 E-mail: dahfl@aol.com.

HOLCOMB, JEFFREY G. lawyer; b. Hamilton, Ohio, Dec. 16, 1971; s. John Frederick and Judith Ellen Holcomb; m. Brandi L. Holcomb, July 13, 2001. BA in History, Xavier U., Cin., 1994; JD, U. Toledo, Ohio, 1998. Bar: Ohio 1998, U.S. Dist. Ct. (so. dist.) Ohio 1999. Law clk. Holcomb & Hyde LLP, Hamilton, Ohio, 1995, County Ct. Common Pleas, 1996—97; legal intern City of Maumee Prosecutor's Office, Ohio, 1998; atty. Holcomb & Hyde LLP, Hamilton, 1998—2000, John A. Garretson Co., LPA, Hamilton, 2000—. Mem.: ABA, Ohio Acad. Trial Lawyers, Butler County Bar Assn., Ohio State Bar Assn., Scottish Rite, Masons. Family and matrimonial, Personal injury (including property damage). Office: John A Garretson Co LPA PO Box 1166 Hamilton OH 45012

HOLCOMB, LYLE DONALD, JR., retired lawyer; b. Miami, Fla., Feb. 3, 1929; s. Lyle Donald and Hazel Irene (Watson) H.; m. Barbara Jean Roth, July 12, 1952; children: Susan Holcomb Davis, Scott H. (deceased), Douglas J., Mark E. BA, U. Mich., 1951; JD, U. Fla., 1954. Bar: U.S. Ct. Appeals (5th and 11th cirs.) 1981, U.S. Supreme Ct. 1966. Ptnr. Holcomb & Holcomb, Miami, 1955-72; assoc. Copeland, Therrel, Baisden & Peterson, Miami Beach, Fla., 1972-75; ptnr. Therrel, Baisden, Stanton, Wood & Setlin, Miami Beach, Fla., 1976-85, Therrel, Baisden & Meyer Weiss, Miami Beach, Fla., 1985-93; pvt. practice Tallahassee, Fla., 1993-95. Organizing pres. So. Fla. Migrant Legal Svcs. Program (now Fla. Rural Legal Svcs.), 1966-68. Mem. exec. coun. So. Fla. coun. Boy Scouts Am., 1958-93; past pres., past counselor Miami chpt. Huguenot Soc. Fla. Served with USNR, 1947-53. Recipient Silver Beaver award So. Fla. coun. Boy Scouts Am., 1966. Fellow Am. Coll. Trust and Estate Counsel, 1980-94, Acad. Fla. Probate and Trust Litigation Attys., 1980-95; mem. Dade County Bar Assn. (dir. 1960-71, sec. 1963-71), Miami Beach Bar Assn. (pres. 1980), Estate Planning Coun. Greater Miami, Soc. Mayflower Descs. (past pres. Miami club, past counselor soc.), SAR (past pres. Miami chpt.), Univ. Yacht Club. Republican. Mem. United Ch. of Christ. Home: 3538 Killarney Plaza Dr Tallahassee FL 32309-3491 E-mail: lholcomb23@aol.com.

HOLDAWAY, RONALD M. retired federal judge; b. Afton, Wyo. m. Judy Janowski, Dec. 1958; children: Denise, Georgia. BA, U. Wyo., 1957, JD, 1959. Bar: Wyo. 1959, U.S. Dist. Ct. (Wyo.), U.S. Ct. Mil. Appeals, 1960, U.S. Army Ct. Mil. Rev., U.S. Supreme Ct., 1967. Commd. 2nd lt. U.S. Army., 1960, advanced through grades to brig. gen., 1989; legal staff officer U.S. Army, Ft. Lewis, Washington, 1960-63, legal staff, 1963-66, instr. criminal law, Judge Advocate Gen.'s Sch., 1966-69, staff judge advocate 1st cav. divsn., 1969-70, chief govt. appellate divsn., 1971-75, chief of pers., 1975-77, staff judge advocate Stuttgart, Germany, 1978-80, exec. to judge advocate gen. Washington, 1980-81, asst. judge advocate gen., 1981-83; judge advocate U.S. Army Europe, Heidelberg, Germany, 1983-87; chief judge Ct. Mil. Review U.S. Army, Washington, 1987-89; judge U.S. Ct. of Vets. Appeals, Washington DC, 1990—2002; ret., 2002. Decorated Bronze Star, Legion of Merit, Disting. Svc. medal with Oak Leaf Cluster, Meritorious Svc. medal with Oak Leaf Cluster, Air medal, Nat. Def. Svc. medal, Vietnam Campaign medal with 4 campaign stars, Vietnam Svc. medal, Overseas medal (3). Mem. Wyo. State Bar Assn., Assn. U.S. Army, Army Navy Club. Office: US Ct of Appeals for Vets Claims 625 Indiana Ave NW Ste 900 Washington DC 20004-2917

HOLDEN, FREDERICK DOUGLASS, JR., lawyer; b. Stockton, Calif., Nov. 21, 1949; s. Frederick Douglass and Sarah Frances (Young) H.; m. Patricia Brierton, June 25, 1988; children: Elizabeth, Andrew. BA, U. Calif., Santa Barbara, 1971; JD, U. Calif., Davis, 1974. Bar: Calif. 1974, U.S. Dist. Ct. (no., cen., ea. and so. dists.) Calif. 1974, U.S. Ct. Appeals (9th cir.) 1974, D.C. 1996, U.S. Dist. Ct. D.C. 1996, U.S. Supreme Ct. 2001. Assoc. Brobeck, Phleger & Harrison LLP, San Francisco, 1974-81, ptnr., 1981—2003; co-chair bench-bar liaison com. U.S. Bankruptcy Ct. No. Dist. Calif., 2002—03; ptnr. Orrick, Herrington & Sutcliffe, LLP, 2003—. Mem. faculty Practising Law Inst., 1990; spkr. Nat. Conf. Bankruptcy Judges, 1987, 91, Banking Law Inst., 1986, Calif. Continuing Legal Edn. of Bar, Calif., 1983-85, Calif. State Bar, 1993; bd. dirs. Bay Area Bankruptcy Forum. Mng. editor U. Calif. Davis Law Rev., 1974. Fellow Am. Coll. Bankruptcy; mem. ABA (bus. bankruptcy com., spkr. 1991, 95), Calif. Bar Assn. (commendation 1983), San Francisco Bar Assn. (cert. appreciation 1985, 88, 90, 95, vice chair 2003—), Turnaround Mgmt. Assn. (dir., sec. 1994-96), Am. Bankruptcy Inst., San Francisco Yacht Club, Sigma Pi (pres. 1970). Democrat. Avocations: triathlons, skiing, sailing. Bankruptcy, Commercial, contracts (including sales of goods; commercial financing), Mergers and acquisitions. Home: 140 Bella Vista Ave Belvedere CA 94920-2466 Office: Orrick Herrington & Sutcliffe LLP Old Fed Res Bank Bldg 400 Sansome St San Francisco CA 94111 E-mail: fholden@orrick.com.

HOLDEN, JULIA, lawyer; b. Liverpool, Eng. BA with Honors in Law and German, U. Sussex, Brighton, Eng., 1986. Bar: Eng. and Wales 1990. Trainee solicitor Pritchard, Englefield & Tobin, London, 1988-90; asst. solicitor Slaughter & May, London, 1990-91; with Trevisan & Cuonzo Avvocati, Milan. Intellectual property, Private international, Trademark and copyright. Office: Trevisan & Cuonzo Avvocati Via Brera 6 Milan 20121 Italy E-mail: jholden@trevisan.inet.it.

HOLDEN, WILLIAM HOYT, JR., lawyer; b. Chgo. s. William Hoyt and Bernice Elizabeth (McKenzie) H.; m. Mary Ann Kula, June 23, 1954 (div. June 1982); children: William, Christopher, Sarah, Peter. BS, U. Ill., 1954; JD, U. Md., Balt., 1965. Bar: Md. 1965, U.S. Supreme Ct. 1969. Assoc. Weinberg and Green, Balt., 1965-72, ptnr., 1973-83; sr. v.p. CRI, Inc., Rockville, Md., 1983-85; sr. advisor Legg Mason Wood Walker, Inc., Balt., 1985-86; pvt. practice Bethesda, Md., 1987—. Pres., bd. dirs. Am. Franchise Cons., Inc., Bethesda, 1987—, Mid-Atlantic Title Closing, Inc.

Capt. USNR, 1977, ret., 1982. Mem. Order of Coif, Rotary. Republican. Corporate, general, Property, real (including real estate development, water), Taxation, general. E-mail: wholden1@cox.net.

HOLDER, JANICE MARIE, state supreme court justice; b. Canonsburg, Pa., Aug. 29, 1949; d. Louis V. and Sylvia (Abraham) H.; m. George W. Loveland II, June 5, 1976 (div. Mar. 1987). Student, Allegheny Coll., 1967-68, Sorbonne, 1970; BS summa cum laude, U. Pitts., 1971; JD, Duquesne U., 1975. Bar: Pa. 1975, Tenn. 1979, D.C. 1988. Sr. law clk. to chief judge U.S. Dist. Ct. for Western Dist. Pa., Pitts., 1975-77; assoc. Catalano & Catalano, P.C., Pitts., 1977-79, Holt, Batchelor, Spicer & Ryan, Memphis, 1980-82; pvt. practice Memphis, 1983-87; assoc. James S. Cox & Assocs., Memphis, 1987-89; pvt. practice law Memphis, 1989-90; judge 30th Jud. Dist., Memphis, 1990-96; justice Tenn. Supreme Ct., 1996—. Solicitor Borough of McDonald (Pa.), 1978-79. Bd. dirs. Alliance for Blind and Visually Impaired, Memphis, 1985—94, Midtown Mental Health Ctr., 1995—97; trustee Memphis Bot. Garden Found., 1996—2002; mem. state coordinating coun. Tenn. Task Force Against Domestic Violence, 1994—96. Fellow: Tenn. Bar Found. (trustee 1995—99); mem.: ABA, Tenn. Trial Judges Assn. (exec. com. 1994—96), Tenn. Lawyers' Assn. for Women, Memphis Trial Lawyers Assn. (bd. dirs. 1988—90), Am. Inns Ct., Tenn. Jud. Conf. (treas. 1993—94, exec. com. 1993—96), Assn. for Women Attys. (treas. 1989, v.p. 1991, Marion Griffin-Frances Loring award 1999), Memphis Bar Assn. (bd. dirs. 1986—87, 1993—94, editor Memphis Bar Forum 1987—91, 1993—94, sec. 1993, treas. 1994, Sam A. Myar award 1990, Judge of Yr. divorce and family law sect. 1992, Chancellor Charles A. Rond award Outstanding Jurist 1992), Tenn. Bar Assn., Am. Bar Found. Office: Tenn Supreme Ct 119 S Main St Ste 310 Memphis TN 38103-3678

HOLIDAY, GREGORY, administrative law judge; b. Detroit, Nov. 27, 1951; s. Christor and Merdis (Jackson) H.; m. Zenobia Ann Watts, Mar. 24, 1985; 1 child, Kai Alano. Student, Ferris State Coll., 1970; BS, Eastern Mich. U., 1974; JD, U. Detroit, 1977; postgrad., U. Mich., Wayne State U., Detroit Coll., 1977-88. Bar: Mich. 1977, U.S. Dist. Ct. (ea. dist.) Mich. 1978, U.S. Supreme Ct. 1983. Staff atty. Oakland County Legal Aid, Royal Oak Twp., Mich., 1977-80; supervising atty. Oakland Livingston Legal Aid, Ferndale, Mich., 1980-81; adminstrv. law judge Mich. Dept. Licensing and Regulation, Lansing, 1981-83, adminstrv. law judge, acting dir., 1983—; adj. prof. Cooley Law Sch., Lansing, 1989—. Faculty advisor Nat. Jud. Coll., Reno, 1982-85, '87-90, mem. faculty, 1999—, chmn. faculty coun. 2001-2002; chmn. state coordinating planning commn. Nat. Conf. Adminstrv. Law Judges, Washington, 1985—; coord., host 1986 Adminstrv. Law Program, Ann Arbor, Mich. Contbr. articles to profl. jours. Arbitrator Better Bus. Bur. Met. Detroit, 1981—; trustee Otis Bryant Jr. Scholarship Fund, Oak Park, Mich., 1981—; chmn. Citizens Task Force for Royal Oak Twp., Oakland County, Mich., 1984—; pres. Huntington Estates Homeowner Assn., Oak Park, 1986—; bd. dirs. Southeast Mich. State Employees Fed. Credit Union, Southfield, 1987-2002, South Oakland County chpt. NAACP, 1990-96. Reginald H. Smith fellow, 1977-79; recipient Spirit of Black Enterprise award Sanders and Assocs., 1985. Mem. ABA (com. chmn. 1985—), Nat. Bar Assn., Oakland County Bar Assn., Wolverine Bar Assn., Assn. Black Judges Mich., Nat. Conf. Adminstrv. Law Judges (exec. com. 1986-88), Mich. Assn. Adminstrv. Law Judges (bd. dirs. 1982-90, pres. 1985-86), Mich. Bar Assn. (exec. coun. adminstrv. law sect. 1986—), Park Place Investment Club (pres. 1982-84), Econ. Club Detroit (jr. exec. 1981-86). Baptist. Avocations: golf, tennis, racquetball, whist, bicycling. Office: MI Dept Labor & Economic Growth Bur Hearings 3026 W Grand Blvd Ste 2-700 Detroit MI 48202

HOLLADAY, ROBERT LAWSON, SR., lawyer; b. Greenwood, Miss., Jan. 28, 1948; s. Robert William and Jo Holladay; children: Rob, Jennifer. BS, Delta State U., 1970; JD, U. Miss., 1973. Bar: Miss. 1973, U.S. Dist. Ct. (no. dist.) Miss. 1973, U.S. Ct. Appeals (5th cir.) 1975, U.S. Supreme Ct. 1991. Ptnr. Towsend, McWilliams & Holladay LLP, Drew, Miss., 1973—. Miss. Bar Found. fellow 1983. Mem. Miss. Trial Lawyers Assn. (bd. dirs. 1975-80). Avocations: hunting, fishing. General civil litigation, Criminal, Personal injury (including property damage). Office: Townsend McWilliams & Holladay LLP PO Box 288 Drew MS 38737-0288 Fax: (662) 745-8518. E-mail: tmh@tecinfo.com.

HOLLAND, CHARLES JOSEPH, lawyer; b. Ottumwa, Iowa, Oct. 6, 1949; m. Nancy Jo Daniels, Aug. 29, 1970; children: Tyler, Emily, Clare. BA, U. Iowa, 1971, JD (with high honors), 1977. Bar: Iowa 1977, U.S. Dist. Ct. (so. dist., no. dist.) Iowa 1977. Assoc. Hayek, Hayek & Hayek, Iowa City, 1977-81; ptnr. Hayek, Hayek, Holland & Brown, Iowa City, 1981—. Dir. Iowa City Downtown Assn., 1988—. Mem. Assn. Trial Lawyers Iowa, Iowa Coun. Sch. Bd. Attys., ABA, Iowa Bar Assn.(pres. 2001-2002), Johnson County Bar Assn. Commercial, contracts (including sales of goods; commercial financing), Education and schools, Property, real (including real estate development, water). Office: 300 Brewery Sq 123 N Linn St PO Box 2820 Iowa City IA 52244-2820

HOLLAND, LYMAN FAITH, JR., lawyer; b. Mobile, Ala., June 17, 1931; s. Lyman Faith and Louise (Wisdom) H.; m. Leannah Louise Platt, Mar. 6, 1954; children: Lyman Faith III, Laura. BS in Bus. Adminstrn, U. Ala., 1953, LLB, 1957. Bar: Ala. 1957, U.S. Supreme Ct. 1992. Assoc. Hand, Arendall & Bedsole, Mobile, 1957-62; ptnr. Hand, Arendall, Bedsole, Greaves & Johnston, 1963-94, mem., 1995, Hand Arendall LLC, 1996—. Mem. Mobile Hist. Devel. Com., 1965-69, v.p., 1967-68; bd. dirs. Mobile Azalea Trail, Inc., 1963-68, chmn. bd., 1963-65; bd. dirs. Mobile Mental Health Ctr., 1969-76, v.p., 1972, pres., chmn. bd., 1973; bd. dirs. Mobile chpt. ARC, 1969-89, 91-97, vice chmn., 1975-77, exec. vice chmn., 1978-80, chmn., 1980-82, life bd. dirs. emeritus, 1997—; bd. dirs. Deep South coun. Girl Scouts U.S., 1965-71, Gordan Smith Ctr. Inc., 1973, Bay Area Coun. on Alcoholism, 1973-76, Comty. Chest Coun. of Mobile County, Inc., 1976-81; bd. dirs. Greater Mobile Mental Health-Mental Retardation Bd., Inc., 1975-81, pres., 1975-77; mem. exec. com. Mobile Estate Planning Coun., 1988-97, pres., 1994-95. 1st lt. USAF, 1953-55; lt. col. USAF ret. Mem.: ABA, Ala. Law Found., Ala. Law Inst. (coun. 1978—), Am. Coll. Trust and Estate Counsel Found., Am. Coll. Trust and Estate Counsel, Am. Counsel Assn., Mobile County Bar Assn., Ala. State Bar (chmn. sect. corp., banking and bus. law 1978—80), Camellia Club of Mobile, Bienville Club, Country Club of Mobile, Athleston Club (Mobile), Lions, Phi Delta Phi, Phi Kappa Alpha. Baptist (deacon, ch. trustee 1968-73, chmn. trustees 1971-73). Estate planning, Probate (including wills, trusts), Property, real (including real estate development, water). Home: 3606 Provident Ct Mobile AL 36608-1534 Office: Hand Arendall LLC PO Box 123 Mobile AL 36601-0123 E-mail: lymanh@handarendall.com.

HOLLAND, MICHAEL WADE, lawyer; b. Louisville, Aug. 20, 1971; s. Roger Dale and Janet Ann Holland; m. Heather Nikkole Holland, July 22, 2002; 1 stepchild, Taylor Logan Horning. BS, Ball State U., 1994; JD, Valparaiso U., 1998. Bar: Tenn. 1998, Ind. 2000, U.S. Dist. Ct. (no. and so. dists.) Ind. 2000. Law clk. Stephen Plopper & Assocs., Indpls., 1999, CMG Worldwide, Inc., Indpls., 2001—02; counsel Action Performance Cos., Inc. - Charlotte, Concord, NC, 2002—. Republican. Corporate, general, Trademark and copyright. Office: Action Performance Cos Inc Charlotte 6301 Performance Dr Concord NC 28027

HOLLAND, RANDY JAMES, state supreme court justice; b. Elizabeth, N.J., Jan. 27, 1947; s. James Charles and Virginia (Wilson) H.; m. Ilona E. Holland, June 24, 1972 BA in Econs., Swarthmore Coll., 1969; JD cum laude, U. Pa., 1972; LLM, U. Va., 1998; Doctor (hon.) , Widener U. Sch. Law, 2001. Bar: Del. 1972. Ptnr. Dunlap, Holland & Rich and predecessors, Georgetown, Del., 1972-80, Morris, Nichols, Arsht & Tunnell, Georgetown, Del., 1980-86; justice Supreme Ct. Del., Georgetown, 1986—. Mem. Del. Bar Examiners, 1978-86; mem. Gov.'s Jud. Nominating Commn., 1978-86, sec., 1982-85, chmn., 1985-86; mem. Del. Supreme Ct. Consol. Com., 1985-86; pres. Terry-Carey Inn of Ct., 1991-94; v.p. Am. Inns of Ct., 1996-2000, pres., 2000—; co-chair Racial and Ethnic Task Force, 1995—; adj. prof. Widener U. Sch. Law, 1991—, U. Pa. Sch. Law, 1993-94, U. Iowa Sch. Law, 1997-, Vanderbilt Law Sch., 2000-; co-chair Del. Cts. Planning Com., 1996; chair nat. jud. adv. com. fed. Office of Child Support Enforcement; Jud. Ethics Adv. Commn., 1994—; del. Code Jud. Conduct Rev. Commn., 1991-94; del. Bar Bench Media Conf., 1990—. Mem. editL. bd. Del. Lawyer Mag., 1981-85; contbr. chpt. Del. Appellate Handbook, 1985—. Pres. adminstrv. bd. Ave. United Meth. Ch., Milford, Del. Bar Found.; hon. chmn. History of the Del. Bar in 20th Century, 1992—. Recipient Henry C. Loughlin prize for legal ethics U. Pa. 1972, St. Thomas More award, 1999, Alumni award of merit U. Pa. Sch. Law, 2002; named Judge of the Yr. Nat. Child Support Enforcement Assn., 1992. Mem. ABA (standing com. on lawyer competence, nat. jud. coll. adv. commn. model rules jud. disclosure enforcement 1996, appellate judge's conf. exec. com. 2001—, chmn. joint com. on lawyer regulation 2002—), Am. Judicature Soc. (nat. trustee 1992—, ctr. for jud. ethics, 1994, chair 1997-, Herbert Harley Award 2003.), Am. Inns of Ct. Found. (trustee 1992—, nat. trustee 1996—, v.p. 1996-2000, nat. pres. 2000—), Am. Law Inst., Del. Bar Found., Am. Law Inst. Republican. Avocations: gardening, swimming, cycling. Office: Del Supreme Ct 22 The Cir Georgetown DE 19947-1500

HOLLAND, ROBERT DALE, retired judge; b. Sayre, Okla., June 10, 1928; s. Claude Henry and Alva Mae (Joyce) H.; children: Arlene, Burton Dale, Rhonda Jo. Student, Tex. A&M, 1946, Internat. Corr. Schs., 1963, 65, 67-68; PhD of Sociology (hon.), Scholars U., 1975. Safety, security, loss prevention officer Copper Queen Br. Phelps Dodge Corp., Bisbee, Ariz., 1946-85; probation officer Cochise County, Bisbee, 1986—87; safety dir., loss prevention dir. Spray Sys. Environ., Phoenix, 1987-93; city magistrate City of Bisbee, 1989-93; pres., owner Copper City Cons., Bisbee, 1989—. Referee & hearing officer Cochise County Juvenile Ct., 1969-78; juvenile ct. judge pro tem, 1990-93; justice ct. judge pro tem, 1991-93; bd. dirs. Southern Ariz. Safety Coun., Tucson, 1986-91. Councilman City of Bisbee, 1973-82; chmn. relief com. Salvation Army, 1980—; chmn., vice chmn. bd. dirs. Copper Queen Hosp. Corp., Bisbee, Ariz. With USMC, 1947-52. Mem. ADHS (water quality com. 1974), Am. Mining Congress (ad-hoc com. 1980), Perfect Ashlar Lodge F&AM (master 1964), Masons. Democrat. Avocations: gun collecting, reading, church work. Home and Office: PO Box 5427 206 Black Knob View Bisbee AZ 85603-5427

HOLLANDER, FRANK, lawyer; b. York, Pa. B in Bus. Adminstrn. magna cum laude, U. Fla., 1984, JD, 1987. Bar: Fla. 1988, U.S. Ct. Appeals (11th cir.) 1989, U.S. Dist. Ct. (so. dist.) Fla. 1993, U.S. Supreme Ct. 1997. Prosecutor Fla. State Atty. Janet Reno, Miami, 1987; atty., pres. Law Offices Frank L. Hollander, Miami, 1988—. Mem.: ATLA, ABA, Nat. Assn. Criminal Def. Lawyers, Acad. Fla. Trial Lawyers, Fed. Bar Assn. Office: 200 S Biscayne Blvd 51st Fl Miami FL 33131-2340 E-mail: fhollander@attyatlaw.org.

HOLLEB, MARSHALL MAYNARD, lawyer; b. Chgo., Dec. 25, 1916; s. A. Paul and Sara (Zaretsky) H.; m. Doris Bernstein, Oct. 15, 1944; children: Alan R., Gordon P., Paul D. BA, U. Wis., 1937; MBA, Harvard U., 1939; IA, 1941, JD, 1942. Bar: Ill. 1947, U.S. Supreme Ct. 1960. Assoc. Levenson, Becker & Peebles, Chgo., 1947-51; ptnr. Yates & Holleb, Chgo., 1952-59, Holleb, Gerstein & Glass, Chgo., 1960-81; sr. ptnr. Holleb & Coff, Chgo., 1982-2000; sr. counsel Wildman, Harrold, Allen & Dixon, 2000—. Chmn. bd. dirs. Urban Assocs. Chgo., Inc. Contbr. articles to profl. jours.; profiled on PBS-TV program Chicago Stories, 2001. Trustee Acorn Fund, 1971-95; life trustee Hull House Assn., pres., 1980-82; trustee emeritus nat. Bldg. Mus., Chgo. Inst. Psychoanalysis; overseer Harvard Bus. Sch. Club Chgo.; founder, life trustee, gen. legal counsel Mus. Contemporary Art Chgo.; mem. adv. bd. Landmarks Preservation Coun., Fair Housing Ctr. Home Investments Fund, Citizens Sch. Com.; mem. vis. coms. Oriental Inst. and Visual Arts U. Chgo.; bd. dirs. Intenat. Visitors Ctr., Mostly Music, Inc., Chgo. Fund. on Aging and Disability; mem. Ill. Internat. Trade and Port Promotion Adv. Com., 1982, Chgo.'s Future Project Com. of Trust, Inc., 1982, Pacific Basing Inst.; mem. nat. adv. bd. on internat. edn. programs U.S. Dept. Edn., 1981, City Chgo. Local Cultural Devel. Commn.; pres. Chgo. Theater Preservation Group Ltd., sec., bd. dirs. Arts Club Chgo.; bd. dirs. Chgo. Maritime Soc.; me. industry sector adv. com. on svcs. for trade policy matters U.S. Dept. Commerce, 1995-98; mem. nat. adv. com. and del. White House Conf. on Aging, 1971, 81; mem. Ill. Coun. Aging, 1961-81, chmn., 1973-81; panel mem. Ill. Statewide Comprehensive Outdoor Recreation Plan; mem. weatherization adv. com. Ill. Dept. Bus. and Econ. Devel., 1975—; mem. Ill. appeal bd. SSS, 1966-73; cons. Vt. rsch. project HUD. 1st lt. U.S. Army, Philippines and Japan, 1943-46. Recipient Humanitarian of Yr. Henry Booth House award Hull House Assn., 1979; Am. Heritage award Am. Jewish Com., 1986, Arts award Mostly Music Inc., 1986, City Brightener award Bright New City Chgo., 1987. Mem. ABA, Ill. Bar Assn., Chgo. Bar Assn., Fed. Bar Assn., Am. Soc. Internat. Law, Am. Arbitration Assn. (nat. panel), Am. Inst. Planners, Nat. Assn. Housign and Redevel. Ofcls., Urban Land Inst., Harvard Law Soc. Ill. (bd. dirs.), Arts Club, Univ. Club, Bryn Mawr Country Club, Execs. Club (Chgo.), Lambda Alpha. Democrat. Corporate, general, Estate planning, Property, real (including real estate development, water). Office: 225 W Wacker Dr Ste 3000 Chicago IL 60606-1229

HOLLENBAUGH, H(ENRY) RITCHEY, lawyer; b. Shelby, Ohio, Nov. 12, 1947; m. Diane Robinson Nov. 21, 1973 (div. 1989); children: Chad Ritchey, Katie Paige; m. Rebecca U., Aug. 8, 1995. BA, Kent State U., 1969; JD, Capital U., 1973. Bar: Ohio 1973, U.S. Dist. Ct. (so. dist.) Ohio 1974, U.S. Ct. Appeals (6th cir.) 1976, U.S. Supreme Ct. 1978. Investigator Ohio Civil Rights Com., Columbus, Ohio, 1969-72; legal intern City Atty.'s Office, Columbus, Ohio, 1972-73, asst. city prosecutor, 1973-75, sr. asst. city atty., 1975-76; ptnr. Hunter, Hollenbaugh & Theodotou, Columbus, Ohio, 1976-85, Delligatti, Hollenbaugh, Briscoe & Milless, Columbus, Ohio, 1985-91, Climaco Seminatore Delligatti & Hollenbaugh, Columbus, 1991-93, Delligatti, Hollenbaugh & Briscoe, Columbus, 1993-95, Draper, Hollenbaugh, Briscoe, Yashko & Carmany, 1996-99, Carlile Patchen & Murphy, Columbus, 1999—. Mem. Ohio Pub. Defender Commn., 1988-94; chmn. Franklin County Pub. Defender Commn., 1986-92. Treas. The Gov's. Com., 1987-96, Friends With Celeste, Friends of Gov's. Residence, 1987-92, Participation 2000, 1987-91, Ohio Legal Assistance Found., 1998—. Fellow ABA Found. (chair commn. on advt. 1993-97, ho. of dels. 1993—, chair nat. conf. lawyers and reps. of media 2000—); mem. Ohio State Bar Assn. (bd. govs. 1989-94, pres. 1992-93), Columbus Bar Assn. (pres. 1987-88), Nat. Conf. Bar Pres., Nat. Assn. Criminal Def. Lawyers, Capital Club. Democrat. Methodist. Avocations: golf, politics. Federal civil litigation, State civil litigation, Criminal. Home: 8549 Glenalmond Ct Dublin OH 43017-9737 Office: Carlile Patchen & Murphy 336 E Broad St Columbus OH 43215-3202 E-mail: HRH@CPMLAW.com.

HOLLENBERG, HARVARD, lawyer, writer; b. N.Y.C., Dec. 14, 1938; s. William Gustave and Harriet Grace (Renault) Von Höllenberg. BA, NYU, 1960; MA in Polit. Sci., Victoria U., Wellington, New Zealand, 1962; JD, Harvard U., 1965. Bar: N.Y. 1967, U.S. Dist. Ct. (so. and ea. dists.) N.Y. 1993. Sr. atty. Supreme Ct. Mental Hygiene Legal Svc., N.Y.C., 1965-70; chief counsel, staff dir. N.Y. State Commn. to Evaluate the Drug Laws, N.Y.C., Albany, N.Y., 1970-76; asst. state atty. gen. litigation N.Y. State Dept. Law, N.Y.C., 1976-78; spl. counsel to speaker N.Y. State Assembly, N.Y.C., Albany, 1978-83; dep. pub. advocate N.J. Dept. Pub. Advocate, 1983-85; gen. counsel N.Y.C. Dept. Mental Hygiene, 1985-88; pvt. practice specializing in litig., contracts, govt. rels., rsch. and writing briefs in developing areas of law N.Y.C., 1988—. Author: Employing the Rehabilitated Addict, 1972, Drug Abuse Prevention, 1973, How People Overseas Deal with Drugs, 1974, A Law of Vengeance, 1993, The Vinyard Diamonds, 1994; contbr. frequent articles to Nat. Law Jour., N.Y. Times, Atlanta Constn., St. Louis Post-Dispatch, Phila. Inquirer, Chgo. Tribune, Manchester (N.H.) Union Leader; regular monthly food and travel columnist World's Fare in Newsday. Vol., Met. Opera Guild, N.Y.C. Fulbright scholar Inst. for Internat. Edn., New Zealand, 1960-62, Felix Frankfurter scholar Harvard Law Sch., 1962-65. Mem. N.Y. State Bar Assn., Assn. of Bar of City of N.Y., N.Y. County Bar Assn., Phi Beta Kappa. Democrat. Jewish.

HOLLEY, STEVEN LYON, lawyer; b. Ft. Wayne, Ind., Apr. 5, 1958; s. Wesley Lewis and Cornelia Alice (Reeder) H. BA in History/Polit. Sci., Ind. U., 1980; JD, NYU, 1983. Bar: N.Y. 1984, U.S. Dist. Ct. (so. and ea. dist.) N.Y. 1985, U.S. Dist. Ct. (no. dist.) N.Y. 1988. Law clk. Hon. Jose' A. Cabranes, Hartford, Conn., 1983-84; assoc. Sullivan & Cromwell, N.Y.C., 1984-90, ptnr., 1991—. Mem. Assn. Bar City of N.Y. (sec. com. on profl. and jud. ethics 1988-90). Democrat. Antitrust, Mergers and acquisitions, Securities. Home: 832 Broadway New York NY 10003-4813 Office: Sullivan & Cromwell 125 Broad St Fl 34 New York NY 10004-2498 E-mail: holleys@sullcrom.com.

HOLLIDAY, THOMAS EDGAR, lawyer; b. Ft. Hood, Tex., July 3, 1948; s. William Lamont and Eileen (Fiebig) H.; m. Linda Loudon, May 7, 1988; children: Devon M., Trey S. BA, Stanford U., 1971; JD, U. So. Calif., 1974. Bar: Calif. 1974. Assoc. Gibson, Dunn & Crutcher LLP, L.A., 1974-81; ptnr. Gibson, Dunn & Crutcher, L.A., 1981—. Editor: (book, desk edition) Antitrust and Trade Regulations. Trustee S.W. Mus., L.A., 1981-98, bd. pres., 1995-97; trustee Found. for People, L.A., 1985-90, Clarkson U., 2000—; mem. L.A. Police Dept. Meml. Found. Bd. Fellow Am. Coll. Trial Lawyers; mem. Fed. Bar Assn. (exec. com. L.A. chpt. 1990, pres. 1998). Avocation: collecting southwestern art. Criminal. Office: Gibson Dunn & Crutcher LLP 333 S Grand Ave Ste 4400 Los Angeles CA 90071-3197

HOLLINGSWORTH, JOHN R. lawyer; b. Fayette, Ala., Sept. 21, 1946; s. John J. and Dixie D. Hollingsworth; m. Rebecca Kay Reeves, Apr. 2, 1968; children: John R. Jr., Robert Brian. BS, Auburn U., 1974; JD, Birmingham U., 1978. Bar: Ala., U.S. Dist. Ct. (ctrl. and no. dists.) Ala. Solo practitioner, Enterprise, Ala., 1978—. E-5 USN, 1969—72. Church Of Christ. Avocations: restoring antiques, fishing. Personal injury (including property damage), Family and matrimonial. Office: Hollingsworth & Hollingsworth 406 Glover Ave POB 311612 Enterprise AL 36331

HOLLINGTON, LARRY N. lawyer; b. Cuthbert, Ga., Mar. 2, 1951; s. Edward Ercel and Ruby White Hollington; m. Judith Denney Hollington, Nov. 30, 1985; children: Sarah Lauren, William Neal. Bachelors, Troy State U., 1973; JD, Mercer U., 1982. Bar: Ga. 1982, U.S. Ct. Appeals 1982. Atty. Swift, Currie, McGhee & Hiers, Atlanta, 1982—85; pvt. practice Augusta, Ga., 1985—. Chmn. sect. workers compensation State Bar Ga. 1st lt. USMC, 1973—76. Mem.: ATLA, ABA, Augusta Bar Assn., Ga. Trial Lawyers. Baptist. Workers' compensation. Office: 1206 George C Wilson Dr Augusta GA 30909 Office Fax: 706-868-9020.

HOLLINGTON, RICHARD RINGS, JR., lawyer; b. Findlay, Ohio, Nov. 12, 1932; s. Richard Rings and Annett (Kirk) H.; m. Sally Stecher, Apr. 4, 1959; children: Florence A., Julie A., Richard R. III. Peter S. BA, Williams Coll., 1954; JD, Harvard U., 1957. Bar: Ohio 1957. Ptnr. Marshman, Hornbeck & Hollington, Cleve., 1958-67, McDonald, Hopkins, Hardy & Hollington, Cleve., 1967-69; law dir. City of Cleve., 1971-72; sr. ptnr. Baker & Hostetler, Cleve., 1969-71, 73—. Lead bd. dirs. Sky Fin. Group; mem. FDIC Advisory Com. on Banking Policy, 2002-, mem. Ohio Banking Commn., 2001—. Mem. Ohio Gen. Assembly, 1967-70, Cuyahoga County Rep. Ctrl. Com., 1962-66; exec. com. Ohio Rep. Fin. Com., 1971-98, Cuyahoga County Rep. Orgn., 1968-98, Geauga County Rep. Orgn., 1998—; trustee Cleve. State U., 1970-73, Greater Cleve. Hosp. Assn., 1976-82, Cleve. Mus. Natural History, 1969-81, Cleve. Zool. Soc., 1970-99, N. E. Ohio Regional Sewer Dist., 1972-73, Cuyahoga County Hosp. Found., 1968-73, Cleve. 500 Found., 1990-95, U. Findlay, 1991—, others; bd. commrs. grievance and discipline Ohio Supreme Ct., 1993-95. Mem. ABA, Ohio Bar Assn., Greater Cleve. Bar Assn., Sixth Cir. Jud. Conf. (life), Eighth Dist. Ohio Jud. Conf. (life), Ct. Nisi Prius, Union Club (Cleve.), The Country Club (Pepper Pike), Pepper Pike Club, Roaring Gap (N.C.) Club, Rolling Rock (Pa.) Club. Banking, General civil litigation, General practice. Home: 13792 County Line Rd Chagrin Falls OH 44022-4008 Office: Baker & Hostetler 3200 National City Ctr 1900 E 9th St Ste 3200 Cleveland OH 44114-3475

HOLLINSHEAD, EARL DARNELL, JR., lawyer; b. Pitts., Aug. 1, 1927; s. Earl Darnell and Gertrude (Cahill) H.; m. Sylvia Antion, June 29, 1957; children: Barbara, Kim, Earl III, Susan. AB, Ohio U., 1948; LLB, U. Pitts., 1951. Bar: Pa. 1952, U.S. Ct. Mil. Appeals 1954, U.S. Dist. Ct. (we. dist.) Pa. 1955, U.S. Supreme Ct. 1956, U.S. Ct. Appeals (3d cir.) 1959, U.S. Dist. Ct. (ea. dist.) Ohio 1978. Sole practice, Pitts., 1955-70; ptnr. Hollinshead and Mendelson, Pitts., 1970-89, Hollinshead, Mendelson, Bresnahan & Nixon, P.C., Pitts., 1990-97; sole practitioner Pitts., 1997—. Mem. Pitts. Estate Planning Council. Contbr. articles to profl. jours. Served to lt. USNR, 1951-55. Fellow Pa. Bar Found. (life); mem. Pa. Bar Assn. (chmn. real property divsn. 1983-85, real property, probate and trust sects. 1985-86), Allegheny County Bar Assn. (chmn. real property sect. 1975-76), Pa. Bar Inst. (lectr., planner, bd. dirs. 1988-94), Am. Coll. Real Estate Lawyers. Bankruptcy, Probate (including wills, trusts), Property, real (including real estate development, water). Home: 2535 Windgate Rd Bethel Park PA 15102-2730 Office: Regional Enterprise Tower 425 Sixth Ave Ste 2490 Pittsburgh PA 15219-1819

HOLLIS, DARYL JOSEPH, judge; b. Pitts., Oct. 22, 1946; s. Joseph and Margaret Clara (Meszar) H.; m. Linda Eardley, July 18, 1970. BS in Edn., Pa. State U., 1968, MEd in Remedial Reading, 1971; JD, Cath. U. Am., 1984. Bar: Pa. 1987, D.C. 1989, U.S. Supreme Ct. Law clk. D.C. Office of Employee Appeals, Washington, 1984-85, adminstrv. law judge, 1985-97, sr. adminstrv. law judge, 1997—. Lectr. D.C. Bar Assn. Pro Bono Svcs., Washington, 1985—; mem. Transplant Recipients Internat. Orgn., Nat. Capital Area Chpt., 1993—. Mem. Columbia Pines Citizens Assn., 1993—. Mem. Transplant Recipients Internat. Orgn. Democrat. Roman Catholic. Avocations: woodworking, hiking, civil war, baseball history, sports. Home: 4002 Rose Ln Annandale VA 22003-1943

HOLLIS, SHEILA SLOCUM, lawyer; b. Denver, July 15, 1948; d. Theodore Doremus and Emily M. (Caplis) Slocum (dec.); m. John Hollis; 1 child, Windsong Emily Lanford. BS in Journalism with honors, BS in Gen. Studies cum laude, U. Colo., 1971; JD, U. Denver, 1973. Bar: Colo. 1974, D.C. 1975, U.S. Supreme Ct. 1980. Trial atty. Fed. Power Commn., Washington, 1974-75; assoc. firm Wilner & Scheiner, Washington, 1975-77; dir. office enforcement Fed. Energy Regulatory Commn., Washington, 1977-80; pvt. practice, 1980—; ptnr. Vinson & Elkins, Washington, 1987-92; sr. ptnr. Metzger, Hollis, Gordon & Alprin, Washington, 1992-97; mng. ptnr. D.C., mem. exec. com. Duane Morris LLP, Washington, 1997—2003. Professorial lectr. in energy law George Washington U., 1980—2000; bd. dirs. U.S. Energy Assn. Co-author: Energy Decision Making, 1983, Energy Law and Policy, 1989; mem. editl. bd. Oil and Gas Reporter, Pub. Utility Fortnightly; contbr. articles to profl. publs. Established and developed enforcement program Fed. Energy Regulatory Commn.; mem. adv. bd. Pub. Utility Ctr. N.Mex. State U., 1986—94; mem. N.Am. Energy Stds. Bd., 1998—; pres. Women's Coun. Energy and Environment, 1997—2003; bd. dirs. Nat. Assn. Vets. Health Care., Wyo. State Soc. U. Denver scholar, 1972-73. Fellow: ABA (chair coord. group energy law 1989—92, mem. ho. dels. 1992—2001, chair standing com. environ. law 1997—2000, mem. bd. editors ABA Jour. 2000—02, immediate past chair sect. environ., energy and resources 2001—02, standing com. on fed. judiciary 2002—); mem.: U.S. Energy Assn. (bd. dirs.), John Carroll Soc., Women's Bar Assn. D.C., D.C. Bar Assn., Colo. Bar Assn., Internat. Legal Edn. Ctr. (trustee), Oil and Gas Ednl. Inst., Energy Bar Assn. (pres. 1991—92), Am. Law Inst., Internat. Bar Assn., Comml. Bar of Eng. and Wales (hon.), Sir Thomas More Soc. (pres.-elect), Cosmos Club, Nat. Press Club. Roman Catholic. Administrative and regulatory, FERC practice, Environmental. Office: DuaneMorris LLP 1667 K St NW Ste 700 Washington DC 20006-1608 E-mail: sshollis@duanemorris.com.

HOLLOWAY, DONALD PHILLIP, lawyer; b. Akron, Ohio, Feb. 18, 1928; s. Harold Shane and Dorothy Gayle (Ryder) H. BS in Commerce, Ohio U., Athens, 1950; JD, U. Akron, 1955; MA, Kent State U., 1962. Bar: Ohio 1955. Title examiner Bankers Guarantee Title & Trust Co., Akron, 1950-54; acct. Robinson Clay Product Co., Akron, 1955-60; libr. Akron-Summit Pub. Libr., 1962-69, head fine arts and music divsn., 1969-71, sr. libr., 1972-82; pvt. practice Akron, 1982—. Payroll treas. Akron Symphony Orch., 1957-61; treas. Friends Libr. Akron and Summit County, 1970-72. Mem. ABA, ALA, Ohio Bar Assn., Akron Bar Assn., Ohio Libr. Assn., Nat. Trust Hist. Preservation, Music Libr. Assn., Soc. Archtl. Historians, Coll. Art Assn., Art Librs. N.Am., Akron City Club, North Coast Soc. Republican. Episcopalian. Avocations: art and architecture, music, travel. Probate (including wills, trusts). Home: 293 Delaware Pl Akron OH 44303-1275

HOLLOWAY, JOHN P. lawyer; b. Boulder, Colo., Oct. 22, 1953; s. John P. Sr. and Sally H.; m. Deborah Sue Bloch, Apr. 2, 1980; children: Tres, Coleman. BA, U. Colo., 1977, JD, 1989. Bar: Colo. 1989. Profl. landman AAPL, Ft. Worth, Tex., 1983—, DAPL, Denver, 1983—. City councilman City of Steamboat Springs, 1991-93, planning commr., 1989-91. Mem. Rotary. Probate (including wills, trusts), Property, real (including real estate development, water). Office: Holloway & Assocs PC PO Box 770908 Steamboat Springs CO 80477-0908

HOLLOWAY, WILLIAM JUDSON, JR., federal judge; b. 1923; AB, U. Okla., 1947; LLB, Harvard U., 1950; LLD (hon.) , Oklahoma City U. Ptnr. Holloway & Holloway, Oklahoma City, 1950—51; atty. Dept. Justice, Washington, 1951—52; assoc., ptnr. Crowe and Dunlevy, Oklahoma City, 1952—68; judge U.S. Ct. Appeals (10th cir.), Oklahoma City, 1968—84, chief judge, 1984—91, sr. judge, 1992—. Mem.: FBA, ABA, Oklahoma County Bar Assn., Okla. Bar Assn. Office: US Ct Appeals 10th Cir PO Box 1767 Oklahoma City OK 73101-1767

HOLLYER, A(RTHUR) RENE, lawyer; b. Wycoff, N.J., July 28, 1938; s. Richard W. and Florence (Vervaet) H.; m. Lauraine Dennis, Apr. 8, 1978; children: James Richard, Jennifer Ashley. BA, Williams Coll., 1961; MPA, Woodrow Wilson Sch., Princeton, 1963; LLB, Columbia U., 1966. Bar: N.J. 1966, U.S. Dist. Ct. N.J. 1966, N.Y. 1968, U.S. Dist. Ct. (so. and ea. dists.) N.Y. 1969, U.S. Ct. Appeals (3rd cir.) 1970, U.S. Ct. Appeals (2d cir.) 1971, D.C. 1972, U.S. Supreme Ct. 1974. Law sec. to judge chancery divsn. N.J. Superior Ct., Newark, 1966-67; assoc. Olwine, Connelly, Chase, O'Donnell & Weyher, N.Y.C., 1968-70, 72-74; asst. U.S. atty. Dist. N.J., 1970-71; ptnr. Hollyer, Brady, Smith & Hines, L.L.P. and predecessor firms, N.Y.C., 1974—. Mem.: Assn. of Bar of City of N.Y. (profl. discipline com. 1990—92, 1995—98, 2001—, chmn. complaint mediation panel 1991—92, ethics com. 1992—95, profl. responsibility com. 1998—2001), N.Y. State Bar Assn. (chair spl. com. on procedures for judicial discipline 2001—). Federal civil litigation, State civil litigation, General practice. Home: 50 Hamilton Rd Glen Ridge NJ 07028-1109 Office: Hollyer Brady Smith & Hines LLP 551 5th Ave New York NY 10176-0001 E-mail: arhesq@worldnet.att.net.

HOLLYFIELD, JOHN SCOGGINS, lawyer; b. Harlingen, Tex., Aug. 20, 1939; m. Penny Pounds, Dec. 27, 1962; children: Jon Scott, Courtney. Bar: Tex. 1968. Assoc. Fulbright & Jaworski, Houston, 1968—75, ptnr., 1975—2002, of counsel, 2002—. Lt. USNR, 1961-65. Recipient Pres.'s award Houston Bar Assn., 1986. Mem. ABA (coun. real property sect. 1986-93, sec. 1993-94, vice chair real property divsn. 1994-96, chair elect 1996-97, chair 1997-98, ho. of dels. 1999—), Am. Coll. Real Estate Lawyers (pres. 1990-91), Anglo-Am. Real Property Inst. (chair 2001). Commercial, contracts (including sales of goods; commercial financing), Landlord-tenant, Property, real (including real estate development, water). Office: Fulbright & Jaworski LLP 1301 Mckinney St Houston TX 77010-3095 E-mail: jhollyfield@fulbright.com.

HOLMAN, BUD GEORGE, lawyer; b. N.Y.C., June 30, 1929; s. Harry and Fannie Abrams (Bass) H.; m. Kathleen Barbara McLean, Sept. 1, 1961; children: Jennifer Jean, Wayne George. BBA, CCNY, 1950; LLB, Yale U., 1956. Bar: N.Y. 1956, Conn. 1979, D.C. 1982. Law sec. to judge N.Y. Ct. Appeals, 1956-58; practice in N.Y.C., 1958—; ptnr. Kelley Drye & Warren (and predecessor firms), 1965—. Pres., chmn. bd. dirs. Sixty Sutton Corp., 1969-97; lectr. Practising Law Inst., Wage Price Inst., Young Pres. Orgn. Editor: The Bar, 1949-50, Yale Law Jour., 1955-56. Trustee U.S. Naval Acad. Found., 1978-85; bd. dirs. USO Met. N.Y. Mem. Naval Res. Assn. (pres. 3d naval dist. chpts. 1973-75, mem. nat. adv. coun. 1975-94), Am. Arbitration Assn. (bd. dirs., mem. exec. com.), Navy League (bd. dirs. coun. N.Y. chpt. 1979-99), Yale U. Law Sch. Assn. (mem. exec. com. 1987-90, 93-96, bd. dirs.), Yale Law Sch. Assn. N.Y.C. (bd. dirs.), Met. Club, Yale Club, Beta Gamma Sigma. Democrat. Presbyterian. Antitrust, General civil litigation, Product liability. Home: 350 Park Ave Box 978 Mattituck NY 11952 Office: Kelley Drye & Warren LLP 101 Park Ave New York NY 10178-0002 E-mail: bholman@kelleydrye.com., holmanbg@aol.com.

HOLMAN, DONALD REID, retired lawyer; b. Astoria, Oreg., Jan. 30, 1930; s. Donald Reuben and Hattie Laveda (Card) H.; m. Susan Muncy Morris, Aug. 31, 1956; children: Donald Reid, Laura Morris Holman O'Brien, Douglas Edward. BA, U. Wash.-Seattle, 1951, JD, 1958; post-grad., U. Oreg.-Eugene, 1955-57. Bar: Oreg. Assoc. Miller Nash LLP, Portland, 1958-63, ptnr., 1963-93, mng. ptnr., 1987-90, sr. counsel, 1994-2001, ret., 2001. Bd. dirs. Copeland Lumber Yards Inc., Portland, Huntair Inc., Portland. Lt. (j.g.) USN, 1951-55; capt. JAGC USNR, 1977-90, ret. Fellow Am. Bar Found.; mem. Order of Coif, Multnomah Athletic club (trustee 1983-85, v.p. 1985-86), Waverley Country Club, Phi Delta Phi. Republican. Avocations: tennis, golf, squash. Home: 8040 SW Broadmoor Ter Portland OR 97225-2121 E-mail: holmor@aol.com.

HOLMAN, JOSEPH FREDERICK, retired lawyer; b. Farmington, Maine, Aug. 15, 1925; s. Currier Carleton and Rosa (Skillings) H.; m. Brenda Hart, June 24, 1977. AB, Bowdoin Coll., 1947; LLB, Boston U., 1950. Bar: Maine 1951, U.S. Dist. Ct. Maine 1963, U.S. Supreme Ct. 1963. Pvt. practice, Farmington, 1951—2002; atty. Franklin County, Farmington, 1953-58. Pres., Farmington Pub. Libr., 1998—; assessor, Farmington Village Corp., 1980—. Sen. State of Maine, 1970; mem. Maine State Claims Comm., 1990-2001. Mem. ABA, Maine Bar Assn. (exec. com. 1963-71, pres. 1971-72), Franklin County Bar Assn. (pres. 1993). Republican. Avocations: hunting, fly fishing. General practice, Probate (including wills, trusts), Property, real (including real estate development, water). Home: 129 Orchard St Farmington ME 04938-5925

HOLMAN, LESLIE ANN, lawyer; b. N.Y.C., Feb. 10, 1962; d. Martin and Agnes Eve Ehrenreich; m. Andrew Keith Holman, June 14, 1990; children: Amanda, Zachary. BA in Psychology, Clark U., 1983; JD with distinction, Hofstra U., 1987. Bar: N.Y. 1988, Vt. 1997. Assoc. Rivkin Radler Dunne & Byan, Uniondale, NY, 1987—90, Milgrim, Tomajan & Lee, N.Y.C., 1990—91, Pierez, Ackerman & Levine, Great Neck, NY, 1991—92, Wilson Powell Lang & Faris, Burlington, Vt., 1996—99, Bothfeld & Volk, Burlington, 1999—2000; pvt. practice Burlington, 2000—. Mem. Flynn Theater Programming Com., 2001—. Mem.: Vt. Bar Assn. (mem. internat. law com.), Am. Immigration Lawyers Assn. (Vt. INS liaison N.E. chpt. 2001—). Avocations: dancing, skiing. Immigration, naturalization, and customs. Office: One Lawsin Ln Burlington VT 05401 Office Fax: 802-860-3337. E-mail: lholman@immigrationvt.com.

HOLMAN, MAUREEN, lawyer; b. Mpls., Jan. 30, 1952; BA, U. Nebr., 1973; JD, U. N.D., 1983. Bar: N.D. 1983, Minn. 1983. Atty. Serkland Law Firm, Fargo, ND. Mem.: ABA, Order of Coif, State Bar Assn. N.D. (bd. govs. 1995—97, joint task force on family law 1995—, disciplinary bd. Supreme Ct. 1997—), Cass County Bar Assn., Minn. State Bar Assn., Phi Delta Phi, Phi Beta Kappa. Family and matrimonial. Office: Serkland Law Firm PO Box 6017 10 Roberts St Fargo ND 58108-6017*

HOLME, HOWARD KELLEY, lawyer, executive; b. Denver, May 5, 1945; s. Peter Hagner Jr. and Lena (Phillips) H.; m. Barbara Lynn Shaw, June 16, 1968; children: Timothy Peter, Lisa. AB in history with distinction and honor, Stanford U., 1967; JD, Yale U., 1972. Bar: Colo. 1972, U.S. Dist. Ct. Colo. 1972, U.S. Ct. Appeals (10th cir.) 1972, U.S. Supreme Ct. 1984. Staff Denver U. Law Sch., 1969-71; assoc. Fairfield & Woods, Denver, 1972-77; ptnr., dir., pres., mng. dir. Fairfield & Woods, PC, Denver, 1977-98; pres. Bandwidth Market Ltd., Denver, 1998—. Cons. Fryingpan-Ark. Project, Southeastern Colo. Water Conservation Dist., 1976-98. Editor: National Water Resources Regulation: Where is the Environment Pendulum Now?, 1994; contbr. articles to profl. jours. Bd. dirs. nat. legal adv. com. Planned Parenthood Fedn. Am., N.Y.C.; active Colo. Supreme Ct. law com., Denver. Mem. Colo. Bar Assn., Denver Bar Assn., Denver Law Club (pres.), Colo. Yale Assn. (pres.)Cactus Club. Federal civil litigation, Environmental. Home: 5833 Montview Blvd Denver CO 80207-3923 Office: Bandwidth Market Ltd 1700 Lincoln St Ste 2400 Denver CO 80203-4524 Fax: 303-830-1033. E-mail: hholme@bandwidthmarket.com.

HOLME, RICHARD PHILLIPS, lawyer; b. Denver, Nov. 6, 1941; s. Peter Hagner Jr. and Lena (Phillips) H.; m. Barbara June Friel, July 17, 1944; children: Daniel Friel, Robert Muir. BA, Williams Coll., Williamstown, Mass., 1963; JD, U. Colo., 1966. Bar: Colo. 1966, U.S. Dist. Ct. Colo. 1966, U.S. Ct. Claims 1990, U.S. Ct. Appeals (10th cir.) 1966, U.S. Ct. Appeals (1st cir.) 1980, U.S. Dist. Ct. D.C. 1988, U.S. Ct. Appeals (D.C. cir.) 1988, U.S. Ct. Appeals (4th cir.) 1989, U.S. Ct. Appeals (fed. cir.) 1995, U.S. Supreme Ct. 1975. Assoc. Davis, Graham & Stubbs, Denver, 1966-68, ptnr., 1972-87, 91—, mng. ptnr., D.C. office Washington, 1987-91; dep. Denver Dist. Atty., 1969-71. Grievance com. Colo. Supreme Ct., Denver, 1979-85, civil rules com., 1994—, civil justice com., 1998—. Fellow Am. Bar Found., Am. Coll. Trial Lawyers (Colo. state chair 1994-96); mem. ABA, ABA Found., Colo. Bar Found., Colo. Bar Assn. (bd. govs. 1974-76, 85-87, 95-99, 2001—), Denver Bar Assn. (trustee 1977-80, 1st v.p. 1997-98), Order of Coif. Republican. Presbyterian. General civil litigation, Labor (including EEOC, Fair Labor Standards Act, labor-management relations, NLRB, OSHA), Libel. Home: 3944 S Depew Way Denver CO 80235-3105

HOLMES, BROOX GARRETT, lawyer; b. Mobile, Ala., Nov. 15, 1932; s. Williams Coghlan and Philomene (Boogaerts) H.; m. Laura Claire Hays, Feb. 21, 1955 (dec. 2000); children: Broox Garrett, Dupree Hays, Williams Coghlan II. BA, U. Ala., 1954, JD, 1960. Bar: Ala. 1960. Since practiced in, Mobile; mem. firm Armbrecht Jackson LLP, 1960—. Trustee St. Paul's Episcopal Sch., chmn. bd., 1980-83. Capt. USMCR, 1954-58. Fellow Am. Coll. Trial Lawyers (state chmn. 1991-92), Am. Bar Found.; mem. ABA, Ala. State Bar (bd. commrs. 1987-93, chmn. litigation sect. 1991, pres. 1994-95), Ala. Bar Found., Mobile Bar Assn. (exec. com. 1987-93), Nat. Assn. R.R. Trial Counsel, Internat. Assn. Def. Counsel, Am. Law Inst., Ala. Law Inst., Ala. Def. Lawyers (pres. 1977-78, named one of Best Lawyers in Am. bus. and personal injury litigation), Mobile Country Club (pres. 1983-84), Mobile Touchdown Club, Athelstan Club, Delta Kappa Epsilon, Phi Delta Phi. Episcopalian. Federal civil litigation, General civil litigation, State civil litigation. Home: 609 Fairfax Rd E Mobile AL 36608-2939 Office: Armbrecht Jackson LLP PO Box 290 Mobile AL 36601-0290

HOLMES, DALLAS SCOTT, lawyer, educator; b. L.A., Dec. 2, 1940; s. Donald Cherry and Hazel (Scott) H.; m. Patricia McMichael, Aug. 21, 1965; children: Mark Scott, Tobin John. AB cum laude, Pomona Coll., 1962; MS, London Sch. Econs., 1964; JD, U. Calif., Berkeley, 1967. Bar: Calif. 1968. Assoc. Best, Best & Krieger, Riverside, Calif., 1968-74, ptnr., 1974-96; mem. Calif. Jud. Coun., 1995-96; adj. prof. Hastings Coll. Law U. Calif., San Francisco, 1990; exec. asst. to Assembly majority fl. leader, Calif. State Legislature, Sacramento, 1969-70; asst. adj. prof. Grad. Sch. Mgmt., U. Calif.-Riverside, 1977-88; lectr. UCLA Extension, 1987—; Superior Ct. judge, 1996—; chair Riverside Superior Ct. Jury Com., 1997-2003; chair Calif. jud. coun. task force jury sys. improvements, 1998-2003; city atty. City of Corona, Calif., 1976-96; lectr. local govt. and univ. extension groups. Pres., Pomona Coll. Alumni Coun., 1973-74, Century Club, Riverside, 1974-76, Citizens Univ. Com., 1983-85, Downtown Riverside Assn., 1987-88; chmn. legal affairs com. Assn. Calif. Water Agys., 1985-91. Mem. bd. govs. State Bar Calif., 1990-93, v.p. 1992-93. Named Man of Yr., Riverside Press-Enterprise, 1962, Young Man of Yr., Riverside Jr. C. of C., 1972. Mem. Riverside County Bar Assn. (pres. 1982), Calif. State Bar Assn. (exec. com. pub. law sect. 1983-86), Am. Judicature Soc. Republican. Presbyterian. Contbr. articles on mass transit, assessment of farmland in Calif., exclusionary zoning and environ. law to profl. jours.; author proposed tort reform initiative for Calif. physicians. Office: Riverside Superior Ct 4050 Main St Riverside CA 92501-3702

HOLMES, HENRY W. lawyer; b. Malden, Mass., Apr. 1, 1943; s. Henry W. Holmes BA, U. Calif., 1966, JD, 1969. Bar: Calif. 1970, U.S. Dist. Ct. (cen. dist.) Calif. 1970, U.S. Ct. Appeals (9th cir.) 1970. Lawyer Pacht, Ross, Warne, Bernhard & Sears, L.A., 1972-78; prin. Schiff, Hirsch & Schreiber, Beverly Hills, Calif., 1978-79; ptnr. Butler, Davidson & Holmes, Beverly Hills, Calif., 1979-84; counsel Cooper, Epstein & Hurewitz, Beverly Hills, Calif., 1984-94; counsel, sports and entertainment law Weissman, Wolff, Bergman, Coleman, Silverman, and Holmes, Beverly Hills, Calif., 1994—2002, Grunberg Traurig LLC, Santa Monica, Calif., 2002—. Spkr. in field; adj. prof. sports UCLA; adj. prof. sports law Pepperdine U. Law Sch. Contbr. articles to profl. jours. Trustee U.S. Womens Sports Found., N.Y., 1984-97; bd. dirs. Surfinder Found., Calif. Wildlife Ctr. Named one of Top 20 Sports Lawyers Daily Jour., 1993; Ford Found. fellowship, New Delhi, India, 1969-70. Mem. SAG, Beverly Hills Bar Assn., L.A. Bar Assn., Calif. Bar Assn., Am. Somoa Bar Assn., Explorer's Club. Roman Catholic. Avocations: surfing, acting, art appreciation, scuba diving. Home: 21096 Pacific Coast Hwy Malibu CA 90265-5242 Office: Weissman Wolff Bergman Coleman & Silverman 9665 Wilshire Blvd Fl 9 Beverly Hills CA 90212-2316

HOLMES, JAMES HILL, III, lawyer; b. Birmingham, Ala., Sept. 10, 1935; s. Houston Eccleston and Celia Lindsey (Wearn) Holmes; m. Julia (Judy) Ryman, Aug. 17, 1963; children: James H. IV, Randell Ryman, Tucker Malone. BBA, So. Meth. U., 1957, LLB, 1959. Bar: Tex. 1959, U.S. Ct. Mil. Appeals 1960, U.S. Dist. Ct. (no. dist.) Tex. 1963, U.S. Dist. Ct. (ea. dist.) Tex. 1966, U.S. Dist. Ct. (we. dist.) Tex. 1979, U.S. Ct. Appeals (5th and 11th cirs.) 1981, U.S. Supreme Ct. 1974. Ptnr. Burford & Ryburn, Dallas, 1962—. Mock trial participant Tex. Nurses Assn., 1978—86; spkr. State Bar Tex. Profl. Devel. Program, 1987—2002; co-chair adv. com. professionalism Supreme Ct. Tex., 1989—90. Contbr. articles to profl. jours. Past mem. University Park (Tex.) Bd. Adjustment; chmn. University Park (Tex.) Planning and Zoning Commn., 1988—94; numerous other offices in civic orgns.; city councilman City of University Park, 1994—2000, mayor pro tem, 1998—2000, 2002—; past dir. Child Guidance Clinic; past bd. dirs. Park Cities Town North YMCA; trustee Tex. Ctr. Legal Ethics & Professionalism, 2001—; past dir., past pres. All Sports Assn., Dallas, 1977; pres. University Park Cmty. League, 1987—88; vice chmn. adminstrv. Tex. Ctr. Legal Ethics and Professionalism, 2001—. With USAF, 1959—62. Recipient Presdl. Citation, State Bar of Tex., 1995, Judge Sam Williams Local Bar Leadership award, 2001, Professionalism award, Coll. of the State Bar Tex., 1999, Morris Harrell Professionalism award, Dallas Bar Assn. and Tex. Ctr. for Ethics and Professionalism, 2000, Lola Wright Found. award, 2002. Fellow: State Bar Tex., Tex. Bar Found., Am. Coll. Trial Lawyers; mem.: Patrick E. Higginbotham Am. Inn of Ct. (master 1989—95), Am. Bd. Trial Advocates (pres. Dallas chpt. 2000), Tex. Bar Assn., Dallas Bar Assn. (numerous coms.), Def. Rsch. Inst. (state chmn. 1994), Internat. Assn. Def. Counsel, Assn. Def. Trial Attys., Tex. Assn. Def. Counsel (pres. 1992—93, Founder's award 1997), Dallas Assn. Def. Counsel (chmn. 1975), ABA, Blue Key, Phi Delta Theta, Phi Alpha Delta. Episcopalian. Avocations: jogging, spectator sports, outdoors. General civil litigation, Personal injury (including property damage), Product liability. Home: 3804 Lovers Ln Dallas TX 75225-7101 Office: Burford & Ryburn LLP 3100 Lincoln Pla 500 N Akard St Ste 3100 Dallas TX 75201-6697

HOLMES, MICHAEL GENE, lawyer; b. Longview, Wash., Jan. 14, 1937; s. Robert A. and Esther S. Holmes; children: Helen, Peyton Robert. AB in Econs., Stanford U., 1958, JD, 1960. Bar: Oreg. 1961, U.S. Dist. Ct. Oreg. 1961, U.S. Ct. Appeals (9th cir.) 1961, Temp. Emergency Ct. Appeals 1976, U.S. Supreme Ct. 1976. Assoc. Spears, Lubersky, Bledsoe, Anderson, Young & Hilliard, Portland, 1961-67, ptnr., 1967-90, Lane Powell Spears Lubersky, Portland, 1990-95, of counsel, 1995. Mem. Oreg. Joint Com. of Bar, Press & Broadcasters, 1982-85, sec., 1983-84, chmn. 1985. Author Survey of Oregon Defamation and Privacy Law, ann., 1982-95. Trustee Med. Rsch. Found. Oreg., Portland, 1985-94, exec. com., 1986-94; hon. trustee Oreg. Health Scis. Found., 1995—; trustee Portland Civic Theatre, 1962-66. Mem. Oreg. Bar Assn., Phi Beta Kappa. Administrative and regulatory, General civil litigation, Labor (including EEOC, Fair Labor Standards Act, labor-management relations, NLRB, OSHA).

HOLMES, WILLIAM JAMES, lawyer; b. Hamilton, Ohio, June 2, 1955; s. William J. and Barbara A. (Huff) H.; m. Traci L. Gossett, Sept. 30, 1995. BA, Ohio No. U., 1977; JD, Capital U., Columbus, Ohio, 1980. Bar: Ohio 1980, Va. 1988, U.S. Ct. Claims 1992, U.S. Ct. Mil. Appeals 1981, U.S. Ct. Appeals (Fed. cir.) 1993, U.S. Supreme Ct. 1986. Pvt. practice, Virginia Beach, Va., 1984—. Note editor Capital U. Law Rev., 1979, symposium editor, 1980. Capt. USMC, 1981-84. Criminal, Family and matrimonial, Military. Home: 2112 Tibberton Ct Virginia Beach VA 23464-7851 Office: 6064 Indian River Rd Ste 203 Virginia Beach VA 23464 E-mail: wjhomesmillaw@erts.com.

HOLSCHUH, JOHN DAVID, federal judge; b. Ironton, Ohio, Oct. 12, 1926; s. Edward A. and Helen (Ebert) H.; m. Carol Eloise Stouder, May 25, 1952; 1 child, John David Jr. BA, Miami U., 1948; JD, U. Cin., 1951. Bar: Ohio 1951, U.S. Dist. Ct. (so. dist.) Ohio 1952, U.S. Ct. Appeals (6th cir.) 1953, U.S. Supreme Ct. 1956. Atty. McNamara & McNamara, Columbus, Ohio, 1951-52, 54; law clk. to Hon. Mell. G. Underwood U.S. Dist. Ct., Columbus, 1952-54; ptnr. Alexander, Ebinger, Holschuh, Fisher & McAlister, Columbus, Ohio, 1954-80; judge U.S. Dist. Ct. (so. dist.) Ohio, 1980—, chief judge, 1990-96. Adj. prof. law Ohio State U. Coll. Law, 1970; mem. com. on codes of conduct Jud. Conf. U.S., 1985-90. Pres. bd. dirs. Neighborhood House, Columbus, 1969-70; active United Way of Franklin County, Columbus. Fellow Am. Coll. Trial Lawyers; mem. Order of Coif, Phi Beta Kappa, Omicron Delta Kappa. Home and Office: US Dist Ct 109 US Courthouse 85 Marconi Blvd Rm 109 Columbus OH 43215-2823

HOLSCHUH, JOHN DAVID, JR., lawyer; b. Columbus, Ohio, Dec. 21, 1955; s. John D. and Carol Elouise (Stouder) H.; m. Wendy G. Ellis, Sept. 22, 1984; children: Heather Elyse, John David III, Jacob Alexander. BS, Miami U., Oxford, Ohio, 1977; JD, U. Cin., 1980. Bar: Ohio 1980, U.S. Dist. Ct. (so. dist.) Ohio 1980, U.S. Ct. Appeals (6th cir.) 1986, U.S. Supreme Ct. 1986, U.S. Dist. Ct. (ea. dist.) Ky. 1987, Ky. 1991. Assoc. Santen, Shaffer & Hughes, Cin., 1980-87, ptnr., 1987-89, Santen & Hughes, Cin., 1989—. Pros. atty. City of Loveland, Ohio, 1987-92, magistrate, 1992—; magistrate Village of Fairfax, Ohio, 1999—; mem. faculty Nat. Inst. Trial Advocacy, 1990, 91, 96; participant Pretrial Civil Litigation Skills Workshop, 1991. Author: Medical Malpractice, 1986, Tort Reform Pleading, 1987, Civil Procedure, 1986, rev. edit., 1989, Damages for Plaintiff and Defense Attorneys in Ohio, 1990, 2d edit., 1991, Tort Reform Update, 1990. Recipient merit award Ohio Legal Ctr. Inst., 1986. Mem.: ATLA, Order of Barristers, Potter Stewart Inns of Ct. (emeritus mem.), Cin. Bar Found. (trustee 2001—), Cin. Bar Assn. (chmn. common pleas ct. 1991—93, trustee 1995—, co-chmn. bench-bar conf. 1997—98, sec. 1999—2000, v.p. 2000—01, pres.-elect 2001—02, pres. 2002—), Hamilton County Trial Lawyers (pres. 1990—92), Ohio State Bar Assn., Ohio Acad. Trial Lawyers (trustee 1991—95, 1998—2000), Am. Bd. Trial Advs., 6th Cir. Jud. Conf. (life; del. 1983—88). Avocations: sports, travel. Federal civil litigation, General civil litigation, Personal injury (including property damage). Office: Santen & Hughes 312 Walnut St Ste 3100 Cincinnati OH 45202-4044

HOLSINGER, JOHN PAUL, lawyer; b. New Kensington, Pa., June 22, 1963; s. Perry Lanson and Jayne (Devine) H.; m. Amy O'Leary, May 20, 1989; children: Sarah Jayne, Thomas O'Leary, Julia Margaret. BBA, George Washington U., 1985, MBA, 1987; JD, U. Va., 1990. Bar: Pa. 1990, U.S. Dist. Ct. (we. dist.) Pa. Counsel Alcoa Inc., Pitts., 1990-2000; dir. Real Estate, Pitts., 2000—02, sr. counsel, 2002—. Corporate, general, FERC practice, Property, real (including real estate development, water). Office: 8550 W Bryn Mawr Ave 10th Fl Chicago IL 60631 E-mail: john.holsinger@alcoa.com.

HOLSTEAD, JOHN BURNHAM, retired lawyer; b. Dallas, Mar. 5, 1938; s. J.B. and Maurice (Cook) H.; m. Marilyn Morris, Nov. 23, 1963; children: Will, Rand, Scott. BA, La. Tech. U., 1959; LL.B., U. Tex.-Austin, 1962. Bar: Tex., U.S. Dist. Ct. Tex. 1965, U.S. Ct. Appeals (5th cir.), U.S. Ct. Appeals (10th cir.), U.S. Supreme Ct. 1974. Briefing clk. Tex. Sup. Ct., 1962-63; assoc. Vinson & Elkins, Houston, 1965-72, ptnr., 1972; ret., 2001. Mem. bd. advisors Biology of Info. Ctr., Baylor Coll. Medicine; spkr. on civil litigation and bus. disputes, disting. alumni, La. Tech. U.. Bd. dirs., trustee Goodwill Industries Houston, Inc. Named Centennial Outstanding Alumni, La. Tech. U., 1998. Fellow Internat. Soc. Barristers, Houston Bar Found., Tex. Bar Found.; mem. ABA, Tex. Bar Assn., Houston Bar Assn., River Oaks Country Club. Episcopalian. Federal civil litigation, State civil litigation. Office: Vinson & Elkins 3200 First City Tower 1001 Fannin St Ste 3300 Houston TX 77002-6706 E-mail: jholstead@velaw.com.

HOLSTEIN, JOHN CHARLES, former state supreme court judge; b. Springfield, Mo., Jan. 10, 1945; s. Clyde E. Jr. and Wanda R. (Polson) H.; m. Mary Frances Brummell, Mar. 26, 1967; children: Robin Diane Camacho, Mary Katherine Link, Erin Elizabeth Lary. BA, S.W. Mo. State Coll., 1967; JD, U. Mo., 1970; LLM, U. Va., 1995. Bar: Mo. 1970. Atty. Moore & Brill, West Plains, Mo., 1970-75; probate judge Howell County, West Plains, 1975-78, assoc. cir. judge, 1978-82; cir. judge 37th Jud. Cir., West Plains, 1982-87; judge so. dist. Mo. Ct. Appeals, Springfield, 1987-88, chief judge so. dist., 1988-89; judge Supreme Ct. Mo., Jefferson City, 1989—2002, chief justice, 1995-97; shareholder Thomson & Kilroy, P.C., Springfield, 2002—. Instr. bus. law S.W. Mo. State Coll., 1976-77, pub. sch. law S.W. Bapt. U., 1999-2000. Lt. col. USAR, 1969-87. Office: Shugart Thomson & Kilroy PC 901 St Louis St Ste 1200 Springfield MO 65806*

HOLT, CHARLES WILLIAM, JR., lawyer, mediator; b. Dallas, Aug. 8, 1951; s. Charles William Sr. and Oleta Ruth (Leonard) H.; m. Claudia Capeau, Dec. 2, 1978; 1 child, Auston Charles. BS, East Tex. State U., 1973; JD, So. Meth. U., 1977. Bar: Tex. 1977, U.S. Dist. Ct. (fed. dist.) 1978. Assoc. Ralph M. Hall Law Office, Rockwall, Tex., 1977-89; pvt. practice Rockwall, 1990—. Chmn. Rockwall Firefighter Support Com., 1996-99. Mem.: Rockwall Bar Assn. (pres. 1986—87), State Bar Tex., Rockwall Area C. of C. (bd. dirs. 1982—84, 1997—), Rockwall Noon Club, Rotary Internat. Methodist. Avocations: video production, camping, outdoors, arts. Commercial, contracts (including sales of goods; commercial financing), Personal injury (including property damage), Property, real (including real estate development, water). Office: 500 Turtle Cove Blvd Ste 140 Rockwall TX 75087-5300 Business E-Mail: holt@charlesholt.com.

HOLT, MARJORIE SEWELL, lawyer, retired congresswoman; b. Birmingham, Ala., Sept. 17, 1920; d. Edward Rol and Juanita (Felts) Sewell; m. Duncan McKay Holt, Dec. 26, 1946; children: Rachel Holt Tschantre, Edward Sewell, Victoria. Grad., Jacksonville Jr. Coll., 1945; JD, U. Fla., 1949. Bar: Fla. 1949, Md. 1962. Pvt. practice, Annapolis, Md., 1962; clk. Anne Arundel County Circuit Ct., 1966-72; mem. 93d-99th Congresses from 4th Dist. of Md., 1973-86; armed services com., vice-chair Office Tech. Assessment, 1977; chair Republican Study com., 1975-76; of counsel Smith, Somerville & Case, Balt., 1986-90. Supr. elections Anne Arundel County, 1963-65; del. Rep. Nat. Conv., 1968, 76, 80, 84, 88; mem. Pres.'s Commn. on Arms Control and Disarmament; mem. ind. commn. USAR; bd. dirs. Annapolis Fed. Savs. Bank; adv. bd. Crestar; co-chair George W. Bush Presdl. campaign, Md., 2000. Co-author: Case Against The Reckless Congress, 1976, Can You Afford This House, 1978. Bd. dirs. Md. Sch. for the Blind, Hist. Annapolis Found. Recipient Disting. Alumna award U. Fla., 1975, Trustees award U. Fla. Coll. Law, 1984, Alumnae Outstanding Achievement award, 1997. Mem. ABA, Md. Bar Assn., Anne Arundel Bar Assn., Phi Kappa Phi, Phi Delta Delta. Presbyterian (elder 1959).

HOLTON, WALTER CLINTON, JR., lawyer; b. Winston-Salem, N.C. s. Walter Clinton and Mabel (Hartsfield) H.; m. Lynne Rowley. BA in Polit. Sci., U. N.C., 1977; JD, Wake Forest U., 1984. Bar: N.C. 1984, U.S. Dist. Ct. (mid. dist.) N.C. 1986, U.S. Ct. Appeals (4th cir.) 1990, U.S. Supreme Ct., 1996. Asst. dist. atty. Office 21st Jud. Dist. Atty., Winston-Salem, 1985-87; assoc. White & Crumpler, Winston-Salem, 1987-88; pvt. practice Winston-Salem, 1989; ptnr. Holton & Menefee, Winston-Salem, 1989-92, Tisdale, Holton & Menefee, PA, Winston-Salem, 1992-94; U.S. atty. Office U.S. Atty. Mid. Dist. N.C., Greensboro, N.C., 1994-2001; pvt. practice Grace Holton Tisdale & Clifton PA, Winston-Salem, 2001—. Democrat. Office: Grace Holton Tisdale & Clifton 301 N Main St Ste 100 Winston Salem NC 27101 Fax: (336) 721-1176. E-mail: wholton@ghtclaw.com.

HOLTZMAN, ELIZABETH, lawyer; b. Bklyn., Aug. 11, 1941; d. Sidney and Filia Holtzman. AB magna cum laude, Radcliffe Coll., 1962; JD, Harvard U., 1965; L.D.S., Regis Coll., 1975, Skidmore Coll., 1980, Simmons Coll., 1981, Smith Coll., 1982. Bar: N.Y. 1966. Assoc. Wachtell, Lipton, Rosen, Katz & Kern, N.Y.C., 1965-67; asst. to mayor N.Y.C., 1968-69; assoc. Paul, Weiss, Rifkind, Wharton & Garrison, 1970-72; mem. 93d-96th Congresses from 16th dist., N.Y.; vis. prof. Law Sch. and Grad. Sch. Pub. Adminstrn. NYU, 1981; dist. atty. Kings County, Bklyn., 1982-89; comptr. City of N.Y., 1990-93. Mem. Am. Jewish Commn. on the Holocaust, Nazi and Japanese War Criminal Records Working Group, 1999—; Dem. nominee U.S. Senate, 1980; N.Y. State Dem. committeewoman, 1970—72; mem. Pres.'s Nat. Commn. on U.S. Observance Internat. Women's Yr., Helsinki Watch Com., 1981—88, Select Com. on Immigration Policy, 1979—80; bd. overseers Harvard U., 1976—82; bd. trustees Radcliffe Coll., Bklyn. Acad. Music Endowment Trust; mem. Lawyers Com. Internat. Human Right, 1981—88. Recipient Nat. Coun. Jewish Women's Faith and Humanity award, YWCA Elizabeth Cutter Morrow award, Maccabean award N.Y. Bd. Rabbis, Alumni recognition award Radcliffe Coll. Alumnae Assn., 1973, N.J. and L.A. ACLU awards for contbns. to def. of Constn. and preservation of civil liberties, 1981, Athena award N.Y.C. Commn. on Status of Women, 1985, Woman of Yr. award N.Y. League Bus. and Profl. Women, 1985, Jan Korzak award 5th Ann. Kent State Holocaust Conf., 1986, Outstanding and Meritorious Svc. award Jewish War Vets. of U.S., 1986, Award of Remembrance Warsaw Ghetto Resistance Orgn., 1987, Gates of Freedom award State of Israel Bonds, 1987; Award of Honor United Jewish Appeal, 1988, Deed of Tzedakah award, 1991. Fellow N.Y. Inst. Humanities; mem. Assn. of Bar of City of N.Y., Nat. Women's Polit. Caucus (Outstanding Svc. award 1987), Phi Beta Kappa. Office: Herrick Feinstein LLP 2 Park Ave Fl 20 New York NY 10016-9302

HOLTZMAN, ROBERT ARTHUR, lawyer; b. L.A., July 17, 1929; s. Ruben and Bertha (Dembowsky) H.; m. Barbara Polis, June 26, 1954 (dec. 1985); children: Melinda, Mark, Bradley; m. Liliane Gurwith Endlich, July 6, 1986. BA, UCLA, 1951; LLB, U. So. Calif., 1954. Bar: Calif. 1955, U.S. Dist. Ct. (cen. dist.) Calif. 1955, U.S. Ct. Appeals (9th cir.) 1958. Assoc. Gang, Tyre & Brown, L.A., 1954, Loeb and Loeb, L.A., 1956-63, ptnr., 1964-95; of counsel, 1996—. Judge pro tem Mcpl. Ct. L.A. Jud. Dist.; lectr. Calif. Continuing Edn. of Bar. Contbr. articles to legal publs. With U.S. Army, 1954-56. Mem. ABA (dispute resolution sect., vice-chmn. arbitration com.), Calif. Bar Assn. (chmn. com. on adminstrn. of justice 1984-85), L.A. County Bar Assn., Am. Arbitration Assn. (panel arbitrators 1974—, panel mediators 1992—, arbitrator large complex case program 1993—). General civil litigation. Office: Loeb & Loeb LLP 1000 Wilshire Blvd Ste 1800 Los Angeles CA 90017-2475 E-mail: rholtzman@loeb.com.

HOLTZMANN, HOWARD MARSHALL, lawyer, judge; b. N.Y.C., Dec. 10, 1921; s. Jacob L. And Lillian (Plotz) H.; m. Anne Fisher, Jan. 14, 1945 (dec. Aug. 1967); children: Susan Holtzmann Richardson, Betsey; m. Carol Ebenstein Van Berg, Dec. 23, 1972 AB, Yale Coll., 1942, JD, 1947; LittD (hon.), St. Bonaventure U., 1952; LLD (hon.), Jewish Theol. Sem., N.Y.C., 1990. Bar: N.Y. 1947. Atty. Colorado Fuel & Iron Corp., Buffalo, N.Y., 1947-49; ptnr. Holtzmann, Wise & Shepard, N.Y.C., 1949-95; judge Iran-U.S. Claims Tribunal, The Hague, Netherlands, 1981-94; arbitrator and dispute resolution cons., 1994—; arbitrator Claims Resolution Tribunal for Dormant Accounts, Zurich, Switzerland, 1998—2002. U.S. del. UN Commn. on Internat. Trade Law, 1975—, Hague Conf. on Pvt. Internat. Law, 1985; advisor U.S.A. Arbitration agreements with USSR, Russian Fedn., China, Hungary, Bulgaria, Czechoslovakia, Poland and German Dem. Republic. Author, editor: A New Look at Legal Aspects of Doing Business with China, 1979; co-author: A Guide to the Unicitral Model Law on International Commercial Arbitration—Legislative History and Commentary, 1988 (cert. of merit Am. Soc. Internat. Law 1991); contbr. chpts. to books and articles to law jours. Mem. governing coun. Downstate Med. Sch. SUNY, Bklyn., 1961-78; trustee St. Bonaventure U., Olean, N.Y., 1968-90, trustee emeritus, 1990—; chmn. bd. Jewish Theol. Sem., N.Y.C., 1983-85, hon. chmn., 1985—; trustee Inst. Internat. Law, Pace U. Sch. Law, 1992—. Mem. ABA (chmn. com. code ethics comml. arbitrators 1973-77), Internat. Coun. for Comml. Arbitration (hon. vice chmn.), Am. Arbitration Assn. (hon. chmn., Gotshal Internat. Arbitration award 1980), Internat. C. of C. (vice chmn. arbitration commn. 1979-2001), Stockholm Arbitration Inst. (adv. bd.), Am. Bar Found., N.Y. County Lawyers Assn., Internat. Law Assn., Am. Fgn. Law Assn. (v.p. 1995—), Internat. Bar Assn., N.Y. State Bar Assn., Assn. of Bar of City of N.Y., Am. Soc. Internat. Law (cert. merit 1991), Soc. Profls. in Dispute Resolution, Indsl. Rels. Rsch. Assn., N.Y. Law Inst., Am. Judicature Soc., Am. Assn. for Internat. Commn. of Jurists. Private international, Public international, Alternative dispute resolution. Office: Ste 2000 630 Fifth Ave New York NY 10111-0100

HOLTZSCHUE, KARL BRESSEM, lawyer, author, educator; b. Wichita, Kans., Mar. 3, 1938; s. Bressem C. and Josephine E. (Landsittel) H.; m. Linda J. Gross, Oct. 24, 1959; children: Alison, Adam, Sara. AB, Dartmouth Coll., 1959; LLB, Columbia U., 1966. Bar: N.Y. 1967, U.S. Dist. Ct. (so. and ea. dists.) N.Y. 1968. Assoc. Webster & Sheffield, N.Y.C., 1966-73, ptnr., 1974-88; ptnr., head real estate dept. O'Melveny and Myers, N.Y.C., 1988-90; pvt. practice N.Y.C., 1990—. Adj. prof. Fordham U. Law Sch., 1990—; adj. prof. Bus. Sch., Columbia U., 1990-96, Law Sch., 1991. Author: Holtzschue on Real Estate Contracts, New York Practice Guide: Real Estate, Vol. 1 on Purchase and Sale, Real Estate Transactions: Purchase and Sale of Real Property; editor: NYSBA's Res. R.E. Forms on Hot Docs. Trustee Soc. of St. Johnland, 1980-86, Ensemble Studio Theatre, 1986-88; bd. dirs. The Bridge, 1990—, pres., 1992-95; mem. alumni bd. Dartmouth Ptnrs. in Cmty. Svc., 1994—, chmn., 1994-99. Lt. (j.g.) USN, 1959-62. Mem. ABA (com. on internat. investment in real estate 1987-97, com. on legal opinions in real estate trans. 1990—), N.Y. State Bar Assn. (exec. com. real property sect. 1998—, com. on attys. opinions 1992—, com. on title and transfer 1998—, co-chmn. 1998—), Assn. Bar City N.Y. (com. on real property law 1977-80, chmn. 1987-90, 95-98, com. ctrl. and East Europe 1998-99), Am. Coll. Real Estate Lawyers (opinions com. 1989—, vice chmn. 1992-95), Tri Bar (opinions com. 1990-99). Episcopalian. Property, real (including real estate development, water). E-mail: kholtzschue@nyc.rr.com.

HOLZ, HARRY GEORGE, lawyer; b. Milw., Sept. 13, 1934; s. Harry Carl and Emma Louise (Hinz) H.; m. Nancy L. Heiser, May 12, 1962; children: Pamela Gretchen, Bradley Eric, Erika Lynn. BS, Marquette U., 1956, LLB, 1958; LLM, Northwestern U., 1960. Bar: Wis. 1958, Ill. 1960. Tchg. fellow Northwestern U. Sch. Law, 1958-59; assoc. Sidley & Austin, Chgo., 1960; ptnr. Quarles & Brady, Milw., 1968—2002, of counsel, 2002—. Lectr. law securities regulation U. Wis. Law Sch., 1971—74; adj. prof. Marquette U. Sch. Law, 1976—91; faculty program on antitrust law Wis. State Bar Sems., 1975—82, 1989, 93; bd. dirs., sec. Creative Sharp Presentations Inc.; lectr. PLI 33rd Antitrust Inst.; lectr., spkr. in antitrust field. Bd. visitors Marquette U. Sch. Law, 1990, 93. Capt. C.E. U.S. Army, 1960-67. Fellow: Am. Bar Found.; mem.: ABA (lectr. nat. antitrust program 1997, Robinson-Patman com., corp. counsel com., antitrust litigation com.), Marquette U. Law Alumni Assn. (bd. dirs.), Milw. Bar Assn., Wis. Bar Assn. (chmn. bus. law com. 1978—79, bd. dirs. 1978—83, chair 180 standing rev. com. 2001—, standing com. bus. law), Marquette U. Sch. Law Woolsack Soc. (bd. dirs., past pres.), Western Racquet Club, Phi Delta Phi, Beta Gamma Sigma. Antitrust, Corporate, general, Mergers and acquisitions. Office: Quarles & Brady 411 E Wisconsin Ave Ste 2550 Milwaukee WI 53202-4497

HOLZ, MICHAEL HAROLD, lawyer; b. Dayton, Ohio, Apr. 10, 1942; s. Harold L. and Norma (Montgomery) Holz; m. Tanya Noffsinger, July 22, 1972 (div. Jan. 1983). BA, Wittenberg U., 1964; JD, U. Cin., 1967; MBA, U. Dayton, 1979. Bar: Ohio 1968, U.S. Dist. Ct. 1971, U.S. Tax Ct. 1975. With office of legal assistance Butler County OEO, Hamilton, Ohio, 1968; legal dep. probate Montgomery County, Dayton, 1971—73; asst. pros. atty. Greene County, Xenia, Ohio, 1973; sole practice Dayton, 1974—. Mem. Dayton Jaycees, 1971—78, Montgomery County Dem. Ctrl. Com., 1972—84. Served with U.S. Army, 1968—70, Vietnam. Mem.: ACLU (dir.), Ohio Bar Assn., Dayton Bar Assn. (ethics com. 1985—89, unauthorized practice of law com. 1990—95, bar exam. and qualifications com. 1996—2003), Mensa, Vietnam Vets. Am., Greater Dayton Real Estate Investors Assn., Phi Alpha Delta. Episcopalian. Criminal, General practice, Property, real (including real estate development, water). Home: 507 Wilmington Ave Apt 1 Dayton OH 45420-1876

HOMER, BARRY WAYNE, lawyer; b. Junction City, Kans., Jan. 13, 1950; BA, U. Kans., 1972; JD, U. Chgo., 1975. Bar: Calif. 1975, U.S. Dist. Ct. (no. dist.) Calif. 1975, U.S. Tax Ct. 1980. Assoc. Brobeck, Phleger & Harrison, San Francisco, 1975-82, ptnr., 1982—2003, Morgen, Lewis & Bockius, LLP, San Francisco, 2003—. Co-author: Attorney's Guide to Pension and Profitsharing Plans, 1985, Compensating the Executive with Stock: Some Planning Possibilities and the Effect of the Parachute Provisions, 1986; contbr. articles to profl. jours. Mem. ABA (employee benefits com. tax sect. 1978—), Western Pension & Benefits Conf. Pension, profit-sharing, and employee benefits, Corporate taxation. Office: Morgan Lewis & Bockius LLP Spear St Tower 1 Market Plz San Francisco CA 94105-1420

HOMESLEY, CLIFTON W. lawyer; b. Bremerhaven, Germany, Mar. 25, 1960; s. Troy Clifton and Jean McCauley Homesley; m. Fariba G. Golkho, Aug. 17, 1985; children: Troy Clifton, Persia Freshteh, Cyrus Walker, Darius Quartes. BS, U. N.C., 1982. Bar: N.C. 1986. Ptnr. Homesley, Jones, Gaines, Homesley & Dudley, Mooresville, NC, 1986—2002, Homesley, Parker & Wingo, PLLC, 2002—02. Chmn. N.C. Law Practice Mgmt. Coun., Cary, 2002—. Facilities chairperson Friends of the Libr., Mooresville, NC, 2000—. General civil litigation, Corporate, general, General practice. Office: Homesley Parker & Wingo PLLC 330 South Main St Mooresville NC 28115 Office Fax: 704-664-0267. E-mail: chomesley@lakenormanlaw.com.

HONAKER, JIMMIE JOE, lawyer, ecologist; b. Oklahoma City, Jan. 21, 1939; s. Joe Jack and Ruby Lee (Bowen) H.; children: Jay Jimmie, Kerri Ruth. BA, Colo. Coll., 1963; MA, U. No. Colo., 1991; JD, U. Wyo., 1966, MS, 1995; postgrad., Utah State U., 1995—. Bar: Colo. 1966, U.S. Dist. Ct. Colo., U.S. Ct. Appeals (10th cir.), Ute Indian Tribal Ct. Utah. Pvt. practice, Longmont, Colo., 1966-91. Incorporator Longmont Boys Baseball, 1969; chmn. Longmont City Charter Commn., 1973; chmn. ch. bd. 1st Christian Ch., Longmont, 1975, 76; chmn. North Boulder County unit Am. Cancer Soc., 1978, 79. Recipient Disting. Svc. award Longmont Centennial Yr., 1971; named Outstanding Young Man, Longmont Jaycees, 1973. Mem.: ABA, Internat. Assn. Landscape Ecology-U.S. Regional Assn., Ecol. Soc. Am., Denver Bar Assn., Colo. Bar Assn. (interprofl. com. 1972—91, environ. law sect. 1999—), Nat. Eagle Scout Assn., Utah Mountain Club, Colo. Mountain Club, Alpha Tau Omega, Xi Sigma Pi, Alpha Kappa Psi, Phi Alpha Delta. Avocations: private pilot, mountain climbing. Commercial, contracts (including sales of goods; commercial financing), Environmental, Property, real (including real estate development, water). Address: Utah State U Box 1320 Logan UT 84322-0199

HONAKER, RICHARD HENDERSON, lawyer; b. Laramie, Wyo., Mar. 10, 1951; s. Hayward E. and Faola I. (Henderson) H.; m. Shannon Kathleen Casey, Dec. 24, 1978; children: Heather, Harmony, Dustin. BA cum laude, Harvard U., 1973; JD, U. Wyo., 1976. Bar: Wyo. 1976, U.S. Dist. Ct. Wyo., 1976, U.S. Ct. Appeals (10th cir.) 1977, U.S. Supreme Ct. 1989. Asst. atty. gen. State of Wyo., Cheyenne, 1976-78, state pub. defender, 1979-81; solo practitioner Honaker Law Offices LC, Rock Springs, Wyo., 1981—. Mem. Wyo. State Ho. of Reps., Sweetwater County, 1986-93. Mem. ATLA, Wyo. State Bar (pres. 2002—), Wyo. Trial Lawyers Assn. (pres. 1986), Am. Bd. Trial Advocates (charter), Nat. Coll. Advocacy (advocate). General civil litigation, Criminal, Personal injury (including property damage). Office: Honaker Law Offices LC PO Box 366 Rock Springs WY 82902-0366

HONEMANN, DANIEL HENRY, lawyer; b. Balt., Oct. 20, 1929; s. Henry Letcher and Maude Elizabeth (Wilson) H.; m. Rose Ann Clark, Mar. 23, 1974; children by previous marriage: Deborah, Dori, Daniel, Donna. AB, Western Md. Coll., Westminster, 1951; JD, U. Md., 1956. Bar: Md. 1956. Practice law, Balt.; partner firm Clapp, Somerville, Honemann & Beach, 1962-85, Whiteford, Taylor & Preston, 1986—; asst. U.S. atty. Dist. Md., 1960-61. Author: (with others) Robert's Rules of Order Newly Revised, 10th edit. Served to 1st lt. inf. AUS, 1951-53. Decorated Bronze Star, Combat Inf. badge. Fellow Am. Coll. Trust and Estate Counsel, Md. Bar Found.; mem. ABA (ho. of dels. 1978-80), Md. Bar Assn. (sec. 1977-84, bd. govs. 1975-84), Balt. Bar Assn. Home: 2318 Harcroft Rd Lutherville Timonium MD 21093-2638 Office: 7 Saint Paul St Ste 1400 Baltimore MD 21202-1654 E-mail: dhonemann@wtplaw.com., dhonemann@comcast.net.

HONG, BYUNG SOO, lawyer; b. Seoul, Republic of Korea, Feb. 26, 1971; arrived in Brazil, 1971; s. Yong Ik and Yong Hee Hong; m. Susana Bae Hong, Nov. 20, 2000. LLB, U. Sao Paulo, 1994. Bar: Sao Paulo chpt. Brazilian Bar Assn. 1994. Legal counsel Anfavea, Sao Paulo, Brazil, 1994—96; assoc. Tavares Guerreiro Adv., Sao Paulo, 1996—97, Ochman Advogados, Sao Paulo, 1997—2000; ptnr. Felsberg & Assocs., Sao Paulo, 2000. Legal cons. Brazilian Venture Capital Assn., 2001—. Mergers and acquisitions, Corporate, general, Private international. Office: Felsberg & Assocs 2d Fl Ave Paulista 1294 01310 915 São Paulo Brazil Office Fax: 55 11 3141 9150. E-mail: byung@felsberg.com.br.

HONG, DONG OH, lawyer; b. Pusan, Republic of Korea, Apr. 18, 1967; s. Hwa Yoon Hong and Duk In Kim. LLB, Seoul (Republic of Korea) Nat. U., 1993; M in Electronic Engring., Yonsei Grad. Sch., Seoul, 2001. Bar: Korea Supreme Ct. 1997. Jud. trainee Jud. Tng. Acad., Korea Supreme Ct., Seoul, 1997; assoc. Yoon & Ptnrs., Seoul, 1997, Ctrl. Internat. Law Firm, Seoul, 1997—. Contbr. articles to profl. jours. Intellectual property, Antitrust. Home: Goryo Academitel 1625 Ahyundong Mapogu Seoul Republic of Korea Office: Ctrl Internat Law Firm Soosongdong 80 Chongnogu Seoul Republic of Korea

HONIG, GÉRARD, lawyer; b. Paris, July 2, 1946; s. François and Hélène Honig. MA in Law, U. Paris II, 1969, DES in Pvt. Law, 1970; MJC in Comparative Law, NYU, 1974. Mng. sr. ptnr., co-founder Honig Buffat Mettetal, Paris, 1979, Honig Preel Metteltal Buffat Coulon, Paris, 2001, HPMBC Clyde & Co., Paris, 2002—. Aviation, Product liability, Professional liability. Office: HPMBC Clyde & Co 19 rue Magellan 75008 Paris France

HONSA, FRANTISEK, lawyer; b. Ceske Budejovice, Apr. 29, 1968; s. Frantisek and Marta Honsa; m. Hedvika Honsa, Mar. 23, 2000; 1 child, Frantisek. M of Law, Charles U., Prague, 1991; LLD, PhD, Charles U., 1998. Counsel Halliburton Co., Czech Republic, 1994—97; sr. atty. Burns & Schwartz, Prague, Czech Republic, 1997—99; ptnr. Brzobohaty, Broz and Honsa, Prague, Czech Republic, 2000—. Mem.: Czech Bar Assn. Personal injury (including property damage), State civil litigation, Criminal. Office: Brzobohaty Broz & Honsa Klimentska 10 Prague 110 00 Czech Republic Office Fax: 00420 234 091 366. Business E-Mail: fhonsa@bbh.cz.

HOOD, EARL JAMES, lawyer, state legislator; b. Spearfish, S.D., Apr. 28, 1947; s. Earl Kenneth and Florence Lorraine (Castor) m. Judith G. Witzel, June 2, 1968 (div. Sept. 1974); children: Jason, Jared Jon; m. Kathleen Gay Donahue, Sept. 13, 1975; 1 child, Stewart Lee. BS, Black Hills State Coll., 1969; JD, U. S.D., 1972. Mem. S.D. Ho. of Reps., Pierre, 1983-92, speaker pro tem, 1989-90, speaker of the house, 1991-92; pvt. practice Spearfish, 1972—; pres., shareholder, bd. dirs. Hood, Nies & Dardis, P.C., Spearfish, 2000—. City atty. City of Spearfish, 1972-76, 87—; mem. S.D. Code Commn., 1989-92. Chief Spearfish Vol. Fire Dept., 1982-83; pres. Black Hills State Coll. Found., Inc., Spearfish, 1986; mem. S.D. Pvt. Industry Coun., 1993-94; mem. S.D. Quality Govt. Commn., 1993-94; chair Kids Voting, Spearfish, 1993-95, bd. dirs., 1994-95; chair Workforce Devel. Coun. S.D., 1994-95; eagle scout Boy Scouts Am., 1961; bd. dirs. High Plains Heritage Soc., 1999—; bd. dirs. No. Hills Tng. Ctr. Found., 1999—, pres., 2001—; del. Rep. Nat. Conv., 1996; bd. dirs. West River Econs. Devel. Corp., 1999-2002. Recipient Vigil Honor Order of Arrow, BSA, 1965, Disting. Alumnus award Black Hills State U., 1990; named S.D. Firefighter of Yr. Keep S.D. Green Assn., 1984, Friend of Edn. S.D. Edn. Assn., 1990. Mem. S.D. Bar Assn., S.D. Trial Lawyers Assn., Lions, Masons (Spearfish Lodge #18), Order Eastern Star (Queen City chpt #89), Black Hills Scottish Rite, Naja Shrine. Republican. Avocations: reading, travel. General practice, Legislative, Probate (including wills, trusts). Home: PO Box 611 Spearfish SD 57783-0611 Office: Hood Nies & Dardis PC PO Box 759 Spearfish SD 57783-0759

HOOD, MARY DULLEA, law librarian; b. Fargo, N.D., Jan. 3, 1947; d. Maurice Eugene and Rosemary (Melican) Dullea; m. Michael L. Hood, May 26, 1974; children: David Patrick, Michelle Marie. BA, U. Santa Clara, 1970, JD, 1975; MLS, San Jose State U., 1979. Bar: Calif. 1976. Libr. asst. Law Libr., U. Santa Clara, Calif., 1970-75, reference libr., 1975-78; instr. legal rsch. Paralegal Inst., 1976-84; head pub. svcs. U. Santa Clara, Calif., 1978-87, assoc. dir., 1987—, mem. univ. automation task force, 1986-91, mem. adj. faculty advanced legal rsch. Law Sch., 1998-99, 2001, acting dir., 2001. Mem. Santa Clara CSC, 1976-78. Mem. Am. Assn. Law Librs. (placement com. 2000-02, awards com. 2002—), No. Calif. Assn. Law Librs. (pres. 1982-83), U. Santa Clara Law Sch. Alumni Assn. (treas. 1983-85). Avocations: needlepoint, reading, stained glass. Office: Santa Clara U Law Libr 500 El Camino Real Santa Clara CA 95053-0430 E-mail: mhood@scu.edu.

HOOD, ROBERT HOLMES, lawyer; b. Charleston, S.C., Oct. 5, 1944; s. James Albert and Ruth (Henderson) H.; m. Mary Agnes Burnham, Aug. 5, 1967; children: Mary Agnes, Elizabeth, Robert Holmes Jr., James Bernard. BA, U. of the South, 1966; JD, U. S.C., 1969. Bar: U.S. Supreme Ct. 1969, S.C. 1969, U.S. Dist. Ct. S.C. 1969, U.S. Ct. Appeals (4th cir.) 1969. Asst. atty. gen. State of S.C., Columbia, 1969-70; ptnr. Sinkler, Gibbs & Simons, Charleston, 1970-85; prin. Hood Law Firm, LLC, Charleston, 1985--. Mem. Assn. Def. Trial Attys. (pres. 1985-86), Am. Bd. Trial Advs. (diplomate, pres. Charleston chpt. 1997), Internat. Assn. Def. Counsel, Def. Rsch. and Trial Inst. (bd. dirs. 1987-90), Fedn. Ins. and Corp. Counsel, S.C. Def. Trial Attys. Assn. (pres. 1980-81), Network of Trial Law Firms. Episcopalian. General civil litigation, Commercial, consumer (including collections, credit), Personal injury (including property damage). Office: 172 Meeting St Charleston SC 29401-3126 E-mail: bobby-hood@hoodlaw.com.

HOOGLAND, ROBERT FREDERICS, lawyer; b. Paterson, N.J., Apr. 3, 1955; s. Robert J. and Lucretia H. BA, U. Fla., 1976; MBA, Rollins Coll., 1977; JD, U. Fla., 1982. Bar: Fla. 1983, U.S. Dist. Ct. (mid. dist.) Fla. 1989; cert. real estate law. Assoc. Giles, Hedrick & Robinson, Orlando, Fla., 1983-89; ptnr. Hoogland & Durket, P.A., Longwood, Fla., 1989-92, Robert F. Hoogland, P.A., Altamonte Springs, Fla., 1992—. Mem. ABA, Fla. Bar Assn., Orange County Bar Assn.,Voile A. Williams Inns of Court, Phi Delta Phi. Republican. Roman Catholic. Avocations: tennis, golf, fishing. Property, real (including real estate development, water), State civil litigation, Commercial, consumer (including collections, credit). Home: 139 Olive Tree Cir Altamonte Springs FL 32714-3240 Office: PO Box 160021 Altamonte Springs FL 32716-0021

HOOK, CHRISTIAN ROBERT MALNACHTAN, solicitor; b. Edinburgh, Scotland, Aug. 16, 1952; s. William Thomson and Margaret (Barr) Hook; m. Stephanie Ann Taylor, Sept. 11, 1981. BA in Law, U. Cambridge, 1975. Bar: England & Wales 1980, Scotland 1988. Clk. Trowers &Hamline, London, 1976—79; with Bahrain Govt., Manama, 1978—79; asst. solicitor Trowers & Hamline, 1980—85, ptnr., 1985—87; with Bahrain Govt., 1982—86; assoc. Dundarn Wilson, Edinbugh, Scotland, 1987—90, ptnr., 1990—2002, Morgon Fraser, 2002—. Mem.: Hollywood High Constables (constable 1995—), New Club. Avocations: skiing, horseback riding, shooting, golf. Corporate, general, Mergers and acquisitions, Commercial, contracts (including sales of goods; commercial financing). Office: Morton Fraser 30-31 Queen St Edinburgh EH2 1JX Scotland Fax: +31 247 1007. E-mail: christian.hook@morton-frazer.com.

HOOKER, WADE STUART, JR., lawyer; b. Brockton, Mass., Sept. 23, 1941; s. Wade S. and Eleanor T. Hooker; m. Susan M. Levine, May 20, 1984; children: Thomas A., Richard P. BA, Harvard Coll., 1963; LLB, U. Va., 1966. Bar: N.Y. 1969. Assoc. Casey, Lane & Mittendorf, N.Y.C., 1968-77; ptnr. Burlingham Underwood LLP, N.Y.C., 1979—2001; ind. practice, 2002—. Spkr. in field. Contbr. articles to profl. jours. Maxwell fellow Syracuse U., Resident scholar Indian Law Inst., New Delhi, 1966-67. Mem. ABA, Assn. Bar City of N.Y. (chair aeronautics com.), Computer Law Assn., Inc., Internat. Bar Assn., Maritime Law Assn. U.S. (chair com. maritime regulation and promotion 1990-94), Mensa. Admiralty, Corporate, general, Finance. Office: 211 Central Park W New York NY 10024 E-mail: wadehooker@post.harvard.com.

HOOPER, SCOTT ALAN, lawyer; b. Huntsville, Ala., May 29, 1963; s. H. L. and Glenna Hooper. BBA, U. Tenn., 1985, JD honors, 1988. Assoc. Vinson & Elkins, Houston, 1988—98; ptnr. Smith & Hooper, Houston, 1998—2000; shareholder Scott Hooper & Assocs., Houston, 2000—. Bd. trustees Houston Symphony. Fellow: Tex. Bar Found., Tex. Trial Lawyers Assn. (dir.); mem.: Houston Bar Found., Houston Trial Lawyers Assn. (dir.). Personal injury (including property damage). Office: 1414 W Clay Houston TX 77019

HOOPS, FREDERICK KURRE, lawyer; b. Highland Park, Mich., July 22, 1939; s. Walter Sawslayer and Kathryn Sylvia (Kurre) Hoops; m. Cynthia Ann Heynen, Jan. 6, 1962; children: Frederick III, Stephanie, Daniel, Haley, Elliot, William. BA in Econs., U. Mich., 1961, JD with distinction, 1966; MBA in Internat. Bus. and Fin., Harvard U., 1968; MTaxation, Wayne State U., 1973. Bar: Mass. 1968, Mich. 1970, U.S. Dist. Ct. D.C. 1969, U.S. Dist. Ct. Mass. 1968, U.S. Dist. Ct. (so. dist.) Mich. 1970, U.S. Ct. Appeals (1st cir.) 1968, U.S. Ct. Appeals (D.C. cir.) 1969, U.S. Ct. Appeals (6th cir.) 1970, U.S. Ct. Appeals (1st cir.) 1968, U.S. Ct. Claims, U.S. Tax Ct., U.S. Supreme Ct. 1972. Assoc. Hale & Dorr, Boston, 1968-69; atty. examiner/fin. SEC, Washington, 1969-70; assoc., ptnr. Evans & Luptak, Detroit, 1970—74; mem., pres., founder Hoops & Drollinger, P.C., Detroit, 1974—84, Hoops, Hoops & Hoops, P.C., Farmington Hills, Mass., 1984—98. Chmn., trustee Novi Found. Performing Arts, Mich., 1975—; chmn., dir. Chrystal Systems, Co., Birmingham, 1982—; dir. Security Bank Oakland County, Novi; mem. Mich. Securities Bur. Adv. Com., Lansing, 1978-; adj. prof. Mich. State/Detroit Coll. Law, 1975-. Author: Family Estate Planning Guide (2 vols.), Planning for Estates and Administration in Michigan (7 vols.). Served to 1st lt. U.S. Army, 1961—63. Mem.: D.C. Bar Assn., Mass. Bar Assn., State Bar Mich., Huron River Hunting and Fishing Club, Meadowbrook Country Club. Securities, Corporate, general, Estate taxation. Home: 22978 Brookforest Novi MI 48375-4420 Office: Kitch Drutchas Wagner et al Principal One Woodward Ave 10th Fl Detroit MI 48228 Personal E-mail: fkhoops22@msn.com. Business E-Mail: hoopf1@kitch.com.

HOOVER, RUSSELL JAMES, lawyer; b. Evanston, Ill., Apr. 27, 1940; s. Russell E and Grace M. (Nolan) H.; m. Judith Devine, Aug. 29, 1973; m. 2d JoAnn Dale Cloud, Sept. 15, 1979. A.B., U. Notre Dame, 1962; J.D. Georgetown U., 1965. Bar: Ill. 1968. Assoc. Jenner and Block, Chgo., 1968-75, ptnr. 1975— . Served to capt. U.S. Army, 1965-67. Decorated Army Commendation medal. Federal civil litigation, State civil litigation, Criminal. Home: 550 Monroe Ave River Forest IL 60305-1902 Office: Jenner & Block 1 E Ibm Plz Ste 5300 Chicago IL 60611-3586

HOPE, JOHN CHARLES, JR., lawyer; b. Cleve., Nov. 12, 1948; s. John Charles and Ruth Marie (Carens) H. BA, U. Nev., Reno, 1974; JD, Western State U., 1977. Bar: Calif. 1977, Nev. 1978, U.S. Dist. Ct. Nev. 1979, U.S. Ct. Appeals (9th cir.) 1981, U.S. Dist. Ct. (so. dist.) Calif. 1982, U.S. Dist. Ct. (ea. dist.) Calif. 1983. Atty. Corn & Hardesty, Reno, 1979-82; sole practice Reno, 1982—. Republican. Roman Catholic. Home: 3820 Piccadilly Dr Reno NV 89509-5625 Office: PO Box 13043 Reno NV 89507-3043 E-mail: jhopelaw@aol.com.

HOPFENBECK, GEORGE MARTIN, JR., lawyer; b. N.Y.C., Mar. 1, 1929; s. George Martin and Margaret Spencer (Felt) H.; m. Ruth Elizabeth Allen, June 27, 1953; children: Ann Elizabeth, James Allen. BA, Williams Coll., 1951; JD, Yale U., 1954. Bar: Colo., 1955. Assoc. Davis, Graham & Stubbs and predecessor Lewis, Grant & Davis, Denver, 1954-59, ptnr., 1959-92, of counsel, 1993—. Bd. dirs. Am. Cancer Soc. Inc., Colo. divsn., Denver, 1966-90, chmn., 1975-77; bd. dirs. Colo. Regional Cancer Ctr. Inc., Denver, 1974-81, pres., 1975-77; bd. dirs. Am. Cancer Soc. Inc., Atlanta, 1984-90, Denver Parks and Recreation Found., 1966-75; bd. dirs. Boys and Girls Clubs of Metro Denver, Inc., 1993—, chmn., 1998-2000; mem. Colo. State Pers. Bd., Denver, 1971-75, chmn., 1971-72; mem. Denver Bd. Parks & Recreation, 1961-69; trustee Kent Sch. for Girls, Denver, 1970-73; chmn. campaign com. for Gov. Love, Colo., 1966, campaign com. for McKevitt for Congress, Denver, 1970. Recipient St. George medal Am. Cancer Soc., 1982. Mem. ABA, Colo. Bar Assn., Denver Country Club (bd. dirs. 1967-70, 2002—), University Club (Denver) (bd. dirs. 1973-82). Republican. Episcopalian. Corporate, general, Finance, Property, real (including real estate development, water). Home: 450 Race St Denver CO 80206-4121 Office: 333 Logan St Ste 108 Denver CO 80203-4089

HOPKINS, HARRY L. lawyer; b. Piggott, Ark., Aug. 11, 1935; s. Marcus Vann and Nellie Mae (Branson) H.; m. Martha Markline, Feb. 4, 1940; children: Peter Ashley, Heather Caroline. BA, U. So. Miss., 1960; LLB, Tulane U., 1964. Bar: Miss. 1964, Ala. 1973. Pvt. practice, Meridian, Miss., 1964-65; trial atty. NLRB, New Orleans, 1965-69, gen. atty., 1969-73; ptnr. Lange, Simpson, Robinson & Somerville, Birmingham, Ala., 1973-97, Ogletree, Deakins, Nash, Smoke and Stewart, Birmingham, 1997—. Adj. prof. econs. U. So. Miss., Hattiesberg, 1968-72; prof. labor law U. Ala. Sch. Law, Tuscaloosa, 1979—; pres. Klondike Cattle Co. Maj. U.S. Army, 1953-56. Fellow Coll. of Labor and Employment Lawyers; mem. Briarwood Country Club, Northwood Country Club, Klondike Hunting Club. Constitutional, Labor (including EEOC, Fair Labor Standards Act, labor-management relations, NLRB, OSHA). Home: 308 17th Ave Tuscaloosa AL 35401 Office: One Federal Place Ste 1000 Birmingham AL 35203-3212 also: 2314 Poplar Springs Dr Meridian MS 39301-2129 E-mail: hhopkins@uofala.l.sch.edu.

HOPKINS, JOHN DAVID, lawyer; b. Memphis, Feb. 8, 1938; s. John and Helen (Sweeney) H.; m. Evelyn Harry, June 8, 1963 (div. Feb. 1985); children: John David III, Katharine Jane, Matthew Joseph; m. Laurie Eileen House, June 3, 1987. BA, Vanderbilt U., 1959; LLB, U. Va., 1965. Bar: Ga. 1966, D.C. 1979. From assoc. to ptnr. King & Spalding, Atlanta, 1965-93; exec. v.p., gen. counsel Jefferson-Pilot Corp., Greensboro, NC, 1993—2003. Bd. dirs., mem. exec. com. Rock-Tenn Co., Atlanta, 1989; mem. Guilford Coll. Bd. of Visitors, 1994-2000; bd. dirs. Univ. N.C. at Greensboro Excellence Found., 1995-2003. Bd. dirs. Atlanta Ballet, 1991-93, Greensboro United Arts Coun., 1994-97, Ea. Music Festival, 1998—; mem. alumni coun. U. Va. Law Sch. Alumni Assn., 2000—; trustee Children's Sch., Inc., Atlanta, 1971-79, 88-89, Nat. Assn. Children's Hosps. and Related Instns., Alexandria, Va., 1973-79. Lt. USN, 1959-62. Mem. Ga. Bar Assn. (chmn. corp. code revision com., corp. and banking sect. 1970-79), D.C. Bar Assn., Greensboro Country Club, Cherokee Town and Country Club (Atlanta), Highlands Country Club, Order of Coif, Omicron Delta Kappa. Episcopalian. Corporate, general, Finance, Mergers and acquisitions. Office: 2660 Peachtree Rd NW Unit 25C Atlanta GA 30305 E-mail: jdhopki@yahoo.com.

HOPKINS, JOHN J. lawyer; b. Sept. 24, 1951; s. Charles Joseph and Evelyne Hopkins; m. Margaret Anne Hopkins; children: Brian, Michael, Bridget. BA in English Lit., St. Louis U., 1973; JD, U. Tulsa, 1977. Bar: Ill. 77, Mo. 77. Spl. asst. atty. gen., 1985—87; asst. city atty. City of Granite City, Ill., 1985—87; pvt. practice John J. Hopkins & Assocs., Edwardsville, Ill. Mem. sch. bd. Marquette Cath. H.S., 1995—96; co-chmn. campaign for equal justice Land of Lincoln Legal Assistance Found., Madison County, Ill. Fellow: Am. Bar Found., Ill. Bar Found. (life); mem.: ATLA (charger mem. Pres. Club 1999—), ABA, Tri City Bar Assn. (pres. 1984), Ill. Trial Lawyers Assn. (mem. civil practice com. 1992—, mem. med. malpractice com. 1992—, bd. mgrs. 1996—, sec. 2001, treas. 2002), Madison County Bar Assn. (pres. 1997), Ill. State Bar Assn. (mem. gen. assembly 1998—, mem. task force on allocation of judges, mem. com. on jud. evaluations, mem. educating the pub. on jud. process com., chmn. com. on atty. fin. responsibility, mem. future of legal profession com.). Avocations: golf, reading, travel. Personal injury (including property damage), Toxic tort. Office: 1120 8th St 157 Ste 200 Edwardsville IL 62025-3602 Home: 1014 Henry Alton IL 62002

HOPP, DANIEL FREDERICK, manufacturing company executive, lawyer; b. Ann Arbor, Mich., Apr. 14, 1947; s. Clayton A. and Monica E. (Williams) H.; m. Maria G. Lopez, Dec. 20, 1968; children: Emily, Daniel, Melissa. BA in English, U. Mich., 1969; JD, Wayne State U., 1973. Bar: Ill. 1974, Mich. 1980. Atty. Mayer, Brown and Platt, Chgo., 1973-79, Whirlpool Corp., Benton Harbor, Mich., 1979-84, asst. sec., 1984-85, sec., asst. gen. counsel, 1985-89, v.p., gen. counsel, sec., 1989-98, sr. v.p., corp. affairs and gen. counsel, 1998—. Past co-chmn. Conf. Bd. Legal Quality Coun. Mem. City of St. Joseph (Mich.) Planning Comm.; bd. dirs. Lakeland Regional Health Sys., Joseph, Mich., St. Joseph Today; mem. Coun. for World Class Cmtys. With U.S. Army, 1969-71. Mem. Am. Soc. Corp. Secs. (past pres., bd. dirs. Chgo. chpt.), Mich. Bar Assn. (mem. Open Justice Commn.), Ill. Bar Assn., Berrien County Bar Assn. Republican. Mem. Ch. of Christ. Avocation: golf. Office: Whirlpool Corp Adminstrv Ctr 2000 N M 63 Benton Harbor MI 49022-2692

HOPP, WALTER JAMES, lawyer; b. Longmont, Jan. 17, 1945; s. Conrad and Frieda (Gies) H.; m. Margaret Ann Warnock, June 17, 1965 (dec. July 1985); children: Elizabeth Ann, Walter David, William John, Martha Jean; m. Vicki S. Lake, Nov. 29, 1985; 1 child, Emily Jean. BA, U. Colo., 1967, JD, 1970. Bar: Colo. 1970, U.S. Dist. Ct. Colo. 1970, U.S. Ct. Appeals (10th cir.) 1970. Law clk. U.S. Dist. Ct., Denver, 1970-71; assoc. Schey & Schey, Longmont, 1971-73, ptnr., 1973-80; sole practice Longmont, 1980-81, Hopp & Assocs., Longmont, 1981-83; mng. ptnr. Hopp, Carlson & Beckmann, P.C., Longmont, 1983—89, Hopp & Assocs., 1989—. Mem. ABA, Colo. Bar Assn., Boulder County Bar Assn., Colo. Trial Lawyers Assn. Republican. Lutheran. General practice, Probate (including wills, trusts), Property, real (including real estate development, water). Office: Hopp & Assocs 1002 17th Ave Longmont CO 80501 Home: 671 Glenarbor Cir Longmont CO 80501-2328

HOPSON, EDWIN SHARP, lawyer; b. Louisville, Apr. 23, 1945; s. Henry Dockins and Martha (Linton) H.; m. Jane Mayo Fitzpatrick, July 20, 1968; children: Edwin Hopson Jr., Martha. BSL, U. Louisville, 1967, JD, 1969; LLM, George Washington U., 1971. Bar: Ky. 1969, Fla. 1969, U.S. Supreme Ct. 1972, U.S. Dist. Ct. (we. dist.) Ky. 1974, U.S. Ct. Appeals (6th cir.) 1977. Atty. Solicitor's Office, U.S. Dept. Labor, Washington, 1969-72; field atty. NLRB, Balt., 1972-74; assoc. Tarrant, Combs, Blackwell & Bullitt, Louisville, 1974-77; ptnr. Tarrant, Combs & Bullitt, Louisville, 1977-80, Wyatt, Tarrant & Combs, L.L.P., Louisville, 1980—. Chair, mem. exec. com. Labor and Employment Practice Group; mem. legal adv. bd. Access Partnership, 2000. Editor: (jour.) Ky. Bench & Bar, 2001—, 1989—91, (chpt.) How Arbitration Works, 1989, 2nd edit., 2001—; contbr. articles. Bd. dirs. Bellewood Presbyn. Children's Home, Louisville, 1988-96, pres., 1991-93; bd. dirs. Louisville Ballet, 1991—, v.p., 1992-93, pres., 1993-94; bd. dirs. Bellewood Children's Found., 1995-2002, pres., 1995-96. Fellow Coll. Labor and Employment Lawyers, Inc.; mem. ABA (co-chmn. pub. of arbitration awards subcom. 2000—, adr. com. of labor and employment sect.), FBA (chpt. pres. 1991-92), Louisville Bar Assn. (co-chmn. labor and employment law sect. 1982-83), Ky. Bar Assn. (co-chmn. labor and employment law sect. 1987-89, mem. ho. of dels. 1996-2002, chair pub. com. 1989-91, 2001—). Republican. Presbyterian. Avocations: flying, various sports, reading. Labor (including EEOC, Fair Labor Standards Act, labor-management relations, NLRB, OSHA). Home: 3003 Lighteart Rd Louisville KY 40222-6138 Office: Wyatt Tarrant & Combs LLP 2600 PNC Plz Louisville KY 40202-2823 E-mail: ehopson@wyattfirm.com.

HOPSON, EVERETT GEORGE, retired lawyer; b. Stillwell, Ill., Sept. 4, 1922; s. Carman Roy and Adella (George) H.; m. Doris May Hutchins, Aug. 15, 1953 (dec.); children: Christine E., Eugene G. AA, Springfield Jr. Coll., 1942; BS, U. Ill., 1947, JD, 1949; MS in Internat. Affairs, George Washington U., 1967; disting. grad., Air War Coll., 1967. Bar: Ill. 1949, U.S. Ct. Mil. Appeals 1957, U.S. Supreme Ct. 1957. Dep. collector U.S. Treasury, IRS, Carlinville, Ill., 1949-51; commd. officer USAF, 1951, advanced to col., judge advocate, 1951-71; spl. asst. to asst. sec. def. Dept. Def., Washington, 1971; sr. atty. U.S. Postal Svc., Washington, 1972-73; dep. chief gen. law divsn. USAF, Washington, 1973-75, chief gen. law divsn., 1975-94, ret., 1994. Trustee USAF JAG Sch. Found. Served with U.S. Army, 1943-46. Decorated Legion of Merit; recipient Presdl. Rank of Meritorious Exec., USAF, 1981, 87, 92, Freedoms Found. award, 1961, 62, 66. Mem. ABA, Ill. Bar Assn. (sr. counsellor 1999), Fed. Bar Assn., Judge Advocates Assn., Am. Inns of Ct., Phi Alpha Delta. Democrat. Methodist. Avocations: coin collecting, gardening. Home: 9719 Limoges Dr Fairfax VA 22032-1115 E-mail: eghdmh@aol.com.

HORAHAN, EDWARD BERNARD, III, lawyer; b. Drexel Hill, Pa., Dec. 30, 1951; s. Edward Bernard and Ann Veronica (Schneeweis) H.; m. Rebecca Joy Fusco, Mar. 13, 1976; 1 child, Elizabeth Joy. BA, LaSalle Coll., Phila., 1973; JD, Yale U., 1976. Bar: D.C. 1976. Staff atty. office of gen. counsel SEC, Washington, 1976-78; staff atty. office of solicitor, plan benefits security divsn. U.S. Dept. Labor, Washington, 1978-80; assoc. Arter & Hadden, Washington, 1980-84; ptnr. Parker, Chapin, Flattau & Klimpl, Washington, 1984-88, Stroock & Stroock & Lavan, Washington, 1988-93; pvt. practice Law Offices of Edward B. Horahan III, Washington, 1993-96; counsel Groom Law Group, Washington, 1996-2001, Dechert, Washington, 2001—. Mem. ABA. Federal civil litigation, Pension, profit-sharing, and employee benefits, Securities. Office: 1775 Eye St NW Washington DC 20006 E-mail: edward.horahan@dechert.com.

HORAN, ADNAN, lawyer; b. Yonkers, N.Y., Feb. 22, 1971; s. Alan and Gail Horan; m. Lisa Horan; 1 child, Brandon Alan. BSBA, U. Phoenix, 1994, MBA, 1996; JD, U. San Diego, 1997. Bar: Ariz. 1997, U.S. Dist. Ct. Ariz. 2000. Atty. Ernst & Young, LLP, Phoenix, 1997—99, O. Joseph Chornenky, P.C., Phoenix, 1999—2002, Horan Law Offices, P.C., 2002—. Comments editor: U. San Diego Law Rev., 1996—97. Mem.: ABA, ATLA, Municopa County Bar Assn., Nat. Assn. Criminal Def. Lawyers, Ariz. Attys. for Criminal Justice. Criminal, Personal injury (including property damage). Home: 22628 N 47th Pl Phoenix AZ 85012 Office: Horan Law Offices PC One Camelback Bldg One East Camelback Rd Ste 650 Phoenix AZ 85012

HORLICK, GARY NORMAN, lawyer, legal educator; b. Washington, Mar. 12, 1947; s. Reuben S. and Gertrude V. (Cooper) H.; m. Kathryn L. Mann, June 1, 1986. AB, Dartmouth Coll., 1968; BA, MA, Diploma in Internat. Law, Cambridge (Eng.) U., 1970; JD, Yale U., 1973. Bar: Conn. 1974, U.S. Ct. Appeals (D.C. cir.) 1975), D.C. 1977, U.S. Supreme Ct. 1977, U.S. Ct. Internat. Trade 1979, U.S. Ct. Customs and Patent Appeals 1980. Asst. to rep. Ford Found., Santiago, Chile, 1973-74, asst. rep. Bogota, Colombia, 1974-76; assoc. Steptoe & Johnson, Washington, 1976-80; internat. trade counsel U.S. Senate Fin. Com., Washington, 1981; dep. asst. sec. U.S. Dept. Commerce, Washington, 1981-83; ptnr. O'Melveny & Myers, Washington, 1983—2002, Wilmer, Cutler & Pickering, Washington, 2002—. Lectr. law Yale U., New Haven, 1983-86, 2001—, World Trade Inst., U. Berne, 2000—; adj. prof. Georgetown U. Law Ctr., Washington, 1986—, World Trade Inst. U. Rome; lectr. various orgns.; adv. com. U.S. Ct. Internat. Trade, 1993-97; mem. permanent group of experts World Trade Orgn., 1996-2001, chmn., 1996-97. Mem. ABA (chmn. standing com. on customs law 1993), Coun. Fgn. Rels., Internat. Law Assn. (mem. exec. coun. Am. br. 1983—), Internat. Bar Assn. (vice chmn. antitrust and trade law 1987-89), D.C. Bar Assn. (chmn. internat. divsn. 1984-85), Am. Soc. of Internat. Law (exec. coun. 1998-99, WTO & NAFTA rules and sidpute resolution 2003). Private international, Public international. Office: Wilmer Cutler & Pickering 2455 M St NW Washington DC 20037- E-mail: gary.horlick@wilmer.com.

HORMEKU, LEBENE ABENA, lawyer; b. Bklyn., Sept. 3, 1974; d. Kofi Hormeku and Gloria Obuobi. BA, Boston U., 1996, MS, JD, Boston U., 1999. Bar: D.C., Mass. Law clk. Mass. Supreme Ct. Jud. Ct., Boston, 1999—2000; corp. counsel Glotel, Inc., Chgo., 2000—. Adj. prof. East-West U., Chgo. Mem.: ABA, Am. Immigration Lawyers Assn., D.C. Bar Assn., Mass. Bar Assn. Corporate, general, Immigration, naturalization, and customs. Office: Glotel Inc 30 S Wacker Dr #3900 Chicago IL 60606 Fax: 312-612-6248. E-mail: lhormeku@glotel.com.

HORN, ANDREW WARREN, lawyer; b. Apr. 19, 1946; s. George H. and Belle (Collin) H.; m. Melinda Fink; children: Lee Shawn, Ruth Belle. BBA in Acctg., U. Miami, 1968, JD, 1971. Bar: Fla. 1971, Colo. 1990, U.S. Dist. Ct. (so. dist.) Fla. 1972, U.S. Tax Ct. 1974. Ptnr. Gillman & Horn P.A., Miami, Fla., 1973-74; pvt. practice Miami, 1974—. Active civic coun. Children's Hosp., Miami, Dade County, Fla., 1994—, Blue Ribbon Aviation Panel-Miami-Dade County, Fla., 2000. Recipient Am. Jurisprudence award Lawyers Coop. Pub. Co., 1970. Mem. ABA, ATLA, Fla. Bar, Acad. Fla. Trial Lawyers. State civil litigation, Commercial, consumer (including collections, credit), Personal injury (including property damage). E-mail: lawofficehorn@msn.com.

HORN, BRENDA SUE, lawyer; b. Beech Grove, Ind., Apr. 22, 1949; d. Donald Eugene Horn and Barbara Joyce (Waggoner) Christie. AB with distinction, Ind. U., 1971; MS, Purdue U., 1975; JD summa cum laude, Ind. U., 1981. Bar: Ind. 1981, U.S. Dist. Ct. (so. dist.) Ind. 1981. Assoc. Ice Miller, Indpls., 1981-87, ptnr., 1988—. Assoc. editor Ind. Law Rev., 1980-81. Bd. dirs. Ballet Internationale, 1995—, treas., 1996-2000; pres. Greenleaf Cmty. Ctr., 1992-93, 96-99, v.p., 1991, sec., 1990; bd. dirs., v.p. Cmty. Alliance for the Far East Side, 1997-98, hon. dir. 1998-2003; bd. dirs. Big Sisters of Ctrl. Ind., 1995-98, hon. dir., 1998—2002; bd. dirs. Indiana Edn. Svcs. Authority, 1996—, Cmty. Orgns. Legal Assistance Project, 2000—, treas., 2001-2003, pres. 2003- Named among Influential Women in Indpls., Ind. Lawyer and Indpls. Bus. Jour., 1998; Disting. fellow Indpls. Bar Fond. Mem. ABA (com. on tax exempt fin.), Am. Coll. Bond Counsel (bd. dirs., v.p. 1995-98, pres. 1998-2001), Ind. Bar Assn., Indpls. Bar Assn. (bd. mgrs. 1992), Ind. Mcpl. Lawyers Assn., Nat. Assn. Bond Lawyers, Skyline Club (bd. dirs.), Phi Beta Kappa. Health, Municipal (including bonds). Office: Ice Miller One American Sq Box 82001 Indianapolis IN 46282 E-mail: horn@icemiller.com.

HORN, CHARLES M. lawyer; b. Boston, Sept. 28, 1951; s. Garfield Henry and Alexandra (Matz) H.; m. Jane Charlotte Luxton, May 29, 1976; children: Andrew L., Caroline C. AB magna cum laude, Harvard Coll., 1973; JD, Cornell Law Sch., 1976. Bar: D.C. 1976, U.S. Dist. Ct. D.C. 1977, U.S. Ct. Appeals (D.C. cir.) 1977, U.S. Supreme Ct. 1980. Atty. U.S. Securities and Exchange Commn., Washington, 1976-82, br. chief divsn. enforcement, 1982-83; asst. dir. securities and corp. practices Office Comptroller of Currency, Washington, 1983-86, dir. securities and corp. practices, 1986-89; ptnr. Stroock & Stroock & Lavan, Washington, 1989-92, Mayer, Brown & Platt, Washington, 1992—2002, Mayer, Brown, Rowe & Maw, Washington, 2002—. Mem. faculty Am. Bankers Assn. Nat. Grad. Compliance Sch., 1991-92, 94, Fed. Fin. Instns. Exam. Coun. (programs off-balance-sheet risk, Trust Exams. Sch.); lectr. in field. Edit. adv. bd. Bank Acctg. and Fin., 1993—; contbr. articles to profl. jours. Mem. ABA (banking law com., com. fed. regulation securities), D.C. Bar Assn., Washington Golf and Country Club. Administrative and regulatory, Banking, Securities. Home: 1918 Massachusetts Ave Mc Lean VA 22101-4907 Office: Mayer Brown Rowe & Maw 1909 K St NW Washington DC 20006 E-mail: chorn@mayerbrownrowe.com.

HORN, JOHN HAROLD, lawyer; b. Eugene, Oreg., Mar. 4, 1927; s. Harold William and Mildred A. (Truesdale) H.; m. Deloris Eileen Davis, Aug. 22, 1948; children: Lorraine, Deborah, Lisa, Darren. BS, U. Oreg., 1949, JD, 1951. Bar: Oreg. 1951, U.S. Dist. Ct. Oreg. 1957. Ptnr. Horn & Slocum, Roseburg, Oreg., 1951-65, Riddlesbarger, Pederson, Young & Horn, Eugene, 1970-74, Young, Horn, Cass & Scott, Eugene, 1974-82; pvt. practice Roseburg, 1965-70, Eugene, 1982—. Chmn. fund raising Douglas County unit ARC, 1966, county chmn., 1968; exec. bd., legal advisor Eugene Mission, 1979—; pres. bd. dirs. Jubilee Ministries, Eugene, 1980—; v.p., bd. dirs. His Word Broadcasting, 1989-91, pres. bd. dirs., 1991—. Recipient Outstanding Svc. award ARC, 1968. Mem. ABA, Oreg. Bar Assn., Douglas County Bar Assn. (pres. 1960, chmn. grievance com. 1961-62), Lane County Bar Assn., Lions (dir. Eugene chpt. 2000-2002). Republican. Avocations: aviation, golf, skiing. General civil litigation, Probate (including wills, trusts), Property, real (including real estate development, water). Home: 640 Elwood Ct Eugene OR 97401-2235 Office: 875 Country Club Rd Eugene OR 97401-2255 E-mail: jhhorn@hotmail.com.

HORN, MARK, lawyer; b. Bronx, N.Y. s. Harry and Sala H.; m. Yael T. Frydman, July 30, 1996; 1 child, Chava. BA, Fla. Internat. U., 1989; JD, Touro Coll., 1990. Bar: Fla. 1990, N.Y. 1991, D.C. 1991, U.S. Dist. Ct. (so. dist.) Fla. 1991, U.S.Ct. Appeals (11th cir.) 1992, U.S. Supreme Ct. 1993. Dir. gen. counsel ALEPH Inst., Surfside, Fla., 1991-96. Apptd. Miami-Dadae Co. traffic hearing officer, 2000. Contbr. articles to profl. jours. Mem. Nat. Assn. Criminal Def. Lawyers, Dade County Bar Assn., Jewish Lawyers Network (vice-chmn. 1998). Jewish. Administrative and regulatory, Constitutional, Criminal. Office: 18800 NW 2nd Ave Ste 211 Miami FL 33169-4044 E-mail: legalZ123@aol.com.

HORNBECK, DAVID ARTHUR, lawyer; b. Reno, Nev., May 9, 1943; s. William Hornbeck and Sarah (Dixon) Ercolini. BS in Physics and Math., U. Nev., Reno, 1968; JD, U. Pacific McGeorge Sch. of Law, Sacramento, 1979. Bar: Nev. 1979, Calif. 1980, U.S. Dist. Ct. Nev. 1980, U. S. Ct. Appeals (9th cir.) 1987. Law clk. 2d Jud. Dist. Ct. Nev., Reno, 1979-80; dep. pub. defender Washoe County Pub. Defender, Reno, 1980-84; pvt. practice Reno, 1984—; dep. atty. gen. Environ. Protection divsn. State of Nev., 1993-95. Bd. dirs. Washoe Legal Svcs., Reno, 1985-88. Bd. dirs. No. Nev. Mental Health Adv. Bd., Reno, 1988-91; founding bd. dirs., pres. Friends of Pyramid Lake, Reno, 1982—; bd. dirs., past treas., past pres. Reno Chamber Orch., Inc., 1987-95; trustee Reno Chamber Orch. Endowment, 2000—02. Lt. USNR, 1968-73. Mem. ABA, Nev. Trial Lawyers Assn., Washoe County Bar Assn. Avocations: skiing, soaring, tennis, racquetball, hiking. General civil litigation, Environmental, Family and matrimonial. Office: 1675 Lakeside Dr Reno NV 89509-3408 Fax: 775-322-0223. E-mail: davidhornbecklaw@msn.com.

HORNBERGER, LEE, lawyer; b. Elizabethtown, Pa., Oct. 31, 1946; s. Lee and Peggy (Mann) H. AB, U. Mich., 1966, JD cum laude, 1968; LLM in Labor Law, Wayne State U., 1982. Bar: Mich. 1969, Ohio 1982, U.S. Dist. Ct. (no. dist.) Ohio 1971, U.S. Dist. Ct. (so. dist.) Ohio 1982, U.S.

Dist. Ct. (we. and ea. dists.) Mich. 1973, U.S. Dist. Ct. (ea. dist.) Ky., U.S. Ct. Mil. Appeals 1970, U.S. Ct. Appeals (6th cir.) 1972, U.S. Supreme Ct. 1998. Atty. Office of Solicitor, U.S. Dept. Labor, Washington, 1971-75; pvt. practice, Cin., 1982—2002, Traverse City, Mich., 2002—. Adj. prof. law U. Cin., 1985-87, Chase Coll., 1992—; presenter Employment Lawyers Assn., Lake Tahoe, 1990, Cin., 1991, Cin. Bar Assn., 1990-93, 95, 97, Ohio State Bar Assn., Cin., 1991, Nat. Employment Lawyers Assn., Cape Cod, 1991, Advanced Ednl. Seminars, Cin., 1991, 2002, Ohio Employment Lawyers Assn., Columbus, 1991, Ohio Edn. Assn., Cin., 1992, Nat. Edn. Network, Cin., 1993, 94, Ky. Employment Lawyers Assn., 1996, U. Ky., 1996, Vail, Colo., 2003, others. Contbr. articles to profl. jours. including Cleve. Law Rev., Capital U. Law Rev., Mich. Lawyers Weekly and Ohio Trial. Dem. candidate spl. election, 2nd dist. Ohio for U.S. Congress. Capt. U.S. Army, 1969-71, Vietnam. Decorated Bronze Star, U.S. Army. Mem. ABA (labor and employment law sect.), Mich. Bar Assn., Ohio State Bar Assn. (cert. labor and employment law specialist), Nat. Employment Lawyers Assn. (chmn. Cin. chpt. 1987-90, mediator Equal Employment Opportunity Commn.), Mich. Dept. Civil Rights; arbitrator Nat. Arbitration Forum. Avocations: camping, sailing, employment law seminars. Labor (including EEOC, Fair Labor Standards Act, labor-management relations, NLRB, OSHA), Alternative dispute resolution, Civil rights. Office: Ste 407 310 W Front St Traverse City MI 49684-2279 E-mail: leehornberger@leehornberger.com.

HORNBY, DAVID BROCK, federal judge; b. Brandon, Manitoba, Can., Apr. 21, 1944; s. William Ralph Hornby and Retha Patricia (Fox) Sword; m. Helaine Cora Mandel, Oct. 9, 1946; children: Kirstin, Zachary. BA, U. Western Ont., 1965; JD, Harvard U., 1969. Bar: Va. 1973, Maine 1974, U.S. Supreme Ct. 1980. Law clk. U.S. Ct. Appeals, New Orleans, 1969-70; assoc. prof. U. Va. Sch. Law, Charlottesville, 1970-74; ptnr. Perkins, Thompson, Hinckley & Keddy, Portland, Maine, 1974-82; U.S. magistrate Dist. Maine, Portland, 1982-88; assoc. justice Maine Supreme Jud. Ct., Portland, 1988-90; judge U.S. Dist. Ct. Maine, 1990—; chief judge, 1996—2003. Contbr. articles to profl. jours.; editor, officer Harvard Law Rev., 1967-69. Fellow Am. Bar Found.; mem. ABA, Am. Law Inst., Maine State Bar Assn., Maine Bar Found. (bd. trustees 1990-94), Cumberland County Bar Assn. Office: US Dist Ct Edward T Gignoux Courthouse 156 Federal St Portland ME 04101-4152

HORNE, MICHAEL STEWART, lawyer; b. Mpls., May 10, 1938; s. Owen Edward and Adeline (DiGeorgio) H.; m. Martha Brean, Sept. 11, 1965; children: Jennifer, Katherine, Sarah, Owen. BA, U. Minn., 1959; LLB, Harvard U., 1962. Bar: D.C. 1963, U.S. Ct. Appeals (D.C. cir.) 1964, U.S. Supreme Ct. 1968, U.S. Ct. Appeals (6th cir.) 1966, U.S. Ct. Appeals (9th cir.) 1978, U.S. Ct. Appeals (4th cir.) 1979, U.S. Ct. Appeals (5th cir.) 1979, U.S. Ct. Appeals (2d cir.) 1980, U.S. Ct. Appeals (11th cir.) 1983, U.S. Ct. Appeals (8th cir.) 1984, U.S. Ct. Appeals (10th cir.) 1997. Assoc. Covington & Burling, Washington, 1964-71, ptnr., 1971—. Co-author (with T.S. Williamson and A. Herman): The Contingent Workforce, Business and Legal Strategies, 2000. Mem. ABA, D.C. Bar Assn., FCC Bar Assn., Am. Judicature Soc. Democrat. Administrative and regulatory, Labor (including EEOC, Fair Labor Standards Act, labor-management relations, NLRB, OSHA), Libel. Home: 9008 Levelle Dr Bethesda MD 20815-5608 Office: Covington & Burling 1201 Pennsylvania Ave NW PO Box 7566 Washington DC 20044-7566 E-mail: hornems@earthlink.net., mhorne@cov.com.

HOROWITZ, DONALD LEONARD, lawyer, educator, researcher, political scientist, arbitrator; b. N.Y.C., June 27, 1939; s. Morris and Yetta (Hibscher) H.; m. Judith Anne Present, Sept. 4, 1960; children: Marshall, Karen, Bruce. AB, Syracuse U., 1959, LLB, 1961; LLM, Harvard U., 1962, AM, 1965, PhD, 1968. Bar: N.Y. 1962, D.C. 1979, U.S. Ct. Appeals (D.C., 6th, 7th and 10th cirs.) 1970, U.S. Supreme Ct. 1969. Law clk. U.S. Dist. Ct. (ea. dist.), Pa., 1965-66; rsch. assoc. Harvard U. Ctr. Internat. Affairs, 1967-69; atty. Dept. Justice, Washington, 1969-71; fellow Coun. on Fgn. Rels./Woodrow Wilson Internat. Ctr. Scholars, Washington, 1971-72; rsch. assoc. Brookings Instn., Washington, 1972-75; sr. fellow Rsch. Inst. on Immigration and Ethnic Studies/Smithsonian, Washington, 1975-81; prof. law and polit. sci. Duke U., Durham, N.C., 1980—, Charles S. Murphy Prof., 1988-93, James B. Duke prof., 1994—. Vis. prof. Charles J. Merriam scholar U. Chgo. Law Sch., 1988; vis. fellow Cambridge U., Eng., 1988; Sticerd Disting. visitor London Sch. Econs., 1998-2000, Centennial prof., 2001; vis. scholar Universiti Kebangsaan Malaysia Law Faculty, 1991; Fulbright sr. specialist, 2002; cons. Ford Found., 1977-82; mem. internat. adv. com. Office of the High Rep., Bosnia, 1998-99; McDonald-Currie Meml. lectr. McGill U., Montreal, 1980; mem. Coun. on Role of Cts., 1978-83; Opsahl lectr. Queen's U., Belfast, 2000. Author: The Courts and Social Policy (Nat. Acad. Public Adminstrn. Louis Brownlow prize for best book in pub. adminstrn. 1977), 1977; The Jurocracy: Government Lawyers, Agency Programs and Judicial Decisions, 1977; Coup Theories and Officers' Motives, 1980, Ethnic Groups in Conflict, 1985, A Democratic South Africa? Constitutional Engineering in a Divided Soc., 1991 (Am. Polit. Sci. Assn. Ralph J. Bunche award for best book in ethnic and cultural pluralism, 1992), The Deadly Ethnic Riot, 2001; mem. editl. bd. Ethnicity, 1974-82, Law and Contemporary Problems, 1983-84, 89-2000, Jour. Democracy, 1993—. Guggenheim fellow, 1980-81; Nat. Humanities Ctr. fellow, 1984; Carnegie scholar, 2001-2002. Fellow Am. Acad. Arts and Scis. Office: Duke University School Law Durham NC 27708-0360

HOROWITZ, ROBERT M. lawyer; b. NYC, Feb. 14, 1963; s. Harold M. and Charlotte R. (Rosenblatt) H. BA, Coll. of William and Mary, 1985; JD, U. Colo., 1988. Bar: Colo. 1988, U.S. Dist. Ct. Colo. 1988, U.S. Ct. Appeals (10th cir.). Instr. People's Law Sch., 1991-93, Nat. Inst. Trial Advocacy, 1993; shareholder Pearson & Poskus PC, Denver, 1991—. Mem. faculty 3rd Ann. Rocky Mountain Child Advocacy Tng. Inst., Million Dollar Advs. Forum. Mem. ABA (litigation sect.), Denver Bar Assn., Colo. Bar Assn. (litigation sect.), Colo. Trial Lawyers Assn. Avocations: backpacking, rock climbing, music. Commercial, contracts (including sales of goods; commercial financing), Property, real (including real estate development, water), General civil litigation. Office: Pearson & Poskus PC 1999 Broadway Ste 2300 Denver CO 80202-5750 E-mail: rhorowitz@ph-law.com.

HORR, WILLIAM HENRY, retired lawyer; b. Portsmouth, Ohio, Sept. 23, 1914; s. Charles Chick and Effie (Amberg) H.; m. Marjorie Bell Marshall, Aug. 31, 1940; children— Robert W., Thomas M., Catherine, James C., Elizabeth; m. 2d Wilma Crawford, Mar. 12, 1988. AB, Ohio Wesleyan U., 1936; JD, U. Cin., 1939. Bar: Ohio 1939. Practice in, Portsmouth, 1939-42, 45-99; atty. Skelton, Kahl, Horr, Marshall & Burton, 1939-42, 45-78; spl. agt. FBI, Louisville, Indpls., Newark, 1942-45; substitute judge Mcpl. Ct., Portsmouth, 1955-80; gen. counsel Ohio Wesleyan U., 1966-70. Mem. Portsmouth Bd. Edn., 1947- 60; pres. Portsmouth YMCA.; trustee Ohio U. Portsmouth Br., Shawnee State C.C., 1975-80, Ohio Wesleyan U., 1953-68; chmn. bd. Hill View Retirement Ctr., 1973-85. Recipient Disting. Svc. award Portsmouth Jr. C. of C., 1947. Mem. Ohio Bar Assn. (past mem. exec. com.), Portsmouth Bar Assn. (past pres.), Phi Delta Phi, Phi Kappa Psi, Omicron Delta Kappa, Rotary (past pres.). Republican. Methodist. Home: 1732 Hillview Cir Portsmouth OH 45662-2673

HORRIGAN, JOSEPH STEWART, lawyer; b. Houston, Nov. 22, 1938; s. Joseph Raymond and Ruth (Mize) H.; (div. Nov. 1986); children: Elizabeth, Katherine, Erin; m. Katherine K. Horrigan, Aug. 20, 1988. BA, Duke U., 1961; LLB, U. Tex., 1964. Bar: Tex. 1964, U.S. Dist. Ct. (we. and so. dists.) Tex., 1966, U.S. Ct. Appeals (5th cir.), 1981, U.S. Supreme Ct. 1995; cert. in estate planning and probate law Tex. Bd. Legal Specialization. Law clk. U.S. Dist. Ct., 1964-65, U.S. Ct. Appeals (5th cir.), 1965-66; assoc. Bryan, Suhr, Bering, & Bailey, Houston, 1966-71; ptnr. Dyche & Wright, Houston, 1973-81, Armogida & Coats, Houston, 1981-84, Coats, Yale, Holm, Horrigan & Lee, Houston, 1984-85, Horrigan & Goehrs, Houston, 1986—. Fellow Am. Coll. Trust and Estate Counsel, Tex. Bar Found., Houston Bar Assn. (charter sustaining); mem. ABA, State Bar Tex., Disability and Elder Law Attys., Houston Ctr. Club. State civil litigation, Probate (including wills, trusts). Home: 2310 Mimosa Dr Houston TX 77019-6024 Office: 1000 Two Houston Ctr Houston TX 77010

HORSLEY, JACK EVERETT, lawyer, writer; b. Sioux City, Iowa, Dec. 12, 1915; s. Charles E. and Edith V. (Timms) H.; m. Sallie Kelley, June 12, 1939 (dec.); children: Pamela, Charles Edward; m. Bertha J. Newland, Feb. 24, 1950 (dec.); m. Mary Jane Moran, Jan. 20, 1973; 1 child, Sharon. AB, U. Ill., 1937, LLB, JD, 1939, Med./Legal Doctorate, 2001. Bar: Ill. 1939. Instr. Sch. of the Solder, U. Ill. ROTC, 1934—36; temp. prof. law NYU, N.Y.C., 1974, N.Y.C., 90, N.Y.C., 99, N.Y.C., 2000—03; mem. Harlan Moore Heart Rsch. Found., 1968—, asst. treas., 1996—; mem. lawyers adv. coun. U. Ill. Law Forum, 1992—96, 1999—2002; lectr. Practicing Law Inst., N.Y.C., 1967—73, 1994—98, U. Ill., Champaign, 1974, Ct. Practice Inst., Chgo., 1974—, Coll. Law Inst. Continuing Legal Edn., U. Mich., 1967, Bankers' Seminar, 1999, 2000, Banker's Seminar, 2002; vis. lectr. Orange County (Fla.) Med. Soc., 1985, San Diego Med. Soc., 1970, 89, lectr., 96; vis. lectr. U. S.C., 1976, 98, Duquesne Coll., 1970, U. Ill. Law Forum and Student Adv. Com., 1984—96; alumni adv. com. U. Ill. Law Forum, 1991—2000; vis. lectr. trial practice NYU Coll. Law, 1972, 94; vis. lectr. faculty banker seminar Wis. Med. Assn., Lake Geneva, 1997; lectr. med./legal seminars on tour Chgo., Cleve., Pa., Orlando, 1995; chmn. rev. bd. Ill. Supreme Ct. Disciplinary Comm., 1973—76, adv. cons., 1976—2003; lectr. Cleve. Hosp., Shelby, NC, 1976; vis. prof. trial practice Fordham Law Sch., N.Y.C., 1989—96; vis. prof. U. Berkeley Coll. Law, 1999, vis. prof, 2002; vis. lectr. John Marshall Sch. Law, Chgo., 1999—2002; vis. lectr. trial practice U. Nebr. Law Sch., 1999—2002, Columbia U., N.Y.C., 1999; vis. lectr. Trial Practice Columbia U., NY, 1999; Trial Laureate Ill. Trial Lawyers Acad., 1996, Laureata-emeritus, 2000. Narrator Poetry Interludes, Sta. WLBH-FM, 1977—91; author: Trial Lawyer's Manual, 1967, Voir Dire Examinations and Opening Statements, Real Estate Foreclosures, 1968, Current Development in Products Liability Law, 1969, Illinois Civil Practice and Procedure, 1970, The Medical Expert Witness, 1973, Testifying in Court, 1973, Testifying in Court, 4th edit., 1992, Testifying in Court, supplement 4th edit, 1993, The Doctor and the Law, 1975, The Doctor and Family Law, 1975, The Doctor and Business Law, 1976, The Doctor and Medical Law, 1977, Anatomy of a Medical Malpractice Case, 1984, Anatomy of a Medical Malpractice Case, 3d edit., 1993, Trilogy: The Frivolous Law Suit, 2000, Lincoln the Lawyer, 2002, Lincoln-Circuit Lawyer, 2002, (municipals) G.O. of Revenue, 1992, World War II, D-Day, 1994, World War II, D-Day, 2d edit., 1998, Life's Challenges Preparation, 1999, World War II Air Mus, Duxford, Eng., 1999, Trial Techniques, 1995, Trial Techniques, 2d edit., 2001, Legal Liability Exposure of Trust Co., 1996, Legal Liability Exposure of Trust Co., 2d edit., 1999, On Trust Dept. Guide-lines and Risks, 1996, On Federal Evidence and Examination, 1995, 1996, 1997, Memories of World War II in the European Theater, 1997, 1999, suppl. on post World War II Reserve officer duties, 2000 (awarded Purple Heart, 1943), suppl. on post World War II Reserve officer duties, 2d edit., 2001, History of the Bar in East Central Illinois, 1997, Remembrances: An Autobiography, 1998, Remembrances: An Autobiography, 2d edit., 2000, Views of Christianity: Origin of Man, 1999, (pamphlet) A Doctor's Duty: Presciption Care, 1999, Thoughts to Ponder, 2001, Heartstrings of the Mind, 2003; co-author: RN Legally Speaking, 1998, Matthew Bender Forensic Sciences, 1988, (2d edit.) , 2000; editor: Med. Econs., 1969—, Fifty Eight Years as Attorney, 1997, Fifty Eight Years as Attorney, 3d update, 2003; legal cons. Mast-Head, 1972—; contbr. Forensic Scis. Texts and Treatises, 1981, Forensic Scis. Texts and Treatises, 2d edit., 1999, Fed. Evidence Rules, 1996, Fed. Evidence Rules, 1998, Fed. Evidence Rules, 2000, Fed. Evidence Rules, 2d term, 2001, Cross-Exam Techniques and Potential Traps, 1996, Eagle Forum (On Pro-Life), Alton, Ill., 1999, Christianity: The Origin of Man Creationism vs. Darwinism, U. Ill. Law Rev., 2000, Selected Poems, Interludes of Poetry, 2001; cons., reviewer Civil Practice State and Fed. Cts., 1998—2001, Thoughts to Ponder, 2001; author: (pamphlet) Thoughts to Ponder, 2d edit., 2002, Thoughts to Ponder, 3d edit.; reviewer Current Developments in Medical Malpractice Law. Alt. del. to Rep. Platform Com., 2000; active Senatorial Reelection Com., 1993; mem. exec. com. Ill. Rep. Election Campaign, 1997; founding mem. U.S. Air Mus., Am. Air Mus., U.S. Supreme Ct. Hist. Soc.; pres. bd. edn. sch. dist. 100, 1946-48; bd. dirs. Harlan Moore Heart Rsch. Found., 1968-91, hon. dir., 1991—; vol. reader in rec. texts Am. Assn. for Blind, 1970-72; chmn. exec. com. U. Ill. Law Forum, 1990-91; founding mem. Home for Law Alumni Found., Chgo., 1998-99; pres. Res. Officers Assn. East Cen. Ill., 1988-89, 99-2000, chair, bd. dirs., 2000-2002; founder Bertha Newland Horsley award St. John's Coll. Nursing, Springfield, Mary Jane Horsley award trophy Mattoon (Ill.) H.S.; mem. exec. com. Ill. Rep. Election Campaign, 1997. Brig. gen. hon. res., 2000; tournament judge Big Ten Debating Contest, 2001, tech. advisor, 2002. Recipient Disting. Svc. award U. Ill., 1995. Fellow Am. Coll. Trial Lawyers (co-chair membership commn. 1998, acting regent 2000-01); mem. ABA, Ill. Bar Assn. (exec. coun. ins. law 1961-63, com. chmn. banking law 1972, lectr. law course for attys. 1962, 64-65, sr. counsellor 1989—, Disting. Svc. award 1982-83), Assn. of Bar of City of N.Y. (non-resident), Coles-Cumberland Bar Assn. (v.p. 1968-2000, pres. 1969-70, chmn. com. jud. inquiry 1976-80, chair meml. com. 1989-2000, mem. exec. com. 1998, sr. counsellor 1989, co-author Forensic Scis. Jour. 1991, 2d edit. 1999, Life-time Achievement award 1999), Am. Arbitration Assn. (nat. panel arbitrators, counsel advisor hearing officers in Ill. 1996-97), U. Ill. Law Alumni Assn. (life mem., pres. 1966-67, Alumni of Month Sept. 1974, exec. com. 1990-91, Sr. Alumni of Month 2001), Ill. Appellate Lawyers Assn. (editl. cons. 2002), Soc. Legal Scribes (chair emeritus 1995-2002), Ill. Def. Counsel Assn. (pres. 1967-88), Soc. Trial Lawyers (chmn. profl. activities 1960-61, bd. dirs. 1966-67, 88-94), Fed. Ct. Hist. Soc. (co-chmn.), Adelphic Debating Soc., Assn. Ins. Attys., Internat. Assn. Ins. Counsel, Am. Judicature Soc., Res. Officers Assn. (pres. 1997-98, chair exec. com., pres. emeritus 2002, hon. brig. gen. JAGD 1997), U. Ill. Alumni Assn. (exec. com. 1990-91), Masons (lectr. ceremonial 32 degree Scottish Rite 2000, Sr. Master award 1992), Scabbard and Blade Soc. U. Ill. (pres. 1936), Delta Phi (exec. com. alumni assn. 1960-61, 67-68), Sigma Delta Kappa. Lutheran. State civil litigation, Health, Personal injury (including property damage). Home: 913 N 31st St Mattoon IL 61938-2271

HORTEN, ERIC KORRE, lawyer; b. Springs, South Africa, July 25, 1953; s. Jorgen and ELse Frede Larsen; m. Jannike Horten, Jan. 6, 1979 (div. Sept. 1988); children: Alexander, Caroline; m. Ulla Pedersen, Oct. 1, 1988. B of Comm., Copenhagen Bus. Sch.; JD, U. Copenhagen. Assoc. Horten & Trier, Copenhagen, 1978—80; sec. COWI/consult Cons. Engrs., Lyngby, 1980—82; contracts mgr. CHR Rovsing A/S, Ballerup, 1982—84; sr. assoc. O. Bondo Svane Law Firm, Copenhagen, 1984—86, ptnr., 1986—2000, Plesner Svane Gronborg, 2000—01, Philip & Ptnrs., 2001—. Bd. dirs. Olicom, Holte, Denmark, Neohorm, Copenhagen, Hymite, Lyngby, PLH Architects, Wapmore, Cander Kemiske, Chempag, 10B Holdings, Titon Capitol Fund Ltd. Mem.: The Danish Bar and Law Soc. Avocations: travel, badminton, skiing. Commercial, contracts (including sales of goods; commercial financing), Corporate, general, Mergers and acquisitions. Office: Philip & Ptnrs Vognmagergade 7 DK-1120 Copenhagen Denmark Fax: +45 3328045. E-mail: eric.horten@philip.dk.

HORTON, JAMES WRIGHT, retired lawyer; b. Belton, S.C., Dec. 24, 1919; s. John Aiken and Emmae (Tate) H.; m. Eunice Rice, Nov. 20, 1948; children— James Wright, Max Rice, Rex Rice. BA, Furman U., 1942; JD, Harvard U., 1948. Bar: S.C. 1948. Ptnr. Nettles & Horton, Greenville, S.C., 1948-52; ptnr. Rainey, Fant & Horton, Greenville, S.C., 1952-70, Horton, Drawdy, Marchbanks, Ashmore, Chapman & Brown, Greenville, S.C., 1970-78, Horton, Drawdy, Ward & Black, Greenville, S.C., 1978-91; ret., 1997. Pres. United Fund Greenville County, 1959; mem. Greenville County Sch. Trustees, 1964-70, vice chmn., 1969; pres. Greenville Family and Children's Service, 1954-55, 68-70; bd. dirs. Salvation Army, 1969— , treas., 1970-71; bd. dirs. Family and Children's Service, Greenville Mental Health Clinic, 1956-59, Greater Greenville Community Found., 1981. Col. USMCR, ret. Decorated Silver Star. Mem. Greenville County Bar Assn. (pres. 1981) Baptist (deacon 1964-69, 71-72, 86-88). General practice. Home: 2 Osceola Dr Greenville SC 29605-3013

HORTON, LINDA RAE, lawyer; b. Louisville, Dec. 1, 1946; d. Raymond Thomas and Marcia Bryan Horton; m. Henry Ninghan Ho (dec. Jan. 1987); 1 stepchild, Michael Ho; children: Jonathan Horton, Colleen Horton; m. Carl V. Nelson Jr.; children: Cassandra Nelson, Douglas Nelson. BA, U. Ky., 1968; JD, George Washington U., 1975; LLM, Georgetown U., 1997. Bar: Md. 1975, D.C. 1975, U.S. Supreme Ct. 1980. Mgmt. intern Food and Drug Adminstrn., Arlington, Va., 1968-69; legis. asst. FDA, Rockville, Md., 1970-74, chief legis. br., 1974-75, trial atty., 1975-76, assoc. chief counsel, 1976-79, dep. chief counsel, 1979-93, dir. internat. policy, 1993-99, dir. internat. agreements, 1999—2001, advisor to acting dep. commr, 2001—02. Adj. prof. George Washington U. Sch. Law, Washington, 1983-85, Georgetown U. Sch. Law, Washington, 1999—. Chair editl. bd. Food and Drug Law Jour., 1985-86; FDA editl. bd. Commerce Clearing House, 2000—; contbr. chpts. to books and articles to profl. jours. Precinct capt. Dem. Party Ky., Jeffersontown, 1968, del. state pres. conv., Louisville, 1968; PTA fgn. lang. coord. Montgomery County Schs., Potomac, Md., 1986-89; dep. mgr., parent swim team Montgomery Swim League, Rockville, Md., 1988-90. Recipient Disting. Svc. award Dept. Health Human Svc., Washington, 1989, Meritorious Svc. award Am. Nat. Stds. Inst., 1997, Disting. Svc. award Food and Drug Law Inst., 1999, Merit award FDA, 1975, 81, 2001. Mem. ABA, Md. Bar Assn., D.C. Bar Assn., Supreme Ct. Bar, Nat. Cooperation Lab. Accreditation (bd. dirs. 1997-99), Am. Nat. Standards Inst. (bd, dirs 1994-99), Regulatory Affairs Profl. Soc. (bd. dirs. 2001-03) Presbyterian. Avocations: travel, bridge, reading, hiking, writing. Office: Hogan & Hartson 555 13th St NW Washington DC 20004 E-mail: lrhorton@hhlaw.com.

HORTY, JOHN FRANCIS, lawyer; b. Johnstown, Pa., Oct. 21, 1928; s. John Frank and Nancy Bolsinger (Dibert) H.; m. Christine Kennamer, June 1979; children: John Francis, Jon Michael, Kathryn Camille, Roger Lawrence, Jason Lawrence. BA cum laude, Amherst Coll., 1950; LLB, Harvard U., 1953. Bar: Pa. 1956, D.C., 1981. Prof. U. Pitts., 1956-68; pres. Aspen Systems Corp., Pitts., 1966-71; mng. ptnr. Horty, Springer & Mattern, P.C., Pitts., 1971—. Pres. Action Kit for Hosp. Law, Pitts., 1971—; chmn. bd. St. Francis Ctrl. Hosp., Pitts., 1973-99, St. Francis Med. Ctr., 1999-2000; vice chmn. St. Francis Health System, 1999-2000; chmn. Estes Park Inst., Denver, 1984—; chmn. Indigo Inst., Washington, 1988—; pres. Nat. Coun. Cmty. Hosps., Washington, 1974-2001; bd. dirs. Hosp. Coun. Western Pa., 1989-2000. Editor and pub. (manuals, newsletters, chpts.) Hospital Law Manual, 1956, Action Kit for Hospital Law, 1973, Action Kit for Hospital Trustees, 1977, Patient Care Law, 1981, Treatise on Hospital Law, 1977, Medical Staff Law, 1984. Named Hon. Fellow Am. Coll. Hosp. Execs., 1965; recipient award of honor Am. Hosp. Assn., 1970. Mem. ABA, Am. Hosp. Assn. (life, hon.), Pa. Bar Assn., D.C. Bar Assn., Allegheny County Bar Assn., Ponte Vedra Country Club, Tournament Players Club. Republican. Avocation: golf. Health. also: 637 Ponte Vedra Blvd Unit D Ponte Vedra Beach FL 32082-2974 Home and Office: Horty Springer & Mattern 4614 5th Ave Pittsburgh PA 15213-3663

HORVITZ, MICHAEL JOHN, lawyer; b. Cleve., Feb. 15, 1950; s. Harry Richard and Lois Joy (Unger) H.; m. Jane Rosenthal, Aug. 25, 1979; children: Katherine R., Elizabeth R. BS in Econs., U. Pa., 1972; JD, U. Va., 1975; LLM in Taxation, NYU, 1980. Bar: Ohio 1975, Fla. 1976. Assoc. Hahn, Loeser, Freedheim, Dean & Wellman, Cleve., 1975-78; counsel Hollywood, Inc., Fla., 1978-79; assoc. Jones, Day, Reavis & Pogue, Cleve., 1980-85, ptnr., 1985-2000, of counsel, 2001—. Mem. adv. bd. Kirtland Capital Ptnrs., L.P., 1992—; chmn. Parkland Mgmt. Co., 1992—; vice chmn. Horvitz Newspapers, Inc., 1994—; pres. H.R.H. Family Found., 1992—; chmn. H.R.H. Family Trust, 1992—; bd. dirs. Zephyr Mgmt., Inc.; corp. advisor Internat. Mgmt. Group, 1999—. Trustee Jewish Cmty. Fedn. Cleve., 1993-99, 2002—, Case Western Res. U., Musical Arts Assn., 1992—, Cleve. Ctr. Econ. Edn., 1992-95, Am. Cancer Soc., Cuyahoga County unit, 1989-95, Hathaway Brown Sch., Mt. Sinai Med. Ctr., Cleve. chpt. Am. Jewish Com., 1984-95, Montefiore Home for the Elderly, 1982-90, Health Hill Hosp. for Children, 1982-95, bd. pres., 1987-89; bd. dirs. Cleve. Mus. Art, 1991—, pres. bd., 1996-2001, chmn. bd., 2001—; bd. dirs. U. Va. Law Sch. Found., 1999—, pres., 2002—. Corporate, general, Estate planning, Taxation, general. Office: Jones Day 901 Lakeside Ave E Cleveland OH 44114-1190 also: Parkland Mgmt Co 1001 Lakeside Ave E Ste 900 Cleveland OH 44114-1172

HORWICH, ALLAN, lawyer; b. Des Moines, Apr. 8, 1944; s. Joseph Maurice and Bernice (Davidson) Horwich; m. Carolyn Ruth Allen, Feb. 28, 1975; children: Benjamin, Diana, Eleanor, Flannery. AB, Princeton U., 1966; JD, U. Chgo., 1969. Bar: Ill. 1969, U.S. Dist. Ct. (no. dist.) Ill. 1969, U.S. Ct. Appeals (7th cir.) 1971, U.S. Supreme Ct. 1976, U.S. Ct. Appeals (10th cir.) 1983, U.S. Dist. Ct. (ctrl. dist.) Ill. 1990, U.S. Dist. Ct. (ea. dist.) Wis. 1995, U.S. Dist. Ct. (ea. dist.) Mich. 1995, U.S. Ct. Appeals (6th cir.) 1996. Assoc. Schiff Hardin & Waite, Chgo., 1969-74; ptnr. Schiff Hardin and Waite, Chgo., 1975—, vice-chmn., 1989-95. Adj. prof. law Northwestern U. Sch. Law, 1999—2000, sr. lectr. law, 2000—; mem. adv. bd. Wall St. Lawyer. Contbr. articles to profl. jours. General civil litigation, Utilities, public. Home: 216 W Concord Ln Chicago IL 60614-5743 Office: Schiff Hardin & Waite 6600 Sears Tower Chicago IL 60606 E-mail: ahorwich@schiffhardin.com.

HORWITZ, DONALD PAUL, lawyer; b. Chgo., Feb. 5, 1936; s. Theodore J. and Lillian H. (Shlensky) H.; m. Judith Robin, Aug. 23, 1964; children: Terry Robin Kass, Linda Diane, Gail Elizabeth. BS, Northwestern U., 1957; JD, Yale U., 1960. Bar: Ill. 1961, D.C. 1961, U.S. Supreme Ct. 1966; CPA, Ill. With atty. gen.'s honors program Dept. Justice, 1961-63; atty. Gottlieb & Schwartz, Chgo., 1963-66; with Arthur Young & Co. CPAs, Chgo., 1966-72, ptnr., 1971-72; exec. v.p., sec., dir. McDonald's Corp., Oak Brook, Ill., 1972-90; ptnr. Sonnenschein, Nath & Rosenthal, Chgo., 1990—. Lectr. Northwestern U. Law Sch., Grad. Sch. Commerce, DePaul U., Chgo.; bd. dirs. Bernard Tech. Inc., 1997—, chmn. bd., 1998-2002; sec. System Capital Corp, 1996. Contbr. articles to profl. jours. Trustee Goodman Theatre/Chgo. Theatre Group, 1993—96, Evans Scholars Found., Western Golf Assn., 1984—87; pres., bd. dirs. Briarwood Country Club, 1972—73; caucus nominating com. Village of Glencoe, Ill., 1975—78, vice-chmn., 1988—89; bd. dirs. Northwestern Healthcare Network, 1990—94; vice-chmn., bd. dirs., chmn. bd. Highland Park Hosp., Lakeland Health Ventures and Northwestern Network, bd. govs., 1994—2000; chief legal officer adv. bd. Northwestern U. Kellogg Bus. Sch., 2000—; chmn. Midwest region Anti-Defamation League, 1994—95, mem. nat. commn., 1994—; exec. com. Yale Law Sch. Assn.; bd. dirs. Lakeland Health Ventures and Northwestern Network, 1986—94, McDonald's Family Charities, Inc., 2001, Scholl Sch. Podiatry, 2001—, Chgo. Med. Sch./Finch U. Health Scis., 1993—, Found. for Podiatric Edn., 2002—. Mem.: ABA, Chgo. Bar Found. (trustee 1990—97), Chgo. Bar Assn., Ill. Bar Assn., Northmoor Country Club, Econs. Club, Standard Club. Corporate, general, Franchising, Trademark and copyright.

HORWITZ, MELVIN, lawyer, physician; b. N.Y.C., Nov. 20, 1926; m. Dorothy G. Horwitz. BA, Columbia U., 1945; MD, Harvard U., 1949; JD, Yale U., 1986. Bar: Conn. 1986. Resident in surgery Yale-New Haven Hosp., New Haven, 1959-52; resident Columbia-Presbyterian Med. Ctr.,

1954-55; surgeon Manchester (Conn.) Meml. Hosp., 1956-86, chief of surgery, 1976-81, sr. surgeon emeritus, 1981—; rsch. cons., vis. lectr. dept. animal pathology and virology U. Conn., Storrs, 1962-73. Adj. prof. Western New Eng. Law Sch., Springfield, Mass., 1986-87; pres. Helapol Assocs., Manchester, 1987—; chmn. Nutmeg Inst. Rev. Bd., 1991-2001; cons. Inst. Medicine, Washington, 1985. Health, Personal injury (including property damage). Office: Helapol Assoc 223 Ludlow Rd Manchester CT 06040-4546

HOSEMAN, DANIEL, lawyer; b. Chgo., Aug. 18, 1935; s. Irving and Anne (Pruzansky) H.; m. Susan H. Myles, Aug. 7, 1960; children: Lawrence N., Joan E., Jonathan W. BS, U. Ill., 1956, JD, 1959. Bar: Ill. 1959, U.S. Dist. Ct. (no. dist.) Ill. 1960, U.S. Ct. of Appeals (7th cir.) 1969, U.S. Supreme Ct. 1976. Atty. pvt. practice, Chgo., 1959—. Mem. panel pvt. atty. trustees U.S. Bankruptcy Ct. No. Dist. Ill., 1979—; arbitrator Cir. Ct. Cook County. Trustee Ill. Legal Svcs. Fund, 1978—; v.p. Allied Jewish Sch. Bd. Met. Chgo., 1977—; v.p. United Synagogue Am., 1978—. With USAFR, 1959-65. Mem. Am. Bankruptcy Inst., Advs. Soc., Decalogue Soc. Lawyers (pres. 1981-82, award of merit 1979-80), Ill. Bar Assn. (gen. assembly, long-range planning com.), Lake County Bar Assn. (com. on bankrutpcy 1980—), Chgo. Coun. Lawyers, Comml. Law League Am., Am. Bankruptcy Inst., Nat. Assn. Bankruptcy Trustees. Bankruptcy, Commercial, consumer (including collections, credit), Commercial, contracts (including sales of goods; commercial financing). Home: 2151 Tanglewood Ct Highland Park IL 60035-4231 Office: 77 W Washington St Ste 1220 Chicago IL 60602-2901

HOSKINS, RICHARD JEROLD, lawyer; b. Ft. Smith, Ark., June 19, 1945; s. Walter Jerold and Emma Gladys Hoskins; children: Stephen Weston, Philip Richard. BA, U. Kans., 1967; JD, Northwestern U., 1970. Bar: N.Y. 1971, Ill. 1976, U.S. Supreme Ct. 1982. Assoc. Davis Polk & Wardwell, N.Y.C., 1970-73; asst. U.S. atty., So. Dist. N.Y., 1973-76; assoc. Schiff Hardin & Waite, Chgo., 1976-77, ptnr., 1978—. Adj. prof. U. Va. Law Sch., 1980-83, Northwestern U. Law Sch., 1992-98, sr. lectr., 1999—. Contbr. articles to profl. jours. Mem. vis. com. U. Chgo. Div. Sch.; Chancellor emeritus Episcopal Diocese of Chgo. Fellow Am. Coll. Trial Lawyers, Am. Bar Found.; mem. ABA, Ill. State Bar Assn., Chgo. Bar Assn., 7th Cir. Bar Assn., Assn. of Bar of City of N.Y., Chgo. Coun. Lawyers, Law Club Chgo., Met. Club (Chgo.), Univ. Club (Chgo.); bd. visitors and govs. St. John's Coll., Antitrust, Federal civil litigation, Patent. Office: 6600 Sears Tower Chicago IL 60606

HOSSLER, DAVID JOSEPH, lawyer, law educator; b. Mesa, Ariz., Oct. 18, 1940; s. Carl Joseph and Elizabeth Ruth (Bills) H.; m. Gretchen Anne, Mar. 2, 1945; 1 child, Devon Annagret. BA, U. Ariz., 1969, JD, 1972. Bar: Ariz. 1972, U.S. Dist. Ct. Ariz. 1972, U.S. Supreme Ct. 1977. Legal intern to chmn. FCC, summer 1971; law clk. to chief justice Ariz. Supreme Ct., 1972-73; chief dep. county atty. Yuma County (Ariz.), 1973-74; ptnr. Hunt, Kenworthy, Meerchaum and Hossler, Yuma, Ariz., 1974—. Instr. in law and banking, law and real estate Ariz. Western Coll.; instr. in bus. law, mktg., ethics Webster U.; instr. agrl. law U. Ariz.; co-chmn. fee arbitration com. Ariz. State Bar, 1990—; instr. employee/employer law U. Phoenix. Editor-in-chief Ariz. Adv., 1971-72. Mem. precinct com. Yuma County Rep. Ctrl. Com., 1974-2000, vice chmn., 1982; chmn. region II Acad. Decathalon competition, 1989; bd. dirs. Yuma County Ednl. Found. (Hall of Fame 2000), Yuma County Assn. Behavior Health Svcs., also pres., 1981; coach Yuma H.S. mock ct. team, 1987-94; bd. dirs. friends of U. Med. Ctr. With USN. Recipient Man and Boy award Boys Clubs Am., 1979, Freedoms Found. award Yuma chpt., 1988, Demolay Legion of Honor, 1991, Francis Woodward award Ariz. Pub. Svc., 2000; named Vol. of Yr., Yuma County, 1981-82, Heart of Yuma award, 2000. Mem. ATLA, Am. Judicature Soc., Yuma County Bar Assn. (pres. 1975-76), Navy League, VFW, Am. Legion, U. Ariz. Alumni Assn. (nat. bd. dirs., past pres., hon. bobcat 1996, Disting. Citizen award 1997), Rotary (pres. Yuma club 1987-88, dist. gov. rep. 1989, dist. gov. 1992-93, findings com. 1996, dist. found. chair 1996-2000, co-chmn. internat. membership retention 2000-01, John Van Houton Look Beyond Yourself award 1995, Roy Slayton Share Rotary Share People award 1996, Al Face You Are the Key award 1997, Ted Day Let Svc. Light the Way award 1998, Rotary Found. citation for meritorious svc., Internat. Svc. Above Self award, Cliff Doctorman Real Happiness is Helping Others award, Disting. Svc. award). Episcopalian (vestry 1978-82). Personal injury (including property damage), State civil litigation, Family and matrimonial. Home: 2802 S Fern Dr Yuma AZ 85364-2919 Office: Hunt Kenworthy Meerchaum and Hossler 330 W 24th St Yuma AZ 85364-6455 also: PO Box 2919 Yuma AZ 85366-2919 E-mail: dhossler@mindspring.com.

HOSTAGE, JOHN BRAYNE ARTHUR, law librarian; b. Hartford, Conn., June 10, 1952; s. John Brayne and Anne (Leonard) H. BA, Columbia U., 1974; MA in German, U. Wis., 1978, MA in LS, 1979. Cataloger U. Ill., Chgo., 1979-82, Harvard U. Law Sch. Libr., Cambridge, Mass., 1982—. Mem. ALA (editor SRRT newsletter 1984-86, coordinator SRRT 1987-89), Am. Assn. Law Libraries. Office: Harvard Law Sch Libr Langdell Hall Cambridge MA 02138 E-mail: hostage@law.harvard.edu.

HOSTNIK, CHARLES RIVOIRE, lawyer; b. Glen Ridge, N.J., Apr. 8, 1954; s. William John and Susan (Rivoire) H. AB, Dartmouth Coll., 1976; JD, U. Puget Sound, 1979. Bar: Wash. 1980, U.S. Dist. Ct. (we. dist.) Wash. 1980, U.S. Dist. Ct. (ea. dist.) Wash. 1982, U.S. Ct. Appeals (9th cir.) 1983, Hoh Tribal Ct. 1984, Nisqually Tribal Ct. 1984, Puyallup Tribal Ct. 1984, Shoalwater Bay Tribal Ct. 1984, Skokomish Tribal Ct. 1984. Asst. atty. gen. Atty. Gen.'s Office State of Wash., Olympia, 1980-84; assoc. Kane, Vandeberg, Hartinger & Walker, Tacoma, 1984-87; ptnr. Anderson, Burns & Hostnik, Tacoma, 1988—. Trial and appellate judge N.W. Intertribal Ct. Sys., Edmonds, Wash., 1986—2000. Author: (chpt.) Washington Practice, 1989. Native American, Personal injury (including property damage), General civil litigation. Office: Anderson Burns & Hostnik 6915 Lakewood Dr W Ste A1 Tacoma WA 98467-3299

HOTH, STEVEN SERGEY, lawyer, educator; b. Jan. 30, 1941; s. Donald Leroy and Ina Dorothy (Barr) H.; m. JoEllen Maly, July 29, 1967; children: Andrew Steven, Peter Lindsey. AB, Grinnell Coll., 1962; JD, U. Iowa, 1966; postgrad., U. Pa., 1968, Oxford (Eng.) U., 1973. Bar: U.S. Ct. Appeals (8th cir.) 1966, U.S. Tax Ct. 1967, U.S. Ct. Claims 1967, U.S. Dist. Ct. Iowa 1968, U.S. Dist. Ct. N.D. 1968, U.S. Dist. Ct. S.D. 1968, U.S. Supreme Ct. 1973, U.S. Ct. Appeals (7th cir.) 1982. Law clk. to chief justice U.S. Ct. Appeals (8th cir.), Fargo, N.D., 1967-68; assoc. Hirsch, Adams, Hoth & Krekel, Burlington, Iowa, 1968-72, ptnr., 1972-91; pvt. practice Burlington, 1992—. Asst. atty. Des Moines County, Burlington, 1968-72, atty., 1972-83; alt. mcpl. judge, Burlington, 1968-69; lectr. criminal law Southeastern C.C., West Burlington, 1972-82; assoc. prof. polit. sci. Iowa Wesleyan Coll., Mt. Pleasant, 1981-82, Iowa Truck Rail, Amerial, Inc.; pres. Burlington Truck Rail, Burlington Short Line RR. Inc., Iowa Internat. Investments, Burlington Storage and Transfer; sec. Burlington Loading Co. Contbr. numerous articles to profl. jours. Chmn. Des Moines County Civil Svc. Commn.; trustee Charles H. Rand Lecture Trust; mem. Des Moines County Conf. Com., Des Moines County Conf. Bd.; dir. Burlington Med. Ctr. Staff Found.; moderator 1st Congl. Ch., Burlington; bd. dirs. UN Assn.; clk. Burlington North Bottoms Levy and Drainage Dist.; bd. mem., pres. Burlington Cmty. Sch. Dist. Bd. Edn., chmn. commn. on ministry, mem. exec. com. Nat. Assn. Congl. Christian Chs., moderator; treas. 1st dist. Dem. Com.; bd. dirs. Legal Aid Soc. Planned Parenthood Des Moines County. Recipient Chmn.'s award ARC, 1980; Reginald Heber Smith fellow in legal aid Cheyenne River Indian Reservation, Eagle Butte, S.D., 1967-68. Mem. Missionary Soc.-Nat. Assn. Congl. Christian Chs., ABA (internat. sect., tax sect.), Iowa State Bar Assn. (liaison to Iowa Med. Soc.), Des Moines County Bar Assn., Am. Judicature Soc., Agrl. Law Com., Iowa Def. Coun., Iowa Archaeol. Soc., Soc. for German Am. Studies, Manorial Soc. Gt. Britain, Grinnell Coll. Alumni Assn. (bd. dirs.), Malawi Soc., Burlington-West Burlington C. of C. (bd. dirs.), Nat. Assn. Congrl. Christian Chs., Burlington Golf Club, New Crystal Lake Club (pres.), Elks, Eagles, Masons, Rotary. Corporate, general, General practice, Private international. Office: PO Box 982 Hoth Bldg 200 Jefferson St Burlington IA 52601

HOUGH, THOMAS HENRY MICHAEL, retired lawyer, educator; b. Midland, Pa., Aug. 4, 1933; s. Bert Patrick and Marguerite (Mullen) H.; m. Jocelyn Peltz, Aug. 20, 1956; children: Jocelyn, Thomas Henry Michael. AB, Dickinson Coll., 1955; JD, Dickinson Sch. Law, 1958. Bar: Pa. 1959, U.S. Ct. Appeals (3d cir.) 1975, U.S. Supreme Ct. 1970. Field atty. NLRB, Pitts., 1959-60; atty. United Steelworkers Am., 1960-68; ptnr. Lucchino, Gaitens & Hough, Pitts., 1968-79, Hough & Gleason, PC, Pitts., 1980-94, Barry Fasulo & Hough, PC, Pitts., 1994—2002; ret., 2003. Adj. assoc. prof. pub. sector arbitration and pub. sector collective bargaining Grad. Sch. Pub. and Internat. Affairs, U. Pitts., 1970-97. Health, Labor (including EEOC, Fair Labor Standards Act, labor-management relations, NLRB, OSHA).

HOULE, JEFFREY ROBERT, lawyer; b. Biddeford, Maine, July 27, 1965; s. Marcel Paul and Lois Marie (Jackson) H.; children: Grace Morgan, Hunter Jackson. AB, Boston Coll., Chestnut Hill, Mass., 1987; JD, Western New Eng. Coll., Springfield, Mass., 1991; LLM in Taxation, Cert. in Employee Benefits Law, Georgetown U., Washington, 1992, LLM in Securities Regulation, 1995. Bar: D.C., N.Y., Conn., Mass., Maine. Pres. A.F.I. Investments, Springfield, Mass., 1988-91, Washington Capital Ventures, LP, Washington, 1995-98; law clk. Stones Solicitors, Exeter, Devon, Eng., 1989; jud. intern to the Hon. Joan Glazer Margolis U.S. Magistrate Judge, New Haven, Conn., 1990; legal intern Office of Atty. Gen. Robert Abrams, N.Y.C., 1990; analyst The Bur. of Nat. Affairs, Inc., Washington, 1992; assoc. Andros, Floyd & Miller PC, Hartford, Conn., 1992-94, Elias, Matz, Tiernan & Herrick LLP, Washington, 1994-98; founding ptnr. Greenberg Traurig LLP, McLean, Va., 1998—. Contbr. articles to profl. jours. With U.S. Army, 1984-86. Mem. ABA, The Army and Navy Club, The Federalist Soc.,The Tower Club, Phi Alpha Delta. Republican. Roman Catholic. Avocations: hiking, horseback riding, swimming, scuba diving, international travel. Corporate, general, Securities, Taxation, general.

HOULIHAN, DAVID PAUL, lawyer; b. Youngstown, Ohio, May 14, 1937; s. Paul V. and Delcie (Norman) H.; m. Marlene K. Betras, Aug. 13, 1960; children: Kevin, Rex, Laura, Brian. BS, Youngstown State U., 1959; postgrad., Purdue U., 1960; LLB, Georgetown U., 1964. Bar: D.C. 1965, U.S. Ct. Appeals (D.C. cir.) 1965, U.S. Supreme Ct. 1968, U.S. Ct. Internat. Trade 1976, U.S. Ct. Customs and Patent Appeals 1976, U.S. Ct. Appeals (Fed. cir.) 1982. Analyst U.S. Internat. Trade Commn., Washington, 1960-64; counsel U.S.-Japan trade council Stitt & Hemmendinger, Washington, 1964-68; ptnr. Daniels, Houlihan & Palmeter P.C., Washington, 1968-84, Mudge, Rose, Guthrie, Alexander & Ferdon, Washington, 1984-95, White & Case, Washington, 1995—. Lectr. Oxford U., Eng., 1972; chmn. Keidanren Seminar: Dumping, Customs and Tax Aspects of Transfer Pricing. Contbr. articles to profl. jours. Mem. ABA, D.C. Bar Assn., British-Am. C. of C. Democrat. Roman Catholic. Avocations: sailing, music. Administrative and regulatory, Private international. Address: White & Case 601 13th St NW Washington DC 20005-3807 Personal E-mail: dholihan@whitecase.com.

HOULIHAN, GERALD JOHN, lawyer; b. Cortland, N.Y., Aug. 26, 1943; s. Robert Emmett and Helen (Corsi) H.; m. Claudia C. Kitchens; children: Andrea, Gerald Jr., Maureen, Katherine, Colleen. BS, U. Notre Dame, 1965; JD, Syracuse U., 1968. Bar: N.Y. 1968, U.S. Dist. Ct. (we. dist.) N.Y. 1968, U.S. Ct. Appeals (2nd cir.) 1972, U.S. Supreme Ct. 1980, U.S. Ct. Appeals (5th cir.) 1981, U.S. Ct. Appeals (11th cir.) 1981, Fla. 1985, U.S. Dist. Ct. (so. dist.) Fla. 1985, U.S. Dist. Ct. (so. dist.) N.Y. 1986, U.S. Dist. Ct. (no. dist.) Fla. 1986, U.S. Ct. Appeals (4th and D.C. cirs.) 1987, U.S. Dist. Ct. (middle dist.) Fla., 1987. Assoc. Harris, Beach, Keating et al., Rochester, N.Y., 1968-72; asst. U.S. atty. U.S. Atty.'s Office, Rochester, 1972-81; sr. litigation counsel U.S. Dept. Justice, Rochester, 1981-82; chief asst. U.S. atty. U.S. Atty.'s Office, Miami, Fla., 1982-85; ptnr. Steel Hector & Davis, Miami, 1985-91; mem. Greenberg, Traurig, Hoffman, Lipoff, Rosen & Quentel, P.A., Miami, 1991-95; ptnr. Houlihan & Ptnrs., P.A., 1995—. Advocate Am. Bd. Trial Advocates. Belle L. Landry scholar Syracuse Soc. Mem. Fed. Bar Assn. (pres. 1993-94, bd. dirs. Miami chpt. 1988—), Order of Coif. Democrat. Antitrust, Federal civil litigation, Criminal. Home: 5191 SW 76th St Miami FL 33143-6015 Office: Houlihan & Ptnrs PA 2600 S Douglas Rd Ste 600 Miami FL 33134-6100 E-mail: gjhoulihan@aol.com.

HOUPT, JAMES EDWARD, lawyer; b. Calif., 1951; m. Leslie Ann Jones Houpt. BA with distinction, Calif. State U., Chico, 1976; JD cum laude, Harvard U., 1992. Bar: Va. 1992, D.C. 1992, U.S. Ct. Appeals (4th cir.) 1992, Md. 1993, Calif. 1997, U.S. Ct. Appeals (9th cir.) 1997. News dir. Sta. KNVR-FM, Paradise, Calif., 1978-80; anchor, reporter Sta. KHSL-AM-TV, Chico, 1980-85; sr. reporter Sta. KOLO-TV, Reno, 1985-89; assoc. Baker & Hostetler, Washington, 1992-97; assoc. of counsel, ptnr. Orrick, Herrington & Sutcliffe LLP, Sacramento, 1997—. Lectr. journalism Calif. State U., 1981, 85; adj. prof. law sch. U. Calif., Davis, vis. prof., 1999, 2000. Author: (booklet) Access to Electronic Records, 1990, The Libel Curtain: A Comparison of Canadian & American Libel Law, 1994, Going On-Line: Is the World Wide Web a Web for the Unwary?, 1996, Boarding a Moving Bus: Developing an Internet Risk Management Strategy, 1997, The Courts and the Internet: A Match Made in Hell?, 2000; contbr. articles to legal and gen. interest publs. With USN, 1970-74. Recipient Cert. of Merit, Calif.-Nev. AP TV-Radio Assn., 1983, 84, 86. Mem. ABA, Va. State Bar Assn., D.C. Bar, Calif. Bar Assn., VFW, Am. Legion. Avocations: photography, hiking, canoeing. General civil litigation, Libel, Trademark and copyright. Office: Orrick, Herrington & Sutcliffe LLP 400 Capitol Mall Ste 3000 Sacramento CA 95814-4497

HOUSER, DOUGLAS GUY, lawyer; b. Oregon City, Oreg., July 11, 1935; s. Roy B. and Shirley (Knight) H.; m. Lucy Anne Latham, Sept. 1, 1961; children: Brooks Bonham, Bradley Knight, Anne Elizabeth. BA, Willamette U., 1957; JD, Stanford, 1960. Bar: Oreg. 1960. Practice in Portland, 1961—; ptnr. Bullivant, Houser PC, 1965—. Chmn. com. on continuing legal edn. Oreg. State Bar, 1969-70, chmn. com. jud. adminstrn., 1975, bd. bar examiners, 1970-72, mem. bd. bar govs., 1977-80, treas., 1979-80; judge protem Circuit Ct., 1973-77; gen. counsel NIKE, Inc., 1972-84, dir, 1972—; bd. overseers RAND Inst. for Civil Justice; gen. counsel Soc. Registered Profl. Adjusters; former gen. counsel Pacific N.W. Life Ins. Co.; lectr. Contbr. articles to profl. publs. Legal adviser Portland Sch. Dist. 1 Race and Edn. Com., 1963-64; mem. Eagle bd. Columbia-Pacific council Boy Scouts Am., 1962-70; past v.p., treas., bd. dirs. Waverley Children's Home; trustee Willamette U.; bd. visitors Stanford U. Sch. Law, 1978-80, 8991, 96-98, 98-2000, Willamette U. Law Sch., 1986; chmn. Oreg. State Jud. Fitness Commn., 1980—. Fellow Am. Bar Found. (life), Am. Coll. Trial Lawyers, Internat. Acad. Trial Lawyers; mem. ABA (past chmn. tort and ins. practice sect.), Multnomah County Bar Assn. (chmn. com. continuing legal edn. 1977), Oreg. Assn. Def. Counsel (dir. 1972-76, pres. 1976-77), Def. Research Inst. (bd. dirs. 1990-93, sec.-treas. 1993—), Fedn. Def. and Corp. Counsel (chmn. bd. dirs. 1991-92), Am. Judicature Soc. (bd. dirs. 1985-88), Internat. Assn. Def. Counsel, Stanford Law Soc. Oreg., Am. Law Inst., Nat. Jud. Coll. (adv. coun. 1990—), Willamette U. Alumni Assn. (pres. 1972-74, bd. trustees 1971—), Beta Theta Pi, Phi Delta Phi, Omicron Delta Kappa, Pi Gamma Mu. Republican. Episcopalian (trustee Diocese Oreg. 1972-75, sr. warden). Clubs: Waverly Country, Arlington, Multnommah Athletic. Federal civil litigation, State civil litigation, Private international. Home: 11621 SW Military Ln Portland OR 97219 Office: Bullivant Houser Bailey PC Portland OR 97204-2089

HOUSLANGER, TODD ERIC, lawyer; b. Franklin Square, N.Y., Oct. 6, 1961; s. William and Rhoda Houslanger. BS in Biochemistry, SUNY, Stony Brook, 1983; JD, Touro Law Sch., 1988. Bar: Conn. 1988, N.Y. 1989, D.C. 1989, U.S. Dist. Ct. (ea. and so. dist.) N.Y. 89, U.S. Ct. Internat. Trade 1989, U.S. Ct. Mil. Appeals 1989, U.S. Ct. Appeals (D.C. cir.) 1993, U.S. Supreme Ct. 1993. Law clk. intern to Hon. Francis Altimari U.S. Cir. Ct. Appeals, 2nd Cir., N.Y.C., 1987; pub. defender Legal Aid Soc. of Nassau County, Hempstead, N.Y., 1988-89; pvt. practice Houslanger & Assocs., Huntington, N.Y., 1989—. Editor-in-chief: Jour. Suffolk Acad. Law, 1987-88. Mem. Stony Brook Coun., 1982-83; chairman, co-founder Citizens Sunday, Huntington, 1995-96; chairman Project C.A.R.E., Huntington, 1993-95. Mem. ABA, N.Y. Bar Assn., N.Y. Assn. Criminal Def. Lawyers, Suffolk County Bar Assn. (chmn. lawyers assistance com. 1993-94, unlawful practice com. 1993-96, chmn. creditors rights law com. 2000—), Nassau Lawyers Assn., Nassau County Bar Assn. (criminal law, lawyers assistance and comml. law coms.), Huntington Lawyers Club (1st v.p. 2002-03). Avocations: scuba diving, travel, acting, culinary delights. Commercial, consumer (including collections, credit), Criminal, Property, real (including real estate development, water). Office: Houslanger & Assocs 372 New York Ave Huntington NY 11743-3311 also: 253 Katonah Ave Katonah NY 10536

HOUSTON, JAMES GORMAN, JR., state supreme court justice; b. Eufaula, Ala., Mar. 11, 1933; s. James Gorman and Mildred (Vance) H.; m. Martha Martin, Dec. 3, 1955; children: Mildred Vance, J. Gorman III. BS, Auburn U., 1955; LLB, U. Ala., 1956, JD, 1969. Bar: Ala. 1956. Law clk. to chief justice Ala. Supreme Ct., Montgomery, 1956-57; ptnr. Houston & Martin, P.C., Eufaula, 1960-85; assoc. justice Ala. Supreme Ct., Montgomery, 1985—. County atty. Barbour County, Clayton, Ala., 1961-79. Contbr. numerous opinions to So. Reporter; contbr. articles to profl. jours. Mayor pro tem, alderman City of Eufaula, 1964-70; pres. Heritage Assn., Eufaula, Ala., 1979-82; mem. Ala. Commn. on Uniform State Laws. 1st lt. JAGC, USAF, 1957-60. Named Citizen of Yr., City of Eufaula, 1979; recipient Alumni Achievement in Humanities award Auburn Univ., 1993. Fellow Am. Bar Found.; mem. ABA, Ala. Bar Assn., Ala. State Bar (examiner 1979-82, disciplinary commn. 1984-85, state bar commr. 1982-85), Barbour County Bar Assn. (pres. 1975), Eufaula C. of C. (pres. 1974). Republican. Methodist. Office: Ala Supreme Ct 300 Dexter Ave Montgomery AL 36104-3741

HOUSTON, JAMIE GILES, III, lawyer, accountant; b. Greenwood, Miss., June 11, 1952; s. Jamie Giles Jr. and Joan (Miller) H.; m. Katherine Elise Smith, Dec. 29, 1979; children: Jamie G. IV, Andrew Phillips. BBA, U. Miss., 1974, JD, 1976; LLM in Taxation, NYU, 1978. Bar: Miss. 1976, U.S. Dist. Ct. (no. dist.) Miss. 1976, U.S. Dist. Ct. (so. dist.) Miss. 1978, U.S. Tax Ct. 1979, U.S. Ct. appeals (5th cir.) 1983; CPA, Miss. Assoc. Knight, Ballew & Van Slyke, Jackson, Miss., 1976-79; ptnr. Van Slyke & Houston, Jackson, 1979; assoc. Watkins & Eager, PLLC, Jackson, 1979-82, mem., 1983—. Spkr. Miss. Tax Inst., Jackson, 1980, chmn. bd. trustees, 1983-84; mem. estate planning coun. Millsaps Coll., Jackson, 1987-93; spkr. Miss. Bankruptcy Conf., Jackson, 1988. Mem. adminstrv. bd. Galloway United Meth. Ch., Jackson, 1983-88, 92-94; bd. dirs. Goodwill Industries, 1992-94, U. Miss. Found., 1996-. Mem. ABA, AICPA, Miss. State Bar (chmn., estates and trusts sect. 2000-01), Hinds County Bar Assn., Miss. Estate Planning Coun., Miss. Soc. CPA's, Am. Coll. Trust and Estate Counsel (state chair 2002-). Avocation: golfing. Corporate, general, Estate planning, Estate taxation. Office: Watkins & Eager PLLC 400 E Capitol St Jackson MS 39201-2610

HOUTCHENS, BARNARD, retired lawyer; b. Johnstown, Colo., Aug. 5, 1911; s. Everet Harrison and Evelyn Mary (Barnard) H.; m. Margaret Belle Colvin, Dec. 28, 1940; children: John Barnard, Marilyn (dec.). BA, U. Nebr., 1933, LL.B., 1935; LL.D., U. No. Colo. at Greeley, 1963. Bar: Colo. 1935. Practiced in, Greeley, 1935-90; ret., 1990; city atty., 1941-47, 49-50. Mem. bar com. Colo. Bd. Law Examiners, 1947-81, chmn., 1968-81 Trustee State Colls., Colo., 1948-65, pres. bd., 1964-65; nat. sec.-treas. Assn. Gov. Bds. State Univs. and Allied Instns., 1960-62; bd. dirs. U. No. Colo. Found., 1975-79, pres., 1978-79. Fellow Am. Coll. Trial Lawyers; mem. ABA, Colo. Bar Assn., Weld County Bar Assn. (pres. 1946-47), Greeley Jr. C. of C., Greeley C. of C. (pres. 1951-52), Blue Key, Sigma Chi. Clubs: Rotary, Elks (past exalted ruler Greeley), Masons. Home: 1020 48th Ave Greeley CO 80634-2316

HOVDA, THEODORE JAMES, lawyer; b. Forest City, Iowa, Oct. 15, 1951; s. Ernest J. and Doris (Goodnight) H.; m. Susan J. Miller, Feb. 24, 1973; children: Theodore James III, Lee Joseph, Margaux Ann. BS, Iowa State U., 1973; JD, U. Iowa, 1977. Asst. county atty. Hancock County, Garner, Iowa, 1977-78, county atty., 1979-98; mem. Riehm & Hovda, Garner, 1977-98, Hovda Law Office, 1998—. County chmn. Hancock County Rep. Ctrl. Com., 1979-98. Mem. Iowa Bar Assn., Hancock County Bar Assn., Dist. 2A Bar Assn., Rotary, Masons. Republican. Methodist. Estate planning, Probate (including wills, trusts), Personal income taxation. Home: 785 11th Street Pl Garner IA 50438-1848 Office: Hovda Law Office PO Box 9 395 State St Garner IA 50438-1236 Fax: 641-923-3108. E-mail: tshovda@kalnet.com.

HOVDE, FREDERICK BOYD, lawyer; b. Mpls., Aug. 7, 1934; s. Frederick L. and Priscilla L. (Boyd) H.; m. Alice Austell, Feb. 22, 1981; children by previous marriage: Frederick R., Debra L., Kristine L., Sarah L. AB, Princeton U., 1956; JD, U. Mich., 1959. Bar: Ind. 1959, U.S. Dist. Ct. (no. and so. dists.) Ind. 1959, U.S. Ct. Appeals (7th cir.) 1960, U.S. Supreme Ct. 1977. Assoc. Ice, Miller, Donadio & Ryan, Indpls., 1959-67, ptnr., 1967-69, Townsend, Hovde & Townsend, Indpls., 1969-77; mem. Townsend, Hovde, Townsend & Montross, P.C., 1977-84, Townsend, Hovde & Montross, P.C., 1984-97, F. Boyd Hovde, P.C., 1985—, Hovde Law Firm, 1997—. Mem. com. on character and fitness Ind. Supreme Ct., 1976-2000, rules of practice and procedure, 1980-92. Mem. Indpls. Bar Assn. (treas. 1969, v.p. 1974, pres. 1979), ABA (del. 1980-83), Ind. Trial Lawyers Assn. (bd. dirs. 1970—, pres. 1976-77), Assn. Trial Lawyers Am., Am. Coll. Trial Laywers, Internat. Acad. Trial Lawyers, Ind. Coll. Trial Lawyers, Indpls. Jaycees (pres. 1963-64), Ind. Golf Assn. (pres. 1974-75), Western Golf Assn. (dir. 1969-81, v.p. 1972-81), Crooked Stick Golf Club (Carmel, Ind.), Pine Valley Golf Club (Celmenton, N.J.), Old Marsh Golf Club (Palm Beach Gardens, Fla.). Personal injury (including property damage), Product liability, Professional liability. Office: Hovde Law Firm Ste 205 10585 N Meridian St Indianapolis IN 46290-1068

HOVDE, FREDERICK RUSSELL, lawyer; b. Lafayette, Ind., Oct. 1, 1955; s. F. Boyd and Karen (Sorenson) H. BBA, So. Meth. U., 1977; JD, Ind. U., 1980. Bar: Ind. 1980, U.S. Dist. Ct. (no. and so. dists.) Ind. 1980, U.S. Ct. Appeals (7th cir.) 1980. Ptnr. Hovde Law Firm, Indpls., 1980—. Bd. visitors Ind. U. Sch. of Law, Indpls., 1993—. Bd. dirs. Ind. Golf Found., 1998—. Fellow Am. Coll. Trial Lawyers, Ind. Coll. Trial Lawyers, Indpls. Bar Found.; mem. ABA, Ind. Bar Assn. (bd. dirs. young lawyers sect. 1983-86), Indpls. Bar Assn. (bd. dirs. young lawyers sect. 1986-89), Assn. Trial Lawyers Am. (sustaining), Ind. Trial Lawyers Assn. (bd. dirs. 1990—, exec. com. 1995—, pres. 2002-03), Am. Bd. Trial Advs., Ind. Golf Assn. (pres. 1995-97), Sagamore Inn of Ct., Crooked Stick Golf Club (pres. 1992-93). Personal injury (including property damage), Product liability. Office: Hovde Law Firm 10585 N Meridian St Indianapolis IN 46290-1069 E-mail: rhovde@hovdelaw.com.

HOWALD, JOHN WILLIAM, lawyer; b. St. Louis, Dec. 21, 1935; s. Herbert John and Irene Dorothy (Weber) H.; m. Nina M. Zierendeng, June 15, 1957 (div. 1970); children: Deborah A., Catherine A., Laura A., John William; m. Betty L. Curtis, Feb. 14, 1971 (div. 1999); 1 stepchild, Tracy L.; m. Nancy J. Owens, Mar. 1, 2003. BS, U. Mo., 1957; JD, St. Louis U.,

1962. Bar: Mo. 1962, U.S. Dist. Ct. (ea. dist.) Mo. 1962, U.S. Ct. Appeals (8th cir.) 1965, U.S. Supreme Ct. 1985. V.p. sales Eureka Svc. and Equip. Co., Eureka, Mo., 1959-62; ptnr. Sheehan, Furtaw & Howald, Hillsboro, Mo., 1963-64, Thurman, Nixon, Smith & Howald, Hillsboro, 1964-70, Thurman, Nixon, Smith, Howald, Weber & Bowles, Hillsboro, 1970-80, Thurman, Smith, Howald, Weber & Bowles, Hillsboro, 1989-91, Thurman, Howald, Weber, Bowles & Senkel, Hillsboro, 1991-95, Thurman, Howald, Weber, Senkel & Norrick, L.L.C., Hillsboro, 1995—. Bd. dirs. LaBarque Ent. of Jefferson County, Hillsboro, 1965-02, Rustic Hills Resort Ltd., Hillsboro, 1968—. Mem. Mo. Ethics Commn., 1994-98, vice-chmn., 1995-96, chmn., 1996-98. Lt. (j.g.) USN, 1957-59. Recipient Spl. award, Meramec Basin Assn., 1967, 69. Fellow Am. Bar Found., Am. Coll. Trust and Estate Counsel (Mo. chmn. 1987-92); mem. ABA, Estate Planning Coun. St. Louis (pres. 1990-91), Mo. Bar Assn. (bd. govs. 1975-87, Pres. Spl. award 1979), Jefferson County Bar Assn. (pres. 1963-64). Avocations: travel, golf. Corporate, general, Estate planning, Property, real (including real estate development, water). Home: 9662 W Vista Dr Hillsboro MO 63050-3112 Office: Thurman Howald Weber Senkel & Norrick LLC PO Box 800 One Thurman Ct Hillsboro MO 63050

HOWARD, ALEX T., JR., federal judge; b. 1924; Student, U. Ala., 1942, student, 1946, Auburn U., 1942-44; JD, Vanderbilt U., 1950. U.S. probation officer, Mobile, Ala., 1950-51; ptnr. Johnstone, Adams, Howard, Bailey & Gordon, Mobile, 1951-86; U.S. commr. U.S. Dist. Ct. (so. dist.) Ala., 1956-70, judge, 1986—, chief judge, 1989-94, sr. judge, 1996—. Assoc. editor Am. Maritime Cases for Port of Mobile. Served to 2d lt. U.S. Army, 1943-46. Mem. ABA, Internat. Soc. Barristers, Internat. Assn. of Ins. Counsel, Maritime Law Assn. of U.S., Southeastern Admiralty Law Inst. (dir. 1978-80), Ala. Bar Assn., Ala. Def. Lawyers Assn. (dir. late 1950's), Mobile Bar Assn. (pres. 1973).

HOWARD, ANDREW BAKER, lawyer; b. Watertown, N.Y., July 26, 1969; s. Courtland Rogers and Maryanne H.; m. Elizabeth Edge, June 8, 1996; children: Christopher Baker, Paul Andrew. BA cum laude, St. Lawrence U., 1991; JD cum laude, Union U., 1994. Bar: N.Y. 1995. Atty. Connor, Curran & Schram, Hudson, N.Y., 1994—; asst. dist. atty. Columbia County Dist. Atty., Hudson, 1995. Instr. Am. Inst. Banking, Albany, 1997—. Mem. N.Y. State Bar Assn., Columbia County Bar Assn., Justinian Soc., Columbia County C. of C. (bd. dirs.). Republican. Roman Catholic. Avocations: mountain biking, skiing, shooting. Banking, General civil litigation, Personal injury (including property damage). Home: 3075 Upper Main St Valatie NY 12184 Office: Connor Curran & Schram PC 441 E Allen St Hudson NY 12534-2422 E-mail: howard@ccslawfirm.com.

HOWARD, BLAIR DUNCAN, lawyer; b. Alexandria, Va. s. T. Brooke and Elizabeth Duncan H.; m. Catherine Cremins; children: Thomas Brooke II, Caitlin Margaret. BA, U. Va., 1960; LLB, American U., 1963. Ptnr. Howard, Leino & Howard, Alexandria, Va., 1966—. Capt. USA, 1963-65. Named in Superstar Ohio Assn. Criminal Defense Lawyers, Columbus, 1994, One of Top Lawyers in Met. Washington, Washingtonian Mag. article, 1997. Fellow Am. Coll. Trial Lawyers; mem. ABA, ATLA, Alexandria Bar Assn., Va. State Bar Assn. (faculty professionalism course 1990-93). Criminal, Federal civil litigation, General civil litigation. Office: Howard Morrison & Howard 1 Wall Street Warrenton VA 20186-3319

HOWARD, CARL, lawyer; b. Chgo., July 23, 1920; m. Kathleen Agnes Costello, May 10, 1953; 1 child, Carl. AB, DePauw U., 1942; JD, U. Calif., San Francisco, 1949. Bar: Calif. 1951. Supervising dep. corps. commr. State of Calif., San Francisco, 1951-69; supervisory asst., asst. house counsel Fed. Home Loan Bank of San Francisco, 1970-75; legal counsel Home Fed. Savs. and Loan Assn., San Francisco, 1976-88, chmn. bd. dirs., 1985-86; assoc. Kerner, Colangelo & Imlay, 1976-86; sole practice, 1987-96. Lt. USNR, 1942-46, PTO. Mem. State Bar Calif., Am. Legion. Republican. Roman Catholic. Avocations: walking, golfing, bicycling. Banking, Corporate, general. Home: 2450 Quintara St San Francisco CA 94116-1139

HOWARD, DAVIS JONATHAN, lawyer, educator, author; b. S.I., N.Y., Dec. 8, 1954; s. Royal Marwin and Muriel Lu (Russell) H. BA summa cum laude, Wagner Coll., 1976; JD, Yale U., 1982. Bar: N.Y. 1983, N.J. 1986, U.S. Dist. Ct. (so. and ea. dists.) N.Y. 1983, U.S. Dist. Ct. N.J. 1986, U.S. Ct. Appeals (3d cir.) 1987, U.S. Ct. Appeals (4th cir.) 1988, U.S. Ct. Appeals (2d cir.) 1994. Assoc. Robson & Miller, N.Y.C., 1983-85, Sills Cummis Zuckerman Radin Tischman Epstein & Gross, P.A., Newark, 1985-92; ptnr. Parry & Howard, P.A., Elizabeth, N.J., 1993-98; pvt. practice Staten Island, NY, 1998—. Lectr. law Rutgers U. Sch. Law, Newark, 1987-89; faculty legal seminars, symposiums; adjunct Coll. of Staten Island, CUNY, 1999. Contbr. articles to legal jours.; editor-in-chief, co-founder Shepard's N.J. Ins. Law and Regulation Reporter, 1991. Dir. alumni sch. com. Yale U., 1989-96. Mem. ATLA, ABA, N.Y. State Bar Assn., N.J. Bar Assn., N.Y. County Lawyers Assn., Def. Rsch. Inst., Am. Soc. Writers on Legal Subjects, Scribes. Federal civil litigation, General civil litigation, Insurance. Home and Office: 46 Longfellow Ave Staten Island NY 10301-4616 Fax: 718-816-4961. E-mail: dajho@aol.com.

HOWARD, GENE CLAUDE, retired lawyer, retired state senator; b. Perry, Okla., Sept. 26, 1926; s. Joe W. and Nell L. (Brown) Howard; m. Belva J. Prestidge, Dec. 28, 1979; children: Jean Ann, Joe Ted, Belinda Janice. JD, U. Okla., 1951. Bar: Okla. 1950, U.S. Ct. Mil. Appeals 1956, U.S. Supreme Ct. 1956. Ptnr. Howard & Widdows & Bufogle PC, and predecessors, Tulsa, 1952—; mem. Okla. Ho. of Reps., 1958-62, Okla. Senate, 1964-82, pres. pro tem, 1974-81. Mem. exec. com. Coun. State Govts., 1974—76; chmn. Okla. State and Edn. employees Group Ins. Bd., 1990—98; bd. dirs. Cubic Energy Corp., Local Okla. Bank; trustee Phila. Mortgage Trust, Okla. Coll. Savs. Plan. Mem. So. Growth Policy Bd., 1972—76; pres. Okla. Jr. Dems., 1954; del. Dem. Nat. Conv., 1964. With U.S. Army, 1944—46, PTO, lt. col. USAF, 1961—62. Mem.: Phi Delta Phi, Tulsa County Bar Assn. (Outstanding Young Atty. 1953), Okla. Bar Assn. Mem. Disciples Of Christ. Federal civil litigation, Corporate, general, Personal injury (including property damage). Home: 2404 E 29th St Tulsa OK 74114-5619 Office: Howard Widdows & Bufogle PC 1500 Nations Bank Ctr 15W6 Tulsa OK 74119 E-mail: howardgc@swbell.net.

HOWARD, GEORGE, JR., federal judge; b. Pine Bluff, Ark., May 13, 1924; Student, Lincoln U., 1951; BS, U. Ark., JD, 1954; LL.D., 1976. Bar: Ark. bar 1953, U.S. Supreme Ct. bar 1959. Pvt. practice law, Pine Bluff, 1953-77; spl. assoc. justice Ark. Supreme Ct., 1976, assoc. justice, 1977; justice U.S. Ct. Appeals, Ark., 1979-80; U.S. dist. judge, Eastern dist. Little Rock, 1980—. Mem. Ark. Claims Commn., 1969-77; chmn. Ark. adv. com. Civil Rights Commn.. Recipient citation in recognition of faithful and disting. svc. as mem. Supreme Ct. Com. of Profl. Conduct, 1980, disting. jurist award Jud. Coun. Nat. Bar Assn., 1980, Wiley A. Branton Issues Symposium award, 1990; voted outstanding trial judge 1984-85 Ark. Trial Lawyers Assn.; inducted Ark.'s Black Hall of Fame, 1994; recipient keepers of the spirit award Univ. Ark., Pine Bluff, 1995, quality svc. award Ark. Dem. Black Caucus, 1995, Drum Major award, Ark. Martin Luther King, Jr., Commn., 2003. Mem. ABA, Ark. Bar Assn., Jefferson County Bar Assn. (pres.) Baptist.

HOWARD, GREGORY CHARLES, lawyer; b. Jan. 20, 1947; s. Robert L. and Nonamae (Lawlor) H.; m. Kathy Arlene Steinbacher, Oct. 1, 1983. Student, Clarkson Coll., 1965-67; BS, Boston U., 1969; JD, New Eng. Sch. Law, 1975. Bar: Mass. 1975, U.S. Dist. Ct. Mass. 1975, U.S. Supreme Ct. 1979. Assoc. Carmen L. Durso, Boston, 1975-77, Norris Kozodoy & Krasnoo, Boston, 1977-79; pvt. practice Boston, 1979-80; ptnr. Hoff Ernstoff & Howard, Boston, 1980-86; pres. Gregory C. Howard, PC, Boston, 1986—. State civil litigation, Personal injury (including property damage), Property, real (including real estate development, water). Home: 5 Eliot Ave Chestnut Hill MA 02467-1455 Office: 28 State St Ste 1100 Boston MA 02109-1775 E-mail: greghoward@earthlink.net.

HOWARD, HARRY CLAY, lawyer; b. Rockwood, Tenn., May 1, 1929; s. Harry Clay and Julia Roe (Cannon) H.; m. Mary Helen Harrison, June 12, 1951 (dec. Dec. 1997); children: Helen Howard Porter, Anne Howard Freihofer; m. Telside Matthews Strickland, Dec. 15, 1998. BA, Vanderbilt U., 1951; LLB, Emory U., 1955. Bar: Ga. 1955. Sr. ptnr. King & Spalding, Atlanta, 1956-92, ret. ptnr., 1993—. Bd. dirs. Avondale Mills Inc. Mem. coun. Emory Law Sch., 1975-85, chmn., 1976-77; bd. dirs. Cen. Atlanta Progress Inc., 1981-85, Wesley Woods Geriatric Hosps., 1987-93, chmn., 1988-92; trustee Wesley Homes Inc., 1961-93, chmn., 1981-86; past trustee Oglethorpe U., The Lovett Sch. 1st lt. USMC, 1951-53. Mem. Am. Law Inst., State Bar Ga., Atlanta Bar Assn., Lawyers Club Atlanta, Piedmont Driving Club, Peachtree Golf Club, Highlands Country Club, Phi Beta Kappa, Omicron Delta Kappa. Office: King & Spalding 191 Peachtree St NE Ste 4900 Atlanta GA 30303-1740

HOWARD, JEFFREY R. judge, lawyer, former state attorney general; b. Claremont, N.H. BA, Plymouth St Coll-Univ N.H., 1978; JD, Law Ctr-Georgetown U, 1981. Assoc. atty. gen. Div. Legal Counsel; atty. Antitrust Div-Atty. Gen. Ofc., 1981; U.S. atty. Dist. of N.H., Concord, 1989—92; atty. gen. State of N.H., 1993—97; ptnr. Choate Hall & Stewart, 1997—2001. Mem. atty. gen. adv. com. Attys. Gen. Thornburg & Barr. Office: 1 Warren Rudman US Courthouse 55 Pleasant St Concord NH 03301*

HOWARD, JOHN WAYNE, lawyer; b. Dec. 17, 1948; s. Joseph Leon and Irene Elizabeth (Silver) H.; m. Kathleen Amanda Busby, Oct. 7, 1978. BA, U. Calif., San Diego, 1971; JD, Calif. Western Sch. Law, 1976; postgrad., San Diego Inn of Ct., 1979, Hastings Coll. Advocacy, 1981; grad. Program of Instrns. for Lawyers, Harvard Law Sch., 1992. Bar: Calif. 1978, U.S. Dist. Ct. (so. dist.) Calif. 1978, U.S. Supreme Ct. 1989, Colo. 1989, U.S. Dist. Ct. (no. dist.) Calif., U.S. Dist. Ct. (ea. dist.) Calif., U.S. Ct. Appeals (9th cir.) 1995, U.S. Ct. Appeals (D.C. cir.) 1996, U.S. Ct. of Claims 1996. Assoc. Robert T. Dierdorff, San Diego, 1978-79; pvt. practice San Diego, 1979-82; ptnr. Howard & Neeb, San Diego, 1982-84; prin. John W. Howard and Assocs., San Diego, 1984-86; gen. counsel Ace Parking, Inc., 1986-89, CCCA Inc., 1989-93; pres. Individual Rights Found. Inc., 1993-95, Inst. for Constitutional Rights, Inc., 1995—, John W. Howard and Assoc., 1995—. Jud. arbitrator Superior Ct. Calif., 1983—. Chmn. San Diego County Indigent Def. Adv. Bd., 1981-84, mem. subcom. on def. monitoring and budget for Office Defender Svcs. of San Diego County; mem. select com. on small bus. Calif. State Assembly, 1983-90; chmn. San Diego Pub. Arts Adv. Bd.; mem. San Diego County Coun. of Com. Chairs; chmn. precinct orgn. Roger Hedgecock for Supt. Campaign Com., 1976, mem. steering com., 1976; chmn. steering com. Hedgecock for Mayor, 1982, Cleator for Mayor, 1986; chmn. Muscular Dystrophy Telethon, San Diego, 1983; vice chmn. San Diego Festival of Arts, 1983-84; pres. Bowery Theatre, San Diego, 1984-89; pres., bd. dirs. La Jolla Stage Co.; founder, bd. dirs. San Diego Theatre League; 1st v.p., bd. dirs. Muscular Dystrophy Assn.; bd. dirs. Patrick Henry Meml. Found., Brookneal, Va., The Poe Mus., Richmond, Va., San Diego Med. Oncology Rsch. Found., Ilan-Lael Found., Multiple Sclerosis Soc., Am. Ballet Found., Wellness Cmty., Teatro Macara Magica; bd. dirs., chmn. legal affairs subcom. Calif. Motion Picture Coun.; mem. adv. bd. dirs. San Diego Motion Picture Bur.; mem. pub. edn. com. Am. Cancer Soc.; founder, bd. dirs. San Diego Theatre Found., 1984—; mem. 44th Congl. Dist. Adv. Com.; mem. Com. to Re-Elect Congressman Bill Lowery; mem. San Diego County 4th Dist. Adv. Com. Mem. ABA, ATLA, Calif. State Bar Assn., Am. Corp. Counsel Assn., San Diego County Bar Assn. (chmn. superior ct. com. 2002—), Consumer Attys. Assn. L.A., U. Calif.-San Diego Alumni Assn. (past v.p., bd. dirs.), Calif. Western Sch. Law Alumni Assn., Friendly Sons of St. Patrick, Delta Kappa Epsilon, Phi Alpha Delta, Enright Inn of Ct., Am. Inns of Ct. Republican. Federal civil litigation, State civil litigation, Constitutional.

HOWARD, LEWIS SPILMAN, lawyer; b. Knoxville, Tenn., Oct. 10, 1930; s. Frank Catlett and Lillian (Spilman) H.; m. Anne Robinson, Dec. 26, 1953 (div. 1976); children: Catherine C., Martha S., Lewis S. Jr., Laura A. (dec.). BSBA, JD, U. Tenn., 1953. Bar: Tenn. 1953, U.S. Ct. Mil. Appeals 1954, U.S. Dist. Ct. Ga. 1954, U.S. Dist. Ct. Tenn. 1956, U.S. Ct. Appeals (6th cir.) 1959. Ptnr. Kennerly, Montgomery, Howard & Finley, Knoxville, 1957-84, Howard & Ridge, Knoxville, 1984-99, Howard & Howard, Knoxville, 2000—. Gen. counsel Coal Creek Mining and Mfg. Co., Knoxville, 1969—, pres., 1971—. Vice chmn. Knoxville Bd. Edn., 1968-71. Capt. JAGC, USAR, 1953-56. Mem. ABA, Tenn. Bar Assn., Knoxville Bar Assn., Cherokee Country Club. Republican. Presbyterian. Avocation: boating. Corporate, general, Mergers and acquisitions, Natural resources. Home: 1604 Kenesaw Ave Knoxville TN 37919-7863 Office: Howard & Howard 4800 Old Kingston Pike Knoxville TN 37919-6478

HOWARD, ROSCOE CONKLIN, JR., lawyer, educator; b. 1952; m. Deborah Ryan Howard; children: Ryan, Adam. Grad., Brown U., 1974, U. Va., 1977. Summer assoc. Brown, Wood, Ivey, Mitchell & Petty, N.Y.C., 1976; law clk. to Hon. Raymond L. Finch, Territorial Ct. V.I., Christiansted, St. Croix, 1977—78; assoc. Jones, Day, Reavis & Pogue, Washington, 1978—79, Crowell & Moring, Washington, 1979—81; staff atty. FTC, Washington, 1981—84; asst. U.S. atty. Office of U.S. Atty. D.C., 1984—87, Office of U.S. Atty. (ea. dist.) Va., Alexandria divsn., 1987—89, Office of U.S. Atty. (ea. dist.) Va., Richmond divsn., 1989—91; assoc. prof. law U. Kans. Sch. Law, Lawrence, 1994—99, prof. law, 1999—; U.S. atty. U.S. Dist. Ct. D.C., 2001—. Faculty advisor Black Am. Law Students Assn., 1994—, The Criminal Procedure Review, 1994—97; assoc. ind. counsel Office of Ind. Counsel, Alexandria, Va., 1997—98. Sec. Lawrence Pub. Libr. Found. Bd., 1997, 1998—; bd. trustees Culver Ednl. Found., Ind., 1989—97; vol. Am. Heart Assn., 1996; v.p. Culver Mil. Acad. Alumni Legion Bd., Ind., 1978—82. Mem.: Assn. Am. Law Schs. (adv. bd. 1996—99, exec. com. 2001—), Kans. Bar Assn. (task force on criminal justice funding 1995—96), D.C. Bar Assn., Va. Bar Assn. Office: Judiciary Ctr Bldg 555 Fourth St NW Washington DC 20530*

HOWBERT, EDGAR CHARLES, lawyer; b. Detroit, June 29, 1937; s. Edgar Cowgill and Martha Viola (Brekke) H.; m. Susan Bartlett Rumsey, July 24, 1974; children: John Edgar, Dana Elizabeth. AB, Princeton U., 1959; LLB, Harvard U., 1965. Bar: Mich. 1966. Assoc. Dickinson Wright, Detroit, 1965-72, ptnr., 1972—. Pres. Franklin Wright Settlements, Inc., Detroit, 1984, Friends Sch. in Detroit, 1986. Lt. USN, 1959-62; trustee Univ. Liggett Sch., 1991-97. Mem. Detroit Bar Assn., Am. Bankruptcy Inst., Turnaround Mgmt. Assn. (bd. dirs. 1989-91, 92—), Country Club of Detroit. Banking, Bankruptcy, Corporate, general. Office: Dickinson Wright PLLC 500 Woodward Ave Ste 4000 Detroit MI 48226-3416

HOWE, DRAYTON FORD, JR., lawyer; b. Seattle, Nov. 17, 1931; s. Drayton Ford and Virginia (Wester) H.; m. Joyce Arnold, June 21, 1952; 1 son, James Drayton. AB, U. Calif., Berkeley, 1953; LLB, U. Calif., San Francisco, 1957. Bar: Calif. 1958. CPA Calif. Atty. IRS, 1958-61; tax dept. supr. Ernst & Ernst, San Francisco, 1962-67; ptnr. Bishop, Barry, Howe, Haney & Ryder, San Francisco, 1968—. Lectr. on tax matters U. Calif. extension, 1966-76. Mem. Calif. Bar Assn., San Francisco Bar Assn. (chmn. client relations com. 1977), Calif. Soc. CPA's. State civil litigation, Estate planning, Corporate taxation. Office: Bishop Barry Howe Haney & Ryder 2000 Powell St Ste 1425 Emeryville CA 94608-1861 E-mail: dhowe@bbhhr.com.

HOWE, JONATHAN THOMAS, lawyer; b. Evanston, Ill., Dec. 16, 1940; s. Frederick King and Rosalie Charlotte (Volz) H.; m. Lois Helene Braun, July 12, 1963; children: Heather C., Jonathan Thomas Jr., Sara E. BA with honors, Northwestern U., 1963; JD with distinction, Duke U., 1966. Bar: Ill. 1966, U.S. Dist. Ct. (no. dist.) Ill. 1966, U.S. Ct. Appeals (7th cir.) 1967, U.S. Tax Ct. 1968, U.S. Supreme Ct. 1970, U.S. Ct. Appeals (D.C. cir.) 1976, U.S. Ct. Appeals (9th cir.) 1980, U.S. Ct. Appeals (4th, 5th, 11th dirs.) 1983, U.S. Claims Ct. 1990. Ptnr. Jenner & Block, Chgo., 1966-85, sr. ptnr. in charge assn. and adminstrv. law dept., 1978-85; founding and sr. ptnr., pres. Howe & Hutton, Chgo., Washington & St. Louis, 1985—. Exec. and adv. coms. to Ill. Sec. of State to revise the Ill. Not for Profit Act, 1983-86; dir. Pacific Mut. Realty Investors, Inc., 1985-86; dir. cable TV options for public Chgo. Access Corp., 1995-97, Bostrom Corp., 2001—. Contbg. editor Ill. Inst. for Continuing Legal Edn., 1973—, Sporting Goods Bus., 1977-91, Meeting News, 1978-88, Meetings Mgr., 1988—, Meetings and Convs., 1991—; contbr. articles to profl. jours.; legal editor Meetings and Convs., 1990—. Mem. Dist. 27 Bd. Edn., Northbrook, Ill., 1969-89, sec., 1969-72, pres., 1973-84; chmn. bd. trustees Sch. Employee Benefit Trust, 1979-85; founding bd. dirs., pres. Sch. Mgmt. Found. Ill., 1976-84; mem. exec. com. Northfield Twp. Rep. Orgn., 1967-71; bd. deacons Village Presbyn. Ch. Northbrook, 1975-78, trustee, 1981-83; mem. Arts and Music Forum, 4th Presbyn. Ch., Chgo., 1990-93; spl. advisor Pres.'s Coun. Phys. Fitness and Sports, 1983-87, Duke Univ. Sch. of Law Bd. of Visitors (life mem.). Named Industry Leader of Yr., Meeting Industry, 1987, Sch. Bd. Mem. Yr. (twice) , Ill. State Bd. Edn.; recipient Internat. Found. PaceSetters award Hospitality Sales Mktg. Assn., 1996. Fellow Internat. Forum of Travel and Tourism Advs., Am. Soc. Assn. Execs. (vice-chmn. legal com. 1983-86), Am. Bar Found.; mem. Internat. Assn. Conv. and Hosp. Indsl. Attys. (founder), ABA (antitrust sect. Nat. Inst. com., trade assn. law com. corp. banking and bus. law sect., sect. on litigation, adminstrv. law sect.; mem. internat. law com., continuing edn. com., tort and ins. practice, vice-chmn. com. sports law 1986—, standing com. meetings and travel 1988-93, spl. advisor 1993—), Task Force on Membership Benefits for Disabled Lawyers, Ill. Bar Assn. (antitrust sect., civil practice sect., sch. law sect., adminstrv. law sect.; co-editor Antitrust Newsletter 1968-70), Chgo. Bar Assn. (def. of prisoners com. 1966-83, antitrust law com. 1971—, continuing edn. com. 1977—, chmn. assn. and non-profit soc. law com. 1984-86), Am. Soc. Assn. Execs. (vice-chmn. legal com., founding mem. legal sect.), N.Y. Soc. Assn. Execs., Acad. Hospitality Industry Attys. (founder, bd. dirs. 1994—, pres. 2001—), Nat. Sch. Bds. Assn. (nat. bd. dirs. 1979-89, exec. com. 1981-89, sec.-treas. 1983-85, 2d v.p. 1985-86, pres. 1987-88, chmn. devel. com. 1982-87, pres. 1987-88), D.C. Bar Assn., Am. Judicature Soc., Ill. Assn. Sch. Bds. (pres. 1977-79, bd. dirs. 1971-88), Chi Bar Found. (life), Assn. Forum Chicagoland (assoc., formerly Chgo. Soc. Assn. Execs.), Nat. Sch. Bds. Found. (pres./trustee 1995-2002), U.S. C. of C. (legal coun. 1998—), Greater Washington Soc. Assn. Execs., Legal Club, Law Club, Mid-Am. Club, Tower Club, Univ. Club Chgo., Order of Coif, Psi Upsilon. General civil litigation, General practice, Non-profit and tax-exempt organizations. Home: 126 W Delaware Pl Chicago IL 60610-3252 Office: 20 N Wacker Dr Ste 4200 Chicago IL 60606-9833 E-mail: jth@howehutton.com.

HOWE, RICHARD CUDDY, state supreme court justice; b. South Cottonwood, Utah, Jan. 20, 1924; s. Edward E. and Mildred (Cuddy) H.; m. Juanita Lyon, Aug. 30, 1949; children: Christine Howe Schultz, Andrea Howe Reynolds, Bryant, Valerie Howe Winegar, Jeffrey, Craig. BS, U. Utah, 1945, JD, 1948. Bar: Utah. Law clk. to Justice James H. Wolfe, Utah Supreme Ct., 1949-50; judge city ct. Murray, Utah, 1951; individual practice law, 1952-80; justice Utah Supreme Ct., Salt Lake City, 1980—. Mem. Utah Constnl. Revision Commn., 1976-85. Chmn., original mem. Salt Lake County Merit Coun.; mem. Utah Ho. of Reps., 1951-58, 69-72, Utah Senate, 1973-78. Named Outstanding Legislator Citizens' Conf. State Legislatures, 1972 Mem. ABA, Utah Bar Assn., Sons of Utah Pioneers. Mem. Lds Ch. Office: Utah Supreme Ct 450 S State St PO Box 140210 Salt Lake City UT 84114-0210

HOWE, RONALD EVANS, lawyer, minister, small business owner; b. Charles City, Iowa, Feb. 17, 1945; s. Evans R. and Elizabeth (Atchison) H.; m. M. Kristin Petersmith, Aug. 16, 1970; children: Sarah Elizabeth O'Brien, Rachel Ellen Wolf, Michael Evans. Cert., Moody Bible Inst., 1966, AB, 1969, U. Iowa, 1968, JD, 1972; ThM, Dallas Theol. Sem., 1975. Lic. to ministry Ind. Mission Ch., 1966, ordained Evang. Free Ch. Am., 1990. Bar: Iowa 1972, Tex. 1973, U.S. Tax Ct. 1974. Atty. Law Offices of Gordon Macdowell, Dallas, 1972-75; sr. min. Elim Chapel, Winnipeg, Man., Can., 1975-85, Evang. Free Ch., Fresno, Calif., 1985—2001; broadcaster weekly radio program Free to Live, 1985—2001; owner, pres. Elimcare Cmty., 1992—, Elim Place, Inc., 1992—, Elim Gardens, LLC, 2000—; pres. Elimcare Ministries, 2001—; exec. dir. The Elimcare Found., 2001—; ch. cons., 2002—. Adj. prof. Winnipeg Theol. Sem., 1975-85, Briercrest Grad. Sch., Caronport, Sask, Can., 1985-87; bd. dirs. Haggai Inst., Winnipeg, 1977-85, Link Care Ctr., Fresno, 1985-2001; bd. govs. Winnipeg Bible Coll. and Sem., 1982-85; mem. exec. com. Fresno Christian Sch., 1985-2001; cons. Evangelical Ministries Found., Fresno, 1999-2001; lectr. in field. Author: (booklet) Breakfast of Champions, 1984. Exec. dir. Cmty. Advocacy Found., 1999-2002. Recipient Mayor's Commendation for 10 Yrs. of Contbn. in Leadership to City of Fresno, 1995, Outstanding Bus. award for leadership in edn. Compact Fresno, 1998. Mem. North Fresno Rotary (bd. dirs. 2003--). Republican. Office: Elimcare 6276 N First St Ste 103B Fresno CA 93710 Business E-Mail: elimcare@sbcglobal.net.

HOWELL, ALLY WINDSOR, lawyer, author, editor; b. Montgomery, Ala., Mar. 10, 1949; s. Elvin and Bennie Merle (Windsor) H.; m. Donna K. Graffander, Sept. 2, 1989; children: Christopher Darby, Joshua Darby, Jeremiah Graffander. BA, Huntington Coll., 1971; JD, Jones Sch. Law, 1974. Bar: Ala. 1974, U.S. Supreme Ct. 1977, U.S. Ct. Appeals (fed. cir.) 1983, U.S. Ct. Appeals (11th cir.) 1981, U.S. Tax Ct. 1979, U.S. Claims Ct. 1982, U.S. Dist. Ct. (mid. dist.) Ala. 1975, U. Dist. Ct. (so. dist.) Ala. 1978. Archivist Hist. Rsch. Ctr. Air U., Maxwell AFB, Ala., 1972-75; pvt. practice Montgomery, 1975-82, 83-01; atty.-editor West Group, Rochester, N.Y., 2001—. Adj. prof. Faulkner U., Montgomery, 1975—, adj. prof. Jones Law Sch. , 1983—85; asst. atty. gen., chief legal sect. Ala. Medicaid Agy., Montgomery, 1982—83. Author: Alabama Civic Practice Forms, 1986, 3d edit., 1992, Alabama Torts Case Finder, 1988, Alabama Personal Injury and Torts, 1996, Trial Handbook for Alabama Lawyers, 2d edit., 1998. Co-founder, bd. dirs. Montgomery Inst., 2000—01; treas. bd. dirs. Gay Alliance of the Genesee Valley. Hon. lt. col., aide de camp Gov. Ala., 1974. Mem. ABA (contbr. editor profl. liability newsletter, litigation sect. 1990-92, co-editor trial techniques comm. newsletter), Assn. Trial Lawyers Am., Montgomery County Bar Assn. (newsletter editorial com. 1984-85), Nat. Bd. Trial Adv. (cert. civil litigation 1981, 86, 91, examiner ethics, evidence and civil procedure), Nat. Lesbian and Gay Law Assn. (bd. dirs. 1999-2001, vice co-chair 2000-2001, editor newsletter 2000—). Presbyterian. Insurance, Personal injury (including property damage), Probate (including wills, trusts).

HOWELL, ARTHUR, lawyer; b. Atlanta, Aug. 24, 1918; s. Arthur and Katharine (Mitchell) H.; m. Caroline Sherman, June 14, 1941; children: Arthur, Caroline, Eleanor, Richard, Peter, James; m. Janet Kerr Franchot, Dec. 16, 1972. AB, Princeton U., 1939; JD, Harvard U., 1942; LLD (hon.), Oglethorpe U., 1972. Bar: Ga. 1942. Assoc. F.M. Bird, 1942-45; ptnr. Alston & Bird (and predecessor firms), 1945-89, of counsel, 1989—. Bd. dirs., gen. counsel Atlantic Steel Co., 1960-93; chmn., bd. dirs. Summit Industries, Inc.; bd. dirs. Enterprise Funds; chmn. emeritus bd. dirs. Crescent Banking Co.; past pres. Atlanta Legal Aid Soc.; emeritus mem. bd. dirs. Crescent Bank and Trust Co. Pres. Met. Atlanta Cmty. Svcs., 1956, dir., 1953—; pres. Cmty. Planning Coun., 1961—63; gen. chmn. United Appeal, 1955; spl. atty. gen. State Ga., 1948—55; spl. counsel, Univ. Sys. Ga. State

Sch. Bldg. Authorities, 1951—70; adv. com. Ga. Corp. Code, 1967—; trustee, past chmn. Oglethorpe U.; trustee Princeton, 1964—68; emeritus trustee Atlanta Speech Sch., Westminster Schs., Atlanta, Episcopal H.S., Alexandria, Va., Morehouse Coll.; past trustee Inst. Internat. Edn., mem. exec. com., 1969—72; elder, trustee, chmn. bd. trustees Presbyn. Ch., 1985—89; past chmn. Atlanta Adv. Com. Pks. Named hon. alumnus Ga. Inst. Tech. Mem.: Am. Judicature Soc., Lawyers Club of Atlanta (past. pres.), Atlanta Bar Assn., Ga. Bar Assn., ABA, Am. Law Inst. (life), Soc. Colonial Wars, Princeton Club of N.Y., Nassau Club, Homosassa Fishing Club, Capital City Club, Phi Beta Kappa. Home: 200 Larkspur Ln Highlands NC 28741-8388 Office: Alston & Bird One Atlantic Ctr 1201 W Peachtree St Atlanta GA 30309-3424

HOWELL, BRIAN GRAHAM, lawyer; b. Phila., May 14, 1954; s. Richard Graham and Rita Gloria (Monastra) H.; m. Lisa Marguerite Maiale, June 6, 1982; children: Meredith, Carl. BA, Dickinson Coll., 1976; JD, Rutgers U., 1979. Bar: N.J. 1979, U.S. Dist. Ct. N.J. 1979. Assoc. Bertman, Johnson & Sahli, Hammonton, N.J., 1979-85; ptnr. Donio, Bertman, Johnson, Sahli & Greco, Hammonton, 1985, Donio, Olivo & Howell, Hammonton, 1985-91, Olivo & Howell, Hammonton, 1992—; pvt. practice Hammonton, 1995—. Mem. Hammonton Bd. Edn., 1982-85, 87, pres., 1991-94. Mem. ABA, N.J. State Bar Assn., Atlantic County Bar Assn., Hammonton C. of C. (dir. 1988-94), Lions. General practice, Personal injury (including property damage). Home: 728 Central Ave Hammonton NJ 08037-1111 Office: Bellevue at Horton St Hammonton NJ 08037

HOWELL, DONALD LEE, lawyer; b. Waco, Tex., Jan. 31, 1935; s. Hilton Emory and Louise Howell; m. Gwendolyn Avera, June 13, 1957; children: Daniel Liege, Alison Avera, Anne Turner. BA cum laude, Baylor U., 1956; JD with honors, U. Tex., 1963. Bar: Tex. 1963. Assoc. Vinson & Elkins, Houston, 1963-70, ptnr., 1970—, mem. mgmt. com., 1980-99. Capt. USAFR, 1956-59. Fellow Am. Bar Found., Tex. Bar Found., Houston Bar Found., Am. Law Inst.; mem. ABA, Am. Coll. Bond Counsel, Houston Bar Assn., Nat. Assn. Bond Lawyers (pres. 1981-82, bd. dirs. 1979-83), Attys. Liability Assurance Soc. (Bermuda bd. dirs. 1992—, chmn. 2000-02, U.S. bd. dirs. 1992—, chmn. 2000-02), Houston Club, Houston Ctr. Club, Order of Coif, Phi Delta Phi. Democrat. Episcopalian. Finance, Municipal (including bonds), Utilities, public. E-mail: dhowell@velaw.com.

HOWELL, GEORGE COOK, III, lawyer; b. New Orleans, June 27, 1956; s. George C. Jr. and Billie Grace (Webb) H.; children: Margaret Sloan, George C. IV. AB magna cum laude, Princeton U., 1978; JD, U.Va., 1981. Bar: Va. 1981, U.S. Dist. Ct. (ea. dist.) Va. 1982, U.S. Ct. Appeals (4th cir.) 1982. Law clk. U.S. Dist. Ct. (ea. dist.) Va., Alexandria, 1981-82; assoc. Hunton & Williams, Richmond, Va., 1982-89, ptnr., 1989—, team head tax & employee benefits, 1999—. Contbr. Va. Law Rev., 1980; editor-in-chief Va. Tax Rev., 1980-81; articles editor The Tax Lawyer, 1983-86, mng. editor, 1987-89. Mem. usher's guild 1st Presbyn. Ch., Richmond, 1986-90; participant Leadership Metro Richmond, 1987-88. Mem. ABA (taxation sect. chmn. remic task force 1987-88, chmn. mini-program on mortgage-backed securities 1988, chmn. subcom. on asset securitization 1988-90, corp. tax shelters tax force 2000-2001, vice chmn. com. on fin. trans. 1990-92, chmn. com. on fin. trans. 1992-94, sec. taxation 1995-97, sect. taxation coun., 1997-2000, vice chmn. comm. 2001—2003), Princeton Assn. Va. (treas. 1987-89, pres. 1989-91), Order of Coif, Phi Beta Kappa. Republican. Avocations: golf, tennis, basketball, running, the stock market. Corporate taxation. Office: Hunton & Williams 951 E Byrd St Ste 200 Richmond VA 23219-4074

HOWELL, JOEL WALTER, III, lawyer; b. Jackson, Miss., Dec. 25, 1949; s. Joel W. and Elizabeth (Harris) H.; m. Wilhelmina C. Pontus, June 25, 1983. BA, Millsaps Coll., 1971; JD, Columbia U., 1974. Bar: Tex. 1974, U.S. Ct. Appeals (5th cir.) 1974, Miss. 1975, U.S. Dist. Ct. (no. and so. dists.) Miss. 1975. Ptnr. Daniel, Coker, Horton, Bell & Dukes, Jackson, 1975-80; pvt. practice, Jackson, 1981—. Adj. faculty law sch. Miss. Coll., Jackson, 1988. Contbg. editor, case notes and comments editor Columbia Jour. Transnat. Law, 1973-74. Mem. ABA, ATLA, Tex. Bar Assn., Miss. Bar, Hinds County Bar Assn. (small firm practice com. 1993-94, chair 1995, computer columnist newsletter 1996—, webmaster 1997—), Miss. Trial Lawyers Assn., Miss. Def. Lawyers Assn., Def. Rsch. Inst., Miss. Bankruptcy Conf. Federal civil litigation, State civil litigation, Personal injury (including property damage). Home: 50 St Andrews Dr Jackson MS 39211-2466 Office: PO Box 16772 5446 Executive Pl Jackson MS 39206-4103 E-mail: jwh3@mindspring.com.

HOWELL, R(OBERT) THOMAS, JR., lawyer, former food company executive; b. Racine, Wis., July 18, 1942; s. Robert T. and Margaret Paris (Billings) H.; m. Karen Wallace Corbett, May 11, 1968; children: Clarinda, Margaret, Robert. AB, Williams Coll., 1964; JD, U. Wis., 1967; postgrad., Harvard U., 1981. Bar: Wis. 1968, Ill. 1968, U.S. Dist. Ct. (no. dist.) Ill. 1968, U.S. Tax Ct. Assoc. Hopkins & Sutter, Chgo., 1967-71; atty. The Quaker Oats Co., Chgo., 1971-77, counsel, 1977-80, v.p., assoc. gen. corp. counsel, 1980-84, v.p., gen. corp. counsel, 1984-96, corp. sec., 1994-96; of counsel Seyfarth Shaw, Chgo., 1997—. Bd. dirs. Ill. Inst. of Continuing Legal Edn., Lawyers for Creative Arts. Editor (mags.) Barrister, 1975-77, Compleat Lawyer, 1983-87. Bd. dirs. Metro. Family Svcs.; bd. dirs. Chgo. Bar Found., 1987—, pres., 1991-93; trustee 4th Presbyn. Ch., Chgo., 1989-92, pres., 1994-96; bd. dirs. Chgo. Equity Fund, 1992-96. Capt. USAR, 1966-72. Mem. ABA, Ill. Bar Assn., Wis. Bar Assn., Chgo. Bar Assn. (bd. mgrs. 1977-79, chmn. young lawyers sect. 1974-75), LawClub Chgo., Econ. Club Chgo., Univ. Club Chgo. (bd. dirs. 1982-85, 87-88, v.p.). Presbyterian. Antitrust, Corporate, general, Mergers and acquisitions. Home: 853 W Chalmers Pl Chicago IL 60614-3233 Office: Seyfarth Shaw 55 E Monroe St Ste 4200 Chicago IL 60603-5863 E-mail: thowell@seyfarth.com.*

HOWELL, STEVEN JOHN, judge; b. Greenville, S.C., Feb. 12, 1952; s. Jack A. and Margaret I. Howell; m. M. Melanie McHugh, Sept. 2, 1972; children: Aaron, Ethan. BA in Philosophy, U. Calif., Davis, 1974; JD magna cum laude, Santa Clara U., 1977. Bar: Calif. 1977, U.S. Dist. Ct. (no. dist.) Calif. 1977, U.S. Dist. Ct. (ea. dist.) Calif. 1979, U.S. Ct. Appeals (9th cir.) 1981, U.S. Dist. Ct. (so. dist.) Calif. 1983, U.S. Supreme Ct. 1983. Atty. Howell & Howell, Oroville, Calif., 1978—87; mcpl. ct. judge South Butte County Mcpl. Ct., Oroville, Calif., 1987—96; superior ct. judge County of Butte, Oroville, Calif., 1996—. Mem.: Calif. Judges Assn. Office: Superior Ct Calif County Butte 1 Court St Oroville CA 95965

HOWELL, WELDON U., JR., lawyer; b. Dallas, July 16, 1947; s. Weldon U. and Betty (Temple) H.; m. Barbara Molina, July 14, 1973; children: Benjamin, Sarah. B.A., U. Ariz., 1969; postgrad. City London Poly. Sch., 1971; J.D., U. Tex., 1973. Bar: Tex. 1973, Calif. 1974, U.S. Dist. Ct. (cen., no., so. and ea. dists.) Calif., U.S. Ct. Appeals (9th cir.) 1984, U.S. Tax Ct. 1981, U.S. Ct. Claims 1981. Briefing atty to assoc. justice Supreme Ct. Tex., Austin, 1973-74; assoc. Schramm & Raddue, Santa Barbara, Calif., 1974-77, sr. ptnr., chmn. bus. and tax dept., 1977—; sr. ptnr. Howell Moore & Gough LLP, Santa Barbara. Bd. dirs., pres. Santa Barbara County Bd. Edn. Mem. Santa Barbara County Bar Assn. (chmn. tax sect. 1984, bd. dirs. 1986-88, pres. 1994), Barristers Club Santa Barbara (pres. 1977-78), Pi Kappa Alpha. Democrat. Clubs: Tennis of Santa Barbara (chmn., 1980). Corporate, general, Securities, Personal income taxation. Home: 2525 Anacapa St Santa Barbara CA 93105-3511 Office: Howell Moore & Gough LLP 812 Presidio Ave Santa Barbara CA 93101-2210

HOWELL, WILLIAM ASHLEY, III, lawyer; b. Raleigh, N.C., Jan. 2, 1949; s. William Ashley II and Caroline Erskine Greenleaf; m. Esther Holland, Dec. 22, 1973. BS, Troy State U., 1972; postgrad., U. Ala., Birmingham, 1974-75; JD, Birmingham Sch. Law, 1977. Bar: Ala. 1977, U.S. Dist. Ct. (no. dist.) Ala. 1977, U.S. Ct. Appeals (5th cir.) 1977, U.S. Supreme Ct. 1982, U.S. Ct. Appeals (11th cir.) 1983, U.S. Dist. Ct. (mid. dist.) Ala. 1987. Atty. pub. defender divsn. Legal Aid Soc. of Birmingham, 1977—78, civil divsn. Legal Aid Soc. of Birmingham, 1978—81; dist. office atty. SBA, Birmingham, 1980—82, supervising atty. Ala. Dist., 1982—; spl. asst. U.S. Atty. (mid. dist.), Ala., 1988—, U.S. Atty. (so. dist.), Ala., 2002—. Part-time instr. legal and social environ. and human resources mgmt. Jefferson State C.C., Birmingham, 1993. Contbr. articles to profl. jours. Vol. reader Radio Reading Svc. Network for Blind, 1991—93; mem. Shelby County Econ. Devel. Coun., 1993—94, Hispanic Outreach Commn., 2000—01, Highland Crest Homeowners Assn., 2002—; del. state conv. Episc. Ch. of Ala., various yrs.; bd. dirs. Hoover Homeowners Assn., 1977—81, Southside Ministries, Inc., 1990—91, v.p. bd. dirs., 1990—91; bd. dirs. SafeHouse of Shelby County, Inc., 1990—93, vice chmn., 1991—93. Recipient Am. Jurisprudence Criminal Procedure Book award. Mem. ABA (sect. corporation, banking and bus. law), Nat. Parks and Conservation Soc. (life), Fed. Bar Assn. (sec. Birmingham chpt. 1980-81, del. nat. conv. 1993, 94, del. mid yr. meeting, 1994-95), Ala. Bar Assn. (com. on future of the profession 1978-81, 83-84, com. on quality of life 1992-93, sect. bankruptcy and corp. law, sect. bankruptcy and comml. law, sect. corp. counsel, sect. banking and bus. law), Nature Conservacy (life), Birmingham Bar Assn., Birmingham Venture Club, Sierra Club (life), Sigma Delta Kappa (v.p., Outstanding Sr. award 1977). Episcopalian. Office: US Small Bus Adminstrn 801 Tom Martin Dr Ste 201 Birmingham AL 35211-4436 Fax: 205-290-7443. E-mail: william.howell@sba.gov.

HOWES, BRIAN THOMAS, lawyer; b. Sioux Falls, S.D., July 23, 1957; s. Thomas A. and Joyce L. (McFarland) H.; m. Robin Kay Schoonover, June 2, 1979; children: Phillip, Adam, Jason. BSBA in Acctg., BA in Polit. Sci., Kans. State U., 1979; JD, U. Kans., 1982. Bar: Mo. 1982, U.S. Dist. Ct. (we. dist.) Mo. 1982, U.S. Supreme Ct. 1989. Assoc. Shughart, Thomson & Kilroy, Kansas City, Mo., 1982-85; exec. v.p., COO, gen. counsel Tenenbaum & Assocs., Inc., Kansas City, 1985-95; ptnr., nat. dir. property tax svcs. Ernst & Young LLP, Kansas City, 1995-99; of counsel Shughart Thomson & Kilroy, P.C., Kansas City, 2000—. Pres. Nat. Coun. Property Taxation, 1999-2000. Contr. articles to profl. jours; writer, speaker in field. Contbg. mem. Dem. Nat. Com.; bd. dirs. Kansas City Wheelchair Athletic Commn., 1987-89, Vol. Atty. Project, 1984—, Nat. Youth Sports Coaches Assn., 1994—. Mem. ABA, Kansas City Met. Bar Assn., Lawyers Assn. Kansas City, Am. Corp. Counsel Assn., Inst. for Profls. in Taxation, Internat. Assn. of Assessing Officers, Urban Land Inst. Episcopalian. Corporate, general, Property, real (including real estate development, water), State and local taxation. Home: 4901 W 130th St Shawnee Mission KS 66209-1864 Office: Shughart Thomson & Kilroy PC Ste 1800 120 W 12th St Kansas City MO 64105-1929 E-mail: bhowes@kc.stklaw.com.

HOWLAND, JOAN SIDNEY, law librarian, law educator; b. Eureka, Calif., Apr. 9, 1951; d. Robert Sidney and Ruth Mary Howland. BA, U. Calif., Davis, 1971; MA, U. Tex., 1973; MLS, Calif. State U., San Jose, 1975; JD, Santa Clara (Calif.) U., 1983; MBA, U. Minn., 1997. Assoc. librarian for pub. svcs. Stanford (Calif.) U. Law Library, 1975-83, Harvard U. Law Library, Cambridge, Mass., 1983-86; dep. dir. U. Calif. Law Library, Berkeley, 1986-92; dir. law libr., Roger F. Noreen prof. law U. Minn. Sch. of Law, 1992—, assoc. dean info. tech., 2001—. Questions and answers column editor Law Libr. Jour., 1986-91; memt. column editor Trends in Law Libr. Mgmt. & Tech., 1987-94. Mem. ALA, ABA (com. on accreditation 2001—), Am. Assn. Law Librs., Am. Assn. Law Schs., Am. Indian Libr. Assn. (treas. 1992—), Am. Law Inst. Office: U Minn Law Sch 229 19th Ave S Minneapolis MN 55455-0400

HOWLAND, RICHARD MOULTON, retired lawyer; b. Glen Cove, L.I., N.Y., Jan. 2, 1940; s. Richard Moulton and Natalie (Fuller) H.; m. Julie Rose Keschl, Sept. 28, 1974 (div.); children: Kimberly Merrill, Gillian Fuller. BA, Amherst Coll., 1961; JD, Columbia U., 1968. Bar: Mass. 1968. Assoc. firm Nutter, McLennen & Fish, Boston, 1968-69, DiMento & Sullivan, Boston, 1969-70; atty. for students U. Mass., Amherst, 1970-74; practice law Amherst, 1974-2000; Legal Infirmary Amherst, 1997-98; ret., 2001. Adj. prof. U. Mass., 1972-76, Western New Eng. Coll. Sch. Law, 1993-94; vis. lectr. Amherst Coll., 1983, mock trial team coach, 1989-98; mock trial team coach Tufts Coll., 1998, Deerfield Acad., 1999-2000, Southwick H.S., 1999-2000; tchr. constnl. law, history, social studies Springfield H.S. Sci. and Tech., 2001—. Co-editor: Mass. Lawyers Weekly, 1979—94; emeritus: , 1994, statistician: New Eng. Blizzard, 1996—98, Conn. Pride, 1999—2000, Springfield Sirens Pro Soccer, 1999—2000. Asst. moderator Town of Leverett, 1988—93, moderator, 1993—96; mem. Leverett Sch. Bldg. Com., 1988—89; trustee Art Inst. Boston, 1990—92, Greenfield C. C. Found., 1991—97, Amherst Regional H.S. Coun., 1993—95, Amherst Hist. Soc., 1990—95; pres. Leverett PTO, 1981—85; mem. devel. com. Pioneer Valley H.S. of the Performing Arts, 1996—97; pres. Interfaith Housing Corp., Amherst, 1984—93; bd. dirs. Leverett Craftsmen and Artists, Inc., 1986—2001, treas., 1988—89, v.p., 1988—89, pres., 1989—2001; bd. dirs. Cmty. Multisvc. Inc., Northampton, Mass., 1987—93; trustee Wildwood Cemetery Assn., 1987—; bd. dirs., sec. Responsible Hospitality Inst., 1990—95; mem. host com. Russia-Amherst Exchange City of Petrozavadsk, 1988—; del. rep. Town of Amherst to Sister City, Kanegasaki, Japan, 1992—95; chair Amherst-Kanegasaki Sister Com., 1994—95; mem. bd. career com. Hampshire-Franklin Sch., 1995—98; cert. nat. ofcl. U.S. Assn. Track and Field, 1996—; Western Mass. track and field ofcl., 1995—; Western Mass. football ofcl., 1995—; referee FIFA Soccer, 1997—; collegiate water polo ofcl., 1997—2000; asst. coach varsity girls soccer Amherst Regional H.S., 1995—99; v.p. Western Mass. track and field, 2002—. Lt. j.g. USNR, 1961—65. Mem. ABA (chmn. profl. liability com. Gen. Practice Sect. 1987-90, chmn. certification and specialization com. Gen. Practice Sect. 1992-95, chmn. family law com. 1995-96, chmn. certification, specialization and law sch. curriculum com. 1996-98, mem. coun. 1997-2001), Mass. Bar Assn. (chmn. com. on chem. dependency, Mass. Community Svc. award 1984), Franklin Bar Assn., Hampshire Bar Assn. (del. to Mass. Bar Assn., sec., v.p. 1986), Mass. Acad. Trial Lawyers, Amherst C. of C. (pres. 1985-93, Dakin medallion 1995), Nat. High Sch. Slavic Honor Soc. (hon.), Amherst Alumni Athletic Assn. (bd. dirs. 1995—), Skating Club (past v.p., treas. 1987-96, Amherst). Democrat. General civil litigation, Family and matrimonial, General practice. Home: 326 N Pleasant St Amherst MA 01002-1706 E-mail: rmh1240@hotmail.com.

HOWLEY, JAMES MCANDREW, lawyer; b. Dunmore, Pa., Oct. 3, 1928; s. Joseph Austin and Mary Helene (Ruddy) H.; m. Mary McDade; 1 child, Maura. BS, U. Scranton, 1952; LLB, U. Pa., 1955. Bar: Pa. 1956, U.S. Dist. Ct. (mid. dist.) Pa. 1956, U.S. Ct. Appeals (3d cir.) 1960. Pvt. practice, Scranton, Northeastern Pa., 1956—. Panel mem. and speaker at various legal symposiums; chmn. and commr. Pa. State Ethics Commn.; chmn. Gov.'s Spl. Trial Ct. nomination commn., Lackawanna County, Pa., 1987; disciplinary bd. Supreme Ct. Pa. hearing com., 1987; lawyer's adv. com. U.S. Ct. Appeals (3d cir.), 1983-86, U.S. Dist. Ct. (mid. dist.) Pa., 1981-86. Chmn. and trustee Marywood Coll., trustee St. Mary's Villa. Fellow Am. Coll. Trial Lawyers; mem. ABA, Pa. Bar Assn., Pa. Def. Inst., Am. Bd. Trial Advs. (cert.), Lackawanna County Bar Assn., Scranton C. of C. (bd. dirs.), Country Club of Scranton (pres. 1974-79), Friendly Sons of St. Patrick (pres. 1986). Roman Catholic. Avocation: golf. Federal civil litigation, General civil litigation, State civil litigation. Home: 115 Maple Ave Clarks Summit PA 18411-2513 Office: 1000 Bank Towers 321 Spruce St Scranton PA 18503-1400 E-mail: jmhowley@aol.com.

HOWORTH, DAVID BISHOP, lawyer; b. Temple, Tex., Feb. 6, 1947; s. Marion Beckett and Mary Hartwell (Bishop) H.; m. Martha Ellen Peacock, Aug. 29, 1970; children: Katherine Somerville, Emily Hartwell. BA, Yale U., 1971; JD, U. Miss., 1975. ar: N.Y. 1976, Oreg. 1990, Wash. 1996, Miss. 2000, U.S. Dist. Ct. (so. and ea. dists.) N.Y. 1977, U.S. Ct. Appeals (2d cir.) 1984, U.S. Dist. Ct. Oreg. 1990, U.S. Ct. Appeals (9th cir.) 1991. Assoc. Dewey Ballantine, N.Y.C., 1975-77, 78-83, ptnr., 1984-90; asst. prof. law U. Miss., University, 1977-78, vis. assoc. prof. law, 2000—. Mem. ABA, N.Y. State Bar Assn., Assn. Bar City of N.Y. General civil litigation. Home: 1420 S 10th St Oxford MS 38655 Office: Sch Law U Miss University MS 38677 E-mail: dhoworth@olemiss.edu.

HOYLE, LAWRENCE TRUMAN, JR., lawyer; b. Greensboro, N.C., Oct. 6, 1938; s. Lawrence Truman and Martha Parks (Lane) H.; m. Molly Hoyle, Oct.1993; children: Eric L., Alison D. AB in History, Duke U., 1960; JD, U. Chgo., 1965. Bar: Pa. 1965, U.S. Dist. Ct. (ea. dist.) Pa. 1966, U.S. Ct. Appeals (3d cir.) 1966, U.S. Dist. Ct. (no. dist.) Miss. 1968, U.S. Supreme Ct. 1970, U.S. Ct. Appeals (4th, 5th and 11th cirs.) 1984, U.S. Ct. Appeals (D.C. cir.) 1988, U.S. Ct. Appeals (6th cir.) 2001. Assoc. Schnader, Harrison, Segal & Lewis, Phila., 1965-71; dep. atty. gen., chief civil litigation divsn. Pa. Dept. Justice, Harrisburg, Pa., 1971-72; exec. dir. Pa. Crime Commn., Harrisburg, Pa., 1972-74; ptnr. Schnader, Harrison, Segal & Lewis, Phila., 1974-85, Hoyle, Morris & Kerr LLP, Phila., 1985—2002, Hoyle, Fickler, Herschel, & Mathes LLP, 2003—. Lectr. Sch. Law, Temple U., 1969-71; mem. vis. com. Law Sch., U. Chgo., 1975-77, 88-90, 96-98, 2000-01; mem. nominating com. Pa. Appellate Ct., 1979-86; mem. Pa. Jud. Inquiry Rev. Bd., 1988-90. Bd. vis. Duke U. Trinity, 1992-99; bd. dirs. The Lighthouse, Phila., 1968-77, United Communities of S.E. Phila., 1983-86, Pub. Interest Law Ctr., Phila., 1976-2002, Fox Chase Cancer Ctr., 1992—; vol. atty. Lawyers' Com. for Civil Rights Under the Law, 1968; trustee Acad. Natural Scis., 1998—. Fellow Am. Bar Found., Am. Coll. Trial Lawyers (chair complex litigation com. 2000-03; mem. ABA, Pa. Bar Assn., Phila. Bar Assn., Racquet Club Phila., Blooming Grove Hunting and Fishing Club. Democrat. General civil litigation, Securities, Toxic tort. Home: 404 Spruce St Philadelphia PA 19106-4216 Office: Hoyle Fickler Herschel & Mathes 1 S Broad St Ste 1500 Philadelphia PA 19107 E-mail: lhoyle@hoylelawfirm.com.

HOYNES, LOUIS LENOIR, JR., lawyer; b. Indpls., Sept. 23, 1935; s. Louis L. and Catharine (Parker) H.; m. Judith E. Kass, Oct. 12, 1958 (div. 1979); children: Thomas M., William D., Ellen B.; m. Virginia Devin, Dec. 9, 1979. AB, Columbia U., 1957; JD cum laude, Harvard U., 1962. Bar: N.Y. 1963, U.S. Supreme Ct. 1967, U.S. Dist. Ct. (so. dist.) N.Y., U.S. Ct. Appeals (2d, 7th and 9th cirs.). Assoc. Willkie Farr & Gallagher, N.Y.C., 1962-68, ptnr., 1969-90; counsel Nat. League Profl. Baseball Clubs, 1970-90; sr. v.p., gen. counsel Wyeth (formerly) Am. Home Products Corp., 1990-2000; exec. v.p. gen. counsel Am. Home Products Corp. (now Wyeth), 2000—. Lectr. law Columbia U., N.Y.C., 1982-91; bd. dirs. Cytec Industries Inc.; trustee Food and Drug Law Inst., 1994-2002. Served to lt. USNR, 1957-59, PTO. Mem. ABA, N.Y. State Bar Assn., Assn. of City of Bar of N.Y., The Assn. Gen. Counsel. Federal civil litigation, Corporate, general, Labor (including EEOC, Fair Labor Standards Act, labor-management relations, NLRB, OSHA). Home: 47 Cornwells Beach Rd Sands Point NY 11050-1305

HOYOS BELMONT, JESUS EDUARDO, lawyer, consultant; b. Mex. City, Mexico, Oct. 18, 1975; s. Jesus Eusebio Hoyos and Patricia Belmont. LLB, Inst. Tech. Autonoma, Mex., Mex. City, 2000. Bar: Sec. Pub, Edn., Mex. 2001. Assoc. Basham, Ringe y Correa, Mex. City, Mexico, 1998—. Mem.: Phi Delta Phi (pres. Palacios Inn chpt. 1997—98). Avocations: golf, music, travel. Labor (including EEOC, Fair Labor Standards Act, labor-management relations, NLRB, OSHA). Office: Basham Ringe y Correa Paseo de la Tamarindos 400-A piso 9 Fed Dist Mexico CS 05120 Mexico Office Fax: (0155)52610496. E-mail: jehoyos@basham.com.mx.

HOYT, KENNETH M. federal judge; b. 1948; AB, Tex. So. U., 1969, JD, 1972. Mem. firm Wickliff, King, Hoyt & Jones, 1972-75, Anderson, Hodge, Jones & Hoyt, 1975-79, Webster & Andrews, 1979-81; presiding judge 125th Civil Dist. Ct., 1981-82; pvt. practice law Kenneth M. Hoyt & Assocs., 1983-85; justice U.S. Ct. Appeals (1st cir.), 1985-88; judge U.S. Dist. Ct. (so. dist.)Tex., Houston, 1988—. Faculty trial advocacy program South Tex. Coll., 1981-82; adj. prof. Thurgood Marshall Sch. Law, 1983-84. Contbr. articles to profl. jours. Former bd. dirs. Bus. and Profl. Men's Club; judge trial advocacy program U. Houston, 1982-84, 87-88; former mem. Juvenile Justice & Delinquency Prevention Adv. Bd., Blue Ribbon Commn., Rev. Criminal Justice Corrections System, Referendum Force, Selection of Judges; former mem. adv. bd. Parents of Murdered Children and Coalition of Victims Rights; formerly active Salvation Army; former chmn. Capital Devel. Com., Wheeler Ave. Bapt. Ch.; past dir. Houston Lawyer's Referral Svc. With USNG, 1972-78. Decorated Am. Spirit medal; recipient Outstanding Community Svc. award Kendleton, Tex., Ethel Ranson Art & Literary Club award, Outstanding Acheivement award Thurgood Marshall Sch. Law Alumni Assn., 1986; named one of Most Outstanding Black Rep. South Tex. Mem. Nat. Bar Assn., State Bar Tex. (task force, minimum continuing legal edn.). Office: US District Courthouse Suite 11144 515 Rusk St Houston TX 77002-2605

HOYT, MONT POWELL, lawyer; b. Oklahoma City, Apr. 3, 1940; s. Lester Dean and Paula (Powell) H.; m. Alice Nathalie Ryan, June 15, 1974; children: Mont Powell Jr., Kathleen, Michael, Caroline. BA, Northwestern U., 1962; JD, Okla. Law Sch., 1965; M in Comparative Law, U. Chgo., 1968. Bar: Okla. 1965, Tex. 1968. Law clk. U.S. Dist. Ct., Oklahoma City, 1965; stagiaire to French advocat Paris, 1967-68; assoc. Baker & Botts, Houston, 1968-75, ptnr., 1975-92; shareholder Verner, Liipfert, Bernhard, McPherson & Hand, Houston, 1993-94; ptnr. Hughes & Luce, Houston, 1994-2001, Shook, Hardy & Bacon, Houston, 2001—. Adj. prof. law U. Houston, 1970-76 Contbr. articles to profl. jours. Bd. dirs. French Am. Found., N.Y.C., 1979-85, Mexican Cultural Inst., 1991-95, Fgn. Policy Assn., 1991-93; mem. Latin Am. adv. bd. Americas Soc., 1992—. Mem. ABA (chmn. sect. internat. law and practice 1984-85), Internat. Bar Assn. (coun. sect. of energy and nat resources law 1983-86), Am. Law Inst., Am. Soc. Internat. Law, Am. Arbitration Assn., German Am. C. of C. (bd. dirs. 1978-94), InterAm. C. of C. (bd. dirs. 1991-99, chmn. 1996-98), U. Chgo. Law Sch. Alumni Assn. (v.p. 1990-91), Coun. on Fgn. Rels. (chmn. Houston 1991-92), Houston Country Club (Houston), Met. Club (Washington). Avocations: spanish language study, running, international affairs, ham radio. Commercial, contracts (including sales of goods; commercial financing), Corporate, general, Private international. Office: PO Box 131026 Houston TX 77219-1026 E-mail: mhoyt@shb.com.

HRANITZKY, RACHEL ROBYN, lawyer; b. Irving, Tex., Mar. 16, 1968; d. Dennis Rogers and Jeanne Beverly (Crooks) H. BA, Tex. Christian U., 1987, U. Tex., 1988; JD, So. Meth. U., 1995. Bar: Tex. 1995, U.S. Dist. Ct. (no. dist.) Tex. 1997, U.S. Dist. Ct. (ea. dist.) Tex. 1999, U.S. Dist. Ct. (so. and we. dists.) Tex. 2000. Tchr. Grapevine (Tex.) H.S., 1988-92; clk. to Hon. Candace Tyson, 44th Dist. Ct., Dallas, 1993; assoc. coun. Mesa, Inc., Dallas, 1995; assoc. Hiersche, Hayward, Drakeley & Urbach, Dallas, 1996—. Rsch. asst. William V. Dorsaneo, III, 1993-95; clinic atty. So. Meth. U. Legal Clinics, Dallas, 1995. Mem. ABA, ATLA, Dallas Bar Assn., Dallas Assn. Young Lawyers, Rotary Club, Jr. League Plano, Delta Theta Phi. Avocations: art, music, sports, cooking, dancing. General civil litigation, Commercial, contracts (including sales of goods; commercial financing), Trademark and copyright. Home: 11251 Newberry Dr Frisco TX 75035-8614 Office: 15303 Dallas Pkwy Ste 700 Addison TX 75001-4610 E-mail: rhranitzky@hhdulaw.com.

HRIBERNICK, PAUL R. lawyer; b. LaGrande, Oreg., Oct. 28, 1954; BS, U. Oreg., 1977, JD, 1980. Bar: Oreg. 1980, U.S. Dist. Ct. Oreg. 1980, U.S. Ct. Appeals (9th cir.) 1985, U.S. Supreme Ct. 1988. Dep. dist. atty. Klamath County, Klamath Falls, Oreg., 1980; rsch. lawyer La. Sea Grant Program,

Baton Rouge, 1981-82; jud. clk. U.S. Dist. Ct. (ea. dist.) La., New Orleans, 1983-84; lawyer Black Helterline LLP, Portland, Oreg., 1984—. Contbg. author: Immigration and Nationality Law Handbook, 1990, 93, 94, 96, 99; assoc. editor: H-1B Toolbox, 1994-98; editor: AILA INS Resource Guide, 1998-2002. Adminstrv. coun. All Saints Parish, Portland; mem. bd. dirs. Oreg. Concrete and Aggregate Prodrs. Assn., Salem. Fulbright scholar USIA/Commn. Fulbright, Lima, Peru, 1982-83. Mem. Am. Immigration Lawyers Assn. (bd. govs. 1992-94, chair nat. membership com.). Avocations: hunting, kayaking, fishing. Immigration, naturalization, and customs, Land use and zoning (including planning). Office: Black Helterline LLP 1900 Fox Tower 805 SW Broadway Portland OR 97205-3359

HRITZ, GEORGE F. lawyer; b. Hyde Park, N.Y., Aug. 28, 1948; s. George F. and Margaret M. (Callahan) H.; m. Mary Elizabeth Noonan; 1 child, Amelia C. Hritz. AB, Princeton U., 1969; JD, Columbia U., 1973. Bar: N.Y. 1974, D.C. 1978, U.S. Supreme Ct. 1979. Law clk. U.S. Dist. Ct. (ea. dist.) N.Y., N.Y.C., 1973; assoc. Cravath, Swaine & Moore, N.Y.C., 1974-77; counsel U.S. Senate Select Com. Ethics Korean Inquiry, Washington, 1977-78; ptnr. Moore & Foster, Washington, 1978-80, Davis, Weber & Edwards, N.Y.C., 1980-2000; assoc. ind. counsel Washington, 1986-89; ptnr. Hogan & Hartson, LLP, N.Y.C., 2000—. Mem. adv. com. U.S. Dist. Ct. (ea. dist.) N.Y., 1990—. Trustee Fed. Bar Found., 1998—; bd. dirs. gen. counsel exec. com. Internat. Rescue Com., 1982—; chmn. planning bd. Village of Sleepy Hollow, N.Y., 1993-97; bd. dirs. exec. com. Princeton in Africa, 2000—. Mem. Fed. Bar Coun., D.C. Bar Assn. Federal civil litigation, State civil litigation, Private international. Home: 29 Guinea Rd Greenwich CT 06830 Office: Hogan & Hartson LLP Ste 2600 875 Third Ave New York NY 10022 E-mail: gfhritz@hhlaw.com.

HRONES, STEPHEN BAYLIS, lawyer, educator; b. Boston, Jan. 20, 1942; s. John Anthony and Margaret (Baylis) H.; m. Anneliese Zion, Sept. 11, 1970; children: Christopher, Katja. BA cum laude, Harvard U., 1964; postgrad., U. Sorbonne, Paris, 1964-65; JD, U. Mich., 1968. Bar: Iowa 1969, Mass. 1972, U.S. Dist. Ct. Mass. 1973, U.S. Ct. Appeals (1st cir.) 1979, U.S. Tax Ct. 1985, U.S. Supreme Ct. 1991. Pvt. practice, Heidelberg, Germany, 1970-72; pvt. practice Boston, 1973-86; ptnr. Hrones and Harwood, Boston, 1986-90, Hrones and Garrity, Boston, 1990—. Clin. assoc. Suffolk U. Law Sch., Boston, 1979-82; faculty advisor Harvard Law Sch., 1988—; instr. Northeastern Law Sch., 1998; Mass. Continuing Legal Edn. Programs, 1988—. Author: How To Try a Criminal Case, 1982, Criminal Practice Handbook, 1995, 2d edit., 1999, Massachusetts Jury (Criminal) Instructions, 2d edit., 1999; contbr. articles to profl. jours. Trustee Orgn. for Assabet River, 1990-99; mem. schs. and scholarship com. Harvard U.; fundraiser Harvard Coll. Fund, 1985—. Recipient Edward J. Duggan Pvt. Counsel award for zealous advocacy and outstanding legal svcs. to the poor Com. for Pub. Counsel Svcs., 2000; Fulbright scholar, 1968-69. Mem. ABA, ACLU, Nat. Assn. Criminal Def. Lawyers, Mass. Assn. Criminal Def. Lawyers, Mass. Bar Assn., Boston Bar Assn., Nat. Lawyers Guild. Democrat. Avocations: squash, skiing, wind-surfing, vegetable gardening, reading. Civil rights, Criminal, Personal injury (including property damage). Home: 39 Winslow St Concord MA 01742-3817 Office: Hrones and Garrity Lewis Wharf Bay 232 Boston MA 02110 Fax: (617) 227-3908. E-mail: azhro@aol.com.

HRUSKA, ALAN J. lawyer; b. N.Y.C., July 9, 1933; BA, Yale U., 1955, LL.B., 1958. Bar: N.Y. 1959, U.S. Supreme Ct. 1970. Assoc. firm Cravath, Swaine & Moore, N.Y.C., 1958-67, ptnr., 1968—; chmn. planning and program com. 2d Circuit Jud. Conf., 1974-80; co-chmn. 2d Circuit Commn. Reduction of Burdens and Costs in Civil Litigation, 1977-80; commr. N.Y. State Exec. Adv. Commn. on Adminstrn. of Justice, 1981-83; chmn. bd. SoHo Press, Inc., 1986—; CEO The Talking Pictures Co., 2001—. Author: Borrowed Time, 1984. Bd. dirs. Legal Action Ctr., 2000—. Mem.: ABA, Fund for Modern Cts. (bd. dirs. 1994—), Inst. Jud. Adminstrn. (trustee 1978—92, pres. 1982—85, bd. dirs. 1992—2002), Fed. Bar Coun. (trustee 1976—, pres. 1984—86), Assn. Bar City of N.Y. (sec. 1965—66), N.Y. State Bar Assn., Am. Coll. Trial Lawyers, Ctr. for Pub. Resources (exec. com. 1984—2002). Antitrust, Federal civil litigation, Securities. Office: Cravath Swaine & Moore 825 8th Ave Fl 38 New York NY 10019-7475

HRYCAK, MICHAEL PAUL, lawyer; b. Mpls., May 12, 1959; s. Peter and Rea Meta (Limberg) Hrycak; m. Rita Hrycak; children: Brandon Paul, Jared Michael. BA, Rutgers U., 1981, JD, 1989; MS, N.J. Inst. Tech., 1983. Bar: N.J. 1990, N.Y. 1990, Conn. 1990, D.C. 1992, U.S. Dist. Ct. N.J. 1990. Systems analyst RCA Astro-Electronics Divsn., Princeton, N.J., 1983-86; prin. atty. Law Office of Michael P. Hrycak, Westfield, N.J., 1990—. Lt. USNG, 1981-87, capt., 1987-96, maj., 1996—. Mem.: Ukrainian Engrs. Soc. Am. (treas. 1984—2002), Ukrainian Am. Bar Assn., Conn. Bar Assn., N.Y. Bar Assn. Republican. Ukrainian Catholic. Avocations: skiing, backpacking, marksmanship, traveling, current events. Computer, Criminal, Family and matrimonial. Home: 129 Beech St Cranford NJ 07016 Office: 316 Lenox Ave Westfield NJ 07090-2138

HSI, EDWARD YANG, lawyer, industrialist, business executive, political advisor; b. Ann Arbor, Mich., May 30, 1957; s. Peter Hwei-Yang and Priscilla Lai-Fong (Lam) H.; m. Denise Chur-Yee Tso, Aug. 3, 1985; 2 children, Edward Yang II, Clarissa Sian Li-Hwa. BS, U. So. Calif., 1980; MBA, Duke U., 1983; JD, U. Calif., Davis, 1986. Bar: Calif. 1986, U.S. Dist. Ct. (cen. dist.) Calif. 1987, U.S. Ct. Appeals (9th cir.) 1987, U.S. Tax Ct. 1988, U.S. Supreme Court 1991. Tax intern Coca Cola Co., L.A., 1983, Lear Siegler Inc., Santa Monica, Calif., 1984; assoc. Lawler, Felix & Hall, L.A., 1986-87, Morrison & Foerster, L.A., 1987-89, Thelen, Marrin, Johnson & Bridges, L.A., 1989, Baker & McKenzie, Hong Kong, Singapore, 1989-92; of counsel Tilleke & Gibbins/Jones, Day, Reavis & Pogue, Bangkok, 1992—, Tilleke & Gibbins Cons., Ltd., Indochina, 1992—; group gen. counsel Humpuss Group Indonesia, Jakarta, Singapore, 1992-94; pres., CEO Humpuss Arun Aromatics Petrochemicals, Jakarta, Arun, Sumatra, 1994—96; exec. dir. Dharmala Group, Jakarta, 1997; vice chmn., CEO Asean Infrastructure Holdings Ltd., Jakarta, 1997—; chmn., CEO Asean Energy Group Ltd., Jakarta, 1998—. Spl. advisor to the shareholders Gunung Sewu Group and Duta Anggada Group, Jakarta, 1997; spl. advisor to chmn. Shingfa Group, Taipei, 2001—02; founder, prin. Grant Thornton Taira Hsi and Taira & Hsi, Internat. in cooperation with Kaye Scholer LLP, Jakarta, 1998—2000, Govt. of Republic of Indonesia on a Policy Proposal for the Econ. Restoration of Province of Aceh; advisor to chmn. of Indonesian Parliament DPR on a Nat. Econ. Revitalization Policy, 1998—99; mng. dir. Asia-Pacific region Mysmart Solutions, Inc., 2000—01; advisor Golkar Parliamentary Party of The Republic of Indonesia Del. to Taiwan to address Bilateral Internat. Cooperation in the Labor and Energy Sectors, 2002; bd. dirs. DEH Asia Ltd., VBP Ltd., AO Asia Ltd., Asia Beta Capital Ltd.; co-founder, CEO, New Template Media Group, L.A., 2003—. Editor: Income Taxation of Foreign Related Transaction, 5 vols., 1987; contbr. articles on tax to profl. jours. Mem.: ABA, L.A. County Bar Assn., State Bar Calif., U. Calif. Alumni Assn., Duke Alumni Assn., Punahou Sch. Alumni Assn., Hong Kong Stanley Residents' Assn., Indonesian Bus. Soc., Hong Kong Assn., Am. C. of C.-Hong Kong, Tuen Ng Dragon Boat Races Festival (co-chmn., ATT and Baker & McKenzie entry), Order of Coif, Phi Kappa Tau, Alpha Mu Alpha, Phi Delta Phi. Democrat. Avocations: southeast asian art, jazz drumming, classical music, anthropology, discipleship. Corporate, general, Private international, Taxation, general. Home: 819 S Ridgeside Dr Monterey Park CA 91754-3724 Office: Chase Plaza 21st Fl Jalan Jenderal Sudirman Kav 21 Jakarta 12910 Indonesia E-mail: eyhsi@yahoo.com.

HSIA, MARTIN EDGAR, lawyer; b. London, Eng., Sept. 30, 1957; came to U.S., 1963; s. Yujen Edward and Juliet Wai Mun (Yuen) H.; children: Robert Edward Tien Ming, Kyla Martina Mei Ming. BA with honors, Brown U., 1978; JD cum laude, Georgetown U., 1981. Bar: Hawaii 1981, U.S. Ct. Appeals (fed. cir.) 1990, U.S. Patent and Trademark Office 1986. Paralegal Drug Enforcement Adminstrn., Washington, 1979-80; cons. Office Tech. Assessment U.S. Congress, Washington, 1980-81; assoc. Cades Schutte Fleming & Wright, Honolulu, 1981-88, ptnr., 1988—. Mem. Licensing Execs. Soc., Internat. Trademark Assn., Patent and Trademark Office Soc., Computer Law Assn., Am. Intellectual Property Law Assn., Hawaii Bar Assn. (intellectual property and tech. sect.), Hawaii Venture Capital Assn. (sec. 1988—), Hawaii Tech. Trad. Assn. (asst. sec. 2000-). Avocations: music, ice hockey, science fiction. Computer, Patent, Trademark and copyright. Office: Cades Schutte LLP 1000 Bishop St Fl 12 Honolulu HI 96813-4212 E-mail: mhsia@cades.com.

HSIAO, JOANNE Y. lawyer; b. Taipei, Taiwan, Nov. 29, 1965; d. Teng-Tzang Hsiao and Ling-Miao Hsu. LLB, Nat. Taiwan U., 1988. Bar: Taiwan 1991. Assoc. Taiwan Comml. Law Offices, Taipei, 1989—94; atty. Taipei, 1994—96; cons. Provisional Engring. Office High Speed Rail, Ministry Transp. and Comm., Taipei, 1996—98; mgr. legal dept. Taiwan High Speed Rail Corp., Taipei, 1998—2000; ptnr. J&J Attys. at Law, Taipei, 1997—. Mem. legal rsch. com. Chinese Inst. Civil and Hydraulic Engring., Taipei, 2000—. Co-author: International Manual of Planning Practice, 1995—. Mem.: Taipei Bar Assn., Internat. Trademark Assn., Internat. Bar Assn., Arbitration Assn. Republic China (arbitrator). Avocation: travel. Construction, Nuclear power, Government contracts and claims. Office: J&J Attys at Law 333 Keelung Rd 20th Fl Ste 2009 Taipei 110 Taiwan

HU, DANIEL DAVID, lawyer; b. N.Y.C., 1960; BA, Rice U., 1982, MA, 1984; Jd, U. Tex., 1986. Bar: Tex. 1986. Jud. clk. Hon. Norman W Black, Houston, 1986-88; assoc. Royston Rayzor, Houston, 1988-91; asst. U.S. atty. U.S. Attys. Office, Houston, 1992—. Mem. State Bar Tex. (bd. mem.), Gulf Coast Legal Found. (bd. mem.), Houston Asian Bar. Avocation: running. Office: US Attys Office PO Box 61129 Houston TX 77208-1129

HUANG, THOMAS WEISHING, lawyer; b. Taipei, Taipan, Feb. 1, 1941; came to U.S., 1967; s. Lienden and Helen (Yen) H. BA, Taiwan U., 1964; JD magna cum laude, Ind. U., Indpls., 1970; LLM, Harvard U., 1971, SJD, 1975. Bar: D.C. 1975, Mass. 1976, U.S. Dist. Ct. Mass. 1976, U.S. Ct. Appeals (1st cir.) 1978, N.Y. 1980. Judge adv. Chinese Army, Taiwan, 1964-65; legal officer treaty and legal dept. Ministry Fgn. Affairs, Taiwan, 1966-67; assoc. Chemung County Legal Svcs., Elmira, N.Y., 1975-76, Taylor Johnson & Wieschhoff, Marblehead, Mass., 1980; prin. Reiser & Rosenberg, Boston, 1982-86, Huang & Assocs., Boston, 1987-88, Hale, Sanderson, Byrnes & Morton, Boston, 1988-96; of counsel Chin, Wright & Branson P.C., Boston, 1996-97; shareholder Sherburne, Powers & Needham, P.C., Boston, 1997-98; ptnr. Holland & Knight, LLP, Boston, 1998—2002, Burns & Levinson LLP, 2002—. Exec. v.p. Excel Tech. Internat. Co., Brunswick, N.J., 1982-88; bd. dirs. Asian Am. Bank & Trust Co., Boston, exec. com., clk., 1993—; legal counsel Nat. Assn. Chinese Ams., Washington, 1979-80. Mem. editl. staff Ind. Law Rev., 1969-70; contbr. articles to legal jours. Bd. dirs. Chinese Econ. Devel. Coun., Boston, 1978-80; mem. Gov.'s Adv. Coun. on Guangdong, 1984-87; mem. minority bus task force Senator Kerry's Office, 1988—. Mem. Boston Bar Assn. (steering com. internat. law sect. 1979-90, ad hoc com. on code profl. conduct), Nat. Assn. Chines Ams. (v.p. Boston chpt. 1984-86, pres. 1986-88, 1st v.p. nat. assn. 1994-97), Taiwan C of C. in New Eng. (clk., bd. dirs. 1996-2000), N.E. Chinese Internet & Network Assn. (bd. dirs. 2000—). Commercial, contracts (including sales of goods; commercial financing), Immigration, naturalization, and customs, Private international. Home: 30 Farrwood Dr Andover MA 01810-5233 Office: Burns & Levinson LLP 125 Summer St Boston MA 02110 E-mail: thuang@b-l.com.

HUBBARD, ELIZABETH LOUISE, lawyer; b. Springfield, Ill., Mar. 10, 1949; d. Glenn Wellington and Elizabeth (Frederick) H.; m. A. Jeffrey Seidman, Oct. 27, 1974 (div. May 1982). BA, U. Ky., 1971; JD with honors, Ill. Inst. Tech.-Chgo. Kent Coll. Law, 1974. Bar: Ill. 1974, U.S. Dist. Ct. (no. dist.) Ill. 1974, U.S. Ct. Appeals (7th cir.) 1976, U.S. Supreme Ct. 1984. Atty. Wyatt Co., Chgo., 1974-75, Gertz & Giampietro, Chgo., 1975-81, Baum, Sigman, Gold, Chgo., 1981-98, Elizabeth Hubbard, Ltd., 1981-98, Hubbard & O'Connor, Ltd., Chgo., 1998—. Legal counsel NOW, Chgo., 1978-94, sec., 1977. Editor: Chgo. Kent Law Rev., 1970; supplement editor: Litigating Sexual Harassment and Sex Discrimination Cases, 1997—2003. Bd. dirs., mem. The Remains Theatre, 1985-94. Mem. Chgo. Bar Assn. (fed. civil procedure com.), Ill. State Bar Assn., Nat. Employment Lawyers Assn. (chair Ill. chpt. 1992-95, sec.-treas. 1997—). Civil rights, Corporate, general, Family and matrimonial. Home: 420 W Grand Ave Apt 4A Chicago IL 60610-4087 Office: Ste Six West 900 W Jackson Blvd Chicago IL 60607-3024 Fax: (312) 421-5310. E-mail: ehubbard@hubbardoconnor.com.

HUBBARD, HERBERT HENDRIX, lawyer; b. Balt., Sept. 20, 1922; s. Amberson Hardy and Louise Virginia (Hendrix) H.; m. Joanne Hileman Nottingham, June 5, 1948 (dec. Sept. 2002); children: Melissa Hubbard O'Donnell, Alison Hubbard. JD, U. Md., Balt., 1950. Bar: Md. 1950, U.S. Dist. Ct. Md. 1950, U.S. Ct. Appeals (4th cir.) 1953, U.S. Supreme Ct. 1963. Clk. to dist. judge U.S. Dist. Ct. Md., Balt., 1950-51; assoc. France, Rouzer & Harris, Balt., 1951-52, 54-59; asst. U.S. atty. Dist. Md., Balt., 1952-53, 1st asst. U.S. atty., 1953-54; atty., ptnr. Weinberg & Green, Balt., 1959—98; gen. counsel Forest Haven Nursing Home, Balt., 2001—; counsel Saul Ewing, Balt., 1998—2001, of counsel, 2001—. Founding dir. Devel. Credit Fund, Inc., Balt., 1984-96. Chmn., corp. devel. coun. Sheppard & Enoch Pratt Hosp., Balt., 1978-86. Mem. ABA, Md. Bar Assn. (founding, chmn. profl. liability ins. com. 1976-82), Bar Assn. Ins. Trust (trustee 1976-88), Legal Mut. Liability Ins. Soc. Md. (sr. v.p., gen. counsel, bd. dirs., exec. com. 1986—, founding dir.), Order of Coif, U. Md. Law Review. Episcopalian. Avocations: tennis, bridge. Corporate, general, Insurance, Mergers and acquisitions. Home: Blakehurst 1055 W Joppa Rd Towson MD 21204 Office: 100 S Charles St Ste 1500 Baltimore MD 21201-2771 also: 701 Edmondson Ave Catonsville MD 21228

HUBBARD, MELISSA, lawyer; b. Chgo., Feb. 4, 1960; d. James Lebeck and Trish Hollingsworth; m. Bruce Hubbard, Aug. 1978 (div. Mar. 1994); 1 child, Mark; m. Anthony Giordano, Mar. 17, 2000; children: Nicolas Giordano, Matthew Giordano. AB in Polit. Sci., Stanford U., 1980; JD, U. Colo., 1983. Bar: Colo. 1983. From assoc. to ptnr. Holland & Hart, Denver, 1982—92; gen. counsel, sr. v.p. Daniels and Assocs., Denver, 1992—2002; shareholder Berenbaum, Weinshienk & Eason PC, Denver, 2003—. Arbitrator Am. Arbitration Assn., Denver, 1987—; bd. dirs. New Frontier Media, Inc. Trustee, mem. corp. com. Legal Aid Found., 2000—; mem. adv. bd. Young Ams. Bank, Denver, 1998—; chair U. Colo. Alumni Found., 2000—. Mem.: ABA, Denver Bar Assn., Women in Telecom., Colo. Bar Assn. Republican. Presbyterian. Avocations: golf, skiing, running, reading, travel. Alternative dispute resolution, Securities, Communications. Home: 7120 W Princeton Ave Denver CO 80235 Fax: 303-629-7610. Personal E-mail: melissa4hubbard@aol.com.

HUBBARD, MICHAEL JAMES, lawyer; b. N.Y.C., Dec. 8, 1950; s. William Neil and Elizabeth (Terleski) H. AB, U. Mich., 1976; JD, Marquette U., 1979. Bar: Wis. 1980, Mich. 1980. Assoc. Kidston, Peterson P.C., Kalamazoo, 1980, Barbier, Goulet & Petersmarck, Mt. Clemens, Mich., 1981; pvt. practice Detroit, 1982-86, Belleville, Mich., 1990-98; assoc. Lawrence J. Stockler, P.C., Southfield, Mich., 1987; staff atty. Hyatt Legal Svcs., Southgate, Mich., 1988; assoc. Dunchock, Linden & Wells, Coruna, Mich., 1989. Mem. State Bar Mich. (criminal law, negligence, gen. practice sects.) Republican. General practice, Other.

HUBBARD, PETER LAWRENCE, lawyer; b. Syracuse, N.Y., Apr. 4, 1946; s. Bardwell B. and Barbara (Bowen) H.; m. Hannah R., June 21, 1967; 1 child, Brian C. BA, Syracuse U., 1968, JD, 1971; postgrad., Judge Advocate Gen.'s Sch., Charlottesville, Va., 1976. Bar: N.Y. 1972, U.S. Dist. Ct. (no. and we. dists.) N.Y. 1972, U.S. Ct. Appeals (2d cir.) 1983. Assoc. Smith & Sovik, Syracuse, N.Y., 1971-72; asst. dist. counsel U.S. SBA, Syracuse, 1972-80; mng. ptnr. Menter, Rudin & Trivelpiece, Syracuse, 1980—. Lectr. in field. Contbr. articles to profl. jours. Pres. Reachout Inc., County Drug Rehab. Agy., Syracuse, 1979; mem. bd. trustees Loretto Mgmt. Corp., Syracuse, 2001. Banking, Bankruptcy, Commercial, contracts (including sales of goods; commercial financing). Office: Menter Rudin & Trivelpiece 500 S Salina St Ste 500 Syracuse NY 13202-3300 E-mail: phubbard@menterlaw.com.

HUBBARD, WILLIAM L. lawyer; b. Farmland, Ind., July 14, 1945; s. Charles and Mary Virginia (Horner) H.; m. Linda Crouse, Jan. 31, 1969 (div.); 1 child, Angela; m. Connie Stewart, Sept. 29, 1984; children: Jameson, Joshua. BSBA, Northwestern U., 1967; JD, Mo. U., 1971. Bar: Mo. 1971, U.S. Dist. Ct. (we. dist.) Mo. 1971, U.S. Ct. Appeals (10th cir.) 1981. Lawyer, shareholder, dir. The Popham Law Firm, PC, Kansas City, Mo., 1971-97, mng. dir., 1996-97; mng. ptnr. Hubbard, Kurtz, Taylor, LLP, Kansas City, 1997—. Spkr. various seminars, 1994—; mem. planning com. Heart of Am. Tax Inst. Contbr. Mo. Law Rev., 1971. Chair edn. work area Ctrl. United Meth. Ch., Kansas City, 1992-97; com. chair Pack 24 Cub Scouts, Kansas City, 1996-98, charter organization rep., 1998. Mem. ABA (probate and tax coms. 1984—), Mo. Bar Assn. (legislative, tax and probate coms. 1994—), Kansas City Met. Bar Assn. (vice chair probate com. 1997, chair 1998), Nat. Acad. of Elder Law Attys. (sec. Mo. chpt. 1997, v.p. 1998, pres. 2000-01). Estate planning, Probate (including wills, trusts), Elder. Office: Hubbard & Kurtz 1718 Walnut St Kansas City MO 64108-1316

HUBBELL, BILLY JAMES, lawyer; b. Pine Bluff, Ark., May 21, 1949; s. Arley E. and Mary M. (Duke) H.; m. Judy C. Webb, Feb. 21, 1981; children: Jennifer Leigh, William Griffin. BE, U. Cen. Ark., 1971; JD, U. Ark, Little Rock, 1978. Bar: Ark. 1978, U.S. Dist. Ct. (ea. dist.) Ark. 1978, U.S. Ct. Appeals (8th cir.) 1987. Tchr. Grady (Ark.) High Sch., 1971-78; assoc. Smith and Smith, McGehee, Ark., 1978-79; ptnr. Smith, Hubbell and Drake, McGehee, 1979-86, Griffin, Rainwater & Draper, P.A., Crossett, Ark., 1987-90; dep. prosecuting atty. Ashley County, Ark., 1989-90; dist. judge Crossett, 1991—; pvt. practice, 1991—. Candidate Ark. Ho. of Reps., Lincoln County, 1984, 10th Jud. Dist. Cir./Chancery Judge, 1998. Sgt. USAR, 1970-76. Mem. Ark. Bar Assn., S.E. Ark. Legal Inst. (chmn. 1984-85, Ashley County Bar Assn. (past pres.), Ark. Trial Lawyers Assn. Democrat. Seventh Day Adventist. Avocations: jogging, computers. General civil litigation, Commercial, contracts (including sales of goods; commercial financing), Personal injury (including property damage). Office: PO Box 574 Crossett AR 71635-0574 E-mail: bjhubbell@alltel.net.

HUBBELL, ERNEST, lawyer; b. Trenton, Mo., Aug. 28, 1914; s. Platt and Maud Irene (Ray) H.; m. Nevah Smith, Apr. 25, 1943; 1 child, Platt Thorpe. AA, North Cen. Mo. Coll. (formerly Trenton Jr. Coll.), 1934; JD, Georgetown U., 1938. Bar: D.C. 1937, Mo. 1938, U.S. Supreme Ct. 1946. Practiced in, Trenton, 1938-39, Jefferson City, Mo., 1939-42; pvt. practice, Kansas City, Mo., 1947-52; ptnr. Hubbell, Sawyer, Peak, O'Neal & Napier (formerly Hubbell, Lane & Sawyer), Kansas City, 1952—. Asst. atty. gen. Mo., 1939-43; first chmn. bench, bar com. 16th Jud. Cir. Ct., Kansas City, 1964-69, mem 16th Cir. Jud. Nominating Commn., 1970-75; mem. U.S. Cir. Judge Nominating Commn., 1977-80. Trustee Legal Aid and Defender Soc. Greater Kansas City, 1964-73; mem. Law Found. U. Mo. Kansas City, 1966-71; chmn. Nat. Council on Crime and Delinquency, 1966-76; pres. Hubbell Family Hist. Soc., 1981-85; mem. Soc. Fellows Nelson Art Gallery. With USAAF, 1943-44, capt. JAGC, 1944-46. Mem. ABA, Kansas City Met. Bar Assn. (pres. 1963-64, ann. Achievement award 1974, 1st ann. Litigator Emeritus award), Mo. Bar Assn., Assn. Trial Lawyers Am. (assoc. editor R.R. law sect. of jour. 1951—), Mo. Assn. Trial Attys. (pres. 1954, editor bull. 1955), Lawyers Assn. Kansas City, Lawyers Assn. St. Louis, Archeol. Inst. Am., Sierra Club (life). Episcopalian. Democrat. Club: Kansas City. General civil litigation, Product liability, Personal injury (including property damage). Home: 1210 W 63d St Kansas City MO 64113-1513 Office: Hubbell Sawyer Peak O'Neal & Napier Power and Light Bldg 106 W 14th St Fl 12 Kansas City MO 64105-1914

HUBEN, BRIAN DAVID, lawyer; b. Inglewood, Calif., May 14, 1962; s. Michael Gerald and Dorothy (Withers) H.; m. Kathy Henson Johnson, Apr. 6, 1991; children: Kaitlin Johnson, Mariana Johnson. BA, Loyola Marymount U., 1984; JD, Loyola Law Sch., 1987. Bar: Calif. 1988, U.S. Dist. Ct. (no., ce., ea. and so. dists.) Calif. 1988, Ariz., 1994, U.S. Ct. Appeals (9th cir.) 1988, D.C. 1989, U.S. Supreme Ct. 1996. Assoc. Steinberg, Nutter & Brent, Santa Monica, Calif., 1988-89, Smith & Hilbig, Torrance, Calif., 1989-95, Robie & Matthai, L.A., 1995-99; spl. master State Bar of Calif., 1995-99; counsel Katten Muchin Zavis Rosenman, L.A., 1999—. Del. L.A. County Bar Assn. State Conv., 1990-99. Mem. instl. rev. bd. Torrance Meml. Med. Ctr., 1990-95. Mem. Calif. Bar Assn., D.C. Bar Assn., L.A. County Bar Assn., Loyola Marymount Univ. Alumni Assn. (dir., bd. dirs. 1995-01). Democrat. Roman Catholic. Avocations: travel, sports, current events. Bankruptcy, General civil litigation, Commercial, contracts (including sales of goods; commercial financing). Office: Katten Muchin Zavis Rosenman 2029 Century Park E 26th Flr Los Angeles CA 90067-3012 E-mail: brian.huben@kmzr.com.

HUBER, RICHARD GREGORY, lawyer, educator; b. Indpls., June 29, 1919; s. Hugh Joseph and Laura Marie (Becker) H.; m. Katherine Elizabeth McDonald, June 21, 1950 (dec.); children: Katherine, Richard, Mary, Elizabeth, Stephen, Mark. BS, U.S. Naval Acad, 1942; JD, U. Iowa, 1950; LLM, Harvard U., 1951; LLD (hon.), New England Sch. Law, 1985, Northeastern U., 1987, Roger Williams U., 1996. Instr. law U. Iowa, 1950; assoc. prof. law U. S.C., 1952-54; assoc. prof. Tulane U., 1954-57, Boston Coll., 1957-59, prof., 1959-90, dean, 1970-85; disting. prof. Roger Williams U., Bristol, R.I., 1993-95; prof. New England Sch. Law, Newton, Mass., 1995-99. Adj. faculty Boston Coll., 1999—. Contbr. articles and book revs. to profl. jours. Past chairperson pers. and fin. coms. Mass. chpt. Multiple Sclerosis Soc.; past pres. bd. trustees Beaver Country Day Sch. With USN, 1941-47, 51-52. Mem. ABA (del., mem. coun. legal edn. 1981-85, trustee law sch. admissions coun 1983-85), Soc. Am. Law Tchrs., Assn. Am. Law Schs. (pres. 1988-89), Coun. Legal Edn. Opportunity (pres. 1975-79), Am. Judicature Soc., Mass. Bar Assn., Mass. Bar Found. Democrat. Roman Catholic. Home: 406 Woodward St Waban MA 02468-1523 Office: 885 Centre St Newton MA 02459-1148 E-mail: richard.huber1@worldnet.att.net., huber@monet.bc.edu.

HUBER, WILLIAM EVAN, lawyer; b. Celina, Ohio, Mar. 10, 1943; s. W. Evan and Genevieve Rose Huber; m. E. Marie Schwaberow, June 24, 1966 (div. Aug. 1994); m. Betty Jo Bowers, Aug. 23, 1999; children: Michael D., Mark William. BSEd, Ohio No. U., 1965, JD, 1968. Bar: Ohio 1968, U.S. Dist. Ct. (no. dist.) Ohio 1972, U.S. Supreme Ct. 1972, U.S. Ct. Appeals (6th cir.) 1990, U.S. Tax Ct. Ohio, U.S. Dist. Ct. (no. dist.) Ohio. Asst. pros. atty. Auglaize County, Ohio, 1969-76; pvt. practice St. Marys, Ohio, 1969—. Asst. law dir. City of St. Marys, Ohio, 1972-79. Past pres., past state dir. St. Marys Jaycees; past state v.p. Ohio Jaycees, 1969; mem. Jr. Chamber Internat. Senate; past trustee Auglaize County Mental Health Assn.; past gen. chmn. St. Mary's Area United Way; past chmn. St. Marys City Recreational Adv. Bd.; past pres. St. Marys Nat. Little League; past chmn. St. Marys Medic-Search Com.; mem., past trustee St. Marys Cmty. Improvement Corp.; past mem. Mayor's Downtown Re-vitalization Com.; past mem., chmn. St. Marys Civil Svc. Commn., 1993-97; mem. Auglaize County Bd. Elections, 1994-97; past mem. Auglaize County Dem. Exec. Com., chmn., 1992-97. Named Outstanding Jaycee, St. Marys Jaycees,

1971; recipient Ohio Jaycees Presdl. award of Honor, 1972, Disting. Svc. award Ohio Dem. Party, 1997. Mem. Ohio State Bar Assn., Auglaize County Bar Assn. (past pres.), St. Marys C. of C. (past trustee, past pres.). General civil litigation, Family and matrimonial, General practice. Office: 137 E Spring St PO Box 298 Saint Marys OH 45885-0298

HUBERMAN, RICHARD LEE, lawyer; b. Lynn, Mass., Dec. 6, 1953; s. Irving Morris and Selma Edythe (Wolk) H. AB, Harvard U., 1975, JD, 1978. Bar: Mass. 1979, D.C. 1979. Atty. Office of Rail Pub. Counsel, Washington, 1978-80; counsel subcom. on commerce, consumer protection and competitiveness (formerly commerce, transp. and tourism) U.S. Ho. of Reps., Washington, 1980-95, mem. prof. staff Com. on Edn. and Workforce, 1995—97; pvt. practice Washington, 1997-98; counsel to commr. and chmn. Occupl. Safety and Health Rev. Commn., Washington, 1998—. Mem. ABA, Mass. Bar Assn., Harvard Law Sch. Assn. Clubs: Harvard (Washington). Democrat. Home: 2141 P St NW Apt 302 Washington DC 20037-1031 Office: Occupl Safety and Health Rev Commn 1120 20th St NW Washington DC 20036 E-mail: rhuberman@oshrc.gov.

HUBSCHMAN, HENRY A. lawyer; b. Newark, N.J., Aug. 12, 1947; s. Morris and Esther (Weissman) H.; m. Joanne L. Goode; children: Lilly, Josie, Ellis, Nathan. BA summa cum laude, Rutgers U., 1969; JD magna cum laude, M Pub. Policy, Harvard U., 1973. Bar: Mass. 1973, N.J. 1974, D.C. 1974, Ohio 1994. Law clk. U.S. Dist. Ct. Mass., Boston, 1973-74; assoc. Fried, Frank, Harris, Shriver & Jacobson, Washington, 1974-77, 79-80, ptnr., 1980-92; v.p., gen. counsel, bus. devel. GE Aircraft Engines, Cin., 1992-97; pres., CEO GE Capital Aviation Svcs., Stamford, Conn., 1997—. Exec. asst. to Sec. HUD, Washington, 1977-79; bd. dir. Fed. Nat. Mortgage Assn., 1979-81. Jewish. Federal civil litigation, Insurance, Securities. Home: 37 Hillside Rd Greenwich CT 06830-4834 Office: GE Capital Aviation Svcs 201 High Ridge Rd Stamford CT 06905-3417

HUCK, L. FRANCIS, lawyer; b. Pittsfield, Mass., May 5, 1947; s. Lewis Francis Joseph and Rosemary (Ahearn) H.; m. Natalie Anne Murphy, June 10, 1978; children: Amelia Emerson, Rosemary Alice, Charles Randolph. AB, Harvard U., 1969; JD, Stanford U., 1972. Assoc. Simpson, Thacher & Bartlett, N.Y.C., 1972-79, ptnr., 1980—. Mem. Harvard Club N.Y.C., Wee Burn Club. Democrat. Banking. Home: 90 Inwood Rd Darien CT 06820-2427 Office: Simpson Thacher & Bartlett 425 Lexington Ave Fl 15 New York NY 10017-3954

HUCKABEE, HARLOW MAXWELL, lawyer, writer; b. Wichita Falls, Tex., Jan. 22, 1918; s. Edwin Cleveland and Gladys Idella (Bonney) H.; m. Gloria Charlotte Comstock, Jan. 10, 1942; children: Bonney M., David C., Stephen M. BA, Harvard U., 1948; JD, Georgetown U., 1951. Bar: U.S. Dist. Ct. D.C. 1952, U.S. Ct. Appeals (D.C. cir.) 1952. Cashier br. office Columbian Nat. Life Ins. Co., Boston, 1935-40; lawyer Fed. Housing Adminstrn., Washington, 1955-56; trial lawyer, criminal sect., tax divsn. U.S. Justice Dept., Washington, 1956-63; lawyer IRS, Washington, 1963-67; trial lawyer organized crime and racketeering sect. U.S. Justice Dept., Washington, 1967-68, trial lawyer criminal sect., tax divsn., 1968-80. Author: Lawyers, Psychiatrists and Criminal Law, 1980, Mental Disability Issues in the Criminal Justice System: What They Are, Who Evaluates Them, How and When, 2000; contbr. articles to profl. jours. and legal publs. including Diminished Capacity Dilemma in the Federal System, 1991. Maj. U.S. Army, 1940-45, 48-55, ETO, Korea; lt. col. USAR, 1961. Methodist. Home: 5100 Fillmore Ave Apt 913 Alexandria VA 22311-5048

HUCKABY, GARY CARLTON, lawyer; b. Lanett, Ala., July 12, 1938; s. Carl Walker and Mary Evelyn (Meriwether) H.; m. Jeanne Davey Huckaby, Feb. 23, 1963; children: Gary Jr., John Stephen, Michael Stewart. BA, U. Ala., 1960, JD, 1962. Bar: U.S. Supreme Ct. 1963, U.S. Ct. of Mil. Appeals 1963, U.S. Ct. Appeals (5th and 11th cirs.) 1963, U.S. Dist. Ct. (no., middle and so. dists) Ala. 1963. Law clk. to chief justice Ala. Supreme Ct., Montgomery, 1962-63; asst. U.S. Sen. Lister Hill, Washington, 1963; ptnr. Smith, Huckaby & Graves, Huntsville, Ala., 1966-85, Bradley, Arant, Rose & White, Huntsville, 1985—; dir. Ala. Ctr. for Law & Civic Edn., 1992—. Dir. coun. Internat. Visitors of Huntsville-Madison County, 1983-89, Tenn. Valley Boy Scouts Am., 1975-79, Mental Health Assn. Madison County, 1970-78, Ala. Law Sch. Found., 1981—; pres. Huntsville-Madison County Mental Health Bd., 1977-80, Madison County Heart Assn., 1968; active Citizens Com. on Higher Edn. of Ala. Legis., 1976, judicial sect. of Huntsville-Madison County Local Govt. Study Com., 1969. Capt. USAF, 1963-66. Fellow Am. Bar Found., Am. Coll. Trial Lawyers; mem. ABA (bd. govs. 1990-91, house of delegates, chmn. standing com. on lawyer referral and info. services 1982-85, chmn. spl. com. on delivery of legal services 1976-79, standing com. on lawyers pub. service responsibility 1987-90, consortium on legal services and the pub. 1976-79, task force on pub. edn. 1978, standing com. on lawyers in the armed forces 1971-73), Ala. State Bar (pres., bd. commrs. 1981-87, exec. com. 1982-83, 84-85, 87-88, chmn. governance com. 1986-87, action group on professionalism, disciplinary bd. 1981-87; recipient award of merit 1986), Huntsville-Madison County Bar Assn. (pres. 1977-78, chmn. grievance com. 1976, bench and bar relations 1981, convention host com. 1971, law day com. 1968), Am. Judicature Soc. (former bd. dirs.), Rotary. Democrat. Episcopalian. Federal civil litigation, State civil litigation, Libel. Home: 701 Greene St SE Huntsville AL 35801-4232 Office: Bradley Arant Rose & White 200 Clinton Ave W Ste 900 Huntsville AL 35801-4900

HUDDLESON, EDWIN EMMETT, III, lawyer; b. Oct. 20, 1945; s. Edwin Emmet and Mary (Taeusch) H.; m. Andra Nan Oakes, July 8, 1978; children: Michael, Jonathan. BS, Stanford U., 1967; JD, U. Chgo., 1970. Bar: Calif. 1970, D.C. 1977, Md. 2001. Law clk. to Judge Charles M. Merrill U.S. Ct. Appeals (9th cir.), 1970-71; civil divsn. U.S. Dept. Justice, Washington, 1971-77. Chmn. Ct. Rules Com. D.C. Bar, 2001—; chmn. com. on procedures U.S. Ct. Appeals (D.C. cir.), 2002—, adv. com. on procedures, 2002—. Author: Waiver of Miranda Rights, 1969, Confidentiality for Editorial Process, 1978, Treatise on Equipment Leasing, 1989—, Appellate Advocacy, 1991, Environmental Law Protections for Lenders, 1994, Leasing Is Distinctive!, 2003; mem. U. Chgo. Law Rev., 1968-70, comment editor, 1969-70; originator Harold Leventhal Talks; contbr. articles on comml. law, 1st Amendment, appellate advocacy to law jours. Fellow Am. Bar Found.; mem. ABA (chmn. com. on leasing 2002—), Am. Law Inst. General civil litigation, Corporate, general, Environmental. Home: 1962 Upshur St NW Washington DC 20011-5354 Office: The Woodward Building 733 15th St NW Ste 719 Washington DC 20005 E-mail: huddlesone@aol.com.

HUDDLESTON, JOSEPH RUSSELL, judge; b. Glasgow, Ky., Feb. 5, 1937; s. Paul Russell and Laura Frances (Martin) H.; m. Heidi Wood, Sept. 12, 1959; children: Johanna, Lisa, Kristina. AB, Princeton U., 1959; JD, U. Va., 1962, LLM, 1997. Bar: Ky. 1962, U.S. Ct. Appeals (6th cir.) 1963, U.S. Supreme Ct. 1970. Ptnr. Huddleston Bros., Bowling Green, Ky., 1962-87; judge Warren Cir. Ct. Divsn. I, Bowling Green, Ky., 1987-91, Ky. Ct. appeals, Bowling Green, Ky., 1991—. Mem. Adv. Com. for Criminal Law Revision, 1969-71; exec. com. Ky. Crime Commn., 1972-77. Named Ky. Outstanding Trial Judge, 1990. Fellow Am. Bar Found.; mem. ABA, Ky. Bar Assn. (ho. of dels. 1971-80), Assn. Trial Lawyers Am. (state del. 1981-82), Ky. Acad. Trial Attys. (bd. govs. 1975-87, pres. 1978), Bowling Green Bar Assn. (pres. 1972), So. Ky. Estate Planning Coun. (pres. 1983), Rotary Internat. (Paul Harris fellow), Bowling Green-Warren County C. of C. (bd. dirs. 1987-91), Port Oliver Yacht Club (commodore). Democrat. Episcopalian. Home: 644 Minnie Way Bowling Green KY 42101-9210 Office: 1945 Scottsville Rd Ste 101 Bowling Green KY 42104-5824

HUDIAK, DAVID MICHAEL, academic administrator, lawyer; b. Darby, Pa., June 27, 1953; s. Michael Paul and Sophie Marie (Glowaski) H.; m. Veronica Ann Barbone, Aug. 28, 1982; children: David Michael, Christopher Andrew, Jonathan Joseph. BA, Haverford Coll., 1975; JD, U. Pa., 1978. Bar: Pa. 1979, U.S. Dist. Ct. (ea. dist.) Pa. 1979, NJ 1981, U.S. Dist. Ct. NJ 1981. Assoc. Jerome H. Ellis, Phila., 1978-79, Berson, Fineman & Bernstein, Phila., 1979-80; pvt. practice Aldan, Pa., 1980-81; dir. tng. paralegal program PJA Sch., Upper Darby, Pa., 1982—, acting dir., 1983-89, dir., 1989—; v.p. The PJA Sch., Inc., 1989—, bd. dirs.; v.p., sec.-treas., bd. dirs. 7900 West Chester Pike Corp., 1994—. Mem. staff Nat. Ctr. Ednl. Testing, Phila., 1982-87; instr. Villanova (Pa.) U., 1985. Mem. Havertown Choristers; active U. Pa. Light Opera Co., 1977—84; mem. 10th Synod Archdiocese of Phila., 2002; active mem., parish coun., lector, cantor St. Eugene Parish. Mem. ABA, Pa. Bar Assn., Founders Club Haverford Coll. Office: PJA Sch 7900 W Chester Pike Upper Darby PA 19082-1917

HUDNER, PHILIP, lawyer, rancher; b. San Jose, Calif., Feb. 24, 1931; s. Paul Joseph and Mary E. (Dooling) H.; m. Carla Raven, Aug. 6, 1966; children: Paul Theodor, Mary Carla. BA with great distinction, Stanford U., 1952, LL.B., 1955. Bar: Calif. 1955. Lawyer Pillsbury, Madison & Sutro, San Francisco, 1958—, ptnr., 1970-99, Botto Law Group, San Francisco, 1999—; rancher San Benito County, Calif., 1970—. Asst. editor: Stanford Law Rev., 1954-55; author articles on estate and trust law. Pres. Soc. Calif. Pioneers, 1976-78, Louise M. Davies Found., 2002—, Drum Found., 1985—. Served with U.S. Army, 1956-58. Fellow Am. Bar Found.; mem. Internat. Acad. Estate and Trust Law (steering com. 1974-75, exec. coun. 1980-85), San Benito County Saddle Horse Assn., Order of Malta, Phi Beta Kappa, Pacific Union Club, Lagunitas Country Club, Frontier Boys, Bohemian Club, Rancheros Visitadores. Democrat. Roman Catholic. Office: Botto Law Group 180 Montgomery St Fl 16 San Francisco CA 94104-3104 Fax: 415-364-0075. E-mail: phudner@bottolaw.com.

HUDSON, DENNIS LEE, lawyer, retired government official, arbitrator, educator; b. St. Louis, Jan. 5, 1936; s. Lewis Jefferson and Helen Mabel (Buchanan) H.; children: Karen Marie, Karla Sue, Mary Ashley. BA, U. Ill., 1958; JD, John Marshall Law Sch., 1972. Bar: Ill. 1972, U.S. Dist. Ct. (so. and no. dists.) Ill. 1972. Ins. IRS, Chgo., 1962-72; spl. agt. GSA, Chgo., 1972-78, spl. agt.-in-charge, 1978-83, regional insp. gen., 1983-87; supervisory spl. agt. Dept. Justice-GSA Task Force, Washington, 1978; arbitrator Circuit Ct. Cook County, Ill., 1987-93; prof. criminal justice Coll. of DuPage, Glen Ellyn, Ill., 1996—. Mem. adv. bd. Suburban Law Enforcement Acad., Glen Ellyn, Ill., 1999—; mem. adv. bd. campus police Coll. DuPage, Glen Ellyn, 1999—; deacon Grace Luth. Ch., La Grange, Ill., 1977—81; lay eucharistic min. All Sts. Episcopal Ch., Western Springs, Ill., 1999—; bd. govs. Theatre Western Springs, Ill., 1978—81, 1991—92; bd. dirs. Pendulum Theatre Co., Chgo., 2001—. With U.S. Army, 1959—61. John N. Jewett scholar, 1972, Am. Jurisprudence shcolar, 1972. Mem. ABA, Ill. Bar Assn. Office: Coll Dupage Bus & Svcs Div 22D St Lambert Rd Glen Ellyn IL 60137 E-mail: hudsond@cdnet.cod.edu.

HUDSON, JEFFREY REID, lawyer; b. Santa Monica, Calif., Mar. 15, 1952; s. Caswell Hadden and Donna Rita (Mazzulla) H.; children: Joan Louise, Reid Adams. BA, Claremont McKenna Coll., 1974; JD, Harvard U., 1978. Bar: Calif. 1978. Assoc. Gibson, Dunn & Crutcher, L.A., 1978-85, ptnr., 1986—. Banking, Commercial, contracts (including sales of goods; commercial financing), Finance. Office: Gibson Dunn & Crutcher 333 S Grand Ave Ste 4400 Los Angeles CA 90071-3197

HUDSON, LEIGH CARLETON, lawyer; b. Fort Scott, Kans., Apr. 18, 1948; s. Howard Carleton and Dorothy Delano H.; m. Marsha Ann Corn, July 30, 1971; children: Tyler William, Ryan Carleton. BS in Bus., Emporia State U., 1971; JD, Washburn U., 1975. Bar: Kans. 1975, U.S. Dist. Ct. Kans. 1975, Kansas Supreme Ct. 1975, U.S. Ct. Appeals (10th cir.) 1997. Mem. White & Hudson, Pittsburg, Kans., 1975-82, Hudson & Mullies, Fort Scott, 1982—. Contbr. articles to profl. jours. Fellow Am. Coll. Trial Lawyers (mem. state com. 1993); mem. Kans. Bar Assn. (bd. govs. 1981-87), Kans. Def. Assn. (pres. 1993), Am Bd. Trial Advs., Rotary. Personal injury (including property damage), Professional liability, Workers' compensation. Home: 601 Fairway Dr Fort Scott KS 66701-3130 Office: Hudson & Mullies LLC 102 S Main St Fort Scott KS 66701-1415

HUDSON, MANLEY O., JR., lawyer; b. Boston, June 25, 1932; s. Manley O. and Janet (Aldrich) H.; m. Olivia d'Ormesson, July 1, 1971 (dec. May 2000); children: Nicholas Aldrich, Antonia Maria Conchita. AB, Harvard U., 1953, LL.B., 1956. Bar: N.Y. 1964. Law clk. Justice Stanley Reed, U.S. Supreme Ct., Washington, 1956-57; assoc. Cleary, Gottlieb, Steen & Hamilton, 1958-68, ptnr., 1968—2001. Contbr. articles to profl. jours. Mem. Assn. Bar City N.Y., Coun. Fgn. Rels., Century Assn. Office: Cleary Gottlieb Steen & Hamilton City Place House 55 Basinghall St London EC2V 5EH England Business E-Mail: mhudson@cgsh.com.

HUDSON, ROBERT FRANKLIN, JR., lawyer; b. Miami, Fla., Sept. 20, 1946; s. Robert Franklin and Jane Ann (Reed) H.; m. Edith Mueller, June 19, 1971; children: Daniel Warren, Patrick Alexander. BSBA in Econs., U. Fla., 1968, JD, 1971; summer cert., U. London, 1970; LLM in Taxation, NYU, 1972. Bar: Fla. 1971, N.Y. 1975. Law clk. to judge Don N. Laramore U.S. Ct. Claims, Washington, 1972-73; assoc. Wender, Murase & White, N.Y.C., 1973-77; ptnr. Arky, Freed, Stearns et al, Miami, 1977-86, Baker & McKenzie, Miami, 1986—, mem. policy com., 1990-93, mem. client credit com., 1992-99, mng. ptnr. Miami office, 1996-98; N. Am. Tax Practice Group Mgmt. com., 2000—. Mem. adv. bd. Tax Mgmt., Inc., Washington, 1986—, Fgn. Investment N.Am., London, 1990-96; legal counsel to her majesty's Britanic Counsel, Miami. Author: Federal Taxation of Foreign Investment in U.S. Real Estate, 1986; contbr. articles to legal publs. Bd. dirs. Fla. Philharmonic, 1996-97, Performing Arts Ctr. Found., 1994—, vice chmn. 2000—; bd. dirs. Concert Assn. Fla., 1992—, exec. com., 1993-98, vice chmn., 1994-98; bd. dirs. Camillus House 2003-. Mem. ABA, Fla. Bar Assn. (chmn. tax sect. 1989-90, Outstanding Spkr. 1995), Internat. Fiscal Assn. (v.p. S.E. region U.S. br. 1985-92, exec. coun. 1987—), Inter-Am. Bar Assn., Internat. Bar Assn., Internat. Tax Planning Assn., Coll. Tax Lawyers, World Trade Ctr. (bd. dirs. 1992-94), S.E./U.S. Japan Assn., Japan Soc. South Fla. (chmn. pub. affairs com. 1991-93, bd. dirs. 1993-2000, treas. 1995-96, pres. 1996-99 Democrat. Methodist. Avocations: skiing, boating, photography, travel, hiking. Private international, Corporate taxation, Taxation, general. Office: Baker & McKenzie 1111 Brickell Ave Ste 1700 Miami FL 33131-3257 E-mail: bob.hudson@bakernet.com.

HUDSPETH, CHALMERS MAC, lawyer, educator; b. Denton, Tex., Oct. 18, 1919; s. Junia Evans and Ethel (Burns) H.; m. Demaris Eleanor De Lange, Jan. 30, 1945; children: Albert James, Thomas Richard, Helen Demaris. BA, Rice U., Houston, 1940; JD, U. Tex., 1946. Bar: Tex. 1946. Pvt. practice, Houston, 1947—; of counsel De Lange Hudspeth McConnell and Tibbets LLP, 1988—; asst. prof. law U. Tex. at Austin, 1946-47; lectr. govt. Rice U., 1947—, bd. govs., 1980-89, trustee, 1982-89, trustee emeritus, 1989—. Bd. dirs. Stewart Info. Services Corp., Stewart Title Guaranty Co. Contbr. articles to profl. jours. Mem. bi-racial com. Houston Ind. Sch. Dist., 1955-56; trustee, v.p. Brown Found., 1983-89. Served to lt. USNR, 1942-45. Fellow Am. Bar Found., Tex. Bar Found.; mem. ABA, Tex. Bar Assn., State Bar Tex. (dir. 1966-68, v.p. 1968-69), Houston Philos. Soc. (pres. 1964-65), Houston Com. on Fgn. Relations (chmn. 1973-74), Petroleum Club of Houston, Chancellors, Order of Coif, Phi Delta Phi. Federal civil litigation, Estate planning, Property, real (including real estate development, water). Office: De Lange Hudspeth McConnell & Tibbets LLP Eight Greenway Plz Ste 1300 Houston TX 77046

HUDSPETH, HARRY LEE, federal judge; b. Dallas, Dec. 28, 1935; s. Harry Ellis and Hattilee (Dudney) H.; m. Vicki Kathryn Round, Nov. 27, 1971; children: Melinda, Mary Kathryn. BA, U. Tex., Austin, 1955, JD, 1958. Bar: Tex. 1958. Trial atty. Dept. Justice, Washington, 1959-62; asst. U.S. atty. Western Dist. Tex., El Paso, 1962-69; assoc. Peticolas, Luscombe & Stephens, El Paso, 1969-77; U.S. magistrate El Paso, 1977-79; judge U.S. Dist. Ct. (we. dist.) Tex., El Paso, 1979—; chief judge U.S. Dist. Ct. (we. dist) Tex., El Paso, 1992-1999. Bd. dirs. Sun Carnival Assn., 1976, Met. YMCA El Paso, 1980-88. Mem. Travis Cnty Bar Assn., U. Tex. Ex-students Assn. (exec. coun. 1980-86), Chancellors, Order of Coif, Phi Beta Kappa. Democrat. Mem. Christian Ch. (Disciples Of Christ). Office: US Dist Ct We Dist Tex 903 San Jacinto Ste 440 Austin TX 78701

HUESTIS, BRADLEY JOHN, law educator; b. Homestead, Fla., Feb. 2, 1967; s. Alfred Victor and Ruth Mary Huestis; m. Ute Pittl, Feb. 14, 1992; children: Sarah Ann, Alexandra Marie, Kevin John. BS (disting. mil. grad.), Ariz. State U., 1989; JD cum laude, U. Ariz., 1995; LLM in Mil. Criminal Law, JAG Sch., Charlottesville, Va., 2001. Bar: Ariz. 1995, U.S. Ct. of Appeals for the Armed Forces 1996, Colo. 1997, U.S. Supreme Ct. 2001. Legal assistance atty., operational law atty., prosecutor XVIII Airborne Corps, Ft. Bragg, NC, 1995—97; task force legal advisor Task Force Tiger, Tuzla, Bosnia-Herzegovina, 1997; chief adminstrv. law and claims 1st Armored Divsn., Baumholder, Germany, 1997—98; def. counsel U.S. Army Trial Def. Svc., Baumholder, 1998—2000; prof. dept. criminal law JAG Sch., Charlottesville, 2001—. Contbr. , articles to profl. jours. Maj. U.S. Army, 1989—2002. Decorated Airborne Wings U.S. Army, Ranger Tab. Mem.: ABA, VFW (life), Nat. Assn. Criminal Def. Lawyers. Office: JAG Sch 600 Massie Rd Charlottesville VA 22911 E-mail: brad.huestis@us.army.mil.

HUETTNER, RICHARD ALFRED, lawyer; b. N.Y.C., Mar. 25, 1927; s. Alfred F. and Mary (Reilly) Huettner; m. Eunice Bizzell Dowd, Aug. 22, 1971; children: Jennifer Mary, Barbara H. Stead. Marine Engrs. License, N.Y. State Maritime Acad., 1947; BS, Yale U. Sch. Engring., 1949; JD, U. Pa., 1952. Bar: D.C. 1952, N.Y. 1954, U.S. Ct. Mil. Appeals 1953, U.S. Ct. Claims 1961, U.S. Supreme Ct. 1969, U.S. Ct. Appeals (fed. cir.) 1982, also other fed. cts, registered to practice U.S. Patent and Trademark Office 1957, Canadian Patent Office 1968. Engr. Jones & Laughlin Steel Corp., 1954-55; assoc. atty. firm Kenyon & Kenyon, N.Y.C, 1955-61, mem. firm, 1961-96, of counsel, 1996-98; specialist patent, trademark and copyright law. Trustee N.J. Shakespeare Festival, 1972-79, sec., 1977-79; trustee Overlook Hosp., Summit, N.J., 1978-84, 86-89, vice chmn. bd. trustees, 1980-82, chmn. bd. trustees, 1982-84; trustee Overlook Found., 1981-89 , chmn. bd. trustees, 1986-89, emeritus trustee, 1991; trustee Colonial Symphony Orch., Madison, N.J., 1972-82, v.p. bd. trustees 1974-76. pres. 1976-79; chmn. bd. overseers N.J. Consortium for Performing Arts, 1972-74; mem. Yale U. Council, 1978-81; bd. dirs. Yale Communications Bd., 1978-80; chmn. bd. trustees Center for Addictive Illnesses, Morristown, N.J., 1979-82; rep. Assn. Yale Alumni, 1975-80, chmn. com. undergrad. admissions, 1976-78, bd. govs., 1976-80, chmn. bd. govs., 1978-80; chmn. Yale Alumni Schs. Com. N.Y., 1972-78; assoc. fellow Silliman Coll., Yale U., 1976—; bd. dirs., exec. com. Yale U. Alumni Fund, 1978-81; mem. Yale Class of 1949 Council, 1980—; bd. dirs. Overlook Health Systems, 1984—. Served from midshipman to lt. USNR, 1945-47, 1952-54; cert. JAGC 1953; Res. ret. Recipient Yale medal, 1983, Disting. Svc. to Yale Class of 1949 award, 1989, Yale Sci. and Engring. Meritorious Svc. award, 1992. Fellow: AAAS, N.Y. Bar Found.; mem.: ABA (life), Fed. Bar Coun., Yale Sci. and Engring. Assn. (v.p. 1973—75, pres. 1975—78, exec. bd. 1972—79), Am. Judicature Soc., Internat. Patent and Trademark Assn., Ret. Officers Assn. (life), N.Y. Intellectual Property Law Assn. (life; chmn. com. mtgs. 1961—64, chmn. com. econ. matters 1966—69, 1972—74), Am. Intellectual Property Law Assn. (life), N.Y. County Lawyers Assn., N.Y. Acad. Scis., Assn. Bar City N.Y., N.Y. State Bar Assn., Yale (N.Y.C.); Yale of Central N.J. (Summit) (trustee 1973-88, pres. 1975-77), Morris County Golf (Convent, N.J.); The Graduates (New Haven). Intellectual property, Patent, Trademark and copyright. Home: 20 Chadwell Place Morristown NJ 07960-6945 Fax: 973-455-7165. E-mail: huettnerrichard@aol.com.

HUFF, BARBARA KAY, lawyer; b. Clarinda, Iowa, Jan. 19, 1957; d. George Robert and Onalea Sharlene Huff; m. Jonathan Kahn, Apr. 8, 1989. BA, Reed Coll., 1979; JD, U. Pa., 1982. Bar: Wash. 1984, N.Y. 1986, Kans. 1989. Law clk. U.S. Ct. Appeals (9th cir.), San Francisco, 1982-83; assoc. Karr, Tuttle and Koch, Seattle, 1984-85; staff atty. Legal Aid Soc., N.Y.C., 1985-88; asst. pub. defender Kansas Indigent Def. Svcs., Topeka, 1989, Olathe, 1989-91; pvt. practice Lawrence, Kans., 1991—. Mem. adj. faculty Kans. Defender Project, Law Sch. U. Kans., Lawrence, 1992-97. Mem. ACLU (chpt. pres. 1996-97), Calif. Water Color Assn. (signature mem.). Civil rights, General civil litigation, Criminal. Office: 1040 New Hampshire St Lawrence KS 66044-3044

HUFFAKER, GREGORY DORIAN, JR., lawyer; b. Phila., Nov. 30, 1944; s. Gregory Dorian Sr. and Suzanne (Adams) H.; m. Katrina Morris, Aug. 28, 1976; 1 child, Gregory D. III. BA, Columbia U., 1973; JD, Harvard U., 1976. Bar: N.Mex. 1977; U.S. Dist. Ct. N.Mex. 1977; U.S. Ct. Appeals (10th cir.) 1978, U.S. Supreme Ct. 1985. Law clk. assoc. justice John Paul Stevens, U.S. Supreme Ct., Washington, 1976-77; atty. Poole, Kelly & Ramo, Albuquerque and Santa Fe, 1977-93; atty. Huffaker & Conway, P.C., Santa Fe, 1993—; mem. com. admissions & grievances U.S. Dist. Ct., N.Mex., 1994-2002, chmn., 2000-02; spl. asst. atty. gen. New Mexico, 1987-88. Author: (with others) Your New Lawyer, 1992. Rep. Coalition Albuquerque Neighborhoods, 1984; active Albuquerque Com. Fgn. Relations, 1983-91; com. mem. N.Mex. First, Albuquerque, 1988-2000; mem. com. Equal Access to Justice Fund, 1998-2000. 1st lt. U.S. Army, 1968-71. Mem. ABA, Rocky Mountain Mineral Law Inst. Federal civil litigation, Environmental, Natural resources. Office: Huffaker & Conway PO Box 1868 Santa Fe NM 87504-1868

HUFFMAN, GREGORY SCOTT COMBEST, lawyer; b. Austin, Tex., Dec. 19, 1946; s. Calvin Combest and Olive Agnes (Weaver) H.; m. Mary L. Murphy, Feb. 1, 1986. Student, Stanford U., France, 1966—67; BA in History with great distinction, Stanford U., 1969; postgrad., London Sch. of Econs., 1971—72; JD, Harvard U., 1973. Bar: Tex. 1973, U.S. Dist. Cts. Tex. 1974, U.S. Ct. Appeals (5th cir.) 1975, U.S. Supreme Ct. 1976. From assoc. to sr. ptnr. Thompson & Knight, Dallas, 1973—, also dir. Chief editor (monographs) Texas Free Enterprise and Antitrust Act, 1984-90, Texas Antitrust and Related Statutes, 1991—. Pres. Northern Hills Neighborhood Assn., 1980; bd. dirs. Common Cause of Tex., 1979-81, Love Field Citizens Action Commn., 1980-83, Appleseed Found., 1996-2001; adminstrv. chmn., bd. dirs. Tex. Appleseed, 1996-2001; active Tex. Supreme Ct. Adv. Com. on Professionalism. Fellow Tex. Bar Found., Dallas Bar Found.; mem. ABA (antitrust and litigation sect.), Tex. Bar Assn. (antitrust and litigation sect., chmn. unlawful practice law com. 1981-83, chmn. lawyer referral svc. com. 1982-83, bd. legal specialization 1974-77, chmn. antitrust and bus. litigation sect. 1991-92, bd. dirs. 1983—, task force on unauthorized practice of law, author of reports, presdl. citation 2000, cert. of merit 2001), Dallas Bar Assn. (antitrust sect., sec.-treas. 1981, chmn. unauthorized practice law com. 1979, chmn. lawyer referral svc. com. 1980-81, chmn. profl. svcs. com. 1986-87, chmn. spkrs. com. 1999-2000, chmn. CLE com. 2001, bd. dirs. antitrust sect. 1981, 89-2002, bd. dirs. litigation sect. 1988), Harvard Law Sch. Assn. Tex. (pres. 1987-88), Tower Club Dallas, Phi Beta Kappa, Sigma Alpha Epsilon. Methodist. Antitrust, Federal civil litigation, State civil litigation. Home: 8234 Garland Rd Dallas TX 75218-4417 Office: Thompson & Knight 1700 Pacific Ave Ste 3300 Dallas TX 75201-4693

HUFFMAN, RICHARD LEE, lawyer; b. Fairfield, Conn., Sept. 6, 1943; s. H. Lee and Anna K. (Johnson) H.; m. Valrae Reynolds, Sept. 14, 1974; children— Elizabeth, Margaret. A.B., Brown U., 1965; J.D., Emory U., 1968. Bar: Ga. 1968, U.S Dist. Ct. (no. dist.) Ga. 1970, N.Y. 1971, U.S. Dist. Ct. (ea. dist.) N.Y. 1972, U.S. Ct. Appeals (2d cir.) 1975, U.S. Dist. Ct. (so. dist.) N.Y. 1979, U.S. Supreme Ct. 1982. Asst. corp. counsel City of N.Y., 1973-75; asst. U.S. atty. U.S. Atty.'s Office, Eastern Dist. N.Y., 1975-79; ptnr. Baden Kramer, Huffman & Brodsky, N.Y.C., 1979—2002, Fox Horan & Camirini, N.Y.C., 2002—. Pres., First Unitarian Congregational Soc., Bklyn., 1984—86; bd. dirs. Bklyn. Legal Services, 1978-81, 2001—. Reginald Heber Smith fellow, 1968-70. Mem. Assn. Bar City of N.Y. Federal civil litigation, Environmental, General practice. Office: Fox Horan & Camerini 825 3d Ave New York NY 10022

HUFFMAN, ROSEMARY ADAMS, lawyer, corporate executive; b. Orlando, Fla., Oct. 18, 1939; d. Elmer Victor and Esther (Weber) Adams; divorced; 1 child, Justin Adams Fruth. A.B. in Econs., Ind. U., 1959, J.D., 1962; LL.M., U. Chgo., 1967. Bar: Ind. 1962, Fla. 1963. Dep. prosecutor Marion County, Ind., 1963; ct. adminstr. Ind. Supreme Ct., 1967-68; pro-tem judge Marion County Mcpl. Ct., 1969-70; jud. coordinator Ind. Criminal Justice Planning Agy., 1969-70; dir. ctr. for Jud. Edn., Inc., 1970-73; pub. Jud. Xchange, 1972-73; instr. bus. law Purdue U., Indpls., 1962-63, Ind. U., Indpls., 1963-64; asst. Ind. Jud. Council, 1965; legis. intern Ford Found., 1965; sole practice, Indpls., 1962— ; pres., owner Abacus, Inc., Indpls., 1980—. Mem. Ind. Bar Assn., Fla. Bar Assn. Home and Office: 6630 E 56th St Indianapolis IN 46226-1781

HUFFSTETLER, PALMER EUGENE, lawyer; b. Shelby, N.C., Dec. 21, 1937; s. Daniel S. and Ethel (Turner) H.; m. Mary Ann Beam, Aug. 9, 1958; children: Palmer Eugene, Ben Beam, Brian Tad. BA, Wake Forest U., 1959, JD, 1961. Bar: N.C. 1961. Practiced in, Kings Mountain, N.C., 1961-62, Raleigh, N.C., 1962-64; with State Farm Ins. Co., Orlando, Fla., 1962; gen. legal counsel Carolina Freight Corp., Cherryville, N.C., 1964-93, sec., 1969-90, sr. v.p., 1969-89, exec. v.p., 1985-93, pres., 1993-95; ret., 1995; pres., CEO Blue Chip Inc., 1997-99. Author, composer: Senior Man on Carolina Line, Fifty Years Ago. Chmn. Cherryville Zoning Bd. Adjustment, 1967-70; active N.C. Gasoline and Oil Insp. Bd., 1974-76; class chmn. Wake Forest Coll. Fund, 1971-79, decade chmn., 1981-82; governing body, chmn. adminstrv. com. So. Piedmont Health Systems Agy., 1975-77; mem. Cherryville Econ. Devel. Commn., 1982-87, Cherryville Econ. Devel. Com., 1995-97; pres. Cherryville Devel. Corp., 1986—; bd. dirs. C. Grier Beam Truck Mus., 1982-2002, pres. 1982-96; bd. dirs. Schiele Mus., Gastonia, N.C., 1985-88, Gaston Meml. Hosp., 1990-93, vice-chmn. bd.; active N.C. Gov.'s Hwy. Safety Commn., 1985-88, Gov.'s Bus. Com., N.C., 1993-95; v.p. Ctrl. and So. Rate Bur., 1984-89; trustee Brevard Coll., 1987-93. Mem. N.C. State Bar, N.C. Bar Assn. (mem. adminstrv. bd. 1965-69, 71-72, chmn. adminstrv. bd., trustee 1970-73, fin. com. 1994-2002). Methodist. Corporate, general, Labor (including EEOC, Fair Labor Standards Act, labor-management relations, NLRB, OSHA), Transportation. Home: 2141 Fairways Dr Cherryville NC 28021-2115

HUFSTEDLER, SETH MARTIN, lawyer; b. Dewar, Okla., Sept. 20, 1922; s. Seth Martin and Myrtle (Younts) H.; m. Shirley Ann Mount, Aug. 16, 1949; 1 child, Steven. BA magna cum laude, U. So. Calif., 1944; LL.B., Stanford U., 1949. Bar: Calif. 1950. Pvt. practice, L.A.; assoc. Lillick, Geary & McHose, 1950-51; with Charles E. Beardsley, 1951-53; ptnr. Beardsley, Hufstedler & Kemble, 1953-81, Hufstedler, Miller, Carlson & Beardsley, 1981-88, Hufstedler, Kaus & Ettinger, L.A., 1988-94; Hufstedler & Kaus, 1994-95; sr. of counsel Morrison & Foerster LLP, 1995—. Mem. Calif. Jud. Coun., 1977—78. Legis. editor Stanford U. Law Rev., 1948-49. Sec. regional planning coun. United Way, 1971-75; co-chmn. Pub. Commn. County Govt., L.A., 1975-76, 89-92; trustee AEFC Pension Fund, 1978-82; mem. Calif Citizens Commn. on Tort Reform, 1976-77; bd. visitors Stanford Law Sch., chmn., 1972-73. Lt. (j.g.) USNR, 1943-46. Mem. ABA (chmn. action commn. to reduce ct costs and delay 1979-81, mem. coun. sr. bar div. 1986-89, chmn. 1987-88), Los Angeles County Bar Assn. (trustee 1963-65, 66-70, pres. 1969-70, Shattuck Price award 1976), State Bar Calif. (bd. govs. 1971-74, pres. 1973-74, Bernard Witlan medal 2002), Am. Judicature Soc., Am. Law Inst., Am. Coll. Trial Lawyers, Am. Bar Found. (bd. govs. 1975-86, pres. 1982-84), Chancery Club (pres. 1974-75), Order of Coif, Phi Beta Kappa, Phi Kappa Phi, Delta Tau Delta. Democrat. Antitrust, General civil litigation, Insurance. Office: Morrison & Foerster 555 W 5th St Ste 3500 Los Angeles CA 90013-1024

HUFSTEDLER, SHIRLEY MOUNT (MRS. SETH M. HUFSTEDLER), lawyer, former federal judge; b. Denver, Aug. 24, 1925; d. Earl Stanley and Eva (Von Behren) Mount; m. Seth Martin Hufstedler, Aug. 16, 1949; 1 son, Steven Mark. BBA, U. N.Mex., 1945, LLD (hon.), 1972; LLB, Stanford U., 1949; LLD (hon.), U. Wyo., 1970, Gonzaga U., 1970, Occidental Coll., 1971, Tufts U., 1974, U. So. Calif., 1976, Georgetown U., 1976, U. Pa., 1976, Columbia U., 1977, U. Mich., 1979, Yale U., 1981, Rutgers U., 1981, Claremont U. Ctr., 1981, Smith Coll., 1982, Syracuse U., 1983, Mt. Holyoke Coll., 1985; PHH (hon.), Hood Coll., 1981, Hebrew Union Coll., 1986, Tulane U., 1988. Bar: Calif. 1950. Mem. firm Beardsley, Hufstedler & Kemble, L.A., 1951-61; practiced in L.A., 1961; judge Superior Ct., County L.A., 1961-66; justice Ct. Appeals 2d dist., 1966-68; circuit judge U.S. Ct. Appeals 9th cir., 1968-79; sec. U.S. Dept. Edn., 1979-81; ptnr. Hufstedler & Kaus, L.A., 1981-95; sr. of counsel Morrison & Foerster LLP, L.A., 1995—. Emeritus dir. Hewlett Packard Co., US West, Inc.; bd. dirs. Harman Internat. Industries. Mem. staff Stanford Law Rev, 1947-49; articles and book rev. editor, 1948-49. Trustee Calif. Inst. Tech., Occidental Coll., 1972-89, Aspen Inst., Colonial Williamsburg Found., 1976-93, Constl. Rights Found., 1978-80, Nat. Resources Def. Coun., 1983-85, Carnegie Endowment for Internat. Peace, 1983-94; bd. dirs. John T. and Catherine MacArthur Found., 1983—2002; chair U.S. Commn. on Immigration Reform, 1996-97. Named Woman of Yr. Ladies Home Jour., 1976; recipient UCLA medal, 1981. Fellow Am. Acad. Arts and Scis.; mem. ABA (medal 1995), L.A. Bar Assn., Town Hall, Am. Law Inst. (coun. 1974-84), Am. Bar Found., Women Lawyers Assn. (pres. 1957-58), Am. Judicature Soc., Assn. of the Bar of City of N.Y., Coun. on Fgn. Rels. (emeritus), Order of Coif. Appellate, Private international. Office: Morrison & Foerster LLP 555 W 5th St Ste 3500 Los Angeles CA 90013-1024

HUG, PROCTER RALPH, JR., federal judge; b. Reno, Mar. 11, 1931; s. Procter Ralph and Margaret (Beverly) H.; m. Barbara Van Meter, Apr. 4, 1954; children: Cheryl Ann English, Procter J., Elyse Marie Pasha. BS, U. Nev., 1953; LLB, JD, Stanford U., 1958. Bar: Nev. 1958. Mem. Springer, McKissick & Hug, 1958—63, Woodburn, Wedge, Blakey, Folsom & Hug, Reno, 1963—77; U.S. judge 9th Circuit Ct. Appeals, Reno, 1977—2002, U.S. chief judge, 1996—2000; sr. judge, 2002—. Dep. atty. gen. State of Nev.; v.p. dir. Nev. Tel. & Tel. Co., 1958—77. Mem. bd. regents U. Nev., 1962—71, chmn., 1969—71; bd. visitors Stanford Law Sch.; mem. Nev. Humanities Commn., 1988—94; vol. civilian aid sect. U.S. Army, 1977. Lt. (j.g.) USNR, 1953—55. Named Alumnus of Yr., U. Nev., 1988; recipient Outstanding Alumnus award, 1967, Disting. Nevadan citation, 1982. Mem.: ABA (bd. govs. 1976—78), Stanford Law Soc. Nev. (past pres.), U. Nev. Alumni Assn. (past pres.), Nat. Assn. Coll. and Univ. Attys. (past mem. exec. bd.), Nat. Judicial Coll. (bd. dirs. 1977—78, 2001—), Am. Judicare Soc. (bd. dirs. 1975—77). Office: US Ct Appeals 9th Cir US Courthouse Fed Bldg 400 S Virginia St Ste 708 Reno NV 89501-2181

HUGE, HARRY, lawyer; b. Deshler, Nebr., Sept. 16, 1937; s. Arthur and Dorothy (Vor de Strasse) H.; m. Reba Kinne, July 2, 1960; 1 child, Theodore. AB, Nebr. Wesleyan U., 1959; JD, Georgetown U., 1963. Bar: Ill. 1963, D.C. 1965, S.C. 1985. Assoc. Chapman & Cutler, Chgo., 1963-65; from assoc. to ptnr. Arnold & Porter, Washington, 1965-76; sr. ptnr. Donovan, Leisure, Rogovin, Huge & Schiller, Washington, 1976-92, Shea and Gould Internat., Washington, 1992-94; ptnr. Powell Goldstein Frazer & Murphy, Washington, 1995—2002, Harry Huge Law Firm LLP , 2002—. Chmn. Oncostasis, Inc., Charleston, S.C.; chmn., trustee United Mine Workers Health and Retirement Funds, 1973-78; chmn. bd. dirs. Hollings Cancer Ctr. Med. U. S.C., Charleston; trustee Shook and Fletcher Asbestos Settlement Trust, Washington, 2002—. Contbr. articles to legal jours. Pres. Voter Edn. Project, Atlanta, 1974-78; mem. Pres.'s Gen. Adv. Com. Arms Control, 1977-81; trustee Nebr. Wesleyan U., 1978—; mem. task force local govt. Greater Washington Rsch. Ctr., 1981-82; spl. master Friends for All Children, Inc., U.S. Dist. Ct. D.C.; mem. Nat. Tobacco Settlement Arbitration Panel, Durham, N.C. With U.S. Army, 1960; officer USNG, 1960-65. Mem.: ABA (co-chmn. legis. com. litigation sect. 1981), Inst. Human Virology (bd. dirs. U. Md. Balt. 1996—2001), D.C. Bar Assn. (bd. profl. responsibility 1976—81). Federal civil litigation, Corporate, general, General practice. Home: 25 E Battery St Charleston SC 29401-2740 Office: Harry Huge Law Firm LLP 901 Ninth St NW Washington DC 20004-2505 Office Fax: 202-318-1261.

HUGGARD, JOHN PARKER, lawyer; b. Midland, Tex., Dec. 7, 1945; s. Peter John and Dorothy (Sampson) H. BA, U. N.C., 1971, JD, 1975; MA, Duke U., 1989. Bar: N.C. 1975, U.S. Dist. Ct. (ea. dist.) N.C. 1975, U.S. Ct. Appeals (4th cir.) 1975, U.S. Tax Ct. 1976, U.S. Ct. Claims 1976, U.S. Ct. Customs 1977, U.S. Ct. Mil. Appeals 1977, U.S. Dist. Ct. D.C. 1979, U.S. Supreme Ct. 1979, U.S. Ct. Internat. Trade 1981, U.S. Ct. Customs and Patent Appeals 1982; cert. fin. planner; chreterd fin. cons. Sr. ptnr. Hensley & Overby, Raleigh, N.C., 1975-88, Huggard, Obiol & Blake, PLLC, Raleigh, 1988—; alumni disting. prof. Law and Econs. N.C. State U., Raleigh, 1975—. Author: The Adminstration of Decedents' Estates in North Carolina, 1985, North Carolina Estate Settlement Guidebook, 1995, Living Trust/Living Hell-Why You Should Avoid Living Trusts, 1998, Investing with Variable Annuities, 2002; contbr. articles to profl. publs. With USMC, 1964-68, capt. USNR. Mem. ABA, Am. Bus. Law Assn., Assn. Trial Lawyers Am., N.C. Bar Assn., N.C. Acad. Trial Lawyers, N.C. Coll. Advocacy, Acad. Outstanding Tchrs., Wake County Bar Assn., Phi Beta Kappa. Democrat. Roman Catholic. Avocation: flying. Finance, Military, Probate (including wills, trusts). Home: 8621 Kings Arms Way Raleigh NC 27615-2029 Office: Huggard Obiol & Blake PLLC 124 Saint Marys St Raleigh NC 27605-1809

HUGHES, BYRON WILLIAM, lawyer, oil exploration company executive; b. Clarksdale, Miss., Nov. 8, 1945; s. Byron B. and Francis C. (Turner) H.; m. Sarah Eileen Goodwin, June 23, 1973 (div.); children: Jennifer Eileen, Stephanie Ann. BA, U. Miss., 1968; JD, Jackson Sch. Law (now Miss. Coll. Law), 1971. Bar: Miss. 1971, U.S. Supreme Ct. 1975; cert. real estate appraiser. Atty., abstractor Miss. Hwy. Dept., 1971-76; atty., ind. landman Byron Hughes Oil Exploration Co., Jackson, Miss., 1976-92; prosecutor, child support enforcement atty. Miss. Dept. Human Svcs., 1992—. Tchr. high sch.; real estate broker. Mem. ABA, Miss. Bar Assn., Hinds County Bar Assn., Bolivar County Bar Assn., Am. Judicature Soc., Nat. Assn. Real Estate Appraisers, Miss. Child Support Assn., Miss. Assn. Petroleum Landmen, Ala. Landmen Assn., Black Warrior Basin Petroleum Landmen Assn., Am. Assn. Petroleum Landmen (cert. profl. landman 1991), Ole Miss. Alumni Assn., Miss. Coll. Alumni Assn., Miss. Art Assn., Cleve. Exch. Club, Sigma Delta Kappa. Methodist. Oil, gas, and mineral, Family and matrimonial, Property, real (including real estate development, water). Home and Office: PO Box 1485 Jackson MS 39215-1485

HUGHES, DAVID ANDREW, lawyer; b. N.Y.C., Jan. 20, 1963; s. John Earl Hughes and Dolores W. Carano; m. Karen Lee Kaplan, Jan. 12, 1985; children: Nicole, Hunter. B in Mech. Engring., Vanderbilt U., 1984, JD, 1991; MS in Mgmt., Troy State U., 1987. Bar: Tenn. 1991, Ark. 1996, U.S. Dist. Ct. (mid. dist.) Tenn. 1996, Ga. 1997, U.S. Dist. Ct. (no. and mid. dists.) Ga. 1997, U.S. Dist. Ct. (ea. dist.) Tenn. 2002. Lawyer Dubois & Mounger, Columbia, Tenn., 1991—95, Ogletree Deakins, Atlanta, 1995—. Grad. Leadership Maury, Maury County, Tenn.; active Boy Scouts Am. Capt. USAF, 1984—88. Mem.: ABA, Ark. Bar Assn., Tenn. Bar Assn., Ga. Bar Assn. Avocation: coaching youth sports. Labor (including EEOC, Fair Labor Standards Act, labor-management relations, NLRB, OSHA), General civil litigation. Office: Ogletree Deakins Nash Smoak & Stewart Ste 2100 600 Peachtree St Atlanta GA 30308

HUGHES, KEVIN JOHN, lawyer; b. St. Cloud, Minn., July 27, 1936; s. Fred James and Valeria Mary (Spaniol) H.; m. Joanne Margaret Robertson, July 27, 1936; children: Anne, Thomas, Jennifer, James, Emily. BA in Philosophy and Polit. Sci., St. John's U., Collegeville, Minn., 1958; JD, U. Minn., 1962. Bar: Minn. 1962, U.S. Dist. Ct. Minn. 1963, U.S. Ct. Appeals (8th cir.) 1973, U.S. Supreme Ct. 1973. Law clerk Minn. Supreme Ct., 1962-63; assoc. Fred J. Hughes Atty., St. Cloud, 1963; ptnr. Hughes Thoreen & Sullivan, Hughes Thoreen Mathews & Knapp, St. Cloud, 1964-94, Hughes Mathews PA, St. Cloud, 1994—. Bd. dirs. Ctrl. Minn. Cmty. Found., United Way, YMCA. 1st lt. U.S. Army, 1959. Mem.: Nat. Health Lawyers Assn., Minn. State Bar, St. Cloud C. of C. General civil litigation, Commercial, contracts (including sales of goods; commercial financing), Labor (including EEOC, Fair Labor Standards Act, labor-management relations, NLRB, OSHA). Home: 295 Waite Ave S Saint Cloud MN 56301-7335 Office: Hughes Mathews PO Box 548 Saint Cloud MN 56302-0548 E-mail: khughes@hughesmathews.com.

HUGHES, KEVIN PETER, lawyer; b. N.Y.C., Sept. 8, 1943; s. George and Mae (Kilduff) H.; m. Margaret Ellen Comiskey, Nov. 18, 1967; children: Erin, Cara, Deirdre. BA, Manhattan Coll., 1965; JD, St. John's U., 1968. Bar: N.Y. 1968, U.S. Dist. Ct. (so. dist., ea. dist.) N.Y. 1971, U.S. Ct. Appeals (2d cir.) 1975, U.S. Supreme Ct. 1980. Law clerk to justice N.Y. Ct. Appeals, Albany, 1968-70; assoc. Weil, Gotshal & Manges, N.Y.C., 1970-77, ptnr., 1977—. Arbitrator Am. Arbitration Assn., N.Y.C., 1984—. Mem. ABA (litigation sect.), N.Y. State Bar Assn., Plandome Country Club (Manhasset, N.Y.), Eagle Creek Golf and Country Club (Naples, Fla.) Republican. Roman Catholic. Avocations: skiing, golf. Bankruptcy, Federal civil litigation, State civil litigation. Home: 27 Chapel Rd Manhasset NY 11030-3601 Office: Weil Gotshal & Manges 767 5th Ave Fl Concl New York NY 10153-0119 E-mail: kevin.hughes@weil.com.

HUGHES, LYNN NETTLETON, federal judge; b. Houston, Sept. 9, 1941; m. Olive (Allen). BA, U. Ala., 1963; JD, U. Tex., 1968; LLM, U. Va., 1992. Bar: Tex., 1966. Pvt. practice, Houston, 1966-79; judge (Dist. Ct.) Tex., Houston, 1979-85; U.S. dist. judge (So. Dist.) Tex., Houston, 1985—. Adj. prof. South Tex. Coll. Law, 1973—, U. Tex., 1990-91, 2000-01; Tex. del. Nat. Conf. State Trial Judges, 1983-85; cons. Tex. Jud. Budget Bd., 1984; lectr. Tex. Coll. Judiciary, 1983; mem. task force on revision rules of civil procedure Supreme Ct. Tex., 1993-94; cons. on constn. Moldova, 1993, European Community, 1989, Ukraine, 1995, Romania, 1996, Albania, 1997; mem. jud. adv. bd. Law and Econs. Ctr., George Mason U., 1999—. Mem. adv. bd. Houston Jour. Internat. Law, 1981—, chmn., 1989-99. Trustee Rift Valley Rsch. Mission, 1978—; mem. St. Martin's Episcopal Ch.; dir. Houston World Affairs Coun., 1997—, co-chair 1999-00. Mem. ABA, FBA (bd. dirs. Houston chpt. 1986-89), Am. Law Inst., Maritime Law Assn., Houston Bar Assn., Tex. State Bar (nominations com. jud. sect. 1983, court cost, delay and efficiency com. 1981-90, vice chmn. 1984-86, selection, compensation and tenure state judges com. 1981-85, vice chmn. 1982-83, liaison with law schs. com. 1987-92, plain lang. com. 1989-96), Am. Judicature Soc., Am. Soc. Legal History (com. on fgn. rels., chmn. 2003—), Am. Anthrop Assn., Houston Com. in Foreign Relations (chmn. 2003-2004), Houston Philos. Soc. (mem. exec. com. 2000-03), Coun. on Fgn. Rels., Am. Inns of Ct. XV (pres. 1986-92). Office: US Ct Hse 11122 515 Rusk St Houston TX 77002-2605 Home: PO Box 61565 Houston TX 77208

HUGHES, MARCIA MARIE, lawyer, consultant, motivational speaker; b. Montrose, Colo., Oct. 12, 1949; d. John Atkinson and Catherine Marie (Buskirk) H.; m. James Terrell, Dec. 26, 1990; 1 child, Julia. BA, U. Colo., 1972; JD with honors, George Washington U., 1976; MA in Psychology, U. Colo. Bar: Colo. 1976, U.S. Dist. Ct. Colo. 1976, U.S. Ct. Appeals (10th cir.) 1976. Adminstrv. aide Bur. Accounts Treasury Dept., Washington, 1972-73; legis. aide to Congresswoman Patricia Schroeder Washington, 1973-74; legal intern Consumer Product Info. Ctr., Washington, 1974-75, Media Access Project, Washington, 1975-76; law clk. to Hon. William E. Doyle U.S. Ct. Appeals (10th cir.), Denver, 1976-77; asst. atty. gen. Colo. Atty. Gen.'s Office, Denver, 1977-79; spl. asst. to dir. Colo. Dept. Health, Denver, 1979-81; assoc. Rothgerber, Appel, Powers & Johnson, Denver, 1982-85; ptnr. Cockrel, Quinn & Creighton, Denver, 1985-87; pres. Hughes, Duncan & Dingess, Denver, 1987-90, Marcia M. Hughes, P.C., Denver, 1990-99, Collaborative Growth, L.L.C., 1993—; exec. dir. Pntrs. Mentoring Assn., 1998-2000. Pub. spkr. on orgnl. growth, interpersonal dynamics, negotiation strategies, spirit in the workplace. Bd. dirs. Jefferson County chpt. ARC, 1999-2000, Influence Denver X, Capitol Hill United Neighborhoods, 1977-86; v.p. Nat. Assn. Neighborhoods, 1980-81; bd. dirs. Ecumenical Housing Corp., 1982-85; participant Leadership Denver, 1984-85; active Big Sisters Colo., Denver, 1987-93; vice chmn. Kempe Children's Found., bd. dirs., 1991-95, chair pub. affairs com.; bd. dirs. Colo. Found. Children and Families, 1993-96, pres., 1995-96; apptd. mem. family issues task force Colo. Legislature. Named one of Outstanding Young Women in Colo., 1980, Big Sister of Yr., 1991. Mem. Colo. Profl. Soc. on Abuse of Children (bd. dirs.), Colo. Bar Assn. (chmn. environ. sect., officer 1982-86), Colo. Hazardous Waste Com. (chmn. 1982-85). Avocations: writing, hiking, gardening, reading. Alternative dispute resolution, Environmental, Family and matrimonial. Home: PO Box 10758 Golden CO 80401-0610

HUGHES, MARY KATHERINE, lawyer; b. July 16, 1949; d. John Chamberlain and Marjorie (Anstey) H.; m. Andrew H. Eker, July 7, 1982. BBA cum laude, U. Alaska, 1971; JD, Willamette U., 1974; postgrad., Heriot-Watt U., Edinburgh, Scotland, 1971. Bar: Alaska 1975. Ptnr. Hughes, Thorsness, Gantz, Powell & Brundin, Anchorage, 1974-95; mcpl. atty. Municipality of Anchorage, 1995-2000; of counsel Hughes, Thorsness, Powell, Huddleston & Bauman, 2001—. Trustee Willamette U., 1997—; bd. visitors WUCL, 1978—2001; bd. dirs. Alaska Repertory Theatre, 1986—88, pres., 1987—88; commr. Alaska Code Revision Commn., 1987—94; active U. Alaska Found., 1985—, trustee, 1990—; bd. visitors U. Alaska, Fairbanks, 1994—2002, bd. regents, 2002—; bd. dirs. Anchorage Econ. Devel. Corp., 1989—, chmn., 1994; active Providence Anchorage Adv. Coun., 1993—, Providence Alaska Found., 1998—, chair, 2002—; lawyer rep. 9th Cir. Jud. Conf., 1995—2000; pres., trustee Alaska Bar Found., 1984—98, trustee, 2001—. Fellow: Am. Bar Found.; mem.: Internat. Mcpl. Lawyers Assn. (state chair 1995—96, regional v.p. 1997—2000), Anchorage Assn. Women Lawyers (pres. 1976—77), Alaska Bar Assn. (bd. govs. 1981—84, pres. 1983—84), Soroptimists (pres. 1986—87), Delta Theta Phi. Republican. Roman Catholic. Home: 1592 Coffey Ln Anchorage AK 99501-4977 E-mail: mkhughes@acsalaska.net.

HUGHES, ROY FREDERICKS, lawyer; b. Honolulu, Nov. 11, 1947; s. John Harold and Marcelle (Figueroa) H.; m. Heidi Catil Schroder, Aug. 18, 1973; children: Hallie, Nathan, Benjamen. BA, Ripon Coll., 1970; JD, Marquette U., 1976. Bar: Wis. 1976, Hawaii 1976, U.S. Dist. Ct. Hawaii 1976. Assoc. Libkuman, Ventura, Honolulu, 1976-82, ptnr., 1982-87; sole practice Honolulu, 1987—. Mem. Assn. Trial Lawyers Am., Def. Research Inst., Fedn. Ins. and Corp. Counsel, Hawaii Assn. Def. Attys. State civil litigation, Insurance, Personal injury (including property damage).

HUGHES, THOMAS MORGAN, III, lawyer; b. Racine, Wis., June 14, 1949; s. Thomas Morgan and Rosemary (Navratil) H.; m. Teresa Lee Cloud, Aug. 10, 1974; 1 child, Gwyneth Leigh. B.B.A., U. Wis.-Madison, 1971; J.D., St. Louis U., 1974. Bar: Ark. 1974, U.S. Dist. Ct. (ea. dist.) Ark. 1974. Sole practice, Beebe, Ark., 1974-78; ptnr., Hughes & Hughes, Searcy, Ark., 1978— ; instr. Ark. State U., Beebe, 1975. City atty. City of Beebe, 1975-76; treas. Beebe Indsl. Devel. Corp., Beebe, 1983— ; judge City Ct., Beebe, 1985-87, Beebe Mcpl. Ct., 1987—. Mem. White County Bar Assn. Prs. 1996), Beebe C. of C. (pres. 1984—), Kiwanis (pres. 1981-82, bd. dirs. 1979—). Democrat. Family and matrimonial, Probate (including wills, trusts), Personal injury (including property damage). Home: 807 W Louisiana St Beebe AR 72012-2623 Office: Hughes & Hughes PO Box 91 Searcy AR 72145-0091

HUGHES, VESTER THOMAS, JR., lawyer; b. San Angelo, Tex., May 24, 1928; s. Vester Thomas and Mary Ellen (Tisdale) H. Student, Baylor U., 1945-46; BA with distinction, Rice U., 1949; LLB cum laude, Harvard U., 1952. Bar: Tex. 1952. Law clk. U.S. Supreme Ct., 1952; assoc. Robertson, Jackson, Payne, Lancaster & Walker, Dallas, 1955-58; ptnr. Jackson, Walker, Winstead, Cantwell & Miller, Dallas, 1958-76, Hughes, Luce, Hennessy, Smith & Castle, Dallas, 1976—, Hughes & Hill, Dallas, 1979-85, Hughes & Luce, Dallas, 1985—. Bd. dirs. Exell Cattle Co., Amarillo, Tex., LX Cattle Co., Amarillo, Austin Industries, Dallas, Sammons Enterprises, Inc.; adv. dir. First Nat. Bank Mertzon; sr. tax counsel Cmtys. Found. of Tex., Inc.; mem. adv. com. Tex. Supreme Ct., 1985-93. Contbr. articles on fed. taxation to profl. jours. Bd. dirs. Juvenile Diabetes Found. Inc., Dallas, 1982—; trustee Dallas Bapt. U., 1967-77; v.p., trustee, exec. com. Tex. Scottish Rite Hosp. for Children, 1967—; bd. overseers vis. com. Harvard Law Sch., 1969-75. 1st lt. JAGC U.S. Army, 1952-55. Mem. ABA (coun. sect. taxation 1969-73), Tex. Bar Assn., Dallas Bar Assn., Am. Law Inst. (coun. 1958—), Am. Coll. Tax Counsel, Ctr. for Am. and Internat. Law, Am. Coll. Trust and Estate Counsel, Met. Club (Washington), Harvard Club (N.Y.C.), Masons, Order Ea. Star, Phi Beta Kappa, Sigma Xi. Democrat. Baptist. Avocations: traveling, community and church activities, reading. Corporate taxation, Estate taxation, Personal income taxation. Office: Hughes & Luce 1717 Main St Ste 2800 Dallas TX 75201-4685

HUGHEY, RICHARD KOHLMAN, author, lawyer; b. Chgo., July 6, 1934; BA cum laude, Santa Clara U., 1958, JD cum laude, 1963. Bar: Calif. 1964, U.S. Ct. Appeals (9th cir.) 1964, U.S. Supreme Ct. 1972. Atty. Pacific Gas & Elec. Co., San Francisco, 1963-69, Berry, Davis & McInerny, Oakland, Calif., 1969-71; ptnr. Caputo, Liccardo, Rossi & Kohlman, San Jose, 1971-75; lectr. law, dir. CLE Santa Clara (Calif.) U., 1975-80; mng. editor Bancroft-Whitney Co., San Francisco, 1980-91, Lawyers Coop. Pub. Co., Rochester, N.Y., 1992-94; history and lit. biography writer, 1995—; columnist Mountain Democrat, Placerville, Calif., 1997—. Author: Jeffers Country Revisited: Beauty Without Price, 1996, Computer Technology in Civil Litigation, 1990, Trial Lawyers Manual, 1978, Jeffers in Antrim, 2003, El Dorado: California's Empire County, 2003; co-author: Petroglyphs: Poetry and Fiction, 1994, Hey Lew: Homage to Lew Welch, 1997; editor: Am. Jury Trials, 1980—90, Proof of Facts, 1982—90; bd. editors Calif. State Bar Jour., 1972—75, editor-in-chief Santa Clara Law Rev., 1961—63. Mem. citizen's adv. commn. U.S. Postal Svc., San Francisco, 1989—92; mem. adv. bd. Commn. on Future of the Cts., Jud. Coun. of Calif., 1992. Avocation: photography.

HUGO, MICHAEL R. lawyer; b. Portland, Maine, May 23, 1952; s. Frank D. and Harriet Hugo; m. Beverly Krauss, June 21, 1975; children: Carly L., Mark A., Matthew L. BS, Boston Coll., 1975; postgrad., Harvard U., 1976—77; JD, New Eng. Sch. Law, Boston, 1982. Bar: Mass., U.S. Dist. Ct. Mass., U.S. Dist. Ct. Colo., U.S. Dist. Ct. Ariz., U.S. Dist. Ct. (ea. dist.) Mich., U.S. Ct. Fed. Claims, U.S. Ct. Appeals (fed. cir.), U.S. Ct. Appeals (1st cir.), U.S. Ct. Appeals (6th cir.). Law clk. Swartz & Swartz, Boston, 1979—82; assoc. Denner & Beyoya, Boston, 1982—85; ptnr. Schlichtmann Conwey Crowley & Hugo, Boston, 1986—94, Hugo & Pollack, Boston, 1995—. Mem. discovery com. In Re Rezulin Litigation, N.Y.C., 2000—, In

Re Baycol Litigation, Phila., 2002; mem. settlement com. In Re Breast Implant Litigation, Birmingham, Ala., 1993—99; mem. adv. com. U.S. Claims Ct., Washington, 1989—92. Composer (movie sound track): Heart of a Champion, 2001; contbr. . Recipient award, Md. Trial Lawyers Assn., 2002. Mem.: ATLA (forum leader, bd. com. chair), Mass. Acad. Trial Lawyers (bd. govs.), Everett C. Benton Lodge AF&AM (master 1984—86). Avocations: music, skiing, boating, writing. Personal injury (including property damage), Product liability, Environmental. Office: Hugo & Pollack LLP 440 Commercial St Boston MA 02107

HUHS, JOHN I. international lawyer; b. Galveston, Tex., Sept. 18, 1944; s. Roy E. and Martha Mae (Hansen) H.; m. Vivian C. Swindley, 1970 (div. 1978). BA, U. Wash., 1966; MBA, JD, Stanford U., 1970. Bar: N.Y. 1971, D.C. 1981. Internat. cons. Satra Cons. Corp., N.Y.C., 1970-73; sr. staff White House Office Mgmt. & Budget Nat. Security, Internat. Affairs, Washington, 1974-75; ptnr. Pisar & Huhs, N.Y.C., 1976-84; sr. v.p., gen. counsel Tendler, Beretz Assocs., Ltd., N.Y.C., 1985-87; pvt. practice N.Y.C., 1987-88; ptnr., chmn. internat. dept. LeBoeuf, Lamb, Greene & MacRae, N.Y.C., 1989—. Prin. Ctr. for Excellence in Govt., 1984—99. Contbr. articles on internat. law, bus. and fin. to profl. jours.; comment editor Stanford Law Rev., 1967-69. Mem. bd. visitors Stanford Law Sch., 1996-98. Mem.: ABA (chmn. com. on Soviet and Ea. European law 1982—85, chmn. com. internat. comml. trans. 1985—90, coun. sect. internat. law and practice 1988—92, rep. to Union Internat. Avocats 1991—94), D.C. Bar Assn., N.Y. State Bar Assn. (chmn. internat. investment devel. com. 1987—91), Assn. of Bar of City of N.Y. (internat. trade com. 1987—89, com. Newly Ind. States of former Soviet Union 1989—2000), 175 E. 74th Corp. (pres.), Univ. Club N.Y.C., Order of Coif. Commercial, contracts (including sales of goods; commercial financing), Private international, Public international. Home: 175 E 74th St New York NY 10021-3218 Office: LeBoeuf Lamb Greene MacRae 125 W 55th St New York NY 10019-5369 E-mail: jhuhs@llgm.com.

HUI, HELEN YUEN HING, lawyer; b. Hong Kong, Jan. 3, 1944; came to U.S., 1964; d. Lap Sam and Shuk Han (Cheng) H.; m. Gordon Lew, July 12, 1969; 1 child, Beverly. BA, Smith Coll., 1967; MSW, U. Calif., Berkeley, 1970; JD, U. Calif., San Francisco, 1974. Bar: Calif. 1975. Intern ACLU, San Francisco, 1973; assoc. Hardesty & Lau, 1973-77; ptnr. Law Office Lau & Lee, 1977-79, Law Office Lee & Hui, 1979-88; prin. Law Offices of Helen Y.H. Hui, San Francisco, 1988—. Spkr., panelist on comty. svc. forums, radio and TV programs, chs. and nonprofit orgns. Officer, dir. East/West Pub. Co., San Francisco, 1968—; dir., pres. Chinese Newcomers Svc. Ctr., San Francisco, 1977-83, 94-2000; v.p. Childcare Law Ctr., 1987-88; officer, dir., mem. adv. bd. Self-Help for Elderly, San Francisco, 1977—; pres. N.E. Med. Svc., 1982-88, Chinatown Cmty. Childrens Ctr., 1986-88; co-chair Chinese Culture Found., San Francisco, 1994-98; pres. San Francisco Bay chpt. Orgn. Chinese Ams., 1996-97; mem. citizen adv. bd. Chinese for Affirmative Action, World Affairs Coun., 1994—; dir. Angel Island Immigration Sta. Found., 1994-97, Am. Lung Assn., 1995-96. Mem. ABA, LWV, Am. Immigration Lawyers Assn. (pres. no. Calif. chpt. 1992-93, editor Key Issues in Immigration Law 1992, writer, spkr. ann. confs. 1995, 96, chair advocacy task force), Nat. Asian Pacific Am. Bar Assn., State Bar Calif. (cert. specialist in immigration and nationality law, commr. immigration law adv. commn. 1991-94, pro bono svc. awards), Asian Am. Bar Assn. Greater Bay Area, Bar Assn. San Francisco, Lions Club (bd. dirs.). Avocation: classical music. Immigration, naturalization, and customs. Office: 456 Montgomery St Ste 700 San Francisco CA 94104-1280

HULBERT, RICHARD WOODWARD, lawyer; b. Cambridge, Mass., Sept. 24, 1929; s. Woodward Dennis and Clifford (Halliday) H.; m. Dorothy Marie Hanni, Apr. 21,1954; children: Jonathan, Ann, Laura, Mary. AB, Harvard U., 1951, LLB, 1955. Bar: N.Y. 1956. Assoc. Cleary, Gottlieb, Steen & Hamilton, N.Y.C., 1955-65, ptnr., 1966-83, 89-96, Paris, 1983-89, mng. ptnr. N.Y.C., 1979-84, of counsel, 1997—. Lectr. in law U. Calif., Berkeley, 1988; adj. prof. NYU Law Sch., 1990—; vice chmn. internat. ct. arbitration Internat. C. of C., 1994-99. Trustee Bklyn. Mus., 1992—, Bklyn. Bot. Garden, 1982-98, 99—; mem. Internat. C. of C. Commn. Internat. Arbitration, 2001—. Sheldon fellow in history Harvard U., 1951-52 Mem. ABA, N.Y. Bar Assn., Assn. of Bar of City of N.Y., Bklyn. Bar Assn., N.Y. County Lawyers Assn., Am. Law Inst., Century Assn., India House, Heights Casino. Democrat. Alternative dispute resolution, General civil litigation, Private international. Home: 141 Henry St Brooklyn NY 11201-2501 Office: Cleary Gottlieb et al 1 Liberty Plz New York NY 10006-1470 E-mail: rhulbert@cgsh.com.

HULIN, FRANCES C. retired prosecutor; AB, Northwestern U., 1957; JD, U. Ill., Urbana, 1971. Bar: Ill. 1973. Asst. states atty. Champaign County, IL, 1973-76, Macon County, Ill., 1977-78; prosecutor U.S. Attys. Office, Ctrl. Dist. Ill., 1978-93; U.S. atty. Dept. Justice, Springfield, Ill., 1993—2001.*

HULL, DAVID JULIAN, lawyer; b. Birmingham, West Midlands, Eng., Oct. 18, 1961; s. Derek and Anne H.; m. Anne Louise Morgan, June 29, 1985 (div.); children: Gabriella, Olivia. LLB with honors, Sheffield U., 1983. Trainee Dibb Lupton & Broomheads, 1984-86; solicitor Hammond Suddards, 1986-87, Edge Ellison, 1987-88; assoc., 1998-90; ptnr., 1990-2000, Hammond Suddards Edge, Birmingham, 2000—, head corp. fin., chmn., 2001—. Spkr. in field. Dir. Birmingham Repertory Theatre, Midlands Art Ctr. Named Leading Expert in Corp. Law Legal 500, Chambers Guide to the Legal Profession, Top 30 Lawyer in the Regions Legal Bus., 1999. Mem. Brit./North Am. Group in the Midlands (founing dir.). Corporate, general, Entertainment, Mergers and acquisitions. Office: Hammond Suddards Edge Rutland House 148 Edmund St Birmingham B3 2JR England Fax: 44 (0) 121 222 3001. E-mail: david.hull@hammondsuddardsedge.com.

HULL, FRANK MAYS, federal judge; b. Augusta, Ga., Dec. 9, 1948; d. James M. Hull Jr. and Frank (Mays) Pride; m. Antonin Aeck, Apr. 16, 1977; children: Richard Hull Aeck, Molly Hull Aeck. AB, Randolph-Macon Women's Coll., 1970; JD cum laude, Emory U., 1973. Bar: Ga. 1973, U.S. Ct. Appeals (5th cir.) 1973, U.S. Dist. Ct. (no. dist.) Ga. 1974, U.S. Ct. Appeals (11th cir.) 1982. Law clk. to Hon. Elbert P. Tuttle U.S. Ct. Appeals (5th cir.), Atlanta, 1973—74; assoc. Powell, Goldstein, Frazer & Murphy, Atlanta, 1974—80, ptnr., 1980—84; judge State Ct. Fulton County, Atlanta, 1984—90, Superior Ct. Fulton County, Atlanta, 1990—94, U.S. Dist. Ct. (no. dist.) Ga., 1994—97, U.S. Ct. Appeals (11th cir.), 1997—. Mem. commn. on family violence State of Ga., 1992—94, commn. on gender bias in jud. sys., 1988—90. Mem. Leadership Atlanta, 1986—, program co-chair criminal justice com., 1988—89; Sunday sch. tchr. Cathedral St. Philip, Atlanta, 1983—88, children's com., 1981—82, outreach com., 1989—91; bd. dirs. Met. Atlanta Mediation Ctr., Inc., 1976—79, Atlanta Vol. Lawyers Assn., 1988—91. Fellow, AAUW, 1973—. Mem.: ABA (fin. sec. long range planning com. tort and ins. practice sect. 1979—82, chmn. contract documents divsn., forum com. on constrn. industry 1983—85, editl. staff jour. 1981—85, vice chmn. fidelity and surety law com. 1978—85), Nat. Assn. Women Judges, Ga. Assn. Women Lawyers, Atlanta Bar Assn., Am. Judicature Soc. (bd. dirs. 1990—96), Ga. Bar Assn., Order of Coif. Office: US Ct of Appeals 56 Forsyth St NWRm 300 Atlanta GA 30303-2289

HULL, J(AMES) RICHARD, retired lawyer, business executive; b. Keokuk, Iowa, Dec. 5, 1933; s. James Robert and Alberta Margaret (Bouseman) H.; m. Patricia M. Kiesner, June 14, 1958; children—Elizabeth Ann Hull Whims, James Robert, David Glen. BA, Ill. Wesleyan U., 1955; JD, Northwestern U., 1958. Bar: Ill. 1958, Fla. 1978. V.p., sec., gen. counsel Honeggers & Co., Inc., Fairbury, Ill., 1959-65, also bd. dirs.; staff atty. Am. Hosp. Supply Corp., Evanston, Ill., 1965-68, chief atty., asst. sec., 1968-70, corp. sec., 1970-71, corp. sec., corp. gen. counsel, 1971-79, gen. counsel, 1979-84; sr. v.p., sec., gen. counsel Household Internat. Inc., Northbrook, Ill., 1984-93, sr. v.p., of counsel, 1993-94; ret. Mem. planning com. Northwestern U. Corp. Counsel Inst., 1992-93, chmn. Northwestern Corp. Counsel Ctr., 1993. Bd. trustees, bd. visitors Ill. Wesleyan U.; pres. Prestancia Cmty. Assn. Fellow Am. Bar Found., Am. Law Inst.; mem. ABA, Ill. Bar Assn., Fla. Bar Assn., Chgo. Bar Assn. (chmn. corp. law dept.), North Shore Gen. Counsels, Northwestern U. Sch. Law Alumni Assn. (pres.), Sigma Chi, Legal Club (Chgo.), Law Club (Chgo.), Skokie Country Club (Glencoe, Ill.), Gator Creek Golf Club (Sarasota, Fla.), T.P.C. Club (Prestancia, Fla.), Prestancia Cmty. Assn. (pres. 1995-96), Champion Hills Golf Club (Hendersonville, N.C.), Hendersonville Country Club. Home (Winter): 4634 Mirada Way #24 Sarasota FL 34238 Home (Summer): 21 LaCoste Dr Hendersonville NC 28739

HULL, JOHN DANIEL, IV, lawyer; b. Washington, Feb. 27, 1953; s. John Daniel III and Arlene (Reemer) Hull. BA cum laude, Duke U., 1975; JD, U. Cin., 1978. Bar: DC 1980, U.S. Dist. Ct. DC 1983, U.S. Ct. Appeals (DC cir.) 1984, U.S. Ct. Appeals (10th cir.) 1986, Md. 1989, Pa. 1989, U.S. Dist. Ct. (we. dist.) Pa. 1989, U.S. Ct. Appeals (3d cir.) 1989, U.S. Supreme Ct. 1989, Calif. 2002, U.S. Dist. Ct. (so. dist.) Calif. 2002. Legis. asst. 93d & 96th U.S. Congresses, Washington, 1974, 78-81; assoc. Rose, Schmidt & Dixon, Washington, 1981-87, ptnr., 1988-92, Hull McGuire PC, Pitts., Washington, and San Diego, 1992—. Mem.: U. Cin. Law Rev., 1976—77, editor student articles: , 1977—78. Fellow Congress of Ctr. for Internat. Legal Studies, Salzburg, Austria. Fellow: Congressional Ctr. Internat. Legal Studies; mem.: ABA, Internat. Bar Assn., Pa. Bar Assn., Md. Bar Assn., Bar Assn. DC, Internat. Bus. Law Consortium, Tara Club, Duke Club. Federal civil litigation, Environmental, Legislative. Office: Hull McGuire PC 32d Fl US Steel Tower 600 Grant St Pittsburgh PA 15219-2702 also: Hull McGuire PC 888 17th St NW Ste 1000 Washington DC 20006 also: Hull McGuire PC 701 B St Fl 10 San Diego CA 92101 E-mail: jdhull@hullmcguire.com.

HULL, PHILIP GLASGOW, lawyer; b. St. Albans, Vt., Feb. 17, 1925; s. Charles Herman and Gladys Gertrude (Glasgow) H.; m. Gretchen Elizabeth Gaebelein, Oct. 24, 1952; children: Jeffrey R., Sanford D., Meredyth Hull Smith. AB, Middlebury Coll., 1949; LLB, Columbia U., 1952. Bar: N.Y. 1952, Fla. 1977. Staff mem. subcom. on adminstrn. internal revenue laws, com. on ways and means U.S. Ho. of Reps., Washington, 1951; assoc. Winthrop, Stimson, Putnam & Roberts, N.Y.C., 1952-63, ptnr., 1964-97, sr. counsel, 1998-2000, Pillsbury Winthrop, N.Y.C., 2001—. Mem. Sch. Revenue Com., Cold Spring Harbor, N.Y., 1963-65; bd. dirs. Eagle Dock Found., Cold Spring Harbor, 1971-74, People's Symphony Concerts, N.Y.C., 1977—, L.I. Philharm., 1979-81; trustee L.Am. Mission, Miami, Fla., 1969-79; elder Ctrl. Presbyn. Ch., Huntington, N.Y., 1956-78; mem. nat. mssions bd. United Presbyn. Ch., U.S.A., 1967-73; trustee Madison Avenue Presbyn. Ch., N.Y.C., 1989-94, pres., 1993-94; mem. Lloyd Harbor Conservation Adv. Coun., 1973-77. With U.S. Army, 1943-46. Ellis fellow, Kent scholar, Stone scholar Columbia U. Mem. Am. Coll. Trust and Estate Counsel, 1979-2002, N.Y. State Bar Assn., Fla. Bar Assn., Christian Legal Soc. (bd. dirs. 1984-97), Fellowship Christians in Univs. and Schs. (trustee 1983-90), Univ. Club N.Y.C. (bd. dirs. 1986-90), Cold Spring Harbor Beach Club, Blue Key, Phi Beta Kappa. Office: Pillsbury Winthrop One Battery Park Plz New York NY 10004-1490

HULL, THOMAS GRAY, federal judge; b. 1926; m. Joan Brandon; children: Leslie, Brandon, Amy. Student, Tusculum Coll.; JD, U. Tenn., 1951. Atty. Easterly and Hull, Greeneville, Tenn., 1951-63; mem. Tenn. Ho. of Reps., 1955-65; atty., prin. Thomas G. Hull, 1951-72; chief clk. Tenn. Ho. of Reps., 1969-70; judge 20th Jud. Cir., Greeneville, Morristown and Rogersville, Tenn., 1972-79; legal counsel to Tenn. Gov. Lamar Alexander, 1979-81; judge U.S. Dist. Ct. (ea. dist.) Tenn., 1983—. Served as cpl. U.S. Army, 1944-46. Mem. Tenn. Bar Assn. (chmn. East dist. com. 1969), Greenville Bar Assn. (pres. 1969-71), Tenn. Jud. Conf. (del. 1972-79, vice chmn. 1974-75, com. to draft uniform charges for trial judges). Republican. Office: Office of US Dist Judge 220 W Depot St Greeneville TN 37743

HULLVERSON, JAMES EVERETT, JR., lawyer; b. St. Louis, Sept. 20, 1953; s. James Everett and Shirley (Shaughnessey) Hullverson; m. Laure Albers Bauer, Oct. 7, 1977; children: Everett James, Leigh Bauer, Elliot. BA, Yale U., 1975; JD cum laude, St. Louis U., 1978. Bar: Mo. 1978, Ill. 1979, U.S. Dist. Ct. (ea. dist.) Mo. 1978, U.S. Ct. Appeals (8th cir.) 1983, U.S. Supreme Ct. 1981, Diplomate Am. Bd. Profl. Liability Attys., cert.: cert. civil trial adv. Nat. Bd. Trial Advocacy. Ptnr. Hullverson, Hullverson & Frank, Inc., St. Louis, 1978—2002, Hullverson & Hullverson, St. Louis, 2003—. Adj. assoc. prof. law St. Louis U., 1983—; faculty Nat. Coll. Advocacy, 1983, 85; lectr., presenter in field. Contbr. chapters to books. Mem.: Am. Soc. Law and Medicine, Mo. Bar Assn., Mo. Assn. Trial Attys., Ill. Trial Lawyers Assn., Assn. Trial Lawyers Am., Yale Club, Masters Swim Club, Mo. Athletic Club. Roman Catholic. Federal civil litigation, State civil litigation, Personal injury (including property damage). Home: 9252 Clayton Rd Saint Louis MO 63124 Office: Hullverson & Hullverson LC Ste 1616 7777 Bonhomme Ave Saint Louis MO 63105

HULSTON, JOHN KENTON, lawyer, director; b. Dade County, Mo., Mar. 29, 1915; s. John Fred and Myrtle Rosa (King) H.; m. Ruth Amis Luster, Dec. 18, 1944; 1 son, John Luster. AB, Drury Coll., Springfield, Mo., 1936; JD, Mo. U., Columbia, 1941, D (hon.), 1997. Bar: Mo. 1941, U.S. Supreme Ct. 1949. Tchr., coach Ash Grove (Mo.) High Sch., 1936-38; pvt. practice law Springfield, 1946—; co-founder, dir., v.p., sec. Royal Oil Co., Big Spring, Tex., 1951-68, Pioneer Oil Co., Ft. Worth, 1954-79; operator, chmn. Copperhead Hill farms (beef production), 1955-98; chmn. Bank of Ash Grove, 1959—, Citizens Home Bank, Greenfield, Mo., 1966—; pres. Bank of Springfield, 1968-69, Bank of Billings, 1987—; vice chmn., dir., mem. exec. com. Centerre Bank of Springfield (now Bank of Am.), 1969-89; sec., dir., v.p., mem. exec. com. Ozark Air Lines Inc. (now Am. Air Lines), St. Louis, 1971-86, sec., dir., v.p., 1984-88. Instr. real estate law Drury Coll., 1948-64; vis. lectr. corp. law E.R. Breech Sch. Bus., 1953. Author: West Point and Wilson's Creek 1861, 1955, An Ozarks Boy's Story, 1971, An Ozarks Lawyer's Story, 1976, History of Bank of Ash Grove, 1883-1983, 1983, A Look at Dade County, Missouri, 1905-85, 1985, Panhandle Profiles, 1889-1989, 1989, Lester E. Cox, 1895-1968, 1992, Moments in Time, 2001; (with Paul W. Barrett) Harry S. Truman v. J. William Chilton, 1991; contbr. articles to profl. jours. Chmn. Wilson's Creek Nat. Battlefield Commn., 1969-79; vice chmn. Springfield Home Rule Charter Commn., 1953; chmn. Springfield City Charter Commn., 1977; pres. Greene County Estate Planning Coun., 1952; trustee Springfield Pub. Libr., 1957-63, Drury Coll., 1966-96, life trustee, 1996--; trustee State Hist. Soc. Mo., 1974—, CoxHealth, 1959—, pres., 1966, chmn., 2001-03; chmn. Greene County Dems., 1947-48; introduced Pres. Harry S. Truman at 1st Whistle Stop Speech, Springfield, July 5, 1948; presdl. elector, 1948; mem. Mo. Civil War Centennial Commn., 1961-65; trustee U. Mo. Jefferson, 1976-82, Mo. U. Law Sch. Found., Columbia, pres., 1985-87; co-founder Civil War Round Table of the Ozarks, 1948, Wilson's Creek Battlefield Found., 1952, Greene County Hist. Soc., 1962, The Hist. Mus. Springfield-Greene County, 1974; mem. devel. fund bd. Mo. U., Columbia, 1986-90. Maj. U.S. Army, WWII, 1941-46. Recipient Springfield Young Man of Year award, 1950, Disting. Alumni award Drury Coll., 1974, Springfieldian of Year award, 1978, The Missourian award, 1998, Spl. commendation U.S. Dept. Interior, Nat. Park Service, 1981, Faculty-Alumni Gold medal award Mo. U., Columbia, 1988, Citation of Merit Mo. U. Law Sch., Disting. Svc. award Mo. U. Alumni Assn., 1993; inductee into Mo. Writers Hall of Fame, 1995. Fellow Am. Bar Found. (life); mem. ABA (real property, probate/trust reporter Mo. 1974-96), Am. Judicature Soc., Am. Acad. Hosp. Attys., Am. Soc. Law, Ethics and Medicine, Mo. Bar Assn. (1st chmn. legal aid 1952), Springfield Met. Bar Assn. (pres. 1973, Disting. Atty. award 2002), Springfield C. of C. (pres. 1950, 51, 54), Supreme Ct. of Mo. Hist. Soc. (co-founder, trustee 1984-90), SAR, Order of Coif, Masons (32 deg.), Shriners (potentate 1963), Jester, Hickory Hills Country Club (Springfield), Phi Delta Phi, Kappa Alpha Order. Democrat. Presbyterian. Home: 1300 E Catalpa St Springfield MO 65804-0134 Office: 2060 E Sunshine St Springfield MO 65804-1815

HULTQUIST, STEVEN JOHN, lawyer; b. Sioux City, Iowa, Jan. 29, 1949; s. Robert Edward and Betty (Van Dyck) H.; m. Judith Ann Raymond, July 10, 1972 (div. May 1981); m. Donna Marie DeMichele, Nov. 18, 1981 (div. Feb. 1995); 1 child, Liana Rose; m. Debra R. Ashe, July 29, 1998. BSChemE, Wash. U., 1970, MSChemE, 1972; JD, Fordham U., 1979. Bar: U.S. Patent and Trademark Office 1976, N.Y. 1980, Calif. 1981, U.S. Dist. Ct. (cen. dist.) Calif. 1982, U.S. Ct. Appeals (9th cir.) 1982, Conn. 1984, U.S. Ct. Appeals (fed. cir.) 1985, N.C. 1987. Lab. researcher Carboline Co., St. Louis, 1969-72; patent engr. Union Carbide Co., Tonawanda, N.Y., 1972-74, patent trainee N.Y.C., 1974-76, patent agt., 1976-80, patent atty., 1980-81, Tosco Corp., L.A., 1981-82; patent counsel Am. Cyanamid Corp., Stamford, Conn., 1982-85; pvt. practice Weston, Conn., 1985-86; assoc. Olive & Olive P.A., Durham, N.C., 1986-87, ptnr., 1988-89; of counsel Harlow, Derr & Stark, Research Triangle Park, N.C., 1990; ptnr. Harlow, Stark, Hultquist, Evans & London, Research Triangle Park, 1990-92; prin. Intellectual Property/Tech. Law, Research Triangle Park, 1992. Adj. prof. engring. N.C. State U., 1994-97; chmn. Incutech Com., 1987, Tech. Exch. Com., 1989; pres. Tri-Letix Corp., 1995-97; v.p. CaroTech LLC, 1995-96, pres., 1996-99; bd. dirs. Coun. Entrepreneurial Devel. Author: North Carolina General Practice Deskbook, 1995—; editor Tech. Exch. Newsletter; patentee in semiconductor mfg., material scis. fields; contbr. articles to profl. jours. Fundraiser YMCA of Wake County, Raleigh, N.C., 1988. Mem. ABA (Intellectual Property Law Chpt. Deskbook award 1998), N.C. Bar Assn. (intellectual property sect., counsel mem. 1992-95), Copyright Law Assn., Durham C. of C., Coun. for Entrepreneurial Devel., N.C. Acad. Trial Lawyers, Licensing Exec. Soc., Sigma Xi (sec. Research Triangle Park chpt. 2000-2002). Republican. Presbyterian. Avocations: civic affairs, bus. devel. and networking, pro bono law, psychology of learning. Commercial, contracts (including sales of goods; commercial financing), Patent, Trademark and copyright. Home: 100 Steeple Chase Ln Chapel Hill NC 27517-7436 Office: 1414 Raleigh Rd Ste 201 Chapel Hill NC 27517-E-mail: hultquist@iptl.com.

HULZEBOS, LEAH KATHERINE, paralegal; b. Windom, Minn., Aug. 14, 1979; d. Verlo and Andrea Adrian; m. Lance Hulzebos, Apr. 10, 1999. AS in Legal Asst., Iowa Lakes C.C., Estherville, Iowa, 1999; BA in Polit. Sci., Buena Vista U., 2001. Paralegal Sunde, Olson, Kircher & Zender, St. James, Minn., 1998—2001, Hughes Law Offices, Sioux Falls, SD, 2001—. Avocation: photography.

HUMBLE, MONTY GARFIELD, lawyer; b. Cameron, Tex., Dec. 20, 1951; s. Don Garfield Humble and Betty Sue (Maedgen) French; m. Donell Lou Moss, Mar. 12, 1976 (div. June 1981); m. Macy A. Melton, Oct. 23, 1993; children: Megan Elizabeth, John Marshall, Nicole Marie, Crawford Melton. BA, U. Tex., 1974, JD, 1976. Assoc. Clark, Thomas, Winters and Shapiro, Austin, Tex., 1972-82, Vinson & Elkins, Houston, 1982-86, ptnr. Dallas, 1986—. Bd. dirs. Ft. Worth Ballet, 1990-94, Dallas Opera, 1987-92, Tex. Gen. Counsel Forum, 2001—, Tex. Nanotech. Initiative, 2002—; mem. external rsch. adv. coun. U. Tex., Dallas; gen. counsel Superconducting Super Collider Devel. Authority, 1987-94; mem. Leadership Dallas, 1988; mem. legal advisors Dallas City Charter Revision Com., 1990; mem. Greater Dallas Planning Coun.; mem. adv. coun. U. Tex. Dallas External Rsch., 2002. Fellow Dallas Bar Found.; mem. ABA, State Bar Tex., Nat. Assn. Bond Lawyers (steering com. 1985-87, 94-96, bd. dirs. 2001—, treas. 2002—), Health Care Fin. Mgrs. Assn. (bd. dirs. 1990-92), Crescent Club, Bent Tree Country Club, Phi Beta Kappa. Republican. Health, Municipal (including bonds), Non-profit and tax-exempt organizations. Office: Vinson & Elkins LLP 2001 Ross Ave Ste 3700 Dallas TX 75201-2975 E-mail: mhumble@velaw.com.

HUMICK, THOMAS CHARLES CAMPBELL, lawyer; b. N.Y.C., Aug. 7, 1947; s. Anthony and Elizabeth Campbell (Meredith) H.; m. Nancy June Young, June 7, 1969; 1 child, Nicole Elizabeth Campbell. BA, Rutgers U., 1969; JD, Suffolk U., 1972; postgrad., London Sch. Econs.-Polit. Sci., 1977-78. Bar: N.J. 1972, U.S. Ct. Appeals (3d cir.) 1976, U.S. Supreme Ct. 1977, N.Y. 1981. Law clk. Superior Ct. N.J., 1972-73; assoc. Riker, Danzig, Scherer & Debevoise, Newark and Morristown, N.J., 1973-77; ptnr. Francis & Berry, Morristown, 1978-84, Dillon, Bitar & Luther, Morristown, 1985-92, Schenck, Price, Smith & King, Morristown, 1992—. Arbitrator U.S. Dist. Ct. N.J., 1985—; del. to Jud. Conf. for 3d Jud. Cir. U.S., 1975-79; mem. dist. X ethics com. N.J. Supreme Ct., 1983-87; mem. jud. selection com. Morris County, 1995-99. Contbg. author: Valuation for Eminent Domain, 1973; mem. editl. bd. Suffolk U. Law Rev., 1970-71, N.J. Lawyer, 1993-94. Trustee Peck Sch., 1993-98; trustee Richmond Fellowship N.J., 1982-89, pres., 1984. Mem. ABA, FBA, N.J. Bar Assn., Morris County Bar Assn. (trustee 1995-2000), Bay Head Yacht Club. Republican. Presbyterian. Federal civil litigation, State civil litigation, Corporate, general. Home: PO Box 191 Oldwick NJ 08858-0191 Office: Schenck Price Smith & King 10 Washington St Morristown NJ 07960-7117 E-mail: tcch@spsk.com.

HUMMEL, GREGORY WILLIAM, lawyer; b. Sterling, Ill., Feb. 25, 1949; s. Osborne William and Vivian LaVera (Guess) H.; m. Teresa Lynn Beveroth, June 20, 1970; children: Andrea Lynn, Brandon Gregory. BA, MacMurray Coll., 1971; JD, Northwestern U., 1974. Bar: Ill. 1974, U.S. Dist. Ct. (no. dist.) Ill. 1974. Assoc. Rusnak, Deutsch & Gilbert, Chgo., 1974-78; ptnr. Rudnick & Wolfe, Chgo., 1978-97; mem. Bell, Boyd & Lloyd LLC, Chgo., 1997—. Editor Jour. Criminal Law & Criminology Northwestern U., 1973-74; co-author: Illinois Real Estate Forms, 1989; contbr. articles to law jours. Mem. gov. coun. Luth. Gen. Hosp. Advocate Health Care Sys.; trustee Mac Murray Coll., Jacksonville, Ill., 1986-2001; trustee, sec.-treas. Homes for Children Found; bd. advisors Chgo. area coun. Boy Scouts Am., ChildServ; trustee Nat. Inst. Constrn. Law and Practice. Mem. Internat. Bar Assn. (past co-chmn. com. internat. constrn. projects), Am. Coll. Constrn. Lawyers (past pres.), Urban Land Inst. (trustee), Urban Land Inst. Found. (gov.), Chgo. Dist. Coun. (past chmn.), Lambda Alpha Internat. (Ely chpt. past pres.). Construction, Municipal (including bonds), Property, real (including real estate development, water). Office: Bell Boyd & Lloyd LLC 3 1st Nat Plaza 70 W Madison St Ste 3300 Chicago IL 60602-4207 E-mail: ghummel@bellboyd.com.

HUMPHERYS, LEGRANDE RICH, lawyer; b. Provo, Utah, May 16, 1949; m. Susan J. Olson, May 28, 1971; children: Daniel, Benjamin, Christa, Alissa, Joseph, Sara. BA, Brigham Young U., 1973, JD, 1976. Bar: Utah 1976, U.S. Dist. Ct. Utah 1976, U.S. Ct. Appeals (10th cir.) 1984, U.S. Claims Ct. 1991, U.S. Supreme Ct. 2002. Shareholder Christensen & Jensen, Salt Lake City, 1980-98, pres., 1998—; v.p. Christensen, Jensen & Powell, Salt Lake City, 1986-98, also bd. dirs. Adj. assoc. prof. U. Utah., Salt Lake City, 1981-1986; v.p. Lo-Vo Tech. Inc., Salt Lake City, 1984-90, also dir. Bd. dirs. Davis County Mental Health Assn., Farmington, Utah, 1985-89; vice chmn. Indian Springs coun. Boy Scouts Am., 1985-86; state and county del. Rep. party, Davis County, 1982; dir. bd. dirs. Utah Alliance for the Mentally Ill; dir. devel. bd. Brigham Young U., Coll. Nursing; mem. LDSP Com. And Justice for All. Named Utah Trial Lawyer of Yr., 1999. Mem. ATLA, Am. Bd. Trial Advocates, Utah State Bar, Def. Rsch. Inst., Barrister Inns of Ct., Utah Trial Lawyers Assn., Am. Coll. Trial Lawyers. Mem. Lds Ch. Avocation: fly fishing. General civil litigation, Insurance, Personal injury (including property damage). Office: Christensen & Jensen 50 S Main St Ste 1500 Salt Lake City UT 84144-2044

HUMPHREY, DUDLEY, lawyer; b. Dec. 1933; AB, Duke U., 1955; JD with honors, U. N.C., 1961. Bar: N.C. 1961. With Kilpatrick Stockton LLP,

Winston-Salem, NC. Mem.: N.C. State Bar (pres.-elect 2002). Construction, Probate (including wills, trusts), Estate planning. Office: Kilpatrick Stockton LLP 1001 W Fourth St Winston Salem NC 27101-2400*

HUMPHREYS, ROBERT RUSSELL, lawyer, consultant, arbitrator; b. Eugene, Oreg., May 7, 1938; s. Russell Wallace and Roberta Lois (Bennett) H.; m. Natalia Dimitrievna Lucenko; children: Tatyana Roberta, Grigori Robert. BA, U. Wash., 1959; LLB, George Washington U., 1965. Bar: Va. 1965, D.C. 1966, U.S. Dist. Ct. (D.C.) 1966, U.S. Ct. Appeals (D.C. cir.) 1985, U.S. Ct. Appeals (4th cir.) 2000, Ct. Fed. Claims 2001. Law clk. Barco, Cook & Patton, Washington, 1963-64, Keller & Heckman, Washington, 1964; mgr. pub. affairs services Air Transport Assn. Am., Washington, 1965-66; asst. to v.p. fed. affairs, 1966-71; spl. counsel com. on labor and human resources U.S. Senate, Washington, 1971-77; commr. Rehab. Services Adminstrn., HEW, Washington, 1977-80; ptnr. Hoffheimer & Johnson, Washington, 1980-83, Humphreys & Mitchell, Washington, 1983-88; cons. MARC Assocs., Inc., Washington, 1988-94; pvt. practice law, Washington, 1988—; pres. The Humphreys Group, Washington, 1991-95; pres., ceo Jennings Randolph Inst., Washington, 1998—; hearing officer State of N.C., 2002. Spkr. nat., internat. confs. Author: Compliance Manual on Americans with Disabilities Act; contbr. articles to profl. jours. Incorporator, bd. dirs., treas., counsel Nat. Ctr. for Barrier-Free Environ., 1975-77, 81-84; bd. dirs. Va. Spl. Olympics, 1982-84. Mem. D.C. Bar Assn., George Washington U. Law Alumni Assn., Va. State Bar, Phi Delta Phi. Achievements include being the prin. Senate draftsman for Black Lung Benefits Act, 1972, Rehab. Act, 1973, Randolph-Sheppard Act Amendments, 1974, Black Lung Benefits Reform Act, 1977. Administrative and regulatory, Alternative dispute resolution, Federal civil litigation.

HUMPHRIES, JAMES NATHAN, lawyer; b. Detroit, Feb. 15, 1958; s. Andrew John and Mary Jane (Leigh) H.; m. Diane D. Rogers, Dec. 14, 1985; children: Charneise, Keyontay, Kailea, Kalon. BGS, U. Mich., 1980, JD, 1984. Bar: Mich. 1986, U.S. Dist. Ct. (ea. dist.) Mich., U.S. Ct. Appeals (6th cir.). Youth agt. Wayne County 4H, Detroit, 1985-87; staff analyst, atty. Detroit City Coun., 1987-89; atty. City of Dearborn, Mich., 1989-95, Detroit Bd. Edn., 1995—. Chmn. Victory Opportunity Trust Polit. Action Com., Detroit, 1986—. Baptist. Avocations: walking, sports. Office: Detroit Bd Edn 3011 W Grand Blvd Fisher Bldg 18th Fl Detroit MI 48202-4050

HUND, EDWARD JOSEPH, lawyer; b. May 3, 1945; s. Edward J. and Josephine A. (Hoover) Hund; m. Marty M. Anderson, June 29, 1970; children: Corie Elizabeth, Cyrus Anthony, Hanna Christine. Student, Creighton U., 1963—64; AB in Polit. Sci., Hays Coll., 1967; JD, Washburn U., 1970. Asst. county atty. Sedgwick County, Wichita, Kans., 1971—72; assoc. Smith, Shay, Farmer, Wetta, Wichita, Kans., 1972—75, ptnr., 1975—84, Focht, Hughey & Hund, Wichita, 1984—. Pres. Legacy of Justice Found., 2002—. 1st lt. NG USAR, 1968—74. Mem.: Wichita Bar Assn. (pres. young lawyers 1978), Kans. Bar Assn. (sec.-treas. 1981), Kans. Trial Lawyers Assn. (pres. 1991), Am. Bd. Trial Advocates (pres. Kans. chpt. 1995), Am. Trial Lawyers Assn. (bd. govs. 1994—95), ABA, Lions (v.p. 1979), East Y Mens Club (Wichita chpt.) (pres. 1980). Democrat. Congregationalist. Federal civil litigation, State civil litigation, Personal injury (including property damage). Home: 325 Brookfield St Wichita KS 67206-1901 Office: Bradshaw Johnson & Hund 200 W Douglas Ave Ste 100 Wichita KS 67202-3001

HUNGATE, MARK EDWARD, lawyer; b. Indpls., June 7, 1951; s. Edward R. and Patti Ruth (Graves) H.; m. Cindy S. White, Jan. 19, 1980 (div. 1981); m. Theresa A. Lonas, May 15, 1987 (div. 1994); m. Kristine A. Ebbesmier, Jan. 10, 1998; children: Zachary Ross, Coley Christopher. BA in Psychology with honors, DePauw U., 1973; JD with honors, Stetson U., 1976. Bar: Fla. 1976, U.S. Dist. Ct. (mid. dist.) Fla. 1976, U.S. Ct. Appeals (5th and 11th cirs.) 1976. Assoc. Fowler, White, Gillen, St. Petersburg, Fla., 1976-81, shareholder, 1981—; leader Workers Compensation Practice Group, 2002—. Mem. Fla. Bar (cert. in worker's compensation), Gold Key, Phi Delta Phi, Beta Theta Pi. Insurance, Workers' compensation. Office: Fowler White Boggs Banker PA PO Box 210 Saint Petersburg FL 33731-0210 E-mail: mhungate@fowlerwhite.com.

HUNKINS, RAYMOND BREEDLOVE, lawyer, rancher; b. Culver City, Calif., Mar. 19, 1939; s. Charles F. and Louise (Breedlove) H.; m. Mary Deborah McBride, Dec. 12, 1967; children: Amanda, Blake, Ashley. BA, U. Wyo., 1966, JD, 1968. Ptnr. Jones, Jones, Vines & Hunkins, Wheatland, Wyo., 1968—. Local rules com. U.S. Dist. Ct., 1990—; spl. counsel U. Wyo., Laramie, State of Wyo., Cheyenne; mem. faculty Western Trial Adv. Inst., 1993-95, Wyo. Supreme Ct. Commn. Jud. Salary and Benefits, 1996-98; ; owner Thunderhead Ranches, Albany and Platte Counties, Wyo.; gen. ptnr. Split Rock Land & Cattle Co.; spl. asst. atty. gen., Wyo.; bd. dirs. Found. for Laramie, Laramie Peak Mus. Chmn. Platte County Reps., Wheatland, 1972-74, chmn. adv. coun. Coll. Commerce and Industry, U. Wyo., 1978-79; bd. dirs. U. Wyo. Found., 1996-2002, Found. Laramie, 2002—, Laramie Peak Mus., 1989—; bd. advisors Am. Heritage Ctr., 1995-99; active Gov.'s Crime Commn., 1970-78; pres. Wyo. U. Alumni Assn., 1973-74, commr. Wyo. Aeronautics Commn., 1987-98; moderator United Ch. Christ, 1997-98; Rep. candidate for Gov. Wyo., 2002. With USMCR, 1956-60. Recipient Big Horn Mountain Roundup Pax Irvine award, 1989, Outstanding Advisor award Phi Delta Theta, 1968. Fellow Am. Coll. Trial Lawyers (Wyo. state chmn. 1998-2000, nat. ethics com. 2000—), Internat. Soc. Barristers, Am. Bd. Trial Advs.; mem. ABA (aviation com. 1980-86, forum com. on constrn. industry litigation sect.), Wyo. Bar Assn. (chmn. grievance com. 1980-86, mem. com. on civil pattern jury instrns. 1999-2002, state bar-law sch. com., bench-bar rels. com.), Wyo. Trial Lawyers Assn. (past pres.), Lions, Elks. Federal civil litigation, Construction, Personal injury (including property damage). Office: Jones Jones Vines & Hunkins PO Drawer 189 9th and Maple Wheatland WY 82201

HUNNICUTT, CHARLES ALVIN, lawyer; b. LaGrange, Ga., Dec. 7, 1950; s. William Oliver and Mary Olivia (Leggett) Hunnicut. BS, Am. U., 1972; JD, U. Ga., 1975; LLM, U. Brussels, Belgium, 1976. Bar: Ga. 1975, D.C. 1978, U.S. Dist. Ct. D.C. 1978, U.S. Ct. Appeals (D.C. cir.) 1978, U.S. Ct. Internat. Trade 1980, U.S. Ct. Appeals (fed. cir.) 1981, U.S. Supreme Ct. 1981. Dep. dir. State of Ga. Office, Brussels, 1975-76; ops. mgr. Presdl. Pers. The White House, Washington, 1976-77; exec. asst. to under sec. internat. trade U.S. Dept. Commerce, Washington, 1977-80; legal advisor to chmn. Internat. Trade Commn., Washington, 1980-87; ptnr. Robins, Kaplan, Miller & Ciresi, Washington, 1987-96, mng. ptnr., 1989-91; advisor to Govt. of Ukraine on accession to Gen. Agreement on Tariffs and Trade World Trade Orgn., Kiev, 1994-95; asst. sec. for aviation and internat. affairs U.S. Dept. Transp., Washington, 1996-99; ptnr. Robins, Kaplan, Miller & Ciresi, Washington, 1999—, mem. exec. bd., 2003—. Adj. prof. Am. U. Coll. Law, Washington, 1988—91. Bd. visitors U. Ga. Sch. Law., 2000—. Mem.: Internat. Bar Assn., Am. Soc. Internat. Law (exec. coun. 1999—2002, chair budget com. 2000—), Washington Fgn. Law Soc. (pres. 1987—88), Ga. State Bar, Bar Assn. D.C., FBA, ABA (internat. trade steering com., air and space law forum). Democrat. Presbyterian. Commercial, contracts (including sales of goods; commercial financing), Private international, Transportation. Office: Robins Kaplan Miller & Ciresi 1801 K St NW Ste 1200 Washington DC 20006-1307 E-mail: cahunnicutt@rkmc.com.

HUNSAKER, RICHARD KENDALL, lawyer; b. L.A., June 2, 1960; s. Richard Allan and Patricia Kendall (Cook) H.; m. Laura Constance Haile, Oct. 8, 1988; children, Charles Nicholas, Laura Caroline. BA, U. Ill., 1982, MA, 1983; JD, Washington U., St. Louis, 1986. Bar: Ill. 1986, U.S. Dist. Ct. (cen. and no. dists.) Ill. 1987, U.S. Ct. Appeals (7th cir.) 1990, Wis. 1992. Speech coach Champaign (Ill.) Central High Sch., 1979-81; instr. speech communications, asst. debate coach U. Ill., Urbana, 1982-83; assoc. Heyl, Royster, Voelker & Allen, Springfield, Ill., 1986-87, Rockford, Ill., 1987-93, ptnr., 1994—2002, Edwardsville, Ill., 2002—. Author: Advanced Real Estate Law in Illinois - Environmental Liabilities, 1992, (with others) Advanced Real Estate Law in Illinois: Environmental Liability, 1992. Mem. ABA (tort and ins. practice, litigation and natural resources, energy and environ. law sects.), Ill. Bar Assn. (assoc., ins. law sect. 1990-92, civil practice and procedure, workers compensation, tort law and environ. control law sects.), Ill. Assn. Def. Trial Counsel (co-chair fall seminar), St. Clair County Bar ASsn., Madison County Bar Assn., Seventh Cir. Bar Assn., Def. Rsch. Inst. Methodist. Avocations: golf, biking, backpacking. General civil litigation, Insurance, Workers' compensation. Home: 14 Saffrin Hill Glen Carbon IL 62034 Office: Heyl Royster Voelker & Allen Mark Twain Plaza II 103 W Vandalia St PO Box 467 Edwardsville IL 62025-0467 E-mail: rhunsaker@hrva.com.

HUNSTEIN, CAROL, state supreme court justice; b. Miami, Fla., Aug. 16, 1944; AA, Miami-Dade Jr. Coll., 1970; BS, Fla. Atlantic U., 1972; JD, Stetson U., 1976, LLD (hon.), 1993. Bar: Ga. 1976; U.S. Dist. Ct. 1978; U.S. Ct. Appeals 1978; U.S. Supreme Ct. 1989. Legal practice, Atlanta, 1976-84; judge Superior Ct. of Ga. (Stone Mt. cir.), 1984-92; justice Supreme Ct. of Ga., Atlanta, 1992—. Chair Ga. Commn. on Gender Bias in the Judicial System 1989—; pres. Coun. of Superior Ct. Judges of Ga., 1990-91; adj. prof. Sch. Law Emory U., 1991—. Bd. dirs. Ga. Campaign Adolescent Pregnancy Prevention, 1992—; chair Ga. Child Support Commn., 1993, 98, Supreme Ct. Equality Commn. Recipient Clint Green Trial Advocacy award 1976, Women Who Made A Difference award Dekalb Women's Network 1986, Outstanding Svc. commendation Ga. Legislature, 1993, Cmty. Svc. award Emory U. Legal Assn. for Women Students., 1993, Gender Justice award Ga. Commn. Family Violence, 1999, Margaret Burns award ABA, 1999; inducted to Fla. Atlantic U. Hall of Fame, 1993. Mem. Ga. Assn. of Women Lawyers, Nat. Assn. of Women Judges (dir. 1988-90), Bleckley Inn of Ct., State Bar Ga. Office: Supreme Ct Ga 244 Washington Street Atlanta GA 30334-9007 E-mail: hunsteic@supreme.courts.state.ga.us.

HUNT, DAVID EVANS, lawyer; b. Wilkes-Barre, Pa., May 10, 1953; s. James Dixon and Twyla (Burkert) H.; m. Denise M. Barbera, Aug. 21, 1976 (div. 1984); 1 child Christopher Evans; m. Elizabeth S. Pearce, Sept. 5, 1987; children: Alexandra Stacy, Thomas Dixon. AB, Dartmouth Coll., 1975; JD, U. Chgo., 1978. Bar: N.Y. 1979, U.S. Dist. Ct. (so. and ea. dists.) N.Y. 1979, Maine 1982, U.S. Dist. Ct. Maine 1982, U.S. Tax Ct. 1982, Fla. 1999. Assoc. Debevoise & Plimpton, N.Y.C., 1978-81; ptnr. Pierce, Atwood, Scribner, Allen, Smith & Lancaster, Portland, Maine, 1981-92, McCandless & Hunt, Portland, Maine, 1992-97; sole practitioner Portland, 1997—. Adj. prof. U. Maine Law Sch., Portland, 1991—92, Portland, 2000—02. Co-author: Maine Will and Trust Forms Annotated, 1994, Maine Estate Administration, 1996. Officer, dir. Maine Estate Planning Coun., Portland, 1986-94. Fellow: Am. Coll. Trust and Estate Counsel (state chair 1997—2001, regent 2001—02); mem.: ABA, Cumberland County Bar Assn., N.Y. State Bar Assn., Maine State Bar Assn., Fla. Bar, Woodlands Club. Episcopalian. Avocations: classical latin, skiing. Estate planning, Probate (including wills, trusts), Taxation, general. Home: 6 Highland St Portland ME 04103-3005 Office: 511 Congress St Portland ME 04101-3411 E-mail: dhunt@mainewills.com.

HUNT, DAVID FORD, lawyer; b. Ft. Worth, Apr. 7, 1931; s. John Greffrey and Bernice (Ford) H. BS, North Tex. State U., 1954; JD, Vanderbilt U., 1960. Bar: Tex. 1961, U.S. Dist. Ct. (no. dist.) Tex., U.S. Dist. Ct. (we. dist.) Tex., U.S. Dist. Ct. (ea. dist.) Tex.U.S. Ct. Appeals (5th and 11th cir.), U.S. Supreme Ct. Law clk. to U.S. dist. judge No. Dist. Tex., 1960-62; pvt. practice, Dallas, 1962-94; ptnr. Jenkens & Gilchrist, P.C., Dallas, 1980-92, of counsel, 1993-94; atty. pvt. practice, Denton County, Tex., 1995—. Chmn. com. on admissions Dist. 6 Tex. State Bd. Law Examiners, 1978-87 Contbr. articles to legal jours. Co-chmn. pollwatchers com. Dallas County Republican Com., 1964; Sec. Bootstrap Ranch, 1972-74; pres. So. Methodist U. Lambda Chi Edn. Found., 1972-76, dir. Internat. Lambda Chi Edn. Found., 1966-68. Served with AUS, 1954-56. Mem. Tex. Bar Assn., Tex. Bar Found., Vanderbilt U. Law Sch. Alumni Assn. (pres. Dallas chpt. 1972-75), Lambda Chi (chancellor 1966-68). Federal civil litigation, State civil litigation, Construction. Home and Office: 1849 Bridle Bit Rd Flower Mound TX 75022-6571

HUNT, GERALD WALLACE, lawyer; b. Portland, Oreg., Oct. 31, 1939; BSBA in Econs., U. Denver, 1961, JD, 1964; LLM in Taxation, Washington U., 1981. Bar: Colo. 1964, Ariz. 1968, Tex. 1996, Alaska 1999, cert.: Ariz. Bd. Legal Specialization (tax specialist). Asst. trust officer The Ariz. Bank, Phoenix, 1967-69; atty. Westover, Keddie, et al, Yuma, Ariz., 1969-73; pvt. practice law Yuma, 1973-74; atty. Hunt & Clark, Yuma, 1974-75, Hunt, Stanley & Hossler, Yuma, 1975-96, Hunt, Tallan & Hossler, Yuma, 1996-97, Hunt, Kenworthy and Hossler, Yuma, 1998—2002, Hunt, Kenworthy, Meerchaum & Hossler, Yuma, 2002—. Treas. Excel Group, Yuma, 1998—99, chair, 2000—02; bd. dirs. Greater Yuma Port Authority, 2000. Fellow: Am. Coll. Trust and Estate Counsel; mem.: ABA, Tex. Bar, Alaska Bar, Colo. State Bar, Ariz. State Bar, Internat. Mcpl. Lawyers Assn. Estate planning, Probate (including wills, trusts), Taxation, general. Office: Hunt Kenworthy Meerchaum & Hossler 330 W 24th St Yuma AZ 85364-6455

HUNT, GORDON, lawyer; b. L.A., Oct. 26, 1934; s. Howard Wilson and Esther Nita (Dempsey) H. BA in Polit. Sci, UCLA, 1956; JD, U. So. Calif., 1959. Bar: Calif. 1960. Law clk. Appellate Dept., Superior Ct. L.A. County, 1959-60; mem. firm Behymer & Hoffman, Los Angeles, 1960-65; partner firm Behymer, Hoffman & Hunt, Los Angeles, 1965-68; ptnr. firm Munns, Kofford, Hoffman, Hunt & Throckmorton, Pasadena, 1969-90, Hunt, Ortman, Blasco, Palffy & Rossell, Pasadena, 1990-95; mem. Hunt, Ortman, Blasco, Palffy & Rossell Inc., 1995—. Lectr. UCLA, various yrs.; chmn. legal adv. com. Assoc. Gen. Contractors Calif., 1985; arbitrator L.A. Superior Ct., State of Calif. Author: Construction Surety and Bonding Handbook; co-author: California Construction Law, 16th edit.; contbr. numerous articles to legal jours. Mem. ABA, Calif. Bar Assn. (del. Conv. 1964-69), L.A. County Bar Assn. (real property com. 1965-66, exec. com. 1970-72, sec. 1972-73, vice chmn. 1972-75, chmn. real property sect. 1975-76, co-chmn. continuing edn. bar com. 1969-71), Am. Arbitration Assn. (arbitrator, mediator). Construction. Office: 301 N Lake Ave Fl 7 Pasadena CA 91101-4108 E-mail: goff@hobpr.com.

HUNT, HEATHER M. lawyer; b. Madison, Wis., June 21, 1971; d. Charles Leonard Wnukowski and Nancy M. Marek; m. Rick J. Hunt, July 11, 1992. BS cum laude, U. Wis., Eau Claire, 1993; JD, U. Wis., Madison, 1997. Bar: Wis. 1997, U.S. Dist. Ct. (we. dist.) Wis. 1997. Intern Legal Assistance to Institutionalized Persons Program, Madison, 1995-96, La-Crosse County Dist. Atty.'s Office, LaCrosse, 1996, Wis. Supreme Ct., Madison, 1996; shareholder Wiley Colbert Norseng Cray Herrell & Flory, S.C., Chippewa Falls, Wis., 1997—. Note and comment editor U. Wis. Law Rev., 1995-97. Bd. dirs. Chippewa Valley Cultural Assn., Inc., 1997—, Leave A Legacy--Chippen Valley. Mem. Chippewa County Bar Assn., State Bar of Wis. Commercial, contracts (including sales of goods; commercial financing), Estate planning, Property, real (including real estate development, water). Home: 921 W Willow St Chippewa Falls WI 54729-2149 Office: Wiley Colbert et al 119 1/2 N Bridge St Chippewa Falls WI 54729-2404 E-mail: hhunt@wileylaw.com.

HUNT, JAMES BAXTER, JR., lawyer, retired governor; b. Guilford County, N.C., May 16, 1937; s. James Baxter and Elsie (Brame) Hunt; m. Carolyn Joyce Leonard, Aug. 20, 1958; children: Rebecca Hunt Hawley, James Baxter Hunt III, Rachel Nilender, Elizabeth Amigh. BS in Agrl. Edn., N.C. State U., 1959, MS in Agrl. Cons., 1962; JD, U. N.C., 1964. Bar: N.C. 1964. Econ. advisor H.M. Govt. of Nepal for Ford Found., 1964—66; ptnr. Kirby, Webb and Hunt, 1966—72; lt. gov. State of N.C., 1973—77, gov., 1977—85, gov., 1993—2001; ptnr. Poyner and Spruill, Raleigh, NC, 1985—93; mem. Womble Carlyle Sandridge & Rice, Raleigh, 2001—. Originator, bd. dirs. Triangle East; chmn. N.C. State U. Emerging Issues Forum; bd. visitors Wake Forst U.; founding chmn. Nat. Bd. for Profl. Tchg. Stds., 1987, Nat. Ctr. for Pub. Policy and Higher Edn., 1998. Author: Rally Around the Precinct, 1968. Trustee Atlantic Christian Coll.; mem. Carnegie Forum on Edn. and Econ. Task Force on Tchg. as a Profl., 1986; chmn. Nat. Commn. on Tchg. and Am.'s Future, 1994; state pres. Young Dems., 1968; del. Dem. Nat. Conv., 1968. Named Outstanding Young Man of Yr., Wilson Jr. C. of C., 1969, Outstanding Govt. Ofcl. in Cmty. Edn., Nat. Assn. Cmty. Edn., 1977; recipient 1st Harry S. Truman award, Nat. Young Dems., 1975, James Bryant Conant award, Edn. Commn. States, 1984, Nat. 4-H Outstanding Alumnus award, 1984, Soil Conservation Honors award, 1986, Child Health Adv. award, Am. Acad. Pediat., 1994, Friend of Edn. award, Horace Mann League, 1999. Mem.: Nat. Govs. Assn. (chmn. task force on technol. innovation mem. exec. com., chmn. edn. com. states and nat. task force on edn. for econ. growth 1982—83, leadership team on controlling crime and violence 1994, chmn. nat. edn. goals panel 1997—). Presbyterian. Office: Womble Carlyle Sandridge & Rice 150 Fayetteville St Mall Ste 2100 PO Box 831 Raleigh NC 27602

HUNT, LYNNE, federal agency administrator; Grad., U. San Diego, 1977. Spl. agt. FBI, 1978, with legal counsel divsn., 1984—89, supr., 1989—91, 1991—95, chief health care fraud unit, 1995—96, asst. spl. agt. in charge Balt. divsn., 1996—98, sect. chief fin. crimes sect., 1998—2000, sgt. agt. in charge Balt. divsn., 2000—02, asst. dir. inspection divsn., 2002—. Office: FBI J Edgar Hoover FBI Bldg 935 Pennsylvania Ave NW Washington DC 20535*

HUNT, RONALD FORREST, lawyer, director; b. Shelby, N.C., Apr. 18, 1943; s. Forrest Elmer and Bruna Magnolia (Brackett) H.; m. Judy Elaine Shultz, May 19, 1965; 1 child, Mary AB, U. N.C., 1966, JD, 1968. Bar: N.C. 1968, D.C. 1973. Mem. staff SEC, Washington, 1968-69, legal asst. to chmn., 1970-71, sec. of commn., 1972-73; dep. gen. counsel, sec. Student Loan Mktg. Assn., Washington, 1973-78, sr. v.p., gen. counsel, sec., 1979-83, exec. v.p., gen. counsel, 1983-90; pvt. practice New Bern, NC, 1991—99. Vice chmn. First Capital Corp., Southern Pines, N.C., 1984-90; bd. dirs. Student Loan Mktg. Assn., Washington., SLM Corp., Reston, Va., e-Numerate Solutions, Inc., McLean, Va.; chmn. bd. dirs. Nat. Student Loan Clearinghouse, Reston, 1993-95, 97—. Trustee Warren Wilson Coll., Asheville, NC; mem. Montgomery County (Md.) Commn. Landlord and Tenant Affairs, 1976—81, chmn., 1979—81; bd. dirs. D.C. chpt. ARC, 1976—83; trustee Arena Stage, Washington, 1984—89, Washington Theatre Awards Soc., 1988—90. Republican. Presbyterian. Avocations: sailing; gardening. Corporate, general, Securities.

HUNT, SEAN ANTONE, lawyer, civil engineer; b. Warrenton, Va., Sept. 6, 1965; s. John Booker, Jr. and Isabelle H. Hunt; m. Clarice Turner, Dec. 2, 1995. BS in Civil Engring., Tenn. State U., 1988; JD, Vanderbilt U. Sch. Law, 1993. Bar: Tenn. 1993, U.S. Dist. Ct. (ea., mid. and we. dists.) Tenn. 1993, Ga. 1994, U.S. Dist. Ct. (no. dist.) Ga. 1994. Assoc. hwy. engr. N.C. Dept. Transportation, Raleigh, 1988-90, bridge design engr., 1990; intern Tenn. Atty. Gen.'s Office, Nashville, 1993, U.S. Dist. Ct. Judge Robert L. Echols, Nashville, 1993; law clerk Law Offices Raymond G. Prince, Nashville, 1993; atty. Leitner, Warner, Moffitt, Williams, Dooley, Carpenter, & Napolitan, PLLC, Chattanooga, 1993-96, Spicer, Flynn & Rudstrom, P.L.L.C., Nashville, 1996—. Com. mem. Martina O'Bryan Ctr., Nashville, 1996-97; com. co-chair Bethlehem Ctrs. Nashville, 1998; treas., Friends in Gen. (Gen. Hosp.), Nashville, 1998—. With USAFR, 1983-87. General civil litigation, Construction, Personal injury (including property damage). Office: Spicer Flynn & Rudstrom 80 Monroe Ave Ste 500 Memphis TN 38103-246 E-mail: sahcthanh@netscope.net., sah@sfrlaw.com.

HUNT, THOMAS REED, JR., lawyer; b. Elkton, Md., Feb. 22, 1948; s. Thomas R. and Marian D. (Decker) H.; children: Reed Thomas, Clifton Bowie, Molly Dustin, Travis John. Ptnr. Morris, Nichols, Arsht & Tunnell, Wilmington, Del., 1972—.

HUNTER, BYNUM MERRITT, lawyer; b. Greensboro, N.C., June 13, 1925; s. Hill McIver and Annie (Merritt) H.; m. Ann Fulenwider, June 22, 1957 (div. 1968); children: Ann Shirley, Mary Parker; m. Mary Lane Yancey, Aug. 7, 1969 (div. 1978); m. Mary Bonneau McElveen, June 13, 1980; 1 son, Bynum Jr. AB, U. N.C., 1945, JD, 1949. Bar: N.C. 1949. Ptnr. Smith & Moore LLP. Served with USNR, 1943-46, 51-53. Fellow Am. Coll. Trial Lawyers, Am. Bar Found. (life mem.); mem. ABA, Internat. Assn. Def. Counsel, Am. Judicature Soc., Greensboro Bar Assn. (pres. 1965-66) 4th Cir. Jud. Conf., N.C. Bar Assn., Zeta Psi, Phi Delta Phi. Clubs: Rotary. Home: 710 Country Club Dr Greensboro NC 27408-5714 Office: Smith & Moore LLP Ste 1400 PO Box 21927 300 N Green St Greensboro NC 27420-1927 E-mail: bynum.hunter@smithmoorelaw.com.

HUNTER, DONALD FORREST, lawyer; b. Mpls., Jan. 30, 1934; s. Earl Harvey and Ruby Cecilia (Lagerson) H.; m. Marlys Ann Zilge; Jeffrey, Cheri, Kathryn. BA, U. Minn., 1961, JD, 1963. Bar: Minn. 1963, U.S. Dist. Ct. Minn. 1965, U.S. Ct. Appeals (8th cir.) 1965, Ill. 1977, U.S. Dist. Ct. (no. dist.) Ill. 1991, U.S. Supreme Ct. 1986. Assoc., then ptnr. Gislason, Dosland, Hunter & Malecki, New Ulm, Minn., 1963-76; exec. v.p., sec., gen. counsel Wirtz Prodn. Ltd. Ice Follies/Holiday on Ice, Chgo., 1976-79; ptnr. Gislason, Dosland, Hunter & Malecki, Mpls., 1979-99; of counsel Gislason & Hunter, 1999—. Chmn. bd. dirs. Chgo. Milw. Corp., 1977-81; pres. Chgo. Milw. R.R., 1977-81; bd. dirs. First Security Bank, Chgo.; bd. dirs., officer First Security Bancorp, Inc., Chgo., 1993—; bd. dirs., sec. Wirtz Corp., Chgo. Blackhawk Hockey Team and related cos. Fellow Am. Coll. Trial Lawyers; mem. ABA, Am. Judicature Soc., Minn. Bar Assn. (bd. of govs. 1973-76), 5th Dist. Bar Assn. (pres. 1971-72), Hennepin County Bar Assn., Minn. Def. Lawyers Assn. (bd. dirs. 1976), Internat. Assn. Ins. Counsel, U.S. Supreme Ct. Hist. Assn. General civil litigation, Commercial, contracts (including sales of goods; commercial financing), Corporate, general. Office: Gislason & Hunter PO Box 5297 9900 Bren Rd E Ste 215E Hopkins MN 55343-9666

HUNTER, FORREST WALKER, lawyer; b. Arlington, Va., Jan. 25, 1950; s. Dallas Walker and Ann Arsell (Wheat) H.; m. Susan Gladys Zsamer, June 8, 1974; children: Andrew Chastain, Alison Christian. BA, U. Va., 1972; JD, Emory U., 1975. Bar: Ga. 1975, U.S. Dist. Ct. (no. dist.) Ga. 1978, U.S. Ct. Appeals (5th cir.) 1978, U.S. Ct. Appeals (11th cir.) 1981, U.S. Dist. Ct. (mid. dist.) Ga. 1982, U.S. Dist. Ct. (so. dist.) Ga. 1983, U.S. Ct. Appeals (6th cir.) 1988, U.S. Dist. Ct. (we. dist.) Mich. 1994, U.S. Ct. Appeals (7th cir.) 1996, U.S. Dist. Ct. (ea. dist.) Tex. 1999, U.S. Dist. Ct. (no. dist.) Ind. 2002. Atty. Office Chief Counsel IRS, Dept. Treasury, Washington, 1975-77, sr. atty. Office. Regional Counsel Atlanta, 1977-81; assoc. Jones, Bird & Howell and Alston & Bird, Atlanta, 1981-85; ptnr. Alston & Bird, Atlanta, 1985—. Bd. dirs. Boys and Girls Clubs of Metro Atlanta, 1984. Mem. Am. Health Lawyers Assn., Ga. Acad. Hosp. Attys., Lawyers Club Atlanta, Atlanta Bar Assn., U. Va. Alumni Assn., Emory U. Alumni Assn. Labor (including EEOC, Fair Labor Standards Act, labor-management relations, NLRB, OSHA). Office: Alston & Bird 1 Atlantic Ctr Atlanta GA 30309-3424

HUNTER, GEORGE S. lawyer; b. Buffalo, N.Y., Jan. 27, 1957; s. George H. Hunter and Manoli Veira-Gantes; m. Montse Alvarez Gonzalez, Apr. 22, 1994; 1 child, Jorge Hunter Alvarez. Student, Atlantic Coll., 1976; BA, NYU, 1978; JD, Boston U., 1982; degree in Law, U. Navarra, 1987. Bar: Mass. 81, Madrid 86. Atty. Garrigues Abogados Y. Asesores, Madrid. Tchr.

Inst. Empresa, Escuela Org. Indsl. Author: Spanish Corporations Law, 1994. Mergers and acquisitions, Commercial, contracts (including sales of goods; commercial financing), Corporate, general. Office: Garrigues C José Abascal 45 28003 Madrid Spain Fax: 34.91 399.24.08. E-mail: george.hunter@garriguesabogados.com.

HUNTER, HAROLD J., JR., legal association administrator; b. L.A., Feb. 14, 1933; m. Sally Hunter. AB, Stanford U., 1955, JD, 1960. Bar: Calif. 1961. Sr. ptnr. Kirtland & Packard, L.A., 1964—97; v.p. Internat. Acad. Trial Lawyers, Pasadena, Calif., 1997—. Reviewing editor: Calif. Continuing Edn. Bar, 1970; contbr. articles to profl. jours. Officer USN, 1955—57. Fellow: Internat. Acad. Trial Lawyers (bd. dirs.), Am. Coll. Trial Lawyers; mem.: Am. Bd. Trial Advs. (diplomate, pres. L.A. chpt. 1990). Office: 251 S Lake Ave Pasadena CA 91101 Office Fax: 626-405-0786.*

HUNTER, HOWARD OWEN, academic administrator, law educator; b. Brunswick, Ga., Oct. 14, 1946; m. Susan Frankel, Nov. 27, 1971; 1 child, Emily Atwood Plotkin. BA in Russian Studies, Yale U., 1968, JD, 1971. Bar: Ga. 1971. Assoc. atty. Hogan & Hartson, Washington, 1971-72, Hansell, Post, Brandon & Dorsey, Atlanta, 1972-76; asst. prof. Emory U. Sch. Law, Atlanta, 1976-79, assoc. prof., 1979-82, assoc. dean, 1979-80, prof., 1982—, prof. law, dean, 1989-2001, provost, exec. v.p. for acad. affairs, 2001—. Dir. Ga. Vol. Lawyers for the Arts, Inc., 1975-89, sec., 1975-77, treas., 1978-80, v.p., 1980-82, pres., 1984-87; vis. prof. law U. Va. Sch. Law, Charlottesville, 1982-83; hon. prof. law U. Hong Kong, 1986; vis. Mills E. Godwin prof. law Coll. William & Mary, Williamsburg, Va., 1989; mem. Chief Justice Commn. on Professionalism, 1990—, Supreme Ct. Commn. on Indigent Def., 2000—; bd. trustees Fed. Def. Program, 1991-97; lectr. in field. Author: Freedom of Information Handbook: Georgia, 1979, Modern Law of Contracts: Breach and Remedies, 1986, supplements, 1987, 88, 89, 90, 91, 92, 93, Modern Law of Contracts: Formation, Performance, Relationships, 1987, supplements, 1988, 89, 90, 91, 92, 93, Modern Law of Contracts, revised edit., 1993, supplements, 1994, 95, 96, 97, 98, 2d rev. edit., 1999, supplements, 2000, 01, (with Mogens Pedersen) Recent Reforms in Swedish Higher Education, 1980; contbr. articles to profl. jours.; mem. editl. bd. Jour. of Contract Law, 1988—. Fulbright Sr. scholar U. Sydney, 1988. Mem. ABA, Assn. Am. Law Schs., Am. Law Inst. (mem. consultative com. on revisions to article 2 of UCC), State Bar Ga. (mem. editl. bd. Ga. State Bar Jour. 1977-82), Decatur-DeKalb Bar Assn., Atlanta Bar Assn. (vol. lawyer project on illegal Cuban immigrants 1985-87, vol. lawyer in representation of Cuban inmates at fed. prison in Talladega, Ala. 1988, bd. dirs. internat. transaction sect. 1995—), Inst. Continuing Legal Edn. (vice-chmn. bd. trustees 1993-97), Inst. Continuing Judicial Edn. (bd. trustees 1989-2001). Avocations: cycling, jogging, fishing, travel. Office: 404 Adminstrn Bldg Emory Univ Atlanta GA 30322 E-mail: hunter@emory.edu.

HUNTER, JAMES AUSTEN, JR., lawyer; b. Phoenix, June 19, 1941; s. James Austen and Elizabeth Aileen (Holt) H.; m. Donna Gabriele, Aug. 24, 1973; 1 child, James A. AB, Cath. U. Am., 1963, LL.B., 1966. Bar: N.Y. 1967, Pa. 1975, U.S. Supreme Ct. 1974. Assoc. firm Sullivan & Cromwell, N.Y.C., 1967-74; assoc. firm Morgan, Lewis & Bockius, LLP, Phila., 1974-77, ptnr., 1977—. Staff: The Yale Law Jour. Banking, Corporate, general, Property, real (including real estate development, water). Home: 1001 Red Rose Ln Villanova PA 19085-2118 Office: Morgan Lewis & Bockius LLP 1701 Market St Philadelphia PA 19103-2903 E-mail: jhunter@morganlewis.com.

HUNTER, JAMES GALBRAITH, JR., lawyer; b. Phila., Jan. 6, 1942; s. James Galbraith and Emma Margaret (Jehl) H.; m. Pamela Ann Trott, July 18, 1969 (div.); children: James Nicholas, Catherine Selene; m. Nancy Grace Scheurwater, June 21, 1992. B.S. in Engring. Sci., Case Inst. Tech., 1965; J.D., U. Chgo., 1967. Bar: Ill. 1967, U.S. Dist. Ct. (no. dist.) Ill. 1967, U.S. Ct. Appeals (7th cir.) 1967, U.S. Ct. Claims, 1976, U.S. Ct. Appeals (4th and 9th cirs.) 1978, U.S. Supreme Ct. 1979, U.S. Dist. Ct. (cen. dist.) Ill. 1980, Calif. 1980, U.S. Dist. Ct. (cen. and so. dists.) Calif. 1980, U.S. Ct. Appeals (5th cir.) 1982, U.S. Ct. Appeals (fed. cir.) 1982. Assoc. Kirkland & Ellis, Chgo., 1967-68, 70-73, ptnr., 1973-76; ptnr. Hedlund, Hunter & Lynch, Chgo., 1976-82, Los Angeles, 1979-82; ptnr. Latham & Watkins, Hedlund, Hunter & Lynch, Chgo. and Los Angeles, 1982— . Served to lt. JAGC, USN, 1968-70. Mem. ABA, State Bar Calif., Los Angeles County Bar Assn., Chgo. Bar Assn. Clubs: Metropolitan (Chgo.), Chgo. Athletic Assn., Los Angeles Athletic. Exec. editor U. Chgo. Law Rev., 1966-67. Antitrust, Federal civil litigation, State civil litigation. Office: Latham & Watkins Sears Tower Ste 5800 Chicago IL 60606-6306 also: 633 W 5th St Los Angeles CA 90071-2005

HUNTER, JOHN LESLIE, lawyer; b. Miss., Aug. 15, 1946; m. Judy G. Hunter; children: John Leslie II, Lee Joseph, Kristy Lynn. BS, Miss. State U., 1969; JD, U. Miss., 1972. Bar: U.S. Dist. Ct. (no. dist.) Miss. 1972, U.S. Dist. Ct. (so. dist.) Miss. 1973, U.S. Ct. Appeals (5th cir.) 1974, U.S. Supreme Ct. 1978, U.S. Dist. Ct. (so. dist.) Ala. 1980, U.S. Ct. Appeals (11th cir.) 1981. Ptnr. Cumbest Cumbest Hunter & McCormick, Pascagoula, Miss., 1973—. Atty. Jackson county Port Authority. Mem. ABA, Assn. Trial Lawyers of Am. (sustaining mem.), Am. Bd. Trail Advocates, Miss. Bar Assn. (past exec. com. bd. commrs.), Miss. Trial Lawyers Assn. (sustaining), Jackson County Bar Assn. Presbyterian. Admiralty, Insurance, Personal injury (including property damage). Office: Cumbest Cumbest Hunter McCormick 729 Watts Ave PO Box 1287 Pascagoula MS 39568-1287 E-mail: jlh@cchmlawyers.com., jlh@cableone.net.

HUNTER, LARRY DEAN, lawyer; b. Leon, Iowa, Apr. 10, 1950; s. Doyle J. and Dorothy B. (Grey) H.; m. Rita K. Barker, Jan. 24, 1971; children: Nathan (dec.), Allison. BS with high distinction, U. Iowa, 1971; AM, JD magna cum laude, U. Mich., 1974, CPhil in Econs., 1975. Bar: Va. 1975, Mich. 1978, Calif. 1992. Assoc. McGuire Woods & Battle, Richmond, Va., 1975-77; asst. counsel, internat. counsel Clark Equipment Co., Buchanan, Mich., 1977-80; ptnr. Honigman, Miller, Schwartz and Cohn, Detroit, 1980-93; asst. gen. counsel Hughes Electronics Corp., L.A., 1993-98, corp. v.p., 1998—; sr. v.p., gen. counsel DIRECTV, Inc., El Segundo, Calif., 1996-98; chmn. pres. DIRECTV Japan Mgmt., Inc., Tokyo, 1998-2000. Mem. faculty Wayne State U. Law Sch., Detroit, 1987-89. Mem. Order of Coif. Commercial, contracts (including sales of goods; commercial financing), Corporate, general, Securities. Home: 1101-B S Catalina Ave Redondo Beach CA 90277 Office: Hughes Electronics Corp 200 N Sepulveda El Segundo CA 90245 E-mail: larry.hunter@hughes.com.

HUNTER, MARK JOHN, lawyer, photographer; b. Alpena, Mich., Dec. 22, 1956; s. Francis Raymond and Evelyn Joan (Hoodlet) Hunter. BA in U.S. History, Mich. State U., 1979, BA in Graphic Design, 1981; A in Concrete Tech., Alpena CC, 1987; JD, Ohio No. U., 1995. Bar: Mich. 1996. Freelance photographer, Alpena, 1974—; mfg. mgr. Concrete Product Industry, Mass., 1987—89; funeral home attendant Hunter Funeral Home, Alpena, 1995—; pvt. law practice Alpena, 1996—. Ex-officio mem. Alpena County Planning Commn., 1999—2002; vice chmn. Alpena County Rep. Com., 2001—02; mem. Alpena County Rep. Exec. Bd., 2003—, mem. exec. com., 2003—04; bd. dirs. Sunrise Mission Shelter, Alpena, 2000. Mem.: World Wildlife Fund, Mich. Land Use Inst., Eagles Club of Ossineke, Moose Lodge. Avocations: political theory, prisoners of conscience, world development, reading biographies. Commercial, contracts (including sales of goods; commercial financing), Probate (including wills, trusts), Property, real (including real estate development, water). Office: 310 W Chisholm St Alpena MI 49707 E-mail: ehunter@i2k.com.

HUNTER, M(ILTON) REED, JR., lawyer; b. Salt Lake City, Oct. 5, 1932; s. Milton Reed and Ferne (Gardner) H.; m. Mary Anne Shumway, Dec. 19, 1968; children: Edward Lund, Anne Leslie, Maria Lynne, Jefferson Reed. BA with honors, Brigham Young U., 1953; JD, U. Utah, 1961. Bar: Utah 1961, Calif. 1969, U.S. Ct. Appeals (10th cir.) 1961, U.S. Ct. Appeals (9th cir.) 1969, U.S. Supreme Ct. 1978. Asst. atty. gen. Utah State Atty. Gen.'s Office, Salt Lake City, 1961-68; staff atty. Continuing Edn. of the Bar, U. Calif., Berkeley, 1968-71; assoc., ptnr. Goldstein, Barceloux & Goldstein, San Francisco, 1971-84; v.p., atty. Fadem, Berger & Norton, Santa Monica, Calif., 1984-89; sole practitioner Encino, Calif., 1989-90; ptnr. Crosby, Heafey, Roach & May, L.A., 1990-2000; sole practitioner, 2000—. Contbr. articles to profl. jours. Sgt. U.S. Army, 1953-55, Germany. Mem. Calif. State Bar, Calif. Acad. Appellate Lawyers (pres. 1979-80; chair state bar com. on appellate cts. 1985), Los Angeles County Bar Assn. (condemnation com.), Mensa, Phi Kappa Phi, Phi Alpha Theta. Republican. Mem. Lds Ch. Avocations: music, film, tennis, travel. Appellate, Land use and zoning (including planning). Home and Office: 1359 Amesbury Cir Salt Lake City UT 84121 E-mail: reed@mariahunter.com.

HUNTER, RICHARD SAMFORD, JR., lawyer; b. Montgomery, Ala., May 8, 1954; s. Richard Samford and Anne (Arendell) H.; m. Jane Messer, June 28, 1981; children: Richard Samford III, Benjamin Arendell. Student, Berklee Coll. of Music, 1974—75; BA, U. N.C., 1977; JD, Cumberland Sch Law of Samford U., 1980. Bar: N.C. 1980, U.S. Dist. Ct. (ea. and ctrl. dists.) N.C. 1981; cert. Am. Bd. Trial Advs. Assoc. Green & Mann, Raleigh, N.C., 1980-82, Smith, Debnam, Hibbert & Pahl, Raleigh, 1982-85; ptnr. Futrell, Hunter & Bingham, Raleigh, 1985-97. Pres., North Carolina Acad. of Trial Lawyers, 1993-94; pres. elect, 1992-93; exec. comm., 1987-94; bd., 1984-87; chair, Auto Torts Sect., 1998—, program chmn. media law U. N.C., Chapel Hill, 1983-84; mem. faculty NCATL Nat. Inst. Trial Advocacy, 1987; lectr. in field. Author: How to Try a Civil Case, 1986, Traumatic Medicine, 1988, Insurance Law for the General Practitioner, 1992, North Carolina Bar Assn. Desk Book, 1992, Traumatic Medicine, 1988, Inadequate Offer? Try that P.I. Case, 1995; composer, performer (TV musical) The Tomorrow Show, 1975; contbr. articles to profl. jours. and mags. including Trial Briefs Mag., Fourth Quarter. Corp. fund raiser United Way, Wake County, N.C., 1984-85; mem. clergy's sermon evaluation com. Christ Episc. Ch., Raleigh; bd. dirs. Raleigh Chamber Music Guild, 1986-88; bd. dirs. Food Bank of N.C., 1990—. Fellow Roscoe Pound Found. Fellow So. Trial Lawyers Assn., Roscoe Pound Found.; mem. ABA (litig. sect.), ATLA, Am. Bd. Trial Advocates (cert.), N.C. Bar Assn. (litig. sect.), Wake County Bar Assn. (bd. dirs. 1987, 88, chmn. 1988), Assn. Trial Lawyers Am. (Stalwart fellow Roscoe Pound Found.), N.C. State Bar, N.C. Acad. Trial Lawyers (speaker various seminars, chmn. speakers bur. 1984-85, bd. govs. 1986—, v.p. pub. svc. and info. com. 1988-90, v.p. membership 1990-91, v.p. legis. 1991—, pres. 1993-94, exec. com. 1987-94, chmn. auto torts sect. 1998—, mem. edn. com. 1985-88, pres.-elect 1992-93, bd. dirs. 1984-87, co-chair auto torts sect. 1998-99, U. N.C. journalism press law seminar, 1983, 84), Kiwanis, Sphinx, Phi Alpha Delta. Democrat. Avocations: sports, music, hunting, fishing. Alternative dispute resolution, General civil litigation, Personal injury (including property damage). Home: 813 Graham St Raleigh NC 27605-1124 Office: 133 Fayetteville Street Mall Ste 300 Raleigh NC 27601-2908 Fax: 919-831-8734. E-mail: hunteratty@aol.com.

HUNTER, ROBERT FREDERICK, lawyer; b. Ft. Worth, June 7, 1937; s. Homer Alexander and Pauline (Steely) H.; m. Elisabeth Loader, July 1, 1961 (div. Sept. 1982); children: Homer Alexander II, Robert Frederick Jr.; m. Barbara Bailey, June 7, 1984. BBA, BS in Civil Engring., Tex. A&M U., 1960; MS, M.I.T., 1964; JD, So. Meth. U., 1974. Bar: Tex. 1975, Mo. 1976. Pres., chief exec. officer Hydro-Air Engring., St. Louis, 1974-84; sole practice Dallas, 1985-86; ptnr. Ashley and Welch, Dallas, 1987-90; pvt. practice Dallas, 1990—. Mem. ABA, ASCE, Tex. Bar Assn., Mo. Bar Assn., Phi Delta Phi. Lodges: Rotary (pres. 1970). Republican. Avocations: cameras, woodworking. Commercial, contracts (including sales of goods; commercial financing), Corporate, general, Private international. Home: 3517 Villanova St Dallas TX 75225-5008

HUNTER, WILLIAM DENNIS, lawyer; b. Boise, Idaho, June 26, 1943; s. William Gregory and Lorene (Persilla) H.; m. Jane Emily Porter, Apr. 30, 1966; children: Keith Alan, Elise Aubrey. BA, Stanford U., 1965; JD, U. Calif., San Francisco, 1973. Bar: Calif. 1973, U.S. Dist. Ct. (no. dist.) Calif. 1974, U.S. Ct. Appeals (9th cir.) 1974, U.S. Supreme Ct. 1996. Assoc. Pettit & Martin, San Francisco, 1973-79, ptnr., 1980-92, counsel, 1993-95, Collette & Erickson LLP, San Francisco, 1995-2000; regional counsel The Nature Conservancy, San Francisco, 2000—. Bd. dirs. City Celebration, Inc., San Francisco, 1984-91, pres., 1989-91. Recipient Service award Calif. Nature Conservancy, 1987. Mem. ABA, Calif. State Bar Assn., San Francisco Bar Assn., Nat. Assn. Installation Devel. (regional dir. 1993-2000), Order of coif. Democrat. Land use and zoning (including planning), Property, real (including real estate development, water). Office: The Nature Conservancy 201 Mission St 4th Fl San Francisco CA 94105

HUNTINGTON, STEPHEN N. lawyer; b. Toledo, Sept. 9, 1943; s. Robert Hubbard and Katharine (Wolf) H.; m. Susan Merkin, Aug. 6, 1977; children: Carey, Samuel, Audrey. B.A., Yale U., 1965; J.D., U. Pa., 1970. Bar: Pa. 1970, U.S. Dist. Ct. (ea. dist.) Pa. 1970, U.S. Ct. Appeals (3d cir.) 1970. Assoc. firm Duane Morris & Heckscher, Phila., 1970-74; ptnr. firm Warner & Huntington, Phila., 1974-77, firm Dougherty & Huntington, Phila., 1977-82, firm Sarner, Franklin, Grodinsky, Margulies & Huntington, Phila., 1982-91, firm Cohen & Huntington, 1991—; instr. dept. legal and real estate studies Temple U., Phila., 1982-91 . Pres. emeritus Center City Residents' Assn., Phila. Mem. Pa. Trial Lawyers Assn., Pa. Def. Inst. Clubs: Racquet, Yale (Phila.). Bankruptcy, Commercial, contracts (including sales of goods; commercial financing), Insurance. Home: 2226 Delancey St Philadelphia PA 19103-6502 Office: Huntington Hodge & Franklin 1500 JFK Blvd Philadelphia PA 19102

HUPP, HARRY L. federal judge; b. L.A., Apr. 5, 1929; s. Earl L. and Dorothy (Goodspeed) H.; m. Patricia Hupp, Sept. 13, 1953; children: Virginia, Karen, Keith, Brian. AB, Stanford U., 1953, LLB, 1955. Bar: Calif. 1956, U.S. Dist. Ct. (cen. dist.) Calif. 1956, U.S. Supreme Ct. Pvt. practice law Beardsley, Hufstedler and Kemble, L.A., 1955-72; judge Superior Ct. of Los Angeles, 1972-84; appointed fed. dist. judge U.S. Dist. Ct. (cen. dist.) Calif., L.A., 1984-97, sr. judge, 1997—. Served with U.S. Army, 1950-52. Mem. Calif. State Bar, Los Angeles County Bar Assn. (Trial Judge of Yr. 1983), Order of Coif, Phi Alpha Delta. Office: US Dist Ct 312 N Spring St Los Angeles CA 90012-4704

HUPPER, JOHN ROSCOE, lawyer; b. N.Y.C., June 16, 1925; s. Roscoe Henderson and Dorothy Wallace (Healy) H.; m. Joyce Shirley McCoy, June 14, 1952; children: John R. Jr., Gail J., Craig W. AB, Bowdoin Coll., 1949; LLB, Harvard U., 1952. Bar: N.Y. 1954, U.S. Supreme Ct. 1960. Assoc. Cravath, Swaine & Moore, N.Y.C., 1952-60, ptnr., 1961-95. Overseer Bowdoin Coll., 1970-82, trustee, 1982-95; trustee Allen-Stevenson Sch., 1968-96; bd. dirs. Legal Aid Soc., N.Y.C., 1971-76, Travelers Aid Soc., N.Y., 1962-79. Served with U.S. Army, 1943-46. Fellow Am. Coll. Trial Lawyers; mem. ABA, N.Y. State Bar Assn., N.Y. County Lawyers Assn., Assn. of Bar of City of N.Y., N.Y. Supreme Ct. (com. character and fitness appellate divsn. 1st dept. 1992—, spl. master appellate divsn. 1st dept. 1982—), Apawamis Club, Down Town Assn., Univ. Club, Union Club. Republican. Home: 105 E 67th St New York NY 10021-5901 Office: Cravath Swaine & Moore 825 8th Ave New York NY 10019-7475

HURD, HEIDI M. law educator, dean; b. Laramie, Wyo., Oct. 19, 1960; d. Carroll Parsons and Jeanne Marie (Lemal) H.; m. Michael S. Moore, Aug. 8, 1987; children: Gillian K.J. and Aidn A. (twins). BA with honors, Queen's U., Kingston, Ont., Can., 1982; MA, Dalhousie U., Halifax, N.S., Can., 1984; JD, U. So. Calif., L.A., 1988, PhD, 1992. Asst. prof. U. Pa. Law Sch., Phila., 1989-94, prof. law and philosophy, 1994—2002, assoc. dean, 1994-96, co-dir. Inst. Law and Philosophy, 1998—2002; dean, prof. philosophy, David Baum prof. law U. of Ill. College of Law, 2002—. Vis. asst. prof. dept. philosophy U. Iowa, Iowa City, 1991-92; vis. prof. law U. Va. Law Sch., Charlottesville, 1997-98. Author: Moral Combat, 1999; contbr. articles to profl. jours. Office: U Illinois College Law Dean Office 504 E Pennsylvania Ave Champaign IL 61820-6909

HURD, JOHN R. lawyer; b. San Francisco, May 4, 1942; BA, Harvard U., 1964; student, U. Ctrl. del Ecuador; LLB, U. Tex., 1967. Bar: Tex. 1967. Mem. Vinson & Elkins L.L.P., Houston. Mergers and acquisitions, Natural resources. Office: Vinson & Elkins 2500 First City Tower 1001 Fannin St Ste 3300 Houston TX 77002-6706 Address: 10 Blenheim San Antonio TX 78209

HURLEY, LAWRENCE JOSEPH, lawyer; b. Plainfield, N.J., Nov. 17, 1946; s. Luke Michael and Gertrude Marie (Bremer) H.; m. Allyson J. Kingsley, May 28, 1977; children: Michael William, Kathryn Elizabeth. BS, U. Dayton, 1969; JD, Cath. U. Am., 1974. Bar: N.J. 1974, U.S. Dist. Ct. N.J., 1974, D.C. 1976, N.Y. 1980, U.S. Ct. Appeals (3rd cir.) 1980, U.S. Dist. Ct. (ea. and so. dists.) N.Y. 1981, U.S. Ct. Appeals (2nd cir.) 1981, U.S. Ct. Appeals (D.C. cir.) 1982. Law clk. Superior Ct. N.J., New Brunswick, 1974-75; assoc. Lynch, Mannion, Lutz & Lewandowski, New Brunswick, 1975-76, Stryker, Tams & Dill, Newark, 1976-79; atty. AT&T , Basking Ridge, NJ, 1979-85; chief asst. prosecutor econ. crimes and ofcl. corruption Morris County Prosecutor's Office, Morristown, NJ, 1985—89; ptnr. Voorhees & Acciavatti, Morristown, 1989-91; sr. atty. AT&T, 1991—96; labor and employment counsel Lucent Techs., Murray Hill, NJ, 1996—99, mng. labor and employment corp. counsel, 1999—2001, mng. litigation, labor and employment counsel, 2001—. With U.S. Army, 1969-71. Decorated Bronze Star and Army Commendation medal U.S. Army. Mem. ABA (litig. sect. 1976-86, labor law sect. 1981-86, criminal law sect. 1985-91, labor law sect. 1991—), N.J. State Bar Assn. (labor law sect. 1981—). Labor (including EEOC, Fair Labor Standards Act, labor-management relations, NLRB, OSHA). Office: Lucent Techs Rm 3C542 600 Mountain Ave New Providence NJ 07974

HURLOCK, JAMES BICKFORD, retired lawyer; b. Chgo., Aug. 7, 1933; s. James Bickford and Elizabeth (Charls) Hurlock; m. Margaret Lyn Holding, July 1, 1961; children: James Bickford III, Burton Charls, Matthew Hunter. AB, Princeton U., 1955; BA, Oxford U., 1957, MA, 1960; JD, Harvard U., 1959. Bar: N.Y. 1960, U.S. Supreme Ct. 1967. Assoc. White & Case, N.Y.C., 1959—66, ptnr., 1967—2000; ret., 2000. Bd. dirs. Orient Express Hotels, Ltd., Stolt Offshore S.A. Trustee N.Y. Presbyn. Hosp., Parker Sch. Fgn. and Comparative Law, Woods Hole Oceanog. Inst.; chmn. Internat. Devel. Law Inst., U.S. Assn. for UNHCR. Recipient Rhodes scholarship, 1955. Mem.: ABA, Am. Assn. Internat. Law, Am. Law Inst., N.Y. State Bar Assn., N.Y. Yacht Club, River Club. Republican. Episcopalian. Antitrust, Corporate, general, Private international. Home: 46 Byram Dr Greenwich CT 06830-7008 Office: White & Case 1155 Avenue Of The Americas New York NY 10036-2787 E-mail: jhurlock46byram@aol.com.

HURNYAK, CHRISTINA KAISER, lawyer; b. Noblesville, Ind., Dec. 22, 1949; d. Albert Michael and Lois Angie (Gatton) Kaiser; m. Cyril Hurnyak, June 24, 1972. BA cum laude, Wittenberg U., 1972; JD, SUNY-Buffalo, 1979. Bar: N.Y. 1980, Pa. 1996, U.S. Dist. Ct. (we. dist.) Pa. 1998. Mem. support staff McKinsey & Co., Inc., mgmt. cons., Chgo., 1972-75; law clk. Justice Norman J. Wolf, N.Y. Supreme Ct., Buffalo, 1980-81; assoc. Dempsey & Dempsey, Buffalo, 1979-80, 81-90, Grossman, Levine & Civiletto, Niagara Falls, N.Y., 1990-95, Tarasi, Tarasi & Fishman, P.C. (formerly Tarasi Law Firm), Pitts., 1998—. Mem. ABA, ATLA, Pa. State Bar Assn., Pa. Trial Lawyers Assn.. Allegheny County Bar Assn. Democrat. Lutheran. Federal civil litigation, State civil litigation, Personal injury (including property damage). Office: Tarasi Tarasi & Fishman PC 510 3rd Ave Pittsburgh PA 15219-2107

HURSH, JOHN R. lawyer; b. Scottsbluff, Nebr., Feb. 16, 1943; s. R. Max and Virginia Hursh; m. Judy Ann Lopez, Mar. 10, 1978; 1 child, Bryan W. BA, U. Wyo., 1965, JD, 1968. BAr: Wyo. 1968, U.S. Dist. Ct. Wyo. 1968, U.S. Ct. Appeals (10th cir.), U.S. Claims Ct., U.S. Supreme Ct. Assoc. atty. Paul Godfrey Law Offices, Cheyenne, Wyo., 1972-73; atty. Ctrl. Wyo. Law Assocs., Riverton, 1973—. Mem. Wyo. State Legislature, Cheyenne, 1974-80. Capt. USMCR, 1968-72. Mem. Wyo Trial Lawyers (pres. 1991-92). Republican. Episcopalian. General civil litigation. Home: 1497 S Hwy 20 Thermopolis WY 82443 Office: Ctrl Wyo Law Assocs 105 S 6th St E Riverton WY 82501-4456

HURST, CHARLES WILSON, lawyer; b. Salt Lake City, July 4, 1957; s. John Vann and Myra (Kasik) Piscane; m. Karen Buck, Jan. 5, 1985; children: Jeanette Q., Daniel C., Brian K., Matthew C., Robert W. Student, U. Chgo., 1975-77; BA cum laude, Wesleyan U., Conn., 1979; JD, Duke U., 1983. Bar: Pa. 1983, U.S. Dist. Ct. (ea. dist.) Pa. 1985, Calif. 1986, U.S. Dist. Ct. (cen. dist.) Calif. 1990. Assoc. Saul, Ewing, Remick & Saul, Phila., 1983-85, Wyman Bautzer Kuchel & Silbert, Orange County, Calif., 1985-89, ptnr., 1990, Snell & Wilmer LLP, Orange County, 1990—. Dir. Pacific Art Found., 1994-2000; trustee Pegasus Sch., 1996—. Mem. ABA (comml. leasing com. of real property, probate and trust law sect.), Orange County Bar Assn. Commercial, contracts (including sales of goods; commercial financing), Land use and zoning (including planning), Property, real (including real estate development, water). Office: Snell & Wilmer 1920 Main St Ste 1200 Irvine CA 92614-7230 E-mail: churst@swlaw.com.

HURT, JENNINGS LAVERNE, III, lawyer; b. Sanford, Fla., Oct. 25, 1952; s. Jennings Laverne Jr. and Virginia (Ludwig) H.; m. Maribeth O'Connor, June 24, 1978; children: Jennings Laverne IV, Matthew Alexander, Natalie Elizabeth, Joseph Connor. AA, Seminole Jr. Coll., 1972; BSBA, U. Fla., 1974; JD with honors, Cumberland Sch. Law, 1977. Bar: Fla. 1977, U.S. Dist. Ct. (mid. dist.) 1978, U.S. Dist. Ct. (no. and so. dists.) Fla. 1982, U.S. Ct. Appeals (11th cir.) 1988; cert. trial lawyer Nat. Bd. Trial Advocacy. Assoc. D'Aiuto, Walker & Buckmaster, P.A., Orlando, Fla., 1977-79; ptnr. Anderson & Hurt, P.A., Orlando, 1979-87; mng. ptnr. Rissman, Weisberg, Barrett & Hurt, P.A., Orlando, 1987—. Contbr. articles to profl. jours. Recipient Am. Jurisprudence award, 1974. Mem. ABA, Orange County Bar Assn., Fla. Bar Assn. (bd. cert. trial lawyer), Fla. Def. Lawyers Assn., Def. Rsch. Inst., Cen. Fla. Med. Malpractice Claims Assn. (treas. 1992-95). Republican. Roman Catholic. Avocations: golf, tennis. General civil litigation, Insurance, Personal injury (including property damage). Home: 1655 Barcelona Way Winter Park FL 32789-5614 Office: Rissman Weisberg Barrett & Hurt PA 201 E Pine St 15th Fl Orlando FL 32801-2738 E-mail: bucky.hurt@rissman.com.

HURTT, HAROLD L. protective services official; BS, Ariz. State U., 1977; M in Orgnl. Mgmt., U. Phoenix, 1991. Joined Phoenix Police Dept., 1968, chief of police, 1998—. Mem. pres. adv. coun. Rio Salado Coll.; bd. dirs. Major Cities Chief's, Yalle of the Sun YMCA, Phoenix Boys Choir, Mercy Health Care West. Mem.: NAACP (life), Police Exec. Rsch. Forum, Nat. Orgn. Black Law Enforcement Execs., Internat. Assn. Chiefs Police. Avocation: golf. Office: Phoenix Police Dept 620 W Washington St Phoenix AZ 85003*

HURWITZ, ANDREW D. judge; AB cum laude, Princeton U., 1968; JD, Yale U., 1972. Bar: Conn. 1973, Ariz. 1974, U.S. Dist. Ct. Ariz. 1975, U.S. Ct. Appeals (9th cir.) 1975, U.S. Supreme Ct. 1976, U.S. Dist. Ct. Conn. 1977, U.S. Ct. Appeals (2d cir.) 1977, U.S. Tax Ct. 1987, U.S. Ct. Appeals (7th cir.) 1987. Law clk. to Hon. Jon O. Newman U.S. Dist. Ct. Conn.,

1972; law clk. to Hon. J. Joseph Smith U.S. Ct. Appeals, 1972—73; law clk. to Hon. Potter Stewart U.S. Supreme Ct., 1973—74, 1984—95; with Meyer Hendricks et. al., 1974—80, 1984—95, 1983—95, Osborn Maledon, 1995—2003; judge Ariz. State Supreme Ct., Phoenix, 2003—; chief of staff Gov. State of Ariz. Office: Ariz State Supreme Ct Adminstrv Office Cts 1501 W Washington Phoenix AZ 85007

HURWITZ, BARRETT ALAN, lawyer; b. New Bedford, Mass., Dec. 9, 1948; s. Harold and Claire (Wollison) H. BA, Colby Coll., 1970; JD, Suffolk U., 1973. Bar: Mass. 1973, U.S. Dist. Ct. Mass. 1974. Intern U.S. Atty.'s Office, Boston, 1972-73; ptnr. Hurwitz and Hurwitz, New Bedford, 1973-97, owner, 1997—. Author weekly newspaper column: The Legal Forum, 1982-84. Bd. dirs. New Bedford Legal Aid Soc., 1976-93. Recipient Achievement award in oral advocacy Suffolk U. Law Sch., 1971, Achievement award in brief writing, 1971, Excellence award in corps. Am. Jurisprudence, 1973. Mem. New Bedford Bar Assn. (bar coun. 1975-82, pres. 1982-84), Bristol County Bar Assn. (bd. dirs. 1982-84), Mass. Bar Assn. Corporate, general, General practice, Probate (including wills, trusts). Home: 74 William St South Dartmouth MA 02748-3703 Office: Hurwitz and Hurwitz 888 Purchase St New Bedford MA 02740-6217

HURYN, CHRISTOPHER MICHAEL, lawyer; b. Akron, Ohio, June 1, 1967; s. Michael Alexander and Eileen Ruth (McFadden) H.; m. Leslie Marie Vitale, Oct. 9, 1993; children: Samuel, Jacob, Natalie. BS in Bus. cum laude, Miami U., Oxford, Ohio, 1989; JD, U. Akron, 1993. Bar: Ohio 1993, U.S. Dist. Ct. (no. dist.) Ohio 1994, U.S. Ct. Appeals (6th cir.) 1994. Jud. law clk. to Hon. Frank J. Bayer, Summit County Ct. Common Pleas, Akron, 1990-93; ptnr. Tzangas, Plakas, Mannos & Recupero, Canton, Ohio, 1993—. Dean's Club scholar, Sch. Law scholar and Judge and Mrs. Charles Sacks scholar U. Akron Sch. Law, 1992-93. Mem. Ohio Bar Assn., Ohio Acad. Trial Lawyers, Stark County Acad. Trial Lawyers (trustee 1997). Personal injury (including property damage). Office: Tzangas Plakas Mannos Et Al 454 Citizens Bldg Canton OH 44702

HUSBAND, BERTRAM PAUL, lawyer; b. L.A., Aug. 15, 1950; s. Bertram Perry and Ruth (Eatough) H.; m. Beverly Ruth Hyams, May 1, 1987, div. March 6, 2003; children: Joseph Bertram, Daniel James, David Paul. BA, Occidental Coll., 1972; JD, UCLA, 1977. Bar: Calif. 1977, U.S. Dist. Ct. (cen. dist.) Calif. 1978, U.S. Ct. Appeals (9th cir.) 1979, U.S. Dist. Ct. (so. dist.) Calif. 1980, U.S. Dist. Ct. (no. dist.) Calif. 1988, U.S. Tax Ct. 1987. Assoc. Coskey, Coskey & Boxer, L.A., 1978-79, Cooper, Epstein & Hurewitz, Beverly Hills, Calif., 1979-81; pvt. practice L.A., 1981-84; ptnr. Husband & Morris, L.A., 1984-89, Husband & Roberts, L.A. and Encino, Calif., 1989-91; pvt. practice Encino, 1991-94, Valencia, Calif., 1994-97, Burbank, Calif., 1997—. Adj. prof. law Pepperdine U., Malibu, Calif.,1978-79. Author equine law column Jour. Agrl. Taxation and Law, 1987-93; writer, producer (ednl. video) Fighting Back: Successfully Representing Your Horse Business to the IRS, 1991; editl. adv. bd. Am. Horse Coun. Tax Bulletin, 1994—. Registered judge Am. Horse Shows Assn., 1975-94; recommended judge Equestrian Trials Inc., 1988-94; dir., gen. counsel Burbank Internat. Children's Film Festival, 2000-03. Mem. ABA (tax sect., agrl. com., forum com. entertainment and sports industry, L.A. County Bar Assn. (chmn. pro bono oversight com. tax sect. 1987-88, officer entertainment tax com. of tax sect. 1993-96, chair 1995-96), Beverly Hills Bar Assn. (exec. com. entertainment sect. 1992-96), San Fernando Valley Bar Assn. (chair tax sect. 1993-94), Calif. State Bar (tax sect., lectr. 1988 seminar), Internat. Arabian Horse Assn. (vice chair fed. tax study com. 1979-92), Association Internationale du Film d'Animation (Hollywood chpt., dir. 1997-2003, gen. counsel 1997—), Media Dist. Intellectual Property Assn., World Arabian Horse Orgn. Mem. Ch. of Christ. Avocation: speculative fiction. Entertainment, Taxation, general, Equine law. Office: 10 Universal City Plz Ste 2000 Universal City CA 91608 E-mail: Paul.Husband@Husbandlaw.com.

HUSBAND, PHILLIP LYLE, lawyer; b. Meridian, Miss., Sept. 25, 1962; s. Billy Ford and Barbara Ann (Byrd) H. AA, Meridian Community Coll., Miss., 1982; BBA, Miss. State U., 1984; JD, Tulane, 1987. Bar: Miss. 1987, La. 1989, US V.I. 1990, Tex. 1990, US Dist. Cts. (no. and so. dists.) Miss. 1987, U.S. Ct. Appeals (5th cir.) 1987, US Ct. Appeals (3d cir.), US Supreme Ct. 1993, DC 1998, Va. 2002. Assoc. Ready & Assocs., Meridian, 1987-88; law clk. to magistrate judge U.S. Dist. Ct., Alexandria, La., 1988-89; assoc. DeVos & Co., St. Thomas, 1989—93; sr. atty. Law Offices of Joel W. Marsh, 1993—98; assoc. gen. counsel DC Health and Hosps. Pub. Benefit Corp., 1999—2000, gen. counsel, 2000—01; spl. counsel DC, 2001—. Instr. Meridian Community Coll., 1987. Mem. ABA, Miss. State Bar Assn., La. State Bar Assn., Tex. Bar Assn., V.I. Bar Assoc., DC Bar Assn. Methodist. Home: 700 7th St SW # 524 Washington DC 20024 Office: Dist Columbia Dept Health 825 N Capitol St NE Washington DC 20002 E-mail: Philip.Husband@dc.gov.

HUSKEY, DOW THOBERN, lawyer; b. Sept. 23, 1946; s. Dow Thobern Huskey and Helen (Weathersbee) Morris; m. Julie Beth Coursin, May 17, 1975; children: Dow, III, Whitney. BS, Samford U., 1970; JD, Cumberland Sch. Law, 1976. Bar: Ala. 1977, U.S. Dist. Ct. (mid. dist.) Ala. 1977, U.S. Ct. Appeals (5th cir.) 1977, U.S. Ct. Appeals (11th cir.) 1981, U.S. Supreme Ct. 1981. Ptnr. Huskey & Etheredge, Dothan, 1977—82, Johnson Huskey Hornsby & Etheredge, Dothan, 1982—87; pvt. practice Dothan, 1987—. Author: (non-fiction) Landlord and Tenant, The Law in Alabama, 1980, Damages, The Law in Alabama, 1985. Pres. Houston County chpt. Am. Cancer Soc., Dothan, Ala., 1979—81, Houston County chpt. Ala. Soc. Crippled Children and Adults, Dothan, 1982—83. Mem.: Soc. Ala. Def. Lawyers Assn., Am. Judicature Soc., Assn. Trial Lawyers Am., Nat. Assn. Coll. and Univ. Attys., Ala. Trial Lawyers Assn. (bd. govs. 1980—85), Rotary (pres. 1990—91). Republican. Episcopalian. Federal civil litigation, Corporate, general, Property, real (including real estate development, water). Home: 27 Hampton Way Dothan AL 36305-6319 Office: 112 W Adams St Dothan AL 36303-4528

HUST, BRUCE KEVIN, lawyer; b. Cin., Aug. 16, 1957; s. George Julius and Shirley Mae (Glaser) H. BA, U. Cin., 1979; JD, No. Ky. U., 1985. Bar: Ohio 1986, U.S. Dist. Ct. (so. dist.) Ohio 1987, U.S. Ct. Appeals (6th cir.) 2000. Pvt. practice, Cin., 1986—; trial counsel Hamilton County Pub. Defender's Office, Cin., 1988—2000. Vol. Lawyers Project, Cin., 1986-87, 90—; precinct exec. mem. Hamilton County Rep. Ctrl. Com., 1988—. With Ohio Naval Militia, 1988-94; journalist USNR, 1994—. Mem. Ohio State Bar Assn., Cin. Bar Assn., Ohio Assn. Criminal Def. Lawyers, Masons, Odd Fellows. Mem. United Ch. of Christ. Avocations: reading, current events, politics, writing and performing comedy. Appellate, Criminal, General practice. Home: 4247 Delridge Dr Cincinnati OH 45205-2025 Office: 30 E Central Pkwy Ste 100 Cincinnati OH 45202-1120 Office Fax: 513-421-7794.

HUSTED, STANLEY NEAL, II, lawyer; b. Ft. Smith, Ark., July 22, 1944; s. Stanley Neal and Dorothy Louise (Lehmann) H.; m. Clara May Howson, Sept. 21, 1974; children: Laura Ann Peck, Sara Beth. BA, Wittenberg U., 1969; JD, Ohio No. U., 1972. Bar: Ohio 1972, Fla. 1973. Dir. Clark County Bd. Elections Springfield, Ohio, 1974-76, dep. dir., 1976-78; sec.-treas., legal counselor Springfield Conservancy Dist., Springfield, Ohio, 1977—; pvt. practice Springfield, Ohio, 1972—. Pres. Clark County Young Rep. Club, Springfield, 1972-74; treas. Clark County Men's Rep. Club, 1979, v.p., 1980; legal counsel, parliamentarian Springfield Jaycees, 1975-76, Northridge Jaycees, Springfield, 1975-80. Mem. ABA, Ohio Bar Assn., Fla. Bar Assn., Clark County Bar Assn., Kiwanis, Masons, Shriners, Scottish Rite. Lutheran. Avocations: waterskiing, boating, travel, gemology, jetskiing. Estate planning, General practice, Probate (including wills, trusts). Home: 1009 Moorefield Rd Springfield OH 45503-5853 Office: 906 National City Bank Bldg Springfield OH 45502

HUSTON, JOHN CHARLES, law educator; b. Chgo., Mar. 21, 1927; s. Albert Allison and Lillian Helen (Sullivan) H.; m. Joan Frances Mooney, Aug. 1, 1954; children: Mark Allison, Philip John, Paul Francis James; m. Inger Margareta Westerman, May 4, 1979. AB, U. Wash., 1950; JD, U. Wash., 1952; LLM, NYU, 1955. Bar: Wash. 1952, N.Y. 1964, U.S. Dist. Ct. (we. dist.) Wash. 1953, U.S. Ct. Appeals (9th cir.) 1953, U.S. Tax Ct. 1977, U.S. Supreme Ct. 1993. Assoc. Kahin, Carmody & Horswill, Seattle, 1952—53; teaching fellow NYU Law Sch., 1953—54; asst. prof. NYU, 1953—57; asst. co-dir. U. Ankara Legal Rsch. Inst., Turkey, 1954—55; asst. prof. Syracuse U., NY, 1957—60, assoc. prof., 1960—65, prof., 1965—67; prof., assoc. dean U. Wash., Seattle, 1967—73, prof. law, 1973—96, prof. emeritus, 1996—. Of counsel Carney, Badley, Smith & Spellman, Seattle, 1987—2002, Smith McKenzie Rothwell & Barlow, P.S., Seattle, 2002—; vis. prof. U. Stockholm, 1986, U. Bergen, 1989, Bond U., Australia, 1991. Author: (with Redden) The Mining Law of Turkey, 1956, The Petroleum Law of Turkey, 1956, (with Mucklestone and Cross) Community Property: General Considerations, 1971, (with Price and Treacy) 4th edit., 1994, (with Sullivan and others) Administration of Criminal Justice, 166, 2d edit., 1969, (with Miyatake and Way) Japanese International Taxation, 1983, supplements through 1997, (with Cross and Shields) Community Property Desk Book, 1977, 2d edit., 1989, supplement, 1997, (with Williams) Permanent Establishment, 1993. With USNR, 1945-46; capt. USAFR. Mem.: ABA, Internat. Fiscal Assn. (past regional v.p., past mem. coun.), Japanese Am. Soc. Legal Studies, King County Bar Assn., Wash. State Bar Assn. (chmn. tax sect. 1984—85), Am. Coll. Trust and Estate Coun. Office: 700 Logan Bldg 500 Union St Seattle WA 98101 Fax: 206-525-1758. E-mail: huston@att.net.

HUSTON, STEVEN CRAIG, lawyer; b. Morris, Ill., June 3, 1954; s. Raymond P. and Evelyn M. (Bass) Huston; m. Nina Huston. BA, Ill. Coll., 1977; JD, John Marshall Law Sch., 1980; MBA, Northwestern U., 1989. Bar: Ill. 1980, U.S. Dist. Ct. (no. dist.) Ill. 1980, U.S. Ct. Appeals (7th cir.) 1980. Assoc. Siegel, Denberg et al, Chgo., 1980-83; staff atty. William Wrigley Jr. Co., Chgo., 1983-84, asst. sec. legal, 1984-94, asst. v.p. legal, 1994-96, counsel North Am., 1996—2001; v.p., gen. counsel Symons Corp., 2002—03; v.p., gen. counsel, sec. Dayton Superior Corp., 2003—. Bd. dirs. SOS Am. Mem.: ABA, Am. Corp. Counsel Assn., Chgo. Bar Assn. Corporate, general, Securities, Trademark and copyright.

HUTCHEON, PETER DAVID, lawyer; b. S.I., N.Y., Sept. 11, 1943; s. Peter and Helen Christine (Buckley) H.; m. Elizabeth Ann Demy, June 8, 1969 (div. Jan. 1986); children: Rececca Leigh, Douglas Ian; m. Barbara Mary Silver, Feb. 14, 1986; 1 child, Peter Silver. BA, Williams Coll., 1965; postgrad., Ludwig-Maximilian Universität, Munich, 1965-66; JD, Harvard U., 1969. Bar: N.Y. 1970, N.J. 1975. Assoc. White & Case, N.Y., 1968-75, Norris, McLaughlin & Marcus, P.A., Somerville, N.J., 1975-76, mem., 1976—. Chmn. N.J. Corp. and Bus. Law Study Commn., 1989—; mem., sec. adv. com. N.J. Bur. Securities, 1993-2001, chmn., 1994-2001. Contbr. articles to profl. jours. Chmn. bd. mgrs. St. Andrews Soc. of N.Y., 1986—87; deacon United Reformed Ch., Somerville, 1977—80; elder Bound Brook Presbyn. Ch., 1996—99. Dankstipendium scholar govt. of the Fed. Republic of Gemany, 1965. Mem. ABA (chmn. sect. of sci. and tech. 1986-87), N.J. State Bar Assn. (chmn. banking law sect. 1982-83, chmn. corp. and bus. sect. 1990-92), N.Y. State Bar Assn., German-Am. Lawyers Assn., Nat. Conf. of Lawyers and Scientists (del. 1988-91), Princeton Area Alumni Assn. of Williams Coll. (pres. 1981-89), Clan Donald (N.Y.). Avocations: wine tasting, singing. Banking, Corporate, general, Securities. Office: Norris McLaughlin & Marcus PA PO Box 1018 721 Rt 202/206 Somerville NJ 08876

HUTCHESON, MARK ANDREW, lawyer; b. Phila., Mar. 29, 1942; s. John R. and Mary Helen (Willis) H.; m. Julie A. Olander, June 13, 1964; children: Kirsten Elizabeth, Mark Andrew II, Megan Ann. BA, U. Puget Sound, 1964; LLB, U. Wash., 1967. Bar: Wash. 1967, U.S. Dist. Ct. (we. and ea. dists.) Wash., U.S. Ct. Appeals (9th cir.), U.S. Supreme Ct. Staff counsel Com. on Commerce U.S. Senate, Washington, 1967-68; assoc. Davis Wright Tremaine, Seattle, 1968-72; ptnr. Davis, Wright Tremaine, Seattle, 1973—; mng. ptnr., chief exec. officer Davis Wright Tremaine, Seattle, 1989-94; chmn. Davis, Wright Tremaine, Seattle, 1994—. Mem., co-founder labor law com. Nat. Banking Industry, 1984—. Co-author: Employer's Guide to Strike Planning and Prevention, 1986; contbr. articles to profl. jours. Chmn., trustee Virginia Mason Hosp., Seattle, 1980—, Overlake Sch., Redmond, Wash., 1984-89, Epiphany Sch., Seattle, 1982-84, Legal Aid for Wash. Fund, 1991—; bd. dirs. Vis. Nurse Svcs., Seattle-King County, 1985-88; trustee Pacific N.W. Ballet, 1991-99, Pacific N.W. Assn. Ind. Schs., 1996-98. Nelson T. Hartson scholar U. Wash., 1966; Deerfield fellow Heritage Found., Deerfield, Mass., 1963. Mem. ABA (health care forum, employment law sect.), Seattle-King County Bar Assn. (employment law sect.), Am. Acad. Hosp. Attys., Am. Hosp. Assn. (labor rels. adv. com. 1978—), Coll. Labor and Employment Lawyers, Greater Seattle C. of C. (bd. dirs. 1991-94), Rainier Club, Seattle Tennis Club, Univ. Club, Order of Coif. Episcopalian. Avocations: sailing, tennis, skiing, reading, travel. Health, Labor (including EEOC, Fair Labor Standards Act, labor-management relations, NLRB, OSHA). Office: Davis Wright Tremaine 2600 Century Sq 1501 4th Ave Seattle WA 98101-1688 E-mail: markhutcheson@dwt.com.

HUTCHINS, PETER EDWARD, lawyer; b. Nashua, N.H., Jan. 20, 1958; s. Edward Peter and Joyce Martha Hutchins; m. Kathy Hutchins; 1 child, Jamie. BA cum laude, Dartmouth Coll., 1980; JD magna cum laude, Boston U., 1983. Bar: N.H. 1983, U.S. Dist. Ct. N.H. 1983. Ptnr. Wiggin & Nourie, P.A., Manchester, N.H., 1983-98, Hall & Hess, PA, Manchester, 1998—. Basketball referee, cert. Internat. Assn. Approved Basketball Officials, N.H., 1992—; girls softball umpire, cert. N.H. Softball Umpires Assn., 1994—. Mem. N.H. Bar Assn. (v.p., pres. 2001-02). Avocation: officiating high school sports. Insurance, Personal injury (including property damage), Product liability. Office: Hall Stewart Murphy Brown & Hutchins 80 Merrimack St Manchester NH 03101

HUTCHINSON, ASA, federal agency administrator; b. Benton County, Ark., Dec. 3, 1950; m. Susan Burrell; children: Asa III, Sarah, John, Seth. BS in Acctg., Bob Jones U.; JD, U. Ark. Atty. U.S. Dist. Ct. (we. dist.) Ark., 1982-85; ptnr. Karr & Hutchinson, Ft. Smith, Ark., 1986-96; rep. Ark. 3rd dist. U.S. House of Reps., 1996—2001; adminr. drug enforcement admin. U.S. Dept. Justice, Washington, 2001—03; under sec. for border and transp. security dept. Homeland Security, Washington, 2003—. Judiciary com. U.S. Congress, subcom. crime, subcom. constitution, transp. and infrastructure com., subcom. Water Resources and Environment, subcom. aviation, intelligence com., ethics com., intellectual property subcom.; co-chair Freshmen Bipartisan Campaign Finance Reform Task Force; apptd. to Speakers Task Force for Drug-Free Am.; co-chmn., chmn. Rep. Ctrl. Com. of Ark., 1990-95; past mem. Ark. Jud. Ethics Commn., Ark. Election Commn., Ark. Election Law Revision Commn.; condr. democracy workshops in Russia, 1994; del. White House Conf. on Aging, 1995; past bd. mem. Western Ark. chpt. Alzheimer's Assn. Named one of Ten Outstanding Young Leaders in Ark., Ark. Jaycees, 1986. Republican. Office: Dept Homeland Security 3801 Nebraska Ave NW Washington DC 20016*

HUTCHINSON, DENNIS JAMES, law educator; b. Boulder, Colo., Dec. 28, 1946; s. Dudley Isom and Jane Wilcox (Sampson) H.; children: Kathryn Wood, David, Jane. Office: U Chgo Law Sch 1111 E 60th St Chicago IL 60637-2776 E-mail: dhutch@law.uchicago.edu.

HUTCHINSON, MARK STEVENSON, lawyer; b. Syracuse, N.Y., Apr. 28, 1965; s. Edward Ross and Jean Marie (King) H.; m. Robin Jones; 1 child: James Mark. BS, Millsaps Coll., 1987; JD, Miss. Coll., 1990. Bar: Miss. 1990, U.S. Dist. Ct. (so. dist.) Miss. 1990. Assoc. Richard Schartz & Assocs., Jackson, Miss., 1990; lawyer Miss. Asbestos Assn., Jackson, 1990-91; pvt. practice Jackson, 1991—. Hall scholar Millsaps Coll., Jackson, 1983, Regents scholar SUNY, Albany, 1983. Mem. ABA, Am. Trial Lawyers Assn., Delta Theta Phi (officer 1988-90). Criminal, Family and matrimonial, Personal injury (including property damage). Home: 315 Cox Crossing Madison MS 39110 Office: 5269 Keele St Ste A Jackson MS 39206-4322

HUTCHISON, STANLEY PHILIP, retired lawyer; b. Joliet, Ill., Nov. 22, 1923; s. Stuart Philip and Verna (Kinzer) H.; m. Helen Jane Rush, July 25, 1945; children: Norman, Elizabeth. BS, Northwestern U., 1947; LLB, Ill. Inst. Tech., 1951. Bar: Ill. 1951. Legal asst. Washington Nat. Ins. Co., Evanston, 1947-51, asst. counsel, 1951-55, asst. gen. counsel, 1955-58, assoc. gen. counsel, 1958-60, gen. counsel, 1960-63, v.p., gen. counsel, dir., 1963-66, exec. v.p., gen. counsel, dir., 1966-67, exec. v.p., gen. counsel, sec., dir., 1967-70, chmn. exec. com., 1970-73, vice-chmn. bd., 1974-75, chmn. bd., CEO, 1976-88; pres. Wash. Nat. Corp., 1970-83, CEO, 1978-88, chmn. bd., 1983-88; ret., 1988-98. Bd. dirs. Washington Nat. Corp. Pres.'s coun. Nat. Coll. Edn., 1977-88, adv. coun. Kellogg Grad. Sch. Mgmt. Northwestern U., 1981-88; bd. dirs. Evanston Hosp. Corp., 1983-88. Lt. (j.g.) USNR, 1942-46. Mem. Assn. Life Ins. Counsel, Am. Coun. Life Ins. (bd. dir. 1977-81, 84-88), Ill. Life Ins. Coun. (bd. dir. 1978-86, pres. 1983-85), Inc. Econs. Soc. Am. (bd. dir. 1977-85, chmn. 1981-82), Health Ins. Assn. Am. (bd. dirs. 1982-88, chmn. 1987-88). Insurance. Home: 7501 E Thompson Peak Pky #501 Scottsdale AZ 85255 E-mail: carefreesh@aol.com.

HUTH, LESTER CHARLES, lawyer; b. Tiffin, Ohio, Nov. 21, 1924. JD, U. Notre Dame, 1951. Bar: Ohio 1951. Pvt. practice, Fostoria, Ohio, 1954-97. Tiffin, Ohio, 1997—; acting mcpl. judge, Fostoria, 1970, city solicitor, 1954-56, 60-64, police prosecutor, 1964-68; magistrate Common Pleas Ct., Seneca County, Ohio, 1995—; legal counsel to St. Wendelin Parish, Fostoria, 1972-96, Cmty. Hospice, 1992—; atty. Selective Svc. Bd. Appeals, 1956-75. Clk. city council, Fostoria, 1957-58; sec.-treas. Karrick Sch. Handicapped Children, 1956-77; adviser to Fostoria Family and Child Svc., 1977-83. Recipient Certs. of Appreciation Pres. Lyndon Johnson, 1966, SSS, 1975. Mem. Mem. Ohio Bar Assn., Senece County Bar Assn., C. of C. (dir. 1970-71), Fostoria Jaycees (founding pres. 1954), Fostoria A.M. Exchange Club. General practice. Home and Office: 80 Northwood Dr Tiffin OH 44883-1997

HUTH, WILLIAM EDWARD, lawyer; b. South Bend, Ind., July 26, 1931; s. Edward Andrew and Margaret Mary (Emonds) H.; m. Mary Pamela Hall, Aug. 11, 1962; children: Katharine Louise, Stephen Edward (dec.), Alan Edward. BS, U. Dayton, 1952; JD, Yale, 1957. Bar: N.Y. 1958, U.S. Dist. Ct. (so. dist.) N.Y. 1959, Hawaii 1961, Mich. 1962, U.S. Dist. Ct. (ea. dist.) Mich. 1962, U.S. Supreme Ct. 1969, Pa. 1975, Conn. 1978. Assoc. Kelley, Drye, Newhall & Maginnes, N.Y.C., 1958-61; group counsel Chrysler Corp., Detroit, 1962-72; ptnr. Ziegler, Dykhouse, Wise & Huth, Detroit, 1973-74; assoc. gen. counsel Westinghouse Electric Corp., Pitts., 1974-76; asst. sec., asst. gen. counsel Combustion Engrng., Inc., Stamford, Conn., 1976-90; ptnr. Huth, Grinnell & Flaherty, Stamford, 1991-2000. Adj. prof. law Wayne State U., Detroit, 1969-74, adj. prof. law Pace U. Sch. of Law, 1999-2001. Contbr. articles to profl. publs. 1st lt. AUS, 1952-54. Mem. ABA (antitrust sect., internat. law sect., bus. law sect.), Am. Soc. Internat. Law, Am. Arbitration Assn. (Blue Ribbon Panel Arbitrators and Mediators, internat. panel, mem. corp. coun. com.), ICC Arbitration Com., U.S. Coun. for Internat. Bus. (ICC arbitration com.), Chartered Inst. Arbitrators (London), Inter-Pacific Bar Assn., Internat. Bar Assn., Conn. Bar Assn. (chmn. corp. coun. sec. 1991-94), Assn. of Bar of City of N.Y., Westchester-Fairfield Corp. Counsel Assn. (pres. 1987, bd. dirs. 1984-88), U.S. C. of C. (mem. antitrust adv. coun.), Yale Club N.Y.C., The Army and Navy Club (Washington), Indian Harbor Yacht Club (Greenwich), Order of Coif. Roman Catholic. Antitrust, Commercial, contracts (including sales of goods; commercial financing), Private international. Home: 39 Balmaha Ct Fairfield CT 06825-1173 Office: PO Box 320298 Fairfield CT 06825 E-mail: huthwe@ix.netcom.com.

HUTSON, JEFFREY WOODWARD, lawyer; b. New London, Conn., July 19, 1941; s. John Jenkins and Kathryn Barbara (Himberg) Hutson; m. Susan Office, Nov. 25, 1967; children: Elizabeth Kathryn, Anne Louise. AB, U. Mich., 1963, LLB, 1966. Bar: Ohio 1966, Hawaii 1971. Assoc. Lane, Alton & Horst, Columbus, Ohio, 1966-74, ptnr., 1974—. Arbitrator commercial construction panel Am Arbitration Asn, 1976—. Trustee, vice-chair 6 Pence Sch, 1983—88; mem comt creeds and professionalism Ohio Supreme Ct, 1989—90; chair, bd dirs NW Counseling Servs, 1990—92; regional vpres Def Research Inst, 1991—93. Lt comdr USNR, 1967—71. Fellow: Columbus Bar Found, Ohio State Bar Found, Am Bar Found, Am Col Trials Lawyers, Am Arbit Asn; mem.: Faculty Def Coun Trail Acad, Int Asn Def Counsel, Columbus Bar Asn, Ohio Asn Civil Trial Attys, Ohio Bar Asn, Athletic Club, Scioto Country Club. Avocations: cycling, reading, music. Alternative dispute resolution, Construction, Insurance. Office: Lane Alton & Horst 175 S 3rd St Ste 700 Columbus OH 43215-5100

HUTSON, MELVIN ROBERT, lawyer; b. Decatur, Ala., Dec. 7, 1947; s. John Robert and Katie Louise (Waddell) H.; m. Margaret Ann Shaddix; children: Melvin, Rachael, Katie, Jamie. BS, U. Ala., 1968, JD, 1971. Bar: Ala. 1971, Ga. 1972, S.C. 1975, D.C. 1978. Atty. NLRB, Atlanta, 1971-73; ptnr. Thompson Mann & Hutson, Greenville, S.C., 1974-98, Melvin Hutson, PA, Greenville, 1998—. Bd. dirs. Primesco, Inc., Mutual Savings Life Ins. Co., Inc., Liquid Server Sys., Inc. Chmn. bd. dirs. World Cancer Rsch. Fund, London, 1994—; chmn. AGC Labor Lawyers Coun., 1989-90, Am. Inst. Cancer Rsch., 1982—. Mem. ABA (mem. com. on devel. of law under nat. labor relations act 1977—, chmn. subcom. on labor mgmt. litigation). Labor (including EEOC, Fair Labor Standards Act, labor-management relations, NLRB, OSHA). Home: 1307 N Main St Greenville SC 29609-4716 Office: PO Box 88 Greenville SC 29602-0088 E-mail: mel.hutson@scbar.org.

HUTT, LAURENCE JEFFREY, lawyer; b. N.Y.C., Dec. 15, 1950; s. George Joseph and Miriam Martha (Cohen) H.; children: Marcie Arin, Ethan Lance, Amanda Rachel, Denver Allison. BA in History, U. Pa., 1972; JD, Stanford U., 1975. Bar: Calif. 1975, Colo., 1995. Assoc. Kadison, Pfaelzer, Woodard, Quinn & Rossi, L.A., 1976-82, ptnr., 1982-87; shareholder Quinn, Kully and Morrow, L.A., 1987-96; ptnr. Arnold & Porter, L.A., 1996—. Judge pro tem L.A. Mcpl. Ctr.; judge pro tem settlement officer L.A. Superior Ct. Bd. dirs. Western Ctr. on Law and Poverty, 1999—2002. Mem. State Bar Calif. (mem. exec. com. conf. del. 1992-95, legis. chair and vice chair 1994-95), L.A. County Bar (del. to Calif. State Bar Conv. 1980-92, 97-98, 2002—, mem. del. exec. com. 1989-92, 2002—, del. chair 1991-92, state cts. com. 1989-93, vice chair 1989-90, chair superior cts. subcom. 1988-89, Calif. jud. sys. com. 1988-90, liaison bench and bar com. 1988-90, mem. jud. elections evaluation com. 1999—), Constnl. Rights Found. (high sch. moot ct. scoring att., coach 1985-90), Order of Coif, Phi Beta Kappa. Avocations: wine tasting, theater, film. General civil litigation, Property, real (including real estate development, water), Sports. Office: Arnold & Porter 777 S Figueroa St Fl 44 Los Angeles CA 90017-5800

HUTT, PETER BARTON, lawyer; b. Buffalo, Nov. 16, 1934; s. Lester Ralph and Louise Rich (Fraser) H.; children: Katherine Zurn, Peter Barton, Sarah Henderson, Everett Fraser. BA magma cum laude, Yale U., 1956; LLB, Harvard U., 1959; LLM, NYU, 1960. Bar: N.Y. 1959, D.C. 1961, U.S. Supreme Ct. 1967. Assoc. Covington & Burling, Washington, 1960-68, ptnr., 1968-71, 75—; chief counsel FDA, Washington, 1971-75. Bd. dirs. Cognetix, Inc., Salt Lake City, CV Therapeutics Inc., Palo Alto, Calif.,

PhaseForward, Inc., Waltham, Mass., Microban Internat. Ltd., N.Y.C., Momenta, Inc., Cambridge, Mass.; mem. adv. com. to dir. NIH, 1976—81; mem. com. on rsch. tng. NAS, 1976—80; bd. dirs. Calif. HealthCare Inst., San Diego; counsel to Alcoholic Beverage Med. Rsch. Found., 1984—85, chmn. bd. dirs., 1986—92; mem. Nat. Com. to Rev. Current Proc. for Approval of New Drugs for Cancer and AIDS, Nat. Cancer Inst., 1988—90; mem. nat. bd. Scripps Clinic and Rsch. Found., La Jolla, 1977—85, La Jolla, 1990—95; mem. internat. bd. Scripps Instns. of Medicine and Sci., 1995—, Ctr. for Study Drug Devel., Tufts U. Ctr., 1976—99, Ctr. for Advanced Studies, U.Va., 1982—, Inst. for Health Policy Analysis, 1982—, Am. Pharm. Inst., Washington, 1988—92; mem. Com. on Food Laws and Regulations, Inst. Food Tech.; mem. adv. com. Progress and Freedom Found., 1994—97; mem. adv. bd. Frazier Healthcare Investments, Seattle, 1993—, Sprout Group, N.Y. and Menlo Park, 1993—, Polaris Venture Ptnrs., Waltham, 1995—, Vanguard Medica Ltd., Guildford, England, 1993—99, Sherbrook Capital Health & Wellness Fund, Lexington, Mass., 1999—, Burrill Neutraceuticals Adv. Bd., San Francisco, 2000—; mem. various panels U.S. Congl. Office Tech. Assessment; lectr. on food and drug law Harvard U., 1994—, Stanford U., 1998; mem. adv. bd. Columbia U. Sch. Pub. Health, 1997—. Author: (with Patricia Wald) Dealing with Drug Abuse, 1972, (with Richard Merrill) Food and Drug Law, 1991, (with Bruce Kuhlik) Understanding Export Law, 1998; editor-in-chief U.S. Food Labeling Law, 1991—; contbg. editor: Legal Times of Washington, 1978-86; mem. editorial bd. various jours.; editor: Food and Drug Law: An Electronic Book of Harvard Law School Student Papers. Bd. dirs. Sidwell Friends Sch., Washington, 1976-84; bd. dirs. Legal Action Ctr., N.Y.C., 1976—, vice-chmn., 1984-98; bd. dirs. Found. for Biomed. Rsch., 1976-2003, vice chmn., 1989— ; trustee Washington Lawyers Com. for Civil Rights & Urban Affairs, 1976—, Food and Drug Law Inst., 2001—; bd. dirs. Soc. Risk Analysis, 1985-88, 89-92, counsel, 1992—; mem. vis. com. Harvard Sch. Pub. Health, 1980-86. Recipient award of merit FDA, 1972, 75, Disting. Svc. award HEW, 1974, Underwood-Prescott award MIT, 1977. Fellow: Soc. Risk Analysis; mem.: Inst. Medicine of NAS (Devel. of Drugs and Vaccines Against AIDS roundtable 1988—94, bd. on health care svcs. 1998—2002), Met. Club (Washington). Episcopalian. Administrative and regulatory, Environmental, Health. Home: 402 Prince St Alexandria VA 22314-3114 Office: Covington & Burling 1201 Pennsylvania Ave NW Washington DC 20004-2401

HUTTO, RICHARD JAY, lawyer; b. Fitzgerald, Ga., Oct. 7, 1952; s. O.J. and Reba Ivalow (Gossett) H.; m. Katherine Anne Johnston, Aug. 3, 1991; children: Katherine Tod, Bradley Martin. BA, U. Ga., 1974; JD, Mercer U., 1984. Bar: Ga., 1984, D.C., 1985. Polit. coord. Jimmy Carter Presdl. Campaign, Atlanta, 1975-76; Carter family appointments sec. The White Ho., Washington, 1977-78; asst. to Lt. Gov. Zell Miller Lt. Gov. Zell Miller, Atlanta, 1978; program coord. White Ho. Conf. on Small Bus., Washington, 1979-80; dir. spl. projects White Ho. Conf. for Children and Youth, Washington, 1980-81; atty. Barrett, Montgomery and Murphy, Washington, 1984-87; v.p. Challenger Ctr. Space Sci. Edn., Alexandria, Va., 1987-89; pvt. practice Alexandria, Va., 1989-93; asst. v.p. devel. Mercer Univ., Macon, Ga., 1995-96. Commr. for Arts, City of Alexandria, 1989-93; mng. dir. The Grand Opera House, Macon, Ga.; Gov.'s appointee Ga. Coun. for Arts, 1995—, chmn., 1997-99; bd. dirs. So. Arts Fedn., 1997-99; pres. Macon-Bibb County Conv. and Visitors Bur.; exec. dir. Jekyll Island Found., 2000—; dir. planned giving Wesleyan Coll., 2001-02; dir. devel. Ga. Music Hall of Fame, 2002—. Decorated knight of merit Sacred Mil. Constantinian Order St. George. Mem. Nat. Assembly State Arts Agys. (bd. dirs.), Royal Overseas Club (London), Macon C. of C. (bd. dirs.). Roman Catholic. Avocations: book collecting, travel. Home: 1269 Jackson Springs Rd Macon GA 31211-1731

HYAMS, HAROLD, lawyer; b. Bklyn., May 19, 1943; s. Frank Charles and Celia (Silverstein) H.; m. Simone Elkeharrat, Nov. 18, 1973; children: Gabriel, Galite, Emilie, Jonathan. BA, U. Vt., 1965; MA in Latin Am. Studies, Georgetown U., 1966; JD, Syracuse U., 1970. Bar: N.Y. 1971, Ariz. 1974, U.S. Dist. Ct. Ariz. 1974, U.S. Ct. Appeals (9th cir.) 1974, U.S. Supreme Ct. 1995. Asst. to the gen. counsel Am. Express Co., N.Y.C., 1970-72; atty. Legal Aid Soc., Bklyn., 1973; ptnr. Harold Hyams and Assocs., Tucson, 1974—. Mem. panel of arbitrators Am. Arbitration Assn., N.Y.C., 1971-73. Mem. Commn. on Ariz. Environ., 1988. Mem. Am. Bd. Trial Advs., Ariz. Trial Lawyers Assn., Pima County Bar Assn., Assn. Trial Lawyers Am. (adv. bd. trial advocates 1990, cert. specialist in personal injury and wrongful death 1991). Avocation: travel. Federal civil litigation, Personal injury (including property damage). Home: 3175 N Elena Maria Tucson AZ 85750-2915 Office: 680 S Craycroft Rd Tucson AZ 85711-7197

HYBL, WILLIAM JOSEPH, lawyer, foundation executive; b. Des Moines, July 16, 1942; s. Joseph A. and Geraldine (Evans) H.; m. Kathleen Horrigan, June 6, 1967; children: William J. Jr., Kyle Horrigan. BA, Colo. Coll., 1964; JD, U. Colo., 1967. Bar: Colo. 1967. Asst. dist. atty. 4th Jud. Dist. El Paso and Teller Counties, 1970-72; pres., dir. Garden City Co., 1973—; dir. Broadmoor Hotel, Inc., 1973—, also vice-chmn., 1987—; chmn., CEO, trustee El Pomar Found., Colorado Springs, Colo., 1973—; pres. U.S. Olympic Com., 1991-92,96-2000. Dir. USAA, San Antonio, Kinder Morgan Inc., Houston, FirstBank Holding Co. of Colo., Lakewood; mem. Colo. Ho. Reps., 1972-73; spl. counsel The White House, Washington, 1981; U.S. rep. to 56th Gen. Assembly of U.N., 2001-02. Pres. Air Force Acad. Found.; sec.; vice chmn. bd. U.S. Adv. Commn. on Pub. Diplomacy, 1990-97; civilian aide to sec. of army, 1986—. Capt. U.S. Army, 1967-69. Republican. Property, real (including real estate development, water).

HYDE, ALAN LITCHFIELD, retired lawyer; b. Akron, Ohio, Nov. 4, 1928; s. Howard Linton Hyde and Katharine (Pennington) Litchfield; m. Charlotte Griffin Ross, July 10, 1954; children: Elizabeth Hyde Moore, Pamela. AB magna cum laude, Amherst Coll., 1950; JD, Harvard U., 1953. Bar: Ohio 1953, U.S. Dist. Ct. (no. dist.) Ohio 1955. Assoc. Thompson, Hine and Flory, Cleve., 1953-64, ptnr., 1964-93; ret., 1993. Hon. consul, Mexico, 1969—74. Contbr. articles to profl. jours. Trustee Planned Parenthood Greater Cleve., Inc., 1960-79, 80-81, pres. bd. trustees, 1977-79; sec., gen. counsel Greater Cleve. Growth Assn., 1972-74, 86-88, bd. dirs., 1974-80, 82-86, 88-93; trustee Cleve. World Trade Assn., 1978-81; trustee Cleve. Coun. World Affairs, 1980-93, mem. exec. com., 1980-83. Mem. ABA, Inter-Am. Bar Assn. (coun., com. on Latin Am. Devel.), Greater Cleve. Internat. Lawyers Group, Tavern Club (Cleve.), Chagrin Valley Hunt Club (Gates Mills, Ohio). Republican. Episcopalian. Corporate, general, Private international, Securities.

HYDE, DAVID ROWLEY, lawyer; b. Norwalk, Conn., Aug. 21, 1929; s. Thomas Arthur and Mary Julia (Sass) H.; m. Valerie Rosemary Worrall, Dec. 30, 1961; children: Meredith Ellen, Timothy Worrall. AB, Yale U., 1951, LL.B., 1954. Bar: Conn. 1954, N.Y. 1956, U.S. Supreme Ct. 1969. Assoc. Cahill Gordon & Reindel, N.Y.C., 1954-59, 64-65, ptnr., 1966-90, sr. counsel, 1991—; chief civil div. U.S. Atty.'s Office, 1961-63. Federal civil litigation, State civil litigation. Home: 35 W 12th St New York NY 10011-8501 Office: Cahill Gordon & Reindel 80 Pine St Fl 17 New York NY 10005-1790

HYDE, HERBERT LEE, lawyer; b. Bryson City, N.C., Dec. 12, 1925; s. Ervin M. and Alice (Medlin) H.; m. Kathryn Long, Dec. 25, 1949; children: Deborah, Lynn, Karen, Benjamin, Jane, William. AB, W. Carolina U., 1951; JD, NYU, 1954. Bar: N.C. 1954, U.S. Dist. Ct. (we. dist.) N.C. 1954, U.S. Ct. Appeals (4th cir.) 1957, U.S. Supreme Ct. 1962, U.S. Dist. Ct. (mid. dist.) N.C. 1975, U.S. Dist. Ct. (ea. dist.) N.C. 1980. Ptnr. Van Winkle, Buck, Wall, Starnes & Hyde, Asheville, N.C., 1954-79; sole practice Asheville, 1979—. Sec. N.C. Dept. Crime Control and Pub. Safety, Raleigh, 1979. Author: Genuine Hyde, 1976, My Home is in the Smoky Mountains, 1998, Of Truth and Freedom, 2001, Living and Learning, Just Natural, 2001, Mountain Speaking, 2002; writer (song) The Cold Icy Waters of Swain. Senator N.C. Senate, Raleigh, 1964-66, 1990-94; mem. N.C. Ho. of Reps., Raleigh, 1972-76; chmn. Dem. Exec. Com. of Buncombe County, Asheville, 1988—; chmn. Dem. Congl. Dist. 11, 1988-90, N.C. State Dems., 1990—, chmn., 1993. Named N.C. Bar Assn. Gen. Practice Hall of Fame, 1999. Mem.: Am. Coll. Trial Lawyers. Democrat. General practice. Home: 93 Eastview Cir Asheville NC 28806-1150 Office: PO Box 7266 Asheville NC 28802-7266

HYDE, HOWARD LAURENCE, lawyer; b. Boston, Sept. 4, 1957; s. Morris Morton and Evelyn Lee (Weinstein) H.; m. Nancy J. Paulu, May 18, 1985; children: Emma Catherine, Benjamin Tuttle. AB, Dartmouth Coll., 1979; JD, Harvard U., 1982. Bar: Mass. 1983, D.C. 1987, U.S. Dist. Ct. Mass. 1984, U.S. Ct. Appeals (1st. cir.) 1984. Jud. clk. Minn. Supreme Ct., St. Paul, 1982-83; assoc. Gaston Snow & Ely Bartlett, Boston, 1983-86, Arnold & Porter, Washington, 1986-91, spl. counsel, 1992—. Mem. ABA (Bus. law sect.). Avocations: fly fishing, canoeing. Banking, Corporate, general, Securities. Office: Arnold & Porter 555 12th St NW Washington DC 20004-1206 E-mail: Howard_Hyde@aporter.com.

HYDE, JAMES DUDLEY, lawyer; b. Oklahoma City, May 20, 1944; s. Homer Clark and Winonah Mae Hyde; m. Sue Ann White, Dec. 28, 1966; children: Heatherlyn Corey Hyde Blake, James Devon. BA, U. Okla., 1966; JD, So. Meth. U., 1969; LLM in Taxation, George Washington U., 1974. Bar: Tex. 1969, Okla. 1974. Ptnr., dir. McAfee & Taft, Oklahoma City, 1974—. Pres. S.W. Benefits Assn., Dallas, 2000—01; charter fellow Am. Coll. Employee Benefits Coun., 2002. Chmn. Oklahoma City Pub. Schs. Found., 2002; bd. dirs. Redbud Classic Found., Oklahoma City, 2002. Capt. JAG, 1969—74. Named Outstanding Alumni, U. Okla. Mem.: ABA, Okla. Bar Assn. Office: McAfee & Taft 10th Fl 211 N Robinson Oklahoma City OK 73102

HYDE, THOMAS D. lawyer; Sr. v.p., sec., gen. counsel Raytheon Co., Lexington, Mass., 1994—2001; exec. v.p. for legal and corp. affairs Wal-Mart Stores, Inc., 2001—. Office: Wal-Mart Stores, Inc 702 SW Eighth St Bentonville AR 72716*

HYLAND, WILLIAM FRANCIS, lawyer; b. Burlington, N.J., July 30, 1923; s. Theodore J. and Margaret M. (Gallagher) H.; m. Joan E. Sharp, Apr. 20, 1946; children: William Francis, Nancy E. Hyland Wiley, Stephen J., Emma L. Hyland McCormack, Margaret M. Hyland Frank, Thomas M. BS in Econs, U. Pa., 1944, LL.B., 1949; D.H.L., Hahnemann Med. Sch. and Hosp., 1976. Bar: N.J. 1949, U.S. Supreme Ct. 1960. Of counsel Riker, Danzig, Scherer, Hyland & Perretti, Morristown, N.J.; atty. gen. N.J., 1974-78. Mem. N.J. Gen. Assembly from Camden County, 1954-61, speaker of house, 1958, acting gov., N.J., 1958; chmn. N.J. Sports and Expn. Authority, 1978-82, commr., 1974-84; pres. N.J. Bd. Pub. Utility Commrs., also mem. cabinet govs. Meyner, Hughes, Byrne, N.J., 1961-68, 74-78; chmn. N.J. Atomic Energy Council, 1968-69, N.J. Commn. Investigation, 1969-71; co-chmn. Reapportionment Commn.; chmn. Brazilian Mission Com., 1962-65; permanent del. Fed. Jud. Conf. 3d Circuit.; del.-at-large Dem. Nat. Conv., 1964, del., 1968; assoc. trustee U. Pa., 1960-74. Served as officer USNR, 1943-46, ETO, PTO. Decorated knight Order of St. Gregory (Pope Paul VI), 1964; recipient Distinguished Service award Camden County Jaycees, 1954, Outstanding Young Man in Govt. N.J. award N.J. Jaycees, 1958, Myrtle Wreath award Camden County So. N.J. region Hadassah, 1977, Pub. Service award Anti-Defamation League of B'nai B'rith, 1982; named Outstanding Citizen of N.J. Advt. Club. N.J., 1979 Mem. ABA (fellow N.J. chpt.), Camden County Bar Assn. (pres. 1959), Nat. Assn. R.R. and Utilities Commrs. (exec. com. 1965-68), Nat. Assn. Attys. Gen. (exec. com. 1975-78, v.p. 1976, pres. elect 1977-78), Phi Kappa Psi. Home: 1 Polo Club Rd Far Hills NJ 07931-2474 Office: Riker Danzig Scherer Hyland & Perretti Headquarters Plz 1 Speedwell Ave Ste 2 Morristown NJ 07960-6823

HYLTON, MYLES TALBERT, lawyer; b. Pearisburg, Va., Apr. 22, 1954; s. Joseph Gordon and Ruby Viola (Clarkson) H.; 1 child, Jessica Kathleen. BSME, U. Mich., 1977, MSME, 1978; JD, U. Va., 1983. Bar: Va. 1983, U.S. Ct. Appeals (4th cir.) 1983, U.S. Patent Office 1985. Mech. engr. White Motor Co., New River, Va., 1979-80; assoc. Gentry, Locke, Rakes & Moore, Roanoke, Va., 1983-86, Stone & Hamrick, Radford, Va., 1986-89; ptnr. Pavin, Wilson, Barnett & Hopper, Roanoke, 1990-95; pvt. practice, Roanoke, 1995—. Mem. Va. Trial Lawyers, Assn. Trial Lawyers Am., Nat. Assn. Criminal Def. Lawyers, Soc. Automotive Engrs. Republican. Avocations: baseball, racquetball, weight lifting, boxing, scuba diving. General civil litigation, Criminal, Personal injury (including property damage). Home: 1812 Sheffield Rd SW Roanoke VA 24015-3022 Office: 23 Franklin Rd SW Roanoke VA 24011-2403

HYMAN, JEROME ELLIOT, lawyer; b. Rosedale, Miss., Dec. 26, 1923; s. Mose and Mary Ann (Sprecher) H.; m. Isabelle Miller, July 1, 1960. AB, Coll. William and Mary, 1944; LL.B. magna cum laude (Fay diploma), Harvard U., 1947. Bar: N.Y. 1949, D.C. 1960. Mem. fgn. funds control staff Dept. Treasury, U.S. Mil. Govt., Frankfurt and Berlin, Germany, 1945-46; law clk. to judge U.S. Ct. Appeals, Boston, 1947-48; assoc. firm Cleary, Gottlieb, Steen & Hamilton, N.Y.C., 1948-58, ptnr., 1959-93, sr. counsel, 1994—; trustee, mem. exec. com. Practising Law Inst., N.Y.C., 1972-97, v.p., 1979-86, pres., 1986-96, chmn. bd. trustees, 1996-97, chmn. emeritus, 1997—; sr. v.p., gen. counsel Pan Am World Airways, Inc., 1982-84. Bd. editors: Harvard Law Rev., 1945-47. Pres. Lexington Dem. Club, N.Y.C., 1956-58; counsel N.Y. Com. for Stevenson, 1956; del. various Dem. state and jud. convs.; alumni mem. Harvard Law Sch. Placement Com., 1976-79; nat. chmn. maj. gifts com. Harvard Law Sch. Fund, 1978-80; mem. overseers com. to visit Harvard Law Sch., 1986-92; trustee Lawyers' Com. for Civil Rights Under Law, 1981—; trustee Citizens Budget Commn., N.Y.C., 1991-94, trustee emeritus, 1994—; trustee Endowment Assn. of the Coll. of William and Mary, 1997—; mem. dean's adv. bd. Harvard Law Sch., 2000—. Fellow Am. Bar Found., Phi Beta Kappa Soc.; mem. ABA, Assn. Bar City N.Y. (chmn. com. corp. law 1984-87), Am. Law Inst., Am. Judicature Soc., N.Y. County Lawyers Assn., Tribar Opinion Commn., Harvard Law Sch. Assn. N.Y.C. (trustee 1980-83, v.p. 1984-85, pres. 1985-86), Nat. Harvard Law Sch. Assn. (mem. coun. 1990-93, mem. exec. com. 1991-93), Sky Club. Home: 1125 Park Ave Apt 10B New York NY 10128-1243 Office: Cleary Gottlieb Steen & Hamilton One Liberty Plaza New York NY 10006-1470 E-mail: jehyman23@hotmail.com., jhyman@cgsh.com.

HYMAN, LESTER SAMUEL, lawyer; b. Providence, July 14, 1931; s. Carl and Alice (Adelman) H.; m. Helen Reeder Sidman, Sept. 19, 1959 (div. 1982); children: David, Andrew, Elizabeth. AB, Brown U., 1952; LLB, Columbia U., 1955. Bar: D.C. 1955, Mass. 1955, U.S. Supreme Ct. 1957. Atty. SEC, Washington, 1955-57; chief asst. to Gov. State of Mass., Boston, 1962-64, sec. commerce, 1964-65; sr. cons. HUD, Washington, 1966-67; ptnr. Leva, Hawes & Symington, Washington, 1969-82; founding ptnr. Swidler & Berlin, Washington, 1982—, sr. of counsel. Lectr. John F. Kennedy Sch. Govt. Harvard U., 1968-69; bd. dirs. CDS Internat., 1988-94. mem. Internat. Oberver Team for nat. election in Haiti, 1990. Bd. dirs. Ctr. Nat. Policy, Washington, 1980—; bd. advisors Close-Up Found.; bd. govs. Am. Jewish Commn., 1980-84; Dem. chmn., Mass., 1967-69, del. Dem. Nat. Conv., 1968, mem. Dem. Charter Reform Commn., 1970, D.C. Cmty. Humanities, 1988-90; bd. dirs. Cmty. Coll. of Brit. V.I., 1989—, Young Artists, 1989-94; mem. adv. bd. Internat. legal Studies Program, Washington Coll. Law, Am. U., 1990—; apptd. by Pres. Clinton to Franklin Delano Roosevelt Meml. Commn., 1994; trustee Norton Simon Mus. of Art, Pasadena, Calif., 1995-97; mem. U.S. Presdl. Del. to Guatamalan Peace Accord Singing, 1996; bd. dirs. Brit VI Natl. Park Trust, 1999, U. of Dist. of Columbia Fdn., 2002. Named Outstanding Young Man of Yr., Greater Boston Jr. C. of C., 1964. Mem. Performing Artists Soc. Am. (mng. dir. 1997), Internat. Intellectual Property Inst. (dir. 1998—). Home: 3826 Van Ness St NW Washington DC 20016-2228 Office: Swidler Berlin Shereff Friedman 3000 K St NW Ste 300 Washington DC 20007-5116 E-mail: lshyman@aol.com., lshyman@swidlaw.com.

HYMAN, MICHAEL BRUCE, lawyer; b. Elgin, Ill., July 26, 1952; s. Robert I. and Ruth (Cohen) H.; m. Leslie Bland, Aug. 14, 1977; children: Rachel Joy, David Adam. BSJ with honors, Northwestern U., 1974, JD, 1977. Bar: Ill. 1977, U.S. Supreme Ct. 1989. Asst. atty. gen. Antitrust div. State of Ill., Chgo., 1977-79; trial atty. Much Shelist Freed Denenberg Ament & Rubenstein, Chgo., 1979-85, ptnr., 1985—. Chmn. panelist various continuing legal edn. seminars. Columnist Editor's Briefcase, CBA Record, 1988-90, 93—, The Red Pencil, 1986-89; contbr. chpt. to book, articles to profl. jours.; host (cable TV program) You and the Law, 1995—. Trustee North Shore Congregation Israel, Glencoe, 1980-89, 95-2001, v.p., 1987-89. Mem.: ABA (sect. litig., chmn. antitrust litig. com. 1987—90, editor-in-chief Litig. News 1990—92, mng. editor 1989—90, assoc. editor 1985—89, chmn. monographs and unpub. papers com. 1992—95, task force on civil justice reform 1991—93, chmn. consumer and personal rights litig. com. 2002—, editor-in-chief Litig. Docket 1995—2001, Tips From the Trenches 2001—02, divsn. mem. chair 2002—, jud. divsn. lawyers conf., membership com. chair 1999—2003, exec. com. 2002—), Decalogue Soc. Lawyers (trustee 2001—, co-chair CLE programs 2001—, fin. sec. 2002—03, sec. 2003—), Am. Soc. Writers on Legal Subjects (chair book award com. 1997—), Ill. Bar Assn. (rep. on assembly 1986—92, 1994—99, 2001—, antitrust coun. 1981—87, chmn. coun. 1985—86, vice chair, sec., co-editor newsletter 1982—85, chmn. bench and bar sect. coun. 1990—91, bench and bar sect. coun. 1998—2003, professionalism com. 1992—95, chair 1993—94, vice chair ARDC com. 1995—96, chair ARDC com. 1996—97, cable TV com. 1995—, chair 1997—99), Chgo. Bar Assn. (editor-in-chief CBA Record 1988—90, 1993—, CBA News 1994—98, bd. mgrs. 1992—94, vice chair class action com. 1999—2000, chair 2000—01, 2d v.p. 2003—). Jewish. Avocations: writing, abraham lincoln. Antitrust, General civil litigation, Commercial, consumer (including collections, credit). Office: Much Shelist Freed Denenberg Ament & Rubenstein 191 N Wacker Dr Ste 1800 Chicago IL 60606-1615 E-mail: mbhyman@muchshelist.com.

HYMAN, MILTON BERNARD, lawyer; b. L.A., Nov. 19, 1941; s. Herbert and Lillian (Rakowitz) Hyman; m. Sheila Goldman, July 4, 1965; children: Lauren Davida, Micah Howard. BA in Econs. with highest honors, UCLA, 1963; JD magna cum laude, Harvard U., 1966. Bar: Calif. 1967. Assoc. Irell & Manella LLP, L.A., 1970-73, ptnr., 1973—. Co-author: Partnerships and Associations: A Policy Critique of the Morrisey Regulations, 1976, Consolidated Returns: Summary of Tax Considerations in Acquisition of Common Parent of Subsidiary Member of Affiliated Group, 1980, Tax Aspects of Corporate Debt Exchanges, Recapitalization and Discharges, 1982, Tax Strategies for Leveraged Buyouts and Other Corporate Acquisitions, 1986, Preservation and Use of Net Operating Losses and Other Tax Attributes in a Consolidated Return Context, rev. edit., 1992, Collier on Bankruptcy Taxation, 1992, Real Estate Workouts and Bankruptcies, 1993, Current Corporate Bankruptcy Tax Issues, 1993, Tax Strategies for Corporate Acquisitions, Dispositions, Financing, Joint Ventures, Reorganizations, and Restructurings, 1995; author: A Transactional Encounter with the Partnership Rules of Subchapter K: The Effects of the Tax Reform Act of 1984, 1984, Net Operating Losses and Other Tax Attributed of Corporate Clients, 1987. Past pres., bd. dirs. Sinai Temple, West Los Angeles, Calif. Capt. JAGC, U.S. Army, 1967-70. Sheldon traveling fellow Harvard U., 1966-67. Mem. ABA (chmn. com. affiliated and related corps. 1981-83, chmn. corp. tax com. 1999-2000), Calif. State Bar Assn., Am. Law Inst. (fed. income tax project tax adv. group 1976—), Masons, Phi Beta Kappa. Jewish. Corporate, general, Corporate taxation, Personal income taxation. Office: Irell & Manella LLP Ste 900 1800 Avenue Of The Stars Los Angeles CA 90067-4276

HYMAN, MONTAGUE ALLAN, lawyer, educator; b. N.Y.C., Apr. 19, 1941; s. Allan Richard and Lilyan P. (Pollock) H.; m. susann Podell, Jan. 25, 1965; children: Jeffrie-Anne, Erik. BA, Syracuse U., 1962; JD, St. Johns U., 1965. Bar: N.Y. 1965, U.S. Dist. Ct. (so. and ea. dists.) N.Y. 1967, U.S. Ct. Appeals (2d cir.) 1982, U.S. Supreme Ct. 1973. Assoc. Warburton, Hyman, Deeley & Connolly, Mineola, NY, 1965-67; ptnr. Hyman & Deeley, 1967-69, Koeppel, Hyman, Sommer, Lesnick & Ross, 1969-72, Hyman & Hyman, P.C., Garden City, 1972-80, Costigan, Hyman, Hyman & Herman, P.C., Mineola, 1980-87, Certilman, Haft, Balin, Buckley, Adler & Hyman, 1988—, Certilman Balin Adler & Hyman, 1988—. Lectr. Hofstra U., Adelphi U., Columbia Appraisal Soc., Practicing Law Inst.; chmn. bd. Edn. and Assistance Corp. Contbr. articles to profl. jours. Bd. trustees North Shore L.I. Jewish Health System. Mem. Nassau County Bar Assn., N.Y. State Bar Assn., Inst. Property Taxation. Federal civil litigation, Property, real (including real estate development, water), State and local taxation. Office: Certilman Balin Adler & Hyman LLP 90 Merrick Ave East Meadow NY 11554-1571 E-mail: ahyman@certilmanbalin.com.

HYMAN, ROGER DAVID, lawyer; b. Oak Ridge, Tenn., Apr. 23, 1957; s. Marshall Leonard and Vera Lorraine (McKinney) H.; m. Elsa Laurencio; children: Cristina Alicia, James Marshall. BA, Vanderbilt U., 1979; JD, U. Tenn., 1984. Clk. Oak Ridge Nat. Lab., 1977-78, 81; air personality, news reporter Stas. WKDA, WKDF, Nashville, 1979; program dir. Sta. WBIR-FM, Knoxville, Tenn., 1979-80; assoc. atty. Hindman & Holt, Attys., Knoxville, Tenn., 1984-85; asst. atty. gen. State of Tenn., Knoxville, 1986-95; with Law Offices of Roger D. Hyman Powell, Tenn., 1995-97; ptnr. Hyman & Carter, PLLC, Powell, Tenn., 1997—. Bd. dirs. Knoxville Christian Sch., 1991-93. Democrat. Mem. Ch. of Christ. Home: 2713 Windemere Ln Powell TN 37849-3782 Office: Hyman & Carter PLLC PO Box 1304 Powell TN 37849-1304 E-mail: RDHymanLAW@aol.com.

HYMEL, L(EZIN) J(OSEPH), lawyer, former prosecutor; b. Baton Rouge, July 2, 1944; s. Lezin Joseph Sr. and Alma K. Hymel; m. Linda N. Hymel, Oct. 6, 1973; children: Traci Lyn, Shea Roach Bonaventure, Kimberly Kaye. BS in Geology, La. State U., 1966, JD, 1969. Bar: La., U.S. Dist. Ct. (ea. dist.) La., U.S. Dist. Ct. (mid. dist.) La., U.S. Dist. Ct. (we. dist.) La., U.S. Ct. Appeals (5th cir.). Pvt. practice, Baton Rouge, 1969—70; staff atty. Office State Atty. Gen., Baton Rouge, 1970—71, asst. atty. gen., 1972—78, dir. criminal divsn., 1992—93; asst. dist. atty. Office 19 Jud. Dist. Attys., Baton Rouge, 1978—79; city judge Baton Rouge City Ct., 1980—83; state dist. ct. judge criminal divsn. 19th Jud. Dist. Ct, Baton Rouge, 1983—90, state dist. ct. judge civil divsn., 1991—92; U.S. atty. Office U.S. Atty., Dept. Justice, Baton Rouge, 1994—2001; ptnr. Sharp Henry Cerniglia Calvin Weaver & Hymel, Baton Rouge, 2001—. Office: Sharp Henry Cerniglia et al Ste C 15171 So Harrells Ferry Rd Baton Rouge LA 70816 Fax: (225) 755-1065. E-mail: ljhymel@sharphenry.com.

HYNES, PATRICIA MARY, lawyer; b. N.Y.C., Jan. 26, 1942; BA, CUNY, 1963; LLB, Fordham U., 1966. Bar: N.Y. 1966, U.S. Dist. Ct. (so. and ea. dists.) N.Y. 1969, U.S. Ct. Appeals (2d cir.) 1982. Law clk. Hon. Joseph C. Zavatt U.S. Dist. Ct. (ea. dist.) N.Y., 1966-67; asst. U.S. atty. U.S. Dist. Ct. (so. dist.) N.Y., 1967-82, exec. asst. U.S. atty., 1980-82, chief ofcl. corruption and spl. pros. unit, 1978-80, chief consumer fraud unit, 1971-78, mem. civil divsn., 1967-71; ptnr. Milberg Weiss Bershad Hynes & Lerach LLP, N.Y.C., 1983-99, of counsel, 2000—. Adj. prof. law Fordham U., 1978—83; lectr. trial advocacy Harvard U. Law Sch., 1983; lectr. Practising Law Inst.; mem. criminal justice act peer rev. panel U.S. Dist. Ct. (so. dist.) N.Y., 1982—83, mem. discovery com., 1982—84, mem. civil litig. com., 1983—84, chmn. merit selection panel for N.Y. magistrate judges, 2002—. Mem. Fordham Law Rev., 1964-66; mem. editl. bd. N.Y. Law Jour.,

1994—. Mem. NYC Charter Revision Commn., 2002, Gov.'s Exec. Adv. Com. on Adminstrn. Criminal Justice, 1981—82, N.Y. Gov.'s Commn. on Govt. Integrity, 1987—90, Mayor's Adv. Com. on Jud., 1994—2001; chairperson N.Y. Regional Consumer Protection Coun., 1971—72. Named one of 50 Top Women Lawyers, Nat. Law Jour., 1998, 2001. Fellow: Am. Coll. Trial Lawyers; mem.: ABA (chair govt. litig. com. litig. sect. 1984—87, chair securities litig. com. 1987—89, coun. litig. sect. 1989—92, chair pre-trial practice and discovery com. 1992—94, standing com. on fed. jud. 1995—2000, chair 2000—01, criminal justice sect.), Legal Aid Soc. (bd. dirs. 1998—), N.Y. Coun. Def. Lawyers, Fed. Bar Coun. (trustee 1983—91, treas. 1987—90, v.p. 1990, 1996—), N.Y. State Bar Assn. (consumer affairs com. 1974—78, criminal law com. 1980—84, police law and policy com. 1981—83, sec. 1982—84, ho. dels. 1983—84, exec. com. 1984—88, second century com. 1988—92, del. to ABA, ho. dels. 1990—94, chair fed. cts. com. 1992—95, del.), Assn. of the Bar of the City of N.Y., Am. Law Inst (spl. adviser 1995—2001), Fordham Law Alumni Assn. Federal civil litigation, General civil litigation, Securities. Office: Milberg Weiss Bershad Hynes & Lerach LLP One Penn Plz New York NY 10119

HYTKEN, FRANKLIN HARRIS, lawyer; b. Memphis, Dec. 25, 1948; s. Mac E. and Florence B. H.; m. Louise Grace Parks, Aug. 11, 1979 (div. 1999); 1 child, Rachel Lee. Student, U. Louisville, 1965-66; BA cum laude, Northwestern U., 1969, JD, 1972. Bar: Tex. 1972, U.S. Dist. Ct. (no., so., ea. and we. dists.) Tex., U.S. Tax Ct., U.S. Ct. Appeals (5th and llth cirs.), U.S. Supreme Ct. 1978; cert. in civil trial law Tex. Bd. Legal Specialization and Nat. Bd. Trial Advocacy. Assoc. Goins & Underkofler, Dallas, 1977-79; pres. Rhodus, Jones & Hytken, P.C., Dallas, 1979-83, 83—, Franklin Harris Hytken, P.C., Dallas, 1983—. Author: Pro-competitive Restraints of Trade, 1972. Chmn. Dem. Legis. Dist. Exec. Com., Dallas, 1984. Served to capt. (chief def. counsel 3d div. 1974, chief prosecutor Camp Zukeran 1975, mil. judge 1976-77) USMCR, 1972-77. Fellow Tex. Bar Found. (life), Dallas Bar Found. (life), Dallas Bar Assn. (libr. com. 1996-97, chmn. legal ethics com. 1983, bylaws com. 1989-90, fee disputes subcom. 1987-89), North Dallas Bar Assn. (sec., treas. 1985-86), Tex. Young Lawyers Assn. (chmn. fed. practice subcom. 1980), North Dallas C. of C. (chmn. membership com. small bus. coun. 1984-85), Com. for Qualified Judiciary (exec. com. 1986—); mem. Coll. State Bar Tex., Am. Legion, B'nai B'rith (pres. couples unit 1980-81), Bench Bar Lodge, (v.p. 2002-03). Avocations: tennis, golf, scuba diving. Federal civil litigation, State civil litigation. Office: 16950 Dallas Pkwy Ste 1000 Dallas TX 75248-1942 Fax: (972)-713-8790.

HYVÖNEN, VEIKKO OLAVI, lawyer, educator; b. Sysmä, Finland, Sept. 18, 1929; s. Aleksander and Elsa (Neoff) H.; m. Reetta Onerva Puhakka; 1 child, Keijo. BCE, U. Tech., Helsinki, Finland, 1955; TechD, U. Tech., 1970; JD, U. Helsinki, 1970. State geodesist Finnish Geodetic Inst., Helsinki, 1954-56; civil engr. Surveyor-Gen.'s Office, Helsinki, 1956-66; assoc. prof. U. Helsinki, 1966-71, prof. land and water law, 1971-96; propr., mng. dir. Commandite Co. VOH, Espoo, Finland, 1974—. Author: Määräalan luovutuksensaajan oikeusasemasta, 1970, Asianosaisten määräämistoimista kiinteistötoimituksessa, 1970, Kaavoitus-ja rakentamisoikeus, 1974, Maapaketti, 1976, Kiinteistöjärjestelmä ja kiinteistönmuodostamisoikeus, 1982, Kaavoitus-ja rakentamisoikeus, 1988, Maaomaisuuden perustuslainsuoja, 1993, Kiinteistönmuodostamisoikeus I, 1998, Kiinteistönmuodostamisoikeus II, 2001. Home: Westendinkuja 19 02160 Espoo Finland

IAMELE, RICHARD THOMAS, law librarian; b. Newark, Jan. 29, 1942; BA, Loyola U., L.A., 1963; MSLS, U. So. Calif., 1967; JD, Southwestern U., L.A., 1976. Bar: Calif. 1977. Cataloger U. So. Calif., L.A., 1967-71; asst. cataloger L.A. County Law Libr., 1971-77, asst. ref. libr., 1977-78, asst. libr., 1978-80, libr. dir., 1980—. Mem. ABA, Am. Assn. Law Librs., Calif. Libr. Assn., So. Calif. Assn. Law Librs., Coun. Calif. County Law Librs. (pres. 1981-82, 88-90). Office: LA County Law Libr 301 W 1st St Los Angeles CA 90012-3140 E-mail: richard@lalaw.lib.ca.us.

IANNAZZONE, JOSEPH CHARLES, judge; b. Camp Kilmer, N.J., Oct. 15, 1954; s. Ralph Louis and Constance Margaret Iannazzone; m. Shirley Angela Williams, July 7, 1990; children: Joseph Adam, Matthew Streicher, Christie Streicher. BS, Ga. Inst. Tech., 1975; JD, Emory U., 1979. Bar: Ga. 1979. Asst. gen. counsel Internat. Ladies' Garment Workers' Union, AFL-CIO, Atlanta, 1979-86; lawyer Lawrenceville, Ga., 1987-95; part-time judge Magistrate Ct. of Gwinnett County, Lawrenceville, 1988-96, judge, 1997—2002, State Ct. Gwinnett County, Lawrenceville, 2002—. Officer Ga. Coun. Magistrate Ct. Judges, pres.-elect, 1999, pres. 1999-2000; dir. Gwinnett County Pro Bono Project, 1990—; mem. Jud. Coun. Ga., 1998-2000; mem. Ga. Cts. Automation Commn., 1997—, vice chair, 1999—. Editor Ga. Magistrate Ct. Newsletter, 1996—; contg. author: Georgia Magistrate Benchbook, 1991—; contbr. aticles to profl. jours. Pres., Flowers Crossing Neighborhood Assn., Lawrenceville, 1998; leader Boy Scouts Am., Lawrenceville, 1997—. Avocations: fly fishing, backpacking, woodworking, photography. Home: 4015 Vicksburg Dr Lawrenceville GA 30044-5986 Office: State Ct Gwinnett County 75 Langley Dr Lawrenceville GA 30045-6935 E-mail: iannazjo@co.gwinnett.ga.us.

IANNUZZI, JOHN NICHOLAS, lawyer, author, educator; b. N.Y.C., May 31, 1935; s. Nicholas Peter and Grace Margaret (Russo) I.; m. Carmen Marina Barrios, Aug. 1979; children: Dana Alejandra, Christina Maria, Nicholas Peter II, Alessandro Luca; children from previous marriage: Andrea Marguerite, Maria Teresa. BS, Fordham U., 1956; JD, N.Y. Law Sch., 1962. Bar: N.Y., U.S. Dist. Ct. (so. and ea. dists.) N.Y. 1964, U.S. Dist. Ct. (no. and we. dists.) N.Y. 1965, U.S. Ct. Appeals (2d cir.) 1965, U.S. Supreme Ct. 1971, U.S. Dist. Ct. Conn. 1978, U.S. Tax Ct. 1978, U.S. Ct. Appeals (5th and 11th cirs.) 1982, U.S. Ct. Appeals (4th cir.) 1988, Wyo. 1994. Assoc. Law Offices of H.H. Lipsig, N.Y.C., 1962, Law Offices of Aaron J. Broder, N.Y.C., 1963; ptnr. Iannuzzi & Iannuzzi, N.Y.C., 1963—. Adj. prof. trial advocacy Fordham U. Law Sch. Author: (fiction) What's Happening, 1963, Part 35, 1970, Sicilian Defense, 1974, Courthouse, 1977, J.T., 1984, (non-fiction) Cross-Examination: The Mosaic Art, 1984, Trial Strategy and Psychology, 1992, Handbook of Cross-Examination, 1999, Handbook of Trial Strategy, 2000. Mem. ABA, N.Y. County Bar Assn., N.Y. Criminal Bar Assn., Columbian Lawyers Assn., Lipizzan Internat. Fedn. (v.p.). Roman Catholic. Federal civil litigation, State civil litigation, Civil rights. Home: 118 Via Settembre 9 Rome Italy Office: Iannuzzi & Iannuzzi 74 Trinity Place New York NY 10006 also: 775 Park Ave Huntington NY 11743-3976 also: 345 Franklin St San Francisco CA 94102-4427 also: 1592 Pine Ave W Montreal QC Canada also: 120 Adelaide St W Toronto ON Canada H3B 3G3 E-mail: jni@iannuzzi.net.

IATESTA, JOHN MICHAEL, lawyer; b. Orange, N.J., Dec. 29, 1944; s. Thomas Anthony and Marie Monica I.; m. Paulina Clare Pascuzzi, July 11, 1971. BS magna cum laude, Seton Hall U., 1967, JD cum laude, 1976; MS, Fordham U., 1968; LLM in Corp. Law, NYU, 1986. Bar: N.J. 1976, U.S. Dist. Ct. N.J. 1976, U.S. Ct. Appeals (3d cir.) 1981, N.Y. 1982, U.S. Supreme Ct. 1985. Law sec. to presiding judge appellate div. Superior Ct. N.J., Trenton, 1976-77; assoc. Wilentz, Goldman & Spitzer, Woodbridge, N.J., 1977-81, D'Alessandro, Sussman & Jacovino, Florham Park, N.J., 1981-83; corp. counsel, 1983—, Rhodia Inc., Cranbury, N.J. Recipient Book prize Tchrs. Coll. Columbia U., 1967. Mem. ABA, N.J. Bar Assn., Am. Corp. Counsel Assn., Order of the Cross & Crescent, Delta Epsilon Sigma, Kappa Delta Pi. Corporate, general, Finance, Property, real (including real estate development, water). Office: Rhodia Inc 259 Prospect Plains Rd Cranbury NJ 08512 E-mail: john.iatesta@us.rhodia.com.

IAVICOLI, MARIO ANTHONY, lawyer; b. Camden, N.J., Aug. 11, 1939; s. Vito Anthony and Angelina Jessie (Marchionese) I.; m. Arlene V. LeDonne, July 6, 1963; children— Michelle, Denise, Laura. BME, Drexel U., 1962; JD, U. Pa., 1965. Bar: N.J. 1965. Assoc. Samuel P. Orlando, Camden, 1965-66, Ballen & Batoff, Camden, 1966-68; ptnr. Maressa, Console & Iavicoli, Berlin, N.J., 1968-72; first asst. prosecutor Camden County, 1972-74; pvt. practice Pennsauken, N.J., 1974-79, Haddenfield, 1980—; counsel to spkr. N.J. Gen. Assembly, 1970-72, N.J. Automobile Ins. Study Commn., 1970-74, Camden County Charter Study Commn., 1974, Camden County Republican party, 1974-76, N.J. Rep. party, 1976—; solicitor Haddenfield Borough, 1980—. Author: No Fault and Comparative Negligence in New Jersey, 1973; Drafter: N.J.'s No Fault Law and other companion legislation, 1970-73. Chmn. Camden County Rep. Com., 1978— ; Rep. state committeeman, 1976— ; mem. Electoral Coll. from, N.J., 1976; solicitor Pennsauken Twp., 1975— ; Vice pres. Haddonfield Home Sch. Assn., 1972-73; Bd. dirs. Drexel U. Class Endowment Fund; trustee Haddonfield Civic Assn. Named One of N.J.'s 5 Outstanding Young Men, 1974; recipient Ocean County Bar Assn. award, 1975 Mem. Camden County Jr. C. of C. (counsel 1967-68), ABA, N.J. Bar Assn., Camden County Bar Assn (trustee 1996-98, sec. 1998-99, treas. 1999-2000, 2d v.p. 2000-01, 1st v.p. 2001-02, pres.-elect 2002-03, pres. 2003—), Sons of Italy, Drexel U. Alumni Assn. (v.p. 1991—), Rotary. Roman Catholic. Home: 340 Marquis Rd Haddonfield NJ 08033-4011 Office: 43 Kings Hwy W Haddonfield NJ 08033-2128 E-mail: mario.iavicoli@verizon.net.

IBAÑEZ, LOPEZ MARIO, lawyer; b. Barcelona, Oct. 7, 1969; s. Mario Ibañez Fina and Teresa Lopez Narvaez; m. Eva Rodriguez Romero, Sept. 16, 2000. Law Degree, U. Barcelona, 1992; M. in Co. Law, U. Pompeu Fabra, Barcelona, 1994. Bar: Barcelona 1992. Asst. Bufete Ibañez, Barcelona, 1987—92, lawyer, 1992—94; assoc. Uria & Menendez, Barcelona, 1994—. Contbr. Mem.: Law Soc. Barcelona (mem. labor law comm. 1992—). Avocations: reading, languages. Labor (including EEOC, Fair Labor Standards Act, labor-management relations, NLRB, OSHA). Office: Uria & Menendez Diagonal 514 08006 Barcelona Spain

IBAÑEZ, MAURICIO, lawyer; b. Mexico City, Nov. 8, 1969; s. José Luis and Magdalena (Campos) Ibañez. LLB, Iberoamericana U, Mexico City, 1994; LLM, Columbia U, NY, NY, 1999. Bar: Mexican Bar Association 1994, ABA 2000. Law clk. Baker & McKenzie, Mexico City, 1990—94, assoc., 1994, White & Case , Mexico City, 1994—97, White & Case, NY, NY, 1997—98, Mexico City, 1999—2001, Jauregui, Navarrete, Nader & Rojas, Mexico City, 2001—. Named thesis, 1994. Avocations: guitar, music, art. Home: 3835 A602 Av Vasco 05340 Quirogo Mexico Office: Jauregui Navarrete Nader y Rojas 400B Paseo de los Tamarindos 05120 Mexico City Mexico

IDE, ROY WILLIAM, III, lawyer; b. Geneva, Ill., Apr. 23, 1940; s. Roy William and Jenny (Coleman) Ide; m. Gayle Marie Oliver, Jan. 21, 1967; children: Logan, Jennifer, Lucienne. BA cum laude, Washington and Lee U., 1962; LLD, U. Va., 1965; MBA, Ga. State U., 1972. Bar: Ga. 1967, D.C. 1994, U.S. Ct. Appeals (5th and 11th cirs.) 1967, U.S. Supreme Ct. 1969. Law clk. Judge Griffin Bell U.S. Ct. Appeals (5th cir.), 1965—66; assoc. King & Spalding, Atlanta, 1966—71; ptnr. Huie, Sterne & Ide, Atlanta, 1971—77, Kutak Rock (and predecessor firm), Atlanta, 1978—92, mng. ptnr., Atlanta office, vice-chair, chmn. fin. dept., chmn. healthcare dept.; ptnr. Long, Aldridge & Norman; sr. v.p., spl. counsel E.F. Hutton and Co., Inc., 1985—87; spl. counsel, mng. dir. Prescott, Ball & Turben, 1988—. Former bd. dirs., mem. exec. com. Atlanta Com. for Olympic Games. Named one of Atlanta's Five Outstanding Men of Yr., 1976; recipient Arthur Van Briesen award, Nat. Legal Aid and Defender Assn., 1977. Mem.: ABA (ho. of dels., chair young lawyer's divsn. 1976, chair genl practice sect. 1983—84, chair spl. com. on drug crisis 1991—92, 1992—93, pres.-elect 1992—93, pres. 1993—94, immediate past pres. 1994—), Ga. Bar Assn. (bd. govs.). Health, Municipal (including bonds). Office: McKenna Long & Aldridge LLP 303 Peachtree St NE Ste 5300 Atlanta GA 30308 Office Fax: 404-527-8566. E-mail: bide@mckennalong.com.

IDING, ALLAN EARL, lawyer; b. Milw., Apr. 29, 1939; s. Earl Herman and Erna Adeline (Albrecht) I.; m. Anne Louise Chaconas, July 9, 1961; children: Kent Earl, Krista Anne Templeman, Bradford A., Andrea Beth Brozynski. BS, Marquette U., 1961, LLB, 1963; DHL (hon.), Nashotah (Wis.) House, 1990. Bar: Wis. 1963, U.S. Dist. Ct. (ea. dist.) Wis. 1963, U.S. Ct. Appeals (7th cir.) 1963. Law clk. U.S. Ct. Appeals (7th cir.), Chgo., 1963-64; assoc. Whyte Hirschboeck Dudek, S.C., Milw., 1964-71, mem., 1971—. Trustee Nashotah House, 1976—; pres., bd. dirs. Wis. DeMolay Found., Milw., 1985—, Wis. Health and Ednl. Facilities Authority, 1978-85, Wis. Masonic Home, Inc.; bd. dirs. Wis. Masonic Home, Inc.; pres., bd. dirs. Todd Wehr Found., Inc.; mem. Wauwatosa (Wis.) Police and Fire Commn., 1978-83. Mem. Blue Mound Golf and Country Club (sec., bd. dirs.), Masons (grand master Wis. 1981-82). Republican. Episcopalian. Avocation: golf. Corporate, general, Estate planning, Probate (including wills, trusts). Home: 9212 Wilson Blvd Milwaukee WI 53226-1729 Office: Whyte & Hirschboeck Dudek SC Ste 2100 111 W Wisconsin Ave Milwaukee WI 53203-2501 E-mail: aiding@whdlaw.com.

IDZIK, DANIEL RONALD, retired lawyer; b. Depew, N.Y., Jan. 20, 1935; s. Daniel Henry and Ann Mary (Kolakowski) I.; m. Kathleen Osborne, Oct. 6 1989; children by previous marriage: Christopher, Rebecca, Laura, Susan. BS, SUNY, Buffalo, 1956; LLB, Harvard U., 1963. Bar: N.Y. 1964. Exec. v.p. U.S. Nat. Student Assn., Phila., 1956-57; assoc. sec. World Univ. Svc., Geneva, 1957-60; chief counsel N.Y. State Senate Commn. on Labor and Industry, Albany, 1965; from assoc. counsel to gen. counsel Booz, Allen & Hamilton, Inc., N.Y.C., 1967-98; ret., 1998. Chmn. Philharmonia Virtuosi, Westchester County, N.Y., 1988-90, pres. 1987-88, bd. dirs. 1985-91; pres. Coun. for Arts in Westchester, 1983-85, bd. dirs., 1980-85; chmn., Friends of Neuberger Mus., Purchase, N.Y., 1991-93, pres., 1990, bd. dirs., 1987-97; bd. dirs. Buffalo State Coll. Found., 1985—, Jacob's Pillow, 1996—, LongBoat Key Ctr. Arts, 2000—, pres., 2002-. Recipient Disting. Alumni award SUNY Buffalo, 1986, Arts award Coun,. for the Arts in Westchester, 1990. Mem. Harvard Club of N.Y. (mem. bd. mgrs. 1997-2000). Commercial, contracts (including sales of goods; commercial financing), Corporate, general, Private international. E-mail: daniel_idzik@post.harvard.edu.

IDZIK, MARTIN FRANCIS, lawyer; b. Depew, N.Y., Apr. 2, 1942; s. Daniel Henry and Ann Mary (Kolakowski) I.; m. Patricia Ann O'Brien, Aug. 7, 1965; children: Andrew, Amy. BS, Canisius Coll., 1963; JD, U. Notre Dame, 1966. Bar: N.Y. 1966. Assoc. Phillips, Lytle et al., Buffalo, 1971-76, ptnr., 1977-78, Jamestown, N.Y., 1979—. Bd. trustees Randolph Children's Home, 1993—99. Acting village justice, East Aurora, N.Y.,1972-79; bd. dirs. Chautauqua County Humane Soc., 1989-93, Downtown Jamestown Devel. Task Force, 1988-92, Jamestown YMCA, 1985-87, N.Y. State affiliate of Am. Heart Assn., 1983-85, Southwestern chpt. Am. Heart Assn., 1981-85, Jamestown Cmty. Learning Coun., 1995—, Roger Tory Peterson Inst., 2000—; chmn. fund for the Arts in Chautauqua County, 1984-88; pres. Arts Coun. Chautauqua County, 1982-84, United Way South Chautauqua County, 2000-01; mem. Jamestown Civic Ctr. Task Force, 1982-86, N.Y. State Mgmt. Atty.'s Conf., 1978—. Capt. JACG, U.S. Army, 1967-71. Mem. ABA, N.Y. State Bar Assn., Erie County Bar Assn., Jamestown Bar Assn. (pres. 1991-92), No. Chautauqua County Bar Assn., Sportsmen's Club (Stow, N.Y.). Civil rights, Labor (including EEOC, Fair Labor Standards Act, labor-management relations, NLRB, OSHA). Office: Phillips Lytle Hitchcock 8 E 3rd St PO Box 1279 Jamestown NY 14702-1279 E-mail: midzik@phillipslytle.com.

IEYOUB, RICHARD PHILLIP, state attorney general; b. Lake Charles, La., Aug. 11, 1944; s. Phillip Assad and Virginia Khoury Ieyoub; m. Caprice Brown, Feb. 3, 1995; children: Amy Claire, Nicole Anne, Brennan Jude, Richard Phillip Jr., Khoury Myhand, Christian Brown. BA in history, McNeese State U., 1968; JD, La. State U., 1972. Bar: La. 1972, U.S. Supreme Ct. Spl. prosecutor to atty. gen. State of La., Baton Rouge, 1972—74; assoc. Camp, Carmouche, Lake Charles, 1974—76; mem. Stockwell, Sievert, Lake Charles, 1976—78, Baggett, McCall, Singleton, Ranier, Ieyoub, Lake Charles, 1978—; pvt. practice Lake Charles; dist. atty. Calcasieu Parish, 1985—92; atty. gen. State of La., 1992—. Instr. criminal law McNeese State U.; chmn. La. Drug Policy Bd. Active La. Commn. on Law Enforcement; apptd. by gov. to adv. bd. D.A.R.E., La.; chmn. New Orleans Met. Crime Task Force, Gov's. Military Adv. Commn.; active President's Commn. on Model State Drug Laws, 1992—; parish coun. Immaculate Conception Cathedral Parish, Lake Charles; bd. dirs. S.W. La. Health Counseling Svcs., Crime Stoppers of Lake Charles, St. Jude Children's Rsch. Hosp., 1998—99; vice-chmn. La. coord. Coun. on the Prevention of Drug Abuse and Treatment of Drug Use; bd. dirs. La. State U. Alumni Assn. Named Outstanding Pub. Ofcl. for Diocese Lake Charles, 1990; recipient Disting. Alumnus award, McNeese State U., 1994, Legis. Leadership award, Nat. Coun. Against Drinking and Driving, 1996, Ochsner Humanitarian award, 1998. Mem.: ABA (vice-chmn. prosecution function com.), So. Attys. Gen. Assn. (elected chmn.), S.W. La. Bar Assn. (exec. com. 1979), Nat. Coll. Dist. Attys. (bd. regents 1991), La. Dist. Attys. Assn. (pres., bd. dirs. 1989—90), Nat. Assn. Attys. Gen. (exec. working group on prosecutorial rels.), Nat. Dist. Attys. Assn. (pres., bd. dirs. 1990—91), La. Bar Assn. (lectr. criminal law), Nat. Assn. Criminal Def. Lawyers, Assn. Trial Lawyers Am., Sierra Club. Democrat. Roman Catholic. Office: Justice Dept PO Box 94095 Baton Rouge LA 70804-4095*

IGLEHEART, TED LEWIS, lawyer; b. Shelbyville, Ky., Feb. 17, 1930; s. James Hayden and Mary Gladys Igleheart; m. Elizabeth Ann Craig, Feb. 5, 1956; children: Gladys Woods, Ted L. II, Margaret Sparks. BA, Centre Coll., 1951; LLB, U. Ky., 1957, JD, 1970. Bar: Ky. 1957, U.S. Dist. Ct. (we. dist.) Ky. 1989. Pvt. practice law, Shelbyville, 1957—; adminstrv. asst. Gov.'s Office, Frankfort, Ky., 1957-59; atty. Shelbyville Water and Sewer Commn., Shelbyville, 1966—, Shelby County Suburban Fire Dist., Shelbyville, 1967-87. Judge City of Shelbyville, 1961-63; county atty. Shelby County, Shelbyville, 1970-78; commonwealth atty. Commonwealth Ky., Shelbyville, 1982-94. Contbr. articles to profl. jours. Pres. Shelby County Hist. Soc., Shelbyville, 1964-65, 97-99; past chmn. bd. Am. Cancer Soc., Ky., 1960—. Cpl. U.S. Army, 1953-55, Korea. Named Outstanding Young Man, Shelbyville Jaycees, 1958. Mem. Ky. Bar Assn., 53rd Jud. Dist. Bar Assn. (sec.), Rotary Club (past pres.), Phi Delta Theta. Democrat. Methodist. Avocations: tennis, golf, fishing, photography, model railroads. Criminal, General practice, Probate (including wills, trusts). Office: 543 Main St Shelbyville KY 40065-1119

IGLESIAS, DAVID CLAUDIO, prosecutor; b. Jan. 1958; B, Wheaton Coll.; JD, U. N.Mex. Asst. atty. gen. N.Mex Atty. Gen. Office; asst. city atty. City of Albuquerque, 1991—94; spl. asst. to sec. transp. White Ho. Fellowship, 1995; chief counsel N.Mex Risk Mgmt. Legal Office, 1995—98; gen. counsel N.Mex Taxation and Revenue Dept., 1998—2001; assoc. Walz and Assoc., Albuquerque; U.S. Atty. Dist. of N.Mex, 2001—. Comdr. JAGC USNR. Office: US Atty PO Box 607 Albuquerque NM 87103 Fax: 505-346-7296.

IHM, STEPHEN LAWRENCE, lawyer; b. Galena, Ill., Apr. 28, 1962; s. Lawrence Charles Ihm and Elvera Ann Schardt; m. Terry Lee Swenson, May 31, 1986; children: Dietrich John, Nathan Paul, Elizabeth Ann. BA, Carthage Coll., 1984; JD magna cum laude, No. Ill. U., 1988. Bar: Ill. 1988, Ill. 1989, N.Y. 1997; U.S. Dist. Ct. (no. dist.) Ill. Asst. counsel Allstate Ins. Co., Northbrook, Ill., 1991-93; gen. counsel Allstate Enterprises, Inc., Arlington Heights, Ill., 1994-95; counsel Allstate Ins. Co., Northbrook, Ill., 1995—99, regional counsel Farmingville, NY, 2000—03, counsel Northbrook, 2003—. Zone rep. Nat. Autp Travel Orgn., 1994; faculty Exec. Enterprises N.Y.C., 1996, 97. Editor: Centrique, 1984, No. Ill. U. Law Rev., 1988; author: Criminal Justice, 1988. Lobbyist Allstate Ins. Co., N.Y., Conn., 1995-97, N.C., S.C., 1989-93; mem. Chgo. Sister Cities Internat., 1998-99, N.Y., 2000-03. Recipient writing award Lexis, 1988, award Am. Juriprudence, 1988. Mem. ABA, N.Y. State Bar Assn., Ill. Bar Assn. Avocations: golf, bicycling. Insurance, Private international, Legislative. Office: Allstate Ins Co 2775 Sanders Rd Northbrook IL 60062-6127

IHRIG, HANS-CHRISTOPH, lawyer; b. Frankfurt, Hessen, Germany, Aug. 23, 1959; m. Anna Ihrig; 3 children. 1st state exam, U. Heidelberg, Germany, 1984; Dr.iur.utr., U. Heidelberg, 1990; 2nd state exam, U. Stuttgart, Germany, 1987. Bar: Germany 1990. Asst. lectr. law U. Heidelberg, 1985—90; assoc. Schilling Zutt & Anschutz, Mannheim, Germany, 1990—94, ptnr., 1995—2000, Allen & Overy, Frankfut, 2000—. Mem.: German Bar Assn. (mem. standing com. on comml. law 2000). Corporate, general. Office: Allen & Overy Taunustor 2 60311 Frankfurt Germany

IIDA, YUKISATO, lawyer; b. Tokyo, Aug. 24, 1918; s. Sueharu and Kazuko I.; m. Turuko Aoki, May 1, 1948; children: Hidesato, Toshiyuki, Fumisato. Lectr. on European Cmty. trademark, 1997. Author: English-Japanese Dictionary of Patent Terms, 1973, Translation of English Patent Specifications, 1981, Japanese-English Dictionary of Patent Terms, 1982, Drafting of English Patent Specifications, 1983, Manual of Foreign Patent Application, 1985, Guideline Concerning the European Community Trademark, 1997, Primer of Japanese Patent Terms, 1999, Preparation of Patent Drawings, 1999. Recipient Yellow Ribbon medal Japanese Govt., 1978, 5th Order of Merit of the Rising Sun, 1988. Mem. Japan Patent Attys. Assn. (Spl. Meritorious Patent Atty. 1999). Home: 5-18-13 Koenji-Minami Suginami-ku Tokyo 166 Japan Office: Kojimachi Bldg 6F 3-3-6 Kudan Minami Chiyoda-Ku Tokyo 102-0074 Japan Office Fax: +81 3 5276 6370.

IIJIMA, AYUMU, lawyer; b. Kobe, Hyogo, Japan, Dec. 14, 1966; LLM, Duke U. Sch. Law, Durham, NC, 2000—01; Diploma to Practice Law, Legal Tng. and Rsch. Inst. Supreme Ct. of Japan, Tokyo, Japan, 1992—94; LLB, Kyoto U., Japan, 1985—92. Bar: NY 2002, Japan 1994. Assoc. Kitahama Law Office, Osaka, Japan, 1994—2000; staff atty. Akin, Gump, Strauss, Hauer & Feld LLP, Washington, 2001—02; spl. counsel Japan Patent Office, Chiyoda-ku, Japan, 2002—03; ptnr. Kitahama Partners LPC, Osaka, Japan, 2003—. Mem.: Info. Network Law Assn. Japan, Japan Fedn. Bar Associations, Osaka Bar Assn., NY Bar Assn. Intellectual property, Computer, Entertainment. Office: Kitahama Partners LPC Keihan Yodoyabashi Bldg 3-2-25 Kitahama Chuo-ku Osaka 541-0041 Japan

IIJIMA, CHRIS K. law educator; b. NYC, Dec. 19, 1948; s. Takeru and Kazuko (Ikeda) I.; m. Karen Asakawa (div. Aug. 1991); m. Jane Ann Dickson, Feb. 17, 1993; children: Alan Kando, Christopher Takeru. BA, Columbia U., 1969; JD, N.Y. Law Sch., 1988. Bar: N.Y. 1989, U.S. Dist. Ct. (so. and ea. dists.) N.Y. 1989. Jud. clk. U.S. Dist. Ct. (so. dist.) N.Y., N.Y.C., 1988-90; litigation assoc. Friedman & Kaplan, N.Y.C., 1990-93; lawyering instr. NYU Sch. Law, N.Y.C., 1993-95; asst. prof., dir. lawyering process program Western New Eng. Coll. Sch. Law, Springfield, Mass., 1995-98; assoc. prof., dir. pre-admission program William S. Richardson Sch. Law, Honolulu, 1998—. Bd. dirs. Na Loio Pub. Interest Legal Ctr., Honolulu; mem. Manoa Network for Minority Students, Honolulu, 1998—. Bd. advisors Rosenberg Fund for Children, Springfield, Mass., 1997—; bd. dirs. Homeless Solutions, Inc., 2001—. Mem.: Soc. Am. Law Tchrs. (bd. dirs. 2002—). Office: William S Richardson Sch Law 2515 Dole St Honolulu HI 96822-2328 E-mail: iijimac@hawaii.edu.

IKARD, FRANK NEVILLE, JR., lawyer; b. Wichita Falls, Tex., June 26, 1942; s. Frank Neville and Jean (Hunter) I.; children: Frank III, Jean, Charles; m. Katherine P. Ikard, Feb. 14, 1998. BA, U. Tex., 1965, JD, 1968. Bar: Tex. 1968; cert. Tex. Estate Planning and Probate Law Bd. of Legal Specialization. Assoc. then ptnr. Clark, Thomas, Winters, & Shapiro,

Austin, Tex., 1968-84; mng. ptnr. Jenkens & Gilchrist, Austin, 1985-88; ptnr. Johnson & Gibbs, Austin, 1988-92, Ikard & Golden, Austin, 1992—. Bd. dirs. Paramount Theatre, Austin, 1988-89, pres. bd. dirs., 1991-92; mem. Greater Austin Crime Commn. Fellow Am. Coll. Probate Counsel, Tex. Bar Found.; mem. Am. Coll. Trust and Estate Coun. (fiduciary litigation com. 1991-2001), Tex. Acad. Real Estate (pres. probate and trust law coun. 1988-89), State Bar Tex. (chmn., sec.-treas. legis. com. real estate, probate trust law sect. 1983-84, coun. chmn.), Travis County Bar Assn., Tarry House, Headliners, U. Tex. Club. Avocations: fly fishing, photography. Estate planning, Probate (including wills, trusts), Estate taxation. Home: 1107 Gaston Ave Austin TX 78703-2507 Office: Ikard & Golden 106 E 6th St Ste 500 Austin TX 78701-3666 E-mail: fni@ikardgolden.com.

IKENBERRY, HENRY CEPHAS, JR., lawyer; b. Cloverdale, Va., Mar. 23, 1920; s. Henry Cephas and Bessie (Peters) I.; m. Margaret Sangster Henry, July 3, 1943; children: Anna Catherine Ikenberry Fawell, Mary Margaret Ikenberry Rauck. BA, Bridgewater Coll., 1947; JD, U. Va., 1947. Bar: Va. 1947, W.Va. 1948, D.C. 1948, U.S. Supreme Ct. 1954, U.S. Ct. Claims 1972, U.S. Ct. Appeals (fed. cir.) 1982. Assoc. firm Steptoe & Johnson, Washington, 1947-49, 50-53, partner, former chmn. exec. com., 1953-85, of counsel, 1986-92; asst. counsel Gen. Aniline & Film Co., N.Y.C., 1949-50. Mem. com. on unauthorized practice D.C. Ct. Appeals, 1972-76. Ruling elder Chevy Chase Presbyn. Ch., Washington, 1970-72; trustee Mary Baldwin Coll., Staunton, Va., 1979-92, mem. exec. com., 1987-92; life mem., dean's counsel Univ. Va. Sch. Law. Lt. comdr. USNR, 1941-46, ETO, PTO, Okinawa, The Philippines. Recipient Alumni citation Bridgewater Coll., 1960; named Ky. col., 1973 Mem. Bar Assn. D.C. (chmn. com. on corp. law 1960-61, com. comml. bus. law 1969-72), Raven Soc., Am. Legion, Metropolitan Club, Chesapeake Bay Yacht Club, Chevy Chase Club, Talbot Country Club (Easton, Md.), Order of Coif, Phi Delta Phi, Tau Kappa Alpha. Corporate, general, Securities. Home: Pine Lodge 26783 Miles River Rd Easton MD 21601-5013 also: PO Box 1518 Easton MD 21601-8929 also: Box N-308 8101 Connecticut Ave Chevy Chase MD 20815

IMBER, ANNABELLE CLINTON, state supreme court justice; b. Heber Springs, Ark., July 15, 1950; m. Ariel Barak Imber (dec. 2001); 1 child, William Pierce Clinton. BA magna cum laude, Smith Coll., 1971; postgrad., Inst. for Paralegal Tng., 1971, U. Houston, 1973-75; JD, U. Ark., 1977. Atty. Wright, Lindsey & Jennings Law Firm, Little Rock, Ark., 1977-88; apptd. cir. judge (5th divsn.) Pulaski and Perry Counties, Ark., 1984, elected chancery and probate judge (6th divsn.), 1989-96; elected assoc. justice Ark. Supreme Ct., 1997—. Bd. dirs. Ark. Advs. for Children and Families, 1985-90, pres. 1986-88; bd. dirs Pulsaki County Hist. Soc., 1992-95, Congregation B'Nai Israel, 1988-92, 2001-, Kiwanis Club 1995-98, YMCA of Greater Little Rock and Pulaski County, Our House-A Shelter for Homeless, 1992—, St. Vincent Devel. Found., 1989-93, UAMS Med. Ctr. Dept. Pastoral Care and Edn., 1996—. Mem. ABA, AAUW, Nat. Assn. Women Judges, Ark. Bar Assn., Ark. Women Exec., Assn. of Ark. Women Lawyers (pres. 1980-81, Judge of the Year award 1994), Pulaski County Bar Assn. (bd. dirs. 1982-84). Office: Ark Supreme Ct Justice Bldg 625 Marshall St Little Rock AR 72201-1054

IMEL, JOHN MICHAEL, lawyer; b. Cushing, Okla., Aug. 4, 1932; s. Arthur Blaine and Hazel Monnet (Kelly) I.; m. Patricia Ann Carney, July 31, 1954; children: Blythe Michele, Kathryn Ann, Dixie Lynn, Sally Louise. BS, U. Okla., 1954, JD, 1959. Bar: Okla. 1959, U.S. Dist. Ct. (no. dist.) Okla. 1961, U.S. Ct. Appeals (10th cir.) 1961, U.S. Supreme Ct. 1962, U.S. Dist. Ct. (we. dist.) Okla. 1967, U.S. Dist. Ct. (ea. dist.) Okla. 1971. Asst. atty. County of Tulsa, 1959—60; mcpl. judge City of Tulsa, 1960—61; U.S. atty. U.S. Dept. Justice, Tulsa, 1961—67; ptnr. Moyers, Martin, Santee Imel & Tetrick, Tulsa, 1967—. Regent U. Okla., Norman, 1981-88, chmn., 1987-88; trustee Children's Med. Ctr., Tulsa, 1979-84. Capt. USNR, 1954-56. Fellow Am. Bar Found., Am. Coll. Trial Lawyers (state chmn. 1987-88); mem. Am. Inns of Ct. (program chmn. 1989-90, Exemplary Leadership award 1996), So. Hills Country Club (bd. govs. 1993-99), Tulsa Club (pres. 1990), Rotary (pres. 1968-69). Democrat. Methodist. Avocations: golf, swimming, tennis, reading. Federal civil litigation, General civil litigation, State civil litigation. Home: 3920 E 58th Pl Tulsa OK 74135-7823 Office: Moyers Martin Santee Imel & Tetrick 401 S Boston Ste 1100 Tulsa OK 74103 E-mail: imel@moyersmartin.com.

IMHOFF, EARL J. lawyer; b. Chgo., Aug. 2, 1950; s. Earl J. Imhoff, Sr. and Lois Olsen Imhoff; m. Judith Rose Lammers, Dec. 1, 1973; children: Elisabeth Rose, Benjamin Winden, Julia Rose. AB, U. Notre Dame, 1972; student, U. Moscow, 1970; MA, U. So. Calif., London, 1977; JD, U. Wis., 1979. Bar: Wis. 1979, (U.S. Dist. Ct. (we. dist.) Wis.) 1979, Calif. 1980, U.S. Dist. (no., cen., so., and ea. dists.) Calif. 1980, U.S. Ct. Appeals (9th and 7th cirs.). Assoc. Hancock Rothert & Bunshoft, San Francisco, 1980—85; ptnr. Hill Betts & Nash, L.A., 1985—88, Ullick McHose & Charles, L.A., 1988—89, Hancock Rothert & Bunshoft, L.A., 1989—2000, Coudert Bros., L.A., 2000—. Cons., counsel KidsPace Mus., Pasadena, Calif., 1995—2000. Contbr. articles to law jours. Cons., vol. Boy Scouts Am., L.A., 1988—95, Pasadena Little League, 1990—2000; cons., vol., com. head Poly. Sch., Pasadena, 1997—2001. Lt. USN, 1972—77. Mem.: State Bar Calif./L.A. County Bar Assn. (del. 1989—99), Inter-Pacific Bar Assn. (charter mem.), Maritime Law Assn. U.S. (proctor on admiralty 1980—2002). Admiralty, Insurance, Private international. Office: Coudert Bros LLP 23d Fl 333 S Hope St Los Angeles CA 90071 Office Fax: 213-229-2999. E-mail: eimhoff@coudert.com.

IMIG, WILLIAM GRAFF, lawyer, lobbyist; b. Omaha, Aug. 13, 1941; s. Jacob H. and Gretchen (Kirk) I.; m. Joyce Stevens, Dec. 18, 1976; children: Scott, Kari, Steven. BA, Cornell U., 1963, LLB, 1965. Bar: Colo. 1965, U.S. Ct. Appeals (10th cir.) 1965, U.S. Supreme Ct. 1969. Assoc. Sherman & Howard, Denver, 1965-66; v.p., shareholder Ireland, Stapleton, Pryor & Pascoe, Denver, 1970-92; pvt. practice, Denver, 1992—. Colo. counsel Nat. Assn. Ind. Insurers, Des Plaines, Ill., 1971—; Colo. legis. counsel Allstate Ins. Cos., 1982—. Bd. editors Cornell Law rev., 1964-65. Chmn. Colo. Gov.'s Auto Insurance Reform Task Force, 2002-03, 1987-90; trustee Colo. chpt. Nat. Multiple Sclerosis Soc., 1995-2000; mem. Auto Ins. Roundtable. Capt. JAGC, U.S. Army, 1966-70. Mem. Colo. Bar Assn. (bd. govs. 1974-77, pro bono award 1985), Colo. Assn. Commerce and Industry (chmn. tort reform coun., chmn. auto ins. roundtable), City Club of Denver, Denver Law Club, Phi Kappa Phi. Republican. Episcopalian. Administrative and regulatory, Legislative. Home and Office: 1795 Monaco Pky Denver CO 80220-1644

IMMERGUT, MEL M. lawyer; b. Bklyn., 1947; BA, U. Pa., 1968; JD, Columbia U., 1971, MBA, 1972. Bar: N.Y. 1972. Ptnr. Milbank, Tweed, Hadley & McCloy, N.Y.C. Mem. ABA, N.Y. State Bar Assn., Assn. Bar City N.Y. Office: Milbank Tweed Hadley & McCloy 1 Chase Manhattan Plz Fl 47 New York NY 10005-1413*

IMMKE, KEITH HENRY, lawyer; b. Peoria, Ill., Jan. 18, 1953; s. Francis William and Pearl Lenora (Kime) I. BA, U. Ill., 1975; JD, So. Ill. U., 1978. Bar: Ill. 1978, U.S. Dist. Ct. (so. and ea. dist.) Ill. 1979. Assoc. Lawrence E. Johnson & Assocs., P.C., Champaign, Ill., 1979-87; staff atty. Dept. Ins. State Ill., Springfield, 1987-88; legal counsel Underground Storage Tank program (now Divsn. Petroleum and Chem. Safety), 1988-98; asst. legal counsel Office Fire Marshal State Ill., 1988—. Legal counsel Underground Storage Tank Program (now Div. Petroleum and Chem. Safety 1988-98), asst. legal counsel; Office Fire Marshal State Ill., 1998—. Mem. ABA, Ill. State Bar Assn., U. Ill. Alumni Assn., Phi Kappa Phi, Pi Sigma Alpha, Phi Alpha Delta. Environmental. Office: State Ill Office Fire Marshal Div Petroleum and Chem Safety 1035 Stevenson Dr Springfield IL 62703-4259

IMPASTATO, DAVID JOHN, III, lawyer; b. Chapel Hill, NC, Feb. 9, 1963; s. David John, Jr. and Nancy Impastato; m. Sally Reed; children: William, Rachel. BA, U. Calif.-Berkeley, 1986; JD, Columbia U., 1991. Bar: N.Y. 1992, Calif. 1999. Assoc. Milbank, Tweed, Hadley & McCloy, various locations, 1991—2000, ptnr. Tokyo, 2000—. Private international, Banking, Corporate, general. Office: Milbank Tweed Hadley & McCloy 2-2-2 Uchisaiwaicho Tokyo 100-0011 Japan

IMRE, CHRISTINA JOANNE, lawyer; b. Gary, Ind., Oct. 25, 1950; d. Joseph and Ruth Leone I.; m. Richard Long, Dec. 31, 1991. BA, Mt. St. Mary's Coll., L.A., 1972; MA, U. Notre Dame, 1974; JD, Loyola Law Sch., L.A., 1980. Bar: Calif. 1980, U.S. Ct. Appeals (ninth cir.) 1982, U.S. Dist. Ct. (ctrl. dist.) Calif. 1983, U.S. Dist. Ct. (no. dist.) Calif. 1988,U.S. Dist. Ct. (so. dist.) Calif. 1995, U.S. Supreme Ct., 2000. Assoc. Lascher & Lascher, Ventura, Calif., 1980-83, Law Office of Errol Berk, Ventura, Calif., 1983-84, Pachter, Gold & Schaffer, L.A., 1984-87; sr. atty. Kornblum & McBride, L.A., 1987-89; ptnr. Horvitz & Levy LLP, Encino, Calif., 1989—2000, Crosby, Heafey, Roach & May, Los Angeles, 2000—02, Sedgwick, Detert, Moran & Arnold, LLP, Los Angeles, 2002—. Bd. govs. Calif. Continuing Edn. of Bar, Berkeley, Calif., 1996-2000; chair Calif. Continuing Edn. of Bar Joint Adv. Com., Berkeley, 1995; editorial bd. L.A. Lawyer Mag., L.A., 1996-99; cons. Handling Civil Appeals, Berkeley, 1996, Calif. Trial Practice, Berkeley, 1995; lectr. in field. Editor-in-chief: Loyola of Los Angeles International & Comparative Law Journal, 1979-80; monthly columnist CEB Civil Litigation Reporter; contbr. articles to profl. jours. and chpts. to books. Named one of 50 Most Powerful Women in L.A. Law, L.A. Business Journal, 1998; Loyola Law Sch. fellow, 1979-80, U. Notre Dame fellow, 1972-74. Mem. L.A. County Bar Assn., Defense Rsch. Inst., So. Calif. Defense Counsel Assn. Avocations: music, shakespeare, history, philosophy. Appellate, State civil litigation, Insurance. Office: Sedgwick Detert Moran & Arnold LLP 801 S Figueroa St 18th Fl Los Angeles CA 90017 E-mail: christina.imre@sdma.com.

INABA, YOSHIYUKI, patent and trademark lawyer; b. Osaka, Japan, Mar. 8, 1950; s. Yoshisada and Kaori (Yokokoji) I.; m. Kayoko Takamatsu, June 10, 1984; children: Kanako, Daisuke. BS, Sophia U., Tokyo, 1973; postgrad., Patent Acad., 1980. Bar: Japan; lic. patent atty. Assoc. Unuma & Assocs., Tokyo, 1974-78, 80-85; assoc., trainee Koda & Androlia, L.A., 1978-80; trainee Stevens, Davis et al, Washington, 1980; prin. Inaba & Assocs., Tokyo, 1985-90; ptnr. TMI Assocs., Tokyo, 1990—. Spkr. Am. Intellectual Property Law Assn., 1983; lectr. Santa Clara U. Sch. Law Summer Program, Tokyo, 1998—. Mem. Internat. Assn. for the Proetction of Indsl. Property, , Internat. Trademark Assn. (spkr.), Asian Patent Atty. Assn. Office: TMI Assocs/37 Mori Bldg 5-1 Toranomon 3-chome 8F Minato-ku Tokyo 105-0001 Japan E-mail: yinaba@tmi.gr.jp.

INDURSKY, ARTHUR, lawyer; b. Bklyn., Jan. 1, 1943; s. David and Anne (Levine) I.; m. Deanne Fiedler, Mar. 26, 1967; 1 child, Blake. BBA, CCNY, 1964; JD, Bklyn. Law Sch., 1967. Bar: N.Y., 1968. Entertainment counsel Columbia Pictures, N.Y.C., 1969-72; mng. ptnr. Grubman Indursky & Schindler P.C., N.Y.C., 1973—. Bd. dirs. Alliance Artists and Rec. Cos.; guest spkr. Can. Rec. Industry Seminar, 1986, Entertainment Law Soc., Bklyn. Law Sch., 1987, 92, Copyright Soc., 1988, Disting. Alumni Lecture Series Bklyn. Law Sch., 1989, Hofstra Law Sch., 1995. Bd. dirs. T.J. Martell Found. for Leukemia, Cancer and AIDS Rsch., 1993—. Recipient 1st Ann. Alumni Achievement award Bklyn. Law Sch., 1992, Outstanding Leadership award Meml. Sloan Kettering Cancer Ctr., 1994, City of Hope award, 1995, Jule Styne Humanitarian award Childrens Hearing Inst., 1998. Entertainment. Office: Grubman Indursky & Schindler PC 152 W 57th St New York NY 10019-3310

INGALLS, EVERETT PALMER, III, lawyer; b. Portland, Maine, Nov. 21, 1947; s. Everett Palmer and Joyce (Iveney) I.; m. Susan Wilson, Feb. 15, 1992; 1 child, Abigail Valentine. AB, Brown U., 1969; JD, Harvard U., 1972. Bar: Maine 1972, U.S. Dist. Ct. Maine 1972. Assoc. Pierce Atwood, Portland, 1972-77, mem., 1977—. Area chmn. Harvard Law Sch. Fund, Cambridge, Mass., 1978-82; pres. Portland Widows' Wood Soc., 1982-86; bd. dirs. Portland Stage Co., 1979-82; pres. Portland Performing Arts, 1992-94; pres. planned giving com. Maine Med. Ctr., 2002—. Fellow Am. Coll. Trust & Estate Counsel; mem. ABA (real property, probate & trust law and taxation), Harvard Law Sch. Assn. in Maine (pres. 1982-85), Phi Beta Kappa. Administrative and regulatory, Corporate, general, Estate planning. Home: 125 Neal St Portland ME 04102-3209 Office: Pierce Atwood One Monument Sq Portland ME 04101 E-mail: eingalls@pierceatwood.com.

INGALSBE, WILLIAM JAMES, lawyer; b. Guam, June 5, 1947; came to U.S., 1953; s. Wilbur and Erma I.; m. Heidi Marie Freed, June 21, 1969; 1 child, James. BA, Calif. State U., San Diego, 1969; JD, Southwestern U., 1975. Bar: Calif., 1975, U.S. Ct. Appeals (9th cir.) 1984, U.S. Dist. Ct. (cen. and so. dist.) Calif. 1976, U.S. Dist. Ct. (no. dist.) Calif. 1984, U.S. Claims Ct. 1979. Assoc. Spray, Gould & Bowers, L.A., 1975-76; ptnr. Monteleone & McCrory, L.A., Calif., 1976—. Editor-in-chief: Southwestern U. Law Rev., 1974. Vol. investigative atty. State Bar Calif., L.A., 1986. Mem. Assoc. Gen. Contractors Calif., L.A. County Bar Assn. (judge pro tem mcpl. ts. com. 1984-86, vol. atty. client rels. com. 1984-90). Avocations: fishing, golf, photography. Federal civil litigation, State civil litigation, Construction. Office: # 130 450 W 4th St Santa Ana CA 92701-4562 E-mail: ingalsbe@mmlawyers.com.

INGERSOLL, RICHARD KING, lawyer; b. Algoma, Wis., Aug. 13, 1944; s. Robert Clive and Bernice Eleanore (Koehn) I.; m. Caroline Soi-Keu Yee, Aug. 31, 1968; children: Kristin Paula Juk-Yee, Karin Eleanor Juk-Ling. BBA, U. Mich., 1966; JD, U. Calif.-Berkeley, Berkeley, 1969. Bar: Ill. 1969, Hawaii 1973. Asst. prof. U. Ill.-Champaign, Champaign, 1969-70; assoc. Sidley & Austin, Chgo., 1970-73; ptnr. Rush, Moore, Craven, Kim & Stricklin, Honolulu, 1973-88, Gelber, Gelber, Ingersoll & Klevansky , Honolulu, 1989—. Spkr. tax law seminars. Author various law materials. Mem. ABA (taxation, bus. and internat. law coms.), Waialae Country Club (sec.). Corporate, general, Private international, Corporate taxation. Home: 944 Waiholo St Honolulu HI 96821-1226 E-mail: ringersoll@ggikf.com.

INGERSOLL, WILLIAM BOLEY, lawyer, real estate developer; b. Washington, Sept. 21, 1938; s. William Brown and Loraine (Boley) I.; m. Carolyn Grace Potter, Sept. 8, 1963; children: William Brett, Courtney Lynn, Wayne Brandon, Dana Lee. BS, Brigham Young U., 1964; JD, Cath. U. Am., 1968. Bar: Va. 1968, D.C. 1969. Atty. Office of Corp. Counsel D.C., 1967-69, Office Gen. Counsel HUD, 1969-70; ptnr. Fried, Klewans, Ingersoll & Bloch, Washington, 1970-72; pres. Ingersoll and Bloch Chartered, Washington, 1972—; of counsel Holland & Knight, Washington, 1998—. Mng. ptnr. JC Assocs. Real Estate Devel., Washington, 1973—; gen. counsel Am. Resort Devel. Assn.; lectr. in field. Co-editor-in-chief Land Devel. Law Reporter, Land Trends, 1973—, The Digest of State Land Sales, 1976—, Time Sharing Law Reporter, 1980—, D.C. Real Estate Reporter, 1982—, Real Estate Opportunity Report, 1986; contbr. in field. Bd. dirs. Nat. Timesharing Coun., 1981—; mem. Garrison Presdl. Commn., 1984; mem. bd. adv. J. Ruben Clark Law Sch., 1987-93, chmn., 1991-93; bishop McLean (Va.) Ward, LDS Ch.; mem. nat. adv. com. Inside Real Estate, 1985—. Mem. ABA, FBA, D.C. Bar Assn., Va. Bar Assn., Va. Assn. Trial Lawyers, Land Devel. Inst. (vice chmn.), Brigham Young U. Alumni Assn. (bd. dirs. 1984-92), Order of Coif, Univ. Club Washington. Administrative and regulatory, Legislative, Property, real (including real estate development, water). Home: 713 Potomac Knolls Dr Mc Lean VA 22102-1421 also: Holland & Knight Ste 100 2099 Pennsylvania Ave NW Washington DC 20006-1816 E-mail: wingerso@hklaw.com.

INGLEZ DE SOUZA, RICARDO NOROUHA, lawyer; b. São Paulo, Brazil, Nov. 8, 1976; s. Sérgio Dias and Rosie Kiehl (Noronha) Inglez de Souza; m. Paula Haddad Troubela, June 17, 2000. Law Degree, Cath. U. São Paulo, 2000; postgrad., U. São Paulo, 2001—. Paralegal Pignalosa Advogados Associados, 1996, Dauro Dórea Advogados Associados, São Paulo, 1996—97, Demarest & Almeida Advogados, São Paulo, 1997—2000, atty., 2001—; internat. lawyer of Demarest Marval, O'Farrel & Mairal, Buenos Aires, 2002. Mem. corp. law commn. Ctr. of Studies of Brazilian Law Firms, São Paulo, 2000—; commr. for antitrust Brazilian Bar Assn., São Paulo, 2001—; founding mem., coord. Studies Group of Econ. Law, GEDECON, São Paulo, 2001—; lectr. in field. Contbr. Vol. Brazilian Orgn. Transplant Assn., São Paulo Sch. Medicine. Recipient Hon. Mention, Brazilian Inst. for Antitrust and Consumer Def., 2001, Nat. Ctr. of Rsch., 1998. Roman Catholic. Avocations: reading, soccer, movies, rafting. Antitrust, Administrative and regulatory, Commercial, contracts (including sales of goods; commercial financing). Office: Demarest & Almeida Aduogados Av Pedroso de Moraes 1201 05419-001 São Paulo Brazil

INGRAM, GEORGE CONLEY, lawyer, judge; b. Dublin, Ga., Sept. 27, 1930; s. George Conley and Nancy Averett (Whitehurst) I.; m. Sylvia Williams, July 26, 1952; children: Sylvia Lark, Nancy Randolph, George Conley. AB, Emory U., 1949, LL.B., 1951. Bar: Ga. 1952. City atty. City of Smyrna, Ga., 1958-64, City of Kennesaw, Ga., 1964; judge Cobb County Juvenile Ct., 1960-64, Superior Ct., Cobb Jud. Cir., 1964-68; justice Supreme Ct. Ga., 1973-77; spl. asst. atty. gen. State of Ga., 1979-86; ptnr. Alston & Bird, Atlanta, 1977-98; sr. judge State of Ga., 1998—. Staff, faculty Judge Advocate Gen. Sch. U.S. Army U. Va., 1952-54. Former trustee Agnes Scott Coll., Kennesaw Coll. Found., Emory U.; trustee Cobb Cmty. Found., The Eleventh Cirs. Hist. Soc. Inc.; emeritus mem. Emory Law Sch. Coun.; past pres. Cobb County YMCA, Cobb Landmarks Soc.; former chmn. ofcl. bd. 1st Meth. Ch. of Marietta, trustee. 1st lt. JAGC, USAR, 1952-54. Recipient Emory U. medal and Disting. Svc. award Kennesaw Mountain Jaycees, 1961, Ga. Jaycees, 1961, Emory Law Sch. Alumni Assn., 1985; Disting. Citizen award City of Marietta, Ga., 1973; Len Gilbert Leadership award Cobb County C. of C., 1985; Cobb County Citizen of Yr. award, 1990; hon. life mem. Ga. PTA. Fellow Am. Bar Assn. Found., Am. Coll. Trial Lawyers, Internat. Soc. Barristers, Am. Acad. Appellate Lawyers, Marietta-Cobb Mus. Art; mem. ABA, Am. Law Inst., State Bar Ga. (Tradition of Excellence award 1987), Cobb and Atlanta Bar Assn., Lawyers Club of Atlanta, Old War Horse Lawyers Club, Cobb County C. of C. (Pub. Svc. award 1970, Turner award in family law 2002) Georgian Club (bd. mem., founding chmn.), Rotary (award for vocat. excellence 1999), Order of Coif (hon.), Phi Delta Phi, Omicron Delta Kappa. Methodist. Federal civil litigation, State civil litigation, General practice. Home: 540 Hickory Dr Marietta GA 30064-3602

INGRAM, JAMES MICHAEL, lawyer; b. Memphis, Tenn., May 23, 1960; s. James Milton Ingram III and Janet Kay (Parker) Ingram Girnius. BS in Psychology, Santa Clara U., Calif., 1982; JD, Pepperdine U., Malibu, Calif., 1985. Bar: (Calif.) 1985, U.S. Dist. Ct., Ctrl. Dist. Calif. 1986, U.S. Ct. of Appeals (9th cir.) 1986, U.S. Dist. Ct., No. Dist. Calif. 1988, US Dist. Ct., Ea. Dist. Calif. 1988, U.S. Ct. of Appeals, Fed. Cir. 1990, U.S. Dist. Ct., So. Dist. Tex. 1997. Law clk. Evanns & Walsh, Beverly Hills, Calif., 1983—85, assoc., 1985—87, Law Offices of Mark I. Rosenberg, Century City, Calif., 1987—88, Mount & Stoelker, San Jose, Calif., 1988—96, Law Offices Lester G. Sachs, San Jose, Calif., 1996—2001; mem. Law Offices of James M. Ingram, Irvine, Calif., 2001—. Sec., bd. dirs. Let Them Play Found., Inc., Santa Clara, Calif., 1994—; advisor to bd. dirs., v.p., sec. The Robert Brownlee Found., Mountain View, Calif., 2001—. Mem. St. Thomas More Soc. of Santa Clara County, Santa Clara, Calif., 1998—. Recipient Am. Jurisprudence Award in Torts, Bancroft Whitney - Lawyers Coop. Pub. Co., 1983. Mem.: ATLA, Orange County Bar Assn., Santa Clara County Bar Assn. Conservative. Roman Catholic. Avocations: intercollegiate athletics, equestrian sports, travel, cooking, sport horse breeding. General civil litigation, Intellectual property, Property, real (including real estate development, water). Office: Law Offices James M Ingram 5405 Alton Parkway Ste 5A-739 Irvine CA 92604 Office Fax: 866-390-0002. E-mail: jmingram@sprynet.com.

INGRAM, KENNETH FRANK, retired state supreme court justice; b. Ashland, Ala., July 7, 1929; s. Earnest Frank and Alta Mary (Allen) I.; m. Judith Louise Brown, Sept. 3, 1954; children: Jennifer Lynn Ingram Malone, Kenneth Frank Jr. BS, Auburn U., 1951; LLB, Jones Law Sch., 1963. Bar: Ala. 1963, U.S. Dist. Ct. (no. dist.) Ala. 1965, U.S. Dist. Ct. (mid. dist.) Ala. 1966. City councilman City of Ashland, Ala., 1956-58; mem. Ho. of Reps., Ala., 1958-66; presiding judge 18th Jud. Cir. Ct., Ala., 1968-87; judge Ala. Ct. Civil Appeals, Montgomery, 1987-89, presiding judge, 1989-91; assoc. justice Ala. Supreme Ct., Montgomery, 1991-97. Mem., chmn. Ala. Jud. Inquiry Commn., 1979-87. Contbr. articles on jud. ethics to profl. pubs. With USMC, 1952-54. Mem. Ala. Bar Assn., Masons. Democrat. Methodist. Avocations: woodworking, metalcrafting, tennis, swimming. Home: 264 1st St N PO Box 729 Ashland AL 36251-0729

INGRAM, SAMUEL WILLIAM, JR., lawyer; b. Utica, N.Y., Mar. 20, 1933; s. Samuel William and Mary Elizabeth (Rosen) I.; m. Jane Austin Stokes, Sept. 30, 1961; children: Victoria, William BS, Vanderbilt U., 1954; LLB, Columbia U., 1960. Bar: N.Y. 1960. Assoc. Sullivan & Cromwell, N.Y.C., 1960-67; assoc. Shea Gallop Climenko & Gould, N.Y.C., 1967-68; ptnr. Shea & Gould and predecessors, N.Y.C., 1968-89, Ingram, Yuzek, Gainen, Carroll & Bertolotti LLP, N.Y.C., 1989—. Bd. dirs. Legal Aid Soc., N.Y.C., 1974-86, sec., 1978-86; trustee Green Mountain Valley Sch., Waitsfield, Vt., 1984-87. Served to 1st lt. USMC, 1954-57 Mem. ABA, N.Y. State Bar Assn., Assn. of Bar of City of N.Y. Avocation: athletic and outdoor activities. Property, real (including real estate development, water). Home: 332 Long Ridge Rd Pound Ridge NY 10576-2005 Office: Ingram Yuzek Gainen Carroll & Bertolotti LLP 250 Park Ave Ste 600 New York NY 10177-0699 E-mail: singram@ingramllp.com.

INKLEY, JOHN JAMES, JR., lawyer; b. St. Louis, Nov. 7, 1945; s. John James Sr. and Morjorie Jane (Kenna) I.; m. Catherine Ann Mattingly, Apr. 13, 1971; children: Caroline Marie, John James III. BSIE, St. Louis U., 1967, JD, 1970; LLM in Taxation, Washington U., St. Louis, 1976. Bar: Mo. 1970, U.S. Dist. Ct. (we. dist.) Mo. 1970, U.S. Dist. Ct. (ea. dist.) Mo. 1975, U.S. Tax Ct. 1975, U.S. Supreme Ct. 1975. Assoc. Padberg, Raack, McSweeney & Slater, St. Louis, 1970-73; ptnr. Summer, Hanlon, Summer, MacDonald & Nouss, St. Louis, 1973-81; city atty. City of Town and Country, Mo., 1979-84, spl. counsel, 1984-88; ptnr. Hanlon, Nouss, Inkley & Coughlin, St. Louis, 1981-83; ptnr., chmn. banking and real estate dept. Suelthaus & Kaplan, St. Louis, 1983-91; ptnr. Armstrong Teasdale LLP (and predecessor firm), St. Louis, 1991—; co-chmn. bus. svcs. group, 1993-2000; exec. com., 1994—. Mem. ABA, Mo. Bar Assn., Bar Assn. Met. St. Louis. Roman Catholic. Banking, Corporate, general, Property, real (including real estate development, water). Home: 35 Muirfield Ln Saint Louis MO 63141-7382 Office: Armstrong Teasdale LLP 1 Metropolitan Sq Ste 2600 Saint Louis MO 63102-2740

INNAMORATO, DON ANTHONY, lawyer; b. Perth Amboy, N.J., Sept. 10, 1961; s. Anthony John Innamorato and Caroline Elizabeth Rusin; m. Laura Ann Russo, Nov. 9, 1996; children: Anthony, Gabriela. BA in Psychology, Columbia U., 1983; JD, Villanova U., 1986. Bar: Pa. 1986, N.J. 1987, U.S. Dist. Ct. (ea. dist.) Pa. 1987, U.S. Dist. Ct. N.J. 1987, U.S. Ct. Appeals (3rd cir.) 1987. Assoc. Reed Smith Shaw & McClay, Phila., 1986-95, ptnr. Princeton, N.J., 1995—. Editor-in-chief The N.J. Labor Letter, 2000—. Labor (including EEOC, Fair Labor Standards Act, labor-management relations, NLRB, OSHA). Office: Reed Smith LLP Princeton Forrestal Village 136 Main St Princeton NJ 08540-5735

INNES, KENNETH FREDERICK, III, lawyer; b. San Francisco, May 15, 1950; s. Kenneth F. Jr. and Jean I.; m. Patricia Ann Graboyes, May 12, 1973; children: Kenneth F. IV, Julia Christine. BA, San Francisco State U., 1972, JD, 1984. Bar: Calif. 1984, U.S. Dist. Ct. (no. dist.) Calif. 1987, U.S. Dist. Ct. (ea. dist.) Calif. 1988. Tchr. secondary schs., Red Bluff, Calif., 1973-74; postal clk. U.S. Postal Svc., Vallejo, Calif., 1977-84, postal insp. Denver, 1984-87; regional atty. U.S. Postal Inspection Svc., Memphis, 1987-90, fin. auditor, 1990-92, regional atty. San Francisco, 1992—. Capt. USMCR, 1974-77. Mem. ABA, Calif. Bar Assn., Mensa, Elks. Democrat. Roman Catholic. Home: 157 Heartwood Ct Vallejo CA 94591-5638 Office: US Postal Insp Svc PO Box 882528 San Francisco CA 94188-2528

INOUE, AKIRA, law educator; b. Japan, 1938; LLB, Hitotsubashi U., Tokyo, 1962, LLM, 1967. Cert. full prof. grad. sch. of law, coun. for establishment of univs., Minister of Edn., Japan. Asst. prof. Seijo U. Faculty Law, Tokyo, 1977-79, prof., 1980—, prof. Grad. Sch. Law, 1987—. Vis. scholar Inst. Comparative Law, U. Jean Moulin (Lyon III), Lyon, France, 1976-77, 89, Inst. Comparative Law Paris, U. Law, Econs. and Social Scis. (Paris 2), 1989. Co-author: (with others) (books) Important Problems of Modern Commercial Law, 1983, Grand Dictionary on Law of Corporations, 1984, Present Problems of Commercial Law, 1985, Powers and Liablilites of Directors, 1994, Jurisprudence and Politics Facing Toward the 21st Century, 1999. Mem. Japan Assn. Private Law, Assn. Econ. Jurisprudence, Japanese Maritime Law Assn., Japan Soc. of Comparative Law. Office: Seijo U Faculty of Law 6-1-20 Seijo Setagaya-ku Tokyo 157 Japan

INOUE, HIDENORI, law educator; b. Kyoto, Dec. 20, 1950; s. Tsuyoshi and Toshiko Inoue. B of Politics, Waseda U., Tokyo, 1975, LLM, 1977. Instr. Mesei U., Tokyo, 1984-89, assoc. prof., 1989-95, prof., 1995—. Committeeman Japan Energy Law Inst., Tokyo, 1984—95, Inst. Developing Economies, Tokyo, 1992—96, Clean Japan Ctr., Tokyo, 1992, Nuc. Material Control Ctr., 1997—98; rapporteur Internat. Bar Assn., London; bd. dirs. Japan Ctr. for Human Environ. Problems, Japanese Assn. Environ. Law and Policy, Japanese Assn. Land and Environment; workshop mem. Ministry of Environment, 2001—; vice chmn. Japan Com. for IUCN, 2002—; expert Environ. Coun., Tochigi Prefecture, 2002—. Mem.: Soc. Environ. Sci. Japan, Japanese Assn. Water Resources and Environment, Japanese Assn. Traffic Law, Japanese Assn. World Law, Japanese Assn. Internat. Law, Am. Soc. Internat. Law, Internat. Bar Assn. Office: Meisei U 1-1 Hodokubo 2 chome 191-8506 Hino Tokyo Japan E-mail: inoueh@econ.meisei-u.ac.jp.

INOUYE, DANIEL KEN, senator; b. Honolulu, Sept. 7, 1924; s. Hyotaro I. and Kame Imanaga; m. Margaret Shinobu Awamura, June 12, 1949; 1 child, Daniel Ken. AB, U. Hawaii, 1950; JD, George Washington U., 1952. Bar: Hawaii 1953. Asst. pub. prosecutor, Honolulu, 1953-54; pvt. practice, 1954—; majority leader Territorial Ho. of Reps., 1954-58, Senate, 1958-59; mem. 86th-87th U.S. Congresses from Hawaii; senator from Hawaii U.S. Senate (now 106th Congress), 1962—; sec. Senate Dem. Conf., 1978-88; chmn. Dem. Steering Com., Senate Com. on Appropriations; chmn. subcom. def., mem. Commerce Com.; chmn. subcom. on communications Select Com. on Intelligence, 1976-77, ranking mem. subcom. budget authorizations, 1979-84; former chmn. Select Com. Indian Affairs; mem. Select Com. on Presdl. Campaign Activities, 1973-74; chmn. Sen. select com. Secret Mil. Assistance to Iran and Nicaraguan Opposition, 1987. Ranking minority mem. Appropriations subcom. on defense, Commerce, Sci., & Transp. subcom on surface transp. & merchant marine; mem. Indian Affairs Com., Rules & Adminstrn. Com. Joint Com. on the Libr. & Congl. Intern Program, Dem. Steering & Coordination Com., Joint Com. on Printing. Author: Journey to Washington. Active YMCA, Boy Scouts Am. Keynoter; temporary chmn. Dem. Nat. Conv., 1968, rules com. chmn., 1980, co-chmn. conv., 1984. Pvt. to capt. AUS, 1943-47. Decorated D.S.C., Bronze Star, Purple Heart with cluster; named 1 of 10 Outstanding Young Men of Yr. U.S. Jr. C. of C., 1960; recipient Splendid Am. award Thomas A. Dooley Found., 1967 Golden Plate award Am. Acad. Achievement, 1968 Mem. DAV (past comdr. Hawaii), Honolulu C. of C., Am. Legion (Nat. Comdr.'s award 1973) Clubs: Lion. (Hawaii), 442d Veterans (Hawaii). Democrat. Methodist. Home: 469 Ena Rd Honolulu HI 96815-1749 Office: US Senate 722 Hart Senate Bldg Washington DC 20510-0001

INSEL, MICHAEL S. lawyer; b. N.Y.C., Apr. 19, 1947; s. Ralph David and Lillian Ruth (Solomon) I.; married; 1 child, Louis Leo. BA, Duke U., 1969; JD, NYU, 1973. Bar: N.Y. 1974, Fla. 1984. Assoc. Kelley Drye & Warren, N.Y.C., 1973-82, ptnr., 1982—; pres. French Am. Vintners LLC. Bd. dirs. Kobrand Corp., N.Y.C., Maison Louis Jadot, S.A., Beaune, France, L & L, S.A., Boe, France, Western Wine Svcs., Inc., North Bergen, N.J., Taittinger C.C.U.C., Reims, France, Kobrand Found., N.Y.C., The Kopf Family Found., Inc., St. Francis Vineyards, Sonoma, Calif., Domaine Carneros, Napa, Calif.; chmn. Goodwill Industries, Astoria, N.Y.; trustee Elsie del Fierro Charitable Trust, N.Y.C., 1985—, Barbara Bell Cumming Found., N.Y.C., 1991—. Mem.: ABA, Fla. Bar Assn., NY State Bar Assn. Avocations: sailing, golf, opera. Office: Kelley Drye & Warren 101 Park Ave Fl 30 New York NY 10178-0062

INTRILIGATOR, MARC STEVEN, lawyer; b. Oceanside, N.Y., July 14, 1952; s. Alan and Sally (Jacobs) I.; m. Roxann Kathleen Hoff, Aug. 28, 1977; children: Seth Adam, Joshua Ross, Daniel Benjamin. BA, SUNY, Binghamton, 1974; JD, Boston U., 1977. Bar: N.Y. 1978. Assoc. Dreyer and Traub, N.Y.C., 1977-83, assoc. ptnr., 1984-85, sr. ptnr., 1985-96; of counsel Fischbein Badillo Wagner Harding, N.Y.C., 1996—. Projects editor: Boston U. law rev., 1976-77. Past pres. Croton Jewish Ctr., Highlands Country Club. Mem. ABA, Assn. Bar City N.Y., The Country Club at Lake MacGregor, Tau Epsilon Phi. Landlord-tenant, Property, real (including real estate development, water). Office: Fischbein Badillo Wagner Harding 909 3rd Ave New York NY 10022-4731 E-mail: mintrili@fbwhlaw.com.

INZETTA, MARK STEPHEN, lawyer; b. N.Y.C., Apr. 14, 1956; s. James William and Rose Delores (Cirnigliaro) I.; m. Sharon Inzetta; children: Michelle, Margot, Mallory. BBA summa cum laude, U. Cin., 1977; JD, U. Akron, 1980. Bar: Ohio 1980, U.S. Dist. Ct. (no. dist.) Ohio 1980. Legal intern City of Canton, Ohio, 1979-80; assoc. W.J. Ross Co., LPA, Canton, 1980-84; v.p., asst. gen. counsel Wendy's Internat. Inc., Columbus, Ohio, 1984—. Instr. real estate law Stark Tech. Coll., Canton, 1983. Case and comment editor: Akron Law Rev., 1979-80. Instr. religious edn. St. Peter's Cath. Ch.; bd. dirs. Brookside Village Civic Assn., 1985-87, treas., 1986-87; bd. dirs. Ct. Apptd. Spl. Advs. of Franklin County, Ohio; chmn. campaign Earle Wise Appellate Judge, North Canton, Ohio, 1982; legis. dir. Children's and Parents' Rights assn., 1996-97, chmn., 1997—, State of Ohio Child Support Guidelines Commn., 1995-97, 99-2001; treas. State of Ohio Task Force on Family Law and Children, 1998-2001; asst. coach Worthington Kilbourne H.S. Varsity Girls Lacrosse Team, 2002. Recipient Am. Jurisprudence award Lawyers Coop. Pub. Co., 1978, Dir. of Yr. award North Canton Jaycees, 1982, Presdl. award of honor, 1984, Dist. Dir. award of honor Ohio Jaycees, 1984, Vol. of Yr. award Children's Rights Coun., 2001. Mem. ABA, Ohio Bar Assn., North Canton Jaycees (bd. dirs. 1981-82, v.p. 1982-83, pres. 1983-84), North Canton C. of C. (bd. dirs. 1983-84). Democrat. Roman Catholic. Corporate, general, Private international, Property, real (including real estate development, water). Home: 295 Weatherburn Ct Powell OH 43065 Office: Wendy's Internat Inc 4288 W Dublin Granville Rd Dublin OH 43017-1442 E-mail: mark_inzetta@wendys.com.

IOANES, JOYCE, lawyer, social worker; b. Washington, Feb. 23, 1944; d. Raymond Andrew and Irma Elizabeth (Blazo) I. BA in French Lit., Dunbarton Coll., 1965; MS in Psychiat. Social Work, Simmons Coll., 1971; JD cum laude, Suffolk U., 1983. Bar: R.I. 1983, U.S. Cts. 1984, Mass. 1985; cert. Acad. Cert. Social Workers, 1978. Social caseworker R.I. Dept. Social and Rehab. Svcs., Cranston, Providence, 1968-74, casework supr. Cranston, Johnston, 1974-77; therapist Northwestern Mental Health Clinic, Greenville, R.I., 1974-75, Washington County Mental Health Clinic, Charlestown, R.I., 1977-79; mental health profl. R.I. Mental Health Advs. Office, Cranston, 1977—, atty., 1983—; sole practice law Jamestown, 1983—. Field instr. R.I. Coll., Roger Williams Coll., 1975-77, Providence Coll., 1975-81; mem. Gov.'s Task Force Community Placement of Geriatric Patients, 1977-81. Recipient Am. Jurisprudence award, 1980-81, R.I. Cmty. Person of Yr. award, 1993. Mem. ABA, Nat. Assn. Social Workers, Mass. Bar Assn., R.I. Bar Assn. Avocations: bicycling, gardening. Home: 78 Columbia Ave Jamestown RI 02835-1345 Office: RI Mental Health Cottage 405 Cranston RI 02920

IPYANA, AMINATA FULANI N. law educator; b. Groton, Mass., Feb. 14, 1962; d. James H. and Justine R. Greene. BA, Howard U. Coll. of Liberal Arts, 1980—84; JD, Wash. U. Sch. of Law, 1986—89. Bar: D.C. 1991. Rsch. asst. Wash. U. Sch. of Law, 1987—87; staff atty. Pub. Defender Svc., Washington, 1989—2001; assoc. prof. of law Howard U. Sch. of Law, 2001—. Bd. mem. D.C. Law Students In Ct., 2001—; chair, edn. com. Bd. of Directors, D.C. Law Students In Ct., 2002—; sect. co-chair Assn. of Am. Law Schools - Clinicians of Color, Washington, 2004—. Mem.: D.C. Bar Assn. (sect. ct., lawyers &adminstrn. justice, criminal law and indiv. right), Clin. Sect. - Assn. of Am. Law Schools, Clin. Legal Edn. Assn. (sect. bar admission, legal edn.), ABA. Office: Howard University School of Law 2900 Van Ness St NW Washington DC 20008 Office Fax: 202-806-8436. E-mail: aipyana@law.howard.edu.

IRAK, JOSEPH S. lawyer; b. Gary, Ind., May 7, 1955; s. John Jr. and Evelyn (Scott) I.; m. Kristi M. Irak, May 21, 1988; children: Christopher Joseph, Nicholas Arthur. BA, Valparaiso U., 1978, JD, 1981. Bar: Ind. 1982, U.S. Dist. Ct. (no. dist.) Ind. 1982, U.S. Supreme Ct. 1982. Pvt. practice, Merrillville, Ind., 1982—; asst. county atty., atty. plan commn. Lake County Ind., Crown Point, 1985—; town atty. Town of New Chicago; atty. Town of Winfield Plan Commn. Mem. precinct com. Lake County Dem. Party, 1983—. Mem.: Lake County Bar Assn. Avocations: fishing, handball, hunting, skiing, boating. General practice, Personal injury (including property damage), Property, real (including real estate development, water). Office: 9219 Broadway Merrillville IN 46410-7046

IRBY, HOLT, lawyer; b. Dodge City, Kans., July 4, 1937; s. Jerry M. and Virgie (Lorean) I.; m. LaVerne Smith, May 27, 1956; children: Joseph, Kathy, Kay, Karon, James. BA, Tex. Tech. U., 1959; JD, U. Tex., 1962. Bar: Tex. 1962, U.S. Dist. Ct. (no. dist.) Tex. 1963. Asst. city atty. City of Lubbock, Tex., 1962-63; assoc. Hugh Anderson, Lubbock, 1963-66; gen. counsel, sec. Merc. Fin. Corp., Dallas, 1966-69; gen. counsel, v.p. Ward Food Restaurants, inc., Dallas, 1969-71; pvt. practice, Garland, Tex., 1971—. Mem. lawyer referal com. State Bar Tex., 1977, 78. Mem. bd. deacons First Bapt. Ch., Garland, 1979-90, chmn., 1976-77; bd. dirs. Garland Assistance Program, 1980, Habitat for Humanity of Greater Garland, Inc., 1997—, Dallas Life Found., 1980-90, Toler Children's Cmty., 1983-85; bd. dirs. Garland Civic Theatre, 1986—, pres., 1990-91, 92-93, v.p., 1991-92; mem. Garland Drug Task Force, 1990; deacon South Garland Bapt. Ch., 1992—, chmn., 1993-94, 98-99, 2002-03. Mem. Tex. Trial Lawyers Assn., Tex. Assn. Bank Counsel, Tex. Bar Assn., Garland Bar Assn. (bd. dirs. 1986-96, sec. 1992-93, v.p. 1993-94, pres. 1995-96), Dallas Bar Assn., Praetor Legal Frat. (named outstanding mem. 1962), Lubbock Jaycees (dir. 1963-65), Kiwanis (dir. 1973-74). State civil litigation, Commercial, contracts (including sales of goods; commercial financing), General practice. Office: Bank of Am Tower 705 W Avenue B Ste 404 Garland TX 75040-6241

IREDALE, EUGENE GERALD, lawyer; b. Louisville, Nov. 16, 1951; children: Danielle, Jake. BA in History and Sociology, Columbia Coll., N.Y.C., 1973; JD, Harvard U., 1976. Bar: Mass. 1977, Calif. 1977. Atty. Fed. Defenders of San Diego, 1977-82, chief trial atty., 1982-83; prin. Law Offices of E. G. Iredale, San Diego, 1983—. Editor: Defending a Federal Criminal Case, 1980-83. Instr. Nat. Coll. for Criminal Def., Houston and Macon, Ga., 1979—. Mem. Nat. Assn. Criminal Def. Lawyers, Calif. Attys. for Criminal Justice, Criminal Def. Lawyers Club. Democrat. General civil litigation, Criminal. Office: 105 W F St Fl 4 San Diego CA 92101-6087 E-mail: iredale@aol.com.

IRELAND, FAITH, state supreme court justice; b. Seattle, 1942; d. Carl and Janice Enyeart; m. Chuck Norem. BA, U. Wash.; JD, Willamette U., 1969; M in Taxation with honors, Golden Gate U. Past assoc. McCune, Godfrey and Emerick, Seattle; pvt. practice Pioneer Square, Wash., 1974; judge King County Superior Ct., 1984—98; justice Wash. Supreme Ct., 1998—. Past dean Washington Jud. Coll.; past mem. Bd. Ct. Edn. Served on numerous civic and charitable bds.; past pro-bono atty. Georgetown Dental Clin.; past bd. dirs. Puget Sound Big Sisters, Inc.; founding mem. Wing Luke Asian Mus., 1967—, past pres., past bd. dirs.; bd. dirs. Youth and Fitness Found., 1998. Named Judge of Yr., Washington State Trial Lawyer's Assn., Man of Yr. for efforts in founding Wing Luke Asian Mus.; recipient Disting. Svc. award, Nat. Leadership Inst. Jud. Edn., 1998. Mem.: Superior Ct. Judges Assn. (past bd. dirs., pres. 1996—97, vice chair bd. dirs. jud. adminstrn. 1996—98), Wash. State Trial Lawyer's Assn. (past chair bd. dirs.), Washington Women Lawyer's (founding mem., Pres.'s award, Vanguard award), Rotary (bd. dirs. Seattle No. 4 1998), Rainer Valley Hist. Soc. (life; founding mem.). Office: Washington Supreme Ct 415 12th St W PO Box 40929 Olympia WA 98504-0929

IRELAND, RODERICK L. state supreme court justice; m. Alice Alexander. Bachelor's degree, Lincoln U., 1966; Master's degree, Harvard U.; JD, Columbia U., 1969; PhD, Northeastern U., 1998. Assoc. justice Mass. Supreme Jud. Ct., 1997—. Judge Boston Juvenile Ct., 1977, 90, Mass. Appeals Ct., 1990-97. Mem. Eliot Congregational Ch. Office: Mass Supreme Jud Ct Pemberton Square 1300 New Courthouse Boston MA 02108-1701

IRENAS, JOSEPH ERON, judge, director; b. Newark, July 13, 1940; s. Zachary and Bessie (Shain) Irenas; m. Nancy Harriet Jacknow, Jan. 1, 1962; children: Amy Ruth, Edward Eron. AB, Princeton U., 1962; JD cum laude, Harvard U., 1965; postgrad., NYU Sch. Law, 1967-70. Bar: N.J. 1965, N.Y. 1982. Law sec. to justice N.J. Supreme Ct., 1965-66; assoc. McCarter & English, Newark, 1966-71, ptnr., 1972-92; judge U.S. Dist. Ct. N.J., 1992—. Trustee Hamilton Investment Trust, Elizabeth, NJ, 1980—83; mem. N.J. Supreme Ct. Dist. Ethics Com., 1984—86, vice chmn., 1986; adj. prof. law Rutgers Sch. Law, Camden, 1985—86, Camden, 1988—97, Camden, 1999—2002, N.J. Bd. Bar Examiners, 1986—88. Contbr. Chmn. bd. trustees United Hosps. of Newark, 1982—83; trustee United Hosps. Found., 1985—92, United Way Essex County, 1988—92, treas., 1990—92. Fellow: Am. Bar Found., Royal Chartered Inst. Arbitrators (London); mem.: ABA, Camden County Bar Assn., N.J. Bar Assn., Am. Law Inst., Union League Club, Nassau Club. Republican. Jewish. Office: Mitchell H Cohen US Courthouse One John F Gerry Plaza PO Box 2097 Camden NJ 08101-2097

IRISH, LEON EUGENE, lawyer, educator, non-profit organization executive; b. Superior, Wis., June 19, 1938; s. Edward Eugene and Phyllis Ione (Johnson) I.; m. Karla W. Simon; children: Stephen T., Jessica L., Thomas A., Emily A. BA in History, Stanford U., 1960; JD, U. Mich., 1964; D.Phil in Law, Oxford (Eng.) U., 1973. Law clk. to Assoc. Justice U.S. Supreme Ct. Byron R. White, 1967; cons. Office Fgn. Direct Investments, Dept. Commerce, 1967-68; spl. rep. sec. def. 7th session 3d UN Conf. Law of Sea; mem. Caplin & Drysdale, chartered, Washington, 1968-85; prof. law U. Mich. Law Sch., Ann Arbor, 1985-88; ptnr. Jones, Day, Reavis & Pogue, Washington, 1988-93; v.p., sr. counsel Aetna Life and Casualty Co., Hartford, Conn., 1993-95; pres., chmn. Internat. Ctr. Not-for-Profit Law, Washington, 1992—2002; pres., CEO United Way Internat., Alexandria, Va., 1996; sr. legal cons. World Bank, 1997—2001. Adj. prof. Georgetown U. Law Ctr., 1975-85; regent Am. Coll. Tax Counsel, 1986-89; mem. IRS Commr.'s Adv. Group, 1987; bd. dirs., sec. Vols. Tech. Assistance, 1978-, Found. for Devel. of Polish Agr. 1988-; vis. fellow World Bank, 1995-96; vis. prof. law Temple U., 2002-2003. Contbr. articles to legal jours. Mem. ABA, D.C. Bar Assn., Am. Law Inst., Am. Coll. Tax Counsel, Coun. on Fgn. Rels. Am. Coll. Employee Benefits Coun. Democrat. Labor (including EEOC, Fair Labor Standards Act, labor-management relations, NLRB, OSHA), Public international, Non-profit and tax-exempt organizations. Home: 304 Kyle Rd Crownsville MD 21032-1843 E-mail: leon.Irish@temple.edu.

IRONS, SPENCER ERNEST, lawyer; b. Chgo., Sept. 15, 1917; s. Ernest Edward and Gertrude Bertwhistle (Thompson) I.; m. Betty M. Chesnut, Jan. 16, 1954; children: Janet L., Nancy G., Edward S. AB, U. Chgo., 1938; JD, U. Mich., 1941. Bar: Ill. 1941, U.S. Dist. Ct. (no. dist.) Ill. 1953, U.S. Supreme Ct. 1962. Assoc. Holmes, Dixon, Knouff & Potter, Chgo., 1946-50, McKinney, Carlson, Leaton & Smalley, Chgo., 1950-54, ptnr., 1955-58; sr. atty. Brunswick Corp., Skokie, Ill., 1959-82; pvt. practice Flossmoor, Ill., 1983-92; ret., 1992. Mem. bd. editors U. Mich. Law Rev., 1939-41. Mem. bd. trustees Flossmoor Pub. Library, 1959-61; mem. Chgo. Crime Commn., 1954-82. Lt. col. U.S. Army, 1941-46, 61-62. Mem. ABA, Ill. Bar Assn., Chgo. Bar Assn. (bd. of mgrs. 1954-56), Law Club. Republican. Unitarian Universalist. Corporate, general, Federal civil litigation, Property, real (including real estate development, water). Home: 2020 Plymouth Ln Northbrook IL 60062-6064

IRONS, WILLIAM LEE, lawyer; b. Birmingham, Ala., June 9, 1941; s. George Vernon and Velma (Wright) I. BA, U.Va., 1963; JD, Samford U., 1966. Bar: Ala. 1966, U.S. Dist Ct. (no. dist.) Ala. 1966, U.S. Ct. Appeals (5th cir.) 1966. Dir. mil. justice Maxwell AFB, Ala., 1963-69; law clk. Speir, Robertson & Jackson, Birmingham, 1964-66; asst. judge adv. Whiteman AFB, Mo., 1966-67, Gunter AFB, 1967-68; ptnr. Speir, Robertson, Jackson & Irons, 1970-71, Speir & Irons, 1971-72, William L. Irons & Assocs., 1972—; U.S. trustee, 1964-86; instr. sr. officers Judge Adv. Gen.'s Sch. Air War coll., Air Univ., Maxwell AFB. Candidate Ala. Ho. Reps. 1966. Deacon, Sunday sch. supt. Mountain Brook Bapt. Ch. Served to capt. USAF Strategic Air Command. Decorated Commendation medal and citation USAF Congl. medal of honor project, Freedon's Found., Valley Forge, Pa., 1968; named Outstanding Jr. Officer Vietnam War, USAF, 1969; DuPont Regional scholar U.Va. Mem. ABA, Birmingham Bar Assn., Assn. Trial Lawyers Am., Nat. Assn. Cert. Judge Advs., Fed. Bar Assn., Nat. Res. Officer Assn., Newcomen Soc., St. Andrews Soc., SAR (pres. Ala. chpt., writer numerous cover stories on Am. Revolution era, Taylor award 1990, U.S. Senate Commendation for Authorship of Colonial Navy 1992, senate commendation state of N.Y. for Chronicles of the Am. Revolutionary War 1995), Descendants of Washington's Army at Valley Forge (capt. of the guard, com. admiral state of Md. 1995), Nat. Lawyers Club, Birmingham Exec. Club (pres. 1978-79), Sigma Delta Kappa. Democrat. Baptist. Bankruptcy, Probate (including wills, trusts), Property, real (including real estate development, water). Home: 3855 Cove Dr Birmingham AL 35213-3801 Office: 1227 City Federal Building Birmingham AL 35203-3714

IRVIN, MICHAEL P. lawyer; b. Ft. Worth, Apr. 29, 1950; BA, U. Tex., 1972; JD, U. Houston, 1975. Bar: Tex. 1975. Ptnr. Fulbright & Jaworski L.L.P., Houston. Mem. ABA, Houston Bar Assn., State Bar Tex., Phi Delta Phi, Order of the Barons. Office: Fulbright & Jaworski LLP 1301 Mckinney St Ste 5100 Houston TX 77010-3031

IRWIN, PHILIP DONNAN, lawyer; b. Madison, Wis., Sept. 6, 1933; s. Constant Louis and Isabel Dorothy (Elfving) I.; m. Sandra L. McMahan, Sept. 14, 1985, div.; children: Jane Donnan, James Haycraft, Victoria Wisnom, Philip Donnan Jr. BA, U. Wyo., 1954; LLB, Stanford U., 1957. Bar: Wyo. 1957, Calif. 1958. Assoc. O'Melveny & Myers, L.A., 1957-65, ptnr., 1965-2000, of counsel, 2000—. Mem. planning com. Inst. Fed. Taxation of U. So. Calif. Law Ctr., 1976—, chairperson, 1995-98; spkr. legal seminars. Contbr. articles legal jours. Trustee Mackenzie Found., Los Angeles, 1969— . Recipient Dana Latham Meml. Lifetime Achievement award, LA County Bar Assn. (Taxation Sect.), 2002. Mem.: Calif. Club (L.A.). Republican. Episcopalian. Office: O'Melveny & Myers 400 S Hope St Rm 1853 Los Angeles CA 90071-2899 E-mail: pirwin@omm.com.

IRWIN, R. ROBERT, lawyer; b. Denver, July 27, 1933; s. Royal Robert and Mildred Mary (Wilson) Irwin; m. Sue Ann Scott, Dec. 16, 1956; children: Lori, Stacy, Kristi, Amy. Student, U. Colo., 1951-54; BS in Law, U. Denver, 1955, LLB, 1957. Bar: Colo. 1957, Wyo. 1967. Asst. atty. gen. State of Colo., 1958-66; asst. divsn. atty. Mobil Oil Corp., Casper, Wyo., 1966-70; prin. atty. No. Natural Gas Co., Omaha, 1970-72; sr. atty., asst. sec. Coastal Oil & Gas Corp., Denver, 1972-83; ptnr. Baker & Hostetler, 1983-87; pvt. practice Denver, 1987—. Mem.: Rocky Mountain Oil and Gas Assn., Colo. Bar Assn., Denver Law Club, Los Verdes Golf Club. Republican. Corporate, general, Oil, gas, and mineral, Property, real (including real estate development, water). Office: 650 S Alton Way Apt 4D Denver CO 80247-1669

ISAACMAN, ALAN L. lawyer; b. Harrisburg, Pa., July 12, 1942; BS, Pa. State U., 1964; JD, Harvard U., 1967. Bar: Calif. 1968, U.S. Ct. Appeals (1st, 2nd, 4th, 9th and 10th cirs.) 1968, U.S. Supreme Ct. 1968. Sr. ptnr. Isaacman, Kaufman & Painter, Beverly Hills, Calif.; law clk. to U.S. Dist. Judge Harry Pregerson Ctrl. Dist., Calif., 1969—70. Lectr. in field. Fellow: Am. Coll. Trial Lawyers. General civil litigation, Entertainment. Office: Isaacman Kaufman & Painter Ste 850 8484 Wilshire Blvd Beverly Hills CA 90211*

ISAACS, LEONARD BERNARD, lawyer; b. Bklyn., Feb. 1, 1951; s. Louis Jack and Sadie (Groman) I.; m. Allison Meryl Grushack, Aug. 23, 1986 (dec.); children: Samantha Nicole, Justin Lance, Adam Tyler. BA, CUNY, 1973; JD, Hofstra U., 1976. Bar: N.Y. 1977, U.S. Dist. Ct. (ea. and so. dists.) N.Y. 1977, U.S. Ct. Appeals (2d cir.) 1978, U.S. Ct. Claims 1978, U.S. Tax Ct. 1978, U.S. Ct. Mil. Appeals 1978, U.S. Customs Ct. 1978, U.S. Ct. Customs and Patent Appeals 1980, U.S. Ct. Internat. Trade 1980, U.S. Supreme Ct. 1980, U.S. Ct. Appeals (fed. cir.) 1982, U.S. Dist. Ct. (no. dist.) N.Y. 1983. Assoc. in law office, Mineola, N.Y., 1977-80; pvt. practice Valley Stream, N.Y., 1980—. Mem. N.Y. State Bar Assn., Nassau County Bar Assn. Republican. Jewish. Criminal, Family and matrimonial, Personal injury (including property damage). Office: 108 S Franklin Ave Ste 16 Valley Stream NY 11580-6105

ISAACS, ROBERT CHARLES, retired lawyer; b. July 16, 1919; s. David and Elsie (Weiss) I.; m. Doris Frances Shapiro, Nov. 20, 1943 (dec. 1982); 1 child, Leigh Richard; m. Mary Lou Anderson, Dec. 12, 1986. BA cum laude, NYU, 1941, JD, 1943. Bar: N.Y. 1943. Dep. asst. atty. gen. N.Y. State Dept. Law, Albany, 1943, spl. asst. atty. gen., 1946; ptnr. Nordlinger Riegelman Benetar, N.Y.C., 1946-71, Aranow Brodsky Bohlinger Benetar & Einhorn, N.Y.C., 1972-79, Benetar Isaacs Bernstein & Schair, N.Y.C., 1979-88. Mem. Lebanon (N.H.) Zoning Bd. Adjustment, 1988—; adj. prof. law St. John's U. Sch. Law, N.Y.C., 1961-72; mem. panel mediators and fact finders N.Y. State Pub. Employment Rels. Bd., 1968-88. Contbr. articles to profl. publs. Capt. U.S. Army, 1943-45, 51. Mem. ABA, ASCAP, Am. Arbitration Assn. (mem. panel arbitrators 1988), N.Y.C. Bar Assn., NYU Law Review Alumni Assn. Home: 5 Village Green West Lebanon NH 03784-1506

ISAACSON, ALLEN IRA, lawyer; b. N.Y.C., Nov. 10, 1938; s. Bernard and Sylvia Isaacson; m. Dena Mishkoff, Mar. 8, 1970; 1 child, David Andrew. AB, Princeton U., 1960; LLB, Yale U., 1963; postgrad., U. Melbourne, Australia, 1963-64; LLM in Taxation, NYU, 1973. Bar: N.Y. 1966. Assoc. Fried, Frank, Harris, Shriver & Jacobson, N.Y.C., 1966-70, ptnr., 1970—. Bd. dirs. FR Holdings, Inc. Fulbright fellow, 1963-64 Mem. ABA, N.Y. State Bar Assn., Assn. of Bar of City of N.Y. Banking, Private international, Mergers and acquisitions. Home: 15 W 81st St New York NY 10024-6022 Office: Fried Frank Harris Shriver & Jacobson 1 New York Plz Fl 22 New York NY 10004-1980 E-mail: allen.isaacson@ffhsj.com.

ISABELLA, MARY MARGARET, lawyer; b. Pitts., Oct. 16, 1947; d. Sebastian C. and Joanna C. (dec.) (Ferris) I. BS in Biology, Duquesne U., 1969; cert. med. technologist, Mercy Hosp., Pitts., 1970; JD, Duquesne U., 1975. Bar: Pa. 1976, U.S. Dist Ct. (we. dist.) Pa. 1976, U.S. Supreme Ct., 1982. Sole practice, Pitts., 1977—. Instr. Wheeling (W.Va.) Coll., 1978-80. Mem. coun. Brentwood Whitehall Assn., Pitts., 1984-90; bd. dirs. Dukes Ct., Duquesne U.; bd. govs. Law Alumni Assn., treas., 1993, sec., 1994-95; sec., treas. Brentwood Bus. Owners' Assn., 2001—. Mem. ABA (vice chair sole practice sect., 1994—), Pa. Bar Assn., Allegheny County Bar Assn., Delta Theta Phi (past asst. dist. chancellor). Lodges: Italian Sons and Daughters of Am. (trustee local chpt.). Republican. Roman Catholic. Family and matrimonial, Estate planning. Office: 4101 Brownsville Rd Bldg 200 Pittsburgh PA 15227-3336 E-mail: mmiesq@juno.com.

ISAF, FRED THOMAS, lawyer; b. Jacksonville, NC, Nov. 18, 1950; s. Thomas Fred and Rowanda (Maloof) I.; m. June J. Jeffcoat, Aug. 18, 1973; children: Julie, Thomas, Christa. BA, Duke U., 1972; JD, Emory U., 1975, LLM in Taxation, 1978. Bar: Ga. 1975. Ptnr. Peterson, Young, Self & Asselin, Atlanta, 1980-86; shareholder Roberts and Isaf, PC, Atlanta, 1986-94, Roberts, Isaf & Summers, PC, Atlanta, 1994-99; ptnr. McGuire Woods LLP, Atlanta, 1999—. Contbr. article to profl. jour. Dir. Pinecrest Acad., 1995—2002. Mem.: State Bar Ga., Cherokee Town and Country Club (sec. 1993, bd. dirs. 1994—2000, v.p. 1997, pres. 1998—99), Order of Barristers, Order of the Coif. Corporate, general, Property, real (including real estate development, water), Securities. Office: McGuire Woods Ste 2100 1170 Peachtree St Atlanta GA 30309 E-mail: fisaf@mcguirewoods.com.

ISBELL, DAVID BRADFORD, lawyer, educator; b. New Haven, Feb. 18, 1929; s. Percy Ernest and Dorothy Mae (Crabb) I.; m. Florence Bachrach, July 21, 1971; children: Christopher Pascal, Virginia Anne, Nicholas Bradford. BA, Yale U., 1949, LLB, 1956. Bar: Conn., 1956, D.C. 1957. Assoc. Covington & Burling, Washington, 1957-59, 61-65, ptnr., 1965-98, sr. counsel, 1998—; asst. staff dir. U.S. Commn. on Civil Rights, Washington, 1959-61. Lectr. Sch. Law U. Va., 1962—, Georgetown U. Law Ctr., 1996—. Bd. dirs. ACLU, 1965-92; chmn. exec. bd. Vets. Consortium Pro Bono Program, 1992—. 2nd lt. U.S. Army, 1951-53. Mem.: ABA (mem. ho. dels. 1986—96, chmn. com. on ethics & profl. responsibility 1991—94), D.C. Bar (gov. 1978—82, pres. 1983—84), Cosmos Club. Probate (including wills, trusts). Home: 3709 Bradley Ln Bethesda MD 20815-4256 Office: Covington & Burling 1201 Pennsylvania Ave NW Washington DC 20004 E-mail: disbell@cov.com.

ISEMAN, JOSEPH SEEMAN, lawyer; b. N.Y.C., May 29, 1916; s. Percy Reginald and Edith Helene (Seeman) I.; m. June Lorraine Bang, Dec. 10, 1966; children: Peter A., Frederick J., Ellen M.; stepchildren: Anne Hamilton, Susan E. Hamilton, William C. Hamilton. BA magna cum laude, Harvard U., 1937; LLB, Yale U., 1941; LHD (hon.), Am. U. of Paris, 1997. Bar: N.Y. State 1941, D.C. 1970, France, 1986. Investigator, clk. Comml. Factors Corp., 1937-38; atty. WPB, 1941-42; mng. dir. Iranian Airways Corp., 1946; asso. Chadbourne, Wallace, Parke & Whiteside, N.Y.C., 1946-50, Paul, Weiss, Rifkind, Wharton & Garrison, N.Y.C., 1950-53, ptnr., 1954-86, counsel, 1987—. Counsel Charles F. Kettering Found., 1965-84. Author: A Perfect Sympathy, 1937; contbr. articles to profl. jours. Trustee Bennington Coll., 1969—81, acting pres., 1976; bd. dirs. Acad. for Ednl. Devel., Safe Horizon, 1980—, also chmn.; bd. dirs. The Hastings Ctr., 1999—, Am. U. , Paris, 1987—2000, also vice chmn. Capt. USAF, 1942—46. Woodrow Wilson vis. fellow Coll. William and Mary, 1977, Ripon Coll., 1979, Rollins Coll., 1980, De Pauw U., 1980, Fisk U., 1981, Albright Coll., 1982, Hood Coll., 1983, Southwestern U., 1984. Mem. ABA, N.Y. State Bar Assn., Assn. of Bar of City of N.Y., Century Assn., Coveleigh Club, Phi Beta Kappa. Democrat. Corporate, general, Private international, Probate (including wills, trusts). Office: 1285 6th Ave Rm 2828 New York NY 10019-6064

ISOTUPA, SIRPA HANNELE, lawyer; b. Espoo, Finland, June 2, 1967; d. Matti Ilmari Isotupa and Helka Marjatta Talvinen; m. Jussi Matti Ilmari; children: Lauri Juhani Petaja, Eero Matti Petaja. LLM, Helsinki U., 1991. Atty. Profl. Enngrs. Union, Helsinki, 1992; trained at bench Lappeenranta Dist. Ct., 1993—94; atty. Krogerus & Pirila, 1994—2000; ptnr. Krogerus & Co., 2000—. Mem.: Internat. Bar Assn., Assn. Internat. des Jeunes Advocates, Finnish Bar Assn. Commercial, contracts (including sales of goods; commercial financing), Labor (including EEOC, Fair Labor Standards Act, labor-management relations, NLRB, OSHA), Alternative dispute resolution. Office: Krogerus & Co PB 143 FIN-00131 Helsinki Finland

ISQUITH, FRED TAYLOR, lawyer; b. N.Y.C., June 6, 1947; s. Stanley and Rita (Hoskwith) I.; m. Susan Nora Goldberg, May 23, 1976: children: Fred, Rebecca. BA, CUNY, 1968; JD, Columbia U., 1971. Bar: N.Y. 1972, D.C. 1976, U.S. Dist. Ct. (so. and ea. dists.) N.Y. 1975, U.S. Dist. Ct. (no. dist.) N.Y. 1988, U.S. Dist. Ct. (we. dist.) Mich. 1992, U.S. Dist. Ct. Ariz. 1994, U.S. Dist. Ct. (ctrl. dist.) Ill. 1996, U.S. Ct. Appeals (2d cir.) 1975, U.S. Ct. Appeals (8th cir.) 1985, U.S. Ct. Appeals (3d cir.) 1986, U.S. Ct. Appeals (4th cir.) 1990, U.S. Supreme Ct. 1983, U.S. Dist. Ct. Colo. 1999, U.S. Dist. Ct. Nebr. 2000, U.S. Ct. Appeals (1st cir.) 2000. Assoc. Fulbright & Jaworski, N.Y.C., 1971-75, Kaye Scholer et al, N.Y.C., 1975-80; ptnr. Wolf Haldenstein Adler Freeman & Herz, N.Y.C., 1980—. Bd. dirs. 103 East 84th St. Corp., N.Y.C., Sheinkopf, Ltd.; lectr. Am. Conf. Inst., N.Y. State Bar Assn., N.Y. County Bar Assn., others; mediator Supreme Ct. State N.Y. County N.Y. Comml. Divsn.; arbitrator Am. Arbitration Assn.; lectr. in field. Author: An Introduction to Securities Arbitration, 1994, Real Estate Exit Strategies, 1994, Fundamental Strategies in Securities Litigation, 2000, Federal Civil Practice, 2000; A Scalpel in Your Hand Litigation As a Tool for Inforcing Responsible Corporate Guidance, 2002, Anatomy of a Deposition:Perparation for a Deposition in a Complex Finacial Case, 2002 editor, weekly columnist The Class Act. Mem. devel. com. Friends Sem., N.Y.C., 1998—; clk., mem. vestry St. Thomas Ch. Fifth Ave., N.Y.C., 2002—. Mem. ABA (mem. internet com. anti-trust law sect.), NASCAT (pres.), N.Y. State Bar Assn. (coms. on securities and legis., arbitrator securities industry disputes sect.), N.Y. County Lawyers Assn. (chmn. bus. torts), D.C. Bar Assn., Assn. of Bar of City of N.Y. (Fed. Cts. com.), Bklyn. Bar Assn. (civil practice law and rules com., legis. com. and fed. cts. com.), Columbia Club. Federal civil litigation, State civil litigation, Securities. Office: Wolf Haldenstein Adler Freeman & Herz 270 Madison Ave New York NY 10016-0601

ISRAEL, STUART MICHAEL, lawyer; b. Detroit, Mar. 13, 1947; m. Cheryll B. Israel, Dec. 23, 1971; children: Alexander, Nicholas. BA, Mich. State U., 1968; JD cum laude, U. Mich., 1971. Bar: Mich. 1972, U.S. Dist. Ct. (ea. dist.) Mich. 1972, U.S. Dist. Ct. (so. dist.) Ohio 1975, U.S. Ct. Appeals (6th cir.) 1976, U.S. Dist. Ct. (we. dist.) Mich. 1981, U.S. Ct. Appeals (1st cir.) 1982, U.S. Ct. Appeals (7th cir.) 1986, U.S. Ct. Appeals (11th cir.) 1987, U.S. Supreme Ct. 1979. Asst. defender Mich. State Appellate Defender Office, Detroit, 1972-75; lectr. law Law Sch., U. Mich., Ann Arbor, 1973-75; of counsel local 423 legal svc. Laborers Internat. Union, Columbus, Ohio, 1975-77; adj. prof., dir. clin. teaching project Coll. of Law Ohio State U., Columbus, 1975-77; counsel, asst. dir. legal svcs. plan UAW, Detroit, 1978-81; assoc. prof. law Wayne State U. Law Sch., Detroit, 1977-79; vis. assoc. prof. law U. Hawaii Sch. of Law, Honolulu, 1981; mem. Martens, Ice, Geary, Klass, Legghio, Israel & Gorchow, P.C., Southfield, Mich., 1981—. Bd. dirs. Nat. Resource Ctr. for Consumers of Legal Svcs., Washington, 1983—. Editor Labor and Employment Lawnotes, 1995—; contbr. articles to profl. jours. With USAR, 1969-75. Mem. ABA, AFL-CIO (lawyers coord. com.). Federal civil litigation, General civil litigation, Labor (including EEOC, Fair Labor Standards Act, labor-management relations, NLRB, OSHA). Office: Martens Ice Geary Klass Legghio Israel & Gorchow 1400 N Park Plz 17117 W 9 Mile Rd Southfield MI 48075-4602

ISRAELITE, DAVID M. prosecutor; b. 1968; BA, William Jewell Coll.; JD, U. Mo. Dir. polit. and govt. affairs Rep. Nat. Com., 1999—2001; dep. chief staff, chief counsel to U.S. Atty. U.S. Dept. of Justice, Washington, 2001—. Campaign mgr., adminstrv. asst. Senator Christopher Bond, Mo., 1998. Office: US Dept Justice Office Atty Gen 950 Pennsylvania Ave NW Washington DC 20530-0001*

ISSELBACHER, RHODA SOLIN, lawyer; b. Springfield, Mass., June 12, 1932; d. Jay Zachary and Theo L. (Michelman) S.; m. Kurt J. Isselbacher, June 22, 1955; children: Lisa Isselbacher-Ramirez (dec.), Karne Isselbacher-Epstein, Jody Isselbacher-Coukos, Eric M. BA, Cornell U., 1954; JD, Harvard U., 1959. Bar: Mass. 1960, U.S. Dist. Ct. Mass. 1984. Assoc. firm Melvin Dangel, Boston, 1960-67, Sherin & Lodgen, Boston, 1965-67, Pollock & Katz, Boston, 1967-70; ptnr. firm Epstein, King & Isselbacher, Boston, 1971-91; gen. counsel Dana-Farber Cancer Inst., Boston, 1979-89; pvt. practice law Newton Centre, Mass., 1989-91; of counsel Edwards and Angell, Boston, 1991-92; legal counsel Mass. Gen. Hosp. Svc. League, 1969-85; legal cons. Children's Sch. of Sci., Woods Hole, Mass., 1969—. Cons. med. programming WGBH-TV, 1972-73. Alderman, Woods Hole, Mass., 1968; chmn. Newton United Fund, Mass., 1961; trustee Beaver Country Day Sch., 1975-77. Mem. Mass. Bar Assn., Boston Bar Assn., Mass. Health Lawyers Assn. Health, Probate (including wills, trusts), Property, real (including real estate development, water). Home and Office: 20 Nobscot Rd Newton MA 02459-1323 E-mail: isselbacher@helix.mgh.harvard.edu.

ISSLER, HARRY, lawyer; b. Cologne, Germany, Nov. 14, 1935; came to U.S., 1937; s. Max and Fanny (Grunbaum) I.; m. Doris Helen Lukow, June 1, 1958; children: Adriane P. Schorr, M. Valerie Priestley, Stephanie L. Beck. BS, U. Wis., 1955; JD, Cornell U., 1958. Bar: N.Y. 1958, U.S. Supreme Ct. 1962, U.S. Ct. Mil. Appeals 1967, U.S. Dist. Ct. (so. and ea. dists.) N.Y. 1960, U.S. Customs Ct. 1964, U.S. Tax Ct. 1964; cert. specialist in civil trial advocacy Nat. Bo. Trial Advocacy. Assoc. Wing & Wing, N.Y.C., 1958-60; assoc. Fuchsberg & Fuchsberg, N.Y.C., 1960-62; ptnr. Issler & Fein, N.Y.C., 1963-68, Shaw, Issler & Rosenberg, N.Y.C., 1968-70; pvt. practice N.Y.C., 1970-79; ptnr. Issler & Scrage, P.C., N.Y.C., 1980-99; sr. ptnr. The Law Firm of Harry Issler PLLC, N.Y.C., 1999—. Arbitrator Civil Ct., N.Y. County, 1979-91; hearing officer N.Y. State Tax Appeals, 1975-77, Supreme Ct. of N.Y., N.Y. County Med. Malpractice Panel, 1980-91; judge advocate N.Y. State; mem. neutral evaluator mediation panel Supreme Ct., N.Y. County, 1997—; charter mem. Trial Lawyers Care, Inc. Trustee N.Y. State Mil. Ednl. Found., 1997-2000; exec. v.p. Sutton Area Cmty., Inc., 2000—; v.p., pres. 50 Sutton Pl. South Owners, Inc., 2002—. With U.S. Army, 1958-59, N.Y. Army N.G., 1963-88, ret. brig. gen., 1988. Ford Found. scholar, 1951-55. Mem. ABA, N.Y. State Bar Assn., Assn. of Bar of City of N.Y., Am. Trial Lawyers Assn., N.Y. State Trial Lawyers Assn., 42d Infantry Divsn. Officers Club (N.Y.C.pres. 1979-80), Officers Club (U.S. Mcht. Marine Acad.), 42d Infantry Rainbow Disn. Assn. (pres. 1989), Phi Alpha Delta, Pi Lambda Phi (Omega chpt. pres. 1953-54). Family and matrimonial, Personal injury (including property damage). Home: 50 Sutton Pl S New York NY 10022-4167 Office: 110 E 59th St 29th Fl New York NY 10022 E-mail: harryissler@lawyer.com.

ITAKURA, HIROSHI, criminal law educator; b. Ohsaka, Japan, Jan. 15, 1934; s. Takeo and Toshie Itakura; m. Akiko Hanawa, July 30, 1961; children: Hiroaki, Hiroyuki. LLD, Tokyo U., 1956, ML, 1958, LLD, 1961. Bar: Japan 1991. Assoc. prof. Coll. Law Nihon U., Tokyo, 1961-70, prof. criminal law Coll. Law, 1970—, dir. Law Inst., 1983-84, dir. Comparative Law Inst., 1984-88, dir. Law Inst., 1990—. Examining commr. Nat. Patent Lawyer Examination Commn., Tokyo, 1976-80, Nat. Bar Examinication Commn., Tokyo, 1989—; mem. security study group for computer systems com. Nat. Police Agy., Tokyo, 1986—. Author: Corporate Crime, 1975, Bribes, 1986, Criminal Law, 1988, The Modern Crime, 1990. Chmn. Coun. Info. Disclosure Systems, Fujisawa City, Japan, 1986—. Mem. Crimianl Law Soc. Japan (auditor 1973-91, dir. 1991—), Japanese Soc. Tax Law (dir. 1974—), Law and Computers Assn. Japan (dir. 1988—), Assn. Internat. Droit Pénal. Home: 12-24-1 Chome Kugenuma-Sakuragaoka Fujisawa 251 Japan Office: Nihon U Coll Law 3-1-2 Chome Misakicho Tokyo Chiyoda 101 Japan

ITZKOFF, NORMAN JAY, lawyer; b. N.Y.C., Oct. 9, 1940; s. Louis and Rose Itzkoff; divorced; 1 child, Francesca Sandra. BS with distinction, U. Buffalo, 1961; LLB cum laude, Columbia U., 1965. Bar: N.Y. 1965, U.S. Dist. Ct. (so. and ea. dists.) N.Y. 1967, U.S. Ct. Appeals (2d cir.) 1967, U.S. Supreme Ct. 1971. Law clk. to judge U.S. Dist. Ct. (so. dist.) N.Y., N.Y.C., 1965-66; assoc. Cravath, Swaine & Moore, N.Y.C., 1966-74, Rosenman & Colin, N.Y.C., 1974-76, ptnr., 1976-86; sr. litigation counsel Siemens Corp., N.Y.C., 1988-93; cons., arbitrator and mediator, 1994—. Gen. counsel Assn. Internat. Photography Art Dealers Inc., N.Y.C., 1981-91. Editor: Dealing with Damages, 1983, Columbia U. Law Rev., 1963-65. Mem. adv. bd. Catskill Ctr. for Photography, Woodstock, N.Y., 1982-87; chmn. adv. bd. Ctr. for Photography at Woodstock, 1987-88. Harlan Fiske Stone scholar. Mem. ABA (jud. adminstrn. div. lawyers conf., com. on jud. qualification and selection, com. jud.compensation, sect. of litigation, com. corp. counsel), Fed. Bar Coun., N.Y. State Bar Assn. (alt. dispute resolution com., antitrust law sect., mem. coms. on court adminstrn. and practice and procedure, comml. and fed. litigation sect., com. on corp. counsel, entertainment arts and sports law sect., com. on fine arts , internat. law and practice sect. coms. internat. dispute resolution and subcom. arbitration, mcpl. law sect., profl. litigation com., trial lawyers sect., com. on fed. cts., com. on litigation mgmt. and econs.), Assn. Bar City N.Y. (alternative dispute resolution com., profl. discipline com., adv. bd. demonstration observation com., com. on nuclear tech. and law, com. on art law, liaison art law com., chmn. subcom. on state legislation 1983-84, Am. Arbitration Assn. (panel), Ctr. Pub. Resources (com. on disputes with distbrs., dealers and franchisees), Columbia Club, Westchester Rugby Club (N.Y.C.), Beta Gamma Sigma. Avocations: fine art photography, running. Alternative dispute resolution. Home and Office: 2600 Netherland Ave New York NY 10463-4801

IVERS, DONALD LOUIS, judge; b. San Diego, May 6, 1941; s. Grant Perrin and Margaret (Ware) I. BA, U. N.Mex., 1963; JD, Am. U., 1971. Bar: U.S. Dist. Ct. (D.C. 1972), U.S. Ct. Appeals (D.C. cir.) 1972, U.S. Ct. Mil. Appeals 1972, U.S. Supreme Ct. 1975. Assoc. Brault, Graham, Scott, Brault, Washington, 1972-78; chief counsel Republican Nat. Com., Washington, 1978-81; gen. counsel 1980 Rep. Nat. Conv. Site Selection Com., 1979-80; chief counsel Fed. Hwy. Adminstrn., U.S. Dept. Transp., 1981-85; counselor to sec., chmn. sec.'s safety rev. task force U.S. Dept. Transp., 1984-85; gen. counsel VA, 1985-89; acting gen. counsel U.S. Dept. Vet. Affairs, 1989-90, asst. to the sec., 1990; judge U.S. Ct. Appeals Vet. Claims, 1990—. Capt. U.S. Army, 1963-68, Vietnam, lt. col. Res., ret. Office: US Ct Appeals Vet Claims 625 Indiana Ave NW Washington DC 20004-2923

IVES, STEPHEN BRADSHAW, JR., retired lawyer; b. N.Y.C., Oct. 6, 1924; AB, Harvard U., 1948; LLB, Yale U., 1951. Bar: R.I. 1952, D.C. 1970, U.S. Supreme Ct. 1960. Assoc. Hinckley, Allen, Salisbury & Parsons, Providence, 1952-57, ptnr., 1957-61; exec. asst. to adminstr. AID, Washington, 1961-62, dir. Office Korea Affairs, 1962-64, dir. Office East Asian Affairs, 1964-66, assoc. asst. adminstr. Far East, 1966-67, dept. asst. adminstr. East Asia, 1967-68, gen. counsel, 1968-70; ptnr. Wald, Harkrader and Ross, Washington, 1970-87; of counsel Pepper, Hamilton & Scheetz, 1987-95. Mem. R.I. Mechanics Lien Law Commn., R.I. Commn. Interstate Coop. Bd. dirs. Providence Community Fund, Children's Friend and Svc. R.I.; mem. U.S. del. U.S.-USSR Comml. Commn., 1975; dir. Bus. Coun. S.E. Europe, 1977-95, vice. chmn. 1991-95. Mem. ABA, D.C. Bar Assn. (chmn. div. internat. law and transactions 1976-77), R.I. Bar Assn. (past mem. exec. com.), Washington Fgn. Law Soc. (past pres.), Am. Soc. Internat. Law, Am. Arbitration Assn. (panel), Order of Coif, Phi Beta Kappa. Commercial, contracts (including sales of goods; commercial financing), Private international, Public international. Home: 3508 Macomb St NW Washington DC 20016-3162

IVEY, STEPHEN DAVID, lawyer; b. Glen Ridge, N.J., Jan. 15, 1953; s. Henry Franklin and Sylvia (Berg) I. BA in History, Polit. Sci., Pa. State U., 1975; JD, Georgetown U., 1978. Bar: Pa. 1978, U.S. Dist. Ct. (ea. dist.) Pa. 1979, U.S. Ct. Appeals (3d cir.) 1979, U.S. Supreme Ct. 1982, U.S. Ct. Appeals (fed. cir.) 1984. Law clk. to judge Supreme Ct. Pa., Phila., 1978-81; pvt. practice Phila., 1981—. Appellate, General civil litigation, Criminal. Office: 325 S 16th St Philadelphia PA 19102-4936

IWAI, WILFRED KIYOSHI, lawyer; b. Honolulu, Aug. 21, 1941; s. Charles Kazuo and Michiko (Sakimoto) I.; m. Judy Tomiko Yoshimoto, Mar. 1, 1963; children: Kyle K., Tiffany Seiko. BS in Bus., U. Colo., 1963, JD, 1966. Bar: Hawaii 1966, Colo. 1966, U.S. Dist. Ct. Hawaii 1966, U.S. Ct. Appeals (9th cir.) 1966. Dep. corp. counsel State of Hawaii, Honolulu, 1966-71; assoc. Kashiwa & Kanazawa, Honolulu, 1971-75; ptnr. Kashiwa, Iwai, Motooka & Goto, Honolulu, 1975-82, Iwai & Morris, Honolulu, 1982—2001; pvt. practice Wilfred K. Iwai Atty. at Law, A Law Corp., Honolulu, 2002—. Mem. ABA, Hawaii Bar Assn., Assn. Trial Lawyers Am., Bldg. Industry Assn., Bldg. Owners & Mgrs. Assn. Hawaii. Clubs: Draftsmen's (Honolulu) (pres.). State civil litigation, Construction, General practice. Office: PO Box 61392 Honolulu HI 96839

IZARD, JOHN, lawyer; b. Hartford, Conn., Mar. 4, 1923; s. John and Elizabeth (Andrews) I.; m. Mary Bailey, apr. 16, 1955; children: Sarah Izard Pariseau, John Jr., David Bailey. BS, Yale U., 1945; LLB, U. Va., 1949. Bar: Ga. 1950. Assoc. King & Spalding, Atlanta, 1949-52, ptnr., 1952-90. Mem. Adminstrv. Conf. U.S., Washington, 1978-82. Author, pub.: A Traveler's Table, 2002; editor-in-chief Va. Law Rev., 1948; contbr. articles to legal periodicals. Mem. Nat. Com. To Study Antitrust Laws and Procedures, Washington, 1978; trustee Episcopal Media Ctr., Atlanta, 1988—, chmn., 1992-96; trustee U. Va. Law Sch. Found., Charlottesville, 1974-97. Lt. (j.g.) USNR, 1944-46, PTO. Mem. ABA (chmn. antitrust sect. 1974-75), Ga. Bar Assn. (chmn. antitrust sect. 1969-71), Atlanta Legal Aid Soc. (pres. 1960), Lawyers Club Atlanta, Capital City Club (bd. dirs. 1976-79), Peachtree Golf Club, Piedmont Driving Club. Democrat. Episcopalian. Antitrust, Corporate, general. Home: 4061 Glen Devon Dr NW Atlanta GA 30327-3613 Office: King & Spalding 191 Peachtree St NE Ste 3900 Atlanta GA 30303-1740

JABLONSKI, JAMES ARTHUR, lawyer; b. Sheboygan, Wis., Nov. 12, 1942; s. John Alfred and Dena (Kaat) J. BBA, U. Wis., 1965, JD, 1968. Bar: Wis. 1968, Calif. 1969, U.S. Ct. Appeals (7th cir) 1969, U.S. Supreme Ct. 1974, Colo. 1976, U.S. Ct. Appeals (8th and 10th cirs.) 1976. Assoc. Pillsbury, Madison & Sutro, San Francisco, 1969-72; asst. prof. law Washington U., St. Louis, 1972-76; ptnr. Gorsuch Kirgis L.L.C., Denver, 1976—. Mem. Colo. Bar Assn., Wis. Bar Assn. (bd. govs. 1990-92), Denver Bar Assn. Clubs: Pinehurst Country (Denver). Democrat. Federal civil litigation, Construction, Labor (including EEOC, Fair Labor Standards Act, labor-management relations, NLRB, OSHA). Office: Gorsuch Kirgis Tower 1 1515 Arapahoe St Ste 1000 Denver CO 80202-2120

JABOCS, STEPHEN E. lawyer; b. N.Y.C., Nov. 21, 1938; BS in Econs., U. Pa., 1959; JD, Columbia U., 1962. Bar: N.Y. 1962. Sr. ptnr. Weil, Gotshal & Manges, N.Y.C., 1962—. Office: Weil Golshal & Manges 1 South Pl The Helicon London EC2M 2WG England

JACK, JANIS GRAHAM, judge; b. 1946; RN, St. Thomas Sch. Nursing, 1969; BA, U. Balt., 1974; JD summa cum laude, South Tex. Coll., 1981. Pvt. practice, Corpus Christi, Tex., 1981-94; judge U.S. Dist. Ct. (so. dist.) Tex., Corpus Christi, 1994—. Jud. mem. The Maritime Law Assn. U.S. Mem. ABA, Fed. Judges Assn., Fifth Cir. Dist. Judges Assn., Nat. Assn. Women Judges, Tex. Bar Found., State Bar Tex., The Philos. Soc. Tex., Order of Lytae, Phi Alpha Delta. Office: US Dist Ct 1133 N Shoreline Blvd Corpus Christi TX 78401

JACKLEY, MICHAEL DANO, lawyer; b. Balt., Oct. 1, 1942; s. Francis Dano and Jean Diantha (Dietz) J.; m. Mary Margaret Mixer, July 5, 1977 (div.); children: Megan, Dano Mixer, Jackley; m. Karen Klare Blocher, Oct. 5, 1987. BA, U. Md., 1965, JD, 1970; LLM in Corp. Law with highest honors, George Washington U., 1977. Bar: D.C., Md. 1971, U.S. Tax Ct. 1973. Assoc. Williams, Brown, Eklund & Baldwin, Washington, 1971-74, Smith, Joseph, Greenwald & Laake and predecessor forms, Hyattsville, Md., 1974-77; prin. Joseph, Greenwald & Laake, PA, 1977—. Mem. Select Com. to Redraft D.C. Corp. Statute, 1977-86; tchr. Paralegal Inst., 1977-80; mem. peer rev. com. Md. Atty. Grievance Commn., 2001—. Adv. bd. Prince George's County Mental Health Assn., 1978-99. Key Delta Theta Phi scholar, 1970. Mem. ABA, Md. State Bar Assn., Prince George's County Bar Assn., DC Bar Assn. Democrat. Unitarian Universalist. Corporate, general, Corporate taxation, Taxation, general. Address: 6404 Ivy Ln Ste 400 Greenbelt MD 20770-1407 Personal E-mail: mdjackley@aol.com. Business E-Mail: mjackley@jgllaw.com.

JACKSON, DARNELL, judge; b. Saginaw, Mich., Feb. 2, 1955; s. Roosevelt and Annie Lois (Pratt) J.; m. Yvonne Kay Givens, July 29, 1978; children: Brandon Darnell, Elliott Stephen. BA, Wayne State U., 1977, JD, 1981; AA, Kalamazoo C.C., 1993. Office mgr., shift supr. Wayne State U., Detroit, 1979-81; mng. ptnr. Allan & Jackson, P.C., Saginaw, 1983-85; asst. city atty. Saginaw City Atty.'s Office, 1985-86; asst. prosecuting atty. Saginaw County Prosecutor's, Saginaw, 1986-89; assoc. Braun, Kendrick, Finkbeiner et al, Saginaw, 1989-90; instr. Paralegal Inst. Delta Coll., University Center, Mich., 1986, instr. Northeastern Basic Police Acad., 1991-96; dep. chief asst. prosecuting atty. Saginaw County Prosecutor's Office, 1990-93; adminstrv. dep. chief of police Saginaw Police Dept., 1993-96; dir. Office of Drug Control Policy State of Mich., Lansing, 1996-2001; dist. ct. judge 70th Jud. Dist. Ct., Saginaw, Mich., 2001—. Mem. Drug Edn. Adv. Com., Lansing, Mich., 1996-2001, DARE Policy Adv. Bd., Lansing, 1996-2001, Mich. Dispute Resolution, Saginaw, 1989-92, Sen. Cisky Adv. Com., Saginaw, 1992-94; co-chair Partnership for Drug Free Mich., 1997-2001; speaker in field. Bd. dirs. United Way of Saginaw County, 1996, Westchester Village/Essex Manor, 1994-96, Saginaw County Child Abuse and Neglect Coun., 1994-96, Mr. Rogers Say No to Drugs Program, 1991-95; mem. Saginaw Valley Sate U. Multicultural Adv. Com., 1991-96; adv. bd. Saginaw St. Mary's Hosp., 1991-94, State Sen. Jon Cisky Minority Affairs Adv. Com., 1992-94. Recipient award for Profl. Excellence, FBI/Saginaw County Gang Crime Task Force, 1995, Frederick Douglass award for Community Svc., Mich. State Legis., 1991, award for Effort in War on Drugs, Saginaw Police Dept. Spl. Ops. Unit, 1989, Spl. Tribute for Community Svc., Mich. State Legis., 1985, Comm. Svc. awards

Wayne State Univ. Free Legal Aid Clin, 1980-81. Mem. Mich. Bar Assn., Saginaw County Bar Assn., Fraternal Order of Police, Internat. Assn. of Chiefs of Police, Mich. Assn. of Chiefs of Police, Nat. Orgn. of Black Law Enforcement Execs. Office: State of Mich Saginaw County Ct Ho Saginaw MI 48602

JACKSON, JAMES G. protective services official; m. Mary Jackson; children: James, Jason, Michelle. Student, Harvard U., FBI Nat. Exec. Inst., Northwestern U. Joined Columbus (Ohio) Police Dept., 1958, patrolman, sgt., 1967—71, lt., 1971—74, capt., 1974—77, dep. chief, 1977—90, chief of police, 1990—. Mem.: Nat. Orgn. Black Law Enforcement Execs., Internat. Assn. Chiefs Police, Major City Chiefs Assn. Office: Columbus Police Dept 120 Marconi Blvd Columbus OH 43215-0009*

JACKSON, JAMES RALPH (JIM JACKSON), lawyer; b. Oakland, Calif., Mar. 20, 1967; s. Thomas Edwin and Lillian Nan J.; m. Lisa Carolyn Ferrell, Feb. 14, 1998. BA in History, Hendrix Coll., 1989; JD, U. Ark., 1993. Bar: Ark. 1993. Office asst. Sen. Dale Bumpers U.S. Senate, Washington, 1990; dep. campaign mgr. Jay Bradford for Congress, Pine Bluff, Ark., 1993-95; assoc. Law Offices of Gary Green, Little Rock, 1995-98, Boswell Law Firm, Bryant, Ark., 1998—. Counsel Dem. Party of Ark., Little Rock, 1998; mentor Big Bros./Big Sisters, Little Rock, 1997-98. Mem. Ark. Bar Assn., Ark. Trial Lawyers Assn., Saline County Bar Assn. Methodist. Avocations: reading, basketball. General civil litigation, Personal injury (including property damage), Product liability. Home: 8601 Cantrell Rd Little Rock AR 72227-2317 Office: Boswell Law Firm PO Box 798 Bryant AR 72089-0798 E-mail: jimjack1@swbell.net.

JACKSON, JOHN HOWARD, lawyer, educator; b. Kansas City, Mo., Apr. 6, 1932; s. Howard Clifford and Lucile (Deischer) J.; m. Joan Leland, Dec. 16, 1962; children: Jeannette, Lee Ann, Michelle. AB, Princeton U., 1954; JD, U. Mich., 1959. Bar: Wis. 1959, Mo. 1959, Calif. 1964, Mich. 1970. Pvt. practice law, Milw., 1959-61; assoc. prof., prof. law U. Calif., 1961-66; prof. law U. Mich., 1966-97; univ. prof. law Georgetown U., Washington, 1998—, dir. Inst. of Internat. Econ. Law. On leave gen. counsel U.S. Office Spl. Trade Rep., 1973-74, acting deputy spl. rep. for trade, 1974; vis. prof. U. Brussels, 1975-76; vis. fellow Inst. for Internat. Econs., Washington, 1983; Hessel E. Yntema prof. law U. Mich., 1983-97, assoc. v.p. acad. affairs, 1988-89; disting. vis. prof. law Georgetown Law Ctr., Washington, 1986-87, 93; Ford Found. cons. legal edn., vis. prof. U. Delhi, India, 1968-69; lectr. in field. Author: World Trade and the Law of GATT, 1969, Contract Law in Modern Society, 1973, 2d edit., 1980, Legal Problems of International Economic Relations, 1977, 4th edit. (with William Davey and Alan Sykes), 2002; (with Jean-Victor Louis and Mitsuo Matsushita) Implementing the Tokyo Round, 1984; (with Edwin Vermulst) Anti-Dumping Law & Practice: Comparative Study, 1989; The World Trading System, 1989, 2d edit., 1997, Restructuring the GATT System, 1990; (with Alan Sykes) Implementing the Urugauy Round, 1997, World Trade Organization, 1998, The Jurisprudence of GATT and the WTO, 2000; editor-in-chief Jour. Internat. Econ. Law; bd. editors: Am. Jour. Internat. Law, Jour. Law and Policy in Internat. Bus., others; contbr. articles to profl. jours. With M.I. U.S. Army, 1954-56. Recipient Wolfgang Friedman Memorial award Columbia U., 1992; Rockefeller Found. fellow for study European community law Brussels, 1975-76 Mem. ABA, Am. Soc. Internat. Law (v.p. 1990-92), Am. Law Inst., Council Fgn. Relations, Phi Beta Kappa, Order of Coif. Office: Georgetown U Law Ctr 600 New Jersey Ave NW Washington DC 20001-2022

JACKSON, JOHN HOLLIS, JR., lawyer; b. Mongomery, Ala., Aug. 21, 1941; s. John Hollis and Erma (Edgeworth) J.; m. Rebecca Mullins, May 27, 1967; 1 child, John Hollis III. AB, U. Ala., 1963, JD, 1966. Bar: Ala. 1966, U.S. Dist. Ct. (no. dist.) Ala. 1969, U.S. Ct. Appeals (11th cir.) 1993. Pvt. practice, Clanton, Ala., 1967—. County atty. Chilton County Commn., Clanton, 1969— ; mcpl. judge Clanton, 1971-99, city atty., 1999—; dir. First Nat. Bank, Clanton, 1974-83; mem. adv. bd. Colonial Bank, Clanton, 1983—; mcpl. judge, Jemison, Ala., 1984—. Bd. dirs. Chilton-Shelby Mental Health Bd., Calera, Ala., 1974-83, pres., 1974-79; mem. State Dem. Exec. Com., Birmingham, Ala., 1974-98, County Dem. Exec. Com., Chilton County, 1982-94; del. Dem. Nat. Conv., N.Y.C., 1976. 1st lt. U.S. Army, 1966-67. Mem. Ala. Young Lawyers Sect. (exec. com. 1969-70), Chilton County Bar Assn. (pres. 1969, 74), Ala. State Bar Assn. (bd. bar commrs. 1984-87, 93-99, chmn. adv. com. to bd. bar examiners 1986-87, 19th cir. indigent def. commn. 1983—, chmn. disciplinary panel II 1997-99), Kiwanis, Phi Alpha Delta. Democrat. Methodist. General practice. Home: Samaria Rd Clanton AL 35045 Office: PO Box 1818 500 2nd Ave S Clanton AL 35046-1818

JACKSON, LOUISE ANNE, lawyer, accountant; b. Bowling Green, Ohio, July 27, 1948; BSBA, Bowling Green State U., 1970; MBA, U. Colo., 1971; JD, U. Toledo, 1976. CPA Ohio; bar: Ohio 1977. Sr. staff acct. Arthur Young and Co., Toledo, 1972—75; ptnr. Marshall & Melhorn, Toledo, 1976—85; pvt. practice Toledo, 1985—95; ptnr. Spengler Nathanson PLL, Toledo, 1995—. Mem. Ohio Bd. Tax Appeals, 1991—. Mem.: Toledo Bar Assn. (treas. 1994—97), Ohio State Bar Assn., Ohio Soc. CPAs (pres. Toledo chpt. 1992—93, state v.p. 1995—97). Estate planning, Probate (including wills, trusts), Taxation, general. Office: Spengler Nathanson PLL 608 Madison Ave Ste 1000 Toledo OH 43604-1169

JACKSON, NEAL A. lawyer; b. Raleigh, N.C., Sept. 6, 1943; s. Irvine L. and Dorothy A. Jackson; m. Louise M. Reggia (div. 1994); children: Adrienne, Kimberly; m. Sandra Willett, 1995. AB, U. N.C., 1965; JD, Georgetown U., 1968. Bar: D.C. 1968, Md. 1979. Pvt. practice, Washington, 1970—96; v.p. for legal affairs, gen. counsel & sec. Nat. Pub. Radio, Inc., 1996—. Mem.: ABA, Univ. Club, Edgemoor Club (pres. 1984—85). Administrative and regulatory, Federal civil litigation, Corporate, general. Home: 3408 Reservoir Rd NW Washington DC 20007-2328 Office: Nat Pub Radio Inc 635 Massachusetts Ave NW Washington DC 20001-3753

JACKSON, NICHOLAS MILLER, lawyer, researcher; b. Colon, Panama, Sept. 23, 1950; came to U.S., 1966; s. William Merrill J. and Barbara Margaret Malo; m. Jennifer Jewel Watson, Feb. 9, 1971 (div. June 1990); children: Nathaniel Todd, Robert Sean. BA, Mich. State U., 1976; JD, Detroit Coll. Law, 1990; LLM, Stetson U., 2001; MLS, U. Ariz., 2002. Bar: Mich. 1991, La. 1998, Fla. 1999, N.Y. 2000, U.S. Supreme Ct. 1997. Law clk. 16th Cir. Ct., Mt. Clemens, Mich., 1990-91, rsch. atty., 1991-2000; reference libr. Law Libr., Stetson U. Coll. Law, Gulfport, Fla., 2000—01; fellow law libr. U. Ariz., James E. Coll. Law, Tucson, 2001—02; ref. law libr. Stetson U. Coll. Law, Gulfport, Fla., 2003—. Cons. in field. Asst. scoutmaster Great Sauk Trail Coun. Boy Scouts Am., Ypsilant, Mich., 1995-99; vol. libr. LDS Family History Ctr., Ann Arbor, Mich., 1990-93; first counselor Ann Arbor, Mich., pres. LDS Stake Mission, 1999-2000; gospel doctrine tchr. Park Ave. LDS Ward, Tucson, Ariz., 2001-2002; priesthood leader asst., LDS br., Gulfport, Fla., 2002-. With U.S. Army Res., 1978-81. Mem. State Bar Mich., La. State Bar Assn., Panama Canal Soc., Fla. Bar Assn. Independent. Mem. LDS Ch. Avocations: genealogy, jogging, amateur radio, photography. Office: Stetson U Coll Law Law Libr 1401 61st St S Gulfport FL 33707-5658 Home: 1200 Hull St So Gulfport FL 33707-3222 E-mail: nmj1950@cswebmail.com.

JACKSON, RAYMOND A. federal judge; b. 1949; BA, Norfolk State U., 1970; JD, U. Va., 1973. Capt. U.S. Army JAGC, 1973-77; asst. U.S. atty. Ea. Dist. Va., Norfolk, 1977-93, chief criminal divsn., civil divsn., exec. asst.; judge U.S. Dist. Ct. (ea. dist.) Va., Norfolk, 1993—. Mem. jud. conf. U.S. Ct. Appeals (4th cir.); adj. faculty Marshall Wythe Sch. of Law, Coll. of William and Mary, 1978—93. Active Day Care and Child Devel. Ctr., Tidewater, 1980—86; mem. exec. com. Va. State Bar, 1991—93; bd. dirs. Peninsula Legal Aid Ctr., 1977. Col. Res. USAR, ret. 1998. Fellow: Va. Bar Found.; mem.: U.S. Judicial Conf. Com. Adminstrn. Magistrate Judge Sys., Va. Law Found., Am. Inn Ct. (Hoffman-l'Anson chpt. pres. 2000—02), South Hampton Rds. Bar Assn., Norfolk-Portsmouth Bar Assn., Old Dominion Bar Assn. (pres. 1984—86), U.S. Dist. Judges Assn. Office: 600 Granby St Norfolk VA 23510-1915

JACKSON, REGINALD SHERMAN, JR., lawyer, educator; b. Oct. 8, 1946; s. Reginald Sherman and Frances (Holland) J.; m. Joanne Marie Warren, Aug. 31, 1968; children: Reginald Sherman III, Michael W., Adam H. BA, Ohio State U., 1968, JD, 1971. Bar: Ohio 1971, U.S. Supreme Ct. 1976; cert. civil trial advocate Nat. Bd. Trial Advocacy. Mem. Fuller, Henry, Hodge Snyder, Toledo, 1971-76; asst. U.S. atty. no. dist. Ohio U.S. Dept. Justice, 1976-78; ptnr. Connelly, Jackson & Collier, Toledo, 1978—. Adj. prof. trial practice U. Toledo Coll. Law, 1976-89. Fellow Am. Bar Found., Ohio State Bar Found. (trustee 1998—), Toledo Bar Found. (pres. 1993-98); mem. ABA (ho. of dels. 1996-99, 2001—, exec. com. nat. caucus state bars, litig. sect.), Am. Bd. Trial Advocates, Ohio State Bar Assn. (pres. 2000-01), Toledo Bar Assn. (pres. 1989-90), Toledo Golf Hall of Fame (founder), Toledo Country Club (trustee 1981-93, pres. 1991-93), Rotary (trustee 1994-96, 1st v.p.). Federal civil litigation, State civil litigation. Home: 2907 River Rd Maumee OH 43537-3740 Office: Connelly Jackson & Collier 405 Madison Ave Ste 1600 Toledo OH 43604-1226 E-mail: rjackson@gcjc-law.com.

JACKSON, THOMAS FRANCIS, III, lawyer; b. Memphis, Oct. 21, 1940; s. Thomas Francis and Sarah Elizabeth (Farris) J.; children: Thomas Francis, Wythe Macrae Bogy. Grad., The Taft Sch.; BA, Rhodes Coll., 1962; LLB, George Washington U., 1967. Bar: Tenn. 1967, U.S. Supreme Ct. 1974. Law clk. to chief judge U.S. Dist. Ct. Western Dist. Tenn., 1967-68; with Armstrong, Allen PLLC, Memphis, 1968-72, Lawler, Humphreys PLLC, Memphis, 1972-83; pvt. practice Memphis, 1983—. Lt. USNR, 1962-67. Mem. ABA, Tenn. Bar Assn., Memphis Bar Assn. Episcopalian. General civil litigation, General practice, Probate (including wills, trusts). Home: 232 S Highland St Memphis TN 38111-4540 Office: PO Box 111221 Memphis TN 38111-1221 Fax: 901-324-6997. E-mail: tfj@lawtenn.com.

JACKSON, THOMAS GENE, lawyer; b. N.Y.C., Mar. 9, 1949; s. Alan Clark and Clare Seena (Werther) J.; m. Beatrice Lafrance Korab, June 11, 1972; children: Sarah Ann, Alan Edward. AB magna cum laude in English, Dartmouth Coll., 1971; JD, U. Va., 1974. Bar: N.Y. 1975, U.S. Dist. Ct. (so. and ea. dists.) N.Y. 1975, U.S. Ct. Appeals (2d cir.) 1975, U.S. Ct. Appeals (5th cir.) 1978, U.S. Supreme Ct. 1978, U.S. Ct. Appeals (D.C. cir.) 1986. Editor The Rsch. Group, Charlottesville, Va., 1973-74; assoc. Phillips Nizer Benjamin Krim & Ballon LLP, N.Y.C., 1974-82; ptnr. Phillips Nizer LLP, N.Y.C., 1982—. Mem. fed. bar coun. com. 2d Cir. Cts., 1997-2000, chmn. subcom. on tech. in the cts., 1997-2000. Mem. Village of Irvington Cable TV Adv. Com., N.Y., 1979-91, 95—, chmn. franchise renewal com., 1991-95; sec. Village of Irvington Environ. Conservation Bd., 1983-87, chmn., 1987—; mem. Dartmouth Coll. Alumni Coun., 1986-89. Mem.: ABA (sect. antitrust law, mergers and acquisitions com.), Assn. Bar City N.Y. (antitrust and trade regulation com. 1988—92, mergers acquisitions and joint ventures subcom. 1991—92), Am. Arbitration Assn. (comml. tribunal 1986—, panel of arbitrators), Dartmouth Coll. Class Secs. Assn. (v.p. 1984—85, pres. 1985—86), Dartmouth Club Westchester (sec. 1984—87, pres. 1987—90), Dartmouth Coll. Club Officers Assn. (exec. com. 1988—91). Antitrust, Federal civil litigation. Home: 32 Hamilton Rd Irvington NY 10533-2311 Office: Phillips Nizer LLP 666 5th Ave New York NY 10103-0084

JACKSON, THOMAS PENFIELD, federal judge; b. Washington, Jan. 10, 1937; s. Thomas Searing and May Elizabeth (Jacobs) J. AB in Govt., Dartmouth Coll., 1958; LLB, Harvard U., 1964. Bar: D.C., Md., U.S. Supreme Ct. 1970. Assoc., ptnr. Jackson & Campbell, P.C., Washington, 1964-82; U.S. dist. judge U.S. Dist. Ct. D.C., Washington, 1982—. Vestryman All Saints' Episcopal Ch., Washington, 1969-75; trustee Gallaudet U., Washington, 1985-99, St. Marys Coll., Md., 2001—. Lt. (j.g.) USN, 1958-61. Fellow Am. Coll. Trial Lawyers; mem. ABA, Bar Assn. D.C. (pres. 1982-83), Rotary. Clubs: Chevy Chase, Metropolitan, Lawyers', Barristers. Republican. Office: US Dist Ct US Courthouse 3rd & Constitution Ave NW Washington DC 20001

JACOB, BRUCE ROBERT, law educator; b. Chgo., Mar. 26, 1935; s. Edward Carl and Elsie Berthe (Hartmann) J.; m. Ann Wear, Sept. 8, 1962; children: Bruce Ledley, Lee Ann, Brian Edward. BA, Fla. State U., 1957; JD, Stetson U., 1959; LLM, Northwestern U., 1965; SJD, Harvard U., 1980; LLM in Taxation, U. Fla., 1995. Bar: Fla. 1959, Ill. 1965, Mass. 1970, Ohio 1972. Asst. atty. gen. State of Fla., 1960-62; assoc. Holland, Bevis & Smith, Bartow, Fla., 1962-64; asst. to assoc. prof. Emory U. Sch. Law, 1965-69; rsch. assoc. Ctr. for Criminal Justice, Harvard Law Sch., 1969-70; staff atty. Cmty. Legal Assistance Office, Cambridge, Mass., 1970-71; assoc. prof. Coll. Law, Ohio State U., 1971-73, prof., dir. clin. programs, 1973-78; dean, prof. Mercer U. Law Sch., Macon, Ga., 1978-81; v.p., dean, prof. Stetson U. Coll. Law, St. Petersburg, Fla., 1981-94, dean emeritus and prof., 1994—. Contbr. articles to profl. jours. Mem. Fla. Bar, Sigma Chi. Democrat. Home: 1946 Coffee Pot Blvd NE Saint Petersburg FL 33704-4632 Office: Stetson U Coll Law 1401 61st St S Saint Petersburg FL 33707-3246 E-mail: jacob@law.stetson.edu.

JACOB, EDWIN J. lawyer; b. Detroit, Aug. 25, 1927; s. A. Aubrey and Estelle R. (Vesell) J.; m. Constance Dorfman, June 15, 1948; children—Louise B., Beth D., Ellen P. AB cum laude, Harvard U., 1948, JD cum laude, 1951. Bar: N.Y. 1951, U.S. Dist. Ct. (so. dist.) N.Y. 1953, U.S. Dist. Ct. (ea. dist.) N.Y. 1953, U.S. Ct. Appeals (2d cir.) 1954, U.S. Supreme Ct. 1963, U.S. Ct. Appeals (8th cir.) 1981, U.S. Ct. Appeals (10th cir.) 1987. Assoc. Davis Polk Wardwell Sunderland & Kiendl, N.Y.C., 1951-62; ptnr. Cabell, Medinger, Forsyth & Decker, N.Y.C., 1962-69, Lauterstein & Lauterstein, N.Y.C., 1969-72, Jacob, Medinger & Finnegan, LLP, N.Y.C., 1973—. Bd. advisors Inst. for Health Policy Analysis, Georgetown U., 1987-90. Contbr. articles to profl. jours. Mem. nat. bd. Assn. Ref. Zionists Am., 1991-97; trustee Stephen Wise Free Synagogue, 1991—, pres., 1994-96. With USN, 1945-46 Mem. Am. Law Inst., Am. Judicature Soc., Assn. Bar City N.Y. Clubs: Harvard of N.Y.C. Federal civil litigation, State civil litigation, Product liability. Office: Jacob Medinger Finnegan LLP 1270 Ave of Americas New York NY 10020

JACOB, MARVIN EUGENE, lawyer; b. N.Y.C., Feb. 4, 1935; s. Sam Jacob and Ann (Garfinkel) Law; m. Atara Binnun, Mar. 27, 1960; children: Shalom J., Aviva, Asher. BA, Bklyn. Coll., 1961; JD cum laude, N.Y. Law Sch., 1964. Bar: N.Y. 1964, U.S. Supreme Ct. 1967. Assoc. regional adminstr. SEC, N.Y.C., 1964-79; ptnr. Weil, Gotshal & Manges, N.Y.C., 1979—. Adj. prof. law N.Y. Law Sch., 1975—. Editor: Restructurings, 1993, Reorganizing Failing Businesses, 1999. Mem. ABA, N.Y. State Bar Assn. Bankruptcy, Federal civil litigation, Securities. Office: Weil Gotshal & Manges 767 5th Ave Fl 29 New York NY 10153-0023

JACOBOWITZ, HAROLD SAUL, lawyer; b. N.Y.C., Aug. 26, 1950; s. William and Miriam (Spector) J.; m. Estrella B. Rivera, Oct. 26, 1972. BA, CUNY, 1972; JD, Rutgers U., 1977. Bar: N.Y. 1977, U.S. Dist. Ct. (so. dist.) N.Y. 1978, U.S. Dist. Ct. (ea. dist.) N.Y. 1978. Assoc. Goldman & Heffernan, N.Y.C., 1977-78; assoc. Zola & Zola, N.Y.C., 1978-79, Goldberg & Lysaght, N.Y.C., 1979-82; from atty. of record to cons. Am. Internat. Group (Jacobowitz, Spessard, Garfinkel & Lesman), N.Y.C., 1982—2001, cons., 2002—. Arbitration panel U.S. Dist. Ct. (ea. dist.) N.Y. Mem. ABA, N.Y. State Bar Assn., Assn. Bar City N.Y., N.Y. County Lawyers Assn., Assn. Trial Lawyers N.Y.C. (bd. dirs.). Alternative dispute resolution, Insurance, Personal injury (including property damage). Office: Am Internat Group 70 Pine St New York NY 10270-0002 E-mail: harold.jacobowitz@aig.com.

JACOBS, ANDREW ROBERT, lawyer; b. Newark, Sept. 18, 1946; s. Seymour B. and Pearle (Flaschen) J.; m. Yardana Steinberg, July 10, 1976; 1 child, Suzanne Michal. BA with high honors, Rutgers U., 1968; JD, Columbia U., 1971. Bar: N.J. 1971, D.C. 1976, U.S. Dist. Ct. N.J. 1971, U.S. Ct. of Appeals (3rd cir.) 1974, U.S. Supreme Ct. 1979, U.S. Dist. Ct. (ea. and so. Dists.) N.Y. 1980, N.Y. 1980, Pa. 1981, U.S. Ct. Appeals (2nd cir.) 1984, U.S. Claims Ct. 1986. Law clk. to chief judge U.S. Dist. Ct., Newark, 1971-72; asst. U.S. atty. U.S. Atty.'s Office, Newark, 1972-76; assoc. Cole Berman & Belsky, Rochelle Park, N.J., 1976, Lanigan O'Connell Jacobs & Chazin, Basking Ridge, N.J. and N.Y.C., 1977-78, ptnr., 1979-82; asst. U.S. atty., chief spl. pros., dep. chief criminal div. U.S. Atty.'s Office (ea. dist.), N.Y., 1983-85; ptnr. Horowitz & Jacobs, Hackensack, N.J. and N.Y.C., 1985-89, Gern, Dunetz, Davison & Weinstein, Roseland, N.J. and N.Y.C., 1990-93, Fitzsimmons Ringle & Jacobs, Newark, N.J., Hackensack, N.J. and N.Y.C., 1993-2000, Epstein, Fitzsimmons, Brown, Gioia, Jacobs and Sprouls, P.C., Chatham, Newark, Hackensack, N.Y.C., 2000—. Faculty Practicing Law Inst., N.Y.C., 1980-82; legal writing instr. N.Y. Law Sch., 1981-82; master Justice William J. Brennan, Jr. Inns of Ct., 1995—. Trustee N.J. YM-YWHA Camps, Fairfield, NJ, Milford, Pa., 1985—, pres., 2001—; trustee Congregation Shomrei Emunah, Montclair, NJ, 1985—96; pres. Rutgers Coll. Alumni Class 1968. Capt. U.S. Army, 1997. Harlan Fiske Stone scholar; recipient U.S. Dept. Justice Spl. commendation award, 1973, 75, U.S. Dept. Treasury ATF cert. of Appreciation, 1976, Jerome Michael prize for Excellence in Trial Advocacy Columbia U. Mem.: ATLA, ABA, Assn. Fed. Bar N.J., Essex County Bar Assn., Bergen County Bar Assn., Morris County Bar Assn., Assn. Criminal Def. Lawyers N.J., N.Y. State Trial Lawyers Assn., N.Y. County Lawyers Assn. (fed. cts. com.), N.J. State Bar Assn., Soc. Loyal Sons and Daus. of Rugers Coll. (elected), Phi Beta Kappa. Federal civil litigation, State civil litigation, Criminal. Home: 47 Haller Dr Cedar Grove NJ 07009 Office: Epstein Fitzsimmons Brown Gioia Jacobs & Sprouls PC Box 901 245 Green Village Chatham NJ 07928 also: 83 Maiden Ln 13th Fl New York NY 10038 also: 2 University Plz Ste 18 Hackensack NJ 07601-6202 also: 50 Park Pl Ste 903 Newark NJ 07102 Fax: 973-593-0179. E-mail: ajacobs@epsteinfitz.com.

JACOBS, ANN ELIZABETH, lawyer; b. Lima, Ohio, July 28, 1950; d. Warren Charles and Virginia Elizabeth (Lewis) J.; m. Mark S. Bush, Nov. 26, 1988; 1 child, Whitney Elizabeth. BA, George Washington U., 1972; JD, Cath. U., 1976. Bar: Ohio 1977, Calif. 1977, U.S. Ct. Appeals (D.C. cir.) 1980, U.S. Dist. Ct. (no. dist.) Ohio 1982, S.C. 2000. Asst. atty. gen. State of Ohio, Columbus, 1977-78; trial atty. EEOC of Ohio, Miami, Fla., 1978-80; sole practice Lima, 1980—. Bd. dirs. Allen County Blackhoof Area Legal Svcs. Assn., Marimor Industries, Inc., Lima. Pres., legal liaison Shawnee Sch. Dist. Bd. Edn., 2002-03; fundraiser Lima Symphony Orch., 1985, pres. legis. liaison, 2002-03; trustee Lima Art Assn., YWCA; bd. dirs. Sr. Citizens; mem. bd. elders Market St. Presbyn. Ch., chairperson mission com., 2001. Recipient Recognition award US Naval Air Sta., Jacksonville, Fla., 1979. Mem. LWV, Ohio Bar Assn., Calif. Bar Assn., D.C. Bar Assn., Allen County Bar Assn. (chmn. juvenile ct. com. 1993). Avocations: sailing, golf, reading. General civil litigation, General practice, Personal injury (including property damage). Home: 1529 Shawnee Rd Lima OH 45805-3801 Office: Jacobs & Von der Embse 558 W Spring St Lima OH 45801-4728

JACOBS, HARVEY S. lawyer; b. Bradley Beach, N.J., 1958; s. Joseph and Leatrice J.; m. Marcia E. Clarke; 2 children. BBA in Acctg., George Washington U., 1980; JD, Bklyn. Law Sch., 1983. Bar: N.Y. 1984, D.C. 1985, Md. 1995. Assoc. Graham & James (merger Austrian, Lance & Stewart and Graham & James), N.Y.C., 1984-87, Mudge Rose Guthrie Alexander & Ferdon, N.Y.C., 1987-88, Ginsburg Feldman & Bress, Washington, 1988-89; ptnr. Joyce & Jacobs, Washington, 1989-2000; mng. dir. Jacobs & Assocs., Attys. at Law, Washington, 2000—. Internet corr. ABC-TV World News Now; gen. counsel stress-free settlements. Author: A Business and Legal Guide to Global E-Commerce; editor: D.C. Bar Practice Manual; contbr. articles on Internet and real estate to Wired Unique Homes, Dist. Lawyer mags., Internet: Legal and Business Aspects, Small Bus. News, Georgetowner. Mem. ABA (sect. on bus. law), D.C. Bar Assn. (steering com. of real estate, housing and land use sect., former chair real property transactions subcom.), George Washington U. Sch. Govt. and Bus. Alumni Assn. (pres. 1986-88), Balt.-Washington Venture Group, Kiwanis (dir.). Computer, Corporate, general, Property, real (including real estate development, water). Office: Jacobs & Assocs Atty at Law Ste 800 2300 M St NW Washington DC 20037-4924 E-mail: jacobs@internet-law-firm.com.

JACOBS, JACK BERNARD, judge; b. July 23, 1942; s. Louis K. and Phoebe J.; m. Marion Antiles, Apr. 2, 1967; 1 child, Andrew Seth. AB, U. Chgo., 1964; LLB, Harvard U., 1967. Bar: Del. 1968, U.S. Dist. Ct. Del. 1968, U.S. Ct. Appeals (3d cir.) 1968, U.S. Supreme Ct. 1975. Law clk. Del. Chancery and Superior Cts., 1967-68; assoc. Young, Conaway, Stargatt & Taylor, Wilmington, Del., 1968-71, ptnr., 1971-85; vice chancellor Ct. of Chancery State of Del., 1985—2003; apptd. justice Supreme Ct. of Del., 2003—. Adj. prof. Widener U. Sch. Law, 1986—; chmn. Bar-Bench-Media Conf. Del., 1992-93; faculty continuing legal edn. programs. Contbr. articles to profl. jours. Vice chmn. Nat. Jewish Cmty. Rels. Adv. Coun., 1985-89; bd. dirs. Jewish Fedn. Del., 1981-87, Del. Symphony Assn., 1991-95, Del. Cmty. Found., 1994-2000, chair grants com., 1998-2000, 02—, chmn. governance com., 2002—; pres. Milton & Hattie Kutz Home, 1990-92. Mem.: ABA (litigation sect., bus. law sect., mem. com. corp. laws 1999—), Harvard Law Sch. Del. (pres. 1986—87), Del. Bar Assn., Am. Judicature Soc. (bd. dirs. 1999—), Am. Law Inst. (advisor Restatement (3d) Restitution), Phi Beta Kappa. Democrat. Jewish. Home: 28 Beethoven Dr Wilmington DE 19807-1923 Office: Ct of Chancery 500 N King St ste 11400 Wilmington DE 19801 E-mail: jjacobs@state.de.us.

JACOBS, JEFFREY LEE, lawyer, education network company executive; b. Boston, Jan. 20, 1951; s. Philip and Millicent T. (Katz) J.; m. Deborah R. Rath, June 7, 1981; children: Alison, Hannah. BA, U. Pa., 1973; MPA, U. So. Calif., 1979; JD, Pace U., 1985. Bar: Conn. 1985, N.Y. 1988. Asst. to comptroller gen. U.S. Gen. Acctg. Office, Washington, 1976-80; sr. rsch. assoc. Nat. Acad. Pub. Adminstrn., Washington, 1980-83; dir. of seminars Prentice Hall, Clifton, N.J., 1985-87; pres. Profl. Edn. Network, Inc., Westport, Conn., 1987—. Lectr. Ga. Tax Inst., Ohio Fed. Tax Inst.; adj. prof. Quinnipiac Coll., Univ. New Haven; cons. SmartPros Ltd. Co-author: GAO: Government Accountability, 1979; producer, writer TV series The CPA Report, 1988-91; producer, writer radio series Legal Practice Alert, 1990—. Trustee Westport Pub. Libr. Mem. ABA (taxation sect.), Acad. Legal Studies in Bus. Home: 16 Janson Dr Westport CT 06880-2568 Office: SmartPros Ltd 12 Skyline Dr Hawthorne NY 10532-2133 E-mail: jeffjacobs@aol.com.

JACOBS, JOHN E. lawyer; b. Detroit, Feb. 13, 1947; s. Morton and Gilberta (Jewell) J.; m. Gilda Gail Zalenko, June 6, 1971; children: Rachel H., Jessica E. BA, Mich. State U., 1968; JD, U. Mich., 1971. Bar: Mich. 1971, U.S. Dist. Ct. (ea. dist.) Mich. 1971, U.S. Ct. Appeals (6th cir.) 1984, U.S. Dist. Ct. (we. dist.) Mich. 1997. Assoc. Butzel, Levin, Winston & Quint, Detroit, 1971-76, ptnr., 1976-81; shareholder Mason, Steinhardt, Jacobs, Perlman & Pesick, P.C., Southfield, Mich., 1981-2000, DKW Law Group, P.C., Southfield, 2000—02, Maddin, Hauser, Wartell, Roth & Heller, P.C., 2002—. Contbr. articles to profl. jours. Pres. Jewish Family Svc., Southfield, 1991-93, Temple Emanu-El, Oak Park, Mich., 1995-97. Mem.

ABA (mem. consumer fin. svcs. com. 1978—), Jewish Fedn. Met. Detroit (bd. govs. 1997—, mem. exec. com. 1998-99, 2002—). Democrat. Avocations: golfing, bicycling. Commercial, contracts (including sales of goods; commercial financing), Corporate, general, Property, real (including real estate development, water). Home: 8353 Hendrie Blvd Huntington Woods MI 48070-1613 Office: Maddin Hauser Wartell Roth & Heller PC Third Fl Essex Ctr 28400 Northwestern Hwy Southfield MI 48034

JACOBS, JOHN PATRICK, lawyer; b. Chgo., Oct. 27, 1945; s. Anthony N. and Bessie (Montgomery) J.; m. Linda I. Grams, Oct. 6, 1973; 1 child, Christine Margaret. BA cum laude, U. Detroit, 1967, JD magna cum laude, 1970. Bar: Mich. 1970, U.S. Dist. Ct. Mich (ea. dist.) 1970, U.S. Ct. Appeals (6th cir.) 1974, U.S. Supreme Ct. 1978, U.S. Ct. Appeals (D.C. cir.) 1988, U.S. Ct. Appeals (4th cir.) 2001. Law clk. to chief judge Mich. Ct. Appeals, Detroit, 1970-71; assoc., then ptnr. Plunkett & Cooney P.C., Detroit, 1972-92, also bd. dirs.; founding ptnr., prin. mem. O'Leary, O'Leary, Jacobs, Mattson, Perry & Mason P.C., Southfield, Mich., 1992-99; prin., owner John P. Jacobs, P.C., 1999—. Investigator Atty. Grievance Com., Detroit, 1975-84; mem. hearing panel Atty. Discipline Bd., Detroit, 1984-87, 94—; adj. prof. law Sch. Law, U. Detroit, 1983-84, faculty advisor, 1984-89, Pres.'s Cabinet, 1982—; elected rep. State Bar Rep. Assembly, Lansing, Mich., 1980-82, 91-92, 93-96; fellow Mich. State Bar Found., 1990-98; treas., mem. steering com. Mich. Bench-Bar Appellate Conf. Com., 1994—; apptd. mem. Mich. Supreme Ct. Com. on Appellate Fees, 1990; spl. mediator appellate negotiation program Mich. Ct. Appeals, 1995—; mem. exec. com. Mich. Appellate Bench-Bar Conf. Found., 1996—; appellate counsel to State Bar of Mich., mem. profl. ethics com., 1998, mem. multi-disciplinary practice com., 1999. Bd. editors Mich. Lawyers Weekly. Bd. dirs. Boysville of Mich., Clinton, 1988-95, 99—, chmn. pub. policy com., 1993-95, pub. policy liaison, 1999—; apptd. mem. State Bar Mich. Blue Ribbon Com. Improving Def. Counsel-Insurer Rels., 1998-99. Named Mgsr. Malloy Cath. Lawyer of Yr., Archdiocese of Detroit, 2001; recipient Robert E. Dice Med. Malpractice Def. Atty. award, Mich. Physicians, 1986; fellow Reginald Heber Smith fellow, 1971—72. Fellow Am. Acad. Appellate Lawyers, Mich. Std. Jury Instn. (subcom. employment law 1984-87); mem. ABA (litigation sect., appellate subcom., torts and ins. practice), Internat. Assn. Def. Counsel (v.p., amicus curiae com., med. and legal malpractice coms., product liability com.), Fedn. Ins. and Corp. Counsel, Mich. Def. Trial Counsel (chmn. amicus curiae com. 1986-88, chmn. future planning com., bd. dirs. 1989—, treas. 1993-94, sec. 1994-95, v.p. 1995-96, program chair 1990, 94, 95, pres., 1996-97), Def. Rsch. Inst. (state rep. 1997-98, Outstanding Performance Citation 1997, nat. appellate com. steering com. 1997—), Cath. Lawyers Soc. (bd. dirs. 1988-98, emeritus dir. 1998—, pres. 1994-95), Supreme Ct. U.S. Historical Soc., Supreme Ct. Mich. Historical Soc., Democrat. Roman Catholic. Avocations: collecting antique law books, film. Appellate, Federal civil litigation, State civil litigation. Office: The Dime Bldg 719 Griswold Ste 600 Detroit MI 48226

JACOBS, JOSEPH JAMES, lawyer, communications company executive; b. Toronto, Ont., Can., Mar. 18, 1925; came to U.S., 1925; s. Sidney and Hildred Veronica (Greenberg) J.; m. Carole Evelyn Bent, Jan. 22, 1946 (div. 1972); children— Carole Lynn Urgenson, Joseph James III; m. Edna Mae Meincke, Jan. 5, 1973. J.D., Tulane U., 1950. Bar: La. 1950, N.Y. 1951, U.S. Dist. Ct. (so. dist.) N.Y. 1953, U.S. Ct. Mil. Appeals 1953, U.S. Ct. Appeals (2d cir.) 1977, U.S. Ct. Appeals (D.C. cir.) 1980. Assoc. Proskauer, Rose, Goetz & Mendelsohn, N.Y.C., 1950-53; asst. gen. counsel, asst. to pres. Am. Broadcasting Co., N.Y.C., 1954-60; gen. atty. Metromedia, Inc., N.Y.C., 1960-61; dir. program and talent negotiations United Artists TV, Inc., 1961-66; atty. United Artists Corp., N.Y.C., 1966-69; v.p., counsel United Artists Broadcasting, Inc., N.Y.C., 1969-71; gen. atty. ITT World Commd. Inc., N.Y.C., 1972-74; v.p., legal dir. ITT Commd. Ops. and Info. Svcs. Group (formerly U.S. Tel. & Tel. Corp.), N.Y.C. and Secaucus, N.J., 1974-83, ITT Comms. and Info. Svcs., Inc., Secaucus, 1983-87; v.p., gen. counsel U.S. Transmission Systems, Inc., Secaucus, 1984-87, ITT World Comms. Inc., Secaucus, 1984-87; of counsel Seyfarth, Shaw, Fairweathr & Geraldson, N.Y.C., 1988-89; v.p., gen. counsel Graphic Scanning Corp., Englewood, N.J., 1989-91; v.p., gen. counsel Ram/BSE, L.P., Woodbridge, N.J., 1992; pvt. practice, Wainscott, N.Y., 1992-95. Bd. editors Tulane Law Rev., 1949, asst. editor-in-chief, 1950; cons. 1996—. Served with parachute inf. U.S. Army, 1943-46, ETO, PTO, to maj. USAFR ret. Mem. Order of Coif. Republican. Jewish. Administrative and regulatory, Corporate, general, Entertainment. Office: 6380 Sweet Maple Ln Boca Raton FL 33433-1933

JACOBS, JULIAN I. federal judge; b. Balt., Aug. 13, 1937; s. Sidney and Bernice (Kellman) J.; m. Donna Buffenstein; children: Richard S., Jennifer K. BA, U. Md., 1958, JD, 1960; LL.M., Georgetown U., 1965. Bar: Md., 1960. Atty. chief counsel's office IRS, Washington, 1961-65, trial atty. regional counsel's office Buffalo, 1965-67; assoc. Weinberg & Green, Balt., 1967-69, Hoffberger & Hollander, Balt., 1969-72, Gordon Feinblatt Rothman Hoffberger & Hollander, Balt., 1972-74, ptnr., 1974-84; judge U.S. Tax Ct., Washington, 1984—. Chmn. study commn. Md. Tax Ct., 1978-79, mem. rules com., 1980; mem. spl. study group Md. Gen. Assembly, 1980; adj. prof. grad. tax program U. Balt., 1991-93; adj. prof. law, U. San Diego, 2001; adj. prof. grad. tax program, U. Denver, 2001—. Mem.: U Md. Law Rev. Bd. Mem. Md. State Bar Assn. (past chmn. taxation sect.), Balt. City Bar Assn. (past chmn. tax legis. subcom.). Office: US Tax Ct 400 2nd St NW Washington DC 20217-0002

JACOBS, LESLIE WILLIAM, lawyer; b. Akron, Ohio, Dec. 5, 1944; s. Leslie Wilson and Louise Francis (Walker) J.; m. Laurie Hutchinson, July 12, 1962; children— Leslie James, Andrew Wilson, Walker Fulton. Student, Denison U., 1962-63; BS, Northwestern U., 1965; JD, Harvard U., 1968. Bar: Ohio 1968, D.C. 1980, U.S. Supreme Ct. 1971, Brussels 1996. Law clk. to Chief Justice Kingsley A. Taft Ohio Supreme Ct., 1968-69; assoc. Thompson, Hine and Flory, Cleve., 1969-76, ptnr., 1976—, chmn. antitrust, internat. and regulatory area, 1988-99; chmn. bus. regulation and trade dept. Thompson Hine LLP and predecessor, Cleve., 1999—. Lectr. conf. bd. Ohio Legal Ctr. Insts., Ohio State Bar Assn. Antitrust and Corp. Counsel Insts., Fed. Bar Assn., ABA, Canadian Inst., Internat. Assn. Young Lawyers, others; mem. Ohio Bd. Bar Examiners, 1990-94. Contbr. articles to profl. jours. Chmn. EconomicsAmerica, 1990-93; mem. vis. com. Case Western Res. U. Sch. Law, 1985-91; mem. Leadership Cleve., 1988. Lt. comdr. USNR, 1967-79. Fellow Am. Bar Found. (life), Ohio State Bar Found. (life, trustee 1985-87, Ritter award 1997); mem. ABA (ho. dels. 1986—, antitrust law sect. coun. 1985-88, officer 1991-97, state del. 1995-2001, nominating com. 1995-2001, bd. gov. 2001—, task force on corp. liability), Ohio State Bar Assn. (pres. 1987, Ohio Bar medal 1990), Cleve. Bar Assn. (chmn. jud. selection com. 1982, trustee 1983-85), Am. Law Inst., Nat. Conf. Bar Pres., Harvard Club (N.Y.C.), Chagrin Valley Hunt Club, Union Club (Cleve.), Castalia Trout Club. Republican. Presbyterian. Antitrust, General civil litigation, Private international. Office: Thompson Hine LLP 3900 Key Ctr 127 Public Sq Cleveland OH 44114-1291

JACOBS, MICHAEL A. lawyer; b. Atlantic City, Mar. 9, 1967; s. Jerrold L. and Carol N. Jacobs; m. Susan G. Lopes, June 19, 1994. BA, Yale U., 1989; LLB, Harvard U., 1992. Bar: Va., D.C., Mass. Assoc. Shaw, Pittman, Potts & Trowbridge, Washington, 1992—96, Choate, Hall & Stewart, Boston, 1996—2000, non-equity ptnr., 2000—. Mem.: ABA (mem. tax sect.), Boston Bar Assn. (mem. tax sect., chair fed. tax and bus. transactions com. 1998—2000). Corporate taxation, State and local taxation, Taxation, general. Office: Choate Hall and Stewart Exch Pl 53 State St Boston MA 02109 Office Fax: 617-248-4000.

JACOBS, PAUL, lawyer; b. N.Y.C., Sept. 29, 1946; s. William R. and Sylvia (Wanshel) J.; m. Lisette Simon, Oct. 10, 1979; children: Alexia, Caroline. BA, Colgate U., 1967; JD, Columbia U., 1971. Bar: N.Y. 1971, U.S. Dist. Ct. (so. dist.) N.Y. 1971. Assoc. Reavis & McGrath, N.Y.C., 1971-78, ptnr., 1978-89, Fulbright & Jaworski, N.Y.C., 1989-96, sr. ptnr., 1996—. Mem. adv. com. Grace Ventures Corp., Cupertino, Calif., 1988-98, Euro-Am.-I C.V., San Bruno, Calif., 1988-98; sec. Zygo Corp., Middlefield, Conn., 1992—. Mem. N.Y. Bar Assn., N.Y.C. Bar Assn., Phi Beta Kappa, The University Club. Corporate, general, Private international. Office: Fulbright & Jaworski 666 5th Ave Fl 31 New York NY 10103-0001 E-mail: p.jacobs@fulbright.com.

JACOBS, RANDALL BRIAN, lawyer; b. N.Y.C., July 8, 1951; s. John and Evelyn Jacobs; 1 child, Jillian. BA, Coll. of Idaho, 1972; JD, U. West L.A., 1978. Bar: Calif., D.C., Wis. Lawyer B. Randall Jacobs Law Corp., Brentwood, Calif., 1978—; real estate broker Morgan Reed & Co., Brentwood, 1979—; pvt. investigator Randy Brian Assocs., Brentwood, 1976—. Reserve deputy sheriff, L.A. County Sheriff, L.A., 1979—. Mem. NRA, IDPA, USPSA, Shom Rim Soc., Calif. Rifle and Pistol Assn., Calif. Police Pistol Assn., Mensa, Masons, Shriners. Insurance, Personal injury (including property damage), Product liability. Office: 654 N Sepulveda Blvd # 17 Los Angeles CA 90049-2169

JACOBS, RANDALL SCOTT DAVID, lawyer; b. Sept. 6, 1944; s. Irving and Lea Sylvia (Kerner) Jacobs; m. Jill Barbara Weiss, June 20, 1981; children: Evan, Todd. BSBA, NYU, 1967, LLM in Corp. Law, 1971; JD, Temple U., 1970. Bar: N.Y. 1977, U.S. Dist. Ct. (ea. dist.) N.Y. 1979, U.S. Dist. Ct. (so. dist.) N.Y. 1979, U.S. Ct. Appeals (2d cir.) 1980, U.S. Supreme Ct. 1980. Assoc. Coudert Brothers, N.Y.C., NY, 1968; with Comml. Coverage Corp., N.Y.C., 1971—78; assoc. Levy, Tandet, Sohn and Loft, N.Y.C., 1978—82; of counsel Harvis and Zeichner, N.Y.C., 1982—84; ptnr. Rich, Krinsly, Dorman & Jacobs, P.C., N.Y.C., 1984—91, Mintz and Fraade, PC, N.Y.C., 1991—94, Branin Investments, Inc., N.Y.C., 1995—96, Recap. Ptnrs., LLC, N.Y.C., 1996—2000, FMG Acquisitions Fund, LLC, N.Y.C., 2000—, Turnaround Capital, LLC , 2003—. Mem. staff Temple Law Quarterly Law Rev., 1969—70. Mem.: Assn. of Bar of City of N.Y., N.Y. State Bar Assn., ABA. Federal civil litigation, State civil litigation, Commercial, consumer (including collections, credit). Office: 67 Wall St Ste 1901 New York NY 10005

JACOBS, REUVEN, lawyer; b. Boston, July 5, 1956; s. James M. and Muriel (Robinson) J.; m. Chana R. Bohensky, Dec. 28, 1982; children: Yoel M., Yisroel C., Shlomo S., Tzvi E., Sara P., Nechama L., Chaya M., Sheva Y., Nochum, M.M., Pinchas D., Devora A., Dina R. JD, Boston U. Bar: N.Y. 1986, U.S. Dist. Ct. (so. and ea. dists.) N.Y. 1986. Assoc. Boyle, Vogeler & Haimes, N.Y.C., 1985-86; pvt. practice Law Offices of Reuven Jacobs, N.Y.C., 1986—. Mem. ABA, N.Y. County Lawyers Assn. (immigration and naturalization com.). Corporate, general, Immigration, naturalization, and customs, Property, real (including real estate development, water). Home: 1907 Avenue I Brooklyn NY 11230-3113 Office: 321 5th Ave Fl 3 New York NY 10016-5015

JACOBS, ROBERT ALAN, lawyer; b. Waco, Tex., June 23, 1937; s. Abe and Ruth (Englander) J.; m. Sue C. Braunstein, Aug. 22, 1961; children: Jacqueline Anne, Michelle Keri. BBA, U. Tex., 1957; LLB cum laude, NYU, 1960, LLM in Taxation, 1963. Bar: N.Y. 1961. Assoc. Greenbaum, Wolff & Ernst, N.Y.C., 1961-63; asst. br. chief, chief counsel IRS, Washington, 1963-67; assoc. Paul, Weiss, Rifkind, Wharton & Garrison, N.Y.C., 1967-69; sr. tax mem. Milgrim Thomajan Jacobs & Lee PC, N.Y.C., 1969-87; tax ptnr. Milbank, Tweed, Hadley & McCloy, LLP, N.Y.C., 1987—2002, cons. ptnr., 2002—; head low income tax clinic Benjamin A. Cardozo Sch. Law, 2002; underwriting dir. Gulf Ins. Group, 2002—. Adj. prof. law NYU, 1976-85; vis. sr. lectr. taxation, U. Calif. Davis, 1977; spl. counsel to sec. treas., Washington, 1965-67. Note and comment editor NYU Law Rev.; contbr. articles to profl. jours. Mem. adv. group Senate Fin. Com. Staff on Subchpt. C Revision, 1983-85; arbitrator Civil Ct. City of N.Y., 1972—; bd. dirs. Community Action Legal Svcs., 1978-82, MFY Legal Svcs., 1991-98, N.Y. County Lawyers, 1990-93. With U.S. Army, 1960-61, 61-62. Root-Tilden scholar; recipient commendation medal U.S. Army. Mem. ABA (tax sect., asst. sec. 1987-88, chmn. com. corp. stockholder relationships 1983-85, chmn. task force on pass-through entities 1986-88), Am. Law Inst., Tax Forum (chmn. 1989-2001), Am. Coll. Tax Counsel, N.Y. State Bar Assn. (tax sect., exec. com. 1980—, chair 2001), Tax Club (chmn. 1987-88). Corporate taxation. Office: Milbank Tweed Hadley & McCloy LLP 1 Chase Manhattan Plz Fl 47 New York NY 10005-1413 E-mail: rjacobs@milbank.com., rajacobs@gulfins.com.

JACOBS, ROLLY WARREN, judge; b. Nashville, Aug. 26, 1946; s. William Clinton Jr. and Eleanor Olive (Warren) J.; m. Karen Lee Ponist, Sept. 16, 1972; children: Collin Wayne, Tyler Warren. BA in Econs., Washington & Lee U., 1968; JD, U. S.C., 1974. Bar: S.C. 1975, U.S. Dist. Ct. for S.C. 1975. Assoc. Carl R. Reasonover, Camden, S.C., 1975-77; ptnr. Reasonover & Jacobs, Camden, S.C., 1977-80; pvt. practice law Camden, S.C., 1980-99; judge family ct. 5th Jud. Cir., S.C., 1999—. Asst. city judge Mcpl. Ct., Camden, 1976-77; master in equity S.C. Jud. Sys., Camden, 1978-99; mem. Jud. Coun. for S.C., Columbia, 1989-2000; mem. fee dispute panel S.C. Bar Assn., 1986-93. Bd. dirs. ARC, Camden, 1976-78, Am. Cancer Soc., Camden, 1976-78, United Way, Camden, 1978-82; active Boy Scouts Am., Camden, 1984-96. Capt. U.S. Army, 1968-72. Recipient Dist. Award of Merit Indian Waters Coun. Boy Scouts Am., 1991; named Scouting Family of Yr., 1990. Mem. ABA, VFW, S.C. Bar Assn., Am. Legion, Res. Officers Assn., Elks. Methodist. Home: 418 Lafayette Way Camden SC 29020-1642 Office: Kershaw County Courthouse PO Box 664 Camden SC 29020-0664

JACOBS, SHARON O. lawyer; b. Oklahoma City, Okla., Jan. 26, 1962; 2 children. BA, U. Ga., 1984; JD, U. Mo. Columbia, 1990. Asst. gen. counsel Tenn. Dept. Environment and Conservation, Nashville, 1991—92; asst. atty. gen. Tenn. Atty. Gen. and Reporter, Nashville, 1992—95; assoc., ptnr. Wyatt, Tarrant and Combs, Nashville, 1995—2003; mem. Bone McAllester Norton PLLC, Nashville, 2003—. Co-author: West's Medical Waste Handbook, 1999, West's Medical Waste Handbook, 2d edit., 2000. Pres. Akiva Sch. Bd. Dirs., 2000—02. Mem.: Nashville Bar Assn. (chair Environ. law sect.), Tenn. Bar Assn. (chair, vice chair, sec. 1997—2002, chair Environ. sect. 2001—02, Outstanding Sect. Chair award 2001—02). Avocations: hiking, reading, camping, skiing. Environmental, Administrative and regulatory. Office: Bone McAllester Norton PLLC 511 Union St Ste 1600 Nashville TN 37219

JACOBS, STEPHEN LOUIS, lawyer; b. Staples, Minn., June 22, 1953; s. James P. and Gertrude G. (Willis) J.; m. Sue E. Bell, June 14, 1975; 2 children. BA, St. John's U., 1975; JD, William Mitchell Coll. of Law, St. Paul, 1979. Bar: Minn. 1979, U.S. Dist. Ct. Minn. 1979. Assoc. Bertie, Bettenburg & Strong, St. Paul, 1979-84; ptnr. Bertie, Bettenberg, Jacobs & Bettenburg, St. Paul, 1984-89; pvt. practice law St. Paul, 1989—. Mem. Minn. Bar Assn., Kiwanis (pres. St. Paul-Midway chpt. 1987-88, 97-98, bd. dirs. 1984-2003). Roman Catholic. General practice, Probate (including wills, trusts), Property, real (including real estate development, water). Office: 190 Midtown Commons 2334 University Ave W Saint Paul MN 55114-1802

JACOBS, WENDELL EARLY, JR., lawyer; b. Detroit, Nov. 15, 1945; s. Wendell E. and Mildred P. (Horton) J.; m. Elaine M. Lott (div.); children: Wendell Early III, Damon R. BFA, Denison U., 1969; JD, Wayne State U., 1972. Bar: Mich. 1972, U.S. Dist. Ct. (ea. dist.) Mich. 1973, Fla. 1974. Asst. prosecutor Jackson County, Mich., 1973-76; ptnr. Jacobs & Engle, Jackson, 1977—. Mem. Mich. Coun. on Crime and Delinquency. Mem. Nat. Assn. Criminal Def. Lawyers, Criminal Def. Attys. Mich., Jackson County Bar Assn., Eagles Club, Grotto Club, Elks. Avocations: paddleball, motorcycling. Criminal, Family and matrimonial, General practice. Home: 9281 Greenwood Rd Grass Lake MI 49240-9590 Office: Jacobs & Engle 1104 W Michigan Ave Jackson MI 49202-4123

JACOBS, WILLIAM MICHAEL, lawyer; b. Las Vegas, Nev., Aug. 17, 1951; s. William Alfred Jr. and Mary Louise (Carmody) J.; m. Andrea Lee Port, Oct. 6, 1974; children: Aviva So Ree, Leah In Hee, Seth Jong Ho. BA magna cum laude, U. Calif.-L.A., 1973, MA, 1976; JD with high honors, George Wash. U., 1983. Bar: Md. 1983, U.S. Dist. Ct. Md. 1984, Bar: D.C. 1992, U.S. Dist. Ct. D.C., 1993, U.S. Cir. Ct. (4th cir.) 1989. Sr. assoc. Semmes, Bowen and Semmes, Balt., 1983-91, Kroll and Tract, Balt., 1991—95, Chaikin & Karp, Washington, 1995—97; pvt. practice Columbia, Md., 1997—. V.p. Tarleton Community Assn., Inc., 1983-84; pres. Howard County Jewish Community Sch., 1990-91. Scholar Nat. Merit Fund, 1969, George Wash. U., 1980; Chancellor's Intern fellow, 1975. Mem. ABA (chmn. com. on rules and procedures, tort and ins. practice sect., 1990-92), Am. Judicature Soc., Order of Coif, Moot Ct. Democrat. Jewish. Aviation, Construction, Insurance. Office: Law Office W Michael Jacobs 10440 Little Patuxent # 300 Columbia MD 21044

JACOBS, WILLIAM RUSSELL, II, lawyer; b. Chgo., Oct. 26, 1927; s. William Russell and Doris B. (Desmond) J.; m. Shirley M. Spiegler, Mar. 21, 1950; children: William R. III, Richard W., Bruce Allen. BS, Northwestern U., 1950, JD, 1953. Bar: Ill. 1953, U.S. Dist. Ct. (no. dist.) Ill. 1958, U.S. Ct. Appeals (7th cir.) 1958, U.S. Supreme Ct., 1962. Atty. Continental Casualty Co., Chgo., 1955-58; assoc. Horwitz and Anesi, Chgo., 1958-62; prin. William R. Jacobs and Assocs., Chgo., 1962—. Adj. prof. Lewis Coll. Law, Glen Ellyn, Ill., 1975-76; dir., tchr. Ct. Practice Inst., Chgo., 1974—; lectr. Ill. Inst. Continuing Legal Edn., Chgo., 1967—. Elected alderman Des Plaines (Ill.) City Coun., 1953-54; mem. Ill. Bar Assembly, 1973—. 1st lt. inf. U.S. Army, 1946-48. Mem. Ill. State Bar Assn., Am. Acad. Matrimonial Lawyers. Congregationalist. General civil litigation, Family and matrimonial, Personal injury (including property damage). Office: William R Jacobs & Assocs 4474 N Little Rock Tucson AZ 85730 E-mail: spregler@yahoo.com.

JACOBSEN, RAYMOND ALFRED, JR., lawyer; b. Wilmington, Del., Dec. 14, 1949; s. Raymond Alfred and Margaret (Walters) J.; m. Marilyn Perry, Aug. 4, 1973; 1 child, Hunter Perry. BA, U. Del., 1971; JD, Georgetown U., 1975. Bar: D.C. 1975, U.S. Supreme Ct. 1982. From assoc. to ptnr. Howrey & Simon, Washington, 1975-97; dir. antitrust/trade regulation group McDermott, Will & Emery, Washington, 1997-, ptnr., 1997—, head regulatory and govt. affairs dept. and mem. mgmt. com. Adj. prof. internat. anti-trust law Am. U. Law Sch. Spl. projects editor Law & Policy in International Business, 1974-75. Served to capt. U.S. Army, 1975. Mem. ABA (antitrust law sect, litigation sect., internat. law sect., pub. contract law sect.), D.C. Bar Assn., U.S. Supreme Ct. Bar Assn., City Club (Washington), Army and Navy Country Club. Republican. Antitrust, Federal civil litigation, Mergers and acquisitions. Home: 4205 Maple Tree Ct Alexandria VA 22304-1035 Office: McDermott Will & Emery 600 13th St NW Fl 12 Washington DC 20005-3096 E-mail: rayjacobsen@mwe.com.

JACOBSEN, VAN PAUL, lawyer; b. Olivia, Minn., Nov. 26, 1954; s. Ivan Robert and Nola Ruth Jacobsen; children: Natalie, Evan. BS, U. Minn., 1977, JD, 1982. Bar: Minn. 1982, U.S. Dist. Ct. Minn. 1986, U.S. Supreme Ct. 1997. Law clk. Dakota County Atty.'s Office, Hastings, Minn., 1980-82; asst. county atty. Renville County, Olivia, Minn., 1982-84; assoc. Simmons, Hunt & Jacobsen, Olivia, Minn., 1985-87, Steward, Perry, Mahler & Bird, Rochester, Minn., 1985-87; ptnr. Bird and Jacobsen, Rochester, Minn., 1987—. Vol. Legal Assistance of Olmsted County, Rochester, 1985—; mem. social concerns com. 1st Presbyn. Ch., Rochester, 1997—; bd. dirs. Vol. Connection, Rochester, 1990-92. Mem. Minn. Trial Lawyers Assn., Minn. State Bar Assn., Nat. Orgn. Social Security Claimant's Reps., Minn. Arabian Horse Assn., Internat. Arabian Horse Assn. Pension, profit-sharing, and employee benefits, Workers' compensation. Home: 628 73rd St NW Rochester MN 55901-5509 Office: Bird and Jacobsen 305 Ironwood Sq 300 3rd Ave SE Rochester MN 55904-4619 E-mail: vpjacobsen@aol.com.

JACOBSON, BARRY STEPHEN, lawyer, judge; b. Bklyn., Mar. 30, 1955; s. Morris and Sally (Ballaban) J.; m. Andrea Jacobson; children: Faith Blair, Matthew Aaron Jacobson. Cert. in drama, Sch. of Performing Arts, N.Y.C., 1973; BA, CUNY, 1977, MA, 1980; JD, Bklyn. Sch. Law, 1980. Bar: N.Y., 1981, U.S. Dist. Ct. (ea. and so. dists.) N.Y. 1981, U.S. Dist. Ct. (we. and no. dists.) N.Y., 1988, U.S. Dist. Ct. D.C., 1988, U.S. Ct. Appeals (2d cir.) 1981, U.S. Ct. Appeals (fed. and D.C. cirs.) 1988, U.S. Supreme Ct. 1984, U.S. Ct. Claims, 1985, U.S. Tax Ct. 1988 and others. Sole practice, Bklyn., 1981; asst. corp. counsel N.Y.C. Law Dept., Bklyn., 1981-84; asst. dist. atty. Borough of Queens, Kew Gardens, N.Y., 1984-85; judge adminstrv. law N.Y. Dept. Motor Vehicles, Bklyn., 1985-86, 87-92; assoc. counsel N.Y. State Dept. Health, N.Y.C., 1986; arbitrator N.Y.C. Small Claims Ct., 1986-91; pvt. practice Bklyn., 1992—. Gen. counsel Amersfort Flatlands Devel. Corp., Bklyn., 1981-82; arbitrator N.Y.C. Civil Ct. 1987-92; adminstrv. law judge N.Y.C. Parking Violators Bur., 1987-93; mem. Indigent Defenders Appeal Panel, 1988-96; sr. adminstrv. law judge N.Y.C. Parking Violation Bur., 1989-93; leader Nat. Jud. Coll., N.Y. Mem. Roosevelt Dem. Party, Bklyn., 1984-95, mem. adv. bd., 1989-92, treas., 1990-92; active Kings Hwy. Dem. Party, Bklyn., 1982-95, Dem. com. 1986-95; active King's County Young Dems., 1985-86; gen. counsel Bklyn. Coll. Hillel, Bklyn. Coll. Student Govts., 1980-90, also advisor; treas. local div. dept. mtr. vehicles pub. employees fedn. AFL-CIO; coun. ldr. div. #255 Pub. Employee's Fedn., 1989-92, conv. del. 1989, 90, 91; chmn. Bklyn. Traffic Employee Assistance Prog., 1989-92. Named one of Outstanding Young Men Am., 1983, 85, 86, 87, 88. Mem. ABA (judicial sect., spl. const. judges traffic cts. com.), Am. Judges Assn. (hwy. safety com.), Bklyn. Bar Found. (trustee, bd. dirs.), Am. Arbitration Assn. (forums 1988—), Am. Judicature Soc., Assn. Adminstrv. Law Judges (pres.), N.Y. State Dept. Motor Vehicles (v.p.), N.Y. State Adminstrv. Law Judges Assn. (pres. bd. dirs. parking violation com., v.p.), N.Y. State Bar Assn. (pres. for DMV, spl. com. juvenile justice, adminstrv. law jud. coms., jud. adminstrn. com.), Bklyn. Bar Assn. (family ct. com., chmn. young lawyers sect., trustee 1991, chmn. adminstrn. law com.), N.Y. County Lawyers Assn. (family Ct. Com.), Bklyn. Coll. Alumni Assn. (gen. counsel student govt. affiliate 1983-92, bd. dirs. 1985-92), Jaycees, B'nai B'rith, Hillel (bd. dirs. 1983-91, gen. counsel 1987-91), many others. Jewish. Avocations: motorcycling, drama, theatre, target shooting, flying. Administrative and regulatory, Criminal, Transportation. Home: 342 Coleridge Ln Jericho NY 11753-2605 Office: 26 Court St Ste 810 Brooklyn NY 11242-1108 E-mail: ticklaw@aol.com.

JACOBSON, BERNARD, lawyer; b. Hartford, Conn., Feb. 27, 1930; s. Samuel Barnard and Lillian Jacobson; m. Florence Ellen Greenberg, Oct. 7, 1956; children: Daniel John, Alice Lash, Nancy Jacobson-Penn. AB, Amherst Coll., 1951; LLB, Columbia U., 1954. Bar: Conn. 1955, Fla. 1957, U.S. Dist. Ct. (so. dist.) Fla. 1957, U.S. Ct. Appeals (11th cir.) 1961. Pvt. practice, Miami, Fla., 1957-68; ptnr. Fine, Jacobson, Miami, Fla., 1968-94, Holland & Knight LLP, Miami, Fla., 1994—2002, Akerman Senterfitt, Miami, 2002—. Pres., CEO Rep. Mortgage Investors, Miami, 1973-81; presenter in field. Contbr. articles to profl. jours. Chmn. Fla. Congl. Partnership, Miami, 1987; vice chmn. Greater Miami C. of C., 1988-92. With U.S. Army Counter Intelligence Corps, 1955-57. Mem. ABA, Fla. Bar Assn. Avocations: tennis, boating, skiing. Mergers and acquisitions, Corporate, general, Securities. Office: Akerman Senterfitt One SE ed Ave Ste 2800 Miami FL 33131 E-mail: bjacobson@akerman.com.

JACOBSON, DAVID EDWARD, lawyer; b. Port Chester, N.Y., May 17, 1949; s. Robert Herzel and Ruth Doris (Rosenzweig) J.; m. Debra Ann Denkensohn, Aug. 10, 1975; 1 child, Andrew. BA in Econs., U. Rochester, 1971; JD, SUNY, Buffalo, 1974; LLM in Taxation, Georgetown U., 1977. Bar: N.Y. 1975, D.C. 1976, U.S. Tax Ct. 1982, U.S. Ct. Appeals (fed. cir.) 1983. Atty.-advisor Office of Chief Counsel, IRS, Washington, 1974-79; tax counsel com. on fin. U.S. Senate, Washington, 1979-81; assoc. firm Thelen Reid & Priest LLP, Washington, 1981-86, ptnr., 1986—. Mem. Partnership Coun., 2001—. Vol. Income Tax Assistance, Arlington, Va., 1977-81; treas. Overlook Townhouse Homeowhers Assn., Arlington. Mem. ABA (mem. tax sect. 1982—, vice chmn. regulated utilities com. 1988-90, chmn. 1990-92), N.Y. State Bar Assn. Utilities, public, Corporate taxation, Personal income taxation. Office: Thelen Reid & Priest LLP 701 Pennsylvania Ave NW Ste 800 Washington DC 20004-2608 E-mail: djacobson@thelenreid.com.

JACOBSON, EDWARD (JULIAN EDWARD JACOBSON), lawyer; b. Chgo., Mar. 18, 1922; s. Lewis Frederick and Pearl (Hoffman) J. BA magna cum laude, Carleton Coll., 1942; Baker Scholar with Distinction, Harvard Bus. Sch., 1943; JD with honors, U. Ariz., 1946; DHL (hon.), Carleton Coll., 1994, Ariz. State U., 1995. Bar: Ariz. 1947, U.S. Dist. Ct. Ariz. 1947, U.S. Ct. Appeals (9th cir.) 1956, U.S. Supreme Ct. 1963. Law clk. to presiding justice Ariz. Supreme Ct., Phoenix, 1947-48; asst. atty. gen. Ariz. Atty. Gen.'s Office, Phoenix, 1948-50; ptnr. Snell and Wilmer, Phoenix, 1950-89, of counsel, 1990—. Author: The Art of Turned Wood Bowls, 1985. Pres. Civic Ctr. Mgmt. Bd., 1960-90, Phoenix Art Mus., 1974-76, Heard Mus., 1962-64, Phoenix Cmty. Coun., 1960-62, Family Svc. Phoenix; mem. Ariz. Commn. on Arts, 1979-88; bd. visitors Coll. Law U. Ariz., Tucson, 1978-80. Recipient Man of Yr. award Phoenix Advt. Club, 1974, Disting. Achievement award Ariz. State U. Law Sch., 1976, Disting. Achievement award Ariz. State U. Coll. Fine Arts, 1982, Gov.'s Arts award State of Ariz., 1983, Centennial Presdl. medal Ariz. State U., 1985, Visionary award Valley Leadership Alumni Assn., 1990, Historymaker award The Hist. League of Ariz. Hist. Soc., 1993. Fellow Ariz. Bar Found. (founding bd. mem. 1980, Walter E. Craig award 1995); mem. ABA, Ariz. Bar Assn., Maricopa County Bar Assn., Law Soc. Ariz. State U. (pres. 1974-75), Am. Judicare Soc., University Club, Phoenix Country Club. Home: 2201 N Central Ave Phoenix AZ 85004-1417 Office: Snell & Wilmer One Arizona Ctr Phoenix AZ 85004-0001 E-mail: bjacobson@swlaw.com.

JACOBSON, JEFFREY E. lawyer, consultant; b. N.Y.C., Aug. 19, 1956; s. Murray and Adele (Ebert) J.; m. Linda Moel, Aug. 11, 1984; children: Justin Myles, Sari Amanda. BA, Fordham U., 1976; JD, N.Y. Law Sch., 1980. Bar: N.Y. 1982, D.C. 1982, U.S. Tax Ct. 1982, U.S. Ct. Internat. Trade 1982, U.S. Dist. Ct. (so. and ea. dists.) N.Y. 1982, U.S. Ct. Appeals (2nd cir.) 1988, U.S. Supreme Ct. 1988. Assoc. SESAC, Inc., N.Y.C., 1980-82; sole practice N.Y.C. and D.C., 1982-85; sr. ptnr. Jacobson & Colfin, P.C., N.Y.C., Washington, L.I., 1985-90, mng. mem., 1991—; exec. v.p., sec. Fifth Ave. Media, Ltd., N.Y.C., 1995—; assoc. prof. Five Towns Coll., N.Y., 1999—. Asst. mgr. Embassy Theatre, N.Y.C., 1975, Victoria Theatre, N.Y.C., 1975; asst. Theatre Confections, Inc., N.Y.C., 1975; mgr. Criterion Theatre, N.Y.C., 1976; mgr., sec. Squirrels Prodns. Ltd., N.Y.C., 1976-88; pres. Aldous Demian Prodns., Ltd., N.Y.C., 1980-82; counsel Box Office Media, N.Y.C., 1982-88, Eggink, N.Y.C., 1982-89, Performance Records, 1988-97, J&J Mus. Enterprises, Ltd., 1982-95,, Anamaze Records, 1982-95, Cynthia Entertainment Group, Ltd., 1989-91, Roir Records, Inc., 1992—, Super Bubble Music Corp., 1992-99, Sergei Artemiev Benefit, 1993, New Riders of the Purple Sage, 1985—, Mick Taylor Music, 1985—, Best Film and Video Corp., 1988-91, Marty Balin, 1988—, Dope Bros. Records, 2001—, Vega Records, Inc., 2003—, Andrew Tosh, 1990—; spkr. CMJ Music Marathon & Musicfest, 1995, Phila. Music Confs., 1993, 94, 95, 96, 97. Mem. editl. bd. Mealey's Intellectual Property Litigation Law Report, 1992-93; contbr. articles to profl. jours.; music and internat. promotion mgmt., 1984-85; columnist IMPS Jour., 1990-95; featured columnist Replication News Medialine, 1998-2002. Mem. Rep. candidate assembly; v.p. Pelham Pkwy., 1983-88; speaker Songwriter's Guild, N.Y.C., 1983-88, NARAS, 1991; entertainment arbitrator Am. Arbitration Assn., N.Y.C., 1984-95; guest speaker Ctr. for Media Arts, N.Y.C., 1985, Fordham U., N.Y.C., 1986, N.Y. Law Sch., 1987, Detroit Sch. Law, 1991, 93; counsel Pelham Pkwy. Block Assn., Inc., 1991; panelist Mid-Am. Music Conf., Detroit, 1993, Black Radio Exclusive, Econs. of Music, 1993; league lawyer Hewlett-Woodmere Little League, 1994-2000; mem. planning bd. Inc. Village of Hewlett Harbor, 2001-02. Recipient Eagle Scout with Silver Palm award Boy Scouts Am., 1972, Cert. of Merit Bronx House, 1973, Nathan Burkan award ASCAP, 1980, Plaque of Appreciation, Am. Arbitration Assn., 1985; named Most Admired Men and Women of Yr., 1993, Two Thousand Notable Am. Men, 1993, Man of Yr., 1996. Mem. ABA (chmn. subcom. on satellites, chmn. subcom. on copyright compliance, chmn. subcom. on copyright renewal, mem. patent trademark, copyright law sect., forum com. on entertainment and sports law sects., mem. spl. com. on corp. practice 1992-97, mem. spl. com. on atty. opinions 1994—, com. on internat. copywright 2002-2003, com. on databases 2002—, mem. spl. com. on internet 1997—, sub. com. on broadcasting and music industry), forum com. on comm. law, young lawyer's divsn., vice chmn. 1992-94, patent, trademark, intellectual property sect. exec. com., 1992-93, media law com., young lawyers divsn., founder Urban Intellectual Property Law seminars 1993-95, dir., 1993-95, mem. com. on atty./client opinions, mem. spl. com. Internet usage, mem. internat. trademark treaties & laws com. 2002—, mem. ethics and profl. responsibility com.), Assn. Bar City N.Y. (entertainment law com. 1992-95, 2001—, trademark law com. 1997-2000), Copyright Soc. USA (com. on Bicentennial of copyright, mem. editl. bd. Jour. of Copyright Soc. 1991-93, 97—, trustee 2001—, exec. com. 2002—, co-chmn. website com. 2002—), Nat. Acad. Rec. Arts and Scis. (edn. com., columnist N.Y. chpt. newsletter 1997-2000), Rock and Roll Hall of Fame and Mus. (founding mem.), Internat. Assn. Entertainment Lawyers, B'nai B'rith (v.p. 1988-91), Order of the Arrow Brotherhood, Sephardic Jewish Brotherhood Am., Masons (officer 1997-2000, planning bd. Village of Hewlett Harbor 2001—), Audubon Soc. Inc., Phi Delta Phi. Jewish. Avocations: music, photography, swimming, stereo equipment, traveling. Federal civil litigation, Entertainment, Trademark and copyright. Office: Jacobson & Colfin PC 19 W 21st St New York NY 10010-6805 also: 1208 W Broadway Hewlett NY 11557 E-mail: jejesq@aol.com., jeff@thefirm.com.

JACOBSON, JEROLD DENNIS, lawyer; b. N.Y.C., Oct. 12, 1940; s. Sidney and Lillian D. (Fink) J.; m.Gertraude M.J. Holle-Suppa, May 4, 1998; children: Diana, Lisa, Pamela. AB, U. Vt., 1962; JD, Cornell U., 1965; LLM in Labor Law, N.Y. U., 1966. Bar: N.Y. 1966, U.S. Dist. Ct. (so. and ea. dists.) N.Y. 1968, U.S. Dist. Ct. (no. dist.) N.Y. 1981, U.S. Ct. Appeals (2d cir.) 1979, U.S. Ct. Appeals (5th cir.), 1980, U.S. Ct. Appeals (11th cir.) 1981, U.S. Supreme Ct. 1982. Assoc. to gen. counsel ILGWU, AFL-CIO, N.Y.C., 1966-69; assoc. Rains, Rogrebin and Scher, N.Y.C. and Mineola, N.Y., 1969-70, Guggenheimer & Untermyer, N.Y.C., 1970-74, ptnr., 1975-85, Summit, Rovins & Feldsman, N.Y.C., 1986-89, Patterson, Belknap, Webb & Tyler, N.Y.C., 1989-91, Proskauer Rose LLP, N.Y.C., 1991—. Lectr. in labor and employment relations law Practising Law Inst., Am. Soc. Law and Medicine, Profl. Edn. Systems, Inc. Contbr. articles to profl. jours. Bd. dirs. Nassau County chpt. N.Y. State Civil Liberties Union; mem. adv. bd. U. Vt. Holocaust Study Ctr., U. Vt. Coll. Arts and Scis.; bd. dirs. Harlem Day Charter Sch. Mem. ABA, Legal Aid Soc., Am. Arbitration Assn., Am. Acad. Hosp. Attys., N.Y. State Bar Assn. (lectr.). Administrative and regulatory, Health, Labor (including EEOC, Fair Labor Standards Act, labor-management relations, NLRB, OSHA). Office: Proskauer Rose LLP 1585 Broadway Fl 20 New York NY 10036-8299 E-mail: jjacobson@proskauer.com.

JACOBSON, MARIAN SLUTZ, lawyer; b. Cin., Nov. 10, 1945; d. Leonard Doering and Emily Dana (Wells) Slutz; m. Fruman Jacobson, Sept. 21, 1975; 1 child, Lisa Wells. BA cum laude, Ohio Wesleyan U., 1967; JD, U. Chgo., 1972. Bar: Ill. 1972, U.S. Dist. Ct. (no. dist.) Ill. 1972, U.S. Ct. Appeals (7th cir.) 1973. Assoc. Sonnenschein Nath & Rosenthal, Chgo., 1972-79, ptnr., 1979—. Vis. com. U. Chgo. Law Sch., 1992-94. Mem. ABA, Chgo. Coun. Lawyers. Corporate, general. Office: Sonnenschein Nath & Rosenthal 233 S Wacker Dr Ste 8000 Chicago IL 60606-6491 E-mail: msj@sonnenschein.com.

JACOBSON, RICHARD JOSEPH, lawyer; b. Ft. Benning, Ga., July 12, 1943; s. Harold Gordon and Ruth Fern (Enenstein) J.; m. Judy Josephine Dunbar, Sept. 17, 1966; 1 child, David Dunbar. AB, Harvard U., 1965, PhD, 1970; JD, U. Va., 1977. Bar: Ill. 1977, Va. 1977, D.C. 1979, U.S. Dist. Ct. (no. dist.) 1977, U.S. Ct. Appeals (7th cir.) 1991. Asst. prof. English U. Va., Charlottesville, 1970-74; assoc. Keck, Mahin & Cate, Chgo., 1977-83, ptnr., 1984-96; prin. Flaherty & Jacobson, P.C., Chgo., 1996—. Author: Hawthorne's Conception of the Creative Process, 1965; contbr. articles to profl. jours. Pres. North Park Condominium assn., Chgo., 1978-80. Woodrow Wilson Nat. fellow, 1965. Mem. Va. State Bar Assn., D.C. Bar Assn., Chgo. Bar Assn. (chmn. com. preventing atty. malpractice 2000-2001), Assn. Profl. Responsibility Lawyers, Cliff Dwellers Club, Lawyers Club Chgo., Chgo. Literary Club. General civil litigation, Construction, Insurance. Home: 850 W Adams St Apt 3D Chicago IL 60607-3088 Office: Flaherty & Jacobson PC 134 N Lasalle St Ste 1600 Chicago IL 60602-1108 E-mail: rjacobson@fljlaw.com.

JACOBSON, RONALD H. lawyer; b. Chgo., July 23, 1963; BA, U. Ill., 1985; JD, Loyola U., Chgo., 1988; M in Mgmt., Northwestern U., 1990. Bar: Ill. 1988. Assoc. Winston & Strawn, Chgo., 1990-96, ptnr., 1997—. Mem. Winston & Strawn Assoc. Evaluation Com., Winston and Strawn Billings and Collections Com. Mem. ABA (bus. law sect.), Comml. Fin. Assn. (founders' leadership coun.), Loan Syndications and Trading Assn. Banking, Commercial, contracts (including sales of goods; commercial financing), Finance. Office: Winston & Strawn 35 W Wacker Dr Chicago IL 60601-1695

JACOBSON, SANDRA W. lawyer; b. Bklyn., Feb. 1, 1930; d. Elias and Anna (Goldstein) Weinstein; m. Irving Jacobson, July 31, 1955; 1 child, Bonnie Nancy. BA, Vassar Coll., 1951; LLB, Yale U., 1954. Bar: N.Y. 1955, U.S. Supreme Ct. 1960, U.S. Dist. Ct. (so., ea. dists.) N.Y. 1972, U.S. Ct. Appeals (2nd cir.) 1975. Ptnr. Mulligan, Jacobson & Langenus, N.Y.C., 1964-88, Hall, McNicol, Hamilton & Clark, N.Y.C., 1988-92; sole practitioner N.Y.C., 1992—2003; atty. NY Sisters Place Legal Counsel Ctr., 2003—. Lectr. in family law. Contbr. articles to profl. jours. and chpts. to books. Mem.: ABA (family law sect.), Internat. Acad. Matrimonial Lawyers, Westchester Women's Bar Assn., Ind. Jud. Screening Panel, Com. to Improve Availability of Legal Svcs., Am. Acad. Matrimonial Lawyers (bd. mgrs. N.Y. chpt. 1987—89, 1991—93, chair lawyer specialization com. 1999—2000, bd. mgrs. N.Y. chpt., 1995-98, 2000-2002, v.p., 1998-2000, 2002-), Westchester County Bar Assn., Assn. of Bar of City of N.Y. (com. women in the cts. 1986—96, sec. 1987—90, state cts. of superior juridiction 1987—90, women in the profession 1989—92, chair 1990—93, chmn. 1990—93, judiciary 1995—99, family law 1999—2000, com. matrimonial law, 1984-87, 2001-, chmn. 1990-98), Women's Bar Assn. of State of N.Y. (chair cts. com. 1987—88, CLE com. 1998—99, by-laws 1999—2001, co-chair amicus com. 2002—, matrimonial com., co-chmn. 1987-89, co-chair task force on ct. reogrn.), N.Y. Women's Bar Assn. (matrimonial and family law com. 1984—2000, chmn. 1986—88, jud. screening com. 1987—88, pres. 1989—90, ethics commn. 1990—), N.Y. State Bar Assn. (co-chair lawyer specialization 1999—, family law sect., legis. and exec. com.), Phi Beta Kappa. State civil litigation, Family and matrimonial. Office: NY Sisters Place 2 Lyon Pl Ste 300 White Plains NY 10601

JACOBUS, CHARLES JOSEPH, lawyer, title company executive, writer; b. Ponca City, Okla., Aug. 21, 1947; s. David William and Louise Graham (Johnson) J.; m. Heather Jeanne Jones, June 6, 1970; children: Mary Helen, Charles J. Jr. BS, U. Houston, 1970, JD, 1973. Bar: Tex. 1973; cert. specialist residential and commerical real estate law Tex. Bd. Legal Specialization. Pvt. practice, Houston, 1973-75; staff counsel Tenneco Realty, Inc., Houston, 1975-78, v.p., gen. counsel, 1979—83; chief legal counsel Speedy Muffler King, Deerfield, 1978-79; v.p. Commerce Title Co., Houston, 1983-85; sr. v.p. Charter Title Co., Houston, 1986—; ptnr. Jacobus & Melamed PC, Houston, 1988-97; shareholder Jenkens & Gilchrist, Houston, 1998-99; pvt. practice Bellaire, Tex., 1999—. Adv. dir.First Prosperity Bank, Houston; adj. faculty Tex. A&M U., 1986-90; adj. prof. U. Houston Law Ctr., Houston C.C., Champions Sch. Real Estate; instr. advanced real estate law State Bar Tex., course dir., 1990, Tex. Land Title Assn. Sch. Author: Real Estate Law, 2d edit., 1996, Texas Real Estate, 8th edit., 2001; co-author: Mastering Real Estate Titles and Title Insurance in Texas, 1996, Georgia Real Estate, 1995, Ohio Real Estate, 2d edit., 1990, Calif. Real Estate, 1989, Keeping Current with Texas Real Estate, updated annually, Real Estate Principles, 9th edit., 2001, Real Estate, An Introduction to the Profession, 9th edit., 2001, Texas Title Insurance, updated annually, Texas Real Estate Brokerage and the Law of Agency, 2002; co-author: Real Estate Brokerage Law and Practice; editor: Building Blocks of a Commercial Transaction, 1992, Building Blocks of a Residential Real Estate Transaction, 1994, Texas Real Estate Law Deskbook, 1995; editor-in-chief Tex. Forms Manual. Chmn. Planning and Zoning Commn., Bellaire, Tex., 1976-77; bd. dirs. Tax Increment Fin. Dist., Bellaire, 1984-91; chmn. task force on edn. Tex. Real Estate Commn.; chmn. profl. adv. com. dept. urban and regional planning Tex. A&M U., 1988-89; 1st asst. scoutmaster Boy Scout World Jamboree, Holland, 1995, scoutmaster, Chile, 1999; scoutmaster Nat. Boy Scout Jamboree, 1997, 1st asst. scoutmaster, 2001; mayor City of Bellaire, 1998-2000; sec.-treas. Harris County Mayors and Coun. Assn. 1999. Recipient Peggy Hayes Tchg. Excellence award TLTA, 1993, Don Roose award of excellence in real estate edn., 2001. Mem. ABA (acquisitions editor books and pubs. com. 1994-2001, chmn. brokers and brokerage com. 1986-93), Internat. Wine Food Soc. (host Houston chpt. 1993-94), Am. Coll. Real Estate Lawyers, Nat. Assn. Corp. Real Estate Execs. (chpt. v.p.), Am. Land Devel. Assn. (bd. dirs.), Tex. Land Title Assn. (chmn. forms manual com., TREC earnest money contract task force), Tex. Land Title Inst. (chmn. 2001), State Bar Tex. (mem. coun. of real estate, probate and trust law sect. 2002—), Tex. Real Estate Tchrs. Assn. (Outstanding Real Estate Educator 1986), Houston Real Estate Lawyers Coun., Real Estate Educator's Assn. (pres. 1987-88, Real Estate Educator of Yr. 1986, 2000), Houston Bar Assn. (chmn. real estate sect. 1987-88), Bellaire/S.W. Houston C. of C. (Outstanding Businessman of Yr. 1990, chmn. Tex. Real Estate Commns. Edn. Task Force, 1999-2000), U. Tex. Mortgage Lending Inst. (faculty), U. Houston Law Alumni Assn. (bd. dirs.). Universal Order Knights of Vine (master barrister Houston chpt.), Rotary, Les Amis Escoffier. Republican. Roman Catholic. Probate (including wills, trusts), Property, real (including real estate development, water). Home: 5223 Pine St Bellaire TX 77401-4820 Office: Ste 615 6750 West Loop S Bellaire TX 77401-4525 E-mail: chuck@chuckjacobus.com.

JACONETTY, THOMAS ANTHONY, lawyer; b. Chgo., May 21, 1953; s. George Bernard and Mary Jane (Sgarioto) J.; m. Judith Hamill; 1 child, Nicole Alicia. AB in History and Polit. Sci. summa cum laude with honors, Loyola U., Chgo., 1975; JD, Northwestern U., 1978. Bar: Ill. 1978, U.S. Dist. Ct. (no. dist.) Ill. 1978, U.S. Ct. Appeals (7th cir.) 1979; cert. rev. appraiser. Adminstrv. asst. Chgo. Dept. Aviation, 1979; asst. corp. counsel Chgo. Dept. Law, 1980; asst. to commr. Cook County Bd. Tax Appeals, Chgo., 1981-83, dep. commr., 1983-87, commr., 1988-89, chief dep. commr., 1989—; sole practice Chgo. Lectr. Ill. Inst. for Continuing Legal Edn.; lectr. and presenter Lorman Edn. Svcs., Lincoln Inst. Land Policy, Internat. Assn. of Assessing Officers, Chgo. Chpt. of Appraisal Inst. Asst. editor, indexer: Corwin on the Constitution, 1981; author book chpts.; editor, author articles on real estate taxation, assessment adminstrn. and election law, including Assessment Jour., Jour. Property Tax Mgmt.; contbr. Commerce Clearing House State Tax Reports, Ill. Inst. for Continuing Legal Edn. Mem. Cook County Dem. Orgn.; pres., bd. dirs. Polish and Am. Citizens Club, 1981—; pres. Italian Am. Cath. Assn., Chgo., 1981—; mem. Old Timers' Baseball Assn., Art Inst. Chgo., Channel 11-PBS, Mus. Sci. and Industry, Ill. Spl. Olympics, Nat. Trust Hist. Preservation, Libr. of Congress, Ill. Alzheimer's Assn., Civic Fedn. Tax Com.; mem. planning com. Nat. Conf. State Tax Judges, 1999—, chair 2002—. Mem. ABA, Ill. Bar Assn. (mem. assembly 1988-91, 92-94, state and local taxation sect. coun. and several subcoms., chmn. 1994-95, vice chmn. 1993-94, ad hoc and 4 separate civic fedn. coms. on property tax reform, 1994-96, 2000-01), Chgo. Bar Assn. (chmn. election law com.), Internat. Assn. Assessing Officers (arbitrator cir. ct. Cook County, 1990-97, various sects., legal coms., chmn. nat. legal com. 1995-96, 97-98, 99-2000, 2000-01, 2001-02, 2002-03, Donohoo Essay award, 1996), Justinian Soc. Italian Lawyers, Northwestern Law Sch. Alumni Assn., Loyola U. Alumni Assn., Pi Sigma Alpha, Alpha Sigma Nu. Avocations: travel, reading. Family and matrimonial, General practice, State and local taxation. Office: Cook County Bd of Review 118 N Clark St Ste 601 Chicago IL 60602-1311

JAFFE, ALAN STEVEN, lawyer; b. Portland, Maine, Nov. 11, 1939; s. Herman and Rose (Simon) J.; m. Elizabeth L. Reiss, Nov. 3, 1943; children: David, Robert, Richard. BS cum laude, Cornell U., 1961; LLB cum laude, Columbia U., 1964. Bar: N.Y. 1964. Assoc. Poletti, Freiden, Prashker and Gartner, N.Y.C., 1964-65; asst. chief counsel N.Y.C. Anti-Poverty Program, 1965-66; ptnr. Proskauer Rose LLP, N.Y.C., 1966—, chmn., 1999—. Bd. dirs. Lincoln Savs. Bank, N.Y.C., 1984-92. Editor Columbia Law Rev., 1962-64. Bd. dirs., v.p. Coun. Jewish Fedns. N.Am., N.Y.C., 1992-99, Jewish Cmty. Rels. Coun., N.Y., 1987-91; bd. dirs., mem. exec. com. Beth Israel Med. Ctr., 1995—, Am. Jewish Joint Distbn. Com., 1991—; bd. govs. Jewish Agy. for Israel, 1999-2001; pres. Altro Health and Rehab. Svcs., Inc., N.Y.C., 1983-86, pres. UJA Fedn. of N.Y., 1992-95, bd. dirs. 1980—, chmn. bd. domestic affairs, 1988-91; bd. dirs. N.Y.C. Coalition for Homeless, 1995-98; mem. N.Y.C. Sports Devel. Corp., 1995-98; bd. dirs. Am. Jewish Com., 2002—, chmn. Nat. Legal Com., 2002—. Office: Proskauer Rose LLP 1585 Broadway Fl 27 New York NY 10036-8299

JAFFE, F. FILMORE, lawyer, retired judge; b. Chgo., May 4, 1918; s. Jacob Isadore and Goldie (Rabinowitz) J.; m. Mary Main, Nov. 7, 1942; children: Jo Anne, Jay. Student, Southwestern U., 1936-39; JD, Pacific Coast U., 1940. Bar: Calif. 1945, U.S. Supreme Ct. 1964. Practiced law, Los Angeles, 1945-91; ptnr. Bernard & Jaffe, Los Angeles, 1947-74, Jaffe & Jaffe, Los Angeles, 1975-91; apptd. referee Superior Ct. of Los Angeles County, 1991-97, apptd. judge pro tem, 1991-97; ret., 1997; atty. in pvt. practice, 1997—. Mem. L.A. Traffic Commn., 1947-48; arbitrator Am. Arbitration Assn., 1968-91; chmn. pro bono com. Superior Ct. Calif., County of Los Angeles, 1980-86; lectr. on paternity; chair family law indigent paternity panel L.A. County Supr. Ct., 2001—. Served to capt. inf. AUS, 1942-45. Decorated Purple Heart, Croix de Guerre with Silver Star, Bronze Star with oak leaf cluster; honored Human Rights Commn. Los Angeles, Los Angeles County Bd. Suprs.; recipient Pro Bono award State Bar Calif., commendation State Bar Calif., 1983. Mem. ABA, Los Angeles County Bar (honored by family law sect. 1983), Los Angeles Criminal Ct. Bar Assn. (charter mem.), U.S. Supreme Ct. Bar Assn., Masons, Shriners State civil litigation, Family and matrimonial, General practice. Office: 433 N Camden Dr Ste 400 Beverly Hills CA 90210-4408 E-mail: filmorejaffe@earthlink.net.

JAFFE, MARK M. lawyer; b. Paterson, N.J., Sept. 18, 1941; s. Irving and Bertha (Margolis) J.; m. June A. Fisher, June 19, 1977. BS in Econs., U. Pa., 1962; JD, Columbia U., 1985. Bar: N.J. 1965, La. 1968, N.Y. 1970, U.S. Dist. Ct. (ea. dist.) N.Y., U.S. Ct. Mil. Appeals, U.S. Ct. Appeals (2d and 5th cirs.), U.S. Dist. Ct. N.J., U.S. Supreme Ct. Assoc. Hill, Betts & Nash, LLP, N.Y.C., 1969-72; ptnr. Hill, Betts & Nash, N.Y.C., 1972—. Lt. USCGR, 1965-68. Mem. ABA, N.J. Bar Assn., La. Bar Assn., Assn. of Bar of City of N.Y., Am. Judicature Soc., Maritime Law Soc. Admiralty, General civil litigation, Corporate, general. Home: 377 Rector Pl New York NY 10280-1432 Office: Hill Betts & Nash 99 Park Ave New York NY 10016

JAFFE, RICHARD S. lawyer; b. N.Y.C., N.Y., Apr. 14, 1968; s. Stanley Robert and Myra Jacqueline Jaffe; m. Lainie Joy Jaffe, Aug. 4, 2002. BA, SUNY, Binghamton, 1990; JD, Touro Coll., Huntington, N.Y., 1994. Bar: N.Y. 1995, N.J. 1995, D.C. 1995, U.S. Dist. Ct. (so. dist.) NY 1995, U.S. Dist. Ct. (ea. dist.) NY 1995. Assoc. atty. Law Office of Stephen M. Cohen, Lake Success, NY, 1995—98, ptnr., 1998—, Cohen & Jaffe, Esquire, 2003—. Arbitrator Small Claims Ct., Bronx, 2000—. Mem.: ATLA, Nassau County Bar Assn., NY State Trial Lawyers Assn., NY State Bar Assn., Trial Lawyers Care, Inns Of Ct. Personal injury (including property damage), Toxic tort, Insurance. Office: Law Office of Stephen M Cohen 2001 Marcus Ave New Hyde Park NY 11042 Office Fax: 516-358-6903.

JAGLOM, ANDRE RICHARD, lawyer; b. N.Y.C., Dec. 23, 1953; s. Jacob and Irene (Moore) J.; m. Janet R. Stampfl, Apr. 12, 1980; children: Peter Stampfl Jaglom, Wendy Stampfl Jaglom. BS in Mgmt., BS in Physics, MIT, 1974; JD, Harvard U., 1977. Bar: N.Y. 1978, U.S. Dist. Ct. (so. and ea. dists.) N.Y. 1978, U.S. Supreme Ct. 1982, U.S. Ct. Appeals (2d cir.) 1987. Assoc. Paul, Weiss, Rifkind, Wharton & Garrison, N.Y.C., 1977-84; mng. ptnr. Stecher Jaglom & Prutzman LLP, N.Y.C., 1984-2000; ptnr. Tannenbaum Helpern Syracuse & Hirschtritt LLP, N.Y.C., 2000—. Bd. dirs. Cmty. Fund of Bronxville, Eastchester and Tuckahoe, Inc., 1988-94. Computer mktg. and distbn. editor Computer Law Reporter, 1984-90; Am. Law Inst. ABA course of study on product distbn. and mktg., mem. faculty 1983—, chmn., 1987—; contbr. article to law jours.; contbr chpt. to Legal Checklists, 1988—. Trustee bd. edn. Bronxville Union Free Sch. Dist., 1997-2001. Mem. NY State Bar Assn., Bar Assn. City N.Y. (computer law com. 1986-89, sec. 1990-94, com. on tech. and practice of law 1993-96), Am. Inst. Wine and Food (bd. dirs. N.Y. chpt. 1991-99, treas. 1992-99, adv. bd. 2000—). Computer, Trademark and copyright, Distribution and Marketing Law. Office: 900 3d Ave New York NY 10022-4728

JAGMETTI, MARCO, lawyer, judge; b. Zurich, Switzerland, July 16, 1935; s. Riccardo James and Anna Marie Esther (Hürlimann) J.; m. Corinne Jagmetti-Giacometti, 1973; children: Luca, Flavia. Lic. law, U. Zurich, 1958, Dr.iur., 1961; diploma, Acad. Internat. Law, The Hague, 1961; M in Comparative Law, U. Mich., 1965. Bar: Canton of Zurich, 1963. Clk. Dist. Ct. of Zurich, 1961-63; from assoc. to sr. ptnr. Lenz & Staehelin, Zurich, 1965—. Tchr. Law Sch. U. Zurich, 1978-86; aux. judge Supreme Ct. of the State of Zurich, 1983, elected judge, 1988, pres. 1997-2002; chmn. bd. dirs. Banca Commerciale Italiana (Suisse), Zurich, 1983—. Mem. Internat. Bar Assn. (past co-chmn. banking com.), Rotary Club (Zurich). Liberal/Conservative. Avocations: cultural activities, golf, tennis. Home: Kurfirstenstr 61 8002 Zurich Switzerland Office: Lenz & Staehelin Bleicherweg 58 8027 Zurich Switzerland

JAHNS, JEFFREY, lawyer; b. Chgo., July 6, 1946; s. Maxim G. and Josephine Barbara (Czernek) J.; m. Jill Metcoff, Sept. 8, 1973; children: Anna Hope, Claire Martine, Elizabeth Grace. AB, Villanova U., 1968; JD, U. Chgo., 1971. Bar: Ill. 1971, U.S. Dist. Ct. (no. dist.) Ill. 1971, U.S. Ct. Appeals (7th cir.) 1973, U.S. Supreme Ct. 1974. Assoc. Roan & Grossman, Chgo., 1971-77, ptnr., 1977-81, Seyfarth Shaw, Chgo., 1981—. Mem. tax mgmt. adv. bd. Bur. Nat. Affairs, Washington, 1981--. Co-author: Corporate Acquisition Debt Interest Deduction, 1973; contbr. numerous articles to legal publs., chpts. to books. Trustee, chmn. Chgo. Architecture Found., 1982—; bd. dirs. Prairie Ave. House Mus., 1995-98; trustee, treas. Graham

Found., 1998—. Ctr. for Urban Studies fellow U. Chgo., 1969-71. Mem. ABA, Chgo. Bar Assn. (chmn. various coms.), Internat. Coun. Shopping Ctrs., Mid-Day Club, Econ. Club Chgo., Lambda Alpha. Construction, Land use and zoning (including planning), Property, real (including real estate development, water). Office: Seyfarth Shaw 55 E Monroe St Ste 4200 Chicago IL 60603-5863

JAKUBOWICZ, ROBERT F. lawyer; b. Providence, June 24, 1932; s. Stephen and Josephine Jakubowicz; m. Sylvia Jakubowicz, May 13, 1961; children: Peter, Caroline Nelson, Susan, Maryann Carroll. AB, Northeastern U., Boston, 1955; JD, Boston Coll., 1960. Bar: Mass. 61. Spl. agt. FBI, Chgo., 1961—62; pvt. practice Pittsfield, 1962—; staff atty. Union Fed. S&L Assn., Pittsfield, Mass.; city councilman City of Pittsfield, 1972—80; asst. dist. atty. Berkshire County, Mass., county commr., 1980—83; state rep. Mass. Legis., Pittsfield. Adj. prof. Williams Coll., Williamstown, Mass., 1997, 99, 2000, 01, Mass. Coll. Liberal Arts, Adams, Mass., 1996; columnist Berkshire Eagle, 1991—, Cape Code Times, 1991—. Bd. dirs. Friends of Berkshire Libr., Pittsfield, Mass., 1999—2002, BCAC, 1998—99. With U.S. Army, 1955—57. Recipient Human Svc. Providers award, Mass. Human Svc. Providers, 1990. Democrat. Avocations: swimming, cross country skiing. Mailing: 88 Northumberland Rd Pittsfield MA 01201 Office: 25 Bartlett Ave Pittsfield MA 01201

JALIL, JAMES PAUL, lawyer; b. N.Y.C., July 4, 1948; s. C. Jacob and Susana (Burbano) Jalil; m. Jane Pennotti, Sept. 9, 1972; children: Catherine, Jane. AB in Econs., Holy Cross Coll., 1970; JD, Columbia U., 1973. Assoc. Cahill Gordon & Reindel, N.Y.C., 1973—81; ptnr. Lane & Mittendorf, N.Y.C., 1981—92, Shustak, Jalil & Heller, N.Y.C., 1992—. Mem.: ABA, N.Y. State Bar Assn. (com. on securities regulation 1985—92), Ecuadorian-Am. Assn. Democrat. Roman Catholic. Corporate, general, Private international, Securities. Home: 25 Fawn Hill Ct Ramsey NJ 07446-1735

JALLINS, RICHARD DAVID, lawyer; b. L.A., Mar. 21, 1957; s. Walter Joshua and Elaine Beatrice (Youngerman) J.; m. Katherine Sue Pfeiffer, June 12, 1982; children: Stephen David, Rachel Marie. BA, U. Calif., Santa Barbara, 1978; JD, Calif. Western Sch. Law, 1981. Bar: Calif. 1988, U.S. Dist. Ct. (so. dist.) Calif. 1988. Panel atty. Bd. Prison Terms, Sacramento, 1989-96, Appellate Defenders, Inc., San Diego, 1989-91, Calif. Dept. Corrections, Parole Hearings Divsn., Sacramento, 1992-94; dep. commr. Bd. Prison Terms, 1996—2001, assoc. chief dep. commr., 2001—. Mem. ABA, Orange County Bar Assn., Phi Alpha Delta.

JAMAR, STEVEN DWIGHT, law educator; b. Ishpeming, Mich., May 11, 1953; s. Dwight W. and Lorraine (Persgard) J.; m. Shelley June Von Hagen-Jamar, May 19, 1979; children: Alexander S., Eric D. BA, Carleton Coll., 1975; JD cum laude, Hamline U., 1979; LLM with distinction, Georgetown U., 1994. Bar: Minn. 1979, D.C. 1993, U.S. Supreme Ct. 1985. Jud. clk. Minn. Supreme Ct., St. Paul, 1979-80; pvt. practice law Minn., 1980—89; prof. law U. Balt., 1989-90; prof. Sch. Law Howard U., Washington, 1990—, dir. legal rsch. and writing program, 1990—2002. Cons. on Environ. Legal Info. Sys. project NASA, 1998-2002; cons. on Global Legal Info. Network to Law Libr. of Congress, 1999—. Co-author: Essential Lawyering Skills: Interviewing, Counseling, Negotiation, and Persuasive Fact Analysis, 1999; contbr. articles to profl. jours. Rsch. fellow Law Libr. Congress, 2000-01. Mem. ABA, ACLU, Legal Writing Inst. (pres. 1997-98), Am. Soc. Internat. Law, Amnesty Internat., Assn. Legal Writing Dirs., Sierra Club. Avocations: canoe camping, soccer, go, photography, guitar. Office: Howard U Sch Law 2900 Van Ness St NW Washington DC 20008-1106

JAMES, CHARLES ALBERT, lawyer; b. Newark, May 2, 1954; s. Charles Albert and Mary Letitia (Baskerville) J.; 1 child, Kathryn E. BA, Wesleyan U., Middletown, Conn., 1976; JD, George Washington U., Washington, 1979. Bar: D.C. 1979. Atty. FTC, Washington, 1979—85; assoc./ptnr. Jones, Day, Reavis & Pogue, Washington, 1986—91; acting asst. atty. gen. U.S. Dept. Justice, Washington, 1991—93; dep. asst. atty. gen. Dept. Justice, Washington, 1991; assoc./ptnr. Jones, Day, Reavis & Pogue, Washington, 1993—2001; asst. atty. gen. Antitrust Divsn. U.S. Dept. Justice, Washington, 2001—02; v.p. & gen. coun. Chevron Texaco, San Ramon, Calif., 2002—. Recipient Chmn.'s award FTC, 1985, Edmund Randolph award Dept. Justice, 1992. Mem. ABA (sect. of bus. law chmn. com. 1999), Fed. Bar Assn. (chmn. antitrust com. 1990), U.S. C. of C. (mem. antitrust coun. 1993—), Psi Upsilon. Republican. Office: Office Gen Coun Chevron Texaco Corp 6001 Bollinger Canyon Rd San Ramon CA 94583*

JAMES, GORDON, III, lawyer; b. Montclair, N.J., Feb. 24, 1947; s. Ernest Gordon Jr. and Betty (Wackerman) J.; m. Adelia Louise Medlin (div. Sept. 1989); children: Deidre Leigh, Diana Catherine, Gordon Daniel; m. Yolanda Trapana. BS, U. Tenn., 1969; JD, Vanderbilt U., 1972. Bar: Fla. 1972, U.S. Dist. Ct. (so. dist.) Fla. 1972, D.C. 1973, U.S. Ct. Appeals (11th cir.) 1980, U.S. Dist. Ct. (mid. dist.) Fla. 1985, U.S. Dist. Ct. (no. dist.) Fla. 1986, U.S. Supreme Ct. 1988. Assoc. Bradford, Williams, Kimbrell, et al, Miami, Fla., 1972-76; ptnr. Druck, Grimmett, Norman, Weaver, Scherer, Ft. Lauderdale, Fla., 1976-77, Druck, Grimmett, Scherer, James, Ft. Lauderdale, 1977-78, Grimmett, Scherer, James, Ft. Lauderdale, 1978-79, Conrad, Scherer, James & Jenne, Ft. Lauderdale, 1979-95, Heinrich Gordon Hargrove Weihe & James, Ft. Lauderdale, 1995—. Eucharistic lay minister, All Saints Episcopal Ch., 1991—; Gueardian Ad Llet Program Broward County, 1995-. Capt. USAR, 1969-77. Mem. ABA, Fla. Bar Assn. (vice chmn. civil rule of procedure com. 1990-91), Nat. Assn. R.R. Counsel, Am. Bd. Trial Advs. (cert., Ft. Lauderdale chpt. pres. 1998), Def. Rsch. Inst., Fla. Def. Lawyers (pres. 1991-92). Republican. Avocations: fishing, snow skiing, scuba diving, physical and aerobics exercise. General civil litigation, Personal injury (including property damage), Product liability. Office: Heinrich Gordon Hargrove Weihe & James 500 E Broward Blvd Fort Lauderdale FL 33394-3000 E-mail: jamesiii@heinrichgordon.com.

JAMES, MICHAEL ANDREW, lawyer; b. Indpls., June 8, 1953; s. Joseph Schell and Dorothy Agnes (Meth) J. BA, U. Va., 1975; JD, Yale U., 1978. Bar: N.Y. 1979. Assoc. Chadbourne & Parke, N.Y.C., 1978-80; assoc. Zimet, Haines, Friedman & Kaplan, N.Y.C., 1980-85, ptnr., 1986-95. Vol. gen. counsel People with AIDS Coalition N.Y., 1991-95. Mem. ABA, Phi Beta Kappa. Democrat. Roman Catholic. Corporate, general, Mergers and acquisitions, Securities.

JAMES, PAUL M. lawyer; b. Providence, Aug. 16, 1963; s. Anita James; m. Rita S. Speziale, Nov. 4, 1988; children: Andrea Katherine, Meghan Elizabeth. BA, Providence Coll.; JD, Boston U., 1988. Bar: Mass. 1988, U.S. Dist. Ct. Mass. 1988. Ptnr. Holland & Knight LLP, Boston, 1988—. Mem.: ABA (Forum on the Constrn. Industry), Boston Bar Assn. (co-chmn. constrn. law com. of real estate sect. 2002—). Construction. Office: Holland & Knight LLP 10 St James Ave Boston MA 02116 Office Fax: 617-523-6850. E-mail: pjames@hklaw.com.

JAMIN, MATTHEW DANIEL, lawyer, magistrate judge; b. New Brunswick, N.J., Nov. 29, 1947; s. Matthew Bernard and Frances Marie (Newburg) J.; m. Christine Frances Bjorkman, June 28, 1969; children: Rebecca, Erica. BA, Colgate U., 1969; JD, Harvard U., 1974. Bar: Alaska 1974, U.S. Dist. Ct. Alaska 1974, U.S. Ct. Appeals (9th cir.) 1980. Staff atty. Alaska Legal Svcs., Anchorage, 1974-75, supervising atty. Kodiak, Alaska, 1975-81; contract atty. Pub. Defender's Office State of Alaska, Kodiak, 1976-82; prin. Matthew D. Jamin, Atty., Kodiak, 1982; ptnr. Jamin & Bolger, Kodiak, 1982-85, Jamin, Ebell, Bolger & Gentry, Kodiak, 1985-97; part-time magistrate judge U.S. Cts., Kodiak, 1984—; shareholder Jamin, Ebell, Schmitt & Mason, Kodiak, 1998—. Part-time instr. U. Alaska Kodiak Coll., 1975—; active Theshold Svcs., Inc., Kodiak, 1985—, pres., 1985-92, 95-96, 99-2000. Mem. Alaska Bar Assn. (Professionalism award 1988), Kodiak Bar Assn. General civil litigation, Family and matrimonial, Probate (including wills, trusts). Office: US Dist Ct 323 Carolyn Ave Kodiak AK 99615-6348 E-mail: matt@jesmkod.com.

JAMISON, DANIEL OLIVER, lawyer; b. Fresno, Calif., Nov. 28, 1952; s. Oliver Morton and Margaret (Ratcliffe) J.; m. Debra Suzanne Parent, May 23, 1981; 1 child, Holly Elizabeth. Student, Claremont Men's Coll., 1970-72; BA in Philosophy, U. Calif., Berkeley, 1974; JD, U. Calif., Davis, 1977. Bar: Calif. 1977, U.S. Dist. Ct. (ea. dist.) Calif. 1977, U.S. Dist. Ct. (no. dist.) Calif. 1982, U.S. Ct. Appeals (9th cir.) 1987. Law clk. to judge M.D. Crocker U.S. Dist. Ct. (ea. dist.) Calif., Fresno, 1977-78; assoc. Stammer, McKnight, Barnum & Bailey, Fresno, 1978-83, ptnr., 1983-95; shareholder Sagaser, Franson, Jamison & Jones (formerly Sagaser, Hansen, Franson & Jamison), 1995—99; pvt. practice Law Offices of Daniel O. Jamison, P.C., Fresno, 1999—. Vol. atty. Calif. H.S., Fresno, 1983-87, 89-94; mem. Assocs. of Valley Children's Hosp., Fresno, 1980-81; co-chmn. Fresno County Law Day, 1995-96; panelist for CEB Selected Issues in Employment Discrimination and Wrongful Discharge Litigation; panelist on indigent care Calif. Soc. for Healthcare Attys.; panelist Lorman Edn. Svcs. on Health Care Corp. and Physician Compliance Programs in Calif., Pres' Circle, Bulldog Found., Quarterback Club, Calif. State U., Fresno; sustaining mem. Fresno Met. Mus., corp. mem. Comty. Med. Found.; mem. Fresno Hist. Soc., Fresno City and County Conv. and Visitor's Bur. Mem. ABA, Fed. Bar Assn., No. Calif. Assn. Def. Counsel, Fresno County Bar Assn. (spkr. to Agrl. sect. on insuring dirs. and officers, bus. law sect. on malpractice risks in failing to address ins. rights), Fresno County C. of C., Calif. C. of C., East Dist. Hist. Soc. (charter mem.), 9th Jud. Cir. Hist. Soc., Calif. Soc. for Healthcare Attys., Am. Health Lawyers Assn. Republican. Avocations: golf, aerobics. General civil litigation, Health, Personal injury (including property damage). Office: 2445 Capitol St Ste 150 Fresno CA 93721-2224 E-mail: dojamison@jamisonpc.com.

JANIGIAN, BRUCE JASPER, lawyer, educator; b. San Francisco, Oct. 21, 1950; s. Michael D. Janigian and Stella (Minasian) Amerian; m. Susan Elizabeth Frye, Oct. 4, 1986; children: Alan Michael, Alison Elizabeth. AB, U. Calif., Berkeley, 1972; JD, U. Calif., San Francisco, 1975; LLM, George Washington U., 1982. Bar: Calif. 1975, U.S. Supreme Ct. 1979, D.C. 1981. Dir. Hastings Rsch. Svcs., Inc., San Francisco, 1973-75; judge adv. in Spain, 1976-78; commr. U.S. Navy and Marine Corps Ct. Mil. Rev., 1978-79; atty. advisor AID U.S. State Dept., Washington, 1979-84; dep. dir., gen. counsel Calif. Employment Devel. Dept., Sacramento, 1984-89; Fulbright scholar, vis. prof. law U. Salzburg, Austria, 1989-90; chmn. Calif. Agrl. Labor Rels. Bd., 1990-95; v.p. Europe, resident dir. Salzburg (Austria) Seminar, 1995-96; U.S. legate European Acad. Scis. and Art, 1996—; Rapporteur, World Economic Forum, 1996; of counsel Weintraub Genshlea Chediak Sproul, Sacramento, 1998—2001; pvt. practice Sacramento, 2001—. Prof. McGeorge Sch. Law, U. Pacific, Sacramento, 1986—, Inst. on Internat. Legal Studies, Salzburg, summer 1987, London Inst. on Comml. Law, summers 1989, 92-93; vis. scholar Hoover Inst. War, Revolution and Peace, Stanford U., 1991-92; dir. Vienna-Budapest East/West Trade Inst., 1993; vis. prof. law U. Salzburg, 1995-96, prof. internat. bus. mgmt., Golden Gate U., 1998—. Editor: Financing International Trade and Development, 1986-87, 89, International Business Transactions, 1989, 92, International Trade Law, 1993-94. Coord. fund raiser March of Dimes, Sacramento, 1987; bd. adv. European-Am. C. of C., 2003, Capt. USNR, JAGC, 1976-79, mem. Res. Fulbright scholar, 1989-90; decorated Meritorious Achievement medal; recipient USAID Meritorious Honor award, Faculty of Yr. award Golden Gate U., 2001. Mem.: Am. Soc. of Internat. Law, Austro-Am. Soc., World Art Forum (v.p. 1996), European Acad. Scis. and Art (U.S. Legate 1996—), Pub. Internat. Law and Policy Group, Anthony M. Kennedy Am. Inn of Ct. (barrister 1998—2001), Sacramento Bar Assn. (exec. com. taxation sect. 1988—89, chair internat. law sect. 1999—2002), D.C. Bar Assn., Calif. Bar Assn., Marine Meml. Assn., Navy League (gen. counsel 1997—), Naval Res. Officers Assn. (life), Knights of Vartan, Sacramento Capitol Club (dir. 1999—2001), Comstock Club (bd. dirs. 1998—99), Sacramento Met. C. of C. (award for program cntbns. and cmty. enrichment 1989), Rotary (chair, internat. found. com. 1999—2002), Fulbright Assoc. (life), Phi Beta Kappa. Avocations: cross-country skiing, tennis, bicycling. Home: 1631 12th Ave Sacramento CA 95818-4146 Office: 400 Capitol Mall Ste 900 Sacramento CA 95814-4407 Business E-Mail: law@janigian.com.

JANKE, RONALD ROBERT, lawyer; b. Milw., Mar. 2, 1947; s. Robert Erwin and Elaine Patricia (Wilken) J.; m. Mary Ann Burg, July 3, 1971; children— Jennifer, William, Emily. B.A. cum laude, Wittenberg U., 1969; J.D. with distinction, Duke U., 1974. Bar: Ohio 1974. Assoc. Jones Day, Cleve., 1974-83, ptnr., 1984—. Served with U.S. Army, 1970-71, Vietnam. Mem. ABA (chmn. environ. control com. 1980-83), Ohio Bar Assn., Greater Cleve. Bar Assn., Environ. Law Inst. Environmental. Office: Jones Day N Point 901 Lakeside Ave E Cleveland OH 44114-1190

JANNEY, DONALD WAYNE, lawyer; b. Clinton, N.C., Jan. 9, 1952; s. Wayne Columbus and Bernice (Talley) J.; m. Sydney Louise Rhame, May 28, 1977; children: Taylor Columbus, Camden St. Clair. BA, Furman U., 1974; JD, U. Va., 1978. Bar: Ga. 1978, U.S. Dist. Ct. (no. dist.) Ga. 1978, U.S. Ct. Appeals (11th cir.) 1982. Assoc. Troutman Sanders, Atlanta, 1978-85; ptnr. Troutman Sanders and predecessor firm, Atlanta, 1985—. Bd. dirs. State YMCA Ga., Atlanta, 1980-91. Mem. ABA, Ga. Bar Assn., Atlanta Bar Assn., Lawyers Club Atlanta, Phi Beta Kappa. Baptist. General civil litigation, Condemnation (eminent domain). Home: 705 E Morningside Dr Atlanta GA 30324-5220 Office: Troutman Sanders Ste 5200 600 Peachtree St NE Atlanta GA 30308-2216 E-mail: donald.janney@troutmansanders.com.

JANNEY, OLIVER JAMES, lawyer, plastics and semiconductor company executive; b. N.Y.C., Feb. 11, 1946; s. Walter Coggeshall and Helen Jennings (James) Janney; m. Suzanne Elizabeth Lenz, June 21, 1969; children: Elizabeth Flower, Oliver Burr. BA cum laude, Yale U., 1967; JD, Harvard U., 1970. Bar: Mass. 1970, N.Y. 1971, Fla. 1991. With Walston & Co., Inc., N.Y.C., 19770-73, asst. v.p., 1971-73; assoc. Cleary Gottlieb, Steen & Hamilton, N.Y.C., 1973-76; with RKO Gen., Inc., N.Y.C., 1976-90, asst. sec., 1977-85, asst. gen. atty., 1978-82, asst. gen. counsel, 1982-85, sec., gen. counsel, 1985-89; exec. v.p., gen. counsel, sec. Uniroyal Tech. Corp., Sarasota, Fla., 1990—. 1st lt. USAR, 1969—77. Mem.: ABA, Assn. Bar of City of N.Y., N.Y. State Bar Assn., Am. Corp. Counsel Assn., Sleepy Hollow Country Club Scarborough. Republican. Corporate, general, Mergers and acquisitions, Securities. Home: 1684 Peregrine Point Dr Sarasota FL 34231-2331 Office: Uniroyal Tech Corp 3401 Cragmont Dr Tampa FL 33619

JANSEN, DONALD ORVILLE, lawyer; b. Odessa, Tex., Nov. 17, 1939; s. Orville Charles and Dolores Elizabeth (Olps) J.; m. E. Janice Law; children: Donald Orville, Lauren, Christine, David, Margaret BBA magna cum laude, Loyola U., New Orleans, 1961, JD cum laude, 1963; LLM, Georgetown U., 1966. Bar: La. 1963, Tex. 1965. Ptnr. Fulbright and Jaworski, Houston, 1966—. Served to capt. JAGC, U.S. Army, 1963-66 Mem. ABA, Fed. Bar Assn. State Bar Tex., La. Bar Assn., Am. Coll. Trust and Estate Counsel Roman Catholic. Estate planning, Pension, profit-sharing, and employee benefits, Probate (including wills, trusts). Home: 5212 Sagesquare St Houston TX 77056-7041 Office: Fulbright & Jaworski 1301 Mckinney St Ste 5100 Houston TX 77010-3031

JANSEN, JAMES STEVEN, lawyer; b. Marshalltown, Iowa, Mar. 16, 1948; s. Virgil Charles and Virginia Rae (Hiatt) J.; m. Patricia Jean Beard, Nov. 24, 1984; children: Katherine, Emily, Ashley, Kristen. BS in Edn., U. Nebr., 1970; JD, Creighton U., 1973. Bar: Nebr. 1974, U.S. Dist. Ct. Nebr. 1974. Dep. county atty. County of Douglas, Omaha, 1974-78, county atty., 1991—; assoc. Naviaux, Kinney, Jansen and Dosek, Omaha, 1979-83; assoc., then ptnr. Stave, Coffey, Swenson, Jansen and Schatz, Omaha, 1984-90. Bd. dirs. Nebr. County Atty.'s Standards Adv. Coun., Lincoln, 1992--. Bd. dirs. Domestic Violence Coord. Coun. Greater Omaha, 1996-- ,co-chair, 1996-97, chmn., 1997-98; bd. dirs. Omaha Community Partnership, 1991—, chmn., 2000-01; mem. Nebr. Drug and Violent Crime Policy Bd., Lincoln, 1991-98, bd. dirs. Project Harmony Child Protection Ctr., 1996—, chmn., 1998. Mem. Nebr. State Bar Assn., Omaha Bar Assn., Nebr. County Atty.'s Assn. (bd. dirs. 1991—, pres. 1997-98), Nat. Dist. Atty.'s Assn. Democrat. Roman Catholic. Avocations: golf, reading. Office: Douglas County Attys Office Rm 100 Hall of Justice Omaha NE 68183

JARBOE, MARK ALAN, lawyer; b. Flint, Mich., Aug. 19, 1951; s. Lloyd Aloysius and Helen Elizabeth (Frey) J.; m. Patricia Kovel, Aug. 20, 1971; 1 child, Alexander. Student, No. Mich. U., 1968-69; AB with high distinction, U. Mich., 1972; JD magna cum laude, Harvard U., 1975. Bar: Minn. 1975, U.S. Dist. Ct. Minn. 1975, U.S. Ct. Appeals (8th cir.) 1975, U.S. Ct. Appeals (7th cir.) 1993. Law clk. to presiding justice Minn. State Ct., St. Paul, 1975-76; from assoc. to ptnr. Dorsey & Whitney LLP, Mpls., 1976-81, ptnr., 1982—. Lectr. U. Minn. Law Sch., Hamline U. Sch. Law. Contbr. articles to profl. jours. Pres. parish coun. Ch. of Christ the King, Mpls., 1981-83. Mem. Fed. Bar Assn., Native Am. Bar Assn., Minn. Am. Indian Bar Assn., Mensa, Phi Beta Kappa. Republican. Roman Catholic. Finance, Native American. Home: 4816 W Lake Harriet Pky Minneapolis MN 55410-1903 Office: Dorsey & Whitney LLP 50 S 6th St Ste 1500 Minneapolis MN 55402-1498 E-mail: jarboe.mark@dorseylaw.com.

JARPE, GEOFFREY PELLAS, lawyer; b. Milw., Aug. 2, 1945; s. Gunnar E. and Laura Johnson (Camp) J.; m. Lezlie J. Myhra, Aug. 10, 1968; children: Nathan M., Rachel K., Joseph S. BA, U. Mich., 1967, JD, 1969. Bar: Minn. 1970, U.S. Dist. Ct. Minn. 1973, U.S. Ct. Appeals (8th cir.), 1973, U.S. Dist. Ct. (ea. dist.) Mich. 1982, U.S. Dist. Ct. (ea. dist.) Wis. 1987, U.S. Claims Ct. 1990, Wis. 1989, U.S. Dist. Ct. (we. dist.) Wis., 1995, U.S. Supreme Ct. 1990; cert. Nat. Bd. Trial Advocacy. Spl. asst atty. gen. State of Minn., St. Paul, 1970-72; assoc. Maun & Simon, St. Paul, 1972-78, ptnr., 1978-2000, Maslon Edelman Borman & Brand, Mpls., 2001—. Mem. ABA, Minn. State Bar Assn. (cert. civil trial specialist, civil litigation sect.), Hennepin County Bar Assn., U. Mich. Club (pres. Twin Cities chpt. 1985-87), Am. Bd. Trial Adv. Lutheran. Federal civil litigation, General civil litigation, State civil litigation. Office: Maslon Edelman Borman & Brand 3300 Wells Fargo Ctr 90 S 7th St Minneapolis MN 55402-4140

JARRETT, ALEXIS, insurance agent, lawyer; b. Independence, Kans., July 2, 1948; d. Robert Patterson and Betty June (Johnson) Jarrett. BS, U. Minn., Duluth, 1970; postgrad., U. Mo., 1974—77; JD, John Marshall Law Sch., 2001. Lic. property and casualty ins. Ind., life and health ins. Ind., cert. Life Underwriting Tng. Coun.; coach Minn. Tchr. Esko (Minn.) Pub. Schs., 1970-74; asst. dir. athletics, head coach basketball, softball, track U. Mo., Columbia, 1974-77; pvt. practice Schererville, Ind., 1984—; pres., CEO INFINITE Sports and Entertainment, Inc., 2002—. Women's basketball and softball color analyst Regional Radio Sports, N.W. Ind., 1992—94; with Moot Ct. Coun., 1999; jud. extern Cir. Ct. Cook County, Chgo., 1999; coord. Women's Sports Info. Dept., U. Mo., 1974—77; v.p. legal affairs Nat. Assn. State Farm Agts., Inc., 1997—2000; contract advisor NFL Players Assn., 2002—, Women's Nat. Basketball Players Assn., 2002—, CFL Players Assn., 2003—. Contbr. articles to newspapers. Sponsor Lake County (Ind.) HS Girls Basketball Banquet, 1989—99; bd. dirs. Samaritan Counseling Ctr. N.W. Ind., pres., 1994; bd. dirs. VNA Found., sec.-treas., 1994; celebrity Am. Heart Assn. Celebrity Dinner; v.p. S.W. Lake divsn. Am. Heart Assn., 1992—94; mem. bd. advisors Basketball Hall of Fame, 1999—; bd. dirs. Boys and Girls Club N.W. Ind.; mem. adv. bd. indsl. rsch. liaison program Ind. U., Bloomington, 1990—96. Recipient Individual with Vision award, Ind. HS Athletic Assn., 1996. Mem.: ABA (entertainment and sports law forum, labor and law com., ins. law com., sports law subcom.), Sports Lawyers Assn., Chgo. Bar Assn. (labor and employment law com., ins. law com., immigration law com., health law com.), Ind. State Med. Assn. Alliance (chair media rels. 1990—91, treas. 1992—93, chair media rels. 1993—94), Am. Bus. Women's Assn. (pres. New Image chpt. 1983, Woman of the Yr. 1983), Lake County Med. Soc. Alliance (pres. 1992—94), Nat. Life Underwriters (bd. dirs. N.W. Ind. chpt. 1995, 1996, 1997). Address: 2330 Wicker Blvd Schererville IN 46375-2810

JARVIS, JAMES HOWARD, II, judge; b. Knoxville, Tenn., Feb. 28, 1937; s. Howard F. and Eleanor B. J.; m. Martha Stapleton, June 1957 (div. Feb. 1962); children: James Howard III, Leslie; m. Pamela K. Duncan, Aug. 23, 1964 (div. Apr. 1991); children: Ann, Kathryn, Louise; m. Gail Stone, Sept. 4, 1992. BA, U. Tenn., 1958, JD, 1960. Bar: Tenn. 1961, U.S. Dist. Ct. (ea. dist.) Tenn. 1961, U.S. Ct. Appeals (6th cir.) 1965. Assoc. O'Neil, Jarvis, Parker & Williamson, Knoxville, Tenn., 1960-68, mem., 1968-70, Meares, Dungan, Jarvis, Knoxville, Tenn., 1970-72; judge Law & Equity Ct., Blount County, Tenn., 1972-77, 30th Jud. Ct., Blount County, Tenn., 1977-84, U.S. Dist. Ct. (ea. dist.) Tenn., Knoxville, 1984—, chief judge, 1991-98. Bd. dirs. Maryville (Tenn.) Coll., 1991-98; mem., past chmn. fin. com. St. Andrews Episc. Ch.; past bd. dirs. Detoxification Rehab. Inst. Knoxville; past mem. com. codes of conduct Jud. Conf. U.S. Mem. Tenn. Bar Assn. (bd. govs. 1983-84), Am. Judicature Soc., Tenn. Trial Judges Assn. (pres. mem. exec. com.), Tenn. Jud. Conf. (pres. 1983-84), Blount County Bar Assn., Knoxville Bar Assn., Great Smoky Mountains Conservation Assn., Phi Delta Phi, Sigma Chi (significant Sigma Chi). Republican. Home: 6916 Stone Mill Rd Knoxville TN 37919-7431 Office: Howard H Baker Jr US Courthouse 800 Market St Knoxville TN 37902-2327

JARVIS, JOHN MANNERS, barrister, judge; b. London, Nov. 20, 1947; s. Donald Manners and Brixie Theodora J.; m. Janet Rona Kitson, May 5, 1972; children: Christopher, Fergus. BA, Emmanuel Coll., Cambridge, Eng., 1969; MA, 1972. Bar: Eng., Wales 1970; apptd. Queens counsel 1989; accredited mediator C.E.D.R. Mem. chambers 3 Verulam Bldgs. Gray's Inn, London, 1970—; asst. recorder, 1987-91; recorder, 1991—; dep. high ct. judge, 1998—; joint head chambers, 1999—. Co-author: Lender Liability, 1993; internat. editor: Jour. Banking and Fin. Law and Practice, 1989—; contbr. author: Banks, Liability and Risk, 2d edit. Gov. King's Coll. Sch., Wimbledon, Eng., 1987—. Mem. Comml. Bar Assn. (treas. 1993-95, chmn. 1995-97), Lincoln's Inn (bencher 1997—). Avocations: horse-riding, tennis, skiing, cycling, sailing. Office: 3 Verulam Bldgs Gray's Inn London WC1R 5NT England Fax: 020 7831 8441. E-mail: jjarvis@3vb.com.

JARVIS, ROBERT GLENN, lawyer; b. San Benito, Tex., Jan. 20, 1938; s. Robert Harral and Helen Aline (Cruse) J.; m. Patricia Joyce Morgan, June ll, 1960; children: Jeffrey, Todd, Tate. BA, Rice U., 1960; JD, U. Tex., 1963. Bar: Tex. 1963, U.S. Dist. Ct. (so. dist.) Tex. 1963, U.S. Ct. Appeals (5th cir.) 1968, U.S. Ct. Appeals (D.C. cir.) 1970, U.S. Supreme Ct. 1975. Assoc. Ewers & Toothaker, McAllen, Tex., 1963-65, ptnr., 1965-85, Jarvis, Schwarz & Kittleman, McAllen, 1985-90; pres. Jarvis & Kittleman, PC, McAllen, 1991-98; pvt. practice McAllen, 1998—. Adv. coun. Tex. Commerce Bank, McAllen, 1981-84; mem., bd. dirs. Internat. Bank McAllen, 1984—. Mem. Watermaster planning adv. com. Tex. Water Commn., Austin, 1987-91; pres. McAllen Ind. Sch. Dist. Bd. Edn., 1979; bd. dirs. McAllen Econ. Devel. Corp., 1987-98; chmn. McAllen Infrastructure Planning Coun., 1989-94; bd. dirs. Tex. Turnpike Authority, 1997-2001; chmn. Tex. Water Devel. Bd., Rio Grande Regional Water Planning Group, 1997—2001. Fellow Tex. Bar Found.; mem. ABA, State Bar Tex. (labor law adv. com. bd. legal specialization 1978-99), Coll. State Bar Tex., Hidalgo County Bar Assn., McAllen C. of C. (bd. dirs. 1987-97, pres. 1995-96), Rio Grande Valley C. of C. (bd. dirs. 1992-95). pres. 1995-96). Administrative and regulatory, Environmental, Property, real (including real estate development, water). Office: PO Box 4828 Mcallen TX 78502-4828

JARVIS, ROBERT MARK, law educator; b. N.Y.C., Oct. 17, 1959; s. Rubin and Ute (Hacklander) J.; m. Judith Anne Mellman, Mar. 3, 1989. BA, Northwestern U., 1980; JD, U. Pa., 1983; LLM, NYU, 1986. Bar: N.Y. 1984, Fla. 1990. Assoc. Haight Gardner Poor & Havens, N.Y.C., 1983-85, Baker & McKenzie, N.Y.C., 1985-87; asst. prof. law ctr. Nova Southeastern U., Ft. Lauderdale, Fla., 1987-90, assoc. prof., 1990-92, prof., 1992—. Chmn. bd. dirs. Miami Maritime Arbitration Bd., 1993-94; vice chmn. bd. dirs. Miami Internat. Arbitration and Mediation Inst., 1993-94; mem. adv. bd. Carolina Acad. Press, 1996—, Sports Law Reporter, 2000—, hospitalitylawyer.com, 2000—. Co-author: AIDS: Cases and Materials, 1989, 3d edit, 2002, AIDS Law in a Nutshell, 1991, 2d edit., 1996, Notary Law and Practice: Cases and Materials, 1997, Travel Law: Cases and Materials, 1998, Sports Law: Cases and Materials, 1999, Art and Museum Law: Cases and Materials, 2002, Gaming Law: Cases and Materials, 2003; author: Careers in Admiralty and Maritime Law, 1993, An Admiralty Law Anthology, 1995; editor: Maritime Arbitration, 1999, Law of Cruise Ships, 2000; co-editor: Prime Time Law: Fictional Television as Legal Narrative, 1998, Bush v. Gore: The Fight for Florida's Vote, 2001; mem. editl. bd. Washington Lawyer, 1988-94, Jour. Maritime Law and Commerce, 1990-92, 2001—, assoc. editor, 1993-95, editor, 1996-2000, Maritime Law Reporter, 1991-99, Hospitality Law, 1999-2001; mem. adv. bd. Transnat. Lawyer, 1991—; mem. adv. bd. World Arbitration and Mediation Report, 1990—, U. San Francisco Maritime Law Jour., 1992-95, 2002—; contbg. editor Preview U.S. Supreme Ct. Cases, 1990-95, 1999-2002. Mem.: ABA (vice chmn. admiralty law com. young lawyers divsn. 1992—93, chair 1993—94), Phi Delta Phi (province pres. 1989—91, coun. 1991—93), Assn. Am. Law Schs. (chmn.-elect maritime law sect. 1991—93, chmn. 1993—94), Maritime Law Assn. U.S., Fla. Bar Assn. (admiralty law com. 1988—95, vice chmn. 1991—92, chmn. 1992—93, exec. coun. internat. law sect. 1992—96), Acacia, Northwestern U. Club South Fla. (v.p. 1992—93, pres. 1993—95), Phi Beta Kappa. Democrat. Jewish. Avocations: theatre, running. Office: Nova Southeastern U Law Ctr 3305 College Ave Fort Lauderdale FL 33314-7721

JASCOURT, HUGH D. lawyer, arbitrator, mediator; b. Phila., Mar. 25, 1935; s. Jacquard A. and Gladys Mae (Bregen) J.; m. Resa B. Zall, Nov. 28, 1963; children: Stephen, Leigh. AB, U. Pa., 1956; JD, Wayne State U., 1960. Bar: Mich. 1961, U.S. Supreme Ct. 1965, D.C. 1967. Atty. advisor U.S. Dept. Labor, Washington, 1960-64; asst. dir. employee-mgmt. rels. Am. Fedn. Govt. Employees, Washington, 1964-65; atty. advisor Nat. Labor Rels. Bd., Washington, 1965-66; exec. dir. Fed. Bar Assn., Washington, 1966-67; house counsel Am. Fedn. of State, County, & Mcpl. Employees, Washington, 1967-69; sr. labor-law counsel Bd. of Gov. Fed. Reserve Bd., Washington, 1969-72; dir. Pub. Employment Rels. Rsch. Inst., Washington, 1972-74; asst. solicitor U.S. Dept. of Interior, Washington, 1974-82; sr. labor-law counsel U.S. Dept. Commerce, Washington, 1982-90; pres. Agency for Dispute Resolutions and Synergistic Rels., Greenbelt, Md., 1991—. Lectr. George Washington U. Law Sch., Washington, 1970—75; chmn. unfair labor practice panel Prince George County Employee Rels. Bd., Upper Marlboro, Md., 1972—83; mem. Greenbelt (Md.) Employee Rels. Bd. , 1977—, chair, 2002—; panel mem. Fed. Mediation and Conciliation Svc., Nat. Mediation Bd., Nat. Assn. Security Dealers, Libr. of Congress, D.C. PERB, Washington, N.J. PERC, N.J. Bd. Mediation, SSA-Am., Fedn. Govt. Employees; arbitrator/mediator, 1973—. Author, editor: Trends in Public Sector Labor Relations, 1973, Government Labor Relations, 1979; author: (with others) Labor Relations, 1978-82; Collective Bargaining, 1980; labor rels. editor Jour. Law and Edn., 1972-2001. Pres. Road Runners Club Am., 1962-66, Prince George's County (Md.) Fedn. of Recreational Couns., 1969, Prince George's County Coun. of PTAs, 1989-90; mem. Prince George's County Cmty. Adv. Coun., 1988—; coach U.S. track and field team AAU So. Games, Trinidad, 1964, Internat. Cross Country Championship, Morocco, 1966; v.p. Am. Running and Fitness Assn., 1968-84. Inductee Road Runners Club Am. Hall of Fame, 1986; initial inductee D.C. Road Runners Club Hall of Fame, 1994; named master ofcl. honoree Penn Relays, 2000. Fellow Coll. of Labor and Employment Lawyers; mem. ABA (com. on state and local labor employment and law, chmn. subcom. 1982—, co-chmn. com. on fed. svc. labor and employment law 1985-97, mem. mediation com., sect. on dispute resolution), ASPA, Soc. Fed. Labor Rels. Profls. (bd. dirs. 1992-93), Assn. for Conflict Resolution (charter mem., co-chair fed. workplace ADR com. 2002-), Indsl. Rels. Rsch. Assn., Internat. Pers. Mgmt. Assn., Am. Arbitration Assn., Md. Coun. on Dispute Resolution. Office: Agency Dispute Resolution & Synergistic Rels 18 Maplewood Ct Greenbelt MD 20770-1907 E-mail: hugh.d.jascourt@verizon.net.

JASEN, MATTHEW JOSEPH, lawyer, state justice; b. Buffalo, Dec. 13, 1915; s. Joseph John and Celina (Perlinski) Jasinski; m. Anastasia Gawinski, Oct. 4, 1943 (dec. Aug. 1970); children: Peter M., Mark M., Christine (Mrs. David K. Mac Leod), Carol Ann (Mrs. J. David Sampson); m. Gertrude O'Connor Travers, Mar. 25, 1972 (dec. Nov. 1972); m. Grace Yungbluth Frauenheim, Aug. 31, 1973. BA, Canisius Coll., 1937; LLB, U. Buffalo, 1939; postgrad., Harvard U., 1944; LLD (hon.), Union U., 1980, N.Y. Law Sch., 1981. Bar: N.Y. 1940. Ptnr. firm Beyer, Jasen & Boland, Buffalo, 1940-43; pres. U.S. Security Rev. Bd., Wurttemberg-Baden, Germany, 1945-46; judge U.S. Mil. Govt. Ct., Heidelberg, Germany, 1946-49; sr. ptnr. firm Jasen, Manz, Johnson & Bayger, Buffalo, 1949-57; justice N.Y. Supreme Ct. (8th jud. dist.), 1957-67; judge N.Y. Ct. Appeals, 1968-85; U.S. Supreme Ct. spl. master S.C. v. U.S., 1987-88; spl. master Ill. vs. Ky. U.S. Supreme Ct., 1989-95; of counsel Moot & Sprague, Buffalo, 1986-90; counsel Jasen, Jasen & Sampson, P.C., Buffalo, 1990-99, Jasen & Jasen, P.C., Buffalo, 1999—. Mem. N.Y. State Jud. Screening Com., 1996—. Contbr. articles to profl. jours. Mem. council U. Buffalo, 1963-66; trustee Canisius Coll. Chair of Polish Culture, also, Nottingham Acad. Served to capt. AUS, 1943-46, ETO. Fellow Hilbert Coll.; recipient Disting. Alumnus award SUNY-Buffalo Sch. Law, 1969, Disting. Alumnus award Alumni Assn., 1976, Disting. Alumnus award Canisius Coll., 1978, Edwin F. Jaeckle award SUNY-Buffalo Sch. Law, 1982. Mem. Nat. Conf. Appellate Judges, State U. N.Y. at Buffalo Law Sch. Alumni Assn. (pres. 1964-65), Am., N.Y. State, Erie County bar assns., Am. Law Inst., Am. Judicature Soc., Lawyers Club Buffalo (pres. 1961-62), Nat. Advocates Club, Profl. Businessmen's Assn. Western N.Y. (pres. 1952), Phi Alpha Delta, DiGamma Soc. Roman Catholic (mem. Bishop's Bd. Govs., Buffalo diocese 1951—). Clubs: K.C. (4 deg.). General civil litigation, Corporate, general, Personal injury (including property damage). Home: 26 Pine Ter Orchard Park NY 14127-3928 Office: Ste 700 69 Delaware Ave Buffalo NY 14202-3805 E-mail: jjatts@buffnet.net.

JASON, J. JULIE, money manager, author, lawyer; b. Owensboro, Ky. d. Richard and Grazina Pauliukonis; m. Marius J. Jason, Dec. 19, 1970; children: Ilona, Leila. BA, Baldwin-Wallace Coll., 1971; JD, Cleve. State U., 1974; LLM, Columbia U., 1975. Bar: Ohio 1974, N.Y. 1976, U.S. Dist Ct. (so. dist.) N.Y. 1976, U.S. Ct. Appeals (2d cir.) 1976, U.S. Supreme Ct. 1978. Pvt. practice, N.Y.C., 1974-78; asst. gen. counsel Paine Webber, N.Y.C., 1978-83; pres. P.W. Trust and Paine Webber Futures Mgmt. Co., N.Y.C., 1983-88; sr. fin. svcs. atty. Donovan, Leisure, Newton & Irvine, N.Y.C., 1988-89; co-founder, mng. dir. Jackson, Grant & Co., Stamford, Conn., 1989—. Arbitrator NYSE; mediator U.S. Bankruptcy Ct., 1997. Author: You and Your 401(K), 1996, The 401(K) Plan Handbook, 1997, Strategic Investing, 2001; columnist: 401-OK. Mem. ABA, AAUW (chair scholarship com. 1992-93), Nat. Assn. Securities Dealers (cert. arbitrator, cert. mediator), Am. Soc. Journalists & Authors, Investment Co. Inst. (sec. regulation com. 1978-83), The Corp. Bar, Columbia U. Alumni Club of Fairfield County (pres. 1993-94, chair pres.'s coun. 1994-96). Office: Jackson Grant & Co 1177 High Ridge Rd Stamford CT 06905-1203

JASPER, SEYMOUR, lawyer; b. N.Y.C., May 15, 1919; s. Louis and Gussie (Levitch) J.; m. Geulah Eidelsberg, Nov. 24, 1940 (dec.); children: Michael, Ronald, Jeffrey, Idylia; m. Barbara Gray, Feb. 11, 1975. BS, NYU, 1939; JD, Columbia U., 1956. Bar: N.Y. 1956. Assoc. Young, Kaplan & Edelstein, N.Y.C., 1956-59; ptnr. Jasper, Sandler & Lipsay, N.Y.C., 1959-62; pvt. practice, N.Y.C., 1962—. With USN. Estate planning, Probate (including wills, trusts). Office: 115 E 87th St New York NY 10128-1136 E-mail: sey1@rcn.com.

JASSY, EVERETT LEWIS, lawyer; b. N.Y.C., Feb. 4, 1937; s. David H. and Florence A. (Pollak) J.; m. Margery Ellen Rose; children: Katherine Savitt Lennon, Andrew Ralph, Jonathan Scott. AB, Harvard U., 1957, JD, 1960. Bar: N.Y. 1960, D.C. 1975. Assoc. Dewey Ballantine, N.Y.C., 1960-68, ptnr., 1968—, chmn. mgmt. com., 1996—. Mem. ABA, N.Y. State Bar Assn., Assn. of Bar of City of N.Y., The Tax Club, Harmonie Club (bd. govs. 1999-2001), Fairview Country Club, Washington Athletic Club. Avocations: golf, travel. Corporate taxation, Personal income taxation. Home: 20 Tompkins Rd Scarsdale NY 10583-2838 Office: Dewey Ballantine LLP 1301 Avenue Of The Americas New York NY 10019-6022

JAUDES, RICHARD EDWARD, lawyer; b. St. Louis, Feb. 22, 1943; s. Leo August Jr. and Dorothy Catherine (Schmidt) J.; m. Mary Kay Tansey, Sept. 22, 1967; children: Michele, Pamela. BS, St. Louis U., 1965, JD, 1968. Bar: Mo. Supreme Ct. 1968, U.S. Dist. Ct. (ea. dist.), Mo. 1973 U.S. Ct. Appeals (8th cir.) 1973, U.S. Supreme Ct. 1990. With Peper, Martin, Jensen, Maichel & Hetlage, St. Louis, 1973-97, mng. ptnr., 1990-93; lawyer, co-chair labor and employment practice group Thompson Coburn LLP, St. Louis, 1997—; mem. mgmt. com. Thompson Coburn, St. Louis, 1997—2000. Bd. dirs. Baldor Electric Co., 1999— Vol. Civic Entrepreneurs Orgn., St. Louis, 1990; vol. counsel St. Louis chpt. MS Soc., 1990—, exec. com. Lt. USN, 1968-73; comdr. USNR, ret. Labor (including EEOC, Fair Labor Standards Act, labor-management relations, NLRB, OSHA). Office: Thompson Coburn LLP US Bank Plz Saint Louis MO 63101-1693 E-mail: rjaudes@thompsoncoburn.com.

JAVITS, ERIC MOSES, lawyer, diplomat; b. N.Y.C., May 24, 1931; s. Benjamin Abraham and Lily Javits; m. Margaretha Espersson, May 24, 1979; children by previous marriage: Jocelyn Ingrid, Eric Moses. Student, Stanford U., 1948-49; AB, Columbia U., 1952, JD, 1955. Bar: N.Y. 1955, U.S. Supreme Ct. 1959. Temp. cons. Office Def. Moblzn., Washington, 1951; assoc. firm Javits & Javits, N.Y.C., 1955-58, mem. firm to ptnr., 1958-82; sr. ptnr. Javits, Robinson, Brog, Leinwand & Reich, P.C. (and successor firms), 1984-89; cons. to Dept. State, amb.-designate to Venezuela, 1989-90; sr. counsel Robinson, Brog, Leinwand, Reich, Genovese & Gluck, P.C. (and successor firms), 1993—2001; U.S. rep. and amb. to Conf. on Disarmament in Geneva, 2002—. Ind. gen. ptnr. ML Venture Ptnrs., 1982-96; spl. dep. to N.Y. Atty. Gen. Elections Frauds Bur., 1958-59; counsel N.Y. Senate Com. on Affairs of City N.Y., 1959; mem. N.Y.C. Commn. for Protocol, 1994-2001; bd. dirs. N.Y. State Conv. Ctr. Oper. Corp., 1995-2001; past dir. N.Y. Stock Exch., Am. Stock Exch., over the counter cos. Author: SOS New York, 1961. Mem. numerous charitable coms.; bd. govs. N.Y. Young Rep. Club, 1955-58, v.p., 1957-58, bd. advisers, 1958-64; trustee French Inst./Alliance Francaise, 1995-2001, Cardozo Law Sch., 1997-2001; mem. exec. com. Jacob K. Javits campaigns, 1954-80; mem. N.Y. Rep. County Com., 1960-64; mem. exec. com. Nat. Rep. Club, 1962-70; exec. sec. U.S. Paper Exporters Coun., Inc., 1964-72; mem. bd. Spain-U.S.A. C. of C., 1993-2001; chmn. emeritus Spanish Inst., N.Y.C.; bd. dirs. Fair Return League, Inc., pres., 1975—; chmn. Republican Eagles, 1999-2001. Decorated Order of Isabel La Catolica (Spain), 1981, 89; recipient Spanish Inst. Gold medal, 1994. Mem.: Nacoms, U. Club N.Y.C., Phi Alpha Delta, Beta Theta Pi, Phi Beta Kappa. Jewish. Office: US Mission Geneva C/D 11 Rte De Pregny 1292 Chambesy Switzerland

JAVITS, JOSHUA MOSES, lawyer; b. N.Y.C., Jan. 2, 1950; s. Jacob Koppel and Marian (Borris) J.; m. Sabina Paula Golding, May 25, 1985. BA, Yale U., 1972; JD, Georgetown U., 1978. Bar: D.C. 1979, Calif. 1983. Trial atty. NLRB, L.A., 1978-83; assoc. Mullholland & Hickey, Washington, 1983-85, Cades, Schutte, Fleming & Wright, Washington, 1985-87; arbitrator Washington, 1985-88; mem., chmn. Nat. Mediation Bd., Wshington, 1988-93; ptnr. Ford & Harrison, Washington, 1993—2001; arbitrator and mediator, 2001—. Mem. ABA, Indsl. Relations Rsch. Assn., Soc. Fed. Labor Relations Profls., Soc. Profls. in Dispute Resolution. Labor (including EEOC, Fair Labor Standards Act, labor-management relations, NLRB, OSHA). Fax: 202-237-2050. E-mail: JJAVITS@aol.com.

JAVORE, GARY WILLIAM, lawyer; b. San Antonio, Apr. 3, 1952; s. Fred Walter and Glennice Jean (Gilbert) J. BA, Kent (Ohio) State U., 1975; JD, Cleve. State U., 1978. Bar: Tex. 1978, U.S. Dist. Ct. (we. dist.) Tex. 1981, U.S. Ct. Appeals (5th cir.) 1981, U.S. Supreme Ct. 1981. Atty. Bexar County Legal Aid, San Antonio, 1979-81; prin. Johnson, Christopher, Javore & Cochran, San Antonio, 1981—. Author, speaker legal seminars. Mem. Leadership San Antonio Class XXIV. Fellow Tex. Bar Found., San Antonio Bar Found.; mem. San Antonio Trial Lawyers Assn. (bd. dirs. 1986—, treas. 1991, pres. 1993, Outstanding Young Lawyer award 1986), Greater San Antonio Builders Assn. (cons., exec. bd. 1990—, v.p. assoc. coun. 1993), Tex. Trial Lawyers Assn., Order of Barristers. Avocations: wood carving, tennis, scuba diving. Alternative dispute resolution, Commercial, consumer (including collections, credit), Construction. Office: Johnson Christopher Javore & Cochran 5802 Northwest Expy San Antonio TX 78201-2851

JAY, SARA D'ORSEY, arbitrator, lawyer; b. Washington, June 1, 1951; d. John Elliott and Martha (Lowsley) J.; m. William Maxwell Dixon, Sept. 26, 1981; 3 children. BA with highest honors, U. Minn., 1977, JD cum laude, 1980. Bar: Minn. 1980, U.S. Dist. Ct. Minn. 1981. From law clk. to staff atty. Mpls. Star and Tribune Co., Minn., 1978-82; assoc. law offices Michael Colloton, Mpls., 1983-87; gen. counsel Maxims Beauty Salons, Mpls., 1987-89; administrv. law judge Minn. Office of Administrv. Hearings, Mpls., 1990—2002; pvt. practice Mpls., 1991—. Mem. Iowa Pub. Rels. Bd. Mem. ABA (labor law sect.), Fed. Mediation and Conciliation Svcs., Nat. Acad. Arbitrators, Wis. Employee Rels. Commn., Minn. Bur. Mediation Svcs., Minn. State Bar Assn., Hennepin County Bar Assn., Am. Arbitration Assn.

JAYNES, GORDON LESLIE, lawyer; b. Spokane, Wash., Feb. 6, 1929; s. Charlie David Jaynes and Jimmie Kathryn Frost; m. Judith Lyle Lawson. AB, Whitman Coll., 1950; LLB, U. Wash., 1954; diploma in internat. law, U. London, 1962. Bar: Wash. 1954, U.S. Dist. Ct. Wash. 1954, U.S. Ct. Appeals (fed. cir.) 1954, U.S. Ct. Appeals (9th cir.) 1954, Calif. 1964. With Little, LeSourd, Palmer, Scott & Slemmons, Seattle, 1954—55; civilian atty. Implementing Office for NATO U.S. Forces, Ruislip, England, 1957—61; civilian atty. ballistic sys. divsn. USAF, Norton AFB, Calif., 1961—64; atty. Kaiser Engrs. and Constructors, Inc., Oakland, Calif., 1964—73; from ptnr. to of counsel Graham James Whitman & Rallsom(and successor firms), London, 1973—99; pvt. practice Virginia Water, England, 1999—. Dir. Internat. Devel. Law Inst., Rome; mem. assessment panel for adjudicators Internat. Fedn. Consulting Engrs., Geneva; lectr. in field; bd. dirs. Internat. Motor Sports Ltd. Mem. editl. adv. bd.: Internat. Constrn. Law Rev., mem. editl. bd.: U. Wash. Law Rev.; contbr. articles to profl. jours. With U.S. Army, 1955—57. Fellow: Chartered Inst. Arbitrators; mem.: Wentworth Club, Royal Automobile Club. Avocations: motor sports, fly fishing. Construction, Private international, Alternative dispute resolution.

JAYSON, MELINDA GAYLE, lawyer; b. Dallas, Sept. 29, 1956; d. Robert and Louise Adelle (Jacobs) J. BA, U. Tex., 1977, JD, 1980. Bar: Tex. 1980, U.S. Dist. Ct. (no. dist.) Tex. 1980, U.S. Ct. Appeals (5th and 11th cirs.) 1981, U.S. Dist. Ct. (so. dist.) Tex. 1989, U.S. Ct. Appeals (8th cir.) 1990, U.S. Supreme Ct. 1991. Assoc. Akin, Gump, Strauss, Hauer & Feld, Dallas, 1980-86, ptnr., 1987-96, Melinda G. Jayson, P.C., 1996—; gen. counsel Hall Fin. Group, Dallas, 1999—. Comml. arbitrator, mem. regional adv. coun. Am. Arbitration Assn.; arbitrator, mediator N.Y. Stock Exch., NASD Regulation, Inc. and Dispute Solutions, Inc.; mediator U.S. EEO Commn., 1999-2000; arbitrator Nat. Arbitration Forum, 2000—. Named one of Outstanding Young Women Am., 1983. Mem. Tex. Bar Assn., Dallas Bar Assn., State Bar of Tex. (mem. dist. 6A grievance com. 1997-99, mem. professionalism enhancement com. 1997-99). Federal civil litigation, State civil litigation. Office: Ste 2015 5445 Caruth Haven Ln Dallas TX 75225-8166 E-mail: mjayson@hallfinancial.com.

JEANSONNE, MARK ANTHONY, judge, mayor; b. Hessmer, La., Oct. 5, 1962; s. Milburn Joseph and Wava (Normand) J.; m. Shannon Descant, Dec. 12, 1992. BA in Polit. Sci., La. State U., 1988; JD, Loyola U., 1991. Bar: La., U.S. Dist. Ct. (we. dist.) La., U.S. Dist. Ct. (mid. dist.) La. Mayor Village of Hessmer, La., 1993—, magistrate, 1993—, Town of Cottonport, La., 1996—, Town of Mansura, La., 1997—; pvt. practice Hessmer, 1998—; judge 12th Jud. Dist. Ct., La., 2003—. Recipient Small Town Leadership award Wal-Mart, 1997. Mem. La. State Bar, Avoyelles Parish Bar (pres. 1995-96). Avocations: collecting gold and silver coinage, antiques. Home: PO Box 301 2540 Main St Hessmer LA 71341-4058 Office: 2472 Main St Hessmer LA 71341-4034

JEFFERIS, PAUL BRUCE, lawyer; b. Barnesville, Ohio, Jan. 11, 1952; s. Maurice D. and Ruth C. (Rinehart) J.; m. Shirley R. Zervos, Sept. 13, 1997; children: Paul M., Elaini Noel Zervos. BA, Ohio State U., 1977; JD, U. Akron, 1980. Bar: Ohio 1980. Asst. prosecutor Belmont County, St. Clairsville, Ohio, 1981-83; pvt. practice, Barnesville, 1983—. Bd. dirs. St. Clairsville Drug and Alcohol Coun., 1982—. With USN, 1975-77. Mem. ABA, Belmont County Bar Assn., Am. Legion, Moose. Roman Catholic. Avocations: reading, hunting. Criminal, Family and matrimonial, General practice. Office: 58884 Wright Rd Barnesville OH 43713-9799

JEFFERS, MICHAEL BOGUE, lawyer; b. Wenatchee, Wash., July 10, 1940; s. Richard G. and Betty (Ball) J. BA, U. Wash., 1962, LLB, 1964; LLM in Taxation, NYU, 1970. Bar: Wash. 1964, N.Y. 1970, Calif. 1988. Ptnr. Hughes & Jeffers, Wenatchee, 1964-65, 68, Hill, Betts & Nash, N.Y.C., 1970-72, Battle Fowler, N.Y.C., 1973-88, Buchalter, Nemer, Fields & Younger, Newport Beach, Calif., 1988-89, Riordan & McKinzie, Costa Mesa, Calif., 1989-90, Phillips, Haglund, Haddan & Jeffers, Newport Beach, 1991-93, Jeffers, Shaff & Falk, LLP, Newport Beach, Calif., 1994—2002, Dechert LLP, Newport Beach, 2002—. Sec. Thornburg Mortgage Inc. Mem. ABA, Calif. Bar Assn., Orange County Bar Assn., Wash. State Bar Assn., U. Wash. Alumni Assn. (pres. Greater N.Y. chpt. 1972-88), Pacific Club, Nat. Wild Turkey Fedn., Ballet Pacifica, Explorers Club, Phi Gamma Delta. Corporate, general, Securities. Office: Dechert LLP 4675 MacArthur Ct Ste 1400 Newport Beach CA 92660 E-mail: michael.jeffers@dechert.com.

JEFFERSON, WADE HAMPTON, IV, lawyer; b. Lexington, Ky., Aug. 20, 1969; s. Wade Hampton Jefferson, III and Linda Jefferson White; m. Linnea Karin Renfer, Dec. 31, 1995; children: Lucy Anne, Wade Hampton V. BS, U. Va., 1992; MBA, JD, U. Ky., 1995. Bar: Ky. 1996. Atty. Frost, Brown, Todd, LLC, Lexington, 1997—. Deacon 1st Presbyn. Ch., Lexington. Corporate, general, Finance, Mergers and acquisitions. Office: Frost Brown Todd LLC 2700 Lexington Fin Ctr Lexington KY 40507 Business E-Mail: jjefferson@fbtlaw.com.

JEFFERSON, WALLACE B. state supreme court justice; BA James Madison Coll., JD U. Tex. Cert.: Tex. Bd. Legal Specialization (in civil appellate law). With Groce, Locke & Hebdon, San Antonio, 1988—91; ptnr. Crofts, Callaway & Jefferson, San Antonio, 1991—2001; justice Supreme Ct. Tex., Austin, 2001—. Mem. bd. dirs. San Antonio Pub. Libr. Found., Alamo Area Big Bros./Big Sisters.; mem. edn. com. San Antonio Area Found. Mem.: San Antonio Bar Assn. (pres. 1998—99). Office: 201 W 14th St Austin TX 78701 also: PO Box 12248 Austin TX 78711

JEFFREY, DOUGLAS JASON, lawyer; b. Chgo., Apr. 15, 1973; m. Marianella A. Jeffrey. BA, Marquette U., 1995; JD cum laude, U. Miami, Coral Gables, 1998. Bar: Fla. 1998, U.S. Ct. Appeals (11th cir.) 1998, U.S. Dist. Ct. (so., ctrl. and no. dists.) Fla. 1998. Atty. Gilbride, Heller & Brown, PA, Miami, 1999—. Mem.: ATLA, ABA (litigation and bus. law sects.), Broward County Bar Assn., Dade County Bar Assn. Commercial, contracts (including sales of goods; commercial financing), Insurance, Construction. Office: Gilbride Heller & Brown PA 2 S Biscayne Blvd 15th Fl Miami FL 33131

JEFFREYS, SIMON BADEN, lawyer; b. London, May 3, 1957; BA with honors, Cambridge U., Eng., 1979. Bar: Supreme Ct. Eng., Wales 1982. Articled clk. McKenna & Co., London, 1980-82; asst. solicitor, 1982-88; ptnr. CMS Cameron McKenna and predecessor firm, 1988—. Author: Hiring and Firing Executives, 1995; co-editor: Employment Precedents and Company Policy Documents, 1996, Transfer of Undertakings, 1997. Mem. Law Soc., Employment Lawyers Assn. Avocation: fly fishing. Labor (including EEOC, Fair Labor Standards Act, labor-management relations, NLRB, OSHA). Home: 35 The Boundary Tunbridge Wells Kent TN3 OYA England Office: CMS Cameron McKenna Mitre House 160 AldersgateSt EC1A 4DD London England E-mail: sbj@cmk.com.

JEFFRIES, JOHN CALVIN, JR., law educator; b. 1948; BA, Yale U., 1970; JD, U. Va., 1973. Bar: Va. 1973, D.C. 1974. Law clk. to Hon. Justice Powell U.S. Supreme Ct., 1973-74; asst. prof. U. Va., Charlottesville , 1975-79, assoc. prof. Charlottesville, 1979-81, prof. law, 1981—, Emerson Spies prof., 1986—, acad. assoc. dean, 1994, Arnold H. Leon prof. law, dean Sch. Law. Vis. asst. prof. Stanford U., fall 1977; vis. prof. Yale U., 1981-82, So. Calif. U., fall 1986, 89, 93; prof. FBI Acad., Quantico, Va., 1976—. Author: Justice Lewis F. Powell, Jr.: A Biography, 1994, (with Low) Model Penal Code and Commentaries, 3 vols., 1980, (with Karlan, Low and Rutherglen) Civil Rights Actions: Enforcing the Constitution, 2000, Federal Courts and the Law of Federal-State Relations, 4th edit., 1998, (with Low and Bonnie) Cases and Materials on Criminal Law, 1982, 2d edit., 1986; editor-in-chief Va. Law Rev. Mem. Am. Law Inst., Va. State Bar (com. for oversight of bar activities). Office: U Va Sch Law Charlottesville VA 22903

JEFFRIES, SEYMOUR BARNARD, lawyer; b. N.Y.C., Oct. 10, 1916; BBA, CUNY, N.Y., 1939; JD, Harvard U., 1948. Bar: N.Y. 1964. Prof., chmn. dept. bus. adminstrn., jurisprudence Bklyn Coll. Pharmacy, 1949-58; trade rels., legis. liason dir. Warner Lambert Pharm. Co., 1958-60; investment, legal cons. Investors Counsel Inc., N.Y.C., 1963-65; pres. Med. Securities Fund Inc., N.Y.C., 1963-65; adviser, dir., ofcl. negotiator govt. Israel Drug and Fine Chem. Indsl. Merger, 1962-70; pvt. practice, 1964—; gen. counsel Pre-Paid Prescription Svcs. Corp., 1966-68. Cons. Family Drugs N.Y.C. Health and Welfare Coun.; specialist, lectr. in health care law field; specialist med. care ethics; lectr. consumer law, corp. and internat. law. Contbr. articles to profl. jours; contbg. author: Remington's Practice of Pharmacy. Mem. ABA, Am. Nassau Bar Assn., (chmn. internat. law com. 1997, chmn. pre-paid legal svcs. com. 1974-76), Am. Phar. Assn., Trial

Lawyers Assn. Nassau County, AAUP, Kings County Pharm. Assn.(Leadership plaque 1955). Home: Island and Ibsen Sts Woodmere NY 11598 Office: 809 Ibsen St PO Box 388 Woodmere NY 11598-0388 E-mail: Dr.Jeffries@worldnet.att.net.

JELKIN, JOHN LAMOINE, lawyer; b. Hildreth, Nebr., Dec. 24, 1952; s. Lamoine George and Verna Mae (DeJonge) J.; m. Diane Louise Davis, June 10, 1978; children: Jessica Jean, Jaclyn Jade. BA, Univ. Nebr., 1975; JD, U. Nebr., 1978. Bar: Nebr. 1978, U.S. Dist. Ct. Nebr. 1978. Assoc. Duncan & Duncan, Franklin, Nebr., 1978-81; ptnr. Duncan, Duncan & Jelkin, Franklin, 1981-87, Duncan, Duncan, Jelkin & Walker, Franklin, 1987—. Bd. dirs. Nebr. Continuing Legal Edn., Inc., 1995—; sec.-treas. Hildreth Area Bus. Devel. Corp., 1983-88; dep. atty. Buffalo County, Kearney, Nebr., 1986. Vol. fireman; chmn. Franklin County Dems., 1984-98; dep. atty. Franklin County, Nebr.; seminar presenter, speaker NCLE, Inc., 1991, 92, 93 94, 98; mem. ch. council St. Peters Luth. Ch., Hildreth, Nebr., 1988, pres., 1989-90; vice-chmn. Trinity Luth. Ch. Endowment Fund, 2002—; pres. Hildreth Alumni Assn., 1990-95, Hildreth Cmty. Improvement Project, 1992-93; active Hildreth Industrial Devel. Com., 1995, chmn., 1997; bd. dirs. Franklin County Cmty. Found., 1995—, Nebr. Child Abuse Prevention Fund, 1996-2000. Mem. ABA (mem. real estate probate and trust sect.), Nebr. Bar Assn. (exec. com. real estate, probate and trust sect. 1992-94, chmn. 1994-95, real estate practice guidelines com. 1991—), Buffalo County Bar Assn., Nebr. Assn. Trial Attys., 10th Jud. Bar Assn. (pres. 1983-84, 98-99), Lions (bd. dirs. 1993—, v.p. 1982-85, pres. 1985-86, 2000-01). Republican. Lutheran. Probate (including wills, trusts), Property, real (including real estate development, water), Personal income taxation. Office: Duncan Duncan Jelkin & Walker PO Box 340 Hildreth NE 68947-0340 E-mail: jelkinlaw@mailcity.com.

JENKINS, ALBERT FELTON, JR., lawyer; b. Madison, Ga., Jan. 18, 1941; s. A. Felton and Jimmie Lucille (Davis) J.; m. Julie Richardson Green, Apr. 16, 1966; children: A. Felton III, Emily Green, Alan Davis. AB, U. Ga., 1963, LLB, 1965. Bar: Ga. 1965, U.S. Dist. Ct. (no. dist.) Ga. 1965, U.S. Ct. Appeals GA. 1965, U.S. Ct. Appeals (4th cir.) 1981, U.S. Ct. Appeals (5th cir.) 1966, U.S. Ct. Appeals (11th cir.) 1981, U.S. Ct. Appeals (D.C. cir.) 1987, U.S. Supreme Ct. 1968. Assoc. King & Spalding, Atlanta, 1965-70, ptnr., 1971-92, ret. ptnr., 1992—. Chmn. bd. visitors U. Ga. Law Sch., Athens, 1974; mem. Gov.'s Appellate Jud. Selection Com., Atlanta, 1972-73, Gov.'s Jud. process Rev. Com., Atlanta, 1984-85, Ga. Joint Study Commn. on Revenue Structure, 1992-95, Ga. Agrl. Exposition Authority; dir. Dundee Mills, Inc., 1994-95. Co-author: (2 vol. treatise) Georgia Civil Procedure Forms-Practice, 1988. Sec. U. Ga. Bd. Trustees, 1979-85; chmn., pres. Atlanta Unit Am. Cancer Soc., 1982-83; trustee Atlanta Fulton Pub. Libr. Sys., 1995-97. Sgt. Air Nat. Guard, 1965-71. Fellow Am. Bar Found.; mem. State Bar of Ga. (pres. Young Lawyers 1972-73, bd. govs. 1983-91), Piedmont Driving Club (Atlanta), Phi Beta Kappa, Omicron Delta Kappa. Methodist. General civil litigation. Office: King & Spalding 191 Peachtree St SW Ste 4100 Atlanta GA 30303-1763

JENKINS, BRUCE STERLING, federal judge; b. Salt Lake City, Utah, May 27, 1927; s. Joseph and Bessie Pearl (Iverson) J.; m. Margaret Watkins, Sept. 19, 1952; children— Judith Margaret, David Bruce, Michael Glen, Carol Alice. BA with high honors, U. Utah, 1949, LLB, JD, U. Utah, 1952. Bar: Utah 1952, U.S. Dist. Ct. 1952, U.S. Supreme Ct. 1962, U.S. Circuit Ct. Appeals 1962. Pvt. practice, Salt Lake City, 1952-59; assoc. firm George McMillan, 1959-65; asst. atty. gen. State of Utah, 1952; dep. county atty. Salt Lake County, 1954-58; bankruptcy judge U.S. Dist. Ct., Utah, 1965-78, judge, 1978—, chief judge, 1984-93. Adj. prof. U. Utah, 1987-88, 95-99. Research, publs. in field; contbr. essays to Law jours.; bd. editors: Utah Law Rev, 1951-52. Mem. Utah Senate, 1959-65, minority leader, 1963, pres. senate, 1965, vice chmn. commn. on orgn. exec. br. of Utah Govt., 1965-66; Mem. adv. com. Utah Tech. Coll., 1967-72; mem. instl. council Utah State U., 1976. Served with USN, 1945-46. Named Alumnus of Yr. award Coll. Law Univ. Utah, 1985; recipient Admiration and Appreciation award Utah State Bar, 1995, Emeritus Merit of Honor award U. Utah Alumni Assn., 1997. Fellow Am. Bar Found.; mem. ABA, Am. Inn Ct., Utah State Bar Assn. (Judge of Yr. 1993), Salt Lake County Bar Assn., Fed. Bar Assn. (Disting. Jud. Svc. awrd Utah chpt. 1993), Order of Coif, Phi Beta Kappa, Phi Kappa Phi, Phi Eta Sigma, Phi Sigma Alpha, Tau Kappa Alpha. Democrat. Mem. Lds Ch. Office: US Dist Ct 462 US Courthouse 350 S Main St Salt Lake City UT 84101-2106

JENKINS, EVERETT WILBUR, JR., lawyer, author, historian; b. Oklahoma City, Nov. 28, 1953; s. Everett Wilbur and Lillie Bell (Ingram) J.; m. Monica Lynn Endsley, June 3, 1978 (sep. Dec. 31, 2000); children: Ryan, Camille, Jennifer, Cristina. BA cum laude, Amherst Coll., 1975; JD, U. Calif., Berkeley, 1978. Bar: Calif. 1979. Dep. county counsel Contra Costa County, Martinez, Calif., 1980-81; dep. city atty. City of Richmond, Calif., 1981-84, asst. city atty., 1984—; bd. atty. West County Agy., Richmond, 1981-90; authority atty. Solid Waste Mgmt. Authority West Contra Costa, Richmond, 1985-87, 88-91. Legal rep. tech. adv. com. Contra Costa County Solid Waste Commn., Martinez, Calif., 1986-87; pub. mem., 1987-88; adv. atty. West Contra Costa Transp. Adv. Com., San Pablo, 1994—; bd. atty. Richmond Housing Authority, 1992-99. Author: Pan-African Chronology, 1996, Pan-African Chronology II, 1998, Pan-African Chronology III, 2001, The Muslim Diaspora, 1999, The Muslim Diaspora, vol. 2, 2000, The Creation, 2003. Rep. Contra Costa County Hazardous Materials Commn., Martinez, 1987-88; bd. dirs. YMCA of the East Bay, Oakland, 1996—; bd. dirs. West Contra Costa YMCA, Richmond, 1987—, chair program com., 1991-92, vice chair bd. dirs. 1992-96, chair bd. dirs., 1996-98, chair cmty. gifts campaign, 1992-94 (named Rita Davis Vol. of the Yr., 1993); umpire Little League Baseball, 1997—, ASA Softball, 1997—. Mem. ABA, State Bar Calif. (exec. bd. pub. law sect. exec. com. 1987-91, editor Pub. Law News 1988-91, liaison to bd. govs. 1991-92), Continuing Edn. Bar (joint adv. com. 1993-96), Contra Costa County Bar Assn., Charles Houston Bar Assn., Nat. Assn. Sports Officials. Independent. Office: City Atty's Office 1401 Marina Way South Richmond CA 94804-1654

JENKINS, JAMES C. lawyer; b. Logan, Utah, July 16, 1948; BA in Fin., U. Utah, 1972; JD, Gonzaga U., 1976. Bar: Utah 1976, U.S. Dist. Ct. Utah 1976, U.S. Ct. Appeals (10th cir.) 1992, U.S. Tax Ct. 1985, U.S. Supreme Ct. 1981. Ptnr. Olson & Hoggan, P.C., Logan, Utah; Rich county atty., 1978-81; Cache county dep. atty., 1981-95; gen. counsel Bear Lake Spl. Svcs. Dist., Rich County, Utah, 1978-2001. Instr. Utah State U., 1976; trustee Utah Bankruptcy Ct., 1977-80. Chair jud. conduct commn. Utah Jud. Coun., 1996-97, mem. jud. performance and evaluation com., mem. adv. bd. Utah State Crime Lab. Mem. ABA (trial practice com., litig. sect. 1986-95), Utah State Bar Assn. (pres.-elect 1997-98, pres. 1998-99, law benefit com. 1978-80, law day com. 1989-90, ethics and discipline com. 1992-93, exec. com., litig. com. 1993-95, bd. commrs. 1993-96), Utah Statewide Assn. Pros., Cache County Bar Assn. (sec.-treas. 1978-81) General civil litigation, Personal injury (including property damage), Property, real (including real estate development, water). Office: Olson & Hoggan PC PO Box 525 88 W Center St Logan UT 84323-0525

JENKINS, JAMES R. lawyer, telecommunications industry executive; b. Bethlehem, Pa., Apr. 18, 1961; s. Richard B. and Margaret Jenkins; m. Nicole Beukers, July 15, 1989; children: Aidan, Charlotte, Pierce. BA in History, Northwestern U., Evanston, Ill., 1983; JD, Northwestern U., Chgo., 1991. Bar: Ill. 1991, U.S. Dist. Ct. (no. dist.) Ill. 1991. Assoc. Laner, Muchin, Chgo., 1991—93, Seyfarth Shaw, Chgo., 1993—96; counsel 360° Comm., Chgo., 1996—98; v.p. law ALLTEL Corp., Little Rock, 1998—2001; v.p. external affairs U.S. Cellular Corp., Chgo., 2002—. Mem.: ABA, Am. Corp. Counsel Assn. Communications, Labor (including EEOC, Fair Labor Standards Act, labor-management relations, NLRB, OSHA), Corporate, general. Office: US Cellular 8410 W Brynmawr Ave Chicago IL 60631 Office Fax: 773-864-3133. Business E-Mail: james.jenkins@uscellular.com.

JENKINS, ROBERT ROWE, lawyer; b. Norwalk, Ohio, Aug. 8, 1933; s. Robert Leslie and Millie Leona (Rowe) J.; m. Francis Jean Cline, June 12, 1955 (div. July 1972); children: Diane Elaine, Katherine Eileen; m. Jean Dingus, July 9, 1972. Student, Lebanon Valley Coll., 1951-55; BS in Chemistry, Eastern Coll. (now U. Balt.), 1967; JD, U. Balt., 1975. Bar: Md. 1976, U.S. Dist. Ct. Md. 1976, U.S. Ct. Appeals (4th cir.) 1979, U.S. Supreme Ct. 1979. Atty. Social Security Adminstrn., Balt., 1975-76; trial atty. Nelson R. Kandel, Balt., 1976-77; sole practice Balt., 1977-81; ptnr. Jenkins Block & Mering, Balt., 1981—. Faculty continuing profl. edn. of lawyers Md. Inst., Balt., 1986—. Ruling elder Redeemer Presbyn. Ch., Presbyn. Ch. Am., Balt., 1982—. Served with U.S. Coast Guard, 1955-59. Mem. ABA, Md. Bar Assn., Balt. City Bar Assn., Assn. Trial Lawyers Am., Md. Trial Lawyers Assn., Christian Legal Soc., Nat. Orgn. Social Security Claimant's Rep. (exec. com.). Republican. Avocations: fishing, boating. Administrative and regulatory, Pension, profit-sharing, and employee benefits, Personal injury (including property damage). Home: 1003 Travers St Cambridge MD 21613-1543 Office: Jenkins Block and Assoc PO Box 739 828 Airpax Rd Ste 300 Cambridge MD 21613 also: 33 W Franklin St Ste 102 Hagerstown MD 21740-4826 E-mail: rjenk5906@aol.com.

JENKINS, RONALD WAYNE, lawyer; b. Johnson City, Tenn., Aug. 14, 1950; s. James Herman and Peggy Sue (Hutchison) J.; children: April Chalice, Kimberly Michelle, Robert Herman, Ronald Wayne II. BSEE, U. Tenn., 1972, JD, 1980. Bar: Tenn. 1980, U.S. Supreme Ct. 1986, U.S. Ct. Appeals (6th cir.) 1986, U.S. Dist. Ct. (ea. dist.) Tenn. 1986. Assoc. M. Lacy West, P.C., Kingsport, Tenn., 1980-83, Andrews, Herndon, Coleman, Brading & McKee, Johnson City, 1984-86, ptnr., 1986—2001, Herrin, Booze, Rambo, Jenkins & Wheeler, Jonesborough, Johnson City, 2001—. Instr. rsch. and writing III U. Tenn. Coll. Law, 1979. Rsch. editor Tenn. Law Rev., 1978-79, editor-in-chief, 1979. Mem. ABA, Tenn. Bar Assn., Washington County Bar Assn., Nat. Aeronautic Assn., Aircraft Owners and Pilots Assn., Am. Bd. Trial Advs. (assoc. 1999), Tau Beta Pi (Tenn. col., engring. honor), Eta Kappa Nu (electrical engring. honor), Spangdahlem AB Aero Club (pres. 1976-77). Avocations: agriculture, aviation. General civil litigation, Insurance, Professional liability. Office: Herrin Booze Rambo Jenkins & Wheeler PO Box 308 806 E Jackson Blvd Jonesborough TN 37659-0308

JENKINSON, WILLIAM ELDRIDGE, III, lawyer; b. Kingstree, S.C., June 27, 1946; s. William Eldridge Jr. and Gordon (Brockington) J.; m. Salley K. Jenkinson, July 20, 1974; children: William E. IV, Anne Gordon, Louisa K. BA, The Citadel, 1968; JD, U. S.C., 1971. Bar: S.C., U.S. Dist. Ct. S.C., U.S. Ct. Appeals (4th cir.), U.S. Supreme Ct. Sr. ptnr. Jenkinson Jarrett & Kellahan PA, Kingstree, SC, 1971—. Chmn. bd. visitors The Citadel, Charleston, S.C., 1992—; trustee The Meth. Oaks, Orangeburg, S.C., 1997—; sec. Williamsburgh Hist. Soc., Kingstree, 1990—. 1st lt. U.S. Army, 1971. Mem. Lions. General civil litigation, Commercial, contracts (including sales of goods; commercial financing), Criminal. Office: Jenkinson & Jenkinson PA 120 W Main St Kingstree SC 29556-3344

JENKS, THOMAS EDWARD, lawyer; b. Dayton, Ohio, May 31, 1929; s. Wilbur L. and Anastasia A. (Ahern) J.; m. Marianna Fischer, Nov. 10, 1961; children— Pamela (dec.), William, David, Christine, Daniel, Douglas Student, Miami U., Oxford, Ohio, 1947-50; JD cum laude, Ohio State U., 1953; hon. grad., U.S. Naval Sch. Justice, 1953. Bar: Ohio 1953, U.S. Dist. Ct. (so. dist.) Ohio 1961, U.S. Supreme Ct. 1971, U.S. Ct. Appeals (6th cir.) 1984. Pvt. practice, Dayton, 1955—; atty. Jenks, Pyper & Oxley, Dayton. Served to 1st lt. USMC, 1953-55 Fellow Am. Coll. Trial Lawyers, Am. Bar Found., Ohio Bar Found.; mem. ABA (ho. of dels. 1985-88), Dayton Bar Assn. (pres. 1978-79), Ohio Bar Assn. (bd. govs. litigation sect., 1990-98), Internat. Assn. Def. Counsel, Ohio Assn. Civil Trial Attys., Am. Bd. Trial Advs. (adv.), Kettering C. of C. (past pres.), Kettering Holiday at Home Found. (past pres.), Order of Coif, Dayton Lawyers Club (pres. 1999-2002), Optimist Club (past pres. Oakwood chpt.), Phi Delta Phi, Sigma Chi. Republican. Roman Catholic. State civil litigation, Insurance, Personal injury (including property damage). Office: Jenks Pyper & Oxley Courthouse Plz SW 10 N Ludlow St Dayton OH 45402

JENNER, EVA C. lawyer; b. Taipei, Taiwan, Feb. 2, 1968; d. William John and Kitty J. BA, U. Calif., 1990; JD magna cum laude, Syracuse U., 1995. Bar: N.Y. 1996. Paralegal Hawaii Lawyers Care, Honolulu, 1992; legal intern Bklyn. Legal Svcs., N.Y.C., 1993; assoc. Rogers & Wells, N.Y.C., 1995-97, Cleary, Gottlieb, Steen & Hamilton, N.Y.C., 1997—99; contract atty. Davis & Gilbert, N.Y.C., 2000, Ingram Yuzek Gainen Carroll & Bertolotti, LLP, N.Y.C., 2001—. Andrews scholar Syracuse U., 1992-95. Democrat. Buddhist. Avocations: painting, photography, baseball. Corporate, general, Mergers and acquisitions, Securities. Office: 1 Liberty Plz Fl 38 New York NY 10006-1404

JENNINGS, ALSTON, lawyer; b. West Helena, Ark., Oct. 30, 1917; s. Earp Franklin and Irma (Alston) J.; m. Dorothy Buie Jones, June 12, 1943; children: Alston, Eugene Franklin, Ann Buie. AB, Columbia U., 1938; JD, Northwestern U., 1941. Bar: Ark. 1941. Practiced law, Little Rock, 1947—; spl. agt. intelligence unit Treasury Dept., 1946; assoc. Wright, Harrison, Lindsey & Upton, 1949-51, mem., 1951-60, Wright, Lindsey, Jennings, Lester & Shults, 1960-65, Wright, Lindsey & Jennings, 1965—. Mem. adv. bd. Salvation Army, Pulaski County. Served to lt. USNR, 1941-45. Fellow Am. Bar Found.; mem. ABA, Ark. Bar Assn., Pulaski County Bar Assn. (past pres.), Internat. Assn. Def. Counsel (pres. 1972-73), Am. Coll. Trial Lawyers (regent 1975-79, treas. 1979-80, pres.-elect 1980-81, pres. 1981-82) Antitrust, Federal civil litigation, State civil litigation. Home: 1801 Beechwood St Little Rock AR 72207-2001 Office: 200 W Capitol Ave Little Rock AR 72201-3605

JENNINGS, THOMAS PARKS, lawyer; b. Alexandria, Va., Nov. 16, 1947; s. George Christian and Ellen (Thompson) J.; m. Shelley Corrine Abernathy, Oct. 30, 1971; 1 child, Kathleen Eayre. BA in History, Wake Forest U., 1970; JD, U. Va., 1975. Bar: Va. 1975. Assoc. Lewis, Wilson, Lewis & Jones, Arlington, Va., 1975-78; atty. First Va. Banks, Inc., Falls Church, 1978-80, gen. counsel, 1980—, sec., 1993-99, sr. v.p., 1995—. Adj. prof. George Mason U. Sch. Law, Arlington, 1987-88. Trustee Arlington Cmty. Found., 1998—, treas., 2001—; dir. Rixey St. Found., Inc., 1997—; deacon Georgetown Presbyn. Ch., Washington, 1980-82, elder, 1983-85, 95-97, trustee, 1988-90, dir. Bd. Pensions, Presbyn. Ch. USA, 2001—. With U.S. Army, 1970-71. Mem. ABA, Am. Soc. Corp. Secs., Va. State Bar Assn., Va. Bankers Assn. (legal affairs com.), Fairfax County Bar Assn., Am. Corp. Counsel Assn., Washington Met. Area Corp. Counsel Assn. (bd. dirs. 1984-87). Avocations: bridge, kayaking. Banking, Commercial, contracts (including sales of goods; commercial financing), Corporate, general. Office: First Va Banks Inc 6400 Arlington Blvd Ste 420 Falls Church VA 22042-2336

JENSCH, CHARLES CAMPBELL, lawyer; b. St. Paul, Apr. 15, 1929; s. Charles C. Jensch and Dorothy Tilden Stoms; m. Helen Joan Alan, Jan. 26, 1957; children: Jeanne, Clifton, Diana, Charles, Marianne, Christine. AB cum laude, Williams Coll., 1950; JD, U. Mich., 1953. Bar: Ill. 1953, Minn. 1978; cert. real property law specialist. Assoc. Wilson & McIlvaine, Chgo., 1953-58; asst. sec. Story & Clark Piano Co., Chgo., 1958-60; v.p., asst. legal counsel A.E. Staley Mfg. Co., Decatur, Ill., 1960-69; exec. v.p., pres., sec. Sunstar Foods, Inc., Mpls., 1969-80; v.p., dir. Petersen, Tews & Squires, St. Paul, 1980-96; of counsel Krass Monroe, P.A., Mpls., 1998—. Mem. Minn. State Bar Assn., Barristers Club. Landlord-tenant, Property, real (including real estate development, water). Home: 197 Avon St S Saint Paul MN 55105-3319 Office: Krass Monroe PA Southpoint Office Ctr 1650 West 82nd St Ste 1100 Minneapolis MN 55431-1447 E-mail: CharlesJ@Krassmonroe.com.

JENSEN, D. LOWELL, federal judge, lawyer, government official; b. Brigham, Utah, June 3, 1928; s. Wendell and Elnora (Hatch) J.; m. Barbara Cowin, Apr. 20, 1951; children: Peter, Marcia, Thomas. AB in Econs, U. Calif.-Berkeley, 1949, LL.B., 1952. Bar: Calif. 1952. Dep. dist. atty., Alameda County, 1955-66; asst. dist. atty., 1966-69; dist. atty., 1969-81; asst. atty. gen. criminal div. Dept. Justice, Washington, 1981-83, assoc. atty. gen., 1983-85, dep. atty. gen., 1985-86; judge U.S. Dist. Ct. (no. dist.) Calif., Oakland, 1986—. Mem. Calif. Council on Criminal Justice, 1974-81; past pres. Calif. Dist. Atty.'s Assn. Served with U.S. Army, 1952-54. Fellow Am. Coll. Trial Lawyers; mem. Nat. Dist. Atty.'s Assn. (victim/witness commn. 1974-81), Boalt Hall Alumni Assn. (past pres.) Office: US Dist Ct 1301 Clay St Rm 490C Oakland CA 94612-5217*

JENSEN, DALLIN W. lawyer; b. Afton, Wyo., June 2, 1932; s. Louis J. and Nellie B. Jensen; m. Barbara J. Bassett, Mar. 22, 1958; children: Brad L., Julie N. BS, Brigham Young U., 1954; JD, U. Utah, 1960. Bar: Utah 1960, U.S. Dist. Ct. Utah 1962, U.S. Supreme Ct. 1971, U.S. Ct. Appeals (10th cir.) 1974, U.S. Ct. Appeals D.C. 1980. Asst. atty. gen. Utah Atty. Gen., Salt Lake City, 1960—83, solicitor gen., 1983—88; shareholder Parsons, Behle & Latimer, Salt Lake City, 1988—. Alt. commr. Upper Colo. River Commn., 1983—; mem. Colo. River Basin Salinity Adv. Coun., 1975—; commr. Utah Reclamation Mitigation and Conservation Commn., 2003—; spl. legal cons. Nat. Water Commn., Washington, 1971—73. Author (with Wells A. Hutchins): The Utah Law of Water Rights, 1965; mem. editl. bd. Rocky Mountain Mineral Law Found., 1983—85; contbr. articles on water law and water resource mgmt. to profl. jours. Served with U.S. Army, 1955—57. Mem. Lds Ch. Administrative and regulatory, Natural resources, Property, real (including real estate development, water). Home: 3565 S 2175 E Salt Lake City UT 84109-2902 Office: PO Box 45898 Salt Lake City UT 84145-0898 E-mail: d.jensen@pblutah.com.

JENSEN, DENNIS LOWELL, lawyer; b. Erie, Pa., July 5, 1951; s. Lowell and Roberta (Umbaugh) J. Student, Cornell Coll., 1969-70; BA, Macalester Coll., 1973; JD, U.Houston, 1973. Bar: Tex. 1977, U.S. Dist. Ct. (so. dist.) Tex. 1978, Calif. 1981. Sole practice, Houston, 1977-78; asst. housing coordinator Santa Ana Housing Authority, Calif., 1979; polit. cons. Huntington Beach, Calif., 1980-81; legis. analyst Tosco Corp., Los Angeles, 1981-82; polit. cons. Lynn Wessell Co., 1982-83, George Young & Assocs., 1983-84; legis. aide Los Angeles City Councilman Ernani Bernardi, 1984-86; dep. atty. Los Angeles City Atty.'s Office, 1986-95; pvt. practice Huntington Beach, 1995—. Lectr. in field. Contbr. articles to profl. jours. Campaign mgr. for Congressman Tom Kindness, Hamilton, Ohio, 1978, Initiative to Abolish Inheritance Tax, Bakersfield, Calif., 1980; alumni admissions rep. Macalester Coll., 1984; mem. bd. dirs. Adult Day Svc. Orange County, 1998-; instr. Calif. State U. Extended Edn. programs gerontology and geriatric care mgmt., 1999-. Mem. Am. Assn. Polit. Cons., Nat. Acad. Elder Law Attys., Orange County Bar Assn. (vice chmn. elder law sect.), Order of Barons, Phi Delta Phi. Republican. Home: 18801 Gregory Ln Huntington Beach CA 92646-1921 Office: Dennis L Jensen Atty at Law 18377 Beach Blvd Ste 212 Huntington Beach CA 92648-1349

JENSEN, DICK LEROY, lawyer; b. Audubon, Iowa, Oct. 25, 1930; s. A.B. and Bernice (Fancher) J.; m. Nancy Wilson, June 30, 1956; children: Charles F., Sarah R. (dec.). LL.B., U. Iowa, 1954. Bar: Iowa 1954. Practice in, Audubon, Iowa, 1958-60; gen. counsel, sec. Walnut Grove Products, Co., Atlantic, Iowa, 1960-64; legal staff W.R. Grace & Co., Atlantic, 1964-66; gen. counsel, v.p., sec. Spencer Foods, Inc., Iowa, 1966-72, dir., 1968-72; mem. Dreher, Simpson and Jensen, Des Moines, 1972—. Notes and legis. editor: Iowa Law Rev, 1953-54. Pres. S.W. Iowa Mental Health Inst., 1964-66. Served to lt. USNR, 1955-58. Mem. Masons, Sigma Nu, Phi Delta Phi. Republican. Presbyterian. Commercial, contracts (including sales of goods; commercial financing), Corporate, general, General practice. Home: 3901 River Oaks Dr Des Moines IA 50312-4638 Office: Dreher Simpson & Jensen The Equitable Bldg Ste 222 Des Moines IA 50309-3723 E-mail: djensen@dreherlaw.com.

JENSEN, JOHN ROBERT, lawyer; b. Rapid City, S.D., Aug. 9, 1946; s. Edwin Robert and Roxina Althier (Hollinger) J.; m. Susan McClelland, Aug. 27, 1977; children: Margaret Marie, Jennifer Jo, Edwin Robert II, James Peder. BA, Calif. State U., Northridge, 1971; JD, Baylor U., 1976. Bar: Tex. 1977, U.S. Dist. Ct. (no. dist.) Tex. 1977, U.S. Ct. Appeals (5th cir.) 1982. Asst. ins. dir. Groesbeck Fin., L.A., 1971-73; v.p. Capital Cons., Dallas, 1973-74; assoc. McConnell & Assocs., Arlington, Tex., 1977; sole practice Arlington, Tex., 1984—. Author: Checklist for Texas Lawyers, 1979, 2d edit., 1981. Served with U.S. Army, 1966-68, Vietnam. Decorated Army Commedation medal. Mem. Arlington Bar Assn., Baylor Order Barristers, Tex. Bd. Legal Specialization (cert. personal injury trial law), Nat. Bd. Trial Adv. (cert. civil trial adv.), Delta Theta Phi (treas. Baylor chpt. 1976). Lutheran. Federal civil litigation, State civil litigation, Personal injury (including property damage). Office: Jensen & Jensen 6025 Interstate 20 W Arlington TX 76017-1077

JENSEN, KEITH MICHAEL, lawyer; b. Huntington, N.Y., Aug. 20, 1964; s. John Joseph and Anne Marie (McCann) J.; 1 child, Olivia. BA in Govt. and Politics, U. Md., 1987; JD, So. Meth. U., 1990. Bar: Tex. 1990, U.S. Dist. Ct. (no. dist.) Tex. 1992, U.S. Ct. Appeals (5th cir.) 1993, U.S. Ct. Appeals (3d cir.). Assoc. Hutcheson & Grundy, Dallas and Houston, 1990-91; ptnr. Liles, Hartley, Jensen & Woods, LLP, Ft. Worth, 1992-94; pvt. practice, Dallas, 1991-92, Ft. Worth, 1994—. Advisor Tex. Exotic Feline Found., Inc., Boyd, Tex., 1996—. Author: Class Actions in Texas, 2000. Mem. ATLA, ACLU, Coll. of State Bar of Tex., Tex. Trial Lawyers Assn., Trial Lawyers for Pub. Justice, Dallas Bar Assn., Tarrant County Bar Assn. Roman Catholic. Avocations: skiing, chess, billiards, tennis. General civil litigation, Personal injury (including property damage), Product liability. Office: 514 E Belknap Fort Worth TX 76102

JENSEN, SAM, lawyer; b. Blair, Nebr., Oct. 30, 1935; s. Soren K. and Frances (Beck) J.; m. Marilyn Heck, June 28, 1959 (div. Jan. 1987); children: Soren R., Eric, Dana; m. Carmen Patton, Apr. 7, 1990. BA, U. Nebr., 1957, JD, 1961. Bar: Nebr. 1961. Mem. Smith Bros., Lexington, Nebr., 1961-63, Swarr, May, Smith and Andersen, Omaha, 1963-83, Erickson & Sederstrom, P.C., Omaha, 1983—. Chmn. bd. dirs., v.p. bd. dirs. Omaha Public Power Dist., 1979-81; chmn. Nebr. Coordinating Commn. for Postsecondary Edn., 1976-78. Del. Nat. Rep. Conv., 1960, mem. Nebr. Rep. Ctrl. Com., 1968-70; mem. Regents Commn. Urban U., U. Nebr., Omaha, chmn. Task Force on Higher Edn.; mem. Hwy Commn. State of Nebr., 1989-95; vice chmn. Opera Omaha, 1992-95, v.p., 1994-96. Recipient Disting. Service award U. Nebr., 1981 Mem. Omaha Bar Assn. (past exec. com.), Nebr. Bar Assn. (chmn. com. public relations 1973-76), Am. Bar Assn., U. Nebr. Alumni Assn. (pres. 1976-78), Rotary Club, Omaha Club, Beta Theta Pi, Phi Delta Phi. Clubs: Rotary, Omaha, Racquet. Federal civil litigation, Labor (including EEOC, Fair Labor Standards Act, labor-management relations, NLRB, OSHA), Trademark and copyright. Office: 1 Regency Westpointe 10330 Regency Parkway Dr Omaha NE 68114-3774 E-mail: sj@eslaw.com., Jensen@cox.net.

JENSEN, WALTER EDWARD, lawyer, educator; b. Chgo., Oct. 20, 1937. AB, U. Colo., 1959; JD, Ind. U., 1962, MBA, 1964; PhD (Univ. fellow), Duke U., 1972. Bar: Ind. 1962, Ill. 1962, D.C. 1963, U.S. Tax Ct. 1982, U.S. Supreme Ct. 1967. Assoc. prof. Colo. State U., 1964-66, U. Conn., Storrs,

1966-67, Ill. State U., 1970-72; prof. bus. adminstrn. Va. Poly. Inst. and State U., beginning 1972, prof. fin., ins. and law, 1972-; with Inst. Advanced Legal Studies, U. London, 1983-84; prof. U.S. Air Force Grad. Mgmt. Program, Europe, 1977-78, 83-85; Duke U. legal rsch. awardee, rschr., Guyana, Trinidad and Tobago, 1967; vis. lectr. pub. internat. law U. Istanbul, 1988, Roberts Coll. U. Bosporous, Istanbul, Uludag U., Turkey, 1988; rschr. U. London Inst. Advanced Legal Studies, London Sch. Econs. and Inst. Commonwealth Studies, 1969, 71-74, 76; Ford Found. Rsch. fellow Ind. U., 1963-64; faculty rsch. fellow in econs. U. Tex., 1968; Bell Telephone fellow in econs. regulated pub. utilities U. Chgo., 1965. Recipient Dissertation Travel award Duke U. Grad. sch., 1968; Ind. U. fellow, 1963, 74, scholar, 1963-64. Mem. D.C. Bar Assn., Ill. Bar Assn., Ind. bar Assn., ABA, Am. Polit. sci. Assn., Am. Soc. Internat. Law, Am. Judicature Soc., Am. Bus. Law Assn., Alpha Kappa Psi, Phi Alpha Delta, Pi Gamma Mu, Pi Kappa Alpha, Beta Gamma Sigma. Contbr. articles to profl. publs.; staff editor Am. Bus Law Jour., 1973— ; vice chmn. assoc. editor for adminstrv. law sect. young lawyers Barrister (Law Notes), 1975-83; book rev. and manuscript editor Justice System Jour: A Mgmt. Rev., 1975— ; staff editor Bus. Law Rev., 1975— . Home: 3358 Glade Creek Blvd 5 Roanoke VA 24012 Office: Va Poly Inst and State U Blacksburg VA 24060

JENTZ, GAYLORD ADAIR, law educator; b. Beloit, Wis., Aug. 7, 1931; s. Merlyn Adair and Delva (Mullen) Jentz; m. JoAnn Mary Hornung, Aug. 6, 1955; children: Katherine Ann, Gary Adair, Loretta Ann, Rory Adair. BA, U. Wis., 1953, JD, 1957, MBA, 1958. Bar: Wis. 1957. Pvt. practice law, Madison, 1957-58; from asst. prof. to assoc. prof. bus. law U. Okla., 1958-65; assoc. prof. U. Tex., Austin, 1965-68, prof., 1968-98, Herbert D. Kelleher prof. bus. law, 1982-98, prof. emeritus, 1998—, chmn. gen. bus. dept., 1968-74, 80-86. From vis. instr. to vis. prof. U. Wis. Law Sch., Wis., 1957—65. Author (with others): (book) Texas Uniform Commercial Code, 1967, rev. edit., 1975, Business Law Text and Cases, 1968, Business Law Text, 1978, Legal Environment of Business, 1989, Texas Family Law, 7th edit., 1992, Business Law Today-Alternate Essentials Edition, 4th edit., 1997, Fundamentals of Business Law, 5th edit., 2002, Business Law Today, 6th comprehensive edit., 2004, Business Law Today, 6th std. edit., 2003, Business Law Today-The Essentials, 6th edit., 2003, West's Business Law: Text and Cases, 9th edit., 2004, West's Business Law: Alternate Edition, 9th edit., 2004, Law for E-Commerce, 2002, West's Business Law-Case Study Approach, 2003, Business Law Today-Interactive Text, 6th edit., 2003; dep. editor: Social Sci. Quar., 1966—82, mem. editl. bd.: , 1982—94, editor-in-chief: Am. Bus. Law Jour., 1969—74, adv. editor: , 1974—. With U.S. Army, 1953—55. Named to CBA Hall of Fames, 1999; recipient Outstanding Tchr. award, U. Tex. Coll. Bus., 1967, Jack G. Taylor Tchg. Excellence award, 1971, 1989, Joe D. Beasley Grad. Tchg. Excellence award, 1978, CBA Found. Adv. Coun. award, 1979, Grad. Bus. Coun. Outstanding Grad. Bus. Prof. award, 1980, James C. Scorboro Meml. award for outstanding leadership in banking edn., Colo. Grad. Sch. Banking, 1983, Utmost Outstanding Prof. award, 1989, CBA award for excellence in edn., 1994, Banking Leadership award, Western States Sch. Banking, 1995, Civitatis award, U. Tex., 1997. Mem.: So. Bus. Law Assn. (pres. 1967), Wis. Bar Assn., Tex. Assn. Coll. Tchrs. (pres. Austin chpt. 1967—68, mem. exec. com. 1979—80, state pres. 1971—72), Acad. Legal Studies Bus. (pres. 1971—72, mem. exec. com. 1989—94), Am. Arbitration Assn. (nat. panel 1966—96), Southwestern Fedn. Adminstrv. Disciples (v.p. 1979—80, pres. 1980—81), Phi Kappa Phi (pres. 1983—84), Omicron Delta Kappa. Home: 4106 N Hills Dr Austin TX 78731-2826 Office: U Tex MSIS Dept McCombs Sch Bus CBA 5 202 1 University S Austin TX 78712

JEPSEN, WILLIAM E. lawyer; b. Omaha, July 1, 1947; s. Herschel Lewis and Ellen (Viola) J.; m. Cynthia Cadden, Aug. 22, 1969 (div. Aug. 1989); children: David, John. BS, U. Nebr., 1969; JD, U. Minn., 1972. Bar: Minn. 1972, U.S. Dist. Ct. Minn. 1973, U.S. Ct. Appeals (8th cir.) 1973. Atty., pres. Hebert, Cass, Jepsen & Doyscher, Stillwater, Minn., 1972-85; atty., ptnr. Karon, Jepsen & Daly, St. Paul, 1985-96; atty. Schwebel, Goetz & Stieben, Mpls., 1996—. Mem., chair Minn. Bd. Continuing Legal Edn., St. Paul, 1993-2000; bd. dirs. Creative Dispute Resolution, Mpls., 1997—. Mem. city coun. Mainre On St. Croix, Minn., 1978-80. Mem. Minn. State Bar Assn. (bd. govs. 1997—), Minn. Trial Lawyers Assn. (pres. 1990-91, Mem. of Yr. 1986). State civil litigation, Personal injury (including property damage). Home: 321 Boutwell Pl Stillwater MN 55082-4518 Office: Schwebel Goetz & Sieben 5120 IDS Center Minneapolis MN 55402 E-mail: wjepsen@schwebel.com.

JERNIGAN, JOHN LEE, lawyer; b. Atlanta, May 29, 1942; s. Alton Lee and Marian (Heidt) J.; m. Virginia McKinney; children: Lee Ashley, Frank McKinney. AB, Davidson Coll., 1964; JD, U. N.C., 1967. Bar: N.C. 1967. Assoc. Smith, Anderson, Blount, Dorsett, Mitchell & Jernigan, Raleigh, N.C., 1969-72, mng. ptnr., 1972—. Bd. adv. U. N.C. Banking Law Inst., U. N.C. Law Sch. Campaign for Carolina Law Steering Com. Bd. visitors Davidson (N.C.) Coll., 1986—; trustee Choate-Rosemary Hall, Wallingford, Conn., 1989-92. Capt. U.S. Army, 1967-69. Fellow N.C. Bar Found.; mem. N.C. Bar Assn. (chmn. bus. law sect. 1985-87, bd. govs. 1989-92, chmn. bar ctr. cabinet 1994-98, pres.-elect 1998-99, pres. 1999-2000, past pres. 2000-2001), Wake County Bar Assn., Cardinal Club (bd. dirs.), So. Conf. Bar Pres., Nat. Conf. Bar Pres., Supreme Ct. Hist. Soc. Episcopalian. Banking, Commercial, contracts (including sales of goods; commercial financing), Corporate, general. Office: PO Box 2611 Raleigh NC 27602-2611

JEROME, JOHN JAMES, lawyer; b. N.Y.C., Oct. 17, 1933; s. Eugene George and Gladys Odette (Conterno) J.; ; children by previous marriage: Christopher J., Jennifer T.; m. Maureen M. Murphy, Sept. 19, 1981; children: Mairin Ashling, Emily Campbell. BBA, St. John's U., N.Y.C., 1958, LLB, 1961. Bar: N.Y. 1962, U.S. Dist. Ct. (so. dist.) N.Y. 2d cir., 3d cir., U.S. Supreme Ct., U.S. Dist. Ct. (ea. dist.) N.Y. 1964. Assoc. Milbank, Tweed, Hadley & McCloy, N.Y.C., 1962-70, ptnr., 1970-98; pres. Jerome Advisors, LLC, N.Y.C., 1999—. Adj. prof. N.Y. Law Sch., 1978-81; lectr. Am. Law Inst., Corp. Strategies, Inc., N.Y. State Bar Assn., Nat. Law Jour., Oreg. Law Sch., Ky. Law Sch. With U.S. Army, 1954-57. Mem. ABA (program chmn.), N.Y. State Bar Assn., Assn. of Bar of City of N.Y. (chmn. com. on bankruptcy and corp. reorgn. 1990-93), Nat. Bankruptcy Conf. Clubs: N.Y. Athletic, Sharon and Norfolk Country. Bankruptcy, Commercial, contracts (including sales of goods; commercial financing), Corporate, general. Home: 1165 5th Ave New York NY 10029-6931 Office: 80 Chambers St New York NY 10007

JERRY, ROBERT HOWARD, II, law educator; b. Lafayette, Ind., July 11, 1953; s. Robert Howard and Marjorie (Collings) J.; m. Lisa Nowak, Sept. 4, 1982; children: John Robert, James Martin, Elizabeth Catherine. BS, Ind. State U., 1974; JD, U. Mich., 1977. Bar: Ind. 1977, U.S. Ct. Appeals (D.C. cir.) 1978, U.S. Ct. Appeals (7th cir.) 1980, U.S. Ct. Appeals (10th cir.) 1989. Law clk. to Hon. George MacKinnon U.S. Ct. Appeals (D.C. cir.), Washington, 1977-78; assoc. Barnes, Hickam, Pantzer & Boyd, Indpls., 1978-81; assoc. prof. law U. Kans., Lawrence, 1981-85, prof., 1985-94, dean sch. law, 1989-94; prof., Herbert Herff chair of excellence law Cecil C. Humphreys Sch. Law U. Memphis, 1989—. Author: Understanding Insurance Law, 1987, 2d edit., 1996; (with Roger C. Henderson) Insurance Law: Cases and Materials, 2d edit., 1996; contbr. numerous articles to profl. jours., chpts. to books. Fellow Am. Bar Found.; mem. ABA, Am. Law Inst. Democrat. Episcopalian. Office: U Memphis Humphreys Sch Law PO Box 526513 Memphis TN 38152-0001*

JESKE, CHARLES MATTHEW, lawyer; b. Bartlesville, Okla., July 16, 1964; s. Arnold Carl and Maudie Marie (Matthews) J.; m. Pamela Kay Paholek, May 20, 1989. BBA in Fin./Acctg., Tex. A&M U., 1986; JD, South Tex. Coll. Law, Houston, 1989. Bar: Tex. 1989, U.S. Dist. Ct. (so. dist.) Tex. 1990, U.S. Ct. Appeals (5th cir.) 1990. Briefing atty. 14th Dist. Ct. of Appeals Tex., Houston, 1989-90, 90-91; sr. assoc. atty. Renneker & Assocs., Houston, 1991-96; pvt. practice Jeske & Assocs. PLLC, Houston, 1996—, mng. ptnr., 1998—. Contractor, investment analyst Jeske Homes, Bryan, Tex., 1986—. Trustee, officer Meml. Hollow Citizens, Inc., Houston, 1994-96. Mem. ABA, Houston Bar Assn., Tex. A&M U. Former Students Assn., Phi Alpha Delta Alumni Assn. Republican. Lutheran. Avocations: photography, travel. Estate planning, Probate (including wills, trusts), Estate taxation. Home and Office: 12407 Barryknoll Ln Houston TX 77024-4113 E-mail: cmjeske@usa.net.

JESPERSEN, ROBERT RANDOLPH, legal consultant; b. N.Y.C., June 17, 1936; s. Randolph Foyen and Marie (Larsen) J.; m. Shirley Dubber, Dec. 20, 1958; children: Robert Randolph Jr., Craig Christopher. AB, Columbia U., 1958, AM, 1964; JD, U. Houston, 1975; LLM, U. Tex., 1987. Bar: Tex. 1975, Ark. 1981, U.S. Supreme Ct., U.S. Ct. Appeals (5th and 8th cirs.), U.S. Dist. Ct. (so. dist.) Tex., U.S. Dist. Ct. (ea. dist.) Ark., U.S. Ct. Mil. Appeals. Pvt. practice law, 1975—. Moderator Am. Arbitration Assn. conf., Little Rock, 1987; asst. atty. gen. Tex., 1975-76; apprentice banker The Bank of N.Y., N.Y.C., 1964-66; mgmt. analyst U.S. Govt., Washington, 1961-62; hon. consul Kingdom of Lesotho, Jurisdiction of Tex., 1972-75; legal cons., 1995—; adj. prof. law U. Ark.-Little rock, 1987-91, prof. bus. law, 1980-95, prof. emeritus, 1995—; vis. prof. law U. Auckland, 1993; vis. sr. lectr. bus. law Massey U., N.Z., 1991; vis. disting. lectr. internat. bus. Calif. State U., Long Beach, 1987; vis. prof. bus. law U. Tex., Austin, 1987; part-time instr. Houston C.C., 1975-76; part-time tchg. fellow U. Houston, 1974-75; sr. advisor Assn. African Univs., Accra, Ghana, 1971-72; headmaster Kurisini Internat. Edn. Ctr., Dar-es-Salaam, Tanzania, 1969-71; dir. devel. African-Am. Inst., N.Y.C., 1967-69; assoc. dir. career svcs. Princeton U., 1966-67; asst. dir. univ. placement Columbia U., 1962-64. Co-author: Business Law: Comprehensive Edit., 1987, Business Law: Text and Cases, 1984, 8th edit., 1996, American Legal System, 1986; editor, contbr.: Industrial Laws, 1980; editl. bd. Jour. Legal Studies Edn., 1983-85, The Houston Lawyer, 1978-80; editor: Proc. of Internat. Legal Studies Assn. Ann. Mtg., 1988; contbr. numerous articles to profl. jours. 1st lt. USMC, 1958—61, col. res. USMC, 1961—88. Recipient Tchg. Excellence award Nat. Conf. of Acad. Bus. Adminstrn., 1993, Faculty Excellence award Coll. Bus. Adminstrn., U. Ark.-Little Rock, 1992; Sam M. Walton Free Enterprise fellow, 1995, Peace Rsch. fellow U. Auckland Ctr. for Peace Studies, 1992.. Mem. Nat. Assn. Scholars, The Federalist Soc. for Law and Pub. Policy Studies (lawyers divsn. Ark. chpt. dir. 1992-93, 94-95, pres. 1991-92), Am. Bus. Law Assn. (pres. 1988-89), So. Reg. Bus. Law Assn. (pres. 1983-84), Ark. Bar Assn. (mem. alternative dispute resolution com. 1987-88, 92-93, internat. law com. 1983-84), State Bar of Tex. (exec. com. mil. law sect. 1978-80), Southwestern Fedn. Adminstrv. Disciplines (bd. dirs. 1982-84), Internat. Consular Acad., Am. Arbitration Assn., Assn. Law Tchrs. G.B., Assn. of Attenders and Alumni of the Hague Acad. Internat. Law, Nat. Arbitration Forum, Order of Barristers, Order of Advocates, Golden Key, Beta Gamma Sigma (chpt. pres. 1985-86), Phi Kappa Phi (chpt. pres. 1984-85), Phi Alpha Delta, Alpha Kappa Psi, Alpha Phi Omega. Republican. Office: PO Box 33471 Pensacola FL 32508

JESSEE, ROY MARK, lawyer; b. Kingsport, Tenn., Feb. 8, 1966; s. Roy Claude and Myrtle Delight (Robinette) J.; m. Cortney Wynn Williams, June 30, 1990. BA, King Coll., 1988; JD, U. Va., 1991. Bar: Va. 1991, U.S. Dist. Ct. (we. dist.) Va. 1992. Law clk. Ct. of Appeals of Va., Bristol, 1991-92; assoc. atty. Mullins, Thomason & Harris, Norton, Va., 1992-94; shareholder, prin. atty. Mullins, Thomason, Harris & Jessee, Norton, Va., 1995-98; shareholder, prin. Mullins, Harris & Jessee, Norton, Va., 1998—. Contbr. articles to legal jours. Chmn. Scott County Dem. Party, 1993-95, 95-97. Named one of Outstanding Young Men in Am., 1989. Mem. ABA, Wise County Bar Assn. (pres.-elect 1998, pres. 1999), Am. Judicature Soc., Va. Assn. Def. Attys. Democrat. Baptist. Avocations: running, weight lifting, reading, writing poetry. General civil litigation, Personal injury (including property damage), Product liability. Home: 157 Fraley Ave Duffield VA 24244 Office: Mullins Harris & Jessee PO Box 1200 30 Seventh St Norton VA 24273

JESSUP, PHILIP CARYL, JR., b. Utica, N.Y., Aug. 30, 1926; s. Philip C. and Lois K. (Kellogg) J.; m. Dorothy A. Kerr, Jan. 15, 1951 (div.); children: Timothy, Nancy, Margaret; m. Helen I. Ibbitson, Jan.24, 1969; stepchildren: Genevieve, Lucinda, Francesca, Alexander. BA, Yale Coll., 1949; JD, Harvard U., 1952. Bar: N.Y. 1954. Atty. Whitman, Ransom & Coulson, N.Y.C., 1952-58; legal officer Internat. Nickel Co., Inc., N.Y.C., 1958-63; gen. solicitor internat. Inco Ltd., N.Y.C., 1963-68; chief legal officer, sec., dir. Inco Europe Ltd., London, 1968-72; pres., mng. dir. P.T. Internat. Nickel Indonesia, Jakarta, 1972-78; v.p., gen. counsel and sec. Inco Ltd., N.Y.C., Toronto, Can., 1978-84; sec., gen. counsel Nat. Gallery Art, Washington, 1985-2000. Dir. Biogen N.V., Geneva, 1981-85; chmn. bd. Inco Gulf, E.C., Bahrain, 1980-84; chmn. bd. Am. Friends Nat. Gallery Art Australia, N.Y.C., 2001—, asst. treas., 2002—; bd. dirs. Norfolk Land Trust, Norfolk, Conn. Trustee Obor, Internat. Book Inst. Inc., Phila., 1978—, sec.-treas., 1989-96, chmn. bd., 1996-2001; mem. adv. commn. H.H. Humphrey Fellowship Program, 1984-89; trustee Asia Soc., 1991-99, sec., 1993-99, mem. adv. com. Washington Ctr., 1985-2000, chmn. adv. com., 1989-2000; pres. Friends of Hosp. for Sick Children, Toronto, 1985—; mem. Coun. on Fgn. Rels., N.Y.C., 1972—; pres. West Brooklyn Ind. Dems., 1956-58. Served to staff/sgt. C.E., U.S. Army, 1944-46. Mem. ABA, Assn. of Bar of City of N.Y., Century Assn. (N.Y.C.). Democrat. Home: 97 Gamefield Rd Norfolk CT 06058-1272

JETTE, ERNEST ARTHUR, lawyer; b. Nashua, N.H., Apr. 19, 1945; s. Fernand Ernest and Jeannette M. (Thibodeau) J.; m. Bridget Belton, Sept. 4, 1977; 1 child, Alexandra. BA, Boston Coll., 1967, JD, 1970. Bar: N.H. 1970, U.S. Dist. Ct. N.H. 1971, U.S. Tax Ct. 1972; diplomate Trial Practice Inst. Mng. atty. N.H. Legal Assistance, Nashua, 1970-72; ptnr. Janelle, Nadeau & Jette, Nashua, 1972-81; dir. Hamblett & Kerrigan, P.A., Nashua, 1981-93; pvt. practice Nashua, 1993—. Lectr. paralegal studies Rivier Coll., Nashua, 1977-78. Chmn. Nashua Regional Planning Commn., 1981-82; mem. Town of Merrimack (N.H.) Master Plan Com., 1981, dir. Nashua Youth Coun., Inc., 1975-80, pres., 1978-79; dir. NEEDS, Inc., 1972-75; chmn. Heart Sunday, N.H. Heart Assn., 1973; mem. pub. affairs com. N.H. Assn. Commerce and Industry, 1983-93; bd. dirs. Cmty. Coun. Nashua, 2002—; mem. sch. bd. Bishop Guertin H.S., 1994-96. Capt. U.S. Army, 1970. Mem. ABA (state com. disaster legal assistance 1973-75, litigation, tort and ins. practice sects.), N.H. Bar Assn. (past mem. law related edn., coop. with the cts., profl. responsibility coms.), N.H. Bar Found., N.H. Trial Lawyers Assn., Nashua Bar Assn. (pres. 1990-91), Greater Nashua C. of C. (dir. 1985-96), Four Seasons Property Owners' Assn. (pres. 1977-78), Rotary Club Nashua (dir. 1978-79, pres. 1992-93). General civil litigation, General practice, Personal injury (including property damage). Home: 9 Westbrook Dr Nashua NH 03060-5314 Office: 187 Main St Nashua NH 03060-2701 E-mail: ejette@ejette.com.

JETTON, GIRARD REUEL, JR., lawyer, retired oil company executive; b. Washington, Feb. 19, 1924; s. Girard Reuel and Hallie (Grimes) J.; m. Mera Riddell, Sept. 4, 1948 (dec. Dec. 1997); children: Mera Elizabeth, Robert Girard, James Thomas. BS in Engring., George Washington U., 1945, BA, 1947; JD, Harvard U., 1950. Bar: D.C. 1951, Md. 1959, Ohio 1960. Elec. engr. in rsch., 1944-45; patent atty., 1950-51; atty. IRS, Washington, 1951-54; trial atty. Dept. Justice, Washington, 1954-55; atty. then ptnr. McClure & McClure, Washington, 1955-60; with Marathon Oil Co., Findlay, Ohio, 1960-85, asst. to chmn. bd., 1969-73, corp. sec., 1973-85; pvt. practice Findlay, 1985—. With USNR, 1945-46. Mem. Bar Assn. D.C., Findlay/Hancock County Bar Assn., Met. Club (Washington). Estate planning, Probate (including wills, trusts), Taxation, general. Home and Office: 170 Orchard Ln Findlay OH 45840-1130

JEWELL, GEORGE BENSON, lawyer, educator, minister; b. Evanston, Ill., Mar. 26, 1944; s. Benson Murray and Ellen Louise (Mahle) J.; m. Pamela Elaine Peterson, Aug. 12, 1967; children: Jeffrey Benson, Brian Edward. BA, Beloit (Wis.) Coll., 1966; MDiv, Gordon-Conwell Theol. Sem., 1978; JD, Washington U., St. Louis, 1971. Bar: Ill. 1971, Mo. 1972, Mass. 1990, U.S. Dist. Ct. (ea. dist.) Mo. 1973, U.S. Dist. Ct. Mass. 1991, Ind. 1998. Trust adminstr. Ill. Nat. Bank, Springfield, 1971; corp. atty. Ralston Purina Co., St. Louis, 1971-75; assoc. pastor Westminster Presbyn. Ch., Bluefield, W.Va., 1978-81, sr. pastor Cape Girardeau, Mo., 1981-86, Evang. Free Ch., Cape Girardeau, 1986-88; pvt. practice Cape Girardeau, 1988-89; counsel, dir. gift planning, adj. assoc. prof. bus. law Gordon Coll., Wenham, Mass., 1989-97; dir. legal support svcs. Renaissance Inc., Carmel, Ind., 1997-98, v.p. legal support svcs., v.p. client svcs., 1998-99, v.p., sr. counsel, 1999—2002; v.p. Wachovia Trust Co., 2003—. Instr. in bus. law S.E. Mo. State U., Cape Girardeau, 1986; cons. Stone, McGhee, Feuchtenberger & Barringer, Bluefield, 1980-81; mng. editor Washington U. Law Quar. Author: Charitable Trusts; contbr. chpts. to Life Insurance Answer Book. Deacon Ctrl. Presbyn. Ch., St. Louis, 1974-75; scoutmaster Appalachian coun. Boy Scouts Am., Bluefield, 1979; bd. advisors Sta. KUGT, Cape Girardeau, 1988, Boston Rescue Mission, 1994-97; baccalaureate spkr. Ctrl. H.S., Cape Girardeau, 1988; workshop presenter Congress '93 and Congress '94, Boston; bd. dirs. Young Life of Cape Girardeau. Mem. ABA, Nat. Assn. Coll. and Univ. Attys. (ad hoc com. on income devel. 1990-91, ad hoc com. svcs. small colls. 1991-93, com. profl. devel., 1993-97), Nat. Assn. Estate Planners and Couns., Ind. State Bar Assn. (mem. probate rev. com. 1999-2002), Mass. Soc. Sons Am. Revolution, Boston Bar Assn. (coll. and univ. com., estate planning com.), Planned Giving Group of New Eng., Christian Fin. Advisors Network (founder), Mo. Bar Assn. (franchise tax subcom. corp. law and bus. orgn. coms.), Evang. Free Ch. Ministerial Assn., Sigma Alpha Epsilon. Avocations: swimming, tennis, sailing. Estate planning, Estate taxation, Probate (including wills, trusts). Office: Wachovia Trust Co 3 Beaver Valley Rd Wilmington DE 19803 E-mail: george.jewell@wachovia.com.

JEWELL, GEORGE HIRAM, lawyer; b. Fort Worth, Jan. 9, 1922; s. George Hiram and Vera (Lee) J.; m. Betty Jefferis, July 21, 1944 (dec. Feb. 2000); children: Susan Jewell Cannon, Robert V., Nancy Jewell Wommack; m. Nancy Hart Glanville, May 19, 2001. BA, U. Tex., 1942, LLB, 1950. Bar: Tex. 1950. With Baker & Botts, LLP, Houston, 1950—; sr. ptnr. Baker & Botts, Houston, 1960-90, counsel, 1990—. Trustee Tex. Children's Hosp., Houston, 1977—, pres., 1982-83, chmn., 1984-86; bd. dirs. Schlumberger Found., N.Y.C., 1982-90. Lt. USNR, 1943-46, 50-53. Fellow Am. Coll. Tax Counsel, Am. Bar Foun.; mem. ABA, Houston Country Club, Coronado Club (pres. 1976-77), Old Baldy Club (chmn. 1993-98), Eldorado Country Club (pres. 1995-96), Blind Brook Club, Order of Coif, Phi Beta Kappa, Phi Delta Phi. Corporate taxation, Personal income taxation. Office: Baker Botts LLP 1 Shell Plz Houston TX 77002 Home: 1000 Uptown Park Blvd Houston TX 77056

JIMENEZ, MARCOS DANIEL, lawyer; b. Havana, Cuba, Dec. 15, 1959; came to U.S., 1961; s. Frank T. and Daisy (D'Clouet) J. BA, U. Miami, Fla., 1980, JD, 1983. Bar: Ill. 1983, U.S. Dist. Ct. (no. dist.) Ill. 1983, Fla. 1984, U.S. Dist. Ct. (so. dist.) Fla. 1984, U.S. Ct. Appeals (11th cir.) 1985. Assoc. Phelan, Pope and John, Ltd., Chgo., 1983-84, Greenberg, Traurig et al, Miami, 1984-89; asst. U.S. atty. U.S. Dist. Ct. (So. dist.) Fla., Fla., 1989—92; partner White & Case LLP, 1992—2002; US atty. south dist. U.S. Dept. of Justice, 2002—. Contbr. articles to profl. jours. Mem. ABA, Fla. Bar Assn. (com. mem.), Dade County Bar Assn. (com. mem.), Hurricane Club. Republican. Baptist. Avocations: basketball, saxophone. General civil litigation, Constitutional. Office: 99 NE 4th Street Miami FL 33132*

JIN, HONG KI, lawyer; b. Seoul, Republic of Korea; s. Joong Kwan and In Ok (Kang) Jin; m. Soo Mi Kim, Apr. 5, 1986; children: Kyoung Hoon, Hye Won, Kyoung Hwi. BA, Seoul Nat. U., 1983, LLM, 1985, U. Coll. London, 2002. Ptnr. Hwang Mok Park, PC, Seoul, 1994—. Sgt., 1976—79, Katusa, Republic of Korea. Mem.: Seoul Bar Assn. (cert.). Commercial, contracts (including sales of goods; commercial financing), Mergers and acquisitions, Property, real (including real estate development, water). Office: Hwang Mok Park 120 Taepyungro Chung Gu 2 Ka 9th Fl Seoul 100-724 Republic of Korea

JOCHNER, MICHELE MELINA, lawyer; b. Naperville, Ill., May 19, 1966; BA summa cum laude, Mundelein Coll., 1987; JD with honors, DePaul U., 1990, LLM in Taxation Law, 1992. Bar: Ill. 1990, U.S. Dist. Ct. (no. dist.) Ill. 1990, U.S. Ct. Appeals (7th cir.) 1996, U.S. Supreme Ct. 1996. Law clk. U.S. Securities & Exch. Commn., Chgo., 1989; legal rsch. asst. to prof. Marlene Nicholson DePaul U. Sch. Law, Chgo., 1989-91, legal rsch. asst. to assoc. dean Vincent Vitullo, 1989-91; law clk. extern U.S. Dist. Ct. (no. dist.) Ill., Chgo., 1989-90; judicial law clk. Cir. Ct. of Cook County, Chgo., 1991-92, staff atty., 1992-93, sr. staff atty., 1993-95, acting supr. legal rsch. divsn., 1995-96; staff atty. permanency project child protection divsn. Cir. Ct. Cook County, Chgo., 1996-97; jud. law clk. to Chief Justice Mary Ann G. McMorrow Ill. Supreme Ct., Chgo., 1997—. Adj. prof. law John Marshall Law Sch., Chgo., 1994—, DePaul U. Coll. Law, 1998—; mem. subcom. money transfers and adminstrv. regulations Ill. Supreme Ct., 1995—96; judge Herzog Moot Ct. Competition, 1997—; spkr. in field. Contbr. articles to profl. jours. Recipient Harold A. Shertz award, Film, Air & Package Carriers Conf., 1990. Mem.: ABA, U.S. Supreme Ct. Hist. Soc., Chgo. Bar Assn., Fed. Bar Assn., Ill. Bar Assn. (elected assembly mem. 2000, bd. govs. 2002—, chair gen. practice sect. coun., chair continuing legal edn. subcom., fmr. mem. standing com. legal edn., admission and competence, mem. tradition of excellence award subcom., mem. bench and bar sect. coun., co-editor Bench and Bar Newsletter, mem. jud. evaluations com., Lincoln award 2d pl. 1994, Lincoln award 1st pl. 1996, Lincoln award 2d pl. 1997, Lincoln award 1st pl. 1999, Lincoln award 2d pl. 2000, Lincoln award 1st pl. 2002, 2001), planning com. 4th Annual Women Everywhere: Partners in Svc. Project, Alliance for Women (mem. constitutional law com., judiciary com.), Order of Coif, Phi Sigma Tau, Kappa Gamma Pi. Avocation: writing fiction, non-fiction.

JOCK, PAUL F., II, lawyer; b. Indpls., Jan. 25, 1943; s. Paul F. and Alice (Sheehan) J.; m. Gail A. Webre, Sept. 16, 1967; children: Craig W., Nicole L. BBA, U. Notre Dame, 1965; JD, U. Chgo., 1970. Bar: Ill. 1970, N.Y. 1990. Ptnr. Kirkland & Ellis, Chgo. and N.Y.C., 1970-2001; v.p., gen. counsel GM Asset Mgmt., N.Y.C., 2000—. V.p. legal affairs Tribune Co., Chgo., 1981. Assoc. editor U. Chgo. Law Rev., 1969-70. Served to lt. USN, 1965-67. Mem. ABA, Chgo. Bar Assn., Assn. of the Bar of City of N.Y. Banking, Corporate, general, Securities. Address: GM Asset Mgmt 767 Fifth Ave New York NY 10153 E-mail: paul.jock@gm.com.

JOELSON, MARK RENÉ, lawyer; b. Paris, Oct. 23, 1934; came to U.S., 1941, naturalized, 1947; s. Michael and Helen (Streicher) J.; m. Anastasia Whelan, June 4, 1967; children: Helen, Daniel, Marisa. BA, Harvard U., 1955, LLB, 1958; diploma in law, Oxford U., Eng., 1962. Bar: D.C. 1958, U.S. Supreme Ct. 1959. Atty. U.S. Dept. Justice, Washington, 1958-63; assoc., then ptnr. Arent, Fox, Kintner, Plotkin & Kahn, Washington, 1963-80; ptnr. Wald, Harkrader & Ross, Washington, 1980-85, Morgan, Lewis & Bockius LLP, Washington, 1986-97; pvt. practice, 1998—. Mem. adv. com. internat. investment, tech. and devel. U.S. Dept. State, 1978-87; cons. UN Conf. Trade and Devel., 1977-79; adj. prof. Georgetown U., Washington; panelist N.Am. Free Trade Agreement, Am. Arbitration Assn., Nat. Arbitration Forum. Author (with Earl W. Kintner): An International Antitrust Primer, 1974; author: An International Antitrust Primer, 2d edit., 2001; editor (with others): Current Legal Aspects of Doing Business in the E.E.C., 1978; editor: Enterprise Law in the 80's, 1980, Joint Ventures in the United States, 1988. Fulbright scholar Oxford U., 1961-62. Mem. ABA (chmn. sect. internat. law and practice 1983-84, del. Internat. Bar Assn. coun. 1984-92), Internat. Bar Assn., Fed. Bar Assn. (pres. D.C. chpt. 1976-77), Washington Inst. Fgn. Affairs, Cosmos Club (Washington), Order of Brit. Empire. Antitrust, Federal civil litigation, Private international. E-mail: joelsonmr@msn.com.

JOERLING, DALE RAYMOND, lawyer; b. St. Louis, Apr. 11, 1949; s. Raymond H. and Opal M. (Hoffman) J.; m. Cozette Joyce Turner, Apr. 7, 1979; children: Jeffrey Dale, Jill Lorraine. BA in Econ. cum laude, Southeast Mo. State U., 1971; JD, U. Mo., 1976. Bar: Mo. 1976, D.C. 1980, U.S. Dist. Ct. (ea. dist.) Mo. 1982, Ill. 1990. Atty. FTC, Washington, 1976-81; assoc. Guilfoil, Petzall & Shoemake, St. Louis, 1981-85; ptnr. Thompson Coburn, LLP, St. Louis, 1985—. Served as sgt. U.S. Army, 1971-73. Mem. ABA, Mo. Bar Assn., Bar Assn. of St. Louis, Ill. Bar Assn. Clubs: Mo. Athletic (St. Louis). Avocation: juggling. Antitrust, General civil litigation, Environmental. Home: 23 S Elm Ave Saint Louis MO 63119-3015 Office: Thompson Coburn LLP One US Bank Plz Mercantile Ctr Saint Louis MO 63101

JOFFE, ROBERT DAVID, lawyer; b. N.Y.C., May 26, 1943; s. Joseph and Bertha (Pashkovsky) J.; children by prior marriage: Katherine, David; m. Virginia Ryan, June 20, 1981; stepchildren: Elizabeth DeHaas, Ryan DeHaas. AB, Harvard U., 1964, JD, 1967. Bar: N.Y. 1970, U.S. Dist. Ct. (so. and ea. dists.) N.Y. 1971, U.S. Ct. Appeals (2d cir.) 1972, U.S. Supreme Ct. 1973. Maxwell Sch. Africa Pub. Svc. fellow (funded by Ford Found.), Republic of Malawi, 1967-69; state counsel, 1968-69; assoc. Cravath, Swaine & Moore LLP, N.Y.C., 1969-75, ptnr., 1975—, dep. presiding ptnr., 1998, presiding ptnr., 1999—. Apptd. to bd. dirs. by Pres. Clinton, Romanian Am. Enterprise Fund, 1994-2003. Bd. dirs. Lawyers Com. for Human Rights, The Jericho Project, 1985—97, Franklin Resources, 2003—; chair Harvard Law Sch. Nat. Fund, 1995—97, dean's adv. bd., 1997—; bd. dirs. Fiduciary Trust Co. Internat., 1999—, The After Sch. Corp. Mem. ABA, N.Y. Bar Assn., Assn. of the Bar of the City of N.Y. (chmn. trade regulation com. 1980-83, exec. com. 1995-99, nominating com. 2001-02, v.p. 2003—), Coun. on Fgn. Rels., Human Rights Watch/Africa (adv. com.), Harvard Club, Century Assn. Antitrust, Federal civil litigation, Communications. Home: 300 W End Ave Apt 13A New York NY 10023-8156 Office: Cravath Swaine & Moore LLP 825 8th Ave Fl 46 New York NY 10019-7475

JOHANNSEN, MARC ALAN, lawyer; b. Victorville, Calif., Feb. 14, 1964; s. Gerald W. and Sharon K. J.; m. Kimberly Kriss, Sept. 29, 1990. BSBA magna cum laude, Carroll Coll., 1986; JD cum laude, U. Minn., 1989. Bar: Minn. 1989, U.S. Dist. Ct. Minn. 1990, Wis. 1997. Jud. clk. Hennepin County Dist. Ct., Mpls., 1989-90, Minn. Ct. Appeals, St. Paul, 1990-91; atty., shareholder Lommen, Nelson, Cole & Stageberg, Mpls., 1991—. Vol. pro bono atty. Vol. Lawyers Network, Mpls., 1991—; mem. city coun. City of Vadnais Heights, Minn., 1995—. AV Rating, Martindale Hubbell. Mem. ABA, Minn. Bar Assn., Hennepin County Bar Assn. Avocations: hiking, gardening, computers, politics. General civil litigation, Family and matrimonial. Office: Lommen Nelson Cole & Stageberg 80 S 8th St 1800 IDS Center Minneapolis MN 55127 E-mail: marc@Lommen.com.

JOHN, DARWIN A. federal agency administrator; BS in Prodn. Mgmt., Utah State U., 1965, MBA, 1971. With Thiokol Chem. Corp., Brigham City, Utah; sr. sys. analyst Honeywell, Inc., Mpls.; dir. info. and comm. sys. devel. and ops. Gen. Mills, Mpls.; v.p. Scott Paper Co.; mng. dir. info. and comm. sys. LDS Ch.; chief info. officer FBI, Washington, 2002—. Office: FBI J Edgar Hoover Bldg 935 Pennsylvania Ave NW Washington DC 20535*

JOHN, IAN GRANT, lawyer; b. Pitts., June 14, 1968; s. T. Grant and Mary A. John; m. Elizabeth D. Stuart, Aug. 11, 1995; 1 child, Kathryn I. AB, Bowdoin Coll., 1990; JD, Ind. U., 1995. Bar: N.Y. 1996, U.S. Dist. Ct. (so. dist.) N.Y. 1997, U.S. Dist. Ct. (ea. dist.) N.Y. 1997. Assoc. Skadden, Arps, Slate, Meagher & Flom LLP, N.Y.C., 1995—. Mem.: ABA (mem. antitrust sect.). Antitrust. Office: Skadden Arps Slate Meagher and Flom LLP 4 Times Sq New York NY 10036 Business E-Mail: ijohn@skadden.com.

JOHN, PHILLIP L.M. lawyer; b. Eng., Nov. 26, 1962; s. Hugh and Vena John. LLB, Bristol (Eng.) U., 1986. Bar: U.K. (solicitor) 1990, Hong Kong 1993. Solicitor Simmons & Simmons, London, 1990—92, Hong Kong, 1992—2000; mng. ptnr. Bangkok office Norton Rose, Bangkok, 2000—. Mem.: Law Soc. Hong Kong, Law Soc. Eng. and Wales. Mergers and acquisitions, Securities, Corporate, general. Office: Norton Rose (Thailand) Ltd 130 Wireless Rd 14th Fl Tower 21 Bangkok 10330 Thailand

JOHN, ROBERT MCCLINTOCK, lawyer; b. Phila., May 21, 1947; s. Lewis Timothy and Marie (McClintock) J.; m. Barbara Ann Weand, May 10, 1975; children: Jennifer, Ryan. BA, Villanova U., 1969, JD, 1972. Bar: Pa. 1972, U.S. Dist. Ct. (ea. dist.) Pa. 1973, U.S. Ct. of Appeals (3d cir.) 1998. Atty. Schneider, Nixon & John, Hatboro, Pa., 1972-74, ptnr., 1975-93, sole proprietor, 1993—. Scoutmaster Boy Scouts Am., Hatboro, 1972—, long range planning com., 1979; lectr. and student loan com. Hatboro-Horsham High Sch., 1972-95, co-chmn. Tip of the Hat Cavalcade of Bands, 1994, 95, 96; co-prs. Hatters for Music, 1997-99; prodr. multi media banquet show Marching Hatters, 1994-2000; mgr. Little League, Horsham, Pa., 1985-96, girls' sr. tournament coach, 1993; referee Hatboro-Horsham Youth Basketball Assn., 1990-91, mgr., 1991-94. Recipient award Hatboro-Horsham Sch. Bd., 1979, medal Hatboro YMCA Triathlon, 1983, Silver Beaver award Boy Scouts Am., 1981, Scoutmaster's award of Merit, 1989, Nat. God and Svc. award, 1991, Hatboro-Horsham H.S. Prin.'s Golden Apple award, 1997, Martin Luther King Humanitarian award Upper Moreland Mid. Sch., 1997, Cmty. Svc. award Borough of Hatboro, 2002, others; named to Hatboro-Horsham H.S. Hall of Fame, 2000. Mem. Pa. Bar Assn., Montgomery County Bar Assn., Greater Hatboro C. of C. (pres. 1983, Honored Citizen Svc. to Youth award 1984, judge advocate 1984—, chmn. awards com. and prod. multimedia awards ceremony biannual borough ball, 86, 89, 97, 99, 2001, 2003), Navy League (sec. southeastern Pa. coun. 1975-89, pres. 1989, S.E. Pa. Coun. Svc. to Youth and Community award 1990, Willow Grove naval Air Sta. svc. award 1986), Rotary (pres. 1984, Dist. Gov.'s Outstanding Pres.'s award 1984, host family foreign exch. students). Republican. Roman Catholic. Avocations: scouting, swimming, cycling, backpacking. Family and matrimonial, General practice, Probate (including wills, trusts). Home: 83 Home Rd Hatboro PA 19040-1830 Office: Schneider Nixon & John 76 Byberry Ave # 698 Hatboro PA 19040-3419 E-mail: legalbeaglermj@juno.com.

JOHNS, MARY E. law librarian; b. Davenport, Iowa, Apr. 27, 1953; d. Donald S. and Elizabeth C. Blackman; m. Christopher K. Johns, Aug. 25, 1973; 1 child, Eric Robert. AB, U. Calif., Berkeley, 1977; MLS, La. State U., 1982. Cataloger La. State U. Law Libr., Baton Rouge, 1982-84, head cataloging, 1984—87, 1989—2001, acting head tech. svcs., 1987-89, electronic info. svcs. libr., 2001—. Mem. Am. Assn. Law Librs. Home: 864 Albert Hart Dr Baton Rouge LA 70808-5807 Office: La State U Law Libr Baton Rouge LA 70803-1010

JOHNS, TIMOTHY ROBERT, judge; b. Aberdeen, S.D., July 17, 1948; s. Frank Edward Johns and Helen Theresa Mock; m. LeAnn L. Thoresen, Nov. 25, 1978; children: Nicholas, Justin. BA, No. State U., 1970; JD, U. S.D., 1974. Dep. states atty. Butte County, S.D., 1974-75; atty. City of Nisland, S.D., 1974-75; pvt. practice Belle Fourche, S.D., 1974-75; magistrate State of S.D., Deadwood, 1975-89, cir. ct. judge, 1989—. Mem. S.D. Jud. Qualifications Commn. , 1997—2001. Mem., pres. Deadwood-Lead (S.D.) Jaycees, 1978-85; bd. dirs. Adv. Coun. Black Hills coun. Boy Scouts Am., Northern Hills Adjustment Tng. Ctr., Spearfish, S.D., Northern Hills YMCA of Lead, State Bd. S.D. Spl. Olympics. Recipient Keyman award Deadwood-Lead Jaycees, 1982-83; named Outstanding Young Man of Am. Mem.: SD Judges Assn. (pres. 1995—96), Kiwanis (pres. 2001—02), KC. Roman Catholic. Avocations: reading, hunting, fishing, boating. Home: 110 S Main St Lead SD 57754-1541 Office: 4th Jud Cir Ct PO Box 626 78 Sherman St Deadwood SD 57732-1341

JOHNS, WARREN LEROI, lawyer; b. Nevada, Iowa, June 9, 1929; s. Varner Jay and Ruby Charlene (Morrison) J.; m. Elaine C. Magnuson, July 24, 1955 (div. June 1983); children: Richard Warren, Lynn Cherie Johns-Pence; m. Ruth Page Scott, Sept. 29, 1985. BA, La Sierra U., 1950; MA, Andrews U., 1951; JD, U. So. Calif., 1958. Bar: Calif. 1959, U.S. Dist. Ct. (cen. dist.) Calif. 1959,U.S. Supreme Ct. 1963, Md. 1976, D.C. 1976, U.S. Dist. Ct. Md. 1976, U.S. Dist. Ct. D.C. 1976, U.S. Tax Ct. 1976, U.S. Ct. Appeals (4th cir.) 1976, U.S. Ct. Appeals (10th cir.) 1977, U.S. Ct. Customs and Patent Appeals 1979. Gen. counsel So. Calif. Conf. Seventh-day Adventists, Glendale, 1959-63, Pacific Union Conf. Seventh-day Adventists, Glendale and Sacramento, 1964-69; pvt. practice Sacramento, 1969-75; gen. counsel Gen. Conf. Seventh-day Adventists, Washington, 1975-92, trustee; pvt. practice Brookeville, Md., 1992-98. Mem. adv. bd. Ctr. for Ch./State Studies, De Paul U. Coll. Chgo., 1987-93, spl. counsel to gen. conf., 1992-95; spl. counsel Adventist HealthCare Corp., Columbia Union HealthCare Corp., 1992-97. Author: Dateline Sunday USA, 1967, Ride to Glory, 1999; editor CreationDigest.com, 2001, Creation Equation Newsletter, 2002; founding editor JD, 1978-92. Chmn. bd. dirs., pres. Sacramento Area Econ. Opportunity Coun., 1974. Recipient Frank Yost award Ch. State Coun., Glendale, Alumnus of Achievement award Andrews U., 1981, Alumnus of Yr. award La Sierra U., 1994. Mem. AAAS, ABA (vice-chmn. com. on torts, non-profit, charitable and religious orgns., sect. of tort and ins. practice 1990-91). Democrat. Avocations: sports, photography, book collecting. Alternative dispute resolution, Corporate, general, General practice. Office: 21320 Georgia Ave Brookeville MD 20833-1132

JOHNSON, ALEX MOORE, lawyer, educator; b. Portland, Oreg., Oct. 5, 1953; s. Alex M. and Margaret (Clark) J.; m. Perdita L. Currie (div. Oct. 1982); 1 child, Reginald Osborne; m. Karen J. Anderson. BA, Claremont U., 1975; JD, UCLA, 1978. Bar: Calif. 1978, U.S. Dist. Ct. (cen. and so. dists.) Calif. 1978. Atty. Latham & Watkins, L.A., 1978-80, 82-84; assoc. prof. law U. Minn., Mpls., 1980-82; asst. prof. U. Va., Charlottesville, 1985-88, prof. law, 1989-93; Mary and Daniel Loughran prof. of law, 1993—; vice provost for faculty, 1995—. Vis. prof. U. Tex., Austin, 1988-89, Stanford Law Sch., 1991. Contbr. articles to profl. jours. Mem. Law Sch. Admission Coun. (bd. trustees 1994, minority affairs com. 1989-94), Assn. Am. Law Schs. (chair curriculum and rsch. com. 1993—), U. Va. Alumni Assn. (chmn. career counseling panel 1987—). Office: U Minn Sch Law Walter F Mondale Hall Rm 381 229-19th Ave S Minneapolis MN 55455*

JOHNSON, ALISE M. lawyer; b. Gainesville, Fla., Dec. 17, 1968; d. Gregory William and Jean Johnson. BA, Vanderbilt U., 1989; JD, U. Fla., 1993. Bar: Fla. 1994, U.S. Dist. Ct. (so., mid. and no. dists.) Fla. Law clk. U.S. Magistrate Chief William Turnoff, Miami, Fla., 1994-97; assoc. Akerman Senterfitt, Miami, 1997—. Articles editor U. Fla. Law Rev., 1993. Mem. Jr. League of Miami, 1995—; participant Leadership Miami, 1998. General civil litigation, Insurance, Municipal (including bonds). Office: Akerman Senterfitt One SE 3d Ave 28th Fl Miami FL 33131

JOHNSON, ALLAN RICHARD, lawyer; b. New Haven, Mar. 25, 1933; s. Karl G. and Anna S. (Nelson) J.; m. Nancy C. Prins, June 23, 1955; children— Joshua W., Gilead G., Abigail A. B.A., Wesleyan U., 1955; J.D., U. Va., 1958. Bar: Conn. 1959, U.S. Dist. Ct. Conn. 1960, U.S. Ct. Appeals (2d cir.) 1966, U.S. Supreme Ct. 1981. Assoc. Willis & Willis, Bridgeport, Conn., 1959-71; ptnr. Tate, Capasse and Johnson, Westport, Conn., 1971-88. Mem. Greater Bridgeport Regional Planning Agy., 1975-88; mem. Sasquanaug Assn., Southport, Conn., past pres., v.p. and bd. dirs., 1961—; mem. Pequot Library, Southport, past v.p. and bd. dirs., 1961— ; chmn. bd., pres. Southport Conservancy, 1982. Mem. Westport Bar Assn., Conn. Bar Assn. (med.-legal com., civil justice sect.), ABA (medicine and law com.), Am. Judicature Assn., Am. Arbitration Assn. Republican. Congregationalist. Club: Pequot Yacht (Southport). State civil litigation, Family and matrimonial, Personal injury (including property damage). Home: 1148 Crystal Lake Dr Virginia Beach VA 23451-3850 Office: 5 Imperial Ave Westport CT 06880-4302

JOHNSON, ANNE STUCKLY, retired lawyer; b. Axtell, Tex., Jan. 8, 1921; d. Arnold Joseph and Angeline (Morris) Stuckly; m. Edward James Johnson, Oct. 9, 1943 (dec. 1967); children: Edward M., Ronald J., Dennis L., Shawn T., Rozlynn Jan, Anne J'lynn, Kevin J, Karal Ian, Donna Lynn. BA, Baylor U., 1940; MA in Econs., St. Mary's U., 1974, JD, 1980. Bar: Tex. 1980. Claims clk. Social Security Adminstrn., Amarillo, Tex., 1940-42; asst. chief divsn. pers. Pantex Ordnance Plant, Amarillo, Tex., 1942-43; chief divsn. pers. Cactus Ordnance Works, Dumas, Tex., 1943-44; citations unit supr. Gen. Hdqrs. Far East Command, Tokyo, 1950-51; v.p., treas. Drive-Safe Corp., San Antonio, 1967-69; counseling psychologist ARC, San Antonio, 1968-69, Divsn. Pers. Office, Ft. Sam Houston, 1969, pers. mgmt. specialist, 1969-77; pvt. practice Oliver B. Chamberlin Offices, San Antonio, 1981-86, San Antonio, 1987-93; ret., 1994. Active Am. Heart Assn., 1983—. Mem. ABA, San Antonio Bar Assn., Tex. Bar Assn., Am. Trial Lawyers Assn., Assn. Social Econs., Tex. Trial Lawyers Assn., Phi Alpha Delta, Pi Gamma Mu, Omicron Delta Epsilon. Home: 3714 Hunters Point San Antonio TX 78230

JOHNSON, BARBARA JEAN, retired judge, lawyer; b. Detroit, Apr. 9, 1932; d. Clifford Clarence and Orma Cecile (Boring) Barnhouse; m. Ronald Mayo Johnson, June 24, 1965; 1 child, Belinda Etezad. BS, U. So. Calif., 1953, JD, 1970. Bar: Calif. 1971. Ptnr. Angela, Burford, Johnson & Tookay, Pasadena, Calif., 1970-77; judge L.A. Mcpl. Ct., 1977-81, L.A. Superior Ct., 1981-97; ret., 1997. Lectr. U. So. Calif. Law Sch. profl. program; adj. prof. Southwestern U. Law Sch. Recipient Ernestine Stahlhut award, 1981. Mem. Calif. Judges Assn., 1977-98, Nat. Assn. Women Judges, 1980-98, Calif. Women Lawyers Assn. (pres. 1976-77), Women Lawyers Assn. LA (pres. 1975-76), Christian Legal Soc. Home: 1000 Prospect Blvd Pasadena CA 91103-2810

JOHNSON, BERNETTE J. state supreme court justice; b. Ascension Parish, La. d. Frank Joshua Jr. and Olivia W. Johnson. BA, Spelman Coll., Atlanta, 1964; JD, La. State U., 1969. Bar: La. Law intern Civil Rights divsn. U.S. Dept. Justice; judge La. Civil Dist. Ct., 1984-94, chief judge, 1994; assoc. justice La. Supreme Ct., New Orleans, 1994—. Legal svc. atty. New Orleans Legal Asst. Corp. Bd. dirs. YMCA, New Orleans; chmn. bd. Learning Ctr., Great St. Stephen Full Gospel Bapt. Ch. Named Woman of Yr., LaBelle chpt. Am. Bus. Women's Assn., 1994. Office: Supreme Ct Bldg 301 Loyola Ave New Orleans LA 70112-1814

JOHNSON, BRUCE EDWARD HUMBLE, lawyer; b. Columbus, Ohio, Jan. 22, 1950; s. Hugo Edward and M. Alice (Humble) J.; m. Paige Robinson Miller, June 28, 1980; children: Marta Noble, Winslow Collins, Russell Scott. AB, Harvard U., 1972; JD, Yale U., 1977; MA, U. Cambridge, Eng., 1978. Bar: Wash. 1977, Calif. 1992. Atty. Davis Wright Tremaine LLP, Seattle, 1977—. Mem. oversight com. King County Gov. Access Channel, 1996—2001. Bd. dirs. Seattle Repertory Theatre, 1993—, pres., 1999-01; bd. dirs. Huntington's Dis. Soc. of Am., N.W. chpt., 2001—. Mem. ABA (tort and ins. practice sect., media law and defamation torts com. chair 1999-2000). General civil litigation, Constitutional, Libel. Home: 711 W Kinnear Pl Seattle WA 98119-3621 Office: Davis Wright Tremaine LLP 2600 Century Sq 1501 4th Ave Seattle WA 98101-1688

JOHNSON, C. TERRY, lawyer; b. Bridgeport, Conn., Sept. 24, 1937; s. Clifford Gustave and Evelyn Florence (Terry) J.; m. Suzanne Frances Chichy, Aug. 24, 1985; children: Laura Elizabeth, Melissa Lynne, Clifford Terry. AB, Trinity Coll., 1960; LLD, Columbia U., 1963. Bar: Ohio 1964, U.S. Ct. Appeals (6th cir.) 1966, U.S. Dist. Ct. (so. dist.) Ohio 1970. Legal dep. probate ct. Montgomery County, Dayton, Ohio, 1964-67; head probate dept. Coolidge Wall & Wood, Dayton, 1967-79, Smith & Schnacke, Dayton, 1979-89, Thompson, Hine and Flory, Dayton, 1989-92; head estate planning and probate group Dayton office Porter, Wright, Morris & Arthur, Dayton, 1992—. Frequent lectr. on estate planning to various profl. orgns. Contbr. articles to profl. jours. Fellow Am. Coll. Trust and Estate Counsel; mem. Ohio Bar Assn. (bd. govs. estate planning, trust and probate law sect., chmn. 1993-95), Dayton Bar Assn. (chmn. probate com. 1992-94), Ohio State Bar Found. (trustee 1995-2000), Ohio CLE Inst. (trustee 1995-99, chair 1998-99), Dayton Legal Secs. Assn. (hon.), Dayton Bicycle Club. Estate planning, Probate (including wills, trusts), Estate taxation. Home: 8307 Rhine Way Centerville OH 45458-3017 Office: Porter Wright Morris & Arthur 1 S Main St Ste 1600 Dayton OH 45402-2028 E-mail: ctjohnson@porterwright.com.

JOHNSON, CAROLYN JEAN, retired law librarian; b. Beaver Dam, Wis., Nov. 7, 1938; d. Henry William and Bernice Mae (Haas) Krueger; m. Robert Edward Johnson, June 19, 1960; children: Eric Steven, Kristin Elizabeth. BS in Edn., Wartburg Coll., 1960. Tchr., various locations, 1960-64, Hennepin County Library, 1972-81; libr. 3M Tech. Libr., St. Paul, 1981-86; law libr. 3M Ctr. Law Libr., St. Paul, 1986-2000; ret., 2000. Mem. Am. Assn. Law Libraries, Minn. Assn. Law Libraries. Lutheran. Avocations: reading, walking, cooking.

JOHNSON, CHARLES RICK, lawyer; b. Burke, S.D., July 29, 1942; s. George Fielding and Corinne (Johnson) J.; m. Frances Ellen Driscoll, 1965; children— Stephanie, Sarah, George, Charlie. J.D., U. S.D., 1966. Bar: S.D. 1966, U.S. Dist. Ct. S.D. 1966, U.S. Ct. Appeals (8th cir.) 1966, U.S. Supreme Ct. 1976. Assoc., Johnson Law firm, 1966-69, ptnr. Johnson & Johnson, 1969-71, sr. ptnr. Johnson, Eklund & Davis, Gregory, S.D., 1971— ; lectr. in field. Contbr. articles to profl. jours. Mem. ABA, Assn. Trial Lawyers Am., Am. Bd. Trial Advocates, Am. Bd. Criminal Lawyers, Am. Assn. Criminal Def. Attys., S.D. Bar Assn. (pres. 1984-85), S.D. Trial Lawyers Assn. (pres. 1976-77), Phi Beta Kappa. Republican. Episcopalian. Club: Three Fingers of Red Eye Soc. (Gregory, S.D.). Criminal. Office: State Bar SD 405 Main St Gregory SD 57533-1639

JOHNSON, CHARLES WILLIAM, state supreme court justice; b. Tacoma, Wash., Mar. 16, 1951; BA in Econs., U. Wash., 1973; JD, U. Puget Sound, 1976. Bar: Wash. 1977. Justice Wash. Supreme Ct., 1991—. Co-chair Wash. State Minority and Justice Commn. Mem. bd. dirs. Wash. Assn. Children and Parents; mem. vis. com. U. Wash. Sch. Social Work; bd. visitors Seattle U. Sch. Law; liaison ltd. practice bd., co-chair BJA subcom. on juc. svcs.; mem. Am. Inns of Ct., World Affairs Coun. Pierce County. Mem. Wash. State Bar Assn., Tacoma-Pierce County Bar Assn. (Liberty Bell award young lawyers sect. 1994). Avocations: sailing, downhill skiing, cycling. Office: Wash State Supreme Ct 415 12th St W PO Box 40929 Olympia WA 98504-0929

JOHNSON, CHERYL ANN, judge; b. Aurora, Ill., Sept. 30, 1946; d. Ellsworth Tower and Vava Vieda (Munson) Johnson; m. Gregory William Lasley, May 27, 1989. BS, Ohio State U., 1968; MS, U. Ill., Urbana, 1970; JD, John Marshall Law Sch., Chgo., 1983. Bar: Tex. 1984, Ill. 1984, U.S. Ct. Appeals (7th cir.) 1986, U.S. Dist. Ct. (we. dist.) Tex. 1991, cert.: Tex. Bd. Legal Specialization (in criminal law). Jud. clk. U.S. Ct. Appeals for 5th Circuit, 1983-84; pvt. practice Austin, 1984-98; judge Tex. Ct. Criminal Appeals, Austin, 1999—. Tutor Literacy Austin, 1997—99; active El Buen Samaritano Episcopal Mission, 2001—. Mem.: State Bar Coll. Office: Tex Ct Criminal Appeals Capitol Sta PO Box 12308 Austin TX 78711-2308

JOHNSON, CHRISTIAN KENT, lawyer; b. Hays, Kans., Dec. 11, 1935; s. Joseph Claude and Arleen (Wilson) J.; m. Jeanne Aldridge, June 16, 1957 (div. 1982); children: Kimberly Ann, Christian Kent Jr.; m. Judith Ann Tucker, Sept. 10, 1982. BS in Acctg., U. Colo., 1957, JD, 1961. Bar: Colo. 1961. Ptnr. Gordon, Gordon & Johnson, Lamar, Colo., 1961-64; trust officer lst Interstate Bank, Denver, 1964-67, sr. v.p., 1967-76, exec. v.p., 1976-79; owner, mgr. Equity Mgmt. Group, Inc., Denver, 1979-80; ptnr. Buchanan, Thomas & Johnson, P.C., Lakewood, Colo., 1980-88; pvt. practice Ouray, Colo., 1988-95; ptnr. Johnson & Link, P.C., Ouray, 1995—2000. Bd. dirs. Craig Hosp., Englewood, Colo., 1978-86, Craig Hosp. Found., 2002—, pres., 1983-85. Mem. ABA, Colo. Bar Assn., Denver Bar Assn., Denver Estate Planning Coun. (bd.d irs. 1965), Lions (bd. dirs. Denver 1966-78), Montrose County Rotary. Methodist. Avocations: reading, outdoor activities. Estate planning, Probate (including wills, trusts), Estate taxation. Home and Office: 6107 Coors Way Arvada CO 80004-6174

JOHNSON, CHRISTOPHER GEORGE, lawyer; b. Aug. 22, 1963; s. Alexander Chester and Virginia Ann J.; m. Diane Marie Dorkey, June 30, 1990; children: Stephanie, Samantha, Ryan. BA (hons.) in History and Polit. Sci., Canisius Coll., 1985; JD, U. Detroit, 1988. Bar: N.Y. 1989, U.S. Dist. Ct. (we. dist.) N.Y. 1993. Pvt. practice, Rochester, N.Y., 1989; assoc. attorney Darweesh, Callen & Lewis, Rochester, N.Y., 1989; asst. dist. attorney Monroe County Dist. Attorney's Office, Rochester, 1989—2001; ptnr. Cellino & Barnes, 2001—. Rschr. Mich. Criminal Law Update, 1988. Mem. CURE Childhood Cancer, Mock Trial Law Explorers (winning coach 1992), Neighborhood Empowerment team, Rochester, 1997—; active Leadership Rochester, 1998—; steering com. Minority Achiever's Program YMCA Metro Rochester, 1996—. Mem. Am. Trial Lawyers Assn. Roman Catholic. Avocations: my children, reading, home brewing, physical fitness.

JOHNSON, CRAIG EDWARD, lawyer; b. Orange, N.J., Oct. 30, 1953; s. Charles Armond Johnson and Ruth Evans Sweeny; m. Kimberley Ellen Young, Oct. 8, 1983; children: Alec Daniel, Evan McFarland, Conor Thomas. BS, Cornell U., 1976; JD, Syracuse U., 1981. Bar: D.C. 1983, N.J. 1991, U.S. Dist. Ct. D.C. 1984, U.S. Dist. Ct. N.J. 1993. Law clk. U.S. Dist. Ct., Norfold, Va., 1981-82; atty. U.S. Dept. Energy, Washington, 1982-86; sr. atty. U.S. Dept. Justice, Washington, 1986-91; of counsel Gibbons Del Deo Dolan Griffinger Vechione, Newark, 1991-94; asst. gen. counsel, dir. litig. ITT Industries, N.Y.C., 1994—. Mem. ABA (chair real estate sect. 1994-96, chair Corp. Environ. Enforcement Coun. 1999-2000 General civil litigation, Environmental. Office: ITT Industries 4 W Red Oak Ln Fl 2 West Harrison NY 10604-3617

JOHNSON, CRANE, writer, lawyer; b. Bayard, Nebr., June 30, 1921; s. Carl Arthur and Pearl (Haskins) J. MA, U. So. Calif., 1948; postgrad., Stanford U., 1949; PhD, Case We. Res. U., 1960; LLB, N.Y. Law Sch., 1960; LLM, NYU, 1968. Bar: N.Y., 1962. Vol. legal aid lawyer. Author: Past Sixty, 1953, Thirty-Five One Act Plays, 1967, Presque Isle Village, 1995, Three Jacumba Tales, 1998, Ten Stories, 1999, Twelve Jacumba Tales, 1999, Jacumba Heidi, 2000, Buckboard to Jacumba, 2001, Mountain Springs Saga, 2002. U.S. rep. at ednl. confs. in London and Vienna. Served with AUS, WWII. Mem. N.Y. Bar Assn. Address: PO Box 158 Jacumba CA 91934-0158

JOHNSON, CYNTHIA L(E) M(AE), lawyer; b. Detroit, Mar. 1, 1952; d. Robert Alexander and Frances Esedell (Peeples) J.; children: Alexandra, Lauren Gayle. BA, U. Mich., 1973, MPH, 1975; JD cum laude, Mich. State

U., 1984. Bar: Mich. 1984, U.S. Dist. Ct. (ea. dist.) 1984, U.S. Supreme Ct. 1989; cert. mediator and arbitrator. Health planning asst. Charles R. Drew Postgrad. Sch. Medicine, L.A., 1974; dep. project dir. Mich. Health Maintenance Orgn. Plans, Detroit, 1975; sr. health program analyst N.Y. Health and Hosps. Corp., N.Y.C., 1975-77; health care cons. UAW, Detroit, 1977-84; jud. law clk. Mich. Ct. Appeals, 1984-86, Mich. Supreme Ct., 1986-87; ptnr. now Clark Hill, PLC, Detroit, 1987-2000; shareholder Couzens, Lansky, et al, P.C., 2000—. Chpt. treas. Jack N Jill Am.; bd. dirs. Mich. Metro Girl Scouts Coun., Ronald McDonald House of Detroit. Mem. ABA, Mich. Bar Assn., Am. Arbitration Assn. (cert.), Detroit Bar Assn., Wolverine Bar Assn., Delta Sigma Theta. Corporate, general, General practice, Health. Office: Couzens Lansky etal PC Penobscot Bldg 645 Griswold St Ste 1300 Detroit MI 48226-3202 Office Fax: 313-967-0344. Business E-Mail: cynthia.johnson@couzens.com.

JOHNSON, DARRYL TODD, lawyer; b. Suttons Bay, Mich., Sept. 7, 1962; s. Roderic M. and Laura J. (Steffens) J.; m. Susan E. Peckham, Sept. 6, 1986; children: Laura A., Austin T., Kelsey A. BS, Ferris State U., 1984; JD, Mich. State U., 1991. Bar: Mich. 1991, U.S. Dist. Ct. (we. dist.) Mich. 1992. Pvt. practice, Suttons Bay, 1991—. Candidate County Bd. Commrs., Leland, Mich., 1995, 2000; v.p. coun. Immanuel Luth. Ch., Suttons Bay, 1994-98. Mem.: Rotary (pres. 2001—02). Republican. Avocations: running, camping, home computing, home repair. Family and matrimonial, General practice, Municipal (including bonds). Home: 1103 Regina St Longview TX 75605-1527 Office: Tourneau Univ PO Box 7001 Longview TX 75607-7001

JOHNSON, DAVID RAYMOND, lawyer; b. Bartlesville, Okla., Sept. 12, 1946; s. Lloyd Theodore and Mary Pauline (Auten) J.; m. Marion Frances Monroe, May 14, 1977; children: Marc, Meredith. BA, Tulane U., 1968; JD, U. Va., 1971. Bar: Tex. 1971, D.C. 1977, U.S. Dist. Ct. D.C. 1979, U.S. Ct. Appeals (D.C. cir.) 1981, U.S. Supreme Ct. 1982, U.S. Claims Ct. 1984. Assoc. Fulbright & Jaworski, Houston, 1971-72, Washington, 1974-78, ptnr., 1978-87; atty.-advisor Office of Gen. Counsel of Air Force, Washington, 1972-74; ptnr. Gibson, Dunn & Crutcher LLP, Washington, 1987—. Trustee Washington Episcopal Sch., 1991-93, McLean Sch. Md., 1994-96. Capt. USAF, 1972-74. Mem. D.C. Bar Assn., Phi Beta Kappa, Raven Soc., Order of Coif, Congressional Country Club. Government contracts and claims, Computer, Commercial, contracts (including sales of goods; commercial financing). Office: Gibson Dunn & Crutcher LLP 1050 Connecticut Ave NW Ste 900 Washington DC 20036-5306

JOHNSON, DAVID WESLEY, lawyer; b. Rochester, N.Y., Mar. 13, 1933; BA, U. Rochester, 1954; LLB, Columbia U., 1959. Bar: N.Y. 1961, U.S. Dist. Ct. (so. dist.) N.Y. 1961, U.S. Dist. Ct. (no. dist.) N.Y. 1971. Counsel, sec., v.p. Textile Banking Co., N.Y.C., 1959-68; legis. counsel CIT Fin. Corp., N.Y.C., 1968-70; ptnr. Otterbourg, Steindler, Houston & Rosen, N.Y.C., 1970-71, Palmer & Johnson, Tupper Lake, N.Y., 1971-74; pvt. practice Tupper Lake, 1974—. Bd. dirs. Adirondack Cmty. Trust Trustee, chmn. bd. North Country C.C., Saranac Lake, N.Y., 1973-82; bd. dirs., pres. High Peaks Hospice, Inc., Saranac Lake, 1988-92; bd. dirs., v.p. Lake Placid (N.Y.) Ctr. for Arts, 1989—, Franklin County Children's Legal Svcs., Inc., pres., 1991—; trustee Nat. History Mus. of the Adirondacks, 1998—; bd. dirs. Adirondack Med. Ctr. Found., 2001—. Mem. Franklin County Bar Assn. (pres. 1979-81), N.Y. State Bar Assn., Lawyers Assn. Textile Industry (bd. dirs., sec.-treas. 1962-71), Assn. Comml. Fin. Attys. (bd. dirs., v.p. 1962-71). General practice. Office: 51 Lake St Tupper Lake NY 12986-1624 E-mail: jnglaw@adelphia.net.

JOHNSON, DENISE REINKA, state supreme court justice; b. Wyandotte, Mich., July 13, 1947; Student, Mich. State U., 1965-67; BA, Wayne State U., 1969; postgrad., Cath. U. of Am., 1971-72; JD with honors, U. Conn., 1974; LLM, U. Va., 1995. Bar: Conn. 1974, U.S. Dist. Ct. Conn. 1974, Vt. 1980, U.S. Ct. Appeals (2d cir.) 1983, U.S. Dist. Ct. Vt. 1986. Atty. New Haven (Conn.) Legal Assistance Assn., 1974-78; instr. legal writing Vt. Law Sch., South Royalton, 1978-79; clerk Blodgett & McCarren, Burlington, Vt., 1979-80; chief civil rights divsn. Atty. Gen.'s Office, State of Vt., 1980-82; chief pub. protection divsn. Atty. Gen.'s Office, Montpelier, Vt., 1982-88; pvt. practice Shrewsbury, Vt., 1988-90; assoc. justice Vt. Supreme Ct., Montpelier, 1990—. Chair Vt. Human Rights Commn., 1988-90. Mem. Am. Law Inst., Am. Judicature Soc. Office: Vt Supreme Ct 109 State St Montpelier VT 05609-0001

JOHNSON, DON EDWIN, lawyer; b. Decatur, Ill., Jan. 29, 1939; s. B. Edwin and Mary Louise (Pitzer) J.; m. Suzanne Curtis, Aug. 23, 1959; children: Jennifer, Marc Wade. BA cum laude, Millikin U., 1959; LLB, U. Ill., 1961, JD, 1968. Bar: Ill. 1961, U.S. Dist. Ct. (so. dist.) Ill. 1961, U.S. Tax Ct. 1986. Law clk. Ill. Supreme Ct., Springfield, 1961-63; assoc. Hohlt, House & DeMoss, Pinckneyville, Ill., 1961-66; ptnr. Johnson Seibert & Bigham, Pinckneyville, 1966—; state's atty. Perry County, Ill., Pinckneyville, 1968-72. Bd. dirs. 1st Nat. Bank, Pinckneyville, First Perry Bancorp, Pinckneyville. Contbr. articles to profl. jours. City atty. DuQuoin, Ill., 1965-68, Pinckneyville, 1983—; bd. dirs. Rend Lake Coll. Found., Ina, Ill., 1981-90; bd. visitors U. Ill. Coll. Law, 1984-88. Fellow Am. Coll. Trust and Estate Counsel, Am. Bar Found., Ill. Bar Found. (chmn. 1986-87); mem. Ill. State Bar Assn. (chmn. fed. tax sect. 1983-84, chmn. mineral law sect. 1984-86, 94-95, 96-97), Energy and Mineral Law Found. (trustee 1985—), Nat. Acad. Elder Law Attys., Pinckneyville C. of C. (pres. 1968), So. Ill. Golf Assn. (pres. 1997—), USGA (sectional affairs com. 1994—), Rotary (pres. 1966, 76), Elks, Scottish Rite, Shriners, Chaine des Rotisseurs, Red Hawk Country Club, Crab Orchard Golf Club, Kelly Greens Golf and Country Club, Delta Sigma Phi. Republican. Presbyterian. Avocations: golf, travel, stamp and coin collecting. Oil, gas, and mineral, Probate (including wills, trusts), Property, real (including real estate development, water). Home: 605 W South St Pinckneyville IL 62274-1236 Office: Johnson Seibert & Bigham One N Main St Pinckneyville IL 62274 Fax: 618-357-3314. E-mail: JSBAttorneys@Midamer.net.

JOHNSON, DONALD EDWARD, JR., lawyer; b. Denver, Sept. 24, 1942; s. Donald Edward and Miriam Bispham (Chester) J.; m. Charlotte Marie Hassett, Aug. 15, 1964; children: Julie Anna, Jenny Marie. Student, Lewis and Clark Coll., 1960-62; BA in History, U. Ariz., 1968; JD, U. Wyo., 1971. Bar: Wyo. 1971, Colo. 1971, U.S. Dist. Ct. Colo. and Wyo. 1971, U.S. Supreme Ct. 1978. Assoc. Hammond and Chilson, Loveland, Colo., 1971-72; dep. dist. atty. 8th Jud. Dist., Loveland and Fort Collins, Colo., 1972-80, chief dep. dist. atty., 1977-80; assoc. Allen, Rogers, Metcalf and Vahrenwald, Ft. Collins, 1980-82, ptnr., 1982—. Asst. city atty., prosecutor City of Loveland, 1971-72; asst. mcpl. judge, Loveland, 1972; instr. bus. law Ames Coll., 1972-74; lectr. Regional Homocide Sch., 1977. Author: Criminal Conspiracy—The Colorado District Attorney's Evidence Manual, 1976; student editor ABA Law Student Jour. Chmn. 45th Republican House Dist., 1977-82; mem. Colo. Rep. Central Com., 1980-85; mem. Loveland Open Space Adv. Bd., 1977-78; bd. dirs. Loveland United Way, 1977-84, pres., 1981-83; bd. dirs. Loveland Midget Athletic Assn., sec., 1974-78; mem. ctrl. com. Parlimentarian Larimer County Rep., 1992-96; mem. local adv. bd. McKee Med. Ctr., Loveland, 1992—, pres., 1995—; mem. adv. bd. Banner Health Sys., Colo., 1996—, pres., 1999-2002; treas. 8th Jud. dist. Victims Assistance Law Enforcement Fund, 1990-96 (8th judicial dist.), mem. nominating commn., 1998—; mem. Larimer County Bench-Bar Commn., 1993-95. Served to sgt. USMC, 1966-68. Mem. ABA (Gold Key award 1970), Larimer County Bar Assn. (exec. com. 1990-2002, pres. 1995-96), Colo. Bar Assn. (bd. govs. 1997-2002), Colo. Trial Lawyers Assn. Episcopalian. Family and matrimonial, Criminal, General practice. Office: Allen Vahrenwald & Johnson LLC Key Bank Bldg 125 S Howes St 1100 Fort Collins CO 80521

JOHNSON, DONALD RAYMOND, lawyer; b. N.Y.C., June 26, 1960; s. Donald Francis and Jacqueline E. (Barnett) J. BA, Liberty U., 1982, MA, 1984; JD, Washington and Lee U., 1989; postgrad., Va. Polytech. Inst., Yale U., U. Va. Bar: Va. 1989, D.C. 1991, N.Y. 1995, U.S. Dist. Ct. (no., so., and ea. dists.) N.Y., U.S. Dist. Ct. (ea. and we. dists.) Va., U.S. Ct. Appeals (fed. cir.), U.S. Supreme Ct., U.S. Ct. Internat. Trade. Pvt. practice, Charlottesville, Va., 1989-96; dir., pres. Internat. Brokerage & Investment Co., Charlottesville, 1991-99; dir., v.p. Internat. Investment Svcs., Inc., Charlottesville, 1991-2000; pvt. practice N.Y.C., 1995—; pres. Real E.S. AG, 2003—. Bd. dirs. Excellence in Edn., Charlottesville, 1990-92, Heritage Soc., Charlottesville, 1990-92, World of Life Internat., 2000—; U.S. del. German-Am. Multiplicitorian Seminars; founder Mission, Inc., 2000—. Named one of Outstanding Young Men of Am., Alumnus of the Yr.; recipient numerous awards and honors for ednl., civic, and social activities. Mem. ABA, ATLA. Republican. Baptist. Avocations: running, sailing, tennis. Commercial, contracts (including sales of goods; commercial financing), Corporate, general, Private international. Office: 90 Schermerhorn St Brooklyn NY 11201-5028 Fax: 801-340-1789. E-mail: drjohnson@att.net.

JOHNSON, DONALD WAYNE, lawyer; b. Memphis, Feb. 2, 1950; s. Hugh Don and Oline (Rowland) J.; m. Jan Marie Mullinax, May 12, 1972 (div. 1980); 1 child, Scott Fitzgerald; m. Cindy L. Walker, Dec. 10, 1988; children: Trevor Christian, Mallory Faith. Student, Memphis State U., 1968, Lee Coll., 1968-72; JD, Woodrow Wilson Coll. Law, 1975. Bar: Ga. 1975, U.S. Dist. Ct. (no. dist.) Ga. 1975, U.S. Ct. Appeals (5th cir.) 1976, U.S. Ct. Appeals (11th, 9th, DC cirs.) 1984, U.S. Ct. Claims 1978, U.S. Tax Ct. 1978, U.S. Supreme Ct. 1979. Ptnr. Barnes & Johnson, Dalton, Ga., 1975-77, Johnson & Fain, Dalton, 1977-80; pvt. practice Dalton, 1975-85, Atlanta, 1985—; city atty. City of Forest Park, Ga., 1996-97. Bd. dirs. Pathway Christian Sch., Dalton, 1978-85, Jr. Achievement of Dalton, 1978-84, Dalton-Whitfield County Day Care Ctrs., Inc.; legal counsel Robertson for Pres. Com., Ga., 1988; bd. chmn. Ga. Family Coun., 1990-97; Rep. chmn. Clayton County, 1993-95; Rep. gen. counsel 3rd Congl. Dist., 1993-95, Clayton County Rep. Com., 1995-96; Rep. candidate for Ga. Senate, 1998; emcee, community prayer breakfast, Proj. Cor. Angel Tree, 1999-. Recipient Power of One award Ga. Family Coun., 1997. Mem. State Bar Ga., Fayette County Bar Assn., Ga. Trial Lawyers Assn., Christian Legal Soc. Mem. Ch. of God. Corporate, general, Personal injury (including property damage), Probate (including wills, trusts). Office: PO Box 187 Fayetteville GA 30214-0187 E-mail: jlfpc@mindspring.com., djohn36755@aol.com.

JOHNSON, DOUGLAS BLAIKIE, lawyer; b. Chgo., Sept. 13, 1952; s. Marvin Melrose and Anne Stuart (Campbell) J.; m. Pamela Jane Tomlinson, Aug. 1, 1975; children: Richard Aaron, Lauren Stuart, Diana Blaikie, Scott Nathaniel, Catherine Joan. BSME, U. Nebr., 1974; JD, Seton Hall U., 1980. Bar: Nebr. 1980, U.S. Dist. Ct. Nebr. 1980; registered profl. engr., Nebr., Ark. Project engr. DuPont, Cleve., 1974-75, Exxon Chems., Linden, N.J., 1975-78, cost engr., 1978-80; sr. engr. InterNorth, Inc., Omaha, 1980-82, market planner, 1982-84, corp. planner, 1984-85, bus. mgr., 1985-86; program mgr. Brunswick Corp., Lincoln, Nebr., 1987-95; product devel. mgr. Lincoln Composites, 1995-98, sr. bus. devel. mgr., 1999-2000, dir. oilfield products, 2000—02; mgr. Gen. Dynamics, 2003—. Mem. ABA, ATLA, Nebr. Bar Assn., Lincoln Bar Assn., Triangle, Sigma Tau, Pi Tau Sigma, Phi Eta Sigma. Republican. Presbyterian. Home: 4600 Birch Hollow Dr Lincoln NE 68516-5107 Office: Gen Dynamics 4300 Industrial Ave Lincoln NE 68504-1107 E-mail: djohnson@gdatp.com.

JOHNSON, DOUGLAS WELLS, lawyer; b. May 31, 1949; s. Robert Douglas and Mildred Irene (Fehr) J.; m. Kathryn Ann Hoberg, Oct. 18, 1980. BA, U. Denver, 1971, JD, 1974. Ptnr. Mellman, Mellman & Thorn, Denver, 1974-80; sr. atty. Amoco Corp., Chgo., 1980-91; mgr. real estate Amoco Oil Co., Chgo., 1991-94; sr. atty. Amoco Corp., Chgo., 1994-98; v.p. and chief counsel BP Pipelines N. Am., Warrenville, Ill., 1998—. U. Denver Alumni scholar, 1967-71. Mem. ABA, Ill. Bar Assn., D.C. Bar Assn., Chgo. Bar Assn., Kappa Delta Pi. Antitrust, Commercial, contracts (including sales of goods; commercial financing), Franchising. Home: 3040 Indianwood Rd Wilmette IL 60091 Office: BP America Inc 4101 Winfield Rd Warrenville IL 60555

JOHNSON, EARL, JR., judge, author; b. Watertown, S.D., June 10, 1933; s. Earl Jerome and Doris Melissa (Schwartz) J.; m. Barbara Claire Yanow, Oct. 11, 1970; children: Kelly Ann, Earl Eric, Agaarn Yanovitch. BA in Econs., Northwestern U., 1955, LL.M., 1961; JD, U. Chgo., 1960. Bar: Ill. 1960, U.S. Ct. Appeals (9th cir.) 1964, D.C. 1965, U.S. Supreme Ct. 1966, Calif. 1972. Trial atty., organized crime sect. Dept. Justice, Washington, Miami, Fla. and Las Vegas, Nev., 1961-64; dep. dir. Neighborhood Legal Svcs. Project, 1964-65, OEO Legal Svcs. Program, 1965-66, dir., 1966-68; vis. scholar Ctr. for Study of Law and Soc. U. Calif., Berkeley, 1968-69; assoc. prof. U. So. Calif. Law Center, L.A., 1969-75, dir. clin. programs, 1970-73, prof. law, 1976-82, dir. Program Study Dispute Resolution Policy, Social Sci. Research Inst., 1975-82; assoc. justice Calif. Ct. Appeal, 1982—; co-dir. Access to Justice Project European U. Inst., 1975-79. Vis. scholar Inst. Comparative Law, U. Florence, Italy, 1973, 75; Robert H. Jackson lectr. Nat. Jud. Coll., 1980; adv. panel Legal Svcs. Corp., 1976-80; legis. impact panel Nat. Acad. Scis., 1977-80; faculty Asian Workshop on Legal Svcs. to Poor, 1974; mem. Internat. Legal Ctr., Legal Svcs. in Developing Countries, 1972-75; founder, bd. mem. Action for Legal Rights, 1971-74; pres., trustee Western Ctr. on Law and Poverty, 1972-73, 76-80; v.p., chmn. exec. com. Calif. Rural Legal Assistance Corp., 1973-74; exec. com. Nat. Sr. Citizens Law Ctr., 1980-82; sec. Nat. Resource Ctr. for Consumers of Legal Svcs., 1974-82; chair Nat. Equal Justice Libr. Com., 1989-92; pres., Consortium for Nat. Equal Justice Libr., Inc., 1992-95, bd. dirs., 1995—; chair Calif. Access to Justice Working Group, 1993-96; mem. Calif. Commn. on Access to Justice, 1997—, co-chmn., 2002-. Author: Justice and Reform: The Formative Years of the American Legal Services Program, 1974, 2d edit., 1978, Toward Equal Justice: A Comparative Study of Legal Aid in Modern Societies, 1975, Outside the Courts: A Survey of Diversion Alternatives in Civil Cases, 1977, Dispute Processing Strategies, 1978, Dispute Resolution in America, 1985, California Trial Guide, 8 vols., 1986, Texas Trial Guide, 6 vols., 1989, New York Trial Guide, 5 vols., 1990, Florida Civil Trial Guide, 5 vols., 1990, Ill. Civil Trial Guide, 5 vols., 1991, Fed. Trial Guide, 5 vols., 1992, Indiana Civil Trial Guide, 5 vols., 1992, California Family Law Trial Guide, 5 vols., 1992, Pennsylvania Civil Trial Guide, 5 vols., 1992, Mich. Trial Guide, 5 vols., 1993, N.C. Civil Trial Guide, 5 vols., 1993, California Criminal Trial Guide, 3 vols., 1994; editor U. Chgo. Law Rev, 1960; mem. editl. bd. Jour. Law and Social Inquiry, 1987—; contbr. articles to books and periodicals. Bd. dirs. Beverly Hills Bar Found., 1972-73, Nat. Legal Aid and Defenders Assn., 1987-91; trustee L.A. Legal Aid Found., 1969-71; mem. L.A. County Regional Planning Commn., 1980-81; bd. visitors U. San Diego Law Sch., 1983-86. Served with USNR, 1955-58. Recipient Dart award for acad. innovation U. So. Calif., 1971, Loren Miller Legal Services award Calif. State Bar, 1977, Appellate Justice of the Yr. award L.A. Trial Lawyers Assn., 1989, Outstanding Jud. Achievement award Calif. Trial Lawyers Assn., 1991, Legal Svcs. Pioneer award L.A. Legal Aid Found., 1999; named So. Calif. Citizen of Week, 1978; Ford Found. fellow, 1960; Dept. State lectr., 1975; grantee Ford Found.; grantee Russell Sage Found.; grantee Law Enforcement Assistance Adminstrn.; grantee NSF. Fellow Am. Bar Found. (rsch. adv. com. 1996—, chair 1999-2002); mem. ABA (com. chmn. 1972-75, spl. com. resolution minor disputes 1976-83, coun. sect. of individual rights and responsibilities 1990-91, consortium on legal svcs. and the pub. 1991-94), Calif. Bar Assn., L.A. Bar Assn. (neighborhood justice ctr. com. 1976-81), Law and Soc. Assn., Nat. Legal Aid and Defender's Assn. (bd. dirs. 1968-74), Am. Acad. Polit. and Social Sci., Calif. Judges Assn. (appellate cts. com. 1983-87, 93-99, ethics com. 1985-89), Internat. Assn. Procedural Law, Order of Coif. Democrat. Office: Ct Appeals Calif 2d Appellate Dist 300 S Spring St Los Angeles CA 90013-1230 E-mail: justej@aol.com.

JOHNSON, EDWARD MICHAEL, lawyer, consultant; b. Waco, Tex., July 12, 1944; s. Edward James and Anne Margaret (Stuchly) J.; m. Yvonne Margaret Hill, May 7, 1977; children: Hilary Yvonne, Megan Joy, Michael David. BA in Polit. Sci., S.W. Tex. State U., 1967; JD, St. Mary's U., 1970. Bar: Tex. 1971, U.S. Dist. Ct. (we. and so. dist.) Tex. 1972, U.S. Ct. Claims, 1972, U.S. Supreme Ct. 1976. Asst. law libr. Bexar County Law Libr., 1968-69; briefing clk. Judge Preston H. Dial, Jr., 1969-70; briefing atty. U.S. Dist. Judge John H. Wood Jr., San Antonio, 1971-72; asst. U.S. atty. Dept. Justice, San Antonio, 1972-76; sole practice San Antonio, 1976-81; sr. atty. Wiley, Garwood, Hornbuckle, Higdon & Johnson, San Antonio, 1980-81; pres. McCabe Petroleum Corp., San Antonio, 1981; chmn. bd., CEO, gen. counsel Blue Chip Petroleum Corp., San Antonio, 1981-83; pres., gen. counsel Harvest Investments Corp., San Antonio, 1983-87, also dir.; gen. ptrn. Med. Mobility Ltd. IV, San Antonio, 1984-87; mgr. Med. Mobility Joint Venture, San Antonio, 1984-87; exec. cons. Advance Tax Representation, Inc., 1987-88; gen. ptrn. Harvest Venture Capital Ltd. I, San Antonio, 1986-87; pres., gen. counsel Blue Chip Securities Corp., San Antonio, 1984-87; rep. First Investors Corp., 1987-88; pres., CEO Johnson, Curney, Garcia, Wise & Farmer P.C., 1990-2000; Diamond direct distbr. Amway Corp., 1997—2000; mem. exec. com. EcoQuest Internat., 2002—. Host radio program The Christian Lawyer, 1990-91, TV program God's Army, 1990-98; mem. adv. bd. Red McCombs Galleria Imports, 1996-98, Network Mktg. Lifestyles Mag., 1999-2002, Hovey Motorcars, 1999—. Co-chmn. fund raising Am. Heart Assn., San Antonio, 1982-84; bd. dirs. Am. Cancer Soc., San Antonio, 1982-84; chmn. San Fernando Cathedral Endowment Fund, San Antonio, 1986; mem. Gideons Internat., San Antonio, 1982-86, mem. exec. bd. San Antonio Christian Schs., 1983-84, San Antonio Christian Legal Soc., 1991-2000, Fed. Bar Licensing Bd., 1976-78; bd. dirs. Tex. Bible Coll., 1984-87, Christian Businessmen's Com., San Antonio, 1981-88, Cornerstone Christian Schs., San Antonio, 1991-92, mem., spkr., pres. Med. Ctr. chpt. 1988-91, mem. Full Gospel Businessmen's Fellowship, 1981-92, pres. 1985-88, field rep., 1988-92; Rep. precinct chmn., 1988-89; bd. dirs. Assn. Spirit Filled Fellowships, 1991-93; pres. God's Army Internat. Found., Inc., 1990-92; gen. counsel, bd. dirs. Four Winds Ministries, Inc., 1992-93; scoutmaster Alamo area coun. Boy Scouts Am., San Antonio, 1973-74; founder, chmn. Christian Businessmen's Focus on the Family, San Antonio, 1984-85. Recipient spl. commendation Dept. Transp. 1973, Dept. Air Force HQ, ATC, 1974, Dept. Treasury, 1974; named Outstanding Asst. U.S. Atty. Dept. Justice, 1974-75, One of Outstanding Young Texans, 1976. Mem. FBA (pres. San Antonio chpt. 1975-76, v.p. 1973-74, sec. 1972-73, treas. 1971-72, Outstanding Chpt. Pres. award 1976), Tex. Bar Assn., San Antio Bar Assn. (spl. asst. to exec. dir. 1968-69). Republican. Federal civil litigation, Insurance, Securities. E-mail: edjohnson@ecoquestintl.com.

JOHNSON, EINAR WILLIAM, lawyer; b. Fontana, Calif., Apr. 6, 1955; s. Carl Wilbur and Judith Priscilla (Orcutt) J.; m. Cynthia Jeanne Bailey, Oct. 9, 1976; children: Brian Mark (dec.), Carl Einar, Gregory Daniel, Christopher James, Shaun Curtis, Bradford Keith. BA in Speech Communications, Brigham Young U., 1980; JD, J. Reuben Clark Law Sch., Provo, Utah, 1983. Bar: Calif. 1983, U.S. Dist. Ct. (cen. dist.) Calif. 1984, U.S. Ct. Appeals (9th cir.) 1986, U.S. Supreme Ct. 1987. Asst. debate coach Brigham Young U., Provo, Utah, 1979-80; fin. committeeman Jed Richardson for Congress, Provo, 1980; sales mgr./salesman Ortho Mattress, Orem, Utah, 1979, 81; law clk. Acret & Perrochet, L.A., 1982; jud. clk. U.S. Cts., Salt Lake City, 1983-84; litigation atty. Smith & Hilbig, Torrance, Calif., 1984-90, litigation ptnr., 1990-93; owner, founder Johnson and Assocs., 1993—. Editor Moot Ct. program J. Reuben Clark Law Sch., 1982-83. Contbr. articles to profl. jours. Missionary, leader Ch. of Jesus Christ of Latter Day Saints, Denver, 197476, Sunday sch. tchr., L.A., 1986-89, stake high counselor, 1989-92, 1st counselor ward bishopric, 1992-93, pres. elders quorum, 1993-94, high counselor, 1994-2000, 2nd counselor bishopric, 2000-2002, 1st Asst. H. Prsts. Grp. Recipient A.H. Christensen award, Am. Jurisprudence awards Bancroft-Whitney, 1981. Mem. ABA, Calif. Bar Assn., L.A. County Bar Assn., Assn. Trial Lawyers Am., Internat. Platofrm Assn., Order Barristers, Kappa Tau Alpha. Republican. Mem. Lds Ch. Avocations: photography, guitar, fishing, house remodeling, automobile restoration. General civil litigation, Labor (including EEOC, Fair Labor Standards Act, labor-management relations, NLRB, OSHA), Landlord-tenant. Office: Johnson & Assocs 3655 Torrance Blvd Ste 470 Torrance CA 90503-4848

JOHNSON, ELMER WILLIAM, lawyer; b. Denver, May 2, 1932; s. Elmer William and Lillian Marie (Nelson) J.; m. Constance Dorothy Mahon, June 18, 1955; children: Julianne Marie, Valerie Lynn, Garrett Douglas. BA, Yale U., 1954; JD, U. Chgo., 1957. Bar: Ill. 1957. Assoc. Kirkland & Ellis, Chgo., 1956-62, ptnr., 1962—99; v.p., group exec. gen. counsel Gen. Motors Corp., Detroit, 1983-87, exec. v.p., dir., 1987-88; gen. counsel Internat. Harvester, Chgo., 1982-83; spl. counsel to chmn. of Ameritech Corp., Chgo., 1982-83; pres., CEO Aspen Inst., Washington, 1999—2002; ptnr. Jenner & Block, Chgo., 2002—. Mem. legal adv. com. N.Y. Stock Exch., 1987-91; v.p., dir. The Econ. Club of Chgo.; chmn. bd. govs. Chgo. Lighthouse for Blind. Author: Avoiding the Collision of Cities and Cars, 1993, Chicago Metropolis 2020, 2001. Trustee U. Chgo., 1977-89, Aspen Inst., Colo., 1988—. Fellow Am. Acad. Arts and Scis.; mem. ABA, Ill. Bar Assn., Chgo. Club, Old Elm. Republican. Presbyterian. Corporate, general. Office: Jenner & Block 1 IBM Plaza Chicago IL 60611

JOHNSON, ERIC HEATH, lawyer; b. Gadsden, Ala., Apr. 2, 1966; s. James Edward and Sherry Lynn (Akin) J.; m. Rexanne T., June 4, 1994. BA, U. Ala., Birmingham, 1989; JD, Cumberland Sch. Law, Birmingham, 1993. Bar: Ala. 1994, U.S. Dist. Ct. (no. dist.) Ala. 1994. Sole practice, Birmingham, 1994—2000; ptnr. Russo & Johnson P.C., Birmingham, 2000—. Served in USAR, 1985-91. Mem. Birmingham Bar Assn. Baptist. Avocations: golf, fishing, stamp and coin collecting. Bankruptcy, Criminal, Family and matrimonial. Office: 315 Gadsden Hwy Ste D Birmingham AL 35235-1000

JOHNSON, GARRETT BRUCE, lawyer; b. Akron, Ohio, Sept. 15, 1946; s. Vincent Hadar and Elizabeth Irene (Garrett) J.; m. Barbara Peters Silver, May 31, 1969; children: Emily Peters, Adam Garrett. A.B., Princeton U., 1968; J.D., U. Mich., 1971. Bar: Ill. 1973, U.S. Dist. Ct. (no. dist.) Ill. 1973, U.S. Ct. Appeals (7th cir.) 1979, U.S. Supreme Ct. 1990. Fellow Max Planck Inst. for Fgn. and Internat. Criminal Law, Freiburg, Germany, 1971-72; assoc. Kirkland & Ellis, Chgo., 1973-78, ptnr., 1978— . Article and book review editor Mich. Law Rev. 1970-71. Humboldt scholar, 1971-72. Federal civil litigation, State civil litigation. Office: Kirkland & Ellis 200 E Randolph St Fl 54 Chicago IL 60601-6636

JOHNSON, GARY M. lawyer; b. 1947; BS, Gustavus Adolphus Coll., 1969; JD, NYU, 1973. Law clk. to justice U.S. Ct. Appeals (3d cir.), Phila., 1973-74; assoc. Dorsey & Whitney, Mpls., 1974-79, ptnr., 1980—. Fellow Am. Coll. Trust and Estate Counsel; mem. Minn. Bar Assn., Hennepin County Bar Assn., Order of Coif. Estate planning, Probate (including wills, trusts). Office: Dorsey & Whitney Ste 1500 50 South Sixth Street Minneapolis MN 55402-1498 E-mail: johnson.gary@dorsey.com.

JOHNSON, GARY THOMAS, lawyer; b. Chgo., July 26, 1950; s. Thomas G. Jr. and Marcia Johnson; m. Susan Elizabeth Moore, May 28, 1978; children: Christopher Thomas, Timothy Henry, Anna Louisa. AB, Yale U., 1972; Hons. BA, Oxford U., 1974, MA, 1983; JD, Harvard U., 1977. Ba: Ill. 1977, U.S. Dist. Ct. (no. dist.) Ill. 1977, U.S. Ct. Appeals (7th cir.) 1985, U.S. Supreme Ct. 1986, N.Y. 1993. Assoc. Mayer, Brown &

Platt, Chgo., 1977-84, ptnr., 1985-94, Jones, Day, Reavis & Pogue, Chgo., 1994—. Mem. Spl. Commn. on Adminstrn. of Justice Cook County, Chgo., 1984-88; v.p. Criminal Justice Project of Cook County, 1987-91; bd. dirs. Lawyers' Com. for Civil Rights Under Law, 1992—, trustee, 1994—, regional co-chair, 1996-2001, co-chair, 2001-2003; mem. Ill. Supreme Ct. Spl. Commn. on the Adminstrn. of Justice, 1992-94. Bd. dirs. Chgo. Lawyers' Com. for Civil Rights Under Law, 1981-90, Legal Assistance Found., Chgo., 1987-96, pres., 1994-96. Rhodes scholar Oxford U., 1972-74. Fellow Am. Bar Found. (life; state chair 2003—), Ill. Bar Found. (life); mem. ABA (Ho. of Dels. 1991-97), Am. Judicature Soc. (bd. dirs. 1987-91), Ill. State Bar Assn., Chgo. Bar Assn., Chgo. Coun. Lawyers (pres. 1981-83), Internat. Bar Assn. Corporate, general, Finance, Securities. Office: Jones Day Reavis & Pogue 77 W Wacker Dr Chicago IL 60601-1692

JOHNSON, GOODYEAR See O'CONNOR, KARL WILLIAM

JOHNSON, HAROLD GENE, lawyer; b. St. Louis, July 20, 1934; s. Edward Henry Johnson and Betty (Burton) Pallister; m. Susan Ann Giesecke, Oct. 10, 1953; children: H. Mark, Deborah S. Johnson Schnitzer, Michael R., Laura A. Johnson Schwent, Mitchell D. BSBA, Washington U., St. Louis, 1961, LLB, 1962. Bar: Mo. 1962, U.S. Dist. Ct. (ea. dist.) Mo. 1964, U.S. Ct. Appeals (8th cir.) 1981. Assoc. Schomburg, Marshall & Craig, St. Louis, 1962-63, Green & Raymond, St. Louis, 1963-64; ptnr. Johnson & Hayes, St. Louis, 1978-85, Law Offices Mitchell D. Johnson, St. Louis, 1988-93, Johnson & Johnson, 1993—. Judge mcpl. ct. City of Bridgeton, Mo., 1973-85. Served with U.S. Army 1954-56. Recipient Spl. Service award City of Bridgeton, 1985; Honored with ann. presentation of The Judge Harold Johnson award Pro-Life Direct Action League, 1985. Bar: Mo. Bar Assn., Met. Bar St. Louis, St. Louis County Bar Assn. Avocation: woodworking. State civil litigation, General practice, Personal injury (including property damage). Office: 500 Northwest Plz Ste 715 Saint Ann MO 63074-2222

JOHNSON, HARRY STERLING, lawyer; b. Havre de Grace, Md., Nov. 10, 1954; s. Harry Durwood and Sarah Gladys (Rice) J.; m. Janet Amanda Thomas, May 14, 1988; 1 child, Amanda Sterling. BA, U. Md., Catonsville, 1976; JD, U. Md., Balt., 1979. Bar: Md. 1979, U.S. Dist. Ct. Md. 1979, U.S. Dist. Ct. D.C. 1986. Assoc. Whiteford, Taylor & Preston, Balt., 1979-86, ptnr., 1986—. Instr. U. Md., Baltimore County, Catonsville, 1982-87; bd. dirs. Bedco Devel. Corp., The Chapman Funds, The Afro Am. Newspapers; mem. com. Rules of Practice and Procedure, Ct. Appeals Md., Annapolis, 1986—. Mem. exec. bd. Balt. Area coun. Boy Scouts of Am., 1990—; pres., chair New Community Coll. Balt. Found., 1988, Greater Balt. Com., 1989. Mem. ABA, Md. State Bar Assn. (bd. govs. 1987-89, 91—, treas. 1999-2002, pres.-elect 2002-03), Bar Assn. Baltimore City, Nat. Bar Assn., Monumental City Bar Assn. (Founder's award 1987). Avocations: music, sports, tennis. Federal civil litigation, State civil litigation, Personal injury (including property damage). Office: Whiteford Taylor & Preston 7 St Paul St Ste 1400 Baltimore MD 21202-1626*

JOHNSON, HAZEL L, law librarian; d. Robert C. and Jimmie L. Johnson; m. Timothy L. Coggins, Sept. 29, 1990. BS, Miss. U. for Women, 1973—76; MLS, U. of Ala., 1976—77. Circulation, reference libr. U. of Ala. Law Sch. Libr., 1977—79; pub. services libr. U. of Ga. Law Libr., 1979—82; law libr. Smith & Hulsey, Jacksonville, Fla., 1982—87; mgr., law libr. and records ctr. Long Aldridge & Norman, Atlanta, 1987—90; social sciences reference libr. N.C. State U., 1990—92; law libr. Sutherland Asbill & Brennan, Atlanta, 1995—96, Lightfoot Franklin & White, Birmingham, Ala., 1996—97; libr. McGuire Woods LLP, Richmond, Va., 1998—. Law libr. services cons., Richmond, Va., 1996—98. Mem.: Va. Assn. of Law Libraries, Southeastern Chpt., Am. Assn. of Law Libraries (pres. 1987—88, Svc. Award 1992), Am. Assn. of Law Libraries, ABA. Office: McGuireWoods LLP 901 E Cary St Richmond VA 23219 Office Fax: 804-775-1061. E-mail: hjohnson@mcguirewoods.com.

JOHNSON, JAMES DOUGLAS (JIM JOHNSON), lawyer; b. Crossett, Ark., Aug. 20, 1924; s. Thomas William and Maudie Myrtle (Long) J.; m. Virginia Morris, Dec. 21, 1947; children: Mark Douglas, John David and Joseph Daniel (twins). LL.B., Cumberland U., 1947. Bar: Ark. 1948. Practice in, Crosset, 1948-58; assoc. justice Supreme Ct. Ark., 1958-66; practice law Little Rock, 1966—; Ark. Senate 22d Senatorial Dist., 1950-54. Served with USMCR, World War II. Mem. Ark. Jud. Council, Lamda Chi Alpha. Republican. Christian Scientist. Home: PO Box 1086 Conway AR 72033-1086

JOHNSON, JAMES J. lawyer; BA, U. Mich.; JD, Ohio State U. Bar: Ohio 1972. V.p., gen. counsel Procter & Gamble Co., Cin., 1991—, now sr. v.p., gen. counsel, 1991—, chief legal officer. Office: Procter & Gamble Co 1 Procter And Gamble Plz Cincinnati OH 45202-3393*

JOHNSON, JAMES JOSEPH SCOFIELD, lawyer, judge, educator, author; b. Washington, Apr. 28, 1956; s. Richard Carl and Harriette (Benson) J.; m. Sherry Bekki Hall; children: Andrew Joel Schaeffer Johnson. AA with high honors, Montgomery Coll., Germantown, Md., 1980; BA with honors, Wake Forest U., 1982; JD, U. N.C., 1984; ThD with highest honors, Emmanuel Coll. Christian Studies, 1996, DASc with highest honors, 2000; PhD with highest honors, Cambridge Grad. Sch., Springdale, Ark., 1996, MSc, M of Liberal Arts, 1999. Bar: Tex. 1985, U.S. Dist. Ct. (no. dist.) Tex. 1986, U.S. Dist. Ct. (ea. dist.) Tex. 1987, U.S. Ct. Appeals (5th cir.) 1989, U.S. Dist. Ct. (we. and so. dists.) Tex. 1990, U.S. Supreme Ct. 2000; bd. cert. bus. bankruptcy law Tex. Bd. Legal Specialization, 1990, 95, 2000, Am. Bankruptcy Bd. Cert., 1992; cert. water quality monitor Tex. Natural Resource Conservation Commn., 1994-1997. Assoc. various orgns., Dallas, 1985—; pvt. practice law Dallas, 1993—. Adj. prof. LeTourneau U., Dallas, 1991—, Dallas Christian Coll., 1995—; lectr. History, Geography, Ecology, Culture, Norwegian Cruise Lines, 1998—; Bibl. langs. instr. Cross Timbers Inst., 2001—. Author: Introduction to Environmental Studies, 1995, 98, Doxological Zoology and Zoogeography, 1998, How Texas is Addressing Administrative Law Issues in School Law Contexts, 2003; sr. editl. staff N.C. Jour. Internat. Law and Comml. Regulation, 1983-84; conf. issue editor Harvard Jour. Law & Pub. Policy, 1984; contbr. articles to profl. jours. Protestant chaplain Boy Scouts Am., Goshen, Va., 1976; libr. vol. N.W. Bible Ch., Dallas, 1991-2000; cmty. program dir. Southwestern Legal Founds. Conf. on Internat. and Am. Law, 1991-92; scripture chmn. Gideons Internat., North Dallas, Tex., 1993-94. Recipient award for excellence in biblical studies and biblical langs. Am. Bible Soc., 1982. Mem. Near East Archaeology Soc., Sangre de Cristo Mountain Coun., Icelandic Geneal. Soc., Creation Rsch. Soc., Evangel. Theol. Soc., Norwegian Soc. Tex., Icelandic Soc. of Dallas, Sons of Norway (historian). Republican. Avocations: reading, writing, birding, traveling, hiking. Bankruptcy, General civil litigation, Environmental. Office: PO Box 2952 Dallas TX 75221-2952

JOHNSON, JAMES TERENCE, lawyer, educator, minister; b. Springfield, Mo., Oct. 25, 1942; s. Clifford Lester and Margaret Jeanne (Wallace) Johnson; m. Martha Susan Mitchell, May 2, 1964; children: Jennifer Jeanne, Emily Jill. BA, Okla. Christian Coll., 1964; JD, So. Meth. U., 1967; LLD (hon.) , Pepperdine U., 1980. Min., Okla., Tex., 1961—; staff counsel, asst. prof. Okla. Christian Coll., Oklahoma City, 1968-72; pvt. practice Oklahoma City, 1969—; v.p. Okla. Christian U., 1972-73, exec. v.p., 1973-74, pres., 1974-95, chancellor, 1995—2000. Co-founder Enterprise Sq., 1982, Cascade Coll., 1993. Mem.: Okla. Bar Assn., Phi Delta Theta.

JOHNSON, JEH CHARLES, lawyer; b. N.Y.C., Sept. 11, 1957; s. Jeh Vincent and Norma (Edelin) J.; m. Susan M. DiMarco, Mar. 18, 1994. BA, Morehouse Coll., Atlanta, 1979; JD, Columbia U., 1982. Bar: N.Y. 1983, D.C. 1999. Litig. assoc. Sullivan & Cromwell, N.Y.C., 1982—84; assoc. Paul, Weiss, Rifkind, Wharton & Garrison, N.Y.C., 1984-88, 92-93; asst. U.S. atty. So. Dist. N.Y., 1989-91; ptnr. Paul, Weiss, Rifkind, Wharton & Garrison, N.Y.C., 1994-98, 2001—; gen. counsel USAF, Washington, 1998—2001. Adj. lectr. law Columbia U. Law Sch., N.Y.C., 1995—97. Trustee Adelphi U., 2001—. Mem.: Coun. Fgn. Rels. Office: Paul Weiss Rifkin Wharton & Garrison 1285 Ave of Americas New York NY 10019 Office Fax: 212-757-3990. Business E-Mail: jjohnson@paulweiss.com.

JOHNSON, JENNIFER ROSE, lawyer; b. Springfield, Mo., Dec. 24, 1959; d. LeRoy Vincent Johnson and Jewell Faye Tykeson. BS in Psychology, Evangel Coll., 1984; AA in Nursing, Mesa C.C., 1987; JD, U. Ariz., 1992. Bar: Calif. 1992, U.S. Ct. Appeals (9th cir.) 1998, U.S. Dist. Ct. (ctrl. dist.) Calif. 1998; RN Ariz. Nurse Mesa Gen. Hosp., Ariz., 1987—89, Tucson Gen. Hosp., 1989—92; assoc. Tuverson & Hallyand, Palm Springs, Calif., 1992—98, Lafollette, Johnson et al, Santa Ana, 1998—99; ptnr. Tuverson & Hillyard, Newport Beach, 1999—2000; atty. Lopez, Hodes et al, 2000—. Bd. dirs. William Hall Master Chorale, Orange, Calif., 2001—03. Contbr. articles to profl. jours. Mem.: ATLA, Consumer Attys. Calif. (at-large bd. dirs. 2001—), Orange County Trial Lawyers Assn. (bd. dirs. 2001—). Avocations: church choir, exercise, piano, sports. Personal injury (including property damage), Product liability. Office: Lopez Hodes Restaino Milman & Skikos 450 Newport Ctr Dr 2d Fl Newport Beach CA 92660 Fax: 949-640-8294. E-mail: jjohnson@lopez-hodes.com.

JOHNSON, JOHN PAUL, lawyer, administrative law judge; b. Omaha, Dec. 4, 1944; s. John and Dorothy (Mullen) J.; m. Suzanne Alice Smiley, July 12, 1974; children: James Thomas, Jennifer Anne. BA, Washburn U., Topeka, 1967; JD, U. Nebr., 1971; postgrad., Fed. Exec. Inst., Charlottesville, Va., 1988. Bar: Nebr. 1972. Claims examiner VA, St. Paul, 1972; staff atty. Bd. Vets. Appeals, Washington, 1973-79, sr. atty., 1979-81; adminstrv. law judge Office of Hearings and Appeals, Des Moines, 1981—, chief adminstrv. law judge, 1988-93. With U.S. Army, 1968-70 (Vietnam). Decorated Bronze Star; recipient Exceptional Svc. award VA, 1974. Mem. Assn. Adminstr. Law Judges, Nebr. State Bar Assn., Kappa Sigma. Episcopalian. Home: 228 39th St West Des Moines IA 50265-3938 Office: Office Hearings and Appeals 4400 Westown Pky West Des Moines IA 50266

JOHNSON, JOSEPH CLAYTON, JR., lawyer; b. Vicksburg, Miss., Nov. 15, 1943; s. Joseph Clayton and Rose Butler (Levy) J.; m. Cherrian Frances Turpin, Oct. 24, 1970; children: Mary Clayton, Erik Cole. BS, La. State U., 1965, JD, 1969. Bar: La. 1969, U.S. Dist. Ct. (ea. and mid. dists.) La. 1969, U.S. Dist. Ct. (we. dist.) La. 1979, U.S. Ct. Appeals (5th cir.) 1982. Ptnr. Taylor, Porter, Brooks & Phillips, Baton Rouge, 1969—. Mem. civil justice reform act com. U.S. Dist. Ct. (mid. dist.) La., 1995-97, chmn. 1996-97; mem. La. Atty. Disciplinary Bd., 1997-99. Bd. editors Oil and Gas Reporter, 1988—. Pres. Baton Rouge area Am. Cancer Soc., 1987—88; adv. bd. Ctr. for Energy Law, 2000—. With U.S. Army, 1969—75. Recipient John Rogers award, 1999, Ctr. for Am. and Internat. Law. Master: Dean Henry George McMahon Am. Inn of Ct.; mem.: Ctr. for Am. and Internat. Law (bd. editors Oil and Gas Reporter), Baton Rouge Bar Assn., La. State Law Inst. (mineral code com.), La. Bar Assn. (mem. ho. of dels. 1979—92, coun. rep. mineral law sect. 1986—94, chmn. mineral law sect. 1992—93). Republican. Methodist. Oil, gas, and mineral, Natural resources, General civil litigation. Office: PO Box 2471 Baton Rouge LA 70821-2471 E-mail: clay@tpbp.com.

JOHNSON, JOSEPH H., JR., lawyer; b. Dothan, Ala., July 14, 1925; Student, La. Poly. Inst.; LLB, U. Va., 1949. Bar: Ala. 1949. Of counsel Adams and Reese/Lange, Simpson LLP, Birmingham, Ala. Recipient Bernard P. Friel medal for disting. svc. in pub. fin., 1997. Mem. ABA (mem. com. 1962-66, 68-72, 73-77, chmn. 1981-82, sec. of urban, state and local govt. law), Assn. of Bar of City of N.Y., Birmingham Bar Assn. (chmn. com. on profl. ethics 1978-79), Ala. State Bar, Nat. Assn. Bond Lawyers (pres. 1988-89), Am. Coll. Bond Counsel (bd. dirs. 1998—). Office: Adams and Reese Lange Simpson LLP Ste 1100 2100 3d Ave N Birmingham AL 35203-3367 E-mail: jjohn2994@charter.net., joseph.johnson@arlaw.com.

JOHNSON, JULIE MARIE, lawyer, lobbyist; b. Aberdeen, S.D., Aug. 7, 1953; d. Howard B. and Jerauldine (Dilly) J.; m. Bryan L. Hisel. BA in Govt., Comm., U. S.D., 1974, MA in Polit. Sci., JD, U. S.D., 1976. Bar: S.D. 1977, U.S. Dist. Ct. S.D. 1977. Assoc. Siegel, Barnett Law Firm, Aberdeen, 1977; law clk. Fifth Judicial Circuit Ct., Aberdeen, 1977-78; ptnr. Maloney, Kolker, Fritz, Hogan & Johnson, Aberdeen, 1978-84; dep. sec. S.D. Dept. Labor, Aberdeen, Pierre, 1983-84, sec. Gov.'s Cabinet, 1985-87; pres. Industry and Commerce Assn. of S.D., Pierre, 1987-95; sec., Gov.'s Cabinet S.D. Dept. Revenue, Pierre, 1995; exec. dir. S.D. Rural Devel. Coun., Pierre, 1995—2003; adminstrv. law judge, 2003—. Treas. S.D. Cmty. Found., Pierre, 1987-95; mem. Pvt. Industry Coun., 1985-87, S.D. Coun. on Vocat. Edn., 1985-87; bd. dirs. Mo. Shores Women's Resource Ctr., Pierre, 1988-89; chmn. S.D. Main St. Adv. Coun., 1987-91; bd. dirs. United Way, 1988-96, chmn., 1991; mem. Shortgrass Arts Coun., 1987—, South Dakotans for the Arts, 1981—, Solid Waste Mgmt. Plan Task Force, 1990, S.D. Citizens Adv. Coun. on Hazardous Waste, 1991-92, gov.'s adv. coun. on health care reform, 1992-93; bd. dirs. Hist. S.D. Found., 1996-99; founding mem., legal counsel Outdoor Women of S.D., Inc., 1995—; bd. trustees USD Found., 1992—; trustee, mem. bus. affairs com., 1996—, com. on trustees, Kelley Ctr. for Entrepreneurship adv. bd., presdl. search com. Dakota Wesleyan U., 1999-2000; founding mem., treas. S.D. Discovery Ctr. and Aquarium, Inc., bd. dirs., 1988-92; mem. S.D. Water Congress, 1990—97, bd. dirs., 1987-95; bd. dirs. Nyoda Girl Scout Coun., 1997-99; mem. adv. bd. W.O. Farber Ctr. for Excellence in Civic Leadership, 1998—; bd. dirs. Farber Fund, 1987—; founding mem. S.D. Chambers & Econ. Devel. Coun., 1989—; mem. Network Mgmt. Team Nat. Rural Devel. Partnership, 1998—2001; mem. Children's Care Hosp. and Sch. Found. Bd., 1997—, investment com., 1999—, bd. devel. com., 2000—; mem. Nat. Rural Devel. Partnership Presdl. Transition Team, 2000-01, Agr. and Econ. Devel. Task Force, 2001, S.D. Habitat for Humanity Bd., 2001—; bd. dir. Historic S.Dak. Found., 1995-98, Genesis of Innovation, 2000-, S.Dak. Habitat for Humanity, 2001-, ; acting exec. dir. S.Dak. Math., Sci. and Tech. Coun., 2000-03; vol. chmn. S.Dak. WWII Meml. Dedication, 2001. RJR Nabisco fellow Women Execs. in State Govt., Harvard, 1986; named Outstanding Young Citizen Jaycees, Aberdeen, 1982, S.D. Jaycees, 1983. Mem. S.D. Bar Assn. (chmn. adminstrv. law com. 2001-, mem. CLE com., Worker's compensation com.), Industry and Commerce Assn. S.D. (bd. dirs. 1985-87), U. S.D. Alumni Assn. (exec. com. 1987-96, pres. 1990-92), AAUW, Bus. and Profl. Women U.S.A. (nat. legis. chmn. 1987-88, 92-94, nat. chmn. issues mgmt. 1991-93, pres. S.D. 1984-85, Woman of Yr. award Aberdeen chpt. 1982), Women Execs. in State Govt. (bd. didrs. 1985-87), Coun. State Mfrs. Assn., S.D. Mining Assn. (bd. dirs. 1991-95, Gold PAC, 1995-), Nat. Indsl. Coun., Coun. State C.'s of C., Ducks Unltd., Rotary, Zonta, ABC Investment Club, Rocky Mountain Elk Found. Republican. Lutheran. Address: 1100 E Church St Apt 352 Pierre SD 57501-2354 Office: Capitol Lake Plz 711 E Wells Ave Pierre SD 57501-3335 Home: 1414 Sharpstone Dr Mitchell SD 57301-6250 E-mail: juliem.johnson@state.sd.us.

JOHNSON, KATHERINE ANNE, health research administrator, lawyer; b. Medford, Mass., Apr. 20, 1947; d. Lester and Eileen Anne (Henaghan) J. BS, La. State U., 1969, MSA, George Washington U., 1972; JD, Cath. U., 1985. Bar: Md. 1985. Pub. health adviser HHS, Washington, 1970-76; dir. plan implementation SE Colo. Health Sys. Agy., Colorado Springs, 1976-78; sr. mng. assoc. CDP Assocs., Inc., Atlanta, 1978-87, dir. legal affairs, 1986-87; v.p. Cancer CarePoint Inc., Atlanta, 1987; sr. mgr. Salick Health Care, Inc., Bethesda, Md., 1987-89; pvt. practice Potomac, Md., 1989-90; assoc. dir. for adminstrn. San Antonio Cancer Inst., 1990-96; assoc. dir. planning and adminstrn. CTRC Rsch. Found., San Antonio, 1996-97, v.p., 1997-98; COO Inst. Drug Devel., San Antonio, 1997-98; prin. biomed. program devel. consulting, 1998-99; dir. rsch./adminstrn. Am. Coll. Surgeons, 1999—2002; asst. prof., assoc. dir. adminstrn. Massey Cancer Ctr., Richmond, 2002—. Spkr. in field. Contbr. articles to profl. jours. Vol. Ct.-Apptd. Spl. Adv. for Abused Children. Mem. Md. Bar Assn., Am. Health Lawyers Assn., Leadership Tex. Class of 1996, Soc. Rsch. Adminstrs. Avocations: skiing, reading, antique collecting. Office: Po Box 980037 Richmond VA 23298 E-mail: kajohns@earthlink.net.

JOHNSON, KENNETH F. lawyer; b. Ft. Bragg, Calif., June 10, 1938; s. Frank W. and Gertrude Johnson; m. Jane Perry Drennan, June 11, 1961; children: Erik, Mark. BSCE, U. Calif., Berkeley, 1962; JD, U. Calif., Hastings, 1969. Bar: Calif. 1970. Of counsel ReedSmith Crosby Heafey, Oakland, Calif., 2003—. Note and comment editor: Hastings Law Jour., 1968-69. Officer USNR, 1962—66. Scholar U. Calif. Hastings, 1967-68, 68-69. Mem. Calif. Bar Assn., Alameda County Bar Assn., Contra Costa County Bar Assn., Bar Assn. San Francisco, Assn. Bus. Trial Lawyers Assn., Order of Coif. General civil litigation, Construction. Office: Reed Smith Crosby Heafey 1999 Harrison St Fl 22 Oakland CA 94612-3520

JOHNSON, KEVIN RAYMOND, lawyer, educator; b. Culver City, Calif., June 29, 1958; s. Kenneth R. Johnson and Angela J. (Gallardo) McEachron; m. Virginia Salazar, Oct. 17, 1987; children: Teresa, Tomás, Elena. AB in Econs. with great distinction, U. Calif., 1980; JD magna cum laude, Harvard U., 1983. Bar: Calif. 1985, U.S. Dist. Ct. (no., ea. and so. dists.) Calif. 1985, U.S. Ct. Appeals (9th cir.) 1985, U.S. Supreme Ct. 1991. From rsch. asst. to Charles Haar prof. Harvard U., Cambridge, Mass., 1982-83, instr. legal writing, 1982; law clk. to Hon. Stephen Reinhardt, U.S. Ct. Appeals (9th cir.), L.A., 1983-84; atty. Heller Ehrman White & McAuliffe, San Francisco, 1984-89; acting prof. law U. Calif., Davis, 1989-92, prof. law, 1992—, assoc. dean for acad. affairs, 1998—, prof. Chicano studies, 2000—, dir. Chicano Studies Program, 2000—01. Instr. civil procedure, complex litigation, immigration law, refugee law, acting dir. clin. legal edn., spring 1992, Latinos and Latines and the Law, 2001, Critical Race Theory, 2003; mem. legal del. to El Salvador, 1987. Author: How Did You Get To Be Mexican? A White/Brown Man's Search for Identity, 1999, Race, Civil Rights, and the Law: A Multiracial Approach, 2001, Mixed Race and the Law: A Need, 2002; editor: Harvard Law Rev., 1981—83; contbr. articles to profl. jours. Bd. dirs. Legal Svcs. No. Calif., 1996—, exec. com., 1997—, v.p., 2001-2003, pres., 2003—; bd. dirs. Yolo County ACLU, 1990-93, chmn. legal com., 1991-93; magistrate merit selection panel U.S. Dist. Ct. for Ea. Dist. Calif.; vol. Legal Svcs. Program, San Francisco, Sacramento, Calif.; mem. Lawyers Com. for Civil Rights of the San Francisco Bay Area, 1991—; various pro bono activies. Recipient commendation Calif. State Bar, 1985-90, Chancellor's Cmty. and Diversity award, 2001. Mem. ABA (coordinators com. immigration 1998—), Calif. Bar Assn. (standing com. legal svcs. for poor 1992-94, gov. com. continuing edn. bar 1993-98, mem. minority affairs com., law sch. admission coun. 1999-2001), U. Calif. Alumni Assn. (class sec. Class of 1980), Phi Beta Kappa. Democrat. Roman Catholic. Office: U Calif Sch Law King Hall Davis CA 95617

JOHNSON, KRAIG NELSON, lawyer, mediator; b. Landstuhl, Germany, July 8, 1959; came to U.S., 1966; s. Howard Arthur and Joy Anne (Nelson) J.; m. AmberJade F. Leca, Nov. 13, 1993. BA with honors, Eckerd Coll., 1981; M in Internat. Mgmt., Am. Grad. Sch. Internat. Mgmt., Glendale, Ariz., 1982; JD, Baylor U., 1992. Bar: Fla. 1993; cert. mediator and arbitrator Supreme Ct. of Fla. Mktg. mgr. Jack Eckerd Corp., Clearwater, Fla., 1982-85; mktg. systems mgr. NCS, Inc., Houston, 1985-87; dir. ops. Petro, Inc., El Paso, 1987-90; atty. and shareholder Zimmerman, Shuffield, Kiser & Sutcliffe, P.A., Orlando, Fla., 1992—2003; atty., mng. ptnr. Goodman McGuffey Lindsey & Johnson LLP, Orlando, Fla., 2003—. Editor: Florida Workers' Compensation Practice, 1994; contbr. articles to profl. jours. Mem. internat. trade and investment adv. bd. Econ. Devel. Commn. of Mid-Fla., Orlando, 1997—; mem. Task Force on Title IX, Baylor U. Bd. of Regents, Waco, 1992-93; bd. dirs. Asian-Am. C. of C., Orlando, 1994-95. Fellow Soc. of Antiquaries of Scotland; mem. Am. Immigration Lawyers Assn., St. Andrew's Soc. of Ctrl. Fla. (bd. dirs., v.p. 1996-98, pres. 1998-2000), Fla. Bar Assn. (sect. on internat. law and litig.), Order of Barristers. Avocations: sailing, flying, shooting sports, mandarin chinese and german languages. General civil litigation, Immigration, naturalization, and customs, Private international. Home: 509 N Hampton Ave Orlando FL 32803-5516 Office: Goodman McGuffey Lindsey & Johnson LLP 1245 W Fairbanks Ave Winter Park FL 32789

JOHNSON, LAEL FREDERIC, lawyer; b. Yakima, Wash., Jan. 22, 1938; s. Andrew Cabot and Gudney M. (Fredrickson) Johnson; m. Eugenie Rae Call, June 9, 1960; children: Eva Marie, Inga Margaret. AB, Wheaton Coll., 1960; JD, Northwestern U., 1963. Bar: Ill. 1963, U.S. Dist. Ct. (no. dist.) Ill. 1964, U.S. Ct. Appeals (7th cir.) 1966. V.p., gen. counsel Abbott Labs., Abbott Park, Ill., 1981-89, sr. v.p., sec., gen. counsel, 1989-94; of counsel Schiff Hardin & Waite, Chgo., 1995—. Mem., past chmn. Law Sch. bd. Northwestern U. Mem.: ABA, Assn. Gen. Counsel. Antitrust, Corporate, general, Securities. Office: Schiff Hardin & Waite 6600 Sears Tower Chicago IL 60606

JOHNSON, LAURENCE MICHAEL, lawyer; b. N.Y.C., Feb. 8, 1940; s. Edgar and Eleanor (Kraus) Johnson; m. Margie Serrano, Mar. 15, 2003; children: Mark Steven, Lisa Arienne, Laura Elizabeth, Daniel Milton, Miguel L., Daniel B. AB cum laude, Harvard U., 1961; LL.B. cum laude, Columbia U., 1964. Bar: Mass. 1964. Research asst. Columbia U., 1962-64; law clk. Supreme Jud. Ct. Mass., 1964-65; from assoc. to ptnr. firm Nutter, McClennen & Fish, Boston, 1965-77; ptnr. firm Newman & Meserve, Boston, 1977-78, Palmer & Dodge, Boston, 1978-83; sole practice law Boston, 1983-85; ptnr. firm Johnson & Polubinski, Boston, 1985-86, Johnson & Schwartzman, Boston, 1986—91; of counsel Fordham & Starrett, Boston, 1991—96; ptnr. Mahoney, Hawkes & Goldings, Boston, 1996—2001, Davis, Malm & D'Agostine, Boston, 2001—. Arbitrator Am. Arbitration Assn., 1976—; tchg. team Harvard Trial Adv. Workshop, 1976—; mem. trial adv. faculty Mass. Contg. Legal Edn. of New Eng. Law Inst., 1979—. Author: 20 Years of Civil Rights: Epilogue and Prologue, Boston Bar Journal, 1988; contbr. articles to profl. jours. Group chmn. larger law firms United Way of Mass. Bay, 1976; mem. Sudbury Human Rights Council, 1964-68, pres., 1965-66, Patriot award, 1976 Fellow: Am. Coll. Trial Lawyers (complex litigation com. 1994—99), Boston Bar Found. (life); mem.: ABA (jud. adminstrn. divsn. , litigation & anti-trust sects.), Mass. Bar Assn., Am. Law Inst., Boston Bar Assn. (steering com. lawyers com. for civil rights under law 1976—). Democrat. Home: 11 Northway Rd Randolph MA 02368-2913

JOHNSON, LAWRENCE WILBUR, JR., lawyer; b. Columbia, S.C., Apr. 17, 1955; s. Lawrence Wilbur and Ruth (Cooper) J.; m. Cindy Ann Small, May 26, 1979. BS in Acctg., U. S.C., 1976, JD, 1979. Bar: S.C. 1979, U.S. Dist. Ct. S.C. 1979, U.S. Ct. Appeals (4th cir.) 1980. Jud. clk. 3d Jud. Cir. Ct., Bishopville, S.C., 1979-80; ptnr. Robinson, McFadden, Moore, Pope, Williams, Taylor & Brailsford, P.A., Columbia, 1980-87; shareholder Adams, Quackenbush, Herring & Stuart, P.A., Columbia, 1987-94; ptnr. Young, Clement, Rivers & Tisdale, LLP, Columbia, 1994-96, Johnson Law Firm, Columbia, 1996—. Mem. S.C. Bar Assn., Richland County Bar Assn. (pres. bankruptcuy law sect. 1982-85), S.C. Bankruptcy Law Assn. (bd. dirs.), S.C. Bar Ho. of Dels., Greater Columbia C. of C. (bd. dirs.), Com. of 100 (chmn.), Forest Lake Club , U. S.C. Alumni Assn. (bd. dirs. 1980-82), Chi Psi, Omicron Delta Kappa. Republican. Baptist. Avocation: golf. Banking, Bankruptcy, Commercial, consumer (including collections, credit). Home: 713 Harborview Ct Chapin SC 29036-7716 Office: Johnson Law Firm PA 1728 Main St Ste 221 Columbia SC 29201-2844 also: PO Box 883 Columbia SC 29202-0883

JOHNSON, LEONARD HJALMA, lawyer; b. Thomasville, Ga., May 22, 1957; s. Hjalma Eugene and Laura Nell (McLeod) J.; m. Nancy Louise Brock, Dec. 13, 1981; children: Brock Hjalma, Paige McLeod. BSBA, U. Fla., 1978, JD, 1980. Assoc. Dayton, Sumner, Luckie and McKnight, Dade City, 1981-83, Greenfelder and Mander, Dade City, 1983-84; pres. East Coast Bank Corp., Ormond Beach, Fla., 1983-2000; pvt. practice Dade City, 1984-89; ptnr. Johnson, Auvil, Brock & Wilson, PA, Dade City, 1990—; vice chmn. Bank of Madison (Fla.) County, 1983—88, N. Fla. Bank Corp., Madison, 1983—88, Bank at Ormond By-the-Sea, 1983-2000. Vice chmn. Lake State Bank, 1989-96. Bd. dirs. Downtown Dade City Main St. Inc., 1987-96, East Pasco Habitat for Humanity, 1998-99; trustee Dade City Hosp., 1994-96, chmn., 1996; mem. Leadership Fla. Mem. ABA, Fla. Bar Assn., Pasco County Bar Assn. (sec. 1982-83), Young Pres. Orgn. (edn. chmn. Fla. chpt. 1997-98, chpt. chmn. 1998-99), Dade City C. of C., Fla. Blue Key. Republican. Methodist. Banking, Corporate, general, Property, real (including real estate development, water).

JOHNSON, MARK ALAN, lawyer; b. Marysville, Ohio, June 5, 1960; s. Neil Raymond and Elizabeth Johnson; m. Deborah Anne Hillis, Sept. 21, 1984. BA, Otterbein Coll., 1982; JD, Ohio State U., 1985. Bar: Ohio 1985, U.S. Dist. Ct. (so. dist.) Ohio 1985, U.S. Ct. Appeals (6th cir.) 1987, U.S. Dist. Ct. (no. dist.) Ohio 1991, U.S. Ct. Appeals (5th cir.) 1998. Assoc. Baker and Hostetler LLP, Columbus, Ohio, 1985-92, ptnr., 1993—. Mem. ABA (litigation sect., mem. bus. torts litigation com., comml. and banking litigation com.), Ohio Bar Assn., Columbus Bar Assn. Federal civil litigation, State civil litigation, Commercial, contracts (including sales of goods; commercial financing). Office: Baker & Hostetler LLP 65 E State St Ste 2100 Columbus OH 43215-4215 E-mail: mjohnson@bakerlaw.com.

JOHNSON, MARK ANDREW, lawyer; b. Plainville, Kans., Feb. 27, 1959; s. Delton Lee and Margaret Ellen (McCracken) J. BA in Chemistry, Reed Coll., 1982; JD, U. Calif., Berkeley, 1987. Bar: Oreg. 1987, U.S. Supreme Ct. 1991. Jud. clk. U.S. Dist. Ct. Oreg., Portland, 1987-88, Oreg. Ct. of Appeals, Salem, 1988-89; assoc. Gevurtz, Menashe, Larson, Kurshner & Yates, PC, Portland, 1989-93; ptnr. Findling & Johnson LLP, Portland, 1993-99; of counsel Bennett Hartman Morris & Kaplan, LLP and predecessor, Portland, 1999—. Mem. ABA, Nat. Lesbian and Gay Law Assn. (co-chmn. 1994-95), Oreg. Gay and Lesbian Law Assn. (co-chair 1990-92), Oreg. State Bar (pres. 1998-99). Appellate, Family and matrimonial. Office: Bennett Hartman Morris & Kaplan LLP 851 SW 6th Ave Ste 1600 Portland OR 97204-1307 E-mail: johnsonm@bennetthartman.com.

JOHNSON, MARK EUGENE, lawyer; b. Independence, Mo., Jan. 8, 1951; s. Russell Eugene and Reatha (Nixon) J.; m. Vicki Ja Lane, June 11, 1983. AB with honors, U. Mo., 1973, JD, 1976. Bar: Mo. 1976, U.S. Dist. Ct. (we. dist.) Mo. 1976, U.S. Ct. Appeals (8th cir.) 1984, U.S. Supreme Ct. 1993. Ptnr. Stinson Morrison Hecker LLP, Kansas City, Mo., 1976—. Editor Mo. Law Rev., 1974-76. Pres. Lido Villas Assn., Inc., Mission, Kans., 1979-81. Mem. ABA, Mo. Bar Assn., Kansas City Bar Assn., Lawyers Assn. Kansas City, Def. Rsch. Inst., Internat. Assn. Def. Counsel, Mo. Orgn. Def. Lawyers, Carriage Club, Order of Coif, Phi Beta Kappa, Phi Eta Sigma, Phi Kappa Phi, Omicron Delta Kappa. Republican. Presbyterian. Federal civil litigation, State civil litigation. Home: 4905 Somerset Dr Shawnee Mission KS 66207-2230 Office: Stinson Morrison Hecker LLP 2600 Grand Blvd Ste 1200 Kansas City MO 64108-4606

JOHNSON, MICHAEL A. lawyer; b. Hornell, N.Y., Mar. 5, 1955; s. Richard C. and Patricia A. J.; m. Katherine A. Sheridan, Aug. 9, 1980; children: Michael Patrick, Kaitlyn Meghan. BA, St. Vincent Coll., 1977; JD, Ohio No. U., 1980. Bar: Pa. 1980, U.S. Dist. Ct. (we. dist.) Pa. 1980, U.S. Ct. Appeals (3rd cir.) 1991, U.S. Supreme Ct. 1988. Assoc. Hammer & Pollins, Greensburg, Pa., 1981-84; pvt. practice Mt. Pleasant, Pa., 1984—. Active Boy Scouts Am., 1969. Recipient Eagle Scout Boy Scouts Am. Mem. Pa. Bar Assn. (zone 6 bd. dels. 1996-99), Pa. Trial Lawyers Assn., Mental Health Assn. (pres. 1996-97, Fred Funari award 1998), Westmoreland Bar Assn. (life, chair planning com. 1990-92, mock trial advisor Mt. Pleasant Sch. 1993-95), Lawyers Abstract Westmoreland County (bd. dirs./ officer 1997-2001, pres. 2000), Ned J. Nakles Am. Inn of Ct. (master, sec., treas. 1997—). Avocations: automotive restoration, reading, coaching soccer, football. Corporate, general, Property, real (including real estate development, water), Workers' compensation. Office: 749 N Church St Mount Pleasant PA 15666-9147 E-mail: tjktmplaw@aol.com.

JOHNSON, NORMA HOLLOWAY, federal judge; b. Lake Charles, La. d. H. Lee and Beatrice (Williams) Holloway; m. Julius A. Johnson, June 18, 1964. BS, D.C. Tchrs. Coll., 1955; JD, Georgetown U., 1962. Bar: D.C. 1962, U.S. Supreme Ct. 1967. Pvt. practice law, Washington, 1963; atty. civil divsn. Dept. Justice, Washington, 1963-67; asst. corp. counsel Office of Corp. Counsel, Washington, 1967-70; judge D.C. Superior Ct., 1970-80, U.S. Dist. Ct. (D.C. dist.), Washington, 1980-97, chief judge, 1997-2001; senior judge U.S. Dist. Ct. (D.C. dist), Washington, 2001. Bd. dirs. Judiciary Leadership Devel. Coun. Fellow Am. Bar Found.; mem. Nat. Bar Assn., Fed. Judges Assn., Am. Judicature Soc., Supreme Ct. Hist. Soc., Am. Inns of Ct. (William Bryant inn). Office: US Dist Ct US Courthouse 333 Constitution Ave NW Washington DC 20001-2802

JOHNSON, OLIVER THOMAS, JR., lawyer; b. San Antonio, July 3, 1946; s. Oliver Thomas and Joan Elizabeth (Edwards) J.; m. Susan Caroline Nelson, Nov. 6, 1976; children: Caroline Elizabeth, Thomas Christian. Student, U. Redlands, 1964-65; BA, Stanford U., 1968, JD, 1971. Bar: Calif. 1972, D.C. 1975, U.S. Ct. Internat. Trade 1983, U.S. Supreme Ct. 1991. Atty. office of legal adviser U.S. Dept. State, Washington, 1971-73, spl. asst. to legal adviser, 1973-75; assoc. Covington & Burling, Washington, 1975-80, ptnr., 1980—. Co-author: The Registration of Foreign Agents in the United States, 1981, Private Investors Abroad: Problems and Solutions, 1987, The North American Free Trade Agreement: Issues, Options, Implications, 1992, The International Lawyer's Deskbook, 1996; contbr. articles to profl. jours. Bd. dir. U.S.-Azerbaijan Coun., Washington, 1995. Mem.: ABA, Inst. Transnat. Arbitration (adv. bd.), Washington Inst. Fgn. Affairs (bd. dirs.), Am. Soc. Internat. Law, Met. Club, Order of Coif. Private international, Public international. Office: Covington & Burling 1201 Pennsylvania Ave NW Washington DC 20004-2401 E-mail: tjohnson@cov.com.

JOHNSON, ORRIN WENDELL, lawyer; b. Mpls., Nov. 7, 1920; s. Elmer Godfrey and Lydia (Carlson) J.; m. Patsy Elizabeth Coons, Apr. 2, 1951; children: Forrest, Wendell, Carol, Laura. BA cum laude, U. Tex., 1942, JD cum laude, 1947. Bar: Tex. 1947, U.S. Ct. Appeals 1948, U.S. Supreme Ct. 1964. Assoc. Karl Gibbon, Harlingen, Tex, 1947-49; ptnr. Gibbon, Coneway, Johnson, Harlingen, 1949-51, Gibbon & Johnson, Harlingen, 1951-53; pvt. practice law Harlingen, 1953-67; ptnr. Johnson & Davis, Harlingen, 1967-95; of counsel Rodriguez, Colvin and Chaney, Brownsville, Tex., 1995—. Assoc. editor Tex. Law Rev., 1946-47; contbr. articles to profl. jours. Pres. Cameron County Good Govt. League, 1979-82, bd. dirs., 1980-86; trustee Marine Mil. Acad., 1964-91, v.p., 1982-86, pres., 1986-89; adv. dir. Valley Baptist Hosp., 1964-72. Maj. USMCR, 1942-57. Recipient Pub. Service Achievement award Common Cause, 1981. Fellow Am. Coll. Trial Lawyers, Am. Coll. Trust and Estate Attys., Tex. Acad. Trust and Probate Lawyers, Am. Bar Found., Tex. Bar Found. (trustee 1977, chmn. fellows 1980-81, sustaining life mem., Lola Wright Found. award 1989, Five Outstanding Fifty Yr. Lawyers in Tex. 1999); mem. ABA (del. Tex. chpt. 1989-90), State Bar Tex. (bd. dirs. 12th dist. 1972-75, pres. 1982-83, chmn. rules ethics com. 1986-88, Pres.' award 1986, Frank J. Scurlock award 1983, trustee Tex. Ctr. for Legal Ethics and Professionalism 1990-94), Immigration Law Reform Inst. (bd. dirs., exec. com. 1987-90), Order of Coif, Masons, Phi Delta Phi. Methodist. State civil litigation, Probate (including wills, trusts). Office: Law Offices of Orrin Johnson 402 E Van Buren Ave Harlingen TX 78550-6834

JOHNSON, PATRICK, JR., lawyer; b. New Orleans, June 6, 1955; s. Patrick and Louise J.; m. Gayle Marie Daniel, Feb. 24, 1979; children: Patrick III, Daniel Hartman, Michael Joseph. BS, U. New Orleans, 1977; JD magna cum laude, Tulane U., 1979; diploma with distinction, U. Stockholm, 1980. Bar: La. 1980, U.S. Dist. Ct. (ea. and mid. dists.) La. 1980, U.S. Ct. Appeals (5th and 11th cirs.) 1981, U.S. Supreme Ct. 1985, U.S. Dist. Ct. (we. dist.) La. 1986. Assoc. Lemle & Kelleher, L.L.P., New Orleans, 1980-85, ptnr., 1985—. Lectr. in field. Articles editor Tulane U. Law Rev., 1978-79, mem. bd. student editors, 1977-78. Mem. ABA (bus. bankruptcy com., chpt. 11 and secured creditors subcom.), Am. Bankruptcy Inst., La. Bar Assn. Bankruptcy, Federal civil litigation, State civil litigation. Home: 403 Atherton Dr Metairie LA 70005-3809 Office: Lemle & Kelleher LLP Pan-Am Life Ctr 21st Fl 601 Poydras St New Orleans LA 70130-6029 E-mail: pjohnson@lemle.com.

JOHNSON, PHILIP WAYNE, judge; b. Greenwood, Ark., Oct. 24, 1944; s. John Luther and Flora (Joyce) J.; m. Carla Jean Newsom, Nov. 6, 1970; children: Betsy, Carl, Jeff, Laura, Philip. BA, Tex. Tech. U., 1965, JD, 1975. Bar: Tex. 1975, U.S. Dist. Ct. (no. and we. dists.) Tex. 1976, U.S. Ct. Appeals (5th cir.) 1984, U.S. Supreme Ct. 1984; cert. in civil trial and personal injury trial law, Tex. Bd. Legal Specialization. Assoc. Crenshaw Dupree & Milam, Lubbock, Tex., 1975-80, ptnr., 1980-98; justice Tex. State Ct. of Appeals (7th dist), Amarillo, 1999—2002, chief justice, 2003—. Bd. dirs., pres. Lubbock County Legal Aid Soc., Tex., 1977-79; bd. dirs., chmn. Trinity Christian Schs., Lubbock, 1978-83, 85-89; bd. dirs., pres. S.W. Lighthouse for Blind, Lubbock, 1978-85. Served to capt. USAF, 1965-72. Decorated Silver Star, D.F.C.; Cross of Gallantry (Vietnam). Fellow: Tex. Bar Found. (life), Am. Bar Found. (life); mem.: ABA, Lubbock County Bar Assn. (pres. 1984—85), Amarillo Bar Assn., Tex. Bar Assn., Phi Delta Phi. Home: 7818 Covington Pkwy Amarillo TX 79121-1940 Office: Seventh Ct of Appeals 501 S Fillmore St Rm 2A Amarillo TX 79101-2449

JOHNSON, PHILIP LESLIE, lawyer; b. Beloit, Wis., Jan. 24, 1939; s. James Philip and Christabel (Williams) J.; m. Kathleen Rose Westover, May 12, 1979; children: Celeste Marie, Nicole Michelle. AB, Princeton U., 1961; JD, U. South Calif., 1973. Bar: Calif. 1973, U.S. Ct. Appeals (9th cir.) 1975, U.S. Ct. of Military Appeals, 1978, U.S. Supreme Ct. 1980. Pilot U.S. Marine Corps., 1961-70; assoc. Law Office Wm. G. Tucker, L.A., 1973-78; ptnr. Engstrom, Lipscomb & Lack, L.A., 1978-92; judge pro tem Calif. State Bar Ct., 1990-95; ptnr. Lillick & Charles, Long Beach, Calif., 1993-99, Shaw, Terhar & LaMontagne, L.A., 2000—. Chmn. aerospace law com. Def. Rsch. Inst. Contbr. articles to profl. jours. Pres., bd. dirs. U. So. Calif. Legion Lex, 1992-93; chmn. com. to nom. alumni trustees Princeton U., 1996-97, mem. exec. com. of alumni coun., 1996-97; chmn. Marine Corps Scholarship Found. L.A. Ball, 1997-99. Mem. ABA, (aviation & space law com., torts & ins. practice section), Princeton Club (So. Calif., bd. dirs.). Avocations: flying, snow skiing, jazz. Aviation, Insurance, Product liability. Home: 5340 Valley View Rd Palos Verdes Peninsula CA 90275-5089 Office: Shaw Terhar & LaMontagne 707 Wilshire Blvd Ste 3060 Los Angeles CA 90017 E-mail: avnlawyer@aol.com.

JOHNSON, PHILIP MCBRIDE, lawyer; b. Springfield, Ohio, June 18, 1938; AB with honors, Ind. U., 1959; LLB, Yale U., 1962. Bar: Ill. 1962, D.C. 1983, N.Y. 1984. Ptnr. Kirkland & Ellis, Chgo., 1962-81; chmn. Commodity Futures Trading Commn., Washington, 1981-83; ptnr. Wiley, Johnson & Rein, Washington, 1983-84, Skadden, Arps, Slate, Meagher & Flom, Washington, 1984—; lectr. on commodities regulation U. Va. Law Sch., 1993—. Spkr. panelist on Commodity Exch. Act Fed. Bar Assn., others; mem. adv. com. definition and regulation Commodity Futures Trading Commn., adv. com. state jurisdiction and responsibility; adv. com. regulatory coordination, adv. com. fin. products, adv. com. tech., adv. com. global markets Commodity Futures Trading Comm. Author: Commodities Regulation, 2 vols., 1997, Derivatives: A Manager's Guide to the World's Most Powerful Financial Instruments, 1999; mng. editor Yale U. Law Jour, 1962, Agrl. Law Jour; contbr. articles to legal jours. Mem. ABA (founder, chmn. com. on futures regulation 1975-81, mem. governing coun. sect. on bus. law 1981-83), Futures Industry Assn. (bd. dirs. 1980-81, 86-87), Internat. Bar Assn. (founder, chmn. subcom. on commodities, futures and options law 1986-90), N.Y. Stock Exch. (mem. regulatory adv. com. 1988—). Administrative and regulatory, Securities, Commodities. Office: Skadden Arps Slate Meagher & Flom 1440 New York Ave NW Ste 700 Washington DC 20005-2111 E-mail: pjohnson@skadden.com.

JOHNSON, PHILLIP EDWARD, lawyer; b. Cleve., Mar. 19, 1950; s. Donald Marquis and Jeannette (Tetinek) Johnson; m. Priscilla Dwinnell, Sept. 12, 1981. BA, Miami U., Oxford, Ohio, 1972; JD, Case Western Res. U., Cleve., 1975. Bar: Ohio 75, U.S. Dist. Ct. (no. dist.) Ohio 75, Maine 77, U.S. Dist. Ct. Maine 77. Assoc. Arter & Harden, Cleve., 1975—77, Pierce, Atwood, Schriber, Allen, Smith & Lancaster, Augusta and Portland, Maine, 1977—82, ptnr., 1983—92, Johnson & Webbert, LLP, Augusta, 1992—. Vice chmn. Maine Bd. of Property Tax Rev., 1992—; mem. Maine Profl. Ethics Commn., 2001—, chmn., 2003—. Mem.: ABA, Maine Profl. Ethics Commn. (chair 2003—), Kennebec County Bar Assn. (pres. 1983—85), Maine Trial Lawyers Assn. (bd. govs. 1993—2003), Maine State Bar Assn., Lawyer-Pilots Bar Assn. Republican. Estate planning, Personal injury (including property damage), Professional liability. Home: 66 Hemlock Ter Augusta ME 04330-6248 Office: PO Box 79 160 Capitol St Augusta ME 04332-0079 E-mail: pjohnson@johnsonwebbert.com.

JOHNSON, REVERDY, lawyer; b. N.Y.C., Aug. 24, 1937; s. Reverdy and Reva (Payne) J.; m. Pamela Forbes, Mar. 10, 1961 (div.); m. Marta Schneebeli, Apr. 4, 1970 (div.); children: Deborah Ghiselin, Reverdy Payne; m. Robbie M. Williams, Feb. 20, 1994. AB cum laude, Harvard U., 1960, LLB, 1963. Bar: Fla. 1963, Calif. 1964, N.Mex. 1997. Assoc. Brobeck, Phleger & Harrison, San Francisco, 1963-66; from assoc. to ptnr. Pettit & Martin, San Francisco, 1966-95; of counsel Steinhart & Falconer LLP, San Francisco, 1995-97, Scheuer Yost & Patterson, Sante Fe, NMex., 1996—, Fenwick and West, LLP, Mountain View, Calif., 1999—. Co-owner Johnson Turnbull Vineyards, Napa Valley, Calif., 1977-93; tech. adv. com., com. open space lands Calif. Joint Legislature, 1968-69, chmn., 1969-70. Bd. dirs. Planning and Conservation League, 1966-72, League to Save Lake Tahoe, 1972-77, Found. for San Francisco's Archtl. Heritage, 1975-84, San Francisco Devel. Fund, 1986-96; bd. dirs. Santa Fe Shakespeare Co.2001—, pres., 2002—. Mem. Urban Land Inst. (vice chmn. recreational devel. council 1975-78, comml. and retail devel. council 1980-99), Napa Valley Vintners Assn. (bd. dirs. 1985-88, v.p. 1987, pres. 1988), Am. Coll. Real Estate Lawyers, Lambda Alpha. also: Scheuer Yost & Patterson 125 Lincoln Ave Ste 223 Santa Fe NM 87501-2053 E-mail: reverdyj@santafelawyers.com.

JOHNSON, RICHARD ARLO, lawyer; b. Vermillion, S.D., July 8, 1952; s. Arlo Goodwin and Edna Marie (Styles) J.; m. Diane Marie Zephier, Aug. 18, 1972 (div. Jan. 1979); m. Sheryl Lavonne Mader, June 5, 1981; 1 stepchild, Chadwick O. Wagner; 1 child, Sarah N. BA, U. S.D., 1974, JD, 1976. Bar: S.D. 1977, U.S. Dist. Ct. S.D. 1977. Ptnr. Pruitt, Matthews, Muilenberg & Strange, Sioux Falls, S.D., 1977-92, Strange, Farrell & Johnson, P.C., Sioux Falls, 1992—. Mem. Pub. Defender Adv. Bd., Sioux Falls, 1983-98; mem. S.D. Dental Peer Rev. Com. S.E. Dist. Fellow Am. Acad. Matrimonial Lawyers; mem. ATLA, ABA, S.D. Trial Lawyers Assn., State Bar S.D. (chmn. family law com. 1989-92), Sioux Falls (S.D.) Jazz and Blues Soc. (bd. dirs., 1998—, pres. 2003), Phi Delta Phi (pres. 1976-77), Masons, Shriners (past potentate). Democrat. Lutheran. Commercial, consumer (including collections, credit), Criminal, Family and matrimonial. Home: 409 E Lotta St Sioux Falls SD 57105-7109 Office: Strange Farrell & Johnson PC 141 N Main Ave Ste 200 Sioux Falls SD 57104-6429

JOHNSON, RICHARD FRED, lawyer; b. July 12, 1944; s. Sylvester Hiram and Naomi Ruth (Jackson) Johnson; m. Sheila Conley, June 26, 1970; children: Brendon, Bridget, Timothy, Laura. BS, Miami U., Oxford, Ohio, 1966; JD cum laude, Northwestern U., 1969. Bar: Ill. 1969, U.S. Dist. Ct. (no. dist.) Ill. 1969), U.S. Dist. Ct. (ctrl. dist.) Ill. 2000, U.S. Ct. Appeals (7th cir.) 1977, U.S. Ct. Appeals (2d cir.) 1980, U.S. Ct. Appeals (9th cir.) 1991, U.S. Ct. Appeals (5th cir.) 1993, U.S. Supreme Ct. 1978. Law clk. U.S. Dist. Ct. (no. dist.) Ill., Chgo., 1969-70; assoc. firm Lord, Bissell & Brook, Chgo., 1970-77, ptnr., 1977—. Lectr. legal edn. Contbr. articles to profl. jours. Recipient Am. Jurisprudence award 1968. Mem. Chgo. Bar Assn., Union League. Admiralty, Insurance, General civil litigation. Home: 521 W Roscoe St Chicago IL 60657-3518 Office: Lord Bissell & Brook 115 S La Salle St Ste 3200 Chicago IL 60603-3902

JOHNSON, RICHARD TENNEY, lawyer; b. Evanston, Ill., Mar. 24, 1930; s. Ernest Levin and Margaret Abbott (Higgins) J.; m. Marilyn Bliss Meuth, May 1, 1954; children: Ross Tenney, Lenore, Jocelyn. AB with high honors, U. Rochester, 1951; postgrad., Trinity Coll., Dublin, Ireland, 1954-55; LLB, Harvard, 1958. Bar: D.C. 1959. Trainee Office Sec. Def., 1957-59; atty. Office Gen. Counsel. Dept. Def., 1959-63; dep. gen. counsel Dept. Army, 1963-67, Dept. Transp., 1967-70; gen. counsel CAB, 1970-73, mem., 1976-77; gen. counsel NASA, 1973-75, ERDA, 1975-76; chmn. organizational integration Dept. Energy Activation, Exec. Office of Pres., 1977; ptnr. firm Sullivan & Beauregard, 1978-81; gen. counsel Dept. Energy, 1981-83; ptnr. Zuckert, Scoutt, Rasenberger & Johnson, 1983-87; prin. Law Offices of R. Tenney Johnson, Esq., Washington, 1987-2001; gen. counsel Assn. of Univs. for Rsch. in Astronomy, 1987—. Lt. USNR, 1951-54. Mem. ABA, Fed. Bar Assn., Cosmos Club, Phi Beta Kappa, Theta Delta Chi. Administrative and regulatory, Aviation, Government contracts and claims. E-mail: marandten@starpower.net.

JOHNSON, RICHARD WESLEY, lawyer; b. Stockton, Calif., Aug. 15, 1933; s. Ralph Wesley and Elizabeth Louise (Pucci) J.; m. Suzanne Marie Waldron, Feb. 18, 1962 (div. 1979); children: Scott Wesley, Elizabeth Nancye, Alexis Marie. BA, U. Calif., San Francisco, 1957, JD, 1961. Bar: Calif. 1961, U.S Dist. Ct. Utah., U.S. Dist. Ct. (no. dist.) Calif., U.S. Ct. Appeals (9th cir.). Assoc. Pillsbury, Madison & Sutro, San Francisco, 1961-65; sole practice A&J Publs., Walnut Creek, 1963—, ptnr., 1985—. Author: Express Your Love, 1986; editor-in-chief: Hastings Law Rev. Founding trustee J.F.K. Univ., Orinda, Calif., 1963-66, sec., dean of law, 1964-66. Served as pvt. U.S. Army, 1953-55. Mem. Calif. Bar Assn. (com. mem. 1972), Calif. Bar Assn., Mt. Diablo Bar Assn. (bd. dirs. 1974), Nat. Ski Patrol (patrol leader), Contra Costa Bar Assn. Republican. Roman Catholic. Avocations: photography, sailing, poetry, songwriting. State civil litigation, Criminal, Personal injury (including property damage).

JOHNSON, ROBERT ALAN, lawyer; b. Harrisburg, Pa., June 18, 1944; s. Harry Andrew and Minna Melissa (Ebert) J.; m. Selina Braham Pedersen, Aug. 25, 1979; children: Isabella P., Robert A. Jr. BA, Washington and Jefferson Coll., 1966; JD, Harvard U., 1969. Bar: Pa. 1969. Assoc. Buchanan Ingersoll, Pitts., 1969-76, ptnr., 1977—. Contbr. legal articles to profl. jours. Pres. Bach Choir Pitts., 1979-81; bd. dirs. Pitts. Opera, 1985-94, River City Brass Band, Pitts., 1986-95, Renaissance and Baroque Soc., Pitts., 1994—, Friends of the Music Libr., Carnegie Libr. of Pitts., 1995—, CTC Found., 1999—, River City Brass Band Charitable Endowment, Pitts., 2000—, Early Music Am., 2002-. Fellow Am. Coll. Tax Counsel, Am. Coll. Employee Benefits Counsel; mem. ABA, Allegheny County Bar Assn., Allegheny Tax Soc. (chmn. 1982-83), Pitts. Tax Club, Duquesne Club. Republican. Presbyterian. Avocation: avid collector classical music recs. Non-profit and tax-exempt organizations, Pension, profit-sharing, and employee benefits. Home: 601 St James St Pittsburgh PA 15232-1434 Office: Buchanan Ingersoll 301 Grant St Ste 20 Pittsburgh PA 15219-1410 E-mail: johnsonra@bipc.com.

JOHNSON, ROBERT MAX, lawyer; b. Thomas, Okla., Aug. 20, 1942; s. Claude L. and Jesse C. (Stimmel) J.; m. Virginia A. LeForce, May 31, 1964; children: Kelli Brook, Brent Matthew. BS, Okla. State U., 1964; JD, U. Okla., 1967; LLD (hon.), Oklahoma City U., 2001. Bar: Okla. 1967. Shareholder Crowe & Dunlevy, Oklahoma City, 1967—, pres., 1985-87, exec. com., 1992—. Spl. lectr. in land fin. and real estate contracts U. Okla. Coll. of Law, Norman, 1973, 84. Mng. editor: Oklahoma Environmental Law Handbook, 1992-96; contbr. to book: The Law of Distressed Real Estate, 1987; case editor Okla. Law Rev., 1966. Bd. dirs. Redbud Found., Oklahoma City, 1987-96, Myriad Gardens Conservatory, Oklahoma City, 1987-89, Myriad Gardens Found., 1993-96, ARC, 1994-96, Arts Coun. Oklahoma City, 1994—, Am. Heart Assn., 1999—; chmn. Oklahoma City Festival of Arts, 1993-94, Murrah Fed. Bldg. Meml. Task Force, 1995-96, Oklahoma City Nat. Meml. Found., 1996-98, Oklahoma City Nat. Meml. Trust, 1998-2001. Capt. U.S. Army, 1968-70. Recipient Outstanding Svc. to the Pub. award Okla. Bar Assn., 1998, Cmty. Svc. award, 2000, Disting. Svc. award, Oklahoma City/County Hist. Soc., 2000, Robert M. Johnson award, Am. Coll. Mortgage Attys., 2001. Fellow Am. Coll. Mortgage Attys. (bd. regents, pres. 1994-95, chmn. exec. com. 1995-96); mem. Am. Coll. Real Estate Lawyers, Oklahoma City Golf and Country Club (bd. dirs. 1981-82, sec. 1982), Order of Coif, Phi Delta Phi (magister 1966-67), Lambda Alpha. Avocations: golf, quail hunting, fly fishing. Finance, Landlord-tenant, Property, real (including real estate development, water). Home: 1608 Mulholland Dr Edmond OK 73003-4114 Office: East Wharf Plz Ste 102 9225 Lake Hefner Pkwy Oklahoma City OK 73120 E-mail: RMJohnson@coxinet.net.

JOHNSON, ROBERT VEILING, II, lawyer; b. Laconia, N.H., Apr. 29, 1939; s. Robert Veiling and Pauline Leora (Roberts) J.; children: Celia Annah, Jared Veiling. BA, Boston U., 1961; diploma, Internat. Grad. Sch., Sweden, 1963; MS, U. Stockholm, 1964; JD, Boston U., 1967. Bar: N.H. 1967, U.S. Dist. Ct. N.H. 1968, U.S. Ct. Appeals (1st cir.) 1971, U.S. Supreme Ct. 1974. Instr. Wilbraham-Monson Acad., Wilbraham, Mass., 1961-62; assoc. Upton, Sanders & Smith, Concord, N.H., 1967-71; asst. atty. gen. Chief of Criminal Div., State of N.H., Concord, 1971-77; chmn. Bd. of Tax and Land Appeals, State of N.H., Concord, 1977-82; sr. ptnr. Law Offices of Robert V. Johnson II, Concord, 1977—. Bd. dirs. Warren Electrical, Inc., Concord; bd. dirs. N.H. Electric Cooperative, Inc., Plymouth, vice chmn. bd. dirs. exec. com., fin., engring. and ops. coms., 1995—. Author: European Economic Community Law, 1964. Instr. Am. Inst. Banking, 1971; chmn. Concord Conservation Commn., 1971-84; bd. dirs. N.H. Assn. Conservation Commns., Concord, 1977-78; vice chmn. Concord Heritage Commn., 1998—; legal counsel State of N.H. Exec. Council, 1974; chmn. bd. trustees First Congl. Ch., Concord, 1998-99. Am.-Scandinavian Found. fellow, Sweden, 1962; recipient leadership award Rotary Internat., Laconia, N.H. Mem. ABA, N.H. Bar Assn., N.H. Trial Lawyers Assn., Assn. Trial Lawyers Am., Internat. Assn. Assessing Ofcls., Boston U. Alumni Assn. Republican. Federal civil litigation, State civil litigation, General practice. Home: 130 Oak Hill Rd Concord NH 03301-8632 Office: 64 N State St Concord NH 03301-4330 Fax: (603) 224-4414. E-mail: rvjiilaw@sprynet.com.

JOHNSON, RUFUS WINFIELD, lawyer; b. Montgomery County, Md., May 1, 1911; s. Charles L. and Margaret (Smith) J.; m. Rosena L. Allen, June 21, 1939 (div. May 1971); m. Vaunda Louise Griffith, May 29, 1971; step-children: Yvonne, Jackie, Karen, Rodney, Michelle. AB, Howard U.,

1934, postgrad., 1934-36, LLB, 1939. Bar: Calif., Ark., Supreme Ct. Ark., Supreme Ct. Calif., D.C. Dist. Ct., U.S. Ct. Appeals, D.C., U.S. Supreme Ct., Supreme Ct. of South Korea; cert. counsel Judge Advocate Gen. Sch., Washington. Pvt. practice, D.C., Calif., Ark., 1945—. Originator Lawyer's Pro Bono Svc. Ret. lt. col. USAR. Decorated Combat Inf. badge, Purple Heart, Bronze Star with 2 oak leaf clusters, Spl. Citation for Bravery. Mem. VFW (life), Am. Judicature Soc., Am. Acad. Polit. and Social Sci., Mil. Order Purple Heart, Internat. Soc. Poets, Am. Kempo Karate Assn., Sr. Citizens Coalition, Ret. Officers Assn., Am. Legion, Masons, Am. Karate Assn. (5th degree Shorin-Ryu Black Belt), Lions. Baptist. Appellate, Criminal, Military. Home: PO Box 776 Mason TX 76856-0776

JOHNSON, SHIRLEY Z. lawyer; b. Burlington, Iowa, Mar. 6, 1940; d. Arthur Frank and Helen Martha (Nelson) Zaiss; m. Charles Rumph, Jan. 19, 1979. BA summa cum laude, U. Iowa, 1962; JD with honors, U. Mich., 1965. Bar: Calif. 1966, D.C. 1976, U.S. Supreme Ct. 1979. Trial atty. antitrust divsn. U.S. Dept. Justice, San Francisco, 1965-72; counsel antitrust subcom. U.S. Senate Jud. Com., Washington, 1973-75; ptnr. Baker & Hostetler, Washington, 1976-85; pvt. practice Washington, 1985-98; ptnr., chair antitrust and trade regulations dept. Greenberg Traurig, Washington, 1998—. Adv. bd. BNA Antitrust & Trade Regulations Reporter, 2000—; mediator U.S. Dist. Ct., Washington, 1990—. Contbr. articles to profl. jours. Trustee The Textile Mus., Washington, 1991—, v.p. bd. trustees, 1994—. Mem. ABA, Women's Bar Assn. (bd. dirs. 1989-91), Am. Law Inst., Order of Coif, Phi Beta Kappa. Democrat. Avocation: collecting asian art. Administrative and regulatory, Antitrust, Legislative. Office: Greenburg Traurig 800 Connecticut Ave NW Washington DC 20006-2709 E-mail: Johnson@gtlaw.com.

JOHNSON, SYLVESTER, protective services official; m. Cynthia Johnson; 3 children. Student, Phila. C.C., Temple U., Harvard U. Joined Phila. Police Dept., 1964, dep. commr. ops., 1998—2002, police commr., 2002—. Recipient George Fencl award, Dirs. award, U.S. Dept. Exec. Office for the Weed & Seed Program. Office: Phila Police Dept One Franklin Sq Philadelphia PA 19106*

JOHNSON, TERRI SUE, lawyer; b. Saginaw, Mich., Sept. 18, 1961; BA, Mich. State U., 1983; JD, U. Fla., 1988. Bar: Fla. 1989. Assoc. Roy J. Morgan & Assocs., P.A., Orlando, Fla., 1980-92; ptnr. Morgan & Johnson, P.A., Orlando, Fla., 1992—2001, Terri S. Johnson, P.A., 2001—. Assoc. editor Acad. Fal. Trial Lawyers Jour., 1994—. Mem. Fla. Bar Assn., Nat. Orgn. Social Security Reps., Acad. Fla. Trial Lawyers, Orange County Bar Assn. (guardian ad litem). Insurance, Personal injury (including property damage). Office: Terri S Johnson PA 221 N Joanna Ave Tavares FL 32778-3217

JOHNSON, THOMAS EDWARD, lawyer; b. Jamestown, N.D., May 26, 1953; s. John Edward and Lorna Genevieve (Kolden) J.; m. Jinx Lee Howell, Sept. 1, 1984; children: Anthony John Howell, Matthew Thomas Howell. BA, St. John's U., Collegeville, Minn., 1975; JD, Duke U., 1978. Bar: Minn. 1979, U.S. Dist. Ct. Minn. 1979, U.S. Ct. Appeals (8th cir.) 1991. Staff atty. Murrin Legal Ctr., Mpls., 1979-81, supervising atty., 1981-87; ptnr. Johnson, McClay & Nelson, St. Paul, 1987-91, Johnson, McClay & Alton, St. Paul, 1991-92; sole practice Mpls., 1992—98; counsel to standing chpt. 13, trustee Dist. Minn., 1999—. Mem. Minn. Bar Assn. (human rights com. 1985-96, chmn. 1988-91). Roman Catholic. Avocations: biking, tennis, music. Home: 4512 Zenith Ave S Minneapolis MN 55410-1423 Address: 12 S 6th St Ste 310 Minneapolis MN 55402-1521 E-mail: tej@ch13mn.com.

JOHNSON, THOMAS STUART, lawyer; b. Rockford, Ill., May 21, 1942; s. Frederick C. and Pauline (Ross) J. BA, Rockford Coll., 1964, LLD, 1989; JD, Harvard U., 1967. Bar: Ill. 1967. Ptnr., past pres. Williams & McCarthy, Rockford, 1967—. Lectr. in field. Contbr. numerous articles to profl. jours. Chmn. bd. trustees Rockford Coll., 1986—89; trustee Eastern Ill. U., 1996—2000, Emanuel Med. Ctr., Turlock, Calif., 1984—86, Swedish Covenant Hosp., Chgo., 1984—86, Lincoln Acad. of Ill., 1999—; chmn. bd. dirs. Ill. Inst. Continuing Legal Edn., Chgo., 1984—86; treas. Lawyers Trust Fund of Ill., Chgo., 1984—86; bd. govs. Regent's Coll., London, 1985—89; bd. dirs., mem. benevolence bd. Covenant Ch. Am., Chgo., 1984—86; chmn. Regent's Found. for Internat. Edn., London; chancellor Ill. Acad. Lawyers, 1999. With U.S. Army, 1968—70. Fellow Am. Bar Found., Am. Coll. Trust and Estate Counsel; mem. ABA (ho. of dels. 1982-89, chmn. commn. on advt. 1984-88), Ill. Bar Assn. (bd. govs. 1976-82, sec. 1981-82, medal of honor 1997), Winnebago County Bar Assn. (pres. 1990), Am. Judicature Soc. (bd. dirs. 1986-90), Rockford Country Club, Rotary (pres. Rockford 1992-93), Univ. Club Rockford. Republican. Corporate, general, Estate planning, General practice. Home: 913 N Main St Rockford IL 61103-7068

JOHNSON, THOMAS WEBBER, JR., lawyer; b. Indpls., Oct. 18, 1941; s. Thomas W. and Mary Lucinda (Webber) J.; m. Sandra Kay McMahon, Aug. 15, 1964 (div. 1986); m. Deborah Joan Collins, May 17, 1987 (div. 1990); m. Barbara Joyce Walter, Mar. 13, 1992. BS in Edn., Ind. U., 1963, JD summa cum laude, 1969. Bar: Ind. 1969, Calif. 1970. Law clk. Ind. Supreme Ct., Indpls., 1968-69; assoc. Irell & Manella, L.A., 1969-76, ptnr., 1976-84, Irell & Manella , Newport Beach, Calif., 1984—99; atty. Irell & Manella, of counsel, 2000—. Chair Com. on Group Ins. Programs for State Bar of Calif., San Francisco, 1978-79; adj. prof. law UCLA, 1996-2001; lectr. for Practicing Law Inst., Calif. Continuing Edn. of the Bar, Calif. Judges Assn., seminars on ins. and bus. litigation. Editor-in-chief: Ind. Law Review, 1968-69; contbr. articles to profl. jours. With USNR, 1959-65. Named Outstanding Grad. Province XII, Phi Delta Phi legal fraternity, 1969. Mem. ABA (lectr. chair ins. coverage litigation com., tort and ins. practice sec. 1995-96), Calif. Bar Assn., Orange County Bar Assn., Masons, Newport Beach Country Club. Republican. Mem. Christian Ch. General civil litigation, Insurance. Office: Irell & Manella 840 Newport Center Dr Ste 400 Newport Beach CA 92660-6323

JOHNSON, TOMMY J. prosecutor, legal association administrator; b. Homer, La., Jan. 19, 1949; s. William Boyd and Louise Crain Johnson; m. Kathryn R. Sweedar, June 13, 1981; children: Jordan, Trevor, Ballard, Spencer. BS, La. Tech U., 1971; JD, La. State U., 1975. Asst. atty. gen. State of La., Baton Rouge, 1975—76; atty. Tyler & Johnson, Shreveport, La., 1978—; asst. dist. atty. Caddo Dist. Atty's Office, Shreveport, La., 1982—; v.p. Shreveport Bar Assn., 2003—. Bd. govs. La. Trial Lawyers Assn., Baton Rouge, 1987—89; bd. dirs. N.W. La. Legal Svcs., Shreveport, 1983—87. With La. NG, 1970—76. Mem.: ATLA, Am. Bd. Trial Advocates. Democrat. Methodist. Office: Tyler & Johnson 1717 Marshall St Shreveport LA 71101 Office Fax: 318-425-8136. E-mail: johnstonT@shreve.net.

JOHNSON, VINCENT ROBERT, law educator, educator; b. Latrobe, Pa., Oct. 10, 1953; s. Harry Paul and Anna Ruth (Gozlick) J. BA, St. Vincent Coll., 1975; JD, U. Notre Dame, 1978; LLM, Yale U., 1979; LLD, St. Vincent Coll., 1991. Bar: Pa. 1978, U.S. Ct. Appeals (7th cir.) 1981, Tex. 1985, U.S. Supreme Ct. 1986. Law clk. Hon. Bernard S. Meyer, N.Y.C., Albany, N.Y., 1979-80, Hon. Thomas E. Fairchild, Chgo., 1980-82; asst. prof. St. Mary's U., San Antonio, 1982-85, assoc. prof., 1985-88, prof., 1988—; assoc. dean for adminstrn., 2001—02; assoc. dean acad. and student affairs, 2002—. Jud. fellow U.S. Supreme Ct., 1988-89; dir. St. Mary's Inst. on World Legal Problems, Innsbruck, Austria, 1989-2001; vis. prof. Vt. Law Sch., 1991, St. Petersburg State U., Russia, 1999, Shandong U., China, 2001. Author: Mastering Torts, 1995, 2d edit., 1999; co-author: Studies in American Tort Law, 1994, 2d edit., 1999, Teaching Torts, 1995, 2d edit., 1999; mem. editl. adv. bd. Carolina Acad. Press, Chinese Rev. Common Law. Chair Mayor of San Antonio's Task Force on Ethics in Govt., 1997-98; mem. adv. bd. Chinese Rev. Common Law, 2002—. Fulbright sr. scholar, Beijing, China, 1998. Mem. ABA, Am. Law Inst., State Bar Tex. (lawyer advt. com. 1985-88, rules of profl. conduct com. 1996-99), Assn. Am. Law Schs. (chmn. teaching methods sect. 1987-88), Order of Art and Culture (Innsbruck, Austria), Phi Delta Phi (Teaching Excellence award 1986), Phi Alpha Delta (Disting. Svc. award 1984). Democrat. Roman Catholic. Home: 124 W Gramercy Pl San Antonio TX 78212 Office: St Marys U Sch Law One Camino Santa Maria San Antonio TX 78228-8602 E-mail: vjohnson@stmarytx.edu.

JOHNSON, WALTER FRANK, JR., lawyer; b. Georgiana, Ala., 1945; s. Walter F. and Marjorie Ellen (Carnathan) J.; m. Emily Waldrep, Nov. 23, 1969; children: Brian W., Stacey E. BS, Auburn U., 1968; JD, Samford U., 1973. Bar: Ala. 1973, Ga. 1974. Acct. Union Camp Corp., 1968-70; assoc. Hatcher, Meyerson, Oxford and Irvin, Atlanta, 1973-74, Thompson and Redmond, Columbus, Ga., 1974-78, pvt. practice, 1978—. Asst. pub. defender, Columbus, 1978. Mem. ABA, Ala. State Bar, State Bar Ga., Columbus Lawyers Club. Methodist. Bankruptcy, Probate (including wills, trusts). Home: 3235 Flint Dr Columbus GA 31907-2029 Office: PO Box 6507 3006 University Ave Columbus GA 31907-2106 E-mail: wfjattorney@earthlink.net.

JOHNSON, WELDON NEAL, lawyer; b. Lovington, N.Mex., Apr. 3, 1961; s. Ben and O. Annette Johnson; m. Kellie Marie Nolfo, June 22, 1962; children: Kaitlyn Elizabeth, Shannon Christine. BS in Bus. Adminstrn., Columbia Coll., 1992; JD, St. Louis U., 1996. Bar: Mo. 1996, Ill. 1997, U.S. Dist. Ct. (ea. dist.) Mo. 1997. With Anheuser-Busch, Inc., St. Louis, 1980-93; assoc. The O'Malley Law Firm, St. Louis, 1996—. Mem. ABA, Mo. Bar Assn., Ill. State Bar Assn., Bar Assn. Met. St. Louis, Alpha Chi. Insurance, Labor (including EEOC, Fair Labor Standards Act, labor-management relations, NLRB, OSHA), Personal injury (including property damage). Office: The O'Malley Law Firm 10 S Brentwood Blvd Ste 102 Saint Louis MO 63105-1694

JOHNSON, WILLIAM ASHTON, retired lawyer; b. St. Louis, June 26, 1933; s. William Stuart and Adele (Balmer) J.; m. Anne Chartrand, Nov. 11, 1961; children: Mark, Anthony, Jocelyn, Jennifer. BA, St. Louis U., 1955, JD, 1957; postdoctoral, Northwestern U., 1969. Bar: Mo. 1957. Asst. sec. Mercantile Bank NA, St. Louis, 1969-73, asst. trust officer, 1973-76, trust officer, 1976-78, asst. v.p., 1978-83, v.p., 1983-86; sr. atty. trust Mercantile Bancorporation Inc., St. Louis, 1996—99; ret., 1999. Author St. Louis U. Law Rev., 1971. Served with U.S. Army, 1957-59. Mem. Alpha Sigma Nu. Democrat. Roman Catholic. Home: 4732 Prague Ave Saint Louis MO 63109-2708

JOHNSON-CHAMP, DEBRA SUE, lawyer, educator, writer, artist; b. Emporia, Kans., Nov. 8, 1955; d. Bert John and S. Christine (Brigman) Johnson; m. Michael W. Champ, Nov. 23, 1979; children: Natalie, John. BA, U. Denver, 1977; JD, Pepperdine U., 1980; postgrad., U. So. Calif., 1983-84. Bar: Calif. 1981. Pvt. practice, Long Beach, Calif., 1981-82, L.A., 1981-87, Woodland Hills, Calif., 1993-99; of counsel Greenbaum & Champ, 1999—. Legal reference librarian, instr. Southwestern U. Sch. Law, L.A., 1982-88; adj. prof. law, 1987-88; atty. Contos & Bunch, Woodland Hills, 1988-93; free lance writer/artist; owner The Purple Iguana, 1997—; of counsel Greenbaum & Champ LLP, 1999—. Editor-in chief: Southern Calif. Assn. Law Libraries Newsletter, 1984-85; mem. law rev. Pepperdine U., 1978-80; contbr. articles to profl. jours. Trustee United Meth. Ch., Tujunga, Calif., 1986-88. West Pub. Co. scholar, 1983; recipient H. Wayne Gillis Moot Ct. award, 1980, Vincent S. Dalsimer Best Brief award 1979. Mem. ABA, So. Calif. Assn. Law Libr., Am. Assn. Law Libr., Calif. Bar Assn., Southwestern Affiliates, Friends of the Libr. L.A. Democrat. General civil litigation, Personal injury (including property damage). Home and Office: 5740 Valerie Ave Woodland Hills CA 91367-3967 E-mail: legaldebi2@prodigy.net.

JOHNSTON, ALAN COPE, lawyer; b. Evanston, Ill., Mar. 4, 1946; S. Alan Rogers and Eleanor Cope (Smith) J.; m. Kathryn Elizabeth Edwards, June 21, 1969; 1 child, Eliza. BA, Yale U., 1968; JD, Harvard U., 1975. BAR: Calif. 1975, D.C. 1979, u.S. Dist. Ct. (no., ea., ctrl. and so. dists.) Calif., U.S. Dist. Ct. D.C., U.S. Ct. Appeals (9th fed. and D.C. cirs.)., U.S. Supreme Ct., Gaikoku Jimu Bengoshi, Japan. Assoc. Morrison & Foerster, San Francisco, 1975-79, Washington, 1979-81, ptnr. San Francisco, 1981-85, Palo Alto, Calif., 1986—2002, Tokyo, 2002—. Lt. USNR, 1969-72. Avocations: sailing, reading. General civil litigation, Intellectual property. Office: Morrison & Foerster 755 Page Mill Rd Palo Alto CA 94304-1018 E-mail: acjohnston@mofo.com.

JOHNSTON, DAVID FREDERICK, lawyer; b. Tiffin, Ohio, Sept. 9, 1943; s. Frederick Walter and Aleta Marguerite (Ruehle) J.; m. Ona Lee Graham, June 18, 1966; children: Matthew, Rebecca, Elisabeth, Benjamin. BA in Chemistry, Oreg. State U., 1965; JD, Golden Gate U., 1971. Bar: Calif. 1972, Oreg. 1973, U.S. Ct. Mil. Appeals 1974, U.S. Supreme Ct. 1983. Commd. officer U.S. Coast Guard, 1965; sea duty U.S. Coast Guard Cutter Magnolia, 1966-67; staff atty. U.S. Coast Guard, 1971-79; dept. chief U.S. Coast Guard Marine Safety Office, Norfolk, Va., 1979-82; appeal decision supr. U.S. Coast Guard Hdqrs., Washington, 1982-85; sole practice Portland, Oreg., 1985-86; workers compensation ins. EBI Ins., Portland, Oreg., 1986-95. Author: Suspension and Revocation of Mariner's Licenses, Certificates and Documents, 1984. Elder, Presbyn. Ch., Green Acres Ch., Portsmouth, Va., 1979, Multnomah Ch., Portland, 1986; com. chmn. Clermont Sch., Fairfax County, Va., 1983, bd. co-chair, 1996-99, land use co-chair, Collins View Neighborhood Assn., Portland, 1999— Mem. Oreg. State Bar, Phi Kappa Phi, Phi Lambda Upsilon. Home and Office: 0550 SW Palatine Hill Rd Portland OR 97219-7830

JOHNSTON, EDWARD ALLAN, lawyer; b. Balt., Sept. 25, 1921; s. William Henry and Hattie Frisby (Sanner) J.; m. Dorothy Janet Swart, June 23, 1951 (dec. Jan. 1994); children: Elizabeth Janet, Jean Taylor; m. Mary Ellen Kinnaird, Apr. 15, 1995. BBA, U. Balt., 1942, BS, 1947, LLB, 1949, LLM, 1957. Bar: Md. 1949; CPA, Md. Assoc. Whiteford, Taylor & Preston, Balt., 1954-62, ptnr., 1962—. Lectr. taxes U. Balt., 1948-65; bd. dirs. Dunbar Armored Express Inc. Pres. Dickeyville Assn., 1960; bd. dirs. Contact-Balt., 1974-80, chmn. bd., 1976-80; trustee Asbury Found., 1970—; trustee The Wesley Home, Inc., 1985-92; v.p., gen. counsel Soc. of Srs., 1983—; gen. counsel Ea. Srs. Golf Assn., Inc., 1988—; chmn. of adminstrv. bd. Meth. Ch., 1965-69, 88-90, trustee, chmn. bd., 1977-87. Recipient Alumnus of Yr. award U. Balt., 1980 Mem. U. Balt. Alumni Assn. (pres. 1975-76), Md. Golf Assn. (v.p. 1960-67, pres. 1968), Mid. Atlantic Golf Assn. (v.p. 1978-81, pres. 1982, gen. counsel 1983—), Balt. Country Club (golf com., house commn., bd. govs. 1989-95, exec. com., treas. fin. com. 1991-95, v.p. 1992-93, pres. 1993-95). Corporate, general, Probate (including wills, trusts), Taxation, general. Home: 4104 Ravenhurst Cir Glen Arm MD 21057-9767 Office: Whiteford Taylor & Preston 210 W Pennsylvania Ave Ste 400 Baltimore MD 21204-5332 Fax: 410-832-2015. E-mail: ejohnston@wtplaw.com.

JOHNSTON, JOCELYN STANWELL, paralegal; b. Evanston, Ill., Feb. 16, 1954; d. Gerald and Dorothy Jeanne (Schoenfield) Stanwell; m. Thomas Patrick Johnston, Nov. 28, 1986. BA, U. Minn., 1981; cert., Phila. Inst. Paralegal Tng., Phila., 1986. Paralegal Fredrikson & Byron PA, Mpls., 1981-84, Reed, Smith, Shaw and McClay, Phila., 1984-85, McCausland, Keen & Buckman, PC, Radnor, Pa., 1985-86, Harris, Guenzel, Meier & Nichols, PC, Ann Arbor, Mich., 1986-87, Conner & Bentley, PC, Ann Arbor, 1987-88, Cichocki & Armstrong, Ltd., Oak Park, Ill., 1988-90, Bishop and Bishop, Oak Brook, Ill., 1994-95, Martin, Breen & Merrick, Oak Park, 1994-95, Saitlin, Patzik, Frank & Samotny, Ltd., Chgo., 1995, Bryson R. Cloon, Esquire, Leawood, Kans., 1996—. Democrat. Home: 14501 Marty St Overland Park KS 66223-2300 Office: Bryson R Cloon Esquire 11350 Tomahawk Creek Pkwy Leawood KS 66211-2670 E-mail: johnstont@umkc.edu.

JOHNSTON, JOHN STEVEN, lawyer; b. Kansas City, Mo., Dec. 5, 1948; s. Herschel Wayne and Dixie June J.; m. Deb Neal, Feb. 19, 1977; children: Benjamin, Will. BA in Math., William Jewel Coll., 1970; MA in Psychology, U. Mo., 1975, JD, 1980; postgrad. in clin. psychology, U. Minn., 1975—77. Bar: Mo., 1980, U.S. Dist. Ct. Kans., 1999. Assoc. Linde, Thomson, Fairchild, Langworthy & Kohn, Kansas City, 1980-81, Shook, Hardy & Bacon LLP, Kansas City, 1981-85, ptnr., 1986—, chmn. tort law sect., 1998—2002. Bd. dirs. Lawyers Encouraging Acad. Performance. Author (contbg.): Missouri Methods of Practice-Litigation Guide, 1991; contbr. articles articles to profl. jours. Bd. dirs. Big Bros. and Big Sisters, Kansas City, 1989—, Ozanam Home for Boys, Kansas City, 1990-2002, Lawyers Encouraging Acad. Progress, 2002—. Recipient Outstanding Contbn. to Cmty Health award S. Kansas City Mental Health Resource Network, 1975, Michael Coburn award for cmty. svc. Legal Aid of We. Mo., 1999; named to William Jewell Coll. Hall of Fame, 1999. Mem.: Kansas City Met. Bar Assn. (chmn. civil law and procedure com. 1991—92, bd. dirs. 1993—, pres. 1998, 7th Ann. Pres. award for bar svc. 1993), Mo. Bar Assn. (bd. govs. 1999—), Kansas City Met. Bar Found. (bd. dirs./exec. com. 1995—, chair lawyers for children com. 1998—2002, v.p. 2000—, 1st Ann. Pres.'s award for bar svc. 2001), Ross T. Roberts Inn of Ct. (master 1995—). General civil litigation, Personal injury (including property damage), Product liability. Home: 25004 Timberlake Trl Greenwood MO 64034 Office: Shook Hardy & Bacon LLP 1200 Main St Kansas City MO 64105 Fax: 816-421-4066. E-mail: jjohnston@shb.com.

JOHNSTON, LOGAN TRUAX, III, lawyer; b. New Haven, Dec. 9, 1947; s. Logan Truax Jr. and Elizabeth (Josey) J.; m. Celeste Linguere; children: Charlotte Hathaway, Logan Truax IV, Owen Conrad, Oritse J., Gboyega P. BA, Yale U., 1969; JD, Harvard U., 1973. Bar: Ill. 1973, Ariz. 1984, U.S. Ct. Appeals (2d cir.) 1982, U.S. Ct. Appeals (7th cir.) 1973, U.S. Ct. Appeals (9th cir.) 1986, U.S. Ct. Appeals (fed. cir.) 1990, U.S. Supreme Ct. 1991. Assoc. Winston & Strawn, Chgo., 1973-79, ptnr., 1979-83, Phoenix, 1983-89; mng. ptnr. Johnston Maynard Grant & Parker, Phoenix, 1989-97, Johnston & Kelly, Phoenix, 1997—2003. Spl. asst. state's atty. Du Page County, Ill., Wheaton, 1976-77; cons. Community Legal Svcs., Phoenix, 1984—. Contbg author: Arizona Appellate Handbook, Vol. III. Served with U.S. Army N.G., 1970-76. Mem. ABA, Maricopa County Bar Found., Maricopa County Bar Assn., Ariz. Bar Found., Ariz. State Bar Assn., Phoenix Heroes Endowment Fund. Presbyterian. Avocations: books, movies, golf, hiking, travel. Administrative and regulatory, General civil litigation, Health. Office: Johnston Law Offices PLC 1 N 1st St Phoenix AZ 85004-2357

JOHNSTON, MURRAY LLOYD, JR., lawyer; b. Lake Charles, La., May 25, 1940; s. Murray Lloyd and Nancy Laura (Perry) J.; m. Jewel Anne Whittenburg, Sept. 4, 1965; children: Murray Lloyd III, Roy Austin. B.A., Austin Coll., 1962; J.D., U. Tex., 1965. Bar: Tex. 1965, U.S. Tax Ct. 1975. Adminstrv. asst. to dir. planning and to exec. dir. Tex. Water Devel. Bd., 1965-6; assoc. gen. counsel H.B. Zachry Co., San Antonio, 1967-75, v.p., gen. counsel, sec., 1975—; mng. ptnr. Johnston, Reed, Watt & Goff, San Antonio, 1977— . Mem. Nat. Republican Senatorial Com., 1980-88; mem. legal adv. bd. Nat. Legal Ctr. for Pub. Interest, Washington; mem. adv. bd. San Antonio Missions, 1987-90, chmn. Los Compadres, 1987-88; active The Zachry Found., 1984—, Cancer Therapy and Rsch. Found., 1992—, Tex. Rsch. Park Found. 1995—, Morningside Ministries Found. Bd., 1998—. Lt. comdr. USNR, 1967-78. Mem. San Antonio Estate Planners Council, ABA, San Antonio Bar Assn. (corp. chmn.), Am. Judicature Soc., Internat. Assn. Def. Counsel (v.p. 1991-93). Methodist. Club: San Antonio Country (bd. govs. 1996-99), Conopus Club, Jr. Achievement 1987-91), Argyle Club, San Antonio Rotary Club. Home: 306 Kennedy Ave San Antonio TX 78209-5250 Office: Zachry Constrn Corp PO Box 21130 San Antonio TX 78221-0130

JOHNSTON, NEIL CHUNN, lawyer; b. Mobile, Ala., Feb. 23, 1953; s. Vivian Gaines and Sara Niel (Chunn) J.; m. Ashley Monroe Hocklander, Dec. 20, 1980; children: Katie, Neil Jr. BA, Southwestern at Memphis (name changed to Rhodes Coll.), 1975; JD, U. Ala., 1978. Atty. Hand, Arendall L.L.C., Mobile, Ala., 1978—. Practice group leader, land use and environment Contbr. articles to profl. jours. Pres. Project CATE Found, Inc., Mobile, 1987—; trustee Nature Conservancy, Ala., 1990-96; bd. dirs. Am. Jr. Miss Program, 1996-2003; bd. dirs., (pres. 2003—),Ala. Coastal Found. Recipient Ala. Gov.'s award-Water Conservationist, Ala. Wildlife Fedn., 1987, EPA Region IV Wetlands Recognition award, 2000, Nat. Wetlands award Environ. Law Inst., 2003. Mem. ABA (vice-chair forestry com. sect. environment, energy, resc.), Ala. State Bar Assn. (chmn. environ. law sect. 1984-91, corp. banking, bus. law sect. 1993), Mobile Bar Assn., Ala. Forestry Assn., Ala. Law Inst., Rotary (pres. Mobile 1996-97). Commercial, contracts (including sales of goods; commercial financing), Environmental, Property, real (including real estate development, water). Office: Hand Arendall LLC 3000 FNB Bldg 107 St Francis St Mobile AL 36602

JOHNSTON, OSCAR BLACK, III, lawyer; b. Tulsa, Oct. 1, 1941; s. Oscar Black Jr. and Carol (VanDerwiele) J.; m. Ruth Archdeacon Darrough; children: Eric Oscar, David Darrough. BBA, Baylor U., 1963; JD, U. Tulsa, 1966. Bar: Okla. 1966, U.S. Dist. Ct. (no., ea., we. dists.) Okla., U.S. Ct. Claims, U.S. Ct. Appeals (10th cir.), U.S. Supreme Ct. Asst. U.S. attorney U.S. Dist. Ct. (we. dist.) Okla., 1970-76; ptnr. Logan & Lowry, L.L.P., Vinita, Okla., 1979—. Assoc. editor Tulsa Law Review, 1964-66. Presiding judge divsn. 54 Okla. Temp. Ct. Appeals, 1980-81, judge divsn. XIV, 1991-93; presiding judge panel VI Lawyer-Staffed Ct. Appeals, 1992. Capt. JAGC, U.S. Army, 1966-70. Fellow Am. Bar Found. (state chair 2001—), Okla. Bar Found. (trustee 1988-96, pres. 1995); mem. ABA (sects. litigation, family law and criminal), Fed. Bar Assn. (pres. Oklahoma City chpt. 1975), Craig County Bar Assn. (pres. 1986-88), Okla. Bar Assn. (adminstrn. of justice, bench and bar coms., assoc. editor, mem. bd. editors Okla. Bar Jour. 2000—), Okla. Trial Lawyers Assn., Rotary (pres. Vinita 1983-84), Phi Alpha Delta. Republican. Methodist. General civil litigation, Criminal, Family and matrimonial. Office: Logan & Lowry PO Box 558 Vinita OK 74301-0558 Home: 116 Westwood Ave Vinita OK 74301-2703

JOHNSTON, RICHARD ALAN, lawyer; b. Buffalo, Mar. 18, 1950; s. Richard W. and Virginia (Holmes) J.; m. Patricia Downing, Aug. 28, 1971; children: Matthew, Sarah, Elizabeth, Michael. BA, Cornell U., 1972; JD, Harvard U., 1976. Bar: Mass. 1977, U.S. Dist. Ct. Mass. 1977, U.S. Ct. Appeals (1st cir.) 1977. Law clk. to presiding justice Mass. Ct. Appeals, Boston, 1976-77; assoc. Hale and Dorr LLP, Boston, 1977-82, sr. ptnr., 1982—. Co-chmn. North Area Task Force, Charlestown, Mass., 1981—; trustee Dennis (Mass.) Conservation Trust, 1988—, pres., 1995—; mem. transition team Mass. Gov. William Weld, 1990-91; internat. election observer Internat. Human Rights Law Group, Nepal, 1991; dir. Friends of City Square Park, 1993—; trustee Hockey Humanitarian Award Found., 1997—; pres. Friends of Tanzanias Schs., Inc., 1997—, Compact of Cape Cod Conservation Trusts, 2001—. Mem. ABA, Internat. Bar Assn., Boston Bar Assn., Nat. Health Lawyers Assn., Mass. Bar Assn. General civil litigation, Environmental, Health. Home: 43 Monument Ave Charlestown MA 02129-3323 Office: Hale & Dorr LLP 60 State St Boston MA 02109-1816

JOHNSTON, RONALD ALLEN, lawyer; b. Vancouver, Wash., Oct. 23, 1950; s. Don E. and Marjorie J. (Blank) J.; m. Deborah M. Riolo, Aug. 4, 1973; children: Christopher, Kayla BA in Polit. Sci. with honors, Pacific U.,

1972; JD, Cath. U. Am., 1976. Bar: Oreg. 1976, U.S. Dist. Ct. Oreg. 1976, U.S. Ct. Appeals (9th cir.) 1976. Assoc. Shannon & Johnson, Portland, 1977-81, McCormick & Reynolds, Portland, 1981-84; ptnr. Reynolds & Johnston, Portland, 1984-86; owner, mgr. Ronald Allen Johnston and Assocs., 1986-88; ptnr. Johnston & Root, 1989—. Legal advisor Father's PAC, Portland, 1985—. Mem. ABA (family law sect.), Oreg. Bar Assn. (family law sect.), Multnomah County Bar Assn. Avocations: boating, fishing. State civil litigation, Commercial, consumer (including collections, credit), Family and matrimonial. Office: Johnston & Root 1500 SW 1st Ave Ste 630 Portland OR 97201-5826

JOHNSTON, THOMAS E. prosecutor; BA, JD, W.Va. U. Atty. Schrader, Byrd and Companion, 1994—96; assoc. Flaherty, Sensabaugh and Bonasso, 1996—98; ptnr. Bailey, Riley, Buch and Harmon, Wheeling, W.Va., 1998—2001; U.S. atty. No. Dist. W.Va. U.S. Dept. Justice, 2001—. Office: PO Box 591 Wheeling WV 26003-0011*

JOHNSTON, WILLIAM DAVID, lawyer; b. Aberdeen, Md., Jan. 31, 1957; s. David Irvine and Nancy (Smith) J.; m. Mary Teresa Miller, May 29, 1983; children: Ellen Christine, Amy Elizabeth. AB, Colgate U., 1979; JD, Washington and Lee U., 1982. Bar: Del. 1982, U.S. Dist. Ct. Del. 1983, U.S. Ct. Appeals (3rd cir.) 1991, U.S. Supreme Ct. 1991. Judicial law clk. to chief justice Daniel L. Herrmann Del. Supreme Ct., Wilmington, 1982-83; assoc. Potter, Anderson and Corroon, Wilmington, 1983-85, Young, Conaway, Stargatt and Taylor, Wilmington, 1985-89, ptnr., 1990—. Contbr. articles to profl. jours. Mem. choir, adminstrv. bd. lay leadership Aldersgate United Meth. Ch., Wilmington, 1970—, chmn. religion and race commn., 1987-89; com. chmn. Boy Scouts of U.S. troop 67, 1982-85, Del. Human Rels. Commn., 1986—; trustee The Pilot Sch., 1995—. Best Brief Worldwide award Am. Soc. Internat. Law, Washington, 1980. Mem. ABA (chmn. indemnification and ins. subcom. 1997—, Am. Judicature Soc. (bd. dirs. 2002—), Del. State Bar Assn. (award for pub. svc. 1991, 93, 99, pres.-elect 2000-2001, pres. 2001-02), Sigma Chi (pres. Colgate U. chpt. 1984-88), Phi Delta Phi, Univ. and Whist Club (bd. govs. 1990-95), Lincoln (Del.) Club, Wilmington Country Club. Methodist. Avocations: running, squash, reading, travel, golf. Federal civil litigation, State civil litigation, Corporate, general. Office: Young Conaway Stargatt and Taylor The Brandywine Bldg 1100 West St PO Box 391 Wilmington DE 19899-0391

JOHNSTONE, DOUGLAS INGE, state supreme court justice; b. Mobile, Ala., Nov. 15, 1941; s. Harry Inge and Kathleen (Yerger) J.; m. Mary Jayne Baynes (div.); 1 child, Francis Inge. BA, Rice U., 1963; JD, Tulane U., 1966. Bar: Ala. 1966, U.S. Dist. Ct. Ala. 1966, U.S. Ct. Appeals (5th cir.) 1968, U.S. Supreme Ct. 1969. Pvt. practice, Mobile, 1966-84; dist. judge Ala. Dist. Ct., Mobile, 1984-85, presiding dist. judge, 1985, cir. judge, 1985-99; justice Supreme Ct. Ala., Montgomery, 1999—. Rep. State of Ala., 1974-78. MKem. Jaycees, Mobile, Mobile County Wildlife; bd. advisors Salvation Army, Mobile, 1989—; bd. dirs. Mental Health Assn., Mobile, 1990-92. Capt. U.S. Army, 1963-72. Elected Outstanding Freshman Rep., Capital Prses Corps., 1975; recipient Meritorious Svc. award Mobile County Bd. of Health, 1968, Humanitarian Svc. award Mobile Cerebral Palsy Assn., 1973. Mem. ABA, Am. Judges Assn., Ala. Bar Assn., Mobile Bar Assn., Internat. Acad. Trial Judges. Democrat. Episcopalian. Home: 205 Government St Ste 4500 Mobile AL 36644-0001 Office: Supreme Ct of Ala 300 Dexter Ave Montgomery AL 36104-3741

JOHNSTONE, MARTIN E. state supreme court justice; BA, Western Ky. U.; JD, U. Louisville. Bar: Ky. Judge 3d Magisterial Dist., Ky., 1976-78; dist. judge Jefferson County, Ky., 1978-83; chief judge, 1987-93; circuit judge, 1985-87; justice Ky. Ct. Appeals, 1993-96, chief judge pro tem, 1996; justice Ky. Supreme Ct., 1996—, dep. chief justice, 1998—. Recipient Outstanding Trial Judge award Ky. Acad. Trial Attys., 1991. Mem. Louisville Bar Assn. (Judge of Yr. 1981). Office: State Capitol Capitol Bldg 700 Capitol Ave, Suite 1000 Frankfort KY 40202-2761

JOHNSTONE, PHILIP MACLAREN, lawyer; b. Sharon, Conn., Mar. 24, 1961; s. Rodney Stuart and Frances Louise (Davis) J.; m. Elizabeth Laird McGovern, Sept. 10, 1988. BA in Econs. magna cum laude, Duke U., 1983; JD, U. Pa., 1986. Bar: Mass. 1986, Conn. 1987, U.S. Dist. Ct. Conn. 1988, R.I. 1998. Ptnr. Waller, Smith & Palmer, P.C., New London, Conn., 1997—. Bd. dirs. J Boats, Inc., Newport, R.I., 1987—. Trustee Denison Pequotsepos Nature Ctr., Mystic, Conn., 1998-2002, Pine Point Sch., Stonington, Conn., 2000—. Mem. ABA, Mass. Bar Assn., Conn. Bar Assn., R.I. Bar Assn. Republican. Episcopalian. Avocations: tennis, golf. Estate planning, Estate taxation, Pension, profit-sharing, and employee benefits. Home: 17 Cliff St Stonington CT 06378-1249 Office: Waller Smith and Palmer PC 52 Eugene Oneill Dr New London CT 06320-6324 E-mail: pmjohnstone@wallersmithpalmer.com.

JOHNSTONE, ROBERT PHILIP, lawyer; b. Bellefonte, Pa., Dec. 1, 1943; s. B. Kenneth and Helene (Hetzel) J.; m. Susan Alice Hardy, June 22, 1968; children: Natalie, Nancy. BS with honors, Denison U., 1966; JD magna cum laude, U. Mich., 1969. Bar: Ind. 1969. Assoc. Barnes, Hickam, Pantzer & Boyd, Indpls., 1969-75, ptnr., 1976-82, Barnes & Thornburg, Indpls., 1982—. Chmn. litigation dept. Barnes & Thornburg, 1988-89, mem. mgmt. com., 1988-89; lectr., panelist legal seminars and trial advocacy programs. Sec.-treas. Contemporary Art Soc. of Indpls. Mus. Art, 1983—84; v.p., bd. dirs. Friends of Herron Gallery, Herron Sch. Art, 1981—85; bd. dirs. Eagle Creek Park Found., 2001—. Fellow Am. Coll. Trial Lawyers (state com. 1992-97, state chair 1995-96); mem. U.S. 7th Fed. Cir. Bar Assn., Ind. Bar Assn., Indpls. Bar Assn., Order of the Coif, Woodstock Club (Indpls., bd. dirs. 1988-90, v.p. 1989, pres. 1990), Indpls. Art Ctr. (bd. dirs. 1991-97), Dramatic Club (Indpls.), Phi Beta Kappa, Omicron Delta Kappa. General civil litigation, Insurance, Libel. Home: 1065 W 52nd St Indianapolis IN 46228-2463 Office: Barnes & Thornburg 11 S Meridian St Indianapolis IN 46204-3535 E-mail: bob.johnstone@btlaw.com.

JOHNTING, WENDELL, law librarian; b. Winchester, Ind., Aug. 30, 1952; s. Ernest K. and Jewell G. (Browning) J. AB, Taylor U., 1974; MLS, Ind. U., 1975. Asst. dir. tech. svcs. Ind. U. Sch. Law Libr., Indpls., 1975—. Project dir. Indpls. Law Cataloging Consortium, 1980-92; vis. libr. Cambridge U., Squire Law Libr., Cambridge, Eng., 1985; founding mem. Info. Online Project Leaders, 1987-90; spkr. in field; mem., sec. Ind. U. Librs. Faculty Coun., 2001-02. Libr. vol. Beech Grove (Ind.) Pub. Libr., 1993-95; reader, vol. Marion County Health Care Home, Indpls., 1989. Mem.: Ind. U. Libr. Faculty Coun. (sec. 2001—02), Indpls. Law Librs. Assn. (sec.-treas. 1999—2000), Ind. Libr. Fedn. (pers. com. 2000—), Ind. Law Librs. Assn. (sec.-treas. 1999—2001), Christian Legal Soc. (faculty adv. 2001—), Ind. U. Librs. Assn. (exec. bd. 1982—85, v.p. 1986—87, treas. 1999—2001), Ohio Region Assn. Law Librs. (sec. 1982, exec. bd. 1982—85), Knights of Pythias, Dramatic Order Knights of Khorassen, Alpha Phi Gamma, Chi Alpha Omega, Beta Phi Mu. Republican. Baptist. Avocations: gardening, astronomy, cooking. Home: 420 N 23rd Ave Beech Grove IN 46107-1032 Office: Ind U Sch Law Libr 530 W New York St Indianapolis IN 46202 E-mail: wjohntin@iupui.edu.

JOINER, CHARLES WYCLIFFE, judge; b. Maquoketa, Iowa, Feb. 14, 1916; s. Melvin William and Mary (von Schrader) J.; m. Ann Martin, Sept. 29, 1939; children: Charles Wycliffe, Nancy Caroline, Richard Martin. BA, U. Iowa, 1937, JD, 1939. Bar: Iowa 1939, Mich. 1947. With firm Miller, Huebner & Miller, Des Moines, 1939-47; part-time lectr. Des Moines Coll. Law, 1940-41; faculty U. Mich. Law, 1947-68, assoc. dean, 1960-65, acting dean, 1964-65; dean Wayne State U. Law Sch., Detroit, 1968-72; U.S. dist. judge, sr. judge, 1972—. Assoc. dir. Preparatory Commn. Mich. Constl. Conv., 1961, co-dir. research and drafting com., 1961-62; civil rules adv. com. U.S. Jud. Conf. Com. Rules Practice and Procedure, 1959-70, evidence rules adv. com., 1965-70; rep. Mich. Atty. Gens. Com. Ct. Congestion, 1959-60 Author: Trials and Appeals, 1957, Civil Justice and the Jury, 1962, Trial and Appellate Practice, 1968; Co-author: Introduction to Civil Procedures, 1949, Jurisdiction and Judgments, 1953, (with Delmar Karten) Trials and Appeals, 1971. Mem. charter rev. com. Ann Arbor Citizens Coun.cil, 1959-61; mem. Mich. Commn. Uniform State Laws, 1963-97; Mem. Ann Arbor City Coun.cil, 1955-59. Served tot lt. USAAF, 1942-45. Fellow Am. Bar Found. (chmn. 1977-78); mem. ABA (chmn. com. specialization 1952-56, spl. com. uniform evidence rules fed. cts. 1959-64, adv. bd. jour. 1961-67, spl. com. on specialization 1966-69, ethics com. 1961-70, council mem. sect. individual rights and responsibilities 1967-77, chairperson 1976-77), State Bar Mich. (pres. 1970-71, chmn. joint com. Mich. procedural revision 1956-62, commr. 1964—), Am. Judicature Soc. (chmn. publs. com. 1959-62), Am. Law Student Assn. (bd. govs.), Am. Law Inst., Scribes (pres. 1963-64)

JOLLES, BERNARD, lawyer; b. N.Y.C., Oct. 5, 1928; s. Harry and Dora (Hirschorn) J.; m. Lenore Madison Jolles, Oct. 11, 1953 (div. Jan. 1984); children: Abbe, Jacqueline, Caroline. BA, N.Y.U., 1951; LLB, Lewis & Clark Coll., 1961. Bar: Oreg. 1963, U.S. Dist. Ct. Oreg. 1964, U.S. Dist. Ct. (no. dist.) Miss. 1968, U.S. Ct. Appeals (9th cir.) 1965, U.S. Supreme Ct. 1979. Assoc. Anderson Franklin Jones & Olsen, Portland, Oreg., 1963-68; ptnr. Franklin Olsen Bennett & Desbarsay, Portland, Oreg., 1968-79, Jolles Bernstein & Garone and predecessor firms Jolles Sokol & Bernstein, Portland, Oreg., 1979—. Editor: Damages, 1974. Bd. dirs. ACLU, Portland, Oreg., 1975—. Fellow Am. Coll. Trial Lawyers; mem. Oreg. State Bar Assn. (pres. 1986-87), Am. Inns of Ct. (sr. barrister 1985—). Avocations: cooking, reading. General civil litigation, Labor (including EEOC, Fair Labor Standards Act, labor-management relations, NLRB, OSHA), Personal injury (including property damage). Office: Jolles & Bernstein 721 SW Oak St Fl 2 Portland OR 97205-3712

JOLLES, JANET K. PILLING, lawyer; b. Akron, Ohio, Sept. 5, 1951; d. Paul and Marjorie (Logue) Kavanaugh; m. Martin Jolles, Mar. 6, 1987; children: Madeleine Sloan Langdon Jolles, Jameson Samuel Rhys Jolles. BA, Ohio Wesleyan U., 1973; JD, U. Mo., 1976; LLM, Villanova U., 1985. Bar: Pa. 1976, U.S. Tax Ct. 1976, U.S. Dist. Ct. (ea. dist.) Pa. 1976, Ohio 1996. Atty. Schnader, Harrison, Segal & Lewis, Phila., 1976-83; gen. counsel Kistler-Tiffany Cos., Wayne, Pa., 1983-95; lawyer Janet Kavanaugh Pilling Jolles & Assocs., Berea, Ohio, 1996-99; v.p. First Union Trust Co., Wilmington, Del., 1999—2002, Wachovia Trust Co., Wilmington, 2002—. Mem. Estate Planning Coun. Del., Wilmington Tax Group, Phila. Estate Planning Coun., Estate Planning Coun. Cleve., Estate Planning Coun. Del. Mem.: ABA, Wilmington Women in Bus., Pa. Bar Assn., Phila. Bar Assn. (probate sect., tax sect.), Cuyahoga County Bar Assn., Cleve. Bar Assn., Ohio State Bar Assn., Berea Women's League, Phi Beta Kappa, Phi Delta Phi. Estate planning, Probate (including wills, trusts), Estate taxation. Office: 3 Beaver Valley 4th Fl Wilmington DE 19803 E-mail: janet.jolles@wachovia.com., jjolleslaw@aol.com.

JOLLS, CHRISTINE MARGARET, lawyer, educator; b. White Plains, N.Y., Oct. 1, 1967; d. Robert Talcott and Cecelia (Thurmaier) Jolls; m. Ranier Gavlilk; 2 children. BA, Stanford (Calif.) U., 1989; JD, Harvard U., Cambridge, Mass., 1993; PhD in Econs., M.I.T., 1995. Bar: Mass. 1997. Law clk. U.S. Ct. Appeals, Washington, 1995—96; law clk. U.S. Supreme Ct., Washington, 1996—97; prof. law Harvard Law Sch., Cambridge, Mass., 1997—. Mem. editl. bd. Am. Law and Econ Rev., New Haven, 1999—; reporter Restatement of Employment Law, Phila., 2001—. Contbr. articles to Univ. Law Revs., Stanford, Harvard, Chgo. Fellow: Nat. Bur. Econ. Rsch., Mind/Brain Behavior Initiative. Office: Harvard Law Sch Griswold 504 Cambridge MA 02138

JONES, B. TODD, lawyer, former prosecutor; s. Paul and Sylvia Jones. Grad., Macalester Coll., 1979; JD, U. Minn., 1983. Mng. ptnr. Greene Espel, Mpls., 1996—97; asst. U.S. atty. for Minn., 1997—98; U.S. atty. Minn. dist. U.S. Dept. Justice, 1998—2001; ptnr. Robins, Kaplan, Miller & Ciresi, Mpls., 2001—. With USMC. Office: Robins Kaplan Miller & Ciresi 2800 LaSalle Plaza 800 LaSalle Ave Minneapolis MN 55402

JONES, BILL, lawyer; b. 1959; BBA, Tex. A&M U., 1981; JD, Baylor U., 1985. Bar: Tex. 1985. With Locke, Liddell & Sapp; ptnr. Cash & Jones, Houston, 1991—2001; gen. counsel to gov. Office Gov. State of Tex., Austin, 2001—. Office: Office Gov PO Box 12428 Austin TX 78711*

JONES, C. PAUL, lawyer, educator; b. Grand Forks, N.D., Jan. 7, 1927; s. Walter M. and Sophie J. (Thorton) J.; m. Helen M. Fredel, Sept. 7, 1957; children— Katherine, Sara H. BBA, JD, U. Minn., 1950; LLM, William Mitchell Coll. of Law, 1955. Assoc. Lewis, Hammer, Heaney, Weyl & Halverson, Duluth, Minn., 1950-51; asst., chief dep. Hennepin County Atty., Mpls., 1952-58; asst. U.S. atty. U.S. Atty's. Office, St. Paul, 1959-60; assoc. Maun & Hazel, St. Paul, 1960-61; ptnr. Dorfman, Rudquist, Jones, & Ramstead, Mpls., 1961-65; state pub. defender Minn. State Pub. Defender's Office, Mpls., 1966-90. Adj. prof. law William Mitchell Coll. of Law, St. Paul, 1953-70, prof. law, 1970—2001, prof. emeritus, 2001-. assoc. dean for acad. affairs, 1991-95; adj. prof. U. Minn., Mpls., 1970-90; mem. adv. com. on rules of criminal procedure Minn. Supreme Ct., 1970—. Author: Criminal Procedure from Police Detention to Final Disposition, 1981; Jones on Minnesota Criminal Procedure, 1955, 64, 70, 75; Minnesota Police Law Manual, 1955, 67, 70, 76 Mem. Minn. Gov.'s Crime Commn., St. Paul, 1970s, Minn. Fair Trial-Free Press Assn., Mpls., 1970s, Citizens League, Mpls., 1955—, Mpls. Aquatennial Assn., Mpls., 1955-60, Minn. Coun. on Crime and Justice, 1991—. Recipient Reginald Heber Smith award Nat. Legal Aid and Defender Assn., 1969 Fellow Am. Coll. Trial Lawyers; mem. Am. Bd. Trial Advs., ABA, Minn. State Bar Assn., Hennepin County Bar Assn., Ramsey County Bar Assn., Nat. Legal Aid & Defender Assn. Clubs: Suburban Gyro of Mpls., Mpls. Athletic. Lodges: Rotary. Democrat. Lutheran. Avocations: fishing; hunting; golfing; desert watching. Home: 5501 Dewey Hill Rd Edina MN 55439-1906 Office: William Mitchell Coll Law 875 Summit Ave Saint Paul MN 55105-3030

JONES, CHARLES E. chief justice supreme court; b. June 12, 1935; BA, Brigham Young U., 1959; JD, Stanford U., 1962. Bar: Calif. 1963, U.S. Dist. Ct. Ariz. 1964, U.S. Ct. Appeals (9th cir.) 1963, Ariz. 1964, U.S. Ct. Appeals (10th cir.) 1974, U.S. Supreme Ct. 1979. Law clk. to Hon. Richard H. Chambers U.S. Ct. Appeals (9th cir.), 1962-63; assoc., ptnr. Jennings, Strouss & Salmon, Phoenix, 1963-96; apptd. justice Ariz. Supreme Ct., Phoenix, 1996, vice chief justice, 1997—2002, chief justice, 2002—. Bd. visitors Brigham Young U. Law Sch., 1973-81, chmn., 1978-81, Univ. Arizona Coll. Law, 2003—. Named Avocat du Consulat-Gen. de France, 1981—; Alumni Dist. Svc. award Brigham Young U., 1982; recipient Aaron Feuerstein award U. Ariz., 1998. Fellow Am. Bar Found., Ariz. Bar Found.; mem. ABA, State Bar Ariz., Fed. Bar Assn. (pres. Ariz. chpt. 1971-73), J. Reuben Clark Law Soc. (nat. chmn. 1994-97), Maricopa County Bar Assn., Am. Coll. Labor & Employment Lawyers, Conf. Chief Justices of Fifty States, Nat. Com. Pub. Trust and Confidence in the Cts. (chmn.), Pi Sigma Alpha. Office: Ariz Supreme Court 1501 W Washington St Phoenix AZ 85007-3222

JONES, CHRISTOPHER ANDREW, lawyer; b. Ann Arbor, Mich., May 19, 1972; s. Roger Allen Jones and Monica Lyn Lundy; m. Amy Butler Jones, May 26, 2001. BS in Sociology, James Madison U., 1997; JD, U. Va., 2000. Bar: Va. 2000, D.C. 2001, U.S. Dist. Ct. (ea. and we. dists.) Va. 2001, U.S. Dist. Ct. D.C. 2001, U.S. Ct. Appeals (4th and D.C. cirs.) 2001. Assoc. Ross, Dixon & Bell, LLP, Washington, 2000—02, Martin & Raynor, P.C., Charlottesville, Va., 2002—. Mem.: ABA, Va. Trial Lawyers Assn., Va. Bar Assn. Avocation: home remodeling. General civil litigation, Construction, Personal injury (including property damage). Office: Martin & Raynor PC 415 4th St NE Charlottesville VA 22902

JONES, CRAIG WARD, lawyer; b. Pitts., June 14, 1947; s. Curtis Edison and Margaret (McFarland) J.; m. Sarah Dowding; children: Laura McFarland, Rebecca Long, Nancy Harper. BA, Carleton Coll., 1969; JD, U. Pitts., 1976. Bar: Pa. 1976, U.S. Dist. Ct. (we. dist.) Pa. 1976, U.S. Ct. Appeals (3d cir.) 1981. Ptnr. Reed Smith LLP, Pitts., 1976—. Served to lt. USNR, 1969-73. Mem. Allegheny County Bar Assn. Presbyterian. Federal civil litigation, State civil litigation. Home: 208 Cornwall Dr Pittsburgh PA 15238-2639 Office: Reed Smith LLP Mellon Sq 435 6th Ave Pittsburgh PA 15219-1886

JONES, DALE EDWIN, public defender; b. Rahway, N.J., Oct. 22, 1948; s. Horatio Gates and Audrey Irma (Morgan) J.; m. Karen Anne Woodhall, June 19, 1971; children: Sharon, Michael, Stephan; m. Maria D. Noto, Aug. 2, 1987 (div. 1989); m. Joan E. DiTullio, Oct. 18, 1991; 1 child, Trevor. BA, Rutgers U., 1970, JD, 1973. Bar: N.J. 1973, U.S. Dist. Ct. N.J. 1973, U.S. Supreme Ct. 1977, N.Y. 1983. 1st asst. pub. defender Office Pub. Defender, Newark, 1974-84, dep. pub. defender in charge of capital litigation, 1984-87; asst. pub. defender, dir. of policy Office of Pub. Defender, Trenton, NJ, 1987—, dir. policy, dir. of policy, 1987—. Mem. model jury charge com., N.J. Supreme Ct., 1983-88, criminal practice com., Trenton, 1983—, com. media rels., 1987-89, strategic planning com., 1996-98, rules of evidence com., 1998-2002. Mem. editorial bd. N.J. Lawyer. Mem. ACDL-N.J., Nat. Assn. Criminal Def. Lawyers (cert. criminal atty.), Amnesty Internat. Democrat. Office: Pub Defender Office PO Box 850 Trenton NJ 08625-0850 Personal E-mail: djones2411@yahoo.com. Business E-Mail: Dale.Jones@opd.state.nj.us.

JONES, DOUGLAS WILEY, lawyer; b. Fort Lauderdale, Fla., 1948; AB, Princeton U., 1970; JD, Harvard U., 1973. Bar: N.Y. 1974. Mem. Milbank, Tweed, Hadley & McCloy LLP, N.Y.C. Mem. ABA, Assn. of the Bar of the City of N.Y. Corporate, general, Private international, Securities. Office: Milbank Tweed Hadley & McCloy LLP 1 Chase Manhattan Plz Fl 47 New York NY 10005-1413

JONES, E. STEWART, JR., lawyer; b. Troy, N.Y., Dec. 4, 1941; s. E. Stewart and Louise (Farley) J.; m. Constance M., Dec. 28, 1968; children: Christopher, Brady, Erin. BA, Williams Coll., 1963; JD, Albany Law Sch., 1966. Bar: N.Y. 1966, U.S. Dist. Ct. (no. dist.) N.Y. 1966, U.S. Dist. Ct. (so. and ea. dist.) N.Y. 1994, U.S. Dist. Ct. (we. dist.) N.Y. 1987, U.S. Claims Ct. 1991, U.S. Ct. Appeals (2d cir.) 1976, U.S. Supreme Ct. 1976. Asst. dist. atty. Rensselaer County (N.Y.), 1968-70, spl. prosecutor, 1974; ptnr. E. Stewart Jones, Troy, 1974—. Lectr. in field; mem. com. on profl. standards of 3d jud. dept. State of N.Y., 1977-80, mem. 3d jud. screening com., Albany County; mem. merit selection panel for selection and appointment of U.S. magistrate for No. Dist. N.Y., 1981, 91; bd. dirs. Univ. Found. at Albany, trustee Troy Savs. Bank. Contbr. numerous articles to profl. jours. Trustee The Albany Acad., Albany Law Sch.; active Nat. Alumni Coun. Albany Law Sch. With USNG. Fellow: Am. Bar Found., N.Y. Bar Found., Inner Circle Advs., Internat. Acad. Trial Lawyers (chmn. Upstate N.Y. 1988—), Am. Bd. Trial Lawyers, Am. Inns. of Ct., Internat. Acad. Trial Lawyers, Am. Coll. Trial Lawyers, Am. Bd. Profl. Liability Attys. (diplomate), Internat. Soc. Barristers; mem.: Coll. Master Advs. and Barristers (sr. counsel), Saratoga County Bar Assn., Am. Coll. Barristers (sr. counsel), Internat. Acad. Litigators (diplomate), Civil Justice Found. (founding sponsor), Trial Lawyers for Pub. Justice (founder), Inst. Injury Reduction (founder), Am. Bd. Trial Advs. (adv.), N.Y. State Assn. Criminal Def. Lawyers, Nat. Assn. Criminal Def. Lawyers, Nat. Bd. Trial Advocacy (diplomate), Fed. Bar Coun., Dispute Resolutions, Inc. (nat. panel of arbitrators), Am. Arbitration Assn. (nat. panel of arbitrators), N.Y. State Defenders Assn., Albany County Bar Assn., Am. Soc. Law and Medicine, Rensselaer County Bar Assn., Am. Judicature Soc. (sustaining), Practising Law Inst., ABA (numerous coms.), Capital Dist. Trial Lawyers Assn. (bd. dirs. 1973—76), N.Y. State Trial Lawyers Assn. (bd. dirs. 1982—91, dir. emeritus 1991), N.Y. State Bar Assn. (mem. exec. com. trial lawyers sect. 1977—90, 1981—94, mem. spl. com. med. malpractice, other coms., Outstanding Practitioner award 1980), Williams Club (N.Y.C.), Stone Horse Yacht Club (Harwich Port, Mass.), Ft. Orange Club, Schuyler Meadows Club. Federal civil litigation, Criminal, Personal injury (including property damage). Home: 46 Schuyler Rd Loudonville NY 12211-1447 Office: 28 2nd St Troy NY 12180-3986 E-mail: info@esjlaw.com.

JONES, E. THOMAS, lawyer; b. Buffalo, July 19, 1950; s. Thomas Kenneth and Marian Arlene (Turk) J.; m. Jennifer Dee Lowery, Oct. 19, 1974; children: Evan Thomas III, Courtney Bree. BA, SUNY, Buffalo, 1972; JD, Cleve. State U., 1981. Bar: N.Y. 1982, U.S. Dist. Ct. (we. dist.) N.Y. 1982, U.S. Ct. Appeals (2d cir.) 1987. Mem. mgmt. staff Marine Midland Bank, Buffalo, 1971-76, M&T Bank, Buffalo, 1976-78, 81-82, Nat. City Bank, Cleve., 1978-81; sole practice Buffalo, 1982—. Hearing officer Buffalo City Ct., 1997—. Committeeman Amherst Rep. Party, N.Y., 1984—; fire fighter Getzville Fire Co., Inc., Amherst, 1988-91; town councilman, Amherst, 1990-91; coach, bd. dirs. Amherst Youth Hockey Assn.; dep. town atty. Town Amherst, N.Y., 1996-2001, town atty., 2002—. Mem. ABA, N.Y. State Bar Assn., Erie County Bar Assn. General civil litigation, General practice, Probate (including wills, trusts). Home: 1375 N French Rd Amherst NY 14228-1908

JONES, EDGAR ALLAN, JR., law educator, arbitrator, lawyer; b. Bklyn., Jan. 8, 1921; s. Edgar Allan and Isabel (Morris) J.; m. Helen Callaghan, Sept. 15, 1945; children: Linda Marie, Anne Marie, Carol Marie, Edgar Allan III, Denis James, Robert Morris, David Llewellyn, Therese Marie, Catherine Marie, Nancy Marie, Daniel Anthony. BA, Wesleyan U., 1942; LLB, U. Va., 1950. Bar: Va. 1948. Faculty UCLA, 1951—, prof. law, 1958-91, emeritus, 1991—, asst. dean, 1957-58; dir. Law-Sci. Rsch. Ctr., 1963-66; labor dispute arbitrator, mediator, fact finder for pvt. and pub. employers and unions, 1953—. Appeared as judge ABC-TV network programs Accused, 1958-59, Traffic Ct., 1958-61, Day in Court, 1958-64; moderator ednl. TV program Forum West, 1966; author: (novel) Mr. Arbitrator, 2000; editor: Law and Electronics: The Challenge of a New Era, 1960; founding editor Va. Law Weekly, 1948-50, NAA Chronicle, 1977-78; contbr. numerous labor law, arbitration and polygraph articles to law revs. Pres. Creddalt Rsch., Inc., 1959-90; dir. Deauville Restaurant, Inc. (Jimmy's 1978-94); pub. mem. Calif. Commn. Manpower Automation and Tech., 1963-67, Calif. Manpower Adv. Com., 1964-67; nat. enforcement commr. WSB, 1951; sec. Californians for Kennedy, 1960. Mem. ABA, Nat. Acad. Arbitrators (pres. 1981). Home: PO Box 1347 Pacific Palisades CA 90272-1347 E-mail: tedjones@ucla.edu.

JONES, FRANCES MARY, law librarian; b. Little Rock, Ark., Dec. 27, 1942; d. Henry George and Ruth O'Donnell Nachtsheim; m. Ronald Benjamin Jones, May 6, 1967 (dec. Nov. 22, 1986). BA, Coll. St. Catherine, 1964; MA, U. Minn., 1982; JD, William Mitchell Coll. Law, 1988. Bar: Minn. 1989. With Calif. State Libr., Sacramento, 1995—99; dir. Maricopa County Law Libr., Phoenix, 1991—94; sr. tax cons. Deloitte & Touche, Mpls., 1987—90; libr. U. Minn. Law Libr., 1990—91; dir. Calif. Jud. Ctr. Libr./Calif. Supreme Ct., San Francisco, 1999—. Mem. State Govt. Adv. Group, WestGroup, Eagan, 2002—. Author: (monograph) Defusing Censorship: The Librarian's Guide to Managing Censorship Conflict, (directory) Directory of Library Staff Organizations. Mem.: Ariz. Assn. Law Librs. (pres. 1994), Women Lawyers Sacramento, Minn. State Bar Assn., No. Calif. Assn. Law Librs., Am. Assn. Law Librs., Phi Kappa Phi. D-Conservative. Catholic. Avocations: music, ice skating, walking. Office:

Calif Judicial Center Libr 455 Golden Gate Ave Rm 4617 San Francisco CA 94102 Home Fax: 916-441-2469; Office Fax: 415-865-7357. Personal E-mail: francesmjones@yahoo.com. E-mail: fran.jones@jud.ca.gov.

JONES, FRANK CATER, retired lawyer; b. Macon, Ga., June 19, 1925; s. Charles Baxter and Carolyn (Cater) J.; m. Annie Gantt Anderson, Mar. 31, 1951; children: Eugenia Anderson Henderson, Annie Gantt Blattner, Carolyn Corley, Frank Cater. BBA, Emory U., 1947; LLB, Mercer U., 1950, LLD (hon.), 1996. Bar: Ga. 1950. Pvt. practice, Macon, 1950—77; mem. firm Jones, Cork & Miller (and predecessor), 1950—77, King & Spalding, Atlanta, 1977—2001. Bd. dirs. So. Trust Corp. Trustee Wesleyan Coll., Macon, 1966—, chmn. bd. dirs., 1981-86; pres. Atlanta Symphony Orch. League, 1982-84; chmn. Ga. Gt. Park Authority, 1980-83, Ga. Pub. Telecom. Commn., 1983-98, Met. Atlanta chpt. ARC, 1987-88; bd. dirs. Carter Ctr., Emory U., 1987—; chmn. Michael C. Carlos Mus., 1991-96; trustee Emory U., Atlanta, 1991-95, trustee emeritus, 1995—. Fellow: ACTL (bd. regents 1986—, sec. 1990—92, pres. 1993—94); mem.: ABA (ho. of dels. 1972—94), U.S. Supreme Ct. Hist. Soc. (pres. 2002—), State Bar of Ga. (pres. 1968—69), Ga. Bar Assn. (pres. young lawyers sect. 1956—57), Macon Bar Assn. (pres. 1954), Greater Macon C. of C. (pres. 1965), Rotary. Federal civil litigation, General civil litigation, State civil litigation. Home: 4957 Wellington Dr Macon GA 31210-4427 Office: King & Spalding 191 Peachtree St Atlanta GA 30303-1763 E-mail: fjones@kslaw.com.

JONES, FRANKLIN CHARLES, judge; b. Hanover, N.H., July 2, 1948; s. Laurence Harry and Dorothy Selma (Covey) J.; m. Jan Lynn Griggs, June 18, 1966; children— Gregory Allen, Matthew Scott, Benjamin Albert, Kathryn Covey. B.A., U. N.H., 1970; J.D., Boston U., 1973. Bar: N.H. 1973, U.S. Dist. Ct. N.H. 1978, U.S. Ct. Appeals (1st cir.) 1978, U.S. Supreme Ct. 1979. Atty. Michael & Wallace, Rochester, N.H., 1973-76; ptnr. Michael & Jones, Rochester, 1976-78, Michael Jones & Wensley, 1979-86, 87-2001; presiding justice Rochester Dist. Ct., 2001—; mng. ptnr. Jones, Wensley, Wirth & Azcrian, 2001—. Office: Rochester Dist Ct 76 N Main St Rochester NH 03867

JONES, GEORGE WASHINGTON, JR., lawyer; b. Balt., July 27, 1953; s. George W. and Mattie Alice (Reed) Jones; m. Loretta Phylis Pleasant, Aug. 5, 1978; children: Melissa Grace, George Charles, Jessica Michelle. BA, U. Chgo., 1975; JD, Yale U., 1980. Bar: D.C. 1980, U.S. Dist. Ct. D.C. 1980, U.S. Ct. Appeals (D.C. cir.) 1983, U.S. Supreme Ct. 1986. Law clk. to judge U.S. Ct. Appeals (7th Cir.), Chgo., 1978-79; assoc. O'Melveny & Myers, Washington, 1979-80; asst. to solicitor gen. U.S. Dept. Justice, Washington, 1980-83; assoc. Sidley & Austin, Washington, 1983-87, ptnr., 1988—. Mem.: NBA, ABA, DC Bar (pres. 2002—03). Administrative and regulatory, Federal civil litigation, General civil litigation. Office: Sidley Austin Brown & Wood LLP 1501 K St NW Washington DC 20005

JONES, GLOWER WHITEHEAD, lawyer; b. Atlanta, May 4, 1936; s. Samuel L. and Alma (Powell) J.; m. Joanna Dayvault, Apr. 5, 1980; children: Mark, Jeff, Tom, Frank, Michael. Grad. Dartmouth Coll. 1958; JD, Emory U., 1963. Bar: Ga. 1962, U.S. Dist. Ct. Ga. 1963, U.S. Ct. Appeals (5th and 11th cirs.), U.S. Ct. Claims, U.S. Supreme Ct. Assoc. Smith, Swift, Currie, McGhee & Hancock, Atlanta, 1963-65; ptnr. Smith Currie & Hancock, Atlanta, 1967-99, of counsel, 2000—. Author: Legal Aspects of Doing Business in North America and Canada, 1987, Alternative Clauses to Standard Construction Contracts, 1990, editor 2d edit., Construction Subcontracting: A Legal Guide for Industry Professionals, 1991, Wiley Construction Law Update, 1992, 93, 94, Construction Contractors: The Right To Stop Work, 1993, Remedies for International Sellers of Goods, 1993; mem. editl. bd. Ga. State Bar Jour.; contbr. articles to profl. jours. Mem. exec. bd. Met. Atlanta Boys' & Girls' Clubs, Inc., asst. sec., 1973-80, sec., 1980-83; bd. dirs. Samuel L. Jones Boys' & Girls' Club, Inc., So. Region Boys Clubs Am.; trustee, past pres. Atlanta Florence Crittendon Svcs., Inc.; bd. dirs. Carrie Steele Pitts Home, Gate City Day Nursery Assn.; treas. IBA Found. Recipient Golden Boy award Met. Atlanta Boys' Club, 1971. Fellow Chartered Inst. Arbitrators; mem. ABA, Fed. Bar Assn., Internat. Bar Assn. (chmn. internat. sales com., chmn. UNCITRAL subcom., chmn. membership com., mem. governing coun. sect. bus. law), Ga. Bar Assn., State Bar Ga., Atlanta Bar Assn. (former chmn. prepaid legal svcs. com., engr. lawyers rels. com.), Lawyers Club Atlanta, Am. Judicature Soc., Assn. Trial Attys. Am., Ga. Assn. Trial Lawyers, Dartmouth Coll. Alumni Club, Baylor Alumni Club, Emory U. Alumni Club, Atlanta Athletic Club, Ansley Park Golf Club, Dartmouth Club, World Trade Club, Phi Delta Theta. Commercial, contracts (including sales of goods; commercial financing), Construction, Public international. Home: 78 Peachtree Cir NE Atlanta GA 30309-3519 Office: Smith Currie & Hancock Harris Tower 233 Peachtree St NE Ste 2600 Atlanta GA 30303-1530

JONES, GRIER PATTERSON, lawyer; b. Ft. Worth, June 26, 1942; s. Kenneth Hugh and Nancy (Culver) J.; m. Mary Ransford, Mar. 17, 1979; children: Allison Culver, Megan Elizabeth. BA, U. of South, 1964; JD, U. Tex., 1967. Bar: Tex. 1967, Ill. 1978. Asst. sec. and counsel Southland Fin. Corp., Dallas, 1969-74; atty. Mobil Oil Corp., Dallas, 1974-77, litigation mgr. Chgo., 1977-79; corp. counsel Hunt Energy Corp., Dallas, 1979-83; pvt. practice Dallas, 1983-95; asst. dist. atty. Dallas County, 1995-2001, asst. atty. gen., 2001—. Mem. Tex. Unauthorized Practice of Law Com., 1987-95; asst. Atty. Gen. Speaker to various groups. Lay reader, vestryman Good Shepherd Episcopal Ch. Fellow Coll. State Bar Tex., Dallas Bar Found.; mem. Dallas Bar Assn. (bd. dirs. 1998-99, chmn. house com. 1996-98), Tex. Steeplechase Club, Phi Gamma Delta. Republican. General civil litigation, Probate (including wills, trusts). Home: 9048 Stone Creek Pl Dallas TX 75243-6213 Office: Office Atty Gen Ste 700 1600 Pacific Ave Dallas TX 75202 Fax: 214-965-7132. E-mail: grier.jones@cs.oag.state.tx.us.

JONES, H(AROLD) GILBERT, JR., lawyer; b. Fargo, N.D., Nov. 2, 1927; s. Harold Gilbert and Charlotte Viola (Chambers) J.; m. Julie Squier, Feb. 15, 1964; children: Lenna Lettice Mills Jones Carroll, Thomas Squier, Christopher Lee. B of Engring., Yale U., 1947; postgrad., Mich. U., 1948-49; JD, UCLA, 1956. Bar: Calif. 1957. Mem., ptnr. Overton, Lyman & Prince, L.A., 1956—61; founding ptnr. Bonne, Jones, Bridges, Mueller & O'Keefe, L.A., 1961—89, of counsel, 1990—92, Lewis, Brisbois, Bisgaard & Smith, 1992—. Bd. dirs. Wilshire YMCA, 1969-75. With U.S. Army, 1950-52. Fellow Am. Coll. Trial Lawyers, Am. Bd. Trial Advs. (nat. pres. 1988-89, nat. exec. com. 1990, 92, 96, nat. bd. dirs. 1977—, pres. L.A. chpt. 1980, Calif. Trial Lawyer of Yr. 1999), Internat. Acad. Trial Lawyers: mem. ABA, Calif. Bar Assn., Los Angeles County Bar Assn. (past. chmn. legal-med. rels. com.), Orange County Bar Assn., So. Calif. Assn. Def. Counsel, Jonathan Club, Transpacific Yacht Club (commodore 1996-98), Newport Harbor Yac ht Club (commodore 1998), Cruising Club Am., L.A. Yacht Club, Univ. Athletic Club, Ctr. Club. Home: 818 Harbor Island Dr Newport Beach CA 92660-7228 Office: 650 Town Center Dr Ste 1400 Costa Mesa CA 92626-7020 E-mail: hg5150@aol.com., gjones@lbbslaw.com.

JONES, HARTWELL KELLEY, JR., lawyer; b. Columbia, S.C., Mar. 4, 1941; s. Hartwell Kelley and Lora (Bussey) J. BA in Journalism, U. S.C., 1963, MA in Internat. Studies, 1966, JD, 1970. Bar: S.C. 1970, U.S. Ct. Appeals (4th cir.) 1974, U.S. Dist. Ct. 1975, U.S. Supreme 1976. Reporter Columbia Record, 1961-64; press sec. to U.S. Rep. A. W. Watson, 1964-67; reporter govt. affairs The State newspaper, Columbia, 1967-68, night city editor, 1968-70; legal asst., press sec. to Gov. of S.C., 1970-74; gen. counsel S.C. Ins. Dept., Columbia, 1974-78; sole practice Cayce, S.C., 1978-83, West Columbia, S.C., 1983-92, Columbia, S.C., 1992—. Exec. v.p., legis. counsel Profl. Ins. Agents S.C.; gen. counsel S.C. Optometric Assn.; exec. dir. and legis. counsel S.C. Assn. Veterinarians; legis. counsel S.C. Child Care Assn., legis. counsel S.C. Soc. of Accountants. Bd. dirs. Riverland Park Neighborhood Assn.; Cayce planning commn. WOLO-TV Citizens Adv. Com., S.C. With U.S. Army, 1964-70. Decorated Order of Palmetto, State of S.C. Highest Civilian award. Mem. S.C. Bar, S.C. Law Enforcement Officers Assn., S.C. Sheriffs Assn., S.C. Soc. Accts. (legis. counsel). Baptist. Insurance, Personal injury (including property damage). Office: 1226 Pickens St Ste 203 Columbia SC 29201-3462 E-mail: kelley@sc.rr.com.

JONES, JAMES ALTON, lawyer; b. Palestine, Tex., Feb. 26, 1956; s. Ralph A. and Jo Nell (Broadway) J. JD magna cum laude, Tulane U., 1983. Bar: Tex. 1985, U.S. Dist. Ct. (so. dist.) Tex. 1985, U.S. Dist. Ct. (no. and eas. dists.) Tex. 1986, U.S. Dist. Ct. (we. dist.) Tex. 1988, U.S. Ct. Appeals (5th cir.) 1985, Minn. 1993, U.S. Dist. Ct. Minn. 1993, U.S. Ct. Appeals (8th cir.) 1993. Law clk. U.S. Ct. Appeals (5th cir.), Houston, 1983-84; assoc. Holtzman & Urquhart, Houston, 1984-86, Johnson & Swanson, Dallas, 1986, Figari & Davenport, Dallas, 1986-89; ptnr. Doke & Riley, Dallas, 1989-92, Sprenger & Lang, Mpls., 1992-95; shareholder Jones & Assocs. P.C., Dallas, 1995—. Instr. legal rsch. and writing Tulane U., 1983. Mem. ABA, State Bar Tex., Dallas Bar Assn., Nat. Employment Lawyers Assn., Tex. Employment Lawyers Assn., Order of Coif. Baptist. Avocations: tennis, skiing. Civil rights, Federal civil litigation, Labor (including EEOC, Fair Labor Standards Act, labor-management relations, NLRB, OSHA). Office: Jones & Associates PC 5015 Tracy St Ste 100 Dallas TX 75205-3400 Fax: 214-219-9309. E-mail: titlevii@direcway.com.

JONES, JAMES EDWARD, JR., retired law educator; b. Little Rock, June 4, 1924; BA, Lincoln U., Mo., 1950; MA, U. Ill. Inst. Labor and Indsl. Relations, 1951; JD, U. Wis., 1956. Bar: Wis., U.S. Supreme Ct. Indsl. relations analyst U.S. Wage Stabilization Bd., Region 7, 1951-53; legis. atty. Dept. Labor, Washington, 1956-63, counsel for labor relations, 1963-66, dir. office labor mgmt., policy devel., 1966-67, assoc. solicitor labor div. labor relations and civil rights, 1967-69; vis. prof. law and indsl. relations U. Wis.-Madison, 1969-70, prof., 1970-93, Bascom prof. law, 1983-91, Nathan P. Feinsinger prof. labor law, 1991-93, prof. emeritus, 1993—. Dir. Inst. Relations, Research Inst., 1971-73, assoc. Inst. for Research on Poverty, 1970, dir. Ctr. for Equal Employment and Affirmative Action, Indsl. Relations Research Inst., 1974-93; mem. research and edn. staff Pulp, Sulphite and Paper Mill Workers, AFL-CIO, 1958; mem. Fed. Service Impasses Panel, 1978-82; mem. pub. rev. bd. Internat. Union UAW, 1970—; mem. adv. com. NRC Nat. Acad. Scis., 1971-73; mem. Wis. Manpower Planning Council, 1971-76; mem. spl. com. on criminal justice, standards and goals Wis. Council Criminal Justice, 1975-76; bd. dirs. labor law sect. Wis. State Bar, 1976; mem. Fed. Mediation and Conciliation Arbitration Panel, 1975—; spl. arbitrator U.S. Steel and United Steel Workers, 1976-86; mem. expert com. on family budget revision Dept. Labor Series, 1978-79; cons. in field. Mem. Madison Police and Fire Commn., 1973-77, 94-95, pres., 1976-77. Recipient Sec. Labor Career Svc. award Dept. Labor, 1963, Hilldale award (Social Sci. Divsn.), 1990-91, Wis. Law Alumni Disting. Svc. award, 1995, tchr. of yr. award Soc. Am. Law Tchrs., 1998, disting. alumni award U. Ill., 1996; John Hay Whitney fellow, 1953, 54. Mem. Labor Law Group Trust (chmn. editorial policy com. 1978-82), Indsl. Relations Research Assn. (treas. Washington chpt. 1968-69, exec. bd. 1977-80), Fed. Bar Assn. (chmn. labor law com. 1967-69, dep. chmn. council on labor law and labor relations 1979-80), State Bar Wis., Nat. Bar Assn. (nat. adv. com. of equal employment clin. project 1970-79, Hall of Fame 1999), Nat. Acad. Arbitrators, Order of Coif, Phi Kappa Phi. Office: Univ Wisconsin Sch of Law Madison WI 53706

JONES, JENIVER JAMES, lawyer; b. Sutton, W.Va., Sept. 24, 1915; s. Lee Jackson J. and Mary Ida (Lewis) J.; m. Maxine Hickman, Oct. 3, 1939 (dec. Dec. 1993); children: Gary Keith, Glendon Kent, Ronnie Dale; m. Mary Frame, July 30, 1994; stepchildren: Debra Frame Brady, Joseph Frame. Student, Glenville (W. Va.) Coll., 1938; JD, W. Va. U., 1947. Bar: W. Va. 1947. Tchr. Braxton County Bd. Edn., Sutton, W. Va., 1936-43, attendance dir., 1947-48; aircraft inspector Glen L. Martin, Middle River, Md., 1943-45; pvt. practice Sutton, 1948-91, Gassaway, 1991—. W. Va. Rep. Supreme Ct. nominee, 1988. Mem. Lions Club Internat. (dist. gov. 1963-64, Sutton, W.Va.). Methodist. Avocations: reading, tennis, baseball, golfing. Family and matrimonial, General practice, Property, real (including real estate development, water). Office: Law Offices of Jeniver J Jones HC 62 Box 75 Gassaway WV 26624-9405

JONES, JOHN FRANK, retired lawyer; b. Carrington, N.D., Feb. 24, 1922; s. Dwight Frank and Veronica Esther (Sheehy) J.; m. Sally Oppegard; children: Janna Jones Bellwin, John M., Jeramy Ridder, Jill Jones Nester, Julie, Jeffrey, J. David. BS, U. N.D., 1946; MS in Organic Chemistry, U. Wis., 1953; JD, U. Akron, 1956. Bar: Ohio 1956, U.S. Patent Office, U.S. Ct. Appeals. Patent atty. B. F. Goodrich Co., Akron, Ohio, 1956-62; sr. patent atty. Standard Oil Co., Cleve., 1962-70, patent counsel, 1970-81, food and drug atty. Vistron Corp. subs. Standard Oil Co., Cleve., 1968-81, ret., 1981; cons. to Standard Oil Co., Cleve. and Ashland Chem. Co. (div. Ashland Oil Co.), Columbus, Ohio, 1981-95, B.F. Goodrich Co. Served with USAAF, 1943-46. Decorated D.F.C., Air medal. Mem. Am. Chem. Soc., Ohio Bar Assn., ABA, Cleve. Intellectual Property Law Assn., CBI Hump Pilots Assn. Republican. Patentee in chem. and polymer fields; contbr. articles on polymer sci. to profl. jours. Patent, Trademark and copyright. Home and Office: 2724 Cedar Hill Rd Cuyahoga Falls OH 44223-1226

JONES, JOHN PAUL, probation officer, psychologist; b. Blanchard, Mich., July 23, 1944; s. Lawrence John and Thelma Blanche (Eldred) J.; m. Joan Margaret Bruder, Aug. 18, 1972; children: Jason John, Justin John, Jessica Joan-Margaret. BS, Cen. Mich. U., 1970, MA, 1974; PhD, Wayne State U., Detroit, 1980. Diplomate Am. Bd. Forensic Medicine, Am. Bd. Cert. Forensic Examiners, Am. Bd. Psychol. Specialties, Am. Acad. of Experts in Traumatic Stress; diplomate in psychotherapy; cert. addictions counselor. Mgr. F. W. Woolworth Co., Bay City, Mich., 1970; probation officer Oakland County Cir. Ct., Pontiac, Mich., 1970-74, probation officer supr., 1974-78, dir. spl. probation program, 1978-80; chief probation officer County of Oakland, Pontiac, 1980-93; outpatient clin. dir. Auro Med. Ctr., Bloomfield Hills, 1993—. Lectr. Oakland U., Rochester, Mich., 1978-82; lic. psychologist Psychol. Svcs. of Bloomfield Hills, Mich., 1980-82, Family Treatment Ctr., Pontiac, Mich., 1983-84, Associated Profls., Bloomfield Hills, 1984-85, Auro Med. Ctr., Bloomfield Hills, 1985—. Pres. Pontiac Lions Club, 1986-87; study subcom. Oakland County Jail, 1982-84; mem. Oakland County Child Sexual Abuse Task Force, 1982-83. With U.S. Army, 1966-68. Mem. APA (bd. govs.), Internat. Neuropsychol. Assn., Am. Correctional Psychologist Assn., Am. Acad. Experts in Traumatic Stress, Am. Coll. Forensic Examiners (BCFE, BCFM), Am. Psychotherapy Assn., Mich. Corrections Assn., Mich. Assn. Probation Officers Svcs., Mich. Psychol. Assn., Fraternal Order of Police, Cen. Mich. U. Alumni Assn. (bd. dirs. Mt. Pleasant chpt. 1989-93), Mich. Neuropsychol. Soc., Am. Psychol. Assn. Republican. Avocations: travel, horseback riding, reading, fencing. Home: 2915 Masefield Dr Bloomfield Hills MI 48304-1951 Office: Auro Med Ctr Ste 102 1711 S Woodwood Ave Bloomfield Hills MI 48302

JONES, JOHNNIE ANDERSON, lawyer; b. Laurel Hill, La., Nov. 30, 1919; s. Henry Edward and Sarah Ann (Coats) J.; m. Sebell Elizabeth Chase, June 1, 1948; children— Johnnie, Adair Darnell, Adal Dalcho, Ann Sarah Bythelda. B.S. in Psychology, So. U., Baton Rouge, 1949; J.D., 1953. Bar: La. 1953, U.S. Dist. Ct. (ea. and mid. dists.) La. 1953, U.S. Ct. Appeals (5th cir.) 1982, U.S. Supreme Ct. 1961. Ins. agt. Universal Life Ins. Co., Baton Rouge, 1947-48; letter carrier U.S. Post Office, Baton Rouge, 1948-50; practice, Baton Rouge, 1953— ; sr. lawyer Jones & Jones, Baton Rouge, 1975— ; asst. parish atty. City-Parish Govt., Baton Rouge, 1969-72. Mem. La. Ho. of Reps., 1972-76; bd. dirs. La. Human Relations Council, Baton Rouge, 1984. Served with U.S. Army, 1942-46, ETO. Recipient Cert. of Appreciation, L.B. Johnson and H.H. Humphrey, Washington, 1964, Plaque, Alpha Kappa Alpha, 1972; named Most Outstanding Man of Yr., Mt. Zion First Bapt. Ch., Baton Rouge, 1970, Frontiersman of Yr., Frontiers Club Internat., Baton Rouge, 1962. Mem. Am. Judicature Soc., ABA, Nat. Bar Assn., Louis A. Marinet Legal Soc., Baton Rouge Bar Assn., Am. Legion, NAACP, Alpha Phi Alpha. Democrat. Baptist. Civil rights, Federal civil litigation, Labor (including EEOC, Fair Labor Standards Act, labor-management relations, NLRB, OSHA). Office: Jones & Jones 251 Florida St Suite 215 Baton Rouge LA 70801

JONES, JOSEPH HAYWARD, lawyer; b. Shamokin, Pa., July 9, 1924; s. Joseph H. and Anna Elizabeth (Lippiatt) J.; m. Grace Loretta Hicks, Mar. 17, 1951; children: Elizabeth Christie, Joseph H. Jr., Gregory H. BA, Ursinus Coll., 1947, LLD (hon.), 1987; JD, Dickinson Sch. Law, Carlisle, Pa., 1950; LLM, NYU, 1954. Bar: Pa. 1950, U.S. Supreme Ct. 1959. Ptnr. Williamson, Friedberg & Jones, Pottsville, Pa., 1950—. Mem. Pa. Judicial Reform Commn., 1987. Past pres. Appalachian Trail coun. Boy Scouts Am., Hawk Mountain coun. Boy Scouts Am.; sec., past pres. Schuylkill Econ. Devel. Corp.; pres. Pottsville Area Devel. Corp., 1986; bd. dirs. Salvation Army, Pa. Lawyers Trust Account Bd., 1989-96. Lt. (j.g.) USN, 1942-45, PTO. Recipient Silver Beaver award Boy Scouts Am., Disting. Citizen award Pa. State U., Schuylkill, 1987, Citizen of Yr. award St. David's Soc. Schuylkill and Carbon Counties; named Young Man of Yr., Pottsville Area Jaycees, Vol. of Yr., So. Schuylkill United Fund, 1972. Mem. Pa. Bar Assn. (pres. 1987-88, recipient Pa. Bar medal, chmn. task force legal svcs. to poor 1989-90, recipient ADL torch of Liberty 1997), Pa. Bar Found. (pres.), Masons (33 deg.), Lions (past pres.). General practice, Probate (including wills, trusts), Taxation, general. Home: 2100 Mahantongo St Pottsville PA 17901-3112 Office: Williamson Friedberg & Jones Ten Westwood Rd Pottsville PA 17901

JONES, JULIE LAURA, lawyer, risk manager; b. Milton, Fla., Nov. 21, 1967; d. Wyman Lloyd and Kathleen Grace Jones. B.S. in Acctg., U. So. Miss., 1990; JD, Emory U., 1993. Bar: Fla. 1993, Ala. 1994, U.S. Dist. Ct. (no. dist.) 1994. Claims and litig. coord. Gulf Power Co., Pensacola, Fla., 2001—, labor rels. coord., 1999—2001; asst. gen. counsel Dept. Juvenile Justice, Pensacola, Fla., 1997—99; asst. pub. defender Office Pub. Defender - First Jud. Cir. Fla., Pensacola, Fla., 1995—97; assoc. Johnson, Green & Locklin, Milton, Fla., 1993—95. Utilities, public, Insurance, General civil litigation, Risk Management. Office: Gulf Power Co One Energy Place Pensacola FL 32520

JONES, KEITH ALDEN, lawyer; b. Tulsa, July 11, 1941; s. Leonard Virgil and Bernadine (Hutchison) J.; m. Renata Skuta, June 15, 1974; children: Emily Isobel, Alden Rivendale. BA, Harvard U., 1963, LLB, 1966. Bar: Mass. 1966, D.C. 1978, U.S. Supreme Ct. 1972. Asst. prof. Boston U. Law Sch., 1966-67; lectr. Harvard U. Law Sch., 1967-68; assoc. Ropes & Gray, Boston, 1968-70; minority counsel U.S. Senate Select Com. on Small Bus., 1970-72; asst. to Solicitor Gen. of U.S., 1972-75; dep. solicitor gen., 1975-78; ptnr. Fulbright & Jaworski, Washington, 1978-94; of counsel Beck, Redden & Secrest, Houston, 1995—. Mem. ABA, Am. Law Inst. Appellate.

JONES, LAUREN EVANS, lawyer; b. Lawrence, Kans., Jan. 10, 1952; s. Kevin Rice and Marcia Jo Ann (Peterson) J.; m. Vivien Craig Long, Mar. 26, 1978; children: Dylan Tyler, Hayden Blake, Carson Reed. BA in History, U. Mich., 1973; JD, Duke U., 1977. Bar: R.I. 1978, U.S. Dist. Ct. R.I. 1978, U.S. Ct. Appeals (1st cir.) 1985, U.S. Ct. Appeals (9th cir.) 1994, U.S. Supreme Ct. 1991. Assoc. Lovett, Morgera, Schefrin & Gallogly, Providence, R.I., 1979-83; ptnr. Jones & Aisenberg, Providence, 1983-89; owner Jones Assocs., Providence, 1990—. Mem. Jud. Performance Eval. Commn., 1993—; mem. R.I. Supreme Ct. Com. on Profl. and Civility, 1995-96. Editor R.I. Bar Jour., 1989-95, 2002-; contbr. articles to profl. jours. Nominee R.I. Supreme Ct., 1993, 95, 96, 97. Mem. R.I. Bar Assn. (exec. com. 1989-2000, 2002—, sec. 1995, v.p. 1996, pres. elect 1997, pres. 1998-99). Appellate, General civil litigation, Personal injury (including property damage). Office: Jones Assocs 72 S Main St Providence RI 02903-2907 E-mail: ljones@appealaw.com.

JONES, LAWRENCE TUNNICLIFFE, lawyer; b. Mineola, N.Y., Jan. 20, 1950; s. Carroll Hudson Tunnicliffe and Florence Virginia (Greene) J. BA, U. Va., 1972; JD, U. Richmond, 1975. Bar: Va. 1975, D.C. 1976, N.Y. 1976, U.S. Dist. Ct. (ea. and so. dist.) N.Y. 1976, U.S. Supreme Ct. 1986. Bus. mgr. law review U. Richmond, Va., 1974-75; ptnr. Carroll Hudson Tunnicliffe Jones and Lawrence Tunnicliffe Jones Attys. at law, Mineola, 1976-91; owner, 1992—. Trustee Nassau County Hist. Soc., 1976—, pres., 1983-89; bd. dirs. Friends of Hist. St. George's Ch., Hempstead, N.Y., 1982—, v.p., 1990-92, pres., 1992-94; bd. dirs. St. Mary's Devel. Fund, Garden City, N.Y., 1983-89, pres., 1987-89; pres. coun. Cathedral Sch. St. Paul Alumni Fund, Inc., Garden City, 1984—; bd. govs. Cathedral Sch. St. Mary, Garden City, 1983-86. Recipient Mineola Bus. Person of Yr. award, 2000. Mem. ABA, Nat. Acad. Elder Law Attys., Va. State Bar Assn., N.Y. State Bar Assn., Nassau County Bar Assn., Nassau County Tax and Estate Planning Coun., Univ. Club (N.Y.C.), Univ. Club (L.I., pres. 1986-87, 93-94, bd. dirs. 1983-86, 89—), Mineola C. of C. (dir. 1993—), Garden City Golf Club, Mineola-Garden City Rotary (dir. 1991-94), Garden City Fellowship (pres. 1993-94, dir. 1994—), Cathedral Club (Garden City) (pres. 1993-95), Garden City C. of C. Episcopalian. Avocation: historic building preservation. General practice, Probate (including wills, trusts), Property, real (including real estate development, water). Home: 158 Cathedral Ave Hempstead NY 11550-1140 Office: Jones & Jones 1000 Franklin Ave Ste 302 Garden City NY 11530-2910

JONES, LINDY DON, lawyer; b. Vernon, Tex., Aug. 20, 1949; s. Earl Irven Jones and Avis June (Koontz) McDowell; m. M. Kathryn Sanders, June 6, 1969; children: Brandi Kim, Megan Dawn, Ty Jeffrey. BBA in Mgmt. with honors, U. Tex., Arlington, 1971; JD, So. Meth. U., 1974. Bar: Tex. 1974, U.S. Ct. Appeals (5th cir.) 1974, U.S. Dist. Ct. (we. dest.) Tex. 1977, U.S. Dist. Ct. (ea. dist.) Tex. 1978, U.S. Dist. Ct. (so. dist.) Tex. 1979. Ptnr. Moseley, Jones, Enoch & Martin and predecessors, Dallas, 1974-81, Moseley, Jones, Allen & Fuquay, Dallas, 1981-86, Jones, Allen & Fuquay, Dallas, 1986—. Pres. Highland Park United Meth. Ch. Mens Club, Dallas, 1979; chmn. bd. dirs. Dickinson Pl. Charitable Corp., Dallas, 1984-86. Recipient hon. life membership Highland Park United Meth. Ch. Mens Club, 1980. Mem. ABA, Dallas Bar Assn. (com. mem. 1974—), State Bar Tex., Delta Theta Phi. Republican. Banking, State civil litigation, Commercial, contracts (including sales of goods; commercial financing). Home: 8068 Moss Meadows Dr Dallas TX 75231-3915 Office: Jones Allen & Fuquay LLP 8828 Greenville Ave Dallas TX 75243-7160 E-mail: ljones@jonesallen.com.

JONES, LUCIAN COX, lawyer; b. Kew Gardens, N.Y., Dec. 22, 1942; m. Ann Waters, Aug. 22, 1964; children— L. Rustin, Norman W., Warren R. AB, Davidson Coll., 1964; JD, Columbia U., 1967. Bar: N.Y. 1967. Assoc. Shearman & Sterling, N.Y.C., 1967-68, 70-76, ptnr., 1976-98; lectr-.Cameron Sch. Bus. U. N.C., Wilmington, 1998—. Served to capt. U.S. Army, 1968-70 Mem. ABA, N.C. State Bar Assn., Assn. Bar City N.Y. Antitrust, Banking, Commercial, contracts (including sales of goods; commercial financing). Office: U NC Cameron Sch Bus 601 S College Rd Wilmington NC 28403-3297

JONES, MICHAEL EARL, lawyer; b. Easton, Md., Oct. 23, 1950; s. Lawrence F. and Marlen N. Jones. BA, Denison U., 1972; MBA, U. Pa., 1974; JD, U. Miami, 1978. Bar: N.H. 1978, U.S. Dist. Ct. N.H. 1978, U.S. Tax Ct. 1978, U.S. Supreme Ct. 1983, U.S. Ct. Internat. Trade 1985, U.S.

Ct. Appeals (D.C. cir.) 1986, U.S. Ct. Appeals (1st cir.) 1986. Sole practice, Pelham, N.H., 1978—; asst. prof. U. N.H., Durham, 1978-82; assoc. prof. law U. Mass., Lowell, 1984—98, prof. law, 1998—; judge Salem (N.H.) Dist. Ct., 1989—. Mem. Ho. of Reps., Concord, N.H., 1982-88. Author: Current Issues in Pro Sports, 1980, Sports Law, Prentice Hall, 1999; editor: Readings in International Law, 1987; exhbns. include N.H. Inst. Arts, 2000--, Denison U. Art Gallery, 2002; contbr. articles on sports, art and entertainment law to profl. jours. Chmn. Pelham Cable TV Adv. Commn., N.H., 1981-85, Pelham Conservation Commn., 1982-83, Pelham Parks and Recreation Commn.; ranking mem. Judiciary Com., 1982-88; bd. dirs. Home Health and Hospice; chmn. bd. Pelham Bank and Trust Co., vice chmn. First Finance Co. 1993-96; trustee N.H. Inst. Art, 2002--; chief judge U.S. Olympic Trials, Triathlon, 2000--. Recipient Tufts Disting. Citizen of N.H. award, 1988. Mem. N.H. Bar Assn., Am. Judges Assn., Am. Bus. Law Assn., Internat. Law Assn. (officer 1984—), Am. Trial Law Assn., Internat. Bar Assn., North Atlantic Bus. Lawyers Assn. (pres. 1990-91), Phi Alpha Delta (clk. 1977-78), Omicron Delta Epsilon (pres. 1971-72). Avocations: oil painting, swimming, triathlons, running. General practice. Home: PO Box 397 Pelham NH 03076-0397 Office: Salem Dist Ct 35 Geremonty Rd Salem NH 03079

JONES, MICHAEL FRANK, lawyer; b. Chgo., May 5, 1948; s. Martin F. and Joan M. (Harvey) J.; m. Susan D. Drozda. AB in Econs., Middlebury Coll., 1970, JD, 1973. Bar: Ill. 1973, Utah 1981. Assoc. Coles & Wise Ltd., Chgo., 1973-78, Rosenberg, Savner & Unikel, Chgo., 1978-80, ptnr., 1980-81; assoc. Fabian & Clendenin, Salt Lake City, 1981-82, mem., 1982-83; assoc. Hansen, Jones, Maycock & Leta, Salt Lake City, 1983-84; ptnr. Tibbals, Howell, Jones & Moxley, Salt Lake City, 1984-88, Jones & Farr, Salt Lake City, 1988-90, Pruitt, Gushee & Bachtell, Salt Lake City, 1990-95, Michael F. Jones P.C., Salt Lake City, 1995-96; mem. Moxley Jones & Campbell, L.C., Salt Lake City, 1996-98, Baird & Jones, L.C., Salt Lake City, 1998—. Chmn. Salt Lake City (Utah) Bd. Adjustment, 2001—. Contbr. articles to profl. jours. Trustee Utah Heritage Found., Salt Lake City, 1984-93; mem. Salt Lake City Bd. Adjustment, 1993—, chmn., 2001—. Mem. ABA, Ill. Bar Assn., Am. Coll. Real Estate Lawyers, Utah State Bar (chmn. real property sect. 1985-86). Commercial, contracts (including sales of goods; commercial financing), Corporate, general, Property, real (including real estate development, water). Home: 1703 Yalecrest Ave Salt Lake City UT 84108-1839 Office: Baird & Jones LC One Utah Ctr Ste 900 Salt Lake City UT 84111 E-mail: mjones@bairdjones.com.

JONES, NANCY LEE, lawyer; b. Washington; d. Joseph Crockett and Ann A. Jones; m. Richard Even Rowberg; children: Jeffrey, Andrew. AB, Georgetown U., 1972, JD, 1975. Bar: Va., U.S. Supreme Ct. Legis. atty. Am. Law divsn. Congrl. Rsch. Svc., Libr. of Congress, Washington, 1975—. Author: A Guide for Educators, Parents and Attorneys, 1999, (with others) Droit et Sida, 1994, The Americans with Disabilities Act: From Policy to Practice, 1991; contbr. articles to profl. jours. Office: Congrl Rsch Svcs Libr Of Congress Washington DC 20540-0001

JONES, NAPOLEON A., JR., judge; b. 1940; BA, San Diego State U., 1962, MSW, 1967; JD, U. San Diego, 1971. Legal intern, staff atty. Calif. Rural Legal Assistance, Modesto, Calif., 1971-73; staff atty. Defenders, Inc., San Diego, 1973-75; ptnr. Jones, Cazares, Adler & Lopez, San Diego, 1975-77; judge San Diego Mcpl. Ct., 1977-82, San Diego Superior Ct., 1982-94, U.S. Dist. Ct. (so. dist.) Calif., San Diego, 1994—. Mem. San Diego County Indigent Def. Policy Bd. Bd. visitors Sch. Social Work San Diego State U.; active Valencia Park Elem. Sch. Mem. San Diego County Bar Assn., Earl B. Gilliam Bar Assn., San Diego Bar Found., Nat. Bar Assn., Calif. Bar Assn., Calif. Black Attys. Assn., Nat. Assn. Women Judges, Masons, Sigma Pi Phi, Kappa Alpha Psi. Office: US Dist Ct So Dist Calif US Courthouse 940 Front St Ste 2125 San Diego CA 92101-8912

JONES, NATHANIEL RAPHAEL, retired federal judge; b. Youngstown, Ohio, May 13, 1926; s. Nathaniel B. and Lillian (Rafe) J.; m. Lillian Graham, Mar. 22, 1974; children: Stephanie Joyce, Pamela Haleystepchildren: William Hawthorne, Rickey Hawthorne, Marc Hawthorne. AB, Youngstown State U., 1951, LL.B., 1955, LL.D. (hon.) (hon.), 1969, Syracuse U., 1972. Editor Buckeye Rev. newspaper, 1956; exec. dir. FEPC, Youngstown, 1956—59; practiced law, 1959—61; mem. firm Goldberg & Jones, 1968—69; asst. U.S. atty., 1961—67; asst. gen. counsel Nat. Adv. Commn. on Civil Disorders, 1967—68; gen. counsel NAACP, 1969—79; judge U.S. Ct. of Appeals, 6th Circuit, 1979—2002, sr. judge, 1995—2002; sr. ptnr. Blank Rome Comisky & McCauley LLP, Cin., 2002—. Adj. prof. U. Cin. Coll. Law, 1983—; trial observer , South Africa, 1985; dir. Buckeye Rev. Pub. Co.; chmn. Con. on Adequate Def. and Incentives in Mil.; mem. Task Force-Vets. Benefits; lectr. South African Judges seminar, Johannesburg. Co-chmn. Cin. Roundtable, Underground R.R. Freedom Ctr.; observer Soviet Union Behalf com. on Soviet Jewry. With USAF, 1945—47. Mem.: FBA, ABA (co-chmn. com. constl. rights criminal sect. 1971—73, chmn. Africa coun., chmn. jud. clerkship initiative 1999—2000, chmn. spl. advisor coun. on racial and ethnic justice 1994—97), Cin. Bar Assn., Nat. Conf. Black Lawyers, Urban League, Am. Arbitration Assn., Nat. Bar Assn., Mahoning County Bar Assn., Ohio State Bar Assn., Houston Law Club (Youngstown), Elks, Kappa Alpha Psi. Baptist. Office: Blank Rome LLP 201 E 5th St Ste 1700 Cincinnati OH 45202 E-mail: Jones-n@blankrome.com.*

JONES, PHILIP KIRKPATRICK, JR., lawyer; b. Baton Rouge, June 26, 1949; s. Philip Kirkpatrick and Mary Jane (Kincade) J.; m. Serena Catherine Cockayne, Apr. 5, 1980; children: Veronica Cockayne, Nicola Kincade, Clare Kirkpatrick, Philip Carruth Elliot. BA in Govt., Dartmouth Coll., 1971; JD, La. State U., 1974; LLB, diploma in legal studies, Cambridge (U.K.) U., 1976. Bar: La. 1974, U.S. Dist. Ct. (ea. and we. dist.) La. 1980, U.S. Ct. Appeals (5th and 11th cirs.) 1981, U.S. Dist. Ct. (mid. dist.) La. 1987, U.S. Supreme Ct. 1992. Law clk. to John A. Dixon Jr. Supreme Ct. La., New Orleans, 1974-75; staff atty. Presdl. Clemency Bd., Washington, 1975; lectr. U. Singapore, 1977-79; from assoc. to ptnr. Liskow & Lewis, New Orleans, 1980—. 1st lt. USAF, 1975. Republican. Presbyterian. Bankruptcy, Federal civil litigation, Private international. Office: Liskow & Lewis PC 50th Fl One Shell Square New Orleans LA 70139 E-mail: pkjones@liskow.com.

JONES, RANDY KANE, lawyer; b. Jacksonville, N.C., Oct. 25, 1957; s. Henry and Julia Mae (Saunders) J.; m. Traci Eileen Williams, Feb. 21, 1998; children: Randy Kane Baker, Ardington Kane. BA in Polit. Sci., U. N.C., 1979, JD, 1982; LLD (hon.), Claflin Coll., 1998. Bar: N.C. 1983, Calif. 1987. Judge adv. Dept. Navy, San Diego, 1982-86; asst. U.S. atty. Dept. Justice, San Diego, 1987—. Counselor Nu-Way Youth Gang Diversion, San Diego, 1990-96; dir. Voices for Children, San Diego, 1992-97; moderator Christian Fellowship Ch., San Diego, 1997—; bd. dirs. San Diego Crime Victims Fund, 1993—. With USNR, 1988-98. Recipient San Diego County Pub. Lawyer of Yr. award, 1994, Disting. Alumni award U. N.C. Chapel Hill, 1998; named one of 100 Most Influential Leaders, Ebony Mag., 1998, among Best Lawyers, Calif. Lawyer mag., 1999, 20 Under 40, Calif. Bus. Lawyer mag., 1994. Mem. ABA, Nat. Bar Assn. (pres. 1997-98), Earl B. Gilliam Bar Assn. (pres. 1990-91). Avocations: singing, mentoring, sports, travel. Office: US Attys Office 880 Front St Fl 6 San Diego CA 92101-8897

JONES, RICHARD MICHAEL, lawyer; b. Chgo., Jan. 16, 1952; s. Richard Anthony and Shirley Mae (Wilhelm) J.; m. Catherine Leona Ford, May 25, 1974. BS, U. Ill., 1974; JD, Harvard U., 1977. Bar: Colo. 1977, U.S. Dist. Ct. Colo. 1977. Assoc. Davis, Graham & Stubbs, Denver, 1977-81; corp. counsel Tosco Corp., Denver, 1981-82; asst. gen. counsel Anschutz Corp., Denver, 1982-88, gen. counsel, v.p., 1989—. Mem. ABA, Colo. Bar Assn., Denver Bar Assn. Corporate, general, Oil, gas, and mineral, Private international. Office: Anschutz Corp 555 17th St Ste 2400 Denver CO 80202-3987

JONES, ROBERT D. judge; b. Ft. Worth, Oct. 16, 1934; s. Algernon S. and F. Marie Jones; m. Beverly A. Jones, Dec. 26, 1965; children: Jennifer S., Michael C., Steven J. BA in Govt., U. Tex., Austin, 1960, JD, 1964. Bar: Tex. 1964, U.S. Dist. Ct. (so., no., ea. and we. dists.) Tex. 1964, U.S. Ct. Appeals (5th cir.) 1964, U.S. Ct. Mil. Appeal 1964. Lawyer Procter, Maloney & Fullerton, Austin, 1964—85; dist. judge State of Tex., Austin, 1985—93, sr. dist. judge, 1993—. Pres. PTA, Austin, 1985; bd. dirs. Hope House, Austin, 1980—84. Lt. col. USMC Reserve, 1952—94, Korea, Austin. Mem.: Tex. Criminal Def. Lawyers Assn. (pres. 1980—81), Tex. State Bar Assn. (bd. dirs. 1982—84), Travis County Bar Assn. (pres. 1981). Democrat. Presbyterian. Home: 1607 Sharon Ln Austin TX 78703 Office: 510 S Congress Ste 310 Austin TX 78704 Office Fax: 512-473-2042 . E-mail: rjones1034@aol.com.

JONES, ROBERT EDWARD, federal judge; b. Portland, Oreg., July 5, 1927; s. Howard C. and Leita (Hendricks) J.; m. Pearl F. Jensen, May 29, 1948; children— Jeffrey Scott, Julie Lynn BA, U. Hawaii, 1949; JD, Lewis and Clark Coll., 1953, LHD (hon.), 1995; LLD (hon.), City U., Seattle, 1984. Bar: Oreg. Trial atty., Portland, Oreg., 1953-63; judge Oreg. Circuit Ct., Portland, 1963-83; justice Oreg. Supreme Ct., Salem, 1983-90; judge U.S. Dist. Ct. Oreg., Portland, 1990—. Mem. faculty Nat. Jud. Coll., Am. Acad. Jud. Edn., ABA Appellate Judges Seminars; former mem. Oreg. Evidence Revision Commn., Oreg. Ho. of Reps.; former chmn. Oreg. Commn. Prison Terms and Parole Stds.; adj. prof. Northwestern Sch. Law, Lewis and Clark Coll., 1963—, Willamette Law Sch., 1988-90. Author: Rutter Group Practice Guide Federal Civil Trials and Evidence, 1999—. Mem. bd. overseers Lewis and Clark Coll., mem. bd. visitors to Northwestern Sch. Law. Served to capt. JAGC, USNR. Recipient merit award Multnomah Bar Assn., 1979; Citizen award NCCJ, Legal Citizen of the Yr. award Law Related Edn. Project, 1988; Service to Mankind award Sertoma Club Oreg.; James Madison award Sigma Delta Chi; named Disting. Grad., Northwestern Sch. Law; Outstanding Profl. Achievement Alumnus award, U.S. Merchant Marine Acad., 1998; Judge Robert E. Jones Oreg. Justice award, Am. Judicature Soc., 1999. Mem. Am. Judicature Soc. (bd. dirs. 1997-2001), State Bar Oreg. (past chmn. Continuing Legal Edn.), Oregon Circuit Judges Assn. (pres. 1967-1968), Oreg. Trial Lawyers Assn. (pres. 1959, chair 9th cir. edn. com. 1996-97). Office: US Dist Ct House 1000 SW 3rd Ave Ste 1407 Portland OR 97204-2944 E-mail: robert_jones@ord.uscourts.gov.

JONES, ROBERT JEFFRIES, lawyer; b. Atlantic City, N.J., Sept. 7, 1939; s. Robert Lewis and Mildred Laura (Jeffries) J.; m. Joan Mary Feichtner, Aug. 17, 1963; children: Christopher, Kendall, Stephen. BA, Colgate U., 1961; LLB with honors, U. Pa., 1964. Bar: Pa. 1965, U.S. Dist. Ct. (ea. dist.) Pa. 1965, U.S. Ct. Appeals (3d cir.) 1965. Assoc. Saul, Ewing LLP, Phila., 1964-71, ptnr., 1971—. Mem. steering com. Bond Atty.'s Workshop, Chgo., 1980. Mem. Montgomery County Rep. Com., Norristown, Pa., 1967-71; chmn. Whitpain Twp. Park and Recreation Bd., Blue Bell, Pa., 1980-84; bd. dirs. Phila. YMCA Camps, 1970-76; trustee Colgate U., 1999—; mem. gen. counsel alumni corp., 1993-99, pres. Phila. chpt., 1980-84. Fellow Am. Coll. Bond Counsel (founder); mem. ABA, Phila. Bar Assn. (chmn. tax exempt fin. com. 1985-86), Pa. Bond Lawyers Assn. (founder Harrisburg, Pa. 1987), Pa. Economy League (bd. dirs. 1994—). Avocations: skiing, golf, history. Finance, Municipal (including bonds), Securities. Office: Saul Ewing LLP 3800 Centre Sq W Philadelphia PA 19102 E-mail: rjjboilerplate@aol.com., rjones@saul.com.

JONES, RONALD DAVID, lawyer; b. Oneida, N.Y., Jan. 2, 1930; s. Keith Walton and Winnie (Thomas) J.; children: Susan D., Stephen T.; m. Hildegard Vetter, June 9, 1984. BS, Yale U., 1951; JD cum laude, Harvard U., 1958. Bar: N.Y. 1958, U.S. Ct. Appeals (1st, 2nd, 4th, 5th, 6th and D.C. cirs.), U.S. Supreme Ct. 1980. Assoc. LeBoeuf, Lamb, Leiby & MacRae, N.Y.C., 1958-64, ptnr., 1965-89, of counsel, 1990—. Pres. Coun. Econ. Regulation, 1988-92; chmn. United Distbn. Cos., 1990-97; chmn. Upper Housatonic Valley Nat. Heritage Area, Inc., 2000—. Served to lt. USNR, 1951-55 Mem. ABA (chmn. sect. on pub. utilities law 1986-87), Internat. Bar Assn. (chmn. SBL com. on utility law 1988-90), Univ. Club (N.Y.C.). Avocations: running, writing, history. Office: 27 Woodcrest Ln PO Box 1942 Lakeville CT 06039 E-mail: rdjones@discovernet.net.

JONES, RONALD LEE, lawyer, writer; b. Ames, Iowa, Apr. 11, 1942; s. L. Meyer and Mary Elizabeth (Homer) J.; m. Cynthia Jane Spitzer, Oct. 1, 1994. BA, Ill. Wesleyan U., 1965; cert., Naval Justice Sch., Camp Pendleton, Calif., 1968; JD, Calif. Western Sch. Law, 1972. Bar: Nebr. 1973, U.S. Ct. Appeals (8th cir.) 1973, U.S. Supreme Ct. 1979. Corp. counsel Gene Fuller, Inc., San Diego, 1972-73; asst. gen. counsel Daniel Internat. Corp., Greenville, S.C., 1974-79; v.p., gen. counsel, sec. Royster Co., Norfolk, Va., 1979-83; writer Virginia Beach, Va., 1983—; counsel Peter Kiewit Sons, Inc., Omaha, 1984-87, Occidental Chem. Corp., Dallas, 1988—, The Williams Cos., 1997, Hall Estill Law Firm, Tulsa, Okla., 2002—. Chmn. lawyers coordinating com. Fla. Phosphate Council, Tampa, 1980. Author: Practice Preventive Corporat Law, 1985, How to Counsel Corporate Clients: Ten Reasons Business People Don't Take Legal Advice (And What You Can Do About It), ALI-ABA, 2000; editor (newsletter) Corp. Counsel Reporter, 1985—; contbr. articles to profl. jours. Capt. USMC, 1965-69. Mem. ABA (corp., banking and bus. law sect., constrn. law forum com.), Fertilizer Inst., Am. Mfrs. Assn. Construction, Corporate, general, Oil, gas, and mineral. Home: 1 Royal Dublin Ln Broken Arrow OK 74011-1127

JONES, SHELDON ATWELL, lawyer; b. Melrose, Mass., Apr. 20, 1938; s. Sheldon Atwell and Hannah Margaret (Andrews) J.; m. Priscilla Ann Hatch, Sept. 10, 1966; children: Sarah Percy, Abigail Atwell. BA, Yale U., 1959; LLB, Harvard U., 1965. Bar: Mass. 1965, U.S. Dist. Ct. Mass. 1967, Calif. 2001. Assoc. Gaston, Snow, Motley & Holt, Boston, 1965-72; ptnr. Gaston Snow & Ely Bartlett, Boston, 1972-87, Dechert LLP, Boston, Newport Beach, 1987—. Past sec. H&Q Healthcare Investors, Boston. Contbr. articles to profl. jours. Lt. (j.g.) USN, 1959-62. Mem. ABA (past chmn. subcom. on investment cos., state regulation of securities com.), Mass. Bar Assn., Boston Bar Assn. (past co-chmn. subcom. on investment cos. and investment advisers), Calif. State Bar Assn., Orange County Bar Assn., Yale Club, Harvard Club. Congregationalist. Avocations: skiing, sailing. Corporate, general, Securities, Investment. Home: 701 Garrett Dr Corona Del Mar CA 92625 Office: Dechert LLP 14th Fl 4675 MacArthur Ct Newport Beach CA 92660 E-mail: sheldon.jones@dechert.com.

JONES, STEPHEN, lawyer; b. Lafayette, La., July 1, 1940; s. Leslie William and Gladys A. (Williams) J.; m. Virginia Hadden (dec.); 1 child, John Chapman; m. Sherrel Alice Stephens, Dec. 27, 1973; children: Stephen Mark, Leslie Rachael, Edward St. Andrew. Student, U. Tex., 1960-63; LLB, U. Okla., 1966. Sec. Rep. Minority Conf., Tex. Ho. of Reps., 1963; personal asst. to Richard M. Nixon N.Y.C., 1964; adminstrv. asst. to Congressman Paul Findley, 1966-69; legal counsel to gov. of Okla., 1967; spl. asst. U.S. Senator Charles H. Percy and U.S. Rep. Donald Rumsfeld, 1968; mem. U.S. del. to North Atlantic Assembly NATO, 1968; staff counsel censure task force Ho. of Reps. Impeachment Inquiry, 1974; spl. U.S. atty. No. Dist. Okla., 1979; spl. prosecutor, spl. asst. dist. atty. State of Okla., 1977; judge Okla. Ct. Appeals, 1982; civil jury instrn. com. Okla. Supreme Ct., 1979-81; adv. com. ct. rules Okla. Ct. Criminal Appeals, 1980; now mng. ptnr. Stephen Jones & Assoc., Enid, Okla. Adj. prof. U. Okla., 1973-76; instr. Phillips U., 1982-90; bd. dirs. Coun. on the Nat. Interest Found. Author: Oklahoma and Politics in State and Nation, 1907-62, 1974, Others Unknown: The Oklahoma City Bombing Case and Conspiracy, 1998; co-author: France and China, The First Ten Years, 1964-74, 1991, Vernon's Oklahoma Forms 2d Criminal Practice & Procedure Vols. I, II, 1999; contbr. articles to various jours. Bd. dirs., coun. mem. Nat. Interest Found.; acting chmn. Rep. State Com., Okla., 1982; Rep. nominee Okla. atty. gen., 1974, U.S. Senate, 1990; spl. counsel to Gov. Okla., 1995; apptd. chief def. counsel by U.S. Dist. Ct., Oklahoma City, U.S. vs. Tim McVeigh, Oklahoma City Bombing Case, 1995-97; mem. vestry St. Matthews Episc. Ch., 1974, sr. warden, 1983-84, 89-90. Mem. ABA, Okla. Bar Assn., Garfield County Bar Assn., Beacon Club. General civil litigation, Criminal, Taxation, general. Office: PO Box 472 Enid OK 73702-0472

JONES, STEPHEN WITSELL, lawyer; b. Honolulu, Aug. 12, 1947; s. Allen Newton Jr. and Maude Estelle (Witsell) J.; m. Judy Kaye Mason, Aug. 13, 1977; children: MaryAnn, Adam, Kathleen. Student, Hendrix Coll., 1965—66; AB with high honors, U. Ill., 1969; JD with highest honors, U. Ark., Little Rock, 1978. Bar: Ark. 1978, U.S. Dist. Ct. (ea. and we. dists.) Ark. 1978, U.S. Ct. Appeals (7th and 8th cirs.) 1978, U.S. Supreme Ct. 1984. Rsch. statistician Ark. Dept. Parks and Tourism, Little Rock, 1971—72, dir. tourist info. ctr., 1972—74; affirmative action specialist Office of the Gov., Little Rock, 1974—75; dir. pers. Ark. Social Svcs. Div., Little Rock, 1975—77; mgmt. info. specialist Ark. Health Dept., Little Rock, 1977—78; assoc. House, Holmes & Jewell, Little Rock, 1978—84; ptnr. House, Wallace, Nelson & Jewell, Little Rock, 1984—86; ptnr., founding mem. Jack, Lyon & Jones, P.A., Little Rock, 1986—2002. Adj. instr. div. lifelong edn. U. Ark., Little Rock, 1992-95. Co-author: Employment Law Deskbook for Arkansas Employers, 1997; editor-in-chief U. Ark. Little Rock Law Rev., 1977; editor Ark. Employment Law Letter, 1996—; contbr. chpt.: Employment Discrimination Law, 2d edit., 1983. Bd. dirs. United Cerebral Palsy of Ctrl. Ark., Little Rock, 1978—; bd. dirs. Ark. Ice Hockey Assn., 1992-2000; pres. Ctrl. Ark. Youth Hockey Assn., 2000. With U.S. Army, 1969-71. Recipient Svc. Recognition award United Cerebral Palsy of Ctrl. Ark., 1986, 95. Fellow Coll. Labor and Employment Lawyers, Greater Little Rock C. of C.; mem. ABA (labor/litigation law practice mgmt. sect.), Ark. Bar Assn., Def. Rsch. Inst., Ark. State C. of C. (bd. dirs., chair health com.). Episcopalian. Avocations: photography, golf. Civil rights, Labor (including EEOC, Fair Labor Standards Act, labor-management relations, NLRB, OSHA), Commercial, contracts (including sales of goods; commercial financing). Home: 1724 S Arch St Little Rock AR 72206-1215 Office: Jack Lyon & Jones PA 3400 TCBY Tower 425 W Capitol Ave Little Rock AR 72201-3405

JONES, SYLVANUS BENSON, adjudicator, consultant, lawyer; b. Southport, N.C., Nov. 21, 1928; s. Thomas Henry and Katie Mable J.; m. Karen Ann Charbonneau, Aug. 10, 1970 (div. May 1975); 1 child, Donovan; m. Brenda Castleyoung-Jones, Sept. 9, 1999. Student, Howard U., 1945-48; AD in Fin., Peter's Bus. Coll., Washington, 1955; postgrad., Fgn. Svc. Inst., Arlington, Va., 1956, George Washington U., 1959-60, Bibliothèque de la Sorbonne U. de Paris, Paris, 1962, Georgetown U., Washington, 1962, Am. U., 1966-68. Lic. real estate agt.; lic. gen. contractor, Md.; lic. ins. agt., Md., D.C. Enumerator, IBM computer operator U.S. Census Bur., Suitland, Md., 1950-51; clk. typist, claims div. VA, Washington, 1951-52; rsch. clk. Bur. Security and Consular Affairs, U.S. Dept. State, Washington, 1952-53, supr. passport processing sect., 1953-56, from jr. to sr. adjudicator domestic adjudication div., 1956-61, consular affairs officer adv. opinions div., 1961-63, chief pvt. bill staff, office of dep. dir. for ops., 1963-68, chief fraud and investigation unit, 1968-72; adjudicator, gen. cons., 1972—. Editor-in-chief The Washington Press, 1957-63; founder, dir. Mut. Fund Investment Program for Govt. Employees, Washingotn, 1969-73; instr. Tennis U. Puebla (Mex.), 1973-75; editor-in-chief The Annapolis (Md.) Press, 1989—; chmn. ad hoc com. to repeal the utilities tax, Annapolis, 1992—. Contbr. articles to profl. jours; grantee hub cap locking device. Treas. Annapolis City Dem. Ctrl. Com., 1992, 97; Dem. candidate for mayor, Annapolis, 1993, 97, 2001; chmn. trans. adv. bd., Annapolis, 1992-98. Recipient Cert. of Disting. Citizenship, City of Annapolis, 1987, 97, 99, Gov.'s Citation for Outstanding Svc. to Citizens, State of Md., 1997, 99, Red Cross Citizenship award, Trailblazer award U.S. Dept. State, 1998; numerous meritorious svc. awards; Howard U. scholar. Home: 16 Bausum Dr Annapolis MD 21401-4309 E-mail: syl_jones@juno.com.

JONES, THOMAS BROOKS, lawyer, educator; b. Atmore, Ala. s. John Maxwell and Marjorie Lee (Brooks) J. BA, U. Ala., 1949, JD, 1951; LLM, Columbia U., 1958; postgrad. legal studies, U. Stockholm, 1973. Bar: Ala. 1951. Sole practice, Escambia County, Ala., 1951-52; judge, 1953-57; interim asst. prof. U. Fla. Law Sch., Gainesville, 1958-60; atty. Dept. of the Army, various cities, 1961-83; instr. Anchorage Community Coll., Chapman Coll., Anchorage, 1982—. Author: Munich, 1977; contbr. articles to profl. jours. With AUS, 1946-47. Mem. ABA, Fla. Bar Assn. Democrat. Baptist. Avocations: foreign travel, sports. Home and Office: 836 M St Apt 208 Anchorage AK 99501-3355

JONES, WILLIAM ALLEN, lawyer, entertainment company executive; b. Phila., Dec. 13, 1941; s. Roland Emmett and Gloria (Miller) J.; m. Margaret Smith, Sept. 24, 1965 (div. 1972); m. Dorothea S. Whitson, June 15, 1973; children— Darlene, Rebecca, Gloria, David. BA, Temple U., 1967; MBA, JD, Harvard U., 1972. Bar: Calif. 1974. Atty. Walt Disney Prodns., Burbank, Calif., 1973-77, treas., 1977-81; atty. Wyman Bautzer et al, L.A., 1981-83, MGM/UA Entertainment Co., Culver City, 1983, v.p., gen. counsel, 1983-86; sr. v.p., corp. gen. counsel, sec. MGM/UA Communications Co., Culver City, Calif., 1986-91; exec. v.p., gen. counsel, sec. Metro-Goldwyn-Mayer Inc., Santa Monica, Calif., 1991-95, exec. v.p. corp. affairs, 1995-97, sr. exec. v.p., 1997—. Bus. mgr. L.A. Bar Jour., 1974-75; bd. dirs. The Nostalgia Network Inc.; mem. bd. of govs. Inst. for Corp. Counsel, 1990-93. Charter mem. L.A. Philharm. Men's Com., 1974-80; trustee Marlborough Sch., 1988-93, Flintridge Preparatory Sch., 1993-96. With USAF, 1960-64. President's scholar Temple U., 1972 Mem. Harvard Bus. Sch. Assn. So. Calif. (bd. dirs. 1985-88). Home: 1557 Colina Dr Glendale CA 91208-2412 Office: Metro Goldwyn Mayer Inc 2500 Broadway Santa Monica CA 90404-3065

JONES, WILLIAM REX, law educator; b. Murphysboro, Ill., Oct. 20, 1922; s. Claude E. and Ivy P. (McCormick) J.; m. Miriam R. Lamy, Mar. 27, 1944; m. Gerri L. Haun, June 30, 1972; children: Michael Kimber, Jeanne Keats, Patricia Combs, Sally Horowitz, Kevin. BS, U. Louisville, 1950; JD, U. Ky., 1968; LLM, U. Mich., 1970. Bar: Ky. 1969, Ind. 1971, U.S. Supreme Ct. 1976. Exec. v.p. Paul Miller Ford, Inc., Lexington, Ky., 1951-64; pres. Bill's Seat Cover Ctr., Inc., Lexington, Ky., 1952-65, Bill Jones Real Estate, Inc., Lexington, Ky., 1965-70; asst. prof. law Ind. U., Indpls., 1970-73, assoc. prof., 1973-75, prof., 1975-80; dean Salmon P. Chase Coll. Law. No. Ky. U., Highland Heights, 1980-85, prof., 1980-93, prof. emeritus, 1993—. Vis. prof. Shepard Broad Law Ctr., Nova Southeastern U., Ft. Lauderdale, Fla., 1994-95; mem. Ky. Pub. Advocacy Commn., 1982-93, 97-2000, chmn., 1986-93; chmn. existing structures appeal bd. Newport, Ky., 2002-. Author: Kentucky Criminal Trial Practice, 3d edit., 2001, Kentucky Criminal Trial Practice Forms, 3d edit., 2000. 1st sgt. U.S. Army, 1940-44. Cook fellow U. Mich., 1969-70, W.G. Hart fellow Queen Mary Coll. U. London, 1985. Mem. Order of Coif. E-mail: jonesw@nku.edu., wrexjones@zoomtown.com.

JONG, JAMES C. (CHUANPING ZHANG), lawyer, educator; b. Wuhan, China; LLB, South Ctrl. U., Wuhan, 1977; LLM, Peking U., Beijing, China, 1982; JD, Columbia U., 1986. Bar: N.Y. 1992, U.S. Dist. Ct. (so. dist.) N.Y. 1993, China 1983. Dir. China Higher Edn. Assn., Beijing, 1981-88, China Civil Law Soc., Beijing, 1983-86; sec.-gen. Grad. Assn. of Peking U., Beijing, 1983-86; legal counsel Longyi Co., Ltd., Beijing, 1985-86; assoc. Menaker & Herrmann, N.Y.C., 1989-95; vis. prof. South Ctrl. U., Wuhan, 1993—; pvt. practice, N.Y.C., 1995—. Legal counsel U.S. China Trade Ctr. in Oakland City, Calif., 1997—; cons. Metro Internat.,

Stockholm, 1998—. Author: Handbook of Chinese Law, 1986; editor Jour. China Law, Columbia U., 1987-89; contbr. articles to profl. jours. Banking, Immigration, naturalization, and customs, Private international. Office: 410 Park Ave New York NY 10022 E-mail: attorney@jcjlaw.net.

JONSEN, ERIC RICHARD, lawyer; b. San Francisco, June 5, 1958; s. Richard William and Ann Margaret (Parsons) J.; m. Ida-Marie, May 8, 1982; children: Kaitlyn, Jeremy, Michelle. BA, Hartwick Coll., 1980; JD, U. Colo., 1985. Bar: Colo., N.Y., U.S. Dist. Ct. Colo., U.S. Ct. Appeals (10th cir., Fed. cir.), U.S. Ct. Appeals (fed. cir.). Assoc. William P. DeMoulin, Denver, 1986-88, Fairfield & Woods, Denver, 1988—91; ptnr. Ciancio & Jonsen PC, Denver, 1994—2001, Jonsen & Assoc. LLC, Broomfield, Colo., 2001—. Bd. dirs. Broomfield Blast Soccer Club, 2000—. Mem. ABA, Colo. Bar Assn., Rotary (pres. Broomfield Crossings 2000--). Federal civil litigation, General civil litigation, Intellectual property. Office: Jonsen & Assocs LLC 10901 W 120th Ave # 240 Broomfield CO 80021 E-mail: erjonsen@jonsen.net.

JONTZ, JEFFRY ROBERT, lawyer; b. Stuart, Iowa, May 28, 1944; s. John Leo Jontz and Leora Burnette (Pittman) Myers; m. Sharyn Sue Kopriva, June 8, 1968; 1 son, Eric Barrett. BA, Drake U., 1966; JD with distinction, U. Iowa, 1969. Bar: Iowa 1969, Fla. 1971, Ohio 1972, U.S. Dist. Ct. (mid. dist.) Fla. 1971, U.S. Ct. Appeals (5th cir.) 1971, fla. 1972, U.S. Ct. Appeals (11th cir.) 1981, U.S. Tax Ct. 1983. Law clk. to Hon. Charles R. Scott U.S. Dist. Ct. (mid. dist.) Fla., Jacksonville, 1969-70; to Hon. Bryan Simpson U.S. Ct. Appeals (5th cir.), Jacksonville, 1970-71; assoc. Jones, Day, Cockley & Reavis, Cleve., 1971-72; asst. U.S. atty. U.S. Dist. Ct. (mid. dist.) Fla., Orlando, 1972-74; pvt. practice Orlando, 1974—; ptnr. Young, Turnbull & Linscott, Orlando, 1974-79, Baker & Hostetler, Orlando, 1979, DeWolf, ward & Morris, Orlando, 1979-84, Jontz, russell & Hull, Orlando, 1985-86, Holland & Knight, 1986-96, Carlton Fields, Orlando, 1996—. Contbr. articles to profl. jours.; mem. editl. bd. Iowa Law Rev., 1968. Chmn. Fed. Judicial Rels. Com., 2001—; Past bd. dirs. The Door Drug Rehab. Ctr. of Ctrl. Fla.; bd. dirs. Fla. Symphony Orch., 1985—93, Jr. Achievement Ctrl. Fla., 1997—; mem. Rollins Coll. Tar Boosters; mem. code enforcement bd. City of Maitland, Fla., 1990—92; chmn bd. adjustment City of Winter Park, Fla., 1995—; mem. parents com. Dartmouth Coll., 1995—99; mem. long range planning com. , former county committeeman Orange County (Fla.) Reps.; past chmn. bd. trustees First Congregational Ch., Winter Park, Fla. Recipient Outstanding Individual Cmty. Leadership award Vol. Ctr. Ctrl. Fla., 1991. Mem. Am. Bankruptcy Inst., Ctrl. Fla. Bankruptcy Lawyers Assn., Fla. Bar (9th cir. grievance com. 1979-82, chmn. comml. litigation com. 1981-82, bankruptcy and creditor's rights com. corp. bus. and banking law sect., com. on jud. adminstrn., selection and tenure 1985-86, mem. jud. nominating procedures com. 1995-96, lectr. seminars), Orange County Bar Assn. (chmn. jud. rels. com. 1995—, bankruptcy com.), ABA (mem. comml. transactions litigation com., others), Drake U. Nat. Alumni Assn. (past chmn. ctrl. Fla. chpt., sec., bd. dirs. 1981-93, pres.'s circle coun.), Iowa State Bar Assn., Order of Coif, Winter Park Racquet Club (mem. bd. govs., sec., v.p., pres. 1989-94, 96-98), Tiger Bay Club Orlando, Citrus Club, Omicron Delta Kappa, Tau Kappa Epsilon, Phi Delta Phi. Banking, Bankruptcy, General civil litigation. Office: 450 S Orange Ave Ste 500 Orlando FL 32801-3370 E-mail: jjontz@carltonfields.com., jontz@worldnet.att.net.

JOPLIN, JULIAN MIKE, lawyer; b. Littlefield, Tex., Aug. 30, 1936; s. Charles Arbie and Gladys (Douglass) J.; m. Barbara Maye McKinney, Sept. 1, 1957; children: Erin Colleen, Jeffrey Miles. BBA in Fin., Tex. Tech U., 1958; JD, U. Tex., 1963. Bar: Tex. 1963. Ptnr. Strasburger & Price, Dallas, 1963—. Bd. dirs. Notre Dame Spl. Sch., 1986-91, Presbyn. Hosp., Dallas, 1988-93, Ctrl. Dallas Assn., 1989-98, Children's Hosp., Dallas, 1998-2001; ruling elder Highland Pk. Presbyn. Ch., Dallas, 1982-2000. Capt. U.S. Army and Tex. N.G., 1958-63. Mem.: U. Tex. Law Sch. Alumni Assn. (bd. dirs. 1987—90, mem. exec. com. 1998—2001), Dallas Bar Found. (bd. dirs., chmn. 1997—98), Dallas Bar Assn. (bd. dirs., pres. 1988), State Bar Tex. (bd. dirs. 1989—92), Riverhill Country Club, Salesmanship Club. Republican. Avocation: racquet sports. Corporate, general. Home: 1542 Saddle Club Dr Kerrville TX 78028 Office: Strasburger & Price 901 Main St 4300 Bank of Am Plz Dallas TX 75202 E-mail: mjoplin@ktc.com.

JORDAN, ALEXANDER JOSEPH, JR., lawyer; b. New London, Conn., Oct. 11, 1938; s. Alexander Joseph and Alice Elizabeth (Mugovero) J.; m. Mary Carolyn Miller, Aug. 8, 1964; children: Jennifer, Michael, Stephanie. BS, U.S. Naval Acad., 1960; LLB, Harvard U., 1968. Ptnr. Gaston & Snow, Boston, 1968-91, Bingham, Dana & Gould, Boston, 1991-93, Nixon Peabody LLP, Boston, 1994—. Mem., past chmn. adv. com. Town of Hingham, Mass., 1989-95, mem. govt. study com., 2000-2001. With USN, 1960-65, capt. USNR, 1965-94, ret. Mem. ABA, Mass. Bar Assn., Boston Bar Assn., U.S. Naval Inst., Naval Res. Assn., Harvard Alumni Assn. (regional dir. 1998-2001), U.S. Naval Acad. Alumni Assn., Harvard Club Hingham (trustee, chmn. com. schs. and scholarships, past pres.), Harvard Club of Boston. Corporate, general, Finance, Securities. Office: Nixon Peabody LLP 101 Federal St Fl 13 Boston MA 02110-1832

JORDAN, CHARLES MILTON, lawyer; b. Houston, Apr. 3, 1949; m. Jeanette Jordan; children: Nicole, John, Rebecca. BBA, U. Tex., 1971, JD, 1975, BBA, 1971, JD, 1975. Bar: Tex. 75, U.S. Dist. Ct. (so. dist.) Tex. 76, U.S. Supreme Ct. 78, U.S. Ct. Appeals (5th cir.) 79, U.S. Dist. Ct. (no. dist.) Tex. 82, U.S. Dist. Ct. (we. and ea. dists.) Tex. 83. Assoc. Troutman, Earle & Hill, Austin, 1975-76, Simpson & Burwell, Texas City, 1976-78, Smith & Herz, Galveston, Tex., 1978-80; ptnr. Dibrell & Greer, Galveston, 1980-85, Barlow, Todd, Crews & Jordan PC, Houston, 1986-88, Barlow, Todd, Jordan & Oliver, LLP, Houston, 1988-99, Barlow, Todd, Jordan & Jones, LLP, Houston, 1999—2002, Daughtry , Scott & Jordan, P.C., Houston, 2003—. Commr. Commn. Texas City/Galveston Ports, 1984. 1st lt. USAF, 1971-77. Recipient Outstanding Young Man Am. award, U.S. Jaycees, 1980. Mem. Tex. Bar Assn., Galveston County Bar Assn. (pres. 1981-82, bd. dirs. 1985-88), Tex. Young Lawyers Assn (bd. dirs. 1982-85, Outstanding Dir. award 1983-84), Galveston County Young Lawyers Assn. (pres. 1979-80, Outstanding Young Lawyer award 1981). Federal civil litigation, State civil litigation. Office: Daughtry Scott & Jordan PC LLP 17044 El Camino Real Ste 400 Houston TX 77058-2768 E-mail: cmjordan@daughtryscott.com.

JORDAN, DAVID FRANCIS, JR., retired judge; b. Apr. 18, 1928; s. David Francis Jordan and Frances Marion (J.) Edebohls; m. Bess Vukas, Aug. 4, 1956; children: Melissa Marie, David Francis III, Dennis Paul. AB, Princeton U., 1950; JD, NYU, 1953, LLM in Taxation, 1970. Law clk. U.S. Ct. Appeals (2d cir.), 1957-58, chief dep., clk., 1958-59; pvt. practice Smithtown, N.Y., 1959-63; ptnr. O'Rourke & Jordan, Central Islip, N.Y., 1963-67; asst. dist. atty. Suffolk County, Riverhead, N.Y., 1969-74; law clk. Supreme Ct., Suffolk County, 1975; investigator N.Y. Supreme Ct. Appellate Divsn. 2d dept., Bklyn., 1976; corp. counsel City of Newburgh, N.Y., 1976-78; acting city mgr., 1978; U.S. magistrate judge Ea. Dist. N.Y., Bklyn., Uniondale, and, Hauppage, N.Y., 1978-94, So. Dist. Calif., San Diego, 1994, So. Dist. Ohio, 1996; mil. judge U.S. Army Judiciary, Washington, 1969-80; legis. analyst Cen. and Ea. European Law Initiative; ret., 1994. With JAGC, U.S. Army, 1954-57; col. USAR. Decorated Meritorious Svc. medal. Mem. ABA (vice chair sr. lawyers divsn. jud. com. 1994-97). Home: 15732 Vista Vicente Dr Ramona CA 92065-4323

JORDAN, EDDIE J. lawyer, former prosecutor; b. Ft. Campbell, Ky., Oct. 6, 1952; BA with honors, Wesleyan U., 1974; JD, Rutgers U., 1977. Bar: Pa. 1977, La. 1982. Law clk. for Hon. Clifford Scott Green U.S. Dist. Ct. (ea. dist.) Pa., Phila.; assoc. Pepper, Hamilton & Scheetz, Phila.; asst. prof. law So. U., Baton Rouge, 1981-83; asst. U.S. atty. U.S. Dept. Justice, New Orleans, 1984-87; assoc. Sessions & Fishman, New Orleans, 1987-91, ptnr., 1991-92; of counsel Bryan Jupiter, New Orleans, 1992-94; U.S. atty. for ea. dist. La. U.S. Dept. Justice, New Orleans, 1994—2001; lawyer Rodney, Bordenave, Boykin & Ehret, New Orleans, 2001; dist. atty. Office Dist. Atty., New Orleans, 2002—. Mem. adv. com. on humam rels. City of New Orleans, 1993; mem. various bds. of dirs. Recipient A.P. Tureaud award Louis A. Martinet Legal Soc., 1992. Office: Office Dist Atty 619 S White St New Orleans LA 70119-7348*

JORDAN, GREGORY B. lawyer; b. Wheeling, W.Va. s. Nicholas M. and Roberta Jordan; m. Ellen Jordan; 2 children. BA magna cum laude, Bethany Coll., 1981; JD cum laude, U. Pitts., 1984. Bar: Pa., W.Va. With Reed Smith, Pitts., 1984—2000, dir. legal pers., dir. practice devel., mng. ptnr., chmn. sr. mgmt. team, 2000—. Mem.: U. Pitts. Law Rev.; contbr. articles to profl. jours. Trustee Bethany Coll. Mem.: Order of Coif, Duquesnes Club (mem. governing com.). Office: Reed Smith 435 6th Ave Pittsburgh PA 15219 Office Fax: 412-288-3063.*

JORDAN, HILARY PETER, lawyer; b. Mineola, N.Y., July 30, 1952; s. Thomas Francis and Clorinda G. (Beltramo) J.; m. Judith Lynn Spencer, Sept. 7, 1984. BA, U. Ariz., 1974; JD, Harvard U., 1977. Bar: Ga. 1977, U.S. Dist. Ct. (no. dist.) Ga. 1977, U.S. Ct. Appeals (5th cir.) 1978. Assoc. Kilpatrick Stockton LLP, Atlanta, 1977-84, ptnr., 1984—. Banking, Commercial, consumer (including collections, credit), Finance. Office: Kilpatrick Stockton LLP 1100 Peachtree St NE Ste 2800 Atlanta GA 30309-4530

JORDAN, JAMES D(EE), lawyer; b. Chattanooga, Oct. 23, 1956; s. Francis L. and Helen Virginia (Slaughter) J.; m. Paula Walker, Nov. 17, 1984. BA, U. Tenn., Chattanooga, 1978; JD, Vanderbilt U., 1981. Bar: Tenn. 1981, U.S. Dist. Ct. (ea. and mid. dists.) Tenn. 1983, U.S. Supreme Ct. 1986. Assoc. Chambliss, Bahner et al, Chattanooga, 1981-83; ptnr. Guenther, Jordan & Price, Nashville, 1983—. Mem. Nashville Estate Planning Council, Cumberland Presbyn. Ch. Mem. Tenn. Bar Assn., Nashville Bar Assn., Order of Coif. Avocations: tennis, woodworking. Probate (including wills, trusts), Property, real (including real estate development, water), Estate taxation. Home: 1892 Old Highway 431 S Greenbrier TN 37073-5172 Office: 1150 Vanderbilt Pla 2100 W End Ave Nashville TN 37203-5200

JORDAN, LILLIAN B. judge; b. Asheboro, N.C., May 19, 1939; d. Obert Charles and Lilly Irene Burrow; m. Thomas Andrew Jordan, Apr. 24, 1999; m. Thomas Lorenzo O'Briant, Sept. 5, 1959 (dec. May 31, 1995); children: Thomas Lorenzo O'Briant, Jr., Patrick Marvin O'Briant, Michael Heilig O'Briant, John Curt O'Briant. BA, Guilford Coll., Greensboro, N.C., 1961; JD, Wake Forest U., Winston Salem, 1979. Bar: N.C. 1979, U.S. Dist. Ct. (mid. dist.) N.C. 1979, U.S. Supreme Ct. 2001, cert.: (specialist in family law) 1995, Adminstrv. Office of the Courts, NC (juvenile ct. judge) 1998, (family law mediator) 2003. Ptnr. O'Briant, O'Briant, Bunch and Robins, Asheboro, NC, 1979—97; dist. ct. judge State of N.C., Asheboro, Troy, Carthage, NC, 1997—2002, emergency dist. ct. judge, 2002—. Bd. of trustees IOLTA N.C. State Bar, Raleigh, 1985—92, bd. of law examiners, 1992—97, bd. of law examiners, emeritus mem. Pres. Guilford Coll. Nat. Alumni Assn., Greensboro, NC, 1982—83; mem., bd. of dirs. Merce Clinic, Asheboro, NC, 2000—; mem., bd. dirs. Randolph County Day Reporting Ctr., Asheboro, NC, 1999—; mem., bd. of dirs. United Way of Randolph County, Asheboro, NC, 1981—93, Asheboro/Randolph C. of C., Asheboro, NC, 1986—89, Women's Aid, Inc., Asheboro, NC, 1980—83; chairperson Randolph County Coun. on the Status of Women, Asheboro, NC, 1975—76; mem. N.C. Cts. Commn., Raleigh, NC, 1987—91, Revenue Laws Study Commn. of the N.C. Legis., Raleigh, NC, 1991—95; mem., bd. of dirs. Randolph Hosp. Cmty. Health Found., Asheboro, NC, 1996—2002; del. Dem. Nat. Conv., N.Y.C., 1980—80. Recipient Athena award, Asheboro/Randolph C. of C., 1994, Paul Harris fellow, Asheboro Rotary Club, 1997, Alumni Excellence award, Guilford Coll., 1998. Mem.: N.C. Ctr. for Justice and Cmty. Devel. (mem. of directors 1997—), 19B Jud. Bar Assn. (former pres.), Randolph Bar Assn. (former pres.), N.C. Bar Assn. (bd. of governors 1985—88), N.C. Assn. of Women Attys. (pres. 1995—96), N.C. State Bar (licentiate). Democrat-Npl. Episcopal. Avocations: travel, reading, gardening. Home: 645 Holly Grove Dr Randleman NC 27317 Personal E-mail: lilliob@yahoo.com.

JORDAN, MICHAEL S. arbitrator, mediator; b. Chgo., Apr. 7, 1942; s. Benjamin and Sally Jordan; m. Maureen Lynn Pearlman, Dec. 29, 1968; children: Eliza, Jeff. BS in Psychology, U. Wis., 1963; JD, DePaul U., 1966. Bar: Ill. 1966, cert.: Nat. Jud. Coll. (mediator). Asst. corp. counsel City of Chgo. Law Dept., 1966—74; judge Cir. Ct. Cook County, Ill., 1974—99; arbitrator, mediator Mediation & Arbitration Svc., Chgo., 1999—. Mediator, arbitrator ADR Sys. Am., Chgo., 1999—, Resolute Sys., Milw., 2000—, Great Neck, NY, 2000—; arbitrator U.S. Postal Svcs., 2000—, Nat. Mediation Bd., Chgo., 2002—, Washington, 2002—. Editor, author: newsletter Ill. State Bar Assn., 1975—2002, editor-in-chief: Ill. Bar Jour., 1988—90. Named Judge of the Month, N.W. Suburban Bar Assn., 1984; recipient Svc. award, N. Suburban Bar Assn., 1992. Mem.: Nat. Assn. R.R. Referees, Ill. State Bar Assn. (editor-in-chief 1988—90, chair bench bar sect. coun. 2002—, Bd. Govs. award). Office: Mediation and Arbitration Svcs 3817 Brett Ln Glenview IL 60025-1201

JORDAN, ROBERT ELIJAH, III, lawyer; b. South Boston, Va., June 20, 1936; s. Robert Elijah and Lucy (Webb) J.; children: Janet Elizabeth, Jennifer Anne, Robert Elijah IV. SB, MIT, 1958; JD magna cum laude, Harvard U., 1961. Bar: D.C. 1962, Va. 1964. Spl. asst. civil rights Office Sec. Def., Washington, 1963-64; asst. U.S. atty. for D.C., 1964-65; exec. asst. for enforcement Office Sec. Treasury, 1965-67; dep. gen. counsel Dept. Army, 1967, acting gen. counsel, 1967-68; gen. counsel of Army, spl. asst. for civil functions to Sec. Army, 1968-71; ptnr. Steptoe & Johnson, Washington, 1971—2003, mng. ptnr., 1988-90. Mem. Jud. Conf., D.C. Cir., 1973, 86—; mem. bd. cert. U.S. Cir. Cts. of Appeals Cir. Execs., 1987-88; pres. Langley Sch., 1981-82; mem. civil pro bono com. U.S. Dist. Ct., 1991-92. Contbr. articles to profl. jours. Mem. bd. dirs. Washington Humane Soc., 2000-03. Served to 1st lt. AUS, 1961-63. Recipient Karl Taylor Compton award, 1958, Arthur S. Flemming award, 1970, award for exceptional civilian svc. Dept. Army, 1971; Sloan Found. scholar; Edward J. Noble Found. fellow. Mem. Va. State Bar, D.C. Bar (chmn. ethics com. 1978-83, spl. com. on model rules profl conduct 1983-89, pres. 1987-88), Calif. State Bar, D.C. Bar Found. (pres. 1993-94, 97-98), Atlantic Coun. (bd. dirs. 1993—, exec. com. 1994—2001, chmn. nominating com. 1997-2001), Tau Beta Pi, Tau Kappa Alpha. Democrat. Antitrust, Federal civil litigation, Oil, gas, and mineral. Home: 5239 Siesta Cove Dr Sarasota FL 34242 Office: 1330 Connecticut Ave NW Washington DC 20036-1795 E-mail: rjordan@steptoe.com.

JORDAN, ROBERT LEON, lawyer, educator; b. Reading, Pa., Feb. 27, 1928; s. Anthony and Carmela (Votto) J.; m. Evelyn Allen Willard, Feb. 15, 1958 (dec. Nov. 1996); children: John Willard, David Anthony BA, Pa. State U., 1948; LLB, Harvard U., 1951. Bar: N.Y. 1952. Assoc. White & Case, N.Y.C., 1953-59; prof. law UCLA, 1959-70, 75-91, prof. law emeritus, 1991—, assoc. dean Sch. Law, 1968-69. Vis. prof. law Cornell U., Ithaca, N.Y., 1962-63; co-reporter Uniform Consumer Credit Code, 1964-70, Uniform Comml. Code Articles 3, 4, 4A, 1985-90; Fulbright lectr. U. Pisa, Italy, 1967-68 Co-author: (with W.D. Warren) Commercial Law, 1983, 5th edit., 2000, Bankruptcy, 1985, 5th edit., 1999. Lt. USAF, 1951-53. Office: UCLA Sch Law 405 Hilgard Ave Los Angeles CA 90095-9000

JORDAN, ROBERT LEON, judge; b. Woodlawn, Tenn., June 28, 1934; s. James Richard and Josephine (Broadbent) J.; m. Dorothy Rueter, Sept. 8, 1956; children: Robert, Margaret, Daniel. BS in Fin., U. Tenn., 1958, JD, 1960. Atty. Goodpasture, Carpenter, Dale & Woods, Nashville, 1960-61; mgr. Frontier Refining Co., Denver, 1961-64; atty. Green and Green, Johnson City, Tenn., 1964-66; trust officer 1st Peoples Bank, Johnson City, 1966-69; v.p., trust officer Comml. Nat. Bank, Pensacola, Fla., 1969-71; atty. Bryant, Price, Brandt & Jordan, Johnson City, 1971-80; chancellor 1st Jud. Dist., Johnson City, 1980-88; dist. judge U.S. Dist. Ct. (ea. dist.) Tenn., Knoxville, 1988—2001, sr. dist. judge, 2001—. Mem. adv. com. U. Tenn. Law Alumni, 1978-80; sec. Tenn. Jud. Conf., 1987-88, mem. exec. com., 1988; del. Tenn. State-Fed. Judicial Coun., 1993—. Bd. dirs., v.p. Tri-Cities estate Planning Coun., Johnson City, 1969; bd. dirs. Washington County Tb Assn., Rocky Mount Hist. Assn., High Rock Camp, Johnson City, Jr. Achievement of Pensacola Inc.; bd. dirs., treas. N.W. Fla. Crippled Children's Assn., Pensacola; chancellor's assoc. U. Tenn. With U.S. Army, 1954-56. Named Boss of Yr. Legal Secs. Assn., Washington, Carter County, Tenn., 1982. Mem. Tenn. Bar Assn., Tenn. Bar Found., Knoxville Bar Assn. (bd. govs. 1999), Washington County Bar Assn. (pres.-elect 1980), Johnson City C. of C., Hamilton Burnett Am. Inn of Ct. (pres. 1993-94), Kiwanis (pres. Met. Johnson City Club 1969, Kiwanian of Yr. award 1986-87). Republican. Mem. Ch. of Christ. Office: Howard H Baker US Courthouse 800 Market St Ste 141 Knoxville TN 37902-2303

JORDAN, VERNON EULION, JR., lawyer, former association official; b. Atlanta, Aug. 15, 1935; s. Vernon Eulion and Mary (Griggs) J.; m. Shirley M. Yarbrough, Dec. 13, 1958 (dec. Dec. 29, 1985); 1 child, Vickee; m. Ann Dibble Cook, Nov. 22, 1986. BA, DePauw U., 1957; JD, Howard U., 1960; hon. degrees, DePauw U., Howard U., Boston Coll., Brandeis U., CUNY, U. Ill. Chgo. Duke U., U. Mass., NYU, Princeton U., Tulane U., Rutgers U., Tuskegee Inst., Yale U., Notre Dame U., Harvard U., plus 50 other instns. higher edn. Bar: Ga. 1960, Ark. 1964. Practice law, Atlanta, 1960-61, Pine Bluff, Ark., 1964-65; Ga. field dir. NAACP, 1961-63; dir. Voter Edn. Project So. Regional Council, 1964-68; atty. OEO, Atlanta, 1969; exec. dir. United Negro Coll. Fund, N.Y.C., 1970-71; pres. Nat. Urban League, 1972-81; sr. ptnr. firm Akin, Gump, Strauss, Hauer & Feld, LLP, Washington, of counsel, 2000—; sr. mng. dir. Lazard Freres & Co., LLC, N.Y.C., 2000—. Bd. dirs. Am. Express Co., Am. Online Latin Am., Asbury Automotive Group, Dow Jones & Co., J.C. Penney Co., Inc., Xerox Corp., Revlon, Inc., Sara Lee Corp; frequent guest on maj. nat. TV programs including Meet The Press, Face the Nation; chmn. Clinton Presdl. Transition Bd.; apptd. to Pres.'s adv. com. Points of Light Initiative Found., 1989. Mem. Nat. Adv. Commn. on Selective Svcs., 1966-67, Am. Revolution Bi-Centennial Commn., 1972—, Presdl. Clemency Bd., 1974; adv. coun. Social Security, 1974; trustee Ford Found., LBJ Found., Urban Inst. (life), Howard U.; mem. steering com. Bilderberg Meetings; mem. Coun. on Fgn. Rels.; adv. trustee DePauw U., bd. dirs. NAACP Legal Def. and Ednl. Fund; hon. mem. Ralph Bunche Inst. on the UN. Fellow 2Met. Applied Research Center, 1968; Fellow Harvard Inst. Politics, 1969; recipient Alexis de Tocqueville award United Way Am., 1977. Mem. ABA, D.C. Bar Assn., Nat. Bar Assn., Nat. Conf. Black Lawyers, Am. Law Inst., University Club, Board Room, Council on Fgn. Relations, Century Assn.. Mem. A.M.E. Ch. Office: Lazard Freres & Co LLC 30 Rockefeller Plz New York NY 10112-0002

JORDAN-HOLMES, CLARK, lawyer; b. Pitts., Sept. 1, 1946; s. Richard K. and Olive J. (Letchworth) Holmes; m. Sarah Jordan-Holmes, Apr. 8, 1981; children: Micah Jordan-Holmes, Todd R. Holmes, Tara L. Holmes. BA, U. Fla., 1968, JD, 1973. Bar: Fla. 1974. Mem. staff Ctr. for Govt. Responsibility U. Fla., Gainsville, 1972-73; law clk. Fla. Ct. Appeals (2d dist.), Lakeland, 1973-74; ptnr. Shackleford, Farrior, Stallings & Evans, P.A., Tampa, Fla., 1974-85; mng. ptnr. Tampa office Lyle & Skipper, P.A., 1985-91; mng. ptnr. Stewart, Joyner & Jordan-Holmes, PA, Tampa, 1991—. Gen. coun. HART Transit Authority, Tampa, 1992—; chmn. bd. Tampa Bay chpt. The Nat. Conf., 1995-96. Editor-in-chief The Verdict, U. Fla., 1972-73. Chmn. bd. Tampa Habitat for Humanity, 1990; chmn. Interfaith Prayer Brunch, 1989; J-5 Project com. Transp. Rsch. Bd., Leadership Fla. Alumni; gen. counsel Fla. Edn. Fund.; bd. dirs. Tampa Met. Ministries, 2002—, Bahai Local Spiritual Assembly, 2002—. Capt. U.S. Army, 1968-71, Vietnam. Decorated Bronze Star with oak leaf cluster. Mem. ABA, Nat. Bar Assn., Fla. Bar (rules of civil procedure com.), NCCJ (Brotherhood/Sisterhood award 1991). Avocation: community activism. General civil litigation, Commercial, consumer (including collections, credit), Government contracts and claims. Office: PO Box 172297 1112 E Kennedy Blvd Tampa FL 33602-0297

JORDEN, DOUGLAS ALLEN, lawyer, zoning hearing officer; b. Ft. Smith, Ark., July 17, 1950; s. James Roy and Gordon P. J.; m. Mary Zoe Arendt, Apr. 23, 1983; children: Michael, Willie, Julia. BA, U. Ark., 1972, JD, 1976. Bar: Ark. 1976, Ariz. 1976, U.S. Dist. Ct. Ariz. 1976, U.S. Ct. Appeals (9th cir.) 1977, Calif. 1992, Colo. 1992, U.S. Supreme Ct. 1996. Assoc. Harold Mott Esq., Phoenix, 1976-78; town atty. Town of Paradise Valley, Ariz., 1978-82; assoc. Fennemore Craig, Phoenix, 1982-84; ptnr. Slavin, Kane & Paterson, Phoenix, 1984-88, Lancy, Scult, McVey, Phoenix, 1988-90, Jorden Law Firm, Phoenix, 1990-92, Kane, Jorden, von Oppenfeld, Phoenix, 1992-98, Jorden, Bischoff, McGuire & Rose, PLC, Phoenix, 1998—. Co-author: Arizona Land Use Law, 1988, 3d rev. edit. 1998. Mem. Paradise Valley Village Planning Com. 1988-90; chmn. Phoenix Environ. Quality Commn., 1988-95. Mem. State Bar Ariz. (continuing legal edn. com. 1990-94), Rocky Mt. Land Use Inst. (regional adv. bd. 1992—). Democrat. Methodist. Avocation: hiking. Environmental, Land use and zoning (including planning), Property, real (including real estate development, water). Office: Jorden Bischoff McGuire & Rose PLC Ste 205 7272 E Indian Sch Rd Scottsdale AZ 85251-6268 E-mail: djorden@jordenbischoff.com.

JORGENSEN, NORMAN ERIC, lawyer; b. Oakland, Calif., July 13, 1938; s. Peter Wesley and Janet Marie Jorgensen; m. Concetta Finocchio, Aug. 3, 1963 (div.); children: Eric Vincent, Joseph Peter, Catherine Ann Jorgensen Martinsen, Lara Lynn; m. Connie Engelking, Feb. 4, 1979. BS in Physics, MIT, 1960; postgrad., Princeton U., 1960-61, U. Calif., Berkeley, 1961-65, JD, 1968. Bar: Calif. 1969, U.S. Dist. Ct. (no. dist.) Calif. 1969, U.S. Ct. Appeals (9th cir.) 1969, Oreg. 1973, U.S. Ct. Claims 1973, U.S.Dist. Ct. (ctrl. dist.) Calif. 1974, U.S. Dist. Ct. Oreg. 1976, U.S. Supreme Ct. 1976, U.S. Ct. Appeals (fed. cir.) 1982, U.S. Patent and Trademark Office 1993. Pvt. practice, Oakland, 1969-71; ptnr. Grose Rose & Jorgensen, Oakland, 1971-73; assoc. gen. counsel Tektronix Inc., Beaverton, Oreg., 1973-90; group counsel Intel Corp., Santa Clara, Calif., 1990-91; pvt. practice, San Jose, Calif., 1991—. Mem. Calif. State Bar, Oreg. State Bar, Santa Clara County Bar Assn. Corporate, general, Intellectual property, Patent. Office: 3465 Sierra Rd Ste 1000 San Jose CA 95132-3000 E-mail: ericjorgensen@alum.mit.edu.

JORGENSEN, RALPH GUBLER, lawyer, accountant; b. N.Y.C., Mar. 12, 1937; s. Thorvald W. and Florence (Gubler) J.; m. Patricia June Spivey, June 21, 1971 (dec. Oct. 1997); 1 child, Misty. AB, George Washington U., 1960, LLB, 1962. Bar: D.C. 1963, Md. 1963, N.C. 1972, U.S. Dist. Ct. D.C. 1963, U.S. Ct. Appeals (D.C. cir.) 1963, U.S. Dist. Ct. Md. 1964, U.S. Dist. Ct. (ea. dist.) N.C. 1972, U.S. Dist. Ct. (mid. dist.) N.C. 1977, U.S. Ct. Appeals (4th cir.) 1974, U.S. Tax Ct. 1976, U.S. Ct. Claims 1979, U.S. Supreme Ct. 1971; CPA, Md., Nev., N.C. Sole practice, Washington, Silver Spring, Md., 1963-71, Tabor City, NC, 1971—. Bd. dirs. Columbus County ARC, N.C., 1974. Mem. ABA, ATLA, Am. Assn. Atty.-CPAs, N.C. Bar Assn., N.C. Acad. Trial Lawyers, Alpha Kappa Psi. Democrat. Baptist. Federal civil litigation, State civil litigation, Taxation, general. Home: 101 Pireway Rd Tabor City NC 28463-2021 Office: 116 W 4th St PO Box 248 Tabor City NC 28463-0248 E-mail: R.G.Jorgensen@weblink.net.

JOSCELYN, KENT B(UCKLEY), lawyer; b. Binghamton, N.Y., Dec. 18, 1936; s. Raymond Miles and Gwen Buckley (Smith) J.; children: Kathryn Anne, Jennifer Sheldon. BS, Union Coll., 1957; JD, Albany (N.Y.) Law Sch., 1960. Bar: N.Y. 1961, U.S. Ct. Mil. Appeals 1962, D.C., 1967, Mich. 1979. Atty. adviser hdqts. USAF, Washington, 1965-67; assoc. prof. forensic studies U. Ind., Bloomington, 1967-76; dir. Inst. Rsch. in Pub. Safety, 1970-75; head policy analysis divsn. Highway Safety Rsch. Inst. U. Mich., Ann Arbor, 1976-81; dir. transp. planning and policy Urban Tech. Environ. Planning Program, Ann Arbor, 1981-84; prin. Joscelyn and Treat P.C., Ann Arbor, 1981—93, Joscelyn, McNair & Jeffrey P.C., Ann Arbor, 1993-2001. Cons. Law Enforcement Assistance Adminstrn., U.S. Dept. Justice, 1969-72; Gov.'s appointee as regional dir. Ind. Criminal Justice Planning Agy., 1969-72; vice chmn. Ind. Organized Crime Prevention Coun., 1969-72; commr. pub. safety City of Bloomington, Ind., 1974-76. Editor Internat. Jour. Criminal Justice. Capt. USAF, 1961-64. Mem. NAS, ABA, NRC, D.C. Bar Assn., N.Y. State Bar Assn., Internat. Bar Assn., Transp. Rsch. Bd. (chmn. motor vehicle and traffic law com. 1979-82), Am. Soc. Criminology (life), Assn. for Advancement Automotive Medicine (life), Soc. Automotive Engrs., Acad. Criminal Justice Scis. (life), Assn. Chiefs Police (assoc.), Nat. Safety Coun., Assn. Former Intelligence Officers (life), Product Liability Adv. Coun., Sigma Xi, Theta Delta Chi. General civil litigation, Estate planning, Product liability. Office: Kent B Joscelyn PC PO Box 130589 Ann Arbor MI 48113-0589 E-mail: kbjpc@earthlink.com.

JOSEPH, ANTHONY AARON, lawyer; b. Birmingham, Ala., Oct. 8, 1953; s. David Joseph and Lucille (Townsend) Tarver; m. Cassandra Andry, July 2, 1994; children: Kevin, Justin Gray, Aaron. BS, Vanderbilt U., 1975; MCP, Howard U., 1977; JD, Cumberland Sch. Law, 1980. Bar: U.S. Dist. Ct. (mid., no. dists.) Ala., U.S. Ct. Appeals (11th cir.). Asst. dist. atty. Dist. Atty.'s Office, Bessemer, Ala., 1980—82; spl. agt. FBI, Birmingham, 1982—86; asst. U.S. atty. U.S. Atty.'s Office, Birmingham, 1986—90; ptnr. Johnston Barton Proctor & Powell, Birmingham, 1991—. Adj. prof. Miles Coll., Birmingham, 1990—94, Cumberland Law Sch., Birmingham, 1993—. Bd. dirs. ARC, Birmingham, 2001, YMCA, Birmingham, 2002—; mem. steering com. Leadership Birmingham, 2002. Mem.: ABA (mem. criminal justice coun. 2001—), Birmingham Bar Assn. (treas. 2002—), Ala. State Bar (bar commr. 2001—). Criminal. Office: Johnston Barton Proctor and Powell LLP 1901 6th Ave N Ste 2900 Birmingham AL 35203 Office Fax: 205-458-9500. Business E-Mail: aaj@jbpp.com.

JOSEPH, DANIEL MORDECAI, lawyer; b. Paterson, N.J., Aug. 20, 1941; m. Susan Fields, July 30, 1972; 1 child, Nicholas. AB, Columbia U., 1963; LLB, Harvard U., 1966. Bar: N.J. 1967, U.S. Supreme Ct. 1970, D.C. 1974. Law clk. to judge U.S. Ct. Appeals (5th cir.), Dallas, 1966-67; atty. civil div. U.S. Dept. Justice, Washington, 1967-71; asst. gen. counsel EPA, Washington, 1971-72; spl. asst. environ. affairs gen. counsel U.S. Dept. Transp., Washington, 1972-74; ptnr. Akin, Gump, Strauss, Hauer & Feld, Washington, 1974—. Mem. D.C. Bar (rules of conduct rev. com. 1991-2000, chmn. 1996-99, spl. com. on multidisciplinary practice 1999—, legal ethics com. 2000—). Federal civil litigation, Environmental. Office: Akin Gump Strauss Hauer & Feld Ste 400 1333 New Hampshire Ave NW Washington DC 20036-1564

JOSEPH, GREGORY PAUL, lawyer; b. Mpls., Jan. 18, 1951; s. George Phillip and Josephine Sheha (Nofel) J.; m. Barbara, Jan. 19, 1979. BA summa cum laude, U. Minn., 1972, JD cum laude, 1975. Bar: Minn. 1975, N.Y. 1979, U.S. Dist. Ct. Minn. 1975, U.S. Dist. Ct. (so. and ea. dist.) N.Y. 1979, U.S. Ct. Appeals (8th cir.) 1976, U.S. Ct. Appeals (2d cir.) 1979, U.S. Ct. Appeals (D.C. cir.) 1980, U.S. Supreme Ct. 1983, U.S. Tax Ct. 1987, U.S. Ct. Appeals (7th cir.) 1989, (5th cir.) 1992, (6th cir.) 1999, (11th cir.) 2002. Pvt. practice, Mpls., 1975-79; assoc. Fried, Frank, Harris, Shriver & Jacobson, N.Y.C., 1979-82, ptnr., 1982-01, chair litigation dept., 2000-01; chmn. Gregory P. Joseph Law Offices, LLC, N.Y.C., 2001—. Asst. U.S. spl. prosecutor N.Y.C., 1981—82, Washington, 1981—82; mem. adv. com. on fed. rules of evidence U.S. Judicial Conf, 1993—99; co-chair 3d Circuit Task Force on Selection of Class Counsel, 2001; chair com. of lawyers to enhance the jury process N.Y. State Cts., 1998—99, mem. adv. com. on civil practice, 1999—2002. Author: Modern Visual Evidence, 1984, Sanctions: The Federal Law of Litigation Abuse, 1989, 3rd edit., 2000, Civil RICO: A Definitive Guide, 1992, 2nd edit., 2000; co-author: Evidence in America, 1987; editor: Emerging Problems Under the Federal Rules of Evidence, 1983, reporter 2d edit., 1991; co-editor: Sanctions: Rule 11 and Other Powers, 1986, 2d rev. edit., 1988; editorial bd. Moore's Fed. Practice, 1995—; contbr. articles to profl. jours. Fellow Am. Bar Found., Am. Coll. Trial Lawyers (chmn. fed. rules of civil procedure com. 2000-02, regent 2002—); mem. ABA (chmn. litig. sect. 1997-98), Am. Law Inst., N.Y. Bar Assn. (chair trial evidence com. 1988-94), Minn. Bar Assn., N.Y. County Lawyers Assn., Assn. of Bar of City of N.Y. (chmn. profl. responsibility com. 1993-96, mem. exec. com. 1999—). Federal civil litigation, State civil litigation. Home: 390 West End Ave Apt 10G New York NY 10024 Office: Gregory P Joseph Law Offices LLC 805 Third Ave Fl 31 New York NY 10022 E-mail: gjoseph@josephnyc.com.

JOSEPH, LEONARD, lawyer; b. Phila., June 8, 1919; s. Harry L. and Mary (Pollock) J.; m. Norma Hamberg, 1942; children: Gilbert M., Stuart A., Janet H. Fitzgerald. BA, U. Pa., 1941; LLB, Harvard U., 1947. Bar: N.Y. 1949. Law clk. to chief judge U.S. Ct. Appeals, Boston, 1947-48; since practiced in N.Y.C.; ptnr. and of counsel Dewey Ballantine, 1957—. Bd. dirs., exec. com. Legal Aid Soc. N.Y., 1986-89; mem. panel of disting. neutrals CPR Inst. for Dispute Resolution. Bd. editors Harvard Law Rev., 1946-47. Served with AUS, 1943-46. Fellow Am. Bar Found., Am. Coll. Trial Lawyers Antitrust, Federal civil litigation, Utilities, public. Office: Dewey Ballantine 1301 Avenue Of The Americas New York NY 10019-6022

JOSEPH, MARIO ALEXIS, lawyer; b. Cordoba, Argentina, Jan. 16, 1971; m. Naomi Joseph, June 24, 1992. Student, Yeshiva U., 1989-90; BA, CUNY, Queens, 1992; JD, Benjamin N. Cordozo Sch. Law, 1995. Bar: N.Y., N.J. Asst. ombudsman Dept. of State, Office of Gov., N.Y.C., 1991-92; clk., liaison Franklin H. Williams, Jud. Commn. on Minorities, N.Y.C., 1993-94; pin. law clk. N.Y. State Supreme Ct., N.Y.C., 1993-94; cons. Interpublic Group, N.Y.C., 1995-96; prin. Law Offices of Mario A. Joseph, N.Y.C., 1997—. Clk., liaison Jud. Commn. on Minorities, N.Y.C., 1993-94; asst. ombudsman Office of the Gov., Dept. State, N.Y.C., 1991-92. Mem. young leadership com. mem. Am. Israel Pub. Affairs, 1999. Recipient Cert. of Achievement Nat. Multiple Sclerosis Soc., 1997, Cert. of Merit N.Y. Acad. Scis., 1994. Mem. AMA, Chinese Am. Bar Assn. (dir., founder 1998-99), N.Y. State Bar Assn. Avocations: skiing, horseback riding, painting. Office: Law Office of Mario A Joseph 401 Broadway New York NY 10013-3005

JOSEPH, PAUL R, law educator; b. Los Angeles, Apr. 30, 1951; s. Lawrence H. Joseph and Barbara A. (Acoff) Brittin; m. Lynn Wolf, 1990. BA, Goddard Coll., 1973; JD, U. Calif., Davis, 1977; LLM, Temple U., 1979. Bar: Calif. 1977, U.S. Supreme Ct. 1981, U.S. Ct. Appeals (9th cir.) 1982, U.S. Ct. Appeals (11th cir.) 1987. Lectr. law, tchg. fellow Temple U., Phila., 1977-79; asst. prof. Salmon Chase Coll. Law No. Ky. U., Highland Heights, 1979-82, assoc. prof., 1982-84, Nova Southeastern U., Ft. Lauderdale, Fla., 1984-88, prof., 1988—, dir. internat. programs, 1996-98, Goodwin prof., 1999, assoc. dean internat. and external programs, 1999—2003. Interview team Benjamin Franklin Fellowship Program, Russia, 1992; spkr. on law topics including search and seizure and civil liberties, and the use of computers in legal edn., law and popular culture; lectr. in field. Author: Warrantless Search Law, 1991 (updated yearly); co-editor: Prime Time Law: Fictional Television as Legal Narrative, 1998; mem. editl. bd. Human Rights mag., 1986-95, Legal Studies Forum, 1998-99; columnist Visions mag., 1995; contbr. articles to profl. jours. Mem. Broward County Human Rights Bd., 1986-92, vice chmn., 1987-88, chmn., 1991-92; trustee Goddard Coll., 1981-90, 95-96, vice chmn. bd. dirs., 1985-86, chmn. fin. com., 1986-89, chmn. presdl. search com., 1989-90, chmn. acad. and student affairs com., 1995-96; mem. Broward County Dem. Exec. Com., 1988-92; bd. dirs. Inter-Am. Ctr. for Human Rights, 1997—. Mem. ABA (chair, liaison to state and local individual rights sects. 1991-95, individual rights and responsibilities sect. liaison to spl. com. on the drug crisis 1991-95, standing com. on Gavel awards 1996-99, Gavel awards screening com. 2000-, legal edn. to admission to bar tech. com. 2001-), ACLU (nat. bd. 1995-97, chmn. Broward County chpt. 1985-86, 90-91, chmn. legal panel 1984-87, Fla. state bd. dirs. 1985-97, chmn. legal programs com. 1986-87, pres. 1990-93, del. to nat. conv. 1987, 89, 91, 95, chair nat. affiliate leadership network 1991-93), Fla. Bar Assn. (faculty affiliate, exec. coun. pub. interest sect. 1990-92, vice-chmn. Broward county fair campaign practices com. 2000-03), NSU Criminal Justice Inst. (exec. com. 2000—, mng. editor Online jour. Law and Popular Culture 2000-). Democrat. Avocations: computers, irish music, travel. Office: Nova Southeastern U Shepard Broad Law Ctr 3305 College Ave Fort Lauderdale FL 33314-7721 E-mail: josephp@nsu.law.nova.edu.

JOSEPH, RAYMOND, lawyer; b. Lansing, Mich., Jan. 21, 1924; s. John Gamel and Lena (Tobia) J.; divorced; children: Gina Marie, Mark Raymond. Student, Mich. State U., 1948; JD, Wayne State U., 1951. Law clk. to Leland Carr, presiding chief justice Mich. Supreme Ct., 1953—54; with Raymond Joseph & Assocs., Lansing, Mich. Former pres. Lansing Symphony Assn.; officer, dir. Opera Co. Mid-Mich., Kresge Art Mus., Lansing Art Gallery, Lansing Ballet Assn., Mich. Orchestral Assn. Lt. USAAF, 1943-45, ETO. Decorated 7 Air medals for combat flying; recipient presdl. citation for 35 combat missions, 1944. Mem. ABA, Mich. Bar Assn., Ingham County Bar Assn. (former sec.), Assn. Trial Lawyers Am., Mich. Trial Lawyers Assn., Am. Judicature Soc. (fed. ct. mediator), Def. Rsch. Inst. Democrat. Mem. Christian Ch. Avocations: art and art history, classical music, reading, tennis. Aviation, Federal civil litigation, Insurance. Home and Office: 713 Applegate Ln East Lansing MI 48823-2109 E-mail: raymond.joseph@eudoramail.com.

JOSEPH, ROBERT THOMAS, lawyer; b. June 12, 1946; s. Joseph Alexander and Clara Barbara (Francis) J.; m. Sarah Granger, May 22, 1971; children: Paul, Timothy. AB, Xavier U., 1968; JD, U. Mich., 1971. Bar: Mich. 1971, Ill. 1976, U.S. Dist. Ct. (no. dist.) Ill. 1976, U.S. Ct. Appeals (7th cir.) 1983. Staff atty. FTC Bur. Competition, Washington, 1971-76, asst. to dir., 1972-74; atty. Sonnenschein Nath & Rosenthal, Chgo., 1976—, ptnr., 1978—. Trustee Northbrook (Ill.) Libr. Bd., 1979-89, pres., 1983-85. Recipient Disting. Svc. award FTC, 1976. Mem. ABA (chair franchising com. of antitrust law sect. 1984-87, chair videotapes com. 1987-90, chair publs. com. 1991-94, coun. 1994-97, program officer 1997-99, com. officer 1999-2000, vice-chair 2000-2001, chair 2001-02, mem. governing bd. forum on franchising), Met. Club. Roman Catholic. Antitrust, State civil litigation, Franchising. Office: Sonnenschein Nath Rosenthal 233 S Wacker Dr Ste 8000 Chicago IL 60606-6491

JOSEPH, STEVEN JAY, lawyer; b. Baker, Oreg., Sept. 7, 1950; s. Jay Hyrum and Patricia Jean (Cahill) J.; m. Melissa Davis Joseph, Jan. 1, 1978; children: Lindsey Joseph, Logan Joseph. BS, Ea. Oreg. State Coll., 1972; JD, U. Oreg., 1975. Bar: Oreg. 1975, U.S. Dist. Ct. Oreg. 1975. Assoc. Willard K. Carey P.C., LaGrande, Oreg., 1975-76; ptnr. Carey & Joseph P.C., LaGrande, Oreg., 1976-88, Carey, Joseph & Mendiguren, LaGrande, Oreg., 1988-95, Joseph & Mendiguren P.C., LaGrande, 1995-96; atty. pvt. practice, LaGrande, 1997—. Pres. La Grande Indsl. Devel. Corp., 1999—. Councilor City of LaGrande, Oreg. 1990-94, 97-98; adv. bd. Salvation Army, 1995-2001; trustee E.O.S.C. Found., 1980-95, pres. 1988-90, East Oreg. U.-East Oreg. U. Found., 2000—, La Grande Sch. Dist. Bd., 2001—. Mem. LaGrande-Union County C. of C. (dir. 1982-84), Rotary, Elks. Republican. Avocations: polo, racquetball, skiing, hunting, golf. General civil litigation, Estate planning, Property, real (including real estate development, water). Home: 806 Highland Pl La Grande OR 97850-3216 Office: PO Box 3230 La Grande OR 97850-7230 E-mail: sjoseph@uwtc.net.

JOSEPHSON, MARK A. lawyer, accountant; b. Bklyn., Aug. 29, 1959; BSBA, Boston U., 1981; JD, NYU, 1997. CPA; bar: N.J. 1997, N.Y. 1999, Fla. 1999; cert. fin. planner. Pvt. practice lawyer, CPA, N.Y.C. Mem.: N.Y.C. Bar Assn. (mem. small law firm com.), New York Soc. CPAs (mem. estate tax com.), New County Lawyers Assn. (mem. tax. com., mem. estate tax and supreme ct. practice com.). Taxation, general, Estate planning, General practice. Office: 425 Madison Ave 9th Fl New York NY 10017 Office Fax: 212-644-9802. Business E-Mail: mj@josephsonco.com.

JOSEPHSON, WILLIAM HOWARD, lawyer; b. Newark, Mar. 22, 1934; s. Maurice and Gertrude (Brooks) J.; m. Barbara Beth Haws, June 18, 1995. AB, U. Chgo., 1952; JD, Columbia, 1955; commoner, St. Antony's Coll., Oxford (Eng.) U., 1958-59. Bar: N.Y. 1956, D.C. 1966, U.S. Supreme Ct. 1959. Assoc. Paul, Weiss, Rifkind, Wharton & Garrison, N.Y.C., 1955-58, Joseph L. Rauh, Jr., Washington, 1959; Far East regional counsel ICA, 1959-61; spl. asst. to dir. Peace Corps, 1961-62, dep. gen. counsel, 1961-63, gen. counsel, 1963-66; assoc. Fried, Frank, Harris, Shriver & Jacobson, N.Y.C., 1966-67, ptnr., 1968-94, counsel, 1994-99; asst. atty. gen. in charge charities bur. N.Y. State Law Dept., 1999—. Spl. counsel N.Y.C. Human Resources Adminstrn., 1966-67, City Univ. Constrn. Fund, 1967-96, N.Y.C. Bd. Edn., 1968-71, N.Y.C. Employees' Retirement Sys., 1975-86; Nat. Dem. vice presdl. campaign coord., 1972; pres. Peace Corps Inst., 1980—; mem. N.Y. State Gov. Task Force Pension and Investment, 1987-89, N.Y. State His. Records Adv. Bd., 1990-96, N.Y. State Archives Preservation Trust, 1994-96. Bd. editors: Columbia Law Rev, 1953-55. Trustee and treas. St. Antony's Coll. trust, 1994-99. Recipient William A. Jump award exemplary achievement pub. adminstrn., 1965, Disting. Svc. award, Valerie Kantor award, Corp. Social Responsibility award Mex. Am. Legal Def. and Edn. Fund, 1980, 81, 93. Mem. Assn. Bar City N.Y. (spl. com. on Congl. ethics 1968-70), Council on Fgn. Relations. Jewish. Non-profit and tax-exempt organizations, Legislative, Municipal (including bonds). Home: 58 S Oxford St Brooklyn NY 11217-1305 Office: Charities Bur NY State Law Dept 120 Broadway Fl 3 New York NY 10271

JOSLYN, ROBERT BRUCE, lawyer; b. Detroit, Jan. 9, 1945; s. Lee Everett, Jr. and Juanita Constance Joslyn; m. Karen Sue Glenny, July 8, 1967; children: Gwendolyn Constance, Robert Bruce. BA, Fla. State U., 1967; JD, Emory U., 1970. Bar: Mich. 1970. Law clk. Gurney, Gurney & Handley, Orlando, Fla., summer 1969; assoc. Joslyn & Keydel, Detroit, 1970-74; ptnr. Joslyn, Keydel & Wallace, 1975-95; pvt. practice Robert B. Joslyn, PC, St. Clair Shores, Mich., 1996—. Vis. instr. Oakland U., Rochester, Mich., 1974-75; faculty Inst. Continuing Legal Edn., Ann Arbor, Michl, 1975—; guest instr. U. Mich. Law Sch. Co-author: Manual for Lawyers and Legal Assistants: Probate and Trust Administration, 1977, Manual for Lawyers and Legal Assistants: Taxation of Trusts and Estates, 1977, 3d edit., 1980. Active U.S. All Am. Prep. Sch. Swim Team, 1963. Mem. ABA, Detroit Bar Assn. (chmn. taxation com. 1985-87), State Bar Mich. (chairperson probate and estate planning sect. 1992-93), Am. Coll. of Trust and Estate Counsel (state chmn. 1987-92, bd. regents 1994-2001), Internat. Acad. Estate and Trust Law, Fin. and Estate Planning Coun. Detroit (bd. dirs. 1988-92, pres. 1992), Grosse Pointe Yacht Club, Phi Delta Phi, Phi Kappa Psi. Estate planning, Estate taxation, Personal income taxation. Home: 11 Waverly Ln Grosse Pointe Farms MI 48236-3123 Office: 200 Maple Park Blvd Ste 201 Saint Clair Shores MI 48081-2211

JOST, LAWRENCE JOHN, lawyer; b. Alma, Wis., Oct. 9, 1944; s. Lester J. and Hazel L. (Johnson) J.; m. Anne E. Fisher, June 10, 1967; children—Peter, Katherine, Susan. BSCE, U. Wis., 1968, JD, 1969. Bar: Wis. 1969, U.S. Dist. Ct. (ea. dist.) Wis. 1969, U.S. Ct. Appeals (7th cir.) 1969, U.S. Supreme Ct. 1980. Law clk. to judge U.S. Dist. Ct., Milw., 1969-70; assoc. firm Brady, Tyrrell, Cotter & Cutler, 1970-74; assoc. Quarles & Brady, 1974-76, ptnr., 1976—, chair real property sect., 2002—, coord. real estate group, 1985—. Vis. tchr. gen. practice Wis. Law Sch. Bd. dirs. Milw. Chamber Theatre, 1998-2001, Marcus Ctr. for the Performing Arts, 2003—; pres. Vis. Nurse Assn. Milw., 1982-85, VNA, Corp., 1982-86; bd. dirs. Wis. Heritage Inc., 1980-82, Vis. Nurse Found., 1986-95, pres., 1993-94; bd. dirs. Milw. Repertory Theater, 1987-95, 2001—, pres., 1990-92; bd. dirs. United Performing Arts Fund, 1989-93. Mem. ABA, Wis. Bar Assn. (lectr. seminars), Milw. Bar Assn., Am. Coll. Real Estate Lawyers, Am. Coll. Mortgage Attys. Mem. Plymouth United Ch. of Christ Land use and zoning (including planning), Landlord-tenant, Property, real (including real estate development, water). Office: Quarles & Brady LLP 411 E Wisconsin Ave Ste 2550 Milwaukee WI 53202-4497

JOST, RICHARD FREDERIC, III, lawyer; b. N.Y.C., Sept. 25, 1947; s. Richard Frederic Jr. and Gertrude (Holoch) J.; m. Sally Ann Galvin, July 29, 1972; children: Jennifer, Richard IV. BA, Dickinson Coll., 1969; JD, Syracuse U., 1975. Bar: N.Y. 1976, Nev. 1978, U.S. Dist. Ct. Nev. 1979, U.S. Supreme Ct. 1984. Dep. dist. atty. Elko (Nev.) County Dist. Atty.'s Office, 1976-80; dep. atty. gen. Nev. Atty. Gen.'s Office, Carson City, 1980-83; ptnr. Jones & Vargas, Las Vegas, Nev., 1983—. Trustee United Meth. Ch., Carson City, Nev., 1982-83; bd. dirs. Ormsby Assn. Retarded Citizens, Carson City, 1982-83. Served to lt. USNR, 1970-74. Mem. ABA (urban, state and local govt. law sect.), Clark County Bar Assn., Nat. Assn. Bond Lawyers, Med. Liability Assn. Nev. (bd. dirs. 2002—. Democrat. Administrative and regulatory, Municipal (including bonds). Home: 2840 S Monte Cristo Way Las Vegas NV 89117-2951 Office: Jones & Vargas 3773 Howard Hughes Pkwy Las Vegas NV 89109-0949 E-mail: rfj@jonesvargas.com.

JOURNEY, DREXEL DAHLKE, lawyer; b. Westfield, Wis., Feb. 23, 1926; s. Clarence Earl and Verna L. Gilmore (Dahlke) Journey Gilmore; m. Vergene Harriet Sandsmark, Oct. 24, 1952; 1 child, Ann Marie. BBA, U. Wis., 1950, LLB, 1952; LLM, George Washington U., 1957. Bar: Wis. 1952, U.S. Dist. Ct. (we. dist.) Wis. 1953, U.S. Supreme Ct. 1955, U.S. Ct. Appeals (4th cir.) 1960, U.S. Ct. Appeals (5th cir.) 1961, U.S. Ct. Appeals (D.C. cir.) 1965, U.S. Ct. Appeals (7th and 9th cirs.) 1967, U.S. Ct. Appeals (1st cir.) 1969, D.C. 1970, U.S. Dist. Ct. D.C. 1970, U.S. Ct. Appeals (2d, 3d, 6th, 8th and 10th cirs.) 1976, U.S. Ct. Appeals (11th cir.) 1981. Counsel FPC, Washington, 1952-66, asst. gen. counsel, 1966-70, dep. gen. counsel, 1970-74, gen. counsel, 1974-77; ptnr. Schiff, Hardin & Waite, Washington, 1977—. Mem. mediation program U.S. Dist. Ct. (D.C. cir.), 1989—, early neutral evaluation program, 1989-95; mem. case evaluation program D.C. Superior Ct., 1991—. Author: Corporate Law and Practice, 1975; contbr. articles to profl. jours. Pres. Am. U. Park Citizens Assn., Washington, 1970-72; trustee Lincoln-Wesmoreland Housing Project, Washington, 1978-79. With Mcht. Marine Res., USNR, 1944-46, USNG, 1948-50. Knapp scholar U. Wis., 1952. Mem. ABA, FBA, Energy Bar Assn., Masons, Army and Navy Club, Phi Kappa Phi, Phi Eta Sigma, Theta Delta Chi. Republican. Congregationalist. Administrative and regulatory, FERC practice, Municipal (including bonds). Home: 4540 Windom Pl NW Washington DC 20016-2452 Office: Schiff Hardin & Waite 1101 Connecticut Ave NW Ste 600 Washington DC 20036-4390

JOVICK, ROBERT L. lawyer; b. Butte, Mont., Oct. 2, 1950; m. Stacy Towle, June 23, 1976; children: Janelle, Torey, Jay. BS in Indsl. Engring., Mont. State U., 1972; JD, U. Mont., 1975. Bar: Mont. 1975, U.S. Dist. Ct. Mont. 1975, U.S. Supreme Ct. Pvt. practice, Livingston, Mont., 1975—. City atty. City of Livingston, 1975-95. Sec. Livingston Community Trust, 1987—. Mem. Livingston Golf Club (pres. 1990). Methodist. Avocations: fly fishing, hiking, history of montana. General civil litigation, Personal injury (including property damage), Property, real (including real estate development, water). Office: PO 1245 227 S 2nd St Livingston MT 59047-3001

JOYCE, MICHAEL PATRICK, lawyer; b. Omaha, Oct. 3, 1960; s. Thomas Hunt and Joan Clare (Berigan) J. Student, Miami U., Oxford, Ohio, 1978-79; BSBA, Creighton U., 1982; JD, U. Houston, 1988. Bar: Mo., Kans., U.S. Dist. Ct. (we. dist.) Mo. 1988, U.S. Dist. Ct. Kans. 1989, U.S. Ct. Appeals (8th and 10th cirs.) 1988, U.S. Supreme Ct. 1994. Assoc. mgr. Avco Fin. Svcs. Internat., Inc., Omaha, 1983-85; assoc. Wyrsch, Atwell, Mirakian, Lee & Hobbs, P.C. (formerly Koenigsdorf & Wyrsch, P.C.), Kansas City, Mo., 1988-94; shareholder Wyrsch, Hobbs, Mirakian, & Lee, PC, Kansas City, Mo., 1995-97; pvt. practice, 1997-98; pres. The Joyce Law Firm, LLC, Kansas City, Mo., 1998-2000; shareholder Van Osdol, Magruder Erickson & Redmond, PC, Kansas City, 2000—. Adj. prof. U. Mo. Kansas City Sch. Law, 1997-2001. Asst. editor (newsletter State Bar Tex.) Caveat Vendor, 1987-88. Grad. NITA, 1992; bd. dirs. Creighton U., 1997-99. Mem. ABA, Nat. Assn. Criminal Def. Lawyers, Am. Health Lawyers Assn., Mo. Bar Assn., Mo. Assn. Criminal Def. Lawyers, Kans. Bar Assn., Kansas City Metro Bar Assn., Johnson County Bar Assn., Creighton U. Alumni Assn. (dir. region IV nat. alumni bd. dirs. 1994-96, pres. 1997-99), Creighton U. Alumni Club (pres. Kansas City area 1992-94). Roman Catholic. Avocations: golf, basketball, community service. General civil litigation, Commercial, consumer (including collections, credit), Criminal. Office: 2400 Commerce Tower 911 Main St Kansas City MO 64105-2009 E-mail: mpjoyce@vomer.com.

JOYCE, STEPHEN MICHAEL, lawyer; b. Los Angeles, Mar. 19, 1945; s. John Rowland and Elizabeth Rose (Rahe) J.; m. Bernadette Anne Novey, Aug. 18, 1973; children: Natalie Elizabeth, Vanessa Anne. BS, Calif. State U., Los Angeles, 1970; JD, U. LaVerne, 1976. Bar: Calif. 1976, U.S. Dist. Ct. (cen. dist.) Calif. 1977, U.S. Ct. Claims 1981. Pvt. practice, Beverly Hills, Calif., 1976-93; ptnr. Gold & Joyce, Beverly Hills, 1982-84. Personal atty. to Stevie Wonder and various other celebrities, 1977—. Contbr. articles to profl. jours. Served to pvt. USAR, 1963-69. Mem.: ABA, San Fernando Valley Bar Assn., Consumer Atty. of So. Calif. Assn., Beverly Hills Bar Assn., L.A. County Bar Assn., Calif. Bar Assn., Calabasas Tennis & Swim Club. Democrat. Roman Catholic. Avocation: long distance running. State civil litigation, Entertainment, General practice. Home: 4724 Barcelona Ct Calabasas CA 91302-1403 Office: 15260 Ventura Blvd Ste 640 Sherman Oaks CA 91403-5340 E-mail: enjoyce2@aol.com.

JOYNER, J(AMES) CURTIS, judge; b. Newberry, S.C., Apr. 18, 1948; s. George C. and Joan C. (Glenn) J.; m. Mildred Ann Carter, Apr. 5, 1975; children: Jennifer Christine, Nicole Marie, Jacqlyn Ann. Student, Peirce Jr. Coll., Phila., 1967; BS in Acctg., Ctrl. State U., Wilberforce, Ohio, 1971; JD, Howard U., 1974. Bar: Pa. 1975, U.S. Dist. Ct. (ea. dist.) Pa. 1981. Contr. D.C. Project, Washington, 1972-73; legal publ. specialist Fed. Register, Washington, 1974-75; asst. dist. atty. Dist. Atty. Office Chester County, West Chester, Pa., 1975-80, chief dep. dist. atty., 1980-84, 1st asst. dist. atty., 1984-87; judge Ct. of Common Pleas, 15th Jud. Dist., West Chester, 1987-92, U.S. Dist. Ct. (ea. dist.) Pa., Phila., 1992—. Mem. coun. trustees West Chester U., 1983-2000, trustee emeritus, 2001. Named Trailblazer in Law Enforcement Gov. Thornburgh, 1986; recipient Outstanding Svc. award to law enforcement Pa. Criminal Investigators, 1987, Disting. Law and Justice award County and State Detectives Assn., 1988, Donald K. Anthony Alumni Achievement Hall of Fame Ctrl. State U., 1994, Pres.' Medallion for Svc. West Chester U., 2001. Mem. Fed. Bar Assn. (hon.), Chester County Bar Assn. Avocations: sports, jazz, golf. Office: US Dist Ct Rm 8613 601 Market St Philadelphia PA 19106-1714

JOYNER, WALTON KITCHIN, lawyer; b. Raleigh, N.C., Apr. 1, 1933; s. William Thomas and Sue (Kitchin) J.; m. Lucy Holmes Graves, Sept. 23, 1955; children: Sue Carson Clark, Walton K. Jr., James Y. II. AB in Polit.

Sci., U. N.C., 1955, JD with honors, 1960. Bar: N.C., cert. mediator:; lic. comml. pilot. Ptnr. Joyner & Howison, Raleigh, 1960-80, Hunton & Williams, Raleigh, 1980—. Sec., treas. N.C. R.R. Co., Raleigh, 1966; bd. dirs. United Title Ins. Co., Raleigh; bd. mgrs. Wachovia Bank, N.C., 1969-98; bd. govs. U.S. Power Squadrons, 1974-81. Assoc. editor U. N.C. Law Rev. Pres. Rehab. and Cerebral Palsy Ctr. Wake County, Raleigh, 1974; trustee St. Mary's Coll., 1990-91; bd. dirs. Peace Coll. Found., 2001—. Mem.: Law Alumni Assn. U. N.C. (bd. dirs.), Wake County Bar Assn. (chmn., bd. dirs. 1977), N.C. Bar Assn. (treas. probate sect. 1983), Carolina Country Club (pres. 1983—84, 2000—01), Order of Coif, Phi Beta Kappa. Presbyterian. Avocation: flying. Corporate, general, Probate (including wills, trusts). Home: 815 Marlowe Rd Raleigh NC 27609-7022 Office: Hunton & Williams 1 Hannover Sq PO Box 109 Fl 14 Raleigh NC 27602-0109

JOYNTON, STANLEY FORREST, lawyer; b. Bethesda, Md., Sept. 12, 1951; s. Harry Dudley Jr. and Mary Ruth (Jordan) J.; m. Lynne Deana Olson, Nov. 21, 1981; children: Carrie Alice, Emily Lynne. BA, Rice U., 1973; JD with honors, U. Tex., 1978. Bar: Tex. 1978, U.S. Dist. Ct. (no. dist.) Tex. 1982, U.S. Tax Ct. 1989; cert. in estate planning and probate law Tex. Bd. Legal Specialization. Ptnr. Shannon Porter & Johnson L.L.P., San Angelo, Tex. Mem. ABA, Tom Green County Bar Assn., Order of Coif. Baptist. Avocations: music, backpacking, running, bicycling, canoe building. Estate planning, Probate (including wills, trusts), Estate taxation. Office: Shannon Porter Johnson LLP PO Box 1272 San Angelo TX 76902-1272 Home: 2802 Palo Duro Dr San Angelo TX 76904-7429

JUCEAM, ROBERT E. lawyer; b. N.Y.C., June 16, 1940; s. Benjamin T. and Amelia B. (Spatz) J.; m. Eleanor Pam, May 24, 1970; children: Daniel, Jacquelyn, Gregory. AB cum laude, Columbia U., 1961, LLB, 1964, JD, 1972; LLM, NYU, 1966. Bar: N.Y. 1965, U.S. Dist. Ct. (so. and ea. dists.) N.Y. 1966, U.S. Tax Ct. 1968, U.S. Ct. Appeals (2d cir.) 1967, U.S. Supreme Ct. 1971, U.S. Ct. Appeals (5th cir.) 1978, U.S. Ct. Appeals (D.C. cir.) 1980, U.S. Ct. Appeals (11th cir.) 1987, U.S. Ct. Appeals (7th cir.) 1989, U.S. Ct. Appeals (9th cir.) 1999. Law clk. U.S. Dist. Ct., N.Y., 1964-66; assoc. Fried, Frank, Harris, Shriver & Jacobson, N.Y.C., 1966-73, ptnr., 1974—. Bd. dirs. Nat. Network Def. of the Right to Counsel, Inc., 1985-89, Lawyers Com. for Human Rights, 1986-94, Bar Assurance and Reins. Ltd., 1991—, Am. Immigration Law Found., 1987—, pres., 1991-2000, treas., 2000—; gen. counsel U.S. Supreme Ct. Hist. Soc., 1995—, trustee, mem. exec. com., 1999—; mem. arbitration panel U.S. Dist. Ct. (ea. dist.) N.Y., 1986—; mem. comml. and constrn. panels Am. Arbitration Assn., 1972-94; dir. civil rights Washington Lawyers Com., 1996-99; mem. bd. advisors D.C. Bar Found., 1996-2001; treas., bd. dirs. Pro Bono Inst., 1997—. Contbr. articles to legal jours. Trustee Mex.-Am. Legal Def. and Edn. Fund, 1986-90, chmn. program and planning com., 1988-90; adv. com. to task force on racial, gender and minority discrimination U.S. Ct. Appeals for 2d Circuit, 1994-96; bd. dirs. Appleseed Found., Inc., 1997-99; mem. bd. advisors Atlantic Legal Found., 2001—. Recipient Lester Zazuly medal, 1958, Columbia Coll. Alumni Achievement award, 1961, Edward Foxx prize Columbia Coll., 1961, Maldef Corp. Responsibility award, 1993, Valerie J. Kantor award for extraordinary achievement, 1997, Am. Immigration Law Found. hon. fellow and Founder's award, 1989, Lifetime Achievement award Ctr. for Human Rights and Constl. Law, 1993. Fellow Am. Bar Found. (life), N.Y. State Bar Found., ABA (ho. of dels. 1983—, chmn. com. on immigration sect. litigation 1985-90, immigration pro bono adv. task force, 1992-98, vice chmn., 1995-96, mem. coordinating com. on immigration law 1984-87, chmn. 1989-92, mem. com. environ. controls sect. banking, 1983-86, vice chmn. com. on constrn., sec. gen. practice 1989-90, mem. standing com. lawyers pub. svc. responsibility 1993-96, mem. coun. fund justice & edn. 1994-2000, adv. mem., 2000—, chmn. major gifts com. 1997-98, Pro Bono award 1992); mem. Internat. Bar Assn. (chmn. Sect. Gen. Practice com. bus. migration 1987-88), N.Y. State Bar Assn., Assn. Bar City of N.Y. (com. on trademarks and unfair competition 1983-86, com. immigration 1986-89, com. on profl. and jud. ethics 1989-92, com. Human Rights Law 1994-96), Nat. Assn. Criminal Def. Lawyers (co-chmn. com. on immigration 1988-90), Am. Judicature Soc. (life), Am. Bar Endowment, Nat. Conf. Bar Presidents (assoc.), Am. Immigration Lawyers Assn. (pres. 1982-83, bd. govs. 1971—, chmn. N.Y. chpt. 1971-72, gen. counsel 1986-91, liaison to ABA commn. on nonlawyer practice 1993-94, editor Ann. Symposium Handbook 1985-88, assoc. editor 1989-90, Edith Lowenstein Meml. award 1981, Pro Bono award 1992), Soc. Sachems, Am. Mgmt. Assn., Fed. Bar Assn., N.Y. County Lawyers Assn. (reporter N.Y. Equitable Distbn. Law Proposals 1968, bd. dirs. 1996-98), Def. Rsch. Inst., N.Y. Criminal Bar Assn., N.Y. State Trial Lawyers Assn., Assn. Profl. Responsibility Lawyers, Assn. Fed. Def. Lawyers, Cow Neck Peninsula Hist. Soc. (life), Italy and Colonies Philat. Soc. of Gt. Brit. (life), Jack Knight Soc. (life), L.I. Postal History Soc. (life), Am. Helvetia Philatelic Soc. (life), Am. Philat. Soc. (life), Internat. Fedn. Postcard Dealers, India House Club, Continental Club, Alpha Epsilon Pi. Administrative and regulatory, General civil litigation, Insurance. Home: 106 Hemlock Rd Manhasset NY 11030-1214 Office: Fried Frank Harris Shriver & Jacobson 1 New York Plz Ste 2500 New York NY 10004-1901

JUDD, DENNIS L. lawyer; b. Provo, Utah, June 27, 1954; s. Derrel Wesley and Leila (Lundquist) J.; m. Carol Lynne Chilberg, May 6, 1977; children: Lynne Marie, Amy Jo, Tiffany Ann, Andrew, Jacquelyn Nicole. BA in Polit. Sci. summa cum laude, Brigham Young U., 1978, JD, 1981. Bar: Utah 1981, U.S. Dist. Ct. Utah 1981. Assoc. Nielson & Senior, Salt Lake City and Vernal, Utah, 1981-83; dep. county atty. Uintah County, Vernal, 1982-84; ptnr. Bennett & Judd, Vernal, 1983-88; county atty. Daggett County, Utah, 1985-89, 91-99; pvt. practice Vernal, 1988—; county atty. Daggett County, 2000—; prosecutor City of Naples, Naples, 1996-99; legal counsel Uintah County Sch. Dist., 1996—; city atty. Naples City, Utah, 1999—, Vernal City, Utah, 2000—; atty. City of Vernal, 2000—. Mem. governing bd. Uintah Basin applied Tech. Ctr., 1991-95, v.p., 1993-94, pres., 1994-95. Chmn. bd. adjustment Zoning and Planning Bd., Naples, 1982-91, 94—; mem. Naples City Coun., 1982-91; mayor pro tem City of Naples, 1983-91; legis. v.p. Naples PTA, 1988-90; sec. Friends of Utah Field House of Natural History, 2000—; v.p. Uintah Dist. PTA Coun., 1990-92; mem. resolution com. Utah League Cities and Towns, 1985-86, small cities com., 1985-86; trustee Uintah Sch. Dist. Found., 1988-97, vice chmn., 1991-93; mem. Uintah County Sch. Dist. Bd. Edn., 1991-95, v.p., 1991-92, pres., 1992-95; chmn. Uintah County Rep. Conv., 1998. Hinkley scholar Brigham Young U., 1977. Mem. Utah Bar Assn., Uintah Basin Bar Assn., Statewide Assn. Prosecutors, Vernal C. of C. Republican. Mem. Lds Ch. Avocations: hunting, photography, lapidary. Home: 460 E 1555 S Naples UT 84078 Office: 461 W 200 S Vernal UT 84078-3049

JUDE, CARLIN M. prosecutor; b. Iron Mountain, Mich. BA in Journalism, BA in Edn., Ea. Wash. U., 1973, M in Bus., 1980; JD, Gonzaga U., 1986. Bar: Idaho 1988, Wash. 1990. Dep. prosecutor Spokane (Wash.) County Pros. Atty., 1991—. Mem.: Wash. Women Lawyers (rep. to state bd. 2003—, treas. 2001—02). Office: Spokane County Prosecutor W 1100 Mallon Spokane WA 99260

JUDELL, HAROLD BENN, lawyer; b. Milw., Mar. 9, 1915; s. Philip Fox and Lena Florence (Krause) J.; m. Maria Violeta van Ronzelen, May 5, 1951 (div.); m. Celeste Seymour Grulich, June 24, 1986. BA, U. Wis., 1936, JD, 1938; LLB, Tulane U., 1950. Bar: Wis. 1938, La. 1950. Mem. Scheinfeld Collins Durant & Winter, Milw., 1938; spl. agt., adminstrv. asst. to dir. FBI, 1939-44; legal attache U.S. Embassy Peru, 1942-44; ptnr. Foley & Judell, LLP, New Orleans, 1950—; v.p., dir. Dauphine Orleans Hotel Corp., 1970—, chmn. bd., 1999—. Mem. Tulane U. Bus. Sch. Coun.; trustee Greater New Orleans YMCA, 1981—; dir. Sizeler Property Investors, Inc., 1986—. Fellow Am. Coll. Bond Counsel (founding); mem. ABA, La. Bar Assn., Nat. Assn. Bond Lawyers (bd. dirs., pres. 1984-85), New Orleans Country Club, Lawn Tennis Club, Met. Club (N.Y.C.). Municipal (including bonds). Office: Foley & Judell LLP 365 Canal St New Orleans LA 70130-1112 E-mail: hjudell@foleyjudell.com.

JUDGE, BERNARD MARTIN, editor, publisher; b. Chgo., Jan. 6, 1940; s. Bernard A. and Catherine Elizabeth (Halloran) J.; m. Kimbeth A. Wehrli, July 9, 1966; children: Kelly, Bernard R., Jessica. Reporter City News Bur., Chgo., 1965-66; reporter Chgo. Tribune, 1966-70, city editor, 1974-79, asst. mng. editor met. news, 1979-83; editor, gen. mgr. City News Bur. Chgo., 1983-84; assoc. editor Chgo. Sun-Times, 1984-88; from editor to pub. Chgo. Daily Law Bull., 1988—; pub. Chgo. Lawyer, 1989—; v.p. Law Bull. Pub. Co., Chgo., 1988—. Bd. dirs. Constnl. Rights Found., Chgo., 1992—, chmn. bd. dirs., 1995-97; trustee Fenwick Cath. Prep. H.S., Oak Park, Ill., 1989—. Named to Chgo. Journalism Hall of Fame, 2000. Mem. Sigma Delta Chi. Home: 360 E Randolph St Apt 1905 Chicago IL 60601-7335 Office: Law Bull Pub Co 415 N State St Chicago IL 60610-4631

JUDICE, GREGORY VAN, lawyer, educator; b. Lake Charles, La., June 14, 1966; s. Richard Edward and Anne Lynne J.; m. Caroline Kaye Zama, May 9, 1992. BS in Polit. Sci., McNeese State U., 1989; JD, Notre Dame Law Sch., London, 1994, Wesleyan U., 1995. Bar: La. 1996; cert. mediator. Staff atty. West Pub., Inc., Dallas, 1994-96; atty. Woodley, Williams, Fenet et al, Lake Charles, 1996-97; atty., cert. mediator Hunt Law Firm, Lake Charles, 1997—. Bd. dirs. vol. ctr. United Way, Lake Charles, 1995—. Named to Order of Barristers, 1994; recipient Am. Jurisprudence award Lawyers Coop. Pub. Co., 1994, 95. Mem. ABA (house dels. 1995), La. Bar Assn., Southwest La. Bar Assn. Episcopalian. Avocations: travelling, writing, reading, teaching, outdoor activities. General civil litigation, Corporate, general, Insurance. Office: Judice Law Firm 616 Broad St Lake Charles LA 70601 also: 616 W Broad St PO Drawer 556 Lake Charles LA 70601 Fax: 337-439-6177.

JUDICE, MARC WAYNE, lawyer; b. Lafayette, La., Oct. 22, 1946; s. Marc and Gladys B. Judice; 1 child, Renee. BS, U. La., 1969; MBA, U. Utah, 1974; JD, La. State U., 1977. Bar: La. 1977; CPA, La.; bd. cert. civil trial law, civil trial advocacy Nat. Bd. Trial Advocacy. Ptnr. Voorhies & Labbe, Lafayette, 1977-85, Juneau, Judice, Hill & Adley, Lafayette, 1985-93, Judice & Adley, Lafayette, 1993—. Bd. dirs. Univ. Med. Ctr., Lafayette, 1991, chmn.; bd. dirs. Home Savs. Bank, Lafayette, 1996—, Women's & Childrens Hosp., Lafayette, 1992-94; bd. trustees Med. Ctr. Southwest La., 1998-2001, chmn. bd. dirs., 1999-2003. Republican. Roman Catholic. Insurance, Personal injury (including property damage), Professional liability. Office: Judice & Adley 926 Coolidge Blvd Lafayette LA 70503-2434 E-mail: mwj@judice-adley.com.

JUDSON, C(HARLES) JAMES (JIM JUDSON), lawyer; b. Oregon City, Oreg., Oct. 24, 1944; s. Charles James and Barbara (Busch) J.; m. Diana L. Gerlach, Sept.11, 1965; children: Kevin, Nicole. BA cum laude, Stanford U., 1966, LLB with honors, 1969. Bar: Wash. 1969, U.S. Tax Ct. 1970, D.C. 1981. Ptnr. Davis Wright Tremaine, Seattle, 1969—. Bd. dirs. Port Blakely Tree Farms, Garrett and Ring, Joshua Green Corp., China Unicom; spkr. in field. Author: State Taxation of Fin. Instns., 1981; contbr. articles to profl. jours., bd. dir., Port Blakely Tree Farms, Garrett and Ring, Joshua Green Corp., China Unicom. Chmn. Bus. Tax Coalition, Seattle, 1987; chmn. lawyers div. United Way, Seattle, 1986, 87, commerce and industry div., 1989-91; trustee Wash. State Internat. Trade Fair, Seattle, 1981-86; bd. dirs. Seattle Prep. Sch., 1986-88; bd. dirs. Olympic Park Inst., 1988—, Yosemite Nat. Insts., 1993—; mem. Assn. Wash. Bus. Tax Com., 1978—; tax advisor Wash. State House Reps. Dem. Caucus; advisor Wash. State Dept. Revenue on Tax and Legis. Matters; mem. Seattle Tax Group, 1983—. Fellow Am. Coll Tax Counsel; mem. ABA (chmn. com. on fin. orgns. tax sect. 1978-82, subcom chmn. state and local tax com. tax sect. 1979—, chmn. excise tax com. 1983-90, interorgn. coordination com. 1985—, chmn. environ. tax com. 1991—), Wash. State Bar Assn. (chmn. tax sect. 1984-86, chmn. western region IRS/bar liaison com. 1987-88, mem. rules com. 1991—), Seattle-King County Bar Assn. (mem. tax sect. 1973-86), Seattle C. of C. (tax com. 1982—), Wash. Athletic Club (Seattle), Broadmoor Golf Club (Seattle), Bear Creek Golf Club (Redmond). Avocations: skiing, golf, basketball, wood working, hiking. Corporate, general, Taxation, general, State and local taxation. Office: Davis Wright Tremaine 2600 Century Sq 1501 4th Ave Seattle WA 98101-1688

JUDSON, PHILIP LIVINGSTON, lawyer; b. Palo Alto, Calif., Oct. 25, 1941; s. Philip MacGregor and Elizabeth Stuart (Peck) J.; m. Dorothy Louisa Lebohner, Sept. 6, 1963 (div. Jan., 1996); children: Wendy Patricia, Philip Lebohner, Michael Lee; m. Danielle DuPuis Kane, May 18, 1996. BA, Stanford U., 1963; JD, U. Calif., Hastings, 1969. Bar: Calif. 1970, Tex. 1999, U.S. Dist. Ct. (no. dist.) Calif. 1970, U.S. Ct. Appeals (9th cir.) 1970, U.S. Dist. Ct. (ctrl. dist.) Calif. 1984, U.S. Dist. Ct. (ea. dist.) Calif. 1985, U.S. Supreme Ct. 1987, D.C. 1988, U.S. Dist. Ct. (so. dist.) Calif. 1989, Tex. 1999, U.S. Dist. Ct. (no. and we. dists.) Tex. 2000, U.S. Dist. Ct. (ea. dist.) Tex. 2002. Assoc. Pillsbury, Madison & Sutro, San Francisco, 1969-76, ptnr., 1977-99, Skjerven Morrill MacPherson, LLP, San Jose, Calif., 1999, Austin, Tex., 1999—2002; shareholder Winstead Sechrest & Minick, P.C., Austin, Tex., 2002—. Lectr. Practising Law Inst., U. Tex. Advanced Intellectual Property Law Inst., Inst. for Am. and Internat. Law Intellectual Property Law Program. Pres. St. Mark's Sch., San Rafael, 1983-85, founding mem. trustee 1980-86; trustee Marin Acad., San Rafael, 1985-91. 1st lt. U.S. Army, 1963-65. Mem. ABA (antitrust and litigation sects.), San Francisco Bar Assn., Am. Judicature Soc., Austin Intellectual Property Law Assn., Travis County Bar Assn., Order of Coif, Phi Delta Theta. Republican. Episcopalian. Antitrust, Federal civil litigation, State civil litigation. Home: 8004 High Hollow Dr Austin TX 78750-7872 Office: 100 Congress Ave Ste 800 Austin TX 78701 E-mail: pjudson@austin.rr.com., pjudson@winstead.com.

JUETTNER, DIANA D'AMICO, lawyer, educator; b. N.Y.C., Jan. 21, 1940; d. Paris T.R. and Dina Adele (Antonucci) D'Amico; m. Paul J. Juettner, June 29, 1963; children: John, Laura. BA, Hunter Coll., 1961; postgrad., Am. U., 1963; JD cum laude, Touro Coll., 1983. Bar: N.Y. 1984, U.S. Dist. Ct. (so. dist.) N.Y. 1984, U.S. Supreme Ct. 1987. Office mgr. Westchester County Dem. Com., White Plains, NY, 1976-79; dist. mgr. for Westchester County U.S. Bur. Census, N.Y.C., 1979-80; pvt. practice Ardsley, NY, 1984—; prof. law, program dir. for legal studies Mercy Coll., Dobbs Ferry, NY, 1985—, co-chair social and behavioral scis. divsn., 2002—, asst. chair dept. law, criminal justice-safety adminstrn., 1994-98, pres. faculty senate, 1996—98, 2000—02. Arbitrator small claims matters White Plains City Ct., 1985-89. Co-author: (booklet) Your Day in Court, How to File a Small Claims Suit in Westchester County, 1976; assoc. editor N.Y. State Probation Officers Assn. Jour., 1990-92; editor-in-chief Jour. Northeast Acad. Legal Studies in Bus., 1996-98; contbr. articles to profl. jours. Councilwoman Town of Greenburgh, N.Y., 1992—; vice chair law com. Westchester County Dem. Com., White Plains, 1987-91; corr. sec. Greenburgh Dem. Town Com., Hartsdale, N.Y., 1986-91; mem. Westchester County Citizens Consumer Adv. Coun., White Plains, 1975-91, chair, 1991; chair Ardsley (N.Y.) Consumer Adv. Commn., 1974-79. Mem. Am. Assn. for Paralegal Edn. (model syllabus task force 1992-95, chair legis. com. 1995-97), N.Y. State Bar Assn. (elder law sect. com. on pub. agy. liaison and legis. 1992-95), Westchester County Bar Assn. (chair paralegal subcom. 1990—, chair bicentennial U.S. Constitution com. 1987-91), Westchester Women's Bar Assn. (v.p. 1989-91, dir. 1994-96, co-chair tech. com. 1996-2000), Women's Bar Assn. State N.Y. (chair profl. ethics com. 1997-98). Avocations: sailing, walking. Probate (including wills, trusts), Property, real (including real estate development, water), Alternative dispute resolution. Office: Mercy Coll 555 Broadway Dobbs Ferry NY 10522-1134 Business E-Mail: djuettner@mercy.edu.

JUHOLA, MICHAEL DUANE, lawyer; b. Ashtabula, Ohio, May 11, 1955; s. Kenneth Duane and Lois Rosemary (England) J.; m. Denise H. Juhola, May 2, 1987. BA, Hiram Coll., 1977; JD, Ohio State U., 1980. Bar: Ohio 1980, U.S. Dist. Ct. (so. dist.) Ohio 1987, U.S. Ct. Appeals (6th cir.) 1992. Asst. dir. Ohio Legal Ctr. Inst., Columbus, 1980-88; staff atty. Smith, Clark & Holzapfel, Columbus, 1988-89; exec. dir. Ohio div. Profl. Edn. System, Inc., Columbus, 1989-91; pvt. practice law Columbus, 1991—. Coun. mem. North Community Luth. Ch., Columbus, 1989-93. Mem. Ohio Bar Assn., Columbus Bar Assn., Worthington Estate Planning Coun., Phi Beta Kappa. Estate planning, Family and matrimonial, Probate (including wills, trusts). Office: 867-B High St Worthington OH 43085

JULIA, KATHERINE DRISCOLL, lawyer; b. Fort Ord, Calif., May 10, 1969; d. Donald John and Patricia (Troberman) Driscoll; m. Luis Manuel Julia, Mar. 22, 1997; children: H. Driscoll, Antonio Duval. BA in Polit. Sci., U. North Tex., 1993; JD, So. Meth. U., 1997. Bar: Tex. 1997, U.S. Dist. Ct. (so. dist.) Tex. 1997. Clk., counsel Law Office of Diana Rivera, McAllen, Tex., 1996—98; counsel Law Office of Preston Henrichson PC, Edinburg, Tex., 1998—. Fellow: Tex. Bar Found.; mem.: ATLA, Tex. Trial Lawyers Assn., Coll. State Bar Tex., Hidalgo County Bar and Young Lawyers Assn., South Tex. Trial Lawyers (pres. 2002, sec. 2000—01), Tex. Trial Lawyers Assn. (spkr. on mediation 2002). Avocations: carpentry, interior decorating, cooking, exercise. Personal injury (including property damage), Product liability. Office: Law Office Preston Henrichson PC 222 W Cano Edinburg TX 78539

JULIAN, J. R. lawyer; b. Wilmington, Del., Apr. 6, 1943; BA, Am U., 1966; JD, Cath. U. Am., 1970. Bar: Del. 1971, U.S. Dist. Ct. Del., U.S. Ct. Appeals (3d cir.), U.S. Supreme Ct. Pvt. practice, Wilmington, Del. Mem. bd. bar examiners Supreme Ct. State Del., 1985-89; mem. rules com. Del. Indsl. Accident Bd. Bd. dirs. Hist. Soc. Ct. Chancery. Mem. ABA (litig. sect., bus. law sect.), ATLA, Del. Bar Assn. (v.p. New Castle County chpt., former vice chair jud. appointments com., exec. com., litig. com., alt. dispute resolution com., ins. com., workers' compensation com., pres.), Am. Bd. Trial Advocates, Def. Rsch. Inst., Am. Judicature Soc., Del. Trial Lawyers Assn., Federalist Soc. for Law and Pub. Policy Studies (bd. adv. Del. chpt. lawyers divsn.), St. Thomas More Soc. Del. (pres.), Pi Sigma Alpha, Delta Theta Pi. General civil litigation, Insurance, Product liability. Office: Ste 1001 Market St Mall PO Box 2171 Wilmington DE 19899-2171*

JULIAN, JIM LEE, lawyer; b. Osceola, Ark., Dec. 14, 1954; s. John Roland and Lucille Angela (Potts) J.; m. Patricia Lynn Roberts, Jan. 26, 1980; 1 child, Kathryn Elizabeth. BA, Ark. State U., 1976; JD, U. Ark., 1979. Bar: Ark. 1979, U.S. Dist. Ct. (ea. and we. dists.) Ark. 1979, U.S. Ct. Appeals (8th cir.). Assoc. Skillman & Durrett, West Memphis, Ark., 1979-82; staff atty. Ark. Power and Light Co., Little Rock, 1982-84; assoc. House, Wallace & Jewell, Little Rock, 1984-85, ptnr., 1986-89, Chisenhall, Nestrud & Julian, Little Rock, 1989—. Pres. Crittenden County (Ark.) Young Dems., 1980-82; chmn. bd. dirs. Northside YMCA, 1992-96, North Little Rock Boys and Girls Club, 1998—. Mem. ABA, Internat. Assn. Def. Counsel, Ark. Bar Assn., Pulaski County Bar Assn., Ark. Assn. Def. Counsel, Major Sports Assn., North Hills Country Club. Avocation: golf. Product liability, Environmental, Insurance. Home: 3711 Lochridge Rd North Little Rock AR 72116-8328 Office: Chisenhall Nestrud & Julian 400 W Capitol Ave Ste 2840 Little Rock AR 72201-3467

JULIANO, JOHN LOUIS, lawyer; b. Oct. 21, 1944; s. John Carmine and Jeannette Helen (Ciotti) J.; m. Maryjane Theresa Groccia, July 4, 1966 (dec.); children: Jennifer, Jonathan. BBA, St. John's U., 1966; JD, Bklyn. Law Sch., 1969. Bar: N.Y. 1970, U.S. Dist. Ct. (ea. and so. dists.) N.Y., U.S. Ct. Appeals (2d cir.), U.S. Supreme Ct. Ptnr. Juliano, Karlson, Weisberg, 1970-72; pvt. practice East Northport, N.Y., 1972—. Pres., dir. Hillside United Van Lines, Inc.; mem. N.Y. State 10th Jud. Grievance Com., 1998—; lectr. Suffolk Acad. Law. Mem. ATLA, N.Y. State Bar Assn., Suffolk County Bar Assn. (pres. 1996-97, v.p. 1995-96, treas. 1994-95, sec. 1993-94, bd. dirs. 1998-2001), N.Y. State Trial Lawyers Assn., ICC Practitioners, Criminal Bar Assn., Columbian Lawyers Assn. (sec. 1972, treas. 1973, pres. 1974-75), Am. Inns of Ct. Criminal, Family and matrimonial, Personal injury (including property damage). Address: 39 Doyle Ct East Northport NY 11731-6404

JUNE, ROY ETHIEL, lawyer; b. Forsyth, Mont., Aug. 12, 1922; s. Charles E. and Elizabeth F. (Newnes) J.; m. Laura Brautigam, June 20, 1949; children: Patricia June, Richard Tyler. BA, U. Mont., 1948, BA in Law, 1951, LLB, 1952. Bar: Mont. 1952, Calif. 1961. Sole practice, Billings, Mont., 1952-57; atty. Sanders and June, 1953-57; real estate developer Orange County, Calif., 1957-61; ptnr. Dugan, Tobias, Tornay & June, Costa Mesa, Calif., 1961-62; city prosecutor Costa Mesa, 1962-63; asst. city atty., 1963-67; city atty., 1967-78; sole practice, 1962—. Atty., founder, dir. Citizens Bank of Costa Mesa, 1972-92; atty. Costa Mesa Hist. Soc., Costa Mesa Playhouse Patron's Assn., Red Barons Orange County, Costa Mesa Meml. Hosp. Aux., Harbor Key, Child Guidance Ctr. Orange County, Fairview State Hosp. Therapeutic Pool Vols., Inc. Active Eagle Scout evaluation team Harbor Area Boy Scouts Am., YMCA; atty. United Fund/Cmty. Chest Costa Mesa and Newport Beach; bd. dirs. Boys' Club Harbor Area, Mardan Ctr. Ednl. Therapy, United Cerebral Palsy Found., Orange County; docent Palm Springs Mus., 1996—. With USAF, WWII. Decorated Air medal with oak leaf cluster, DFC. Mem. Calif. Bar Assn., Costa Mesa C. of C. (bd. dirs.), Masons, Scottish Rite, Shriners, Santa Ana Country, Amigos Viejos, Los Fiestadores, Palm Springs Calif. Air Mus. (docent). Banking, Corporate, general, Municipal (including bonds). E-mail: RoyJune655@cs.com.

JUNEWICZ, JAMES J. lawyer; b. Oct. 1, 1950; s. John and Genevieve J.; m. Virginia Bornyas. BS, Georgetown U., 1972; JD, Duquesne U., 1976; LLM, NYU, 1978. Bar: Pa. 1977, D.C. 1978, Ill. 1984. Asst. gen. counsel SEC, Washington, 1982—84; ptnr. Mayer, Brown, Rowe & Maw, Chgo., 1987—. Corporate, general, Securities. Office: Mayer Brown Rowe & Maw 190 S La Salle St Ste 3900 Chicago IL 60603-3410

JUNG, HARALD H. lawyer; b. Duesseldorf, Germany, May 31, 1948; s. Reinhard A. and Elsa J. Jung; m. Marianne A. Heinz, Aug. 2, 1974; children: Martin, Alice. Bar: Frankfurt 1978, Appellate Ct. Frankfurt 1984; cert. notary 1996. Asst. lectr. U. Marburg, Germany, 1974—75, U. Frankfurt, Germany, 1975; legal trainee Appelate Ct., Frankfurt, 1975—77; assoc. Peltzer & Riesenkampff, Frankfurt, 1978—81; ptnr. Pltzer & Riesenkampff (now CMS Hasche Sigle), Frankfurt, 1981—. Author: Starting Business Operations in Germany, 1993; co-author: German Employment Law, 1983, Commentary to the German Banking Act, 1988. With Germany Mil., 1967—68. Mem.: Steuben-Squrz Soc. (bd. mem.), Am. C. of C. in Germany (chmn. legal com.). Mergers and acquisitions, Commercial, contracts (including sales of goods; commercial financing), Corporate, general. Office: CMS Hasche Sigle Friedrich-Ebert-Anlage 44 60325 Frankfurt Germany

JUNG, KAREN EUNKYUNG, lawyer, consultant; b. Seoul, Republic of Korea, July 21, 1971; BA, U. Calif., Berkeley, 1995; JD, UCLA, 2000. Bar: Calif. 01, U.S. Dist. Ct. (cen. dist.) Calif. 01. V.p. ACRESWorld, Inc, Santa Monica, Calif., 2000—. Republican. Methodist. Property, real (including real estate development, water), Probate (including wills, trusts). Office: ACRESWorld Inc 937 12th St # 109 Santa Monica CA 90403 Fax: 310-576-0747. E-mail: Karjung@aol.com.

JUNGEBERG, THOMAS DONALD, lawyer; b. Berea, Ohio, June 12, 1950; s. Wilbert Donald and Carolyn Francis (Gaube) J.; m. Kathleen Ann Killmer, Oct. 5, 1973; children: Kimberlee Ann, Allison Lynn, Zebulun Thomas, Nathan Aaron. BA, Kent State U., 1972; JD, Cleve. State U., 1976. Bar: Ohio 1976, Mass. 2001, U.S. Dist. Ct. (no. dist.) Ohio 1977, U.S. Tax Ct. 1980, U.S. Supreme Ct. 1980. Tchr. Berea City Schs., Ohio, 1972-75; staff atty. Palmquist & Palmquist, Medina, Ohio, 1977-80, Gibbs & Craze, Parma Heights, Ohio, 1980-81; sole practice Medina, 1981-87; v.p., gen. counsel, corp. sec. Shelby (Ohio) Ins. Co., 1987-95; prin. Lexington (Ohio) Ins. Cons., 1995-96; sole practice Lexington, 1995-96; v.p. legal Reliance Nat., Cleve., 1996-98; asst. v.p., asst. gen. counsel Commerce Ins. Group, Webster, Mass., 1999—. Tchr. First Bapt. Christian Sch., Medina, 1981-84; elder, sec. First Bapt. Ch. of Medina, 1979-86, chmn. First Bapt. Christian Sch., Medina, 1984; bd. govs. Ohio Med. Profl. Liability Underwriting Assn., 1993-95; dir. Inst. Inst. Ind., 1994-95. Mem. Ohio State Bar Assn.Mass. Bar Assn., Am. Corp. Counsel Assn., Gideons Internat. Republican. Avocations: piano, archery, gospel music composition, flying. Corporate, general, Insurance, Labor (including EEOC, Fair Labor Standards Act, labor-management relations, NLRB, OSHA). Home: 66 Westview Dr Danielson CT 06239 E-mail: tdjungeberg@aol.com., tjungeb@commerceinsurance.com.

JUNO, CYNTHIA, lawyer; b. Lubbock, Tex., Feb. 19, 1958; B in Music Edn., Tex. Tech. U., 1980; JD, Georgetown U., 1989. Bar: Calif. 1989, D.C. 1990. Assoc. atty. Hufstedler, Kaus & Ettinger, L.A., 1989-91, Jeffer, Mangels, Butler & Marmaro, L.A., 1991-93; pres., owner Juno Law Offices, L.A., 1993—. Civil rights, State civil litigation, General practice. Office: Juno Law Offices 8306 Wilshire Blvd Ste 7000 Beverly Hills CA 90211-2382 E-mail: junolaw@aol.com.

JUREWICZ, RICHARD MICHAEL, lawyer; b. Phila., Jan. 4, 1958; s. Leo Peter and Margaret Carol Jurewicz; m. Susan Mary McElwee, May 18, 1991; children: Kelsey Ann, Kaitlyn Nicole, Karly Renee. BS in Adminstrn. Justice, Pa. State U., 1980; JD, Temple U., 1983. Bar: Pa. 1983, U.S. Dist. Ct. (ea. dist.) Pa. 1984, U.S. Ct. Appeals (3d cir.) 1985. Judicial law clk. Pa. Supreme Ct., Phila., 1983-84; assoc. Galfand Berger Lurie Senesky & March, Phila., 1984—; ptnr. Galfand Berger, LLP, Phila., 1989—. Pres., bd. dirs. Kids Chance Penn. Inc., Phila., 1997—. Mem. Nat. Bd. Trial Advocacy (cert. in civil trial law and advocacy), Phil. Trial Lawyers Assn. (pres., bd. dirs. 2002-), Million Dollar Advocates Forum. Democrat. Avocations: racketball, camping, biking. General civil litigation, Construction, Product liability. Office: Galfand Berber LLP 1818 Market St Ste 2300 Philadelphia PA 19103-3648

JURKOWITZ, DANIEL S. lawyer, prosecutor, judge; b. Tucson; s. Harvey and Chaya Jurkowitz; m. Lisa A. Klein. BA, U. Ariz., 1994, JD, 1997. Bar: Ariz. 1997, U.S. Dist. Ct. Ariz. 1998, U.S. Ct. Appeals (9th cir.) 1998, U.S. Supreme Ct. 2000. Intern Ariz. Atty. Gens. Office, Dept. Econ. Security, Tucson, 1994; appeals clk. criminal divsn. Pima County Attys. Office, Tucson, 1995—96, student prosecutor criminal divsn., 1996; Westlaw student rep. West Pub. Corp., Tucson, 1996—97; law clk. civil divsn. Pima County Attys. Office, Tucson, 1997, dep. county atty. criminal divsn., 1997—98, dep. county atty. civil divsn., law clk. supr., 1998—2001; adminstrv. law judge Ariz. Dept. Transp., Tucson, 2001—; judge pro tempore Ariz. Superior Ct., 2003—; arbitrator State Bar of Ariz. Fee Arbitration Pgm, 2003—; hearing officer Sunnyside Unified Sch. Dist., 2002—. Legal columnist: Daily Jour. Corp., 2000. Teen ct. judge Pima County Teen Ct., 2001—02; treas. Fountain Park Homeowners Assn., 2002—03; mem. City of Tucson Citizens' Transp. Adv. Com., 2001—03; state and precinct committeeman Ariz. Rep. Party, Tucson, 1994—2001; vice chmn., sec. exec. com. Pima County Rep. Party, 1999—2001; v.p, pres. Sienna Homeowners Assn., Tucson, 1998—2000. Nat. merit scholar. Mem.: ABA, Pima County Bar Assn. (co-chair, sch. coord., tutor Lawyers for Literacy, Young Lawyers div. 1997—2002, bd. dirs. Young Lawyers divsn. 1999—2003, bd. dirs. 2002—), Mensa, Phi Beta Kappa. Jewish. Avocations: guitar, tennis, reading. Office: Arizona Dept Trans Motor Vehicle Exec Hearing Office 3565 S Broadmont Dr Second Fl Tucson AZ 85713-5240 Fax: 520-838-2779. E-mail: daniel.jurkowitz@azbar.org.

JUROW, GEORGE, judge; b. N.Y.C., Feb. 3, 1943; m. Barbara Hertzberg, Jan. 25, 1995; 1 child, John Ross. BS, U. Pa., 1963; JD, Yale U., 1966; PhD, Adelphi U., 1971. Dep. commr. N.Y.C. Dept. Mental Health, 1972-79; judge N.Y. State Family Ct., N.Y.C., 1982—. Contbr. numerous articles to profl. jours. Office: NY State Family Ct 60 Laayette St New York NY 10013

JUST, CHRISTOPH OLIVER THOMAS, lawyer; b. Harderberg, Lower Saxony, Germany, July 26, 1968; s. Hans-Guenther and Christine M. Elizabeth (Czech) Just. 1st exam, U. Saarbruecken, 1993; 2d exam, Palatine Ct. Appeals, 1996. Bar: Regional Cts. Germany, Regional ct. Frankfurt/Main, Ct. Appeals Frankfurt/Main, cert.: tax law specialist 2002, adminstrv. law specialist 2003. Assoc. Feddersen Laule Scherzberg Ohle Hansen Ewerwahn, Frankfurt, Germany, 1996—2000, Schulte Lawyers, Frankfurt/Main, 2000—01, ptnr., 2001—. Co-author: Export Law, 2002, Handbook Tax and Law in e-business, 2002; contbr. Administrative and regulatory, FERC practice, Environmental. Office: Schulte Lawyers Hochstrasse 49 60313 Frankfurt Hessen Germany

JUSTICE, JACK BURTON, retired lawyer, writer; b. Hardy, Ky., Aug. 2, 1931; s. George Edward and Goldia (Alley) J.; m. Martha Monser, Dec. 28, 1957 (dec. Feb. 1974); m. Judith Farquhar Lang, Apr. 26, 1975; children—Jonathan Burton, George Lewis, Paul Williamson. AB in Polit. Sci, W.Va. U., 1952, postgrad. in law, 1954-55; BA in Jurisprudence, Oxford (Eng.) U., 1954, MA, 1960. Bar: Pa. 1956. Assoc. firm Drinker Biddle & Reath, Phila., 1956-62, ptnr., 1962-82, White & Williams, Phila., 1982-96. Bus. mgr. Am. Oxonian, 1967-86; lectr. in field. Contbr. articles to profl. and lit. jours. Pres. Youth Svc., Phila., 1962-65; chmn. Phila. Com. on City Policy, 1966-67, Southeastern Pa. chpt. Ams. for Democratic Action, 1968-70; bd. overseers William Penn Charter Sch., Phila., 1978-91, clk., 1986-89. Rhodes scholar, 1952-54. Mem. Assn. Am. Rhodes Scholars (sec. 1967-86, pres. 1986-94). Democrat. Banking, Bankruptcy, Commercial, contracts (including sales of goods; commercial financing). Home: 10 Coyote Pass Rd Santa Fe NM 87508

KABAK, DOUGLAS THOMAS, lawyer; b. Elizabeth, N.J., Nov. 19, 1957; s. Aaron and Marilyn Virginia (Johnson) K.; m. Elisabeth Wiggin McDuffie, Oct. 21, 1989; 1 child, Matthew Thomas McDuffie Kabak. BA, Rutgers U., 1979, MBA, MBA, Rutgers U., 1990; postgrad., U. Exeter, Eng., 1980; JD, Seton Hall U., 1982. Bar. N.J. 1982, U.S. Dist. Ct. N.J. 1982. Law clk. Superior Ct. N.J., Elizabeth, 1982-83; assoc. Z. Lance Samay, Morristown, N.J., 1983-86; asst. dep. pub. defender Office Pub. Defender, Elizabeth, 1986—. Legal rep. St. Joseph's the Carpenter Bd. Edn., Roselle, N.J., 1985-87. Dir. St. Joseph the Carpenter Cath. Youth Orgn., Roselle, 1986-88, coach, 1981-88. Mem. KC. Roman Catholic. Home: 16 Indian Spring Rd Cranford NJ 07016-1616 Office: Pub Defender Office 65 Jefferson Ave Ste 3 Elizabeth NJ 07201-2441 E-mail: mckabak@juno.com.

KABALA, EDWARD JOHN, lawyer, corporate executive; b. Phila., Mar. 21, 1942; s. Stan and Margaret (Toner) K.; m. Gail L., DEc. 28, 1963; children: Courtenay, Paxson. BS, Pa. State U., 1964; JD, Duquesne U., 1970. Bar: Pa. 1970, U.S. Dist. Ct. (we. dist.) Pa., U.S. Ct. Appeals (3rd cir.) 1970, U.S. Tax Ct. 1970. Indsl. engr. Allegheny Ludlum Steel Co., 1964-67; sr. indsl. engr. Titanium Metals Corp. Am., 1967-68; patent engr. U.S. Steel Corp., 1969; atty., 1970, Houston, Cooper, Speer and German, Pitts., 1970-73; pres. Kabala & Geeseman and predecessor firm, 1973—2002; office mng. ptnr. Fox & Rothschild. Counsel Allegheny Med. Soc.; author, lectr. pensions, estate planning, taxation, fin. planning health care law various univs. and profl. orgns. of physicians, attys., accts., dentists, 1976—; editl. bd. MD News, 2001—, Best Lawyers in Am., 2001—; bd. dirs., chmn. Cancer Support Network, 1994-96. Author: Defending Your Practice in a Blue Shield Audit, 1992. Bd. dirs. Cancer Support Network, 1992-96, chmn., 1994-96; fund raiser Muscular Dystrophy Assn., 1998—. Recipient Crystal award, Cancer Support Network, 1993—95, Muscular Dystrophy Millenium Diamond award, 2001. Fellow Allegheny County Bar Found.; mem. ABA (sect. taxation com. on closely held corps., com. on profl. svc. corps., sec. bus. banking and corp. law com. on employee benefits), Am. Soc. Med. Assn. Counsel, Am. Health Lawyers Assn., Pa. Bar Assn., Allegheny County Bar Assn., Am. Acad. Hosp. Attys. Estate planning, Health, Pension, profit-sharing, and employee benefits. Home: 4405 Bayard St Pittsburgh PA 15213-1505 Office: 2900 Dominion Twr 625 Liberty Ave Pittsburgh PA 15222 E-mail: ekabala@frof.com.

KABEL, ROBERT JAMES, lawyer; b. Burbank, Calif., Nov. 30, 1946; s. Herman James and Margaret Elizabeth (Doyle) K. BA, Denison U., 1969; JD, Vanderbilt U., 1972; LL.M. in Taxation, Georgetown U., 1979. Bar: D.C., Tenn., Ohio, U.S. Supreme Ct. Adminstrv. asst. to Gov. Winfield Dunn of Tenn., Nashville, 1972-75; legis. asst. to Senator Paul Fannin, Washington, 1975-77; legis. dir. Senator Richard G. Lugar of Ind., Washington, 1977-82; spl. asst. to pres. White House, Washington, 1982-84; ptnr. Manatt, Phelps & Phillips and precedessor firm, Washington, 1985—2002, Baker & Daniels, Washington, 2002—; sr. v.p. Sagamore Assoc., Washington, 2002—. Part-time mem. Fgn. Claims Settlement Commn., 1987-91; chair Greater Washington Bd. Trade Task Force Internat. Trade & Intellectual Property, 1996-97. Mem. Bretton Woods Commn.; Vanderbilt Law Sch. Alumni Bd., 1997-2000; bd. trustees Denison U., 1999—; chmn. bd. dirs. Log Cabin Reps., 1994-99; chmn. Liberty Edn. Fund, 1999—; mem. D.C. Rep. Com., vice chmn. Recipient citation Denison U. Alumni. Mem. ABA, Rep. Lawyers Assn., Denison U. Alumni Soc. (pres. 1994-96), Met. Club Washington, The Federalist Soc. Republican. Presbyterian. Office: Baker & Daniels 805 15th St NW Ste 700 Washington DC 20005 E-mail: RKabel@bakerd.com.

KACHWAHA, SUMEET, lawyer, consultant; b. Agra, India, Dec. 19, 1955; s. Ranjeet Singh and Kushal Kachwaha; m. Mamta Sarin Kachwaha, Oct. 6, 1984; children: Samar Singh, Shivani. BA in English with honors, U. Delhi, India, 1976; LLB, U. Delhi, 1979. Pvt. practice, Delhi, 1979—98; ptnr. Rajinder Narain & Co., Delhi, 1998—2002; sr. ptnr. Kachwaha & Ptnrs., Delhi, 2002—. Mem.: Inter Pacific Bar Assn., Internat. Bar Assn., Supreme Ct. Bar Assn. India. Avocations: reading, swimming, travel, music. Corporate, general, Environmental, Intellectual property. Office: Kachwaha & Ptnrs 1/6 Shanti Niketan New Delhi 110023 India

KADEN, LEWIS B. law educator, lawyer; b. 1942; AB, Harvard U., 1963, LLB, 1967. Bar: N.Y. 1970, N.J. 1974. Harvard scholar Emmanuel Coll., Cambridge U., 1963-64; law clk. U.S. Ct. Appeals, 1967; legis. asst. Senator Robert F. Kennedy, 1968; ptnr. Battle, Fowler, Stokes & Kheel, 1969-73; chief counsel to gov. State of N.J., 1974-76; assoc. prof. Columbia U., 1976-79, prof., 1979-84, adj. prof., 1984—, dir. Ctr. for Law and Econ. Studies, 1979-83; ptnr. Davis, Polk & Wardwell, N.Y.C., 1984—. Bd. dirs. Bethlehem Steel Corp.; chmn. U.S. Govt. Overseas Presence Adv. Panel, 1999. Chmn. N.Y. State Indsl. Coop. Coun., 1986-92. Office: Davis Polk & Wardwell 450 Lexington Ave Fl 31 New York NY 10017-3982 E-mail: kaden@dpw.com.

KADISH, SANFORD HAROLD, law educator; b. N.Y.C., Sept. 7, 1921; s. Samuel J. and Frances R. (Klein) K.; m. June Kurtin, Sept. 29, 1942; children: Joshua, Peter. B Social Scis, CCNY, 1942; LLB, Columbia U., 1948; JD (hon.), U. Cologne, 1983; LLD (hon.), CUNY, 1985, Southwestern U., 1993. Bar: N.Y. 1948, Utah 1954. Pvt. practice law, N.Y.C., 1948-51; prof. law U. Utah, 1951-60, U. Mich., 1961-64, U. Calif., Berkeley, 1964-91, dean Law Sch., 1975-82, Morrison prof., 1973-91, prof. emeritus, 1991—. Fulbright lectr. Melbourne (Australia) U., 1956; vis. prof. Harvard U., 1960-61, Freiburg U., 1967; lectr. Salzburg Seminar Am. Studies, 1965; Fulbright vis. lectr. Kyoto (Japan) U., 1975; vis. fellow Inst. Criminology, Cambridge (Eng.) U., 1968. Author: (with M.R. Kadish) Discretion to Disobey— A Study of Lawful Departures from Legal Rules, 1973, (with Schulhofer) Criminal Law and Its Processes, 6th edit., 1995, Blame and Punishment—Essays in the Criminal Law, 1987; editor-in-chief Ency. Crime and Justice, 1983; contbr. articles to profl. jours. Reporter Calif. Legis. Penal Code Project, 1964-68; pub. mem. Wage Stblzn. Bd., region XII, 1951-53; cons. Pres.'s Commn. Adminstrn. of Justice, 1966; mem. Calif. Coun. Criminal Justice, 1968-69. Lt. USNR, 1943-46. Fellow, Ctr. Advanced Study Behavioral Scis., 1967—68, Guggenheim fellow, Oxford U., 1974—75, vis. fellow, All Souls Coll. Oxford U., 1983. Fellow AAAS (v.p. 1984-86), Brit. Acad. (corr.); mem. AAUP (nat. pres. 1970-72), Am. Assn. Law Schs. (exec. com. 1960, pres. 1982), Order of Coif (exec. com. 1966-67, 74-75), Phi Beta Kappa. Home: 774 Hilldale Ave Berkeley CA 94708-1318 E-mail: shk@law.berkeley.edu.

KADISHA, SHEILA, lawyer; b. Tehran, Iran, Aug. 30, 1969; arrived in U.S., 1978; d. Rudy Kadisha and Nina Moradi. BA, U. Calif., Santa Barbara, 1991; JD, Loyola U., L.A., 2000. Bar: Calif. 2000, U.S. Dist. Ct. (cen. dist.) Calif. 2000. Hearing rep. City Interpreting, Sherman Oaks, Calif., 1991—97. Bd. dirs. Advancement Rsch. Myopathics, L.A., 2000—, Together Forever, L.A., 2002. Mem.: ABA, L.A. County Bar Assn. Jewish. General practice, General civil litigation. Address: 115 N Kings Rd Los Angeles CA 90048-2624 Office: Law Offices of Nownejad & Jaramillo 433 N Camden Ste 400 Beverly Hills CA 90210

KADISON, STUART, lawyer, educator; b. Richmond, Va., Nov. 17, 1923; s. Elliot Theodore and Rebecca (Lesser) K.; m. Carita Silverman, June 23, 1946; children: Dana, Brian, Warne. Student, NYU, 1938-40; AB, U. Md., 1942; LL.B., Stanford U., 1948. Bar: Calif. 1948. Practiced law, Los Angeles; now ret. ptnr. Sidley & Austin, Los Angeles. Lectr. Southwestern U. Sch. Law, L.A., 1948-52, Stanford U. Sch. Law, 1977-82; Herman Phleger vis. prof. Stanford Law Sch., 1994; vis. prof. Brigham Young U. Law Sch., 1995-99, U. Chgo. Law Sch., 2000; co-chmn. ABA-Am. Newspaper Pubs. Assn. Task Force, 1977-83. Bd. visitors Stanford Law Sch., 1964-72, chmn., 1969-70; bd. dirs. Friends of Huntington Libr., v.p. and treas., 1977-82, pres., 1983-85, bd. overseers, 1978-91; chmn. lawyers adv. com. Constl. Rights Found., 1978-81; trustee Santa Barbara Mus. Art, 1991-97, 2001--. Lt. USNR, 1942-46. Elected to Townsend Harris Hall of Fame, 1994. Fellow Am. Coll. Trial Lawyers, Am. Bar Found.; mem. ABA (chmn. spl. com. on delivery of legal svcs. 1973-75, chmn. resource devel. coun. 1983-84), Am. Law Inst. (life), L.A. County Bar Assn. (pres. 1971-72, chmn. com. on judiciary 1976-77, Shattuck-Price Meml. award 1986), State Bar Calif. (gov. 1973-76), Destroyer Escort Commanding Officers WWII. Home: 4853 Glencairn Rd Los Angeles CA 90027-1135

KAESTNER, RICHARD DARWIN, lawyer; b. Milw., Feb. 10, 1934; s. Henry B. and Sophia (Schley) K.; m. Shirley Sue Higgins, Sept. 16, 1961; children: Richard, Kurtis. BS, Marquette U., 1956; JD, 1961. Bar: Wis. 1961, U.S. Dist. Ct. (ea. dist.) Wis. 1961, U.S. Supreme Ct. 1971. Assoc. Wiernick & Zurlo, Milw., 1961-63, Beaudry & Kershek, Milw., 1963-67; sole practice Milw., 1976-77; ptnr. Harris & Kaestner, Wauwatosa, Wis., 1977-80; sole practice Elm Grove, Wis., 1980—. Ct. commr. Circuit Ct. Wis., 1981-2000, Waukesha County, Wis., 1987—. Examiner, Milwaukee County Civil Svc. Commn., 1983—; officer, bd. dirs. Willaura West Homeowners Assn., 1976-84. Served with AUS, 1956-58. Mem. State Bar of Wis. (bd. attys. profl. responsibility com. 1976-85), Wis. Bar Assn., Milw. Bar Assn., Waukesha Bar Assn., Am. Coll. Trust and Estate Counsel, Delta Theta Phi. Lutheran. Family and matrimonial, Probate (including wills, trusts). Home: N30w28935 W Lakeside Dr Pewaukee WI 53072-3312 Office: PO Box 619 Elm Grove WI 53122-0619 E-mail: attyrdk@execpc.com.

KAFANTARIS, GEORGE NICHOLAS, lawyer; b. Kardamyla, Chios, Greece, May 11, 1953; came to U.S., 1966; s. Nicholas George and Evangelia M. (Frangias) K.; m. Maria G. Gampieris, June 3, 1977; children: Nicholas, Theologos, Mark, Constantine-Evangelos. BS, Youngstown State U., 1976; JD, U. Toledo, 1979. Bar: Ohio, 1981, U.S. Dist. Ct. (no. dist.) Ohio 1982. Pvt. practice, Warren, Ohio, 1981—. Sec. United Chios Soc., Agia Markela, Warren, 1984-85; bd. dirs. St. Demetrios Orthodox Ch., Warren, 1984-85; Trumbull County Rep. Precinct Committeeman, Warren, 1984-85. Mem. ABA, Assn. Trial Lawyers Am., Ohio State Bar Assn. (mem. computer com. 1989—), Ohio Acad. Trial Lawyers, Mahoning County Bar Assn., Trumbull County Bar Assn., Mahoning-Trumbull Acad. Trial Lawyers. Avocations: photography, computers, swimming. State civil litigation, Labor (including EEOC, Fair Labor Standards Act, labor-management relations, NLRB, OSHA), Personal injury (including property damage). Home: 734 N Park Ave Warren OH 44483-4821 Office: 720 N Park Ave Warren OH 44483-4821

KAFIN, ROBERT JOSEPH, lawyer; b. Phila., Jan. 1, 1942; s. Jacob A. and Anna C. (Cohen) K.; m. Carol A. Friedman, June 20, 1965; children: Tammy Ellen, Peter Douglas. AB, Franklin & Marshall Coll., 1963; JD, Harvard U., 1966. Bar: N.Y. 1967, U.S. Dist. Ct. (so. dist.) N.Y. 1968, U.S. Dist. Ct. (no. dist.) N.Y. 1971, U.S. Dist. Ct. (we. dist.) N.Y. 1974, U.S. Ct. Appeals (2d cir.) 1971, U.S. Supreme Ct. 1972, D.C. 1997. Ptnr. Kafin and Needleman, Glens Falls, N.Y., 1971-78; prin. Miller, Mannix, Lemery & Kafin, Glens Falls, N.Y., 1978-87; assoc. Proskauer Rose LLP, N.Y.C., 1967-71, ptnr., 1987-91, chief operating officer, ptnr., 1991—. Trustee Adirondack Conservancy Com., Elizabethtown, N.Y., 1980-87; judge Glens Falls City Ct., 1976; counsel N.Y. State Senate, Albany, N.Y., 1973-87. Editor: N.Y. Environmental Law Handbook, 1988, 92. Bd. dirs. Environ. Planning Lobby, Albany, 1977-88; active Manhattan Solid Waste Adv. Bd., N.Y.C., 1987—; dir. N.Y. Parks and Conservation Assn., 1995—, chmn., 1999; trustee Preservation League N.Y. State, 1997—. Mem. N.Y. Bar Assn. (sec. environ. law sect. 1988, treas. 1989, 1st vice chmn. 1991, chair 1992-93), Assn. Bar City N.Y. (environ. law com. 1987-89). Democrat. Jewish. Environmental, Land use and zoning (including planning). Home: 340 E 72d St Apt 3-SE New York NY 10021 Office: Proskauer Rose LLP 1585 Broadway Fl 27 New York NY 10036-8299

KAFKA, GERALD ANDREW, lawyer; b. Martins Ferry, Ohio, Sept. 9, 1951; s. Andrew and Mary (Spustek) K.; m. Rita A. Cavanagh; children: Andrea, Sarah, Justin. BA, Wheeling Jesuit Coll., 1972; JD, U. Cin., 1975; LLM in Taxation, Georgetown U., 1979. Bar: Ohio 1975, D.C. 1982, Md. 1984, U.S. Tax Ct. 1977, U.S. Claims Ct. 1978, U.S. Supreme Ct. 1979, D.C. 1982, U.S. Dist. Ct. (D.C. dist.) 1983, U.S. Ct. Appeals (D.C., fed., 3d, 4th, 5th, 6th, 7th 8th and 9th cirs.). Trial atty. honors program tax div. U.S. Dept. Justice, Washington, 1975-79; ptnr. Scribner, Hall & Thompson, Washington, 1979-84, Steptoe & Johnson, Washington, 1984-92, Dewey Ballantine, Washington, 1992-2000, Mokee Nelson, LLP, Washington, 2000—. Mem. adj. faculty Georgetown U. Law Ctr., Washington, 1979—; master J. Edgar Murdoch Am. Inn of Ct., U.S. Tax Ct., 1989—. Author: Litigation of Federal Tax Civil Controversies, 1996; editor procedure dept. Jour. Taxation; contbr. articles to profl. jours. Named Outstanding Atty., Tax Divsn. U.S. Dept. Justice, Washington, 1977. Fellow Am. Coll. Tax Counsel; mem. ABA (chair ct. procedure com. tax sect. 1993-95, chmn. task force civil tax litigation process 1989-90, task force on large case audits and litigation 1990-91, ad hoc joint com. tax ct. jurisdiction 1987, task force on taxpayer bill of rights legis 1987-88), D.C. Bar Assn. (steering com. tax sect. 1986-91, chmn. com. audits and litigation tax sect. 1987). Federal civil litigation, Taxation, general, Personal income taxation. Office: 1919 M St NW Washington DC 20036-3816 E-mail: gkafka@mckeenelson.com.

KAGAN, ELENA, law educator; b. 1960; BA summa cum laude, Princeton, 1981; MPhil, Worchester Coll., Oxford, 1983; JD magna cum laude, Harvard Law School, 1986. Law clk. US Ct. of Appeals for Judge Abner Mikva of the US Supreme Ct. for the DC Circuit, 1986—87, US Ct. of Appeals for Justice Thurgood Marshall of the US Supreme Ct., 1987—88; assoc. Williams & Connolly, Wash., DC, 1989—91; faculty mem. Univ. of Chgo. Law Sch., Chgo., 1991—99; nominated to serve as judge US Supreme Ct. of Appeals, Wash., DC, 1999; asst. prof. Univ. of Chgo. Law Sch., 1991, prof. of Law tenure, 1995; Assoc. Coun. to the Pres. White House, Wash., DC, 1995—96, Dep. Asst. to the Pres. for Domestic Policy, 1997—99, Dep. Dir. of the Domestic Policy Coun., 1997—99; vis. prof. Harvard Law Sch., 1999, prof. of Law, 2001—. Author: (article) Harvard Law Rev. Article, "Pres. Admin.", 2001 (honored as the year's top scholarly article by the Am. Bar Assoc. Section on Admin. Law and Reg. Pract., 2001). Kagan has also written on a range of First Amendment issues, including the role of governmental motive in different facets of First Amendment doctrine, and the interplay of libel law and the First Amendment. Mem.: Harvard Law Sch. faculty appt. comm., Harvard Law Sch. Locational options comm. (chair 2001—02). Kagan is a prof. of law at Harvard fLaw Sch. where she teaches admin. law, constitutional law, and civil procedure. Her recent sholarship focuses primarily on the role of the Pres. of the US in formulating and influencing fed. admin. and regulatory law. Office: Harvard Law Sch Griswold 507 1563 Mass Ave Cambridge MA 02138*

KAHARICK, JEROME JOHN, lawyer; b. Johnstown, Pa., Apr. 15, 1955; s. Stanley Joseph and Emily (Solic) K.; m. Carolyn Marie Safko, Aug. 7, 1977; children: Natalie, Allison. BA summa cum laude, U. Pitts., 1977; JD, Duquesne U., 1991. Bar: Pa. 1991, N.Y. 2000, U.S. Dist. Ct. (we. dist.) Pa. 1991, U.S. Dist. Ct. (we. dist.) Mich. 1998, U.S. Dist. Ct. (no. dist.) N.Y. 1998, U.S. Ct. Appeals (3d cir.) 1992, U.S. Supreme Ct., 1997. Sales rep. Met. Life, Johnstown, Pa., 1977-84; owner, stockholder Planned Fin. Svcs., Johnstown, Pa., 1984-88; law clk. Wayman, Irvin & McAuley, Pitts., 1988-89; legal analyst Elliott Co., Jeannette, Pa., 1989-92; pvt. practice Johnstown, 1992-95, 97—; asst. pub. defender Cambria County, Pa., 1993-99; ptnr. Weaver and Kaharick, 1995-97; atty. in pvt. practice Johnstown, Pa., 1997—. Exec. production editor Duquesne Law Rev., 1990-91. Mem. ABA, ATLA, N.Y. Bar Assn., Nat. Assn. Criminal Def. Lawyers, Pa. Bar Assn., N.Y. State Bar Assn., Order of Barristers. Republican. Roman Catholic. Civil rights, General civil litigation, Criminal. Office: Wallace Bldg 406 Main St Ste 301-302 Johnstown PA 15901-1906

KAHLENBECK, HOWARD, JR., lawyer; b. Ft. Wayne, Ind., Dec. 7, 1929; s. Howard and Clara Elizabeth (Wegman) K.; m. Sally A. Horrell, Aug. 14, 1954; children: Kathryn Sue, Douglas H. BS with distinction, Ind. U., 1952; LLB, U. Mich., 1957. Bar: Ind. 1957. Ptnr. Krieg DeVault, LLP, Indpls., 1957—. Sec., bd. dirs. Maul Tech. Corp. (formerly Buehler Corp.), Indpls., 1971-81, Am. Monitor Corp., Indpls., 1971-86, Am. Interstate Ins. Corp. Wis., Milw., 1973-84, Am. Interstate Ins. Co. Ga., Am. Underwriters Group, Inc., Indpls., 1973-86, Pafco Gen. Ins. Co., 1987-88. With USAF, 1952-54. Mem. ABA, Ind. Bar Assn., Indpls. Bar Assn., Alpha Kappa Psi, Delta Theta Phi, Beta Gamma Sigma, Delta Upsilon Internat. (sec., bd. dirs. 1971-83, chmn. 1983-86, trustee found. 1983-98). Lutheran. Commercial, contracts (including sales of goods; commercial financing), Corporate, general, Mergers and acquisitions. Home: 6320 Old Orchard Rd Indianapolis IN 46226-1041 Office: Krieg DeVault LLP One Indiana Sq Ste 2800 Indianapolis IN 46204 Business E-mail: hk@kdlegal.com.

KAHLER, RAY WILLIAM, lawyer; b. Longview, Wash., Oct. 29, 1970; s. Ray E. and Karen G. Kahler. BA in English, U. Puget Sound, 1993; JD, Harvard U., 1996. Bar: Wash. 1996, U.S. Dist. Ct. (we. dist.) Wash. 1997.

Lawyer Stritmatter Kessler Whelan Withey Coluccio, Hoquiam, Wash., 1996—. Personal injury (including property damage), Product liability, Toxic tort. Office: Stritmatter Kessler Whelan Withey Coluccio 413 8th St Hoquiam WA 98550-3607 E-mail: ray@skwwc.com.

KAHN, ANTHONY F. lawyer; b. Washington, Apr. 29, 1954; s. Henry and Claudia F.; m. Cynthia Marie Farhart, Aug. 11, 1979; children: Brian, Andrew, Stephen. BA, Wake Forest U., 1976; MBA summa cum laude, JD magna cum laude, U. Notre Dame, 1980. Bar: N.Y. 1981. Ptnr. White & Case LLP, N.Y.C., 1980—. Finance, Mergers and acquisitions, Municipal (including bonds). Office: White & Case LLP 1155 Avenue of the Americas New York NY 10036-2711 E-mail: AKAHN@WHITECASE.com.

KAHN, BENJAMIN ALEXANDER, lawyer; b. Boston, July 8, 1970; s. Michael David and Ruth Jacobson Kahn. BA cum laude, Tufts U., 1992; vis. law student, U. Colo., 1994; JD, U. Mich., 1995. Bar: Colo. 1997, U.S. Dist. Ct. Colo. 1998, U.S. Ct. Appeals (10th cir.) 1999. Clk. to Hon. Justice George E. Lohr, Denver, 1995-96; assoc. Kennedy & Christopher, P.C., Denver, 1998-2001, Brownstein, Hyatt & Farber, P.C., Denver, 2001—. Contbr. articles to profl. jours. including Stanford Jour. of Internat. Law, ABA Tort and Ins. Law Jour., William Mitchell Law Rev. Clara Belfield-Henry Bates Law Travel fellow, 1997. Mem. Colo. Bar Assn. (environ., natural resources, water, litigation, and other coms.), Adminstrn. Law Forum Com., Denver Bar, Colo. Def. Lawyers Assn., Colo. Indian Bar Assn. Avocations: art, music, outdoor activities, antiques, travel. Administrative and regulatory, Appellate, General civil litigation. Home: 2590 Cherry St Denver CO 80207-3145 Office: 410 17th St Ste 2200 Denver CO 80202-4437 E-mail: bkahn@bhf-law.com.

KAHN, BERT L. lawyer; b. Milw., July 5, 1938; s. David and Rose (Glusman) K.; m. Erika Apt, Sept. 1, 1963; children: Rita, Mitchell, Abigail. BBA, U. Wis., 1960, JD, 1963. Bar: Wis. 1964, Ill. 1971, U.S. Tax Ct. 1966. Atty. Estate & Gift Tax div., IRS, Chgo., 1963-65; trial aty. Reg. Counsels Office-U.S. Treasury Office, St. Paul and Chgo., 1965-72; ptnr. Hirschtritt, Hirschtritt, Gold, P.C., Chgo., 1972-77, Mardell & Kahn, Ltd., Chgo., 1977-81; pvt. practice Bert L. Kahn, Ltd., Skokie, Ill., 1981—. Lectr. in field. Pres. Religious Zionists of Chgo., 1979-80, co-nat. pres. 1996-98; bd. dirs. Airie Crown Hebrew Day Sch., Chgo., 1981; chmn. subcom. lawyers div. Jewish United Fund, 1989-90; v.p., past co-pres. Religious Zionists of Am. Mem. ABA (tax com.), Chgo. Bar Assn. (tax com.). Estate planning, Probate (including wills, trusts), Personal income taxation. Office: 8707 Skokie Blvd Ste 107 Skokie IL 60077-2200

KAHN, DAVID MILLER, lawyer, educator; b. Port Chester, N.Y., Apr. 21, 1925; m. Barbara Heller, May 9, 1952; children: William, James, Caroline. BA, U. Ky., 1947; LLB cum laude, N.Y. Law Sch., 1950. Bar: N.Y. 1951, U.S. Dist. Ct. (ea. and so. dists.) N.Y. 1953, U.S. Supreme Ct. 1958. Sole practice, White Plains, N.Y., 1951-60; ptnr. Kahn & Rubin, White Plains, 1960-66, Kahn & Goldman, White Plains, 1967-80; sr. ptnr. Kahn & Landau, White Plains, Palm Beach, Fla., 1980-88, Kahn and Kahn, Fla., N.Y., 1988-95, Kahn, Kahn & Scutieri Esq., Palm Beach Gardens, 1995—. Lectr. N.Y. Law Sch., 1982—; spl. counsel Village Port Chester, N.Y., 1960-63; commr. of appraisal Westchester County Supreme Ct., 1973-77; counsel Chemplex Industries, Inc., BIS Communications Corp., Bilbar Realty Co. Chmn. Westchester County Citizens for Eisenhower, 1950-52; pres. Westchester County Young Reps. Clubs, 1958-60; founder, chmn. bd. dirs. Port Chester-Rye Town Vol. Ambulance Corps, 1968-77; pres. Driftwood Corp., Amagansette, L.I., N.Y., 1984-91. Served with Counter Intelligence Corps USAF, 1942-46. Recipient John Marshall Harlan fellow N.Y. Law Sch., 1990-93, lifetime achievement award Westchester County Bar Assn, 2001. Fellow Am. Acad. Matrimonial Lawyers (bd. govs. N.Y. chpt. 1976-79); mem. ABA, N.Y. State Bar Assn., Westchester County Bar Assn., White Plains Bar Assn., N.Y. Law Sch. Alumni Assn. (bd. dirs. 1970-80), Elmwood C.C. (legal counsel), Eastpointe Country Club. Family and matrimonial, Probate (including wills, trusts), Property, real (including real estate development, water). Home and Office: 6419 Eastpointe Pines St Palm Beach Gardens FL 33418 also: 175 Main St White Plains NY 10601-3105

KAHN, EDWIN LEONARD, lawyer; b. N.Y.C., Aug. 1, 1918; s. Max L. and Julia (Rich) K.; m. Myra J. Green, Oct. 20, 1946 (dec. 1994); children: Martha L., Deborah K. Spiliotopoulos. AB, U. N.C., 1937; LLB cum laude, Harvard U., 1940. Bar: N.C. 1940, D.C. 1949. Atty., asst. head legislation and regulations div. Office Chief Counsel IRS, 1940-52, dir. tech. planning div., 1952-55; ptnr. Arent, Fox, Kintner, Plotkin & Kahn, Washington, 1955-86, of counsel, ret., 1986—. Lectr. NYU Tax Inst., mem. adv. bd., 1959-70; lectr. tax insts. Coll. William and Mary, U. Chgo., U. Tex. Editor: Harvard Law Rev, 1939-40; editorial adv. bd. Tax Advisor of Am. Inst. CPA's, 1974-86. Bd. dirs. Jewish Community Ctr. Greater Washington, 1972-78; trustee Cosmos Club Found., 1989-93, chmn., 1989-91. With U.S. Army, 1943-46, ETO. Decorated Bronze Star. Fellow Am. Bar Found. (life); mem. ABA (coun. 1963-66, vice chmn. sect. taxation 1965-66), Fed. Bar Assn. (chmn. taxation com. 1967-68), D.C. Bar Assn., Nat. Tax Assn.-Tax Inst. Am. (adv. coun. 1967-69, bd. dirs. 1969-73), Am. Law Inst. (life), Am. Coll. Tax Counsel, J. Edgar Murdock Am. Inn Ct. (master bencher 1988-91), Phi Beta Kappa (life mem. fellows). Jewish. Home: 4104 40th St N Arlington VA 22207-4805 Office: 1050 Connecticut Ave NW Washington DC 20036-5303

KAHN, EDWIN SAM, lawyer; b. N.Y.C., Jan. 22, 1938; m. Cynthia Chutter, May 30, 1966; children: David, Jonathan, Jennifer. BA, U. Colo., 1958; JD, Harvard U., 1965. Bar: Colo. 1965, U.S. Dist. Ct. (Colo.) 1965, U.S. Ct. Appeals (10th cir.) 1965, U.S. Supreme Ct. 1968. Assoc. Holland & Hart, Denver, 1965-70, ptnr., 1970-77; ptnr., shareholder Kelly, Haglund, Garnsey & Kahn, LLC, Denver, 1978—. 1st lt. USAF, 1959-62. Fellow Am. Coll. Trial Lawyers; mem. Denver Bar Assn. (pres. 1984-85). Federal civil litigation, State civil litigation, Libel. Home: 2345 Leyden St Denver CO 80207-3441 Office: Kelly Haglund Garnsey & Kahn LLC 1441 18th St Ste 300 Denver CO 80202-1255 E-mail: edkahn@4dv.net.

KAHN, ELLIS IRVIN, lawyer; b. Charleston, S.C., Jan. 18, 1936; s. Robert and Estelle Harriet (Kaminski) Kahn; m. Janice Weinstein, Aug. 11, 1963; children: Justin Simon, David Israel, Cynthia Kahn Nirenblatt. AB in Polit. Sci., Citadel, 1958; JD, U. S.C., 1961. Bar: S.C. 1961, U.S. Ct. Appeals (5th cir.) 1963, U.S. Ct. Appeals (4th cir.) 1964, U.S. Supreme Ct. 1970, DC 1978, U.S. Claims Ct. 1988, diplomate: Nat. Bd. Trial Advocacy, Am. Bd. Profl. Liability Attys. (trustee 1989-), cert.: (civil ct. mediator). Law clk. U.S. Dist. Ct. S.C., 1964—66; prin. Kahn Law Firm, Charleston. Adj. prof. med.-legal jurisprudence Med. U. S.C., 1978—87; mem. rules com. U.S. Dist. Ct., 1984—96. Mem. nat. coun. Am. Israel Pub. Affairs Com., 1982—88, Hebrew Benevolent Soc., pres., 1994—96; mem. Hebrew Orphan Soc., S.C. Organ Procurement Agy., 1989—94; chmn. campaign Charleston Jewish Fedn., 1986—87, pres., 1988—90. Capt. USAF, 1961—64. Fellow: Internat. Soc. Barristers; mem.: ATLA (state committeeman 1970—74), ABA, S.C. Trial Lawyers Assn. (pres. 1976—77), 4th Cir. Jud. Conf. (life), S.C. Bar. Federal civil litigation, State civil litigation, Personal injury (including property damage), Libel, General civil litigation. Home: 316 Confederate Cir Charleston SC 29407-7431 Office: PO Box 31397 Charleston SC 29417-1397

KAHN, LAURENCE MICHAEL, lawyer, business consultant; b. Chgo., May 15, 1947; s. Ernest Newman and Louise (Schoenberg) K.; m. Geraldine Marie Hirsch, July 31, 1971 (div. Oct. 1985); children: Eric M., Melissa M.; m. Candace L. Ross, Sept. 7, 1991. BA magna cum laude, U. Pa., 1969, MS in Edn., 1971; JD cum laude, U. Mich., 1977. Bar: Mich. 1977, D.C. 1980, Md. 1981, U.S. Dist. Ct. Md. 1981, U.S. Dist. Ct. D.C. 1981, U.S. Ct. Claims 1989, U.S. Ct. Appeals (D.C. cir) 1992, Calif. 1994. Tchr. Northbrook (Ill.) Sch. Dist. 27, 1969-70, Abington (Pa.) Sch. Dist., 1971-73, Phila. Sch. Dist., 1973-74; staff atty. FTC, Washington, 1977-81; from assoc. to ptnr. Sherman Meehan & Curtin, PC, Washington, 1981-91; pres. Negotiated Solutions, Jacksonville, Oreg., 1991—, Washington, 1991—, Jacksonville, Oreg., 1991—; dep. city atty. San Diego City Atty.'s Office, 1994-95; bus. cons. The Thomas Group, Medford, Oreg., 2001—. Adj. prof. U. Md., College Park, 1981, Nat. U., San Diego, 1997, San Diego State U., 1999-2001. Bd. dirs. San Diego Urban League, San Diego Civic Light Opera Assn. Mem. ATLA, Phi Beta Kappa. Avocations: jogging, participating in team sports, canoeing, hiking, ornithology. Alternative dispute resolution, Commercial, contracts (including sales of goods; commercial financing).

KAHN, RICHARD DREYFUS, lawyer; b. N.Y.C., Apr. 25, 1931; s. David Effrian and Lucille (Kahn) K.; m. Judith Raff, Sept. 10, 1961 (div. 1977); children— Jason, Adam, Alexander; m. Elaine H. Peterson, July 21, 1983 AB, Harvard U., 1952, JD, 1955. Bar: N.Y. 1955. Assoc. Debevoise & Plimpton, N.Y.C., 1955-62, ptnr., 1963-90, of counsel, 1991-93. Editor Harvard Law Rev., 1953-55 Trustee Am. Soc. Psychical Rsch., N.Y.C., 1966-73; bd. dirs. The Emerson Sch., N.Y.C., 1968-71, J. M.R. Barker Found., N.Y.C., 1968—, C. G. Jung Found. Analytical Psychology, 1984-90, Concerned Citizens of Montauk, 1991—, Group for the South Fork, 1993—; bd. dirs. Found. Child Devel, N.Y.C., 1970-88, coun. vice chmn., 1996-2000; mem. Montauk Citizens Adv. Com., 1992—. Mem. Assn. of Bar of City N.Y. (chmn. com. atomic energy 1965-68), Harvard Club N.Y.C. (bd. mgrs. 1991-93), Phi Beta Kappa. Corporate, general, Securities, Non-profit and tax-exempt organizations. Home: 224 W Lake Dr Montauk NY 11954-5235 E-mail: arcon@optonline.net.

KAHN, SCOTT HARRIS, lawyer; b. Chgo., Dec. 28, 1955; s. Lee K. and Jeannett Kahn; m. Janice M. Aveni, July 28, 1979; children: Justin R., Adam Kadan, Jamie Victoria. BS/BA, John Carroll U., 1979; JD, Cleve. U., 1982. Bar: Ohio 1982. With Moore Bus. Forms, Cleve., 1979-81, Magna Form, Inc., Cleve., 1981-83; ptnr. McIntyre, Kahn & Kruse Co. LPA, Cleve., 1982—, mng. ptnr., 1986—. Karate tchr. Kwanmuzendikia, Cleve., 1988; youth soccer coach Mayfield (Ohio) Soccer Club, 1992. Commercial, contracts (including sales of goods; commercial financing), Construction, Property, real (including real estate development, water). Office: McIntyre Kahn & Kruse The Galleria & Towers 1301 E 9th St Ste 1200 Cleveland OH 44114-1823 E-mail: skahn@mkkglaw.com.

KAHRL, ROBERT CONLEY, lawyer; b. Mt. Vernon, Ohio, June 2, 1946; s. K. Allin and Evelyn Sperry (Conley) K.; m. LaVonne Elaine Rutherford, July 12, 1969; children: Kurt Freeland, Eric Allin, Heidi Elizabeth. AB, Princeton U., 1968; MBA, JD, Ohio State U., 1975. Bar: Ohio 1975, U.S. Ct. Appeals (6th cir.) 1976, U.S. Dist. Ct. (no. dist.) Ohio 1977, U.S. Ct. Appeals (9th cir.) 1979, U.S. Ct. Appeals (fed. cir.) 1984, U.S. Ct. Appeals (D.C. cir.) 1986. Law clk. to presiding judge U.S. Ct. Appeals (6th cir.), Cleve., 1975-76; assoc. Jones, Day, Reavis & Pogue, Cleve., 1976-84, ptnr., 1985—, chair intellectual property sect., 1991—. Mem. Hudson Park Bd. Served to lt. USN, 1968-72. Mem. Ohio State Bar Assn. (chmn. emeritus intellectual property sect.), Am. Intellectual Property Law Assn., Order of Coif, Am. Guild Organists. Republican. Presbyterian. Federal civil litigation, Computer, Intellectual property. Home: 7624 Red Fox Trl Hudson OH 44236-1926 Office: Jones Day Reavis & Pogue 901 Lakeside Ave E Cleveland OH 44114-1190 E-mail: rckahrl@jonesday.com.

KAIER, EDWARD JOHN, lawyer; b. Sewickley, Pa., Sept. 23, 1945; s. Edward Anthony and Mary Patricia (Crimmins) K.; m. Annette Thomas, July 31, 1976; children: Elizabeth Anne, Charles Crimmins, Thomas Edward. AB, Harvard U., 1967; JD, U. Pa., 1970. Bar: D.C. 1970, Pa. 1970, U.S. Dist. Ct. (ea. dist.) Pa. 1971, U.S. Ct. Appeals (3rd and D.C. cirs.) 1971, U.S. Dist. Ct. D.C., 1971. Law clk. to presiding justice U.S. Dist. Ct. for D.C., Washington, 1970-71; assoc. Dechert Price & Rhoads, Phila., 1971-74; ptnr. Kaier and Kaier, Phila., 1974-77, Hepburn Willcox Hamilton & Putnam, Phila., 1977—. Pres. Savoy Co., Phila., 1978-80; bd. dirs. Mgrs. Funds, Norwalk, Conn., Mgrs. AMG Funds, Boston, Third Avenue Funds, N.Y. Vice chmn. Rosemont (Pa.) Sch. of Holy Child, 1981-90. Mem. ABA, Phila. Bar Assn. (chmn. office practice com. probate sect. 1987-90, exec. com. 1990-92, 2002-2003), Merion Cricket Club, Phila. Club, Phila. Country Club, Avalon Yacht Club (trustee 1987-90, 92-93, treas. 1990-92), Harvard-Radcliffe Club (Phila., sec. 1989—). Republican. Roman Catholic. Avocations: sailing, golf. Estate planning, Probate (including wills, trusts), Estate taxation. Home: 111 N Lowrys Ln Bryn Mawr PA 19010-1408 Office: Hepburn Willcox Hamilton & Putnam 1100 One Penn Ctr Philadelphia PA 19103 E-mail: ejkaier@hepburnlaw.com, macoejk@aol.com

KAIGHEN, SONDRA, lawyer; b. Pasadena, Tex., Nov. 23, 1958; d. Gerard Alan and Veronica Walker; m. Rodney John Kaighen, May 19, 1979; children: Cortney Michelle, Kyle Rodney. BA, U. Houston, 1983; JD, South Tex. Coll. Law, 1986. Bar: Tex. 1986, Colo. 1993, cert.: Tex. Bd. Legal Specialization (bd. cert. family law) 1994. Pvt. practice, Houston. Adj. prof. family law Southwestern Paralegal Inst., 1988, Clear Lake Paralegal Inst., 1988; spkr. in field. Asst. mng. editor: South Tex. Coll. Law Rev., 1986. Contbr. Planned Parenthood. Fellow: Royal Acad. Matrimonial Lawyers; mem.: ABA, Houston Bar Assn. (mentorship program, dir. family law divsn. 1993—95, past chair QDRO book com.), Coll. State Bar Tex., Galveston County Bar Assn., Gulf Coast Family Law Specialists, Assn. Women Attys., Tex. Acad. Family Law Specialists, State Bar Colo., State Bar Tex. (mem. grievance com. dist. 4 1993—99), Amnesty Internat., Delta Theta Phi. Avocations: soccer, martial arts, reading. Family and matrimonial, Alternative dispute resolution. Office: Sondra Kaighen & Assoc PC 17210 Mercury Dr Houston TX 77058

KAILAS, LEO GEORGE, lawyer; b. N.Y.C., May 28, 1949; s. George and Evanthia (Skoulikas) K.; m. Merle S. Duskin; children: Arianne, George, Shirley. AB, Columbia U., 1970, JD, 1973. Bar: N.Y. 1974. Assoc. Olwine, Connelly, Chase, O'Donnell and Weyher, N.Y.C., 1973-77; ptnr. specializing in internat., comml.-admiralty litigation Milgrim Thomajan Jacobs & Lee, PC (now Piper & Marbury LLP), N.Y.C., 1977-2000, mem. internat. trade and litigation group, until 2000; ptnr. Reitler Brown LLC, N.Y.C., 2000—. Mem. ABA, Assn. Bar City N.Y. (chmn. admiralty com. 1985-88). Public international, Commodities. Office: Reitler Brown LLC 800 3d Ave 21st Fl New York NY 10022 E-mail: lkailas@reitlerbrown.com.

KAIMOWITZ, GABE HILLEL, lawyer; b. N.Y.C., May 5, 1935; s. Abraham and Esther (Bialogursky) K.; children: David, Beth. BS, U. Wis., 1955; MA, U. Cen. Fla., 1988; LLB, NYU, 1967. Bar: N.Y. 1969, Mich. 1971, Fla., 1987, U.S. Dist. Ct. (mid. dist.) Fla., 1987, U.S. Ct. Appeals (6th cir.) 1971, U.S. Ct. Appeals (3d cir.) 1982, U.S. Ct. Appeals (2d cir.) 1983, U.S. Ct. Appeals (11th cir.), 1989 U.S. Ct. Appeals (7th cir.) 1990, U.S. Ct. Appeals (D.C. cir.) 1998. Atty. Ctr. Social Welfare, Politics and Law, N.Y.C., 1967-70; sr. atty. Mich. Legal Services, Detroit, 1971-79; assoc. P.R. Legal Def., N.Y.C., 1980-84; exec. dir. Greater Orlando (Fla.) A. Legal Services, 1985-86; equal opportunity investigator Alachua County, Fla., 1999—2002. Atty. Attys. Against Am. Apartheid, Fla. and various other civil rights orgns., 1969—; lectr., adj. prof. numerous univs. Contbr. articles to profl. jours.; author poems. Served with U.S. Army, 1956-57, with Res. 1958-60. Smith fellow, 1970-71, Legal Services Corp. fellow, 1979-80. Mem. N.Y. State Bar Assn., Fla. Bar Assn. Jewish. Avocation: writing and editing. Home: 4411 SW 34th St Gainesville FL 32608-2562 Office: PO Box 140119 Gainesville FL 32614-0119 E-mail: gabehk@aol.com.

KAINE, TIMOTHY M. lieutenant governor; m. Anne Holton; children: Annella, Woody, Nat. AB summa cum laude, U. Mo., 1979; JD cum laude, Harvard U., 1983. Law clk. to judge R. Lanier Anderson III U.S. Ct. Appeals (11th cir.); mem. law firm; mem. City Council, Richmond; mayor City of Richmond, 1998—2001; lt. gov. State of Virginia, 2002—. Mem. local and state govt. adv. com. FCC. Contbr. articles to profl. jours. Bd. dirs. Historic Jackson Ward Found. Mem. ABA, Va. Bar Assn., Richmond Bar Assn. Democrat. Office: Office Lt Gov 900 E Main St Ste 1400 Richmond VA 23219*

KAISER, LINDA SUSAN, lawyer; b. Alexandria, Va., Apr. 7, 1956; d. Thomas Raymond Kaiser and Joanne May (Wilber) Raynolds. BA, Pa. State U., 1978; JD, U. Pitts., 1981. Asst. counsel Pa. Ins. Dept., Harrisburg, 1981-85; sr. counsel Cigna Corp., Phila., 1985-92; asst. gen. counsel Reliance Ins. Co., Phila., 1992-95; ins. commr. Commonwealth of Pa., Harrisburg, 1995-97; sr. v.p., gen. counsel and sec. Reliance Ins. Co., Phila., 1997-2000; ptnr. Saul Ewing, LLP, 2000—. Property casualty steering com. Ins. Fedn. Pa., Phila., 1992-95; alternate Pa. Workers Compensation Gov. Bd., 1993-95; bd. dirs. Nat. Assn. Ind. Insurers, 1997-2000, vice-chair membership com., 1999-2000; bd. dirs. Ins. Fedn. Pa., 1998-2000; vice chair Issues Com., 2003—. Pres. Huntington's Disease Soc. Am., Delaware Valley, Phila., 1993-96, v.p., 1996-2002; bd. dirs. Phila. Theatre Co., 2002—; mem. Com. of Seventy, 2002—. Mem. ABA, Soc. CPCU, Soc. Nat. Assn. Ins. Commrs. (vice chair N.E. zone 1997), Order of Coif, Barristers, Com. of Seventy. Office: Centre Square West 3d Fl Philadelphia PA 19102-2186 E-mail: lkaiser@saul.com.

KALDER, FRANK M. federal agency administrator; married; 4 children. B in Forensic Sci. and Psychology, Ind. U., 1974; MPA, Mich. State U., 1983. Presdl. mgmt. intern Office Mgmt. and Budget, 1983; dir. budget and liaison Office Nat. Drug Control Policy; from asst. dir. to dep. dir. Dept. Justice Budget Staff; dep. dir. exec. office U.S. Attys.; CFO Drug Enforcement Adminstrn., Alexandria, Va., 2000—. Office: Drug Enforcement Adminstrn 2401 Jefferson Davis Hwy Alexandria VA 22301*

KALER, ROBERT JOSEPH, lawyer; b. Boston, July 20, 1956; s. Robert Joseph and Joanne (Bowen) K. BA, Dartmouth Coll., 1978; JD, Am. U., 1981. Bar: D.C. 1981, Mass. 1983, U.S. Dist. Ct. D.C. 1982, U.S. Dist. Ct. Mass. 1984, U.S. Ct. Appeals (D.C. cir.) 1983, U.S. Dist. Ct. Appeals (1st cir.) 1984, U.S. Supreme Ct. 1986. Law clk. Sullivan & Cromwell, Washington, 1979-80, U.S. Dept. Justice, Washington, 1980-81; assoc. McKenna, Connor & Cuneo, Washington, 1981-83; ptnr. Gadsby & Hannah, Boston, 1983—. Contbr. articles to profl. jours. Mem. ABA, Internat. Bar Assn., Mass Bar Assn. General civil litigation, Private international, Trademark and copyright. Office: Gadsby & Hannah 225 Franklin St Boston MA 02110-2804

KALIKOW, RICHARD R. lawyer; b. N.Y.C., 1949; BS, Cornell U., 1971; JD, Fordham U., 1974; LLM, NYU, 1979. Bar: N.Y. 1975, Fla. 1979. Mem. Skadden, Arps, Slate, Meagher & Flom, N.Y.C. Property, real (including real estate development, water). Office: Skadden Arps Slate Meagher & Flom 4 Times Sq Fl 24 New York NY 10036-6595

KALIL, DAVID THOMAS, lawyer; b. Detroit, Sept. 22, 1926; s. David A. and Rose Kalil; m. Helga A. Kalil, Nov. 1, 1958; children: David E., John T. BSE in Chem. Engring., U. Mich., 1948; LLB, Mich. State U., Detroit, 1951. Bar: Mich. 1951, Pa. 1989, U.S. Dist. Ct. (we. dist.) Pa. 1989, U.S. Dist. Ct. (ea. dist.) Mich. 1951. Examiner U.S. Patent Office, Washington, 1951-52; pvt. practice, Detroit, 1952-58; patent lawyer Internat. Nickel Co., Inc., N.Y.C., 1959-63; gen. and patent lawyer Kaynar Mfg. Co., Inc., Fullerton, Calif., 1963-64; asst. dir. law dept. Amax, Inc., N.Y.C., 1964-77; v.p., gen. counsel Jones & Laughlin Steel, Pitts., 1977-83; pvt. practice, Pitts., 1989—. Cons. D.E. Cummings, Inc., Bethlehem, Pa., 1985—; gen. mgr. Mindlin Co., Pitts., 1983-85. Cpl. USAAF, 1945-46, ETO. Roman Catholic. Avocations: golf, reading, lecturing, mentoring. Commercial, contracts (including sales of goods; commercial financing), Corporate, general, Natural resources. Home: 111 Shannon Dr Pittsburgh PA 15238-1713 Office: 260 Alpha Dr Pittsburgh PA 15238-2906

KALISH, ARTHUR, lawyer; b. Bklyn., Mar. 6, 1930; s. Jack and Rebecca (Biniamofsky) K.; m. Janet J. Wiener, Mar. 7, 1953; children: Philip, Pamela. BA, Cornell U., 1951; JD, Columbia U., 1956. Bar: N.Y. 1956, D.C. 1970. Assoc. Paul, Weiss, Rifkind, Wharton & Garrison, N.Y.C., 1956-64, ptnr., 1965-95, of counsel, 1996—. Lectr. NYU Inst. Fed. Taxation, Hawaii Tax Inst., Law Jour. Seminars Contbr. articles to legal jours. Assoc. trustee L.I. Jewish Med. Ctr., New Hyde Park, N.Y., 1978-82, trustee, 1982-95, hon. trustee, 1995-97; trustee emeritus North Shore - L.I. Jewish Health Sys., 1997-98, life trustee, 1998-2003, trustee, 2003—; bd. dirs. Cmty. Health Program of Queens Nassau Inc., New Hyde Park, 1978-94, pres., 1981-89, chmn. emeritus, 1994-97; bd. dirs. Managed Health, Inc., New Hyde Park, 1990-98, chmn., 1994-95. Fellow Am. Coll. Tax Counsel; mem. ABA, N.Y. State Bar Assn., Assn. Bar City N.Y., Columbia Law Sch. Assn. (bd. dirs. 1990-94). Corporate taxation, Personal income taxation. Home: 2 Bass Pond Dr Old Westbury NY 11568-1307 Office: Paul Weiss Rifkind Wharton & Garrison 1285 Avenue Of The Americas New York NY 10019-6064 E-mail: akalish@paulweiss.com.

KALISH, DANIEL A. lawyer; b. N.Y.C., Aug. 22, 1958; m. Hildie Kalish, Oct. 28, 1988; children: Jordan, Ryan. BA, Duke U., 1980; JD, Washington U., St. Louis, 1985. Assoc. Kelner & Kelner, N.Y.C., 1985-86, Rheingold & Golomb, N.Y.C., 1987, pvt. practice, White Plains, N.Y., 1988—. Bd. govs. Ardsley (N.Y.) - Secor Vol. Ambulence Corps, 1995—. Mem. ATLA, N.Y. State Trial Lawyers Assn., Westchester County Bar Assn., Trial Lawyers for Pub. Justice. Avocations: family, juggling, tennis, reading. State civil litigation, Personal injury (including property damage). Office: 175 Main St Ste 207 White Plains NY 10601-3128

KALISH, MYRON, lawyer; b. N.Y.C., Dec. 3, 1919; s. Louis and Bertha (Nacht) K.; m. Evelyn J. Zobler, Apr. 1, 1944; children— Nita Jane, Pamela Sue. BS in Social Sci., CCNY, 1940; LLB cum laude, Harvard U., 1943. Bar: N.Y. bar 1944. Since practiced in, N.Y.C.; sr. ptnr. Arthur, Dry & Kalish and predecessor firms, 1961-84; gen. counsel UNIROYAL, Inc., 1961-84; spl. ptnr. Shea & Gould, N.Y.C., 1985-91, of counsel, 1992-94, Parker Duryee Rosoff & Haft, N.Y.C., 1994—2002; sole practice, 2002—. Editor: Harvard Law Rev, 1942-43. Adv. bd. Southwestern Legal Found. Lt. USNR, 1943-46. Mem. ABA, N.Y. State Bar Assn., Assn. Bar City N.Y., NAM (mem. lawyers adv. com. to gen. cousnel), Harvard Club, Bellport Country Club, Rockefeller Ctr. Luncheon Club, Westhampton Yacht Squadron. Antitrust, Corporate, general, Product liability. Home and Office: 50 E 79th St New York NY 10021-0232 E-mail: mkalish@earthlink.net.

KALKSTEIN, JOSHUA ADAM, lawyer; b. Phila., Oct. 1, 1943; s. Abraham and Helen (Ponemone) K.; children: Aleta K., Trevor W., Maxim J. AB, Brown U., 1965; JD, U. Pa., 1968. Bar: N.Y. 1968, N.J. 1971, Mass. 1978, U.S. Dist. Ct. N.Y. 1968, U.S. Dist. Ct., N.J. 1971, U.S. Dist. Ct., Mass. 1978, U.S. Ct. of Appeals (3d cir.) 1973, U.S. Ct. Mil. Appeals 1969. Asst. gen. counsel Pfizer Inc., Groton, Conn., 1978—; assoc. Hellring, Lindeman & Landau, Newark, 1972-75; corp. counsel Hooper Holmes Inc., Basking Ridge, N.J., 1975-78. Vis. counsel Harvard U., MIT Ctr. for Exptl. Pharmacology and Therapeutics, Cambridge, 1995—. Bd. dirs. Howland Art Ctr., Beacon, N.Y., 1987-91, Congregation Beth El, New London, Conn., 1995-96, Main Street New London, 2000—; commr. Waterfront Redevel. Commn., Beacon, 1990-91. Lt. USNR, 1969-72. Mem. N.Y. State Bar Assn., N.J. Bar Assn., Mass. Bar Assn. Jewish. Avocations: art collecting, book collecting, golf. Home: 76 Library St Mystic CT 06355-2420 Office: Pfizer Inc 50 Pequot Ave New London CT 06320 E-mail: joshua_a_kalkstein@groton.pfizer.com.

KALLGREN, EDWARD EUGENE, retired lawyer; b. San Francisco, May 22, 1928; s. Edward H. and Florence E. (Campbell) K.; m. Joyce Elaine Kislitzin, Feb. 8, 1953; children: Virginia K. Pegley, Charles Edward. AB, U. Calif., Berkeley, 1951, JD, 1954. Bar: Calif. Assoc., ptnr. Brobeck, Phleger & Harrison LLP, San Francisco, 1954-93, of counsel, 1993—2003; ret., 2003. Bd. dirs. Olivet Meml. Park, Colma, Calif., 1970-98, pres., 1991-98; chair, pres. Five Bridges Found., 1998—; mem. Berkeley City Council, 1971-75; bd. dirs., v.p./treas. Planned Parenthood Alameda/San Francisco, 1984-89. Served to sgt. USMC, 1945-48. Mem. ABA (ho. of dels. 1985-2000, state del. 1997-98, coun. sr. law divsn. 1996-2001, chair 1999-2000), State Bar of Calif. (bd. govs. 1989-92, v.p. 1991-92), Found. of State Bar Calif. (bd. dirs. 1993-98, v.p., 1994-96, chair fellows soc. 1996-98), Bar Assn. San Francisco (pres. 1988, bd. dirs.), San Francisco Lawyers Com. Urban Affairs (co-chair 1983-85), Lawyers Com. Civil Rights Under Law (trustee 1985—), The TenBroek Soc. (chair bd. dirs. 1992-95). Democrat. Commercial, contracts (including sales of goods; commercial financing), Corporate, general. E-mail: ekallgren@brobeck.com.

KALLICK, DAVID A. lawyer; b. Chgo., Nov. 7, 1945; s. Joseph N. and Elizabeth A. (Just) K.; m. Arline E. Chizewer, Nov. 26, 1972; children: Michelle, Robert. AB in History, Princeton U., 1967; JD, Northwestern U., 1971. Bar: Ill. 1971, Calif. 1972. Law clk. to presiding justice Ill. Appellate Ct., Chgo., 1971-72; assoc. McCutchen, Doyle, Brown & Enersen, San Francisco, 1972-74; asst. dean U. So. Calif. Law Ctr., L.A., 1974-76, Ill. Inst. Tech.-Kent Coll. Law, Chgo., 1976-79; ptnr. Hurley Kallick & Schiller, Ltd., Deerfield, Ill., 1979-92, Tishler & Wald, Ltd., Chgo., 1992—. Past bd. dirs. Congregation Solel, Highland Park, Ill., Birchwood Club, Highland Park; past bd. mem., pres. Sch. Dist. 107, Highland Park; former trustee Legacy 107 Edn. Found., Highland Park. With USAR, 1968-74. Mem. ABA, Calif. Bar Assn., Ill. Bar Assn., Chgo. Bar Assn., Princeton Univ. Club. Banking, Corporate, general. Home: 1887 Spruce Ave Highland Park IL 60035-2150 Office: 200 S Wacker Dr Ste 3000 Chicago IL 60606-5807

KALLMANN, STANLEY WALTER, lawyer; b. Bklyn., June 6, 1943; s. Silve and Erna Kallmann; m. Carolee A. McDonald, Aug. 23, 1969; 1 child, Alexander;1 child, Andrew. BA, Rutgers U., New Brunswick, 1964; LLB, Rutgers U., Newark, 1967. Bar: N.J. 1967, U.S. Dist. Ct. N.J. 1967, N.Y. 1984. Law clk. to judge U.S. Dist. Ct. N.J., Newark, 1967-69; assoc. Stryker, Tams & Dill, Newark, 1969-71; asst. U.S. atty. U.S. Atty.'s Office, Newark, 1971-75; ptnr. Gennet, Kallmann, Antin & Robinson, Parsippany, N.J., 1975—. Mem. ABA, N.J. Bar Assn. Federal civil litigation, State civil litigation, Insurance. Office: Gennet Kallmann Antin & Robinson 6 Campus Dr Parsippany NJ 07054-4406

KALLSTROM, JAMES DAVID, lawyer; b. Akron, Ohio, Sept. 20, 1950; s. David H. and Mary (Joshua) K.; m. Phebe Gay Zimmerman, Jan. 2, 1982; 1 child, Adam J. BA, Kenyon Coll., 1973; JD, Case Western Res. U., 1976. Bar: Ohio 1976, Okla. 1982. Gen. counsel Kallstrom Real Estate, Akron, Ohio, 1976-81; ptnr. Kallstrom & Ming, Edmond, Okla., 1982-84, Reed, Kallstrom, Shadid & Pipes, Oklahoma City, 1984-86; of counsel Speck, Philbin, Fleig, Trudgeon & Lutz, Oklahoma City, 1987-99, Lynn & Neville, Oklahoma City, 1999-2000, Hartzog,Conger, Cason & Neville, Oklahoma City, 2000—. Instr. real estate law Akron U., 1979-81, Cen. State U., Edmond, 1982-84; instr. bus. law Okla. Christian Coll., Edmond, 1984. Mem. Okla. Bar Assn., Oklahoma City Real Property Lawywers Assn., Federalist Soc. Oil, gas, and mineral, Property, real (including real estate development, water). Office: Hartzog Conger et al 1600 Bank of Okla Plz 201 Robert S Kerr Ave Oklahoma City OK 73102 E-mail: jkallstrom@hartzoglaw.com.

KALOOSDIAN, ROBERT ARAM, lawyer; b. Watertown, Mass., Oct. 29, 1930; s. Paul and Grace (Mugrditchian) K.; m. Marianne Kaloosdian, June 30, 1957; children: Paul, Lori, Sonia. AB, Clark U., 1952; JD, Boston U., 1957, LLM, 1962. Bar: Mass. 1957, U.S. Supreme Ct. 1962. Assoc. Miles, Curran & Malkasian, Boston, 1958-60; pvt. practice Watertown, 1960—; assoc. Kaloosdian, Ciccarelli & Lerman, Watertown, 1982-99; law offices Robert A. Kaloosdian, 1999—. Corporator Watertown Savs. Bank, 1972—, trustee, 1976—, mem. cmty. reinvestment com. Corporator Mt. Auburn Hosp., Cambridge, Mass., 1978— ; pres. Armenian Nat. Inst., Washington, 1996—, Kaloosdian/Mugar Chair of Genocide and History Clark U., 2002. Bd. dirs. Armenian Assembly of Am., 1972-2000, co-chmn., 1974-83, chmn., 1990-92; assoc. dir. State Dept. AID Grant to Lebanon, 1978—; mem. Gov.'s Task Force on Ethinic Heritage, Boston, 1976. With U.S. Army, 1952-54. Recipient Prince of Cilicia award, Catholosate of Antelias, Beirut, 1980, Dist. Svc. award Armenian Assembly, 2000. Mem. ATLA, Middlesex Bar Assn., Mass. Bar Assn. (spl. asst. to pres. 2000), Rotary (pres. 1975-76), Delta Theta Phi. Democrat. Mem. Armenian Apostolic Ch. General practice, Probate (including wills, trusts), Property, real (including real estate development, water). Home: 25 Fletcher Rd Belmont MA 02478-2014 Office: 43 Mount Auburn St Watertown MA 02472-3924 E-mail: kaloosdian@aol.com.

KALSI, SWADESH SINGH, lawyer, educator; b. Nairobi, Kenya, Apr. 10, 1943; came to U.S., 1971; s. Ujagar Singh and Kailash Kalsi; m. Sarla Mirchandani, Aug. 27, 1977; children: Surekha, Sanjay, Sandeep. BS in Econs. cum laude, London Sch. Econs., 1965; Barrister-at-law, Lincoln's Inn, London, 1970; LLM, George Washington U., 1972. Bar: Eng. & Wales 1970, Ind. 1977, U.S. Dist. Ct. (so. dist.) Ind. 1977. Statistician East African Statis Dept. East African Community, Nairobi, 1965-70; barrister-at-law S. Gautama, Esq., Nairobi, 1970-71; sr. atty. Cummins Engine Co., Inc., Columbus, Ind., 1973-92; ptnr. in charge of internat. bus. practice Krieg DeVault LLP, Indpls., 1992—. Adj. prof. Ind. U. Law Sch., Indpls., 1984—. Contbr. articles to profl. jours. Co-chair Ind. U. India Studies Chair Campaign, 1994-2000; vice chmn., pres. Internat. Sch. Ind., 1993-; bd. dirs. Internat. Ctr. Indpls., Internat. Violin Competition Indpls., Christel House India. Mem. ABA, Am. Soc. Internat. Law, Ind. Bar Assn. (chmn. Internat. Law Sect. 1982-84, chmn. Corp. Counsel Sect. 1991-92). Corporate, general, Private international. Home: 4970 Washington St Columbus IN 47203-1140 Office: Krieg DeVault LLP 1 Indiana Sq Ste 2800 Indianapolis IN 46204-2079

KALUSTIAN, RICHARD PETER, judge; b. LA, May 31, 1936; s. Richard Hatchadour and Lueda Adele (Peterson) Kalustian; m. Pamela Diane Holmes. BSME, U. So. Calif., 1958; LLB, Loyola U., LA, 1963. Bar: Calif., U.S. Dist. Ct. (ctrl. dist.) Calif. Head dep. dist. atty. City of LA, 1964—85; judge Superior Ct., LA, 1985—2001; assigned judge Assigned Judge Program, Calif., 2001—. Republican. Avocations: golf, tennis, travel, computers. Mailing: PO Box 469 Gualala CA 95445

KAMERICK, EILEEN ANN, corporate financial executive, lawyer; b. Ravenna, Ohio, July 22, 1958; d. John Joseph and Elaine Elizabeth (Lenney) K.; m. Victor J. Heckler, Sept. 1, 1990; 1 child, Connor Joseph Heckler. AB in English summa cum laude, Boston Coll., 1980; postgrad., Exeter Coll., Oxford, Eng., 1981; JD, U. Chgo., 1984, MBA in Finance and Internat. Bus. with honors, 1993. Bar: Ill. 1984, U.S. Dist. Ct. (no. dist.) Ill. 1985, Mass. 1986, U.S. Ct. Appeals (7th cir.) 1988, U.S. Supreme Ct. 1993. Assoc. Reuben & Proctor, Chgo., 1984-86, Skadden, Arps et al, Chgo., 1986-89; atty. internat. Amoco Corp., Chgo., 1989-93, sr. fin. mgr. corp. fin., 1993—96, dir. banking and fin. svcs., 1996-97, v.p., treas., 1998-99, Whirlpool Corp., Benton Harbor, Mich., 1997; v.p., gen. counsel GE Capital Auto Fin. Svcs., Barrington, Ill., 1997-98; v.p., CFO BP Am., 1998—2000; exec. v.p. & CFO United Stationers Inc., Des Plaines, Ill., 2000—01; exec. v.p., CFO Bcom3, Chgo., 2001—. Advisor fin. com. Am. Petroleum Inst., 1992; bd. dirs. Heartland Alliance, Info. Resources, Inc. Vol. adv. 7th Cir. Bar Assn., Chgo., 1987—; bd. dirs. Boys & Girls Clubs of Chicago. Mem. Phi Beta Kappa. Roman Catholic. Home: 2627 N Greenview Ave Chicago IL 60614 Office: Bcom3 Ste 2200 35 W Wacker Dr Chicago IL 60601

KAMIN, CHESTER THOMAS, lawyer; b. Chgo., July 30, 1940; s. Alfred and Sara (Liebenson) K.; m. Nancy Schaefer, Sept. 8, 1962; children—Stacey Allison, Scott Thomas AB magna cum laude, Harvard Coll., 1962; JD, U. Chgo., 1965. Bar: Ill. 1965, U.S. Dist. Ct. (no. dist.) Ill. 1965, U.S. Dist. Ct. D.C. 1994, U.S. Ct. Appeals (fed. cir.) 1967, U.S. Ct. Appeals (7th cir.) 1970, U.S. Ct. Appeals (5th cir.) 1975, U.S. Ct. Appeals (2d cir.) 1987, U.S. Ct. Appeals (6th cir.) 1996, U.S. Supreme Ct. 1971. Law clk. Ill. Appellate Ct., 1965-66; assoc. Jenner & Block, Chgo., 1966-72, ptnr., 1975—; spl. counsel to Gov. Ill., Springfield, 1973-74. Mem. steering com. Com. on Cts. and Justice, 1971— ; mem. Ill. Law Enforcement Commn., 1975-77; adj. prof. U. Chgo. Law Sch. Contbr. articles to profl. jours. Fellow Am. Bar Found., Am. Coll. Trial Lawyers; mem. ABA, Ill. State Bar Assn., Chgo. Bar Assn., Chgo. Coun. Lawyers, Lawyers Club, Quadrangle Club. Antitrust, Federal civil litigation, State civil litigation. Office: Jenner & Block 1 E Ibm Plz Fl 4700 Chicago IL 60611-3599 E-mail: ckamin@jenner.com.

KAMIN, SHERWIN, lawyer; b. N.Y.C., Feb. 5, 1927; s. Theodore and Esther K.; children: Lawrence O., Samuel N., Janet C., David W., Julia E.; m. S. Jeanne Hall, Oct. 1, 1993. BBA, CCNY, 1948; LLB, Harvard U., 1951. Bar: N.Y. 1953. Asst. to reporter Fed. Income Tax Project, Am. Law Inst., Cambridge, Mass., 1951—52; assoc. Botein, Hays, Sklar & Herzberg, N.Y.C., 1952—62, ptnr., 1962—68, Kramer, Levin, Naftalis & Frankel, N.Y.C., 1968—93, of counsel, 1993—2001, Fulton, Rowe & Hart and predecessors, N.Y.C., 2002—. Served with USN, 1945-46. Mem. ABA, Assn. of Bar of City of N.Y., N.Y. State Bar Assn., Am. Law Inst., Am. Coll. Tax Counsel. Taxation, general, Estate planning. Home: 163 W 76th St New York NY 10023-8325 Office: Fulton Rowe & Hart One Rockefeller Plz New York NY 10020-2002 E-mail: sherwink@aol.com.

KAMINS, BARRY MICHAEL, lawyer; b. Oct. 3, 1943; s. Abe and Evelyn Bertha (Goffen) K.; m. Fern Louise Kamins, Mar. 30, 1968; 1 child, Allyson. BA, Columbia U., 1965; JD, Rutgers U., 1968. Bar: N.Y. 1969, U.S. Dist. Ct. (ea. and so. dists.) N.Y. 1973, U.S. Supreme Ct. 1974. Asst. dist. atty., 1969-73; dep. chief Criminal Ct. Bur., 1971-73; ptnr. Flamhaft, Levy, Kamins & Hirsch, 1973—. Chmn. grievance com. 2d and 11th Jud. Dist., 1994-98; adj. prof. Fordham Law Sch., Bklyn. Law Sch., Bklyn. Law Sch.; adj. prof. in criminal law N.Y. Tech. Coll.; apptd. spl. prosecutor, Kings County, 1990-92; chmn. oversight com. Criminal Def. ORgn. 2d Appellate Divsn., 1997—. Author: The Social Studies Student Investigates the Criminal Justice System, 1978, New York Search and Seizure, 1991; contbr. numerous articles on criminal law to profl. jours. Mem. ABA, N.Y. State Bar Assn. (mem. ho. dels., chair com. prof. discipline 1999—), Bklyn. Bar Assn. (past pres., chair jud. com. 1994-98), Kings County Criminal Bar Assn. (past pres.), Assn. Bar City of N.Y. (chair jud. com. 1998-2001, exec. com. 2001—). Criminal. Office: 16 Court St Brooklyn NY 11241-0102

KAMINSKI, LEON R. lawyer; b. LaPorte, Ind., Nov. 21, 1924; s. Stanley A. and Stephanie L. Kaminski; m. Norma Jean Lynn Kaminski, Oct. 28, 1950; children: Daniel, Anne, Lynn, Paul, James, William. AB, Ind. U., 1946; JD, Ind. U., Indpls., 1950. Bar: Ind. 1950, U.S. Dist. Ct. (no. and so. dists.) Ind. 1950, U.S. Ct. Appeals (7th cir.) 1967, U.S. Supreme Ct. 1980. Pvt. practice, LaPorte, 1950—57; dep. pros. atty. Prosecutor's Office, LaPorte, 1953—58; ptnr. Newby, Lewis, Kaminski & Jones, LaPorte, 1958—94, sr. counsel, 1995—. Pres. LaPorte City Bar Assn., 1967, LaPorte County Bar Assn., 1972, Ind. State Bar Assn., 1982—83; mem. Ind. Supreme Ct. Bd. Bar Examiners, 1971—75, Ind. Supreme Ct. Character and Fitness Com., 1991—. Charter mem. LaPorte County Sheriff's Merit Bd., 1970—81; chmn. LaPorte City March of Dimes Dr., 1960; v.p. men's coun. Roman Cath. Diocese Gary, Ind., 1968—76. Named diplomat, Def. Trial Counsel Ind., 1982; recipient Disting. Alumni Svc. award, Ind. U. Sch. Law, Indpls., 1988, Sagamore of the Wabash, 1999. Fellow: Ind. Bar Found. (fellows chair 1991—92, 50 Yr. award 2000), Am. Bar Found., Internat. Soc. Barristers (state chair 1985), Am. Coll. Trial Lawyers (state chair 1981—82). Roman Catholic. Avocations: golf, tennis, travel. Alternative dispute resolution. Office: Newby Lewis Kaminski & Jones 916 Lincolnway La Porte IN 46350

KAMINSKY, RICHARD ALAN, lawyer; b. Toledo, Nov. 15, 1951; s. Jack and Sally (Kale) K. BA, Johns Hopkins U., 1973; JD, U. Mich., 1975. Bar: Ill. 1976, U.S. Dist. Ct. (no. dist.) Ill. 1976. Assoc. Vedder, Price, Kaufman & Kammholz, Chgo., 1976-83; atty. Borg-Warner Corp., Chgo., 1983-89; v.p., assoc. gen. counsel CNA Ins. Cos., Chgo., 1989—. Bd. dirs. DePaul U. Inst. Bus. & Profl. Ethics. Contbr. chpt. to book. Mem. ABA, Chgo. Bar Assn., Ill. State C. of C. General civil litigation, Labor (including EEOC, Fair Labor Standards Act, labor-management relations, NLRB, OSHA). Home: 47 Williamsburg Rd Evanston IL 60203-1813 Office: CNA Ins Cos Cna Pla Chicago IL 60685-0001 E-mail: richard.kaminsky@cna.com.

KAMISAR, YALE, lawyer, educator; b. N.Y.C., Aug. 29, 1929; s. Samuel and Mollie (Levine) K.; m. Esther Englander, Sept. 7, 1953 (div. Oct. 1973); children: David Graham, Gordon, Jonathan; m. Christine Keller, May 10, 1974 (dec. 1997); m. Joan Russell, Feb. 28, 1999. AB, NYU, 1950; LLB, Columbia U., 1954; LLD, CUNY, 1978. Bar: D.C. 1955. Rsch. assoc. Am. Law Inst., N.Y.C., 1953; assoc. Covington & Burling, Washington, 1955-57; assoc. prof., then prof. law U. Minn., Mpls., 1957-64; prof. law U. Mich., Ann Arbor, 1965-92, Clarence Darrow disting. univ. prof., 1992—. Vis. prof. law Harvard U., 1964-65, San Diego U., 2000-02; disting. vis. prof. law Coll. William and Mary, 1988; cons. Nat. Adv. Commn. Civil Disorders, 1967-68, Nat. Commn. Causes and Prevention Violence, 1968-69; mem. adv. com. model code pre-arraignment procedure Am. Law Inst., 1965-75. Reporter-draftsman: Uniform Rules of Criminal Procedure, 1971-73; author: (with J.H. Choper, S. Shiffrin and R.H. Fallon), Constitutional Law: Cases, Comments and Questions, 9th edit., 2001; (with W. LaFave, J. Israel and N. King) Modern Criminal Procedure: Cases and Commentaries, 10th edit., 2002, Criminal Procedure and the Constitution: Leading Cases and Introductory Text, 2002; (with F. Inbau and T. Arnold) Criminal Justice in Our Time, 1965; (with J. Grano and J. Haddad) Sum and Substance of Criminal Procedure, 1977, Police Interrogation and Confessions: Essays in Law and Policy, 1980; contbr. articles to profl. jours. Served to 1st lt. AUS, 1951-52. Recipient Am. Bar Found. Rsch. award, 1996. Home: 2910 Daleview Dr Ann Arbor MI 48105-9684 Office: U Mich Law Sch 625 S State St Ann Arbor MI 48109-1215

KAMM, LINDA HELLER, lawyer; b. N.Y.C., Aug. 25, 1939; d. Seymour A. and Mary Heller; children: Lisa, Oliver. BA in History, Brandeis U., 1961; LLB, Boston Coll., 1967. Bar: Mass. 1967, D.C. 1978, U.S. Supreme Ct. 1985. Counsel Dem. Study Group, Washington, 1968-71; counsel select com. on coms. U.S. Ho. of Reps., Washington, 1973-75, gen. counsel budget com., 1975-77; gen. counsel U.S. Dept. Transp., Washington, 1977-80; ptnr. Foley and Lardner, Washington, 1980-84, of counsel, 1984-95; pvt. practice, 1995—; of counsel Boies, Schiller & Flexner, 2001—.

KAMMERER, ADRIAN W. lawyer; b. Zurich, Switzerland, Apr. 26, 1964; LLB, Zurich U., 1991, PhD, 1997. Bar: Zurich 1999. Asst. to prof. U. Zurich, 1992—95; asst. to gen. sec. Cantrade Pvt. Bank, Zurich, 1995—96; judges asst. County Ct. Uster, Switzerland, 1997—99; assoc. Niederer Kraft & Frey, Zurich, 1999—2003. Author: Undefeasible Competences of Board of Directors, 1997. Officer Can. Infantry, 1990—2003. Mem.: Zurich Bar Assn., Swiss Bar Assn. Avocations: sports, music, political literature. Aviation, Bankruptcy, Corporate, general. Office: Niederer Kraft & Frey Bahnhofstr 13 8001 Zürich Switzerland

KAMMERER, KELLY CHRISTIAN, lawyer; b. N.Y.C., Nov. 29, 1941; s. William Henry and Edith (Langley) K.; m. Nancy Davis Frame, Oct. 2, 1999. BA, U. Notre Dame, 1963; LLB, U. Va., 1968. Bar: Va. 1968, N.Y. 1969, D.C. 1969, Fla. 1969. Peace Corps vol., Colombia, 1963-65; Reginald Heber Smith atty./fellow U. Pa., Washington, 1968-70; atty.-advisor, dep. gen. counsel Peace Corps, Washington, 1970-74; atty.-advisor AID, Dept. State, Washington, 1975-76, asst. gen. counsel, 1976-78, sr. dep. gen. counsel, 1978-82, legal counselor, 1981-82, dir. congl. rels., 1983-89; mission dir. Kathmandu, Nepal, 1989-93, counselor to the agy., 1994-99; vice chmn., U.S. rep. OECD/DAC, Paris, 1999—. Recipient Disting. Honor award AID, 1979, 83, Equal Opportunity award, 1982; presdl. rank of Disting. Sr. Exec., 1984, 89, Meritorious Sr. Exec., 1997. Mem. Inter-Am. Bar Assn., Soc. Internat. Law. Address: Psc 116 Box Oecd/aid Apo AE 09777-5000 also: 11 bis Blvd Jules Sandeau 75016 Paris France

KAMP, ARTHUR JOSEPH, JR., lawyer; b. July 22, 1945; s. Arthur Joseph and Irene Catherine (Ehrstein) K.; m. Barbara Hays, Aug. 24, 1968; children: Sara, Nathaniel. BA, SUNY, 1968, JD, 1970. Bar: N.Y. 1971, U.S. Dist. Ct. (we. dist.) N.Y. 1971, Va. 1973, U.S. Dist. Ct. (ea. dist.) Va. 1973. Atty. Neighborhood Legal Svcs., Buffalo, 1971; assoc. Diamonstein & Drucker, Newport News, 1972-77; ptrn. Diamonstein, Drucker & Kamp, Newport News, 1977-84, Kamp & Kamp, Newport News, 1984-87, Kaufman & Canoles, 1987-96, David, Kamp & Frank, L.L.C., 1996—; v.p. Peninsula Legal Aid Ctr., Inc., 1978-92. Chmn. Newport News Planning Commn., 1994-95, commr., 1990-97; mem. bd. visitors Ea. Va. Med. Sch., 1997—, vice rector, 2001, rector, 2002. Lt. USAF, 1971-72. Mem. Va. State Bar Assn., Newport News Bar Assn. (past bd. dirs., chmn. legal aid com.), Va. Bar Assn., Va. Peninsula C. of C. (bd. dirs., exec. com., chmn. 1997, gen. counsel 1999-2001). Democrat. Corporate, general, Finance, Property, real (including real estate development, water). Office: David Kamp & Frank LLC 301 Hiden Blvd Ste 200 Newport News VA 23606-2939 E-mail: ajkamp@davidkampfrank.com.

KANAI, MICHIKO, lawyer; b. Miyazaki, Japan, June 19, 1955; BA in Sociology, Kyoto (Japan) U., 1979; LLB, Kobe (Japan) U., 1984; LLM, Harvard U., 1986. Bar: Osaka, Japan 1990. Programmer Woodland K.K., Osaka, 1979—81; vis. rschr. Harvard Law Sch., Mass., 1986—87; assoc. Oh-Ebashi LPC & Ptnrs., Osaka, 1990—98, ptnr., 1998—. Secondment Nabarro Nathanson, London, 1994—95; com. mem. Kobe Nat. Consumer Conf., 1996—. Author: Tax and Law Business Transfer, Stock Transfer, Meager, Reorganization and Liquidation, 1995, Touron (Discussion) Sexual Harassment, 1998. Commercial, contracts (including sales of goods; commercial financing), Corporate, general, Intellectual property. Office: Oh-Ebashi LPC & Ptnrs 8F Umedashinmishi Bldg 1-5 Dojima 1-chome Kita-ku Osaka 530-0003 Japan

KANDEL, ALAN HAROLD, lawyer; b. St. Louis, Mar. 8, 1955; AB universali cum honore, Washington U., St. Louis, 1983; JD cum laude, St. Louis U., 1986. Bar: Mo. 1986. Assoc. Popkin & Stern, St. Louis, 1986-91, Lewis, Rice & Fingersh, St. Louis, 1991-95; of counsel Farnam Law Firm, St. Louis, 1995-96; sr. atty. Peper, Martin, Jensen, Maichel & Hetlage, St. Louis, 1996-97; ptnr. Blackwell Sanders Peper Martin LLP, St. Louis, 1998—2003; instr. Fontbonne U., 2000—. Sr. v.p. H.F. Epstein Hebrew Acad., St. Louis, 1999-2001, pres. 2001-2003; pres. Tpheris Israel Chevra Kadisha Congregation, Chesterfield, Mo., 1997-98, Vaad Hoeir of St. Louis, 1998-2000. Mem. Mo. Bar (chmn. employee benefits com. 1991-93), Bar Assn. Met. St. Louis (chmn. employee benefits law com. 1995-96). Pension, profit-sharing, and employee benefits. Office: Blackwell Sanders Peper Martin LLP 720 Olive St Fl 24 Saint Louis MO 63101-2338 E-mail: akandel@blackwellsanders.com.

KANDEL, CHRISTOPHER NELSON, lawyer; b. Balt., May 11, 1960; s. Nelson Robert and Brigitte Kleemaier; m. Tanya Marie Neill Cox, 1994; children, Edward Neill Alexander, Claudia Charlotte Neill. BA magna cum laude with distinction, Yale U., 1982; JD cum laude, Cornell U., 1985. Bar: Calif. 1985, Md. 1986, D.C. 1987, Eng. and Wales 1999. Assoc. O'Melveny and Myers, L.A., 1985-88, London, 1988-90, 92-94; spl. counsel O'Melveny & Myers, London, 1994-97, ptnr., 1998-2000; assoc. Piper and Marbury, London, 1990-92; ptnr. Fried, Frank, Harris, Shriver & Jacobson, London, 2000—02, Cadwalader Wickersham & Taft, 2002—. Panelist Bond Atty.'s Workshop, Chgo., 1987, SMI conf., 1994, Euroforum conf., 1994, Internat. Bar Assn. Conf., 1997. Former assoc. editor Cornell Internat. Law Jour.; contbr. articles to profl. jours. Former dir. Yale Alumni Schs. Com., Eng. and Wales. Democrat. Lutheran. Avocation: mountain climbing. Office: Cadwalder Wickersham & Taft 265 Strand London WC2R 1BH England E-mail: christopher.kandel@cwt.com.

KANDEL, NELSON ROBERT, lawyer; b. Balt., Sept. 15, 1929; m. Brigitte Kleemaier, Feb. 28, 1957; children: Katrin, Christopher, Peter. BA, U. Md., 1951, LLB, 1954. Bar: Md. 1954, U.S. Supreme Ct. 1964, D.C. 1980. Pres. Kandel & Assocs. P.A., Balt., 1957—. With U.S. Army. Mem. Md. Bar Assn., Balt. Bar Assn. Democrat. Lutheran. General civil litigation, Commercial, contracts (including sales of goods; commercial financing), General practice. Office: The World Trade Ctr Ste 1252 401 E Pratt St Baltimore MD 21202

KANDEL, WILLIAM LLOYD, lawyer, mediator, arbitrator, educator, writer; b. N.Y.C., Apr. 25, 1939; s. Morton H. and Lottie S. (Smith) K.; m. Joyce Roland, Jan. 27, 1974; 1 child, Aron Daniel (Ari). AB cum laude, Dartmouth Coll., 1961; JD, Yale U., 1964; LLM in Labor Law, NYU, 1967. Bar: N.Y. 1965, U.S. Dist. Ct. (ea. dist.) N.Y. 1978, U.S. Dist. Ct. (so. dist) N.Y. 1980, U.S. Dist. Ct. (no. dist.) N.Y. 1988, U.S. Ct. Appeals (2nd cir.) 1982, U.S. Dist. Ct. (no. dist.) Calif. 1988, U.S. Ct. Appeals (3rd cir.) 1997, U.S. Ct. Appeals (5th cir.) 2000. Assoc. Lorenz, Finn & Giardino, N.Y.C., 1964-66; labor atty. NAM, N.Y.C., 1966-68; with Singer Co., N.Y.C., 1968-79, asst. v.p. pers. dept., 1973-76, mng. counsel pers. office of gen. counsel, 1976-79; assoc. Skadden, Arps, Slate, Meagher & Flom, N.Y.C., 1979-85; ptnr. Finley, Kumble, Wagner, Heine, Underberg, Manley, Myerson & Casey, N.Y.C., 1985-87, Myerson & Kuhn, N.Y.C., 1987-89, McDermott Will & Emery, 1989-97, Orrick, Herrington & Sutcliffe, 1997-2000; full-time mediator and arbitrator, 2000; mediator U.S. Dist. Ct. (so. and ea. dists.), Supreme Ct., NY, 2001—; pvt. mediator and arbitrator, 2000—. Adj. prof. employment law Fordham U., 1983-86; lectr. Practising Law Inst.'s Ann. Inst. on Employment Law, 1980—, co-chair, 1995, chair, 1996-2002; vol. mediator U.S. EEO Commn., 2000—; spl. master Appellate Divsn. of Supreme Ct., N.Y., 2002—; panelist comml. and employment, Am. Arbitrator Assn., 2002—; arbitrator Nat. Assn. Securities Dealers, 2002—. Contbg. editor: Employee Rels. Law Jour., 1975—; contbr. over 100 articles to profl. jours. V.p., bd. dirs. Assn. for Integration Mgmt., 1979-85; bd. dirs. N.Y. chpt. Am. Jewish Com., 1980-82; mem. human resources com. N.Y. YMCA, 1994—. Recipient award of Merit, Nat. Urban Coalition, 1979. Mem.: Am. Arbitration Assn. (comml. and employment paneel 2001—), Bar Assn. of City of N.Y., University Club. Democrat. Jewish. Alternative dispute resolution, Federal civil litigation, Labor (including EEOC, Fair Labor Standards Act, labor-management relations, NLRB, OSHA). Home and Office: Mediator/Arbitrator 880 Fifth Ave New York NY 10021 E-mail: wlkandel@hotmail.com.

KANDRAVY, JOHN, lawyer; b. Passaic, N.J., May 9, 1935; s. Frank and Anna (Chan) K.; m. Alice E. Sullivan, Feb. 17, 1962; children: Elizabeth Ann (Mrs. Joseph P. Cassidy), Katherine Ann. BA, Wesleyan U., Middletown, Conn., 1957; JD, Columbia U., 1960. Bar: N.J. 1960, D.C. 1969, U.S. Supreme Ct. 1973, N.Y. 1982. From assoc. to ptnr. Shanley & Fisher, Newark, 1961-80, ptnr. Morristown, N.J., 1980-99, mng. ptnr., 1983-85, 89-99; ptnr. Drinker Biddle & Reath LLP, Florham Park, NJ, 1999—. Bd. dirs. Tingue, Brown & Co., GAR Internat. Corp.; mem. adv. bd. Ridgewood Savs. Bank of N.J. (divsn. Boiling Springs Savings Bank). Mem. Gov.'s Mgmt. Commn., State of N.J., 1970; chmn. Planning Bd., Ridgewood, N.J., 1981-85, Zoning Bd. Adjustment, 1979-81; mem. bd. advisors Coll. Bus. Adminstrn., Fairleigh Dickinson U., 1983-87, chmn. bd. advisors, 1985-86; mem. Soc. of Valley Hosp., Ridgewood, 1971—, chmn. bd. trustees Cen. Bergen Comty. Mental Health Ctr., N.J., 1970-73; trustee Palisades Counseling Ctr., Rutherford, 1968-81, The Forum Sch., Waldwick, N.J., 1987—, The Forum Sch. Found., Waldwick, 1978—; trustee The Valley Hosp., Ridgewood, 1992—, chmn. 2001—; trustee Peer Found. for Plastic Surgery and Rehab., Florham Park, 1996—, Valley Health Sys., Inc., Paramus, 1997—, Children's Aid and Family Svcs., Inc., Paramus, N.J., 1998—; lawyers' adv. coun. Rutgers Law Sch., Newark, 1994-98, vis. com., 1994-98. Edward John Noble Found. grant, 1957-60. Mem. ABA, N.J. Bar Assn., Essex County Bar Assn., D.C. Bar Assn., Morris County Bar Assn., Essex Club (gov. 1976-85), Wesleyan U. Alumni Assn. (chmn. 1981-83), Ridgewood Country Club, Park Ave. Club (gov. 1992-97). Republican. Presbyterian. Corporate, general, Finance, Mergers and acquisitions. Home: 56 Monte Vista Ave Ridgewood NJ 07450-2428 Office: Drinker Biddle & Reath LLP 500 Campus Dr Fl 4 Florham Park NJ 07932-1047 E-mail: john.kandravy@dbr.com.

KANE, ALICE THERESA, lawyer; b. N.Y.C., Jan. 16, 1948; AB, Manhattanville Coll., 1969; JD, NYU, 1972; grad., Harvard U. Sch. Bus. Program Mgmt. Devel., 1986. Bar: N.Y. 1973, U.S. Dist. Ct. (so. dist.) N.Y. 1974. Atty. N.Y. Life Ins. Co., N.Y.C., 1972-83, v.p., assoc. gen. counsel, 1983-85, v.p. dept. pers., 1986, sr. v.p., gen. counsel, 1986-89, corp. sec., 1989-94, exec. v.p., gen. counsel, sec., 1992-95, exec. v.p. asset mgmt., 1995-98; exec. v.p. Am. Gen. Investment Mgmt. Corp., N.Y.C., 1998—. Mem. ABA (chmn. employee benefits com., tort and ins. practice sect. 1984-85, mem. corp., banking and bus. law sects., tort and ins. practice sects.), NASD, Assn. Life Ins. Counsel (deps. solvency com.). Corporate, general. Office: Am Gen Investment Mgmt Corp 390 Park Ave 6th Fl New York NY 10022 E-mail: alice_kane@agfg.com.*

KANE, JOANNA DAWN, lawyer; b. Valley Stream, N.Y., Aug. 28, 1975; d. Stephen John and Barbara Ellen Kane. BS, Fla. State U., 1997; JD, U. Miami, 2000. Bar: Fla. 2000. Lawyer Greenspoon Marder, Ft. Lauderdale, Fla., 2000—. Mem.: Broward County Bar Assn., Jr. League Greater Ft. Lauderdal. Home: 541 SW 9th Ter Fort Lauderdale FL 33312 Personal E-mail: joannakane@yahoo.com.

KANE, JOHN LAWRENCE, JR., judge; b. Tucumcari, N.Mex., Feb. 14, 1937; s. John Lawrence and Dorothy Helen (Bottler) K.; m. Stephanie Jane Shafer, Oct. 5, 1993; children: Molly Francis, Meghan, Sally, John Pattison. BA, U. Colo., 1958; JD, U. Denver, 1961, LL.D. (hon), 1997. Bar: Colo. 1961. Dep. dist. atty., Adams County, Colo., 1961-62; assoc. firm Gaunt, Byrne & Dirrim, 1961-63; ptnr. firm Andrews and Kane, Denver, 1964; pub. defender Adams County, 1965-67; dep. dir. eastern region of India Peace Corps, 1967-69; with firm Holme Roberts & Owen, 1970-77, ptnr., 1972-77; judge U.S. Dist. Ct. Colo., Denver, 1978-88, U.S. sr. dist. judge, 1988—. Adj. prof. law U. Denver, U. Colo., 1996—; vis. lectr. Trinity Coll., Dublin, Ireland, winter 1989; adj. prof. U. Colo., 1996. Contbr. articles to profl. jours. Recipient St. Thomas More award Cath. Lawyers Guild, 1983, U.S. Info. Agy. Outstanding Svc. award, 1985, Outstanding Alumnus award U. Denver, 1987, Lifetime Jud. Achievement award Nat. Assn. Criminal Def. Lawyers, 1987, Civil Rights award B'nai B'rith, 1988, Justice Gerald Le Dain award Drug Policy Found., 2000. Fellow Internat. Acad. Trial Lawyers, Am. Bd. Trial Advs. (hon.). Roman Catholic. Office: US Dist Ct US Courthouse 901 19th St Denver CO 80294-1929 E-mail: john_L_Kane@cod.uscourts.gov.

KANE, MARY KAY, dean, law educator; b. Detroit, Nov. 14, 1946; d. John Francis and Frances (Roberts) K.; m. Ronan Eugene Degnan, Feb. 3, 1987 (dec. Oct. 1987). BA cum laude, U. Mich., 1968, JD cum laude, 1971. Bar: Mich. 1971, N.Y., Calif. Rsch. assoc., co-dir. NSF project on privacy, confidentiality and social sci. rsch. data sch. law U. Mich., 1971-72, Harvard U., 1972-74; asst. prof. law SUNY, Buffalo, 1974-77; mem. faculty Hastings Coll. Law U. Calif., San Francisco, 1977—, prof. law, 1979—, assoc. acad. dean, 1981-83, acting acad. dean, 1987-88, acad. dean., 1990-93, dean, 1993—; chancellor U. Calif., San Francisco, 2001—. Vis. prof. law U. Mich., 1981, U. Utah, 1983, U. Calif., Berkeley, 1983-84, sch. law U. Tex., 1989; cons. Mead Data Control, Inc., 1971, 74, Inst. on Consumer Justice, U. Mich. Sch. Law, 1972, U.S. Privacy Protection Study Commn., 1975-76; lectr. pretrial mgmt. devices U.S. magistrates for 6th and 11th cirs. Fed. Jud. Ctr., 1983; Siebenthaler lectr. Samuel P. Chase Coll. Law, U. North Ky., 1987; reporter ad hoc com. on asbestos litigation U.S. Jud. Conf., 1990-91, mem. standing com. on practice and procedure, 2001—; mem. 9th Cir. Adv. Com. on Rules Practice and Internal Oper. Procedures, 1993-96; spkr. in field. Author: Civil Procedure in a Nutshell, 1979, 5th edit., 2003, Sum and Substance on Remedies, 1981; co-author: (with C. Wright and A. Miller) Pocket Supplements to Federal Practice and Procedure, 1975—, Federal Practice and Procedure, vols. vol. 7, 3d edit., 2001, 10, 10A and 10B, 3d edit., 1998, vols. 7-7C, 2d edit., 1986, vols. 6-6A, 2d edit., 1990, vols. 11-11A, 2d edit., 1995, (with J. Friedenthal and A. Miller) Hornbook on Civil Procedure, 3d edit., 1999, (with C. Wright) Hornbook on the Law of Federal Courts, 2002, Federal Practice Deskbook, 2002; mem. law sch. divsn. West. Adv. Editl. Bd., 1986—; contbr. articles to profl. jours. Mem. standing com. on rules of practice and procedure U.S. Jud. Conf., 2000—. Mem. ABA (mem. bar admissions com. 1995-2000), Assn. Am. Law Schs. (com. on prelegal edn. statement 1982, chair sect. remedies 1982, panelist sect. on prelegal edn. 1983, exec. com. sect. on civil procedure 1983, 86, panelist sect. on tchg. methods 1984, spkr. new tchrs. conf. 1986, 89, 90, chair sect. on civil procedure 1987, spkr. sects. civil procedure and conflicts 1987, 91, chair planning com. for 1988 Tchg. Conf. in Civil Procedure 1987-88, nominating com. 1988, profl. devel. com. 1988-91, planning com. for workshop in conflicts 1988, planning com. for 1990 Conf. on Clin. Legal Edn. 1989, chair profl. devel. com. 1989-91, exec. com. 1991-93, 2000-02, pres.-elect 2000, pres. 2001), Am. Law Inst. (co-reporter complex litigation project 1988-93, coun. 1998—), ABA/Assn. Am. Law Schs. Commn. on Financing Legal Edn., State Bar Mich. Home: 8 Admiral Dr Ste 421 Emeryville CA 94608-1567 Office: U Calif Hastings Coll Law 200 Mcallister St San Francisco CA 94102-4707

KANE, PAULA, lawyer; b. Burbank, Calif. BS, U. So. Calif., 1971, M, 1973; JD, Southwestern U. of Law, 1980. Bar: Calif. 1980. Atty. Law Offices Stuart Walzer, L.A., 1980-82, Greenberg, Glusker, Claman, Machtinger & Fields, L.A., 1982-84, pvt. practice, L.A., 1984—. Lectr. Winter Education Inst. Calif. State Bar, 2003. Mem. adv. bd. Harriett Buhai Ctr. Family Law. Mem. L.A. County Bar Assn. (exec. com. 1990-92), Beverly Hills Bar Assn. Family and matrimonial. Office: 1801 Century Park E Los Angeles CA 90067-2302

KANE, SIEGRUN DINKLAGE, lawyer; b. N.Y.C., Sept. 21, 1938; d. Ralph Dieter and Lisbeth (Adam) Dinklage; m. David H.T. Kane, Jan. 24, 1964; children: David D., Brendon T. BA cum laude, Mt. Holyoke Coll., 1960; LLB, Harvard U., 1963. Bar: N.Y. 1963, U.S. Ct. Appeals (2d cir.) 1964, U.S. Supreme Ct. 1967, U.S. Ct. Appeals (7th cir.) 1984, U.S. Ct. Appeals (5th cir.) 1997. Ptnr. Kane, Dalsimer, Sullivan, Kurucz, Levy, Eisele & Richard, N.Y.C., 1970—99, Morgan & Finnegan, N.Y.C., 1999—. Bd. mem. Bur. Nat. Affairs Adv. Com., Washington, 1988—; mem. U.S. Patent and Trademark Office Pub. Adv. Com., Washington, 1989-95, 2000-; lectr. trademarks Practicing Law Inst., N.Y.C., 1980—; designated mem. INTA Panel Neutrals, 2000-; mem. adv. bd. McCarthy Ctr. Intellectual Property and Tech. Law, U. San Francisco, 2001-. Author: Trademark Law: A Practitioner's Guide, 1987, 4th edit., 2002, annual supplements, 1998—; contbr. articles on trademark law to profl. jours. Mem. Briarcliff Zoning Bd. Appeals, Briarcliff Manor, N.Y., 1978-90, Briarcliff Hist. Soc. Bd., Briarcliff Manor, 1986-90. Mem. ABA, Internat. Trademark Assn., N.Y. Patent Law Assn. Avocations: aerobics, tennis, travel. E-mail: skane@morganfinnegan@com. Trademark and copyright. Office: Morgan & Finnegan LLP 345 Park Ave Fl 22 New York NY 10154-0053

KANE-VANNI, PATRICIA RUTH, paleo-educator, lawyer; b. Phila., Jan. 12, 1954; d. Joseph James and Ruth Marina (Ramirez) Kane; m. Francis William Vanni, Feb. 14, 1981; 1 child, Christian Michael. AB, Chestnut Hill Coll., 1975; JD, Temple U., 1985; postgrad., U. Pa. Bar: Pa. 1985, U.S. Ct. Appeals (3d cir.) 1988. Freelance art illustrator, Phila., 1972-80; secondary edn. instr. Archdiocese of Phila., 1980-83; contract analyst CIGNA Corp., Phila., 1983-84; jud. aide Phila. Ct. of Common Pleas, 1984; assoc. atty. Anderson and Dougherty, Wayne, Pa., 1985-86; atty. cons. Bell Telephone Co. of Pa., 1986-87; sr. assoc. corp. counsel Independence Blue Cross, Phila., 1987-96; pvt. practice law, 1996-97; dinosaur educator Acad. Natural Scis., Phila., 1997—. Atty. cons., 1996-2003; counsel Reliance Ins. Co., Phila., 1998-2000, contract atty., 2000-2003; counsel Westmont Law Assocs., 2002; atty. Westmont Assocs., Haddonfield, N.J., 2002; legal counsel Phila. Ho. Authority, 2003-; cons. Coll. Consortium on Drug and Alcohol Abuse, Chester, Pa., 1986-89; paleo-sci. educator Pa. Acad. Natural Scis., 1997—; paleontology field expdns. include Mont., 1999. 2000, Isle of Wight, Eng., 1999, Bahariya Oasis, Egypt, 2000; spkr. in field. Contbr. articles and illustrations to profl. mags.; performer: Phila. Revels. Judge Del. Valley Sci. Fairs, Phila., 1986, 87, 98, 99; Dem. committeewomen, Lower Merion, Pa., 1983-87; ch. cantor, soloist, mem. choir Roman Cath. Ch.; bd. dirs. Phila. Assn. Ch. Musicians. Recipient Legion of Honor award Chapel of the Four Chaplins, 1983. Mem. ABA, Pa. Bar Assn., Phila. Bar Assn. (Theatre Wing), Phila. Assn. Def. Counsel, Phila. Vol. Lawyers for Arts (bd. dirs.), Nat. Health Lawyers Assn. (spkr. 1994 ann. conv.), Hispanic Bar Assn., Soc. Vertebrate Paleontology, Pa. Acad. Nat. Scis. (vol.), Delaware Valley Paleontol. Soc. (v.p. 1998—). Democrat. Avocations: choral and solo vocal music, portrait painting and illustrating, paleontology. Home: 119 Bryn Mawr Ave Bala Cynwyd PA 19004-3012 E-mail: pkv1@erols.com., Paleopatti@hotmail.com.

KANGAS, URPO PEKKA ANTERO, civil law educator; b. Sammatti, Finland, Aug. 31, 1951; s. Rainer Antero Johannes and Eini Marjatta (Pohjolainen) K.; m. Helena Orvokki Pikkarainen, Sept. 27, 1971; children: Riikka, Aino. M in Laws, U. Helsinki, Finland, 1975, Lic. in Laws, 1978, D in Laws, 1982. Vice dean Faculty of Law U. Helsinki, Finland, 1992—2000; rschr. Acad. Finland, Finland, 1972-75; assoc. prof. in civil law U. Helsinki, Finland, 1975-83, prof. in civil law, 1989—; assoc. prof. in private law U. Turku, Finland, 1983-87. Author 20 books, 80 articles on civil law, ins. law, jurisprudence. Vice chmn. Finnish Cultural Found., 1993-2001. Named Mother of the Yr., Save the Mothers' Assn., Finland, 1990. Mem. Finnish Acad. Sci. and Letters, 1994. Avocations: lit., red wine. Office: U Helsinki Dept Pvt Law Box 4 00014 Helsinki Finland

KANNER, GIDEON, lawyer; b. Lwów, Poland, Apr. 15, 1930; came to U.S., 1947; s. Stanley and Claire Kanner; children: Jonathan, Jesse. B of Mech. Engring., The Cooper Union, 1954; JD, U. So. Calif., 1961. Bar: Calif. 1962, U.S. Supreme Ct. 1967. Rocket engr. USN, N.J., 1954-55, Rocketdyne, Calif., 1955-64; assoc. Fadem & Kanner, L.S., 1964-74; prof. law Loyola U., L.A., 1974-90; assoc. Crosby, Heafey, Roach & May, L.A., 1990-95; lawyer Berger & Norton, Santa Monica, Calif., 1995—. Cons. Calif. Law Revision Commn., 1968-77, 97—. Co-editor: Nichols on Eminent Domain, Compensation for Expropriation-A Comparative Study, Vol. II, 1990, After Lucas: Land Use Regulation and the Taking of Property Without Compensation, 1993; editor, pub. Just Compensation, 1974—; contbr. articles and revs. to profl. law jours. Recipient Shattuck prize Am. Inst. Real Estate Appraisers, 1973, Harrison Tweed Spl. Merit award for continuing legal edn. Am. Law Inst.-ABA, 1999. Appellate, State civil litigation, Condemnation (eminent domain). Home: PO Box 1741 Burbank CA 91507-1741 Office: Berger & Norton 12121 Wilshire Blvd Ste 1300 Los Angeles CA 90025 E-mail: gkanner@bergernorton.com.

KANOV, JONATHAN E. lawyer; b. Chgo., Jan. 22, 1970; s. Arnold Lloyd and Penny (Bookschester) Kanov. BBA in Fin., U. Tex. Austin, 1992; JD, U. Miami, 1996. Bar: Fla. 1986, U.S. Dist. Ct. (so. dist.) Fla. 1997, U.S. Dist. Ct. (no. dist.) Fla. 1997, U.S. Ct. Appeals (11th cir.) 1999. Litigation assoc. Rosenthal, Rosenthal, Rasco, Stok, Denberg & Wolf, Aventura, Fla., 1996—98, Goldstein, Tanen & Trench, Miami, Fla., 1999—2001, Fischman, Harvey & Dutton, Miami, 2001—. Spkr. CLE Seminars Internet Rsch., Miami, 2000—; pro bono counsel Pup Something Back, Miami, 1999—. Mem.: ATLA, ABA, Miami-Dade County Bar Assn. Commercial, contracts (including sales of goods; commercial financing), Appellate, Intellectual property. Office: Fischman Harvey & Dutton PA 3050 Biscayne Blvd Ste 600 Miami FL 33137

KANREK, VICTORIA JANE, lawyer; b. N.Y.C., June 9, 1955; d. Sidney and Aurelia (Valice) K. BA in Music, Brandeis U., 1976; JD cum laude, Suffolk U., 1990; LLM in Taxation, NYU, 1992. Bar: Mass. 1990, N.Y. 1991; U.S. Dist. Ct. Mass., 1991; U.S. Tax Ct. 1992. Law clerk to Hon. Roderick L. Ireland, Mass. Appeals Ct., Boston, 1990-91; atty., Manhattan Dist. Counsel IRS, N.Y.C., 1992-96, sr. atty., Manhattan Dist. Counsel, 1996-2000, sr. atty. Office of Chief Counsel, Large and Mid-Sized Bus. Divsn., 2000—. Democrat. Jewish. Avocations: travel, fitness, music, animal rights. E-mail: Victoria.J.Kanrek@irscounsel.treas.gov.

KANTER, ALAN MICHAEL, lawyer; b. Detroit, Apr. 24, 1954; s. Erwin Jack and Geraldine Ruth (Harvey) K.; m. Deborah Helen Avery, Dec. 11, 1983; children: Amanda Danielle, Steven Joseph. BA with high distinction, Wayne State U., 1976, JD, 1979. Bar: Mich. 1979, U.S. Dist. Ct. (ea. dist.) Mich. 1979, U.S. Dist. Ct. (we. dist.) Mich. 1981, U.S. Ct. Appeals (6th cir.) 1982. Assoc. Robert F. Wick, P.C., Rochester, Mich., 1979-80, Shapack, Singer & McCullough, P.C., Bloomfield Hills, Mich., 1980-85; ptnr. Shapack, McCullough & Kanter, P.C. (formerly Shapack, McCullough & Frank, P.C.), Bloomfield Hills, 1986—; shareholder Strobl, Cunningham, Caretti & Sharp PC, 2001. Adv. bd. Greater West Bloomfield Cable TV, 1987. Mem. ABA, Oakland County Bar Assn. (chmn. pub. rels. com. 1985-86, chmn. case evaluation com. 1999-2000, alternative dispute resolution com., 1999—, cir. ct. com. 2001—, membership com. 2002—, computer tech. com. 2002—), Am. Arbitration Assn. (cert. and ct. approved arbitrator, mediator, case evaluator, nat. complex coml. panel, coml. law panel, employment law panel), Assn. Comml. Arbitrators (mem. arbitration panel), Internat. Acad. Mediators (assoc.), Phi Beta Kappa. Jewish. Avocations: music, photography, sports. Alternative dispute resolution, Commercial, contracts (including sales of goods; commercial financing), Health. Office: Ste 200 300 E Long Lake Rd Bloomfield MI 48304-2376

KANTER, CARL IRWIN, retired lawyer; b. Jersey City, Feb. 17, 1932; s. Morris and Beatrice (Wilson) K.; m. Gail Herman, Nov. 27, 1963; children— Deborah, David, Andrew, Aaron AB, Harvard U., 1953, LL.B., 1956. Bar: Calif. 1956, N.Y. 1959. Assoc. Stroock & Stroock & Lavan, N.Y.C., 1959-67, ptnr., 1967-92; sr. v.p., co-gen. counsel Merck-Medco Managed Care L.L.C., Montvale, N.J., 1992-97, spl. counsel, 1997-99; ret. Served with U.S. Army, 1957-58 Banking, Corporate, general. Home: 19 Tompkins Rd Scarsdale NY 10583-2839 E-mail: kanterart@yahoo.com.

KANTER, SEYMOUR, lawyer; b. Phila., Feb. 4, 1931; s. William and Elizabeth (Huberman) K.; m. Rhoda Rosen, Aug. 19, 1956; children: Cynthia, Gregg, Lawrence, Brad. BS, Temple U., 1953; LLB, U. Pa., 1956. Bar: Pa. 1957, U.S. Dist. (ea. dist.) Pa. 1957, U.S. Supreme Ct. 1965, U.S. Ct. Appeals (3rd cir.) 1980. Ptnr. Halbert & Kanter, Phila., 1958-74; sr. ptnr. Kanter, Bernstein, & Kardon, Phila., 1974—. Contbr. articles to profl. jours. Bd. dirs. Melrose (Pa.) Park Improvement Assn., Pa., 1967-72, Greater Basketball Assn., Melrose, 1966-70, Melrose Park Town Watch (treas. 1994-2000). Mem. ABA, Phila. Bar Assn. (chmn. fee disputes com. 1984, 87-91), Acad. of Advocacy (faculty 1981, 84), Pa. Bar Assn., Phila. Trial Lawyers Assn., Pa. Trial Lawyers Assn., Assn. Trial Lawyers Am., Pine Tree Rifle Club (sec., treas. 1970-75). Democrat. Jewish. Personal injury (including property damage), Product liability, Professional liability. Home: 1420 Locust St Apt 35K Philadelphia PA 19102-4222

KANTER, STEPHEN, law educator, dean; b. Cin., June 30, 1946; s. Aaron J. and Edythe (Kasfir) K.; m. Dory Jean Poduska, June 24, 1972; children: Jordan Alexander, Laura Elizabeth. BS in Math., MIT, 1968; JD, Yale U., 1971. Spl. asst. Portland (Oreg.) City Commr., 1971-72; from staff atty. to asst. dir. Met. Pub. Defender, Portland, 1972-77; prof. law Lewis and Clark Coll., Portland, 1977—, assoc. dean, 1980-81, acting dean, 1981-82, dean, 1986-94. Fulbright prof. law Nanjing (China) U., 1984-85, U. Athens (Greece) Faculty of Law, 1993; bd. dirs. Northwest Regional China Coun., 1996-00, pres.- elect, 1997-98, pres., 1998-99; exec. com. Owen M. Panner Am. Inns of Ct., pres., 1994-95; mem. judicial selection com. U.S. Dist. Ct. Oreg., 1993; cons. on drafting and implementation of Kazakhstan Constn., 1992, 94, cons. on Sch. Police funciton, Portland Sch. Dist. Author: The Bear and the Blackberry, 1999; contbr. articles to profl. jours. Mem. bd. overseers World Affairs Coun. Oreg., Portland, 1986-89; mem. Oreg. Criminal Justice Coun., Salem, 1987-92, Oreg. Bicentennial Commn., Portland, 1986-89; pres. Portland Baseball Group, 2000—. Named One of 10 Gt. Portlanders, Willamette Week newspaper, 1980; recipient E.B. MacNaughton Civil Liberties award, 1991. Fellow Am. Bar Found.; mem. ACLU (bd. dirs. Oreg. chpt. 1976-82, pres. 1979-81, lawyers com. 1976—), Oreg. State Bar Assn., Am. Law Inst. (ex-officio 1986-94), Fulbright Assn. (bd. dirs. 1987-93, exec. com. 1989-93). Home: 3142 SW Fairview Blvd Portland OR 97205-1831 Office: Lewis & Clark Coll Northwestern Sch Law 10015 SW Terwilliger Blvd Portland OR 97219-7768

KANTOR, DAVID, lawyer; b. Riverside, Calif., Aug. 10, 1952; BA, U. Mich., 1974, JD, 1980; MA, Stanford U., 1975. Bar: Minn. 1980, U.S. Dist. Ct. Minn. 1981. Assoc. O'Connor & Hannan, Mpls., 1980-85, ptnr., 1985-87; assoc. Leonard, Street and Deinard, Mpls., 1987-88, ptnr., 1989—. Vol. Peace Corps, 1975-77, Legal Advice Clinics, Mpls., 1980—. Mem. ABA, Minn. Bar Assn., Hennepin County Bar Assn. Banking, Commercial, consumer (including collections, credit), Property, real (including real estate development, water). Office: Leonard Street & Deinard 150 S 5th St Ste 2300 Minneapolis MN 55402-4238

KANTOR, ISAAC NORRIS, lawyer; b. Charleston, W.Va., Aug. 29, 1929; s. Israel and Rachel (Cohen) K.; m. Doris Sue Katz, June 17, 1956; children: Mark B., Cynthia Kantor Kraft, Beth Kantor Zachwieja. BA, Va. Mil. Inst., 1953; JD, W.Va. U., 1956. Bar: W.Va. 1956, U.S. Dist. Ct. (so. dist.) W.Va. 1956, U.S. Ct. Mil. Appeals 1957, U.S. Ct. Appeals (4th cir.) 1978, U.S. Dist. Ct. (no. dist.) W.Va. 1991, U.S. Ct. Fed. Claims 1996. Ptnr Katz Katz and Kantor, Bluefield, W.Va., 1958-70, Katz Kantor Katz Perkins and Cameron, Bluefield, W.Va., 1970-82, Katz Kantor and Perkins, Bluefield, 1982—. Town atty. Town of Bramwell, W.Va., 1970-75, Town of Peterstown, W.Va., 1981-85; bd. dirs. First Cmty. Bank, First Cmty. Bancshares Inc., Bluefield, Va.; mem. vis. com. W.Va. U. Coll. Law, Morgantown, 1986-89; mem. dean's adv. coun. Appalachian Sch. of Law, Grundy, Va., 1998— Parliamentarian W.Va. Dem. Exec. Com., 1964-68; co-chmn. W.Va. Gov.'s Jud. Selection Com., 1988-97; chmn. W.Va. Ethics Commn., 1998-2000; chmn. W.Va. divsn. Am. Cancer Soc., 1990-92, pres. New River Pkwy. Authority, 1996—; mem. adv. bd., chmn. Bluefield State Coll., 1997-2001, chmn. bd. govs. 2001—; vice-chair Governmental Affairs Bluefield C. of C., 1999-01; chmn. of bd., Greater Bluefield C. of C., 2002; chmn. Mercer County W.Va. Dem. Exec. Comm., 1966-70. Capt. JAGC, USAF, 1956-58; mem. USAFR, 1953-61. Paul Harris fellow Rotary Internat., 1999; recipient Citizen of Yr. award Greater Bluefield Jaycees, 1980, Boss of Yr. award, 1992, St. George medal, Nat. Divsnl. award Am. Cancer Soc., 1993. Mem. W.Va. Trial Lawyers Assn. (pres. 1980-81), B'nai B'rith (pres. W.Va. coun. 1975-76), Rotary Internat. Jewish. Avocations: golf, reading, travel, civic activities. Administrative and regulatory, Family and matrimonial, Personal injury (including property damage). Home: 231 Oakdell Ave Bluefield WV 24701-4840 Office: PO Box 727 Bluefield WV 24701-0727

KANZIG, DAVID FREDERIC, lawyer; b. Niskayuna, N.Y., Jan. 2, 1959; s. Werner and Erika (Huber) Kanzig; m. Susan Steger; children: Sophie, Max, Kathy. Degree in Law, U. Zurich, Switzerland, 1983, NYU, 1990. Bar: Switzerland, N.Y. 1987. Assoc. Steptoe & Johnson, N.Y.C., 1990—91, Law Firm in Zurich, Switzerland, 1987—89, Bär & Karrer, Zurich, Switzerland, 1991—96; ptnr. Thouvenin Stutzer Eggimann & Ptnrs., Zurich, 1997—. Asst. prof. Internat. Inst. for Mgmt. in Telecom., Fribourg, Switzerland, 1999—. Co-author: International Asset Securitization, 1997, Introduction to the New Swiss Act on Cartels, 2000, Cross Border-Collateral, 2002. Fellow: Ctr. for Internat. Legal Studies; mem.: Internat.. Assn. of Bus. Leaders. Commercial, contracts (including sales of goods; commercial financing), Private international, Mergers and acquisitions. Office: Thouvenin Attys at Law Klausstrasse 33 Zürich 8034 Switzerland Office Fax: +41 1 421 45 00. E-mail: d.kaenzig@thouvenin.com.

KAPLAN, CARL ELIOT, lawyer; b. N.Y.C., Apr. 17, 1939; s. Lawrence S. and Pearl (Eisenberg) K.; m. Diane L. Garvin, Dec. 16, 1965; children: Lynn, Jonathan. BA, Columbia Coll., 1959; LLB, 1962. Bar: U.S. Dist. Ct. (so. and ea. dists.) N.Y. 1964, U.S. Ct. Appeals (2nd cir.) 1966, U.S. Supreme Ct. 1970. Assoc. Fulbright & Jaworski L.L.P., N.Y.C., 1963-69; ptnr., 1969—. Bd. dirs. Bio Tech. Gen. Corp., East Brunswick, N.J. Bd. editors: Columbia Law Rev., 1961-62. Mem. ABA, N.Y. Bar Assn., Assn. of Bar City of N.Y., Am. Soc. Corp. Secs., Univ. Club (N.Y.C.), Phi Beta Kappa. Avocations: biking, jogging. Corporate, general, Finance, Securities. Office: Fulbright & Jaworski LLP 666 5th Ave Fl 31 New York NY 10103-3198 E-mail: ckaplan@fulbright.com.

KAPLAN, GILBERT B. lawyer; b. Endicott, N.Y., July 9, 1951; s. Marek and Helene Christine (Freund) K.; m. Elizabeth Ann Piserchia, June 26, 1983; children: Katharine, Nicholas. Grad., Phillips Exeter Acad., 1969; AB, Harvard U., 1974, JD, 1977. Bar. Mass. 1977, D.C. 1989. Dir. office of investigations U.S. Dept. Commerce, Washington, 1983-85, dep. asst. sec. import adminstrn., 1985-87, acting asst. sec., 1987-88; sr. ptnr., head internat. trade practice Hale and Dorr, Washington, 1990—; chmn. Govt. and Regulatory Affairs Dept., 2001—. Sec. Washington Exeter Alumni Assn., 1989-92; Rep. nominee and candidate state rep. BackBay-Beacon Hill Sect., Boston, 1982. Mem. ABA (co-chmn. com. on China, internat. law sect. 1989-91). Republican. Private international, Public international, Administrative and regulatory. Office: Hale and Dorr Ste 1000 1455 Pennsylvania Ave NW Washington DC 20004-1085 Business E-Mail: gilbert.kaplan@haledorr.com.

KAPLAN, HARVEY L. lawyer; b. Kansas City, Mo., Nov. 11, 1942; BS in Pharmacy, U. Mich., 1965; JD, U. Mo., 1968. Bar: Mo. 1968, U.S. Tax Ct. 1971, U.S. Supreme Ct. 1971. Ptnr. Shook, Hardy & Bacon LLP, Kansas City. Faculty mem. NITA Advanced Advocacy Program, 1988-89; mem. Kansas City-St. Louis Panel, CPR Inst. Dispute Resolution, 1989—. Mem. bd. editors Mo. Law Rev., 1967-68. Fellow Internat. Acad. Trial Lawyers (bd. dirs. 1991-97, 98—, sec.-treas. 2001-02), Internat. Soc. Barristers, Am.

Bar Found.; mem. Am. Soc. Pharmacy Law, Mo. Orgn. Def. Lawyers (bd. dirs. 1985-93), Internat. Assn. Def. Counsel (exec. com. 1991-94, def. counsel trial acad. 1989, dir.-elect 1992, dir. 1993, v.p., found. bd. dirs. 2001-03), Def. Rsch. Inst. (chmn. drug and med. device litigation com. 1991-94, bd. dirs. 1995-98, Law Inst. 1998-2001), Nat. Judicial Coll. (mem. adv. coun. 1993—),Phi Delta Phi. Product liability. Office: Shook Hardy & Bacon LLP 1 Kansas City Pl 1200 Main St Ste 2700 Kansas City MO 64105-2118 E-mail: hkaplan@shb.com.

KAPLAN, HOWARD GORDON, lawyer; b. June 1, 1941; s. David I. and Beverly Kaplan. BS, U. Ill., 1962; JD, John Marshall Law Sch., Chgo., Ill., 1967. CPA Ill.; bar: Ill. 1967, D.C. 1980, N.Y. 1982, Wis. 1983, U.S. Supreme Ct. 1971. CPA Ill. Acct., Chgo., 1962—67; sr. ptnr. The Kaplan Group Ltd., Chgo., 1967—, The Kaplan Ptnrs. L.L.P., Chgo., 1975—. Asst. prof. Chgo. City Colls., 1967—78. Contbr. articles to profl. jours. Treas. Ill. Devel. Fin. Authority. Mem.: ABA, AICPA, Ill. Soc. CPAs, Decalogue Soc., Bar Assn. 7th Cir., Chgo. Bar Assn., Ill. Bar Assn., B'nai B'rith, Friars Club (L.A.), Bryn Mawr Country Club (Chgo.), Standard Club, Chgo. Athletic Assn. Commercial, contracts (including sales of goods; commercial financing), Probate (including wills, trusts), Corporate taxation. Office: 180 N La Salle St 25th Fl Chicago IL 60601-2501

KAPLAN, HOWARD M(ARK), lawyer; b. Bklyn., Apr. 4, 1938; s. Isaac M. and Dorothy M. (Penn) K.; m. Carol Rose Silber, Aug. 11, 1963; children: Rachel Dale, Deborah Michelle, Sarah Beth. BA cum laude, U. Pa., 1960; JD, Yale U., 1963. Bar: N.J. 1963, U.S. Dist. Ct. N.J. 1963, U.S. Supreme Ct. 1980. Dep. atty. gen. State of N.J., 1966-70; pvt. practice Teaneck, 1967—99; ptnr. Kaplan, Radol, Fields & Kaplan, LLP, Teaneck, 1999—. Chmn. ann. Cmty. Blood Dr., Teaneck, 1980—, Cmty. Scholarship Fund, Teaneck, 1976—. Named Teaneck Man of Yr., 1979. Mem. ABA, N.J. Bar Assn., Bergen County Bar Assn., Assn. Trial Lawyers Am., Yale Law Sch. Assn. N.J. (pres. 1988-90). Democrat. Jewish. Commercial, contracts (including sales of goods; commercial financing), Estate planning, Personal injury (including property damage). Home: 370 Churchill Rd Teaneck NJ 07666-3008 Office: 1086 Teaneck Rd PO Box 78 Teaneck NJ 07666-0078

KAPLAN, JARED, lawyer; b. Chgo., Dec. 28, 1938; s. Jerome and Phyllis Enid (Rieber) K.; m. Rosellen Engstrom, Dec. 28, 1964 (div. 1978); children: Brian F., Philip B.; m. Maridee Quanbeck, June 2, 1990. AB, UCLA, 1960; LLB, Harvard, 1963. Bar: Ill. 1963, U.S. Dist. Ct. (no. dist.) Ill. 1969, U.S. Tax Ct. 1978. Assoc. Ross & Hardies, Chgo., 1963-69, ptnr., 1970, Roan & Grossman, Chgo., 1970-83, Keck, Mahin & Cate, Chgo., 1983-94, McDermott, Will & Emery, Chgo., 1994—. Bd. dirs. ESOP (Employee Stock Ownership Plan) Assn., Washington, 1987-90, Family Firm Inst., Boston, 1996-99; adv. coun. Ill. Employee-Owned Enterprise, Chgo., 1984-98; chmn. Ill. Adv. Task Force on Ownership Succession and Employee Ownership, 1994-95. Editor in chief: Callaghan's Fed. Tax Guide, 1988; author: Employee Stock Ownership Plans, 1999. Nat. pres. Ripon Soc., Washington, 1975-76; adv. council mem. Rep. Nat. Com., Washington, 1978-80; alt. delegate Rep. Nat. Conv., Detroit, 1980; bd. dirs. Family Firm Inst., 1996-99. Mem. ABA (chmn. section of taxation, adminstrv. practice com. 1978-80), City Club, Chgo. (bd. govs. 1982-92), Univ. Club, Met. Club. Republican. Jewish. Mergers and acquisitions, Pension, profit-sharing, and employee benefits, Corporate taxation. Home: 105 W Delaware Pl Chicago IL 60610-3200 Office: McDermott Will & Emery 227 W Monroe St 47th Fl Chicago IL 60606-5018 E-mail: jkaplan@mwe.com., jkaplan0@aol.com.

KAPLAN, KEITH EUGENE, insurance company executive, lawyer; b. Rahway, N.J., Apr. 6, 1960; s. Eugene Aloysius and Barbara Ann (Dempski) K.; m. Rita Maria Baker, Aug. 8, 1987; children: Matthew Joseph Kaplan, William Alexander Kaplan (dec.). BS, U. Pa., 1982; JD, Temple U., 1992. Bar: Pa. 1992. Underwriter Home Ins. Co., Phila., 1982-85, underwriting supr., 1985-86, product line mgr. N.Y.C., 1987; underwriting dir. Reliance Ins. Co., Phila., 1987-88; asst. v.p. Reliance Nat., Phila., 1988-90, N.Y.C., 1990-92, v.p., 1992-96, mng. v.p., 1996-2000, exec. v.p., 2000—. Mem.: ABA, Pa. Bar Assn. Home: 1240 Pickering Ln Chester Springs PA 19425-1423 Office: Reliance National 5 Hanover Sq New York NY 10004 also: Reliance Ins Co Three Parkway Philadelphia PA 19102

KAPLAN, LEE LANDA, lawyer; b. Houston, Jan. 26, 1952; s. Charles Irving and Ara Celine (Seligman) K.; m. Diana Morton Hudson, Feb. 6, 1982. AB, Princeton U., 1973; JD, U. Tex., 1976. Bar: Tex., U.S. Dist. Ct. (no., we., ea. and so. dists.) Tex., U.S. Ct. Appeals (5th, 11th and Fed. cirs.), U.S Supreme Ct. Law clk. to sr. cir. judge U.S. Ct. Appeals (5th cir.), Houston, 1976-77; assoc. Baker & Botts, L.L.P., Houston, 1977-84, ptnr., 1985-94, Smyser Kaplan & Veselka, L.L.P., Houston, 1995—. Mem. Tex. Aerospace Commn., 1994-99. Mem. ABA, State Bar Tex., Houston Bar Assn., Am. Bd. Trial Advs. (assoc.), Am. Intellectual Property Law Assn., Houston Intellectual Property Law Assn. Democrat. Jewish. Avocation: history. Federal civil litigation, State civil litigation, Patent. Office: Smyser Kaplan & Veselka LLP 700 Louisiana St Ste 2300 Houston TX 77002-2728 E-mail: lkaplan@skv.com.

KAPLAN, MADELINE, legal administrator; b. N.Y.C., June 20, 1944; d. Leo and Ethel (Finkelstein) Kahn; m. Theodore Norman Kaplan, Nov. 14, 1982. AS, Fashion Inst. Tech., N.Y.C., 1964; BA in English Lit. summa cum laude, CUNY, 1982; MBA, Baruch Coll., 1990. Free-lance fashion illustrator, N.Y.C., 1965-73; legal asst. Krause Hirsch & Gross, Esquires, N.Y.C., 1973-80; mgr. communications Stroock & Stroock & Lavan Esquires, N.Y.C., 1980-86; dir. adminstrn. Cooper Cohen Singer & Ecker Esquires, N.Y.C., 1986-87, Donovan Leisure Newton & Irvine Esquires, N.Y.C., 1987-93, Proskauer Rose Goetz & Mendelsohn, N.Y.C., 1993-95, Kaye Scholer LLP, N.Y.C., 1995—. Mem. adv. bd. Grad. Sch. Human Resources Mgmt. Mercy Coll., 1997—; bd. dirs. Suitability. Contbr. articles to profl. jours. Founder, pres. Knolls chpt. of Women's Am. Orgn. Rehab. Through Tng., Riverdale, N.Y., 1979-82, v.p. edn., Manhattan region, 1982-83; adv. bd. Suitability; vol. Starlight Found. Mem. ASTD, Assn. Legal Adminstrs. (program com.), MBA Alumni Assn. (bd. dirs.), Sigma Iota Epsilon (life). Office: 425 Park Ave New York NY 10022-3506

KAPLAN, MARC J. lawyer; b. Phila., Mar. 12, 1957; s. Ronald L. Kaplan and Sylvia B. (Meyers) Price; m. Mary J. Dulacki, Sept. 16, 1984; children: Alexandra Zoe, Rini Isadora. BA, Duke U., 1979; JD, U. Denver, 1983. Bar: Colo. 1984, Mont. 1999, U.S. Dist. Ct. Colo. 1984, U.S. Ct. Appeals (10th cir.) 1984; cert. civil trial advocate Nat. Bd. Trial Advocacy. Asst. for polit. ops. Dem. Nat. Com., Washington, 1979-80; asst. to spl. asst. to pres. White House, Washington, 1980-81; atty. Aisenberg & Kaplan, Denver, 1984-94, Rossi, Cox, Kiker & Inderwish, P.C., Denver, 1994-98; special counsel Gutterman, Carlton & Heckenbach LLP, 1998-2000; pvt. practice Denver, 2000—. Polit. cons. Washington, 1981, lawyering process adj. prof. U. Denver Coll. of Law, 1990-92, faculty basic civil litig. skills continuing legal edn. of Denver, 1990-92, Colo, Supreme Ct. Greivance Com. Hearing Bd., Denver, 1993-98; mem. Supreme Ct. Colo., com. county and dist. ct. cir. and jud. access issues, 1998-99. Contbr. Colo. Auto Litigator's Handbook. Pres. Duke Club of Denver, 1990-92, chmn. Children of Violence Com., Denver, 1993-94; bd. dirs. United Citizens of Arapahoe Neighborhoods, 1997-2001. Named Young Polit. Leader U.S. State Dept., Washington, 1979. Mem.: Am. Coll. of Barristers (sr. coun. mem.), Faculty of Fed. Advocates, Thompson G. Marsh Inn of Ct., Denver and Arapahoe Bar Assn., Colo. Trial Lawyers Assn. (pres. 1998—99), Colo. Bar Assn. (gov. 1990—93, Pro Bono award 1993), ATLA (state del. 1997—99). General civil litigation, Family and matrimonial, Personal injury (including property damage). Office: Atty at Law LLC 2300 15th St Ste 320 Denver CO 80202-1184 E-mail: marc@kaplan-law.com.

KAPLAN, MARK NORMAN, lawyer; b. N.Y.C., Mar. 7, 1930; s. Louis and Ruth (Hertzberg) K.; m. Helene L. Finkelstein, Sept. 7, 1952; children: Marjorie Ellen, Sue Anne. AB, Columbia, 1951, JD, 1953. Bar: N.Y. 1953. Assoc. Garey & Garey, N.Y.C., 1953; law clk. to Hon. William Bondy U.S. Dist. Ct. for So. Dist. N.Y., 1953-54; assoc. Columbia Law Sch., 1954-55, Wickes, Riddell, Bloomer, Jacobi & McGuire, N.Y.C., 1955-59; from assoc. to sr. ptnr. Marshall, Bratter, Greene, Allison & Tucker, N.Y.C., 1959-70; sr. ptnr. Burnham & Co., N.Y.C., 1970-71; pres. Drexel Burnham Lambert Inc., N.Y.C., 1972-77, also CEO, 1976-77; pres. Engelhard Minerals & Chem. Corp., N.Y.C., 1977-79; mem. firm Skadden, Arps, Slate, Meager & Flom, N.Y.C., 1979—. Bd. dirs. Am. Biltrite, Grey Advt., Inc., REFAC Tech. Devel. Corp., DRS Techs. Inc., Volt Info. Sci., Inc., Jim Pattison, Ltd., Internat. Creative Mgmt., Inc., Monte Carlo Grand Hotel, Congoleum Corp., Worldwide Securities Ltd., Smith Barney World Wide Spl. Fund N.V.; vice-chmn. Am. Stock Exch., N.Y.C., 1974, bd. govs., 1975, vice-chmn. bd. govs., 1975-76; trustee Bard Coll.; chmn. audit com. City of N.Y. Co-chmn. audit adv. com. Bd. Edn. of City of N.Y.; chmn. Early Edn. Leadership Group; bd. dirs. New Alternatives for Children. Mem. Coun. Fgn. Rels., Century Assn., Econ. Club N.Y. Corporate, general, Securities. Home: 146 Central Park W New York NY 10023-2005 Office: Skaden Arps 4 Times Sq Fl 24 New York NY 10036-6595 E-mail: mkaplan@skadden.com.

KAPLAN, RICHARD ALAN, government official; b. San Francisco; s. Murray M. and Beatrice (Ray) K. AA, Canada Coll., 1973; BA, San Francisco State U., 1975, BA, 1976, MA, 1981; postgrad., U. London, 1978—80. Intelligence analyst US Govt., Washington, 1986—. Adv. bd. U.S. Congress, Washington, 1982—85; program mgr. Balance Tech. Initiative Office of Sec. of Def., 1988—89; with office of dep. chief of staff intelligence, conv. arms control support group, strategic def. intelligence working group, change working group Def. Intelligence Agy., 1988—89. Author: An Interdisciplinary Study of the International Law of Armed Conflict, 1981; author 62 intelligence documents and studies for Army and nat. intelligency cmty. With U.S. Army, 1968. Recipient Commdrs. award for civilian svc., Dept. of the Army, 1991, Superior Civilian Svc. award, 1991, Civilian award for humanitarian svc., 1992, Superior Civilian Svc. award, 1995, Meritorious Civilian Svc. award, 1996, Commdrs. award for civilian svc., 1996, others. Fellow Inter-Univ. Seminar on Armed Forces and Soc., Internat. Inst. Air and Space Law; mem. Am. Fgn. Law Assn., Internat. Law Assn. (com. on internat. terrorism 1983—, com. on armed conflict 1983—), Internat. Inst. Humanitarian Law, Am. Soc. Internat. Law, Royal Inst. Internat. Affairs. Home: Apt I 5701 Woodlawn Green Cir Alexandria VA 22309-4609

KAPLAN, SHELDON, lawyer, director; b. Mpls., Feb. 16, 1915; s. Max Julius and Harriet (Wolfson) K.; m. Helene Bamberger, Dec. 7, 1941; children— Jay Michael, Mary Jo, Jean Burton, Jeffrey Lee. BA summa cum laude, U. Minn., 1935; LLB, Columbia U., 1939. Bar: N.Y. 1940, Minn. 1946. Pvt. practice, N.Y.C., 1940-42, Mpls., 1946—; mem. firm Lauterstein, Spiller, Bergerman & Dannett, N.Y.C., 1939-42; ptnr. Maslon, Kaplan, Edelman, Borman, Brand & McNulty, Mpls., 1946-80. Chmn. Kaplan, Strangis and Kaplan, Mpls., 1980—; bd. dirs. Stewart Enterprises Inc., Creative Ventures Inc. Decisions editor Columbia Law Review, 1939. Served to capt. AUS, 1942-46. Mem. Minn. Bar Assn., Hazeltime Nat. Golf Club, Mpls. Club, Phi Beta Kappa. Corporate, general, Mergers and acquisitions, Corporate taxation. Home: 2950 Dean Pkwy Minneapolis MN 55416-4446 Office: Kaplan Strangis & Kaplan 5500 Wells Fargo Ctr Minneapolis MN 55402

KAPLAN, SUSAN, lawyer; BA summa cum laude, Hofstra U., 1971; JD, Columbia U., 1974. Bar: N.Y. 1975, U.S. Dist. Ct. (so. and ea. dists.) N.Y. 1975. Assoc. Patterson Belknap & Webb, N.Y.C., 1974-76; asst. dist. atty. Nassau County, N.Y., 1976-81; asst. chief prosecution Office Profl. Discipline, State of N.Y., 1981-83; dep. dir. prosecution Office Profl. Discipline State of N.Y., 1983-85; pvt. practice N.Y.C., 1985—. Mem. adv. bd. Employee Assistance Program Health Care Network, 1988-2002; lectr. in field. Contbr. articles to profl. jours. Mem. adminstrv. bd. Soc. Meml. Sloan-Kettering Cancer Ctr., 1975-78; mem. adv. coun. Nassau County Boy Scouts Am., 1977-87, v.p., 1981-84; sec., bd. dirs. Harkness Ballet Found., 1980-86. Assoc. fellow N.Y. Acad. Medicine 1990-91, fellow 1992—. Fellow N.Y. Bar Found.; mem. N.Y. State Bar Assn. (com. on pub. health 1975-78, com. on profl. discipline 1983-90, com. on health law 1985-88, 92-96, com. to confer with state med. soc. 1985-96, vice chair 1986-87, chair 1987-92, mem. health law sect. 1996—). Health, Professional liability. Office: 165 W End Ave Ste 27P New York NY 10023-5515

KAPLOW, LOUIS, law educator; b. Chgo., June 17, 1956; s. Mortimer and Irene (Horwich) K.; m. Jody Ellen Forchheimer, July 11, 1982; children: Irene Miriam, Leah Rayna. BA, Northwestern U., 1977; AM, JD, Harvard U., 1981, PhD, 1987. Bar: Mass. 1983. Prof. law Harvard U., Cambridge, Mass., 1982—, assoc. dean for rsch. and spl. programs, 1989-91. Co-author: Antitrust Analysis, 1997, Fairness Versus Welfare, 2002; contbr. articles to profl. jours.; mem. editl. bd. Jour. of Law, Econs. and Orgn., 1989—, Nat. Tax Jour., 1995—, Legal Theory, 1995—. Jour. Pub. Econs., 2001—. Faculty rsch. assoc. Nat. Bur. Economic Rsch., Cambridge, Mass., 1985—. Mem. AAAS, Am. Econ. Assn., Nat. Tax Assn., Am. Law and Econs. Assn., Am. Philos. Assn. Jewish. Office: Harvard U 1575 Mass Ave Rm 322 Cambridge MA 02138-2801

KAPLOW, ROBERT DAVID, lawyer; b. Bklyn., Feb. 6, 1947; s. Herbert and Geraldine Rhoda Kaplow; m. Lois Susan Silverman, May 22, 1971; children: Julie, Jeffrey. BS, Cornell U., 1968; JD, U. Mich., 1971; LLM, Wayne State U., 1978. Bar: Mich. 1972, U.S. Dist. Ct. (ea. dist.) Mich. 1972, U.S. Tax Ct. 1976, U.S. Ct. Appeals (6th cir.) 1991. Assoc. Milton Y. Zussman, Birmingham, Mich., 1972-75, Rubenstein, Isaacs, Lax & Bordman, Southfield, Mich., 1975-89; ptnr. Maddin, Hauser, Wartell, Roth & Heller P.C., Southfield, 1989—. Mem. Fin. and Estate Planning Coun. Met. Detroit, Inc.; bd. dirs. Jewish Assn. Retarded Citizens. Mem.: ABA, Oakland County Bar Assn., Mich. Bar Assn., Cornell Club Mich. Corporate, general, Estate planning, Personal income taxation. Office: Maddin Hauser Wartell Roth and Heller PC 28400 Northwestern Hwy Fl 3 Southfield MI 48034-1839 also: PO Box 215 Southfield MI 48037-0215 E-mail: rdk@maddinhauser.com.

KAPNICK, RICHARD BRADSHAW, lawyer; b. Chgo., Aug. 21, 1955; s. Harvey E. and Jean (Bradshaw) Kapnick; m. Claudia Norris, Dec. 30, 1978; children: Sarah Bancroft, John Norris. BA with distinction, Stanford U., 1977; MPhil in Internat. Rels., U. Oxford, 1980; JD with honors, U. Chgo., 1982. Bar: Ill. 1982, N.Y. 1993. Law clk. to justice Ill. Supreme Ct., Chgo., 1982—84; law clk. to Justice John Paul Stevens U.S. Supreme Ct., Washington, 1984—85; assoc. Sidley, Austin, Brown & Wood, Chgo., 1985—89, ptnr., 1989—. Mng. editor: U. Chgo. Law Rev., 1981—82. Vestryman Christ Ch., Winnetka, Ill., 2000—03; trustee Chgo. Symphony Orch., 1995—, vice chmn., 2001—03; bd. dirs., chmn. Civic Orch. Chgo., 1999—2001; bd. dirs. Cabrini Green Legal Aid Clinic, 1990—94, chmn. bd., 1991—93; mem., advisor, bd. dirs. Stanford Inst. Econ. Policy Rsch., 1999—. Fellow, Leadership Greater Chgo., 1989—90; Marshall scholar, 1978—80. Mem.: Order Coif, Lawyers Club Chgo., Econ. Club Chgo., Chgo. Club, Phi Beta Kappa. Republican. Episcopalian. General civil litigation, Libel, Mergers and acquisitions.

KAPP, C. TERRENCE, lawyer; b. Pine Bluff, Ark., Oct. 1, 1944; s. Robert Amos and Guenevere Patricia (DeVinne) Kapp; m. Betsy Langer, May 2, 1987. BA, Colgate U., 1966; JD, Cleve. State U., 1971; MA summa cum laude, Holy Apostles Coll., 1984. Bar: Ohio 1971, U.S. Dist. Ct. (no. dist.) Ohio 1973, U.S. Supreme Ct. 1980, U.S. Tax Ct. 1996. Ptnr. Kapp & Kapp, East Liverpool, Ohio, 1971-84; pvt. practice Cleve., 1984—; ptnr. Marshman, Snyder & Kapp, Cleve., 1991-93, Kapp Law Offices, Cleve., 1994—. Contbr. articles to profl. jours. Chair St. John's Cathedral Endowment Trust, Cleve., 1992—94; pres., bd. dirs. Lake Erie Nature and Sci. Ctr., Bay Village, Ohio, 1991—92. Mem.: ABA (judge finals nat. appellate adv. competition 1987, taxation com. exec. 1988—, nat. chmn. divorce laws and procedures com. family law sect. 1989—93, vice-chmn. step families com. 1991—93, task force client edn. 1991—, commr. presdl. commn. non-lawyer practice 1992—96, chmn. alternative funding com. 1992—, chair nat. symposium image family law atty-fact or myth 1993, domestic rels. taxatoin problems com. exec. tax sect., lit. sect., cert. Outstanding Svc. 1988, 1989, 1993, 1995), Cuyahoga County Bar Assn. (bar admissions com. exec. 1986—, cert. grievance com. 1990—, chair family law sect. 1991—92, jud. selection com. 1991—, unauthorized practice law com. 1992—, cert. Outstnading Leadership 1992), Ohio State Bar Assn. (family law com. exec. 1987—, family law curriculum com. Ohio CLE Inst. 1992—), Bay Men's Club, Cleve. Athletic Club (pres., bd.dirs.). Roman Catholic. Avocations: sailing, handball, racquet sports, dog training. Family and matrimonial. Office: Kapp Law Offices PO Box 40447 Bay Village OH 44140-0447 Business E-mail: kapplawoffices@ameritech.net.

KAPP, JOHN PAUL, lawyer, physician, educator; b. Galax, Va., Feb. 22, 1938; s. Paul Homer and Jesse Katherine (Vass) K.; m. Emily Lureese Evans, June 23, 1961; children: Paul Hardin, Emily Camille. MD, Duke U., 1963, BS, 1966, PhD in Anatomy, 1967; JD, Wake Forest U., 1990. Bar: N.C. 1990, Va. 1991, Fla. 1991. Intern Med. Coll. Va., Richmond, 1963; resident in surgery Duke U., Durham, N.C., 1964, resident in neurosurgery, 1964-69; asst. prof. neurosurgery U. Tenn., Memphis, 1971-72; attending neurosurgeon Bay Meml. Med. Ctr., Panama City, Fla., 1972-80, Gulf Coast Cmty. Hosp., 1977-80; assoc. prof. neurosurgery U. Miss., Jackson, 1980-83, prof., 1983-85; prof., chmn. dept. neurosurgery SUNY, Buffalo, 1985-87; pvt. practice as lawyer Galax, 1990—, Winston-Salem, NC, 1990—, Panama City, Fla., 1990—. Editor: The Cerebral Venous System and Its Disorders, 1984; contbr. articles to profl. jours. and chpts. to books; patentee arterial pressure control system, prosthetic vertebral body, cranial sensor attaching device. Major U.S. Army, 1969-71. USPHS Neurosurgy fellow, 1965-67; recipient Rsch. award Am. Acad. Neurol. Surgery, 1967. Republican. Methodist. Avocations: hunting, dog training. Personal injury (including property damage). Office: 105 W Grayson St Galax VA 24333 E-mail: kappoffice728@cs.com.

KAPP, MICHAEL KEITH, lawyer; b. Winston-Salem, N.C., Nov. 28, 1953; s. William Henry and Betty Jean (Minton) K.; m. Mary Jo Chancy McLean, Aug. 13, 1977; 1 child, Mary Katherine. AB with honors, U. N.C., 1976, JD with honors, 1979. Bar: N.C. 1979, U.S. Dist. Ct. (ea. dist.) N.C. 1980, U.S. Ct. Appeals (4th cir.) 1982, U.S. Dist. Ct. (mid. dist.) N.C. 1986, U.S. Supreme Ct. 1988. Law clk. to presiding justice N.C. Ct. Appeals, Raleigh, 1979-80, N.C. Supreme Ct., Raleigh, 1980-81; assoc. Maupin, Taylor & Ellis, Raleigh, 1981-85; ptnr. Maupin, Taylor P.A. (formerly Maupin, Taylor & Ellis, P.A.), Raleigh, 1985—, mng. dir., 2002—. Research editor U. N.C. Jour. Internat. Law and Comml. Regulation, 1978-79; editor Survey of Significant Decisions of North Carolina Court of Appeals and North Carolina Supreme Court, 1979-81, 2d vol., 1981-82. N.C. teen Dem. advisor, 1983-85; mem. exec. council N.C. Dem. Party, 1983-85; founding dir. N.C. Vol. Lawyers for Arts, Raleigh, 1982-85; counsel Moravian Music Found., Winston-Salem, 1982-85, trustee, 1985-90, pres., 1990-92; counsel Raleigh Little Theatre, 1996-98, bd. dirs., 1998—, pres.-elect, 2002; bd. dirs. Moravian Ch. Archives, Winston-Salem, 1984-89, Soc. for Preservation of Historic Oakwood, Raleigh, 1981-83, Carolina Charter Corp., 1990—, dir. 1995—. Morehead scholar U. N.C., 1972. Mem. ABA, N.C. Bar Assn. (chmn. young lawyer div. continuing legal edn. 1980-82, membership 1984-86, bd. govs. 1983-86), N.C. State Bar (ethics com. 1981-91, com. on professionalism 1986-87, jud. dist. councilor 2001—), Wake County Bar Assn. (bd. dirs. 1988-90, pres.-elect 1995, pres. 1996), Kiwanis (Raleigh Kiwanis Found. dir., 1996-98), Raleigh Execs. Club (pres. 1998-99), Phi Beta Kappa, Phi Delta Phi, Pi Lambda Phi. Avocations: historic preservation, hiking, gardening. Administrative and regulatory, General civil litigation, Franchising. Home: 1615 Craig St Raleigh NC 27608-2201 Office: Maupin Taylor PA Highwoods Tower One 3200 Beech Leaf Ct Ste 500 Raleigh NC 27604-1670 E-mail: KKapp@maupintaylor.com.

KAPPEL, MATTHEW JAY, lawyer; b. Atlanta, Mar. 14, 1970; s. Stephen Barnett and Linda Hagedorn Kappel; m. Jennifer Sasser Kappel, Nov. 21, 1998. BA, Coll. Charleston, 1992; JD, U. S.C., 1997. Bar: S.C. 1998. Asst. solicitor 13th Cir. Solicitor's Office, Greenville, SC, 1998—2001; ptnr. Bannister, Wyatt & Kappel, L.L.C., Greenville, 2002—. Mem.: Greenville Assn. Criminal Def. Lawyers. Family and matrimonial, State civil litigation, Criminal. Office: Bannister Wyatt & Kappel LLC 401 Pettigru St Greenville SC 29601 Office Fax: 864-298-0146.

KAPPES, PHILIP SPANGLER, lawyer; b. Detroit, Dec. 24, 1925; s. Philip Alexander and Wilma Fern (Spangler) K.; m. Glendora Galena Miles, Nov. 27, 1948; children: Susan Lea, Philip Miles, Mark William. Bar: Ind. 1948. Assoc. Armstrong and Gause, 1948-49, C.B. Dutton, 1950-51; ptnr. Dutton, Kappes & Overman, 1952-85, of counsel, 1983-85; ptnr. Lewis Kappes Fuller & Eads, Indpls., 1985-89, Lewis & Kappes, Indpls., 1989-92, Lewis & Kappes PC, Indpls., 1993—, Labeco Properties, Creston Group, Indpls.; pres., dir. K&K Realty, Inc., Indpls. Sec., dir., mem. Ind. Machine Works, Inc.(formerly named Laboratory Equipment Corp.), Mooresville, Ind.; instr. bus. law Butler U., 1948-49, chmn. bd. govs., 1965-66, bd. trustees, 1987-90; chmn. Ovid Butler Soc., 1982-83. Life bd. dirs. Crossroads Am. coun. Boy Scouts Am., 1965—, v.p. fin., mem. exec. com., pres., 1977-79, chmn. trustees endowment fund, 1987-92, trustee, 1987—, chmn. Gathering of Eagles dinner, 2000; bd. dirs. Fairbanks Hosp., Indpls., 1986-94, chmn. bd., 1988-91, exec. com., 1987-94, mem. audit and fin. com., 1992-94, life dir. emeritus, 1994—, chmn. nominating com., 1991; trustee Butler U., 1987-90, Children's Mus., Indpls., 1969-88, pres. bd. trustees, 1984-85, bd. disting. advisors, 1990-01, hon. trustee, 2001—; mem. First Meridian Heights Presbyn. Ch., 1933—, chmn. bd. trustees, 1958-61, 69-72, 1996— ruling elder 1982-85, 94-99, deacon, 1950-58; mem. planning com. and dir. Indpls. 32-Degree Masonic Learning Ctr. for Children, 1997-98, dir., 1998—, chmn. bd., 2002-2002, vice chmn., 2002—; chmn. Dyslexia Tutor Tng. Inst., 2000—. Recipient Paul H. Buchanan award of excellence Indpls. Bar Found. Mem. ABA (ho. of dels. 1970-71), Ind. State Bar Assn. (ho. dels. 1959—, chmn. pub. rels. exec. com. 1966-69, sec. 1973-74, bd. mgrs. 1975-77, chmn. law practice mgmt. com. 1991-92), Indpls. Bar Assn. (treas., 1st v.p. 1965, pres. 1970, bd. mgrs. 1968-71, 75-77, chmn. law day com. 1991-92, settlement week com. 1989-95, co-chair Family Law Study Commn., co-chmn. ct. liaison com. 1992-93, family law implementation com. 1993-97, exec. com. bd. mgrs. 1994-96, counsel bd. mgrs. 1994, chmn. sr. lawyers divsn. 1999-2000), Am. Judicature Soc., Indpls. Legal Aid Soc., Indpls. Jr. C. of C. (past 1st v.p., dir. ct. unification implementation com., chmn. 1995-98), Butler U. Alumni Assn. (past pres.), Mich. Alumni Assn., Meridian Hills Country Club, Lawyers Club, Gyro Club (pres. 1966), Masons (worshipful master 1975), Valley Scottish Rite (33d degree, most wise master 1982-84, trustee 1996-2002, chmn. bd. trustees 1998-99, 2001— pres. Indpls. Scottish Rite Cathedral Found., dir. 1996— chmn. 2001— dir. Indpls. Scottish Rite Found., 1996—, Shriners, Phi Delta Theta (chpt. advisor 1950-82), Tau Kappa Alpha. Republican. Presbyterian. Corporate, general, Property, real (including real estate development, water), Taxation, general. Home: 624 Somerset Dr W Indianapolis IN 46260-2924 Office: 1 American Square PO Box 82053 Indianapolis IN 46282-0003 E-mail: pkappes@lewis-kappes.com.

KAPPLER, ANN M. lawyer, finance company executive; b. New Brunswick, N.J., Dec. 24, 1957; AB magna cum laude, Darmouth Coll., 1979; JD, NYU, 1986. Bar: N.Y. 1988, DC 1989. Law clk. to Hon. Abner J. Mikva U.S. Ct. Appeals (DC cir.), Washington, 1986—87; law clk. to Hon. Harry Blackmun U.S. Supreme Ct., 1987—88; assoc. Jenner & Block, 1989—93, ptnr., 1994—98; sr. v.p., gen. counsel Fannie Mae, Washington, 1998—. Editor-in-chief: NYU Law Rev., 1985—86. Mem.: ABA, Order of Coif, DC Bar Assn., Internat. Human Rights Law Group (bd. dirs. 1999—2001), Coun. Ct. Excellence (bd. dirs. 1999—2001), Wash. Lawyers Com. Civil Rights and Urban Affairs (bd. dirs. 1999—2001). Office: Fannie Mae Legal Dept 3900 Wisconsin Ave NW Washington DC 20016 Office Fax: 202-752-5023.*

KAPSNER, CAROL RONNING, state supreme court justice; b. Bismarck, N.D. m. John Kapsner; children: Mical, Caithlin. BA in English lit., Coll. of St. Catherine; postgrad., Oxford U.; MA in English lit., Ind. U.; JD, U. Colo., 1977. Pvt. practice, Bismarck, 1977-98; justice N.D. Supreme Ct., 1998—. Mem. N.D. Bar Assn. (past bd. govs.), N.D. Trial Lawyers Assn. (past bd. govs.), Big Muddy Bar Assn. (past pres.). Office: Supreme Ct State Capitol 600 E Boulevard Ave Dept 180 Bismarck ND 58505-0530 Fax: 701-328-4480. E-mail: ckapsner@ndcourts.com.

KARAGEORGE, THOMAS GEORGE, lawyer; b. Louisville, Sept. 26, 1950; s. George D. and Betty D. Karageorge. JD, U. Louisville, 1977. Bar: Ky. 1977. Assoc. Stallings & Stallings, Louisville, 1976-80; pvt. practice, Louisville, 1980-93; assoc. Borowitz & Goldsmith, Louisville, 1993—. Mem.: Louisville Bar Assn., Ky. Bar Assn., Am.Hellenic Ednl. Progressive Assn. (treas.). State civil litigation, Family and matrimonial. Office: Borowitz & Goldsmith 1 Riverfront Plz # 1100 Louisville KY 40202 E-mail: tkarageorge@bglaw.com.

KARAM, ERNEST, chief magistrate; b. Cleve., Apr. 3, 1909; s. Henry Harvey and Frieda K.; m. Lucille Himebaugh, Nov. 23, 1934 (dec. 1985). BS in Bus. Adminstrn., Ohio State U., 1933; LLB, Chase Coll. Law, Cin., 1947; JD, Chase Coll. Law, 1968. Bar: Ohio, U.S. Ct. Mil. Appeals, 1955, U.S. Tax Ct., 1976, U.S. Supreme Ct., 1955. Circulation exec. Cin. Post, 1933-74; referee Hamilton County Domestic Rels. Ct., Cin., 1976-77, chief referee, 1977-97, dir., 1978-97, chief magistrate, 1997—. Lectr. Am. Press Inst., 1961-73; spl. counsel Atty. Gen. Ohio, 1983. Lt. cmdr. U.S. Navy, 1943-46, USNR, 1947-74. Named Citizen of Day and Citizen of Decade, Radio WLW-700, Cin., 1968, Ky. Col., 1969—, Hon. Col., Office of Gov. Okla.,1 969—; Ernest Karam Day named in his honor, Apr. 2, 1999, City of Cin. Mem. ABA, Assn. Trial Lawyers Am., Ohio State Bar Assn., Ohio Circulation Mgrs. Assn., Cin. Bar Assn. Home: 5105 Graves Rd Cincinnati OH 45243-3807

KARAMANIAN, KIRK EDWARD, lawyer; b. Detroit, July 8, 1969; s. Edward Karamanian and Marilyn Joyce Elam; m. Kathleen Ann Tripp, Dec. 30, 1995. BA, Mich. State U., 1991; JD, U. Detroit, 1994. Bar: Ohio 1994, U.S. Dist. Ct. (no. dist.) Ohio 1994, Mich. 1995, U.S. Ct. Appeals (7th cir.) 1998, U.S. Dist. Ct. (no. dist.) Ill. 1999, U.S. Ct. Appeals (6th cir.) 1999, U.S. Dist. Ct. (ctrl. dist.) Ill. 2000, U.S. Supreme Ct. 2002, U.S. Dist. Ct. (so. dist.) Ohio 2002. Lawyer Fuller & Henry, Toledo, 1994—95, O'Bryan, Baun, Cohen, and Kuebler, Birmingham, Mich., 1995—. Mem.: ABA, Ohio State Bar, State Bar Mich., Maritime Law Assn. U.S., Justice Frank Murphy Honor Soc. Admiralty. Office: O'Bryan Baun Cohen Kuebler 401 S Old Woodward Ste 320 Birmingham MI 48009 Office Fax: 248-258-6047. Business E-Mail: kkaramanian@obryanlaw.net.

KARAN, PAUL RICHARD, lawyer; b. Providence, June 12, 1936; s. Aaron Arnold and Sadye (Persky) K.; m. Susan Clare Brody, Jan. 3, 1964 (dec. Apr. 1986); children: Jennifer Hilary, Steven Lee; m. Linda Doris Adler, July 2, 1987. BA, Brown U., 1957; JD, Columbia U., 1960. Bar: NY 1961, U.S. Dist. Ct. (so. dist.) N.Y. 1962, U.S. Supreme Ct. 1967, U.S. Tax Ct. 1975, U.S. Claims Ct. 1976. Assoc. Demov & Morris, N.Y.C., 1960-65, ptnr., 1966-85, Gordon Altman Weitzen Shalov & Wein, N.Y.C., 1985-2000, Tofel, Karan & Ptnrs., P.C., N.Y.C., 2000—. Contbr. articles to profl. jours. Chmn. Bd. Assessment Rev., Greenburgh, N.Y., 1978-86; mem. Planning Bd., Greenburgh, 1975-78, Bd. Edn., Greenburgh, 1980-83. Fellow Am. Bar Found., Am. Coll. Trust and Estate Counsel (chmn. downstate N.Y. 1996-2001), N.Y. Bar Found.; mem. ABA, N.Y. State Bar Assn. (chmn. trusts and estates law sect. 1990-91), Assn. of Bar of City of N.Y. Avocation: golf. Estate planning, Probate (including wills, trusts), Estate taxation. Office: Tofel Karan & Ptnrs PC 780 3d Ave New York NY 10017 E-mail: prkaran@tkplaw.com.

KARASOV, PHYLLIS, lawyer; b. St. Paul, Oct. 3, 1951; d. Elliott and Doris (Unger) K.; m. Alan David Olstein, Sept. 2, 1979; children: Samuel Louis, Joshua Charles, Adam Bernard. Student, Eastman Sch. Music, Rochester, N.Y., 1969-73, U. Minn., 1972; BA with distinction, U. Rochester, 1973; JD, Emory U., 1976. Bar: Minn. 1976, Ga. 1976, U.S. Dist. Ct. Minn. 1976, U.S. Dist. Ct. (no. dist.) Ga. 1976. Field atty. NLRB, Mpls., 1976-81; assoc. Moore, Costello & Hart, St. Paul, 1981-84, ptnr., 1984—. Lectr. in field. Contbr. articles to profl. publs. Bd. dirs. Talmud Torah, St. Paul, 1982-86, pres., 1983-85; bd. dirs. U. Minn. Student Legal Svcs., 1982-85, United Arts Coun., 1994—; bd. dirs. Resources for Child Caring, Inc., St. Paul, 1985—, sec.-treas., 1992-95; bd. dirs. United Jewish Fund and Coun. St. Paul, 1999—, mem. exec. com., 2001—. Recipient Miriam Kaplan Young Leadership award United Jewish Fund and Coun. St. Paul, 1987. Mem. ABA, Nat. Assn. Coll. and Univ. Attys. (chair employment law sect. 1995—1997), Ramsey County Bar Assn. (pres. 1999-2000), Minn. Bar Assn. (mem. exec. com. 2001-2003, editor labor law sect. newsletter 1983-84, com. on non-criminal sexual harassment 1988-89, com. on rules profl. conduct 1989-92, chmn. com. on discrimination 1990-91), Minn. Women Lawyers (pres. 1979-80, trustee polit. action com. 1982-84), pres. Corporate, general, Labor (including EEOC, Fair Labor Standards Act, labor-management relations, NLRB, OSHA). Office: Moore Costello & Hart Suite 1400 55 5th St E Ste 1400 Saint Paul MN 55101-1792

KARASZ, PETER, lawyer; b. Budapest, Hungary, June 18, 1941; came to U.S., 1949. s. Arthur and Eva Karasz; m. Marilyn Sobel, Apr. 20, 1986; children: Andrew, Valerie, Alexandra, Matthew. BA, Johns Hopkins U., 1962; JD, U. Chgo., 1965. Bar: Ill. 1965, N.Y. 1968. Ptnr. Cleary, Gottlieb, Steen & Hamilton, N.Y.C., 1967—. Mem. ABA, N.Y.C. Bar Assn., Heights Casino. Office: Cleary Gottlieb Steen & Hamilton 1 Liberty Plz Fl 38 New York NY 10006-1470*

KARAZIN, EDWARD ROBERT, JR., judge; b. NYC, Feb. 24, 1940; s. Edward R. and Ann L. (Kampe) Karazin; m. Irene M. Karazin, May 8, 1965; children: Edward, Deborah, Michael. BA, Boston Coll., 1961; LLB, Fordham U., 1964, LLD, 1968. Bar: Conn. 1964, U.S. Supreme Ct. 1971. Ptnr. Senie, Stock, LaChance, Karazin & Thiemann, Westport, Conn., 1964—74; pvt. practice Westport, 1974—75; ptnr. Schine, Julianelle, Bozelko & Karazin, Westport, 1975—90; judge Conn. Superior Ct., Stamford, 1990—. Asst. pros. atty. State of Conn., 1969—76, criminal justice adv. bd., 1972—73. Chmn. profl. divsn. United Fund, Westport, 1972; bd. govs. ARC, 1977—79; ct. rules adv. com. Bench-Bar; active Westport Bd. Fin., 1983—90; governing bd. Levitt Pavilion, 1980—90. Capt. U.S. Army, 1965—67. Decorated Bronze Star. Mem.: Westport Bar Assn. (pres.), Conn. Bar Assn. (civil justice sect. exec. com. 1980—86), Conn. Trial Lawyers Assn. (gov. 1976—87). Home: 3 Wisteria Ln Westport CT 06880-2208 Office: Court House 123 Hoyt St Stamford CT 06905

KARCHER, STEVEN MICHAEL, lawyer; b. San Diego, Oct. 25, 1956; s. Carl Michael and Margaret Ruby (Hayden) K.; m. Dana C. Karcher, June 8, 1985. BS summa cum laude, Calif. State U., Hayward, 1984; JD, Emory U., 1988. Bar: Calif. 1989, U.S. Dist. Ct. (ea. and no. dist.) Calif. 1990, U.S. Dist. Ct. (ctrl. dist.) Calif. 1992. Legal rschr. S.M. Karcher Co., Decatur, Ga., 1985-88; atty. Ericksen Arbuthnot et al, Sacramento, 1988-92, 2000—; ptnr. Borton Petrini & Conron, Bakersfield, Calif., 1992—2000, Pacific Coast Bus. Group, LLC, Bakersfield, Calif., 1999—2001; founder, mng. ptnr. Ericksen, Kilduft et al., 2000—. Contbr. articles to profl. jours. Chmn. site coun. Franklin Elem. Sch., Bakersfield, 1998; bd. dirs. Bakersfield City Sch. Edn. Found., 1993-2000, Bakersfield Boys & Girls Club, 2000—; cand. City Schs. Bd. Trustees, Bakersfield, 1996. Mem. Kern County Bar Assn. (co-chmn. Spkrs. Bur. 1997-98), Greater Bakersfield C. of C., Downtown Bus. Assn., East Bakersfield Rotary. Republican. Episcopalian. Avocations: history, horsemanship and cowboying, reading, domestic travel, cowboy work. General civil litigation, Commercial, consumer (including collections, credit), Property, real (including real estate development, water). Office: Ericksen Arbuthnot et al 1830 Truxtun Ave Ste 200 Bakersfield CA 93301

KARDOS, MEL D. lawyer, educator; b. Phila., Feb. 6, 1947; s. Julius S. and Rose (Klein) K.; children: Lindsay Dara, Matthew Daniel. BS, Temple U., 1970; MEd, Trenton State Coll., 1972; JD, U. Balt., 1975. Bar: Pa. 1975, N.J. 1975, U.S. Dist. Ct. (ea. dist.) Pa. 1975, U.S. Dist. Ct. N.J. 1975, U.S. Supreme Ct. 1984. Asst. pub. defender Bucks County, Doylestown, Pa., 1975-80; ptnr. Kardos & Lynch, Newtown, Pa., 1980, Kardos & Heley, Newtown, 1980-87, Kardos, Rickles, Sellers & Hand, Newtown, 1988-. Adj. prof. Temple U., Phila., 1987, Bucks County C.C., 1995. Sec., bd. dirs. Lower Bucks County Pa. chpt. ARC; mem. exec. bd. Bucks chpt. ARC; supr. Middletown Twp., Bucks County, 1998—, chmn. Mem. ABA, Bucks County Bar Assn., Assn. Trial Lawyers Am., Soc. for Am. Baseball Research. Democrat. Avocations: sports broadcasting, sports, history, politics. General civil litigation, Criminal, Personal injury (including property damage). Office: Kardos Rickles Sellers & Hand 626 S State St Newtown PA 18940-1509 also: 194 S Broad St Trenton NJ 08608-2405

KARIUKI, PAUL KIHARA, lawyer, director; b. Kiambu, Kenya, May 11, 1954; s. Obadiah and Lilian Wairimu Kariuki; m. Sarah Njoki Kimingi Kariuki, Sept. 4, 1976; children: Marion Wairimu, Andrew, Zazira Njeri. LLB (upper 2nd class honors), U. Nairobi, 1977. Bar: High Ct. Kenya 1978. Legal asst. Hamilton Harrison and Matthews, Nairobi, 1977—80, ptnr., 1981—86, Ndungu Njoroge and Kwach, Nairobi, 1986—2000; group mng. dir. Internat. Controls Group Cos., Nairobi, 2000—. Chancellor Anglican Ch. Kenya, Nairobi, 1980—2001. Commr. Nairobi City Commn., Nairobi, 1985—86; mem. Kenya Anti-Corruption Authority Adv. Bd., Nairobi, 1997—98. Mem.: Law Soc. Kenya, Nairobi Club, Nairobi Safari Club, Muthaiga Country Club. Anglican. Avocations: acting, theater , squash, cricket, gardening. Office: Internat Controls Ltd Loita St Po Box 28035 Nairobi Kenya 00200 Fax: 254-2 217840. E-mail: aml@africanoline.co.ke.

KARLIN, CALVIN JOSEPH, lawyer; b. Hutchinson, Kans., Oct. 31, 1952; s. Norman Joseph and Edith Lucille (Biggs) K.; m. Janice Miller, May 25, 1975. BA, U. Kans., 1974, JD, 1977. Bar: Kans. 1977, U.S. Dist. Ct. Kans. 1977. Mem. Barber, Emerson, Springer, Zinn & Murray, L.C., Lawrence, Kans., 1977—. Adj. faculty Sch. Law U. Kans. Note and comments editor U. Kans. Law Rev.; contbr. articles to profl. jours. Bd. dirs. United Way, Lawrence, 1983-85, drive chair, 1993, pres., 1995-96; bd. dirs. Kaw Valley Dance Theatre, Lawrence, 1982-85, Vis. Nurses Assn., 1987-93, Lawrence Pub. Libr., 1989-94; coun. pres. Lawrence Free State H.S. Site, 2001-03. Mem. Am. Coll. Trust and Estate Counsel, Kans. Bar Assn. (exec. com. corp. bus. and banking law sect. 1985-88, exec. com. real estate, probate and trust law sect. 1998—), Douglas County Bar Assn. (sec. 1982-83, v.p. 1986-87, pres. 1987-88, chair ethics com. 2002—), Lawrence C. of C. (bd. dirs. 1997-2000), Swarthout Soc. (corp. and bus. com. 1983-91), Order of Coif, Phi Beta Kappa. Democrat. Avocations: travel, biking. Probate (including wills, trusts), Commercial, consumer (including collections, credit), Estate planning. Office: Barber Emerson Springer Zinn & Murray LC PO Box 667 Lawrence KS 66044-0667 E-mail: ckarlin@beszm.com.

KARLIN, MICHAEL JONATHAN ABRAHAM, lawyer; b. London, Eng., Aug. 27, 1952; came to U.S., 1980; s. Eli Karlin and Miriam (Stahl) Henderson; m. Fiona Jane Wilson, July 20, 1973; children: Laura, Toby. BA with Hons., Cambridge (Eng.) U., 1973, MA, 1977. Bar: Calif. 1980, U.S. Dist. Ct. (cen. dist.) Calif. 1980, U.S. Tax. Ct. 1981; solicitor, Eng. and Wales 1977. Asst. solicitor D.J. Freeman & Co., London, 1975-80; assoc. Gelles, Singer & Johnson, L.A., 1980-83, Morgan, Lewis & Bockius LLP, L.A., 1983-88, ptnr., 1988—97, KPMG LLP, 1998—2000. Contbr. articles to profl jours., 1980—. Mem. ABA (co-chmn. subcom. on tax treaties, tax sect. com. on U.S. Activities of Foreigners and Tax Treaties 1987-92), Calif. State Bar Assn., L.A. County Bar Assn. (chmn. fgn. tax law com. taxation sect. 1989-90). Private international, Corporate taxation. Office: Karlin & Co 150 S Rodeo Dr # 220 Beverly Hills CA 90211-2408

KARLTON, LAWRENCE K. federal judge; b. Bklyn., May 28, 1935; s. Aaron Katz and Sylvia (Meltzer) K.; m. Mychelle Stiebel, Sept. 7, 1958 (dec.); m. Sue Gouge, May 22, 1999. Student, Washington Sq. Coll., 1952-54; LL.B., Columbia U., 1958. Bar: Fla. 1958, Calif. 1962. Acting legal officer Sacramento Army Depot, Dept. Army, Sacramento, 1958-60, civilian legal officer, 1960-62; individual practice law Sacramento, 1962-64; mem. firm Abbott, Karlton & White, 1964, Karlton & Blease, 1964-71, Karlton, Blease & Vanderlaan, 1971-76; judge Calif. Superior Ct. for Sacramento County, 1976-79, U.S. Dist. Ct. (ea. dist.) Calif., Sacramento, 1979-83; formerly chief judge U.S. Dist. Ct., Sacramento, 1983-90, chief judge emeritus, 1990-2000, sr. judge, 2000—. Co-chmn. Central Calif. council B'nai B'rith Anit-Defamation League Commn., 1964-65; treas. Sacramento Jewish Community Relations Council, chmn., 1967-68; chmn. Vol. Lawyers Commn. Sacramento Valley ACLU, 1964-76. Mem. Am. Bar Assn., Sacramento County Bar Assn., Calif. Bar Assn., Fed. Bar Assn., Fed. Judges Assn., 9th Cir. Judges Assn. Clubs: B'nai B'rith (past pres.). Office: US Dist Ct 501 I St Sacramento CA 95814-7300

KARMALI, RASHIDA ALIMAHOMED, lawyer; b. Uganda, May 12, 1948; came to U.S., 1978; d. Alimahomed and Sakina (Govani) K. BSc, MakerereU., 1971; MSc, Aberdeen U., 1973; PhD, U. Newcastle Upon Tyne, 1976; JD, Rutgers U., 1993. Bar: N.Y. 1994; registered to practice U.S. Patent Office. Fellow Clin. Rsch. Inst., Montreal, 1976-78; rsch. assoc. E. Carolina U., Greenville, N.C., 1978-80, Meml. Sloan-Kettering Inst., N.Y.C., 1980-84; adj. assoc. prof. Cook Coll., New Brunswick, N.J., 1984-90; practice in tech. law N.Y.C., 1991—. Bd. dirs. Skin Rsch. Found., N.Y.C. Grantee NIH, Am. Cancer Soc. Mem. ABA, Assn. Bar City N.Y. (com. on patents), Am. Intellectual Property Law Assn. (internat. and fgn. law com.), Licensing Execs. Soc. Antitrust, Federal civil litigation, Intellectual property. Office: 99 Wall St 10th Fl New York NY 10005 E-mail: karmali@aol.com.

KARMEL, ROBERTA SEGAL, lawyer, educator; b. Chgo., May 4, 1937; d. J. Herzl and Eva E. (Elin) Segal; m. Paul R. Karmel, June 9, 1957 (dec. Aug. 1994); children: Philip, Solomon, Jonathan, Miriam; m. S. David Harrison, Oct. 29, 1995. BA, Radcliffe Coll.; LLB, NYU, 1962; HHD (hon.), King's Coll., 1998. Bar: N.Y. 1962, U.S. Dist. Ct. (so. and ea. dists.) N.Y. 1964, U.S. Ct. Appeals (2d cir.) 1968, U.S. Supreme Ct. 1968, U.S. Ct. Appeals (3d cir.) 1987. Asst. regional adminstr. SEC, Washington, 1962-69, commr., 1977-80; assoc. Willkie Farr & Gallagher, N.Y.C., 1969-72; ptnr. Rogers & Wells, N.Y.C., 1972-77, of counsel, 1980-85; ptnr. Kelley Drye & Warren, N.Y.C., 1987-94, of counsel, 1995—2002. Adj. prof. law Bklyn. Law Sch., 1973-77, 82-85, prof., 1985—, co-dir. Ctr. for Study of Internat. Bus. Law; bd. dirs. Kemper Ins Cos.; trustee Practicing Law Inst. Author: Regulation by Prosecution, 1982; contbr. articles to profl. jours. Fellow Am. Bar Found.; mem. ABA, Assn. Bar City N.Y., Am. Law Inst., Fin. Women's Assn. Home: 66 Summit Dr Hastings On Hudson NY 10706-1215 Office: Bklyn Law Sch 250 Joralemon St Brooklyn NY 11201-3700 E-mail: roberta.karmel@brooklaw.edu.

KARNEZIS, JOHN T. lawyer; b. Chgo., July 23, 1966; s. Themis Nicholas and Margaret Melodie (Johnson) Karnezis. BS, U. Ill., 1988; JD, Loyola U., Chgo., 1991. Atty. Cook County States Attys. Office, Chgo., 1991—2000; assoc. Clifford Law Offices, Chgo., 2000—. Personal injury (including property damage). Office: Clifford Law Office 120 N LaSalle # 3100 Chicago IL 60602 E-mail: jtk@cliffordlaw.com.

KARNIEL, YUVAL, lawyer; b. Jerusalem, June 15, 1963; s. Hanania and Ilana Karniel; m. Tamar Olanda Mordahovich, July 2, 1993; children, Adi, Michal, Jonathan. LLB, Hebrew U., Jerusalem, 1988, LLD, 1997; LLM, Am. U., Washington, 1990. Legal adviser Police and Communication Minister, Jerusalem, Tel Aviv, 1992-93, 2d TV and Radio Authority, Jerusalem, 1993-95; lectr. Hebrew U., Jerusalem, 1996-2000; head communicaion and media law sector Zysman, Aharoni, Gayer & Co., Tel Aviv, 1999—2001; of counsel Shibolet, Yisraeli, Roberts, Zisman & Co., 2001—. Mem. Freedom Info. Pub. Commn., Israel, 1994-95, Copyright and Patent Enactment Commn., Israel, 1997—. Contbr. articles to profl. jours. Chmn. Keshev - Protection Democracy in Israel, 1990-2001; mem. Assn. Civic Rights Israel, 1990-2001. Sgt. maj. Israeli Def. Force Air Force, 1981-84. Recipient Outstanding Acad. Achievement award Golda Meir Fund, 1989; grantee New Israel Fund, 1989-90. Mem. Israel Bar Assn., Internet Soc. Communications, Corporate, general, Intellectual property. Office: Shibolet Yisraeli Roberts Zisman & Co 46 Montefiore St 65201 Tel Aviv Israel Office Fax: 972-3-710-3322. Business E-Mail: manager@shibolet.com.

KARNO, NORTON STANLEY, lawyer; b. Chgo., June 29, 1936; s. Phillip and Rose (Sukert) K.; children: Stephanie Lynn, Valerie Ann, Mitchell Perry. BS, UCLA, 1956; JD, U. So. Calif., 1960, cert. advanced studies, 1962. Bar: Calif. 1961; CPA, Calif. Sr. ptnr. Karno, Schwartz & Friedman and predecessors, Encino, Calif., 1961—. Assoc. editor So. Calif. Law Rev., 1958-60. Recipient commendation Calif. State Senate, 1976. Mem. Apt. Owners Assn. San Fernando Valley (pres. 1975-76), Order of Coif, Phi Beta Kappa, Beta Gamma Sigma, Phi Eta Sigma. Republican. Office: Karno Schwartz & Friedman Ste 1200 16255 Ventura Blvd Suite 1200 Encino CA 91436 E-mail: nsk@cal-am.com.

KAROL, NATHANIEL H. lawyer, consultant; b. N.Y.C., Feb. 16, 1929; s. Isidore and Lillian (Orlow) K.; m. Liliane Leser, July 20, 1967; children: David, Jordan. BS in Social Sci, CCNY, 1949; MA (fellow), Yale U., 1950; LL.B., N.Y. U., 1957, LL.M., 1959, JD, 1966. Bar: N.Y. 1957. Mgmt. trainee Curtiss Wright Corp., Wood-Ridge, N.J., 1956-57; practiced in N.Y.C., 1957-58; contracting officer USAF, N.Y.C., 1958-62; chief contract mgmt. survey and cost adminstrn. Office of Procurement, NASA, Washington, 1962-64; asst. dir. cost reduction, 1964-66; dep. asst. sec. Grants Adminstrn., HEW, Washington, 1966-69; univ. dean City U. N.Y.; exec. dir. Research Found., 1969-73; v.p. Hebrew Union Coll., Cin., 1973-75; partner, nat. chmn. cons. services for edn. Coopers & Lybrand (C.P.A.s), Chgo., 1975-81; pres. Nathaniel H. Karol & Assocs. Ltd., 1981—. Cons. to govt. agys. and ednl. instns., 1969— Author: Managing the Higher Education Enterprise. Served with U.S. Army, 1953-56. Recipient Outstanding Performance award HEW, 1968, Superior Performance award, 1969 Mem. N.Y. Bar, Nat. Assn. Coll. and Univ. Bus. Officers, Nat. Assn. Coll. and Univ. Attys. Home and Office: 1228 Cambridge St Highland Park IL 60035-1014

KARON, SHELDON, lawyer; b. Superior, Wis., Mar. 1, 1930; s. Bert and Betty Karon; m. Lee Goldwasser, Aug. 6, 1950; children: Maureen Byron, Laurie Feig, Peggy Pattis. BS, Northwestern U., 1952; JD, Harvard U., 1955. Bar: Ill. 1955. Assoc. Jenner & Block, Chgo., 1955-61; ptnr. Friedman & Koven, Chgo., 1962-75; ptnr., chmn. Karon, Morrison & Savikas, Chgo., 1975-88, Keck, Mahin & Cate, Chgo., 1988-97; of counsel Foley & Lardner, Chgo., 1997—. Arbitrator CPR Inst. Dispute Resolution, N.Y.C.; mem. Ill. Supreme Ct. Commn. for Jud. Reform, 1993-95. Bd. dirs. Kohl CHildren's Mus., Wilmette, Ill., 1988—, Highland Park (Ill.) Cmty. Edn., 1995—. Fellow Am. Coll. Trial Lawyers; mem. ABA, Ill. State Bar Assn., Chgo. Bar Assn., Fed. Cir. Bar Assn., Am. Arbitration Assn. (chair large complex case panel), Law Club, Legal Club. Alternative dispute resolution, Federal civil litigation, Intellectual property. Office: Foley & Lardner 321 N Clark St Chicago IL 60610 E-mail: skaron@foleylaw.com.

KARP, DAVID BARRY, lawyer; b. Milw., Dec. 12, 1955; s. Joseph and Sally P. (Nashinsky) K.; m. Donna L. Boorse, Apr. 8, 1984. BA, U. Wis., Milw., 1977; postgrad., Am. U., 1978; JD, Marquette U., 1982. Bar: Wis. 1982, U.S. Dist. Ct. (we. and ea. dist.) Wis. 1982, U.S. Cir. Ct. (7th cir.) 1982. Assoc. Karp Law Offices, S.C., Milw., 1990—. Mem. ABA, Wis. Assn. Trial Lawyers, Wis. State Bar, ATLA Inns of Ct., Matrimonial Divsn., Soc. Family Lawyers. Avocations: golf, running, music. Family and matrimonial, Personal injury (including property damage). Office: Karp Karp & Zirgibel 2675 N Mayfair Rd Ste 300 Milwaukee WI 53226

KARP, MARVIN LOUIS, lawyer; b. Milo, Maine, June 12, 1934; s. Harry and Rose Helen (Kiersh) K.; m. Lesley M. Ulevitch, Aug. 11, 1963; children: Harlan, Elissa, Douglas. BA, Yale U., 1955, JD, 1958. Bar: Ohio 1958, U.S. Dist. Ct. (no. dist.) Ohio 1960, U.S. Ct. Appeals (6th cir.) 1963, U.S. Supreme Ct. 1974. Ptnr. Ulmer & Berne, Cleve., 1958—, head litigation dept., 1968—. Pres. Park Synagogue. Fellow Internat. Acad. Trial Lawyers, Am. Coll. Trial Lawyers; mem. ABA (chmn. torts and ins. practice sects., ins. law commn.), Cleve. Bar Assn. (trustee 1981-84, pres. 1988-89, professionalism award, 2001), Fedn. Ins. and Corp. Counsel (pres., chmn. standing com. on ethics), Am. Judicature Soc., Def. Rsch. Inst. Federal civil litigation, State civil litigation, Insurance. Home: 3180 Lander Rd Cleveland OH 44124 Office: 900 Bond Court Blvd Cleveland OH 44114

KARPINSKI, IRENA IZABELLA, lawyer; b. Phila., July 6, 1950; d. Zygmunt Karpinski and Izabella Styczek; m. Walter Charles Johnston, Sept. 17, 1988; 1 child, Aleksander Styczek Johnston. BA, Manhattanville Coll., 1968-72; JD, Temple U., 1972-75; student, Leningrad (USSR) State U., 1970, U. Fribourg, Switzerland, 1970-71. Bar: Pa., 1975, D.C., 1976, N.Y., 1982, Md., 1982; U.S. Dist. Ct. D.C., 1977, U.S. Dist. Ct. (ea. dist.) Pa., 1978, U.S. Dist. Ct. Md., 1986. Spl. asst. to E.G. Biester U.S. Congress, Washington, 1975-76; assoc. atty. Samuel J. Levine, Esq., Washington, 1976-77; pvt. practice Washington, 1977—. Chairperson D.C. Bd. Appeals Rev., Washington, 1984-91; cons. bd. govs. Fed. Res., Washington, 1992-94. Mem. Women's Bar Assn. (chair standing com. 1993—). Avocations: languages, traveling, bridge, chess, tennis. Family and matrimonial, Immigration, naturalization, and customs, Private international. Office: # 111 1330 New Hampshire Ave NW Washington DC 20036

KARPINSKI, JOHN STANLEY, lawyer; b. Elgin, Ill., June 17, 1956; s. Adolph Leon and Carolyn Jean (Garafalo) K.; m. Diane Marie Anicker, Sept. 6, 1987; 2 children. BS, No. Ill. U., 1978; JD, U. Oreg., 1982. Bar: Wash. 1983, U.S. Dist. Ct. (we. dist.) 1983, U.S. Ct. Appeals (9th cir.) 1994. Atty. Miles & Miles, Vancouver, Wash., 1983-84; pvt. practice Vancouver, 1984—. Mem. exec. com. Clark County Dem. Party, Vancouver, 1985-91; mem. paralegal adv. com. Clark Coll., Vancouver, 1987-98; co-founder, mem. Clark County Natural Resources Coun., Vancouver, 1986—, chair, 1986, 97—; mem. legal com. Wash. Environ. Coun., 1990-96, v.p., 1998—. Mem. Sierra Club (chair S.W. Wash. club 1983-84, bd. dirs. Pacific N.W. 1983-85, citizen lobbyist Columbia Gorge Nat. Scenic Area 1983-85).

Democrat. Avocations: golf, wine tasting, games, sports. Environmental, Land use and zoning (including planning), Personal injury (including property damage). Office: 2612 E 20th St Vancouver WA 98661-4641 E-mail: karpjd@pacifier.com.

KARPOFF, MICHAEL STEVEN, lawyer; b. Newark, Aug. 27, 1950; s. Emanuel and Rebecca (Seidman) K.; m. Susan Nancy Lehrer, Dec. 29, 1973; children: Alana, Joshua, Rachel. AB, Rutgers Coll., 1972, JD, 1980; MS, Boston U., 1974. Bar: N.J. 1980, N.Y. 1989, Pa. 1992, U.S. Dist. Ct. N.J. 1980, U.S. Ct. Appeals (3d cir.) 1988, U.S. Supreme Ct. 1987; cert. civil trial atty., N.J. Pub. rels. account exec. William G. Hetherington and Co., Newark, 1974; pub. rels. asst. Newark Beth Israel Med. Ctr., 1974-76; comm. coord. Apollo Technologies, Inc., Whippany, N.J., 1976-80; law asst. Div. of Law N.J. Dept. of Law and Pub. Safety, Newark, 1980, dep. atty. gen., 1980-84; assoc. atty. Lane and Perl, Esq., Hillsborough, N.J., 1984-89; prin., atty. Perl, Karpoff & Kessler, P.C., Hillsborough, 1989-96; ptnr. Hill Wallack, Princeton, N.J., 1996—. Spkr., co-author N.J. Inst. for Continuing Legal Edn. seminar: "Community Association Collections-Practice, Pointers, and Pitfalls", 1993; spkr. N.J. State Bar Assn. Spkrs. Bur., New Brunswick, 1988—. Atty. Zoning Bd. of Adjustment, Highland Park, N.J., 1987-95; mem. Rent Leveling Bd., Highland Park, 1986-95, chmn., 1994-95; trustee Rutgers Hillel, New Brunswick, 1980-2000, v.p. resources, 1997-2000; chmn. pack com. Cub Scout Pack 5 Boy Scouts Am., Highland Park, 1992-96, chmn. troop com. troop 55, 1997—; judge h.s. mock trial competition N.J. Bar Found., 1991, 95, 97-2002; coach mock trial team Yeshiva H.S. Sch. Ctrl. N.J. (now Moshe Aaron Yeshiva H.S.), 1996—; bd. dirs. Congregation Ahavas Achim, Highland Park, 2000—. Mem. ATLA, ABA, N.J. State Bar Assn., Pa. Bar Assn., Middlesex County Bar Assn., Cmty. Assocs. Inst., Coll. Cmty. Assn. Lawyers. Avocations: cycling, playing drums, model railroading. General civil litigation, Land use and zoning (including planning), State civil litigation. Office: Hill Wallack 202 Carnegie Ctr Princeton NJ 08540-6239

KARR, CHARLES, lawyer; b. Coal Hill, Ark., Aug. 3, 1941; s. William Joe and Doris Jane (Coats) K.; m. Suzanne Mary Stoner, Dec. 23, 1962; children: Stephanie, Jennifer, Jeffrey. BA, U. Ark., 1965, LLB, 1967. Bar: Ark. 1968, U.S. Dist. Ct. (we. dist.) Ark. 1979, U.S. Ct. Appeals (8th cir.), 1982, U.S. Supreme Ct. 1985. Law clk. to assoc. justice Ark. Supreme Ct., Little Rock, 1968; dep. pros. atty. Sebastian County, Fort Smith, Ark., 1969-72; pros. atty. 12th Jud. Cir., Fort Smith, 1973-78; ptnr. Law Offices Charles Karr, PA, Fort Smith, 1979—. Mem. Criminal Detention Facilities Bd., Pine Bluff, Ark., 1976-78, Gov.'s Commn. on Prisons, Little Rock, 1977; bd. dirs. United Way Fort Smith, Inc., 1977-79, Bost Human Devel. Svcs., Inc., Fort Smith, 1983-88. Mem.: ABA (speedy trial com. 1976—77, prosecution discretion com. 1983—84), Ark. Pros. Attys. Assn. (pres. 1977), Ark. Bar Assn. (chmn. criminal law sect. 1976—77), W.B. Putnam Am. Inn of Ct. (pres. 1999), Assn. Trial Lawyers Am. Democrat. Mem. Ch. of Christ. Personal injury (including property damage), Product liability, Professional liability. Home: 7415 Westminster Pl Fort Smith AR 72903-4250 Office: Law Offices Charles Karr PA 1st Nat Bank Bldg 602 Garrison Ave Ste 650 Fort Smith AR 72901-2535 E-mail: karrlawfirm@aol.com.

KARR, DAVID DEAN, lawyer; b. Denver, Sept. 3, 1953; s. Dean Speece and Jean (Ransbottom) K.; m. Laura A. Foster, Apr. 10, 1982; children: Emily Ann, Bradley Foster. BA, U. Puget Sound, 1975; JD, Loyola U., 1979. Bar: Colo. 1979, U.S. Dist. Ct. 1979, U.S. Ct. Appeals (10th cir.) 1981, U.S. Supreme Ct. 1983. Assoc. Pryor Carney & Johnson, P.C., Englewood, Colo., 1979-84, ptnr., 1984-95, Pryor, Johnson, Montoya, Carney and Karr, P.C., Englewood, Colo., 1995—. Mem. ABA (lead atty. pro bono team death penalty project Tex. chpt. 1988—), Colo. Bar Assn. (interprofl. com. 1990—), Arapahoe County Bar Assn., Denver Bar Assn., Def. Rsch. Inst. Federal civil litigation, Insurance, Personal injury (including property damage). Home: 5474 E Hinsdale Cir Littleton CO 80122-2538 Office: Pryor Johnson Montoya Carney and Karr PC 5619 DTC Pkwy Ste 1200 Greenwood Village CO 80111-

KART, EUGENE, lawyer; b. Dec. 4, 1911; s. Isaac and Sarah (Beym) K.; m. Ruth Becker, Apr. 29, 1937; children: Lawrence, Judith Kart Hazan. BS with distinction, Northwestern U., 1933; JD, 1936. Bar: Ill. 1936, U.S. Dist. Ct. (no. dist.) Ill. 1937, U.S. Ct. Mil. Appeals 1963, U.S. Ct. Claims 1963, U.S. Supreme Ct. 1963. Assoc. Remer and Shapiro, Chgo., 1936-37; ptnr. Fisk and Kart, Ltd., Chgo., 1937-71; pres., 1971—. Chmn. lawyers div. Jewish United Fund Met. Chgo., 1977; v.., bd. dirs. Schwab Rehab. Hosp.; bd. dirs. North Shore Congregation Israel, 1967-76. Bd. editors Northwestern U. law Rev., 1935-36. Lt. (s.g.) USNR, 1944-46. Recipient Svc. award Northwestern U., 1984. Mem. ABA, Ill. Bar Assn., Chgo Bar Assn., Am. Jud. Soc., Decalogue Soc., Law Club Chgo., Phi Beta Kappa (fellow), Tau Epsilon Rho Law Soc. (past nat. chancellor). Democrat. Clubs: Winnetka Golf, John Evans of Northwestern U. (chmn. membership 1985-87). State and local taxation. Office: Fisk Kart Katz & Regan Ltd 77 W Washington St Ste 900 Chicago IL 60602-2804

KARTIGANER, JOSEPH, retired lawyer; b. Berlin, June 5, 1935; came to U.S., 1939; s. Harold and Lilly (Wolkowitz) K.; m. Audrey Gertsman Amdursky; children: Deborah Lynn, Alison Beth. AB, CCNY, 1955; LL.B., Columbia U., 1958. Bar: N.Y. 1960, Fla. 1978, D.C. 1979. Assoc. White & Case, N.Y.C., 1960-69, ptnr., 1969-88, Simpson Thacher & Bartlett, N.Y.C., 1988-99; ret., 1999. Lectr. law Columbia Law Sch., N.Y.C., 1973-80; vis. lectr. Sch. Law Yale U., 1997-2000; mem adv. com. N.Y. Estates, Powers and Trust Law-Surrogate's Ct. Procedure Act, 1997—. Mem.: Columbia Law Rev. Fellow Am. Bar Found., Am. Coll. Trust and Estate Counsel (regent 1978-84), Am. Coll. Tax Counsel, N.Y. State Bar Found.; mem. ABA (chmn. real property, probate and trust law sect. 1986-87, co-chair sect. standing com. on govt. submissions 1995—), N.Y. State Bar Assn., Assn. of Bar of City of N.Y. (chmn. com. on trusts, estates and surrogate's cts. 1990-92), Nat. Conf. Lawyers and Corp. Fiduciaries (co-chair 1991-93), Am. Law Inst., Internat. Acad. Estate and Trust Law (exec. coun. 1980-94, 98-2002), Scarsdale Golf Club (Hartsdale, N.Y.). Estate planning, Probate (including wills, trusts), Estate taxation. Home: 812 5th Ave # 5B New York NY 10021-7253 Office: Simpson Thacher & Bartlett 425 Lexington Ave Fl 15 New York NY 10017-3954 E-mail: joekart@yahoo.com.

KARWACKI, ROBERT LEE, former judge; b. Balt., Aug. 2, 1933; s. Lee Daniel and Marie Ann (Budzynski) K.; m. Patricia Ann Deal, Nov. 3, 1956 (dec. May 1972); children: Ann Elizabeth, Lee Daniel, John Robert; m. Marion Elizabeth Harper, June 16, 1973. AB, U. Md., 1954; LLB, U. Md., Balt., 1956. Bar: Md. 1956, U.S. Supreme Ct. 1963, U.S. Dist. Ct. Md. 1957, U.S. Ct. Appeals (4th cir.) 1960. Law clk. to Hon. Stephen R. Collins Ct. Appeals Md., Annapolis, 1956-57; assoc. Miles & Stockbridge, Balt., 1957-63, ptnr., 1965-73; asst. atty. gen. State of Md., Balt., 1963-65; assoc. judge Cir. Ct. Balt. City, 1973-84, Ct. Spl. Appeals Md., Annapolis, 1984-90, Ct. Appeals Md., Annapolis, 1990-97. Pres. Balt. City Sch. Bd., 1970-72. Sgt. USAR, 1956-62. Recipient Man for All Seasons award St. Thomas More Soc., 1977. Fellow Md. Bar Found.; mem. Lawyer's Roundtable, Wednesday Law Club (pres. 1984). Democrat. Roman Catholic. Avocations: golfing, boating, fishing, hunting. Home: 1013 Calvert St Baltimore MD 21202-3823*

KASANIN, MARK OWEN, lawyer; b. Boston, June 28, 1929; s. Jacob Sergei and Elizabeth Owen (Knight) K.; m. Anne Camilla Wimbish, Dec. 18, 1960; children: Marc S., James W. BA, Stanford U., 1951; LL.B., Yale U., 1954. Bar: Calif. Assoc. Bignham McCutchen, San Francisco, 1957-62, 63-67; ptnr. McCutchen, Doyle, Brown & Enersen, 1967—. Mem. planning commn. City of Belvedere, Calif., 1974-76; chair tech. adv. com. San Francisco Bay Area Water Transit Authority, 2001--. Served with USNR, 1955-57 Named among Best Lawyers in Am., 2001—02. Fellow Am. Coll. Trial Lawyers; mem. Maritime Law Assn. U.S. (exec. com. 1984-87), Product Liability Adv. Coun. Found. (trustee 1990—), Jud. Conf. U.S. (mem. fed. civil rules adv. com. 1992-2002). Admiralty, Insurance, Product liability. Home: PO Box 698 Belvedere Tiburon CA 94920-0698 Office: Bingham McCutchen 3 Embarcadero Ctr San Francisco CA 94111-4003 Fax: 415-393-2286.

KASHANI, HAMID REZA, lawyer, computer consultant; b. Tehran, Iran, May 1, 1955; came to U.S., 1976; s. Javad K. BSEE with highest distinction, Purdue U., 1978, MSEE, 1979; JD, Ind. U., 1986. Bar: Ind. 1986, U.S. Dist. Ct. (so. and no. dists.) 1986, U.S. Ct. Appeals (7th cir.) 1986, U.S. Supreme Ct. 1994, U.S. Ct. Appeals (9th cir.) 1996. Rsch. asst. Purdue U., West Lafayette, Ind., 1978-79, 80-81; engr. Cummins Engine Co., Columbus, Ind., 1981-82; assoc. faculty Ind. U.-Purdue U., Indpls., 1983-84; sr. software engr. Engineered System Devel., Indpls., 1985-87; computer cons. Hamid R. Kashani, Indpls., 1986—; pvt. practice law Indpls., 1986—; cons. Good Techs., Indpls., 1987-90; pres. Virtual Media Techs., Inc., 1998—. Cons. Prism Imaging, Denver, 1990-93, Ind. Bar Assn., 1989-95. Editor: Computer Law Desktop Guide, 1995. Mem., bd. dirs. ACLU, 1997—, Ind. Civil Liberties Union, Indpls., 1987—, mem. legis. com., 1987—, mem. screening com., 1985—, del., 1989, 91, 93, 95, 97, 99, 2001, acting v.p. fundraising, 1995-96, v.p. edn., 1996—, chair long-range planning com., 1991-92, 96—, chmn. nominating com., 1997—, pres., 1999—; bd. dirs. ACLU, 1997—. Fellow Ind. U. Sch. Law, 1984; recipient Cert. of Appreciation Ind. Correctional Assn., 1988; named Cooperating Atty. of Yr. Ind. Civil Liberties Union, 1990, 95, 98. Mem. ABA (vice chmn. YLD computer law com. 1990-91, chmn. computer law exec. com. 1991-93, litigation exec. com. 1987-89, 90-93, YLD liaison standing com. on jud. selection, tenure and compensation 1992-94, 95-96, sci. and tech. co-chair first amendment rights in the digital age com. 1997—, vice chair com. on opportunities for minorities and women 1997-99, YLD liaison to ABA tech. coun. 1992-93, vice chmn. nat. info. infrastructure com. sect. sci. and tech. 1993-97, chair privacy info. and civil liberties ABA sect. of individual rights and responsibilities 1998-2002, co-chair technology com., mem. standing com. on jud. selection, tenure and compensation 1995-96, chair privacy info. and civil liberties sect. of individual rights and responsibilities 1998-2002), IEEE (Outstanding Contbns. award 1983), Indpls. Bar Assn. (chmn. articles and bylaws coms. 1994-95), Ind. State Bar Assn. (vice chair computer comms. com. 1995-98, chair computer comms. com. 1998—, chair computer comm. com. 1998—), Eta Kappa Nu, Tau Beta Pi, Phi Kappa Phi, Phi Eta Sigma. Civil rights, Federal civil litigation, Computer. Office: 445 N Pennsylvania St Ste 600 Indianapolis IN 46204-1818 E-mail: hkashani@kashanilaw.com.

KASISCHKE, LOUIS WALTER, lawyer; b. Bay City, Mich., July 18, 1942; s. Emil Ernst and Gladys Ann (Stuady) K.; m. Sandra Ann Colosimo, Sept. 30, 1967; children: Douglas, Gregg. BA, Mich. State U., 1964, JD, 1967; LLM, Wayne State U., 1971. Bar: Mich. 1968, U.S. Dist. Ct. (southeastern dist.) Mich. 1968; CPA. Acct. Touche Ross & Co., Detroit, 1967-71; atty. Dykema Gossett, Detroit, 1971—; pres. Pella Window and Door Co., West Bloomfield, Mich., 1990-98. Bd. dirs. Barton Malow Co., Southfield. Author: Michigan Closely Held Corporations, 1986; contbr. articles to profl. jours. Mem. ABA, AICPA, State Bar Mich. (editor column Mich. Bar Jour. 1971-83), Mich. Assn. CPAs, Am. Coll. Tax Counsel Republican. Lutheran. Avocations: mountaineering, skiing, running, squash, golf. Corporate, general, Corporate taxation, Taxation, general. Home: 3491 N Lakeshore Harbor Springs MI 49740 Office: Dykema Gossett 39577 Woodward Ave Ste 300 Bloomfield Hills MI 48304-5086

KASS, BENNY LEE, lawyer; b. Chgo., Aug. 20, 1936; s. Herman and Ethel (Lome) K.; m. Salme Lundstrom, Aug. 30, 1963; children: Gale, Brian. BS, Northwestern U., 1957; LLB, U. Mich., 1960; LLM, George Washington U., 1967. Bar: D.C. 1960. Atty. Maritime Adminstrn., 1960-61; counsel House Info. Subcom., 1962-65; asst. counsel Senate Adminstrv. Practice Subcom., Washington, 1965-69; pvt. practice law Washington, 1969—; mem. Kass, Mitek & Kass, PLLC, 2001; prof. communication law Am. U.; pub. mem. Nat. Advt. Rev. Bd., 1971-74. Life mem. Conf. on Uniform State Laws. Columnist Washington Post, L.A. Times; contbr. articles to profl. jours. Chmn. consumer affairs subcom. Mayors Econ. Devel. Com., 1968-70; chmn. Ad Hoc Com. on Consumer Protection, 1965—. With USAF, 1961-62. Am. Polit. Sci. Assn. Congl. fellow, 1966. Mem. ABA, FBA, Am. Polit. Sci. Assn., Sigma Delta Chi. Commercial, consumer (including collections, credit), General practice, Property, real (including real estate development, water). Office: Kass & Skalet PLLC 1050 17th St NW Ste 1100 Washington DC 20036-5596 E-mail: bkass@kmklawyers.com.

KASS, DAVID NORMAN, accountant, lawyer; b. N.Y.C., Mar. 8, 1951; s. Joseph Zane and Rosalind (Sperber) K.; m. Esta Gail Millman, Nov. 26, 1977; children: Sean N., Joshua A. BS in Acctg., SUNY, Albany, 1973; JD, St. John's U., Jamaica, N.Y., 1982. Bar: N.Y. 1983. Staff acct. Touche Ross & Co., N.Y.C., 1972-74; sr. acct. Reich Weiner & Co., N.Y.C., 1974-76; ptnr. Brandt, Pollack, Kass & Wilkins, N.Y.C., 1976-79, Kass & Kass CPAs PC, Roslyn, N.Y., 1979—; pvt. practice Roslyn, 1983—. Seminar leader Nassau Acad. Law, Mineola, N.Y., 1993, seminar leader/lectr., 1995. Contbr. articles to The Nassau Lawyer. Baseball coach Roslyn Little League, 1990-95; active in alumni fund campaign SUNY, Albany, 1994. Mem. Am. Arbitration Assn. (comml. law arbitrator), N.Y. State Bar Assn., Nassau County Bar Assn. (mentor), Nat. Assn. CPA Practitioners, N.Y. State Soc. CPAs. E-mail: dkass@mindspring.com.

KASSNER, HERBERT SEYMORE, lawyer; b. N.Y.C., Dec. 3, 1931; s. Abraham and Rose (Rosenblatt) K.; m. Sheilah Goodwin, 1957 (div. 1965); children: Andrew, Kenneth; m. Marjorie Fern Golding, 1974 (div. 1992); children: Robin, Jeffrey; m. Linda Rubinstein Finder, 1993. BA (hon.), Franklin and Marshall U., 1952; cert., Hague (Netherlands) Acad. of Internat. Law, 1953; MA, NYU, 1955; LLB (hon.), Harvard U., 1955. Bar: N.Y. 1955, Conn. 1986. Atty. Gallap, Climenko & Gould, N.Y.C., 1955, Otterbourg, Steindler, Huston & Rosen, N.Y.C., 1956; pvt. practice law N.Y.C., 1957-65, 1969; atty. Dryer & Traub, N.Y.C., 1966-68, Kassner & Detsky, N.Y.C., 1970-80, Kassner & Haigney, N.Y.C., 1981-90. Instr. Ohio State U., Columbus, 1956-57; asst. prof. Ark. State U., Pine Bluff, 1965. Contbr. articles to profl. jours. on 1st amendment law. Mem. Phi Beta Kappa. Antitrust, Constitutional, Property, real (including real estate development, water). Home: 7221 Montrico Dr Boca Raton FL 33433-6931

KASSON, CONSTANTINE D. lawyer; b. Aug. 14, 1929; s. Tracy and Helen Kasson; m. Constance L. Kezios; children: Tracy, Lynee M. BA, DePaul U., 1950; JD, U. Mich., 1954. Ptnr. Klein, Thorpe, Kasson & Jenkins, Chgo., 1954—78, Burdutt & Calkins (then Burditt & Kadzuis), 1978—98, Bulwinkel Ptnrs., Ltd., 1998—. Adj. prof. law John Marshall Law Sch., Chgo., 1980—; arbitrator Cir. Cts., 1990—. Mem.: Trial Lawyers Assn., Chgo. Bar Assn., Ill. Bar Assn. Greek Orthodox. General civil litigation, Commercial, contracts (including sales of goods; commercial financing), Product liability. Home: 746 McKinley Ln Hinsdale IL 60521 Office: Bullwinkel Ptnrs Ltd 19 S LaSalle St Ste 1300 Chicago IL 60603 Fax: 312-201-0737. E-mail: cdk@bullwinkel.com.

KASWELL, STUART JOEL, lawyer, trade association executive; b. Brookline, Mass., Oct. 17, 1954; s. Ernest Ralph and Yolande Marilyn (Romsey) K.; m. Sherry L. Kinland, Nov. 9, 1985; children: Alisa Joy, Noah Kinland. AB in Polit. Sci. with gen. and dept. honors, Vassar Coll., 1976; JD, Am. U., 1979. Bar: Va. 1979, D.C. 1980, U.S. Dist. Ct. D.C. 1981, Md. 1981, U.S. Ct. Appeals (4th cir.) 1981, U.S. Ct. Appeals (D.C. cir.) 1981, U.S. Supreme Ct. 1983. Staff atty. SEC, Washington, 1979-83, spl. counsel, 1983-84, branch chief div. market regulation, 1984-86; minority Rep. counsel Com. on Energy and Commerce, U.S. Ho. of Reps., Washington, 1986-90; sr. assoc. Winthrop, Stimson, Putnam & Roberts, Washington, 1990-94; sr. v.p., gen. counsel Securities Industry Assn., Washington, 1994—. Spkr. at profl. confs.; interviewed by major news madia; co-chmn. task force NASD. Contbr. articles to profl. jours. Co-chmn. spl. gifts Vassar 10th Reunion Fund, Poughkeepsie, 1984-86; alumnus interviewer Vassar Coll., 1984—; mem. Vassar Club of Washington, 1976—; bd. dirs. B'nai Israel Synagogue, Rockville, Md., 1998-2001. Mem. ABA (co-chair internat. securities transaction com. internat. law sect. 1994-95), Va. State Bar Assn., Md. Bar Assn., SEC Hist. Soc. (mem. adv. com.). Office: Securities Industry Assn 1401 Eye St NW Washington DC 20005-2225

KATAYAMA, ROBERT NOBUICHI, lawyer; b. Honolulu, Oct. 11, 1924; s. Sanji K.; married; children: Alyce A. Katayama Jenkins, Robert Nobuichi, Kent J., Susan H. Ono, Carole Y. Kaneshiro, Wendy L. Lee. BA, U. Hawaii, 1950; LLB, Yale U., 1955; grad., Command and Gen. Staff Coll., 1964; LLM, George Washington U., 1967; grad., Indsl. Coll. Armed Forces, 1971. Bar: Calif. 1956, Ill. 1973, Hawaii 1989. Commd. 1st lt. JAGC U.S. Army, 1958, advanced through grades to col., 1973, ret., 1973; gen. counsel Overseas Mdse. Inspection Co., San Francisco, 1956-58, Army Contract Adjustment Bd., Washington, 1964-68; prof. law JAG Sch. U. Va., 1968-70; from assoc. to ptnr. Baker & McKenzie, Chgo., Tokyo and San Francisco, 1973-85; ptnr. Seki & Jarvis, San Francisco and San Jose, 1985-86, Nutter, McClennen & Fish, San Francisco, 1986-88; spl. counsel, sr. advisor Crosby, Heafey, Roach & May, Oakland, Calif., 1988; ptnr. Carlsmith Ball, Honolulu, 1988-95, counsel, 1995—. Chmn., CEO Kapolei People's Inc. dba Kapolei Golf Course, Honolulu, 1996-99, Kapolei Holding Corp. Trustee Nat. Japanese Am. Meml. Found., 1995—97, gov., 1997—; mem. Hawaii Adv. Coun. to Japanese Am. Nat. Mus., 2001—03; bd. dirs. Japanese Cultural Ctr. Hawaii, 1997—98, bd. govs., 1998—. Named Real Dean, U. Hawaii, Honolulu, 1950; recipient Disting. Alumni award, 2001. Mem.: ABA, Ill. Bar Assn., 442d Regimental Combat Team Found. (trustee 1993—, pres. 1999—2002), Hawaii Army Mus. Soc. (trustee 2001—), Ret. Officers Assn., Japanese Am. Soc. Legal Studies, Nat. Japanese Am. Hist. Soc. (legal officer 1984—89), Japan Am. Soc. Hawaii, Hawaii Bar Assn., Calif. Bar Assn., Oahu AJA Vets. Coun. (pres. 1997), Japanese C. of C. of No. Calif. (bd. dirs. 1987—89), 442d Vets. Club (legal advisor 1994—95, pres.-elect 1996, pres. 1997—98, legal advisor 2000—). Democrat. Buddhist. Corporate, general, Government contracts and claims, Private international. Office: Carlsmith Ball ASB Tower Ste 2200 1001 Bishop St Honolulu HI 96813-3676

KATCHER, RICHARD, lawyer; b. N.Y.C., Dec. 17, 1918; s. Samuel and Gussie (Applebaum) K.; m. Shirley Ruth Rifkin, Sept. 24, 1944; children: Douglas P., Robert A., Patti L. BA, U. Mich., 1941, JD, 1943. Bar: Mich. 1943, N.Y. 1944, Ohio 1946. Assoc. Noonan, Kaufman & Eagan, N.Y.C., 1943-46; from assoc. to ptnr. Ulmer, Berne & Laronge, Cleve., 1946-72; ptnr. Baker & Hostetler, Cleve., 1972-95. Lectr. in fed. income taxation Case Western Res. U. Sch. Law, Cleve., 1953-69, 71-72; mem. bd. in control of intercollegiate athletics, U. Mich., 2001—. Contbr. articles on fed. tax to profl. jours. Recipient Disting. Alumni Service award U. Mich., 1987, Leadership medal Pres.' Soc. of U. Mich., 1991. Fellow ABA (coun. sect. taxation 1973-76), Am. Coll. Tax Counsel (regent); mem. Am. Bar Retirement Assn. (bd. dirs., v.p. 1986-87, pres. 1987-88), U. Mich. Pres. Soc. (chmn. exec. com. 1987-90), U. Mich. Cleve. Club (pres. 1959, Outstanding Alumnus award 1987), U. Mich. Alumni Assn. (dir. 1994-98, sec. 1997-98). Avocation: tennis. Probate (including wills, trusts), Corporate taxation, Estate taxation. Home: 26150 Village Ln Apt 104 Beachwood OH 44122-7527 Office: Baker & Hostetler 3200 National City Ctr 1900 E 9th St Ste 3200 Cleveland OH 44114-3475 E-mail: RKatcher@baker-hostetler.com.

KATKIN, ELIZABETH LYNN, lawyer; b. Buffalo, N.Y., Mar. 28, 1968; arrived in Eng., 2001; m. Richard H. Waryn, Sept. 12, 1995. BA, Yale Coll., 1989; MIA, Columbia U., 1992, JD, 1995. Bar: Calif. 1995, D.C. 1996. Assoc. Cugly, Gottleib, Steen & Hamilton, Washington, 1995—2000; v.p., gen. counsel Findlaw, Washington, 2000; assoc. Hogan & Hartson, London, 2001—. Mem. adv. bd. Leading Edge LLC, Washington, 1999—2001, Smoke Clinic, Palo Alto, Calif., 2001—. Corporate, general, Private international. Office: Hogan & Hartson One Angel Ct London W1H 2LL England

KATSH, SALEM MICHAEL, lawyer; b. NYC, May 5, 1948; s. Abraham Isaac and Estelle (Wachtell) K.; m. Jennette Williams, Sept. 4, 1983; children: Halley Rachel, Emmet Walker. BA, NYU, 1970, JD cum laude, 1972. Bar: N.Y. 1973, U.S. Dist. Ct. (so., ea., no. dists. N.Y.) 1975, U.S. Ct. of Appeals (2d cir.) 1975, U.S. Ct. of Appeals (9th cir.) 1977, U.S. Supreme Ct. 1983, U.S. Ct. Appeals (fed. cir.) 1990, U.S. Dist. Ct. (no. dist.) Calif. 1993. Assoc. Weil, Gotshal & Manges, N.Y.C., 1972-80, ptnr., 1980-97, Shearman & Sterling, N.Y.C., 1997—. Adj. prof. New York Law Sch., 1980-84. Author: Industrial Power and the Law, 1980, (with others) The Limits of Corporate Power, 1981; founder Jour. Proprietary Rights; contbr. articles to profl. jours. Mem.: ABA, NY State Bar Assn., Order of Coif. General civil litigation, Intellectual property, Patent. Office: 599 Lexington Ave New York NY 10022-6030

KATSORIS, CONSTANTINE NICHOLAS, lawyer, consultant; b. Bklyn., Dec. 5, 1932; s. Nicholas C. and Nafsika (Klonis) K.; m. Ann Kanganis, Feb. 19; children: Nancy, Nicholas, Louis. BS in Acctg., Fordham U., 1953; JD cum laude, 1957; LLM, NYU, 1963. Bar: N.Y. 1957, U.S. Dist. Ct. (so. and ea. dist.) N.Y. 1959, U.S. Tax. Ct. 1959, U.S. Ct. Appeals (2nd cir.) 1959, U.S. Supreme Ct. 1961. Assoc. Cahill, Gordon, Reindel & Ohl, N.Y.C., 1958-64; asst. prof. Law Sch. Fordham U., N.Y.C., 1964-66, assoc. prof., 1966-69; prof., 1969—; apptd. Wilkinson prof. law, 1991. Cons. N.Y. State Temporary Commn. on Estates, 1964-67; arbitration panelist N.Y. Stock Exchange, 1971—, Nat. Assn. Securities Dealers, 1968—, 1st Jud. Dept., 1972—; pub. mem. Securities Industry Conf. on Arbitration, 1977-97, 2003-, chairperson, 2003-; pvt. judge adjudication ctr. Duke U. Law Sch., 1989—. Contbr. articles to profl. jours. Mem. sch. bd. Greek Orthodox Parochial Sch. St. Spyridon, 1975-89, chmn. sch. bd., 1983-89. With U.S. Army, 1963. Recipient Cert. Appreciation Nat. Assn. Securities Dealers, 1982, Ellis Is. Medal of Honor award, 1999. Mem. ABA (fed. estate and gift tax com. 1966-68), N.Y. State Bar Assn. (sect. on trust and estates 1969—), Assn. Bar City of N.Y. (trusts, estates and surrogates' cts. com. 1968-70, legal assistance com. 1965-67), Fordham U. Law Alumni Assn. (bd. dirs. 1972—), Fordham U. Law Rev. Alumni Assn. (pres. 1962-64). Republican. Greek Orthodox. Office: 140 W 62nd St New York NY 10023-7407

KATZ, AYA, jurist, linguist, writer; b. Rehovot, Israel, July 30, 1960; came to U.S., 1961; d. Amnon and Ora (Minkowitz) K. BA, U. Tex., Arlington, 1979; JD, Baylor Law Sch., 1982; PhD, Rice U., 1996. Bar: Tex. 1982. Sole practice, Grand Prairie, Tex., 1983—91; asst. prof. Providence U., Taiwan, 1999—2001; primate lang. rschr., 2001—. V.p. Inverted-A, Inc., Grand Prairie, 1979—, pres. Inverted-A, Inc., 2002-,bus. cons., 1984—. Author (novel): The Few Who Count, 1985, (poetry) The Blake Bunch, 1988. Andrews, Korth, Campbell & Jones scholar, 1981-82. Republican. Office: PO Box 267 Licking MO 65542-0267 E-mail: amnfn@well.com.

KATZ, DONALD H. lawyer; b. Boston, May 16, 1942; s. Jacob and Pearl Katz; m. Phyllis Bessler Katz, Aug. 22, 1964; children: Stephanie Dana, Jeffrey Evan. BA, Boston U., 1963, JD, 1965. Bar: Mass. 1965, U.S. Dist. Ct. Mass. 1967, U.S. Ct. Appeals (1st cir.) 1980, U.S. Supreme Ct. 1982. Assoc. Bernkopf, Goodman & Baseman, Boston, 1967—68, Fanger & Birnbaum, 1968—75, ptnr., 1975—78; atty. pvt. practice, 1978—82; mng. ptnr. Katz, Fanger & Greely, 1982—92, Katz & Rudnick, PC, 1992—. Pres. bd. trustees Agassiz Village, Lexington, Mass. and Poland, Maine, 2000—. 1st lt. U.S. Army, 1968—70. Avocations: golf, cooking. General practice,

Family and matrimonial, Landlord-tenant. Home: 35 Dunster Rd Sudbury MA 01776 Office: Katz & Rudnick PC 73 Tremont St Boston MA 02108 Fax: 617-973-1520. E-mail: dhk@katzrucnick.com.

KATZ, HAROLD AMBROSE, lawyer, former state legislator; b. Shelbyville, Tenn., Nov. 2, 1921; s. Maurice W. and Gertrude Evelyn (Cohen) K.; m. Ethel Mae Lewison, July 21, 1945; children: Alan, Barbara, Julia, Joel. AB, Vanderbilt U., 1943; JD, U. Chgo., 1948, MA, 1958. Bar: Ill. 1948. Ptnr. Katz, Friedman, Eagle Eisenstein & Johnson, Chgo., 1948—; spl. legal cons. to Gov. of Ill., 1961-63; master-in-chancery, circuit ct. Cook County, Ill., 1963-67; mem. Ill. Ho. of Reps., 1965-83, chmn. judiciary com., co-chmn. rules com. Lectr. U. Coll., U. Chgo., 1959-64; Chmn. Ill. Commn. on Orgn. of Gen. Assembly, 1966-82; del. nat. Democratic conv., 1972 Author: Liability of Auto Manufacturers for Unsafe Design of Passenger Cars, 1956; (with Charles O. Gregory) Labor Law: Cases, Materials and Comments, 1948, Labor and the Law, 1979, Harold A. Katz Memoirs, 1988; editor: Improving the State Legislature, 1967; contbr. articles to mags. Recipient Jurisprudence award, Chgo. Am. Orgn. for Rehab. through Tng., 2000, Laureate, Ill. Acad. Lawyers, 2001. Fellow Coll. Labor and Employment Lawyers; mem. ABA, Ill. Bar Assn. (chmn. labor law sect. 1979-80), Internat. Soc. for Labor Law and Social Legislation (U.S. chmn. 1961-67), Am. Trial Lawyers Assn. (chmn. workmen's compensation sect. 1963-64. Jewish. Federal civil litigation, State civil litigation, Labor (including EEOC, Fair Labor Standards Act, labor-management relations, NLRB, OSHA). Home: 1180 Terrace Ct Glencoe IL 60022-1241 Office: Katz Friedman Eagle Eisenstein & Johnson 77 W Washington St Fl 20 Chicago IL 60602-2904

KATZ, JANYCE C(HARLENE), lawyer; b. Cin., Aug. 19, 1949; d. Louis and Ida (Schreiber) K.; m. Mark Glazman. BA, Boston U., 1971; MA in History, U. Cin., 1974, ABD, 1976, JD, 1989. Teaching asst., instr. history dept. U. Cin., 1973-76; prodr., writer, announcer Sta. WGUC-FM, Cin., 1976-78, Sta. WCET-Pub. TV, Cin., 1978; pub. rels. dir. Nat. Women's Polit. Caucus, Washington, 1979-82; mktg. and pub. rels. mgr. AAUW, Washington, 1982-83; pres. Janyce Katz Prodns., Washington, L.A. and Cin., 1983-89; asst. atty. gen. taxation sect. Ohio Atty. Gen. Office, Columbus, 1989—. Cons. in field; organizer tax seminar for new Ams.; speaker at profl. confs. Writer, producer radio documentaries: Oil in America, 1977 (award), 100 Yrs. of Music Hall, 1977 (award), Employment at Will, 1988 (1st prize), others. Dem. precinct exec., Cin., 1986-89; bd. dirs. Cin. Am. Jewish Com., 1986-92, Columbus Women's Polit. Caucus, 1992—, New Am. Assn., 1992—, founding mem. bd.; PAC treas., 1992-94; mem. bd. Columbus Women's Pol Caucus, 1992-96; state pres. edn. fund Nat. Abortion Rights Action League, 1991-94; founding mem. bd. Franklin County Consortium Good Govt., chmn. bd., 1991-; v.p. Columbus Coun. Jewish Women; nat. v.p., capitol com. Nat. Coun. Jewish Women (chmn. 1991-97, 2003-, pres. DC sect., co-pres. VP Columbus Sect.); mem. bd. League Women Voters; Columbus rep. State Jewish Community Rels. Coun.; chmn. Noontime Showtime Art at Lunch, 1998-2000. Recipient Best Pub. Rels. Effort award Pub. Rels. Soc. Am., 1983, Nat. Women's Polit. Caucus, 1981. Mem. Ohio Bar Assn. (mem. media com. 1990—, chmn. pub. understanding law com. 1995-97, mem. editl. bd.), Columbus Bar Assn. (co-chairperson media com. 1991-92, community svcs., mem. editl. bd. Columbus Bar Breifs 2002-, mem. bd., bylaws chmn. Franklin County Women Lawyers 1992-95), Law Women of U. Cin. Law Sch. (pres. 1989), Phi Delta Phi. Avocations: horseback riding and jumping, reading, writing, painting, guitar. Office: Ohio Atty Gen Taxation Sect 30 E Broad St Columbus OH 43215

KATZ, JASON LAWRENCE, lawyer, insurance executive; b. Chgo., Sept. 28, 1947; s. Irving and Goldie (Medress) K.; 2 children. B.A., Northeastern Ill. U., 1969; J.D., DePaul U., 1973. Bar: Calif. 1976, Ariz. 1973, U.S. Ct. Appeals (9th cir.) 1976. Sole practice, Scottsdale, Ariz., 1973-76; v.p., corp. counsel Mission Ins. Group, Inc., Los Angeles, 1976-84; exec. v.p., gen. counsel Farmers Group, Inc., Los Angeles, 1984—, bd. dirs., 1986—; v.p., bd. dirs. Calif. Def. Counsel, 1986-88. Mem. Calif. Bar Assn. (exec. bd. ins. law subcom. 1991-94), Los Angeles County Bar Assn. (mem. exec. bd. corp. law sect. 1993—), Conf. Ins. Counsel (v.p., pres. L.A. chpt. 1981-82), Assn. Calif. Tort Reform (bd. dirs. 1990—), The Ins. Coun. So. Calif. (City of Hope chpt. 1991—). Administrative and regulatory, Corporate, general, Insurance. Office: Farmers Group Inc 4680 Wilshire Blvd Los Angeles CA 90010-3807

KATZ, JEROME CHARLES, lawyer; b. Boston, Sept. 25, 1950; s. Ralph and Thelma M. (Clark) K.; m. Nancy M. Green, Aug. 29, 1976; children: Jonathan Green, Elizabeth Rachel. AB magna cum laude, Duke U., 1972; JD, Columbia U., 1975. Bar: N.Y. 1976, U.S. Dist. Ct. (so. and ea. dists.) N.Y. 1976, U.S. Supreme Ct. 1979, U.S. Ct. Appeals (2d cir.) 1981, U.S. Dist. Ct. (we. dist.) N.Y. 1990. Assoc. Chadbourne & Parke, N.Y.C., 1975-83, ptnr., 1983—. Ct.-apptd. neutral mediator U.S. Dist. Ct. (so. dist.) N.Y., 2001—; bd. dirs. The Legal Aid Soc., 2002--. Assoc. editor Columbia Jour. Transnat. Law, 1974-75. Harlan Fiske Stone scholar Columbia U., 1974. Mem. ABA, Assn. of the Bar of the City of N.Y., Phi Beta Kappa. Federal civil litigation, General civil litigation, State civil litigation. Home: 77 E 12th St New York NY 10003-5002 Office: Chadbourne & Parke 30 Rockefeller Plz Fl 31 New York NY 10112-0129 E-mail: jkatz@chadbourne.com.

KATZ, JOEL ABRAHAM, lawyer, music consultant; b. Bronx, N.Y., May 27, 1944; s. Harry and Hilda (Wiesenthal) K.; Kane Swims, 1994; children from previous marriage: Leslie Helaine, Jeni Michelle. BA in Econs., Hunter Coll., 1966; JD, U. Tenn., 1969. Bar: Tenn. 1969, D.C. 1970, Ga. 1971, U.S. Dist. Ct. (ea. dist.) Tenn. 1970, U.S. Dist. Ct. Appeals (11th cir.) 1971. Co-mng. shareholder, chair entertainment practice Greenberg Traurig, Atlanta. Gen. coun., bd. dirs. Farm Aid Inc., T.J. Martell Found.; bd. contbg. editors Entertainment Law & Finance. Mem. exec. coun. T.J. Martell Found. for Leukemia Rsch., N.Y.C.; mem. Ga. Music Hall of Fame Authority; bd. dirs. Very Special Arts. Mem. NARAS (gen. counsel, past v.p., past nat. trustee, dir. found. bd., nat. chmn. bd. trustees, trustee Atlanta chpt., chmn. emeritus), ABA, Fed. Bar Assn., Ga. Bar Assn., Tenn. Bar Assn., Atlanta C. of C. (bd. advisors), D.C. Bar Assn., Atlanta Bar Assn. Home: 675-8 W Paces Ferry Rd Atlanta GA 30327 Office: 3290 Northside Pkwy Ste 400 Atlanta GA 30327 E-mail: katzj@gtlaw.com.

KATZ, JOETTE, state supreme court justice; b. Bklyn., Feb. 3, 1953; BA, Brandeis U., 1974; JD, U. Conn., 1977. Bar: Conn. 1977. Pvt. practice, 1977-78; asst. pub. defender Office Chief Pub. Defender, 1978-83; chief legal svcs. Pub. Defender Svcs., 1983-89; judge Superior Ct., 1989-92; assoc. justice Conn. Supreme Ct., Hartford, 1992—; adminstrv. judge Appellate Sys., Hartford, 1994-2000. Instr. U. Conn. Sch. Law, 1981-84; instr. ethics and criminal law Quinnipiac Coll. Sch. Law, 1999—. Mem. Justice Edn. Ctr. Mem. Am. Law Inst.; Chair Evidence Code Drafting Com., Chair Adv. Com. for Appellate Rules; Am. Inns Ct. (past pres. Fairfield County br.), Assn. Reproductive Tech. (mem. com.). Office: Conn Supreme Ct Drawer N Sta A 231 Capital Ave Hartford CT 06106-1548

KATZ, JOHN W. lawyer, state official; b. Balt., Md., June 3, 1943; s. Leonard Wallach and Jean W. (Kane) K.; m. Joan Katz, June 11, 1969 (div. 1982); 1 child, Kimberly Erin. BA, Johns Hopkins U., Balt., 1965; JD, U. Calif., Berkeley, 1969; DDL (hon.) , U. Alaska, 1994. Bar: Alaska 1971, Pa. 1971, U.S. Dist. Ct. D.C. 1971, U.S. Ct. Appeals (D.C. cir.), U.S. Tax Ct., U.S. Ct. Claims, U.S. Ct. Mil. Justice, U.S. Supreme Ct. Legis. and adminstrv. asst. to Congressman Howard W. Pollock of AK, Washington, 1969—70; legis. asst. US Sen. Ted Stevens of AK, Washington, 1971; assoc. McGrath and Flint, Anchorage, 1972; gen. counsel Joint Fed. State Land Use Planning Commn. for AK, Anchorage, 1972—79; spl. counsel Gov. Jay S. Hammond of AK, Anchorage and Washington, Alaska, 1979—81; commr. AK Dept. Natural Resources, Juneau, Alaska, 1981—83; dir. state fed. rels. and spl. counsel Gov. Bill Sheffield of AK, Washington and Juneau, 1983—86; dir. state-fed. rels., spl. counsel to Gov. Steve Cowper of AK, Washington, 1986—90, Gov. Walter J. Hickel of AK, Washington, 1990—94, Gov. Tony Knowles, 1994—2002, Gov. Frank Murkowski, 2002—. Mem. Alaska Power Survey Exec. Adv. Com. of FPC, Anchorage, 1972—74; com. hard rock minerals Gov.'s Coun. of Sci. and Tech., Anchorage, 1979—80; guest lectr. on natural resources U. Alaska, U. Denver. Contbr. ; columnist Anchorage Times, 1991. Acad. supr. Alaska Externship Program, U. Denver Coll. Law, 1976—79; mem. Reagan-Bush transition team, U.S. Dept. Justice, 1980. Recipient Superior Sustained Performance award, Joint Fed. State Land Use Planning Commn. for Alaska, 1978, Resolution of Commendation award, Alaska Legis., 1988, Citation for svc. to people of Alaska, 2003. Republican. Office: State of Alaska Office of Gov 444 N Capitol St NW Ste 336 Washington DC 20001-1529

KATZ, JONATHAN, lawyer; b. Syracuse, NY, Aug. 18, 1953; s. Abraham Robert and Margaret (Volosin) Katz. BA, U. Conn., 1975; JD, Northeastern U., 1979. Bar: Conn. 1979, U.S. Dist. Ct. Conn. 1979, U.S. Tax Ct. 1981, U.S. Ct. Appeals (2d cir.) 1981, U.S. Supreme Ct. 1990. Atty. Jacobs, Grudberg, Belt & Dow, P.C., New Haven, 1979—. Personal injury (including property damage). Office: Jacobs Grudberg Belt & Dow PC 350 Orange St New Haven CT 06510 Fax: 203-772-1691. Business E-Mail: jkatz@jacobslaw.com.

KATZ, KENNETH ARTHUR, lawyer, accountant; b. N.Y.C., Apr. 4, 1955; s. Bernard and Shirley Anne (Schachter) K.; m. Gillian Lynn Bagg, Nov. 29, 1986; children: Melissa Lee, Ashley Dawn. AB in Econs. cum laude, Harvard U., 1976; JD, Yeshiva U., 1980; MBA in Pub. Acctg., Pace U., 1987. Bar: N.Y. 1994, U.S. Tax Ct. 1994, D.C. 1995; CPA, N.Y. Legal asst. Law Offices of Jerome A. Wisselman, Manhasset, N.Y., 1980-81, Law Offices of S. Mac Gutman, Forest Hills, N.Y., 1981-82; asst. contr. Tauck Tours, Inc., Westport, Conn., 1982-84; pvt. practice acct. Eastchester, N.Y., 1984-87; tax specialist KPMG Peat Marwick, White Plains, N.Y., 1987-88; atty., acct., ptnr. Bernard Katz & Co, P.C., Eastchester, 1988—. Mem. ABA (taxation and internat. law sects.), N.Y. State Bar Assn. (tax sect.), D.C. Bar Assn. (taxation and sect. on corps., fin. and securities law), Westchester County Bar Assn. (tax and trusts and estates coms.), N.Y. State Soc. CPAs, Nat. Tax Assn.-Tax Inst. Am. (com. on internat. pub. fin.), Harvard-Radcliffe Club of Westchester. Avocations: sports, music, personal investing. Corporate taxation, Estate taxation, Personal income taxation. Office: Bernard Katz & Co PC 1 Mayfair Rd Eastchester NY 10709-2701 E-mail: bkatzcopc@aol.com.

KATZ, LAWRENCE EDWARD, lawyer; b. Norfolk, Va., Sept. 15, 1947; s. Hyman and Beatrice (Kellert) K.; m. Susan Dubick, Mar. 24, 2002. BA, U. Richmond, Va., 1969; JD, U. Balt., 1973. Contract specialist U.S. Dept. Energy, Washington, 1979-80; law clk. various attys., Fla., 1980-86; atty. Richard M. Labovitz, Balt., 1986-87; pvt. practice law Balt., 1987—. Movie critic Sta. WTTR, Westminster, Md., 1987—, Prestige Cablevision, Westminster, 1988—, Montgomery County Cable TV, 1991—, Crix Pix Variety, 1991, Labor Herald Weekly mag., 1991, Norfolk City News, L.A., Navy Voice, North Orange County News; entertainment critic Landmark News, Reisterstown, Md., 1987—; host Pro Wrestling Talk, Radio Sta. WCAO, Balt., 1989-92 Fundraiser Jewish Nat. Fund, Balt., 1988; vol. Assoc. Jewish Charities, Balt., 1985—, Zionist Orgn. Am., Balt., 1987—. With U.S. Army Res., 1969-75. Mem. B'nai B'rith. Bankruptcy, Entertainment, Personal injury (including property damage). Home and Office: PO Box 32060 Baltimore MD 21282-2060

KATZ, LAWRENCE SHELDON, lawyer; b. Newark, N.J., Jan. 30, 1943; s. Edward and Pearl (Weiss) K.; married; 1 child, Scott. BBA in Govt., U. Miami, 1965, JD, 1968. Assoc. Hoffman & St. Jean, Miami Beach, Fla., 1968-70, Jack R. Nageley Law Office, Miami Beach, Fla., 1970-72, Swickle, Katz & Brotman, Miami Beach, Fla., 1972-77; pvt. practice Miami Beach, Fla., 1977—90, Coconut Grove, Fla., 1990—2001, Miami, 2001—. Gen. counsel Fraternal Order of Police, Hialeah, Fla., 1972-89; gen. counsel U.S. Shooting Team Found., Colorado Springs, 1978-95, chmn., 1978-83; mem. U.S. Olympic Commn. Ho. Dels., 1978-83. 2d lt. U.S. Army, 1965-69. Recipient Pres.'s award Nat. Assn. Criminal Def. Atty.'s, 1977. Mem. ABA (com. on internat. criminal law 1971-94, criminal def. function com. 1989-98, family law sect. com. on internat. law and procedure, 1996-, internat. child abduction atty. network 1997-, 11th Cir. Pro Bono Award), NRA (bd. dirs. 1977-83), Fla. Sportshooting Assn. (pres. 1985), The Fla. Bar (narcotics practice com. 1988-92, mental health profl. in litigation com. 1994-96, domestic violence com. 1994-98, legislation com. 1998-2003), Acad. Fla. Trial Lawyers (vice chmn. criminal law sect.), Fla. Assn. Criminal Def. Attys. (sec. 1978-79, v.p. 1979-80), Fla. Smallbore Rifle Assn. (pres. 1968-70), Safari Club Internat. Found. (pres. 1999-2000, pres. S. Fla. chpt, 1990-92, Mem. of Yr. award 1999-2000, Presdl. award 1996, 98), Phi Epsilon Pi (pres. 1964), Phi Alpha Delta, World Forum for Future of Sportshooting (v.p. 2000-01). Jewish. Avocations: flying, photography, scuba, skiing, hunting. Criminal, Family and matrimonial, Public international. Office: 1 Datran Ctr Penthouse 1-Ste 1702 9100 S Dadeland Blvd Miami FL 33156-7814 Office Fax: 305-670-1314.

KATZ, MELISSA, plaintiff attorney; b. Blytheville, Ark., Nov. 25, 1973; d. Mort Allen and Linda Lou (Laughlin) Katz. BS Journalism, U. Tex., Austin, 1995; JD, South Tex. Coll. Law, 1998. Bar: Tex. 1998. Intern child abuse Dallas County Dist. Attys. Office, 1996; law clk. Coblenz & Smith, Houston, 1996—97; selected intern Tex. Ct. Criminal Appeals, Austin, 1997; legal asst. Weyer & Markoff, Houston, 1997—98; ind. contractor Vinson & Elkins, 1998; asst. dist. atty. Tarrant County Dist. Attys. Office, Ft. Worth, 1999—2000; with Cowles & Thompson, P.C., 2000—01, Waters & Kraus, LLP, Dallas, 2002—. Vol. Kids in Ct., 1999, Stonegate Nursing Ctr., Ft. Worth, 1999, Child Advs. Soc. Am., SPCA of Dallas. Scholar, Vison & Elkins, Houston, 1996, 1997, 1998. Mem.: ATLA, ABA, Dallas Trial Lawyers Assn., Tex. Dist. & County Attys. Assn. Methodist. Avocations: travel, exercise, skiing, water skiing. Office: Waters & Kraus LLP 3219 McKinney Ave Dallas TX 75204

KATZ, MICHAEL ALBERT, lawyer; b. Bklyn., May 8, 1942; s. Emanuel and Miriam (Fassler) K.; 1 child, Nathaniel P. BS, Bklyn. Coll., 1963; LLB, NYU, 1966; LLM, George Washington U., 1973. Bar: N.Y. 1966, D.C. 1970, Ill. 1976, N.J. 1995, U.S. Supreme Ct. 1975. Asst. U.S. atty., D.C., 1971-75; trial atty. United Airlines, Chgo., 1975-78; div. counsel ea. divsn. N.Y.C., 1978-81; counsel indsl. rels. Trans World Airlines, Inc., N.Y.C., 1981-86, asst. gen. counsel, 1986-91, assoc. gen., counsel, 1991-94; assoc. gen. counsel GAF/ISP Corp., Wayne, N.J., 1994-96; of counsel Pfaltz & Woller PA, Summit, N.J., 1996—. Capt. JAGC, U.S. Army, 1967-71, ret. col. res. Decorated Bronze Star. Federal civil litigation, Labor (including EEOC, Fair Labor Standards Act, labor-management relations, NLRB, OSHA), Property, real (including real estate development, water). Home: 94 Canterbury Rd Chatham NJ 07928-1771 Office: 382 Springfield Ave Ste 217 Summit NJ 07901-2707 E-mail: makatz@att.net.

KATZ, MICHAEL JEFFERY, lawyer; b. Detroit, May 11, 1950; s. Wilfred Lester and Bernice (Ackerman) K. BE with honors, U. Mich., 1972; JD, U. Colo., 1976; cert. mgmt., U. Denver, 1985, cert. fin. mgmt., 1990. Bar: Colo. 1978. Rsch. atty., immigration specialist Colo. Rural Legal Svcs., Denver, 1976-77, supervising atty. migrant farm lab., 1977-78; ind. contractor Colo. Sch. Fin., Denver, 1978-79; sole practice Denver, 1978-86; assoc. Levine and Pitler, P.C., Denver, 1986-88; gen. counsel, sec. Grease Monkey Internat., Inc., Denver, 1988-92; prin. Katz & Co., Denver, 1992—; ptnr. Corprorn, Eyler & Katz LLC, Denver, 1999—. Lectr. on incorporating small bus. and real estate purchase agreements Front Range Coll., 1986—, condr. various seminars on real estate and landlord/tenant law, 1980—; lectr. on real estate Lorman Ednl. Svcs., Inc., 2001--; of counsel Levine and Pitler, P.C., Englewood, Colo., 1985—. Contbr. Action Line column Rocky Mountain News; contbr. articles to profl. jours. Mem. ATLA, Am. Arbitration Assn. (mem. panel of arbitrators 1989), Denver Bar Assn. (mem. law day com. 1985—, mem. real estate com. 1980—, mem. pro bono svcs. com. 1984—), Colo. Assn. Bus. Intermediaries, U.S. Yacht Racing Assn., Dillon Yacht Club. Avocations: sailing, bicycling, swimming, art collecting, reading. Commercial, contracts (including sales of goods; commercial financing), Corporate, general, Property, real (including real estate development, water). Office: 13710 E Rice Pl Aurora CO 80015-1058 Fax: 303-790-0927. E-mail: bizlaw@ix.netcom.com.

KATZ, MORTON HOWARD, lawyer; b. New Orleans, Feb. 5, 1945; s. David and Belle (Estes) K.; m. Carole Rae Deutch, Dec. 22, 1966; children: Brian David, Andrew Blair, Jonathan Ryan. BA, U. So. Miss., 1966; JD, Loyola U., New Orleans, 1969. Bar: La. 1969, U.S. Dist. Ct. (ea. dist.) La., U.S. Ct. Appeals (5th and 11th cirs.) 1970. Assoc. Law Offices of Ivor Trapolin, New Orleans, 1969-71, Herman & Herman, New Orleans, 1971-72; ptnr. Herman, Herman, Katz & Cotlar, New Orleans, 1972—. Former owner New Orleans Saints Football Club; lectr. various univs. Prof. Jr. Achievement bd. dirs. Assembly Ctr., U. New Orleans, 1982—; bd. dirs., pres. Jewish Cmty. Ctr., New Orleans, 1993-95, New Orleans Alcohol Beverage & Control Bd., 1986-87; adv. bd. Ponchartrain Bank; mem. exec. bd. La. Mental Health Assn.; trustee Met. Pk. Country Day Sch.; mem. vis. com. Loyola U. Law Sch. Lt. USNG, 1969-74. Recipient first place award Local and Regional World LAw Fund Writing Contest, 1966. Mem. ATLA, Am. Arbitration Assn. (bd. dirs.), La. Trial Lawyers Assn. (bd. govs.), So. Trial Lawyers Assn. (bd. govs.), Loyola Law Sch. Alumni Assn. (pres.), Endymion Club (New Orleans). Democrat. Avocations: jogging, woodworking, wine. Construction, Corporate, general, Personal injury (including property damage). Home: 6034 Hurst St New Orleans LA 70118-6130 Office: Herman Herman Katz & Cotlar 820 Okeefe Ave New Orleans LA 70113-1125

KATZ, STEVEN MARTIN, lawyer, accountant; b. Washington, Feb. 8, 1941; s. Joseph and Pauline (Weinberg) K.; m. Lauri Gail Berman, Aug. 23, 1964; children: Benjamin, Aaron, Rebecca, Joshua. BS, U. Md., College Park, 1962; JD, George Washington U., 1965. Bar: D.C. 1966, Md. 1971; CPA, Md. Ptnr. Euzent, Katz & Katz, Washington, 1969-72; sr. ptnr. Katz, Frome & Bleecker, P.A., and predecessors, Rockville, Md., 1972-95; pvt. practice Rockville, 1995—. Mem. Md. State Grievance Commn., 1991—. Mem. Am. Soc. Atty.-CPAs, Md. Bar Assn., Md. Assn. CPAs, D.C. Bar, Montgomery County Bar Assn., Md. Soc. Accts., Md. State Bar Found. Jewish. Corporate, general, Estate planning, Probate (including wills, trusts), Taxation, general. Office: 401 E Jefferson St Ste 208 Rockville MD 20850-2613 Fax: 301-294-9484. E-mail: smkatz@intr.net.

KATZ, STUART MICHAEL, lawyer; b. N.Y.C., Sept. 24, 1967; BA cum laude, Brandeis U., 1989; JD, Boston U., 1992. Bar: Conn. 1992, U.S. Dist. Ct. Conn. 1993. Assoc. Cohen and Wolf P.C., Bridgeport, Conn., 1992—2000, shareholder, 2000—. Contbr. articles to profl. newspapers. Commr. Human Rights and Rels. Commn., Hamden, Conn., 2002. Mem.: Anti Defamation League (exec. com. 1998—, Daniel Ginsburg Leadership award 1997). Labor (including EEOC, Fair Labor Standards Act, labor-management relations, NLRB, OSHA), General civil litigation, Criminal. Office: Cohen and Wolf PC 1115 Broad St Bridgeport CT 06604

KATZ, STUART Z. lawyer; b. N.Y.C., July 14, 1942; s. David B. and Sally (Wieder) K.; m. Jane Martin, Sept. 10, 1977; children: Amanda, Sally; children from a previous marriage: Jennifer, Emily. BA, CCNY, 1964; JD, NYU, 1968. Bar: N.Y. 1968. Ptnr. Fried, Frank, Harris, Shriver & Jacobson, N.Y.C., 1968—. Lectr. Practicing Law Inst., Prentice Hall, N.Y.C. and Mile, Minn., 1984-92. Mem. ABA. Corporate, general, Mergers and acquisitions, Securities. Office: Fried Frank Harris Shriver & Jacobson 1 New York Plz Fl 22 New York NY 10004-1980

KATZ, THOMAS OWEN, lawyer; b. Killeen, Tex., Jan. 15, 1958; s. Herbert D. and Eleanor (Meyerhoff) K.; m. Elissa Ellant, Nov. 6, 1983; children: Joseph, Peyton, Jacob. BS in Econs., U. Pa., 1979; JD, Georgetown U., 1982. Bar: Fla. 1982, U.S. Tax Ct. 1983. Shareholder, chair income tax dept. Ruden, McClosky, Smith, Schuster & Russell, P.A., Ft. Lauderdale, Fla., 1982—. Bd. dirs. CLAL-Ctr. for Jewish Learning and Leadership, N.Y., 1993—, chmn., 2002—, Donors Forum S.Fla., 1998—, exec. com. 2000—, Cmty. Found. of Broward, 2000—; mem. bd. overseers Ctr. Advanced Judaic Studies U. Pa., 2001—. Estate planning, Probate (including wills, trusts), Taxation, general. Office: Ruden McClosky Smith Sch PO Box 1900 Fort Lauderdale FL 33302-1900 E-mail: thomas.katz@ruden.com.

KATZEN, SALLY, lawyer, educator; b. Pitts., Nov. 22, 1942; d. Nathan and Hilda (Schwartz) K.; m. Timothy B. Dyk, Oct. 31, 1981; 1 child, Abraham Benjamin BA magna cum laude, Smith Coll., 1964; JD magna cum laude, U. Mich., 1967. Bar: D.C. 1968, U.S. Supreme Ct. 1971. Congl. intern Sente Subcom. on Constl. Rights, Washington, 1963; legal rsch. asst. civil rights div. Dept. Justice, Washington, 1965; law clk. to Judge J. Skelly Wright U.S. Ct. Appeals (D.C. cir.), 1967-68; assoc. Wilmer, Cutler & Pickering, Washington, 1968-75, ptnr., 1975-79, 81-93; gen. counsel Coun. on Wage and Price Stability, 1979-80; dep. dir. for policy, 1980-81; adminstr. Office of Info. and Regulatory Affairs, Office of Mgmt. and Budget, Washington, 1993-98; dep. dir. Nat. Econ. Coun., The White House, Washington, 1998-99; counsellor to the dir. Office Mgmt. and Budget, Washington, 1999-2000, dep. dir. mgmt., 2000-2001. Adj. prof. Georgetown U. Law Ctr., 1988, 1990—92; vis. lectr. Smith Coll., 2001—, Johns Hopkins U., 2002—, U. Pa. Law Sch., 2003; pub. mem. Adminstrv. Conf. U.S., 1988, govt. mem. and vice chair, 1993—95; mem. exec. com. Prettyman-Leventhal Inn of Ct., 1988—90, counselor, 1990—91; mem. Jud. Conf. for D.C. Cir., 1972—91. Editor-in-chief U. Mich. Law Rev., 1966-67 Mem. com. visitors U. Mich. Law Sch., 1972—. Fellow ABA (ho. of dels. 1978-80, 89-91, coun. adminstrv. law sect. 1979-82, chmn. adminstrv. law and regulatory practice sect. 1988-89, governing com. forum com. communications law 1979-82, chmn. standing com. Nat. Conf. Groups 1989-92); mem. D.C. Bar Assn., Women's Bar Assn., FCC Bar Assn. (exec. com. 1984-87, pres. 1990-91), Women's Legal Def. Fund (pres. 1977, v.p. 1978), Order of Coif. Home: 4638 30th St NW Washington DC 20008-2127

KATZENBACH, NICHOLAS DEBELLEVILLE, lawyer; b. Phila., Jan. 17, 1922; s. Edward Lawrence and Marie Louise (Hilson) K.; m. Lydia King Phelps Stokes, June 8, 1946; children— Christopher Wolcott, John Strong Minor, Maria Louise Hiltson, Anne deBelleville. BA, Princeton U., 1945; LL.B., Yale U., 1947; Rhodes scholar, Balliol Coll., Oxford (Eng.) U., 1947-49. Bar: N.J. 1950, Conn. 1955, N.Y. 1972. With firm Katzenbach, Gildea & Rudner, Trenton, N.J., 1950; atty.-adviser Office Gen. Counsel Air Force, 1950-52, part-time cons., 1952-56; asso. prof. law Yale Law Sch., 1952-56; prof. law U. Chgo. Law Sch., 1956-60; asst. atty. gen. Dept. Justice, 1961-62; dep. atty. gen., 1962-64; acting atty. gen., 1964; atty. gen., 1965-66; under sec. state, 1966-69; sr. v.p., gen. counsel IBM Corp., 1969-84, sr. v.p. law and external relations, 1984-86, also bd. dirs.; ptnr. Riker, Danzig, Scherer, Hyland & Perretti, Morristown, N.J., 1986-91. Author: (with Morton A. Kaplan) The Political Foundations of International Law, 1961; editor-in-chief: Yale Law Jour, 1947; contbr. articles to profl. jours. Served to 1st lt. USAAF, 1941-45. Decorated Air medal with three clusters; Ford Found. fellow, 1960-61 Mem. AAAS, Am. Law Inst. (mem. coun.), Am. Bar Assn., Am. Judicature Soc., Am. Philos. Soc. Democrat. Episcopalian. Corporate, general. Home: 33 Greenhouse Dr Princeton NJ 08540-4802 E-mail: nkatzenbac@aol.com.

KATZENSTEIN, ROBERT JOHN, lawyer; b. Phila., May 2, 1951; s. Lawrence and Joan I. (Hassall) K.; children: Jeffrey Hunt, Erick Hill. BA, Yale U., 1973; JD, U. Pa., 1976. Bar: Del. 1976, DC 1979. Trial atty. antitrust div. U.S. Dept. of Justice, Washington, 1976-78; assoc. Richards, Layton & Finger, Wilmington, Del., 1978-84; ptnr. Katzenstein & Furlow, Wilmington, 1984-85, Lassen, Smith, Katzenstein & Furlow, Wilmington, 1985-91, Smith, Katzenstein & Furlow LLP, Wilmington, 1992—. Asst. disciplinary counsel to Del. Bd. Profl. Responsibility, 1986-92; mem. Richard S. Rodney Inn of Court, 1993—, Product Liability Adv. Coun.; mem. bd. bar examiners Del. Supreme Ct., 2003--. Mem. ABA (litig. sect., bus. law sect.), Del. State Bar Assn. (jud. appts. com. 1991—, co-chair 1999—, corp. law, litig. sect.), Internat. Assn. Def. Coun., Def. Counsel of Del. (pres. 1997-99), Yale Club of Del., ARC (bd. dirs. Delmarva peninsula, sec. 1998-99, vice chair 1999-2001, chair 2001-03), Mass for the Homeless Inc. (pres. 1998—). Democrat. General civil litigation, Insurance. Office: Smith Katzenstein & Furlow LLP PO Box 410 800 Delaware Ave The Corp Plz Wilmington DE 19899-0410 Home: 2522 W 18th St Wilmington DE 19806-1208 E-mail: rjk@skfdelaware.com.

KATZMAN, IRWIN, lawyer; b. Windsor, Ont., Can., June 29, 1931; s. Aaron and Rose (Tarnow) K.; m. Helen Frances Blecher, Dec. 20, 1952 (dec. Feb. 1998); children: Barry, Harriet, Kenneth, Rhonda, Aaron; m. Toby Lyman, Aug. 15, 1999. BS, Wayne State U., 1953, MBA, 1963; JD cum laude, Loyola U., L.A., 1974. Bar: Calif. 1974, U.S. Dist. Ct. (cen. dist.) Calif. 1974, U.S. Ct. Appeals (9th cir.) 1980, U.S. Supreme Ct. 1980, U.S. Tax Ct. 1988. Chemist E.I. Dupont de Nemours, Phila., 1953-54; asst. quality mgr. Chrysler Corp., Detroit, 1956-63; mfg. plans mgr. Ford Motor Co., Newport Beach, Calif., 1963-70; prodn. control mgr. Dresser Industries, Huntington Park, Calif., 1970-73; purchasing mgr. Hughes Aircraft Co., Inglewood, Calif., 1973-74; v.p. First Alliance Mortgage Co., Santa Ana, Calif., 1976-77; pvt. practice Anaheim, Calif., 1975-94, San Jose, Calif., 1995—. Pres. Temple Beth Emet, Anaheim, 1988-90. With U.S. Army, 1953-56. Mem. State Bar of Calif., Orange County Bar Assn., Santa Clara County Bar Assn., Alpha Epsilon Pi (life). Avocations: sailing, golf, amateur radio. Bankruptcy, Family and matrimonial, Personal injury (including property damage). Office: 8346 Riesling Way San Jose CA 95135-1435

KATZMANN, ROBERT ALLEN, judge; b. N.Y.C., 1953; AB summa cum laude, Columbia U., 1973; MA in Govt., Harvard U., 1975, PhD in Govt., 1978; JD, Yale U., 1980. Bar: Mass. 1982, U.S. Ct. Appeals (1st cir.) 1983, D.C. 1984, U.S. Dist. Ct. Mass. 1984, N.Y. Law clk. to judge U.S. Ct. Appeals (1st cir.), Concord, N.H., 1980-81; rsch. assoc. Brookings Instn., Washington, 1981-85, fellow, 1985-99; adj. prof. law, pub. policy Georgetown U., Washington, 1984-92, William J. Walsh prof. govt., prof. law, 1992-99; pres. Governance Inst., Washington, 1986-99; acting dir. govt. studies Brookings Instn., Washington, 1998; judge U.S. Ct. Appeals (2nd cir.), 1999—; adjunct prof. of Law New York University, New York, 2001—. Vis. prof. polit. sci. UCLA, Washington program, 1990-92; vis. chair, Wayne Morse prof. law and politics U. Oreg., 1992; cons. Fed. Cts. Study Com., 1990; adj. prof. law N.Y. U., 2001-. Author: Regulatory Bureaucracy: The Federal Trade Commission and Antitrust Policy, 1980, Institutional Disability, 1986, Courts and Congress, 1997; co-editor: Managing Appeals in Federal Courts, 1988; editor: Judges and Legislators, 1988, The Law Firm and the Public Good, 1995; article and book editor Yale U. Law Jour., 1979-80. Fellow: Am. Acad. Arts and Scis.; mem.: ABA (adminstrv. law sect., vice chair com. on govt. ops. and separation of powers 1991—94, pub. mem. adminstrn. conf. 1992—95), Am. Polit. Sci. Assn. (Charles E. Merriam award 2001), Am. Judicature Soc. (bd. dirs. 1992—98), Phi Beta Kappa. Office: US Ct Appeals 2d Cir 40 Foley Sq New York NY 10007-1502

KAUCHER, JAMES WILLIAM, lawyer; b. Belleville, Ill., Oct. 20, 1958; s. Robert Frederick and Mary Ellen (Shepard) K.; m. Janine Kaucher, Oct. 24, 1993. BA, U. Colo., 1980; JD, U. Ill., 1983. Bar: Ariz. 1983, U.S. Dist. Ct. Ariz. 1983. Assoc. Evans, Kitchel & Jenckes, Phoenix, 1983—85, Teilborg, Sanders & Parks, Phoenix, 1985—92; ptnr. Cavett and Kaucher, Tucson, 1992—98; dir. Goodwin Raup PC, Tucson, 1998—2002, Shughart, Thomson, Kilroy, P.C., Tucson, 2002—. Chmn. human rsch. rev. bd. Humana Hosp., Phoenix, 1989-94. Mem. bioethics com. Northwest Hosp., Tucson, 1993—. Mem. Am. Assn. Health Lawyers, Maricopa Bar Assn., Def. Rsch. Inst., Forum on Health Law, Ariz. Soc. Health Care Risk Mgrs. (bd. dirs. 1989-91), Ariz. Assn. Def. Counsel, Ariz. Mountaineering Club, Am. Alpine Club. Avocations: mountaineering, flying, bicycle racing. Health, Labor (including EEOC, Fair Labor Standards Act, labor-management relations, NLRB, OSHA), Personal injury (including property damage). Office: Shughart Thomson & Kilroy PC Ste 2130 One S Church Ave Tucson AZ 85701 E-mail: jamesw@kaucher.com.

KAUFFMAN, STEPHEN BLAIR, law librarian; b. St. Louis, Sept. 25, 1948; s. William Porter and Patricia Mary (Cain) Kauffman Supernois; m. Susan Heffernan, Jan. 24, 1971 (dec. Aug. 1972); m. Mary Ann Royle, Aug. 24, 1979; children: Ashley, Stephanie, Cameron. B.S., U. Mo., St. Louis, 1971; J.D., U. Mo., Kansas City, 1975, LL.M., 1976; M.L.L., U. Wash. 1977. Law librarian Reiderer, Eisberg, Kansas City, Mo., 1973-75; law library asst. U. Wash., Seattle, 1976-77; law librarian Nat. Jud. Coll., Reno, 1977-81; law library dir. No. Ill. U., DeKalb, 1981-88; prof. law, law libr. dir. U. Wis., Madison, 1988-94; prof. law, law libr. Yale U., 1994—. Bd. dirs. Ill. Bar Automated Research, Chgo., 1982-88, Oceana Publs., 1990—; mem. adv. bd. Washoe County Law Library, Reno, 1978-81. Contbr. articles to profl. jours. Mem. Am. Assn. Law Libraries, Law Library Assn. Wis., Chgo. Assn. Law Libraries, Mid Am. Assn. Law Libraries, Spl. Libraries Assn., Mo. Bar Assn. Democrat. Office: Yale Law Sch 127 Wall St New Haven CT 06511-6636 Home: 152 Waite St Hamden CT 06517-2526

KAUFMAN, ALBERT I. lawyer; b. N.Y.C., Oct. 2, 1936; s. Israel and Pauline (Pardes) K.; m. Ruth Feldman, Jan. 25, 1959; 1 son, Michael Paul. AA, L.A. City Coll., 1957; BA, U. San Fernando Valley, 1964, JD, 1966. Bar: Calif. 1967, U.S. Ct. Appeals (9th cir.) 1968, U.S. Supreme Ct. 1971, U.S. Dist. Ct. (cen. dist.) Calif. 1967, U.S. Tax Ct. 1971, U.S. Ct. Internat. Trade 1981. Sole practice, Woodland Hills, Calif., 1967—; judge pro tem L.A. Mcpl. Ct., 1980—, L.A. Superior Ct., 1991—; family law mediator L.A. Superior Ct., 1980—. Mem. Pacific S.W. regional bd. Anti-Defamation league of B'nai B'rith, 1970-91. Served with USAF, 1959-65, to col. CAP, 1956—. Recipient Disting. Svc. award B'nai B'rith, 1969; Exceptional Svc. award CAP, 1977, 95. Mem. ABA, L.A. County Bar Assn., San Fernando Valley Bar Assn., Consumer Atty. of Calif., Consumer Atty. Assn. L.A. Republican. Clubs: Toastmasters, Westerners 1117 (pres. 1969), B'nai B'rith (pres. 1971-72), Santa Monica Yacht (judge adv.) Civil rights, Family and matrimonial, Personal injury (including property damage). Office: 22900 Ventura Blvd Ste 205 Woodland Hills CA 91364 E-mail: lawyer4@earthlink.net.

KAUFMAN, ANDREW LEE, law educator; b. Newark, Feb. 1, 1931; s. Samuel and Sylvia (Meltzer) K.; m. Linda P. Sonnenschein, June 14, 1959; children: Anne, David, Elizabeth, Daniel. AB, Harvard U., 1951, LL.B., 1954. Bar: D.C. 1954, Mass. 1979, U.S. Supreme Ct. 1961. Assoc. Bilder, Bilder & Kaufman, Newark, 1954-55; law clk. to Justice Felix Frankfurter U.S Supreme Ct., 1955-57; ptnr. Kaufman, Kaufman & Kaufman, Newark, 1957-65; lectr. in law Harvard U., Cambridge, Mass., 1965-66, prof., 1966-81, Charles Stebbins Fairchild prof. law, 1981—, assoc. dean, 1986-89. Author: (with others) Commercial Law, 1971, 82, Problems in Professional Responsibility, 1976, 84, 89, 2002, Cardozo, 1998. Treas. Shady Hill Sch., 1969-76; treas. Hillel Found. Cambridge, Inc., 1977-86. Mem. Mass. Bar Assn. (chmn. com. profl. ethics 1982—). Office: Harvard U Law Sch Cambridge MA 02138 E-mail: kaufman@law.harvard.edu.

KAUFMAN, ANDREW MICHAEL, lawyer; b. Boston, Feb. 19, 1949; s. Earle Bertram and Miriam (Halpern) K.; m. Michele Moselle, Aug. 24, 1975; children: Peter Moselle, Melissa Lanes, Caroline Raney. BA cum laude, Yale U., 1971; JD, Vanderbilt U., 1974. Bar: Tex. 1974, Ga. 1976, Ill. 1993, U.S. Ct. Appeals (5th and 11th cirs.) 1981. Assoc. Vinson & Elkins, Houston, 1974-76, ptnr., 1982-83, Austin, 1983-92, Dallas, 1992; assoc. Sutherland, Asbill & Brennan, Atlanta, 1976-80, ptnr., 1980-81, Kirkland & Ellis, Chgo., 1993—. Editor in chief Vanderbilt U. Law Rev., 1973-74. Mem. nat. alumni bd. Vanderbilt U.Law Sch., 1994—2000; Alumi fund raiser Yale U., 1971—; mem. Alumni Schs. Com. Yale U., 1986—92; mem. med. ethics coun. Seton Hosp. , 1988—92; participant Leadership Austin, 1987—88; bd. dirs. KLRU-TV, 1989—93; mem. Austin (Tex.) Entrepreneurs Coun., 1991—92; mem. adv. bd. Dallas Bus. Com. Arts Leadership Inst., 1992—93; governing bd. mem. Chgo. Symphony Orch.; bd. dirs. United Way, Austin, Tex.; pub. TV Ballet Austin, Tex., 1986—92; mem. adv. bd. Austin Tech. Incubator, 1989—93. Mem. ABA (bus. law sect. 1978—, chmn. lease financing and secured transactions subcom. of com. devels. in bus. financing 1993-99, UCC com., legal opinions com., comml. fin. svcs. com.), Tex. Bar Assn., Yale U. Alumni Assn., Order of Coif, Headliners Club, Yale Club, N.Y.C. and Chgo., Knights of the Symphony Austin. Avocation: sailing. Banking, Corporate, general, Finance. Office: Kirkland & Ellis 200 E Randolph St Fl 54 Chicago IL 60601-6636 E-mail: Andrew.Kaufman@chicago.kirkland.com.

KAUFMAN, CHRISTOPHER LEE, lawyer; b. Chgo., Mar. 17, 1945; s. Charles R. and Violet-Page (Koteen) K.; m. Carlyn A. Clement, Jan. 25, 1986; children: Charles Alexander, Caroline Clement. BA, Amherst Coll., 1967; JD, Harvard U., 1970. Bar: Ill. 1970, Calif. 1972. Law clk. to judge U.S. Ct. Appeals (2d cir.), N.Y.C., 1970-71; from assoc. to ptnr. Heller, Ehrman, White and McAuliffe, San Francisco, Palo Alto, Calif., 1974-90; ptnr. Latham & Watkins, Menlo Park, Calif., 1990—. Editor: Harvard Law Review., 1968-70. Mem. ABA (com. on negotiated acquisitions, com. on fed. regulation of securities). Corporate, general, Mergers and acquisitions, Securities. Office: Latham & Watkins 135 Commonwealth Dr Menlo Park CA 94025-1105 E-mail: christopher.kaufman@lw.com.

KAUFMAN, JAMES JAY, retired lawyer; b. Newark, N.Y., Jan. 23, 1939; s. Joseph Julius and Ann Gertrude (Quick) K.; m. Patricia Ann Patterson, Sept. 3, 1966; children: Kristine, Jeffrey. BA, Bucknell U., 1960; LLB, JD, Union Coll., Albany, 1964. Bar: N.Y. 1965, U.S. Ct. Appeals (2nd cir.) 1966, U.S. Dist. Ct. (we. and no. dists.) N.Y. 1968, N.C. 1985, Pa. 1985, U.S. Supreme Ct. 1985, U.S. Dist. Ct. (ea. dist.) N.C. 1991, U.S. Ct. Appeals (4th cir.) 1991, U.S. Ct. Appeals (7th cir.) 1992, U.S. Dist. Ct. (mid. dist.) N.C. 1993; certified mediator, Wilmington, Conn. Legal counsel, legis. and adminstrv. asst. Rep. Theodore R. Kupferman, U.S. Congress, Washington, 1965-67; assoc. Houghton, Pappas & Fink, Rochester, N.Y., 1967-70; ptnr. Culley, Marks, Rochester, 1970-75; sr. ptnr. James J. Kaufman, P.C., Newark, 1975-84, Kaufman & Forsyth, Rochester, 1984-91, Barefoot & Kaufman, Wilmington, N.C., 1991-93, Kaufman, Barefoot & Green, Wilmington, 1993-94; of counsel Hancock & Estabrook, Syracuse, N.Y., 1994-96; sr. ptnr. Kaufman & Green, L.L.P., Wilmington, 1994-2001, Maupin, Taylor & Ellis, P.A., 2001—. V.p. Fed. Bar Coun., 1968; mem. 7th Jud. Dist. Grievance Com., 1983-89; del. U.S./China Joint Session on Trade, Investment and Econ. Law, Beijing, 1987; strategic planning cons., Rochester, 1994-95; panel mem. Commerce Tech. Adv. Bd. on Noise Abatement, Washington, 1968; chmn. noise task force Genesee Region Health Planning, Rochester, 1970-71, mem./counsel noise task force, mem./counsel environ. health planning com., 1972-73. Author: What to Do Before the Money Runs Out—A Road Map for America's Automobile Dealers, 1993; contbr. articles to profl. publs. Justice Town of Arcadia, Newark, 1976-89. Mem. N.Y. State Bar Assn. (mem. spl. com. on environ. law 1974-77, mem. com. on profl. discipline, mem. com. on ct. in cmty. banking com. 1986—), Wayne County Bar Assn. (pres. 1986-87, v.p. 1985-86, chmn. family law sect. 1975-80, chmn. com. on profl. discipline 1975-89), N.C. Bar Assn., Pa. Bar Assn., New Hanover County Bar Assn., Monroe County Bar Assn., Wilmington Inns of Ct. (pres. 1994-97). Republican. Presbyterian. Avocations: boating, scuba diving, fishing. Banking, Commercial, contracts (including sales of goods; commercial financing), Health. E-mail: jjkauf123@aol.com.

KAUFMAN, LEONARD LEE, retired lawyer; b. Butte, Mont., May 8, 1939; s. Leonard Carl and Madeline (Marx) K.; m. Mary F. Culleton; children: Jennifer Lee, Julie Lee, Jody Lee. BA, Middlebury Coll., 1961; JD, U. Mont., 1964; LLM in Taxation, Denver U., 1976. Bar: Mont. 1961, U.S. Tax Ct. 1978. Trial atty. Mont. Dept. Hwys., Helena, 1967-69; asst. county atty. County of Lincoln, Mont., 1969-72; ptnr. Murray & Kaufman, P.C. (now Kaufman, Vidal & Hileman, P.C.), Kalispell, Mont., 1972—. Ct. appointed mediator, arbitrator and settlement worker, Mont. Contbr. articles to agrl. and comml. code publs. Pres., bd. dirs. Flathead Valley Ski Found., Kalispell, 1978-88. Capt. U.S. Army, 1964-66. Mem. Mont. Bar Assn. (bd. trustees), Northwest Mont. Bar Assn. (pres. 1978), U.S. Ski Assn. (cert. ofcl.), No. Div. Ski Assn. (v.p. 1988-89). Republican. Avocations: alpine skiing, hunting, fishing. Alternative dispute resolution, Property, real (including real estate development, water), Taxation, general. Office: Kaufman Vidal & Hilman PC 22 2nd Ave E Kalispell MT 59901-4567

KAUFMAN, MARK DAVID, lawyer; b. St. Louis, Feb. 24, 1949; s. Rudolf Ernst and Edith (Greiderer) K.; m. Margaret Taylor James, June 1, 2002; 1 child, Mark David. BA, Northwestern U., 1971; JD, Duke U., 1974. Bar: Ga. 1974, U.S. Ct. Appeals (11th cir.) 1974, U.S. Dist. Ct. (no. dist.) Ga. 1974. Assoc. Sutherland Asbill & Brennan LLP, Atlanta, 1974-81, ptnr., 1981—, exec. com., 1996-2000. Contbr. articles to profl. jours. Mem. ABA, Ga. Bar Assn., Atlanta Bar Assn. (legal counsel 1979-2000, Exceptional Svc. award 1987, Pres.'s Disting. Svc. award 1979-80, Charles E. Watkins Jr. award 1989), Atlanta Bar Found. (legal counsel 1985-2000), Order of Coif. Lutheran. Corporate, general, Mergers and acquisitions, Securities. Home: 3181 Habersham Rd NW Atlanta GA 30305

KAUFMAN, ROBERT MAX, lawyer, director; b. Vienna, Nov. 17, 1929; came to U.S., 1939, naturalized, 1945; s. Paul M. and Bertha (Hirsch) K.; m. Sheila Seymour Kelley. BA with honors, Bklyn. Coll., 1951; MA, NYU, 1954; JD magna cum laude, Bklyn. Law Sch., 1957. Bar: N.Y. 1957, U.S. Supreme Ct. 1961. Successively jr. economist, economist, sr. economist N.Y. State Div. Housing, 1953-57; atty. antitrust div. U.S. Dept. Justice, 1957-58; legis. asst. to U.S. Senator Jacob K. Javits, 1958-61; assoc. Proskauer Rose LLP, N.Y.C., 1961-69, ptnr., 1969—. Past chmn. bd. Pirelli Cables & Systems, LLC, Pirelli Tires LLC; chmn. bd. Old Westbury Funds, Inc.; bd. dirs. Roytex Inc., Meadowbrook Equity Fund, L.L.C.; mem. N.Y. State Legis. Adv. Com. on Election Law, 1973-74; chmn. adv. com. N.Y. State Bd. Elections, 1974-78; chmn. N.Y. State Bd. Pub. Disclosure, 1981-82, U.S. Army Chief of Staff's Spl. Commn. on Honor System, 1988-89, N.Y. Chief Judge's Com. on Availability of Legal Svcs., 1988-90; referee Commn. on Jud. Conduct; spl. master N.Y. Supreme Ct. Appellate Divsn., 1999—; mem. Adminstrv. Conf. U.S. (chair com. regulations), 1988-95; chmn. Fund for Modern Cts., 1990-95; mem. Def. Adv. Com. on Women in the Svcs., 1997-99, vice chair com. on equality mgmt., mem. exec. com. 1998. Co-author: Congress and the Public Trust, 1970, Disorder in the Court, 1973; co-gen. editor: Matthew Bender Treatise on Health Care Law, 4 vols., 1992—. Bd. dirs., mem. exec. com. Lawrence M. Gelb Found., Inc., Lawyers in the Public Interest, 1986-95, Am. Judicature Soc., pres. 1995-97, Citizens Union of N.Y.C., vice chair, 1997-2000, bd. dirs., 1987—, Citizen's Union Found., 1993—; bd. dirs., chmn. exec. com. Cmty. Action for Legal Svcs., Inc., 1976-78; dir., mem. exec. com. Legal Aid Soc., 1985-90, mem. exec. com. Vols. of Legal Svc., 1986-94; mem. platform com. N.Y. Rep. State Com., 1974; mem. jud. selection adv. coms. Senator Javits, 1972-80, and Senator Moynahan, 1977-2000; N.Y.C. Quadrennial Comm. on compensation of elected officials, 1995, 99; mem. distbn. com., vice chair, 2001—, N.Y. Cmty. Trust; bd. dirs. N.Y. Cmty. Funds, James Found.; bd. vis. U.S. Mil. Acad., 1976-79; dir., mem. exec. com., past chmn. bd. Times Square Bus. Improvement Dist.; trustee Bklyn. Law Sch. With U.S. Army, 1957-58. Fellow Am. Bar Found., N.Y. State Bar Found.; mem. ABA, Assn. of Bar of City N.Y. (pres. 1986-88, chmn. house com., co-chmn. com. on campaign fin. reform 1997-2001, past chmn. com. on 2d Century; past chmn. exec. com., past chmn. com. profl. responsibility, past chmn. spl. com. on campaign expenditures, past chmn. com. civil rights, past vice chmn. com. grievances, past chmn. delegation to state bar ho. dels.), N.Y. State Bar Assn. (ho. of dels. 1978, 86-90), N.Y. County Lawyers Assn. (past chmn. com. on civil rights), Am. Law Inst. Corporate, general, Health, Non-profit and tax-exempt organizations. Office: Proskauer Rose LLP 1585 Broadway New York NY 10036-8299 E-mail: kaufman@proskauer.com.

KAUFMAN, SANFORD PAUL, lawyer; b. N.Y.C., Jan. 4, 1928; s. Max and Rose (Kornitzky) K.; m. Bernice R. Sulkis, June 17, 1956; children—Leslie Keith, Brad Leigh, Rona Sheryl, Jeffrey Scott, Adam Ira. BBA in Accounting, Coll. City N.Y., 1948; LL.B., N.Y. U., 1952, LL.M. in Taxation, 1957. Bar: N.Y. bar 1953, Calif. bar 1962. With firm Garey & Garey, N.Y.C., 1953-55; asst. gen. counsel Olympic Radio & TV, L.I. City, 1961-63; sec., gen. counsel Tel-Autograph Corp., L.A., 1961-63; asst. gen. counsel Nat. Gen. Corp., L.A., 1963-74; sec., gen. counsel Familian Corp., L.A., 1974-77; pvt. practice Torrance, Calif., 1977—. Bd. dirs. Temple Ner Tamid, S. Bay, Calif. Mem. Am. Soc. Corporate Secs., Los Angeles County Bar Assn., Beverly Hills Bus. Men's Assn. Clubs: K.P. (past chancellor). Corporate, general, Family and matrimonial, General practice. Home: 28412 Golden Meadow Dr Rancho Palos Verdes CA 90275-2926 Office: 23505 Crenshaw Blvd Ste 246 Torrance CA 90505-5223

KAUFMAN, STEPHEN EDWARD, lawyer; b. N.Y.C., Feb. 16, 1932; s. Herbert and Gertrude Kaufman; m. Marina Pinto, June 22, 1967; children: Andrew H. and Douglas P. BA, Williams Coll., 1953; LLB, Columbia U., 1957. Bar: N.Y. 1958, U.S. Ct. Appeals (2d cir.) 1958, U.S. Dist. Ct. (so. and ea. dists.) N.Y. 1960, U.S. Supreme Ct. 1963. Asst. U.S. Atty. U.S. Attys. Office, So. Dist., N.Y., 1964-69, chief of criminal div., 1964-69; pres. Stephen E. Kaufman, P.C., N.Y.C., 1976—. Bd. dirs. Smith Barney Mut. Funds. Trustee Mus. Jewish Heritage; dir. Police Athletic League. Fellow Am. Coll. Trial Lawyers; mem. ABA, N.Y. State Bar Assn., Assn. of Bar of City of N.Y. Federal civil litigation, State civil litigation. Office: 277 Park Ave New York NY 10172-0003

KAUFMAN, STEVEN MICHAEL, lawyer; b. Spokane, Wash., July 2, 1951; s. Gordon Leonard and Terri (Thal) K.; m. Connie Hoopes, June 7, 1973; children: Kristopher, Shana. BS magna cum laude, U. Utah, 1973; JD cum laude, Gonzaga U., 1977. Bar: Utah 1977, U.S. Dist. Ct. Utah 1977, U.S. Ct. Appeals (10th cir.) 1977, U.S. Supreme Ct. 1985. Founding ptnr. Farr, Kaufman, and Hamilton, 1979-89; mng. ptnr. Farr, Kaufman, Sullivan, Gorman, Jensen, Medsker, Nichols & Perkins, 1989—; judge pro tem, 1981-98; bar commr. Utah State Bar Commn., 1991-98. Chmn. Commn. on Pub. Defenders, Ogden, 1984. Mem. ATLA, ABA, Utah Bar Assn. (pres.-elect 1995-96, pres., 1996-97, bar commr. 1992-98, rep. Utah Jud. Coun. 1998-99), Weber County Bar Assn. (pres. 1981-82), Rex E. Lee Inn of Ct. (master), Utah Jud. Coun. Jewish. Criminal, Family and matrimonial, Personal injury (including property damage). Home: 5878 S 1050 E Ogden UT 84405-4959 Office: Farr Kaufman Sullivan Gorman Jensen Medsker Nichols & Perkins 205 26th St Ste 34 Ogden UT 84401-3109

KAUFMAN, THOMAS FREDERICK, lawyer, legal educator; b. Buffalo, Sept. 10, 1949; s. Frederick J. and Edna M. (Kilian) K.; children: Alycia, Thomas, Jonathan. BSEE, SUNY, Buffalo, 1971; JD, Georgetown U., 1976; MBA, U. Pa., 2001. Bar: Va. 1976, U.S. Ct. Appeals (6th cir.) 1976, D.C. 1977, U.S. Dist. Ct. D.C. 1981, Md. 1996. Law clk. to chief judge U.S. Ct. Appeals (6th cir.), 1976-77; assoc. Melrod, Redman & Gartlan, Washington, 1977-81, Willkie Farr & Gallagher, Washington, 1981-84, ptnr., 1985-95, Hunton & Williams, Washington, 1995—. Adj. prof. law Georgetown U., Washington, 1986—. Mem. Am. Coll. Real Estate Lawyers. Banking, Property, real (including real estate development, water). Office: Hunton and Williams 1900 K St NW Washington DC 20006-1110 E-mail: tkaufman@hunton.com.

KAUFMANN, PHILIP SEIL, lawyer; b. Akron, Akron, Ohio, July 18, 1946; s. Frank Philip and Clare Wilmont Kaufmann; m. Patricia Mary Kaufmann, Dec. 6, 1985; 1 child, Cbristopher. BA, Loyola U., Chgo., 1968; JD, U. Akron, 1971. Bar: Ohio 1971, U.S. Ct. Appeals (6th cir.) 1975, U.S. Dist. Ct. (no. dist.) Ohio 1975, U.S. Tax Ct. 1988, U.S. Supreme Ct. 1989. Mng. ptnr. Kaufmann & Kaufmann, Akron, 1972—. Mem. Salvation Army Bd. Summit County, North Coast Cmty. Homes; mem. cabinet United Way Alexis de Tocqueville of Summit County; trustee Cath. Diocese of Cleve. Found.; past chair Ohio Assn. County Bds. MR/DD, Summit County Bd. MR/DD; bd. dirs. Village at St. Edward, Cmty. Fund Mgmt. Found.; trustee Cummit County Hhist. Soc. trust adv. com.; bd. overseers Blossom Music Ctr.; bd. trustees U. Akron; past chair, bd. trustees Cath. Charities Corp. Recipient Disting. Svc. award, Ohio Assn. Retarded Citizens, 1979, Heart to God, Hand to Man award, Salvation Army, 1986, Apostolate for Persons with Devel. Diksabilities Svc. 1st award, 1993, Citizen of Yr. award, Akron Area Bd. Realtors, 1996, Alumni award, St. Vincent-St. Mary H.S., 1996, Alumni of Yr. award, U. Akron Law Sch., 2000, Citizen of Yr. award, Fairlawn Area C. of C., 2002, Thomas More award, Cath. Diocese and St. Bernard Ch., 2002. Fellow: Am. Coll. Trust and Estate Planning; mem.: Akron Bar Assn. Found., Union Club of Cleve., Kiwanis. Avocations: travel, golf. Estate planning, Probate (including wills, trusts), Estate taxation. Home: 880 Sovereign Rd Akron OH 44303 Office: Kaufmann & Kaufmann 106 S Main St Ste 1200 Akron OH 44308

KAUGER, YVONNE, state supreme court justice; b. Cordell, Okla., Aug. 3, 1937; d. John and Alice (Bottom) K.; m. Ned Bastow, May 8, 1982; 1 child, Jonna Kauger Kirschner. BS magna cum laude, Southwestern State U., Weatherford, Okla., 1958; cert. med. technologist, St. Anthony's Hosp., 1959; JD, Oklahoma City U., 1969, LLD (hon.), 1992. Med. technologist Med. Arts Lab., 1959-68; assoc. Rogers, Travis & Jordan, 1970-72; jud. asst. Okla. Supreme Ct., Oklahoma City, 1972-84, justice, 1984-94, vice chief justice, 1994-96, chief justice, 1997-98, justice, 1998—. Mem. appellate div. Ct. on Judiciary; mem. State Capitol Preservation Commn., 1983-84; mem. dean's adv. com. Oklahoma City U. Sch. Law; lectr. William O. Douglas Lecture Series Gonzaga U., 1990. Founder Gallery of Plains Indian, Colony, Okla., Red Earth (Down Towner award 1990), 1987; active Jud. Day, Girl's State, 1976-80; keynote speaker Girl's State Hall of Fame Banquet, 1984; bd. dirs. Lyric Theatre, Inc., 1966— , pres. bd. dirs., 1981; past mem. bd. dirs. Civic Music Soc., Okla. Theatre Ctr., Canterbury Choral Soc.; mem. First Lady of Okla.'s Artisans' Alliance Com. Named Panhellenic Woman of Yr., 1990, Woman of Yr. Red Lands Coun. Girl Scouts, 1990, Washita County Hall of Fame, 1992. Mem. ABA (law sch. accreditation com.), Okla. Bar Assn. (law schs. com. 1977—), Washita County Bar Assn., Washita County Hist. Soc. (life), St. Paul's Music Soc., Iota Tau Tau, Delta Zeta (Disting. Alumna award 1988, State Delta Zeta of Yr. 1987, Nat. Woman of Yr. 1988). Episcopalian.

KAUPPI, MATTI RISTO SAKARI, lawyer, researcher; b. Helsinki, Finland, June 29, 1963; s. Risto and Ellen Kauppi; m. Anne Palo-Kauppi, Aug. 26, 2000; 1 child, Sonja. Baccalaureate, Munkkiniemi Sch., Helsinki, 1983; LLM, U. Helsinki, 1992; LLM in European Bus. Law, Amsterdam Sch. Internat. Rels., 1994. Bar: Internat. Bar Assn. 1999. Euro civil servant trainee Ministry Trade and Industry, Helsinki, 1994—95; lawyer Borenius & Kemppinen Law Firm, Helsinki, 1995; ct. trainee Helsinki City Ct., 1995—96; legal advisor on European Union law Ministry for Fgn. Affairs, Helsinki, 1996—97; lawyer Bercona Trust Law Firm, Helsinki, 1997, Hirvi,

Penttila & Varhela Law Firm, Helsinki, 1997—99; asst. prof. European law U. Helsinki, 1998—99; practising atty. Nordic Law Sundström Oy, Helsinki, 1999—. Mem. entrance examination bd. faculty law U. Helsinki, Finland, 1998; sec. gen. Nordic Conf. of the European Union, 1998; sec. gen. conf. Helsinki Internat. Fedn. for European Law, 2000. Author: The Legal Personality of the European Union, 1996; editor: XIX F.I.D.E. Congress Reports, 2000; co-editor: The Nordic Conference on the European Union-Access to Justice, 1999. Sgt. Finnish Antitank Def., 1983—84. Mem.: Legal Soc. Finland, Union Finnish Lawyers, Finnish Assn. European Law. Commercial, contracts (including sales of goods; commercial financing), Private international, Antitrust. Office: Nordic Law Oy Ab Unioninkatu 39 A 9 00170 Helsinki Finland

KAUTTER, DAVID JOHN, lawyer; b. Wilkes-Barre, Pa., Mar. 20, 1948; s. William George and Mary (Flanagan) K.; m. Kathy Jane Price, May 22, 1976; children: Hilary, David Jr. BBA, Notre Dame U., 1971; JD, Georgetown U., 1974. Bar: D.C. 1975, U.S. Dist. Ct. D.C. 1981, U.S. Tax Ct. 1981, U.S. Supreme Ct. 1981. Staff acct. Coopers & Lybrand, Washington, 1971-74; mgr. Arthur Young and Co., Washington, 1974-78; legis. asst. Senator John Danforth, Washington, 1979-82; ptnr. Arthur Young and Co., Washington, 1982-89, dir. Wash. Nat. Tax Group, 1986-89; nat. dir. compensation and benefits tax svcs. Ernst & Young, Washington, 1989-98, mem. ptnrs. adv. coun., 1993-96, nat. dir. human resource svcs., 1998-2001, dir. nat. tax, 2001—. Contbr. articles to profl. jours. Mem. ABA, Fed. Bar Assn., AICPA's. Republican. Roman Catholic. Avocation: cabinet making. Legislative, Pension, profit-sharing, and employee benefits, Personal income taxation. Home: 8312 Summerwood Dr Mc Lean VA 22102-2212 Office: Ernst & Young 1225 Connecticut Ave NW Ste 700 Washington DC 20036-2621

KAUTZMAN, JOHN FREDRICK, lawyer; b. Indpls., Aug. 23, 1959; s. Fred L. and Barbara J. (Seeger) K. BA, Ind. U., 1981; JD, Ind. U., Indpls., 1984. Bar: Ind. 1985, U.S. Dist. Ct. (no. and so. dists.) Ind. 1985, U.S. Ct. Appeals (7th cir.) 1992. Law clk. Marion County Pros. Office, Indpls., 1981; bailiff Marion County Cir. Ct., Indpls., 1981-84, commr., judge pro tempore, 1985-89; assoc. Ruckelshaus, Roland, Hasbrook & O'Connor, Indpls., 1985-89, ptnr., 1990-98, Ruckelshaus, Roland, Kautzman, Blackwell & Hasbrook, Indpls., 1998—. Mem. faculty Ind. Trial Advocacy Coll., 1998—. Contbg. author The Indiana Lawyer newspaper, 1991—. Mem. bd. assocs. Ind. U. Found., Bloomington, 1993—, v.p. 1997-99, pres., 2000—; precinct commiteeman Marion County Rep. Party, Indpls., 1994-96. Mem.: ABA, Indpls. Bar Assn. (chmn. young lawyers divsn. 1988—89, bd. mgrs. 1994—2002, v.p. 1998, first v.p. 2003, Disting. fellow 1993), Ind. State Bar Assn., Phi Delta Phi. Methodist. Avocations: professional piano, golf. General civil litigation, Criminal, General practice. Office: Ruckelshaus Roland Kautzman Blackwell & Hasbrook Ste 900 107 N Pennsylvania St Indianapolis IN 46204-2424 Fax: (317) 634-8635.

KAUTZSCH, CHRISTOF, lawyer; b. Frankfurt, Germany, Feb. 4, 1970; s. Mathias and Ortrud Kautzsch; m. Christiane Torley, July 3, 1999; 1 child, Philipp. JD, U. Muenster, 2001. Bar: Dist. Ct. Berlin 1998. Assoc. Haarmann Hemmelrath, Berlin, 1998—2001, jr. ptnr., 2001—. Author: Unternehmenssanierung, 2001, Muenchener Anwaltshandbuch, 2002. Mergers and acquisitions, Corporate, general. Office: Haarmann Hemmelrath Markgrafenstrasse 33 D-10117 Berlin Germany Fax: +4930 26473133. E-mail: christof.kautzsch@haarmannhemmelrath.com.

KAVOUKJIAN, MICHAEL EDWARD, lawyer; b. Mpls., Apr. 19, 1958; s. Antranik M. and Leikny Dorthea (Oines) K. AB with distinction, Stanford U., 1980; JD cum laude, Harvard U., 1984. Bar: Minn. 1984, N.Y. 1986, U.S. Dist. Ct. Minn. 1985, U.S. Dist. Ct. (so. dist.) N.Y. 1988, Fla. 1999. From assoc. to ptnr. White & Case, N.Y.C. and Miami, Fla., 1985—. Mem.: ABA (chmn. com. estate planning and drafting 1992—94), Soc. Trust and Estate Practitioners (UK), Assn. Bar City N.Y., The Fla. Bar, Minn. State Bar Assn., Lincoln's Inn Soc. of Harvard Law Sch. (bd. govs. 1982—84), Nat. Press Club (Washington), Harvard Club (N.Y.C., Washington, Boston). Republican. Presbyterian. Estate planning, Probate (including wills, trusts), Estate taxation. Office: White & Case 1155 Avenue Of The Americas New York NY 10036-2787 also: White & Case 200 S Biscayne Blvd Miami FL 33131-2352

KAWACHIKA, JAMES AKIO, lawyer; b. Honolulu, Dec. 5, 1947; s. Shinichi and Tsuyuko (Murashige) K.; m. Karen Keiko Takahashi, Sept. 1, 1973; 1 child, Robyn Mari. BA, U. Hawaii, Honolulu, 1969; JD, U. Calif., Berkeley, 1973. Bar: Hawaii 1973, U.S. Dist. Ct. Hawaii 1973, U.S. Ct. Appeals (9th cir.) 1974, U.S. Supreme Ct. 1992. Dep. atty. gen. Office of Atty. Gen. State of Hawaii, Honolulu, 1973-74; assoc. Padgett, Greeley & Marumoto, Honolulu, 1974-75, Law Office of Frank D. Padgett, Honolulu, 1975-77, Kobayashi, Watanabe, Sugita & Kawashima, Honolulu, 1977-82; ptnr. Carlsmith, Wichman, Case, Mukai & Ichiki, Honolulu, 1982-86, Bays, Deaver, Hiatt, Kawachika & Lezak, Honolulu, 1986-95; propr. Law Offices of James A. Kawachika, Honolulu, 1996—2002; ptnr. Reinwald, O'Connor & Playdon LLP, Honolulu, 2002—. Mem. Hawaii Bd. of Bar Examiners, Honolulu; arbitrator Cir. Ct. Arbitration Program State of Hawaii, Honolulu, 1986—. Chmn. Disciplinary Bd. Hawaii Supreme Ct., 1991-97; mem. U.S. Dist. Ct. Adv. Com. on the Civil Justice Reform Act of 1990, 1991—. Mem. ABA, ATLA, Am. Judicature Soc. (bd. dirs. Hawaii chpt. 2003-), Hawaii State Bar Assn. (bd. dirs. 1975-76, young lawyers sect. 1983-84, 92-93, treas. 1987-88, v.p./pres.-elect 1997-98, pres. 1998-99), 9th Cir. Jud. Conf. (lawyer rep. Honolulu chpt. 1988-90). Avocations: running, tennis, skiing. General civil litigation, Insurance, Personal injury (including property damage). Office: Pacific Guardian Ctr Makai Tower 733 Bishop St 24th Flr Honolulu HI 96813-4070

KAWANO, ARNOLD HUBERT, lawyer; b. Phila., Mar. 27, 1948; s. James Tadao and Shigeko (Sakamoto) K.; m. Sandra K. Lee, July 1, 1970; children: Thomas L., Mark L. BS magna cum laude, Columbia U., 1975, JD, 1977. Bar: N.Y. 1978, D.C. 1979, Pa. 1981, U.S. Dist. Ct. (ea. and so. dists.) N.Y. 1978, U.S. Ct. Appeals (fed. cir.) 1992, U.S. Ct. Internat. Trade 1992, U.S. Supreme Ct. 1981. Assoc. Reid & Priest, N.Y.C., 1977-80, Weil, Gotshal & Manges, N.Y.C., 1980-81; counsel Sumitomo Corp. of Am., N.Y.C., 1981-84; pvt. practice N.Y.C., Mineola, N.Y., 1984-87; v.p. J.P. Morgan, N.Y.C., 1987-91; ptnr. Inouye & Ogden, N.Y.C., 1992-93; sr. v.p., gen. counsel ORIX USA Corp., N.Y.C., 1993-98; mng. dir. Harold L. Lee & Sons, Inc., N.Y.C., 1999—. Bd. dirs. Harold L. Lee & Sons, Inc., N.Y.C. Bd. dirs. Asian-Am. Legal Def. and Edn. Fund, N.Y.C., 1977-88, N.Y. Civil Liberties Union, 1992-94. Harlan Fiske Stone scholar Columbia Law Sch., 1976, Internat. fellow Columbia U. Sch. Internat. Affairs, 1976. Fellow Am. Coll. Investment Counsel; mem. ABA, NAACP, N.Y. State Bar Assn., D.C. Bar, Assn. of Bar of City N.Y., Asian Pacific Am. Bar Assn. N.Y. (bd. dirs. 1992-93), Am. Corp. Counsel Assn., Computer Law Assn., Internat Wine Law Assn., Assn. for Computing Machinery, Nat. Press Photographers Assn., Evidence Photographers Internat. Coun., Japanese Am. Citizens League, Phi Beta Kappa. Avocations: photography, skiing. Commercial, contracts (including sales of goods; commercial financing), Corporate, general, Property, real (including real estate development, water). Office: 31 Pell St New York NY 10013-5148 E-mail: kawano@abanet.org.

KAWITT, ALAN, lawyer; JD, Chgo.-Kent Coll. Law, 1965; postgrad. Lawyers Inst., John Marshall Law Sch., 1966-68. Bar: Ill. 1966, U.S. Dist. Ct. (no. dist.) Ill. 1967, U.S. Ct. Appeals (7th cir.) 1971, U.S. Supreme Ct. 1971. Sole practice, 1970—. Mem. Am. Arbitration Assn. (arbitrator). Commercial, consumer (including collections, credit), Insurance, Landlord-tenant. Office: 226 S Wabash Ave Ste 905 Chicago IL 60604-2319

KAY, HERMA HILL, education educator; b. Orangeburg, S.C., Aug. 18, 1934; d. Charles Esdorn and Herma Lee (Crawford) Hill. BA, So. Meth. U., 1956; JD, U. Chgo., 1959. Bar: Calif. 1960, U.S. Supreme Ct. 1978. Law clk. to Hon. Roger Traynor Calif. Supreme Ct., 1959-60; from asst. prof. to assoc. prof. law U. Calif., Berkeley, 1960-62, prof., 1963, dir. family law project, 1964-67, Jennings prof., 1987-96, dean, 1992-2000, Armstrong prof., 1996—; co-reporter uniform marriage and div. act Nat. Conf. Commrs. on Uniform State Laws, 1968-70. Vis. prof. U. Manchester, England, 1972, Harvard U., 1976; mem. Gov.'s Commn. Family, 1966. Author (with Martha S. West): (book) Text Cases and Materials on Sex-Based Discrimination, 5th edit., 2002; author: (with D. Currie and L. Kramer) Conflict of Laws: Cases, Comments, Questions, 6th edit., 2001; contbr. articles to profl. jours. Trustee Russell Sage Found., NY, 1972—87, chmn. bd. trustees, 1980—84; trustee, bd. dirs. Equal Rights Advs., Calif., 1987—88, chmn., 1976—83; pres. bd. dirs. Rosenberg Found., Calif., 1987—88, bd. dirs., 1978—. Recipient Rsch. award, Am. Bar Found., 1990, Margaret Brent award, ABA Commn. Women in Profession, 1992, Marshall-Wythe medal, 1995; fellow, Ctr. Advanced Study Behavioral Sci., Palo Alto, Calif., 1963. Mem.: ABA (sect. legal edn. and admissions to bar coun. 1992—99, sec. 1999—2001), Order of Coif (nat. pres. 1983—85), Am. Philos. Soc., Am. Acad. Arts and Scis., Assn. Am. Law Schs. (exec. com. 1986—87, pres.-elect 1988, pres. 1989, past pres. 1990), Am. Law Inst. (mem. coun. 1985—), Calif. Women Lawyers (bd. govs. 1975—77), Bar U.S. Supreme Ct., Calif. Bar Assn. Democrat. Office: U Calif Law Sch Boalt Hall Berkeley CA 94720-7200 E-mail: kayh@law.berkeley.edu.

KAY, JOEL PHILLIP, lawyer; b. Corsicana, Tex., Aug. 27, 1936; m. Marilyn Soltz, July 9, 1961; children: Arthur Hyman, Sarah Anne, Leslie Anette. BS in Econs., Wharton Sch., U. Pa., 1958; LLB, U. Tex., 1961; LL.M., Georgetown U., 1967. Bar: Tex. 1961, U.S. Dist. Ct. (so. and we. dists.) Tex., U.S. Dist. Ct (so. dist.) Ala., U.S. Ct. Appeals (5th cir.), U.S. Supreme Ct. Trial atty. tax div. Dept. Justice, 1963-67; U.S. atty. So. Dist. Tex., 1967-69; ptnr. Sheinfeld, Maley & Kay, P.C., Houston, 1969—2001; of counsel Hughes, Watters & Askanase, LLP , Houston, 2001—. Mem. Tex. Bd. Pub. Accountancy, 1984-85, quality rev. oversight bd., 1992-93; speaker at numerous institutes on comml. and bankruptcy law. With AUS, 1961-63. Fellow Am. Bar Found., Am. Coll. Bankruptcy (5th cir. regent 1997-2003); mem. ABA, Tex. Bar Assn. (dir. 1979-81, chmn. bd. 1981-82), Houston Bar Assn., Tex. Bar Found. (trustee 1983-86), Houston Bar Found. (dir. 1995-98), Tex. Supreme Ct. (grievance oversight com. 1987-94). Bankruptcy, Commercial, contracts (including sales of goods; commercial financing). Office: 1415 Louisiana 37th Fl Houston TX 77002-6709 E-mail: jkay@hwallp.com.

KAY, RICHARD BROUGHTON, lawyer; b. Cleve., Apr. 7, 1918; s. Joseph Stanley and Frances Anna (Broughton) Kay; m. Ellen Fletcher, June 7, 1992. BBA, Miami U. of Ohio, 1939; LLB, Case Western Res. U., 1948. Bar: Fla., U.S. Supreme Ct. Pvt. practice, Tequesta, Fla. Field organizer Eisenhower for Pres., N.Y.C., 1952; exec. sec. Stassen for Pres., Cleve., 1948; nat. v.p. Wilkie Young Voters, N.Y.C., 1940. Lt. USNR, 1941-61. Mem.: Attys. Bar of Palm Beach County, North Palm Beach County Bar Assn. (pres. 1988), Palm Beach County Bar Assn., Fla. Bar Assn., Am. Legion, VFW, Elks. Avocation: travel. Home: 19800 Us Highway 1 Apt 506 Tequesta FL 33469-2357 Office: 222 US Hwy # 208 Tequesta FL 33469

KAY, STEPHEN WILLIAM, lawyer; b. Omaha, Dec. 27, 1953; s. Harold Wallace and Patricia Lou (Larson) K.; m. Jean Marie Lawse, Aug. 5, 1978; children: Melissa Marie, Stephen William II, Robert Andrew. BS, U. Nebr., 1975; JD, Creighton U., 1978. Bar: Nebr. 1978, U.S. Dist. Ct. Nebr. 1978, U.S. Ct. Claims 1987, U.S. Ct. Appeals (8th cir.) 1978, U.S. Ct. Appeals (Fed. cir.) 1984, U.S. Ct. Appeals (D.C. cir.) 1987, U.S. Supreme Ct. 1984., U.S. Ct. Appeals 1990, U.S. Ct. Internat. Trade 1990. Assoc. Kay & Satterfield, North Platte, Nebr., 1978-80; ptnr. Kay & Kay, North Platte, 1980—. Mem. standing com. Episcopal Diocese of Nebr., 1985-89, mem. com. on legis., 1990-95, exec. com., 1992-95; exec. bd. dirs. Tri Trails coun. Boy Scouts Am., North Platte, 1982-93, Overland Trails coun., Grand Island, 1993—, v.p. adminstrn., 1996-2001; dist. chmn. Buffalo Bill Dist., 1994-96, vice chmn., 1996-98; chmn. Lincoln County Reps., North Platte, 1982-84; cen. committeeman Nebr. Reps., 1984-98, asst. chmn., 1986, mem. exec. com., 1986; bd. dirs. Mid-Nebr. Cmty. Found., 1998-93, 95-97; provisional dep. Gen. Conv., Episcopal Ch., 1991, 94, 97. Recipient Dist. award of Merit Boy Scouts Am., 1996, Silver Beaver award, 1998. Fellow: Nebr. State Bar Found.; mem.: ABA, Assn. Def. Trial Attys., Nat. Assn. R.R. Trial Coun., Am. Judicature Soc., Nebr. Bar Assn., Western Nebr. Bar Assn., Lincoln County Bar Assn. Episcopalian. Federal civil litigation, Insurance, Personal injury (including property damage). Home: 1111 Custer Ct North Platte NE 69101-6305 Office: Wells Fargo Bank Bldg 315 N Dewey St Ste 205 North Platte NE 69103

KAYDEN, JEROLD S. lawyer, urban planner; b. N.Y.C., Sept. 12, 1953; AB, Harvard U., 1975, JD, MCRP, Harvard U., 1979. Bar: Mass. 1985, D.C. 1991, N.Y. 1992. Law clk. to judge U.S. Ct. Appeals for 2nd Cir., 1979-80; law clk. to Justice William J. Brennan, Jr. U.S. Supreme Ct., Washington, 1980-81; lectr. Harvard Grad. Sch. Design, Cambridge, Mass., 1981-84, assoc. prof. urban planning, 1995—, dir M. in Urban Planning program, 1998—2000; of counsel Warner & Stackpole, Boston, 1987—99. Gerald D. Hines lectr. Harvard Grad. Sch. Design, 1986-87; sr. fellow Lincoln Inst. Land Policy, Cambridge, 1988-92; sr. advisor on land reform PADCO/U.S. Agy. for Internat. Devel., 1992-94; pres. Masterclass, Inc., L.A., 1976—; bd. dirs. PADCO, Inc. Co-author: Landmark Justice, 1989, Privately Owned Public Space, 2000; co-editor: Zoning and the American Dream, 1989; contbr. articles to profl. jours. Bd. dirs. Kathmandu Valley Pres. Trust. Guggenheim fellow, 1989-90; grantee Nat. Endowment for Arts, 1979, 88, 20th Century Fund, 1989-92. Home: 11 Clement Cir Cambridge MA 02138-2205 Office: Harvard U Grad Sch Design 48 Quincy St Cambridge MA 02138 E-mail: jkayden@gsd.harvard.edu.

KAYE, JUDITH SMITH, judge; b. Monticello, N.Y., Aug. 4, 1938; d. Benjamin and Lena (Cohen) Smith; m. Stephen Rackow Kaye, Feb. 11, 1964; children: Luisa Marian, Jonathan Mackey, Gordon Bernard BA, Barnard Coll., 1958; LLB cum laude, NYU, 1962; LLD (hon.), St. Lawrence U., 1985, Union U., 1985, Pace U., 1985, Syracuse U., 1988, L.I. U., 1989. Assoc. Sullivan & Cromwell, N.Y.C., 1962-64; staff atty. IBM, Armonk, N.Y., 1964-65; asst. to dean Sch. Law NYU, 1965-68; ptnr. Connelly Chase O'Donnell & Weyher, N.Y.C., 1969-83; assoc. judge N.Y. State Ct. Appeals, N.Y.C., 1983-93, chief justice, 1993—. Bd. dir. Sterling Nat. Bank. Contbr. articles to profl. jours. Former bd. dirs. Legal Aid Soc. Recipient Vanderbilt medal NYU Sch. of Law, 1983, Medal of Distinction, Barnard Coll, 1987. Fellow Am. Bar Found.; mem. Am. Law Inst., Am. Coll. Trial Lawyers, Am. Judicature Soc. (bd. dirs. 1980-83). Democrat. Office: NY Court of Appeals Court of Appeals Hall 20 Eagle St Albany NY 12207-1009 also: NY Court of Appeals 230 Park Ave Rm 826 New York NY 10169-0007

KAYE, MARC MENDELL, lawyer; b. Irvington, N.J., Nov. 25, 1959; s. Aaron Morton and Sandra (Hoch) K. AA, BA, Rutgers U., 1980; JD, U. Toledo, 1983. Bar: N.J. 1984, Fla. 1987, D.C. 1991, N.Y. 1998, U.S. Dist. Ct. N.J. 1984, U.S. Supreme Ct. 1992; cert. civil trial atty. 1991. Trial atty. Shevick, Ravich, Koster et al, Rahway, N.J., 1984-85, Greenberg, Margolis et al, Roseland, N.J., 1985-86, Brian Granstrand, Fairfield, N.J., 1986-90; pvt. practice Livingston, N.J., 1986-94, Short Hills, 1994—. Counsel CNA Ins. Co., Fairfield, 1986-90; apptd. arbitrator Union County Arbitrator Program, 1993, Essex County Arbitrator and Mediator Programs, 1995, Millburn Citizen Budget Com., 1998—; adv. coun. mem. Chmn.'s Club Summit Bank, 1989-91. Mem. exec. com. Young Leadership div. United Jewish Appeal, Metrowest, N.J, 1988-91; bd. dirs. Jewish Cmty. Ctr. of MetroWest, 1998—, Opera Music Theatre Internat., 1999—. Mem. N.J. Bar Assn., Essex County Bar Assn. (subcom. chmn. legal med. com. 1992-94), Union County Bar Assn., Fla. Bar Assn., D.C. Bar Assn., Assn. Trial Lawyers Am., N.J. Trial Lawyers Assn., Lions Club (v.p. 1993-95), Prime Ministers Club, Israel Bonds. Avocations: golf, swimming, scuba diving, travel. General civil litigation, Insurance, Personal injury (including property damage). Office: One N Brook Dr at S Orange Ave Short Hills NJ 07078-3126 E-mail: Kayemarc@hotmail.com.

KAYE, STEPHEN RACKOW, lawyer; b. Nyack, N.Y., May 4, 1931; s. Edward and Florence (Karp) K.; m. Judith Smith, Feb. 11, 1964; children: Luisa Marian, Jonathan Mackey, Gordon Bernard. AB, Cornell U., 1952, LL.B. with honors, 1956. Bar: N.Y. 1956, U.S. Supreme Ct. 1961. Assoc. Sullivan & Cromwell, N.Y.C., 1956-63, Proskauer Rose Goetz & Mendelsohn, N.Y.C., 1964-68, ptnr., past chair, co-chmn. lit. dept., 1968—. Mem. Judicial Inst. on Professionalism in the Law, 1999—. Author treatise texts on trials and appeals of comml. cases; mng. editor Cornell Law Quar.; contbr. to profl. publs. Served to 1st lt. AUS, 1952-54, Korea. Mem. ABA, N.Y. State Bar Assn., Assn. of Bar of City of N.Y. (past chmn. com. on profl. and jud. ethics, chmn. com. on profl. discipline), N.Y. County Lawyers Assn. (past vice chmn. com. on Supreme Ct.), 1st Dept. Disciplinary Commn. (hearing panel chair, policy com. 1991-96, 1999-2002), Order of Coif, Phi Kappa Phi. Antitrust, Federal civil litigation, State civil litigation. Office: Proskauer Rose LLP 1585 Broadway New York NY 10036-8299

KAYLOR, GAY L. paralegal, food company administrator; b. Cin., Sept. 6, 1961; d. Kenneth E. and Esther M. Umberger; m. Keith E. Kaylor, Oct. 27, 1984; children: Megan, Mark. Paralegal, Harrisburg (Pa.) Area C.C., 1995. Stockholder rels. adminstr. Hershey Foods Corp., Hershey, Pa., 1992-95, assoc. stockholder rels. rep., 1995-97, stockholder rels. rep., 1998—2000, sr. stockholder rels. rep. Mem. client adv. bd. Mellon Investor Svcs., N.Y.C., 1998—. Mem. Pa. Assn. Notaries, Ctrl. Pa. Corp. Rels. Soc. Republican. Office: Hershey Foods Corp 100 Crystal A Dr Hershey PA 17033-9702

KAYSER, KENNETH WAYNE, lawyer; b. N.Y.C., Apr. 28, 1947; s. William Gilbert and Joan Phyliss (Bach) K.; m. Linda Calcote, Apr. 13, 1968; 1 child, Christopher R. BA, Syracuse U., 1969; JD, Seton Hall, 1977. Bar: N.J. 1977, U.S. Dist. Ct. N.J. 1977, U.S. Cir. Ct. (3d cir.) 1988, U.S. Ct. Internat. Trade 1990. Asst. prosecutor Essex County Prosecutor's Office, Newark, 1978-82; assoc. Brach, Eichler, Rosenberg, Silver, Bernstein & Hammer, Roseland, N.J., 1982-83; sole practice West Orange, N.J., 1984—. Mem. ABA, N.J. State Bar Assn., Essex County Bar Assn., Assn. Criminal Def. Lawyers N.J. Democrat. General civil litigation, Criminal, Property, real (including real estate development, water). Home: PO Box 2087 Livingston NJ 07039 Office: 120 Eagle Rock Ave East Hanover NJ 07936-3105 E-mail: kenkayser@cs.com.

KAZANJIAN, PHILLIP CARL, lawyer; b. Visalia, Calif., May 15, 1945; s. John Casey and Sat-ten Arlene K.; m. Wendy Coffelt, Feb. 5, 1972; 1 child, John. BA with honors, U. So. Calif., 1967; JD with honors, Lincoln U., 1973. Bar: Calif. 1979, U.S. Dist. Ct. (ctrl. dist.) Calif. 1980, U.S. Tax Ct. 1980, U.S. Ct. Appeals (9th cir.) 1980, U.S. Mil. Ct. Appeals 1980, U.S. Supreme ct. 1983. Ptnr. Brakefield & Kazanjian, Glendale, Calif., 1981-87; sr. ptnr. Kazanjian & Martinetti, Glendale, Calif., 1987—. Judge pro tem L.A. County Superior Ct., 1993—; instr. U.S. Naval Acad., Annapolis, Md., 1981; adj. prof. Glendale C.C., 1997—. Author: The Circuit Governor, 1972; editor-in-chief Lincoln Law Rev., 1973. Mem. Calif. Atty. Gen.'s Adv. Commn. on Cmty.-Police Rels., 1973; bd. dirs. L.A. County Naval Meml. Found., Inc,. 1981-85; pres., bd. trustees Glendale C.C. Dist., 1981-97, L.A. World Affairs Coun., Town Hall Calif., Rep. Assocs. (dir.), Rep. Lincoln Club; vice chmn. bd. govs. Calif. Maritime Acad., 1986-94. Capt. USNR, 1969-99. Decorated Navy Commendation medal, Navy Achievement medal, knight Order of Knights Templar, 1990; recipient Patrick Henry medal Am. Legion, 1963, Congl. Record tribute U.S. Ho. of Reps., 1974, Centurion award Chief of Naval Ops., 1978; commendatory resolutions Mayor of L.A., L.A. City Coun., L.A. County Bd. Suprs., Calif. State Assembly and Senate, and Govt. of Calif., 1982, 2003, Justice award Calif. Law Student Assn., 1973. Mem. ABA (Gold Key 1972), Calif. Bar Assn., L.A. County Bar Assn., Am. Judicature Soc., ATLA, Glendale C. of C. (bd. dirs., Patriot Yr. 1986), Res. Officers Assn. (nat. judge adv., award 1981), Naval Res. Assn. (nat. adv. com.), U.S. Naval Inst., Interallied Confedn. Res. Officers (internat. chmn. 1987-94), Explorers Club, Commonwealth of Calif. Club. Republican. Episcopalian. State civil litigation, Personal injury (including property damage). Office: Kazanjian & Martinetti 520 E Wilson Ave Ste 250 Glendale CA 91206-4346

KAZEN, GEORGE PHILIP, federal judge; b. Laredo, Tex., Feb. 29, 1940; s. Emil James and Drusilla M. (Perkins) K.; m. Barbara Ann Sanders, Oct. 27, 1962; children: George Douglas, John Andrew, Elizabeth Ann, Gregory Stephen. BBA, U. Tex., 1960, JD with honors, 1961. Bar: Tex. 1961, U.S. Supreme Ct., U.S. Ct. Claims, U.S. Ct. Appeals (5th cir.), U.S. Dist. Ct. (so. dist.) Tex. Briefing atty. Tex. Sup. Ct., 1961-62; founder, first pres. Laredo Legal Aid Soc., 1966-69; assoc. Mann, Freed, Kazen & Hansen, 1965-79; judge U.S. Dist. Ct. (so. dist.) Tex., Laredo, 1979-96; founder, first pres. Laredo Legal Aid Soc., 1966-69; chief judge U.S. Dist. Ct. (so. dist.) Tex., Laredo, 1996—. Mem. Jud. Conf. Com. Criminal Law, 1990-96, chair com., 1996-99; mem. 5th Cir. Jud. Coun., 1991-94, 96—; adj. prof. law St. Mary's U. Sch. Law, 1990—. Pres. Laredo Civic Music Assn.; chmn. St. Augustine-Ursuline Consol. Sch. Bd.; bd. dirs. Boys' Clubs Laredo; trustee Laredo Jr. Coll., 1972-79; bd. dirs., v.p., pres. Econ. Opportunities Devel. Corp., 1968-70; past bd. dirs. D.D. Hachar Found. With USAF, 1962-65. Decorated Air Force Commendation medal; named Outstanding Young Lawyer, Larado Jaycees, 1970. Mem. ABA, Tex. Bar Found., Tex. Bar Assn., Tex. Criminal Def. Lawyers Assn., Tex. Assn. Bank Counsel, Tex. Assn. Def. Counsel, Laredo C. of C. (bd. dirs. 1975-76), 5th Cir. Dist. Judges Assn. (v.p. 1984-85, pres. 1986-88), U. Tex. Law Sch. Alumni Assn. (bd. dirs. 1976-77). Roman Catholic. Office: US Dist Ct PO Box 1060 Laredo TX 78042-1060

KEADY, GEORGE CREGAN, JR., judge; b. Bklyn., June 16, 1924; s. George Cregan and Marie (Lussier) K.; m. Patricia Drake, Sept. 2, 1950; children: Margaret Keady Goldberg, Marie E., George Cregan, Catherine A. Keady Dunn, Kathleen V. Student, U. Kans., 1943-44; BS, Fordham U., 1949; JD, Columbia U., 1950; LL.D., Western New Eng. Coll., 1973. Bar: Mass. 1950. Since practiced in, Springfield, Mass.; asso. firm Ganley & Crook, 1950-53; assoc. firm Peter D. Wilson, 1953-57; partner firm Wilson, Keady & Ratner, 1958-79; justice Dist. Ct., Springfield, 1979-82; assoc. justice Superior Ct., Springfield, 1982-93; ret., 1993; freelance mediator and arbitrator, 1993—. Dean Western New Eng. Coll. Law Sch., 1970-73; dir. Western Mass. Bar Rev., 1956-63, Western New Eng. Coll. Bar Rev., 1965-72; chmn. Mass. Continuing Legal Edn., Inc., 1977-80; mem. Mass. Commn. on Jud. Conduct, 1988, chmn., 1990-93. Active United Fund, Springfield, 1950-72, Joint Civic Agys.; chmn. fund drive Am. Cancer Soc., 1962, selectman, Longmeadow, Mass., 1958-68, chmn. selectmen, 1960-61, 63-64, 66-68, moderator, 1968-73; vice chmn. Rep. Town Com., Longmeadow, 1956-60; alt. del. Rep. Nat. Conv., 1960, del., 1964; pres. Hampden Dist. Mental Health Clinic, Inc., 1966-71, Child Guidance Clinic, Springfield, 1962-64; corporator, trustee, chmn. bd. Baystate Med. Center, 1985-87, trustee, 1984-92, 94-99; chmn. bd. Baystate Health System, 1987-90; trustee Western New Eng. Coll., 1978-84, Baypath Jr. Coll., 1972-87, Baystate Health Systems, 1993-98; dir. BHIC, 1993—. Served with AUS, 1943-46. Decorated Bronze star. Mem. Am. Law Inst., Mass. Bar Assn., Hampden County Bar Assn. (exec. com. 1960-79, pres. 1965-67), Supreme Ct. Hist. Soc., Longmeadow Country Club, Phi Delta Phi. Roman Catholic. Home: 16 Meadowbrook Rd Longmeadow MA 01106-1341

KEAN, HAMILTON FISH, lawyer; b. NYC, Mar. 1, 1925; s. Robert Winthrop and Elizabeth Stuyvesant (Howard) K.; m. Ellen Shaw Garrison, Mar. 25, 1950 (div. 1976); children: Leslie K. McKim, Elizabeth Douglas , Lloyd Garrison, Lewis Morris; m. Alice Kay Newcomer, July 6, 1981 (dec. 1986); m. Edith Williamson Bacon, Sept. 23, 1989. AB cum laude, Princeton U., 1949; JD, Columbia U., 1954. Bar: NY 1954, NJ 1955. Asst. counsel Waterfront Commn. NY Harbor, 1954; law sec. NJ Supreme Ct., 1954-55; asst. U.S. atty. NJ Dist., 1955-57; ptnr. Clapp and Eisenberg and predecessors, Newark, 1957-62; trustee various funds, 1963—; lectr. law Rutgers U. Sch. Law, 1960; lectr. environ. law SUNY at Purchase, Westchester Cmty. Coll., 1974-76. Supervising atty. clin. program environ. law NYU Sch. Law, 1972-76; chmn. Livingston Nat. Bank, 1984; bd. dir. Realty Transfer Co. Bd. dir. Morris County Urban League, 1956-51; mem. Urban Crisis Task Force, 1976; bd. dir. Youth Counseling League, 1969-93, pres., 1979-83, hon. dir.; bd. dir. Citizens Com. for Children NY, 1971-2002, now hon. dir., pres., 1972-77, Eleanor Roosevelt award, 2001; chmn. Joint Action for Children, 1976; trustee Natural Resources Def. Coun., 1973-2002, hon. trustee, 2002—, treas., 1973-76; bd. dir., sec. Environ. Advocates, 1972-78, hon. bd. dir., 1999–; bd. dir. Fountain House, 1966—, pres., 1975-78; mem. Adv. Coun. to NY State Office Mental Health, 1979-83; mem. Mental Health Svc. Coun., 1983-90; trustee Coro Found., 1979-85; mem. NY State Mental Hygiene Planning Coun., 1981-85; trustee Alice Desmond and Hamilton Fish Libr., 1981-98; trustee Schuyler Ctr. for Analysis and Avocacy, 1982—, pres., 1985-92; mem. adminstrv. bd. Lab. Ornithology Cornell U., 1982-87; trustee Hancock Shaker Village, 1986-92; mem. adv. bd. Panel of Ams., 1986—; bd. dir., sec. Episc. Charities, 1995-2002; trustee World Federalist Assn. Endowment Fund, 1998—, chmn., 2001—. 2d lt. US Army, 1943-46. Decorated Purple Heart Mem.: ABA, Assn. Bar City NY, NY State Bar Assn. (chmn. conf. on pub. interest law 1975), Columbia Law Sch. Alumni Assn. (treas. 1958—62), New Bedford Yacht Club, Millbrook Golf and Tennis Club, NY Health and Racquet Club, Princeton Club, Knickerbocker Club, Century Assn. Home: 130 East End Ave New York NY 10028-7553 Office: 120 E 56th St New York NY 10022

KEAN, JOHN VAUGHAN, retired lawyer; b. Providence, Mar. 12, 1917; s. Otho Vaughan and Mary (Duell) Kean. AB cum laude, Harvard U., 1938, JD, 1941; grad., U.S. Army War Coll., 1970. Bar: R.I. 1942, U.S. Dist. Ct. R.I. 1946, U.S. Ct. Appeals (1st cir.) 1950, U.S. Ct. Appeals (4th cir.) 1955, U.S. Ct. Claims 1963, U.S. Supreme Ct. 1982. With Edwards & Angell, Providence, 1941—, ptnr., 1954-87, ret. ptnr., 1987—. Bd. dirs. Greater Providence YMCA, 1964—76; chmn. Downtown Providence YMCA, 1964—67, Providence Com. on Fgn. Rels., 1994—2000. Capt. AUS U.S. Army, 1943—46, capt. AUS U.S. Army, 1950—52, brig. gen. R.I. Nat. Guard U.S. Army, 1964—72. Decorated Legion of Merit. Mem.: ABA, R.I. Bar Assn., Res. Officers Assn., N.G. Assn., Soc. Cin. (hon.; R.I.), The Robbins Co. (bd. dirs. 1988—2000), Assn. U.S. Army, Nature Conservancy (hon.), Urban League R.I., Alexis de Tocqueville Soc. R.I., Soc. Colonial Wars in R.I., Harvard R.I. Club (pres. 1964—66), Sakonnet Golf Club (Little Compton, R.I..), Army and Navy Club (Washington), Hope Club (bd. govs. 1996—2000, v.p.), Agawam Hunt Club. Home: 2 Angell St Providence RI 02903 Office: c/o Edwards & Angell 2800 Financial Plz Providence RI 02903-2499

KEAN, SHARON BITTNER, lawyer; b. Ridgewood, N.J., Oct. 30, 1965; d. Thomas Raymond Bittner and Dorothy Mae O'Connell; m. James Gerald Kean, July 8, 1998; children: Fiona Annette, Grace O'Connell. BS, Northeastern U., 1988; JD, Rutgers U., 1995. Bar: N.J. 1996, N.Y. 1996, U.S. Dist. Ct. N.J. 1996. Law clk. Hon. Sybil R. Mosses, Hackensack, NJ, 1995—96; assoc. Law Offices Alan L. Zegas, Chatham, NJ, 1996—. Mem.: ABA, Assn. Criminal Def. Lawyers, N.J. Bar Assn., Willard C. Heckel Inn of Ct. Criminal, Appellate, Juvenile. Office: Law Offices Alan L Zegas 552 Main St Chatham NJ 07982

KEANE, THOMAS J. lawyer; b. N.Y.C., Mar. 12, 1953; s. Raymond T. and Catherine (Mcloughlin) K.; m. Alyson M. Krohne, July 24, 1976; children: Raymond G., Kristen M., Danielle M. BA, St. Anselm Coll., Manchester, N.H., 1975; JD magna cum laude, Western New Eng. Coll., Springfield, Mass., 1980. Bar: Mass. 1980, NY 1981, U.S. Dist. Ct. (so. and ea. dists.) NY 1983. Claims Royal Globe Ins. Cos., White Plains, NY, 1975—76; staff atty. Ins. Co. N.Am., Springfield, Mass., 1980—82; assoc. Law Offices of Joseph Conklin, N.Y.C., 1982—84; in house assoc. Cigna Corp., N.Y.C., 1982—84; asst. gen. counsel Liberty Lines Cos., Yonkers, NY, 1984—93; atty., ptnr. Nesci, Keane, Piekarski, Keogh & Corrigan, White Plains, 1993—. V.p. Specialized Risk Mgmt. Inc., White Plains, 1993—. Mem. Mass. Jud. Internship Program, Boston, 1980; mem. Rep. Congl. Task Force, Washington, 1995-96. Mem. N.Y. State Bar Assn., Westchester County Bar Assn., Soc. Friendly Sons of St. Patrick in the County of Westchester. Avocations: history, golf. General civil litigation, Insurance, Personal injury (including property damage). Home: 348 Fort Washington Ave Hawthorne NY 10532-1452 Office: Nesci Keane et al 245 Main St Ste 600 White Plains NY 10601 E-mail: tjkeane@nesci-keane.com.

KEANY, SUTTON, lawyer; b. Limon, Costa Rica, Feb. 19, 1943; s. Francis Xavier and Winsome (Scoltock) K.; m. Susanne Elvera Andover, June 12, 1965; children: Damian Winsome, Alison Arwen, Courtney Vanessa, Sutton Andover. AB, Yale U., 1963; JD, Harvard U., 1966. Bar: P.R. 1967, N.Y. 1971, U.S. Supreme Ct. 1977. Assoc. McConnell, Valdes, Kelly & Sifre, San Juan, P.R., 1966-70, Winthrop, Stimson, Putnam & Roberts, N.Y.C., 1970-75, ptnr., 1976—. Mediator, early neutral evaluator U.S. Dist. Ct. (ea. dist.) N.Y., 1992—. Author: (with Jay M. Vogelson) Complying with International Antitrust Regulations; contbr. articles to Bklyn. Law Rev. Trustee Aperture Found., N.Y.C., 1988-92; dir. The Fund for Modern Cts., 1992-99, The Legal Aid Soc., 1995-2001. Mem. ABA, Assn. Bar City N.Y., Am. Arbitration Assn. (arbitrator 1990-2000), Yale Club of N.Y. Avocation: squash. Antitrust, General civil litigation. Home: 157 Duane St New York NY 10013-3836 Office: Pillsbury Winthrop LLP One Battery Park Pla New York NY 10004 E-mail: skeany@pillsburywinthrop.com.

KEARNEY, DOUGLAS CHARLES, lawyer, journalist; b. Gloucester, Mass., June 24, 1945; s. Charles Matthew Kearney and Jean (Tarr) Thomas. Student, Brown U., 1963-64; BA, Fla. State U., 1971, JD with high honors, 1973. Bar: Fla. 1974, Calif. 1976, U.S. Ct. Appeals (5th cir.) 1977, U.S. Dist. Ct. (mid. and so. dists.) Fla. 1978, U.S. Ct. Appeals (11th cir.) 1981, U.S. Supreme Ct. 1982, U.S. Dist. Ct. (no. dist.) Tex. 1985, Tex. 1986. Asst. pub. defender Office of Pub. Defender 2d Jud. Cir., Tallahassee, 1973-76; asst. atty. gen. Atty. Gen.'s Office State of Fla., Tallahassee, 1977-78, chief antitrust enforcement unit Atty. Gen.'s Office, 1978-79; prin. Law Offices of Douglas C. Kearney, Tallahassee, 1979-85; assoc. Brice & Mankoff, P.C., Dallas, 1985-87, mem., 1987-89, Choate & Lilly, P.C., Dallas, 1989-92; prin. Kearney & Assocs., Dallas, 1992—. Pres. Legal Aid Found. of Tallahassee, Inc., 1984. With U.S. Army, 1965-68, Vietnam. Mem. Fla. Bar Assn., Tex. Bar Assn., Calif. Bar Assn. Episcopalian. Avocations: sailing, tennis, swimming, gardening. Antitrust, Banking, Federal civil litigation. Office: Kearney & Assocs 15105 Cypress Hills Dr Dallas TX 75248-4914

KEARNEY, PATRICIA ANN, lawyer; b. Warren, Ohio, Nov. 23, 1951; d. Peter Sauricki and Orpha Maxine Slick; m. F. Thomas Kearney Jr., May 21, 1982. BA, Youngstown State U., 1973; JD, Akron State U., 1991. Bar: Ohio 1991, U.S. Dist. Ct. (no. dist.) Ohio 1993. Escrow officer Trumbull Co. Abstract, Warren, 1976-85; mgr. Valley Title, Warren, 1985-88, Youngstown, Ohio, 1988-91, Title Co. Warren, 1991-94; owner Title Profls., Warren, 1994—. Estate planning, Probate (including wills, trusts), Property, real (including real estate development, water). Office: Title Profls Inc 295 Harmon Ave NW Warren OH 44483-4804 E-mail: titleprof@onecom.com.

KEARNS, JOHN J., III, lawyer; b. Jersey City, Apr. 24, 1951; s. John J. Jr. and Beverly (Bailey) K.; m. Maria C. DelFemine, May 15, 1976. AB, Columbia U., 1972; JD cum laude, Fordham U., 1976. Bar: N.J. 1976, N.Y. 1977, Pa. 1985. Assoc. firm White and Case, N.Y.C., 1976-84; mem. firm Eckert, Seamans, Cherin and Mellott, LLC, Pitts., 1984—, mem. exec. com., 1989-93, chmn. tax dept., 1994-96, mem. fin. com., 1994—, CFO, 2000—01. Contbr. articles to profl. publs. Mem. ABA, Pitts. Tax Club. Avocations: thoroughbred racing, softball, reading. Mergers and acquisitions, Pension, profit-sharing, and employee benefits, Corporate taxation. Office: Eckert Seamans Cherin & Mellot 600 Grant St Ste 4400 Pittsburgh PA 15219-2702 E-mail: jjk@escm.com.

KEARNS, JOHN W. lawyer; b. Sept. 9, 1933; s. John W. and Frances R. (Forch) Kearns; m. Karen E. Swanson, May 3, 1990 (div. 1979); children: Jennifer F., John W., Charles S. BA, Yale U., 1955; JD, Harvard U., 1958. Bar: Ill. 58, Fla. 70, U.S. Dist. Ct. (no. dist.) Ill. 58, U.S. Ct. Appeals (7th, 5th., 3d and 11th cirs.), U.S. Supreme Ct. 71. With Peterson, Ross, Rall, Barber & Seidel, Chgo., 1958—61, Kirkland & Ellis, Chgo., 1961—69, Paul & Thompson, Miami, Fla., 1969—73; pvt. practice Miami, 1973—. Bd. dirs. Fla. Zool. Soc., 1974—79. Mem.: ABA, Chgo. Bar Assn., Dade County Bar Assn., Fla. Bar Assn., Coral Feef Yacht Club, Chgo. Yacht Club. Antitrust, State civil litigation, General practice. Office: 431 Gerona Ave Coral Gables FL 33146-2807

KEARNS, KEVIN LAWRENCE, political association executive, lawyer; b. Bklyn., Sept. 5, 1947; s. John C. and Alice C. (Kelleher) K.; m. Judith A. Daly, May 20, 1995; children: Nicole, Leah, Monique, Kathleen, Christopher, Kevin Michael. BA, Fordham U., 1969; MA, SUNY, Stony Brook, 1970; JD, Bklyn. Law Sch., 1976. Bar: N.Y. 1977, D.C. 1977. Legis. counsel State Senator Sheldon Farber, Queens, N.Y., 1976-77; fgn. svc. officer U.S. Dept. State, Washington, 1977-90; assigned to Am. Consulate Gen., Frankfurt, Germany, 1977-79, Am. Embassy, Bonn, Germany, 1979-80, Seoul, 1981-83, Tokyo, 1986-88; congrl. fellow Senate Fgn. Rels. Com., 1988—89; didr. Office Strategic Trade, 1989—90; sr. rsch. fellow Econ. Strategy Inst., Washington, 1990-92, Mfg. Policy Project, Washington, 1992-93; pres. U.S. Bus. and Industry Coun., Washington, 1993—. Roman Catholic. Office: US Bus & Industry Coun 910 16th St NW Ste 300 Washington DC 20006-2903 E-mail: council@usbusiness.org., kearns@usbusiness.org.

KEARSE, AMALYA LYLE, federal judge; b. Vauxhall, N.J., June 11, 1937; d. Robert Freeman and Myra Lyle (Smith) K.. BA, Wellesley Coll., 1959; JD cum laude, U. Mich., 1962. Bar: N.Y. 1963, U.S. Supreme Ct. 1967. Assoc. Hughes, Hubbard & Reed, N.Y.C., 1962—69, ptnr., 1969—79; judge U.S. Ct. Appeals (2d cir.), 1979—. Lectr. evidence NYU Law Sch., 1968—69. Author: Bridge Conventions Complete, 1975, Bridge Conventions Complete, 3d edit., 1990, Bridge at Your Fingertips, 1980; transl., editor: Bridge Analysis, 1979; editor: Ofcl. Ency. of Bridge, 3d edit., 1976; mem. editl. bd.: Charles Goren, 1974—. Trustee N.Y.C. YWCA, 1976—79, Am. Contract Bridge League Nat. Laws Commn., 1975—; mem. Pres.'s Com. on Selection of Fed. Jud. Officers, 1977—78; Bd. dirs. NAACP Legal Def. and Endl. Fund, 1977—79, Nat. Urban League, 1978—79. Named Women's Pairs Bridge Champion Nat. div., 1971, 1972, World div., 1986, Nat. Women's Teams Bridge Champion, 1987, 1990, 1991. Mem.: ABA, Lawyers Com. for Civil Rights Under Law (mem. exec. com. 1970—79), Am. Law Inst., Assn. of Bar of City of N.Y. Office: US Ct Appeals US Courthouse 40 Foley SqRm 2001 New York NY 10007

KEATING, FRANCIS ANTHONY, II, former governor, lawyer; b. St. Louis, Feb. 10, 1944; s. Anthony Francis and Anne (Martin) K.; m. Catherine Dunn Heller, 1972; children: Carissa Herndon, Kelly Martin, Anthony Francis III. AB, Georgetown U., 1966; JD, U. Okla., 1969. Bar: Okla. 1969. Spl. agt. FBI, 1969-71; asst. dist. atty. Tulsa County, 1971-72; mem. Okla. Ho. of Reps., 1972-74, Okla. Senate, 1974-81; U.S. atty. No. Dist. Okla., 1981-84; asst. sec. U.S. Treasury Dept., Washington, 1985-88; assoc. atty. gen. Dept. Justice, 1988-89; gen. counsel, acting dep. sec. Dept. Housing and Urban Devel., Washington, 1989-93; gov. State of Okla., 1995—2003; pres. Am. Coun. Life Insurers, Washington, 2003—. Mem. Okla. Bar Assn. Republican. Office: Am Coun Life Insurers 101 Constitution Ave NW Washington DC 20001*

KEATING, MICHAEL BURNS, lawyer, educator; b. Cambridge, Mass., May 17, 1940; s. John Stuart and Anne Veronica (Burns) K.; m. Martha Harrison McGuire, OCt. 12, 1974; children: Michael Burns, Andrew Wade, Lucy Harrison. BA, Williams Coll., 1962; LLB, Harvard U., 1965. Bar: Mass. 1965, U.S. District Ct. Mass. 1966. Law clk. to presiding justice Superior Ct. Mass., Boston, 1965-66, U.S. Dist. Ct. Mass., Boston, 1966-67; assoc. Foley Hoag, Boston, 1967-74, ptnr., 1974—. Adj. prof. trial practice Northeastern Law Sch., Boston, 1985—. Trustee Brooks Sch., North Andover, Mas., 1978—, Foley, Hoag & Eliot Found., Boston, 1981-89, Williams Coll., Williamstown, Mass., 1996—; pres. Crime & Justice Found., Boston, 1985-94; bd. dirs. Navy Meml. Found., 1994—. Lt. (j.g.) USNR, 1967-72. Fellow Am. Coll. Trial Lawyers, Harvard Club; mem. Boston Bar Assn. (pres. 2001-02). Democrat. Roman Catholic. Avocations: tennis, squash, skiing, sailing. Federal civil litigation, General civil litigation, Criminal. Home: 3 W Cedar St Boston MA 02108-3535 Office: Foley Hoag 155 Seaport Blvd Boston MA 02210-2600

KEATINGE, ROBERT REED, lawyer; b. Berkeley, Calif., Apr. 22, 1948; s. Gerald Robert and Elizabeth Jean (Benedict) K.; m. Katherine Lou Carr, Feb. 1, 1969 (div. Dec. 1981); 1 child, Michael Towne; m. Cornelia Elizabeth Wyma, Aug. 21, 1982; 1 child, Courtney Elizabeth. BA, U. Colo., 1970; JD, U. Denver, 1973, LLM, 1982. Bar: Colo. 1974, U.S. Dist. Ct. Colo. 1974, U.S. Ct. Appeals (10th cir.) 1977, U.S. Tax Ct. 1980. Ptnr. Kubie & Keatinge, Denver, 1974-76; pvt. practice Denver, 1976; assoc. Richard Young, Denver, 1977-86; counsel Durham & Assoc. P.C., Denver, 1986-89, Durham & Baron, Denver, 1989-90; project editor taxation Shepard's/McGraw-Hill, Colorado Springs, Colo., 1990-96; of counsel Holland & Hart, LLP, Denver, 1992—. Lectr. law U. Denver, 1982-92, adj. prof. grad. tax program, 1983-94. Author, cons. (CD-ROM) Entity Expert, 1996; co-author: Ribstein and Keatinge on Limited Liability Companies, 1992; contbr. articles to profl. jours. and treatises. Spkr. to profl. socs. and univs. including AICPA, ALI-ABA, U. Tex., 1984—. Recipient Law Week award U. Denver Bur. Nat. Affairs, 1974. Fellow: Am. Coll. of Tax Counsel; mem.: Am. Law Inst., Denver Bar Assn., Colo. Bar Assn. (taxation sect. exec. coun. 1988—94, sec.-treas. 1991—92, chmn. 1993—94, bd. govs. 1996—, bus. law sect. sec 2001—, ethics com., corp. code revision com., co-chmn. ltd. liability co. revision com.), ABA (chmn. subcom. ltd. liability cos. of com. on partnerships 1990—95, ABA adviser to Uniform Ltd. Liability Co. Act 1995, chmn. com. on taxation 1995—99, mem. ho. of dels. 1996—2002, ABA/Nat. Conf. Commrs. on Uniform State Laws joint editl. bd. on uninc 1996—, editl. bd. ABA/BNA Lawyer's Manual on Professional Conduct 1998—2002, chmn. com. on partnerships 2000—, chair 2000—, ABA adviser to Revision of Uniform Ltd. Partnership Act 2001). Home: 460 S Marion Pky Apt 1904 Denver CO 80209-2544 E-mail: rkeatinge@hollandhart.com.

KEDDIE, ROLAND THOMAS, physician, hospital administrator, lawyer; b. Altoona, Pa., Oct. 21, 1928; s. John Barkeley and Jessie E. (Keddie) Isenberg; m. Suzanne M. Seno, Feb. 6, 1978; 1 child, Dawn Michelle; children by previous marriage: Roland, Thomas, Francis, Robert, Michael, Karen, Andrew, Rosemary. BS cum laude, U. Pitts., 1956, MD, 1957, JD, 1970. Diplomate Am. Bd. Family Practice. Bar: Pa. 1970. Intern St. Josephs Hosp., Pitts., 1958; practice medicine specializing in emergency medicine and family practice. Med. dir. Westmoreland Manor, Greensburg, Pa., 1971; dir. emergency dept. Connemaugh Valley Meml. Hosp., Johnston, Pa., 1976-77, Shadyside Hosp., Pitts., 1978-80, chmn. dept. emergency services McKeesport (Pa.) Hosp., 1980-83, dir. emergency medicine residency program; pres. EmergiCenters Inc., 1983-97; chmn. dept. family practice St. Clair Hosp., Pitts., 1990-93; pres. Emergency Med. Svcs. Inst., 1982-85; adj. prof. U. Pitts. Sch. Nursing; cons. in field. Served with USN, 1946-47, 50-52. Mem. Am. Coll. Emergency Physicians (life, bd. dirs. Pa. chpt. 1977-81, 83-86, v.p. 1980-81, pres. 1985-86), Pa. Med. Soc., Hosp. Assn. Pa. (mem. profl. practice com. 1981-82), Allegheny County Bar Assn., AMA (Physicians Recognition award 1974, 77, 80), Allegheny County Med. Soc., Pa. Emergency Health Services Council (dir. 1980), Soc. Tchrs. Emergency Medicine, Beta Beta Beta. Roman Catholic. Home and Office: 45 Meadowcrest Dr Cecil PA 15321-1118 E-mail: RTKeddie@msn.com.

KEEDY, CHRISTIAN DAVID, lawyer; b. Worcester, Mass., Jan. 9, 1945; BBA, Tulane U. La., 1967, JD, 1972. Bar: Fla. 1972; bd. cert. in admiralty and maritime law, Fla. Pvt. practice Christian D. Keedy, P.A., Coral Gables, Fla., 1981—. Mem. ABA, Maritime Law Assn. U.S., Southeastern Admiralty Law Inst. (dir. 1982-83), The Fla. Bar (chmn. 1981-82, 2003—, admiralty law com.), Miami Maritime Arbitration Coun. (dir.). Admiralty, Federal civil litigation, State civil litigation. Office: Christian D Keedy PA 7931 SW 59th Ave South Miami FL 33143-5513

KEEFFE, JOHN ARTHUR, lawyer, director; b. Bklyn., Apr. 5, 1930; s. Arthur John and Mary Catherine (Daly) K.; m. Frances Elizabeth Rippetoe, July 24, 1952; children: Virginia Frances, Cynthia Louise, Amy Marie. AB, Cornell U., 1950; JD, U. Va., 1953. Bar: Va. 1953, NY 1956. Asst. U.S. atty. so. dist. State of N.Y., 1955-57; assoc. Rogers, Hoge & Hills, N.Y., 1957-63; of counsel Havens, Wandless, Stitt & Tighe, N.Y., 1963-65; ptnr. Keeffe & Costikyan, N.Y.C. and Washington, 1965-74, Keeffe Bros., N.Y.C. and Washington, 1974-77; sec., mng. dir. Saud Al-Farhan Inc., N.Y.C., 1979-80; pres., dir. J.A. Keeffe, PC, Eastchester, NY, 1981—2000. Bd. dirs., sec. The Street Theater, White Plains, N.Y., 1973—. 1st lt. USAF, 1953-55. Mem. ABA, ATLA, N.Y. State Bar Assn., Va. Bar Assn., Westchester County Bar Assn. (dir. 1989-90, chmn. com. on fed. courthouse plans and procedures 1994-2000), N.Y. State Trial Lawyers Assn., Eastchester Bar Assn. (v.p. 1988-89, pres. 1989-90, bd. dirs. 1990-2000), Rotary (bd. dirs. 1991-2000, sec. 1991-92, pres.-elect 1992-93, pres. 1993-94, co-chair Eastchester Rotary Gift of Life 1993-94, co-chair dist. 7230 Gift of Life 1995-97). Republican. Congregationalist. Avocations: golf, reading. General civil litigation, Corporate, general, Estate planning. Home: 315A Heritage Hls Somers NY 10589-1716

KEENAN, BARBARA MILANO, judge; Judge Gen. Dist. Ct., Fairfax County, Va., 1980-82, Circuit Ct., Fairfax County, Va., 1982-85, Court of Appeals of Va., 1985-91; justice Supreme Court Va., Richmond, 1991—. Office: Ste 425 200 Golden Oak Ct Virginia Beach VA 23452-8509

KEENAN, JOHN FONTAINE, judge; b. N.Y.C., Nov. 23, 1929; s. John Joseph and Veronica (Fontaine) K.; m. Diane R. Nicholson, Oct. 6, 1956; 1 child, Marie Patricia BBA, Manhattan Coll., N.Y., 1951; LLD (hon.), Manhattan Coll., 1989; LLB, Fordham U., 1954; LLD (hon.), Mt. St. Vincent Coll., 1989. Bar: N.Y. 1954, U.S. Dist. Ct. (so. dist.) N.Y. 1983. From asst. dist. atty. to chief asst. dist. atty. N.Y. County Dist. Atty.'s Office, 1956-76; spl. prosecutor, dep. atty. gen. City of N.Y., 1976-79; chmn. bd., pres. N.Y.C. Off-Track Betting Corp., 1979-82; criminal justice coord. City of N.Y., 1982-83; judge U.S. Dist. Ct. So. Dist. N.Y., N.Y.C., 1983—; chief asst. dist. atty. Queens County Dist. Atty.'s Office, N.Y., 1973. Adj. prof. John Jay Coll. Criminal Justice, N.Y.C., 1979-83, Fordham U. Sch. Law, N.Y.C., 1992, 93; mem. Fgn. Intelligence Svc. Ct., 1994-2001, Judicial Panel on Multi-Dist. Litigation, 1998—. Contbr. articles to law jours. Chmn. Daytop Village, Inc., N.Y.C., 1981-83. Served with U.S. Army, 1954-56. Recipient Frank S. Hogan award Citizens Com. Control of Crime in N.Y., 1975, Emory R. Buckner award Federal Bar Coun., 1993; cert. of recognition Patrolmen's Benevolent Assn., 1976; 1st Ann. Hogan-Morgenthau Assocs. award N.Y. County Dist. Atty.'s Office, 1976, Medal of Achievement, 1992; Excellence award N.Y. State Bar Assn., 1978, award N.Y. Criminal Bar Assn., 1979, Disting. Faculty award Nat. Coll. Dist. Attys., 1978, Louis J. Lefkowitz award Fordham Urban Law Jour., 1983, Charles Carroll award Guild Cath. Lawyers, 1994, Ellis Island medal of honor, Nat. Ethnic Coalition of Orgns. Found., Inc., 1998. Mem.: Brehon Soc. (award 2002), Skytop Club, Amackassin Club. Republican. Roman Catholic. Office: US Dist Ct US Courthouse 500 Pearl St Rm 1930 New York NY 10007-1312

KEENE, JOHN CLARK, lawyer, educator; b. Phila., Aug. 17, 1931; s. Floyd Elwood and Marthe (Bussiere) K.; m. Ana Maria Delgado, July 21, 1973; children: Lisa Keene Kerns, John, Suzanna Tonra, Katharine, Peter; stepchildren: Carlos, René, Mario, Raúl, Silvio Navarro, Carmen Peláez. BA, Yale U., 1953; JD, Harvard U., 1959; M in City Planning, U. Pa., 1966. Bar: Pa. 1960. Assoc. Pepper, Hamilton & Scheetz, Phila., 1959-64; prof. city and regional planning U. Pa., Phila., 1968—, chmn., 1989-93, univ. ombudsman, 1978-84, chmn. faculty senate, 1998-99; ptnr. Coughlin, Keene & Assocs., Phila., 1981—2000, Keene and Assocs., Phila., 2001—; chair doctoral program in city and regional planning U. Pa., 2002—. Vis. prof. U. Paris X, 1991. Author: (with Robert E. Coughlin) The Protection of Farmland, 1981, Growth Without Chaos, 1987, (with others) Untaxing Open Space, 1976, (with Samuel Hamill) Growth Management in New Jersey, 1989, (with Robert Coughlin and Joanne Denworth) Guiding Growth: Managing Urban Grown in Pennsylvania, 1991, 93, (with Julia Freedgood) Saving American Farmland: What Works, 1997. Trustee ex officio Phila. Mus. Art, 1978-80; mem. sci. and tech. adv. com. Chesapeake Bay Program. Lt. USN, 1953-56. Fulbright fellow Tunisia, 1985. Mem. Am. Inst. Cert. Planners, Phila. Club, Merion Cricket Club. Property, real (including real estate development, water). Home: 1527 Montgomery Ave Bryn Mawr PA 19010-1659 Office: U Pa 127 Meyerson Hall Philadelphia PA 19104 E-mail: keenej@pobox.upenn.edu.

KEENE, KENNETH PAUL, lawyer; b. Torrington, Wyo., Oct. 29, 1940; s. Lyndell Franklin and Marion (Morgan) K.; m. Katherine LaHeist Keith Bell, Sept. 10, 1966 (div. May 1992); children: Elizabeth LaHeist Keene Lusby, Kenneth Paul Jr., Susan Morgan. BS, U. Nebr., 1962, JD cum laude, 1965. Bar: Nebr. 1965, Colo. 1968, Ariz. 1989. Shareholder Hecox, Tolley, Keene & Beltz, PC, Colorado Springs, Colo., 1970-94; ptnr. Rothgerber, Johnson & Lyons LLP, Colorado Springs, 1995—. Bd. dirs. Cheyenne Mountain Zoo, Colorado Springs, 1997—. Capt. JAGC, U.S. Army, 1965-69. Mem. Colo. Bar Assn., Nebr. Bar Assn., Ariz. Bar Assn., El Paso County Bar Assn. (probate sect., past pres.), Colorado Springs Estate Planning Coun. (past pres.), Cheyenne Mountain Country Club, El Paso Club, Kissing Camels Club. Republican. Estate planning, Probate (including wills, trusts), Estate taxation. Office: Rothgerber Johnson & Lyons 90 S Cascade Ave Ste 1100 Colorado Springs CO 80903-1677 E-mail: kkeene@rothgerber.com.

KEENE, LONNIE STUART, lawyer; b. Milw., Sept. 13, 1954; s. Harold William and Phyllis K. BS, U.S. Mil. Acad., 1976; MPA, Harvard U., 1984; JD, NYU, 1998. Bar: N.Y. Asst. prof., instr. U.S. Mil. Acad., West Point, N.Y., 1984-87; asst. army attache U.S. Embassy, Beijing, 1988-90; mem. policy planning staff U.S. Dept. State, Washington, 1990-94; sr. policy analyst, office sci. & tech. policy The White House, Washington, 1994-95; assoc. Linklaters, London, 1998-99, Milbank, Tweed, Hadley & McCloy, London, Hong Kong, 1999—2001, Wollmuth Maher & Deutsch, NYC, 2002; v.p., asst. gen. counsel Goldman, Sachs & Co., N.Y.C., 2002—. Lt. col. U.S. Army, 1976—95, ret. U.S. Army. Decorated Legion of Merit; Olmsted scholar George and Carol Olmsted Found., Beijing, 1981-83. Mem. Coun. Fgn. Rels. (Internat. Affairs fellow 1990-91), Harvard Club N.Y.C. Avocations: golf, art, travel, skiing. Corporate, general. Office: One New York Plz New York NY 10004 E-mail: Lonnie.Keene@gs.com.

KEENEY, JOHN CHRISTOPHER, JR., lawyer; b. Washington, Aug. 29, 1951; s. John Christopher and Eugenia M. (Brislin) K.; m. Kathleen V. Gunning; children: Katherine, Jaclyn. AB summa cum laude, U. Notre Dame, 1973; JD cum laude, Harvard U., 1976. Bar: Md. 1976, D.C. 1977, U.S. Dist. Ct. D.C. 1978, U.S. Dist. Ct. Md. 1977, U.S. Ct. Appeals (4th cir.) 1977, U.S. Ct. Appeals (D.C. cir.) 1978, U.S. Ct. Appeals (7th cir.) 1984, U.S. Ct. Appeals (10th cir.) 1989, U.S. Ct. Appeals (11th cir.) 1990, U.S. Ct. Appeals (9th cir.) 1997, U.S. Ct. Appeals (6th cir.) 1999, U.S. Supreme Ct. 1980. Law clk. to presiding judge U.S. Dist. Ct. Md., Balt., 1976-78; assoc. Hogan & Hartson, Washington, 1978-84, ptnr., 1985—. Ptnr. in charge pro bono community svcs. dept. Hogan & Hartson, Washington, 1989-93 (rated best in pro bono in U.S. by ABA, 1991); adj. instr. legal ethics Am. U. Law Sch., 2000-2002. Co-author: Civil and Criminal Remedies for Racially and Religiously Motivated Violence, 1983, 2d edit., 1999. Co-chair Dem. Nat. Lawyers Coun., 1999—; dir. Pub. Justice Ctr., Balt., 1990—95, 1997—2000; counsel for del. selection Babbitt for U.S. Pres. campaign, 1987—88; counsel Dem. credentials com., 1989—91; hearing officer Dem. Nat. Conv., 1992, 1996; chmn. Berlage for County Coun. campaign, Montgomery County, Md., 1989—94; bd. dirs. Washington Lawyers Com. for Civil Rights and Urban Affairs, 1999—. Mem. ABA (former co-chair adjudication com., Ad. Law and Regulatory Practice sect. 1999-2002), D.C. Bar (bd. govs. 2000—, exec. com., former chmn. subcom. legal needs, pub. svc. activities com., former chmn. pro bono subcom. task force on reproductive cancers, nom. pres. elect, 2003), Phi Beta Kappa. Roman Catholic. Civil rights, Federal civil litigation, Political campaigns. Home: 5516 Lincoln St West Bethesda MD 20817-3724 Office: Hogan & Hartson 555 13th St NW Ste 10W-206 Washington DC 20004-1109 E-mail: jckeeney@hhlaw.com.

KEEPHART, LYDIA FABBRO, lawyer, mediator; b. Trenton, N.J., Apr. 19, 1952; d. Leo Fabbro and Elide Agnes Romano; m. William Joseph Keephart; 1 child, Jonathan Fabbro. BA, Coll. N.J., 1973; MA, Rider U., 1978; JD, Seton Hall U., 1991; diploma in mediation, Rutgers U., Newark, 1998, Harvard U., 2000. Bar: N.J., Pa., Colo. Tchr. East Windsor Bd. Edn., Hightstown, NJ, 1973—81; test developer, program adminstr. Ednl. Testing Svc., Princeton, 1981—87; ptnr. Pellettieri, Rabstein & Altman, Princeton, 1991—. Mem. adv. bd. Fleet Bank Boston, NJ, 1995—, St. Lawrence & Morris Hall, NJ, 1999—. Mem.: ABA, N.J. Bar Assn., Pa. Bar Assn., Colo. Bar Assn., Green Acres Country Club. Family and matrimonial, General practice. Office: Pellettieri Rabstein and Altman 100 Nassau Park Blvd Ste 111 Princeton NJ 08540 Office Fax: 609-452-8796. Business E-Mail: lkeephart@pralaw.com.

KEESLING, KAREN RUTH, lawyer; b. Wichita, Kans., July 9, 1946; d. Paul W. and Ruth (Sharp) Keesling. BA, Ariz. State U., 1968, MA, 1970; JD, Georgetown U., 1981. Bar: Va. 1981, Fla. 1981. Asst. dean of women U. Kans., Lawrence, 1970-72; exec. sec. , sec.'s adv. com. on rights and responsibilities of women HEW, Washington, 1972-74; dir. White House Office of Women's Programs, Washington, 1974-77; head civil rights and equal opportunity sect., Gov. Div., Congl. Rsch. Svc. Libr. Congress, Washington, 1977-80; legis. aide Sen. Nancy Kassebaum, Washington, 1979-81; mem. pers. office staff Office of Pres.-elect, Washington, Jan. 1981; pvt. practice Falls Church, Va. and Peoria, Ariz., 1981-88, 90—; dept. for equal opportunity dept. Dept. Air Force, Washington, 1981-82, dep. asst. sec. manpower res. affairs and installations, 1982-83, prin. dep. asst. sec. manpower res. affairs, 1983-87, prin. dep. asst. sec. readiness support dept., 1987-88, prin. dep. asst. sec. manpower and res. affairs, 1988, asst. sec. manpower and res. affairs, 1988-89; acting wage and hour adminstr. U.S. Dept. Labor, Washington, 1992-93; pvt. practice Falls Church, Va., Peoria, Ariz. Bd. advisers Outstanding Young Women Am., 1983—90. Mem. Nat. Women's Polit. Caucus, Washington, 1980, Nat. Fedn. Rep. Women's Club, Washington, 1975; chair pers. com. Faith Presbyn. Ch., 2000—. Named One of Ten Outstanding Young Women of Am., 1975; recipient Alumni Achievement award, Ariz. State U., 1976, Elizabeth Boyer award, Women's Equity Action League, 1986, Meritorious Civilian award, USAF, 1987, Woman of Distinction award, Nat. Conf. Coll. Women, Student Leaders and Women of Distinction, 1988, Exceptional Civilian Svc. award, USAF, 1988. Mem.: Va. Bus. and Profl. Women's Found. (trustee 1985—93), The Women's Inst. Inc. (adv. coun. 1985—96), No. Va. Women atty.'s Assn. (steering com. 1990—95), Va. Fedn. Bus. and Profl. Women's Clubs (2d v.p. 1987—88, 1st v.p. 1988—89, pres.-elect 1989—90, pres. 1990—91), Fla. Bar Assn., Va. Bar Assn., Ariz. Bar Assn., P.E.O., U.S. Com. for UNIFEM (gen. counsel 1983—), Pi Beta Phi. Avocation: Avocation: golf (Kans. Women's Golf Champion 1966, Wichita Women's Champion 1968, 70, Outstanding Woman Golfer in Kans. 1966). Home: 9606 W Lindgren Ave Sun City AZ 85373 E-mail: Keeslingkr@aol.com.

KEETON, ROBERT ERNEST, federal judge; b. Clarksville, Tex., Dec. 16, 1919; s. William Robert and Ernestine (Tuten) K.; m. Elizabeth E. Baker, May 28, 1941; children: Katherine, William Robert. BBA, U. Tex., 1940, LLB, 1941; SJD, Harvard U., 1956; LLD (hon.), William Mitchell Coll., 1983, Lewis and Clark Coll., 1988. Bar: Tex. 1941, Mass. 1955. Assoc. firm Baker, Botts, Andrews & Wharton (and successors), Houston, 1941-42, 45-51; assoc. prof. law So. Meth. U., 1951-54; Thayer teaching fellow Harvard U., 1953-54, asst. prof., 1954-56, prof. law, 1956-73, Langdell prof., 1973-79; assoc. dean Harvard, 1975-79; judge Fed. Dist. Ct., Boston, 1979—. Commr. on Uniform State Laws from Mass., 1971-79; trustee Flaschner Jud. Inst., 1979-86; exec. dir. Nat. Inst. Trial Advocacy, 1973-76; ednl. cons., 1976-79; mem. com. on ct. adminstrn. U.S. Jud. Conf., 1985-87, mem. standing com. on rules, 1987-90, chmn., 1990-93. Author: Trial Tactics and Methods, 1954, 2d edit., 1973, Cases and Materials on the Law of Insurance, 1960, 2d edit., 1977, Legal Cause in the Law of Torts, 1963, Venturing To Do Justice, 1969, (with Jeffrey O'Connell) Basic Protection for the Traffic Victim: A Blueprint for Reforming Automobile Insurance, 1965, After Cars Crash: The Need for Legal and Insurance Reform, 1967, (with Page Keeton) Cases and Materials on the Law of Torts, 1971, 2d edit., 1977, Basic Text on Insurance Law, 1971, (with others) Tort and Accident Law, 1983, 2d edit., 1989, (with others) Prosser & Keeton, Torts, 5th edit., 1984, Pocket Part, 1988, (with Alan Widiss) Insurance Law, 1988, Judging, 1990, Judging the American Legal System, 1999, Guidelines for Drafting, Editing, and Interpreting, 2002; also articles. Served to lt. comdr. USNR, 1942-45, PTO, 1945-56. Recipient Wm. B. Jones award Nat. Inst. Trial Advocacy, 1980; recipient Leon Green award U. Tex. Law Rev., 1981, Francis Rawle award Am. Law Inst.-ABA, 1983, Samuel E. Gates litigation award Am. Coll. Trial Lawyers, 1984 Fellow Am. Bar Found., mem., Am. Acad. Arts and Scis., Am. Bar Assn., Mass. Bar Assn., State Bar Tex., Am. Law Inst., Am. Risk and Ins. Assn., Chancellors, Friars, Order of Coif, Beta Gamma Sigma, Beta Alpha Psi, Phi Delta Phi, Phi Eta Sigma. Office: US Dist Ct 1 Courthouse Way Ste 3130 Boston MA 02210-3005

KEGEL, GERHARD, retired law educator; b. Magdeburg, Germany, June 26, 1912; s. Martin and Wilhelmine (Schönbach) K.; m. Irmgard Vethake, Jan. 2, 1940; children: Irmelis, Charlotte, Marianne, Joachim. Dr.iur., U. Berlin, 1936, U. Mannheim, Germany, 1983; Prof. (hon.) , U. Rosario, Bogota, Colombia, 1983. Asst. Kaiser Wilhelm Inst. Fgn. and Internat. Pvt. Law Berlin, 1936-45; lectr. U. Cologne, Germany, 1946—50, prof. law, 1950—78; prof. emeritus U. Cologne (Fed. Republic Germany), 1978—. Author: Soergel Commentary Civil Code, Vol. X, 1996, Internationales Privatrecht, 2000, Vertrag und Delikt, 2002. Lst lt. arty. German Army, 1941-45. Decorated Gt. Cross of Merit (Fed. Republic Germany); recipient citation U. Calif., Berkeley, 1981. Home: Am Steinrausch 3 D-5533 Hillesheim Germany Office: Gottfried-Keller-Strasse 2 D-5000 Cologne Germany

KEHOE, TERRENCE EDWARD, lawyer; b. Washington, June 21, 1955; s. Edward Thomas and Dorothy (Dunbar) K.; m. Priscilla Joan O'Brien, Nov. 24, 1984; children: Ryan Edward, Brendan Charles. BA, U. N.C., 1976; JD, Georgetown U., 1981. Bar: Fla. 1981, U.S. Supreme Ct. 1987; bd. cert. criminal appellate lawyer. Assoc. James M. Russ P.A., Orlando, Fla., 1981-85, Haas Boehm Brown Rigdon Seacrest & Fischer P.A., Orlando, 1985-88; pvt. practice Orlando, 1988—. Mem. Nat. Assn. Criminal Def. Lawyers, Fla. Assn. Criminal Def. Lawyers. Appellate, Criminal. Home: 1911 Ivanhoe Rd Orlando FL 32804-5938 Office: 18 W Pine St Orlando FL 32801-2612 E-mail: tekehoelaw@aol.com.

KEHOE, WILLIAM FRANCIS, lawyer; b. Stoneham, Mass., Dec. 3, 1933; s. William Andrew and Josephine Agnes (Crowley) K.; m. Dorothy Landry Kehoe; children by previous marriage: John William, Kathleen Emily. AB summa cum laude, Dartmouth Coll., 1955; MA, Yale U., 1956; LLB, Harvard U., 1963. Bar: Mass. 1963, U.S. Dist. Ct. Mass. 1964. Instr. English Middlebury (Vt.) Coll., 1956-57; ptnr. Gaston & Snow, Boston, 1970-91; counsel Hutchins, Wheeler & Dittmar, Boston, 1991-94, Taylor, Ganson & Perrin, Boston, 1995—. Mng. trustee Katharine L.W. and Winthrop Murray Crane, 3d Charitable Found.; mem. standing adv. com. on rules of civil procedure Supreme Jud. Ct.; lectr., panelist Mass. Continuing Legal Edn. Program and Mass. Jud. Inst. Author: Enjoying Ireland, 1966; contbr. articles and revs. to profl. jours. Served with U.S. Army, 1957-59. Fulbright scholar, Trinity Coll., Dublin, Ireland, 1959-60. Fellow Am. Coll. Trust and Estate Counsel; mem. Boston Bar Assn., Phi Beta Kappa. Office: Taylor Ganson & Perrin 160 Federal St Fl 20 Boston MA 02110-1722

KEINER, CHRISTIAN MARK, lawyer; b. Omaha, Mar. 16, 1953; s. John Frederick Keiner and Geraldine Elizabeth (Smith) Eadie; m. Rosemary Monique White, Nov. 21, 1980; 1 child, Colin MacGregor. BA with high honors, U. Calif., Santa Barbara, 1977; JD with distinction, U. of Pacific, 1980. Bar: Calif. 1980, U.S. Ct. Appeals (9th cir.) 1988, U.S. Supreme Ct. 1991. Assoc. Biddle, Walters, Bukey, Sacramento, 1980-82, Biddle and Hamilton, Sacramento, 1982-92; pvt. practice, Sacramento, 1992-98; ptnr. Girard and Vinson, Sacramento, 1998—. Contbr. articles to law jours. Bd. dirs. Calif. Found. for Improvement Employer-Employee Rels., Sacramento, 1994-99, Calif. Coun. Sch. Attys., Sacramento, 1996-98; instr., mem. labor-mgmt. adv. com. U. Calif. Davis Ext., Sacramento, 1986-99. Recipient award for adminstrv. law Am. Jurisprudence, 1979. Mem. ABA (pub. law sect.), Sacramento County Bar, Harry S. Truman Club (pres. 1992), Order of Coif. Democrat. Roman Catholic. Administrative and regulatory, Appellate, Education and schools. Office: Girard and Vinson 1006 4th St 8th Fl Sacramento CA 95814-3326 E-mail: keiner@gandv.com.

KEINER, R(OBERT) BRUCE, JR., lawyer; b. Washington, July 12, 1942; s. R. Bruce and Alice Miriam (Draeger) K.; m. Suellen Terrill, June 15, 1968; children: Scott, Grant, Terrill. BA, Dickinson Coll., 1964; LLB, U. Va., 1967. Bar: D.C. 1968, U.S. Supreme Ct. 1980. Assoc. to ptnr. Jones, Day, Reavis & Pogue, Washington, 1970-79; ptnr. Crowell & Moring, Washington, 1979—; pres. Internat. Aviation Club of Washington, 1995. Pres., bd. trustees Maret Sch., 2000—. Capt. U.S. Army, 1968-69. Mem.: Internat. Aviation Club Washington (pres. 1995). Aviation, Private international, Transportation. Home: 1730 Crestwood Dr NW Washington DC 20011-5334 Office: Crowell & Moring 1001 Pennsylvania Ave NW Fl 10 Washington DC 20004-2595 E-mail: rbkeiner@crowell.com.

KEINER, SUELLEN TERRILL, lawyer; b. Cin., Sept. 29, 1944; d. William A. and Lois (Hamilton) Terrill; m. R. Bruce Keiner Jr., June 15, 1968; children: Scott, Grant, Terrill. Student, Inst. Polit. Studies, Paris, 1964-65; BA, Bryn Mawr Coll., 1966; JD, Georgetown U., 1971. Bar: D.C. 1971, U.S. Supreme Ct. 1975. Fgn. documents analyst CIA, Washington, 1966-67; rsch. analyst Civil Rights divsn. U.S. Dept. Justice, Washington, 1968, 70; law clk. Weyerhaeuser Co., Tacoma, 1968-69, D.C. Superior Ct., Washington, 1971; atty. Terris & Assocs., Washington, 1972-78; asst. solicitor U.S. Dept. Interior, Washington, 1978-81; cons. for natural resources mgmt. Coun. of State Planning Agys., Washington, 1982-84; dir. litigation project Environ. Policy Inst., Washington, 1984-86; dir. program on environ. governance and mgmt. Environ. Law Inst., Washington, 1988-2000; dir. Ctr. for Economy and Environment Nat. Acad. Pub. Adminstrn., Washington, 2000—. Pres. Crestwood Citizens Assn., Washington, 1982-84. Environmental. Office: Nat Acad of Pub Adminstrn Ste 1090 E 1100 New York Ave NW Washington DC 20005

KEISERUD, ERIK, lawyer; b. Oslo, Mar. 20, 1945; s. Egil and Anne Merete Keiserud; m. Anne Seljsestad Keiserud, Apr. 11, 1945; children: Thomas, Martin, Jørgen. Degree in Law, U. Oslo; Degree in Comparative Law, U. Cambridge, Eng. Cert.: Supreme Ct. (advocate) 1988. Dept. dir. Ministry Justice, Oslo, 1971—86; adv. with atty. gen. Oslo, 1986—89; ptnr. Hjort Law Firm, Oslo, 1989—. Chmn. pub. adminstrn. Uni Storebrand, Oslo, 1992—93; chmn. Govt. Bank Investment Fund, Oslo, 1998—, Norway's Land Info., Oslo, 1999—. Co-author: Commentary on Criminal Procedure Act, 2001. General civil litigation, Commercial, contracts (including sales of goods; commercial financing), General practice. Office: Hjort Law Firm PB 471 Sentrum 0105 Oslo Norway Home: Lonnasen 5 1362 Hosle Norway

KEITH, ALEXANDER MACDONALD, retired state supreme court chief justice, lawyer; b. Rochester, Minn., Nov. 22, 1928; s. Norman and Edna (Alexander) K.; m. Marion Sanford, April 29, 1955; children: Peter Sanford (dec.), Ian Alexander, Douglas Scott. BA, Amherst Coll., 1950; JD, Yale U., 1953. Assoc. counsel, mem. Mayo Clinic, Rochester, 1955-60; state sen. Olmstead County, St. Paul, 1959-63; lt. gov. State of Minn., St. Paul, 1963-67; pvt. practice, Rochester, 1960-73; ptnr. Dunlap Keith Finseth Berndt and Sandberg, Rochester, 1973-89; assoc. justice Minn. Supreme Ct., St. Paul, 1989-90, chief justice, 1990-98; ret., 1998; of counsel Dunlap & Seeger P.A., Rochester, Minn., 1998—. Sen. del. White House Conf. on Aging, Washington, 1960; U.S. del. UN Delegation for Funding Developing Countries, Geneva, 1966; bd. dirs. Rochester Grad. Edn. Adv. Com., 1988-89, Ability Bldg. Ctr. Inc. 1st lt. USMC, 1953-55, Korea. Named Outstanding Freshman Senator, Minn. Senate, St. Paul. Home: 5225 Meadow Crossing Rd SW Rochester MN 55902-3506 Office: Dunlap & Seeger PA PO Box 549 Rochester MN 55903-0549 Fax: 507-288-9342.*

KEITH, JOHN A.C. lawyer; b. Washington, Aug. 22, 1946; BA, U. Va., 1968, JD, 1974. Bar: Va. 1975, D.C. 1976. Law clk. Hon. Albert V. Bryan, Jr. U.S. Dist. Ct. (ea. dist.) Va., 1974-75; ptnr. Blankingship & Keith, Fairfax, Va. Fellow Am. Bar Found.; mem. ABA, Am. Counsel Assn., Va. State Bar (10th dist. com. 1983-86, chmn. 1985-86, chmn. standing com. on legal ethics 1996-97, bar coun. 1991—, exec. com. 1993—, pres.-elect 1997-98, pres. 1998—), Fairfax Bar Assn. General civil litigation, Personal injury (including property damage), Property, real (including real estate development, water). Office: Blankingship & Keith PC 4020 University Dr Ste 312 Fairfax VA 22030-6802 E-mail: JKeith@blankeith.com.

KEITHLEY, BRADFORD GENE, lawyer; b. Nov. 23, 1951; s. Sanderson Irish and Joan G. (Kenneday) K.; m. Ginger W. Wilhelmi, Mar. 26, 1994; children: Paul Michael, Rachel Austin Bernstein. BS, U. Tulsa, 1973; JD, U. Va., 1976. Bar: Va. 1976, Okla. 1978, D.C. 1979. Atty. Office of Gen. Counsel to Sec. USAF, Washington, 1976-78; ptnr. Hall, Estill, Hardwick, Gable, Collingsworth and Nelson, Tulsa, 1978-84; sr. v.p. gen. counsel natural gas divsn. Arkla, Inc. (now CenterPoint Energy, Inc.), Shreveport, La., 1984—90; ptnr. co-head global oil and gas practice team Jones Day, Dallas, 1990—. Mem. ABA, Fed. Energy Bar Assn., Va. State Bar, Okla. Bar Assn., D.C. Bar Assn., Am. Gas Assn. (mem. legal sect.), Dallas Petroleum Club. Federal civil litigation, FERC practice, Oil, gas, and mineral. Home: 12652 Sunlight Dr Dallas TX 75230-1856 Office: Jones Day 2727 N Harwood Dallas TX 75201-1515

KEITHLEY, ROGER LEE, judge; b. Macomb, Ill., July 19, 1946; s. Gilbert Lee and Mary Jane (Torrance) K.; m. Karen Sue Metzger, Apr. 1, 1973; children: Roger Livingston, Terrance Christopher, Kathryn Suzanne. BS, U. Ill., 1968; JD, Harvard U., 1973. Bar: Colo. 1973, U.S. Dist. Ct. Colo. 1973, U.S. Ct. Appeals (10th cir.) 1976. Law clk. to justice Colo. Supreme Ct., Denver, 1973-74; trial atty. SEC, Denver, 1974-76; assoc. Morrato, Gueck & Colantuno, Denver, 1976-80; ptnr. Krys, Boyle, Golz & Keithley, Denver, 1980-86, Law, Knous & Keithley, Denver, 1986-90, Law, Keithley & Tuttle, Denver, 1990-93; pvt. practice Roger L. Keithley, P.C., Denver, 1993-98; presiding disciplinary judge Colo. Supreme Ct., 1998—. Prof. physics U. Asmara, Eritrea, Ethiopia, 1969-70. With U.S. Army, 1968-70. Mem.: ABA, Am. Law Inst., Denver Bar Asn., Colo. Bar Assn. Home: 5239 E 17th Ave Denver CO 80220-1313 E-mail: rlkeithley@aol.com.

KELAHER, JAMES PEIRCE, lawyer; b. Orlando, Fla., Oct. 28, 1951; s. Philip James and Neva Cecelia (Peirce) K. BA, U. Cen. Fla., 1973; JD, Fla. State U., 1981. Bar: Fla. 1981, U.S. Dist. Ct. (mid. dist.) Fla. 1982, U.S. Ct. Appeals (11th cir.) 1983, U.S. Supreme Ct.; cert. civil trial law. Assoc. Law Office of Nolan Carter, P.A., Orlando, 1981-83, Law Office of James Kelaher, P.A., Orlando, 1983-87; ptnr. Kelaher & Wieland, P.A., Orlando, 1987—, Kelaher, Wieland and Hilado, P.A., Orlando, 1996-98, Kelaher Law Offices, P.A., Orlando, 1998—. Contbr. articles to profl. jours. Eagle benefactor Rep. Party. Mem. ABA, ATLA (sustaining), Orange County Bar Assn., Acad. Fla. Trial Lawyers (sec. 1994-95, treas. 1995-96, pres. 1997-98, bd. dirs. coll. diplomates, membership exec. com. bd. trustees Fla. lawyers action group), Ctrl. Fla. Trial Lawyers Assn. (pres. 1992-94). Roman Catholic. Avocations: tennis, golf, snow skiing, fishing. General civil litigation, Personal injury (including property damage). Office: Kelaher Law Offices 800 N Magnolia Ave Ste 1301 Orlando FL 32803-3255 E-mail: jim@kelaherlaw.com.

KELEHEAR, CAROLE MARCHBANKS SPANN, senior legal secretary; b. Morehead City, N.C., Oct. 2, 1945; d. William Blythe and Gladys Ophelia (Wilson) Marchbanks; m. Henry M. Spann, June 5, 1966 (div. 1978); children: Lisa Carole, Elaine Mabry; m. Zachariah Lockwood Kelehear, Sept. 15, 1985. Student, Winthrop Coll., 1963-64; grad., Draughon's Bus. Coll., 1965; cert. in med. terminology, Greenville Tech. Edn. Coll., 1972; grad., Millie Lewis Modeling Sch. Office mgr. S.C. Appalachian Adv. Commn., Greenville, 1965-68, Wood-Bergheer & Co., Newport Beach and Palm Springs, Calif., 1970-72; asst. to Dr. J. Ernest Lathem Lathem & McCoy, P.A., Greenville, 1972-75; asst. to Gov. Robert E. McNair, McNair, Konduros, Corley, Singletary and Dibble Law Firm, Columbia, S.C., 1975-77; office mgr. Dr. James B. Knowles, Greenville, 1977-78, Constangy, Brooks & Smith, Columbia, 1978-83; legal asst. to sr. ptnr. William L. Bethea Jr., Bethea, Jordan & Griffin, P.A., Hilton Head Island, 1983—88; legal asst. Rajko D. Medenica, MD, PhD, 1988—95; adminstr. Dibble Law Offices, Columbia, 1995-96; sr. legal sec. Haynsworth Sinkler Boyd, P.A., Columbia, 1997—. Notary pub.; vol. Ladies aux. Greenville Gen. Hosp., 1966-72, South Coast Hosp., Laguna Beach, Calif., 1973, St. Francis Hosp, Greenville, 1974-76, Hilton Head Hosp., 1983-92. Mem. Hilton Head Hosp. Aux., Profl. Women's Assn. Hilton Head Island, Am. Bus. Women's Assn., Nat. Assn. Female Execs., Am. Soc. Notaries, Beta Sigma Phi.

KELEHER, MICHAEL LAWRENCE, lawyer; b. Albuquerque, Sept. 21, 1934; s. William A. Keleher and Loretta Barrett; m. Margaret Anne Wills, June 10, 1961; children: Anne Barrett, Elizabeth Katherine, Margaret Mary, Mary Ann, Loretta Wills, Michael Wills. BA, U. N. Mex., 1956; MA, NYU, 1958; JD, U. Miss., 1962. Bar: N.Mex. 1962. Atty. Keleher & McLeod PA, Albuquerque, 1962—2001, of counsel, 2001—. Mem. N.Mex. Old Lincoln County Meml. Commn., 1969—76; chmn. N.Mex. Diamond Jubilee/U.S. constl. Bicentennial Commn., 1986—89; bd. dirs. Bernalillo County unit Am. Cancer Soc., 1966—74, pres., 1969—70; mem. Albuquerque Environ. Planning Commn., 1973—75, chair land controls bd., 1974—75; mem. Shared Vision, Inc., 1994—98; trustee U. Albuquerque, 1970—78, sec., 1974—78; chair N.Mex. State U. Rio Grande Hist. Collectors, 1978—79; chmn. Archdiocese Santa Fe Devel. Coun., 1990—93; v.p. Archdiocese Santa Fe Cath. Found., 1991—2003, pres., 1997—99; spiritial affiliate Order of Friars Minor; pres. Guadalupe Inst.; bd. dirs. Robert O. Anderson Schs. Mgmt. Found., 1995—99. Lt. (j.g.) USNR, 1956—58. Mem.: ABA, N.Mex. Bar Assn., U. N.Mex. Alumni Lettermen's Assn., Phi Theta Phi, Sigma Chi. Democrat. Roman Catholic. Estate planning, Probate (including wills, trusts), Property, real (including real estate development, water). Office: Keleher & McLeod PA 201 3rd St NW Albuquerque NM 87102-3370 E-mail: mlk@keleher-law.com.

KELL, SCOTT K. lawyer; b. Lake Worth, Fla., Jan. 11, 1928; s. Scott Kell and Frances (Aborn) Jefferson; m. Virginia Kell, Sept. 30, 1990. BA, Ill. Wesleyan U., 1953; student, U. Ill., 1953—54; JD, Lincoln Coll. Law, 1953. Bar: Ill. 1953, Ohio 1963, Mo. 1967. Pvt. practice, Montgomery City, Mo., 1967—, Hermann and Montgomery City, Mo., 1997—. Mem. Assn. Trial Lawyers Am., Mo. Bar Assn., St. Louis Met. Bar Assn. Family and matrimonial, Personal injury (including property damage), Workers' compensation. Office Fax: 573-564-1500. E-mail: kellaw@ktis.net.

KELL, VETTE EUGENE, retired lawyer; b. Marengo, Iowa, Oct. 17, 1915; s. Eugene S. and Florence (Vette) K.; m. Alice Eaton, Sept. 3, 1938; 1 child, Michael V. JD, U. Iowa, 1940. Bar: Iowa 1940, Ill. 1948. Ptnr. Joslyn, Parker & Kell, Woodstock, Ill., 1948-67, Kell, Conerty & Poehlmann, Woodstock, 1967-84; sr. ptnr. Kell, Nuelle & Loizzo, Woodstock, 1985-97; ret., 1997. Lectr. Ill. Continuing Edn. Inst. Lt. USN, 1943-45, PTO. Mem. Ill. Bar Assn., Soc. Trial Lawyers, Am. Coll. Trial Lawyers, Internat. Coll. Trial Lawyers. Episcopalian.

KELLEHER, DANIEL FRANCIS, lawyer; b. Wilmington, Del., May 8, 1935; s. Harry James and Marjorie (Lancaster) K.; children: Hillary, Brendan, Peter; m. Jane Mignanelli, Dec. 27, 1991. AB, St. Marys Sem. and U., 1958; LLB, Georgetown U., 1961. Bar: D.C. 1962, Del. 1962. Ptnr. Theisen, Lank & Kelleher, Wilmington, 1962-72; assoc. judge Del. Family Ct., 1972-78; ptnr. Trzuskowski, Kipp & Kelleher PA, Wilmington, 1978—. Atty. Del. State Senate, 1967-68. Bd. dirs. YMCA, 1974-81; active Del. Alcoholism Coun., 1974-81, pres., 1977-80; bd. dirs. Beechwood Sch., 1973-80, pres., 1975-80; trustee, chmn. Del. Childrens Trust Fund, 1985-02. Mem. ABA, Del. State Bar Assn., Am. Judicature Soc., Nat. Coun. Juvenile Ct. Judges, Greenville Country Club (Wilmington, v.p. 1980-82). Roman Catholic. Family and matrimonial, General practice, Personal injury (including property damage). Address: PO Box 429 Wilmington DE 19899-0429 E-mail: dkelleher@tkkp.com.

KELLEHER, ROBERT JOSEPH, judge; b. N.Y.C., Mar. 5, 1913; s. Frank and Mary (Donovan) K.; m. Gracyn W. Wheeler, Aug. 14, 1940; children: R. Jeffrey, Karen Kathleen Kelleher King. AB, Williams Coll., 1935; LL.B., Harvard U., 1938. Bar: N.Y. 1939, Calif. 1942, U.S. Supreme Ct 1954. Atty. War Dept., 1941-42; asst. U.S. atty. So. Dist. Calif., 1948-50; pvt. practice Beverly Hills, 1951-71; U.S. dist. judge, 1971-83; sr. judge U.S. Dist. Ct. 9th Cir., 1983—. Mem. So. Calif. Com. Olympic Games, 1964; capt. U.S. Davis Cup Team, 1962-63; treas. Youth Tennis Found. So. Calif., 1961-64. Served to lt. USNR, 1942-45. Recipient Bicentennial Medal award Williams Coll., 2001; enshrined in Internat. Tennis Hall of Fame, 2000. Mem. So. Calif. Tennis Assn. (v.p. 1958-64, pres. 1983-85), U.S. Lawn Tennis Assn. (pres. 1967-68), Internat. Lawn Tennis Club

U.S.A., Gt. Britain, France, Can., Mex., Australia, India, Israel, Japan, All Eng. Lawn Tennis and Croquet (Wimbledon), Harvard Club (N.Y./So. Calif.), Williams Club (N.Y.), L.A. Country Club, Delta Kappa Epsilon. Home: 2311 Roscomare Rd #5 Los Angeles CA 90077 Office: US Dist Ct 255 E Temple St Ste 830 Los Angeles CA 90012-3334

KELLER, BRENDA ANN SCHRADER, lawyer; b. Corpus Christi, Tex., Jan. 31, 1952; d. Bernard William and Barbara Ann (Freeman) Schrader; m. James Allen Keller, Feb. 2, 1974. BBA, S.W. Tex. State U., 1973; JD, U. Houston, 1981. Bar: Tex. 1981. Mgr. br. office Gibraltar Savs. Assn., Houston, 1974-78; probate trust officer Tex. Commerce Bank, Houston, 1981-84; staff atty., ct. coord. Harris County Probate Ct. 4, Houston, 1985—. Contbg. author Disability & Elder Law Attys. Assn. Practice Manual, 1991. Discussion leader Bible Study Fellowship, Houston, 1987-94. Fellow Houston Bar Found.; mem. Houston Bar Assn., Coll. State Bar Tex.. Women Attys. in Tax and Probate (pres. 1997-98). Republican. Baptist. Office: Harris County Probate Ct 4 1115 Congress St Fl 5 Houston TX 77002-1927

KELLER, JAMES, state supreme court justice; b. Harlan, 1942; m. Elizabeth Keller; 2 children. Student, Ea. Ky. U.; JD, U. Ky. Pvt. practice; master commr. Fayette Cir. Ct., 1969-76, judge, 1976-99; justice Ky. Supreme Ct., 1999—. Mem. Ky. Bar Assn., Fayette County Bar Assn. Office: Supreme Ct Ky 155 E Main St Ste 200 Lexington KY 40507-1332 E-mail: JamesKeller@mail.aoc.state.ky.us.

KELLER, JANICE N. lawyer, councilwoman; b. L.A., Nov. 29, 1947; d. Max B. and Ruth (Dobris) Musicer. BA, U. Calif., Santa Barbara, 1969; JD, U. Pacific, 1984. Bar: Calif. 1986; cert. C.C. tchg. Campaign cons. various candidates, Santa Barbara, 1978—88; mng. atty. Legal Aid Found., Lompoc, 1988—91; dep. pub. defender Santa Barbara County, Santa Maria, Calif., 1991—; councilwoman City of Lompoc, Calif., 1998—. Instr. Allan Hancock C.C., Lompoc, 1989—98. Environ. rev. commr. City of Santa Barbara, 1985—88; human svcs. commr. City of Lompoc, 1991—92, planning commr., 1992—98. Recipient Cmty. Svc. award, Citizens Planning Found., 2001, Sadie West Pub. Servant award, No. Santa Barbara County Women's Polit. Com., 2001, Cert. Congl. Recognition, U.S. Congress, 2001. Mem.: No. Santa Barbara County Bar Assn. Avocations: photography, travel. Home: PO Box 504 Lompoc CA 93438

KELLER, JOHN WARREN, lawyer; b. Niagara Falls, Aug. 6, 1954; s. Joseph and Edith Lilian (Kilvington) K.; m. Sandra D. Hubbard, Dec. 18, 1981; children: Sean, Christopher. BA, Rider U., 1976; JD, Coll. William and Mary, 1979. Bar: Ky. 1980. Staff atty. Appalachian Rsch. & Def. Fund Ky., Inc., Barbourville, 1979-82; assoc. F. Preston Farmer Law Offices, London, Ky., 1982-88; ptnr. Farmer, Keller & Kelley, London, 1988-91, Taylor, Keller & Dunaway, London, 1991—. Mem. Fla. Adv. Com. on Arson Prevention, 1990—; chair bd. dirs. Appalachian Rsch. & Def. Fund Ky., 1994-96; founder, chmn. bd. dirs. Ky. Lawyers for Legal Svcs. to the Poor; mem. editl. adv. bd. Ky. West Publ. Group, 1997. Contbg. editor: ABA Annotations to Homeowner's Policy, 3rd edit., 1995, ABA Bad Faith Annotations, 2d edit., 2001. Pres. Access to Justice Found., 1996—; bd. dirs. Christian Ch. in Ky., 1994—98; elder First Christian Ch., London, 1994—97, 2002—, chmn. bd. elders, 2002—. Recipient Access to Justice award Ky. Legal Svcs. Programs, 1995, Outstanding Svc. award Ky. chpt. Nat. Soc. Profl. Ins. Investigators, 2000. Fellow: Ky. Bar Found. (bd. dirs. 2000—); mem.: ABA (vice chair property ins. law com. 1992—97), Nat. Soc. Profl. Ins. Investigators (bd. govs. 2001—, 2d v.p. 2002—), Laurel County Bar Assn. (pres. 1992—93), Ky. Bar Assn. (bd. govs. 1996—2002, Donated Legal Svcs. award 2001), The Honorable Order of Ky. Cols. General civil litigation, Insurance. Office: Taylor Keller & Dunaway 1306 W 5th St London KY 40741-1615 E-mail: wkeller@tkdlaw.com.

KELLER, JUAN DANE, lawyer; b. Cape Girardeau, Mo., Jan. 30, 1943; s. Irvin A. and Mercedes (Crippen) K.; m. Sandra Anne Solomon; children: Mary, John, Katharine, Robert, Michael, Cassandra. AB in History, U. Mo., l965, JD, l967; LLM, Georgetown U., 197l. Bar: Mo. Assoc. Bryan, Cave, St. Louis, 1971-78, ptnr., 1979—. Contbg. author: Missouri Bar Taxation Handbook, 1988-95. Capt. JAGC, U.S. Army, 1967-71. Mem. ABA, Mo. Bar (tax com. 1971—), Met. St. Louis Bar Assn., Order of Coif. Methodist. Corporate taxation, Taxation, general, State and local taxation. Office: Bryan Cave 1 Metropolitan Sq Ste 3600 Saint Louis MO 63102-2750 E-mail: jkeller@bryancave.com.

KELLER, MARILYN B. lawyer; b. Covina, Calif., Nov. 20, 1964; m. John Patrick Keller, Oct. 8, 1988; children: Thomas P., Elizabeth A., Mary Christine, William J. BS in Acctg., William Jewell Coll., Liberty, Mo., 1986; JD, U. of Mo.- Kans. City, 1991. Bar: Mo. 1991, U.S. Dist. Ct. (we. dist.) Mo. 1991, U.S. Ct. Appeals (8th cir.) 1991, Kans. 1992, U.S. Dist. Ct. Kans. 1992. Assoc. Wyrsch Hobbs & Mirakian, P.C., Kansas City, Mo., 1991—. Criminal. Office: Wyrsch Hobbs & Mirakian PC 1101 Walnut Ste 1300 Kansas City MO 64106 Office Fax: 816-221-3280. E-mail: mbkeller@whmlaw.net.

KELLER, SHARON FAYE, judge; Presiding judge Tex. Ct. Criminal Appeals. Office: Tex Ct Criminal Appeals PO Box 12308 Austin TX 78711-2308

KELLER, STANLEY, lawyer; b. N.Y.C., Aug. 16, 1938; s. Irving S. and Ceil (Silverstein) K.; m. Sandra Freshman, Dec. 25, 1960; children: Andrew J., Eric L., Matthew A. AB, Columbia U., 1959; LLB, Harvard U., 1962. Bar: Mass. 1962. Assoc. Palmer & Dodge LLP, Boston, 1962-68, ptnr., 1969—. Lectr. Boston U. Law Sch., 1969-79; treas., trustee Mass. Continuing Legal Edn., Inc., Boston, 1985-91; panelist continuing legal edn. programs for profl. orgns. Chmn. legal sect. United Way of Boston, 1982. Fellow Am. Bar Found., Mass. Bar Found.; mem. ABA (chair fed. regulation of securities com.), Mass. Bar Assn. (chmn. bus. law sect. 1983-85), Boston Bar Assn. (chmn. corp. law com. 1988-89, chmn. bus. law sect. 1989-91, co-chair legal opinions com. 1992-95, co-chair com. to revise Mass. Bus. Corp. Law 1992—), Tri Bar Opinion Com. Jewish. Corporate, general, Finance, Securities. Office: Palmer & Dodge LLP 111 Huntington Ave Boston MA 02199-7613 E-mail: skeller@palmerdodge.com.

KELLERMAN, EDWIN, lawyer, physician; b. Phila., Feb. 9, 1932; AB, U. Pa., 1954; MD, Northwestern U., 1959; JD, Temple U., 1984. Bar: Pa. 1984, U.S. Dist. Ct. (ea. dist.) Pa. 1984, U.S. Ct. Appeals (3d cir.) 1985, U.S. Ct. Claims 1995; diplomate Am. Bd. Internal Medicine, Am. Bd. Nephrology. Intern Jersey City Med. Ctr., 1959-60; resident Mt. Sinai Hosp., 1962-63, Jackson Meml. Hosp., 1963-64; NIH fellow Hahnemann Med. Coll., 1964-65; pvt. practice medicine NJ, 1965-72, 1995—, 1972-86; sole practice health care law, 1984—. Cons. in medicine, Social Security Adminstrn., 1979-84. Contbr. to Legal Medicine, 1988, 90, 95. Capt. M.C., U.S. Army, 1960-62. Fellow Am. Coll. Legal Medicine. State civil litigation, Health, Personal injury (including property damage).

KELLEY, FRANK JOSEPH, lawyer, former state attorney general; b. Detroit, Dec. 31, 1924; s. Frank Edward and Grace Margaret (Spears) Kelley; m. Nancy Courtier; children: Karen Ann, Frank Edward II, Jane Francis. Pre-law cert., U. Detroit, 1948, JD, 1951. Bar: Mich. 1952. Pvt. practice law, Detroit, 1952—54, Alpena, 1954—61; atty. gen. State of Mich., Lansing, 1962—98; pvt. practice Lansing, 1998—. Instr. econs. Alpena CC, 1955—56; instr. pub. adminstrn. Alpena County, 1956; atty. city real estate law U. Mich. Extension, 1957—61. Mem. Alpena County Bd. Suprs., 1958—61; pres. Alpena Cmty. Svcs. Coun., 1956; chmn. Gt. Lakes Commn., 1971; founding dir., 1st sec. Alpena United Fund, 1955; founding dir., 1st pres. Northeastern Mich. Child Guidance Clinic, 1958; pres. bd. dirs. Northeastern Mich. Cath. Family Svc., 1959. Mem.: ABA, Nat. Assn. Attys. Gen. (pres. 1967), State Bar Mich., 26th Jud. Cir. Bar Assn. (pres. 1956), Internat. Movement Atlantic Union, KC (4 deg., past legal adv.), Alpha Kappa Psi. Address: 101 S Washington Sq Fl 9 Lansing MI 48933-1731

KELLEY, JAMES FRANCIS, lawyer; b. Dec. 30, 1941; s. James O'Connor and Marcella Cecilia (Salb) K.; children: Sarah, Leah, Laurence. AB, Yale U.; JD, U. Chgo. Bars: N.Y. 1967, Tex. 1981. Assoc. Breed, Abbott & Morgan, NYC, 1967-75; dep. gen. counsel United Tech. Corp., Hartford, Conn., 1975-81; sr. v.p., gen. counsel Diamond Shamrock Corp. (name now Maxus Energy Corp.), Dallas, 1981-88; ptnr. Jones, Day, Reavis & Pogue, Dallas and Paris, 1988-93; sr. v.p. law, gen. counsel Georgia-Pacific Corp., 1993-2000; currently holds the position of exec. v.p. & Gen. coun., 2000-pres.; Gov. Dallas Symphony Assn., 1985-89; bd. dir. North Tex. Pub. Broadcasting Found., Dallas, 1983-91, mem. exec. com., 1988-91; bd. dirs. Atlanta Symphony Orch., 1994—, mem. exec. com., 1996—, vice chair fin. com., 1996—; bd. dirs. Ga. Trust Hist. Preservation, 1994—; mem. bd. visitors Emory U., 1999—. Mem. ABA, Assn. Gen. Counsel. Corporate, general, Private international, Mergers and acquisitions. Office: Georgia-Pacific Corp 133 Peachtree St NE Ste Bsmt Atlanta GA 30303-1847*

KELLEY, JOHN JOSEPH, JR., lawyer; b. Cleve., June 17, 1936; s. John Joseph and Helen (Meier) K.; m. Gloria Hill, June 20, 1959; children: John Joseph III, Scott MacDonald, Christopher Taft, Megan Meredith. BS cum laude in Commerce, Ohio U., 1958; LL.B., Case Western Res. U., 1960. Bar: Ohio bar 1960. Clk. firm Walter & Haverfield, Cleve., 1957-60; assoc. Walter, Haverfield, Buescher & Chockley, Cleve., 1960-66, partner, 1967-72; chief exec. officer Fleischmann Enterprises, Cin., 1972-77; pvt. practice law Cin., 1977-87; ptnr. Kohnen & Patton, Cin., 1988—. Chmn. bd. Basic Packaging Systems, Inc., 1982-87; dir. Orgamac Leasing Ltd; pres. Naples Devel. Inc., 1974-87, Yankee Leasing Co. Mem. Lakewood (Ohio) City Council, 1965-72, pres., 1972; mem. exec. com. Cuyahoga County (Ohio) Republican Central Com., 1965-72; mem. Hamilton County (Ohio) Rep. Policy Com.; Ohio chmn. Robert Taft, Jr. Senate Campaign Com., 1970, 76; bd. govs. Case Western Res. U., 1961, 84-87. Mem. Assn. Ohio Commodores, ABA, Ohio State Bar Assn., Cin. Bar Assn. Clubs: Cin. Country, Queen City (Cin.); Naples Bath and Tennis. Administrative and regulatory, Corporate, general, Mergers and acquisitions. Home: 5 Woodcreek Dr Cincinnati OH 45241-3255 E-mail: jkelley@kohnenpatton.com.

KELLEY, THOMAS JOSEPH, lawyer; b. L.A., Dec. 9, 1936; s. Thomas Joseph and Mary Pauline (O'Dea) K.; m. Kaye Saxon Baker, June 25, 1966; children: Sean, Thomas Joseph III, Scott. BS in History, U. Santa Clara, 1958; JD, Loyola U., Los Angeles, 1966. Bar: Calif. 1966, U.S. Dist. Ct. (so. dist.) Calif. 1966, U.S. Supreme Ct. 1970. Assoc. Schell and Delamer, Los Angeles, 1966-73; assoc. Musick, Peeler & Garrett, Los Angeles, 1973-76, ptnr., 1976-84; ptnr. Moneymaker & Kelley, 1984-91, Dear & Kelley, 1992—; hearing officer state bar cts., 1976-82. Served to maj. USMCR, 1958-78. Mem. ABA, Los Angeles County Bar Assn., Assn. Bus. Trial Lawyers, So. Calif. Def. Counsel, Lawyer-Pilots Bar Assn., Santa Clara Alumni Assn. (pres. 1981-82). Republican. Roman Catholic. Bankruptcy, General civil litigation, Commercial, contracts (including sales of goods; commercial financing). Home: 35 Aloha Dr Pacific Palisades CA 90272-4639 Office: 35 Aloha Dr Pacific Palisades CA 90272-4639

KELLY, ANASTASIA DONOVAN, lawyer; b. Boston, Oct. 9, 1949; d. Charles A. and Louise V. Donovan; m. Thomas C. Kelly, Aug. 23, 1980; children: Michael, Brian. BA cum laude, Trinity Coll, 1971; JD magna cum laude, George Washington U., 1981. Bar: D.C. 1982, Tex. 1982. Analyst Air Line Pilots Assn., 1971-74; dir. employee benefits Martin Marietta Corp., Bethesda, Md., 1974-81; assoc. Carrington, Coleman, Sloman & Blumenthal, Dallas, 1981-85, Wilmer, Cutler & Pickering, Washington, 1985-90, ptnr., 1990-95; sr. v.p., gen. counsel, sec. Fannie Mae, Washington, 1995-99, Sears, Roebuck & Co., 1999—2003. Named one of Outstanding Young Women of Am., 1980. Mem. Am. Bar Found., Order of Coif. Republican. Roman Catholic. Banking, Corporate, general.*

KELLY, CHARLES ARTHUR, lawyer; b. Evanston, Ill., Mar. 2, 1932; s. Charles Scott and Bess (Loftis) K.; m. Frances Kates, Sept. 9, 1961 (div. 1979); children: Timothy, Elizabeth, Mary; m. Patricia Lynn Francis, June 28, 1979. BA with honors, Amherst Coll., 1953; LLB, Harvard U., 1956. Bar: D.C. 1956, Ill. 1956. Assoc. Hubachek & Kelly, Chgo., 1956-64, ptnr., 1964-82, Chapman & Cutler, Chgo., 1982—99, of counsel, 1999—. Sec.l Speedfam Internat., Inc., 1992-99, gen. counsel, 1998-99. Bd. dirs. Gads Hill Ctr., Chgo., pres., 1977—82; bd. dirs. Quetico Superior Found., Mpls., v.p., 1964—; bd. dirs. Lakeland Found., Chgo., 1960—96, pres., 1970—85, Ernest C. Oberholtzer Found., Mpls., 1962—2002, v.p., treas., 1998—2002; bd. dirs. Chgo. Hearing Found., 1990—94, Wilderness Rsch. Found., Chgo. Recipient Legion of Merit, USAF, 1982. Fellow Am. Coll. Trust and Estate Counsel; Mem. ABA, Chgo. Bar Assn., Ill. Bar Assn., Fed. Bar Assn., Univ. Club, Mid-Am. Club, Mich. Shores Club (Wilmette, Ill.), Harvard Club (Boston). Republican. Presbyterian. Corporate, general, Probate (including wills, trusts), Property, real (including real estate development, water). Office: Chapman and Cutler 111 W Monroe St Ste 1800 Chicago IL 60603-4096 E-mail: ckelly@chapman.com.

KELLY, CHRISTOPHER RICHARD, lawyer; b. Brisbane, Australia, Sept. 26, 1967; s. Richard Eason and Christine Temple Kelly; m. Susan Jane Leggett, Oct. 5. B of Commerce, B of Laws, U. Queensland. Clk. Feez Ruthning, Queensland, Australia, 1990—95; atty. Linklaters, London, 1995—2000, ptnr., 2000—. Avocations: cricket, photography, skiing. Mergers and acquisitions, Oil, gas, and mineral, Corporate, general. Office: Linklaters 1 Silk St London EC2Y 8HQ England Fax: 44207 4562222. E-mail: ckelly@linklaters.com.

KELLY, DANIEL GRADY, JR., lawyer; b. Yonkers, N.Y., July 15, 1951; s. Daniel Grady and Helene (Coyne) K.; m. Annette Susan Wheeler, May 8, 1976; children— Elizabeth Anne, Brigid Claire, Cynthia Logan. Grad., Choate Sch., Wallingford, Conn., 1969; BA magna cum laude, Yale U., 1973; JD, Columbia U., 1976. Bar: N.Y. 1977, U.S. Dist. Ct. (so. and ea. dists.) N.Y. 1977, Calif. 1986, U.S. Dist. Ct. (cen. dist.) Calif. 1987. Law clk. to judge U.S. Ct. Appeals (2d cir.), N.Y.C., 1976-77; assoc. Davis Polk & Wardwell, N.Y.C., 1977-83; sr. v.p. Lehman Bros., N.Y.C., 1983-85; sr. v.p., gen. counsel Kaufman & Broad, Inc., L.A., 1985-87; ptnr. Manatt, Phelps, Rothenberg & Phillips, L.A., 1987-90, Sidley & Austin, L.A. and N.Y., 1990-99, Davis Polk & Wardwell, N.Y.C. and Menlo Park, Calif., 1999—. Mem. editl. bd. Columbia Law Rev., 1975-76. Finance, Mergers and acquisitions, Securities. Office: Davis Polk & Wardwell 1600 El Camino Real Menlo Park CA 94025-4119 E-mail: dankelly@dpw.com.

KELLY, DENNIS MICHAEL, lawyer; b. Cleve., May 6, 1943; s. Thomas Francis and Margaret (Murphy) K.; m. Marilyn Ann Divoky, Dec. 28, 1967; children: Alison, Meredith. BA, John Carroll U., 1961-65; JD, U. Notre Dame, 1968. Bar: Ohio 1968. Law clk. U.S. Ct. Appeals (8th cir.), Cleve., 1968-69; assoc. Jones, Day, Reavis & Pogue, Cleve., 1969-75, ptnr., 1975—. Mem. Ohio Bar Assn., Bar Assn. Greater Cleve. Federal civil litigation, General civil litigation, State civil litigation. Office: Jones Day Reavis & Pogue North Point 901 Lakeside Ave E Cleveland OH 44114-1190 E-mail: dmkelly@jonesday.com.

KELLY, EDMUND JOSEPH, lawyer, investment banker; b. Mount Vernon, N.Y., May 18, 1937; s. Hugh Joseph and Catherine (Rice) K.; m. Joan Anne Fee, Nov. 18, 1961; children: Kathleen Kelly Broomer, Edmund Murphy, Thomas More, Mary Kelly Mehr, Michael McNaboe. AB cum laude, Coll. of Holy Cross, 1959; JD (James Kent scholar), Columbia U., 1962. Bar: N.Y. 1962. Sec. of Air Force Office of Gen.Counsel, Washington, 1962-65; assoc. White & Case, N.Y.C., 1965-70, ptnr., 1971-84; vice chmn. Dominick & Dominick Co., N.Y.C., 1984-91, Eighteen Seventy Corp., Purchase, N.Y., 1991—. Lectr. Practicing Law Inst., Am. Mgmt. Assn.; bd. dirs. Fed. Paper Bd. Co., Inc., Montvale, N.J., 1981-96; bd. dirs., mem. exec. com. Chgo. Pneumatic Tool Co., N.Y.C., 1980-86. Author: The Takeover Dialogues, A Discussion of Hostile Takeovers, 1987; editor Columbia Law Rev., 1961-62; contbr. articles to legal jours. Air Force mem. Armed Services Procurement Regulation Com., 1964-65. Corporate, general. Office: Eighteen Seventy Corp Two Manhattanville Rd Purchase NY 10577-2118

KELLY, EDWIN FROST, prosecutor; b. Kearney, Nebr., Jan. 3, 1946; s. Edwin F. and Eora Louise (Ludlum) K.; m. Susan E. Kelly; children: Christopher, Summer, Matthew. BA, Wayne (Nebr.) State Coll., 1968; JD, U. Iowa, 1971. Bar: Iowa 1971, U.S. Dist. Ct. (so. dist.) Iowa 1972, U.S. Ct. Appeals (8th cir.) 1975, U.S. Supreme Ct. 1975, U.S. Dist. Ct. (no. dist.) Iowa 1980. Sole practice, Fairfield, Iowa, 1971-73; ptnr. Kelly & Morrissey, Fairfield, 1974-91; fed. prosecutor, asst. U.S. atty. U.S. Dist. Ct. (So. Dist.) Iowa, Des Moines, 1991—. Prosecutor Jefferson County, Fairfield, 1971-83; lectr. Parsons Coll., 1971-72. Author: Iowa Legal Forms; Creditors Remedies, 1983, 2d rev. edition, 1986, 3d rev. edition, 1990. Chmn. Jefferson County Reps., Fairfield, 1984-85, Iowa Rep. Platform Com., 1988; Rep. nominee for Atty. Gen. of Iowa, 1990. Mem. Masons, Midwest Cruising Sailors Assn. (commodore 1999-2000). Methodist. Avocations: private pilot, sailing. Home: 692 48th St Des Moines IA 50312-1955 Office: US Courthouse Annex 110 E Court Ave Des Moines IA 50309-2044 E-mail: ed.kelly@usdoj.gov.

KELLY, HUGH RICE, retired lawyer; b. Austin, Tex., Dec. 16, 1942; s. Thomas Philip and Cecilia Elizabeth (Rice) K.; m. Marguerite Susan McIntosh, Dec. 27, 1971; children: Susan McIntosh, Cecilia Rice. BA, Rice U., 1965; JD, U. Tex., 1972. Bar: Tex. 1972, U.S. Dist. Ct. (so. dist.) Tex. 1974; U.S. Ct. Appeals (5th cir.), U.S. Supreme Ct. 1975. Assoc. Baker & Botts, Houston, 1972-78, ptnr., 1979-84; sr. v.p., gen. counsel Reliant Resources Inc. (formerly Houston Lighting & Power Co.), 1984—, ret., 2003—. 1st lt. U.S. Army, 1966-69. Fellow Tex. Bar Found., Houston Bar Found.; mem. ABA, State Bar Tex., Houston Bar Assn., Coronado Club. Republican. FERC practice, Administrative and regulatory, Corporate, general. Home: 1936 Rice Blvd Houston TX 77005-1635

KELLY, J. MICHAEL, lawyer; b. Hattiesburg, Miss., Dec. 5, 1943; BA, Emory U., 1966; LLB, U. Va., 1969. Bar: Ga. 1969, U.S. Supreme Ct. 1978, D.C. 1980, Utah 1982, Calif. 1988. Law clerk to Judge Griffin B. Bell (5th cir.) U.S. Ct. Appeals, Atlanta, 1969-70; ptnr. Alston & Bird (formerly Alston, Miller & Gaines), Atlanta, 1970-77, 81-82; counselor to atty. gen. U.S. Dept. Justice, Washington, 1977-79; counselor to sec. U.S. Dept. Energy, Washington, 1979-81; ptnr., shareholder, dir. Ray, Quinney & Nebeker, Salt Lake City, 1982-87; ptnr. Cooley Godward LLP, San Francisco, 1987—. Mem. Omicron Delta Kappa, Phi Alpha Delta. Bankruptcy, Commercial, consumer (including collections, credit). Office: Cooley Godward LLP 1 Maritime Plz Fl 20 San Francisco CA 94111-3510

KELLY, JAMES HOWARD, JR., lawyer; b. Florence, S.C., Dec. 26, 1942; s. James Howard and Mary Neal (Saunders) K.; m. Louise Rankin, April 5, 1969; children: James Howard III, Elizabeth Rankin. AB in English, Political Sci., Davidson (N.C.) Coll., 1965; JD, Duke U., 1968. Bar: N.C. 1968, U.S. Dist. Ct. (ea., we. and ctrl. dists.) 1972, U.S. Supreme Ct. 1974. Assoc. Hudson Petree Stockton Stockton & Robinson, Winston-Salem, N.C., 1972-76; ptnr. Petree Stockton/Kilpatrick Stockton, Winston-Salem, N.C., 1977—. Capt. U.S. Army, 1969-72, Vietnam. Fellow Am. Coll. Trial Lawyers; state chmn, DRI, 1978-1980, mem., NC Assn. of Defense Attys., 1985-86. Methodist. Avocations: water sports, automobiles, reading, hiking, dogs. General civil litigation, Insurance, Personal injury (including property damage). Office: Kilpatrick Stockton LLP 1001 W 4th St Winston Salem NC 27101-2410 E-mail: jkelly@kilpatrickstockton.com.

KELLY, JANET G. retail executive; b. 1953; BA, Morehead State U.; JD, U. Ky. Bar: Ky. 1978. V.p., sr. counsel The Limited, INc.; exec. v.p., gen. counsel Kmart, Troy, Mich., 2001—. Office: Kmart Corp 3100 W Big Beaver Rd Troy MI 48084-3163*

KELLY, JOHN FLEMING, lawyer; b. Denver, Mar. 13, 1926; s. Charles James and Marjorie (Fleming) K.; children: Maureen Kelly Barker, Johanna Elizabeth, Alinka Flaminia, John Fleming Jr. B.A., Yale U., 1947, LL.B., 1950. Bar: Colo. 1950, U.S. Supreme Ct. 1957. Assoc., Holland & Hart, Denver, 1950-54, ptnr., 1954-89; pvt. practice, 1989—, sr. cons. CPR Inst. for Dispute Resolution, 1995—; legal counsel, dir., mem. exec. com. Colo. Assn. Commerce and Industry, 1965-87; mem. Denver panel for dispute resolution Ctr. for Pub. Resources, 1988-95; gen. counsel Univ. Corp. for Atmospheric Research, Boulder, Colo., 1974-84, spl. counsel, 1984-89. Mem. legis. com. Am. Pub. Transit Assn., 1970-81; pres. Central City Opera House Assn., 1972-74, chmn. bd. dirs., 1974-76, hon. dir., 1976— ; bd. dirs. Regional Transp. Dist. Colo., 1969-81; chmn., 1969-74, mem. exec. com., 1969-79; chmn. Gov.'s Spl. Com. on Schs., 1970-71; bd. dirs. Boys' Clubs of Denver, Inc., 1961-71, treas., 1961-66; trustee Kent Sch., Denver, 1971-74; chm. Found. for the Denver Performing Arts Complex, 1988-94 (cert. appreciation Denver City Coun. 1991, dedication of lobby of Buell Theatre 1991). Served with USNR, 1943-46, 52-53. Named Colo. Bus. Leader, Colo. Assn. Commerce and Industry, 1984; recipient Yale medal for outstanding service, 1985. Mem. ABA, Colo. Bar Assn. (bd. govs. 1961-65, v.p. 1964-65), Denver Bar Assn., Fed. Energy Bar Assn., Assn. Yale Alumni (bd. govs. 1977-82, vice chmn. 1978-80, chmn. 1980-82). Republican. Roman Catholic. Clubs: University, Colo. Arlberg; Yale of N.Y.C. Corporate, general, FERC practice, Legislative. Home: 9488 E Florida Ave Apt 2094 Denver CO 80231-7822 Office: 366 Madison Ave New York NY 10017

KELLY, JOHN FRANCIS, lawyer, law educator; b. Buffalo, N.Y., Mar. 14, 1929; s. John James and Catherine McGeever Kelly; m. Louise Mary Heretick; children: Michael J., Catherine E. Cabell, Martin P., Theresa A. Poland, Timothy P., Mary L. Gressens, John F. Jr., Christopher D. BA, U. Richmond, 1951, LLB, 1956; LLM, William and Mary, 1980. Bar: (Va.) 1956. From assoc. to mng. ptnr. Cohen, Cox & Kelly, Richmond, Va., 1956—70; ptnr., mng. ptnr. Hirschler Fleischer, Richmond, 1970—81; mgr. Kelly & Lewis, PC, Richmond, 1981—98; mgr., mem. Kelly & Kelly, PLC, Richmond, 1998—. Adj. prof. William and Mary Law Sch., Williamsburg, Va., 1986—95, U. Richmond Law Sch., 1996—2001. Cpl. U.S. Army, 1951—53. Fellow: Am. Coll. Tax Counsel. Roman Catholic. Avocations: golf, sports. Corporate taxation, Estate taxation, State and local taxation. Home: 4315 Northwich Ct Midlothian VA 23112 Office: Kelly & Kelly PLC Ste 300 7400 Beaufont Springs Dr Richmond VA 23225

KELLY, JOHN JAMES, lawyer; b. Rockville Centre, N.Y., July 4, 1949; s. John James Sr. and Eleanor Grace (Vann) K.; m. Clara Sarah Gussin; 1 child, John James III. AB in Govt., Georgetown U., 1971, JD, 1975. Bar: Pa. 1976, D.C. 1979, U.S. Dist. Ct. D.C. 1980, U.S. Claims Ct. 1982, U.S. Ct. Appeals (D.C. cir.) 1980, U.S. Ct. Appeals (fed. cir.) 1982. Law clk. to judge U.S. Dist. Ct., Washington, 1975-77; assoc. Corcoran, Youngman & Rowe, Washington, 1977-80, Capell, Howard, Knabe & Cobbs, Washington, 1980-83, Loomis, Owen, Fellman & Howe, Washington, 1983-86, ptnr., 1986-90; v.p., sec., gen. coun. Electronic Industries Alliance, Arlington, Va., 1990-96, exec. v.p., gen. counsel, 1997—; pres. JEDEC Solid State Tech. Assn., 2000—; counsel Howe, Anderson & Steyer, Washington, 1990—. Mem. Jud. Conf., D.C. Cir., Washington, 1983, Jud. Conf. Fed.

Cir., Washington, 1988—. Contbr. articles to legal and profl. publs. Mem. ABA, D.C. Bar, Pa. Bar Assn., Am. Soc. Assn. Execs. (bd. dirs. legal section 1989-94, chmn. 1992-93), Fed. Bar Assn., Met. Club. Democrat. Roman Catholic. Antitrust, Federal civil litigation, Corporate, general. Office: Electronic Industries Alliance 2500 Wilson Blvd Arlington VA 22201-3834

KELLY, JOHN MARTIN, lawyer; b. Oshkosh, Wis., Dec. 13, 1948; s. Martin Paul and Ivy Cecile (James) Kelly; m. Teresa Jean Wendland, July 24, 1982. BA, U. Wis., Madison, 1971; JD, Georgetown U., 1974; postgrad. in bus., Harvard U., 1976-77. Bar: Wis. 1974, D.C. 1975. Atty. office chief counsel IRS, Washington, 1974-76; assoc. Dempsey Law Office, Oshkosh, 1977-82, ptnr., 1983—. Mem. ABA, Wis. Bar Assn., D.C. Bar Assn., Winnebago County Bar Assn. General practice, General civil litigation, Personal injury (including property damage). Office: Dempsey Law Office PO Box 886 Oshkosh WI 54903-0886 E-mail: jmkelly@dempseylaw.com.

KELLY, MARILYN, state supreme court justice; b. Apr. 15, 1938; m. Donald Newman. BA, Ea. Mich. U., 1960, JD (hon.); postgrad., U. Paris.; MA, Middlebury Coll., 1961; JD with honors, Wayne State U., 1971. Assoc. Dykema, Gossett, Spencer, Goodnow & Trigg, Detroit, 1973-78; ptnr. Dudley, Patterson, Maxwell, Smith & Kelly, Bloomfield Hills, Mich., 1978-80; owner Marilyn Kelly & Assocs., Bloomfield Hills, Birmingham, Mich., 1980-88; judge Mich. Ct. of Appeals, 1989-96; justice Mich. Supreme Ct., 1997—. Tchr. lang., lit. Grosse Pointe Pub. Schs., Albion Coll., Ea. Mich. U.; past mem. rep. assembly, comms. com., family law coun. Mich. State Bar, now co-chair Open Justice Commn. Active Mich. Dem. Party, 1963—. Recipient Disting Alumni award Ea. Mich. U., Disting. Svc. award Mich. Edn. Assn. Mem. Soc. Irish-Am. Lawyers, Women Lawyers Assn. (past pres.), Oakland County Bar Assn. (past chair family law com.) Office: Mich Supreme Ct PO Box 30052 Lansing MI 48909*

KELLY, MAURA PATRICIA, lawyer; b. St. Louis; d. Martin J. and Kathleen A. Kelly; m. Joshua D. Holden, June 17, 2000. BA cum laude, St. Louis U., 1995, JD cum laude, 1998. Bar: Mo. 1998. Corp. counsel McCarthy Bldg. Cos., Inc., St. Louis, 1996—. Mem.: Young Ireland Club, St. Louis Gateway Feis Soc. Construction, Labor (including EEOC, Fair Labor Standards Act, labor-management relations, NLRB, OSHA), Corporate, general. Office: McCarthy Bldg Cos Inc 1341 N Rock Hill Rd Saint Louis MO 63124

KELLY, MICHAEL JOSEPH, lawyer; b. Bklyn., Apr. 24, 1947; s. Patrick and Bridget Kelly; m. Sharon Ann Erwin, Aug. 8, 1970; children: Tara Bridget, Liam Patrick, Cristin Jane, Devon Michael. BA, Syracuse U., 1969; JD, SUNY, Buffalo, 1972. Bar: N.Y. 1972. Assoc. Sam Greene, Syracuse, N.Y., 1972-73; ptnr. Bayer, Dupee & Smith, Rochester, N.Y., 1973-79, Gates & Kelly, Perry, N.Y., 1979-81; pvt. practice, Perry, 1981—. Judge Town and Village of Warsaw, N.Y., 1990-91; asst. dist. atty. Wyoming County, Perry, 1991-97. Pres. Arts Coun. Wyoming County, 1983-84. Mem. ABA, N.Y. State Bar Assn. (bd. dirs. grievance com. 1986-92, svc. recognition award 1986, 92), Wyoming County Bar Assn. (pres. 1985-86, co-coord.Retrouvaille of Buffalo, 2002-), Rotary (bd. dirs., pres. Perry 1995-96), Retrouvaille Buffalo (coord. 2002-). Avocations: tennis, biking, music, reading, gardening. General civil litigation, General practice, Probate (including wills, trusts). Office: 24 Lake St Perry NY 14530-1516

KELLY, PAUL JOSEPH, JR., judge; b. Freeport, N.Y., Dec. 6, 1940; s. Paul J. and Jacqueline M. (Nolan) Kelly; m. Ruth Ellen Dowling, June 27, 1964; children: Johanna, Paul Edwin, Thomas Martin, Christopher Mark, Heather Marie. BBA, U. Notre Dame, 1963; JD, Fordham U., 1967. Bar: N.Mex. 1967. Law clk. Cravath, Swaine & Moore, N.Y.C., 1964—67; assoc. firm Hinkle, Cox, Eaton, Coffield & Hensley, Roswell, N.Mex., 1967—71, ptnr., 1971—92; judge U.S. Ct. Appeals (10th cir.), Santa Fe, 1992—. Mem. N.Mex. Bd. Bar Examiners, 1982—85, N.Mex. Ho. of Reps., 1976—81, chmn. consumer and pub. affairs com., mem. judiciary com.; mem. N.Mex. Pub. Defender Bd., U.S. Jud. Conf. Com. on the Jud. Br., 1994—99, U.S. Jud. Conf. Civil Rules Adv. Com., 2002—; chair 10th Cir. Rules com., 10th Cir. Uniform Criminal Jury Instrn. Com.; mem. Civil Rules Adv. Com. U.S. Jud. Conf. Bd. visitors Fordham U. Sch. Law, 1992—; pres. Oliver Seth Inn of Ct., 1993—, Roswell Drug Abuse Com, 1970—71; mem. Appellate Judges Nominating Commn., 1989—92, Eastern N.Mex. State Fair Bd., 1978—83; pres. Chaves County Young Reps., 1971—72; vice chmn. N.Mex. Young Reps., 1969—71, treas., 1968—69; pres. parish coun. Roman Cath. Ch., 1971—76; bd. dirs. Zia coun. Girl Scouts Am., Roswell Girls Club; bd. dirs.. Chaves County Mental Health Assn., 1974—77; bd. dirs. Santa Fe Orch., 1992—93, Roswell Symphony Orch. Soc., 1969—82, treas., 1970—73, pres., 1973—75. Mem.: State Bar N.Mex. (v.p. young lawyers sect. 1969, co-chmn. ins. sub-com. 1972—73, mem. continuing legal edn. com. 1970—73), Fed. Bar Assn., ABA. Office: US Court Appeals 10th Circuit Federal Courthouse PO Box 10113 Santa Fe NM 87504-6113

KELLY, PETER MCCLOREY, II, lawyer; b. Chgo., Mar. 23, 1948; s. John Stephen and Helen (Patterson) K.; m. Susan Barrett, Aug. 17, 1995; children: Peter, Eli, Eamon, Liam. A.B., U. Notre Dame, 1970; J.D. cum laude, Ind. U., 1973. Bar: Ill. 1973. Assoc. McDermott, Will & Emery, Chgo., 1973-78, ptnr., 1979-81; ptnr. Kirkland & Ellis, Chgo., 1981-84, Bell, Boyd & Lloyd, Chgo., 1984-91, Murphy, Smith & Polk, Chgo., 1991-98, Ogletree Deakins (formerly Murphy Smith & Polk), 1999—; adj. prof. Sch. of Law, Loyola U., Chgo., 1976-84, Ind. U. Law Sch., Bloomington, 1985; speaker to various profl. groups and orgns. Mem. U.S. C. of C. (employee benfits council 1981—), ABA (life fellow), charter fellow, bd. govs., Am. Coll. Employee Benefits Counsel Chgo. Bar Assn. (sec. employee benefits com. 1982-83, vice chmn. employee benefits com. 1983-84, chmn. 1984-85), Midwest Pension Conf. (exec. bd. 1984—), Order of Coif. Pension, profit-sharing, and employee benefits. Home: 1316 Davis St Evanston IL 60201-4104 Office: Ogletree Deakins 2 1st Nat Plz Fl 25 Chicago IL 60603 E-mail: kellypm@odnss.com.

KELLY, ROBERT EDWARD, JR., lawyer; b. Pitts., Nov. 28, 1950; s. Robert E. Sr. and Adelaide Cecelia (Harris) K.; m. Noreen Theresa Quinn, Oct. 23, 1976; children: Robert E. III, Christopher Patrick, Andrew Clifford. BA, Siena Coll., 1972; JD, Georgetown U., 1975. Bar: Pa. 1975, U.S. Dist. Ct. (we. dist.) Pa. 1975, U.S. Dist. Ct. (ea. and mid. dist.) Pa. 1978, U.S. Ct. Appeals (3d cir.) 1979, U.S. Supreme Ct. 1980, U.S. Dist. Ct. (no. dist.) N.Y. 1992, U.S. Dist. Ct. (no. dist.) Calif. 1994. Assoc. Houston, Harbaugh, Cohen & Lippard, Pitts., 1975-77; assoc., dep. atty. gen. Commonwealth of Pa., Harrisburg, 1977-80; assoc. Duane, Morris & Heckscher, Harrisburg, 1980-86, ptnr., 1986—2002, Kelly, Hoffman & Goduto, LLP, 2002—. Mem. ABA, FBA, Pa. Bar Assn., Pa. Def. Inst., Dauphin County Bar Assn., Pa. Soc., Am. Inns of Ct., St. Thomas More Soc., West Shore Country Club (Camp Hill, Pa.). Republican. Roman Catholic. Administrative and regulatory, Federal civil litigation, State civil litigation. Home: 3610 Horsham Dr Mechanicsburg PA 17050-2204 Office: Kelly Hoffman & Goduto LLP Commerce Towers 10th Fl 300 N 2d St Harrisburg PA 17101 E-mail: rkelly@khgllp.com.

KELLY, ROBERT F. federal judge; b. 1935; BS, Villanova U., 1957; LLB, Temple U., 1960. Pvt. practice law, Media, Pa., 1961-62, 64-76, Chester, Pa., 1962-64; law clk. to Hon. Francis J. Catania Ct. Common Pleas, Delaware County, Pa., 1964-72; prothonotary Delaware County, 1972-76; former judge Ct. Common Pleas 32d Jud. Dist. Pa.; judge U.S. Dist. Ct. (ea. dist.) Pa., Phila., 1987—, sr. judge, 2001—. Lectr. law Villanova U. Law Sch. Voluntary defender Delaware County, 1962; chmn. Delaware County Rep. Exec. Com., 1972-76, Subcom. on Libr. Programs; mem. Judicial Coun. com. on Automation and Tech., 1989—. Mem. ABA, Am. Judicature Soc., Pa. Bar Assn., Pa. Trial Judges Assn., Delaware County Bar Assn. (judicial counsel's com. automation and tech., 1989—, chmn. subcom. libr. programs). Office: US Dist Ct 11613 US Courthouse 601 Market St Philadelphia PA 19106-1713

KELLY, ROBERT QUAINE, law librarian; b. Chgo., Apr. 3, 1922. B.A., St. Mary of the Lake U., 1945; M.A. in Library Sci., Rosary Coll., 1950; J.D., DePaul U., 1956. Bar: Ill. 1957, Nebr. 1975. Librarian, DePaul U. Coll. Law, 1950-73; prof. law Creighton U., Omaha, dir. law library, 1973—90, ret. 1990. Trustee, North Riverside, Ill., 1969-72. Mem. ABA, Am. Assn. Law Libraries (treas. 1964-66), Bibliog. Soc. Am. Home: 717 Sunset Trl Omaha NE 68132-1919 Office: Creighton U Law Sch Klutznick Law Libr 2133 California St Omaha NE 68102-4537

KELLY, SHAWN PAUL, lawyer; b. N.Y.C., Feb. 9, 1952; s. John Donald and Kathleen Marie (O'Leary) K.; m. Carol Ann Baumgarth, Sept. 24, 1989; children: Sean, Ryan. BA, U. Notre Dame, 1974; JD, St. John's Sch. Law, 1977. Bar: N.Y. 1977. Ptnr. Kelly, Rode & Kelly L.L.P., Mineola, N.Y., 1977—. Chmn. Nassau, Suffolk (N.Y.) Trial Lawyer's Assn., 1987—. Vol. (pro-bono) Lawyer's Initiative St. Mary's Parish, Manhasset, N.Y., 1998—. Fellow Am. Coll. Trial Lawyers; mem. N.Y. Bar Assn., N.Y. State Med. Def. Bar Assn., Nassau Bar Assn. Insurance, Personal injury (including property damage), Product liability. Office: Kelly Rode & Kelly LLP 330 Old Country Rd Ste 305 Mineola NY 11501-4170 E-mail: spkelly@krklaw.com.

KELLY, T. CHRISTOPHER, lawyer; b. Cedar Falls, Iowa, Aug. 12, 1955; s. Ryan and Harriett Kelly. BA, U. Wis., 1977, JD, 1980. Bar: Wis. 1980, U.S. Dist. Ct. (we. and ea. dists.) Wis. 1980, U.S. Ct. Appeals (7th cir.) 1983, U.S. Supreme Ct. 1991. Law clk. Wis. Ct. Appeals, Madison, 1980-82; ptnr. Dewa, Beardin & Kelly, Madison, 1983-86; sole practitioner Kelly Law Offices, Madison, 1987-94; ptner. Kelly & Habermehl & S.C., Madison, 1995—. V.p., bd. dirs. Mercados Ltd., Madison, 1991-94; instr. U. Wis. Law Sch., Madison, 1994-97. Mem. Nat. Assn. Criminal Def. Lawyers, Wis. Assn. Criminal Def. Lawyers. Criminal, Labor (including EEOC, Fair Labor Standards Act, labor-management relations, NLRB, OSHA), Personal injury (including property damage). Office: Thomas Kelly et al 145 W Wilson St Madison WI 53703-3254

KELLY, THOMAS PAINE, JR., lawyer; b. Tampa, Fla., Aug. 29, 1912; s. Thomas Paine and Beatrice (Gent) K.; m. Jean Baughman, July 25, 1940; children: Carla (Mrs. Henry Dee), Thomas Paine III, Margaret Jo (Mrs. Jeffrey Holmes). AB, U. Fla., 1935, JD, 1936. Bar: Fla. 1936, U.S. Dist. Ct. (no. dist.) Fla. 1936, U.S. Ct. Appeals (5th cir.) 1936, U.S. Dist. Ct. (mid. dist.) Fla. 1940, U.S. Dist. Ct. (so. dist.) Fla. 1939, U.S. Ct. Appeals (11th cir.) 1983, U.S. Supreme Ct. 1990. Since practiced in, Tampa; assoc. McKay, Macfarlane, Jackson & Ferguson, 1939-40; ptnr. McKay, MacFarlane, Jackson & Ferguson, 1940-48, Macfarlane, Ferguson, Allison & Kelly, 1948-83, sr. ptnr., 1983-91; of counsel Shear, Newman, Hahn & Rosenkranz, 1992-95; shareholder MacFarlane Ferguson & McMullen, P.A., Tampa, Fla., 1996—. Chmn. Tampa Com. 100, 1960-61; pres. Tampa Citizens' Safety Coun., 1961-62; Bd. dirs. Tampa chpt. ARC, 1955-62, pres., 1958-59; bd. dirs. Boys Clubs Tampa, 1956-67, pres., 1966-67. Col. F.A. AUS, 1940-45. Decorated Silver Star. Fellow Am. Coll. Trial Lawyers, Internat. Acad. Trial Lawyers; mem. Am. Bar Assn., Bar Assn. Hillsborough County, Fla. Bar (chmn. com. profl. ethics 1953-58, chmn. com. ins. and negligence law 1962-63, chmn. fed. rules com. 1969-70) Republican. Home: 5426 Lykes Ln Tampa FL 33611-4747 Office: McFarlane Ferguson & McMullen PO Box 1531 Tampa FL 33601-1531 E-mail: tpk@mac.com.

KELLY, TIMOTHY WILLIAM, lawyer; b. Apr. 27, 1953; s. George Raymond and Mary Therese (Kelly) K.; m. Mary Teresa Harms, May 24, 1980; children: Ryan Timothy, Colin Patrick, Kaitlynn Elizabeth. BS in Bus. Adminstrn., U. Dayton, 1975, JD, 1978. Bar: Ill. 1978, U.S. Dist. Ct. (cen. and no. dists.) Ill. 1979. Staff counsel Prairie State Legal Aid, Bloomington, Ill., 1978-81; felony asst. McLean County Pub. Defenders, Bloomington, 1981-83; assoc. Jerome Mirza & Assocs., Bloomington, 1983-88; asst. prof. polit. sci. Ill. State U., Normal, 1980-83; faculty mem. Ill. Inst. Continuing Legal Edn. Lectr. in field. Contbr. articles to profl. jours. Bd. dirs. Bloomington/Normal Day Care Assn., 1982-83; civil actions arbitrator and mediator McLean County, 1996—. Named one of Top Three Attys. in McLean, Bus. to Bus. Mag., 1997. Fellow Ill. Bar Found.; mem. ATLA, Ill. State Bar Assn. (mem. civil practice and procedure sect. coun. 1992—, chmn. 1998, Allerton house steering com. 1994, 96, 98, tort law sect. coun. 1995—, assembly mem. 1995—), Ill. Trial Lawyers Assn. (mem. bd. mgrs. 1992—, continuing legal edn. com. 1995-96, exec. com. 1996, chmn. ins. law com. 1996-98), Chgo. Bar Assn., McLean County Bar Assn. (sec. 1984-85), McLean County Inns of Ct., IICLE (bd. dirs. 2000—). Democrat. Roman Catholic. Personal injury (including property damage). Office: 205 N Williamsburg Dr Ste A Bloomington IL 61704-7721 E-mail: twkelly271@aol.com.

KELLY, WILLIAM CHARLES, JR., lawyer; b. Mpls., June 9, 1946; s. William Charles and Marian Eileen (Moritz) K.; m. Cynthia Ann Churchill, June 28, 1969; children: Patrick, Brian. AB, Harvard U., 1968; JD, Yale U., 1971. Bar: Maine 1972, D.C. 1973, U.S. Supreme Ct. 1973. Law clk. to Judge Coffin U.S. Ct. Appeals (1st cir.), Portland, Maine, 1971-72; law clk. to Justice Powell U.S. Supreme Ct., Washington, 1972-73; exec. asst. to sec. HUD, Washington, 1975-77; ptnr. Latham & Watkins, Washington, 1978—. Bd. dirs. Nat. Low Income Housing Coalition, Washington, 1983-94, The Governance Inst., 1986—, Washington Legal Clinic for the Homeless, 1999—; trustee Sheridan Sch., 1992-98; mem. Ashoka World Coun., 1997—; dir. Ashoka Innovators for the Public, 1999—. Lt. USNR, 1973-75. Mem. ABA, D.C. Bar Assn. Commercial, contracts (including sales of goods; commercial financing), Property, real (including real estate development, water), Transportation. Office: Latham & Watkins Ste 1000 555 11th St NW Washington DC 20004-1304

KELLY, WILLIAM GARRETT, judge; b. Grand Rapids, Mich., Nov. 30, 1947; s. Joseph Francis and Gertrude Frances (Downes) K.; m. Sharon Ann Diroff, Aug. 11, 1979; children: Colleen, Joseph, Caitlin, Meaghan and Patricia. BA, U. Detroit, 1970, JD, 1975. Bar: Mich. 1975, U.S. Dist. Ct. (we. dist.) Mich. 1975. Tchr. Peace Corps, Ghana, Republic of West Africa, 1970-72; asst. prosecutor Kalamazoo (Mich.) Prosecutor's Office, 1975-77; atty. Office of Defender, Grand Rapids, 1977-78; judge 62d B Dist. Ct., Kentwood, 1979—. Faculty Mich. Jud. Inst., Lansing, 1985—, 2d Nat. Conf. on Ct. Tech., Denver, 1988, Nat. Jud. Coll., 2001--; chmn.-elect Jud. Conf. State Bar Mich., 1990-91, chmn., 1991-92. Bd. dirs. Nat. Ctr. for State Cts., 1994-2000; pres. Kentwood Jaycees, 1979-80. Named one of Five Outstanding Young Men of Mich., Mich. Jaycees, 1982. Mem. ABA (chmn. nat. conf. spl. ct. judges 1992-93, chmn. traffic ct. program 2002-), State Bar Mich., Grand Rapids Bar Assn., Cath. Lawyers Assn. Western Mich. (pres. 1987), Mich. Dist. Judges Assn. (pres. 1989). Roman Catholic. Office: 62d B Dist Ct 4740 Walma SE Kentwood MI 49512

KELMACHTER, LESLIE DEBRA, lawyer; b. Bklyn. d. Meyer and Jean Muraskin (Metcalf) K. BA magna cum laude, SUNY, New Paltz, 1974; JD, Albany Law Sch., 1977. Bar: N.Y. 1978, U.S. Dist. Ct. (no. dist.) N.Y., U.S. Dist. Ct. (ea. dist.) N.Y. 1989, U.S. Dist. Ct. (so. dist.) N.Y. 1995. Atty. Legal Aid Soc., Schenectady, 1977—79, atty., juvenile rights divsn. N.Y.C., 1979—86; atty., asst. corp. counsel Law Dept., City of N.Y., 1986—90; ptnr. Schneider, Kleinick, Weitz, Damashek & Shoot, N.Y.C., 1990—99, Meyers, Meyers and Kelmachter, N.Y.C., 1999—2002, The Jacob D. Fuchsberg Law Firm, LLP, N.Y.C., 2000—. Dean N.Y. State Trial Lawyers Inst.; co-chair Decisions, Mealey's Nat. Lead Litigation Conf., 1999. Participant, fund raiser Race for the Cure, N.Y.C., 1995—98; competitor N.Y.C. Ctrl. Park Triathalon, 1999. Mem.: Met. Women's Bar, N.Y. State Trial Lawyers Assn. (bd. dirs.), Bar Assn. City of N.Y. (chair tort litigation com. 2001—). State civil litigation, Personal injury (including property damage), Toxic tort. Office: 500 Fifth Ave 45th Flr New York NY 10010

KELMAN, EDWARD MICHAEL, lawyer; b. N.Y., Aug. 29, 1943; s. Jack H. and Evelyn (Karp) K.; children: Matthews S., Joshua K. AB, Cornell U., 1965; JD, NYU, 1968. Bar: N.Y. 1969, Conn. 1972. Asst dist. atty. N.Y. County Dist. Atty.'s Office, 1968-71; assoc. Glazer & Wechsler, Stamford, Conn., 1971-72, Squadron, Gartenberg, Elenoff & Plesent, N.Y., 1972-73; sr. atty. CBS Records, CBS, Inc., N.Y., 1973-76; asst. gen. atty. CBS Pub., CBS, Inc., N.Y., 1976-77; v.p. law Chappell Music Co., N.Y., 1977-80; of counsel Law Offices of Michael Sukin, N.Y., 1980-82; v.p. bus. affairs and acquisitions Thorn EMI Video & TV, N.Y., 1982-83; pvt. practice entertainment and media law N.Y., 1983—. Vice chmn. Mayor's TV & Film Commn., Stamford, 1986—; cons. First Night Entertainment Com., Stamford, 1990. Recipient Spl. award Rec. Ind. Assn. Am., 1975. Mem. NARAS, Assn. Bar City N.Y., Conn. Bar Assn., Nat. Acad. Popular Music, Cornell Club of N.Y. Avocations: sports, movies, theatre. Office: 521 Fifth Ave 26th Fl New York NY 10175 Fax: 212-750-1356. E-mail: Emknyc@aol.com.

KELSO, LINDA YAYOI, lawyer; b. Boulder, Colo., 1946; d. Nobutaka and Tai Ike; m. William Alton Kelso, 1968. BA, Stanford U., 1968; MA, U. Wis., 1973; JD, U. Fla., 1979. Bar: Fla. 1980. Assoc. Mahoney, Hadlow & Adams, Jacksonville, Fla., 1979-82, Commander, Legler, Werber, Dawes, Sadler & Howell, Jacksonville, 1982-86, ptnr., 1986-91, Foley & Lardner, Jacksonville, 1992—. Mem. ABA (bus. law sect.), Jacksonville Bar Assn., Phi Beta Kappa, Order of Coif. Avocations: music, gardening, cooking. Corporate, general, Securities. Office: Foley & Lardner 200 N Laura St Jacksonville FL 32202-3500 E-mail: lkelso@foleylaw.com.

KELSON, RICHARD B. metal products executive; b. Pitts., Nov. 20, 1946; B in Polit. Sci., U. Pa.; JD, U. Pitts. Atty. Alcoa, Pitts., 1974-77, gen. atty., 1977-83, mng. gen. atty., 1983-84, asst. sec., mng. gen. atty., 1984-89, asst. gen. counsel, 1989-91, sr. v.p. environ. health and safety, 1991-94, exec. v.p. environ., health and safety, gen. counsel, 1994-97, exec. v.p., CFO, 1997—. Bd. dirs. Meadwestvaco. Bd. dirs. Alcoa Found., U. Pitts. Law Sch. Bd. Visitors, Pitts. Civic Light Opera; mem. Fin. Exec. Inst. the Officers Conf. Group, The Pvt. Sector Coun.'s CFPs; mem. bd. trustees Carnegie Mellon. Mem. ABA. Office: Alcoa 390 Park Ave New York NY 10022

KEMLER, R(OBERT) MICHAEL, lawyer; b. Boston, Oct. 25, 1945; s. Charles and Evelyn (Jaffe) K.; m. Deborah Glaser, Aug. 20, 1970 (div. 1980); 1 child, Matthew Alex Kemler Nelson. AB, U. Pa., 1967; JD, Boston Coll., 1970; LLM, U. Pa. (partial fellowship-grad. law student), 1972; postgrad., U. Oxford, Eng., 1970-71. Guest lectr. Hosp. U. Pa., Phila., 1972; atty. law reform health law Community Legal Svcs., Phila., 1973-79; lectr. health law Vallanova (Pa.) Law Sch., 1980; atty. Pub. Interest Law Ctr. of Phila., 1979-80; asst. regional atty. Office of Civil Rights, U.S. Dept. Health & Human Svcs., Phila., 1980-82; asst. dep. pub. advocate N.J. Dept. Pub. Advocate, Trenton, N.J., 1982-87; assoc. litigation dept. Duane, Morris & Heckscher, Phila., 1987-88; of counsel Monaghan & Gold, Phila., 1990-94; pvt. practice health law Phila., 1994—. Pvt. practice health law guest lectr. U. Pa. Med. Sch., Phila., 1972—; cons. legal medicine Wood Inst., Coll. Physicians of Phila., 1990-92; guest lectr. forensic psychiatry U. Pa. Sch. Medicine; gen. lectr. in health law field; apptd. mediator U.S. Dist. Ct. (ea. dist.) Pa. 1992—. Author: A Handbook on the Medicaid Boycott and Antitrust, 1981, Mock Medical Malpractice Trial, U. Pa. Med. Sch., 1989, Health Care Reform: Post Election Look at Congress's Unfinished Agenda, 1994, Medical Malpractice Liabilty and the HMO, 1993, Rationing in Health Care, 1998; contbr. articles to profl. jours. Bd. dirs. Pa. Pro Musica, Phila., 1990—; bass II Mendelssohn Club of Phila., 1990; asst. mgr. Pa. Ballet, Phila., 1985-88. Nat. Legal Svc. Corp. rsch. fellow, 1981. Fellow Coll. Physicians of Phila.; mem. Phila. Bar Assn. (Medico-legal com. 1989—, health law com. 1992), Pa. Soc. Healthcare Attys. Democrat. Avocations: harpsichord, choral singing, yachting, swimming, tennis. Home: 1914 Waverly St Philadelphia PA 19146-1425 Office: 2207 Chestnut St Fl 2D Philadelphia PA 19103-3010

KEMP, BARRETT GEORGE, lawyer; b. Dayton, Ohio, Feb. 22, 1932; s. Barrett M. and Gladys M. (Linkhart) K.; children: Becky A., Barrett George II; m. Shirley, 1997. BSC, Ohio U., 1954; JD, Ohio No. U., 1959. Bar: Ohio 1959. With FBI, 1959-61; mem. B.G. Kemp Law Firm, St. Marys, Ohio, 1961—. Law dir. City of St. Marys, 1964-80. Sec., treas. Cmty. Improvement Corp., 1967-79; founder St. Marys Sister City, Inc.; founder, organizer sister city with Ho Kudan-cho, Japan, 1985. Recipient Outstanding Citizen award City of St. Marys, 1973, Builder of Bridges award St. Mary's C. of C., 1995. Mem. Ohio Bar Assn., Auglaize County Bar Assn., Rotary (v.p. 1968, pres. 1969, Lifetime achievement 1997, Four Aves. of Cvs. citation 1999), Masons, Shriners, Scottish Rite. General practice. Office: Ste 203 Cmty First Bank & Trust Bldg Saint Marys OH 45885

KEMP, ROLAND CONNOR, lawyer; b. Dallas, May 29, 1943; s. William Thomas and Martha Belle (Arney) K.; m. Carol Ann DeRosa, Dec. 12, 1966 (div. Oct. 13, 1989); children: Thomas Roland, Patrick Michael. BA, Baylor U., 1965, postgrad., 1966; JD, U. Tex., 1972. Bar: Tex. 1972, U.S. Dist. Ct. (so. dist.) Tex. 1973, U.S. Dist. Ct. (we. dist.) Tex. 1973, U.S. Ct. Appeals (5th cir.) 1973, U.S. Supreme Ct. 1977. Law clk. U.S. Dist Ct. So. Dist. Tex., Houston, 1972-74; assoc. Schlanger, Cook, Cohn & Mills, Houston, 1974-76, Fred Parks & Assocs., Houston, 1977-80; sole practice Houston, 1980-87; ptnr. Henderson & Kemp, Houston, 1988—. Chmn. bd. dirs. Timberlane Mcpl. Utility Dist., Harris County, Tex., 1973. Served to capt. USAF, 1966-70. Mem. State Bar Tex., Houston Bar Assn., Phi Delta Phi. Bankruptcy, Family and matrimonial, Probate (including wills, trusts). Office: PO Box 90775 Houston TX 77290-0775

KEMPER, EDWARD CRAWFORD, lawyer; b. Seattle, Dec. 7, 1942; s. Edward C. and Sarah (Tolman) K.; m. Joleen Osterling, Sept. 5, 1964; children: Kevin, Kirsten. BA, George Washington U., 1965, JD with honors, 1968. Bar: Hawaii 1969, U.S. Dist. Ct. Hawaii 1969, U.S. Ct. Appeals (9th cir.) 1974, U.S. Supreme Ct. 1974. Assoc. Cades, Schutte, Fleming & Wright, Honolulu, 1968-71; ptnr. Mattoch, Kemper & Brown, Honolulu, 1971-77, Kemper & Watts, Honolulu, 1977—. Editor-in-chief Hawaii Bar Jour., 1972-1992, editor 1992-; author articles. Pres. Kokua Kalihi Valley, Honolulu, 1983, Friends of Kailua (Hawaii) High Sch., 1985-, pres. Hawaii Family Support Ctr. 2001-, v.p., dir. Epilepsy Found. Hawaii, 2002-. Mem. Hawaii Bar Assn. (bd. dirs. 1974). Clubs: Honolulu. Federal civil litigation, State civil litigation, Personal injury (including property damage). Home: 1307 Onaona Pl Kailua HI 96734-3752 Office: Kemper & Watts Pacific Guardian Ctr 737 Bishop St #1455 Honolulu HI 96813

KEMPER, JAMES DEE, lawyer; b. Olney, Ill., Feb. 23, 1947; s. Jack O. and Vivian L. Kemper; m. Diana J. Deig, June 1, 1968; children: Judd, Jason. BS, Ind. U., 1969, JD summa cum laude, 1971. Bar: Ind. 1971. Law clk. U.S. Ct. Appeals (7th cir.), Chgo., 1971-72; mng. ptnr. Ice Miller, Indpls., 1972—. Note editor Ind. U. Law Rev., 1970-71; contbr. articles to profl. jours. Past officer, bd. dirs. Marion County Assn. for Retarded Citizens, Inc., Indpls.; past bd. dirs. Cen. Ind. Easter Seal Soc., Indpls., Crossroads Rehab. Ctr., Inc, Indpls.; pres., bd. govs. Orchard Country Day Sch., Indpls.; mem. bd. Eiteljorg Mus. Native Americans, Butler U. Fellow Ind. Bar Found.; mem. ABA (employee benefit com.), Ind. Bar Assn., The

Group, Inc., Midwest Pension Conf., U.S. C. of C. (employee benefit com.), Stanley K. Lacy Leadership Alumni. Health, Pension, profit-sharing, and employee benefits, Corporate taxation. Office: Ice Miller 1 American Sq Indianapolis IN 46282-0020

KEMPF, DONALD G., JR., lawyer; b. Chgo., July 4, 1937; s. Donald G. and Verginia (Jahnke) K.; m. Nancy Kempf, June 12, 1965; children: Donald G. III, Charles P., Stephen R. AB, Villanova U., 1959; LLB, Harvard U., 1965; MBA, U. Chgo., 1989. Bar: Ill. 1965, U.S. Supreme Ct. 1972, N.Y. 1986, Colo. 1992. Assoc. Kirkland & Ellis, Chgo., 1965-70, ptnr., 1971-2000; exec. v.p., chief legal officer, sec. Morgan Stanley, N.Y.C., 2000—. Trustee Chgo. Symphony Orch., 1995—, Am. Inns of Ct., 1997-, v.p., 2002—; bd. govs. Chgo. Zool. Soc., 1975—, Art Inst. Chgo., 1984—; bd. dirs. United Charities Chgo., 1985—, chmn. bd., 1991-93. Capt. USMC, 1959-62. Fellow Am. Coll. Trial Lawyers; mem. Am. Econ. Assn., ABA, Chgo. Club, Econ. Club, Univ. Club, Mid-Am. Club, Saddle and Cycle Club (Chgo.), Snowmass (Colo.) Club, Quail Ridge (Fla.) Club, Westmoreland Club. Roman Catholic. Antitrust, General civil litigation, Mergers and acquisitions. Address: Morgan Stanley 1585 Broadway Fl 39 New York NY 10036-8200 E-mail: donald.kempf@morganstanley.com.

KENDALL, FRANK RUSSELL, SR., lawyer; b. Houston, June 14, 1920; s. William E. and Theodora Dudley (Kuker) K.; m. Anne Benson, Sept. 9, 1942; children: Theodora, Bernard, Frank, John, Thomas. Student, Gregorian U., Rome, 1937-40, U. Houston, 1940-42; LLB, South Tex. Coll. Law, 1949. Bar: Tex. 1949, U.S. Dist. Ct. (so. dist.) Tex. 1949, U.S. Ct. Appeals (5th cir.) 1949, U.S. Supreme Ct. 1969, U.S. Ct. Claims 1974. Asst. dist. atty. Harris County State of Tex., Houston, 1948-52; ptnr. Vinson & Elkins, Houston, 1953—. Vice gov. Gen. Equestrian Order of the Holy Sepulchre of Jerusalem, Protection of Holy See. Lt. (s.g.) USNR, 1942-45, PTO. Mem. ABA, Am. Coll. Trial Lawyers, Tex. Bar Assn., Tex. Bar Found., Houston Bar Assn. Roman Catholic. Condemnation (eminent domain). Office: Vinson & Elkins 1001 Fannin St Ste 3300 Houston TX 77002-6706

KENDALL, PHILLIP ALAN, lawyer; b. Lamar, Colo., July 20, 1942; s. Charles Stuart and Katherine (Wilson) K.; m. Margaret Roe Greenfield, May 2, 1970; children: Anne, Timothy. BS in Engring., Stanford U., 1964; JD, U. Colo., Boulder, 1969; postgrad., U. Freiburg (Germany), 1965-66. Engr. Siemens Halske, Munich, 1965; of counsel Kraemer, Kendall & Benson LLC, Colorado Springs, Colo., 1969—. Gen. counsel Peak Health Care, Inc., Colorado Springs, 1979-87; bd. dirs. Wells Fargo Banks Colorado Springs. Pres. bd. Colorado Springs Symphony Orch. Assn., 1977-80; bd. dirs. Penrose Hosps., Colorado Springs, 1982-88; pres. bd. Citizen's Goals, Colorado, 1984-86; bd. dirs. Legal Aid Found., Denver, 1988-94, chmn., 1991-93; bd. dirs. Colo. chpt. Nature Conservancy, 1996—, chair 2001—. Recipient Medal of Distinction-Fine Arts, Colorado Springs C. of C., 1983. Mem. ABA, Am. Bar Found., Colo. Bar Found., Colo. Bar Assn. (bd. govs. 1985-88, outstanding young lawyer 1977), El Paso County Bar Assn. (bd. trustees 1983-85), Colorado Springs Estate Planning Coun.(lectr charitable estate planning). Avocations: triathlons, helicopter skiing, marathon swimming, windsurfing, sailing. Estate planning, Probate (including wills, trusts), Estate taxation. Home: 1915 Wood Ave Colorado Springs CO 80907-6714 Office: Kraemer Kendall & Benson LLC Ste 300 430 N Tejon St Colorado Springs CO 80903-1167 E-mail: pkendall@k2blaw.com.

KENDE, CHRISTOPHER BURGESS, lawyer; b. N.Y.C., Apr. 28, 1948; s. Herbert Alexander and Helga Henrietta (Wieselthier) K.; m. Barbara Gonzales, May 22, 1976. BA, MA, Brown U., 1970; JD, NYU, 1973. Bar: N.Y. 1974, Mass. 1975, D.C. 1988, Calif. 1996, U.S. Dist. Ct. (So. and Ea. dists.) N.Y. 1974, U.S. Ct. Appeals (2nd cir.) 1976, U.S. Ct. Appeals (9th cir.) 1996, U.S. Supreme Ct. 1978. Staff atty. Legal Aid Soc., N.Y.C., 1973-76; assoc. Dewey, Ballantine et al., N.Y.C., 1976-78, Hill Betts & Nash, N.Y.C., 1978-82, ptnr., 1982-89, Holtzmann, Wise & Shepard, N.Y.C., 1989-96, Cozen O'Connor, N.Y.C., 1996—. Contbr. articles to profl. jours. Recipient Silver medal Caisse des Depots, 1984. Mem. ABA, N.Y. County Lawyers Assn. (past chmn. com. on admiralty and maritime law 1998-99), Maritime Law Assn. (marine ecology com., com. on the CMI), French Maritime Law Assn., India House, Edgartown Yacht Club, Univ. Club N.Y., The Travellers (Paris), Yacht Club de France, Order of Coif, Phi Beta Kappa. Democrat. Presbyterian. Avocations: sailing, motorcycling, tennis, fitness, gardening. Admiralty, Federal civil litigation, Insurance. Home: 545 W End Ave Apt 2B New York NY 10024-2723 Office: Cozen & O'Connor 45 Broadway New York NY 10006-3007 E-mail: ckende@cozen.com.

KENDE, MARK STEVEN, law educator; b. White Plains, N.Y., Mar. 31, 1960; s. Andrew Steven and Frances Boothe Kende. BA, Yale U., 1982; JD, U. Chgo., 1986. Bar: Ill. 1988, U.S. Dist. Ct. (no. dist.) Ill. 1988, U.S. Ct. Appeals (7th cir.) 1990, Mich. 1996. Law clk. to Hon. Julian A. Cook, Jr. U.S. Dist. Ct., Detroit, 1986—88; atty. Miner, Barnhill & Galland, Chgo., 1988—93; assoc. prof. Thomas M. Cooley Law Sch., Lansing, Mich., 1993—99; prof. U. Mont., Missoula, 1999—. Vis. prof. U. Stellenbosch, South Africa, 1999—; cons. Internat. Found. Election Sys., Democratic Republic of Congo, 2000. Bd. dirs. Chgo. Lawyers Commn. Civil Rights, 1991—93; chair Mich. Acad. Sci., Arts & Letters, 1998. Fulbright scholar, 2000. Fellow: Mich. Bar Found.; mem.: ABA, Assn. Am. Law Schs. (chair-elect Africa sect. 2002). Democrat. Roman Catholic. Avocations: chess, tennis, softball, basketball, travel. Office: U Mont Sch Law Missoula MT 59812

KENDRICK, NISBET S., III, lawyer; b. Ga., Apr. 04; m. Bambi Kendrick; children: Harris, Merideth. BA in Philosophy, U. Ga., 1974, JD, 1977. Pvt. practice, Marietta, Ga., 1977—82; ptnr. Fishman, Kendrick & Gordon, Atlanta, 1982—88, Parker, Johnson & Montgomery, Atlanta, 1988—96, Womble, Carlyle, Sandridge & Rice, PLLC, Atlanta, 1996—. Bd. dirs. Primier/First Alliance Bankshares. Mem.: ABA (co-chair ADR Inst.), Ga. Bar Assn. (mem. alt. dispute resolution sect.). Republican. Episcopalian. Avocation: iron man triathalon. Office: Womble Carlyle Sandridge and Rice PLLC 1 Atlantic Ctr 1201 W Peachtree St Ste 3500 Atlanta GA 30309 Office Fax: 404-870-4861. Business E-Mail: kkendrick@wcsr.com.

KENEALLY, KATHRYN MARIE, lawyer; b. Dayton, Ohio, Apr. 30, 1958; d. William Henry and Joanna Gertrude K.; m. Thomas Marshall, Oct. 16, 1992. BA, Cornell U., 1979; JD, Fordham U., 1982; LLM in Taxation, NYU, 1993. Bar: N.Y., 1983, U.S. Dist. Ct. (so., ea. dists.) N.Y., 1983, U.S. Ct. Appeal (2d, 3d, 11th cirs.), U.S. Tax Ct. Law clk. to Hon. E. R. Neaher U.S. Dist. Ct. (ea. dist.) N.Y., Bklyn., 1982-83; assoc. Skadden Arps Slate Meagher & Flom, N.Y.C., 1983-85, Kostelanetz Ritholz Tigue & Fink, N.Y.C., 1985-90, ptnr., 1990-93, Kostelanetz & Fink, LLP, N.Y.C., 1993-99; mem. Owen & Davis, PC, N.Y.C., 2000—02; ptnr. Fulbright & Jaworski, L.L.P., N.Y.C., 2002—. Columnist The Champion, 1996—, Jour. Tax Practice and Prodecure, 1999--; co-author: Practice Under Federal Sentencing Guidelines, 1998; contbr. articles to profl. jours. Mem. practitioners adv. group U.S. Sentencing Commn., 1993—. Mem. ABA (chmn. taxation sect., civil and criminal tax penalties com. 2000-02), Nat. Assn. Criminal Def. Lawyers (life). Federal civil litigation, Criminal, Taxation, general. Home: 48 Charlotte Pl Hartsdale NY 10530-2602 Office: Fulbright & Jaworski LLP 660 Fifth Ave New York NY 10103 E-mail: kkeneally@fulbright.com.

KENNARD, JOYCE L. judge; b. Bandung, West Java, Indonesia, May 6, 1941; AA, Pasadena City Coll., 1970; BA, U. So. Calif., 1971, MPA, JD, U. So. Calif., 1974. Former judge L.A. Mcpl. Ct., Superior Ct., Ct. Appeal, Calif.; assoc. justice Calif. Supreme Ct., San Francisco, 1989—. Office: Calif Supreme Ct 350 Mcallister St San Francisco CA 94102-4783

KENNEDY, ANTHONY MCLEOD, United States supreme court justice; b. Sacramento, July 23, 1936; AB, Stanford U., 1958; student, London Sch. Econs.; LLB, Harvard U., 1961; JD (hon.), U. Pacific, 1988, U. Santa Clara, 1988. Bar: Calif. 1962, U.S. Tax Ct. 1971. Former ptnr. Evans, Jackson & Kennedy; prof. constl. law McGeorge Sch. Law, U. of Pacific, 1965-88; judge U.S. Ct. Appeals (9th cir.), Sacramento, 1976-88; assoc. justice U.S. Supreme Ct., Washington, 1988—. Mem. bd. student advisors Harvard Faculty, 1960-61. Fellow Am. Bar Found. (hon.), Am. Coll. Trial Lawyers (hon.); mem. Sacramento County Bar Assn., State Bar Calif., Phi Beta Kappa. Office: US Supreme Ct Supreme Ct Bldg 1 1st St NE Washington DC 20543-0001

KENNEDY, CHARLES ALLEN, lawyer; b. Maysville, Ky., Dec. 11, 1940; s. Elmer Earl and Mary Frances Kennedy; m. Patricia Ann Louderback, Dec. 9, 1961; 1 child, Mimi Mignon. AB, Morehead State Coll., 1965, MA in Edn., 1968; JD, U. Akron, 1969; LLM, George Washington U., 1974. Bar: Ohio 1969. Asst. cashier Citizens Bank, Felicity, Ohio, 1961-63; tchr Triway Local Sch. Dist., Wooster, Ohio, 1965-67; with office of gen. counsel Fgn. Agr. and Spl. Programs Divsn. USDA, Washington, 1969-71; ptnr. Kauffman, Eberhart, Cicconetti & Kennedy Co., Wooster, 1972-86, Kennedy, Cicconetti, Knowlton & BuyTendyk, LPA, Wooster, 1986—. Mem. ABA, FBA, ATLA, Am. Coll. Barristers, Ohio State Bar Assn., Ohio Acad. Trial Lawyers, Wayne County Bar Assn., Exch. Club, Lions, Elks, Phi Alpha Delta, Phi Delta Kappa. Republican. General civil litigation, State civil litigation, Personal injury (including property damage). Home: 275 W Henrietta Wooster OH 44691 Office: Kennedy Cicconetti & Know Ken 558 N Market St Wooster OH 44691-3406 E-mail: Knndy558@netscape.net.

KENNEDY, CORNELIA GROEFSEMA, federal judge; b. Detroit, Mich., Aug. 4, 1923; d. Elmer H. and Mary Blanche (Gibbons) Groefsema; m. Charles S. Kennedy, Jr. (dec.); 1 son, Charles S. III. BA, U. Mich., 1945, JD with distinction, 1947; LL.D. (hon.), No. Mich. U., 1971, Eastern Mich. U., 1971, Western Mich. U., 1973, Detroit Coll. Law, 1980, U. Detroit, 1987. Bar: Mich. bar 1947. Law clk. to Chief Judge Harold M. Stephens, U.S. Ct. of Appeals, Washington, 1947-48; assoc. Elmer H. Groefsema, Detroit, 1948-52; partner Markle & Markle, Detroit, 1952-66; judge 3d Judicial Circuit Mich., 1967-70; dist. judge U.S. Dist. Ct., Eastern Dist. Mich., Detroit, 1970-79, chief judge, 1977-79; circuit judge U.S. Ct. Appeals, (6th cir.), 1979-99, sr. judge, 1999—. Mem. Commn. on the Bicentennial of the U.S. Constitution (presdl. appointment). Recipient Sesquicentennial award U. Mich. Fellow Am. Bar Found.; mem. ABA, Mich. Bar Assn. (past chmn. negligence law sect.), Detroit Bar Assn. (past dir.), Fed. Bar Assn., Am. Judicature Soc., Nat. Assn. Women Lawyers, Am. Trial Lawyers Assn., Nat. Conf. Fed. Trial Judges (past chmn.), Fed. Jud. Fellows Commn. (bd. dirs.), Fed. Jud. Ctr. (bd. dirs.), Phi Beta Kappa. Office: US Ct of Appeals 6th Circuit 532 Potter Stewart US Courthouse 100 E Fifth St Cincinnati OH 45202

KENNEDY, CORNELIUS BRYANT, retired lawyer; b. Evanston, Ill., Apr. 13, 1921; s. Millard Bryant and Myrna Estelle (Anderson) K.; m. Anne Martha Reynolds, June 20, 1959; children: Anne Talbot, Lauren K. Mayle. AB, Yale U., 1943; JD, Harvard U., 1948. Bar: Ill. 1949, D.C. 1965. Assoc. Mayer Meyer Austrian & Platt, Chgo., 1949-54, 55-59; asst. to U.S. atty. Dept. Justice, Chgo., 1954-55; counsel to minority leader U.S. Senate, 1959-65; sr. ptnr. Kennedy & Webster, Washington, 1965-82; of counsel Armstrong, Teasdale, Schlafly & Davis, Washington, 1983-88; public mem. Adminstrv. Conf. U.S., 1972-82, sr. conf. fellow, 1982-90, chmn. rulemaking com., 1973-82; ret., 1988. Contbr. articles to law jours. Fin. chmn. Lyric Opera Co., Chgo., 1954; chmn. young adults group Chgo. Coun. Fgn. Rels., 1958-59; pres. English Speaking Union Jrs., Chgo., 1957-59; trustee St. John's Child Devel. Ctr., Washington, 1965-67, 75-87, pres., 1983-85 ; exec. dir. Supreme Ct. Hist. Soc., 1984-87. 1st lt., AC U.S. Army, 1942-46. Fellow Am. Bar Found.; mem. Am. Law Inst., ABA (coun. sect. adminstrv. law 1967-70, chmn. sect. 1976-77), Fed. Bar Assn. (chmn. com. adminstrv. law 1963-64), Legal Club Chgo., Explorers Club, N.Y.C. Club, Capitol Hill Club, Chevy Chase Club, Sailing Club of Chesapeake, Adventurer's Club. Home: 8462 Brook Rd Mc Lean VA 22102-1703

KENNEDY, DAVID J. lawyer; b. N.Y.C., July 11, 1971; s. James Joseph and Anne Veronica (Hearne) K.; m. Aldina Maria Vazao, Apr. 11, 1997; 1 child, Dylan Jeronimo. BA, Harvard U., 1993; JD, Yale U., 1997. Bar: Conn. 1997, N.Y. 1998, U.S. Ct. Appeals (2d cir.) 1998, U.S. Dist. Ct. (so. dist.) N.Y. 1999. Pub. Interest Law fellow Alliance for Justice, Washington, 1997-98; law clk. to Hon. Kimba M. Wood U.S. Dist. Ct. (so. dist.) N.Y., N.Y.C., 1998-99; law clk. to hon. Wilfred Feinberg U.S. Ct. Appeals (2d cir.), 1999-2000; asst. U.S. Atty., So. Dist. N.Y., 2000—. Mem. grad. rev. bd. Harvard Lampoon, 1993—; contbr. articles to law rev. Contbg. mem. Dem. Nat. Com., Washington, 1995—. Harry S Truman scholar, 1992, Henry Luce scholar, 1993. Roman Catholic. Avocations: cooking, reading, bears. Home: 3235 Cambridge Ave Bronx NY 10463-3622

KENNEDY, EMILY KATHRYN, paralegal; b. Indpls., June 14, 1978; d. James Douglas and Anne Ellen Allen; m. Matthew Montgomery Kennedy, Jan. 20, 2001. BA, Ind. U., 2000. Sales rep. Western-Southern Life, Indpls., 2000—01; paralegal Ice Miller, Indpls., 2001—. Republican. Presbyterian. Avocations: reading, travel, British comedy, French language, volunteer work. Office: Ice Miller One American Sq Box 82001 Indianapolis IN 46282

KENNEDY, GEORGE WENDELL, prosecutor; b. Altadena, Calif., Aug. 5, 1945; s. Ernest Campbell Kennedy and Mildred (Onstott) Stuckey; m. Janet Lynn Stites, Aug. 3, 1978; children: Campbell, Britton. BA, Claremont Men's Coll., 1968; postgrad., Monterey Inst. Fgn. Studies, 1968; JD, U. So. Calif., 1971; postgrad., Nat. Coll. Dist. Attys., 1974, F.B.I. Nat. Law Inst., 1989. Bar: Calif. 1972, U.S. Dist. Ct. (no. dist.) Calif. 1972, U.S. Ct. Appeals (9th cir.) 1972. Dep. dist. atty. Santa Clara County, San Jose, Calif., 1972-87, asst. dist. atty., 1987-88, chief asst. dist. atty., 1988-90, dist. atty., 1990—. Author: California Criminal Law Practice and Procedure, 1986. Active NAACP, 1989—, police chiefs' assn. Santa Clara County, San Jose, 1990—; chair domestic violence coun. Santa Clara County, San Jose, 1990-92; bd. dirs. Salvation Army, 1993. Recipient commendation Child Advocates of Santa Clara & San Mateo Counties, 1991, Santa Clara County Bd. Suprs., 1992, Valley Med. Ctr. Found., 1992, 93; elected Ofcl. of Yr. award Am. Electronics Assn., 1998. Mem. Nat. Dist. Attys. Assn., Calif. Dist. Attys. Assn. (bd. dirs. 1988-90, officer 1993-97, pres. 1997-98), Santa Clara County Bar Assn., Rotary Club. Avocation: sailing. Office: 70 W Hedding St 5th Flr West Wing San Jose CA 95110

KENNEDY, JACK LELAND, lawyer; b. Portland, Oreg., Jan. 30, 1924; s. Ernest E. and Lera M. (Talley) K.; m. Clara C. Hagans, June 5, 1948; children: James M., John C. Student, U.S. Maritime Commn. Acad., Southwestern U., L.A.; JD, Lewis and Clark Coll., 1951. Bar: Oreg. 1951. Pvt. practice, Portland; ptnr. Kennedy & King, Portland, 1971-77, Kennedy, King & McClurg, Portland, 1977-82, Kennedy, King & Zimmer, Portland, 1982-98, Kennedy, Watts, Arellano & Ricks L.L.P., Portland, 1998—. Trustee Northwestern Coll. Law, Portland; dir. Profl. Liability Fund, 1979-82. Contbr. articles to legal jours. Mem. bd. visitors Lewis and Clark Coll. With USNR, 1942-46. Recipient Disting. Grad. award Lewis and Clark Coll., 1983; named Best Lawyers in Am. Fellow Am. Coll. Trial Lawyers, Am. Bar Found. (life), Oreg. Bar Found. (charter); mem. ABA (ho. of dels. 1984-88), Oreg. State Bar (bd. govs. 1976-79, pres. 1978-79), Multnomah Bar Assn., City Club, Columbia River Yacht Club. Republican. General civil litigation, Insurance, Personal injury (including property damage). Office: Kennedy Watts Arellano & Ricks LLP 2850 Pacwest Ctr 1211 SW 5th Ave Portland OR 97204-3713

KENNEDY, JEANNE ELIZABETH, lawyer; b. 1947; d. Richard Bernard and Rosalie Ann Ryan; m. James N. Kennedy; children by previous marriage: Margaret, Robbie. AA, Mira Costa Coll., 1970; BA, Calif. State U., San Diego, 1973, MA, 1975; JD, Citrus Belt Law Sch., 1983. Bar: Calif. 1984, U.S. Dist. Ct. (cen. dist.) Calif. 1984. Instr. Victor Valley Coll., Victorville, Calif., 1975-78; project coord. Cropsey Constrn., Adelanto, Calif., 1978-81; law clerk Delatore, Caldwell & Hanson, Victorville, 1980—83; assoc. Caldwell & Hansen, Victorville, 1983-86; ptnr. Caldwell & Cropsey, Victorville, 1986-91, Caldwell & Kennedy, Victorville, 1991-2000, Caldwell, Kennedy & Porter APC, Victorville, 2000—. Trustee Victor Elem Sch. Dist., 1983-2001. Mem.: Victor Valley Bus. and Profl. Women (treas. 1985—86), San Bernardino County Bar Assn. (bd. dirs. 1993—99), Hi Desert Bar Assn. (bd. dirs. 1984—87, treas. 1987—88, bd. dirs. 1996—97), Victorville C. of C. (bd. dirs. 1986—92), Soroptimists Internat. of Victor Valley (bd. dirs. 2000—02). Republican. Roman Catholic. Avocations: snow skiing, camping, reading. Estate planning, Family and matrimonial, Probate (including wills, trusts). Office: Caldwell Kennedy & Porter 15476 W Sand St Victorville CA 92392-2349 E-mail: cklaw@mscomm.com.

KENNEDY, JERRY WAYNE, lawyer; b. Murphy, N.C., Nov. 18, 1947; s. Almon T. and Ruby Mae (McCalla) K.; m. Maura Comerford, July 15, 1978. BA, Birmingham So. Coll., 1970; MA, Am. U., 1977; JD, Samford U., 1984; postgrad., Georgetown U., 1983-84. Bar: Ala. 1985, D.C. 1986. Press sec. Rep. Ronnie Flippo, 5th dist. Ala., 1977-80; chief of staff, legis. dir. Rep. Ben Erdreich, 6th dist. Ala., 1982-86; assoc. Heron, Burchette, Ruckert & Rothwell, Washington, 1987-90; of counsel Tuttle & Taylor, Washington, 1990-94; owner Kennedy Govt. Rels., Washington, 1995—. Adj. prof. Sch. Communication, Am. U., Washington, 1979. Assoc. editor Am. Jour. Trial Advocacy, 1982-82. With USAF, 1970-74. Mem. ABA, Ala. Bar Assn., D.C. Bar Assn., Ala. State Soc. (bd. dirs.), Soc. Profl. Journalists (Sigma Delta Chi), Delta Theta Phi. Democrat. Unitarian Universalist. Legislative. Home and Office: Kennedy Govt Rels 313 S Carolina Ave SE Washington DC 20003-4213

KENNEDY, JOHN EDWARD, lawyer; b. Mpls., Feb. 18, 1947; s. John Edward and Margaret (Greathouse) K.; m. Linda Bagwell, June 22, 1968; children: John Harlan, Linda Elizabeth. AB cum laude, Harvard U., 1968, JD magna cum laude, 1971. Bar: Tex. 1971, U.S. Dist. Ct. (so. dist.) Tex. 1972, U.S. Ct. Appeals (5th cir.) 1972, U.S. Supreme Ct. 1975, U.S. Ct. Appeals (D.C. cir.) 1984. Assoc. Vinson & Elkins, Houston, 1971-80, ptnr., 1980—. Served to 2d lt. USAR, 1972. Mem. ABA, Houston Bar Assn., Fed. Energy Bar Assn. Clubs: Houston Ctr. Presbyterian. Administrative and regulatory, Appellate, FERC practice. Home: 2617 Pemberton Dr Houston TX 77005-3441 Office: Vinson & Elkins LLP 2500 First City Tower Houston TX 77002-6760 E-mail: jkennedy@velaw.com.

KENNEDY, JOSEPH WINSTON, lawyer; b. Marshalltown, Iowa, June 5, 1932; s. Roy Wesley and Julia Harriet (Plum) K.; m. Barbara B. Bowman, July 11, 1954 (div. June 1982); children: Kimberle Ann, Kamella Lucille; m. Paula Terry Smith, Nov. 24, 1984. BS cum laude, McPherson (Kans.) Coll., 1954; JD with honors, George Washington U., 1958. Bar: Kans. 1958, U.S. Dist Ct. Kans. 1958, U.S. Ct. Appeals (10th cir.) 1976, U.S. Supreme Ct. 1970. Spl. agt. Office of Naval Intelligence, Washington, 1954-58; assoc. Morris, Laing, Evans & Brock, Wichita, Kans., 1958-62; ptnr. Morris, Laing, Evans, Brock & Kennedy, Wichita, 1962—. Chmn. profl. divsn., atty. United Way of the Plains, Wichita, 1990-93. Recipient Best Lawyers in Am. award, 1987, 89-90, 91-92, 93-94, 95-96. Mem. ABA, Kans. Bar Assn. (bd. law examiners 1993-2002), Wichita Bar Assn. (bd. govs. 1964-66). Federal civil litigation. Office: Morris Laing Evans Brock & Kennedy 200 W Douglas Ave Fl 4 Wichita KS 67202-3013 E-mail: jkennedy@morrislaing.com.

KENNEDY, MARC J. lawyer; b. Newburgh, N.Y., Mar. 2, 1945; s. Warren G. K. and Frances F. (Levinson) K.; m. Karen Karatsu; children: Michael L., Kayla R., Shawna D. BA cum laude, Syracuse U., 1967; JD, U. Mich., 1970. Bar: N.Y. 1971. Assoc. Davies, Hardy, Ives & Lawther, N.Y.C., 1971-72, London, Buttenweiser & Chalif, N.Y.C., 1972-73, Silberfeld, Danziger & Bangser, N.Y.C., 1973; counsel Occidental Crude Sales, Inc., N.Y.C., 1974-75; v.p., gen. counsel Internat. Ore & Fertilizer Corp., N.Y.C., 1975-82; asst. gen. counsel Occidental Chem. Corp., Houston, 1982; v.p., gen. counsel Occidental Chem. Agrl. Products Inc., Tampa, Fla., 1982-87; v.p., gen counsel agrl. products group Occidental Chem. Corp., Tampa, 1987-91, assoc. gen. counsel Dallas, 1991—. Faculty mentor Columbia Pacific U., Mill Valley, Calif., 1981—88. Contbr. articles to profl. jours. Mem. governing bd. Ctr. for Brain Health U. Tex. Dallas, 2001—; trustee Bar Harbor Festival Corp., N.Y.C., 1974-87; bd. dirs. Am. Opera Repertory Co., 1982-85; mem. com. planned giving N.Y. Foundling Hosp., 1977-88; Explorer post advisor Boy Scouts Am., 1976-78. Mem. ABA (vice-chmn. com. internat. law liaison young lawyers sect. 1974-75, chmn. sub-com. proposed trade barriers to the importation of products into U.S. 1985-88, vice chmn. corp. counsel com. 1992-93, co-chmn. corp. counsel com. 1993-98), N.Y. State Bar Assn., Am. Corp. Counsel Assn., Tex. Bar Assn. Admiralty, Corporate, general, Private international. Office: Occidental Chem Corp PO Box 809050 Dallas TX 75380-9050

KENNEDY, MICHAEL JOHN, lawyer; b. Spokane, Wash., Mar. 23, 1937; s. Thomas Dennis Kennedy and Evelyn Elizabeth (Forbes) Gordon; m. Pamalee Hamilton, June 14, 1959 (div. July 1968); children: Lisa Marie, Scott Hamilton; m. Eleanore Renee Baratelli, July 14, 1968; 1 child, Anna Rosario. AB in Econs., U. Calif., Berkeley, 1959; JD, U. Calif., San Francisco, 1962. Bar: Calif. 1963, N.Y. 1976, U.S. Ct. Appeals (9th cir. 1963), U.S. Supreme Ct. 1967, U.S. Ct. Appeals (5th cir.) 1975, U.S. Ct. Appeals 2d cir.) 1977, U.S. Ct. Appeals (1st 3d and 4th cirs.) 1979, U.S. Ct. Appeals (3d and D.C. cirs.) 1982. Assoc. Hoberg & Finger, San Francisco, 1962-67; staff counsel Emergency Civil Liberties, N.Y.C., 1967-69; ptnr. Kennedy & Rhine, San Francisco, 1969-76; sole practice N.Y.C., 1976—. Served to 1st lt. U.S. Army, 1963-65. Mem. ABA, N.Y. Criminal Bar Assn., Nat. Assn. Criminal Defenders. Clubs: N.Y. Athletic. Democrat. Roman Catholic. Civil rights, Criminal, Libel. Office: 425 Park Ave New York NY 10022-3506 Home: 150 Central Park S New York NY 10019

KENNEDY, RICHARD JOSEPH, lawyer; b. Joliet, Ill., Aug. 31, 1942; BA in Econs., U. Notre Dame, 1964; JD, Northwestern U., 1967. Bar: Ill. 1967, Colo. 1975, U.S. Dist. Ct. Colo. 1976. Assoc. Barr & Barr, Joliet, 1968-69, Schutts & Hutchison, Joliet, 1969-71; atty. Schutts & Schutts, Joliet, 1971-75, Rector, Melat & Wheeler, Colorado Springs, 1975-77; pvt. practice Colorado Springs, 1977—. Bd. dirs. Colorado Springs Osteopathic Found., 1990-97; mem. Skyway subdivisions archtl. control com. Skyway Archtl. Control Com., Colorado Springs, 1988-99. Mem. Skyway Assn. (v.p. 1988-98), Broadmoor Rotary Club (dir. 1994-97), Notre Dame Club (pres. 1982-83). Roman Catholic. General civil litigation, Personal injury (including property damage), Probate (including wills, trusts). Office: 324 S Cascade Ave Colorado Springs CO 80903-3804

KENNEDY, THOMAS J. lawyer; b. Milw., July 29, 1947; s. Frank Philip and June Marian (Smith) K.; m. Cathy Ann Cohen, Nov. 24, 1978; children: Abby, Sarah. BA, U. Wisc., 1969, JD cum laude, 1972. Bar: Wis. 1972, U.S. Dist. Ct. (ea. and we. dists.) Wis. 1972, Ariz. 1981, U.S. Dist. Ct. Ariz.

1981, U.S. Ct. Appeals (7th cir.) 1980, U.S. Ct. Appeals (9th cir.) 1981, U.S. Ct. Appeals (D.C. cir.) 1983, U.S. Supreme Ct. 1984, U.S. Ct. Appeals (11th cir.) 1986. Assoc. Goldberg, Previant, Milw., 1972-79, Brynelson, Herrick, Madison, Wisc., 1979-81; ptnr. Snell & Wilmer, Phoenix, 1981-93, Lewis and Roca, Phoenix, 1993-96, Ryley, Carlock and Applewhite, Phoenix, 1996-99, Gallagher & Kennedy, 1999—2000, Sherman & Howard, 2000—. Contbg. editor The Developing Labor Laws, 2d, 3d edits., The Fair Labor Standards Act. Mem. ABA, Ariz. State Bar, State Bar Wisc., Maricopa County Bar Assn. Avocations: tennis, reading, hiking. Administrative and regulatory, Labor (including EEOC, Fair Labor Standards Act, labor-management relations, NLRB, OSHA).

KENNELLY, DENNIS L. lawyer; b. Jersey City, N.J., July 23, 1948; s. Lawrence William and Florence (Taylor) Kennelly; m. Anne Marie Gilles, Jan. 14, 1978; children: Margaret Anne, Maureen Elizabeth. AB cum laude, Coll. of Holy Cross, 1970; JD, Duke U., 1973. Bar: Iowa 1973, Hawaii 1974, Calif. 1975. Labor rels. mgr., counsel San Francisco Newspaper Agy. (Chronicle/Examiner), 1976—79; dir. employee rels., labor counsel Peninsula Times Tribune, Palo Alto, 1979—85; prin. Dennis L. Kennelly Law Office, Menlo Park, 1985—. Lt. USNR, 1973—76. Republican. Roman Catholic. Avocations: golf, sports, basketball. Labor (including EEOC, Fair Labor Standards Act, labor-management relations, NLRB, OSHA). Office: 1030 Curtis St Ste 200 Menlo Park CA 94025-4501

KENNEY, FRANK DEMING, lawyer; b. Chgo., Feb. 20, 1921; s. Joseph Aloysius and Mary Edith (Deming) K.; m. Virginia Stuart Banning, Feb. 12, 1944; children: Claudia Kenney Carpenter, Pamela Kenney Voetberg, Sarah Kenney Swanson, Stuart Deming Kenney AB, U. Chgo., 1948, JD, 1949. Bar: Ill. 1948, U.S. Dist. Ct. (no. dist.) Ill. 1949. Assoc. J.O. Brown, Chgo., 1948-49; assoc., ptnr. Winston & Strawn, and predecessors, Chgo., 1949-92, ret., 1992. 1st lt. AUS, 1942-46, CBI, PTO. Mem. ABA, Ill. Bar Assn., Chgo. Bar Assn. (chmn. real property law com. 1982-83), Lawyers Club Chgo., Fox River Valley Hunt Club, Quadrangle Club, Nat. Beagle Club Am. (bd. dirs. 1981-92), Spring Creek Basset Hunt Club (master 1977-93, chmn. bd., 1993-98, hon. chmn. bd. 1998-2002, hon. master 2002-), Kappa Sigma (nat. housing fin. commr. for U.S. and Can., 1959-91). Republican. Roman Catholic. Corporate, general, Property, real (including real estate development, water). Home: PO Box 581 333 Old Sutton Rd Barrington IL 60010-9368 Office: Winston & Strawn 35 W Wacker Dr Ste 3800 Chicago IL 60601-1695

KENNEY, JAMES ALBERT, III, judge; b. Salisbury, Md. m. Karen H. Abrams. BA, Dickinson Coll., 1959; postgrad., Yale U., 1959—60; JD, George Washington U., 1963. Bar: Md. Ct. Appeals 1963, U.S. Dist. Ct. D.C. 1964, U.S. Dist. Ct. Md. 1965, U.S. Ct. Appeals 1974, U.S. Supreme Ct. 1977. Assoc. Barco Cook Patton (now Patton Boggs), Washington, 1963—64; asst. state atty. State Atty. for St. Mary's County, Leonardtown, Md., 1964—67; ptnr. Briscoe Kenney and successors, Lexington Park, Md., 1966—97; judge Ct. Spl. Appeals Md., Leonardtown, 1997—. Adj. prof. St. Mary's Coll. Md., St. Mary's City, 1964—. Contbr. Mem.: ABA, Md. Bar Assn., Am. Coll. Real Estate Lawyers. Episcopalian.

KENNEY, JOHN ARTHUR, lawyer; b. Oklahoma City, Aug. 3, 1948; s. Jack H. and Betty Jo (Hill) K.; m. Jane Francis, Sept. 4, 1971; children: John Graham, Lauren Elizabeth. BS in Indsl. Engring. with distinction, U. Okla., 1971, JD, 1975. Bar: Tex. 1975, U.S. Dist. Ct. (so. dist.) Tex. 1976, U.S. Ct. Appeals (5th cir.) 1977, Okla. 1981, U.S. Dist. Ct. Okla. 1981, U.S. Ct. Appeals (10th cir.) 1983. Assoc. Baker & Botts, Houston, 1975-81; shareholder McAfee & Taft, Oklahoma City, 1982—. Temp. judge Okla. Ct. of Appeals, atty. appointed panels, Leadership Oklahoma City; magistrate judge merit selection com. and civil justice reform act adv. com. U.S. Dist. Ct. (we. dist.) Okla. Bd. advisors dept. indsl. engring.; past trustee Westminster Presbyn. Ch.; dir., past pres. Rebuilding Together with Christmas in April, Oklahoma City. Mem. ABA, Okla. Bar Assn. (adminstrn. of justice com. 1990-2000), Fed. bar Assn. Okla. City (chpt. pres. 2001-03), Okla. County Bar Assn. (dir. 1997-98, pres. 1999-2000), Order of Coif, Tau Beta Pi. Federal civil litigation, State civil litigation, Intellectual property. Office: McAfee & Taft Two Leadership Sq 10th Fl Oklahoma City OK 73102

KENNEY, JOHN JOSEPH, lawyer; b. N.Y.C., July 13, 1943; s. Joseph Charles and Regina Elizabeth (Hulbert) K.; m. Charlotte O'Brien, May 23, 1971; 1 child, Alexander Hulbert. BA, St. Michael's Coll., 1966; JD, Fordham U., 1969. Bar: N.Y. 1970, U.S. Dist. Ct. (so. dist.) N.Y. 1973, U.S. Ct. Appeals (2d cir.) 1973, U.S. Dist. Ct. (ea. dist.) N.Y. 1980, U.S. Supreme Ct. 1991. Assoc. Dunnington, Bartholow & Miller, N.Y.C., 1969-71; asst. U.S. atty. U.S. Dist. Ct. (so. dist.) N.Y., N.Y.C., 1971-80; assoc. Simpson, Thacher & Bartlett, N.Y.C., 1980-81, ptnr., 1981—. Mem. deptl. disciplinary com. Appellate Divsn. 1st Dept., 2002—. Counsel, Village of Bronxville, 1983-86; mem. Planning Bd. of Bronxville, 1992-98, counsel, 1981-83; trustee Hist. Deerfield Inc., 1992-98, Bennington Coll., 1999—, Bronxville Pub. Libr., 2003-; bd. dirs. Citizens Crime Commn., 1998—, Am. Assn. for Internat. Commn. Jurists, 2000—. Recipient John Marshall award U.S. Dept. Justice, 1980. Fellow Am. Coll. Trial Lawyers; mem. ABA, Fed. Bar Coun. (pres. 1994-96), Assn. Bar City N.Y. (chmn. criminal law com. 1992-95), New York County Lawyers Assn. (pres. 1996-97), N.Y. State Bar Assn. (exec. com. 1997-2000). Republican. Roman Catholic. Federal civil litigation, Criminal, Securities. Home: 8 The Byway Bronxville NY 10708-4934 Office: Simpson Thacher & Bartlett 425 Lexington Ave 15th Fl New York NY 10017-3954 E-mail: jkenney@stblaw.com.

KENNEY, RAYMOND JOSEPH , JR., lawyer; b. Boston, Aug. 3, 1932; m. Claire L. Ducey; children: Marianne Lordi, Raymond Joseph III, Stephen V., John M. AB cum laude, Boston Coll., 1953, JD, 1958. Bar: Mass. 1958, U.S. Dist. Ct. 1960, U.S. Ct. Appeals (1st cir.) 1969, U.S. Supreme Ct. 1985, U.S. Ct. Appeals (11th cir.) 1995. Mem. firm Martin, Magnuson, McCarthy & Kenney (and predecessor firms), Boston, 1958—. Instr. law Mass. Dept. Edn., U. Ext., 1958-60, Boston U., 1961-66; corporator Winchester Savs. Bank, 1973—, Winchester Hosp., 1980—; lectr. continuing legal edn.; mem. Winchester Fin. Com., 1967-70, chmn., 1970-71; moderator Town of Winchester, 1972-77; chmn. Mass. Jud. Nominating Commn., 1975-77; mem. standing com. on civil rules Supreme Jud. Ct., 1977—; mem. time standards com. Mass. Superior Ct., 1990—; chmn. Mass. Clients Security Bd., 1984-87; dir. Mt. Vernon House, Winchester, 1990—. Author: Mass. Practice series (West), 1998—, Mass. Law Rev.; editor-in-chief, 1973-76; contbr. articles to legal jour. Bd. dirs. Winchester chpt. ARC, 1968-71; pres. Mass. Continuing Legal Edn., 1980-83. Fellow Am. Coll. Trial Lawyers (state committeeman 1982-86), Am. Bar Found., Mass. Bar Found. (pres. 1984-88, trustee 1994-96); mem. ABA (del. 1976-78), Am. Judicature Soc. (dir. 1978-81), New Eng. Bar Assn. (pres. 1980-81), Mass. Bar Assn. (pres. 1977-78, founding chmn. sr. lawyers sect. 1999-2001), Middlesex Bar Assn., Mass. Def. Lawyers Assn. (Def. Lawyer of Yr. 1995), Internat. Assn. Def. Counsel, Boston Coll. Alumni Assn. (pres. 1983-84, 50th Ann. Disting. Law Alumnus award). Personal injury (including property damage), Product liability, Professional liability. Home: 5 Salisbury St Winchester MA 01890-2409 Office: Martin Magnuson McCarthy Kenney 101 Merrimac St Boston MA 02114-4716

KENNEY, WILLIAM FITZGERALD, lawyer; b. San Francisco, Nov. 4, 1935; s. Lionel Fitzgerald and Ethel Constance (Brennan) K.; m. Susan Elizabeth Langfitt, May 5, 1962; children: Anne, Carol, James. BA, U. Calif.-Berkeley, 1957, JD, 1960. Bar: Calif. 1961. Assoc. Miller, Osborne Miller & Bartlett, San Mateo, Calif., 1962-64; ptnr. Tormey, Kenney & Cotchett, San Mateo, 1965-67; pres. William F. Kenney, Inc., San Mateo, 1968—; gen. ptnr. All Am. Self Storage, 1985—, Second St. Self Storage, 1990-96, Cochrane Rd. Self Storage, 1996—, Marine Bus. Ctr., 1998—; pres. The Positive Edge, 2000—. Trustee San Mateo City Sch. Dist., 1971-79, pres., 1972-74; pres. March of Dimes, 1972-73; bd. dirs. Boys Club San Mateo, 1972-90, Samaritan House, 1989—, Lesley Found., 1992—. With U.S. Army, 1960-62. Mem. State Bar of Calif. (taxation com. 1973-76), San Mateo County Bar Assn. (bd. dirs. 1973-75), Calif. Assn. Realtors (legal affairs com. 1978—), San Mateo C. of C. (bd. dirs. 1987-93), Self Storage Assn. (we. region, pres. 1989-90, nat. bd. dirs. 1990-97, nat. v.p 1994-95, pres. 1996), Rotary (pres. 1978-79), Elks (exalted ruler 1974-75). Republican. Roman Catholic. Property, real (including real estate development, water), Estate taxation. Home: 221 Clark Dr San Mateo CA 94402-1004 Office: 120 N El Camino Real San Mateo CA 94401-2705 E-mail: bill1135@rcn.com.

KENNY, GEORGE JAMES, lawyer; b. Jersey City, Feb. 18, 1935; s. George W. and Alice M. Kenny; m. Sandra B. Kenny, Oct. 10, 1959; children: Erin, Michael, Thomas, Patricia, Brendan, Mary, Timothy. BS in Econs., Seton Hall U., 1956; LLB, Rutgers U., 1959. Bar: N.J. 1961, U.S. Dist. Ct. N.J. 1961, U.S. Dist. Ct. (so. and ea. dists.) N.Y., 1991, U.S. Supreme Ct. 1966, N.Y. 1983, U.S. Ct. Appeals (3d cir.) 1987, U.S. Ct. Appeals (4th cir.) 1988; cert. Civil Trial Atty. N.J. Supreme Ct. 1982. Jud. clerkship to Hon. Theodore J. Labrecque N.J. Superior Ct., 1960-61; assoc. Connell & Foley, LLP, Roseland and Newark, 1961-68; ptnr. Connell, Foley & Geiser, 1968—. Adj. faculty Rutgers U. Sch. Law Mem. editl. bd. N.J. Law Jour., 1984—; author: New Jersey Insurance Law, 2d edit, 2001; contbr. articles to profl. jours. Trustee Essex County Coll. 1971-78 (chmn. 1973-74), Legal Svcs. Found. Essex County, 1989-2001. Fellow Am. Coll. of Trial Lawyers, Am. Bar Found.; mem. ABA (sec. of litigation, coun. mem. 1991-94, chmn. ins. coverage litigation com. 1988-91, fed. judiciary com. 1999-2002), N.J. State Bar Assn. (trustee 1968-69, 89-93), Essex County Bar Assn. (trustee, officer 1974-81, pres. 1981-82), Practicing Law Inst. N.J. Supreme Ct. coms.; Inst. Continuing Legal Edn., Adv. Am. Bd. Trial Advs., Internat. Assn. Def. Counsel. Democrat. Roman Catholic. Avocation: reading. General civil litigation. Office: Connell Foley LLP 85 Livingston Ave Roseland NJ 07068-3702 E-mail: gkenny@connellfoley.com.

KENNY, MARY ALICE, lawyer, law librarian; b. Evergreen Park, Ill., July 5, 1961; d. Ronald Stanley and Kathleen Regina (Fawcett) Adams; m. James Michael Kenny, Sept. 3, 1988; children: Daniel Patrick, Eileen Anne. BS, Ill. State U., 1984; JD, DePaul U., 1988; M of Libr. and Info. Sci., Rosary Coll., River Forest, Ill., 1997. Bar: Ill. 1988, U.S. Dist. Ct. (no. dist.) Ill. 1988, U.S. Cir. Ct. (7th cir.) Ill. 1988; cert. instr. h.s. grades 6-12, Ill. Br. law libr., dir. Cook County Law Libr., Bridgeview, Ill., 1989-97; paralegal educator Am. Inst. Paralegal Studies, Oakbrook Terrace, Ill., 1990-97; pvt. practice Oak Lawn, Ill., 1992—; adj. prof. law, ref. libr. Sch. Law Libr. Loyola U., Chgo., 1998—. Mem. adv. bd. Am. Inst. Paralegal Studies, Oakbrook Terrace, 1994-96. Contbg. author: Bar None: 125 Years of Women Lawyers in Illinois, (booklet) Union List of Holdings of the Branch Libraries of the Cook County Law Library, 1995, 96; contbr.: (book) Legal Research and Writing Exercises for Paralegals, 1992. Bd. dirs. Queen of Peace H.S. Alumnae Assn., Burbank, Ill., 1996—. Mem. ABA, Am. Assn. Law Librs. (Chgo. chpt.), Am. Assn. Law Schs., Chgo. Assn. Law Librs. Democrat. Roman Catholic. Estate planning, Property, real (including real estate development, water). Office: 16335 Harlem Ave Ste 400 Tinley Park IL 60477-2594 E-mail: mkenny@luc.edu.

KENNY, PHILIP WILLIAM, lawyer; b. Mt. Vernon, N.Y., Nov. 9, 1946; s. Paul James and Ethel Roma (Dooley) K.; m. Ellen Goldberg, Feb. 16, 1974 (div. Nov. 1980); m. Christine Madge Dockum, Nov. 29, 1980; children: Merideth, Jason, Matthew. BA, Fordham U., 1968; JD, N.Y. Law Sch., 1973. Bar: N.Y. 1974. Sole practice, Star Lake, N.Y., 1975-80; atty. Nationwide Ins. Co., Syracuse, N.Y., 1980-83; assoc. Meiselman, Farber, Poughkeepsie, N.Y., 1983-84, Grogan & Botti, P.C., Goshen, N.Y., 1984-86; atty. Office of Ct. Adminstrn., Poughkeepsie, NY, 1986—92; pvt. practice Poughkeepsie, 1992—. Served with U.S. Army, 1968-70. Roman Catholic. Home: 505 Stanton Ter Poughkeepsie NY 12603-1165 Office: Dutchess County Ct Market St Poughkeepsie NY 12601

KENNY, ROBERT, lawyer; b. Bklyn., June 26, 1947; s. Raymond John and Madeline Catherine (McNally) K.; children: Kaitlin Simon, Brendan William. BBA, Manhattan Coll., 1968; JD, Northeastern U., 1973. Bar: Mass. 1973, Ill. 1975, Mich. 1983, U.S. Dist. Ct. (no. dist.) Ill. 1975, U.S. Tax Ct. 1976, N.J. 1994, U.S. Dist. Ct. N.J. 1997; CPA, N.Y. Dir. taxes and tax counsel Whirlpool Corp., Benton Harbor, Mich., 1981-87; dir. taxes and asst. sec. Rhone-Poulenc Inc., Princeton, N.J., 1987-93; dir. corp. tax strategy Ricoh Corp., West Caldwell, N.J., 1994-95; pvt. practice Princeton, 1995—. Adj. prof. Seton Hall U. Sch. of Law, 1997, Rider U., Lawrenceville, N.J., 1996—; mediator Mercer County Superior Ct., Trenton, N.J., 1996—. Contbr. articles to profl. jours. Counsel, Friends West Windsor Open Space, 1996-. Mem. Rotary Internat. (bd. dirs. 1996-97), N.J. State Bar Assn. (tax com. 1999—), Princeton Bar Assn., N.J. Soc. CPAs (tax com., bd. Mercer Chpt. 1999—), Mercer County Estate Planning Coun., Tax Execs. Inst. N.J. (pres. 1985, program chair 1984, membership chair 1992, IRS liaison chair 1993). Roman Catholic. Avocations: jogging, theatre, volleyball, scuba, tennis. Corporate, general, Estate planning, Taxation, general. Office: 212 Carnegie Ctr Ste 206 Princeton NJ 08540-6236 E-mail: taxdefender@lawyer.com.

KENRICK, CHARLES WILLIAM, lawyer; b. Chgo., June 16, 1946; s. Ralph Schwarting and Angela Augusta (Shostrom) K.; m. Patricia June Ogilvie, Dec. 27, 1969; children: Hugh, Alex, Graham, Charlotte, Blair. AB cum laude, Kenyon Coll., 1968; JD, Duquesne U., 1972. Bar: Pa. 1972, U.S. Dist. Ct. (we. dist.) Pa. 1972, U.S. Ct. Appeals (3rd cir.) 1977, U.S. Supreme Ct. 1984, U.S. Ct. Appeals (6th, 7th and 10th cirs.), 1988. From assoc. to ptnr. Dickie, McCamey & Chilcote, Pitts., 1972—98, mng. ptnr., 1993-97; ptnr. Gorr Moser Dell & Loughney, Pitts., 1999-2000, Grogan & Graffam, Pitts., 2000—. Articles editor Duquesne U. Law Rev., 1971; editor Pitts. Legal Jour., 1980-84. Fellow: ABA, Allegheny Bar Found. (ho. of dels. 1980—2000), Pa. Bar Found.; mem.: Pa. Bar Assn., Allegheny County Bar Assn. (bd. govs. 1984—, adminstrv. v.p. 1986—, pres.-elect 1990, pres. 1991), Duquesne U. Law Alumni Assn. (pres. 1985—86), Kenyon Coll. Alumni Assn. Pitts. (pres. 1983—84), Duquesne Club, Valley Brook Club, Rivers Club. Democrat. Federal civil litigation, General civil litigation, State civil litigation. Office: Grogan & Graffam 4 Gateway Ctr 12th Fl Pittsburgh PA 15222-1000

KENSINGTON, ANDREW JUSTUS, litigation consultant, practitioner, property manager, small business owner; b. Elmhurst, Ill., Oct. 3, 1950; s. Walter Alan Kerr and Esther Elizabeth Blanton. Cert. litigation specialist, Roosevelt U., 1981; BA in Psychology and Sociology, Ill. State U., 1984; grad., Gabriel Richard Inst., 1984. Cert.: (Westlaw specialist). Pres. U.S. Justice Party Americále, 1976—; owner Orion Inst., Buckingham, Va., 2001; asst. Niro, Scavone, Haller & Niro, Chgo., 1983—85; with Johnson, Cusack & Bell, Chgo., 1986—87; legal asst. Trexler-Bushnell, et al, Chgo., 1987—88; patent cons. Legal Pers., Northbrook, Ill., 1990; sales rep. Radio Am./APAC Corp., Chgo., 1991—93; litigation cons., asst. Paul Armstrong, Atty. at Law, Chgo., 1993—94; resident property mgr. Joel Kaplan, Herbert G. Dorsey III, Sedona, Ariz., 1994—98; patent cons. Office Tech. Develop. Office Vice Chancellor U. Ill. Asst. project mgr. Amoco Corp., Chgo., Olsten Svcs., Inc. , Chgo., 1989—90; lead litig. asst. Niro, Scavone, Chgo.; rschr. in field. Author 300 page reports of custom rsch.; contbr. free verse poetry; creator, producer, engr., arranger (personalized audio tapes), ; author press releases. Participant anti-war movement Vietnam War, 1968—76; candidate U.S. Presidency U.S. J.P.A., Va., 2003—; co-founder, advocate N.A.C.G., Va., 1993—. Capt. USAR. Named Excellence in Mil. Sci., U.S. Army, Howe, Ind., 1995; U. Ill. scholarr. Mem.: NACDL, ATLA (assoc.), ABA (assoc.). Episcopalian. Avocations: music, game collecting , walking. Home and Office: Rt 1 Box 1392 Buckingham VA 23921

KENT, ALAN HEYWOOD, lawyer; b. N.Y.C., Apr. 15, 1946; s. George and Rose (Polakoff) K.; m. Jane Alice Jacoby, Apr. 9, 1972; 1 child, Jennifer. BSBA, Boston U., 1967, JD, 1969; Cert. d' Application, L'Acad. de Droit Internat., The Hague, Netherlands, 1969; LLM, George Washington U., 1979. Bar: N.Y. 1969, D.C. 1974, Md. 1975, Pa. 1975, U.S. Dist. Ct. D.C., U.S. Dist. Ct. Md. 1978, U.S. Dist. Ct. (no. dist.) Tex. 1979, U.S. Ct. Appeals (fed. cir.) 1978, U.S. Ct. Appeals (D.C. cir.) 1979, U.S. Ct. Appeals (4th cir.) 1981, U.S. Claims Ct. 1978, U.S. Supreme Ct. 1974. Trial counsel Office of Gen. Counsel U.S. Gen. Svcs. Adminstrn., Washington, 1971-73; assoc. Greenberg, Trayman, Cantor, Reiss & Blasky, Washington, 1974-76, ptnr., 1976-80, Schnader, Harrison, Segal & Lewis, Washington, 1981—96; of counsel Tighe Patton Armstrong Teasdale Washington, 1996—; counsel D.C. Ct. Appeals com. on admissions, 2000—. Mem. nat. constrn., commercial, and large complex case panels Am. Arbitration Assn., Washington, 1982—; faculty mem. Fed. Pubs. Inc., Washington, 1980-1998, The Cambridge Inst., Washington, 1989—. Co-author: Construction Arbitration, 1981, Litigating Against the Federal Government, 1987, Construction Claims Under Maryland Law, 1990; editor (law jour.) Insurance Counsel Journal, 1978; contbr. articles to prof. jours. Recipient Platinum award United Way Campaign, Washington, 1987,'88. Mem. ABA, Fed. Bar Assn. (chmn. Govt. Constrn. Cont. Com. 1984-92), Md. State Bar Assn., D.C. Bar Assn.; fellow ABA. Avocations: opera, travel. Construction, Corporate, general, Government contracts and claims. Home: 7013 Nevis Rd Bethesda MD 20817-4763 Office: Tighe Patton Armstrong Teasdale PLLC 1747 Pennsylvania Ave NW Ste 300 Washington DC 20006-2106

KENT, DAVID CHARLES, lawyer; b. Shreveport, La., July 23, 1953; s. Keith C. and Louise (Goode) K.; m. Carol Elizabeth Hittson, July 3, 1976; children: John, Meredith, Robert. BA, Baylor U., 1975, JD, 1978. Bar: Tex. 1978, U.S. Dist. Ct. (no. dist.) Tex. 1980, U.S. Ct. Appeals (5th cir.) 1980, U.S. Dist. Ct. (so. and we. dists.) Tex. 1981, U.S. Ct. Appeals (11th cir.) 1981, U.S. Dist. Ct. (ea. dist.) Tex. 1981; bd. cert. civil trial law, personal injury trial law. Briefing atty. Supreme Ct. Tex., Austin, 1978-79; ptnr. Hughes & Luce L.L.P., Dallas, 1979-2000, Diamond McCarthy Taylor Finley Bryant & Lee, LLP, 2000—. Bd. dirs. Law Focused Edn., Inc. Editor: Managing Scarce World Resources, 1975, Crime and Justice in America, 1976, Medical Care and Health in America, 1977, Meeting America's Energy Needs, 1978; contbr. articles to profl. jours. Coord. employee campaign United Way Dallas, 1981-90, teamwalk March of Dimes, Dallas, 1981-87; nat. exploring com. Boy Scouts Am., Irving, Tex., 1982-92; mem. HOBY Tex. North, bd. dirs., 1999-2003, sec., 2000-03; mem. Baylor Parents League, pres. North Dallas Area chpt., 1999-2001; pres. Twin Bridge Homeowners Assn., 2000-02. Named Outstanding Young Lawyer Dallas, Dallas Assn. Young Lawyers, 1989; recipient Cert. Recognition United Way, 1983. Fellow: Tex. Bar Found., Dallas Bar Found.; mem.: ATLA, ABA, Coll. of State Bar of Tex., Dallas Bar Assn. (chair Tex. h.s. mock trial program 1994—99, chair Law Day com. 2000—01, chair Speakers Com. 2002, Outstanding Com. Chair award 1998), Baylor U. Alumni Assn. (scholarship com. 1980—81). Republican. Methodist. General civil litigation, Insurance, Personal injury (including property damage). Office: Diamond McCarthy Taylor Finley Bryant Lee 1201 Elm St 34th Flr Dallas TX 75270 E-mail: dkent@diamondmccarthy.com.

KENT, JOHN BRADFORD, lawyer; b. Jacksonville, Fla., Sept. 5, 1939; s. Frederick Heber and Norma Cleveland (Futch) K.; m. Monett Powers, Dec. 18, 1969; children: Monett, Susan, Sally, Katherine. AB, Yale U., 1961; JD, U. Fla., 1964; LLM in Taxation, NYU, 1965. Bar: Fla., 1964, U.S. Dist. Ct. (mid. dist.) Fla. 1965, U.S. Tax Ct., 1965, U.S. Dist. (so. dist.) Fla., 1981, Neb., 1995, U.S. Ct. Appeals (11th cir.), U.S. Supreme Ct., 1973. Assoc. Ulmer, Murchison, Kent, Ashby & Ball, Jacksonville, 1965-67; ptnr., shareholder Kent, Watts & Durden, P.A. and predecessor firms, Jacksonville, 1967-85; shareholder Carlton, Field, Ward, Emmanuel, Smith, Cutler & Kent, Jacksonville, 1985-88, Kent, Crawford, P.A., Jacksonville, 1988—. Jacksonville Legal Aid Soc. (past bd. dirs.), Fla. Cmty. Coll Found. (past pres., trustee), Children's Home Soc. Fla. NE Divsn. (past pres., bd. dirs.). Mem. Nat. Assn. Theatre Owners Fla. (bd. dirs., officer 1969-2000), Rotary (past officer, Paul Harris Fellow). Banking, Commercial, contracts (including sales of goods; commercial financing), Corporate, general. Office: Kent & Crawford PA 225 Water St Ste 900 Jacksonville FL 32202-5142

KENT, M. ELIZABETH, lawyer; b. N.Y.C., Nov. 17, 1943; d. Francis J. and Hannah (Bergman) K. AB, Vassar Coll. magna cum laude, 1964; AM, Harvard U., 1965, PhD, 1974; JD, Georgetown U., 1978. Bar: D.C. 1978, U.S. Dist. Ct. D.C. 1978, U.S. Ct. Appeals (D.C. cir.) 1978, U.S. Supreme Ct. 1983, U.S. Dist. Ct. Md. 1985. From lectr. to asst. prof. history U. Ala., Birmingham, 1972-74; assoc. Santarelli and Gimer, Washington, 1978; sole practice Washington, 1978—. Mem. Ripon Soc., Cambridge and Washington, 1968-93; rsch. dir. Howard M. Miller for Congress, Boston, 1972; vol. campaigns John V. Lindsay for Mayor, 1969, John V. Lindsay for Pres., 1972, John B. Anderson for Pres., 1980. Woodrow Wilson fellow 1964-65; Harvard U. fellow 1968-69. Mem.: ACLU, ABA, Superior Ct. Trial Lawyers Assn., DC Assn. Criminal Def. Lawyers (bd. dirs. 2001—), Women's Bar Assn., DC Bar Assn., Phi Beta Kappa. Republican. Avocations: history, politics. Appellate, General civil litigation, Criminal. Home: 35 E St NW Apt 810 Washington DC 20001-1520 Office: 601 Indiana Ave NW Ste 500 Washington DC 20004-2918 E-mail: kentlaw@earthlink.net.

KENT, STEPHEN SMILEY, lawyer; b. Reno, July 6, 1952; s. Robert Roe and Muriel (Smiley) K.; m. H. Mayla Walcutt, Dec. 19, 1976; children: Kristopher, Kimberly, Alisa. BS (hons.), U. Nev., 1975; JD, U. of the Pacific, 1980. Bar: Nev. 1980. Law clk. to Hon. William N. Forman, Reno, 1980-81; assoc. Vargas & Bartlett, Reno, 1981-86, Beckley, Singleton, Jemison & List, Reno, 1986-89, shareholder, 1989-97, Woodburn & Wedge, Reno, 1997—. Mem. exec. coun. Nev. State Bar Young Lawyers Assn., Reno, 1987-89; mem. fee dispute com. Nev. State Bar, Reno, 1985-88, mem. ins. com., 1986-87. Co-author: (manuals/seminars) Nevada Uninsured Motorist Insurance, 1985, Controlling Damages, 1991, Enforcing Judgments, 1989, Pretrial Discovery, 1988, Default Judgements, 1994, Insurance Coverage Law in Nevada, 1998, Advanced Personal Injury Practice, 2001. Mem. Neighborhood Adv. Coun., Reno, 1992-98. Mem. ABA (litigation sect.), Internat. Assn. Def. Counsel, Nat. Bd. Trial Advocacy (cert. civil trial advocate), Reno Rodeo Assn., Rotary Club Reno. Federal civil litigation, Personal injury (including property damage), Insurance. Office: Woodburn & Wedge 6100 Neil Rd PO Box 2311 Reno NV 89505-2311 Home: 7029 Heatherwood Dr Reno NV 89523-2094 Fax: 775-688-3088. E-mail: skent@woodburnandwedge.com.

KENTRIS, GEORGE LAWRENCE, lawyer; b. Detroit, Mich., Nov. 3, 1949; s. Michael Nicholas and Mary (Cassimatis) K.; m. Susan Jo Van Dorn, Nov. 18, 1972; children: Emily Joya, Vanessa, Ann Alexia. BA, Ohio State U., 1971; JD, U. Toledo Coll. Law, 1976. Bar: Ohio 1976, U.S. Dist. Ct. (no. dist.) Ohio 1977, U.S. Supreme Ct. 1980, U.S. Ct. Appeals (6th cir.) 1989. Asst. pros. atty. Hancock County Ohio Prosecutors Office, Findlay, Ohio, 1977-85; assoc. Noble, Bryant & Needles, Findlay, Ohio, 1977-81; pvt. practice Findlay, Ohio, 1981-87, 99—; sr. ptnr. Kentris & Wolph, Findlay, Ohio, 1987-92; sr. atty. Kentris & Assoc., Findlay, Ohio, 1992-96; sr. ptnr. Kentris, Brown & Powell, Findlay, Ohio, 1996-97; pres. Kentris, Brown, Powell & Balega Co., LPA, Findlay, Ohio, 1997-98. Franchisee Taco Bell Corp., Ohio, 1982—; licensee Pizza Hut Inc., 1999—; officer, dir. Findlay TV Corp., 1991-97. Bd. trustees Am. Cancer Soc. Hancock County, Findlay, 1980-94, pres., 1985-86; mem. Hancock County Rep. Exec. Com., 1982-98, treas., 1984-86; bd. dirs. Jr. Achievement of Hancock Co., Inc., 1991-98, Franchisee Choice Hotels, 1998—; dir. Unified Foodservice Purchasing Coop, LLC, 1999-2003; rep. Franmac, 2001—; chmn. Franchise Rels., Integrated Expansion and Devel. Com., 2001—. Mem. Findlay/Hancock County Bar Assn. (cert. grievance com. 1987-98, chmn.

1995, sec. 1993, treas. 1980-81). Mem. Greek Orthodox. Avocations: golf, sports cars. General civil litigation, Criminal, Personal injury (including property damage). Office: George L Kentris Atty at Law 431 E Main Cross St Findlay OH 45840-4822 E-mail: gkentris@aol.com.

KENWORTHY, WILLIAM EUGENE, judge; b. Las Animas, Colo., Apr. 27, 1933; s. William Sydner and Joyce Lovelle (Thedford) K.; m. Lucille Nicoletta Capozzola, July 20, 1963; children: William D., Kathryn J., Randal A. BS, U. Denver, 1955, LLB, 1956. Bar: Colo. 1957, U.S. Dist. Ct. Colo. 1957, U.S. Ct. Appeals (10th cir.) 1962, U.S. Supreme Ct. 1972. Assoc. Fugate & Mitchem, Denver, 1960-63, ptnr., 1964-67; counsel Navajo Freight Lines, Denver, 1967-69; gen. counsel Rocky Mountain Motor Tariff Bur., Denver, 1970-87; ptnr. Rea, Cross & Auchincloss, Washington, 1988-97; adminstrv. law judge Office of Hearings and Appeals Social Security Adminstrn., Pitts., 1997—. Instr. Coll. Law, U. Denver, 1965-66. Author: Transportation of Hazardous Materials, 2d edit., 1992, Corporate Counsel's Guide to Occupational Safety and Health Law, 1993, with supplements, Transportation Safety and Insurance Law, 2 vols., 1998, with ann. supplements, Killer Roads, 1999; writer columns Electric Light and Power, 1966-84, Heavy Duty Trucking, 1993—; also articles. Served with USNR, 1957-60; comdr. Res. ret. Mem. Assn. Transp. Practitioners (pres. 1985-86), Denver Bar Assn., Colo. Bar Assn., Transp. Lawyers Assn., Fed. Bar Assn., Mil. Officers Assn., Exch. Club, Kiwanis (pres. local club 1965-66). Republican. Roman Catholic.

KENYON, EDWARD TIPTON, lawyer; b. Summit, N.J., Jan. 27, 1929; s. Theodore S. and Martha (Tipton) K.; m. Dolores Cetrule, July 11, 1953; children: David S., James N., Jonathan W., Theodore H. AB, Harvard U., 1950; LL.B., Columbia U., 1953. Bar: N.Y. 1956, N.J. 1957. Assoc. Thacher, Proffitt, Prizer, Crawley & Wood, N.Y.C., 1955-56; law clk. to presiding judge U.S. Dist. Ct. N.J., Newark, 1956-57; assoc. Jeffers, Mountain & Franklin, Morristown, N.J., 1957-59, Bourne, Noll and Kenyon and predecessor firm, Summit, 1959-62, ptnr., 1962-97, of counsel, 1997—. Bd. dirs. Atlantic Mgmt. Corp., 1990-98. Trustee Summit Art Ctr., 1960-72, Trinity-Pawling Sch., Pawling, N.Y., 1977-2003, Pingry Sch., Martinsville, N.J., 1970-97, Martha's Vineyard Preservation Trust, 1999—; deacon Cen. Presbyn. Ch., Summit, 1960-65, trustee, 1965-72, 87-93, pres., 1970-72, 88-91; deacon First Congl. Ch., West Tisbury, Mass., 2000—; trustee Overlook Hosp., Summit, 1967-75, pres., 1973-75; trustee Overlook Hosp. Found., 1975-84, sec., 1977-80, v.p., 1980-81, pres., 1981-84; trustee Winston Sch., Summit, 1986-93, v.p., 1987-90, pres., 1990-92; bd. dirs. Overlook Mgmt. Corp., 1988-97; mem. planning bd. Town of Chilmark, 1998—, chmn., 2000—. With M.C., U.S. Army, 1953-55. Mem. ABA, N.Y. State Bar Assn., N.J. Bar Assn., Summit Bar Assn. (pres. 1983-84), Union County Bar Assn., Am. Coll. Trust and Estate Counsel, Am. Law Inst. Clubs: Beacon Hill (trustee 1977-81, pres. 1979-81), Edgartown Yacht Club, Harvard of N.Y.C, Harvard of N.J. (trustee 1958-69, pres. 1968-69). Education and schools, Estate planning, Estate taxation. Home: 49 N Abels Hill Rd Chilmark MA 02535-2026 Office: 382 Springfield Ave Summit NJ 07901-2707

KEPKE, CARLOS ERWIN, lawyer; b. Austin, Tex., July 19, 1939; s. Robert Ernest and Elizabeth Rosalyce (Schoenewolf) K.; m. Patricia Marie Jones, Aug. 9, 1975; children: Bethelyn Ann, Melissa Marie, Amanda Patricia. BA, U. Tex., 1961, JD, 1964. Bar: Tex. 1964, Ohio 1970, U.S. Supreme Ct. 1971. Tax atty. Exxon Co., Houston, 1964-67, Esso Inter-Am., Inc., Miami, Fla., 1967-69; sr. tax atty. Marathon Oil Co., Findlay, Ohio, 1969-71; ptnr. in charge of internat. Chamberlain, Hadlicka, White, Williams, Martin, Houston, 1972-89; ptnr. head tax sect. Shank, Irwin, Conant, Lipshy & Casterline, Dallas, 1989-90; ptnr. Margraves & Schueler, Houston, 1990-92; pvt. practice Houston, 1992—. Editor internat. dept. The Tax Times, 1985-89; contbr. articles to profl. jours. Adv. bd. dirs., Houston Grand Opera Assn., 1973-78, Baylor Coll. Medicine, 1981-83; mem. Japan Soc. Houston 1975-89, Asia Soc. Houston, 1975-89; bd. visitors adv. U. Tex. Sch. Law, Austin, 1989-90. With U.S. Marine Corps, 1957-58. Mem. River Oaks Country Club (audit and fin. com.), Plaza Club, Allegro. Republican. Episcopalian. Avocations: racewalking, reading, collecting books. Estate planning, Private international, Estate taxation. Home: 5161 San Felipe #320 Houston TX 77056 Office: Three Riverway Ste 470 Houston TX 77056

KEPLINGER, BRUCE (DONALD KEPLINGER), lawyer; b. Kansas City, Kans., Feb. 4, 1952; s. Donald Lee and Janet Adelheit (Viets) K.; children: Mark William, Lisbeth Marie, Kristen Michelle, Kailyn Emily, Courtney Nicole; m. Carol Ann Heinz, Apr. 12, 1991. BA with highest distinction, U. Kans., 1974; JD cum laude, So. Meth. U., 1977. Bar: Kans. 1977, U.S. Dist. Ct. Kans. 1977, Mo. 1980, U.S. Dist. Ct. Mo. 1980, U.S. Ct. Appeals (10th cir.) 1985, U.S. Supreme Ct. 1989. Assoc. Clark, Mize & Linville, Salina, Kans., 1977-79, Blackwell, Sanders et al, Kansas City, Mo., 1979-82; ptnr. Payne & Jones, Overland Park, Kans., 1982-94, Norris, Keplinger & Hillman, LLC, Overland Park, 1994—. Master Kansas Inns of Ct.; chmn. Kansas Lawyer Svcs Corp., 1992-01. Contbr. articles to profl. jours. V.p. Friends of Libr., Johnson County, Kans., 1980-85; deacon Village Presbyn. Ch., 1982-86; trustee United Meth. Ch. of Resurrection, trustee, 2002—. Mem.: ABA, Fedn. Def. and Corp. Counsel, Def. Rsch. Inst., Kans. Assn. Def. Counsel (pres.-elect 1992—93, pres. 1993—94), Mo. Bar Assn., Kans. Bar Assn. (chmn. Kans. lawyer svc. corp. 1992—2001), Assn. Def. Trial Attys. (state chmn. 1996—, exec. coun. 1999—2002), Internat. Assn. Def. Counsel, Hallbrook Country Club. Republican. Avocations: reading, golf. Federal civil litigation, State civil litigation, Personal injury (including property damage). Office: Norris Keplinger & Hillman LLC 6800 College Blvd Ste 630 Overland Park KS 66211-1556 E-mail: bkeplinger@k-c-lawyers.com.

KEPLINGER, MICHAEL SCOTT, lawyer; b. Martinsburg, W.Va., Mar. 26, 1940; s. Raymond Lester and Bertha Louise (Kidwiler) K.; m. Helen Bunten, Dec. 27, 1963; children: Michael Scott, Gregory Thomas. BS in Chemistry, W.Va. U., 1963; JD, Georgetown U., 1971. Bar: Md. 1972. Computer scientist Nat. Bur. Stds., Washington, 1967-76; asst. exec. dir. Nat. Commn. on New Technol. Uses of Copyrighted Works, Washington, 1976-78; spl. legal asst. to register U.S. Copyright Office, Washington, 1978-80, chief info. and rev. divsn., 1980-83, policy planning advisor, 1983-84; sr. counselor Office Legis. and Internat. Affairs U.S. Patent and Trademark Office, Washington, 1984—. Cons. World Intellectual Property Orgn.; dep. head Del. to Diplomatic Conf. on Certain Copyright and Neighboring Rights Matters, 1996; chief copyright negotiator for Agreement on Trade Related Aspects of Intellectual Property (TRIPS) for the U.S., 1990-95; negotiator for Diplomatic Conf. on Protection of Audiovisual Performers, Dec. 2000. Home: 5001 Nahant St Bethesda MD 20816-2462 E-mail: michael.keplinger@uspto.gov.

KEPPEL, WILLIAM JAMES, lawyer, educator, writer; b. Sheboygan, Wis., Sept. 25, 1941; s. William Frederick and Anne Elizabeth (Cinealis) K.; m. Polly Holmberg, June 26, 1965; children: Anne Rusert, Timothy, Matthew. BA, Marquette U., 1963; JD, U. Wis., Madison, 1970. Bar: Minn. 1970, U.S. Dist. Minn. 1970, U.S. Ct. Appeals (8th cir.) 1973, U.S. Dist. Ct. (we. dist.) Wis. 1979, U.S. Supreme Ct. 1979, U.S. Ct. Claims 1982. Assoc. Dorsey & Whitney, Mpls., 1970-76, ptnr., 1979-96; assoc. prof. Hamline U. Sch. Law, 1976-79, disting. practitioner in residence, 1996-2000. Instr. U. Minn. Law Sch.; adj. prof. William Mitchell Coll. Law, St. Paul; state adminstrv. law judge, 1977-79, 98—; chmn., dir. Legal Advice Clinics, Ltd.; dir. Legal Assistance of Minn., Inc.; head Hennepin County Pub. Defender's Office for Misdemeanors. Author: (with Mc Farland) Minnesota Civil Practice (4 vols.), 1979, 3d edit., 1999, Administrative Practice and Procedure, 1999; co-author, editor: Minnesota Environmental Law Handbook, 2nd edit., 1995; contbr. articles and monographs to legal jours. Lt. USN, 1963-67, Vietnam. Mem. ABA, Minn. Bar Assn. Roman Catholic. Administrative and regulatory, Federal civil litigation, Environmental. Home: 10 Luverne Ave Minneapolis MN 55419-2612

KEPPELER, H(ERBERT) K(ARL) BRUSS, lawyer; b. Honolulu, Jan. 13, 1937; s. Herbert Kealoha and Doris Kahikilani (Mossman) K. BA, U. Wash., 1959, JD, 1966. Bar: Hawaii 1966, U.S. Dist. Ct. Hawaii 1966, U.S. Ct. Appeals (9th cir.) 1969, U.S. Supreme Ct. 1972. Planning aide R.M. Towill Corp., Honolulu; mgmt. trainee Peoples Nat. Bank, Seattle, 1960-61; records and document analyst land dept. Amfac/JMB Inc. (formerly Am. Factors Ltd.), Honolulu, 1961-63; dep. atty. gen. State of Hawaii, Honolulu, 1966-69, asst. state hwy. safety coord., 1969-71; atty. Dillingham Corp., Honolulu, 1971-75; v.p., coun., sec. The Hawaii Corp., Honolulu, 1975-76; sole practice Honolulu, 1976-90, 94—; of counsel Lyons, Brandt, Cook & Hiramatsu, Honolulu, 1990-94. Mem. Commn. for Hawaii State Pub. Defender's Office, 1976-86, chmn. 1980-86; bd. dirs. Native Hawaiian Legal Corp., 1985-98. Active Prince Kuhio Hawaiian Civic Club, Hawaiian Civic Club Honolulu, Hawaii Emergency Medical Svcs. Program 1972-74; bd. dirs. Kuliouou Cmty. Assn. 1973-74, 75-77, Hawaiian Scholars Program Na Poki'i 1974-84; bd. dirs. Moanalua Gardens Found., 1975—, pres. 1990-92; bd. dirs. Assn. of Hawaiian Civic Clubs 1976-86, 88-2000, pres. Oahu Coun. 1984-86, 1st v.p. 1988-92, pres. 1992-96; bd. dirs Aloha Festivals, 1977-89, 91-94, 96-97, pres., 1980-81; mem. coun. Bishop Mus. Assn. 1987—, pres. 1989-90; mem. adv. coun. Queen Lili'uokalani Children's Ctr., 1991-97; trustee Historic Hawaii Found. 1979-82; bd. dirs. The Friends of 'Iolani Palace, 1978—, Hale Ola o Ho'opakolea, 1989-92; bd. dirs., treas. Hui Na'auao, 1991-92; mem. adv. com. Ford Found. Diversity Project Hawaii Cmty. Found.; mem. Hawaiian Sovereignty Elections Coun., 1993-96; del. Native Hawaiian Conv., 1999—, Royal Order Kamehameha I. 2d lt. U.S. Army, 1960, capt. USAR, 1969. Mem. ABA, Hawaii State Bar Assn. (pres. Young Lawyers sect. 1972, Sec. of Bar 1973), Legal Aid Soc. of Hawaii (bd. dirs. 1971-72), Polynesian Voyaging Soc. (adv. bd. 1973-75), Hawaii C. of C. (chmn. land use and housing com., armed svcs. com. 1977), Punahou Alumni Assn., U. Wash. Alumni Assn., Native Hawaiian C. of C. (dir. 1977-94, 97—, pres. 1980-81), Native Hawaiian Bar Assn., Phi Kappa Sigma, Phi Delta Phi, The Pacific Club. Corporate, general, Estate planning, Property, real (including real estate development, water). Office: PO Box 1319 Honolulu HI 96807-1319 E-mail: kepplaw.hawaii@juno.com.

KEPPELMAN, NANCY, lawyer; b. Abington, Pa., June 28, 1950; d. H. Thomas and Helene A. (Harrow) Keppelman; m. Michael E. Smerza, Sept. 9, 1978. Student, Oberlin (Ohio) Coll., 1968-70; BA, U. Mich., 1972, JD, 1978; Cert., Inst. for Paralegal Trg., Phila., 1972. Bar: Mich. 1978, U.S. Dist. Ct. (ea. dist.) Mich. 1978, U.S. Tax Ct. 1986. Legal asst. Dykema, Gossett et al, Detroit, 1972-75; assoc. Butzel, Keidan et al, Detroit, 1978-80, Law Offices of Brook McCray Smith, Ann Arbor, Mich., 1980-82, Miller, Canfield et al, Detroit, 1982-89, Stevenson Assocs., Ann Arbor, 1989-90; shareholder/lawyer Stevenson Keppelman Assocs., Ann Arbor, 1991—. Condr. seminars in field. Co-author, editor QDROs, EDROs and Division of Employee Benefits in Divorce, A Guide for Michigan Practitioners, 2002; contbr. articles to profl. jours. James B. Angell scholar, U. Mich., 1972. Fellow Mich. State Bar Found., Am. Coll. Benefits Counsel; mem. ABA, State Bar Mich. (mem. taxation coun. 1991-94), Washtenaw County Bar Assn., Women Lawyers Assn. Mich. (bd. dirs., pres. Washtenaw region 1990-93). Avocations: birdwatching, music, hiking. Corporate, general, Pension, profit-sharing, and employee benefits, Taxation, general. Office: 444 S Main St Ann Arbor MI 48104-2304 E-mail: kep@skalaw.com.

KERBY, YALE LELAND, lawyer; b. Corunna, Mich., Apr. 11, 1925; s. Yale H. Harrington and Eltha M. (Bias) K.; m. Grace G. Cutler, June 30, 1956; children: Marla Lynn, Paula Louise, Kevin Yale. Student, Mich. State U., 1946—49; JD, Ohio No. U., 1952. Bar: Ohio 1952, Mich. 1952, U.S. Dist. Ct. (ea. dist.) Mich. 1958, U.S. Dist. Ct. (no. dist.) Ohio 1964, Tex. 1983, U.S. Dist. Ct. (we. dist.) Tex., U.S. Ct. Appeals (6th cir.). Practice Morenci and Adrian, Mich.; judge Mich. (State) dist. Ct. Mich., 1968-78; sole practice Adrian, 1978-83; assoc. E.D. Kincaid, III, Uvalde, Tex., 1983; elected GOP county and regional chmn. Uvalde. Founder Alcohol Info. Ctr., Bixby Hosp., Adrian, Vols. in Probation, Lenawee Traffic Safety Sch., Lenawee Substance Abuse, Inc.; councilman Morenci City, 1960-63. With USMC, 1944-46. Mem. ABA, Tex. Bar Assn., Mich. Bar Assn. (life), Am. Judicature Soc., Am. Legion (1st comdr., county commr., dist. chaplain, dist. judge adv.), ADV, Am. Contract Bridge League, Elks, Kiwanis. Personal injury (including property damage), Probate (including wills, trusts), Property, real (including real estate development, water). Home: 1245 N Park Sr PO Box 5158 Uvalde TX 78802-5158 Office: 220 E Main St Ste 100 Uvalde TX 78801-5639

KERIAN, JON ROBERT, retired judge; b. Grafton, N.D., Oct. 23, 1927; s. Cyril Robert and Elizabeth Antoinette (Kadlec) K.; m. Sylvia Ann Larson, Dec. 28, 1959; children: John, Ann. PhB, U. N.D., 1955, LLB, 1957, JD, 1971. Bar: N.D. 1957, U.S. Dist. Ct. N.D. 1958, U.S. Ct. Appeals (8th cir.) 1971, U.S. Supreme Ct. 1963. Pvt. practice law, Grand Forks, N.D., 1958-61; asst. atty. gen. State of N.D., Bismarck, 1961-67; ptnr. Bosard, McCutcheon, Kerian, Schmidt, Minot, N.D., 1967-80; dist. judge State of N.D., Minot, 1980-92, surrogate judge, 1993—. History instr. Bismarck State Coll., 1965-67; asst. city atty. City of Minot, 1968-76; atty. Zoning & Planning Commn., Minot, 1969-76; lectr. in field. Contbr. articles to profl. jours.; editor ABA newsletter, The Judges News, 1990—95. Mem. ABA (bd. editors Judges Jour. 1990-95), Western States Bar Conf. (pres. 1982-83), N.D. Bar Assn. (pres. 1979-80), Nat. Conf. State Trial Judges (exec. com. 1983-89). Home: 1800 8th St SW Minot ND 58701-6410 Office: PO Box 340 Minot ND 58702-0340

KERLIN, GILBERT, lawyer; b. Camden, NJ, Oct. 10, 1909; s. Ward Dix Sr. and Jenny (Gilbert) K.; m. Sarah Morrison, Aug. 23, 1941; children: Sarah Kerlin Gray, Gilbert Nye, Jonathan Otis. BA, Harvard U., 1933, LLB, 1936. Bar: U.S. Ct. Appeals (2d cir.) 1937, U.S. Supreme Ct. 1945. Of counsel Shearman & Sterling, NYC, 1936—. Chmn. bd. dirs. Wave Hill Inc. Served to lt. col. USAF, 1942-46. Democrat. Unitarian Universalist. Home: Dodgewood Rd Bronx NY 10471 Office: Shearman & Sterling 153 E 53rd St New York NY 10022

KERN, GEORGE CALVIN, JR., lawyer; b. Balt., Apr. 19, 1926; s. George Calvin and Alice (Gaskins) K.; m. Joan Shorell, Dec. 22, 1962; 1 child, Heath. BA, Princeton U., 1947; LLB, Yale U., 1952. Bar: N.Y. 1952. Chief U.S. Info. Ctr., Mannheim, W.Ger., 1947-48; dep. dir. pub. info. Office U.S. Mil. Govt. for Germany, Berlin and Nurnberg, 1948-49; assoc. Sullivan & Cromwell, N.Y.C., 1952-60, ptnr., 1960—. Publ. Cub newspaper, Tehachapi, Calif., 1974—; bd. dirs. McJunkin Corp., Charleston, W.Va. Lt. USN, 1944-46. Corporate, general, Mergers and acquisitions, Securities. Home: 830 Park Ave New York NY 10021-2757 Office: Sullivan & Cromwell 125 Broad St Fl 28 New York NY 10004-2489

KERN, JOHN WORTH, III, judge; b. Indpls., May 25, 1928; s. John Worth and Bernice (Winn) K.; children: John, Stephen. BA, Princeton U., 1949; LLB, Harvard U., 1952. Bar: D.C. 1953, U.S. Ct. Appeals (D.C. cir.) 1955. With CIA, 1952-54; law clk. to chief judge U.S. Ct. Appeals D.C. Cir. Ct., 1954-55; asst. U.S. atty. D.C. Dist. Dept. Justice, Washington, 1955-59; assoc. Kilpatrick, Ballard & Beasley, Washington, 1959-65; with Dept. of Justice, Washington, 1965-68; judge D.C. Ct. Appeals, Washington, 1968-84, sr. judge, 1987—. Dean Nat. Jud. Coll., Reno, 1984-87. Mem. D.C. Bar. Presbyterian. Office: DC Ct Appeals 500 Indiana Ave NW Washington DC 20001-2138

KERN, TERRY C. judge; b. Clinton, Okla., Sept. 25, 1944; s. Elgin L. Kern and Lora Lee (Miller) Renegar; m. Charlene Heinen, Dec. 26, 1970; children: Lauren, Suzanne, Justin Hunter. BS, Okla. State U., Stillwater, 1966; JD, U. Okla., 1969. Bar: Okla. 1969, U.S. Dist. Ct. (ea. dist.) Okla. 1974, U.S. Dist. Ct. (we. dist.) Okla. 1979, U.S. Dist. Ct. (no. dist.) Okla. 1993, U. S. Ct. Appeals (10th cir.) 1979. Gen. atty. FTC, Washington, 1969—70; ptnr. Fischl, Culp, McMillin, Kern and Chaffin, Ardmore, Okla., 1971—86; founding ptnr., pres. Kern, Mordy and Sperry, Ardmore, 1986—94; dist. judge U.S. Dist. Ct. (no. dist.) Okla., Tulsa, 1994—, chief judge, 1996—. Mem. Jud. Conf. Com. on Security and Facilities, 10th Cir. Jud. coun. Chmn. bd. dirs. Southern Okla. Meml. Hosp., Ardmore, 1982—92, chmn., 1989—91. Served with USAR, 1970—75. Named to, Beta Theta Pi Hall of Fame, 2000; recipient Leadership Legacy award, Okla. State U., 2000, Disting. Alumnus award, 2001. Fellow: Okla. Bar Found. (pres. 1991, Disting. Svc. award 1992), Am. Bar Found.; mem.: ABA, Tulsa City Bar Assn. (bd. dirs.), Fed. Judges Assn., U. Okla. Coll. Law Assn., Okla. Bar Assn., Am. Bd. Trial Advocates (Okla. chpt.), W. Lee Johnson Inn of Ct. (master of bench). Democrat. Episcopalian. Office: US Dist Courthouse 333 W 4th St Tulsa OK 74103-3839

KERNEN, WILL, lawyer; b. Boston, July 4, 1951; s. Judson and Olive (Bardsley) K.; m. Cindy M. Krueger, June 21, 1970; children: Kerry, Kurt, Kyle, Kasey, Kathy. BA, Bridgewater State Coll., 1974; JD, Ohio State U., 1976. Bar: Ohio, U.S. Dist. Ct. (so. dist.) Ohio 1978. Assoc. Lappen & Lilley, Logan, Ohio, 1977-78; ptnr. Lappen, Lilley, Kernen & Co., L.P.A., Logan, 1978-96. Law dir. City of Logan, 1978-79; law librarian Hocking County Law Library, 1980-83; acting judge Hocking County Mcpl. Ct., Logan, 1983-87. Bd. dirs. Logan-Hocking City Sch. Dist., 1979-83; counsel Hocking County Rep. Party, 1979. Served with U.S. Army, 1968-71, Germany. Mem. ABA, Ohio Bar Assn., Hocking County Bar Assn. (v.p. 1978-79, pres. 1989—), Jaycees (pres. Logan 1983-84 dist. dir. Ohio 1984-85). State civil litigation, General practice, Property, real (including real estate development, water). Home: 26816 Darl Rd Rockbridge OH 43149-9601 Office: PO Box 388 Logan OH 43138-0388 E-mail: kernenlaw@hocking.net.

KERNER, MICHAEL PHILIP, lawyer; b. N.Y.C., July 21, 1953; s. Arthur and Rosalind (Mehr) K. BA, Antioch Coll., 1976; JD, Lewis & Clark U., 1979; LLM in Taxation with honors, Golden Gate U., 1995. Bar: Calif. 1980 (cert. specialist probate, trusts & estate planning), U.S. Dist. Ct. (no. and ea. dists.) Calif. 1983, U.S. Ct. Appeals (9th cir.) 1983, U.S. Tax Ct., 1996. Staff atty. U.S. EPA, Washington, 1979-80, asst. regional counsel region 9 San Francisco, 1980-83; ptnr. Kerner, Weppner & Rosenbaum, San Francisco, 1983-95; prin. Kerner & Assocs., San Francisco, 1996-2000; ptnr. Janin, Morgan & Brenner, San Francisco, 2000—. Bd. dirs. Solano County Legal Assistance, Vallejo, Calif., 1983-86; arbitrator San Francisco Superior Ct., 1991-94. Editor law rev. and law jours. Mem. ABA, Solano County Bar Assn., Bar Assn. of San Francisco, Nat. Assn. of Trust & Estate Profls. Democrat. Jewish. Avocations: windsurfing, snowboarding, road and mountain biking. Estate taxation, Estate planning, Taxation, general. E-mail: mpk@jmblaw.com.

KERNOCHAN, JOHN MARSHALL, lawyer, educator; b. New York, Aug. 3, 1919; s. Marshall Rutgers and Caroline (Hatch) K. BA, Harvard U., 1942; JD, Columbia U., 1948. Bar: N.Y. 1949. Asst. dir. Legis. Drafting Research Fund Columbia U., N.Y.C., 1950-51, acting dir., 1951-52, dir., 1952-69, lectr. law, 1951-52, assoc. prof., 1952-55, prof., 1955-77, Nash prof. law, 1977-89, Nash prof. law emeritus, 1990—; spl. lectr., 1991—2000; co-dir., 1999—. Cons. Temporary State Commn. to Study Orgnl. Structure of Govt. N.Y.C., 1953; exec. dir. Coun. for Atomic Age Studies, 1956—59, co-chmn., 1960—62; chmn. bd. Galaxy Music Corp., 1956—89; bd. dir. E.C. Schirmer Music Co., Inc.; pres. Gaudia Music & Arts, Inc., 1987—; co-dir. Ctr. for Law and Arts (now Kernochan Ctr. Law, Media & Arts), 1999. Author: The Legislative Process, 1980; co-author: Legal Method Cases and Materials, 1980; contbr. articles to profl. jour. Mem. civil and polit. rights com. President's Commn. on Status of Women, 1962-63; dir. emeritus Vol. Lawyers for the Arts; mem. legal and legis. com. Internat. Confedn. Soc. Authors and Composers. Mem. Assn. Bar City of N.Y. Internat. Lit. and Artistic Assn. (mem. d'honneur, internat. exec. com., mem. U.S.A. group), Copyright Soc. U.S.A. (exec. com. 1986-89), Assn. Tchrs. and Rschr. in Intellectual Property. Office: Columbia Univ Sch Law 435 W 116th St New York NY 10027-7297

KERNS, DAVID VINCENT, lawyer; b. Jan. 29, 1917; s. Clinton Bowen and Ella Mae (Young) K.; m. Dorothea Boyd, Sept. 5, 1942; children: David V., Clinton Boyd. BPh, Emory U., 1937; JD, U. Fla., 1939. Bar: Fla. 1939, U.S. Dist. Ct. (mid. dist.) Fla. 1939, (so. dist.) Fla. 1978, (no. dist.) Fla. 1981, U.S. Ct. Appeals (11th cir.) 1981, U.S. Supreme Ct. 1988. Assoc. Sutton & Reeves, Tampa, Fla., 1939-41, Fowler & White, Tampa, 1945-47; ptnr. Moran & Kerns, Tampa, 1948-49; resident atty. Fla. Road Dept., 1949-53; rsch. asst. Supreme Ct. Fla., 1953-58; dir. Fla. Legis. Reference Bur., 1958-68, Fla. Legis. Svc. Bur., 1968-71, Fla. Legis. Libr. Svcs., 1971-73; gen. counsel Fla. Dept. Adminstrn., 1973-82; mem. Fla. Career Svc. Commn., 1983-86; spl. master Fla. Senate, 1987-96; legal cons. chief inspector gen. Fla. Gov. Office, 1995-98. Contbr. articles to profl. jours. Served with U.S. Army, 1941-45. Mem. Fla. Govt. Bar Assn. (pres. 1966, J. Ernest Webb Meml. award 1982), Fla. Bar (bd. govs. 1978-84), Tallahassee Bar Assn. (spl. dir. 1993-95). Democrat. Methodist. Home: 418 Vinnedge Ride Tallahassee FL 32303-5140

KERR, ALEXANDER DUNCAN, JR., lawyer; b. Pitts., May 6, 1943; s. Alexander Duncan Sr. and Nancy Greenleaf (Martin) K.; m. Judith Kathleen Mottl, May 25, 1969; children: Matthew Jonathan, Joshua Brandon. BS in Bus., Northwestern U., 1965, JD, 1968. Bar: Ill. 1968, Pa. 1969, U.S. Dist. Ct. (ea. dist.) Pa. 1969, U.S. Dist. Ct. (no. dist.) Ill. 1969, U.S. Ct. Appeals (3rd and 7th cirs.) 1969, U.S. Supreme Ct. 1969. Assoc. Clark, Ladner, Fontenbaugh & Young, Phila., 1968-69, 73-74; asst. U.S. atty. U.S. Dept. Justice, Chgo., 1974-79; assoc., ptnr. Keck, Mahin & Cate, Chgo., Oak Brook, Ill., 1979-90; shareholder Tishler & Wald, Ltd., Chgo., 1990—. Staff atty. Park Dist. La Grange, Ill., 1985-2001; active Ill. St. Andrew Soc., North Riverside, 1982—, pres., 1995-97; vestryman, lay reader, chancellor, chalice bearer Emmanuel Episcopal Ch., 1980-99; mem. Pack 177, Troop 19, Order of the Arrow, Boy Scouts Am., La Grange, 1980—. With USN, 1969-75. Mem. Am. Legion, DuPage Club, Atlantis Divers. Bankruptcy, General civil litigation, Corporate, general. Home: 709 S Stone Ave La Grange IL 60525-2725 Fax: 708-354-1208. E-mail: akerr@tishlerandwald.com.

KERR, BAINE PERKINS, JR., lawyer, writer; b. Houston, June 23, 1946; s. Baine Perkins and Mildred Pickett (Caldwell) Kerr; m. Cynthia Anne Carlisle; children: Dara, Baine. BA, Stanford U., 1968; MA, U. Denver, 1976, JD, 1979. Bar: Colo. 1979, U.S. Dist. Ct. (Colo.) 1979, U.S. Ct. Appeals 1979. Editor-in-chief Place Mag., Palo Alto, Calif., 1971—74; ptnr. Hutchinson, Black, Hill & Cook, Boulder, Colo., 1979—. Elections supr., Bosnia-Herzegovina, 1997; fiction writer. Author: Jumping Off Place, 1981, Harmful Intent, 1999, Wrongful Death, 2002. Recipient Editor's prize, Mo. Rev., 1992; fellow, Nat. Endowment for the Arts, 1983. Mem.: ABA, Boulder County Bar Assn., Colo. Bar Assn. Democrat. Office: 921 Walnut St Ste 200 Boulder CO 80306

KERR, GARY ENRICO, lawyer, educator; b. Kewanee, Ill., Feb. 8, 1948; s. Roy Harrison and Marietta (Dani) K.; m. Eileen Elizabeth Straeter, Aug. 18, 1978; 1 child, Victoria Elizabeth. BA, No. Ill. U., 1970; JD, Northwestern U., Chgo., 1973. Bar: Ill. 1974, U.S. Dist. Ct. (cen. dist.) Ill. 1982, U.S. Ct. Appeals (7th cir.) 1983, U.S. Supreme Ct. 1983. Adminstrv. asst. Office Supt. Pub. Instrn. State Ill., Chgo., Springfield, 1971-74; asst. legal advisor Ill. State Bd. Edn., Springfield, 1974-78; spl. counsel Ill. State Comptroller,

Springfield, 1978-79; pvt. practice Springfield, 1979—. Adj. faculty Sangamon State U. (now Ill. State U.), Springfield, Ill., 1994; pres., dir. counsel Kerr Products, Inc., Kewanee, Ill., 1980—; instr. paralegal program Robert Morris Coll., Springfield, 1992. Atty. South County Democrats, Sangamon County, Ill. Fellow Ednl. Policy program Inst. Ednl. Leadership, George Washington U., 1976-77. Mem. Ill. State Bar Assn. (chmn. sch. law sect. coun. 1983-84), Sangamon unty Bar Assn., Automotive Parts and Accessories Assn. (mem. govtl. affairs and internat. trade com. 1997). Avocations: snow skiing, tennis, fishing. Education and schools, Labor (including EEOC, Fair Labor Standards Act, labor-management relations, NLRB, OSHA). Office: Gary Kerr Ltd 1020 S 7th St Springfield IL 62703-2417 E-mail: kerrltd@aol.com.

KERRICK, DAVID ELLSWORTH, lawyer; b. Caldwell, Idaho, Jan. 15, 1951; s. Charles Ellsworth and Patria (Olesen) K.; m. Juneal Casper, May 24, 1980; children: Peter Ellsworth, Beth Anne, George Ellis, Katherine Leigh. Student, Coll. of Idaho, 1969-71; BA, U. Wash., 1972; JD, U. Idaho, 1980. Bar: Idaho 1980, U.S. Dist. Ct. Idaho 1980, U.S. Ct. Appeals (9th cir.) 1981. Mem. Idaho Senate, 1990-96, majority caucus chmn., 1992-94, majority leader, 1994-96. Mem. S.W. Idaho Estate Planning Coun. Mem. ABA, Assn. Trial Lawyers Am., Idaho Bar Assn. (3d dist. pres. 1985-86), Idaho Trial Lawyers Assn., Canyon County Lawyers Assn. (pres. 1985). Lodges: Elks. Republican. Presbyterian. Avocations: skiing, photography. Estate planning, Personal injury (including property damage), Property, real (including real estate development, water). Office: PO Box 44 Caldwell ID 83606-0044

KERRIDGE, RONALD DAVID, lawyer; b. Houston, Mar. 23, 1962; s. Isaac Curtis and Ruth Stewart Kerridge; m. Elisabeth Michele Crook, June 20, 1987 (div. Aug. 1997); children: Merritt Cottrell, Wynne Banning. AB summa cum laude, Princeton U., 1984; JD magna cum laude, Harvard U., 1987. Bar: Tex. 1987, U.S. Tax Ct. 1991. Assoc. Carrington, Coleman, Sloman & Blumenthal, Dallas, 1987-93; ptnr. Sayles & Lidji, Dallas, 1994-96, Hughes & Luce, LLP, Dallas, 1996—. Episcopalian. Corporate taxation, Taxation, general. Office: Hughes & Luce LLP 1717 Main St Ste 2800 Dallas TX 75201-4605 E-mail: rkerridge@hughesluce.com.

KERSH, DEWITTE TALMADGE, JR., lawyer; b. Balt., June 1, 1930; s. DeWitte Talmadge and Marianna (Snyder) K.; m. Sharon R. Doherty, Aug. 2, 1986; children: DeWitte III, Sarah Anne. BS, Cornell U., 1952, LLB, 1957. Bar: R.I. 1958, N.H. 1991, U.S. Dist. Ct. R.I. 1959, U.S. Dist. Ct. N.H. 1991. Ptnr. Tillinghast, Collins & Graham, Providence, 1965-93; counsel Tillinghast, Licht, Perkins Smith & Cohen, Providence, 1993—. Adj. instr. Law Sch. Roger Williams U. Mem. planning bd. Town of Waterville Valley, selectman; co-chair, sec. Waterville Valley Found. Fellow Am. Acad. Matrimonial Lawyers; mem. R.I. and N.H. Bar Assns. (pro bono svc. 1987-94), R.I. Family Ct. Bench and Bar (past. pres.), Rotary (pres. 1989-90). Republican. Unitarian Universalist. Home: PO Box 346 Waterville Valley NH 03215-0346 Office: Tillinghast Licht et al 10 Weybosset St Providence RI 02903

KERSKER, PETER WHEELER, lawyer, travel consultant, restaurant consultant; b. St. Petersburg, Fla., Dec. 27, 1942; s. Peter Benjamin and Marjorie (Wheeler) K. BA, Johns Hopkins U., 1965; JD, Tulane U., 1969. Bar: Fla., 1969, U.S. Tax Ct., 1980, U.S. Supreme Ct., 1973, U.S. Bankruptcy Ct., 1993. Pvt. practice, St. Petersburg, 1969—; restaurant owner Peter's Pl. Café Internat., St. Petersburg, 1973-93; travel agy. owner Fantasy Adventures Travel, St. Petersburg, 1979-91. Cons. Anita Travel, St. Petersburg, 1991—. Bd. dirs. The Fla. Orch., Tampa Bay, 1974-76, The Fla. Opera, Tampa Bay, 1990-96, Royal Marsden Cancer Appeal, London, Eng., 1991-92. Mem. Fla. Bar Assn., St. Petersburg Yacht Club (cons. 1973—). Avocations: reading, travel, magnet collecting, miniature collecting. Bankruptcy, General practice, Personal income taxation. Home: Bayfront Twr 1 Beach Dr SE Saint Petersburg FL 33701-3963 Office: 1 Beach Dr SE Apt 1201 Saint Petersburg FL 33701-3954 Address: 25 Mallard Point Rainhill Way BOW London E3 3JE England Mailing: PO Box 3180 Saint Petersburg FL 33731-3180

KERSTETTER, WAYNE ARTHUR, law educator, lawyer; b. Chgo., Dec. 1, 1939; s. Arthur Edward and Lillian (Asplund) K. BA, U. Chgo., 1964, JD, 1967. Bar: Ill. 1968. Asst. commr. N.Y. Police Dept., N.Y.C., 1972-73; supt. Ill. Bur. Investigation, Chgo., 1973-76; assoc. dir. Ctr. for Studies in Criminal Justice, U. Chgo., 1976-78; assoc. prof. criminal justice, dept. criminal justice U. Ill., Chgo., 1978-2000. Sr. rsch. fellow Am. Bar Found., Chgo., 1982-93, fellow, 1993—; cons. U.S. Civil Rights Commn., U. Chgo., ABT Assocs., Univ. Research Assocs., Police Found. Mem. transition team Mayor Washington, Chgo., 1983, Criminal Justice Project of Cook County, 1987. Served with USNR, 1962-64. Rsch. grantee Nat. Inst. Justice, 1976, Chgo. Bar Found., 1979-80, Am. Bar Found., 1983; fellow Ctr. for Studies in Criminal Justice, U. Chgo. Law Sch., 1978-82.

KERYCZYNSKYJ, LEO IHOR, county official, educator, lawyer; b. Chgo., Aug. 8, 1948; s. William and Eva (Chicz) K.; m. Alexandra Irene Okruch, July 19, 1980; 1 child, Christina Alexandra. BA, BS, DePaul U., 1970, MS in Pub. Svc., 1975; JD, No. Ill. U., 1979; postgrad., U. Ill., Chgo., 1980-82. Bar: Ill. 1981, U.S. Dist. Ct. (no. dist.) Ill. 1981, U.S. Ct. Appeals (7th cir.) 1981, U.S. Tax Ct. 1981, U.S. Ct. Claims 1982, U.S. Ct. Mil. Appeals 1982, U.S. Ct. Appeals (fed. cir.) 1983, U.S. Supreme Ct. 1984. Condemnation awards officer Cook County Treas.'s Office, Chgo., 1972-75, adminstrv. asst., 1975-77, dep. treas., 1977-87, chief legal counsel, 1987-96, dir. fin. svcs., 1988-96; pvt. practice, 1996-98; adv. Office of Profl. Stds. Chgo. Police Dept., 1998—. Adj. prof. DePaul U., Chgo., 1979-95; elected chmn. bd. dirs., 1st Security Fed. Savs. Bank Chgo., 1992-93. Capt. Ukrainian Am. Dem. Orgn., Chgo., 1971. Recipient Outstanding Alumni award Phi Kappa Theta, 1971. Mem. ABA, Ill. State Bar Assn., Ill. Trial Law Assn., Ukrainian Am. Bar Assn., Chgo. Bar Assn., Ill. Assn. County Ofcls., Internat. Assn. Clerks, Recorders, Election Ofcls. and Treas., Shore Line Interurban Hist. Soc. (bd. dirs., legal counsel 1987-2001, pres. and chmn., 1993-98), Theta Delta Phi. Ukrainian Catholic. Home: 2324 W Iowa St Apt 3R Chicago IL 60622-4720 Office: Office Profl Stds 10 W 35th St Chicago IL 60616

KESHIAN, RICHARD, lawyer; b. Arlington, Mass., Aug. 11, 1934; s. Hamayak and Takuhe (Malkesian) K.; m. Jacqueline C. Cannilla, Sept. 11, 1965; children: Carolyn D., Richard M. (dec. 1999). BSBA, Boston U., 1956, JD, 1958. Bar: Mass. 1958. Pvt. practice law, Arlington, 1964-71; ptnr. Keshian & Reynolds, P.C., Arlington, 1971—. Instr. bus law George Washington U., 1961-63; mem. adv. bd. Coop. Bank Concord, Arlington, 1983-86; corporator Bank Five for Savs., Arlington, 1984-91; bd. dirs., gen. counsel Arlington Coop. Bank, 1978-83. Chmn. Arlington Zoning Bd. Appeals, 1972-76; pres. Arlington C. of C., 1976; v.p. Mass. Fedn. Planning Bds., 1978-85; mem. Arlington Contributory Retirement Bd., 1984—. With USMC, 1958-64; maj. Res. ret. Mem. ABA, Mass. Bar Assn., Am. Arbitration Assn. (arbitrator 1975—), Mass. Conveyancers Assn. (bd. dirs. 1996—, chmn. title standards com. 1996-2000, clk. 1999-2001, pres. 2003—), Mass. Assn. Bank Counsel (bd. dirs. 1985-2002, pres. 1992-95). Democrat. Congregationalist. Banking, Probate (including wills, trusts), Property, real (including real estate development, water). Home: 93 Falmouth Rd W Arlington MA 02474-1007 Office: 1040 Massachusetts Ave Arlington MA 02476-0052 E-mail: rkeshian@krtlawfirm.com.

KESLER, JOHN A. lawyer, land developer; b. Clark County, Ill., Apr. 25, 1923; s. Hal H. and Clara (Hurst) K.; m. Maxine Ruth Weaver, May 13, 1948; children: Nicki Kesler Cotsworth, Bradley Weaver, John A. II. AB, Ind. State U., 1948; JD, Ind. U., 1951. Bar: Ind. 1951, Ill. 1951. Chief dep. prosecutor County Vigo, Terre Haute, Ind., 1954-58; probate commr. Cir. Ct., 1971-74; mem. ho. reps. Ind. Legis., 1969-73; asst. state atty. County Madison, Edwardsville, Ill., 1985-88; pvt. practice law Terre Haute, 1951—. Pres. Wabash Valley Land Developers, Inc., Terre Haute, 1979—. Staff sgt. U.S. Army, 1943-46. Recipient Legion of Honor; recipient Good Govt. award West Vigo Jaycees, 1971, Civic Svc. award U.S. Jaycees, 1957; named Outstanding Pub. Offcl. Terre Haute Jaycees. Mem. ABA, Nat. Assn. Criminal Def. Lawyers, Ill. State Bar Assn., Ind. Bar Assn., VFW, Am. Legion, United War Vets. Coun. Vigo County (past commdr.), SAR (state pres.), Exchange Club (pres.), Shriners, Grand Soc. Sycamores, Honorable Order of Ky. Cols., Grotto. Democrat. Methodist. Avocations: bowling, geneology, reading. General civil litigation, Criminal, General practice. Home: 76 S Thorpe Pl West Terre Haute IN 47885 Office: 219 Ohio St Terre Haute IN 47807-3420

KESS, LYDIA E. retired lawyer; b. Bklyn., Sept. 17, 1935; BBA, Pace U., 1954; MBA, CUNY, 1958; LLB, Bklyn. Law Sch., 1962. Bar: N.Y. 1963. With Davis Polk & Wardwell, N.Y.C., 1964—2003, ptnr., 1971—2003. Mem. ABA, N.Y. State Bar Assn., Assn. of the Bar of the City of N.Y. Office: Davis Polk & Wardwell 99 Gresham St London EC2V 7NG England

KESSEL, MARK, lawyer; b. Krasnik, Poland, June 14, 1941; arrived in U.S., 1948; s. Leo and Erna (Friedman) Kessel; m. Elaine Keit, Aug. 29, 1966; children: Greer Kessel Hendricks, Robert W. BA with honors in Econs., CUNY, 1963; JD magna cum laude, Syracuse U., 1966. Bar: N.Y. Assoc. Shearman & Sterling, N.Y.C., 1971-77, ptnr., 1997—2001, mng. ptnr., 1990-94; mng. dir. Symphony Capital LLC, N.Y.C., 2002—. Bd. dirs. Harrods Ltd., Antigenics, Inc. Bd. visitors Syracuse U. Coll. Law; bd. dirs. San Francisco Psychoanalytic Inst., 1988—90, Mus. City of N.Y., W.M. Keck Found., L.A., 1985—86; dir. Heller Fin., Inc., 1992—2001. Capt. JAGC U.S. Army, 1963—71. Avocations: reading, running. Corporate, general, Mergers and acquisitions, Securities. Office: Symphony Capital LLC 117 E 55th St New York NY 10022

KESSINGER, B.L., JR., lawyer; b. Oct. 30, 1922; s. Ben L. and Martha B. Kessinger; m. Martha Bishop, Oct. 23, 1950; children: Martha Sanford, Kendall, Ben III. BS, U. Ky., 1940, JD, 1948. Bar: Ky. 1948, U.S. Supreme Ct. 1948, U.S. Dist. Ct. (ea. and we. dists.) Ky. 1948. With Harbison, Kessinger, Lisle & Bush, 1948—83; ptnr. Stites & Harbison, Lexington, Ky., 1983—. Spkr. in field; spl. judge Ct. Appeals Ky.; spl. justice Supreme Ct. Ky.; U.S. commr. Ea. Dist. Ky., 1950—72; chmn. Jud. Retirement and Removal Commn., 1980—84. Contbr. articles to profl. jours. Past. bd. govs. Shriner's Hosp. Lexington; past bd. dirs. Bank of Lexington, Liberty Nat. Bank and Trust Co.; past chmn. bd. dirs. Manchester Ctr. 1st lt. USAF, 1943—46, PTO. Fellow: Ky. Bar. Assn. Found., Am. Coll. Trial Lawyers, ABA Found.; mem.: ABA, Nat. Conf. Bar Pres., Ky. Def. Counsel Assn., Am. Bd. Trial Advocates, 6th U.S. Jud. Conf. (life; chmn. 1989), Internat. Assn. Def. Counsel, Nat. Assn. Railroad Trial Counsel, Ky. Bar Assn. (chmn. 1965, bd. govs. 1966—67, pres. 1975—76, ho. of dels.), Fayette County Bar Assn. (pres. 1958), U. Ky. Coll. Law Alumni Assn., Oleika Temple, Spendletop Hall, Inc., Idle Hour Country Club, Grand Lodge Ky., Sigma Alpha Epsilon. Methodist. General civil litigation, Insurance, Libel. Office: Stites & Harbison 2300 Lexington Fin Ctr 250 W Main St Lexington KY 40507-1758 Home: 1361 Cooper Dr Lexington KY 40502

KESSLER, ALAN CRAIG, lawyer; b. Washington, Sept. 16, 1950; s. Alfred Milton and Josephine (Taub) K.; m. Gail Elaine Strauss, June 16, 1974; children: Stacy Ilana, Mark Jay, Daniel Jordan. BA with honors, U. Del., 1972; JD with honors, U. Md., 1975. Bar: Pa. 1975, U.S. Dist. Ct. (ea. dist.) Pa. 1975, U.S. Ct. Appeals (3d and 6th cirs.) 1975. Assoc. Dilworth, Paxson, Kalish, Levy & Kauffman, Phila., 1975-77, Berger & Montague, P.C., Phila., 1977-81; ptnr. Mesirov, Gelman, Jaffe, Cramer & Jamieson, Phila., 1981-91, Buchanan Ingersoll, P.C., Phila., 1991-99, Wolf, Block, Schorr & Solis-Cohen, 1999—. Instr. Inst. for Paralegal Tng., Phila., 1977-96. Fin. com. Dem. City Com. Phila., 1981-84, dep. counsel, 1980-84; chmn. bd. Bldg. Stds. City of Phila., 1983-84, bd. licenses and inspections rev., 1984-91; mem. City Planning Commn., Phila., 1992-97, Presdl. Transition Team, 1992-93; commr. Lower Merion (Pa.) Twp., 1988-2000, Mayors Comm. Homelessness, 1990—, Mayors Com. on Spl. Svcs. Dist., 1989—; vice-chmn. Pres. Commn. on Risk Assessment and Risk Mgmt., 1993-97; bd. dirs., pres. Randolph Ct. Assn., Phila., 1980-85; bd. dirs., v.p. South St. Neighbors Assn., Phila., 1983-87, Park Towne Pl. Tenants Assn., 1977-79; bd. dirs. Support Ctr. for Child Advs., 1983-94, Phila. Indsl. Devel. Corp.; exec. com. Ctrl. Phila. Devel. Corp., 1989—, Jewish Employment Vocat. Svcs., 1989—, Phila. 2000.; chair Supreme Ct. of Pa. Commn. on CLE, 1999—; mng. trustee Dem. Nat. Com., 1992—, fin. vice-chair, 2000—; bd. govs. U.S. Postal Svc., 2000—. Mem. ABA, Pa. Bar Assn., Phila. Bar Assn. (exec. bd. dirs. young lawyers sect., legis. liaison com., officer various coms.), Racquet Club, Radnor Valley Country Club. Democrat. Jewish. Antitrust, Federal civil litigation. Home: 204 Daisy Ln Wynnewood PA 19096-1654 Office: Wolf Block Schorr & Solis-Cohen 1650 Arch St Fl 22 Philadelphia PA 19103-2097 E-mail: akessler@wolfblack.com.

KESSLER, JEFFREY L. lawyer; b. N.Y.C., Feb. 19, 1954; s. Milton M. and Edith H. Kessler; m. Regina T. Dessoff, May 21, 1977; children: Andrew Zalman, Leora Miriam. BA, JD summa cum laude, Columbia U., 1977. Bar: N.Y. 1978, U.S. Dist. Ct. (so. dist.) N.Y. 1978, U.S. Supreme Ct. 1985. Assoc. Weil, Gotshal & Manges, N.Y.C., 1977-85, ptnr., 1985—. Adj. assoc. prof. Fordham Law Sch., 1988—; founder, bd. advisors study pvt. antitrust litig. Georgetown U., 1983-85. Mem. editl. bd.: Columbia U. Law Rev., 1976—77, Competition Laws Outside the U.S., 2001; editor (in chief): State Antitrust Practice Statutes, 1999; contbr. articles to profl. jours.; co-editor: International Trade and U.S. Antitrust Law. Kent scholar, 1975-76, Stone scholar, 1976-77. Mem. ABA (antitrust law sect., vice-chmn. Sherman Act Sect. 2 com. 1989-90, chmn. internat. law com. 1990-94, co-chmn. pub. com. 1994-96, coun. mem. 1996-99, internat. task force 2001-03), Columbia Coll. Alumni Assn. (bd. dirs. 1996-99), Phi Beta Kappa. Democrat. Jewish. Antitrust, Federal civil litigation, Private international. Office: Weil Gotshal & Manges 767 5th Ave Ste 3406 New York NY 10153-0023 E-mail: jeffrey.kessler@weil.com.

KESSLER, JUDD LEWIS, lawyer; b. Newark, Apr. 10, 1938; s. Samuel W. and Ethel S. (Shapiro) K.; m. Marian Osterweis, Jan. 7, 1979 (div. 1986); m. Carol Ann Farris, Oct. 19, 1987; 1 child, Samuel Farris. AB, Oberlin Coll., 1960; LLB, Harvard U., 1963. Bar: N.J. 1963, D.C. 1972, Md. 1989, U.S. Dist. Ct. N.J., U.S. Dist. Ct. D.C., U.S. Dist. Ct. Md., U.S. Ct. Appeals (4th cir.), U.S. Supreme Ct. 1968. Assoc. Toner, Crowley, Woelper and Vanderbilt, Newark, 1963-66; asst. gen. counsel U.S. Agy. for Internat. Devel., Washington, 1966-82; ptnr., chmn. internat. bus. practice group Porter, Wright, Morris & Arthur, Washington, 1982—. Author: (with others) Legal Aspects of Exporting, 1986; contbr. articles to profl. jours. Bd. dirs. Congregation Har Shalom, Potomac, Md., 1998-2001. Recipient Outstanding Career Achievement award U.S. Agy for Internat. Devel. 1982; named Presdl. Appointment to Sr. Fgn. Svc., 1982. Master: London Court Internat. Arbitration; mem.: ABA, Fed. Bar Assn. (chmn. internat. sect. 1983—87, nat. coord. Export Legal Assistance Network 1985—, Pres.'s E Excellence Export Svc. award 1997), Am. Soc. Internat. Law, Internat. C. of C. (mem. U.S. arbitration com. 2000), Inter-Am. Bar Found. (pres. 1994—), Inter-Am. Bar Assn., Am. Arbitration Assn. (mem. internat. panel arbitrators 1997—), Cosmos Club. Government contracts and claims, Private international, Public international. Office: Porter Wright Morris & Arthur 1919 Penn Ave NW Washington DC 20006-3434

KESSLER, KEITH LEON, lawyer; b. Seattle, July 18, 1947; s. Robert Lawrence and Priscilla Ellen (Allbee) K.; m. Lynn Elizabeth Eisen, Dec. 24, 1980; children: William Moore, Christopher Moore, Bradley Moore, Jamie Kessler. BA in Philosophy, U. Wash., 1969, JD, 1972. Bar: Wash. 1972, U.S. Dist. Ct. (we. dist.) Wash. 1973, U.S. Dist. Ct. (ea. dist. 1992); U.S. Ct. Appeals (9th cir.) 1973, U.S. Supreme Ct. 1975. Law clk. to Hon. Robert Finley Wash. Supreme Ct., Olympia, Wash., 1972-73; ptnr. Kessler, Tegland & Urmston, Seattle, 1973-75, Kessler & Urmston, Seattle, 1975-76, Kessler, Urmston & Sever, Seattle, 1976-77, Kessler & Sever, Seattle, 1977-79; assoc. Stritmatter & Stritmatter, Hoquiam, Wash., 1980-83; ptnr. Stritmatter, Kessler & McCauley, Hoquiam, Wash., 1983-93, Stritmatter Kessler, Hoquiam, Wash., 1993-97, Stritmatter, Kessler, Whelan, Withey, Hoquiam, 1997—. Chmn. LAW PAC, Seattle, 1991-93; mem. pattern jury instrns. com. Wash. Supreme Ct., 2000—. Editor: Trial Evidence, 1996, author: (with others) Motor Vehicle Accident Litigation Desk Book, 1988, 1995, 97; contbr. chpt. to book. Pres. Kairos Ctr., Aberdeen, Wash., 1984-86; co-founder Grays Harbor Support Group; bd. dir. Wash. State Head Injury Found., Bellevue, Wash., 1993-96. Recipient Founders award Wash. State Head Injury Found., 1990, Silver award United Way, 1992. Mem. Am. Bd. Trial Advocates, (pres. Wash. chpt. 1997), Wash. State Trial Lawyers Assn. (pres. 1990-91, named trial lawyer of yr., 1994, outstanding plaintiff trial lawyer), Damage Attys. Round Table (pres. 2002-03), Wash. Trial Attys. Political Forum (chmn. 1993-95), Wash. Def. Trial Lawyers, Trial Lawyers for Public Justice (state exec. com. 1994—). Personal injury (including property damage), Aviation. Office: Stritmatter Kessler Whelan Withey 413 8th St Hoquiam WA 98550-3607 E-mail: keith@skww.com.

KESSLER, MARK, political scientist, educator; b. McKeesport, Pa., Jan. 9, 1955; s. Robert and Rae Kessler; m. Stephanie Weko Kessler, Aug. 14, 1983; children: Robert, Jennifer, Hannah. BA, U. Pitts., 1976; PhD, Pa. State U., 1985. Prof. polit. sci. Bates Coll., Lewiston, Maine, 1983—. Chair divsn. social sci. Bates Coll., 2000—, chair dept. polit. sci., 1994—98. Author: Legal Services for the Poor, 1987; co-author: The Play of Power, 1997; contbr. articles to profl. jours. Mem.: Law & Soc. Assn., Am. Polit. Sci. Assn. Democrat. Jewish. Office: Bates Coll Dept Polit Sci 174 Pettengill Hall Lewiston ME 04240 E-mail: mkessler@bates.edu.

KESSLER, MARK ALLEN, political scientist, educator; b. McKeesport, Pa., Jan. 3, 1955; s. Robert and Rae (Alpern) K.; m. Stephanie Weko, Aug. 14, 1983. BA, U. Pitts., 1977; MA, Pa. State U., 1979, PhD, 1985. Prof. politi. sci. Bates Coll., Lewiston, Maine, 1983—, chair polit. sci., 1993-97, chair divsn. social sci., 2000—. Author: Legal Services for the Poor, 1987; co-author: The Play of Power, 1996; contbr. articles to profl. jours. NSF grantee, 1981. Mem.: Law and Soc. Assn., Am. Judicature Soc., Am. Polit. Sci. Assn. Democrat. Jewish. Home: 241 5th St Providence RI 02906-3763 Office: Bates Coll 174 Pettingill St Lewiston ME 04240-5324 E-mail: mkessler@bates.edu.

KESSLER, RICHARD PAUL, JR., lawyer; b. Latrobe, Pa., July 11, 1945; s. Richard Paul Sr. and Dorothy Henrietta (Comp) K.; m. Kathleen Jane Parker, June 17, 1973 (dec. May 11, 1996); 1 child, Grace Elizabeth; m. Susan Kessler, Oct. 2000. BA, Fairfield (Conn.) U., 1968; JD, Emory U., 1971. Bar: Ga. 1971, U.S. Dist. Ct. (no. dist.) Ga. 1973, U.S. Ct. Appeals (5th cir.) 1974, U.S. Ct. Appeals (11th cir.) 1981, U.S. Supreme Ct. 1995. Law clk. to presiding justice U.S. Dist. Ct. (no. dist.) Ga., 1971-73; ptnr. Macey, Wilensky, Cohen, Wittner & Kessler, LLP, Atlanta, 1973—. Lectr. Practising Law Inst., 1981, 83, Fin. Svc. Corp. Career Conf., Atlanta, 1986, Ga. and Ala. Insts. of Continuing Legal Edn., 1993-95; panelist Credit Union Nat. Assn., Inc. League Attys. Conf., 1980-82, 87, 88-93, ABA, 1990-91; participant Nat. Conf. Commrs. on Uniform State Laws Drafting Com. on U.C.C. Articles, 3, 4, 4A, 1985-90; chair corp. and banking law sect. State Bar Ga., 1995-96. Author: What You Should Know About the New Bankruptcy Code, 1979, Guide to the Bankruptcy Laws: The Bankruptcy Reform Act of 1978, 79, Guide to the Bankruptcy Laws: The Bankruptcy Reform Act of 1978 (Bankruptcy Code) as Amended by the Bankruptcy Amendments and Federal Judgeship Act of 1984, The Bankruptcy Judges, U.S. Trustees and Family Farmer Bankruptcy Act of 1986; contbr. articles to profl. jours. Mem.: East Lake Golf Club. Banking, Bankruptcy, Commercial, consumer (including collections, credit). Office: Ste 600 285 Peachtree Center Ave NE Atlanta GA 30303-1234 E-mail: rkessler@maceywilensky.com.

KESSLER, ROBERT MARK, lawyer; b. St. Louis, Jan. 19, 1968; s. Neil and Diane Kessler; m. Patti Davis Kessler; 1 child, Arielle Rose. AB, U. So. Calif., L.A., 1990; JD, Chgo.-Kent Coll. Law, 1994. Bar: Ga. 1994, Calif. 1996. Atty. K&R Law Group LLP, L.A., 1996—. Bd. dirs. Clinica Para Las Americas, L.A., 2000—. Contbr. articles to profl. jours. Mem.: Am. Health Lawyers Assn. Health. Office: K&R Law Group LLP 350 S Grand Ave Los Angeles CA 90071

KESSLER, STEVEN FISHER, lawyer; b. McKeesport, Pa., June 29, 1951; s. Robert and Rae (Alpern) K.; children: Matthew, Katie. BA, U. Pitts., 1973, JD, 1976. Bar: Pa. 1976, U.S. Dist. Ct. (we. dist.) Pa. 1976. Staff atty. Neighborhood Legal Services, McKeesport, Pa., 1976-79; solicitor City of McKeesport, 1980-82; sole practice, McKeesport, 1982—; solicitor McKeesport Housing Corp., 1985—; chmn. bd. dirs. McKeesport Devel. Corp., 1984—. Mem. Am. Arbitration Assn. (panel arbitrators 1981—). Democrat. General practice, Personal injury (including property damage), Probate (including wills, trusts). Home: 1337 Foxwood Dr Monroeville PA 15146-4436 Office: 332 5th Ave Mc Keesport PA 15132-2616

KESTENBAUM, HAROLD LEE, lawyer; b. Bronx, N.Y., Sept. 27, 1949; s. Murray Louis and Yetta (Weiner) K.; m. Felice Gail Kravit, Aug. 11, 1973; children: Michelle, Benjamin. BA, Queens Coll., 1971; JD, U. Richmond, 1975. Bar: N.Y. 1976, N.J. 1977, U.S. Dist. Ct. (so. and ea. dist.) N.Y. Assoc. Wayne and Reiss, N.Y.C., 1975-76, Natanson, Reich and Barrison, N.Y.C., 1976-77, Goldstein and Axelrod, N.Y.C., 1977-81; pvt. practice N.Y.C. and L.I., 1981—2002; counsel Farrell Fritz, P.C., 2003—; chmn. of the bd. Franchise It Corp., Bohemia, N.Y., 1984-89; pres., chief exec. officer Mr. Sign Franchising Corp., 1987-89. Bd. dirs. Sbarro Inc., RezConnect Techs., Inc. GarageTek, Inc., Ultimate Francluse Sys., Inc., Wall St. Deli Sys., Inc.; cons. in field. Mem. ABA, N.Y. Bar Assn., N.J. Bar Assn., Nassau County Bar Assn. Republican. Jewish. Avocations: softball, weight training. Corporate, general, Franchising, Property, real (including real estate development, water). Office: 14th Fl EAB Plz West Tower Uniondale NY 11556-0120

KESTER, CHARLES MELVIN, lawyer; b. Batesville, Ark., Jan. 19, 1968; s. Monty Charles and Phyllis Smith Kester; m. Cheryl Goodwin, June 1, 1991. BA in Philosophy summa cum laude, Liberty U., 1991; JD magna cum laude, Georgetown U., 1994. Bar: Ark. 1994, U.S. Dist. Ct. (ea. and we. dists.) Ark. 1995, U.S. Ct. Appeals (8th cir.) 1995, U.S. Ct. Fed. Claims, 2002, U.S. Supreme Ct. 1998. Law clk. U.S. Ct. Appeals 8th Cir., Fargo, N.D., 1994-95; atty. Lingle Law Firm, Rogers, Ark., 1995-96; pvt. practice law Fayetteville, Ark., 1996—. Assoc. editor Georgetown Law Jour., 1993-94; contbr. articles to profl. jours. Mem. Ark. Bar Assn. (appellate practice com. 1997-2002, young lawyers sect. adv. coun. 1998-99, sec. labor and employment law sect. 2002, treas. 2001), Ark. Trial Lawyers Assn. (amicus curiae com. 1997-2003, labor and employment sect. 2001-03), Phi Alpha Delta. Avocations: camping, rock climbing, spelunking. Appellate, Civil rights, Criminal. Home: 13602 White Oak Ln Fayetteville AR 72704-8312 Office: 1160 N College Ave Ste 1 Fayetteville AR 72703-1907

KESTER, RANDALL BLAIR, lawyer; b. Vale, Oreg., Oct. 20, 1916; s. Bruce R. and Mabel M. (Judd) K.; m. Rachael L. Woodhouse, Oct. 20, 1940; children: Laura, Sylvia, Lynne. AB, Willamette U., 1937; JD, Columbia U., 1940. Bar: Oreg. 1940, U.S. Dist. Ct. Oreg. 1940, U.S. Ct. Appeals (9th cir.) 1941, U.S. Supreme Ct. 1960. Assoc., then partner firm

Maguire, Shields, Morrison & Bailey, Portland, 1940-57; justice Oreg. Supreme Ct., Salem, 1957-58; partner Maguire, Shields, Morrison, Bailey & Kester, 1958-66, Maguire, Kester & Cosgrave, 1966-71, Cosgrave & Kester, Portland, 1972-78, Cosgrave, Kester, Crowe, Gidley & Lagesen, Portland, 1978-89, Cosgrave, Vergeer & Kester, Portland, 1989—. Instr. Northwestern Coll. Law, 1947-56; gen. solicitor northwestern dist. U.P. R.R., 1958-79; sr. counsel UPRR Co., 1979-81 Co-author: The First Duty: History of the U.S. District Court of Oregon, 1993; contbr. articles to profl. jours. Past v.p. Portland area council Boy Scouts of Am.; past pres. Mountain Rescue and Safety Council Oreg.; past trustee Willamette U.; past bd. dirs. Oreg. Symphony Soc., Oreg. Mus. Sci. and Industry. Recipient Silver Beaver award Boy Scouts Am., 1956, alumni citation Willamette U., 1987. Fellow Am. Acad. Appellate Lawyers; mem. ABA, Am. Bar Found. (life), Multnomah Bar Assn. (past pres. 1956, Professionalism award 1991), Oreg. State Bar (treas. 1965-66, Disting. Svc. award pub. utility sect. 1991), Am. Law Inst. (life), Nat. Ski Patrol, Mt. Hood Ski Patrol (past pres.), Mazamas (past pres., climbing chmn.), Wy'east Climbers, Portland C. of C. (pres. 1973, chmn. bd. 1974), U.S. Dist. Ct. Oreg. Hist. Soc. (past pres, bd. dirs.) Oreg. Ethics Commons (co-founder, sec.), Phi Delta Phi, Beta Theta Pi, Tau Kappa Alpha. Clubs: Arlington (Portland), City (Portland) (v.p. 1978-80, pres. 1986-87), University (Portland), Multnomah Athletic (Portland). Republican. Unitarian Universalist. General civil litigation, Insurance, Transportation. Office: Cosgrave Vergeer & Kester LLP 805 SW Broadway 8th Fl Portland OR 97205 E-mail: rkester@cvk-law.com.

KETCHAM, ORMAN WESTON, lawyer, former judge; b. Bklyn., Oct. 1, 1918; s. Walter Seymour and Arline May (Weston) K.; m. Anne Phelps Stokes, Dec. 22, 1947; children: Anne Weston Ketcham Felder, Helen Phelps Ketcham Ryan, Elizabeth Miner Ketcham Mercogliano, Susan Stokes Ketcham. BA, Princeton U., 1940; postgrad., Yale U., 1940-41, LLB, 1947, JD, 1971. Bar: D.C. 1948. With Covington & Burling, Washington, 1947-53; asst. gen. counsel Fgn. Ops. Adminstrn., Washington, 1953-55; trial atty. antitrust div. Justice Dept., 1955-57; judge Juvenile Ct. D.C., 1957-71, Superior Ct. D.C., 1971-77; sr. staff atty. Nat. Center State Cts., 1977-81; sr. fellow Washington Coll. Law Inst., 1981-83. Adj. prof. law Georgetown U., 1963-67, U. Va., 1971-77, William and Mary Coll., 1978-80, Am. U., 1981-92; mem. U.S. Edn. Appeal Bd., 1982-90. acting chmn., 1984-85; mem. coun. of judges Nat. Coun. on Crime and Delinquency, 1959-83, bd. dirs., 1974-83; mem. U.S. del. UN Congress on Crime, Stockholm, 1965, Geneva, 1975; mem. Nat. Com. on Secondary Edn., 1970-74; chmn. adv. coun. to Select Com. on Crime, Ho. of Reps., 1969-70 Author: (with others) Justice for the Child, 1961, Changing Faces of Juvenile Justice, 1978, (with Monrad G. Paulsen) Cases and Materials Relating to Juvenile Courts, 1967. Washington rep. Fund for the Republic, 1953; mem. vis. com. Brookings Instn., 1971-76; bd. dirs. Children's Nat. Med. Ctr., 1987-90. Mem. ABA, Bar Assn. D.C., Am. Law Inst., Nat. Coun. Juvenile and Family Ct. Judges (pres. 1965-66), Internat. Assn. Youth Magistrates (v.p. 1966-74) Clubs: Cosmos, Princeton (Washington), Chevy Chase. Congregationalist. Home: 2 E Melrose St Chevy Chase MD 20815-4204

KETCHAM, RICHARD SCOTT, lawyer; b. Columbus, Ohio, Jan. 8, 1948; s. Victor Alvin and Dorothy Eloise (Becher) K.; m. Kim Michelle Halliburton, Apr. 7, 1984 (div. 1989); 1 child, Kate Erin; m. Christy M. Canaday, Sept. 9, 1990 (div. 1994). BS, Bowling Green (Ohio) State U., 1970; JD cum laude, Capital U., Columbus, 1974. Bar: Ohio 1974, U.S. Dist. Ct. (so. dist.) Ohio 1979. Asst. pros. atty. Franklin County (Ohio) Pros., Columbus, 1974-79, sr. asst. pros. atty., 1979-84; ptnr. Ketcham & Ketcham, Columbus, 1984—. Mem. task force Legal Aid Referral Project, Columbus Bar Assn. Homeless Project, 1989—. Mem. Gov.'s Task Force on Family Violence, 1984-86. Mem. Nat. Assn. Criminal Def. Lawyers, Ohio Assn. Criminal Def. Lawyers (bd. dirs. 1989—, v.p. CLE, sec.), Ctrl. Ohio Assn. Criminal Def. Lawyers (pres. 1994-95, bd. dirs. 2001—), Ohio State Bar Assn., Columbus Bar Assn. (chmn. criminal law com. 1994-95, 95-96), Franklin County Trial Lawyers. Avocations: fishing, basketball, model railroads, gardening. Criminal. Home: 1937 Elmwood Ave Columbus OH 43212-1112 Office: Ketcham & Ketcham 755 S High St Columbus OH 43206-1908 E-mail: rsketch@msn.com.

KETCHAND, ROBERT LEE, lawyer; b. Shreveport, La., Jan. 30, 1948; s. Woodrow Wilson and Attie Harriet (Chandler) K.; m. Alice Sue Adams, May 31, 1969; children: Peter Leland, Marjory Attie. BA, Baylor U., 1970; JD, Harvard U., 1973. Bar: Tex. 1973, Mass. 1973, D.C. 1981. Assoc., ptnr. Butler & Binion, Houston, 1976-85, Washington, 1981-82; shareholder Brodsky & Ketchand, Houston, 1985-88; ptnr. Webster & Sheffield, Houston, 1988-90; atty. pvt. practice, Houston, 1990-92; ptnr. Short & Ketchand, Houston, 1992-2001; dir. Boyer & Ketchand, P.C., Houston, 2001—. Founder, chmn. bd. dirs. Rolling Waters, d/b/a Houston Legal Clinic. Pres. Prisoner Svcs. Com. Houston, 1986; deacon South Houston Bapt. Ch., 1976—; gen. counsel, dir. Houston Met. Ministries, 1986-88; dir. Interfaith Ministries Greater Houston, 1996-98; gen. counsel Houston Bus. Roundtable, 1988—. Lt. USNR, 1973-76. Mem. ABA, Tex. Bar Assn., Houston Bar Assn. (chmn. dispute com. 1989-90). Avocations: reading, family. Federal civil litigation, General civil litigation, State civil litigation. Home: 2707 Carolina Way Houston TX 77005-3423 Office: Boyer & Ketchand PC 9 Greenway Plz Ste 3100 Houston TX 77046 Fax: 713-871-2024. E-mail: rketchand@boyerketchand.com.

KETTER, DAVID LEE, lawyer; b. Portsmouth, Ohio, Jan. 7, 1929; s. William Leslie and Dorothy Aileen (Weidner) K.; m. Beverly Jane Kinker, June 10, 1951; children— Michael David, Sandra Lee, Beth Ann, Richard Douglass AB, Ohio U., 1953; JD, U. Cin., 1955. Bar: Ohio 1955, Pa. 1964. Trial lawyer Dept. Justice, Washington, 1955-56; trial lawyer Chief Counsel's Office, IRS, Pitts., 1956-62; assoc. Kirkpatrick, Pomeroy, Lockhart & Johnson, Pitts., 1962-65; ptnr. Kirkpatrick & Lockhart, LLP, Pitts., 1965-94, of counsel, 1995—. Served as sgt. USMC, 1946-47, 50-52 Mem. ABA (tax sect.), Pa. Bar Assn. (tax sect.), Allegheny County Bar Assn. (chmn. tax sect. 1964-66), Estate Planning Coun. (bd. dirs. 1975-77), Pitts. Tax Club (pres. 1985-86), Order of Coif, Duquesne Club, Rivers Club, Valley Brook Country Club (sec. 1977-78). Clubs: Duquesne, Rivers, Valley Brook Country (McMurray, Pa., sec. 1977-78). Republican. Methodist. Avocations: golf, tennis, shooting. Corporate taxation, Estate taxation, Personal income taxation. Home: 160 Canterbury Rd Mc Murray PA 15317-2802 Office: Kirkpatrick & Lockhart LLP Henry W Oliver Bldg 535 Smithfield St Pittsburgh PA 15222-2312 E-mail: dketter@kl.com.

KETTERER, ANDREW, state commissioner, former state attorney general; b. Trenton, N.J., Jan. 17, 1949; s. Frederic and Loretta (Mehan) Ketterer; m. Susanne Powell, 1978; 1 child, Andrew Powell. BA magna cum laude, Conn. Coll., 1971; JD, Northeastern U., 1974. Former mem. Maine Ho. of Reps.; atty. gen. State of Maine, 1995—2001; commr. State of Maine's Comm. on Govtl. Ethics and Election Practices, Augusta, Maine, 2002—. Dir., vice chmn. Norridgewock Indsl. Com., 1982; dir. Ctrl. Maine Airport Authority, 1982—; sec., treas. Youth and Family Svcs., Skowhegan, Maine, 1980; chmn. Madison Dem. Town Com., Maine, 1980—; del. Somerset County Dem. Com., 1980—, Dem. State Conv., 1980—82. Mem.: ATLA, ABA, Somerset County Bar Assn., Maine Bar Assn., Norridgecock C. of C. (pres. 1982—83), Elks. Democrat. Home: 10 Laney Rd Skowhegan ME 04976-9400 Office: 135 State House Station Augusta ME 04333-0135

KEYES, GEORGE PETER, lawyer; b. Jan. 18, 1936; s. George Joseph and Evelyn Marion (Ashton) K.; m. Elizabeth D. De Houst, July 18, 1965; children: Elizabeth, Sheila, Brendan. AB, U. Notre Dame, 1957; LLB, JD, Columbia U., 1960; postgrad., SUNY, Binghamton, 1982—. Bar: N.Y. 1962, U.S. Dist. Ct. (no. dist.) N.Y. 1963, U.S. Ct. Appeals (2d cir.) 1969. Assoc. Coughlin, Dermody & Guy, Binghamton, 1961-62, Levene, Gouldin & Thompson, Binghamton, 1962-67, ptnr., 1967-2001, counsel, 2001—. Master arbitrator N.Y. State Ins. Dept., 1978—. Mem. N.Y. State Bar Assn. (chair workers' compensation divsn. 1991-93), Broome County Bar Assn., Blind Work Assn., Inc. (bd. dirs. 2003—), USATF (1st v.p. Niagara dist. 1994-98, 2001—, pres. 1998-2000), Triple Cities Runners Club (sec. 1980—). Roman Catholic. Workers' compensation. Home: 46 Matthews St Binghamton NY 13905-4013 Office: Levene Gouldin & Thompson PO Box 13902-1563 Bache Bldg 71 State St Binghamton NY 13901 E-mail: gkeyes@binghamtonlaw.com.

KEYES, JEFFREY J. lawyer; BA magna cum laude, U. Notre Dame, 1968; JD cum laude, U. Mich., 1972. Bar: Minn. 1972. Shareholder Briggs and Morgan, P.A., Mpls.; fellow Am. Coll. Trial Lawyers, Mpls. Mem. Gov.'s Task Force on Tort Reform, 1986; chmn. fed. practice com. U.S. Dist. Ct. Minn., 1990-93, 2002—, chmn. adv. group on civil justice reform act, 1991-93; trainer U.S. Magistrate Judges Tng. Conf. on Settlement, Mpls., 1992; lectr. in field. Contbr. articles to law jours. Mem. ABA (chmn. antitrust sect. franchise com. 1989-90, contbg. editor Antitrust Monograph 1987, co-editor Antitrust Sect. State Antitrust Law Handbook, Minn. chpt. 1990), Minn. State Bar Assn. (co-chair Women in the Legal Profn. task force 1996-97, chmn. civil litigation sect. 1985-86), Hennepin County Bar Assn. Office: Briggs and Morgan 2400 Ids Ctr Minneapolis MN 55402

KEYS, JERRY MALCOM, lawyer; b. Childress, Tex., Dec. 5, 1947; s. Earl Milas and Mary Maud (Furr) K. BSEE with honors, U. Tex., 1970, JD with honors, 1975. Bar: Tex. 1975, U.S. Dist. Ct. (so. and we. dists.) Tex. 1980, U.S. Patent and Trademark Office. Assoc., Pravel & Wilson, Houston, 1975-76; assoc. Brown, Maroney, Rose, Baker & Barber, Austin, Tex., 1975-81; ptnr. Brown, Maroney, Rose, Barber & Dye, Austin, 1981-88; prin. Hagans/Keys PC, Austin, 1988-90; sr. shareholder Thompson & Knight, P.C., 1990-94, Locke Purnell Rain Harrell, P.C., 1994-98; ptnr. Locke Liddell & Sapp LLP, 1999; sr. v.p. and gen. counsel, FundsXpress, Inc., 1999-2001; shareholder Winstead Sechrest & Minick PC, 2001—; adj. asst. prof. U. Tex., 1979-85; mem. tech. adv. com. Supreme Ct. Tex. 1983-85. Mem. exec. coun. Greater Austin-San Antonio Corridor Coun., 1993—. Mem. Tex. Bar Assn. (profl. efficiency and econ. research com., chmn. office automation subcom. 1982-86), Austin Intellectual Property Law Assn. (pres. 1989-90). Computer, Intellectual property, Corporate, general.

KEYSER, FRANK RAY, JR., lawyer, former governor; b. Chelsea, Vt., Aug. 17, 1927; s. Frank Ray and Ellen L. (Larkin) K.; m. Joan Friedgen, July 15, 1950; children: Christopher Scott, Carol Ellen, Frank Ray III. Student, Tufts Coll., 1946-49, LLD, 1961; LLB, Boston U., 1952; LLD, Norwich U., 1962. Bar: Vt. 1952. Practiced in, Chelsea, 1952-65; mem. Vt. Ho. of Reps., 1955-59, speaker, 1959-60; gov. Vt., 1961-63; mem. Wilson & Keyser, 1952-65; v.p., pres., chmn. Vt. Marble Co., 1965-79. Of counsel Keyser, Crowley P.C..; chmn. bd. dirs. Hitchcock Clin. Ctrl. Dir. Green Mt. Coun. BSA. With USNR, WWII. Named Outstanding Young Vermonter Vt. Jr. C. of C., 1959; One of 10 Outstanding Young Men in in Nation, Jr. C. of C., 1961 Mem. ABA, Vt. Bar Assn., Vt. Golf Assn. (past pres.), Am. Legion, Masons. Republican. Address: 64 Warner Ave Proctor VT 05765-1322 E-mail: frkeyser@aol.com.

KEZSBOM, ALLEN, lawyer; b. N.Y.C., July 5, 1941; BA cum laude, Bklyn. Coll., 1962; LLB magna cum laude, Harvard U., 1965. Bar: N.Y. 1966, U.S. Dist. Ct. (so. dist.) N.Y. 1968, U.S. Dist. Ct. (ea. dist.) N.Y. 1972, U.S. Ct. Appeals (1st cir.) 1982, U.S. Ct. Appeals (2d cir.) 1971, U.S. Ct. Appeals (6th cir.) 1986, U.S. Ct. Appeals (8th cir.) 1981, U.S. Ct. Appeals (11th cir.) 1983, U.S. Supreme Ct. 1978. Assoc. Kaye, Scholor, Fierman, Hays & Handler, N.Y.C., 1966-71, ptnr., 1972-86, Fried, Frank, Harris, Shriver & Jacobson, N.Y.C., 1986—. Vis. lectr. Yale Law Sch., New Haven, Conn., 1992-93. Mem. Harvard Law Rev., 1963-65; contbr. articles to profl. jours. Knox fellow Harvard Law Sch., 1965-66. Mem. ABA (antitrust sect., litigation sect., nat. resources, energy & environ. law), N.Y. State Bar Assn. (antitrust sect., litigation, environ.), Assn. Bar City N.Y. Antitrust, Environmental, Intellectual property. Office: Fried Frank Harris Shriver & Jacobson 1 New York Plz Fl 22 New York NY 10004-1980

KHOREY, DAVID EUGENE, lawyer; b. Pitts., Oct. 5, 1959; s. Eugene George and Margaret (Yanyo) K.; m. Jennifer Ann Robinson, Dec. 29, 1983; children: Christopher David, Katherine Ann, Joanna Dale. BA with honors, U. Notre Dame, 1981; JD, Vanderbilt U., 1984. Bar: Mich. 1984, U.S. Dist. Ct. (we. dist.) Mich. 1984, U.S. Ct. Appeals 1989, U.S. Dist. Ct. (ea. dist.) Mich. 1990, U.S. Supreme Ct. 1999. Assoc. Varnum, Riddering, Schmidt & Howlett, Grand Rapids, Mich., 1984-89, ptnr., 1989—, chair labor practice group, 2000—. Instr. seminars Mich. Inst. of Continuing Legal Edn., Nat. Bus. Inst., Stetson Coll., NACUA Conf. Co-author: Developing Labor Law; mem. editl. bd. State Bar Mich. Mem. ABA (labor sect., com. devels. law under the nat. labor rels. act), State Bar Assn. Mich. (vice chair labor and employment sect.). Labor (including EEOC, Fair Labor Standards Act, labor-management relations, NLRB, OSHA). Office: Varnum Riddering Schmidt & Howlett PO Box 352 Bridgewater Pl Grand Rapids MI 49501-0352

KIBLINGER, CINDY JO, lawyer; b. Lynchburg, Va., July 27, 1972; d. Robert William Sr. and Susan Jane Kiblinger. BA, Vanderbilt U., 1994; JD, W.Va. U., 1997. Bar: W.Va. 1997, U.S. Dist. Ct. (so. dist.) W.Va. 1997, D.C. 1998, U.S. Dist. Ct. (no. dist.) W.Va. 2000. Assoc. James Humphreys & Assocs., L.C., Charleston, W.Va., 1997—. Mem. ATLA, W.Va. Trial Lawyers. State civil litigation, Personal injury (including property damage), Product liability. Home: 4110 Washington Ave SE Charleston WV 25304-2430 Office: James Humphreys & Assocs LC United Center St Ste 800 500 Virginia St E Charleston WV 25301 E-mail: cindykiblinger@aol.com.

KIDD, JOHN EDWARD, lawyer, corporate executive; b. Jan. 17, 1936; s. Edward F. and Mary (Feczko) K.; m. Elaine Mitchell, Feb. 23, 1963; children: John Mitchell, David Alan, Cynthia Lorraine. BS in Physics, LeMoyne Coll., 1957; LLB, Georgetown U., 1961. Bar: Va. 1961, U.S. Supreme Ct. 1966, U.S. Tax Ct. 1966, N.Y. 1968, U.S. Ct. Appeals (2d cir.) 1968, U.S. Ct. Appeals (4th cir.) 1968, U.S. Dist. Ct. (so. and ea. dists.) N.Y. 1969, U.S. Dist. Ct. (no. dist.) Calif. 1980, U.S. Ct. Appeals (3d, 5th, 9th, and 11th cirs.) 1981, U.S. Dist. Ct. (ea. dist.), Va. 1993. Patent examiner U.S. Patent Office, Washington, 1957-60; patent advisor USN, Washington, 1960-62; trial atty. Dept. Justice, Washington, 1963-67; counsel to Copyright Office, Washington, 1966-67; spl. counsel Dept. Justice, 1967; assoc. Kenyon & Kenyon, N.Y.C., 1967-70; assoc., ptnr. Pennie & Edmonds, N.Y.C., 1971-85, Anderson, Kill, Olick & Oshinsky, P.C., 1986-91; mng. ptnr. group and exec. com. Shea & Gould, 1991-94; sr. ptnr. Rogers & Wells, 1994-99, exec. com., mng. ptnr. intellectual property and tech. group, 1996—2000; counsel Baseball Hall of Fame, 1995-2001; sr. ptnr., global leader intellectual property Clifford, Chance, Rogers & Wells, 2000—; patent examiner U.S. Patent Office, Washington, 1957-60; sr. ptnr. Clifford Chance US, LLP, 2002—. Referee 9th Jud. Dept. N.Y. Supreme Ct., 1968-69; exec., chmn. bd. E.M. Kidd, Ltd.; chmn. Symposium on Presdl. Patent Reform Commn., 1966; lectr., mem. faculty Practicing Law Inst., 1967, 84-96; mem. Bicentennial Commn. U.S. Claims Ct., 1987-89; guest lectr. Inventor Hall of Fame, 1996-2000; patent litigation lectr. Practicing Law Inst., 2001, Am. Intellectual Property Law Assn., 2001. Contbr. over 40 articles to profl. jours. Active United Fund of Westchester, Comty. Fund of Bronxville, Westchester coun. Boy Scouts Am.; trustee LeMoyne Coll. Alumni. Mem. ABA (lectr. 1984-94), ATLA, Am. Intellectual Property Assn., U.S. Trademark Assn., Copyright Soc. Am., N.Y. State Bar Assn. (chmn. spl. com. on patents and trademarks 1982-86), Fed. Cir. Bar Assn., N.Y. Intellectual Property Assn. (bd. dirs. 1998-91, chmn. arbitration com., 1999-2002), Licensing Exec. Soc. (co-chmn. N.Y.C. sect. 2002-03), Assn. of Bar of City of N.Y., The Law Soc., London, Eng., The Oaks Country Club (Sarasota, Fla.), Yale Club, Sky Club, Rockefeller Club, Delta Theta Phi. Federal civil litigation, Patent, Trademark and copyright. Office: Clifford Chance US LLP 200 Park Ave Fl 8E New York NY 10166-0899 Home (Winter): 538 Dove Pointe, The Oaks Osprey FL 34229 E-mail: john.kidd@cliffordchance.com.

KIDDER, FRED DOCKSTATER, lawyer; b. Cleve., May 22, 1922; s. Howard Lorin and Virgina (Milligan) K.; m. Eleanor (Hap) Kidder; children— Fred D. III, Barbara Anne Donelson, Jeanne Louise Haffeman. BS with distinction, U. Akron, 1948; JD, Case Western Res. U., 1950. Bar: Ohio 1950, Tex. 1985, U.S. Dist. Ct. (no. dist.) Ohio 1950, U.S. Dist. Ct. (no. dist.) Tex. 1985. Assoc. Arter & Hadden and predecessors, Cleve., 1950-79, ptnr., 1960-79, Jones, Day, Reavis and Pogue, Cleve., 1980-89, regional mng. ptnr. Tex., 1985-86; gen. counsel Lubrizol Corp., Cleve., 1989-92, spl. counsel, 1993—. Contbr. articles to profl. jours. Mem. Cleve. Growth Assn., Shaker Heights Citizens Com., Citizens League Cleve.; former pres. Estate Planning Coun.; former co-chmn. bd. trustees Lake Erie Coll.; former bd. trustees, v.p., Alzheimer's Assn., Cleve.; mem., bd. trustees Cleve. Sight Ctr.; past mem. alumni coun. U. Akron; past. corp. coun. Dallas Mus. Art; past pres. Case Western Reserve U. Law Sch. Alumni Assn.; past chmn. Shaker Heights Recreation Bd. Mem. ABA, Am. Soc. Corp. Secs., Tex. Bar Assn., Ohio State Bar Assn., Estate Planning Coun. (past pres.), Blue Coats, Soc. Benchers (past chmn.), Union Club, Pepper Pike Club (past sec.), The Country Club, Cleve. Skating Club, Order of Coif, Ct. of Nisi Prius (former judge), Phi Eta Sigma, Beta Delta Psi, Phi Sigma Alpha, Phi Delta Theta, Phi Delta Phi. Commercial, contracts (including sales of goods; commercial financing), Corporate, general, Mergers and acquisitions. Office: The Lubrizol Corp 29400 Lakeland Blvd Wickliffe OH 44092-2298

KIDDER, GEORGE HOWELL, lawyer; b. Boston, June 14, 1925; s. Henry Purkitt and Julia Edwards (Howell) K.; m. Ellen Windom Warren, Aug. 17, 1946 (dec. May 1956); children: Susan Warren, George Howell, Stephen Wells; m. Priscilla Peele Hunnewell, Sept. 3, 1958 (dec. Nov. 1993); children: Priscilla Hunnewell, Timothy Hurd, Peter Arnold; m. Nancy D. Kidder, June 3, 1995. Grad., St. Mark's Sch., Southborough, Mass., 1943; student Navy V-12 program, Williams Coll., 1943-44; B in Naval Sci., Tufts Coll., 1945; LLB, Harvard, 1950; DD (hon.), Episcopal Div. Sch., 1987. Bar: Mass. 1951. With Office Gen. Counsel CIA, 1952-54, 1950-52; assoc. Hemenway & Barnes, 1950—52, 1954—55, ptnr., 1956-97, of counsel, 1997—. Mem. panel neutral mediators and arbitrators Jud. Arbitration and Mediation Svc./Endispute, 1997—. Trustee Episcopal Ch. Found., Episcopal Divinity Sch., Cambridge, Mass., 1967—86, 1998—, pres. bd. trustees, 1977—86, hon. trustee, 1986—98; chancellor Episcopal Diocese of Mass., 1988—, dir., Trustees of Donations; trustee St. Mark's Sch., 1959—84, pres. bd. trustees, 1974—84; trustee Fenn Sch., Concord, 1956—77, pres. bd. trustees, 1960—73; trustee Concord Acad., 1963—78, pres. bd. trustees, 1971—78; trustee Boston Symphony Orch., 1977—94, pres. bd. trustees, 1987—94, life trustee, 1994—; trustee Children's Med. Ctr. and Children's Hosp. Corp., 1982—97, chmn. bd. dirs., 1992—97; trustee Wellesley Coll., 1962—80, trustee emeritus, 1980—; bd. dirs. Greater Boston Legal Svcs., 1961—87; dir. Controlled Risk Ins. Co., Ltd., 1988—99, chmn. bd. dirs., 1991—98; dir. Risk Mgmt. Found. Harvard Med. Instns., Inc., 1988—98, chmn. bd. dirs., 1991—98; trustee Harvard Med. Ctr. Inc., 1989—; trustee, mem. exec. com. WGBH Ednl. Found., 1987—, vice chmn., 1998—2003. Fellow Am. Coll. Probate Counsel; mem. Am. Law Inst., Internat. Acad. Estate and Trust Law; Mem. Tau Beta Pi. General practice, Probate (including wills, trusts), Estate planning. Home: 110 Spencer Brook Rd Concord MA 01742-5206 Office: 60 State St Boston MA 02109-1800 E-mail: gkidder@hembar.com.

KIDWELL, WAYNE L. state supreme court justice; b. Council, Idaho, 1938; m. Shari Linn; children: Vaughn, Blair. BA, JD, U. Idaho. Bar: Idaho 1964, Hawaii, former U.S. Trust Territories. Past atty. law firms, Idaho and Hawaii; past pvt. practice Idaho and Hawaii; past atty. gen. State of Idaho; past majority leader Idaho Senate; past prosecuting atty. Ada County, Idaho; past assoc. dep. atty. gen. Pres. Reagan adminstrn., past liason Dept. Justice U.S. Govt.; past atty. gen. Republic of Marshall Islands; judge Idaho Supreme Ct. Photographer pvt. shows; one-man shows include galleries in Hawaii. Active numerous civic and profl. orgns. Served USMCR, U.S. Army Mil. Police Corps. Office: Idaho Supreme Ct Supreme Ct Bldg PO Box 83720 Boise ID 83720-0101

KIEF, PAUL ALLAN, lawyer; b. Montevideo, Minn., Mar. 22, 1934; s. Paul G. and Minna S. K. BA, LLB, U. Minn., 1957. Bar: Minn. 1957, U.S. Dist. Ct. Minn. 1964, U.S. Tax Ct. 1968, U.S. Supreme Ct. 1981; cert. criminal trial law specialist Nat. Bd. Trial Advocacy. Gen. practice, Bemidji, Minn., 1959—; ptnr. Kief, Fuller, Baer & Wallner, Ltd., Bemidji, Minn., 1973-97; owner Paul A. Kief Law Firm, Bemidji, Minn., 1998—; pub. defender 9th Jud. Dist. Minn., Bemidji, Minn., 1966-98. Chief pub, defender, Benudji, Minn., 1968—94; vol. atty. Minn. Civil Liberties Union; mem. adv. bd. Innocence Project of Minn.; panel atty Legal Svcs., Northwest, Minn. Vice chmn. Beltrami County Planning Commn., 1964-68; chmn. adv. com. Gov.'s Crime Commn., 1971-77; mem. Minn. Task Force on Standards and Goals in Criminal Justice, 1975-76, Crime Victims Task Force, 1985, Jud. Selection Com., 1987, Com. on Criminal Jury Instrn. Guides, 1988-90; bd. dirs. Legal Svcs. Northwest Minn., 1990-96; capt. CAP, 1969—. Served with USAR, USNG, 1958-64. Mem. ABA, ATLA, NACDL, MACDL, Nat. Bd. Trial Advocacy (cert. crim. law trial specialist 1998), Minn. Bar Assn., Minn. Trial Lawyers Assn., 15th Dist. Bar Assn. (past sec.), Beltrami County Bar Assn. (past pres.), Lawyer-Pilots Bar Assn., Minn. Criminal Def. Lawyers Assn. Clubs: Toastmasters. Democrat. Congregationalist. Criminal, General practice. Home: PO Box 212 Bemidji MN 56619-0212 Office: 514 America Ave NW PO Box 212 Bemidji MN 56619-0212 E-mail: paky@paulbunyan.net.

KIEFER, KAREN LAVERNE, lawyer; b. Lancaster, Ohio, Nov. 8, 1952; d. Ray E. and Marilyn L. (Keister) K. BA in Econs., Chatham Coll., 1974; MBA in Fin., George Washington U., 1977; JD in Internat. Law, U. Balt., 1982. Bar: Md. 1987, D.C. 1988, Pa. 1998. Counsel Europe, Israel and Am. Westinghouse Elec. Corp., Balt., 1974-84; mgr. Internat. Ops. Gould Inc., Washington, 1985-87; pvt. practice law Annapolis, Md., 1987—, Scottdale, Pa., 1987—. Founder, owner Mainsail of Annapolis Yacht Chartering, 1979—; incorporator, legal counsel Scottdale Cmty. Pool. Pub.: The Cormany Diaries, A Northern Family in the Civil War, 1982. Sponsor U.S. Naval Acad. Midshipmen, Annapolis 1981-97; coach Naval Acad. Sailing Squadron, 1991-97. Mem. ABA, D.C. Bar Assn., Md. Bar Assn., Pa. Bar Assn., Am. Soc. Internat. Law, Am. Mgmt. Assn., Westmoreland County Bar Assn. Avocations: swimming, sailing, music, arts. Family and matrimonial, General practice, Probate (including wills, trusts).

KIEFNER, JOHN ROBERT, JR., lawyer, educator; b. Peoria, Ill., May 31, 1946; s. John Robert and Luna Merle (Froment) K.; m. B.C. Clayton, Feb. 14, 1989; 1 child, John William. BA, Johns Hopkins U., 1968; JD, Stetson U., 1971. Bar: Fla. 1971, U.S. Ct. Appeals (D.C. cir.) 1971, U.S. Ct. Appeals (11th cir.) 1981, U.S. Dist. Ct. (no. dist.) Fla. 1971, U.S. Dist. Ct. (mid. dist.) Fla. 1981, U.S. Ct. Mil. Appeals 1971, U.S. Tax Ct. 1979, U.S. Supreme Ct. 1979. Staff atty. SEC, Washington, 1971-74, br. chief, 1974-77, regional trial counsel, 1977-82; mem. Robbins, Gaynor, Burton, Hampp, Burns, Bronstein & Shasteen, St. Petersburg, Fla., 1982-86; ptnr. Riden, Earle & Kiefner, P.A., St. Petersburg, 1986-99, Harris, Barrett, Mann & Dew, L.L.P., St. Petersburg, 1999—2001, Kiefner & Renaldo, P.A., St. Petersburg, 2001—. Adj. prof. law Stetson U., St. Petersburg, 1982—. Past chmnn. Combined Fed. Campaign, 1976-77. Capt. U.S. Army, 1968-76. Recipient Cert. of Merit, SEC, 1982; Charles A. Dana scholar, 1970-71. Mem. ABA, ATLA, Fla. Bar Assn., St. Petersburg Bar Assn., Fla. Acad. Trial Lawyers, Pinellas County Trial Lawyers Assn., Fed. Bar Assn., Nat.

Assn. Colls. and Univs. (recruitment com.), St. Petersburg Area C. of C., Johns Hopkins U. Alumni Assn., Masons, Shriners. Lutheran. Administrative and regulatory, Federal civil litigation, Securities. Home: 227 126th Ave E Treasure Island FL 33706 Office: Kiefner & Renaldo PA Ste 300 146 2nd St N Saint Petersburg FL 33701 E-mail: JKiefner@Kiefnerrenaldolaw.com.

KIEL, FREDERICK ORIN, lawyer; b. Columbus, Feb. 22, 1942; s. Fred and Helen Kiel; m. Vivian Lee Naff, June 2, 1963; 1 child, Aileen Vivian. AB magna cum laude, Wilmington Coll., 1963; JD, Harvard U., 1966. Bar: Ohio 1966, U.S. Supreme Ct. 1972. Assoc. Peck, Shaffer & Williams, Cin., 1966-71, ptnr., 1971-80, Taft, Stettinius & Hollister, Cin., 1980-89; pvt. practice law Cin., 1990—. Lectr. and expert witness in field; co-founder Bond Attys.' Workshop, 1976. Editor: Bond Lawyers and Bond Law: An Oral History, 1993, Bondletter, 1991—, Anderson Insights, 1992—; contbr. articles on mcpl. bond fin. to profl. jours. Arbitrator Mcpl. Securities Rulemaking Bd., 1985-92; mem. Anderson Twp. Govtl. Task Force, 1986—; sec. Anderson Twp. Greenspace Adv. Com., 1990—; rep. precinct exec. Precinct H Anderson Twp., 1991-92, 94-2001, Precinct X Anderson Twp., 2001—; twp. atty. Anderson Twp., 1997—; sec. Anderson Twp. Rep. Screening Com., 1999 Mem. Ohio State Bar Assn., Cin. Bar Assn., Nat. Assn. Bond Lawyers (dir. 1979-84, pres. 1982-83, hon. dir. 1984—, editor The Quar. Newsletter and The Bond Lawyer 1982—, Bond Atty.'s Workshop steering com. 1976, 83, 85, scrivener com. stds. of practice 1987-89), Queen City Club. Municipal (including bonds). Office: 1095 Nimitzview Dr Ste 103 Cincinnati OH 45230-4392

KIENBAUM, THOMAS GERD, lawyer; b. Berlin, Nov. 16, 1942; came to U.S., 1957; s. Gerd Wilhelm Kienbaum and Albertine Brigitte (Kramm) Kettler; m. Karen Smith, June 24, 1966 (div.); 1 child, Ursula; m. Elizabeth Hardy, Jan. 22, 1992. AB, U. Mich., 1965; JD magna cum laude, Wayne State U., 1968. Bar: Mich. 1968, Ill. 1991, U.S. Supreme Ct. 1983. Assoc. Dickinson, Wright, Moon, Van Dusen & Freeman, Detroit, 1968-76, ptnr., 1976-97; ptnr., founder Kienbaum Opperwall Hardy & Pelton, Detroit and Birmingham, 1997—. Contbr. legal articles to profl. publs. Bd. dirs. Wayne County Neighborhood Legal Svc., 1972-76, 87-88. Fellow ABA, State Bar of Mich. Found.; mem. Am. Judicature Soc., Coll. Labor and Employment Lawyers, State Bar Mich. (pres. 1995-96), Detroit Bar Assn. (pres. 1985-86), Barristers Assn. (pres. 1978-79), Oakland County Bar Assn., Order of the Coif. Avocations: reading, skiing, squash, sailing. Labor (including EEOC, Fair Labor Standards Act, labor-management relations, NLRB, OSHA). Office: Kienbaum Opperwall Hardy & Pelton 325 S Old Woodward Ave Birmingham MI 48009-6202

KIENER, JOHN LESLIE, judge; b. Ft. Madison, Iowa, June 21, 1940; s. Cyril Joseph and Lucille Olive (Golden) K.; m. Carol Lynn Winston, June 4, 1966; children: Susan, Gretchen. BA cum laude, Loras Coll., 1962; JD, Drake U., 1965. Bar: Iowa 1965, Tenn. 1972, U.S. Supreme Ct. 1974. Practice law, Decorah, Iowa, 1965-68; asst. atty. gen. State of Iowa, 1968-72; ptnr. Cantor & Kiener, 1972-80; city judge City of Johnson City, Tenn., 1975-80, gen. sessions judge, 1980—. Continuing edn. tchr., bus. law East Tenn. State U., 1975—. Contbr. and articles editor in Jonesborough Herald and Tribune. Mem. ABA, Tenn. Bar Assn., Washington County Bar Assn., Rotary, Elks. Republican. Avocations: stamp collecting, genealogy. Home: 2403 Camelot Cir Johnson City TN 37604-2938 Office: Gen Sessions Ct Downtown Ctr Courthouse 101 E Market St Ste 7 Johnson City TN 37604-5722 E-mail: ckiener@preferred.com.

KIERNAN, THOMAS EDWARD, lawyer; b. Buffalo, Minn., Apr. 6, 1962; s. Daniel Patrick and Ardis Jane Kiernan; m. Julie R. Nilson, June 25, 1988. BA in Polit. Sci., U. Wis., Eau Claire, 1986; JD, William Mitchell Coll. Law, St. Paul, 1990. Bar: Minn. 1990. Assoc. Rinke-Noonan, St. Cloud, Minn., 1990-94; ptnr. Roes, Larsen & Kiernan, Annandale, Minn., 1994-99; pvt. practice Kiernan Personal Injury Atty. P.A., Buffalo, Minn., 1999—. Named Super Lawyer, Law and Politics mag., 1999, named Rising Star, 2002. Mem. Minn. Bar Assn. (cert. civil trial specialist 1997). Democrat. Roman Catholic. Avocations: reading, golf, movies, boating. Office: PO Box 433 Buffalo MN 55313-0433

KIES, KENNETH J. lawyer; b. Ft. Benning, Ga., Jan. 4, 1952; s. Robert Herman K.; m. Kathleen Barbara Clark, Oct. 11, 1986. BA, Ohio U., 1974; JD, Ohio State U., 1977; LLM in Taxation, Georgetown U., 1986. Bar: Ohio 1977, U.S. Tax Ct. 1978, D.C. 1987, U.S. Supreme Ct. 1992. Assoc. Baker & Hostetler, Cleve., 1977-81; asst. minority tax counsel Com. on Ways & Means U.S. Ho. of Reps., Washington, 1981-82, chief minority tax counsel, 1982-87; ptnr. Baker & Hostetler, Washington, 1987-95; chief of staff joint com. on taxation U.S. Congress, Washington, 1995-98; mng. ptnr. Price Waterhouse Coopers, Washington, 1998—2002; mng. dir. Fed. Policy Group, Clark Cons., Washington, 2002—. Contbr. articles to profl. jours. Mem. Capitol Hill Club, Washington Golf and Country Club, Robert Trent Jones Golf Club. Republican. Taxation, general. Office: Fed Policy Group 101 Constitution Ave NW 701E Washington DC 20001-2133

KIHLE, DONALD ARTHUR, lawyer; b. Noonan, N.D., Apr. 4, 1934; s. J. Arthur and Linnie W. (Ljunngren) K.; m. Judith Anne, July 18, 1964; children: Kevin, Kirsten, Kathryn, Kurte. BS in Indsl. Engring., U. N.D., 1957; JD, U. Okla., 1967. Bar: Okla. 1967, U.S. Dist. Cts. (we. and no. dists) Okla. 1967, U.S. Ct. Appeals (10th cir.) 1967, U.S. Supreme Ct. 1971. Assoc. Huffman, Arrington, Scheurich & Kincaid, Tulsa, 1967-71, ptnr., 1971-78; shareholder, dir., officer Arrington Kihle Gaberino & Dunn, Tulsa, 1978-97, pres., 1994-97; shareholder, dir. Gable & Gotwals, Tulsa, 1997-99, advisor, dir., 1999-2001. Dist. chmn. Boy Scouts Am., 1983-85, cubmaster, 1986-88, coun. coms., 1988-96, campiree chmn., 1990; mem. Statewide Law Day Com., 1982-86, chmn., 1983-85; trustee Brandon Hall Sch., Atlanta, 1991—, chmn., 1995-99. Lt. U.S. Army, 1957-59. Recipient Silver Beaver award Boy Scouts Am. Mem.: ABA, Tulsa County Bar Assn., Okla. Bar Assn. (chmn. constl. bicentennial com. 1986—89), Tulsa Club (bd. govs. 1987—94, pres. 1992), So. Hills Country Club, Q Club (scribe 1991—), Rotary, Order of Arrow (vigil), Order or Coif, Sigma Chi (Tulsa alumni pres. 1995—97), Phi Delta Phi, Sigma Tau. Republican. Corporate, general, Oil, gas, and mineral, Securities. Home: 4717 S Lewis Ct Tulsa OK 74105-5135 Office: 1100 ONEOK Plz 100 W 5th St Tulsa OK 74103-4240 E-mail: dkihle@gablelaw.com.

KIKOLER, STEPHEN PHILIP, lawyer; b. N.Y.C., Apr. 24, 1945; s. Sigmund and Dorothy (Javna) K.; m. Ethel Lerner, June 18, 1967; children: Jeffrey Stuart, Shari Elaine. AB, U. Mich., 1966, JD cum laude, 1969. Bar: Ill. 1969, U.S. Dist. Ct. (no. dist.) Ill. 1969, U.S. Ct. Appeals (7th cir.) 1988, U.S. Ct. Appeals (11th cir.) 1994, U.S. Ct. Appeals for the Armed Forces 1970, U.S. Supreme Ct. 1994. Capt. Judge Advocate Gen.'s Corps U.S. Army, 1970-73; with Much, Shelist, Freed, Denenberg, Ament & Rubenstein PC, Chgo. Mem. ABA, Ill. State Bar Assn., Chgo. Bar. Assn. (real property law com., mechanics' liens subcom.). General civil litigation, Construction, Property, real (including real estate development, water). Home: 2746 Norma Ct Glenview IL 60025-4661 Office: Much Shelist Freed Denenberg Ament & Rubenstein PC 191 N Wacker Dr Chicago IL 60606-1615 E-mail: skikoler@muchshelist.com.

KILBANE, ANNE L. judge; b. Cleve., Sept. 22, 1941; d. Thomas Bryan and Nora (Coyle) K. BA in Chemistry, Seton Hill Coll., Greensburg, Pa., 1963; JD, Cleve. Marshall Coll. Law, 1976. Bar: Ohio 1977, U.S. Dist. Ct. (so. dist.) Ohio 1977, U.S. Dist. Ct. (no. dist.) Ohio 1978), U.S. Ct. Appeals (6th cir.) 1978, U.S. Supreme Ct. 1985. Sr. chemist Dept. of Health City of Cleve., 1963-66; chief brewing chemist, asst. quality control mgr. Carling Brewing Co., Cleve., 1966-71; chemist, plant mgr. Phillips Syrup Corp., Parma, Ohio, 1971-75; asst. to dir. law City of Cleve., 1975-77; assoc. Kilbane & Kilbane, Columbus, Ohio, 1977-78, Nurenberg, Plevin, Heller, Cleve., 1978-86, ptnr., 1986-99; judge Ohio Ct. of Appeals (8th dist.), Cuyahoga County, Ohio, 1999—. Lectr. in field. Mem. Ohio State Bar Assn. (negligence subcom.), Ohio Women's Bar Assn. (founding), Ohio Jud. Conf., Ohio Ct. Appeal Judge's Assn., Cuyahoga County Bar Assn. (appellate sect.), Cleve. Bar Assn. (appellate sect., commn. on women in the law), Nat. Lawyers Assn., 6th Cir. Jud. Conf. (life), Cleve. Marshall Alumnae Assn. (life), Am. Chem. Soc., Delta Theta Phi. Office: Cuyahoga County Ct House 1 W Lakeside Ave Cleveland OH 44113-1023

KILBANE, THOMAS M. lawyer; b. Cleve., Mar. 1, 1953; s. Thomas M. and Kathleen K.; m. Helen Crowley, June 26, 1976; children: Catherine Ann, Patrick Thomas, Michael Crowley. BA magna cum laude, Xavier U., 1974; postgrad., Miami U., Ohio, 1975; JD with highest distinction, John Marshall Law Sch., 1978. Bar: Ill. 1978, Wash. 1980, U.S. Dist. Ct. (no. dist.) Ill. 1978, U.S. Dist. Ct. (we. dist.) Wash. 1980, U.S. Ct. Appeals (5th and 9th cirs.) 1981, U.S. Dist. Ct. (ea. dist.) Wash. 1992. Jud. extern U.S. Dist. Ct. Ill., Chgo., 1977; jud. clk. to presiding justice Ill. Appellate Ct., Chgo., 1978-80; assoc., shareholder Garvey, Schubert & Barer, P.C., Seattle, 1980-85, 86-89; shareholder Ater Wynne LLP, Seattle, 1990—. Editor-in-Chief John Marshall Law Rev., 1977-78. Trustee Queen Anne Cmty. Coun., Seattle, 1983-85; mem. Queen Anne Land Use Rev. Com., 1983-85; mem. branch bd. Sammamish Family YMCA, 1993-95. Chgo. Bar Found. grantee, 1978. Mem. ABA (bus., environment and energy, sects.), Wash. State Bar Assn. (bus., , environment and land use sects.), King County Bar Assn., Alpha Sigma Nu. Corporate, general, Environmental, Property, real (including real estate development, water). Home: 7551 Madrona Dr NE Bainbridge Island WA 98110-2901 Office: Ater Wynne LLP 601 Union St Ste 5450 Seattle WA 98101-2327 E-mail: tmk@aterwynne.com.

KILBANE, THOMAS STANTON, lawyer; b. Cleve., Mar. 7, 1941; s. Thomas Joseph and Helen (Stanton) K.; m. Sally Conway Kilbane, June 4, 1966; children: Sarah, Thomas, Eamon, James, Carlin. BA magna cum laude, John Carroll U., 1963; JD, Northwestern U., 1966. Bar: Ohio 1966, U.S. Dist. Ct. (no. dist.) Ohio 1969, U.S. Supreme Ct. 1975, U.S. Ct. Claims 1981, U.S. Ct. Appeals (6th cir.) 1982, U.S. Ct. Appeals (3d cir.) 1990, U.S. Ct. Appeals (5th cir.) 1998, U.S. Ct. Appeals (2d, 7th and 9th cirs.) 2002, U.S. Ct. Appeals (4th cir.) 2003. Assoc. Squire, Sanders & Dempsey, Cleve., 1966-76, ptnr., 1976—, adminstrv. com., 1979-80, mgmt. com., 1981-83, 87-90, mng. ptnr. litigation practice area, 1991—. Fed. ct. panelist U.S. Dist. Ct. (no. dist.) Ohio. Mem. editl. bd. Northwestern U. Law Rev., 1965-66. Active Rep. Presdl. Task Force; bd. dirs. United Way Svcs. Capt. U.S. Army, 1967-69, Vietnam. Decorated Bronze Star; named Greater Cleve. Cath. Man of Yr., 1996. Fellow ABA, Am. Coll. Trial Lawyers, Internat. Acad. Trial Lawyers, Master Bencher of Anthony J. Celebrezze Inns of Ct.; mem. Fed. Bar Assn., Am. Coll. Barristers, Ohio Bar Assn. (AAA corp. counsel com., ctr. for pub. resources constrn. com.), Greater Cleve. Bar Assn., Def. Rsch. Inst., Jud. Conf. 8th Jud. Dist. Ohio (life), Union Club, The 50 Club, The Club, Alpha Sigma Nu. Republican. Roman Catholic. Federal civil litigation, State civil litigation, Construction. Office: Squire Sanders & Dempsey 4900 Key Tower 127 Public Sq Cleveland OH 44114-1304 E-mail: tkilbane@ssd.com.

KILBOURN, JOSEPH A. lawyer; b. Providence, June 16, 1926; s. Jonathan Francis Kilbourn and Clara Vivell Kent; m. Elaine Mary Deran, Aug. 1, 1959; children: Mary, Pamela, Kent, Connor, Andrew. BA, Yale U., 1948; LLB, Columbia U., 1952. Bar: N.Y. 1953. Assoc. Bigham, Englar, Jones & Houston, N.Y.C., 1953-63, ptnr., 1963-98, of counsel, 1998—. Chmn. excess, surplus lines, reins. com. tort and ins. practice sect. ABA, 1991-92. Pres. Rowayton (Conn.) Hose Co. vol. fire co., 1975-80, 83-84. Staff sgt. U.S. Army, 1944-46. Mem. Comml. Bar Assn. (London, hon.), Order of Founders and Patriots Am. (atty. gen. 1994-96, sec. gen. 1996-98, gov. gen. 1998-2000, Disting. Svc. award 2000), Soc. Colonial Wars in State of Conn. (mem. coun. 1977—), Norwalk Yacht Club. Avocation: sailing. Home: Apt 206 114 Strawberry Hill Ave Stamford CT 06902 Office: Bigham Englar Jones & Houston 40 Wall St New York NY 10005 E-mail: jkilbourn@bejh.com.

KILBOURN, WILLIAM DOUGLAS, JR., law educator; b. Colorado Springs, Colo., Dec. 9, 1924; s. William Douglas and Clara Howe (Lee) K.; m. Barbara Ruth Neff, Sept. 16, 1950; children: Jonathan VI, Katharine Ann. BA, Yale U., 1949; postgrad., Columbia U., 1949-50, LLB, 1953. Bar: Mass. 1962, Oreg. 1953, Minn. 1974. Acct. Arthur Andersen & Co., 1949-50; assoc. Davies, Biggs, Strayer, Stoel & Boley, Portland, Oreg., 1953-56; asst. prof. law U. Mont., 1956-57; assoc. prof. law U. Mo., 1957-59; prof. law, founding dir. grad. tax program Boston U., 1959-71; prof. law U. Minn., 1971-98, prof. emeritus, 1998—. Dir. U. Mont. Tax Inst., 1956; of counsel Palmer & Dodge, Boston, 1964-75, Oppenheimer, Wolff & Donnelly, St. Paul and Mpls., 1980-94; mem. exec. com. Fed. Tax Inst. New Eng., 1966-72; mem. adv. com. Western New Eng. Coll. Tax Inst; vis. prof. law Duke U., 1974-75, U. Tex., 1977, Washington U., St. Louis, 1977; past ednl. advisor Tax Execs. Inst.; lectr. in 31 states, Mex., The Caribbean, D.C.; expert witness in field. Editor: Estate Planning and Income Taxation, 1957; contbr. articles to profl. jours. Dist. dir. United Fund, Belmont, Mass., chair fair practices com. Recipient numerous tchg. awards; Kent scholar, Stone scholar Columbia U. Law Sch. Mem. ABA (tax sect., corp. stockholder rels. com. 1962-76, chair subcom. inc. 1968-73), Boston Bar Assn. (chair tax sect. 1967-70), Boston Tax Forum, Boston Tax Coun. Avocations: tennis, botany, landscape gardening. Home: 2681 E Lake Of The Isles Pkwy Minneapolis MN 55408-1051

KILBOURNE, GEORGE WILLIAM, lawyer; b. Berea, Ky., Mar. 29, 1924; s. John Buchanan and Maud (Parsons) K.; m. Helen Spooner, Dec. 25, 1945 (div. 1968); m. Carole Marko, June 12, 1970 (div. 1984); children: Stuart (dec.), Charles; m. Anne F. Lavine, Aug. 19, 1996. Student, Berea Coll., 1941-42, Denison U., 1944; BS in Mech. Engring., U. Mich., 1946; JD, U. Calif., Berkeley, 1951. Bar: Calif. 1952, U.S. Dist. Ct. (no. dist.) Calif. 1952, Ind. 1957, U.S. Appeals (9th cir.). Sole practice, Berkeley, 1952-57; assoc. Hays & Hays, Sullivan, Ind., 1957-59, Boyle & Kilbourne, Sullivan, 1961-63, Bernal, Rigney & Kilbourne, Berkeley, 1963-68, Sherbourne & Kilbourne, Pleasant Hill, Calif., 1968-75; sole practice Pleasant Hill and Martinez, Calif., 1975—. Lectr. Lincoln Law Sch., San Francisco, 1956-57, John F. Kennedy Law Sch., Orinda, Calif., 1977-78. Served to 2d lt. USMC, 1942-46, PTO. Mem.: Elks. Episcopalian. Avocations: tennis, bowling, outdoors. Environmental, Personal injury (including property damage), Toxic tort. Office: 661 Augusta Dr Moraga CA 94556-1035 E-mail: gwkilbourn@aol.com.

KILBRIDE, THOMAS L. judge; m. Mary Kilbride; 3 children. BA magna cum laude, St. Mary's Coll., 1978; JD, Antioch Sch. Law, 1981. Practicioner U.S. Dist. Ct., Ill., U.S. Seventh Cir. Ct. Appeals; Supreme Ct. justice Ill. State Supreme Ct., 2000—. Former mem. bd. dirs., former v.p., former pres. Ill. Twp. Attys. Assn. Vol. legal adv. Cmty. Caring Conf., Quad City Harvest Inc.; charter chmn. Quad Cities Interfaith Sponsoring Com.; former mem. Rock Island Human Rels. Com.; former vol. lawyer, charter mem. Ill. Pro Bono Ctr. Mem.: Rock Island County Bar Assn., Ill. State Bar Assn.

KILGORE, GARY LYNN, lawyer; b. Chattanooga, July 17, 1953; s. James Velton Jr. and Frankie Jean (Eggert) K. BA, U. Va., 1975; JD, U. Tex., 1978. Bar: Tex. 1978, U.S. Dist. Ct. (no. dist.) Tex. 1979, U.S. Dist. Ct. (we. dist.) Tex. 1980, U.S. Ct. Appeals (5th cir.) 1979, U.S. Ct. Appeals (11th cir.) 1981, U.S. Dist. Ct. Hawaii 1984, U.S. Supreme Ct. 1985; bd. cert. personal injury tiral lawyer. Assoc. Garcia & Ganne, Austin, 1978-81; pres. Garcia & Kilgore, P.C., Austin, 1981-83, Garcia, Kilgore & Hickman, P.C., Austin, 1983—93; appeals judge Tex. Workers Compensation Commn., 1993—. Pres. Am. Inst. Defensive Driving, Inc. 1981-84. Author, research editor Am. Jour. Criminal Law, 1977-78. Del. Travis County Dem. Conv., Austin, 1980, 84, Tex. State Dem. Conv., Houston, 1984. Mem. ABA, Tex. State Bar Assn. Avocations: tropical fish, computers. State civil litigation, Personal injury (including property damage), Workers' compensation. Home: 1605A Southgate Cir Austin TX 78704-7747 Office: Tex Workers Compensation Commn 4000 IH-35 Austin TX 78704-7491

KILGORE, JERRY, state attorney general; m. Marty Kilgore; children: Klarke, Kelsey. JD, Coll. William & Mary, 1986; grad., U. Va. Prin. Richmond law firm Sands Anderson Marks & Miller; asst. Commonwealth atty. Scott County; asst. U.S. atty. gen. Western Dist. Va.; state, fed. prosecutor State of Va.; sec. pub. safety former Gov. George Allen's Cabinet , 1994—97; atty. gen. State of Va., 2001—. Republican. Office: 900 E Main St Richmond VA 23219*

KILGORE, TERRY LEE, lawyer; b. Mansfield, Ohio, May 5, 1948; s. Kenneth Burr and Velma (Gatton) K.; m. Renee Mary Bassak, Sept. 16, 1972; children: Todd Lee, Michelle Renee. BA in Polit. Sci. cum laude, Wittenberg U., 1970; JD cum laude, Ohio State U., 1973. Bar: Ohio 1973, U.S. Dist. Ct. (no. dist.) Ohio 1974, U.S. Ct. Appeals (6th cir.) 1975. Ptnr. Weldon, Huston & Keyser, Mansfield, 1973-94; pvt. practice Columbus, 1994—. Mem. Interprofl. Edn. and Practice Commn., Ohio State U., Columbus, 1978—; chmn/ Mansfield CSC, 1976-85. Mem.: ABA, Ohio Bar Assn., Liederkranz Club (Mansfield). Republican. Lutheran. Avocations: sailing, biking. Home and Office: 3031 Birch Hollow Way Columbus OH 43231-7674 Fax: 614-794-6993. E-mail: tkilgore13@ameritech.net.

KILLEEN, MICHAEL JOHN, lawyer; b. Washington, Oct. 5, 1949; s. James Robert and Georgia Winston (Hartwell) K.; m. Therese Ann Goeden, Oct. 6, 1984; children: John Patrick, Katherine Therese, Mary Clare, James Philip. BA, Gonzaga U., 1971, JD magna cum laude, 1977. Bar: Wash. 1977, U.S. Dist. Ct. (we. dist.) Wash. 1979, U.S. Ct. Appeals (9th cir.) 1984, U.S. Supreme Ct. 1990. Jud. clk. Wash. State Ct. Appeals, Tacoma, 1977-79; assoc. Davis Wright Tremaine, Seattle, 1979-85, ptnr., 1985—. Bd. dirs. Seattle Goodwill, 1987—, sec., 1998-02. Author: Guide to Strike Planning, 1985, Newsroom Legal Guidebook, 1996, Employment in Washington, 1984—. Active Gonzaga Law Bd. Advisors, Spokane, Wash., pres., 1992-96. Recipient Freedom's Light award Washington Newspaper Pub. Assn., 1999, Disting. Alumni award Gonzaga U., 2002. Mem. ABA, Wash. State Bar Assn., King County Bar Assn. (treas. 1987-89, pres. award 1989). Democrat. Roman Catholic. General civil litigation, Communications, Labor (including EEOC, Fair Labor Standards Act, labor-management relations, NLRB, OSHA). E-mail: mikekilleen@dwt.com.

KILLIAN, ROBERT KENNETH, JR., judge, lawyer; b. Hartford, Conn., Jan. 29, 1947; s. Robert Kenneth Sr. and Evelyn (Farnan) K.; m. Candace Korper, Oct. 6, 1979; children: Virginia, Carolyn. BA, Union U., 1969; JD, Georgetown U., 1972. Bar: Conn. 1972, U.S. Ct. Appeals (2nd cir.) 1973, D.C. 1974, U.S. Ct. Appeals (D.C. cir.) 1974. Bur. chief Sta. WTIC-AM-FM-TV, Washington, 1969-72; spl. asst. Senator Abe Ribicoff, Washington, 1972-73; ptnr. Gould, Killian, Wynne et al, Hartford, 1972-84; judge Conn. Probate Ct., Hartford, 1984—; ptnr. Killian & Donohue, Hartford, 1985—98, Killian Donohue & Shipman LLC, Hartford, 1998—2001, Killian Donohue & Jaff LLC, 2001—. Spl. counsel Lt. Gov. Conn., Hartford, 1974-78; mem. exec. com. Conn. Probate Assembly, 1987—, pres.-judge, 1997-99; mem. investment adv. coun. State of Conn., 1995-99; mem. Jud. Commn. on Attys.' Ethics, 1990—. Author: Basic Probate in Connecticut, 1990, 8th edit., 2002. Regent, U. Hartford; trustee Hartt Sch. Music; chmn. Conn. chpt. March of Dimes, 1986—; bd. dirs. Yeats Drama Found., 1989—; incorporator St. Francis Hosp. and Med. Ctr. Recipient 1st Pl. award New England Conv. Magicians, 1965; named Conn.'s Outstanding Probate Judge, Conn. Probate Assembly, 1990. Mem. ABA, ATLA, Nat. Coll. Juvenile and Family Ct. Judges, Nat. Conf. Probate Judges, Conn. Bar Assn., Conn. Trial Lawyers Assn., Psychic Entertainer's Assn., Internat. Brotherhood Magicians, Soc. Am. Magicians (chmn. nat. conv. 1977). Democrat. Roman Catholic. Home: 83 Bloomfield Ave Hartford CT 06105-1007 Office: Killian Donohue & Jaff LLC 363 Main St Hartford CT 06106-1885 E-mail: bob@kdjlaw.com.

KILLORIN, ROBERT WARE, lawyer; b. Atlanta, Nov. 12, 1959; s. Edward W. and Virgina (Ware) K. AB cum laude, Duke U., 1980; JD, U. Ga., 1983. Bar: Ga. 1984, U.S. Dist. Ct. (no. dist.) Ga. 1984, U.S. Ct. Appeals (11th cir.) 1984. Ptnr. Killorin & Killorin, Atlanta, 1984—. Mem. Atlanta Bar Assn., Ga. Def. Lawyers Assn., State Bar Ga. (chair SCOPE com. 1986, young lawyers sect. legis. affairs com. 1989-91, instr. mock trial program 1989—), Ga. C. of C. (govtl. affairs com.), Internat. Assn. Def. Counsel, 11th Cir. Hist. Soc., Assn. Trial Lawyers Am., Nat. Assn. Underwater Instrs., Nat. Speliological Soc., Mil. Order of Carabao, U. Ga. Pres.'s Club, Explorer's Club. Avocations: forestry, scuba diving, basketball, tennis. Antitrust, General civil litigation, Environmental. Office: Killorin & Killorin 5587 Benton Woods Dr NE Atlanta GA 30342-1308

KILROY, JOHN MUIR, lawyer; b. Kansas City, Mo., Apr. 12, 1918; s. James L. and Jane Alice (Scurry) K.; m. Lorraine K. Butler, Jan. 26, 1946; children: John Muir, William Terence. Student, Kansas City Jr. Coll., 1935-37; AB, U. Kansas City, 1940; JD, U. Mo., 1942. Bar: Mo. 1942. Practice in, Kansas City, 1946—; ptnr. Shughart, Thomson & Kilroy, 1948—, pres., 1977-86, chmn. bd. dirs., 1980-88, chmn. emeritus, 1988—. Instr. med. jurisprudence U. Health Scis., 1973-93; panelist numerous med.-legal groups ACS, Mo. Med. Assn., Kans. U. Med. Sch., S.W. Clin. Soc. Contbr. articles to profl. jours. Chmn. bd. dirs. Kansas City Heart Assn.; mem. adv. bd. Midwest Christian Counseling Svc.; bd. dirs., pres. Della Lamb Cmty. Svc., 1991, chmn. bd. dirs., 1993; bd. dirs. Laubach Literacy Coun., 1998-2001, Kingswood Manor, 1992-94, Mo. Meth. Found., 1993-2002. Named Man of Yr., Sigma Chi, 1989. Fellow Am. Coll. Trial Lawyers; mem. ABA, Mo. Bar Assn. (chmn. med. legal com.), Kansas City Bar Assn. (Litigator Emeritus award 1990), Internat. Assn. Barristers, Internat. Assn. Def. Counsel, Am. Coll. Legal Medicine, Am. Bd. Profl. Liability Attys., Fedn. Ins. Counsel, Law Soc. U. Mo., Order Barristers U. Mo., Lawyers Assn., Kansas City (pres. 1968), Kansas City C. of C., Univ. Club (v.p. 1984, pres. 1985), Indian Hills Country Club, Kansas City Club. Federal civil litigation, State civil litigation, Personal injury (including property damage). Home: 6860 Tomahawk Rd Shawnee Mission KS 66208-2176 Office: Shughart Thomson & Kilroy 120 W 12th St Ste 1800 Kansas City MO 64105-1922

KILSCH, GUNTHER H. lawyer; b. N.Y.C., Jan. 8, 1930; s. Frederick and Toni (Becher) K.; m. Kathryn A. Severance, Mar. 28, 1959; children: Nancy, Peter, Ann, Sarah. AB, Queens Coll./CUNY, 1957; LLB, NYU, 1963. Bar: N.Y. 1964, U.S. Dist. Ct. (so. and ea. dists.) 1966, U.S. Ct. Appeals (2d cir.) 1993; diplomate Am. Bd. Profl. Liability Attys. Assoc. Schaffner D'Onofrio, N.Y.C., 1964-68, John J. Tullman, N.Y.C., 1968-71, Kroll, Edelman & Lanzone, N.Y.C., 1971-73, Martin, Clearwater & Bell, N.Y.C., 1973-75, Montfort, Healy, McGuire & Salley, Mineola, N.Y., 1975-77; mem. firm McAloon & Friedman, P.C., N.Y.C., 1977-99, of counsel, 2000—; sole practice, 1999—. Warden, mem. vestry Christ Ch. Riverdale, Bronx, N.Y. Cpl. AUS, 1953-55. Fellow Am. Bar Found. (life), N.Y. Bar Found. (life); mem. N.Y. State Bar Assn. (mem.-at-large exec. com. 2001—, mem. Ho. of Dels. 1979-80, 93-94, 98--, chair tort reparations com. 1992-97, sec. trial lawyers sect. 1976-77, vice chair 1977-78, chair 1978-79, life mem. exec. com. 1968—), Am. Bd. Trial Advs. (pres. N.Y.C. chpt. 1998, 99, del. nat. bd. dirs. 2001—), N.Y. County Lawyers Assn. Episcopalian. Avocations: photography, boating, hiking, choir. General civil litigation, Personal injury (including property damage), Professional liability. Home: 46 Sunnyside Dr Yonkers NY 10705-1731 Office: McAloon & Friedman PC 116 John St Fl 29 New York NY 10038-3498 E-mail: guntherkilsch@mcf-esq.com., g.kilschp.c@worldnet.att.net.

KIM, CHARLES CHANGYOUNG, trade association executive, lawyer; b. Seoul, South Korea, Apr. 16, 1962; came to U.S., 1964; s. Jinak and Kero Lee K. BA, Columbia U., 1987; JD, Cath. U., Washington, 1996. Bar: Md. 1997. Instr. English Hyundai Engring. & Constrn. Co., Seoul, 1987-88; from asst. to chmn. to v.p. internat. Olympic Cultural Ctr., Seoul, 1988-91; dep. nat. dir. Asian Pacific Am. coalition Bush/Quayle Presdl. Campaign, Washington, 1992; from asst. dir. to dir. state legis. programs Am. Cons. Engrs. Coun., Washington, 1998-99, dir. state legis. programs, asst. gen. counsel, 1999-2000, dir. state legis. programs, gen. counsel, 2000—01, gen. counsel, 2001—. Law rev. staff mem., law sch. commencement class spkr. Vol. fl. mgr. Rep. Nat. Conv., San Diego, 1996; vol. asst. to the deputy spl. asst. to pres. for pub. liaison, The White House, Washington, 1992. Mem.: Md. Bar Assn., Am. Soc. Assn. Execs., Capital Toastmasters (v.p. edn. 1999—2000, pres. 2000—01), Univ. Club Washington. Republican. Avocations: history, heraldry, fencing. Office: Am Coun Engring Cos 1015 15th St NW 8th Fl Washington DC 20005-2605 E-mail: ckim@acec.org.

KIM, DANIEL J. publishing executive, editor; B, JD, U. Mich. TV prodr., writer, Detroit; pub., editor-in-chief Mich. Lawyers Weekly; interim exec. dir. State Bar Mich., Lansing; pub., editor ABA Jour., Chgo., 2000—. Office: ABA Jour 750 N Lake Shore Dr 6th Fl Chicago IL 60611 Office Fax: 312-988-6014. Business E-Mail: kimd@staff.abanet.org.*

KIM, MICHAEL CHARLES, lawyer; b. Honolulu, Mar. 9, 1950; s. Harold Dai You and Maria Adrienne K. Student, Gonzaga U., 1967-70; BA, U. Hawaii, 1971; JD, Northwestern U., 1976. Bar: Ill. 1977, U.S. Dist. Ct. (no. dist.) Ill. 1977, U.S. Ct. Appeals (7th cir.) 1981, U.S. Supreme Ct. 1986. Assoc. counsel Nat. Assn. Realtors, Chgo., 1977-78; assoc. Rudnick & Wolfe, Chgo., 1978-83, Rudd & Assocs., Hoffman Estates, Ill., 1983-85; ptnr. Rudd & Kim, Hoffman Estates and Chgo., 1985-87; prin. Michael C. Kim & Assocs., Chgo. and Schaumburg, Ill., 1987-88; ptnr. Martin, Craig, Chester & Sonnenschein, Chgo. and Schaumburg, 1988-91, Arnstein & Lehr, Chgo., 1991—. Gen. counsel Assn. Sheridan Condo-Coop Owners, Chgo., 1988—; adj. prof. John Marshall Law Sch., Chgo. Author column Apt. and Condo News, 1984-87; co-author Historical and Practice Notes; contbr. articles to profl. jours. Bd. dirs. Astor Villa Condo Assn., Chgo., 1987-91, 2002—, treas. 1987-89, 2002—, sec., 2002. Mem. ABA, Chgo. Bar Assn. (chmn condominium law subcom. 1990-92, chmn. real property legis. subcom. 1995-97, vice chmn. real property law com., 1998-99, chmn. real proprty law com. 1999-2000), Ill. State Bar Assn. (real estate law sect. coun. 1990-94, corp. and securities law sect. coun. 1990-92), Asian Am. Bar Assn. Greater Chgo. Area (bd. dirs. 1987-88, 90-91), Cmty. Assns. Inst. Ill. (bd. dirs. 1990-92, pres. 1992), Coll. Cmty. Assn. Lawyers (bd. govs. 1994-98), Univ. Club (Chgo.). Avocations: squash, photography, travel. General civil litigation, Construction, Property, real (including real estate development, water). Office: Arnstein & Lehr 120 S Riverside Plz Ste 1200 Chicago IL 60606-3910

KIM, YOO YIK, former law firm adviser; b. Ulsan, Korea, May 24, 1929; s. Sang Eon Kim and Won Seong Li; m. Sun Yong Chu, June 26, 1974 (div. Aug. 1978); 1 child, Han Yong. Student, Seoul Nat. U., 1946-51, Seoul Journalism Acad., 1952-53. Fgn. news reporter Kukje Newspaper Co., Pusan, Korea, 1953-55; fgn. news editor Sekye News Agy., Seoul, 1960-61, Chosun Ilbo Newspaper Co., Seoul, 1963-65, Orient Press Co., Seoul, 1965-70, Korea Herald, Seoul, 1970-73; spl. adviser Law Offices of Kim, Shin & Yu, Seoul, 1973-2000. Rschr. Mass. Comm. Rsch. Inst., Seoul Nat. U., 1967-69; prof. Korea U. Fgn. Studies, Seoul, 1971-75. Sec. Korea League of World Fedn., 1976-85. Mem. Nat. Geog. Soc. Avocations: mountain climbing, skiing, partook game. Home: AID Apt 24-103 50 Samseongtong 2 Kangnamku Seoul 135-877 Republic of Korea

KIMBALL, CATHERINE D. state supreme court justice; b. Alexandria, La., Feb. 7, 1945; m. Clyde W. Kimball; 3 children. JD, La. State U., 1970. Law clerk US Dist. Court, Western Dist. La., 1970; spec. coun. La. Attorney Gen. Office, 1971—73; gen coun. La. Commn. Law Enforcement & Admin. Crim. Just., 1973—81; priv. law prac., 1975—82; judge La. Dist. Ct. (18th dist.), 1982—92; assoc. justice Supreme Ct. of La., 1992—. Office: Supreme Ct of La 301 Loyola Ave New Orleans LA 70112-1814

KIMBALL, SPENCER LEVAN, lawyer, educator; b. Thatcher, Ariz., Aug. 26, 1918; s. Spencer Woolley and Camilla (Eyring) K.; m. Kathryn Ann Murphy, June 12, 1939; children: Barbara Jean (Mrs. Thomas Sherman), Judith Ann (Mrs. William Stillion), Kathleen Louise, Spencer David, Kent Douglas, Timothy Jay; m. Virginia Barrus Johnson, June 4, 1994. BS, U. Ariz., 1940; postgrad., U. Utah, 1946-47; BCL, Oxford (Eng.) U., 1949; SJD, U. Wis., 1958. Bar: Utah 1950, Mich. 1965, Wis. 1968, U.S. Dist. Ct. (we. dist.) Wis. 1968, U.S. Supreme Ct. 1982, U.S. Ct. Appeals (9th cir.) 1986. Assoc. prof. U. Utah Coll. Law, Salt Lake City, 1949-50, dean, 1950-54, prof., 1954-57, rsch. prof. emeritus, 1993—; prof. U. Mich., 1957-68, dir. legal rsch. Law Sch., 1962-67; staff dir. Wis. Ins. Law Revision Project, 1966-79; prof. law, dean U. Wis. Law Sch., 1968-72; exec. dir. Am. Bar Found., Chgo., 1972-82; prof. law U. Chgo., 1972-88, Seymour Logan prof., 1978-88, Seymour Logan prof. emeritus, 1988—. Author: Insurance and Public Policy (Elizur Wright award), 1960, Introduction to the Legal System, 1966, Essays in Insurance Regulation, 1966, Cases and Materials on Insurance Law, 1992; (with Werner Pfenningstorf) The Regulation of Insurance Companies in the United States and the European Communities: A Comparative Study, 1981; editor: (with Herbert Denenberg) Insurance, Government and Social Policy, 1969, (with Werner Pfenningstorf) Legal Service Plans, 1977; bd. editors: Jour. Ins. Regulation, Internat. Jour. Ins. Law, Assicurazioni; contbr. articles to profl. jours. Lt. USNR, 1943-46. Recipient Rsch. award Am. Bar Found.; award Outstanding Rsch. in Law and Gov't, 1984, Am. Bar Assn. Sect. of Torts and Ins. Practice, Robert B. McKay award Lifetime contbns. to Ins. and Tort Law, 1991. Fellow Am. Bar Found., Wis. Bar Found.; mem. ABA, Mich. State Bar, Utah State Bar, Wis. State Bar, Internat. Assn. Ins. Law (hon. pres., past pres. U.S. chpt., mem. presdl. coun.) Phi Beta Kappa, Phi Kappa Phi. Home: 241 N Vine Apt 1001W Salt Lake City UT 84103-1936

KIMBERLING, JOHN FARRELL, retired lawyer; b. Shelbyville, Ind., Nov. 15, 1926; s. James Farrell and Phyllis (Casady) K. B of Naval Sci. and Tactics, Purdue U., 1946; AB, Ind. U., 1947, JD, 1950. Bar: Ind. 1950, Calif. 1954. Assoc. Bracken, Gray, DeFur & Voran, 1950-51, Lillick McHose & Charles, and predecessor firms, 1953-63, ptnr., 1963-86, Dewey Ballantine, L.A., 1986-89; ret., 1989. Bd. visitors Ind. U. Sch. Law, 1987—; bd. dirs. Ind. U. Found., 1988—. Lt. (j.g.) USNR, 1951-53. Fellow Am. Coll. Trial Lawyers, Acad. Law Alumni Sch. Law Indiana U. (Disting. Alumni Svc. award, 2001); mem. ABA (charter, litigation sect.), State Bar Calif., LA Bar Assn., LA Jr. C. of C. (past pres.), Beta Theta Pi, Phi Delta Phi., Calif. Club, Chancery Club, Lincoln Club. Democrat. Home: 1180 Los Robles Dr Palm Springs CA 92262-4124 E-mail: jackkim323@aol.com.

KIMBLE, WILLIAM EARL, lawyer; b. Denver, May 4, 1926; s. George Wilbur and Grace (Fick) K.; m. Jean M. Cayia, Dec. 27, 1950; children: Mark, Cary, Timothy, Stephen, Philip, Peter, Michael. LL.B., U. Ariz., 1951. Bar: Ariz. 1951. Spl. agt. FBI, 1951-52; pvt. practice Bisbee, 1952-60, Tucson, 1962—; judge Superior Ct. Ariz., 1960-62; ptnr. Kimble, Nelson, Audilett, McDonough & Molla, 1962—. Commr. Ariz. Oil and Gas Commn., 1958-60; adj. prof. law U. Ariz. Coll. Law, 1962-86. Author: The Consumer Product Safety Act, 1973, Products Liability, 1977; sr. editor Consumer Products Alert newsletter, 1980-81; editor, pub. In Def. of Elec. Accidents newsletter, 1993—. Founder Naval War Coll. Found.; Rep. nominee Ariz. atty. gen., 1956; Rep. nominee Ariz. U.S. Congress, 1964. Served with USNR, 1944-46. Fellow Am. Coll. Trial Lawyers; mem. Sigma Chi, Phi Alpha Delta. Federal civil litigation, State civil litigation, Insurance. Home: 3544 E Placita de Pipo Tucson AZ 85718 Office: Kimble Nelson Audilett McDonough & Molla 335 N Wilmot Rd Ste 500 Tucson AZ 85711-2636

KIMBROUGH, ROBERT AVERYT, lawyer; b. Sarasota, Fla., Nov. 2, 1933; s. Verman T. and Edith (Averyt) K.; m. Emilie Hudson, Aug. 24, 1957; children: James E., Robert A. Jr. BS, Davidson Coll., 1955; LLB to JD, U. Fla., 1960. Bar: Fla. 1960, U.S. Dist. Ct. Fla. 1962. Pvt. practice, Sarasota, 1960—. Chmn., bd. trustees, Ringling Sch. Art & Design, Sarasota, 1983-85; chmn. Sarasota Welfare Home Inc., 1986-89; pres. Fla. West Coast Symphony, Sarasota, 1986-90. Recipient Champion Higher Edn. in Fla., Ind. Coll. and Univs. of Fla., 1984-85, Alumnus of Yr. award Phi Delta Theta, 1997. Mem. ABA, Fla. Bar, Sarasota County Bar Assn., Sarasota Yacht Club, Kiwanis. Republican. Presbyterian. Avocations: flying, fishing, boating. Home: 7100 S Gator Creek Blvd Sarasota FL 34241-9729 Office: 1530 Cross St Sarasota FL 34236-7015 E-mail: rak@KimbroughKoach.com.

KIMM, MICHAEL S. lawyer; b. Seoul, July 12, 1963; came to U.S., 1974; s. Chun Teak and Chong Sim K. BA, Fordham U., 1987; JD, Boston U., 1991. Bar: N.J. 1991, N.Y. 1992, U.S. Dist. Ct. N.J. 1991, U.S. Dist. Ct. (so. and ea. dists.) N.Y. 1993, U.S. Ct. Appeals (2nd, 3rd and Fed cirs.) 1994, U.S. Supreme Ct. 1995. Pvt. practice, Hackensack, NJ. Mng. editor: Boston U. Internat. Law Jour., 1990-91; contbr. articles to profl. jours. Gen. counsel Korean-Am. Assn. for Rehab. of Disabled, Queens, N.Y., 1992-94. Mem. ABA, N.J. State Bar Assn., N.Y. State Bar Assn. Federal civil litigation, Intellectual property, Trademark and copyright. Office: 185 Great Neck Rd Great Neck NY 11021 Address: 190 Moore St # 272 Hackensack NJ 07601

KIMMITT, ROBERT MICHAEL, executive, banker, diplomat, lawyer; b. Logan, Utah, Dec. 19, 1947; s. Joseph Stanley and Eunice L. (Wegener) K.; m. Holly Sutherland, May 19, 1979; children: Kathleen, Robert, William, Thomas, Margaret. BS, U.S. Mil. Acad., 1969; JD, Georgetown U., 1977. Bar: D.C. 1977. Commd. 2d lt. U.S. Army, 1969, advanced through grades to maj., 1982, served in Vietnam, 1970-71; maj. gen. USAR, 1999—; law clk. U.S. Ct. Appeals, Washington, 1977-78; sr. staff mem. NSC, Washington, 1978-83, dep. asst. to Pres. for nat. security affairs and exec. sec. and gen. counsel, 1983-85; gen. counsel U.S. Dept. Treasury, Washington, 1985-87; ptnr. Sidley & Austin, Washington, 1987-89; undersec. for polit. affairs Dept. State, Washington, 1989-91, ambassador to Germany, 1991-93; mng. dir. Lehman Bros., Washington, N.Y.C., 1993-97; sr. ptnr. Wilmer, Cutler & Pickering, Washington, 1997-00; vice-chmn., pres. Commerce One, Pleasanton, Calif., 2000-01; exec. v.p. AOL Time Warner, Washington, 2001—. U.S. mem. panel of arbitrators Ctr. Settlement of Investment Internat. Disputes, 1988—89. Bd. dirs. German Marshall Fund, Atlantic Coun., Mike Mansfield Found., Am. Inst. Contemporary German Studies, Georgetown U. Decorated Bronze star (3), Purple Heart, Air medal, Vietnamese Cross of Gallantry, German Svc. Cross, German Army Cross in Gold; recipient Arthur Flemming award Downtown Jaycees, 1987, Alexander Hamilton award U.S. Dept. Treasury, 1987, Presdl. Citizens medal, 1991, Def. Disting. Civilian Svc. medal, 1993. Mem. Am. Acad. Diplomacy, Assn. Grads. U.S. Mil. Acad. (trustee 1976-82), Coun. Fgn. Rels. Roman Catholic. Office: AOL Time Warner 800 Connecticut Ave NW Washington DC 20006

KIMURA, KEVIN, lawyer; b. Newton, N.J., June 1964; s. K. S. Kimura. BA, U. Hawaii, 1991, MA, 1994, JD, 1999. Bar: Hawaii 2000, DC 2002. Staff atty. Vol. Legal Svc. Hawaii, Honolulu, 1999—. Mem. coun. Statewide Ind. Living Ctr. Hawaii, Honolulu, 2002—. Mem.: ABA, Toastmasters, Lions, Phi Delta Phi. Family and matrimonial. Home and Office: 2333 Kapiolani Blvd # 610 Honolulu HI 96826

KINAKA, WILLIAM TATSUO, lawyer; b. Lahaina, Hawaii, Apr. 4, 1940; s. Toshio and Natsumi (Hirouji) K.; m. Jeanette Louisa Ramos, Nov. 23, 1968; children: Kimberly H., Kristine N.Y. BA in Polit. Sci., Whittier Coll., 1962; MA in Internat. Rels., Am. U., 1964, JD, 1973. Bar: D.C. 1975, U.S. Ct. Appeals (D.C. cir.) 1975, U.S. Dist. Ct. D.C. 1975, U.S. Tax Ct. 1975, U.S. Ct. Mil. Appeals 1975, Hawaii 1976, U.S. Dist. Ct. Hawaii 1976, U.S. Ct. Appeals (9th cir.) 1976. Career trainee CIA, Langley, Va., 1966; legis. asst. Sen. Hiram L. Fong, Washington, 1966-76; assoc. Ueoka & Luna, Wailuku, Hawaii, 1977-85; pvt. practice law Wailuku, Hawaii, 1985—; grand jury counsel 2d Cir. Ct., 1985-86. Ct. arbitrator, 1989—; legal cons. Hale Mahaolu Elderly Housing, Kahului, 1976—. Active Dem. Party of Hawaii, Wailuku, 1988-89; pres. Nat. Eagle Scout Assn. of Boy Scouts Am., Wailuku, 1983-91; bd. dirs. Wailuku Main St. Assn., 1988-94, Maui Adult Day Care Ctr., Puunene, pres. 2000—; bd. dirs. Kahului; Maui Coun., Boy Scouts of Am.; bd. dirs. Maui Youth Intervention Program, Inc., pres. 1993—; bd. dirs. Iao Intermediate Sch. Renaissance Ednl. Found., pres. 1999—. Mem. Hawaii Bar Assn., Maui Bar Assn., Maui Japanese C. of C., Maui C. of C., Nat. Eagle Scout Assn. (pres. Wailuku 1983-91). United Ch. of Christ. Avocations: scouting, gardening, swimming, poetry writing. Commercial, consumer (including collections, credit), Family and matrimonial, Landlord-tenant. Home: 639 Pio Dr Wailuku HI 96793-2622 Office: 24 N Church St Ste 201 Wailuku HI 96793-1606

KINCANNON, RONALD LYNN, judge; b. Guymon, Okla., Feb. 7, 1948; s. Jesse Leroy and Audrey Elizabeth (Tidwell) Kincannon; m. Betty Carol Littau, May 22, 1975; children: Erin Dawn, Dustin Mark. BS in Psychology, Okla. Panhandle State U., 1970; JD, Okla. City U., 1982. Bar: Okla. 1983, U.S. Dist. Ct. (we. dist.) Okla. 1983. Min. Ch. of God, Kans., 1969—70; probation and parole officer Okla. Dept. Corrections, Oklahoma City, 1975—81; ptnr. Manske & Kincannon, Boise CIty, 1984—93; atty. pvt. practice, 1983—94; assoc. dist. judge 1st Jud. Dist., 1995—. Adj. prof. bus. law Okla. Panhandle State U., Goodwell. Lt. comdr. U.S. Army, 1971—98. Mem.: Mil. Intelligence Corps Assn., No Man's Land Hist. Soc. (dir., vice chmn. 1992—), Gideons, Rotary (dist. gov. 2001—02). Avocations: writing, painting, drawing, genealogy, photography. Office: PO Box 788 Boise City OK 73933

KIND, KENNETH WAYNE, lawyer, real estate broker; b. Missoula, Mont., Apr. 1, 1948; s. Joseph Bruce and Elinor Joy (Smith) K.; m. Diane Lucille Jozaitis, Aug. 28, 1971; children: Kirstin Amber, Kenneth Warner. BA, Calif. State U., Northridge, 1973; JD, Calif. Western U., 1976. Bar: Calif. 1976, U.S. Dist. Ct. (ea., so., no. dists.) Calif., 1976, U.S. Cir. Ct. Appeals (9th cir.), U.S. Supreme Ct.; lic. NASCAR driver, 1987. Mem. celebrity security staff Brownstone Am., Beverly Hills, Calif., 1970-76; tchr. Army and Navy Acad., Carlsbad, Calif., 1975-76; real estate broker Bakersfield, Calif., 1978—; sole practice, 1976—. Lectr. mechanic's lien laws, Calif., 1983—. Staff writer Calif. Western Law Jour., 1975. Sgt. U.S. Army, 1967-70. Mem. ABA, VFW, Nat. Order Barristers, Rancheros Visitadores. Libertarian. State civil litigation, Insurance, Property, real (including real estate development, water). Office: 4042 Patton Way Bakersfield CA 93308-5030

KINDEL, JAMES HORACE, JR., lawyer; b. L.A., Nov. 8, 1913; s. James Horace and Philipina (Butte) K.; children: William, Mary, Robert, John. AB, UCLA, 1934; LLB, Loyola U., Los Angeles, 1940. Bar: Calif. 1941; CPA, Calif. Pvt. practice Kindel & Anderson, L.A., 1945—96; of counsel McKenna, Long & Ald, L.A., 1997—. Former ptnr. Coopers-Lybrand; co-owner gravel and poultry bus., Guatemala; co-owner Sunnymead Poultry Ranch, Calif. Trustee UCLA Found. Mem. ABA, L.A. Bar Assn., Orange County Bar Assn., State Bar Calif., AICPA, Chancery Club, Calif. Club, Phi Delta Phi, Theta Xi. Home: 800 W 1st St Apt 2405 Los Angeles CA 90012-2432 Office: 444 S Flower St Fl 7 Los Angeles CA 90071-2901

KINDLER, JEFFREY B. lawyer; b. May 13, 1955; JD, Harvard Law Sch., 1980; BA, Tufts Univ., 1977. Bar: D.C. 1980. V.p. and sr. counsel, litig. and legal policy Gen. Electric; ptnr. Williams and Connolly, Wash., DC; law clk. US Supreme Ct. Justice, william J. Brennan, Jr.; pres. ptnr. brands McDonald's Corp., 1996-97, exec. v.p., gen. counsel, 1997—2002; chmn., CEO Boston Market, Oak Brook, Ill., 2000-2001; pres., ptnr. Brands McDonalds Corp., 2001—02; chmn., CEO Boston Market, 2001—02; sr. v.p. & Gen. Coun. Pfizer, Inc., NYC, 2002. Mem.: Nat. Ctr. for State Cts., Corp. Coun. Adv. Bd., Council of Chief Legal Officers, Civil Justice Reform Group, Am. Bar Assoc., Assoc. of Gen. Coun., City Bar Fund., US Chamber, Atlantic Legal Found., Citizens Crime Comm., Jane Addams Juvenile Ct. Found., Am. Arbitration Assoc. Office: Pfizer Office of Gen Coun 235 E 42nd St New York NY 10017 E-mail: jeff.kindler@mcd.com.*

KINDREGAN, CHARLES PETER, law educator; b. Phila., June 18, 1935; s. Charles Peter and Catherine (Delaney) K.; m. Patricia Ann. Patterson, Aug. 18, 1962 (dec. 1998); children: Chad, Helen, Tricia, Brian. BA, LaSalle U., 1957, MA, 1958; JD, Chgo.-Kent Coll. Law, 1966; LLM, Northwestrn U., 1967. Bar: Ill. 1966, Mass. 1968, U.S. Dist. Ct. Mass. 1970. Instr. Va. Mil. Inst., 1960-62, Loyola U., Chgo., 1964-67; prof. law Suffolk U., Boston, 1967—, assco. dean, 1990-94. Author: The Quality of Life, 1969, Malpractice and the Lawyer, 1981, professional Responsibility of the Lawyer, 1995; co-author: Massachusetts Family Law and Practice, 3d edit., 2003, (with M. Inker) Mass. Domestic Relations Rules Annotated, 2003; contbr. articles to law revs., jours. Mem. Hull Bd. Zoning Appeals, Mass., 1969; pres. Beacon Hill PTA, Boston, 1974-75. Mem. ABA (academic rep. to publications bd. family law sect.), Mass. Bar Assn. (task force on model rules of profl. conduct 1982-84, co-chair com. on crisis in probate and family ct. 1994-97), Suffolk Ctr. for Advanced Legal Studies (dir. 1982-87). Democrat. Roman Catholic. Home: 150 Staniford St Apt 710 Boston MA 02114-2597 Office: Suffolk U Law Sch 120 Tremont St Boston MA 02108-4910

KINDT, JOHN WARREN, lawyer, educator, consultant; b. Oak Park, Ill., May 24, 1950; s. Warren Frederick and Lois Jeannette (Woelffer) K.; m. Anne Marie Johnson, Apr. 17, 1982; children: John Warren Jr., James Roy Frederick. AB, Coll. William and Mary, 1972; JD, U. Ga., 1976, MBA, 1977; LLM, U. Va., 1978, SJD, 1981. Bar: D.C. 1976, Ga. 1976, Va. 1977. Advisor to gov. State of Va., Richmond, 1971-72; asst. to Congressman M. Caldwell Butler, U.S. Ho. of Reps., Washington, 1972-73; staff cons. White House, Washington, 1976-77; asst. prof. U. Ill., Champaign, 1978-81, assoc. prof., 1981-85, prof., 1985—. Cons. 3d UN Conf. on Law of Sea; lectr. exec. MBA program U. Ill. Author: Marine Pollution and the Law of the Sea, 4 vols., 1981, 2 vols., 1988, 92, Economic Impacts of Legalized Gambling, 1994; contbr. articles to profl. jours. Caucus chmn., del. White House Conf. on Youth, 1970; co-chmn. Va. Gov.'s Adv. Coun. on Youth, 1971; mem. Athens (Ga.) Legal Aid Soc., 1975-76. Rotary fellow, 1979-80; Smithsonian ABA/ELI scholar, 1981; sr. fellow London Sch. Econs., 1985-86. Mem. Am. Soc. Internat. Law, D.C. Bar Assn., Va. Bar Assn., Ga. Bar Assn. Home: 801 Brookside Ln Mahomet IL 61853-9545 Office: U Ill 350 Commerce W Champaign IL 61820

KING, ADRIENNE SEPANIAK, lawyer; b. Detroit, Nov. 4, 1947; d. Edward Aloysius and Irene (Kapuchinski) Szczepaniak; m. Samuel Pailthorpe King, Jr., Oct. 19, 1974; children: Christopher, Samuel Wilder. BS in Biology, U. Detroit, 1969, JD, 1972. Bar: Hawaii 1972, U.S/ Dist. Ct. Hawaii 1972, Mich. 1973, U.S. Ct. Appeals (9th cir.) 1974. Dep. prosecuting atty. City and County of Honolulu, 1972-75; dep. corp. counsel City Atty's. Office, Honolulu, 1975-85; pvt. practice King & King, Honolulu, 1985-90; chief trials divsn. City Atty's. Office, Honolulu, 1990-93; pvt. practice King & King, Honolulu, 1993—. Guest lecturer U. Hawaii Law School, 1997-98. Arbitrator Hawaii's Ct. Annexed Arbitrtion Program, 1987—; chair Chamber Music Hawaii's Fundraiser, 1988-90; chair County of Honolulu Zoning Bd. Appeals, 1989; vice-chancellor Episcopal Diocese Honolulu, 1989-96 (appointed spl. coun. Episcopal Ch. Eccles. Ct., 1996); active Jr. League Honolulu, 1981-87 (chair rummage sale fundraiser, projects com., bd. mem.); chair St. Andrews Episcopal Cathedral Newcomer Com., 1990, Heritage Fundraising Com., 1991, elected governing Bd. Cathedral, 1991-96, elected chair By-laws Revision Com., 1991-96, elected Bd. Workers St. Andrews, 1991-96 (chair 1992-96); elected Diocesan Coun., 1995-96, 1997-1999; elected Sec. Coun., 1995-99; elected to Spl. Investigating Com. regarding losses in the matter of Episcopal Homes, 1998; mem. Fundraiser Native Hawaiin Legal Corp., 1993-96 (most money raised 1993); sec. Republican 8th Senate Dist., 1994-95 (precinct sec. 1993, pres. 1994-95, v.p. 1995-96); del. to state conventions, 1992-98 (platform com. 1993); alt. del. Republican Nat. Convention in Houston, 1992, Philadelphia, 2000; vol. Punahou Sch. Theatrical Performances, 1993-; mem. Ka Iwi Action Coun.1993—, elected spokesman, 2000-; chairperson Women Lawyers for Bush/Quayle, 1992; mem. Team Hawaii Rep. donors cir., 1998, mem., campaign for Repub. Com. Barbara Marumoto state legis., 2002. Mem. Hawaii State Bar Assn. (bd. dirs. 1991-92), Consumer Lawyers Hawaii (bd. govs. 1988-90), Hawaii Women Lawyers, Hawaii Assn. Criminal Def. Lawyers (co-founder, bd. dirs. 1987-90, pres. 1989). Republican. Home: 1163 Kaeleku St Honolulu HI 96825-3007 Office: King & King 735 Bishop St Ste 304 Honolulu HI 96813-4819

KING, BERNARD T. lawyer; b. Gouverneur, N.Y., Feb. 28, 1935; BS, Le Moyne Coll., 1956; JD cum laude, Syracuse U., 1959. Bar: N.Y. 1959. Ptnr. Blitman and King, Syracuse, N.Y. Assoc. editor Syracuse Law Rev., 1958-59; Syracuse Law Sch., bd. of visitors, 1980-; lectr. Labor Studies Program, N.Y. State Sch. Indsl. and Labor Rels., Cornell U., 1974; sec. Onondaga County Indsl. Devel. Agy., 1978-81. Mem., bd. dirs. Syracuse Model Neighborhood Corp., 1972-75, Regents, 1973—, sec., 1983—1984, bd. trustees, 1984-90. vice chmn., bd. trustees, 1988, LeMoyne Coll., 1974-80, v.p. 1977-79, pres., 1979-80; bd. trustees Manlius Pebble Hill Sch. Corp.; mem. United Way Cen. N.Y., 1971-75, bd. dirs., 1981-87; com. mem. 33rd Congl. Dist. Naval Academise Selection Bd., 1980-83. With USAF, 1961-62, Air NG, 1959-65, Salvation Army, mem. bd. 1995. Recipient Disting. Alumni award LeMoyne Coll., 1979, Whitney M. Seymour award Am. Arbitration Assn., 1986. Fellow Am. Bar Found.; mem. ABA (labor law and employment law com. 1963-, chmn. labor and employment sect. 1987-88, sect. del. to ho. of dels., mem. joint com. on employee benefits), Soc. Profls. in Dispute Resolution, Panel of Arbitrators, Am. Arbitration Assn. (bd. dirs. 1988), Onondaga County Bar Assn., N.Y. State Bar Assn. (exec. com., labor law sect. 1976—, chmn. 1980-81), Am. Judicature Soc., ABA Standing comm. on substance abuse; fel. ABA Coll. Labor and Employment Lawyers, ABA Am. Coll. Employment Benefits. Labor (including EEOC, Fair Labor Standards Act, labor-management relations, NLRB, OSHA), Pension, profit-sharing, and employee benefits, Personal injury (including property damage). Office: Franklin Ctr Ste 300 443 N Franklin St Syracuse NY 13204

KING, CAROLYN DINEEN, federal judge; b. Syracuse, N.Y., Jan. 30, 1938; d. Robert E. and Carolyn E. (Bareham) Dineen; children: James Randall, Philip Randall, Stephen Randall. AB summa cum laude, Smith Coll., 1959; LLB, Yale U., 1962. Bar: D.C. 1962, Tex. 1963. Assoc. Fulbright & Jaworski, Houston, 1962—72; ptnr. Childs, Fortenbach, Beck & Guyton, Houston, 1972—78, Sullivan, Bailey, King, Randall & Sabom, Houston, 1978—79; judge U.S. Ct. Appeals (5th cir.), Houston, 1979—99, chief judge, 1999—; with U.S. Jud. Conf., 1999—, exec. com., 2000—, chmn. exec. com., 2002—. Trustee, exec. com., treas. Houston Ballet Found., 1967—70; Houston dist. adv. coun. SBA, 1972—76; Dallas regional panel Pres.'s Commn. White House Fellowships, 1972—76, mem. commn., 1977; bd. dirs. Houston chpt. Am. Heart Assn., 1978—79; nat. trustee Palmer Drug Abuse Program, 1978—79; trustee, sec., treas., chmn. audit com., fin. com., mgmt. com. United Way Tex. Gulf Coast, 1979—85; trustee, exec. com., chmn. bd. trustees U. St. Thomas, 1988—98. Recipient

Smith Coll. medal, 1997, Outstanding Alumnus award, Phi Beta Kappa Alumni of Greater Houston, 1998; rsch. fellow, Ctr. for Am. and Internat. Law, 1989—. Mem.: ABA, Philos. Soc. Tex., Houston Bar Assn., State Bar Tex., Am. Law Inst. (coun. 1991—, chmn. membership com. 1997—99), Fed. Bar Assn. Roman Catholic. Office: US Ct Appeals 11020 US Courthouse 515 Rusk Avenue Houston TX 77002-2694

KING, GARR MICHAEL, federal judge; b. Pocatello, Idaho, Jan. 28, 1936; s. Warren I. King and Geraldine E. (Hanlon) Appleby; m. Mary Jo Rieber, Feb. 2, 1957; children: Mary, Michael, Matthew, James, Margaret, John, David. Student, U. Utah, 1957-59; LLB, Lewis and Clark Coll., 1963. Bar: Oreg. 1963, U.S. Dist. Ct. Oreg. 1965, U.S. Ct. Appeals (9th cir.) 1975, U.S. Supreme Ct. 1971. Dep. dist. atty. Multnomah County Dist. Atty.'s Office, Portland, Oreg., 1963-66; assoc. Morrison, Bailey, Dunn, Carney & Miller, Portland, 1966-71; ptnr. Kennedy & King, Portland, 1971-77, Kennedy, King & McClurg, Portland, 1977-82, Kennedy, King & Zimmer, Portland, 1982-98; judge U.S. Dist. Ct. Oreg., Portland, 1998—. Active various pvt. sch. and ch. bds. Served as sgt. USMC, 1954-57. Fellow Am. Coll. Trial Lawyers (regent 1995-98), Am. Bar Found.; mem. ABA, Oreg. Bar Assn., Multnomah County Bar Assn. (pres. 1975), Jud. Conf. 9th Cir. (del.), Northwestern Coll. Law Alumni Assn. (pres.), Multnomah Athletic Club. Democrat. Roman Catholic. Avocations: tennis, reading, gardening. Office: 907 US Courthouse 1000 SW 3rd Ave Portland OR 97204-2930 E-mail: garr-king@ord.uscourts.gov.

KING, HENRY LAWRENCE, lawyer; b. N.Y.C., Apr. 29, 1928; s. H. Abraham and Henrietta (Prentky) K.; m. Barbara Hope, 1949 (dec. May 1962); children: Elizabeth King Robertson, Patricia King Cantlay (dec.), Matthew Harrison.; m. Alice Mary Sturges, Aug. 1, 1963 (div. 1978); children: Katherine Masury King Baccile, Andrew Lawrence, Eleanor Sturges; m. Margaret Gram, Feb. 14, 1981 AB, Columbia U., 1948; LLB, Yale U., 1951. Bar: N.Y. 1952, U.S. Supreme Ct., other fed. cts. 1952. With Davis Polk & Wardwell, N.Y.C., 1951—, ptnr., 1961—, mng. ptnr., chmn., 1982-96. Mng. editor Yale Law Jour., 1951. Trustee, chmn. bd. Columbia U., 1983-95, chmn. emeritus, 1995—; chmn. bd. Columbia Presbyn. adv. coun.; pres. Assn. Alumni Columbia Coll., 1966-68, Alumni Fedn. Columbia U., 1973-75; chmn. Coll. Fund, 1972-73; pres. Yale Law Sch. Assn., 1984-86, chmn., 1986-88; pres. Cathedral of St. John the Divine, N.Y.C.; bd. dirs. N.Y. Acad. of Medicine, Citizen's Com. for N.Y.C., Inc., Am. Skin Assn., Fishers Island Devel. Co., Episcopal Charities; vestryman Trinity Ch., N.Y.C., 1991-98; trustee Chapin Sch., 1977-89, Columbia U. Press, 1978-92. Recipient Columbia Alumni medal for conspicuous service, 1968, John Jay award, 1992. Fellow Am. Coll. Trial Lawyers; mem. ABA, Coun. on Fgn. Rels., Am. Law Inst., N.Y. State Bar Assn. (pres. 1988-89), Assn. Bar City N.Y., Am. Judicature Soc., Fishers Island Club, Century Assn., Union Club (N.Y.C.), Jupiter Island Club, Blind Brook Club, Fishers Island Yacht Club, Pilgrims, Church Club (N.Y.C.), Links Club. Antitrust, Federal civil litigation, Private international. Home: 115 E 67th St New York NY 10021-5951 also: East End Rd Fishers Island NY 06390 Office: Davis Polk & Wardwell 450 Lexington Ave 27th Fl New York NY 10017-3982 also: 61 Links Rd Hobe Sound FL 33455 E-mail: hking@dpw.com.

KING, JACK A. lawyer; b. Lafayette, Ind., July 29, 1936; s. Noah C. and Mabel E. (Pierce) K.; m. Mary S. King, Dec. 10, 1960; children: Jeffrey A., Janice D., Julie D. BS in Fin., Ind. U., 1958, JD, 1961. Bar: Ind. 1961. Ptnr. Ball, Eggleston, King & Bumbleburg, Lafayette, 1961-70; judge Superior Ct. 2 of Tippecanoe County, Ind., 1970—78; v.p., assoc. gen. counsel Dairyland Ins. Co., 1978—79, v.p., gen. counsel, asst. sec., 1980—85; asst. gen. counsel Sentry Corp., 1979—85; v.p., gen. counsel, asst. sec. Gt. S.W. Fire Ins. Co., 1980-85; v.p., gen. counsel Dairyland County Mut. Ins. Co. Tex., 1980-85; v.p., counsel Sentry Ctr. West, 1981-85; v.p., gen. counsel, asst. sec. Gt. S.W. Surplus Lines Ins. Co., 1981-85; v.p. legal, asst. sec. Scottsdale Ins. Co., 1985-95; asst. sec. Nat. Casualty Co., 1985-95; v.p. Ariz. Ins. Info. Assn., 1988-96; v.p. legal, asst. sec. Scottsdale Indemnity Co., 1992-95; sr. v.p., gen. coun. TIG Excess & Surplus Lines, Inc., 1995-96; exec. dir. Ariz. Ins. Guaranty Funds, 1998-2001. Cons., mediator and arbitrator, 1996-97, 2001—; exec. com. Ariz. Joint Underwriting Plan, 1980-81; mem. Ariz. Property & Casualty Ins. Commn., 1985-86, vice-chmn., 1986; mem. Ariz. Study Commn. on Ins., 1986-87, Ariz. Task Force on Ct. Orgn. and Adminstrn., 1988-89; adv. com. Ariz. Ho. Rep. Majority Leaders, 1989, Ariz. Dept. Ins. Fraud Unit, 1997-97; mem. Ariz. Dept. Ins. Comml. Lines Ins. Market Task Force, 2002. Contbr. to The Law of Competitive Business Practices, 2d edit. Bd. dirs. Scottsdale Art Ctr. Assn., 1981-84. Mem. ABA, Ind. Bar Assn., Maricopa County Bar Assn. Corporate, general, Insurance.

KING, JAMES LAWRENCE, federal judge; b. Miami, Fla., Dec. 20, 1927; s. James Lawrence and Viola (Clodfelter) K.; m. Mary Frances Kapa, June 1, 1961; children— Lawrence Daniel, Kathryn Ann, Karen Ann, Mary Virginia BA in Edn., U. Fla., 1949, JD, 1953; LHD (hon.), St. Thomas U., 1992. Bar: Fla. 1953. Assoc. Sibley & Davis, Miami, Fla., 1953-57; ptnr. Sibley Giblin King & Levenson, Miami, 1957-64; judge 11th Jud. Cir. Dade County, Miami, 1964-70; temp. assoc. justice Supreme Ct. Fla., 1965; temp. assoc. judge Fla. Ct. Appeals (2d, 3d and 4th dist.), 1965-68; judge U.S. Dist. Ct. (so. dist.) Fla., Miami, 1970-84, chief judge, 1984-91, sr. judge, 1991—. Temp. judge U.S. Ct. Appeals 5th cir., 1977-78; mem. Jud. Conf. U.S., 1984-87, mem. adv. commn. jud. activities, 1973-76, mem. joint commn. code jud. conduct, 1974-76, mem. commn. to consider stds. for admission to practice in fed. cts., 1976-79, chmn. implementation com. for admission attys. to fed. practice, 1979-85, mem. com. bankruptcy legis., 1977-78; mem. Jud. Conf. U.S., 1984-87; mem. Jud. Coun. 11th Cir., 1989-92; pres. 5th cir. U.S. Dist. Judges Assn., 1977-78; chief judge U.S. Dist. Ct. C.Z., 1977-78; long range planning commn. Fed. Judiciary, 1991-95. Mem. state exec. council U. Fla., 1956-59; mem. Bd. Control Fla. Governing State Univs. and Colls., 1964. Served to 1st lt. USAF, 1953-55 Recipient Outstanding Alumnus award U. Fla. Law Rev., 1980, Lifetime Achievement award Greater Miami Jewish Fedn. Commerce and Professions Attys. Divsn., 1992, 18th Annual Edward J. Devitt Disting. Svc. to Justice award, 2000; The James Lawrence King Fed. Justice Bldg. named in his honor, 1996. Mem. Fla. Bar Assn. (pres. jr. bar 1963-64, bd. govs. 1958-63, Merit award young lawyer sect. 1967), ABA, Am. Law Inst., Inst. Jud. Adminstrn., Fla. Blue Key, Pi Kappa Tau, Phi Delta Phi Democrat. Home: 11950 SW 67th Ct Miami FL 33156-4756 Office: US Dist Ct James King Fed Justice Bldg 99 NE 4th St Rm 1127 Miami FL 33132-2139

KING, JAMES R. lawyer; b. Geneva, Ill., Oct. 24, 1946; BA, Miami U., 1968; JD, Ohio State U., 1974. Bar: Ohio 1974. Ptnr. Jones Day Reavis & Pogue, Columbus. Office: Jones Day Reavis & Pogue 1900 Huntington Ctr Columbus OH 43215-6103

KING, MICHAEL HOWARD, lawyer; b. Chgo., Mar. 10, 1943; s. Warren and Betty (Fine) K.; m. Candice M. King, Aug. 18, 1968; children— Andrew, Julie. B.S. Washington U., St. Louis 1967, J.D. 1970. Bar: Ill. 1970, U.S. Dist. Ct. (no. dist.) Ill. 1970, U.S. Dist. Ct. (ea. dist.) Wis. 1972, U.S. Ct. Appeals (7th cir.) 1974, U.S. Ct. Appeals (5th cir.) 1979, U.S. Supreme Ct. 1975, U.S. Ct. Appeals (3d cir.) 1983, U.S. Tax Ct. 1987, U.S. Ct. Appeals (10th cir.) 1987, U.S. Dist. Ct. (no. dist.) Calif. 1987, U.S. Dist. Ct. Nebr. 1988, U.S. Dist. Ct. (ctrl. dist.) Ill. 1992, U.S. Dist. Ct. (no. dist.) N.Y. 1992, U.S. Ct. Appeals (2nd cir.) 1994. Spl. atty. organized crime, racketeering sect. U.S. Dept. Justice, Washington, 1970-73; asst. U.S. atty. No. Dist. Ill., Chgo., 1973-75; assoc. Antonow & Fink, Chgo., 1976, ptnr., 1977-79; ptnr. Ross & Hardies, Chgo., 1979-95; chmn. Bd. Commr. Office of State Appellate Defender. Co-author Model Jury Instructions in Criminal Antitrust Cases, 1982, Handbook on Antitrust Grand Jury Investigations, 1988. Bd. dirs. Chgo. Youth Ctrs., 1977-82; trustee Cove Sch., 1984-88, the Goodman Theatre, 1993—. Mem. ABA (litigation sect., antitrust sect., criminal practice procedure com.), Ill. Bar Assn., Chgo. Bar Assn. (judiciary com., antitrust com.), Am. Judicature Soc., Fed. Bar Assn., Assn. Trial Lawyers Am., Mid-Am. Club (bd. govs.), Econ. Club, Chgo. Inn of Cts., Phi Delta Phi, Alpha Epsilon Pi. Antitrust, Federal civil litigation, Criminal. Home: 2025 Windy Hill Ln Highland Park IL 60035-4233 Office: Ross & Hardies 150 N Michigan Ave Ste 2500 Chicago IL 60601-7567 E-mail: michael.king@rosshardies.com.

KING, NICHOLAS SPENCER, lawyer; b. L.A., May 6, 1963; s. Walter Herbert and Patricia Ann King; m. Eugene Alkeng, Sept. 18, 1982; children: Victoria Maraiah, Bjorn Alexander, Karl Torstein. BS in Geography, U. Calif., Riverside, 1989; JD, Calif. We. Sch. Law, 1995. Bar: Calif. 1995, U.S. Dist. Ct. Calif. - Southern Dist. 2001, U.S. Dist. Ct. Calif. - Ctrl. Dist. 2002, U.S. Ct. Appeals (9th cir.) 2001, U.S. Supreme Ct. 2002. 2nd lt. U.S. Army, 1989, advanced through grades to maj., 2000; with U.S. Army Res., 2001; legal assistance atty. U.S. Army, Ft. Lewis, Wash., 1995—96, trial counsel, 1996—97, chief, legal assistance, 1997—98, base camp legal advisor Camp Bedrock, Bosnia-Herzegovina, 1998, operational law trainer, Nat. Tng. Ctr. Ft. Irwin, Calif., 1998—2000, chief of client svcs., 2000—01; solo practitioner San Diego, 2001—. Judge advocate USAR, 2001. Mem.: San Diego Bar Assn. (military liaison com. 2001—), Kiwanis. Democrat. Avocations: Tae Kwon Do, cross country skiing, sailing. General practice, Personal injury (including property damage), Criminal. Office: 707 Broadway Ste 1800 San Diego CA 92101 Office Fax: 619-232-3914. E-mail: nskingja@cs.com.

KING, PETER NELSON, lawyer; b. Marblehead, Mass., Nov. 1, 1958; s. Robert Paul and Janice Lee K. BA in Internat. Trade and Transp., U. Wash., 1984; JD, Willamette U., 1987; student in Real Estate Studies, U. Calif., L.A., 1993—; postgrad., Pepperdine U., Malibu, Calif., 1995—. Bar: Calif. 1989, U.S. Supreme Ct. 1993, U.S. Dist Ct. (so. and ctrl. dists.) Calif. 1989, U.S. Ct. Appeals (9th cir.) 1989, Calif. Supreme Ct. 1989; lic. real estate broker, Calif.; lic. yacht capt. USCG. Rsch. atty. South Bay Ct., Torrance, Calif., 1988-89; prosecutor L.A. City Atty.'s Office, 1989-90, dep. city atty., civil liability divsn., 1990-92, dep. city atty., police litigation divsn., 1992-93, gen. counsel Housing Authority of L.A., 1993-94, gen. counsel land use divsn., 1994—. Contbr. articles to profl. jours. Founder Blitzsnell Alpine Athletic Devel. Found., Big Bear, Calif., 1997; dir. Advancement of Alpine Ski Racing. Recipient Excellence in Lawyering recommendation L.A. City Coun., 1996. Mem. ABA, L.A. City Atty's. Assn. (dir. 1994, 95), U.S. Ski Assn. (master Alpine skier/racer), Phi Alpha Delta. Avocations: alpine ski racing, sailing, biking, hiking, photography. Home: PO Box 53737 Los Angeles CA 90053-0737 Office: LA City Attorney Attorney's Office 800 CHE 200 N Main St Los Angeles CA 90012 E-mail: pnelson@atty.lacity.org.

KING, REBECCA J. lawyer, consultant; b. Hazard, Ky., Aug. 7, 1951; d. Roger William and Fannie Jane Richmond; m. Colbert Sylvester King, Nov. 10, 1982; children: Justin, Allison. BA, Wright State U., 1977; MA, Miami U., Oxford, Ohio, 1978; JD, Tulane U., 1988. Bar: La. 1988, U.D. Dist. Ct. (ea. dist.) La. 1989, U.S. Dist. Ct. (we. dist.) La. 1992, U.S. Ct. Appeals (5th cir.) 1992, U.S. Dist. Ct. (ctrl. dist.) La. 1998. Law clk. Civil Dist. Ct., New Orleans, 1988—91; assoc. Carter & Cates, New Orleans, 1991—92; sr. law clk. La. Supreme Ct., New Orleans, 1992—94; ptnr. Middleberg Riddle & Gianna, New Orleans, 1994—. V.p. King Consulting, Inc., New Orleans, 1999—. Corp. counsel Union Bethel Cmty. Devel. Corp., New Orleans, 1994—; chair pro tem, bd. trustees Union Bethel AME Ch., New Orleans, 1999—. Recipient Black Achiever in Bus. and INdustry award, Dryades YMCA, New Orleans, 1992. Mem.: ABA (award, sect. urban, state and local govt. 1988), ATLA, New Orleans Bar Assn., La. State Bar Assn., Louis A. Martinet Legal Soc., Nat. Bar Assn. Democrat. African Methodist Episcopal. Aviation, Family and matrimonial, General practice. Office: Middleberg Riddle & Gianna 201 St Charles Ave 31st Fl New Orleans LA 70170 E-mail: rking@midrid.com.

KING, RICHARD ALLEN, lawyer; b. St. Joseph, Mo., July 4, 1944; s. Allen Welden and Lola (Donelson) K.; m. Deedee Gershenson, Apr. 19, 1986; children from previous marriage: Mary, Suzanne, Allen. BA, U. Mo., Columbia, 1966, JD cum laude, 1968. Bar: Mo. 1968. Law clk. Office of Chief Counsel, IRS, 1967; assoc. Reese, Constance, Slayton, Stewart & Stewart, Independence, Mo., 1968-73; ptnr. Constance, Slayton, Stewart & King, Independence, 1973-80, Cochran, Kramer, Kapke, Willerth & King, Independence, 1980-81; exec. asst. to gov. State of Mo., Jefferson City, 1981-82, dir. revenue, 1982-85; ptnr. Smith, Gill, Fisher and Butts, Inc., Kansas City, Mo., 1985-87, Wirken & King, Kansas City, 1988-93; chmn., CEO King Hershey, Kansas City, Mo., 1993—. Asst. city counselor City of Independence, 1968—69, mayor, 1974—78; vice chmn. Nat. Conf. Rep. Mayors, 1975—77; chmn. Mo. Gov.'s Task Force on Cmty. Crime Prevention, 1975—76, Kansas City Pub. Improvements Adv. Com., 1991—96, KC Team Effort, 1991—95; pres. Good Govt. League, Independence, 1972—73; mem. Mo. Commn. Human Rights, 1973—74; bd. dirs. Multistate Tax Commn., 1983—85, Chrisman Sawyer Bank, 1989—95. Contbr. articles to profl. jours. Bd. dirs. Am. Cancer Soc., Independence, 1973-79, chmn. crusade, 1973; bd. dirs. Independence Boys Club, 1972-79, Independence Cmty. Assn. Arts, 1973-76, Independence Sanitarium and Hosp., 1974-78, Jefferson City Meml. Hosp., 1981-85, NE Jackson County Mental Health Ctr., 1978-80, Greater Kansas City Nat. Coun. on Alcoholism, 1978-81, Am. Legion Boys State Mo., 1975—, Jefferson City United Way, 1982-85, Multi-State Tax Commn., 1982-85, Jackson County Hist. Soc., 1999—; pres. Friends U. Mo. Truman Campus, 1979-80, Kansas City Consensus, 1989-90; trustee Harry S. Truman Scholarship Found., 1975-78, Kansas City U., 1979-80, Andrew Drumm Inst., 1990—, pres. bd. trustees, 1992-94. Capt. U.S. Army, 1969-72. Recipient Outstanding Young Man of Mo. award Mo. Jaycees, 1975, award Mo. Inst. Pub. Adminstrn., 1983 Mem.: ABA, Independence C. of C. (pres. 1980—81), Mo. Econ. Devel. Fin. Assn. (pres. 1999—2001), Kansas City Bar Assn., Internat. Assn. Gaming Attys., Nat. Assn. Bond Lawyers, Kansas City Bar Assn. (chmn. real estate law com. 1988—89), Ea. Jackson County Bar Assn., Mo. Bar Assn., Order of Coif, Beta Theta Pi, Phi Delta Phi. Unitarian Universalist. Administrative and regulatory, Property, real (including real estate development, water), State and local taxation. Home: 206 E 30th St Kansas City MO 64108-3213 Office: King Hershey Ste 2100 2345 Grand Blvd Kansas City MO 64108-2619 E-mail: rking@kinghershey.com.

KING, ROBERT BRUCE, federal judge; b. White Sulphur Springs, W.Va., Jan. 29, 1940; m. Julia Kay Doak, Apr. 16, 1965. BA, W.Va. U., 1961; JD, W.Va. Coll. of Law, 1968. Bar: W.Va. 1968, U.S. Dist. Ct. (so. dist.) W.Va. 1968, U.S. Ct. Appeals W.Va. 1968, U.S. Ct. Appeals (4th cir.) 1970, U.S. Dist. Ct. (no. dist.) W.Va. 1972, U.S. Supreme Ct. 1974, U.S. Dist. Ct. (ea. dist.) Ky. 1975, U.S. Claims Ct. 1985, U.S. Tax Ct. 1991. Asst. mgr. Sam Snead All-Am. Golf Course, Sharpes, Fla., 1965; rsch. asst. State and Cmty. Planning Office, Office of R&D, W.Va. U., Morgantown, W.Va., 1966—68; law clk. Chief Judge John A. Field, Jr. U.S. Dist. Ct. (so. dist.) W.Va., Charleston, 1968—69; assoc. Haynes and Ford, Lewisburg, W.Va., 1969—70; asst. U.S. atty. So. Dist. of W.Va., Charleston, 1970—74; assoc. Spilman, Thomas, Battle and Klostermeyer, Charleston, 1975, ptnr., 1976—77, 1981; U.S. atty. So. Dist. of W.Va., Charleston, 1977—81; ptnr. King Allen Guthrie & McHugh, 1981—98; judge U.S. Ct. Appeals (4th cir.), Richmond, Va., 1998—. Mem. Jud. Investigation Commn. of W.Va., 1990—94; vis. com. Coll. of Law of W.Va. U., 1997—. Scholar Patrick Duffy Koontz. Fellow: Am. Bar Found., Am. Coll. Trial Lawyers; mem.: ABA, Am. Bd. Trial Advocates (W.Va. chpt. pres. 1986—90), Jud. Conf. of 4th Cir. Ct. Appeals, W.Va. Law Sch. Assn., W.Va. U. Alumni Assn., Greenbrier County Bar Assn., Kanawha County Bar Assn., W.Va. Bar Assn., W.Va. Golf Assn., U.S. Golf Assn., Order of the Coif, Phi Alpha Delta, Pi Sigma Alpha. Presbyterian. Office: Ste 7602 300 Virginia St Charleston WV 25301

KING, ROBERT LEWIS, lawyer; b. Johnson City, Tenn., June 20, 1950; s. Herbert and Ruth Marie (Dulaney) K. BA, Earlham Coll., 1973; MS, Columbia U., 1974; JD, U. Tenn., 1985; SJD, Widener U., 2003. Bar: Tenn. 1986, D.C. 1989. Fgn. corr. AP, Paris, 1971-72; reporter The Miami (Fla.) Herald, 1974-75; polit. editor The Courier-Post, Cherry Hill, N.J., 1975-78; prof. communications East Tenn. State U., Johnson City, 1978-88; mem. Tenn. Legislature, Nashville, 1978-84; sole practice Johnson City, 1986—. Chmn. law revision subcom. Tenn. Ho. Reps., 1978—84. Recipient Scripps-Howard Pub. Svc. citation, 1977, citation 1990 Dist. Judges for Pro Bono Svcs. to Poor. Mem. ABA (Silver Gavel award 1976), Assn. Trial Lawyers Am., Tenn. Trial Lawyers Assn., N.J. Soc. Profl. Journalists (Investigative Reporting award 1976), Am. Health Lawyers Assn. General civil litigation, Health, Personal injury (including property damage). Home: 1302 Sunset Dr Johnson City TN 37604-3620 Office: PO Box 4055 CRS Johnson City TN 37602-4055 E-mail: KingLaw@chartertn.net.

KING, ROBERT WILSON, lawyer; b. Durant, Miss., Sept. 30, 1926; s. Norman Edwards and Ethel (Pearson) K.; m. Bobbie Haynie, Aug. 10, 1950; children: Robin, Lowrey, Christian, Kimberley. BA, Cumberland U., 1948, JD, 1950. Bar: Miss. 1950, U.S. Dist. Ct. (so. dist.) Miss. 1950, U.S. Ct. Appeals (5th cir.) 1969. Ptnr. King & Spencer, Jackson, Miss., 1979—. Pres. Miss. Bankruptcy Conf., 1982-83. Pres. Jackson Library Bd. 1973-76; pres., trustee Bapt. Children's Village, Jackson; bd. dirs. Jackson Prep. Sch., 1972-79. Served to capt. USAFR, 1944-53. Named one of Best Lawyers in Am., Harvard Law '77, 1983, 1991, 1993, 1995, 1997. Fellow Miss. Bar Found.; mem. ABA, Miss. Bar Assn., Hinds County Bar Assn. (bd. dirs.), Am. Judicature Soc., Blue Key. Lodges: Masons (32 degree). Republican. Avocations: hunting, fishing, cooking. Bankruptcy, State civil litigation, General practice. Home: 3671 Woodward Pl Jackson MS 39216-3525

KING, RONALD BAKER, federal judge; b. San Antonio, Aug. 16, 1953; s. Donald Dick and Elaine (Baker) K.; m. Cynthia Sauer, June 7, 1975; children: Karen Elizabeth, Ronald Baker Jr., Kelsey Ann. BA with high honors, So. Meth. U., 1974; JD with high honors, U. Tex., 1977. Bar: Tex. 1977, U.S. Dist. Ct. (we. dist.) Tex. 1980, U.S. Ct. Appeals (5th cir.) 1981, U.S. Tax Ct. 1985. Briefing atty. Supreme Ct. Tex., Austin, 1977-78; assoc. Foster, Lewis, Langley, Gardner & Banack Inc., San Antonio, 1978-82, ptnr., 1982-88; judge U.S. Bankruptcy Ct. (we. dist.) Tex., San Antonio, 1988—. Mem. Tex. Bar Assn., Nat. Conf. Bankruptcy Judges. Presbyterian. Avocation: basketball. Office: US Bankruptcy Ct PO Box 1439 San Antonio TX 78295-1439

KING, TROY, lawyer; b. Elba, Ala., Aug. 22, 1968; m. Paige King; children: Briggs, Colden. B In History and Social Scis., Troy State U., 1990; JD, U. Ala., 1994. Dep. exec. sec. Gov. Fob James, 1995—99; asst. atty. gen. State of Ala., 1999—2003; legal adviser to gov. Office Gov. State of Ala., Montgomery, 2003—. Office: Office Gov State Capitol 600 Dexter Ave Rm N104 Montgomery AL 36130*

KING, WILLIAM BRUCE, retired lawyer; b. Boston, June 3, 1932; s. Gilbert and Frances (Hood) K.; m. Sheila Malone, July 9, 1955; children: Stephen Bruce, Rachel Creath, Christopher Bruce. AB, Harvard U., 1954, LL.B., 1959. Bar: Mass. 1959. Assoc. firm Goodwin Procter, Boston, 1959-67, ptnr., 1968-99, of counsel, 2000—; prin. William B. King P.C., 1981-99. Mem. bd. investment Cambridge Savs. Bank, 1973—, trustee, 1969—, corporator, 1965—; sec. Bradley Real Estate, Inc., 1963-99; trustee Cambridge Heritage Trust, 1984—; dir. mem. exec. com. Cambridge Fin. Group, Inc., 1998—, Cambridge Appleton Trust, N.A., 1999—. Author: (with others) Real Estate Investment Trusts: Structures, Analysis, and Strategy, 1997. Trustee Buckingham Browne and Nichols Sch., 1970-76, sec., 1970-73, vice chmn., 1974-76; mem. Cambridge (Mass.) Hist. Commn., 1973—, vice chmn., 1973-86, chmn., 1986—; pres Cambridge Civic Assn., 1963-65; bd. govs. Nat. Assn. Real Estate Investment Trusts, 1982-88, chmn. state regulation subcom. of govt. rels. com., 1989-91. Served with USN, 1954-56. Recipient 4th Ann. Industry Leadership award Nat. Assn. Real Estate Investment Trusts, 1995. Mem. ABA, Mass. Bar Assn., Boston Bar Assn., Cambridge-Arlington-Belmont Bar Assn. (pres. 1974-75) Corporate, general, Property, real (including real estate development, water), Securities. Home: 25 Hurlbut St Cambridge MA 02138-1603 Office: Exchange Pl Boston MA 02109-2803 E-mail: basking@attbi.com.

KING, WILLIAM H., JR., lawyer; b. Richmomd, Va., Nov. 4, 1940; AB, Dartmouth Coll., 1963; LLB, U. Va., 1967; MA (hon.), Dartmouth Coll., 1992. Bar: Va. 1967, Tex. 1993. Mem. McGuireWoods LLP, Richmond. Fellow Am. Bar Found., Am. Coll. Trial Lawyers; mem. ABA. General civil litigation, Product liability, Toxic tort. Office: McGuireWoods One James Ctr Richmond VA 23219-4030 E-mail: wking@mcguirewoods.com.

KINGHAM, RICHARD FRANK, lawyer; b. Lafayette, Ind., Aug. 2, 1946; s. James R. and Loretta C. (Hoenigke) Kingham; m. Justine Frances McClung, July 6, 1968; 1 child, Richard Patterson. BA, George Washington U., 1968; JD, U. Va., 1973. Bar: D.C. 1973, U.S. Dist. Ct. D.C. 1974, U.S. Ct. Appeals (8th cir.) 1977, U.S. Supreme Ct. 1977, U.S. Ct. Appeals (5th cir.) 1980, registered: Law Soc. Eng. and Wales (fgn. lawyer) 1994. Edtl. asst. Washington Star, 1964-68, 69-70; assoc. Covington & Burling, Washington, 1973-81, ptnr., 1981—, mng. ptnr. London office, 1996-2000; mem. mgmt. com., co-head Life Scis. Industry Group, 2000—. Lectr. law U. Va., Charlottesville, 1977—90; mem. com. issues and priorities new vaccine devel. Inst. Medicine, NAS, 1983—86, Nat. Adv. Allergy and Infectious Diseases Coun. NIH, 1988—92; mem. adv. bd. World Pharms. Report, 1990—96; mem. WHO Coun. Internat. Orgns. Med. Scis. and Working Party in Pharmacovigilance, 1997—99; mem. com. on accelerating biowarfare countermeasures Inst. of Medicine, NAS, 2002—; lectr. grad. program in pharm. medicine U. Wales, 1999—. Contbr. articles to profl. jours. Pres. Am. Friends of St. Peter's Eaton Square, 2001—; treas., mem. parochial ch. coun. St. Peter's Ch. Eaton Sq., London, 1998—2001. With U.S. Army, 1968—69. Mem.: ABA, European Forum for Good Clin. Practice, Soc. Vertebrate Paleontology, Food Law Group (U.K.), European Soc. Pharmacovigilance, Food and Drug Law Inst., Drug Info. Assn., Brussels Pharm. Law Group, Reform Club (London), Order of Coif. Republican. Episcopalian. Avocation: vertebrate paleontology. Administrative and regulatory, Health. Home: 4821 Dexter St NW Washington DC 20007 E-mail: rkingham@cov.com.

KINLIN, DONALD JAMES, lawyer; b. Boston, Nov. 29, 1938; s. Joseph Edward and Ruth Claire (Byrne) K.; m. Donna C. (McGrath), Nov. 29, 1959; children: Karen J., Donald J., Joseph P., and Kevin S. BS in acctg., Syracuse U., 1968, MBA, 1970; JD, U. Nebr., 1975. Bar: Nebr., 1976, Ohio, 1982, U.S. Supreme Ct., 1979, U.S. Claims Ct., 1982, U.S. Tax Ct., 1982, U.S. Ct. Appeals (5th and fed. cir.), 1982. Atty. USAF, Mather AFB, Calif., 1976-78; sr. trial atty. Air Force Contract Law Ctr., Wright Patterson AFB, Ohio, 1978-86, dep. dir., 1986-87; ptnr. Smith and Schnacke, Dayton, Ohio, 1987-89, Thompson and Hine LLP, Dayton, Ohio, 1989—. Mem. adv. bd. Fed. Publ. Inc., Govt. Contract Costs, Pricing & Acctg. Report. Contbr. articles to legal jours. Pres. Forest Ridge Assn., Dayton,Ohio, 1984-96; sec., gen. counsel U.S. Air and Trade Show, 1994-98, chmn., 1998—; bd. dir. Nat. Aviation Hall of Fame, 1998—. Mem. ABA (chmn. sect. pub. contract law 1993-94), sec., budget and fin. officer sect., coun. mem., chmn. fed. procurement divsn., vice chmn. acctg., cost and pricing com., truth in negotiations com., chmn. cost acctg. stas. sub com.), Fed. Bar Assn., Ohio Bar Assn., Nebr. Bar Assn., Contracts Appeals Bar Assn. (bd. govs. 1998-2001). Avocation: travel. Administrative and regulatory, Commercial, contracts (including sales of goods; commercial financing), Military. Office: Thompson and Hine LLP 10 W 2nd St Dayton OH 45402-1758

KINNALLY, WILLIAM LEE, JR., lawyer; b. Nov. 20, 1947; s. William Lee and Rita (Cleary) K.; m. Susan Cronin, July 1, 1978; 1 son, William Denis. BA magna cum laude, Niagara U., 1969; JD, Cornell U., 1972. Bar: N.Y. 1973, U.S. Dist. Ct. (ea. and so. dists.) N.Y. 1974, U.S. Ct. Appeals (2d cir.) 1974, U.S. Dist. Ct. (no. dist.) N.Y. 1975, U.S. Ct. Appeals (3d cir.) 1975. Assoc. Javits & Javits, N.Y.C., NY, 1972-73, Parker, Duryee, Zunino, Malone & Carter, N.Y.C., NY, 1973-81, ptnr., 1981-86, Engel & Milholland, N.Y.C., NY, 1986-89, Gibney, Anthony & Flaherty, LLP, N.Y.C., NY, 1989—. Village trustee Village of Hastings-on-Hudson, NY, 1978—90, 1992—93, mayor, 1993—. Mem. ABA, Bar Assn. City N.Y., Westchester County Bar Assn. Federal civil litigation, State civil litigation, Intellectual property. Home and Office: Gibney Anthony & Flaherty 665 5th Ave New York NY 10022-5305 E-mail: wlkinnally@gibney.com.

KINNAN, DAVID EMERY, lawyer; b. Columbus, Ohio, May 15, 1946; BA, Pa. State U., 1968; JD, U. Tex., 1970. Bar: Tex. 1971. Assoc. gen. counsel Shell Oil Co., Houston, 1977—. Served to capt. USAF, 1971-76. Federal civil litigation, Corporate, general, Oil, gas, and mineral. Office: PO Box PO Box 2463 Houston TX 77252-2463

KINNEBREW, JACKSON METCALFE, lawyer; b. Oklahoma City, June 29, 1941; s. Jackson A. and Mary Lucille (Metcalfe) K.; m. Carole A. Vadner, Sept. 23, 1967; children: Scott, Sarah. BBA in Acctg., U. Okla., 1963; JD, So. Meth. U., 1967, LLM in Taxation, 1973. Bar: Tex. 1968, U.S. Dist. Ct. (no. dist.) Tex. 1968, U.S. Tax Ct. 1970, U.S. Ct. Appeals (5th cir.) 1971, U.S. Supreme Ct. 1971; CPA, Tex. Assoc. Strasburger & Price, Dallas, 1968-74, ptnr., 1975—. Lectr. Wills and Probate Inst., 1980, 81, 83, 89, Practicing Law Inst., 1983; bd. trustees Ctr. Am. and Internat. Law (formerly Southwestern Legal Found.), 1987-. Contbr. legal articles to profl. jours. Gen. counsel Cmtys. Found. of Tex., Dallas, 1987—; fund raising chmn. Boy Scouts Am., Dallas, 1984—86; chmn. legacy com. Am. Cancer Soc., Dallas, 1978—82; interim exec. dir. Cmtys. Found. Tex., Dallas, 2001—. Lt. U.S. Army, 1963—65. Recipient Disting. Alumni award Pub. Interest, So. Meth. U. Sch Law, 2002. Fellow Am. Coll. Trust and Estate Counsel (state chmn. 1984-89, bd. regents 1988-94, membership selection com. 1993-99), Internat. Acad. Estate and Trust Law (academician 1990—); mem. ABA (subcom. chmn. 1979), State Tex. Bar Assn. (lectr. 1981, 82), Dallas Bar Assn. (chmn. probate sect. 1985), Tex. Soc. CPAs, Dallas Estate Planning Coun. (pres. 1985, program v.p. 1984, treas. 1982, sec. 1981), Tex. Bd. Legal Specialization (cert.). Avocations: golf, sports, bridge. Office: Strasburger & Price LLP Bank Am Plz 901 Main St Ste 4300 Dallas TX 75202-3724

KINNEY, GREGORY HOPPES, lawyer; b. Anderson, Ind., July 15, 1947; s. Dalton Roth and Effie Eleanor (Hoppes) K. BA, Mich. State U., 1969, M in Labor Rels., 1971; JD, U. Detroit, 1974. Bar: Mich. 1975, U.S. Dist. Ct. (ea. dist.) Mich. 1975, U.S. Dist. Ct. (we. dist.) Mich. 2000, U.S. Ct. Appeals (D.C. cir.) 1975, U.S. Ct. Appeals (6th cir.) 1987. Labor law editor Bur. Nat. Affairs, Washington, 1974; pension cons. Edward H. Friend & Co., Washington, 1975, Wyatt Co., Detroit, 1976-84; pvt. practice Detroit, 1984-86, Troy, Mich., 1986-99, Decatur, Mich., 1999—. General practice, Probate (including wills, trusts), Property, real (including real estate development, water). Office: PO Box 243 Decatur MI 49045-0243

KINNEY, JAMES HOWARD, lawyer; b. Oklahoma City, Mar. 2, 1937; s. William Edgar and Chrissie (Ballingall) K.; m. June Lassick, Mar. 26, 1961; children: Karen Jill, Scott James. BS in Bus. Mgmt., Calif. State U., Long Beach, 1963; JD, UCLA, 1966. Bar: Calif. 1966, U.S. Dist. Ct. (so. dist.) Calif. 1966. Dep. dist. atty. Ventura (Calif.) County, 1966-68; ptnr. Collins, Gleason & Kinney, Torrance, Calif., 1968-85, O'Melveny & Myers, Los Angeles, 1985—2000. Lectr. Harbor Coll., L.A., 1971-72. Councilman City of Palos Verdes Estates, Calif., 1983-1990, Mayor, 1985-86, 88-89. With USMC, 1955-58. Mem. Los Angeles County Bar Assn., Internat. Council Shopping Ctrs., Sigma Alpha Epsilon. Republican. Property, real (including real estate development, water). also: O'Melveny & Myers 400 S Hope St Los Angeles CA 90071-2801 Office: Ste 700 401 Wilshire Blvd Santa Monica CA 90401-1452

KINNEY, LISA FRANCES, lawyer; b. Laramie, Wyo., Mar. 13, 1951; d. Irvin Wayne and Phyllis (Poe) Kinney; m. Rodney Philip Lang, Feb. 5, 1971; children: Cambria Helen, Shelby Robert, Eli Wayne. BA, U. Wyo., 1973, JD, 1986; MLS, U. Oreg., 1975. Reference libr. U. Wyo. Sci. Libr., Laramie, 1975-76; outreach dir. Albany County Libr., Laramie, 1975-76, dir., 1977-83; mem. Wyo. State Senate, Laramie, 1984-94, minority leader, 1992-94; with documentation office Am. Heritage Ctr. U. Wyo., 1991-94; assoc. Corthell & King, 1994-96, shareholder, 1996-99; owner Summit Bar Rev., 1987—; fin. planner VALIC, 2001—. Author: (with Rodney Lang) Civil Rights of the Developmentally Disabled, 1986; (with Rodney Lang and Phyllis Kinney) Manual For Families with Emotionally Disturbed and Mentally Ill Relatives, 1988, rev. 1991, 99, 2003, Lobby For Your Library, Know What Works, 1992; contbr. articles to profl. jours.; editor, compiler pub. rels. directory of ALA, 1982. Bd. dirs. Big Bros./Big Sisters, Laramie, 1980-83, Children's Mus., 1993-97; bd. dirs. Am. Heritage Ctr., 1993-97, Citizen of the Century, 1997-99, govt. chmn. 1997-99. Recipient Beginning Young Profl. award Mt. Plains Libr. Assn., 1980; named Outstanding Wyo. Libr. Assn., 1977, Outstanding Young Woman State of Wyo., 1980, Arts and Scis. Disting. Alumni award U. Wyo., 1997, Making Democracy Work award Wyo. LWV, 2000. Mem.: ABA, Nat. Conf. State Legislatures (various coms. 1985—90), Laramie Area C. of C. (bd. dirs. 1996—2000, pres. 1999, Top Hand award 1997), Zonta, Kiwanis. Democrat. Avocations: photography, dance, reading, travel, languages. Estate planning, General practice, Legislative. Home: 1415 E Baker St Laramie WY 82072 Office: PO Box 1710 Laramie WY 82073-1710 E-mail: lfkl@aol.com.

KINNEY, STEPHEN HOYT, JR., lawyer; b. Albuquerque, Feb. 27, 1948; s. Stephen Hoyt and Harriet May (Gadsden) K.; m. Leslie vanLiew, June 10, 1972; 1 child, Erin. BS, MIT, 1970; JD, Harvard U., 1973. Bar: N.Y. 1974, U.S. Dist. Ct. (so. dist.) N.Y. 1974, U.S. Dist. Ct. (ea. dist.) N.Y. 1974, U.S. Dist. Ct. (no. dist.) N.Y. 1978, U.S. Ct. Appeals (2d cir.) 1975, U.S. Supreme Ct. 1982. Programmer, analyst MIT, 1968-70; law clk. N.J. Organized Crime Unit, Trenton, 1972; assoc. Reid & Priest, N.Y.C., 1973-85, sr. atty., 1985-86, ptnr., 1986-98, Thelen Reid & Priest LLP, N.Y.C., 1998—. Author, editor: Outline of Arbitration, 1984; contbr. articles to profl. jours.; creator software. Mem. ABA, MB Yacht Club (Port Washington, N.Y.). Commercial, contracts (including sales of goods; commercial financing), Computer, Securities. Office: Thelen Reid & Priest 875 Third Ave New York NY 10022-6225 E-mail: skinney@thelenreid.com.

KINSER, CYNTHIA D. state supreme court justice; b. Pennington Gap, Dec. 20, 1951; d. Morris and Velda (Myers) Fannon; m. H. Allen Kinser, Jr., March 17, 1974; children: Charles Adam, Terah Diane. Student, Univ. of Ga., 1970-71; BA, Univ. of Tenn., 1974; JD, Univ. of Va., 1977. Bar: Va. 1977, U.S. Dist. Ct. (we. dist.) Va. 1977, U.S. Ct. Appeals (4th cir.) 1977, U.S. Supreme Ct. 1988. Law clk. to Judge Glen M. Williams U.S. Dist. Ct., 1977-78; pvt. law practice, 1978-90; commonwealth's atty. Lee County, Va., 1980-83; magistrate judge U.S. Dist. Ct. (we. dist.) Va., Abingdon, 1990-98; justice Va. Supreme Ct., Richmond, 1998—. Trustee Chapter 7 Panel, U.S. Bankruptcy Ct., 1979-90. Mem. Va. Bar Assn., Va. Trial Lawyers Assn., Am. Bar Assn. Methodist. Office: Supreme Court 100 North 9th Street, 5th Floor Richmond VA 23219

KINSEY, ROBERT STANLEIGH, III, lawyer; b. Highland Park, Ill., Dec. 31, 1944; s. Robert Stanleigh, Jr. and Jane Kinsey; m. Kathleen Ann Smith, Oct. 14, 1972; children: Jessica, Catlain, Kristoffer. BA, Grinnell Coll., 1967; JD with distinction, U. Iowa, 1973. Bar: Iowa 1973, U.S. Dist. Ct. (no. dist.) Iowa 1973, U.S. Dist. Ct. (so. dist.) Iowa 1982, U.S. Ct. Appeals (8th cir.) 1979, U.S. Supreme Ct. 1979. Mem. Brown, Kinsey & Funnkhouser P.L.C., Mason City, Iowa, 1973—. Mem. Iowa Bar Assn. (chair workers compensation sect. 1990-91, 2000-01), Iowa Assn. of Workers Compensation Attys. (pres., v.p., sec., treas., bd. dirs. 1978—), Rotary (pres. 1990-91). Democrat. Congregationalist. Avocations: tennis, biking, sailing, travel, reading. Civil rights, Personal injury (including property damage), Workers' compensation. Office: Brown Kinsey & Funkhouser PLC 214 N Adams Ave Mason City IA 50401-3120

KINSEY, RONALD C., JR., lawyer; b. Washington, June 28, 1942; s. Ronald C. Kinsey; m. Maria Emma Pikon, July 20, 2002; children: Kyle, Cara. AB, Dartmouth Coll., 1964; JD, U. Wash., 1967. Bar: Wash. 1970, U.S. Dist. Ct. (we. dist.) Wash. 1973. Dep. pros. atty. King County, Seattle, 1970-71; mcpl. legal cons. Assn. of Wash. Cities, Seattle, 1971-81; mcpl. atty. Holt Law Offices, Issaquah, Wash., 1981-83; pvt. practice law Seattle, 1983-89; marine investigator USCG, Seattle, 1989—; chief Coast Guard Casualty Investigations, Seattle, 1996—. Capt. U.S. Army, 1968-70. Mem. Rotary of Univ. Dist., Seattle Yacht Club, Dartmouth Club of Western Wash. Home: 4346 NE 58th St Seattle WA 98105-2250 E-mail: rkinsey@pacnorwest.uscg.mil.

KINTZELE, JOHN ALFRED, lawyer; b. Denver, Aug. 16, 1936; s. Louis Richard and Adele H. Kintzele; children: John A., Marcia A., Elizabeth A.; m. Suzanne Hinsberger; stepchildren: William Karp III, Christopher Karp. BS in Bus., U. Colo., 1958, LLB, 1961. Bar: Colo. bar 1961. Assoc. James B. Radetsky, Denver, 1962-63; pvt. practice law Denver, 1963—. Corp. officer, dir. Kintzele, Inc.; rep. 10th cir. U.S. Ct. of Claims Bar. Chmn. Colo. Lawyer Referral Service, 1978-83, Election commr., Denver, 1975-79, 83-86. Mem. ABA, Colo. Bar Assn., Denver Bar Assn., Am. Judicature Soc. Democrat. Roman Catholic. General civil litigation, Personal injury (including property damage), Workers' compensation. Home: 10604 E Powers Dr Englewood CO 80111-3957 Office: 1317 Delaware St Denver CO 80204-2704 E-mail: kintzeles@aol.com., jkintlaw@aol.com.

KINZER, WILLIAM LUTHER, lawyer; b. Mifflintown, Pa., Jan. 25, 1929; s. John Raymond and Ethel Naomi (Sellers) K.; m. Ann Marie Rosato, May 3, 1958; children: Karen, Carolyn, Cynthia, Matthew, Mark. BA, Dickinson Coll., Carlisle, Pa., 1950; LLB, Temple U., 1956; LLM, Georgetown U., 1961. Bar: D.C. 1957, Ga. 1962. Atty. IRS, Washington, 1956-62; assoc. Powell, Goldstein, Frazer & Murphy, Atlanta, 1962-65, ptnr., 1965-2000, of counsel, 2000—. Author miscellaneous tax articles, 2 BNA Tax Portfolios. Capt. USAF, 1951-53. Mem. ABA (com. chmn. 1987-89), Fed. Bar Assn., Ga. Bar Assn., Atlanta Bar Assn., Atlanta Tax Forum (pres. 1980, trustee 1978-81), Cherokee Town and Country Club (Atlanta). Roman Catholic. Avocation: golf. Home: 904 Spring Valley Woodstock GA 30189-6102 Office: Powell Goldstein Frazer & Murphy 191 Peachtree St NE Ste 16 Atlanta GA 30303-1740 E-mail: wkinzer@pgfm.com.

KINZIE, RAYMOND WYANT, banker, lawyer; b. Chgo., Oct. 20, 1930; s. Raymond Allen and Florence (Wyant) K.; m. Dorothy Cherry Beek, Sept. 17, 1955; children: Diana K. Wieczorek, Dorothy K. Tedeschi, Raymond Wyant Jr., Susan Hawthorne (dec.). BA, Carleton Coll., 1952; LLB, Yale U., 1955, JD, 1964. Bar: Ill. 1956, U.S. Dist. Ct. (no. dist.) Ill. 1959, U.S. Ct. Appeals (7th cir.) 1961, U.S. Supreme Ct. 1964. Assoc. McBride and Baker, Chgo., 1955-56; atty. Continental Ill. Nat. Bank & Trust Co. (now Bank Am. Chgo.), Chgo., 1956-59; trust officer Lake View Trust and Savs. Bank, Chgo., 1959-65, asst. v.p. loans and credit, 1965-71, v.p., trust officer, 1971-82, sr. v.p., sr. trust officer, 1982-88; sr. v.p., sr. trust officer LaSalle Bank Lake View subs. Algemene Bank Nederland (now known as ABN-AMRO Bank), Chgo., 1988-90; sr. v.p. trust svcs. ABN-AMRO Bank subs. LaSalle Nat. Trust, N.A., Chgo., 1990-92; sr. v.p. wealth mgmt. group Lasalle Nat. Trust, N.A., Chgo., 1993-97; sr. v.p. Wealth Mgmt. Group LaSalle Nat. Bank, Chgo., 1997-98, cons., 1998—. Mem. adv. bd. Nat. Coll. Edn. (Lewis U.), Evanston, Ill., 1975—; commentator radio editl. rebuttals Sta. WBBM; talk shows commentator WLS. Contbr. Bd. dirs., sec.-treas. Ravenswood Hosp. Med. ctr., Chgo., 1975-85; bd. dirs., sec. Ravenswood Health Care Found., 1975-80. Mem. Am. Mgmt. Assn., Ill. State Bar Assn., Chgo. Bar Assn., Chgo. Estate Planning Coun., Land Trust Coun. Ill. Home: 1027 N Marion St Oak Park IL 60302-1374 E-mail: kinzie@ameritech.net.

KINZLER, THOMAS BENJAMIN, lawyer; b. N.Y.C., June 19, 1950; s. David and Rhoda Lenore (Wolgel) K.; m. Carol Ada Loebel, Aug. 24, 1975; children: Katherine Diane, David James. BA, Columbia Coll., 1971; JD, Boston U., 1975. Bar: N.Y. 1976, U.S. Dist. Ct. (no., so., ea. and we. dists.) N.Y. 1976, U.S. Ct. Appeals (2d cir.) 1976. Assoc. Kreindler, Relkin & Goldberg, N.Y.C., 1975-77, Arthur, Dry & Kalish, N.Y.C., 1977-80, Kelley Drye & Warren LLP, N.Y.C., 1980-85; ptnr. Kelley Drye & Warren, N.Y.C., 1985—. Mem. ABA, Assn. of the Bar of City of N.Y.C. (products liability com. 1983-86, com. on state legis. 1978-80). Bankruptcy, Federal civil litigation, State civil litigation. Office: Kelley Drye & Warren 101 Park Ave Fl 30 New York NY 10178-0062

KIOK, JOAN STERN, lawyer; b. N.Y.C., Dec. 19, 1929; d. Milton William and Pauline (Bauer) Stern; children: Paul, Pter. BA, Cornell U., 1951; LLB, Columbia U., 1954. Bar: N.Y. 1955, Colo. 1958, U.S. Dist. Ct. (so. and ea. dists.) N.Y., U.S. Ct. Appeals (2nd cir.) 1961, U.S. Supreme Ct. 1961, 1968-78. Assoc. gen. counsel D.C.37 AFSCME, AFL-CIO, N.Y.C.; sole practitioner N.Y.C., 1978—. Gen. counsel Mgr. Employees Assn., N.Y.C., 1980-02, Uniformed Sanitation chiefs Assn., N.Y.C., 1988—, EMS Chiefs Assn., N.Y.C., 1986—, Orgn. Staff Analysts, N.Y.C., 1985—, Fire Alarm Dispatchers, N.Y.C., 1988—; chair bd. dirs. MFY Legal Svcs., N.Y.C., 1980-85. Mem. N.Y. County Lawyers Assn. (labor law com. 1975—). Labor (including EEOC, Fair Labor Standards Act, labor-management relations, NLRB, OSHA). Home and Office: 442 E 20th St New York NY 10009-8120 E-mail: kiok@earthlink.net.

KIPPERMAN, LAWRENCE I. lawyer; b. Chgo., Nov. 22, 1941; s. Solomon and Idelle (Goldman) K.; m. Carol A. Kipperman, Jan. 29, 1967 (div. Sept. 1985); children: Anna, Lynne. BA, U. Ill., 1963, JD, 1966; LLM, George Washington U., 1968. Bar: Ill. 1966, U.S. Dist. Ct. (no. dist.) Ill. 1966, U.S. Supreme Ct. 1968, Ohio 1970, U.S. Ct. Appeals (7th cir.) 1973, U.S. Ct. Appeals (8th cirs.) 1986. Atty. NLRB, Washington, 1966-70; assoc. Burke, Haber & Berick, Cleve., 1970-71, Sidley & Austin, Chgo., 1971-73, ptnr., 1973-2000, sr. counsel, 2000—. Lectr. Ill. Continuing Legal Edn., 1985, Am. Arbitration Assn. Mem. Chgo. Bar Assn., Legal Club Chgo. Jewish. Avocations: architectural history, baseball, basketball, jazz. Labor (including EEOC, Fair Labor Standards Act, labor-management relations, NLRB, OSHA). Office: Sidley Austin Brown & Wood Bank One Plz Chicago IL 60603-2000 E-mail: lkipperman@sidley.com.

KIPPUR, MERRIE MARGOLIN, lawyer; b. Denver, July 24, 1962; d. Morton Leonard and Bonnie (Seldin) Margolin; m. Bruce R. Kippur, Sept. 7, 1986. BA, Colo. Coll., 1983; JD, U. Colo., 1986. Bar: Colo. 1986, U.S. Dist. Ct. Colo. 1986, U.S. Ct. Appeals (10th cir.) 1987. Assoc. Sterling & Miller, Denver, 1985-88, McKenna & Cuneo, Denver, 1989-94; sr. v.p., gen. counsel, dir. First United Bank, Denver, 1994-96; prin. Merrie Margolin Kippur Assocs., PC, Denver, 1997—2002. Lectr. in field; clk. Hon. Elizabeth E. Brown, 2001—. Author: Student Improvement in the 1980's, 1984; (with others) Ethical Considerations in Bankruptcy, 1985, Partnership Bankruptcy, 1986, Colorado Methods of Practise, 1988; lectr. in field. Pres.-elect, then pres. Jr. League Denver, 2001—; bd. mgrs. Met. Mayors and Commrs. Youth Award; active Jr. League Denver, 1992—. Mem. ABA, Colo. Bar Assn., Denver Bar Assn., Gamma Phi Beta, Phi Delta Phi, Pi Gamma Mu. Democrat. Avocations: reading, scuba diving, wine collecting. Bankruptcy. E-mail: merrie_kippur@cob.uscourts.gov.

KIRBY, JOHN JOSEPH, JR., lawyer; b. Washington, Oct. 22, 1939; s. John Joseph and Rose Elizabeth (Mangan) Kirby; children: John Pickens, Timothy James, Perrin Patricia Lucia. BA, Fordham Coll., 1961; BA (Rhodes scholar), Oxford U., 1964, MA, 1967; LLB, U. Va., 1966. Bar: Va 1966, NY 1969. Asst. prof. law U. Va., 1966-67; spl. asst. civil rights divsn. U.S. Dept. Justice, Washington, 1967-68; assoc. Mudge Rose Guthrie Alexander & Ferdon, N.Y.C., 1968-70, ptnr., 1971-95, chmn., 1991-95; ptnr. Latham & Watkins, N.Y.C., 1995—. Dep dir Pres's Comn Campus Unrest, 1970. Bd dirs Georgetown Univ, 1976—92, Fordham Univ, 1994—2000, Merton Col Charitable Corp, 1995—, Fund Modern Cts, 1998—. Mem.: ABA, DC Bar, Va State Bar, Asn Bar City NY. Antitrust, Federal civil litigation, Trademark and copyright. Home: 115 E 87th St Apt 6F New York NY 10128-1101 also: 64 Beach Rd Westhampton Beach NY 11978-2339 Office: Latham & Watkins 885 3d Ave Ste 1000 New York NY 10022-4834

KIRCHER, JOHN JOSEPH, law educator; b. Milw., July 26, 1938; s. Joseph John and Martha Marie (Jach) K.; m. Marcia Susan Adamkiewicz, Aug. 26, 1961; children: Joseph John, Mary Kathryn. BA, Marquette U., 1960, JD, 1963. Bar: Wis. 1963, U.S. Dist. Ct. (ea. dist.) Wis. 1963, U.S. Ct. Appeals (7th cir.) 1992. Sole practice, Port Washington, Wis., 1963-66; with Def. Research Inst., Milw., 1966-80, research dir., 1972-80; with Marquette U., 1970—, prof. law, 1980—, assoc. dean acad. affairs, 1992-93. Chmn. Wis. Jud. Council, 1981-83. Author: (with J.D. Ghiardi) Punitive Damages: Law and Practice, 1981, 2d edit (with C.M. Wiseman), 2000; editor Federation of Defense and Corporate Counsel Quarterly; mem. editorial bd. Def. Law Jour.; contbr. articles to profl. jours. Recipient Teaching Excellence award Marquette U., 1986, Disting. Service award Def. Research Inst., 1980, Marquette Law Rev. Editors' award, 1988. Mem. ABA (Robert B. McKay Professor award 1993), Am. Law Inst., Wis. Bar Assn., Wis. Supreme Ct. Bd. of Bar Examiners (vice chair 1989-91, chair 1992), Am. Judicature Soc., Nat. Sports Law Inst. (adv. com. 1989—), Assn. Internationale de Droit des Assurances, Scribes. Roman Catholic. Office: PO Box 1881 Milwaukee WI 53201-1881

KIRCHHEIMER, ARTHUR E(DWARD), lawyer, business executive; b. N.Y.C., June 26, 1931; s. Arthur and Lena K.; m. Esther A. Jordan, Sept. 11, 1965. BA, Syracuse U., 1952, LL.B., 19S4. Bar: N.Y. 1954, Calif. 1973. Ptnr. Block, Kirchheimer, Lemax & Failmezger, Syracuse, N.Y., 1954-70; corp. counsel Norwich Pharmacal Co., N.Y., 1970-72; sr. v.p., gen. counsel Wickes Cos., Inc., San Diego, 1972-84; prin. Arthur E. Kirchheimer, Inc., P.C., San Diego, 1984-90; writer, cons. in bus. matters La Jolla, Calif., 1990—. Sec., dir. Corp. Fin. Council San Diego, 1975 Pres. Mental Health Assn. Onondaga County, 1970; chmn. Manlius (N.Y.) Planning Commn., 1969-72; mem. Alternatives to Litigation Spl. Panel, 1984—; mem. San Diego County Grand Jury, 1991-92. Mem. ABA, Calif. Bar Assn. Antitrust, Corporate, general, Securities. Home and Office: 2876 Palomino Cir La Jolla CA 92037-7066

KIRCHHOFF, BRUCE C. lawyer; b. Rochester, Pa., Sept. 23, 1959; s. Peter Olsen and Harriet (Heiden) K.; m. Andrea Jean Brady, June 1, 1985; children: Andrew Christopher, Tyler Michael. BA, Colo. Coll., 1981; JD, U. Denver, 1984; MSc in Mineral Econs., Colo. Sch. Mines, Golden, 1985. Bar: Colo. 1985, U.S. Dist. Ct. Colo. 1996. Gen. atty. Cyprus Amax Minerals Co., Englewood, Colo., 1986-92, Tempe, Ariz., 1992-96; mem. Alfers & Carver, Denver, 1996—. Adj. prof. law U. DenverColl. Law, 1997-98. Mem. ABA, Colo. Bar Assn., Denver Bar Assn. Republican. Methodist. Avocations: bicycling, golf, skiing. Commercial, contracts (including sales of goods; commercial financing), Corporate, general, Oil, gas, and mineral. Office: Carver & Kirchhoff LLC 730 17th St Ste 340 Denver CO 80202-3513 Fax: 303-592-7680.

KIRCHMAN, ERIC HANS, lawyer; b. Washington, May 2, 1962; s. Charles Vincent and Erika Ottilie (Knoeppel) K.; m. Hillary Bronkie Hutson, Apr. 19, 1991; children: Erika B., Thomas E. BA, Univ. Md., 1985; JD, Univ. Balt., 1990. Bar: Md. 1990, U.S. Dist. Ct. Md. 1991. Assoc. Hillel Abrams, Rockville, Md., 1990-92; ptnr. Kirchman & Kirchman, Wheaton, Md., 1992—. Of counsel Md. Coun. for Gifted and Talented Children, Inc., Silver Spring, 1994. With U.S. Army Reserve, 1985-98. Mem. ATLA, Md. Criminal Def. Attys. Assn., Montgomery County Bar Assn. General practice. Office: Kirchman & Kirchman 11141 Georgia Ave Ste 403 Wheaton MD 20902-4659

KIRGIS, FREDERIC LEE, law educator; b. Washington, Dec. 29, 1934; s. Frederic Lee Sr. and Kathryn Alice (Burrows) K.; children: Julianne, Paul Frederic. BA, Yale U., 1957; JD, U. Calif.-Berkeley, 1960. Bar: Colo. 1961, Va. 1983. Atty. Covington & Burling, Washington, 1964-67; from asst. prof. to prof. law U. Colo., Boulder, 1967-73; prof. law UCLA, 1973-78, Washington & Lee U., Lexington, Va., 1978—, dir. Frances Lewis Law Ctr., 1978-83, dean law sch., 1983-88. Author: International Organizations in their Legal Setting, 1977, 2d edit. 1993, Prior Consultation in International Law, 1983; contbr. articles to profl. jours. Pres. Maury River Soccer Club, Lexington, 1978-85. Served to capt. USAF, 1961-64 Recipient Deak award 1974; research fellow NATO, Brussels, 1978 Mem. Am. Soc. Internat. Law (v.p. 1985-87, sec. 1994—), Am. Law Inst., Internat. Law Assn. (Am. br.), Am. Jour. Internat. Law (bd. editors 1984-96, 98-2003, hon. editor 2003—), State Bar Va., Order of Coif. Democrat. Presbyterian. Home: 15 Grey Dove Rd Lexington VA 24450-2269 Office: Washington and Lee U Sch of Law Lexington VA 24450

KIRK, DENNIS DEAN, lawyer; b. Pittsburg, Kans., Dec. 13, 1950; s. Homer Standley and Maida Corena (Rouse) K.; 1 child, Dennis Dean II. AA, Hutchinson Cmty. Jr. Coll., 1970; BS with distinction, No. Ariz. U., 1972; JD, Washburn U., 1975. Bar: Kans. 1975, U.S. Dist. Ct. Kans. 1975, D.C. 1977, U.S. Ct. Appeals (D.C. cir.) 1978, U.S. Supreme Ct. 1979, U.S. Ct. Appeals (5th cir.) 1981, U.S. Dist. Ct. Md. 1984, U.S. Tax Ct. 1984, U.S. Claims Ct. 1984, U.S. Ct. Appeals (fed. cir.) 1984, U.S. Ct. Mil. Appeals 1984, Va. 1990, U.S. Ct. Appeals (4th cir.) 1990; lic. pvt. investigator; lic. personal protection specialist. Trial atty. ICC, Washington, 1975-77; assoc. Goff, Sims, Cloud & Stroud, Washington, 1977-82; pvt. practice Washington, 1982-90; ptnr. Slocum, Boddie, Murry & Kirk, Falls Church, Va., 1990-93; pvt. practice Falls Church, Va., 1993—. Pres. Law Facilities, Inc., Washington, 1982—. Vol. parole and probation officer Shawnee County, Kans., 1973-74; citizens adv. task force group Md. Nat. Park and Planning Commn., 1978-80; citizens task force on gen. plan amendments study Fairfax County coun., Va., 1981-82; active Seven Corners Task Force, Fairfax County, 1981-82, chmn. transp. and housing subcoms.; pres. Seven Springs Tenants Assn., College Park, Md., 1976-80, Ravenwood Park Citizens Assn., 1981-82; dir. Greenwood Homes, Inc., Fairfax County Dept. Housing and Cmty. Devel., 1983—; active Gala Com. Spotlight the Kennedy Ctr., Pres. Adv. Com. on the Arts, 1986-87, Mason Dist. Rep. Com., 1981-91, Fairfax County Young Reps., Fairfax County Rep. Com., 1982—; founding chmn., charter mem. Mason Dist. Jaycees, 1984-86; sec., gen. counsel, bd. dirs. U.S. Assocs. for the Cultural Triangle in Sri Lanka, 1983-90; commr. Consumer Protection Commn., Fairfax County, 1982—, chmn., 1996-97; towing adv. bd. Fairfax County, 1993—; Ravenwood precinct chmn. Rep. Orgn., Falls Church, Va., 1982-90, 97—; bd. dirs. PTA Baileys Elem. Magnet Sch., 1995-99, v.p., 1996-97. Named to Honorable Order Ky. Cols. Mem. ABA, NRA (life), Am. Fedn. Musicians (life, emeritus), Assn. Former Intelligence Officers, Masons (Grand Sword Bearer 1992), Shriners, Tall Cedars, Scottish Rite, Moose, Royal Arch, Phi Kappa Phi, Phi Alpha Delta (nat. capital area alumni chpt. justice 1984-86, 94-96). Methodist. Avocation: music. Administrative and regulatory, Corporate, general, General practice. Home: 6315 Anneliese Dr Falls Church VA 22044-1620 Office: 5201 Leesburg Pike Ste 1108 Falls Church VA 22041-3268 E-mail: kirklaw@fcc.net.

KIRK, JOHN MACGREGOR, lawyer; b. Flint, Mich., Mar. 9, 1938; s. R. Dean and Berenice E. (Mac Gregor) K.; m. Carol Lasko, June 8, 1971; children: John M. Jr., Caroline Dwyer. BA, Washington & Lee U., 1960, LLB, 1962; LLM in Taxation, NYU, 1967. Bar: Mich. 1962, U.S. Ct. Mil. Appeals 1966, U.S. Supreme Ct. 1966, U.S. Tax Ct. 1969, U.S. Dist. Ct. (ea. dist.) Mich. 1982, U.S. Ct. Appeals (6th cir.) 1983. Trial atty. tax divsn. U.S. Dept. Justice, Washington, 1967-72; assoc. Boyer & Briggs, Bloomfield Hills, Mich., 1972-74; ptnr. Butzel, Long, Gust, Klein & Van Zile, Detroit, 1975-78; mem. Meyer, Kirk, Snyder & Lynch P.L.L.C., Bloomfield Hills, 1978—. Mem., past pres. Friends of Baldwin Pub. Libr., Birmingham, Mich., 1972—. Mem. ABA, State Bar Mich., Oakland County Bar Assn., Detroit Bar Assn., Birmingham Rotary, Walloon Yacht Club (treas., past commodore 1960—). Republican. Presbyterian. Estate planning, Probate (including wills, trusts), Estate taxation. Home: 4350 Yale Ct Bloomfield Hills MI 48302-1669 Office: Meyer Kirk Snyder and Lynch PLLC 100 W Long Lake Rd Ste 100 Bloomfield Hills MI 48304-2773 E-mail: jkirk@meyerkirk.com.

KIRK, JOHN ROBERT, JR., lawyer; b. Stuart, Va., June 21, 1935; s. John Robert and Mary Elise (Mustaine) K.; m. Margarite Conover Kirk; children: Karen Louise, Laura Elise, Rebecca Elizabeth. Student, Rice Inst., 1953-56; BSChemE, U. Tex., 1959; JD, U. Houston, 1966. Bar: Tex. 1966, U.S. Patent and Trademark Office 1967, U.S. Supreme Ct. 1973, U.S. Dist. Ct. (so. dist.) Tex. 1974, U.S. Ct. Claims 1975, U.S. Dist. Ct. (no. dist.) Tex. 1977, U.S. Ct. Appeals (5th cir.) 1980, U.S. Ct. Appeals (11th cir.) 1981, U.S. Ct. Appeals (Fed. cir.) 1983. Patent atty. Jefferson Chem. Co., Houston, 1966-69; mgr. patent divsn., 1969-72; mem. Pravel, Gambrell, Hewitt, Kirk & Kimball, P.C., Houston, 1972-84; ptnr., 1973-84, Baker & Kirk, P.C., 1984-87, Baker, Kirk & Bissex, P.C., 1987-90, Baker, Kirk & Lindsay, P.C., 1990-93, Jenkens & Gilchrist, 1993—. Dir. Nat. Inventors Hall of Fame Found, Inc., 1979-82, 87-97, treas., 1983-84, v.p., 1984-86, pres., 1986-87; adv. bd. Intellectual Property Law Program U. Houston, 1991-2000, John Marshall Law Sch., 1999—, chair; adv. bd. Gulf Coast Regional Small Bus. Devel. Ctr., 1994—, Tex. Mfg. Assistance Ctr., Inc., 1995—. Lt. USMCR, 1958-60. Fellow: Coll. State Bar Tex., Houston Bar Found. (life), Tex. Bar Found. (life); mem.: ABA (com. chair 1982—90, intellectual property law sect. coun. 1990—94, vice chmn. 1994—95, chmn. 1996—97, standing com. on specialization 2002—, com. chair 2002—), Am. Intellectual Property Law Assn., State Bar Tex. (chair intellectual property law sect. 1977—78), Nat. Inventive Thinking Assn. (adv. dir. 1990—2000), Licensing Exec. Soc., Houston Bar Assn., Houston Intellectual Property Law Assn. (bd. govs. 1986—92, pres. 1990—91), Commn. of Patents Edn. Roundtable (commr. 1987—95), Nat. Coun. Intellectual Property Law Assns. (vice chmn. 1986—87, chmn. 1987—88), Garden of the Gods Club, Lakeside Country Club, Union League Club Chgo. Republican. Baptist. Intellectual property, Patent, Trademark and copyright. Office: 1100 Louisiana St Ste 1800 Houston TX 77002-5215 E-mail: jkirk@jenkens.com.

KIRK, PATRICK LAINE, lawyer; b. South Bend, Ind., May 12, 1948; s. Jerry W. and Vivian E. (Evans) K.; m. Cheryl A. Ensminger, Dec. 30, 1967; children: Kevin P., Travis S. BA, Valparaiso U., 1970, JD, 1973. Bar: N.Y. 1974, U.S. Dist. Ct. (no. dist.) N.Y. 1977, U.S. Supreme Ct. 1986. Ptnr. Grilli & Kirk, Herkimer, N.Y., 1974-89; asst. dist. atty. Herkimer County, Herkimer, N.Y., 1976-78, chief asst. dist. atty., 1978-86, 1978-86, dist. atty., 1986-91, county judge and county surrogate, 1992—; acting justice Supreme Ct. of N.Y., 1997—2001. Counsel Herkimer Cen. Sch., 1974-76; asst. counsel Village of Herkimer, N.Y., 1981-89; lectr. Police Tng. Sch., Utica, N.Y., 1979-91, Arson Seminar, 1987, Rape Crisis Tng.; tchr. Herkimer County C.C., 1981; criminal justice com. Nat. Conf. State Trial Ct. Judges. Advisor Law Explorer Post, Herkimer, 1974-76; bd. dirs. Martin Luther Home, Clinton, N.Y., 1980, Herkimer County Drug Task Force; chmn. sect. Mohawk Valley United Fund, Ilion, N.Y., 1985; mem. Arson Task Force, 1986-91. Mem. ABA (N.Y. del. to nat. conf. of spl. court judges 1995), N.Y. State Bar Assn. (jud. adminstrn. com.), Internat. Narcotics Enforcement Officers Assn., Drug Enforcement Assn. N.Y. (v.p. 1990-91), N.Y. State County Judges Assn., N.Y. State Surrogate Judges Assn., Am. Judges Assn., Elks. Republican. Lutheran. Criminal. Home: 840 W German St Herkimer NY 13350-2136 Office: Herkimer County Facility 301 N Washington St Herkimer NY 13350

KIRK-DUGGAN, MICHAEL ALLAN, retired law, economics and computer sciences educator; b. Stevens Point, Wis., Dec. 15, 1931; s. Frank E. and Dorothy Ada (Darrow) Duggan; married July 1956 (div. Jan. 1981); children: Michelle, Cheryl, Michael, Christopher, Robert, Siobhan, Mary; m. Cheryl Ann Kirk, Jan. 1, 1983. BS in Math., Coll. Holy Cross, 1953; postgrad., U. Minn., 1953—56; JD, LLB, Boston Coll., 1956; M in Patent Law, Georgetown U., 1959. Bar: Mass. 1956, U.S. Supreme Ct. 1961; qualified trial/def. counsel Gen. Cts. Martial, 1965; cert. cmty. based conflict resolution, 1994. Sr. engr. Sylvania Programming Lab., Needham, Mass., 1960—61; trial atty. antitrust divsn. U.S. Dept. Justice, 1961—67; asst. prof. econs. Whittemore Sch., U. N.H., Durham, 1967—69; comdr. U.S. Naval Intelligence Res., 1956—78; adminstrv. judge Atomic Safety and Licensing Bd. Panel, Washington, 1972—89; prof. bus. law and computer scis. U. Tex., Austin, 1969—93, prof. emeritus, 1993—. Apptd. adv. procurator Tribunal, Diocese of Raleigh, 1995-97; editor-in-chief Computing Revs., N.Y.C., 1969-74. Author: Antitrust & U.S. Supreme Court, 1829-1984, 1984, Computer Utility, 1972, Law and the Computer, 1973, Paul Robeson Movies and Discography, 1998, Amazon Reviews; editor: Legal Developments, J. Marketing, 1967-93, Legal Comments; contbr. numerous articles to profl. jours. Head Profs. for Johnson, Durham, 1968; eucharistic min., lector, lay pres. St. Columba Cath. Ch., Oakland, Calif., 1997—; del. Tex. Dem. Com., Austin, 1972; IRS Vol. Income Tax Assistance, 1993-97. Mem. Mensa, Friend of Bill W. Democrat. Avocations: computer guru/hacker, semi-pro photographer, choral. Home: 4872 Reno Ln Richmond CA 94803-3850 E-mail: kirkdugg@attbi.com.

KIRKPATRICK, ANDREW BOOTH, JR., lawyer; b. Asheville, N.C., Jan. 16, 1929; s. Andrew Booth and Gertrude Elizabeth (Ingle) K.; m. Frances Gordon Cone, Oct. 9, 1954; children: Christine, Melissa, Charles. BS cum laude, Davidson Coll., 1949; LLB magna cum laude, Harvard U., 1954. Bar: Del. 1954, Fla. 1955. Law clk. U.S. Ct. Appeals 3d Cir., 1954-55; assoc. Morris, Nichols, Arsht & Tunnell, Wilmington, Del., 1955-58, ptnr., 1958-95, of counsel, 1995—. Chmn. censor com. Supreme Ct. Del., 1970-78. Trustee U. Del.; trustee Unidel Found., Inc.; pres. Young Republicans of New Castle County, 1957-58; chmn. Kennett Pike Assn., Wilmington, 1967-68; chmn. Gov.'s Commn. on Organized Crime, 1972-73; trustee Tatnall Sch., Inc., 1972-82. 1st lt. inf. U.S. Army, 1951-53. Fellow Am. Coll. Trial Lawyers; mem. Del. Bar Assn. (pres. 1978-79), Wilmington Club, Wilmington Country Club, Vicmead Hunt Club, Phi Beta Kappa. Presbyterian. Federal civil litigation, State civil litigation, Corporate, general. Home: 9 Barley Mill Dr Wilmington DE 19807-2217 Office: Morris Nichols Arsht & Tunnell PO Box 1347 Wilmington DE 19899-1347

KIRKPATRICK, CARL KIMMEL, prosecutor; b. Kingsport, Tenn., Aug. 2, 1936; s. Carl Kimmel and Alice (Rowland) K.; m. Barbara G. Kirkpatrick, Aug. 7, 1992; 1 child, Carl Kimmel III. BA, Vanderbilt U., 1959, JD, 1962. Bar: Tenn. 1962, U.S. Dist. Ct. (ea. dist.) Tenn. 1964. Pvt. practice, Kingsport, 1962-66; asst. dist. atty. 20th Jud. Dist. Sullivan County, Tenn., 1963-64; dist. atty. gen. 2d Jud. Dist. Tenn., 1966-93; U.S. atty. U.S. Dept. of Justice, Knoxville, Tenn., 1993-2001; ret., 2001. Mem. Nat. Dist. Attys. Assn. (bd. dirs. 1983-93), Knoxville Bar Assn., Phi Delta Phi. Democrat. Baptist. Avocations: motorcycle riding, sport shooting, gardening. Office: US Attys Office 800 Market St Ste 211 Knoxville TN 37902-2342*

KIRKPATRICK, JOHN EVERETT, lawyer; b. Meadville, Pa., Aug. 20, 1929; s. Francis Earl and Marjorie Eloise (Roudebush) K.; m. Patricia Ann Benkert, Aug. 9, 1952 (div. June 1963); children: Amy Kirkpatrick Fidler, John Scot, Ann Kirkpatrick Mullen; m. Phyllis Jean Daeuble, Aug. 31, 1963. AB, Amherst Coll., 1951; JD, Harvard U., 1954. Bar: Ohio 1955, Ill. 1962. Assoc. Squire, Sanders & Dempsey, Cleve., 1954-61, Kirkland, Ellis, Hodson, Chaffetz & Masters, Chgo., 1962-64; sr. ptnr. Kirkland & Ellis, Chgo., 1965—. Contbr. articles on tax and estate planning to profl. jours. Mem. Cen. DuPage Hosp. Devel. Commn., Winfield, Ill.; elder 1st Presbyn. Ch., Wheaton, Ill., 1983—. Mem. ABA, Ill. State Bar Assn., Chgo. Bar Assn.,Glen Oak Club (Glen Ellyn, Ill.), Lago Mar Club (Plantation, Fla.). Clubs: Chgo. Golf (Wheaton), Mid Am. (Chgo.). Republican. Avocation: golf. Corporate, general, Estate planning, Probate (including wills, trusts). Office: Kirkland & Ellis 200 E Randolph St Fl 54 Chicago IL 60601-6636

KIRSCH, FLORENCE WEITZ, lawyer; b. Bklyn., Feb. 16, 1922; d. Harry and Rose (Copland) Weitz; m. Seymour D. Kirsch, Nov. 28, 1946; children: Roberta K. Feldman, Kenneth C., Harold F. BBA, Baruch Coll., 1943; JD, Bklyn. Law Sch., 1945. Bar: N.Y. 1945, Mass. 1965. Pvt. practice, Marblehead, Mass., 1965—. CPA, Marblehead, 1966-2002. Estate planning, Probate (including wills, trusts), Property, real (including real estate development, water). Home and Office: 20 Homestead Rd Marblehead MA 01945-1123

KIRSCH, LAURENCE STEPHEN, lawyer; b. Washington, July 20, 1957; s. Ben and Bertha (Gomberg) K.; m. Celia Goldman, Aug. 19, 1979; children: Rachel Miriam, Max David. BAS, MS, U. Pa., 1979; JD, Harvard U., 1982. Bar: D.C. 1982, U.S. Ct. Appeals (3d cir.) 1983, (5th cir.) 1997, (9th cir.) 2001, U.S. Dist. Ct. D.C. 1985, U.S. Ct. Appeals (D.C. cir.) 1985, U.S. Supreme Ct. 1987; registered environ. assessor, Calif. 1988. Law clk. to presiding judge Pa. Dist. Ct., Phila., 1982-83; vis. asst. prof. law U. Bridgeport (Conn.) Law Sch., 1983-84; assoc. Cadwalader, Wickersham & Taft, Washington, 1984-90, ptnr., 1991—2002; with Shea Gardner, Washington, 2002—. Chmn. steering coms. Superfund. Editor-in-chief Indoor Pollution Law Report, 1987-91; mng. editor Harvard Environ. Law Rev., 1981-82; contbr. articles to profl. jours. Mem. ABA, Fed. Bar Assn., AAAS, Air and Waste Mgmt. Assn. (indoor air quality com.), Environ. Law Inst., Nat. Inst. Bldg. Scis. (indoor air quality com.), Am. Soc. Testing and Measurement (indoor air quality com.), Phi Beta Kappa. Administrative and regulatory, Federal civil litigation, Environmental. Home: 7212 Longwood Dr Bethesda MD 20817-2122 Office: Shea & Gardner 1800 Massachusetts Ave NW Washington DC 20036 E-mail: lkirsch@sheagardner.com.

KIRSCH, LYNN, lawyer; b. New Orleans, Oct. 31, 1964; d. Henry C. and Therese M. ((Guenther) K. BS in Bus. Mgmt., Fla. State U., Panama City, 1992; JD, U. Ariz., 1995. Bar: Nev. 1995, U.S. Dist. Ct. Nev. 1995, U.S. Ct. Fed. Claims 1997, U.S. Ct. Appeals (9th cir.) 1998, U.S. Supreme Ct. 1999. Law clk. U.S. Atty.'s Office, Phoenix, 1993, Slutes, Sakrison, Evan, Grant & Pelander, Tucson, 1993-94, Lionel, Sawyer & Collins, Las Vegas, 1994; judicial extern Fed. Dist. Ct., Tucson, 1994; rsch. asst. U. Ariz., Tucson, 1994-95; law clk. Jacob & Fishbein, Tucson, 1994-95; assoc. Goold, Patterson, DeVore & Rondau, Las Vegas, 1995-97, Curran & Parry, Las Vegas, 1997-99, Bernhard & Bradley, Las Vegas, 1999—2001; gen. counsel Unlt. Holdings, Inc., 2001—. Mem. Justice of the Peace pro-tempore panel, Las Vegas Twp., County of Clark, 1998-2000; alt. mcpl. ct. judge City of Las Vegas, 1999—; vol. mediator clerk county social svs. Neighborhood Justice Ctr.; arbitrator BBB AutoLine; instr. The Nonprofit Corp., Nevada, UNLV Continuing Edn., 2002, 2003. Article editor U. Ariz. Law Rev., 1994-95. Mem. Jr. League of Las Vegas, 1998—, league atty., 2000—; mem. State of Nev. Commn. on Postsecondary Edn., 1998-01, Social Register of Las Vegas, House of Blues Found. Adv. Bd. Recipient Cert. Appreciation, U.S. Atty.'s Office, Phoenix, 1993, AmJur award Lawyers Coop. Publ., Tucson, 1993. Mem. ABA (litigation sect., assoc. editor The Affiliate 1999-2000), ATLA, State Bar Nev. (chair young lawyers sect. 1999-2000, so. Nev. disciplinary bd., fee dispute arbitration com.), Clark County Bar Assn. (trial by peers com., cmty. svc. com.), Nev. Trial Lawyers Assn., So. Nev. Assn. Women Attys. Avocations: horseback riding, hiking, skydiving. General civil litigation, Construction, Government contracts and claims. Office: 2685 S Jones Blvd Las Vegas NV 89146

KIRSCHBAUM, MYRON, lawyer; b. N.Y.C., Nov. 20, 1949; s. Jonas and Doris (Rose) K.; m. Esther Weiner, June 23, 1971; children: Rachel, Shoshana Stein, Yisrael. BA, Yeshiva U., 1971; JD, Harvard U., 1974. Bar: N.Y. 1975, U.S. Dist. Ct. (so. dist.) N.Y. 1975, U.S. Dist. Ct. (no. dist.) Calif. 1989, U.S. Ct. Appeals (2d cir.) 1975, U.S. Ct. Appeals (9th cir.) 1990, U.S. Ct. Appeals (fed. cir.) 1994, U.S. Ct. Appeals (3d cir.) 2001. Law clk. U.S. Ct. Appeals (2d cir.), N.Y.C., 1974-75; assoc. Kaye, Scholer, Fierman, Hays & Handler, N.Y.C., 1975-82, ptnr., 1983—. Editor Harvard Law Rev., 1972-73, case and comment editor, 1973-74. Mem. ABA, Assn. Bar City N.Y. General civil litigation, Insurance, Securities. Office: Kaye Scholer LLP 425 Park Ave New York NY 10022-3506 Business E-Mail: mkirschbaum@kayescholer.com.

KIRSCHNER, RICHARD, lawyer; b. Phila., Apr. 3, 1932; s. Walter and Rebekah (Muller) K.; m. Beverly Yanoff, June 7, 1953; children— Stefi Lynn, Lee Scott, Linda Sue, Jason Alan; m. M. Kay Gartrell, July 30, 1978; 1 dau., Meredith Anne. B.A., Pa. State U., 1954; J.D., U. Pa., 1957; LLM, Am. U. Wash. Coll. Law, 2002. Bar: Pa. 1958, D.C. 1982. Practice labor law, 1958— ; sr. ptnr. Kirschner Weinberg & Dempsey, Washington, 1982—90 ; ptnr. Kirschner & Gartrell P.C., 1990-; adj. prof. labor law Temple U., Phila., 1976-82; lectr., speaker in field. Mem. ABA, Pa. Bar Assn., Phila. Bar Assn., D.C. Bar Assn. Author articles on labor law. Labor (including EEOC, Fair Labor Standards Act, labor-management relations, NLRB, OSHA).

KIRSCHNER, WILLIAM STEVEN, lawyer; b. Los Angeles, Jan. 9, 1950; s. Robert and Ethel Ada (Bershad) K.; m. Sandy Bernstein, Aug. 31, 1976 (div. 1981); m. Laurie Kay Miller, Aug. 11, 1983; 1 child, Beryl Susan Elizabeth Miller. BA, Bklyn Coll., 1971; JD, Fordham U., 1976. Bar: N.D. 1980, Minn. 1981, Ga. 1977, N.Mex. 1995, U.S. Dist. Ct. N.D. 1981, U.S. Dist. Ct. Minn. 1985, U.S. Ct. Appeals (8th cir.) 1985. Assoc. Brian Nelson, Fargo, N.D., 1980-82; sole practice Fargo, 1982-84; ptnr. Kirschner & Baker Legal Clinic, Fargo, 1984-86; mng. atty. William Kirschner & Assocs., Fargo, 1986—2001; asst. county atty. Dona Ana County, N.Mex., 2001—02; city atty. City of Alamogordo, N.Mex., 2002—; assoc. Holt & Babington, Las Cruces, N.Mex., 2003—. Bd. dirs. Alcohol Out Reach, Fargo, 1983-85, Youth Depot, Fargo, 1985, Temple Beth El, Fargo, 1986-88; sec. legal com. N.D. ACLU, 1986-95. Francis Kneller scholar Bklyn. Coll., 1969. Mem. Cass County Bar Assn., Nat. Lawyers Guild, N.D. Trial Lawyers Assn., Fargo Criminal Def. Lawyers Assn. (organizer), N.D. State Bar Assn. (ethics com. 1987-91). Avocations: sailing, skiing, tennis. Criminal, Family and matrimonial, General practice. Office: Holt & Babington PO Box 2699 Las Cruces NM 88004

KIRSHBAUM, HOWARD M. retired judge, arbiter; b. Oberlin, Ohio, Sept. 19, 1938; s. Joseph and Gertrude (Morris) K.; m. Priscilla Joy Parmakian, Aug. 15, 1964; children— Audra Lee, Andrew William. BA, Yale U., 1960; AB, Cambridge U., 1962, MA, 1966; LL.B., Harvard U., 1965. Ptnr. Zarlengo and Kirshbaum, Denver, 1969-75; judge Denver Dist. Ct., Denver, 1975-80, Colo. Ct. Appeals, Denver, 1980-83; justice Colo. Supreme Ct., Denver, 1983-97; arbiter Jud. Arbiter Group, Inc., Denver, 1997—, sr. judge, 1997—; adj. prof. law U. Denver, 1970—. Dir. Am. Law Inst. Phila., 1982-2002, Am. Judicature Soc., Chgo., 1979-2002, Colo. Jud. Inst. Denver, 1979-89; pres. Colo. Legal Care Soc., Denver, 1974-75. Bd. dirs. Young Artists Orch., Denver, 1976-85; pres. Community Arts Symphony, Englewood, Colo., 1972-74; dir. Denver Opportunity, Inc., Denver, 1972-74; vice-chmn. Denver Council on Arts and Humanities, 1969 Mem.: ABA (standing com. pub. edn. 1996—2001), Soc. Profls. in Dispute Resolution, Denver Bar Assn. (trustee 1981—83), Colo. Bar Assn. Avocation: music performance. Office: Jud Arbiter Group Inc 1601 Blake St Ste 400 Denver CO 80202-1328

KIRTLEY, JANE ELIZABETH, law educator; b. Indpls., Nov. 7, 1953; d. William Raymond and Faye Marie (Price) K.; m. Stephen Jon Cribari, May 8, 1985. BS in Journalism, Northwestern U., 1975, MS in Journalism, 1976; JD, Vanderbilt U., 1979. Bar: N.Y. 1980, D.C. 1982, Va. 1995, U.S. Dist. Ct. (we. dist.) N.Y. 1980, U.S. Dist. Ct. D.C. 1982, U.S. Ct. Claims 1982, U.S. Ct. Appeals (4th cir.) 1982, U.S. Ct. Appeals (D.C. cir.) 1985, U.S. Ct. Appeals (10th cir.) 1996, U.S. Ct. Appeals (5th cir.) 1997, U.S. Ct. Appeals (6th cir.) 1998, U.S. Ct. Appeals (6th and 11th cir.) 1998, U.S. Supreme Ct. 1985. Assoc. Nixon, Hargrave, Devans & Doyle, Rochester, N.Y., 1979-81, Washington, 1981-84; exec. dir. Reporters Com. for Freedom of Press, Arlington, Va., 1985-99; Silha prof. media ethics & law U. Minn. Sch. Journalism & Mass Comm., Mpls., 1999—; dir. Silha Ctr. for Study of Media Ethics and Law, Mpls., 2000—; mem. affiliated faculty U. Minn. Law Sch., 2001—. Mem. adj. faculty Am. U. Sch. Comm., 1988-98; mem. affiliated law faculty U. Minn., 2001—. Exec. articles editor Vanderbilt U. Jour. Transnat. Law, 1978-79; editor: The News Media and the Law, 1985—, The First Amendment Handbook, 1987, 4th edit., 1995, Agents of Discovery, 1991, 93, 95, Pressing Issues, 1998-99; columnist NEPA Bull., 1988-99, Virginia's Press, 1991-99, Am. Journalism Rev., 1995—, W.Va.'s Press, 1997-99, Tenn. Press, 1997-99; mem. editl. bd. Comm. Law and Policy. Bd. dirs. Sigma Delta Chi Found., Indpls. Mem. ABA, N.Y. State Bar Assn., D.C. Bar Assn., Va. State Bar Assn., Sigma Delta Chi. Home: 3645 46th Ave S Minneapolis MN 55406-2937 Office: 111 Murphy Hall 206 Church St SE Minneapolis MN 55455-0488 E-mail: kirtl001@tc.umn.edu.

KIRVELAITIS, VYTENIS P. lawyer, accountant; b. Chgo., Aug. 3, 1963; s. Justinas and Vilune Kirvelaitis. BSBA, Roosevelt U., Chgo., 1981—85; JD, U. Ill., Coll. Law, Champaign, 1985—88. Cert. Pub. Acct., Ill., 1988, lic. Ill. Dept. Profl. Regulation, 1990; bar: Ill. 1988, U.S. Dist. Ct. (no. dist.) 2002. Sr. tax cons. Arthur Andersen LLP, Chgo., 1988—91; mgr., state & local taxes R. R. Donnelley & Sons Co., Downers Grove, Ill., 1991—. Trustee, treas., chmn. fin. com., chmn. policy & pers. com. Lemont Pub. Libr. Dist., Ill., 1999—; dir., chmn. by-laws com. Lithuanian Found., Inc., Lemont, Ill., 1990—; dir. Lithuanian Scouts Assn., Inc., Lemont, Ill., 2000—, Vydunas Youth Fund, Inc, Lemont, Ill., 2000—03. Mem.: Chgo. Bar Assn. (corr.; chmn., state and local tax com. 2000—01). Roman Catholic. Avocations: college sports, camping. State and local taxation, Corporate taxation, Personal income taxation. Home: 1 E Custer St Lemont IL 60439-3801 Office: R R Donnelley & Sons Co 3075 Highland Pkwy Downers Grove IL 60515-1261 Office Fax: 630-322-6155. Personal E-mail: vytenis_kirvelaitis@hotmail.com. E-mail: vytenis.kirvelaitis@rrd.com.

KIRVEN, TIMOTHY J. lawyer; b. Buffalo, Wyo., May 26, 1949; s. William J. and Ellen F. (Farrell) K.; m. Elizabeth J. Adams, Oct. 31, 1970; 1 child, Kristen B. BA in English, U. Notre Dame, 1971; JD, U. Wyo., 1974. Bar: Wyo. 1974. Ptnr. Kirven & Kirven, PC, Buffalo, 1974—. Author Rocky Mountain Mineral Law, 1982. Mem. Johnson County Libr. Br., Buffalo. Mem. ABA (ho. of dels. 2002—), Wyo. State Bar (pres. 1998-99), Johnson County Bar Assn., Western States Bar Conf. (pres. 1998-99), Rotary (pres. Buffalo club 1988-89, youth exch. program chmn. 1993-98). Home: PO Box C Buffalo WY 82834-0060 Office: Kirven & Kirven PC PO Box 640 Buffalo WY 82834-0640

KIRWAN, R. DEWITT, lawyer; b. Albany, Calif., Aug. 30, 1942; s. Patrick William and Lucille Anne (Vartanian) K.; m. Betty-Jane Elias, June 29, 1969 (div. 1982); children: Katherine DeWitt, Andrew Elias; m. Nancy Jane Evers, Oct. 27, 1984; 1 child, Fletcher Evers. BA, U. Calif., Berkeley, 1966; JD, U. San Francisco, 1969. Bar: Calif. 1971, U.S. Dist. Ct. (ctrl. dist.) Calif. 1971, U.S. Ct. Appeals (9th cir.) 1971. Assoc. Schell & Delamer, L.A., 1971-73; ptnr. Lillick & McHose, L.A., 1973-90, Pillsbury Madison & Sutro, L.A., 1990-98, Akin, Gump, Strauss, Hauer & Feld, L.A., 1998—. Chmn., exec. bd. U. Calif., Berkeley, 1988-97, trustee U. Calif. Berkeley Found., 1995-98; bd. dirs., trustee Pacific Crest Outward Bound Sch., 1993-99; bd. dirs. L.A. Philharm. Assn., 1985-89, pres., 1986-88, mem. bus. and profl. com.; bd. dirs. Pasadena (Calif.) Symphony Assn., 1978-82; adv. bd. OpusAlliance.com., 1999-2001. Capt. USAR, 1966-71. Mem. ABA, Am. Bd. Trial Advs., Calif. Club. Democrat. Roman Catholic. Avocations: fly fishing, mountaineering, hunting, skiing. Federal civil litigation, General civil litigation, State civil litigation. Office: Akin Gump Strauss Hauer & Feld Ste 2400 2029 Century Park E Los Angeles CA 90067-3012

KIRWIN, THOMAS F. prosecutor; Interim U.S. atty. no. dist., Fla., 2001; prosecutor U.S. Atty. Off., Fla., 2003—. Office: 315 S Calhoun St Ste 510 Tallahassee FL 32301 Office Fax: 850-942-8429.*

KISER, JACKSON L. federal judge; b. Welch, W.Va., June 24, 1929; m. Carole Gorman; children: Jackson, William, John Michael, Elizabeth Carol. BA, Concord Coll., 1951; JD, Washington and Lee U., 1952. Bar: Va. Asst. U.S. atty. Western Dist. Va., 1958-61; assoc., then ptnr. R.R. Young, Young, Kiser, Haskins, Mann, Gregory & Young P.C., Martinsville, Va., 1961-82; judge U.S. Dist. Ct. (we. dist.) Va., 1982-93, chief judge, 1993-97, sr. judge, 1997—. Mem. Martinsville City Sch. Bd., 1971-77. With JAGC U.S. Army, 1952-55, capt. Res., 1955-61. Mem. Am. Coll. Trial Lawyers (state com.), Va. Bar Assn. (exec. com.), Va. State Bar, Va. Trial Lawyers Assn., 4th Cir. Jud. Conf. (permanent), Martinsville-Henry County Bar Assn., Order of Coif. Office: US Dist Ct PO Box 3326 700 Main St Danville VA 24543-3326

KISSEL, PETER CHARLES, lawyer; b. Watertown, N.Y., Sept. 29, 1947; s. Laurence Haas and Catherine Cantwell (Weldon) Kissel; m. Sharon Darlene Murphy, June 14, 1970. AB, Syracuse U., 1969; JD, Am. U., 1972. Bar: DC 1973, US Court Claims 1976, US Court Appeals (3d cir) 1976, US Supreme Court 1978, US Dist Ct DC 1979, US Ct Appeals (9th cir) 1979, US Ct Appeals (DC cir) 1983, US Ct Appeals (5th cir) 1988. Atty.-advisor Fed. Power Commn., Washington, 1972-74; atty. pub. utilities, 1974-77; assoc. O'Connor & Hannan, Washington, 1977-79, ptnr., 1979-87, Baller Hammett, Washington, 1987-93; ptnr., CFO, Grammer, Kissel, Robbins, Skancke & Edwards (GKRSE), Washington, 1993—. Co-bus mgr Energy Law Jour, Washington, 1981, asst editor, 1982—89, bus. mgr., 1989—92. Contbr. articles profl jours. Mem Washington adv. bd. Syracuse U., 1995—; mem. adv. bd. Maxwell Sch. Citizenship and Pub. Affairs, 2002—; bd. dirs. Episcopal Caring Response to AIDS Inc., 1988—93, v.p., 1990—91, pres., 1992, mem. exec. com., 1990—93; mem vestry St Patrick's Episcopal Ch, Washington, 1975—78, chmn. ann. fundraising campaign, 1987—89; bd. dirs. PRISM, 1996—97, Waterpower XII Steering Com., 2000—01. Recipient Spl Award, Fed Power Comn, 1973. Mem.: Syracuse Univ. Soc. Fellows, Bar Assn. DC, John Sherman Myers Soc., Nat. Hydropower Assn., Energy Bar Assn. (vice chmn com on publs 1984—85, chmn com on hydroelectric regulation 1991—92), Phi Kappa Psi. Democrat. Episcopalian. Avocations: gardening, American history, Irish history. Administrative and regulatory, Appellate, FERC practice. Home: 5604 Utah Ave NW Washington DC 20015-1230 Office: GKRSE 1500 K St NW Ste 330 Washington DC 20005 E-mail: pckissel@GKRSE-law.com.

KITAGAWA, AUDREY EMIKO, lawyer, retired; b. Mar. 31, 1951; d. Yonoichi and Yoshiko (Nagaishi) K. BA cum laude, U. So. Calif., 1973; JD, Boston Coll., 1976. Bar: Hawaii 1977, U.S. Dist. Ct. Hawaii 1977. Assoc. Rice, Lee & Wong, Honolulu, 1977-80; pvt. practice Honolulu, 1980-96; head Sri Ramakrishna Spiritual Family, 1992—. Advisor Office of Spl. Rep. of Sec. Gen. for Children and Armed Conflict (UN); mem. internat. adv. coun. Internat. Caring Comtys., Toda Inst. for Peace and Global Policy Rsch.; exec. coun. World Commn. Global Consciousness and Spirituality. Coun. Global Action to Stop War; founder, dir. Vision for Humanity; bd. dirs. Wall St. Rotary; co-facilitator United Religions Initiative, UN Cooperation Circle; co-dir. Mereon Inst. Mem.: ABA, Religious Initiative at the UN Cooperation Cir., Women in Internat. Security, Hawaii Bar Assn., Spiritual Caucus at the UN, Honolulu Club. Republican. Family and matrimonial. Office: 327 E 48th St #31A New York NY 10017 E-mail: dmaudrey@verizon.net.

KITAY, HARVEY ROBERT, lawyer, investment manager; b. Bklyn., Oct. 16, 1931; s. David and Celia (Sherman) K.; m. Betty Finkelstein, Sept. 3, 1956; children: Robin Ann, William Douglas. BA, NYU, 1953; JD, Harvard U., 1956. Bar: N.Y. 1957. Acct. Peat Marwick Mitchel, N.Y.C., 1956-57; assoc. Law Office Gustave Simons, N.Y.C., 1957-70; ptnr. Kolleeny, Kitay & Hort, N.Y.C., 1970—. Mgr. Sahabe Securities Co., Scarsdale, N.Y., 1960—. Mem. ABA, N.Y. State Bar Assn., N.Y. Co. Bar Assn., Assn. of Bar of City of N.Y. Estate planning, Probate (including wills, trusts), Taxation, general. Home: 38 Montrose Rd Scarsdale NY 10583-1127 Office: Kolleeny Kitay & Hort 500 Fifth Ave Ste 1610 New York NY 10110 E-mail: hkitayesq@aol.com.

KITCH, EDMUND WELLS, lawyer, educator, private investor; b. Wichita, Kans., Nov. 3, 1939; s. Paul R. and Josephine (Pridmore) K.; m. Joanne Steiner, 1966 (div. 1976); 1 child, Sarah; m. Alison Lauter, Jan. 29, 1978 (div. 2000); children: Andrew, Whitney; m. Gail Lettwich Apr. 26, 2003. BA, Yale U., 1961; JD, U. Chgo., 1964. Bar: Kans. 1964, Ill. 1966, U.S. Supreme Ct. 1973, Va. 1986. Asst. prof. law Ind. U., 1964-65; mem. faculty U. Chgo., 1965-82, prof., 1971-82; prof., mem. Ctr. Advanced Studies U. Va., Charlottesville, 1982-85, Joseph M. Hartfield prof., 1985—, Sullivan and Cromwell rsch. prof., 1996-99. Vis. prof. Bklyn. Law Sch., 1995, Northwestern U., 1996, Georgetown U., 2002, U. Nebr., 2002; spl. asst. solicitor gen. U.S. Dept. Justice, 1973-74; exec. dir. Adv. Com. on Procedural Reform CAB, 1975-76; reporter Com. on Pattern Jury Instruction, Ill. Supreme Ct., 1966-69; mem. com. on pub.-pvt. sector rels. in vaccine innovation Inst. of Medicine, NAS, 1982-85, mem. com. on evaluation polio vaccine, 1987-88. Author: (with Harvey Perlman) Intellectual Property, 5th edit., 1997; Regulation, Federalism and Interstate Commerce, 1981. Contbr. articles to profl. jours. Mem. Va. Bar Assn., Am. Law Inst., Order of Coif, Phi Beta Kappa. Office: U Va Sch Law 580 Massie Rd Charlottesville VA 22903-1738

KITCHEN, CHARLES WILLIAM, lawyer; b. July 17, 1926; s. Karl K. and Lucille W. (Keynes) K.; m. Mary Applegate, July 22, 1950; children: Kenneth K., Guy R., Anne Kitchen Campbell. BA, Western Res. U., 1948, JD, 1950. Bar: Ohio 1950, U.S. Dist. Ct. Ohio 1952, U.S. Ct. Appeals (6th cir.) 1972, U.S. Supreme Ct. 1981. Ptnr. Kitchen, Derry & Barnhouse Co., LPA, Cleve., 1950-97, sr. ptnr., 1972, ret., 1997; life mem., exec. com. 8th Jud. Dist. Ct., 1988-91. Mem. Regional Coun. on Alcoholism, 1981-86, chmn., 1985-86; bd. dirs. Scarborough Hall, 1992-94. With A.C., U.S. Army, 1944-45. Fellow Internat. Acad. Trial Lawyers, Am. Coll. Trial Lawyers (sr. mem.); mem. ABA (sect. tort and ins. practice, sec. litigation), Am. Arbitration Assn. (panelist 1961-91), Am. Bd. Trial Advocates (advocate), Cleve. Assn. Civil Trial Attys. (pres. 1971-72), Ohio Assn. Civil Trial Attys. (pres. 1975-76), Greater Cleve. Bar Assn. (chmn. med.-legal com. 1974-75, chmn. lawyers assistance program 1981-83, chmn. mentor com. 1988-95, jud. campaign com. chmn. 1993-95, trustee 1984-87), Am. Legion, Order of Coif, Beta Theta Pi, Phi Delta Phi. Presbyterian. Federal civil litigation, State civil litigation. Home: 8755 E Old Spanish Ter Dr Tucson AZ 85710 E-mail: ckitch26@aol.com.

KITCHEN, E.C. DEENO, lawyer; b. Tallahassee, May 1, 1942; s. Oscar Edward and Rose (Deeb) K.; m. Patricia Gautier, June 22, 1968; children: Anne-Elizabeth K. Williams, Kimberly Gautier K. Robson, William Gautier, Deeb-Paul II. JD cum laude, U. Fla., 1967. Bar: 1968, U.S. Dist. Ct. (no. and ctrl. dists.) Fla., U.S. Ct. Appeals (3d and 11th cirs.), U.S. Supreme Ct., 1975. Ptnr. Ervin, Varn, Jacobs, Odom & Kitchen, Tallahassee, 1971-88, Kitchen & High, Tallahassee, 1988-93; founding ptnr. Kitchen, Judkins, Simpson & High, Tallahassee, 1993—. Past mem. editl. bd. U. Fla. Law Rev. Chmn. exec. com., Leon County (Fla.) Dem. Party, 1971-73, mem. state exec. com., 1971-75; trustee U. Fla. Law Ctr. Assn.; vol. karate instr., City of Tallahassee. Master Tallahassee Am. Inn of Ct. (charter mem.); fellow Am. Coll. Trial Lawyers, Internat. Soc. Barristers, Am. Bar Found., Fla. Bar Found.; mem. ABA (bd. regents Nat. Coll. Criminal Def., 1981-84, mem. litigation and criminal justice sects.), Am. Bd. Trial Advocates (charter mem. Tallahassee chpt., advocate, pres. 1996), Nat. Assn. Criminal Def. Lawyers, Acad. Fla. Trial Lawyers (bd. dirs. 1983-85, past Eagle sponsor), Florida Bar (bd. cert. trial lawyer 1983, exec. coun. trial lawyers sect. 1980-88, chmn. steering com. trial lawyers sect., chmn. trial advocacy program 1982, 88, faculty mem. and lectr. 1979—, faculty mem. advanced trial advocacy program, exec. coun. criminal law sect. 1976-85, chmn. legis. com., chmn. grievance com. 2d Jud. Cir. Fla. 1979-80, mem. 1977-80), Leading Fla. Attys. (adv. bd.), Order of Coif, Phi Kappa Phi, Phi Alpha Delta (past pres.). Avocations: karate (black belt cuong nhu oriental martial arts, black belt isshin-ryu karate). General civil litigation, Criminal, Personal injury (including property damage). Office: Kitchen Judkins Simpson & High PO Box 10368 Tallahassee FL 32302-2368 and: 1102 N Gadsden St Tallahassee FL 32303-6328 Fax: (850) 561-1471. E-mail: dkitchen@kishlaw.com.

KITCHENS, JOYCE ELLEN, lawyer; b. Jesup, Ga., Oct. 8, 1948; d. Arthur Ellis and Ray Lucille (Burton) K.; m. Larry Keith Brumfield, Aug. 23, 1969 (div. July 1973); m. Jerry Baxter Barnes; stepchildren: Craig Randall Barnes, Suzanne Cynthia Barnes. BA in English Lit., Purdue U., 1970, MA in English Lit., 1972; JD, Emory U., 1982. Bar: Ga. 1982, U.S. Dist. Ct. (no. dist.) Ga. 1982, U.S. Dist. Ct. (mid. dist.) Ga. 1992, U.S. Ct. Appeals (11th cir.) 1982, U.S. Ct. Mil. Appeals 1996, U.S. Tax Ct. 1995, U.S. Ct. Appeals (fed. cir.), 1999. Staff atty. Dept. Vet. Affairs, Atlanta, 1982-89, asst. dist. counsel, 1989-91; pvt. practice Atlanta, 1991—. Adj. faculty Emory U. Sch. Law Mem. Fed. Bar Assn. (pres. Atlanta chpt. 1991-92, 11th cir. officer 1992-98, dep. sec. 1998-99, sec. 1999-2000, pres.-elect, 2002, pres. 2003--), Ansley Kiwanis (past pres. 1992-93, Disting. Svc. award 1991). Democrat. Methodist. Avocations: reading, travel, adventure. General civil litigation, Estate planning, Labor (including EEOC, Fair Labor Standards Act, labor-management relations, NLRB, OSHA). Office: 2973 Hardman Ct Atlanta GA 30305

KITCHIN, JOHN JOSEPH, lawyer; b. Kansas City, Mo., Mar. 23, 1933; s. John Bernard and Delia Clare (White) K.; m. Mary A. Medill, Feb. 15, 1958; children: Teresa M., Nancy J., John T., Barbara A. BA, Rockhurst Coll., 1954; JD cum laude, St. Louis U., 1957. Bar: Mo. 1957. Assoc. Swanson, Midgley Law Firm, Kansas City, 1961-65; ptnr. Swanson, Midgley, Gangwere, Kitchin and McLarney, Kansas City, 1966—, mng. ptnr., 1983—2001. Gen. counsel Nat. Collegiate Athletic Assn. Contbr. articles to profl. jours. Chmn. Kansas City Bd. Liquor Rev.; mem. Avila Coll. Bd. Councillors, Kansas City, 1972-90, pres., 1989-90; trustee Avila Coll., 1991-2000; mem. Seton Ctr., Inc., Kansas City, 1980-99; trustee St. Joseph Health Ctr. Found., 1994-2000, chmn., 2000. Capt. USAF, 1957-61. Mem. ABA, Kansas City Bar Assn., Lawyers Assn. of Kansas City, Am. Judicature Soc., Mo. Bar Assn., Nat. Sports Law Inst. (bd. advisors), Sports Lawyers Assn., Serra Club (pres. 1978-79), St. Teresa Acad. Club (pres. 1976-77), Rotary. Democrat. Roman Catholic. Avocations: golfing, travel, reading. Corporate, general, Entertainment, Sports. Home: 11548 Baltimore Ave Kansas City MO 64114-5554 Office: Swanson Midgely LLC 2420 Pershing Rd Ste 400 Kansas City MO 64108 E-mail: jkitchin@swansonmidgley.com.

KITCHINGS, ALTON DWITH, lawyer; b. Candler County, Ga., Nov. 7, 1923; s. Arthur Mandozier and Eulalia Bolen Kitchings; m. Charlotte Guy, 1946 (div. 1956); 1 child, Rhonda Sutlive; m. Gloria McCall Collins, Aug. 10, 1957; children: Billie Sigmon, Allison Hearn. JD, U. Ga., 1949. Bar: Ga. 1949, U.S. Supreme Ct. 1968. Pvt. practice, Savannah, Ga., 1949—; atty. Office of Price Adminstrn., Savannah, 1950, Dickey, Futrel & Kitchings, Savannah, 1957. Contbr. articles to profl. jours.; author: Cross-Currents in the Winds of Life, 2002. Asst. city atty. City of Savannah, 1959—65. 1st class seaman USN, 1943—45, PTO. Mem.: Ga. Trial Lawyers Assn. (sec., pres. 1985—86, Heritage award 2001), State Bar Ga. (Tradition of Excellence award trial sect. 1989). Baptist. Avocations: golf, hunting, fishing, dancing, travel. Home and Office: 7 Indian Summer Ct Savannah GA 31410 Fax: 912-897-4333.

KITE, MARILYN S. state supreme court justice, lawyer; b. Laramie, Wyo., Oct. 2, 1947; BA with honors, U. Wyo., 1970, JD with honors, 1974. Bar: Wyo. 1974. Mem. Holland & Hart, Jackson, Wyo., 1979—2000; justice Wyo. Supreme Ct., 2000—. Contbr. articles to profl. jours. Mem. ABA (nat. resources sect., litigation sect.), Wyo. State Bar. Address: Wyo Supreme Ct 2301 Capitol Ave Cheyenne WY 82002

KITE, STEVEN B. lawyer; b. Chgo., May 30, 1949; s. Ben and Dolores (Braver) K.; m. Catherine Lapinski, Jan. 13, 1980; children: David, Julia. BA, U. Ill., 1971; JD, Harvard U., 1974. Bar: Ga. 1974, U.S. Dist. Ct. Ga. 1974, U.S. Ct. Appeals (5th and 11th cirs.) 1981, Ill. 1985, Fla. 1986. Ptnr. Kutak Rock, Atlanta, 1974-84, Gardner, Carton & Douglas, Chgo., 1984—. Author, editor: Law For Elderly, 1978; author: Tax-Exempt Financing for Health Care Organizations, 1996; co-author: Bond Financing, 1994. Bd. dirs. Atlanta Legal Aid Soc., 1979-84; trustee Sr. Citizens Met. Atlanta, 1980-83. Mem. ABA, Ill. Bar Assn., State Bar Ga., Chgo. Bar Assn., Fla. Bar Assn., Nat. Assn. Bond Lawyers. Avocations: travel, sports, reading. Municipal (including bonds). Office: Gardner Carton & Douglas LLC 191 N Wacker Dr Ste 3700 Chicago IL 60606 E-mail: skite@gcd.com.

KITTA, JOHN NOAH, lawyer; b. San Francisco, Aug. 26, 1951; s. John E. and Norma Jean (Noah) K. BS, U. Santa Clara, 1973, JD, 1976. Bar: Calif. 1976. Asst. mgr. Transamerica Title Co., Dublin, Calif., 1977-78; assoc. Rhodes, McKeehan & Bernard, Fremont, Calif., 1978-79, sr. atty., 1979—. V.p. Californians Against Fraud, 1996—. Author: Wrongful Discharge...Look Before You Leap, 1990. Commr. Calif. Crime Resistance Task Force, Sacramento; trustee Alameda County Bd. Edn.; del. Dem. Cen. Com., Alameda County, 1980-81, 83-84. Democrat. Corporate, general, Personal injury (including property damage), Property, real (including real estate development, water). Home: 2135 Ocaso Camino Fremont CA 94539-5645 Office: 39560 Stevenson Pl Ste 217 Fremont CA 94539-3074 E-mail: jkitta@aol.com.

KITTELSEN, RODNEY OLIN, lawyer; b. Albany, Wis., Mar. 11, 1917; s. Olen B. and Nellie Winifred (Atkinson) K.; m. Pearle M. Haldiman, Oct. 12, 1940; children: Gregory S., James E., Bradley J. PhB, U. Wis., 1939, LLB, 1940. Spl. agt. FBI, Washington, 1940-46; ptnr. Kittelsen, Barry, Ross, Wellington & Thompson, Monroe, Wis., 1946—. Dist. atty. Green County, Monroe, 1947-53; pres. State Bar Wis., Madison, 1976-77, 83-85; dir. Wis. Law Found., Madison, 1992—. Pres. Monroe Police and Fire Commn., 1947—; legal counsel X-FBI Inc., Quantico, Va., 1986—; mem. Am. Coll. Trust and Estate Coun., Chgo., 1983—. Recipient Outstanding Citizen award Monroe Jaycees, 1977, Outstanding Svc. award Albany FFA, 1991, Disting. Svc. award U. Wis. Law Sch., 1995, Disting. Svc. award U. Wis. Law Alumni Assn., 1995. Fellow: Am. Bar Found.; mem.: Wis. Bar Found., Wis. Law Found. (life), Wis. Bar Assn. Education and schools, General practice, Probate (including wills, trusts). Home: 708 26th Ave Monroe WI 53566-1620 Office: 916 17th Ave Monroe WI 53566-2003

KITTRELL, PAMELA R. lawyer; b. Athens, Ga., June 15, 1965; d. John Edison and Anne (Hagins) K. AB summa cum laude, U. Miami, 1987; JD, U. Mich., 1990. Bar: Fla. 1990, U.S. Dist. Ct. (so. dist.) Fla. 1991, D.C. 1992, Colo. 1994, U.S. Ct. Appeals (11th cir.) 1994, U.S. Dist. CT. (mid. dist.) Fla. 1995. Assoc. Stearns, Weaver, Miller, Weissler, Alhadeff & Sitterson, PA, Miami, 1990-93; sr. assoc. Cooney, Mattson, Lance, Blackburn, Richards & O'Connor, P.A., Ft. Lauderdale, Fla., 1994-98. Mem. Fla. Bar (appellate practice sec.), Fla. Def. Lawyers Assn. Democrat. Appellate.

KITZES, WILLIAM FREDRIC, lawyer, safety analyst, consultant; b. Bklyn., Nov. 24, 1950; s. David Louis and Rhoda Rachel (Feldman) K.; m. Sandra Shimasaki, Apr. 7, 1979: children: Justin, Dana. BA, U. Wis., 1972; JD, Am. U., 1975. Bar: D.C. 1977. Legal advisor on product recalls U.S. Consumer Products Safety Commn., Washington, 1975-77, program mgr., 1977-80, regulatory counsel, 1980-81; v.p., gen. mgr. Inst. for Safety Analysis, Rockville, Md., 1981-83; prin. Consumer Safety Assocs., Potomac, Md., Boca Raton, Fla., 1983—. Cons. Toro Co., Bloomington, Minn., 1987, Vendo Co., Fresno, Calif., 1987, Nat. Assn. Attys. Gens., Washington, 1987, Arctic Cat, Inc., Thief River Falls, Minn., 1995—, Global Furniture, Toronto, Ont., 1997, Product Safety Online, Boca Raton, 1997—, Cisco Sys., Inc., San Jose, Calif., 2001-. Contbg. columnist CCH Product Safety Guide and Products Liability Reporter, 2000-01. Counsel Friends of Charlie Gilchrist, Montgomery County, Md., 1983; chmn. Fla. Consumers Coun., 1995—. Recipient silver medal for meritorious svc. U.S. Consumer Products Safety Commn., 1976. Mem. Am. Soc. Safety Engrs., Human Factors Soc., System Safety Soc., Nat. Safety Coun., Internat. Consumer Product Health and Safety Orgn. Personal injury (including property damage). Home and Office: Consumer Safety Assocs 4501 NW 25th Way Boca Raton FL 33434-2506

KITZMILLER, HOWARD LAWRENCE, lawyer; b. Shippensburg, Pa., May 6, 1930; s. Franklin Leroy and Emma Corrinna (Bedford) K.; m. Shirley Mae Pine, Apr. 4, 1953; children: David Lawrence, Diane May. BA summa cum laude, Dickinson Coll., 1951; JD, Dickinson Sch. of Law, 1954; LLM, George Washington U., 1958. Bar: Pa. 1955, D.C. 1984. Commr. U.S. Ct. Mil. Appeals, Washington, 1958-59; various positions to assoc. gen. counsel FCC, Washington, 1959-80; various positions to dir., sr. v.p. and sec. Washington Mgmt. Corp., 1983—. Editor Dickinson Law Rev., 1954. Deacon, elder Westminster Presbyn. Ch., Alexandria, Va.; bd. dirs. S.E. Fairfax Devel. Corp., Fairfax County, Va., 1977-98, also past pres.; various positions including pres., parents adv. coun., bd. assocs., trustee, investment com. Randolph-Macon Coll., Ashland, Va., 1984-95. Capt. JAGC, U.S. Army, 1955-58. Mem. ABA, FBA, City Club Washington, Masons, Phi Beta Kappa. Republican.

KJAELDGAARD, JOERGEN, lawyer; b. Copenhagen, June 20, 1952; s. Carl Johan and Ingrid Rita Kjaeldgaard; m. Annette Staugaard, June 19, 1982; children: Johan Christian, Gregers Frederik. LLM, U. Copenhagen, 1976. Bar: Denmark 1978. Asst. mgr. Danske Bank, Copenhagen, 1976—78; assoc. Elvin Petersen, Axel Kirkegaard, 1978—83, Nielsen & Norager, 1983—86, ptnr., 1986—99, Mazanti-Andersen, Korso, Jensen & Ptnrs., 2000—. Avocations: hunting, hiking, flying, organ. Finance, Mergers and acquisitions, Alternative dispute resolution. Home: Bakkediget 3 DK-2970 Hoesterkoeb Denmark Office: Mazanti-Andersen Korso Kensen & Ptnrs St Kongensgade 69 DK-1264 Copenhagen Denmark Fax: +45 30193770. E-mail: jok@mazanti.dk.

KLAAS, PAUL BARRY, lawyer; b. St. Paul, Aug. 9, 1952; s. N. Paul and Ruth Elizabeth (Barry) K.; m. Barbara Ann Bockhaus, July 30, 1977; children: James, Ann, Brian. AB, Dartmouth Coll., 1974; JD, Harvard U., 1977. Bar: Minn. 1977, U.S. Dist. Ct. Minn. 1977, U.S. Ct. Appeals (8th cir.) 1979, U.S. Ct. Appeals (10th cir.) 1980, U.S. Supreme Ct. 1982, U.S. Ct. Appeals (9th cir.) 1989, U.S. Ct. Appeals (fed. cir.) 1994. Assoc. Dorsey & Whitney, Mpls., 1977-82, ptnr., 1983—. Chair trial dept., co-chair Internat. Arbitration and Litigation Practice Group; adj. prof. William Mitchell Coll Law, St. Paul, 1980-85. Fellow: Am. Coll. Trial Lawyers. Federal civil litigation, General civil litigation, Intellectual property. Office: Dorsey & Whitney 50 S 6th St Ste 1500 Minneapolis MN 55402-1498 E-mail: klaas.paul@dorseylaw.com.

KLAFTER, CARY IRA, lawyer; b. Chgo., Sept. 15, 1948; s. Herman Nicholas and Bernice Rose (Maremont) K.; m. Kathleen Ann Kerr, July 21, 1974; children: Anastasia, Benjamin, Eileen. BA, Mich. State U., 1968, MS, 1971; JD, U. Chgo., 1972. Bar: Calif. 1972. Assoc. Morrison & Foerster, San Francisco, 1972-79, ptnr., 1979-96; v.p. legal and govt. affairs, dir. corp. affairs, corp. sec. Intel Corp., Santa Clara, Calif., 1996—. Lectr. law Stanford Law Sch., 1990-99. Capt. USAR, 1971-78. Mem. Am. Soc. Corp. Secs. (bd. dirs.). Corporate, general, Securities.

KLAHR, GARY PETER, retired lawyer; b. N.Y.C., July 9, 1942; s. Fred and Frieda (Garson) K. Student, Ariz. State U., 1958-61; LL.B. with high honors, U. Ariz., 1964. Bar: Ariz. 1967, U.S. Dist. Ct. Ariz. 1967. Assoc. Brazlin & Greene, Phoenix, 1967-68; sr. ptnr. Gary Peter Klahr, P.C., Phoenix, 1968—2002. Asst. editor Ariz. Law Rev., 1963-64; contbr. articles to profl. jours. Bd. dirs. CODAMA, 1975-89, pres., 1980-81; bd. dirs. Tumbleweed Runaway Ctr., 1972-76; mem. bd. dirs. Internat. Found. Anti-Cancer Drug Discovery, 1998-2002, chair exec. com., 1999-2002; chmn. Citizens Criminal Justice Commn., 1977-78; elected Phoenix City Coun., 1974-76; co-chmn. delinquency subcom. Phoenix Forward Task force; vol. referee Juvenile Ct., 1969; mem. City Coun., Phoenix, 1974-1976; vol. adult probation officer; vol. counselor youth programs Dept. Econ. Security and Dept. of Corrections, Phoenix; ex-officio mem., spl. cons. Phoenix Youth Commn.; mem. citizen adv. coun. Phoenix Union H.S. Dist., 1985-90, 95-99, co-chmn. 1998-99, elected governing bd., 1991-95, 2000—, v.p., 1992-95, co-chmn. citizens adv. com., 1970-72; mem. rev. bd. Phoenix Police Dept., 1985-94; bd. dirs. Metro Youth Ctr., 1986-87, Svc./Employment/Redevel. (SER) Jobs for Progress, Phoenix, 1985-90, pres., 1986-87; bd. dirs. East McDowell Youth Assn., 1992-94; v.p. local chpt. City of Hope, 1985-86; Justice of the Peace pro tem Maricopa County Cts., 1985-89, City License Appeals Bd., 1987-97, vice chmn. 1988-93, chmn. 1993-97; juvenile hearing officer Maricopa County Juvenile Ct., 1985-89; v.p., co-founder Cmty. Leadership for Youth Devel. (CLYDE); del. Phoenix Together Town Hall on Youth Crime, 1982. Named 1 of 3 Outstanding Young Men of Phoenix, Phoenix Jaycees, 1969; recipient Disting. Citizen award Ariz. chpt. ACLU, 1976. Mem. ACLU (v.p. ctrl. chpt. Ariz. 1990-95, pres. 1995-2001, mem. state bd. 1990-2001), Ariz. State Bar (past sec., bd. dirs. young lawyers sect., co-chmn. unauthorized practice com. 1988-89, mem. other coms.), Maricopa County Bar Assn. (past sec., bd. dirs. young lawyers sec., vice-chmn. juvenile practice com. 1998-99), Am. Judicature Soc., Jewish Children's and Family Svc., Common Cause, NAACP, Ariz. ConsumersCoun., Phoenix Jaycees, Order of the Coif, Phi Alpha Delta. Democrat. Jewish. Criminal, Juvenile, Personal injury (including property damage). Office: 317 E Berridge Ln Phoenix AZ 85012

KLAMANN, JOHN MICHAEL, lawyer; b. Fresno, Calif., Aug. 23, 1952; s. Michael J. and Jacqueline C. K.; m. Brigid A. Cleary, Apr. 17, 1982; children: Conor, Seth, Zachary, Hannah, Kaitlin, Abbye. BS in Psychology, Kans. State U., 1974; JD, U. Kans., 1978. Bar: Mo. 1978, Kans. 1979. Atty. Popham Law Firm, Kansas City, Mo., 1978-88, Payne and Jones, Overland Park, Kans., 1989-96, Klamann and Hubbard, P.A., Overland Park, 1996—. Adj. prof. U. Mo., Kansas City Sch. of Law, 1998-2001. Author: (with others) Am Jur Trials, 1988, 90, 92. Mem. ABA, ATLA, Mo. Assn. Trial Attys., Kans. Trial Lawyers Assn., Mo. Bar Assn., Kans. Bar Assn. Federal civil litigation, State civil litigation, Personal injury (including property damage). Home: 4105 W 123rd St Leawood KS 66209 Office: Klamann and Hubbard PA 7101 College Blvd Ste 120 Overland Park KS 66210 Fax: 913-327-7800. E-mail: jklamann@kh-law.com.

KLAMON, LAWRENCE PAINE, lawyer; b. St. Louis, Mar. 17, 1937; s. Joseph Martin and Rose (Schimel) K.; m. Jo Ann Karen Beatty, Nov. 1957 (div. Feb. 1974); children: Stephen Robert, Karen Jean, Lawrence Paine; m. Frances Ann Estes, Mar. 1980. AB, Washington U., St. Louis, 1958; JD, Yale U., 1961. Bar: N.Y. 1964, Ga. 1990. Confidential asst. Office Sec. Def., Washington, 1961-62, spl. asst. to gen. counsel, 1962-63; asso. Cravath, Swaine & Moore, N.Y.C., 1963-67; v.p., gen. counsel Fuqua Industries, Inc., Atlanta, 1967-73, sr. v.p. fin. and adminstrn., 1971-81, pres., 1981-89, chief exec. officer, 1989-91; chmn., 1991; sr. counsel Alston & Bird, Atlanta, 1991-95; pres., CEO Fuqua Enterprises, Inc., Atlanta, 1995-97. Chmn. Gov.'s Internat. Adv. Coun., 1992-95. Mem. bd. editors Yale Law Jour., 1959-61. Mem. State Bar Ga., Order of Coif, Phi Beta Kappa, Omicron Delta Kappa. Home: 2665 Dellwood Dr NW Atlanta GA 30305-3519

KLAPER, MARTIN JAY, lawyer; b. Chgo., Jan. 12, 1947; s. Carl and Kate F. (Friedman) K.; m. Julia Warner, Nov. 14, 1973. BS in Bus. summa cum laude, Ind. U., 1969, JD summa cum laude, 1971. Bar: Ind. 1971, U.S. Dist. Ct. (no. and so. dists.) Ind. 1971, U.S. Ct. Appeals (7th cir.) 1972, U.S. Supreme Ct. 1979. Law clk. to justice U.S. Ct. Appeals (7th cir.), 1971-72; ptnr. Ice Miller, Indpls., 1972—. Mem. ABA, Ind. Bar Assn. Civil rights, Labor (including EEOC, Fair Labor Standards Act, labor-management relations, NLRB, OSHA). Office: Ice Miller PO Box 82001 Indianapolis IN 46282-2001 E-mail: Klaper@iquest.net., Klaper@Icemiller.com.

KLAPPER, GAIL HEITLER, lawyer; b. Denver, May 26, 1943; d. Emmett H. and Dorothy (Shwayder) Heitler; m. Jack A. Klapper, June 25, 1965; children: Dana, Stacy, Amy, Lisa. BA in Polit. Sci., Wellesley (Mass.) Coll., 1965; JD, U. Colo., 1968. Bar: Colo. 1968, U.S. Dist. Ct. Colo. 1968. Pvt. practice, Denver, 1968-76, 1983—; White House fellow U.S. Dept. of Interior, Washington, 1976-77; exec. dir. Colo. Dept. Regulatory Agencies, Denver, 1977-81, Colo. Dept. Pers., Denver, 1981-82; candidate Colo. atty. gen. ptnr. Klapper Zimmermann, Denver, 1983-86; of counsel Moye, Giles, O'Keefe, Vermeire & Gorrell, Denver, 1986-89; founder, mng. prin. The Klapper Firm, Denver, 1989—. Bd. dirs. Boston, Gold, Inc., Denver, Orchard Trust, Denver. Trustee Wellesley Coll., 1986—, chair, 1993-99; founder, bd. dirs. Pub. Edn. Coalition, Denver, 1984-95; bd. dirs. Nat. Jewish Ctr. for Immunology and Respiratory Medicine, Denver, 1986-96, Downtown Denver Partnership, chair, 1996-97; trustee Denver Mus. Nature and Sci., 1999—. Recipient Leadership Denver Assn. award, 1984, Norlin award U. Colo., 1987, Pub. Svc. award U. Colo. Grad. Sch. Pub. Affairs, 1987; White House fellow, 1976-77. Mem. Colo. Bar Assn., Denver Bar Assn., Colo. Forum (dir.), Colo. Women's Forum (pres. 1980-81), Denver Met. C. of C. (chair bd. dirs. 1997-98), Order of Coif. Democrat. Avocations: marathon running, quarter horses. Administrative and regulatory, Private international, Legislative.

KLAPPER, MOLLY, lawyer, educator; b. Berlin; came to U.S., 1950; d. Elias and Ciporah (Weber) Teicher; m. Jacob Klapper; children: Rachelle Hannah, Robert David. BA, CUNY, MA, 1964; PhD, NYU, 1974; JD, Rutgers U., 1987. Bar: N.J. 1987, U.S. Dist. Ct. N.J. 1987, N.Y. 1989, U.S. Dist. Ct. (so. and ea. dists.) N.Y. 1989, D.C. 1989, U.S. Supreme Ct. 1991, U.S. Ct. Appeals (2d cir.) 1992; cert. arbitrata, Better Bus. Bur., 2000, cert. arbitrator (NASD) Nat. Assn. of Security Dealers, 2003. Prof. English Bronx C.C., CUNY, 1974-84; law intern U.S. Dist. Ct. N.J., Newark, 1987;

law sec. to presiding judge appellate div. N.J. Supreme Ct., Springfield, 1987-88; assoc. Wilson, Elser, Moskowitz, Edelman and Dicker, N.Y.C., 1988-96; adminstrv. law judge Dept. Finance, N.Y.C., 1997—; adj. prof. law Touro Law Ctr., Huntington, N.Y., 2001—. Small claims ct. arbitrator, 1994—; mediator N.Y. State Supreme Ct., comml. divsn., 2000—; cert. arbitrator Better Bus. Bur., 2000—; jud. nominee State Supreme Ct., 2d dist., 1999; mediator Nat. Assn. Sec. Dirs., 2002—. Author: The German Literary Influence on Byron, 1974, 2d edit., 1975, The German Literary Influence on Shelley, 1975; contbr. to profl. publs. NEH fellow, 1978; grantee Am. Philos. Soc., 1976. Mem. Assn. Bar of City of N.Y., Adminstr. Law Com., 2003. Avocations: bicycling, skiing, roller skating, walking, hiking. Alternative dispute resolution, Administrative and regulatory, Insurance. Office: 720 Ft Washington Ave New York NY 10040-3708

KLARFELD, PETER JAMES, lawyer; b. Holyoke, Mass., Aug. 19, 1947; s. David Nathan and Gloria (Belsky) K.; m. Mary Myrtle, July 7, 1985; children: Peter Marcus (dec.), Mary Elizabeth, Louis Edward. BA, U. Va., 1969, JD, 1973; MA, U. Chgo., 1970. Bar: Va. 1973, D.C. 1975, U.S. Dist. Ct. D.C. 1977, U.S. Dist. Ct. (ea. dist.) Va. 1977, U.S. Dist. Ct. (ea. dist.) Wis. 1987, U.S. Dist. Ct. (no. dist.) Calif. 1990, U.S. Ct. Appeals (4th cir.) 1978, U.S. Ct. Appeals (3rd & 9th cirs.) 1986, U.S. Ct. Appeals (2d cir.) 1998, U.S. Ct. Appeals (7th cir.) 2003, U.S. Supreme Ct. 1977. Law clk. to Hon. Robert R. Merhige, Jr. U.S. Dist. Ct. (ea. dist.) Va., Richmond, 1973-74; atty., office of legal counsel U.S. Dept. Justice, Washington, 1974-76; ptnr. Brownstein Zeidman & Lore, Washington, 1977-96, Wiley, Rein &Fielding LLP, Washington, 1996—. Editor: Covenants Against Competition in Franchise Agreements, 2002; contbr. articles to profl. jours. Trustee Dalkon Shield Other Claimants Trust, Richmond, 1990-96, chmn., 1991-96. Mem. ABA. Antitrust, General civil litigation, Franchising. Home: 434 E Columbia St Falls Church VA 22046-3501 Office: Wiley Rein & Fielding 1776 K St NW Washington DC 20006-2304 E-mail: pklarfeld@wrf.com.

KLARQUIST, KENNETH STEVENS, JR., lawyer; b. Washington, Aug. 18, 1948; s. Kenneth S. and Lois M. (Boening) K.; m. Linda L. Arndt, Sept. 18, 1971; children: Josef, Peter, Jared. AB, Princeton U., 1970; JD, U. Oreg., 1973. Bar: Va. 1974, Oreg. 1975, Wash. 2003, U.S. Supreme Ct. 1980. Atty. estate tax U.S. Dept. Treasury, Richmond, Va., 1973-76; assoc. McMurry & Nichols, Portland, Oreg., 1976-77, Dahl, Zalutsky, Nichols & Hinson, P.C., Portland, Oreg., 1977-80; shareholder Zalutsky & Klarquist, P.C., Portland, Oreg., 1980—. Dir., past pres. Oreg. Wildlife Heritage Found., Portland, 1981—; dir., treas. KBPS Pub. Radio Found., Portland, 1991-99; bd. dirs. Nat. Alliance for Mentally Ill-Oreg., 1999—, pres., 2001—, Mem. Rotary (Rotarian of Month Portland 1996). Avocation: competitive rowing. Estate planning, Pension, profit-sharing, and employee benefits, Probate (including wills, trusts). Office: Zalutsky & Klarquist PC 215 SW Washington St Portland OR 97204-2636

KLASKO, HERBERT RONALD, lawyer, law educator, writer; b. Phila., Nov. 26, 1949; s. Leon Louis and Estelle Lorraine (Baratz) K.; m. Marjorie Ann Becker, Aug. 27, 1977; children: Brett Andrew, Kelli Lynn. BA, Lehigh U., 1971; JD, U. Pa., 1974. Bar: Pa. 1974, U.S. Dist. Ct. (ea. dist.) Pa. 1974, U.S. Ct. Appeals (3d cir.) 1981. Assoc. Fox, Rothschild, O'Brien & Frankel, Phila., 1974-75; ptnr., chmn. immigration dept. Abrahams & Loewenstein, Phila., 1975-88, Dechert, Price & Rhoads, Phila., 1988—. Instr., mem. adv. bd. Inst. for Paralegal Tng., Phila., 1974-81; instr. Temple Law Sch. Grad. Legal Studies, Phila., 1984; adj. prof. Villanova U. Law Sch., Pa., 1985-90. Co-author: (with Matthew Bender and Hope Frye) Employer's Immigration Compliance Guide, 1985; bd. editors: Immigration Law and Procedure Reporter. Exec. committeeman, bd. dirs. Jewish Community Rels. Coun., Phila., 1977—; chmn. exec. com., com. on unprosecuted Nazi war criminals Nat. Jewish Community Rels. Adv. Coun., N.Y.C., 1983-90; v.p. Hebrew Immigrant Aid Soc., Phila., 1977—; pres. Coun. of Tenants Assn., Southeastern Pa., 1980-81. Recipient Legion of Honor award Chapel of Four Chaplains, 1977. Mem. ABA (coordinating com. on immigration), Phila. Bar Assn., Am. Immigration Lawyers Assn. (chmn. Phila. chpt. 1980-82, bd. govs. 1980—, nat. sec. 1984-85, 2d v.p. 1985-86, 1st v.p. 1986-87, pres.-elect 1987-88, pres. 1988-89, exec. com. 1984-90, 96-99, gen. counsel, 1996-99, Founders award 1999), Am. Immigration Law Found. (bd. dirs. 1987-90). Avocations: politics, sports, traveling, organizations. Immigration, naturalization, and customs. Office: Dechert Price & Rhoads 4000 Bell Atlantic Tower 1717 Arch St Lbby 3 Philadelphia PA 19103-2713 E-mail: ronald.klasko@dechert.com.

KLATSKY, FRED M. lawyer; b. Red Bank, N.J., Sept. 25, 1951; s. William and Ann Klatsky; m. Kathy Sue Klatsky; children: Michael, David, Jaclyn. BA cum laude, Emory U., 1973, JD, 1976. Judge West Long Branch Mcpl. Ct., 1980—83; ptnr. Klatsky and Klatsky, Red Bank, 1976—. Pres. Holmdel (N.J.) Sch. Bd., 1983; basketball coach AAU, NJ. Avocation: basketball coaching. State civil litigation, Family and matrimonial, Sports. Home: 7 Pheasant Run Holmdel NJ 07733 Office: Klatsky and Klatsky 320 Broad St Red Bank NJ 07701 Office Fax: 732-758-0799.

KLAUS, CHARLES, retired lawyer; b. Freiburg, Baden, Germany, Feb. 11, 1935; came to U.S., 1939; children: Charles, Kathryn, Richard; m. Elaine S. Jones, Jan. 6, 2002. BA, Cornell U., 1956, MBA, JD with distinction, 1961; postdoctoral, Case Western Res. U., 1964, Lakeland Community Coll., 1976. Bar: Ohio 1961, U.S. Dist. Ct. (no. dist.) Ohio 1962. Assoc. Baker & Hostetler, Cleve., 1961-71, ptnr., 1972-94, retired, 1995. Past hon. trustee and pres. Cleve. Music Sch. Settlement; past trustee Cleve. Audubon Soc.; past trustee, sec. Cleve. Area Arts Coun., Lake Erie Opera Theatre, N.E. Ohio chpt. Arthritis Found.; former mem. Group Svc. Coun. Welfare Fedn. Cleve.; corp. mem. The Holden Arboretum, 1993—. Recipient Award of Merit, Cleve. Audubon Soc., 1979. Mem. Millard Fillmore Soc., Rowfant Club (past sec.), Kirtland Country Club (past dir., past sec., Willoughby, Ohio). Commercial, contracts (including sales of goods; commercial financing), Corporate, general, Environmental.

KLAUS, WILLIAM ROBERT, lawyer; b. Phila., Jan. 19, 1926; s. William Anthony and Amanda (Pusey) K.; m. Janet Lois Scoggins, Aug. 18, 1951; 1 child, Kenneth Springfield. LLB, Temple U., 1951. Bar: Pa. 1952. Assoc. Pepper, Hamilton & Scheetz, Phila., 1952-59, ptnr., 1959—95, retired, chmn. emeritus, 1995—. Bd. dirs. Westmoreland Coal Co., Colorado Springs, Perna Warehousing, Co., Phila. Co-author: Practical Guide to U.C.C., 1969. Chmn. Phila. Comm. Legal Svcs., Inc., 1966-83, Phila. Legal Assistance Corp., 1995-2000. Staff sgt. U.S. Army, 1943-46, ETO. Faculty fellow U. Pa. Law Sch., 1973. Mem. ABA (chmn. com. legal aid 1978-79), Nat. Legal Aid Defenders Assn. (pres. 1978), Pa. Bar Assn., Phila. Bar Assn. (chancellor 1974), Phila. Club (chmn. house com. 1979-2002), Little Egg Harbor Yacht Club (commodore 1991), Merion Cricket Club. Avocations: skiing, sailing, archeology, music, antiques.

KLAUSNER, JACK DANIEL, lawyer; b. N.Y.C., July 31, 1945; s. Burt and Marjory (Brown) K.; m. Dale Arlene Kreis, July 1, 1968; children: Andrew Russell, Mark Raymond. BS in Bus., Miami U., Oxford, Ohio, 1967; JD, U. Fla., 1969. Bar: N.Y. 1971, Ariz. 1975, U.S. Dist. Ct. Ariz. 1975, U.S. Ct. Appeals (9th cir.) 1975, U.S. Supreme Ct. 1975. Assoc. counsel John P. McGuire & Co., Inc., N.Y.C., 1970-71; assoc. atty. Hahn & Hessen, N.Y.C., 1971-72; gen. counsel Equilease Corp., N.Y.C., 1972-74; assoc. Burch & Cracchiolo, Phoenix, 1974-78, ptnr., 1978-98; judge pro tem Maricopa County Superior Ct., 1990—, Ariz. Ct. Appeals, 1992—; ptnr. Warner Angle Roper & Hallam, Phoenix, 1998—. Bd. dirs. Hunter Contracting Co. Bd. dirs. Santos Soccer Club, Phoenix, 1989-90; bd. dirs., pres. south Bank Soccer Club, Tempe, 1987-88. Antitrust, General civil litigation, Property, real (including real estate development, water). Home: 9146 N Crimson Canyon Fountain Hills AZ 85268 Office: Warner Angel Roper & Hallam 3550 N Central Ave Ste 1500 Phoenix AZ 85012-2112

KLAY, ANNA NETTIE, lawyer; b. Palo Alto, Calif., Aug. 27, 1940; BA, U. Colo., Boulder, 1962; JD, Golden Gate Law Sch., 1976. Bar: Calif. 1976. Ptnr. Edson & Klay, Eureka, Calif., 1977-82; atty. Anna N. Klay Law Firm, 1982-87, Conrad F. Gullixson Law Firm, Palo Alto, 1987-93; sole practice, 1993—. Vol. chaplain Stanford U. Hosp., Palo Alto, 1996—. Named one of Silicon Valley's Best Lawyers, San Jose Mag., 1999, 2000, 2001, 2002. Democrat. Episcopalian. Avocations: music, opera, gardening. Administrative and regulatory. Office: 550 Hamilton Ave Ste 300 Palo Alto CA 94301 Office Fax: 650-326-2404.

KLECKNER, ROBERT GEORGE, JR., lawyer; b. Reading, Pa., Mar. 14, 1932; s. Robert George and Elizabeth (Endlich) K.; m. Carol Espie, June 15, 1955; children: Anthony Savage, Susan Duffield. BA, Yale U., 1954; LLB, U. Pa., 1959. Bar: Pa. 1960, N.Y. 1964. Pvt. practice, Reading, 1960-63; assoc. Sullivan & Cromwell, N.Y.C., 1963-70; house counsel Goldman, Sachs & Co., N.Y.C., 1970-78; cons. N.Y.C., 1978-80; house counsel Johnson & Higgins, N.Y.C., 1980-97; sr. atty. legal dept. Marsh & McLennan Cos., Inc., N.Y.C., 1997; ret., 1997. 1st lt. USAR, 1955-57, Korea. Mem. ABA, Assn. Bar City N.Y., Berks County Bar Assn., Union Club, Univ. Club, Mill Reef Club, Phi Beta Kappa. Republican. Lutheran. Home: 80 East End Ave New York NY 10028-8004

KLEE, ANN, lawyer; BA in Ancient History, Swarthmore Coll., 1983; JD, U. Pa., 1986. Assoc. Crowell & Moring, Washington, 1986—90; ptnr., chair environ. group Preston, Gates, Ellis & Rouvelas Meeds, Washington, 1990—95; chief counsel Senate Environment and Pub. Works Com., Washington, 1997—2001; counselor to sec. U.S. Dept. of Interior, Washington, 2001—. Office: US Dept Interior Office Sec 1849 C St NW Washington DC 20240 Office Fax: 202-208-6956.*

KLEFF, PIERRE AUGUSTINE, JR., lawyer; b. Washington, Oct. 28, 1942; s. Pierre A. Sr. and Mary Emily (Hayes) K.; m. Cheryl S. Henk, June, 1965 (div.); 1 child, Pierre A. III; m. Rosemarie F. Lockmer, Mar. 17, 1973 (div.); 1 child, Amber Marie. BA, U. Dayton, 1968; JD, No. Ky. State U., 1973. Bar: Ohio, 1973, Tex., 1976, U.S. Ct. Appeals (5th cir.) 1981, U.S. Ct. Mil. Appeals 1974, U.S. Dist. Ct. (we. dist.) Tex., 1979, U.S. Dist. Ct. (no. dist.) Tex. 1993, U.S. Supreme Ct. 1986. Ptnr. Kleff and Assocs. P.C., Killeen, Tex. Mem. Nat. Rep. Orgn., Rep. Orgn. Tex.; alt. del. Rep. Nat. Conv., Detroit, 1980. Served to capt. U.S. Army, 1973-77, lt. col. USAR, 1977-95, ret., 1995. Named Texas Businessman of the Year, Natl. Republican Congressional Com., 2003. Fellow Tex. Bar Found.; Mem. Tex. Bar Assn., Bell-Lampasas-Mills Counties Bar Assn. (bd. dirs. 1986-89, reporter 1989-90, sec.-treas. 1990-91, pres. 1992-93), Rotary (treas. Killeen club 1984). Roman Catholic. Avocations: weightlifting, boating. Commercial, contracts (including sales of goods; commercial financing), General practice, Property, real (including real estate development, water). Office: PO Box 11329 Killeen TX 76547-1329

KLEIMAN, BERNARD, lawyer; b. Chgo., Jan. 26, 1928; s. Isidore and Pearl (Wikoff) Kleiman; m. Gloria Baime, Nov. 15, 1986; children: Leslie, David. BS, Purdue U., 1951; JD, Northwestern U., 1954. Bar: Ill. 1954. Practice law in assn. with Abraham W. Brussell, 1957-60; dist. counsel United Steel Workers Am., 1960-65, spl. counsel, 1997—, gen. counsel, 1965-97; ptnr. Kleiman, Cornfield & Feldman, Chgo., 1960-75; prin. B. Kleiman (P.C.), 1976-77, Kleiman, Whitney, Wolfe & Elfenbaum, P.C., 1978-99. Mem. collective bargaining coms. for nat. labor negotiations in basic steel, tire mfg., and shipbuilding industries. Contbr. articles to legal jours. Served with U.S. Army, 1946—48. Mem.: ABA, Allegheny County Bar Assn. Labor (including EEOC, Fair Labor Standards Act, labor-management relations, NLRB, OSHA).

KLEIMAN, DAVID HAROLD, lawyer; b. Kendallville, Ind., Apr. 2, 1934; s. Isadore and Pearl (Wikoff) K.; m. Meta Dene Freeman, July 6, 1958; children: Gary, Andrew, Scott, Matthew. BS, Purdue U., 1956; JD, Northwestern U., 1959. Bar: Ind. 1959. Assoc. firm Bamberger & Feibleman, Indpls., 1959-61; ptnr. Bagal, Talesnick & Kleiman, Indpls., 1961-73, Dann Pecar Newman & Kleiman, Indpls., 1973—; dep. pros. atty., 1961-62; counsel Met. Devel. Commn., 1965-75; Ind. Heartland Coordinating Commn., 1975-81. Editor: Jour. of Air Law and Commerce, 1958-59. Chmn. Young Leadership Coun., 1967; v.p. Indpls. Hebrew Congregation, 1973, bd. dirs., 2003—; pres. Jewish Cmty. Ctr. Assn., 1972-75; pres. Jewish Welfare Fedn., 1981-84; v.p. United Way Ctrl. Ind., 1982-86, pres., 1986, chmn. bd. dirs., 1987; bd. dirs. Jewish Fedn., 1972—, Ind. Symphony Soc., 1991-96; bd. dirs. Ind. Repertory Theatre, 1986—, pres. 1991-94; trustee Indpls. Found., 2000—; bd. dirs. Ctrl. Ind. Cmty Found., 2000—, English Found., 2000—. Recipient Young Leadership award, 1968, Isadore Fiebleman Man of Yr. award, 1987, Mossler Cmty. Svc. award, 1988, Chalfie Cmty. Svc. award, 1998. Mem. ABA, Ind. State Bar Assn., Indpls. Bar Assn., Comml. Law League Am., Am. Coll. Bankruptcy, Columbia Club, Skyline Club (bd. dirs. 1993—), B'nai B'rith, Broadmoor Country Club. Office: Dann Pecar Newman & Kleiman One American Square PO Box 82008 Indianapolis IN 46282-2008

KLEIMAN, MARY MARGARET, lawyer; b. Norfolk, Va., May 26, 1959; d. William Edward and Patricia Mae Holste; m. David James Kleiman, June 29, 1991; children: Amanda Grace, Amy Elizabeth. BA in History summa cum laude, Marian Coll., Indpls., 1981; JD cum laude, Ind. U., Indpls., 1984. Bar: Ind. 1985, U.S. Dist. Ct. (no. and so. dists.) Ind. 1985. Bailiff, law clk. Marion County Mcpl. Ct., Indpls., 1983-84; counsel Am. Fletcher Nat. Bank (now Bank One, Ind. N.A.), Indpls., 1985-88; assoc. Krieg DeVault Alexander & Capehart, Indpls., 1989-95; ptnr. Krieg Devault Alexander & Capehart, Indpls., 1995-2000; v.p. and assoc. gen. counsel Federal Home Loan Bank of Indianapolis, 2000—. Bd. dirs. Ind. Bus. Devel. Corp., 1994-97; spkr. at banking confs. Contbr. articles to profl. jours. Pro bono atty. Cmty. Orgns. Legal Assistance Project, Indpls., 1994—; vol. com. chair, mem. client programs com. Ind. chpt. Nat. Multiple Sclerosis Soc., 1997-2001, trustee Ind. chpt., 1999-2001; mem. mission com. Castleton United Meth. Ch., Indpls., 1993-2000, acolyte coord., mem. worship com., 1998-99, mem. chancel choir, 1999—, chair staff-parish rels. com., 2000-02; bd. dirs. Circle Area Comm. Devel. Corp., 2000—, Downtown Area Comm. Devel. Corp., 2000—, Mass. Ave. Commn. Devel. Corp., 2000—, Naval Air Warfare Center Reuse Planning Authority. Recipient Leadership award Nat. Multiple Sclerosis Soc., 1998, Nat. Vol. of Yr. award Nat. Multiple Sclerosis Soc., 1999, Outstanding Vol. award Ind. Ronald McDonald House, 1990; named to Outstanding Young Women in Am., 1981, 87. Mem. ABA, Ind. State Bar Assn., Indpls. Bar Assn. (chair printed forms com. 1987), Phi Delta Phi. Democrat. Avocations: gardening, cross-stitch, reading science fiction, calligraphy. Banking, Commercial, contracts (including sales of goods; commercial financing), Securities. Office: Federal Home Loan Bank of Indianapolis PO Box 60 Indianapolis IN 46206 E-mail: mkleiman@fhlbi.com.

KLEIN, ARNOLD SPENCER, lawyer; b. N.Y.C., Mar. 10, 1951; s. Paul and Ethel (Cooper) K.; m. Arlene Sandra Feinberg, Aug. 14, 1977; children: Jeffrey Daniel, Rachel Pauli. BA, SUNY, Stony Brook, 1974; JD cum laude, N.Y. Law Sch., 1977. Bar: N.Y. 1978, Fla. 1984, U.S. Dist. Ct. (so. and ea. dists.) N.Y., U.S. Dist. Ct. (so. dist.) Fla., U.S. Ct. Appeals (2d cir.), U.S. Supreme Ct. Mem. Kelley, Drye & Warren, N.Y.C., 1977-85, ptnr., 1986-94, Meltzer, Lippe, & Goldstein, LLP, Mineola, 1994—. Mem. ABA, N.Y. State Bar Assn., Nassau County Bar Assn. Federal civil litigation, State civil litigation, Alternative dispute resolution. Office: Meltzer Lippe 190 Willis Ave Mineola NY 11501-2693 E-mail: aklein@mlg.com.

KLEIN, COLEMAN EUGENE, lawyer; b. Chgo., Apr. 8, 1938; BBA, Wayne State U., 1960, JD magna cum laude, 1967. Bar: Mich. 1968, U.S. Dist. Ct. (ea. dist.) Mich. 1968, U.S. Tax Ct. 1968, U.S. Ct. Appeals (6th cir.) 1970, U.S. Supreme Ct. 1989. Ptnr. Shere & Klein, Detroit, 1968-82; pvt. practice Southfield, Mich., 1982-2000, Bloomfield Hills, Mich., 2000—. Contbr. articles to profl. jours. Recipient Disting. Cmty. Svc. award Alzheimer's Assn., Detroit, 1984, 91. Mem. ABA, State Bar of Mich., Oakland County Bar Assn. Corporate, general, Estate planning, Taxation, general. Office: 39533 Woodward Ave Ste 210 Bloomfield Hills MI 48304-5103

KLEIN, HENRY LEONARD, lawyer; b. Hopkinsville, Ky., Apr. 23, 1932; s. Mose and Dorothy Klein; m. Elizabeth Levine, Dec. 1960 (div. Nov. 1969); children: Henry Leonard Jr., John Stuart, Roger Bennett; m. Jane Elizabeth Walker, Nov. 7, 1986; children: William Maxwell Mose, Barbara Alexandra. BA, Vanderbilt U., 1954, LLB, 1960. Bar: U.S. Supreme Ct. 1979. Atty. Winchester & Winchester, Memphis, 1960-65; asst. U.S. atty. Dept. Justice, Memphis, 1965-69; asst. city atty., staff atty. City of Memphis, 1972—; atty. Rickey Shankman, Memphis, 1969-85, Harkary Shainberg, Memphis, 1985-91, Apperson Crump Duzane & Maxwell, Memphis, 1991—. With U.S. Army, 1954-56, Korea. Named one of the Best Lawyers in Am., 2001, 2002, 2003. Fellow Tenn. Bar Found., Memphis Bar Assn. (pres. 1983); mem. ABA, Tenn. Bar Assn. (ho. of dels. 1984-90), Jour. Club Memphis, Kiwanis Club, B'nai B'rith (lodge pres.). Jewish. Avocations: golf, tennis. Civil rights, General civil litigation, Criminal. Office: Apperson Crump & Maxwell 6000 Poplar Ave Ste 400 Memphis TN 38119

KLEIN, HOWARD BRUCE, lawyer, law educator; b. Pitts., Pa, Feb. 28, 1950; s. Elmer and Natalie (Rosenzweig) K.; m. Lonnie Jean Wilets, Dec. 12, 1977; children: Zachary B., Eli H. Student, Northwestern U., 1968-69; BA, U. Wis., 1972; JD, Georgetown U., 1976. Bar: Wis. 1976, Pa. 1981, U.S. Ct. Appeals D.C., 1978, U.S. Dist. Ct. Pa. 1981, U.S. Ct. Appeals (3rd cir.) 1982, U.S. Supreme Ct. 1983. Law clk. to justice Robert Hansen Wis. Supreme Ct., Madison, 1976-77; asst. atty. gen. dept. justice State of Wis., 1977-80; chief criminal divsn. U.S. Atty.'s Office, Phila., 1980-87; ptnr. Blank, Rome & McCauley, Phila., 1987-96, chmn. litigation dept., 1991-94; prin. Law Offices of Howard Bruce Klein, Phila., 1996—; dir. in house tng. Am. Law Inst.-ABA, 1996—. Regional, nat. instr. Nat. Inst. Trial Advocacy, Phila. and Boulder, Colo., 1987-98; adj. prof. evidence and trial advocacy Temple U. Law Sch., 1984—; instr. Atty. Gen. Advocacy Inst., Washington, 1983-87; lectr. pub. corruption and trial advocacy; cons. Pa. Valley Neighborhood Assn., 1984—. Contbr. to profl. jours. Advisor Phila. Police Dept. Reform Commn., 1986—; campaign issues dir. Pa. Atty. Gen. campaign, Phila., 1988, 92; bd. dirs. Citizens Crime Commn. Delaware Valley, Phila. Mem. Fed. Bar Assn. (chmn. criminal law com.), Phila. Bar Assn., Wis. Bar Assn., D.C. Bar Assn., U.S. Attys. Alumni Assn. (co-founder, exec. bd.), Vesper Club (Phila.). Democrat. Jewish. Avocations: golf, basketball, hiking. Federal civil litigation, Criminal. Office: 1700 Market St Ste 2632 Philadelphia PA 19103-3903 E-mail: howbrklein@aol.com.

KLEIN, IRWIN GRANT, lawyer; b. Bklyn., June 6, 1949; s. Melvin Morton and Gladys (Mandel) K.; m. Charlene Elena Perez, July 31, 1988; children: Robert Matthew Perez, Gabriella Margaux Perez. BS, U. Wis., 1971; JD, Vt. Law Sch., 1977. Bar: N.Y., 1977, U.S. Dist. Ct. (so. & ea. dist.) N.Y., 1977, Vt., 1977, U.S. Supreme Ct., 1988. Assoc. atty. Hein, Waters, Klein & Zurkow, Far Rockaway, N.Y., 1977-78; asst. dist. atty. Queens County Dist. Atty., Kew Gardens, N.Y., 1979-82; ptnr. Hein, Waters & Klein, Cedarhurst, NY, 1982—89, Lapp & Klein, Cedarhurst, 1989-91, Hein, Waters & Klein, Cedarhurst, 1991—. Mem. Vt. Law Rev., N.Y. State Defenders Assn., N.Y. State Bar Assn., Nassau County Bar Assn., Queens County Bar Assn., Phi Delta Phi. Corporate, general, Criminal, Estate planning. Office: Hein Waters & Klein 123 Grove Ave Cedarhurst NY 11516-2302 E-mail: igkny@earthlink.net.

KLEIN, JERRY A. lawyer; b. Chillicothe, Mo., Jan. 10, 1937; s. Melvin H. and Gertrude K.; m. Mary Sharon, Apr. 15, 1967; children: Suzanne Klein Randolph, Jordan M. AB, JD, Washington U., St. Louis, 1961. Bar: Mo. 1961, U.S. Dist. Ct. (ea. dist.) Mo. 1962, U.S. Ct. Appeals (8th cir.) 1978, U.S. Supreme Ct. 1979. Ptnr. Taub & Klein, St. Louis, 1962-76; prin. Dolgin, Beilenson & Klein, St. Louis, 1977-81; atty. pvt. practice, St. Louis, 1981—. Avocations: golf, racquetball, travel, investments. General civil litigation, Personal injury (including property damage), Workers' compensation. Office: 7777 Bonhomme Ave Ste 1910 Clayton MO 63105-1911 E-mail: jaklein@inlink.com.

KLEIN, JUDAH BAER, retired lawyer; b. Bklyn., Feb. 9, 1923; s. Kolman Karl and Gladys Ruth (Edelson)) K.; m. Paula Berk, Nov. 8, 1953; 1 child, Caryn Ann. BS, U. Md., 1947; LLB, Bklyn. Law Sch., 1950. Bar: N.Y. 1951, U.S. Dist. Ct. (so. and ea. dists.) N.Y. Ptnr. Klein & Klein, N.Y.C., 1952-58; gen. counsel Paragon Industries Inc., Mineola, N.Y., 1959-70; pvt. practice, 1970-71; asst. chief counsel, sr. v.p. The Title Guarantee Co., N.Y.C., 1972-79; v.p., gen. counsel LTIC Assoc., Inc., N.Y.C., 1979-93; ret., 1993. 1st lt. U.S. Army, 1943-46, 51-52. Mem. ABA, Assn. Bar City N.Y., Nassau County Bar Assn., Am. Coll. Real Estate Lawyers, N.Y. State Bar Assn., Masons. Jewish. Insurance, Property, real (including real estate development, water).

KLEIN, LINDA ANN, lawyer; b. N.Y.C., Nov. 7, 1959; d. Gerald Ira Klein and Sandra Florence (Kimmel) Fishman; m. Michael S. Neuren, Sept. 23, 1985. BA cum laude, Union Coll., 1980; JD, Washington & Lee U., 1983. Bar: Ga. 1983, D.C. 1984, U.S. Dist. Ct. (no. and mid. dist.) Ga. 1985, U.S. Ct. Appeals (11th cir.) 1986. Assoc. Nall & Miller, Atlanta, 1983-86, Martin, Cavan & Andersen, Atlanta, 1986-90, ptnr., 1990-93; mng. ptnr. Gambrell & Stolz, 1993—. Instr. Nat. Ctr. Paralegal Tng., Atlanta, 1986. Mem.: ABA (editor Trial Techniques newsletter 1989, vice chmn. trial techniques com. 1989—90, chair 1991—92, vice chair fidelity and surety com. 1994—97, chair ann. meeting 1996—97, mem. coun. tort and ins. practice sect. 1998—, ho. of dels. 1998—, chair elect tort and ins. practice sect. 2002—), Am. Law Inst. (mem. 2003—), Coun. of Superior Cts. Judges (ex-officio uniform rules com.), Atlanta Bar Assn. (chair commn. on uniform rules of ct. 1986, bd. dirs. Atlanta Coun. on Young Lawyers 1986—89), Inst. for CLE (chair Ga. br. 1998—2000), Nat. Conf. Bar Pres. (exec. coun. 1998—2001), State Bar of Ga. (chair study com. on rules of practice 1987—94, bd. govs. 1989—, mem. exec. com. 1992—99, sec. 1994—96, pres. 1997—98, vice chair profl. liability com.), Pi Sigma Alpha, Phi Alpha Delta. General civil litigation, Construction, Personal injury (including property damage).

KLEIN, MARTIN I. lawyer; b. N.Y.C., Nov. 12, 1947; m. Diane Levbarg. BA, Lehigh U., 1969; JD, Am. U., 1972. Bar: N.Y. 1973, Fla. 1978, Calif. 1981, D.C. 1981; solicitor Supreme Ct. Eng., 1996—. Mem. profl. staff U.S. Senate Com. on Labor and Pub. Welfare, 1969-72; legis. aide U.S. Senator Jacob K. Javits, 1969-72; ptnr., head creditors' rights dept. Dreyer & Traub, N.Y.C., 1980-93; ptnr., head dept. bankruptcy Shea & Gould, N.Y.C., 1993—95; pvt. practice Martin I. Klein, P.C., 1995—. Lectr. Am. Law Inst.-ABA Com. on Continuing Profl. Edn., 1975—, The Practising Law Inst., 1975—, Mathematica, 1981—; adj. assoc. prof. law Benjamin Cardozo Sch. Law, Yeshiva U., 1980—; lectr. Columbia U. Sch. Law, 1980—; mem. med. malpractice mediation panel appellate div. Supreme Ct. State N.Y. 1980—; trustee, treas., pres. Cen. Synagogue, N.Y.C., 1986—; arbitrator, N.Y.C. Small Claims Ct. Contbr. articles on fin. real estate and comml. law to profl. jours. Del. White House Conf. on Youth, 1971; chmn. Town of Palm Beach Zoning Commn., 1994—. Mem. ABA, N.Y. State Bar Assn., Fla. Bar Assn., Calif. Bar Assn., D.C. Bar Assn., N.Y. County Lawyers Assn. (mem. com. on bankruptcy), Am. Arbitration Assn. (mem. comml. panel). Bankruptcy, Federal civil litigation, General practice. Address: 21st Fl 780 Third Ave New York NY 10017

KLEIN, MICHAEL D. lawyer; b. Wilkes-Barre, Pa., June 9, 1951; BA magna cum laude, King's Coll., 1973; JD, Dickinson Sch. Law, 1976. Bar: Pa. 1976, U.S. Ct. Appeals (3rd cir.) 1984, U.S. Dist. Ct. (mid. dist.) Pa. 1984, U.S. Dist Ct. (ea. dist.) Pa. 1994. Asst. atty. gen. Commonwealth of Pa., Harrisburg, 1976-82; mgr. corp. affairs, corp. sec. Pa. Am. Water Co., Hershey, 1982-89; ptnr. LeBoeuf, Lamb, Greene & MacRae LLP, Harrisburg, Pa., 1991—. Mem. Pa. Bar Assn., Am. Water Works Assn. Office: LeBoeuf Lamb Greene & MacRae LLP PO Box 12105 Harrisburg PA 17108-2105 E-mail: mklein@llgm.com.

KLEIN, PAUL E. lawyer; b. N.Y.C., Apr. 26, 1934; AB, Cornell U., 1956; JD, Harvard U., 1960. Bar: Mich. 1960, Ill. 1965, N.Y. 1967, U.S. Supreme Ct. 1977, U.S. Ct. Appeals (2d cir.) 1980. Atty. Dow Chem. Co., Midland, Mich., 1960-65; assoc. Gunther & Choka, Chgo., 1965-66; atty. Esso Rsch. & Engring. Co., Linden, N.J., 1966-67; sr. mng. editor Matthew Bender & Co., N.Y.C., 1967-72; assoc. gen. counsel N.Y. Life Ins. Co., N.Y.C., 1972-80, v.p., assoc. gen. counsel, 1980-84; v.p., counsel Huggins Fin. Svcs., Inc., N.Y.C., 1984-86; exec. corp. tax. div. Ernst & Young, N.Y.C., 1986-95; pvt. practice White Plains, N.Y., 1995—. Adj. asst. prof. L.I. U., 1972-79, adj. assoc. prof., 1979-80; adj. assoc. prof. acctg. and taxation, Fordham U. at Lincoln Ctr. grad. sch. of bus. adminstrn., 1995—. Former columnist Jour. Real Estate Taxation; writer; editor. Mem. ABA (past chmn. subcom. on life ins. products/ins. cos. com., sect. taxation), Assn. Bar City N.Y. (past chair subcom. on life and health ins. of the com. on ins. law), Assn. Life Ins. Counsel (sec.-treas. 1979-83, bd. govs. 1983-87), N.Y. State Bar Assn. Insurance, Pension, profit-sharing, and employee benefits, Corporate taxation. Office: 58 Midchester Ave White Plains NY 10606-3817 E-mail: pek34@optonline.net.

KLEIN, PETER WILLIAM, lawyer, corporate officer, investment company executive; b. Lorain, Ohio, Sept. 22, 1955; s. Warren Martin Klein and Barbara (Lesser) Pomeroy; m. Jennifer Lynn Ungers, Aug. 3, 1984. Student, U. Sussex, 1975-76; BA, Albion Coll., 1976; JD, Cleve. Marshall Coll. Law, 1981; LLM, NYU, 1982. Bar: Ohio 1981, Ill. 1984. Assoc. Guren, Merritt, Feibel, Sogg & Cohen, Cleve., 1982-84, Siegan, Barbakoff, Gomberg & Gordon, Ltd., Chgo., 1984-86; mng. dir., gen. counsel Trivest Inc., Miami, Fla., 1986-2000; ptnr., gen. counsel Brockway, Moran & Ptnrs., Inc., Boca Raton, Fla., 2000—. Mem. ABA (taxation sect., corp. sect., banking and bus. law). Corporate, general, Mergers and acquisitions, Corporate taxation. Home: 3618 Palmetto Ave Miami FL 33133-6221 Office: Brockway Moran & Ptnrs Inc 7th Fl 225 NE Mizner Blvd Fl 7 Boca Raton FL 33432-4078

KLEIN, RICHARD DENNIS, lawyer; b. Far Rockaway, N.Y., Nov. 8, 1950; m. Ellen Klein. BA, SUNY, Stony Brook, 1972; MPS in Hosp./Health Svcs. Adminstrn., Cornell U., 1975; JD, Ill. Inst. Tech., 1985. Bar: Ill. 1985, U.S. Dist. Ct. (no. dist.) Ill. 1987. Dir. membership Am. Coll. Healthcare Execs., Chgo., 1984-89; atty. Richard D. Klein & Assocs., Attys. at Law, Naperville, Ill., 1989—. Recipient fellowship Am. Coll. Healthcare Execs., 1988. Mem. Ill. State Bar Assn., Dupage County Bar Assn. (real estate com. 1995—). Estate planning, Family and matrimonial, Property, real (including real estate development, water). Office: 500 E Ogden Ave Ste 200 Naperville IL 60563-3281 E-mail: lawyers@wans.net.

KLEINBARD, EDWARD D. lawyer; b. N.Y.C., Nov. 6, 1951; s. Martin L. and Joan K.; m. Norma F. Cirincione, Oct. 17, 1947. BA, MA, Brown U., 1973; JD, Yale U., 1976. Bar: N.Y. 1977. Ptnr. Cleary, Gottlieb, Steen & Hamilton, N.Y.C. Book rev., article editor Yale Law Jour., 1975-76; contbr. articles to profl. jours. Fellow Am. Coll. Tax Counsel; mem. ABA, N.Y. State Bar Assn. (co-chmn. fin. instruments com. 1989-91), Assn. Bar City of N.Y., Internat. Assn. Fin. Engrs., Internat. Fiscal Assn. Office: Cleary Gottlieb Steen & Hamilton 1 Liberty Plz Fl 38 New York NY 10006-1470

KLEINBERG, NORMAN CHARLES, lawyer; b. Phila., July 18, 1946; s. Frank and Mildred Brosnan (Hill) K.; m. Marcia Sue Topperman, Jan. 31, 1971; children: Lauren Blythe, Joanna Leigh. AB, Tufts U., 1968; JD, Columbia U., 1972. Bar: N.Y. 1973, U.S. Supreme Ct., U.S. Ct. Appeals (1st, 2d, 3d, 5th, and fed. cirs.), U.S. Dist. Ct. (so. and ea. dists.) N.Y., U.S. Tax Ct., U.S. Dist. Ct. (ea. dist.) Wis., U.S. Dist. Ct. (no. dist.) Calif., U.S. Dist. Ct. (ea. dist.) Mich. Law clk. to judge U.S. Dist. Ct. (so. dist.) N.Y., N.Y.C., 1972-74; assoc. Hughes Hubbard & Reed, N.Y.C., 1974-80, ptnr., 1980—. Articles editor Columbia Jour. Law and Social Problems, 1971-72. Served to staff sgt. USAR, 1968-74. Fellow Am. Coll. Trial Lawyers; mem. ABA, Fed. Bar Coun., Assn. Bar of City of N.Y. (com. on state cts. of superior jurisdiction, com. profl. responsibility, com. profl. and jud. ethics., com. on jud., coun. on jud. adminstrn.), Internat. Bar Assn., N.Y. State Bar Assn., Def. Rsch. Inst. Antitrust, General civil litigation, Insurance. Home: 460 E 79th St New York NY 10021-1443 Office: Hughes Hubbard & Reed 1 Battery Park Plz Fl 12 New York NY 10004-1482 E-mail: kleinber@hugheshubbard.com.

KLEINFELD, ANDREW J. federal judge; b. 1945; BA magna cum laude, Wesleyan U., 1966; JD cum laude, Harvard U., 1969. Law clk. Alaska Supreme Ct., 1969—71; U.S. magistrate U.S. Dist. Ct. Alaska, Fairbanks, 1971—74; pvt. practice law Fairbanks, 1971—86; judge U.S. Dist. Ct. Alaska, Anchorage, 1986—91, U.S. Ct. Appeals (9th cir.), San Francisco, 1991—. Contbr. articles to profl. jours. Mem.: Tanana Valley Bar Assn. (pres. 1974—75), Alaska Bar Assn. (pres. 1982—83, bd. govs. 1981—84), Phi Beta Kappa. Republican. Office: US Ct Appeals 9th Cir Courthouse Sq 250 Cushman St Ste 3-a Fairbanks AK 99701-4665

KLEMANN, GILBERT LACY, II, lawyer; b. New Rochelle, N.Y., July 26, 1950; s. N. Robert and Rosemary Virginia (Gerard) K.; m. Patricia Louise Hild, June 16, 1973; children: Tricia Rosemary, Gilbert Hild. AB, Coll. Holy Cross, 1972; JD, Fordham U., 1975. Bar: N.Y. 1976, U.S. Dist. Ct. (so. and ea. dists.) N.Y. 1976, Conn. 1988, U.S. Supreme Ct. 1991. Assoc. Chadbourne & Parke, N.Y.C., 1975-83, ptnr., 1983-90, of counsel, 2000; sr. v.p., gen. counsel Fortune Brands, Inc. (formerly Am. Brands Inc.), Old Greenwich, Conn., 1991-97, exec. v.p. strategic and legal affairs, 1998, exec. v.p. corp., mem. bd. dirs., 1999; sr. v.p., gen. counsel, sec. Avon Products, Inc., N.Y.C., 2001—. Editor Fordham Law Rev., 1974-75. Mem. Conn. Bar Assn., Greenwich (Conn.) Country Club, Nassau Club (Princeton, N.J.), Longboat Key Club (Fla.). Republican. Roman Catholic. Avocation: golf. Corporate, general, General practice. Home: 25 Hope Farm Rd Greenwich CT 06830-3331 also: 415 L'Ambiance Dr Longboat Key FL 34288 Office: Avon Products Inc 1345 Ave of the Americas New York NY 10105-0196 E-mail: gilbert.klemann@avon.com.

KLEMIN, LAWRENCE R. lawyer; b. New Rockford, N.D., Mar. 31, 1945; s. Lawrence R. Klemin and Carol M. (Cook) Roaldson; m. Rita R. DiPalma, Sept. 2, 1970; children: Laura K., Peter L. BA in English, U. N.D., 1967, JD with distinction, 1978. Bar: N.D. 1978, U.S. Dist. Ct. N.D. 1978, U.S. Ct. Appeals (8th cir.) 1987, U.S. Supreme Ct. 1988. Hearing officer N.D. Employment Security Bur., Bismarck, 1971-75; assoc. Atkinson & Dwyer, Bismarck, 1978-81; ptnr. Atkinson, Dwyer & Klemin, Bismarck, 1981-82, Dwyer & Klemin, Bismarck, 1982-86; pres. Lawrence R. Klemin, P.C., Bismarck, 1986-92, Bucklin & Klemin, P.C., Bismarck, 1992-96, Bucklin, Klemin & McBride, P.C., Bismarck, 1996—. Pres. Title and Escrow Co., Bismarck, 1988-98, Litigation Svcs., Inc., Bismarck, 1995—; state rep. N.D. legis assembly, 1998—; commr. Nat. Conf. of Commrs. on Uniform State Laws, 1999—; mem. state adv. coun. N.D. Office Adminstrv. Hearings, Bismarck, 1993-98; lectr. on real property law Nat. Bus. Inst., 1989—. Author, editor Civil Practice of North Dakota, 1993—. Bd. dirs. N.D. March of Dimes, Bismarck, 1994-2002, Burleigh-Morton chpt. Am. Red Cross, 2002—; mem. Corpus Christi Parish Coun., Bismarck, 1996-2002. With U.S. Army, 1967-70, Vietnam. Mem. State Bar Assn. N.D. (chair adminstrv. law com. 1996-98), N.D. Land Title Assn. (legis. com. 1990-99), Bismarck Mandan C. of C. (bd. dirs. 1996-98), Optimist Internat. (bd. dirs. 1985-86), Elks, Eagles, Am. Legion. Roman Catholic. Avocations: antique auto restoration, astronomy, camping. Administrative and regulatory, General civil litigation, Property, real (including real estate development, water). Home: 1709 Montego Dr Bismarck ND 58503-0856 Office: Bucklin Klemin & McBride PC 400 E Broadway #500 PO Box 955 Bismarck ND 58502-0955 E-mail: lklemin@bkmpc.com.

KLEPPER, FAITH CHEREE, lawyer; b. Houston, Feb. 5, 1972; d. Jack Houston and Cheryl Louise Klepper. AB in Internat. Rels., AB in Polit. Sci., Brown U., 1993; JD, Ariz. State U., 1997. Bar: Ariz. 1997. Dep. pub. defender Maricopa County Pub. Defender, Phoenix, 1998—2001; dep. county atty. Maricopa County Atty.'s Office, Phoenix, 2001—. Bd. dirs. DNA-People's Legal Svcs., Window Rock, Ariz., 1999—, v.p. bd. dirs., 2002—; mem. continuing legal end. com. State Bar of Ariz., Phoenix, 1998—; mem. steering com. Ariz. Minority Bar Conv., Phoenix, 1999—, chair steering com., 2000. Editl. bd. Ariz. Atty. mag., 1999—. Vol. Habitat for Humanity, Phoenix, 1999—2000; vol. admissions interviewer Brown U. Alumni Assn., Providence, 2000—02. Mem.: Maricopa County Bar Assn. (mem. bench/bar rels. com. 2001—). Avocations: reading, hiking, sports. Office: Maricopa County Attys Office 301 W Jefferson 8th Fl Phoenix AZ 85003

KLERX, OLIVER, lawyer; b. Wuerselen, Germany, June 7, 1970; Student, Trinity Coll., Dublin, Ireland, 1993—94; staatsexamen, U. Wuerzburg, Germany, 1991—96; Dr. jur., U. Wuerzburg. Bar: Germany 2000. Rsch. and tchg. asst. U. Wuerzburg, 1996—97; rechtsanwalt/lawyer Dietrich & Ptnrs. GbR, Bonn, Germany, 2000—01, Schneider-Schwegler GbR, Duesseldorf, Germany, 2001—02, White & Case, Frankfurt am Main, Germany, 2002—. Contbr. articles to profl. jours. Corporate, general, Mergers and acquisitions, Finance. Office: White & Case Stiftstraße 9-17 60313 Frankfurt Germany

KLETT, EDWIN L. lawyer; b. Clearfield, Pa., Dec. 8, 1935; s. John L. and Gertrude Elizabeth (Larson) K.; m. Janis Lynn Gibson; children: David, Lauren, Krista, Kirklin, Keenan. BS in Commerce and Finance, Bucknell U., 1957; JD, Dickinson Sch. Law, Carlisle, Pa., 1962. Bar: Pa. 1963, U.S. Dist. Ct. (we. dist.) Pa. 1963, U.S. Dist. Ct. (mid. dist.) Pa. 1995, U.S. Dist. Ct. (ea. dist.) Pa. 2000, U.S. Ct. Appeals (3d cir.) 1967, U.S. Ct. Appeals (6th cir.) 1985, U.S. Ct. Appeals (11th cir.) 2001, U.S. Supreme Ct. 1983. Assoc. Eckert, Seamans, Cherin & Mellott, Pitts., 1962, ptnr., 1969; sr. ptnr., chmn. Klett Rooney Lieber & Schorling P.C., Pitts., 1989—. Trustee Dickinson Sch. Law, 1982—; mem. civil procedural rules com. Pa. Supreme Ct., 1986-99, vice chair, 1989-92, chair, 1993-99. Mem. Pa. State Transp. Adv. Bd., Harrisburg, Pa., 1985-88, Rep. State Fin. Com., Harrisburg, 1986-91, Allegheny County Rep. Fin. Com., Pitts., 1987-92. Fellow Internat. Acad. Trial Lawyers, Am. Coll. Trial Lawyers (Pa. state com. 1994-99, state chair 1996-98), Am. Bd. Trial Advs., Am. Bar Found., Am. Bar Inst., Pa. Bar Found., Alletheny County Bar Found.; mem. ABA (ho. dels. 1999-2000), Am. Bd. Trial Advs., Acad. Trial Lawyers Allegheny County (bd. govs. 1986-89, pres. 1988-89), Am. Judicature Soc., Allegheny County Bar (bd. govs. 1989-92, 99-02, pres. 1999-01). Federal civil litigation, State civil litigation, Securities. Home: 151 Ordale Blvd Pittsburgh PA 15228-1525 Office: Klett Rooney Lieber & Schorling 1 Oxford Ct Fl 40 Pittsburgh PA 15219-1407 E-mail: elklett@klettrooney.com.

KLEWANS, SAMUEL N. lawyer; b. Lock Haven, Pa., Mar. 2, 1941; s. Morris and Ruth N. Klewans; children: Richard Bennett, Ruth Elise, Paul Henry, Margo Ilene. AB, U. Pa., 1963; JD, Am. U., 1966. Bar: Va. 1966, U.S. Dist. Ct. (ea. dist.) Va. 1966, U.S. Dist. Ct. D.C. 1967, U.S. Ct. Appeals D.C. 1967, U.S. Ct. Appeals (4th cir.) 1967, U.S. Supreme Ct. 1971. Law clk. U.S. Dist. Ct. (ea. dist.) Va., 1966-67; ptnr. Fried, Fried & Klewans, Springfield, Va., 1970-86; prin. Klewans & Assocs., 1986-91; shareholder, ptnr. Grad, Logan & Klewans, P.C., Alexandria, Va., 1991—. Lectr. No. Va. Inst. Continuing Med. Edn., No. Va. Ctr. Quality and Health Edn. Contbr. articles to profl. jours. 1st lt. JAGC-USAR, 1966-72. Corporate, general, Health, Corporate taxation. Office: 1421 Prince St Ste 320 Alexandria VA 22314-2805 E-mail: sklewans@glklawyers.com.

KLIEBENSTEIN, DON, lawyer; b. Marshalltown, Iowa, May 3, 1936; s. Donald B. and Gertrude E. (Skeie) K.; m. Mary L. Delfs, June 11, 1960; 1 child, Julie Ann. Student, Grinnell Coll., 1953-55; BA, U. Iowa, 1957, JD, 1961. Bar: Iowa 1961, U.S. Dist. Ct. (no., so. dists.) Iowa 1961, U.S. Supreme Ct. 1971. Pvt. practice, Grundy Center, Iowa, 1961-67; ptnr. Kliebenstein & Heronimus, Grundy Center, 1967-77, Kliebenstein, Heronimus & Schmidt, Grundy Center, 1977-98, Kliebenstein Heronimus Schmidt and Harris, Grundy Center, 1999—. Bd. dirs. Grundy Nat. Bank, Grundy Ctr.; county atty. Grundy County, 1965-98. Mem. ABA, Iowa State Bar Assn., Grundy County Bar Assn. (pres. 1979-80), 1st Jud. Dist. Bar Assn. (pres. 1975-76). Republican. Methodist. General practice. Home: 701 9th St Grundy Center IA 50638-1238 Office: Kliebenstein Heronimus Schmidt & Harris 630 G Ave Grundy Center IA 50638-1500

KLIMEK, JAMES, lawyer; b. South Bend, Ind., Apr. 19, 1967; s. Thomas F. and Anne (Foley) Klimek. BA, Colby Coll., 1989; JD, Ind. U., 1992. Dep. commr. Ind. Securities Divsn., Indpls., 1992—95, chief counsel, 1995—97; assoc. counsel Std. Mgmt. Corp., Indpls., 1997—99; assoc. Maddox Koeller Hargett & Caruso, Indpls., 2000—02; of counsel Lewis & Kappes, Indpls., 2002—. Mem.: ABA (state and fed. securities coms. 2000—). Securities, Corporate, general, Franchising. Office: Lewis & Kappes PC 1700 One American Sq Indianapolis IN 46282 Fax: 317-639-4882.

KLINE, ALLEN HABER, JR., lawyer; b. Houston, June 17, 1954; s. Allen H. Sr. and Maude Rose (Brown) K.; m. Barbara Ann Byrd, July 24, 1982; children: Allison Ashley, Allen III. BA, U. Denver, 1976; JD, U. Miami, 1979. Bar: Tex. 1980, U.S. Dist. Ct. (so. dist.) Tex. 1980, U.S. Ct. Appeals (5th cir.) 1980, U.S. Ct. Appeals (11th cir.) 1983, U.S. Supreme Ct. 1985; bd. cert. personal injury trial law Tex. Bd. Legal Specialization. Sole practice, Houston, 1980—. Mem. Houston Bar Assn., Coll. of the State Bar of Tex. Clubs: City Wide (Houston) (life). Avocations: tennis, water, snow skiing. General civil litigation, Personal injury (including property damage), Probate (including wills, trusts). Office: 440 Louisiana St Ste 2050 Houston TX 77002-4205

KLINE, DAVID ADAM, lawyer, educator, writer; b. Keota, Okla., Sept. 27, 1923; s. David Adam and Lucy Leila (Wood) K.; m. Ruthela Deal, Aug. 25, 1947; children: Steven, Timothy, Ruthanna. JD, Okla. U., 1950. Bar: Okla. 1949. Law clk., spl. master U.S. Dist. Ct. Okla., 1952-61; 1st asst. U.S. atty. We. Dist. Okla., 1961-69; judge We. Dist. Okla. U.S. Bankruptcy Ct., Oklahoma City, 1969-82; sr. shareholder Kline Kline Elliott Castleberry & Bryant, P.C., Oklahoma City, 1983—. Pres. Nat. Conf. Bankruptcy Judges 1977-78; mem. arbitration panel program U.S. Dist. Ct. (we. dist.) Okla., 1985— mem. faculty Fed. Jud. Ctr., Washington, Nat. Seminar Bankruptcy Judges, 1971-86; adj. prof. law Oklahoma City U., 1980-84; cons. Norton Bankruptcy Law and Practice, 1986, Callaghan & Co.; bd. dirs. Consumer Credit Counseling Svc. Ctr., Okla., 1973-2001, chmn., 1992. Author: A Little Book (A New Thing in the Earth), 1993, A Little Book II (The Blood of the Lion), 1995, A Little Book III (The Revelation), 1997, A Little Book IV (A Still Small Voice), 1998, A Little Book V (Law and Liberty), 2003; digest editor Am. Bankruptcy Law jour., 1974—77; contbr. ; cont. co-author Briefcase, 1988—2000. Fellow Am. Coll. Bankruptcy. Bankruptcy, General civil litigation, Criminal. Office: Kline Kline Elliott Castleberry & Bryant PC Kline Law Bldg 720 NE 63rd St Oklahoma City OK 73105-6405 E-mail: dkline@klinefirm.org.

KLINE, JAMES EDWARD, lawyer; b. Fremont, Ohio, Aug. 3, 1941; s. Walter J. and Sophia Kline; m. Mary Ann Bruening, Aug. 29, 1964; children: Laura Anne Kline, Matthew Thomas, Jennifer Sue. BS in Social Sci., John Carroll U., 1963; JD, Ohio State U., 1966; postgrad., Stanford U., 1991. Bar: Ohio 1966, NC 1989, US Tax. Ct. 1983. Assoc. Eastman, Stichter, Smith & Bergman, Toledo, 1966-70; ptnr. Eastman, Stichter, Smith & Bergman (name now Eastman & Smith), Toledo, 1970-84, Shumaker, Loop & Kendrick, Toledo, 1984-88; v.p., gen. counsel Aeroquip-Vickers, Inc. (formerly Trinova Corp.), Toledo, 1989-99; exec. v.p. Cavista Corp., 2000—01; dir. devel. Toledo Mus. Art, 2002—03; v.p., gen. counsel, sec. Cooper Tire and Rubber Co., Findlay, Ohio, 2003—. Corp. sec. Sheller-Globe Corp., 1977—84; adj. prof. U. Toledo Coll. Law, 1988—94; bd. dirs. Plastic Techs., Inc.; trustee Promedica Health Edn. and Rsch. Corp., 2002—. Author: (with Robert Seaver) Ohio Corporation Law, 1988. Trustee Kidney Found. of Northwestern Ohio, Inc., 1972-81, pres., 1979-80; bd. dirs. Toledo Botanical Garden (formerly Crosby Gardens), 1974-80, pres., 1977-79; bd. dirs. Toledo Zool. Soc., 1983-96, 99—, pres., 1991-93; bd. dirs. Toledo Area Regional Transit Authority, 1984-90, pres., 1987-88; bd. dirs. Home Away From Home, Inc. (Ronald McDonald House NW Ohio), 1983-88; trustee Toledo Symphony Orch., 1981—, St. John's H.S., 1988-91, Ohio Found. Ind. Colls., 1991-2000; trustee Lourdes Coll., 1988-96, chmn., 1994-96; trustee ProMedia Health Edn. and Rsch. Corp., 2002--. Fellow Ohio Bar Found.; mem. ABA, Nat. Assn. Corp. Dirs., Ohio Bar Assn. (corp. law com. 1977—, chmn. 1983-86), NC Bar Assn., Toledo Bar Assn., Mfrs. Alliance (chair Law Coun. II 1997-99), Toledo Area C. of C. (trustee 1994—, chmn. 2000-01), Inverness Club, Toledo Club (trustee 1990-97), Stone Oak Country Club, Ottawa Skeet Club, Answer Club. Roman Catholic. Corporate, general, Securities, Corporate taxation. Home: 216 Treetop Pl Holland OH 43528-8451 Office: Cooper Tire & Rubber Co 701 Lima Ave Findlay OH 45840 E-mail: jekline@coopertire.com.

KLINE, NORMAN DOUGLAS, federal judge; b. Lynn, Mass., Dec. 28, 1930; s. Samuel and Ida (Luff) K.; m. Betty Toba Feldman, Feb. 27, 1966; children: Sarah, Samuel. AB, Harvard Coll., 1952, postgrad., 1952-53; JD, Boston U., 1959. Bar: Mass. 1959. Pvt. practice, Boston, 1959-60; atty. U.S. Dept. Army, Cleve., 1960; trial atty. FMC, Washington, 1960-72, adminstrv. law judge, 1972-92, chief adminstrv. law judge, 1992—. With U.S. Army, 1953-55. Mem. Fed. Adminstrv. Law Judges Conf. Avocations: classical music, collecting cds. Office: Fed Maritime Commn 800 N Capitol St NW Washington DC 20573-0001 E-mail: normank@fmc.gov.

KLINE, PHILLIP D. state attorney general; b. Kansas City, Kans., Dec. 31, 1959; s. James R. and Janet S. (Shirley) K.; m. Deborah Suzanne Shattuck, July 22, 1989; 1 child, Jacqueline Hillary. BS in Pub. Rels. and Polit. Sci., Cen. Mo. State U., 1982; JD, U. Kans., 1987. Bar: Kans. 1987, U.S. Ct. Appeals (10th cir.), U.S. Dist. Ct. Kans. News reporter WHB Radio, Kansas City, Mo., 1981-82; pub. rels. rep. Mid-America, Inc., Kansas City, Mo., 1982-84; assoc. Blackwell, Sanders, Matheny, Weary & Lombardi, Overland Park, Kans., 1987—; legislator State of Kans., 1992—2000, atty. gen., 2003—. Nominee Kans. 2d Congl. Dist., 1986; mem. Kans. State Ho. of Reps. from 18th Dist., 1993—; chmn. taxation com., 1995—; fin. chmn. Johnson County Reps., 1990-91; chmn. Shawnee Reps., 1991-92; chmn., co-chmn. Corp. Woods Charity Jazz Festival, Overland Park, 1991-95; bd. dirs. Shawnee Mission Edn. Found., 1994-95, Rep. Ho. Campaign Com. Mem. Johnson County Bar Assn., Kans. Bar Assn., Rotary (bd. dirs., v.p. 1991-93, pres. 1994-95, Disting. Svc. award 1991). Republican. Methodist. Avocations: history, reading, athletics. Home: 10624 W 61st St Shawnee KS 66203-3016 Office: Atty Gen 120 SW 10th Ave, 2nd Fl Topeka KS 66612*

KLINE, SIDNEY DELONG, JR., lawyer; b. West Reading, Pa., Mar. 25, 1932; s. Sidney D. and Leona Clarice (Barkalow) K.; m. Barbara Phyllis James, Dec. 31, 1955; children: Allison S. McCanney, Leslie S. Davidson, Lisa P. Gallen. BA, Dickinson Coll., 1954, LLD (hon.) , 1998; LLB, The Dickinson Law Sch., 1956, LLD (hon.) , 1994. Bar: Pa. 1956, U.S. Dist. Ct. (ea. dist.) Pa. 1961, U.S. Supreme Ct. 1967. Assoc. Stevens & Lee, Reading, Pa., 1958-62, ptnr., shareholder, 1963-97, pres., 1977-93, chmn., 1993-97, counsel, 1998—. Bd. dirs. Reading Eagle Co. Pres., United Way of Berks County, Reading, 1972-74, campaign chmn., 1986; bd. dirs. Reading Ctr. City Devel. Fund, 1976-98, pres., 1992-97; gov. Dickinson Sch. Law, 1978—, sec., 1988—; trustee Dickinson Coll., 1979—, chmn., 1990-98; bd. dirs. Greater Berks Devel. Fund, 1998—. Served with U.S. Army, 1956-58. Recipient Doran award United Way Berks County, 1978, Richard J. Caron Cmty. Svc. award Caron Found., 1993, Thun Cmty. Svc. award, 1995, William Strong Cmty. Svc. award, 2002. Fellow Am. Coll. Trust and Estate Coun., Nat. Soc. Fund Raising Execs. (Outstanding Vol. Fund Raiser Greater Northeastern Pa. chpt. 1992), Pa. Bar Assn., Berks County Bar Assn., Berkshire Country Club (Reading), Moselem Springs Golf Club (Fleetwood, Pa.), The Club at Pelican Bay (Naples, Fla.). Republican. Lutheran. Banking, Probate (including wills, trusts), Property, real (including real estate development, water). Office: PO Box 679 111 N 6th St Reading PA 19603-0679 E-mail: sdk@stevenslee.com.

KLINE, THOMAS RICHARD, lawyer; b. Hazleton, Pa., Dec. 18, 1947; s. Isadore J. and Jeanne (Levin) K.; m. Paula Wolf, Dec. 25, 1972; children: Hilary, Zachary. AB, Albright Coll., 1969; MA, Lehigh U., 1971; JD, Duquesne U., 1978. Bar: Pa., N.Y., U.S. Supreme Ct., U.S. Dist. Ct. (ea. dist.) Pa., U.S. Dist. Ct. (we. dist.) Pa., U.S. Ct. Appeals (3rd cir.). Tchr. Hazleton Area Sch. Dist., 1969-74; lectr. Lehigh U., Bethlehem, Pa., 1974; law clk. to Hon. Thomas W. Pomeroy Pa. Supreme Ct., Pitts., 1978; atty. Beasley Casey Colleran Erbstein Thistle & Kline, Phila., 1980-94; ptnr. Kline & Specter, 1995—. Adj. prof. sch. law Temple U; chmn. Fed. Judicial Nominations Comm., U.S. Dist. of Pa. Recipient Top Ten Litigators in Am., Nat. Law Jour., 2000. Master Of Bench, U. Pa. Inn of Cts.; fellow: Internat. Acad. Trial Lawyers, Am. Coll. Trial Lawyers; mem.: Inner Circle of Advocates, Phila. Trial Lawyers Assn., Pa. Trial Lawyers Assn., Assn. Trial Lawyers Am., Phila. Bar Assn., Pa. Bar Assn., ABA. Republican. General civil litigation, Personal injury (including property damage). Office: 1525 Locust St Philadelphia PA 19102-3732

KLINE, TIMOTHY DEAL, lawyer; b. Oklahoma City, July 16, 1949; s. David Adam and Ruthela (Deal) K.; m. Alyssa Lipp Krysler, Aug. 29, 1985. BA, U. Okla., 1971, JD, 1976. Bar: Okla. 1976, U.S. Dist. Ct. (we. dist.) Okla. 1977, U.S. Ct. Appeals (10th cir.) 1977; cert. in bus. bankruptcy law and consumer bankruptcy Am. Bankruptcy Bd. of Certification. Law clk. to presiding justice U.S. Dist. Ct. (we. dist.) Okla., Oklahoma City, 1976-80; assoc. Linn, Helms, Kirk & Burkett, Oklahoma City, 1980-83; ptnr. Kline & Kline, Oklahoma City, 1983—2001; shareholder Kline, Kline, Elliott, Castleberry & Bryant PC, Oklahoma City, 2001—. Adj. prof. law Oklahoma City U., 1980-84, 90. Mem. Am. Coll. Bankruptcy, Okla. County Bar Assn. (pres. 1998-99), Phi Delta Phi. Democrat. Bankruptcy. Office: Kline Kline Elliott Castleberry & Bryant PC 720 NE 63rd St Oklahoma City OK 73105-6405 E-mail: tkline@klinefirm.org.

KLINEDINST, JOHN DAVID, lawyer; b. Washington, Jan. 20, 1950; s. David Moulson and Mary Stewart (Coxe) K.; m. Cynthia Lynn DuBain, Aug. 15, 1981. BA cum laude in History, Washington and Lee U., 1971, JD, 1978; MBA in Fin. and Investments, George Washington U., 1975. Bar: Calif. 1979, U.S. Dist. Ct. (so. dist.) Calif. 1979, U.S. Ct. Appeals (9th cir.) 1987. With comml. lending dept. 1st Nat. Bank Md., Montgomery County, 1971-74; assoc. Ludecke, McGrath & Denton, San Diego, 1979-80; ptnr. Whitney & Klinedinst, San Diego, 1980-83, Klinedinst & Meiser, San Diego, 1983-86; mng. ptnr. Klinedinst, Fliehman & McKillop, San Diego, 1986—. Mem. law coun. Washington and Lee U., 1993-97, vice chmn. law campaign, 1991-94, bd. trustees, 2001—; vice chmn. bd. dirs. ARC of San Diego/Imperial, 1991-97; pres. House Corp. Calif. Lambda, Phi Kappa Psi, 1999—. Recipient Disting. Alumnus award Washington and Lee U., 1993.

Mem. ABA (standing com. on legal profl. liability), Calif. Bar Assn., San Diego Bar Assn., San Diego Def. Lawyers, San Diego/Tijuana Sister Cities Soc., Washington Soc. (bd. dirs. 1997—), Washington and Lee U. Alumni Assn. (bd. dirs. 1986-90, pres. 1989-90), Washington and Lee U. Club (pres. San Diego chpt. 1980-87, San Diego dialogue of U. Calif. San Diego), La Jolla Beach and Tennis Club, Fairbanks Ranch Country Club, Phi Kappa Psi. Republican. Episcopalian. Federal civil litigation, State civil litigation. Home: 6226 Via Dos Valles Rancho Santa Fe CA 92067-9999 Office: Klinedinst Fliehman & McKillop 501 W Broadway Ste 600 San Diego CA 92101-3584 E-mail: jdk@kfmlaw.com.

KLINEFELTER, JAMES LOUIS, lawyer; b. L.A., Oct. 8, 1925; s. Theron Albert and Anna Marie (Coffey) K.; m. Joanne Wright, Dec. 26, 1957 (div.); children: Patricia Anne, Jeanne Marie, Christopher Wright; m. Mary Lynn S. Klinefelter, Aug. 19, 1971; 1 child, Mary Katherine. BA, U. Ala., 1949, LLB, 1951. Bar: Ala. 1951, U.S. Dist. Ct. (no. dist.) Ala. 1959, U.S. Ct. Appeals (11th cir.) 1983. Regional claims rep. State Farm Mut. Auto Ins. Co., Anniston, Ala., 1951-54; ptnr. Burnham & Klinefelter, Anniston, 1954—. Mem. adv. com. Supreme Ct. Ala. Mem. Ala. Dem. Exec. Com., 1964—, chmn. legis. rev. com., 1964—; past chmn. Calhoun County Dem. Exec. Com., 1964—; mem. Anniston City Sch. Bd. Lt. (j.g.) USNR, 1943-46. Mem. ABA, Assn. Def. Trial Attys., Ala. Bar Assn. (mem. task force on jud. selection, mem. long-range planning task force), Calhoun County Bar Assn., Ala. Def. Lawyers Assn. (past pres.), Ala. Law Inst. (bd. dirs.), Ala. Sch. Bd. Attys. (past pres.), Internat. Assn. Def. Counsel, Kiwanis (past pres.), Anniston Country Club, Phi Kappa Sigma, Phi Alpha Theta. Avocations: tennis, swimming, reading. General civil litigation, Education and schools, Insurance. Home: 1412 Christine Ave Anniston AL 36207-3924 Office: Burnham & Klinefelter So Trust Nat Bank Bldg PO Box 1618 Anniston AL 36202-1618 E-mail: jlkbkpc@bellsouth.net.

KLINGENBERG, OLAV E. lawyer; b. Oslo, July 24, 1944; s. Erik O. and Gunvor Klingenberg; m. Ellen Skottun Klingenberg, Jan. 9, 1970; children: Peder O., Kaja Marie. Cand. juris., U. Oslo, 1969. Bar: Norway 1973. Legal sec. Dir. Taxes, Oslo, 1970—71; deputy dist. judge Lier, Royken & Huruk County Ct., Frammen, 1971—72; legal cons. Oslo Tax Office, 1973—75; mgr. tax divsn. Arthur Andersen & Co., 1975—79, ptnr., 1980—88, Wikborg Rein & Co., 1989—. Chmn. Norwegian Tax Payer Assn., Oslo, 1988—98. Co-author: Your In-House Lawyer, 1997; editor: Ask You Lawyer, 1988; contbr. articles to profl. jours. With Norwegian Air Force, 1967—68. Mem.: Internat. Fiscal Assn., Norwegian Law Soc., Norwegian Bar Assn., Norwegian Yacht Assn. (mem. appeals bd. 1974—), Hanko Yacht Club, Royal Norwegian Yacht Club. Avocations: sailing, travel, history, photography, model building. Corporate taxation, General civil litigation. Office: Wilkborg Rein & Co Kronprinsesse Martha Pl 1 N-0117 Oslo Norway Fax: 47 22 82 75 01/02. E-mail: oek@wr.no.

KLINGLE, PHILIP ANTHONY, law librarian; b. Bklyn., July 24, 1950; s. Lorin Russell and Therese Margaret (Meehan) K.; m. Rachelle Phyllis Miller, Nov. 20, 1977; children: David Adam, Michael Matthew, Anne Elizabeth. BA, Fordham U., 1971; MA, NYU, 1973; MS, Columbia U., 1976. Asst. reference libr. N.Y. Hist. Soc., N.Y.C., 1973-77; libr. Bklyn. Pub. Libr., 1977-78; reference libr., asst. prof. John Jay Coll. Criminal Justice CUNY, 1978-81; libr. Inst. Jud. Adminstrn. Sch. of Law NYU, 1981-82; sr. law libr. ct. libr. N.Y. State Supreme Ct., S.I., 1982—. Editor: jour. The Literature of Criminal Justice, 1980-81, IJA Report, 1981-82. Mem. ALA, Am. Assn. Law Librs., Law Libr. Assn. Greater N.Y., Libr. Assn. CUNY (mem. exec. coun. 1978-81). Office: NY State Supreme Ct Libr Richmond County Courthouse Staten Island NY 10301

KLINGSBERG, DAVID, lawyer; b. N.Y.C., Feb. 4, 1934; m. Fran Sue Morganstern, Aug. 16, 1959; 3 children. LL.B., Yale U., 1957; BS, NYU, 1954. Bar: N.Y. 1958. Law clk. to U.S. Dist. Judge, N.Y., 1957-58; atty. U.S. Dept. Justice, Office Dep. Atty. Gen., Washington, 1958-59; asst. U.S. atty. criminal div. So. Dist. N.Y., 1959-61; chief appellate atty. U.S. Atty. Office, NY, 1961-62; assoc. Kaye Scholer LLP, N.Y.C., 1962—65, ptnr., 1966—, chmn. exec. com., 1999—. Contbr. articles to legal jours.; mem. editorial bd. Yale Law Jour, 1956-57. Bd. dirs. Legal Aid Soc. NY , 2001—. Recipient Pub. Interest Leadership award, Legal Aid Soc. 2001. Fellow Am. Coll. Trial Lawyers; mem. ABA, Assn. Bar City N.Y. (chmn. anti-trust and trade regulation com. 1986-89, mem. com. on diversity in legal profession 1998—, Thurgood Marshall award for representation in death sentence cases 1998), N.Y. State Bar Assn., Legal Aid Soc. (dir. 1999—), Fed. Bar Coun. Federal civil litigation, State civil litigation. Office: Kaye Scholer LLP 425 Park Ave New York NY 10022-3506

KLINK, FREDRIC J. lawyer; b. N.Y.C., Oct. 4, 1933; s. Frederick Carl and Sophia Adelaide (Wolf) K.; m. Sandra Scott, 1979; children: Christopher, Charles; stepchildren: Kirsten Morehouse, Trina Morehouse. AB, Columbia U., 1955, LL.B., 1960. Bar: N.Y. 1960. Practiced in, N.Y.C.; ptnr. firm Dechert, Price & Rhoads, 1989—. Editor: Columbia U. Law Rev, 1959-60. Served as lt. (j.g.) USNR, 1955-57. Mem. Am. Law Inst., Am., Internat., N.Y. C. bar assns. Corporate, general, Private international, Securities. Office: Dechert LLP 30 Rockefeller Plz New York NY 10021 Home: 265 Riverside Dr New York NY 10024

KLINKOSUM, MAITRI (MIKE KLINKOSUM), lawyer; b. Winston-Salem, N.C., Mar. 18, 1970; s. Nithi and Elizabeth Hopkins Klinkosum. BA, U. N.C., Chapel Hill, 1992; JD, U. Miami, 1995. Bar: Ill. 1995, U.S. Dist. Ct. (no. dist.) Ill. 1997, N.C. 1998, U.S. Dist. Ct. (we. dist.) N.C. 1998. Asst. pub. defender Kane County Pub. Defender's Office, St. Charles, Ill., 1996, Cook County Pub. Defender's Office, Chgo., 1996—98; assoc. Willardson, Lipscomb & Beal, Wilkesboro, NC, 1998—99, Vannoy, Colvard, Tripelett & Vannoy, North Wilkesboro, NC, 1999—2001; solo practitioner Wilkesboro, 2001—03; asst. capital defender Forsyth regional office Office of the Capital Defender, Winston-Salem, 2003—. Author articles to profl. jours. Mem.: ACLU, ATLA, Fla. Assn. Criminal Def. Lawyers (Student Award for Outstanding Advocacy), N.C. Acad. Trial Lawyers, Nat. Assn. Criminal Def. Lawyers. Democrat. Avocations: racquetball, martial arts. Criminal. Home: 625 Taylor Ridge Rd Winston Salem NC 27106 Office: PO Box 20308 Winston Salem NC 27120-0808 Fax: 336-761-2515. E-mail: MKlinkosum@triad.rr.net.

KLIPP, TODD LAMONT CAUSEY, lawyer; b. Syracuse, N.Y., June 27, 1950; s. David Lawrence and Joyce (Axtell) K.; m. Anne MacRae Causey, Aug. 21, 1982; children: Austin, Hillary, Nathan. AB, Hamilton Coll., 1972; JD, Fordham U., 1976. Bar: N.Y. 1977, U.S. Dist. Ct. (so. and ea. dists.) N.Y. 1977, U.S. Tax Ct. 1978, Mass. 1980, U.S. Dist. Ct. Mass. 1980. Assoc. Mudge Rose Guthrie & Alexander, N.Y.C., 1976-79, Goodwin, Procter & Hoar, Boston, 1979-83; asst. gen. counsel Boston U., 1984-85, dep. gen. counsel, 1985-87, gen. counsel, 1987-97, v.p., gen. counsel, 1997—. Adj. prof. law, Boston U. Sch. Law, 2000-; counsel Vol. Lawyers Project, Boston, 1982—. Notes editor Fordham U. Law Jour., 1975-76. Clarinetist, Lexington Bicentennial Band; trustee Lexington Christian Acad., 2002—; chmn. ch. coun. Trinity Covenant Ch., 2000—. Mem. Nat. Assn. Coll. and Univ. Attys. (publs. com. 1987-88, ann. conf. program com. 1988-89, continuing legal edn. com. 1990-92), Mass. Bar Assn., Boston Bar Assn. Avocations: reading, running, swimming. Home: 19 Holmes Rd Lexington MA 02420-1916 Office: Boston U Office Gen Counsel 125 Bay State Rd Boston MA 02215-1708

KLIPSTEIN, ROBERT ALAN, lawyer; b. N.Y.C., Sept. 23, 1936; s. Harold David and Hyacinth (Levin) K. AB, Columbia U., 1957, JD, 1960; LLM in Taxation, NYU, 1965. Bar: N.Y. 1960, U.S. Supreme Ct. 1964. Practice of law Saxe Bacon & O'Shea, N.Y.C., 1961—, assoc., 1961, Rosenman, Colin, Kaye, Petschek & Freund, 1962-63; law sec. to justice N.Y. County Supreme Ct., 1963-64; assoc. Bernays & Eisner, 1965-70; ptnr. Eisner, Klipstein & Klipstein, 1971-77, Danziger, Bangser, Klipstein, Goldsmith, Greenwald & Weiss (now Bangser Klein Rocca & Blum), N.Y.C., 1977-92; counsel Sullivan & Donovan, 1992—2001; ptnr. Ballon, Stoll, Bader & Nadler, N.Y.C., 2002—. Arbitrator City of N.Y. Small Claims Ct., 1971—. With U.S. Army, 1960—62. Mem. ABA, N.Y. State Bar Assn., Assn. Bar City of N.Y., N.Y. County Lawyers Assn., Am. Immigration Lawyers Assn., Westchester County Bar Assn., Am. Judges Assn., Univ. Glee Club (N.Y.C.), Phi Alpha Delta. Immigration, naturalization, and customs, Probate (including wills, trusts), Estate taxation. Home: 401 E 74th St Apt 6G New York NY 10021-3931 Office: Ballon Stoll Bader & Nadler 1450 Broadway New York NY 10018 E-mail: raklip@aol.com.

KLOBASA, JOHN ANTHONY, lawyer; b. St. Louis, Feb. 15, 1951; s. Alan R. and Virginia (Yager) K. BA in Econs., Emory U., 1972; JD, Wash. U., 1975. Bar: Mo. 1975, U.S. Dist. Ct. (ea. dist.) Mo. 1975, U.S. Ct. Appeals (8th cir.) 1976, U.S. Supreme Ct. 1979, U.S. Tax Ct. 1981, U.S. Ct. Appeals (9th cir.) 1990, U.S. Ct. Appeals (10th cir.) 1993. Assoc. Kohn, Shands, Elbert, Gianoulakis & Gilium LLP, St. Louis, 1975—80, ptnr., 1981—. Spl. counsel City of Town and Country, Mo., 1987; spl. counsel City of Des Peres, Mo., 1987, alderman, 1989-91. Mem.: ABA, Met. St. Louis Bar Assn., Mo. Bar Assn., Order of Coif, Phi Beta Kappa. Republican. General civil litigation, Family and matrimonial, Probate (including wills, trusts). Office: Kohn Shands Elbert Gianoulakis & Gilium LLP One US Bank Plz Ste 2410 Saint Louis MO 63101-1643 E-mail: jklobasa@ksegg.com.

KLOCH, JOHN E. judge, educator; b. Angora, Nebr., Apr. 2, 1941; m. Donna C. Kloch, Mar. 24, 1973; children: Aaron, Andrew. BS in Econs., U. Md., 1967; JD, Am. U., Washington, 1970. Assoc. Middleton, Jason & Cadeaux, Washington, 1970—72; pvt. practice Alexandria, Va., 1972—74; dep. commonwealth's atty. City of Alexandria, 1974—78, commonwealth's atty., 1978—97; judge 18th Jud. Cir. Ct., Alexandria, 1997—. Vis. lectr. Georgetown Law Sch., Washington, 1979—83; lectr. No. Va. Regional Police Acad., Va. State Bar, 1986—90; instr. Va. Supreme Ct., Commonwealth's Attys. Svcs. Coun., Va.; adj. faculty No. Va. CC, 1998—. Mem. Atty. Gen.'s Task Force Domestic Violence, 1990—93, Va. Commn. Reduction Sexual Assault, 1991—94; mem. adv. bd. Salvation Army, 1979—97, past chmn.; mem. Rosemont Civic Assn., 1982—; bd. dirs. Found. Alexandria Bar Assn., 1989—; vice chmn. Va. Bd. Health Professions, 1994—96; mem. adv. bd. Va. Lab. Svcs., 1986—90; asst. Rape Victim Companion Program, 1975; founder Alexandria Victim/Witness Program, 1984, Career Criminal Program, 1979, Alexandria Alcohol Safety Action Program, 1986; mem. bd. advisors women's empowerment program Alexandria Correctional Ctr., 1996—97. Recipient Crime Victims and Witnesses award, Va. Network Victims and Witnesses, 1988, Robert F. Horan Jr. award, Va. Assn. Commonwealth's Attys., 1992. Mem.: Alexandria Bar Assn. (bd. dirs. 1977—79, 1983—86). Home: 300 North View Ter Alexandria VA 22301 Office: 520 King St 4th Fl Alexandria VA 22314 Business E-Mail: jkloch@netzero.net.

KLOCK, JOHN HENRY, lawyer; b. Gouverneur, N.Y., Mar. 29, 1944; s. John F. and Patricia M. (Chateau) K.; m. Connie E. McLaughlin, May 31, 1969; children: Thomas, Jacqueline. BA, St. Bonaventure U., 1966; postgrad., U. Va., 1967; MA, NYU, 1970; JD, Rutgers U., 1976. Bar: N.J. 1976, U.S. Dist. Ct. N.J. 1976, N.Y. 1977, U.S. Ct. Appeals (3d cir.) 1979, U.S. Dist. Ct. (ea. dist.) N.Y. 1981, U.S. Supreme Ct. 1981, U.S. Dist. Ct. (so. dist.) N.Y. 1982, U.S. Dist. Ct. (no. dist.) N.Y. 1988, U.S. Dist. Ct. (we. dist.) N.Y. 2002; cert. civil trial atty. N.J. Law clk. to judge U.S. Dist. Ct. N.J., Newark, 1976-77; assoc. Gibbons, Del Deo, Dolan, Griffinger & Vecchione, Newark, 1977-83, ptnr., 1983—. Author: New Jersey Practice Court Rules (5th edit.), vol. 1, 1A, 2, 2A, 2000, New Jersey Practice Evidence Rules, 4th edit., 2002, New Jersey Practice Trial Lawyers Manual, vol. 2E, 2003; contbr. articles to profl. jours. Active Scotch Plains Hist. Commn. Mem. ABA, N.J. Bar Assn., N.Y. Bar Assn., U.S. Supreme Ct. Hist. Soc., N.J. Hist. Soc., Plainfield Country Club. Roman Catholic. Achievements include patents for quick release automatic chaulk gun. Avocations: golf, gardening. General civil litigation, Construction, Environmental. Home: 1800 Lake Ave Scotch Plains NJ 07076-2920 E-mail: jklock@gibbonslaw.com.

KLOCK, JOSEPH PETER, JR., lawyer; b. Phila., Mar. 14, 1949; s. Joseph Peter and Mary Dorothy (Fornace) K.; m. Susan Marie Girsch, Mar. 17, 1979; children: Susan Elizabeth, Kathleen Marie, Robert Charles, Peter Joseph II. BA in Philosophy with honors, LaSalle Coll., 1970; JD cum laude, U. Miami, Fla., 1973; DHL (hon.), LaSalle U., 1999. Bar: Fla. 1973, Pa. 1973, D.C. 1978. Ptnr. Steel, Hector & Davis LLP, Miami, Fla., 1977-79, adminstrv. ptnr., 1978-82, chmn., mng. ptnr., 1983—; gen. counsel, chief legal officer Flo-Sun, Inc., 1991—. Adj. prof. U. Miami Law Sch., 1974-84; bd. dirs. Nat. Beverage Corp., Premier Hotel Corp., Fla. Partnership for the Americas, FTAA Adminstrv. Secretariat, Inc., St. Thomas Human Rights Inst.; vice chmn. bd. dirs. Baypoint Sch., Inc.; mem. Fed. Jud. Nominating Com. of Fla., 1993-97. Trustee Belen Jesuit Prep. Sch., St. Joseph's Preparatory Sch., Barry U., Collins Ctr., Miami Art Mus., Fundacion Mir, New Hope Charities, Inc.; chmn. bd., trustee Carrollton Sch., 1982-98. Fellow Am. Bar Found.; mem. ABA (chmn. Caribbean law com. internat. law sect. 1991-92), Fla. Bar (chmn. civil procedure rules com. 1979-82), D.C. Bar, Dade County Bar Assn., Assn. Bar City of N.Y., Am. Law Inst., Am. Assn. Sovereign Mil. Order Malta, Iron Arrow Honor Soc., Westview Country Club, Sailfish Club Palm Beach, Govs. Club West Palm Beach, Miami City Club (pres. 1994-97), Phi Alpha Delta, Phi Kappa Phi, Omicron Delta Kappa. Democrat. Roman Catholic. General civil litigation, General practice, Private international. Home: 5095 SW 82nd St Miami FL 33143-8503 Office: 200 S Biscayne Blvd Fl 41 Miami FL 33131-2310 also: 2nd Fl One North Clematis St West Palm Beach FL 33401 E-mail: klock@steelhector.com.

KLOESS, LAWRENCE HERMAN, JR., retired lawyer; b. Mamaroneck, N.Y., Jan. 30, 1927; s. Lawrence H. and Harriette Adelia (Holly) K.; m. Eugenia Ann Underwood, Nov. 10, 1931; children: Lawrence H. III, Price Mentzel, Branch Donelson, David Holly. AB, U. Ala., 1954, JD, 1956; grad., Air Command & Staff Coll., 1974, Air War Coll., 1976; grad. Indsl. Coll. of the Armed Forces, Nat. Def. U., 1977. Bar: Ala. 1956, U.S. dist. Ct. (no. dist.) Ala. 1956, U.S. Ct. Appeals (5th cir.) 1957, U.S. Ct. Mil. Appeals 1971, U.S. Supreme Ct. 1971, U.S. Ct. Appeals (11th cir.) 1981. Sole practice, Birmingham, Ala., 1956-60, 62-66; corp. counsel Bankers Fire and Marine Ins. Co., 1961-62; dist. counsel for Ala. Office Dist. Counsel U.S. Dept. Vets. Affairs, Montgomery, 1966-95. Contbr. articles on law to profl. jours. Vice chmn. Salvation Army adv. bd., 1981, mem. bd., 1978-81; mem. nat. conf. bar pres.'s ABA, 1981—; mem. adminstrn. bd. Frazer Meml. United Meth. Ch., 1987-90, 92—; mem. adv. coun. Ret. and Sr. Vol. Program, Montgomery, 1997—; mem. Montgomery Symphony League, 2000—. Col. Judge Adv. Gen. USAFR, 1954-86, ret. Bd. dirs., sec. Air Force Judge Adv. Gen. Sch. Found., 1996—. Decorated Legion of Merit, Meritorious Svc. medal with oak leaf cluster, USAF Commendation medal; named Outstanding Judge Advocate USAFR, 1977, 79. Mem.: ABA (pres. nat. conf. bar 1981—), Wynlakes Residential Homeowners Assn. (bd. dirs), English Speaking Union (bd. dirs. 1997), Ala. Spl. Camp for Children and Adults (bd. dirs. 1999), Svc. Corps of Ret. Execs. Assn. (bd. dirs. 1996—), Farrah Law Soc., Citizens Conf. on Criminal and Juvenile Justice (staff mem. 1974), Citizens Conf. on Ala. Ct. (exec. com., sponsor new jud. article to state constitution 1973), Fed. Bar Assn. (pres. Montgomery chpt. 1973), Montgomery County Bar Assn. (chmn. law day com. 1972, chmn.state bar liason com. 1975, chmn. bd. dirs. 1977, bd. dirs. 1979, chmn. and editor Montgomery County Bar Jour. (ABA Merit award) 1979—80, v.p. 1980, pres. 1981), Ala. Law Found. (trustee), Ala. State Bar Assn. (editl. bd. 1970—82, chmn. law day com. 1973, chmn.citizen edn. com. 1974, chmn. editl. adv. bd. Ala. Lawyer 1975—79, mem. adv. com. CLE 1983, character and fitness com.), Mystic Soc. (krewe of phantom host), Blue-Gray Cols. Assn., Montgomery Country Club, Maxwell-Gunter Officers, Montgomery, Res. Officers Assn. of U.S. (chpt. pres. 1978, state pres. 1982), Ret. Officers Assn. (life), Air War Coll. Alumni Assn. (life), Air Force Ret. Judge Advocate Assn., Capital City Club, The Club, Inc Birmingham, Montgomery Rotary Club (v.p. 1996, pres. 1998), Montgomery Capital Rotary Club (pres. 1979, Paul Harris fellow), Hon. Order Ky. Cols., Theta Chi (Outstanding Alumni award 1976), Sigma Delta Kappa (pres. U. Ala. chpt.). Republican. Home: 7157 Pinecrest Dr Montgomery AL 36117-7413 E-mail: kloess2@aol.com.

KLOS, JEROME JOHN, lawyer, director; b. La Crosse, Wis., Jan. 17, 1927; s. Charles and Edna S. (Wagner) K.; m. Mary M. Hamilton, July 26, 1958; children— Bryant H., Geoffrey W. BS, U. Wis., 1948, JD, 1950. Bar: Wis. 1950. Pres. Klos, Flynn and Papenfuss, La Crosse, 1950—. Bd. dirs. Union State Bank, West Salem, Wis. Mem. LaCrosse County Bd., 1957-74, vice chmn., 1972-74; pub. adminstr. La Crosse County, 1962-73; bd. dirs. West Salem Area Growth, Inc., La Crosse Area Growth, Inc.; trustee Sander and McKinly Scholarship Funds of West Salem Sch. Dist. Fellow Am. Coll. Real Estate Lawyers, Am. Coll. Probate Counsel, Wis. Law Found.; mem. Wis. Bar Assn., Elks, KC. Banking, Corporate, general, Probate (including wills, trusts). Home: 346 N Leonard St West Salem WI 54669-1238 Office: 800 Lynn Tower Bldg La Crosse WI 54601 E-mail: kfpatts@aol.com.

KLOTT, DAVID LEE, lawyer; b. Vicksburg, Miss., Dec. 10, 1941; s. Isadore and Dorothy (Lipson) Klott; m. Maren J. Randrup, May 25, 1975. BBA summa cum laude, Northwestern U., 1963; JD cum laude, Harvard U., 1966. Bar: Calif. 1966, U.S. Ct. Claims 1968, U.S. Supreme Ct. 1971, U.S. Tax Ct. 1973, U.S. Ct. Appeals (fed. cir.) 1982. Ptnr. Pillsbury Winthrop, San Francisco, 1966—. Mem. tax adv. group to sub-chpt. C J and K, Am. Law Inst.; instr. Calif. Continuing Edn. Bar, Practising Law Inst., Hastings Law Sch.; bd. dirs., counsel Marin Wind and Food Soc.; exec. v.p., sec. Global Ctr. Inc., 2000—01; vice-chmn. HL Ventures, LLC, 2000—. Commentator Calif. Nonprofit Corp. Law. Mem.: ABA, San Francisco Bar Assn., Calif. State Bar Assn., Internat. Wine and Food Soc. (coun. mgmt., bd. dirs., exec. com., sr. vice chmn., bd. govs. Ams.), Am.-Korean Taekwondo Friendship Assn. (1st dan-black belt), Harbor Point Racquet and Beach Club, Olympic Club, Harvard Club, Northwestern Club, Beta Alpha Psi, Beta Gamma Sigma (pres. local chpt.). Corporate taxation. Office: Pillsbury Winthrop 50 Fremont St San Francisco CA 94105-2230

KLOWDEN, MICHAEL LOUIS, think-tank executive; b. Chgo., Apr. 7, 1945; s. Roy and Esther (Siegel) K.; m. Patricia A. Doede, June 15, 1968; children: Kevin B., Deborah C. AB, U. Chgo., 1967; JD, Harvard U., 1970. Bar: Calif. 1971. From assoc. to ptnr. Mitchell, Silberberg & Knupp, L.A., 1970-78; mng. ptnr. Morgan, Lewis & Bockius, L.A., 1978-95; vice chmn. Jefferies & Co., Inc., L.A., 1995-96; pres., COO Jefferies Group, Inc. and Jefferies Co., Inc., L.A., 1996-2000, vice chmn., 2000—01; pres., CEO Milken Inst., 2001—. Trustee U. Chgo., 1986—. Office: Milken Institute 1250 Fourth St Santa Monica CA 90401 Office Fax: 310-998-2695. E-mail: mklowden@milkeninstitute.org.

KMIEC, STEVEN GERARD, lawyer; b. West Allis, Wis., Jan. 28, 1965; s. Marjan Ralph and Jeannie Rose K.; m. Kathi Jo Anderson, Oct. 22, 1994; children: Abigail Jo, Zoie Jo. BA, U. Wis. (Milw.), 1988; JD, Marquette U., 1991. Bar: Wis. 1991, we. and ea. dist. cts. Wis. 1991. Office mgr. Kmiec Law Offices, Milw., 1984-91, atty., 1991—. Presenter Moot Ct. presentation State Bar Wis., West Allis, 1996; sec. Layton Blvd. West Neighbors divsn. Sch. Sisters of St. Francis, 2002. Mem. ABA, ATLA, Wis. Acad. Trial Lawyers, Milw. Bar Assn. (chair lawyer referral divsn. 2002—). Roman Catholic. Personal injury (including property damage), Product liability, Workers' compensation. Office: 3741 W National Ave Milwaukee WI 53215-1050

KNAG, PAUL EVERETT, lawyer; b. Flushing, N.Y., Feb. 26, 1948; s. Howard Alf and Charlotte (Rausch) K.; m. Maryann McCaffrey, June 27, 1970; children: Paul Everett, Peter, Kathleen, John. BA magna cum laude, Queens Coll., 1967; JD cum laude, Harvard U., 1970. Bar: N.Y. 1970, Conn. 1971, D.C. 1983. Law clk. U.S. Ct. Appeals (2nd cir.), N.Y.C., 1970-71; ptnr. Cummings & Lockwood, Stamford, 1979—2002, Murtha Cullina LLP, New Haven, 2002—. Author: HIPAA: A Guide to Healthcare Privacy and Security Law, 2002. Mem. Mass. Bar Assn., Boston Bar Assn., Conn. Bar Assn., Regional Bar Assn., Am. Health Lawyers Assn., Conn. Health Lawyers Assn., Officer's Club Hartford, Dunes Club (Naragansett, R.I.), Middlesex Club Darien, Harvard Club Fairfield County, Quinnipiack Club. Republican. Federal civil litigation, Health. Office: Murtha Cullina LLP Box 704 2 Whitney Ave New Haven CT 06503-0704 also: 99 High St Boston MA 02110-2320

KNAPP, CHARLES LINCOLN, law educator; b. Zanesville, Ohio, Oct. 22, 1935; s. James Lincoln and Laura Alma (Richardson) K.; m. Beverley Earle Trott, Aug. 23, 1958 (dec. 1995); children: Jennifer Lynn, Liza Beth. BA, Denison U., 1956; JD, NYU, 1960. Bar: N.Y. 1961. Assoc. Paul, Weiss, Rifkind, Wharton & Garrison, N.Y.C., 1960-64; asst. prof. law NYU Law Sch., N.Y.C., 1964-67, assoc. prof., 1967-70, prof. law, 1970-88, Max E. Greenberg prof. contract law, 1988-98, Max E. Greenberg prof. emeritus contract law, 1998—, assoc. dean, 1977-82. Vis. prof. law U. Ariz. Law Sch., Tucson, 1973, Harvard U. Law Sch., Cambridge, Mass., 1974-75; vis. prof. law Hastings Coll. Law, San Francisco, 1996-97, disting. prof. law, 1998-2000, Joseph W. Cotchett Disting. prof. law, 2000—. Author: Problems in Contract Law, 1976, (with N. Crystal and H. Prince) 5th edit., 2003; editor-in-chief: Commercial Damages, 1986. Mem. Am. Law Inst., Order Coif, Phi Beta Kappa. Office: Hastings Coll Law 200 McAllister St San Francisco CA 94102-4707 E-mail: knappch@uchastings.edu.

KNAPP, JAMES IAN KEITH, judge; b. Bklyn., Apr. 6, 1943; s. Charles Townsend and Christine (Grange) K.; m. Joan Elizabeth Cunningham, June 10, 1967 (div. Mar. 1971); 1 child, Jennifer Elizabeth; m. Carol Jean Brown, July 14, 1981; children: Michelle Christine, David Michael Keith AB cum laude, Harvard U., 1964; JD, U. Colo., 1967; M in Law in Taxation, Georgetown U., 1989. Bar: Colo. 1967, Calif. 1968, U.S. Supreme Ct. 1983, D.C. 1986, Ohio 1995. Dep. dist. atty. County of L.A., 1968-79; head dep. dist. atty. Pomona br. office, 1979-82; dep. asst. atty. gen. criminal divsn. U.S. Dept. Justice, Washington, 1982-86, dep. assoc. atty. gen., 1986-87, dep. asst. atty. gen. tax divsn., 1988-89, acting asst. atty. gen. tax divsn., 1989, acting dep. chief organized crime sect. criminal divsn., 1989-91, dep. dir., asset forfeiture office criminal divsn., 1991-94; adminstrv. law judge Social Security Adminstrn., 1994—. Editor: California Uniform Crime Charging Standards and Manual, 1975 Vice chmn. Young Reps. Nat. Fedn., 1973-75; pres. Calif. Young Reps., 1975-77; mem. exec. com. Rep. State Ctrl. Com., Calif., 1975-77. Mem.: DC Bar Assn., Calif. Bar Assn. Episcopalian. Avocations: travel, reading. Office: Office of Hearings & Appeals 110 N Main St Ste 800 Dayton OH 45402-1786

KNAPP, WHITMAN, federal judge; b. N.Y.C., Feb. 24, 1909; s. Wallace Percy and Caroline Morgan (Miller) K.; m. Ann Fallert, May 17, 1962; 1 son, Gregory Wallace; children by previous marriage— Whitman Everett, Caroline Miller (Mrs. Edward M. W. Hines), Marion Elizabeth. Grad., Choate Sch., 1927; BA, Yale, 1931; LLB, Harvard U., 1934; LLD (hon.), CUNY City Coll., 1992. Bar: N.Y. 1935. With firm Cadwalader, Wickersham & Taft, N.Y.C., 1935-37; dep. asst. dist. atty. N.Y.C., 1937-41; with firm Donovan, Leisure, Newton & Lumbard, N.Y.C., 1941; mem. staff dist. atty. N.Y.C., 1942-50; chief indictment bd., 1942-44; chief, appeal bur., 1944-50; partner firm Barrett Knapp Smith Schapiro & Simon (and predecessors), 1950-72; U.S. dist. judge So. Dist. N.Y., 1972-87, sr. dist. judge, 1987—. Spl. counsel N.Y. State Youth Commn., 1950-53; Waterfront Commn. N.Y. Harbor, 1953-54; mem. temp. commn. revision N.Y. State penal law and criminal code, 1964-69; chmn. Knapp Commn. to Investigate Allegations of Police Corruption in N.Y.C., 1969-72; gen. counsel Urban League Greater N.Y., 1970-72. Editor: Harvard Law Rev. 1933-34. Sec. Community Council Greater N.Y., 1952-58; pres. Dalton Schs., N.Y.C., 1950-53, Youth House, 1967-68; Trustee Univ. Settlement, 1945-64, Moblzn. for Youth, 1965-70. Mem. ABA, Am. Law Inst., Am. Bar Found., Am. Coll. Trial Lawyers, Assn. Bar City N.Y. (sec. 1946-49, chmn. exec. com. 1971-72). Office: 1201 US Courthouse 40 Foley Sq New York NY 10007-1502

KNAUER, JAMES A. lawyer; b. Terre Haute, Ind., Sept. 18, 1946; s. Eugene A. and Dorothy R. K.; m. Jill A. Knauer, Apr. 25, 1988. BS, Ind. U., Bloomington, 1968, Ind. U., Indpls., 1972. Bar: Ind. 1972, U.S. Dist. Ct. (so. dist.) Ind. 1972, U.S. Ct. Appeals (7th cir.) 1972, U.S. Supreme Ct. 1977. Assoc. Kroger Gardis & Regas, Indpls., 1972-70, mng. ptnr., 1979—. Adj. prof. law Ind. U., 1987-88, 90-91; trustee U.S. Bankruptcy panel, 1980-88; pres. bd. dirs. Alpha Tau Omega, Inc., 1997-99; pres. The Lakeridge Group, 1998-2002; SEC receiverships Heartland Fin. Svcs., Wellington Bank, Concord Devel., About Trading. Contbr. articles to profl. jours. Capt. U.S. Army, 1971-72. Mem. ABA, ATLA, Comml. Law League of Am., Indpls. Bar Assn., Am. Bankruptcy Inst., Columbia Club, Woodstock Club. Republican. Bankruptcy, Federal civil litigation, Commercial, contracts (including sales of goods; commercial financing). Office: Kroger Gardis & Regis 900 Bank One Ctr Indianapolis IN 46204 E-mail: jak@kgrlaw.com.

KNEBEL, DONALD EARL, lawyer; b. Logansport, Ind., May 26, 1946; s. Everett Earl and Ethel Josephina (Hultgren) K.; m. Joan Elizabeth Vest, June 5, 1976 (div. 1980); 1 child, Mary Elizabeth; m. Jennifer Colt Johnson, Sept. 25, 1999. BEE with highest distinction, Purdue U., 1968; JD magna cum laude, Harvard U., 1974. Bar: Ind. 1974, U.S. Ct. Appeals (7th cir.) 1980, U.S. Ct. Appeals (3rd cir.) 1986, U.S. Ct. Appeals (6th cir.) 1987, U.S. Ct. Appeals (fed. cir.) 1988. Assoc. Barnes, Hickam, Pantzer & Boyd, Indpls., 1974-81; ptnr. Barnes & Thornburg, Indpls., 1981—. Dir. Tech Point, Inc., 2002—. Contbr. articles on intellectual property, antitrust and distbn. law to profl. publs. Trustee Indpls. Civic Theatre, 1986—95, chmn., 1988—91, hon. trustee, 1995—2002, Trustee, 2002—, chmn., 2002—. Mem.: ABA, TechPoint (dir. 2003—), TechLaw Group (v.p. 2002—), 7th Cir. Bar Assn., Indpls. Bar Assn., Ind. Bar Assn., Columbia Club, Kiwanis (pres. 1991—92). Presbyterian. Antitrust, Federal civil litigation, Intellectual property. Office: Barnes & Thornburg 11 S Meridian St Ste 1313 Indianapolis IN 46204-3535

KNEBEL, JACK GILLEN, lawyer; b. Washington, Jan. 28, 1939; s. Fletcher and Amalia Eleanor (Rauppius) K.; m. Linda Karin Ropertz, Feb. 22, 1963; children: Hollis Anne (dec.), Lauren Beth. BA, Yale Coll., 1960; LLB, Harvard U., 1966. Bar: Calif. 1966, U.S. Dist. Ct. (no. dist.) Calif. 1966, U.S. Ct. Appeals (9th cir.) 1966. Assoc. McCutchen, Doyle, Brown & Enersen, San Francisco, 1966-74, ptnr., 1974-94, of counsel, 1994-99; owner Artema, 1999—; lectr. in law Stanford Law Sch., 1998-2001, Harvard U. Sch. Law, 2002—; dir. litigation tng. Brigham, McCutchen, San Francisco, 2002—. Exec. com. San Francisco Lawyers Com. for Urban Affairs, 1991-93; adv. coun. Hastings Coll. Trial Advocacy, San Francisco, 1981-91, chair, 1990-91; mediator, arbitrator Am. Arbitration Assn., 1989—. Bd. dirs., pres. Orinda (Calif.) Assn., 1972-74, Sea Ranch (Calif.) Assn., 1978-79; co-chmn. Citizens to Preserve Orinda, 1983-85. Lt. (j.g.) USN, 1960-66. Fellow Am. Coll. Trial Lawyers (mem. com. on fed. rules civ. pro 1990-93); mem. ABA, Maritime Law Assn. of U.S. Democrat. Admiralty, General civil litigation, Product liability. Home: PO Box 1133 Gualala CA 95445 Office: Bingham McCutchen Three Embarcadero Ctr Ste 1800 San Francisco CA 94111 E-mail: jknebel@Bingham.com., knebeljack@juno.com.

KNEBEL, JOHN ALBERT, lawyer, former government official; b. Tulsa, Oct. 4, 1936; s. John Albert and Florence Julia (Friend) K.; m. Zenia Irene Marks, June 6, 1959; children— Carrie, John Albert III, Clemens. BS, U.S. Mil. Acad., 1959; MA in Econs, Creighton U., 1962; JD, Am. U., 1965. Bar: D.C. bar 1966, U.S. Ct. Appeals bar 1966. Asst. to Rep. J.E. Wharton of N.Y., Washington, 1963-64; asso. mem. law firm Howrey, Simon, Baker & Murchison, Washington, 1965-68; asst. counsel Com. on Agr., U.S. Ho. Reps., Washington, 1968-71; gen. counsel SBA, Washington, 1971-74, U.S. Dept. Agr., Washington, 1973-75; under sec. Dept. Agr., 1975-76, sec. of agr., 1976-77; ptnr. firm Baker & McKenzie, Washington, 1977-86; pres. Am. Mining Congress, Washington, 1986-95; exec. v.p. Nat. Assn. Broadcasters, Washington, 1995—. Served to 1st lt. USAF, 1959-62. Mem. Fed. Bar Assn. (past pres.), Am., D.C. bar assns., Delta Theta Phi, Omicron Delta Gamma. Home: 1418 Laburnum St Mc Lean VA 22101-2523 Office: Nat Assn Broadcasters 1771 N St NW Washington DC 20036-2891

KNECHT, JAMES HERBERT, lawyer; b. Los Angeles, Aug. 5, 1925; s. James Herbert and Gertrude Martha (Morris) K.; m. Margaret Paton Vreeland, Jan. 3, 1953 (dec. 1994); children— Susan, Thomas Paton, Carol. BS, UCLA, 1947; LLB, U. So. Calif., 1957. Bar: Calif. bar 1957, U.S. Supreme Ct. bar 1969. Mem. firm Forster, Gemmill & Farmer, Los Angeles, 1957-84; sole practice, 1985—. Chmn. bd. Templeton (Calif.) Nat. Bank, 1992-95. Fellow Am. Bar Found. (life); mem. ABA, San Luis Obispo County Bar Assn., Legion Lex, Caltech Assocs., L.A. Area C. of C. (dir. 1979-83), Beta Theta Pi. Probate (including wills, trusts), Corporate taxation, Estate taxation. Home: 5030 Vineyard Dr Paso Robles CA 93446-9682 Office: PO Box 2280 Paso Robles CA 93447-2280 E-mail: jknecht@ccaccess.net.

KNECHT, WILLIAM L. lawyer; b. Lock Haven, Pa., Jan. 15, 1946; s. Clair N. and Betty R. (Harter) K.; m. Margaret E. O'Malley, June 10, 1972; children: William E., Jennifer M. BA, Pa. State U., 1967; JD, Dickinson Sch. Law, 1970. Bar: Pa. 1970, U.S. Supreme Ct. 1976, U.S. Tax Ct. 1981, U.S. Dist. Ct. (middle dist.) Pa. 1973, Ct. Common Pleas 1970. Assoc. McCormick, Lynn, Reeder, Nichols & Sarno, Williamsport, Pa., 1973-76; ptnr. McCormick, Reeder, Nichols, Bahl, Knecht & Person, Williamsport, 1976-96; ptnr. McCormick Law Firm, Williamsport, 1996—. Bankruptcy trustee U.S. Justice Dept., Williamsport, Pa., 1978-91. Editor Lycoming Reporter, 1976—. 1st lt. U.S. Army, 1971-73. Fellow Pa. Bar Found. (life); mem. ABA, Pa. Bar Assn., Lycoming County Law Assn. (exec. com. 1976—), Lycoming Law Assn. (pres. 1995), Ross Club. Republican. United Ch. of Christ. Avocation: stamps and first day cover collecting. Banking, Bankruptcy, Property, real (including real estate development, water). Home: 253 Lincoln Ave Williamsport PA 17701-2237 Office: McCormick Law Firm 835 W 4th St Williamsport PA 17701 E-mail: bknecht@mcclaw.com.

KNEIPPER, RICHARD KEITH, lawyer; b. Kenosha, Wis., June 18, 1943; s. Richard F. and Esther E. (Beaster) K.; m. Sherry Hayes, Dec. 16, 1977; children: Ryan Hayes, Lindsey Merrill. BS, Washington and Lee U., 1965; JD, Cornell U., 1968. Bar: Tex. 1982, U.S. Dist. Ct. (so. dist.) N.Y. 1968, U.S. Ct. Appeals (2d cir.) 1971. Atty. Chadbourne & Parke, N.Y.C., 1968-81, Jones, Day, Reavis & Pogue, Dallas, 1981-99; chief adminstrv. officer Provider HealthNet Svcs. Inc., Dallas, 1999—. Mem. adv. com. Nat. Mus. Am., Smithsonian, Nat. Arts Edn. Initiative, Nat. Mus. Am. Art, Smithsonian Instn. Contbr. numerous articles to profl. jours. Bd. trustees The Dallas Parks Found.; mem. profl. adv. group Save Outdoor Sculpture!; chmn. Dallas Adopt-a-Monument; bd. dirs., mem. adv. coun. Appalachian Coll. Assn., Inc., Sch. Visual Arts, U. North Tex.; former mem. new bus. task force, former mem. internat. task force Health Industry Coun. Dallas-Ft. Worth Region. Mem. ABA, N.Y. Bar Assn., Tex. Bar Assn., Tex. Sculpture Assn., Assn. of Bar of City of N.Y. Episcopal. Banking, Mergers and acquisitions, Securities. Office: Provider HealthNet Svcs Inc 15851 Dallas Pkwy Ste 925 Addison TX 75001-6022

KNEISEL, EDMUND M. lawyer; b. Atlanta, Feb. 21, 1946; s. John F. and Mary E. (Moore) K.; m. Leslie A. Jones, June 19, 1976; 1 child, Mary Kathleen. AB, Duke U., 1968; JD, U. Ga., 1974. Bar: Ga. 1974, U.S. Dist. Ct. (no. and mid. dists.) Ga., U.S. Ct. Appeals (2d, 4th, 5th, 6th and 11th cirs.), U.S. Supreme Ct. 1984. Law clk. to Hon. R.C. Freeman U.S. Dist. Ct. (no. dist.) Ga., Atlanta, 1974-76; assoc. Kilpatrick & Cody, Atlanta, 1976-82; ptnr. Kilpatrick Stockton LLP, 1982—. Mng. editor Ga. Law Rev., Athens, 1973-74; contbr. articles to profl. jours. Lt. USNR, 1968-71. Mem. ABA, Lawyers Club Atlanta, Druid Hills Golf Club. Federal civil litigation, Insurance, Labor (including EEOC, Fair Labor Standards Act, labor-management relations, NLRB, OSHA). Office: Kilpatrick Stockton LLP 1100 Peachtree St NE Ste 2800 Atlanta GA 30309-4530 E-mail: ekneisel@kilstock.com.

KNICKERBOCKER, ROBERT PLATT, JR., lawyer; b. Hartford, Conn., Sept. 23, 1944; s. Robert P. and Audrey Jane (Stempel) K.; m. Kathleen A. Sakal (div. May 1985); children: Sarah, Abigail, Jonathan; m. Barbara Denise Whinnem, Oct. 3, 1987. BA, Cornell U., 1966; JD, U. Conn., 1969. Bar: Conn. 1969, U.S. Dist. Ct. Conn. 1969, U.S. Ct. Appeals (2d cir.) 1970. Law clk. to presiding justice Conn. Supreme Ct., Hartford, 1968-69; ptnr. Day, Berry & Howard, Hartford, 1969—. Mem. State Implementation Plan Regulation Adv. Commn., 1979-90. Chmn. Town Plan and Zoning Commn., Glastonbury, Conn., 1975-79, Glastonbury Bd. Edn., 1982-86. Mem. Conn. Bar Assn., Greater Hartford C. of C. (state legis. com.). Republican. Episcopalian. Administrative and regulatory, Communications, Nuclear power. Office: Day Berry & Howard Cityplace Hartford CT 06103-3499 E-mail: rpknickerbocker@dbh.com.

KNIGHT, TOWNSEND JONES, lawyer; b. N.Y.C., Aug. 10, 1928; s. Jesse and Marguerite H. (Jones) K.; m. Elise Heck; children: Margaret Knight Dudley, Elise Knight Wallace, Jessica Knight Casoni. BS, Harvard U., 1949; JD, Columbia U., 1952. Bar: N.Y. 1952. Assoc. Curtis, Mallet-Prevost, Colt & Mosle, N.Y.C., 1953-65, ptnr., 1965—2001, of counsel, 2001—. Trustee Metropolitan Coll. of NY, 1969—, Cold Spring Harbor (N.Y.) Lab., 1970-76, 82-88, 89-95, hon. trustee, 1995—. Mem. ABA, N.Y. State Bar Assn., Assn. of Bar of City of N.Y., Downtown Assn., Harvard Club, Cold Spring Harbor Beach Club. Episcopalian. Avocation: photography. Banking, Non-profit and tax-exempt organizations, Probate (including wills, trusts). Office: Curtis Mallet-Prevost Colt & Mosle 101 Park Ave Fl 35 New York NY 10178-0061

KNIGHT, W.H., JR., (JOE KNIGHT), dean, law educator; m. Susan Mask; children: Michael Mask, Lauren Mask. BA in Econs., Speech and Polit. Sci., U. N.C., 1976; JD, Columbia U., 1979. Prof. U. Iowa Coll. Law, vice provost, 1997—2000, dean, 2001—, law educator, 2001—. Vis. prof. Washington U., St. Louis, Duke U. Schs. Law; assoc. counsel, asst. sec. Colonial Bancorp, New Haven, Waterbury, Conn. Mem.: ABA, Nat. Bar Assn., Nat. Conf. on Black Lawyers, Soc. Am. Law Tchrs., Am. Law Inst., N.Y. Bar, State Farm Mutual Automobile Ins. Co. Office: U Washington Sch Law 1100 NE Campus Pkwy Seattle WA 98105-6617 Office Fax: 206-616-5305. E-mail: whknight@u.washington.edu.

KNIGHT, ESQUIRE, J. BARRON, mediator, lawyer; m. Bernice Ann Calderon-Knight, May 27, 2000; 1 child, Crystal Elise Girona. JD, U. Md., 1996. Bar: Md. 1999, U.S. Ct. Appeals 1993. Staff atty. Md. Office of the Atty. Gen., Balt., 1999—2002; asst. dir. Dept. Ins. and Securities Regulation, Washington, 2002—. Mediator Sheppard Pratt Family Mediation Services, Balt., 1997—. Mem.: ABA. Republican. Office: Dept Ins & Securities Regulation 810 First St NE Washington DC 20002 Home Fax: 202-442-8661; Office Fax: 202-442-8661. Personal E-mail: night777@earthlink.net.

KNOBBE, LOUIS JOSEPH, lawyer, educator; b. Carroll, Iowa, Apr. 6, 1932; s. Louis C. and Elsie M. (Praeger) Knobbe; m. Jeanette M. Sganga, Apr. 3, 1954; children: Louis, Michael, Nancy, John, Catherine. BSEE, Iowa State U., 1953; JD, Loyola U., L.A., 1959. Bar: Calif. 1960, U.S. Supreme Ct. 1963, U.S. Patent and Trademark Office. Tech. staff Bell Tel. Labs., 1953-54; patent engr. GE, Washington, 1955—56, N.Am. Aviation, Downey, Calif., 1956-59; patent lawyer Beckman Instruments, Fullerton, Calif., 1959-62; co-founder, ptnr. Knobbe, Martens, Olson & Bear, Newport Beach, Calif., 1962—2002, of counsel, 2003—. Lectr. Computer Law Assn., Inc., L.A., L.A. Intellectual Property Law Assn., San Diego Bar Assn.; adj. prof. Sch. Law San Diego U., 1987—. Co-author: (book) Attorney's Guide to Trade Secrets, 1972, 2d edit., 1996, update, 2002, How to Handle Basic Patent, 1992; contbg. author (book) Using Intellectual Property Rights to Protect Domestic Markets, 1986; contbr. articles to profl. jours. Bd. dirs. Orange County (Calif.) Performing Arts Ctr., 1975—83; past pres. Philharm. Soc. Orange County; past bd. mem., past v.p. Opera Pacific, Orange County; bd. visitors Loyola Law Sch., 2000—. Recipient Jurisprudence award, Anti-Defamation League, 1988. Fellow: Inst. Advancement Engring.; mem.: IEEE (past chmn. Orange County sect., Centennial medal 1984), ABA, Licensing Execs. Soc., San Diego Patent Law Assn., Orange County Patent Law Assn. (lectr.), Orange County Bar Assn., State Bar Calif., Am. Arbitration Soc. (panel neutrals), Am. Intellectual Property Law Assn. (lectr.), Balboa Yacht Club, First Friday Friars, Santa Ana North Rotary, Pacific Club, Eta Kappa Nu, Tau Beta Pi, Phi Kappa Phi. Avocations: boating, still and video photography, travel and exploration in lake powell, death valley, deserts of Arizona and Baja California. Intellectual property, Patent, Trademark and copyright. Office: 2040 Main St Fl 14 Irvine CA 92614 E-mail: LKnobbe@kmob.com.

KNOLL, JEANNETTE THERIOT, state supreme court justice; b. Baton Rouge; m. Jerold Edward Knoll; children: Triston Kane, Eddie Jr., Edmond Humphries, Blake Theriot, Jonathan Paul. BA in Polit. Sci., Loyola U., 1966, JD, 1969; LLM, U. Va., 1996; studied with Maestro Adler, Mannes Coll. of Music, 1962-63. Criminal defense atty., first asst. dist. atty. Twelfth Jud. Dist. Ct. Avoyelles Parish, 1972-82; gratuitous atty., advisor U.S. Selective Svc., Marksville, La.; judge (3d cir.) U.S. Ct. of Appeal, 1982-93; justice La. Supreme Ct., 1997—. Instr. La. Jud. Coll.; chair CLE La. Ct. of Appeal Judges; mem. vis. com. Loyola U. Sch. of Law, Loyola Music Sch.; bd. dirs. Loyola U. Alumni Assn.; former mem. state bd. of La. commn. on law enforcement and criminal justice. Past pres. Bus. and Profl. Women's Club; Marksville C. of C.; active Am. Legion Aux. Recipient scholarship Met. Opera Assn., New Orleans Opera Guild. Office: La Supreme Ct 301 Loyola Ave New Orleans LA 70112-1814

KNOLLER, GUY DAVID, lawyer; b. N.Y.C., July 23, 1946; s. Charles and Odette Knoller; children: Jennifer Judy, Geoffrey David. BA cum laude, Bloomfield (N.J.) Coll., 1968; JD cum laude, Ariz. State U., 1971. Bar: Ariz. 1971, U.S. Dist. Ct. Ariz. 1971, U.S. Supreme Ct. 1976. Trial atty. atty. gen.'s hons. program Dept. Justice, 1971-72; atty., adv. NLRB, 1972-73, field atty. region 28, 1972-74; assoc. Powers, Ehrenreich, Boutell & Kurn, Phoenix, 1974-79; ptnr. Froimson & Knoller, Phoenix, 1979-81; sole practice Phoenix, 1985—; of counsel Burns & Burns. Mem. bd. visitors Ariz. State U. Coll. Law, 1975-76; pres. Ariz. Theatre Guild, 1990, 91. Fellow Ariz. Bar Found.; mem. ABA, State Bar Ariz. (chmn. labor rels. sect. 1977-78), Ariz. State U. Coll. Law Alumni Assn. (pres. 1977). Federal civil litigation, State civil litigation, Labor (including EEOC, Fair Labor Standards Act, labor-management relations, NLRB, OSHA). Office: 2828 N Central Ave Ste 1110 Phoenix AZ 85004-1028

KNOPF, BARRY ABRAHAM, lawyer, educator; b. Passaic, N.J., May 11, 1946; s. Edward and Sonia (Sameth) K.; children: Elisa, Scott. Student, Rutgers U., 1968, JD, 1972. Bar: N.J. 1972, U.S. Dist. Ct. N.J. 1972, U.S. Tax Ct. 1975, U.S. Supreme Ct. 1975, U.S. Ct. Appeals (3d cir.) 1981; cert. civil trial atty. Nat. Bd. Trial Advocacy, N.J. Supreme Ct. Assoc. Cohn & Lifland, Saddle Brook, N.J., 1972-75, ptnr., 1975—. Instr. N.J. Inst. for Continuing Legal Edn., 1982—, Nat. Inst. Trial Advocacy, 1989—; adj. faculty Hofstra U. Sch. of Law, 2000. Co-author: Professional Negligence, Law of Malpractice in New Jersey, 1979, 5th edit., 2001, Personal Injury Litigation Practice in New Jersey, 1990, Civil Trial Preparation, Practical skills Series, 1992, 2d edit., 1996, New Jersey Product Liability Law, 1994. V.p. Temple Beth Tikvah, Wayne, N.J., 1985-93, pres. 1993-95. Mem. Morris Pashman Inn of Ct. (master 1998—). Federal civil litigation, State civil litigation, Personal injury (including property damage). Home: 1014 Smith Manor Blvd West Orange NJ 07052-4227 Office: Cohn Lifland Pearlman Herrmann & Knopf Park 80 West 1 Saddle Brook NJ 07663 E-mail: bak@njlawfirm.com.

KNOWLES, MARJORIE FINE, lawyer, educator, dean; b. Bklyn., July 4, 1939; d. Jesse J. and Roslyn (Leff) Fine; m. Ralph I. Knowles, Jr., June 3, 1972. BA, Smith Coll., 1960; LLB, Harvard U., 1965. Bar: Ala., N.Y., D.C. Teaching fellow Harvard U., 1963-64; law clk. to judge U.S. Dist. Ct. (so. dist.), N.Y., 1965-66; asst. U.S. atty. U.S. Atty.'s Office, N.Y.C., 1966-67; asst. dist. atty. N.Y. County Dist. Atty., N.Y.C., 1967-70; exec. dir. Joint Found. Support, Inc., N.Y.C., 1970-72; asst. gen. counsel HEW, Washington, 1978-79; insp. gen. U.S. Dept. Labor, Washington, 1979-80; assoc. prof. U. Ala. Sch. Law, Tuscaloosa, 1972-75, prof., 1975-86, assoc. dean, 1982-84; law prof., dean Ga. State U. Coll. Law, Atlanta, 1986-91, law prof., 1986—. Cons. Ford Found., N.Y.C., 1973-98, 2000-03, trustee Coll. Retirement Equities Fund, N.Y.C., 1983-2002; mem. exec. com. Conf. on Women and the Constn., 1986-88; mem. com. on continuing profl. edn. Am. Law Inst.-ABA, 1987-93. Contbr. articles to profl. jours. Am. Council Edn. fellow, 1976-77, Aspen Inst. fellow, Rockefeller Found., 1976. Mem. ABA (chmn. new deans workshop 1988), Ala. State Bar Assn., N.Y. State Bar Assn., D.C. Bar Assn., Am. Law Inst., Tchrs. Ins. Annuity Assn. (trustee Coll. Equities Ret. Equities Fund 2002—). Office: Ga State U Coll Law University Plz Atlanta GA 30303

KNOWLTON, KEVIN CHARLES, lawyer; b. Syracuse, N.Y., Oct. 19, 1957; s. Erwin Leslie and Arlene Grace (Morgan) K.; m. Lois Jean Clair, July 21, 1979; children: Andrew, Keith, Lauren. BA cum laude, Houghton Coll., 1979; JD, Syracuse U., 1982. Bar: Fla. 1982, U.S. Dist. Ct. (mid. dist.) Fla. 1982, U.S. Ct. Appeals (11th cir.) 1982, U.S. Supreme Ct. 1986. Law clk. to judge 2nd Dist. Ct. Appeals, Lakeland, Fla., 1982-85; ptnr. Peterson & Myers P.A., Lakeland, 1985—, mgmt. com. Treas. Phoenix (N.Y.) Rep. Com., 1980-82, Planning Bd., 1980-82, Town of Schroeppel Planning Bd., 1980-82; chmn. bd. dirs. Lakeland Christian Sch.; chmn. pres.'s adv. bd. Houghton Coll.; vice-chmn. Fla. Bar 10th Jud. Cir. Grievance Com.; mem. instnl. rev. bd. Lakeland Regional Med. Ctr., mem. ethics com.; chmn. exec. bd. dirs. Lake Morton Cmty. Ch., 1995-99, elder. N.Y. State Regents scholar 1975-79. Mem. ABA, Fla. Bar Assn., Lakeland Bar Assn. (chmn. law day legal forum 1986), Fla. Acad. Healthcare Attys., Am. Health Lawyers Assn., Christian Legal Soc., Houghton Coll. Alumni Assn. (pres. Orlando, Fla. chpt. 1985, 91—), Willson Inn of Ct., Lakeland Yacht and Country Club, Phi Alpha Theta. Avocations: basketball, snow skiing. General civil litigation, Health. Home: 1143 E Highland Dr Lakeland FL 33813-1774 Office: Peterson & Myers PA 225 E Lemon St ste 300 Lakeland FL 33801-4655

KNOX, JAMES EDWIN, lawyer; b. Evanston, Ill., July 2, 1937; s. James Edwin and Marjorie Eleanor (Williams) K.; m. Rita Lucille Torres, June 30, 1973; children: James Edwin III, Kirsten M., Katherine E., Miranda G. BA in Polit. Sci., State U. Iowa, 1959; JD, Drake U., 1961. Bar: Iowa 1961, Ill. 1962, Tex. 1982. Law clk. to Justice Tom C. Clark, U.S. Supreme Ct., Washington, 1961-62; assoc., then ptnr. Isham, Lincoln & Beale, Chgo., 1962-70; v.p. law N.W. Industries, Inc., Chgo., 1970-80; exec. v.p., gen. counsel Lone Star Steel Co., Dallas, 1980-86; sr. v.p. law Anixter Internat. Inc., Chgo., 1986—2002. Instr. contracts and labor law Chgo. Kent Coll. Law, 1964—69; arbitrator Nat. Ry. Adjustment Bd., 1967—68; ptnr. Mayer, Brown & Platt, Chgo., 1992—96; gen. counsel Arris Group, Inc., 1996—2002. Mem. ABA, Ill. Bar Assn., Order of Coif, Phi Beta Kappa. Corporate, general. Office: Anixter Internat Inc 2301 Patriot Blvd Glenview IL 60025-8020 E-mail: jeknoxie@aol.com.

KNOX, JAMES MARSHALL, lawyer; b. Chgo., Jan. 12, 1944; s. Edwin John and Shirley Lucille (Collett) K.; m. Janine Foster, July 18, 1964; children: Erik M., Christian S. BA, U. Ill., 1968; MA in Libr. Sci., Rosary Coll., 1973; JD, DePaul Coll. Law, 1979. Bar: Ill. 1979, U.S. Dist. Ct. (no. dist.) Ill. 1979, U.S. Ct. Appeals (7th cir.) 1980. Head reference Northbrook (Ill.) Pub. Libr., 1973-76; asst. dir. hdqrs. Jackson (Miss.) Met. Libr. Sys., 1976-77; assoc. Fishman & Fishman, Ltd., Chgo., 1979-91; prin. Law Office James M. Knox, 1991—. Gen. counsel Deerfield (Ill.) Pub. Libr., 1994—. Commr. Evanston Preservation Commn., 1991-98; sustaining mem. Miss. Hist. Soc. Mem. ABA, Ill. State Bar Assn., Ill. Trial Lawyer's Assn., Chgo. Bar Assn., U. Ill. Alumni Assn. (dir. 1986-91). General practice, Personal injury (including property damage), Workers' compensation. Home: 121 W Chestnut #3202 Chicago IL 60610 Office: Chestnut Tower 121 W Chestnut Chicago IL 60610 E-mail: KawOxford@aol.com.

KOBAK, JAMES BENEDICT, JR., lawyer, educator; b. Alexandria, La., May 2, 1944; s. James Benedict and Hope (McEldowney) K.; m. Carol Johnson, June 11, 1966; children: James Benedict III, Katherine Jean, Marcie Ann. BA magna cum laude, Harvard U., 1966; LLB, U. Va., 1969. Bar: U.S. Dist. Ct. (so. and ea. dists.) N.Y. 1972, U.S. Supreme Ct. 1977, U.S. Ct. Appeals (2nd cir.) 1973, (5th cir.) 1982, U.S. Dist. Ct. (no. dist.) Calif. 1983, N.J. 1996. Asst. prof. U. Ala., 1969-70; assoc. Hughes Hubbard & Reed LLP, N.Y.C., 1970-77, ptnr., 1977—. Lectr. in law U. Va., 1986-2000; adj. assoc. prof. Fordham U., 1986—; arbitrator Am. Arbitration Assn. Editor: Misuse: Licensing and Litigation, 2000; mem. bd. editors Va. Law Rev., 1967-69, assoc. editor, 1968-69; contbr. articles to profl. jours., mags., treatises and newspapers. Trustee Morristown-Beard Sch., 1995—2001, Jersey City Mus., 2002—. Mem. ABA (antitrust sect., former chair intellectual property com.), Assn. Bar City N.Y., N.Y. County Lawyers Assn. (bd. dirs. 1988-93, 95-97, 2001—, chmn. trade regulation com. 1987-88, chmn. com. on changing trends in the profession 1990-93, chmn. com. on law reform 1994-98, exec. com. 1996-98, chair libr. com. 1998—), Order of Coif, Am. Law Inst., Adirondack 46ers Club, Keene Valley Country Club (trustee 1995-98), Harvard Club (N.Y.). Antitrust, Federal civil litigation, Trademark and copyright. Home: 206-95 W Shearwater Ct Jersey City NJ 07305 Office: Hughes Hubbard & Reed 1 Battery Park Plz Fl 12 New York NY 10004-1482 E-mail: kobak@hugheshubbard.com.

KOBAYASHI, BERT TAKAAKI, JR., lawyer; b. Honolulu, Feb. 4, 1940; s. Bert Takaaki Sr. and Victoria Ruth (Tsuchiya) K.; m. Harriet Sanae Ishimine, Aug. 11, 1962; children: Christopher T., Jonathan A., Matthew H., Jennifer Sanae. Student, U. Hawaii, 1958-62; BA, Gettysburg (Pa.) Coll., 1962; JD, U. Calif., Hastings, 1965. Bar: Hawaii 1965, U.S. Dist. (fed. dist.) Hawaii 1965. Assoc. Chung, Vitousek, Chuck & Fujimana, Honolulu, 1967-69, Kono, Ariyoshi, Honolulu, 1969-71; sr. ptnr. Kobayashi, Sugita & Goda, Honolulu, 1971—. Bd. dirs. First Hawaiian Bank, Honolulu, Bank West Corp., Schuler Homes; exec. com. Bank West Corp. Honolulu; mem. State Jud. Selection Comm., Honolulu, 1985-01, chmn., 1987-89. Mem. ABA, Am. Coll. Trial Lawyers, Hawaii Bar Assn., Assn. Trial Lawyers Am., Am. Bd. Trial Advs., Japah-Hawaii Econ. Coun., Pub. Schools Found. State civil litigation, Construction, Property, real (including real estate development, water). Office: Kobayashi Sugita & Goda 999 Bishop St Ste 2600 Honolulu HI 96813-4430

KOBDISH, GEORGE CHARLES, lawyer; b. Casper, Wyo., June 30, 1950; s. Richard Matthew and Jo Earl (Uttz) K.; m. Mary Ellen Griffith, Jan. 24, 1969; children: George Charles, Jr., Kelly Rebecca, Kimberlee Nelle. BBA with honors, U. Tex., 1971, JD, 1974. Bar: Tex. 1974, U.S. Dist. Ct. (no. dist.) Tex. 1975. Asst. atty. gen. State of Tex., Austin, 1974-76; assoc. McCall, Parkhurst & Horton LLP, Dallas, 1976-80, ptnr., 1981—. Bd. dir. North Dallas Shared Ministries, 1993—2000, pres., 1996—98; bd. dir. Notre Dame of Dallas Schs, Inc., 2000—; lay gen. chairperson Cath. Cmty. Appeal, 2000—01. Mem. Am. Coll. Bond Counsel, Nat. Assn. Bond Lawyers, Tex. Bar Assn., Dallas Bar Assn., Royal Oaks Country Club, Tower Club, Dallas Friday Group, Serra Internat. (Dallas bd. dirs., pres. 1998-99, U.S.A. coun., gov. Dist. 46, 2002-03), Phi Delta Theta. Roman Catholic. Municipal (including bonds). Home: 7147 Araglin Ct Dallas TX 75230-2097 Office: McCall Parkhurst & Horton LLP 717 N Harwood St Ste 900 Dallas TX 75201-6586

KOBELL, GERALD, lawyer; b. N.Y.C., Oct. 4, 1941; s. Irving and Mary Kobell; m. Helen Berglas, Nov. 28, 1968; children: Deena, Rona, Aliza, Daniel. BS, U. Pa., 1963, JD, 1966; LLM, NYU, 1967. Bar: Pa. 1967, N.J. 1970, U.S. Dist. Ct. N.J. 1970, U.S. Supreme Ct. 1971, N.Y. 1982, U.S. Dist. Ct. Pa. 1983, U.S. Ct. Appeals (3rd cir.) 1991. Atty. Nat. Labor Rels. Bd., Newark, 1967—71, supervising atty., 1972—74, asst. gen. counsel Washington, 1974—82, regional dir. Pitts. region, 1982—. Adj. prof. U. Pitts. Law Sch., 2000—. Chmn. Fed. Exec. Bd., Pitts., 1986—88. Named Lawyer of Yr., FBA, Pitts., 1997; recipient Presdl. Meritorious Exec. award, Pres. U.S., Washington, 1989. Mem.: Sr. Exec. Svc. (charter). Labor (including EEOC, Fair Labor Standards Act, labor-management relations, NLRB, OSHA), Administrative and regulatory. Office: Nat Labor Rels Bd 1000 Liberty Ave Pittsburgh PA 15222

KOBER, JANE, lawyer; b. Shamokin, Pa., May 17, 1943; d. Jeno Daniel and Angela Agnes (Kogut) DiRienzo; m. Arthur Kober, June 20, 1970 (div. 1975). AB, Pa. State U., 1965; MA, U. Chgo., 1966; JD, Case Western Res. U., 1974. Bar: Ohio, N.Y. Lectr. U. Baghdad, Iraq, 1966-67; editor, cons. Ernst & Young, Washington, 1968-70; law clk. to Hon. William K. Thomas, U.S. Dist. Ct. for No. Dist. Ohio, Cleve., 1974-75; atty., ptnr. Squire, Sanders & Dempsey, Cleve. and N.Y.C., 1975-87; ptnr. Shea & Gould, N.Y.C., 1987-89, LeBoeuf, Lamb, Greene & MacRae, L.L.P., N.Y.C., 1989-98; sole practitioner, 1998—; sr. v.p., gen. counsel, sec. Biopure Corp., Cambridge, Mass., 1998—. Mem. vis. com. Case Western Res. U. Sch. Law, Soc. of Benchers. Office: Jane Kober Law Offices 125 W 55th St New York NY 10019-5369 also: Biopure Corp 11 Hurley St Cambridge MA 02141-2110 E-mail: jkober@biopure.com.

KOBERT, JOEL A. lawyer; b. Newark, Oct. 4, 1943; BA, Norwich U., 1965; JD, Howard U., 1968. Bar: D.C. 1968, N.J. 1971. Atty. U.S. Dept. Justice, Washington, 1968; ptnr. Courter, Kobert, Laufer & Cohen P.C., Hackettstown, N.J. Active Supreme Ct. Ad Hoc Com. on Legal Svcs. 1982-88, Supreme Ct. Com. on Interests and Trust Accts., 1984-86, Supreme Ct. Com. on Computerization of Ct. System, 1984-86; chmn. bd. trustees Interest on Lawyers Trust Accts., 1988-91. Capt. U.S. Army, 1968-70. Reginald Heber Smith fellow, 1970-71. Fellow Am. Bar Found.; mem. ABA (mem. dist XIII ethics com. 1982-86), D.C. Bar, N.J. State Bar Assn. (treas. 1987, sec. 1988, 2d v.p. 1989, 1st v.p. 1990, pres. elect 1991, pres. 1992, bd. trustees 1981-87, bd. trustees N.J. Lawyer, bd trustees N.J. State Bar Found., 1986-93, mem. ops. com. 1985-91, chmn. com. law adminstrn. and econs. 1981-86, mem. membership com., 1986-87, mem. com. fin. and ops, 1990-93, mem. travel com. 1990-93), N.J. League Mcpl. Attys. Office: Courter Kobert Laufer & Cohen PC 1001 County Road 517 Ste 1 Hackettstown NJ 07840-2709

KOBLENTZ, ROBERT ALAN, lawyer; b. Columbus, Ohio, Aug. 20, 1946; s. Maurice Charles and Martha (Levelle) K.; m. Kathryn Anderson, Oct. 20, 1973; children: Maureen, Robert. BA, Ohio State U., 1967, JD, 1970. Bar: Ohio 1970, U.S. Dist. Ct. (so. dist.) Ohio 1971, U.S. Supreme Ct. 1992; cert. family law specialist. Legal rsch. Bancroft-Whitney Co., San Francisco, 1970-71; atty. Tracy, DeLibera, Lyons & Collins, Columbus, 1971-78, DeLibera, Lyons, Koblentz & Scott, Columbus, 1978-80, Scott, Koblentz & Binau, Columbus, 1980-86; pvt. practice Columbus, 1986—. Bd. dirs. Friends of WOSU, Columbus, 1982-88, Opera Columbus, 1984-87, Upper Arlington Civic Assn., Columbus, 1988-90. Mem. ABA, Ohio State Bar Assn. (cert. family rels. specialist, del. family law sect. 1979—), Ohio Acad. Trial Lawyers (chmn. family law sect. 1983), Columbus Bar Assn. (chmn. family law com. 1976-78), Franklin County Trial Lawyers (pres. 1985-86). Family and matrimonial. Office: 35 E Livingston Ave Columbus OH 43215-5762

KOBLENZ, MICHAEL ROBERT, lawyer; b. Newark, Apr. 9, 1948; s. Herman and Esther (Weisman) K.; m. Bonnie Jane Berman, Dec. 22, 1973; children: Adam, Alexander, Elizabeth. B.A., George Washington U., 1969, LL.M., 1974; J.D., Am. U., 1972. Bar: N.J. 1972, D.C. 1973, N.Y. 1980, U.S. Dist. Ct. N.J. 1972, U.S. Dist. Ct. D.C. 1973, U.S. Dist. Ct. (so. dist.) N.Y. 1980, U.S. Ct. Appeals (7th cir.) 1976, U.S. Ct. Claims 1973, U.S. Tax Ct. 1973, U.S. Mil. Ct. Appeals 1974. Atty., U.S. Dept. Justice, Washington, 1972-75; lectr. Am. U., 1975-78; spl. asst. U.S. atty. Office of U.S. Atty., Chgo., 1976-78; atty. Commodity Futures Trading Commn., Washington, 1975-77; spl. counsel, 1977, asst. dir., 1977-78; regional counsel, N.Y.C., 1978-80; assoc. Rein, Mound & Cotton, N.Y.C., 1980-82, ptnr., Mound, Cotton & Wollan (and predecessor firms), 1983—. Contbr. articles to legal jours. Mem. bd. appeals Village of Flower Hill, Manhasset, N.Y., 1983-84, trustee, 1984-86; trustee Village of East Hills, 1988—, Dep. Mayor, 1993-94, Mayor, 1994—; mem. Roslyn Little League, 1991—, bd. dirs., 1992. Recipient Cert. of Appreciation for Outstanding Service U.S. Commodity Futures Trading Commn., 1977. Commercial, contracts (including sales of goods; commercial financing), Corporate, general, Securities. Home: East Hills 20 Hemlock Dr Roslyn NY 11576-2303 Office: Mound Cotton & Wollan 1 Battery Park Plz New York NY 10004-1405

KOBLENZ, N(ORMAN) HERSCHEL, lawyer; b. Albany, NY, Nov. 19, 1934; s. Edmund Akiba and Tillie (Paul) K.; m. Maxine Doris Levy, Aug. 12, 1956; children: Marci, Brian. BA, Cornell U., 1956; JD, Yale U., 1960. Bar: N.Y. 1960, Ohio 1960, U.S. Dist. Ct. (no. and ea. dists.) Ohio 1960, U.S. Ct. Appeals (6th cir.) 1960, U.S. Tax Ct. 1982. Assoc. Hahn Loeser & Parks LLP and predecessor firms, Cleve., 1960-67, ptnr., 1967—, mng. ptnr., 1985-89, exec. ptnr., 1989-91, COO, CFO, 1991-98. Pres. Bur. Jewish Edn. Cleve., 1977-82; mem. exec. com. Park Synagogue, Cleveland Heights, 1986-2000; trustee Jewish Cmty. Fedn. Cleve., 1997-2002. Capt. U.S. Army, 1956-57. Recipient Marvin and Milton Kane award Jewish Community Fedn., Cleve., 1972, A.H. Friedland award Bur. Jewish Edn., 1993; named Centerite of Yr. Park Synagogue, 1990. Mem. ABA, Ohio Bar Assn., Cleve. Bar Assn., Lomond Assn. (pres. 1969), Oakwood (South Euclid, Ohio), City (Cleve.). Democrat. Avocation: golf. Corporate, general, Health, Taxation, general. Home: 18000 S Woodland Rd Cleveland OH 44120-1773 Office: Hahn Loeser & Parks LLP 3300 BP Tower Cleveland OH 44114 E-mail: nhkoblenz@hahnlaw.com.

KOBLISKA, LINDA E. lawyer; b. New Hampton, Iowa, Feb. 17, 1956; d. Hubert J. and Hildegarde M. Zweibohmer; m. James J. Kobliska, Nov. 8, 1975; children: Rebecca, Ryan, Emily. BA, U. No. Iowa, 1993; JD, U. Iowa, 1995. Bar: Iowa 1999, U.S. Dist. Ct. (no. dist.) Iowa 1999. Staff atty. Ag Svcs. Am., Inc., Cedar Falls, Iowa, 1999—2000, gen. counsel, 2000—. Mem. city counsel City of Atla Vista, Iowa, 1999—. Mem.: ABA, Am. Bankruptcy Inst. Office: Ag Svcs Am Inc 1309 Tech Pky Cedar Falls IA 50613 Fax: 319-277-0277. E-mail: linda.kobliska@agservices.com.

KOBRIN, LAWRENCE ALAN, lawyer; b. N.Y.C., Sept. 14, 1933; s. Irving and Hortense (Freezer) K.; m. Ruth E. Freedman, Mar. 5, 1967; children: Jeffrey, Rebecca, Debra. AB in History suma cum laude, Columbia U., 1954, JD, 1957. Bar: N.Y. 1957, U.S. Dist. Ct. (sou. dist.) N.Y. 1958, U.S. Dist. Ct. (ea. dist.) 1958, U.S. Ct. Appeals (2d cir.) 1959, U.S. Supreme Ct. 1966. Assoc. Cahill, Gordon, Reindel & Ohl, N.Y.C., 1958-59, Arthur D. Emil, N.Y.C., 1959-63; ptnr. Emil & Kobrin, N.Y.C., 1963-79, Milgrim, Thomajan, Jacobs and Lee, N.Y.C., 1979-83, Cahill Gordon & Reindel, N.Y.C., 1984—. Bd. dirs. Wurzweiler Sch. of Social Work, vice-chmn., 1994-98; dir. UMB Bank and Trust Co., 1978-91; treas. The Jewish Week, N.Y.C., 1992-96, chmn., 1996—. Notes editor Columbia U. Law Rev.; mng. editor Tradition, 1961-64, editl. com. 1964—; contbr. articles to profl. jours. V.p., assoc. treas., chmn. dist. com. Fedn. Jewish Philanthropies, N.Y.C., 1981-84, com. long range planning, 1985-86, com. inner city, 71-76; chmn. Ramaz Sch., N.Y.C., 1978-83; sec. to bd. Bar Ilan U., N.Y.C., 1972-80; pres. The Jewish Ctr., N.Y.C., 1987-90; dir. N.Y.C. UJA-Fedn., chmn. communal planning com., 1988-91, chmn. com. on cmty. couns., 1996-98; v.p. Union Orthodox Jewish Congregations, 1968-74, dir. 1962—; chmn. campus com., 1962-66, chmn. Israel com., 1967-72, chmn. pub. com., 1972-78; pres. Massad Camps, 1971-77; bd. dirs. Am. Friends Pardes, 1991-96, Histadrut Ivrit., 1991—; pres. Ariel Am. Friends of Midrasha and United Instns., 1991-95, chmn., 1995-2001; sec. Beth Din of Am., 1994-96, chmn. exec. com., 1997—02, exec. com. Orthodox Caucus, 1995—, bd., exec. com., Edah, 1994—; mem. exec. com. Columbia Barnard Hillel, 1995—. Kent scholar, 1954-55, Stone scholar, 1954-55. Mem.: N.Y. State Bar Assn. (com. coops.and condominiums), N.Y. County Lawyers Assn. (chmn. real property law sect. 1991—93), Assn. Bar City N.Y. (com. on philanthropic orgns. 1974—79, edn. and law com. 1985—88, com. on legal edn. 1988—91, com. on legal problems of elderly 1991—94), Coop. Housing Lawyers Group (exec. com. 1972—80), Am. Coll. Real Estate Lawyers, Cream Hill Lake Assn., The Down Town Assn., Columbia Coll. Alumni Assn. (bd. dirs. 1990—2001, v.p. 1996—98), Phi Beta Kappa. Corporate, general, General practice, Property, real (including real estate development, water). Home: 15 W 81st St New York NY 10024-6022 also: 8 Popple Swamp Rd Cornwall Bridge CT 06754-1135 Office: Cahill Gordon & Reindel 80 Pine St Fl 17 New York NY 10005-1790 E-mail: kobrinL@mindspring.com., Lkobrin@cahill.com.

KOCH, EDNA MAE, lawyer, nurse; b. Terre Haute, Ind., Oct. 12, 1951; d. Leo K. and Lucille E. (Smith) K.; m. Mark D. Orton. BS in Nursing, Ind. State U., 1977; JD, Ind. U., 1980. Bar: Ind. 1980, U.S. Dist. Ct. (so. dist.) Ind. 1980. Assoc. Dillon & Cohen, Indpls., 1980-85; ptnr. Tipton, Cohen & Koch, Indpls., 1985-93, LaCava, Zeigler & Carter, Indpls., 1993-94, Zeigler Cohen & Koch, Indpls., 1994—. Leader seminars for nurses, Ind. U. Med. Ctr., Ball State U., Muncie, Ind., St. Vincent Hosp., Indpls., Deaconess Hosp., Evansville, Ind., others; lectr. on med. malpractice Cen. Ind. chpt. AACCN, Indpls. "500" Postgrad. Course in Emergency Medicine, Ind. Assn. Osteo. Physicians and Surgeons State Conv., numerous others. Mem. ABA, ANA, Ind. State Bar Assn., Indpls. Bar Assn., Am. Soc. Law and Medicine, Ind. State Nurses Assn. Republican. State civil litigation, Insurance, Personal injury (including property damage). Office: Zeigler Cohen & Koch 9465 Counselors Row Ste 104 Indianapolis IN 46240-3816

KOCH, EDWARD RICHARD, lawyer, accountant; b. Teaneck, N.J., Mar. 25, 1953; s. Edward J. and Adelaide M. K.; m. Cora Susan Koch, Apr. 12, 1997; children: Edward Peter, William John. BS in Econs. magna cum laude, U. Pa., 1975; JD, U. Va., 1980; LLM in Taxation, NYU, 1986. Bar: N.J. 1980, U.S. Dist. Ct. N.J. 1980, U.S. Tax Ct. 1981, U.S. Ct. Claims 1981. Staff acct. Touche Ross & Co. (now Deloitte & Touche), Newark, 1975-77; assoc. Winne, Banta & Rizzi, Hackensack, N.J., 1980-82; tax atty. Allied Corp. (now Honeywell Internat. Inc.), Morristown, 1982-87; asst. v.p. ChemBank (now Chase Manhattan), N.Y.C., 1987-90; tax mgr. Paul Scherer & Co. LLP, N.Y.C., 1990-97, ptnr., 1998—. Vice chmn. law and legis. com. U.S.A. Track and Field, Indpls., 1985-89, chmn., 1989-2000, chmn. ins. com., 1984-88, bd. dirs., 1989—, treas., 2000—; pres. N.J. Athletics Congress, Red Bank, 1986-90; mem. Jury of Appeals, 1988, U.S. Olympic Men's Marathon Trials, Holy Family Sch. Edn. Coun., 1992-96; Olympic Track and Field ofcl., 1996. Mem. AICPA, N.J. Soc. CPAs, Am. Assn. Attys.-CPAs, N.J. State Bar Assn., N.J. Striders Track Club (chmn. 1981-96), Magazine Publishers Am. (chair tax comm., 2002-). Republican. Roman Catholic. Avocation: running track and field. Corporate taxation, Personal income taxation, State and local taxation. Home: 130 Grant St Haworth NJ 07641-1951 Office: Paul Scherer & Co 335 Madison Ave Fl 9 New York NY 10017-4605 E-mail: ekoch@pscherer.com.

KOCH, RICHARD PHILLIPS (TERRY KOCH), lawyer; b. N.Y.C., Oct. 19, 1947; s. Richard Frederick and Janet Doris (Phillips) K.; m. Cynthia A. Brams, 1968 (div. 1972); m. Linda Pultman, Oct. 14, 1988. BA, Washington U., 1970; JD, Golden Gate U., 1978. Bar: Calif. 1979, U.S. Dist. Ct. (no. dist.) Calif. 1979. Pvt. practice, Berkeley, Calif., 1979—89, Oakland, Calif., 1989—, San Francisco, 1989—. Adj. prof. Golden Gate U., San Francisco, 1980; bd. dirs. Bonita House, Berkeley, 1980-84; co-founder, Left Bank Books, St. Louis; assoc. with Rostenberg & Stern Rare Books, N.Y.C., 1988-2001. Bd. dirs. Bonita House, Berkeley, 1980—84. Mem. State Bar Calif. (Wiley Manuel award 1994), Conf. Dels. (del. chair 1995—, del. 1993, 94), Nat. Lawyers Guild (exec. bd. 1987—), Nat. Assn. Counsel Children, San Francisco Bar Assn. Avocation: rare and fine books. Criminal, Health, Juvenile. Office: 1611 Telegraph Ste 719 Oakland CA 94612 Address: 760 Market St Ste 524 San Francisco CA 94102 E-mail: rpkoch@dnai.com.

KOCH, ROBERT CHARLES, lawyer, community activist; b. Berwyn, Ill., Apr. 7, 1947; s. Eugene William and Ellen Marie (Hudec) K.; m. Sharon Smith, June 27, 1970; children: Jason, Ryan, Lindsay. BS, Ill. Inst. Tech., 1969; JD, Coll. William and Mary, 1972. Bar: Ill. 1972, Okla. 1978, N.Y. 2003. Assoc. Bell, Boyd & Lloyd, Chgo., 1972-78; staff atty. Phillips Petroleum Co., Bartlesville, Okla., 1978-81, sr. atty., 1986-90, sr. counsel, 1990—2002; counsel Phillips Petroleum Co. Europe & Africa, London, 1981-86; mng.ptnr. Koch Law Office, 2002—. Author of Sunday sch. curriculums. Chmn. Washington County Dem. Party, Bartlesville, 1993-97; pres., dir. Westside Cmty. Assn., Bartlesville, 1997—2002. Mem. ABA, ATLA, Okla. Bar Assn., Am. Legion. Democrat. Presbyterian. Avocations: church youth ministry, travel. Corporate, general, Mergers and acquisitions, Securities. Home: 6972 Palmetto Circle S Apt 507 Boca Raton FL 33433 Office: 1699 W Adams Blvd Bartlesville OK 74004 Mailing: PO Box 81041 Boca Raton FL 33481-0841 E-mail: BobKoch@KochLawOffice.com.

KOCHEMS, ROBERT GREGORY, lawyer; b. Cleve., Aug. 6, 1951; s. Roy George and Virginia Mae (Budniak) K.; m. Georgann Ryan; 1 child, Alane Carin. BA cum laude, John Carroll U., 1973; JD, St. Louis U., 1976. Bar: Pa. 1976, U.S. Dist. Ct. (we. dist.) 1978. Sole practice, Mercer, Pa., 1976-81, 88-92; ptnr. Bogaty, McEwen, Sparks, & Kochems, P.C., Mercer, 1981-87, Nelson, Ryan & Kochems, 1992—. Asst. pub. defender Mercer County, 1977-88; asst. dist. atty., 1988—; sub-com. chairperson Mercer County Juvenile Ct. Adv. Com., 1986-88, chair child death rev. com., 1999—, leader dist. atty.'s child abuse prosecution unit, 1996-2001; solicitor Mercer County Regional Planning Commn., 1991—; law enforcement coord. Sharon/Farrell Weed and Seed Program, 2001--. Assoc. editor St. Louis U. Law Jour., 1975-76. Bd. dirs. Transfer Harvest Home Assn., 1986-88; solicitor Mcpl. Corp., 1996—; co-chairperson Mercer County Sexual Assault Response Team, 2000—. Mem. Pa. Bar Assn., Mercer County Bar Assn. (sec. 1977-79, bench bar com. 1982, 84), KC (adv. 1978-88). Republican. Criminal, Family and matrimonial, Juvenile. Home: PO Box 226 Mercer PA 16137-0226

KOEGEL, WILLIAM FISHER, lawyer; b. Washington, Aug. 18, 1923; s. Otto Erwin and Rae (Fisher) K.; m. Barbara Bixler, Feb. 2, 1946 (dec. 1968); children: John Bixler, Robert Bartlett; m. Ruth Swan Boynton, June 21, 1969 (dec. 1983); m. Irene Lawrence, Aug. 4, 1984. BA, Williams Coll., 1944; LL.B., U. Va., 1949. Bar: N.Y. 1950. From assoc. to ptnr. Clifford & Chance (formerly Rogers & Wells), N.Y.C., 1949—88, head litigation dept., 1977-88, sr. counsel, 1989—. Chmn. Scarsdale (N.Y.) Republican Town Com., 1965-71; pres. trustees Hitchcock Presbyn. Ch., Scarsdale, 1970-73, 78-79, 82-83. Served with AUS, 1943-45, ETO. Fellow ACTL; mem. ABA, N.Y. State Bar Assn., Bar Assn. City N.Y., Order of Coif. Clubs: Town (Scarsdale) (pres. 1976-77); Sky (N.Y.C.), Williams (N.Y.C.); Shenorock Shore, Fox Meadow Tennis, The Moorings. Federal civil litigation, State civil litigation. Home: 7 Chesterfield Rd Scarsdale NY 10583-1619 Office: Clifford Chance US LLP 200 Park Ave New York NY 10166-0005

KOEHLER, REGINALD STAFFORD, III, lawyer; b. Bellevue, Pa., Dec. 29, 1932; s. Reginald S. and Esther (Hawken) K.; m. Ann Ellsworth Rowland, June 15, 1956; children: Victoria Elizabeth, Cynthia Rowland, Robert Steven. BA, Yale U., 1956; JD, Harvard U., 1959. Bar: N.Y. 1960, Calif., Fla., D.C. 1979, Wash. 1984, Oreg. 1985, Alaska 1985, U.S. Supreme Ct. 1973. Assoc. Davis Polk & Wardwell, N.Y.C., 1959-68; ptnr. Donovan Leisure Newton & Irvine, N.Y.C., 1968-84, Perkins Coie, Seattle, 1984—. Author: The Planning and Administration of a Large Estate, 1982, 5th edit. 1986. Chmn. bd. trustees Fred Hutchinson Cancer Rsch. Ctr. With U.S. Army, 1952-54. Fellow Am. Coll. Trust and Estate Counsel; mem. N.Y. State Bar Assn., Calif. Bar Assn., D.C. Bar Assn., Wash. Bar Assn., Oreg. Bar Assn., Alaska Bar Assn., Chi Psi. Episcopalian. Estate planning, Family and matrimonial, Probate (including wills, trusts). Office: Perkins Coie 1201 3rd Ave Fl 40 Seattle WA 98101-3029

KOEHN, WILLIAM JAMES, lawyer; b. Winterset, Iowa, Mar. 24, 1936; s. Cyril Otto and Ilene L. (Doop) K.; m. Francia C. Leeper, Sept. 6, 1958; children: Cynthia Rae, William Fredric, James Anthony. BA, JD cum laude, U. Iowa, 1963. Bar: Iowa 1963, U. S. Ct. Appeals (8th cir.) 1971, U.S. Ct. Appeals (10th cir.) 1972, U.S. Ct. Appeals (2d cir.) 1972, U.S. Ct. Appeals (5th cir.) 1977, U.S. Supreme Ct. 1971. Mem. Davis, Brown, Koehn, Shors & Roberts, P.C., Des Moines, 1963—. Prof., lectr. in U.S., Can., Europe. Bd. editors Iowa Law Rev., 1961-63; contbr. articles to profl. jours. C0-founder Big Bros.-Sisters of Greater Des Moines, 1969, pres., 1976-77; chmn. Des Moines Friendship Commmn., 1970-71; bd. dirs. Greater Des Moines YMCA, 1983-90; co-chmn. Des Moines Bicentennial Commn., 1975-76; chmn. Environ. and Pub. Works Commn.; mem. adv. com. civil justice reform act, 1990; chmn. worldwide dispute resolution com., Lex Mundi, 1989-94, bd. dirs., 1992-96. Lt. USNR, 1958-61. Mem. ABA (environ. litigation sub-com., construction com., internat. lit. environ. commn.), Iowa Bar Assn. (environ. coun. 1989-92, 1999-2001, litigation com. 1992-95, proflism. com. 1994-2002), Polk County Bar Assn., Iowa Trial Lawyers Assn., Order of Coif. Republican. Federal civil litigation, State civil litigation, Construction. Office: Fin Ctr 666 Walnut St Des Moines IA 50309-3904 Home: Unit 1801 3305 Ep True Pkwy West Des Moines IA 50265-7677

KOELLER, ROBERT MARION, lawyer, director; b. Quincy, Ill., Apr. 8, 1940; s. Marion Alfred and Ruth (Main) K.; m. Marlene Meyer, June 1962; children: Kristin, Katherine, Robert. AB, MacMurray Coll., 1962; LLB, Vanderbilt U., 1965. Bar: Ind. 1968. Asst. gen. counsel Nat. Homes Acceptance Corp., Lafayette, Ind., 1967-70; gen. counsel, sec. Herff Jones Co., Indpls., 1970-74; ptnr. Warren, Snider, Koeller & Warren, Indpls., 1974-76; sole practice Indpls., 1976—; mem. Coons, Maddox & Koeller, Indpls., 1993-96, Maddox, Koeller Hargett & Caruso, 1996—2002, Sheeks Ittenbach Johnson Trettin & Koeller, Indpls., 2002—. Dir. various cos. Mem. ABA, Ind. Bar Assn., Indpls. Bar Assn., Hillcrest Country Club. Republican. Methodist. Corporate, general, Probate (including wills, trusts), Securities. Office: Ste 4 6350 N Shadeland Ave Indianapolis IN 46220 E-mail: rkoeller@sheeks-ittenbach.com.

KOELLING, THOMAS WINSOR, lawyer; b. Jefferson City, Mo., Oct. 10, 1951; s. Oscar Alvin and Helen Louise (Shields) K.;m. Rebecca Ann Nentwig, Nov. 24, 1973; children: Zachary Thomas, Mathew Garret. BS in Criminal Justice Adminstrn., Ctrl. Mo. State U., Warrenburg, 1978; JD, U. Mo., 1981. Bar: Mo. 1981, Colo. 1982, U.S. Dist. Ct. (we. dist.) Mo. 1981, U.S. Dist. Ct. Colo. 1981, U.S. Ct. Appeals (8th cir.) 1982, U.S. Ct. Appeals (10th cir.) 1981, U.S. Supreme Ct. 1992. Assoc. Tinsley, Frantz et al, Lakewood, Colo., 1981-82, Rex Johnson Law Office, Colorado Springs, Colo., 1982-85; ptnr. Koelling & Crawford, P.C., Kansas City, Mo., 1985—. Legal advisor Kansas City Ski Club, 1987, Competitors Assn., Kansas City, 1995—; adj. prof. dept. criminal justice and legal studies Mo. Western State Coll., St. Joseph, Mo., 1998—. With USAF, 1972-76. Mem. ABA, Am. Coll. Legal Medicine, Am. Soc. Law, Medicine Ethics, Am. Trial Lawyers Assn., Mo. Assn. Trial Lawyers, Clay County Bar Assn. Roman Catholic. Avocations: snow skiing, fly fishing, backpacking. Personal injury (including property damage), Professional liability, Toxic tort. Home: 9617 N Campbell St Kansas City MO 64155-2056 Office: Koelling & Crawford PC 5950 N Oak Trfy Ste 202 Kansas City MO 64118-5164

KOELTL, JOHN GEORGE, judge; b. N.Y.C., Oct. 25, 1945; s. John J. and Elsie (Bender) K. AB summa cum laude, Georgetown U., 1967; JD magna cum laude, Harvard U., 1971. Bar: N.Y. 1972, U.S. Dist. Ct. (so. and ea. dists.) N.Y. 1975, U.S. Ct. Appeals (2d cir.) 1975, U.S. Supreme Ct. 1978, U.S. Ct. Appeals (5th and 11th cirs.) 1981, U.S. Ct. Appeals (4th cir.) 1992, U.S. Dist. Ct. (no. dist.) N.Y. 1982. Law clk. to Judge U.S. Dist. Ct. (so. dist.), N.Y.C., 1971-72; law clk. to Justice Potter Stewart U.S. Supreme Ct., Washington, 1972-73; asst. spl. prosecutor Watergate Spl. Prosecution Force, Dept. Justice, Washington, 1973-74; assoc. Debevoise & Plimpton, N.Y.C., 1975-78, ptnr., 1979-94; judge U.S. Dist. Ct. (so. dist.), N.Y.C., 1994—. Adj. prof. law NYU Law Sch., 1999—. Mem. bd. editors Manual for Complex Litigation 4th edit.; contbr. articles to profl. jours. Mem.: ABA (bd. editors jour. 1991—97, vice chmn. securities com. adminstrv. law sect. 1979—81, co-dir. divsn. publs. litigation sect. 1982—84, coun. mem. litigation sect. 1984—87, assoc. editor Litigation jour. 1975—78, exec. editor 1978—80, editor-in-chief 1980—82, chmn. 1st amendment com. 1987—89, chmn. spl. pubs. com. 1989—92, dir. divsn. publs. litigation sect. 1992—93), Am. Law Inst., Harvard Law Sch. Assn. N.Y. (v.p. 1993—94), N.Y. County Lawyers Assn. (mem. fed. cts. com. 1984—87), N.Y. State Bar Assn., Assn. Bar N.Y.C. (mem. com. on fed. legislation 1976—78, sec. 1978—81, mem. com. profl. and jud. ethics 1981—84, fed. cts. com. 1984—86, chmn. 1986—89, mem. com. on profl. responsibility 1991—94, mem. com. on internat. dispute resolution 2000—). Office: US Courthouse 500 Pearl St Rm 1030 New York NY 10007-1316

KOENIG, HANS-JOACHIM, lawyer; b. Singen, Germany, May 3, 1955; s. Hermann and Ida Koenig; m. Eleonore Reichert; children: Maximiliane, Fabian. State exam, Ruprecht-Karls U., Heidelberg, Germany, 1982, LLD, 1991; state exam, State Baden-Wuerttemberg, Germany, 1985. Bar: LG Konstanz 1988. Lawyer Kanzlei Schrade, Villingen-Schwenningen, Germany, 1989—93; founder, mng. sr. ptnr. Schrade & Ptnr. Rechtsanwaelte, Villingen-Schwenningen, 1993—. Chmn., mem. various supervisory and governing bds., Germany, 1993—, Switzerland, 1993—. Author: Der Verein im Verein, 1992. 1st lt. German Army Reserves, 1974—76. Mem.: Golf Club Steisslingen (pres. 1994—). Avocations: golf, soccer. Mergers and acquisitions, Corporate, general, Health. Office: Schrade & Ptnr Rechtsanwaelte Karlsruher Str 21 78048 Villingen Germany

KOEPKE, SCOTT PAUL, lawyer; b. Utica, N.Y., Feb. 5, 1959; s. H. Paul Koepke Jr. and Janet Allen. BS with honors, U. Mich., 1981; JD, U. So. Calif., 1984. James B. Angell scholar. Mem. L.A. Bar Assn., Assn. Bus. Trial Lawyers. Office: One Bunker Hill 601 W 5th St Fl 8 Los Angeles CA 90071-2004

KOEPPEL, JOHN A. lawyer; b. Jersey City, Aug. 9, 1947; s. A.J. and Florence (McDonald) K.; m. Susan Lynn Rothstein, Nov. 12, 1972; children: Adam, Leah. BA in Govt. cum laude, U. Notre Dame, 1969; MA in Internat. Law, Tufts U., 1970; JD, U. Calif., San Francisco, 1976. Bar: Calif. 1976, D.C. 1980, U.S. Dist. Ct. (no. dist.) Calif. 1976, U.S. Supreme Ct. 1980. Assoc. Barfield, Barfield, Dryden & Ruane, San Francisco, 1976-80; from assoc. to shareholder Ropers, Majeski, Kohn & Bentley, San Francisco, 1980—, resident dir., 1992-95, 97-99. Arbitrator San Francisco Superior Ct., 1979—; legal counsel San Francisco Jaycees, 1980-81, Amigos de los Americas, San Francisco, 1982-84, St. Francis Homes Assn., 1987-89, treas.; instr. Hastings Coll. Advocacy, San Francisco, 1988-91; lectr. U. Calif., San Francisco, 1990-95; sec. San Francisco Casualty Claims Assn., 1993-95; bd. dirs. and legal counsel Or Shalom, 2002—; bd. dirs. Ropers Majeski Kohn & Bentley, 1992-99, 2003—. Bd. dirs. San Francisco Sch., 1998-2000, active youth sports coaching, 1990-2000. Mem. Nat. Bd. Trial Advocacy, Calif. State Bar (certificate of recognition for pro bono legal work, 1989), D.C. Bar, San Francisco Bar Assn. Avocations: running, skiing, hiking, rowing, travel. General civil litigation, Construction, Product liability. Office: Ropers Majeski Kohn & Bentley 333 Market St Ste 3150 San Francisco CA 94105-2132 E-mail: jkoeppel@ropers.com., johna1k@aol.com.

KOESTER, BERTHOLD KARL, lawyer, law educator, retired honorary German consul; b. Aachen, Germany, June 30, 1931; s. Wilhelm P. and Margarethe A. (Witteler) K.; m. Hildegard Maria (Buettner), June 30, 1961; children: Georg W., Wolfgang J., and Reinhard B. Doctor of Laws, U. Muenster, Fed. Republic Germany, 1957. Cert.in Real Estate Brokerage, Ariz. Asst. prof. civil and internat. law U. Muenster, Germany, 1957-60; v.p. Bank J. H. Vogeler and Co., Duesseldorf, Germany, 1960-64; atty. Ct. of Duesseldorf, Germany, 1960-82; pres. Bremer Tank-u, Kuehlschiffahrtsges, M.B.H., Germany, 1964-72; prof., internat. bus. law Am. Grad. Sch. Internat. Mgmt., Glendale, Ariz., 1978-81; coun. Tancer Law Offices, Phoenix, 1978-86; chmn., CEO Arimpex, Inc., Phoenix, 1979—; ptnr. Applewhite, Laflin, and Lewis, Real Estate Investments, Scottsdale, Ariz., 1981-88; atty., trustee internat. corp. Duesseldorf, Germany and Phoenix, 1983—; chief exec. officer, chmn. bd. German Consultants in Real Estate Investments, Phoenix, 1988—; prof., internat. bus. law, chmn. dept. Western Internat. U., Phoenix, 1996—. Bd. dirs. Ariz. Partnership for Air Transp., 1988-92; chmn. Finvest Corp., Phoenix, 1990—; hon. German cons. for Ariz., 1982-92. Author: The Refinancing of the Banking System, 1963, Long Term Finance, 1968, International Joint Ventures, 1974, History and Economy of the Middle East, 1975, Bauhaus and the Expresssionism, 1983; contbr. articles to profl. jour. Pres. Parents Assn., Humboldt Gymnasium, Duesseldorf, Germany, 1971-78; active German Red Cross, from 1977. Mem. Duesseldorf Chamber of Lawyers, Bochum, Fed. Republic Germany, Assn. Tax Lawyers, Bonn German-Saudi Arabian Assn. (pres. 1976-79), Bonn German-Korean Assn., Assn. for German-Korean Econ. Devel. (pres. 1974-78), Ariz. Consular Corp. (sec., treas. 1988-89), Nat. Soc. Arts and Letters (Greater Ariz. chpt., bd. dirs. 1997—), German-Am. C. of C., Phoenix Met., C. of C., Rotary, Scottsdale, Ariz. Finance, Public international, Property, real (including real estate development, water). Home: 6201 E.Cactus Rd Scottsdale AZ 85254-4409 Office: PO Box 15674 Phoenix AZ 85060-5674

KOFF, HOWARD MICHAEL, lawyer; b. Bklyn., July 25, 1941; s. Arthur and Blanche Koff; m. Linda Sue Bright, Sept. 10, 1966; 1 son, Michael Arthur Bright. BS, NYU, 1962; JD, Bklyn. Law Sch., 1965; LLM in Taxation, Georgetown U., 1968. Bar: N.Y. 1965, D.C. 1966, U.S. Supreme Ct. 1969, U.S. Ct. Appeals (2d, 3d, 4th, 5th, 7th, 9th and D.C. cirs.), U.S. Dist. Ct. (no. dist.) N.Y. 1981. Appellate atty. tax divsn. U.S. Dept. Justice, Washington, 1965-69; tax supr. Chrysler Corp., Detroit, 1969-70; chief tax counsel Conn. Gen. Life Ins. Co., Hartford, Conn., 1970-77, Rohm & Haas Co., Phila., 1977-78; ptnr. Dibble, Koff, Lane, Stern and Stern, Rochester, 1978—81; pres. Howard M. Koff, P.C., Albany, N.Y., 1981—. Lectr. tax matters. Editor-in-chief Bklyn. Law Rev., 1964-65; charter mem. editl. adv. bd. Jour. Real Estate Taxation; contbr. articles to legal jours. Chmn. pub. adv. coun. N.Y. State Ethics Commn. Recipient Founders Day award NYU, 1962, Lawyers Coop. award for gen. excellence Lawyers Coop. Pub. Co., 1965. Mem. ABA (past chmn. subcom. on partnerships tax sect.), FBA (past pres. Hartford County chpt.), Albany County Bar Assn., Estate Planning Coun. Ea. N.Y., Albany Area C. of C., Rotary, Colonie Guilderland N.Y. Club. Republican. Corporate taxation, Personal income taxation, State and local taxation. Home: 205 W Bentwood Ct Albany NY 12203-4905 Office: 600 Broadway Albany NY 12207-2205

KOFFLER, WARREN WILLIAM, lawyer; b. N.Y.C., July 21, 1938; s. Jack and Rose (Conovich) K.; m. Barbara Rose Holz, June 11, 1959; m. Jayne Audri Goetzel, May 15, 1970; children: Kevin, Kenneth, Caroline. BS, Boston U., 1959; JD, U. Calif., Berkeley, 1962; LLD, NYU, 1972. Bar: D.C. 1962, N.Y. 1963, U.S. Dist. Ct. D.C. 1963, Fla. 1980, Va. 1981, Pa. 1982. Atty. FAA, Washington, 1964; pvt. practice law Washington, 1964, 78—, Hollywood, Palm Beach, Miami, Fla., 1978—; atty. Fed. Home Loan Bank Bd., Washington, 1964-66; ptnr. Koffler & Spivack, Washington, 1967-77. Mem. ATLA, ABA, FBA, Inter-Am. Bar Assn., D.C. Bar Assn., Fla. Bar Assn., Va. Bar Assn., Brit. Inst. Internat. and Comparative Law, Univ. Club (Washington), Bankers Club (Miami), Membership Club PGA Nat. (Palm Beach), City Club (Palm Beach). Administrative and regulatory, Banking, Private international. Office: 4521 PGA Blvd Ste 361 West Palm Beach FL 33418 also: 1730 K St NW Washington DC 20006-3868 E-mail: wwkvip@msn.com.

KOGOVSEK, DANIEL CHARLES, lawyer; b. Pueblo, Colo., Aug. 4, 1951; s. Frank Louis and Mary Edith (Blatnick) K.; m. Patricia Elizabeth Connell, June 30, 1979; 1 child, Ryan Robert. BA, U. Notre Dame, 1973; JD, Columbia U., 1976. Bar: Colo. 1976, U.S. Dist. Ct. Colo. 1976, U.S. Ct. Appeals (10th cir.) 1978, U.S. Supreme Ct. 1983. Ast. atty. gen. Colo. Dept. Law, Denver, 1976-79; campaign mgr. Congressman Kogovsek, Pueblo, 1980, 82; dir. Office Consumer Svcs., Denver, 1981; mem. firm Fish & Kogovsek, Denver, 1983-84; sr. assoc. Petersen & Fonda, P.C., Pueblo, 1985-89; mem. firm Kogovsek & Higinbotham, P.C., Pueblo, 1989—2002; mem. firm. Kogovsek Law Firm, P.C., Pueblo, 2002—; county atty. Pueblo County, 2001—. Mem. ABA, Colo. Bar Assn., Pueblo Bar Assn. Commercial, consumer (including collections, credit). Home: 584 W Spaulding Ave S Pueblo West CO 81007-1874 Office: Ste 202 830 N Main St Pueblo CO 81003-0202 E-mail: kog-law@aculink.net.

KOH, CHYE HOCK, lawyer; b. Taiping, Malaysia, Sept. 23, 1961; BA, U. Utah, 1983, MA, 1986; LLB, U. Wales, 1989; LLM, Georgetown U., 1991. Bar: Va. 1993, U.S. Ct. Appeals (4th cir.) 1993, Malaysian Cert. Legal Practice 1996. Profl. legal specialist Cleary, Gottlieb, Steen & Hamilton, Washington, 1992—94; legal mgr. Occidental Oil and Gas Corp., Malaysia and Bangladesh, 1994—99; legal dir., internat. counsel Unocal Offshore Svcs., Ltd., Sugarland, Tex., 1999—. Avocations: reading, writing, music, cooking. Private international, Commercial, contracts (including sales of goods; commercial financing), Nuclear power. Office: Unocal Offshore Svcs Ltd 14141 Southwest Fwy Sugar Land TX 77478 E-mail: ckoh@unocal.com.

KOHL, KATHLEEN ALLISON BARNHART, lawyer; b. Ft. Leavenworth, Kans., Jan. 11, 1955; d. Robert William and Margaret Ann (Snowden) Barnhart. BS, Memphis State U., 1978; JD, Loyola U., New Orleans, 1982. Bar: La. 1982, U.S. Dist. Ct. (ea. dist.) La. 1982, U.S. Dist. Ct. (no. dist.) Tex. 1985, U.S. Ct. Appeals (5th cir.) 1986, U.S. Ct. Appeals (11th cir.) 1988, U.S. Supreme Ct. 1994. Assoc. Garrity & Webb, Harahan, La., 1982; revenue officer IRS, Dallas, 1984; sr. trial atty. EEOC, Dallas, 1984-86; sr. criminal enforcement counsel U.S. EPA, Dallas, 1986-91, chief water enforcement sect., office regional counsel, 1991-92, dep. dir. criminal enforcement counsel divsn. Washington, 1992-93, dir. criminal enforcement counsel divsn., 1993-94, sr. criminal enforcement counsel Dallas, 1994—99; spl. asst. U.S. atty. U.S. Atty.'s Office, Montgomery, Ala., 1988-89; chief, criminal enforcement unit Office of regional counsel, Dallas, 1999—. Vis. instr. Fed. Law Enforcement Tng. Ctr., Glynco, Ga., 1987—; adj. prof. environ. crimes seminar Cornell U. Law Sch., spring 1993, environ. law Sch. Law Tex. Wesleyan U., fall 1998; instr. EPA Nat. Acad., 1997—. Vol. instr. New Orleans Police Acad., 1981. Mem. La. Bar Assn. Office: EPA 1445 Ross Ave Ste 1200 Dallas TX 75202-2733

KOHLI, ULRICH A. lawyer; b. Schwarzenburg, Switzerland, Dec. 31, 1947; s. Werner and Cecile Kohli; m. Verena Hostettler; m. Stefanie, Markus, Thomas. PhD in law, U. Bern, 1969. Journalist Berner Zeitung, Bern, 1971; legal advisor Chem. Bank, N.Y.C., 1972-73; legal counsel Bank Julius Baer, Zurich, 1974-79; owner Law Firm of Kohli & Ptnr., Zurich, 1979—. Pres. Kohli Comm. Inc., N.Y.C., 1997— Author (as James Douglas): (novels) Brennpunkt Philadelphia, 1994, Goldauge, Zero Philadelphia, 1997, Der Sintfluter, 1998, Atemlos nach Casablanca, 2000; author: Breathless to Casablanca, 2002; prodr.: (films) Mindbender, 1996, A Million to One, 2002, Breathless to Casablanca, 2002; , co-author movie scripts. Justice of Zurich Tax Ct., 1987-93; pres. Dem. Party of Zollikon-Zurich, 1975-79. Col. Tanks, 1987-95. Mem. Swiss Rifle Assn. (shooting medals), Swiss Ski Fedn. (instr.), Swiss Officer Assn., Swiss Bar Assn. Avocations: golfing, skiing, shooting, yachting. Home: Im Hausacher 10 8706 Feldmeilen Switzerland Office: Kohli & Ptnrs 10 General Willestrasse 8027 Zurich Switzerland E-mail: ulikohli@aol.com.

KOHN, HENRY, lawyer, director; b. St. Louis, May 2, 1917; s. Henry and Hannah (Lederer) K.; m. Anne Frankenthaler, Sept. 23, 1945; children: Margaret, Barbara, Alice. BA, Yale U., 1939, LL.B., 1942. Bar: Mo. 1942, N.Y. 1946. With Bd. Econ. Warfare, 1942; practice with George Frankenthaler, N.Y.C., 1946-48; pvt. practice N.Y.C., 1949-56; sr. ptnr. Frankenthaler, Kohn, Schneider & Katz, N.Y.C., 1957—. Former pres., dir. Fiduciary Mut. Investing Co., Mercer Fund Inc.; bd. dirs. Meta Health Tech., Inc. Chmn. bd., founder Am. Jewish Soc. for Service; former treas. and bd. dirs. Nat. Jewish Welfare Bd.; bd. dirs. Lavanburg Corner House Found.; pres. Ed. Lee and Jean Campe Found., Sam and Louise Campe Found.; dir., past pres. and chmn. bd. dirs. 92d St. YM-YWHA; former dir. Edison Bros. Stores Inc., Graphic Sci. Inc. Served to capt. AUS, 1942-46. Mem. ABA, N.Y. County Lawyers Assn., Assn. Bar City N.Y., Order of Coif, Phi Beta Kappa. Clubs: New York Lawn Bowling, Harmonie, The India House (N.Y.C.). Jewish. Home: 155 E 72nd St New York NY 10021-4371 also: Strawberry Hill Ackert Hook Rd Rhinebeck NY 12572

KOHN, SHALOM L. lawyer; b. Nov. 18, 1949; s. Pincus and Helen (Roth) K.; m. Barbara Segal, June 30, 1974; children: David, Jeremy, Daniel. BS in Acctg. summa cum laude, CUNY, 1970; JD magna cum laude, MBA, Harvard U., 1974. Bar: Ill. 1975, U.S. Dist. Ct. (no. dist.) Ill. 1975, U.S. Ct. Appeals (7th cir.) 1976, U.S. Supreme Ct. 1980, N.Y. 1988, U.S. Dist. Ct. (so. dist.) N.Y. 1988. Law clk. to chief judge U.S. Ct. Appeals (2d cir.), N.Y.C., 1974-75; assoc. Sidley & Austin, Chgo., 1975-80, ptnr., 1980—. Exec. com. Adv. Coun. Religious Rights in Eastern Europe and Soviet Union, Washington, 1984-86; bd. dirs. Brisk Rabbinical Coll., Chgo. Contbr. articles to profl. jours. Mem. ABA, Chgo. Bar Assn. Bankruptcy, Federal civil litigation, General practice. Office: Sidley Austin Brown & Wood Bank One Plz 10 South Dearborn Chicago IL 60603 also: 787 Seventh Ave New York NY 10019

KOHN, WILLIAM IRWIN, lawyer; b. Bronx, N.Y., June 27, 1951; s. Arthur Oscar and Frances (Hoffman) K.; m. Karen Mindlin, Aug. 29, 1974; children: Shira, Kinneret, Asher. Student, U. Del., 1969-71; BA with honors, U. Cin., 1973; JD, Ohio State U., 1976. Bar: Ohio 1976, U.S. Dist. Ct. (no. dist.) Ohio 1982, Ind. 1982, U.S. Dist. Ct. (no. and so. dists.) Ind. 1982, D.C. 1992, U.S. Supreme Ct., 1992, Ill. 1994; cert. Bus. Bankruptcy Law Am. Bankruptcy Bd. Cert. Ptnr. Krugliak, Wilkins, Griffith & Dougherty, Canton, Ohio, 1976-82, Barnes & Thornburg, Chgo., 1982—2001, Sachnoff & Weaver Ltd., Chgo., 2002, Schiff Harden & Waite, Chgo., 2002—. Adj. prof. law U. Notre Dame, Ind., 1984-90. Author: West's Indiana Business Forms, West's Indiana Uniform Commercial Code Forms; contbr. articles to profl. jours. Bd. dirs. Family Svcs., South Bend, 1985-94, Jewish Fedn., Highland Park United Way, Jewish Family and Cmty. Svcs. Mem. ABA (bus. bankruptcy subcom.), Am. Bankruptcy Inst. (insolvency sect., bd. dirs.), Ill. Bar Assn., Chgo. Bar Assn., Comml. Law League, Am. Bd. Certification (dir., std. com.). Banking, Bankruptcy, Commercial, contracts (including sales of goods; commercial financing). Office: Schiff Hardin & Waite 6600 Sears Tower Chicago IL 60606 E-mail: wkohm@schiffhardin.com.

KOLA, ARTHUR ANTHONY, lawyer; b. New Brunswick, N.J., Feb. 16, 1939; s. Arthur Aloysius and Blanche (Raym) K.; m. Jacquelin Lou Draper, Sept. 3, 1960; children— Jill, Jean, Jennifer; m. Anna Molnar, Apr. 15, 1977 AB, Dartmouth Coll., 1961; LLB, Duke U., 1964. Bar: Ohio 1964, U.S. Dist. Ct. (no. dist.) Ohio 1969, U.S. Ct. Appeals (6th cir.) 1971, U.S. Supreme Ct. 1972. Assoc. Squire, Sanders & Dempsey, Cleve., 1964-65, assoc., 1968-74, ptnr., 1974-94; pvt. practice Kola Law Office, Cleve., 1994—. Asst. prof. law Ind. U., Bloomington, 1967-68; instr. labor law Case Western Res. U., Cleve., 1976 Bd. visitors Duke U. Sch. Law, 1985—. Served to capt. U.S. Army, 1965-67 Mem. Ohio Bar Assn., Cleve. Bar Assn. (chmn. labor and employment law sect. 1993-94), Am. Arbitration Assn. (bd. dirs. 1991-97). Administrative and regulatory, Federal civil litigation, Labor (including EEOC, Fair Labor Standards Act, labor-management relations, NLRB, OSHA). Office: Kola Law Office Park Ctr I Ste 200 6100 Oak Tree Blvd Cleveland OH 44131

KOLB, JOHN E. lawyer; b. Argenta, Tex., Aug. 19, 1928; s. Luther T. and Gladys (Bomer) K.; m. Joy Voltz, Aug. 16, 1947; children: Susan Kolb Dunwoody, Jay T., Paul M., Ellen Kolb Klepacki, Ann Kolb Cuclis. BBA, U. Tex., 1949; LLB, U. Houston, 1955. From assoc. to ptnr. Vinson & Elkins, Houston, 1955—. Bd. dirs. Adobe Resources Corp., N.Y.C. Regent U. Houston System, 1981-87; bd. dirs. W.M. Keck Found., Los Angeles, 1986—. Recipient Disting. Alumnus award U. Houston Alumni Assn., 1984. Mem. ABA, Tex. Bar Assn., Houston Bar Assn. Mem. Disciples of Christ Ch. Clubs: Ramada (Houston), River Oaks Country. Address: 10 S Briar Hollow Apt 59 Houston TX 77027

KOLBE, KARL WILLIAM, JR., lawyer; b. Passaic, N.J., Sept. 29, 1926; s. Karl William Sr. and Edna Ernestine (Rumsey) K.; m. Barbara Louise Bogart, Jan. 28, 1950 (dec. Aug. 1992); children: Kim E., William B., Katherine B.; m. Patricia L. Coward, Apr. 30, 1994. BA, Princeton U., 1949; JD, U. Va., 1952. Bars: N.Y. 1952, D.C. 1976, U.S. Supreme Ct. 1966. Ptnr. Thelen, Reid & Priest, N.Y.C., 1966-92, of counsel, 1993—. Dir. Bessemer Trust Co. (N.A.), N.Y.C.,1977-97, Carolinas Cement Co., 1994-98, World Trade Corp., 1987-2002; vice-chmn. The Friends of Thirteen Inc. Bd. dirs. N.J. Ballet Co., West Orange, 1970-98, Ocean Liner Mus., 1992-2003. With USN, 1944-46. Mem. ABA (chmn. pub. utility law sect. 1984-85). Clubs: Univ. (N.Y.C.); Metro. (Washington). Republican. Episcopalian. Taxation, general. Home: PO Box 278 111 Old Chester Rd Essex Fells NJ 07021-1625 Office: Thelen Reid & Priest 875 Third Ave New York NY 10022 E-mail: wkolbe@thelenreid.com.

KOLBER, RICHARD A. lawyer; b. Wantagh, N.Y., Aug. 2, 1961; s. Leonard and Yola Kolber. BA, SUNY, Binghamton, 1983; JD, U. Calif., 1986. Bar: Calif. 1986, U.S. Dist. Ct. (so. and ea. dists.) Calif. 1987. Assoc. Haight, Brown & Bonesteel, Santa Monica, Calif., 1986-88, Barash & Hill, L.A., 1988-93; pvt. practice Law Offices of Richard A. Kolber, L.A., 1993—. General civil litigation. Office: Ste 900 2029 Century Park E Los Angeles CA 90067-2910 Fax: 310-203-0821.. E-mail: rakolber@pacbell.net.

KOLE, JANET STEPHANIE, lawyer, writer, photographer; b. Washington, Dec. 20, 1946; d. Martin J. and Ruth G. (Goldberg) K. AB, Bryn Mawr Coll., 1968; MA, NYU, 1970; JD, Temple U., 1980. Bar: Pa. 1980, N.J. 1994. Assoc. editor trade books Simon & Schuster, N.Y.C., 1968-70; publicity dir. Am. Arbitration Assn., N.Y.C., 1970-73, freelance photojournalist, 1973-76; law clk. Morgan Lewis & Bockius, Phila., 1977-80; assoc. Schnader, Harrison, Segal & Lewis, Phila., 1980-85; ptnr. Cohen, Shapiro, Polisher, Shiekman & Cohen, Phila., 1985-95; ptnr., chmn. environ. practice group Klehr, Harrison, Harvey, Branzburg & Ellers, Phila., 1995-97; pvt. practice, 1997-2001; chmn. environ. dept. Cooper, Levenson, April, Niedelman & Wagenheim, Atlantic City/Cherry Hill, NJ, 2001—. Author: Post Mortem, 1974; editor Environmental Litigation, 1991, 99; contbr. numerous articles to profl. jour.; past mem. editl. bd. New Am. Rev. Mem. Mayor's Task Force on Rape, N.Y.C., 1972-77; adv. Support Ctr. Child Advs., Phila., 1980—; mem. Phila. Vol. Lawyers for Arts. Fellow Acad. Advocacy, Am. Bar Found.; mem. ABA (former co-chair individual and small firm, former co-chair environ. litigation com., former dir., publs., former coun. mem. sect. litigation, dir. publs., former co-divsn. dir. substantive areas litigation, former editor litigation news, former chmn. com. monographs and unpublished papers, com. spl. pubs., co-chair electronic publ. com.), ATLA. Federal civil litigation, State civil litigation, Environmental. Office: 1415 Rte 70 E Ste 600 Cherry Hill NJ 08034 E-mail: jkole@cooperlevenson.com.

KOLENIC, ANTHONY JAMES, JR., lawyer, educator; b. Muskegon, Mich., Nov. 25, 1953; s. Anthony J. and Frances M. (Kulesza) K.; m. Margaret A. Dougherty, Aug. 21, 1976; children: Bethany A., Anthony J. III. AA, Muskegon C.C., 1973; BS, Mich. State U., 1975; JD, U. Mich., 1977. Bar: Mich. 1978, U.S. Dist. Ct. (we. dist.) Mich. 1979. Assoc., then ptnr. Landman, Latimer, Clink & Robb, Muskegon, 1977-86; ptnr. Lague, Newman & Irish, Muskegon, 1986—95, Warner Norcross & Judd LLP, Grand Rapids, 1995—. Instr. Muskegon C.C., 1979-83, Western Mich. U., Grand Rapids, 1987—. Vice pres. Muskegon County Cath. Edn. Found., 1992—. Mem. Kiwanis (pres. Muskegon 1978, dist. lt. gov. 1989), Rotary. Health, Non-profit and tax-exempt organizations, Pension, profit-sharing, and employee benefits. Home: 3925 Lake Point Dr Muskegon MI 49441-4690 Office: Warner Norcross & Judd LLP 900 5th 3rd Bldg Grand Rapids MI 49443 E-mail: akolenic@wnj.com.

KOLESNYK, OLEG IVANOVICH, lawyer; b. Kiev, Ukraine, Nov. 2, 1964; s. Ivan Petrovich and Yadviga Andreevna K.; m. Tatiana Andreevna Smorgonskaya Kolysnyk, Aug. 21, 1998. Law degree, Kiev State U., Ukraine, 1988; student, Leeds U., Eng., 1995. Kiev bar: 1994—. Atty. Grischenko & Part, Kiev, Ukraine, 1992-98; cons. Hewett & Co., London, 1995; sr. lawyer Nch Advisors, Kiev, Ukraine, 1998-99; lawyer Dejure, Kiev, Ukraine, 1999—. Aviation, Commercial, contracts (including sales of goods; commercial financing), Corporate taxation. Home: 12 Geroev Dnepra Apt 59 Kiev 04209 Ukraine Office: Bar Assn of DeJure G Grushevskogo St Kiev Ukraine

KOLKEY, DANIEL MILES, judge; b. Chgo., Apr. 21, 1952; s. Eugene Louis and Gilda Penelope (Cowan) K.; m. Donna Lynn Christie, May 15, 1982; children: Eugene, William, Christopher, Jonathan. BA, Stanford U., 1974; JD, Harvard U., 1977. Bar: Calif. 1977, U.S. Dist. Ct. (ea. dist.) Calif. 1978, U.S. Dist. Ct. (cen. dist.) Calif. 1979, U.S. Ct. Appeals (9th cir.) 1979, U.S. Dist. Ct. (no. dist.) Calif. 1980, U.S. Supreme Ct. 1983, U.S. Dist. Ct. Ariz. 1992, U.S. Dist. Ct. (so. dist.) Calif. 1994. Law clk. U.S. Dist. Ct. judge, N.Y.C., 1977-78; assoc. Gibson Dunn & Crutcher, L.A., 1978-84, ptnr., 1985-94; counsel to Gov., legal affairs sec. to Calif. Gov. Pete Wilson, 1995-98; assoc. justice Calif. Ct. Appeal, 3rd Appellate Dist., Sacramento, 1998—. Arbitrator bi-nat. panel for U.S.-Can. Free Trade Agreement, 1990—94; commr. Calif. Law Revision Commn., 1992—94, vice chair, 1993—94, chair, 1994; mem. Blue Ribbon Commn. on Jury Sys. Improvement, 1996; adj. prof. McGeorge Sch. Law, 2001—; mem. Calif. State-Fed. Jud. Coun., 2001—. Co-editor: Practitioner's Handbook on International Arbitration and Mediation, 2002; contbr. articles to profl. jours. Co-chmn. internat. rels. sect. Town Hall Calif., L.A., 1985—90; chmn. internat. trade legis. subcom., internat. commerce steering com. L.A. Area C. of C., 1983—91, law and justice com., 1993—94; adv. coun., exec. com. Asia Pacific Ctr. for Resolution of Internat. Bus. Disputes, 1991—94; mem. L.A. Com. on Fgn. Rels., 1983—95, Pacific Coun. Internat. Policy, 1999—; gen. counsel Citizens Rsch. Found., 1990—94; assoc. mem. ctrl. com. Calif. Rep. Party, 1983—94, mem. ctrl. com., 1995—98; dep. gen. coun. credentials com. Rep. Nat. Conv., 1992, alt. Calif. Delegation, 1992, Calif. del., 1996; bd. dirs. L.A. Ctr. for Internat. Comml. Arbitration, 1986—94, treas., 1986—88, v.p., 1988—90, pres., 1990—94. Master Anthony Kennedy Inns. of Ct., 1996-99. Mem. Am. Arbitration Assn. (panel of arbitrators, arbitrator large complex case dispute resolution program 1993-94), Chartered Inst. Arbitrators, London (assoc. 1986-94), Friends of Wilton Park So. Calif. (chmn. exec. com. 1986-94, exec. com. 1986—). Office: Calif Ct of Appeal 3d Appellate Dist 914 Capitol Mall Sacramento CA 95814-4802

KOLLAR, LINDA RANDLETT, lawyer; b. Malden, Mass., Nov. 24, 1944; d. Arthur Myrle and Nathalie Marie Randlett. BA with honors, Scripps Coll., 1966; JD cum laude, Pepperdine U., 1985. Bar: Calif. 1986, U.S. Dist. Ct. (ctrl. dist.) Calif. 1988, U.S. Ct. Appeals (9th cir.) 1990. Staff family crisis intervention Dept. Social Svcs., L.A., 1967—76; juvenile ct. dependency case worker L.A. County, 1976—79; investigator Juvenile Ct., L.A., Calif., 1979—82; extern, pub. defender Ventura County, 1983; clk. Nordman, Cormany, Hair & Compton, Oxnard, Calif., 1984; assoc. Price Postel & Parma, Santa Barbara, Calif., 1985—87, Silver & Arsht, Westlake Village, Calif., 1987—93; ptnr. Weinhart & Riley, L.A., 1993—97, Hooper, Lundy & Bookman, L.A., 1997—. Mem. Alliance Children and Family Svcs., Sacramento, 1999—; pres., bd. dirs., co-founder Western Child Welfare Law Ctr., Pasadena, Calif., 1999—; bd. profl. stds. Pepperdine U. Sch. Law; presenter in field. Contbr. chapters to books, articles to profl. jours. Recipient award for contbn. to providers of foster care and role model for young women, David and Margaret Home, LaVerne, Calif., 2000. Mem.: ABA, L.A. County Bar Assn., Calif. Acad. Health Care Attys., State Bar Calif., Phi Delta Phi. Administrative and regulatory, Professional liability, Health, General practice. Office: Hooper Lundy & Bookman 1875 Century Park East #1600 Los Angeles CA 90067

KOLODEY, FRED JAMES, lawyer; b. LaCoste, Tex., Mar. 5, 1936; s. Raymond and Mamie V. (Newman) K.; children: Trecia Anne Estep, Michele Leigh Kolodey; m. Helen Gable McIntosh, June 10, 1989. BA, Tex. Christian U., 1962; LL.B., So. Methodist U., 1964. Bar: Tex. 1964. Since practiced in, Dallas; ptnr. Kolodey & Thomas, 1975-83, of counsel, 1983-94, Thomas, Sheehan & Culp, 1994—2001, Kolodey, Thomas & Blackwood, 2001—. Pres. Dallas Jr. Bar Assn., 1969 Comments editor: Southwestern Law Jour, 1963-64. Mem. dist. hearing office panel Dallas Community Coll., 1974, Democratic precinct chmn., 1968-73. Mem. Tex., Dallas bar assns., Delta Theta Phi (pres. 1963, Nat. award 1964), Alpha Chi, Pi Sigma Alpha. Home: 540 Mariah Bay Dr Heath TX 75032-7626

KOLOSTIAN, RICHARD GEORGE, SR., judge; b. L.A., Dec. 2, 1931; s. Kalost Der Kolostian and Rose Koumrian; m. Joan R. Gabriel, Aug. 22,

1964; children: Richard Jr., Jon Kalost Der. BBA, Loyola U., 1954, LLB, 1963. Bar: Calif. 1964. Dep. city atty. trial and appellat dept. L.A. City Attys. Office, 1964-68; pvt. practice trial/appellat L.A., 1968—74; ct. commr. L.A. Mcpl. Ct., L.A., 1974—80; judge L.A. Superior Ct., 1980—. Supr. judge Van Nuys Dist. of L.A. Superior Ct., 1989-90. Bd. dirs., pres. Vols. Am. Alcohol Program, L.A.; bd. dirs. Salvation Army, L.A. Capt. USAFR, 1955-57; scoutmaster Boy Scouts Am., Van Nuys, 1978—. Named Judge of Yr., San Fernando Valley Criminal Bar, 1988, Constitutional Rights Found. of L.A., 1989. Armenian Orthodox. Avocations: woodwork, house maintenance, backpacking, golf. Office: LA Superior Ct 6230 Sylmar Ave Van Nuys CA 91401-2712

KOMAROFF, STANLEY, lawyer; b. Bklyn, Apr. 1, 1935; s. William Ralph and Fanny (Wein) K.; m. Rosalyn Steinglass, Dec. 25, 1960; children: William Charles, Andrew Steven. BA, Cornell U., 1956, JD, 1958. Bar: N.Y. 1959. Assoc. Proskauer Rose LLP, N.Y.C., 1958-68, ptnr., 1968—, chmn., 1991-99. Mem. rev. and planning coun. N.Y. State Hosp., 1982-92; trustee Beth Israel Med. Ctr., 1984—, vice chair, 1999—; trustee St. Lukes-Roosevelt Hosp. Ctr., Continuum of Health Ptnrs. Inc.; mem. bd. regents L.I. Coll. Hosp., 2001—; bd. dirs. Edmond de Rothschild Found., Club Med, Inc., 1984-95, Overseas Shipholding Group, Inc., Westhampton Beach Performing Arts Ctr.; chmn. ann. fund Cornell U. Law Sch., 1991-93, mem. adv. coun. 1st lt. USAR, 1958. Fellow Am. Bar Found.; mem. N.Y. State Bar Assn., Assn. of Bar of City of N.Y., N.Y. County Lawyers Assn., Order of Coif, Sunningdale Country Club, Phi Kappa Phi. Corporate, general, Private international, Mergers and acquisitions. Home: 910 Park Ave Apt 5-s New York NY 10021-0255 Office: Proskauer Rose LLP 1585 Broadway New York NY 10036-8299 E-mail: skomaroff@proskauer.com.

KOMEN, LEONARD, lawyer; b. St. Louis, May 31, 1943; s. Meyer and Yetta (Ellman) K.; m. Sandra Gail Cytron, June 8, 1969; children: Douglas Steven, Matthew Todd. BA, U. Mo., 1965, JD, 1970. Bar: Mo. 1970, U.S. Dist. Ct. (ea. dist.) Mo. 1971, U.S. Supreme Ct. 1973, U.S. Ct. Appeals (8th cir.) 1985, U.S. Claims Ct. 1992, U.S. Ct. Appeals (3d cir.) 1995. Assoc. Susman, Willer & Rimmel, St. Louis, 1970-74, Susman Schermer Rimmel & Parker, St. Louis, 1974-77, ptnr., 1977-80; prin., v.p. Selner, Glaser, Komen, Berger & Galganski, P.C., St. Louis, 1980-96; prin. mgr. Komen, Berger & Cohen, L.C., 1996-99; prin. Law Offices of Leonard Komen, P.C., 1999—. Ct.-apptd. trustee, examiner, receiver U.S. Bankruptcy Ct., 1988—. bd. dirs. Zeta Beta Tau Frat. Inc., 1984—, nat. sec., 1989-90, nat. v.p., 1990-92, nat. pres., 1992-94; mem. supervisory bd. Nat. Interfraternity Coun. Legal Advocacy Fund, 1993-98. Pres. Creve Coeur Hockey Club Inc., St. Louis, 1987-88, bd. dirs., 1989-93; coord. Parkway North Hockey Club, 1989-91; pres., bd. dirs. Roswell Messing Ednl. Found., 1989—; bd. dirs. Zeta Beta Tau Centennial Found. 1990-98. Recipient Merit citation Zeta Beta Tau Frat., Inc., 1977, 91, 92, 2002. Mem.: ATLA, Mo. Bankers Assn., Comml. Law League Am. Jewish. Bankruptcy, General civil litigation, Commercial, contracts (including sales of goods; commercial financing). Home: 14385 Stablestone Ct Chesterfield MO 63017-2502 Office: Law Offices of Leonard Komen PC 222 S Central Ave Ste 1101 Saint Louis MO 63105-3575 E-mail: lenkomen@komenlaw.com.

KOMITOVA, EMILIA ENEVA, lawyer; b. Lovetch, Bulgaria, Jan. 26, 1953; d. Eonyo Dimov Komitov and Jordanka Jotova Komitova; m. Nikolay Stefanov Petrounova; 1 child, Denitza Nikolaeva Petrounova. LLM, Sofia (Bulgaria) U., 1978. Bar: Sofia 1979. Lawyer Chernev Komitova and Ptnrs., Sofia. Corporate, general, Commercial, consumer (including collections, credit), Civil rights. Office: Chernev Komitova & Ptnrs Parensov 51 Fl 2 1000 Sofia Bulgaria

KONDRACKI, EDWARD JOHN, lawyer; b. Elizabeth, N.J., Sept. 27, 1932; s. John and Catherine Chudio (Saas) K.; m. Barbara Terese Caruso; children: Carol Ann, Maryanne, Christopher. BSEE, N.J. Inst. Tech., 1959; JD with honors, George Washington U., 1963. Bar: Va. 1964, DC 1964, U.S. Dist. Ct. D.C. 1964, U.S. Dist. Ct. (ea. dist.) Va. 1964, U.S. Dist. Ct. (ctrl. dist.) Calif., U.S. Dist. Ct. (so. dist.) Ala., U.S. Dist. Ct. (no. dist.) Fla., U.S. Dist. Ct. (no. dist.) Ga., U.S. Dist. Ct. (we. dist.) La., U.S. Dist. Ct. (ea. dist.) Mich., U.S. Dist. Ct. (no. dist.) Okla., U.S. Dist. Ct. (ea. dist.) Pa., U.S. Dist. Ct. (no. dist.) N.Y., U.S. Dist. Ct. (ea. dist.) Tex., U.S. Dist. Ct. (no. dist.) Tex., U.S. Ct. Appeals (fed. cir.) 1983, U.S. Ct. Claims 1976, U.S. Ct. Customs and Patent Appeals 1976. Patent atty. Gen. Electric Co., Washington, 1959-63; assoc. Kerkam, Stowell Kondracki & Clarke, P.C. and predecessor, Arlington, Va., 1963-65; dir., prin. Kerkam, Stowell Kondracki & Clarke, P.C., Arlington, 1965-99; prin. Miles & Stockbridge, McLean, Va., 2000—. Owner, dir. Patmark Paralegal Svcs., 1975—90, chmn., 1999—, gen. counsel, 2003—. Author: Trademarks-Servicemarks, Use, Usage and Protection, 1990, Proper Use of Trademarks and Servicemarks, 1982, Common Pitfalls Encountered in Patenting Inventions, 1983, Copyright Protection of Computer Software, 1989, Intellectual Property, Rights Acquisition and Protection Conference World Trade Assn. N.J., 1989; contbr. article to Voice of Tech. Bd. dirs. The Amadeus Concerts, Inc., 2003—. Served with USN, 1951—55. Mem. ABA, Am. Intellectual Property Law Assn., Internat. Assn. Protection Indsl. Property, Fed. Bar Assn., Va. Bar Assn., Internat. Trademark Assn., Washington Patent Lawyers Club, D.C. Bar Assn. (chmn. com. internat. affairs 1973), Gt. Falls Hist. Soc., Marmota Farm Assn., KC, Tau Beta Pi, Eta Kappa Nu, Omicron Delta Kappa, Phi Eta Sigma. Private international, Patent, Trademark and copyright. Office: 1751 Pinnacle Dr Ste 500 Mc Lean VA 22102-3833 Fax: (703) 610-8686. E-mail: ekondracki@milesstockbridge.com.

KONENKAMP, JOHN K. state supreme court justice; b. Oct. 20, 1944; m. Geri Konenkamp; children: Kathryn, Matthew. JD, U. S.D., 1974. Dep. state's atty., Rapid City; pvt. practice, 1977-84; former and presiding judge S.D. Cir Ct. (7th cir.), 1988-94; assoc. justice S.D. Supreme Ct., Pierre, 1994—. Bd. dirs. Alt. Dispute Resolution Com., Adv. Bd. for Casey Family Program. With USN. Mem. Am. Judicature Soc., State Bar S.D., Pennington County Bar Assn., Nat. CASA Assn., Am. Legion. Office: SD Supreme Ct 500 E Capitol Ave Pierre SD 57501-5070

KONSTANTAKIS, GEORGIA L. lawyer; b. Chgo., Feb. 2, 1970; BBA cum laude, Loyola U., Chgo., 1992; JD, Mass. Sch. Law, 1996. Bar: Mass. 1996. Law clk. Peter F. Geraci Law Office, Chgo., 1991-92; auditor Lake Shore Bank, Chgo., 1992-92; law clk., atty. Law Office Christos C. Tsiotos, Somerville, Mass., 1995—97; pvt. practice Boston, 1997—. V.p., exec. bd. AXION, Boston, 1996—; v.p., co-founder Hellenic Bus. Network, Boston, 1997—. Mem. Women's Bar Assn., Mass. Bar Assn., Boston Bar Assn., Golden Key. Avocations: reading, public speaking, dancing, tennis, running. Personal injury (including property damage), Property, real (including real estate development, water). Office: 7969 S Forest Meadows Dr Franklin WI 53132-8735

KONVITZ, MILTON RIDBAZ, law educator; b. Safad, Israel, Mar. 12, 1908; came to U.S., 1915, naturalized, 1926; s. Rabbi Joseph and Welia (Ridbaz-Willowski) K.; m. Mary Traub, June 18, 1942; 1 son, Josef. BS, NYU, 1928, AM, JD, NYU, 1930; PhD (Sage fellow in philosophy 1932-33), Cornell U., 1933; LittD, Rutgers U., 1954, Dropsie U., 1975; DCL, U. Liberia, 1962; LHD, Hebrew Union Coll-Jewish Inst. Religion, 1966, Yeshiva U., 1972; LLD, Syracuse U., 1971, Jewish Theol. Sem., 1972. Bar: N.J. 1932. Practice law, Jersey City and Newark, 1933-46; lectr. on law and pub. adminstrn. NYU, 1938-46; asst. gen. counsel NAACP Legal Def. and Edn. Fund, 1943-46; mem. faculty New Sch. for Social Rsch., 1944-46; prof. indsl. and labor rels. N.Y. State Sch. Indsl. and Labor Rels., Cornell U., 1946-73; prof. Law Sch. Cornell U., 1956-73, prof. emeritus, 1973—. Vis. prof., assoc. dir. Truman Ctr. for Peace Rsch., Hebrew U., 1970; dir. Liberian Codification of Laws project, 1952-80; gen. counsel Newark Housing Authority, 1938-43, N.J. State Housing Authority, 1943-45; Pub. rep. Nat. War Labor Bd. region 2, 1943-46; mem. enforcement commn. and hearing commn. Wage Stablzn. Bd., 1952-53; chmn. nat. com. study of Jewish Edn. in U.S., 1958-59; faculty Salzburg (Austria) Seminar Am. Studies, 1952; panel Fed. Mediation and Conciliation Svc., N.Y. Mediation Bd., Am. Arbitration Assn., N.Y. State Pub. Employment Rels. Author: On the Nature of Value: Philosophy of Samuel Alexander, 1946, The Alien and the Asiatic in American Law, 1946, Constitution and Civil Rights, 1946, Civil Rights in Immigration, 1953, Bill of Rights Reader, 1954, Fundamental Liberties of a Free People, 1957, A Century of Civil Rights, 1961, Expanding Liberties: Freedom's Gains in Postwar America, 1966, Religious Liberty and Conscience, 1968, Judaism and Human Rights, 1972, Judaism and the American Idea, 1978, Torah and Constitution, 1998, Nine American Jewish Thinkers, 2000, Fundamental Rights: History of a Constitutional Doctrine, 2001; founding editor: Industrial and Labor Relations Rev. (vols. 1-5), 1947-52, Liberian Code of Laws (5 vols.), 1958-60, Liberian Code of Laws Revised, 1973—, Liberian Law Reports (27 vols.); co-founder and chmn. editl. bd. Midstream Mag.; co-chmn. emeritus adv. editl. bd. Jour. Law and Religion; co-editor: Jewish Social Studies, 1975-93; co-founder: Judaism Mag.; mem. editl. bd. Ency. Judaica. Chmn. Hebrew Culture Found., 1956-95; mem. commn. for reorgn. World Zionist Orgn. Decorated comdr. Order Star of Africa, grand band (Liberia); recipient NYU Washington Sq. Coll. Disting. Alumni award, 1964, Mordecai ben David Disting. award Yeshiva U., 1965, Morris J. Kaplun internat. prize for scholarship Hebrew U., 1969, Tercentenary medal Jewish Community of Essex County, N.J., 1954; Ford Found. Faculty fellow, 1952-53, Guggenheim fellow, 1953-54, Fund for the Republic fellow, 1955, Inst. Advanced Study fellow, 1959-60, Ctr. Advanced Study Behavioral Scis. fellow, 1964-65, NEH fellow, 1975-76. Fellow Am. Acad. Arts and Scis.; mem. AAUP (mem. coun. 1961-64), ACLU (mem. nat. com.), Am. Philos. Assn., Am. Acad. Jewish Rsch., Law and Soc. Assn., Indsl. Rels. Rsch. Assn., Workers Def. League (mem. adv. bd.), Am. Jewish League for Israel (mem. adv. bd.), Internat. Assn. Jewish Law, Internat. Assn. Jewish Lawyers and Jurists, Order of Coif, Phi Beta Kappa. Home: 150 Norwood Ave Oakhurst NJ 07755-1604

KOOB, CHARLES EDWARD, lawyer; b. Kansas City, Mo., Aug. 31, 1944; s. Charles H. and Adeline (Meinert) K.; m. Pamela Ann Nabseth, June 26, 1971; children: Jason Wyeth, Peter Nabseth. BA, Rockhurst Coll., 1966; JD, Stanford U., 1969. Bar: Calif. 1970, N.Y. 1972, U.S. Dist. Ct. (so. and ea. dists.) N.Y. 1973, U.S. Ct. Appeals (2d cir.) 1975, U.S. Ct. Appeals (5th cir.) 1979, U.S. Supreme Ct. 1988, U.S. Ct. Claims 1988, U.S. Ct. Appeals (3d cir.) 1985. Assoc. Simpson, Thacher & Bartlett, N.Y.C., 1970-76, ptnr., 1976—. Mem. ABA, N.Y. State Bar Assn., Calif. Bar Assn. Antitrust, Federal civil litigation, Personal injury (including property damage). Office: Simpson Thacher & Bartlett 425 Lexington Ave Fl 15 New York NY 10017-3954

KOONCE, NEIL WRIGHT, lawyer; b. Kinston, N.C., July 8, 1947; s. Harold Wright and Edna Earle (Regan) K.; m. Virginia Gayle Evans, Feb. 27, 1993; children: Channing, Carl Younger, Ginny Younger. AB, U. N.C., 1969; JD, Wake Forest U., 1974; postgrad. exec. program, U. Va., 1983. Bar: N.C. 1973, U.S. Dist. Ct. (mid. dist.) N.C. 1975, U.S. Ct. Appeals (4th cir.) 1978, U.S. Supreme Ct. 1981. Atty. Cone Mills Corp., Greensboro, N.C., 1974-81, sr. atty., 1981-85, asst. gen. counsel, 1985-87, gen. counsel, 1987—, v.p., 1989—, v.p., gen. counsel, corp. sec., 1999—. Bd. dirs. Family and Children's Svcs., Greensboro, 1981-89, S.C. Energy Users Com., Columbia, S.C., 1984-89, Carolina Utility Customer's Assn., Raleigh, 1983-90, 94—, N.C. Found. for Rsch. and Econ. Edn., 1986-87, 93—, Electricity Consumers Resource Coun., Washington, 1987, 92—, vice chmn., 1990, chmn., 1991; bd. dirs. N.C. Citizens for Bus. and Industry, Raleigh, 1991-96, Met. YMCA, Greensboro, 1991-95, Salvation Army Boys and Girls Clubs, Greensboro, 1996—, S.C. Mfrs. Alliance, 1998—, N.C. Mfrs. Assn., 1998—. With AUS, 1970-71. Mem. ABA, N.C. Bar Assn., N.C. Textile Mfrs. Assn., Greensboro Bar Assn., Rotary (sec. 1983-86, bd. dirs. 1985-90, pres. 1988). Democrat. Presbyterian. Administrative and regulatory, Corporate, general, Personal injury (including property damage). Home: 200 Irving Pl Greensboro NC 27408-6510 Office: Cone Mills Corp # 300 804 Green Valley Rd Greensboro NC 27408-7020

KOONTZ, LAWRENCE L., JR., state supreme court justice; b. Roanoke, Va, Jan. 25, 1940; BS, Va. Polytech. U., 1962. Asst. commonwealth's atty., Roanoke, 1967—68; judge Va. Juvenile & Domestic Rels. Dist. Ct., 1968—76, Va. Cir. Ct. (23rd cir.), 1976—85, Ct. Appeals of Va., 1985—95, Supreme Ct. of Va., 1995—. Mem.: ABA. Office: PO Box 687 Salem VA 24153-0687

KOPEL, DAVID BENJAMIN, lawyer; b. Denver; s. Gerald Henry and Dolores B. Kopel; m. Deirdre Frances Dolan, Apr. 5, 1987. BA in History, Brown U., 1982; JD, U. Mich., 1985. Bar: Colo. 1986, N.Y. 1986, U.S. Dist. Ct. (ea. and so. dists.) N.Y. 1986, U.S. Ct. Appeals (2d cir.) 1986, U.S. Dist. Ct. Colo. 1988, U.S. Ct. Appeals (10th cir.) 1988, U.S. Supreme Ct., 1991, U.S. Ct. Appeals (D.C. cir.) 1997, U.S. Ct. Appeals (5th cir.) 1999, U.S. Ct. Appeals (4th cir.) 2003, U.S. Ct. Appeals (4th cir.) 2003. Assoc. Sullivan & Cromwell, N.Y.C., 1985-86; asst. dist. atty. Manhattan Dist. Atty., N.Y.C., 1986-88; asst. atty. gen. Colo. State Atty. Gen., Denver, 1988-92; rsch. dir. Independence Inst., Golden, Colo., 1992—. Adj. prof. NYU Sch. of Law, 1998-99. Democrat. Avocations: skiing, ham radio.. Office: Independence Inst Ste 185 14142 Denver West Pkwy Golden CO 80401-3119

KOPELMAN, LEONARD, lawyer; b. Cambridge, Mass., Aug. 2, 1940; s. Irving and Frances Estelle (Robbins) K.; m. Carol Hunsberger. BA cum laude, Harvard U., 1962, JD, 1965. Bar: Mass. 1966. Assoc. Warner & Stackpole, Boston, 1965-73; sr. ptnr. Kopelman and Paige, Boston, 1974—. Lectr. Harvard U., 1965— ; permanent master Mass. Superior Ct., 1971— ; gen. counsel Emerson Coll.; hon. consul gen. of, Finland, Mass., 1975— ; U.S. del. Soc. for Internat. Devel.; Chmn. Mass. Jud. Selection Com. for the Fed. Judiciary, 1971— ; chief counsel AAUP; dean consular corps of Boston, 2001—. Trustee Cathedral of the Pines, 1972; pres. Hillel Found. of Cambridge, Inc., 1973— ; trustee Faulkner Hosp., 1974— , Parker Hill Med. Ctr., 1976—; dir. gen. Consular Corps Coll. NEH grantee, 1975; named one of the 12 most powerful lawyers in Mass. Nat. Law Jour. Mem. ABA (exec. coun. 1969—), Mass. Bar Assn. (chmn. mcpl. law sect.), Am. Judges Assn., Mass. C. of C. (pres. 1974-77), Harvard Faculty Club, Algonquin Club (pres.), Harvard Club, Union Club, Hasty Pudding Club, St. Botolph Club. Private international, Public international, Municipal (including bonds). Home: 33 Yarmouth Rd Chestnut Hill MA 02467-2815 Office: Kopelman and Paige 31 St James Ave Boston MA 02116-4101

KOPF, RICHARD G. federal judge; b. 1946; BA, U. Nebr., Kearney, 1969; JD, U. Nebr., Lincoln, 1972. Law clk. to Hon. Donald R. Ross U.S. Ct. Appeals (8th cir.), 1972-74; ptnr. Cook, Kopf & Doyle, Lexington, Neb., 1974-87; U.S. magistrate judge, 1987-92; fed. judge U.S. Dist. Ct. (Nebr. dist.), 1992—, chief judge, 1999—. Mem. ABA, ABA Found., Nebr. State Bar, Nebr. State Bar Found. Office: US Dist Ct 586 US Courthouse 100 Centennial Mall N Lincoln NE 68508-3859

KOPLAN, ANDREW BENNET, lawyer; b. Birmingham, Ala., Apr. 12, 1971; Student, U. Sidney (Australia), 1991; BS in Fin. cum laude, Birmingham-Southern Coll., 1993; JD, U. Ala., 1996. Bar: Ala. 1996, Ga. 1997, U.S. Dist. Ct. (so. dist.) Ga., U.S. Dist. Ct. (no. dist.) Ga., U.S. Dist. Ct. (so. dist.) Ala. 1997. Legal intern Ala. Supreme Ct., Montgomery, 1995, Ala. Dept. Fin., Montgomery, 1995; jud. extern U.S. Dist. Ct. (no. dist.) Ala., Birmingham, 1995-96; clk. for Hon. Assoc. Justice Janie Shores Supreme Ct. Ala., Montgomery, 1996-97; assoc. Post & Pond, LLP, Atlanta, 1997-98, Drew, Elkl, & Farnham, LLP, Atlanta, 1998—2000, Mathis & Adams, Atlanta, 2000—. Jr. editor: Law & Psychology Rev., 1995-96. Mem. ABA, Ga. Trial Lawyers Assn. Avocations: music, sports, art, cooking, exercising. General civil litigation, Commercial, contracts (including sales of goods; commercial financing), Entertainment. Office: Mathis & Adams 100 Peachtree St Ste 1400 Atlanta GA 30303

KOPLIN, BERNICE JUDITH, lawyer; b. Lynn, Mass., Oct. 6, 1943; d. Harold and Rita (Cohen) Berzof; m. Joseph K. Koplin, June 4, 1972; children: Jonathan, Joshua. BA, Douglass Coll., 1965; MA, Brandeis U., 1970; MS, Simmons Coll., 1972; JD, Temple U., 1981, LLM in Taxation, 1984, LLM in Trial Advocacy, 1994. Bar: Pa. 1981, U.S. Dist. Ct. (ea. dist.) Pa. 1982, U.S. Tax Ct. 1982, U.S. Ct. Appeals (3d cir.) 1982, U.S. Ct. Claims 1986, U.S. Supreme Ct. 1986, D.C. 1987, Fla. 1987, N.J. 1987, N.Y. 1993. Assoc. Meltzer & Schiffrin, Phila., 1981-82; sole practice Phila., 1982-83, 86-88; ptnr. Goldman, Koplin & Marshall, P.C., Phila., 1983-86, Levine and Koplin, Phila., 1988-91, Schachtel, Gerstley, Levine & Koplin, Phila., 1991—. Enrolled agt. IRS. Contbr. articles to profl. jours. Mem. Ctl. Women's Com., Phila. Orch., 1978—, chmn., 2001—; bd. dirs. Settlement Music Sch., Phila., 1985-1987. Mem. ABA, Pa. Bar Assn., N.J. Bar Assn., Fla. Bar Assn., Phila. Bar Assn., Camden County Bar Assn., Cosmopolitan Club (Phila., bd. govs. 1985-87, chmn. fin. com. 1985-1987). Jewish. Avocation: bird watching. Corporate, general, Probate (including wills, trusts), Taxation, general. Home: 251 Saint Josephs Way Philadelphia PA 19106-3806 also: 20 Kings Hwy W Haddonfield NJ 08033-2116 Office: So Bepad St Ste 2170 Philadelphia PA 19109-1029

KOPP, EUGENE PAUL, lawyer; b. Charleston, W.Va., Nov. 20, 1934; s. Eugene Alexander and Virginia Elizabeth (King) K.; m. Katherine Patricia Rogers, July 1, 1967; 1 son, Eugene Paul. BA, U. Notre Dame, 1957, MA, 1958; JD, W.Va. U., 1961. Ba: W.Va. 1961, D.C. 1977, Tex. 1980. Law clk. U.S. Dist. Ct. W.Va., 1961-62; trial atty. Dept. Justice, Washington, 1962-69; dep. dir. USIA, 1973-77, acting dir., 1976-77; assoc. gen. counsel Champlin Petroleum Co., Ft. Worth, 1977-81; v.p. Washington affairs Union Pacific Corp., Washington, 1981-87; dep. dir. U.S. Info. Agy., 1989-93; exec. dir. MFJ Task Force, 1993-94; of counsel Clarendon Assocs., Inc., 1995-97, Ruddy and Muir, 1998—; vice chmn. Nexphase Comms., Inc., 2000—01. Cons. nat. Security Council, Washington, 1981, mem. transition team, 1980. Mem.: Washington Inst. Fgn. Affairs, DC Bar Assn., Tex. Bar Assn., W.Va. Bar Assn., Dacor Club (Washington), Met. Club (Washington), Belle Haven Country Club. Roman Catholic. Home: 508 Cathedral Dr Alexandria VA 22314-4706

KOPPANG, BAARD IVAR, lawyer; b. Oslo, Apr. 23, 1966; s. Saeming M. and Berit Karin Koppang; m. Grethe Thesen Koppang, Mar. 6, 1993; children: Lisa, Nora. Candidatis Juris, U. Oslo, 1992. Bar: Norway 1994. Assoc. Hjort, Eriksrud & Co., Oslo, 1992—93, Law Firm Kluge, Stavanger, Norway, 1993—97; asst. judge Sandnes (Norway) Dist. Ct., 1994—96; lawyer Coopers & Lybrand, Stavanger, 1997—2001; lectr. in tax law Peoples' Univ., Rogaland, Norway, 1998—99; ptnr. Pricewaterhousecoopers, Stavanger, 2001—. Quartermaster Norwegian Navy, 1987. Mem.: Norwegian Bar Assn. (bd. mem. Rogaland br. 2002—), Rotary Internat. Avocations: skiing, hunting, fishing, hiking, reading. Mergers and acquisitions, Corporate taxation, Commercial, contracts (including sales of goods; commercial financing). Office: Pricewaterhousecoopers Vassbotnen 15 PO Box 150 N-4065 Stavanger Norway

KORAL, MARK A. lawyer; b. Phila., Apr. 7, 1945; m. Margaret M. Koral, Oct. 15, 1977. BSBA, Drexel U., 1967; JD, Temple U., 1970. Bar: Pa. 1970, D.C.; U.S. Dist. Ct. (ea. dist.) Pa.; U.S. Ct. Appeals (3d cir.); U.S. Supreme Ct. Pvt. practice, Phila., 1970—. General civil litigation, Personal injury (including property damage), Product liability. Office: 1628 John F Kennedy Blvd Fl 18 Philadelphia PA 19103-2102

KORCHIN, JUDITH MIRIAM, lawyer; b. Kew Gardens, N.Y., Apr. 28, 1949; d. Arthur Walter and Mena (Levisohn) Goldstein; m. Paul Maury Korchin, June 10, 1972; 1 son, Brian Edward. BA with high honors, U. Fla., 1971, JD with honors, 1974. Bar: Fla. 1974, U.S. Ct. Appeal (2d, 5th and 11th cirs.), U.S. Dist. Ct. (so., mid. and no. dists) Fla. Law clk. to judge U.S. Dist. Ct., 1974-76; assoc. Steel, Hector & Davis, Miami, Fla., 1976-81, ptnr., 1981-87, Holland and Knight, Miami, 1987—. Author, exec. editor U. Fla. Law Rev., 1973-74. Mem. U. Fla. Law Ctr. Coun., 1980-83; pres. alumni bd. U. Fla. Law Rev., 1983; bd. dirs. Fla. Film & Rec. Inst., 1982-84. Recipient Trail Blazer Award The Women's Com. of 100, 1988. Fellow: Am. Bar Found.; mem.: ABA (sect. alternative dispute resolution, vice chmn. 1994—95, co-chmn. fed. ct. mediation com. 1995, sect. labor and employment law, sect. litig.), Fla. Bar Found. (subcom. legal assistance for poor 1988—90), Fla. Bar Assn. (vice chmn. jud. nominating procedures com. 1982, civil procedure rules com. 1984—89, 1993—95), Nat. Assn. Bank Women (TV panelist greater Miami chpt. 1987), Nat. Assn. Women Bus. Owners (adv. coun. 1987—88), Dade County Bar Assn. (bd. dirs. 1981—82, treas. 1982, sec. 1983, 3d v.p. 1984, 2d v.p. 1985, 1st v.p. 1986, pres. 1987), CPR Inst. for Dispute Resolution (nat. panelist 1994—, exec. com. 2003—), Am. Arbitration Assn. (employment law panel, s.e. 1993—, comml. law panel 1993—), Greater Miami C. of C. (com. profl. devel. 1988—90), Rabbinical Assn. Greater Miami (TV panelist Still Small Voice 1987), City Club (bd. dirs. 1988—93), Phi Kappa Phi, Phi Beta Kappa, Order of Coif. General civil litigation, Labor (including EEOC, Fair Labor Standards Act, labor-management relations, NLRB, OSHA), State and local taxation. Office: Holland & Knight PO Box 015441 701 Brickell Ave Ste 3000 Miami FL 33131-2898

KORDONS, ULDIS, lawyer; b. Riga, Latvia, July 9, 1941; came to U.S., 1949; s. Evalds and Zenta Alide (Apenits) K.; m. Virginia Lee Knowles, July 16, 1966. AB, Princeton U., 1963; JD, Georgetown U., 1970. Bar: N.Y. 1970, Ohio 1978, Ind. 1989. Assoc. Whitman, Breed, Abbott & Morgan, N.Y.C., 1970-77, Anderson, Mori & Rabinowitz, Tokyo, 1973-75; counsel Armco Inc., Parsippany, N.J., 1977-84; v.p., gen. counsel, sec. Sybron Corp., Saddle Brook, N.J., 1984-88, Hillenbrand Industries Inc., Batesville, Ind., 1989-92; pres. Plover Enterprises, Cin., 1992-95, Kordons & Co., LPA, Cin., 1996—. Lt. USN, 1963-67. Mem. N.Y. Bar Assn., Ohio Bar Assn., Ind. Bar Assn. Office: 8238 Wooster Pike Cincinnati OH 45227-4010 E-mail: ukordlaw@aol.com.

KORIN, JOEL BENJAMIN, lawyer, educator; b. Phila., Apr. 15, 1945; s. Leon Aaron and Charlotte Sylvia (Snyder) K.; m. Kallen Stillwell, Aug. 11, 1968; children: Saul, Steven. AB, Dickinson Coll., 1967; JD, Rutgers U., 1971. Bar: N.J. 1971, U.S. Ct. Appeals (3d cir.) 1978, U.S. Supreme Ct. 1978. Assoc. Stransky & Poplar, Camden, N.J., 1971-72, James F. Florio, Camden, 1972-73; asst. dep. pub. defender State of N.J., Camden, 1973-74; assoc. Brown, Connery, Kulp, Willie, Purnell & Greene, Camden, 1975-77, ptnr., 1977-82, George, Korin, Quattrone, Blumberg and Chant, P.A., Woodbury, N.J., 1982-99, Kenney and Kearny LLP, Cherry Hill, 1999—. Lectr. Rutgers U. Sch. Law, Camden, 1982—. Author: (with others) Clinical Correspondence Course, 1983, (with Steven Selbst) Preventing Malpractice Lawsuits in Pediatric Emergency Medicine, 1999; editor: Pediatric Emergency Care, 1985; contbr. articles to profl. publs. Bd. of Govs. Haddonfield (N.J.) Civic Assn. Recipient Martin F. Caulfield Disting. Svc. award Gloucester County Bar Found., 2001. Fellow Am. Coll. Trial Lawyers, Am. Bd. Trial Advocacy, Am. Inns of Ct.; mem. ABA, N.J. Bar Assn. (trustee 1994-2000), N.J. Trial Attys. Assn. (Trial Bar award 2000), Assn. Criminal Def. Attys., Woodbury C. of C. Democrat. Jewish. Federal civil litigation, State civil litigation, Criminal. Home: 127 N Hinchman Ave Haddonfield NJ 08033-2725 Office: Kenney and Kearney LLP PO Box 5034 220 Lake Dr E Ste 210 Cherry Hill NJ 08034-0421 E-mail: jkorin@kenneylaw.com.

KORIN, OFFER, lawyer; b. Jerusalem, Nov. 24, 1964; came to U.S., 1972; s. Uri and Sarah Korin; m. Michelle L. Korin, Nov. 2, 1991; children: Ariel L., Tahlia E., Yael S. BA, Ind. U., Bloomington, 1985; JD, Ind. U., Indpls., 1988. Co-founding ptnr. Katz & Korin, Indpls., 1994—. Mem.

seminar faculty Nat. Bus. Inst., Indpls., 1994, Peoples Law Sch., 1992-94, Indpls. Bar Assn., Indpls., 1998; panelist Ind. U. Sch. of Law, Bloomington, 1998. Bd. dirs. Congregation Shaarey Tefilla, Indpls., 1994-96, Jewish Fedn. Greater Indpls., 1997—; bd. dirs. Jewish Cmty. Rels. Coun., Indpls., 1991—, v.p., 1997-2002, pres., 2002—. Mem. ABA, ATLA, Ind. State Bar Assn., Ind. Trial Lawyers Assn., Indpls. Bar Assn., Fed. Bar Assn.(sec. Indpls. chpt., 2003—) Constitutional, Environmental, Estate planning. Office: Katz & Korin PC 10 W Market St Ste 1120 Indianapolis IN 46204-2964 E-mail: okorin@katzkorin.com.

KORMAN, EDWARD R. federal judge; b. N.Y.C., Oct. 25, 1942; s. Julius and Miriam K.; m. Diane R. Eisner, Feb. 3, 1979; children: Miriam M., Benjamin E. BA, Bklyn. Coll., 1963; LL.B., Bklyn. Law Sch., 1966; LL.M., NYU, 1971. Bar: N.Y. 1966, U.S. Supreme Ct. 1972. Law clk. to judge N.Y. Ct. Appeals, 1966-68; assoc. Paul, Weiss, Rifkind, Wharton and Garrison, 1968-70; asst. U.S. atty. Eastern Dist. N.Y., N.Y.C., 1970-72; asst. to solicitor gen. of U.S., 1972-74; chief asst. U.S. atty. Eastern Dist. N.Y., 1974-78, U.S. atty., 1978-82; ptnr. Stroock & Stroock & Lavan, N.Y.C., 1982-84; prof. Bklyn. Law Sch., 1984-85; U.S. dist. judge Eastern Dist. N.Y., 1985—, chief judge, 2000—. Chmn. Mayor's Com. on N.Y.C. Marshals, 1983-85; mem. Temporary Commn. of Investigation of State of N.Y., 1983-85. Jewish. Office: US Dist Ct US Courthouse 225 Cadman Plz E Brooklyn NY 11201-1818

KORMAN, JAMES WILLIAM, lawyer; b. Washington, Apr. 29, 1943; s. Milton D. and Bernice (Rosensweig) K.; m. Barbara Dale Lewis, June 11, 1967; 1 child, Katherine Korman Frey. AB, Coll. William & Mary, 1965; JD, George Washington U., 1968. Bar: Va. 1968, D.C. 1970, U.S. Supreme Ct. 1972, U.S. Ct. Appeals (4th cir.) 1974, U.S. Dist. Ct. (ea. dist.) Va. 1975. Assoc. Kinney, Smith and Barham, Arlington, Va., 1968-73, ptnr., 1973-78; pres. Bean, Kinney & Korman, Arlington, 1979—; neutral case evaluator Fairfax Cir. Ct., 1995—. Mem. Va. Bar Coun., 1983-89, 98—, 10th dist. grievance com., 1978-81; mem. adv. bd. Bank of Arlington, Va., 1977-78; lectr. various civil litgation topics continuing legal edn.; contbg. atty. Mathew Bender's Fed. Practice Forms, 1978; panelist Va. Conf. Nat. Assn. Bank Women, 1984; adj. prof. George Mason U. Law Sch., 1996—; mem. faculty Va. State Bar Profl. Course, 1998-2001. Contbr. articles to profl. jours. Bd. dirs. No. Va. Jewish Cmty. Ctr., 1985-91; mem. adv. bd. Sch. Contemporary Edn., Springfield, Va., 1985-91; mem. Va. Commn. on Women and Minorities in the Law, 1988-92. Capt. USAR, 1972-74. Recipient Meritorious Svc. award Legal Aid Bur., 1968, Adult Leadership award Boy Scouts Am., 1972; named One of 50 Top Divorce Lawyers Washingtonians Mag., 2000, One of Best Lawyers in Am., 1999-. Fellow: Va. Bar Found., Va. Law Found., Am. Acad. Matrimonial Lawyers (Va. chpt. v.p. 1996—99, pres. 2001—, cert. arbitrator); mem.: ATLA, ABA, Plaintiffs Bar Ltd., Va. Trial Lawyers Assn. (jud. task force 1998—), Arlington Bar Found. (bd. dirs. 1990—, pres. 2000—01), Arlington Bar Assn. (bd. dirs. 1977—81, pres. 1981—82, Robert J. Arthur Disting. Svc. award 2002), Va. State Bar (pro bono steering com. 1992—93). Democrat. Avocation: collecting political buttons. General civil litigation, Family and matrimonial, Personal injury (including property damage). Home: 2450 N Wakefield Ct Arlington VA 22207-3554 Office: Bean Kinney & Korman 200 14th N St Ste 100 Arlington VA 22201-2552

KORMES, JOHN WINSTON, lawyer; b. N.Y.C., May 4, 1935; s. Mark and Joanna P. Kormes; m. Frances W. Kormes, Aug. 19, 1978; 1 child, Mark Vincent. BA in Econs., U. Mich., 1955, JD, 1959. Bar: Pa. 1961, D.C. 1961, U.S. Supreme Ct. 1968. With License and Inspection Rev. Bd. Phila., 1972-73; asst. dist. atty. City of Phila., 1973-74; pvt. practice Phila., 1961—. Moot ct. advisor. Mem. staff Re-elect the Pres. Com., 1972, Rizzo for Mayor Com., 1971, 75, Phila. Flag Day Assn., 1965—. Served with USAF, 1956-57. Recipient N.Y. Intercoll. Legis. Assmebly award, 1954, R.I. Model Congress award, 1954, Queens Coll. Speech Guild award; Eminent Wisdom fellow Wisdom Hall of Fame. Fellow Lawyers in Mensa (charter), Triple Nine Soc. (elections officer 1992-93, legal officer, new mem. welcome program officer 1993—, com. to revise constitition 1993—, ombudsman 1994—), Internat. Soc. Phlos. Enquiry (sr. fellow, pub. Best Telicom 1986, 87, legal officer 1986-91, v.p. 1990-91), Wisdom Soc.; mem. Am. Legion (life mem.), Phila. Bar Assn., Phila. Trial Lawyers Assn., N.Y. State Trial Lawyers Assn., Am. Arbitration Assn., Fed. Bar Assn., Pitts. Inst. Legal Medicine, Assn. Trial Lawyers Am., Intertel, Internat. Platform Assn., Cincinnatus soc., Top One Percent Soc., Collegium Soc. 99.5 (charter), Poetic Genius Soc. 99.5 (charter), Masons, Shriners, KP, Lions, Delta Sigma Rho. Republican. State civil litigation, Family and matrimonial, Personal injury (including property damage). Home: 1070 Edison Ave Philadelphia PA 19116-1342 Office: 8122 Lister St Philadelphia PA 19152

KORN, MICHAEL JEFFREY, lawyer; b. Jersey City, Dec. 22, 1954; s. Howard Leonard and Joyce Ellen Korn; m. Pamela Ann VanZandt, May 29, 1983; children: David Harold, Suzanne Faye. BA, U. Va., 1976; JD, U. Fla., 1979. Bar: Fla. 1980, U.S. Dist. Ct. (no. and mid. dists.) Fla., U.S. Ct. Appeals (5th and 11th cirs.). Jud. law clk. Fla. 1st Dist Ct. Appeal, Tallahassee, 1980-81; assoc. Boyer, Tanzler & Boyer, Jacksonville, Fla., 1981-84; pvt. practice Jacksonville, 1984-87; ptnr. Prom, Korn & Zehmer, P.A., Jacksonville, 1987-95, Korn & Zehmer, P.A., Jacksonville, 1995—. Rules com. Fla. Appellate Ct., 1991-2002. Bd. dirs. North Fla. coun. Camp Fire, 1983-86, Jacksonville Jewish Fedn., 1985, v.p., 1994-99, treas., 1999-2003; bd. dirs. Youth Leadership Jacksonville, 1989-93, Jacksonville Cmty. Coun., 1989-94, 96-98, pres., 1995; Mandarin Cmty. Club, Jacksonville, 1988-91; cmty. adv. bd. WJCT-TV, Jacksonville, 1996—, chmn., 1999-2000; bd. dirs. United Way of N.E. Fla., 1999—, Nonprofit Ctr. of N.E. Fla., Inc., 2003—; trustee North Fla. Family Housing Found., 1999-2003. Recipient Young Leadership award Jacksonville Jewish Fedn., 1992. Mem. Fla. Bar (litig, appellate and health law sects., grievance com. 2001—, chair 2003), Jacksonville Bar Assn. (fee arbitration com. 1987-90, CLE chair 1995-99, vice chair appellate practice sect.), Acad. Fla. Trial Lawyers. Jewish. Avocations: running, reading, golf. Appellate, General civil litigation, Health. Office: Korn & Zehmer PA Ste 200 6620 Southpoint Dr S Jacksonville FL 32216-0940 Fax: 904-296-0384. E-mail: mkorn@kornzehmer.com.

KORNBERG, ALAN WILLIAM, lawyer; b. N.Y.C., Dec. 11, 1952; s. Peter and Selma (Borden) K. AB, Brandeis U., 1974; JD, NYU, 1977. Bar: N.Y. 1978, D.C. 1993. Assoc. Milbank, Tweed, Hadley & McCloy, N.Y.C., 1977-86, ptnr., 1986-90, Paul, Weiss, Rifkind, Wharton & Garrison, LLP, N.Y.C., 1990—. Fellow Am. Coll. Bankruptcy, 1995; adj. instr. law Yeshiva U., N.Y.C., 1984-85. Bd. dirs. Lubovitch Dance Found., Inc., 1988-98, Photographers & Friends United Against AIDS, 1989-92, Classical Action, 1993-98. Mem. ABA, N.Y. Bar Assn., Assn. of Bar of City of N.Y., Akin Hall Assn. Bankruptcy, Commercial, contracts (including sales of goods; commercial financing), Corporate, general. Home: 71 E 77th St New York NY 10021-1849 Office: Paul Weiss Rifkind Wharton & Garrison LLP 1285 Avenue Of The Americas New York NY 10019-6064 E-mail: akornberg@paulweiss.com.

KORNBERG, JOEL BARRY, lawyer, emergency physician; b. Bklyn., June 17, 1953; s. Bernard Fred and Ada (Ritterstein) K.; m. Melinda Michelle Kornberg;children: Dana Nicole, Jordan Reid. AB, Boston U., 1975; MD, N.Y. Med. Coll., 1980; JD, Nova U., 1989. Bar: Fla. 1989, D.C. 1990, U.S. Dist. Ct. (so. dist.) Fla. 1989, U.S. Supreme Ct. 1994; cert. mediator, Fla. 1995; cert. Am. Bd. Emergency Medicine, healthcare risk mgr., Fla. Resident Long Island Jewish-Hillside Med. Ctr., New Hyde Park, N.Y., 1980-81; emergency physician Emergency Med. Svcs. Assocs., Inc., Plantation, Fla., 1981-83, Joel B. Kornberg, M.D. P.A., Coral Springs, Fla., 1983-90, EMSA Ltd. Partnership, Plantation, 1990—; med. dir. Dept. Emergency Svcs. Humana Hosp., Pompano Beach, Fla., 1985-92, regional med. dir., 1992-94; pvt. practice Joel Kornberg, M.D., J.D., Boca Raton, Fla., 1994—; med. dir. dept. emergency medicine Cedars Med. Ctr., Miami, 1993-94; pvt. practice Joel Kornberg MD, JD, Boca Raton, Fla., 1994—. Mem. exec. com. Humana Hosp. Cypress, Pompano Beach, 1985-92, corp. counsel med. affairs; risk mgmt. cons. EMSA Ltd. Partnership, Plantation, 1989-94; dir. edn. Voice Billstat, Plantation, 1992-94. Head coach Coral Springs Youth Soccer Assn., 1989—, mgr. North Springs Little League, 1995-97. Fellow Am. Coll. Legal Medicine, Am. Coll. Emergency Physician; mem. ABA, Nat. Health Lawyers Assn., Am. Soc. Law and Medicine, Nat. Bd. Med. Examiners. Avocations: skiing, piano, tennis, baseball, bicycle. Commercial, contracts (including sales of goods; commercial financing), Corporate, general, Health. Office: Ste 305C 7301A W Palmetto Park Rd Boca Raton FL 33433-3466 E-mail: jkmdjd@aol.com.

KORNBLUM, GUY ORVILLE, lawyer; b. Indpls., Oct. 29, 1939; s. Guy J. and Gilmette Gilberta (Damart) K.; m. Carol Kornblum (div.); m. M. Victoria Adams, Apr. 15, 1977; children: Anna Victoria, Guy Laurence. AB, Ind. U., 1961; JD, U. Calif., San Francisco, 1966. Cert.: Nat. Bd. Trial Advocacy (trial advocate). Assoc. Ice, Miller, Donadio & Ryan, Indpls., 1966-67, Bledsoe, Smith et al, San Francisco, 1967-70; asst. dean, prof. law U. Calif., San Francisco, 1970-72; ptnr. Pettit & Martin, San Francisco, 1972-79; sr. ptnr. Kornblum et al, San Francisco, 1979—96; ptnr. Bailey & Kornblum, San Francisco, 1996—2000, Guy Kornblum & Assocs., San Francisco, 2000—. Assoc. prof. law U. Calif., San Francisco, 1972-79; lectr. Rutter Group, Encino, Calif., 1979—, Calif. Continuing Edn. of the Bar, 1979, ABA Nat. Insts., 1979-88, 89—; co-founder Hastings Ctr. Trial and Appellate Advocacy, San Francisco, 1970-80. Co-author: California Practice Guide: Bad Faith, 1986, Litigating Insurance Claims, 1990; contbr. articles to profl. jours. Served to 1st lt. M.I., U.S. Army, 1960-61. Ford Found. fellow NYU, 1971 Fellow Am. Bar Found.; mem. ABA (award of merit for exceptional svc. sr. lawyer divsn.), ATLA, Consumer Attys. Calif., Calif. Bar Assn., San Francisco Bar Assn., Ind. Bar Assn., Order of Coif, Million Dollar Advocates Forum, Phi Eta Sigma. Clubs: Olympic (San Francisco). Republican. Episcopalian. Avocations: jogging, yachting, tennis, photography. General civil litigation, Insurance, Personal injury (including property damage). Home: 2255 Clay St San Francisco CA 94115 Office: Guy Kornblum & Assocs 1388 Sutter St Ste 820 San Francisco CA 94109 E-mail: gkornblum@kornblumlaw.com.

KORNFELD, JULIAN POTASH, lawyer; b. Dallas, May 1, 1934; s. Abraham L. and Abbie (Potash) K.; children— Meredith, Nancy. BBA, Tex. U., 1955, LL.B., 1957; LL.M. in Taxation, N.Y. U. (1962). Bar: Tex. 1958, Okla. 1963, U.S. Ct. Appeals (10th cir.), U.S. Tax Ct., U.S. Supreme Ct. Assoc. Potash, Cameron, Bernat & Studdard, El Paso, Tex., 1959-61, Mosteller, Fellers et al, Oklahoma City, 1962-63, Mosteller, Andrews et al, Oklahoma City, 1963-68, Andrews, Mosburg, Davis, Elam, Legg & Kornfeld, Oklahoma City, 1968-73; ptnr. Kornfeld, Mcmillin, Phillips & Upp, Oklahoma City, 1973-80, Kornfeld, Lester, Franklin, Renegar & Bryant, Oklahoma City, 1980-82, Kornfeld, Franklin, Renegar & Randall, Oklahoma City, 1982—. Served to 1st lt., Q.M.C. AUS, 1957-59. Mem. Am., Okla., Tex. bar assns. Corporate taxation, Estate taxation, Taxation, general. Home: 3404 Partridge Rd Oklahoma City OK 73120-8907 Office: Kornfeld Renegar & Randall 4100 Perimeter Center Dr Oklahoma City OK 73112-2326

KORNREICH, EDWARD SCOTT, lawyer; b. Brooklyn, Apr. 18, 1953; s. Lawrence and Selma K.; m. Shirley (Werner), Feb. 28, 1982; children: Mollie, Davida, Lawrence. BA(hon.) , Columbia U., 1974; JD, Harvard U., 1977. Appellate atty. Legal Aid Soc., N.Y.C., 1977-79; assoc. atty. Rosenman and Colin, N.Y.C., 1979-84; v.p., legal affairs, gen. counsel St. Luke's-Roosevelt Hosp. Ctr., N.Y.C., 1984-87; mem. Garfunkel , Wild, and Travis, P.C., Gt. Neck, NY, 1987-90; ptnr. Proskauer and Rose, LLP, N.Y.C., 1990—. Joint com. on health care decisions near end of life ABA and Hastings Ctr., 1992-95; sr. adv. com. Robert Wood Johnson N.Y. Acad. Medicine Project. Trustee, post grad. Ctr. Mental Health, N.Y.C., 1992-99. Mem. Am. Health Lawyers Assn.; N.Y. State Bar Assn. (chair provider's com. health care sect. 2002-03); Assn. of Bar City of N.Y. (com. on medicine and law 1985-88, chmn. health law com. 1991-94, AIDS com. 1986-97); Phi Beta Kappa. Avocations: running (completed N.Y.C. Marathon 1978, 83, 86, 95, 97). Commercial, contracts (including sales of goods; commercial financing), Health, Non-profit and tax-exempt organizations. Office: Proskauer & Rose LLP 1585 Broadway Fl 27 New York NY 10036-8299

KOROI, MARK MICHAEL, lawyer; b. Grosse Pointe, Mich., May 22, 1963; s. Remus M. and Eleanor Barbara Koroi. AA, Macomb C.C., Warren, Mich., 1983; Assoc of Gen. Studies, Macomb C.C., Warren, Mich. , 1984; BA in Psychology, Wayne State U., 1986; JD, Thomas M. Cooley Sch. Law, 1990. Bar: Mich. 1991, U.S. Dist. Ct. (ea. dist.) Mich. 1991. Law clk. Law Offices of Roger Leemis, Southfield, Mich., 1986-88, Samaan, Mashni & Assocs., Dearborn, Mich., 1988-89, Law Offices of Salem Samaan, Plymouth, Mich., 1989-91; atty. Law Offices of Mark Koroi, Plymouth, 1991—. Lectr. Mich. Head Injury Alliance, Ann Arbor, 1996. Recipient Prix d'Accessit, French Consulate, Detroit, 1985. Mem. State Bar Mich. Pentecostal. Avocations: weight lifting, reading. Commercial, contracts (including sales of goods; commercial financing), General practice, Personal injury (including property damage). Home: 12131 Champaign Ave Warren MI 48089-1246 Office: 150 N Main St Plymouth MI 48170-1236

KOROTKIN, MICHAEL PAUL, lawyer; b. N.Y.C., Oct. 5, 1937; m. Marcia Ellen, Aug. 28, 1960; children: Darryl, Alan, Alyssa. AB, Duke U., 1959; LLB, NYU, 1962. Bar: N.Y. 1963. Ptnr. Kramer, Levin, Naftalis & Frankel LLP, N.Y.C., 1973—. Office: Kramer Levin Naftalis & Frankel LLP 919 3rd Ave New York NY 10022-3902 E-mail: mkorotkin@kramerlevin.com.

KORS, MURRAY DANIEL, lawyer; b. N.Y.C., Jan. 17, 1927; s. Sydney E. and Bertha (Sussman) Kors; m. Frances Biala, Jan. 5, 1957; children: Robert, Geoffrey, Stacey. BS, NYU, 1948, JD, 1950. Bar: (N.Y.) 1950. Atty. Samuel Brill, N.Y.C., 1950—52; pvt. practice N.Y.C., 1952—64; ptnr. Arye & Kors P.C., N.Y.C., 1964—96; ret., 1996. Spl. master N.Y. Civil Ct., N.Y.C., 1970—72, arbitrator, 1975—83. Fund raiser NYU Law Sch., 1979—83; pres. Crusade Against Communism, New Brunswick, NJ, 1960—65. Mem.: Nassau County Bar Assn., N.Y. County Lawyers Assn., N.Y. State Trial Lawyers, Nat. Trial Lawyers Assn., Am. Arbitration Assn., B'nai B'rith. Jewish. Personal injury (including property damage). Home: 60 Cooper Dr Great Neck NY 11023-1930 E-mail: mfkors@aol.com.

KORTH, FRITZ-ALAN, lawyer; b. Ft. Worth, Aug. 29, 1938; s. Fred and Vera (Connell) K.; m. Penne Percy, Dec. 15, 1965 (div. 1997); children: Fritz-Alan Jr., Maria Eleanor, James Frederick. AB, Princeton U., 1961; LLB cum laude, U. Tex., 1964; HHD (hon.), U. Americas, 1982. Bar: Tex. 1964, D.C. 1964. Asst. sec. OKC Corp., Dallas, 1964-65; ptnr. Korth & Korth, Washington, 1965—; pres. Wilmar Corp., Port Chester, N.Y., 1980—. Founder, sec., bd. dirs. Women's Nat. Bank, Washington, 1978-85, chmn. bd. First WNB Corp., 1982-85; bd. dirs. Trans Leisure Corp., N.Y.C., 1970-75, chmn. bd., 1973-75; bd. dirs. Del Norte Tech., Inc., Dallas., 1969—, chmn., 1982-98, vice chmn. bd. dirs., 1998—; bd. dirs. Del Norte Tech. Ltd., Swindon, Eng., Wilmar Corp.; trustee Meridian Internat. Ctr., 2003—. Registrar St. John's Episcopal Ch., Washington, 1968-70, vestryman, 1970-74, treas., 1973-77; chmn. fin. com., mem. diocesan coun. Episcopal Diocese Washington, 1973-77; trustee, treas. Cathedral chpt. Washington Nat. Cathedral, 1977-84; pres. U. Americas Found., 1969-84; bd. assocs. U. Americas, Puebla, Mex., 1969—; bd. dirs. Travelers Aid Soc. Washington, 1969-86, pres., 1973-75; dir. Southwestern Exposition and Livestock Show, 1987—; charter commr. U.S.-Mex. Commn. for Edn!. and Cultural Exch., 1991-97; pres. AMMA Found., Inc., 1994—, dir. 1989. Mem. ABA, Inter-Am. Bar Assn., D.C. Bar, Tex. Bar Assn., Am. Law Inst., Am. Soc. of Most Venerable Order of Hosp. of St. John of Jerusalem, Phi Delta Phi. Clubs: Met. (Washington), Chevy Chase (Washington); Argyle (San Antonio); Steeplechase (Ft. Worth); Princeton (N.Y.C.); Gymkhana Club (Mauritius). Mailing: PO Box 65482 Washington DC 20035-5482 also: 888 17th St NW Ste 208 Washington DC 20006-3313

KORTHALS, CANDACE DURBIN, lawyer; b. Tampa, Fla., Oct. 3, 1948; d. Robert F. and Geraldine B. Durbin; children: John Kristofor, Kathryn Elizabeth. BA in Internat. Studies, Ohio State U., 1969, BS in Edn., 1970; JD cum laude, Nova U., 1982. Bar: Fla. 1982. Tchr. Palatka (Fla.) Mid. Sch., 1970-72, Dillard H.S., Ft. Lauderdale, Fla., 1974-79; atty. Broward County Pub. Defenders, Ft. Lauderdale, 1982-84, Grimmett & Korthals, Ft. Lauderdale, 1984-90, Gunther & Whittaker, Ft. Lauderdale, 1990-94, Law Office of John Camillo, Ft. Lauderdale, 1994-99, Neale & De Almeida, Ft. Lauderdale, 1999-2000, Heinrich, Gordon, Hargrove, Weihe & James, Ft. Lauderdale, 2000—02, Barnett & Barnard, Hollywood, Fla., 2002—. Staff mem. Nova Law Rev., 1981, 82. Insurance, Personal injury (including property damage), Professional liability. Office: Barnett & Barnard 4601 Sheridan St #505 Hollywood FL 33021 Business E-Mail: ckorthals@bbslawfirm.com.

KORY, MARIANNE GREENE, lawyer; b. N.Y.C., 1931; d. Hyman Louis and Belle (Rome) Greene; children: Erich Marcel, Lisa. BA, CCNY; JD, N.Y. Law Sch., 1976; LLM, U. Wash., 1986. Bar: Ohio 1977, D.C. 1979, N.Y. 1983, Vt. 1994, U.S. Dist. Ct. (so. and ea. dists.) N.Y. 1983, U.S. dist. Ct. Vt. 1994. Hearing examiner Ohio Bd. Employee Compensation, Columbus, 1977; atty. advisor Office Hearings and Appeals Social Security Adminstrn., Cin. and N.Y.C., 1977-78; gen. atty. labor Office of Solicitor U.S. Dept. of Labor, N.Y.C., 1978-82; pvt. practice N.Y.C., 1983—; adminstrv. Seattle, 1989-91, Burlington, Vt., 1994—. Grad. faculty New SCh. Social Rsch. Founder Cin. chpt. Amnesty Internat., 1977. Alvin Johnson fellow in Philosophy; grad. faculty New Sch. for Social Rsch. Mem. Nat. Abortion Rights Action League, Feminist Majority Found., Vt. Bar Assn., Planned Parenthood, Wilderness Soc., Defenders of Wildlife, Ctr. for Marine Conservation, Nat. Wildlife Fedn., Audubon Soc., Emily's List, Phi Beta Kappa. Administrative and regulatory, General practice. Office: 1361 S Ocean Blvd #202 Pompano Beach FL 33062-8022

KORZENIK, ARMAND ALEXANDER, lawyer; b. Hartford, Conn., Oct. 31, 1927; s. Bernard and Dorothy (Goldman) K.; m. Ursula Guttmann, June 30, 1956; children: Peter Brent, Jeffrey Dean, Andrea Diane. AB magna cum laude, Harvard Coll., 1951; JD, Harvard U., 1951; LL.M., Yale U., 1952. Bar: Conn. 1951, U.S. Supreme Ct. 1959. Practiced in Hartford, 1951—; asst. corp. counsel, 1966-72; counsel Hartford Redevel. Agy., 1966-68, Hartford Bd. Edn., 1968-72; instr. bus. law Hartford Inst. Accounting, 1974-75. Editor: Amicus Curiae, 1956-59; bd. editors: Conn. Bar Jour., 1971-79. Mem. Hartford Bd. Edn., 1953-59, Hartford Zoning Bd. Appeals, 1960-66, Hartford Dem. Town Com., 1985-92; justice of peace, Hartford, 1960-73, 84—; Mayor's rep. to Libr. Bd., 1989-91; bd. dirs. YMCA, Boy Scouts Am., PTA, Urban League, Am. Youth Hostels, Jr. C. of C.; founder Blue Hills Civic Assn., West End Civic Assn., Hartford. With USAF, 1946-48, 50, Conn. Air Nat. Guard, 1953-82, brig. gen., 1982-. Mem. Conn. Bar Assn. (ho. of dels. 1975-78, 89-90, exec. com. gen. practice sect. 1983—, chmn. 1997-2001), Hartford County Bar Assn. (editor Bar-Fly 1976-78), Conn. Criminal Def. Lawyers Assn., Harvard Club, Yale Club, Mensa Internat., Phi Beta Kappa. Democrat. Home: 120 Terry Rd Hartford CT 06105-1111 Office: 436 Farmington Ave Hartford CT 06105-4423

KORZENIK, SIDNEY S. lawyer; b. N.Y.C., Jan. 12, 1909; s. Adolph and Sally (Seiden) K.; m. Emily Faust K., June 23, 1949; children: David, Jeremy, Deborah, Joshua. BA, Harvard U., 1929; MA, Columbia U., 1931; LLB, NYU, 1939. Bar: N.Y., Federal Bar, U.S. Supreme Ct. Pvt. practice, N.Y.C., 1946—. With N.Y. State Unemployment Adv. Coun., 1936-41; mem. U.S. Govt. Mgmt.-Labor Textile adv. com.; mem. gen. arbitration coun. of Textile Industry; counsel to various apparel, textile and fur interest orgns., including Nat. Knitted Outerwear Assn., Fedn. Apparel Mfrs., Knitted Textile Assn., Am. Transfer Printing Inst., others; formerly adj. asst. prof. NYU Law Sch.; advisor to govt. textile trade missions; adviser in field. Bd. dirs. Ednl. Found. of Fashion Inst. of Technology, N.Y.C. With U.S. Army, 1941-46. Mem. Phi Beta Kappa. Home: 120 Carthage Rd Scarsdale NY 10583-7202

KOSAKOW, JAMES MATTHEW, lawyer; b. New London, Conn., Apr. 12, 1954; s. Leonard Louis and Lois Ann (Rosen) K.; m. Yvonne Manijeh Bokhour, June 4, 1978; 1 child, Jonathan Daniel. BA, Conn. Coll., 1976; JD, Yeshiva U., 1984. Bar: N.Y. 1985, Conn. 1985, D.C. 1985, Fla. 1991, U.S. Dist. Ct. (so. and ea. dists.) 1985, U.S. Tax Ct. 1993. Assoc. Vittoria & Forsythe, N.Y.C., 1986-92, Gregory and Adams, Wilton, Conn., 1992-94; pvt. practice N.Y.C. and Westport, Conn., 1994-97; ptnr. Kove & Kosakow, LLC, 1997—; vice-chancellor Cambridge Theol. Seminary, Carthage, Ill., 1996—. Guardian and litem N.Y. County Surrogate's Ct., N.Y.C., 1987—, Norwalk Probate Ct., 1993—; mem. faculty, instr. estate planning & personal planning program Albertus Magnus Coll.; lectr. in field; arbitrator BBB, N.Y.C., 1988-89. Co-author: Handling Federal Estate and Gift Taxes, 6th edit., 2000; asst. editor Insights and Strategies; contbr. articles to profl. jours. Trustee, bd. dirs. Internat. Nursery Sch., Queens, N.Y., 1987-89; mem. estates & trusts specialty group lawyers divsn. United Jewish Appeal-Fedn. Jewish Philanthropies of N.Y., Inc., 1990-94; commr. Wilton Water Commn., 1995-96, Wilton Fire Commn., 1996-2000; ptnr. Creative Philanthropic Resources, 1995—; chmn. membership com. Mid-Fairfield Substance Abuse Coalition, 1995-96; dir. Thee Art Tree Source, Inc., 1995—; adv. com. The Unicorn Archive. Mem. N.Y. Bar Assn. (legis. com., trusts and estates sect. 1987—), Conn. Bar Assn. (elder law com.), Fla. Bar (real property, probate and trust law, out-of-state mem. rels. com. 1994—), Assn. of Bar of City of N.Y., Exch. Club (bd. dirs. Wilton club). Estate planning, Probate (including wills, trusts), Estate taxation. Office: 265 Post Rd W Westport CT 06880-1261 also: 685 3d Ave 30th Fl New York NY 10013 E-mail: jmk@kovkos.com.

KOSARIN, JONATHAN HENRY, lawyer, consultant; b. Bklyn., Aug. 13, 1951; s. Lester and Norma (Higger) K.; m. Gayle C. Skarupa, Nov. 27, 1982. BA in History magna cum laude, Syracuse U., 1973; JD, Bklyn. Law Sch., 1976; LLM in Govt. Contract Law, George Washington U., 1984; postgrad., U.S. Army Command and Gen. Staff Coll., 1990, U.S. Army War Coll., 1997. Bar: N.Y. 1977, D.C. 1978, U.S. Supreme Ct. 1980, U.S. Ct. Claims 1981, U.S. Ct. Appeals (Fed. cir.) 1982. Commd. 2d lt. U.S. Army, 1973, advanced through grades to col., 1997, prosecutor trial counsel, 1977-78, adminstrv. law officer, 1978-79, instr. law, 1979-80, trial atty. contract appeals div. Washington, 1980-84; contracts atty. U.S. Army Hdqrs., Heidelberg, Fed. Rep. Germany, 1985-87; assoc. gen. counsel, dir. procurement law Fed Home Loan Bank Bd., Washington, 1987-89; assoc. counsel USN, Washington, 1989-94, dep. counsel, 1994—. Adj. asst. prof. contract law JAG Sch., Charlottesville, Va., 1988-93, adj. assoc. prof., 1993-95, adj. prof., vice chmn., 1995-99, adj. prof., chmn., 1999-2002; dep. gen. counsel def. prisoner of war Missin Pers. Office, 2002—; acting chief contract law U.S. Army Europe, Heidelberg, Germany, 2003; adj. faculty contract law U. Va., 1989—; mem. faculty Fed. Publs. Seminars, 1995—, ESI Internat., 1999-2002. Vol. info. specialist Smithsonian Instn. Washington, 1993—, pres. Temple Rodef Shalom, Falls, Church, Va., 2000-02; mem. Mid-Atlantic coun. Union of Am. Hebrew Congregations, 2002—; para-Rabinnic fellow Temple Rodef Shalom, Falls Church, 1998—. Mem. ABA, D.C. Bar Assn., Titanic Hist. Soc., No. Va. Football Ofcls. Assn., Nat. Assn. Sports Ofcls., Phi Alpha Delta, Phi Beta Kappa, Phi Kappa Phi, Phi Delta Kappa. Democrat. Office: USN Office Of Gen Counsel Washington DC 20350-0001

KOSSAR, RONALD STEVEN, lawyer; b. Ellenville, N.Y., May 30, 1948; s. Emanuel and Helen (Panken) K.; m. Sandra Perlman, Aug. 25, 1973. BA cum laude, Boston U., 1970; JD, Am. U., 1973. Bar: N.Y. 1974, D.C. 1974, U.S. Dist. Ct. (no. dist.) N.Y. 1974, U.S. Tax Ct. 1974, U.S. Ct. Appeals D.C. 1974. Tax law specialist Office Asst. Commr. (Tech.), IRS, Washington, 1973-75; sole practice Middletown, NY, 1976—. Dir. Newburgh (N.Y.) Realty Corp. Mem. ABA, N.Y. State Bar Assn., Orange County Bar Assn., Middletown Bar Assn., D.C. Bar. Jewish. Corporate, general, General practice, Property, real (including real estate development, water). Office: 402 E Main St Middletown NY 10940-2516 Office Fax: 845-343-5222. E-mail: rsklaw@warwick.net.

KOSTELANETZ, BORIS, lawyer; b. St. Petersburg, Russia, June 16, 1911; came to U.S., 1920, naturalized, 1925; s. Nachman and Rosalia (Dimschetz) K.; m. Ethel Cory, Dec. 18, 1938; children: Richard Cory, Lucy Cory. B.C.S., N.Y. U., 1933, BS, 1936; JD magna cum laude, St. John's U., 1936, LL.D. (hon.), 1981. Bar: N.Y. 1936; CPA, N.Y. With Price, Waterhouse & Co., C.P.A.'s, N.Y.C., 1934-37; asst. U.S. atty. So. Dist. N.Y.; also confidential asst. to U.S. atty, 1937-43; spl. asst. to atty. gen. U.S., 1943-46; chief war frauds sect. Dept. Justice, 1945-46; spl. counsel com. investigate crime in interstate commerce U.S. Senate, 1950-51; ptnr. Kostelanetz Ritholz Tigue & Fink, N.Y.C., 1946-89, of counsel, 1990-94, Kostelanetz & Fink, N.Y.C., 1994—. Instr. acctg. N.Y. U., 1937-47, adj. prof. taxation, 1947-69; Mem. com. on character and fitness Appellate div. Supreme Ct. N.Y., 1st dept., 1974— , chmn., 1985-98. Author: (with L. Bender) Criminal Aspects of Tax Fraud Cases, 1957, 2d edit., 1968, 3d edit., 1980; Contbr. articles to legal, accounting and tax jours. Chmn. Kefauver for Pres. Com. N.Y. State, 1952. Recipient Meritorious Svc. award NYU, 1954, John T. Madden Meml. award, 1969, Pietas medal St. John's U., 1961, medal of honor, 1983, James Madison award, 1988, Torch of Learning award Am. Friends of Hebrew U. Law Sch., 1979, N.Y.U. Presdl. citation, 1990, N.Y. State Bar Assn. Fifty-Yr. Lawyer award, 1990, ABA Sect. Taxation Distinguished Svc. award, 1999. Fellow Am. Coll. Trial Lawyers, Am. Coll. Tax Counsel, Am. Bar Found.; mem. ABA (coun. sect. taxation 1978-81, ho. of dels. 1984-89), Fed. Bar Assn., Internat. Bar Assn., Soc. King's Inn, Ireland (hon. bencher 1995), N.Y. State Bar Assn., N.Y. State CPAs, N.Y. County Lawyers Assn. (v.p. 1966-69, pres. 1969-71, bd. dirs. 1958-64, 66-69, 71-74, chmn. judiciary com. 1965-69), Assn. of Bar of City of N.Y., NYU Sch. Commerce Alumni Assn. (pres. 1951-52), NYU Alumni Fedn. (pres. 1989-92), St. John's U. Law Sch. Alumni Assn. (pres. 1955-57), India House. General civil litigation, Criminal. Home: 37 Washington Sq W New York NY 10011-9181 Office: Kostelanetz & Fink 530 5th Ave Fl 22 New York NY 10036-5101

KOSTELNY, ALBERT JOSEPH, JR., lawyer; b. Phila., July 11, 1951; s. Albert Joseph and Margaret (Naile) K. BA, U. Pa., 1973, MA, 1974; JD, Fordham U., 1979. Bar: N.Y. 1980, U.S. Dist. Ct. (so. dist.) N.Y. 1983, U.S. Ct. Claims 1983, U.S. Supreme Ct. 1983, U.S. Ct. Internat. Trade 1985, U.S. Ct. Appeals (2d cir.) 1985. Atty. N.Y. State Divsn. Human Rights, N.Y.C., 1980-81, sr. atty., 1981-89, acting chief adminstrv. law judge, 1989-91, adjudication counsel to commr., 1990-98, supr. atty., dir. prosecutions unit, 1998—2001, assoc. atty., 2001—. Mem. ABA, N.Y. State Bar Assn., N.Y. County Lawyers Assn., Assn. Trial Lawyers Am. Republican. Roman Catholic. Office: NY State Div Human Rights One Fordham Plz Bronx NY 10458-5871 E-mail: kostelna@nysnet.net.

KOSTYO, JOHN FRANCIS, lawyer; b. Findlay, Ohio, Feb. 9, 1955; s. Albert Robert and Mary Agnes (Welsh) K.; m. Shirley Ann Allgyre, June 9, 1984. BA in Polit. Sci. and Philosophy magna cum laude, John Carroll U., 1978; JD, Case Western Res. U., 1981. Bar: Ohio 1981, U.S. Dist. Ct. (no. dist.) Ohio 1982, U.S. Dist. Ct. (ea. dist.) Mich. 1991, U.S. Supreme Ct. 1991, U.S. Dist. Ct. (so. dist.) Mich. 1992, U.S. Dist. Ct. (we. dist.) Mich. 1992. Assoc. Weasel & Brimley, Findlay, 1981-89; ptnr. Brimley, Kostyo & Elliott, L.P.A., Findlay, 1989-91, Brimley & Kostyo Co., L.P.A., Findlay, 1991, Brimley, Kostyo & Lather Co., L.P.A., 1991-93, Brimley & Kostyo Co. L.P.A., 1993-99; v.p. Mid-Am. Title Agy., Inc., Findlay, Ohio, 1989—; mem. Kostyo & Clark, PLL, Findlay, Ohio, 1999—, Fuller & Henry, Ltd., 2001—. Lectr. contracts and negotiable instruments U. Findlay, 1981-84, sr. lectr. 1984-96. Mem. ABA (corp. banking and bus. law, litigation div.), Ohio Bar Assn., Toledo Bar Assn., William Taft Am. Inn of Ct., Alpha Sigma Nu. Clubs: Rockwell Springs Trout. Lodges: Elks, K.C. (4th degree). Roman Catholic. Avocations: sports, comml. trans., books, theater. State civil litigation, Commercial, contracts (including sales of goods; commercial financing), General practice. Home: 462 Penbrooke Dr Findlay OH 45840-7472 Office: Fuller & Henry Ltd 1995 Tiffin Ave Ste 312 Findlay OH 45840-6772 also: MidAm Title Agy Inc 100 E Main Cross St Findlay OH 45840-4861

KOSUB, JAMES ALBERT, lawyer; b. San Antonio, Jan. 8, 1948; s. Ernest Pete and Lonie (Doege) K.; divorced; 1 child, James Jr.; m. Jane Stevens Cain, Aug. 11, 1979; children: Kathryn, Nicholas (dec.). Student, East Carolina U., 1970, San Antonio Coll., 1971-72; BS, SW Tex. State U., 1974; JD, St. Mary's U., San Antonio, 1977. Bar: Tex. 1978, U.S. Dist. Ct. (we. dist.) Tex. 1980, U.S. Ct. Appeals (5th cir.) 1981, U.S. Dist. Ct. (so. dist.) 1986, U.S. Supreme Ct. 1988, U.S. Dist. Ct. (no. and ea. dists.) Tex. 1990. Ptnr. Kosub & Langlois, San Antonio, 1978-79, Kosub, Langlois & Van Cleave, San Antonio, 1979-83; mng. ptnr. Kosub & Langlois, San Antonio, 1983-86; sr. ptnr. James A. Kosub, San Antonio, 1986-94; pvt. practice Eldorado, Tex., 1994—2002; sr. ptnr. Kosub & Griffin, 2002—. Bd. dirs. Judson Ind. Sch. Bd. Trustees, Converse, Tex., 1975-81, Bexar County Fedn. Sch. Bds., San Antonio, 1977-80. Sgt. USMC, 1966-70. Fellow Tex. Bar Found., San Antonio Bar Found.; mem. ABA (EEOC liaison com. San Antonio chpt. 1987-93), San Antonio Bar Assn. (bd. dirs. 1990-92, sec. 1992-93), Fed. Bar Assn. 5th Cir. Bar Assn., Coll. of State Bar of Tex., State Bar of Tex. (coun. labor and employment sect. 1993-97, sec. 1997-98, vice chair 1998-99, chair 1999-2000, past chair 2000-01), Schleicher County C. of C. (pres. 1998-2000), Schleicher County Lions Club. Episcopalian. Avocations: carpentry, gardening, golf. Civil rights, Constitutional, Labor (including EEOC, Fair Labor Standards Act, labor-management relations, NLRB, OSHA). Office: 105 S Main Eldorado TX 76936-0460

KOTELMAN, LAURA MARY, lawyer; b. Chgo., Apr. 5, 1972; Student, Am. U., 1992; BA, Lake Forest Coll., 1993; JD, U. Ill., 1997. Bar: Ill. 1997. Legis. analyst Ill. Senate Majority Staff, Springfield, 1993-94; program legal specialist Ill. Atty. Gen., Chgo., 1997-98; counsel Nat. Assn. Ind. Insurers, Des Plaines, Ill., 1998—. Mem. Ill. State Bar Assn., Federalist Soc. (chpt. pres. 1996-97), Phi Delta Phi (chpt. pres. 1995-96, Most Active Chpt. award 1996). Roman Catholic. Administrative and regulatory, Insurance, Legislative. Office: Nat Assn Ind Insurers 2600 S River Rd Des Plaines IL 60018-3203

KOTLARCHUK, IHOR O. E. lawyer; b. Ukraine, July 31, 1943; came to U.S., 1946, naturalized, 1957; s. Emil and Lidia N. (Maceluch) K. BS in Fin., Fordham U., 1965, JD, 1968; LLM, Georgetown U., 1974, MA in Govt., 1982. Bar: N.Y. 1969, D.C. 1972, Va. 2001, U.S. Ct. Mil. Appeals, U.S. Tax Ct., U.S. Supreme Ct. Sr. trial atty. criminal sect. tax divsn. U.S. Dept. Justice, Washington, 1973-78, civil sect. tax divsn., 1978-80, fraud sect. criminal divsn., 1980-84, internal security sect. criminal divsn., 1984-97; ret., 1999; sr. internat. law enforcement adv. on tax policy/enforcement U.S. Treasury Dept., 2000—; pvt. practice law Alexandria, Va., 2001—. Pres. The Washington Group, 2001—. With U.S. Army, 1969-73, Vietnam; judge advocate gen.; ret. col. USAR. Decorated Bronze star, Legion of Merit. Mem. ABA, N.Y. State Bar Assn., Va. State Bar Assn., Va. Trial Lawyers Assn., D.C. Bar Assn., Res. Officers Assn., Ukrainian Assn. Washington D.C. (pres. 2000-01), Phi Alpha Delta. Ukrainian Catholic. Address: 205 S Lee St Alexandria VA 22314-3307 Office: 109 S Fairfax St Alexandria VA 22314-3307 Fax: 703-548-1861.

KOURIDES, PETER THEOLOGOS, lawyer; b. Istanbul, Turkey, July 24, 1910; came to U.S., 1912, naturalized, 1931; s. Theologos and Zafiro (Gurlides) K.; m. Anna E. Spetseris, Aug. 4, 1938; children— Ione A., P. Nicholas. BA, Columbia, 1931, JD, 1933; HHD (hon.), Hellenic Coll., 1985. Bar: N.Y. 1933. Mem. firm Seward, Raphael & Kourides, N.Y.C., 1935—; gen. counsel Greek Archdiocese of North and South Am., 1938-96; trustee Hellenic Cathedral City N.Y., 1938-98; trustee, counsel St. Basil's Acad., Garrison, N.Y., 1946-97, United Greek Orthodox Charities, 1965-70; counsel World Conf. Religion for Peace, 1970-82; dir., counsel Hellenic Am. C. of C., 1955—; dir. Atlantic Bank N.Y., 1974-97; counsel Consultate Gen. of Greece, N.Y.C., 1963-90. Nat. sec. Greek War Relief Assn., 1941-46; rep. Greek Archdiocese of North and South Am. at enthronement Athenagoras I, Istanbul, 1949; pres. Hellenic U. Club, 1951-52. Author: The Evolution of the Greek Orthodox Church in America and its Current Problems, 1959, The Centennial History of the Archdiocesan Cathedral of the Holy Trinity, 1992. Nat. v.p. Order of Ahepa, 1960; mem. gen. bd. Nat. Coun. Chs., 1960-82, v.p., 1969-72; counsel Columbia U. Cancer Clinic in Greece, 1965-70; del. 3d Assembly World Coun. Chs., New Delhi, India, 1961, 4th Assembly, Uppsala, Sweden, 1968, 5th Assembly, Nairobi, Kenya, 1975, World Conf. Religion on Peace, Kyoto, Japan, 1971; mem. internat. affairs com. World Coun. Chs., 1968-74; trustee Hellenic Coll., Brookline, Mass., 1968-97. Decorated Gold Cross Order of Phoenix by King Constantine II Greece, 1967, Titular Archon Megas Nomophylax by Ecumenical Partriarchate of Eastern Orthodox Ch., 1968, grand comdr. Knights of Holy Sepulchre Jerusalem Patriarchate of Eastern Orthodox Ch., 1961. Mem. ABA, N.Y. Bar Assn., Consular Law Soc., Am. Judicature Soc., Columbia Alumni Assn. Home: 46 Groton St Forest Hills NY 11375-5921 Office: 110 E 59th St New York NY 10022-1304

KOURLIS, REBECCA LOVE, state supreme court justice; b. Colorado Springs, Colo., Nov. 11, 1952; d. John Arthur and Ann (Daniels) Love; m. Thomas Aristithis Kourlis, July 15, 1978; children: Stacy Ann, Katherine Love, Aristithis Thomas. BA with distinction in English, Stanford U., 1973, JD, 1976; LLD (hon.), U. Denver, 1997. Bar: Colo. 1976, D.C. 1979, U.S. Dist. Ct. Colo. 1976, U.S. Ct. Appeals (10th cir.) 1976, Colo. Supreme Ct., U.S. Ct. Appeals (D.C. cir.), U.S. Claims Ct., U.S. Supreme Ct. Assoc. Davis, Graham & Stubbs, Denver, 1976-78; sole practice Craig, Colo., 1978-87; judge 14th Jud. Dist. Ct., Craig, Colo., 1987-94; arbiter Jud. Arbiter Group, Inc., 1994-95; justice Colo. Supreme Ct., 1995—. Water judge divsn. 6, 1987-94; lectr. to profl. groups. Contbr. articles to profl. jours. Chmn. Moffat County Arts and Humanities, Craig, 1979; mem. Colo. Commn. on Higher Edn., Denver, 1980-81; mem. adv. bd. Colo. Divsn. Youth Svcs., 1988-91; mem. com. civil jury instructions, 1990-95, standing com. gender and justice, 1994-97, chair jud. adv. coun., 1997-2002, chair com. on jury reform, 1996—; co-chair com. on atty. grievance reform, 1997-2002; mem. long range planning com. Moffat County Sch., 1990; bd. visitors Stanford U., 1989-94, Law Sch. U. Denver, 1997-2002; trustee Kent Denver Sch., 1996-2002. Named N.W. Colo. Daily Press Woman of Yr., 1993; recipient Trailblazer award AAUW, 1998, Mary Lathrop award, 2001, Jud. Excellence award Acad. Matrimonial Lawyers, 2002, Champion for Children award, Rocky Mt. Children's Law Ctr., 2003. Fellow: Colo. Bar Found., Am. Bar Found.; mem.: N.W. Colo. Bar Assn. (Cmty. Svc. award 1993—94), Dist. Ct. Judges' Assn. (pres. 1993—94), Colo. Bar Assn. (bd. govs. 1983—85, mineral law sect. bd. dirs. 1985, sr. v.p. 1987—88), Rocky Mountain Mineral Found. Office: State Jud Bldg 2 E 14th Ave Denver CO 80203-2115

KOUTOUJIAN, PETER JOHN, lawyer; b. Newton, Mass., Sept. 17, 1961; s. Peter and Cornelia (Cassidy) K. Student, U. Coll., Dublin, Ireland, 1981; BA in Psychology, Bridgewater (Mass.) State Coll, 1983; JD, New Eng. Sch. of Law, 1989. Rsch. asst. Commonwealth of Mass., Boston, 1984-86; pvt. practice Waltham, Mass., 1990—; asst. dist. atty. Mass. Ho. Reps., Boston, 1997-98, state rep. Bar adv. Middlesex County Bar Advs., Waltham, 1990—. Mem. Dem. City Com., Waltham, 1983—; big brother Big Bros. Assn. of Boston, 1990—. Roman Catholic. Avocations: tennis, basketball. General civil litigation, Entertainment, Personal injury (including property damage). Home: 154 Waltham St Newton MA 02465-1333 Office: Ho of Reps State House Rm 448 Boston MA 02133*

KOUTSOGIANE, PHILLIP CHARLES, lawyer; b. Woonsocket, R.I., Sept. 26, 1944; m. Joyce Ann Hindle, July 28, 1984. BA, Brown U., 1966; JD, Boston U., 1973. Bar: R.I. 1973, Mass. 1973, U.S. Dist. Ct. R.I. 1974, U.S. Supreme Ct. 1980, U.S. Dist. Ct. Mass. 1996. Pvt. practice, Woonsocket. 1st lt. U.S. Army, 1968-70. Mem. ABA, R.I. Bar Assn., Pawtucket Bar Assn., Assn. Trial Lawyers Am., R.I. Trial Lawyers. General civil litigation, Personal injury (including property damage), Probate (including wills, trusts). Office: Stadium Bldg 313 Woonsocket RI 02895-3024

KOVACHEVICH, ELIZABETH ANNE, judge; b. Canton, Ill., Dec. 14, 1936; d. Dan and Emilie (Kuchan) Kovachevich. AA, St. Petersburg Jr. Coll., 1956; BBA in Fin. magna cum laude, U. Miami, 1958; JD, Stetson U., 1961, LLD (hon.) , 1993. Bar: Fla. 1961, U.S. Dist. Ct. (mid. and so. dists.) Fla. 1961, U.S. Ct. Appeals (5th cir.) 1961, U.S. Supreme Ct. 1968. Rsch. and adminstrv. aide Pinellas County Legis. Del., Fla., 1961; assoc. DiVito & Speer, St. Petersburg, Fla., 1961—62; house counsel Rieck & Fleece Builders Supplies, Inc., St. Petersburg, 1962; pvt. practice St. Petersburg, 1962—73; judge 6th Jud. Cir., Pinellas and Pasco Counties, Fla., 1973—82, U.S. Dist. Ct. (mid. dist.) Fla., Tampa, 1982—96, chief judge, 1996—. Chmn. St. Petersburg Profl. Legal Project-Days in Ct., 1967, Supreme Ct. Bicentennial Com. 6th Jud. Cir., 1975—76. Prodr., coord. (TV prodn.) A Race to Judgement. Bd. regents State of Fla., 1970—72; legal advisor, bd. dirs. Young Women's Residence, Inc., 1968; mem. Fla. Gov.'s Commn. on Status of Women, 1968—71; mem. Pres.'s Commn. on White House Fellowships, 1973—77; mem. def. adv. com. on Women in Svc. Dept. Def., 1973—76; Fla. publicity chmn. 18th Nat. Rep. Women's Conf., Atlanta, 1971; lifetime mem. Children's Hosp. Guild, YWCA of St. Petersburg; charter mem. Golden Notes, St. Petersburg Symphony; hon. mem. bd. of overeers Stetson U. Coll. of Law, 1986. Recipient St. Petersburg Panhellenic Appreciation award, 1964, Pinellas United Fund award in recognition of concern and meritorious effort, 1968, Disting. Alumni award, Stetson U., 1970, Woman of Yr. award, Beta Sigma Phi, 1970, 1970, Am. Legion Aux. Unit 14 Pres. award cmty. svc., 1970, Dedication to Christian Ideals award and Man of Yr. award, KC Dists. 20-21, 1972, USN Recruiting Command Appreciation award, 1975, Woman of Yr. award, Fla. Fedn. Bus. and Profl. Women, 1981, ann. Ben C. Willard Meml. award, Stetson Lawyers Assn., 1983, Alumni of Yr. award, St. Petersburg Jr. Coll., 1994, Cath. Law Person of Yr., Greater Tampa Cath. Lawyer's Guild, 1998, Disting. Svc. award, Fla. Coun. on Crime and Delinquency, 1999, J-Ben Watkins award, Stetson U. Coll. of Law, 1999, Woman of Achievement award, Delta Delta Delta, 2000, Outstanding Jurist award, Hillsborough County, 2000—01, Pub. Svc. award, William Reece Smith, Jr., 2001, Mrs. Charles Ulrick Bay award, St. Petersburg Rotary award, St. Petersburg Quarterback Club award, President's Award, Fed. Bar. Assn., 2001, Presidential Special Recognition Award, 2002. Mem.: ABA, St. Petersburg Bar Assn. (chmn. bench and bar com., sec. 1969), Am. Judicature Soc., Pinellas County Trial Lawyers, Fla. Bar Assn., ATLA. Office: US Dist Ct 801 N Florida Ave Tampa FL 33602-3849

KOVACIC, WILLIAM EVAN, law educator; b. Poughkeepsie, N.Y., Oct. 1, 1952; s. Evan Carl and Frances Katherine (Crow) K.; m. Kathryn Marie Fenton, May 18, 1985. AB with honors, Princeton U., 1974; JD, Columbia U., 1978. Bar: N.Y. 1979. Law clk. to sr. dist. judge U.S. Dist. Ct. Md., Balt., 1978-79; atty. planning office bur. competition FTC, Washington, 1979-82, atty. advisor to commr., 1983; assoc. Bryan, Cave, McPheeters & McRoberts, Washington, 1983-86; prof. George Mason U. Sch. Law, Arlington, Va., 1986-99, George Washington U. Law Sch., Washington, 1999—; gen. counsel U.S. FTC, 2001—. Cons. in field; mem. U.S. Senate Judiciary Subcom. on Antitrust and Monopoly, Washington, 1975-76. Contbr. legal articles to profl. jours. Assoc. Father Ford Found. Columbia U. Cath. Campus Ministry, N.Y.C. 1985—. Harlan Fiske Stone fellow Columbia U., 1976-78. Mem. ABA (antitrust law and pub. contract law sects.), Fed. Bar Assn. Roman Catholic. Avocations: hiking, camping, photography. Office: George Washington U Law Sch 720 20th St NW Washington DC 20052-0001 E-mail: wkovacic@main.nlc.gwu.edu.

KOVACS, PAUL EUGENE, lawyer; b. Newmark, N.J. s. Eugene A. and Mary (Betell) K.; m. Susann, Aug. 3, 1968; children: Paul Scott, Kristin, Karen, John Paul. AA, Monmouth Coll., 1964, BS, 1966; JD, U. Mo., 1969. Ptnr. Brinker Doyen & Kovacs, Clayton, Mo., 1969-97, Armstrong, Teasdale, LLP, St. Louis, 1997—. Adj. prof. Washington U., St. Louis, 1991-96. Fellow Am. Coll. Trial Lawyers, Internat. Soc. Barristers; mem. ABA, ATLA, Mo. Bar, County Bar Assn., St. Louis, Mo. Assn. Defence Council, Old Warson Country Club. Office: Armstrong Teasdale LLP 1 Metropolitan Sq Ste 2600 Saint Louis MO 63102-2740

KOVACS, WILLIAM LAWRENCE, lawyer; b. Scranton, Pa., June 29, 1947; s. William Lawrence and Jane Claire (Weiss) K.; m. Mary Katherine Maras, Dec. 2, 1979; children: Katherine Elizabeth, William Lawrence III, Margaret Ellen, Tyler Alexander. BS magna cum laude, U. Scranton, 1969; JD, Ohio State U., 1972. Bar: Pa. 1972, D.C. 1973, U.S. Ct. Appeals (D.C. cir.) 1974, U.S. Supreme Ct. 1976, Va. 1981. Legis. asst., staff atty. Congressman Fred B. Rooney, Washington, 1972-74; chief counsel U.S. Ho. of Reps. Subcom. on Transp. and Commerce, Washington, 1975-77; assoc. Liebert, Short, FitzPatrick & Lavin, Phila., 1977-78; environ., litigation atty. Nat. Chamber Litigation Ctr., Washington, 1979; ptnr. Abrams, Kovacs, Westermeier & Goldberg, Washington, 1980-84, Kovacs & Bury, Fairfax, Va., 1984-85, Jaeckle, Fleischmann & Mugel, Washington, 1986-87, Eckert, Seamans, Cherin & Mellott, Washington, 1987-89, Dunn, Carney, Allen, Higgins & Tongue, Portland, Oreg., 1990, Keller & Heckman, Washington, 1991-97; pres. Clean States Found., Inc., 1997-98; dir. legal affairs Worldwide Sunshine Makers, Inc., Washington, 1997-98; v.p. environ. tech. and regulatory affairs U.S. C. of C., Washington, 1998—. Contbr. articles to profl. jours. Mem. Hazardous Waste Facilities Siting Bd., Richmond, Va., 1984-86; vice chmn., 1984-85, chmn., 1985-86. Mem. ABA (vice chmn. energy resources law com. sect. on torts and ins. practice 1981-83, chmn. 1983-84), U.S. C. of C. (mem. environ. law adv. com. 1986-92). Roman Catholic. Administrative and regulatory, Environmental, Legislative. Home: 9805 Arnon Chapel Rd Great Falls VA 22066-3908 Office: 1615 H St NW Washington DC 20062-0001 E-mail: WKovacs@uschamber.com.

KOWALSKY, JOSEPH Z. lawyer, financial consultant; b. Detroit, Aug. 9, 1964; s. Eugene and Cherna R. Kowalsky; m. Jennifer, 1998. Vis. student, Columbia U., 1986-87; BA magna cum laude, Wayne State U., 1987; JD, U. Mich., 1991. Bar: Mich. 1992, D.C. 1993, Mich. 1994; licensed financial adv. 1999, life and health ins. Account exec. Telesaver, Corp., Southfield, Mich., 1981-84; pres., founder Kwality Systems Long Distance, Southfield, 1984-86; v.p. Affordable Vacations Unlimited, Inc., Oak Park, Mich., 1987-88; legis. rsch. asst. U.S. Senator Carl Levin, Washington, 1991-92; staff asst. Presdl. Transition Team, Washington, 1992-93; scheduler Brodhead for Senate, Detroit, 1993-94; atty., ombudsman The Red-tape Machete, Lathrup Village, Mich., 1994—99; fin. advisor life and health ins., bd. dirs. The Cryonics Inst., Clinton, Mich., 1999—; fin. adv. Fahnestock & Co., Inc., West Bloomfield, Mich., 1999—. Pub. The Joseph Z. Kowalsky Securities Newsletter, 1991-94. Campaign worker Tsongas for Pres., Washington and Detroit, 1991-92, Abraham for Senate, Southfield, 1994; youth leader Nat. Conf. Synagogue Youth, Oak Park, 1981-84; founder, bd. dirs. Tomorrow, Inc. Pro-bono Legal Assistance Orgn., Lathrup Village, 1997-99. Avocations: biking, hiking, swimming, research. Office: Fahnestock & Company 6230 Orchard Lake Rd West Bloomfield MI 48322

KOZAK, JOHN W. lawyer; b. Chgo., July 25, 1943; s. Walter and Stella (Palka) K.; m. Elizabeth Mathias, Feb. 3, 1968; children: Jennifer, Mary Margaret, Suzanne. BSEE, U. Notre Dame, 1965; JD, Georgetown U., 1968. Bar: Ill. 1968, D.C. 1968. Patent advisor Office of Naval Rsch., Corona, Calif., 1968-69; assoc. Leydig, Voit & Mayer, Ltd. and predecessor firms, Chgo., 1969-74, ptnr., 1974—, chmn. mgmt. com., 1982-91, pres., 2001—. Mem. United Charities Legal Aid Soc., 1989-2002. Fellow Am. Coll. Trial Lawyers; mem. ABA, Am. Intellectual Property Law Assn., Licensing Execs. Soc., Chgo. Intellectual Property Law Assn., Univ. Club (Chgo.), The Lawyers Club Chgo., Winter Club (Lake Forest, Ill.), Knollwood Club (Lake Forest). Federal civil litigation, Patent, Trademark and copyright. Office: Leydig Voit & Mayer Ste 4900 2 Prudential Pla Chicago IL 60601 E-mail: jkozak@leydig.com.

KRACKE, ROBERT RUSSELL, lawyer; b. Decatur, Ga., Feb. 27, 1938; s. Roy Rachford and Virginia Carolyn (Minter) K.; m. Barbara Anne Pilgrim, Dec. 18, 1965; children: Shannon Ruth, Robert Russell, Rebecca Anne, Susan Lynn. Student, Birmingham So. Coll.; BA, Samford U., 1962; JD, Cumberland Sch. Law, 1965. Bar: Ala. 1965, U.S. Tax Ct. 1971, U.S. Supreme Ct. 1971. Individual practice law, Birmingham, Ala., 1965—; founding ptnr. Kracke and Thompson, Birmingham, 1980—. Editor, Birmingham Bar Bull, 1974—; bd. editors Ala. Lawyer, 1980-86; contbr. articles to profl. jours. Active Dem. Exec. Com., 1970-96; deacon Ind. Presbyn. Ch., Birmingham, 1973-76, elder, 1999—, pres. adult choir, 1968-99, chief adminstrv. officer, 1970-99, pres., treas. Nov. Organ Recital Series, 1999—, Housing Agy. Retarded Citizens; pres. Ala. chpt. Nat. Voluntary Health Agys., 1988-89; mem. exec. com. legal counsel Birmingham Opera Theatre, 1983-95; bd. dirs. Ala. Assn. Retarded Citizens, Jefferson County Assn. Retarded Citizens, 1983-91, pres.-elect, 1994-96, pres. 1996-98, past pres., 1998-2000; coord. com. mem. Nat. Conv. of the ARC of U.S., 1999—; bd. dirs., founding pres. Ala. chpt. Juvenile Diabetes Rsch. Found. Internat., bd. dirs. The ARC of Ala., 1996-98, Found. of ARC, 1998—. With USNR, 1955-61. Mem. Birmingham (exec. com., law libr. chmn., law day 1976, bull., history and archives com.), Ala. Bar Assn., ABA (award merit law day 1976), Am. Judicature Soc., U.S. Supreme Ct. Hist. Soc., Dem. Exec. Com., Ala. Hist. Assn., So. Hist. Assn., The Club, Phi Alpha Delta (pres. chpt. 1964-65), Rotary (pres. Shades Valley club 1988-89, Paul Harris fellow, sec. dist. 6860 1990-91, dist. coord. comm., bd. dir., sec. ednl. found.), Sigma Alpha Epsilon. State civil litigation, Family and matrimonial, Insurance. Home: 4410 Briar Glen Dr Birmingham AL 35243-1743 Office: Kracke and Thompson Lakeview Sch Bldg 808 29th St S Birmingham AL 35205-1004 E-mail: rkracke@ktlegal.com.

KRAEMER, LILLIAN ELIZABETH, lawyer; b. N.Y.C., Apr. 18, 1940; d. Frederick Joseph and Edmee Elizabeth (de Watteville) K.; m. John W. Vincent, June 22, 1962 (div. 1964). BA, Swarthmore Coll., 1961; JD, U. Chgo., 1964. Bar: N.Y. 1965, U.S. Dist. Ct. (so. dist.) N.Y. 1967, U.S. Dist. Ct. (ea. dist.) N.Y. 1971. Assoc. Cleary, Gottlieb, Steen & Hamilton, N.Y.C., 1964-71, Simpson Thacher & Bartlett, N.Y.C., 1971-74, ptnr., 1974-99, of counsel, 2000—. Mem. vis. com. U. Chgo. Law Sch., 1988-90, 91-94, 97-99. Bd. mgrs. Swarthmore Coll., 1993—; warden St. Francis Episcopal Ch., Stamford, Conn., 2001—. Fellow Am. Coll. Bankruptcy; mem. Lawyers Alliance for N.Y. (bd. dirs. 1996-2001), Assn. of Bar of City of N.Y. (mem. various coms.), Coun. on Fgn. Rels., N.Y. State Bar Assn., Order of Coif, Phi Beta Kappa. Democrat. Avocations: travel, reading, word games. Banking, Bankruptcy. Home: 2 Beekman Pl New York NY 10022-8058 also: 62 Pheasant Ln Stamford CT 06903-4428 E-mail: lkraemer@stblaw.com.

KRAEMER, LISA RUSSERT, lawyer; b. Fayetteville, Ark., Dec. 6, 1954; d. William S. and Louise R. (Russert) K.; m. Richard S. Lang, Dec. 30, 1977; children: Jonathan Kraemer Lang, Katherine Kraemer Lang, William Kraemer Lang, Daniel Kraemer Lang. BA, Harvard U., 1976; JD, U. Cin.,

1979; M in Conflict Resolution, Antioch U., 1996. Bar: Ohio 1979, U.S. Dist. Ct. (no. dist.) Ohio 1979. Staff atty. FTC, Cleve., 1980-85; assoc. Madorsky & Katz, Cleve., 1985-86; dir. CLE Case Western Law Sch., Cleve., 1986-88; assoc. Thomas and Boles, Chagrin Falls, Ohio, 1988-89; pvt. practice Cleve., 1989—. Contbg. author: Ohio Family Law Handbook-Mediation, 1996. Councilwoman Village of Chagrin Falls, 1989—; vol. magistrate juvenile divsn. program, 1999—. Mem. Cuyahoga County Bar Assn. Family and matrimonial. Office: Three Commerce Park Square 23230 Chagrin Blvd Ste 740 Cleveland OH 44122-5499

KRAEMER, WALDRON, lawyer; b. Newark, Apr. 13, 1937; s. Manfred Kraemer and Evelyn C. Waldron; m. Jean A. Rosenberg, June 17, 1962; children: Adam, Elise. BA, Colgate U., 1958; LLB, Harvard U., 1961. Bar: N.J. 1961. Law clk. N.J. Supreme Ct., 1962—63; from assoc. to ptnr. Kraemer, Burns, Mytelka, Lovell & Kulka, P.A. and predecessor firms, Newark/Springfield, NJ, 1963—. Mem., chmn. N.J. Bd. Bar Examiners, 1969—78; pres. Essex County Bar Assn., Newark, 1982—83; mem. N.J. Supreme Ct. Disciplinary Rev. Bd., 1984—87. With USAR. Corporate, general. Office: Kraemer Burns Mytelka Lovell & Kulka PA 675 Morris Ave Springfield NJ 07081

KRAEUTER, R. SCOT, lawyer; b. Winchester, Mass., Apr. 25, 1970; s. Lincoln David and Sheila Anne (Buckley) Kraeuter. BA, Vanderbilt U., 1992; JD, Emory U., 1995. Assoc. Savage, Turner, Pinson & Karsman, Savannah, Ga., 1995—2002, ptnr., 2002—. Personal injury (including property damage), Product liability, Professional liability. Office: Savage Turner Pinson and Karsman 304 E Bay St Savannah GA 31401 Office Fax: 912-232-4212.

KRAFT, HENRY ROBERT, lawyer; b. L.A., Apr. 27, 1946; s. Sylvester and Freda (Shochat) K.; m. Terry Kraft, July 21, 1968; children: Diana, Kevin. BA in History, San Fernando Valley State Coll., 1968; JD, U. So. Calif., 1971. Bar: Calif. 1972, U.S. Dist. Ct. (ctrl. dist.) Calif. 1985, U.S. Ct. Appeals (9th cir.) 1998, U.S. Dist. Ct. (so. and no. dists.) Calif 1998. Dep. pub. defender San Bernardino (Calif.) County, 1972-78; pvt. practice, Victorville, Calif., 1979-96; city atty. Victorville, 1987—2002; of counsel Best Best & Krieger LLP, Victorville, 1996-98; assoc. Parker, Covert & Chidester, Tustin, Calif., 1999-2000; ptnr. Parker & Covert LLP, Tustin, 2000—. Atty. City of Barstow, Calif., 1980-97; instr. Victor Valley Coll., Victorville, 1986—. Atty. Barstow Community Hosp., 1980-88. Mem. FBA, San Bernardino Bar Assn. (fee dispute com., jud. evaluation com.), High Desert Bar Assn. (pres., v.p., sec. 1979-81), Calif. Soc. Health Care Attys., League Calif. Cities, Am. Arbitration Assn. (panel neutral arbitrators). Democrat. Jewish. Avocations: bicycling, travel, wine enthusiast. Office: Parker & Covert LLP East Bldg Ste 204 17862 E Seventeenth St Tustin CA 92780-2164 E-mail: ffraft@comcast.com.

KRAFT, RICHARD LEE, lawyer; b. Lassa, Nigeria, Oct. 14, 1958; m. Tanya Kraft, July 14, 1984; children: Devin, Kelsey. BA in Fgn. Svc., Baylor U., 1980, JD, 1982. Bar: N.Mex. 1982, U.S. Dist. Ct. N.Mex., U.S. Ct. Appeals, U.S. Supreme Ct. Assoc. Sanders, Bruin & Baldock, Roswell, N.Mex., 1982-87, ptnr., 1987-98, Kraft & Stone, LLP, Roswell, 1998-2000; owner The Kraft Law Firm, 2000—. Vol. lawyer Ea. N.Mex. U. Roswell, 1984-98; bd. dirs. Roswell YMCA, 1983-87, Crimestopper, 1991-94; pres. Roswell Mens Ch. Basketball League; participant Roswell Mens Ch. Softball League; asst. chair legal div. United Way Drive, 1990. Recipient Outstanding Contribution award N.Mex. State Bar, 1987. Mem. ABA, N.Mex. Trial Lawyers Assn., N.Mex. Bar Assn. (bd. dirs. young lawyers div. 1983-91, pres. 1986-87, chmn. membership com., bar commr. 1986-87, 91—, pres. 1998-99, Outstanding Young Lawyer award 1990), Chaves County Bar Assn. (chair law day activities, chair ann. summer picnic com., rep. bench and bar com.), Roswell Legal Secs. Assn. (hon.), Roswell C. of C. (participant and pres. Leadership Roswell, exec. dir., bd. dirs. 1991-), Sertoma (bd. dirs. Roswell club 1989-91). Baptist. General civil litigation, Family and matrimonial, Personal injury (including property damage). Office: The Kraft Law Firm 111 W Third St Roswell NM 88201-4783 E-mail: thekraftlawfirm@aol.com.

KRAFT, ROBERT MORRIS, lawyer; b. Seattle, Sept. 17, 1954; s. Harry Jay and Leatrice Mae Kraft; m. Lori Sue Kraft, Nov. 9, 1985. BA in Bus. Adminstrn., U. Puget Sound, 1976, JD, 1980. Bar: Wash. 1980. Shareholder Levinson Friedman, P.S. and predecessor firm, Seattle. Mem. Wash. State Bar Assn., Wash. State Trial Lawyers Assn. Admiralty, Personal injury (including property damage), Product liability. Office: Levinson Friedman PS Ste 1800 720 3rd Ave Seattle WA 98104-1845 E-mail: rmk@admiralty.com.

KRAHMER, DONALD LEROY, JR., lawyer; b. Hillsboro, Oreg., Nov. 11, 1957; s. Donald L. and Joan Elizabeth (Karns) Krahmer; m. Suzanne M. Blanchard, Aug. 16, 1986; children: Hillary, Zachary. BS, Willamette U., 1981, MBA, 1987, JD, 1987. Bar: Oreg. 1988, Wash. 2003. Fin. analyst U.S. Bancorp, Portland, 1977-87; intern U.S. Senator Mark Hatfield, 1978; legis. aide State Sen. Jeannette Hamby, Hillsboro, Oreg., 1981-83, State Rep. Delna Jones, Beaverton, Oreg., 1983; bus. analyst Pacificorp, Portland, 1987; mgr. mergers/acquisitions Pacificorp Fin. Svcs., Portland, 1988-89, dir., 1990; CEO, pres. Atkinson Group, Portland, 1991—2002; ptnr. Black Helterline, LLP, Portland, 1991—2001; shareholder Schwabe Williamson & Wyatt, P.C., Portland, 2002—. Bd. dirs. Self-Enhancement, Inc.; chmn. Willamette Forum; with Oreg. Entrepreneur Forum, 1993, chmn. adv. bd., 95, chmn. bd., 98; founder, co-chmn. Oreg. Emerging Bus. Initiative, 1997—, New Economy Coalition, 2001—; bd. dirs. Portland Bus. Alliance, 2001—; chmn. audit com., chmn. corp. gov. com. Pacific Continental Bank, 2003—; chmn. Oreg. Tech. Alliance. Treas. Com. to Re-Elect Jeannette Hamby, 1986; bd. dirs. fin. com., devel. com. Am. Diabetes Assn., Portland, 1990—96; founder Needle Bros., 1994; chmn. Atkinson Grad. Sch. Devel. Com., Salem, 1989—92; bd. visitors Coll. Law Willamette U., 1997—2002; adv. bd. Ctr. for Law and Entrepreneurship U. Oreg. Sch. Law, 1997—2002; founder Conf. of Entrepreneurship, Salem, 1984; chmn. Entrepreneurship Breakfast Forum, Portland, 1993; chmn., founder Oreg. Conf. on Entrepreneurship and Awards Dinner, 1994—99, sr. v.p., 1999—; exec. com., bd. dirs. Cascade Pacific Coun. Boy Scouts Am., chmn. cmty. fund dir., 1997; chmn. Scoutrageous, 2000; vice-chmn. Gov.'s Coun. on Small Bus. State of Oreg.; mem. Gov.'s Econ. Devel. Joint Bds. Working Group, 1999—2002; co-chair Com. for Oreg.'s Future, 2002; steering com. Oreg. Opportunity; tech. advisor Oreg. Coun. on Knowledge and Econ. Devel., 2002—; mem. Greater Portland Innovation Network; mem. ch. coun. Our Savior Luth. Ch., 2000—01. Named one of Top 50 Leaders to Watch, Oreg. Bus. Mag., 2003; recipient Pub.'s award, 1987, Founders award, Willamette U., 1987, award, Scripps Found., 1980, 40 Under 40 award, Bus. Jour., 1996. Mem.: RAINS, ABA, Orgn. Tech. Alliance, Micro2Nano Collaborative, Am. Electronics Assn. (orgn. coun.), Portland Soc. Fin. Analysts, Multnomah County Bar Assn., Software Assn. of Oreg., Oreg. Biotech. Assn., Japan-Am. Soc. Oreg., Oreg. Biosci. Assn., Oreg. Bar Assn. (sec. 1998, chmn. 1999, chmn. exec. com., fin. instns. com. sec., exec. com., bus. law sect., Pres.'s award 1999, James B. Castles Leadership award 2002), Assn. for Corp. Growth, Assn. Investment Mgmt. and Rsch., Arlington Club (treas. 2002, bd. dirs., 1st v.p. 2003), Multnomah Athletic Club, City Club. Republican. Lutheran. Corporate, general, Mergers and acquisitions, Securities. Home: 16230 SW Copper Creek Dr Portland OR 97224-6500 Office: Schwabe Williamson & Wyatt 1211 SW 5th Ave Ste 1800 Portland OR 97204-3718

KRAKOWSKI, RICHARD JOHN, lawyer, public relations executive; b. Meppen, Fed. Republic of Germany, Apr. 3, 1946; came to U.S., 1951, naturalized, 1962; s. Feliks and Maria (Chilinski) K. MBA, DePaul U., 1979; JD, John Marshall Law Sch., 1983. Bar: Ill. 1984. Personnel dir. Andy Frain, Inc., Chgo., 1973-78; pub. rels. dir. Chgo. Health Sys. Agy., 1978-84; assoc. firm Mangum, Smietanka & Johnson, Chgo., 1984-87; asst. atty. gen. Ill. Atty. Gen.'s Ofc., 1987-96. Bd. dirs., St. Mary of Nazareth Hosp., Holy Trinity H.S.; lectr. in field. Co-author: Health Care Financing and Policy Making in Chicago and Illinois, 1982. Fundraising and pub. rels. dir. Cabrini-Green Sandlot Tennis Program, Chgo., 1979-83; sustaining mem. Rep. Nat. Com., 1981—; bd. dirs. Internat. Latino Cultural Ctr. Capt. U.S. Army, 1969-72. Mem. ABA, Nat. Advocates Soc., Ill. Bar Assn., Chgo. Bar Assn., Chgo. Coun. Fgn. Rels., Lyric Opera Guild, Art Inst. Chgo., Chgo. Soc. Polish Nat. Alliance, Publicity Club (Chgo.). Roman Catholic. Home: 1350 N Lake Shore Dr Apt 1215 Chicago IL 60610-5143 Office: Cook County Human Resources Divsn 118 N Clark St Ste 824 Chicago IL 60602-1312 E-mail: rjkrak1350@hotmail.com.

KRAM, RICHARD COREY, lawyer; b. N.Y.C., Oct. 8, 1942; BA in Polit. Sci., Syracuse U., 1964, MA in Polit. Sci., 1972, JD, 1973. Bar: N.Y. 1975, U.S. Dist. Ct. (no. dist.) N.Y. 1975, U.S. Ct. Appeals (2d cir.) 1980, U.S. Supreme Ct. 1982. Assoc. Nottingham Law Firm, Syracuse, N.Y., 1975-76; sole practice Syracuse, 1976—. Adj. prof. law Syracuse U., 1987-88, 89-90. Mem. Syracuse James Joyce Soc., 1996—. Fellow Am. Acad. Matrimonial Lawyers (N.Y. chpt. bd. mgr. 1993-97, 99-2001, v.p. 1997-98), Onondaga County Bar Assn. (bd. dirs. 1984-88, chair family law com. 1997-98). Avocations: reading, aerobics, bicycling, nordic skiing. Family and matrimonial, General practice. Office: 120 E Washington St Syracuse NY 13202-4000

KRAMER, ALAN SHARFSIN, lawyer; b. N.Y.C., Apr. 28, 1934; s. Michael and Alene (Sharfsin) K. BA, Dickinson Coll., 1956; LL.B., Columbia, 1962, JD, 1969. Bar: N.Y. 1962. Practice in, N.Y.C., 1962-69, 73—; sr. v.p. Am. Medicorp, Inc., N.Y.C., 1969-72; individual practice, 1974-78; pres. Alan S. Kramer (p.c.), 1978—; sr. mng. dir. Bear, Stearns & Co., Inc., 1990-96. Editor: Columbia Law Rev, 1960-62. Mem. nat. council Salk Inst. Served with M.I. AUS, 1956-58. Mem. Assn. of Bar of City of N.Y. Finance, Insurance, Securities. Home: 315 E 86th St New York NY 10028-4714 Office: 780 3d Ave 16th Fl New York NY 10017

KRAMER, DANIEL JONATHAN, lawyer; b. Cin., Dec. 20, 1957; s. Milton and Fradie (Ehrlich) K.; m. Judith L. Mogul; children: Ilona, Hannah, Joshua. BA magna cum laude, Wesleyan U., Middletown, Conn., 1980; JD, NYU, 1984. Bar: N.Y. 1985, U.S. Dist. Ct. (so. and ea. dists.) N.Y. 1985, U.S. Ct. Appeals (2d cir.) 1989. Assoc. Cravath, Swaine & Moore, N.Y.C., 1985-86; law clk. to Chief Judge Wilfred Feinberg, U.S. Ct. Appeals for 2d Cir., N.Y.C., 1986-87; assoc. Schulte Roth & Zabel LLP, N.Y.C., 1987-92, ptnr., 1993—2002, Paul, Weiss, Rifkind, Wharton & Garrison, LLP, N.Y.C., 2002—. Mem. pro se discretionary panel U.S. Ct. Appeals for 2d Cir., 1988—. Author: Federal Securities Litigation: Commentary and Forms, A Deskbook for the Practitioner, 1997, Regulation of Market Manipulation, Federal Securities Exchange Act of 1934, 2002; contbr. articles to law jours. and newspaper. Bd. dirs. Leukemia Soc., N.Y.C., 1995-98; Big Apple Greeter, 2001—. Mem. ABA, Assn. Bar City N.Y., N.Y. Lawyers for Pub. Interest. Federal civil litigation, Professional liability, Securities. Office: Paul Weiss Rifkind Wharton & Garrison LLP 1285 Avenue of the Ams New York NY 10019

KRAMER, DONALD BURTON, lawyer; b. St. Louis, Oct. 21, 1928; s. Allen Samuel and Mae (Sachar) K.; m. Elaine Ruth Phillips, Sept. 7, 1952; children: Jeffrey Scott, Janet Sue. BBA, Wash. U., St. Louis, 1950, JD, 1952. Bar: Mo., 1952. Assoc. Kramer & Chused, St. Louis, 1954-60; ptnr. Kramer, Chused & Kramer, St. Louis, 1960-73; owner Kramer and Frank, St. Louis, 1974-86; pres. Kramer and Frank, P.C., St. Louis, 1987—, Attorneyfind Internet Dir., 1997—. Author: Mastering Commercial Collections, 1991; contbr. articles to profl. jours. Cpl. U.S. Army, 1952-54. Named Outstanding Trustee, Zeta Beta Tau, 1970. Mem. Bar Assn. Met. St. Louis, Mo. Bar Assn. (chmn. com. unauthorized practice of law 1969-73), Comml. Law League Am. (co-chmn. bankruptcy com. 1977-78, chmn. nominating com., 1985-86, chmn. midwest dist., 1982-83, practices com. fair debt collection 1986-88), Nat. Assn. Retail Collection Attys. (founder, pres. 1993-95). Commercial, consumer (including collections, credit). Office: Kramer & Frank PC 9300 Dielman Industrial Saint Louis MO 63132-3080 E-mail: dkramer@lawusa.com.

KRAMER, EDWARD GEORGE, lawyer; b. Cleve., July 15, 1950; s. Archibald Charles and Katherine Faith (Porter) K.; m. Roberta Darwin, June 15, 1974. BS in Edn., Kent State U., 1972; JD, Case Western Res. U., 1975. Bar: Ohio 1975, U.S. Dist. Ct. (no. dist.) Ohio 1975, U.S. Ct. Appeals (6th cir.) 1980, U.S. Supreme Ct. 1980. Assoc. dir. The Cuyahoga Plan of Ohio, Cleve., 1975-76; exec. dir. The Housing Advs., Inc., Cleve., 1976—; sr. ptnr. Kramer & Assocs., LPA, Cleve., 1981—. Spl. counsel atty. gen. State of Ohio, Columbus, 1983-95; pres. Atty. Svcs., Inc., 1987-2002, ASI Info. Sys.; dir. Housing Law Clinic, 1989-95; dir. Fair Housing Law Clinic, 1995—; adj. lectr. Cleve. State U., 1991-94, adj. prof., 1994—; alt. consumer rep., FTC, Washington, 1976-77; cons. HUD, Washington, 1978-80, joint select com. sch. desegregation, Ohio Gen. Assembly, Columbus, 1979; visitors com., Case Western Res. U. Sch. Law, Cleve., 1977-83; chmn. Ford Motor Consumer Appeals Bd., 1989-93; bd. advisors Brownstone Pub. Author: How to Settle Small Claims: A Guide to The Use of Small Claims Courts, 1973, (with others) A Guide to Regional Housing Opportunities, 1979, (with Buchanan) Mobile Home Living: A Guide to Consumers' Rights, 1979; contbr. articles to legal jours. Chmn. Ohio Protection and Advocacy System for Developmentally Disabled, Columbus, 1978-80; trustee Muscle Disease Soc., Cleve., 1979-81; sec. Cuyahoga County Housing and Econ. Devel. com., Cleve., 1983—; mem. Cleve. Mayor's Com. on Employment of Handicapped, 1978-79; mem. fair housing adv. bd. John Marshall Law Sch. Named Disting. Recent Grad. Case Western Reserve U. Law Alumni Assn., 1985; Roscoe Pound fellow; recipient Fair Housing Pioneer Award Cuy County Commisioners, 2001. Mem.: ATLA (chair 2001—02, employment rights sect. chair 2001—02, chair sections leaders coun. 2002—03, chair-elect civil rights sect. 2003—, newsletter editor), ACLU (litigation com.), ABA (sect. on urban state and local govt. law, com. on housing and urban devel., forum on constrn. industry), Trial Lawyers for Pub. Justice, Am. Arbitration Assn., Ohio State Bar Assn., Million Dollar Adv. Forum, Planetary Soc., Assn. Am. Law Schs. (com. on clin. legal edn.), Nat. Employment Lawyers Assn., Cleve. Bar Assn. (trustee 1995—98, com. on homeless, chmn. law sch. liaison), Am. Coll. Barristers (life), Masons (Tyrian worshipful master 1989, 1991), Old River Yacht Club, Palm Beach Club (London), Cleve. Grays, Order of Ea. Star (James A. Garfield chpt.). Democrat. Mem. United Ch. Christ. Avocations: softball, scuba diving, collecting coins and stamps, chess, reading. Civil rights, Federal civil litigation, Labor (including EEOC, Fair Labor Standards Act, labor-management relations, NLRB, OSHA). Office: Kramer & Assocs LPA 3214 Prospect Ave E Cleveland OH 44115-2614

KRAMER, EUGENE LEO, lawyer; b. Barberton, Ohio, Nov. 7, 1939; s. Frank L. and Portia I. (Acker) Kramer; m. JoAnn Stockhausen, Sept. 19, 1970; children: Martin, Caroline, Michael. AB, John Carroll U., 1961; JD, U. Notre Dame, 1964. Bar: Ohio 1964. Law clk. U.S. Ct. Appeals (7th cir.), Chgo., 1964-65; ptnr. Squire, Sanders & Dempsey, Cleve., 1965-91, Roetzel & Andress, A Legal Profl. Assn., Cleve. and Akron, Ohio, 1992-97. Cons. Ohio Constl. Revision Commn., Columbus, 1970—74. Trustee Regina Health Ctr., 1997—, pres., 2001—; past pres. HELP Found., Inc., HELP, Inc., Cleve., 1981—92, Playhouse Sq. Assn., Cleve., 1980—84; pres. N.E. Ohio Transit Coalition, 1992—; mem. policy com. Build-Up Greater Cleve. Program, 1982—98; mem. Greater Cleve. Growth Assn.; trustee Consultation Ctr. Diocese Cleve., 1990—96, Citizens League Greater Cleve., 1984—90, 1993—, Citizens League Rsch. Inst., 1995—97, St. Ann Found., 1990—92, Lyric Opera Cleve., 1995—. Recipient Disting. Leadership award, HELP, Inc., 1986, Pioneer Achievement award, HELP-Six Chimneys, Inc., 1986, Disting. Svc. award, Assn. Retarded Citizens, 1990, Vol. Svc. award, City of Lakewood, 2001. Mem.: ABA, Cleve. Bar Assn., Ohio State Bar Assn. (chmn. local govt. law com. 1986—90), Club Key Tower. Democrat. Roman Catholic. Avocations: music, theater, sports, travel. Municipal (including bonds), State and local taxation. Home and Office: 1422 Euclid Ave Ste 706 Cleveland OH 44115-2001

KRAMER, GARY P. judge; b. Pontiac, Ill., Aug. 14, 1947; s. John Vincent and Dorothy Maxine Kramer; m. Alice Lee Childress, Jan. 17, 1971; children: John Lloyd, Robin Marie, Daniel Paul. BA, Carleton Coll., 1969; JD, Washington U., 1972. Bar: Mo., U.S. Dist. Ct. (we. dist.) Mo. 1972, U.S. Dist. Ct. (ea. dist.) Mo. 1973, U.S. Supreme Ct. 1977. Asst. pros. atty. St. Louis County, Clayton, Mo., 1972; assoc. Bahn & Saitz Law Firm, St. Louis, 1972—74; asst. pros. atty. Jefferson County, Hillsboro, Mo., 1972—74; prosecutor Village of Wilbur Park, Mo., 1972—74; from assoc. to ptnr. Law Office of Branson Hollingsworth, Hillsboro, 1974—82; assoc. cir. judge 23rd Jud. Cir., Hillsboro, 1983—90, cir. judge divsn. 2, 0991—. Faculty advisor Nat. Jud. Coll., Reno, 1992, faculty mem., 93. Recipient Equal Justice award, Legal Svcs. Ea. Mo., 1990. Mem.: Mo. Assn. Probate and Assoc. Cir. Judges (bd. dirs. 1986—91). Democrat. Avocations: golf, landscape gardening, skiing. Office: 23rd Jud Cir PO Box 100 Hillsboro MO 63050

KRAMER, GEORGE P. lawyer; b. Holyoke, Mass., Feb. 22, 1927; m. Elizabeth M. Truax, Oct. 13, 1973; children: Alice S. Truax, R. Hawley Truax, Charles W. Truax. AB, Harvard U., 1950, LL.B., 1953; Cert., Sorbonne, 1948. Bar: N.Y. 1954. Assoc. Watson Leavenworth Kelton & Taggart, N.Y.C., 1953-59, partner, 1960-65, Conboy, Hewitt, O'Brien & Boardman, N.Y.C., 1965-86, Hunton & Williams (merger Conboy, Hewitt, O'Brien & Boardman), N.Y.C., 1986—. Lectr. Practising Law Inst.; bd. dirs. Burleson Corp.; mem. vis. com. Peabody Mus. of Harvard U., 1974-80; mem. N.Y. Cotton Exch., N.Y. Bd. Trade. Author: Misleading Trademarks and Consumer Protection. Trustee Hancock Shaker Village, 1982—; trustee Harvard U. Law Sch. Assn. of N.Y., 1985-87, v.p. 1987-89. Served to lt. USNR, 1945-46. Recipient Congl. Antarctic medal, 1977 Mem. ABA, Internat. Bar Assn., Assn. Bar City N.Y. (sec. 1963-65, exec. com. 1970-74, chmn. various coms.), Am. Law Inst., Internat. Trademark Assn. (dir. 1975-78), Assn. Internationale pour la Protection de la Propriete Industrielle, Harvard U. Alumni Assn. (bd. dirs. 1983-89), Mass. Speleological Soc. (pres.), Antarctican Soc., Am. Polar Soc., Century Assn., Harvard Club (sec. 1972-83, 88-90, bd. mgrs. 1983-86), Harvard Faculty Club. Trademark and copyright, Intellectual property. Home: 151 E 79th St New York NY 10021-0417 Office: Hunton & Williams 200 Park Ave Fl 43 New York NY 10166-0005

KRAMER, KENNETH BENTLEY, federal judge, former congressman; b. Chgo., Feb. 19, 1942; s. Albert Aaron and Ruth (Pokrass) K.; m. Louise Kramer; children: Kenneth Bentley, Kelly J. BA magna cum laude in Polit. Sci., U. Ill., 1963; JD, Harvard U., 1966. Bar: Ill. 1966, Colo. 1969. Dep. dist. atty. El Paso County, Colo., 1970-72; pvt. practice law Colorado Springs, 1972-78; mem. Colo. Ho. of Reps., 1973-78, 96th-99th Congresses from 5th Colo. Dist., 1978-86; asst. sec. Dept. Army, Washington, 1988-89; judge U.S. Ct. of Appeals for Vets. Claims, Washington, 1989-2000, chief judge, 2000—. Chmn. com. on vets. benefits ABA, 1990-94. Bd. visitors U.S. Air Force Acad., 1979-86; bd. dirs. Pikes Peak Mental Health Ctr., 1976-78, Mountain Valley chpt. March of Dimes, 1983-85, U.S. Space Found., 1983—; founder U.S. Space Found.; commr. Nat. Coun. on Uniform State Laws, 1977-78. Capt. U.S. Army, 1967-70. Recipient Disting. Civilian Svc. medal. Mem. Phi Beta Kappa. Office: US Ct Appeals for Vets Claims 625 Indiana Ave NW Ste 900 Washington DC 20004-2923

KRAMER, PAUL R. lawyer; b. Balt., June 6, 1936; s. Phillip and Lee (Labovitz) K.; m. Janet Amitin, Sept. 1, 1957; children: Jayne, Susan, Nancy. BA, Am. U., 1959, JD, 1961. Bar: Md. 1961, D.C. 1962, U.S. Supreme Ct. 1965, U.S. Ct. Appeals (6th cir.) 1992, U.S. Dist. Ct. 1963, U.S. Ct. Appeals (4th cir.) 1964, U.S. Ct. Appeals (9th cir.) 1996. Staff atty., dep. dir. Legal Aid Agy. Fed. Pub. Defender's Office, Washington, 1962-63; asst. U.S. atty. Dist. Md., 1963-69; dep. U.S. atty. Md. Balt., 1969-83; exec. bd. Balt. area coun. Boy Scouts Am., 1970-83, exec. bd., 1983—, mem. N.E. regional adv. bd., 1999—. Instr. U. Md. Sch. Law, 1975-80; assoc. prof. law Villa Julie Coll., 1976-80; assoc. professorial lectr. George Washington U., 1979; instr. Nat. Coll. Dist. Attys., 1979; permanent mem. 4th cir. fed. jud. conf. Mem. ABA, Fed. Bar Assn. (pres. Md. chpt. 1973-74, nat. dep. sec. 1981-82, nat. sec. 1982-83, nat. cir. v.p. 1973-81, 86-87, cir. officer 4th cir. 1992-93, v.p. 4th cir. 1996-02, chmn. nat. cir. v.p. 1978-80, nat. coun. 1973—, jud. selection com. 1971-79, 88—, faculty Fed Practice Inst. 1981-86, strategic long range planning com. 1995-96), Md. Bar Assn. (subcom. litig. dist. ct. 1990—), Balt. Bar Assn. (jud. selection com. 1992—, chair judiciary sub-com. on policy 1993-94, chair criminal law com. 1994-95, grievance commn. Md. 1993—, drug ct. com. 1994-95, dist. ct. com. 1990—), Nat. Assn. Criminal Trial Attys., Md. Trial Lawyers Assn., Md. Criminal Def. Atty.'s Assn., U.S. Atty. Alumni Assn. (bd. dirs. 2003), Masons (past master). Federal civil litigation, State civil litigation, Criminal. Office: Jefferson Bldg 101 North Charles St #700 Baltimore MD 21201-3342

KRAMER, PHILIP JOSEPH, lawyer; b. Binghamton, N.Y., May 1, 1936; s. Donald W. and Gladys M. (Dorion) K.; m. Barbara E. Fisher, July, 1960; children: Perry, Donald, Matthew, Sharon. BA, Yale U., 1958; LLB, Cornell U., 1961. Bar: N.Y. 1961, U.S. Dist. Ct. (no. dist.) N.Y. 1961. Assoc. Kramer, Wales & Robinson, Binghamton, 1961-64, ptnr., 1964-78; justice, 6th Jud. Dist. N.Y. Supreme Ct., 1978; ptnr. Kramer, Wales & McAvoy, Binghamton, 1979-84, Kramer, Wales & Wright, Binghamton, 1984-95, Kramer & Kenyon, 1996-98; spl. counsel Hinman, Howard & Kattell. Pres. Binghamton Local Devel. Agy., 1982-87. Fellow Am. Coll. Trial Lawyers; mem. N.Y. State Bar Assn., Broome County Bar Assn. (pres. 1982). Democrat. Roman Catholic. Avocations: fishing, hunting. General civil litigation, Environmental, Personal injury (including property damage). Office: 700 Security Mut Bldg 80 Exchange St PO Box 5250 Binghamton NY 13902-5250 Fax: (607) 723-6605. E-mail: pkramer@hhk.com.

KRAMER, WILLIAM DAVID, lawyer; b. Anniston, Ala., Feb. 2, 1944; s. John Robert and Janice Marian (Dye) K.; m. Johanna Scalzi, Dec. 1, 1973; children: Elizabeth Annemarie, David MacLaren. Student, Case Western Res. U., 1959-60; AB in Govt. with honors magna cum laude, Oberlin Coll., 1965; JD, M in Pub. Adminstrn., Harvard U., 1969. Bar: Mass. 1969, D.C. 1973, U.S. Ct. Appeals (D.C. cir.) 1974, U.S. Dist. Ct. D.C. 1976, U.S. Ct. Appeals (10th cir.) 1978, U.S. Ct. Internat. Trade 1983, U.S. Ct. Appeals (fed. cir.) 1983. Assoc. dir. Gov.'s Com. on Law Enforcement and Adminstrn. Criminal Justice, Boston, 1969-71, dep. dir., 1971-73; assoc. Squire, Sanders & Dempsey, Washington, 1973-79, ptnr., 1979-92, Baker Botts LLP, Washington, 1992-2000; mem. Verner, Liipfert, Bernhard, McPherson and Hand, Chartered, Washington, 2000—02; ptnr. Piper Rudnick LLP, 2002—. Mem. internat. law sect. D.C. Bar. Chmn. bd. dirs. Children's Chorus of Washington, 1995-97, mem. adv. bd., 1997—. Mem. Phi Beta Kappa. Administrative and regulatory, Private international, Legislative. Home: 3512 Leland St Chevy Chase MD 20815-3904 Office: Piper Rudnick LLP 901 15th St NW Washington DC 20005-2301 Fax: 202-371-6279. E-mail: bill.kramer@piperrudnick.com.

KRAMPEN, INGO, lawyer, notary, mediator; b. Witten, Germany, Sept. 28, 1950; s. Wilhelm and Lore (Krumm) K.; m. Christiane L. Krampen, Aug. 11, 1972; children: Saskia G., Anja M., Laura L., Christoph M. Degree in law, Ruhr U., Bochum, Germany, 1975, Landesprufungsamt, Düsseldorf, Germany, 1978. Law pvt. practice, Bochum, 1978—; notary, 1991—; mediator, 2000—; supervisory bd. Gemeinnützige Treuhanstelle E.V., 2000—, also bd. dirs., 1977—99; chmn. supervisory bd. Hannoversche Kassen Wag, 1995—. Cons. GLS Gemeinschaftsbang e.G., Bochum,

1980—, Corp. Waldorf Schs. Nordrhein-Westflen, Germany, 1983—. Co-editor: Self-governed Schools, 1992. Chmn. European Forum Freedom in Edn., 1989—. Mem. Anthroposophical Soc. Germany (bd. dirs. 1986-99), Deutscher Anwaltverein. Avocation: political activities. Office: Husemannplatz 3/4 D-44787 Bochum NRW Germany

KRANE, STEVEN CHARLES, lawyer; b. Far Rockaway, N.Y., Jan. 20, 1957; s. Harry and Gloria (Christle) K.; m. Faith Marston, Oct. 1, 1983; children: Elizabeth Jordan, Cameron Marston. BA, SUNY, Stony Brook, 1978; JD, NYU, 1981. Bar: N.Y. 1982, U.S. Dist. Ct. (so. and ea. dists.) N.Y. 1982, U.S. Ct. Appeals (2d and 6th cirs.) 1987, U.S. Supreme Ct. 1987, U.S. Ct. Appeals (1st and 3d cir.) 2000. Ptnr. Proskauer Rose LLP, N.Y.C.; law clk. to Assoc. Judge Judith S. Kaye N.Y. Ct. Appeals, N.Y.C. and Albany, 1984-85. Lectr. in law Columbia U. Sch. Law, N.Y.C., 1989-92; vis. prof. Ga. Inst. of Tech., 1994-96; mem. departmental disciplinary com. Appellate divsn. 1st Jud. dept. Supreme Ct. N.Y., 1996-2000, spl. trial counsel, 1991-93. Editor articles, NYU Jour. Internat. Law and Politics, 1980-81. Securities Inst. NYU fellow, 1980-81; recipient Vol. Counsel award Legal Aid Soc., 1984. Fellow Am. Bar Found. (chmn. N.Y. state), N.Y. Bar Found.; mem. ABA, N.Y. Bar Assn. (com. on stds. of atty. conduct, chmn. 1999-, com. on profl. ethics 1990-94, spl. com. to rev. the code of profl. responsibility 1992-95, chmn. 1995-99, vice chair spl. com. on future of profession 1997-2000, ho. of dels. 1996—, com. on mass disaster response 1997—, com. on multidisciplinary practice and legal profession 1998-99, exec. com. 1998-2003, mem.-at-large, exec. com. 1998-2000, spl. com. on law gov. firm structure and ops., vice chair 1999—2002, chair 2002-, pres. 2001-02, pres. com. on access to justice, co-chair 2000-01, spl. assn. ho. com. chair 2000-2001), Assn. of Bar of City of N.Y. (com. on profl. and jud. ethics 1990-93, chmn. 1993-96, sec 1985-88, com. on profl. responsibility, chmn. subcom. provision legal svcs. 1985-88, com. on fed. cts. 1996-99, com. Marden Meml. lecture 2000—, chmn. del. to N.Y. State Bar Assn. ho. dels. 1997-98, internat. security affairs 2001-03), Am. Law Inst., Federalist Soc. (profl. responsibility practice group exec. com. 1999—), Hist. Soc. Cts. of State of NY (trustee 2001—), Phi Beta Kappa, Pi Sigma Alpha. Republican. Avocations: military history, meteorology, boston red sox baseball. Federal civil litigation, Sports. Office: Proskauer Rose LLP 1585 Broadway 17th Fl New York NY 10036-8299 E-mail: skrane@proskauer.com.

KRANIS, MICHAEL DAVID, lawyer, judge; b. N.Y.C., Aug. 17, 1955; s. Herbert and Mildred (Swartz) K.; m. Patricia Ann Pagano, Sept. 29, 1989. BA, SUNY, Albany, 1977; JD, Union U., 1980. Bar: N.Y. 1981, U.S. Dist. Ct. (so. and ea. dists.) N.Y. 1983. Law clk. to hon. judge Robert C. William N.Y. Supreme Ct., Monticello, 1980-82; prin. Michael D. Kranis, P.C., Poughkeepsie, N.Y., 1982-88; ptnr. Coombs, Kranis & Wing, Poughkeepsie, 1988-94; sole practitioner Poughkeepsie, 1995—. Asst. corp. counsel City of Poughkeepsie, 1983-85, hearing officer, 1985—; adj. prof. D.C. C.C., Poughkeepsie, 1984-87; judge Town of Pleasant Valley, N.Y., 1988-97; gen. counsel Grace Smith House, Inc., Poughkeepsie, 1983-95; adj. prof. Marist Coll., 1993. Mem. exec. com. Dutchess County Rep. Com., Pleasant Valley, 1997-2000, 2001-, Jud. Nominating Com., Dutchess County, 1987, 97-2000; mem. D.C. Republican Com., 1985-87, 97—; mem. Pleasant Valley Planning Bd., 1984-86; bd. dirs., chmn., vice chmn. Task Force for Child Protection, Inc., 1992-2000; mem. bd. dirs. Dutchess County Econ. Devel. Corp., 1994-2003, Child Abuse Prevention Ctr., Inc., 1994-2003, Pleasant Valley Little League, v.p., 2002—, Child Abuse Prevention Ctr., 2002—; chmn. Town of Pleasant Valley Rep. Com., 2001—. Mem. N.Y. State Bar Assn. (ho. of dels.), Dutchess County Bar Assn. (pres. 1998-99, treas., v.p. 1996, pres.-elect 1997, chmn. fee dispute com., chmn. bar endowment, v.p.), Dutchess County Magistrates Assn., N.Y. State Magistrates Assn., Rotary (pres., bd. dirs. Pleasant Valley chpt. 1985-97, Paul Harris fellow 1987). Family and matrimonial, Personal injury (including property damage), Property, real (including real estate development, water). Office: 2 Jefferson Pl Poughkeepsie NY 12601

KRANITZ, THEODORE MITCHELL, lawyer; b. St. Joseph, Mo., May 27, 1922; s. Louis and Miriam (Saferstein) K.; m. Elaine Shirley Kaufman, June 11, 1944; children: Hugh David, Karen Gail and Kathy Jane (twins). Student, St. Joseph Jr. Coll., 1940-41; BS in Fgn. Svc., Georgetown U., 1948, JD, 1950. Bar: Mo. 1950, U.S. Supreme Ct. 1955. Pres., sr. ptnr. Kranitz & Kranitz, PC, St. Joseph, 1950—. Author articles in field Pres. St. Joseph Comty. Theatre, Inc., 1958-60; bd. dirs. United Jewish Fund St. Joseph, 1957—, pres., 1958-63; sec. Boys' Baseball St. Joseph, 1964-68; trustee Temple Adath Joseph, 1970-74, 77-80; bd. dirs. B'nai Sholem Temple, 1976—, Lyric Opera Guild Kansas City, 1980-91; founder, pres. St. Joseph Light Opera Co., Inc., 1989-90; mem. St. Joseph Postal Customers Adv. Coun., 1993—, chmn., 1993-95; mem., sec. St. Joseph Downtown Assn., 1995-97. Mem. Mo. Bar, St. Joseph Bar Assn. (pres. 1977-78), Am. Legion, Air Force Assn., B'nai B'rith (dist. bd. govs. 1958-61). Family and matrimonial, General practice, Personal injury (including property damage). Home: 2609 Gene Field Rd Saint Joseph MO 64506-1615 Office: Kranitz & Kranitz PC Boder Bldg 107 S 4th St PO Box 968 Saint Joseph MO 64502-0968 Fax: (816) 232-8558. E-mail: kranitz@ponyexpress.net.

KRANSELER, LAWRENCE MICHAEL, lawyer; b. Newton, Mass., Oct. 28, 1958; s. Arthur Sheldon and Barbara Joan (Siegel) K.; m. Wendy Kranseler; children: Alex, Jenna, Lucas. BS in Econs., Boston Coll., 1980; MBA, JD, U. Pa., 1984. Bar: Mass. 1985, U.S. Dist. Ct. Mass. 1985. Assoc. Hale and Dorr, Boston, 1984-89; supervising sr. counsel Hasbro, Inc., Pawtucket, R.I., 1989-95, mng. atty., 1995-2000; v.p. Hasbro Inc., Pawtucket, R.I., 2001—; v.p., sec. Hasbro Interactive, Inc., Pawtucket, 1997—2000. Vol. mentor UCAP Mentoring Program. Bd. dirs., treas., chmn. fin. com., mem. exec. com., vol. Big Brother/Big Sister Assn.; fundraising capt. Am. Heart Assn., Combined Jewish Philanthropies; coach Town of Sharon Baseball, Town of Sharon Soccer, Town of Sharon Basketball. Recipient James E. Shaw Meml. award Pres. Boston Coll., 1980. Mem. ABA, Mass. Bar Assn., Boston Bar Assn., Phi Delta Phi. Corporate, general, General practice, Mergers and acquisitions. Home: 30 Sentry Hill Rd Sharon MA 02067-1522 Office: Hasbro Inc 1027 Newport Ave Pawtucket RI 02861-2500 E-mail: LKranseler@hasbro.com.

KRAPP, FRANZJOSEPH, lawyer; b. Mainz, Germany, Apr. 27, 1931; D Pub. and Canon Law, U. Mainz, Speyer, and Inssbruck, Austria, 1956, D Polit. Sci., 1965. Barrister; specialized solicitor in tax law; dep. head Mainz (Germany) Police Dept., 1959-61; adminstrv. advisor, 1961-66; pvt. practice, 1967-71; adj. prof., 1976—. Hon. mem. U.S. Ct. Mil. Appeals, Washington, 1986—. Office: Moritzstr 59 55130 Mainz Germany

KRASNER, DANIEL WALTER, lawyer; b. N.Y.C., Mar. 18, 1941; s. Nathan and Rose Krasner; m. Ruth Pollack, Dec. 20, 1964; children: Jonathan, Lisa, Noah, Rebecca. BA, Yeshiva Coll., 1962; LLB, Yale U., 1965. Bar: N.Y. 1966, U.S. Dist. Ct. (so. dist.) N.Y. 1967, U.S. Dist. Ct. (ea. dist.) N.Y. 1968, U.S. Supreme Ct. 1978, U.S. Ct. Appeals (1st, 2d, 3d, 5th, 6th, 8th-11th dists.). Assoc. Pomerantz Levy Houdek & Block, N.Y.C., 1965-76; sr. ptnr. Wolf Haldenstein Adler Freeman & Herz, N.Y.C., 1977—. Vice chmn. Westchester Day Sch., Mamaroneck, N.Y., 1979-86; v.p., trustee Bd. Jewish Edn., N.Y.C., 1981—. Democrat. Avocations: tennis, golf, sailing. Federal civil litigation, Securities. Office: Wolf Haldenstein Adler Freeman & Herz 270 Madison Ave New York NY 10016-0601 E-mail: krasner@whafh.com.

KRASNOW, JORDAN PHILIP, lawyer; b. Malden, Mass., May 14, 1944; s. Louis and Roslyn (Packer) K.; children: Laura, Joshua, Abbey, Abigail. AB, Clark U., 1965; JD magna cum laude, Boston U., 1968. Bar: Mass. 1970. Law clk. to Presiding Justice Mass. Superior Ct., Boston, 1968-69; assoc. atty. Peabody & Arnold, Boston, 1969-71, Gaston Snow & Ely Bartlett, Boston, 1971-75, ptnr., 1975-86; officer, dir. Goulston & Storrs, Boston, 1986—; co-mng. dir., 1994-97. Lectr. Mass. Continuing Legal Edn., Boston, 1975-85; adv. com. Boston U. Real Estate Program, 1988—; charter mem. Greater Boston Real Estate Bd.-Real Estate Fin., 1989. Mem. Mayor's Adv. Com. Housing Linkage, Boston, 1984; mem. exec. com. Anti Defamation League New Eng.; trustee Roxbury Prep. Charter Sch. Recipient Disting. Achievement award B'nai B'rith Realty Unit, 1995. Fellow Mass. Bar Found.; mem. Mass. Bar Assn., Boston Bar Assn., B'nai Brith (trustee realty unit New Eng. chpt.). Jewish. Avocations: travel, sports. Finance, Land use and zoning (including planning), Property, real (including real estate development, water). Home: 94 Beacon St Apt 2 Boston MA 02108-3329 Office: Goulston & Storrs 400 Atlantic Ave Boston MA 02110-3333 E-mail: jkrasnow@goulstonstorrs.com.

KRASNOW, RICHARD P. lawyer; b. Bklyn., Feb. 12, 1947; s. Nathan A. and Doris (Pearson) K.; m. Nancy Meyrich, Oct. 3, 1982. AB, U. Chgo., 1968; JD, NYU, 1972. Assoc. Shereff, Friedman, Huffman & Goodman, N.Y.C., 1972-73; ptnr. Weil, Gotshal & Manges, N.Y.C., 1972—. Mem. ABA, N.Y. State Bar Assn., Assn. Bar City of N.Y. Bankruptcy. Office: Weil Gotshal & Manges 767 5th Ave Fl Concl New York NY 10153-0119

KRATOCHVIL, L(OUIS) GLEN, lawyer; b. Highland, Wis., Oct. 11, 1922; s. John A. and Emma (Pusch) K.; m. Evelyn Gregory, Sept. 12, 1946; 1 son, Louis Glen Jr. LLB, U. Wis., 1951; JD. Bar: Wis. 1951, Tex. 1952, U.S. Dist. Ct. (so. dist.) Tex. 1956, U.S. Ct. Appeals (5th cir.) 1956, U.S. Supreme Ct. 1956, U.S. Dist. Ct. (ea. dist.) Tex. 1961. Landman Shell Oil Co., Houston, 1951-52; assoc. firm Murphy & Crystal, Houston, 1953-55; asst. U.S. atty. So. Dist. Tex., 1955-57; pvt. practice Houston, 1957—99. Pres. McGregor Terr. Civic Club, Houston, 1954, Young Rep. Club U. Wis., 1950. Lt. USNR, 1941-46, PTO. Mem.: FBA, ABA, U. Wis. Alumni Assn. (pres. Houston chpt. 1972—73), Maritime Law Assn., Houston Bar Assn., Wis. Bar Assn., Tex. Bar Assn., Brazos River Club (treas. 1970—99), Lions (pres. 1955), Phi Alpha Delta (chief justice 1950). Admiralty. Home: 302 Kickerillo Dr Houston TX 77079-7412 Office: Kratochvil and Powell 3303 Main St Ste 207 Houston TX 77002-9321

KRAUS, ALAN EDWARD, lawyer; b. Orange, N.J., June 18, 1953; s. Edward W. and Elizabeth (Clark) K.; m. Mary Anne Kraus, July 24, 1976; children: Michael, Matthew. BA with honors, Wesleyan U., 1975; JD with high honors, U. N.C., 1978. Bar: N.Y. 1979, U.S. Dist. Ct. (so. and ea. dists.) N.Y. 1979, U. S. Ct. Appeals (2d cir.) 1984, (6th cir.) 1986, (3d cir.) 1989, N.J. 1986, U.S. Dist. Ct. N.J. 1986, U.S. Supreme Ct. 1990, U.S. Ct. Appeals (9th cir.) 1992. Assoc. Cravath, Swaine & Moore, N.Y.C., 1979-85; ptnr. Riker, Danzig, Scherer, Hyland & Perretti, Morristown, NJ, 1985—91, Latham & Watkins, Newark, 1991—. Mem. ABA, N.J. Bar Assn., Am. Coll. Trial Lawyers, Order of Coif. General civil litigation, Product liability, Securities. Office: Latham & Watkins 1 Newark Ctr 16th Fl Newark NJ 07101-3174

KRAUS, LESLIE JAY, lawyer; b. Bklyn., Sept. 6, 1943; s. George E. and Sylvia (Hornreich) K; adopted s. Bobbi (Needleman) K.; m. Susan J. Rosenthal, Dec. 21, 1968; 1 child, Erica. BS, Northeastern U., Boston, 1966; JD, Suffolk U., 1969. Bar: Mass. 1969. Assoc. Cohn, Riemer & Pollack, Boston, 1970; atty. estate tax IRS, Bridgeport, Conn., 1970-71; field atty. NLRB, Mpls., 1971-76; v.p. Indsl. Rels. Assocs., Mpls., 1976-82; pres. Leslie J. Kraus & Assocs., Inc., Edina, Minn., 1982—. Instr. U. Minn., Mpls., 1977-94. Co-chmn. YWCA Parent Coun., Mpls., 1985-86; vice chmn. Lake Fellowship of Unitarian Universalists, Excelsior, Minn., 1986-87, chmn. 1987-89, social action chair 1990—; mem. Southview Mid. Sch. Site Coun., 1993-97, chair, 1994. Mem. ABA (labor law sect.), Mass. Bar Assn., Northwest Athletic Club. Unitarian Universalist/Jewish. Labor (including EEOC, Fair Labor Standards Act, labor-management relations, NLRB, OSHA). Office: Leslie J Kraus & Assocs Inc 4375 Thielen Ave Minneapolis MN 55436-1522 E-mail: leskraus@aol.com.

KRAUS, PETER LEO, librarian, educator; b. Mineola, N.Y., June 18, 1968; s. Leo Emil Kraus and Barbara Luise (Hausser) Kessler; m. Kristin Louise Borden, July 22, 1995. BA in History, Fla. State U., 1991, MS in Library Sci., 1993. Rsch. asst. Ctr. for Local Govt. U. North Fla., Jacksonville, 1991-92; libr. N.Y. Pub. Libr., N.Y.C., 1994-99; asst. libr. Marriott Libr., U. Utah, Salt Lake City, 1999—2003, asst. libr. Technology Assisted Curriculum Ctr., 2003—. Adj. instr. Salt Lake City C.C., 2002—. Mem. ALA, Am. Assn. Coll. and Rsch. Librs., Spl. Librs. Assn., Utah Libr. Assn., Mountain Plains Libr. Assn., We. Assn. Map Librs., Utah Mus. Assn., Utah Hist. Soc. Office: U Utah Marriott Libr Dept Documents & Microforms 295 S 1500 E Salt Lake City UT 84112 E-mail: peter.kraus@library.utah.edu.

KRAUS, SHERRY STOKES, lawyer; b. Richmond, Ky., Aug. 11, 1945; d. Thomas Alexander and Callie (Ratliff) Stokes; m. Eugene John Kraus, Aug. 27, 1966. Student, U. Ky., 1962-64; BS, Roosevelt U., 1966; JD cum laude, Albany Law Sch., 1975; LLM in Taxation, NYU, 1981. Bar: N.Y. 1976, U.S. Dist. Ct. (we. dist.) N.Y. 1976, U.S. Tax Ct. 1986. Law clk. U.S. Tax Ct., Washington, summer 1974; law clk. 4th dept. appellate divsn. N.Y. State Supreme Ct., Rochester, 1975-77; assoc. Nixon, Hargrave, Devans & Doyle, Rochester, 1977-81, 83-84, Harter, Secrest & Emery, Rochester, 1984-86; pvt. practice Rochester, 1986—. Faculty grad. tax program Sch. Law, NYU, N.Y.C., 1981-82; prin. tech. adv. to assoc. chief counsel - tech. IRS, Washington, 1983-84; mem. N.Y. State Tax Appeals Adv. Panel on Practice & Procedure, 1998—. Articles editor ABA Tax Articles Periodical, The Tax Lawyer, 1984-88; mng. editor NYU Tax Articles Periodical, NYU Tax Law Rev., 1981-82; lead articles editor Tax Articles Periodical, Albany Law Rev., 1973-75; contbr. articles to profl. jours. David J. Brewer scholar Albany Law Sch., 1973. Mem. ABA, N.Y. State Bar Assn. (tax sect. exec. com. 1984—), Monroe County Bar Assn. (treas. 1990-92), Monroe County Bar Found. (pres. 1994-95), Justinian Soc. Avocations: watercolors, guitar, dulcimer. Corporate taxation, Taxation, general, Personal income taxation. Office: 513 Times Square Bldg Rochester NY 14614-2078 E-mail: sskraus@frontiernet.net.

KRAUS, STEVEN GARY, lawyer; b. Newark, Aug. 22, 1954; s. Leon Judah Kraus and Rose (Cohen) Turchin; m. Jane Susan Sukoneck, June 29, 1980; children: Adam. AB, Brandeis U., 1976; JD, Rutgers U., 1979. Bar: N.J. 1979, Pa. 1979, U.S. Dist. Ct. N.J. 1979, U.S. Supreme Ct. 2002. Jud. law sec. to assignment judge Charles A. Rizzi, Superior Ct. N.J., Camden, 1979-80; assoc. Kavesh & Basile, Vineland, N.J., 1980-81, Bennett & Bennett, West Orange, N.J., 1981-82; pvt. practice, Warren, N.J., 1982—. Mem. ABA, N.J. State Bar Assn., Nat. Assn. Subrogation Profls. State civil litigation, Insurance, Personal injury (including property damage). Home: 17 Regent Cir Basking Ridge NJ 07920-1900 Office: 122 Mount Bethel Rd Warren NJ 07059-5127 E-mail: steven.kraus@subrogationlawyer.com.

KRAVITCH, PHYLLIS A. federal judge; b. Savannah, Ga., Aug. 23, 1920; d. Aaron and Ella (Wiseman) K.. BA, Goucher Coll., 1941; LLB, U. Pa., 1943; LLD (hon.) (hon.) , Goucher Coll., 1981, Emory U., 1998. Bar: Ga. 1943, U.S. Dist. Ct. 1944, U.S. Supreme Ct. 1948, U.S. Ct. Appeals (5th cir.) 1962. Practice law, Savannah, 1944—76; judge Superior Ct., Eastern Jud. Circuit of Ga., 1977—79, U.S. Ct. Appeals (5th cir.), Atlanta, 1979—81, U.S. Ct. Appeals (11th cir.), 1981—, sr. judge, 1996—. Mem. Jud. Conf. Standing Com. on Rules, 1994—2000. Trustee Inst. Continuing Legal Edn. in Ga., 1979—82; mem. Bd. Edn., Chatham County, Ga., 1949—55; mem. coun. Law Sch., Emory U., Atlanta, 1985—; mem. vis. com. Law Sch., U. Chgo., 1990—93; bd. visitors Ga. State U. Law Sch., 1994—; mem. regional rev. panel Truman Scholarship Found., 1993—2000; mem. vis. com. Goucher Coll., 2000—. Recipient Hannah G. Solomon award, Nat. Coun. Jewish Women, 1978, Trailblazer award, Greater Atlanta Hadassah, 2000, James Wilson award, U. Pa. Law Alumni Soc., 1992, Kathleen Kessler award, Ga. Assn. Women Lawyers, 2001, Shining Star award, Atlanta Women's Found., 2002. Fellow: Am. Bar Found.; mem.: ABA (Margaret Brent award 1991), Nat. Assn. Women Lawyers (Arabella Babb Mansfield award 1999), U. Pa. Law Soc., Am. Law Inst., Am. Judicature Soc. (Devitt award com. 1998—99), State Bar Ga., Savannah Bar Assn. (pres. 1976). Office: US Ct Appeals 11th Cir 56 Forsyth St NW # 202 Atlanta GA 30303-2205

KRAVITT, JASON HARRIS PAPERNO, lawyer; b. Chgo., Jan. 19, 1948; s. Jerome Julius and Shirley (Paperno) K.; m. Beverly Ray Niemeier, May 11, 1974; children: Nikola Wedding, Justin Taylor Paperno. AB, Johns Hopkins U., 1969; JD, Harvard U., 1972; diploma in comparative legal studies, Cambridge U., Eng., 1973. Bar: Ill. 1973, N.Y. 2002, U.S. Dist. Ct. (no. dist.) Ill. 1973, U.S. Dist. Ct. (so. dist.) N.Y. 2002. Assoc. Mayer, Brown Rowe & Maw (formerly Mayer, Brown & Platt), Chgo., 1973-78, ptnr., 1979—, co-chmn., 1998-2001. Adj. prof. law Northwestern U., Evanston, Ill., 1994—, adj. prof. fin. Kellogg Sch. Mgmt., 1998—; sec. and chair Legal Reg. Accounting and Tax Com. Editor: Securitization of Financial Assets, 2d edit., 1996. Bd. dirs. Chgo. Met. YMCA, 1998-2001, Mus. Contemporary Art, Chgo., 1974-75; dir., chmn. The Cameron Kravitt Found., 1984—; sec., chair legal, regulatory tax and acctg. com. Am. Securitization Forum. Fellow Am. Coll. Comml. Lawyers; mem. ABA, Chgo. Coun. Lawyers, Chgo. Bar Assn., N.Y. Bar Assn., Econ. Club of Chgo., Execs. Club Chgo. Banking, Commercial, contracts (including sales of goods; commercial financing), Securities. Home: 250 Sheridan Rd Glencoe IL 60022-1948 Office: Mayer Brown Rowe & Maw 190 S La Salle St Ste 3100 Chicago IL 60603-3441 E-mail: jkravitt@mayerbrownrowe.com.

KRAW, GEORGE MARTIN, lawyer, essayist; b. Oakland, Calif., June 17, 1949; s. George and Pauline Dorothy (Herceg) K.; m. Sarah Lee Kenyon, Sept. 3, 1983 (dec. Nov. 2001). BA, U. Calif., Santa Cruz, 1971; student, Lenin Inst., Moscow, 1971; MA, U. Calif., Berkeley, 1974, JD, 1976. Bar: Calif. 1976, U.S. Supreme Ct. 1980, D.C. 1992. Pvt. practice, 1976—; ptnr. Kraw & Kraw, San Jose, 1988—. Mem. adv. com. Pension Genefit Guaranty Corp., 2002—. Mem. ABA, Internat. Soc. Cert. Employee Benefit Specialists, Nat. Assn. Health Lawyers, Inter-Am. Bar Assn. Corporate, general, Private international, Pension, profit-sharing, and employee benefits. Office: Kraw & Kraw 333 W San Carlos St Ste 200 San Jose CA 95110-2735

KREBS, LEO FRANCIS, lawyer; b. Botkins, Ohio, June 9, 1937; s. Eugene L. and Velma L. K.; m. Paula Anne Calvert, Nov. 4, 1961; children: Matthew, Mark, Thomas, Peter. BA, U. Dayton, 1959; JD, Georgetown U., 1965. Bar: Ohio 1966, U.S. Dist. Ct. (so. dist.) Ohio 1966, U.S. Ct. Appeals (6th cir.) 1974, U.S. Supreme Ct. 1975. Legal dep. Montgomery Probate Ct., 1966-68; assoc. Bieser, Greer & Landis, Dayton, Ohio, 1968-74, ptnr., 1974—. Assoc. editor Georgetown Law Rev., 1964-65. Chmn. fin. com. Holy Angels, 1986-98, former chmn., bd. dirs. parish coun.; former bd. dirs. Cath. Social Svcs. Dayton, 1987-90; former mem. Oakwood YMCA Baseball Commn.; coach YMCA baseball. 1st lt. U.S. Army, 1959-62. Fellow Am. Coll. Trial Lawyers, Ohio State Bar Found.; mem. ABA, Ohio State Bar Assn., Ohio Assn. Trial Attys., Dayton Bar Assn., Phi Delta Phi. Avocations: hiking, tennis. General civil litigation, Personal injury (including property damage), Probate (including wills, trusts). Office: Bieser Greer & Landis 6 N Main St Ste 400 Dayton OH 45402-1914 E-mail: lfr@bgl.com.

KREBS, ROBERT ALAN, lawyer; b. Pitts., Dec. 12, 1958; s. James Arthur and Helen Marie (McGrogan) K.; m. Elizabeth Ann Bedford, Apr. 20, 1985; children: Stephen Vladimir, Diane Kathleen. BA, Pa. State U., 1981; student, U. Exeter, U.K., 1981; JD, Capital U., 1984. Bar: Pa. 1984, D.C. 1989, U.S. Dist. Ct. (ea. dist.) Pa. 1990, U.S. Dist. Ct. (we. dist.) Pa. 1984, U.S. Dist. Ct. (no. dist.) Ohio 1990, U.S. Dist. Ct. (D.C.) 1989, U.S. Ct. Appeals (D.C. cir.) 1989, U.S. Ct. Appeals (3d cir.) 1986, U.S. Supreme Ct. 1988. Assoc. Henderson & Goldberg, Pitts., 1985-87, Messer Shilobod & Crenney, Pitts., 1987-89, Klett Lieber Rooney & Schorling, Pitts., 1989-91, Conte, Melton & D'Antonio, Conway, Pa., 1992—2002, Morella & Assocs., Pitts., 2002—. Articles editor Capital Law Rev., 1983-84. Mem. Pa. Dem. State Com., 37th Dist., 1994-, Allegheny County Dem. Com., Pitts., 1991—; mem. com. on jud. issues Pa. Gov.-Elect Edward G. Rendell Transition Team, 2003; vol. Pitts-; mem. Pa. Workers Compensation Appeal Bd., 2003. Recipient Am. Jurisprudence award Lawyers Coop. Pub. Co., 1982. Mem. ABA, FBA, D.C. Bar Assn., Pa. Trial Lawyers Assn. (amicus curiae com. 1996--), Allegheny County Bar Assn. (fed. ct. sect. coun. 1996-99), Capital U. Law Sch. Alumni Assn. (bd. dirs. 1995-2001, v.p. 1996-2001), Western Pa. Trial Lawyers Assn. (bd. govs. 1994—, chair edn. com. 1994-95, co-chair pres.'s scholarship com. 2001-03, co-chair comeback award com. 2001-03). Democrat. Roman Catholic. Appellate, Commercial, consumer (including collections, credit), Personal injury (including property damage). Home: 3235 Comanche Rd Pittsburgh PA 15241-1138 Office: 8150 Perry Hwy Ste 100 Pittsburgh PA 15237 E-mail: kakrebs@morellalaw.com.

KREEK, LOUIS FRANCIS, JR., lawyer; b. Washington, Aug. 24, 1928; s. Louis F. and Esperance (Agee) K.; m. Gwendolyn Schoepfle, Sept. 12, 1970. BS, MIT, 1948; JD, George Washington U., 1952. Bar: D.C. 1952, U.S. Dist. Ct. D.C. 1952, U.S. Ct. Appeals (D.C. cir) 1952, Ohio 1955, N.Y. 1964, U.S. Dist. Ct. (so. and ea. dists.) N.Y. 1964, N.J. 1972. Patent examiner U.S. Patent Office, Washington, 1948-53; patent atty. Pitts. Plate Glass Co., 1953-54, Battelle Meml. Inst., Columbus, Ohio, 1954-56, Merck & Co., Inc., Rahway, N.J., 1956-60; divsn. patent counsel Air Reduction Co., Murray Hill, N.J., 1960-63; assoc. Kenyon & Kenyon, N.Y.C., 1963-66; patent atty. Johns-Manville Corp., Manville, N.J., 1967-68; sr. patent atty. Esso Rsch. and Enginrg. Co., Linden, N.J., 1968-73, ICI Ams. Inc, Wilmington, Del., 1973-85; assoc. Hahn Loeser & Parks LLP and predecessor firms, Akron, Ohio, 1985-94, of counsel, 1994—. Mem. ABA, Am. Intellectual Property Law Assn., N.Y. Intellectual Property Law Assn. (assoc.), Cleve. Intellectual Property Law Assn. (bd. dirs. 1991-92), Akron Bar Assn., MIT Alumni Assn. (bd. dirs. fund bd. 1977-80, officers conf. com. 1981-84, chmn. 1983), MIT Club Del. Valley (pres. 1978-80), MIT Club NE Ohio (pres. 1986-89), Am. Diabetes Assn. (bd. dirs. Akron chpt. 1989-90), Akron Roundtable (bd. dirs. 1989-90, 2001-02), Kiwanis (pres. 1989-90, 2001-02, lt. gov. 1992-93). Intellectual property, Patent, Trademark and copyright. Home: 2321 Stockbridge Rd Akron OH 44313-4512

KREGER, MELVIN JOSEPH, lawyer; b. Buffalo, Feb. 21, 1937; s. Philip and Bernice (Gerstman) K.; m. Patricia Anderson, July 1, 1955 (div. 1963), children: Beth Barbour, Arlene Roux; m. Renate Hochleitner, Aug. 15, 1975. JD, Mid-valley Coll. Law, 1978; LLM in Taxation, U. San Diego, 1988. Bar: Calif. 1978, U.S. Dist. Ct. (cen. dist.) Calif. 1979, U.S. Tax Ct. 1979, U.S. Supreme Ct. 1995; cert. specialist in probate law, trust law and estate planning law, taxation law, Calif. Life underwriter Met. Life Ins. Co., Buffalo, 1958-63; bus. mgr. M. Kreger Bus. Mgmt., Sherman Oaks, Calif., 1963-78, enrolled agt., 1971—; pvt. practice North Hollywood, Calif., 1978—. Mem. Nat. Assn. Enrolled Agts., Calif. Soc. Enrolled Agts., State Bar Calif., L.A. Bar Assn., San Fernando Valley Bar Assn. (probate sect., tax sect.). Jewish. Avocations: computers, travel. Estate planning, Probate (including wills, trusts), Taxation, general. Office: 11424 Burbank Blvd North Hollywood CA 91601-2301 E-mail: mel@meltaxlaw.com.

KREIDLER, FRANK ALLAN, lawyer; b. Cleve., Jan. 20, 1947; s. Emil J. and Dorothy M. K.; m. Mary Ann Kreidler, Oct. 4, 1980; children: Catherine Allison, James Fredrick, Kristine Anne, Kimberly Jaclyn. AA, Palm Beach Jr. Coll., Lake Worth, Fla., 1968; BS, Fla. State U., 1970, JD, 1973. Bar: Fla. 1973, U.S. Dist. Ct. (so. dist.) Fla. 1974, U.S. Tax Ct. 1974, U.S. Ct. Appeals (5th cir.) 1976, U.S. Supreme Ct. 1977, U. S. Ct. Mil.

Appeals 1977, U.S. Dist. Ct. (mid. dist.) Fla. 1981, U.S. Ct. Appeals (11th cir.) 1982, U.S. Ct. Fed. Claims 1994; diplomate Congress of Cert. Cir. Mediators. Asst. state atty. 15th Circuit, West Palm Beach, Fla., 1973-75, asst. pub. defender Belle Glade, Fla., 1976-78; pvt. practice Belle Glade, 1975-78; city atty. City of Lake Worth, Fla., 1978-82; gen. couns. Lake Worth Utilities Authority, 1980-85; pvt. practice Lake Worth, 1982—. Adj. prof. Fla. Atlantic U., Boca Raton, 1984—; mediator Supreme Ct. Fla., Tallahassee, 1989—, U.S. Dist. Ct. Trial Bar (so. dist.) Fla., Miami, 1982—. Chmn. human rights adv. com. Dist. 9 State of Fla., West Palm Beach, 1992-96; chmn. adv. bd. Palm Beach Kidney Assn., West Palm Beach, 1985-87; mem. Criminal Justice Commn. Corrections Task Force, 1995-97, Nat. Com. for Employer Support of Guard and Res., 1998—, Palm Beach County Emergency Shelter Grants Program adv. bd., 1997-2001; mem. adv. coun. Lake Worth H.S., 1998—. Comdr. USNR, 1977—. Recipient Cmty. Svc. award Palm Beach Blood Bank, 1979, Donor of Month award, 1991, Harriette Glasner Freedom award Pal Beach chpt. ACLU, 2000. Mem. ABA, Am. Arbitration Assn., Palm Beach County Seminole Boosters (bd. dirs. 1990—, Pres.' award 1998), Leadership Palm Beach, Naval Res. Assn. (pres. Palm Beach chpt. 1991—), Legal Aid Soc., Palm Beach County Bar Assn. (Human Rights Advocacy award 1995), Fla. Bar Assn. (Pro Bono Svc. award 1997). Avocation: 1967 chrysler. Administrative and regulatory, General civil litigation, Criminal. Office: 1124 S Federal Hwy Lake Worth FL 33460-5244 E-mail: faklaw@yahoo.com.

KREIG, ANDREW THOMAS, trade association executive; b. Chgo., Feb. 28, 1949; s. Albert Arthur and Margaret Theresa (Baltzell) K. AB, Cornell U., 1970; MSL, Yale U., 1983; JD, U. Chgo., 1990. Bar: D.C. 1991, Mass. 1991, Ill. 1991. Writer, editor Hartford (Conn.) Courant, 1970-84; media dir. Conn. House Spkr., Hartford, 1984; freelance author, journalist, lectr. Hartford and Chgo., 1985-89; law clk. U.S. Dist. Judge Mark L. Wolf, Boston, 1990-91; assoc. Latham & Watkins, Washington, 1991-93; v.p., comms. dir. Wireless Comms. Assn. Internat., Inc., Washington, 1993-96, v.p., gen. counsel, 1996, pres., CEO, 1997—. Ethics com. Soc. Profl. Journalists, 1987-90. Author: Spiked: How Chain Management, 1987, 2d edit., 1988; editor Spectrum, 1994—; bd. editors Pvt. & Wireless Cable, 1994—, Wireless Internat., 1996—; contbr. articles to profl. jours. V.p. Residences Market Square, Washington, 1993-98; co-chair Fixed Wirless Com. Coalition, 2000—. Ford Found. fellow Yale Law Sch., New Haven, 1982-83. Mem. Fed. Com. Bar Assn. (legis. com.). Home: PH8 701 Pennsylvania Ave NW Washington DC 20004-2608 Office: Wireless Comms Assn Ste 700 W 1333 H St Washington DC 20005 E-mail: president@wcai.com.

KREINDLER, PETER MICHAEL, lawyer; b. 1945; BA, Harvard U., 1967, JD, 1971. Bar: D.C. 1971, N.Y. 1989. Assoc. Hughes, Hubbard & Reed, 1975-77, ptnr., 1977-88, Arnold & Porter, 1990-91; sr. v.p., gen. counsel and sec. AlliedSignal, Morristown, NJ, 1992—95; sr. v.p., gen. counsel Honeywell Internat., 1999—. General civil litigation, Corporate, general. Office: Honeywell Inc 101 Columbia Rd Morristown NJ 07960-4640*

KREINER, MARGARET HELEN, sales/marketing executive; b. Cleve., Nov. 15, 1944; d. Abraham Lincoln and Helen M. (Hrusovsky) Hott; m. James G. Kreiner, May 17, 1986. BS in Chemistry, Kent State U., 1966; MBA, U. Akron, 1976, JD, 1985. Cert.: (elderlaw atty.). Engr. B.F. Goodrich Corp., Akron, 1966-74, mktg. tech. svc. staff Cleve., 1974-81; tech. sales rep. Burton (Ohio) Rubber, 1981-92; dir. sales/mktg. Rauh Rubber, Akron, 1992—. Lectr. in field. Dir. alumni bd. U. Akron, 1986-89, co-chmn., 1989; tchr. Jr. Achievement Project Bus., Warrensville Heights, Ohio, 1979; vol. Akron Safe Landing Runaway Shelter, 1980, Summit County Probate Ct. Mem. N.Y. Rubber Group (dir. 1982-91, sec.-treas. 1991, chmn. 1993), Ohio Bar Coll., Akron Rubber Group (reception com. 1992—), Ohio Bar Assn., Fla. Bar Assn., nat. Assn. Elder Law Attys. Roman Catholic. Avocations: reading, travel, sports, cooking, gardening. Office: 2020 Front St Ste202 Cuyahoga Falls OH 44221-3200

KREIS, ELIZABETH SUSAN, lawyer; b. N.Y.C., Nov. 8, 1963; d. Willi and Emily Rutledge Kreis. BS in Biochemistry, U. Wis., 1986; JD, Ohio State U., 1991. Bar: N.Y. 1991, Conn. 1992, D.C. 1992, Colo. 1994. Biochemist Sandoz Pharm., Basel, Switzerland, 1986-88; pvt. practice Stamford, Conn., 1991-93, Arvada, Colo., 1993—. Mem. ABA, Am. Bus. Women's Assn. (chairperson for spkrs.), Colo. Bar Assn., N.Y. State Bar Assn., Conn. Bar Assn., D.C. Bar Assn., Arvada Garden Club (pres. 1997-98). Commercial, consumer (including collections, credit), Family and matrimonial, General practice. Home and Office: 9277 W 56th Pl Ste 12 Arvada CO 80002-2158

KREISLER, DAVID P. lawyer; b. Port Jefferson, N.Y., Oct. 29, 1966; s. Michael N. and Barbara H. Kreisler; m. Gwyn Williams, Aug. 21, 1993; children: Jack Elliot, Emma Catherine. AB in Econs., Princeton U., 1988; JD, Syracuse U., 1991. Bar: Mass. 1991, U.S. Dist. Ct. Mass. 1992. Atty. Nutter, McClerren & Fish, Boston, 1991—93, Hutchins, Wheeler & Dittmar, Boston, 1993—2002, Weil, Gotshal & Manges, LLP, Boston, 2002—. Republican. Jewish. Avocations: golf, skiing. Corporate, general, Mergers and acquisitions, Securities. Office: Weil Gotshal and Manges LLP 100 Federal St 34th Fl Boston MA 02110 Office Fax: 617-772-8333. Business E-Mail: david.kreisler@weil.com.

KREITZMAN, RALPH J. lawyer; b. N.Y.C., Nov. 11, 1945; s. Emanuel M. and Hannah G. (Steinhardt) K.; m. Wendy A. Karpel, Nov. 24, 1968; children: Susan Beth, Emily Meg. BS in Acctg., Rider U., 1967; JD cum laude, Bklyn. Law Sch., 1970. Bar: N.Y. 1971, U.S. Dist Ct. (so. dist.) N.Y. 1971, U.S. Dist. Ct. (ea. dist.) N.Y. 1973, U.S. Ct. of Appeals (2nd cir.) 1975, U.S. Supreme Ct. 1976. Assoc. Hughes Hubbard & Reed LLP, N.Y.C., 1970-80; sr. ptnr. real estate group Hughes Hubbard & Reed LLC, N.Y.C., 1980—. Trustee Village of Great Neck, 2001-, former chair planning bd., mem. archtl. rev. com., 2001-. Served with U.S. Army Res., 1968-74. Mem. ABA (real property law sect. and com. on fgn. investment in U.S. real estate), N.Y. State Bar Assn. (real property law sect., com. on comml. leases and com. on financings), Assn. of Bar of City of N.Y. (com. on real property law, former chair leasing subcom.). Private international, Property, real (including real estate development, water), Administrative and regulatory. Office: Hughes Hubbard & Reed LLP 1 Battery Park Plz New York NY 10004-1482 E-mail: kreitzman@hugheshubbard.com.

KREJCI, KVETOSLAV, lawyer; LLM, PhD, Charles U., Prague, Czech Republic, 2001. Assoc. Beiten Brukhardt Mittl & Wegener, Prague, 1995—97, White & Case Prague, 1998—2000, ptnr., 2001—. Banking, Mergers and acquisitions, Finance. Office: White & Case LLP Staromestske nam 15 110 00 Prague Czech Republic Office Fax: +420-25577 1122. E-mail: kkrejci@whitecase.com.

KREMBS, PETER JOSEPH, lawyer; b. Dec. 12, 1944; s. John G. and Mary m. (Felker) Krembs; m. Nancy Smythe, June 8, 1974; children: Joshua, Marcus. BS, U. Wis., Madison, 1968; JD, Case Western Reserve U., 1973. Bar: Ohio 1973, U.S. dist. Ct. (no. dist.) Ohio 1974, U.S. Ct. Appeals (6th cir.) 1975, U.S. Ct. Appeals (3d cir.) 1998. Assoc. Ford, Whitney, Cleve., 1973—77; corp. atty. Midland-Ross Corp., Cleve., 1977—81; ptnr. Gruber, Moriarty, Fricke & Jaros, Cleve., 1981—92, Hermann, Cahn & Schneider, Cleve., 1992—. Legal officer, dir. several small bus.; diplomate Ct. Practice Inst. Mem.: ABA, Am. Trial Lawyers Assn., Ohio State Bar Assn., Greater Cleve. Bar Assn., Am. Arbitration Assn. (arbitrator 1981—). Federal civil litigation, State civil litigation, Corporate, general. Office: Hermann Cahn and Schneider 1301 E 9th St Ste 500 Cleveland OH 44114-1800

KREMER, CHRISTIAN, lawyer; b. Gent, Belgium, Feb. 25, 1965; arrived in Luxembourg, 1977; m. Danièle-Christine Giglio; 4 children. Lic. droit, Free U. Brussels, 1985. Bar: Brussels 1990, Luxembourg 1990. Collaborator Arendt and Nedernoch, Luxembourg, 1989—94, ptnr., 1994—98, Faltz and Kremer, Luxembourg, 1998—99; mng. ptnr. Kremer Assocs. and Clifford Chance, Luxembourg, 1999—. With various directorships. Contbr. articles to profl. jours. Banking, Commercial, contracts (including sales of goods; commercial financing), Mergers and acquisitions. Home: 68 Ave Gaston Dieolerich Luxembourg L-1420 Luxembourg Office: Kremer Assocs & Clifford Chance 4 Place de Paris BP 1147 Luxembourg Luxembourg L-1011 Office Fax: +352 48 13 85. Business E-Mail: christian.kremer@kremer.cliffordchance.com.

KREPPEL, MILTON MARK, lawyer; b. N.Y.C., June 30, 1951; s. Irving I. and Eva (Gross) K.; m. Geraldine Rienzi, Nov. 23, 1974; children: Rachel, Rebecca, Robyn. BS, U. Bridgeport, 1973; JD, South Tex. Coll. Law, 1978; MS, Pace U., 1985. Bar: Tex. 1978, U.S. Ct. Appeals (5th cir.) 1978, U.S. Dist. Ct. (so. dist.) Tex. 1978, U.S. Tax Ct. 1978, U.S. Ct. Claims 1978, Fla. 1978, U.S. Ct. Mil. Appeals 1978, U.S. Ct. Customs and Patent Appeals 1979, N.Y. 1979, U.S. Dist. Ct. (ea. and so. dists.) N.Y. 1979, Temp. Emergency Ct. Appeals U.S. 1980, U.S. Ct. Internat. Trade 1981, U.S. Supreme Ct. 1981, U.S. Dist. Ct. (middle dist.) Fla. 1981, U.S. Ct. Appeals (11th cir.) 1981, U.S. Ct. Appeals (fed. cir.) 1983, U.S. Ct. Appeals (2d cir.) 1988. Assoc. Brown, Goodman & Kreppel, New Rochelle, N.Y., 1978-85, Irving I. Kreppel, New Rochelle, 1985—2001; pvt. practice New Rochelle, 2001—. Adj. prof. Mercy Coll., Dobbs Ferry, N.Y., 1986-92; instr. paralegal Mercy Coll., White Plains, N.Y., 1996—. Merit badge counselor Boy Scouts Am., White Plains, N.Y., 1985—. Mem. N.Y. State Bar Assn., Fla. Bar Assn., Tex. Bar Assn., New Rochelle Bar Assn. (bd. dirs. 1986-87, treas. 1987-94, v.p. 1994-96, pres. 1996-98, bd. dirs. 1998—). Republican. Jewish. Avocations: water skiing, auto mechanics, reading. Corporate, general, General practice, Personal injury (including property damage). Office: 271 North Ave Ste 919 New Rochelle NY 10801-5117

KRETCHMER, KATHY L. lawyer; b. Ohio, Mar. 28, 1952; BA, U. Mich., 1974; JD, Hastings Coll., 1977. Bar: Calif. 1977, Wis. 1980. Assoc. Spease & Day, Oakland, Calif., 1978-80; project manager State of Wis., Madison, 1980-83; staff lawyer Environ. Cons. Firm, Palo Alto, Calif., 1985-85; dep. county counsel County of Santa Clara, San Jose, Calif., 1985—. Mem. Santa Clara County Bar Assn. (environ. law exec. com.). Office: Office County Counsel 70 W Hedding St Fl 9 San Jose CA 95110-1705

KRIEGER, PAUL EDWARD, lawyer; b. Fairmont, W.Va., Mar. 30, 1942; s. Paul Julius Krieger and Martha Frances (Graham) Ralph; m. Nora Elizabeth Krieger, July 28, 2001; children: Andrew, Thomas. BS in Mining Engring., U. Pitts., 1964; postgrad., Pa. State U., 1964-65; LLB, U. Md., 1968; LLM, George Washington U., 1971. Bar: Md. 1968, U.S. Patent and Trademark Office 1970, D.C. 1973, Tex. 1979. Faculty rsch. asst. U. Md., 1967-70; assoc. Brumbaugh, Graves, Donohue & Raymond, N.Y.C., 1970-71; ptnr. Lane, Aitken, Dunner & Ziems, Washington, 1971-78; sr. pat. atty. Dresser Industries Inc., Dallas, 1978-79; ptnr. Pravel, Hewitt, Kimball & Krieger, Houston, 1979-98, Fulbright & Jaworski, Houston, 1998—. Adj. prof. U. Houston Law Ctr., 1985—. Mem. ABA, Am. Bar Found., Am. Pat. Law Assn., Tex. Bar Found., Tex. Bar Assn., Houston Bar Found., Internat. Assn. of Defense Coun. Federal civil litigation, Patent, Trademark and copyright. Office: Fulbright & Jaworski 1301 Mckinney St Ste 5100 Houston TX 77010-3031 Home: 4116 Coleridge Houston TX 77005 E-mail: pkrieger@fulbright.com.

KRIEGMAN, BRUCE PETER, lawyer; b. Richmond, Va., Aug. 5, 1954; s. George and Lois Kriegman. BA cum laude, Carleton Coll., 1975; JD, Georgetown U., 1984. Bar: Wash. 1984, U.S. Dist. Ct. (we. dist.) Wash. 1985, U.S. Dist. Ct. (ea. dist.) Wash. 1987. Pvt. practice Law Office of Kriegman, Seattle, 1991—2001; ptnr. Gordon, Thomas, Honeywell, Seattle, 2001—. Mem. panel of trustees Western Dist. Wash., U.S. Bankruptcy Ct., 1989—; legis. asst. U.S. Ho. of Reps., Washington, 1976-80. Bankruptcy, Property, real (including real estate development, water), Commercial, contracts (including sales of goods; commercial financing). Office: 600 University St Ste 2100 Seattle WA 98101-1176 Fax: 206-676-7575.

KRIEGSMAN, EDWARD MICHAEL, lawyer; b. Bridgeport, Conn., Oct. 29, 1965; s. Irving Martin and Marlene Sonya (Kates) K.; m. Meryl Gail Dennis, June 11, 1989; children: Barry Alan, David Jacob, Rachel Lynn. BS in Biology, MIT, 1986; JD, U. Pa., 1989. Bar: Pa. 1989, U.S. Patent and Trademark Office 1989, Mass. 1990, U.S. Ct. Appeals (Fed. cir.) 1990, U.S. Dist. Ct. Mass. 1992. Assoc. Finnegan, Henderson, Farabow, et al, Washington, 1989-90; ptnr. Kriegsman & Kriegsman, Framingham, Mass., 1990—. Mem. ABA, Am. Intellectual Property Law Assn., Mass. Bar Assn., Fed. Cir. Bar Assn., Boston Patent Law Assn., South Middlesex Bar Assn. Jewish. Avocations: reading, sports. Patent, Trademark and copyright. Home: 103 Richard Rd Holliston MA 01746-1213 Office: Kriegsman & Kriegsman 665 Franklin St Framingham MA 01702 E-mail: kriegspat@aol.com.

KRIESBERG, SIMEON M. lawyer; b. Washington, June 4, 1951; s. Martin and Harriet M. K.; m. Martha L. Kahn, Jan. 9, 1994. AB, Harvard U., 1973; M in Pub. Affairs, Princeton U., 1977; JD, Yale U., 1977. Bar: D.C. 1977, U.S. Dist. Ct. D.C. 1978, U.S. Ct. Appeals (D.C. cir.) 1978, U.S. Ct. Internat. Trade 1979, U.S. Ct. Appeals (Fed. cir.) 1981, U.S. Supreme Ct. 1982. Assoc. Leva, Hawes, Symington, Martin & Oppenheimer, Washington, 1977-83; sr. counsel internat. trade Sears World Trade Inc., Washington, 1983-85, v.p., gen. counsel, 1985-87; ptnr. Mayer Brown Rowe & Maw, Washington, 1987—. Professorial lectr. Nitze Sch. Advanced Internat. Studies, Johns Hopkins U., 1991-93; mem. binat. dispute resolution panel under U.S.-Can. Free Trade Agreement, 1990-92; guest scholar Brookings Inst., 1992-93; mem. roster of dispute resolution panelists under NAFTA, 1996—. Mem. editorial adv. com. Internat. Legal Materials, 1991-97; article and book rev. editor Yale Law Jour., 1976-77. Officer or dir. Washington Hebrew Congregation, 1980-94, Jewish Cmty. Coun. Greater Washington, 1986-94, Interfaith Conf. of Met. Washington, 1989—, D.C. Jewish Cmty. Ctr., 1994—, Mid-Atlantic coun. Union Am. Hebrew Congregations, 1994—2002. Recipient Pro Bono Svc. award Internat. Human Rights Law Group, 1991, Lawrence L. O'Connor medal Sears, Roebuck and Co., 1984. Mem. ABA, Am. Law Inst., Am. Soc. Internat. Law, D.C. Bar. Administrative and regulatory, Private international, Public international. Office: Mayer Brown Rowe & Maw 1909 K St NW Washington DC 20006-1101

KRINSLY, STUART Z. lawyer, manufacturing company executive; b. N.Y.C., May 19, 1917; m. Charlotte Wolf, Aug. 18, 1944; children: EllinJane, Joan Susan. BA, Princeton U., 1938; LLB, Harvard U., 1941. Bar: N.Y. 1941. Asst. U.S. atty. So. Dist. N.Y., 1942-45; mem. firm Schlesinger & Krinsly, 1945-57; sec. Sun Chem. Corp., N.Y.C., 1957-65, v.p., gen. counsel, 1965-76, sr. v.p., gen. counsel, 1976-78, exec. v.p., gen. counsel, 1978-82, also bd. dirs.; sr. exec. v.p., gen. counsel Sequa Corp., N.Y.C., 1982—, also bd. dirs. Mem. Beach Point Club, Princeton Club N.Y. Corporate, general. Home: 1135 Greacen Point Rd Mamaroneck NY 10543-4612 Office: Sequa Corp 200 Park Ave Fl 44 New York NY 10166-0005

KRISS, ROBERT J. lawyer; b. Cleve., Dec. 15, 1953; BA summa cum laude, Cornell U., 1975; JD cum laude, Harvard U., 1978. Bar: Ill. 1978, U.S. Dist. Ct. (no. dist.) Ill. 1978, U.S. Ct. Appeals (7th cir.) 1983, U.S. Dist. Ct. (no. dist. trial bar) Ill. 1982, U.S. Ct. Appeals (5th cir.) 1984. Ptnr. Mayer, Brown, Rowe & Man, Chgo. Presenter in field; adj. prof. trial practice Northwestern U. Law Sch. Author short story. Chmn. consent degree task force Chgo. Park Dist., 1986-87; bd. dirs. Chgo. Legal Assistance Found., 1996-2000. Mem. Nat. Inst. Trial Advocacy (faculty midwest regional program 1988-91, 94), Winnetka Caucus (chmn. schs. candidate selection com. 1997). Office: Mayer Brown Rowe & Man 190 S La Salle St Ste 3100 Chicago IL 60603-3441

KRISTOL, DANIEL MARVIN, lawyer; b. July 7, 1936; s. Abraham Louis and Pearl Cecile (Oltman) K.; m. Katherine Fairfax Chinn, Nov. 4, 1968; children: Sarah Douglas, Susan Fairfax. BA, U. Pa., 1958, LLB, 1961. Bar: Del. 1961, U.S. Dist. Ct. Del. 1962. Assoc., ptnr. Killoran & VanBrunt, Wilmington, Del., 1961-76; dir. Prickett, Jones, Elliott & Kristol, Wilmington, 1976-99; ptnr. predecessor Prickett, Ward Burt & Sanders, Wilmington, 1976-99; dir. Richards, Layton & Finger, Wilmington, 1999—. Pub. defender Ct. Common Pleas, Wilmington, 1966-69; asst. solicitor City of Wilmington, 1970-73; spl. counsel Div. Housing State of Del., 1972-87, gen. counsel Del. State Housing Authority, 1973-99. With USAR, 1964-67. Mem. ABA, Del. State Bar Assn. (chmn. real and personal property com. 1974-78, chmn. world peace through law com. 1980-81, chmn. sr. lawyers com. 1999—), Am. Coll. Real Estate Lawyers, Wilmington Country Club, Greenville Country Club, Mill Reef Club (Antigua, W.I.), Wilmington Club, Penn Club of N.Y.. Republican. Jewish. Commercial, contracts (including sales of goods; commercial financing), Landlord-tenant, Property, real (including real estate development, water). Office: PO Box 551 Wilmington DE 19899-0551 E-mail: kristol@rlf.com.

KRITZER, GLENN BRUCE, lawyer; b. Newark, June 13, 1947; s. Julius B. and Ethyl (Rosenthal) K.; children: Rebecca, Gary. Student, Lehigh U., 1965-67; BA with distinction, U. Wis., 1969; JD, NYU, 1972. Bar: N.Y. 1973, U.S. Dist. Ct. (so. dist.) N.Y. 1974, U.S. Dist. Ct. (ea. dist.) N.Y. 1975, U.S. Ct. Appeals (2d cir.) 1975, Calif. 1977, Fla. 1980, U.S. Ct. Appeals (5th cir.) 1980, U.S. Dist. Ct. (so. dist.) Fla. 1981, U.S. Ct. Appeals (11th cir.) 1981, U.S. Dist. Ct. (trial bar) Fla. 1982, U.S. Supreme Ct. 1985, U.S. Dist. Ct. (ea. dist.) Wis. 1985, U.S. Ct. Appeals (7th cir.) 1986, U.S. Dist. Ct. (mid. dist.) Fla. 1990. Examining atty. N.Y.C. Dept. Investigation, 1972-73, dep. dir. bur. city marshals, 1973-74, dir. bur. city marshals, 1974-76, spl. asst. dist. atty., 1975, spl. asst. corp. counsel, 1976; assoc. Herzfeld & Rubin P.C., N.Y.C., 1976-77; asst. U.S. atty. Office of U.S. Atty. (ea. dist.) N.Y., 1977-79, Office of U.S. Atty. (so. dist.) Fla., 1979-82; pvt. practice Miami, 1982—. Mem. Nat. Assn. Criminal Def. Lawyers, Fla. Assn. Criminal Def. Lawyers (bd. dirs. Miami chpt.), Fed. Bar Assn., Asst. U.S. Attys. Assn., Dade County Bar Assn. Criminal, Insurance, Personal injury (including property damage). Office: 799 Brickell Plz Ste 700 Miami FL 33131-2805 E-mail: glennbkritzeresq@aol.com.

KRITZER, PAUL ERIC, media executive, communications lawyer; b. Buffalo, May 5, 1942; s. James Cyril and Bessie May (Biddlecombe) K.; m. Frances Jean McCallum, June 20, 1970; children: Caroline Frances, Erica Hopkins. BA, Williams Coll., 1964; MS in Journalism, Columbia U., 1965; JD, Georgetown U., 1972. Bar: U.S. Supreme Ct. 1978, Wis. 1980. Reporter, copy editor Buffalo Evening News, 1964, 69, 70; instr. English Augusta (Ga.) Coll., 1968-69; law clk. Office of FCC Commr., Washington, 1971, MCI, Washington, 1972; counsel U.S. Ho. of Reps., Washington, 1972-77; assoc. counsel Des Moines Register & Tribune, 1977-80; editor, pub. Waukesha (Wis.) Freeman, 1980-83; legal v.p., sec. Jour. Communications Inc., Milw., 1983—. Trustee Carroll Co., Waukesha, 1981-89; producer Waukesha Film Festival, 1982; bd. dirs. Des Moines Metro Opera, Inc., 1979-80; bd. dirs. Milw. Youth Symphony Orch., 1992-2001, pres. 1994-97; bd. dirs. Milw. Symphony Orch., 1997—; bd. dirs. United Performing Arts Fund, 1994-97. With U.S. Army, 1965-68. Presbyterian. Avocations: bridge, gardening. Home: 211 Oxford Rd Waukesha WI 53186-6263 Office: Jour Communications Inc 333 W State St PO Box 661 Milwaukee WI 53201-0661 Business E-Mail: pkritzer@jc.com.

KROBLIN, LUCY S. lawyer; b. St. Louis, July 16, 1947; d. Clement J. and Frances S. Sullivan; m. Thomas E. Kroblin, June 28, 1969; children: Christopher A., Jonathan S. BA, St. Mary's Coll., South Bend, Ind., 1969; JD, U. Tulsa, 1987. Bar: Okla. 1987, U.S. Dist. Ct. (no. dist.) Okla. 1987. Atty. La Sorsa, Weber & Miles, Tulsa, 1987—92; ptnr. Kroblin & Crutchfield, P.C., Tulsa, 1992—94; atty. Howard, Widdow, Bufogle, P.C., Tulsa, 1994—2002, J. Kenton Francy & Assocs., Tulsa, 2002—. Campaign mgr. state senate seat, Okla., 1992; campaign mgr. state ho. seat, 1996. Mem.: ABA, Tulsa County Bar Assn., Okla. Acad. Mediators & Arbitrators, Okla. Bar Assn. Democrat. Roman Catholic. Avocation: sailing. Family and matrimonial, Alternative dispute resolution. Office: 1861 E 15th St Tulsa OK 74104 Office Fax: 918-747-6300.

KROENER, WILLIAM FREDERICK, III, lawyer; b. N.Y.C., Aug. 27, 1945; s. William Frederick Kroener Jr. and Barbara (Mitchell) Kroener; m. Evelyn Somerville Bibb, Sept. 3, 1966; children: William F. Kroener IV(dec.) , Mary Elizabeth, Evangeline Alberta, James Mitchell. AB, Yale Coll., 1967; JD, MBA, Stanford U., 1971. Bar: Calif. 1972, N.Y. 1979, D.C. 1983. Assoc. Davis, Polk & Wardwell, N.Y.C., London, 1971-79, ptnr. N.Y.C., 1979-82, Washington, N.Y.C., 1982-94; gen. counsel Fed. Deposit Ins. Corp., Washington, 1995—. Lectr. Stanford (Calif.) U. Law Sch., 1993—94, George Washington U. Law Sch., 1994—, Washington Coll. Law, Am. U. Law Sch., Washingon, 1996—; chmn. legal adv. group Fed. Fin. Instns. Exam. Coun., 2001—. Pres. Kroener Family Found.; gov. bd. mem. St. Albans Sch., 1991—95; fin. com. mem. Protestant/Episcopal Cathedral Found.-Wash. Nat. Cathedral, 1992—95; bd. visitors mem. Stanford U. Law Sch., 1983—92, deans adv. coun., 1992—93; nat. chair Stanford Law Fund, 1990—92; dir., gen. counsel Kenwood Citizens Assn., Inc., 1993—94. Mem.: ABA, N.Y. Law Inst., Assn. of Bar of City of N.Y., Am. Law Inst., Kenwood Golf Club, Yale Club. Republican. Episcopalian. Home: 6412 Brookside Dr Chevy Chase MD 20815-6649 Office: Fed Deposit Ins Corp 550 17th St NW Washington DC 20429-0001

KROFT, MICHAL, lawyer; b. Pilsen, Czech Republic, Nov. 24, 1969; 1 child, Barbara. M, Charles U., Prague, 1993. Assoc. law firm, Pilsen, 1990-93, trainee Prague, 1994-96; sole practice Prague, 1996; ptnr. Weinhold Andersen Legal, Prague; co-mng. ptnr. Dewet Ballantine V.O.S., 2002—. Lectr. in field. Contbr. articles to profl. jours. Mem. Czech Bar Assn., Slovak Bar Comml. Lawyers. Avocations: reading, cinema, theater, car racing, golf. Patent, Trademark and copyright, Information Technology. Office: Dewey Ballantine VOS Jungmannova 31 110 00 Prague 1 Czech Republic Fax: 2440 7389. E-mail: mkroft@deweyballantine.com.

KROLL, ARTHUR HERBERT, educator, consultant; b. N.Y.C., Dec. 2, 1939; s. Abraham and Sylvia Kroll; m. Lois Handmacher, June, 1964; children: Douglas, Pamela. BA, Cornell U., 1961; LLB cum laude, St. John's U., 1965; LLM in Taxation, NYU, 1969. Bar: D.C. Assoc. Patterson, Belknap, Webb & Tyler, N.Y.C., 1965-72, ptnr., 1972-90, Pryor, Cashman, Sherman & Flynn, N.Y.C., 1990-95; CEO KST Cons. Group, Inc. Adj. prof. U. Miami Sch. Law, NYU; lectr. numerous confs.; mem. adv. bd. Bur. Nat. Affairs Tax Mgmt., Inc., Practising Law Inst. Tax Adv. Bd., U. Miami Inst. Estate Planning, Bus. Laws, Inc.; mem. adv. com. NYU Ann. Inst. on Fed. Taxation. Author: Executive Compensation, 3 vols., Compensating Executives; monthly newsletter Family Bus. Profl.; mem. bd. contbg. editors and advisers Corporate Taxation; mem. editl. adv. bd. Jour. Compensation and Benefits. Mem. ABA (subcom. exec. compensation), Am. Pension Conf. (mem. steering com.). Pension, profit-sharing, and employee benefits, Probate (including wills, trusts), Corporate taxation. Office: KST Consulting Group Inc 250 E Hartsdale Ave Ste 30 Hartsdale NY 10530 E-mail: kstconsultinggroup@att.net.

KROLL, BARRY LEWIS, lawyer; b. Chgo., June 8, 1934; s. Harry M. and Hannah (Lewis) K.; m. Jayna Vivian Leibovitz, June 20, 1956; children: Steven Lee, Joan Lois Kroll Dolgin, Nancy Maxine Kroll Richardson. AB in Psychology with distinction, U. Mich., 1955, JD with distinction, 1958. Bar: Ill. 1958. Assoc. firm Jacobs & McKenna, Chgo., 1958-66, Epstein, Manilow & Sachnoff, Chgo., 1966-68, Schiff, Hardin, Waite Dorschel & Britton, Chgo., 1968-69; ptnr. Wolfberg & Kroll, Chgo., 1970-74, Kirshbaum & Kroll, Chgo., 1972-74; of counsel Jacobs, Williams & Montgomery, Ltd., Chgo., 1973-74; ptnr. Jacobs, Williams & Montgomery Ltd., Chgo., 1974-85, Williams & Montgomery Ltd., Chgo., 1985—2001; of counsel Williams Montgomery & John, Ltd., 2002—. Faculty John Marshall Law Sch., Chgo., 1969-73; atty. for petitioner in U.S. Supreme Ct. decision Escobedo vs Ill., 1964; mem. legal and legis. com. Internat. Franchise Assn., 1976-80 Asst. editor: Mich. Law Rev, 1957-58. Chmn. Park Forest Bd. Zoning Appeals, 1971-78. Served to capt. AUS, 1959-62. Named Outstanding Young Man Park Forest Jr. C. of C., 1966. Mem. Ill. Bar Assn., Chgo. Bar Assn. (chmn. legis. com. 1974-75), Ill. Appellate Lawyers Assn. (treas. 1978-79, sec. 1979-80, pres. 1981-82), Bar Assn. 7th Fed. Circuit, Order of Coif, Tau Epsilon Rho, Alpha Epsilon Pi. Jewish (trustee congregation 1966-70, 72-75, 90—, pres. men's club 1965-66). Appellate, State civil litigation, Insurance. Home: 1440 N State Pkwy Chicago IL 60610-1564 E-mail: blk@willmont.com.

KROLL, MARTIN N. lawyer; b. N.Y.C., Nov. 30, 1937; s. Jack and Ruth (Strassman) K.; m. Rita Evangeline Grossman, Aug. 14, 1965; children: Spencer, Jonathan, Evan. BA, Cornell U., 1959; JD, U. Pa., 1963. Sr. ptnr. Kroll, Levy, Baron & Feinstein, N.Y.C., 1972-80, Snow, Beeker, Kroll, Klaris & Kraus, N.Y.C., 1980-86, Kroll, Moss and Kroll, LLP, Garden City, N.Y., 1987—. Receiver Chrysler Bldg., N.Y.C., 1975-77; village atty. Village of East Hills (N.Y.), 1988-95; counsel Town of North Hempstead, 1987-2001, counsel Econ. Devel. Agy. Town of North Hempstead, 1992—; pres. Jewish Lawyers Assn. of Nassau County, N.Y., 1980. Vice chmn. Nassau County Republican Party, Westbury, N.Y., 1986—. Recipient Torch of Liberty, B'Nai Brigh-ADL, 1982; named Master Builder Conf. of Jewish Educators, 1990. Mem. ABA, N.Y. State Bar Assn., Nassau County Bar Assn. Federal civil litigation, General civil litigation, Municipal (including bonds). Office: Kroll Moss & Kroll 400 Garden City Plz Garden City NY 11530-3322 E-mail: mkroll100@aol.com.

KROLL, SOL, lawyer; b. Russia, Aug. 10, 1918; m. Ruth Saslow; children: Gerald, Judy, Elise, Elliott. LLB, St. John's U., 1942. Bar: N.Y. 1942, U.S. Supreme Ct. 1956. Former U.S. counsel to Assn. Francaise des Socs. D'Assurances Transports; former mem. com. of interfraud task force N.Y. Ins. Dept.; sr. ins. counsel. County atty. Putnam County, N.Y. Contbr. articles on Am. ins. law to various ins. mags. Mem. ABA, Fed. Bar Assn., N.Y. State Bar Assn., N.Y.C. Bar Assn., Internat. Assn. Ins. Counsel, Industry Adv. Com. on Ins., Ins. Fedn. NY (bd. dirs.). Insurance, Product liability, Professional liability. Home: 600 Cantitoe St Bedford NY 10506-1107 Office: 1365 York Ave New York NY 10021 Fax: 212-755-9892.

KRONE, NORMAN BERNARD, commercial real estate developer, lawyer; b. Memphis, Sept. 13, 1938; s. Irving and Eva (Sauer) K.; m. Norma Lee Moon; children: John, Christine, David. LLB, Stetson U., 1964. Bar: Fla. 1964, Ohio 1987, U.S. Dist. Ct. (mid. dist.) Fla. 1965, U.S. Ct. Appeals (7th cir.) 1968; lic. real estate broker, Ohio, Mich., Ala. Atty. Lifsey & Johnston, Tampa, Fla., 1964—65; pvt. practice Tampa, Fla., 1965—66; property mgmt. atty. Ford Motor Co., Dearborn, Mich., 1966—67; audit mgr. Montgomery Ward & Co., Chgo., 1967—68, corp. real estate mgr., 1968—75; exec. v.p. Montgomery Ward Properties Corp., Chgo., 1970—75; from v.p. to sr. v.p. Walgreen Co., Deerfield, Ill., 1975—85; pres., CEO The Hausman Cos., Cleve., 1987—2001; sr. exec. v.p. Henry S. Miller, Grubb & Ellis Comml./Retail Svcs., 1985—87; mng. prin. NK Devel. Ltd., 1996—2002; prin. NK Real Estate Adv. Ltd., 2002—. Trustee Internat. Coun. Shopping Ctrs., N.Y.C., 1976-79; dir. Myers Industries, Lincoln, Ill., 1976-83; instr. Intercoun. Shopping Ctrs.-Inst. Profl. Devel.; dean U. Shopping Ctrs., ednl. adv. com., small ctr. com., chmn. retail adv. com., 1975-76, cert. leasing specialist, 1995-; cons. Krone Group LLC, 2001—; instr., spkr. in field, Law for Non-Lawyers. Author, editor: The Lease and Its Language, 1996, ICSC Study Lease, 2000, Anatomy of a Lease, 2001; contbr. articles to mags. Acting judge City of Tampa, 1964-66; bd. dirs. Met. Housing and Planning Coun., Chgo., 1977-80, New City YMCA, 1976-78; mem. sch. bd. Palisades Cmty. Sch. Dist., 1968-69; mem. strategic planning com. Met. Chgo. YMCA, 1976-77; 1st pres. Cleve. Pops Orch.; bd. dirs. Walgreen Hist. Found., 1984-87; co-founder, pres., mem. exec. com. Realty Resources (a network of comml. brokerage firms), 1987-2001. Named Entrepreneur of Yr. Operation Breadbasket, 1977. Mem. Cleve. Bar Assn., Real Estate Inst., Beachwood C. of C. (pres. 1996, exec. com. 1992—, life bd. dirs.), Acacia Country Club (bd. dirs. 1997-99, chmn. planning com. 1998-99, sec. 1998). Avocations: woodworking, golf. Office: NK Real Estate Advisors Ltd 9391 Mentor Ave PMB 281 Mentor OH 44060 Fax: 440-256-8360. E-mail: nbkrone@netscape.net.

KRONMAN, ANTHONY TOWNSEND, law educator, dean; b. 1945; m. Nancy I. Greenberg, 1982 BA, Williams Coll., 1968, PhD, 1972; JD, Yale U., 1975. Bar: Minn. 1975, N.Y. 1983. Assoc. prof. U. Minn., 1975-76; asst. prof. U. Chgo., 1976-79; vis. assoc. prof. Yale U. Law Sch., New Haven, 1978-79, prof., 1979—, Edward J. Phelps prof. law, 1985—, dean, 1994—. Editor: (with R. Posner) The Economics of Contract Law, 1979 (with F. Kessler and G. Gilmore) Cases and Materials on Contracts, 1986; past mem. editorial bd. Yale Law Jour.; author: Max Weber, 1983, The Lost Lawyer, 1993. Danforth Found. fellow, 1968-72 Fellow ABA, Am. Acad. Arts and Scis.; mem. Selden Soc., Conn. Bar Assn. (Cooper fellow), Coun. on Fgn. Rels. Office: Yale U Law Sch PO Box 208215 New Haven CT 06520-8215

KRONSTEIN, WERNER J, lawyer; b. Heidelberg, Germany, Dec. 12, 1930; came to U.S., 1935; s. Heinrich D. and Kate (Brodnitz) K.; m Ilse Marie Engel, Feb. 10, 1962; 1 child, Phillip D. AB, Georgetown U., 1953, L.L.B., 1956. Bar: 1956. Law clk. U.S. Ct. Appeal for D.C. Circuit, Washington, 1956-57; ptnr. Arnold & Porter, Washington, 1957—. Trustee, Internat. Law Inst., Washington, 1983—, vice chmn., 1989—. Contbr. articles to profl. jours. Roman Catholic. Private international, Securities. Office: Arnold & Porter 555 12th St NW Washington DC 20004-1206

KRONZEK, CHARLES MICHAEL, lawyer; b. Pitts., Feb. 11, 1954; s. Morris and Shirley (Gorin) K.; m. Judith W.; children: Allison F., Jill L. BS, Geneva Coll., Pitts., 1991; JD, Mich. State U., 1994. Bar: Mich. 1995. Sr. ptnr. Kronzek & Cronkright PLLC, Lansing, Mich., 1994—. Criminal, Family and matrimonial, Personal injury (including property damage). Office: Kronzek & Cronkright PLLC 4601 W Saginaw Ste 100 Lansing MI 48917-2741 E-mail: Kronzek@lawyer.com.

KROOT, JASON M. lawyer; b. St. Petersburg, Fla., Jan. 20, 1972; s. Jerry M. and Charlotte A. Kroot. BSci. in Speech Comm., U. of Tex. at Austin, 1993—95; JD, Chicago-Kent Coll. of Law, Chgo., 1996—99. Bar: Ill. 1999, US Dist. Ct. (no. dist.) 1999, US Dist. Ct. (no. dist.) 2001. Law clk. Herbert F. Stride, Ltd. / Stride, Craddock, & Stride, Chgo., 1996—99; lawyer Sussman, Selig & Ross, Chgo., 1999—. Mem.: ABA (assoc.), Chgo. Bar Assn. (assoc.), Ill. Bar Assn. (assoc.), Ill. Trial Lawyers Assn. (assoc.), Am. Assn. of Trial Lawyers (assoc.). State civil litigation, Professional liability, Personal injury (including property damage). Office: Sussman Selig & Ross One E Wacker Drive Suite 2920 Chicago IL 60601

KROUT, MICHAEL SETH, lawyer; b. N.Y.C., Oct. 2, 1945; s. Percy Maurice and Ruth Krout; m. Susan Krout, June 28, 1975; children: Jeremy Charles, Ethan Loren. BS, U. Pa., 1966; JD, Boston U., 1969. Bar: N.Y. 1970, Nev. 1970, Calif. 1972. Dir. atty. Inner Tribal Coun. of Nev., Reno, 1969-71; house counsel Honeywell Farms, Jamaica, N.Y., 1971-73; assoc. George De Wolfe, N.Y.C., 1973-75; pvt. practice San Luis Obispo, Calif., 1975—. Counsel San Luis Obispo Bicycle Club, 1975—, San Luis Obispo Blues Soc., 1979—. Mem. San Luis Obispo County Bar Assn., Elks. Estate planning, General practice, Property, real (including real estate development, water). Home: PO Box 1028 San Luis Obispo CA 93406-1028 Office: Michael S Krout A Law Corp 1264 Higuera St San Luis Obispo CA 93401-3124

KRSUL, JOHN ALOYSIUS, JR., lawyer; b. Highland Park, Mich., Mar. 24, 1938; s. John A. and Ann M. (Sepich) K.; m. Justine Oliver, Sept. 12, 1958; children: Ann Lisa, Mary Justine. BA, Albion Coll., 1959; JD, U. Mich., 1963. Bar: Mich. 1963. Assoc. Dickinson Wright PLLP, 1963-71, ptnr., 1971-99, consulting ptnr., 2000—. Asst. editor: U. Mich. Law Rev, 1962-63. Recipient Disting. Alumnus award Albion Coll., 1984; Sloan scholar, 1958-59; Fulbright scholar, 1959-60; Ford. Found. grantee, 1964 Fellow: Am. Bar Found. (life; chmn. Mich. chpt. 1988—89); mem.: ABA (ho. of dels. 1979—2002, chmn. standing com. on membership 1983—89, exec. coun. 1984—91, chmn. sect. gen. practice 1989—90, tort and ins. practice sect., exec. coun. 1991—94, bd. govs. 1991—99, chmn. fin. com. 1993—94, exec. com. 1993—94, 1996—99, treas. 1996—99, editl. bd. ABA Jour. 1996—99, chmn. audit com. 2003—), Am. Bar Ins. Cons. Inc. (bd. dirs. sec. 1988—95), Am. Bar Endowment (bd. dirs. 1996—99), Nat. Conf. Bar Pres. (exec. coun. 1986—89), Am. Judicature Soc. (dir. 1971—79, exec. com. 1973—74), Fellows of Young Lawyers Am. Bar (bd. dirs. 1977—86, pres. 1983—84, chmn. bd. 1984—86), Mich. State Bar Found. (trustee 1982—83, 1985—99, chmn. fellows 1986—87), State Bar Mich. (commr. 1973—83, pres. 1982—83), Detroit Bar Assn. Found. (dir. 1971—84, pres. 1979—80), Detroit Bar Assn. (dir. 1971—80, pres. 1979—80), Am. Bar Retirement Assn. (bd. dirs. 1999—2003), Sixth Cir. Jud. Conf. (life), Detroit Club, Orchard Lake Country Club, Delta Tau Delta, Phi Eta Sigma, Omicron Delta Kappa, Phi Beta Kappa. Antitrust, Corporate, general. Home: 7094 Huntington Dr Sawyer MI 49125-9319 Office: Dickinson Wright PLLC 500 Woodward Ave Ste 4000 Detroit MI 48226-3416

KRUCKS, WILLIAM NORMAN, lawyer; b. Chgo., Oct. 28, 1949; s. William and Lorraine (Rauland) K.; m. Linda C. Robertson; children: Kathryn Leigh, Greta Anne, Laura Elizabeth. BA, Tulane U., 1972; JD, U. Miss., 1976. Bar: Ill. 1976, Miss. 1976, U.S. Dist. Ct. (no. dist.) Ill. 1976, U.S. Dist. Ct. (no. dist.) Miss. 1976, U.S. Ct. Appeals (5th and 7th cirs.) 1976, U.S. Supreme Ct. 1980, U.S. Dist. Ct. (cen. dist.) Ill. 1984. Assoc. Rooks, Pitts and Poust, Chgo., 1976-83; founding ptnr. Freeborn & Peters, Chgo., 1983—. Chmn., gen. counsel, bd. dirs., corp. sec. Rauland Borg Corp. Editor Miss. Law Jour., 1974-76; contbr. articles to law jours. Atty. Chgo. Vol. Legal Svcs., 1982—. Named Outstanding Young Man Am., U.S. Jaycees, 1976; recipient Dean Robert T. Farley award U. Miss., 1977. Mem. Ill. Self-Insured Assn., Def. Rsch. Inst., Chgo. Assn. Commerce and Industry, Nat. Coun. Self-Insured, Beter Govt. Assn., Am. Jud. Soc., Tulane U. Alumni Assn., U. Miss. Alumni Assn., ABA, Ill. Bar Assn., Chgo. Bar Assn., Miss. Bar Assn., Workers Compensation Lawyers Assn., Legal Club Chgo., Union League Club (Chgo.), Chgo. Yacht Club, Internat. Assn. of Def. Counsel, Phi Delta Phi, Sigma Nu. Methodist. State civil litigation, Labor (including EEOC, Fair Labor Standards Act, labor-management relations, NLRB, OSHA), Workers' compensation. Home: 920 Sunset Rd Winnetka IL 60093-3623 E-mail: bkrucks@freebornpeters.com, wnk@krucks.com.

KRUEGER, HERBERT WILLIAM, lawyer; b. Milw., Apr. 20, 1948; s. Herbert William Sr. and Lily (Kuphall) K.; m. Judith Ann Wanserske, July 20, 1970; children— Kara, Dana, Andrew, Christopher. B.A., U. Wis.-Milw., 1970; J.D., U. Chgo., 1974. Bar: Fla. 1974, Ill. 1975, U.S. Dist. Ct. (no. dist.) Ill. 1975. Instr. in law U. Miami Sch. Law, Coral Gables, Fla., 1974-75; assoc. Mayer, Brown & Platt, Chgo., 1975-80, ptnr., 1981— , head compensation dept., 1984—, mem. mgmt. com., 1989—. Contbg. author Continuing Legal Education Pension Practice and Securities Laws handbooks, Practising Law Inst. handbook Acquiring and Selling Privately Held Companies, Pension Investment Handbook; contbr. articles to profl. jours. State dir. Wis. Coll. Reps., 1969-70; exec. dir. Com. to Reelect Pres., Wis. Young Voters Campaign, 1972; chmn. fiduciary standards com. Ill. Study Commn. on Pub. Pension Investment Policies, 1981-82; mem. nat. adv. bd. NYU Real Estate Inst. Pension Fund Investment in Real Estate Conf. Mem. ABA, Pension Real Estate Assn. (mem. govt. affairs com.). Pension, profit-sharing, and employee benefits. Office: Mayer Brown & Platt 190 S La Salle St Ste 3100 Chicago IL 60603-3441

KRUEGER, JAMES A. lawyer; b. Sept. 21, 1943; s. A.A. and Margaret E. (Hurley) K.; m. Therese Eileen Connors, Aug. 2, 1968; 1 child, Colleen. BA cum laude, Gonzaga U., 1965; JD, Georgetown U., 1968; LLM, NYU, 1972. Bar: Wash. 1969, U.S. Supreme Ct. 1972, U.S. Tax Ct. 1972, U.S. Dist. Ct. (we. dist.) Wash. 1980, U.S. Ct. Appeals (9th cir.) 1982. Mem. staff U.S. senator from Wash., 1967-68; assoc. Kane, Vandeberg & Hartinger, Tacoma, 1972-76; ptnr. Kane, Vandeberg, Hartinger & Walker, Tacoma, 1976-90; shareholder Vandeberg & Johnson PS, Tacoma, 1990—. Spl. dist. counsel Wash. State Bar Assn., 1984-94; adj. prof. law, U. of Puget Sound, 1974-76. Co-author: Representing the Close Corporation, 1979, Partnership Agreements, 1981, Planning for the Small Business Enterprise, 1982, The Partnership Handbook, 1984. Chmn. bd. Cath. Cmty. Svcs. of Pierce and Kitsap Counties, 1983-84; bd. dirs. United Way of Pierce County, 1973-82, 99—. Capt. U.S. Army, 1968-72. Decorated Bronze star. Mem. ABA, Wash. State Bar Assn. (spl. dist. counsel), Tacoma-Pierce County Bar Assn. Roman Catholic. General civil litigation, Corporate, general, Estate planning. Office: 1201 Pacific Ave Ste 1900 Tacoma WA 98402-4315

KRUPANSKY, ROBERT BAZIL, federal judge; b. Cleve., Aug. 15, 1921; s. Frank A. and Anna (Lawrence) K.; m. Marjorie Blaser, Nov. 13, 1952. BA, Case Western Res. U., 1946, LLB, 1948, JD, 1968. Bar: Ohio 1948, Supreme Ct. Ohio 1948, Supreme Ct. U.S. 1948, U.S. Dist. Ct. (no. dist.) Ohio 1948, U.S. Ct. Appeals (6th cir.) 1948, U.S. Ct. Customs and Patent Appeals 1948, U.S. Customs Ct. 1948, ICC 1948. Pvt. practice law, Cleve., 1948—51; asst. atty. gen. State of Ohio, 1951—57; mem. Gov. of Ohio cabinet and dir. Ohio Dept. Liquor Control, 1957—58; judge Common Pleas Ct. of Cuyahoga County, 1958—60; sr. ptnr. Metzenbaum, Gaines, Krupansky, Finley & Stern, 1960—69; U.S. atty. U.S. Dist. Ct. (no. dist.) Ohio, Cleve., 1969—70, U.S. dist. judge, 1970—82; judge U.S. Ct. Appeals (6th cir.), Cleve., 1982—91, sr. judge, 1991—. Legal cons. City of Mayfield Heights, Ohio, 1960—64; spl. counsel Atty. Gen. Ohio, 1964—68; adj. prof. law Case Western Res. U. Sch. Law, 1969—70. 2d lt. U.S. Army, pilot USAAC, 1942—46, col. USAF Res. ret. Mem.: FBA, ABA, Assn. Asst. Attys. Gen. State Ohio, Am. Judicature Soc., Cuyahoga County Bar Assn., Cleve. Bar Assn. Office: Carl B Stokes US Courthouse 801 W Superior Ave Cleveland OH 44113-1832

KRUPKA, ROBERT GEORGE, lawyer; b. Rochester, N.Y., Oct. 21, 1949; s. Joseph Anton and Marjorie Clara (Meteyer) Krupka; m. Pamela Banner Krupka; children: Kristin Nicole, Kerry Melissa. BS, Georgetown U., 1971; JD, U. Chgo., 1974. Bar: Ill. 1974, Colo. 1991, D.C., 1991, Calif. 1998, U.S. Dist. Ct. (no. dist.) Ill. 1974, U.S. Dist. Ct. (ea. dist.) Wis. 1974, U.S. Ct. Appeals (7th cir.) 1976, U.S. Supreme Ct. 1978, U.S. Dist. Ct. (cen. dist.) Ill. 1980, U.S. Dist. Ct. (no. dist.) Calif. 1980, U.S. Dist. Ct. (ctrl. and so. dists.) Calif. 1999, U.S. Ct. Appeals (4th and fed. cirs.) 1982, U.S. Ct. Appeals (6th cir.) 1985, U.S. Ct. Appeals (1st, 2d, 3d, 5th, 8th, 9th, 10th and 11th dists.) 1999. Assoc. Kirkland & Ellis, Chgo., 1974-79, ptnr., 1979—. Author: Infringement Litigation Computer Software and Database, 1984, Computer Software, Semiconductor Design, Video Game and Database Protection and Enforcement, 1984. Mem. bd. trustees Francis W. Parker Sch., 1987-98, pres., 1994-97. Mem. ABA (chmn. sec. com. 1982-88, chmn. div. 1988-90, 98—, coun. 1994-97), Computer Law Assn., U.S. Patent Quar. Adv. Bd., Am. Intellectual Property Law Assn. (chmn. subcom. 1988—), Mid-Am. Club. Federal civil litigation, Patent, Trademark and copyright. Office: Kirkland & Ellis 777 S Figueroa Ste 3700 Los Angeles CA 90017- E-mail: bob_krupka@kirkland.com.

KRUPMAN, WILLIAM ALLAN, lawyer; b. Cleve., Aug. 14, 1936; s. Joel and Betty (Button) K; m. Anne deLemos, June 19, 1960; children: Pamela, Theodore, Sally. BA, Amherst Coll., 1958; LLB, U. Mich., 1961; LLM in Labor Law, N.Y.U., 1962. Bar: Ohio 1961, N.Y. 1962. Ptnr. Jackson Lewis LLP, N.Y.C., 1962-75, mng. ptnr., 1975—. Author: Winning NLRB Elections, 1997. Bd. dirs. Children's Village, Dobbs Ferry, N.Y. Mem. N.Y. State Bar Assn. Labor (including EEOC, Fair Labor Standards Act, labor-management relations, NLRB, OSHA). Home: 2 Ponds Ln Purchase NY 10577 Office: Jackson Lewis LLP 59 Maiden Ln New York NY 10038-4502

KRUSE, F. MICHAEL, judge; Now chief justice High Ct. Am. Samoa, Pago Pago. Office: The High Ct Am Samoa Cthse Chief Justice PO Box 309 Pago Pago AS 96799*

KRUSE, JOHN ALPHONSE, lawyer; b. Detroit, Sept. 11, 1926; s. Frank R. and Ann (Nestor) K.; m. Mary Louise Dalton, July 14, 1951; children: Gerard, Mary Louise, Terence, Kathleen, Joanne, Francis, John, Patrick. BS, U. Detroit, 1950, JD cum laude, 1952. Bar: Mich. bar 1952. Ptnr. Alexander, Buchanan & Conklin, Detroit, 1952-69, Harvey, Kruse, PC, Detroit, 1969—. Guest lectr. U. Mich., U. Detroit, Inst. Continuing Legal Edn.; city atty. Allen Park, Mich., 1954-59; twp. atty., Van Buren Twp., Mich., 1959-61. Co-founder Detroit and Mich. Cath. Radio. Past pres. Palmer Woods Assn.; mem. pres.'s cabinet U. Detroit; bd. dirs. Providence Hosp. Found.; trustee Ave Maria Coll. Named one of 5 Outstanding Young Men in Mich., 1959, Outstanding Alumnus, U. Detroit Sch. Law, 1989, Humanitarian award Neuromuscular Inst. 1988. Mem. Detroit Bar Assn., State Bar Mich. (past chmn. negligence sect.), Assn. Def. Trial Counsel (bd. dirs. 1966-67), Am. Judicature Soc., Internat. Assn. Def. Counsel, Equestrian Order of the Holy Sepulchre. Clubs: Detroit Golf (past pres.). Roman Catholic. State civil litigation, Insurance, Personal injury (including property damage). Home: 5569 Hunters Gate Dr Troy MI 48098-2342 Office: 1050 Wilshire Dr Ste 320 Troy MI 48084-1526 E-mail: jkruse@harveykruse.com., johnakruse@comcast.net.

KRUSE, LAYNE E. lawyer; b. Emporia, Kans., Aug. 15, 1951; BA, Tex. A&M U., 1973; MSc, London Sch. Econs., 1974; JD, Yale U., 1977. Bar: Tex. 1978, cert.: Tex. Bd. Legal Specialization (civil trial law). Law clk. to Hon. John R. Brown U.S. Ct. Appeals (5th cir.); mem. Fulbright & Jaworski, L.L.P., Houston. Chair antitrust and bus. litigation sect. State Bar Tex. Mem.: ABA, Houston Bar Assn. Antitrust, General civil litigation. Office: Fulbright & Jaworski LLP 1301 Mckinney St Ste 5100 Houston TX 77010-3031

KRUSE, PAMELA JEAN, lawyer; b. Miami, Fla., June 3, 1950; d. Robert Emil and Irma G. Kruse. BS, Mich. State U., 1973, MA, 1975, PhD, 1979; JD, U. Mich., 1985. Bar: Mich. 1986. Grad. asst. Mich. State U., East Lansing, 1976-77, asst. intramural dir., 1977-79, labor rels. rep., 1979-81, asst. dir. labor rels., 1981-82; resident mgr. 719 Oakland, Ann Arbor, Mich., 1982-83; rsch. asst. Law Sch. U. Mich., Ann Arbor, 1982-85; jud. clk. U.S. Dist. Ct. (we. dist.) Mich., 1985-86; assoc. Clary, Nantz, Wood, Hoffius, Rankin & Cooper, Grand Rapids, Mich., 1986-91; with Village Bike Shops, 1991—. Bd. dirs. Babe Zaharias Golf Tournament, Am. Cancer Soc., 1987-91. Recipient Gold and Silver medals U.S. Pan Am. Team, Winnipeg, Man., Can., 1967, Silver medal U.S. Olympic Team, Mexico City, 1968; holder world records swimming 400 meters freestyle, 1967, 200 meters freestyle, 1967, 440-yard freestyle, 1966; inducted to Greater Fort Lauderdale Sports Hall of Fame, 1979. Mem. ABA, State Bar Mich. (exec. coun. young lawyers sect. 1987-90), Grand Rapids Bar Assn. (chairperson, exec. bd. dirs. young lawyers sect. 1987-91), Mich. Pub. Employer Labor Rels. Assn. (bd. dirs. 1981-82, chmn. manual revision com. 1982), Mich. State U. Alumni Assn. (1st v.p., bd. dirs. 1988-89), U.S. Olympians, Phi Delta Kappa, Kappa Alpha Theta. Labor (including EEOC, Fair Labor Standards Act, labor-management relations, NLRB, OSHA). Office: Village Bike Shop Ltd 450 A Baldwin St Jenison MI 49428

KRUTTER, FORREST NATHAN, lawyer; b. Boston, Dec. 17, 1954; s. Irving and Shirley Krutter. BS in Econs., MS in Civil Engring., MIT, 1976; JD cum laude, Harvard U., 1978. Bar: Nebr. 1978, U.S. Supreme Ct. 1986, N.Y. 1991. Antitrust counsel Union Pacific R.R., Omaha, 1978-86; sr. v.p. law, sec. Berkshire Hathaway Group, Omaha, 1986—; pres. Republic Ins., Dallas, 2000—. Co-author: Impact of Railroad Abandonments, 1976, Railroad Development in the Third World, 1978; author: Judicial Enforcement of Competition in Regulated Industries, 1979; contbr. articles Creighton Law Rev. Mem. ABA, Phi Beta Kappa, Sigma Xi. Administrative and regulatory, Corporate, general, Insurance. Office: Berkshire Hathaway Group 4016 Farnam St Omaha NE 68131-3016 Business E-Mail: fkrutter@berkre.com.

KRYGOWSKI, WALTER JOHN, lawyer; b. Detroit; s. Walter Robert and Joann Virginia Krygowski. BA, Oakland U., 1992; JD, U. Dayton, 1996. Bar: Ohio 1996, U.S. Dist. Ct. (so. dist.) Ohio 1996, U.S. Ct. Appeals (6th cir.) 1998. Law clk. Banc One Corp., Dayton, Ohio, 1995; contract atty. Dwight D. Brannon & Assocs., Dayton, 1996-99; ast. city atty. City of Dayton, 1999—. Arbitrator Montgomery County Ct. Common Pleas-Compulsory Arbitration, Dayton, 1996-99. Mem. Ohio State Bar Assn., Airport Coun. Internat., Am. Assn. Airport Execs., Ohio Acad. Trial Lawyers. Roman Catholic. Commercial, contracts (including sales of goods; commercial financing), Municipal (including bonds). Home: 4037 Loyala Chase Ln Dayton OH 45424-8004 Office: City of Dayton Law Dept PO Box 22 Dayton OH 45401-0022 Fax: 937-333-3628. E-mail: chanelka@aol.com.

KRZYZANOWSKI, RICHARD L. lawyer, corporate executive; b. Warsaw, Mar. 25, 1932; came to U.S., 1967, naturalized, 1972; s. Andrew and Mary K.; children: Suzanne, Peter, Christine. BA, U. Warsaw, 1956; ML, U. Pa., 1960; PhD, U. Paris, 1962. Bar: Pa. With Crown Cork & Seal Co., Inc., Phila., 1967—, dir., exec. v.p. gen. counsel, 1990-2001. Counselor John Paul II Found., Vatican, Rome, Italy; exec. trustee, founder Krzyzanowski Found., Phila. Mem. Int. Bar Assn. (London). Corporate, general, Private international, Public international. Office: Crown Cork & Seal Co Inc 1 Crown Way Philadelphia PA 19154-4599

KUBALE, BERNARD STEPHEN, lawyer; b. Reedsville, Wis., Sept. 5, 1928; s. Joseph and Josephine (Novak) K.; m. Mary Thomas, Apr. 21, 1956, (dec. Jan. 13, 2001); children: Caroline, Catherine, Anne. BBA, U. Wis., 1950, LLB, 1955; LLD (hon.), St. Norbert Coll., 1985. Bar: Wis. 1955; CPA, Wis. Acct. John D. Morrison and Co., Marquette, Mich., 1950-51; atty., ptnr. Foley and Lardner, Milw., 1955—, chmn. mgmt. com., 1985-94. Bd. dirs. Green Bay Packers, Wis. E.R. Wagner Mfg. Co., Milw., Wausau, Homes, Wis. Chmn. bd. dirs. St. Norbert Coll., DePere, Wis., 1980-84, Children's Hosp. Wis., Milw., 1982-91. 1st lt. USAF, 1951-53. Mem. ABA, Wis. Inst. CPAs, Wis. Bar Assn., Milw. Bar Assn., Chenequa Country Club, Milw. Country Club, The Milw. Club. Republican. Roman Catholic. Avocations: fishing, skiing, baseball. Corporate, general, Mergers and acquisitions, Securities. Home: 5935 Monclaire Rd Hartland WI 53029 Office: Foley & Lardner 1st Wisconsin Ctr 777 E Wisconsin Ave Ste 3800 Milwaukee WI 53202-5367

KUBICZKY, STEPHEN RALPH, lawyer; b. North Braddock, Pa., Oct. 8, 1947; s. Stephen Ralph and Helen (Kish) K. BS, U. Notre Dame, 1969, MS, 1977; JD, Northwestern U., 1972. Bar: Ill. 1972, U.S. Dist. Ct. (no. dist.) Ill. 1972, U.S. Ct. Claims 1978, U.S. Tax Ct. 1978, U.S. Ct. Appeals (7th cir.) 1979. Assoc. Altheimer & Gray, Chgo., 1973-75, 77-80, ptnr., 1980-91, counsel, 1991-92; pvt. practice Riverside, Ill. Chmn. planning com., materials author Ill. Inst. Continuing Legal Edn., 1983, 94, 87-88, 93, 97; pub. witness Pres.'s Commn. on Pension Policy, 1981; mem. instnl. rev. bd. Rush-Presbyn. St. Luke's Med. Ctr., 1999—. Vol. coord. Ill. state Bush/Quayle '92 Presdl. campaign; pres. Riverside Twp. Regular Rep. Orgn., 1994-98; trustee Triton Coll., 1995—. Recipient Hero of the Heart award, 2001, Caught in the Act of Caring award, 2003. Mem. ABA, Ill. State Bar Assn. (chmn. employee benefits sect. 1981-83, sect. coun. fed. taxation sect. 1980-84, contbr. newsletter 1980-85), Wigmore Club (exec. com. 1992-96), Henry Wade Rogers Soc., Ill. Cmty. Coll. trustees Assn. (sec. 1999-2000, chmn. north suburban region 1998-99, Spl. Achievement award 2000, Leadership award 2000, Edn. award 2000). Pension, profit-sharing, and employee benefits. Office: PO Box 86 Riverside IL 60546-0086

KUBO, EDWARD HACHIRO, JR., prosecutor; b. Honolulu, July 9, 1953; s. Edward H. and Rose M. (Coltes) K.; children: Diana K., Dawn M., Edward H. III. BA in Polit. Sci., U. Hawaii, 1976; JD, U. San Diego, 1979. Bar: Hawaii 1979. Legal asst. Legal Aid Soc. Hawaii, 1975-76; law clk. Kobayashi & Watanabe, Honolulu, 1979; dep. pros. atty. Honolulu City Prosecutor's Office, 1980-83, 85-90; assoc. Carlsmith & Dwyer, Honolulu, 1983-85; asst. U.S. atty. U.S. Atty.'s Office, Honolulu, 1990—2001; US atty. U.S. Dept. of Justice, Hawaii, 2001—. Instr. Honolulu Police Dept. Acad., Waipahu, Hawaii, 1986-89; lectr. U.S. Dept. Justice, Lincoln, Neb., 1997, Pearl Harbor Police Acad., 1995, Western State Vice Investigators Assn. Conf., Houston, 1997, Las Vegas, 1998; spkr. teleconf. U.S. Dept. Justice Violence Against Women Act, 1998, Hawaii Bar Assn. H.S. Mock trial adv., 1996-99. Co-author: Concurrent Jurisdiction for Civil RICO, 1987. Recipient Nat. Art medal (France), 1992, Cert. of Appreciation, U.S. Immigration and Naturalization Svc., 1992, Drug Enforcement Adminstrn., 1997, Plaque of Appreciation, U.S. Border Patrol, 1995, cert. appreciation Bureau Alcohol, Tobacco & Firearms, 1999. Mem. Hawaii Bar Assn., Order of Barristers.*

KUBY, RONALD LAWRENCE, lawyer; b. Cleve., July 31, 1956; s. Donald Joseph Kuby and Ruth Miller; m. Marilyn Vasta; 1 child, Emma Sojourner Vasta-Kuby. BA, U. Kans., 1979; JD magna cum laude, Cornell U., 1983. Bar: N.Y. 1984. Assoc. Kunstler & Kuby, N.Y.C., 1994—95, Law Office William M. Kunstler, N.Y.C., 1984—94; ptnr. Law Office Ronald L. Kuby, N.Y.C., 1996—. Contbr. articles to profl. jours. Mem. adv. bd. police misconduct task force N.Y. Civil Liberties Union, 1999—. Recipient Thurgood Marshall award, N.Y. City Bar Assn., 1998, N.Y. Metro Achievement in Radio award for best talk show host, 2000, N.Y. Metro Achievement in Radio award for best talk show, 2001, award for excellence in 9/11 broadcasting, UFA/UFOA (N.Y. Firefighters), 2003. Communist. Office: 740 Broadway Fl 5 New York NY 10003-9518 E-mail: ronkuby@aol.com.

KUCZWARA, THOMAS PAUL, postal inspector, lawyer; b. Dec. 21, 1951; s. Stanley Leo and Eleanore (Pawelko) K.; m. Diana Lynn Rychtarczyk, Sept. 8, 1979; 1 child, Paul Stanley. BA, Loyola U., Chgo., 1973; JD, U. S.C., 1976. Bar: Ill. 1976, U.S. Dist. Ct. (no. dist.) Ill. 1982. Assoc. Doria Law Offices, Chgo., 1977-78; asst. corp. counsel City of Chgo., 1978-80; asst. city atty. City of Aurora, Ill., 1980-82; postal insp. U.S. Postal Inspection Svc., Salt Lake City, 1982-85, regional insp. atty. cen. region Chgo., 1985—. Mem. St. Bartholomew's Parish Coun., Chgo., 1978; vol. atty. Lawyers for Creative Arts, 1978. Ill. state scholar, 1969. Mem. Sierra Club, Pi Sigma Alpha. Roman Catholic. Office: US Postal Inspection Svc Chgo Divsn 433 W Harrison 6th Fl Chicago IL 60669-2201 E-mail: tpkuczwara@uspis.gov.

KUDER, ARMIN ULRICH, lawyer; b. Phila., Nov. 14, 1935; s. David Dennis and Ethel Rose (Strasburger) Kuder; m. Patricia A. Hipple, June 28, 1959 (div. Mar. 1968); children: Carlyn Elizabeth, Eric David, Keith Ulrich; m. Margaret A. Trossen, July 26, 2002. AB, Lafayette Coll., 1956; LLB, Harvard U., 1959. Bar: D.C. 1959, Md. 1987, U.S. Ct. Mil. Appeals 1962, U.S. Dist. Ct. Md. 1968. Assoc. Coles & Goertner, Washington, 1963-65, Mehler, Smollar et al., Washington, 1965-67; ptnr. Smollar & Kuder, Washington, 1967-68, Kuder, Sherman et al., Washington, 1968-78, Kuder, Smollar & Friedman P.C., Washington, 1978—. Lectr. continuing legal edn., various locations. Chmn. Nat. Health Agys., NCAC, 1977—78, Ctr. Marine Conservation, Washington, 1981—83, NIMH human subjects rev. panel, 1978—83; vice chmn. Arthritis Found., Atlanta, 1979—80, 1990—92, chmn., 1992—94; pres. Arthritis and Rheumatism Internat., 1996—98, treas., 1998—; mem. internat. steering com. The Bone and Joint Decade, Lund, Sweden, 2000—; bd. dirs. Can. Arthritis Network, 2001—02; chmn. Hyde Sch., Bath, Maine, 1984—87, New Art Assn., Washington, 1986—87; sec. Combined Health Appeal, Washington, 1984; mem. Gov.'s Adv. Coun. on the Future of Nursing in Va., 2002—. Served to lt. comdr. JAGC USNR, 1959—63. Fellow Am. Acad. Matrimonial Lawyers, Internat. Acad. of Matrimonial Lawyers; mem. ABA, D.C. Bar Assn. (trustee client security fund 1984-92, chmn. 1991-92, hearing com. chmn. bd. on profl. responsibility 1985-91), Md. Bar Assn., Montgomery County Bar Assn., Bar Assn. D.C. State civil litigation, Family and matrimonial, Health. Office: Kuder Smollar & Friedman PC 1925 K St NW Washington DC 20006-1105 E-mail: akuder@ksflaw.com.

KUDRAVETZ, DAVID WALLER, lawyer; b. Sumter, S.C., Feb. 2, 1948; s. George and Barbara (Waller) K.; m. Eleanor McCrea Snyder, June 21, 1969; 1 child, Julia McCrea. BS, U. Va., 1971, JD, 1974. Bar: Va. 1974, U.S. Tax Ct. 1974; CPA, Va. Assoc. Robert M. Musselman, Charlottesville, Va., 1974; ptnr. Carwile & Kudravetz, Charlottesville, Va., 1975-78, McClure, Callaghan & McCallum, Charlottesville, Va., 1979-81, McCallum & Kudravetz, P.C., Charlottesville, Va., 1982—. Instr. fed. income taxation U. of Va. Sch. Continuing Edn., 1975-79. Mem. AICPA, Va. State Bar Assn., Charlottesville-Albemarle Bar Assn., Am. Assn. Atty.-CPAs, Va. Soc. CPAs. Estate planning, Property, real (including real estate development, water), Personal income taxation. Office: McCallum & Kudravetz PC 250 E High St Charlottesville VA 22902-5178 E-mail: DWK@MKPC.com.

KUEBLER, MARGARET PATRICIA, lawyer; b. Memphis, Sept. 21, 1956; d. Charles William Kuebler and Emilie Stanford Smythe. BA in English and Art History cum laude, Hollins Coll., 1975; cert. in corp. law, Adelphi U., 1978; ScD student Sch. of Hygiene/Pub. Health, Johns Hopkins U., 1982-83; MPH, MBA, U. Ala., 1984; postgrad., U. Miss., 1987, 88; postgrad. Faculty of Laws, U. Coll., London, 1988; JD, Pace U., 1989. Bar: Tenn. 1997. Lawyer's asst. Legal Aid Soc., Staten Island, N.Y., 1975, Roanoke, Va., 1975; asst. to treas. Realty Assocs., Inc., Bklyn., 1975-78; legal asst. Davis Polk & Wardwell, N.Y.C., 1978-79; rsch. asst. U. Ala. Hosps., Birmingham, 1982; rsch. asst. divsn. gynecologic oncology Johns Hopkins Hosp., Balt., 1983; rsch. analyst II Bapt. Meml. Hosp., Memphis, 1985; lawyer's asst. Borod & Huggins, Attys., Memphis, 1985-86, Glankler Brown, PLLC, Memphis, 1986; executrix Estate of Charles W. Kuebler, 1986—. Asst. to technical dir.and merchandising mgr. plastics divsn. Toray Industries (America), Inc., N.Y.C., 1976; paralegal Morgan Guarantee Trust Co.; rsch. asst. pharmacology com. WHO, London, 1988. Contbr. short story and two poems to literary mag. Mem. Hollins' Art Assn. and Orgn. Women; counselor S.I. Acad. Day Camp; vol. Edn. and Rsch. Dept. Mus. Modern Art, Birmingham Mus. Art, S.I. Hosp.; nurses aide Silver Lake Nursing Home. Acad. scholar Hollins Coll., 1972-75, Johns Hopkins U., 1982-83, Pace U., 1986-87. Mem. ABA, APHA, Am. Trial Lawyers Assn., Tenn. Bar Assn., Shelby County Bar Assn., Nat. Health Lawyers Assn., Pace U. Sch. Law's Health Law Soc., Hollins' Lit. Soc., Nat. Honor Soc., Population Assn. Am., Student Liaison Com., Model UN Security Coun. Debate Team, Pi Delta Phi. Episcopalian. Home: PO Box 487 Batesville MS 38606-0487

KUEHLING, ROBERT WARREN, lawyer, accountant; b. Madison, Wis., Aug. 31, 1952; s. Warren Ernest and Mary Alice (Jenkins) K.; m. Susan Mary O'Brien, July 8, 1978; children: Megan Ann, Jeffrey Robert. BBA, U. Wis., JD, 1976. Bar: Wis. 1977, U.S. Dist. Ct. (we. dist.) Wis. 1977; CPA. Ptnr. Kuehling & Kuehling, Madison, 1977—. Lawyer, accountant; b. Madison, Jr. Aug. 31, 1952; s. Warren Ernest and Mary Alice (Jenkins) K.; m. Susan Mary O'Brien, July 8, 1978; children— Megan Ann, Jeffrey Robert. B.B.A., U. Wis., J.D., 1976. Bar: Wis. 1977, U.S. Dist. Ct. (we. dist.) Wis. 1977; C.P.A. Ptnr. Kuehling & Kuehling, Madison, 1977— . Probate (including wills, trusts), Property, real (including real estate development, water). Office: Kuehling & Kuehling 131 W Wilson St Ste 501 Madison WI 53703-3243 E-mail: kuehling@execpc.com.

KUEHN, GEORGE E. lawyer, former beverage company executive; b. N.Y.C., June 19, 1946; m. Mary Kuehn; children: Kristin, Rob, Geoff. BBA, U. Mich., 1968, JD, 1973. Bar: Mich. 1974. Assoc. Hill, Lewis et al, Detroit, 1974-78; ptnr. Butzel, Long et al, Detroit, 1978-81; exec. v.p., gen. counsel, sec. The Stroh Brewery Co., Detroit, 1981-99—; shareholder Butzel Long, Detroit, 2000—. With U.S. Army, 1969-71. Corporate, general, Mergers and acquisitions. Office: Butzel Long Ste 900 150 W Jefferson Ave Detroit MI 48226 E-mail: Kuehn@butzel.com.

KUELTHAU, PAUL STAUFFER, lawyer; b. West Bend, Wis., Mar. 31, 1912; s. George Herman and Marie Louise (Rix) K.; m. Laura Parish, Aug. 16, 1937; children: Karen Allan, Marline Holmes. AB, U. Wis., 1934, JD, 1936. Bar: Wis. 1936, U.S. Ct. Appeals (10th cir.) 1941, U.S. Ct. Appeals (7th cir.) 1947, Mo. 1953, U.S. Dist. Ct. (ea. dist.) Mo. 1954, U.S. Ct. Appeals (8th cir.) 1962, U.S. Dist. Ct. (so. dist.) Ill. 1964, U.S. Supreme Ct. 1973, U.S. Ct. Appeals (D.C. cir.) 1974. Regional atty. NLRB, various locations, 1939-46, chief counsel to chmn. Washington, 1946-53; assoc. Lewis, Rice, Tucker, Allen & Chubb, St. Louis, 1953-62; ptnr. Moller, Talent, Kuelthau, & Welch, St. Louis, 1962-88. Contbr. articles to profl. jours. Mem. ABA, Mo. Bar Assn., Bar Assn. St. Louis, Indsl. Relations Research Assn. Presbyterian. Labor (including EEOC, Fair Labor Standards Act, labor-management relations, NLRB, OSHA). Home: 3 Rehabilitation Way Apt 417 Woburn MA 01801-6025

KUH, RICHARD HENRY, lawyer; b. N.Y.C., Apr. 27, 1921; s. Joseph Hellmann and Fannie Mina (Rees) K.; m. Joyce Dattel, July 31, 1966; children: Michael Joseph, Jody Ellen. BA, Columbia Coll., 1941; LLB magna cum laude, Harvard U., 1948. Bar: N.Y. 1948, U.S. Dist. Ct. (so. dist.) N.Y. 1948, U.S. Dist. Ct. (ea. dist.) N.Y. 1967, U.S. Supreme Ct. 1968. Assoc. firm Cahill, Gordon & Reindel, 1948-53; asst. dist. atty. N.Y. County Dist. Attys. Office, 1953-64, dist. atty., 1974; pvt. practice law N.Y.C., 1966-71; ptnr. firm Kuh, Goldman, Cooperman & Levitt, N.Y.C., 1971-73, Kuh, Shapiro, Goldman, Cooperman & Levitt, P.C., N.Y.C., 1975-78, Warshaw Burstein Cohen Schlesinger & Kuh, N.Y.C., 1978—. Adj. prof. NYU Law Sch. Author: Foolish Figleaves, 1967; mem. bd. editors: Harvard Law Rev, 1947-48; mem. adv. bd.: Contemporary Drug Problems, 1975—, Criminal Law Bull, 1976— ; contbr. articles to popular and profl. jours. Trustee Temple Israel, N.Y.C., 1975-84, Grace Ch. Sch., 1981-85. With U.S. Army, 1942-45, ETO. Walter E. Meyer Research and Writing grantee, 1964-65 Mem. ABA (chair criminal justice sect. 1983-84, chair spl. com. on evaluation jud. performance 1983-90, ho. dels. 1988-93, mem. jud. evaluation adv. com. Nat. Ctr. State Cts. 1990-91, chair 1st nat. conf. gun violence 1994), Assn. Bar City N.Y., Am. Bar Found., Harvard Law Sch. Assn. N.Y. (trustee 1989-92), Harvard Club (mem. admissions com. 1998-01), Phi Beta Kappa. Democrat. Jewish. Federal civil litigation, State civil litigation, Criminal. Home: 14 Washington Pl New York NY 10003-6609 Office: 555 5th Ave New York NY 10017-2416

KUHLMANN, FRED MARK, lawyer, business executive; b. St. Louis, Apr. 9, 1948; s. Frederick Louis and Mildred (Southworth) K.; m. Barbara Jane Nierman, Dec. 30, 1970; children: F. Matthew, Sarah Ann. AB summa cum laude, Washington U., St. Louis, 1970; JD cum laude, Harvard U., 1973. Bar: Mo. 1973. Assoc. atty. Stolar, Heitzmann & Eder, St. Louis, 1973-75; from tax counsel to staff v.p. McDonnell Douglas Corp., St. Louis, 1975—87, sr. v.p., gen. counsel, 1991—97; exec. v.p. McDonnell Douglas Health Systems Co., 1987—89; pres. McDonnell Douglas Systems Integration Co., 1989—91; of counsel Bryan Cave, St. Louis, 1997-98; pres. Sys. Svc. Enterprises, St. Louis, 1998—. Bd. dirs. Republic Health Corp., Dallas, 1988-90; mem. governing bd. Luth. Med. Ctr., 1989-95, chmn., 1990-92. Bd. dirs. Luth. Charities Assn., 1982-91, sec. 1984-86, chmn. 1986-89; elder Lutheran Ch. of Resurrection, 1977-80; mem. Regents Coun. Concordia Sem., 1981-84; chmn. cub scout pack 459 Boy Scouts Am., 1984-86; bd. dirs. Luth. High Sch. Assn., 1978-84, 91-97, pres. 1992-97, long range planning com. 1990-92, chmn. alumni assn. 1981; chmn. north star dist. Boy Scouts Am., 1990-93; bd. dirs. Mcpl. Theatre Assn., St. Louis, 1991—; chmn. long range planning com. St. Paul's Luth. Ch., 1988-91, 98-2001, pres., 1996-97, 2002-; bd. dirs., mem. exec. com. United Way of Greater St. Louis, 1994-97, chmn. Vanguard divsn., 1994-97; mem. amb. coun. Luth. Family and Children's Svcs. of St. Louis, 1998—; bd. dirs. Luth. Charities Found., 1998—; mem. adv. bd. Webster U. Bus. and Tech. Sch., 1999-2001; mem. bd mgrs. worker benefit plans Luth Ch.-Mo. Synod, 2001—. Recipient Disting. Leadership award Luth. Assn. for Higher Edn., 1981. Mem. ABA, Mo. Bar Assn., Bar Assn. Met. St. Louis, Bellerive Country Club, Phi Beta Kappa, Omicron Delta Kappa. Republican. Avocations: tennis, golf, racquetball. Home: 1711 Stone Ridge Trails Dr Saint Louis MO 63122-3546 Office: Sys Svc Enterprises 77 Westport Plz Ste 500 Saint Louis MO 63146-3126 E-mail: fmkuhlmann@sseinc.com.

KUHN, BRIAN LAWRENCE, lawyer; b. Memphis, Feb. 16, 1948; s. Edward William and Mattie (Mahaffey) K.; m. Nancy Brandenburg, June 17, 1970; children: Matthew Lawrence, Andrew Ryan, Anthony Mitchell. BSBA, U. Tenn., 1971, JD, 1974. Bar: Tenn. 1974, U.S. Dist. Ct. (we. dist.) Tenn. 1974. Asst. county atty. Shelby County, Memphis, 1974-81; ptnr. Kuhn, Kuhn & Kuhn, Memphis, 1980-82; county atty. Shelby County, Memphis, 1982-94; sr. counsel Ford & Harrison LLP, Memphis, 1998—. Chief adminstrv. officer, 1981. Bd. dirs. Boys' Clubs of Memphis, 1983—; chmn. bd. trustees, Raleigh United Meth. Ch., Memphis, 1982; parliamentarian, legal adviser, Shelby County Charter Commn., 1984. Mem. ABA, Memphis and Shelby County Bar Assn. (law libr. commn. 1982-92), Tenn. Bar Assn., Kiwanis of La.-Miss.-Tenn. (pres. Memphis, lt. gov., dist. chmn. 1976-80). Office: Ford & Harrison LLP 6750 Poplar Ave Ste 600 Memphis TN 38138 E-mail: bkuhn@fordharrison.com.

KUHN, JAMES E. judge; b. Hammond, La., Oct. 31, 1946; s. Eton Percy and Mildred Louise (McDaniel) K.; m. Cheryl Aucoin, Dec. 27, 1969; children: James M., Jennifer L. BA, Southeastern La. U., 1968; JD, Loyola U. of South, 1973. Bar: La. 1973, Colo. 1995, U.S. Supreme Ct. 1978. Asst. dist. atty. 21st Jud. Dist., La., 1980-90, judge, 1990-95, Ct. Appeals (1st cir.), Baton Rouge, 1995—. Instr. history, and polit. sci. Southeastern La. U., Hammond, 1991—; past mem. appellate ct. performance and standards com. La. Supreme Ct.; lectr. in field. Founder For Our Youth; past bd. dirs. La. Coun. Child Abuse, past sec.-treas. Conf. of Ct. Appeal Judges for State of La. Recipient Am. Jurisprudence award Loyola Law Sch. Mem. ABA, La. State Bar Assn. (Professionalism and Quality of Life com.), 21st Jud. Bar Assn., Livingston Parish Bar Assn., Baton Rouge Bar Assn., Covington Bar Assn., Inns of Ct., Delta Theta Phi. Home: 253 W Oak St Ponchatoula LA 70454-3330

KUHN, THOMAS, lawyer; b. Winterthur, Zurich, Switzerland, Dec. 24, 1958; s. Werner Richard and Dora (Keller) Kuhn; children: Angelo Vasilev, Mario Shumanov, Thomas, Alexander, Maximilian Alexandrov. Lic. iur., U. St. Gallen, Switzerland, 1985, LLD, 1986. Bar: Zurich, 1989. Assoc. V.N.J. Landmann, L.L.D., Zurich, 1985-86; law clk. to presiding justice Dist. Ct. of Justice, Pfäffikon ZH, 1986-88; pvt. practice law Zurich, 1988—; law clerk High Ct. Schaffhausen, 1990. Mem.: Am. Econ. Assn., Masons. Office: PO Box 128 CH-8411 Winterthur Switzerland Home: Badstr 6 CH-6423 Seewen Switzerland

KUHRAU, EDWARD W. lawyer; b. Caney, Kans., Apr. 19, 1935; s. Edward and Dolores (Hardman) Kuhrau; m. Janiece Christal (div. 1983); children: Quentin, Clayton; m. Sandy Shreve. BA, U. Tex., 1960; JD, U. So. Calif., 1965. Bar: Calif. 1966, Wash. 1968, Alaska 1977. With Perkins Coie (and predecessor firms), Seattle, 1968—, ptnr., 1973—. Editor-in-chief Wash. Real Property Deskbook; contbr. articles to profl. jours. With USAF, 1955-58. Mem. ABA, Wash. Bar Assn., Am. Coll. Real Estate Lawyers, Pacific Real Estate Inst. (pres., founding trustee), Order of Coif, Seattle Yacht Club, Wing Point Golf and Country Club, Poulsbo Yacht Club. Banking, Finance, Property, real (including real estate development, water). Office: Perkins Coie 1201 3rd Ave Fl 40 Seattle WA 98101-3029 E-mail: kuhre@perkinscoie.com.

KUKLIN, ANTHONY BENNETT, lawyer; b. N.Y.C., Oct. 9, 1929; s. Norman B. and Deane (Cable) K.; m. Vivienne May Hall, Apr. 4, 1964; children: Melissa, Amanda. AB, Harvard U., 1950; JD, Columbia U., 1953. Bar: N.Y. 1953, D.C. 1970. Assoc. Dwight, Royall, Harris, Koegel & Caskey, N.Y.C., 1955-61, Paul, Weiss, Rifkind, Wharton & Garrison, N.Y.C., 1961-69, ptnr., 1969-95, counsel, 1995—. Lectr. in Law, Columbia Law Sch., 1997-2001; bd. dirs. Chgo. Title & Trust Co., Chgo. Title Ins. Co., 1986-96. Contbr. articles to legal jours. Mem. ABA (chmn., sec. real property, probate and trust law 1987-88), Internat. Bar Assn. (chmn. div. one 1985-88), N.Y. State Bar Assn. (chmn. sect. real property 1981-82), Assn. of Bar of city of N.Y., Am. Coll. Real Estate Lawyers (pres. 1981-82), Anglo-Am. Real Property Inst. (chmn. 1989), Am. Coll. Constrn. Lawyers. Property, real (including real estate development, water). Home: 22 Pryer Ln Larchmont NY 10538-4022 Office: Paul Weiss Rifkind Wharton & Garrison Ste # 4200 1285 Ave of Ams Fl 22 New York NY 10019-6065

KUKLIN, SUSAN BEVERLY, law librarian, lawyer; b. Chgo., Nov. 25, 1947; d. Albert and Marion (Goodman) K. BA in English and History with honors, U. Ariz., 1969, JD, 1973; MLS, Ind. U., 1970; LLM in Taxation, DePaul U., 1981. Bar: Ariz. 1973, Ill. 1980, Calif. 1984, U.S. Dist. Ct. (no. dist.) Ill. 1980. Asst. city atty. City of Phoenix, 1974-75; dep. county atty. County of Pima, Ariz., 1975-76; polit. sci., law libr. asst. prof. law No. Ill. U., 1976-78; law libr., assoc. prof. U. S.D., 1978-79; dir. law libr., asst. prof. DePaul U., 1979-83; law libr. Santa Clara County, San Jose, Calif., 1983—. Sec. bd. trustees Law Library Santa Clara County. Mem. Am. Assn. Law Libr. (cert. law libr.), Coun. Calif. County Law Libr. (newsletter editor 1983-84), No. Calif. Assn. Law Libr., Phi Beta Kappa, Phi Kappa Phi, Alpha Lambda Delta, Phi Alpha Theta, Phi Delta Phi. Office: Santa Clara County Law Library 360 N 1st St San Jose CA 95113-1004

KULINSKY, LOIS, lawyer; b. Chgo., Mar. 17, 1946; d. Ben Albert and Florence Sylvia (Barth) Kay; m. Fred Martin Kulinsky, Sept. 4, 1967 (div. 1980); 1 child, Jeffrey. BS, U. Minn., 1967; MAT, U. Chgo., 1970; JD, Ill. Inst. Tech., 1980. Bar: Ill. 1980, U.S. Dist. Ct. (no. dist.) Ill. 1980, U.S. Supreme Ct. 1995. Tchr. Chgo. Pub. Schs., 1967-70, Maine Twp. Schs., Des Plaines, Ill., 1971-80; atty. John P. Biestek & Assocs., Arlington Heights, Ill., 1980-83; pvt. practice Wheeling, Ill., 1983—. Mem. Ill. Bar Assn., Chgo. Bar Assn., Lake County Bar Assn. Avocations: photography, art. Family and matrimonial, General practice, Probate (including wills, trusts). Office: 395 E Dundee Rd Ste 200 Wheeling IL 60090-7003 Fax: (847) 459-4448. E-mail: lois@kulinskylaw.com.

KULLEN, RICHARD CHARLES, JR., lawyer; b. Detroit, June 22, 1938; s. Richard Charles and Margaret Mary (DeConinck) K.; m. Barbara Elizabeth Catoggio, Nov. 7, 1970; children— Richard C., Michael V.S., B. Elizabeth, V. Anthony. A.B., (Nat. Merit scholar) Georgetown U., 1960; J.D. (Root-Tilden Scholar), N.Y.U., 1963. Bar: N.Y. 1967, U.S. Dist. Ct. (so. dist.) N.Y. 1972. Assoc., Townley & Updike, N.Y.C., 1964-73, ptnr., 1974-88; v.p., sr. assoc. counsel The Chase Manhattan Bank, N.A., N.Y.C., 1989-96; sr. counsel Met. Life Ins. Co., 1996-2002. Mem. Cath. Big Bros. of N.Y., 1964—89, bd. dirs. 1970—89, pres. 1979-81. Served with USMCR, 1963. Mem. ABA, N.Y. State Bar Assn., Assn. Bar City of N.Y., Shoreham (N.Y.) Country Club. Republican. Roman Catholic. Banking, Commercial, contracts (including sales of goods; commercial financing), Corporate, general. Home: 61 Maple Hill Dr Larchmont NY 10538-1630 E-mail: dickkullen@yahoo.com.

KULLER, JONATHAN MARK, lawyer; b. Paterson, N.J., Jan. 2, 1951; George and Muriel (Kaplan) K.; m. Mardi Risa Adelman, Oct. 8, 1977; children: Brett Louis, Devin Howard. BS, Livingston Coll., 1972; JD, Rutgers U., 1976. Bar: N.J. 1976, U.S. Dist. Ct. N.J. 1976, U.S. Supreme Ct. 1985. Law clk. to presiding judge N.J. Superior Ct., Hackensack, 1976-77; assoc. Miller & Platt, Paterson, 1977-78; ptnr. Markus, Kuller & Cohen, Parsippany, N.J., 1978-87, Blaustein & Wasserman, Woodbridge, N.J., 1987-98, L'Abbate, Balkan, Colavita & Contini, L.L.P., Livingston, NJ, 1998—, Podvey, Sachs, Meanor, Catenacci, Hildner & Cozziello, P.C., Newark, 2001—. Mem.: N.J. Bar Assn. Jewish. Avocation: tennis. Office: Podvey Sachs Meanor Catenacci Hildner & Cocziello PC One Riverfront Plz Fl 8 Newark NJ 07102 E-mail: jkuller@podveysachs.com.

KULONGOSKI, THEODORE RALPH, governor, former judge, retired judge; b. Nov. 5, 1940; married; 3 children. BA, U. Mo., 1967, JD, 1970. Bar: Oreg., Mo., U.S. Dist. Ct. Oreg., U.S. Ct. Appeals (9th cir.). Legal counsel Oreg. State Ho. of Reps., 1973-74; founding and sr. ptnr. Kulongoski, Durham, Drummonds & Colombo, Oreg., 1974-87; deputy dist. atty. Multnomah County, Oreg., 1992—; atty. gen. State of Oreg., 1993-97; justice Oreg. Supreme Ct., 1997—2001. State rep. Lane County (Oreg.), 1974-77, state senator, 1977-83; chmn. Juvenile Justice Task Force, 1994, Gov.'s Commn. Organized Crime; mem. Criminal Justice Coun.; exec. dir. Met. Family Svc., 1992; dir. Oreg. Dept. Ins. and Fin., 1987-91. Mem. Oreg State Bar Assn., Mo. Bar Assn. Office: Gov's Office 254 Capitol Bldg 900 Court St NE Salem OR 97301

KULZICK, KEN STAFFORD, retired lawyer, travel writer; b. Milw., July 20, 1927; s. Earl Joseph and Claire Agnes (Blask) K.; m. Patricia Louise Siekert, June 19, 1949; 1 child, Kate Kulzick Stafford. PhB, Marquette U., Milw., 1950; JD, UCLA, 1956. Bar: Calif. 1956, U.S. Dist. Ct. (no. and cen. dists.) Calif. 1956, U.S. Ct. Appeals (9th cir.) 1956. Tchg. asst., rschr. UCLA, 1953—56; asst. U.S. atty. (honor grad program) Dept. Justice, L.A., San Francisco, 1956-58; ptnr. Lillick, McHose & Charles, L.A., 1958-86, Liebig & Kulzick, L.A., 1987-91, Gipson, Hoffman & Pancione, L.A., 1991-94; copyright lawyer, past pres. L.A. Copyright Soc. Media cons. specializing in dramatic documentaries, 1958—; media advisor League of Women Voters, L.A., 1986, 90; lectr. UCLA, 1987—. Contbr. articles to L.A. Lawyer mag., EMMY mag., Entertainment Law Reporter, others; bd. editors UCLA Law Rev., 1954-56. Served to lt. USN, 1950-53; Korea Home: PO Box 1926 Eagle River WI 54521-1926 Home (Winter): 1520 Scenic Dr Felton CA 95018-9642

KUMP, KARY RONALD, lawyer; b. Provo, Utah, Apr. 27, 1952; s. Ronald and Ann (Thomas) K.; m. Terri Renee Farley, Sept. 24, 1980; children: Kasey Ronald, Kyle Thomas, Kristopher Lewis, Kolby Lawrence, Karson Jack. AA, Rio Hondo Coll., 1972; BA, U. Calif., Fullerton, 1976;

JD, Western State U., Fullerton, 1980; cert. trial advocacy, Hastings Law Sch., 1982. Bar: Calif. 1982, Utah 1995, U.S. Dist. Ct. (ctrl. dist.) Calif. 1982, (no. and so. dists.) Calif. 1985. Assoc. William G. Kellen & Assocs., Riverside, Calif., 1980-83, Kellen & Luchs, Riverside, 1983-84; ptnr. Luchs, Kump & Milelich, Riverside, 1984-85, Carter & Kump, Riverside, 1985-87; sole practice Riverside, 1987-90; ptnr. Kump & Kennedy, 1990-98, Kump & Earven, 1998-99, Law Offices of Farley & Kump, LLP, Carpinteria, Calif., 1999—2001, Ventura, Calif., 2001—. Panel atty. Lawyer Referral Svc., Riverside, 1982—, Coll. Legal Clinic, Riverside, 1984—, Montgomery Ward Legal Svcs. Plan, Riverside, 1986—; judge pro tem Riverside Mcpl. Ct.; arbitrator Riverside Superior Ct.; mediator 4th Dist. Ct. Appeals; hearing officer City of Riverside. Exec. post advisor Boy Scouts Am. Fellow Roscoe Pound Inst.; mem. ABA, State Bar Calif. (bd. govs., Svc. Contbn. award 1984), Riverside Bar Assn. (panel atty. 1982, co-chair pub. bar rels., fee arbitrator, mediator client rels.), Assn. Trial Lawyers Am., Santa Barbara Bar Assn., Inland Empire Bankruptcy Forum, Ventura/Santa Barbara Trial Lawyers Assn., Consumer Attys. Calif., Calif. Trustees Assn. Republican. Mem. L.D.S. Ch. Avocations: golf, tennis, fishing, scuba. Bankruptcy, State civil litigation, Personal injury (including property damage). Office: 592 Poli St Ventura CA 93001 E-mail: kary@j.farley.com.

KUNDINGER, MATHEW HERMANN, lawyer, engineer, author, entrepreneur; b. Wuerzburg, Fed. Republic Germany, Aug. 7, 1955; s. Joseph and Erika (Endres) K. MSME, Inst. Tech., Wuerzburg-Schweinfurt, 1982; PhD, Greenwich U., 1990; JD, U. West Los Angeles Sch. Law, 1991. Bar: Calif. 1991. Sales rep. Michelin Tire Corp., Karlsruhe, Fed. Republic Germany, 1977; trainee Mercedes-Benz, Wuerzburg, Fed. Republic Germany, 1983; sales/project engr. Gerhard Schubert Machinery, Crailsheim, W.Ger., 1983-84; tech. support mgr. F&E Hedman-LA, Inc., L.A., 1984-87; gen. mgr. Diamond Copy Products, Gardena, Calif., 1987; pres. 140 Plus Mgmt. Cons., Inc., L.A., 1985-90; pvt. practice L.A., 1991—; prin. Am.-German Legal Svcs., Santa Monica, Calif., 1996—2001. Author: California Here I Come, 1987. Avocation: writing. Home and Office: PO Box 34793 Los Angeles CA 90034-0793 E-mail: mathew@kundinger.net.

KUNDTZ, JOHN ANDREW, lawyer; b. Cleve., June 23, 1933; s. Ewald E. and Elizabeth (O'Neill) K.; m. Helen Margaret Luckiesh, Aug. 31, 1957; children— John M., Helen E., Margaret L. BS in Social Studies, Georgetown U., 1955; JD, Case Western Reserve U., 1958. Bar: Ohio 1958, U.S. Dist. Ct. (no. dist.) Ohio 1961. Ptnr. Falsgraf, Kundtz, Reidy & Shoup, Cleve., 1961-69; ptnr. Thompson Hine and Flory, Cleve., 1970-90; pvt. practice Cleve., 1990—. Dir. Investment Advisors Internat., Inc., Cleve. Trustee Hathaway Brown Sch., Shaker Heights, Ohio, Chagrin River Land Conservancy, Chagrin Falls, Ohio, Cleve. Soc. for the Blind. 1st lt. USAF, 1958-60. Mem. Ohio State Bar Assn., Assn. Transp. Practitioners. Republican. Roman Catholic. Probate (including wills, trusts), Transportation. Home: 32540 Creekside Dr Pepper Pike OH 44124-5224 Office: 3000 Aurura Rd Ste 250 Cleveland OH 44139

KUNERT, PAUL CHARLES, lawyer; b. Hankinson, N.D., Jan. 14, 1935; s. Harry Firdinand Kunert and Mary Bernice Sisson; m. Sandra Kathryn Rood, Nov. 19, 1962 (dec. June 1994); children: Melissa, Kathryn, Miles Joseph; m. Paricia Joan McGraw, Oct. 11, 1997. Student, St. John's U., 1954-55; BA, U. Minn., 1957, JD cum laude, 1960. Bar: Minn. 1961, U.S. Dist. Ct. Minn. 1972. Assoc. Robins, Davis & Lyons, St. Paul, 1961-66; ptnr. Sahr, Kunert & Tambornino, Mpls., 1967-96, Kunert, Tambornino & Kuhar, Mpls., 1996-2000; sole practice Minnetonka, Minn., 2000—. Mem. Minn. Def. Lawyers Assn., Hennepin County Bar Assn. General civil litigation, Insurance, Corporate, general. Office: 10285 Yellow Circle Dr Minnetonka MN 55343 Fax: (952) 933-8298.

KUNKEL, DAVID NELSON, lawyer; b. Rochester, N.Y., Apr. 5, 1943; s. Frederick W. and Dorothy Jean (Smith) K.; m. Gayle Kellogg Van Dussen, Aug. 21, 1965; children: Jennifer Dawn, Nelson Charles. BA with high honors, U. Va., 1965; LLB, U. Pa., 1968. Bar: Pa. 1969, N.Y. 1972. Assoc. Montgomery, McCracken, Walker & Rhoads, Phila., 1968, Nixon, Hargrave, Devans & Doyle, Rochester, N.Y., 1971-78, ptnr., 1978-95, sr. counsel, 1995; vice chair, exec. v.p. PSINet, Inc., Ashburn, Va., 1995—2000; cons. internat. and tech. cos., 2000—02; pres., CEO Hopeman Bros. Marine Interiors LLC; pres., COO AWH Corp., 2002—. Mem. Bd. Edn. Bloomfield Ctrl. Sch., East Bloomfield, N.Y., 1982-85. Lt. USNR, 1969-71. Mem. ABA, Internat. Bar Assn. Commercial, contracts (including sales of goods; commercial financing), Computer, Construction. E-mail: davek@hopeman-brothers.com.

KUNKEL, LEAH R. lawyer, composer, producer; b. Washington, June 15, 1948; d. Philip Zachary and Bessie Joan (Levine) Cohen. AB in Govt., Smith Coll., 1988; JD, Western New Eng. Coll., 1992. Bar: Mass. 1992, U.S. Dist. Ct. Mass. 1994, Calif. 1997, U.S. Dist. Ct. (cen. dist.) Calif. 1997. Composer, prodr., L.A., 1968-90; assoc. Kim C. Rosen, Esq., Northampton, Mass., 1992-93; pvt. practice Northampton, 1993—; assoc. Fischbach, Perlstein and Lieberman, L.A., 2000. Chmn. Human Rights Com., Northampton, 1994-1999; v.p. Northampton Ctr. for the Arts, 1994-98, pres. bd. dirs., 1998-1999. Criminal, Entertainment. Office: 17 New South St Northampton MA 01060-4073

KUNKEN, KENNETH JAMES, lawyer; b. Mineola, N.Y., July 15, 1950; s. Leonard Yale and Judith Mae Kunken. BS, Cornell U., 1973, MA, 1977; MEd, Columbia U., 1976; JD, Hofstra U., 1982. Bar: U.S. Dist. Ct. (ea. and so. dist.) N.Y. 1983, U.S. Supreme Ct. 1997, U.S. Ct. Appeals (fed. cir.) 1997. Vocat. rehab. counselor Human Resources Ctr., Albertson, N.Y., 1977-79; asst. dist. atty. Nassau County Dist. Attys. Office, Mineola, N.Y., 1982—, dep. bur. chief, 1997—. Instr. Nat. Inst. Trial Advocacy, Hempstead, N.Y., 1993—. Recipient Judge Thomas E. Ryan award Nassau County Ct. Officers Benevolent Assn., 1996, George M. Estabrook Disting. Svc. award Hofstra Alumni Assn., Inc., 1999. Mem. N.C. Bar Assn., Hofstra U. Sch. of Law Alumni (adv. com. 1993-96). Office: Nassau County Dist Attys Office 262 Old Country Rd Mineola NY 11501-4251

KUNKLE, WILLIAM JOSEPH, lawyer; b. Lakewood, Ohio, Sept. 3, 1941; s. William Joseph and Georgia (Howe) K.; m. Sarah Florence Nesti, July 11, 1964; children: Kathleen Margaret, Susan Mary. BA, Northwestern U., Evanston, Ill., 1963; Jd, Northwestern U., 1969. Bar: Ohio 1969, U.S. Dist. Ct. (no. dist.) Ill. 1969, Ill. 1969, U.S. Ct. Appeals (7th cir.) 1991, U.S. Supreme Ct. 1991. Process control engr. Union Carbide Corp., Cleve., 1964-65, prodn. supr. Greenville, S.C., 1965-66; assoc. Hauxhurst, Sharp, Mollison & Gallagher, Cleve., 1969-70; asst. pub. defender Cook County Pub. Defender, Chgo., 1970-73; asst. states atty. Cook County States Atty., Chgo., 1973-85; ptnr. Phelan, Cahill & Quinlan, Ltd., Chgo., 1985-96, Cahill, Christian & Kunkle, Ltd., Chgo., 1996—2002, Wildman, Harrold, Allen & Dixon, Chgo., 2002—. Chmn. The Ill. Gaming Bd., 1990—93; dep. spl. outside counsel U.S. Ho. Reps., Washington, 1988—89; adj. prof. I.I.T. Chgo. Kent Sch. Law, 1980—84; instr. Nat. Inst. Trial Advocacy, 1978—82, 1986; lectr. Nat. Coll. Dist. Attys., 1978—85, Nat. Law Enforcement Inst., 1983—85; 1st asst. states atty. of Cook County, 1983—85; spl. state's atty. 18th Jud. Cir., DuPage County, 1995—99. Contbg. author: Punishment Prosecutor's Viewpoint, 1983, 1989, Trial Techniques Compendium, Nat. College of Dist. Attys. (2d, 3rd, 4th, 5th, 6th eds.). Recipient Disting. Faculty award Nat. Coll. Dist. Attys., 1980, Award for Prosecution Svc. Chgo. Assn. Commerce & Industry, 1981. Fellow Am. Coll. Trial Lawyers, ABA; mem. Internat. Soc. Barristers, Nat. Dist. Attys. Assn. (bd. dirs. 1984-85), Assn. Govt. Attys. in Capital Litigation (pres. 1983-84), Chgo. Bar Assn. (bd. mgrs. 1983-84), Ill. State Bar Assn. (LAWPAC trustee 1989-95), Internat. Assn. Gaming Attys., Chgo. Crime Commn. (bd. dirs.). Avocations: golf, softball, carpentry, motorcycling. General civil litigation, Criminal, Personal injury (including property damage). Office: Wildman Harrold Allen & Dixon 225 W Wacker Dr Chicago IL 60606-1229

KUNTZ, CHARLES POWERS, lawyer; b. L.A., May 7, 1944; s. Walter Nichols and Katherine (Powers) K.; m. June Emerson Moroney, Dec. 23, 1969; children: Michael Nicholas, Robinson Moroney, Katie Moroney. AB with honors, Stanford U., 1966, JD, 1969; LLM, NYU, 1971. Bar: Calif. 1970, N.Y. 1970, U.S. Dist. Ct. (no. dist.) Calif. 1970, U.S. Ct. Appeals (9th cir.) 1970, U.S. Supreme Ct. 1979. Staff atty. project for urban affairs Office Econ. Opportunity, N.Y.C., 1969-71; dep. pub. defender Contra Costa County Pub. Defender's Office, Martinez, Calif., 1971-75; assoc. Treuhaft, Walker & Brown, Oakland, Calif., 1976-78; ptnr. Hirsch & Kuntz, San Rafael, Calif., 1979-85; pvt. practice San Rafael, 1985-89; ptnr. Coombs & Dunlap, Napa, Calif., 1989—. Mem.: ABA, Napa County Bar Assn., Calif. Attys. Consumer Justice, Inns of Ct. General civil litigation, Insurance, Personal injury (including property damage). Home: 48 Wild Rye Way Napa CA 94558-7014 Office: Coombs & Dunlap 1211 Division St Napa CA 94559-3372 E-mail: ckuntz@coombslaw.com.

KUNTZ, JOEL DUBOIS, lawyer; b. Dennis, Mass., Feb. 5, 1946; s. Paul Grimley Kuntz and Harriette (Hunter) Ainsworth; m. Karan Judd, June 29, 1968; children: Matthew Christopher, Kristin Lara. BA, Haverford Coll., 1968; JD, Yale U., 1971; LLM in Taxation, NYU, 1980. Bar: Conn. 1972, Oreg. 1974. Assoc. Stoel, Rives, Boley, Jones & Grey, Portland, Oreg., 1974-79, ptnr., 1979-94; v.p., gen. counsel Entek Internat. LLC, Lebanon, Oreg., 1994—. Author (with James S. Eustice): Federal Income Taxation of S Corporations, 1982, 4th edit., 2001; author: (with James S. Eustice, Charles S. Lewis, Thomas P. Deering) Tax Reform Act of 1986: Analysis and Commentary, 1987; author: (with Robert J. Peroni) U.S. International Taxation, 1992. Capt. USMC, 1971-74. Mem. Am. Coll. Tax Counsel, Internat. Fiscal Assn. Democrat. Corporate, general, Corporate taxation, Personal income taxation. Home: 3910 Lakeview Blvd Lake Oswego OR 97035-5561 Address: PO Box 39 Lebanon OR 97355-0039 E-mail: jdkuntz@attglobal.net.

KUNTZ, LEE ALLAN, lawyer; b. Nashville, July 9, 1943; s. Irwin and Lucy (Kornman) K.; 1 child, Douglas. BA, Duke U., 1965; LLB, Columbia U., 1968. Bar: N.Y. 1968, U.S. Dist. Ct. (so. dist.) N.Y. 1973, U.S. Tax Ct. 1973. Assoc. Shearman & Sterling, N.Y.C., 1968-76, ptnr., 1976—, mng. ptnr., 1994-98, sr. ptnr. Real Estate Group, 1988-93. Mem. policy com. Shearman and Sterling, 1991-99. Contbr. articles to profl. jours. Bd. visitors Columbia Law Sch., 1998—; dir. Vols. Legal Svcs., 2000—, Am. Coll. Real Estate Lawyers, 2002-. Mem. ABA, Assn. Bar City N.Y., Am. Coll. Real Estate Lawyers. Property, real (including real estate development, water), Private international, Property, real (including real estate development, water). Office: Shearman & Sterling 599 Lexington Ave Fl C2 New York NY 10022-6069

KUNTZ, WILLIAM FRANCIS, II, lawyer, educator; b. N.Y.C., June 24, 1950; s. William Francis I and Margaret Evelyn (Brown) K.; m. Alice Beal, May 20, 1978; children: William Thaddeus, Katharine Lowell, Elizabeth Anne. AB, Harvard U., 1972, AM, 1974, JD, 1977, PhD, 1979. Bar: N.Y. 1978. Assoc. Shearman & Sterling, N.Y.C., 1978-86; mem. Milgrim, Thomajan & Lee, N.Y.C., 1986-94; ptnr. Seward & Kissel, N.Y.C., 1994-2001, The Torys Law Firm, 2001—. Assoc. prof. Bklyn. Law Sch., 1987-2002. Author: Criminal Sentencing, 1988. Bd. dirs. MFY Legal Svcs., Inc., N.Y.C., 1984-90, Boys Brotherhood Republic, N.Y.C., 1986-90, Habitat for Humanity, N.Y.C., 1987-90; chmn. Resources for Children with Spl. Needs, N.Y.C., 1986-89; mem. N.Y. Civilian Complaint Rev. Bd., 1987—, chmn., 1994. Mem. ABA, N.Y. State Bar Assn., N.Y. County Lawyers Assn. (bd. dirs. 1991-96), Assn. of Bar of City of N.Y. (chmn. mcpl. affairs com. 1992-95, judiciary com., exec. com. 2002—), Bklyn. Bar Assn. (judiciary com. 1995—), Met. Black Bar Assn. Democrat. Roman Catholic. Office: The Torys Law Firm 237 Park Ave New York NY 10017-3142 Business E-Mail: wkuntz@torys.com.

KUNTZ, WILLIAM RICHARD, JR., lawyer; b. New Rochelle, NY, Oct. 6, 1949; s. William Richard and Mary Margaret (Kerkvliet) Kuntz. BSE, Princeton U., 1971; JD, U. So. Calif., 1974. Bar: Calif. 1974, US Dist. Ct. (cen. dist.) Calif. Assoc. McKenna & Fitting, LA, 1974—75, Stroock, Stroock & Lavan, LA, 1975—81, Hahn, Cazier & Leff, LA, 1981—82; ptnr. Hahn, Cazier & Smaltz, LA, 1982—87, Morgan, Lewis & Bockius, LA, 1987—88; from v.p. gen. coun. to exec. v.p., CFO Chart House Enterprises Inc., Solana Beach, Calif., 1988—97; mng. dir. CB Richard Ellis, Inc., Newport Beach, Calif., 1997—99; of counsel Merrill, Schultz & Wolds, San Diego, 1999—. Mem.: ABA, State Bar Calif. Assn. Corporate, general, Mergers and acquisitions, Securities. Home: 13536 Kibbings Rd San Diego CA 92130-1242 Office: Merrill Schultz & Wolds Ltd 401 West A St Ste 2550 San Diego CA 92101 Business E-Mail: wrk@mswltd.com.

KUNZE, VIOLETTA DETKOVA, lawyer; b. Russe, Bulgaria, Mar. 5, 1971; d. Shalarmanov Peiko Semednov and Shalamanova Elena Pavlova; m. Axel Kunze, Aug. 17, 2002. LLM, Sofia (Bulgaria) U., 1996. Bar: Sofia. Jr. assoc. Borislav Dialstrov Legal Office, Sofia, 1993—95; law clk. Sofia (Bulgaria) City Ct., 1996—97; in-house counsel Interlease Corp., Sofia, 1996—97; sr. assoc. Djingov, Gouginksi, Kyutchukov & Velichkov, Sofia, 1997—. Contbr. articles to profl. jours. Mem.: Internat. Bar Assn. Avocations: skiing, tennis, music. Corporate, general, Communications, Mergers and acquisitions. Office: Djingov Gouginski Kyutchukov & Veltchkov 10 Tsar Dsuoboditel Blvd 1000 Sofia Bulgaria Fax: +3592 980 3586. E-mail: violetta.kunze@dgkv.com.

KUPCHAK, KENNETH ROY, lawyer; b. Forrest Hills, Pa., May 15, 1942; s. Frank V. and Anne B. (Ruzanic) Kupchak; m. Patricia K. Geer, Jan. 27, 1967; children: Lincoln K., Robinson K. AB, Cornell U., 1964; BS, Pa. State U., 1965; JD in Internat. Affairs, Cornell U., 1971. Bar: Hawaii 1971, U.S. Dist. Ct. Hawaii 1971, U.S. Supreme Ct. 1988. Meteorology staff U. Hawaii, Honolulu, 1968; ptnr. Damon Key Leong Kupchak & Hastert, Honolulu, 1971—, also bd. dirs. Chief minority counsel 8th legis. Hawaii Ho. Reps., Honolulu, 1974—75; legis. coord. Hawaii State Assn. Counties, Honolulu, 1988; bd. dirs. Fletcher Constrn. Co., N.Am. Ltd.; adj. prof. William S. Richardson Sch. Law, U. Hawaii, 1993; mem. Honolulu Common Fgn. Rels., 1995—; vice chair bd. counselors Mid-Pacific Inst., 1993—95, trustee, 1995—, chmn. pers. com., 1998—99, chmn. edn. com., 2000—; lectr. on constrn. law. Co-author: Fifty State Construction Lien and Bond Laws, 2000, The Design/Build Process, 1997, A State-By-State Guide to Architect, Engineer and Contractor Licensing, 1998, A State-By-State Guide to Construction and Design Law, 1998; contbr. articles to profl. jours. Chair agenda com. C.Z.M. Statewide Adv. Com., Hawaii, 1980—92; pres., bd. dirs. Hawaii Cmty. Svc. Coun., Honolulu, 1982—88; trustee Moanalua Gardens Found., 1985—88, Operation Raleigh (N.C.) U.S.A., 1986—90; bd. dirs. Hawaii Nature Ctr., 1989—, sec., 2001—02, pres., 2002—; chair Hawaii State Commn. on Korean and Vietnam War Meml., 1992—95. Capt. USAF, 1964—68, Vietnam. Fellow Centennial, Pa. State U., 1996. Fellow: Am. Coll. Constrn. Lawyers; mem.: ABA (constrn. industry forum, dispute resolution steering com. 1994—, chair 1998—2000, chair ann. meeting 2001, governing com. 2002—), USAF Assn. (v.p. Hawaii chpt. 1994—97), Am. Arbitration Assn. (panel arbitrators), Internat. Bar Assn., Hawaii Bar Assn., Cornell Law Alumni Assn. (exec. com. 1990—93), Hawaii Lacrosse Club (founder, dir., sec. 1990—2000), Volcano Golf and Country Club, Oahu Country Club, Cornell Club Hawaii (bd. dirs., chair scholarship com. 1994—2000). Avocations: lacrosse, hiking, photography. Construction, Land use and zoning (including planning), Property, real (including real estate development, water). Office: 1600 Pauahi Tower 1001 Bishop St Honolulu HI 96813-3429 E-mail: krk@hawaiilawyer.com.

KUPIETZKY, MOSHE J. lawyer; b. N.Y.C., May 17, 1944; s. Jacob Harry and Fanny (Dresner) K.; m. Arlene Debra Usdan, June 22, 1966; children: Jay, Jeff, Jacob. BBA cum laude, CCNY, 1965; LLB, JD magna cum laude, Harvard U., 1968. Bar: N.Y. 1969, Calif. 1970. Law clerk to Hon. William B. Herlands U.S. Dist. Ct., N.Y.C., 1968-69; assoc. Mitchell Silberberg & Knupp, L.A., Calif., 1969-74, ptnr., 1974-80; ptnr., prin. Hayutin Rubinroit Praw & Kupietzky, L.A., 1980-87; ptnr. Sidley, Austin, Brown & Wood, L.A., 1987—. Bd. dirs. Nat. Inst. Jewish Hospice, Beverly Hills, Calif., 1986-98, L.A. Econ. Devel. Corp.; bd. advisors Graziadio Sch. Bus. and Mgmt. Pepperdine U., L.A., 1996-98. Mem. ABA, Beverly Hills Bar Assn., L.A. County Bar Assn. Commercial, contracts (including sales of goods; commercial financing), Corporate, general. Office: Sidley Austin Brown & Wood 555 W 5th St Ste 4000 Los Angeles CA 90013-3000 E-mail: mkupietzky@sidley.com.

KUPPERMAN, LOUIS BRANDEIS, lawyer; b. Augusta, Ga., Dec. 16, 1946; s. Herbert Spencer and Mollie (Kleven) K.; children: David Evan, Robert Dennis; m. Eileen Spadafina, Oct. 24, 1992. BS, Fairleigh Dickinson U., 1972; JD, Bklyn. Law Sch., 1975. Bar: Pa. 1975, U.S. Dist. Ct. (ea. dist.) Pa. 1978, U.S. Ct. Appeals (3d cir.) 1978, U.S. Supreme Ct. 1982. Jud. law clk. to Judge Jacob Kalish Ct. of Common Pleas of Phila. County, 1975-76, jud. law clk. to Judge Eugene Gelfand, 1976-77; corp. counsel Health Corp. Am., Wayne, Pa., 1977-78; ptnr. Dilworth, Paxson, Kalish & Kauffman, Phila., 1978-86; mem. firm, chmn. real estate dept. Baskin Flaherty Elliott & Mannino, P.C., Phila., 1986-90; ptnr., vice chmn. environ. law dept. Obermayer, Rebmann, Maxwell & Hippel, Phila., 1990—. Lectr. Pa. Bar Inst. Author: Real Estate Tax Assessment Appeals, 1987. Chancellor's del. to Phila. Fairleigh Dickinson U., 1983, 86. Recipient Disting. Alumnus award Fairleigh Dickinson U., 1983. Mem. ABA, Pa. Bar Assn., Phila. Bar Assn., (chmn. real estate litigation com. 1983-85), Pyramid Club of Phila. General civil litigation, Land use and zoning (including planning), Property, real (including real estate development, water). Home: 80 Delancy Ct Phoenixville PA 19460-5741 Office: Obermayer Rebmann Maxwell & Hippel 1 Penn Ctr 19th Fl 1617 John F Kennedy Blvd Philadelphia PA 19103-1821 E-mail: Louis.Kupperman@Obermayer.com.

KUPPERMAN, STEPHEN HENRY, lawyer; b. New Orleans, Sept. 17, 1953; s. Abraham Bernard and Jo-Ellyn (Levy) K.; m. Mara Rothstein, Oct. 18, 1980; children: Zachary Hart, Shane Levi, Jake Benjamin. BA, Duke U., 1974; JD, Tulane U., 1977. Bar: La. 1977, U.S. Dist. Ct. (ea. dist.) La. 1977, U.S. Dist. Ct. (mid. dist.) La. 1978, U.S. Dist. Ct. (we. dist.) La. 1981, U.S. Ct. Appeals (5th cir.) 1977, U.S. Ct. Appeals (11th cir.) 1982, U.S. Supreme Ct. 1980. Assoc. Stone Pigman Walther Wittmann & Hutchinson, New Orleans, 1977—81, ptnr., 1981—2003; assoc. Barrasso Usdin Kupperman Freeman & Sarver, L.L.C., New Orleans, 2003—. Adj. prof. Tulane Law Sch., 1988—; mem. Tulane Law Rev., 1975-77, adv. bd., 1992—. Articles editor Tulane Law Rev., 1976-77, mem. 1975-76; contbr. articles to law revs., profl. jours. Bd. dirs. Goodwill Industries, 1980-87, mem. adv. bd. 1987-91; bd. dirs. Jewish Family Svcs., New Orleans, 1978-93, treas. 1986, v.p. 1987-88, pres., 1988-90; bd. dirs. Jewish Fedn., New Orleans, 1989-93, 95-2001, treas. 1991-93; mem. adv. bd. Jewish Endowment Found., New Orleans, 1979—, Tulane Continuing Legal Edn. Program, 1983—; mem. adv. bd. B'nai B'rith Anti-Defamation League S. Ctrl. Region, 1987—, vice-chmn., 1991-95, chmn. 1995-99; mem. Young Leadership Cabinet United Jewish Appeal, 1990-92; bd. dirs. Touro Infirmary Found., 1998—, Touro Synagogue, New Orleans, 1991-2000, sec. 1995-97, v.p. 1997-99, Touro Infirmary, 2000—, vice-chmn., 2002—. Fellow Am. Bar Found.; mem. ABA, La. Bar Assn. (continuing legal edn. com. 1986-88, disciplinary conduct com. 1995—), New Orleans Bar Assn. (mem. Inn of Ct. 1994—), Fed. Bar Assn. (bd. dirs. New Orleans chpt. 1989-94), Securities Industry Assn., Order of Coif. Democrat. Jewish. Federal civil litigation, State civil litigation, Securities. Office: Barrasso Isdin Kupperman Freeman & Server 909 Poydras St Ste 1800 New Orleans LA 70112 E-mail: skupperman@brarrassousdin.com.

KURLAND, PAUL CARL, lawyer, educator; b. Bklyn., May 28, 1946; s. Marvin and Beatrice (Marmer) K.; m. Phyllis Pfeffer, Sept. 1, 1968; children: Joshua Ethan, Abigail Sara. BA, Bklyn. Coll., 1967; JD, NYU, 1970. Bar: N.Y. 1971, U.S. Ct. Appeals (2d cir.) 1971, U.S. Dist. Ct. (so. and ea. dists.) N.Y. 1972, U.S. Supreme Ct. 1974. Assoc. Cahill, Gordon & Reindel, N.Y.C., 1970-73, Emil, Korbin, Klein & Garbus, N.Y.C., 1973-77; ptnr. Kurland and Scheiman, N.Y.C., 1977-79, Baer, Marks & Upham, N.Y.C., 1979-85, Snow, Becker & Krauss, P.C., N.Y.C., 1986—. Mem. faculty Nat. Inst. Trial Advocacy, 1980—, faculty trial techniques program Hofstra U., 1980—, Emory U.., 1982-91, Cardozo Law Sch., 1987—; arbitrator U.S. Dist. Ct. (ea. dist.) N.Y., Am. Arbitration Assn. Pres. Manhasset (N.Y.) Dem. Club; mem. Nassau County Dem. Com.; bd. dirs. World Hunger Yr.; bd. dirs. Sing Out mag., 1998-2000. Mem. ACLU, ABA, Assn. Bar City of N.Y., N.Y. U. Law Sch. Alumni Assn. (v.p. bd. dirs.). Federal civil litigation, State civil litigation. Home: 142 Hemlock Rd Manhasset NY 11030-1216 Office: Snow Becker & Krauss PC 605 3rd Ave Fl 25 New York NY 10158-0125 E-mail: pkurland@sbklaw.com.

KURLANDER, NEALE, accounting and law educator, lawyer; b. Bklyn., Jan. 1, 1924; s. Sol and Eleanor Kurlander; m. Honey Wachtel, June 25, 1949; children: Harold M., Susan L. BS, Long Island U., 1948; JD, N.Y. Law Sch., N.Y.C., 1951; MBA, Adelphi U., 1967. Bar: N.Y. 1952; CPA, N.Y. V.p., chief fin. officer Profit Motivation Svcs., Inc., Garden City, N.Y., 1967-71; cons.-reviewer Ernst & Ernst, Garden City, 1967-72; lectr. Practicing Law Inst., N.Y.C., 1974; chmn. dept. acctng and law Adelphi U., Garden City, 1964-82; cons. Regent's External Degree, Albany, N.Y., 1974-87; pvt. practice law Old Westbury, N.Y., 1952—; pvt. practice acct., CPA, 1960—; prof. acctg. and law Adelphi U., Garden City, 1962—. Profl. developer Harris, Kerr, Forster & Co., N.Y.C., 1969-71; treas. Fin. Execs. Inst., Long Island, N.Y., 1974-76, chmn. acad. rels., 1975—, bd. dirs. 1975—; faculty Found. for Acctg. Edn., 1975—, bd. trustees, 1976-79. Author: Basic Accounting, 1962, Auditing, Vol. I and II, 1978; contbr. articles to profl. jours. Cmdr. post 6081 VFW, Bklyn., 1953-54; mem. Bd. Elections, Nassau County, N.Y., 1964-70, Citizens' Adv. Com. N.Y. State Dept. Taxation, Albany, 1975-87, Bd. Appeals, Old Westbury, 1988-93; legis. adv. coun. N.Y. State Assembly 15th Dist., 1991-93. Recipient cert. Delta Mu Delta, 1982, Dr. Emanuel Saxe Outstanding CPA in Edn. award N.Y. State Soc. Cert. Pub. Accts., 2000; named Outstanding Acctg. Educator, Found. for Acctg. Edn., N.Y., 1982, Acct. of Yr. Acctg. Soc., 1992. Mem. AICPA, N.Y. State Soc. CPA's (Dr. Emanuel Saxe Outstanding CPA in Edn. award 2000), Am. Acctg. Assn., Nassau County Bar Assn., N.Y. State Assembly 15th Dist. (legis. adv. coun.). Avocations: reading, woodworking, traveling, walking, swimming. Home: 6185 Wooded Run Dr Columbia MD 21044 E-mail: nkurlander@aol.com.

KURNIT, RICHARD ALAN, lawyer, educator; b. N.Y.C., Mar. 22, 1951; s. Shepard and Jean (Zinsher) Kurnit; m. Diane Ruth Katzin, Sept. 9, 1979; 1 child, Katrina. AB magna cum laude, Columbia U., 1972; JD cum laude, Harvard U., 1975. Bar: N.Y. 1976, U.S. Dist. Ct. (so. dist.) N.Y. 1976, U.S. Ct. Appeals (D.C. cir.) 1977, U.S. Ct. Appeals (2d cir.) 1978, U.S. Supreme Ct. 1980, U.S. Dist. Ct. (ea. dist.) N.Y. 1981. Law clk. to Thomas P. Griesa U.S. Dist. Ct. (so. dist.) N.Y., N.Y.C., 1975-76; assoc. Paul, Weiss, Rifkind, Wharton & Garrison, N.Y.C., 1976-81; ptnr. Frankfurt Kurnit Klein & Selz, N.Y.C., 1981—. Instr. advt. law New Sch., N.Y.C., 1981—; lectr. Am. Assn./Advt. Agys., ABA, Am. Promotional Mktg. Assn., ALI, 1985—, Am. Advt. Fedn., 1988—. Author: Libel Claims Based on Fiction, 1985. Recipient Citizens Communications Ctr. award, 1975. Mem. ABA, N.Y.C. Bar Assn. (advt. industry subcom.), Phi Beta Kappa. Intellectual property, Libel, Trademark and copyright. Home: 110 Riverside Dr Apt 16F New York NY 10024-3734 Office: Frankfurt Kurnit Klein & Selz 488 Madison Ave Fl 9 New York NY 10022-5754

KURRUS, THOMAS WILLIAM, lawyer; b. Carmel, N.Y., May 13, 1947; s. Theo Hornsby and Jean Ellen (Cumming) K. BS magna cum laude, U. Fla., 1975, JD, 1979. Bar: Fla. 1980, U.S. Dist. Ct. (no. dist.) Fla. 1980, U.S. Ct. Appeals (5th cir.) 1980, U.S. Dist. Ct. (mid. dist.) Fla. 1981, U.S. Ct. Appeals (11th cir.) 1981, U.S. Ct. Appeals (4th cir.) 1984, U.S. Supreme Ct. 1984. Assoc. Law Firm Larry G. Turner, Gainesville, Fla., 1981-83; ptnr. Turner, Kurrus & Griscti, Gainesville, 1983-88; prin. Law Offices of Thomas W. Kurrus, Gainesville, 1988—. Mem. Fla. Supreme Ct. commn. on jury instructions, 1995. Contbr. articles to profl. jours. Mem. ACLU (Gainesville chpt. legal panel chmn. 1999), Nat. Assn. Criminal Defense Lawyers (Fla. chpt. bd. dirs., chmn. continuing legal edn. com., local legis. liaison, pres. award 1993, appreciation award 1998). Avocations: fishing, art, horses. General civil litigation, Criminal, Personal injury (including property damage). Office: PO Box 838 Gainesville FL 32602-0838

KURTZ, HARVEY A. lawyer; b. Baraboo, Wis., July 9, 1950; s. Walter R. and Henrietta M. (Hinze) K.; m. Yvonne Larme, Jan. 28, 1978; children: Benjamin L., Leah L. BA, U. Wis., 1972; JD, U. Chgo., 1975. Bar: Wis. 1975, U.S. Dist. Ct. (ea. dist.) Wis. 1980. Atty. Whyte & Hirschboeck S.C., Milw., 1975-89, shareholder, 1981-89; ptnr. Foley & Lardner, Milw., 1989—. Mem. ABA, State Bar of Wis. Assn., Milw. Bar Assn. (chmn. employee benefits sect. 1993-94), Greater Milw. Employee Benefit Coun., Wis. Retirement Plan Profls. (pres. 1987-88), Internat. Pension and Employee Benefits Lawyers Assn., Kiwanis, Phi Beta Kappa. Corporate, general, Pension, profit-sharing, and employee benefits, Corporate taxation. Home: 3927 N Stowell Ave Milwaukee WI 53211-2461 Office: Foley & Lardner Ste 3800 777 E Wisc Ave Milwaukee WI 53202 E-mail: hkurtz@foleylaw.com.

KURTZ, HOWARD ARTHUR, lawyer; b. Philadelphia, Pa., Apr. 30, 1967; s. Spencer Charles and Carolyn Kurtz. BA, U. of NC, Chapel Hill, 1989—92, JD, 1992. Bar: N.C. 1992, U.S. Dist. Ct. (ea. dist.) N.C. 1997, U.S. Ct. Appeals (4th cir.) 1999. Asst. pub. defender Fayetteville Pub. Defender's Office, NC, 1992—98; founding ptnr. Kurtz & Blum, Raleigh, NC, 1998—. Editor: (Newsletter) The True Bill (the publ. of the Criminal Justice Sect. of N.C. Bar Assn.). Mem.: ATLA, ABA, NC Acad. of Trial Lawyers, Nat. Assn. of Criminal Def. Attorneys, NC Bar Assn., NC State Bar. General civil litigation, Civil rights, Constitutional, Criminal. Office: Kurtz & Blum 16 W Martin St 10th Fl Raleigh NC 27601 Office Fax: 919-832-2740. E-mail: h.kurtz@kurtzandblum.com.

KURTZ, JAMES P. administrative law judge; b. Highland Park, Mich., Dec. 5, 1932; s. A.T. and Virginia C. (Riley) K.; m. Barbara A. Gonczy, Feb. 2, 1957; children: Mary T., Christina M., Ann V., J. Peter, Karen M., Eileen M. AB, U. Detroit, 1955, JD, 1958. Bar: Mich. 1958, U.S. Dist. Ct. (ea. dist.) Mich. 1958, U.S. Ct. Appeals (6th cir.) 1964. Supervisory atty. 7th region NLRB, Detroit, 1958-67; ptnr. firm Brennan & Kurtz, Detroit, 1967-69; adminstrv. law judge Employment rels. commn. State of Mich. Dept. CIS, Detroit, 1969-2001; retired, 2001. Instr. labor and real estate Detroit Coll. Bus., Dearborn, 1968-73; adj. prof. adminstrv. law U. Detroit, 1969-72. Editor-in-chief U. Detroit Law jour., 1957-58; editor procs. Nat. Acad. Arbitrators, 1971-75. Mem. Mich. Bar Assn. (Labor Law sect.). Roman Catholic. Home: RR 1 Craig Beach 401 Erieview Harrow ON Canada N0R 1G0 E-mail: jpkurtz@sympatico.ca.

KURTZ, JEROME, lawyer, educator; b. Phila., May 19, 1931; s. Morris and Renee (Cooper) K.; m. Elaine Kahn, July 28, 1956; children: Madeleine, Nettie Kurtz Greenstein. BS with honors, Temple U., 1952; LLB magna cum laude, Harvard U., 1955. Bar: Pa. 1956, N.Y. 1981, D.C. 1982; CPA, Pa. Assoc. Wolf, Block, Schorr & Solis-Cohen, Phila., 1955-56, 57-63, ptnr., 1963-66, 68-77; tax legis. counsel Dept. Treasury, Washington, 1966-68; commr. IRS, 1977-80; ptnr. Paul, Weiss, Rifkind, Wharton & Garrison, 1980-90; prof. law NYU, 1991-2001, dir. grad. tax program, 1995-98. Instr. Villanova Law Sch., 1964-65, U. Pa., 1969-74; vis. prof. law Harvard U., 1975-76; mem. adv. group to commr. IRS, 1976. Editor: Harvard Law Rev, 1953-55; contbr. numerous articles to profl. jours. Pres. Ctr. Inter-Am. Tax Adminstrn., 1980; bd. dirs. Common Cause, 1984-90, chmn. fin. com., 1985-88; bd. dirs. Nat. Capitol Area ACLU, 1990-91; mem. adv. bd. NYU Tax Inst., 1988-97, Little, Brown Tax Practice Series, 1994-96. Recipient Exceptional Service award Dept. Treasury, 1968, Alexander Hamilton award, 1980 Mem. ABA (chmn. tax shelter com. 1982-84), N.Y. Bar Assn. (exec. com. tax sect. 1981-82), Pa. Bar Assn., Phila. Bar Assn. (chmn. tax sect. 1975-76), Assn. of the Bar of the City of N.Y. (chmn. tax coun. 1993-95), Am. Law Inst. (cons. fed. inc. tax project taxation of pass through entities), Am. Coll. Tax Counsel, Beta Gamma Sigma. Taxation, general. Home: 17 E 16th St New York NY 10003-3116 E-mail: jeromekurtz2@aol.com.

KURTZ, PAUL MICHAEL, law educator; b. Bronx, NY, Sept. 22, 1946; s. Louis and Helen (Mechanic) K.p m. Carol Porter, June 6, 1971; 1 child, Benjamin. BA, Vanderbilt U., 1968, JD, 1972; LLM, Harvard U., 1974. Bar: Tenn. 1972, U.S. Ct. Appeals (6th cir.) 1973, U.S. Ct. Appeals (5th cir.) 1977, U.S. Supreme Ct. 1978. Law clk. to chief judge U.S. Ct. Appeals (6th cir.), 1972-73; instr. Boston U. Law Sch., 1973-74, Boston Coll. Law Sch., 1974-75; asst. prof. law U. Ga., Athens, 1975-78, assoc. prof., 1978-83, prof., 1983-94, assoc. dean, 1991—, J. Alton Hosch prof., 1994—. Vis. prof. U. Mo. Law Sch., 1982, Mercer Law Sch., 1984, U. Tex., 1986, Vanderbilt U., 1987; commr. on Uniform State Laws, 2001—; reporter Nat. Conf. Commrs. on Uniform State Laws, Com. on Interstate Child Support Enforcement, Com. on Status of Children of Aided Conception; reporter Ga. Supreme Ct. Com. on Indigent Def. Reform, 2000-03. Author: Criminal Offenses in Georgia, 1980, Family Law: Cases, Text, Problems, 1986, 3d edit., 1998; contbr. articles to profl. jours.; mem. editl. bd. Family Law Quar., 1983—. Mem. Am. Assn. Law Schs. (chmn. sect. family and juvenile law), ACLU, Am. Humane Assn. (bd. dirs. 1998—), Common Cause, Soc. Am. Law Tchrs., Am. Law Inst. (reporter 1995-96), Supreme Ct. Hist. Soc., Order of Coif, B'nai B'rith (Ga. state sec., pres. Athens lodge). Democrat. Avocations: reading, travel, bowling, politics. Home: 362 W Cloverhurst Ave Athens GA 30606-4212 Office: U Ga Law Sch Athens GA 30602 E-mail: pmkurtz@arches.uga.edu.

KURY, FRANKLIN LEO, lawyer; b. Sunbury, Pa., Oct. 15, 1936; s. Barney and Helen (Witkowski) K.; m. Elizabeth Heazlett, Sept. 14, 1963; children: Steven, David, James. Bar: Pa. 1962. Atty. Pa. Dept. Justice, Harrisburg, 1961-62; ptnr. Kury & Kury, Sunbury, 1963-80, Tive, Hetrick & Pierce, Harrisburg, 1981-82, Reed, Smith, Shaw & McClay, Harrisburg, 1983—. Adj. prof. immigration law, Harrisburg, Widener Law Sch., 1999-2000. Mem. Pa. Ho. of Reps., Harrisburg, 1967-72, Pa. Senate, Harrisburg, 1973-80; del. at large Dem. Nat. Conv., San Francisco, 1984; bd. dirs. Hawk Mountain Sanctuary Assn. 1st lt. USAR, 1962-66. Mem.: Pa. Bar Assn. (chmn. environ. sect. 1984, 1st award for Outstanding Contbn. to Profession of Environ. Law Practice 1993), Am. Immigration Lawyers Assn. Democrat. Avocation: golf. Administrative and regulatory, Environmental, Property, real (including real estate development, water). Office: Reed Smith LLP 213 Market St Ste 900 Harrisburg PA 17101-2108 E-mail: fkury@reedsmith.com.

KURYK, DAVID NEAL, lawyer; b. Balt., Aug. 24, 1947; s. Leon and Bernice G. (Fox) K.; m. Alice T. Lehman, July 8, 1971; children: Richard M., Robert M., Benjamin A. BA, U. Md., 1969; JD, U. Balt., 1972. Bar: Md. 1972, U.S. Dist. Ct. Md. 1973, U.S. Ct. Mil. Appeals 1973, D.C. 1974, U.S. Ct. Appeals (4th cir.) 1974, U.S. Supreme Ct. 1976, U.S. Ct. Appeals (Fed. cir.) 1982. Assoc. Harold Buchman, Esq., Balt., 1970-76; pvt. practice Balt., 1976—. Mem. editl. bd. Md. Bar Jour., 1973-76. Sgt. USAF, 1967-73. Mem. ABA (products gen. liability and consumer law com. 1976—, com. auto law 1977), Md. State Bar Assn., Bar Assn. Balt. City, ATLA, U. Balt. Alumni Assn., Zeta Beta Tau. Democrat. Jewish. State civil litigation, Commercial, contracts (including sales of goods; commercial financing), Personal injury (including property damage). Home: 11200 5 Springs Rd Lutherville MD 21093-3520 Office: Am Bldg 231 E Baltimore St Ste 702 Baltimore MD 21202-3446 E-mail: david@kuryk.com.

KURZ, MARY ELIZABETH, lawyer; b. Scranton, Pa., May 13, 1944; m. William H. Bright III. Student, U. Paris, Sorbonne, summer 1965; BA in French magna cum laude, Marywood Coll., 1966; postgrad., U. Md., 1966-67, U. N.C., 1967, U. Wis., 1969; JD with honors, U. Md., 1971. Bar: Md. 1972, D.C. 1978, Mont. 1982, Mich. 1988, Tex. 1994, N.C. 1996, U.S. Dist. Ct. (we. dist.) Mich., U.S. Supreme Ct., U.S. Ct. Appeals (4th, 6th, D.C. cirs.), U.S. Dist. Ct. Mont. Law clk. to presiding justice Ct. Spl. Appeals Md., 1971-72; asst. atty. gen. criminal div. State of Md., 1972-74, asst. legis. officer to gov., 1974-75, asst. atty. gen. representing U. Md., 1975-82; legal counsel U. Mont., Missoula, 1982-87; gen. counsel, v.p. legal affairs Mich. State U., East Lansing, 1987-94; vice chancellor and gen. counsel Tex. A&M U. System, 1994-96; vice chancellor, gen. coun. N.C. State U. , Raleigh, 1996—. Speaker numerous confs. and profl. meetings; mem. Commn. to Study Sovereign Immunity, 1975. Mem. staff Md. Law Rev. Reginald Heber Smith fellow, 1969. Mem. ABA, Nat. Assn. Coll. and Univ. Attys. (mem. numerous coms., chmn. com. site selection 1985-86, chmn. com. continuing legal edn. 1986-89, bd. dirs. 1985-88, 2d v.p. 1989-90, 1st v.p. 1990-91, pres.-elect 1991-92, pres. 1992-93) Home: 102 King George Loop Cary NC 27511-6334 Office: NC State U 3rd Fl Holladay Hall Raleigh NC 27695

KURZBAN, IRA JAY, lawyer; b. Bklyn., May 9, 1949; s. Benjamin and Irene (Weiss) K.; m. Magda Montiel Davis, Apr. 15, 1989; children: Kathryn Montiel Davis, Paula Lindsay Davis, Magda Marie Davis, Sadie Bethany Kurzban, Benjamin Kurzban. BA magna cum laude, Syracuse U., 1971; MA, U. Calif., Berkeley, 1973, JD, 1976; hon. fellow, U. Pa. Law Sch., 1987. Bar: Calif. 1976, Fla. 1976, U.S. Dist. Ct. (no. dist.) Calif., 1976, U.S. Dist. Ct. (so. dist.) Fla., 1976, U.S. Ct. Appeals (5th cir.) 1978, U.S. Ct. Appeals (11th cir.) 1981, U.S. Supreme Ct. 1980. Ptnr. Kurzban, Kurzban, Weinger & Tetzeli P.A., Miami, Fla., 1977—99; Fla. counsel Nat. Energy Civil Liberties Com., 1979-98; gen. counsel Am. Immigration Lawyers Assn., 1992-93. Adj. prof. immigration and nationality law U. Miami Sch. of Law, 1979—, Nova Southeastern Law Sch., 1982—; instr. polit. sci. U. Calif. Berkeley, 1973; mem. civil justice adv. com. U.S. Dist. Ct. (so. dist.) Fla., 1993-94; mem. certification com. in immigration and nationality law Fla. Bar, 1994-96; lectr. in field. Author: Kurzban's Immigration Law Sourcebook: A Comprehensive Outline and Reference Tool, 8th edit., 2002; contbr. articles to profl. jours. Founder Berkeley Law Found. Recipient Tobias Simon pro bono svc. award Fla. Supreme Ct., 1982, Trial Lawyer of Yr. award Trial Lawyers for Public Justice, Carol King award Nat. Lawyers Guild, 1996, Lawyer of the Ams. award U. Miami Sch. Law, 1992, Edith Lowenstein Meml. award for excellence in immigration scholarship, 2002; Polit. Sci. Dept. fellow U. Calif., Berkeley, 1971, Kent fellow Danforth Found., 1974-77, Law and Society fellow U. Calif., Berkeley, 1975-76. Fellow Am. Immigration Law Found. (hon.); mem. ABA (chair refugee legal assistance com. 1983-84, mem. immigration coord. com. 1991-93), Am. Immigration Lawyers Assn. (pres. so. Fla. chpt. 1980-81, nat. pres. 1987, Jack Wasserman award for excellence in federal litigation 1983, Edith Lawenstein award for excellence in writing in immigrant law 2002), Am. Inns of Ct., Phi Beta Kappa, Phi Kappa Phi. Civil rights, Immigration, naturalization, and customs, Public international. Office: Kurzban Kurzban Weinger & Tetzeli PA 2650 SW 27th Ave Miami FL 33133-3003 E-mail: ira@kkwtlaw.com.

KURZMAN, ROBERT GRAHAM, lawyer, educator; b. N.Y.C., July 3, 1932; s. Benjamin E. and Betty Kurzman; m. Carol Ellis, Aug. 26, 1956; children: Marc, Nancy, Amy. BA, Hofstra U., 1954; JD, Cornell U., 1957. Bar: N.Y. 1959, U.S. Dist. Ct. (no., so., ea. and we. dists.) N.Y. 1964, U.S. Supreme Ct. 1964. Assoc. Wynn, Blattmachr & Campbell, N.Y.C., 1959-63; ptnr. Leaf, Kurzman, Deull & Drogin, N.Y.C., 1963-79, Goldschmidt, Fredericks, Kurzman & Oshatz, 1979-83, Kurzman & Eisenberg and precedessor firms, White Plains, N.Y., 1982—. Adj. prof. law NYU; dir. Stratton Industries, Inc.; acting city ct. judge City of New Rochelle (N.Y.), 1981. Author: (with Rita Gilbert) Paralegals and Successful Law Practice, 1981; contbr. articles to profl. jours. Mem. adv. bd. So. Meth. U. Sch. Law, Estate Planning Inst.; coord. estates and trusts paralegal program Manhattanville Coll., 1974-75; pres. West Putnam coun. Boy Scouts Am., 1981; trustee, pres. Temple Israel; former chmn. New Rochelle Rep. Com. Capt. USAR, 1957-59. Recipient Silver Beaver award Boy Scouts Am., Silver Antelope aawrd; named Man of Yr., New Rochelle B'nai B'rith, 1977. Fellow Am. Coll. Probate Counsel; mem. ABA, N.Y. State Bar Assn., Assn. Bar City N.Y., Masons, Ridgeway Country Club (White Plains), Cornell Club of N.Y.C. (pres.). Family and matrimonial, Probate (including wills, trusts), Estate taxation. Home: 166 Tewksbury Rd Scarsdale NY 10583-6036 Office: 1 N Broadway White Plains NY 10601-2310 E-mail: rkurzman@kelaw.com.

KURZWEIL, HARVEY, lawyer; b. Bklyn., Mar. 23, 1945; s. Martin E. Kurzweil and Muriel (Krause) Kanow; m. Barbara Kramer, Aug. 17, 1969; children: David, Paul (dec.), Emily, Elizabeth. AB, Columbia Coll., 1966, JD, 1969. Bar: N.Y. 1970. Assoc. Dewey, Ballantine, Bushby, Palmer & Wood, N.Y.C., 1969-77, ptnr., 1977-90, Dewey Ballantine, N.Y.C., 1990—, chmn. litigation dept., mem. mgmt. and exec. coms. Bd. dirs. Menninger Clinic; trustee Menninger Found.; bd. visitors Columbia Law Sch. Fellow Am. Bar Found., Internat. Acad. Trial Lawyers; mem. ABA, N.Y. State Bar Assn., D.C. Bar Assn., Assn. of Bar of City of N.Y. (trade regulation com. 1982-85), Univ. Club. Jewish. Avocations: sports cars, reading, gardening, sports. Antitrust, General civil litigation. Home: 1025 5th Ave New York NY 10028 Office: Dewey Ballantine 1301 Avenue Of The Americas New York NY 10019-6022 also: PO Box 370 Saddle River NJ 07458-0389 E-mail: hkurzweil@deweyballantine.com.

KUSHEL, GLENN ELLIOT, lawyer; b. Bklyn., May 5, 1945; BME, CUNY, 1968; MSME, Columbia U., 1970; JD, Seton Hall U., 1974; LLM, NYU, 1978; cert., Coll. Fin. Planning, 1987. Bar: N.J. 1974, N.Y. 1977, U.S. Supreme Ct. 1978. Mem. tech. staff Bell Telephone Labs., Whippany, N.J., 1968-71; cost engr. Exxon Resource and Engr. Co., Florham Park, N.J., 1971-72; dep. atty. gen. State of N.J., Trenton, 1974-76; assoc. Rosenman and Colin, N.Y.C., 1976-81; pvt. practice Bklyn., 1981—2001; assoc. Bivona & Cohen, N.Y.C., 2001—. Mem. N.Y. State Sum/Um Arbitrators, 1995-2001. Assoc. mem. malpractice panel N.Y. State Supreme Ct., Kings County, 1986-90. Atomic Energy Commn. fellowship, 1968. Mem. Pi Tau Sigma, Tau Beta Pi. Avocations: skiing, running, financial planning. State civil litigation, Insurance, Personal injury (including property damage). Office: Wall Street Plz New York NY 10005

KUSHNER, GORDON PETER, lawyer; b. Calgary, Alta., Can., Nov. 3, 1966; came to U.S., 1984; s. H. Peter and V. Marlene (Shatilla) K.; m. Patti A. Yakich, Aug. 10, 1991; children: Brantley Peter, Katerina Mari. BA summa cum laude, U. N.D., 1988; JD cum laude, U. Dayton, 1991. Bar: Ohio 1991, U.S. Dist. Ct. (so. dist.) Ohio 1991. Atty. Dinsmore & Shohl, Cin., 1991-94; atty. internat. ops. LensCrafters Internat., Inc., Cin., 1994-95; corp. atty. Structural Dynamics Rsch. Corp., Milford, Ohio, 1995-98—; v.p., chief tech. counsel Baan Co. N.V., Herndon, Va., Barneveld, Netherlands, 1998-2000; v.p., gen. counsel the Platform for Media, Herndon, 2000—. Dir. Rite Track Equipment Svcs., Inc., Cin., 1994-95; mem. Vision Coun. of Can., Toronto, Ont., 1994-95; spkr. U. Cin. Law Sch., 1993. Author: (newsletter) Cincinnati Small Business Newsletter, 1993; contbr. articles to profl. jours. Mem. Big Bros. and Big Sisters, Dayton, 1990-91; dir. Housing Network of Hamilton County, Cin., 1993-94; coach Lakota Sports Orgn., West Chester, Ohio, 1997-98; treas. Woodlea WaterMocs Swim Team, 2000—. Recipient Yale in Can. Outstanding Can. award Yale U. Can. Alumni Assn., 1990. Mem. ABA, Ohio Bar Assn., Cin. Bar Assn. (presenter NAFTA seminar 1992), Phi Alpha Delta, Phi Beta Kappa. Corporate, general, Intellectual property, Private international. Home: 1409 Moore Pl SW Leesburg VA 20175-5820 E-mail: gordonkushner@theplatform.com.

KUSMA, KYLLIKKI, lawyer; b. Tartu, Estonia, Dec. 8, 1943; came to U.S., 1951; d. August and Helju (Traat) K. BA, Ohio U., 1966; MA (VA Rehab. fellow), Ohio State U., 1967; JD, Ohio No. U., 1976; MLT, Georgetown U., 1980. Bar: Ohio 1977, D.C. 1978. Speech and hearing therapist Lima (Ohio) Meml. Hosp., 1967-70, Tipp City (Ohio) Schs., 1970-74; atty.-adv. Office Chief Counsel, IRS, Washington, 1977-81; v.p., assoc. tax counsel Security Pacific Nat. Bank., L.A., 1981-83; ptnr. Brownstein Zeidman & Lore, Washington, 1983-95, Ernst & Young LLP, Columbus, Ohio, 1995—2002. Instr. Wright State U., 1972-76. Author: (with others) Mortgage-Backed Securities Special Update: REMICs, 1988; contbr. articles to profl. jours. Vol. local civic and polit. activities. Mem. ABA, Ohio Bar Assn., Columbus Bar Assn., Columbus Women Execs. (v.p., sec.), Phi Kappa Phi. Taxation, general, Corporate taxation, Personal income taxation. E-mail: llikki@msn.com.

KUSTER, LARRY DONALD, lawyer; b. Kewanee, Ill., July 27, 1947; s. Donald Carl and Rosemary Ann (Riggins) Kuster; m. Mary Catherine Whitmore, July 11, 1970; children: David, Ryan. BA, Augustana Coll., 1969; JD with honors, U. Iowa, 1973. Bar: Ill. 1973, U.S. Dist. Ct. (cen. dist.) : Ill. 1980, U.S. Dist. Ct. (so. dist.): Ill. 1996, U.S. Ct. Appeals (7th cir.) : 1982, U.S. Tax Ct. : 1979. Assoc. Rammelkamp, Bradney, Kuster, Keaton, Fritsche & Lindsay PC, Jacksonville, Ill., 1973—75, ptnr., 1976—. Moderator continuing legal edn. program Ill. Inst. Continuing Legal Edn., 1985—86; lectr. in field; master barrister Lincoln-Douglas Inn of Ct., 1993—. Contbr. articles to profl. jours. Active Am. Coun. on Germany, 1982—2002, City of Jacksonville Heritage Cultural Ctr. Bd., 1986—91, Fedn. Def. and Corp. Coun., 1989—; pres. West Central Ill. Council on World Affairs, 1982—83; bd. dirs. Sherwood Eddy Meml. YMCA, 1975—80, Jacksonville Area C. of C., 1981—84, pres., 1990; bd. dirs. Jacksonville Area Visitors and Tourism Bur., 1986—91; trustee MacMurray Coll., Jacksonville, 1991—2001; pres. Ill. Assn. Hist. Preservation Commns., 1982; vice-chmn. Jacksonville Hist. Preservation Commn., 1981—83, chmn., 1983—84. Mem.: Ill. Bar Assn. (civil practice and procedure coun. 1976—77, 1986—90, sec. workers' compensation sect. 1982—83, vice-chmn. 1983—84, chmn. 1984—85), Morgan County Bar Assn. (pres. 1977—78), Am. Arbitration Assn. General civil litigation, Municipal (including bonds), Personal injury (including property damage). Home: RR 1 Box 19 Chapin IL 62628-9801 Office: Rammelkamp Bradney 232 W State St Jacksonville IL 62650-2002

KUSZ, MICHAEL JOSEPH, judge; b. Ironwood, Mich., May 17, 1953; s. Walter James and Mary Jean Kusz; m. Christine M. Kusz, Oct. 30, 1976; children: Erin Elizabeth, Kerry Lynn. AA, Gogebic C.C., 1973; BA, U. Minn., 1975, JD, 1978; MBA, Colo. State U., 2001. Assoc. McNeil Mouw & Torrence, Iron Mountain, Mich., 1978—82; prosecuting atty. Dickinson County, 1983—90; dist. judge State of Mich., 1991—. Pres. Habitat for Humanity Menominee River, Iron Mountain, 2001—. Recipient Pathfinder award, Mich. Coalition Against Domestic Violence, Lansing, 1997. Mem.: Am. Judges Assn., Kiwanis (bd. dirs. 200[illegible]—). Mailing: PO Box 609 Iron Mountain MI 49801-0609

KUTCHER, ROBERT A. lawyer; b. N.Y.C., Dec. 27, 1950; s. Joseph L. and Renee M. (Durben) K.; m. Renee Bauchat, Oct. 29, 1985; children: J.C. Rosenbloom, Skylar Rosenbloom, Andrea Kutcher, Jessica Kutcher. BS, Cornell U., 1972; JD cum laude, Loyola U., New Orleans, 1975; postgrad., Tulane U., 1975-77. Bar: N.Y. 1976, La. 1976, U.S. Dist. Ct. (ea., we. and mid. dists.) La., U.S. Ct. Appeals (5th and 11th cirs.) 1976, U.S. Supreme Ct. 1976. Law clk. U.S. Dist. Ct. (ea. dist.) La., New Orleans, 1975-77; assoc. Bronfin & Heller, New Orleans, 1977-82; ptnr. Bronfin, Heller, Steinberg & Berins, New Orleans, 1982-96, Chopin, Wagar, Cole, Richard, Reboul & Kutcher, LLP, Metairie, 1996—. Mem. La. Atty. Disciplinary Bd., 1993-99, chmn. 1999. Contbr. articles to profl. publs. Bd. dirs. Jewish Cmty. Ctr., New Orleans, 1983-92, treas., 1986-89, v.p., 1989-91, pres., 1991-92; bd. dirs. south cen. region Anti-Defamation League, New Orleans, 1985—, vice chmn., 1988-91, chmn., 1991-95, mem. nat. civil rights com., nat. legal affairs com.; chmn. state adv. com. U.S. Civil Rights Commn., 1990; mem. Syr Lindasy Conservative Synagogue (bd. dirs. 1998-, pres. 1999-2001.). Mem. Fed. Bar Assn. (bd. dirs. New Orleans chpt. 1984-91, pres. 1991), N.Y. Bar Assn., 5th Cir. Bar Assn. Republican. Antitrust, Federal civil litigation, Commercial, contracts (including sales of goods; commercial financing). Home: 12 Swan St New Orleans LA 70124-4405 Office: Chopin Wagar Cole Richard Reboul & Kutcher LLP 3850 N Causeway Blvd Ste 900 Metairie LA 70002-8130

KWAKWA, EDWARD KWAKU, lawyer; b. Kumasi, Ghana, Apr. 19, 1961; s. Benjamin and Helena (Donkor) K.; m. Diana Rutiba, June 6, 1992; children: Afia, Sibo, Kofi, Koby. LLB, U. Ghana, 1984; LLM, Queen's U., Kingston, Ont., Can., 1986, Yale U., 1987, JSD, PhD, 1990. Bar: Conn. 1989, D.C. 1991. Legal rsch. asst. State Ins. Corp. of Ghana, Accra, 1983-84; summer assoc. Lawyers' Com. for Civil Rights Under Law, Washington, 1986; vis. lectr. law U. Denver, 1989; assoc. O'Melveny & Myers, Washington, 1990-93; internat. legal advisor Commn. on Global Governance, Geneva, 1993-94; sr. legal advisor UN High Commr. for Refugees, Geneva, 1994-96; legal affairs officer World Trade Orgn., Geneva, 1996; asst. legal counsel World Intellectual Property Orgn., Geneva, 1997—2003, dep. legal counsel, 2003—. Internat. law cons. Lawyers' Com. for Civil Rights Under Law, Washington, 1988-94; rapporteur Am. Soc. Internat. Law, 1988-92; dir. Integrated Bar Project, New Haven, Pretoria, South Africa, 1990-93; dir. Integrated Bar Project, South Africa, 1990-93; vis. prof. law Fletcher Sch. Law and Diplomacy, 2000, U. Pretoria, 2002. Author: The International Law of Armed Conflict, 1992; sr. editor Yale Jour. Internat. Law, 1986-88; bd. editors African Soc. Internat. and Comparative Law, London, 1995—. Mem. internat. observer del. South African Elections, 1994; mem. European Assn. Devel. and Tng. Insts. Working Group on Refugees, Switzerland, 1995, Ghana UN Students Assn., 1980-84. Yale U. Grad. fellow, 1986-89. Mem. ABA, Am. Soc. Internat. Law (rapporteur 1985-92, mem. exec. coun. 2001--), African Soc. Internat. and Comparative Law. Methodist. Avocations: chess, Scrabble, soccer, dancing, travel. Office: WIPO 34 Chemin Colombettes 1211 Geneva 20 Switzerland E-mail: edward.kwakwa@wipo.int.

KWEE, PATTY, lawyer; b. Jakarta, Indonesia; BA, U.C. Riverside, 1990; JD, Southwestern U., 1999. Bar: Calif., U.S. Dist. Ct. Paralegal Farmers Insurance Group, Los Angeles, Calif., 1992—97; judicial extern U.S. Bankruptcy Ct., Woodland Hills, Calif., 1998; law clerk U.S. Small Bus. Admin., Glendale, Calif.; atty. Law Offices of Richard L. Albert, No. Hollywood, Calif. Income tax preparation Volunteer Income Tax Assistance Program, 1999. Mem.: ABA, Orange County Asian-Am. Bar Assn., L.A. County Bar Assn.

KYHOS, THOMAS FLYNN, lawyer; b. Cheverly, Md., May 13, 1947. B.A. in Econs., DePauw U., 1969; J.D., Cath. U., 1973. Bar: Md. 1974, D.C. 1974, U.S. Tax Ct. 1974, U.S. Supreme Ct. 1978. sole practice, Washington, 1974— ; pres. First Oxford Corp., Washington, 1976— . Mem. ABA, Md. Bar Assn., D.C. Bar Assn. Taxation, general. Home: 5714 Massachusetts Ave Bethesda MD 20816-1929 Office: 3528 K St NW Washington DC 20007-3503

KYLE, HENRY CARPER, III, lawyer; b. San Antonio, Dec. 19, 1937; s. Henry C. and Marian Morris (Camp) K.; m. Brenda Joyce Gary, Sept. 4, 1965; children— Katherine, Allen. B.A., Rice U., 1959; J.D., U. Tex.-Austin, 1964. Bar: Tex. 1964. Ptnr. Kyle, Walker & Gossett and predecessor firm, San Marcos, Tex., 1967— . Served to lt. (j.g.) USNR, 1959-61. Mem. State Bar of Tex., Hays County Bar Assn. (past pres.), Rotary Club (past pres.). Republican. Methodist. Banking, Probate (including wills, trusts), Property, real (including real estate development, water). Home: 711 W San Antonio St San Marcos TX 78666-4321 Office: Kyle Walker & Gossett East Side of Square San Marcos TX 78666

KYLE, RICHARD HOUSE, federal judge; b. St. Paul, Apr. 30, 1937; s. Richard E. and Geraldine (House) K.; m. Jane Foley, Dec. 22, 1959; children: Richard H. Jr., Michael F., D'Arcy, Patrick G., Kathleen. BA, U. Minn., 1959, LLB, 1962. Bar: Minn. 1962, U.S. Dist. Ct. Minn. 1992. Atty. Briggs & Morgan, St. Paul, 1963-68, 1970-92; solicitor gen. Minn. Atty. Gen. Office, St. Paul, 1968-70; judge U.S. Dist. Ct., St. Paul, 1992—. Pres. Minn. Law Rev., Mpls., 1962. Mem. Minn. State Bar Assn., Ramsey County Bar Assn. Republican. Episcopal. Office: US Dist Ct Federal Courts Bldg 316 Robert St N Saint Paul MN 55101-1495

LABAY, EUGENE BENEDICT, lawyer; b. El Campo, Tex., July 20, 1938; s. Ben F. and Cecelia M. (Orsak) L.; m. Katherine Sue Ermis, Dec. 29, 1962; children: Michael, Joan, John, Paul, David, Patrick, Steven. BBA, St. Mary's U., San Antonio, 1960; JD, St. Mary's U., 1965. Bar: Tex. 1965, U.S. Dist. Ct. (we. dist.) Tex. 1968, U.S. Dist. Ct. (no. dist.) Tex. 1973, U.S. Dist. Ct. (ea. dist.) Tex. 1986, U.S. Ct. Appeals (5th cir.) 1968, U.S. Ct. Appeals (11th cir.) 1981, U.S. Supreme Ct. 1980. Briefing atty. Supreme Ct. Tex., Austin, 1965-66; assoc. Cox & Smith Inc., San Antonio, 1966-71, ptnr., 1972-83, v.p., 1972-94; pvt. practice, 1994—. Contbr. articles to profl. jours. Served to 1st lt. U.S. Army, 1960-62. Mem. ABA, State Bar Tex. (chmn. sect. internat. law 1979-80), San Antonio Bar Assn., Fed. Bar Assn., Am. Judicature soc., Cath. Lawyers Guild San Antonio, KC (coun. grand knight 1982-83), Phi Delta Phi. State civil litigation, Oil, gas, and mineral, Environmental. Home: 31720 Post Oak Trl Boerne TX 78015-4133 Office: PO Box 15244 112 W Craig Pl San Antonio TX 78212-3416

LABINGER, LYNETTE J. lawyer; m. Ross A. Eadie, Jan. 21, 1972; 1 child, Loren Labinger Eadie. AB magna cum laude, Mt. Holyoke Coll., 1971; JD cum laude, NYU, 1974. Bar: Mass. 1974, R.I. 1975, U.S. Dist. Ct. R.I. 1975, U.S. Ct. Appeals (1st Cir.) 1978, U.S. Supreme Ct. 1980. Law clk. U.S. Dist. Ct. R.I., Providence, 1974-76; assoc. Abedon, Michaelson, Standzler, Biener, Skolnik & Lipsey, Providence, 1976-82; ptnr. Roney & Labinger, Providence, 1983—. Mem. U.S. Dist. Ct. Bar Examiners, 1981—, Commn. . on Jud. Tenure and Discipline, 1983-86. Bd. dirs., vol. atty. R.I. affiliate ACLU, 1978—; bd. dirs. R.I. Legal Svcs. Inc., 1980-83. Recipient Vol. Atty. award ACLU, 1982, Charles Potter award Planned Parenthood R.I., 1982, NYU Prize, 1974, Alumnae Key award NYU Law Sch., 1974, Sorrentino award Nat. Women's Polit. Caucus, 1988, Civil Libertarian of Yr. award R.I. ACLU, 1989; Root-Tilden scholar, 1971-74. Fellow Am. Coll. Trial Lawyers, R.I. Bar Found. (bd. dirs. 1992—); mem. R.I. Bar Assn., Order of Coif, Phi Beta Kappa. Democrat. Civil rights, Federal civil litigation, Labor (including EEOC, Fair Labor Standards Act, labor-management relations, NLRB, OSHA). Office: Roney & Labinger 344 Wickenden St Providence RI 02903-4469 E-mail: office@roney-labinger.com.

LABOVITZ, PRISCILLA, lawyer; b. Lynn, Mass., May 4, 1946; d. Jack Oscar and Barbara Helene (Small) L.; m. Joseph Cirincione, June 25, 1978; children: Amy Labovitz Cirincione, Peter Vincent Labovitz Cirincione. BA, Wellesley Coll., 1968; JD, Northeastern U., 1972. Bar: Mass. 1973, U.S. Ct. Appeals (D.C. cir.) 1983. Ptnr. Geller, Miller, Taylor, Weinberg & Labovitz, Cambridge, Mass., 1973-78; assoc. Bastone & Kaplan, Boston, 1978-81, Law Offices of Jan Pederson, Washington, 1981, Paul Shearman Allen & Assocs., Washington, 1982-84; pvt. practice law Washington, 1988—. Contbr. articles to profl. jours. Literacy vol. Mem. Am. Immigration Lawyers Assn., Amnesty Internat. (legis. coord. 1990-96). Immigration, naturalization, and customs. Office: 6856 Eastern Ave NW Ste 354 Washington DC 20012-2165

LACER, ALFRED ANTONIO, lawyer, educator; b. Hammonton, N.J., Feb. 14, 1952; s. Vincent and Carmen (Savall) L.; m. Kathleen Visser, June 15, 1974; children: Margaret, James, Matthew. BA in Polit. Sci., Gordon Coll., 1974; JD, Cath. U. Am., 1977. Bar: Md. 1977, U.S. Dist. Ct. Md. 1980, U.S. Ct. Appeals (4th cir.) 1980, U.S. Supreme Ct. 1997. Law clk. to Honorable Joseph A. Mattingly, Sr. Cir. Ct. St. Mary's County, Leonardtown, Md., 1977-78; ptnr. Lacer, Sparling, Densford & Reynolds PA and predecessors, Lexington Park, Md., 1978-99; county atty. St. Mary's County, Md., 1999-2000, CEO, county adminstr., 2000—. Adj. prof. bus. law Fla. Inst. Tech., Patuxent, Md., 1989-92, 95-99; vis. instr. St. Mary's Coll. of Md., 1988, 91; mem. bd. edn. St. Mary's County (Md.) Pub. Schs., 1989-94, pres., 1991-92; mem. inquiry panel Atty. Grievance Commn. of Md., 1984-90. Bd. dirs. St. Mary's Hosp., Leonardtown, 1982-88, v.p., 1985-88; bd. dirs. So. Md. Cmty. Action, Inc., Hughsville, Md., 1982-84, St. Mary's County Tech. Coun., 1997-99. Mem. ABA, Md. Bar Assn. (com. on jud. appointments 1982-85), St. Mary's County Bar Assn. (v.p. 1979-80, pres. 1980-81). Episcopalian. General civil litigation, Commercial, contracts (including sales of goods; commercial financing), Corporate, general. Office: Office of the County Adminstr PO Box 653 Leonardtown MD 20650-0653

LACEY, HENRY BERNARD, lawyer; b. Aurora, Colo., Nov. 30, 1963; s. Leonard Joseph and Colleen Trece (Ryan) L. BS, Ariz. State U., 1988, JD, 1991. Bar: Ariz. 1991, Oreg. 1996; U.S. Dist. Ct. Ariz. 1991, U.S. Ct. Appeals (9th cir.) 1992, U.S. Dist. Ct. Oreg. 1999. Jud. law clk. to Hon. Cecil F. Poole U.S. Ct. Appeals 9th Cir., San Francisco, 1991-92; assoc. Kimball & Curry, P.C., Phoenix, 1992-93, Wilenchik & Bartness, P.C., Phoenix, 1996—97; atty. Law Office of Henry B. Lacey, Phoenix, 1993-94, Portland, Oreg., 1997—99, Flagstaff, Ariz., 1999—; vis. fellow Natural Resources Law Inst. Northwestern Sch. Law, Lewis and Clark Coll., Portland, 1994-95. Counsel/ environ. group adv. bd. dirs. Coalition to Reform the Ctrl. Ariz. Project, Phoenix, 1993; vol. lawyer Land and Water Fund of the Rockies, Boulder, Colo., 1993—, Portland Audubon Soc., 1996—99; adj. prof. No. Ariz. U., 2000—. Gen. counsel Maricopa County, Ariz. Dem. Party, 1992-94. Mem.: Order of Coif, Phi Delta Phi. Roman Catholic. Avocations: hiking, bicycling, reading, photography. Intellectual property, Environmental, Natural resources. Office: PO Box 115 Flagstaff AZ 86002-0115 E-mail: henry.lacey@azbar.org.

LACH, SUSAN MARIE, lawyer; b. Mpls., Aug. 4, 1948; d. Edward T. and Delores T. (Baillargeon) L. BA summa cum laude, U. Minn., 1970; JD magna cum laude, U. Ga., 1975. Ptnr. Lach & Elliott PC, Ft. Collins, Colo., 1976-82; owner Susan M. Lach PC, Ft. Collins, Colo., 1982-86; ptnr. Frey, Lach & Michaels PC, Ft. Collins, Colo., 1986-93; assoc. Lang, Pauley, Gregerson & Rosow, Ltd., Mpls., 1992-96; shareholder Messerli & Kramer P.A., Mpls., 1996—. Contbr. chpt. to book. Bd. dirs. U. Minn., YMCA, Mpls., 1995-2000. Fellow Am. Acad Matrimonial Lawyers (chair Minn. chpt. 2001-02, bd. mgrs. Minn. chpt. 1996—); mem. ATLA (chair family law sect. 1994-95), Colo. Bar Assn. (exec. coun. 1982-93), Hennepin County Bar Assn. (exec. coun. family law sect. 1995—, co-chair 1998-99), Order of Coif, Phi Kappa Phi. Democrat. Roman Catholic. Family and matrimonial. Office: Messerli & Kramer PA 1800 5th St Towers 150 S 5th St Ste 1800 Minneapolis MN 55402-4218 Fax: 612-672-3777. E-mail: slach@mandklaw.com.

LACHCIK, NANCY LOU MARSHALL, lawyer, educator; b. Biloxi, Miss., July 25, 1957; d. Joseph John and Ruth Elaine (Glidden) Marshall; m. Joseph A. Lachcik. AA, St. Clair County C.C., 1977; BA, U. Mich., 1979; JD, Thomas M. Cooley Law Sch., 1982. Bar: Mich. 1983. Assoc. Dietrich & Cassavaugh, Port Huron, Mich., 1983-84; atty., referee St. Clair County Probate Ct., Port Huron, 1984-94; substitute tchr. Fraser (Mich.) Area Schs., Mich., 2000—. Deaconess 1st Congl. Ch., Port Huron, 1975-77; campaign worker William T. Fischer for County Commr., 1983; active Pleasant Valley Schs. PTO; mem. Pleasant Valley Sch. Edn. in Excellence Bd. Mem. ABA, ATLA, Mich. Bar Assn., St. Clair County Bar Assn., St. Clair County Coun. for Prevention Child Abuse and Neglect, Women Lawyers Assn. (treas. Blue Water region), Phi Theta Kappa. Republican.

LACK, ROBERT JOEL, lawyer; b. Glen Ridge, N.J., Mar. 7, 1955; s. Walter and Carolyn Lack; m. Colleen Phyllis Kelly, June 9, 1979; children: Kelly Ann, Jonathan Andrew. AB, Princeton U., 1977, M in Pub. Affairs, 1978; JD, Harvard U., 1981. Bar: N.Y. 1982, N.J. 1990, U.S. Dist. Ct. (so. and ea. dist.) N.Y. 1982, U.S. Ct. Appeals (3d cir.) 1982, U.S. Ct. Appeals (1st cir.) 1984, U.S. Ct. Appeals (2d cir.) 1985, U.S. Supreme Ct. 1986, U.S. Ct. Appeals (7th cir.) 1987, U.S. Ct. Appeals (D.C. and 9th cirs.) 1988, U.S. Dist. Ct. (no. dist.) Calif. 1988, U.S. Dist. Ct. N.J. 1991. Law clk. to judge U.S. Ct. Appeals (3d cir.), Newark, 1981-82; assoc. Sullivan & Cromwell, N.Y.C., 1982-90; ptnr. Friedman Kaplan Seiler & Adelman LLP, N.Y.C., 1991—. Editor Harvard Law Rev. 1979-81. Recipient Whitney North Seymour medal Columbia U. Law Sch., 1981. Mem. ABA, N.Y. State Bar Assn. (mem. com. on civil rights 1984-90, mem. securities litigation com. 1998—), N.Y.C. Bar Assn. (sec. com. on lectures and continuing edn. 1984-86, mem. com. on antitrust and trade regulation 1991-94, mem. com. on fed. cts. 1998-2001), Fed. Bar Coun. Federal civil litigation, State civil litigation, Securities. Office: Friedman Kaplan Seiler & Adelman LLP 1633 Broadway New York NY 10019-6708

LACKEY, MICHAEL E., JR., lawyer, educator; b. Hopkinsville, Ky., May 3, 1961; s. Michael E. Lackey, Sr. and Linda L. Sterling; m. Cynthia L. Sheppard, May 23, 1987; children: Michael E. III, Ashleigh L. BS in Aero. and Astronautical Engring., MIT, 1983; JD with high honors, George Washington U., 1993. Bar: Fla. 1993, DC 1994, U.S. Supreme Ct. 1999. Assoc. atty. Arnold & Porter, Washington, 1993—94, Mayer, Brown & Platt, Washington, 1995—97; law clk. to Hon. Jacques L. Wiener U.S. Ct. Appeals, Shreveport, La., 1994—95; assoc. atty. Mayer, Brown & Platt, Washington, 1998—2001; assoc. ind. counsel Office David Barrett Ind. Counsel, Washington, 1997—98; ptnr. Mayer, Brown, Rowe & Maw, Washington, 2002—. Adj. prof. George Washington U., Washington, 1995—. Contbr. articles to profl. jours.; guest commentator (TV series) Supreme Court Watch with Fred Graham. Lt., naval aviator USN, 1983—90. Named Top Gun, USN, 1987; Nat. Merit scholar. Mem.: Fed. Bar Assn. (vice chmn. antitrust and trade regulation 2001—). Episcopalian. Avocations: golf, running, coaching children's sports teams. Antitrust, Appellate, General civil litigation. Office: Mayer Brown Rowe and Maw 1909 K St NW Washington DC 20006

LACKLAND, JOHN, lawyer; b. Parma, Idaho, Aug. 29, 1939; AB, Stanford U., 1962; JD, U. Wash., 1964; master gardener, Colo. State U., 1996. Bar: Wash. 1965, U.S. Dist. Ct. (we. dist.) Wash. 1965, (ea. dist.) Wash. 1973, U.S. Ct. Appeals (9th cir.) 1965, Conn. 1981, U.S. Dist. Ct. Conn. 1983, U.S. Supreme Ct. 1973, U.S. Dist. Ct. (so. dist.) N.Y. 1988. Assoc. firm Lane Powell Moss & Miller, Seattle, 1965-69; asst. atty. gen. State of Wash., Seattle, 1969-72; asst. chief State of Wash. (U. Wash. div.), 1969-72; v.p., sec., gen. counsel Western Farmers Assn., Seattle, 1972-76, Fotomat Corp., Stamford, Conn., 1976-80; ptnr. Leepson & Lackland, 1981-88, Lackland and Nalewaik, 1988-92; pvt. practices Westport, Conn., 1992-94; prin. Lackland Assocs., Grand Junction, Colo., 1994—2002. Bd. dirs. Mercer Island (Wash.) Congl. Ch., 1967-70, pres. bd. dirs., 1970; mem. land use plan steering com. City of Mercer Island, 1970-72; bd. dirs. Mercer Island Sch. Dist., 1970-73, v.p. bd. dirs., 1972, pres. 1973; trustee Mid-Fairfield Child Guidance Ctr., 1982-84, Norfield Congl. Ch., 1982-84; bd. dirs. Grand Junction Symphony Orch., 1995-99.

LACKLAND, THEODORE HOWARD, lawyer; b. Chgo., Dec. 4, 1943; s. Richard and Cora Lee (Sanders) L.; m. Dorothy Ann Gerald, Jan. 2, 1970; 1 child, Jennifer Noel. BS, Loyola U., Chgo., 1965; MA, Howard U., 1967; JD, Columbia U., 1975; grad., U.S. Army Ranger Sch., 1968. Bar: N.J. 1975, U.S. Dist. Ct. N.J. 1975, Ga. 1982, U.S. Tax Ct. 1983, U.S. Supreme Ct. 1979, U.S. Dist. Ct. (no. dist.) Ga. 1982, U.S. Dist. Ct. (mid. dist.) Ga. 1985. Assoc. Dewey, Ballantine, Bushby, Palmer & Wood, N.Y.C., 1975-78; asst. U.S. atty. Dist. N.J., Newark, 1978-81; ptnr. Arnall Golden & Gregory, Atlanta, 1981-93, Lackland & Assoc., Atlanta, 1993-95, Lackland & Heyward, Atlanta, 1995-2000, Lackland & Assocs., LLC, Atlanta, 2000—. Adj. prof. law Ga. State U. Law Sch., 1989-99. Assoc. editor Columbia Human Rights Law Rev., 1974-75; contbr. articles to profl. jours. Adv. dir. Atlanta Bus. Devel. Ctr., Minority Bus. Devel. Coun., Atlanta, 1983-91; mem. exec. com. Leadership Atlanta, 1986, 1990-91. Capt. U.S. Army, 1967-71. Decorated Bronze Star with 1 oak leaf cluster, Purple Heart, Air medal. Mem.: Atlanta Bar Assn., Gate City Bar Assn., Fed. Bar Assn., Ga. Bar Assn., ABA. Democrat. Roman Catholic. General civil litigation, Commercial, contracts (including sales of goods; commercial financing), Corporate, general. Home: 4400 Oak Ln Marietta GA 30062-6355 Office: Lackland & Assocs LLC 230 Peachtree St NW Atlanta GA 30303-1562

LACOSTE, THIERRY C. lawyer; b. Paris, June 19, 1959; s. Robert L. and Nadia M. (Marculescu) L.; m. Lynda M. Heinemann, Sept. 12, 1992. Student, U. Broussais, 1978; M Bus. Law, U. Nanterre, 1982; Grad. in English and U.S. Bus. Law, U. Pantheon-Sorbonne, 1983; LLM, George Washington U., 1985. Bar: France. Jr. assoc. Law Offices of S.G. Archibald, Paris, 1986-89; sr. assoc. Simmons and Simmons, Paris, 1989-93; ptnr. Law Offices of Meyrier, Fayout, Lacoste, Paris, 1993—. Contbr. articles to profl. jours. Mem. Racing Club of France, Club 89 of Washington. Office: 74 Ave Paul Doumer 75116 Paris France E-mail: t.lacoste@mflbar.net.

LACOVARA, MICHAEL, lawyer; b. Bklyn., Oct. 21, 1963; s. Philip Allen and Madeline Estelle (Papio) L.; m. Carla J. Foran, Sept. 9, 1989; children: Claire Elizabeth, Edward Christopher. BA, U. Pa., 1984; MPhil, Cambridge (U.K.) U., 1985; JD, Harvard U., 1988. Law clk. Hon. Stephen Reinhardt, L.A., 1988-89; assoc. Sullivan & Cromwell, N.Y.C., 1989-96, ptnr., 1997-2000, Palo Alto, Calif., 2000—. Bd. dirs. Lower Manhattan Cultural Coun., N.Y.C., 1995-2002, chair, 1998; trustee Cambridge U. in Am. Thouron Found. fellow, 1984. Mem. ABA, Assn. of Bar of City of N.Y., San Francisco Bar Assn., Phi Beta Kappa. Democrat. Roman Catholic. Home: 345 Folsom St San Francisco CA 94105 Office: Sullivan & Cromwell 1870 Embarcadero Rd Palo Alto CA 94303 E-mail: lacovaram@sullcrom.com.

LACY, ALEXANDER SHELTON, lawyer; b. South Boston, Va., Aug. 18, 1921; s. Cecil Baker and Lura Elizabeth (Byram) L.; m. Carol Jemison, Aug. 8, 1952; children: John Blakeway, Joan Elizabeth Chancey, Alexander Shelton. BS in Chemistry, U. Ala., 1943; LL.B., U. Va., 1949. Bar: Ala. 1949, U.S. Ct. Appeals (5th, 11th and D.C. cirs.) 1981, U.S. Supreme Ct. 1979. Assoc. Bradley, Arant, Rose & White, Birmingham, Ala., 1949-54; with Ala. Gas Corp., Birmingham, 1954-86; v.p., asst. sec., atty. Ala. Gas Corp./Energen Corp., 1969-86; v.p., sec., atty. Ala. Gas Corp., 1974-86; with Patrick and Lacy, Birmingham, 1986-96. Pres., chmn. bd. Birmingham Symphony Assn., 1964-67; chmn. Birmingham-Jefferson Civic Center Authority, 1965-71. Served with USN, 1943-46. Mem. ABA, Ala. Bar Assn. (chmn. energy law com. 1984-86), Birmingham Bar Assn., Am. Gas Assn. (chmn. legal sect. 1983-85), Fed. Energy Bar Assn., Fed. Bar Assn., Am. Judicature Soc., Mountain Brook Club, Phi Gamma Delta, Phi Delta Phi. Episcopalian. Corporate, general, FERC practice, Finance. Home: 3730 Montrose Rd Birmingham AL 35213-3824

LACY, ELIZABETH BERMINGHAM, state supreme court justice; b. 1945; BA cum laude, St. Mary's Coll., Notre Dame, Ind., 1966; JD, U. Tex., 1969; LLM, U. Va., 1992. Bar: Tex. 1969, Va. 1977. Staff atty. Tex. Legis. Coun., Austin, 1969-72; atty. Office of Atty. Gen., State of Tex., Austin, 1973-76; legis. aide Va. Del. Carrington Williams, Richmond, 1976-77; dep. atty. gen. jud. affairs div. Va. Office Atty. Gen., Richmond, 1982-85; mem. Va. State Corp. Commn., Richmond, 1985-89; justice Supreme Ct. Va., Richmond, 1989—. Office: Va Supreme Ct 100 North 9th Street, 5th Floor Richmond VA 23219

LACY, ROBINSON BURRELL, lawyer; b. Boston, May 7, 1952; s. Benjamin Hammett and Jane (Burrell) L. AB, U. Calif., Berkeley, 1974; JD, Harvard U., 1977. Bar: N.Y. 1978, U.S. Dist. Ct. (so. and ea. dists.) N.Y. 1979, U.S. Dist. Ct. (we. dist.) N.Y. 1992, U.S. Ct. Appeals (2d cir.) 1983, U.S. Ct. Appeals (10th cir.) 1990, U.S. Ct. Appeals (3d cir.) 2002, U.S. Supreme Ct. 1986. Law clk. to judge U.S. Dist. Ct. (so. dist.) N.Y., N.Y.C., 1977-78; law clk. to chief justice Warren Burger U.S. Supreme Ct., Washington, 1978-79; assoc. Sullivan & Cromwell, N.Y.C., 1979-85, ptnr., 1985—. Mem. ABA, Assn. of Bar of City of N.Y., N.Y. State Bar Assn. Bankruptcy, Federal civil litigation. Office: Sullivan & Cromwell 125 Broad St Fl 28 New York NY 10004-2489

LADAR, JERROLD MORTON, lawyer; b. San Francisco, Aug. 2, 1933; AB, U. Wash., 1956; LLB, U. Calif., Berkeley, 1960. Bar: Calif. 1961, U.S. Supreme Ct. 1967. Law clk. to judge U.S. Dist. Ct. (no. dist.) Calif., 1960-61; asst. U.S. atty. San Francisco, 1961-70; chief criminal div., 1968—71; mem. firm MacInnis & Donner, San Francisco, 1971—73; prof. criminal law and procedure U. San Francisco Law Sch., 1962-83; pvt. practice San Francisco, 1971—; ptnr. Ladar & Ladar, San Francisco, 1994—. Lectr. Hastings Coll. Law, Civil and Criminal Advocacy Programs, 1985-2002; chair pvt. defender panel U.S. Dist. Ct. (no. dist.) Calif., 1980-90; ct. apptd. chair stats. and tech. subcom. Fed. Civil Justice Reform Act Com. (no. dist.) Calif., 1990-95; ct. apptd. mem. Fed. Ct. Civil Local Rules Revision Com. (no. dist.) Calif., 1994—; ct. apptd. chmn. Criminal Local Rules Revision Com. (no. dist.) Calif., 1991-99; mem. continuing edn. of bar criminal law adv. com. U. Calif., Berkeley, 1978-83, 89-2001; panelist, mem. nat. planning com. ABA Nat. Ann. White Collar Crime Inst., 1996—; ct. apptd. mem. Local Disciplinary Rule Draft com., 1998-99 Author: (with others) Selected Trial Motions, Grand Jury Practice, Asset Forfeiture, 6 edits., California Criminal Law and Procedure Practice, 3d edit. 4th edit., 5th edit., 6th edit., 2002, Collateral Effects of Federal Convictions, 1997, Insult Added to Injury: The Fallout From Tax Conviction, 1997, Give Me A Break-Finding Federal Misdemeanors, 1998, The Court: We're Here to Seek the Truth; Defense Counsel: Excuse Me, That's Not My Job, 1999, A Day At The Grand Jury, 2000, The Art of Direct Examination, 2002. Trustee Tamalpais Union High Sch. Dist., 1968-77, chmn. bd., 1973-74; mem. adv. com. Nat. PTA Assn., 1972-78; apptd. mem. criminal justice act com. U.S. Ct. Appeals (9th cir.) Fellow Am. Bd. Criminal Lawyers; mem. ABA, San Francisco Bar Assn. (editor in Re 1974-76), State Bar Calif. (pro-tem disciplinary referee 1976-78, vice chmn. pub. interest and edn. com. criminal law sect., mem. exec. com. criminal law sect. 1980-87, editor Criminal Law Sect. News 1981-87, chmn. exec. com. 1983-84), Am. Inns. of Ct. (exec. com. 1994-97), Fed. Bar Assn. (panelist), Nat. Sentencing Inst. (contbr.) Federal civil litigation, State civil litigation, Criminal. Office: 1916 Vallejo St San Francisco CA 94123-4918

LADD, JEFFREY RAYMOND, lawyer; b. Mpls., Apr. 10, 1941; s. Jasper Raymond and Florence Marguerite (DeMarce) L.; m. Kathleen Anne Crosby, Aug. 24, 1963; children: Jeffrey Raymond, John Henry, Mark Jasper, Matthew Crosby. Student, U. Vienna, Austria; BA, Loras Coll.; postgrad., U. Denver; JD, Ill. Inst. Tech. Bar: Ill. 1973, U.S. Dist. Ct. 1973. V.p. mktg. Ladd Enterprises, Des Plaines, Ill., 1963-66, v.p. mktg. and fin. Crystal Lake, Ill., 1966-70; ptnr. Ross & Hardies, Chgo., 1973-81, Boodell, Sears, et al., 1981-86, Bell, Boyd & Lloyd, Chgo., 1986—. Spl. asst. atty. gen. for condemnation State of Ill., 1977-82; chmn. Metra, 1984—. Del. 6th Ill. Constnl. Conv., 1969—70. Recipient W. Graham Claytor, Jr. award for disting. svc. to passenger transp., 1995, Disting. Svc. award IIT/Chgo.-Kent Law Sch., 1997; named Citizen of Yr., Chgo. City Club, 1995. Mem. ABA, Chgo. Bar Assn., Nat. Assn. Bond Lawyers, Ill. Assn. Hosp. Attys., Am. Acad. Hosp. Attys., Crystal Lake Jaycees (Disting. Svc. award), Crystal Lake C. of C. (past pres.), Econ. Club, Legal Club, Union League Club, Bull Valley Golf Club, Woodstock Country Club, Alpha Lambda. Roman Catholic. Avocations: golf, hunting, fishing, tennis, skiing. Corporate, general, Health, Municipal (including bonds). Office: Bell Boyd & Lloyd 3 First National Pla 70 W Madison St Ste 3300 Chicago IL 60602-4284

LADDAGA, LAWRENCE ALEXANDER, lawyer; b. New Hyde Park, N.Y., Aug. 12, 1957; s. Carmine Michael and Adeline (Lauricella) L.; m. Beth Jane Goodlove, Nov. 12, 1983; children: Amanda May, Rachel. BA cum laude, U. S.C., 1978, JD, 1981. Bar: S.C. 1981, U.S. Dist. Ct. S.C. 1981, U.S. Ct. Appeals (4th cir.) 1981, U.S. Tax Ct. 1982, U.S. Supreme Ct. 1989. Assoc. Wise & Cole, P.A., Charleston, S.C., 1981-83; founding shareholder, sr. ptnr. Laddaga-Garrett PA, Charleston, 1983—; adj. asst. prof. dept. health adminstrn. and policy Med. U. S.C., Charleston, 1999—. Bd. dirs., 1st v.p. Charleston chpt. Am. Cancer Soc., 1987-88. Fellow Healthcare Fin. Mgmt. Assn. (advanced mem., bd. dirs. 1991-94, sec., v.p. 1991-95, pres. 1997-98, nat. principles and practices bd. 2002—), S.C. Bar Assn. (chairperson health care law com. 1995-97), Charleston County Bar Assn., Am. Health Lawyers Assn., S.C. Hosp. Assn., Order Ky. Cols., Kiwanis, Elks, Masons, Phi Beta Kappa. Commercial, contracts (including sales of goods; commercial financing), Health. Home: 1391 Madison Ct Mount Pleasant SC 29466-7961 Office: 5300 International Blvd Ste B 203 North Charleston SC 29418 E-mail: LADDAGA@sehealthlaw.com.

LADNER, THOMAS E. lawyer; b. Vancouver, B.C., Can., Dec. 8, 1916; BA, U. B.C., 1937; LLB, Osgoode Hall. Bar: B.C. bar 1940. Ret. partner firm Borden Ladner Gervais LLP (formerly Ladner Downs), Vancouver, Can. Mem. Canadian, Vancouver bar assns., Law Soc. B.C. Office: PO Box 48600 1200-200 Burrard St Vancouver BC Canada V7X 1T2

LADNER, THOMAS F. lawyer; b. Zurich, Switzerland, Mar. 8, 1968; Lic. iur. HSG, U. St. Gallen, Switzerland, 1993; Dr. iur./PhD, U. St. Gallen, 1996. Bar: Switzerland 1996. Trainee Homburger, Zurich, 1994—95, assoc., 1995—97; ptnr. Nick & Ineichen, Zug, Switzerland, 1997—2002, Meyer Lustenberger, Zurich, 2002—. Corporate, general, Mergers and acquisitions, Commercial, contracts (including sales of goods; commercial financing). Office: Meyer Lustenberger Forchstr 452 8029 Zürich Switzerland

LADSON, M. BRICE, lawyer; b. Moultrie, Ga., Jan. 18, 1952; s. John E. and Margaret (Brice) L.; m. Anna Montgomery, Aug. 15, 1976; children: M. Brice Jr., Laurie Marie. BA, Emory U., 1974, JD, 1977. Ptnr. Bouhan, Williams & Levy, Savannah, Ga., 1977-96, Ladson, Odom & Des Roches, Savannah, 1996-98, Ladson & Suthers, Savannah, 1998—2000; pvt. practice Savannah, 2000—. Mem. ABA, ATLA, Ga. Bar Assn., Ga. Trial Lawyers Assn. Federal civil litigation, State civil litigation, Personal injury (including property damage). Home: 537 Starr Creek Rd Richmond Hill GA 31324 Office: 408 E Bay St Savannah GA 31401

LAFOND, THOMAS JOSEPH, lawyer; b. Chgo., Feb. 25, 1941; s. Charles J. and Marie F. (Lane) LaF.; m. Karen Kent, June 13, 1964; children: Julia, Jennifer, Laura, Susan. BSBA, John Carroll U., 1963; JD, Case Western Res. U., 1966. Assoc. Henderson, Quail, Schneider & Smeltz, Cleve., 1968-75; ptnr. Schneider, Smeltz, Ranney & LaFond, Cleve., 1975—. Pres. Citizens League, Cleve., 1984-86; grad. Leadership Cleve., 1985. Capt. U.S. Army, 1966-68. Mem. ABA, Ohio State Bar Assn., Cleve. Bar Assn. (bd. trustees 1983-86, chmn. young lawyers 1972, ethics com. 1979, profl. trends com. 1982, pres. 1991—). State civil litigation, Family and matrimonial, General practice. Office: Schneider Smeltz Ranney & LaFond 1111 Superior Ave E Ste 1000 Cleveland OH 44114-2568 E-mail: tlafond@ssrl.com.

LAFONT, WILLIAM HAROLD, lawyer, farmer; b. Plainview, Tex., May 14, 1940; s. Harold Matthews and Jane Powell L.; m. Susan Chandler, 1961 (div. Oct. 1984); m. Ellie Agnus Dardis, Dec. 27, 1984; children: Christopher Chapman, Emily, Christopher Lafont, Nicole Smock, Matthew. BBA, U. Tex., 1961, JD, 1964. Bar: Tex. 1964, Am. Bar, Ctrl. Plains Bar. Ptnr. Lafont, Tunnell & Formby, Plainview, Tex., 1964—. Pres. Ctrl. Plains, Plainview, 1980-82. Pres. Plainview C. of C., Plainview, 1964—, Optimist Club, Plainview, 1975. Mem. Toastmasters Internat. (pres. 1964-78), YMCA (dir. 1998—), Plainview Country Club (pres. 1998—). Democrat. Methodist. Banking, General civil litigation, Criminal. Home: 310 Mesa Cir Plainview TX 79072-6508 Office: Lafont Tunnell Formby Lafont Skaggs Bldg 701 Broadway St Fl 1 Plainview TX 79072-7353

LA FORCE, PIERRE JOSEPH, lawyer; b. Berlin, N.H., Mar. 29, 1936; s. F. Maurice and Marie R. (Montminy) La F. AB, St. Anselm Coll., 1957; JD, Georgetown U, 1960. Bar: D.C. 1960, U.S. Supreme Ct. 1972, U.S. Ct. Appeals (D.C. Cir.) 1960, (6th Cir.) 1976, (9th Cir.) 1984, Fed. Cir. 1966. Assoc. Hogan & Hartson, D.C., 1960-69; ptnr. Wilkinson, Cragun & Barker, D.C., 1970-82, Baenen, Timme, D.C., 1982-84, Wilkinson, Barker, Knauer LLP, D.C., 1984—. Mem. D.C. Bar Assn., Barristers, Univ. Club. Republican. Roman Catholic. Avocations: tennis, squash. Administrative and regulatory, Federal civil litigation, Private international. Office: Wilkinson Barker Knauer LLP 2300 N St NW Ste 700 Washington DC 20037-1191

LAFUZE, WILLIAM L. lawyer; b. Washington, Feb. 21, 1946; children: Molly, Betsy, William Jr. BS in Physics, U. Tex., Austin, 1969, JD, 1973; MS in applied Sci., So. Meth. U., 1971; postgrad., U. London, 1973. Rsch. scientist Ctr. for Nuclear Studies, Austin, 1966-69; instr. computer sci. U. Tex., Austin, 1968-69, 71-73; assoc. Vinson & Elkins, Houston, 1973-80, ptnr., 1980—. Speechwriter; contbr. articles to profl. jours. Fellow State Bar Tex. (life, intellectual property sect., coun. 1979-83, chmn. 1984-85, consumer law sect., coun. 1981-88, computer sect., coun. 1990-97), ABA (IPL sect. bd. dirs., vice chair 2002-03), Houston Bar Assn., Am. Intellectual Property Law Assn. (pres. 1992-93, bd. dirs. 1983, chmn. amicus brief com. 1986-88), U.S. Trademark Assn. (bd. editors Trademark Reporter 1976-78), Nat. Coun. Patent Law Assn. (del. 1982—, bd. dirs. 1987-90), Nat. Inventors Hall of Fame (pres. 1984-85, bd. dirs. 1987—), Licensing Exec. Soc., Tex. Assn. Def. Counsel, MIT Ent. Forum Tex. (bd. dirs.), Houston Tech. Ctr. (bd. dirs.); mem. patent pub. adv. com. U.S. Patent and Trademark Office 2002-. General civil litigation, Intellectual property. Office: Vinson & Elkins 1001 Fannin 2720 First City Towers Houston TX 77002 also: 2300 First City Tower 1001 Fannin St Houston TX 77002-6760 E-mail: blafuze@velaw.com.

LAGLE, JOHN FRANKLIN, lawyer; b. Kansas City, Mo., Jan. 22, 1938; s. Ernest J. and Hilda B. Lagle; m. Nina E. Weston, Aug. 1, 1959; m. Diana G. Fogle, July 14, 1962 (dec. 1992); children: Robert, Gregory. BS, UCLA, 1961, JD, 1967. Bar: Calif. 1967, U.S. Dist. Ct. (no. dist.) Calif. 1967. Assoc. Hindin, McKittrick & Marsh, Beverly Hills, Calif., 1967-70, Macco Corp., Newport Beach, Calif., 1970, Rifkind & Sterling, Beverly Hills, 1971; mem. Fulop & Hardee, and predecessor firm, Beverly Hills, 1971-82; ptnr. Leff & Stephenson, Beverly Hills, 1983; sole practice Los Angeles, 1984; ptnr. Barash & Hill (formerly Wildman, Harrold, Allen, Dixon, Barash & Hill) L. A., 1985-91; of counsel Barbosa Garcia, 1998—2000, Hill, Farrer & Burrell, LLP, 2000—01; atty. pvt. practice, 1991—. Arbitrator NASD Regulation, Inc. Contbr. to Practice Under the California Corporate Securities Law of 1978. Served with U.S. Army, 1961-63. Mem. ABA, Calif. Bar Assn., Los Angeles County Bar Assn. Republican. Corporate, general, Property, real (including real estate development, water), Securities. Office: 16750 Marquez Ave Pacific Palisades CA 90272-3240 E-mail: j_lagle@msn.com.

LAGUEUX, RONALD RENE, federal judge; b. Lewiston, Maine, June 30, 1931; s. Arthur Charles and Laurette Irene (Turcotte) L.; m. Denise Rosemarie Boudreau, June 30, 1956; children: Michelle Simone, Gregory Charles, Barrett James. AB, Bowdoin Coll., 1953; LLB, Harvard U., 1956. Assoc. then ptnr. Edwards and Angell Law Firm, Providence, R.I., 1956-68; assoc. justice Superior Ct. State of R.I., Providence, 1968-86; judge U.S. Dist. Ct., Providence, 1986—; chief judge, 1992-99. Exec. counsel to Gov. Chafee, R.I., 1963-65. Rep. candidate for U.S. Senate, 1964; corporator R.I. Hosp., Providence, 1965-01; solicitor Southeastern New Eng. Province United Way, 1957-68. Mem. Bowdoin Coll. Alumni Council (past v.p., pres.), Am.-French Geneal. Soc. Home: 90 Greenwood Ave Rumford RI 02916-1934 Office: US Dist Ct 1 Exchange Ter Providence RI 02903-1744

LAHOUD, NINA JOSEPH, lawyer, international organization assistant; b. Littleton, N.H., July 10, 1956; d. Joseph and Loretta Lahout. Student, Smith Coll., 1975-76; BA, Harvard U., 1978; JD, U. Pa., 1981; postgrad., Am. U., Cairo, 1982. Bar: N.Y. 1981. Assoc. Shearman & Sterling, N.Y.C., 1982-83; legal advisor Office of the Force Comdr., UN Interim Force in Lebanon, Naqoura, 1983-86; dep. legal advisor UN Transition Assistance Group in Namibia, Windhoek, 1989-90; sr. legal officer UN Transitional Authority in Cambodia, Phnom Penh, 1992-93; spl. asst. to asst. sec.-gen. for mgmt. and coordination UN Peace Forces in the Former Yugoslavia, Zagreb, Croatia, 1995-96; legal officer Office of Legal Affairs, UN Hdqrs., N.Y.C., 1986-93, sr.legal officer, 1993-97; spl. asst. to asst. sec.-gen. for planning and support Dept. Peacekeeping Ops., UN Hdqrs., 1997—98, spl. asst. to under-sec.-gen. for peacekeeping ops., 1998—2001, chief of peacekeeping best practices unit Office of Under Sec.-Gen. for Peacekeeping Ops., 2001—. Chief of staff to Spl. Rep. of Sec.-Gen. in Kosovo, UN Mission in Kosovo, Jan.-Sept. 2000; dir. to dep. spl. rep. of sec.-gen. in East Timor, UN Transitional Adminstrn. in East Timor, 2001 . Contbr. articles to profl. jours. Mem. Assn. Bar City N.Y. (com. on internat. human rights 1987-90, com. on internat. law 1996—), Internat. Law Assn. (human rights com. 1983-87), Am. Soc. Internt. Law, U. Pa. Law Sch. Alumni Assn., Harvard U. Alumni Assn. Office: UN Hdqrs Dept Peacekeeping Ops One UN Plz Rm S-2290 A New York NY 10017 E-mail: lahoud@un.org.

LAIDLAW, ANDREW R. lawyer; b. Durham, N.C., Aug. 28, 1946; BA, Northwestern U., 1969; JD, U. N.C., 1972. Bar: Ill. 1972. Chair exec com., mem. Seyfarth, Shaw, Chgo., CEO Chicago. Contbr. articles to profl. jours. Mem. ABA (antitrust and securities law coms. 1982—), Barristers. Commercial, contracts (including sales of goods; commercial financing). Office: Seyfarth Shaw Mid Continental Plz 55 E Monroe St Ste 4200 Chicago IL 60603-5863

LAIRD, EDWARD DEHART, JR., lawyer; b. Pitts., July 14, 1952; s. Edward D. Sr. and Miriam (Hellman) L.; m. Ellen Armstrong, July 30, 1977; children: Megan, Edward, Peter. BA, SUNY, Oswego, 1974; JD, Western New Eng. Sch. Law, 1977. Bar: N.Y. 1978, U.S. Dist. Ct. (no. dist.) N.Y. 1978, U.S. Dist Ct. (so. dist.) N.Y. 1989, U.S. Dist. Ct. Vt. 1995, U.S. Ct. Appeals (2d cir.) 1985, U.S. Supreme Ct. 1986. Shareholder Carter, Conboy, Case, Blackmore, Maloney and Laird, P.C., Albany, NY, 1977—. Instr. legal rsch. and writing Western New Eng. Sch. Law, Springfield, Mass., 1976-77. Master Am. Inns Ct. Albany Law Sch. chpt.; mem. ABA, N.Y. State Bar Assn., Albany County Bar Assn., Def. Rsch. Inst., Def. Rsch. Inst. of Northeastern N.Y. General civil litigation, Insurance, Personal injury (including property damage). Office: Carter Conboy Case Blackmore Maloney and Laird PC 20 Corporate Woods Blvd Albany NY 12211-2350

LAJCHTER, MARCELO ANDRÉ, lawyer; b. Rio de Janeiro, Dec. 10, 1970; s. Julio and Dulce Lajchter; m. Cristina de Araujo Goes, Aug. 11, 2000. Atty. Price WaterhouseCoopers, Rio de Janeiro, 1993—95; ptnr. Barbosa, Mussnich & Aragao, Rio de Janeiro, 1995—. Office: Barbosa Mussnich & Aragão Av Alm Barroso 52-320 20031 Rio de Janeiro Brazil Fax: 21 2262-5536. Business E-Mail: lajchter@bmalaw.com.

LAKATOS, HOLLY ANNE, law librarian, researcher; b. Geneva, Ohio, Oct. 23, 1974; d. Linda and Julius J. Lakatos. MS, U. North Tex., 2000. Libr. access svcs. Tarlton Law Libr. Univ. Tex. , Austin, Tex., 2000—. Mem.: Tex. Libr. Assn., Am. Assn. Law Librs. Office: Tarlton Law Libr Univ of Tex 727 E Dean Keeton St Austin TX 78705 Office Fax: 512-471-0243. Personal E-mail: hlakatos@ev1.net. E-mail: hlakatos@mail.law.utexas.edu.

LAKE, DAVID ALAN, investments lawyer; b. El Campo, Tex., Jan. 15, 1938; s. Cortus L. and Ottis W. (Noland) L.; m. Shirley L. Hill, Dec. 20, 1966; children: Joel, Jonathan, Jeffrey Kyle, Kristi. BA, Baylor U., 1960; BD, Southwestern Seminary, 1963; JD, So. Methodist U., 1966. Bar: Tex. 1966. Lawyer Nickerson & Lake, Pittsburg, Tex., 1966-68; pvt. practice Tyler, Tex., 1967—. Gen. ptnr. Colonial Manor, Tyler, 1968-90, Golden Manor, Pittsburg, 1968-82; pres. Gardendale, Inc., Jacksonville, Tex., 1973-93, Am. Health Svcs., Inc., Tyler, 1977—, N.E. Tex. Contracting Co., Tyler, 1982—; sec., bd. dirs. Sunset Care Ctr., Jacksonville, 1973-79; chmn. bd. dirs. Cypress Bank, Fed. Savs. Bank, Pittsburg. Bd. dirs. Way of Life, Inc., Tyler, 1972-75, Smith County Heart Assn., Tyler, 1974-75; bd. dirs., chmn. Smith County Red Cross, Tyler, 1972-77; deacon, Sunday sch. tchr. 1st Bapt. Ch., Tyler, 1972—; bd. dirs., v.p. Tex. Health Care Assn., 1975-76; trustee East Tex. Bapt. U., Marshall, 1993-99. Mem. Tex. and Smith County Bar Assn., Baylor Univ. Devel. Coun., Jacksonville Jaycees (bd. dirs. 1965-66), Petroleum Club, Emerald Bay club, Lee Booster Club (pres. 1987-88), Rotary Internat. (Paul Harris fellow 1990—, bd. dirs. South Tyler chpt. 1971-74, pres. 1978-79). Avocations: reading, fishing, hunting. Banking, Health, Property, real (including real estate development, water). Home: 815 Pinedale Pl Tyler TX 75701-9645 Office: 6101 S Broadway Ave Ste 450 Tyler TX 75703-4400 E-mail: D-Slake@Tyler.net.

LAKE, I. BEVERLY, JR., judge; b. Raleigh, NC, 1934; s. I. Beverly, Sr. and Gertrude L.; m. Susan Deichmann Smith; children: Lynn Elizabeth, Guy, Laura Ann, I. Beverly III. Student, Mars Hill Coll., 1951; BS, Wake Forest U., 1955, JD, 1960. Bar: N.C. Pvt. practice, 1960-69, 76-85; asst. atty. gen. State of N.C., 1969-74, dep. atty. gen., 1974-76; Gov.'s legis. liason, chief lobbyist, 1985; judge Superior Ct., 1985-91; assoc. justice N.C. Supreme Ct., 1992—2000, chief justice, 2001—. Chmn. bd. trustees Ridge Rd. Bapt. Ch., 1968-69; mem. N.C. Senate, 1976-80, chmn. Senate Judiciary Com.; Rep. nominee Gov. N.C., 1979-80; del. Rep. Nat. Convention, 1980; Rep. state fin. chmn., mem. ctr. com., mem. exec. com., 1980-82; N.C. eastern chmn. Reagan-Bush Campaign, 1984; bd. visitors Wake Forest U. Sch. Law, 1995—; bd. vis. Southeastern Bapt. Theol. Sem.; Intelligence staff officer U.S. Army, 1956-58; capt. USAR, 1958-68; col. N.C. State Militia, 1989-92. Mem. AMVETS, N.C. Bar Assn., Wake County Bar Assn., Assn. Interstate Commerce Commn. Practitioners, Navy League, Am. Legion, Masons, Shriners, Phi Alpha Delta. Office: NC Supreme Ct PO Box 1841 Raleigh NC 27602-1841*

LAKE, SIM, federal judge; b. Chgo., July 4, 1944; BA, Tex. A&M, 1966; JD, U. Tex., 1969. Bar: Tex. 1969, U.S. Dist. Ct. (so. dist.) Tex. 1969, U.S. Ct. Appeals (5th cir.) 1969, U.S. Supreme Ct. 1976. From assoc. to ptnr. Fulbright & Jaworski, Houston, 1969-70, 72-88; judge U.S. Dist. Ct. (so. dist.) Tex., Houston, 1988—. Past editor Houston Lawyer. Capt. U.S. Army., 1970-71. Fellow Tex. Bar Found., Houston Bar Assn., State Bar Tex., Am. Law Inst. Office: US Courthouse 515 Rusk Ave Rm 9535 Houston TX 77002-2605

LAKHDHIR, DAVID KARIM, lawyer; b. N.Y.C., Jan. 12, 1958; s. Noor Mohamed and Ann (Hallan) Lakhdhir; m. Linda Bradshaw; children: Daniel, Rachel. AB, Harvard Coll., Cambridge, Mass., 1980; JD, Harvard Law Sch., Cambridge, Mass., 1983. Admitted gaikokuho jimubengoshi: Japan 1993, bar: N.Y. 1984, D.C. 1994. Assoc. Paul, Weiss, Rifkind, Wharton & Garrison, N.Y.C., NY, 1984—91, ptnr., 1992—, ptnr.-in-charge Tokyo, 1993—97, co-head London, 2002—. Vis. scholar Indian Law Inst., New Delhi, India, 1983-84. Finance, Private international, Mergers and acquisitions. Office: Paul Weiss Rifkind Wharton & Garrison 10 Noble St London EC2V 7JU England

LALLA, THOMAS ROCCO, JR., lawyer; b. Bronxville, N.Y., July 23, 1950; s. Thomas R. and Vincie Catherine (Cremona) L. BA, Fordham U., 1972; JD, Temple U., 1975. Bar: N.Y. 1986, U.S. Dist. Ct. (so. dist.) N.Y. 1978. Asst. dist. atty. Office of Dist. Atty. Westchester County, White Plains, N.Y., 1975-81; assoc. Buchman & O'Brien, N.Y.C., 1981-85, ptnr., 1985-91; mng. ptnr. Buchman Buchman & O'Brien, N.Y.C., 1986-90; gen. counsel Pernod Ricard U.S.A., N.Y.C., 1991—; v.p. adminstrn. and legal affairs Austin, Nichols & Co., Inc., N.Y.C. Mem. ABA, N.Y. State Bar Assn. Republican. Episcopalian. Avocations: running, swimming, cycling. Administrative and regulatory, Commercial, contracts (including sales of goods; commercial financing), Corporate, general. E-mail: tlalla@pernod-ricard-usa.com.

LALLI, MICHAEL ANTHONY, lawyer; b. N.Y.C., Sept. 14, 1955; s. Joseph and Maria (Magnacca) L.; m. Marigrace Ann Esposito, May 19, 1979; children: Elena Marie, Marissa Ann. BA, Fordham Coll., 1976, JD, 1979; LLM, NYU, 1984. Bar: N.Y. 1980, U.S. Dist. Ct. (so. dist.) N.Y. 1981. Assoc. counsel Equitable Life Assurance Soc. U.S., N.Y.C., 1979—85; sr. tax atty. Chevron Texaco Corp., White Plains, NY, 1985—2002; dir., benefits counsel Pitney Bowes Inc., Stamford, Conn., 2002—. Mem. moot ct. bd. 1977-79. Mem. Fordham Urban Law Jour., 1977-79. Mem. ABA, N.Y. State Bar Assn., Phi Beta Kappa, Pi Sigma Alpha. Roman Catholic. Pension, profit-sharing, and employee benefits, Health. Home: 16 Thomas St Scarsdale NY 10583-1031 Office: Pitney Bowes Inc 1 Elmcroft Rd Stamford CT 06926-0700

LALLY-GREEN, MAUREEN ELLEN, superior court judge, law educator; b. Sharpsville, Pa., July 5, 1949; d. Francis Leonard and Charlotte Marie (Frederick) Lally; m. Stephen Ross Green, Oct. 5, 1979; children: Katherine Lally, William Ross, Bridget Marie. BS, Duquesne U., 1971, JD, 1974. Bar: Pa. 1974, D.C., U.S. Dist. Ct. (we. dist.) Pa. 1974, U.S. Ct. Appeals (3d cir.) 1974, U.S. Supreme Ct. 1978. Atty. Houston Cooper, Pitts., 1974-75, Commodity Futures Trading Commn., Washington, 1975-78; counsel Westinghouse Electric Corp., Pitts., 1978-83; adj. prof. law Duquesne U., Pitts., 1983-86, 2000—, prof. law, 1986-2000; judge Superior Ct, 1998, Superior Ct., 2000—. Fed. dist. ct. arbitrator; mem. criminal procedure rules com. Supreme Ct. Pa., 1994-97; dir. European Union Law Conf., Dublin, 1995-97, Intellectual Law Conf., Italy, 1997; panel Discipline Bd. of Commonwealth of Pa.; adj. prof. law Duquesne U., 2000—. Chair Cranberry Twp. Zoning Hearing Bds., Pa., 1983-98; counsel Western Pa. Ptnrs. of Ams., 1987-90, pres. 1993-95, bd. dirs., 1995—; active Elimination of World Hunger Project, 1977-85, Bishop's Com. on Dialogue with Cath. Univs.; co-chair Millenium com. Duquesne U., 1997-2000; bd. regents St. Vincent Sem., Latrobe, Pa., 2002—. Fellow Kellogg Found. (for Ptnrs. of Ams.), 1990-92. Mem. Pa. Bar Assn. (ethics com. 1987-94, commn. on women in the law 1994—, chair quality of work life com. 2002, mem. exec. com.), Allegheny County Bar Assn. (women in law com., professionalism com., ethics com., sec. bd. dirs. 1992-2001), Duquesne U. Alumni Assn. (bd. dirs. 1982-89, sec. 1988-89), Duquesne U. Law Alumni Assn. (bd. dirs. 1987, treas. 1991, v.p. 1992), St. Thomas More Soc. (bd. dirs. 2002—). Republican. Roman Catholic. Avocations: children's activities, sports. Office: 2420 Grant Bldg 330 Grant St Pittsburgh PA 15219-2202

LALONDE, MARC, lawyer, former Canadian government official; b. Ile Perrot, Que., Can., July 26, 1929; s. J. Albert and Nora (St-Aubin) L.; m. Claire Tetreau, Sept. 8, 1955; children: Marie, Luc, Paul, Catherine. BA, Coll. St. Laurent, Montreal, 1950; LLB, U. Montreal, 1964, LLM, 1955; MA in Econs. and Polit. Sci., Oxford (Eng.) U., 1957; PhD honoris causa, Limburg U., The Netherlands, 1989, DhD. Bar: Que. 1955, Queen's Coun. 1971, Order of Can, 1988. Prof. bus. law and econs. U. Montreal, 1957-59; spl. asst. to Minister of Justice, Ottawa, Ont., Can., 1959-60; partner firm Gelinas, Bourque, Lalonde & Benoit, Montreal, 1960-68; policy adviser to Prime Minister Lester B. Pearson, Ottawa, 1967-68; prin. sec. to Prime Minister Pierre E. Trudeau, Ottawa, 1968-72; elected to House of Commons for Montreal-Outremont, 1972; minister of nat. health and welfare, 1972-77; minister of state for fed.-provincial relations, 1977-78; minister responsible for status of women, 1975-78; minister of justice and atty. gen. Can., 1978-79; minister of energy, mines and resources, 1980-82; minister of finance, 1982-84; sr. counsel Stikeman, Elliott, Montreal. Bd. dirs. Citibank of Can., O&Y Properties, Inc., Sherritt Internat. Corp., Oxbow Equities Corp.; ad hoc judge Internat. Ct. Justice, 1995—. Author: The Changing Role of the Prime Minister's Office, 1971. Decorated officer Order of Can.; Queen's Counsel; recipient Dana award APHA, 1978. Mem. Internat. Coun. on Comml. Arbitration, Am. Arbitration Assn., London Ct. Internat. Arbitration, Privy Coun. Can. Mem. Liberal Party. Home: 1477 boul Perrot Ile Perrot QC Canada J7V 7P2 E-mail: mlalonde@stikeman.com.

LAM, CAROL C. lawyer; b. N.Y. m. Mark Burnett; 4 children. BA, Yale U., 1981; JD, Stanford U., 1985. Asst. pros. atty. So. Dist. Calif., 1986—90, chief, Major Fraud Sect., 1997—2000; judge Calif. Superior Ct., 2000—02; U.S. atty. So. Dist. Calif., 2002—. Office: So Dist Calif 880 Front St Rm 6293 San Diego CA 92101-8893*

LAMAR, HOWARD HENRY, III, lawyer; b. Greenville, S.C., Mar. 16, 1961; s. Howard Henry, Jr. and Betty (Shepherd) Lamar; m. Elizabeth Urquhart Bass, Aug. 15, 1992; children: David Hall, Edwin Warner, Thomas Trent. BA, Vanderbilt U., 1983, JD, 1989. Bar: Tenn. 1989. Comml. banking officer NCNB Nat. Bank, Charlotte, NC, 1983—86; assoc. Bass, Berry & Sims, P.C., Nashville, 1989—96, mem., 1997—. Mem. adv. bd. Headwaters MB - Rio Grande Ltd. Partnership, Denver, 2000—. Elder, session mem. Westminster Presbyn., Nashville, 1996—; chmn., pres. Tenn. Repertory Theatre, Nashville, 1998—2000. Mem.: ABA, Nashville Bar Assn. Avocations: hiking, hunting, golf, scuba diving. Corporate, general, Securities, Mergers and acquisitions. Office: Bass Berry and Sims PLC 315 Deaderick St Ste 2700 Nashville TN 37238 Office Fax: 615-742-2709. Business E-Mail: hlamar@bassberry.com.

LAMB, KEVIN THOMAS, lawyer; b. Quincy, Mass., Nov. 14, 1956; s. John Phillip and Kathleen Elaine (O'Brien) L. BA, Washington and Lee U., 1978, JD, 1982. Bar: Va. 1982, D.C. 1988, Mass. 1990. Law clk. to presiding justice U.S. Bankruptcy Ct. (we. dist.) Va., Lynchburg, 1982-84; atty. U.S. Dept. Justice, Los Angeles, 1984-85; assoc. Jones, Day, Reavis & Pogue, Los Angeles, 1985-86, Ballard, Spahr, Andrews & Ingersoll, Washington, 1986-89, Testa, Hurwitz & Thibeault, L.L.P., Boston, 1989-91, ptnr., 1992—. Mem. ABA (com. on cons. fin. svcs., subcom. on securities products, com. on bus. bankruptcy), Am. Bankruptcy Inst. (com. on legis.), Comml. Law League Am. Bankruptcy, Commercial, contracts (including sales of goods; commercial financing). Office: Testa Hurwitz & Thibeault LLP High St Tower 125 High St Fl 22 Boston MA 02110-2704 E-mail: lamb@tht.com.

LAMB, MARK CHRISTOPHER, lawyer; b. Seattle, Nov. 13, 1972; s. George Ervin and Linda Harris Lamb; m. Kimberly Kay Ruef, Apr. 7, 2001; 1 child, Lars Christopher. BA, Duke U., Durham, N.C., 1995; JD, UCLA, 1998. Bar: Calif. 1998, Wash. 2000. Assoc. Foley & Lardner, L.A., 1998—99, Perkins Coie LLP, Seattle, 1999—2001, Preston Gates & Ellis LLP, Seattle, 2002—. Policy com. mem. Econ. Devel. Coun. of Snohomish County, Everett, Wash., 2002—; founder and bd. mem. Citizens for a Safe Snohomish County, Mill Creek, Wash.; vice chmn. 44th Legis. Dist. Rep. Com., Woodinville, Wash., 2001—02; mem. Wash. State Rep. Party; state committeeman; exec. bd. mem. (1st Congl. Dist.), 2003—; bd. mem. Canterbury Westwood Found., L.A., 1998—99. Mem.: ABA, Wash. State Soc. of Health Care Attys., Wash. State Bar Assn., Calif. Bar Assn. Christian. Health, Corporate, general, Finance. Office: Preston Gates & Ellis LLP 925 Fourth Ave Seattle WA 98104 Office Fax: 206-623-7022. E-mail: marklamb@prestongates.com.

LAMB, WILLIAM H. judge; b. Bryn Mawr, Pa., 1940; m. Patricia Kelly Lamb; children: Amanda, Joshua, Kate. BA(hon.) , Duke U.; JD (hon.) , U. Pa., 1965. Bar: Pa., U.S. Tax Ct., U.S. Ct. Appeals (3d cir.), U.S. Supreme Ct. Law clk. to presiding justice Pa. Supreme Ct., 1965-66; asst. dist. atty. Chester County, 1967-72, dist. atty., 1972-80; ptnr. Lamb, Windle & McErlane P.C., West Chester, Pa., 1980—2003; Supreme Ct. Justice State Supreme Ct. Justice, Pa., 2003. Mem. Supreme Ct. Fund for Client Security; bd. dir. Jefferson Bank, Downingtown, Pa. Solicitor Reps. of Chester County, campaign chmn. 1966; campaign mgr. congressman John H. Ware, 1968; chmn. Chester County Reps., 1983—; del. Rep. Nat. Convention, 1984; former chmn. Upper Main Line Young Reps.; former vice chmn. Chester County Fedn. Young Reps.; mem. Rep. Exec. Com. Chester County; pres. Little People's Nursery Sch., Paoli, Pa.; past bd. dir. Chester Valley Little League, Upper Main Line Red Cross; bd. dir. St. Davids Ch. Nursery Sch., Devon, Pa., lay server, St. David's Episcopal Ch., Devon; vice chmn., trustee bd. Alumni mgrs. Episc. Acad. Recipient Citizen of the Yr., Chester County Chamber of Bus. & Industry, 2003. Fellow Am. Coll. Trial Lawyers; mem. ABA, Pa. Bar Assn., Chester County Bar Assn., Pa. Bar Inst. (lectr.), Pa. Trial Lawyers Assn. (lectr.). Lodges: Lions. Home: 355 Pond View Rd Devon PA 19333-1732*

LAMBE, CATHERINE VAN DE VELDE, law librarian; b. Norwalk, Conn., Sept. 5, 1950; d. Louis du Rest and Neltje Scofield (Weston) van de Velde; m. Philip Cadbury Lambe, Aug. l6, 1980; children: Stephanie Scofield, David van de Velde. BA, William Smith Coll., 1972; MSLS, Simmons Coll., 1977. Monographs asst. Humanities Libr. MIT, Cambridge, l974-76, interlibr. loan asst., 1976-78; reference libr. Bentley Coll., Waltham, Mass., l978-79, head reader svcs., 1979-82; libr. Maupin, Taylor & Ellis, P.A., Raleigh, N.C., l984—. Mem. Am. Assn. Law Librs., Raleigh Area Law Librs. Assn. (sec. 1988-89, v.p., pres.-elect 1990, pres. 1991, sec., treas. 1997-2000), Southea. Assn. Law Librs. Office: Maupin Taylor PA 3200 Beechleaf Ct Ste 500 Raleigh NC 27604-1064

LAMBE, JAMES PATRICK, lawyer; b. Washington, June 4, 1952; s. John Joseph and Patricia Ann (Job) Lambe; m. Marie Barbara Giardino, May 21, 1977; children: Katherine Mary, Joseph Patrick. AB with distinction, U. Mich., 1974; JD, U. Ill., 1977. Bar: Calif. 1977, U.S. Dist. Ct. (ea. dist.) Calif. 1977, U.S. Ct. Appeals (9th cir.) 1978, U.S. Supreme Ct. 1981, U.S. Dist. Ct. (ctlr. dist.) Calif. 1983, DC 1985, cert.: State Bar Calif. Bd. Legal Specialization (specialist in criminal law), Nat. Bd. Trial Advocacy (specialist in criminal trial advocacy). Assoc. Wagner & Wagner, Fresno,

Calif., 1978-79, Parichan, Renberg, Crossman & Eliason, Fresno, 1979; claims atty. CIGNA Corp., Fresno, 1979-85; dep. city atty. City of Fresno, 1985-86; dep. pub. defender County of Fresno, 1986—. Cons., author Continuing Edn. Bar, U. Calif./State Bar Calif., Oakland, 1992—; judge pro tem Fresno County Superior Ct., 2000—; instr. Summer Trial Skills Inst., San Diego, 2001—, State Bar Sect. Edn. Inst., Berkeley, 2003. Cons. (book) California Criminal Law Procedure and Practice, update, 1992, 3d edit., 1996, California Criminal Law Forms Manual, 1995, rev., 2001; co-author: (book) California Criminal Law Procedure and Practice, 6th edit., 2002. Mem.: Nat. Assn. Criminal Def. Lawyers, State Bar Calif. (conf. of dels. 1996—99, criminal law sect. exec. com. 2001—), Calif. Pub. Defenders Assn., Calif. Attys. for Criminal Justice (bd. govs. 2003—), D.C. Bar, Fresno County Bar Assn. (bd. dirs. 1998—99), Am. Mensa, Phi Alpha Delta. Democrat. Avocation: running. Office: Fresno County Pub Defenders Office 2220 Tulare St Ste 300 Fresno CA 93721-2130

LAMBERT, DALE JOHN, lawyer; b. Lethbridge, Alberta, Can., Mar. 1, 1946; s. Theron M. and Verl (Johansen) L.; m. Janice Noreen Clitheroe, July 29, 1975; children: Kristin, Kimberly, Tamara. BS, Brigham Young U., 1970; JD, U. Utah, 1973. Bar: Utah 1973, U.S. Dist. Ct. Utah 1975, U.S. Supreme Ct 1991, U.S. Ct. Appeals (10th cir.) 1976. Legis. asst. Congressman Gunn McKay, Washington, 1973-75; dir. Christensen Jensen P.C., Salt Lake City, 1978—. Contbr. articles to profl. jours.; presenter legal seminars. State chmn. Utah State Dem. Party, 1979—81, chmn. platform com., 1982, chmn. state conv., 1983; councilman Salt Lake City, 2002—; bd. trustees Dixie State Coll., St. George, Utah, 1983—93. Recipient Golden Key award Gov.'s Commn. on Employment, 1978; named one of Outstanding Young Men of Am., Jr. C. of C., 1979. Fellow Am. Coll. Trial Lawyers; mem. Internat. Assn. of Def. Counsel, ABA (litigation sect.), Utah State Bar Assn. (litigation sect.), Def. Rsch. Assn. (Utah chair 1989-90), Internat. Assn. Def. Counsel (state chair 2001—). Mem. Lds Ch. Avocations: golf, teaching, traveling. Civil rights, General civil litigation, Personal injury (including property damage). Home: 2563 Maywood Dr Salt Lake City UT 84109-1657 Office: Christensen & Jensen 50 S Main St Ste 1500 Salt Lake City UT 84144-2044 E-mail: dale.lambert@chrisjen.com.

LAMBERT, DAVID, lawyer; b. Clevel., Nov. 9, 1965; m. Julie H. Beamish. BA, Duke U., 1988; JD, N.C. Ctrl. U., 1993; LLM, NYU, 1995. Bar: N.C. 1993, D.C. Law clk. N.C. Ct. Appeals, Raleigh, 1993—94, U.S. Bankruptcy Ct. (ea. dist.) N.C., Raleigh, 1995—96; ptnr. Kirkland & Ellis, Washington, 2001—. Contbr. articles to law jours. Securities, Mergers and acquisitions. Office: Kirkland & Ellis 655 15th St NW Ste 1200 Washington DC 20005

LAMBERT, GEORGE ROBERT, lawyer; b. Muncie, Ind., Feb. 21, 1933; s. George Russell and Velma Lou (Jones) L.; m. Mary Virginia Alling, June 16, 1955; children: Robert Allen, Ann Holt, James William. BS, Ind. U., Bloomington, 1955; JD, Chgo.-Kent Coll. Law, 1962. Bar: Ill. 1962, U.S. Dist. Ct. (no. dist.) Ill. 1962, Iowa 1984, Pa. 1988, Ind. 1999. V.p., gen. counsel, sec. Washington Nat. Ins. Co., Evanston, Ill., 1970-82; v.p., gen. counsel Washington Nat. Corp., Evanston, 1979-82; sr. v.p., sec., gen. counsel Life Investors Inc., Cedar Rapids, Iowa, 1982-88; v.p., gen. counsel Provident Mut. Life Ins. Co., Phila., 1988-95; pres. Lambert Legal Consulting, Inc., Wilmington, Del., 1995—2002; realtor Coldwell Banker, North Palm Beach, Fla., 1996—2001, Cressy and Everett GMAC Real Estate, South Bend, Ind., 1999-2000; owner, broker Lambert Realty, Granger, Ind., 2001—02; realtor Martinique II Realty Inc., Port St. Lucie, Fla., 2002—. Alderman Evanston City Coun., 1980-82. Served to lt. USAF, 1955-57. Mem. Assn. of Life Ins. Counsel (past pres.). Administrative and regulatory. Home: 7958 Poppy Hills Ln Port Saint Lucie FL 34986

LAMBERT, JEREMIAH DANIEL, lawyer, educator; b. N.Y.C., Sept. 11, 1934; s. Noah D. and Clara (Ravage) L.; m. Vicki Anne Asher, July 25, 1959 (div.); children: Nicole Stirling, Alix Stewart, Leigh Asher; m. Sanda Kayden, Dec. 3, 1983; children: Clare Kayden, Hilary Kayden. AB magna cum laude, Princeton U., 1955; LL.B., Yale U., 1959. Bar: N.Y. 1960, D.C. 1964, U.S. Ct. Appeals (5th cir.) 1964, U.S. Supreme Ct. 1964. Assoc. Cravath, Swaine & Moore, N.Y.C., 1959-63; sr. ptnr. Peabody, Lambert & Meyers, Washington, 1969-84; ptnr. Shook, Hardy & Bacon, Washington, 1997—2002; co-chmn. bd. dirs. Global Crossing, Ltd., 2002—; chmn. bd. dirs. Asia Global Crossing, Ltd., 2002—03. Adj. prof. law Georgetown U., Washington, 1978-79; trustee Internat. Law Inst., Washington, 1983-88; mem. adv. com. on Electricity Futures Contracts, N.Y. Merc. Exch., 1994-95; mem. bd. editors Yale Law Jour., 1958-59. Author (editor): Economic and Political Incentives to Petroleum Development , 1990; author: Creating Competitive Markets: The PJM Model, 2001; co-author (with Lawrence White): Handbook of Modern Construction Law, 1982; mem. editl. adv. bd., contbr. The Impact of Competition, 2000; contbr. articles to legal publs. 1st lt. USAR, 1963-66. Fulbright scholar U. Copenhagen, 1955-56. Mem. ABA, Am. Soc. Internat. Law, D.C Bar Assn., Bar Assn. of City of N.Y., Cosmos Club, Princeton Club, Yale Club, Chevy Chase Club, Phi Beta Kappa. Corporate, general, FERC practice, Private international. Office: Law Offices of Jeremiah D Lambert 1615 L St NW Ste 450 Washington DC 20036-5666 E-mail: jlambertlaw@aol.com.

LAMBERT, JOSEPH EARL, state supreme court chief justice; b. Berea, Ky., May 23, 1948; s. James Wheeler and Ruth (Hilton) L.; m. Debra Hembree, June 25, 1983; children: Joseph Patrick, John Ryan. BS in Bus. and Econs., Georgetown Coll., 1970; JD, U. Louisville, 1974; PhD (hon.) , Eastern Ky. U., 1999, Georgetown Coll., 1999, Northern Ky. U., 2002. Bar: Ky. 1974. Staff Sen. John Sherman Cooper U.S. Senate, Washington, 1970-71; law clk. to judge U.S. Dist. Ct., Louisville, 1974-75; ptnr. Lambert & Lambert, Mt. Vernon, Ky., 1975-87; justice Supreme Ct. Ky., Frankfort, 1987-98, chief justice, 1998—. Chmn. Jud. Form Retirement Commn., 1996—. Mem. Bd. Regents Eastern Ky. U., Richmond, 1988-92. Recipient Disting. Alumni award U. Louisville Sch. Law, 1988; named Outstanding Judge of Ky., 2000. Mem.: ABA, Ky. Bar Assn. Republican. Baptist. Office: State Ky State Capitol Bldg Office Chief Justice Rm 231 Frankfort KY 40601 E-mail: cjlambert@mail.aoc.state.ky.us.

LAMBERT, JUDITH A. UNGAR, lawyer; b. N.Y.C., Apr. 13, 1943; d. Alexander Lawrence and Helene (Rosenson) Ungar; m. Peter D. Leibowits, Aug. 22, 1965 (div. 1971); 1 child, David Gary. BS, U. Pa., 1964; JD magna cum laude, U. Miami, 1984. Bar: N.Y. 1985, Fla. 1990. Assoc. Proskauer Rose Goetz & Mendelsohn, N.Y.C., 1984-86, Taub & Fasciana, N.Y.C., 1986-87, Hoffinger Friedland Dobrish Bernfeld & Hasen, N.Y.C., 1987-88; pvt. practice N.Y.C., 1988—. Mem. ABA, N.Y. State Bar Assn., Assn. Bar of City of N.Y., N.Y. Women's Bar Assn. (family law and trusts and estates com.), N.Y. County Lawyers Assn. Avocations: travel, music, theater. Family and matrimonial, Probate (including wills, trusts), Property, real (including real estate development, water). Office: 245 E 54th St New York NY 10022-4707

LAMBERT, LYN DEE, library media specialist, law librarian; b. Fitchburg, Mass., Jan. 5, 1954; m. Paul Frederick Lambert, Aug. 11, 1979; children: Gregory John, Emily Jayne, Nicholas James. BA in History, Fitchburg State Coll., 1976, MEd in History, 1979; JD, Franklin Pierce Law Ct., 1983; MLS, Simmons Coll., 1986. Law libr. Fitchburg Law Libr., Mass. Trial Ct., 1985-96; media specialist libr. Samoset Sch., Leominster, Mass., 1996—. Instr. paralegal studies courses Fisher Coll., Fitchburg, 1989-94, Anna Maria Coll., Paxton, Mass., 1995—, Atlantic Union Coll., Lancaster, Mass., 1995—, pre-law coll. courses Fitchburg State Coll., 1995—; tech. com. City of Leominster Shc., Net Day Participant and trainer/leader, Leominster H.S., Northwest, Johnny Appleseed, Fall Brook, Southeast and Samoset. Mem. Am. Legion Band, Fitchburg, 1959—, Westminster (Mass.) Town Band, 1965—, Townsend Town Band, 1999—; appt. to Mass. Strategic Plan Com. for delivery of libr. svcs. among multi-type librs. within the commonwealth; mem. Patrick S. Gilmore Cmty. Honor Band, Hatch Shell, Boston, 2000—02. Recipient Community Leadership award Xi Psi chpt. Kappa Delta Pi-Fitchburg State Coll. chpt., 1993. Mem. ALA, Am. Assn. Law Librarians (copyright com. 1987-89, publs. rev. com. 1990-92, state, ct. and county law librs. spl. interest sect. publicity com. 1993—), Law Librarians New Eng. (conf. com. 1988), Mass. Libr. Assn. (edn. chair 1991-93, freedom of info. com., legislation com.), New Eng. Libr. Assn., New Eng. Microcomputer Users Group (profl. assoc.), North Cen. Mass. Libr. Alliance (newsletter editor 1990—), Spl. Libr. Assn., Beta Phi Mu, Phi Alpha Delta, Phi Delta Kappa (newsletter editor Montachusett chpt. 1998-2000, pres. Montachusett chpt. 2000-02). Avocations: singing, guitar, clarinet, hiking, camping. Office: Samoset Libr Media Ctr 100 Decicco Dr Leominster MA 01453-5161

LAMBORN, LEROY LESLIE, law educator; b. Marion, Ohio, May 12, 1937; s. LeRoy Leslie and Lola Fern (Grant) Lamborn. AB, Oberlin Coll., 1959; LLB, Western Res. U., 1962; LLM, Yale U., 1963; JSD, Columbia U., 1973. Bar: N.Y. 1965, Mich. 1974. Asst. prof. law U. Fla., 1965-69; prof. Wayne State U., Detroit, 1970-97, prof. emeritus, 1997—. Vis. prof. State U., Utrecht, 1981. Author: (book) Legal Ethics and Professional Responsibility, 1963; contbr. articles on victimology to profl. jours. Mem.: World Soc. Victimology, Nat. Orgn. Victim Assistance (exec. com. 1982—94, bd. dirs. 1979—88), Am. Law Inst. Home: Apt 2502 1300 E Lafayette St Detroit MI 48207-2924 Office: Wayne State U Law Sch Detroit MI 48202

LAMIA, CHRISTINE EDWARDS, lawyer; b. Hollywood, Fla., Dec. 8, 1962; BS in Comms., Fla. State U., 1984; JD, Mercer U., 1987. Lawyer Byrd & Murphy, Ft. Lauderdale, 1987-92, Abel, Band et al, Sarasota, Fla., 1992-97, Becker & Poliakoff, Sarasota, 1997—2002. General civil litigation, Construction. Office: 1745 Shoreland Dr Sarasota FL 34239

LAMKIN, MARTHA DAMPF, lawyer; b. Talladega, Ala., May 20, 1942; d. Keith J. and Neva (Magness) Dampf; m. E. Henry Lamkin Jr., Aug. 28, 1968; children: Melinda Lamkin Magaddino, Matthew Davidson. BA in English summa cum laude, Calif. Baptist U., 1964; MA in English and Am. Lit., Vanderbilt U., 1966; JD, Ind. U., 1970. Bar: Ind. 1970. Assoc. Joseph D. Geeslin, Indpls., 1971-72, Lowe, Gray, Steele & Hoffman, Indpls., 1976-82; field office mgr. U.S. Dept. Housing and Urban Devel., Indpls., 1982-87; exec. dir., corp. rep. responsibility and govtl. affairs Cummins Engine Co., Inc., Columbus, Ind., 1987-91; exec. v.p. corp. advancement USA Group, Inc., Indpls., 1991-2000; pres., CEO, bd. dirs. USA Group Found., Inc., 2000-2001; CEO, pres., bd. dirs. Lumina Foundation for Education Inc., 2001—. Pres., bd. dirs. Cummins Engine Found., 1989-91; bd. dirs. Meridian Mut. Ins. Co., Indpls., 1989-98, USA Group, Inc., USA Group Loan Svcs., Inc., United Student Aid Funds, 1994-2000; bd. dirs. Citizens Gas & Coke Utility, Inc., vice chair, 1990-. Commr., sec., chmn. Indpls. Human Rights Commn., 1971-79; commr. Indpls. Housing Authority, 1979-82; chmn. exec. com. S.K. Lacy Exec. Leadership Alumni, Indpls., 1986-87; chmn. Ind. Leadership Celebration, Indpls., 1985-87; sec. Gov.'s Mansion Commn., Indpls., 1981-89; bd. dirs. Great Indpls. Progress Commn., 1986-87, Indpls. Symphony Orch., 1983-89, 98-99, Indpls. Project, 1986-91, Ind. Fiscal Policy Inst., 1998—, Ind. Colls. Ind., 1997-2000; bd. dirs., sec. COMMIT, Inc., COMMIT Found., 1990-97; chmn. bd. trustees Christian Theol. Sem., Indpls., 1983-93; hon. gov. Richard C. Lugar Excellence Pub. Svc. Series, 1990—; chair, 1997, trustee Indpls. Found., 1992—; mem. exec. com. Mayor's Task Force on Housing, 1987, exec. com., Ind. Sports Corp., 1997-2000; sec., bd. dirs. Indpls. Econ. Devel. Corp., 1997-2000; chair, dir. Ctrl. Ind. Cmty. Found., 1998-; mem. Hoosier Capitol Girl Scouts Adv. Bd., 1996-2002. Recipient Presdl. Rank award 1985, Mental Health Initiative Gov. Ind., 1986, Matrix award Women in Communication, 1987. Mem. State Assembly Women (pres. 1977-79), Indpls. Jr. League, Indpls. C. of C. (bd. dirs. 1986-87). Republican. Mem. Christian Ch. (Disciples Of Christ). Office: Lumina Found for Edn 30 S Meridian Ste 700 Indianapolis IN 46204

LAMM, CAROLYN BETH, lawyer; b. Buffalo, Aug. 22, 1948; d. Daniel John and Helen Barbara (Tatakis) L.; m. Peter Edward Halle, Aug. 12, 1972; children: Alexander P., Daniel E. BS, SUNY Coll. at Buffalo, 1970; JD, U. Miami (Fla.), 1973. Bar: Fla., 1973, D.C., 1976, N.Y. 1983. Trial atty. frauds sect. civil div. U.S. Dept. Justice, Washington, 1973-78, asst. chief comml. litigation sect. civil div., 1978, asst. dir., 1978-80; assoc. White & Case, Washington, 1980-84, ptnr., 1984—. Mem. Sec. State's Adv. Com. Pvt. Internat. law, 1987-2002, Secs. Study Com. on Proposal Hague Conv. on Jurisdiction and the Enforcement of Judgements, 1992-2002; arbitrator U.S. Panel of Arbitrators, Internat. Ctr. Settlement of Investment Disputes, 1995-2002; mem. com. on pvt. dispute resolution NAFTA. Mem. editl. adv. bd. Inside Litigation; contbg. editor: Internat. Arbitration Law Rev., 1997—; contbr. articles to legal publs. Fellow Am. Bar Found., Am. Coll. Trial Lawyers; mem. ABA (chmn. young lawyers divsn., bd. govs. 2002—, rules and calendar com., chmn. house membership com., chmn. assembly resolution com., sec. 1984-85, chmn. internat. litigation com. coun. 1991-94, sect. litigation, ho. dels. 1982—, nomination com. 1984-87, chair 1995-96, past D.C. Cir. mem., standing com. fed. judiciary 1992-95, chmn. com. scope and correlation of work 1996-97, commn. on multidisciplinary practice, bd. govs. 2002—), Am. Coll. Trial Lawyers, Am. Arbitration Assn. (bd., arbitrator, adv. com. internat. arbitration, gen. counsel's law com., bd. dirs.), Fed. Bar Assn. (chmn. sect. on antitrust and trade regulation), Bar Assn. D.C. (bd. dirs., sec., found. bd.), D.C. Bar (pres. 1997-98, bd. govs. 1987-93, steering com. litigation sect.), Am. Law Inst. (mem. coun., named Women Laywer of the Yr., 2002), Women's Bar Assn. D.C., Am. Soc. Internat. Law, Am. Indonesian C. of C. (bd. dirs.), Am. Uzbekistan C. of C. (bd. dirs., sec., gen. counsel), Am. Turkish Friendship Coun. (bd. dirs., chair), Nat. Women's Forum, Columbia Country Club, Manchester Country Club, Stratton Mountain Club. Democrat. Administrative and regulatory, Federal civil litigation, Private international. Home: 2801 Chesterfield Pl NW Washington DC 20008-1015 Office: White and Case 601 13th St NW Washington DC 20005-3807 E-mail: clamm@whitecase.com.

LAMME, KATHRYN ANNE, lawyer; b. Dayton, Ohio, Aug. 7, 1946; d. Herschel R. and Lola G. (Recknor) L.; m. James V. Johnson, Sept. 3, 1982; children: Anna R. Tucker, Molly E. Raske. AB, Cornell U., 1968; MSW, U. Mich., 1971; JD, U. Dayton, 1980. Bar: Ohio 1980, U.S. Ct. Appeals (6th cir.) 1986, U.S. Dist. Ct. (so. dist.) Ohio 1980. Assoc. Turner Granzow & Hollenkamp, Dayton, 1980-83, ptnr., 1983-98; corp. v.p., sec., dep. gen. counsel The Standard Register Co., Dayton, 1998—2002, v.p., gen. counsel & sec., 2002—. Bd. advisors U. Dayton Scho. Law, 1992-2001; pres., trustee Bldg. Bridges Inc., Dayton, 1995-2001. Mem. ABA, Dayton Bar Assn. (trustee 1995-96), Lawyers Club. Corporate, general, Labor (including EEOC, Fair Labor Standards Act, labor-management relations, NLRB, OSHA), Mergers and acquisitions. Office: Standard Register Co PO Box 1167 Dayton OH 45401-1167 E-mail: klamme@stdreg.com.

LAMMERT, THOMAS EDWARD, lawyer; b. Pitts., Mar. 26, 1947; s. John Albert and Gladys Irene (Miller) L.; m. Anita N. Kelm, Sept. 25, 1976; children: Brian, Andrew. BS, U. Pitts, 1969; JD, U. Akron, 1976. Bar: Ohio 1976, Fla 1983, U.S. Ct. Appeals (6th cir.) 1983, U.S. Supreme Ct., 1982. Assoc. Guy, Mentzer & Towne, Akron, Ohio, 1976-84, ptnr., 1984-85, Guy, Lammert & Towne, Akron, 1985—. Mem. ABA, Ohio State Bar Assn., Fla. Bar Assn., Stark County Bar Assn., Akron Bar Assn. Republican. Bankruptcy, General civil litigation, Commercial, contracts (including sales of goods; commercial financing). Office: Guy Lammert & Towne 2210 1st National Towers Akron OH 44308

LAMON, HARRY VINCENT, JR., lawyer, director; b. Macon, Ga., Sept. 29, 1932; s. Harry Vincent and Helen (Bewley) L.; m. Ada Healey Morris, June 17, 1954; children: Hollis Morris, Kathryn Gurley. BS cum laude, Davidson Coll., 1954; JD with distinction, Emory U., 1958. Bar: Ga. 1958, D.C. 1965. Of counsel Troutman Sanders LLP, Atlanta, 1995—. Adj. prof. law Emory U., 1960-79. Contbr. articles to profl. jours. Mem. adv. bd. Metro Atlanta Salvation Army, 1963-97, chmn., 1975-79, life mem., 1997—, mem. nat. adv. bd., 1976-96, chmn. 1991-93, emeritus, 1996—; mem. adv. coun. on employee welfare and pension benefit plans U.S. Dept. Labor, 1975-79; mem. pension and benefits reporter adv. bd. Bur. Nat. Affairs, 1972-; mem. bd. visitors Davidson Coll., 1979-89; founding trustee, pres. So. Fed. Tax Inst., Inc., 1965—, emeritus, 2000—; trustee Am. Tax Policy Inst., Inc., 1989-96, Embry-Riddle Aero U., 1989-2001, emeritus, 2001—, Cathedral of St. Philip Endowment Fund, Atlanta, 1989—. 1st lt. AUS, 1954-56. Recipient Others award Salvation Army, 1979, Centennial honoree, 1990. Fellow Am. Bar Found. (life), Am. Coll. Trust and Estate Counsel, Am. Coll. Tax Counsel, Internat. Acad. Estate and Trust Law, Ga. Bar Found. (life), Am. Coll. Employee Benefits Counsel (charter); mem. ABA, Atlanta Bar Assn. (life), Am. Bar Retirement Assn. (bd. dirs. 1989-96, pres. 1994-95), Am. Law Inst. (life), Am. Employee Benefits Conf., So. Employee Benefits Conf. (pres., 1972, hon. life mem.), State Bar Ga. (chmn. sect. taxation 1969-70, vice chmn. comm on continuing lawyer competency 1982-89, emeritus 2002), Am. Judicature Soc., Atlanta Tax Forum, Lawyers Club Atlanta, Nat. Emory U. Law Sch. Alumni Assn. (pres. 1967), Practicing Law Inst., ALI-ABA Inst., CLUs Inst., The Group, Inc. (hon. life), Kiwanis Club Atlanta (hon. mem.; pres. 1974), Peachtree Racket Club (pres. 1986-87), Atlanta Coffee House Club, Capital City Club, Cosmos Club (Washington), Phi Beta Kappa (fellow), Omicron Delta Kappa, Phi Delta Phi, Phi Delta Theta (chmn. nat. cmty. svc. day 1969-72, legal commr. 1973-76, province pres. 1976-79, Golden Legion 2001). Episcopalian. Estate planning, Pension, profit-sharing, and employee benefits, Taxation, general. Home: 4415 Paces Battle NW Atlanta GA 30327-3023 Office: Lamon & Sherman Consulting LLC 1950 N Park Pl Ste 125 Atlanta GA 30339 Fax: 770-933-0065. E-mail: Harry.Lamon@Lamonsherman.com.

LAMONACA, JOSEPH MICHAEL, lawyer, pilot; b. Phila., Feb. 25, 1962; 1 child, Debra; (div.); children: Jennifer, Jessica, Debra. JD, Widener U., 1990. Bar: Pa., U.S. Ct. Appeals (3d cir.), U.S. Dist. Ct. (western and ea. dist.) Pa., U.S. Dist. Ct. (D.C.), Pa. Cert. Aircraft Owners and Pilots Assn., Nat. Transp. Safety Bd., U.S. Supreme Ct. Pvt. practice, Chadds Ford, Pa. Airline transporter pilot, turbine rated flight safety internat. instr. Mem. ABA (family law sect.), Pa. Bar Assn. (family law sect.), Lawyer Pilot Bar Assn., NTSB Bar Assn., AOPA (panel lawyer). Roman Catholic. Aviation, Family and matrimonial. Home: 42 Solitude Way Wilmington DE 19808-2029 Office: G&M Bldg Ste 303 Chadds Ford PA 19317 E-mail: avlaw@prodigy.net.

LAMPE, ERNST-JOACHIM, law educator; b. Oppeln, Schlesien, Germany, Jan. 4, 1933; s. Hermann and Margarete L.; m. Mathilde Röth; m. Ortrun Pongratz (div.); children: Selma Schaefer, Vilma Buchali. Dr.iur.utr, U. Mainz, 1955. Pub. prosecutor Pub. Prosecutor's Office, Berlin, 1960-61; asst. lectr. U. Mainz, Rheinland-Pfalz, Germany, 1961-66; prof., chair penal law and philosophy of law U. Bielefeld, Germany, 1970-98, dean faculty of law, 1985-86. Mem. adv. bd. Konzepta Unternehmensgruppe, Berlin, 1972—; bd. dirs. Petrol Properties Oil and Gas Ltd., Calgary, Can., 1980-92. Author: Fälschung von Gesamturkunden, 1957, Das personale Unrecht, 1967, Rechtsanthropologie, 1970, Juristische Semantik, 1970, Der Kreditbetrug, 1980, Genetische Rechtstheorie, 1987, Grenzen des Rechtspositivismus, 1988, Strafphilosophie, 1999; editor: Beiträge zur Rechtsanthropologie, 1985, Das sogenannte Rechtsgefühl, 1985, Persönlichkeit Familie Eigentum, 1987, Verantwortlichkeit und Recht, 1989, Deutsche Wiedervereinigung, vol. I & II, 1993, Rechtsgleichheit und Rechtspluralismus, 1995, Entwicklung von Rechtsbewusstsein, 1997, Meinungsfreiheit als Menschenrecht, 1998; contbr. articles to profl. jours. Mem.: Internat. Vereinigung für Rechts- und Sozialphilosophie. Home: An der schwarzen Hecke 25 55270 Ober-Olm Germany Office: Universitaetsstr Fak fuer Rechtswiss 33501 Bielefeld Germany E-mail: palmsteern@aol.com.

LAMPE, RONALD L. lawyer, arbitrator; b. Bellevue, Iowa, Oct. 29, 1940; s. Benjamin R. and Margaret C. Lampe; m. Sharon J. Lampe, June 12, 1965; children: James E., Douglass B. BA, Loras Coll., 1963; JD, Marquette U., 1966. Bar: Wis. Assoc. Williams, Williams & Meyer, Oshkosh, Wis., 1966—68, Williams & Lampe, Oshkosh, Wis., 1968—71; ptnr. Dempsey, Magnusen, Williamson & Lampe, Oshkosh, Wis., 1971—. Pres. Winnebago County Bar Assn., Oshkosh, 1978. Bd. dirs., pres. Bd. Edn., Oshkosh, 1994—97, Boys and Girls Club Oshkosh, 1970—; bd. dirs., chmn. Salvation Army, Oshkosh, 1978—84. Named one of Outstanding Young Men of Am., Jaycess of Am.; recipient Bronze medallion, Boys and Girls Club Am., Man and Youth award. Avocations: birding, hiking, reading, travel. Alternative dispute resolution, Personal injury (including property damage). Office: Dempsey Williamson Lampe Young Kelly & Hertel LLP One Pearl Ave Ste 302 Oshkosh WI 54901 Office Fax: 920-235-2011. Business E-Mail: dmwl@dempseylaw.com.

LAMPERT, MICHAEL ALLEN, lawyer; b. Phila., May 6, 1958; s. Arnold Leonard and Marilyn Lampert; 1 child, David Max. AB in Econs. cum laude, U. Miami, Coral Gables, Fla., 1979, postgrad., 1980; JD, Duke U., 1983; LLM in Taxation, NYU, 1984. Bar: Fla. 1983, D.C. 1984, Pa. 1984, U.S. Tax Ct. 1984, U.S. Ct. of Appeals for the Armed Forces 1995; U.S. Dist. Ct. (S. Dist. Fla.), 2000, bd. cert. tax lawyer, Fla. Bar. Assoc. Cohen, Scherer, Cohn & Silverman, P.A., North Palm Beach, Fla., 1984-88; instr. divsn. continuing edn. Fla. Atlantic U., Boca Raton, Fla., 1988—98; prin. Jacobson & Lampert, P.A., Boca Raton, 1988—91; pvt. practice West Palm Beach, 1991—. Mem. editl. bd. Southeastern Tax Alert, 1993-97, Sales and Use Tax Alert, 1997—. Instr., trainer, past chpt. vice-chair, sect. bd. dirs. ARC, Palm Beach County, Fla.; bd. dirs. Jewish Fedn. Palm Beach County, 1989-91, 97-99, Jewish Family and Children's Svc. Palm Beach County, 1988—, treas., 1991-94, pres., 1997-99; pres. Jewish Residential and Family Svc., Inc., 1997—, T & M Ranch Cmty., Inc., 2000--; commr. Commn. for Jewish Edn.-Palm Beach, 1997-99; past mem. nat. planned giving com. Weismann Inst., Israel; mem. exec. bd., past v.p. planned giving Am. Soc. for Tech., Palm Beach. Recipient Young Leadership award, 1988, Safety award ARC, 1989, Cert. of Merit, Am. Radio Relay League, West Palm Beach Club, 1988, Cert. of Appreciation for Leadership, ARC Disaster Svcs., Palm Beach County, 1989, Disaster Svc. award, 1994, Human Resources award, 1993, Tax Law award Legal Aid Soc. of Palm Beach County and Palm Beach County Bar Assn., 1993, Young Leadership award Jewish Fedn. of Palm Beach County, 1998. Mem. Palm Beach Tax Inst. (pres., bd. dirs. 1993-94), Fla. Bar (exec. coun., mem. dirs. com. tax sect., taxation cert. com., bd. legal specialization and certification), Palm Beach County Bar Assn. (chair bus. and corp. continuing legal edn. com. 1989-90, chair legal asst. com. 1988-91, Tax Law award 1993), Legal Aid Soc. of Palm Beach County, Inc. Avocations: aquatics, amateur radio, running. Estate planning, Taxation, general. Office: Ste 900 1655 Palm Beach Lakes Blvd West Palm Beach FL 33401-2211 E-mail: lamperttaxlaw@att.net.

LAMPTON, DUNN O. prosecutor; married; 2 children. JD, U. Miss., 1975. Ptnr. Phillips, Regan & Lampton, 1976—80; dist. atty. 14th Cir. Ct. Dist., 1976—2001; U.S. atty. U.S. Dept. Justice, So. Dist. Miss., Jackson, 2001—. Staff judge adv. USNG. Office: So Dist Miss 188 E Capital St Ste 500 Jackson MS 39201 Office Fax: 601-965-4409.*

LAMSON, MICHAEL ALAN, lawyer; b. Ann Arbor, Mich., Mar. 15, 1952; s. Frederick William and Nancy (McComb) Lamson; m. Loree Ann Lamson, Apr. 21, 1984. BA, Mich. State U., 1974; JD, U. Ariz., 1977. Bar: Ariz. 1977, Tex. 1978, U.S. Supreme Ct. 1985. Atty. Evans & Brinberg, Houston, 1977—78, Prappas & Lamson, 1978—79, Michael A. Lamson Atty. at Law, 1980—93; ptnr. Lamson & Looney, 1999—. Mem.: Nat. Assn.

Criminal Def. Lawyers, Am. Trial Lawyers Assn. Democrat. Criminal, Personal injury (including property damage). Office: Lamson & Looney 11767 Katy Fwy #740 Houston TX 77079 Fax: 281-597-8284. E-mail: sharklaw@texas.net.

LAMSON, WILLIAM MAXWELL, JR., lawyer; b. Laramie, Wyo., June 28, 1943; s. William Maxwell Lamson and Neville A. Troutman; m. Michaela A. Wright; children: Kelly, Bill, Jill, Katie. BA, Wayne State Coll., 1965; JD, U. Nebr., 1969. Bar: Nebr. 1969, U.S. Ct. Appeals (8th cir.) 1973. Assoc. Kennedy, Holland, Omaha, 1969-74, ptnr., 1974—. Fellow Am. Coll. Trial Lawyers; mem. ABA, Nebr. Bar Assn., Omaha Bar Assn., Def. Rsch. Inst. Avocations: reading, golf. Federal civil litigation, General civil litigation. Office: Lamson Dugan & Murray 10306 Regency Parkway Dr Omaha NE 68114-3748 E-mail: wlamson@ldmlaw.com.

LAN, DONALD PAUL, JR., lawyer; b. Orange, N.J., July 19, 1952; s. Donald Paul and Hannah Paula (Resnik) L.; m. Deborah Sue Rothenberg, Aug. 20, 1978; children: Jennifer Robyn, Adam Christopher, Eric Jacob. BS in Acctg., U. R.I., 1974; JD, Rutger U., 1977; LLM in Taxation, Georgetown U., 1982. Bar: N.J. 1977, D.C. 1978, Tex. 1983, U.S. Dist. Ct. N.J. 1977, U.S. Dist. Ct. (no., so., we. and ea. dists.) Tex. 1983, U.S. Ct. Claims 1978, U.S. Tax Ct. 1977, U.S. Ct. Appeals (fed. cir.) 1978, U.S. Ct. Appeals (5th cir.) 1984, U.S. Ct. Appeals (8th cir.) 1997. Clk. to spl. trial judge U.S. Tax Ct., Washington, 1977-78; trial atty. tax div. U.S. Dept. Justice, Washington, 1978-82; assoc., ptnr. Shank, Irwin & Conant, Dallas, 1982-87; ptnr. Finley, Kumble Wagner et al, Dallas, 1987, Strasburger & Price, Dallas, 1988-96; shareholder Kroney, Mincey, Inc., Dallas, 1996—. Adj. prof. law So. Meth. U., 1990—; lectr. on tax controversy and litigation, 1983—. Named Outstanding Atty. tax div. U.S. Dept. Justice, 1980. Fellow: Am. Coll. Trust and Estate Counsel; mem.: ABA (ct. procedures com. tax sect. 1987—, stds. in tax practice com. tax sect. 1992—, chmn. 2001—03), D.C. Bar Assn., Dallas Bar Assn., State Bar Tex. (chmn. ct. procedures com. tax sect. 1995—97, coun. mem. 1997—2000), Beta Gamma Sigma, Beta Alpha Psi, Phi Kappa Phi. Jewish. Avocation: all sports. Corporate taxation, Taxation, general, Personal income taxation. Office: Kroney Mincey 12221 Merit Dr Ste 1210 Dallas TX 75251-2244

LANAM, LINDA LEE, lawyer; b. Ft. Lauderdale, Fla., Nov. 21, 1948; d. Carl Edward and Evelyn (Bolton) L. BS, Ind. U., 1970, JD, 1975. Bar: Ind. 1975, Pa. 1979, U.S. Dist. Ct. (no. and so. dists.) Ind. 1975, U.S. Supreme Ct. 1982, Va. 1990. Atty., asst. counsel Lincoln Nat. Life Ins. Co., Ft. Wayne, Ind., 1975-76, 76-78; atty., mng. atty. Ins. Co. of N.Am., Phila., 1978-79, 80-81; legis. liaison Pa. Ins. Dept., Harrisburg, 1981-82, dep. ins. commr., 1982-84; exec. dir., Washington rep. Blue Cross and Blue Shield Assn., Washington, 1984-86; v.p. and sr. counsel Union Fidelity Life Ins. Co., Am. Patriot Health Ins. Co., etc., Trevose, Pa., 1986-89; v.p., gen. counsel, corp. sec. The Life Ins. Co. Va., Richmond, 1989-97, sr. v.p., gen. counsel, corp. sec., 1997-98, also bd. dirs.; v.p., dep. gen. counsel Am. Coun. Life Ins., Washington, 1999—. Chmn. adv. com. health care legis. Nat. Assn. Ins. Commrs., 1985-87, chmn. long term care, 1986-87, mem. tech. resource com. on cost disclosure and genetic testing, 1993-98; mem. tech. adv. com. Health Ins. Assn. Am., 1986-89; mem. legis. com. Am. Coun. Life Ins., 1994-96, mem. market conduct com., 1997-98. Contbr. articles to profl. jours. Pres. Phila. Women's Network, 1980—81; chmn. city housing code bd. appeals Harrisburg, 1985—86; bd. dirs. Shakespeare Theatre Guild, 2001—. Mem. ABA, Richmond Bar Assn. Republican. Presbyterian. Corporate, general, Insurance, Legislative. Office: Am Coun Life Ins 1001 Pennsylvania Ave NW Washington DC 20004-2505

LANCASTER, JOAN ERICKSEN, state supreme court justice; b. 1954; BA magna cum laude, St. Olaf Coll., Northfield, Minn., 1977; spl. diploma in social studies, Oxford U., 1976; JD cum laude, U. Minn., 1981. Atty. LeFevere, Lefler, Kennedy, O'Brien & Drawz, Mpls., 1981-83; asst. U.S. atty. Dist. Minn., Mpls., 1983-93; shareholder Leonard, Street and Deinard, Mpls., 1993-95; dist. ct. judge 4th Jud. Dist., Mpls., 1995-98; assoc. justice Minn. Supreme Ct., 1998—2002; judge U.S. Dist. Ct., St. Paul, 2002—.

LANCASTER, KENNETH G. lawyer; b. Stafford Springs, Conn., Dec. 6, 1949; s. Talbot Augustin and Helen Collier (McRae) L.; m. Margaret Jane Royer, Aug. 25, 1973; children: Kimberly Jane, John Talbot, Christopher Andrew. BA, U. Miami, 1971, JD, 1974. Bar: Fla. 1974, U.S. Dist. Ct. (so. dist.) Fla. 1975, U.S. Dist. Ct. (mid. dist.) Fla. 1976. Adminstr. Met. Dade County, Miami, Fla., 1971-73; assoc. Robert A. Spiegel, Coral Gables, Fla., 1973-78; sole practice South Miami, Fla., 1978-80; ptnr. Clark, Dick & Lancaster, South Miami, Fla., 1980-87, King & Lancaster PA, South Miami, Fla., 1987—. Cons. 1st City Bank Dade County, Miami, 1983-84; dir. U. Miami Bus. Sch. Bd. dirs., pres. U. Miami Sports Hall Fame, Coral Gables, 1984—, mem. U. Miami endowment com., 1982—; mem. Atty.'s Title Ins. Fund, 1982—. V.p. , trustee South Fla. coun. Boy Scouts Am. Mem. ABA, Fla. Bar Assn., Dade County Bar Assn. (Disting. Svc. award 1984), Nat. Acad. Elder Law Attys., Fla. Acad. Elder Law Attys., Dade County Attys. Real Property Coun., Hurricane Club/U. Miami (bd. dirs. 1984—, pres. 1996-97). Estate planning, Probate (including wills, trusts), Property, real (including real estate development, water). Home: 10241 SW 141st St Miami FL 33176-7005 Office: King & Lancaster PA 5975 Sunset Dr Ste 703 Miami FL 33143-5198

LANCASTER, RALPH IVAN, JR., lawyer; b. Bangor, Maine, May 9, 1930; s. Ralph I. and Mary Bridget (Kelleher) L.; m. Mary Lou Pooler, Aug. 21, 1954; children: Mary Lancaster Miller, Anne, Elizabeth Peoples, Christopher, John, Martin. AB, Coll. Holy Cross, 1952; LLB, Harvard U., 1955; LLD (hon.), St. Joseph's Coll., 1991. Bar: Maine 1955, Mass. 1955. Law clk. U.S. Dist. Ct. Dist. Maine, 1957-59; ptnr. firm Pierce Atwood, Portland, Maine, 1961—, mng. ptnr., 1993-96; ind. counsel In Re Herman apptd. by spl. divsn. D.C. Ct. Appeals, 1998—2001. Condr. trial advocacy seminar Harvard U.; lectr. U. Maine; chmn. merit selection panel U.S. Magistrate for Dist. of Maine, 1982, 88; bd. visitors U. Maine Sch. Law, 1991-96, chair, 1991-93; spl. master by appointment U.S. Supreme Ct. in State of N.J. vs. State of Nev. et al, 1987-88; mem. 1st Ctr. Adv. Com. on Rules, 1991-96, legal adv. bd. Martindale Hubbell, Lexis Nexis, 1990—; represented U.S. in Gulf of Maine in World Ct. at The Hague, 1984; U.S. Supreme Ct. apptd. spl. master Commonwealth of Va. vs. State of Md., 2000-, chmn. bd. trustees, Davis Family Found., 2001-; chmn. Maine Lawyers Assistance Program, 2002-; nat. membership chair, Supreme Ct. Hist. Soc., 2002-. Former mem. Diocese of Portland Bur. Edn. With U.S. Army, 1955-57. Mem. Maine Jud. Coun., Am Coll. Trial Lawyers (chmn. Maine 1974-79, bd. regents 1982-87, treas. 1985-87, pres. 1989-90), Maine Bar Assn. (pres. 1982), Cumberland County Bar Assn., Canadian Bar Assn. (hon.). Republican. Roman Catholic. Federal civil litigation, State civil litigation, Insurance. Home: 162 Woodville Rd Falmouth ME 04105-1120 Office: 1 Monument Sq Portland ME 04101-4033 E-mail: RLancaster@PierceAtwood.com.

LANCE, ALAN GEORGE, former state attorney general; b. McComb, Ohio, Apr. 27, 1949; s. Cloyce Lowell and Clara Rose (Wilhelm) Lance; m. Sheryl C. Holden, May 31, 1969; children: Lisa, Alan Jr., Luke. BA, S.D. State U., 1971; JD, U. Toledo, 1973. Bar: Ohio 1974, U.S. Dist. Ct. (no. dist.) Ohio 1974, U.S. Ct. Mil. Appeals 1974, Idaho 1978, U.S. Supreme Ct. 1996. Asst. pros. atty. Fulton County, Wauseon, Ohio, 1973—74; ptnr. Foley and Lance, Chartered, Meridian, Idaho, 1978—90; prin. Alan G. Lance, Meridian, 1990—94; rep. Idaho Ho. of Reps., Boise, 1990—94, majority caucus chmn., 1992—94; atty. gen. State of Idaho, 1995—2001. Capt. U.S. Army, 1974—78. Mem.: Idaho Trial Lawyers Assn., Idaho Bar Assn., Ohio Bar Assn., Nat. Assn. Attys. Gen. (vice-chmn. conf. western attys. gen. 1998, chmn. 1999), Meridian C. of C. (pres. 1983), Elks, Am. Legion (judge adv. 1981—90, state comdr. 1988—89, alt. nat. exec. com. 1992—94, nat. exec. com. 1994—96, chmn. nat. fgn. rels. commn. 1996—97, ex-officio mem. nat. POW/MIA com. 1996—, nat. comdr. 1999—2000, chmn. nat. adv. com. 2000—01). Republican. Avocation: fishing.*

LANCIONE, BERNARD GABE, lawyer; b. Bellaire, Ohio, Feb. 3, 1939; s. Americus Gabe and June (Morford) L.; m. Rosemary C., Nov. 27, 1976; children: Amy, Caitin, Gillian, Bernard Gabe II, Elizabetta Marie. BS, Ohio U., 1960; JD, Capitol U., 1965. Bar: Ohio 1965, U.S. Dist. Ct. (so. dist.) Ohio 1967, U.S. Supreme Ct. 1969, U.S. Ct. Appeals (4th cir.) 1982, U.S. Dist. Ct. (no. dist.) Ohio 1989. Pres. Lancione Law Office, Co., L.P.A., Bellaire, Ohio, 1965-87; mng. atty. Cichon Lancione Co., L.P.A., St. Clairsville, Ohio, 1982-85; of counsel Ward, Kaps, Bainbridge, Maurer, Bloomfield & Melvin, Columbus, Ohio, 1987-88; Ohio Asst. Atty. Gen. Columbus, 1988-91; pvt. practice, 1991—2002; assoc. Mills & Mills Law Office, Westerville, Ohio, 2003—. Spl. counsel Ohio Atty. Gen's. Office, 1991-95; solicitor Bellaire City (Ohio), 1968-72; asst. prosecutor County of Belmont (Ohio), 1972-76. Pres. Young Dems. Ohio, 1970-72; pack com. chmn. Pack 961, Westerville, Ohio Cub Scouts Am., 1992-93. Mem. ABA, Assn. Trial Lawyers Am., Ohio State Bar Assn., Columbus Bar Assn., Ohio Acad. Trial Lawyers (award of merit 1972). Democrat. Roman Catholic. Bankruptcy, Family and matrimonial, General practice. Home: 1108 Acillom Dr Westerville OH 43081-1104 Office: 1935 W Schrock Rd Westerville OH 43081 E-mail: blancion@columbus.rr.com.

LANCKTON, ARTHUR VAN CLEVE, lawyer; b. New London, Conn., Sept. 7, 1942; m. Alice Elizabeth Keidan, Aug. 31, 1967; children: Benjamin E., Samuel F. BA cum laude, Yale U., 1964; JD cum laude, Harvard U., 1967. Bar: Mass. 1967, U.S. Dist. Ct. Mass. 1968, U.S. Tax Ct. 1969, U.S. Ct. Appeals (1st cir.) 1982, U.S. Supreme Ct. 1986. Atty., dir. Harvard Law Sch. Community Legal Assistance Office, Cambridge, Mass., 1967-71; teaching fellow Harvard Law Sch., Cambridge, 1970-71; dep. gen. counsel Mass. Exec. Offices of Human Svcs., Boston, 1971-75; gen. counsel Dept. of Pub. Welfare, Boston, 1975-78; assoc. Bingham, Dana & Gould, Boston, 1978-83, Craig and Macauley, Boston, 1983-85, ptnr., 1985—. Democrat. Jewish. General civil litigation, Health, Insurance. Office: Craig and Macauley 600 Atlantic Ave Ste 2900 Boston MA 02210-2215 E-mail: lanckton@craigmacauley.com.

LAND, JOHN CALHOUN, III, lawyer, state senator; b. Manning, S.C., Jan. 25, 1941; s. John Calhoun, Jr. and Anna Abbott (Weisiger) L.; m. Marie Mercogliano, Oct. 23, 1965; children— John Calhoun IV, Frances Ricci, William Ceth. Student vocat. forestry U. Fla., 1960-62; B.S., U. S.C., 1965, J.D., 1968. Bar: S.C. 1968. Mem. Land, Parker and Welch, P.A., Manning, 1968— ; mem. S.C. Ho. of Reps., 1975-76, mem. S.C. Senate, 1977— . Sec. Clarendon County Democratic Com., 1968-70; commr. S.C. Hwys. and Pub. Transp., 1971-74. Mem. ABA, Clarendon County Bar Assn., S.C. Bar Assn., S.C. Trial Lawyers Assn. Avocations: hunting; fishing. Office: 504 Gressette Bldg Columbia SC 29202

LANDAU, MICHAEL B. law educator, musician, writer; b. Wilkes-Barre, Pa., July 3, 1953; s. Jack Landau and Florence (Rabitz) Simon. BA, Pa. State U., 1975; JD, U. Pa., 1988. Vis. prof. law Dickinson Sch. Law, Pa. State U., Carlisle; assoc. Cravath, Swaine and Moore, N.Y.C., 1988-90, Skadden, Arps, N.Y.C., 1990-92; assoc. prof. Coll. Law Ga. State U., Atlanta, 1992-99, prof. law, 1999—. Vis. prof. law U. Ga. Law Sch., 1998; guest lectr. Johannes Kepler U., Linz, Austria, summer 1994, 95, 96; vis. scholar Univ. Amsterdam, 2000. Contbr. articles to law jours. on copyright, art, patent, entertainment law. Mem. ABA, N.Y. State Bar Assn., Internat. Bar Assn., Vol. Lawyers for Arts, Am. Fedn. Musicians, Am. Intellectual Property Law Assn., Copyright Soc. U.S. Am., Phi Kappa Phi, Omicron Delta Epsilon. Democrat. Avocations: photography, jazz guitar, jazz piano. Office: Ga State U Coll Law University Pla Atlanta GA 30303 E-mail: mlandau@gsu.edu.

LANDE, DAVID STEVEN, lawyer; b. N.Y.C., Aug. 1, 1944; s. Jerome J. and Selma (Segal) L.; m. Fern Margolis, Aug. 17, 1975; children: Jill, Jeffrey, Jerome J. BS, Cornell U., 1966; JD, NYU, 1969. Bar: N.Y. 1969, U.S. Dist. Ct. (so. dist.) N.Y. 1971, U.S. Dist. Ct. (ea. dist.) N.Y. 1971, U.S. Supreme Ct. 1976. Aide Office of Mayor, N.Y.C., 1967-69; assoc. Javits & Javits, N.Y.C., 1970-71, Kreindler, Relkin, Olick & Goldberg, N.Y.C., 1971-74; pvt. practice N.Y.C., 1974—. Apptd. chmn. N.Y.C. Loft Bd., 1994-96; commr., vice-chmn. N.Y.C. Civil Svc. Commn., 1996—. Contbr. articles to profl. jours. Dist. leader 69th A. Dist. South N.Y.C. Reps., 1975-94; mem. state com. N.Y. Reps., Albany, 1976-94. Recipient Meritorious Service to Nation award U.S. Selective Service System, 1976. Mem. N.Y. State Bar Assn. (chmn. subcommittee auditing attys. trust accounts; com. on profl. discipline, 1987-93). Jewish. General practice, Probate (including wills, trusts). Office: 305 Madison Ave New York NY 10165-0006

LANDERS, SHARON L. transportation management and policy consultant; b. N.Y.C., May 18, 1953; d. Sidney and Sylvia E. Landers; m. Joe Gagliano. BS, SUNY, Stony Brook, 1974; JD, Union U., 1977; cert. environ. mgmt. inst., U. So. Calif., 1979. Bar: N.Y. 1978. Asst. counsel N.Y. State Dept. Transp., Albany, 1977-82; transp. program assoc. N.Y. State Office Gov., Albany, 1982-83; dep. dir., counsel N.Y.C. Dept. Transp., 1983—86, gen. counsel, dep. commr., 1986—89; transp. advisor Mayor of N.Y.C., 1989—91; counsel legis. and regulatory affairs Orange & Rockland Utilities Inc., Rockland County, N.Y., 1991-94; dep. commr. N.J. Dept. Transp., Trenton, 1994-97; dep. chief exec. officer Los Angeles County Metro. Transp. Authority, L.A., 1998, transp. mgmt. and policy cons., 1999—2001; asst. exec. dir. San Jose (Calif.) Redevel. Agy., 2002—. Bd. dirs. Am. Youth Hostels, Washington, 1982-93. Mem. N.Y. State Bar Assn. Avocations: scuba diving, cross-country and downhill skiing, bicycling.

LANDES, WILLIAM M. law educator; b. 1939. AB, Columbia U., 1960, PhD in Econs., 1966. Asst. prof. econs. Stanford U., 1965-66; asst. prof. U. Chgo., 1966-69; asst. prof. Columbia U., 1969-72; assoc. prof. Grad. Ctr., CUNY, 1972-73; now prof. U. Chgo. Law Sch.; founder, chmn. Lexecon Inc., 1977-98, chmn. emeritus, 1998—; mem. bd. examiners GRE in Econs., ETS, 1967-74. Mem. Am. Econ. Assn., Am. Law and Econ. Assn. (v.p. 1991-92, pres. 1992-93), Mont Pelerin Soc. Author: (with Richard Posner) The Economic Structure of Tort Law, 1987; editor: (with Gary Becker) Essays in the Economics of Crime and Punishment, 1974; editor Jour. Law and Econs., 1975-91, Jour. Legal Studies, 1991—. Office: U Chgo Sch Law 1111 E 60th St Chicago IL 60637-2776 also: Lexecon Inc 332 S Michigan Ave Ste 1300 Chicago IL 60604-4406

LANDESBERG, LEE JAY, lawyer; b. Yonkers, N.Y., Dec. 7, 1948; s. Samuel L. and Rita (Dreschler) L.; m. Carol I. Powdermaker, Oct. 14, 1979. BA, So. Conn. State Coll., 1972; JD, Tulane U., 1975; LLM, Georgetown U., 1978. Bar: La. 1975, D.C. 1976, N.Y. 1980, Md. 1981. Staff atty. office chief counsel IRS, Washington, 1975-78; pvt. practice Washington, 1978-88; adminstrv. law judge City of N.Y., 1988-89.

LANDESS, FRED STONE, lawyer; b. Memphis, Jan. 27, 1933; s. Sterling Stone and Beulah Elizabeth (Melton) L.; m. Catherine Sue Lee, Dec. 27, 1953; children— Susan Elinor, Charles Barton, Catherine Elizabeth Student, Wake Forest Coll., 1951-53; AB, George Washington U., 1955; LL.B., U. Va., 1958. Bar: Va. 1958. Enforcement atty. NLRB, Washington, 1958-60; assoc., then ptnr. McGuire, Woods, Battle & Boothe LLP, Charlottesville, VA., 1960-99, ret., 1999. Sec. Bd. Zoning Appeals, City of Charlottesville, Va., 1967-69; bd. dirs. YMCA, Charlottesville, 1975, Westminster Child Care Ctr., Charlottesville, 1978 Fellow Am. Coll. Real Estate Lawyers; mem. Charlottesville-Albemarle Bar Assn. (pres. 1983-84), Va. Bar Assn. (real estate com.), Va. State Bar (7th dist. disciplinary com. 1986-88, sec. 1987, chmn. 1987-88), Charlottesville-Albemarle Bd. Realtors (assoc.), Blue Ridge Homebuilders Assn. (assoc.). Clubs: Boar's Head Sports (Charlottesville). Democrat. Presbyterian. Avocations: tennis, sailing, gardening. Home: 515 Wiley Dr Charlottesville VA 22903-4650

LANDFIELD, RICHARD, lawyer; b. Chgo., Jan. 16, 1941; s. Joseph D. and Donna (Mayberg) L.; m. Ilona Kiraldi, Aug. 6, 1965; children: Anne, Katharine, Sarah. BA, Amherst Coll., 1962; LLB cum laude, Harvard U., 1965. Bar: N.Y. 1966, D.C. 1972. Asoc. Breed, Abbott & Morgan, N.Y.C., 1965-66, 69-72, Washington, 1972-75; ptnr. Dunnells, Duvall & Porter, 1975-79, Landfield, Becker & Green, Washington, 1979-89, Breed, Abbott & Morgan, 1989-92, Landfield & Becker, Chartered, 1992-94; shareholder Sanders, Schnabel, Brandenburg & Zimmerman, P.C., 1995-97; ptnr. Berliner, Corcoran & Rowe, L.L.P., 1997—. Bd. dirs. Carlson Holdings Corp., 1984-89; gen. counsel The European Inst.; active numerous Amherst Coll. alumni groups; mem. lawyers com. The Washington Opera, 1984-86, 87—; trustee Holton-Arms Sch., Bethesda, Md., 1984-86, 87-96, chmn. bldgs., grounds com., 1985-91, chmn. fin com., 1993-95, past pres. Parents' Assn., trustee emeritus, 1996—. 1st lt. U.S. Army, 1966-69. Decorated Army Commendation medal; John W. Simpson Law fellow Amherst, 1963. Mem. ABA, N.Y. State Bar Assn., Met. Club (Washington), Kenwood Country Club (Bethesda). Republican. Corporate, general, Private international, Property, real (including real estate development, water). Home: 5101 Baltan Rd Bethesda MD 20816-2309 Office: Berliner Corcoran & Rowe LLP 1101 17th St NW Ste 1100 Washington DC 20036-4798 E-mail: rlandfield@bcr-dc.com., rlandfield@yahoo.com.

LANDIN, DAVID CRAIG, lawyer; b. Jamestown, N.Y., Aug. 1, 1946; s. David Carl and Rita Mae (Felthaus) L.; m. Susan Ann Gregory, July 11, 1970; children: Mary Stuart, Alexander Craig, David Reed. BA, U. Va., 1968, JD, 1972. Bar: Va. 1972, Pa. 1991, Tex. 1992, U.S. Supreme Ct. 1979. Ptnr. McGuire, Woods & Battle, Richmond, Va., 1972-95, mgr. of product liability and litigation mgmt. group, 1987-95; gen. counsel Va. Assn. Ind. Schs., 1989—, Coun. for Religion in Ind. Schs., 1990—; ptnr. Hunton & Williams, Richmond, Va., 1995—. Pres. The Landin Cos., 1994—. Chmn. ctrl. Va. chpt. Nat. MS Soc., 1995-96. With USAR, 1968-74. Fellow: Va. Law Found. (pres. 1987—88, DRI Exceptional Performance award 1988); mem.: ABA, Greater Richmond C. of C. (bd. dirs. 1998—2000), Va. Assn. Def. Attys. (pres. 1987—88), Va. Bar Assn. (chmn. young lawyers sect. 1979—80, pres. 1999—2000). Roman Catholic. Avocations: squash, tennis, golf. Environmental, Product liability, Toxic tort. Home: 310 Oak Ln Richmond VA 23226-1639 Office: Hunton & Williams Riverfront Plaza East Tower PO Box 1535 Richmond VA 23218-1535

LANDMAN, CATHERINE R. lawyer; b. Racine, Wis., Mar. 20, 1963; BSFS, Georgetown U., 1985; JD, U. Wis., 1988. Bar: Wis. 1988, Minn. 1988, Tex. 1999. Office: The Pampered Chef 1 Pampered Chef Ln Addison IL 60101

LANDON, WILLIAM J. intelligence officer; b. Menno, S.D., June 23, 1939; s. Helmuth Samuel and Violet A. (McPherson) Neuharth. LLB, Blackstone Sch. Law, 1962, JD, 1968; AA in Bus. Mgmt., Coastline C.C., 1984; postgrad., Am. Mil. U., 2001—. Criminal investigator Internat. Acad. Police Sci., Oklahoma City, Southwestern Inst. Criminology, Lawton, Okla.; criminal investigator, intelligence officer ASI divsn. Internat. Investigators and Police, St. John, N.B., Can., 1964-94; intelligence officer, analyst Internat. Investigators & Police, Rapid City, SD, 1990—2001, ret., 2001. Student Am. Mil. U., Manassas Park, Va., 2000—. Sponsor Robin Anne Syperda Benedict meml. scholarship Calif. State U., Fullerton, 1990—. With USMC, 1957-65. Mem.: Nat. Mil. Intelligence Assn., Am. Soc. Criminology, Assn. Former Intelligence Officers, Internat. Investigators Police Assn., Internat. Assn. Study Organized Crime. Avocations: martial arts, classical music, fencing.

LANDRETH, KATHRYN E. lawyer; U.S. atty. Dept. Justice, Las Vegas, 1993—2001; chief of policy and planning Met. Police Dept., Las Vegas, Nev., 2001—02; metro counsel Las Vegas, 2003—. Office: Las Vegas Metro Police Dept 400 E Stewart Ave Las Vegas NV 89101

LANDRON, MICHEL JOHN, lawyer; b. Santurce, P.R., June 15, 1946; s. Francis Xavier and Francisca (Carretero) Healy; m. Carol McQuade, Apr. 22, 1989; children: Michael Francis, Ryan McQuade. BA, Lehman Coll., 1968, postgrad., 1969-73; JD, Fordham U., 1977. Bar: N.Y. 1978, U.S. Dist. Ct. (so. dist.) N.Y. 1978, U.S. Dist. Ct. (ea. dist.) N.Y. 1978. Asst. atty. gen. Office of Atty. Gen., N.Y. State Dept. Law, N.Y.C., 1978-80; enforcement atty. N.Y. Stock Exch., N.Y.C., 1980-81; pvt. practice, 1981-82, 84—; mem. Leaf, Duell, Drogin P.C., N.Y.C., 1982-84; gen. counsel Rockcom, Inc., 1985-87; adminstrv. law judge City of N.Y., 1987; counsel Berger and Paul, N.Y.C., 1984-85; assoc. area counsel Digital Equipment Corp., 1988-89; v.p., trust adminstrn. officer S.I. Bank & Trust, 2002—; v.p. SIB Fin. Svcs. Corp., 2002—. Adj. instr. N.Y. Law Sch., Ramapo Coll.; master arbitrator, Am. Arbitration Assn., U.S. Dist. Ct. (ea. dist.) N.Y.; mediator U.S. Dist. Ct. (ea. dist.) N.Y.; guest lectr. Lehman Coll.; cons. in field; arbitrator Civil Ct. N.Y.C., No Fault Ins. Panel State of N.Y., Nat. Assn. Securities Dealers, Inc.; arbitrator, mem. arbitration appeals panel Am. Arbitration Assn. Author: Conflicts of Law, 1992; (with others) Personal Injury: Actions, Defenses and Damages, 1992, Choice of Law; contbr. chpts. to books, articles to profl. jours. Mem. N.Y. State Bar Assn., Assn. Arbitrators City of N.Y., KC, Phi Alpha Delta (Disting. Svc. award 1977). Republican. Roman Catholic. Avocations: music, reading, sports. General civil litigation, General practice, Trademark and copyright. Office: SI Bank & Trust Trust Dept 1535 Richmond Ave Staten Island NY 10314

LANDRUM, BEVERLY HOLLOWELL, nurse, lawyer; b. Goldsboro, N.C., Jan. 28, 1960; d. Joseph Bryant and Doris Helen (Barnett) Hollowell; m. Tim Landrum; children: Amber, Justin, Caitlyn. ADN with honors, Florence-Darlington Tech., 1989; BSN summa cum laude, Med. U. S.C., 1995; JD, U. S.C., 2001. RN, S.C.; cert. BLS, ACLS, NALS; bar: S.C. Charge nurse Carolinas Hosp. System, Florence, SC, 1989—98; with Health South Rehab. Hosp., 1998—99; atty. S.C. Judicial Dept., 2002—03; asst. solicitor Fifteenth Jud. Cir., 2003—. Neighborhood campaign organizer March of Dimes, Am. Heart Assn., Atlantic Beach, Fla. and Florence, 1982—; active Assn. Parents and Tchrs., Florence, 1993—. Mem.: ABA, ANA, S.C. Am Bar Assn., S.C. Nurses Assn., Health Law Soc., Women in Law, Sigma Theta Tau.

LANDRUM, MICHAEL ARTHUR, lawyer, educator, mediator; b. Kirksville, Mo., Feb. 10, 1941; s. Lester Arthur and Edna Margaret Landrum; m. Ylva Anna-Greta Grund, July 11, 1994; 1 child, Lynette Janine stepchildren: Marcus Anderberg, Louise Anderberg. BA in Polit. Sci., N.E. Mo. State U., 1963; JD, U. Mo., 1966. Bar: Mo. 1966, Ill. 1968, U.S. Dist. Ct. (no. dist.) Ill. 1975, Minn. 1979, Calif. 1986, U.S. Dist. Ct. Minn. 2002. Asst. to exec. dir., labor counsel Associated Gen. Contractors Ill., Springfield, 1966—68; ind. rels. counsel Jewel Food Stores divsn. Jewel Cos. Inc., Melrose Park, Ill., 1968—72; v.p. indsl. rels. Osco Drug Eisner Food Stores and Turnstyle Family Ctrs. divsn. Jewel Cos. Inc., Chgo., 1972—75; atty. Arnold & Kadjan, Chgo., 1975—76, Berman & Landrum, Chgo., 1976—79; dir. employee rels. Target Stores, Mpls., 1979—83; v.p. adminstrn. Gemco Dept. Store divsn. Lucky Stores, Buena Park, Calif., 1983—84; mediator, pres. Americord, Inc., Sausalito, Calif., 1984—98, Mpls., 1984—98; dir. Ctr. Conflict Mgmt. William Mitchell Coll. Law, St. Paul, 1998—2001; atty., ptnr. Burke & Landrum, P.A., Edina, Minn., 2001—. Adj. prof. William Mitchell Coll. Law, St. Paul, 1986—, U. St. Thomas, Mpls., 2000—; mem. rev. bd. Minn. Supreme Ct., St. Paul, 1994—. Contbr. articles to profl. jours. Bd. dirs. Cedar Isle Homeowners Assn., Apple Valley, Minn., 2001—. Master: Warren E. Burger Inn Ct.; fellow: Internat.

Acad. Mediators; mem.: ABA (mem. dispute resolution, labor and employment), Minn. State Bar Assn. (mem. labor and employment sect., mem. constrn. sect.). Avocations: reading, classical music, automobiles, films. Alternative dispute resolution, Labor (including EEOC, Fair Labor Standards Act, labor-management relations, NLRB, OSHA), Construction. Office: Burke and Landrum PA 7400 Metro Blvd Ste 100 Edina MN 55439 Office Fax: 952-835-1867. Business E-Mail: mlandrum@burklandrum.com.

LANDRY, WALTER JOSEPH, lawyer; b. Willswood, La., Jan. 23, 1931; s. John Theodore and Lelia Lucille (Peltier) L.; m. Carolyn Margaret Kruschke, Nov. 24, 1962; children: Celeste, John, Josepn, Catherine, Walter Jr., James. BSME, U. Notre Dame, 1952; JD, Tulane U., 1958; MA, Am. U., 1969, PhD, 1975. Bar: La. 1958, U.S. Supreme Ct. 1961. Legis asst. to U.S. Sen. Russell B. Long, Washington, 1956-57; pvt. practice law New Orleans, 1958-61; fgn. svc. officer Dept. State, 1961-70; mem., action officer U.S. del. to San Jose Conf. Am. Conv. on Human Rights, 1969; ptnr. Landry, Poteet, and Landry, 1979-90; Futures Broker, 1990-99, U.S. Patent Office, 1999—2001. Asst. prof. U. Southwestern La., 1970-74; chmn. U.S. Lang. Policy Conf., Chgo., 1983; pres. Fedn. Am. Cultural and Lang. Communities, Inc., 1984—. Editor: La. Donkey, 1977-79; contbr. articles to profl. jours. Mem. Lafayette Parish Dem. Exec. Com., 1971—, chmn., 1976-83; mem. Dem. State Ctrl. Com. La., 1971—, past state co-chmn. affirmative action, 1975-76; counsel Bill of Rights Com. La. Constnl. Conv., 1973-74; del. Dem. Nat. Mid-Term Conf., 1974, 78, alt. del. Dem. Nat. Conv., 1980; organizer La. Assn. Parish Dem. Exec. Coms., 1976-77, pres., 1977-78; chmn. Dem. Caucus, 7th Congl. Dist. La., 1985-87. Maj. USMCR, Korea. Mem. Internat. Rels. Assn. of Acadiana (pres. 1974-75), ABA (internat. law working group 1971-76), Am. Soc. Internat. Law, Internat. Good Neighbor Coun. (organizer, pres. Acadiana chpt. 1978-81), Think-Tank for Nat. Self-Determination (exec. dir. 1994—). Intellectual property, Public international, Patent. Home and Office: 3835 9th St N # 201E Arlington VA 22203-1910 E-mail: waltlandry@comcast.net.

LANDSBERG, DENIS NEVILLE, lawyer, consultant; b. Witbank, South Africa, Aug. 24, 1951; s. Melville and Petronella Johanna (Dutoit) L.; m. Penelope Ann Philp, Apr. 2, 1977; 1 child, Robyn. BA, Stellenbosch U., South Africa, 1975; LLB, Stellenbosch U., 1977. Atty. Supreme Ct. of South Africa; conveyancer, commr. of small claims ct., appraiser. Articles clk. Buchanan Boyes, Cape Town, South Africa, 1978-80; ptnr. Groenewald, Landsberg & Pollard, Somerset West, South Africa, 1980-82, Ince & Wood, Stellenbosch, 1983-84; sr. ptnr. Landsberg, Carinus & Brand, Stellenbosch, 1985-91; prin. ptnr. Landsberg & Assocs., Somerset West, 1991-95; pvt. practice. Bd. dirs. Felstead Ltd., Rustenburg, Dariada N.V., St. Maarten, Verhoef Internat. Computer Svcs. Inc., U.S., various cos. in South Africa and U.K.; cons. to various internat. corps. Bd. dirs. Stellenbosch Coll., 1990—, Somerset Coll., Parklands Coll.; trustee Tygerberg Zool. Preservation Trust, Cape Town, 1987—; mem. Lawyers for Human Rights, South Africa; sponsor Magendavidadom, Cape Town; coun. mem. Cape Regional C. of C. and Industry. Lt. South Africa commandos, 1968-79. Recipient B.G. Heydenrych scholarship, 1976. Mem. Law Soc. of the Cape of Good Hope, Stellenbosch C. of C. (pres.), Round Table Assn. (chmn. 1984-85), Hottentots Holland Beach Sailing Club (commodore 1983-85). Avocations: sailing, hiking, constructing kites. Office: Landsberg & Assocs 8 Stuart St Somerset West 7130 South Africa E-mail: dnl@landsberglaw.com., info@landsberglaw.com.

LANDSBERG, JILL WARREN, lawyer, educator, arbitrator; b. N.Y.C., Oct. 11, 1942; d. George Richard and Evelyn (Schepps) Warren; m. Lewis Landsberg, June 14, 1964; children: Alison, Judd Warren. BA, George Washington U., Washington, 1964; MAT, Yale U., 1965; JD, Boston Coll., 1976. Bar: Mass., 1977, Ill., 1991. Assoc., dir. (ptnr.) Widett, Slater & Goldman PC, Boston, 1976-90; pvt. practice Chgo., 1991-94; faculty Med. Sch. Ethics and Human Values Dept. Northwestern U., Chgo., 1991-94; exec. asst. spl. counsel for child welfare svcs. Office of the Gov., Chgo., 1994-95, acting spl. counsel for child welfare svcs., 1995-96; cons. in field, 1996—2002; adj. prof. law Northwestern U., 2000—. Govt. agys. cons.; mem. Legis. Com. on Juvenile Justice, Chgo., 1995—96, Task Force on Violence Against Children, Chgo., 1995—99, Citizens Com. on the Juvenile Ct., Chgo., 1995—. Tutor Ptnrs. in Edn., 4th Presbyn. Ch., Chgo., 1993—; mem. steering com. Ill. Ct. Improvement Program, 1995-99; Ill. Jud. Inquiry Bd., 2000—; adv. bd. Libr. Internat. Rels., Chgo., 1993-94; bd. trustees Children's Home and Aid Soc. of Ill. Mem. Chgo. Bar Assn., Ill. State Bar Assn., , Am. Arbitration Assn. (cons. 1989—),Phi Beta Kappa, Order of the Coif. Home and Office: 70 E Cedar St Chicago IL 60611-1179

LANDY, BURTON AARON, lawyer; b. Chgo., Aug. 16, 1929; s. Louis J. and Clara (Ernstein) L.; m. Eleonora M. Simmel, Aug. 4, 1957; children: Michael Simmel, Alisa Anne. Student, Nat. U. Mex., 1948; BS, Northwestern U., 1950; postgrad. scholar, U. Havana, 1951; JD, U. Miami, 1952; postgrad. fellow, Inter-Am. Acad. Comparative Law, Havana, Cuba, 1955-56. Bar: Fla. 1952. Practice law in internat. field, Miami, 1955—; ptnr. firm Ammerman & Landy, 1957-63, Paul, Landy, Beiley & Harper, P.A. and predecessor firm, 1964-94, Steel Hector & Davis, 1994-97; ptnr. firm, chmn. emeritus Internat. Practice Group Akerman, Senterfitt & Eidson, P.A., 1997—. Lectr. Latin Am. bus. law U. Miami Sch. Law, 1972-75; also internat. law confs. in U.S. and abroad; mem. Nat. Conf. on Fgn. Aspects of U.S. Nat. Security, Washington, 1958; mem. organizing com. Miami regional conf. Com. for Internat. Econ. Growth, 1958; mem. U.S. Dept. Commerce Regional Export Expansion Council, 1969-74, mem. Dist. Export Council, 1978— ; mem. U.S. Sec. State Adv. Com. on Pvt. Internat. Law; dir. Fla. Council Internat. Devel., 1977—, chmn. 1986-87, 99; mem. U. Miami Citizens Bd., 1977— ; chmn. Fla. del. S.E. U.S.-Japan Assn., 1980-82; mem. adv. com. 1st Miami Trade Fair of Ams., 1978; dir., v.p. Greater Miami Fgn. Trade Zone, Inc., 1978—; mem. organizing com., lectr. 4 Inter-Am. Aviation Law Confs.; bd. dirs. Inter-Am. Bar Legal Found., VIII FTAA Ministerial, Am. Bus. Forum; participant Aquaculture Symposium Sci. and Man in the Ams., Mexico City, Fla. Gov's Econ. Mission to Japan and Hong Kong, 1978; mem. bd. exec. advisors Law and Econs. Ctr.; mem. vis. com., internat. adv. bd. U. Miami Sch. Bus.; mem. internat. fin. council Office Comptroller of Fla.; founding chmn. Fla.-Korea Econ. Coop. Com., 1982— , Southeast U.S.-Korea Econ. Com., 1985—; chmn. Expo 500 Fla.-Columbus Soc., 1985-87; founding co-chmn. So. Fla. Roundtable-Georgetown U. Ctr. for Strategic and Internat. Studies, 1982-85; chmn. Fla. Gov.'s Conf. on World Trade, 1984— ; founding gen. counsel Fla. Internat. Bankers Assn.; dir., former gen. counsel Fla. Internat. Ins. and Reins. Assn., chmn. Latin Am. Carribbean Bus. Promotion Adv. Counc. to U.S. Sec. of Commerce and Aid Adminstr; appointee Fla. Internat. Trade and Investment Coun.; mem. steering com. Summit of Ams., 1994—, co-chair post summit planning com.; strategic planning com. Mayor Miami Dade County Internat. Trade Commn. Contbg. editor Econs. Devel. Lawyers of the Ams., 1969-74; contbr. numerous articles to legal jours. in U.S. and fgn. countries. Chmn. City of Miami Internat. Trade and Devel. Com., 1984-86; chmn. internat. task force Beacon Coun. of Dade County, Fla., 1985, dir., chmn., 1991—; bd. dirs., exec. com. Internat. Comml. Dispute Resolution Ctr., Miami Internat. Arbitration and Mediation Inst.; chmn. Comml. Dispute Resolution Ctr. for the Ams., Miami, 1995—; apptd. by Gov. of Fla. to Internat. Currency and Barter Commn., 1986; lectr. U. Miami Inter-Ban course for Latin Am. bankers; steering com. Summit of the Americas, Miami, 1994, co-chair post Summit Planning Com., 1994; co-chair mayor Miami-Dade County Strategic Planning for Internat. Trade, 1998—; co-chair strategic planning com. Mayor of Miami Dade County Internat. Trade Commn.; bd. dirs. Trade Mission Ctr. Am., 2000—, Internat. Trade Coun. Miami-Dade County, Fla., Fla. Free Trade Area Agreement, Inc.; mem. internat. adv. com. Enterprise Fla., 2000—; bd. trustee Fla. Free Trade Area of the Americas; bd. dirs. Fla. Free Trade AGreement Ams., Inc. With JACGC, USAF, 1952-54, Korea; to maj. Res. Named Internat. Trader of Yr., Fla. Council Internat. Devel., 1980, Bus. Person of Yr., 1986; recipient Pan Am. Informatica Comunicaciones Expo award, 1983, Lawyer of Americas award U. Miami, 1984, Richard L. McLaughlin award Fla. Econ. Devel. Coun., 1993; named hon. consul gen. Republic of Korea, Miami, 1983-88, State of Fla., 99—, recipient Heung-in medal (Order of Diplomatic Service), 1986, Ministerial Citation, Min. of Fgn. Affairs, 1988; apptd. Hon. consul Ft. Lauderdale, Fla., 1991-98; apptd. Hon. consul gen. State of Fla., 1999—. Fellow ABA Found. (chmn. com. arrangements internat. and comparative law sect. 1964-65, com. on Inter-Am. affairs of ABA 1985-87); mem. Inter-Am. Bar Assn. (asst. sec.-gen. 1957-59, treas. 11th conf. 1959, co-chmn. jr. bar sect. 1963-65, mem council 1969—, exec. com. 1975—, pres. 1982-84, Diploma de Honor 1987, William Roy Vallance award 1989), Spanish Am. Bar Assn., Fla. Bar Assn. (vice chmn. adminstrv. law com. 1965, vice chmn. internat. and comparative law com. 1967-68, chmn. aero. law com. 1968-69), Dade County Bar Assn. (chmn. fgn. laws and langs com. 1964-65), Internat. Ctr. Fla. (World Trade Ctr., pres. 1981-82), World Peace Through Law Ctr., Miami Com. Fgn. Rels., Inst. Ibero Am. Derecho Aero., Am. Soc. Internat. Law, Coun. Internat. Visitors, Am. Fgn. Law Assn. (pres. Miami 1958), Bar of South Korea (hon. mem.), Greater Miami C. of C. (bd. govs. 1986—), Colombian-Am. C. of C. (bd. dirs. 1986—), Peruvian-Am. C. of C. (bd. dirs.), Norwegian Am. C. of C. (bd. dirs.), Phi Alpha Delta. Alternative dispute resolution, Corporate, general, Private international. Home: 605 Almeria Ave Coral Gables FL 33134-5602 Office: One SE Third Ave 28th Flr Miami FL 33131 E-mail: blandy@akerman.com.

LANDY, LISA ANNE, lawyer; b. Miami, Fla., Apr. 20, 1963; d. Burton Aaron and Eleonora Maria (Simmel) L. BA, Brown U., 1985; JD cum laude, U. Miami, 1988. Bar: Fla. 1988, U.S. Dist. Ct. (so. dist.) Fla. 1988. Atty. Paul, Landy, Beiley & Harper, P.A., Miami, Fla., 1988-94, Steel Hector & Davis, Miami, Fla., 1994-97, ptnr., 1996-97; shareholder Akerman Senterfitt & Eidson P.A., Miami , 1997—. Bd. dirs. Miami City Ballet, 1992-97, pres., 1996; bd. dirs. Women in Internat. Trade, Miami, 1992—, pres., 1994; bd. dirs. Orgn. Women in Internat. Trade, 1994—, v.p., 1997, 98, pres. 1998-2000; bd. dirs. Women in Tech. Internat. South Fla, The Next Step Youth Cmty. Ctr., Inc., IT Women, Inc., 2002—. Mem. ABA, Inter-Am. Bar Assn. (asst. sec. 1997-2000). Avocations: sports, arts, fluent in spanish, french. Commercial, contracts (including sales of goods; commercial financing), Private international, Trademark and copyright.

LANE, ARTHUR ALAN, lawyer; b. N.Y.C., Dec. 2, 1945; s. George and Delys L.; m. Jane Ficocella, Dec. 30, 1972; 1 child, Eva B. BA, Yale U., 1967; JD, Columbia U., 1970, MBA, 1971. Bar: N.Y. 1971. Assoc. Webster, Sheffield, Fleischmann, Hitchcock & Brookfield, N.Y.C., 1971-72; asst. to divsn. counsel Liggett & Myers, Inc., N.Y.C., 1973; assoc. Wickes, Riddell, Bloomer, Jacobi & McGuire, N.Y.C., 1974-78, Morgan, Lewis & Bockius, N.Y.C., 1979; ptnr. Eaton & Van Winkle, N.Y.C., 1980—94, DeForest & Duer, N.Y.C., 1994-99, Lamb & Barnosky, Melville, 1999—. Mem. ABA, Assn. of Bar of City of N.Y. Avocation: gardening. Banking, Corporate, general, General practice. Home: 103 Brooksite Dr Smithtown NY 11787-4456 Office: Lamb & Barnosky 534 Broadhollow Rd Melville NY 11747

LANE, BRADLEY GLENN, lawyer; b. Chgo., July 12, 1963; m. Therese L. Egan, Mar. 9, 1991; children: Megan Elizabeth, Kara Kathleen. BS, U. Ill., 1985; JD, U. Mich., 1988. Bar: Ill. 1988, U.S. Dist. Ct. (no. dist.) Ill. 1988, U.S. Ct. Appeals (fed. cir.) 1992, U.S. Dist. Ct. (e. dist.) Mich. 2002. Assoc. William Brinks Olds Hofer, Chgo., 1988-95; shareholder Brinks Hofer Gilson & Lione, Chgo., 1996—. Mem. ABA, Chgo. Bar Assn., Am. Intellectual Property Law Assn. Avocations: golfing, hiking, skiing. Federal civil litigation, Intellectual property, Patent. Office: Brinks Hofer Gilson & Lione Ste 3600 455 N Cityfront Plaza Dr Chicago IL 60611-5599 E-mail: blane@brinkshofer.com.

LANE, BRUCE STUART, lawyer; b. New London, Conn., May 15, 1932; s. Stanley S. and Frances M. (Antis) L.; m. Ann Elizabeth Steinberg, Aug. 10, 1958; children: Sue Ellen, Charles M., Richard I. Student, Boston U., 1948-49; AB magna cum laude, Harvard U., 1952, JD, 1955. Bar: Ohio 1955, D.C. 1966, U.S. Ct. Claims 1960, U.S. Tax Ct. 1961, U.S. Supreme Ct. 1961. Assoc. Squire, Sanders & Dempsey, Cleve., 1955-59; sr. trial atty. tax div. Dept. Justice, Washington, 1959-61; tax atty. Dinsmore, Shohl, Barrett, Coates & Deupree, Cin., 1961-65; sec., asst. gen. counsel corp. and tax matters Communications Satellite Corp., Washington, 1965-69; v.p., gen. counsel Nat. Corp. Housing Partnerships, Washington, 1969-70; pres. Lane and Edson P.C., Washington, 1970-89; ptnr. Kelley Drye & Warren, Washington, 1989-93, Peabody & Brown, Washington, 1993-99, Nixon Peabody LLP, Washington, 1999-2000, sr. cousnel, 2001—. Co-editor-in-chief Housing and Devel. Reporter; author publs. and articles on tax, partnership and real estate. Incorporator, bd. dirs., past pres. D.C. Inst. Mental Health; past chmn. citizens Com. sect. 5 Chevy Chase, Md.; past mem. Montgomery County Hist. Preservation Commn., Md.,mem. Nat. Adv. Coun., Smithsonian Nat. Mus. of the Am. Indians; mem. chmn. coun. Crow Canyon Archeol. Ctr., Cortez, Colo. Maj. JAG, USAR, 1952-68. Mem.: ABA, Anglo-Am. Real Property Inst., Am. Coll. Real Estate Lawyers (pres. 1986—87), Am. Law Inst., Phi Beta Kappa. Alternative dispute resolution, Property, real (including real estate development, water), Corporate taxation. Home: 5630 Wisconsin Ave #1003 Chevy Chase MD 20815 Office: Nixon Peabody LLP 401 9th St NW Ste 900 Washington DC 20004-2134

LANE, CHARLOTTE, lawyer; b. 1948; AB, Marshall U., 1966—69; JD, W.Va. U., 1969—72. Bar: W.Va. 1972. Delegate W.Va. House of Delegates, 1978—80, 1990—92; commr. W.Va. Pub. Svc. Commn., 1985—89, chmn., 1997—2001, commr., 2001—. Mem. W.Va. Bar Assn. (pres.-elect), Charleston Chamber of Commerce (bd. dirs.), Charleston Rotary (bd. dirs.), former mem. W. Va. Ho. Del., 1978-80, chmn. Public Svc. Commn. 1997-2001 Government contracts and claims, Utilities, public. Office: Public Svc Comm 201 Brooks St Charleston WV 25301*

LANE, FIELDING H. lawyer; b. Kansas City, Mo., May 6, 1926; s. Ralph Fielding and Nancy Lee (Greene) L.; m. Patricia Cecil Parkhurst, Jan. 25, 1980 BS in Bus. Adminstrn., U. Mo.-Columbia, 1948; LL.B. cum laude, Harvard U., 1951. Bar: Mo. 1951, Calif. 1956. Assoc. Watson Ess Marshall & Enggas, Kansas City, Mo., 1951-55; assoc. Thelen Marrin Johnson & Bridges, San Francisco, 1955-66, ptnr., 1967-95, of counsel, 1996—. Served with USN, 1944-46; PTO; lt. comdr. Res. (ret.) State and local taxation. Home: PO Box 1495 Aptos CA 95001-1495 Office: Thelen Reid & Priest LLP 101 2d St Ste 1800 San Francisco CA 94105 E-mail: fhlane@thelenreid.com.

LANE, FRANK JOSEPH, JR., lawyer; b. St. Louis, May 10, 1934; s. Frank Joseph and Virginia Laurette (Hausman) L.; m. Margaret Ann Dwyer, Mar. 2, 1957; children: Mary, Stephen, Thomas, Michael. BS in Commerce, JD, St. Louis U., 1956; LLM, Georgetown U., 1960; grad. Parker Sch. Internat. Law, Columbia U., 1970; cert., Coll. Fin. Planning, Denver, 1988. Bar: Mo. 1956, U.S. Dist. Ct. (ea. dist.) Mo. 1956, U.S. Ct. Appeals (8th cir.) 1960, U.S. Supreme Ct. 1959, U.S. Ct. Mil. Appeals, 1957. Ptnr. Goldenhersh, Goldenhersh, Fredericks, Newman & Lane, St. Louis, 1960-64, Lane & Leadlove, St. Louis, 1964-66, Dill & Lane, St. Louis, 1978-79; counsel Ralston Purina Co., St. Louis, 1966-78; pres.'s adv. bd., 1967-69; of counsel Petrolite Corp., St. Louis, 1979-83; v.p., trust officer Gravois Bank, St. Louis, 1983-85; regional v.p., trust officer Merc Bank N.A., St. Louis, 1985-89; of counsel Dill, Wamser, Bamvakais & Newsham PC, St. Louis, 1989—. Instr. internat. law St. Louis U., 1979. Bd. dirs. Met. St. Louis Sewer Dist., 1965-73, chmn., 1968-69; bd. dirs. Webster Groves KC Home Assn., 1999-01; mem. St. Louis Regional Commerce & Growth Assn. environ. com., 1978-82; mem. planned giving com. Am. Heart Assn., St. Louis, 1986-88, St. Louis Soc. for Crippled Children, 1991; bd. dirs. Midwestern Braille Vols., Inc., chmn., 1995—; atty. St. Louis Geneal. Soc., 1996—; pres. Ozark Cmties. Coun. St. Louis County, 1964-65. Capt. U.S. Army JAGC, Pentagon, 1957-60. Mem. Mo. Bar Assn., Met. St. Louis Bar Assn. (chmn. rels. with law schs. com. 1961-62, enrollment com. 1962-63, chmn. office practice com. 1963-64, elected admissions com. 1967), Estate Planning Coun. St. Louis, Rotary (bd. dirs. Crestwood, Mo. chpt. 1988-89), KC (grand knight 1964-66, adv. West County 1983-90, Webster Groves 1991-2001). Republican. Roman Catholic. Avocations: oil painting, golf, travel, investment analysis. Home: 520 Lering Dr Ballwin MO 63011-1588 Office: 9939 Gravois Rd Saint Louis MO 63123-4211 E-mail: frank_j_lane@juno.com.

LANE, JOHN DENNIS, lawyer; b. Norwalk, Conn. s. John J. and Theresa A. (Donnelly) L.; m. Elizabeth J. Galliher, Apr. 28, 1949; children: Elizabeth J., John Dennis, Margaret A., Robert E., Paul G. BS, Georgetown U., 1943, JD, 1948. Bar: D.C. 1948, Conn. 1950. Atty. Office Chief Counsel, Bur. Internal Revenue, Washington, 1948-49; exec. sec. to U.S. Senator Brien McMahon, 1949-50; adminstrv. asst., 1950-52; pvt. practice, 1953-2001; ptnr. Hedrick & Lane, 1954— 82, Wilkes, Artis, Hedrick & Lane, 1982-2000, Wilkes Artis, 2000-2001. Mem. coun. Adminstrv. Conf. U.S., 1961; bd. regents Georgetown U., 1979—. Served to capt. USMCR, 1943-45. Recipient Citation of Merit. Fellow Am. Bar Found.; mem. ABA (chmn. standing com. unauthorized practice of law 1971-73, chmn. standing com. nat. conf. groups 1973-75, D.C. cir. mem. standing com. on fed. judiciary 1984-86, Fed. cir. mem. 1987-90), Fed. Commn. Bar Assn. (pres.-elect 1990, pres. 1991-92, alt. rep. to UN 1997-99), Am. Law Inst., Met. Club, Columbia Country Club (Chevy Chase, Md.). Communications. Home: 5045 Van Ness St NW Washington DC 20016-1960 Office: 8th Fl 1200 New Hampshire Ave NW Washington DC 20036-6802

LANE, MARK, lawyer, educator, writer; b. N.Y.C., Feb. 24, 1927; s. Harry Arnold and Elizabeth Lane; m. Patricia Ruth Erdner, 1987; children: Anne-Marie, Christina. LLB, Bklyn. Law Sch., 1951. Bar: N.Y. 1951, D.C. 1995. Mng. mem. The Lane Law Firm, LLC, N.Y.C. , Washington, N.J., pvt. practice law, founding mem., sr. ptnr., 1952—; founder Mid-Harlem Community Parish Narcotics Clinic, 1953, East Harlem Reform Dem. Club, 1959; prof. law Cath. U., Washington, 1975—76. Founder and dir. Citizens Commn. Inquiry; founder Wounded Knee Legal Def.-Offense Com., 1973, The Covered Wagon, Mountain Home, Idaho, 1971. Author: (books) Rush to Judgment, 1966, A Citizen's Dissent, 1968, Chicago Eye-Witness, 1969, Arcadia, 1970, Conversations with Americans, 1970, Executive Action, 1973, (with Dick Gregory) Code Name Zorro, 1977, The Strongest Poison, 1980, Plausible Denial, 1991, Murder in Memphis, 1993; prodr. films Rush to Judgment, 1967, Two Men in Dallas, 1987, 92; writer, prodr. plays Trial of James Earl Ray, 1978, Plausible Denial, 1992, Winds of Doctrine, 1994; writer, prodr. screenplays, Arcadia, 1992, Slay the Dreamer, 1992, Plausible Denial, 1993; founder publs. Citizens Quar., 1975, Helping Hand, 1971. Mem. N.Y. State Assembly, 1960-62. With AUS, 1945-47. Civil rights, Constitutional, Libel. Home and Office: 272 Tindall Island Rd Greenwich NJ 08323

LANE, MATTHEW JAY, lawyer; b. Cin., Mar. 6, 1955; s. Joseph Alan and Adele (Stacks) L.; m. Susan Carol. BA, Emory U., 1977; JD, Northwestern U., 1980. Bar: Ohio 1981, U.S. Dist. Ct. (so. dist.) Ohio 1981, U.S. Ct. Appeals (6th cir.) 1981, Fla. 1982, U.S. Ct. Appeals (11th cir.) 1982. Law clk. to chief judge U.S. Dist. Ct. (so. dist.) Ohio, Cin., 1980-82; prin. Matthew Lane & Assocs., P.A., West Palm Beach, Fla.; v.p., gen. counsel PPI, Inc., North Palm Beach, Fla., 1996—. Legal counsel Juvenile Diabetes Assn., Cin., 1984-92; legal counsel MADD, 1986-92, pres. S.W. Ohio chpt., 1988-91, pres. Palm Beach County chpt., 1993-95; active Big Bros./Big Sisters Devel. Com., 1985-88; mem. Palm Beach County Dem. Exec. Com., 1993—; mem. civil rights com. Anti-Defamation League; trustee Temple Israel, 1999-2000; mem. Palm Beach County Bar Employment Law Com., Fla. Bar Labor and Employment Law Com. Mem. Nat. Employment Lawyers Assn., Phi Beta Kappa. General civil litigation, State civil litigation, Corporate, general. Home: 2840 Gettysburg Ln West Palm Beach FL 33409-7212 Office: 777 S Flagler Dr Ste 800 West West Palm Beach FL 33401

LANE, NEWTON ALEXANDER, retired lawyer; b. Boston, June 16, 1915; s. Samuel B. and Eva (Robbins) L. AB, Harvard U., 1936, JD, 1939. Bar: Mass. 1939. Ptnr. emeritus Lane Altman & Owens, Boston. Served with AUS, 1942-46. Mem. Phi Beta Kappa. Home: 704 Dedham St Newton MA 02459-2937 E-mail: newtl@aol.com.

LANER, RICHARD WARREN, lawyer; b. Chgo., July 12, 1933; s. Jack E. and Esther G. (Cohon) L.; m. Barbara Lee Shless, Aug. 15, 1954 (dec. Oct. 1997); children: Lynn, Kenneth; m. Daryl Lynn Homer, Sept. 17, 1998. Student, U. Ill., 1951-54; BS, Northwestern U., 1955, LLB, 1956. Bar: Ill. 1956. Assoc. Laner, Muchin, Dombrow, Becker, Levin & Tominberg, Ltd., Chgo., 1956-62, ptnr., 1962-99, of counsel, 1999. Editor Northwestern Law Rev., 1954-56; contbr. articles to profl. jours. Mem. Chgo. Bar Assn. (chmn. com. labor law 1972-73), Chgo. Assn. Commerce and Industry, Order of Coif. Labor (including EEOC, Fair Labor Standards Act, labor-management relations, NLRB, OSHA). Home: 161 E Chicago Ave Unit 41de Chicago IL 60611-2601 Office: Laner Muchin Dombrow Becker Levin & Tominberg Ltd 515 N State St Fl 28 Chicago IL 60610-4325 E-mail: rlaner@lmdblt.com.

LANEY, JOHN THOMAS, III, federal judge; b. Columbus, Ga., Mar. 27, 1942; s. John Thomas Jr. and Leila (Davis) L.; m. Louise Pierce, Nov. 23, 1974; children: Thomas Whitfield, Elizabeth Davis. AB, Mercer U., 1964, JD magna cum laude, 1966. Bar: Ga. 1965, U.S. Dist. Ct. (mid. dist.) Ga. 1966, U.S. Ct. Appeals (5th cir.) 1966, U.S. Ct. Mil. Appeals 1967, U.S. Ct. Appeals (11th cir.) 1981. Assoc. Swift, Pease, Davidson & Chapman, Columbus, 1970-73; ptnr. Page, Scrantom, Harris & Chapman, Columbus, 1973-86; judge mid. dist. Ga. U.S. Bankruptcy Ct., Columbus, 1986—. Co-editor-in-chief Mercer Law Rev., 1965-66; contbr. articles to profl. jours. Former pres., dir. Metro. Boys Club of Columbus. Capt. U.S. Army, 1966-70. Mem. ABA (judge adminstrv. divsn. Nat. Conf. Fed. Trial Judges), State Bar Ga. (chmn. gen. practice and trial sect. 1983-84, chmn. state disciplinary bd. 1984-85), Am. Judicature Soc., Nat. Conf. Bankruptcy Judges, Columbus Bar Assn., Inc. (pres. 1985-86), Rotary. Presbyterian. Office: US Bankruptcy Ct 1 Arsenal Pl 901 Front Ave Ste 309 Columbus GA 31901-2797 E-mail: k4bai@worldnet.att.net.

LANG, GORDON, JR., retired lawyer; b. Evanston, Ill., July 27, 1933; s. Gordon and Harriet Kendig Lang; m. Clara Bates Van Derzee, Sept. 26, 1970; children: Elizabeth K., Gordon III, Harriet B. BA, Yale U., 1954; MA in History, U. Ariz., 1958; LLB, Harvard U., 1960. Bar: Ill. 1960. Assoc. Gardner, Carton & Douglas, Chgo., 1960-67, ptnr., 1967-98, ret., 1998. Cons., 1999—. Dir. North Side Boys' Clubs, Chgo., 1961-67, Yale Scholarship Trust Ill., 1966-69, pres., 1967; mem. Assocs. Rush-Presbyn.-St. Luke's Med. Ctr., Chgo., 1962—, Assocs. Northwestern U., Evanston, 1970—; dir. Chgo. Youth Ctrs., 1967—, pres., 1982-84; trustee Chgo. Latin Sch. Found., 1978—, pres., 1995—; trustee Groton (Mass.) Sch., 1982-93; dir. United Way of Chgo., 1984-90, United Way/Crusade of Mercy (Met. Chgo.), 1989-95; apptd. Bush/Cheney elector 2000 presdl. election. 1st lt. USAF, 1955-57. Mem. ABA (sect. bus. law), Ill. State Bar Assn., Chgo. Bar Assn. (mem. corp. law com. 1975-98, mem. fin. instns. com. 1985-98), Chgo. Club (former dir. and sec.), Econ. Club Chgo. (former dir. and sec.), Onwentsia Club, Racquet Club Chgo., Chgo. Commonwealth Club, Yale Club Chgo. (former dir., past pres.). Republican. Episcopalian. Avocations: golf, skiing, hiking. Corporate, general, Finance, Securities. Home: 1520 N Astor St Chicago IL 60610-1610 Office: Gardner Carton & Douglas 191 N Wacker Dr Ste 3700 Chicago IL 60606-1698 E-mail: glang@gcd.com.

LANG, JOHN ERNEST, lawyer; b. Arkansas City, Kans., Dec. 27, 1936; s. Ernest R. and Ruth (Evans) L.; m. Joleen C. Jilka, Nov. 22, 1959; children: Jill Kay Lang Gobble, Jeffrey R. BS, U. Kans., 1958; JD, Washburn U., 1962. Bar: Kans. 1962, U.S. Dist. Ct. Kans. 1962, U.S. Ct. Appeals (10th cir.) 1969. Mcpl. judge City of Wamego, Kans., 1967-78; county atty. Pottawatomie County, Kans., 1967-70, county counselor, 1977—2002; pvt. practice, Wamego, 1961—. Bd. dirs. First Nat. Bank, Wamego. Trustee The Stormont Found., Topeka, 1989-95; trustee Wamego City Hosp., 1969-89, chmn. bd. trustees, 1988-89; chair Gov.'s Com. on Instnl. Mgmt. and Comty. Mental Health, Topeka, 1974-80; mem. Gov.'s Adv. Com. on Criminal Adminstrn., Topeka, 1970-72. With USAR, 1956-62. Mem. Kans. Bar Assn., Pottawatomie County Bar Assn. Democrat. Methodist. Avocation: golf. Office: PO Box 2 Wamego KS 66547-0002 E-mail: langlaw@wamego.net.

LANG, RICHARD ARNOLD, JR., lawyer; b. New Rochelle, N.Y., Dec. 18, 1938; s. Richard Arnold and Muriel Herold (Goetz) Lang; m. Nancy Elizabeth Caravajal, Apr. 12, 1966; children: Richard A III, Jessica B. BA, Cornell U., 1960, LLB, 1964. Bar: N.Y. 1965, U.S. Ct. Appeals (2d cir.) 1972, Vt. 1973, U. S. Dist. Ct. Vt. 1973, Fla. 1981. Law clk. to judge U.S. Ct. Appeals (2d cir.), N.Y.C., 1964—65; assoc. McCutcheon, Doyle et al, San Francisco, 1965—67, Whitman, Ransom et al, N.Y.C., 1967—70, Appleton, Rice & Perrin, 1970—72; ptnr. Samuelson, Portnow et al., Burlington, Vt., 1972—80, Hoff, Wilson, Powell & Lang, Burlington, 1980—2002. Mem. Chittenden County Transp. Authority, Burlington; trustee Fletcher Libr., Burlington, Vt. Mem.: ABA, Crittenden County Bar Assn., Vt. Bar Assn. Republican. Episcopalian. General civil litigation, Bankruptcy, Commercial, contracts (including sales of goods; commercial financing). Home: 805 S Prospect St Burlington VT 05401-6168 Office: Bauer, Anderson & Gravel 40 Coll St Ste 100 Burlington VT 05402-0607 Office Fax: 802-864-7779. E-mail: richardlang.esq@verizon.net.

LANGE, C. WILLIAM, lawyer, educator; b. St. Louis, June 15, 1946; s. Carl W. and Marion M. (Guenther) L.; m. Catherine L. Janowiak, June 7, 1981; children: Courtney Anne, Carl William IV. BA, Westminster Coll., 1968; MBA, St. Louis U., 1972; JD, Oklahoma City U., 1974. Bar: Mo. 1975, U.S. Dist. Ct. Mo. 1975, U.S. Ct. Appeals (8th cir.) 1986. With claims dept. MFA Ins. Cos., Columbia, Mo., 1968-71; ptnr. Lange & Lange, Cuba, Mo., 1976-81; pvt. practice Cuba, 1981-88; ptnr. Lange & Lange, Cuba, 1989—. Pros. atty. Crawford County (Mo.), 1979-80; city atty. City of Cuba, 1978-80, 82-88; prof. mgmt. Maryville U., St. Louis, 1974—; instr. East Central Coll., Union, Mo., 1975. Mem. Crawford County Child Welfare Adv. Com., 1979-88, pres. 1984-86; mem. Crawford County Child Abuse and Neglect Team, 1981-90; treas. Sixteenth Senatorial Dist. Rep. Com., 1993-94. Served with Air N.G., 1967-74. Mem. ABA, Mo. Bar Assn., 42d Jud. Cir. Bar Assn., St. Louis Met. Bar Assn., Cuba C. of C. Lodges: Optimists. Presbyterian. Corporate, general, Family and matrimonial, General practice. Home: PO Box 88 Cuba MO 65453-0088 Office: Lange and Lange Attys PO Box 280 Cuba MO 65453-0280 E-mail: langelaw@fidnet.com.

LANGER, BRUCE ALDEN, lawyer; b. N.Y.C., Mar. 17, 1953; s. Samuel S. and Yvette Langer. BA summa cum laude with distinction, Boston U., 1975, JD cum laude, 1978. Bar: N.Y. 1979, U.S. Dist. Ct. (so. and ea. dists.) N.Y. 1979, U.S. Tax Ct. 1979, U.S. Ct. Appeals (2d cir.) 1983, U.S. Supreme Ct. 1985. Law clk. to presiding chief justice U.S. Bankruptcy Ct. (ea. dist.) N.Y., summers 1976-77; with Breed Abbott & Morgan, N.Y.C., 1978-81, White & Case, N.Y.C., 1981-84, Fishman Forman & Landau, N.Y.C., 1984-85, Fishman Forman & Langer, N.Y.C., 1985-86, Paradise & Alberts, N.Y.C., 1986-89; pvt. practice N.Y.C., 1989—. Editor Boston U. Law Rev., 1977-78; contbg. author: Pensions and Investments, 1979; contbr. articles to profl. jours. Harold C. Case Presdl. scholar, 1974-75. Mem. Phi Beta Kappa, Phi Alpha Theta. Bankruptcy, Federal civil litigation, State civil litigation. Office: Law Office of Bruce A Langer Esq 488 Madison Ave 5th Floor New York NY 10022

LANGFORD, JAMES JERRY, lawyer; b. Birmingham, Ala., May 19, 1933; S. N.B. and Margaret Elizabeth (Fuller) L.; m. Mary Elizabeth Fryant, Mar. 21, 1958; children: Jan Carol Langford Hammett, Joel Fryant L. BS, U. So. Miss., 1955; JD, U. Miss., 1970. Bar: Miss. 1970, U.S. Dist. Ct. (no. and so. dists.) Miss. 1970, U.S. Ct. Appeals (5th cir.) 1971, U.S. Ct. Appeals (11th cir.). Agt. Met. Life Ins. Co., Jackson, Miss., 1957-58; sales rep. Employers Mut. of Wausau, Jackson, 1958—64; v.p. Reid-McGee Ins. Co., Jackson, 1964-67; from assoc. to sr. ptnr., mng. ptnr. Wells Marble & Hurst, Jackson, 1970-97, sr. ptnr., 1997—. Editor-in-chief Miss. Law Jour., 1969-70. 1st lt. U.S. Army, 1955-57. Fellow. Miss. Bar Found.; mem. ABA, Fed. Bar Assn. (pres. Miss. chpt. 1981-82), Fedn. Def. and Corp. Counsel, Nat. Assn. RR Trial Counsel, Miss. Bar Assn. (mem. ethics com. 1998—), Miss. Def. Lawyers Assn. (pres. 1992-93), Country Club Jackson, Phi Delta Phi, Omicron Delta Kappa, Pi Kappa Alpha. Presbyterian. Avocations: military history, baseball. General civil litigation, Insurance, Product liability. Home: 12 Plum Tree Ln Madison MS 39110-9620 Office: Wells Marble & Hurst PO Box 131 Jackson MS 39205-0131 E-mail: jlangfordesq@aol.com.

LANGLOIS, JOHN EMILE, lawyer, politician; b. Leicester, Eng., Oct. 31, 1942; s. Emile and Anita Eunice (Bourgaize) L.; m. Patricia Battersby, Jan. 5, 1975; children: Mark, Paul. Assoc., London Bible Coll., 1969; LLB hons., U. London, 1970, Dip.Th., 1969. Barrister, Gray's Inn, London, 1971; advocate Royal Ct. Guernsey, 1971. Ptnr. Carey Langlois, Guernsey, 1973—2003; cons. Carey Olsen, 2003. Bd. dirs. Credit Suisse (Guernsey) Ltd., S.G. Hambros Bank, Guernsey. Contbr. articles to profl. jours., chpts. to books. Dep. States of Guernsey, 1980-; treas. World Evang. Alliance, chmn. World Evang. Alliance Religious Liberty Commn., 1992—; chmn. Advocates Internat., Washington, 1996-2001, chmn. Advocates Europe, 2001—, Care for Children, 1998—. Fellow,arbitrator and mediator, Chartered Inst. Arbitrators. Avocations: motor boating, reading, travel. Home: Les Emrais de Bas Castel Guernsey Channel Islands GY5 7YF England Fax: 44 1481-711052.

LANGTON, JEFFREY H. judge; b. Hamilton, Mont., Apr. 22, 1953; s. Richard L. and N. Louise (Mittower) L.; m. Patricia L. Stanbery, June 17, 1978 (div. Feb. 1999); children: Melanie, Matthew, Stephen, Thomas. BA in history with high honors, U. Mont., 1975, JD, 1978. Bar: Mont. 1978, U.S. Dist. Ct. Mont. 1978. Assoc. Schultz Law Firm, Hamilton, 1978-82; pvt. practice Hamilton, 1982-92; dist. judge 21st Dist. Ct., Hamilton, 1993—. Bd. clin. visitors Law Sch., U. Mont., Missoula, 1993-99; Mont. Sentence Review Divsn., 1998-2001, chmn., 2000-01; chmn. self represented litigants Mont. Supr. Ct. Commn., 2000— Author: The Victor Story, 1985. Bd. dirs. Victor Heritage Mus., 1990-95. Named Man of Yr. Victor Booster Club, 1988, 93. Mem. ABA (Mont. del. 1994—), Am. Jud. Soc., Mont. Bar Assn., Mont. Judges Assn. Presbyterian. Avocations: montana history, fly fishing, environmental issues. Home: 2975 Mittower Rd Victor MT 59875-9542 Office: 21st Jud Dist 205 Bedford St Hamilton MT 59840-2853

LANGWORTHY, ROBERT BURTON, lawyer; b. Kansas City, Mo., Dec. 24, 1918; s. Herman Moore and Minnie (Leach) L.; m. Elizabeth Ann Miles, Jan. 2, 1942; children: David Robert, Joan Elizabeth Langworthy Tomek, Mark Burton. AB, Princeton U., 1940; JD, Harvard U., 1943. Bar: Mo. 1943, U.S. Supreme Ct. 1960. Practiced in, Kansas City, 1943—; assoc., then mem. and v.p. Linde, Thomson, Langworthy, Kohn & Van Dyke, P.C., 1943—91; pres., mng. shareholder Blackwood, Langworthy & Schmelzer, P.C., Kansas City, Mo., 1991—96; mng. mem. Blackwood, Langworthy & Tyson, L.C., and predecessor, Kansas City, Mo., 1996—. Lectr. on probate, law sch. CLE courses U. Mo., Kansas City. Mem. bd. editors Harvard Law Rev., 1941-43; contbr. chpts. to Guardian and Trust, Powers, Conservatorships and Nonprobate Desk Books of Mo. Bar. Mem. edn. appeal bd. U.S. Dept. Edn., 1982-86; commr. Housing Authority Kansas City, 1963-71, chmn., 1969-71; chmn. Bd. Election Commrs. Kansas City, 1973-77; chmn. bd. West Ctrl. area YMCA, 1969—; mem. bd. Mid-Am. region YMCA, 1970-83, vice chmn., 1970-73, chmn., 1973-78; pres. Met. Bd. Kansas City (Mo.) YMCA (now YMCA of Greater Kansas City), 1965, bd. dirs., 1965—, mem. nat. bd. 1971-78, 79-83; bd. dirs. YMCA of the Rockies, 1974—, bd. sec., 1994-99; mem. Sioux Indian YMCAs, 1983-2002, chmn. bd. trustees, 1983-2002, chmn. hon. trustees, 2003—; bd. dirs. Armed Svcs. YMCA, 1984-85; pres. Met. Area Citizens Edn., 1969-72; chmn. Citizens Assn. Kansas City (Mo.), 1967, bd. dirs., 1995-96; bd. dirs. Project Equality Kans.-Mo., 1967-80, pres., 1970-72, treas., 1972-73, sec., 1973-76; 1st v.p. Human Resources Corp. Kansas City, 1969-71, 72-73, bd. dirs., 1965-73; hon. v.p. Am. Sunday Sch. Union (now Am. Missionary Fellowship), 1965—; vice chmn. bd. trustees Kemper Mil. Sch., 1966-73; U.S. del. YMCA World Coun., Buenos Aires, 1977, Estes Park, Colo., 1981, Nyborg, Denmark, 1985; bd. dirs. Mo. Rep. Club, 1960—; del., mem. platform com. Rep. Nat. Conv., 1960; Rep. nominee for U.S. Congress, 1964; mem. gen. assembly Com. on Representation Presbyn., 1991-97, moderator, 1993-94; commr. to gen. assembly Presbyn. Ch., 1984, mem. gen. assembly com. on location of hdqs. 1984-87; moderator Heartland Presbyn., 1984. Lt. (j.g.) USNR, 1943-46, capt. Res. ret. Mem.: ABA, Harvard Law Sch. Assn. Mo. (v.p. 1973—74, pres. 1974—75, 1985—87), Lawyers Assn. Kansas City, Mo. State Bar (chmn. probate and trust com. 1983—85, chmn. sr. lawyers com. 1991—93), Met. Kan. Met. City Bar Assn. (chmn. probate law com. 1988—90, 1999—2000, living will com. 1989—91), Kansas City Club. Presbyterian (Elder). Estate planning, Non-profit and tax-exempt organizations, Probate (including wills, trusts). Home: Claridge Ct Apt 305 8101 Mission Rd Prairie Village KS 66208-5238 Office: 1220 Washington St Ste 300 Kansas City MO 64105-1439 E-mail: robert.langworthy@blackwoodlaw.com.

LANKOWSKY, ZENON P. lawyer; V.p., gen. counsel, sec. CVS Corp., Woonsocket, R.I. Office: CVS Corp One CVS Dr Woonsocket RI 02895*

LANNING, LINDA LEE, lawyer; b. Dearborn, Mo., Apr. 18, 1941; d. George DeWayne and Nannie Mae (Waller) Furbeck; m. Charles Thomas Lanning, July 15, 1961 (dec. Nov. 1986); children: Jeffrey M., Michael A. AA, Mo. Western Coll., St. Joseph, 1961; BS, S.D. State U., 1988; JD, U. Nebr., 1990. Bar: Mo. 1991, Nebr. 1991, Kans. 1992, U.S. Dist. Ct. (we. dist.) Mo. 1991, U.S. Dist. Ct. Nebr. 1991, U.S. Dist. Ct. Kans. 1992. Broker, owner Lanning Real Estate, Watertown, S.D., 1981-88; law clk. Knudsen Berkheimer, Lincoln, Nebr., 1991, Kenneth W. Schutt, Jr., P.C., Phoenix, 1991; atty. Mo. Dept. Revenue, Jefferson City, 1991—. Mem. Mo. Bar Assn., Nebr. Bar Assn., Kans. Bar Assn., Delta Theta Phi. Baptist. Avocations: running, swimming. Home: 109 Terra Bella Ct Jefferson City MO 65109-4973 Office: Dept of Revenue 301 W High St Jefferson City MO 65101-1580

LANS, DEBORAH EISNER, lawyer; b. N.Y.C., Oct. 26, 1949; d. Asher Bob and Barbara (Eisner) L. AB magna cum laude, Smith Coll., 1971; JD cum laude, Boston U., 1974. Bar: N.Y. 1975, U.S. Dist. Ct. (so. and ea. dists.) N.Y. 1975, U.S. Ct. Appeals (2d cir.) 1975, U.S. Supreme Ct. 1983. Assoc. Lans, Feinberg & Cohen, N.Y.C., 1975-80, ptnr., 1980-84, Morrison Cohen Singer & Weinstein, N.Y.C., 1984-2000; counsel Morrison Cohen Singer & Weinstein LLP, N.Y.C., 2000—01, Wasserman Grubin & Rogers LLP, 2001—. Exec. dir. Mentoring USA, 2000-02; mem. Supreme Ct. appellate divsn. first departl. disciplinary com., 2000-; b. dirs. St. Jean Baptiste Sch., Mark and Helene Eisner Found., Marie Christian Giordano Dance Co. Mem. ABA (bd. editors comml. banking litigation sects 1998-2000), Nat. Arbitration Forum (comml. panel arbitrators), Assn. Bar City N.Y. (chmn. young lawyers com. 1981-83, joint com. fee disputes, 1982, judiciary com. 1984-85, exec. com. 1985-89, spl. com. bioethical issues, 1992-94, coun. on judicial adminstrn. 1996—), N.Y. State Bar Assn. (ho. of dels. 1984-87, comml. & fed. litigation sect. com. on judiciary, alternative dispute resolution 1992—, environ. law sect. 1995—, family law sect., co-chair women in cts. com. 1994—), N.Y. Bar Found. Federal civil litigation, State civil litigation. Office: Wasserman Grubin & Rogers LLP 1700 Broadway New York NY 10019 E-mail: dlans@wgrlaw.com .

LANTZ, WILLIAM CHARLES, lawyer; b. Rochester, Minn., July 3, 1946; s. Charles E. and Doris (Greenwood) L.; m. Vickie L. Erickson, May 17, 1972; children: Charles Eric, Andrew William. BA, Hamline U., 1968; JD, U. Minn., 1971. Bar: Minn. 1971. From assoc. to ptnr. Dorsey & Whitney, Rochester, 1975—2002, of counsel, 2002—; inhouse counsel So. Minn. Mcpl. Power Agy., 2002—. Served to lt. JAGC, USNR, 1971-75. Mem. Minn. Bar Assn., Olmsted Bar Assn. Methodist. Commercial, contracts (including sales of goods; commercial financing), Landlord-tenant, Property, real (including real estate development, water). Home: 807 Sierra Ln NE Rochester MN 55906-4230 Office: Dorsey & Whitney LLP 807 Sierra Ln NE Rochester MN 55906 also: SMMPA 500 1st Ave SW Rochester MN 55902 E-mail: lantz.chuck@dorseylaw.com.

LAPIDUS, LAWRENCE SEARLE, lawyer; b. Brownsville, Pa., June 4, 1945; s. Herbert Maurice and Rose Florence (Friedlander) L.; m. Marilyn Lenore Naftalis, Aug. 20, 1972; children: Sivia, Michael. AB, George Washington U., 1967; JD, Am. U., 1970; LLM, Georgetown U., 1976. Bar: D.C. 1973, Pa. 1973, U.S. Dist. Ct. D.C. 1973, U.S. Ct. Appeals (D.C. cir.) 1973, U.S. Ct. Appeals (fed. cir.) 1982, U.S. Ct. Appeals (4th cir.) 1984, U.S. Dist. Ct. Md. 1986, Md. 1989. Ptnr. Law Offices L.S. Lapidus, 1975-81, Sherman & Lapidus, 1981-86, Chaikin & Karp, P.C., Washington and Rockville, Md., 1986-96, Karp, Frosh, Lapidus & Woodsky, Bethesda, Md., 1996—. Capt. USAF, 1970-74. ROTC scholar George Washington U., 1964. Mem.: ABA, Nat. Employment Lawyer's Assn., DC Trial Lawyers Assn. (bd. govs.), Assn. Trial Lawyers Am., DC Bar Assn. Democrat. Jewish. Commercial, contracts (including sales of goods; commercial financing), Labor (including EEOC, Fair Labor Standards Act, labor-management relations, NLRB, OSHA), Personal injury (including property damage). Home: 3707 Yuma St NW Washington DC 20016-2211 Office: Karp Frosh Lapidus Wigodsky & Norwind PA Ste 250 1133 Connecticut Ave NW Washington DC 20036-4307

LAPIN, ANDREW WILLIAM, lawyer; b. Chgo., Feb. 2, 1953; s. Robert Allan and Elaine (Muhlrad) L.; m. Debra Nan Goldberg, July 7, 1979; children: Lauren Elyse, Marisa Anne. BA, Ind. U., 1975; JD, John Marshall Law Sch., 1978. Bar: Ill. 1978, U.S. Dist. Ct. (no. dist.) Ill. 1978. Pvt. practice law, Chgo., 1978-79, 81-87; assoc. Tash & Slavitt, Ltd., Chgo., 1979-81; of counsel Siegan, Barbakoff & Gomberg, Chgo., 1987-89, Lapin & Assocs., Chgo., 1989-2000; ptnr. Much, Shelist, Freed, Denenberg, Ament & Rubenstein, P.C., Chgo., 2000—. Lectr. Nat. Assn. Govt. Guaranteed Lenders. Author: Closing and Funding the SBA Loan. Mem. Nat. Assn. Small Bus. Investment Cos., Chgo. Bar Assn. (real property com., real property fin. subcom.), Ill. Bar Assn., Chgo. Mortgage Attys. Assn. Commercial, contracts (including sales of goods; commercial financing), Franchising, Property, real (including real estate development, water). Office: Much Shelist Freed Denenberg Ament & Rubenstein 191 N Wacker Dr Ste 1800 Chicago IL 60606 E-mail: alapin@muchshelist.com.

LAPIN, HARVEY I. lawyer; b. St. Louis, Nov. 23, 1937; s. Lazarus L. and Lillie L.; m. Cheryl A. Lapin; children: Jeffrey, Gregg. BS, Northwestern U., 1960, JD, 1963. Bar: Ill. 1963, Fla. 1980, Wis. 1985; cert. tax lawyer, Fla.; CPA, Ill. Atty. Office Chief Counsel, IRS, Washington, 1963-65; trial atty. Office Regional Counsel, IRS, Washington, 1965-68; assoc., then ptnr. Fiffer & D'Angelo, Chgo., 1968-75; pres. Harvey I. Lapin, P.C., Chgo., 1975-83; mng. ptnr. Lapin, Hoff, Spangler & Greenberg, Chgo., 1983-88, Lapin, Hoff, Slaw & Laffey, Chgo., 1989-91; ptnr. Gottlieb and Schwartz, Chgo., 1992-93; prin. Harvey I. Lapin & Assocs., P.C., Northbrook, Ill., 1993—. Instr. John Marshall Law Sch., 1969—; facility adv. lawyers asst. program Roosevelt U., Chgo.; mem. cemetery adv. bd. Ill. Comptroller, 1974-96, 99—; mem. IRS Great Lakes TE/EO Coun., 2001—. Asst. editor Fed. Bar Jour., 1965-67; contbg. editor Cemetery and Funeral Service Business and Legal Guide; contbr. articles to profl. jours. Mem. ABA, Fla. Bar Assn., Wis. Bar Assn., Ill. Bar Assn., Chgo. Bar Assn., (mem. tax exempt orgns. subcom., sect. taxation 1988—). Jewish. Corporate, general, Corporate taxation. Office: Harvey I Lapin & Assocs PC PO Box 1327 Northbrook IL 60065-1327

LAPORTE, CLOYD, JR., lawyer, retired manufacturing executive; b. N.Y.C., June 8, 1925; s. Cloyd and Marguerite (Raeder) L.; m. Caroline E. Berry, Jan. 22, 1949; children— Elizabeth, Marguerite, Cloyd III. AB, Harvard U., 1946, JD, 1949. Bar: N.Y. 1949. Assoc. mem. firm Cravath, Swaine & Moore, N.Y.C., 1949-56; dir. adminstrn. Metals div. Olin Corp., N.Y.C., 1957-66; legal counsel Dover Corp., N.Y.C., 1966-93, sec., 1971-93. Dir. Putnam Hosp. Ctr., 2000—. 2d lt. A.C. AUS, WWII. Mem. Harvard Club (N.Y.C.). Home: Gipsy Trail Club Carmel NY 10512

LAPORTE, GERALD JOSEPH SYLVESTRE, lawyer; b. Windsor, Ont., Can., Oct. 16, 1946; came to U.S., 1948, naturalized, 1954; s. Rosaire Joseph and Catherine Rose (Sylvestre) L. BA, Sacred Heart Sem. Coll., 1968; STB, St. Paul U., Ottawa, Ont., 1971; BTh, U. Ottawa, 1971; MA, Georgetown U., 1974; JD, George Washington U., 1976. Bar: Mich. 1976, D.C. 1977. Legis. asst. to U.S. Congressman William J. Randall, Washington, 1971-75; law clk. to U.S. Dist. Judge, 1976-77; assoc. Wilmer, Cutler & Pickering, Washington, 1977-82; sr. spl. counsel Office Gen. Counsel, SEC, Washington, 1982-85, counsel to commr., 1985-87; assoc. Nutter, McClennen & Fish, Washington, 1987; assoc., then ptnr. Patton Boggs, LLP, Washington, 1988-96; counsel Hogan & Hartson LLP, Washington, 1996—2002; chief Office of Small Bus. Policy, SEC, Washington, 2002—. Chmn. steering com. sect. corp., fin. and securities law D.C. Bar, 1997-98; vice chmn. securities law & disclosure com., Nat. Assn. Bond lawyers, 1994-96. Mng. editor George Washington Law Rev., 1975-76. Mem. Arlington County Hist. Affairs and Landmark Rev. Bd., 2001—. Mem. ABA (sect. on bus. law, fed. regulation of securities com.), Arlington Hist. Soc. Inc. (bd. dirs. 1997—, pres. 2001-03). Democrat. Roman Catholic. Corporate, general, Securities, Finance. Home: 3154 Key Blvd Arlington VA 22201-5037 Office: SEC 450 5th St NW Washington DC 20549-0310 E-mail: g.laporte@verizon.net., LaporteG@SEC.gov.

LAPPAS, SPERO THOMAS, lawyer; b. Danbury, Conn., Oct. 20, 1952; s. Tom John and Alexandria (Manolakes) L.; m. Josephine Wahrendorf, Nov. 8, 1981 (div. 1986); 1 child, Thom Spero; m. Julie Marie Waugh, July 12, 1986 (div. 1995); 1 child, Alexandria Julia. BA cum laude, Allegheny Coll., Meadville, Pa., 1974; JD cum laude, Dickinson Sch. Law, Carlisle, Pa., 1977. Bar: Pa. 1977, U.S. Dist. Ct. (mid. dist.) Pa. 1977, U.S. Ct. Appeals (3rd cir.) 1980, U.S. Supreme Ct. 1991. Assoc. Law Office of Arthur Kusic, Harrisburg, Pa., 1977-79; atty. Kusic & Lappas, P.C., Harrisburg, 1979-84; pvt. practice Harrisburg, 1984-85; ptnr. Stefanon & Lappas, Harrisburg, 1985-88; prin. Law Offices Spero T. Lappas, Harrisburg, 1988—2002; ptnr. Serrifiscci, Schiffman, Brown & Calhoon P.C., Harrisburg, 2002—. Mem. ATLA, Pa. Bar Assn., Dauphin County Bar Assn., Pa. Assn. Criminal Def. Lawyers, Mensa, Am. Hellenic Ednl. and Progressive Assn. Civil rights, General civil litigation, Criminal. Office: 2080 Linglestown Rd Ste 201 Harrisburg PA 17110 E-mail: slappas@sstsc-law.com.

LAPPEN, CHESTER I. lawyer; b. Des Moines, May 4, 1919; s. Robert C. and Anna (Sideman) L.; m. Jon Tyroler Irmas, June 29, 1941; children— Jonathan Bailey, Timothy, Andrea L., Sally Morris. AB with highest honors in Econs, U. Calif., 1940; LL.B. magna cum laude (Faye diploma), Harvard, 1943. Bar: Calif. bar 1943. Practice in, Los Angeles, 1946—; sr. partner firm Mitchell, Silberberg & Knupp, 1949—; advisory bd. Bank Am., 1962-65; chmn. bd., dir. Zenith Nat. Ins. Corp., 1975-77. Bd. dirs. Arden Group, Inc. (chmn. exec. com. 1978), 1963-91, Data Products Corp. (chmn. fin. com.), 1965-93, City Nat. Bank Corp., 1967-92; trustee, pres. Citinat, Devel. Trust; bd. dirs., chmn. bd. Pacific Rim Holding Corp., 1987-94. Editor-in-chief: Harvard Law Rev, 1942-43. Chmn. bd. trustees Immaculate Heart Coll., 1981-88; trustee UCLA Found.; v.p., dir. Ctr. for Childhood. Served as spl. agt. CIA ,U.S. Army, 1943-46. Special agent, counter intelligence U.S. Army, 1943—46. Named to Artus Econs. Honor Soc., U. Calif., 1939. Mem. ABA, Los Angeles Bar Assn. (dir. 1953), Los Angeles Jr. Bar Assn. (pres. 1953), Beverly Hills (Calif.) Bar Assn., Harvard Law Sch. Alumni Assn. So. Calif. (pres. 1973-82). Republican. Office: Mitchell Silberberg & Knupp 11377 W Olympic Blvd Los Angeles CA 90064-1625

LAPPEN, TIMOTHY, lawyer, investor; b. L.A., Dec. 26, 1947; s. Chester Irwin and Jon Tyroler (Irmas) L.; children: Amy Elizabeth, Jay Robert, Tyler Lewis. AB, U. Calif., Berkeley, 1972; JD, UCLA, 1975. Bar: Calif. 1975, U.S. Dist. Ct. (no. dist.) Calif. 1975, U.S. Ct. Appeals (9th cir.) 1975. Assoc. Lillick, McHose & Charles, San Francisco, 1975-77; ptnr. Lappen & Lappen, L.A., 1977-84; of counsel Jeffer, Mangels, Butler & Marmaro, L.A., San Francisco, 1984—; pres., chmn. Family Office Practice Group Lappen Realty and Investment Corp., Santa Monica, Calif., 1987—. Sec. Dee Constrn. Co., L.A., 1968—, also bd. dirs. Exec. coms. D.A.R.E., 1992—95; founder, bd. dirs. chmn. Lawyers Against Hunger, 1994—; mem. bd. advisors Am. Acad. for Dance and Kindred Arts, 1995—99; bd. dirs., pres. Santa Monica Protective Assn., Calif., 1981—90, pres., 1991—93; bd. dirs. L.A. Regional Food Bank, 1988—95, pres., 1992—93; trustee Sch. Law UCLA, 1990—94, pres., 1992; mem. bd. dirs. Ctr. for Childhood, 1995—; mem. Chancellor's Assocs. UCLA, 1980—90; exec. coms. L.A. County D.A.'s Office, 1993—2001; former mem. Calif. Lexington Group, L.A. World Affairs Coun. Mem. ABA, Calif. Bar Assn., L.A. County Bar Assn., Century City Bar Assn. Office: Jeffer Mangels Butler & Marmaro 1900 Ave of the Stars 7th Fl Los Angeles CA 90067-4308

LAPPING, RICHARD A. lawyer; b. San Diego, Nov. 5, 1951; s. Alvin W. and Anna M. Lapping; m. Carolyn L. Wright, Aug. 23, 1980; children: Erin H., Zachary T., Hilary C. BA, U. Calif., San Diego, 1979; JD, U. Calif., San Francisco, 1982. Bar: Supreme Ct. Calif. 1982, U.S. Dist. Ct. (no. dist.) Calif. 1982, U.S. Ct. Appeals (9th cir.) 1984, U.S. Dist. Ct. (ea. dist.) Calif. 1990, U.S. Dist. Ct. (so. dist.) Calif. 1993, U.S. Dist. Ct. (ctrl. dist.) Calif. 1995. Assoc. Thelen, Marrin, Johnson & Bridges, San Francisco, 1982—89; ptnr. Thelen Reid & Priest LLP, San Francisco, 1990—. Contbr. articles to profl. jours. Sponsoring ptnr. Lawyers Com. for Civil Rights of the San Francisco Bay Area, 1990—2000. Specialist 5 U.S. Army, 1972—75. Decorated Army Commendation medal U.S. Army. Mem.: ABA (bus. bankruptcy com. sect. bus. law 1990—), Am. Bankruptcy Inst. (program faculty 2001—). Avocations: golf, travel. Bankruptcy, General civil litigation, Corporate, general. Office: Thelen Reid & Priest LLP 101 Second St San Francisco CA 94105-3606 Office Fax: 415-369-8678. Personal E-mail: rlapping@thelenreid.com. E-mail: rlapping@thelenreid.com.

LAREAU, RICHARD GEORGE, lawyer; b. Woonsocket, R.I., June 11, 1928; s. Hector R. and Agnes P. (Valley) L.; m. Thelma Johnson, Aug. 11, 1970; 1 son, Alan Hartland; 1 son by previous marriage, William Wheeler Mohn. BA, St. Michael's Coll., Winooski Park, Vt., 1949; JD, U. Minn., 1952. Bar: Minn. 1952. Ptnr. Oppenheimer, Wolff & Donnelly, St. Paul, Mpls., 1956—. Bd. dirs. Ceridan, Bloomington, Minn., Nash Finch Co., Mpls., Merrill Corp., St.Paul, No. Techs. Internat. Corp., Lino Lakes; trustee Mesabi Trust, N.Y.C.; sec. AVECOR Cardiovascular Inc., Plymouth, Minn. Sec., bd. dir. Minn. Cooperation Office for Small Bus. and Job Creation, Mpls.; bd. dirs. Minn. Project on Corp. Responsibility, Mpls. 1st lt. USAF, 1952-56. Mem. ABA, Minn. Bar Assn., Hennepin County Bar Assn., Mpls. Club. Avocation: fishing. Home: 20750 Linwood Rd Excelsior

MN 55331-9386 Office: Oppenheimer Wolff & Donnelly LLP 3400 Plz VII 45 S 7th St Ste 3400 Minneapolis MN 55402-1609

LARIMORE, TOM L. lawyer; b. Ft. Worth, Sept. 21, 1937; s. T.R. and Mildred Elizabeth (Angell) L.; m. Bobbie Jeanne Wingo, Dec. 20, 1999; children: Thomas Lee, Robert Karl, Susan Lynne, Natalie Jeanne. BA, Washington and Lee U., 1959; LLB, So. Meth. U., 1962. Bar: Tex. 1962, U.S. Dist. Ct. (no. dist.) Tex. 1965, U.S. Dist. Ct. (so. dist.) Tex. 1975, U.S. Ct. Appeals (5th cir.) 1977. Assoc. Walker & Bishop, Ft. Worth, 1962-66; ptnr. Walker, Bishop & Larimore, Ft. Worth, 1966-73, Bishop, Larimore, Lamsens & Brown, Ft. Worth, 1973-79; v.p., gen. counsel, sec. Western Co. of N.Am., Ft. Worth, 1979-80, v.p. law and adminstrn., sec., 1980-86; ptnr. Whitaker, Chalk, Swindle & Sawyer, LLP, Ft. Worth. Pres., bd. dirs. YMCA (West), Ft. Worth, 1966-68; sr. warden, vestryman All Saints Episcopal Ch., Ft. Worth, 1973-74, named Churchman of Yr., 1969; pres., bd. dirs. Sr. Citizens Ctrs., Ft. Worth, 1974-78. Fellow Tex. Bar Found.; mem. ABA, Tarrant County Bar Assn. (bd. dirs. 1978-80), Am. Corp. Counsel Ass.n, Ft. Worth Bar Assn. (chmn. dist. admissions com. 1975-77), Ft. Worth C. of C. (bd. dirs. 1985—, chmn. West area coun. 1985-86), Tex. Rsch. League (bd. dirs. 1980-86), Shady Oaks Country Club (Ft. Worth), Rotary (pres., bd. dirs. West Ft. Worth 1974-75, Paul Harris fellow 1982). Federal civil litigation, State civil litigation, Corporate, general. Home: 11 Lombardy Terr Fort Worth TX 76132 Office: Whitaker Chalk Swindle & Sawyer LLP 301 Commerce St Ste 3500 Fort Worth TX 76102-4186

LARIO, FRANK M., JR., lawyer, judge; b. Phila., July 1, 1937; s. Frank M. and Marie Ann (Mandarino) L.; m. Kathleen A. Cowan, July 1, 1961; children: Michael James, Kathleen Marie, Frank M. III. AB cum laude, Georgetown U., 1959; postgrad., Harvard U., 1959; JD cum laude, Rutgers U., 1962. Bar: N.J. 1962, U.S. Dist. Ct. N.J. 1963, U.S. Ct. Appeals (3d cir.) 1978, U.S. Supreme Ct. 1969. Law sec. to assoc. justice Vincent S. Haneman N.J. Supreme Ct., 1962-63; ptnr. Lario, Nardi & Gleaner, Haddonfield, N.J., 1973-93; mcpl. judge Borough of Magnolia, N.J., 1969-93, Borough of Audubon Park, N.J., 1970-93, Borough of Woodlynne, N.J., 1971-76, Borough of Bellmawr, N.J., 1976-93; superior ct. judge State of N.J., 1993—. Instr. estate planning Inst. Continuing Legal Edn., 1962-69, instr. legal ethics, 1973-78; com. on mcpl. cts. N.J. Supreme Ct., 1980-92, com. on character, 1983-92; bd. govs. Georgetown U., 1978-81, alumni senate, 1981—. Mem. editl. bd. Rutgers Law Rev., 1961-62. Mem. ABA, N.J. Bar Assn. (chmn. mcpl. cts. of N.J. com. 1978-81), Camden County Bar Assn. (bd. mgrs. 1973-76, chmn. immigration and naturalization com. 1974-83, long range planning com. 1976-78, sec. 1979-80, treas. 1980-81, v.p. 1982-83, pres. 1984-85), Camden County Mcpl. Judges Conf. (sec. 1975, pres. 1976-77), Rutgers U. Law Sch. Alumni Assn. (chmn. scholarship com. 1971-82), Rutgers U. Law Sch. Alumni Assn. South Jersey (chancellor 1968-69, bd. mgrs. 1970-82), Georgetown U. Alumni Assn. (gov. 1976—), Men of Malvern (assoc. capt. 1968—), Vesper Club (Phila.), Tavistock Country Club (Haddonfield), Union League of Phila., KC, Georgetown U. Alumni South Jersey (pres. 1970-72). Corporate, general, General practice, Probate (including wills, trusts). Office: Hall of Justice 101 S Fifth St Camden NJ 08103-4001

LARKIN, DAVID JOSEPH, lawyer; b. Oakland, Calif., July 7, 1949; s. Robert J. and Emily S. (Arnold) L.; m. Patricia Cirigliano, July 17, 1976; children: David Joseph, Thomas Francis. BA in English, Calif. State U., Chico, 1972; JD, John F. Kennedy U., 1980. Bar: Calif., U.S. Ct. Appeals (9th cir.). Owner, founder Law Offices David Larkin, Walnut Creek, Calif., 1980—. With USMC, 1970-72. Mem. Calif. Trial Lawyers Assn., Calif. Attys. for Criminal Justice, Calif. Pub. Defenders Assn., Alameda Contra-Costa County Trial Lawyers Assn. Democrat. Roman Catholic. Criminal, Personal injury (including property damage). Office: 1806 Bonanza St Walnut Creek CA 94596-4318

LARKIN, LEE ROY, retired lawyer; b. Oklahoma City, Aug. 11, 1928; s. William Patrick and Agnes (Matthis) L.; m. Mary Jane Langston, Apr. 17, 1965; children— James William, John Patrick (dec.). BS, Oklahoma A&M U., Stillwater, 1950; MA, Vanderbilt U., 1952; LLB, William Mitchell U., St. Paul, 1959. Bar: Minn. 1959, Tex. 1963, D.C. 1963. Economist U.S. Dept. Agr., Washington, 1953; economist, lawyer Pillsbury, Mpls., 1953-62; ptnr. Harris & Larkin, Houston, 1963-65; sr. ptnr. Andrews & Kurth, Houston, 1966-93; retired, 1994. Speaker Continuing Legal Edn. Officer Sharpstown Civic Assn., Houston, 1966-94; elder St. Philip Presbyn. Ch., Houston; moderator Presbytery of New Covenant, Houston, 1980. Served to capt. USAR, 1951-58. Fellow Tex. Bar Found., Houston Bar Found.; mem. ABA, State Bar Tex., Houston Bar Assn., Riverbend Country Club, Rotary (pres. 1978-79), Delta Theta Phi. Avocations: golf, tennis, travel. General civil litigation, Patent, Trademark and copyright. Home: 3725 Wickersham Ln Houston TX 77027-4013

LARKY, SHELDON GLEN, lawyer; b. Detroit, Sept. 16, 1941; s. Irving and Lucille C. (Ziegler) L.; m. Barbara T., Apr. 25, 1965; children: Adam, Howard. BA, U. Mich., 1964; postgrad. Wayne State U., 1964-65; JD, U. Detroit, 1970. Bar: Mich. 1970, U.S. Dist. Ct. (ea. dist.) Mich. 1970, U.S. Ct. Apls. (6th cir.) 1972. Claims adjuster Liberty Mut. Ins. Co., Chgo., Detroit, 1962-64; personnel dir. ITT Continental Baking Co., Detroit, 1964-69; law clk. to judge 6th Jud. Cir. Ct. Mich., Pontiac, 1969-70; ptnr. Leib & Leib, Southfield, Mich., 1970-76; v.p. Hiller, Larky, Hoekenga & Amberg, P.C., Southfield, 1976-87, sole practice law, 1987—. Lic. soccer referee, bd. dirs. Royal Oak Youth Soccer Assn. 1985-88, v.p. 1988; dir. Southeast Oakland Cmty. Credit Union. Contbr. articles over 100 to profl. jours. Mem. ABA, Mich. Bar Assn. (chmn. com. on character and fitness 1980-82, com. on plain English 1981-83, sec. profl. liability ins. com. 1985-91, profl. devel. task force com. 1985—), Oakland County Bar Assn. (dir. 1974-84, pres. 1983-84, editor Laches 1974-82, chmn. law office mgmt. and econs. com. 1986-87, editor Chpt. Leaders 1992—), Soccer Referees Assn. (pres.). General practice, Legal malpractice, Alternative dispute resolution, Family and matrimonial, Professional liability. Office: 30600 Telegraph Rd Ste 3350 Bingham Farms MI 48025-4533

LARO, DAVID, judge; b. Flint, Mich., Mar. 3, 1942; s. Samuel and Florence (Chereton) L.; m. Nancy Lynn Wolf, June 18, 1967; children: Rachel Lynn, Marlene Ellen. BA, U. Mich., 1964; JD, U. Ill., 1967; LLM, NYU, 1970 Bar: Mich. 1968, U.S. Dist. Ct. (ea. dist.) Mich. 1968, U.S. Tax Ct. 1971. Ptnr. Winegarden Booth Shedd and Laro, Flint, Mich., 1970-75; sr. ptnr. Laro and Borgerson, Flint, 1975-86; prin. David Laro, P.C., Flint, 1986-92; apptd. judge U.S. Tax Ct., Washington, 1992—. Of counsel Dykema Gossett, Ann Arbor, Mich., 1989-90; pres., CEO, Durakon Industries, Inc., Ann Arbor, 1989-91, chmn., Lapeer, Mich., 1991—; chmn. Republic Bank, 1986—, vice chmn. Republic Bancorp, Inc., Flint, 1986—; instr. Nat. Inst. Trial Advocacy, vis. prof. U. San Diego Law Sch., adj. prof. law Georgetown Law Sch., 1994—; cons. lectr. on tax reform and litigation in Moscow Harvard U., 1997, Ga. State U., 1998. Regent U. Mich., Ann Arbor, 1975-81; mem. Mich. State Bd. Edn., 1982-83; chmn. Mich. State Tenure Commn., 1972-75; commr. Civil Svc. Commn., Flint, 1984—. Mem. Am. Coll. Tax Counsel, State Bar Mich., Phi Delta Phi. Republican. Office: US Tax Ct 400 2nd St NW Rm 217 Washington DC 20217-0002

LA ROCCA, PHILLIP R. lawyer, educator; b. Newark, Sept. 25, 1934; s. Raymond O. La Rocca and Susan Kauchek; m. Teresa Louise Garcia, Aug. 11; children: Lisa, Dominic. JD, Southwestern U. Law, L.A., 1965. Assoc. prof. law Chapman U., Palm Desert, 1988—; legal liaison to Azerbaijan ABA, 1999—2000. With USN, 1951—55, Europe. Named Judge of Yr., Riverside County Bar Assn., 1978, Inland Empire Bar Assn., 1978, Desert Bar Assn., Coachella Valley, Calif., 1980—81. Avocations: reading, golf. Criminal. Office: 44489 Town Center Way Palm Desert CA 92260 Office Fax: 760-776-1587 . E-mail: judgel@aol.com.

LAROSA, JOSEPH J. lawyer; b. Bklyn., June 15, 1958; BA in Psychology magna cum laude, NYU, 1980, JD, 1983. Bar: N.Y. 1984. V.p., sec., assoc. gen. counsel Schering-Plough Corp., Kenilworth, NJ, 1984—. Mem.: ABA, N.Y. State Bar Assn., Assn. of Bar of City of N.Y. Commercial, contracts (including sales of goods; commercial financing), Corporate taxation, Securities. Office: Schering-Plough Corp 2000 Galloping Hill Rd Kenilworth NJ 07033-0530

LAROSE, LAWRENCE ALFRED, lawyer; b. Lowell, Mass., Oct. 26, 1958; s. Alfred M. and Rita B. (Plunkett) L.; m. Janet G. Yedwab, Aug. 12, 1984. BA summa cum laude, Tufts U., 1980; JD magna cum laude, Georgetown U., 1983. Bar: N.Y. 1984. Assoc. Sullivan & Cromwell, N.Y.C., 1983-85, 87-90, Melbourne, Australia, 1985-87, Cadwalader, Wickersham & Taft, N.Y.C., 1990-92, ptnr., 1993-2001, King & Spalding, N.Y.C., 2001—. Vis. fellow Faculty of Law, U. Melbourne, 1986-87. Co-author: Public Companies, 2002; contbr. articles to profl. publs. Mem. ABA, N.Y. State Bar Assn., N.Y. County Lawyers Assn., Assn. Bar City N.Y., Am. Soc. Internat. Law, Georgetown U. Nat. Law Alumni Bd. (exec. com., sec.), Down Town Assn. in City of N.Y., Phi Beta Kappa. Avocations: art collecting, art history. Corporate, general, Private international, Mergers and acquisitions. Office: King & Spalding 1185 Ave of the Americas New York NY 10036-4003

LARRY, R. HEATH, lawyer, director; b. Huntingdon, Pa., Feb. 24, 1914; s. Ralph E. and Mabel (Heath) L.; m. Eleanor Ketler, Sept. 10, 1938; children: David Heath, Dennis Ketler, Thomas Richard. AB, Grove City Coll., 1934, LL.D., 1964; JD, U. Pitts., 1937. Bar: Pa. 1937, D.C. 1937. Pvt. practice, 1937-38; atty. Nat. Tube Co., 1938-44, sec., dir., 1944-48; gen. atty. U.S. Steel Corp., Pitts., 1948-52, asst. gen. solicitor, 1952-58, adminstrv. v.p. labor relations, 1958-66, exec. v.p., asst. to chmn., 1966-69, vice chmn. bd., 1969-77; pres. N.A.M., 1977-80; of counsel Reed Smith Shaw & McClay, Washington, 1980—. Dir. emeritus Textron, Inc. Trustee emeritus Grove City Coll.; former trustee Conf. Bd. Mem. Am. Iron and Steel Inst. Clubs: Met. (Washington); Economic (N.Y.C.); Gulf Stream Golf, Delray Beach Yacht, Gulf Stream Bath and Tennis, Little. Presbyterian. Home: 4333 N Ocean Blvd Apt A53 Delray Beach FL 33483-7559

LARSON, BRYAN A. lawyer; s. Byron Ancedus and Betty Marilyn Larson; m. Kathy Stevenett; children: Aaron, Adam, Conor, Kaden, Sara, Aubrey. BA, Brigham Young U., 1980, JD, 1983. Bar: Utah 1983. Assoc. Christensen, Jensen & Powell, Salt Lake City, 1983-86, McKay, Burton & Thurman, Salt Lake City, 1986-91; ptnr. Larson, Jenkins & Halliday, Salt Lake City, 1991-95, Larson, Kirkham & Turner, Salt Lake City, 1995-99, Larson, Turner, Fairbanks and Dalby, Salt Lake City, 1999—. Editor: Backtalk Newsletter, 1995—, Utah Auto Body Watch Dawg, 2002—. Mem. ATLA (mem. polit. action com. 1991—), Utah Bar Assn. (com. chmn. 1990-92), Utah Trial Lawyers Assn. (plaintiffs exhange, spkrs. bur., bd. govs.), Plaintiffs' Exchange, Spkrs. Bur., Order of Barristers. Mem. Lds Ch. Avocations: boating, snow skiing. Insurance, Personal injury (including property damage). Office: Larson Turner Fairbanks & Dalby 1218 W South Jordan Pkwy Ste B South Jordan UT 84095

LARSON, CHARLES W. prosecutor; Grad., Kans. State U., U. Iowa Sch. Law. Magistrate Iowa 5th Judicial Ct., 1973; commr. Iowa Dept. Public Safety, 1973—79; mgr. law enforcement Sanders and Assocs., Kingdom of Saudi Arabia, 1979—82; ptnr. Walker, Larson and Billingsley, Newton, Iowa, 1982—86; U.S. atty. No. Dist of Iowa, Cedar Rapids, 1986—93, No. Dist. of Iowa, Cedar Rapids, 2001—; dir. Iowa Office Drug Control, 1993—98; chmn. Iowa Bd. Parole, 1998—2001. Office: PO Box 74950 Cedar Rapids IA 52407-4950

LARSON, EDWARD, state supreme court justice; m. Mary Loretta Thompson; children: Sarah, John, Mary Elizabeth. BS, Kans. State U., 1954; JD, Kans. U., 1960. Pvt. practice, Hays, Kans., 1960—87; judge Kans. Ct. Appeals, 1987—95; justice Kans. Supreme Ct., Topeka, 1995—2003; ret., 2003. Mcpl. judge City of Hays, 1965—72. 2nd lt. USAF. Home: 2761 SW Plass Ave Topeka KS 66611

LARSON, JERRY LEROY, state supreme court justice; b. Harlan, Iowa, May 17, 1936; s. Gerald L. and Mary Eleanor (Patterson) L.; m. Debra L. Christensen; children: Rebecca, Jeffrey, Susan, David. BA, State U. Iowa, 1958, JD, 1960. Bar: Iowa. Partner firm Larson & Larson, 1961-75; dist. judge 4th Jud. Dist. Ct. of Iowa, 1975-78; justice Iowa Supreme Ct., 1978—. Office: Supreme Ct Iowa PO Box 109 Des Moines IA 50319-0001

LARSON, JOHN WILLIAM, lawyer; b. Detroit, June 24, 1935; s. William and Sara Eleanor (Yeatman) L.; m. Pamela Jane Wren, Sept. 16, 1959; 1 dau., Jennifer Wren. BA with distinction, honors in Economics, Stanford, 1957; LLB, Stanford U., 1962. Bar: Calif. 1962. Assoc. Brobeck, Phleger & Harrison, San Francisco, 1962-68, ptnr., 1968—71, 1973—2003, CEO, 1988—96; asst. sec. Dept. Interior, Washington, 1971-73; exec. dir. Natural Resources Com., Washington, 1973; counsellor to chmn. Cost of Living Coun., Washington, 1973; ptnr. Morgan, Lewis & Backius LLP, 2003—. Faculty Practising Law Inst.; bd. dirs. Sangamo Bio Scis., Inc. Mem. 1st U.S.-USSR Joint Com. on Environment; mem. bd. visitors Stanford U. Law Sch., 1974-77, 85-87, 95-96; pres. bd. trustees The Katherine Branson Sch., 1980-83. With AUS, 1957-59. Mem. ABA, Calif. Bar Assn., San Francisco C. of C. (bd. dirs., chmn. 1996), Bay Area Coun., Calif. Acad. Sci., Order of Coif, Pacific Union Club, Burlingame Country Club, Bohemian Club, Lagunitas Country Club. Corporate, general, Mergers and acquisitions, Securities. Home: PO Box 349 Ross CA 94957-0349 Office: Brobeck Phleger & Harrison Spear St Tower 1 Market Plz San Francisco CA 94105-1420

LARSON, MARK EDWARD, JR., lawyer, educator, financial advisor; b. Oak Park, Ill., Dec. 16, 1947; s. Mark Edward and Lois Vivian (Benson) L.; m. Patricia Jo Jekerle, Apr. 14, 1973; children: Adam Douglas, Peter Joseph, Alex Edward, Gretchen Elizabeth. BS in Acctg., U. Ill., 1969; JD, Northwestern U., 1972; LLM in Taxation, NYU, 1977. Bar: Ill. 1973, N.Y. 1975, D.C. 1976, Minn, 1982, Tex. 1984, U.S. Dist. Ct. (no. dist.) Ill. 1973, U.S. Dist. Ct. (so. dist.) N.Y. 1975, U.S. Ct. Appeals (2d cir.) 1975, U.S. Ct. Appeals (7th cir.) 1976, U.S. Dist. Ct. D.C. 1977, U.S. Ct. Appeals (D.C. cir.) 1977, U.S. Dist. Ct. Minn. 1982, U.S. Ct. Appeals (8th cir.) 1982, U.S. Tax Ct. 1976, U.S. Supreme Ct. 1976; CPA, Ill. Acct. Deloitte & Touche (formerly Haskins & Sells), N.Y.C., 1973—76, Chgo., 1978—81; atty., ptnr. Larson, Perry & Ward, P.C. and former firms, Chgo., 1983—; prin. Winfield Fin. Svcs. and affiliates, Houston, Austin and Chgo., 1986—. Adj. faculty U. Minn., Mpls., 1982-83, Aurora (Ill.) U., 1990-98, St. Xavier U., Chgo., 2000—; exec. dir. UFG Inst. for Profl. Edn., 1996—; dir. Rush-Wood Imaging Ptnrs., Ltd., 1993-. Contbr. articles to profl. jours. Mem. ABA, AICPA, AHLA, Am. Assn. Atty.-CPAs, Acad. Fin. Svcs., Am. Acctg. Assn. Private international, Securities, Corporate taxation. Office: 1212 S Naper Blvd Ste 119-131 Naperville IL 60540-7349 E-mail: larsgen@usa.net.

LARSON, OLIVE ELIZABETH, lawyer; b. Newark, N.J., Jan. 24, 1955; s. Joseph N. and Barbara W. (Paterson) L.; m. Jeffrey S. Larson, Sept. 14, 1991; 1 child, Allegra J. AB cum laude, Boston Coll., 1976; MS in Taxation, Bentley Coll., 1982; JD cum laude, Suffolk U., 1988. Bar: Mass. 1988, U.S. Tax Ct. 1989, U.S. Dist. Ct. Mass. 1989. Tax mgr. Gen. Cinema Corp., Chestnut Hill, Mass., 1977-84, Barry Wright Corp., Newton, Mass., 1984-86; sr. tax. cons. Digital Equipment Corp., Acton, Mass., 1986-88; prin. Olive E. Larson, Boston, 1988-96, Friedman & Atherton, Boston, 1996—. Cons. in field. Mem. Boston Bar Assn. Avocations: photography, music, art. Entertainment, Family and matrimonial, Taxation, general. Home: 25 Way To The River Rd West Newbury MA 01985-1217 Office: The New Law Ctr LLC 99 Summer St Boston MA 02109-2807

LARSON, PAUL MARTIN, lawyer; b. Tacoma, June 8, 1949; s. Charles Philip and Margeret (Kobervig) L.; m. Kristina Simonson, June 19, 1971; children: Kristin Ilene, Paul Philip, Erika Louise. AB, Stanford U., 1971; JD, Gonzaga U., 1974. Bar: Wash. 1975, U.S. Dist. Ct. (we. dist.) Wash. 1975, U.S. Dist. Ct. (ea. dist.) Wash. 1978, U.S. Ct. Appeals (9th cir.) 1981. Assoc. Hoff & Cross, Tacoma, 1975-76; ptnr., prin. Brooks & Larson, P.S., Yakima, Wash., 1976-87; ptnr. Bogle & Gates, Yakima, 1987-93, Larson & Perkins, 1994—. Author: (with others) Commercial Law Deskbook, 1981. Pres. Cardio & Pulmonary Inst., Yakima, 1981; bd. dirs. Yakima YMCA, 1981-98, pres.-elect bd. dirs. 2000, pres., 2001-2003; bd. dirs. Yakima Youth Commn., 1989-93, Yakima Valley chpt. ARC, 1990-93; bd. dirs. Sisters of Providence Med. Ctr.-Yakima Found., 1986-96, pres., 1992-93, Area Svc. bd. mem., 2000—; bd. dirs. Yakima Schs. Found., 1993-2000, pres., 2000; bd. dirs. EPIC, 2003-. Fellow ABA (standing com. lawyer's responsibility for client protection 1984-89); mem. Wash. State Bar Assn. (spl. dist. counsel, 1985-96, pres. corp. bus. and banking sect. 1987-88, chmn. unauthorized practice of law task force 1995-96), Yakima Estate Planning Coun. (pres. 1981), Rotary. Avocations: tennis, fishing. Commercial, contracts (including sales of goods; commercial financing), Estate planning, Property, real (including real estate development, water). Office: Larson & Perkins PO Box 550 Yakima WA 98907-0550 E-mail: paul@lplaw.com.

LARUE, PAUL HUBERT, retired lawyer; b. Somerville, Mass., Nov. 16, 1922; s. Lucien H. and Germaine (Choquet) LaR.; m. Helen Finnegan, July 20, 1946; children: Paul Hubert, Patricia Seward, Mary Hogan. PhB, U. Wis., 1947, JD, 1949. Bar: Ill. 1955, Wis. 1949, U.S. Supreme Ct. 1972. Grad. asst. instr. public sci. dept. U. Wis., 1947-48; mem. staff Wis. Atty. Gen., 1949-50; trial atty., legal advisor to commr. FTC, 1950-55; pvt. practice Chgo.; mem. Chadwell & Kayser, Ltd., 1958-90; ptnr. Vedder, Price, Kaufman & Kammholz, 1990-93; of counsel, 1993-99; ret., 1999. Spkr. profl. meetings; mem. Com. Modern Cts. in Ill., 1964; mem. Com. for Constl. Conv. Ill., 1968, Better Govt. Assn., 1966-70 Contbr. articles to profl. jours. Mem. lawyers com. Met. Crusade of Mercy, 1967-68, United Settlement Appeal, 1966-68; apptd. pub. mem. Ill. Conflict of Interest Laws Commn., 1965-67. With AUS, 1943-45, ETO; capt. JAGC, USAFR, 1950-55. Fellow Ill. Bar Found. (life); mem. ABA (mem. coun. sect. antitrust law 1980-83, chmn. Robinson-Patman Act com. 1975-78), Ill. State Bar Assn., Chgo. Bar Assn. (chmn. antitrust com. 1970-71), Wis. State Bar, Rotary. Roman Catholic. Antitrust, Alternative dispute resolution, Federal civil litigation. Home: 250 Cuttriss Pl Park Ridge IL 60068 E-mail: phlarue@aol.com.

LARZELERE, KATHY LYNN HECKLER, paralegal; b. Sellersville, Pa., Dec. 4, 1955; d. Harold Tyson and Hannah Ruth (Wile) Heckler; m. Lawrence Sollanek, Nov. 1984 (div.); m. Loel Harry Larzelere, Aug. 27, 1992; 1 stepdaughter, Lindsie M. AAS magna cum laude, Columbus State C.C., 1991. From sales person to dept. mgr. Macy's New York, North Wales, Pa., 1977-83; store mgr. Bathtique, Wilmington, Del., Towson, Md., 1983-86; customer svc. person Marshall Fields, Chgo., 1987; word processor Franklin County Children Svcs., Columbus, Ohio, 1988-89; legal sec., paralegal M. Cohen and Assocs., Columbus, 1989-94; paralegal Calig and Handelman LPA, Columbus, 1994-97, Weltman, Weinberg & Reis, Columbus, 1997—. Author: (poetry) American High School Poets, 1973. Ward coord. Amelia Salerno for City Coun., Columbus, 1993; co-chmn. Columbus Christmas in Apr. Home Amb. Com., Columbus Christmas in Apr. Materials and In-Kind Donations Com.; vol. Ohio Bicentennial Commn. Mem. award Phi Theta Kappa. Mem. Paralegal Assn. Cen. Ohio (writer newsletter The Citator, co-chair student outreach com. 1994-95, chair 1995-97, 1st v.p. 1995-97, 2000-2001, pres. 1997-99, mem. adv. bd. 1999-2000, chair student outreach com. 1999-2000), Columbus Bar Assn. (assoc.). Lutheran. Avocations: handcrafts, reading, walking, watercolor painting, counted cross-stitch. Home: 2119 Kingsglen Dr Grove City OH 43123-1252 Office: Weltman Weinberg & Reis 175 S 3rd St Ste 900 Columbus OH 43215-5177 E-mail: klarzele@columbus.rr.com., klarzelere@weltman.com.

LASA-FERRER, ARMANDO, lawyer; BA, U. Miami, 1962; JD, Interamerican U., 1966. Bar: P.R. Sr. ptnr. Lasa Monroig & Veve, Guaynabo, PR. Mem. sub-com. on universal svc. com. Assn. Competitive Providers Telecom.; mem. task force in charge of drafing the P.R. telecom. act of 1996 P.R. Ho. Reps.; prof. Interamerican U. Sch. Law, PR; mem. Gov. P.R. Task Force on Health Care Reform; gen. counsel Rep. Nat. Hispanic Assembly. Nat. advisor New Majority Coun., Rep. Nat. Com. Mem.: ABA (bd. govs. 18th dist. 2001—, chair and mem. numerous coms.). Office: Lasa Monroig & Veve Buchanan Office Ctr 40 Road 165 Ste 304 Guaynabo PR 00968*

LASCHER, ALAN ALFRED, lawyer; b. N.Y.C., Dec. 8, 1941; s. Morris Julius and Sadie Lillian (Chassen) L.; m. C. Amy Weingarten, July 12, 1969; children: David, Lauren, Alexandra, Carlyn. BS, Union Coll., 1963; LLB, Bklyn. Law Sch., 1967. Bar: N.Y. 1967. Assoc. Kramer, Leven et al, N.Y.C., 1969-75; ptnr. real estate dept. Weil, Gotshal & Manges, N.Y.C., 1975—. Mem. law com. N.Y. Real Estate Bd., N.Y.C., 1981—; bd. advisors Chgo. Title Ins. Co., 1995—; Leasing Com. Am. Coll. Real Estate Lawyers 2002-. Served to sgt. USAF, 1968-69. Named Real Estate Lawyer of Yr. Am. Lawyer, 1982. Mem. Am. Coll. Real Estate Lawyers (mem. Resolution Trust Corp. and Bankruptcy coms.). Property, real (including real estate development, water). Office: Weil Gotshal & Manges 767 5th Ave Fl Concl New York NY 10153-0119

LASH, DOUGLAS STEVEN, lawyer; b. Council Bluffs, Iowa, July 15, 1948; s. Donald Robert and Frances (Marshall) L.; m. Susan Marie Thompson, July 23, 1983; children: Rebecca, Sarah, Laura. Student, Lawrence U., 1966-67, Dana Coll., 1967-70; JD, Creighton U., 1973. Bar: Iowa 1973, U.S. Dist. Ct. (so. dist.) Iowa 1973, U.S. Dist. Ct. Nebr. 1978, U.S. Ct. Claims 1979, Nebr. 1987. Assoc. Porter, Heithoff, Pratt & Reilly, Council Bluffs, 1973-76; ptnr. Porter, Lash & Tauke, Council Bluffs, 1976-82; v.p., gen. counsel Knudson, Inc., Council Bluffs, 1982-85; sole practice Council Bluffs, 1985-87, Omaha, 1987-90; counsel Brown & Brown, P.C., Omaha, 1990—. Pres. CRE, Inc. (constrn. industry cons.), 1987—. Chmn., bd. dirs. Chem. Dependency Agy., Council Bluffs, 1975-78; chmn. City of Council Bluffs Hist. Commn., 1979-82; bd. dirs. County Hist. Soc., Council Bluffs, 1986-87. Mem. ABA (forum com. on construction), Iowa Bar Assn., Nebr. Bar Assn. Avocations: golf, gardening, racquetball. Construction, Corporate, general, Property, real (including real estate development, water). Office: PO Box 40 501 Scoular Bldg 2027 Dodge St Omaha NE 68101-0040 E-mail: dslash@bblaw.us.

LASH, WILLIAM HENRY, III, federal agency administrator, law educator, lawyer; b. Jersey City, Jan. 21, 1961; s. William H. Jr. and Vivian G. Lash; m. Sharon K. Zackula, Dec. 31, 1992; 1 child, William H. IV. BA, Yale U., 1982; JD, Harvard U., 1985. Bar: N.J. 1986, Washington 1988. Law clk. Justice Alan B. Handler, Trenton, N.J., 1985-86; assoc. Fried, Frank, Harris et al, Washington, 1986-88, 88-89; counsel to chmn. U.S. Internat. Trade Commn., Washington, 1988; asst. prof. law Western New Eng. Coll., Springfield, Mass., 1989-90, St. Louis U., 1990-93; prof. law George Mason U., Arlington, Va., 1993—; asst. sec. commerce Dept. Commerce, Washington, 2001—. U.S. econ. commr. Orgn. for Security and Cooperation in Europe, 2001—; dir. Nostalgia TV Network, Washington, 1993-98, Carlton Maritime Fund; mem. adv. bd. World TV Program, Washington, 1998; disting. sr. fellow Ctr. for Study of Am. Bus., St. Louis, 1993—; bd. dirs. Virtual Credit Svcs.; adj. fellow Citizens for a Sound Economy, 2000—01. Author: Regulating Securities, 1996, International Trade Law, 1998. Bd. dirs., treas. Internat. Law Students Assn., 1996-2001; vice chmn. fin. instns. Federalist Soc., Washington, 1997-2001; mem. Va. Commn. for Environ., Richmond, 1996; bd. dirs. Trade Policy Ctr. Cato

Inst.; adj. fellow Citizens Sound Economy. Mem. ABA (editl. bd. Bus. Law for Today 1997—), Yale Club N.Y.C. Republican. Lutheran. Office: US Dept of Commerce 14th & Constitution Washington DC 20230

LASHLEY, CURTIS DALE, lawyer; b. Urbana, Ill., Nov. 3, 1956; s. Jack Dale and Janice Elaine (Holman) L.; m. Tamara Dawn Yahnig, June 14, 1986. BA, U. Mo., Kansas City, 1978, JD, 1981. Bar: Mo. 1981, U.S. Dist. Ct. (we. dist.) Mo. 1981, U.S. Tax Ct. 1982, U.S. Ct. Appeals (8th cir.) 1992. Assoc. Melvin Heller, Inc., Creve Coeur, Mo., 1982; ptnr. Domjan & Lashley, Harrisonville, Mo., 1983-86; asst. gen. counsel Mo. Dept. Revenue, Independence, 1986-89, assoc. gen. counsel, 1989-92, sr. counsel, 1992—, adminstrv. hearing officer, 1995—; spl asst. atty. gen., 1986—; spl. asst. prosecutor Jackson County, Mo., 1990—. City atty., Adrian and Strasburg, Mo., 1985-86. V.p. Cass County Young Reps., Harrisonville, 1985. Recipient honor Senate Resolution 830 and Mo. Ho. Resolution 2314, 2001, Cert. of Appreciation, Kansas City Bd. Police Commrs., 2001, Legis. Resolution honor, Jackson County Mo., 2001. Mem. ABA, NRA, Kiwanis (treas. Harrisonville chpt. 1985-86, Harrisonville Disting. Svc. award 1985), Phi Alpha Delta. Republican. Presbyterian. Office: Mo Dept Revenue 16647 E 23rd St S Independence MO 64055-1922 E-mail: CurtisL752@excite.com.

LASHMAN, SHELLEY BORTIN, retired judge; b. Camden, N.J., Aug. 18, 1917; s. William Mitchell and Anna (Bortin) L.; m. Ruth Horn, Jan. 3, 1959; children: Karen E. Lashman Hall, Gail A. McBride, Mitchell A., Christopher R. BS, William and Mary Coll., 1938; postgrad., Columbia U., 1938, 39; JD, U. Mich., 1946. Bar: N.Y. 1947, N.J. 1968. Judge N.J. Workers Compensation, 1981-2001. With USNR, 1940-70. Mem. Atlantic County Bar Assn., Am. Judges Assn., Atlantic County Hist. Soc., Am. Judicature Soc., U.S. Navy League, Mil. Officers Assn. Am., VFW, Fleet Res. Assn., USS Yorktown CV-5 Club, Mil. Order World Wars. Republican. Home: 1209 Old Zion Rd Egg Harbor Township NJ 08234-7667 Home Fax: 609-653-6686.

LASKER, MORRIS E. judge; b. Hartsdale, N.Y., July 17, 1917; m. Helen M. Schubach; 4 children. BA magna cum laude, Harvard U., 1938; LLB, JD, Yale U., 1941. Bar: N.Y. 1941. Atty. Nat. Def. Com., U.S. Senate, 1941-42, Battle, Fowler, Jaffin & Kheel, 1946-68; fed. judge U.S. Dist. Ct. (so. dist.) N.Y., 1968-94, U.S. Dist. Ct., Boston, 1994—. Contbr. articles to profl. jours. Hon. trustee, bd. dirs. Vera Inst. Justice. Maj. U.S. Army, 1942-46. Recipient Learned Hand medal Fed. Bar Coun., Edward Weinfeld award N.Y. County Lawyers Assn. Mem. ABA, Assn. of Bar of City of N.Y. (exec. com. 1985-89). Avocations: gardening, reading, history, english and american literature. Office: US Dist Ct US Courthouse 1 Courthouse Way Boston MA 02210-3002

LASKEY, JAMES HOWARD, lawyer; b. N.Y.C., Dec. 19, 1953; s. Herbert M. and Mina (Yohalem) L.; m. Mary C. Jacobson, Oct. 1, 1983; children: Michael Henry, Kevin Connor, Katherine Anne. BS, MIT, 1975; JD, Yale U., 1978. Bar: N.J. 1978, U.S. Tax Ct. 1982. Law sec. to Hon. Sidney M. Schreiber N.J. Supreme Ct., Newark, 1978-79; atty. antitrust divsn. U.S. Dept. Justice, Washington, 1979-82; assoc. Rosen, Gelman & Weiss, Newark, 1982-84, Norris, McLaughlin & Marcus, Somerville, N.J., 1984-86, ptnr., 1986—. Contbr. articles to profl. jours. Mgmt. com. RideWise Raritan Valley, Somerville, N.J., 1993—. Mem. ABA (mem. antitrust sect., pub. utility law sects.), N.J. State Bar Assn. (chair pub. utility law sect. 1997-98), Somerset County C. of C. (bd. dirs. 1997—), Fed. Comms. Bar Assn., Yale Law Sch. N.J. Alumni Assn. (pres.). Administrative and regulatory, Antitrust, Utilities, public. Office: Norris McLaughlin & Marcus 721 Rt 202-206 PO Box 1018 Somerville NJ 08876-1018 E-mail: jlaskey@nmmlaw.com.

LASSAR, SCOTT R. prosecutor; b. Evanston, Ill., Apr. 5, 1950; s. Richard Ernest and Jo (Ladenson) L.; m. Elizabeth Levine, May 22, 1977; children: Margaret, Kate. B.A., Oberlin Coll., 1972; J.D., Northwestern U., 1975. Bar: Ill. 1975. Former dep. chief spl. prosecutions divsn. no. dist. Office U.S. Atty., Chgo.; former ptnr. Keck, Mahin & Cate, Chgo.; former U.S. atty. North Dist. Dept. Justice, Chgo.; now partner, Sidley, Austin, Brown & Wood. Office: Bank One Plaza 10 South Dearborn St Chicago IL 60603*

LAST, MICHAEL P. lawyer; b. Chgo., July 31, 1946; s. Jules Hilbert and Muriel Esther (Ruekberg) L.; m. Yong-Hee Chyun, Dec. 1970 (div.); m. Jane Antoinette Nooy Bunnell, May 29, 1983. BA magna cum laude, Lawrence U., 1968; JD cum laude, Harvard U., 1971. Bar: Mass. 1971. Ptnr., head real estate, environ. law dept. Warner & Stackpole, Boston, 1972-84; ptnr., head environ. law dept. Gaston & Snow, Boston, 1984-91; ptnr., co-chair environ. law sect. Mintz, Levin, Cohn, Ferris, Glovsky and Popeo P.C., Boston, 1991-99; mng. dir. ML Strategies, Inc., Boston, 1991-99, v.p., 1999; co-counsel Rackemann, Sawyer & Brewster, Boston, 1999—; prin. Nexus Environtl. Ptnrs., Boston, 1999—. Bd. dirs. Newell Enterprises Inc., 1983-87; co-chair Am. Law Inst./ABA Ann. Course Study Minimizing Liability for Hazardous Waste Mgmt.; lectr. in field. Contbr. articles to profl. jours. Chair wetlands regulation rev. bd. Mass. Dept. Environ. Quality Engring., 1983-85, Town Wellesley Wetlands Protection Com., 1980-82; mem. Town Wellesley Planning Bd., 1983-88; rep. Town Meeting, Wellesley; mem. rev. bd. Mass. Dept. Environ. Protection, 1991-92; mem. bd. environ. mgmt. Mass. Dept. Environ. Mgmt., 1991—, chmn., 1994-97, 2000—; founder, pres. Santa Fe Coun. Environ. Excellence, 1991—; founder, pres. Berkshire Inst., Inc.; mem. corp. gifts com. Boston Mus. Fine Arts Capital Fund Dr., 1979; vice chair open space plan implementation com. Town Wellesley, 1978-79; trustee, bd. govs. New Eng. Aquarium, 1995—, chmn. David B. Stone award com.; trustee Mass. Eye and Ear Infirmary, 1990-98, Mt. Kearsarge Indian Mus., 1997-2002; trustee, bd. govs., exec. com. Newton-Wellesley Hosp., 1987-94, hon. trustee, 1994—, chmn. joint trustee staff com., 1992-93; mem. corp. Ptnrs. Healthcare Sys., Inc., 1999—; bd. dirs. Environ. Bus. Coun. New Eng., Inc., 1997—, chmn. Brownfields Com., chmn. ann. retreat, mem. exec. com., 2001—. 1st lt. USAF, 1971-72. Warren Hurst Stevens scholar Lawrence U., 1964. Mem. ABA (standing com. environ. law 1989-91, natural resources sect., corp., banking, bus. law sect., real property, probate, trust law sect.), Boston Bar Assn. (bd. dirs. 1984-87, chair environment com. 1979-81, chair urban affairs sect. 1983-87, co-chair mcpl. planning process com. 1983-87), Greater Boston C. of C. (real estate devel. com. 1979-80, co-chair Boston 2000 project review com. 1982-90, Boston 2000 steering com. 1983-90, co-chair adv. com. Devel. Design Guideline Study Downtown Boston 1983-92), Phi Beta Kappa. Avocations: canoeing, cross country skiing, camping. Environmental, Property, real (including real estate development, water). Office: One Financial Center Boston MA 02111 E-mail: mlast@lastlaw.com.

LA STAITI, ELIZABETH O'NEILL, judge; b. New Bedford, Mass., Jan. 27, 1943; d. Walter James O'Neill and Elizabeth Barbara Goodin; m. Ronald S. La Staiti, Aug. 24, 1968 (dec. Mar. 1998); children: Angela E. Crowley, R. Scott, Monica C.; m. Edward R. Dufresne, Dec. 29, 2001. BA, George Washington U., 1964; JD magna cum laude, Boston Coll., 1968. Bar: Mass. 1968, U.S. Dist. Ct. Mass. 1969. Law clk. Hon. Andrew Caffrey, U.S. Dist. Ct., Boston, 1968—69; assoc. Choate, Hail, Stewart, Boston, 1969—70; pvt. practice New Bedford, Mass., 1970—88; legal asst. dist. atty. Commonwealth of Mass. so. dist., Boston, 1973—74; asst. town counsel Town of Dartmouth, Mass., 1979—88; assoc. justice trial ct., probate and family ct. Commonwealth of Mass., Bristol County, 1988—94, first justice, 1994—. Mem. exec. com. Mass. Judges Conf., 1993—97; jud. exch. to Romania U.S. State Dept., 2000; jud. exch. to China Mass. Judges Conf., 2001. Contbg. editor: Mass. Family Law Jour., 1990—. Trustee S.W. Health Sys., New Bedford, 1997—; bd. dirs., past pres. I.H. Schwartz Rehab. Ctr., New Bedford, 1980—. Recipient Jud. Excellence award, Mass. Judges Conf., 1998, Social Justice award, YWCA, New Bedford, 1999. Fellow: Mass. Bar Found.; mem.: Mass. Bar Assn. Avocations: bicycling, skiing, travel, boating. Office: Bristol County Probate Family Ct 505 Pleasant St New Bedford MA 02740 Fax: 508-991-7421.

LASTER, JUDITH EVE, lawyer; b. Washington, Nov. 20, 1959; d. Leonard and Ruth Ann L. BA, Bowdoin Coll., 1981; JD, Lewis and Clark Coll., 1986; LLM, Boston U., 1987. Bar: Mass. 1987. Exec. dir. Spl. Commn. on Fin. Svcs. for Mass. Legislature, Boston, 1987-96; dep. gen. counsel ways and means com. Mass. Senate, 1996-99; hearing officer Mass. Dept. Telecom. and Energy, Boston, 1999—. Dir. Bowdoin Club of Boston; founding mem. Falmouth Community Fund; trustee Wood Hole Community Assn.; dir. Woods Hole Film Festival; mem. alumni cou.n bd., B.U. Law Sch. Democrat. Avocations: photography, windsurfing, running, politics, filmmaking. Office: Office of Atty Gen 200 Portland St Boston MA 02114

LATCHUM, JAMES LEVIN, federal judge; b. Milford, Del., Dec. 23, 1918; s. James H. and Ida Mae (Robbins) L.; m. Elizabeth Murray McArthur, June 16, 1943; children: Su-Allan, Elizabeth M. AB cum laude, Princeton U., 1940; JD, U. Va., 1946. Bar: Va. 1942, Del. 1947. Assoc. Berl, Potter & Anderson, Wilmington, 1946-53, partner, 1953-68; judge U.S. Dist. Ct. Del., Wilmington, 1968-73, chief judge, 1973-83, sr. judge, 1983—. New Castle County atty. Del. Hwy. Dept., 1948-50; asst. U.S. atty., 1950-53; atty. Del. Interstate Hwy. Div., 1955-62, Delaware River and Bay Authority, 1962-68 Chmn. New Castle County Democratic Com., 1953-56, Wilmington City Com., 1959-63. Served to maj. Insp. Gen. Corps AUS, 1942-46, PTO. Mem. ABA, Del. Bar Assn., Va. Bar Assn., Order of Coif, Sigma Nu Phi. Clubs: Wilmington, Univ. Presbyterian. Office: US Dist Ct 844 N King St # 34 Wilmington DE 19801-3519

LATHAM, PATRICIA HORAN, lawyer; b. Hoboken, N.J., Sept. 5, 1941; d. Patrick John and Rosemary (Moller) Horan; m. Peter Samuel Latham, June 12, 1965; children: John Horan, Kerry Patricia. BA, Swarthmore Coll., 1963; JD, U. Chgo., 1966. Bar: D.C. 1967, U.S. Dist. Ct. D.C. 1967, U.S. Ct. Appeals 1967, U.S. Supreme Ct. 1970, Va. 1989, U.S. Dist. Ct. (ea. dist.) Va. 1989, U.S. Dist. Ct. Md. 1991. Assoc. Fried, Frank, Harris, Shriver & Kampelman, Washington, 1966-69; atty. Office of Gen. Counsel, SEC, Washington, 1969-71; assoc. Martin & Smith, Washington, 1971—, ptnr., 1974-85, Latham & Latham, Washington, 1986—. Lectr. Columbus Sch. Law, Cath. U. Am., Washington, 1978-92; mem. panel of arbitrators N.Y. Stock Exch., 1985—; co-founder, co-dir. Nat. Ctr. Law and Learning Disabilities, 1992—; mem. disability adv. com. GED Testing Svc., 1999—. Co-author: Attention Deficit Disorder and the Law, 1992, Attention Deficit Disorder and the Law, 2d edit., 1997, Learning Disabilities and the Law, 1993, Learning Disabilities and the Law, 2d edit., 2000, Succeeding in the Workplace, 1994, Higher Education Services for Students with Learning Disabilities and Attention Deficit Disorder: A Legal Guide, 1994, Documentation and the Law, 1996, Tales from the Workplace, 1997, Terrorism and the Law: Bringing Terrorists to Justice, 2002; contbg. author: ADD and the College Student, 1993, A Comprehensive Guide to ADD in Adults, 1995, Managing Attention and Learning Disorders in Late Adolescence and Adulthood, 1996, Textbook of Pediatric Neuropsychiatry, 1998, Learning Disabilities and Employment, 1997, ADD in Children and Adults, 1999. Co-founder, trustee Beacon Coll., 1989-93, chmn. bd. trustees, 1990-92; mem. adv. bd. Disability Law Reporter Svc., 1996-2001. Mem.: ABA, Learning Disabilities Assn. Am. (nat. adv. bd. 1996—2000, nat. bd. dirs. 2000—), Nat. Attention Deficit Disorders Assn. (bd. dirs. 1993—98, nat. adv. bd. 1998—), Am. Arbitration Assn. (panel arbitrators and mediators 1982—), Va. Bar Assn., DC Bar Assn., Ft. Myer and Ft. McNair Club. Roman Catholic. Corporate, general, Alternative dispute resolution. Home: The Watergate 2700 Virginia Ave NW #707 Washington DC 20037

LATHAM, PETER SAMUEL, lawyer; b. Boston, July 23, 1940; s. Earl Gansen and Margaret (Perrier) L.; m. Patricia Ann Horan, Sept. 5, 1941; children: John Horan, Kerry Patricia. BA with honors, Swarthmore Coll., 1962; LLB, U. Pa., 1965. Bar: D.C. 1966, U.S. Ct. Appeals (D.C. cir.) 1982, U.S. Dist. Ct. Md. 1991. Atty. SEC, Washington, 1965-66; assoc. firm Vom Baur, Coburn, Simmons & Turtle, Washington, 1969-71; mem. firm Wachtel, Ross and Matzkin, Washington, 1971-80; ptnr. Latham & Latham and predecessor firms, Washington, 1980—. Arbitrator Am. Arbitration Assn., 1978-2001. Author: Government Contract Disputes, 1981, 86; co-author: Attention Deficit Disorder and the Law: A Guide for Advocates, 1992, Learning Disabilities and the Law, 1993, Succeeding in the Workplace, 1994, Higher Education Services for Students with Learning Disabilities and Attention Deficit Disorder: A Legal Guide, 1994, Documentation and the Law, 1996, Tales from the Workplace, 1997, Attention Deficit Disorder and the Law, 2d edit., 1997, Learning Disabilities and the Law, 2d edit., 2000, Terrorism and the Law-Bringing Terrorists to Justice, 2002; contbg. author ADD and the College Student, 1993, A Comprehensive Guide to ADD in Adults, 1995, Managing Attention and Learning Disorders in Late Adolescence and Adulthood, 1996, Textbook of Pediatric Neuropsychiatry, 1998, Learning Disabilities and Employment, 1997, ADD in Children and Adults, 1999; producer, dir. The ABC's of ADD, other videos on legal topics. Co-founder, trustee Beacon Coll., 1989-93; co-founder Nat. Ctr. for Law and Learning Disabilities. Lt. USN, 1966-69. Decorated Navy Achievement medal with combat V. Mem. ABA, Nat. Attention Deficit Disorders Assn. (bd. dirs. 1993-97), DC Procurement Reform Taskforce (mem. Alternate Dispute Resolution subcom. 1995—), Ft. Myer and Ft. McNair Club. Republican. Roman Catholic. Avocations: tennis, swimming. General civil litigation, Government contracts and claims. Home: The Watergate 2700 Virginia Ave NW #707 Washington DC 20037 Office: Latham and Latham PO Box 40157 Washington DC 20016-0157

LATHAM, WELDON HURD, lawyer; b. Bklyn., Jan. 2, 1947; s. Aubrey Geddes and Avril (Hurd) L.; m. Constantia Beecher, Aug. 8, 1948; children: Nicole Marie, Brett Weldon. BA, Howard U., 1968; JD, Georgetown U., 1971; postgrad., George Washington U., 1975-76. Bar: D.C. 1972, U.S. Ct. Appeals (D.C. cir.) 1972, U.S. Ct. Mil. Appeals 1974, U.S. Ct. Claims 1975, U.S. Supreme Ct. 1975, Va. 1981, U.S. Ct. Appeals (fed. cir.) 1988. Mgmt. cons. Checchi & Co., Washington, 1968-71; atty. Covington & Burling, Washington, 1971-73; sr. atty. Fed. Energy Adminstrn., Washington, 1974; asst. gen. counsel Exec. Office Pres. Office Mgmt. and Budget The White House, Washington, 1974-76; atty. Hogan & Hartson, Washington, 1976-79; gen. dep. asst. sec. HUD, Washington, 1979-81; v.p., gen. counsel Sterling Sys., Inc. (subs. PRC.); exec. asst., counsel to chmn., CEO and assoc. gen. counsel Planning Rsch. Corp., McLean, Va., 1981-86; mng. ptnr. Reed, Smith, Shaw & McClay, McLean, Va., 1986-91; sr. ptnr. Shaw Pittman, Washington, 1992-2000; sr. ptnr., practice area leader corp. diversity counseling Holland & Knight, Washington, 2000—. Chmn. diversity adv. bd. Deloitte & Touche, 2002--; bd. visitors Georgetown U. Law Ctr., 2002--; mem. adv. coun. Coca-Cola Procurement, 2000--; adj. prof. Howard U. Law Sch., Washington, 1972-82; guest prof. U. Va., Charlottesville, 1976-90; mem. Va. Govs. Bus. and Industry Adv. Com. on Crime Prevention, 1983-85, Va. Govs. Regulatory Reform Adv. Bd., 1982-84; chmn. task force SBA, 1982; legal counsel Md. Mondale for Pres. Campaign, 1984; gen. counsel Nat. Coalition Minority Bus., 1993—; trustee The Am. Univ., 1999-2002; bd. dirs. Metro Washington Airports Authority, 1997-, Telecomms. Sys., Inc., 1999-; bd. govs. Joint Ctr. Polit. and Econ. Studies, 1998--. Columnist Minority Bus. Entrepreneur Mag., 1991—, Diversity Jour., 2002--; mem. editl. adv. bd. Washington Bus. Jour., 1985-87. Washington steering com. NAACP Legal Def. Fund, 1975-95, Fairfax County Airports Adv. Com., 1987-88; bd. dirs., gen. counsel Northern Va. Minority Bus. and Profl. Assn., 1985-92; trustee Va. Commonwealth U., Richmond, 1986-90, George Mason U., Fairfax, Va., 1990-94; bd. dirs. Washington Urban League, 1986-90, U. D.C. Found., 1982-87, Washington Coun. Lawyers, 1973, Profl. Svcs. Coun., 1983-88, Minority Bus. Enterprise Legal Def. and Edn. Fund, 1989-91, Wash. Hosp. Ctr. Found., 1996-98; appointee Greater Washington Bd. Trade, Blue Ribbon Task Force on Home Rule, 1985-86, bd. dirs., exec. com., chmn. regional affairs com., corp. sec. Greater Wash. Bd. Trade, 1990-95; adv. bd. First Union Nat. Bank, 1995-99; civilian aide to Sec. of Army, 1995-2000; mem. Small Bus. Adminstrn. Nat. Adv. Coun., 1993—, Burger King Corp. Diversity Action Coun., 1996-98, Diversity Best Practices Coun., 2001--, Md. Econ. Devel. Commn., 1996-98, Gov. Bd. Transition Team, 1995, Dem. Nat. Com., 1996, Platform Drafting Com., 1996; prin. coun. for Excellence in Govt., 1989-95; at-large mem. Dem. Nat. Com., 2001--; mayor D.C. Internat. Ins. Adv. Commn., 1994-95; chmn. D.C. Mayors Bus. Adv. Coun., 1994-96; vice-chmn. Dem. Bus. Coun. DNC, 1994-98; co-chmn. UNCF Sportsfest Fundraiser, 1994; hon. vice-chmn. Clinton-Gore Campaign, 1996; mem. corp. adv. coun. Congrl. Black Caucus Found., 1999—; gen. counsels Honors Program Office Sec. Capt. USAF, 1973-74. Recipient SES Effective Mgr. award HUD, 1980, Nat. Assn. for Equal Achievement Opportunity in Higher Edn. award, 1987, A. Philip Randolph award Amtrak, 2001, Ron Brown Legacy award Nat. Black MBA Assn., 2002. Mem. ABA (vice-chmn. subcom. pub. contract law sect. 1988-93), Fed. Bar Assn., Nat. Bar Assn., D.C. C. of C. (gen. counsel 1979), State Va. Bar Assn., Washington Bar Assn.(elected to Hall of Fame, 2001), Bar Assn. D.C., Nat. Contract Mgmt. Assn., Econ. Club Washington. Administrative and regulatory, Corporate, general, Government contracts and claims. Home: 7004 Natelli Woods Ln Bethesda MD 20817-3924 Office: Holland & Knight LLP 2099 Pennsylvania Ave NW Washington DC 20006-1813

LATIFUR RAHAMAN, RASUL BOAKSH, legal profession executive; b. Kushita, Bangladesh, Jan. 1, 1945; arrived in India, Jan. 3, 1945; s. Fazlur Rahman and Rabya Khatun Ruby Rabia Khatun; married; children: Rassel, Boaksel. Diploma, Kushtia Coll., 1963, LLB, 1966; M Commerce, Dhaka U., 1967. Headmaster Talberia High Sch., Kushtia Dist., 1961; head asst. Indsl. Promo Svcs., Dacca, 1966-67; income tax cons. Bangladesh Bar Assn., Segun Bagicha/Dacca, 1967-69; pres. Kushtia Income Tax Bar Assn., 1970-90, Padma Devel., Kushtia, 1980—. Chmn. Bangladesh Coms., Padma, Kushtia, 1971—; chmn. Cen. Capital, Padma; leader of party/chmn., Bangladesh Internat. Moisen Order Internat. Command Party, Padma, 1980—; chmn. Ctrl. Capital of Bangladesh, Padma, 299100; trade consulate Bangladesh Trade, Padma, 1980—; chmn. Bazar com., Padma. Mem. Pub. Libr., Kushtia, 1965-66. Office: The Income Tax Bar Assn B06000 Kushtia Padma Bangladesh

LATTINVILLE, ROBERT HENRY, lawyer, educator; b. Kansas City, Mo., Feb. 8, 1963; s. Henry Elmer and Marie Anna Lattinville. BS, U. Mo., 1985; MBA, St. Louis U., 1987; JD, Ind. U., 1990. Bar: Mo. 1990, Ill. 1991. Assoc. Lewis, Rice & Figersh, St. Louis, 1990-95; ptnr. Stinson, Morrison & Hecker, St. Louis, 1995—. Bd. dirs. St. Louis Sports Commn., 1997—; contract adivsor Nat. Football League Players Assn., 1990—, Can. Football League Players Assn., 1992—. Bd. dirs. Mary Grove Home for Abused Children, St. Louis, 1997-2000, Cardinal Glennon Children's Hosp., St. Louis, 1997—. Mem. Mo. Bar Assn. (chmn. sports and entertainment com. 1997—). Avocations: water sports, running, golf. Corporate, general, Intellectual property, Sports. Home: 8411 Kingsbury Blvd Clayton MO 63105-3629 Office: Stinson Morrison & Hecker 100 S 4th St Saint Louis MO 63102-1800 E-mail: blattinville@stinsonmoheck.com.

LAU, EUGENE WING IU, lawyer; b. Canton, China, Sept. 23, 1931; came to U.S., 1939; s. Eugene K. F. and Ann (Leung) L.; m. Dierdre Florence, July 20, 1962; children: Elyse M., Jennifer M. AB, U. Mich., 1953; LLB, Yale U., 1960. Bar: Hawaii 1960, U.S. Supreme Ct. 1965. Dep. Pros. Attys. Office, Honolulu, 1960-63; pvt. practice Honolulu, 1963-67, 73—; v.p. Hawaii Corp., Honolulu, 1967-73. Del. People to People Legal Del. to China, 1987; mem. Commn. on Manpower and Full Employment, Honolulu, 1965-67. With U.S. Army, 1954-55. Mem. ABA, Hawaii Bar Assn., Punahou Tennis Club (Honolulu). Property, real (including real estate development, water), General civil litigation. Home: 3079 La Pietra Cir Honolulu HI 96815-4736 Office: 1188 Bishop St Ste 1912 Honolulu HI 96813-3308 E-mail: EL923@aol.com.

LAU, JEFFREY DANIEL, lawyer; b. Honolulu, May 2, 1948; s. Daniel B.T. and Evelyn (Yee Quil) L.; m. Susan Elizabeth Tilden, June 1, 1974; 1 child, Daniel Prescott Tilden. BSBA in Econs., Lehigh U., 1970; MBA in Fin., Temple U., 1973; JD, U. Calif., San Francisco, 1977. Bar: Hawaii, U.S. Dist. Ct. Hawaii, U.S. Ct. Appeals (9th cir.) 1978. Legis. asst. to U.S. Senator Hiram L. Fong, Washington, 1971-72; law clk. to presiding justice U.S. Dist. Ct. Hawaii, Honolulu, 1975, U.S. Ct. Appeals (9th cir.), Honolulu, 1976; assoc. Frank D. Padgett, Honolulu, 1977-80; ptnr. Chung, Lau, MacLaren and Lau, Honolulu, 1980-81, Fong and Miho, Honolulu, 1981-84; past pres., , v.p., dir. Oliver, Lau, Lawhn, Ogawa & Nakamura, Honolulu, 1985—. Bd. dirs., asst. corp. sec. audit com. Fin. Factors, Ltd., Honolulu, Fin. Realty, Ltd., Honolulu; bd. dirs., corp. sec. Grand Pacific Life Ins., Ltd., 1984-2000; apptd. ct. arbitrator State of Hawaii, 1987—. Dir. Honolulu Bulls Soccer Club, 1993-2000, Hawaii Youth Soccer Assn., 1998—; hon. consul of Belgium in Honolulu, 1999—. Mem. ABA, Assn. Trial Lawyers Am., Am. Bankruptcy Inst., Hawaii State Bar Assn. (del. to Hawaii Congress on Small Bus. 1994—, dir. collection law sect.), Lehigh U. Alumni Assn. Hawaii (pres.), Hawaii Soc. Corp. Planners (dir. 1997—). Mem. United Ch. of Christ. Avocations: skiing, volleyball, softball, coaching youth soccer, basketball and baseball. Commercial, consumer (including collections, credit), General civil litigation, Insurance. Office: Ocean View Ctr 707 Richards St Ste 600 Honolulu HI 96813-4693 E-mail: ollon@gte.net.

LAU, MARY APPLEGATE, lawyer; b. Washington, Dec. 17, 1952; d. Robert Lee and Barbara Edith (Pressler) Applegate; m. James Victor Lau, Apr. 1, 1982; 1 child, Chelsea Nicole. BA magna cum laude, Mich. State U., 1974; JD with honors, Fla. State U., 1976. Bar: Fla. 1977, U.S. Dist. Ct. (mid. dist.) Fla. 1977, U.S. Ct. Appeals (11th cir.) 1977. Assoc. atty. Holland and Knight, Tampa, Fla., 1977-82, ptnr., 1982-86; shareholder Lau, Lane, Pieper, Conley & McCreadie, P.A., Tampa, 1986—. Mem. Fed. Bar Assn., (treas. Tampa Bay chpt. 1993), Hillsborough County Bar Assn. Republican. Roman Catholic. Bankruptcy, Federal civil litigation, Labor (including EEOC, Fair Labor Standards Act, labor-management relations, NLRB, OSHA). Office: Lau Lane Pieper Conley & McCreadie PA 100 S Ashley Dr Tampa FL 33602-5360

LAUCHENGCO, JOSE YUJUICO, JR., lawyer; b. Manila, Philippines, Dec. 6, 1936; came to U.S., 1962; s. José Celis Sr. Lauchengco and Angeles (Yujuico) Sapota; m. Elisabeth Schindler, Feb. 22, 1968; children: Birthe, Martina, Duane, Lance. AB, U. Philippines, Quezon City, 1959; MBA, U. So. Calif., 1964; JD, Loyola U., L.A., 1971. Bar: Calif. 1972, U.S. Dist. Ct. (cen. dist.) Calif. 1972, U.S. Ct. Appeals (9th cir.) 1972, U.S. Supreme Ct. 1975. Banker First Western Bank/United Calif. Bank, L.A., 1964-71; assoc. Demler, Perona, Langer & Bergkvist, Long Beach, Calif., 1972-73; ptnr. Demler, Perona, Langer, Bergkvist, Lauchengco & Manzella, Long Beach, 1973-77; sole practice Long Beach and L.A., 1977-83; ptnr. Lauchengco & Mendoza, L.A., 1983-92; pvt. practice L.A., 1993—. Mem. commn. on jud. procedures County of L.A., 1979; tchr. Confraternity of Christian Doctrine, 1972-79; counsel Philippine Presdl. Commn. on Good Govt., L.A., 1986. Chmn. Filipino-Am. Bi-Partisan Polit. Action Group, L.A., 1978. Recipient Degree of Distinction, Nat. Forensic League, 1955. Mem. Calif. Pub. Defenders Assn., Philippine-Am. Bar Assn., U. Philippines Vanguard Assn. (life), Consumer Attys. Assn. L.A., K.C., Beta Sigma. Roman Catholic. Avocations: classical music, opera, romantic paintings and sculpture, camping, shooting. Federal civil litigation, Criminal, Personal injury (including property damage). Office: 3545 Wilshire Blvd Ste 247 Los Angeles CA 90010-2388

LAUDERDALE, KATHERINE SUE, lawyer; b. Wright-Patterson AFB, Ohio, May 30, 1954; d. Azo and Helen Ceola (Davis) L. BS in Polit. Sci., Ohio State U., 1975; JD, NYU, 1978. Bar: Ill. 1978, U.S. Dist. Ct. (no. dist.) Ill. 1978, Calif. 1987. Assoc. Schiff, Hardin & Waite, Chgo., 1978-82; from dir. bus. and legal affairs to sr. v.p. Sta. WTTW-TV, Chgo., 1982—2000, sr. v.p. strategic partnerships and gen. counsel, 2000—02; sr. v.p. and gen. counsel PBS, Alexandria, Va., 2002—. Mem. Lawyers Com. for Harold Washington, Chgo. 1983; bd. dirs. Midwest Women's Ctr., Chgo., 1985-94; active Chgo. Coun. Fgn. Rels., 1981—, mem. fgn. affairs com., 1985—; mem. adv. bd. Malcolm X Coll. Sch. Bus., 1996-99. Mem. ABA, Chgo. Bar Assn. (bd. dirs. TV Prodns., Inc. 1986—2002), Lawyers for Creative Arts (bd. dir. 1984—2002, v.p. 1998—2002), ACLU (bd. dirs. 1987-94), Nat. Acad. TV Arts and Scis., NYU Law Alumni Assn. Midwest (mem. exec. bd. 1982—86), The Ohio State U. Pres.'s Nat. Adv. Coun. on Pub. Affairs (Chgo. com., 1994—), The U. Chicago Women's Bd., 1996—2002. Democrat. Corporate, general, Entertainment, Communications. Office: PBS 1320 Braddock Place Alexandria VA 22315

LAUER, ELIOT, lawyer; b. N.Y.C., Aug. 17, 1949; s. George and Doris (Trenk) L.; m. Marilyn Steinberg, June 5, 1977; children: Tamar Rachel, Ilana Jennifer, Michael Jonathan, Samuel Geoffrey. BA, Yeshiva U., 1971; JD cum laude, Fordham U., 1974. Bar: D.C. 1975, N.Y. 1975, U.S. Dist. Ct. (so. and ea. dists.) N.Y. 1975, U.S. Ct. Appeals (2d cir.) 1975, U.S. Supreme Ct. 1984. Assoc. Curtis, Mallet-Prevost, Colt & Mosle, N.Y.C., 1974-82, ptnr., 1982—. Counsel Keren-Or Inc., N.Y.C., 1985—; bd. dirs. Hebrew Acad. Long Beach, N.Y., 1985—, Young Israel Lawrence, Cedarhurst, N.Y., 1984—. Mem.: ABA, N.Y. State Bar Assn., Fed. Bar Coun., Nat. Futures Assn. (arbitrator 1983—), Assn. of Bar of City of N.Y. Republican. Federal civil litigation, Criminal. Office: Curtis Mallet-Prevost Colt & Mosle 101 Park Ave Fl 34 New York NY 10178-0061 E-mail: elauer@cm-p.com.

LAUFER, JACOB, lawyer; b. Munich, Feb. 28, 1949; came to the U.S., 1951; s. Moritz and Felicja (Pruszanowska) L.; m. Clara G. Schwabe, Jan. 27, 1983; children: Samara, Aviva, Mia. BS, CUNY, 1971; JD cum laude, Fordham U., 1974. Bar: N.Y. 1975, D.C. 1975, U.S. Ct. Appeals (2d cir.) 1975, U.S. Dist. Ct. (so. and ea. dists.) N.Y. 1976, U.S. Ct. Appeals (5th cir.) 1979, U.S. Supreme Ct. 1980, U.S. Ct. Appeals (3d cir.) 1985, U.S. Ct. Appeals (D.C. cir.) 1994. Spl. atty. Organized Crime and Racketeering Sect., U.S. Dept. Justice, 1974-77; asst. U.S. atty. So. Dist. N.Y., N.Y.C., 1977-79; of counsel Bartels, Pykett & Aronwald, White Plains, N.Y., 1979-81; ptnr. Bornstein & Laufer, N.Y.C., 1981-85, Laufer & Farkash LLP, N.Y.C., 1986—96; with Laufer & Halberstam LLP, N.Y.C., 1996—. Mem., contbr. Fordham Law Rev., 1973-74. Mem. D.C. Bar Assn., Bklyn. Bar Assn., Assn. Bar City of N.Y (com. criminal advocacy 1998—). Democrat. Jewish. Notable cases include: Pavelic & LeFlore vs. Marvel Entertainment Group; and Allen vs. National Video, Inc. General civil litigation, Criminal, Entertainment. Office: Laufer & Halberstam LLP Ste 1440 39 Broadway New York NY 10006-3003 E-mail: jlaufer@lauferhalberstam.com.

LAUGHLIN, DREW ALAN, lawyer; b. McKeesport, Pa., Feb. 28, 1952; s. Edward Stanley L. and Delores Easton Weiler. BA, U. Va., 1974; JD, U. S.C., 1977. Bar: S.C., 1977, U.S. Dist. Ct. S.C., 1978, U.S. Ct. Appeals (4th, 1986, 5th, 1983, and 11th cirs.). Atty. Laughlin & Bowen, Hilton Head Island, SC. Pres. Hilton Head Plantation, Property Owner's Assn, 1996; chmn. Hilton Head Island Planning Commn., 1994-96, Hilton Head Island Corridor Revs. Com., 1992-94; commr. Hilton Head Island Pub. Svc. Dist., 1998—. General civil litigation, Construction, Property, real (including real estate development, water). Home: 6 Oyster Reef Cv Hilton Head Island SC 29926-1800 Office: Laughlin & Bowen PO Drawer 21119 Hilton Head Island SC 29925-1119 E-mail: drew@laughlinandbowen.com.

LAUGHLIN, FELIX B. lawyer; b. New Orleans, Dec. 4, 1942; m. Betty Gayle Laughlin. BS with honors, JD with honors, U. Tenn., 1967; LLM, Georgetown U., 1971. Bar: Tenn. 1967, D.C. 1972, U.S. Ct. Claims 1969, U.S. Tax Ct. 1968, U.S. Dist. Ct. D.C. 1972, U.S. Ct. Appeals (D.C. cir.) 1988, U.S. Ct. Appeals (fed. cir.) 1992, U.S. Supreme Ct. 1970. With interpretation divsn. Office Chief Counsel IRS, 1967-71; assoc. Dewey Ballantine LLP, Washington, 1972-74, mem., 1975—. Dir. Friends of U.S. Nat. Arboretum, Nat. Bonsai Found. (pres.). Mem. ABA (tax sect.), Fed. Bar Assn. (chmn. tax sect. 1989), Met. Club (Washington), George Town Club (Washington), Order of Coif, Sigma Alpha Epsilon, Phi Eta Sigma, Phi Kappa Phi, Phi Delta Phi. Corporate taxation. Office: Dewey Ballantine LLP 1775 Pennsylvania Ave NW Washington DC 20006-4605 E-mail: Flaughlin@dbllp.com.

LAUGHLIN, JAMES HAROLD, JR., lawyer; b. Charleston, W.Va., July 18, 1941; s. James Harold and Pearl Ruby L; m. Eleanor Blackford Watson, II, Aug. 3, 1968; children: C. Michelle, Jeanette C., Cheryl Adele. BS in Chem. Engring., W.Va. U., 1964; JD, Am. U., 1968. Bar: D.C. 1968, Va. 1969. Atty. Am. Cyanamid Co., Wayne, N.J., 1968-70, Xerox Corp., Rochester, N.Y., 1971-77; ptnr. Benoit, Smith & Laughlin, Arlington, Va., 1977-93, Lane & Mittendorf, LLP, Washington, 1993-97, Shook, Hardy & Bacon, LLP, Washington, 1997-99, Arter & Hadden, LLP, Washington, 2000-01, Swidler Berlin Shereff Friedman, LLP, 2001—. Mem. ABA, Am. Intellectual Property Law Assn. (bd. dirs. 1976-79, treas. 1982-85, councilman 1993-94), Va. State Bar (chmn. PTC sect. 1982-83), Nat. Coun. Patent Law Assns. (Va. del. 1983-2002), Nat. Inventors Hall of Fame Found. (bd. dirs. 1988-93, pres. 1991-92). Federal civil litigation, Legislative, Patent. Office: The Washington Harbour 3000 K St NW Ste 300 Washington DC 20007 E-mail: jim.laughlin@jlaughlin.com.

LAULICHT, MURRAY JACK, lawyer; b. Bklyn., May 12, 1940; s. Philip and Ernestine (Greenfield) L.; m. Linda Kushner, Apr. 4, 1965; children: Laurie Hasten, Pamela Hirt, Shellie Davis, Abigail Herschmann. BA, Yeshiva U., 1961; LLB summa cum laude, Columbia U., 1964. Bar: N.Y. 1965, N.J. 1968, U.S. Supreme Ct. 1976. Legal staff Warren Commn., Washington, 1964; law clk. Hon. Harold R. Medina U.S. Ct. Appeals, 1964-65; assoc. Kaye, Scholer, Fierman, Hays & Handler, N.Y.C., 1965-68; ptnr. Lowenstein, Sandler, Brochin, Kohl & Fisher, Newark, N.J., 1968-79, Pitney, Hardin, Kipp & Szuch, Florham Park, N.J., 1979—. Mem. N.J. Consumer Affairs Adv. Com., 1991-93; mem. N.J. Commn. on Holocaust Edn., 1991—, chmn. 1992-95; mem. N.J. Commn. on Character Edn., 2002; pres. Jewish Edn. Assn., 1981-84, Jewish Fedn. Metro West, 1996-99, Edah, 2001-02, chmn. Cmty. Rels. Com., 1988-91, chmn. com. on religious pluralism, 1999-2002; exec. comm. Coun. of Jewish Fedn., 1996-99; trustee United Jewish Cmtys., 1999—. Recipient Julius Cohn Young Leadership award Jewish Fedn. Metrowest, 1976. Mem. ABA, N.J. State Bar Assn. (dist. X ethics com. 1986-89, bd. editors N.J. Law Jour. 1986-93), N.J. Lawyer Mag. (chmn. 1993-95). Democrat. Avocations: jewish studies, communal activities. Antitrust, General civil litigation, Intellectual property. Home: 18 Crestwood Dr West Orange NJ 07052-2004 Office: Pitney Hardin Kipp & Szuch PO Box 1945 200 Campus Dr Florham Park NJ 07932-1007 E-mail: mlaulicht@pitneyhardin.com.

LAURA, ELAINE S. lawyer; b. Newark, Sept. 11, 1973; d. Gabriel Frank and Mary Ann S. Laura. BA, NYU, 1995; JD, Nova U., 2001. Bar: Fla. 2001. Legal asst. Skadden, Aarps et al, N.Y.C., 1997; guaridan ad litem Broward County Ct. House, Ft. Lauderdale, Fla., 2000; legal intern Impact Sports, Boca Raton, Fla., 2001; atty. Flaxman & Lopez, P.A., Hollywood, Fla., 2001—. Scholar, NYU, 1991—95. Mem.: Broward County Bar Assn., Phi Alpha Delta, Nat. Hispanic Honor Soc. Lutheran. Avocations: Tae Kwon Do, travel, reading, piano, guitar. Personal injury (including property damage), Labor (including EEOC, Fair Labor Standards Act, labor-management relations, NLRB, OSHA). Office: Flaxman & Lopez PA 5715 Johnson St Hollywood FL 33021

LAURICELLA, PETER ALAN, lawyer; b. Syracuse, N.Y., May 17, 1971; m. Lori Lauricella, June 8, 1997; 1 child, Andrew. JD, Albany Law Sch., N.Y., 1996. Bar: N.Y. 1997. Assoc. Crane, Greene & Parente, Albany, NY, 1996—. Com. mem. Capital Leadership Amb. Program, Albany, NY, 2000—02; committeeman Bethlehem Rep. Com., Delmar, NY, 1999—2002; bd. dir. Women's Employment and Resource Ctr., Albany, NY, 2002. Mem.: ABA, Nat. Italian-Am. Bar Assn., Albany County Bar Assn., N.Y. State Bar Assn. General civil litigation, Civil rights, Commercial, consumer (including collections, credit). Office: Crane Greene & Parente 90 State St Albany NY 12207 Office Fax: 518-432-0086. E-mail: plauricella@cgplaw.com.

LAURIE, ROBIN GARRETT, lawyer; b. Mobile, Ala., June 10, 1956; s. George and Margaret Eloise (Garrett) L.; m. Deborah Dockery; children: Elizabeth Anne, Robin Garrett. AA, Marion (Ala.) Mil. Inst., 1976; BS in Bus., U. Ala., Tuscaloosa, 1978; JD, U.Ala., Tuscaloosa, 1988. Bar: Ala. 1988, U.S. Dist. Ct. (no., mid. and so. dists.) Ala. 1988, U.S. Ct. Appeals (11th cir.) 1988. Ptnr. Balch & Bingham LLP, Montgomery, Ala., 1988—. Lead articles editor Ala. Law Rev., 1986-88. Recipient Outstanding Svc. award Ala. Law Rev., 1988. Mem. ABA, Ala. State Bar, Montgomery County Bar Assn., Montgomery Rotary Club, Order of the Coif. Methodist. Avocations: flying small airplanes, fishing, hunting. Administrative and regulatory, General civil litigation, Utilities, public. Office: Balch & Bingham LLP PO Box 78 Montgomery AL 36101-0078 E-mail: rlaurie@balch.com.

LAUSE, MICHAEL FRANCIS, lawyer; b. Washington, Mo., Aug. 3, 1948; s. Walter Francis and Junilla Rose (Marquart) L.; m. Ann G. Hellman, Aug. 29, 1981; children: Andrew Edward, Scott Michael. BA, St. Benedict's Coll., 1970; JD, U. Ill., 1973. Bar: Mo. 1973. Ptnr. Thompson Coburn LLP, St. Louis, 1973—. Mem. mgmt. com. Thompson Coburn LLP, St. Louis, 1988-90. Gen. counsel Mo. Health and Ednl. Facilities Authority, 1986—, St. Louis Zoo, 1992—. Mem. ABA, Mo. Bar Assn., St. Louis Bar Assn., Nat. Assn. Bond Lawyers, Bellerive Country Club. Roman Catholic. Corporate, general, Municipal (including bonds), Property, real (including real estate development, water). Home: 9822 Old Warson Rd Saint Louis MO 63124-1066 Office: Thompson Coburn LLP One US Bank Plz Saint Louis MO 63101

LAUTENSCHLAGER, PEGGY A. state attorney general; b. Fond du Lac, Wis., Nov. 22, 1955; d. Milton A. and Patsy R. (Oleson) L.; m. Rajiv M. Kaul, Dec. 29, 1979 (div. Dec. 1986); children: Joshua Lautenschlager Kaul, Ryan Lautenschlager Kaul; m. William P. Rippl, May 26, 1989; 1 child, Rebecca Lautenschlager Rippl. BA, Lake Forest Coll., 1977; JD, U. Wis., 1980. Bar: Wis., U.S. Dist. Ct. (we. dist.). Pvt. practice atty., Oshkosh, Wis., 1981-85; dist. atty. Winnebago County Wis., Oshkosh, 1985-88; rep. Wis. Assembly, Fond du Lac, 1988-92; U.S. atty. U.S. Dept. of Justice, Madison, Wis., 1992—2000; atty. gen. State of Wis., 2003—. Apptd. mem. Govs. Coun. on Domestic Violence, Madison, State Elections Bd., Madison; bd. dirs. Blandine House, Inc. Active Dem. Nat. Com., Washington, 1992-93; com. Wis., 1989-92. Named Legislator of Yr., Wis. Sch. Counselors, 1992, Legislator of Yr., Wis. Corrections Coalition, 1992. Mem. Wis. Bar Assn., Dane County Bar Assn., Western Dist. Bar Assn., Fond du lac County Bar Assn., Phi Beta Kappa. Avocations: gardening, house renovation, sports, cooking. Office: State Capitol Ste 114 E PO Box 7857 Madison WI 53707

LAUTERBACH, PAUL D. lawyer; b. Centralia, Wash., Dec. 19, 1954; s. Paul G. and Lucy G. Lauterbach; married, Mar. 27, 1997; children: Paul J., Abigail O. BS in Chemistry, Oreg. State U., 1979; MS in Pub. and Internat. Affairs, U. Pitts., 1993; JD, Duquesne U., 1998. Bar: Pa. 1998, NJ 1998, NY 1999, U.S. Supreme Ct. 2002, U.S. Patent Office. Environ. lawyer Sci. Applications Internat. Corp., Pitts., 1999—. Atty. Neighborhood Legal Svc. Assn., Pitts., 1998—. Contbr. articles to profl. jours. Mem.: ABA, Allegheny County Bar Assn. Republican. Private international, Intellectual property, Corporate taxation. Office: SAIC PO Box 18689 Pittsburgh PA 15236-0681 Office Fax: 412-386-4736. E-mail: paul_lauterbach@hotmail.com.

LAVAL, JUAN ESTEBAN, lawyer; b. Santiago, Chile, Mar. 20, 1967; s. Enrique Laval and Josefina Zaldívar; m. María Carolina Bannen, June 25, 1971; children: Juan Esteban, José Tomás. LLB, Diego Portales Law Sch., Santiago, Chile, 1989; MA in Pub. Policy, Georgetown U., Washington DC, 1995. Bar: Chile Supreme Ct. 1992. Chief of staff to the min. Ministry of Housing and Urbanism, Santiago, Chile, 1992—93; lawyer Ctrl. Bank of Chile, Santiago, Chile, 1996—2000, Carey y Cía. Ltd., Santiago, Chile, 2000—. Cons. Interam. Devel. Bank, Washington DC, 1995. Legal rschr. Commn. of Truth and Reconciliation, Santiago, Chile. Fellow Pres. of the Republic award, 1993-1995. Banking, Finance, Mergers and acquisitions. Home: Santa Inés 1427 - Huechuraba Santiago Chile Office: Carey y Cía Ltda Miraflores 222 Fl 24 Santiago 6500786 Chile Home Fax: (562) 633 1980; Office Fax: (562) 633 1980. E-mail: jelaval@carey.cl.

LAVECCHIA, JAYNEE, state supreme court justice; b. Paterson, N.J. m. Michael R. Cole. Grad., Douglass Coll., 1976, Rutgers U., 1979. Bar: N.J. 1980. Pvt. law practice; dep. atty. gen. divsn. of law State of N.J., dir. divsn. of law dept. law anf pub. safety, 1984-98, commr. banking and ins., 1998-99; asst. counsel to Gov. Thomas H. Kean Office of Counsel, dep. chief counsel to Gov. Thomas H. Kean; dir., chief adminstrv. law judge Office of Adminstrv. Law, 1989-94; assoc. justice N.J. Supreme Ct., Trenton, 2000—. Chair various N.J. Supreme Ct. Coms. Fellow ABA; mem. Dougls Coll. Alumnae Assn. Office: North Tower 158 Headquarters Pla Morristown NJ 07960

LAVECCHIA, JOHN B. lawyer; b. Newark, Feb. 4, 1932; s. Nicholas and Mary (Boylan) L.; m. Emma Louise Cahill, Feb. 2, 1957; children: John, Emy, Michael, Catherine, Elizabeth, Vincent, Nicholas. BA, Princeton U., 1954; LLB, Columbia U., 1957. Bar: N.J. 1957, U.S. Dist. Ct. N.J. 1957. Assoc. Connell & Foley LLP, Newark, 1957-65; ptnr. Connell, Foley & Geiser LLP, Roseland, NJ, 1965—2001; of counsel, 2002—. Mem. Supreme Ct. Fee Arbitration Com., 1978-79; mem. Essex dist. Supreme Ct. Ethics Com., 1981-86. With N.J. N.G., 1957. Harlan Fiske Stone scholar Columbia U., 1957. Fellow Am. Coll. Trial Lawyers; master William J. Brennan Inn Ct.; diplomate Am. Bd. Trial Atys.; mem. ABA, Fed. Ins. and Corp. Counsel, N.J. State Bar Assn., Trial Attys. N.J., Essex County Bar Assn. Avocations: golf, cross-country skiing, platform tennis. General civil litigation, Environmental, Insurance. Home: PO Box 172 Dorset VT 05251-0172 Office: Connell Foley & Geiser LLP 85 Livingston Ave Roseland NJ 07068-3702

LAVELLE, BETTY SULLIVAN DOUGHERTY, legal professional; b. Omaha, Nov. 12, 1941; d. Marvin D. and Marie C. Sullivan; children from previous marriage: Clayton B. Dougherty, Lance A. Dougherty; m. James S. LaVelle, 1986; 1 child, Lindsay L. A of Pre-Law, U. Nebr., 1960; student, U. Colo., 1964-66; BA in Philosophy, Metro State Coll., 1979; cert. legal assistant, U. San Diego, 1979. Teaching asst. Metro State Coll., Denver, 1978; paralegal Holland and Hart, Denver, 1979-85; litigation paralegal Rothgerber, Appel, Powers and Johnson, Denver, 1985-88; pres., cons. Vivant, Inc., Boulder, 1987—; owner, adminstr. Homestead Group Home for Elderly, Longmont, 1987-92; ptnr. LaVelle & McMillan, Boulder, 1989-90; water law and litigation paralegal Moses, Wittemyer, Harrison and Woodruff, P.C., Boulder, 1990-2001, mediation, water rights, real property and litigation contractor, 2001—. Mediator domestic relations 20th Jud. Dist., Boulder, 1984-85. Contbr. articles to profl. jours. Vol. legal aid Thursday Night Bar, Denver Bar Assn., 1979-86, paralegal coordinator, panelist, speaker, 1983-85; sr. paralegal Boulder County Legal Svcs., 1988-89; mediator landlord/tenant project City of Boulder, 1983-87; coach, trainer Ctr. for Dispute Resolution, Denver and Boulder, 1984-86; vol. Shelter for Homeless, Boulder, 1988. Recipient cert. U. Denver Coll. Law, 1981, Hoagland award Colo. Bar Assn., 1984. Mem. Colo. Bar Assn., Soc. Profls. in Dispute Resolution, Rocky Mountain Paralegal Assn. (mem. adv. bd. 1980-81, bd. dirs. 1983-85, 94-96, rep. to Colo. Bar Assn. 1994-96, dir. pro bono svcs. 1984-85). Democrat. Avocations: vol. legal services for the indigent, computer applications. Home: 1660 Bradley Ct Boulder CO 80305-7300

LAVELLE, BRIAN FRANCIS DAVID, lawyer; b. Cleve., Aug. 16, 1941; s. Gerald John and Mary Josephine (O'Callaghan) L.; m. Sara Hill, Sept. 10, 1966; children: S. Elizabeth, B. Francis D. Jr., Catherine H. BA, U. Va., 1963; JD, Vanderbilt U., 1966; LLM in Taxation, NYU, 1969. Bar: N.C. 1966, Ohio 1968. Assoc. VanWinkle Buck, Wall, Starnes & Davis, Asheville, N.C., 1968-74, ptnr., 1974—. Lectr. continuing edn. N.C. Bar Found., Wake Forest U. Estate Planning Inst., Hartford Tax Inst., Duke U. Estate Planning Inst. Contbr. articles on law to profl. jours. Trustee Carolina Day Sch., 1981-92, sec., 1982-85; bd. dirs. The Salvation Army, 1986—; bd. dirs. Western N.C. Cmty. Found., 1986—, sec., 1987-90; bd. advs. U. N.C. Ann. Tax Inst., 1981—. Capt. JAG USAF, 1966-67. Mem. ABA, Am. Coll. Trust and Estate Counsel (state chmn. 1982-85, regent 1984-90, lectr. continuing edn.), N.C. Bar Assn. (bd. govs. 1979-82, councillor tax sect. 1979-83, councillor estate planning law sect. 1982-85, v.p. 1997—), N.C. State Bar (splty. exam. com. on estate planning and probate law 1984-90, chmn. 1990-91, cert. 1987), Rotary. Clubs: Biltmore Forest Country, Asheville Downtown City. Episcopalian. Estate planning, Probate (including wills, trusts), Taxation, general. Home: 45 Brookside Rd Asheville NC 28803-3015 Office: 11 N Market St PO Box 7376 Asheville NC 28802-8506 E-mail: blavelle@vwlawfirm.com.

LAVELLE, JOSEPH P. lawyer; b. Scranton, Pa., Sept. 7, 1957; s. Patrick Leo and Anne M. (Antal) L.; m. Kathy A. Mlodzienski, Aug. 14, 1982; children: Remy, Joseph, Taylor. BS in Physics, Wilkes Coll., 1979; JD summa cum laude, U. Pitts., 1982. Bar: D.C. 1982, U.S. Ct. Appeals (Fed. cir.) 1982, U.S. Patent and Trademark Office 1982, U.S. Ct. Appeals (3d, 2d and 6th cir.). Assoc. Howrey & Simon, Washington, 1982-90, ptnr., 1991—. Adj. prof. Georgetown U. Law Ctr., 1995—. Editl. bd. ABA Antitrust Law Developments, III, 1992; contbr. articles to profl. jours.; mng. editor U. Pitts. Law Rev., 1981-82. Mem. ABA, AAAS, Am. Phys. Soc., Order of the Coif. Republican. Antitrust, Federal civil litigation, Patent. Office: Howrey Simon Arnold & White Ste 1 1299 Pennsylvania Ave Washington DC 20004-2420 E-mail: lavellej@howrey.com.

LAVELLE, WILLIAM AMBROSE, lawyer, judge; b. Athens, Ohio, Jan. 18, 1925; s. Francis Anthony and Belle Elizabeth (Schloss) L.; m. Marion Helen Yanity, Aug. 7, 1954 (dec. Feb. 10, 2002); children: Frank A., John P., Lydia E., Amy M. BBA, Ohio U., 1949; JD, Ohio State U., 1952. Bar: Ohio 1952, U.S. Dist. Ct. (so. dist.) Ohio 1952. Sr. ptnr. Lavelle Law Offices, Athens, Ohio, 1952-91; judge probate/juvenile divsn. Athens County Common Pleas Ct., 1991-94; assigned judge Supreme Ct. of Ohio, 1994; pvt. practice estate planning, trusts, probate, 1994—. Former solicitor City of Nelsonville, Villages of Albany, Chauncey, Coolville, Glouster, Trimble and Zaleski; counsel Margaret Creek Conservancy Dist., L-Ax Water Distbn. Co., Sunday Creek and Hollister Water Assns.; instr. wills, trusts, estate planning Ohio U., Athens, 1991—; mem. commn. on cert. as atty. specialists Supreme Ct. Ohio, 1994. Former chmn. Athens County and Ohio Dem. Party; former mem. Dem. Nat. Com.; chmn. Athens County Bd. Elections, 1967-80; chmn. pers. rev. bd. State of Ohio, 1983-91; trustee, chmn. trustees Ohio U., 1975-81; mem. parish fin. com., parish coun., sch. bd., diocesan bd. lay consultors St. Paul's Cath. Ch., Athens. Served with inf. U.S. Army, 1943-46, ETO, PTO. Mem. ABA, Ohio State Bar Assn. (bd. govs. 1989-92, probate and trust law sect. 1993—, coun. of dels. 1986-89), Athens County Bar Assn. (past pres.), Nat. Acad. Elder Law Attys., Ohio Horse Coun., Tenn. Walking Horse Breeders and Exhibitors Assn., Walking Horse Owners Assn., Athens Symposiarch Club (past pres., Symposiarch of Yr. 1996), Athens Cotillion Club, Athens Country Club, Athens Rotary Club, VFW, Am. Legion, Am. Vets, Sons of Union Vols., Ohio U. Green and White Club, KC (3d and 4th deg.), St. Francis Soc. Avocations: breeding, raising, riding and driving tennessee walking horses. Probate (including wills, trusts), Property, real (including real estate development, water), Probate (including wills, trusts). Home: 39 Cable Ln Athens OH 45701-1304 Office: 449 E State St Athens OH 45701 Fax: 740-797-1058. E-mail: walavelle@eurekanet.com.

LAVENDER, JAY LAWRENCE, lawyer; b. Wellston, Ohio, Jan. 21, 1949; s. Elbert Jack and Alma Edith (Davis) L.; m. Joy Annette Landis, May 27, 1982; children: Courtney Jaye, Derek Blake. BA, Otterbein Coll., 1971; JD, Capital U., 1982. Bar: Ind. Sole practice, Warsaw, Ind., 1982—. Home: 104 Southfield Rd Winona Lake IN 46590-1718 Office: 116 N Buffalo St Warsaw IN 46580-2728 E-mail: lavenderlaw@kconline.com.

LAVENDER, ROBERT EUGENE, state supreme court justice; b. Muskogee, Okla., July 19, 1926; s. Harold James and Vergene Irene (Martin) L.; m. Maxine Knight, Dec. 22, 1945; children— Linda (Mrs. Dean Courter), Robert K., Debra (Mrs. Thomas Merrill), William J. LL.B., U. Tulsa, 1953; grad., Appellate Judges Seminar, 1967, Nat. Coll. State Trial Judges, 1970. Bar: Okla. bar 1953. With Mass. Bonding & Ins. Co., Tulsa, 1951-53, U.S. Fidelity & Guaranty Co., Tulsa, 1953-54; asst. city atty. Tulsa, 1954-55; practice, 1955-60, Claremore, Okla., 1960-65; justice Okla. Supreme Ct., 1965—, chief justice, 1979-80. Guest lectr. Okla. U., Oklahoma City U., Tulsa U. law schs. Republican committeeman, Rogers County, 1961-62. Served with USNR, 1944-46. Recipient Disting. Alumnus award U. Tulsa, 1993. Mem. ABA, Okla. Bar Assn., Rogers County Bar Assn., Am. Judicature Soc., Okla. Jud. Conf., Phi Alpha Delta (hon.) Methodist (adminstrv. bd.). Club: Mason (32 deg.). Home: 2910 Kerry Ln Oklahoma City OK 73120-2507 Office: US Supreme Ct Okla State Capitol Room 208 Oklahoma City OK 73105

LAVES, ALAN LEONARD, lawyer; b. Austin, Tex., June 17, 1960; s. Benard and Cecile Laves; married, 1987; 3 children. BSEE, MIT, 1982; JD with honors, U. Tex., 1985. Bar: Tex. 1985. Assoc. Akin, Gump, Strauss, Hauer & Feld, LLP, Dallas, 1985-94, ptnr., 1994—. Contbr. articles to profl. jours. Banking, Mergers and acquisitions, Securities. Office: Akin Gump Strauss Hauer & Feld Ste 2100 300 W 6th St Austin TX 78701 Fax: 512-499-6290. E-mail: alaves@akingump.com.

LAVES, BENJAMIN SAMUEL, lawyer; b. Bklyn., Aug. 2, 1946; BBA, Temple U., 1968; JD, Am. U., 1971. Bar: N.J. 1971, U.S. Dist. Ct. 1971. Intern Select Com. U.S. Senate, Washington, 1969; atty. Newark-Essex Joint Law Reform Project, N.J., 1971-74; dep. pub. advocate N.J. Dept. Pub. Advocate, Newark, 1974-83, Rate Counsel Pub. Advocate, Newark, 1983-84; pvt. practice West Orange, N.J., 1984—, 1996—. Active Essex County Estate Planning Coun. Bd. dirs. N.J. Maclaw, 1987—. Mem. ABA (gen. practice, econs. law sects.), N.J. State Bar Assn. (real property, probate and trust law sect., taxation sect.), Essex County Bar Assn. (chair computer/Internet com. 1999-00, chmn. gen. practice com. 1987-89), Essex County Estate Planning Coun., Inc., Tax Commn. Estate planning, Probate (including wills, trusts), Estate taxation. Office: 100 Executive Dr Ste 330 West Orange NJ 07052-3309

LAVIGNE, PETER MARSHALL, environmentalist, lawyer, educator; b. Laconia, N.H., Mar. 25, 1957; s. Richard Byrd and D. Jacquiline (Cobleigh) L.; m. Nancy Gaile Parent, Sept. 20, 1979; 1 child, Rhiannon Genevra Lavigne Parent. BA, Oberlin Coll., 1980; MSEL cum laude, Vt. Law Sch., 1983, JD, 1985. Bar: Mass. 1987. History tchr. Cushing Acad., Ashburnham, Mass., 1983-84; rsch. writer Environ. Law Ctr., Vt., 1985; lobbyist Vt. Natural Resources Coun., Montpelier, 1985; exec. dir. Westport (Mass.) River Watershed Alliance, 1986-88, Merrimack River Watershed Coun., West Newbury, 1988-89; environ. cons. Mass., N.H., Vt., and Oreg., 1990—2001; N.E. coord. Am. Rivers, Washington, 1990-92; dir. river leadership program River Network, Portland, Oreg., 1992-95, dir. spl. programs, 1995-96; dep. dir. For the Sake of the Salmon, Portland, 1996-97; pres. Watershed Cons., Portland, 1997-2001; pres., CEO Rivers Found. of the Ams., 2001—. Adj. prof. Antioch New Eng. Grad. Sch., Keene, N.H., 1991-92; mem. Portland Willamette River Task Force, 1997-99; chair adv. bd. Cascadia Times, Portland, 1995-99, Amigos Bravos, Taos, N.Mex., 1993-98; trustee Rivers Coun. Washington, Seattle, 1993-98; bd. dirs. Alaska Clean Water Alliance, 1995-98, acting pres. 1997-98; adv. bd. Glen Canyon Inst., 2000-01, bd. dirs., 2002—; Watershed adv. group Natural Resources Law Ctr. U. Colo., 1995-96; coastal resources adv. bd. Commonwealth of Mass., Boston, 1987-91; adj. assoc. prof. Portland State U., 1997—; Watershed Mgmt. Profl. program dir., Portland State U., 1999-01, sr. fellow exec. leadership inst., 2001—; pres. Cascadia Times Rsch. Fund, 1998-99. Co-author: Vermont Townscape, 1987; contbr. articles to profl. jours. Dir. Mass. League of Environ. Voters, Boston, 1988-92; mem. steering com. N.H. Rivers Campaign, 1988-92; co-founder, co-chair New England Coastal Campaign, 1988-92; EMT South Royalton (Vt.) Vol. Rescue Squad, 1982-86; dir., chairperson Vt. Emergency Med. Svcs. Dist. 8, Randolph, 1984-86; co-founder, v.p. Coalition for Buzzards Bay, Bourne, Mass., 1987; housing renewal commn. City of Oberlin, Ohio, 1980-81; mem. properties com. First Unitarian Ch., 1995. Recipient Environ. Achievement award Coalition for Buzzards Bay, 1988; land use rsch. fellow Environ. Law Ctr., Vt. Law Sch., 1984-85; Mellon found. rsch. grantee Oberlin Coll., 1980. Mem. Natural Resources Def. Coun., River Alliance of Wis., River Network, Idaho River United, League of Conservation Voters, Amigos Bravos, Glen Canyon Inst. Democrat. Unitarian-Universalist. Avocations: sea kayaking, mountaineering, woodwork, reading, photography. Home: 3714 SE 11th Ave Portland OR 97202-3724 Office: Rivers Found of Ams 3619 SE Milwaukie Ave Portland OR 97202-3858 Fax: (503) 232-2887. E-mail: watershed@igc.org.

LAVIN, LAURENCE MICHAEL, lawyer; b. Upper Darby, Pa., Apr. 27, 1940; s. Michael Joseph and Helen Clair (McGonigle) L. BS, St. Joseph's U., Phila., 1962; JD, Villanova (Pa.) U., 1965. Bar: Pa., S.C. Vol. U.S. Peace Corps, Thika, Kenya, 1966-67; atty. Community Legal Svcs., Phila., 1968-70, exec. dir., 1971-79, Palmetto Legal Svcs., Columbia, S.C., 1981-85; dir. Law Coordination Ctr., Harrisburg, Pa., 1985-88, Nat. Health Law Program, L.A., 1988—; chmn. bd. dirs. L.A. Poverty Dept. Bd. dirs., chmn. civil com. Nat. Legal Aid and Defender, Washington, 1976-78. Founding mem. Pa. Coun. to Abolish Death Penalty, Harrisburg, 1986; bd. dirs. L.A. Poverty Dept., 1996—, Health Care Justice Found., 2002—. Mem. ABA, Pa. Bar Assn. (chmn. legal svcs. to pub. com. 1985-88). Democrat. Civil rights, Health. Home: 3677 Wellington Rd Los Angeles CA 90016 Office: Nat Health Law Program 2639 S La Cienega Blvd Los Angeles CA 90034-2675 E-mail: lavin@healthlaw.org., llavin@boop.com.

LAVIN, TERRENCE J. lawyer; b. May 1954; m. Cynthia Sykes; children: Hillary, Chelsea. Grad. in Journalism, U. Ill.; grad., Chgo.-Kent Coll., 1983. Bd. dirs. , claims com., underwriting com. Ill. State Bar Assn. Mut. Ins. Co.; adj. prof. med. malpractice Chgo.-Kent Coll.; lectr. in field. Contbr. articles to profl. jours.; editor: ITLA's Medical Malpractice Trial Notebook, 1990. Mem.: Ill. Trial Lawyers Assn. (bd. mgrs., amicus curiae com., publs. com.), Ill. State Bar Assn. (chair task forces on multidisciplinary practice and allocation of judg, scope and correlation, budge and fin., and space and properties coms., 3d v.p. 2000—). Personal injury (including property damage). Office: 0 S LaSalle St 2102 Chicago IL 60603*

LAVINE, HENRY WOLFE, lawyer; b. Phila., Apr. 21, 1936; s. Samuel Phillips and Sarah Pamela (Leese) Lavine; m. Meta Landreth Doak, Feb. 20, 1960 (div. Feb. 1980); children: Lisa, Lindsay; m. Martha Putnam Cathcart (div. Feb. 1995); children: Samuel Putnam, Gwenn Cathcart. BA, U. Pa., 1957, JD, 1961. Assoc. Squire, Sanders & Dempsey L.L.P., Cleve., 1961-70, ptnr. Washington, 1970-85, mng. ptnr. Washington office, 1985-91, sr. mng. ptnr., 1991—2002, counsellor to the firm, 2003—. Pres. Sawyer & Co. Mem. The Bretton Woods Com. Mem. Met. Club. Corporate, general, Private international. Office: Squire Sanders & Dempsey 1201 Pennsylvania Ave NW PO Box 407 Washington DC 20044-0407

LA VINE, ROBERT L. lawyer; b. San Francisco, Dec. 24, 1929; s. Jack and Fay L.V.; m. Betty Ann La Vine, June 2, 1951; 1 child, Barbra. BS, U. Calif., 1952; JD, U. Calif. (Hastings), 1959. Bar: Calif., 1959; CPA, Calif. Ptnr. La Vine & Shain, San Francisco, 1961—. Capt. U.S. Army, 1952-54. Mem. San Francisco Bar. Assn., San Francisco Lawyers Club. Corporate, general, Property, real (including real estate development, water), Taxation, general. Office: 5 3rd St Ste 415 San Francisco CA 94103-3205 Fax: 415-777-0222. E-mail: sfolaw@earthlink.net.

LAVORATO, LOUIS A. state supreme court chief justice; s. Charles Lavorato; m. Janis M. Lavorato; children: Cindy, Natalie, Anthony, Dominic. BS in Bus. Adminstrn., Drake U., 1959, JD, 1962. Judge Iowa Supreme Ct., Des Moines, 1986—; sole practice Des Moines, 1962-79; judge Iowa Dist. Ct., Des Moines, 1979-86; justice Iowa Supreme Ct., Des Moines, 1986—2000, chief justice, 2000—. Office: Iowa Supreme Ct St Capitol Bldg Des Moines IA 50319-0001

LAW, MICHAEL R. lawyer; b. Rochester, N.Y., Nov. 30, 1947; s. George Robert and Elizabeth (Stoddart) L.; m. Cheryl Heller. BS, St. John Fisher Coll., 1969; JD, U. Louisville, 1975. Bar: N.Y. 1976, U.S. Supreme Ct. 1982. Assoc. Wood, P.C., Rochester, N.Y., 1976-77; pvt. practice Rochester, 1977-78; assoc. Sullivan, Peters, et al, Rochester, 1978-80; ptnr., 1980-81, Phillips, Lytle, Hitchcock, Blaine & Huber, Rochester, 1982—. Served with USAR, 1968—74. Mem.: ABA (alternate dispute resolution com. 1995—, trial law sect., trial techniques com., editor 1986 Trial Techniques), Genesee Valley Trial Lawyers Assn. (treas. 1992—93, pres.-elect 1993—95, pres. 1995—98), Monroe County Bar Assn. (judiciary com. 1981—88, personal injury com. 1988—, profl. responsibility com. 1996—), N.Y. State Trial Lawyers (bd. dirs.), N.Y. State Bar Assn. (trial sec., ins. negligence com.), Am. Bd. Trial Advocates. Republican. Roman Catholic. Federal civil litigation, State civil litigation, Personal injury (including property damage). Home: 3373 Elmwood Ave Rochester NY 14610-3425 Office: Phillips Lytle Et Al 1400 1st Federal Plz Rochester NY 14614-1981 E-mail: mlaw@phillipslytle.com.

LAWIT, JOHN WALTER, lawyer; b. Phila., Aug. 13, 1950; Student, U. Bridgeport, 1968-70; B of Univ. Studies, U. N.Mex., 1972; JD, Franklin Pierce Law Ctr., Concord, N.H., 1977. Bar: Pa. 1978, N.Mex. 1980, Tex. 1992, U.S. Dist. Ct. (ea. dist.) Pa. 1978, U.S. Dist. Ct. N.Mex. 1980. Investigator Franklin Pierce Law Ctr., 1976-77; sole practitioner N.Y.C., 1978-79; atty., assoc. McCallister, Fairfield, Query, Strotz & Stribling, Albuquerque, 1979-80; sole practitioner Albuquerque, 1980—. Adj. prof. immigration law U. N.Mex. Sch. Law, 1983, 84, 88; spl. immigration counsel U. N.Mex., Albuquerque, 1987—; U.S. immigration judge US. Dept. Justice, 1985; apptd. mem. N.Mex. Internat. Trade/Investment Coun., 1984-87, N.Mex. Border Commn., 1982-86; hon. cons. atty. Ministry Fgn. Affairs Republic of Mex., 1983; lobbyist, author, drafter N.Mex. Immigration & Nationality Law Practice Act. Presenter in field. Founder, profl. cons. Jewish Family Svcs. of Albuquerque, 1988—; bd. dirs., pres. Rainbow House Internat. Adoption, Belen, N.Mex., 1987-2000; v.p. N.Mex. Refugee Assn., Albuquerque, 1979-84; bd. dirs. N.Mex. Civil Liberties Union, 1988-90; mem. adv. bd. Healing the Children, Albuquerque, 1989—; bd. dirs. Inst. for Spanish Arts, 1994-96. Recipient Disting. Svcs. award Cath. Social Svcs., 1988. Mem. N.Mex. State Bar (chair internat. and immigration lawyers sect. 1990-91, bd. dirs. 1988-90), Albuquerque Bar Assn., Am. Immigration Lawyers Assn., El Paso Assn. Immigration and Nationality Lawyers. Avocations: biking, travel, whitewater rafting, hiking. Immigration, naturalization, and customs. Office: 2305 Renard Pl SE Ste 210 Albuquerque NM 87106 Fax: 505-244-1834. E-mail: jlawit@jlawit.com.

LAWLER, THOMAS ALBERT, lawyer; b. Eldora, Iowa, June 10, 1946; s. Lewis W. and Mary C. (Schafer) L.; m. Elaine E. Bruch, June 29, 1968; children: Erin Elizabeth, Loretta Mary. BA, St. Ambrose U., 1968; JD, Cath. U. Am., 1971. Bar: Iowa 1972, U.S. Dist. Ct. (no. and so. dists.) Iowa 1974, U.S. Tax Ct. 1985, U.S. Supreme Ct., 1990, U.S. Ct. Appeals (10th cir.) 1998, U.S. Ct. Appeals (8th cir.) 2002. Pvt. practice, Greene, Iowa, 1972-73; atty., asst. to acct. O's Gold Seed Co., Parkersburg, Iowa, 1972-73; ptnr. Klinkenborg, Lawler, Hansmann & Mansheim, Parkersburg, 1973-85; pvt. practice Parkersburg, 1985-97; mem. Lawler & Swanson, P.L.C., 1997—. Lectr. on taxation and fin. planning for agr. at State Agrl. Acad., Nizhni, Nougorod, Russia, 1995. Author: Iowa Legal Forms, Probate, 1991, Income Tax Consequences of Real Estate Leasing, 1995; contbr. articles to profl. jours. Atty. City of Parkersburg, 1973-91, City of New Hartford, Iowa, 1973—, City of Stout, Iowa, 1973-91, City of Aredale, Iowa, 1981—, City of Greene, Iowa, 2000—, Parkersburg Hist. Soc., 1973—; active Parkersburg Econ. Devel. Fellow Iowa State Bar Assn. Found., Am. Coll. Trust and Estate Coun.; mem. ABA, Iowa Bar Assn. (bd. govs., chair agrl. law sect.), Am. Agrl. Law Assn. (past pres.), Butler County Bar Assn., 2A Bar Assn., Parkersburg C. of C. (pres. 1979-80, Citizen of Yr. 1983), Rotary. Democrat. Roman Catholic. Avocations: gardening, reading, woodworking. Probate (including wills, trusts), Property, real (including real estate development, water), Taxation, general. Office: 601 Coates St Parkersburg IA 50665 Home: PO Box 280 Parkersburg IA 50665-0280 E-mail: tlawler@forbin.com.

LAWLER, WILLIAM E., III, lawyer; b. Washington, May 21, 1960; BA cum laude, U. Notre Dame, 1982; JD cum laude, Georgetown U., 1985. Bar: Md. 1985, D.C. 1986. Asst. U.S. atty. U.S. Atty.'s Office, DC, 1989—96; ptnr. Vinson & Elkins LLP, Washington. Lectr. FBI Tng. Acad., Quantico, Va. Contbr. articles to profl. jours. Named Young Lawyer of Yr., D.C., 1992. Mem.: ABA (Ho. of Dels. 1992—93, 2001—), Bar Assn. D.C. (bd. dirs. 1993—, pres.-elect 2000—01, chair Young Lawyers sect. 1994—95). Federal civil litigation. Office: Vinson and Elkins LLP Willard Office Bldg 1455 Pennsylvania Ave NW Washington DC 20004-1008*

LAWLESS, JANINE A. lawyer; m. Greg Lawless. Cert.: Nat. Elder Law Found. (elder law atty.). Ptnr. Lawless Partnership, Seattle. Fellow: Nat. Acad. Elder Law Attys. (bd. dirs., pres.-elect Wash. chpt.); mem.: Wash. State Bar Assn. (chair elder law sect.). Probate (including wills, trusts), Family and matrimonial. Office: Lawless Partnership 6018 Seaview Ave NW Seattle WA 98107-2657 Office Fax: 206-782-9569. Business E-Mail: jlawless@lawless2.com.*

LAWLESS, WILLIAM BURNS, lawyer, retired judge, academic administrator; b. Buffalo, June 3, 1922; s. William B. and Margaret H. (Welton) L.; children: Sharon, Barbara, William, Cathy, Gregory, Richard, Robert, Jeannie, Therese, John, Maria, Thomas. JD, Notre Dame U., 1944; AB, U. Buffalo, 1950; LLM, Harvard U., 1950. Bar: N.Y. 1946, U.S. Dist. Ct. (we. dist.) N.Y. 1946, U.S. Tax Ct. 1947, U.S. Supreme Ct. 1956, D.C. 1972, U.S. Dist. Ct. (ea. and so. dists.) N.Y. 1972, U.S. Ct. Appeals (2d cir.) 1972, Mass. 1976, U.S. Ct. Appeals (D.C. cir.) 1978, U.S. Ct. Appeals (7th cir.) 1979. Assoc. Kenefick, Cooke, Mitchell, Bass & Letchworth, Buffalo, 1946-50; ptnr. Williams, Crane & Lawless, Buffalo, 1950-54, Lawless, Offermann, Fallon & Mahoney, Buffalo, 1956-60; justice N.Y. State Supreme Ct. 8th Jud. Dist., 1960-68; dean Notre Dame Law Sch., 1968-71; ptnr. Mudge Rose Guthrie & Alexander, N.Y.C., 1971-75; pvt. practice Hawkins, Delafield & Wood, 1976—81; pres. We. State U., Fullerton, Calif., 1982-87; dean Nat. Jud. Coll., 1987-90; pres. Judges Mediation Network, Newport Beach, Calif., 1992—; of counsel Capretz & Assoc., Newport Beach, 1994—2002. Vis. scholar Cambridgge U., Eng., 1990-91; mem. facutly U. Buffalo Law Sch., 1950-59, Notre Dame Law Sch., 1968-71, Fordham U. Law Sch., 1974-81; spl. counsel to Gov. N.Y. State, 1956-58; del., sec. to judiciary com. N.Y. State Constl. Conv., 1967; founder Notre Dame Law Ctr., London, 1968; pub. mem. N.Y. State Joint Legis. Com on Ct. Reorgn., 1973-82; mem. N.Y. State Temporary Commn. on Jud. Conduct, 1974-75; mem. N.Y. State Gov.'s Adv. Panel on Ethical Disclosure Standards, 1974-75; trustee Pace U. Co-author: New York Pattern Jury Instruction, vol. I, 1965, vol. II, 1968; contbr. articles to law revs.; editor-in-chief Notre Dame Lawyer, 1943-44. Bd. dirs. We. State U., Encino, Calif.; corp. city counsel City of Buffalo, 1954-56; pres. Buffalo City Coun., 1956-59. Served to lt. s.g. USNR, World War II, PTO. Mem. ABA, N.Y. State Bar Assn., Am. Law Inst., Am. Coll. Trial Lawyers, Bar N.Y.C., Harvard of N.Y.C. Club, University Club Newport Beach. Office: Judges Mediation Network 1977 Pt Cardiff Newport Beach CA 92660-2151

LAWNICZAK, JAMES MICHAEL, lawyer; b. Toledo, Sept. 11, 1951; m. Christine Nielsen, Dec. 31, 1979; children: Mara Katharine, Rachel Anne, Amy Elizabeth. BA, U. Mich., 1974, JD, 1977. Bar: Mich. 1977, Ill. 1979, Ohio 1989. Law clk. to the Honorable Robert E. DeMascio U.S. Dist. Ct. (ea. dist.) Mich., Detroit, 1977-79; assoc. Levy and Erens, Chgo., 1979-83; assoc. then ptnr. Mayer, Brown & Platt, Chgo., 1983-88; ptnr. Calfee, Halter & Griswold, LLP, Cleve., 1988—. Contbg. author: Collier on Bankruptcy, 15th rev. edit., 1997—. Mem. Chgo. Bar Assn. (subcom. on bankruptcy 1983-88), Cleve. Bar Assn. (bankruptcy com.). Banking, Bankruptcy, Commercial, contracts (including sales of goods; commercial financing). Home: 14039 Fox Hollow Dr Novelty OH 44072-9773 Office: Calfee Halter & Griswold 800 Superior Ave E Ste 1400 Cleveland OH 44114-2601 E-mail: jlawniczak@calfee.com.

LAWRENCE, BETTY TENN, lawyer; b. Memphis, Tenn., Feb. 3, 1949; d. William Harvey and Margaret Amrhein Lawrence. AB, Rollins Coll., 1971; JD, Duke U., 1983. Bar: N.Y. 1984, N.C. 1986. Curator Pack Meml. Pub. Libr., Asheville, N.C., 1974-80; assoc. Davis Polk and Wardwell, N.Y.C., 1983-86; pvt. practice Asheville, 1986—. Mem. Preservation Soc. Asheville and Burcombe Co., Asheville, 1976—, v.p. 1978-80, pres. 1986-89; Commr. Hist. Resources Commn. of Asheville and Buncombe County, 1978-80, 86-92, 94—, chair, 1999. Mem. N.C. Bar Assn. Environmental, Land use and zoning (including planning), Probate (including wills, trusts). Home and Office: 142 Hillside St Asheville NC 28801-1206 E-mail: btlawrence@juno.com.

LAWRENCE, CHARLES EDWARD, JR., lawyer, judge; b. Beaumont, Miss., July 29, 1955; s. Charles Edward and Mattie Mae Lawrence; m. Shirley A. Sutton, June 5, 1977; children: Charles E. III (CJ), Chari E. B, U. So. Miss., 1976; JD, Howard U., 1979. Bar: Miss. 1979. Pvt. practice atty., counselor at law, Hattiesburg, Miss., 1979—; mcpl. ct. judge City of Hattiesburg, 1997—. Bd. dirs. BancorpSouth Cmty. Adv. Coun. Contbg. columnist, 1983-85. V.p. Forrest County br. NAACP, Hattiesburg, 1980; councilmember City of Hattiesburg, 1985-97; pres. Hattiesburg City Coun., 1991-97; bd. dirs. Wesley Med. Ctr. Meth. Hosp., Hattiesburg, 1995-97, United Way, Hattiesburg, 1997—. Recipient Svc. award Optimist International, 1986, New Medinah Islamic Retreat, 1996. Mem. ATLA, Miss. Bar Assn., Miss. Mcpl. Judge Assn., Magnolia Bar Assn. (so. dist. rep. 1986-87). Baptist. Avocations: camping, reading, bike riding, photography. Home: 606 John St Hattiesburg MS 39401-3948 Office: 606 1/2 John St Hattiesburg MS 39401-3966 Fax: 601-544-9279.

LAWRENCE, EDWARD JACK, III, lawyer; b. Beaumont, Tex., Sept. 23, 1949; s. Edward Jack and Nelda Rae (McClure) L. BA in Govt., Lamar U., 1971; JD, U. Houston, 1988. Bar: U.S. Dist. Ct. (ea. dist.) Tex. 1993, U.S. Supreme Ct. 1995. Atty. East Tex. Legal Svcs., Beaumont, 1989; pvt. practice Beaumont, 1990—. Bd. dirs. ACLU, Beaumont, 1978—, Clean Air and Water Orgn., 1996—. Mem. Tex. Bar Assn., Jefferson County Bar Assn. Democrat. Methodist-Unitarian. Avocations: golf, tennis, poetry, astronomy, guitar. Criminal, Education and schools, Family and matrimonial. Home and Office: 5570 Winfree St Beaumont TX 77705-5939

LAWRENCE, JAMES KAUFMAN LEBENSBURGER, lawyer; b. New Rochelle, N.Y., Oct. 8, 1940; s. Michael Monet and Edna (Billings) L.; m. George-Ann Adams, Apr. 5, 1969; children: David Michael, Catherine Robin. AB, Ohio State U., 1962, JD, 1965. Bar: Ohio. 1965, U.S. Dist. Ct. (so. dist.) Ohio 1971, U.S. Ct. Appeals (6th cir.) 1971, U.S. Ct. Appeals (4th cir.) 1978. Field atty. NLRB, Cin., 1965-70; ptnr. Frost Brown Todd LLC, Cin., 1970—. Adj. prof. econs. dept. and Coll. Law U. Cin., 1975—; adj. prof. econs. dept. and Moritz Coll. Law Ohio State U., 1995—; adj. prof. econs. dept. and Coll. Law Xavier U., 1995, McGregor Sch., Antioch U., 1993—98; adj. prof. MBA program Otterbein Coll., 2002—; treas. Potter Stewart Inn of Ct., Cin., 1988—90; tchg. fellow Harvard Negotiation Project, 1991; chmn. adv. panel on appointment of magistrate judges U.S. Dist. Ct. for So. Dist. Ohio, 1993—97. Contbr. articles to profl. jours.; editor: (newsletter) Pass the Gavel, 2002—. Mem. nat. coun. Ohio State U. Coll. Law, 1974—; mem. steering com. Leadership Cin., 1985-89; mem. Seven Hills Neighborhood Houses, Cin., 1973-95, pres., 1992-94; bd. dirs. Beechwood Home, Cin., 1973-85; mem. adv. bd. Emerson Behavioral Health Svcs., 1990-95, chmn., 1995; chmn. Labor Dept., 1978-89, Franciscan Hosp. Devel. Coun., 1995-99, chmn., 1996-97; trustee Ctr. for Resolution of Disputes, Inc., 1988-91, treas., 1990-91; mem. Ohio Gov.'s Ops. Improvement Task Force, 1991. Recipient Outstanding Adj. Faculty award, U. Cin., 1998. Fellow Coll. Labor and Employment Lawyers; mem. ABA, Cin. Bar Assn. (chmn. labor law com. 1979-82, comm. adv. com. 1994-96, alternative dispute resolution com. 1996—), Ohio Bar Assn. (vice chmn. labor and employment law sect. 1987-90, chmn. 1990-92, Ohio's Friend of Legal Edn. award 2003), Indsl. Rels. Rsch. Assn. (bd. govs. 1977-80), Alumni Assn. Coll. Law Ohio State U. (pres. 1984-85), Assn. for Conflict Resolution, Cincinnatus Assn. (pres. 1985-86), Collaborative Law Ctr. (steering com. 1996—), Univ. Club; master Potter Stewart Inn of Ct. Avocations: collecting movie posters, biking. Alternative dispute resolution, Labor (including EEOC, Fair Labor Standards Act, labor-management relations, NLRB, OSHA), Education and schools. Home: 3300 Columbia Pkwy Cincinnati OH 45226-1044 Office: Frost Brown Todd LLC 2500 PNC Ctr 201 E 5th St Cincinnati OH 45202-4182 E-mail: jlawrence@fbtlaw.com.

LAWRENCE, JOHN KIDDER, lawyer; b. Detroit, Nov. 18, 1949; s. Luther Ernest and Mary Anna (Kidder) L.; m. Jeanine Ann DeLay, June 20, 1981. AB, U. Mich., 1971; JD, Harvard U., 1974. Bar: Mich. 1974, U.S. Supreme Ct. 1977, D.C. 1978. Assoc. Dickinson, Wright, McKean & Cudlip, Detroit, 1973-74; staff atty. Office of Judge Adv. Gen., Washington, 1975-78; assoc. Dickinson, Wright, McKean, Cudlip & Moon, Detroit, 1978-81; ptnr. Dickinson, Wright, Moon, VanDusen & Freeman, Detroit, 1981-98, Dickinson Wright PLLC, Detroit, 1998—. Exec. sec. Detroit Com. on Fgn. Rels., 1988—; trustee Ann Arbor (Mich.) Summer Festival, Inc., 1990—; patron Founders Soc. Detroit Inst. Arts, 1979—; dir. Mich. C. of C., 2002—. With USN, 1975-78. Mem. AAAS, ABA, Am. Law Inst., State Bar Mich., D.C. Bar Assn., Am. Judicature Soc., Internat. Bar Assn., Am. Hist. Assn., Mich. C. of C. (bd. dirs. 2002—), Detroit Athletic Club, Econ. Club Detroit, Phi Eta Sigma, Phi Beta Kappa. Democrat. Episcopalian. Banking, Private international, Mergers and acquisitions. Office: Dickinson Wright PLLC 500 Woodward Ave Ste 4000 Detroit MI 48226-3416

LAWRENCE, STEVEN THOMAS, lawyer; b. Sacramento, Calif., Feb. 28, 1968; s. Thomas George and Sharon Lee L.; m. Jodi Lynd Hipps, Aug. 8, 1993. BS, Calif. State U., Sacramento, 1990; JD, U. Pacific, 1994. Fin. cons. Govt. Fin. Strategies, Inc., Sacramento, 1990-91; jud. clk. Ariz. Ct. Appeals, Phoenix, 1994-95; dep. county atty. Maricopa County Atty.'s Office, Phoenix, 1995-96; assoc. atty. Felix & Holohan, Phoenix, 1996-98; assoc. gen. counsel JDA Software Group, Inc., Phoenix, 1998-99; corp. counsel SkyMall, Inc., Phoenix, 1999-2000; assoc. Gallagher & Kennedy, P.A., Phoenix, 2000—02, shareholder, 2003—. Active First Christian Ch., Phoenix. Mem. ABA, Maricopa County Bar Assn. Republican. Avocations: golf, physical fitness, training hunting dogs. Home: 2108 E Marshall Ave Phoenix AZ 85016 Office: Gallagher & Kennedy PA 2575 E Camelback Rd Phoenix AZ 85016 E-mail: stl@gknet.com.

LAWRENCE, WILLIAM CLARENCE, business executive, lawyer, mediator, politician; b. Tuskegee, Ala., Dec. 15, 1945; s. James Clarence and Nellie Mae James Lawrence; m. Audrey Rochelle Diggs Rackley, Dec. 30, 1973 (div. Sept. 1979); 1 child, Kimberly Ann; m. Grace Louise McDonald, June 23, 1984; children: Antoinette, Robert David. BS in Polit. Sci., Tuskegee U., 1968; M in Pub. Adminstrn., St. Mary's U., 1976; JD, Ind. U., 1979; M in Mgmt., U. Dallas, 1993. Tax atty. audit divsn. U.S. Treasury Dept., Indpls., 1979-80; commodities mgr. Cummins Engine Co., Columbus, Ind., 1980-82; staff mgr. GTE Network Svcs. Planning, Stamford, Conn., 1982-86; product mgr.-consumer GTE Product Mgmt., Irving, Tex., 1986-89, group product mgr.-wireless, 1989-92, group product mgr.-devel., 1992-96; group mktg. mgr.-systems GTE Bus. Sales Ops., Irving, 1996-99; pres., CEO Dakiman Co., Highland Village, Tex., 1999—. Chmn., bd. dirs. GTE Hdqrs. PAC, Irving, 1995-98. Pres., bd. dirs. Boston Home Childrens Found., Dallas, 1988-93; commr. Planning and Zoning Commn., Highland Village, 1996-99; chmn. Irving Sch. Dist. Improvement Com., 1998—; mem. Tex. State Textbook Rev. Adv. Panel, 2000; city coun. and mayor pro tem Highland Village, 1999-2000; mayor City of Highland Village, 2000-. Col. USAF Res., 1976—. Mem. ABA (assoc., alternate disputes resolution sect.), New Product Devel. Assn., Project Mgmt. Inst., Tex. St. Bd. Prfl. Engrg., 2002-, Nat. Council Examiners for Engrg. Surveying, 2002-, Alpha Phi Alpha, Phi Alpha Delta. Republican. Baptist. Avocations: golf, racquetball, volleyball. Home: 2800 Woodlake Ct Highland Village TX 75077-6496

LAWSON, A. PETER, lawyer; AB, Dartmouth Coll., 1968; JD, Columbia U., 1971. Bar: N.Y. 1971, Ill. 1979. Assoc. Sullivan & Cromwell, 1971-78; sr. counsel Baxter Internat., 1978-79; various positions Motorola Corp., 1979-89, corp. v.p., asst. gen. counsel, 1989-95, sr. v.p., asst. gen. counsel, 1995-96, sr. v.p., sec., gen. counsel, 1996-98, exec. v.p., gen. counsel, sec., 1998—. Office: Motorola Inc 1303 E Algonquin Rd Schaumburg IL 60196-1079*

LAWSON, JACK WAYNE, lawyer; b. Decatur, Ind., Sept. 23, 1935; s. Alva W. and Florence C. (Smitley) L.; m. Sarah J. Hibbard, Dec. 28, 1961; children: Mark, Jeff. BA in Polit. Sci., Valparaiso U., 1958, JD, 1961. Bar: Ind. 1961, U.S. Dist. Ct. (no. and so. dists.) Ind. 1991, U.S. Ct. Appeals (7th cir.) 1991, U.S. Supreme Ct. 1970. Ptnr. Beckman, Lawson LLP, Ft. Wayne, Ind., 1961-84, sr. ptnr., 1984—. Seminar presenter and writer Ind. CLE Forum, Indpls., 1970—, Nat. Health Lawyers Assn., Washington, 1986. Editor-in-chief Indiana Real Estate Transactions; contbr. articles to profl. jours. Mem. Ft. Wayne C. of C., 1975—; small claims ct. judge, Allen County, Ind., 1963-67. Recipient Sagamore Wabash award, Gov. State of Ind., 2001. Mem. Am. Coll. Real Estate Lawyers. Republican. Lutheran. Avocations: sailing, teaching religious seminars, antique consulting. Corporate, general, Finance, Property, real (including real estate development, water). Office: Beckman Lawson LLP 800 Standard Federal Plaza PO Box 800 Fort Wayne IN 46801-0800

LAWSON, THOMAS SEAY, JR., lawyer; b. Montgomery, Ala., Oct. 30, 1935; s. Thomas Seay and Rose Darrington (Gunter) L.; m. Sarah Hunter Clayton, May 27, 1961; children: Rose Gunter, Gladys Robinson, Thomas

Seay III. AB, U. Ala., 1957, JD, 1963. Bar: Ala. 1963, U.S. Supreme Ct. 1969. Law clk. to chief judge U.S. Dist. Ct. (no. dist.) Ala., 1963-64; assoc. Steiner, Crum & Baker, Montgomery, 1964-68; ptnr. Capell, Howard, Knabe & Cobbs P.A., Montgomery, 1968-98; asst. dist. atty. 15th jud. cir. of Ala., 1969-70; ptnr. Capell & Howard, P.C., Montgomery, 1999—. Mem. lawyers adv. com. U.S. Ct. Appeals, 5th cir. 1978, 11th cir. 1979-82. Pres. The Lighthouse, 1978-79. Lt. USNR, 1957-60. Fellow Ala. Law Found.; mem. ABA, FBA, Ala. State Bar (pres. young lawyers sect. 1970-71), Montgomery County Bar Assn. (pres. 1980), Am. Judicature Soc., 11th Cir. Hist. Soc. (pres. 1999-2001), Lawyers Adv. Com. U.S. Dist. Ct. (mid. dist.) Ala. (chmn. 2000—), Soc. of Pioneers of Montgomery (pres. 1983), Farrah Law Soc. (pres. 1986-88, Outstanding Alumnus award U. Ala. student chpt. 1989), Montgomery Inn of Ct. (master bencher, bd. dirs. 1989-93, chancellor 1991, pres. 1992-93, emeritus 1994—), Ala. Law Inst. (bd. dirs. 1986—), Ala. Law Sch. Found. (trustee 1985—), Montgomery Country Club. Episcopalian. Alternative dispute resolution, Federal civil litigation, General civil litigation. Home: 1262 Glen Grattan Montgomery AL 36111-1402 Office: Capell & Howard PC PO Box 2069 150 S Perry St Montgomery AL 36102-2069 E-mail: tsl@chlaw.com.

LAWSON, WILLIAM HOMER, lawyer; b. Champaign, Ill., Jan. 14, 1953; s. Joel Smith and Grace Lawson; m. Laurie, Nov. 24, 1979; children: William S., Amy R., Bradley C. BA, Trinity Coll., Hartford, Conn., 1974; JD, Stanford U., 1977. Bar: Hawaii 1977. Assoc. Cades, Schutte, Honolulu, 1977-79; sole practice Honolulu, 1979—. Mem. ABA, ATLA., Hawaii Bar Assn., Consumer Lawyers of Hawaii. Personal injury (including property damage), Product liability, Professional liability. Office: 1188 Bishop St Ste 2902 Honolulu HI 96813-3312

LAXON, WILLIAM ALLAN, lawyer; b. Auckland, New Zealand, Jan. 28, 1936; s. William Ash and Alice Margaret Laxon; m. Lorna Delytus Kirk, Nov. 2, 1963; children: Andrew William, Alison Patricia, Iain Allan. LLB, U. Auckland, 1959. Bar: New Zealand; notary public. Ptnr. Brookfields (and predecessor firms), Auckland, 1962-97, cons., 1998—. Bd. dirs. Mount Wellington Trust Hotels Ltd. Author: The Shire Line, 1972, The British India Steam Company Ltd., 1994, Davey and the Awatea, 1997, Crossed Flags, 1997. Chmn. Presbyn. Support, Auckland, 1981-90; pres. Auckland Inst. and Mus., 1989-91. With New Zealand Army, 1955-58. Named MBE, 1988. Mem. Auckland Dist. Law Soc. (convenir libr. com. 1980-88, benevolent fund 1994-97), Northern Club, Auckland Soc. Notaries (councillor). Avocations: shipping history, music, reading, walking. Admiralty, Corporate, general, , Alternative dispute resolution. Office: Brookfields 19 Victoria St W Auckland New Zealand E-mail: laxon@brookfields.co.nz.

LAY, DONALD POMEROY, federal judge; b. Princeton, Ill., Aug. 24, 1926; s. Hardy W. and Ruth (Cushing) L.; m. Miriam Elaine Gustafson, Aug. 6, 1949; children: Stephen Pomeroy(dec.) , Catherine Sue, Cynthia Lynn, Elizabeth Ann, Deborah Jean, Susan Elaine. Student, U.S. Naval Acad., 1945—46; BA, U. Iowa, 1948, JD, 1951; LLD (hon.) (hon.) , Mitchell Coll. Law, 1985. Bar: Nebr. 1951, Iowa 1951, Wis. 1953. Assoc. Kennedy, Holland, DeLacy & Svoboda, Omaha, 1951—53, Quarles, Spence & Quarles, Milw., 1953—54, Eisenstatt, Lay, Higgins & Miller, 1954—66; judge U.S. Ct. Appeals (8th cir.), 1966—, chief judge, 1980—92, senior judge, 1992—. Faculty mem. on evidence Nat. Coll. Trial Judges, 1964—65, U. Minn. Law Sch., William Mitchell Law Sch.; mem. U.S. Jud. Conf., 1980—92. Mem. editl. bd.: Iowa Law Rev., 1950—51; contbr. With USNR, 1944—46. Recipient Hancher-Finkbine medal, U. Iowa, 1980, Disting. Alumni award, 2000. Mem.: ATLA (bd. govs. 1963—65, Jud. Achievement award), ABA, Am. Judicature Soc., Wis. Bar Assn., Iowa Bar Assn., Nebr. Bar Assn., Internat. Acad. Trial Lawyers, Order of Coif, Sigma Chi, Phi Delta Phi, Delta Sigma Rho (Significant Sig award 1986, Herbert Harley award 1988). Presbyterian. Office: US Ct Appeals 8th Cir 316 Robert St N Ste 560 Saint Paul MN 55101-1461

LAYDEN, CHARLES MAX, lawyer; b. Lafayette, Ind., Nov. 10, 1941; s. Charles E. and Elnora M. (Parvis) L.; m. Lynn D. McVey, Jan. 28, 1967; children: David Charles, Kathleen Ann, John Michael, Daniel Joseph. BA in Indsl. Mgmt., Purdue U., 1964; JD, Ind. U., 1967. Bar: Ind. 1967, U.S. Dist. Ct. (no. and so. dists.) Ind. 1967, U.S. Ct. Appeals (7th cir.) 1970. U.S. Tax Ct. 1986. Assoc. Vaughan & Vaughan, Lafayette, 1967-70; ptnr. Vaughan, Vaughan & Layden, Lafayette, 1970-86, Layden & Layden, Lafayette, 1986—. Chmn. profl. div. United Way Lafayette, 1986. Mem. ABA, Ind. Bar Assn., Tippecanoe County Bar Assn. (pres. 1994-95), Am. Bd. Trial Advs. (charter mem. Ind. chpt. 1984—), Ind. Trial Lawyers Assn. (bd. dirs. 1983—). Republican. Roman Catholic. Avocations: photography, classic cars, flying. Federal civil litigation, State civil litigation, Personal injury (including property damage). Home: 2826 Ashland St West Lafayette IN 47906-1510 Office: Layden & Layden PO Box 909 Lafayette IN 47902-0909

LAYMAN, DAVID MICHAEL, lawyer; b. Pensacola, Fla., July 28, 1955; s. James Hugh and Winifred (Smith) L. BA with high honors, U. Fla., 1977, JD with honors, 1979. Bar: Fla. 1980. Assoc. Gunster, Yoakley, Criser & Stewart, West Palm Beach, Fla., 1980-83, Wolf, Block, Schorr & Solis-Cohen, West Palm Beach, 1983-87, ptnr., 1987-88; shareholder Shapiro and Bregman P.A., 1988-91, Greenberg, Traurig, Hoffman, Lipoff, Rosen & Quentel, P.A., West Palm Beach, Fla., 1991-93, Prom, Korn & Zehmer, P.A., Jacksonville, Fla., 1993-94, Mahoney Adams & Criser, P.A., Jacksonville, Fla., 1994-96, Greenberg, Traurig, P.A., West Palm Beach, Fla., 1996—. Mem. Attys. Title Ins. Fund. Contbg. editor U. Fla. Law Rev.; contbr. articles to profl. jours. Del. Statewide Rep. Caucus, Orlando, Fla., 1986; mem. Blue Ribbon Zoning Rev. Com., West Palm Beach, 1986; bd. dirs., pres. Palm Beach County Planning Congress, 1984-89; trustee South Fla. Sci. Mus., 1994-96; bd. dirs., sec., v.p. Ronald McDonald House, Jacksonville, 1994-96, Cultural Coun. of Greater Jacksonville; bd. dirs., v.p. Children's Pl. at Home Safe Inc., 1996—; mem. vestry, jr. warden Holy Trinity Episcopal Ch., West Palm Beach, 2002—. Named one of Outstanding Young Men in Am., 1980. Mem. ABA, Fla. Bar Assn. (bd. govs. young lawyers divsn. 1989-91), Palm Beach County Bar Assn. (pres. young lawyers sect. 1987-88), Fla. Blue Key, Palm Beach County Gator Club (pres., bd. dirs.), Omicron Delta Kappa, Sigma Chi, Phi Kappa Phi. Episcopalian. Landlord-tenant, Property, real (including real estate development, water). Office: 777 S Flagler Dr Ste 300E West Palm Beach FL 33401-6161 E-mail: laymand@gtlaw.com.

LAYTON, ROBERT, lawyer; b. N.Y.C., Feb. 19, 1931; s. Benjamin and Ruth (Beck) L.; m. Joan Levy, May 17, 1967 (div. Jan. 1976); children: Elisabeth, Julie; m. Christine Lambert, Dec. 31, 1988. BA, U. Mich., 1951; LLB, Yale U., 1954. Teaching fellow Stanford Law Sch., Palo Alto, Calif., 1957-58; atty. U.S. Dept. Justice, Washington, 1958-62; assoc., ptnr. Gilbert, Segall & Young, N.Y.C., 1962-73; ptnr. Layton and Sherman, N.Y.C., 1973-84, Surrey & Morse, N.Y.C., 1984-85, Jones, Day, Reavis & Pogue, N.Y.C., 1986-93. Contbr. articles to internat. profl. jours. Mem. exec. com. Yale Law Sch. Assn., 1992-95. Served to sgt. U.S. Army, 1954-56. Fourth Am. recipient Diploma of The Hague Acad. Law, 1959. Mem.: Yale (N.Y.C.). E-mail: rlayton@laytonbh.com.

LAZAR, RAYMOND MICHAEL, lawyer, educator; b. Mpls., July 16, 1939; s. Simon and Hessie (Teplin) L; children: Mark, Deborah. BBA, U. Minn., 1961, JD, 1964. Bar: Minn. 1964, U.S. Dist. Ct. Minn. 1964. Spl. asst. atty. gen. State of Minn., St. Paul, 1964-66; pvt. practice Mpls., 1966-72; ptnr. Lapp, Lazar, Laurie & Smith, Mpls., 1972-86; ptnr., officer Fredrikson & Byron P.A., Mpls., 1986—. Lectr. various continuing edn. programs, 1972—; adj. prof. law U. Minn., Mpls., 1983-99. Fellow Am. Acad. Matrimonial Lawyers; mem. ABA (chair divorce laws and procedures com. family law sect. 1993-94), Minn. Bar Assn., Hennepin County Bar Assn. (chair family law sect. 1978-79). Alternative dispute resolution, Family and matrimonial. Home: 400 River St Minneapolis MN 55401 Office: Fredrikson & Byron PA 4000 Pillsbury Ctr Minneapolis MN 55402-3314 E-mail: rlazar@fredlaw.com.

LAZARUS, ARTHUR, JR., retired lawyer; b. Bklyn., Aug. 30, 1926; s. Arthur and Frieda (Langer) L.; m. Gertrude Chiger, Jan. 8, 1956; children: Andrew Joseph, Edward Peter, Diana Ruth. BA with honors, Columbia U., 1946; JD, Yale U., 1949. Bar: N.Y. 1951, D.C. 1952, U.S. Supreme Ct. 1954. Assoc. Fried, Frank, Harris, Shriver & Jacobson, Washington, 1950-57, ptnr., 1957-91, mng. ptnr. Washington office, 1974-86; of counsel Sonosky, Chambers, Sachse, Endreson & Perry, Washington, 1994—. Vis. lectr. Yale Law Sch., 1973-81. Trustee Arena Stage, 1987-98, Georgetown Day Sch., 1963-71. Federal civil litigation. Home: 3201 Fessenden St NW Washington DC 20008-2032 E-mail: ALazarus@Sonosky.com.

LAZARUS, BRUCE I. restaurant and hotel management educator; b. Pitts. s. Arnold H. and Belle Lazarus. BS, Pa. State U., 1975; JD, U. Pitts., 1980. Bar: Pa. 1980. Ops. analyst ARA Services, Phila., 1976-77; legal intern Pa. Human Relations Commn., Pitts., 1978-79; food service dir. Martin's Run Life Care, ARA Services, Phila., 1980-81; asst. dir. dept. nutrition Bryn Mawr (Pa.) Hosp., ARA Services, 1981-84; prof. restaurant and hotel mgmt. Purdue U., West Lafayette, Ind., 1984—96, prof. emeritus, 1996—. Council Hotel, Restaurant and Instnl. Edn. (membership com. 1984—, paper rev. com. 1988—). Contbr. articles to profl. pubs. Nat. Inst. Food Service Industry grantee, 1986, Internat. Franchise Assn., 1987; recipient Mary Mathew award for Outstanding Undergraduate teaching Consumer anf Family Svcs., 1993, Purdue Univ. award Outstanding Undergraduate Teaching, 1993. Mem. ABA, Ind. Bar Assn., Pa. Bar Assn., Nat. Restaurant Assn., Phi Kappa Phi. Office: Purdue U 1266 Stone Hall Lafayette IN 47907-1266

LAZARUS, KENNETH ANTHONY, lawyer; b. Passaic, N.J., Mar. 10, 1942; s. John Joseph and Margaret (Di Cenzo) L.; m. Marylyn Jane Flemming, Aug. 13, 1966; children: Maggi Ann, John, Joseph. BA, U. Dayton, 1964; JD, U. Notre Dame, 1967; LLM in Taxation, George Washington U., 1971. Bar: N.J. 1967, U.S. Tax Ct. 1970, U.S. Ct. Claims 1970, U.S. Supreme Ct. 1971, D.C. 1976. Trial atty. U.S. Dept. Justice, 1967-71; assoc. counsel and chief counsel to Minority Com. on Judiciary, U.S. Senate, 1971-74; assoc. counsel to Pres. U.S., 1974-77; ptnr. Bierbower & Rockefeller, 1977—81, Ward, Lazarus & Grow, Washington, 1981—91; of counsel Dixon & Jessup, Washington, 1991-97, Krooth & Atlman, 1997—. Mem. adv. bd. Sch. Law Dayton U., 1975-85; adj. prof. Sch. Law Georgetown U., 1979—; mem. U.S. Adv. Com. on Trade Negotiations, 1983-87; chmn. Sailors and Mchts. Bank and Trust Co., Vienna, Va., 1987-89. Mem. adv. bd. Houston Jour. Internat. Law, 1983-90; contbr. numerous articles to profl. publs. U.S. reporter to UN, 1975-77; mem. adv. coun. Rep. Nat. Com., 1977-80; mem. Presdl. transition team Office of Pres.-Elect, 1980-81; caucus mgr. George Bush, Rep. Conv., 1988; trustee Internat. Law Inst., pres., 1990-92. Mem.: ABA, Am. Judicature Soc., N.J. Bar Assn., Fed. Bar Assn., Bar Assn. D.C., D.C. Bar Assn., Am. Law Inst. (life). General civil litigation, Private international, Taxation, general. Home: 4501 Connecticut Ave NW Apt 716 Washington DC 20008-3712 Office: Lazarus & Assocs 1850 M St NW Ste 400 Washington DC 20036-5815

LAZARUS, LINDA IRIS, lawyer; b. Bklyn., Aug. 7, 1951; m. Andrew Jay Schwartzman, June 8, 1986. BA in Philosophy, CCNY, 1972; JD, Am. U., 1976. Bar: D.C. 1976, U.S. Dist. Ct. D.C. 1977, U.S. Ct. Appeals (DC cir.) 1988. Assoc. Lobel, Novins & Lamont, 1977—79; spl. asst. to dir. Office for Civil Rights U.S. Dept. HHS, Washington, 1979—80; spl. counsel Batzell, Nunn & Bode, 1981; assoc. Miller, Loewinger & Assoc., Washington, 1982; trial atty. Office of Corp. Counsel, Washington, 1982—87; atty.-advisor pub. works sect., profl. ethics advisor Office. of Corp Counsel, Washington, 1994—95; asst. gen. counsel Wash. Met. Area Transit Authority, 1987—93; lead atty. examiner/hearing officer Office Hearings and Appeals U.S. Dept. Energy, Washington, 1995—. Vol. mediator U.S. Dist. Ct., Washington, 1991—; trainer mediation workshop U.S. Dept. Energy, 1995, trainer mediation of workplace disputes, 97; conferee Jud. Conf. U.S. Ct. Appeals, Washington, 1996; spkr., lectr. in field. Dean's fellow, Washington Coll. Law, Am. U., 1974. Mem.: ABA (judge regional client counseling competition 2001), Women's Bar Assn., Fed. ADR Network, Am. Soc. Law, Medicine and Ethics, Assn. Conflict Resolution (sect. spirituality, environ. pub. policy). Avocations: qi gong, yoga, tai chi.

LAZERUS, GILBERT, lawyer; b. N.Y.C. s. Jacob and Bessie Lazerus; m. Judith Lazerus, Dec. 25, 1940 (dec.); children: Bruce, June. PhB, Yale U., 1931; JD, Columbia U., 1934. Bar: N.Y. 1934, U.S. Dist. Ct. (so. dist.) N.Y. 1940, U.S. Dist. Ct. (ea. dist.) N.Y. 1940, U.S. Supreme Ct. 1940. Assoc. Joseph V. McKee, 1938-45; ptnr. Strook & Strook & Lavan, N.Y.C., 1945-83, of counsel, 1983—. Master arbitrator Dept. Ins., State of N.Y.; adminstrv. law judge Transit Dept., City of N.Y.; mem. panel of arbitrators Civil Ct. City N.Y., Am. Arbitration Assn., N.Y. Stock Exch., Am. Stock Exch., Nat. Assn. Security Dealers. Mem. Yale Club (N.Y.C.), Columbia Club (N.Y.C.) Home: 1175 York Ave New York NY 10021 Office: 180 Maiden Ln New York NY 10038

LAZROE, JEFFREY ALAN, lawyer, radio host; b. Buffalo, Oct. 9, 1947; s. Martin L. and Ann G. (Skolnick) L.; m. Althea M. Darner, Sept. 23, 1977; children: Mathew, Seth. BA, U. Buffalo, 1968; JD, U. Toledo, Ohio, 1971. Bar: N.Y., U.S. Dist. Ct. (we. dist.) N.Y. Law guardian County of Erie Family Ct., Buffalo, 1971-75; pvt. practice Buffalo, 1971—. Assoc. prof. medicine U. Buffalo, 1971-75; lectr. bus. law Bryant & Stratton Bus. Sch., Buffalo, 1974; lectr. in field. Moderator radio program, 1976-77. General civil litigation, Personal injury (including property damage). Office: 118 W Mohawk St 3d Fl Buffalo NY 14202

LEA, LORENZO BATES, lawyer; b. St. Louis, Apr. 12, 1925; s. Lorenzo Bates and Ursula Agnes (Gibson) L.; m. Marcia Gwendolyn Wood, Mar. 21, 1953; children— Victoria, Jennifer, Christopher. BS, MIT, 1946; JD, U. Mich., 1949; grad. Advanced Mgmt. Program, Harvard U., 1964. Bar: Ill. 1950. With Amoco Corp. (formerly Standard Oil Co. Ind.), Chgo., 1949—89, asst. gen. counsel, 1963-71, assoc. gen. counsel, 1971-72, gen. counsel, 1972-78, v.p., gen. counsel, 1978-89. Trustee Village of Glenview, Ill., 1963-64, mem. Zoning Bd., 1961-63; bd. dirs. Chgo. Crime Commn., 1978— , Midwest Coun. for Internat. Econ. Policy, 1973— , Chgo. Bar Found., 1981— , Chgo. Area Found. for Legal Svcs., 1981— ; bd. dirs. United Charities of Chgo., 1973—, chmn., 1985—; bd. dirs. Cmty. Found. Collier County, 1997—, Naples Bot. Garden, 2000—. Served with USNR, 1943-46. Mem. ABA, Am. Petroleum Inst., Am. Arbitration Assn. (dir. 1980—), Ill. Bar Assn., Chgo. Bar Assn., Assn. Gen. Counsel (bd. dirs. 1983-89), Order of Coif, Law Club, Econs. Club, Legal, Mid-Am. (Chgo.), Glen View, Wyndemere, Hole-In-The-Wall, Sigma Xi. Republican. Mem. United Ch. of Christ. Administrative and regulatory, Antitrust, Corporate, general.

LEACH, DONALD LEE, lawyer, sole practice; b. Talmage, Nebr., Oct. 10, 1934; s. Geraldine Lucille (Cleckner) L.; m. Mary Marie Rowe, June 28, 1953; children:Cindi-Jo Lehman, Kimberly, Lisa Mc Gowan, Troy, Terrence. BA, Humboldt State Col., 1956; MPA, U. Southern Calif., 1973; JD, Ventura Col. Law, 1989. Bar: Calif. 1989, U.S. Dist. Ct. (ctrl. dist.) Calif. 1989, U.S. Ct. Appeals (9th. cir.) 1989. News caster, announcer Sta. KIEM-TV, KIEM Radio, Eureka, Calif., 1956-57, 61-62; area comdr. Calif. Highway Patrol, Ventura, Calif., 1978-91; assoc. Scott F. Dool Inc., Thousand Oaks, Calif., 1989-94; pvt. practice Ventura, Calif., 1994—. Instr. Col. of the Redwoods, Eureka, 1968-70, lectr. Golden Gate U., Sacramento/Santa Barbara, 1973-79; dir. Estate Planning Coun., Ventura County, Calif., 1989—; judge pro tem. Ventura Mcpl. and Superior Cts., 1997—. Mem adv. bd. Salvation Army, Ventura, 1981—; bd. dirs. Am. Cancer Soc., Ventura, 1981—, pres. 2000-01; dir., past pres. 31st Dist. Agrl. Assn., Ventura, 1985-93; commr. Ventura City Planning Comm., 1985-86; trustee, v.p. Ventura Law Libr., 1994—; Capt. USMC, 1957-61, Okinawa, 1966-67, Vietnam. Mem. ABA, Calif. Bar Assn., L.A. County Bar Assn., Ventura County Bar Assn., Rotary Club (sect. 1984-90, pres. 2000-01), Scottish Rite (sect. 1996—, KCCH award 1983, 33-degree IGH award 1995), Masons (master 1978, Insp. 1987—). Republican. Methodist. Avocations: photography, hunting, fishing, gardening. General civil litigation, Probate (including wills, trusts), Property, real (including real estate development, water). Office: Law Office of Donald Leach 425 Day Rd Ventura CA 93003-2045 E-mail: leacht@vcss.k12.ca.us.

LEACH, JAMES GLOVER, lawyer; b. Panama City, Fla., Jan. 26, 1948; s. Milledge Glover and Thelma Louise (Hamilton) L.; m. Judith A. Leach, Feb. 26, 1972 (div. 1987); children: Allison, Arica; m. January Parker, Dec. 1997. AS, Gulf Coast Coll., 1968; BA, Duke U., 1970; MBA, Ga. State U., 1974, MI, 1976; JD, Drake U., 1989. Bar: Iowa 1990; CPCU, CLU. Bank officer Bank South, Atlanta, 1972-75; asst. v.p. Johnson & Higgins, Atlanta, 1975-78; pres. Nat. Gen. Ins. Co., St. Louis, 1978-85, AOPA Svc. Corp., St. Louis, 1985-87, Kirke-Van Orsdel Specialty, Des Moines, 1987-89, Gallagher Specialty, St. Louis, 1990-92; prin., dir., counsel Pauli & Co. Inc., St. Louis, 1992-93; sr. v.p., gen. counsel Am. Safety Ins., Atlanta, 1993-98; pres., CEO, gen. counsel, dir. Unistar Fin. Svc. Corp., Dallas, 1998—2001; exec.-in-residence U. Hartford, 2001; sr. v.p., gen. counsel Bldrs. Ins. Group, Atlanta, 2001—. Cons. McDonnell Douglas, St. Louis, 1987; dir. Gateway Ins. Co., St. Louis, 1992; corp. assembly Blue Cross/Blue Shield, St. Louis, 1991-92. Contbr. articles to profl. jours. 1st lt. USAF, 1970-72, Korea. Avocations: pilot, golf. General civil litigation, Corporate, general, Insurance. Office: Builders Insurance Group PO Box 723099 Atlanta GA 31139-0099 Office Fax: 678-309-4315. E-mail: jleach@buildersinsurancegroup.com.

LEACH, TERRY RAY, lawyer, judge; b. Ft. Worth, Apr. 6, 1949; s. Herbert W. and Catherine A. L.; m. Dixie Gail Day, Jan 8, 1972; children: Michelle Rene, David Richard, Jennifer Anne. BS in Indsl. Engring., Tex. Tech U., 1971, JD with honors, 1975. Bar: Tex. 1975, U.S. Dist. Ct. (no. dist.) Tex. 1976. Engr. Southwest Bell Telephone, San Antonio, 1970; assoc. Whitley, Boring & Morrison, Bedford, Tex., 1975-76; ptnr. Evans, Leach & Ames, Hurst, Tex., 1976-82; sr. ptnr. Leach & Ames PC, Hurst, 1982—. Judge City of Bedford, 1979-93, City of Lakeside, Tex., 1984—, Halton City, Tex., 1986-94; lectr. real estate law Tarrent County Jr. Coll., Hurst, 1980-81; instr. bus. law Tarrent County Jr. Coll., Hurst, 1991-96. Mem. Hurst Zoning Bd. Adjustment, 1985-88, Hurst Planning and Zoning Commn., 1988-93, Hurst Found. Com., 1986; deacon Frist Bapt. Ch., Colleyville, 1997; bd. dirs. N.E. Tarrant County Community Trust, 1987-93, Hurst-Euless-Bedford Ind. Sch. Dist. Edn. Found., 1995—. Mem. ABA, Tex. Bar Assn., N.E. Tarrant County Bar Assn. (pres. 1980-81), Coll. State Bar Tex., Tex. Bd. Specialization (cert., estate planning and probate law 1989—), Tex. Acad. Probate and Trust Attys. Estate planning, Probate (including wills, trusts), Estate taxation. Office: Leach & Ames PC 460 Harwood Rd Hurst TX 76054-2939

LEACHMAN, RUSSELL DEWITT, lawyer; b. Amarillo, Tex., Aug. 8, 1965; s. William D. and Alexia (Hall) L.; m. Margaret Feuille, July 8, 1989; children: William Benton, Richard Boone. BA in Polit. Sci., Tex. Tech. U., 1986, JD, 1990. Bar: Tex. 1990, U.S. Dist. Ct. (we. dist.) Tex. 1992, U.S. Dist. Ct. (no. dist.) Tex. 1994, U.S. Dist. Ct. (ea. dist.) Tex. 1998, U.S. Ct. Appeals (5th cir.) 1994; Bd. cert. criminal law, 1996. Asst. dist. atty. 34th Judicial Dist. Tex., El Paso, 1990-92; atty. Leachman & Escobar LLP, El Paso, 1992-94, Diamond Rash Gordon & Jackson, El Paso, 1994—2001, Mounce, Green, Myers, Safi & Galatzan, P.C., El Paso, 2001—. Dir. El Paso Young Lawyers Assn. Mock Trial Competition, El Paso, 1990-95; mem. Ducks Unltd. Area Com., El Paso, 1991—, area chmn., 1999-2000, dist. chmn., 2001—. Mem. Lodge 130 (mason), Phi Gamma Delta, Delta Theta Phi, Delta Phi Epsilon, Phi Rho Pi, Pi Sigma Alpha. Methodist. General civil litigation, Criminal. Office: Mounce Green et al PO Box 1977 El Paso TX 79950-1977 E-mail: Leachman@mgmsg.com.

LEADER, ROBERT JOHN, lawyer; b. Syracuse, N.Y., Oct. 14, 1933; s. Henry John and Dorothy Alberta (Schad) L.; m. Nancy Bruce, Sept. 23, 1960; children: Henry, William, Catherine, Thomas, Edward. AB, Cornell U., 1956; JD, Syracuse U., 1962. Bar: N.Y. 1963. Assoc. Ferris, Hughes, Dorrance & Groben, Utica, N.Y., 1962-64; ptnr. Cole Leader & Elmer, Gouverneur, N.Y., 1964-66, Case & Leader, Gouverneur, 1966—. Sec. North Country Hosps. Inc., 1972— ; atty. Village of Hermon (N.Y.), 1968— , Town of Gouverneur, 1967-94, Town of Pitcairn (N.Y.), 1974— , Town of Edwards, 1974— , Town of Rossie, 1985—, Town of Fowler, 1978—; corp. counsel Village of Gouverneur, 1973— ; counsel Gouverneur Ctrl. Sch. Dist., 1980—; bd. dirs. Gouverneur Savs. and Loan. Trustee Edward John Noble Hosp., Gouverneur, 1972—, Gouverneur Libr., 1973-83, Governeur Nursing Home Co., Inc., 1972—, past pres., 1979-81, past chmn. bd. trustees, 1979-81; Republican chmn. Town and Village of Gouverneur, 1969-72; del. N.Y. State Jud. conv., 1981—. Served to capt. USAF, 1956-59. Mem. Rotary (pres. 1988-89). Roman Catholic. State civil litigation, Construction, General practice. Home: 27 Howard St Gouverneur NY 13642-1220 Office: 107 E Main St Gouverneur NY 13642-1408

LEAF, FREDERICK PETER, lawyer, educator; b. New Haven, Dec. 4, 1946; s. Milton John and Jane (Collins) L.; m. Kimmy Jin, June 1, 1973; children: Alicia Jin, Thomas Collins. BBA in Acctg. cum laude, Niagara U., 1968; JD, Boston Coll., 1971. Bar: Conn. 1971, U.S. Dist. Conn. 1971, U.S. Ct. Mil. Appeals 1972. Assoc. Gitlitz, Ronai & Bercham P.C., Milford, Conn., 1976-79; ptnr. Altham & Leaf, New Haven, 1980-84; pvt. practice New Haven, 1984—. Atty. City of New Haven, 1980-84; spl. asst. corp. counsel, New Haven, 1980-84; adj. prof. N.H. Coll., 1981—. Capt. JAGC, USAR, 1972-76, lt. col., 1981-96, ret. Democrat. Roman Catholic. Family and matrimonial, Personal injury (including property damage), Property, real (including real estate development, water).

LEAF, MARTIN NORMAN, lawyer; b. N.Y.C., Feb. 19, 1932; s. Jack and Shirley L.; m. Louise Sarkin, Dec. 29, 1956 d. 1995; children— Marc, Jenifer, Clifton. B.A., Washington U., St. Louis, 1952; J.D., NYU, 1958. Bar: N.Y., U.S. District Ct. 1958, U.S. Ct. Customs and Patent Appeals 1964, U.S. Ct. Mil. Appeals 1964, U.S. Ct. Claims 1964, U.S. Supreme Ct. 1964. Sr. assoc. Jacob D. Fuchsberg, N.Y.C., 1958-63; sr. ptnr. Leaf, Sternklar & Drogin, N.Y.C., 1963— ; spl. master N.Y. State Supreme Ct. Arbitrator, Am. Arbitration Assn.; village atty. Hastings-on-Hudson (N.Y.), 1969-82; spl. asst. dist. atty. Westchester Country. Lecturer, Far Eastern Law and Business Studies, Washington U., Bd. dirs. Buckminster Fuller Inst., Echo Hills Mental Health Clinic, 1973-87 , Trailblazers, 1979— , Nat. Black Theatre, 1973— , Am. Arab Affairs Council, 1983— ; mem. internat. adv. bd. World Sikh Centre, 1980— ; Hunger Project del. NGO, UN; mem. N.Y. State Conf. Village Ofcls. Served to 1st lt. U.S. Army, 1955-57. Recipient Disting. Service award VFW, 1983. Mem. Fed. Bar Council, ABA, N.Y. State Bar Assn., New York County Lawyers Assn., N.Y. Trial Lawyers Assn., Union Internationale des Avocats. Clubs: Players, St. Anthony (N.Y.C.). Assoc. editor Am. Trial Lawyers Assn. Jour., 1963-73. State civil litigation, Corporate, general, Private international. Home: 165 W End Ave Apt 19G New York NY 10023-5511 Office: 440 Park Ave S New York NY 10016-8012

LEAKE, LARRY BRUCE, lawyer; b. Asheville, N.C., May 19, 1950; s. A.E. and Ann (McDevitt) L. BA, U. N.C., 1971, JD, 1974. Ptnr. Uzzell and Dumont, Asheville, 1974-80, Harrell & Leake, Asheville, 1980—2001, Leake & Scott, 2001—. Chmn. 11th Congl. Dist. YD, 1974-77; nat.

committeeman Young Dems. of N.C., 1977-79, pres. 1979-80; gen. counsel Young Dems. of Am., 1981-83; state sen. N.C., 1979-80; mem. State Goals and Policy Bd., N.C., 1978-84, Commn. on the Future, N.C., 1981-83; mem. N.C. State Bd. of Elections, 1993-97, chmn., 1997—; mem. bd. advisors Mars Hill Coll., 1992-2001, chmn., 2001—. Named 1 of 10 Outstanding Young Dems. N.C., 1977, Mountain Dem. of Yr., 2002; recipient Ella Grasso award, Outstanding Young Dem. in Am., 1983, Order of Long Leaf Pine, Gov. James B. Hunt, 1981, 2000. Mem. Phi Beta Kappa. Presbyterian. Avocations: bowling, spectator sports, tennis. General civil litigation, Insurance, Personal injury (including property damage). Home: 122 Ridgeway Dr Mars Hill NC 28754-9707 Office: Leake & Scott 501 BB&T Plz Asheville NC 28801

LEAPHART, W. WILLIAM, state supreme court justice; b. Butte, Mont., Dec. 3, 1946; s. Charles William and Cornelia (Murphy) L.; m. Barbara Berg, Dec. 30, 1977; children: Rebecca, Retta, Ada. Student, Whitman Coll., 1965—66; BA, U. Mont., 1969, JD, 1972. Bar: Mont. 1972, U.S. Dist. Ct., U.S. Ct. Appeals (9th cir.) 1975, U.S. Supreme Ct. 1975. Law clk. to Hon. W.D. Murray U.S. Dist. Ct., Butte, 1972—74; ptnr. Leaphart Law Firm, Helena, Mont., 1974—94; justice Mont. Supreme Ct., Helena, 1995—. Office: Mont Supreme Ct Justice Bldg 215 N Sanders St Rm 315 Helena MT 59601-4522 also: PO Box 203001 Helena MT 59620-3001

LEARD, DAVID CARL, lawyer; b. Hartford, Conn., Dec. 9, 1958; BA, Bucknell U., 1981; JD, U. Conn., 1984. Bar: Conn. 1984, U.S. Dist. Ct. Conn. 1985; cert. specialist in workers' compensation law. Assoc. Podorowsky and Wladimer, Hartford, 1985, Manasse, Slaiby & Leard, Torrington, Conn., 1985-88, ptnr., 1989—. Contbr. articles to profl. jours. Dir., past pres. Winchester (Conn.) Land Trust, 1988-93; chmn. allocations com. United Way Torrington, 1989—. Mem.: Nat. Orgn. Social Security Claimants REps., Conn. Bar Assn. (workers compensation sect., cert. specialist in worker's compensation). General civil litigation, Personal injury (including property damage), Workers' compensation. Office: Manasse Slaiby & Leard PO Box 1104 Torrington CT 06790-2958

LEARY, MARGARET, law librarian, library director; Dir. Law Libr. U. Mich., Ann Arbor. Office: U Mich Law Sch S180A Legal Rsch Bdlg S State St Ann Arbor MI 48109-1215 Business E-Mail: mleary@umich.edu.*

LEARY, THOMAS BARRETT, federal agency administrator; b. Orange, NJ, July 15, 1931; s. Daniel and Margaret (Barrett) L.; m. Stephanie Lynn Abbott, Dec. 18, 1954, June 3, 1991; children: Thomas A., David A., Alison Leary Estep. AB, Princeton U., 1952; JD magna cum laude, Harvard U., 1958. Bar: N.Y. 1959, Mich. 1972, D.C. 1983. Assoc. White & Case, N.Y.C., 1958-68, ptnr., 1968-71; atty.-in-charge antitrust Gen. Motors Corp., Detroit, 1971-77, asst. gen. counsel, 1977-82; ptnr. Hogan & Hartson, Washington, 1983-99; commr. FTC, Washington, 1999—. Served to lt. USNR, 1952-55 Mem. ABA (antitrust sect., coun. mem. 1979-83, mem. antitrust adv. bd., BNA antitrust & trade reg. rep., 1981-99. Office: Fed Trade Commn 600 Pennsylvania Ave NW # 520 Washington DC 20580-0002 Business E-Mail: tleary@ftc.gov.

LEASE, ROBERT K. lawyer; b. Cleve., 1948; AB magna cum laude, Dartmouth Coll., 1970; JD cum laude, U. Conn., 1976. Bar: Ohio. Ptnr. Baker & Hostetler LLP, Cleve. Mem. Phi Beta Kappa. Estate planning, Probate (including wills, trusts), Estate taxation. Office: Baker & Hostetler LLP 3200 Nat City Ctr 1900 E 9th St Ste 3200 Cleveland OH 44114-3485 E-mail: rlease@bakerlaw.com.

LEATH, WILLIAM JEFFERSON, JR., lawyer; b. Oakland, Calif., Sept. 9, 1945; s. William and Margaret (Jeffreys) L.; children: Catherine, Zoe, Eugenia, Susanne, Mason, Davis. BA, U. N.C., 1967; diplome, U. Lyon (France), 1966; JD, George Washington, 1971. Bar: D.C. 1971, Md. 1972, S.C. 1975. Atty. U.S. Internat. Trade Commn., Washington, 1971-73; ptnr. Plaia & Leath, Wheaton, Md., 1973-74, Barnwell, Whaley, Patterson, Charleston, S.C., 1974-80, Young, Clement, Rivers, Tisdale, Charleston, 1980-98, Leath, Bouch & Crawford, LLP, Charleston, 1998—. Chmn. Charleston City Rep. Party, 1981; pres. Charleston Neighborhood Assn., 1982. Mem. ABA, Charleston County Bar Assn. (chmn. legal med. com. 1988—), Maritime Law Assn., S.C. State Bd. Archtl. Examiners (vice chmn.), Southeastern Admiralty Law Inst., Internat. Assn. Def. Counsel. Episcopalian. Admiralty, General civil litigation, Construction. Office: Leath Bouch & Crawford LLP PO Box 59 134 Meeting St Charleston SC 29401-2224 Home: 106 Tradd St Charleston SC 29401-2421 Fax: 843-937-0606. E-mail: wjleath@leathbouchlaw.com.

LEAVELL, JULITA ANN, lawyer; JD, U. N.Mex., 1998. Bar: N.Mex. 1998, U.S. Dist. Ct. N.Mex. 2002. Owner and mng. atty. Leavell & Assocs., Albuquerque, 1998—. Commn. appointee Jud. Evaluation Performance Commn., Albuquerque, 2000—. Author: CYFD, Nightmare for Families and Children. Soccer coach AYSO, Albuquerque, 2001—02. Fellow UNM Grad. fellow, U. of N.Mex, 1996—98; scholar Phi Alpha Delta Hon. scholar, Phi Alpha Delta Frat., 1987. Mem.: N.Mex. Women's Bar Assn. (bd. dirs. 2000—). None. Avocations: swimming, bicycling, soccer. Family and matrimonial, Juvenile, Criminal. Home: 300 Central SW Ste 2500W Albuquerque NM 87102 Office: Leavell & Assocs 300 Central SW Ste 2500 W Albuquerque NM 87102

LEAVITT, JEFFREY STUART, lawyer; b. Cleve., July 13, 1946; s. Sol and Esther (Dolinsky) L.; m. Ellen Fern Sugerman, Dec. 21, 1968; children: Matthew Adam, Joshua Aaron. AB, Cornell U., 1968; JD, Case Western Res. U., 1973. Bar: Ohio 1973. Assoc. Jones, Day, Reavis & Pogue, Cleve., 1973-80, ptnr., 1981—. Contbr. articles to profl. jours. Trustee Bur. Jewish Edn., Cleve., 1981-93, v.p., 1985-87; trustee Fairmount Temple, Cleve., 1982-2002, v.p., 1985-90, pres., 1990-93; trustee Citizens League Greater Cleve., 1982-89, 92-94, pres., 1987-89; trustee Citizens League Rsch. Inst., Cleve., 1989-98, Great Lakes Region of Union Am. Hebrew Congregations, 1990-93; mem. bd. govs. Case Western Res. Law Sch. Alumni Assn., 1989-92; sec. Kulas Found., 1986-88, 93-99, asst. treas., 1989-92. Mem. ABA (employee benefits coms. 1976—), Nat. Assn. Pub. Pension Attys. Jewish. Non-profit and tax-exempt organizations, Pension, profit-sharing, and employee benefits, Personal income taxation. Home: 7935 Sunrise Ln Novelty OH 44072-9404 Office: Jones Day Reavis & Pogue N Point 901 Lakeside Ave E Cleveland OH 44114-1190

LEAVITT, MARTIN JACK, lawyer; b. Detroit, Mar. 30, 1940; s. Benjamin and Annette (Cohen) L.; m. Janice C. McCreary; children: Michael J., Paul J., David A., Dean N., Keleigh R. LLB, Wayne State U., 1964. Bar: Mich. 1965, Fla. 1967. Assoc. Robert A. Sullivan, Detroit, 1968-70; officer, bd. dirs. Law Office Sullivan & Leavitt, Northville, Mich., 1970—, pres., 1979—. Bd. dirs. Tyrone Hills of Mich., Premiere Video, Inc., others. Lt. comdr. USNR, 1965-68. Detroit Edison upper class scholar, 1958-64. Mem. ABA, Mich. Bar Assn., Fla. Bar Assn., Transp. Lawyers Assn., ICC Practitioners, Meadowbrook Country Club, Huron River Hunting and Fishing Club (past pres.), Rolls Royce Owners Club (bd. dirs.). Jewish. Federal civil litigation, Corporate, general, Labor (including EEOC, Fair Labor Standards Act, labor-management relations, NLRB, OSHA). Office: Sullivan and Leavitt PC PO Box 5490 Northville MI 48167-5490 E-mail: mjl@sullivanleavitt.com.

LEAVITT, MYRON E. judge; b. Las Vegas; Justice Nev. Supreme Court, Carson City, 1999—; dist. judge Carson City, Nev. Office: Supreme Ct 201 S Carson Ste 300 Carson City NV 89701-4702*

LEAVY, EDWARD, federal judge; b. 1929; m. Eileen Leavy; children: Thomas, Patrick, Mary Kay, Paul. AB, U. Portland, 1950; LLB, U. Notre Dame, 1953. Dist. judge Lane County, Eugene, Oreg., 1957—61, cir. judge, 1961—76; magistrate U.S. Dist. Ct. Oreg., Portland, 1976—84, judge, 1984—87; cir. judge U.S. Ct. Appeals (9th cir.), 1987—97, sr. judge, 1997—. Office: US Ct Appeals Pioneer Courthouse 555 SW Yamhill St Ste 232 Portland OR 97204-1323

LEB, ARTHUR STERN, lawyer; b. Cleve., June 26, 1930; s. Ernest A. and Bertha (Stern) L.; m. Lois Shafron, Jan. 31, 1954; children: Gerald P., Judith A., Robert B. AB, Columbia Coll., 1952; JD, Case Western Res. U., 1955. Bar: Ohio 1955, U.S. Supreme Ct. 1965. Ptnr. Leb & Halm, Canton, Ohio, 1961-84, Amerman, Burt & Jones, L.P.A., Canton, 1985—90; principal Buckingham, Doolittle & Burroughs, L.L.P., 1991—2001, of counsel, 2001—. Founding mem., exec. com. Ohio Coun. Sch. Bd. Attys., 1976-84, pres. 1983. Served to 1st lt. JAGC, USAF, 1955-57. Recipient Merit award Ohio Legal Ctr. Inst., 1964. Fellow Ohio Bar Found.; mem. ABA, Ohio Bar Assn., Stark County Bar Assn. (pres. 1985-86). Education and schools, General practice, Estate planning. E-mail: asleb@bdblaw.com.

LEBAMOFF, IVAN ARGIRE, lawyer; b. Ft. Wayne, Ind., July 20, 1932; s. Argire V. and Helen A. (Kachandov) L.; m. Katherine S. Lebamoff, June 9, 1963; children— Damian I., Jordan I., Justin A. AB in History, Ind. U., 1954, JD, 1957. Bar: Ind. 1957, U.S. Ct. Dist. Ct. (no. and so. dists.) 1958, U.S. Supreme Ct. 1963. Sole practice, Ft. Wayne, Ind., 1957-68; ptnr. Lebamoff, Ver Wiebe & Snow, Ft. Wayne, Ind., 1968-71; mayor City of Ft. Wayne, 1972-75; sole practice Lebamoff Law Offices, Ft. Wayne, 1975—. U.S. commr. No. Dist. Ind., 1957-62; fgn. service officer USIA Dept. Commerce, Bulgaria, 1964; vis. prof. dept. urban affairs Ind. U.-Purdue, Ft. Wayne, 1976-77 Chmn. Allen County Democratic Com., 1968-75, Ft. Wayne Dept. Parks and Recreation, 1984-88; nat. pres. Macedonian Patriotic Orgn. of U.S. and Can., 1983-94. Served with USAF, 1958-64 Mem. ABA, Allen County Bar Assn., Ind. Bar Assn., Am. Trial Lawyers Assn., Ind. Trial Lawyers Assn. Lodges: Kiwanis. Eastern Orthodox. General practice, Personal injury (including property damage). Home: 205 E Packard Ave Fort Wayne IN 46806-1014 Office: Lebamoff Law Offices 918 S Calhoun St Fort Wayne IN 46802-2502

LEBARON, EDWARD WAYNE, JR., retired lawyer; b. San Rafael, Calif., Jan. 7, 1930; s. Edward Wayne and Mabel Butler (Sims) LeB.; m. Doralee M. LeBaron, June 4, 1954; children: Edward Wayne, William Bruce, Richard Wilson. BA, Coll. Pacific, 1950; LLB, George Washington U., 1959. Bar: Calif. bar 1960, Tex. bar 1960, Nev. bar 1967. Football quarterback Washington Redskins, 1952-59; with Dallas Cowboys, 1960-63; exec. v.p. Nevada Cement Co., 1964-65; mem. firm Wynne & Wynne, Dallas, 1960-63, Bible, McDonald & Carano, Reno, 1966-68, Laxalt & Berry, Carson City, Nev., 1969-70; partner firm Jones, Jones, Bell, LeBaron and Brown, Las Vegas, Nev., 1970-76; gen. mgr. Atlanta Falcons Football team, 1977-85; ptnr. Powell, Goldstein, Murphy & Frazer, 1986-89, Pillsbury, Madison & Sutro, 1989-94; ret., 1994. Bd. dirs. Tom Brown, Inc.; ptnr LeBaron Ranches. Served with USMC, 1950-52. Decorated Purple Heart, Bronze Star.; named Sportsman of Year in Ga., 1978-79; named to Coll. Football Hall of Fame, 1980. Mem. ABA, Sutter Club, Northridge Country Club. Republican.

LE BAULT DE LA MORINIERE, ANNE, lawyer; b. Landemont, France, June 5, 1950; d. René Le Bault de La Moriniere and Bernadette de Francqueville. BA, Law Sch. U. Nantes, France, 1973. Lawyers profl. aptitude cert.: 1973, registered: Paris Bar (lawyer) 1973. Assoc. Ribadeau Dumas LeCocq Courteault Law Firm, Paris, 1973—75, Rambaud-Martel, Paris, 1975—, ptnr., 1983—. Mem. Coun. of the Order of the Paris Bar, 1995—97. Named chevalier, Nat. Order Merit, 1999. Avocations: reading, swimming, outdoor activities. Labor (including EEOC, Fair Labor Standards Act, labor-management relations, NLRB, OSHA). Home: 14 Avenue Elisée Reclus 75007 Paris France Office: Rambaud Martel 25 Bd de L Amiral Bruix 75782 Paris France E-mail: a.lamoriniere@rambaud-martel.com.

LEBEAU, CHARLES PAUL, lawyer; b. Detroit, Dec. 11, 1944; s. Charles Henry Jr. and Mary Barbara (Moran) L.; m. Victoria Joy (Huchin), May 16, 1970; children: Jeffrey Kevin, Timothy Paul. AA, Macomb County Community Coll., Warren, Mich., 1967; BA, Wayne State U., 1969; JD, U. Detroit, 1972; grad. tax program, NYU Sch. Law, 1972-73. Bar: Mich. 1973, U.S. Tax Ct. 1973, Calif. 1987, U.S. Ct. Internat. Trade. 1988, U.S. Supreme Ct. 1988, U.S. Dist. Ct. (so. dist.) Calif. 1988. Corp. and tax atty. Ford Motor Co., Dearborn, Mich., 1973-75; assoc. Miller, Canfield, Paddock & Stone, Detroit, 1976-78; tax cons. Oceaneering Internat., Santa Barbara, Calif., 1978-79; tax counsel and internat. Signal Cos. Inc., Beverly Hills and La Jolla, Calif., 1979-83; tax and internat. assoc. Gray, Cary, Ames & Frye, San Diego, 1983-84; of counsel James Watts Esq., La Jolla, Calif., 1985, Murfey, Griggs & Frederick, La Jolla, Calif., 1986; pvt. practice La Jolla and Palm Desert, Calif., 1987—, Detroit. Lectr. grad. tax program Golden Gate U., San Diego, 1979-87; adj. prof. law U. San Diego, 1982-85, 88-89; mem. Law Rev., U. Detroit, 1971-72; lectr. in taxation. Contbr. articles on internat. tax to profl. jours.; monthly tax case commentator Taxes Internat., London, 1981-85. Campaign coord. United Way, Santa Barbara, 1979. Recipient Congrl. Medal of Merit, 1999, Presdl. Medal of Honor, 2000, Rep. of Yr., Calif., 2000, 03. Mem. ABA, Mich. Bar Assn., Calif. Bar Assn., San Diego County Bar Assn., Pi Sigma Alpha. Republican. Roman Catholic. Avocations: sailing, tennis, walking. Corporate, general, Private international, Taxation, general. Home: 1999 Via Segovia La Jolla CA 92037-6441 Office: Law Offices Charles LeBeau Hist 1887 Hayward Patterson Bldg 2148 Broadway San Diego CA 92102-1829 also: The Ford Bldg 615 Griswold Ste 200 Detroit MI 48226 also: The Portola Centre 74-040 Hwy 111 Ste L Palm Desert CA 92260

LEBEDOFF, JONATHAN GALANTER, federal judge; b. Mpls., Apr. 29, 1938; s. Martin David and Mary (Galanter) L.; m. Sarah Sargent Mitchell, June 10, 1979; children: David Shevlin, Ann McNair. BA, U. Minn., 1960, LLB, 1963. Bar: Minn. 1963, U.S. Dist. Ct. Minn. 1964, U.S. Ct. Appeals (8th cir.) 1968. Pvt. practice, Mpls., 1963-71; judge Hennepin County Mcpl. Ct., State Minn., Mpls., 1971-74; dist. ct. judge State of Minn., Mpls., 1974-91; U.S. magistrate judge U.S. Dist. Ct., Mpls., 1991—2002, chief U.S. magistrate judge, 2002—. Mem. Gov.'s Commn. on Crime Prevention, 1971-75; mem. State Bd. Continuing Legal Edn.; mem. Minn. Supreme Ct. Task Force for Gender Fairness in Cts., mem. implementation com. of gender fairness in cts.. Jewish. Avocations: reading (biographies, history), family, bridge. Office: 300 S 4th St Minneapolis MN 55415-1320

LEBEDOFF, RANDY MILLER, lawyer; b. Washington, Oct. 16, 1949; m. David Lebedoff; children: Caroline, Jonathan, Nicholas. BA, Smith Coll., 1971; JD magna cum laude, Ind. U., 1975. Assoc. Faegre & Benson, Mpls., 1975-82, ptnr., 1983-86; v.p., gen. counsel Star Tribune, Mpls., 1989—2001; asst. sec. Star Tribune Cowles Media Co., Mpls., 1990—98; pvt. practice Mpls., 2001—02; v.p., gen. counsel Twin Cities Public Television, 2002—. Bd. dirs. Milkweed Editions, 1989-96. Bd. dirs. Minn. Opera, 1986-90, YWCA, 1984-90, Planned Parenthood Minn., 1985-90, Fund for Legal Aid Soc., 1988-96, Abbott-Northwestern Hosp., 1990-94. Mem. Newspaper Assn. Am. (legal affairs com. 1991-2002), Minn. Newspapers Assn. (bd. dirs. 1995-2002, pres. 2002). Home: 1738 Oliver Ave S Minneapolis MN 55405-2222 Office: 172 E Fourth St Saint Paul MN 55101

LEBEL, LOUIS, judge; b. Quebec City, Can., Nov. 30, 1939; s. Paul LeBel and Marguerite Sasseville; m. Louise Poudrier, Aug. 28, 1965; children: Paul, Catherine, Françoise. BA, Coll. des Jesuites, Quebec City, 1958; LLL, Laval U., 1961, grad. degree in pvt. law, 1965, LLD (hon.) , 2000; LLM, U. Toronto, 1966. Bar: 1962. With LeBel, Letarte, Bilodeau, Boily, 1963—64, Désilets, Grondin, LeBel & Assocs., 1964—71; ptnr. Grondin, LeBel, Poudrier, Isabel, Morin & Gagnon, 1971—84; apptd. mem. Que. Ct. Appeal, 1984—2000, Supreme Ct. Can., 2000—. Lectr. U. Ottawa, Laval U. Co-author (with Robert-P. Gagnon and Pierre Verge): Le droit du travail en vigueur au Québec; mem. editl. bd.: Revue du Barreau, 1976—82, chair editl. bd.: , 1979—82; contbr. articles to profl. jours. Mem.: Bar Que. (mem. various coms. including legal aid com., v.p. 1982—83). Office: Supreme Ct Can 301 Wellington St Ottawa ON Canada K1A 0J1*

LEBLANC, RICHARD PHILIP, lawyer; b. Nashua, N.H., Aug. 5, 1946; s. Ronald Arthur and Jeanette G. (Chomard) LeB.; m. Doris Julie Lavoie, May 25, 1968; children: Justin D., Renée M., Anne-Marie. AB summa cum laude, Coll. of the Holy Cross, 1968; JD cum laude, Harvard U., 1972. Bar: Maine 1972, U.S. Dist. Ct. Maine 1972. Assoc. Bernstein, Shur, Sawyer & Nelson, Portland, Maine, 1972-75, shareholder, 1976-95, LeBlanc & Young, Portland, 1995—. Mem. Probate Law Revision Commn., Augusta, Maine, 1975-80; mem. probate rules and forms adv. com. Maine Supreme Ct. Pres. United Way Greater Portland, 1982-84; trustee Cleverus H.S., Portland, 1982-88; bd. dirs. Habitat for Humanity, Portland, 1984-92, Cumberland County Affordable Housing Venture, Portland, 1987-94, Maine Spl. Olympics, 1988-94, United Way Found. of Greater Portland, 1997—. Fellow Am. Coll. Trust and Estate Counsel; mem. ABA, Maine Bar Assn., Maine Estate Planning Coun. Democrat. Roman Catholic. Estate planning, Probate (including wills, trusts), Estate taxation. Home: 142 Longfellow St Portland ME 04103-4027 Office: LeBlanc & Young PO Box 7950 Portland ME 04112-7950

LEBLANG, SKIP ALAN, lawyer; b. Phila., Jan. 14, 1953; s. Morton and Leah LeB.; m. Beth Siegel, Nov. 27, 1977; children: Kaitlyn Alexa, Chelsey Jenna. BA magna cum laude, U. Pitts., 1974; JD, U. San Diego, 1977. Bar: Pa. 1977, U.S. Dist. Ct. (we. dist.) Pa. 1977, D.C. 1980, N.Y. 1980, U.S. Dist. Ct. (so. and ea. dists.) N.Y. 1980. Jud. clk. Pa. Ct. Common Pleas, Pitts., 1977-78; atty. FTC, N.Y.C., 1978-81; asst. corp. counsel law dept. City of N.Y., 1981-84; assoc. Kramer, Dillof, N.Y.C., 1984-87; pvt. practice law N.Y.C., 1987—, 1987—. Mem. faculty N.E. regional seat Nat. Inst. Trial Advocacy, Hofstra U., Uniondale, N.Y., 1984-2001; mem. faculty advanced trial program Law Sch., Hofstra U., 1984-93, ABA/USTA Trademark Trial Advocacy Inst., 1993; spkr. in field. Author: Police Misconduct, 1981, Emergency Vehicle Liability, 1981, Sidewalks and Roadways, 1981. Co-dir. Coalition to Save Hempstead Harbor, Sea Cliff, N.Y., 1987-2001, pres., 1998—; mem. Environ. Leaders Network, Hicksville, N.Y., 1988; mem. adv. com. Internat. Environ. Conf., Hofstra U., 1990; pres., North Country Reform Temple, 2002—. Recipient award of merit N.Y. State Gov., 1990. Mem. ATLA, N.Y. State Trial Lawyers Assn., Pa. Bar Assn., Assn. of Bar of City of N.Y., Million Dollar Advocates Forum (elected life mem.). Avocations: family, running, basketball, skiing, fly fishing. General civil litigation, Insurance, Personal injury (including property damage). Office: 325 Broadway Ste 401 New York NY 10007-1112 Fax: 212-267-5813.

LEBOW, MICHAEL JEFFREY, lawyer; b. Detroit, Apr. 4, 1956; s. David and Thelma (Shainack) L. BA, Wayne State U., 1978; JD, Detroit Coll. Law, 1981. Bar: Mich. 1982, D.C. 1986, U.S. Dist. Ct. (ea. dist.) Mich. 1982, U.S. Supreme Ct. 2000; diplomate Nat. Bd. Trial Advocacy; cert. civil trial specialist. Litigation assoc. Kemp Klein Endelman & Beer, Birmingham, Mich., 1982-83; pvt. practice Southfield, Mich., 1983—85; ptnr. Lebow & Tobin, Birmingham, 1985-86, Gropman, Lebow & Tobin, Birmingham, 1986-89, Lebow & Tobin, Birmingham, 1989—2001, Harnisch, Lebow, Gerlach, Steffl & Gadd, PLC, Bingham Farms, Mich., 2001—. State coord. Nat. Bd. Trial Advocacy, 1994—, bd. law examiners, 1993—, bd. dirs., v.p., 2001. Contbr. articles to profl. jours. Bd. dirs. Mich. Com. Human Rights, Oak Park, 1976—. Mem. ABA (Excellence Nat. Appellate Advocacy award 1981), Mich. Bar Assn., Am. Inns of the Ct. (barrister Oakland County chpt.), Mto Guzzi Nat. Owners Assn., Mich. Handball Assn. Jewish. Avocations: handball, motorcycle collecting, 1950's jazz. General civil litigation, Professional liability. Office: Harnish Lebow Gerlach Steffl & Gadd PLC 30700 Telegraph Rd Ste 3475 Bingham Farms MI 48025 Office Fax: 248-644-8344. E-mail: mjl@harnischlaw.com.

LEBOWITZ, ALBERT, lawyer, writer; b. St. Louis, June 18, 1922; s. Jacob and Lena (Zemmel) L.; m. Naomi Gordon, Nov. 26, 1953; children— Joel Aaron, Judith Leah. AB, Washington U., St. Louis, 1945; LL.B., Harvard U., 1948. Bar: Mo. bar 1948. Assoc. Frank E. Morris, St. Louis, 1948-55; partner firm Morris, Schneider & Lebowitz, St. Louis, 1955-58, Crowe, Schneider, Shanahan & Lebowitz, St. Louis, 1958-66; counsel firm Murphy & Roche, St. Louis, 1966-67, Murphy & Schlapprizzi, St. Louis, 1967-81; partner firm Murphy, Schlapprizzi & Lebowitz, 1981-86; editor lit. quar. Perspective, 1961-80; of counsel Donald L. Schlapprizzi, P.C., 1986—, John T. Murphy, Jr., 1986-88. Author: novel Laban's Will, 1966, The Man Who Wouldn't Say No, 1969, A Matter of Days, 1989; also short stories. Served as combat navigator USAAF, 1943-45, ETO. Decorated Air medal with 3 oak leaf clusters. Mem. ABA, Mo., St. Louis bar assns., Phi Beta Kappa. Home: 743 Yale Ave Saint Louis MO 63130-3120 Office: Gateway One On The Mall 701 Market St Ste 1550 Saint Louis MO 63101-1897

LEBOWITZ, WALTER BERNARD, lawyer, consultant; b. Newark, May 7, 1930; s. George and Sarah Lebowitz; m. Rhoda E. Kovacs, Feb. 14, 1954 (div. Dec. 1990); children: Terry Lynn Shepard, Toby Jane McConnell, Jeffrey H. BBA, JD, U. Miami, 1954. Bar: Calif.; lic. and bonded pub. adjuster Fla., real estate agt. Fla., mortgage broker Fla., bus. broker. Pub. defender City of Miami Beach, Fla., 1968; mcpl. judge City of Sweetwater, Fla., 1969; dem. committeeman Dem. Party, Dade County, Fla., 1970, atty., 1971; owner, chief legal officer Stardust Prodns., Inc.; legal cons. Law instr. U. Miami, 1969—70, Tel Aviv U., 1988; cons. State of Israel Cable Assn. Author: Law for the Layman, 1980, (newsletter) Tax Planning Newsletter, 1981—82, Money Maker Mag., 1982—83; contbr. articles to profl. jours.; prodr.: 3 TV shows. Adminstrv. aide Dade County Commr., 1987; chmn. Biscayne Shores Cmty. Coun., Dade County, 1998—2000; mem. Film & Entertainment Bd., Dade County, 2000—02. With U.S. Army, 1954—56, France. Named Outstanding Citizen, Dade County, Fla., 1971. Mem.: ABA. Avocation: music. Family and matrimonial, Criminal, Personal injury (including property damage). Home: 4000 Towerside Terr Apt 407 Miami FL 33138-2236 Office: 12555 Biscayne Blvd #924 Miami FL 33181

LEBRAY, XAVIER, lawyer; b. Amiens, Somme, France, Feb. 27, 1950; s. Pierre Lebray and Françoise Vignon; m. Catherine Hache, July 25, 1975; children: Sebastien, Thibault, Vincent, Camille. Licence en droit, Univ. de Lille II, Lille, France, 1973; Des de droit des affaires, DES de sci. econs, Univ. Paris, France, 1975; JD, N.Y. Univ., N.Y., 1976. Bar: Paris 1979. Assoc. White & Case, N.Y., 1976—77, Paris, 1977—80; ptnr. Michaud Brizay Pestel-Debord, Paris, 1981—83, Bignon & Lebray, Paris, 1984—2001, Bignon Lebray Delsol & Assocs., Paris, 2001—. Elected mem. Regional Coun., Ile de France, 1998—2001, City Coun., St. Germain-en-Laye, 1989—. 1st class, 1973—74, Paris. Recipient Chevalier, Ordre Nat. du Merite, 1996. Mem.: Appeal Commn. Football French Fedn. (pres. 1993—). Ump. Roman Cath. Office: Bignon Lebray Delsol & Assocs 14 Rue Pergolese 75116 Paris France

LE CAMUS, GUILLAUME, lawyer, law educator; b. France, Aug. 3, 1970; M in commercial law and tax, U. Paris, 1992; postgrad. diploma in commercial law and tax, U. Montpellier, 1993. Bar: Paris. Tax mgr., internat. tax svcs. Landwell, Paris, 1994—97, Pricewaterhouse Coopers,

N.Y.C., 1997—2000; ptnr. Baker & McKenzie, Paris, 2000—. Lecturer Paris I U., 1999—2003. Mem.: Institut de Avocats Conseils Fiscaux. Office: Baker & McKenzie 32 Ave Baker BP2112 75771 Paris France

LECHNER, ALFRED JAMES, JR., judge; b. Elizabeth, N.J., Jan. 7, 1948; s. Alfred J. and Marie G. (McCormack) L.; m. Gayle K. Peterson, Apr. 3, 1976; children: Brendan Patrick, Coleman Thomas, Mary Kathleen. BS, Xavier U., Cin., 1969; JD, U. Notre Dame, 1972. Bar: N.J. 1972, U.S. Dist. Ct. N.J. 1972, N.Y. 1973, U.S. Dist. Ct. (so. and ea. dists.) N.Y. 1974, U.S. Ct. Appeals (2d cir.) 1974, U.S. Supreme Ct. 1975, U.S. Ct. Appeals (3d cir.) 1980. Assoc. Cadwalader, Wickersham & Taft, N.Y.C., 1972-75, MacKenzie, Welt & Duane, Elizabeth, 1975-76, MacKenzie, Welt, Duane & Lechner, Elizabeth, 1976-84; judge Superior Ct. State N.J., 1984-86, U.S. Dist. Ct. N.J., 1986—. Note and comment editor Notre Dame Law Rev., 1972; contbr. articles to profl. jours. Mem. Union County (N.J.) Adv. Bd. Cath. Cmty. Svcs., 1981-83, chmn., 1982. Lt. col. USMCR. Fellow Am. Bar Found.; mem. Assn. Fed. Bar of State N.J., Friendly Sons of St. Patrick (pres. 1982), Union County Club. Office: US Dist Ct Martin Luther King Jr Fed Bldg PO Box 999 Newark NJ 07101-0999

LEDBETTER, MICHAEL RAY, lawyer; b. San Bernardino, Calif., June 13, 1956; s. Raymond Leonard and Anna Laura Ledbetter; m. Diane Elizabeth Burger, Jan. 16, 1987 (div. Aug. 1991); 1 child, Lauren Ann; m. Diane Lorraine Errick, June 30, 1993. BA, U. Calif., Irvine, 1978; JD, U. So. Calif., 1981. Bar: Calif. 1981, U.S. Dist. Ct. (ctrl. dist.) Calif. 1982, U.S. Dist. Ct. (ea. dist.) Calif. 1992, U.S. Ct. Appeals (9th cir.) 1990, U.S. Supreme Ct. Assoc. atty. Roger J. Rosen Law Office, L.A., 1981-83; dep. pub. defender Office of Pub. Defender, Santa Barbara, Calif., 1983-90; sr. dep. counsel Office of County Counsel, Santa Barbara, 1990—. Bd. dirs. Calif. Joint Powers Ins. Authority, La Palma, 1992-94, 96-2002. Contbg. editor: California County Counsels Benchbook, 1996, 97, 98. Mem. City Coun., City of Carpinteria, Calif., 1990-94, 96—, mayor, 1991-93. Avocations: music (keyboards), computers, automobiles. Office: Office of County Counsel 105 E Anapamu St Rm 201 Santa Barbara CA 93101-6060 E-mail: ldbttr@co.santa-barbara.ca.us., MLdbttr@Netscape.net.

LEDBETTER, PAUL MARK, lawyer, writer; b. San Francisco, Oct. 14, 1947; s. John Paul and Joyce (Mayo) L.; m. Jerald Ann Broyles, Sept. 18, 1971; children: Paul Mark, Sarah Broyles. BA in English, Ouachita Bapt. U., 1970; JD, U. Ark., 1973. Bar: Ark. 1974, Tenn. 1995, U.S. Dist. Ct. (ea. dist.) Ark. 1974, U.S. Ct. Appeals (8th cir.) 1974, U.S. Ct. Appeals (6th cir.) 1991, U.S. Dist. Ct. (mid. dist.) Tenn. 1995. From assoc. to ptnr. Frierson, Walker, Snellgrove & Laser, Jonesboro, Ark., 1974-82; regional def. counsel Sq. D. Co., 1980-82; pres. Mark Ledbetter, P.A., Jonesboro, 1982-86; ptnr. Gerber, Gerber & Agee, Memphis, 1986-89, Taylor, Halliburton, Ledbetter & Caldwell, Memphis, 1989—2002, Taylor, Halliburton & Ledbetter, Memphis, 2003—. Author: The Hearing, 1994, The Thayer Class, 1998, The Wait, 2000. Co-founder St. Mark's Episcopal Day Sch., Jonesboro, 1978; mem. vestry St. Mark's Episcopal Ch., 1979; mem. Forum Commn. City of Jonesboro, 1978-80. Conservation Found. grantee, 1976; Rotary Internat. grantee, Japan, 1979. Mem. ATLA, Am. Bd. Trial Advs. (assoc.), Tenn. Bar Assn., Ark. Bar Assn. (mem. tort reform com. 1980, ho. of dels. 1979-80), Ark. Trial Lawyers Assn. (chmn. amicus curiae com. 1980-81, gov. 1980—), Tenn. Trial Lawyers Assn., Jonesboro C. of C. (bd. dirs. 1978-80), Human Factors and Ergonomics Soc., Rotary. Personal injury (including property damage), General civil litigation, Product liability. Office: Taylor Halliburton Ledbetter 254 Court Ave 3d Fl Memphis TN 38103 E-mail: mark794@aol.com.

LEDEMAN, GORDON NATHANIEL, lawyer; b. Rochester, NY, Dec. 7, 1971; AB, Harvard Coll., 1993; JD, Harvard U., 1997. Bar: D.C., NY. Atty. nat. security law and policy group Arnold & Porter, Washington, 1998—. Author: Reorganizing the Joint Chiefs of Staff, 1998; co-author: Combatting Chemical, Biological, Radiological and Nuclear Terrorism, 2001. Mem.: Cosmos Club. Private international, Government contracts and claims, Computer. Office: Arnold & Porter 555 12th St NW Washington DC 20004-1200

LEDERER, MAX DONALD, JR., lawyer; b. Plattsburgh, N.Y., June 21, 1960; s. Max Donald and Mary Lilian (Adie) L. BA magna cum laude, Marshall U., Huntington, W.Va., 1982; JD, U. Richmond, 1985. Bar: Pa. 1986, U.S. Army Ct. Mil. Rev. 1986. Commd. 2d lt. U.S. Army, 1982-86, advanced through grades to capt., 1987—; def. counsel Ft. Sill, Okla., 1986-87; command judge advocate CP Red Cloud, Korea, 1987-88; sr. trial counsel Combined Field Army, 1989; chief adminstrv. law div. Combined Field Army- 2d armored div. (forward), 1989-90; command judge adv. Op. Desert Storm 2d armored div. (forward), 1991; officer-in-charge Bremerhaven Legal Ctr., Fed. Republic of Germany, 1991-92; gen. counsel European Stars and Stripes, 1992-96, gen. mgr., 1996-2000; gen. mgr., gen. counsel European and Pacific Stars and Stripes, 2000—. Fellow ABA, Pa. Bar Assn. Avocation: running. Home: 4850 Middleton Dr Lockport NY 14094-1616 Office: 2427 Pondside Ter Silver Spring MD 20906-5752 E-mail: ledererm@stripes.usd.mil.

LEDERER, PETER DAVID, lawyer; b. Frankfurt, Germany, May 2, 1930; came to U.S., 1938; s. Leo and Alice Lederer; m. Midori Shimanouchi, Dec. 16, 1966. BA, U. Chgo., 1949, JD, 1957, M in Comparative Law, 1958. Bar: Ill. 1959, U.S. Supreme Ct. 1966, N.Y. 1967. Law and behavioral sci. rsch. fellow U. Chgo. Law Sch., 1958-59; ptnr. Baker & McKenzie, Zurich, Switzerland, 1960-66, N.Y.C., 1966-94, of counsel, 1994—2002. Chmn. bd. dirs. Coverage Connect, Inc., 1999-2002; mem. adv. bd. TeslaLab LLC, 2002-. Dir. Asian-am. Legal Def. and Edn. Fund, N.Y.C.; chmn. emeritus bd. dirs. The Midori Found.; pres. bd. trustees The Calhoun Sch., N.Y.C., 1980—83; mem. vis. com. U. Miami Law Sch., Coral Gables, Fla., 1974—, U. Chgo. Law Sch., 1988—91, 2000—; mem. adv. coun. Wildlife Trust, Phila., 2000—. With AUS, 1951—53. Fellow Am. Bar Found.; mem. ABA, Assn. of Bar of City of N.Y., Internat. Nuc. Law Assn. Insurance, Private international. E-mail: peterdlederer@att.net.

LEDERMAN, BRUCE RANDOLPH, lawyer; b. N.Y.C., Oct. 12, 1942; s. Morris David and Frances Lederman; m. Ellen Kline, Aug. 4, 1979; children: Eric, Jeffrey, Joshua. Cert., U. London, 1963; BS Econs. cum laude, U. Pa., 1964; LLB cum laude, Harvard U., 1967. Bar: U.S. Dist. Ct. (cen. dist.) Calif. 1967. Law clk. to Hon. Irving Hill U.S. Dist. Ct. Cen. Dist., L.A., 1967-68; sr. ptnr. Latham & Watkins, L.A., 1968—. Avocations: bicycle riding, real estate investments. Communications, Corporate, general. Office: Latham & Watkins 633 W 5th St Ste 3800 Los Angeles CA 90071-2007

LEDERMAN, LAWRENCE, lawyer, writer, educator; b. N.Y.C., Sept. 8, 1935; s. Herman Jack and Lillian (Rosenfeld) L.; children: Leandra, Evin. B.A., Bklyn. Coll., 1957; LL.B., N.Y.U., 1966. Bar: N.Y. 1968; Law clk. chief justice Calif. Sup. Ct., 1966-67; assoc. Cravath, Swaine & Moore, N.Y.C., 1968-74; ptnr. Wachtell, Lipton, Rosen & Katz, N.Y.C., 1975-91; ptnr., chmn. corp. practice Milbank, Tweed, Hadley & McCloy, 1991—; adj. prof. law N.Y.U. Sch. Law, 1974—; Chmn. bd. Phoenix House Devel. Corp., mem. Phoenix House Found.; bd. dirs. The Nat. Mentoring Partnership, N.Y. Bot. Garden, Tails In Need. Author: Tombstones: A Lawyer's Tales from the Takeover Decades, 1992; contbr. articles to profl. jours. Served with U.S. Army, 1957-59. Mem. ABA, N.Y. State Bar Assn., Order of the Coif. Corporate, general. Office: Milbank Tweed Hadley & McCloy 1 Chase Manhattan Plz Fl 47 New York NY 10005-1413

LEDWIDGE, PATRICK JOSEPH, lawyer; b. Detroit, Mar. 17, 1928; s. Patrick Liam and Mary Josephine (Hooley) L.; m. Rosemary Lahey Mervenne, Aug. 3, 1974; stepchildren: Anne Marie, Mary Clare, John, David, Sara Mervenne. AB, Coll. Holy Cross, 1949; JD, U. Mich., 1952. Bar: Mich. 1952. Assoc. firm Dickinson, Wright, Moon, Van Dusen & Freeman, Detroit, 1956-63; ptnr. Dickinson Wright PLLC, Bloomfield Hills, Mich., 1964—. Served to lt. j.g. U.S. Navy, 1952-55. Mem. Mich. Bar Assn., Detroit Bar Assn., Am. Law Inst. Clubs: Detroit Athletic, Detroit Golf. Roman Catholic. Banking, Corporate, general, General practice. Office: Dickinson Wright PLLC 38525 Woodward Ave Ste 2000 Bloomfield Hills MI 48304-5092

LEDWITH, JOHN FRANCIS, lawyer; b. Phila., Oct. 3, 1938; s. Francis Joseph and Jane Agnes (White) L.; m. Mary Evans, Aug. 28, 1965; children: Deirdre A., John E. AB, U. Pa., 1960, JD, 1963. Bar: Pa. 1965, N.Y. 1984, U.S. Dist. Ct. (ea. dist.) Pa. 1965, U.S. Ct. Appeals (3d cir.) 1965, U.S. Supreme Ct. 1970. Assoc. Joseph R. Thompson, Phila., 1965-71; mem. Schubert, Mallon, Wallheim & deCindis, Phila., 1971-81, LaBrum & Doak, Phila., 1981-95, Marshall, Denchey, Warner, Coleman & Goggins, Phila., 1995—. Author: (with others) Philadelphia CP Trial Manual, 1982. Bd. dirs. Chestnut Hill Cmty. Assn., Pa., 1975-76. With USCG, 1963-71. Mem. ABA, Pa. Bar Assn., Phila. Bar Assn., Def. Rsch. Inst., Fedn. Ins. Corp. Coun., Racquet Club (Phila.), Phila. Cricket Club, Avalon Yacht Club (commodore 1982). Republican. Roman Catholic. Federal civil litigation, State civil litigation, Insurance. Office: Marshall Dennehey Warner Coleman & Goggins 1845 Walnut St Philadelphia PA 19103-4708

LEDYARD, ROBINS HEARD, lawyer; b. Nashville, Oct. 14, 1939; s. Quitman Robins and Alma Elizabeth (Stevenson) L.; m. Julia Bordeaux Gambill, Dec. 19, 1962; children: Stevenson Gambill, Quitman Robins II, Margaret Dabney. BA, Vanderbilt U., 1965, JD, 1966. Bar: Tenn. 1966, U.S. Supreme Ct. 1975. Atty. Nat. Life & Accident Ins. Co., Nashville, 1966-68, asst. counsel, 1968-69, assoc. counsel, 1969-70, counsel, 1970-72, assoc. gen. counsel, 1972-75, gen. counsel, 1975-80; partner Bass, Berry & Sims, 1980—. Tchr. C.L.U.s, 1967-75 Asst. editor: Vanderbilt Law Rev., 1965-66; contbr. articles to profl. jours. Active United Way, Nashville, 1967— , Heart Fund, 1970-73; vice chmn. United Diocesan Givers, 1975; bd. dirs. St. Thomas Hosp., 1990—. With USMC, 1958-61. Recipient Bennett Douglas Bell Meml. prize, 1966; Marr scholar, 1965-66 Mem. ABA, Am. Coun. Life Ins. (chmn. tax com. 1978-80), Assn. Life Ins. Counsel (chmn. tax com. 1979-80), Tenn. Bar Assn., Nashville Bar Assn., Internat. Assn. Ins. Counsel, Global Leaders for the South, Order of Coif, Phi Delta Phi, Alpha Tau Omega. Clubs: Belle Meade Country, Capitol of Nashville, KC. Democrat. Roman Catholic. Home: 1215 Chickering Rd Nashville TN 37215-4519 Office: 2700 First American Ctr Nashville TN 37238

LEE, BRIAN EDWARD, lawyer; b. Oceanside, N.Y., Feb. 29, 1952; s. Lewis H. Jr. and Jean Elinor (Andrews) L.; m. Eleanor L. Barker, June 5, 1982; children: Christopher Martin, Alison Ruth, Danielle Andrea. AB, Colgate U., 1974; JD, Valparaiso U., 1976. Bar: N.Y. 1977, U.S. Dist. Ct. (so. and ea. dists.) N.Y. 1978, U.S. Ct. Appeals (2nd cir. 1992). Assoc. Marshall, Bellofatto & Callahan, Lynbrook, N.Y., 1977-80, Morris, Duffy, Ivone & Jensen, N.Y.C., 1980-84; sr. assoc. Ivone, Devine & Jensen, Lake Success, N.Y., 1984-85, ptnr., 1985—. Pres., trustee Trinity Christian Sch. of Montville Inc., N.J., 1985—, also track coach. Mem. ABA, N.Y. State Bar Assn., N.Y. County Lawyers Assn., Christian Legal Soc. Republican. Baptist. General civil litigation, Personal injury (including property damage), Product liability. Home: 292 Jacksonville Rd Pompton Plains NJ 07444-1511 Office: Ivone Devine & Jensen LLP 2001 Marcus Ave New Hyde Park NY 11042-1024 E-mail: brianelee@aol.com., blee@idjlaw.com.

LEE, DALE W. lawyer; b. Spokane, Wash., Sept. 16, 1948; AB, Brown U., 1970; JD, So. Meth. U., 1974. Bar: Hawaii 1974. Atty. Kobayashi, Sugita & Goda, Honolulu. Mem.: Hawaii State Bar Assn. (treas. Young Lawyers sect. 1979—80), Delta Theta Phi. Commercial, consumer (including collections, credit), Personal injury (including property damage). Office: Kobayashi, Sugita & Goda Ste 2600 999 Bishop St Honolulu HI 96813*

LEE, DAN M. retired state supreme court chief justice; b. Petal, Miss., Apr. 19, 1926; s. Buford Aaron and Pherbia Ann (Camp) L.; m. Peggy Jo Daniel, Nov. 27, 1947 (dec. 1952); 1 child, Sheron Lee Anderson; m. Mary Alice Gray, Sept. 30, 1956; 1 child, Dan Jr. Attended, U. So. Miss., 1946; LLB, Jackson Sch. Law, 1949; JD, Miss. Coll., 1970. Bar: Miss. 1948. Ptnr. Franklin & Lee, Jackson, Miss, 1948-54, Lee, Moore and Countiss, Jackson, Miss., 1954-71; county judge Hinds County, 1971-77; cir. judge Hinds-Yazoo Counties, 1977-82; assoc. justice Miss. Supreme Ct., Jackson, 1982-87, presiding justice, 1987-95, chief justice, 1995-98; ret., 1998; of counsel Dogan & Wilkinson, PLLC, Jackson, 1999. With U.S. Naval Aviation, 1944-46. Mem. ABA, Hinds County Bar Assn., Miss. State Bar Assn., Aircraft Owners and Pilots Assn., Am. Legion, VFW, Kiwanis Internat. Baptist. E-mail: judgeanddr@aol.com.

LEE, DAVID HAROLD, lawyer; b. N.Y.C., May 27, 1947; AB cum laude, Tufts Coll., 1969; JD, Boston U., 1973. Bar: Mass. 1973, U.S. Dist. Ct. Mass. 1974, U.S. Ct. Appeals (1st cir.) 1974, U.S. Supreme Ct. 1977, U.S. Tax Ct. 1984. Assoc. Mahoney, Atwood & Goldings, Boston, 1973-75; ptnr. Atwood & Wright, Boston, 1975-84, Bowser & Lee, Boston, 1984-88, Lee & Levine, Boston, 1988-91, Lee, Levine & Bowser, Boston, 1991—. Contbr. articles to profl. jours. Fellow IAML, Am. Coll. Family Trial Lawyers (dip.); mem. ABA (family law sect.), Mass. Bar Assn. (family law sect. council, continuing legal edn. adv. com. 1979—, various continuing legal edn. coms.), Boston Bar Assn., Middlesex County Bar Assn., Norfolk County Bar Assn., Norfolk County Bench Bar Com. (chmn. 1985-88), Mass. Acad. Trial Attys. (faculty 1979), Am. Acad. Matrimonial Lawyers (Mass. chpt. 1979—, bd. mgrs. 1981-84, treas. 1984-88, v.p. 1988-90, pres. elect 1990-91, pres. 1991-92). State civil litigation, Family and matrimonial, Probate (including wills, trusts). Office: Lee Levine & Bowser 222 Berkeley St Ste 1400 Boston MA 02116-3750 Home: 375 Heath St Chestnut Hill MA 02467

LEE, DENNIS PATRICK, lawyer, judge; b. Omaha, Feb. 12, 1955; s. Donald Warren and Betty Jean (O'Leary) L.; children: Patrick Michael, Katherine Marie, Megan Elizabeth. BA, Creighton U., 1977, JD, 1980. Bar: Nebr. 1980, U.S. Dist. Ct. Nebr. 1980, U.S. Ct. Appeals (8th cir.) 1980, Iowa 1990. Assoc. Thompson Crounse & Pieper, Omaha, 1980-84; ptnr. Lee Law Offices, Omaha, 1984-87, Silverman, Lee & Crounse Law Offices, 1987-94, Lee & Jones Law Offices, P.C., L.L.O., 1994—. Atty. Nebr. State Racing Commn., Lincoln, 1984-87, commr. 1988—, chmn., 1991—; adminstrv. law judge, State of Nebr., 1985-87; lectr. Creighton U., Omaha, 1982-85. Author: Law of Conservatorships, 1981: Legal Aspects of Equine Veterinary Practice, 1984, Planning Opportunities with Living Trusts in Nebraska, 1995; others. Trustee Holy Name Cath. Ch., Omaha, 1980-84; chmn. nat. enforcement officers com. Nat. Assn. State Racing Commrs., Lexington, Ky., 1984-87; commr. Nebr. State Racing Commn., 1988—. Mem. ABA, Nat. Assn. Trial Attys., Comml. Law League Am., Nebr. State Racing Commn. (chmn. 1991), Assn. Racing Commrs. Internat. (treas. 1996-97, v.p. 1997-2000, chmn. and CEO 2000——), Nebr. Bar Assn, Omaha Bar Assn. (chmn. conservatorship com. 1981—), Nebr.-Iowa Referees Assn. (v.p. 1981-88), Omaha C. of C. (Outstanding Young Omahan 1993). Administrative and regulatory, State civil litigation, Commercial, consumer (including collections, credit). Home: 608 S 123d St Omaha NE 68154-1944 Office: Lee & Jones 12165 W Center Rd Ste 52 Omaha NE 68144-3974

LEE, DONALD JOHN, federal judge; b. 1927; AB, U. Pitts., 1950; LLB, Duquesne U., 1954. Bar: Pa. Supreme Ct. 1955; U.S. Supreme Ct. 1984. Assoc. George Y. Meyer and Assocs., 1954-57; law clk. to Hon. Rabe F. Marsh Jr. U.S. Dist. Ct., Pa., 1957-58; assoc. Wilner, Wilner and Kuhn, 1958-61; ptnr. Dougherty, Larrimer & Lee, Pitts., 1961-84, 86-88; judge Ct. Common Pleas of Allegheny County, Pa., 1984-86, 88-90, U.S. Dist. Ct. (we. dist.) Pa., Pitts., 1990—. Councilman Borough of Green Tree, 1961-63, solicitor, 1963-84, 86-88; spl. asst. atty. gen. Office of Atty. Gen. Commonwealth of Pa., 1963-74; spl. legal counsel Home Rule Study Commn., Municipality of Bethel Park and Borough of Green Tree, 1973-74, City of Pitts., 1978-80, various municipalities, 1970-86; chmn. Home Rule Charter Transition Com. Bethel Park, 1978; bd. dirs. Soldiers' and Sailors' Meml. Hall and Mus. Trust. Mem. ad hoc com. Salvation Army; bd. dirs. Soldiers and Sailors Meml. Hall and Mus. Trust, Inc. With USN, 1945-47. Mem. ABA, Allegheny County Bar Assn., St. Thomas More Legal Soc., Ancient Order of Hibernians, Woodland Hills Swim Club, Gaelic Arts Soc., Tin Can Sailors. Office: US Dist Ct 7th Grant St Rm 916 Pittsburgh PA 15219

LEE, ERNEST J., SR., lawyer; b. Ft. Bragg, N.C., June 21, 1956; s. Major Lee, Sr. and Lucille L. Lee; 1 child, Ernest L. Lee, Jr. BA in Mass Comm., U. Mo., St. Louis, 1996; JD, U. Mo., Kansas City, 1999. Bar: Calif. 2001, U.S. Dist. Ct. (so. dist.) Calif. 2001, U.S. Dist. Ct. (central dist.) Calif. 2003. Mgr., owner Queensway Dry Cleaning Co., St. Louis, 1981—88; owner, operator Ernest Lee Bail Surety Co., St. Louis, 1988—90; pres., CEO, chmn. LEECORP Corp., Inc., St. Louis, 1990—98; pvt. practice San Diego, 2001—. Founder, chmn., 1st pres. Liberty Coalition, San Diego, L.A., 2002—. Avocations: horseback riding, dogs, jogging, golf, tennis, reading. Product liability, Personal injury (including property damage), Communications. Office: 269 E Lexington Ave Ste A El Cajon CA 92020

LEE, EUN HWA, lawyer; b. Seoul, Republic of Korea, Sept. 3, 1971; d. Kwang Hyun and So Ja L.; m. Olivier Jean Louis Ravel. BA in Internat. Rels. with honors and distinction, MA in Sociology, Stanford U., 1992; JD, Georgetown U., 1996. Bar: NY 1997. Dean Acheson Legal Stagiaire Ct. Justice European Cmtys., Luxembourg, 1996; assoc. Rosenman & Colin LLP, N.Y.C., 1997—98, Weil Gotshal & Manges, London, 1998—2000, Debevoise & Plimpton, Paris, 2001—. Jean Monnet fellow Sollac S.A., Paris, 1992—93. Co-author: 1998 Update, Going Private, 1998. Stanford in Government summer fellow State Senator Becky Morgan, Sacramento, 1992. Staff Award and Scholarship, World Affairs Coun., 1991, internat. rels. dept. scholar, Stanford U., 1992, Vos. in Asia Cross-Cultural fellow, 1992, Undergrad. Rsch. Opportunities major grantee, 1992. Mem.: World Assn. Internat. Studies, Internat. Bar Assn., Cap and Gown Women's Honors Soc. Avocations: travel, languages, cinema. Corporate, general, Mergers and acquisitions, Private international. Office: Debevoise & Plimpton 21 ave George V 75008 Paris France Office Fax: 0033 1 47 20 50 82. Business E-Mail: Ehlee@debevoise.com.

LEE, FREDERICK DREXEL, lawyer; b. Savannah, Ga., Sept. 27, 1937; d. Frederick Charles and Geneva (Futch) Drexel; m. Julian Ralson Lee, June 7, 1959; children: Dawn, Courtney. BS in Edn., U. Ga., 1959, MEd, 1960; JD summa cum laude, Woodrow Wilson Coll. Law, Atlanta, 1978. Bar: Ga. 1979. Pvt. practice, Atlanta, 1978-92, Ellabell, Ga., 1992—. Editor Ga. Profl. Engr., 1982-86. Pres. Pembroke (Ga.) Garden Club, 1996-99. Recipient Chief Justice Robert Benham's Supreme Ct. of Ga. award for cmty. svc., 1998. Mem. Phi Beta Kappa, Phi Kappa Phi, Kappa Delta Pi. Methodist. Avocations: gardening, reading, bible study, exercise. General practice. Home: 505 Bill Futch Rd Ellabell GA 31308-4600

LEE, GARY, lawyer; b. Feb. 1955; BA, JD, U. N.D. Bar: N.D. 1980. With Olson Burns Lee, P.C., Minot, ND. Mem.: State Bar Assn. N.D. (pres. 2002). Address: PO Box 1180 Minot ND 58702*

LEE, GEORGE TERRY, JR., lawyer; b. Dallas, Oct. 28, 1935; s. George Terry and Isabel (Breckenridge) T.; m. Natalie Blythe Henderson, Aug. 17, 1957; children: George Terry III, Blythe, Rebecca, Hamilton. BA, Yale U., 1957; LLB, Stanford U., 1960. Assoc. Goldberg, Fonville, et al, Dallas, 1960-65; gen. counsel George A. Fuller Co. and OKC Corp., Dallas, 1965-73; ptnr. Akin, Gump, Strauss, Hauer & Feld, L.L.P., Dallas, 1973—. Trustee Found. for Arts, Dallas, 1963—, St. Mark's Sch. of Tex., Dallas, 1966-72; bd. dirs. Dallas Mus. Fine Arts; pres. Brit.-Am. Commerce Assn., Dallas, 1986. Fellow (life) Tex. Bar Found.; mem. ABA, University Club (N.Y.C.)., Brook Hollow Golf Club (Dallas), Koon Kreek Klub (Athens, Tex.), Crescent Club (Dallas). Home: 3101 Greenbrier Dr Dallas TX 75225-4603 Office: Akin Gump Strauss Hauer & Feld LLP 1700 Pacific Ave Ste 4100 Dallas TX 75201-4675

LEE, HENRY, lawyer; b. N.Y.C., Dec. 18, 1952; s. Tong Shong and Toy (Wong) L. BA, Bklyn. Coll., 1973; JD, U. Iowa, 1977. Bar: Calif. 1979, N.Y. 1980, N.J. 1993. Research atty. Calif. Ct. Appeal, San Bernardino, 1977-78; assoc. Mendes & Mount, N.Y.C., 1980-85, ptnr., 1985-91; legal cons. Am. law Peruvian pvt. corps., 1991-92; of counsel Mendes & Mount, N.Y.C., 1992-95, ptnr., 1996-98, L.A., 1998—2002; pres. FGH Corp SAC, Lima, Peru, 2003—; corp. coun. Textiles San Sebastian SAC, Lima, Peru, 2003—. Note editor Jour. Corp. Law, U. Iowa Coll. Law, 1976-77. General civil litigation, Commercial, contracts (including sales of goods; commercial financing), Private international. Office: Manuel del Valle rax A Lote 3 Pachacamac Lima 19 Peru Home: Casilla Postal 09-0178 Chorrilas Lima 9 Peru E-mail: henry.lee@fghcorp.com.

LEE, IN-YOUNG, lawyer; b. In-Cheon, Kyonggi-do, Korea, Dec. 5, 1952; came to U.S. 1978; s. In-Seok and Hyun-Bo (Rim) L.; m. Young-Lae Hong, July 1, 1978; children: Casey K., Brian K. LLB, Seoul Nat. U., Korea, 1975; LLM, Harvard U., 1980; JD, UCLA, 1983. Bar: Ill. 1983, N.Y. 1987, D.C. 1989, U.S. Ct. Internat. Trade. Assoc. Baker & McKenzie, Chgo., 1983-86, Marks & Murase, N.Y.C., 1986-87, Baker & McKenzie, N.Y.C., 1987-91; ptnr. Marks & Murase, N.Y.C., 1991-96, McDermott, Will & Emory, N.Y.C., 1996—. Gen. counsel Korean C. of C. and Industry in USA, Inc., 1993—, Assn. Korean Fin. Instns. Am., Inc. Articles editor Pacific Basin Law Jour. Presbyterian. Avocations: fishing, golf. Banking, Commercial, contracts (including sales of goods; commercial financing), Private international. Office: McDermott Will & Emery 50 Rockefeller Plz Fl 12 New York NY 10020-1600 E-mail: ilee@mwe.com.

LEE, JAMES B. lawyer; BS in Civil Engring., U.S. Mil. Acad., 1952; JD with honors, George Washington U., 1960. Bar: Utah 1961, U.S. Dist. Ct. Utah 1961, U.S. Supreme Ct. 1971. Sr. atty. Parsons, Behle & Latimer, Salt Lake City, pres., 1979—93. Trustee KUED, 1990—97, chair, 1996—97; mem. State Exec. and Jud. Compensation Commn., 1992—96; chmn. Family Ct. Task Force, 1992—94; chmn. adv. com. on rules of evidence Utah Supreme Ct., 1987—91; chmn. Utah State Bar Future Comms., 1992—93. Bd. dirs. Legal Aid Soc. Salt Lake, 1994—97. Fellow: Am. Bar Found.; mem.: ABA (chmn. Utah chpt. 1994—99, bd. officer 17th dist. 2000—03), Salt Lake County Bar Assn. (pres. 1968—69), Utah State Bar (bar commr. 1971—78, pres. 1977—78), Salt Lake Area C. of C. (bd. govs., v.p. 1991—93), Utah Bar Found. (trustee 1990—96, pres. 1994—96, energy and natural resources sect., Disting. Svc. award 1989—90), Utah Nat. Guard Assn. (pres. 1966—67). Corporate, general, Natural resources, Alternative dispute resolution. Office: Parsons Behle & Latimer Ste 1800 201 S Main St PO Box 45898 Salt Lake City UT 84145-0898*

LEE, JEROME G. lawyer; b. Chgo., Feb. 23, 1924; m. Margo B. Lee, Dec. 23, 1947; children: James A., Kenneth M. BSChemE, U. Wis., 1947; JD, NYU, 1950. Bar: N.Y. 1950, U.S. Supreme Ct. 1964. Assoc. firm Jeffery, Kimball, Eggleston, N.Y.C., 1950-52; assoc. firm Morgan, Finnegan, Durham & Pine, N.Y.C., 1952-59; ptnr. Morgan, Finnegan, Pine, Foley & Lee, N.Y.C., 1959-86; sr. ptnr. Morgan & Finnegan, N.Y.C., 1986-95, of counsel, 1995—. Lectr. in field. Author: (with J. Gould) Intellectual Property Counseling and Litigation, 1988, USPTO Proposals to Change Rule 56 and the Related Rules Regarding a Patent Applicant's Duty of

Candour, Patent World, 1992; contbr. articles to legal jours. in patent and trademark litigation splty. Fellow Am. Bar Found.; mem. ATLA, ABA (mem. coun. Intellectual Property Law sect., chmn. com. fed. practice and procedure, chmn. com. Ct. of Appeals Fed. Cir., chmn. com. on ethics and profl. responsibility, stds. com., mem. fed. cir. adv. com. 1992-97), Am. Intellectual Property Law Assn. (bd. dirs. 1984-90, pres. 1991, Am. Judicature Soc., Internat. Fedn. Indsl. Property Attys., Found. for Creative Am. (bd. dirs.), N.Y. Bar Assn., Assn. of Bar of City of N.Y., N.Y. County Bar Assn., N.Y. Patent, Trademark and Copyright Law Assn. (bd. dirs. 1975-80, pres. 1981), others. Federal civil litigation, Patent, Trademark and copyright. Home: 3328 Sabal Cove Ln Longboat Key FL 34228-4157 Office: Morgan & Finnegan 345 Park Ave Fl 22 New York NY 10154-0053

LEE, LANSING BURROWS, JR., lawyer, corporate executive; b. Augusta, Ga., Dec. 27, 1919; s. Lansing Burrows and Bertha (Barrett) L.; s. Natalie Krug, July 4, 1943; children: Melinda Lee Clark, Lansing Burrows III, Bothwell Graves, Richard Hancock. BS, U. Va., 1939; postgrad., U. Ga. Sch. Law, 1939-40; JD, Harvard U., 1947. Bar: Ga. 1947. Corp. officer Ga.-Carolina Warehouse & Compress Co., Augusta, 1957-89, pres., CEO; co-owner Ga.-Carolina Warehouse; pvt. practice, Augusta, 1947—. Chmn. bd. trustees James Brice White Found., 1962—; sr. warden Episcopal Ch., also chancellor, lay min.; sr. councillor Atlantic Coun. U.S. Capt. USAAF, 1942-46. Fellow Am. Coll. Trust and Estate Counsel; mem. Ga. Bar Found., Harvard U. Law Sch. Assn. Ga. (pres. 1966-67), Augusta Bar Assn. (pres. 1966-67), Soc. Colonial Wars Ga., State Bar Ga. (former chmn. fiduciary law sect.), U.S. Supreme Ct. Hist. Soc., U. Va. Thomas Jefferson Soc. Alumni, Internat. Order St. Luke the Physician, Augusta Country Club, Harvard Club Atlanta, President's Club Med. Coll. Ga. Corporate, general, Estate planning, Probate (including wills, trusts). Office: Wachovia Bldg 699 Broad St Ste 1001 Augusta GA 30901-1448 Office Fax: 706-722-8902. E-mail: lawlee@worldnet.att.net.

LEE, MARILYN MODARELLI (IRMA LEE), lawyer, retired library director; b. Jersey City, Dec. 8, 1934; d. Alfred E. and Florence Olga (Koment) Modarelli; m. Alfred McClung Lee III, June 8, 1957 (div. July 1985); children: Leslie Lee Ekstrand, Alfred McClung IV, Andrew Modarelli. BA, Swarthmore (Pa.) Coll., 1956; JD, Western New Eng. Sch. of Law, 1985. Bar: Mass. 1986. Claims rep., supr. region II Social Security Adminstrn., Jersey City, 1956—59; law libr. County of Franklin, Greenfield, Mass., 1972—78; head law libr. Mass. Trial Ct., Greenfield, 1978—2001. Mem. Franklin County Futures Lab Project (Mass. Cts.), 1994—. Vice chmn. Greenfield Planning Bd., 1987—95; clerk bldg. com. Greenfield Sch., 2002—; mem. Franklin Regional Planning Bd., 1988—98; moderator All Souls Unitarian Ch., 1996—2000, asst. treas., 1997—98, treas., 1998—2001; exec. bd. Franklin Regional Planning Bd., 1992—95; mem.western regional bd. Mass. Soc. for Prevention of Cruelty to Children, 2002—; chmn. Franklin County (Mass.) Tech., Turners Falls, 1974—76; bldg. com. chair Franklin County (Tech) Sch., Turners Falls, 1974—76; clk. Franklin County (Mass.) Tech., Turners Falls, 1976—81; mem. Greenfield C.C. Found., 1990—, Franklin Regional Transp. Com., 1992—; mem. alumni coun. Swarthmore Coll., 1994—97. Mem. Mass. Bar Assn., Franklin County Bar Assn. (chmn. lawyer referral com. 1992-94, 97-99, vice-chmn. 1994-97, chmn. libr. com. 1992—), Law Librs. of New Eng. (treas. 1993-97), Am. Assn. Law Librs. (mem. state ct. and county law librs. sect. 1972—, bylaws com. 1996-99, chair bylaws com. 1997-98), Greenfield Charter (commn. clk. 1979-83). Avocations: swimming, gardening.

LEE, MICHAEL GREGORY, lawyer; b. Berkeley, Calif., June 23, 1951; s. General and Lucy Elizabeth Lee; m. Patricia Anne Spears, Aug. 10, 1974; children: Jared Ahmad, Derrek Jordan. AA, Contra Costa Coll., San Pablo, Calif., 1972; BA, U. Calif., Davis, 1976, JD, 1979. Bar: Calif. 1979, , U.S. Dist. Ct. (no. dist.) Calif. 1985, U.S. Dist. Ct. (ea. dist.) Calif. 1986, U.S. Dist. Ct. (ctrl. dist.) Calif. 1990, U.S. Ct. Appeals (9th cir.) 1988, U.S. Supreme Ct. 1999. Dep. solicitor Calif. Agrl. Labor Rels. Bd., Sacramento, 1979-87; staff counsel II Calif. Sec. State, Sacramento, 1987, Calif. State Water Resources Control Bd., Sacramento, 1987-88; supervising dep. atty. gen. Calif. Dept. Justice, Sacramento, 1988—. Mem. 100 Black Men of Sacramento, Inc., 1996—; mgr., coach Northgate PeeWee League, Sacramento, 1987, Nat. Pony Baseball, Sacramento, 1988-91, Pocket Little League, Sacramento, 1992-98. Fellow U. Calif., 1976-79; recipient Donor's award Calif. State Employees' Campaign, 1991-98, Tournament Team Mgr. award Pocket Little League, 1996, Tournament Coach award Natomas Pony Baseball, 1991. Democrat. Baptist. Office: Atty Gen State of Calif PO Box 944255 1300 I St Ste 1101 Sacramento CA 94244-2550

LEE, PAUL LAWRENCE, lawyer; b. N.Y.C., 1946; AB, Georgetown U., 1969; JD, U. Mich., 1972. Bar: N.Y. 1974. Editor-in-chief Mich. Law Rev., 1971-72; law clk. to Hon. Walter R. Mansfield U.S. Ct. Appeals (2d cir.), 1973-74; spl. asst. to gen. counsel U.S. Treasury Dept., 1977-78, exec. asst. to dep. sec., 1978-79; dep. supt. and counsel N.Y. State Banking Dept., 1980-81; ptnr. Shearman & Sterling, N.Y.C., 1982-94; exec. v.p., gen. counsel Republic N.Y. Corp., N.Y.C., 1994-2000; sr. exec. v.p., gen. counsel HSBC USA Inc., N.Y.C., 2000—. Office: HSBC USA Inc 452 5th Ave Fl 7 New York NY 10018-2786 E-mail: paul.l.lee@us.hsbc.com.

LEE, PAUL P. ophthalmologist, educator, consultant, lawyer; b. Taipei, Taiwan, Sept. 8, 1960; s. Pei-Fei and Julia Lee. BA, U. Mich., 1981, MD, 1986; JD, Columbia U., 1986. Bar: Md. 1987, D.C. 1988. Congl. intern U.S. House Select Commn. on Aging, Washington, 1980; biologist NASA, Cape Canaveral, Fla., 1981; med. intern Beth Israel Hosp., Boston, 1986-87; resident in ophthalmology Johns Hopkins Hosp., Balt., 1987-90; fellow glaucoma Mass. Eye & Ear Infirmary, Boston, 1990-91; asst. prof. U. So. Calif., L.A., 1991-95, assoc. prof., 1995-97; prof. Duke U., Durham, N.C., 1997—, James Pitzer Gills III and Joy Gills prof. ophthalmology. Cons. health scis. program Rand Corp., Santa Monica; bd. dirs. Ctr. Partially Sighted, Blind Children's Ctr.; med. dir. Duke Eye Care, LLC. Mem. editl. bd. Archives Ophthalmology, Evidence-Based Ophthalmology, Chinese Jour. Ophthalmology; contbr. articles to profl. jours. Bd. trustees Am. Acad. Ophthalmology, 2000—. Rsch. fellowship Brookdale Inst. on Aging, 1985, sr. fellow Ctr. Aging Duke U.; Stone scholar Columbia U. Law Sch., 1985. Mem. AMA, ABA, APHA, Am. Acad. Ophthalmology (trustee), Assn. Health Svcs. Rsch., Chinese-Am. Ophthalmology Soc., Assn. for Rsch. in Vision and Ophthalmology. Office: Duke U Eye Ctr Dept Ophthalmology Erwin Rd Durham NC 27710-0001 E-mail: lee00106@mc.duke.edu.

LEE, PAUL W. lawyer; BS in Elec. Engring. and Computer Sci., Columbia U., 1972; JD cum laude, Cornell U., 1976. Ptnr. Goodwin Procter LLP, Boston, chair corp. dept., assoc. compensation and legal pers. supervision com. Apptd. mem. Govs. Asian Am. Commn. Editor: Cornell INternat. Law Jour. Mem.: ABA (minority members-at-large 2000—03, bd. govs., former mem. commn. on opportunities for minorities in the profession), Asian Am. Lawyers Assn. Mass. (founder, first pres.), Nat. Asian Pacific Am. Bar Assn. (pres. 1995—96). Office: Goodwin Procter LLP Exchange Place 53 State St Boston MA 02109*

LEE, RICHARD DIEBOLD, law educator, legal publisher, consultant; b. Fargo, N.D., July 31, 1935; s. Sidney Jay and Charlotte Hannah (Thompson) L.; m. Patricia Ann Taylor, June 17, 1957; children: Elizabeth Carol, Deborah Susan, David Stuart. BA with distinction, Stanford U., 1957; JD, Yale U., 1960. Bar: Calif. 1961, U.S. Dist. Ct. (no. dist.) Calif. 1961, U.S. Ct. Appeals (9th cir.) 1961. Dep. atty. gen. Office of Atty. Gen., Sacramento, 1960-62; assoc. McDonough, Holland, Schwartz, Allen & Wahrhaftig, Sacramento, 1962-66, ptnr., 1966-69; asst. dean U. Calif. Sch. Law, Davis, 1969-73, assoc. dean, 1973-76; assoc. prof. law Temple U. Sch. Law, Phila., 1976-77, vis. prof., 1975-76, prof., 1977-89; dir. profl. devel. Baker & McKenzie, Chgo., N.Y.C., 1981-83; dir. Am. Inst. for Law Tng., Phila., 1985-89, mem. adv. bd., 1989—; dir. profl. devel. Morrison & Foerster, San Francisco, 1989-93; dir. Continuing Edn. of the Bar, Berkeley, 1993-97; v.p. JusLaw.com, 2000—01, LawyersTV Continue Learning Networks L.L.C., 2002. Mem. Grad. and Profl. Fin. Aid Coun., Princeton, N.J., 1974-80; trustee Law Sch. Admission Council, Washington, 1976-78; mem. internat. adv. com. Internat. Juridical Org., Rome, 1977-88; mem. bd. advisors Lawyer Hiring and Tng. Report, Chgo., 1983-95; vis. prof. law sch. law Golden Gate U., San Francisco, 1988-89; v.p. JusLaw.com, 2000-01. Author: (coursebook) Materials on Internat. Efforts to Control the Environment, 1977, 78, 79, 80, 84, 85, 87. Co-editor: Orientation in the U.S. Legal System annual coursebook, 1982-92. Contbr. articles to profl. jours. Bd. dirs. Lung Assn. of Sacramento-Emigrant Trails, 1962-69, pres., 1966-68; bd. dirs. Sacramento County Legal Aid Soc., 1968-74, pres., 1971-72; chmn. bd. overseers Phila. Theol. Inst., 1984-88, bd. overseers, 1979-80, 84-88; mem. bd. of council Episcopal Community Services, Phila., 1984-88; trustee Grace Cathedral, San Francisco, 1989—, chair bd. trustees, 1992-95; mem. bd. visitors John Marshall Law Sch., Chgo., 1989-93; trustee Grad. Theol. Union, Berkeley, 1991-2000, vice chair, 1994-99; trustee Coll. of Preachers, Washington Nat. Cathedral, 1999—; chair, bd. dirs. The Ghiberti Found., 2002--. Mem. ABA (chmn. various coms., spl. cons. on continuing legal edn. MacCrate Task Force on Law Schs. and the Profession: Narrowing the Gap, 1991-93, standing com. on specialization 1998-2001, standing com. legal assts. 2003-), State Bar Calif. (chair standing com. on minimum continuing legal edn. 1990-92, com. mem. 1990-93), Bar Assn. San Francisco (legal ethics com., conf. of delegates 1987—), co-founder and chair, Profl. Devel. Consortium (chair 1991-93), Am. Law Inst., Yale Club (N.Y.C., San Francisco. Democrat. Episcopalian. Home and Office: 2001 Sacramento St Ste 4 San Francisco CA 94109-3342 E-mail: RichardDLee@earthlink.net.

LEE, RICHARD H(ARLO), lawyer; b. Glen Falls, N.Y., June 5, 1947; s. Donald D. and Jeanne M. (Uthus) L.; m. Mary Ahearn, June 10, 1972; children: Christine Marie Ahearn Lee, Andrea Elizabeth Ahearn Lee. BS with honors, Mich. State U., 1972; JD magna cum laude, Ariz. State U., 1976. Bar: Ariz. 1977, U.S. Ct. Appeals (6th cir.) 1977, U.S. Dist. Ct. Ariz. 1978, U.S. Ct. Appeals (9th cir.) 1981. Law clk. to Judge George Edwards U.S. Ct. Appeals (6th cir.) Ohio, Cin., 1976-77; assoc. Sparks & Siler, Scottsdale, Ariz., 1977-78, Murphy & Posner, Phoenix, 1979-82, ptnr., 1983-86; assoc. Storey & Ross, Phoenix, 1986-88; prin. McDaniel & Lee, Phoenix, 1989-91, Law Office of Richard H. Lee, Phoenix, 1992—; of counsel Martin & Patterson, Ltd., 1992-98, Martin & Assocs., 1998-99. Comment and notes editor Ariz. State U. Law Jour., 1975-76; bd. editors Maricopa County Lawyer, 1990-91. Chmn. Ariz. Canal Divershion Channel task force City of Phoenix, 1985—86, mem. exec. com., mem. citizens bond com., 1975, chmn. solid waste bond com., 1987—88, mem. bond adv. com., 1988—2000; mem. adv. com. City of Phoenix Neighborhood Orgn. Divsn., Ariz., 1974—75; vo. VISTA Crow Indian Tribe, Crow Agy., Mont., 1969—71; state committeeman Ariz. Dem.s, Phoenix; bd. dirs. Valley of the Sun Sch. and Habilitation Ctr., 1991—95, treas., 1992—93, chair fin. com., 1993—94. Mem. Ariz. Bar Assn. (chmn. com. on CLE bankruptcy sect. 1985-87, chmn. bankruptcy sect. 1987-88), Ariz. State U. Coll. Law Alumni Assn. (pres. 1981), Ariz. State U. Alumni Assn. (bd. dirs. 1981-82), Kappa Sigma. Bankruptcy, Landlord-tenant, Property, real (including real estate development, water). Home: 331 W Orangewood Ave Phoenix AZ 85021-7249 Office: PO Box 7749 Phoenix AZ 85011-7749 E-mail: lee@azbar.org.

LEE, ROBERT E. lawyer; b. Nashville, Oct. 4, 1963; s. Sherwood C. and Vada Ann Lee; m. Catherine Irene Kunkle, Sept. 16, 1986; children: Frances Margaret Ann, Robert E. Jr. BBA, Francis Marion U., Florence, S.C., 1987; JD, U. S.C., 1990. Bar: S.C. 1991, U.S. Dist. Ct. S.C. 1991, U.S. Ct. Appeals (4th cir.) 1991, cert.: S.C. Supreme Ct. (lead counsel in capital litigation), lic.: (arbitrator). Assoc. McIntosh & Lee, Florence, SC, 1990—2000; mng. shareholder Aiken, Bridges, Nunn, Elliott & Tyler, P.A., Florence, 2000—. Mem. ho. of dels. S.C. Bar, 1998. Chmn. bd. trustees Francis Marion U., Florence, 1998—, 1999—; bd. mgrs. S.C. Hist. Soc., 2002—. Recipient Pres.'s award, Nat. Assn. Criminal Def. Lawyers, 1996. Mem.: Am. Kennel Club (mem. test rules adv. com. 1999—). Appellate, Construction, Federal civil litigation. Home: 2658 Trotter Rd Florence SC 29501 Office: Aiken Bridges Nunn Elliott & Tyler PA 181 E Evans St Ste 409 Florence SC 29506

LEE, SAMUEL S. lawyer; b. Seoul, Korea, Nov. 7, 1965; s. Yong Hae and Jung K. Lee; m. Moriah M. McStay, Dec. 30, 1994; children: Madeleine Elizabeth, Samantha Jane, Claire Beatrice. BS, U. Mich., 1988; MBA, Loyola U., Chgo., 1996; JD, Loyola U., 1996. Bar: Ill. 1996, U.S. Dist. Ct. (no. dist.) Ill. 1996, Tenn. 1997, U.S. Dist. Ct. (we. dist.) Tenn. 1997. Assoc. Fagel & Haber, Chgo., 1996—97; sr. atty. Fed. Express Corp., Memphis, 1997—. Capt. U.S. Army, 1987—97. Mem.: ABA. Avocations: lacrosse, tennis. Aviation, Corporate, general, Finance. Office: Fed Express Corp 3620 Hacks Cross Rd Memphis TN 38125 Office Fax: 901-434-7831. E-mail: sslee1@fedex.com.

LEE, TOM STEWART, judge; b. 1941; m. Norma Ruth Robbins; children: Elizabeth Robbins Maron, Tom Stewart Jr. BA, Miss. Coll., 1963; JD cum laude, U. Miss., 1965. Ptnr. Lee & Lee, Forest, Miss., 1965-84; pros. atty. Scott County, Miss., 1968-71; judge Scott County Youth Ct., Forest, 1979-82, U.S. Dist. Ct. (so. dist.) Miss., Jackson, 1984-96, chief judge, 1996—. Asst. editor: Miss. Law Jour. Pres. Forest Pub. Sch. Bd., Scott County Heart Assn.; bd. trustees Miss. Coll. Named one of Outstanding Young Men Am. Mem.: 5th Cir. Jud. Coun. (CACM com. Jud. Conf., Disting. Svc. award), Fed. Judges Assn., Fed. Bar Assn., Hinds County Bar Assn., Scott County Bar Assn., Miss. Bar Assn., Ole Miss. Alumni Assn. (pres.), Am. Legion. Office: US Dist Ct 245 E Capitol St Ste 110 Jackson MS 39201-2414 E-mail: JoyceWorrell@mssd.uscourts.gov-SCA-I.

LEE, WAYNE J. lawyer; b. New Orleans, Jan. 26, 1950; BA, Tulane U., 1971, JD, 1974. Bar: La. 1974. Atty. Stone Pigman Walther Wittmann LLC, New Orleans, 1974—. Mem. La. Indigent Defender Bd.; chair Civil Justice Reform Act Adv. Group, Fed. Dist. Ct. for Ea. Dist. La.; appointed La. Bd. of Regents for Higher Edn., 1989—94; bd. dirs. Attys.' Liability Assurance Soc., Ltd.; spkr. in field. Adv. bd. editors Tulane Law Review; contbr. La. Appellate Procedure Handbook. Fellow: Am. Coll. Trial Lawyers; mem.: ABA (sect. on litigation and antitrust), Tulane U. Inn of Ct., Fifth Cir. Bar Assn., New Orleans Bar Assn., La. State Bar Assn. (bd. govs. 1993—96, Ho. of Dels. 1997—2002, pres.-elect 2002—03, Pres.'s award 1993, 1998), Def. Rsch. Inst., Nat. Bar Assn., Louis A. Martinet Soc., Order of Coif. Commercial, consumer (including collections, credit), Insurance, Antitrust. Office: Stone Pigman Walther Wittmann 546 Carondelet St New Orleans LA 70130-3588*

LEE, WILLIAM CHARLES, judge; b. Ft. Wayne, Ind., Feb. 2, 1938; s. Russell and Catherine (Zwick) L.; m. Judith Anne Bash, Sept. 19, 1959; children: Catherine L., Mark R., Richard R. AB, Yale U., 1959; JD, U. Chgo., 1962; LLD (hon.), Huntington Coll., 1999. Bar: Ind. 1962. Ptnr. Parry, Krueckeberg & Lee, Ft. Wayne, 1963-69, chief dep., 1966-69; U.S. atty. No. Dist. Ind., Ft. Wayne, 1970-73; ptnr. Hunt, Suedhoff, Borror, Eilbacher & Lee, Ft. Wayne, 1973-81; U.S. dist. judge U.S. Dist. Ct. (no. dist.) Ind., Ft. Wayne, 1981—. Instr. Nat. Inst. Trial Advocacy; lectr. in field. Co-author: Business and Commercial Litigation in Federal Courts, 1998; author: Volume I Federal Jury Practice and Instructions, 1999; contbr. to numerous publs. in field. Co-chmn. Fort Wayne Fine Arts Operating Fund Drive, 1978; past bd. dirs., v.p., pres. Fort Wayne Philharm. Orch.; past bd. dirs., v.p. Hospice of Fort Wayne, inc.; past bd. dirs. Fort Wayne Fine Arts Found., Fort Wayne Civic Theatre, Neighbors, Inc., Embassy Theatre Found.; past bd. dirs., pres. Legal Aid of fort Wayne, Inc.; past mem. chm. coun., v.p. Trinity English Lutheran Ch. Coun.; past trustee, pres. Fort Wayne Cmty. Schs., 1978-81, pres., 1980-81; trustee Fort Wayne Mus. Art, 1984-90; past bd. dirs., pres. Fort Wayne-Allen County Hist. Soc. Griffin Scholar, 1955-59; chmn. Fort Wayne Cmty. Schs. Scholarship Com.; bd. dirs. Arts United of Greater Fort Wayne, Fort Wayne Ballet. Weymouth Kirkland scholar, 1959-62; named Ind. Trial Judge of Yr., 1988. Fellow Am. Coll. Trial Lawyers, Ind. Bar Found.; mem. ABA, Allen County Bar Assn., Ind. State Bar Assn., Fed. Bar Assn., Seventh Cir. Bar Assn., Benjamin Harrison Am. Inn of Ct., North Side High Alumni Assn. (bd. dris., pres.), Fort Wayne Rotary Club (bd. dirs.), Phi Delta Phi (past bd. dirs., 1st pres.). Republican. Lutheran. Office: US Dist Ct 2145 Fed Bldg 1300 S Harrison St Fort Wayne IN 46802-3495

LEE, WILLIAM JOHNSON, lawyer; b. Jan. 13, 1924; s. William J. and Ara (Anderson) L. Student, Akron U., 1941-43, Denison U., 1943-44, Harvard U., 1944-45; JD, Ohio State U., 1948. Bar: Ohio 1948, Fla. 1962, U.S. Dist. Ct. (no. dist.) Ohio 1960, U.S. Dist. Ct. (so. dist.) Fla. 1965, U.S. Dist. Ct. (so. dist.) Ohio 1970. Research asst. Ohio State U. Law Sch., 1948-49; asst. dir. Ohio Dept. Liquor Control, chief purchases, 1956-57, atty. examiner, 1951-53, asst. state permit chief, 1953-55, state permit chief, 1955-56; asst. counsel, staff Hupp Corp., 1957-58; spl. counsel City Attys. Office, Ft. Lauderdale, Fla., 1963-65; asst. atty. gen. Office Atty. Gen. State of Ohio, 1966-70; administr. State Med. Bd. Ohio, Columbus, 1970-85. Mem. Federated State Bd.'s Nat. Commn. for Evaluation of Fgn. Med. Schs., 1981-83; mem. Flex 1/Flex 2 Transitional Task Force, 1983-84; pvt. practice law, Ft. Lauderdale, 1965-66; acting municipal judge, Ravenna, Ohio, 1960; instr. Coll. Bus. Adminstrn., Kent State U., 1961-62. chmn. legal aid com. Portage County, Ohio, 1960. Mem. Editl. bd. Ohio State Law Jour., 1947-48; contbr. articles to profl. jours. Mem. pastoral relations com. Epworth United Meth. Ch., 1976; troop awards chmn. Boy Scouts Am., 1965; mem. ch. bd. Melrose Park (Fla.) Meth. Ch., 1966. Served with USAAF, 1943-46. Mem. ATLA, Exptl. Aviation Assn. S.W. Fla., Franklin County Trial Lawyers Assn., Am. Legion, Fla., Columbus, Akron, Broward County (Fla.) bar assns., Delta Theta Phi, Phi Kappa Tau, Pi Kappa Delta. Administrative and regulatory, General practice, Health. Home: Apple Valley 704 Country Club Dr Howard OH 43028-9530

LEE, WILLIAM MARSHALL, lawyer; b. N.Y.C., Feb. 23, 1922; s. Marshall McLean and Marguerite (Letts) L.; m. Lois Kathryn Plain, Oct. 10, 1942; children: Marsha (Mrs. Stephen Derynck), William Marshall Jr., Victoria C. (Mrs. Larry Nelson). Student, U. Wis., 1939-40; BS, Aero. U., Chgo., 1942; postgrad., UCLA, 1946-48, Loyola U. Law Sch., L.A., 1948-49; JD, Loyola U., Chgo., 1952. Bar: Ill. 1952, U.S. Supreme Ct., 1972. Thermodynamicist Northrop Aircraft Co., Hawthorne, Calif., 1947-49; patent agt. Hill, Sherman, Meroni, Gross & Simpson, Chgo., 1949-51, Borg-Warner Corp., Chgo., 1951-53; ptnr. Hume, Clement, Hume & Lee, Chgo., 1953-72; pvt. practice Chgo., 1973-74; ptnr. Lee and Smith (and predecessors), Chgo., 1974-89, Lee, Mann, Smith, McWilliams, Sweeney & Ohlson, Chgo., 1989—2002; ind. expert intellectual property Barrington, Ill., 1999—. Cons. Power Packaging, Inc., 1982-2002. Speaker and contbr. articles on legal topics. Pres. Glenview (Ill.) Citizens Sch. Com., 1953-57; v.p. Glenbrook High Sch. Bd., 1957-63. Lt. USNR, 1942-46, CBI. Recipient Pub. Svc. award Glenbrook High Sch. Bd., 1963 Mem. ABA (chmn. sect. intellectual property law 1986-87, sect. fin. officer 1976-77, sect. sec. 1977-80, sect. governing coun. 1980-84, 87-88), Ill. Bar Assn., Chgo. Bar Assn., 7th Fed. Cir. Bar Assn., Am. Intellectual Property Law Assn., Intellectual Property Law Assn. Chgo., Licensing Execs. Soc. (pres. 1981-82, treas. 1977-80, trustee 1974-77, 80-81, 82-83, internat. del. 1980—), Phi Delta Theta, Phi Alpha Delta. Republican. Antitrust, Patent, Trademark and copyright. Office: 84 Otis Rd Barrington IL 60010-5128

LEEBRON, DAVID WAYNE, dean, law educator; b. Phila., Feb. 12, 1955; BA, Harvard U., 1976, JD, 1979. Bar: Hawaii 1980, Pa. 1981, N.Y. 1982. Law clk. Judge Shirley Hufstedler, L.A., 1979—80; assoc. Cleary, Gottlieb, Steen & Hamilton, N.Y.C., 1981—83; prof. Sch. Law NYU, 1983—89, Columbia U., N.Y.C., 1989—, dean, Lucy G Moses prof. law, 1996—. Office: Columbia U Sch Law Box B12 801 Jerome Greene Hall 435 W 116th St New York NY 10027-7297

LEECH, CHARLES RUSSELL, JR., lawyer; b. Coshocton, Ohio, July 29, 1930; s. Charles Russell and Edna (Henry) L.; m. Patricia Ann Tubaugh, June 20, 1953; children— Charles Russell III, Timothy David (dec.), Wendy Ann. AB cum laude, Kenyon Coll., 1952; JD, Ohio State U., 1955; MA, U. Toledo, 1969. Bar: Ohio 1955. Assoc. Fuller & Henry Ltd. and predecessors, Toledo, 1957-64, ptnr., 1964-97, counsel, 1997-99. Mng. editor: Ohio State Law Jour, 1955. Mem. exec. com. alumni council Kenyon Coll., 1967-72, trustee coll., 1974-80. Served with USNR, 1955-57. Fellow Ohio State Bar Found.; mem. ABA, Ohio Bar Assn., Kenyon Coll. Alumni Assn. Maumee Valley (past pres.), Beta Theta Pi, Phi Delta Phi. Republican. Home: 20285 Zion Rd Gambier OH 43022-9643

LEECH, JEFFREY JAMES, lawyer; b. Pitts., Apr. 19, 1946; s. James R. and Lois E. (Hartness) L.; m. Lynne R. Townsend, Dec. 26, 1970; children: David, Michael. BA, U. Pitts., 1968, MA, 1969; JD, Ind. U., 1974. Bar: Pa. 1974, U.S. Dist. Ct. (we. dist.) Pa. 1974, U.S. Ct. Appeals (3d cir.) 1980, U.S. Supreme Ct. 1980. Assoc. Tucker Arensberg, P.C., Pitts., 1974-80, shareholder, 1980—, also bd. dirs. Sch. dir. Penn Trafford Sch. Dist., Harrison City, Pa., 1976-80. With U.S. Army, 1969-71. Mem. Acad. of Trial Lawyers, Allegheny County Bar Assn. Presbyterian. Federal civil litigation, General civil litigation, Pension, profit-sharing, and employee benefits. Home: 25 Overlook Ct Pittsburgh PA 15222-4708 Office: Tucker Arensberg PC 1 Ppg Pl Ste 1500 Pittsburgh PA 15222-5413 E-mail: jleech@tuckerlaw.com.

LEECH, NOYES ELWOOD, lawyer, educator; b. Ambler, Pa., Aug. 1, 1921; m. Louise Ann Gallagher, Apr. 19, 1954; children: Katharine, Gwyneth. AB, U. Pa., 1943, JD, 1948. Bar: Pa. 1949. Assoc. Dechert, Price & Rhoads (and predecessors), Phila., 1948-49, 51-53; mem. faculty law sch. U. Pa., Phila., 1949-57, prof., 1957-78, Ferdinand Wakeman Hubbell prof. law, 1978-85, William A. Schnader prof. law, 1985-86, prof. emeritus, 1986—. Co-author: The International Legal System, 3d edit., 1988; gen. editor: Jour. Comparative Bus. and Capital Market Law, 1978-86. Mem. Order of Coif, Phi Beta Kappa. Office: U Pa Law Sch 3400 Chestnut St Philadelphia PA 19104-6204

LEED, ROGER MELVIN, lawyer; b. Green Bay, Wis., July 15, 1939; s. Melvin John and Veronica Sarah (Flaherty) L.; m. Jean Ann Burg, Mar. 1967; children: Craig, Maren, Jennifer. AB, Harvard U., 1961; JD cum laude, U. Mich., 1967. Bar: Wash. 1967, U.S. Dist. Ct. (we. dist.) Wash. 1968, U.S. Ct. Appeals (9th cir.) 1969, U.S. Supreme Ct. 1973. Law clk. Wash. Supreme Ct., Olympia, 1967-68; assoc. Perkins, Coie et al, Seattle, 1968-70; ptnr. Schroeter, Goldmark et al, Seattle, 1970-76; sole practice Seattle, 1976—. Adj. prof. law U. Puget Sound, Tacoma, 1974-77. Editor Shorelines Mgmt., the Wash. Experience, 1972. Pres. Cen. Seattle Community Council Fedn., 1972, Wash. Environ. Council, 1980-82; bd. dirs. Allied Arts, Seattle, 1971-72, Downtown Human Services Council, Seattle, 1985-92. Mem. ABA (standing com. on environtl. law 1980-84), Wash. State Bar Assn., King County Bar Assn., Assn. Trial Lawyers Am., Montlake Cmty. Club (v.p., bd. dirs. 1994-98), Seattle Tilth (bd. dirs. 1990-2001). Clubs: Met. Dem., Washington Athletic. Environmental, Land use and zoning (including planning), Personal injury (including property damage). Office: 2003 Western Ave Ste 600 Seattle WA 98121-3126 E-mail: leedlaw@pipeline.com.

LEEHEY, PAUL WADE, lawyer; b. Johnson AFB, Japan, Sept. 9, 1954; s. Donald James and Sara Aileen (Britton) L.; m. Gail Marie Krafft, Aug. 8, 1987; children: Whitney Kaileen, Shara Michele, Wade Jarik. BA in Polit. Sci./Sociology, Loyola U. L.A., 1976; JD, U. San Diego, 1979. Bar: Calif. 1980, U.S. Dist. Ct. (so. dist.) Calif., U.S. Ct. Appeals (9th cir.), U.S.

Supreme Ct.; cert. specialist family law, State Bar of Calif. Bd. of Legal Specializations, San Diego, No. San Diego County. Pvt. practice law, Fallbrook, Calif., 1980—. Past pres., mem. Fallbrook chpt., Am. Heart Assn., 1988, dir. San Diego chpt., 1990-95; v.p. Zion Luth. Ch,. 1996-2000. Mem. Calif. Bar Assn., San Diego County Bar Assn., San Diego Consumer Attys., Bar Assn. No. San Diego County, Southwest Riverside County Bar Assn., Fallbrook C. of C., Rotary (Fallbrook Village chpt., sec. 1989-2000). Democrat. Avocations: skiing, volleyball, mountain biking, family, church. General civil litigation, Family and matrimonial, Pension, profit-sharing, and employee benefits. Office: 205 W Alvarado St Fallbrook CA 92028-2002 E-mail: pleehey@TFB.com.

LEEKLEY, JOHN ROBERT, lawyer; b. Phila., Aug. 27, 1943; s. Thomas Briggs and Dorothy (O'Hora) L.; m. Karen Kristin Myers, Aug. 28, 1965 (dec. Mar. 1997); children: John Thomas, Michael Dennis; m. Gerry Lee Gildner, June 5, 1999. BA, Boston Coll., 1965; LLB, Columbia U., 1968. Bar: N.Y. 1968, Mich. 1976. Assoc. Curtis, Mallet-Prevost, Colt & Mosle, N.Y.C., 1968-69, Davis Polk & Wardwell, N.Y.C., 1969-76; asst. corp. counsel Masco Corp., Taylor, Mich., 1976-77, corp. counsel, 1977-79, v.p., corp. counsel, 1979-88, v.p., gen. counsel, 1988-96, sr. v.p., gen. counsel, 1996—. Bd. visitors Columbia U. Law Sch., N.Y.C., 1994-96; mem. Freedom Twp. Bd. Tax Appeals, 1984-85. Mem. ABA (com. long range issues affecting bus. practice 1976-96), Mich. State Bar Assn. Democrat. Roman Catholic. Avocations: percheron horse breeding, hunting, fishing, outdoor activities. Office: Masco Corp 21001 Van Born Rd Taylor MI 48180-1300

LEESON, SUSAN M. state supreme court judge; Law clerk U.S. 9th Cir. Ct. of Appeals; Tom. C. Clark judicial fellow U.S. Supreme Ct.; prof. polit. sci., assoc. prof. law Willamette U., Salem, Oreg.; judge Oreg. Ct. Appeals, 1993—98; justice Oreg. Supreme Ct., 1998—. Former mem. Oreg. Criminal Justice Coun., Marion-Polk Local Govt. Boundary Commn. Office: Supreme Ct Bldg 1163 State St Salem OR 97310-1331

LEFCO, KATHY NAN, law librarian; b. Bethesda, Md., Feb. 24, 1949; d. Ted Lefco and Dorothy Rose (Fox) Harris; m. Stephen Gary Katz, Sept. 2, 1973 (div. May 1984); m. John Alfred Price, Nov. 24, 1984 (dec. Jan. 1989); m. Richard Louis Edmonds, Apr. 12, 2002. BA, U. Wis., 1971; MLS, U. Wis., Milw., 1975. Rsch. asst. Ctr. Auto Safety, Washington, 1971-73; asst. to dir. Ctr. Consumer Affairs, Milw., 1973-74; legis. libr. Morgan, Lewis & Bockius, Washington, 1976-78; dir. library Mulcahy & Wherry, Milw., 1978; paralegal Land of Lincoln Legal Assistance, Springfield, Ill., 1979-80; reference and interlibrary loan libr. So. Ill. U. Sch. Medicine, Springfield, 1980; reader svcs. libr. Wis. State Law Library, Madison, 1981-83; ref. libr. Mudge Rose Guthrie Alexander & Ferdon, N.Y.C., 1983-85; sr. legal info. specialist Cravath, Swaine & Moore, N.Y.C., 1985-86; asst. libr. Kaye, Scholer, Fierman, Hays & Handler, N.Y.C., 1986-89; head libr. Parker Chapin Flattau & Klimpl, N.Y.C., 1989-94; dir. libr. svcs. Winston & Strawn, Chgo., 1994—. Author: (with others) Mobile Homes: The Low-Cost Housing Hoax, 1973. Mem. Chgo. Assn. Law Librs., Am. Assn. Law Librs. Democrat. Jewish. Avocations: biking, backgammon, politics. Home: 543 Oakdale Ave Glencoe IL 60022 Office: Winston & Strawn 35 W Wacker Dr Ste 4200 Chicago IL 60601-1695 E-mail: klefco@winston.com.

LEFKOWITZ, ALAN ZOEL, lawyer; b. Pitts., Dec. 1, 1932; s. Curtis and Lily Rose Lefkowitz; m. Francine Marcia Kaplan, Feb. 5, 1956; children: Curtis Robert, Gail Ann, David Edward. AB, U. Pitts., 1953; JD, U. Mich., 1955. Bar: Pa. 1956, U.S. Supreme Ct. 1959, U.S. Ct. Appeals (3d cir.), U.S. Dist. Ct. (we. dist.) Pa., U.S. Tax Ct. Assoc. Kaplan, Finkel & Roth, Pitts., 1955-72; mng. ptnr. Kaplan, Finkel, Lefkowitz, Roth & Ostrow, Pitts., 1972-82, Finkel Lefkowitz Ostrow & Woolridge, Pitts., 1982-88; ptnr., head corp. sect. Tucker Arenberg, P.C., Pitts., 1988-93; dir. Kabala & Geeseman, Pitts., 1993-99. Adj. prof. arts and law Heinz Sch. Pub. Policy and Adminstrn./Carnegie Mellon U., instr. Shakespeare, Acad. Lifelong Learning, 2001—; sec. TPC Comm., Inc., Pitts., 1970-91, Computer Rsch., Inc., Pitts., 1969-92, Star-Tron Tech., Inc., Pitts., 1986-92. Mem. Pitts. Coun. Internat. Visitors; trustee United Jewish Fedn. Pitts., 1964-68, Rodef Shalom Congregation, Pitts., 1962-64, 90-98; bd. dirs., treas., v.p. Jewish Family and Childrens Svcs., Pitts., 1967-68; bd. dirs. Family Resources, 1986X, U.S. Counter-Intelligence Corp. With U.S. Army, 1956-59. Mem. ABA, Internat. Assn. Fin. Planners (Pitts. chpt. v.p. ethics regulation), Internat. Assn. Jewish Lawyers, Pa. Bar Assn., Allegheny County Bar Assn. (former chair arts law sect., former chair, coun. corp. sec., chair securities regulation com., former chair internat. com.), Photoimagers Guild, Acad. Arts and Scis. (photography sect., bd. dirs. 1994X), Silver Eye Ctr. for Photography (trustee, sec.). Avocations: photography, theatre. Corporate, general, Mergers and acquisitions, Securities.

LEFKOWITZ, HOWARD N. lawyer; b. Utica, N.Y., Oct. 28, 1936; s. Samuel I. and Sarah Lefkowitz; m. Martha Yelon, June 16, 1958; children: Sarah, David. BA, Cornell U., 1958; LLB, Columbia U., 1963. Bar: N.Y. 1963. Ptnr. Proskauer Rose LLP, N.Y.C., 1963—. Tri-bar opinion com. Author: New York LLC and LLP Forms and Practice Manual, Data Trace, rev. edit. 2003; co-author: Transactional Lawyers Deskbook: Advising Business Entities West, 2001; editor Columbia Law Rev., 1963. Lt. (j.g.) USN, 1958-61. Kent scholar Columbia U. Law Sch. Fellow: Am. Coll. Investment Counsel; mem.: Pvt. Investment Fund Forum (vice chmn.), N.Y. County Lawyers Assn. (chmn. com. on comm. entertainment and arts-related law 1983—86), Assn. of Bar of City of N.Y. (chmn. com. on corp. law 1990—93, com. on corp. law 1997—2000), ABA (mem. partnership and uninc. bus. orgns. 1993—). Commercial, contracts (including sales of goods; commercial financing), Computer, Corporate, general. Office: Proskauer Rose LLP 1585 Broadway Fl 23 New York NY 10036-8299

LEFKOWITZ, IVAN MARTIN, lawyer; b. Winston-Salem, N.C., Jan. 4, 1952; s. Ernest W. and Matilda C. (Center) L.; m. Fern Deutsch, Apr. 14, 1972; children: Aaron M., Shira B. BBA, U. Cen. Fla., 1973; JD, U. Miami, 1979, LLM Estate Planning, 1980. Bar: Fla. 1979, U.S. Dist. Ct. (mid. dist.) 1980, U.S. Tax. Ct. 1980; CPA, Fla. Sr. acct. Alexander Grant & Co. CPA, Orlando, Fla., 1974-76; assoc. Gray, Harris & Robinson P.A., Orlando, 1980-82; pvt. practice, Orlando, 1982-88; ptnr. Lefkowitz & Miner, P.A., Orlando, 1988-93; sr. ptnr. Lefkowitz & Bloom, P.A., Orlando, 1993—. Adj. prof. Am. Coll., Denver, 1984-90, Mgmt. Inst., U. Cen. Fla., Orlando, 1988—; sec., dir. Employee Benefits Coun. Fla., 1987-89, pres., 1990. Mem. dean's exec. coun. U. Ctrl. Fla. Coll. of Bus., 2000—; mem. governing bd. Princeton Hosp., Orlando, 1997—98; mem. Ctrl. Fla. Estate Planning Coun.; treas. Holocaust Meml. Resource and Edn. Ctr. Ctrl. Fla., 2000—01; mem. U. Ctrl. Fla. Found. Orlando, 1981—96, 2001—; U. Ctrl. Fla. Found. Orlando, 1981—96; bd. dirs., pres. Nat. Kidney Found. Ctrl. Fla., Orlando and Tampa, 1984—91. Recipient Induction to Coll. of Bus. Adminstrn. Hall of Fame, U. Ctrl. Fla., 2001. Democrat. Estate planning, Pension, profit-sharing, and employee benefits, Corporate taxation. Office: 430 N Mills Ave Orlando FL 32803-5746

LEFKOWITZ, JEROME, lawyer; b. N.Y.C., Mar. 24, 1931; s. Jack and Sue (Horowitz) L.; m. Myrna Judith Weishaut, Aug. 12, 1956; children: Jay, Mark, Miriam, Alan. Student, Jewish Theol. Sem., N.Y.C., 1948-51; BA, NYU, 1952; JD, Columbia U., 1955. Bar: N.Y. 1955, U.S. Dist. Ct. (so. and ea. dists.) N.Y. 1990. Asst. atty. gen. N.Y. State Dept. of Law, Albany, 1958-60; counsel, dep. commissioner N.Y. State Dept. of Labor, N.Y.C., Albany, 1960-67; dep. chmn., mem. N.Y. Pub. Rels. Bd., Albany, 1967-87; adj. faculty Albany Law Sch. Columbia U., N.Y.C., Albany, 1968-89; dep. counsel Civil Svc. Employment Assn., Albany, 1987—. Cons. State of Mich., 1969, State of Hawaii, 1970, State of Pa., 1976, State of Mass., 1978. Author: Public Employee Unionism In Israel, 1971; editor: Public Sector Labor & Employment Law, 1988, 2d edit., 1998, supplement, 2002, The Evolving Process--Collective Negotiations In Public Employment, 1985. Chmn. community rels. com. Albany Jewish Fedn., 1980-84, 86-87; pres. Massad Hebrew Speaking Camps. Mem. N.Y. State Bar Assn. (chmn. com. on pub. sector labor rels. 1975-79, chmn. com. on legis. 1980-83, chmn. labor law sect. 1991-92). Republican. Avocations: tennis, skiing, reading, history. Home: 54 Maxwell St Albany NY 12208-1639 Office: Civil Svc Employment Assn 143 Washington Ave Albany NY 12210-2303 E-mail: lefkowitz@cseainc.org.

LEFTWICH, JAMES ASBURY, JR., lawyer, entrepreneur; b. Chesapeake, Va., Dec. 11, 1962; s. James Asbury and Eleaner (Otto) L.; m. Renee Doreen Frey, Sept. 11, 1993; children: Logan Alexander, Austin Reid, Faith Elizabeth, Hope Marie. BS, James Madison U., 1985; JD, U. Richmond, 1988. Bar: Va. 1988, U.S. Dist. Ct. 1988, U.S. Bankruptcy Ct. 1988. Assoc. atty. Basnight, Creekmore, Wright, Jones, Kinser and successors, Chesapeake, Va., 1988-95; ptnr. Basnight, Kinser, Telfeyan, Leftwich, & Nuckolls, P.C., Chesapeake, 1996—. Bd. dirs. Chesapeake Care Free Clinic, 1995—, Am. Cancer Soc., Chesapeake/Portsmouth, Va., 1994-98; mem. bd. dirs. Chesapeake Pub. Schs., 2002--; mem. Va. Inst. Polit. Leadership at U. Va., 1996—. Recipient Multiple Sclerosis Leadership award; named among Top 40 Under 40 in Hampton Roads, Inside Bus. Mag., 2000. Mem. Chesapeake Bar Assn. (pres. 1999), Va. Bar Assn., Hampton Roads Family Law Assn., Great Bridge Jaycees (pres. 1992), Deep Creek Ruritan Club (pres. 2000). Avocations: family, tennis, golf. Family and matrimonial, Health. Office: Basnight Kinser Telfeyan Leftwich & Nuckolls PC 308 Cedar Lakes Dr Chesapeake VA 23322-8343

LEGERE JR, HENRY J. lawyer; b. Orange, N.J., Apr. 3, 1951; s. Henry J. and Rose Legere; m. Pamela Marie Heemer, Mar. 31, 1995; m. Edmona Kay Tschetter, July 2, 1971 (div.); children: Henry J. Legere III, Joseph E. Legere, Monique K. Legere, Sasha L. Legere. DS in Preventive Medicine, Met. Collegiate Inst., London, 1980; MPA, U. of Tex., 1990; JD, Thomas M. Cooley Law Sch., 1993. Bar: Mich. 1994, U.S. Ct. Appeals (6th cir.) 1996, U.S. Dist. Ct. (we. dist) Mich. 1996, U.S. Dist. Ct. (ea. dist.) Mich. 1997, U.S. Supreme Ct. 2003. Of counsel Sheikh & Associates, Mount Clemens, Mich., 1993—; atty. Law Office of Henry J Legere, Jr, Holt, 1997—; contract atty. Miller & Associates, L.L.P., Santa Monica, Calif., 1999—. Mem. Capital Area Rail Coun., East Lansing, Mich., 2001—02. With U.S. Army. Mem.: ABA, Mich State Bar Assn., Macomb County Bar Assn. (chair juvenile law com. 2001—02), Am. Immigration Lawyers Assn., Nat. Assn. Counsel for Children, Nat. Assn. Criminal Def. Lawyers, Criminal Def. Attorneys Mich. (dir. 2000—), Thomas M. Cooley Alumni Assn. (class rep., bd. govs. 1996—), Thomas M. Cooley Law Sch. Alumni Assn. (treas., bd. govs. 2001—). Republican. Methodist. Avocation: travel. Juvenile, Immigration, naturalization, and customs, Criminal. Office: Law Office of Henry J Legere Jr 4523 Willoughby Rd Holt MI 48842 Home Fax: 517-699-5021; Office Fax: 517-699-5021. Personal E-mail: legerelaw@aol.com. E-mail: legerelaw@aol.com.

LEGG, BENSON EVERETT, federal judge; b. Balt., June 8, 1947; s. William Mercer Legg and Beverly Mason; m. Kyle Prechtl Legg; children: Jennifer, Charles, Matthew. AB magna cum laude, Princeton U., 1970; JD, U. Va., 1973. Bar: Md. 1973. Law clk. to Hon. Frank A. Kaufman, Balt., 1973-74; assoc. Venable, Baetjer & Howard, Balt., 1975-81, ptnr., 1982-91; judge U.S. Dist. Ct., Dist. Md., Balt., 1991—. Spl. reporter appeals com. and standing com. on rules of practice and procedure Ct. Appeals Md., 1983-85; faculty mem. nine day intensive trial advocacy program Md. Inst. Continuing Profl. Edn. for Lawyers, Inc., 1987, program on appellate advocacy, 1988; lectr. and panelist in field. Mem. editl. bd. Va. Law Rev., 1973-74; contbr. articles to profl. jours. Bd. dirs. Ctrl. Md. chpt. ARC, 1979-88, past chpt. gen. counsel; mem. adv. bd. Nat. Aquarium in Balt., 1987—; trustee Balt. Zoo. Mem. ABA (bus. torts litigation com. 1987), Md. State Bar Assn., Inc. (chmn. econs. of litigation com. 1981-82), Bar Assn. Balt. City (vice chmn. CLE com. 1986-87, chmn. 1987-88, exec. coun. 1987-88, judiciary com. 1989-90), The Serjeant's Inn Law Club, Order of Coif. Office: US Dist Ct 101 W Lombard St Ste 3D Baltimore MD 21201-2605

LEGON, FAUSTINO JUAN, lawyer, educator; b. Buenos Aires, Sept. 25, 1941; s. Faustino and Maria Erilda (Hargouas) L.; m. Maria Cecilia Cullen, Sept. 15, 1966; children: Cecilia, Ana, María de la Paz. Degree in law, Cath. U., Argentina, 1964. Admitted to bar 1965. Judge Nat. Civil Ct. Appeal, Buenos Aires; prof. civil law Nat. U. Buenos Aires Law Sch., Argentine Cath. U. Law Sch., Buenos Aires. Mem. consulting com. Nat. Ministry Justice for Family Trial Cts., Buenos Aires. Rep. Salvador U., Orgn. Universidades Católicas de America Latina; mem. several civil law congresses. Mem. Buenos Aires Bar Assn., Cath. Lawyers Corp. Argentina. Office: Piso 8 Marcelo T de Alvear 1381 C 1058AAU Buenos Aires Argentina E-mail: estudiolegon@escape.com.ar.

LE GRAND, CLAY, lawyer, former state justice; b. St. Louis, Feb. 26, 1911; s. Nicholas and Mary Margaret (Leifield) Le G.; m. Suzanne Wilcox, Dec. 30, 1935, (wid.); children: Mary Suzanne Le Grand Murray, Julie A. Le Grand Ekstrand, Nicholas W.; m. Margaret Morris Burrows, Dec. 11, 1993. Student, St. Ambrose Coll., Davenport, Iowa, 1928-31; LL.B., Catholic U. Am., 1934. Bar: Iowa 1934. Practice law, Davenport, 1934-57; judge Dist. Ct., 1957-67; justice Supreme Ct. Iowa, Davenport, 1967-83; of counsel Stanley, Rehling, Lande & Van Der Kamp, Davenport, 1983-92, Noyes, O'Brien, Gosma and Brooke, Davenport, 1992-95, Noyes & Gosma, Davenport, 1995-98, Gosma & Gallagher, Davenport, 1998—. Lectr. St. Ambrose Coll., 1957-67 Recipient award for outstanding achievement in field of law and the cts. Cath. U. Am., 1969; award of merit for profl. achievement St. Ambrose Coll., 1976 Mem. Am., Iowa, Scott County bar assns., Am. Judicature Soc., Inst. Jud. Adminstrn. Home: 4130 Northwest Blvd Apt 32 Davenport IA 52806-4234 Office: Gosma & Gallagher 4301 E 53rd St # 300 Davenport IA 52807-3040

LEGRO, STANLEY WAYNE, environmental lawyer; b. Muskogee, Okla., July 3, 1936; s. Wayne Leo and Monta Catherine (Cottingham) L.; m. Marcia Louise West, Aug. 17, 1963 (div. Aug. 1986); children: Susan Louise, Stanley Wayne Jr. BS in Engring. with distinction first in class, U.S. Naval Acad., 1959; JD cum laude, Harvard U., 1966. Bar: Calif. 1967, D.C. 1977, U.S. Supreme Ct. 1971. Pvt. practice law, San Diego, 1967-75, 77-82, Washington, 1983—; asst. adminstr. U.S. EPA, Washington, 1975-77; of counsel Piper Rudnick, Washington, 2002—. Adj. prof. U. San Diego Law Sch., 1968-75; adj. fellow Ctr. for Strategic and Internat. Studies, Washington, 1989-93. Author (movie and teaching materials) ; author: A Model Criminal Trial, 1975 (Golden Gavel award); bd. advisors Harvard Environ. Law. Rev., 1977—88. Appt. by pres. mem. Nat. Adv. Com. on Oceans and Atmosphere, Washington, 1985-89; mem. San Diego Planning Commn., 1971-73; mem. bd. visitors U. San Diego Law Sch., 1974-83, 2001—; mem. Select Com. to Rev. Calif. Postseconary Edn., 1971-73; mem. bd. overseers U. Calif. at San Diego, 1980-84. Officer USMC, 1959-63. Recipient Cert. of Appreciation City of San Diego, 1973; named San Diego's Outstanding Young Man, San Diego Jaycees, 1971. Mem. Harvard Club of N.Y.C., U. Calif. San Diego Med. Sch. Assocs. (pres. 1972-74), Rancho Santa Fe Golf Club, Harvard Faculty Club. Republican. Methodist. Avocations: golf, running, reading, music. Environmental. Office: Piper Rudnick 901 15th St NW Ste 700 Washington DC 20005-2327 E-mail: stanley.legro@piperrudnick.com.

LEHAN, JONATHAN MICHAEL, judge; b. Los Angeles, Apr. 25, 1947; s. Bert Leon and Frances (Shapiro) L.; m. Annett Jean Garrett, Aug. 1, 1970; children: Joshua Michael, Melanie Janine. BA, Calif. State U., Fullerton, 1968; JD, Calif. Western Sch. Law, 1971; grad., Nat. Drug Ct. Inst., 2000, Nat. Ctr. for State Cts., Williamsburg, Va. Bar: Calif. 1972, U.S. Dist. Ct. (no. dist.) Calif. 1973, U.S. Supreme Ct. 1975. Law clk. to presiding and assoc. justice Calif. Dist. Ct. Appeals, San Bernardino, 1971-73; dep. dist. atty. Mendocino County, Ukiah, Calif., 1973-76, coast asst. dist. atty. Fort Bragg, Calif., 1976-83; pvt. practice Fort Bragg, 1983-84; ptnr. Lehan & Kronfeld, Fort Bragg, 1984-90; judge Mendocino County Superior Ct., Ft. Bragg, 1990—. Instr. Barstow C.C., Calif., 1972, Mendocino C.C., Ukiah, 1974-75, Coll. Redwoods, Ft. Bragg, 1981-82; seminar faculty Calif. Jud. Coll., U. Calif., Berkeley, 1993; faculty Calif. Judges Assn. Mid-Year Conf., 1998, ann. conf., 1999; contbr. Calif. Drunk Driving Law, Kuwatch, 1995. Bd. dirs. Salmon Restoration Assn., Fort Bragg, Gloriana Opera Co., Mendocino, Mendocino Art Ctr. Editor Calif. Western Sch. Law Law Rev., 1971. Mem. ABA, Mendocino County Bar Assn. (pres. 1989), Phi Delta Phi, Mendocino C. of C. (bd. dirs.). Democrat. Avocations: violist Mendocino string quartet, violist Osprey string quartet. Office: Mendocino Superior Ct 700 S Franklin St Fort Bragg CA 95437-5464 E-mail: judgejon@judgejon.com.

LEHERISSEL, HERVE, lawyer; b. Paris, May 7, 1953; s. Andre and Annie (Van De Poll) L.; m. Anne Crebassa, Dec. 20, 1980; children: Sophie, Arnaud. Diploma, Polit. Studies Inst., Paris, 1973; law degree, U. Paris 7, 1974; postgrad., Ecole Nat. Adminstrn., 1978. Head office dir. tax rulings bur. Min. of Fin., France, 1978-83; dep. fin. officer Commr. Atomic Energy, France, 1983-86; dep. commr. tax legislation svc. Svc. de la Legis. Fiscale, Paris, 1987-91; ptnr. Archibald, Paris, 1991—. Author: Slavery Games or Citizenship, 1985. Nat. del. Club 89, Paris, 1983-86. Roman Catholic. Taxation, general, Corporate taxation, Estate taxation. Home: 18 Bis Ave Marechal Douglas Haig 78000 Versailles France Office: Archibald 41 Rue Ybry 92576 Neuilly-sur-Seine France

LEHMAN, JEFFREY SEAN, academic administrator, educator; b. Bronxville, N.Y., Aug. 1, 1956; s. Leonard and Imogene (McAuliffe) L.; children: Rebecca Colleen, Jacob Keegan, Benjamin Emil. AB, Cornell U., 1977; M of Pub. Policy, U. M of Pub. Policy, JD, U. Mich., 1981. Bar: D.C. 1983, U.S. Ct. Appeals (fed. cir.) 1984, U.S. Ct. Appeals (D.C. cir.) 1987, U.S. Supreme Ct. 1987. Law clk. to chief judge U.S. Ct. Appeals (1st cir.), Portland, Maine, 1981-82; law clk. to assoc. justice U.S. Supreme Ct., Washington, 1982-83; assoc. Caplin & Drysdale, Chartered, Washington, 1983-87; asst. prof. U. Mich. Law Sch., Ann Arbor, 1987-92, prof., 1992-93, prof. law and pub. policy, 1993—2003, dean, 1994—2003; pres. Cornell U., Ithaca, NY, 2003—. Vis. prof. Yale U., 1993, U. Paris II, 1994. Co-author: Corporate Income Taxation, 1994; editor-in-chief: Mich. Law Rev., 1979-80. Trustee Skadden Fellowship Found., 1995—. Mem. Am. Law Inst., Order of Coif. Office: Cornell University Office of the President 300 Day Hall Ithaca NY 14853 E-mail: president@cornell.edu.

LEHMAN, LARRY L. state supreme court justice; Judge Wyo. County Ct., 1985-88, Wyo. Dist. Ct. (2nd dist.), 1988-94; chief justice Wyo. Supreme Ct., Cheyenne, 1998—2002, justice, 1994—. Office: Supreme Court Bldg 2301 Capitol Ave Cheyenne WY 82002-0001

LEHMAN, LEONARD, lawyer, consultant; b. Bklyn, July 5, 1927; s. Samuel and Marcy (Dolgenas) L.; m. Imogene McAuliffe, June 11, 1954; children— Jeffrey, Toby, Amy, Zachary. B.A., Cornell U., 1949; J.D., Yale U., 1952. Bar: N.Y. 1953, U.S. Supreme Ct. 1969, D.C. 1979, U.S. Ct. Internat. Trade 1981, U.S. Ct. Appeals (fed. cir.) 1982. Atty.-advisor U.S. Tax Ct., Washington, 1952-55; sole practice, N.Y.C., 1955-63; sr. counsel Office Tax Legis. Counsel, U.S. Dept. Treasury, Washington, 1963-65; asst. to chief counsel U.S. Customs Service, 1965-67, dep. chief counsel, 1968-71, asst. commr. 1971-79; ptnr. Barnes, Richardson and Colburn, N.Y.C., Washington and Chgo., 1979-89, counsel, 1989-95; mem. industry functional adv. com. on customs/trade policy U.S. Dept. Commerce, 1989-95. Recipient U.S. Treasury Meritorious Service award, 1971, Exceptional Service award, 1979; U.S. Customs Honor award, 1977. Mem. ABA (standing com. on customs law 1974-80, chmn. 1980, customs and tariff com., adminstrv. law sect. 1971-88, vice chmn. 1981-83, chmn. 1984-88), Phi Beta Kappa, Phi Kappa Phi. Contbr. articles to profl. jours. Administrative and regulatory, Immigration, naturalization, and customs, Private international. Home and Office: 18 Rich Branch Ct North Potomac MD 20878-2461

LEHR, DENNIS JAMES, lawyer; b. N.Y.C., Feb. 7, 1932; s. Irwin Allen and Teeny (Scofield) L.; m. Enid J. Auerbach, June 10, 1956; children— Austin Windsor, Bryant Paul, Amy Lynn BA, NYU, 1954, LLM, 1961; LLB, Yale U., 1957. Bar: N.Y. 1959, D.C. 1967. Atty. Allstate Ins. Co., N.Y.C., 1958-59; atty. Regional Office SEC, N.Y.C., 1959-61; assoc. Borden and Ball, N.Y.C., 1961-63; atty. Office Spl Counsel Investment Co. Act Matters SEC, Washington, 1963-64; assoc. chief counsel Office Comptroller Currency U.S. Treasury Dept., Washington, 1964-67; assoc. Hogan & Hartson, Washington, 1967-69, ptnr., 1969-94, of counsel, 1994—. Bd. advs. So. Meth. U. Grad. Sch. Banking; adj. prof. Georgetown Law Sch., 1964-68; legal adv. com. Nat. Ctr. on Fin. Svcs., U. Calif.; lectr. Practicing Law Inst.; adv. coun. Banking Law Inst.; pub. mem. Adminstrv. Conf. of the U.S. Bd. contbrs. Fin. Services Law Report. Contbr. articles to profl. jours. Mem. ABA (coun. mem. sect. bus. law, former chmn. com. on Long Range Issues Affecting Bus. Law Practice, former chmn., com. on devels. in investment svcs, chmn. standing com. on Gavel Awards.). Office: Hogan and Hartson 555 13th St NW Ste 800E Washington DC 20004-1161

LEIBOLD, ARTHUR WILLIAM, JR., lawyer; b. Ottawa, Ill., June 13, 1931; s. Arthur William and Helen (Cull) L.; m. Nora Collins, Nov. 30, 1957; children: Arthur William III, Alison Aubry, Peter Collins. AB, Haverford Coll., 1953; JD, U. Pa., 1956. Bar: Pa. 1957. With Dechert, Price & Rhoads, Phila., 1956—69, ptnr., 1965—69, Washington, 1972—97. Gen. counsel Fed. Home Loan Bank Bd. and Fed. Savs. & Loan Ins. Corp., Washington, 1969-72, Fed. Home Loan Mortgage Corp., 1970-72; lectr. English St. Joseph's Coll., Phila., 1957-59 Contbr. articles to profl. publs. Mem. Pres. Kennedy's Lawyers Com. Civil Rights, 1963, Adminstrv. Conf. U.S., 1969-72; bd. dirs. Marymount Coll. Va., 1974-75; Mem. Phila. Com. 70, 1965-74, Fellowship Commn. Mem. ABA (mem. ho. dels. 1967-69, 79-88, treas. 1979-83, mem. fin. com., mem. bd. govs. 1977-83), Fed. Bar Assn. (mem. nat. coun. 1971-80), D.C. Bar Assn., Phila. Bar Assn., Am. Bar Found. (treas. 1979-83), Am. Bar Ret. Assn. (dir. 1978-83), Am. Bar Endowment (bd. dirs. 1984-97, pres. 1995-97), Am. Bar Ins. (bd. dirs. 1999—), Phila. Country Club (Gladwyne, Pa.), Chester River Yacht and Country Club (Chestertown, Md.), Skating Club Phila., Order of Coif, Phi Beta Kappa. Republican. Roman Catholic. Administrative and regulatory, Banking. Home: 200 River Shore Rd Chestertown MD 21620 Office: Dechert 1775 Eye St NW Ste 1100 Washington DC 20006-2424 E-mail: leibold1@aol.com., aleibold@dechert.com.

LEIBOWITT, SOL DAVID, lawyer; b. Bklyn., Feb. 18, 1912; s. Morris and Bella (Small) Leibowitt; m. Ethel Leibowitt, June 18, 1950 (dec. Aug. 1985); m. Babs Lee, Dec. 28, 1986 (dec. June 2000). BA, Lehigh U., 1933; JD, Harvard U., 1936. Bar: N.Y. 1937, Conn. 1970. Pvt. practice, N.Y.C., 1937-84, Stamford, Conn., 1970-78, Milford, Conn., 1978-79; gen. counsel New Haven Clock and Watch Co., 1955-59, pres., 1958-59, Diagnon Corp., 1981-83, vice chmn., 1983-86. Chmn. Card Tech. Corp., 1983-85; dir. Data Card Internat. Corp., Hevant, Eng., 1977-79. Pres. Ethel and David Leibowitt Found.; dir. Am. Com. for Weizmann Inst. Sci.; mediator family law Supreme Ct. State Fla. 15th Jud. Ct., 1990—; arbitrator Am. Arbitration Assn., Fla.; chmn. Israel Cancer Assn. USA; dir. Am. Assocs., Ben-Gurion U., 1999. Recipient Human Rels. award Anti-Defamation League, 1969, Ethel Leibowitt Fund Johns Hopkins U. Sch. Medcine Meml. award Anti-Defamation League, 1971, Tikvah award Israel Cancer Assn., 1995. Mem.: ABA, Am. Soc. for Technion U. (bd. dirs., v.p., Conn. pres., life trustee), Anti-Defamation League (commr.), NY State Bar Assn., Assn. Bar N.Y.C., Banyon Country Club (West Palm Beach, Fla.), Harvard Club (N.Y.C.), Lotos Club. Corporate, general.

LEIBOWITZ, MARVIN, lawyer; b. Phila., Jan. 24, 1950; s. Aaron and Ethel (Kashoff) L.; m. Faye Rebecca Liepack, Nov. 12, 1983; children: Cheryl Renée, Ellen Paulette. BA, Temple U., 1971, postgrad., 1971-72; JD, Widener U., 1976. Bar: Pa. 1977, N.J. 1977, U.S. Dist. Ct. N.J. 1977, U.S. Dist. Ct. (we. dist.) Pa. 1980. Atty.-advisor SSA, Pitts., 1977-95, sr. atty., 1995—2001; quality assurance reviewer Office of Program and Integrity Revs., 1997; pvt. practice Pitts., 1979—. Active Phila. Dem. Com., 1973—77. Pa. State Scholar Pa. Higher Edn. Assistance Agy., Harrisburg, 1967-71; recipient U.S. Dept. Health and Human Svcs. Assoc. Commr.'s citation, 1994. Mem. Nat. Treasury Employees Union (regional steward 1982-99, regional v.p. 1999-2001), Pa. Bar Assn., Allegheny County Bar Assn. Democrat. Jewish. Administrative and regulatory, Bankruptcy, Workers' compensation. Home: 6501 Landview Rd Pittsburgh PA 15217-3000

LEICHTLING, MICHAEL ALFRED, lawyer; b. N.Y.C., Mar. 30, 1943; s. Stanley Arthur and Roslyn Priscilla (Fuhr) L.; m. Arlene Dorf, July 30, 1966; children: Julie Karen Nacos, Nina Anastasia, Noah James. BA, SUNY, Binghamton, 1963; JD, Northwestern U., 1966; postgrad., Columbia U., 1968. Bar: N.Y. 1969, U.S. Ct. Appeals (2d cir.) 1969. Assoc. Aranow Brodsky Bohlinger Einhorn & Dann, N.Y.C., 1966, Parker Chapin & Flattau, N.Y.C., 1969-77; ptnr. Parker Chapin Flattau & Klimpl, LLP, N.Y.C., 1977-2001; mem. exec. com. Parker Chapin Flattau & Klimpl, N.Y.C., 1987-92; ptnr. Jenkens & Gilchrist Parker Chapin LLP, N.Y.C., 2001—. Bd. dirs. H. Warshow & Sons Inc., N.Y.C. Editor Northwestern U. Law Rev., 1965-66, Equipment Leasing Jour., 1986—; co-editor Commercial Finance Guide, 1997—, Commercial Loan Documentation Guide, 1997—. Bd. dirs., exec. com. Friends of Israel Disabled Vets., N.Y.C., 1986—; bd. trustees, vice chmn., exec. com. Equipment Leasing and Fin. Found., Arlington, Va., 1998—. With U.S. Army, 1966-68; Vietnam. Decorated Bronze Star; Regents scholar, 1963, Newman scholar, 1963-66. Mem. N.Y. State Bar Assn. (corp. law sect.), N.Y. County Lawyers Assn. (banking law com., secured lending com.), Equipment Leasing Assn. Am. (bd. dirs., exec. com., industry future coun., 2001), Ea. Assn. Equipment Lessors (gen. counsel 1986—). Avocations: reading, painting, swimming, golf. Banking, Corporate, general, Equipment leasing. Home: 148 Quinn Rd Briarcliff Manor NY 10510-2133 Office: 405 Lexington Ave New York NY 10174-0002 E-mail: mleichtling@jenkens.com.

LEIGHTON, GEORGE NEVES, retired federal judge; b. New Bedford, Mass., Oct. 22, 1912; s. Antonio N. and Anna Sylvia (Garcia) Leitao; m. Virginia Berry Quivers, June 21, 1942; children: Virginia Anne, Barbara Elaine. AB, Howard U., 1940; LLB, Harvard U., 1946; LLD, Elmhurst Coll., 1964; LLD., John Marshall Law Sch., 1973; LLD, U. Mass., 1975, New Eng. U. Sch. Law, 1978, R.I. Coll., 1992, So. New Eng. Sch. Law, 2000; LLD (hon.), Loyola U., Chgo., 1989. Bar: Mass. 1946, Ill. 1947, U.S. Supreme Ct. 1958. Ptnr. Moore, Ming & Leighton, Chgo., 1951-59, McCoy, Ming & Leighton, Chgo., 1959-64; judge Cook County Circuit Ct., Chgo., 1964-69, Ill. App Ct. (1st dist.), 1969-76; U.S. dist. judge U.S. Dist. Ct. (no. dist.) Ill., 1976-86, sr. dist. judge, 1986-87; ret.; of counsel Earl L. Neal & Assocs., 1987—. Adj. prof. John Marshall Law Sch., Chgo., 1965—; commr., mem. character and fitness com. for 1st Appellate Dist., Supreme Ct. Ill., 1955-63, chmn. character and fitness com., 1961-62; joint com. for revision Ill. Criminal Code, 1959-63; chmn. Ill. adv. com. U.S. Commn. on Civil Rights, 1964; mem. pub. rev. bd. UAW, AFL-CIO, 1961-70; Asst. atty. gen. State of Ill., 1950-51; pres. 3d Ward Regular Democratic Orgn., Cook County, Ill., 1951-53; v.p. 21st Ward, 1964; spl. counsel to chmn. bd. Chgo. Transit Authority, 1988. Contbr. articles to legal jours. Bd. dirs. United Ch. Bd. for Homeland Ministries, United Ch. of Christ, Grant Hosp., Chgo.; trustee U. Notre Dame, 1979-83, trustee emeritus, 1983—; bd. overseers Harvard Coll., 1983-89. Capt., inf. AUS, 1942-45. Decorated Bronze Star; recipient Civil Liberties award Ill. div. ACLU, 1961, U.S. Supreme Ct. Justice John Paul Stevens award, 2000, Father Agustus Tolton awardCath. Archdioceses Chgo., 2000; named Chicagoan of Year in Law and Judiciary Jr. Assn. Commerce and Industry, 1964, Laureate, Acad. Ill. Lawyers, 2000. Fellow ABA (chmn. coun. 1976, mem. coun. sect. legal edn. and admissions to bar), Am. Coll. Trial Lawyers; mem. NAACP (chmn. legal redress com. Chgo. br.), John Howard Assn. (bd. dirs.), Chgo. Bar Assn., Ill. Bar Assn. (joint com. for revision jud. article 1959-62, sr. counselor 1996), Nat. Harvard Law Sch. Assn. (mem. coun.), Howard U. Chgo. Alumni Club (chmn. bd. dirs.), Phi Beta Kappa. Office: Earl L Neal & Assocs Ste 2300 203 N LaSalle St Chicago IL 60601-1213

LEIKIN, MITCHELL, retired judge; b. Chgo., July 31, 1921; s. Irving and Fannie Leikin; m. Evelyn Leikin, Aug. 10, 1952; children: Jerrold Blair, Robin Cheryl Pomeroy. BS, U. Ill., 1943; JD, DePaul U., 1949. Pvt. practice law, 1950; judge Cir. Ct. of Cook County, Chgo., 1980—2000; ret. Comdr. USNR, 1942—81. Mem.: Decalogue Soc. Lawyers (bd. dirs.), N.W. Suburban Bar Assn., North Suburban Bar Assn. (pres. 1968), Ill. Judges Assn. Home: 3741 Mission Hills Dr # 301 Northbrook IL 60062

LEINENWEBER, HARRY D. federal judge; b. Joliet, Ill., June 3, 1937; s. Harry Dean and Emily (Lennon) L.; m. Lynn Morley Martin, Jan. 7, 1987; 5 children; 2 stepchildren. AB cum laude, U. Notre Dame, 1959; JD, U. Chgo., 1962. Bar: Ill. 1962, U.S. Dist. Ct. (no. dist.) Ill. 1967. Assoc. Dunn, Stefanich, McGarry & Kennedy, Joliet, Ill., 1962-65, ptnr., 1965-79; city atty. City of Joliet, 1963-67; spl. counsel Village of Park Forest, Ill., 1967-74; spl. prosecutor County of Will, Ill., 1968-70; spl. counsel Village of Bolingbrook, Ill., 1975-77, Will County Forest Preserve, 1977; mem. Ill. Ho. of Reps., Springfield, 1973-83, chmn. judiciary I com., 1981-83; ptnr. Dunn, Leinenweber & Dunn, Joliet, 1979-86; fed. judge U.S. Dist. Ct. (no. dist.) Ill., Chgo., 1986—. Bd. dirs. Will County Bar Assn., 1984-86, State Jud. Adv. Coun., 1973-85, sec. 1975-76; tchr. legis. process seminar U. Ill., Chgo., 1988-2001; coord. U. Ill. Disting. Lecture Series, 2002--; mem. U. Ill. Inst. Govt. and Pub. Affairs Nat. Adv. Com., 1998-2001. Bd. dirs. Will County Legal Assistance Found., 1982-86, Good Shepard Manor, 1981—, Am. Cancer Soc., 1981-85, Joliet (Ill.) Montessori Sch., 1966-74; del. Rep. Nat. Conv., 1980; precinct committeeman, 1966-86; mem. nat. adv. com. U. Ill. Inst. Govt. and Pub. Affairs, 1998-2001. Recipient Environ. Legislator Golden award. Mem. Will County Bar Assn. (mem. jud. adv. coun., 1973-85, sec. 1975-76, bd. dirs. 1984-86), Nat. Conf. Commrs. on Uniform State Laws (exec. com. 1991-93, elected life mem. 1996), The Law Club of Chgo. (bd. dirs. 1996-98). Roman Catholic. Office: US Dist Ct 219 S Dearborn St Ste 1946 Chicago IL 60604-1801

LEINWAND, HARRIS DONALD, lawyer; b. Mt. Vernon, N.Y., Dec. 5, 1944; s. Isidor E. and Florence M. Leinwand; 1 child, Joseph Gabriel. BA, U. Pitts., 1965; JD, Cornell U., 1968. Bar: N.Y. 1969, U.S. Dist. Ct. (so. and ea. dists.) N.Y. 1970, U.S. Ct. Appeals (2d cir.) 1982. Ptnr. Leinwand Maron Hendler & Krause, N.Y.C., 1973-80; pvt. practice N.Y.C., 1980—. Bankruptcy. Office: 9 E 40th St New York NY 10016-0402 E-mail: hleinwand@aol.com.

LEIPHAM, JAY EDWARD, lawyer; b. Wilbur, Wash., Dec. 24, 1946; s. Albert Ellsworth and Margaret Lucille (Thomson) L.; m. Arlene R. Fegles, July 31, 1976; children: Hunter, Celeste. BA in Polit. Sci. with high honors, Wash. State U., 1969; JD, U. Chgo., 1972. Bar: Wash. 1973, U.S. Dist. Ct. (we. dist.) Wash. 1973, U.S. Dist. Ct. (ea. dist.) Wash. 1979. Assoc. Hullin, Roberts, Mines, Fite & Riveland, Seattle, 1973-76, Skeel, McKelvy, Henke, Evenson & Betts, Seattle, 1976-79, Underwood, Campbell, Brock, & Cerutti P.S., Spokane, Wash., 1979-80, prin., v.p., 1980-91, chmn. bd. dirs., CEO, 1991-93; prin., v.p., sec. Richter-Wimberley, P.S., Spokane, 1995—. Mem. ABA, ATLA, Wash. State Bar Assn., Spokane Bar Assn., Wash. State Trial Lawyers Assn., Def. Rsch. Inst., Wash. Def. Trial Lawyers, Phi Beta Kappa, Phi Kappa Phi. Presbyterian. General civil litigation, Personal injury (including property damage). Home: 1028 N Summit Blvd Spokane WA 99201-3042 Office: Richter-Wimberley PS 1300 Seafirst Fin Ctr Spokane WA 99201 E-mail: jayleipham@richter-wimberley.com.

LEISURE, PETER KEETON, federal judge; b. N.Y.C., Mar. 21, 1929; s. George S. and Lucille E. (Pelouze) L.; m. Kathleen Blair; Feb. 27, 1960; children: Lucille K. (dec.), Mary Blair, Kathleen K. BA, Yale U., 1952; LL.B., U. Va., 1958. Bar: N.Y. 1959, U.S. Supreme Ct. 1966, D.C. 1979, U.S. Dist. Ct. Conn. 1981. Assoc. Breed, Abbott & Morgan, 1958-61; asst. U.S. atty. So. Dist. N.Y., 1962-66; partner firm Curtis, Mallet-Prevost, Colt & Mosle, 1967-78; ptnr. Whitman & Ransom, N.Y.C., 1978-84; judge U.S. Dist. Ct. So. N.Y., New York, NY, 1984—. Bd. dirs. Retarded Infants Svcs., 1968-78, pres., 1971-75; bd. dirs. Community Coun. of Greater N.Y., 1972-79, Youth Consultation Svcs., 1971-78; trustee Ch. Club of N.Y., 1973-81, 87-90; mem. jud. ethics com. Jud. Conf., 1990-93, fin disclosure com. 1st lt. USAR, 1953-55. Recipient Ellis Island medal of honor, 2000. Fellow: Am. Coll. Trial Lawyers, Am. Bar Found.; mem.: ABA, Fed. Bar Coun. (trustee, v.p. 1973—78), D.C. Bar Assn., Am. Judges Assn., Fed. Judges Assn., Am. Law Inst., Nat. Lawyers Club (hon.). Office: US Dist Ct 1910 US Courthouse 500 Pearl St New York NY 10007-1316

LEITAO, MARIA DA GLORIA, lawyer; b. Rio de Janeiro, Nov. 1, 1955; d. Jaime De Almeida and Maria Manuela (De Almeida) Leitao. Grad., U. Coimbra, 1979. Bar: Portugal. Legal advisor Regional Govt. Açores, Portugal, 1980; lectr. Portuguese Cath. U. Law Sch., Lisbon, 1980—87, Tech. U. Lisbon, 1987—91; legal advisor Fgn. Investment Inst., 1988—89; ptnr. Gonçalves Pereira Castelo Branco E Assocs., 1989—. Pension, profit-sharing, and employee benefits, Labor (including EEOC, Fair Labor Standards Act, labor-management relations, NLRB, OSHA), Workers' compensation. Office: Gonçalves Pereira Castelo Branco E Assocs Praca Marques De Pombal No 1 - 8th Fl 1250-160 Lisbon Portugal Fax: +351 213549784. E-mail: glorialeitao@gpcb.pt.

LEITCH, RYAN L. lawyer; b. Ft. Wayne, Ind., July 18, 1962; s. Richard D. and Nancy E. L.; m. Amy L. Kilfoil, June 6, 1987; children: Jessica, Matthew, Jake, Hannah. BS in Fin., Ind. U., 1984, JD, 1987. Bar: U.S. Dist. Ct. (so. dist.) Ind. 1987. Assoc. Hunt & Suedhoff, Ft. Wayne, 1987-89; with Riley, Bennett & Egloff, Indpls., 1989—, ptnr., 1995—, mng. ptnr., 2002—. Bd. dirs. N. Willow Farms, Inc., Indpls., 1996-98, pres., 1998; mem. devel. com., bd. dirs. Prevent Child Abuse Ind., Indpls., 1988. Mem. ABA, Ind. State Bar Assn., Indpls. Bar Assn. Republican. Avocations: golfing, coaching sports. General civil litigation, Estate planning, Probate (including wills, trusts). Office: Riley Bennett & Egloff One American Sq Box 82035 Indianapolis IN 46282 E-mail: rleitch@rbelaw.com.

LEITER, RICHARD ALLEN, law librarian, law educator; b. Sacramento, Mar. 21, 1952; s. Lionel and Lois Rose Leiter; m. Wendy Ellin Werges, Dec. 30, 1978; children: Emily Grace, Madeline Rose, Anna Joy, Rebecca Hope. BA in Anthropology and Religious Studies with honors, U. Calif., Santa Cruz, 1976; JD, Southwestern U., 1981; M of Libr. and Info. Sci., U. Tex., 1986. Libr. asst. Irell & Manella, L.A., 1977-78; libr. Hopkins, Mitchell & Carley, San Jose, Calif., 1982-84; head of reference Law Sch., U. Tex., Austin, 1984-86; pub. svcs. libr. Law Sch., U. Nebr., Lincoln, 1986-88; head libr. Littler, Mendelson, Fastiff & Tichy, San Francisco, 1988-91; dir. law libr., assoc. prof. law Regent U. Sch. Law, Virginia Beach, Va., 1991-94; assoc. prof. law Howard U. Sch. Law, A.M. Daniels Law Libr., Washington, 1994-98, dir. law libr., 1994—2000; assoc. dean, prof. Howard U., Washington, 1998-2000; dir. Schmid Law Libr., prof. law U. Nebr., Lincoln, 2000—. Mem. Westlaw Acad. Adv. Bd., 1990-93; sec. bd. dirs. StoneBridge Sch., 1993-94; mem. adv. bd. Oceana Publs., Inc., 1994-98. Editor: (book sect.) Yellow Pads to Computers, 1986, 91; author: (bibliography) New Frontiers of Forensic & Demonstrative Evidence, 1985; editor: Automatome, 1987-89, The Spirit of Law Librarianship, 1991, 2d edit., 2003, National Survey of State Laws, 1993, 4th edit., 2002; (with A. White) Concordance of Federal Legislation, 1999; editor Southwestern U. Law Review; contbr. articles to profl. jours. Mem. adv. com. StoneBridge Ednl. Found. Mem. ABA, Am. Assn. Law Librs. (so. chpt., automation and sci. devel. spl. interest sect. 1986—, chair 1989-90, indexing of periodical lit. adv. com. 1990-91, 2001—, chair 1990-91, mem. spl. com. to promote development of resources for legal info. cmty. 1994-96, recruitment com. 1995-97, chair rsch. com. 1998-99), San Francisco Pvt. Law Librs. (steering com. 1989), Mid Am. Law Sch. Libr. Consortium, Scribes. Avocations: bicycling, reading, running. Home: 1301 N 37th St Lincoln NE 68503-2015 Office: U Nebr Schmid Law Libr Coll Law Lincoln NE 68583-0902 E-mail: rleiter@unl.edu.

LEITNER, ANTHONY JOSEPH, lawyer; b. Bklyn., Dec. 16, 1943; s. Anthony J. and Doris (Burns) L.; m. Jennifer A., Aug. 10, 1968; children: Megan M., Wendy A., Helen E. BA, Columbia U., 1965; JD, Northwestern U., 1969. Bars: N.Y. 1970, U.S. Dist. Ct. (so. dist.) N.Y. 1971, U.S. Ct. Appeals (2d cir.) 1971. Assoc. Curtis Mallet-Prevost Colt & Mosle, N.Y.C., 1969-79; spl. counsel Goldman, Sachs & Co., N.Y.C., 1979—. Mem. Bd. Edn. South Orange Maplewood Sch. Dist., 1983-87. Mem. ABA (mem. futures regulation sub-com. of corp. banking and bus. law sect.), N.Y. State Bar Assn. (mem. commodity and futures regulation com.), Assn. of Bar of City of N.Y. Roman Catholic. Avocations: sailing, fishing. Office: Goldman Sachs & Co One New York Plz New York NY 10004-2456

LEITNER, PAUL REVERE, lawyer; b. Winnsboro, S.C., Nov. 11, 1928; s. W. Walker and Irene (Lewis) L.; m. Jeannette C. Card, Mar. 16, 1985; children by previous marriage: David, Douglas, Gregory, Reid, Cheryl. AB, Duke U., 1950; LLB, McKenzie Coll., 1954. Bar: Tenn. 1954; cert. civil trial specialist Nat. Bd. Trial Advocacy and Tenn. Commn. on CLE and Specialization. Pvt. practice law, Chattanooga, 1954; assoc. Leitner, Williams, Dooley & Napolitan and predecessor firms, 1952-57; ptnr. Leitner, Williams, Dooley & Napolitan and predecessor firms, 1957—. Tenn. chmn. Def. Rsch. Inst., 1978-89. Bd. dirs. Family Service Agy., 1957-63, Chattanooga Symphony and Opera Assn., 1986-89, sec., 1987-89, Prison and Prevention Ministries, 1992—, chmn. 1996-99; mem. Chattanooga-Hamilton County Community Action Bd.; mem. Juvenile Ct. Commn., Hamilton County, 1955-61, chmn., 1958-59; chmn. Citizens Com. for Better Schs.; mem. Met. Govt. Charter Commn. Served with U.S. Army, 1946-47. Named Young Man of Yr. Chattanooga Area, 1957 Fellow Am. Coll. Trial Lawyers, Tenn. Bar. Found, Chattanooga Bar Found. (founding); mem. ABA, Tenn. Bar Assn., Jaycees (Chattanooga, pres. 1956-57), Chatanooga Bar Assn., Fed. Bar Assn., Fed. Def. Corp. Counsel, Internat. Assn. Def. Coun., Trial Attys. Am., Tenn. Def. Lawyers Assn. (pres. 1975-76), Am. Bd. Trial Advs. (advocate), U.S. Sixth Cir. Jud. Conf. (life), Am. Inns of Ct. Methodist. Federal civil litigation, State civil litigation, Personal injury (including property damage). Home: 3926 Windward Ln Soddy Daisy TN 37379 E-mail: pleitner@leitnerfirm.com.

LEITZELL, TERRY LEE, lawyer; b. Williamsport, Pa., Apr. 15, 1942; s. Ernest Richard and Inez Mae (Taylor) L.; m. Lucy Acker Emmerich, June 18, 1966; children: Thomas Addison, Charles Taylor, Robert Davies. AB, Cornell U., 1964; JD, U. Pa., 1967. Bar: D.C. bar 1967. Consular officer Dept. State, Bombay, India, 1968-70, atty.-adv. for oceans affairs Washington, 1970-77, chief U.S. negotiator UN law of sea negotiations Geneva, also N.Y.C., 1974-77; asst. adminstr. for fisheries and dir. Nat. Marine Fisheries Service, NOAA, Dept. Commerce, Washington, 1978-81; practice law Washington, 1981-92, Seattle, 1992—; gen. counsel Icicle Seafoods, Seattle. Mem.: Wash. Bar Assn. Democrat. Private international, Legislative. Home: 3150 W Laurelhurst Dr NE Seattle WA 98105-5346 Office: Icicle Seafoods 4019 21st Ave W Ste 300 Seattle WA 98199-1299 E-mail: terryl@icicleseafoods.com.

LEITZKE, RANDY LEE, law firm executive; b. Seattle, June 16, 1958; s. Harold A. and Eloise C. Leitzke; m. Janice K. Oswald, Apr. 12, 1980; children: Danielle, Robin, Jamie. BA in Bus. Adminstrn., U. Wash., 1980, MBA, 1984. CPA, Wash. Fin. adminstr. GTE, Stamford, Conn., 1980-83; mgr. fin. planning and cost acctg. Fairchild Semicondr. Corp., Puyallup, Wash., 1984-87; CFO, ESCA Corp., Bellevue, Wash., 1987-94; exec. dir., COO Lane Powell Spears Lubersky LLP, Seattle, 1994—. Mem. Am. Mgmt. Assn., Fin. Execs. Inst., Wash. Soc. CPAs, Assn. Legal Adminstrs. Office: Lane Powell Spears Lubersky LLP 1420 5th Ave Ste 4100 Seattle WA 98101-2338

LELAND, DAVID CHARLES, former lawyer, record producer, talent agent; b. Berkeley, Calif., Mar. 26, 1953; s. Richard William and Carol Arlene (Plumly) L.; m. Jo-Ann Charak, Nov. 23, 1982; 1 child, Benjamin Nathan; m. Loretta A. Smith, Aug. 12, 1989 (div. Dec. 1991); m. Penelope Irene Barsley Challans, Aug. 26, 1996. Student, New Coll. Calif., 1974-75; BA, U. Calif., Berkeley, 1978; postgrad., Paris, summer 1979; JD, Golden Gate U., 1981. Bar: Mass. 1986, U.S. Dist. Ct. (no. dist.) Calif. 1987, U.S. Dist. Ct. Mass. 1994, U.S. Supreme Ct. 1994, U.S. Ct. Appeals (1st cir.) 1994, U.S. Tax Ct. 1996. Hearing officer San Francisco Residential Rent Bd., 1981-82; pvt. investigtor Pat Kohn Detective Agy., San Francisco, 1980-83; pres. Wilbur & Son, Boston and San Francisco, 1982-84; mktg. mgr. Nat. Bus. Cons., Santa Monica, Calif., 1984-85; sales cons. Entre Computer Corp., San Francisco, 1985; legal asst. Kuvara Law Firm, San Jose, Calif., 1986-87; assoc. Parrish & Assocs., San Francisco, 1987-88; cons. atty. Goshkin, Pollatsek, Meredith & Lee, San Francisco, 1988; cons. Compulaw, Inc., Culver City, Calif., 1987-90, Law Office of David Leland, 1992-98; markup lang. expert Xerox Lang. Svcs., 1998-99; markup analyst FT.com, 1999—. Legal counsel, bd. dirs. Friends of Newton Free Libr., 1993-95; bd. mem. Boston Music Fest, 1994; bd. dirs. Boston Music Fest, 1994; presenter XML 2000 AsiaPacific. Mem. ABA (lt. gov. law student div. 1980-81, Silver Key award 1981), Assn. Trial Lawyers Am., Phi Alpha Delta. Democrat. Avocations: painting, photography, writing, cooking. Office: 20 Chandlers Ho 38 Old London Rd Kingston-Upon-Thames Surrey KT2 6QF England

LEMANN, THOMAS BERTHELOT, lawyer; b. New Orleans, Jan. 3, 1926; s. Monte M. and Nettie E. (Hyman) L.; m. Barbara M. London, Apr. 14, 1951 (dec. 1999); children: Nicholas B., Nancy E.; m. Sheila Bosworth Bell, June 1, 2000. AB summa cum laude, Harvard U., 1949, LL.B., 1952; M.C.L., Tulane U., 1953. Bar: La. 1953. Assoc. Monroe & Lemann, New Orleans, 1953-58, ptnr., 1958-98; of counsel Liskow & Lewis, New Orleans, 1998—. Bd. dirs. B. Lemann & Bro., Mermentau Mineral and Land Co., Avrico Inc.; adv. bd. dirs. Riviana Foods. Contbr. articles to profl. publs. Mem. council La. State Law Inst., sec. trust adv. com.; chmn. Mayor's Cultural Resources Com., 1970-75; pres. Arts Coun. Greater New Orleans, 1975-80, bd. dirs.; mem. vis. com. art museums Harvard U., 1974-80; trustee Metairie Park Country Day Sch., 1956-71, pres., 1967-70, New Orleans Philharmonic Symphony Soc., 1956-78, Flint-Goodridge Hosp., 1960-70, La. Civil Service League, pres., 1974-76, New Orleans Mus. Art, 1986-92; bd. dirs. Zemurray Found., Hever Found., Parkside Found., Azby Fund, Azby Art Fund, Greater New Orleans Found., Arts Coun. New Orleans, Musica da Camera. Served with AUS, 1944-46, PTO. Mem. ABA, La. Bar Assn. (bd. govs. 1977-78), New Orleans Bar Assn., Assn. Bar City N.Y., Am. Law Inst., Soc. Bartolus, Phi Beta Kappa. Clubs: New Orleans Country, Wyvern (New Orleans). Jewish. Estate planning, Probate (including wills, trusts), Estate taxation. Home: 6020 Garfield St New Orleans LA 70118-6039 Office: Liskow & Lewis 701 Poydras St Ste 5000 New Orleans LA 70139-5099 E-mail: tblemann@liskow.com.

LEMAY, JACQUES, lawyer; b. Quebec City, Can., July 10, 1940; s. Gerard and Jacqueline (Lachance) LeM. BA, Que. Sem., 1959; LL.L., Laval U., 1962; postgrad., U. Toronto, 1964; D.E.S., 1965. Bar: Que. 1963. Practice in, Quebec City, 1964—; mem. firm Prevost, Gagne, Flynn, Chouinard & Jacques, 1964-67; ptnr. Flynn, Rivard, Jacques, Cimon, Lessard & LeMay, 1968-86, Flynn, Rivard, 1986—; legal adviser Societe des Ajusteurs d'Assurance, 1969. Bd. dirs. Can. 88 Energy Corp., 1991—2000. Mem. Societe des Etudes Juridiques (pres. 1969) Clubs: Cercle de la Garnison (Que.). Home: 265 ch duBout de l'Ile Sainte-Petronille QC Canada G0A 4CO Office: 70 Dalhousie Bureau 500 Quebec QC Canada G1K 7A6 E-mail: jlemay@flynn.qc.ca.

LEMENS, WILLIAM VERNON, JR., banker, finance company executive, lawyer; b. Austin, Tex., Oct. 26, 1935; s. William Vernon and Lylia (Engberg) L.; m. Jean Lemens, May 31, 1959; children: William Vernon III, Shandra Christine. BA, U. Tex., 1958, LLB, JD, U. Tex., 1962. Bar: Tex. 1962; lic. real estate broker, Tex. Pvt. practice, Austin, 1962—; pres. Standard Fin. Co., Austin, 1963-67, First State Loan, Austin, 1967—; chief exec. officer Southwest Computer Svcs., Inc., Austin, 1965—. Pres., chief instr., mgmt. cons. Decision Dynamics, Inc., Austin, 1965-75; exec. v.p., atty. Northwest Savs. Assn., Austin, 1975-78; chmn. bd. First State Bank, Jarrell, Tex., 1975-87; pres., chief exec. officer First Am. Fin. Co., Ft. Worth, 1982—, Eagle Bank, Jarrell, 1987—. Author: Elements of Objective Orientation, 1971, SSAM-The Power of Perfect Decisions, 1972, Successful Financial Institution Operation, 1978, National Standard Financial Company Operations, 1981. Pres. Ballet Austin, 1967, Southwest Regional Ballet Assn., 1968; deacon Univ. Bapt. Ch., Austin, 1979—. Mem. State Bar Tex., Austin Bd. Realtors, Tex. Fin. Inst. (bd. dirs. 1975—), Tex. Consumer Fin. Asns. (bd. dirs. 1995—). Office: 1509 Guadalupe St Ste 200 Austin TX 78701-1608

LEMIRE, JEROME ALBERT, lawyer, geologist; b. Cleve., June 4, 1947; s. George A. and Matilda (Simon) Lemire; m. Sandra Marsick, Oct. 1, 1976; children: Laura, Lesley, Thomas. BS in Geology, Ohio State U., 1969, MS in Geology, 1973, JD, 1976. Bar: Ohio 1976; cert. fin. planner. Geologist United Petroleum Co., Columbus, Ohio, 1976—77; assoc. Brownfield, Bowen & Bally, Columbus, 1977—79; land mgr. POI Energy Inc., Cleve., 1979—81; cons. Jefferson, Ohio, 1981—83; v.p. Carey Resources Inc., Jefferson, 1984—86; pres. Lemire & Assocs Inc., Jefferson, 1986—. Cons. in field. Vice chmn. Tech. Adv. Coun., Columbus, 1984—94; solicitor Village of Jefferson. Served to 1st lt. U.S. Army, 1970—72. Mem.: VFW, Astabula County Bar Assn. (pres. 2002—), Ohio Bar Assn., Rotary. Corporate, general, Oil, gas, and mineral, Environmental. Home: 838 N State Route 46 Jefferson OH 44047-9785

LEMLE, ROBERT SPENCER, lawyer; b. N.Y.C., Mar. 6, 1953; s. Leo Karl and Gertrude (Bander) L.; m. Roni Sue Kohen, Sept. 5, 1976; children: Zachary, Joanna. AB, Oberlin Coll., 1975; JD, NYU, 1978. Bar: N.Y. 1979. Assoc. Cravath, Swaine & Moore, N.Y.C., 1978—82; assoc. gen. counsel Cablevision Sys. Corp., Woodbury, NY, 1982—84, v.p., gen. counsel, 1984—86, sr. v.p., gen. counsel, sec., 1986—94, exec. v.p., gen. counsel, sec., 1994—2001, vice chmn., gen. counsel, sec., 2001—02, vice chmn., sec., 2002—03; vice chmn. Madison Sq. Garden, N.Y.C., 1999—2002. Bd. editors Cable TV and New Media Law and Fin., N.Y.C., 1983-99, bd. dirs. Cablevision Systems Corp., 1988—. Trustee L.I. Children's Mus., 1990—, pres., 1996—; trustee Oberlin Coll., 1996—, vice chair, 2001--. Mem. ABA, N.Y. State Bar Assn. Avocation: real estate. Corporate, general, Entertainment. Office: Cablevision Systems Corp 1111 Stewart Ave Bethpage NY 11714-3581 E-mail: rlemle@cablevision.com.

LEMLY, THOMAS ADGER, lawyer; b. Dayton, Ohio, Jan. 31, 1943; s. Thomas Moore and Elzabeth (Adger) L.; m. Kathleen Brame, Nov. 24, 1984; children: Elizabeth Hayden, Joanna Marsden, Isabelle Stafford, Kate Brame. BA, Duke U., 1970; JD with honors, U. N.C., 1973. Bar: Wash. 1973, U.S. Dist. Ct. (we. dist.) Wash. 1973, U.S. Ct. Appeals (9th cir.) 1975, U.S. Supreme Ct. 1980. Assoc. Davis Wright Tremaine, Seattle, 1973-79, ptnr., 1979—. Contbg. editor Employment Discrimination Law, 1984-87, 94—; editor Wash., Oreg., Alaska and Calif. Employment Law Deskbooks, 1987—. Chmn. Pacific Coast Labor Conf., Seattle, 1983; trustee Plymouth Congregational Ch., 1980-84, Seattle Opera Assn., 1991—. Fellow Am. Coll. Trial Lawyers; mem. ABA (labor employment law sect. 1975—, subcom. chmn. 1984-90, govt. liaison com. 1982—), Seattle-King County

Bar Assn. (chmn. labor sect.), Assn. Wash. Bus. (sec.-treas. 2002-03, trustee 1992—, vice chair 2003—, chmn. human resources coun. 1993-2002, chmn. employment law task force 1987-93), U. N.C. Bar Found. (bd. dirs. 1973-76), Seattle Duke Alumni Assn. (pres. 1979-84), Order of Coif, Wash. Athletic Club (Seattle), Rotary. Republican. Presbytarian. General civil litigation, Labor (including EEOC, Fair Labor Standards Act, labor-management relations, NLRB, OSHA). Home: 1614 7th Ave W Seattle WA 98119-2919 Office: Davis Wright Tremaine 2600 Century Sq 1501 4th Ave Seattle WA 98101-1688 E-mail: tomlemly@dwt.com.

LEMON, WILLIAM JACOB, lawyer; b. Covington, Va., Oct. 25, 1932; s. James Gordon and Elizabeth (Wilson) L.; m. Barbara Inez Boyle, Aug. 17, 1957; children: Sarah E. Lemon Ludwig, William Tucker, Stephen Weldon. BA, Washington & Lee U., 1957, JD, 1959. Bar: Va. 1959. Assoc. Martin, Martin & Hopkins, Roanoke, Va., 1959-61; ptnr. Martin, Hopkins & Lemon, Roanoke, 1962—. Trustee Washington and Lee U., Lexington, Va., 1988-97, North Cross Sch., Roanoke, 1995—; pres. Specific Reading and Learning Difficulties Assn. Shedd Early Learning Ctr., 1985-86, George C. Marshall Found., Lexington, Va., 1997—. With U.S. Army, 1952-54. Mem. Va. Bar Assn., Roanoke Bar Assn. (pres. 1982-83), Va. State Bar, Shenandoah Club. Presbyterian. Avocations: farming, hunting, travel. Health, Probate (including wills, trusts), Property, real (including real estate development, water). Office: Martin Hopkins Lemon First Union Tower 10 S Jefferson St Ste 1000 Roanoke VA 24011-1314 also: PO Box 13366 Roanoke VA 24033-3366

LEMONS, DONALD W. state supreme court justice; b. Feb. 22, 1949; Justice Supreme Ct. Va., 2000—. Office: Supreme Ct Bldg 100 N Ninth St, 5th Floor Richmond VA 23219 also: PO Box 1315 Richmond VA 23218-1315

LEMOS GODINHOS, MARIA EDUARDA, lawyer; b. Lisbon, Portugal, Aug. 16, 1968; d. Jorge Alberto and Angela Júlia Lemos Godinho. LLM, Coll. Europe, Brussels, 1993; Law Degree, Lisbon U., 1993. Lawyer Luis Brito Correia, Lisbon, 1993—2000; assoc. Vasconcelos F Sao Carneiro Fontes and A, Lisbon. Tchr. internat. pub. law U. Moderna, Lisbon, 1993—2000. Office: Vasconcelos F Sao Carneiro Fontes and A Rua Castilho 20 - 1250-069 Lisbon Portugal

LENAGH, THOMAS HUGH, lawyer, financial advisor; b. Lawrence, Mass., Nov. 1, 1920; s. Frank Albert and Bethia (Coultar) L.; m. Leila Semple Fellner; children: Katherine, Thomas C., Jessie W. BA, Williams Coll., 1941; LLB, Columbia U., 1948. Analyst Cyrus J. Lawrence, N.Y.C., 1953-59; mgr. research service Goodbody & Co., N.Y.C., 1959-61; asst. treas. Ford Found., N.Y.C., 1961-64, treas., 1964-78; fin. v.p. Aspen Inst., N.Y.C., 1978-80; chmn., chief exec. officer Greiner Engring., Los Angeles, 1982-85; chmn. bd. Inrad Corp. Bd. dirs. Gintel Fund, Adams Express, Petroleum & Resources Fund, Inrad Inc., Cornerstone Strategic Fund, Progressive Return Fund. Chmn. N.Y. YWCA, N.Y.C., 1975-92. Served with USN, 1941-46, capt. USNR, 1950-53. Mem. Chartered Fin. Analyst, N.Y. Soc. Security Analyst, Conn. Bar Assn. Clubs: Williams. Republican. Home: 13 Allens Corner Rd Flemington NJ 08822-5620

LENARD, GEORGE DEAN, lawyer; b. Joliet, Ill., Aug. 26, 1957; s. Louis George and Jennie (Helopoulos) L.; m. Nancy Ilene Sundquist, Nov. 11, 1989. BS, Ill. State U., 1979; JD, Thomas Cooley Law Sch., 1984. Bar: Ill. 1984, U.S. Dist. Ct. (no. dist.) Ill. 1984, U.S. Ct. Appeals (6th cir.) 1998, U.S. Supreme Ct. 1990, Mich. 1998, Ariz. 1999, Calif. 2001. Asst. states atty. Will County States Attys. Office, Joliet, 1984-88; pvt. practice law Joliet, 1988—. Mem. ABA (mem. Ill. capital litigation trial bar, lead counsel), ATLA, Nat. Assn. Criminal Def. Lawyers, State Bar Ariz., State Bar Mich., State Bar Calif., Phi Alpha Delta (Isaac P. Christiancy chpt.). Avocation: golf. Constitutional, Criminal. Office: 81 N Chicago St Ste 206 Joliet IL 60432-4383

LENART, LYNN MARIE, law librarian; b. Cleve., Aug. 1, 1957; d. Marshall and June Berger. BA in Secondary Edn., U. Akron, 1982; MLS, Kent State U., 1990; JD, U. Akron, 1999. Bar: Ohio 2000. Clerical specialist Bierce Libr. U. Akron, Ohio, 1982—83, reference assoc. Govt. Documents Bierce Libr., 1984—92, asst. prof. bibliography Bierce Libr., 1993—94, asst. law libr. reference svcs. Sch. Law Libr., 1994—. Mem.: ABA, Ohio Regional Assn. Law Libr., Am. Assn. Law Libr. Office: Univ Akron Sch Law Libr 150 University Ave Akron OH 44325-2902

LENDI, MARTIN, law educator; b. Zurich, Switzerland, Sept. 23, 1933; s. Christian and Emma (Wolff) L.; m. Heidi Bräker; 1 child, Stephan. Dr.iur.utr., U. Zurich, 1958; Dr.h.c. (hon.) , U. Vienna. State exam, lawyer, 1960. Sec. state Dept. Constrn., St. Gall, Switzerland, 1961-69; prof. Swiss Fed. Inst. Tech., Zurich, 1969—98; dean Dept. Law and Economic, Zurich; dir., Swiss Fed. Inst. Urban and Country Planning Swiss Fed. Inst. Tech. Zurich, 1969-87. Author: Planungsrecht und Eigentum, 1976, Recht und Politik der Raumplanung, 1984, Raumplanung in der Schweiz, eine Einfuhrung, 1987, Theorie der Raumplanung, 1988, Verkelerund Recht, 1998, Politisch Sachlian und Ethisch in Dijuth Raumplanung-am Beispiel du Schweiz, 1998, Jerellschafthian Verelyter Recht, 1999. Lebensraum -Technik-Recht, 1988; Bewährung des Rechts, 1992; Rechtsordnung, 1992. Oberst lt. 1 Gst, Gen. Staff, 1968-93, Swiss Mil. Recipient Camillo Sitte-Price award, U. Vienna, 1987. Mem. Germany Acad. Planning (corr. mem. 1976—), Swiss Orgn. Planning, Swiss Acad. Tech. Sci. Swiss Liberals. Protestant. Home: Weinmanngasse 21 Kusnacht CH-8700 Zürich Switzerland Office: Swiss Fed Inst Tech Rämistrasse 101 H 8092 Zürich Switzerland

LENGA, ROBERT ALLEN, lawyer; b. Cleve., Jan. 2, 1938; s. Alexander Richard and Florence (Gessner) Lenga; m. Nancy Ann Dobina, Oct. 6, 1968; children: Jennifer Ann, Kenneth Robert. BA, Bowling Green State U., 1960; JD, Case Western Res. U., 1964. Bar: Ohio 1965, U.S. Dist. Ct. (no. dist.) Ohio 1966. Mem. Harrington Hoppe & Mitchell Ltd., Youngstown, Ohio, 1966—. Mem. Poland (Ohio) Bd. Edn., 1988-91, pres., 1991; trustee Mahoning Shenango Estate Planning Coun., Youngstown, Ohio, 1996-98. Mem. Ohio State Bar Assn. (bd. govs. estate planning trust and probate sect. 1985-91, 97—), Mahoning County Bar Assn. (pres. 1990-91), Rotary Club (Paul Harris fellow 1997). Corporate, general, Estate planning, Probate (including wills, trusts). Office: Harrington Hoppe Mitchell Ltd 26 Market St 1200 Sky Bank Bldg Youngstown OH 44503 E-mail: rlenga@hhmlaw.com.

LENZI, ALBERT JAMES, JR., lawyer; b. Chgo., Feb. 15, 1955; s. Albert Joseph Sr. and Helen Lenzi; adopted children: April Lynn Sorensen, Sean Patrick Sorensen. Student, U.S. Naval Acad., 1972-74; BA, Loyola U., Chgo., 1976; JD, U. of the Pacific, 1979. Bar: Calif. 1979, U.S. Dist. Ct. (ea. dist.) Calif. 1982, U.S. Supreme Ct. 1990. Asst. prof. law Willamette U., Salem, Oreg., 1979-80; assoc. Thompson Mayhew & Michel, Sacramento, 1980-81, Goldstein, Barceloux & Goldstein, Chico, Calif., 1981-82, Brislain & Zink, Chico, 1982-84; ptnr. Brislain, Zink & Lenzi, Chico, 1984-94, Zink & Lenzi, Chico, 1994—. Mem. Big. Bros., Big Sisters, 2002—. Served with USN, 1972-74. Mem. ABA, Calif. Trial Lawyers, Consumer Attys. Calif. (bd. dirs. 1997-98), Calif. Bar Assn., 3d Dist. Agrl. Assn. (bd. dirs. 2002—), Chico Kiwanis Club (pres. 1998-99). Democrat. Roman Catholic. Avocations: bowling, reading. Insurance, Personal injury (including property damage), Workers' compensation. Office: Zink & Lenzi 250 Vallombrosa Ave Ste 175 Chico CA 95926-3973

LEON, RICHARD J. federal judge; b. South Natick, Mass., Dec. 3, 1949; s. Silvano B. and Rita (O'Rorke) L.; m. M-Christine Costa; Nicholas Cavanagh. AB, Holy Cross Coll., 1971; JD cum laude, Suffolk Law Sch., 1974; LLM, Harvard U., 1981. Bar: R.I. 1975, U.S. Ct. Appeals (2d cir.) 1977, U.S. Dist. Ct. R.I. 1976, U.S. Supreme Ct. 1984, D.C. 1991, U.S. Dist. Ct. D.C. 1991, U.S. Ct. Appeals (D.C. cir.) 1991. Law clk. to justices Superior Ct. Mass., 1974-75, to justice R.I. Supreme Ct., 1975-76; spl. asst. U.S. atty. U.S. Attys. Office (so. dist.) N.Y., 1977-78; asst. prof. law St. John's U. Law Sch., 1979-83; adj. prof. law Georgetown U. Law Ctr., 1997—; sr. trial atty., criminal sect., tax div. U.S. Dept. Justice, Washington, 1983-87, dep. asst. atty. gen. environment and natural resources divsn., 1988-89; ptnr. Baker & Hostetler, Washington, 1989-99,Vorys, Sater, Seymour and Pease, Washington, 1999-2002; judge U.S. Dist. Ct., 2002—; dep. chief minority counsel House Select "Iran-Contra" Com., 1987; active Jud. Conf. D.C. cir., 1991—, mem. Commn. on White House Fellowships, 1990-93; chief minority counsel House Fgn. Affairs Com. 'October Surprise' Task Force, 1992; spl. counsel House banking com. "Whitewater investigation", 1994; spl. counsel House ethics reform task force, 1997; mem. Jud. Rev. Commn. on Fgn. Asset Control, 2000-01. Author: (chpt.) Environmental Crime, Lawyers' Desk Book on White Collar Crime, 1991; contbr. articles to legal jours. Trustee Suffolk U., 1990-98. Mem. ABA, Order of Barristers, R.I. Bar Assn., Fed. Bar Coun., Suffolk Law Sch. Assn. Met. N.Y. (past pres.), Suffolk Law Sch. Assn. Met. Washington (past pres.), Harvard Club of N.Y.C., Chevy Chase Club. Republican. Roman Catholic. Office: US Courthouse 333 Constitution Ave NW Washington DC 20001

LEONARD, EDWIN DEANE, lawyer; b. Oakland, Calif., Apr. 22, 1929; s. Edwin Stanley and Gladys Eugenia (Lee) L.; m. Judith Swatland, July 10, 1954; children: Garrick Hillman, Susanna Leonard Hill, Rebecca Leonard McCauley, Ethan York. BA, The Principia, 1950; LLB, Harvard U., 1953; LLM, George Washington U., 1956. Bar: D.C. 1953, Ill. 1953, N.Y. 1957. Assoc. Davis Polk Wardwell Sunderland & Kiendl, N.Y.C., 1956-61; ptnr. Davis Polk & Wardwell, N.Y.C., 1961-97, sr. counsel, 1998—. Trustee the Brearley Sch., N.Y.C., 1980-90; pres. Millbrook Equestrian Ctr., 1983-98. Served to 1st lt. JAGC, 1953-56. Mem. ABA, N.Y. Bar Assn., N.Y. County Bar Assn., Assn. of Bar of City of N.Y. (chmn. various coms.). Corporate, general, Mergers and acquisitions, Securities. Home: 157 Conklin Hill Rd Stanfordville NY 12581-5639 Office: Davis Polk & Wardwell 450 Lexington Ave New York NY 10017-3982 E-mail: deaneleonard@worldnet.att.net.

LEONARD, JEFFREY S. lawyer; b. Bklyn., Sept. 14, 1945; m. Maxine L. Bortnick, Dec. 28, 1967; children: Deborah, Jennifer. AB in History, U. Rochester, 1967; JD, U. Ariz., 1974. Bar: Ariz. 1974; U.S. Dist. Ct. Ariz. 1974, U.S. Ct. Appeals (9th cir.) 1974, U.S. Supreme Ct. 1985. Law clk. to judge U.S. Dist. Ct. Ariz., 1974-75. Mem. editl. bd. Ariz. Law Rev., 1973-74. Mem. Order of Coif. Federal civil litigation, State civil litigation. Office: Leonard Collins & Gillespie PC Two Renaissance Sq 40 N Central Ave Ste 2100 Phoenix AZ 85004-4405 E-mail: jleonard@lcg-law.com.

LEONARD, THOMAS, lawyer; b. Phila., Sept. 5, 1946; s. Thomas Aloysius and Mary Teresa (Kelly) L.; m. Kathleen Mary Duffy; children: Sarah, Mary Kate, Tom. BS, Drexel U., 1968; JD, Temple U., 1971. Bar: Pa., U.S. Supreme Ct., U.S. Ct. Appeals (3d cir.), U.S. Dist. Ct. (ea., mid., we. dists.) Pa., U.S. Dist. Ct. (so. dist.) N.J., U.S. Dist. Ct. Utah, U.S. Dist. Ct. (so. dist.) N.Y. Assoc. Dilworth, Paxson, Kalish & Kauffman, Phila., 1972-76, ptnr., 1976—79, 1983—91, sr. ptnr., mem. exec. com., 1979—83; controller City of Phila., 1991—; chmn. litigation dept., sr. ptnr., permanent mem. mgmt. com. Obermayer, Rebmann, Maxwell and Hippel, Phila., 1991—. Bd. dirs. Fed. Nat. Mortgage Assn., Independence Blue Cross, World Affair Coun. Phila., Cora Social Svcs., Pa. Bus. Bank, U.S. Facilities, Hahnemann Hosp.; vice chmn. Phila. Gas Commn., 1979-83; register of wills City of Phila., 1976-79; mem. disciplinary bd. Supreme Ct., Pa., 1991-95, vice chmn., 1995-96, chmn., 1996—; chmn. Delaware Valley Real Estate Investment Fund, 1999—; chmn. Permalith Plastics. Mem. editorial bd. Amran's Pa. Practice, 1972; contbr. articles to profl. publs. Mem. Dem. Nat. Com., Washington, 1976-83, mem. fin. com., 1988, vice chair fin., 1993—, Pa. fin. chair, 1993—, bd. dirs.; del. Dem. Nat. Conv., 1976, 80, 92, 96; chmn. Pa. fin. com. Clinton for Pres., 1992, 96; co-chair Rendell for Mayor, 1991, 95; mem. coun. Phila. Orch., 1981-86; bd. dirs. Acad. Scis., Phila., 1981-85; pres. Pa. chpt. Irish Am. Partnership. Capt. U.S. Army, 1971-77. Recipient Man of Yr. award Emerald Soc., 1979, Korean-Am. Friendship Soc., 1982, Carmel Humanitarian award Haifa U., 1981, Merit award Chapel of Four Chaplains, 1983. Mem. ABA, Pa. Bar Assn., Phila. Bar Assn. (bd. govs. 1979-82), Union League, Phila. Racquet Club, Serra Club (past pres.). Roman Catholic. General civil litigation, Corporate, general, Environmental. Office: Obermayer Rebmann Maxwell and Hippel 1617 John F Kennedy Blvd Fl 19 Philadelphia PA 19103-1821 E-mail: thomas.leonard@obermayer.com.

LEONARD, TIMOTHY DWIGHT, judge; b. Beaver, Okla., Jan. 22, 1940; s. Dwight and Mary Evelyn Leonard; m. Nancy Louise Laughlin, July 15, 1967; children: Kirstin Dione, Ryan Timothy, Tyler Dwight. BA, U. Okla., 1962, JD, 1965; student, Mil. Naval Justice Sch., 1966. Bar: Okla. 1965, U.S. Dist. Ct. (no. and we. dists.) Okla. 1969, U.S. Ct. Appeals (10th cir.) 1969, U.S. Supreme Ct. 1970. Asst. atty. gen. State of Okla., 1968-70; mem. Okla. Senate, 1979-88; ptnr. Blankenship, Herrold, Russell et al, Oklahoma City, 1970-71, Trippet, Leonard & Kee, Beaver, 1971-88; of counsel Huckaby, Fleming et al, Oklahoma City, 1988-89; U.S. atty. Western Dist. Okla., 1988-92; judge U.S. Dist. Ct. (we. dist.) Okla., 1992—. Guest lectr. Oklahoma City U., 1988—89; mem. U.S. Atty. Gen.'s Adv. Com., 1990—92, chmn. office mgmt. and budget subcom., 1990—92, jud. conf. com. on fin. disclosure, 1998—, jud. coun. of 10th cir., 1999—2001, 10th cir. adv. coun., 2002—; adj. prof. Okla. U. Sch. Law, 2000—. Co-author: 4 Days, 40 Hours, 1970. Rep. Party candidate for lt. gov. of Okla.; minority leader Okla. State Senate, 1985-86; White House mil. aide, Washington, 1966-67; ex officio mem. Okla. State Fair Bd., Oklahoma City, 1987-90; mem. Gov.'s Coun. on Sports and Phys. Edn., Oklahoma City, 1987-89; mem. Donna Nigh Found., Edmond, Okla., 1987-9. Lt. USN, 1965-68. Named Outstanding Legislator, Okla. Sch. Bd. Assn., 1988. Fellow ABA; mem. Okla. Bar Assn., Okla. County Bar, Phi Alpha Delta, Beta Theta Pi. Republican. Presbyterian. Avocations: golf, basketball, running, reading. Office: US Courthouse 200 NW 4th St Ste 5012 Oklahoma City OK 73102-3031

LEONARD, WILL ERNEST, JR., lawyer; b. Shreveport, La., Jan. 18, 1935; s. Will Ernest and Nellie (Kenner) L.; m. Maureen Laniak; children—Will Ernest III, Sherry Elizabeth, Robert Scott, Stephen Michael, Christopher Anthony, Colleen Mary, Leigh Alison. BA, Tulane U., 1956, LLB, 1958; LLM, Harvard U., 1966. Bar: La. 1958, D.C. 1963, U.S. Supreme Ct. 1963. Announcer sta. WVUE-TV, New Orleans, 1958-60; legislative asst. to U.S. Senator Russell B. Long, 1960-65; profl. staff mem. com. fin. U.S. Senate, 1966-68; mem. Internat. Trade Commn. (formerly U.S. Tariff Commn.), 1968-77, chmn., 1975-76; ptnr. Adduci, Mastriani & Schaumberg, LLP, Washington, 2001—. Congl. staff fellow Am. Polit. Sci. Assn., 1965-66 Administrative and regulatory, Private international, Public international. Home: 7324 Bradley Blvd Bethesda MD 20817-2130 Office: Adduci Mastriani & Schaumberg LLP Ste 500 1200 17th St NW Washington DC 20036

LEONHARD, MATTHEW BRENT, prosecutor; s. George Ludwig and Rubye Hannah Leonhard; m. Carolyn E. Eyestone, Aug. 10, 1997. BA, West. Wash. U.; JD, U. of Wash., Seattle, 1997. Bar: Wash. 1997. Lead pub. defender Confederated Tribes of the Colville Reservation, Nespelem, Wash., 1997—99; chief prosecutor White Mountain Apache Tribe, Whiteriver, Ariz., 1999—2002; spl. asst. u.s. atty. US Atty Office, Phoenix, 2000—02; dep. pros. atty. City of Walla Walla, Walla Walla, Wash., 2002—; pvt. practice Walla Walla, Wash., 2003—. Mem. promotions com. Downtown Walla Walla Found., Wash., 2002—03; v.p. cmty. devel. Walla Walla Jaycees, 2002—03; commr. Walla Walla Planning Commn., 2003—; bd. mem. Blue Mt. Land Trust, Walla Walla, 2003—. Recipient Outstanding Grad. in Philosophy, Western Wash. U., 1993. Mem.: ABA. Democrat. Office: 128 N 2nd Ste 201 Walla Walla WA 99362 Office Fax: 509-525-5982. Personal E-mail: mbleonhard@hotmail.com.

LEON-SOTOMAYOR, JOSE RAFAEL, lawyer, engineer, educator; b. Ponce, P.R., Aug. 27, 1930; s. Jose León and Olga Sotomayor; m. Carmen D. Ribas-Rivera, Dec. 11, 1954; children: Jose R., Teresa, Allen L., Carlos J., Carmen L., Candida M., David A., Juan E., Glorimar, Carmen D., Olga G. BSME, U. P.R., 1954; JD magna cum laude, Cath. U., P.R., 1970. Bar: P.R. 1970, U.S. Dist. Ct. P.R. 1973, U.S. Supreme Ct., 1985, U.S. Ct. Mil. Appeals, 1987. Pvt. practice, Ponce, P.R., 1970—; assoc. prof. Cath. U. Sch. Law, Ponce, P.R., 1977-93, prof., 1993-99. Spl. cons., v.p. fin. affairs, 1977-84; cons., lectr. in law. Author: Casebook on Notarial Law, 1984, Puerto Rico Real Property Law Manual, 1984, Family Law in Puerto Rico; contbr. articles to profl. jours. V.p., bd. trustees Ponce Med. Sch. Found., 1979-93; legal cons. com. on civil legislation Ho. of Reps. of Legislature P.R., 1982-84. Capt. USAF. Decorated Knight Cmdr. Equestrian, Order Holy Sepulcher Jerusalem; recipient Ponce Bar Assn. award 1970, Outstanding Alumni award Cath. U. P.R., 1983. Mem. ATLA, ASME, P.R. Bar Assn. (award 1970), Acad. Arts, History and Archaeology P.R., Coll. Engrs. and Surveyors P.R., Deportivo de Ponce (treas. 1975-77, v.p. 1977-78), Ponce Yacht & Fishing Club, Williams Shooting Club, KC, Phi Delta Kappa, Phi Alpha Delta, Nu Sigma Beta. Republican. Roman Catholic. Personal injury (including property damage), Product liability, Property, real (including real estate development, water). Home: 1162 Avila St La Rambla Ponce PR 00730-4026 Office: Marvesa Bldg 472 Tito Castro Ave Ste 201 Ponce PR 00716-4702

LEONTSINIS, GEORGE JOHN, lawyer; b. St. Louis, Feb. 23, 1937; s. John Peter and Lula (Lorandos) L.; m. Patricia Marie Demetrulias, July 9, 1967; children: Anne Marie, Michelle Lynne. BSBA, Washington U., St. Louis, 1958, JD, 1961; LLM, NYU, 1964. Bar: Mo. 1961. Ptnr. Greensfelder, Hemker & Gale, P.C., St. Louis, 1964—. Bd. dirs. Ahepa Apts., St. Louis, 1985-95, Citizens for Modern Transit, St. Louis, 1988-96, Citizen's com. high speed rail Chgo.-St. Louis Corridor, Springfield, Ill., 1992-96. Capt. U.S. Army, 1961-63. Mem. Am. Hellenic Ednl. and Profl. Assn., Racquet Club. Avocation: tennis. Commercial, contracts (including sales of goods; commercial financing), Corporate, general, Private international. Office: Greensfelder Hemker & Gale P C 10 S Broadway Saint Louis MO 63102-1712

LEOPOLD, MARK F. lawyer; b. 1950; s. Paul F. and Corinne (S.) L.; m. Jacqueline Rood, June 9, 1974; children: Jonathan, David. BA, Am. U., Washington, 1972; JD, Loyola U., 1975. Bar: Ill. 1975, U.S. Dist. Ct. (no. dist.) Ill. 1975, Fla. 1976, U.S. Ct. Appeals (7th cir.) 1976, U.S. Ct. Appeals (8th cir.) 1979. Assoc. McConnell & Campbell, Chgo., 1975-79; atty. U.S. Gypsum Co., Chgo., 1979-82, sr. litigation atty., 1982-84, USG Corp., Chgo., 1985-87, corp. counsel, 1987, sr. corp. counsel, 1987-89; asst. gen. counsel G.D. Searle & Co., 1989-93, Household Internat., Inc., Prospect Heights, Ill., 1993—. Mem. adv. bd. Roosevelt U. Legal Asst. Program, 1994-2000; legal writing instr. Loyola U. Sch. Law, Chgo., 1978-79. Pres., bd. dirs. Internat. Policyholders Assn., 1992-93; del. candidate Rep. Nat. Conv., 1996; mem. Lake County Study Commn. II, Waukegan, Ill., 1989-90; commr. Lake County, Waukegan, 1982-84, Forest Preserve, Libertyville, Ill., 1982-84, Pub. Bldg. Commn., Waukegan, 1980-82; chmn. Deerfield Twp. Rep. Cen. Com., Highland Park, Ill., 1984-86, officer, 1981-89; vice chmn. Lake County Rep. Cen. Com., Waukegan, 1982-84; bd. dirs. Am. Jewish Com., Chgo., 1988-91, A Safe Place, Lake County, Ill., 2001—. Recipient Disting. Svc. award Jaycees, Highland Park, 1983. Mem. ABA, (antitrust com. 1976—, litigation com. 1980—, torts and ins. practice com. 1989—), Pi Sigma Alpha, Omicron Delta Kappa. Republican. Antitrust, Commercial, consumer (including collections, credit), Labor (including EEOC, Fair Labor Standards Act, labor-management relations, NLRB, OSHA). Office: Household Internat 2700 Sanders Rd Prospect Heights IL 60070-2701

LEPELSTAT, MARTIN L. lawyer; b. Bklyn., Apr. 10, 1947; s. Larry and Nana (Citrin) L.; m.. Audrey A. Fireman, Jan. 18, 1975; children: Rachel M., Michael H. BBA, CCNY, 1968; JD, Cornell U., 1971; MBA, U. Mich., 1970; LLM, NYU, 1976. Bar: N.J. 1978, N.Y. 1972, Fla. 1972. Tax cons. Touche Ross, N.Y.C., 1971-73; assoc. Weil, Gotshal & Manges, N.Y.C., 1973-78, Greenbaum, Rowe, Smith, Woodbridge, N.J., 1978—. Bd. dirs. Winston Towers 300 Assn., Inc., Cliffside Park, N.J., 1978-86. Fellow Am. Coll. of Trust and Estate Counsel, 1991—; mem. ABA (tax and real estate probate com.), N.J. State Bar Assn., Middlesex County Bar Assn. (pres. tax com. 1987-88, pres. probate com. 1986-87, trustee 1988-92), Fla. Bar Assn. Estate planning, Corporate taxation, Estate taxation. Home: 20 Snoden Ln Watchung NJ 07069-6253 Office: Greenbaum Rowe Smith PO Box 5600 Woodbridge NJ 07095-0988 E-mail: mlepelstat@greenbaumlaw.com.

LEPER, PAUL, lawyer; b. Newark, Jan. 2, 1940; JD, Seton Hall Law Sch., 1962. Pvt. practice, 1995—2001; ptnr. O'Hansen, Meriks, & Barrington, 2001—03. Mem. editl. bd. Rev. Law Jour. Mem.: ABA, Kiwanis (pres. local chpt.), Rotary. Banking, Bankruptcy. Office: O'Hansen Meriks & Barrington 1220 Franklin Ave Ashland OH 44805

LERER, NEAL M. lawyer; b. Chelmsford, Mass., June 20, 1954; m. Rose P. Meegan, July 28, 1991; children: Scott Harold, Benjamin Joseph. BA, Brown U., 1976; JD, Duke Law Sch., 1979. Bar: Mass. 1979, U.S. Dist. Ct. Mass. 1980, U.S. Ct. Appeals (1st cir.) 1991. With Martin, Magnuson, McCarthy & Kenney, Boston, 1980-96; mng. atty., pvt. practice Chelmsford, Mass., 1996—. Corporator Lowell (Mass.) 5 Cents Savings Bank, 1985—. Co-author: Personal Injury and Death, 1980, Damages in Massachusetts, 1990, Personal Injury Litigation in Massachusetts, 1991, Premises Liability, 1994. Reader Recording for the Blind, Cambridge, Mass., 1987-94; bd. dirs. Goodwin Fund; dir. Town of Chelmsford Scholarship Com. Mem. Mass. Bar Assn., Mass. Bar Found., Greater Lowell Bar Assn., Brown Club of Boston (bd. dirs., co-pres. 1998-2000). General civil litigation, Insurance, Personal injury (including property damage). Home: 4 Manahan St Chelmsford MA 01824-2844 E-mail: neallerer@aol.com.

LERMAN, AVERIL, lawyer, legal historian; b. Denver, Aug. 11, 1953; d. Leonard Solomon and Claire (Lindegren) L.; m. Sen Kwang Tan, June 16, 1984; children: Rushi Lerman-Tan, Yinshi Lerman-Tan. BA, Brandeis U., 1976; JD, Northeastern U., 1982. Bar: Alaska 1983. Law clk. Alaska Superior Ct., Anchorage, 1982-83; assoc. Middleton, Timme & McKay, Anchorage, 1983-87; sole practitioner Anchorage, 1987-89; assoc. Preston, Gates & Ellis, Anchorage, 1989-92; sole practitioner Anchorage, 1993-98; asst. pub. advocate Office of Pub. Advocate, Anchorage, 1998—. Legal historian, Anchorage, 1993—; adj. lectr. U. Alaska, Anchorage, 1995, Justice Dept., Anchorage, 1996; speaker in field. Author articles, hist. papers. NEH grantee, 1995. Mem. Alaska Bar Assn. (law examiners com. 1989-92, historians com. 1998-2002). Appellate, Constitutional, Criminal. Office: Office of Pub Advocacy 900 W 5th Ave Ste 525 Anchorage AK 99501-2048 E-mail: averil_lerman@admin.state.ak.us.

LERMAN, HERBERT S. lawyer; b. Cambridge, Mass., Mar. 15, 1938; s. Isaac and Anna (Wilner) L.; m. Ellen, July 1, 1962; children: David, Jonathan, Jennifer. AB, Brown U., 1959; LLB, New Eng. Sch. Law, 1962. Bar: Mass. 1962, U.S. Dist. Ct. Mass. 1963, U.S. Tax Ct. 1972, U.S. Ct. Appeals (1st cir.) 1985, U.S. Supreme Ct. 1986. Assoc. Nathanson & Rudofsky, Boston, 1962-64, Stanley Barron, Boston, 1964-66; ptnr. Lerman & Mann, Brookline, Mass., 1966—; lectr. real estate assns. including Rental Housing Assn. and Boston Real Estate. Bd. dirs. Congregation Mishkan Tefila, Newton, Mass., 1979—, dir. Brotherhood, 1966—, pres., 1972-73; mem. Brookline Ct. Centennial Com., 1982, Oak Hill Park Assn., Newton,

1963-95; apptd. to Newton Ambulance Com., 1976; mem. Jewish Big Bros. Assn.; trustee Boston Children's Theatre, 1980-90, corporator, 1990—; v.p. B'nai B'rith Realty Lodge, 1985-91; mem. Framingham Zoning Bd. of Appeals, 2001—. Recipient Am. Jurisprudence prize, 1962, Jack Wilson Meml. award, 1984, B'nai B'rith awards 1985, 87, spl. citation Sec. of Commonwealth of Mass., 1984, Spl. citation State Senate, 2001. Fellow Mass. Bar Assn. (trustee, property sect., condominium law subcom., chmn. landlord-tenant law subcom., 21st Century Club); mem. Norfolk County Bar, Am. Judicature Soc., Am. Arbitration Assn., Mens Aux. (life), Recuperative Ctr. Assn. Author: Residential Landlord-Tenant Law: A Modern Massachusetts Guide, 1977; contbg. author: Residential and Commercial Landlord-Tenant Practice in Massachusetts, 2002; developer standard leasing form for Rental Housing Assn. Landlord-tenant, Probate (including wills, trusts), Property, real (including real estate development, water). Home: 44 Dinsmore Ave Framingham MA 01702-6010 Office: 1415 Beacon St Brookline MA 02446-4816

LERMAN, KENNETH B. lawyer; s. Robert Allan and Ellen Lerman. BA in Bus. Mgmt. and Govt., Clark U., 1983; JD, Emory U., 1986. Bar: Conn. 1987, U.S. Dist. Ct. Conn. 1987, Fla. 1997. Assoc. Siegel, O'Connor, Schiff, Zangari & Kainen, Hartford, Conn., 1986-88; pvt. practice Kenneth B. Lerman, P.C., Windsor, Conn., 1988—, Boca Raton, Fla., 1997—. Counsel Conn. chpt. Sickle Cell Disease Assn. of Am., 1991—. Co-founder, v.p. Wadsworth Atheneum Art Club, Hartford, 1990-93; exec. com. Hartford chpt. Anti-Defamation League, 1993—; founder, coach, pres. Lacrosse team Clark U., 1981-83; bd. dirs. S. Plumb Dance Co., Hartford, 1999-2001; dir. amb. recruitment Hugh O'Brian Youth Leadership Found. of Conn., 1999-2000; v.p., dir. club divsn. New Eng. Intercollegiate Lacrosse Assn., 1983. Mem. ABA, Fla. Bar Assn., Conn. Bar Assn., Hartford County Bar Assn. Corporate, general, Property, real (including real estate development, water), Securities. Office: 651 Day Hill Rd Windsor CT 06095-1719 also: 6100 Glades Rd Ste 310 Boca Raton FL 33434

LERNER, ALAN JAY, lawyer; b. Scranton, Pa., July 29, 1949; s. Jack and Dorothy Rene (Golob) L.; m. Mary Alicia Kincaid, Nov. 9, 1979; children— Hailey, Joan; m. Estelle Fields, Dec. 21, 1970 (div. Apr. 1978); children— Sonia, Bernadette. B.A. in Polit. Sci. cum laude, San Fernando Valley Coll., 1971; J.D. magna cum laude, U. Toledo, 1974. Bar: Mont. 1974, U.S. Dist. Ct. Mont. 1975, U.S. Ct. Appeals (9th cir.) 1975, U.S. Supreme Ct. 1984. Assoc. Crowley Law Firm, Billings, Mont., 1974-75, Hartelius & Lewin, Great Falls, Mont., 1975-76; ptnr. Richter & Lerner, 1976-81; sole practice, Bigfork, Mont., 1981-88; sole practice Kalispell, Mont., 1988-2002; ptnr. Lerner & Danno, Kalispell, 2002--. Author U. Toledo Law Rev., 1973, editor, 1974. Author: (novel) Spare Parts, 1980. Teaching fellow U. Toledo, 1973; Ohio State Bar scholar, 1972, PAD Nat. scholar, 1973. Mem. Assn. Trial Lawyers Am., Mont. Trial Lawyers Assn., Mont. Bar Assn., N.W. Mont. Bar Assn. Democrat. Jewish. State civil litigation, Insurance, Personal injury (including property damage). Home: 88 Stafford St Kalispell MT 59901-2729 Office: PO Box 1158 Kalispell MT 59901-7532 E-mail: lerner@centurytel.net.

LERNER, MAX KASNER, lawyer; b. N.Y.C., Dec. 27, 1916; s. Louis Lerner and Beckie Kasner; m. Lila Schachner, Oct. 5, 1943; children: Helene, Beth. LLB, Bklyn. Law Sch., 1939. Bar: N.Y. 1940, U.S. Supreme Ct. 1952. Author: ABA Journal of Limitations Imposed on Radio and TV, 1949. Criminal, Probate (including wills, trusts), Trademark and copyright. Home: 350 1st Ave New York NY 10010-4902

LERNER, WILLIAM C. lawyer; b. Phila., July 17, 1933; s. Al and Tillie (Goodman) L.; BA, Cornell U., 1955; LLB, NYU, 1960; m. G. Billie Campbell, Aug. 15, 1957; children: Bonnie, Edwina. Bar: N.Y. 1961, Pa. 1992. Atty. SEC, 1960-65; asst. v.p. Am. Stock Exch., 1965-68; sr. v.p., sec. Carter, Berlind & Weill, Inc. (predecessor to Smith Barney, Inc.), N.Y.C., 1968-71; practicing atty., Buffalo, 1971-85, counsel Snow, Becker & Krauss, P.C., N.Y.C., 1990-95, practicing atty. Washington, Pa., 1990—; v.p., gen. counsel The Geneva Cos., Irvine, Calif., 1986-89, Hon. Devel. Co., Laguna Hills, Calif., 1990-91; bd. dir. Seitel, Inc., Rent-Way, Inc., Micros-to-Mainframes, Inc., The Cortland Fund. Chmn. Erie County Pub. Utilities Task Force, 1974-75; mem. Art Coll. Coun. Cornell U. , 1977-85, N.Y. Gov.'s Hazardous Waste Facilities Task Force, 1983-85. 1st lt. Q.M.C., U.S. Army, 1955-57. Mem. ABA, N.Y. State Bar Assn. Corporate, general, Securities. Office: 423 E Beau St Washington PA 15301-3605 also: 5905 La Rosa Ln Apollo Beach FL 33572-2908

LEROY, DAVID HENRY, lawyer, state and federal official; b. Seattle, Aug. 16, 1947; s. Harold David and Lela Fay (Palmer) L.; 2 children. BS, U. Idaho, 1969, JD, 1971; LL.M., NYU, 1972; JD (hon.), Lincoln Coll., 1993. Bar: Idaho 1971, N.Y. State 1973, U.S. Supreme Ct. 1976. Law clk. Idaho 4th Dist. Ct., Boise, 1969; legal asst. Boise Cascade Corp., 1970; asso. firm Rothblatt, Rothblatt, Seijas & Peskin, N.Y.C., 1971-73; dep. prosecutor Ada County Prosecutor's Office, Boise, 1973-74, pros. atty., 1974-78; atty. gen. State of Idaho, Boise, 1978-82, lt. gov., 1983-87; ptnr. Runft, Leroy Coffin & Matthews, 1983-88, Leroy Law Offices, 1988—. Candidate for Gov. of Idaho, 1986, U.S. Congress, 1994; U.S. nuc. waste negotiator, 1990-93; U.S. Presdl. elector, 1992; chmn. com. on improving practices for regulatory and mng. low-activity radioactive waste NAS, 2002--; lectr., cons. in field. Mem. State Task Force on Child Abuse, 1975; mem. Ada County Coun. on Alcoholism, 1976; del. Rep. Nat. Conv., 1976, 80, 84; chmn. Nat. Rep. Lt. Gov.'s Caucus, 1983-86; bd. dirs. United Fund, 1975-81; del. Am. Coun. Young Polit. Leaders, USSR, 1979, Am. Coun. for Free Asia, Taiwan, 1980, U.S./Taiwan Investment Forum, 1983; del. leader Friendship Force Tour USSR, 1984; legal counsel Young Reps., 1974-81; candidate for Gov. Idaho, 1986; presdl. elector, 1992; candidate U.S. Ho. Reps. 1st Dist, Idaho, 1994. Mem. Nat. Dist. Attys. Assn., Idaho Prosecutors Assn., Am. Trial Lawyers Assn., Idaho Trial Lawyers Assn., Nat. Assn. Attys. Gen. (chmn. energy subcom., exec. com., del to China 1981), Western Attys. Gen. Assn. (vice chmn. 1980-83, chmn. 1981), Nat. Lt. Govs. Assn. (exec. bd. 1983), Idaho Bar Assn., Ada County Lincoln Day Assn. (pres. 2000), Found. for Idaho History (pres. 2001--), NAS (chmn. com. on improving practices for regulating and mng. low activity radioactive waste 2002-), Sigma Alpha Epsilon. Presbyterian. Administrative and regulatory, Government contracts and claims, Legislative. Office: The Leroy Offices PO Box 193 Boise ID 83701-0193 E-mail: dave@dleroy.com.

LESAGE, TRACY ROCHELLE, lawyer; b. Upland, Calif., Mar. 16, 1969; d. Thomas Raphael and Barbara Jean (Douglas) McKinney; m. Robert W. LeSage, Jan. 14, 1995; children: Taylor W., Carson T. BA, UCLA, 1991; JD, Western State U., Fullerton, Calif., 1995. Bar: Calif. 1996, U.S. Dist. Ct. (ctrl. dist.) Calif. 1997, U.S. Ct. Appeals (9th cir.) 1998. Dep. pub. defender Orange County Pub. Defender's Office, Newport Beach, Calif., 2000—. Contbr. to Western State U. Law Rev., 1994. Mem. ATLA, Orange County Bar Assn., William P. Gray Legion Lex Inns of Ct. Personal injury (including property damage). Office: Orange County Pub Defender 4601 Jamboree Rd Ste 101 Newport Beach CA 92660

LESCH, MICHAEL OSCAR, lawyer; b. Berlin, May 28, 1938; came to U.S., 1940, naturalized, 1946; s. Adolf F. and Maria E. Leschnitzer; m. Judith Willis, Aug. 31, 1965; children: Sara, Benjamin. AB, Columbia U., 1958; LLB, Harvard U., 1961. Bar: N.Y. 1961, U.S. Dist. Ct. (so. dist.) N.Y. 1963, U.S. Dist. Ct (ea. dist.) N.Y. 1965, U.S. Ct. Appeals (2d cir.) 1968, U.S. Supreme Ct. 1975, U.S. Ct. Appeals (3d cir.) 1979, U.S. Ct. Appeals (7th cir.) 1979, U.S. Ct. Appeals (9th cir.) 2001. Assoc. Shea & Gould and predecessors, N.Y.C., 1961-69, ptnr., 1970-94, LeBoeuf, Lamb, Greene & MacRae, N.Y.C., 1994—. Dir. Apple Bank for Savs., N.Y.C., 2001—. Contbr. articles to profl. jours. Mem. ABA, N.Y. State Bar Assn., Assn. Bar City N.Y., Fed. Bar Coun., Am. Arbitration Assn. (panel of arbitrators). Federal civil litigation, State civil litigation. Office: LeBoeuf Lamb Greene & MacRae 125 W 55th St New York NY 10019-5369

LESHER, STEPHEN HARRISON, lawyer; b. Tucson, Dec. 31, 1953; s. Robert Overton and June Ruth (Huffer) L. BA, U. Vt., 1975; JD, U. Ariz., 1978. Bar: Ariz. 1978, U.S. Dist. Ct. Ariz. 1978, U.S. Ct. Appeals (9th cir.) 1991. Assoc. Lesher & Kimble PC, Tucson, 1978-79; ptnr. Lesher, Clausen & Borodkin PC, Tucson, 1980-83, Lesher & Borodkin PC, Tucson, 1983-91, Lesher & Williams, Tucson, 1991-93, Lesher & Lesher, Tucson, 1993-99, Kimble, Lesher & Corradini, Tucson, 1999—. Mem. Am. Bd. Trial Advocates, Def. Rsch. Inst. Republican. Avocation: computers. Appellate, General civil litigation, Insurance. Home: 5667 N Via Salerosa Tucson AZ 85750-1154 E-mail: shl@klclaw.com.

LESHNER, STEPHEN I. lawyer; b. N.Y.C., Sept. 26, 1951; s. Leo and Gloria (Perlman) L.; m. Mary Ann Relles, Oct. 28, 1978; children: Samuel Joseph, Harry Jacob. BA, SUNY, Stony Brook, 1973; JD, Northeastern U., 1976. Bar: Ariz. 1976, U.S. Dist. Ct. Ariz. 1977, U.S. Ct. Appeals (9th cir.) 1981, U.S. Supreme Ct. 1980. Assoc. Legal Clinic Bates & O'Steen, Phoenix, 1977; ptnr. O'Steen Legal Clinic, Phoenix, 1977-80, Van, O'Steen and Ptnrs., Phoenix, 1980—. Criminal law specialist, Ariz. Bd. Legal Specialization, 1982-95, injury and wrongful death litigation specialist, 1991—; judge pro tem Maricopa County Superior Ct., 1993—. Mem. Assn. Trial Lawyers Am., Ariz. Trial Lawyers Assn. (bd. dirs., pres. 1999), Am. Bd. Trial Advocates, State Bar Ariz. Assn., Nucleus Club (chmn. 1995-96). Personal injury (including property damage), Product liability. Office: Van O'Steen and Ptnrs 3605 N 7th Ave Phoenix AZ 85013-3638 E-mail: sleshner@vanosteen.com.

LESHY, JOHN DAVID, lawyer, legal educator, government official; b. Winchester, Ohio, Oct. 7, 1944; s. John and Dolores (King) L.; m. Helen M. Sandalls, Dec. 15, 1973; 1 child, David Alexander. AB cum laude, Harvard U., 1966, JD magna cum laude, 1969. Trial atty. Civil Rights Divsn. Dept. Justice, Washington, 1969-72; atty. Natural Resources Def. Coun., Palo Alto, Calif., 1972-77; assoc. solicitor energy and resources Dept. Interior, Washington, 1977-80; prof. law Ariz. State U., Tempe, 1980—2002; spl. counsel to chair Natural Resources Com. U.S. Ho. Reps., Washington, 1992-93; solicitor (gen. counsel) Dept. Interior, 1993-2001. Cons. Calif. State Land Commn., N.Mex. Atty. Gen., Western Govs. Assn., Congl. Rsch. Svc., Ford Found., Hewlett Found., Pew Charitable Trusts, Wyss Found.; mem. com. Onshore Oil & Gas Leasing, NAS Nat. Rsch. Coun., 1989-90; vis. prof. Sch. Law U. San Diego, 1990; disting. vis. prof. law U. Calif. Hastings Coll. Law, 2001-02; disting. prof. law, U. Calif. Hastings, 2002-. Author: The Mining Law: A Study in Perpetual Motion, 1987, The Arizona State Constitution, 1993; co-author Federal Public Land and Resources Law, 5th edit., 2002, Legal Control of Water Resources, 3rd edit., 2000; contbr. articles, book chpts. to profl. jours., environ. jours. Bd. dirs. Ariz. Ctr. Law in Pub. Interest, 1981—86, Grand Canyon Trust, 1987—92, 2002—, Natural Heritage Inst., 2002—, Ariz. Raft Adventures, 1982—92, 2002—; mem. Gov.'s Task Force Recreation on Fed. Lands, 1985—86, Gov.'s Task Force Environ. Impact Assessment, 1990, City of Phoenix Environ. Quality Commn., 1987—90; pres. Wyss Found., 2002—. Robinson Cox vis. fellow U. Western Australia Law Sch., Perth, 1985, rsch. fellow U. Southampton, Eng., 1986; Ford Found. grantee, Resources for the Future grantee. Democrat. Avocations: piano, hiking, whitewater rafting, photography. Office: Hastings Coll Law 200 McAllister St San Francisco CA 94102-4978 E-mail: leshyj@uchastings.edu.

LESICK, JOHN RICHARD, lawyer, consultant, retired lawyer; b. Homestead, Pa., June 11, 1917; s. Michael Joseph Lesick and Mary Teresa Gavalek; m. Mary Eleanor Gillespie, May 29, 1942; children: John Richard II, Lawrence Thomas. BA, Ohio Wesleyan U., 1941; grad., U.S. Naval Sch., Port Hueneme, Calif., 1946; LLB, U. Cin., 1948. Bar: Ohio 1949. Lawyer, Cin., 1949—; ins. salesman W.E. Lord Co., Cin., 1952—56; assoc. C.L. Scroggins Assocs., Cin., 1957—62; pres. Profl. Mgmt. Assn. Inc., Cin., 1963—90; ret. Contbr. articles to profl. jours. Co-founder Village of Forest Park; vol., chmn. bd. Forest Park Hist. Soc.; mem. Forest Park Hall of Fame Commn.; pres. pro-tem City of Forest Park, Ohio, coun. mem. Maj. USMC, 1941—46, PTO. Republican. Avocations: writing, sports, public speaking. Home: 509 Curly Maple Sq Cincinnati OH 45246-4170

LESK, ANN BERGER, lawyer; b. N.Y.C., Feb. 7, 1947; d. Alexander and Eleanor A. (Dickinson) Berger; m. Michael E. Lesk, June 30, 1968. AB cum laude, Radcliffe Coll., 1968; JD with high honors, Rutgers U., 1977. Bar: N.Y. 1979. Law clk. to justice N.J. Supreme Ct., Mountain, 1977-78; assoc. Fried, Frank, Harris, Shriver & Jacobson, N.Y.C., 1978-84, ptnr., 1984—. Editor-in-chief Rutgers Law Rev., 1976-77. Mem.: ABA, Assn. of the Bar of City of N.Y. (com. trusts, estates and surrogates cts. 1992—95, 2000—), N.Y. State Bar Assn., New York County Lawyer's Assn. (co-chair com. trusts and estates sect. 1998—2001, co-chair com. trusts and estates legislation and govtl. affairs 1995—98). Estate planning, Probate (including wills, trusts). Office: Fried Frank Harris Shriver & Jacobson 1 New York Plz Fl 22 New York NY 10004-1980

LESLIE, HENRY ARTHUR, lawyer, retired banker; b. Troy, Ala., Oct. 15, 1921; s. James B. and Alice (Minchener) L.; m. Anita Doyle, Apr. 5, 1943; children: Anita Lucinda Leslie Bagby, Henry Arthur Jr. BS, U. Ala., 1942, JD, 1948; JSD, Yale U., 1959; grad., Rutgers U., 1964. Bar: Ala. 1948. Asst. prof. bus. law U. Ala., 1948-50, 52-54; prof., asst. dean U. Ala. Sch. Law, 1954-59; v.p. trust officer Birmingham Trust Nat. Bank, Ala., 1959-64; sr. v.p., trust officer Union Bank & Trust Co., Montgomery, Ala., 1964-73, sr. v.p., sr. loan officer, 1973-76, exec. v.p., 1976-78, pres. CEO, 1978-91, also bd. dirs.; ret., 1991; pvt. practice, 1991—. Mem. Ala. Oil and Gas Bd., 1984-85. Pres. Downtown Unltd., 1983-84; mem. Ala. Bd. Bar Examiners, 1973-78, bd. dirs. YMCA, 1992—; mem., vice-chmn. Ala. Jud. Campaign Oversight Com., 1999-2001. Decorated Bronze Star. Mem. ABA, Ala. Bar Assn., Montgomery Bar Assn. (Liberty Bell award 1989), Ala. Ind. Bankers (chmn. 1983-84), Ala. Bankers Assn. (trust div. pres. 1963-65), Ind. Bankers Assn. Am. (dir. 1983-90), Farrah Order Jurisprudence (pres. 1973), Order of Coif Alumni, Newcomen Soc. N.Am., Montgomery C. of C. (dir. 1983-84, pres. 1987-88), Maxwell Officers Club, Montgomery Country Club, Kiwanis, Delta Sigma Pi, Phi Delta Phi, Omicron Delta Kappa, Pi Kappa Phi. Episcopalian (past sr. warden). Banking, Estate planning, Probate (including wills, trusts). Home: 3332 Boxwood Dr Montgomery AL 36111-1702

LESLIE, ROBERT LORNE, lawyer; b. Adak, Ala., Feb. 24, 1947; s. J. Lornie and L. Jean (Conelly) L.; children: Lorna Jean, Elizabeth Allen. BS, U.S. Mil. Acad., 1969; JD, U. Calif., San Francisco, 1974. Bar: Calif. 1974, D.C. 1979, U.S. Dist. Ct. (no. dist.) Calif. 1974, U.S. Ct. Claims 1975, U.S. Tax Ct. 1975, U.S. Ct. Appeals (9th and D.C. cirs.) 1974, U.S. Ct. Mil. Appeals 1980, U.S. Supreme Ct. 1980. Commd. 2d lt. U.S. Army, 1969, advanced through grades to maj., 1980; govt. trial atty. West Coast Field Office, Contract Appeals, Litigation and Regulatory Law divsns., Office JAG, Dept. Army, San Francisco, 1974-77; sr. trial atty., team chief Office of Chief Trial Atty., Dept. of Amry, Washington, 1977-80; ptnr. McInerney & Dillon, Oakland, Calif., 1980—, 1980—. Lectr. on govt. contracts CSC, Continuing Legal Edn. Program; lectr. in govt. procurement U.S. Army Material Command. Served to col. USAR, ret. Decorated Purple Heart, Silver Star. Mem. ABA, Fed. Bar Assn., Associated Gen. Contractors, The Beavers. Commercial, contracts (including sales of goods; commercial financing), Construction, Government contracts and claims. Office: McInerney & Dillon Ordway Bldg Fl 18 Oakland CA 94612-3610

LESMAN, MICHAEL STEVEN, lawyer; b. N.Y.C., May 26, 1953; s. Herman and Estelle (Levy) L.; m. Gail R. Grossman, May 26, 1980; children: Adam, Laura. BA magna cum laude, CUNY, 1975; JD, Bklyn. Law Sch., 1982. Bar: N.Y. 1983. From assoc. to supervising atty. Jacobowitz & Lysaght, N.Y.C., 1983-88; atty. of record, mng. atty. Jacobowitz, Garfinkel & Lesman, N.Y.C., 1989—. Staff counsel Am. Internat. Cos., N.Y.C., 1989—. Mem. ABA, N.Y. State Bar Assn., N.Y. County Lawyers Assn., Def. Rsch. Inst., N.Y. State Trial Lawyers Assn. State civil litigation, Insurance, Personal injury (including property damage). Office: Jacobowitz Garfinkel & Lesman 110 William St Fl 17 New York NY 10038-3914 E-mail: michael.lesman@aig.com.

LESOURD, NANCY SUSAN OLIVER, lawyer, writer; b. Atlanta, Aug. 22, 1953; d. Carl Samuel and Jane (Meadows) Oliver; m. Jeffrey Alan LeSourd, Oct. 18, 1986; children: Jeffrey Luke, Catherine Victoria. BA in Polit. Sci., Agnes Scott Coll., 1975; MA in History, Edn., Tufts U., 1977; JD, Georgetown U., 1984. Bar: Pa. 1985, D.C. 1986, Va. 1992, Fed. Cir. Ct. Appeals., 1988, U.S. Claims Ct., 1988, U.S. Supreme Ct. Instr. Newton (Mass.) High Sch., 1976-78, The Stony Brook (N.Y.) Sch., 1978-81; assoc. Gammon and Grange, Washington, 1984-88; shareholder Gammon and Grange, P.C., 1988—; mgr. Marshall-LeSourd L.L.C., 1996—. Legal commentator (radio shows) UPI News, Washington, 1985-91, Focus on the Family (Washington corr.), Colorado Springs, Colo., 1987-94; legal columnist Christian Mgmt. Rev., Downers Grove, Ill., 1987-90; spkr. numerous confs. Author: No Longer The Hero, 1992, Underground Railroad, 2003, Story of Pocahontas, 2003, Civil War Spies, 2003, Pearl Harbor, 2003, (children's book) Christmastime in Cutter Gap, 2003; editor: Georgetown Law Jour., 1982-84; contbr. articles to profl. jours.; cons./prodr. three tv movies based on "Christy", 2000—. Founder, vice-chmn. bd. trustees Ambleside Sch., 1998—2001; Bd. dirs. Arlington County Equal Employment Opportunity Commn., 1985. William Robertson Coe fellow SUNY, Stony Brook, 1978. Mem. D.C. Bar Assn., Va. Bar Assn., Christian Legal Society (bd. dirs. 1990-93). Republican. Intellectual property, Trademark and copyright, Non-profit and tax-exempt organizations. Home: 2624 New Banner Ln Herndon VA 20171-2659 Office: Gammon and Grange PC 8280 Greensboro Dr Fl 7 Mc Lean VA 22102-3807 E-mail: nol@gandglaw.com.

LESSENCO, GILBERT BARRY, lawyer; b. Balt., June 19, 1929; s. Jacob David and Sarah (Bank) L.; m. Elaine Beitler, Sept. 3, 1952; children: Susan Donna, Amy Gail, Robert Howard. BS, Johns Hopkins U.; LLB, Harvard U. Bar: D.C. 1953, Md. 1955. Atty. Wilner and Bergson, Washington, 1955-60; ptnr. Wilner & Scheiner, Washington, 1960-90, Semmes, Bowen & Semmes, Washington, 1990-95, mng. ptnr., 1992-95; of counsel Thompson & Hine , Washington, 1995—. Prof. bus. law and mktg. law Johns Hopkins U. Sch. Profl. Studies in Bus. and Edn., 1997—. Chmn. Internat. Visitors Svc. Coun., 1962; bd. dirs. Mental Health Assn. Montgomery County, 1996, pres., 1981—82; mem. Johns Hopkins U. Com. for Washington, 1996; trustee Meridian Ho. Found.; commr. Washington Suburban San. Commn., 1987—93, chmn., 1989—90; co-chmn., fundraiser St. Luke's Ho., 1989; mem., treas. Dem. Ctrl. Com., Montgomery County, Md., 1970—74; bd. dirs. Jewish Social Svc. Agy. Greater Washington, 1978—, pres., 1984—86. Lt. USAF, 1953—55. Named Outstanding Young Lawyer of Yr., D.C. Jr. Bar, 1965, St. Luke's Ho. Cmty. Leadership award, 2002. Mem. Phi Sigma Delta (v.p.). Administrative and regulatory, Legislative, Probate (including wills, trusts). Home: 10731 Gloxinia Dr Rockville MD 20852-3442 Office: Thompson Hine 1920 N St NW Washington DC 20036-1601 E-mail: gil.lessenco@thompsonhine.com.

LESSER, HENRY, lawyer; b. London, Feb. 28, 1947; came to U.S., 1976; s. Bernard Martin and Valerie Joan (Leslie) L.; m. Jane Michaels, June 29, 1969. BA with honors, Cambridge (Eng.) U., 1968, MA with honors, 1972; LLM, Harvard U., 1973. Bar: Eng. 1969, N.Y. 1977, U.S. Dist. Ct. (so. and ea. dists.) N.Y. 1977, Calif. 1984, U.S. Dist. Ct. (cen. dist.) Calif. 1984. Pvt. practice, London, 1969-71; assoc. Spear & Hill, N.Y.C. and London, 1974-75, Webster & Sheffield, N.Y.C. and London, 1976-77, Wachtell, Lipton, Rosen & Katz, N.Y.C., 1977-80, ptnr., 1980-83, Gibson, Dunn & Cutcher, L.A., 1983-87, Fried, Frank, Harris, Shriver & Jacobson, L.A., 1987-91, Irell & Manella, LLC, L.A., 1991-97, Heller, Ehrman, White & McAuliffe, Palo Alto, Calif., 1997-2000, Gray, Cary, Ware & Freidenrich, Palo Alto, 2000—. Lectr. law Oxford (Eng.) U., 1968-69, Cambridge U., 1970-71, UCLA, 1989. Editor-in-chief emeritus (bi-monthly) Corporate Governance Adviser; contbr. articles to profl. publs. Harkness fellow Commonwealth Fund, N.Y., 1971. Mem. ABA, Internat. Bar Assn., Calif. Bar Assn. (chmn. corps. com. 1990-91, vice chmn. bus. law sect. exec. com. 1993-94), Am. Law Inst., Assn. Bar City N.Y. Avocations: running, golf. Corporate, general, Mergers and acquisitions, Securities. Office: Gray Cary Ware & Freidenrich 400 Hamilton Ave Palo Alto CA 94301-1833 E-mail: hlesser@graycary.com.

LESSER, JOAN L. lawyer; b. L.A. BA, Brandeis U., 1969; JD, U. So. Calif., 1973. Bar: Calif. 1973, U.S. Dist. Ct. (cen. dist.) Calif. 1974. Assoc. Irell and Manella LLP, L.A., 1973-80, ptnr., 1980—. Mem. planning com. Ann. Real Property Inst., Continuing Edn. of Bar, Berkeley, 1990-96; speaker at profl. confs. Trustee Windward Sch., 1994-2000, UCLA Design for Sharing; grad. Leadership L.A., 1992; bd. dirs. L.A. chpt. Legion Lex. Mem. Orgn. Women Execs. (past pres., bd. dirs.), Order of Coif. Corporate, general, Finance, Property, real (including real estate development, water). Office: Irell & Manella LLP 1800 Avenue Of The Stars Los Angeles CA 90067-4276 E-mail: jlesser@irell.com.

LESSER, SETH RICHARD, lawyer; b. N.Y.C., Nov. 14, 1960; s. Joseph and Arlyne (Deutsch) L.; m. Ellis Rosen. AB summa cum laude, Princeton U., 1983; PhD History, Oxford U., 1985; JD magna cum laude, Harvard Law Sch., 1988. Bar: N.J. 1988, N.Y. 1989, D.C. 1990, U.S. Dist. Ct. N.J. 1988, U.S. Dist. Ct. (so. and ea. dists.) N.Y. 1989, U.S. Dist. Ct. D.C. 1990, U.S. Dist. Ct. (D.C. cir.) 1994, U.S. Dist. Ct. (9th cir.) 1997, U.S. Supreme Ct. 1998, U.S. Dist. Ct. (2d cir.) 1998, U.S. Dist. Ct. Colo. 2000, U.S. Dist. Ct. (6th cir.) Colo. 2001, U.S. Dist. Ct. (1st cir.) Colo. 2002. Assoc. atty. Davis Polk & Wardwell, N.Y.C., 1988—96; ptnr. Bernstein Litowitz Berger & Grossmann LLP, N.Y.C., 1996—2002, Law Offices of Gene Locks PLLC, N.Y.C., 2002—. Author: articles to various profl. jours. Recipient Marshall Scholar Marshall Scholarship Commn., U.K., 1983. Mem. ABA, Assn. Bar N.Y.C., Nat. Assn. Consumer Advocates, Assn. of Trial Lawyers Am. Avocations: travel, reading, skiing. General civil litigation. Office: Law Offices of Gene Locks 110 E 55th St New York NY 10022

LESTER, ANDREW WILLIAM, lawyer; b. Mpls., Feb. 17, 1956; s. Richard G. and Marion Louise (Kurtz) L.; m. Barbara Regina Schmitt, Nov. 22, 1978; 1 child, Susan Erika. Student, Ludwig-Maximilians Univ., Munich, 1975-76; BA, Duke U., 1977; MS in Fgn. Service, JD, Georgetown U., 1981. Bar: Okla. 1981, D.C. 1985, Tex. 1990, U.S. Supreme Ct. 1992, Colo. 1995. Cons. Dresser Industries, Inc., Washington, 1979-81; assoc. Conner & Winters, Tulsa, 1981-82; asst. atty. City of Enid, Okla., 1982-84; ptnr. various law firms Enid, Oklahoma City, 1984-96; ptnr. Lester, Loving & Davies P.C., Edmond, 1996—. Adj. prof. Okla. City Univ. Sch. of Law; lectr. in field; U.S. magistrate judge Western Dist. Okla., 1988-96; constl. law specialist Ctrl. and East European Law Initiative, ABA, Ukraine, Belarus and Moldova, 1993; adj. scholar Okla. Coun. Pub. Affairs. Author: Constitutional Law and Democracy, 1994; contbr. book revs. and articles to profl. jours. Intern Office of Senator Bob Dole, Washington, 1977-78; mem. transition team EEOC Office Pres.-Elect Reagan, Washington, 1980-81; chmn. law enforcement and corrections transition team, mem. budget and fin. transition team Office of Gov.-Elect Brad Henry, 2002-03; chmn. Enid Police Civil Service Commn., 1985-87; bd. dirs. Enid Habitat for Humanity, 1986-88, Booker T. Washington Cmty. Ctr., Enid, 1987-90, St. Mary's Episcopal Sch. of Edmond, 1999-2001; mem. bd. advisors Oklahoma City Command Salvation Army, 2002—; mem. Martin Luther King, Jr. Holiday

Commn. of Enid, 1988-91; deacon First Bapt. Ch. of Oklahoma City. Fellow Okla. Bar Found.; mem. Okla. Bar Assn., Colo. Bar Assn., Okla. Assn. Mcpl. Attys. (bd. dirs. 1987-91, 94-98, 2000—, gen. counsel 1987-88, pres. 1988-90), Oklahoma County Bar Assn., Def. Rsch. Inst. (govt. liability com.), Federalist Soc. (vice chmn. civil rights practice group 1996—, pres. Ctrl. Okla. chpt. 1996-99). Republican. Avocations: german language, cartography. Civil rights, General civil litigation, Constitutional. Office: Lester Loving & Davies PC 1505 S Renaissance Blvd Edmond OK 73013-3018 E-mail: alester@lldlaw.com.

LESTER, ARTHUR H. lawyer, obstetrician and gynecologist; b. Cleve., Mar. 5, 1939; s. Samuel and Stella P. (Schwartz) L.; m. Linda A. Wheeler, Feb. 8, 1964; children: Martin, Rebecca, Joseph. BA, Oberlin (Ohio) Coll., 1961; MD, Finch U. Health Scis., 1965; JD, Fla. State U., 1988. Bar: Fla. 1989; diplomate Am. Bd. Ob-Gyn. Intern Albany (N.Y.) Med. Ctr., 1965-66, asst. resident in pathology, 1966-67; resident in ob-gyn. George Washington U., Washington, 1969-72, chief resident, 1971-72; pvt. practice ob-gyn. Ft. Walton Beach, Fla., 1972-98; pvt. practice law, 1989—. Past assoc. med. dir. White Wilson Med. Ctr., also exec. com.; lectr. in field. Contbr. articles to profl. jours. Bd. dirs. Boys Club, Assn. for Retarded Citizens, Cmty.-Based Mental Health Orgn., others. Capt. USAF, 1967-69. Mem. ACOG, Okaloosa-Walton Bar Assn., Fla. Bar Assn., Order of the Coif Avocations: gardening, music, fishing. Health, Personal injury (including property damage). Home: 813 Wagonwheel Rd Fort Walton Beach FL 32547-7304 Office: 88 Eglin Pkwy NE Fort Walton Beach FL 32548-4957

LESTER, ROY DAVID, lawyer; b. Middletown, Ohio, Jan. 16, 1949; s. Edgel Celsus and Norma Marie (Elam) L.; children: Justin David, Benjamin, Jackson. BS, We. Ky. U., 1970; JD, U. Ky., 1975. Bar: Ky. 1975, U.S. Tax Ct. 1979, U.S. Dist. Ct. (ea. dist.) Ky. 1976, U.S. Supreme Ct. 1979. With Stoll, Keenon & Park, Lexington, Ky., 1975—. Mem. YMCA (Lexington), Fayette County Bar Assn., Order of Coif, Lexington Country Club. Republican. Commercial, contracts (including sales of goods; commercial financing), Corporate, general. Office: Stoll Keenon & Park LLP 300 West Vine St Suite 2100 Lexington KY 40507-1380 E-mail: lester@skp.com.

L'ESTRANGE, TIMOTHY I. lawyer; b. Sydney, Australia, Nov. 24, 1955; s. Vincent Joseph and Pamela Mary (McGuigan) L.; m. Elizabeth Jill Campbell; children: Adelaide, Alistair, Alexandra. B of Commerce, U. New South Wales, Sydney, Australia, 1976, LLB, 1978. Assoc. to Justice J.S. Lockhart Fed. Ct. of Australia, Sydney, Australia, 1979-80; ptnr. Allen, Allen & Hemsley, Sydney, Australia, 1987—2001, mng ptnr., 1993-96; ptnr. Allens, Arthur & Robinson, 2001—03; group gen. counsel Anz Bank Ltd., 2003—. Permanent sec. Ct. of Arbitration for Sports, Oceania Divsn., 1996—; bd. mem. Allen, Allen & Hemsley, Sydney, Australia, 2000—. Mem. Internat. Bar Assn., Insolvency Practitioners Assn., Australian Inst. Arbitrators and Mediators. Avocations: golf, rugby union, swimming, walking. Office e-mail: tim.l'estrange@allens.com.au. Antitrust, Alternative dispute resolution, Bankruptcy. Home: 5 Huntington Rd Toorak Melbourne Victoria Australia Office: Allens Arthur & Robinson 2 Chifley Tower Sydney 2000 Australia

LETELIER, JOSE LUIS, lawyer; b. Santiago, Chile, Aug. 6, 1957; s. Francisco Letelier and Lucia Azzari; m. Florencia Larrain, May 16, 1987; children: Jose Vicente, Josefina, Ignacio, Lucia, Maria Teresa, Pedro. LLB, U. Chile, Santiago, 1983; LLM, U. Calif., L.A., 1988. Bar: Chile. Sr. tax dept. Prive Waterhouse, Santiago, 1982—84; atty. Cariola-Sargent & Krahn, Santiago, 1984—87, ptnr., 1987—91; mng. ptnr. Cariola Diez Perez-Cotapos/Sargent & Krahn, Santiago, 1991—. Chmn. bd. dirs. DSM Chile S.A., Santiago, 2000—, Carrefour Chile S.A., Santiago, 2001—; alt. bd. dir. Soprole S.A., Santiago. Mem.: Inst. Trademark Atty., Union Internat. des Avocats, Internat. Bar Assn., Licensing Execs. Soc., European Cmty. Trademark Assn., Internamerican Assn. Intellectual Property. Avocations: golf, skiing, movies, reading. Commercial, contracts (including sales of goods; commercial financing), Corporate, general, Antitrust. Office: Cariola Diez Perez-Cotapos Av Andres Bello 2711 Piso 19 Santiago Chile

LETO, FRANCIS JOSEPH, lawyer, educator; b. Phila., Nov. 3, 1959; s. Francesco and Alice Joan (DeMasi) L.; m. Anita Simone, June 2, 1984; children: Francis Joseph Jr., Christopher Andrew. BA, St. Joseph U., Phila., l98l; JD cum laude, Widener U., l984. Bar: Pa. l984, N.J. 1984. Law clk. Superior Ct. Pa., Norristown, l984-85, sr. rsch. counsel, administrv. asst. to pres. judge Bala Cynwyd, l985-86; ptnr. Celli and Leto LLP, Rosemont, Pa., 1995—. Pres. Brandywine Abstract Co. Ltd., Rosemont, 1988—; prof. law Phila. Inst., l987-98; bd. dirs. Baker Industries, Inc. Contbr. articles to legal publs. Bd. dirs. Southeastern chpt. ARC., Bryn Mawr Trust Co.; bd. trustees Episcopal Acad, Bryn Mawr Hosp. Found. Mem. ABA (subcom. on title ins. l987-88), Pa. Bar Assn., Phila. Bar Assn., Union League, Merion Cricket Club. Republican. Roman Catholic. Avocations: fishing, reading, outdoor activities, squash. Office: 1062 E Lancaster Ave Ste 15L Bryn Mawr PA 19010-1565

LETRÉGUILLY, HERVÉ, lawyer; b. Roven, France, Jan. 1, 1962; s. Alfred Letréguilly and Jacqueline Noailly; m. Sandrine Binet Letréguilly, Apr. 23, 1989; children: Julien, Morgane, Paul. M in Law, U. Rouen, France, 1983; DEA de Droit des Affaires, U. Paris I, 1986. Bar: Paris 1991. Assoc. Hughes, Hubbard & Reed, Paris, 1986—87, Shearman & Sterling, Paris, 1987—96, European counsel, 1997, ptnr., 1998—. Tchr. bus. law U. Paris I, 1996, 97, U. Paris II-Assas, 2001—. Contbr. articles to profl. jours. Mem.: Racing Club de France. Securities, Mergers and acquisitions, Corporate, general. Office: Shearman & Sterling 114 ave des Champs Elysées 75008 Paris France Office Fax: (33-1) 53897070. E-mail: hletreguilly@shearman.com.

LETSON, WILLIAM NORMAND, lawyer; b. N.Y.C., Mar. 24, 1930; s. Benjamin Hugle and Ellen (Skon) L.; m. Barbara C. Briggs, Jan. 22, 1956 (div. May 1980); children: Benjamin B., Katherine L., William C.; m. Brenda Powell, Oct. 10, 1981 (div. Oct. 1995); m. Linda White, Nov. 20, 1999. AB cum laude, Harvard U., 1952, JD magna cum laude, 1955. Bar: Ohio 1955, N.Y. 1956, D.C. 1973, Pa. 1975. Assoc. Shearman & Sterling, N.Y.C., 1955-62; ptnr. Letson, Letson & Kightlinger, Warren, Ohio, 1962-71; gen. counsel U.S. Dept. Commerce, Washington, 1971-73; v.p. gen. counsel, sec. Westinghouse Electric, Pitts., 1973-76; ptnr. Schiff, Hardin & Waite, Washington, 1977-79, Letson, Griffith, Woodall & Lavelle, Warren, Ohio, 1979-86, Letson & Jarrett, Warren, 1986-95, Letson, Griffith, Woodall Lavelle & Rosenberg, L.P.A., 1995—. Mem. Pres. Commn. on Personnel Interchange, Washington, 1976-80; mem. U.S.-USSR Sci. and Tech. Commn., Washington, 1972-73; mem. Harvard Law Review, 1953-55. Mem. State Com. to elect Clarence Brown Gov., 1982; mem. law sch. adv. com. U. Akron, 1981—. Mem. ABA, Ohio State Bar Assn., Warren Area C. of C. (dir. 1984-87), Fox Chapel Golf Club (Pitts.), Trumbull Country Club, Buckeye Club (Warren). Republican. Avocations: skiing, sailing, fly fishing, tennis, golf. Corporate, general, Estate planning, Pension, profit-sharing, and employee benefits. Home: 700 The Greens Warren OH 44484 Office: Letson Griffith Wooddall Lavelle & Rosenberg LPA PO Box 151 155 S Park Ave Warren OH 44482 E-mail: lawfirm@lgwlr.com.

LETTEN, JAMES, prosecutor; married; 2 children. Degree, U. New Orleans, 1976; JD, Tulane Law Sch., 1979. With New Orleans Dist. Attys. Office, 1979—82; with Organized Crime and Racketeering Strike Force Dept. Justice, La., 1982—94; asst. U.S. atty., 1994; interim U.S. atty. ea. dist., 2000—. Office: Hale Boggs Fed Bldg Rm 210 501 Magazine St New Orleans LA 70130 Office Fax: 504-589-4510.*

LETTOW, CHARLES FREDERICK, lawyer; b. Iowa Falls, Iowa, Feb. 10, 1941; s. Carl Frederick and Catherine (Reisinger) L.; m. Sue Lettow, Apr. 20, 1963; children: Renee, Carl II, John, Paul. BS in Chem. Engring., Iowa State U., 1962; LLB, Stanford U., 1968; MA, Brown U., 2001. Bar: Calif. 1969, Iowa 1969, D.C. 1972, Md. 1991. Law clk. to Hon. Ben C. Duniway U.S. Ct. Appeals (9th cir.), San Francisco, 1968-69; law clk. to Hon. Warren E. Burger U.S. Supreme Ct., Washington, 1969-70; counsel Council on Environ. Quality, Washington, 1970-73; assoc. Cleary, Gottlieb, Steen & Hamilton, Washington, 1973-76, ptnr., 1976—. Pres. Busy Way Farms, Inc., 1989—. Contbr. articles to profl. jours. Trustee Potomac Sch., McLean, Va., 1983-90, chmn. bd. trustees, 1985-88. 1st lt. U.S. Army, 1963-65. Mem. ABA, Am. Law Inst., D.C. Bar, Iowa Bar Assn., Order of Coif. Clubs: University. Federal civil litigation, Environmental. Office: 2000 Pennsylvania Ave NW Washington DC 20006-1801 E-mail: clettow@cgsh.com.

LETWIN, JEFFREY WILLIAM, lawyer; b. Pitts., Nov. 26, 1953; s. Myron Harvey and Phyllis Harriet (Unatin) L.; m. Roberta Lee Rosenbloom, July 24, 1983; 1 child, S. Ari; stepchildren: Andrew B. Filipek, Amanda H. Filipek. BA in History and Lit., U. Pitts., 1975; JD, Am. U., 1979. Bar: Pa. 1980, D.C. 1980. Staff atty. Dept. Justice, Washington, 1979-80; assoc. Gilloti, Goldberg & Capristi, Pitts., 1980-83, Finkel, Lefkowitz & Ostrow, Pitts., 1983-85, Rosenberg & Kirshner, Pitts., 1986-94; assoc. v.p. Doepken Keevican & Weiss, Pitts., 1994—2001, bd. dirs.; mng. ptnr. Pitts. office Schnader Harrison Segal & Lewis, 2002—. Lectr. Pa. Bar Inst., 1983, 87, 88; mem. Pitts. High Tech. Council, 19855, Enterprise Group, Pitts., 19855; arbitrator N.Y. Stock Exch; solicitor Allegheny County Airport Authority, 19995. Bd. dirs. Holocaust Commn., Pitts., 19835, Jewish Family and Children's Svc., Pitts., 1983-86, Cmty. Coll. Allegheny County Found., Allegheny County Sanitary Authority, 20005; bd. dirs. United Jewish Fedn., Pitts., 1984-86, 985, chmn. young bus. and profl. divsn., 1985-87, chmn. exec. and profl. divsn. 1987-88; mem. Young Leadership Cabinet USA, 1984-87; participant Leadership Pitts., 1995; chmn. Holocaust Commn. of Greater Pitts., 1991-94, Pitts. Israel C. of C. 1991-97; commr. City of Pitts. Planning Commn., 19965; bd. dirs., vice chmn. Pitts. Film Office, 1965; bd. dirs. Leadership Pitts., Jewish Assn. on Aging, 1975; v.p. C.C. of Allegheny County Edn. Found., 1965; mem. exec. com. United Jewish Fedn., 19975; solicitor Allegheny County Airport Authority, 1999—; bd. dirs. Allegheny County Sanitary Authority, 2000—. Named one of Outstanding Young Men in Am., 1985; recipient Stark Young Leadership award, 1989. Mem. ABA, Pa. Bar Assn., D.C. Bar Assn., Alleghany County Bar Assn. (bus., banking, and comml. sect., continuing legal edn. com.), Nat. Assn. Securities Dealers (arbitrator). Democrat. Jewish. Avocations: golf, tennis, films. Corporate, general, Property, real (including real estate development, water), Securities. Office: Schnader Harrison Segal Lewis LLP 270 5th Ave Pittsburgh PA 15222-3010

LEUCHTEROVA, DARINA, lawyer; b. Prague, Czech Republic, June 23, 1970; d. Ondrej Durej and Daniela Durejova; m. Tomas Leuchter, Sept. 4, 1993; 1 child, Anna. ML, Charles U, Prague, Czech Rep., 1996. Bar: Czech Bar 1996, Slovak Bar Comml. Lawyers 2001. Jr. atty. at law Klein, Holec, Doskova, Prague, Czech Republic, 1992—96; assoc. atty. Ondrej Peterka, Prague, Czech Republic, 1996—2000; ptnr. Peterka & Leuchterova v.o.s., Prague, Czech Republic, 2000—01, Peterka, Leuchterova & Ptnrs. v.o.s., Prague, Czech Republic, 2001—. Avocations: sports, travel. Corporate, general, Labor (including EEOC, Fair Labor Standards Act, labor-management relations, NLRB, OSHA), Trademark and copyright. Office: Peterka Leuchterova & Partners vos Na Prikope 15 Prague 11000 Czech Republic

LEUCHTMAN, STEPHEN NATHAN, lawyer; b. Detroit, Oct. 14, 1945; s. Alexis C. and Frances J. (Boucher) L.; m. Jacque Ward, Nov. 29, 1991; children: Stephen, John II, Lucinda. BA, U. Mich., 1967, JD, 1970. Bar: Mich. 1970, Calif. 1993, U.S. Dist. Ct. (ea. and so. dists.) Mich. 1970, U.S. Ct. Appeals (6th cir.) 1982. Assoc. Eggenberger, Eggenberger, McKinney & Weber, Detroit, 1970-75, Tyler & Canham, Detroit, 1975-80; ptnr. Sommers, Schwartz, Silver & Schwartz, Southfield, 1980-97; founding ptnr. Trowbridge Law Firm, P.C., Detroit, 1997-2001; atty. Stephen N. Leuchtman, P.C., Detroit, 2001—. Contbr. articles to profl. jours. Mem. ABA, ATLA, Am. Bd. Trial Advocates, Million Dollar Advocates Forum, Consumer Attys. of Calif., Mich. Bar Assn., Calif. Bar Assn. Democrat. Achievements include Alll-Big-Ten, Track, 1965, 1966. Avocations: writing, golf, travel. Civil rights, State civil litigation, Personal injury (including property damage). Home: 241 Strathmore Rd Bloomfield Hills MI 48304-3667 Office: 1380 E Jefferson Ave Detroit MI 48207 E-mail: leuchlaw@attglobal.net.

LEVANDER, ANDREW JOSHUA, lawyer; b. N.Y.C., Aug. 15, 1953; s. Seymour S. and Ellenore B. L.; m. Carol A. Loewenson, Sept. 18, 1983; children: Samuel, Benjamin. BA summa cum laude, Tufts U., 1973; JD, Columbia U., 1977. Bar: N.Y. 1978, D.C. 1978, U.S. Supreme Ct., U.S. Ct. Appeals (2d, 3d, 4th, 5th, 7th and D.C. cirs.), U.S. Dist. Ct. (so. and ea. dists.) N.Y. Law clk. Judge Wilfred Feinberg, U.S. Ct. Appeals, N.Y.C., 1977-78; asst. Solicitor Gen.'s Office, U.S. Dept. Justice, Washington, 1978-81; asst. U.S. atty. U.S. Attys. Office, N.Y.C., 1981-85; ptnr. Shereff, Friedman, Hoffman & Goodman, N.Y.C., 1985-98; assoc. ind. counsel Washington, 1987; ptnr. Swidler Berlin Shereff Friedman LLP, N.Y.C., 1998—. Bd. dirs. Swidler, Berlin, Shereff Friedman, mem. exec. com., 1998—. Co-author: The Prosecution and Prevention of Computer and High Technology Crime, 1986, Settling Commercial Litigation, 1999; contbr. articles to profl. jours. Chmn. scholar com. Westside Youth Soccer League, N.Y.C., 1996—. Mem. ABA (white collar com. 1997—, lectr. white collar convention 2002), Bar Assn. City of N.Y. (securities regulation com. 1997-99). Avocations: tennis, travel, coaching. General civil litigation, Criminal, Securities. Office: Swidler Berlin Shereff Friedman 405 Lexington Ave New York NY 10174-0002 E-mail: ajlevander@swidlaw.com.

LEVANDER, HAROLD POWRIE, JR., lawyer; b. St. Paul, Aug. 28, 1940; s. Harold and Iantha (Powrle) L.; m. Carla Ann August, Nov. 15, 1969; children: Eric, Wade, Laura. BA in Polit. Sci., Gustavus Adolphus Coll., 1962; JD, Harvard U., 1965. Bar: Minn. 1965. Ptnr. LeVander Gillen Miller Anderson & Kuntz, St. Paul, 1965-88, Maun & Simon, St. Paul, 1989-2000, Felhaber, Larson, Fenlon & Vogt, St. Paul, 2000—. Chmn., pres. Ford Commn., Minn. Del. Nat. Rep. Conv., Kansas City, 1976; chmn. St. Paul Area ARC, 1985-87; bd. govs. ARC, 1988-94; mem. Gov.'s Coun. Red River Valley Flood Control, 1997. Named one of Outstanding Young Men of Am., U.S. Jaycees, 1972. Mem. ABA, Dakota County Bar Assn. (pres. 1983-86), Nat. Rural Electric Coop. Assn. (region 6 rep. lawyer's com. 1986-88, 1993-96), Electric Coop. Bar Assn. (bd. advs. 2000-). Lutheran. Avocations: public speaking, tennis, squash, hunting, politics. Utilities, public. Home: 8086 Somerset Knls Saint Paul MN 55125-2362 Office: Felhaber Larson Fenlon & Vogt #2100 30 7th St E # 2100 Saint Paul MN 55101-4914

LEVENFELD, MILTON ARTHUR, lawyer; b. Chgo., Mar. 18, 1927; s. Mitchell A. and Florence B. (Berman) L.; m. Iona R. Wishner, Dec. 18, 1949; children— Barry, David, Judith Ph.B., U. Chgo., 1947, JD, 1950. Bar: Ill. 1950. Ptnr. Altman, Levenfeld & Kanter, Chgo., 1961-64, Levenfeld and Kanter, Chgo., 1964-80, Levenfeld, Eisenberg, Janger & Glassberg, Chgo., 1980-99; of counsel Levenfeld Pearlstein, Chgo., 1999—. Former dir. Bank of Chgo., Garfield Ridge Trust & Savs. Bank; lectr. in fed. taxation Contbr. articles to profl. jours. Bd. dirs. Spertus Coll. Judaica, Jewish Fedn. Chgo., 1975-84, Am. Israel C. of C., 1st nat. v.p.; chmn. legacies and endowments com., 1982-84; co-gen. chmn. Chgo. Jewish United Fund, 1977, vice chmn. campaign, 1979; gov. mem. Orchestral Assn. Chgo. Symphony Orch.; vis. com. U. Chgo. Law Sch., 1989-91; pres. Am. Israel C. of C. of Met. Chgo., 1993-95, 96-98. With USNR, 1944-45. Recipient Keter Shem Tov award Jewish Nat. Fund, 1978 Mem. ABA, Ill. Bar Assn., Chgo. Bar Assn., Am.-Israel C. of C. (past pres.). Home: 866 Stonegate Dr Highland Park IL 60035-5145 Office: 2 N LaSalle St Chicago IL 60602 E-mail: mlevenfeld@lplegal.com.

LEVENSON, ALAN BRADLEY, lawyer; b. Long Beach, N.Y., Dec. 13, 1935; s. Cyrus O. and Jean (Kotler) L.; m. Joan Marlene Levenson, Aug. 19, 1956; children: Scott Keith, Julie Jo. AB, Dartmouth Coll., 1956; BA, Oxford U., Eng., 1958, MA, 1962; LLB, Yale U., 1961. Bar: N.Y. 1962, U.S. Dist. Ct. D.C. 1964, U.S. Ct. Appeals (D.C. cir.) 1965, U.S. Supreme Ct. 1965. Law clk., trainee div. corp. fin. SEC, Washington, 1961-62, gen. atty., 1962, trial atty., 1963, br. chief, 1963-65, asst. dir., 1965-68, exec. asst. dir., 1968, dir., 1970-76; v.p. Shareholders Mgmt. Co., L.A., 1969, sr. v.p., 1969-70, exec. v.p., 1970; ptnr. Fulbright & Jaworski, Washington, 1976—. Lectr. Cath. U. Am., 1964-68, Columbia U., 1973; adj. prof. Georgetown U., 1964, 77, 79-81, U.S. rep. working party OECD, Paris, 1974-75; adv. com. SEC, 1976-77; mem. adv. bd. Securities Regulation Inst., U. Calif., San Diego, 1973—, vice chmn. exec. com., 1979-83, chmn., 1983-87, emeritus chmn., 1988—; mem. adv. coun. SEC Inst., U. So. Calif., L.A., Sch. Acctg., 1981-85; mem. adv. com. Nat. Ctr. Fin. Svcs,. U. Calif.-Berkeley, 1985-89; mem. planning com. Ray Garrett Ann. Securities Regulation Inst. Northwestern U. Law Sch.; mem. adv. panel to U.S. compt.-gen. on stock market decline, 1987, panel of cons., 1989-98; mem. audit adv. com. GAO, 1992—. Mem. bd. editl. advisors U. Iowa Jour. Corp. Law, 1978—; Bur. Nat. Affairs adv. bd. Securities Regulation and Law Report, 1976—; bd. editors N.Y. Law Jour., 1976—; bd. advisors, corp. and securities law advisor Prentice Hall Law & Bus., 1991-95; contbr. articles to profl. jours.; mem. adv. bd. Banking Policy Report. Trustee, chair audit com., chair oral history com. SEC Hist. Soc. Recipient Disting. Service award SEC, 1972; James B. Richardson fellow Oxford U., 1956 Mem. ABA (adv. com., fed. regulation securities com., task force rev. fed. securities laws, former chair subcom. on securities activities banks), Fed. Bar Assn. (emeritus mem. exec. com. securities law com.), Am. Law Inst., Practicing Law Inst. (nat. adv. com. 1974, adv. com. ann. securities reg. inst.), AICPA (pub. dir., bd. dirs. 1984-91, fin. com. 1984-91, chmn. adv. coun. auditing standards bd. 1979-80, future issues com. 1982-85), Nat. Assn. Securities Dealers (corp. fin. com. 1981-87, nat. arbitration com. 1983-87, gov.-at-large, bd. govs. 1984-87, exec. com. 1986-87, long range planning com. 1987-90, chmn. legal adv. bd. 1988-93, spl. com. governance and structure 1989-90, numerous adv. coms.), Transparency Internat. USA (bd. dirs.). Banking, Securities. Home: 12512 Exchange Ct S Potomac MD 20854-2431 Office: Fulbright & Jaworski LLP 801 Pennsylvania Ave NW Washington DC 20004-2615 E-mail: alevenson@fulbright.com.

LEVENTHAL, HOWARD G. lawyer; b. N.Y.C., Aug. 15, 1946; BA cum laude, CCNY, 1968; JD, NYU, 1971. Bar: N.Y. 1971, U.S. Ct. Appeals (2d cir.) 1972, U.S. Dist. Ct. (ea. and so. dists.) N.Y. 1973, U.S. Supreme Ct. 1975. Assoc. Cahill, Gordon & Reindel, N.Y.C., 1971-75, Arrow, Silverman & Parcher, N.Y.C., 1975-76; sr. law asst. Supreme Ct. State N.Y., N.Y.C., 1976-80, law sec. to Justice Hortense W. Gabel, 1981-87, spl. referee; bd. dirs., pres. sec. Park Reservior Housing Corp., Bronx, 1974—; v.p. Van Cortlandt Jewish Ctr.; treas. Law Secs. and Law Assts. Collegium. Author: Charges to the Jury and Requests to Charge in a Criminal Case, 1983, Byer's Civil Motions, rev. edit., 1994; contbr. articles to profl. jours. Mem. Law Secs. Assn. (dir.), Sigma Alpha.

LEVETOWN, ROBERT ALEXANDER, lawyer; b. Bklyn., July 20, 1935; s. Alfred A. and Corinne L. (Cohen) L.; m. Roberta S. Slobodkin, Oct. 18, 1959. Student, U. Munich, Fed. Republic Germany, 1954-55; AB, Princeton U., 1956; LLB, Harvard U., 1959. Bar: D.C. 1960, N.Y. 1982, Va. 1984, Pa. 1985. Assoc. Pierson, Ball & Dowd, Washington, 1960-62; asst. U.S. atty. Washington, 1962-63; atty. Chesapeake & Potomac Telephone Cos., Washington, 1963-66, gen. atty., 1966-68, gen. solicitor, 1968-73, v.p., gen. counsel, 1975-83; exec. v.p., gen. counsel Bell Atlantic, 1983-91, vice chmn., 1991-92, also bd. dirs., 1989-92. Chmn. H.R. com., 1995-99; bd. dirs. Telecom NZ. Mem. ABA (vice chmn. comm. com., pub. utility law sect. 1986-93), Washington Met. Corp. Counsels' Assn. (bd. dirs. 1981-83), Nat. Legal Ctr. (legal adv. coun. 1986-92). Republican. Jewish. Address: PMB 606 10645 N Tatum Blvd #200 Phoenix AZ 85028-3053

LEVI, DAVID F. federal judge; b. 1951; BA, Harvard U., MA, 1973; JD, Stanford U. Bar: Calif. 1983. U.S. atty. ea. dist. State of Calif., Sacramento, 1986-90; judge U.S. Dist. Ct. (ea. dist.) Calif., 1990—. Chmn. task force on race, religious and ethnic fairness U.S. Ct. Appeals (9th cir.), 1994-97, mem. jury com., 1993-95. Adv. com. on Civil Rules, 1994—, chair, 2000—; vis. com. U. Chgo. Law Sch., 1995-98. Mem. Am. Law Inst., Milton L. Schwartz Inn of Ct. (pres. 1992-95). Office: 501 I St Rm 14-230 Sacramento CA 95814-7300

LEVIN, A. THOMAS, lawyer; b. Rockville Centre, NY, Dec. 27, 1942; s. Irving and Belle Levin; m. Iris Saletsky, Aug. 13, 1967; children: Amy Beth, Karen Jill. AB in Philosophy, Brown U., Providence, 1964; JD, NYU, 1967, LLM, 1968. Bar: N.Y. 1967, U.S. Dist. Ct. (ea. and so. dists.) N.Y. 1969, U.S. Ct. Appeals (2d cir.) 1970, U.S. Supreme Ct. 1971, Fla. 1980, U.S. V.I. 1991. Sr. dep. county atty. Nassau County Atty.'s Office, Mineola, NY, 1968-70; law sec. NY State Supreme Ct., Mineola, NY, 1970-72; ptnr. Jaspan, Ginsberg, Ehrlich & Levin, Garden City, NY, 1972-88, Blodnick, Schultz & Abramowitz, Lake Success, NY, 1988-89, Meyer, Suozzi, English & Klein, Mineola, NY, 1989—. Reporter to pubs. com. N.Y. State Assn. Supreme Ct. Justices, 1970—; counsel N.Y. State Assembly Jud. Com., Joint Legis. Com. on State's Economy; lectr. in field. Editor: Bench Book for Trial Judges, 1971—; contbr. Village atty. Village of Great Neck Estates, Hewlett Neck, North Hills, Saddle Rock, Thomaston, Woodsburgh; spl. counsel Great Neck Cable Commn., Pub. Access TV Corp., Inc., Nassau County, City of Long Beach, Village of East Hills, Village of Freeport, Village of Great Neck Plaza, Village of Kensington, Village of Kings Point, Village of Lake Success, Village of Laurel Hollow, Village of Munsey Park, Village of Plandome, Village of Plandome Heights, Village of Plandome Manor, Village of Rockville Centre, Village of Russell Gardens, Village of Sea Cliff, We. Suffolk Bd. Coop. Ednl. Svcs., Town of North Hempstead, Town of Brookhaven, Hempstead Sch. Dist.; gen. counsel Child Care Coun. Nassau County, 1972—, Rosa Lee Young Childhood Ctr., Inc., 1972—; mem. Land Use Law Ctr. Conf. Bd., Pace U. Sch. Law; bd. trustees L.I. Cmty. Found., 1995—2000; past counsel Nassau County Planning Commn.; bd. dirs. Nassau Symphony Orch.; trustee Ctrl. Synagogue Nassau County; Village atty. Oyster Bay Cove, Hewlett Bay Pk.; spl. counsel Flower Hill. Fellow: NY Bar Found., Am. Bar Found.; mem.: ABA, Nat. Inst. Mcpl. Law Officers, Nassau Bar Tech. Ctr. Inc. (founding dir. 1994—96, v.p. 1995—96), Suffolk County Bar Assn. (mcpl. law com.), Fla. Bar Assn. (out-of-state practitioners divsn.), V.I. Bar Assn., Nassau Acad. Law (assoc. dean, counsel, lectr.), Nassau County Bar Assn. (1st v.p. 1989—90, pres. 1991—92, chmn. exec. com. 1991—92, bd. dirs., life), NY State Conf. Bar Leaders (exec. coun. 1990—95, chair 1992—93), NY State Bar Assn. (ho. of dels. 1984—87, 1990—, exec. com. 1995—, mcpl. law sect. exec. com. 1995—, v.p. 1998—2001, sec. 2001—02, pres-elect 2002—03, pres. 2003—04), Brown U. Club L.I. (pres. 1972—80, sec.-treas. 1980—88, pres. 1988—98, sec.-treas. 1998—, pres. 1999—, bd. dirs.). General practice, Land use and zoning (including planning), Municipal (including bonds). Office: Meyer Suozzi English Klein 1505 Kellum Pl Mineola NY 11501-4824 E-mail: atlevin@msek.com.

LEVIN, ALLEN JAY, lawyer; b. Bridgeport, Conn., May 27, 1932; s. Simon H. and Adele Miriam (Rossinoff) L.; m. Judith Ann Rubinstein, Aug. 18, 1957 (div. 1987); children: Jennifer Suzanne, Miriam Adele, David Newmark, Michael Aaron; m. Gabrielle Hasson-Azar, Feb. 24, 1995. BA, NYU, 1954; postgrad., Boston U., 1954-55; JD, U. Miami, 1957. Bar: Fla. 1957, Conn. 1958, U.S. Dist. Ct. Conn. 1960, U.S. Dist. Ct. (so. dist.) Fla.

1962, U.S. Dist. Ct. (mid. dist.) Fla. 1969, U.S. Ct. Appeals (11th cir.) 1981, U.S. Supreme Ct. 1972. Small claims ct. judge County of Charlotte, Punta Gorda, Fla., 1962-72; legal counsel Port Charlotte-Charlotte Harbor (Fla.) Fire Control Dist., 1965-86; mcpl. judge City of North Port, Fla., 1973-76, city atty., 1977-87; pvt. practice Charlotte, Fla. Legal counsel Charlotte County Habitat for Humanity, Inc. Mem.: ABA, Port Charlotte-Charlotte County C. of C., Charlotte County Bar Assn., Fla. Bar Assn. (probate law com., real property probate and trust laws sect.), Port Charlotte-Charlotte County Bd. of Realtors (assoc.), Kiwanis (pres. 1984—85, youth svcs. chmn. Port Charlotte Club 1986—, pres. 1998—99, lt. gov.- elect divsn.18 so. Fla. dist. 1999—2000, lt. gov. 2000—01, trustee Fla. dist. found. 2002—, dist. chair com. on bylaws, practice & procedure, protocol Fla. Dist. 2002—), Elks. Avocation: stamp collecting. Estate planning, Probate (including wills, trusts), Property, real (including real estate development, water). Home: 125 Graham St SE Port Charlotte FL 33952 Office: 3440 Conway Blvd Ste 1A Port Charlotte FL 33952 E-mail: ajlgal@juno.com.

LEVIN, DEBBE ANN, lawyer; b. Cin., Mar. 11, 1954; d. Abram Asher and Selma Ruth (Herlands) L. BA, Washington U., St. Louis, 1976; JD, U. Cin., 1979; LLM, NYU, 1983. Bar: Ohio 1979. Staff atty. U.S. Ct. Appeals (6th cir.), Cin., 1979-82; shareholder Schwartz, Manes & Ruby, Cin., 1983-2002; of counsel Drew & Ward Co., LPA, Cin., 2002—. Editor: U. Cin. Law Rev., 1972-79. Trustee Cin. Estate Planning Coun. Mem. ABA, Ohio Bar Assn., Cin. Bar Assn. (chair advanced estate planning inst. 2001), Nat. Acad. Elder Law Attys., Greater Cin. Planned Giving Coun., Order of Coif. Jewish. Pension, profit-sharing, and employee benefits, Corporate taxation, Estate taxation. Office: Drew & Ward Co LPA One W Fourth St Ste 2400 Cincinnati OH 45202 E-mail: dlevin@drewlaw.com.

LEVIN, EDWARD M. lawyer; b. Chgo., Oct. 16, 1934; s. Edward M. and Anne Meriam (Fantl) L.; children from previous marriage: Daniel Andrew, John Davis; m. Margot Aronson, Apr. 4, 1993. BS, U. Ill., 1955; LLB, Harvard U., 1958. Bar: Ill. 1958, U.S. Supreme Ct. 1968. Mem. firm Ancel, Stonesifer, Glink & Levin and predecessors, Chgo., 1958, 61-68; draftsman Ill. Legis. Reference Bur., Springfield, 1961; spl. asst. to regional adminstr. HUD, Chgo., 1968-71, asst. regional adminstr. community planning and mgmt., 1971-72; asst. dir. Ill. Dept. Local Govt. Affairs, Chgo., 1973-77; of counsel Holleb, Gerstein & Glass, Ltd., Chgo., 1977-79; chief counsel Econ. Devel. Adminstrn., U.S. Dept. Commerce, Washington, 1979—85, 1997—2001; sr. fellow Nat. Gov's. Assn., 1985-86; sr. counsel U.S. Dept. Commerce, Washington, 1987-96. Lectr. U. Ill., 1972—73, adj. assoc. prof. urban scis., 1973—79; lectr. Loyola U., 1976—79, No. Va. Law Sch., 1988; instr. Mgmt. Concepts, Inc., Vienna, 2001—. Assoc. editor Assistance Mgmt. Jour., 1990-95; contbr. articles to profl. jours. Mem. Ill. Nature Preserves Com., 1963-68, Northea. Ill. Planning Commn., 1974-77, Ill.-Ind. Bi-State Commn., 1974-77; bd. dirs. Cook County Legal Assistance Found., 1978-79, D.C. Appleseed Ctr., 1994—; bd. dirs. Ill. divsn. ACLU, 1965-68, 77-79, v.p., 1977-78; chmn. ABA fed. assistance com., 1995-96. With AUS, 1958-60. Recipient Lincoln award Ill. Bar Assn., 1977, Gold medal U.S. Dept. Commerce, 2000, Corrigan award Econ. Devel. Adminstrn., 2000. Mem. FBA (chmn. fed. grants com. 1991-95), Nat. Grants Mgmt. Assn. (bd. dirs. 1988-92, Pres.'s award 1994), Appleseed Found. (bd. dirs. 1994—, mem. exec. com. 1994-2002). Home: 3201 Porter St NW Washington DC 20008-3212 E-mail: elevin111@erols.com.

LEVIN, EZRA GURION, lawyer; b. Bklyn., Feb. 10, 1934; s. Harry and Bertha Levin; m. Batya Ann Schaefer, June 19, 1960; children: Zachary Abraham, Ayala Deborah Levin-Kruss. AB, Columbia U., 1955; postgrad., U. Chgo., 1955-56; LLB, Columbia U., 1959. Bar: N.Y. 1961. Assoc., then ptnr. Marshall, Bratter, Greene, Allison & Tucker, N.Y.C., 1961-79; ptnr. Kramer Levin Naftalis & Frankel LLP, N.Y.C., 1979—. Bd. dirs. Kaiser Aluminum Corp., MAXXAM, Inc., Houston; adj. prof. sociology Columbia U., 1973-77, 87, 93; adj. faculty U. Conn. Law Sch., 1970-73; vis. prof. U. Wis. Law Sch., 1967, 98. Contbr. articles to profl. jours. Mem.-at-large Jewish Cmty. Rels. Coun., N.Y.C., 1983—, pres., 2001—; vice chmn. Coalition for Soviet Jewry, N.Y.C., 1984—93, co-chair, 1994—2001; counsel Am. Friends Sarah Herzog Meml. Hosp.-Jerusalem, Inc., N.Y.C., 1975—; sec., bd. dirs. Scholarship, Edn. and Def. Fund for Racial Equality, N.Y.C., 1961—70; founding chair Solomon Schechter High Sch. N.Y., 1992—96. Mem.: Hebrew Free Loan Soc. (bd. dirs.), Law and Soc. Assn., ABA. Avocation: tennis. Corporate, general, Mergers and acquisitions, Securities. Office: Kramer Levin Naftalis & Frankel LLP 919 3rd Ave New York NY 10022-3902 E-mail: elevin@kramerlevin.com.

LEVIN, HERVEY PHILLIP, lawyer, director; b. Oct. 22, 1942; s. Julius L. and Gertrude (Cohen) L.; m. Madeleine J. Raskin, Sept. 22, 1970; children: Arianne, Nicole, David. BBA, U. Mich., 1964, MBA, 1968; JD, DePaul U., 1969. Bar: Ill. 1969, Tex. 1979, U.S. Dist. Ct. (no. dist.) Ill. 1970, U.S. Ct. Appeals (5th cir.) 1981, U.S. Ct. Appeals (7th cir.) 1971, U.S. Supreme Ct. 1972. Assoc. Potts Randall & Horn, Chgo., 1970-71; assoc., jr. ptnr. Mehlman, Ticho, Addis, Susman, Spitzer, Randall, Horn & Pyes, Chgo., 1971-75; pvt. practice, 1975—78, Dallas, 1979—. Dir. Leedal Inc., Chgo.; cons. in workers' compensation, occupational disease and gen. practice. Bd. dirs. Solomon Schecter Acad. of Dallas, 1979—, Cong. Shearith Israel, Dallas, 1981-88, Am. Jewish Congress, Dallas, 1980-85, Nat. Assn. Mortgage Planners, 1995—. Named Ky. Col. Mem. ABA (workers compensation com. torts and ins. practices sect., chmn. 1989-90, sr. vice-chair 1990—, coun. mem. torts and ins. practices sect. 1995-98, 99—, ho. of dels. 1999—, various adminstrv. coms., torts and ins. practices sect. 1990—, liaison to Internat. Assn. Indsl. Accident Bds. and Comms. 1989—, cons. labor stds. subcom., house edn. and labor com., U.S. Congress, chmn. solo and small firm practices com. 1994-95), Ill. Bar Assn., Tex. Bar Assn., Dallas Bar Assn., Chgo. Bar Assn. General practice, Property, real (including real estate development, water), Workers' compensation. Office: 6918 Blue Mesa Dr Ste 115 Dallas TX 75252-6140 Fax: 972-733-3269. E-mail: hervey@airmail.net.

LEVIN, JACK S. lawyer; b. Chgo., May 1, 1936; s. Frank J. and Judy G. (Skerball) L.; m. Sandra Sternberg, Aug. 24, 1958; children: Lisa, Laura, Leslie, Linda. BS summa cum laude, Northwestern U., 1958; LL.B. summa cum laude, Harvard U., 1961. Bar: Ill. 1961; C.P.A. (gold medalist), Ill., 1958. Law clk. to chief judge U.S. Ct. of Appeals 2d Circuit, N.Y.C., 1961-62; asst. for tax matters to Solicitor Gen. of U.S., Washington, 1965-67; assoc. law firm Kirkland & Ellis, Chgo., 1962-65, ptnr., 1967—. Frequent lectr. on legal aspects of venture capital transactions, mergers, acquisitions, buyouts, workouts, fed. income tax matters; vis. com. Harvard Law Sch., 1987-93, lectr., 1997—; lectr. Law Sch. U. Chgo., 1988—. Author book on structuring venture capital, pvt. equity and entrepreneurial transactions; co-author multi-volume treatise on mergers, acquisitions and buyouts; case editor Harvard Law Rev., 1959-61; contbr. numerous articles to legal jours. and chpts. to law books. Parliamentarian Winnetka (Ill.) Town Meetings, 1974-83, 89, 93-96; chmn. nat. fundraising drives Harvard Law Sch., 1985-86, 90-91, 95-96, 2001, chmn. lawyer's divsn. Jewish United Fund Chgo., 1993-95. Mem. ABA (chmn. subcom. 1968-79), Fed. Bar Assn., Chgo. Bar Assn. (exec. com. 1985—), Am. Coll. Tax Counsel. Clubs: Mid-Am. (bd. dirs. 1985-88), Birchwood (Highland Park, Ill.) (pres. 1980-82). Corporate, general, Mergers and acquisitions, Corporate taxation. Home: 985 Sheridan Rd Winnetka IL 60093-1558 Office: Kirkland & Ellis 200 E Randolph St 57th Fl Chicago IL 60601-6608 Business E-Mail: jack.levin@kirkland.com.

LEVIN, MICHAEL DAVID, lawyer; b. Chgo., Oct. 11, 1942; s. Joseph F. and Libbie (Landman) L.; children: Victoria, David, Elizabeth, Emma, Madeline; m. Carol A. McErlean, Oct. 10, 1993. AB, U. Mich., 1964, JD, 1967. Bar: Ill. 1967. Assoc. Arnstein, Gluck, Weitzenfeld & Minow, Chgo., 1967-73, ptnr., 1973-81, Latham & Watkins, Chgo., 1982-95; sr. v.p., sec. & gen. counsel Sears Roebuck & Co., Hoffman Estates, Ill., 1996-98; ptnr. Latham & Watkins, 1998—. Mem. ABA, Chgo. Bar Assn. (chmn. securities law 1982-83), Met. Club. Republican. Jewish. Corporate, general, Securities. Office: Sears Roebuck & Co 5800 Sears Tower Chicago IL 60684-0001

LEVIN, MURRAY SIMON, lawyer; b. Phila., Feb. 8, 1943; s. Sidney Michael and Eva (Goldstein) L.; m. Jalond Marie Robinson, June 9, 1968; children— Adrianne Lesley, Alexandra Amber-Rose. BA, Haverford Coll., 1964; MA, LLB, Harvard U., 1968; cert., Hague Internat. Acad. Law, 1967. Bar: Pa. 1968, U.S. Dist. Ct. (ea. dist.) Pa. 1970, U.S. Ct. Appeals (3d cir.) 1970, U.S. Supreme Ct. 1979. Instr. English Harvard U., 1965-68; law clk. to U.S. Dist. Ct. Judge, 1968-70; instr. govt. Haverford Coll., 1970-71; litigation ptnr. Pepper, Hamilton LLP, Phila., 1970—, mem. firm exec. com., 1993-95. Mem. mng. bd. dirs. Atlas Pipeline Ptnrs.; overseas lectr., U.K., Sweden, Germany, Senegal, Kenya, Cameroon, Morocco, Israel, Vietnam, Italy, 1988—; law seminar speaker. Weekly commentator radio Sta. WCAU Dick Clayton Show, TV program Morningside, 1973-76; weekly host, interviewer Sta. WHYY, 1974-79; TV commentator O.J. Simpson trial, 1995; contbr. articles to profl. jours. Chmn. Phila. Coun. Experiment in Internat. Living, 1968-70; mem. Phila. Urban Coalition Housing Task Force, 1968-80; chmn. coll. divsn. Allied Jewish Appeal, 1968-70; pres. Ctrl. Phila. Reform Dems., 1973-74; bd. dirs. Grad. Hosp. Phila., 1976-96 (patient safety com. 2002-), Friends Ctrl. Sch., 1988-96, divsn. Fgn. Policy Rsch. Com. Mid. East Coun., 1992-94, mem. mng. bd. dirs. Atlas Pipeline Partners L.P., Mid. East Forum, 1994—; bd. dirs. French Internat. Sch. Phila., 2002—; candidate for Dem. Party nomination for U.S. Senate from Pa., 2000; mem. exec. com. Pa. Dem. Party State Com., 2002; chair Dem. Party Lower Merion/Narberth, 2003—. Root-Tilden fellow, 1964. Mem. ABA, Pa. Bar Assn. (ho. of dels.), Phila. Bar Assn. (young lawyers exec. bd. 1973, bd. govs. 1985-88, zone del. 1988—, chmn. profl. guidance com. 1989-92, co-chmn. internat. human rights com. 1990-91), Phila. Trial Lawyers Assn., Assn. Internat. des Jeunes Avocats Brussels (bd. dirs. 1981-85, 1st Am. pres. 1985-88), Union Internationale des Avocats Paris (advisor to pres., mem. exec. com. 1993—, pres. Am. chpt. 1995-97, congress pres. 1997), Am. Law Inst., Am. Judicature Soc., Phi Beta Kappa. Federal civil litigation, Private international, Product liability. Office: Pepper Hamilton LLP 3000 2 Logan Sq 18th & Arch Sts Philadelphia PA 19103-2799 E-mail: levinm@pepperlaw.com.

LEVIN, RICHARD BARRY, lawyer; b. Chgo., Nov. 26, 1956; s. Stanley H. and Dorothy Louise (Goldman) L. BS, U. New Orleans, 1981; JD, La. State U., 1984. Bar: La. 1984, U.S. Dist. Ct. (ea., mid., we. dists.) La. 1985, U.S. Ct. Appeals (5th cir.) 1984, U.S. Supreme Ct. 1990, U.S. Dist. Ct. (eastern dist.) Tex. 1997. Law clk. to judge La. Dist. Ct., New Orleans, 1984-85; ptnr. Goldman & Levin, New Orleans, 1985-93, Levin Law Offices, New Orleans, 1993—; judge pro tempore 1st Parish Ct. Jefferson Parish, 2003—. Bd. dirs. Congregation Gates of Prayer, New Orleans, 2002—. Mem. ABA (dist. rep. 1990-95), La. Bar Assn., New Orleans Bar Assn. (sec.-treas. young lawyers sect. 1987-88, vice-chair 1988-89, chair-elect 1989-90, chair 1990-91, chmn. law day legal clinics 1987, mem. pub. rels. com. 1987—, bd. dirs.). Republican. Avocations: golf, bowling, sailing, reading, tennis. General civil litigation, Commercial, consumer (including collections, credit), Family and matrimonial. Office: Levin Law Offices 1515 Poydras St Ste 2070 New Orleans LA 70112-4506 E-mail: Rick@LevinLawOffices.com.

LEVIN, SUSAN BASS, lawyer; b. Wilmington, Del., July 18, 1952; d. Max S. and Harriet C. (Rubin) Bass; children: Lisa, Amy. BA, U. of Rochester, 1972; JD, George Washington U., 1975. Bar: D.C. 1975, U.S. Ct. Claims 1975, N.J. 1976, Pa. 1981, U.S. Ct. Appeals (3rd cir.) 1983, U.S. Supreme Ct. 1984. Law clk. to assoc. justice U.S. Ct. Claims, Washington, 1975-76; assoc. Covington & Burling, Washington, 1976-79; pvt. practice Cherry Hill, N.J., 1979-87; counsel Ballard, Spahr, Andrews & Ingersoll, Phila., Camden (N.J.), 1993-96, Pepper Hamilton LLP, Phila. and Cherry Hill, Pa., 1996-2000; spl. counsel Fox Rothschild OBrien Frankel, 2001—02; commr. NJ Dept. Cmty. Affairs, 2002—. Pres. Cherry Hill (N.J.) Twp. Coun., 1986—88; mayor City of Cherry Hill, 1988—2002; trustee N.J. Coalition of Small Bus. Orgns., 1985—87; del. to President's Summit on Am.'s Future, chair Pam's List; commr. N.J. Dept. Cmty. Affairs, 2002—; del. Dem. Presdl. Conv., 1992, 1996; bd. dirs. N.J. Alliance for Action, South Jersey Devel. Coun., U.S. Holocaust Coun., Big Bros./Big Sisters, Boys and Girls Club, trustee; bd. dirs. N.J. League Municipalities. Recipient Woman of Achievement award Camden County Girl Scouts, 1986, Barbara Boggs Sigmuno award N.J. Women Polit. Caucus, 1996, Gov.'s award on volunteerism, 1998. Mem. Tri County Women Lawyers (pres. 1984-85), N.J. Assn. Women Bus. Owners (state pres. 1984-85 named Woman of Yr. 1985), Phi Beta Kappa, Order of Coif. General practice, Probate (including wills, trusts), Property, real (including real estate development, water). Office: 1001 Broad St Trenton NJ 08002

LEVIN, WILLIAM EDWARD, lawyer; b. Miami, Fla., June 13, 1954; s. Harold A. and Phyllis (Wolfson) L.; m. Mary Catherine Egan, June 25, 1994; 1 child: Sean Alexander. Student, Corn. Coll., 1972-74; BA, Emory U., Atlanta, 1976; JD, U. Miami, 1979. Bar: Fla. 1979, Calif. 1982; lic. real estate broker, Calif. Distbr. N.Y. Times, Atlanta, 1975-76; legis. intern Congressman William Lehman, Washington, 1974; law clk. Superior Ct. Hillsborough County, Tampa, Fla., 1974; legal asst./law clk. U. Miami Sch. Law, 1977-78; law clk. Shevin, Shapo & Shevin, Miami, 1977-79; assoc. Law Offices of John Cyril Malloy, Miami, 1979-82; assoc./ptnr. Flehr, Hohbach, Test, Albritton & Herbert, San Francisco, 1982-87; ptnr. Cooper, White & Cooper, San Francisco, 1987-88; pvt. practice trademark and copyright law San Francisco, 1988-92, Irvine, Calif., 1993-96; broker/sole proprietor Levin Realty, San Francisco, 1987-92; of counsel Goldstein & Phillips, San Francisco, 1988-91, Hawes & Fischer, Newport Beach, Calif., 1992-93, Gauntlett & Assocs., Irvine, Calif., 1995-96; mng. partner Levin & Gluck, Laguna Beach, Calif., 1996-97; founding ptnr. Levin & Hawes, Laguna Beach, Calif., 1997—. Co-chmn. trademark com. San Francisco Patent & Trademark Assn., 1985-86; moot ct. judge Giles Rich Moot Ct. Competition, San Francisco, 1986; ofcl. arbitrator Am. Arbitration Assn., 1987-96; mem. exec. com. L.A. Complex Inns of Ct., 1994-96; lectr. in field. Author: Trade Press Protection, 1996; mem. editorial bd. Trademark World, London, 1987-90, Trademark Reporter, 1987-89, 93-2000, Trademark Reporter Task Force, 1994-97, San Francisco Atty., 1986-89; mem. adv. bd. United States Patents Quarterly, 2000—; contbr. articles to profl. jours. Mem. adminstrv. bd. Californians for Missing Children, San Francisco, 1989-92, Hebrew Inst. Law, San Francisco, 1986-88; atty's. steering com. Jewish Cmty. Fedn., San Francisco, 1987-88; fin. com. Temple Emanu-el, San Francisco, 1985-86; bd. dirs. Ctr. 500, Orange County Performing Arts Ctr. Support Group, 1996, Anti-Defamation League Orange County and Long Beach Region, 1998—; trustee Shir Ha Ma'lot Temple, 1997-2002; mem. intellectual property adv. bd. Whittier Law Sch., 2002—. Named Rep. of Yr., Nat. Rep. Congl. Com., 2001. Mem. ABA, Internat. Trademark Assn., Orange County Bar Assn., Orange County Patent Law Assn. Jewish. Lead trial counsel in case resulting in $143 million trademark infringement jury verdict, largest award of this type in the world, Oct. 1999. E-mail: william.levin@levinhawes.com.

LEVINE, A. KENNETH, lawyer; b. Charleston, W. Va., June 21, 1965; BS in Mgmt. and Fin., Tulane U., 1987, JD, 1990. Bar: Fla. 1990, D.C. 1991, U.S. Dist. Ct. (no., mid. and so. dists.) Fla., U.S. Ct. Appeals (2nd, 4th, 5th, 6th, 7th, 9th, 11th cirs.), U.S. Ct. Appeals (D.C. cir.), U.S. Ct. Appeals (fed. cir.), U.S. Claims Ct., U.S. Supreme Ct., cert.: ins. mediator. Part-time law clk./extern Judge Robert F. Collins U.S. Dist. Ct. (ea. dist.) La., New Orleans, 1989—90; atty. Fla. Dept. Ins. and Treas., Tallahassee, 1990—92, sr. atty., 1992—95; gen. counsel ACSI, Inc., Clearwater, Fla., 1995; assoc. Blank, Rigsby & Meenan, P.A., Tallahassee, 1996—98; ptnr. Pennington, Moore, Wilkinson, Bell & Dunbar, P.A., Tallahassee, 1998—2001, Tew Cardenas Rebak Kellogg Lehman DeMaria Tague Raymond & Levine, LLP, Tallahassee, 2001—. Gen. counsel Am. Mfrs. Warranty Assn., Inc.; mem. adv. coun. Calif. Bur. Electronic and Appliance Repair, mem. svc. contract task force. Editor: Tulane Environ. Law Jour.; contbr. articles to profl. jours. Named to, Nat. Order of the Barristers. Mem.: ABA, Nat. Alliance Life Companies, Assn. Insurance Compliance Profls., Internat. Assn. Insurance Receivers, Tulane Bus. Assn., Capital City Country Club, Govs. Club. Insurance, Corporate, general. Office: Tew Cardenas Rebak et al 101 N Monroe St Ste 725 Tallahassee FL 32301

LEVINE, ALAN, lawyer; b. Middletown, N.Y., Jan. 17, 1948; s. Jacques and Florence (Tananbaum) L.; children: Emily Jane, Malcolm Andrew. BS in Econs., U. Pa., 1970; JD, NYU, 1973. Bar: N.Y. 1974, U.S. Dist. Ct. (so. dist.) N.Y. 1974, U.S. Dist. Ct. (ea. dist.) N.Y. 1980, U.S. Tax Ct. 1980, U.S. Ct. Appeals (2d cir.) 1975, U.S. Supreme Ct. 2000. Law clk. U.S. Dist. Ct. (so. dist.) N.Y., N.Y.C., 1973-75; asst. U.S. atty. U.S. Attys. Office, so. dist. N.Y., Dept. Justice, N.Y.C., 1975-80; assoc. Kronish, Lieb, Weiner & Hellman, N.Y.C., 1980-82, mem., 1982—, mng. ptnr., 1998—. Chmn. bd. dirs. Park Ave. Synagogue, N.Y.C., 1993-98; bd. dirs. Jewish Theol. Sem., 1998, MYF Legal Svcs. Inc., 1990-93; law chmn. N.Y. County Rep. Com., 1991-93. Recipient Atty. Gen. Dirs. award U.S. Dept. Justice, 1980, Torch of Learning award Am. Friends Hebrew U., 1995, Human Rels. award ADL, 2001. Fellow Am. Bar Found., Am. Coll. Trial Lawyers; mem. ABA (ho. of dels. 1983-84, chmn. spl. com. for youth edn. for citizenship, 1988-91, vice chmn. white collar crime com. 1996—), N.Y. State Bar Assn. (chmn. com. on citizenship edn. 1979-84, ho. of dels. 1982-84, award of achievement 1984), Sunningdale Country Club (bd. trustees 1988-90 Scarsdale, N.Y.), Mask and Wig Club (Phila.). Republican. Jewish. Federal civil litigation, Criminal. Home: 22 E 82d St New York NY 10128-1308 Office: Kronish Lieb Weiner & Hellman 1114 Avenue Of The Americas New York NY 10036-7703

LEVINE, DAVID ETHAN, lawyer; b. Niagara Falls, N.Y., Feb. 28, 1955; s. Morree Morell Levine and Marbud Juel (Gagen) Prozeller; m. Ann Lee Ruhlin, May 23, 1981. BS in Bus., Miami U., 1977; JD, Capital U., 1981. Bar: N.Y. 1982, U.S. Dist. Ct. (we. dist.) N.Y. 1982. Assoc. Grossman, Levine and Civiletto, Niagara Falls, 1981-89, Cummings and Levine, Niagara Falls, 1989-92; pvt. practice Niagara Falls, 1992—. Bd. dirs. Niagara County Legal Aid Soc., Niagara Area Habitat for Humanity. Mem. N.Y. State Bar Assn., Erie County Bar Assn., Niagara Falls Bar Assn., Pitt. Ski Club., Recumbenteers Bicycle Club. Unitarian Universalist. Avocations: skiing, photography, bicycling, camping. Probate (including wills, trusts), Property, real (including real estate development, water), Workers' compensation. Home: 22 Hemlock Dr Grand Island NY 14072-3315 Office: PO Box 922 669 Main St Niagara Falls NY 14302 E-mail: del14072@aol.com.

LEVINE, HAROLD, lawyer; b. Newark, Apr. 30, 1931; s. Rubin and Gussie (Lifshitz) L.; children: Brenda Sue, Linda Ellen Levine Gersen, Louise Abby, Jill Anne Levine Lipari, Charles A., Cristina Gussie, Harold Rubin II; m. Cristina Cervera, Aug. 29, 1980. BS in Engring., Purdue U., 1954; JD with distinction, George Washington U., 1958. Bar: D.C. 1958, Va. 1958, Mass. 1960, Tex. 1972, U.S. Patent Office 1958. Naval arch., marine engr. U.S. Navy Dept., 1954-55; patent examiner U.S. Patent Office, 1955-58; with Tex. Instruments, Inc., Attleboro, Mass., 1959-77, asst. sec. Dallas, 1969-72, asst. v.p. and gen. patent counsel, 1972-77; ptnr. Sigalos & Levine, Dallas, 1977-93; prin. Levine & Majorie LLP, Dallas, 1994-2000, Levine & Starr LLP, 2001—. Chmn. bd. Vanguard Security, Inc., Houston, 1977—; chmn. Tex. Am. Realty, Dallas, 1977—; lectr. assns., socs.; del. Geneva and Lausanne (Switzerland) Intergovtl. Conf. on Revision, Paris Pat. Conv., 1975-76. Editor George Washington U. Law Rev., 1956-57; mem. adv. bd. editors Bur. Nat. Affairs, Pat., Trdmk. and Copyright Jour.; contbr. chpt. to book and articles to profl. jours. Mem. U.S. State Dept. Adv. Panel on Internat. Tech. Transfer, 1977. Mem. ABA (chmn. com. 407 taxation pats. and trdmks. 1971-72), Am. Patent Law Assn., Dallas Bar Assn., Assn. Corp. Pat. Csl. (sec.-treas. 1971-73), Dallas-Ft. Worth Patent Law Assn., Pacific Indsl. Property Assn. (pres. 1975-77), Electronic Industries Assn. (pres. pat. com. 1972), NAM, Southwestern Legal Inst. on Patent Law (planning com. 1971-74), U.S. C. of C., Dallas C. of C., Kiwanis, Alpha Epsilon Pi, Phi Alpha Delta. Republican. Jewish. Intellectual property, Patent, Trademark and copyright. Office: Levine & Starr LLP Bank Am Pl Tower 101 E Park Blvd Ste 755 Plano TX 75074

LEVINE, HERBERT, lawyer; b. June 5, 1924; s. Barnet and Mollie (Morris) L.; m. Pearl H. Kahn, Mar. 30, 1946; children: Barbara, Susan, Deborah, Steven. BBA, JD, U. Wis., 1950. Bar: Wis. 1950, U.S. Dist. Ct. (ea. dist.) Wis. 1950. Pvt. practice, Milw., 1950-66; assoc. Bernstein, Wessel & Lewis, Milw., 1967-75; shareholder Stupar, Schuster & Cooper S.C., Milw., 1976-2000; sole practitioner Milw., 2000—. Instr. Am. Inst. Banking, Milw., 1964-88 ; lectr. Marquette U., 1968-79, Milw. Bd. Realtors, 1961. Pres. Bayside PTA, Wis., 1965-66; active Indian Guides, Bayside, Wis., 1972-73. Sgt. USAAF, 1943-46. Mem. Wis. Bar Assn., Milw. Bar Assn. Personal injury (including property damage), Probate (including wills, trusts), Property, real (including real estate development, water). Home: 9055 N King Rd Milwaukee WI 53217-1848 Office: 633 W Wisconsin Ave Milwaukee WI 53203-1918 E-mail: ssc@ssclaw.com.

LEVINE, HOWARD ARNOLD, state supreme court justice; b. Mar. 4, 1932; m. Barbara Joan Segall, July 25, 1954; children: Neil Louis, Ruth Ellen, James Robert. BA, Yale U., 1953, LLB, 1956; LLD (hon.), Union U., 1994. Bar: N.Y. 1956. Asst. in instrn., research assoc. in criminal law Yale Law Sch., 1956-57; assoc. firm Hughes, Hubbard, Blair, Reed, N.Y.C., 1957-59; practiced in Schenectady, 1959-70; asst. dist. atty., 1961-66, dist. atty., 1967-70; judge Schenectady County Family Ct., 1971-80; acting judge Schenectady County Ct., 1971-80; adminstrv. judge family cts. N.Y. State 4th Jud. Dist., 1974-80; assoc. justice appellate div. 3d dept. N.Y. State Supreme Ct., 1982-93; assoc. judge N.Y. Ct. of Appeals, 1993—2003; Robert H. Jackson disting. prof. law Albany Law Sch., Union U., 2003—; sr. counsel Whiteman, Osterman & Hanna, Albany, NY, 2003—. Vis. lectr. Albany Law Sch., 1972-81; mem. N.Y. Gov.'s Panel on Juvenile Violence, N.Y. State Temp. Commn. on Child Welfare, N.Y. State Temp. Commn. on Recodification of Family Ct. Act, N.Y. State Juvenile Justice Adv. Bd., 1974-80; mem. ind. rev. bd. N.Y. State Div. for Youth, 1974-80; mem. rules and adv. com. on family ct. N.Y. State Jud. Conf., 1974-80 Contbr. articles to law revs. Bd. dirs. Schnecatady County Child Guildance Ctr., Carver Community Ctr., Freedom Forum of Schnectady. Mem. ABA, Am. Law Inst., N.Y. State Bar Assn. (chmn. spl. com. juvenile justice), Assn. Family Ct. Judges State N.Y. (pres. 1979-80) Home: 2701 Rosendale Rd Niskayuna NY 12309-1300 Office: County Jud Bldg 612 State St Schenectady NY 12305-2113

LEVINE, JULIUS BYRON, lawyer, legal educator; b. Waterville, Maine, Feb. 8, 1939; s. Lewis Lester and Celia G. (Gurewitz) L.; m. Diane Groner, Aug. 26, 1965 (div.); children: Rachel A., Sarah L.; m. Susan M. Ginns, Sept. 7, 1980 (div.); 1 child, James G. AB summa cum laude, Harvard U., 1960, JD cum laude, 1964; PhD, Oxford (Eng.) U., 1969. Bar: Maine 1963, Mass. 1964, U.S. Ct. Appeals (1st cir.) 1964. Law clk. U.S. Dist. Ct. Maine, Portland, 1964-65; ptnr., of counsel Levine, Brody & Levine, Boston and Waterville, 1963-80; of counsel Levine, Bishop & Levine, Boston and Waterville, 1980—; assoc. prof. law Boston U., 1969-72, prof. law, 1972—. Master Superior Ct. Mass., Boston, 1972—, coord. jud. intern program, 1979—; asst. dist. atty. Nofrolk County, Mass., 1976; lectr. New Eng. Law Inst.-Mass. Continuing Legal Edn., Boston, 1977-93, Nat. Coll. Probate Judges, Williamsburg, Va., 1979-82. Author: Discovery: A Comparison between English and American Civil Discovery Law with Reform Proposals, 1982, Winning Trial Advocacy, 1989; co-author: Supplements to Massachusetts Pleading and Practice, 1981; faculty editor Probate Law Jour., 1985-89; legal editor Nat. Coll. Probate Judges Newsletter, 1979-82;

mem. exec. com., master bencher Boston Inn of Ct., 1990-95; contbr. to legal jours. and books. Chmn. Citizens for Better Urban Renewal Plan, Waterville, 1962-63; mem. No. Kennebec Valley Regional Planning Commn., 1966-68, Maine Com. to Select Rhodes Scholars, 1971—; co-chmn. Aspinwall Hill Neighborhood Assn., Brookline, Mass., 1974-76; v.p. Ellis (South End) Neighborhood Assn., Boston, 1980-82, 87-88, bd. dirs., 1986-92, pres., 1989-90; chmn. Mass. Victims of Crime, Boston, 1983—; legal dir. Nat. Victims of Crime, Washington, 1983-85; candidate for Mass. Ho. of Reps., 1994, 96. John Harvard scholar Harvard U., 1957-59; Rhodes scholar Oxford U., 1960-61, 67-69. Mem. ABA (mem. adv. coun. real property, probate and trust sect. 1972-81, contbg. editor jour. of litigation sect. 1974-77), Mt. Auburn Club (Watertown, Mass.), Masons, Phi Beta Kappa, Omicron Chi Epsilon. Criminal, Personal injury (including property damage), Probate (including wills, trusts). Home: 40 Williams St Brookline MA 02446-4707 Office: Boston Univ Law Sch 765 Commonwealth Ave Boston MA 02215-1401

LEVINE, MARILYN MARKOVICH, lawyer, arbitrator; b. Bklyn., Aug. 9, 1930; d. Harry P and Fannie L (Hymowitz) Markovich; m. Louis L Levine, June 24, 1950; children: Steven R, Ronald J, Linda J Morgenstern. BS summa cum laude, Columbia U., 1950; MA, Adelphi U., 1967; JD, Hofstra U., 1977. Bar: NY 1978, US Dist Ct (no and ea dists) NY 1978, DC 1979, US Supreme Ct 1982. Sole practice, Valley Stream, N.Y., 1978—. Panel arbitrator retail food indust, New York, NY, 1980—; arbitrator NY Dist Cts, Nassau County, 1981—; contract arbitrator bldg serv indust, New York, NY, 1982—; mem Nat Acad Arbitrators, 1992—. Panel arbitrator Suffolk County Pub Employee Relations Bd, 1979—, Nassau County Pub Employee Relations Bd, 1980—, Nat Mediation Bd, 1986—; mem adv coun Ctr Labor and Indust Relationa, NY Inst Technology, 1985—; counsel Nassau Civic Club, 1978—. Mem.: ABA, Fed Mediation Bd (arbitrator 1980—), Am Arbit Asn (arbitrator 1979—), NJ Bd Mediation (panel arbitrator), Nassau County Bar Asn, DC Bar Asn, NY State Bar Asn. Alternative dispute resolution, Labor (including EEOC, Fair Labor Standards Act, labor-management relations, NLRB, OSHA). Home and Office: 1057 Linden St Valley Stream NY 11580-2135 E-mail: mmllevine@yahoo.com., ml-levine@worldnet.att.net.

LEVINE, MELDON EDISES, lawyer, former congressman; b. Los Angeles, June 7, 1943; s. Sid B. and Shirley B. (Blum) L.; children: Adam Paul, Jacob Caplan, Cara Emily. AB, U. Calif., Berkeley, 1964; MPA, Princeton U., 1966; JD, Harvard U., 1969. Bar: Calif. 1970, D.C. 1972. Assoc. Wyman, Bautzer, Rothman & Kuchel, 1969-71; legis. asst. U.S. Senate, Washington, 1971-73; ptnr. Levine Krom & Unger, Beverly Hills, Calif., 1973-77; mem. Calif. Assembly, Sacramento, 1977-82, 98th-102d Congresses from 27th Calif. dist., Washington, 1983-93; ptnr. Gibson, Dunn & Crutcher, L.A., 1993—. Author: The Private Sector and the Common Market, 1968; contbr. articles to various publs. Mem. governing bd. U.S.-Israel Sci. and Tech. Commn., U.S. Holocaust Meml. Mus.; mem. amateur baseball team Hollywood Stars, 1971—. Mem. Calif. Bar Assn., Los Angeles Bar Assn. Office: Gibson Dunn & Crutcher 2029 Century Park E Ste 4000 Los Angeles CA 90067-3032 E-mail: mlevine@gibsondunn.com.

LEVINE, MELVIN CHARLES, lawyer; b. Bklyn., Nov. 12, 1930; s. Barnet and Jennie (Iser) L. BCS, NYU, 1952; LLB, Harvard U., 1955. Bar: N.Y. 1956, U.S. Supreme Ct. 1964. Assoc. Kriger & Haber, Bklyn., 1956-58, Black, Varian & Simons, N.Y.C., 1959; sole practice N.Y.C., 1959—. Devel. multiple dwelling housing; dir. Am. ORT; mem. Am. ORT Nat. Campaign Com.; trustee Bramson ORT Coll.; mem. housing ct. adv. coun. N.Y. State Unified Ct. Sys.; mem. ind. dem. jud. screening panel N.Y.C civil ct. judges; mem. Character and Fitness Com., First Jud. Dept. Trustee Jewish Ctr. of the Hamptons. Recipient N.Y. Ort Scholarship Fund Cmty. Achievement award. Mem. N.Y. County Lawyers Assn. (dir., co-chair civil ct. practice sect., civil ct. com., housing ct. com., uniform housing ct. rules com., liaison to Assn. Bar City of N.Y. on selection of housing, civil and criminal ct. judges, com. on jud., task force on tort reform, Civil Ct. Practice Sect. Disting. Svc. award), Assn. Bar of City of N.Y. (adj. mem. jud. com.) Democrat. Jewish. State civil litigation, Landlord-tenant, Property, real (including real estate development, water). Home: 146 Waverly Pl New York NY 10014-3848 Office: 271 Madison Ave Ste 1404 New York NY 10016-1001

LEVINE, RICHARD L. lawyer; b. Englewood, N.J., Feb. 28, 1958; s. Alfred H. and Gladys Hurwitt Levine; m. Jill LaZare, Mar. 9, 2002; children: Alan, Samuel, Danielle, Brooke, David, Jamie. BA, Wesleyan U., 1980; JD, NYU, 1983. Bar: N.Y. 1984, U.S. Dist. Ct. (so. and ea. dists.) N.Y., U.S. Ct. Appeals (2d cir.), U.S. Supreme Ct. Assoc. Weil, Gotshal & Manges LLP, N.Y.C., NY, 1983—90, ptnr., 1991—. Alternative dispute resolution, Securities, General civil litigation. Office: Weil Gotshal & Manges LLP 767 5th Ave New York NY 10153 Office Fax: 212-833-3898. E-mail: richard.levine@weil.com.

LEVINE, ROBERT JAY, lawyer; b. Hackensack, NJ, Aug. 7, 1950; s. Nathan R. and Naomi (Bendel) Levine; m. Joan Beth Mirviss, Aug. 10, 1975. AB, Brown U., 1972; JD, U. Pa., 1975. Bar: N.Y. 1976, U.S. Dist. Ct. (so. and ea. dists.) N.Y. 1976. Assoc. Davis Polk & Wardwell, N.Y.C., 1975-82, ptnr., 1983—2002, sr. counsel, 2003—. Pres., bd. dirs. Sylvan Winds, Inc. Trustee N.Y. Youth Symphony, Inc. Mem.: ABA, Assn. Bar City of N.Y., N.Y. State Bar Assn., Brown Club N.Y.C., Phi Beta Kappa. Democrat. Jewish. Avocations: golf, travel, cooking, film. Banking, Bankruptcy, Corporate, general. Home: 115 Central Park W New York NY 10023-4153 Office: Davis Polk and Wardwell 450 Lexington Ave New York NY 10017-3982

LEVINE, ROBERT JEFFREY, lawyer; b. Miami Beach, Fla., Nov. 27, 1956; s. I. Stanely and Elaine (Martz) L. BSBA magna cum laude, U. Fla., 1978; JD, George Washington U., 1981. Bar: Fla. 1981, U.S. Dist. Ct. (so. dist.) Fla. 1981, U.S. Ct. Appeals (5th and 11th cirs.) 1981, U.S. Supreme Ct. 1986; cert. mediator, Fla.; lic. sea capt. USCG. Assoc. Barron, Lehman & Cardenas, Miami, 1981-82; ptnr. Haves & Levine, Miami, 1982-83; pvt. practice law Miami, 1983-85; ptnr. Toland & Levine, Miami, 1985-90, Levine & Geiger, P.A., Miami, 1990-94, Levine & Ptnrs., P.A., Miami, 1994—2002. Mem.: ATLA, Acad. Fla. Trial Lawyers, Fla. Bar Assn. Avocations: diving, fishing, skiing, golf, tennis. General civil litigation, Insurance. Office: Levine & Ptnrs PA 1110 Brickell Ave 7th Fl Miami FL 33131-3132 E-mail: RJL@levinelawfirm.com.

LEVINE, RONALD JAY, lawyer; b. Bklyn., June 23, 1953; s. Louis Leon and Marilyn Priscilla (Markovich) L.; m. Cindy Beth Israel, Nov. 18, 1979; children: Merisa, Alisha. BA summa cum laude, Princeton U., 1974; JD cum laude, Harvard U., 1977. Bar: N.Y. 1978, U.S. Dist. Ct. (so. and ea. dists.) N.Y. 1978, D.C. 1980, N.J. 1987, U.S. Supreme Ct. 1982, U.S. Ct. Apeals (2d cir.) 1983, N.J. 1987, U.S. Dist. Ct. N.J. 1987, U.S. Dist. Ct. (we. dist.) N.Y. 1991, U.S. Ct. Appeals (3d cir.) 1991, Pa. 1995. Assoc. Phillips, Nizer, Benjamin, Krim & Ballon, N.Y.C., 1977-80, Debevoise & Plimpton, N.Y.C., 1980-84, Herrick, Feinstein, N.Y.C., 1984-85, ptnr., 1985—. Gen. counsel Greater N.Y. Safety Council, N.Y.C., 1979-81; arbitrator Small Claims Ct. of Civil Ct. of City of N.Y., 1983-85; chmn. fee arbitration com. Mercer County, N.J. Mem. Site Plan Rev. Adv. Bd., West Windsor, N.J., 1986, planning bd., 1987. Mem. ABA (litigation sect.), N.Y. State Bar Assn. (chmn. com. on legal edn. and bar admission 1982-92, com. on profl. discipline 1989-90), N.J. State Bar Assn. (product liability com. 1991—, profl. responsibility com. 1992-96), Assn. of Bar of City of N.Y. (coun. jud. adminstrn. 1994-95, com. on profl. responsibility 1980-83, com. on legal assistance 1983-86, product liability com. 1987-91, trustee career devel. awards 1989-90), Phi Beta Kappa. General civil litigation, Environmental, Product liability. Home: 6 Arnold Dr Princeton Junction NJ 08550-1521 Office: Herrick Feinstein 2 Park Ave Fl 20 New York NY 10016-9302

LEVINE, SAMUEL MILTON, lawyer, retired judge, mediator, arbitrator; b. Syracuse, N.Y., Feb. 24, 1929; s. Joseph and Sophie Levine; m. Leona Miller, Sept. 9, 1950; children: Judith, Donald, Gary. BBA, Syracuse U., 1950; JD, Bklyn. Law Sch., 1953. Bar: N.Y. 1953, U.S. Supreme Ct. 1960, U.S. Dist. Ct. (ea. and so. dists.) N.Y. 1962; cert. mediator, arbitrator. Assoc. Law Office of William S. Miller, Esq., N.Y.C., 1954-62, Law Office of Ferdinand I. Haber, Esq., Mineola, N.Y., 1958-62; pvt. practice Nassau County, N.Y., 1962-65; counsel English, Cianciulli, Reisman & Peirez, 1962-65; supt. of real estate Nassau County, 1965-84; pvt. practice Garden City, N.Y., 1984—. Pres., past pres. bd. of judges Dist. Ct. Nassau County; N.Y. state hearing officer; lectr. in field. Contbr. articles to profl. jours. Past chmn. Sch. Aid Coun. L.I., Citizens Com. for Elmont Schs., N.Y.; former counsel, trustee Temple Bnai Israel, Elmont; former bd. visitors Pilgrim State Hosp.; treas., counsel N.Y. State Coun. Orgns. for Handicapped; past pres. Nassau County Epilepscy Found.; former chmn. Health and Welfare Coun. Nassau County; former mem. Nassau-Suffolk Health Sys. Agy.; del. White House Conf. on Children and Youth, 1960; candidate N.Y. State Senate, 1964; Dem. candidate Dist. Ct. Judge, 1985; candidate N.Y. State Supreme Ct., 1990; counsel Health Advs., Voice for Handicapped, Fedn. Parent Orgns., League of Voters for Handicapped; del. White House Conf. on Disabilities, 1970, White House Conf. on Sr. Citizens, 1980, White House Conf. on Mental Health, 1999. With U.S. Army, 1948. Recipient Adv. of Yr. award L.I. Coun. Fedn. Parents Orgns., 1978. Mem. Nat. Acad. Elder Law Attys., N.Y. State Bar Assn., Nassau County Bar Assn. (former chmn. social svc. and health law com., legis. com.), Syracuse U. Alumni Club, Kiwanis, Knights of Pythias, B'nai B'rith. Home: 711 Shore Rd Apt 2E Long Beach NY 11561-4707 E-mail: adkjdgsamny@aol.com.

LEVINE, SANFORD HAROLD, lawyer; b. Troy, N.Y., Mar. 13, 1938; s. Louis and Reba (Semegren) L.; m. Margaret R. Appelbaum, Oct. 29, 1967; children: Jessica Sara, Abby Miriam. AB, Syracuse U., 1959, JD, 1961. Bar: N.Y. 1961, U.S. Dist. Ct. (no. dist.) N.Y. 1961, U.S. Dist. Ct. (we. dist.) N.Y. 1979, U.S. Dist. Ct. (ea. and so. dists.) N.Y. 1980, U.S. Ct. Appeals (2d cir.) 1962, U.S. Supreme Ct. 1967. Law asst. to assoc. judge N.Y. Ct. Appeals, Albany and to justice N.Y. Supreme Ct., 1962-66, N.Y. Ct. Appeals, Albany, 1964; asst. counsel N.Y. State Temporary commn. on Constl. Conv., N.Y.C., 1966-67; assoc. counsel SUNY System, Albany, 1967-70, dep. univ. counsel, 1970-78, acting counsel, 1970-71, acting univ. counsel, 1978-79, univ. counsel and vice chancellor legal affairs, 1979-97, prof. Sch. of Edn., dir. program in edn. and law, 1997—. Adj. prof. Sch. of Edn. State U. N.Y., Albany, 1992-97; mem. paralegal curriculum adv. com. Schenectady County Community Coll., 1975— . Editl. bd. Syracuse U. Law Rev., 1960-61; editl. adv. bd. Jour. Coll. and Univ. Law, 1977-81. Fellow Am. Bar Found., N.Y. Bar Found., State Acad. for Pub. Adminstrn.; mem. ABA (ho. dels. 1987-89), N.Y. State Bar Assn., Albany County Bar Assn., Nat. Assn. Coll. and Univ. Attys. (exec. bd. 1979-82, bd. dirs. 1982-89, pres. 1986-87), Am. Soc. Pub. Adminstrn. Home: 1106 Godfrey Ln Schenectady NY 12309-2712

LEVINE, STEVEN JON, lawyer; b. N.Y.C., Sept. 27, 1942; s. Irving I. and Freda S. (Silverman) Levine; m. Linda Jane Silberman, Apr. 23, 1967; 1 child, Lawrence Alan. BS, Syracuse U., 1964; JD, St. John's U., 1966; MA, CCNY, 1973; LLM, NYU, 1978. Bar: NY 1967. Associate Augustin J. San Filippo & Steven Jon Levine, PC, predecessor, N.Y.C., 1966-78; mem. Vittoria & Forsythe and predecessor, N.Y.C., 1978-93, Levine & Zelman, 1993—. Arbitrator N.Y. County Civil Ct. Panel, 1980-93; asst. csl. N.Y. State Senate Judiciary Com., 1977. Author: of legal column Tomorrow newspapers, 1991-2000; co-author: Divorce Q & A: Answers to Questions about Divorce, Equitable Distribution, Maintenance, Custody and Child Support; host weekly radio law program Sta. WVOX, 1990-91; creator, narrator: (audio cassette program) Coping with Separation and Divorce. Committeeman, Bronx County, 1970-76; bd. dirs. Jewish Conciliation Bd. Am., 1973-93. Mem. ABA, N.Y. State Bar Assn., Westchester County Bar Assn., Assn. Bar City N.Y. (sect. vice chmn. matrimonial com. 1977-80), Am. Arbitration Assn. (no-fault, comml. panels 1975-88). Family and matrimonial, General practice, Probate (including wills, trusts). Office: 50 Main St Ph White Plains NY 10606-1901 also: Levine & Zelman 630 5th Ave New York NY 10111-0100

LEVINE, STEVEN MARK, lawyer; b. N.Y.C., Feb. 1, 1956; s. Arthur Morton and Selma (Aber) L.; m. Patricia Mary Petersilia, Sept. 2, 1990; children: Caitlin, Ryan. BA, Clark U., 1978; JD, George Washington U., 1981. Bar: D.C. 1981, Md. 1987, Va. 1994, U.S. Dist. Ct. D.C. 1982, U.S. Dist. Ct. Md. 1985, U.S. Dist. Ct. (ea. dist.) Va. 1995, U.S. Ct. Appeals (D.C. cir.) 1982, U.S. Ct. Appeals (1st cir.) 1991, U.S. Ct. Appeals (2d cir.) 1986, U.S. Ct. Appeals (3d cir.) 1987, U.S. Ct. Appeals (4th cir.) 1983, U.S. Supreme Ct. 2000. Atty. Wilson, Elser, Moskowitz, Edelman & Dicker, Washington, 1981-93; prin. The Law Office of Steven M. Levine, Alexandria, Va., 1993—. Bd. dirs. SOC Enterprises, Inc., Arlington, Va., 1994-2000. Contbr. chpt. to book. Officer of Election, Arlington County Bd. Elections, Arlington, Va., 1990-97. Democrat. Jewish. Civil rights, General civil litigation, Personal injury (including property damage). Home: 2631 S Grant St Arlington VA 22202-2519 Office: 2825 Duke St Alexandria VA 22314-4512 E-mail: slevinelaw@aol.com.

LEVINE, THOMAS JEFFREY PELLO, lawyer; b. Santa Monica, Calif., Mar. 6, 1952; s. Allan Lester and Shirley Elaine (Pello) L.; children: Marissa, Matthew, Molly. Student, U. Denver, 1970-71, Calif. State U., Northridge, 1971-73, Uppsala U., Sweden; BA, Calif. State U., Sacramento, 1974; JD, Southwestern U., 1977; postgrad., Yale U., 1999. Bar: Calif. 1977, U.S. Dist. Ct. (cen. dist.) Calif. 1978. Ptnr. Levine & Levine, L.A., 1977-83; staff atty. Fed. Deposit Ins. Corp., Newport Beach, Calif., 1983-85; v.p., assoc. counsel Imperial Bank, Inglewood, Calif., 1985-88; v.p., counsel Community Bank, Pasadena, Calif., 1988; gen. counsel, sr. v.p., sec. Calif. Commerce Bank, Banamex USA Bancorp, L.A., 1988-2001; gen. counsel, sr. v.p. Banamex-Citibank, 2001; spl. counsel, office of the gen. counsel L.A. Unified Sch. Dist., 2002—. Legal affairs com. mem. Calif. Bankers Assn., San Francisco, 1990—; chmn. Am. Bankers Assn. Bank Counsel Com. 1993-97. Dir. Angelino Heights Historic Preservation Assn., L.A., 1985-95; sec., dir. Carroll Ave. Restoration Found., L.A., 1979-87; dir. Wilshire C. of C., L.A., 1982. Mem. L.A. County Bar Assn., Braemar Country Club (bd. govs. 1979-83). Jewish. Avocations: running, golf, aztec history, historic preservation. Banking, Commercial, consumer (including collections, credit), Private international. Office: Levine & Levine 5460 White Oak Ave Ste A330 Encino CA 91316

LEVINE, WALTER DANIEL, lawyer, accountant; b. Paterson, N.J., July 19, 1941; s. Samuel M. and May (Zaretzky) LeV.; m. Joy Herman, Dec. 24, 1964 (div. 1972); children: Lee Jason, Stephen Ian; m. Ellen R. Ignatoff, Feb. 12, 1976 (div. 2000); children: Elissa Whitney, Evan Harris. BA, Rutgers U., 1962; JD, Temple U., 1965; BS, Fairleigh Dickinson U., 1967. Bar: N.J. 1965. Assoc. Gutkin & Miller, Newark, 1965-72; ptnr. firm Gutkin Miller Shapiro Berson, Millburn, N.J., 1972-78; sole practice Fairfield, N.J., 1978-88; sr. ptnr. Friedman LeVine & Brooks, Florham Park, N.J., 1988-91; sole practice Florham Park, 1991—. Author: Prentice Hall Tax Reports, 1971. Bd. dirs., v.p. Men's Club, Congregation B'nai Jeshurun, 1991, pres., 1993-95; coach, mgr. Livingston (N.J.) Am. Little League, 1988-95. Mem. N.J. Bar Assn. (mem. taxation com. 2000—), Passaic County Bar Assn. (chmn. tax com. 1989), K.P. (chancellor-comdr. Passaic chpt. 1987), Mensa. Democrat. Jewish. Avocations: sports autographs, sports memorabilia. Estate planning, Probate (including wills, trusts), Taxation, general. Home: 345 Walnut St Livingston NJ 07039 Office: 23 Vreeland Rd Florham Park NJ 07932-1510 E-mail: taxlaw1@aol.com.

LEVINGS, THERESA LAWRENCE, lawyer; b. Kansas City, Mo., Oct. 24, 1952; d. William Youngs and Dorothy (Neer) Frick; m. Darryl Wayne Levings, May 25, 1974; children: Leslie Page, Kerry Dillon. BJ, U. Mo., 1973; JD, U. Mo., Kansas City, 1979. Bar: Mo. 1979, U.S. Dist. Ct. (we. dist.) Mo. 1979, U.S. Ct. Appeals (8th cir.) 1982, U.S. Ct. Appeals (10th cir.) 1986, U.S. Dist. Ct. (ea. dist.) Mo. 1989. Copy editor Kansas City Star, 1975-78; law clk. to judge Mo. Supreme Ct., Jefferson City, 1979-80; from assoc. to ptnr. Morrison & Hecker, Kansas City, 1980-94; founding ptnr. Badger & Levings, L.C., Kansas City, 1994—2003. Mem. fed. practice com. U.S. Dist. Ct. (we. dist.), 1990-95; mem. fed. adv. com. U.S. Ct. Appeals (8th cir.), 1994-97. Mem. Mo. Bar (bd. govs. 1990—03, pres. 2001-02, young lawyers coun. 1982-89, chair 1988-89, Pres. award 1989, Outstanding Svc. award young lawyers coun. 1985, 86), Assn. Women Lawyers Greater Kansas City (pres. 1986-87, Woman of Yr. 1993), Lawyers Assn. Greater Kansas City (bd. dirs. young lawyers sect. 1982-83), Kansas City Met. Bar Assn. (chair civil practice and procedure com. 1988-89, chair fed. practice com. 1990-91). Federal civil litigation, Insurance, Product liability. Office: Badger & Levings LC 1101 Walnut St Kansas City MO 64106-2134

LEVINSON, DAVID LAWRENCE, lawyer; b. Bklyn., Jan. 9, 1945; s. Herman and Bertha (Fuchs) L.; m. Marjorie Joan Friedman, June 18, 1967; children: Andrew, Joshua, Lauren. BA, Bklyn. Coll., 1966; JD, Bklyn. Law Sch., 1969. Bar: N.Y. 1969, U.S. Dist. Ct. (so. dist.) N.Y. 1971, U.S. Supreme Ct. 1976. Asst. dist. atty. N.Y. County Dist. Atty.'s Office, N.Y.C., 1969-73; ptnr. law firm Rider, Weiner & Loeb, P.C., Newburgh, N.Y., 1973-80; ptnr. Levinson, Zeccola, Reineke, Ornstein & Selinger, P.C., 1980—2001, Levinson, Reineke & Ornstein, P.C., 2001—. Pres. Monroe (N.Y.) Temple of Liberal Judaism, 1981-83; justice Town of Woodbury, 1978—, Village of Tuxedo Park, 1994--; mem. Zoning Bd. Appeals, 1976-77; atty. Village of Monroe Planning Bd., 1988—, Village of Goshen Zoning Bd. Appeals, 1988—, Village of Goshen, 1989—; mem. Orange County Charter Rev. Commn., 1985. Mem. Orange County Bar Assn. (mem. judiciary com. 1980-90, mem. grievance com. 1983-88, bd. dirs. 1988—, pres. 1993), N.Y. State Bar Assn., Newburgh Bar Assn., Lions Club (publicity com. 1983-84), Woodbury Cmty. Assn. State civil litigation, Criminal, Family and matrimonial. Home: 4 Jones Dr Highland Mills NY 10930-2710 Office: Levinson Reineke & Ornstein PC 11 Abrams Rd Central Valley NY 10917-4101

LEVINSON, PAUL HOWARD, lawyer; b. N.Y.C., Nov. 9, 1952; s. Saul and Gloria (Samson) L.; m. Susan Norine Morley, May 29, 1983; children: Lauren Hope, David Ross. BA in Sociology, Northwestern U., 1973; JD, Columbia U., 1977. Bar: N.Y. 1978; U.S. Dist. Ct. (so. and ea. dist.) N.Y. 1983, U.S. Dist. Ct. (no. dist.) N.Y. 1992; U.S. Ct. Appeals (2d cir.) 1986, U.S. Ct. Appeals (3rd cir. 1987), U.S. Supreme Ct. 1986. Asst. dist. atty., supervising sr. trial atty. Kings County, Bklyn., 1977-84; assoc. Blodnick, Schultz & Abramowitz, P.C., Lake Success, N.Y., 1984-85; ptnr. Leavy, Rosensweig & Hyman and predecessor firms, N.Y.C., 1985-99, McLaughlin & Stern, LLP, N.Y.C., 2000—. Trustee Cmty. Synagogue, Rye, N.Y., 1996-2002, exec. com. (corr. sec. 2000-); mem. adv. coun. parks and recreation Village of Rye Brook, N.Y., 1994-97. Harlan Fiske Stone scholar. Mem. ABA, N.Y. State Bar Assn., Assn. of Bar of City of N.Y. (com. on criminal justice ops. and budget 1992-94, com. on criminal cts. 1995—, chmn. sub-com. on the N.Y.C. civilian complaint rev. bd., moderator), Bklyn. Bar Assn. (continuing legal edn. seminars in criminal trial advocacy and matrimonial practice), Columbia Law Sch. Alumni Assn., Northwestern U. Entertainment Alliance East (treas. 1998—, pres. 2000-2002), Northwestern U. Alumni Assn., Clubs: Northwestern U. Alumni of N.Y.C. Democrat. Jewish. Avocations: tennis, skiing, swimming. General civil litigation, Criminal, Entertainment. Home: 312 Betsy Brown Rd Rye Brook NY 10573-1901 Office: McLaughlin & Stern LLP 260 Madison Ave 18th Fl New York NY 10016 E-mail: plevinson@mclaughlinstern.com.

LEVINSON, PETER JOSEPH, retired lawyer; b. Washington, June 11, 1943; AB in History cum laude, Brandeis U., Waltham, Mass., 1965; JD, Harvard U., 1968. Summer supr. Harvard Legal Aid Bur., Cambridge, Mass., 1968; rsch. asst. Harvard Law Sch., 1968-69; tchg. fellow Osgoode Hall Law Sch. York (Can.) U., 1969-70, rsch. assoc., 1969-70, asst. prof., 1970-71; dep. atty. gen. State of Hawaii, 1971-75; vis. fellow Harvard U., 1976-77; ptnr. Levinson and Levinson, Honolulu, 1977-79; spl. asst. to dir. office program support Legal Svcs. Corp., Washington, 1979; cons. Select Commn. on Immigration and Refugee Policy, Washington, 1980-81; minority counsel subcom. on immigration, refugees and internat. law com. on judiciary U.S. Ho. of Reps., Washington, 1981-85, minority counsel subcom. monopolies and comml. law, 1985-89, minority counsel subcom. econ. and comml. law, 1989-95, counsel com. on judiciary, 1995-2001, ret., 2001. Mem. ABA, Hawaii State Bar Assn. (chmn. standing com. on continuing legal edn. 1972, chmn. standing com. on jud. adminstrn. 1979).

LEVINSON, STEVEN HENRY, state supreme court justice; b. Cin., June 8, 1946; BA with distinction, Stanford U., 1968; JD, U. Mich., 1971. Bar: Hawaii 1972, U.S. Dist. Ct. Hawaii 1972, U.S. Ct. Appeals (9th cir.) 1972. Law clk. to Hon. Bernard H. Levinson Hawaii Supreme Ct., 1971-72; pvt. practice Honolulu, 1972-89; judge Hawaii Cir. Ct. (1st cir.), 1989-92; assoc. justice Hawaii Supreme Ct., Honolulu, 1992—. Staff mem. U. Mich. Jour. Law Reform, 1970-71. Active Temple Emanu-El. Mem. ABA (jud. adminstrn. divsn. 1989—), Hawaii State Bar Assn. (dir. young lawyers divsn. 1975-76, dir. 1982-84), Nat. Jud. Coll., Am. Judges Assn., Am. Judicature Soc. Jewish. Office: Supreme Ct Hawaii Aliiolani Hale 417 S King St Honolulu HI 96813-2912

LEVISS, STEWART MICHAEL, lawyer; b. 1967; JD, Wash. Coll., 1992. Shareholder Budd Larner Rosenbaum Greenberg & Sade, Short Hills, NJ, 1992—2002. Professional liability, Personal injury (including property damage), General civil litigation. Office: Budd Larner Rosenbaum Greenberg & Sade 150 John F Kennedy Parkway Short Hills NJ 07078 E-mail: sleviss@budd-larner.com.

LEVIT, JAY J(OSEPH), lawyer; b. Phila., Feb. 20, 1934; s. Albert and Mary Levit; m. Heloise Bertman, July 14, 1962; children: Richard Bertman, Robert Edward, Darcy Francine. AB, Case Western Res. U., 1955; JD, U. Richmond, 1958; LLM, Harvard U., 1959. Bar: Va. 1958, D.C. Ct. Appeals 1961, U.S. Ct. Appeals (4th cir.) 1967, U.S. Ct. Appeals (11th cir.) 1989, U.S. Supreme Ct. 1961. Trial atty. U.S. Dept. Justice, Washington, 1960-64; sr. atty. Gen. Dynamics Corp., Rochester, N.Y., 1965-67; ptnr. Stallard & Levit, Richmond, Va., 1968-77, Levit, Mann, Halligan & Warren, Richmond, 1978—. Instr. U. Mich. Law Sch., Ann Arbor, 1964-65; adj. assoc. prof. U. Richmond Law Sch., 1974-77; adj. lectr. Va. Commonwealth U., Richmond, 1970-85; lectr. in field. Contbg. editor The Developing Labor Law, 4th edit., Bur. Nat. Affairs, 1974—. Recipient ABA and Bur. Nat. Affairs Books cert. of appreciation for significant contbns. to advancement of the law, 1999—2002. Mem. ABA (labor com.), Va. Bar Assn. (labor and employment com., Chair's award for extraordinary contbns. to labor and employment law sect. 1999), Fed. Bar Assn. (labor and employment com.). Avocations: art collecting, jogging, swimming, travel. Labor (including EEOC, Fair Labor Standards Act, labor-management relations, NLRB, OSHA), General civil litigation, Personal injury (including property damage). Home: 419 Dellbrooks Pl Richmond VA 23233-5559 Office: Levit Mann Halligan & Warren 1301 N Hamilton St Richmond VA 23230-3959 also: Levit Mann Halligan & Warren 127 Thompson St Ashland VA 23005-1511 E-mail: levmanhal@mindspring.com.

LEVIT, WILLIAM HAROLD, JR., lawyer; b. San Francisco, Feb. 8, 1938; s. William Harold and Barbara Janis Kaiser L.; m. Mary Elizabeth Webster, Feb. 13, 1971; children: Alison Jones Baumler, Alexandra Bradley Kovacevich, Laura Elizabeth Fletcher, Amalia Elizabeth Webster Todryk,

William Harold, III. BA magna cum laude, Yale U., 1960; MA Internat. Rels., U. Calif., Berkeley, 1962; LLB, Harvard U., 1967. Bar: N.Y. 1968, Calif. 1974, Wis. 1979. Fgn. service officer Dept. State, 1962-64; assoc. Davis Polk & Wardwell, N.Y.C., 1967-73; assoc. ptnr. Hughes Hubbard & Reed, N.Y.C., L.A., 1973-79; sec. and gen. counsel Rexnord Inc., Milw., 1979-83; ptnr., dir., chair internat. practice group Godfrey & Kahn, Milw., 1983—. Substitute arbitrator Iran-U.S. Claims Tribunal, The Hague, 1984-88; lectr. Practicing Law Inst., ABA, Calif. Continuing Edn. of Bar, State Bar of Wis. Contbr. to: Mergers and the Private Antitrust Suit: The Private Enforcement of Section 7 of the Clayton Act, 1977. Bd. dirs. Wis. Humane Soc., 1980-90, pres., 1986-88; bd. dirs. Vis. Nurse Corp., Milw., 1980-90, chmn., 1985-87; bd. dirs. Vis. Nurse Found., 1986-95, chmn., 1989-91; bd. dirs. Aurora Health Care Inc., 1988-93, Wis. Soc. to Prevent Blindness, 1981-91, Aurora Health Care Ventures, 1993—, chair, 1998-2000, 2002-03; bd. trustees Columbia Coll. Nursing, 1992-98, chair, 2002—; trustee Mt. Mary. Coll. 2002-, dir.; adv. bd. Med. Coll. Wis. Cardiovasc. Ctr., 1994—, chmn., 1999-2002, chmn. Bd. Ad Oversight Supreme Ct. Wis. Office Lawyer Regulation, 2000—; rep. Assn. Yale Alumni, 1976-79, 81-84, 90-93; pres. Yale Club So. Calif., 1977-79; neutral advisor panel and franchise, and ins. panels CPR Inst. for Dispute Resolution. Ford Found. fellow U. Pa., 1960-61, NDEA fellow U. Calif., Berkeley, 1961-62. Mem.: ABA, Am. Arbitration Assn. (comml. panel, internat. panel 1977—), Inst. Jud. Adminstrn., Am. Soc. Internat. Law, N.Am. Coun. London Ct. of Internat. Arbitration, N.Y. Stock Exch. (panel arbitrators 1988—), Chartered Inst. Arbitrators (London), Nat. Assn. Security Dealers (panel arbitrators 1988—), Am. Br. Internat. Law Assn., Bar Assn. 7th Cir. (pres. 2002—03), State Bar Wis. (dir. internat. bus. transactions sect. 1985—92, dist. 2 Wis. Supreme Ct. bd. attys. profl. responsbility com. 1985—94, chmn. 1993—94), L.A. County Bar Assn. (ethics com. 1976—79), State Bar Calif. (com. on continuing edn. of bar 1977—79), Assn. Bar City N.Y., Am. Soc. Corp. Secs. (dir. 1981—92, pres. Wis. chpt. 1982—83), Am. Law Inst., Town Club, Milw. Athletic Club, Milw. Club, Phi Beta Kappa. Antitrust, Federal civil litigation, State civil litigation. Office: 780 N Water St Ste 1500 Milwaukee WI 53202-3512 E-mail: walevit@gklaw.com.

LEVITAN, DAVID M(AURICE), lawyer, educator; b. Tver, Lithuania, Dec. 25, 1915; (parents Am. citizens); m. Judith Morley; children: Barbara Lane Levitan, Stuart Dean Levitan. BS, Northwestern U., 1936, MA, 1937; PhD, U. Chgo., 1940; JD, Columbia U., 1948. Bar: N.Y. 1948, U.S. Dist. Ct. (so. dist.) N.Y. 1948, U.S. Supreme Ct. 1953. Various U.S. Govt. adminstrv. and advisory positions with Nat. Youth Adminstrn., Office Price Adminstrn., War Prodn. Bd., Fgn. Econ. Adminstrn. Supreme Hdqrs. Allied Expeditionary Force, and Cen. European div. Dept. State, 1940-46; cons., sec. joint-com. of 5th and 6th coms., 2d Gen. Assembly, dir. com. of experts for establishing adminstrv. tribunal UN, 1946-47; cons. pub. affairs dept., producer series of pub. affairs programs on TV and radio ABC, 1946-53; pvt. practice N.Y.C., 1948-66; counsel Hahn & Hessen, N.Y.C., 1966-68, ptnr., 1968-86, counsel, 1986-96; instr. U. Chgo., 1938-41; adj. prof. public law Columbia U., 1946-65; adj. prof. John Jay Coll. Criminal Justice, CUNY, 1966-75; adj. prof. polit. sci. Post Coll., 1964-66; adj. prof. law Cardozo Sch. Law, 1978-82; pvt. practice, N.Y.C., 1996—. Asst. to Ill. state adminstr. Nat. Youth Adminstrn., chief budget sect., Washington, 1940-41; mgmt. analyst Office of Price Adminstrn., 1941; spl. asst. to chmn. War Prodn. Bd., 1942-43; chief property control divsn. Fgn. Econ. Adminstrn., Washington, 1944-45; with U.S. Group of Control Coun. for Germany at SHAEF, London, 1944; advisor Ctrl. European divsn. U.S. Dept. State, 1945; cons. UN, 1946-47, Sect. Joint Com. 5th and 6th Coms., 1946-47, 2d session of 1st Gen. Assembly, 1946-47; dir. Com. of Experts on Establishment of Adminstrn. Tribunal, 1946-47; cons. pub. affairs dept. ABC, 1946-53. Contbr. articles to legal jours. Mem. Nassau County (N.Y.) Welfare Bd., 1965-69; chmn. Planning Bd., Village of Roslyn Harbor, N.Y., 1965-66; chmn. Bd. of Zoning Appeals, Village Roslyn Harbor, 1967-86. Recipient Demobilization award Social Sci. Rsch. Coun., 1946-48. Fellow Am. Coll. Trust and Estate Counsel; mem. ABA, Am. Polit. Sci. Assn., Am. Soc. Internat. Law, Am. Law Inst., Assn. Bar City N.Y. Constitutional, Probate (including wills, trusts), Estate taxation. Home: 103 NE 19th Ave Deerfield Beach FL 33441-6106 Office: Ste 704 455 North End Ave New York NY 10282

LEVITAN, JAMES A. lawyer; b. N.Y.C., Mar. 24, 1925; s. Leo and Della (Brody) L.; m. Ruth Terry White, Jan. 30, 1951; children— Deborah A., Judith T., Susan J. BS in Chem. Engring, M.I.T., 1948; LL.B. (mem. bd. Law Rev. 1950-51), Columbia U., 1951. Bar: N.Y. bar 1951. Since practiced in, N.Y.C.; ptnr. Skadden, Arps, Slate, Meagher & Flom, 1965-95, of counsel, 1995—. Life mem. MIT Corp., Cambridge, Mass., 1995-99, emeritus, 2000, chmn. audit com., 1994-2000; regional chmn. N.Y.C. MIT Ednl. Coun., 1974-90; lectr. in field of tax. Served with USNR, 1944-46. Stone scholar, 1948-51; Kent scholar, 1950 Mem. N.Y. State Bar Assn., Assn. Bar City N.Y., Tau Beta Pi. Corporate taxation, Estate taxation, Personal income taxation. Home: 26 Wake Robin Ln Stamford CT 06903-4611 Office: Skadden Arps Slate Meagher & Flom 4 Times Sq Fl 33 New York NY 10036-6522 E-mail: jlevitan@optonline.net., jlevitan@skadden.com.

LEVITAN, KATHERINE D. lawyer; b. Vienna, Austria, July 8, 1933; came to U.S. 1938, naturalized 1942; d. Otto and Hedweega (Saltzer) Lenz; m. Leonard Levitan, Sept. 12, 1952; children— Joel, Jeffrey, Debbie, Diane. B.A. cum laude, N.Y.U. 1952, J.D. cum laude, 1955, LL.M. in Criminal and Family Law, 1977. Bar: N.Y. 1956, U.S. Dist. Ct. (ea. dist.) N.Y. 1972, U.S. Supreme Ct. 1974. Tchr. bus. law N.Y. Inst. Tech., Old Westbury, 1968-69; assoc. Bennett Reiss, Great Neck, N.Y., 1969-70, Malone and Dorfman, Freeport, N.Y., 1970-71; sole practice, Jericho, N.Y., 1971-80; practice with assocs., Mineola, N.Y., 1980— ; also lectr.; assoc. prof. Hofstra Law Sch. Bd. dirs., legal counsel For Our Children and Us, Inc., Nassau chpt. ACLU, 1975— ; mem. Nassau County Democratic Com., 1969— , law guardian adv. panel 2d dept. Human Rights Adv. Commn. Nassau County; past pres. Nassau chpt. N.Y. Civil Liberties Union. Mem. Nassau Bar Assn. (grievance com., martim com.), Nassau/Suffolk Women's Bar Assn. (past pres., legal counsel), Nassau Civil Liberties Union, L.I. Women's Network, Acad. Matrimonial Lawyers, Contbr. articles to profl. publs. Civil rights, Family and matrimonial, General practice. Home: PO Box 846 New Lebanon NY 12125-0846 Office: 83 Prospect St Huntington NY 11743-3306

LEVITIN, MICHAEL JAY, lawyer; b. Norfolk, Va., July 26, 1960; s. Jordan S. and Carol A. (Hyman) L.; m. Caryn F. Ginsberg, Oct. 7, 1990. AB, Harvard U., 1982, JD, 1986; MA in Law and Diplomacy, Fletcher Sch. Law & Diplomacy, 1990. Bar: N.Y. 1987, D.C. 1988. Atty.-advisor Office of Gen. Counsel, U.S. Dept. Treas., Washington, 1986-88; assoc. Sidley & Austin, Washington, 1988-94, Winthrop, Stimson, Putnam & Roberts, Washington, 1994-2000; adj. prof. Georgetown U. Law Ctr., 1999—; sr. ptnr. Hale and Dorr LLP, Washington, 2000—. Co-author: Export and Trade Finance, 2d edit., 2000. Office: Hale and Dorr LLP 1455 Pennsylvania Ave NW Washington DC 20004-1008

LEVMORE, SAUL, law educator, dean; b. 1953; BA, Columbia Coll., 1973, PhD, 1978; JD, Yale U., 1980; LLD (hon.) , Ill. Inst. Tech. Chgo.-Kent Law Sch., 1995. Bar: Va. 1983. Dean Jonathan Edwards Coll. Yale U., 1979-80; asst. prof. U. Va. , Charlottesville, 1980-84; prof. U. Va., Charlottesville, 1984—98, Brokaw prof. of law; William B. Graham prof. law U. Chgo. Law Sch., 1998—, dean, 2001—. Lectr. econs. Yale U., 1976-80, vis. prof., 1986-87; vis. prof. Harvard U., 1990-91, U. Chgo., 1993. Office: U Chgo Law Sch 1111E 60th St Chicago IL 60637

LEVY, ADAM B. lawyer; b. Bklyn. BA, SUNY, Albany, 1989; JD, Hofstra U., 1992. Bar: N.Y., U.S. Dist. Ct. (so. and ea. dists.) N.Y. Asst. dist. atty. Suffolk County Atty.'s Office, Riverhead, NY, 1992—96; ptnr. Maher & Broyman, LLP, Carmel, NY, 1996—98, Levy, Santoro & Santoro, Carmel, 1998—. Mem.: Putman County Bar Assn. (pres. 2000—02). Criminal, Family and matrimonial. Office: Levy Santoro and Santoro 105 Gleneida Ave Carmel NY 10512 Business E-Mail: ablevy@rcn.com.

LEVY, ALAN M. lawyer; b. Milw., Nov. 10, 1940; s. Sam and Emma (Gold) L.; m. Tee Gee Azine, Mar. 3, 1964; children: Shawn, Joshua, Pamela, Jonathan. AB, U. Chgo., 1963, JD, 1965. Bar: Wis. 1965, Ill. 1982, U.S. Ct. Appeals (2d, 5th, 6th, 7th, 8th, 9th and 10th cirs.) 1968, U.S. Dist. Ct. (ea. dist.) Wis. 1965, (no. dist.) Ill. 1982, (so. dist.) Ill. 1969, U.S. Supreme Ct. 1980, U.S. Dist. Ct. (we. dist.) Mich. 2001. Ptnr. Goldberg, Previant, Uelman, Gratz, Miller et al, Milw., 1965-82; sr. legal counsel, dir. plan devel./compliance Central States, S.E. and S.W. Areas Pension Fund, Chgo., 1982-85; assoc. O'Neil, Cannon & Hollman, S.C., Milw., 1985-91, Lindner & Marsack, S.C., Milw., 1991—. Bd. incorporators Commonwealth Mutual Savs. Bank, Milw., 1977-82; adj. prof. labor law U. Wis., Milw., 1974—. Contbr. articles to profl. jours. Chmn. U. Chgo. Alumni Schs. Com., Milw., 1987-2003; trustee Congregation Emanu-El B'Ne Jeshurun, Milw., 1978-82, 86-92; campaign co-chmn. Urban Day Sch., Milw., 1988; active ACLU, Milw., 1966-82. Named Page scholar, U. Chgo., 1961, Iron Mask, 1961-64. Mem. ABA (labor law sect. 1967—), Wis. Bar Assn. (labor law sect. chmn. 1979-80), Ill. Bar Assn., Iron Mask Soc., U. Chgo. Alumni Assn. of Milw. (chmn. 1996-98), U. Chgo. Alumni Assn. (bd. govs. 1998—, v.p. 2002--). Labor (including EEOC, Fair Labor Standards Act, labor-management relations, NLRB, OSHA), Municipal (including bonds), Pension, profit-sharing, and employee benefits. Office: Lindner & Marsack SC 411 E Wisconsin Ave Ste 1000 Milwaukee WI 53202-4416 E-mail: amluclaw@aol.com., alevy@lindner-marsack.com.

LEVY, CHARLOTTE LOIS, law librarian, educator, consultant, lawyer; b. Cin., Aug. 31, 1944; d. Samuel M. and Helen (Lowitz) L.; m. Herbert Regenstreif, Dec. 11, 1980; 1 dau., Cara Rachael Regenstreif. B.A., U. Ky., 1966; M.S., Columbia U., 1969; J.D., No. Ky. U., 1975. Bar: Colo. 1979, N.Y. 1985, Ky. 1985, U.S. Ct. Appeals (6th cir.) 1986. Law librarian No. Ky. U., 1971-75; law librarian, assoc. prof. law Pace U., 1975-77; mgr. Fred B. Rothman & Co., Littleton, Colo., 1977-79; law librarian, prof. Bklyn. Law Sch., 1979-85; adj. prof. Pratt Inst. Grad. Sch. Library and Info. Sci., 1982-85; atty. Cabinet for Human Resources, Frankfort, Ky., 1985-87, atty., pres. Vantage Info. Cons., Inc., Lexington, 1983—; cons. to various libraries, pubs. 1st v.p. Ohavay Zion Synagogue; pres. bd. trustees, Syncopated, Inc. Mem. Am. Assn. Law Libraries (cert. law librarian), ABA, Ky. Bar. Assn., Fayette County Bar Assn. Democrat. Jewish. Author: The Human Body and the Law (Am. Jurisprudence Book award in domestic relations 1974, in trusts 1975), 1974, 2d edit., 1983; Computer-Assisted Litigation Support, 1984; mem. editorial bd. No. Ky. U. Law Rev., 1974-75. Home: 200 McDowell Rd Lexington KY 40502-1896

LEVY, DAVID, consultant, retired lawyer, insurance company executive; b. Bridgeport, Conn., Aug. 3, 1932; s. Aaron and Rachel (Goldman) L. BS in Econs., U. Pa., 1954; JD, Yale U., 1957. Bar: Conn. 1958, U.S. Supreme Ct. 1963, D.C. 1964, Mass. 1965, N.Y. 1971, Pa. 1972; CPA, Conn. Acct. Arthur Andersen & Co., N.Y.C., 1957-59; sole practice Bridgeport, 1959-60; specialist tax law IRS, Washington, 1960-64; counsel State Mut. Life Ins. Co., Worcester, Mass., 1964-70; assoc. gen. counsel taxation Penn Mut. Life Ins. Co., Phila., 1971-81; sole practice Washington, 1982-87; v.p., tax counsel Pacific Life Ins. Co., Newport Beach, Calif., 1987-2001; ret., 2001. Author: (with others) Life Insurance Company Tax Series, Bureau National Affairs Tax Management Income Tax, 1970-71. Mem. adv. bd. Tax Mgmt., Washington, 1975-90, Hartford Inst. on Ins. Taxation, 1990-97; bd. dirs. Citizens Plan E Orgn., Worcester, 1966-70. With AUS, 1957. Mem. ABA (vice-chmn. employee benefits com. 1980-86, ins. cos. com. 1984-86, torts and ins. practice sect., subcom. chair ins. cos. com. tax sect. 1994—), Assn. Life Ins. Counsel, AICPA, Beta Alpha Psi. Jewish. Insurance, Corporate taxation, Taxation, general.

LEVY, HERBERT MONTE, lawyer; b. NYC, Jan. 14, 1923; s. Samuel M. and Hetty D. L.; m. Marilyn Wohl, Aug. 30, 1953; children: Harlan A., Matthew D., Alison Jill. BA, Columbia U., 1943, LLB, 1946. Bar: N.Y. 1946, U.S. Dist. Ct. (so. dist.) N.Y. 1946, U.S. Ct. Appeals (2d cir.) 1949, U.S. Dist. Ct. (ea. dist.) N.Y. 1949, U.S. Supreme Ct. 1951, U.S. Ct. Appeals (10th cir.) 1956, U.S. Tax Ct. 1973, U.S. Ct. Appeals (4th cir.) 1988. Assoc. Rosenman, Goldmark, Colin & Kaye, 1946-47, Javits & Javits, 1947-48; staff counsel ACLU, 1949-56; pvt. practice, 1956-64; ptnr. Hofheimer, Gartlir, Hofheimer, Gottlieb & Gross, 1965-69; pvt. practice N.Y.C., 1969—. Bd. dirs. Music Outreach; faculty N.Y. County Lawyers Assn.; past lectr. Practising Law Inst. Author: How to Handle an Appeal (Practicing Law Inst.), 1968, 4th edit., 1999, now pub. annually; contbr. articles to profl. jours. Exec. com. on law and social action Am. Jewish Congress, 1961-66; trustee Congregation B'nai Jeshurun, 1987-98, chmn. bd. trustees, 1988-91, gen. counsel bd. trustees, 1991-92. Mem. Fed. Bar Coun. (past trustee), Bar Assn. City N.Y., N.Y. County Lawyers Assn., 1st Amendment Lawyers Assn. Democrat. Appellate, Commercial, contracts (including sales of goods; commercial financing), General practice. Home: 285 Central Park W Apt 12W New York NY 10024-3006 Office: 551 Fifth Ave Ste 2700 New York NY 10176 E-mail: hmlnyc@aol.com.

LEVY, JACK B. lawyer; b. Atlanta, Mar. 4, 1951; s. Julian J. and Emily F. Levy; m. Esther Gerson, June 17, 1973; children: Jennifer, Lauren, David. BA, Emory U., 1973, JD, 1976; LLM, NYU, 1977. Bar: Ala. 1977, Ga. 1976. Atty. Berkowitz, Lefkovitz & Patrick, Birmingham, Ala., 1977—79, Sirote & Permutt, 1979—2000, Berkowitz, Lefkovitz & Kushner, 2000—. Author: Owner Dominated Plans Top-Heavy and HR-10 Plans, 1984; co-author: Tax Planning for Professionals, 1986. Mem.: So. Employee Benefit Conf., Am. Health Lawyers Assn. Avocations: golf, skydiving. Corporate taxation, Pension, profit-sharing, and employee benefits, Health. Office: Berkowitz Lefkowitz Isom & Kushner 420 N 20th St Ste 1600 Birmingham AL 35203

LEVY, JEFFREY LAWRENCE, lawyer; b. N.Y.C., Sept. 18, 1949; s. Melville Henry and Esther Levy; m. Lynn Margaret Blowfield, July 26, 1972. BS in Econs., U. Pa., 1970; MBA, U. Chgo., 1973; JD, Vanderbilt U., 1997. Bar: Tenn. 1997, U.S. Dist. Ct. (mid. dist.) Tenn. 1997. Dir. Bank of Montreal, Toronto, 1973—91, Interfaith Housing Corp., North York, 1991—93; v.p. Citicapital Fin., Toronto, 1994; assoc. Bruce Weathers Corley & Lyle, Nashville. Mem.: ABA, Williamson County Bar Assn., Nashville Bar Assn. (reporter Tenn. Law Quarterly), Tenn. Bar Assn. Family and matrimonial, Juvenile, Appellate. Office: Bruce Weathers Corley & Lyle PLLC 315 Deaderick St #2075 Nashville TN 37238-2075 Fax: 615-244-7957. E-mail: levyjl@bellsouth.net.

LEVY, JOSEPH, lawyer; b. N.Y.C., June 9, 1928; s. Morris Joseph and Dora (Cohen) L.; m. Gertrud C. Roeder, Jan. 20, 1967; children— Diana N., Susan R. BBA cum laude, CCNY, 1950; JD cum laude, NYU, 1954. Bar: N.Y. 1955, D.C. 1968. Assoc. Parker, Chapin and Flattau, N.Y.C., 1954-62; ptnr. firm Rivkin, Sherman & Levy (and predecessors), N.Y.C., 1962-84, Schnader, Harrison, Segal & Lewis, 1984-93; v.p., sec., dir. Trecom Bus. Sys., Inc., Edison, N.J., 1993-97. Sec., dir. Horizons Comms. Corp., 1970-78, Quad Typographers, Inc., 1965-79; sec. Savin Bus. Machines Corp., 1959-84, On-Line Systems, Inc., 1968-78, Lambda Tech., Inc., 1970-78, Programming Methods, Inc., 1969-72, Kreisler Mfg. Cor., 1969-72, Peck & Peck, 1970-73, v.p., sec., dir. Trecom Bus. Systems, Inc., 1985-97, Business Edge Solutions, Inc., Edison, N.J., 1999—. Served to capt. AUS, 1951-53. Home: 254 University Way Paramus NJ 07652-5516

LEVY, KENNETH ST. CLAIR, barrister, psychologist, criminologist, accountant; b. Brisbane, Australia, Dec. 23, 1949; s. Francis and Grace (Ferguson) L.; m. Veronica Mary Forster, Jan. 7, 1978; children: Clare, Gregory. BA, U. Queensland, Australia, 1978; B in Commerce, U. Queensland, 1980, PhD, 1994; LLB, Queensland U. Tech., 1986. Barrister at Law High Ct. Australia, Supreme Ct. Queensland; registered tax agt., Queensland. Numerous mgmt. and organizatioal positions, 1974—; dir. gen. Dept. Justice, Queensland, 2000—. Mem. bd. mgmt. Australian Inst. Criminology, 1991—, Criminology Rsch. Coun., Australia, 1991—. Founding mem. Rental Bond Authority, 1989—90; pres. Alternative Dispute Resolution Coun., 1994—2000. Col. Australian Army Res. Fulbright scholar, 1995; recipient Outstanding Law Alumni award Queensland U. Tech., 2002, Res. Force decoration, 1990, Centenary medal, Australia, 2003. Fellow: CPA Australia (v.p. prof. devel. 1996—97, dep. chair 1997, dep. pres. 1998, dep. chmn. disciplinary com. Queensland divsn. 1998—99, pres. 1999, chmn. Queensland divisional coun. 1999—2000, chair disciplinary com. Queensland divsn. 2000—01, nat. v.p. corp.gov. 2002, nat. dep. pres. 2003); mem.: APA, Coll. Forensic Psychology, Bar Assn. Queensland (spl.), Australian Psychol. Soc., United Svcs. Club. Avocations: music, reading, travel. Civil rights, Criminal, Government contracts and claims. E-mail: kslevy@optusnet.com.au., ken.levy@justice.qld.gov.au.

LEVY, ROBERT MORRIS, judge; BA, Harvard Coll., 1971; JD, NYU, 1975. Bar: N.Y., U.S. Dist. Ct. (so. and ea. dists.) N.Y., U.S. Ct. Appeals (D.C. and 2nd cirs.), U.S. Supreme Ct. Staff atty. juvenile rights divsn. Legal Aid Soc., N.Y.C., 1976-77; staff atty. mental health law project N.Y. Civil Liberties Union, N.Y.C., 1977-80, dir. mental health law project, 1980-85, sr. staff atty., 1985-93; gen. counsel N.Y. Lawyers for the Pub. Interest, N.Y.C., 1993-94; U.S. magistrate judge Ea. Dist. N.Y., Bklyn., 1995—, overseer ct.'s mediation and arbitrator programs, 2000—; cons. ADR design program Fed.Jud. Ctr., 2003—. Advisor criminal prosecution, Thailand, 2002; advisor on jud. reform in the Republic of Georgia, Ctrl. and East European Law Initiative ABA, 1998; adj. prof. Bklyn. Law Sch., 1989—, NYU Law Sch., 1991—, Columbia U. Law Sch., 1993—. Author: (with V. Rosenthal) Rights of Nursing Home Residents in New York, 1984, (with L. Rubenstein) Rights of People with Mental Disabilities, 1996. Bd. dirs. NYU Pub. Interest Law Found., N.Y.C., 1980-82; mem. Gov.'s Task Force on Advocacy, N.Y., 1988-91; mem. adv. bd. Protection and Advocacy Svcs. for the Mentally Ill, N.Y.C., 1991-93; vol. factfinding missions Human Rights Watch, No. Ireland and Romania, 1990, 91, 92, 93. Mem. Fed. Bar Coun. (2nd cir. cts. com. 1998—, com. on pub. svc. 2001—), Assn. Bar of the City of N.Y. (sect. ethics and profl. responsibilities 2002-), com. on internat. human rights 1995-98). Office: 225 Cadman Plz E # 621 Brooklyn NY 11201-1818 Fax: 718-260-2647.

LEVY, STANLEY HERBERT, lawyer; b. Phila., Apr. 11, 1922; s. Max and Rose (Cohen) L.; m. Gloria Kamber, Dec. 20, 1953; children: Steven M., Peter B. BA, Cornell U., 1943; LL.B., Harvard U., 1949, JD, 1968. Bar: N.Y. 1949, U.S. Dist. Ct. (ea. and so. dists.) N.Y., U.S. Treasury 1949, U.S. Supreme Ct. 1961. Practiced in N.Y.C., 1949—. Mem. Republican Town Com., Scarsdale, 1963-65, Temple Emanu-el, Westchester, N.Y. Served to 1st lt. F.A., AUS, 1943-47. Mem. Assn. Bar City N.Y., Confrérie des Chevaliers du Tastevin (officier commandeur), Commanderie de Bordeaux (comdr.), Harvard Club, Yale Club, Century Country Club (Purchase, N.Y.), Mashomack Fish and Game Preserve (Pine Plains, N.Y.). Home: 3 Richbell Rd Scarsdale NY 10583-4421 Office: 521 5th Ave New York NY 10175-0003 E-mail: stanley@kamberinc.com.

LEVY, STEVEN B. lawyer; b. Chgo., Sept. 3, 1954; BA, U. Ill., 1975; JD, IIT, 1978. Bar: Ill. 1979, Fla. 1980, U.S. Dist. Ct. (no. dist.) Ill. 1979, U.S. Ct. Appeals (7th cir.) 1979, U.S. Dist. Ct. (so. and mid. dists.) Fla. 1980, U.S. Ct. Appeals (10th and 11th cirs.) 1980, U.S. Supreme Ct. 1993. Pvt. practice, Chgo., 1983—. Lectr. in field; apptd. to com. on profl. responsibility Ill. Supreme Ct., 1996—98, apptd. rules com., 1998—2001. Contbr. articles to profl. publs. Founding mem. DuPage County chpt. Am. Inns of Ct. Mem. Ill. State Bar Assn. (mem. editl. bd. Bar Jour. 1996—, standing CLE 1997—), Fla. Bar Assn., DuPage County Bar Assn. (editor-in-chief Bar Jour. 1995-99, recipient 20th ann. Lawyer of Yr. award, 2d ann. Professionalism award). General civil litigation, Personal injury (including property damage), Professional liability. Office: 40 Shuman Blvd Ste 151 Naperville IL 60563-8224

LEWAND, F. THOMAS, lawyer; b. San Diego, July 24, 1946; s. Barbara (Boening) L.; m. Kathleen Sullivan, Aug. 3, 1968; children: Thomas, Kevin, Kristen, Carrie. BA, U. Detroit, 1968; JD, Wayne State U., 1970. Bar: Mich. 1970, U.S. Dist. Ct. (ea. dist.) 1970. Law clk. to judge U.S. Ct. Appeals (6th cir.), Detroit, 1970; commr. Oakland County, Pontiac, Mich., 1978-80; chief of staff to Gov. J. Blanchard Lansing, Mich., 1982-83; ptnr. Jaffe, Raitt & Heuer, Detroit, 1970-92, Bodman, Longley & Dahling, Detroit, 1992—. Trustee Gov. Blanchard Found., Lansing, 1982—; dir. Wayne County Econ. Devel. Corp., 1997—, Nat. Conf. on Cmty. and Justice, 1999—; trustee U. Detroit Mercy., 1996—, chmn., 2001—. Campaign mgr. Gov. James J. Blanchard, MIch., 1978; chmn. Mich. Dems., 1989-91. Mem. State Bar Mich., Nat. Assn. Bond Lawyers. Corporate, general, Government contracts and claims, Municipal (including bonds). Office: Bodman Longley & Dahling 100 Renaissance Ctr Fl 34 Detroit MI 48243-1001

LEWIN, WERNER SIEGFRIED, JR., lawyer; b. San Francisco, Apr. 13, 1954; s. Werner Siegfried and Libby (Lewis) L.; married. BS, Cornell U., 1975; JD, U. Calif., Hastings, 1980. Bar: Calif. 1980. Assoc. Lynch, Loofburrow et al, San Francisco, 1980-82, Rudy Rapoport & Holden, San Francisco, 1982-86, Hanson, Bridgett, Marcus, Vlahos & Rudy, San Francisco, 1986-87; prin. Werner S Lewin Jr., Esq., Novato, Calif., 1987—. Founder, pres. Attorney Assistance, San Francisco Bay Area, 1986—. General practice. Office: Atty Assistance Co Hdqs 55 Cavalla Cay Novato CA 94949-5341

LEWIS, ALEXANDER INGERSOLL, III, lawyer; b. Detroit, Apr. 10, 1946; s. Alexander Ingersoll Jr. and Marie T. (Fuger) L.; m. Gretchen Elsa Lundgren, Aug. 8, 1970; children: Jennifer L., Katherine F., Elisabeth M., Alexander Ingersoll IV. BA with honors, Johns Hopkins U., 1968; JD cum laude, U. Pa., 1971. Bar: Md. 1972, U.S. Dist. Ct. Md. 1972, U.S. Ct. Appeals (4th cir.) 1975, U.S. Supreme Ct. 1976, D.C. 1982. Assoc. Venable, Baetjer & Howard, LLP, Balt., 1972-75, 78-80, ptnr., 1981—, head estate and trust practice group, 1993-99, sr. ptnr. estate and trust practice group, 1993—; asst. atty. gen. State of Md., 1975-77. Cons. subcom. on probate rules, standing com. on rules and procedures Md. Ct. Appeals, 1976—2003; mem. Md. Gov.'s Task Force to Study Revision of Inheritance and Estate Tax Laws, 1987—88; lectr. Md. Inst. Continuing Profl. Edn. Lawyers, 1978—2001, Nat. Bus. Inst., 1986—87, 1992—99, Cambridge Inst., 1986—90, Nat. Law Found., 1988—99. Contbr. articles to legal jours. Vice chmn. Md. Gov.'s Task Force on Long-Term Fin. Planning for Disabled Individuals, 1990-94. 1st lt. U.S. Army, 1972. Fellow Am. Coll. Trust and Estate Counsel (state laws coord. for Md. 1991-2001); mem. ABA, Md. Bar Assn. (chmn. probate reform and simplification com. estates and trusts coun. 1984-86, sec. 1987-88, chmn. 1989-90, com. on laws 1994-98), D.C. Bar Assn., Bar Assn. City Balt., Balt. Estate Planning Coun., Johns Hopkins Club. Republican. Roman Catholic. Avocations: canoeing, camping, tennis. Estate planning, Probate (including wills, trusts), Estate taxation. Home: 922 Army Rd Ruxton MD 21204-6703

LEWIS, ALVIN BOWER, JR., lawyer; b. Pitts., Apr. 24, 1932; s. Alvin Bower Sr. and Ethel Weidman (Light) L.; m. Elizabeth Therese O'Shea; children: Alvin B. III, Judith W., Robert B. II. BA, Lehigh U., 1954; LLB, Dickinson Sch. Law, 1957. Bar: Pa. 1957, U.S. Dist. Ct. (mid. and ea. dists.) Pa. 1958, U.S. Ct. Appeals (3d cir.) 1958, D.C. 1979. Ptnr. Lewis & Lewis, Lebanon, Pa., 1957-66, Lewis, Brubaker, Whitman & Christianson, Lebanon, 1967-76; spl. counsel, acting chief counsel, dir. select com. on assassinations of M.L. King, and J.F. Kennedy U.S. Ho. of Reps., Washington, 1976-77; ptnr. Lewis & Kramer, Phila., 1977-78, Hartman,

Underhill & Brubaker, Lancaster, Pa., 1979-95, Sprague & Lewis, Ltd., Lancaster, 1995-99, Stevens & Lee, Lancaster, 1999—. Dist. atty. County of Lebanon, Pa., 1962-70; chmn. Gov.'s Justice Commn., Pa., 1969-74; mem., chmn. Pa. Crime Commn., Pa., 1979-85. Fin. chmn., mem. exec. com. Rep. County Com., Lebanon, 1959-76; chmn. Lancaster City Rep. Com., 1994-98; co-chmn. Lancaster Crime Commn., 2000-03; mem. Rep. State Com., 1998-2000; bd. dirs., chmn. adv. com., mem. nominating com. Urban League Lancaster County, 1986-91; elected Rep. State Com., 1998—; co-chmn. Lancaster Crime Commn., 2000; chmn. Lehigh U. Scholar-Athletes Fund Drive, 1990-94; bd. govs. Lancaster County Found. Recipient Furtherance of Justice award Mercyhurst Coll., 1979, Dist. Service award Ho. of Reps. Pa., 1982, Award of Distinction Pa. Senate, 1982, Outstanding Service award Gov. and Atty. Gen. Pa., 1974, Alumni of the Yr. award Lehigh U., 1999. Mem. ABA, Pa. Bar Assn. Lancaster County Bar Assn. (chmn. trial law sect. 1995—), Preservation Fund Pa., Inc., Lebanon County Bar Assn. (pres. 1974-76, bd. dirs. 1982-90), Nat. Dist. Attys. Assn. (bd. dirs. 1966-68), Pa. Dist. Attys. Assn. (officer, pres., bd. dirs. 1964-68), Lancaster County Found. (bd. govs.). Lodges: Masons. Lutheran. Avocations: pilot, small airplanes. Federal civil litigation, State civil litigation, Corporate, general. Office: Stevens & Lee One Penn Sq Lancaster PA 17602-1594

LEWIS, CHERIE SUE, lawyer, English language and journalism educator; b. Cleve., Feb. 6, 1951; d. Samuel D. and Evelyne P. L. BA, U. Mich., 1973; MS, Boston U., 1975; PhD, U. Minn., 1986; JD, Southwestern U., L.A., 1996. Cert. ESL tchr., Calif. Prof. Pa. State U., State College, 1988-89, Nat. Chengchi U., Taipei, Taiwan, 1989-91, Syracuse U., 1992-93, Nat. U., L.A., 1993—; atty.-advisor U.S. Social Security Adminstrn., L.A., 1998—. Cons. Pacific Rim Inst., L.A., 1992-95. Author: (book chpt.) Disability Rights, International, 1994, ednl. brochures, 1994; mng. editor Southwestern U. Jour. Law and Trade, 1995-96. Mem. AAUP, ABA. Avocations: music, skiing, internat. travel. Office: 6 Kenwood Ct Beachwood OH 44122-7501 E-mail: Cherie0206@hotmail.com.

LEWIS, DAVID JOHN, lawyer; b. Zanesville, Ohio, Feb. 4, 1948; s. David Griff and Barbara Ann (Hoy) L.; m. Susan G. Smith; 1 child, Ann Elizabeth. BS in Fin., U. Ill., 1970, JD, 1973. Bar: Ill. 1973, D.C. 1974. Law clk. to Judge Philip W. Tone U.S. Dist. Ct. For North Dist. Ill., Chgo., 1973-74; assoc. Sidley Austin Brown & Wood, LLP, Washington, 1974-80, ptnr., 1980—. Comml. arbitrator Am. Arbitration Assn.; mem. Washington panel CPR Inst. Dispute Resolution. Mem. ABA. Alternative dispute resolution, Federal civil litigation, Product liability. Office: Sidley Austin Brown & Wood LLP 1501 K St NW Washington DC 20005 E-mail: dlewis@sidley.com.

LEWIS, FELICE FLANERY, lawyer, educator; b. Plaquemine, La., Oct. 5, 1920; d. Lowell Baird and E. Elizabeth (Lee) Flanery; m. Francis Russell Lewis, Dec. 22, 1944. BA, U. Wash., 1947; PhD, NYU, 1974; JD, Georgetown U., 1981. Bar: N.Y. 1982. Dean Liberal Arts and Scis. L.I. Univ., Bklyn., 1974-78; assoc. Harry G. English, Bklyn., 1983-85, 91-01; adj. prof. polit. sci. L.I. Univ., Bklyn., 1983-2000. Author: Literature, Obscenity and Law, 1976; co-editor: Henry Miller, Years of Trial & Triumph, 1962-64, 1978. Constitutional, General practice, Probate (including wills, trusts). Home: 28 Whitney Cir Glen Cove NY 11542-1316

LEWIS, GERALD JORGENSEN, judge; b. Perth Amboy, N.J., Sept. 9, 1933; s. Norman Francis and Blanche M. (Jorgensen) L.; m. Laura Susan McDonald, Dec. 15, 1973; children by previous marriage: Michael, Marc. AB magna cum laude, Tufts Coll., 1954; JD, Harvard U., 1957. Bar: D.C. 1957, N.J. 1961, Calif. 1962, U.S. Supreme Ct. 1968. Atty. Gen. Atomic, La Jolla, Calif., 1961-63; ptnr. Haskins, Lewis, Nugent & Newnham, San Diego, 1963-77; judge Mcpl. Ct., El Cajon, Calif., 1977-79, Superior Ct., San Diego, 1979-84; assoc.. justice Calif. Ct. of Appeal, San Diego, 1984-87; dir. Fisher Scientific Group, Inc., 1987-98, Bolsa Chica Corp., 1991-93, Gen. Chem. Group, Inc., 1996—; of counsel Lathan & Watkins, 1987-97; dir. Invesco Mut. Funds, Denver, 2000—. Adj. prof. evidence Western State U. Sch. Law, San Diego, 1977-85, exec. bd., 1977-89; dir. Invesco Mutual Funds, 2000—; faculty San Diego Inn of Ct., 1979— , Am. Inn of Ct., 1984— . Cons. editor: California Civil Jury Instructions, 1984. City atty. Del Mar, Calif., 1963-74, Coronado, Calif., 1972-77; counsel Comprehensive Planning Orgn., San Diego, 1972-73; trustee San Diego Mus. Art, 1986-89; bd. dirs. Air Pollution Control Dist., San Diego County, 1972-76. Served to lt. comdr. USNR, 1957-61. Named Trial Judge of Yr. San Diego Trial Lawyers Assn., 1984. Mem. Am. Judicature Soc., Soc. Inns of Ct. in Calif., Confrerie des Chevaliers du Tastevin, Order of St. Hubert (knight comdr.), Friendly Sons of St. Patrick (Irishman of Yr. 2000), The Irisn 50 Aztec Big 50, Bohemian Club, La Jolla Country Club (dir. 1980-83), Prophets, The K Club (County Kildare), Pauma Valley Country Club. Republican. Episcopalian. Home: PO Box 325 Pauma Valley CA 92061 Office: 701 B St Ste 2100 San Diego CA 92101-8197

LEWIS, GLENN C. lawyer; b. N.Y.C., Oct. 20, 1952; BA in Politics and Pub. Affairs, U. Miami, 1973; JD, George Mason U., 1977. Bar: Va. 1977, U.S. Dist. Ct. (ea. dist.) Va. 1977, U.S. Ct. Appeals (4th cir.) 1977, DC 1978, U.S. Dist. Ct. DC 1978, U.S. Ct. Appeals (DC cir.) 1978, Md. 1999. Prin. Lewis Firm, Washington. Moderator Va. Bar Leader's Inst., Richmond, 1997; neutral case evaluator Fairfax Cir. Ct.; spkr. in field. Exec. prodr., host (TV series) Law Weekly, Washington. Mem. task force domestic rels. delay reduction Fairfax Cir. Ct., 1988—90; mem. Adv. Work Group Legis. Implementation Family Ct., Va., 1992; trustee William B. Fitzgeralad Scholarship Fund. Recipient Telly award for Outstanding Ednl. Series, Local Cable TV Industry, 1990, Outstanding Live Cable Talk Show, Nat. Fedn. Local Cable Programmers, 1991. Mem.: Fairfax County Bar Assn. (mem. family law sect. 1988—, bd. dirs. 1991—, mem. budget com. 1994—, mem. child advocacy task force, mem. legis. com. 1994—, pres. 1995—96, others, Pres.'s award for outstanding svc., Exceptional Svc. award 1990), DC Bar (mem. domestic rels. counsel, mem. family law com., mem. civil litig. com., mem. chief judge's task force maintaining ofcl. ct. record 1994—), Va. State Bar (bd. govs. family law sect. 1989—93, mem. coun., chair family law sect. 1992—93, mem. domestic rels. counsel, others, Oustanding Achievement award 1990, award of merti 1996, Local Bar Leader of the Yr. award 1997). Family and matrimonial. Office: Lewis Firm 805 15th St NW Ste 200 Washington DC 20005*

LEWIS, GUY A. prosecutor; b. Chattanooga, Tennessee; m. Loyda Lewis; 1 child, Rose Marie. BS, U. Tennessee, 1983; Juris Doctor, U. Memphis Sch. of Law, 1986. Law clerk Hon. Thomas E. Scott, U.S. Dist. Ct., Fla., Hon. William Cowen. U.S. Ct. Appeals, Federal Circuit, Washington; prosecutor State's Atty.'s Office, 1988—, first asst.; U.S. atty. so. dist. U.S. Dept. Justice, 2000—02; dir. Exec. Off. for U.S. Atty., 2002—. Co-counsel trial U.S. vs. Gen. Manuel Noreiga, Matthew Block Prosecution; deputy chief Narcotics Section. Office: EOUSA 950 Pennsylvania Ave NW Rm 2616 Washington DC 20530*

LEWIS, JOHN FRANCIS, lawyer; b. Oberlin, Ohio, Oct. 25, 1932; s. Ben W. and Gertrude D. Lewis; m. Catharine Monroe, June 15, 1957; children: Ben M., Ian A., Catharine G., William H. BA, Amherst Coll., 1955; JD, U. Mich., 1958. Bar: Ohio 1958, U.S. Dist. Ct. (no dist.) Ohio 1959, U.S. Supreme Ct. 1973. Assoc. firm Squire, Sanders & Dempsey, Cleve., 1959—67; ptnr. Squire, Sanders & Dempsey LLP, 1967—, mng. ptnr. Cleve. office, 1985—2002. Co-author: Baldwin's Ohio School Law, 1980-91, Ohio Collective Bargaining Law, 1983. Trustee Ohio Found. Ind. Colls., Case Western Res. U., chmn., 1995-2001; trustee Playhouse Sq. Found., chmn., 1980-85; trustee, chmn. Ohio Aerospace Coun., 2001-03; former mem. exec. com. Greater Cleve. Growth Assn.; trustee Musical Arts Assn., Univ. Circle, Inc., Ohio Found. Independent Coll.; hon. trustee Found. for Sch. Bus. Mgmt., Leadership Cleve., 1977-78; chmn. Cleanland Cleve., 1992-95. Recipient Malcolm Daisley Labor-Mgmt. Rels. award, 1991, Tree of Life award Jewish Nat. Fund, 1993, NCCJ award, 1995, Franklin D. Roosevelt March of Dimes award, 1999, Case Western Reserve U. Presidl. medal, 2001. Mem. Cleve. Bar Assn., Ohio Bar Assn., ABA, Nat. Sch. Bd. Assn., Edn. Law Assn. (past pres.), Ohio Assn. Sch. Bus. Ofcls. (hon. life, Marion McGehey Edn. Law award 1998), Fifty Club of Cleve., Ohio Council Sch. Bd. Attys. (founding chair). Episcopalian. Education and schools, Labor (including EEOC, Fair Labor Standards Act, labor-management relations, NLRB, OSHA). Home: 2 Bratenahl Pl Ste 7ef Bratenahl OH 44108-1183 Office: Squire Sanders & Dempsey 4900 Key Tower 127 Public Sq Ste 4900 Cleveland OH 44114-1304 E-mail: capeoceans@aol.com., Jlewis@ssd.com.

LEWIS, R. FRED, judge; b. Beckley, W.Va., Dec. 14, 1947; m. Judith Lewis, 1969; children: Elle, Lindsay. Grad. cum laude, Fla. So. Coll., 1969; JD cum laude, U. Miami, 1972; grad., U.S. Army A.G. Sch.; D (hon.) in Pub. Svc., Fla. So. Coll., 2000. Pvt. practice, Miami; justice Fla. Supreme Ct., 1998—. Contbr. pubs. Continuing Edn. Legal Program. Bd. dir. Miami Children's Hosp.; inventory atty. The Fla. Bar. Recipient of Friends of Justice award ABOTA, 1999; Jud. Pub. Trust & Confidence award FLREA, 2001; NCAA postgrad. grantee, 1969; Citizen of the Yr., Fla., 2001; Everyday Hero award for his outstanding contrib. to cmty. svc. in Fla.; Justice R. Fred fLewis Award from the Univ. of Ctrl. Fla., 2002; the inaugural award for his svc. to the youth of Fla.; hon. Dr. of Pub. Svc. degree from Fla. So. Coll., 2000; hon. Dr. of Law degree from St. Thomas Univ., 2002; Certificate of Apprec. for Outstanding Contrib. to We the People, the Citizens and the Constitution; a State Univ. Coll. of Law Award for Contrib. to the Summer Law Program; Guardian of the Constitution Citizenship Award for Law-Related fEd.; Dade County Bar Assoc., Young Lawyer's Section Dedication to Children Award; Award for Outstanding Contrib.to the Study of Law, Legal and Pub. Affairs, by Miami Sr. HS. Mem. Omicron Delta Kappa, Psi Chi, Sigma Alpha Epsilon. Address: 500 S Duval St Tallahassee FL 32399-6556 E-mail: supremecourt@mail.flcourts.org.*

LEWIS, RICHARD M. lawyer; b. Gallipolis, Ohio, Dec. 11, 1957; s. Denver E. and Mary Esther (Mobley) L.; m. Cheryl F. Hickman (div.); m. Diane K. Williams, Apr. 26, 1986. BA in Polit. Sci., Ohio State U., 1979; JD, Capital U., 1982. Bar: Ohio 1982, U.S. Dist. Ct. (so. dist.) Ohio 1984, U.S. Supreme Ct. 1986, U.S. Ct. Appeals (6th cir.) 1999; cert. civil trial advocacy Nat. Bd. Trial Advocacy. Pvt. practice law, 1982-83; assoc. Mary Bone Kunze, Jackson, Ohio, 1983-85; pvt. practice law Jackson, 1985-86; ptnr. Ochsenbein, Cole & Lewis, Jackson, 1986-96, Cole & Lewis, Jackson, 1996-2000, The Law Firm of Richard M. Lewis, Jackson, 2001—. Lectr. in field; expert witness; appt. to Ohio Sup. Ct. Commn. Cert. of Attys. as Specialists, 2002-03. Co-editor: Book of Complaints, 2002. Mem. ABA, Assn. Trial Lawyers Am., Ohio State Bar Assn. (com. for Independent Judicracy and Unjust Criticism of Judges, 2001—), Jackson County Bar Assn. (past pres.), Ohio Acad. Trial Lawyers (bd. trustees 1993—, budget com. 1993-94, supreme ct. screening com. 1994, vice-chairperson family law com. 1994-95, chairperson-elect family law com. 1995—, chairperson family law com. 1995-96, exec. com., chair mem. com. 1996-97, co-chair regional CLE seminars 1997, exec. com. 1998-99, chair ADOPT task force 1998, editor Book of Complaints 2002). General civil litigation, Family and matrimonial, Personal injury (including property damage). Home: 603 Reservoir Rd Jackson OH 45640-8714 Office: The Law Firm of Richard M Lewis 295 Pearl St Jackson OH 45640-1748

LEWIS, ROBERT LAWRENCE, lawyer, educator; b. N.Y.C., Sept. 25, 1919; s. Isador and Sadie (Holzinger) L.; m. Frieda Friedman, Nov. 24, 1940 (dec. 1961); children— Brian S., Paul E., David N.; m. Joanne Marcia Waxman, June 16, 1963; children— Pavia S., Eraclea S. AB, Hamilton Coll., 1940; LL.B., Case Western Res. U., 1948. With firm Ulmer & Berne, Cleve., 1948-64, ptnr., 1956-64; ret., 1964. Prof. law, dir. grad. div. Cleve.-Marshall Law Sch. (now Cleve. State U.), 1948-53; bd. dirs. Banner Industries, Inc., Cleve.; scholar-in-residence, prof. classics Cuayhoga C.C.; adj. prof. nonprofit governance Case Western Res. U., Cleve. Author: Five Angry Women, 1990, Agatharcus, 1993. Cons., evaluator North Central Assn. Colls. and Schs., Middle States Assn. Mem. Cleve. Area Arts Council, 1971-73; pres. Fairmount Center for Creative and Performing Arts, 1973-75; trustee, chmn. bd. Cuyahoga Community Coll.; trustee Cuyahoga Community Coll. Found., Playhouse Sq. Found., Cleve., Cleve. Commn. Higher Edn., Lake Erie Coll., Council for Interinstnl. Leadership, Pace Assn., New Orgn. for Visual Arts; bd. dirs. Assn. Governing Bds. Univs. and Colls.; bd. advisers Cleve. Ballet; trustee, v.p. New Cleve. Opera Co. Served to 1st lt., arty. and ordnance corps AUS, 1942-46, NATOUSA. Decorated Legion of Merit, Purple Heart Mem. Exec. Order Ohio Commodore, Phi Beta Kappa. Home: 2425 N Park Blvd Apt 4 Cleveland OH 44106-3154 Office: 900 Bond Ct Bldg Cleveland OH 44114

LEWIS, ROBERT LEE, lawyer; b. Oxford, Miss., Feb. 26, 1944; s. Ernest Elmo and Johnice Georgia (Thirkield) L.; children: Yolanda Sherice, Robert Lee Jr., Dion Terrell, Viron Lamar, William Lovell, Tremaine Donnell Lewis. BA, Ind. U., 1970, JD, 1973; M in Pub. Service, West Ky. U., 1980. Bar: Ind. 1973, Ky. 1979, U.S. Ct. Claims, U.S. Ct. Internat. Trade, U.S. Tax. Ct., U.S. Ct. Mil. Appeals, U.S. Ct. Appeals (fed. cir.), U.S. Supreme Ct. Sole practice, Evansville, Ind., 1973-75, Gary, Ind., 1980—; atty., army officer U.S. Army, Ft. Knox, Ky., 1975-78; appellate referee Ind. Employment Security Div., Indpls., 1978-80. Mem. adv. com. Vincennes (Ind.) U., 1983—; bd. dirs. Opportunities Industrialization Ctr., Evansville, 1973-75. Served to sgt. JAGC, USMC, 1962-66, Vietnam, sgt. U.S. Army, 1975-78, lt. col. USAR. Named Ky. Col. Mem. ABA, Ind. Bar Assn., Ky. Bar Assn., Nat. Bar Assn., Ind. Bd. Realtors, Ind. U. Alumni Assn., Phi Alpha Delta. Methodist. Criminal, Family and matrimonial, Personal injury (including property damage). Home and Office: 2148 W 11th Ave Gary IN 46404-2306

LEWIS, RONALD WAYNE, lawyer; b. Buffalo, Wyo., May 13, 1943; s. George Weber and Marianne (Parsons) L.; children: Joshua Byron, Kristopher Byron, Katherine Byron, Annalise N. AB, Dartmouth Coll., Hanover, N.H., 1965; MAT in French, Harvard U., 1969; JD, U. Miss., Oxford, 1978. Bar: Miss. 1978, U.S. Dist. Ct. (no. dist.) Miss. 1978, U.S. Ct. Appeals (5th cir.) 1979, U.S. Dist. Ct. (so. dist.) Miss. 1985, U.S. Supreme Ct. 1990, U.S. Claims Ct. 1991. Pvt. practice, Oxford, 1978-81; assoc. Hill, Lewis & Bell, Oxford, 1981-83, Hill & Lewis, Oxford, 1983-86, Holcomb, Dunbar, Connell, Chaffin & Willard, Oxford, 1986-88; pvt. practice Oxford, 1988—. CJA criminal def. tng. coord. No. Jud. Dist., Miss., 1991-2002, CJA panel rep. to nat. confs., 1995-2003. Mem. Lafayette County Dem. Exec. Com., Oxford, 1985-96, chmn., 1987-91; bd. dirs. ACLU of Miss., 1989-90, Miss. Assn. for Children with Learning Disabilities, 1990-91; mem. instnl. rev. bd. U. Miss., 1999—. Mem.: Miss. Bar Assn. Civil rights, Criminal, Labor (including EEOC, Fair Labor Standards Act, labor-management relations, NLRB, OSHA). Office: 2621 W Oxford Loop Ste C Oxford MS 38655

LEWIS, WILLIAM HENRY, JR., lawyer; b. Durham, N.C., Nov. 12, 1942; s. William Henry Sr. and Phyllis Lucille (Phillips) L.; m. Jo Ann Whitsett, Apr. 17, 1965 (div. Sept. 1982); 1 child, Kimberly N.; m. Peyton Cockrill Davis, Nov. 28, 1987. Student, N.C. State U., 1960-63; AB in Polit. Sci., U. N.C., 1965, JD with honors, 1969. Bar: Calif., D.C., U.S. Dist. Ct. (cen. dist.) Calif., U.S. Ct. Appeals (D.C. cir., 2nd and 5th cirs.), U.S. Supreme Ct. Assoc. Latham & Watkins, Los Angeles, 1969-74; exec. officer Calif. Air Resources Bd., Los Angeles and Sacramento, Calif., 1975-78; dir. Nat. Com. on Air Quality, Washington, 1978-81; counsel Wilmer, Cutler & Pickering, Washington, 1981-84; ptnr. Morgan, Lewis & Bockius LLP, Washington, 1984—, mgr. nat. environ. practice, 1999—2000. Spl. advisor on environ. policy State of Calif., L.A. and Sacramento, 1975; lectr. Law Sch. U. Va., 1993-97. Bd. dirs. For Love of Children, Inc., Washington, 1985-95, pres., 1987-91; bd. dirs. Advs. for Families, Washington, 1985-87, Hillandale Homeowners Assn., Washington, 1986-87, Thurgood Marshall Ctr. Trust, Washington, 1989-95; mem. EPA Clean Air Act Adv. Com., 1994—; chmn. bd. dirs., co-founder The Montpelier Found., 1998—. Mem. ABA. Federal civil litigation, Environmental. Home: 3900 Georgetown Ct NW Washington DC 20007-2127 also: 18454 Monteith Farm Rd Gordonsville VA 22942-7560 Office: Morgan Lewis and Bockius LLP 1111 Pennsylvania Ave NW Washington DC 20004

LEWYN, THOMAS MARK, lawyer; b. N.Y.C., July 2, 1930; s. Oswald and Agnes (Maas) L.; m. Ann Salfeld, July 15, 1955; children— Alfred Thomas, Mark Henry. BA, Stanford, 1952, postgrad., 1952-54; LL.B., Columbia, 1955. Bar: N.Y. 1957. Assoc. Simpson, Thacher & Bartlett, N.Y.C., 1957-64, ptnr., 1965-75, sr. ptnr., 1976-90, of counsel, 1991—95. Bd. dirs. Metro-Goldwyn-Mayer, Inc. Contbr. articles to profl. jours. Served to 1st lt., F.A. AUS, 1955-57. Mem. ABA, Assn. of Bar of City of N.Y., N.Y. State Bar Assn. Home: 911 Park Ave New York NY 10021-0337 Office: Simpson Thacher & Bartlett 425 Lexington Ave Fl 15 New York NY 10017-3954

LEYCEGUI, GARDOQUL BEATRIZ, lawyer; b. Orizaba, Veracruz, Mex., Nov. 10, 1964; d. Manuel Ignacio Leycegui Aiza and Amanda Gardoqui Zurita; children: Tomas Ruiz, Paulina Ruiz, Miguel Ruiz. M of Internat. Affairs, Columbia U., 1988—90; JD, Escuelalibre de Derecho, Mex. City, 1982—87. Legal asst. and counsel during NAFTA negotiations Ministry of the Interior, Mex. City, Mexico, 1984—98; rsch. asst. Columbia U., N.Y.C., 1989—90; legal counsel in consular affairs Ministry of Fgn. Affairs, Mex. City, 1990; dir. legal analysis Ministry of Trade and Indsl. Devel., Mex. City., 1990—92; prof., rschr. ITAM, Mex. City., 1993—99; binational panel asst. NAFTA, Mex. City., 1994—95; sr. assoc. Serra & Assocs. Internat., Mex. City., 1999—. Adv. bd. mem. Inst. Latin Am., Columbia U., N.Y.C., 1999—, Centro De Investigacion y Docencia Economicas, Mex. City, 2002—, U. Iberoamericana, Mex. City, 2002—; panelist NAFTA. Co-editor (with William Robson and Dhalia Stein): Trading Punches: Trade Remedy Law and Disputes under NAFTA-U.S., 1995, Trading Punches: Trade Remedy Law and Disputes under NAFTA-Mexico, 1997; co-editor: (with Rafael Fernández de Castro) Natural Partners? Five Years of the North American Free Trade Agreement, 2000; contbr. articles to profl. jours. Scholar, Ford Found., Columbia U., 1998. Mem.: N.Am. Com. (acad. dir. 1995—99), Mex. Bar, Law Coll., Mex. Coun. for Fgn. Affairs (founding counselor 2002—). Avocations: dancing, music, tennis, travel. Public international. Home: Bernardo Quintana 51 Casa 18 DF 01340 Mexico City Mexico Office: Serra Assocs Internat Pol Reforma 600-103 DF 01210 Mexico City Mexico Fax: 5255 52593928. E-mail: blg@sai.com.mx.

LEYDORF, FREDERICK LEROY, lawyer; b. Toledo, June 13, 1930; s. Loftin Herman and Dorothy DeRoyal (Cramer) L.; m. Mary MacKenzie Malcolm, Mar. 28, 1953; children: Robert Malcolm, William Frederick, Katherine Ann, Thomas Richard, Deborah Mary. Student, U. Toledo, 1948-49; BBA, U. Mich., 1953; JD, UCLA, 1958. Bar: Calif. 1959, U.S. Supreme Ct. 1970. Assoc. Hammack & Pugh, L.A., 1959-61; ptnr. Willis, Butler, Scheifly, Leydorf & Grant, L.A., 1961-81, Pepper, Hamilton & Scheetz, L.A., 1981-83, Hufstedler & Kaus, L.A., 1983-95. Lectr., cons. Calif. Continuing Edn. of Bar, 1965-92; mem. planning com. Probate and Trust Conf., U. So. Calif., 1984-92. Contbg. author: California Non-Profit Corporations, 1969; contbr. articles to profl. jours. Chmn. pub. adminstr.-pub. guardian adv. commn. Los Angeles County Bd. Suprs., 1972-73; v.p. J.W. and Ida M. Jameson Found., 1995—, bd. dirs., 1967—; bd. dirs. Western Ctr. on Law and Poverty, Inc., 1980-82, L.A. Heart Inst., 1988-90; mem. legal com. Music Ctr. Found., 1980-95; mem. lawyers adv. coun. Constl. Rights Found., 1982-85; mem. devel. adv. bd. U. Mich. Sch. Bus. Adminstrn., 1984-90; mem. adv. bd. UCLA-CEB Estate Planning Inst., 1979-92; Lt. USNR, 1953-55. Mem. Libbey H.S. Hall of Fame (Toledo), 1999. Mem. ABA, L.A. County Bar Assn. (bd. trustees 1973-75), State Bar Calif. (chmn. conf. dels. 1977, Alumnus of Yr. award, conf. of dels. 1983, mem. exec. com. estate planning, trust and probate law sect. 1979-80), L.A. County Bar Found. (pres. 1977-79, bd. dirs. 1975-87), Internat. Acad. Estate and Trust Law (v.p. N.Am. 1978-82), Life Ins. and Trust Coun. L.A. (pres. 1983-84), UCLA Law Alumni Assn. (pres. 1982), L.A. World Affairs Coun. (mem. internat. cir.), Chancery Club (pres. 1991-92), Jonathan Club, Laguna Woods Golf Club, Sunrise Country Club (Rancho Mirage, Calif.), Phi Delta Phi, Phi Delta Theta. Republican. Lutheran. Estate planning, Probate (including wills, trusts), Estate taxation. Home: 75 Majorca Dr Rancho Mirage CA 92270-3826

LEYHANE, FRANCIS JOHN, III, lawyer; b. Chgo., Mar. 29, 1957; s. Francis J. and Mary Elizabeth (Crowley) L.; m. Diana M. Urizarri, May 8, 1982; children: Katherine, Francis J. IV, Joseph, Brigid Rose, James Matthew. BA, Loyola U., Chgo., 1977, JD, 1980. Bar: Ill. 1980, U.S. Dist. Ct. (no. dist.) Ill. 1980, U.S. Ct. Appeals (7th cir.) 1986. Assoc. Condon, Cook & Roche, Chgo., 1980-87; ptnr. Condon & Cook, Chgo., 1988-98, Boyle & Leyhane, Ltd., Chgo., 1998—. Contbr. articles to profl. jours. Mem. Sch. bd. Immaculate Conception Parish, Chgo., 1993-96. Fellow Ill. Bar Found.; mem. Appellate Lawyers Assn. Ill., Ill. State Bar Assn. (mem. assembly 1987-90), Chgo. Bar Assn., Blue Key. Appellate, State civil litigation, Insurance. Office: Boyle & Leyhane Ltd 11 E Adams Set 1600 Chicago IL 60603 E-mail: leyhane329@aol.com.

LEZAK, SIDNEY IRVING, lawyer, mediator; b. Chgo., Nov. 8, 1924; s. Manny and Celia (Weiner) L.; m. Muriel Deutsch, June 26, 1949; children: Anne, David, Miriam. PhB, U. Chgo., 1946, JD, 1949. Bar: Oreg. 1949, U.S. Supreme Ct. 1962. Pvt. practice, Portland, Oreg., 1949—61; ptnr. Bailey, Lezak, Swink & Gates, Portland, 1953—61; U.S. atty. for Oreg., U.S. Dept. Justice, Portland, 1961—82; counsel Newcomb, Sabin, Schwartz & Landsverk, Portland, 1982—; mediator, Portland, 1982—. Mem. Oreg. Dispute Resolution Commn., Portland, 1989-91; mem. Dispute Resolution Adv. Coun. Oreg., Portland, 1987-89. 1st lt. USAAF, 1942-45, ETO. Decorated DFC, Air medal with three oak leaf clusters; recipient individual achievement award Willamette U. Dispute Resolution Ctr., 1990. Mem. ABA (cons. com. on dispute resolution 1989-92), Oreg. State Bar (chmn. dispute resolution com. 1986-88), Fed. Bar Assn. (pres. Oreg. 1963-64, chmn. alternative dispute resolution com. 1984-85). Democrat. Avocations: skiing, travel, hiking, france. Home: 1811 SW Boundary St Portland OR 97239 Office: Newcomb Sabin Schwartz Landsverk 111 SW 5th Ave Ste 4040 Portland OR 97204-3643 E-mail: lezak@nsslaw.com.

LI, WINIFRED I. lawyer; b. Boston, Dec. 19, 1950; married; 3 children. BA, Yale U., 1972; JD, U. Calif., Berkeley, 1976. Bar: Mass. 1977, U.S. Dist. Ct. Mass., 1977, U.S. Ct. Appeals (1st cir.) 1977. Ptnr., mem. Hill & Barlow, Boston, 1976—2002; ptnr. Ropes & Gray LLP, Boston, 2003—. Mem. ABA, Mass. Bar Assn., Asian Am. Lawyers Assn. Mass., Boston Estate Planning Council, Boston Bar Assn., Mass. Continuing Legal Edn. Inc. (estate planning and adminstrn. curriculum adv. com. 1986-87), Am. Coll. Trust and Estate Counsel. Estate planning, Probate (including wills, trusts), Estate taxation. Office: Ropes & Gray 1 Internat Pl 100 Oliver St Boston MA 02110-2624

LIBBIN, ANNE EDNA, lawyer; b. Phila., Aug. 25, 1950; d. Edwin M. and Marianne (Herz) L.; m. Christopher J. Cannon, July 20, 1985; children: Abigail Libbin Cannon, Rebecca Libbin Cannon. AB, Radcliffe Coll., 1971; JD, Harvard U., 1975. Bar: Calif. 1975, U.S. Dist. Ct. (cen. dist.) Calif. 1977, U.S. Dist. Ct. (no. dist.) Calif. 1979, U.S. Dist. Ct. (ea. dist.) Calif. 1985, U.S. Ct. Appeals (2d cir.) 1977, U.S. Ct. Appeals (5th cir.) 1982, U.S. Ct. Appeals (7th cir.) 1976, U.S. Ct. Appeals (9th cir.) 1976, U.S. Ct. Appeals (D.C. cir.) 1978, U.S. Supreme Ct. 2001. Appellate atty. NLRB, Washington, 1975-78; assoc. Pillsbury Madison & Sutro LLP, San Francisco, 1978-83, ptnr., 1984-99; sr. counsel SBC Pacific Telesis Group, San

Francisco, 1999—; dir. Jewish Vocat. Svcs., San Francisco, 2002—. Three Guineas fellow Harvard Law Sch., 1997; dir. Alumnae Resources, San Francisco, 1991-97. Mem. ABA (labor and employment sect.), State Bar Calif. (labor law sect.), Bar Assn. San Francisco (labor law sect.), Radcliffe Club (San Francisco). Labor (including EEOC, Fair Labor Standards Act, labor-management relations, NLRB, OSHA). Office: SBC Pacific Telesis Group 140 New Montgomery St San Francisco CA 94105-3705

LIBERT, DONALD JOSEPH, lawyer; b. Sioux Falls, S.D., Mar. 23, 1928; s. Bernard Joseph and Eleanor Monica (Sutton) L.; m. Jo Anne Murray, May 16, 1953; children: Cathleen, Thomas, Kevin, Richard, Stephanie. BS magna cum laude in Social Scis., Georgetown U., 1950, LL.B., 1956. Bar: Ohio. From assoc. to ptnr. Manchester, Bennett, Powers & Ullman, Youngstown, Ohio, 1956-65; various positions to v.p., gen. counsel and sec. Youngstown Sheet & Tube Co., 1965-78; assoc. group counsel LTV Corp., Youngstown and Pitts., 1979; v.p. and gen. counsel Anchor Hocking Corp., Lancaster, Ohio, 1979-87; pvt. practice Lancaster, 1987—. Served to lt. (j.g.) USN, 1951-54. Mem. Ohio Bar Assn. (former chmn. sr. lawyers com.), Fairfield County Bar Assn. (mem. alt. dispute resolution com.), Lancaster Country Club, Rotary. Republican. Roman Catholic. Administrative and regulatory, Antitrust, Corporate, general. Office: 1846 Northshire Dr Lancaster OH 43130-1567

LIBERTH, RICHARD FRANCIS, lawyer; b. Bklyn., Mar. 1, 1950; s. S. Richard and Frances J. (Falconer) L.; m. Lisa M. Feenick, June 8, 1974; children: Andrew R., Erica M. BS in Bus. Adminstrn., U. Denver, 1972; JD, Bklyn. Law Sch., 1976. Bar: N.Y. 1977, U.S. Dist. Ct. (so. and ea. dists.) N.Y. 1981, U.S. Dist. Ct. (no. dist.) N.Y. 1991. Staff atty. Mental Health Legal Svcs., Poughkeepsie, N.Y., 1976-78; sr. asst. dist. atty. Rockland County Dist. Attys. Office, N.Y.C., 1978-81; prin. Drake, Sommers, Loeb, Tarshis Catania & Liberth PLLC, Newburgh, NY, 1981—. Atty. Fraternal Order of Police Lodge #957. Dir. Legal Aid Soc. Orange County, Goshen, N.Y., 1982-84, Orange County Cerebral Palsy Assn., Goshen, 1986-89; mem. Rep. Nat. Com., Washington, 1990—; Rep. chmn. Town of Woodbury, 1997-99. Mem. N.Y. Bar Assn., Newburgh Bar Assn. (pres. 1991), Orange County Bar Assn. (v.p. 1995, pres. 1997), Woodbury Lions Club (Central Valley, N.Y.) (past pres.). Avocations: golf, tennis, reading, collecting. General civil litigation, Product liability, Personal injury (including property damage). Home: 134 Hasbrouck Rd Goshen NY 10924 Office: Drake Sommers Loeb Tarshis Catania & Liberth One Corwin Ct Newburgh NY 12550 E-mail: rliberth@dsltc.com.

LIBERTY, ARTHUR ANDREW, judge; b. Oak Park, Ill., Nov. 7, 1954; s. Arthur and Patricia (Horton) L.; m. Jean Liberty, Nov. 22, 1980; children: Rebecca, Rachael. BS, Excelsior Coll., Albany, 1983; JD with honors, Ill. Inst. Tech., Chgo., 1987. Bar: Ill. 1987, U.S. Dist. Ct. (no. dist.) Calif. 1988, U.S. Dist. Ct. (no. dist.) Ill., 1992, U.S. Dist. Ct. (cen. dist.) Ill., 1995, U.S. Ct. Appeals (7th cir.) 1992, U.S. Ct. Appeals (9th cir.) 1989. Asst. dist. counsel U.S. Immigration and Naturalization Service, San Francisco, Chgo., 1987-88, 91-92; sector counsel U.S. Border Patrol, Livermore, Calif., 1988-91; ptnr. Azulay & Azulay, Chgo., 1992-95; pvt. practice Chgo. and Joliet, Ill., 1995-97; U.S. adminstrv. law judge Office of Hearings and Appeals, Detroit, 1997-98, chief U.S. adminstrv. law judge Evansville, Ind., 1998—2002; nat. chief U.S. adminstrv. law judge Dept. of Housing and Urban Devel., Washington, 2002—. Spl. asst. U.S. atty. ea dist. Calif., Fresno, 1988—91; instr. law and legal proc. Fed. Law Enforcement Tng. Ctr., Artesia, N.Mex., 1989—91; Assn. Pres. Hearing Office Chief Judges, 2001—02; law and jud. proc. Office Hearings and Appeals Nat. Tng. Cadre, Falls Church, Va., 2001—02. Contbr. articles to profl. books. Maj., pilot, comdr. Evansville sr. squadron Civil Air Patrol, 1999—2002, dep. comdr. and inspector gen. Group IV Md. Wing. Mem. Fed. Bar Assn. (jud. divsn.). Avocations: flying, music, cooking. Office: HUD OALJ 409 3rd St SW Suite 320 Washington DC 20024

LIBSTER, JACQUELINE BRENDA, lawyer; b. Bay Shore, N.Y., July 13, 1975; d. Stuart A. and Sara A. Libster. BA, U. of Albany, 1997; JD, Albany Law School, 2000. Bar: N.Y. (admission) 2001, U.S. Dist. Ct. (so. and ea. dists.) N.Y. 2002. Staff atty. Paul Weiss, Rifkind, Wharton & Garrison LLP, N.Y.C., 2001—. New York State Mediator, NY, 1999—2002. Fellow Charles H. Revson Fellow, 1999. Mem.: ABA, N.Y. State Bar Assn. Home: 15 Erin Ct Islip Terrace NY 11752 Personal E-mail: jlibster@aol.com.

LICATA, ARTHUR FRANK, lawyer; b. N.Y.C., June 16, 1947; BA in English, Le Moyne Coll., 1969; postgrad., SUNY, Binghampton, 1969-71; JD cum laude, Suffolk U., 1976. Bar: Mass. 1977, N.Y. 1985, U.S. Ct. Appeals (1st cir.) 1977, U.S. Dist. Ct. Mass. 1977, admitted Frank B. Murray, Jr. Inns of Ct. 1990-92. Assoc. Parker, Coulter, Daley & White, Boston, 1977-82; pvt. practice Arthur F. Licata P.C., Boston, 1982—. Prin. Ardlee Internat. Trading Co., Ea. and Ctrl. Europe and Russia, 1989-99; del. White House Conf. on Trade and Investment in Ctrl. Europe, Cleve., 1995; lectr. Mass. Continuing Legal Edn., Boston, 1982-2001, mem. trial adv. com., 1984-88; mem. working group on drinking and drunk driving Harvard Sch. Pub. Health Ctr. for Health Comms., 1986; spkr. Conv. Nat. Fedn. Paralegal Assns., Boston, 1987; del. U.S.-People's Republic of China Joint Session on Trade, Investment and Econ. Law, Beijing, 1987; co-sponsor Estonian legal del. visit to Mass. and N.H. correctional instns., 1990; Boston host former Soviet legal del. visit, 1989; legal advisor Czech Anglo-Am. Bus. Inst., Prague, Czech Republic, 1989-2000, Russian Children's Fund, 1992-94, Estonia Acad. for Pub. Safety, 1992-94; adv. bd. Ford Found.'s Legal Resource Ctr., Czech Republic, 1994-96; participant U.S.-Russian Investment Symposium, Harvard U.; spkr. Conf. on Proposed Tobacco Settlement and Tort Law, Harvard Law Sch., 1997; guest WGBH-Ch 2, TV, Greater Boston With Emily Rooney, 1999, 2001; chair seminar Mass. CLE, Boston, 2000. Panel mem. sta. WBZ TV, Boston; contbr. articles to profl. jours. U.S. Del. 6th People to People Juvenile Justice Program to USSR, Moscow, 1989; legal advisor Mass. chpt. MADD, Plymouth County, 1984-87; mem. State Adv. Com. Med. Malpractice, Boston, 1985; bd. dirs. Boston Ctr. for the Arts, 1990-94; mem. profl. adv. bd. Mass. Epilepsy Assn., 1986-93; counsel state coord. commn. MADD, Mass., 1984-86; partticipant Harvard Law Ach. Seminar Program on Negotiation and Mediation, 2000-01. Recipient Outstanding Citizen award Mothers Against Drunk Driving, 1986, Sacred Angelic Imperial Constanian Order of Saint George awarded by the Duke of Parma, Italy, 2000. Fellow Mass. Bar Found.; mem. ABA, ATLA, Mass. Bar Assn. (bd. dirs., young lawyers sect. 1979-80, 21st Century Club 1984), Mass. Acad. Trial Attys. (bd. dirs. 1991-99, exec. com. 1997-99), Nat. Bd. Trial Advocacy (bd. cert. civil trial advocate 1992— Avocation: travel. General civil litigation, Private international, Personal injury (including property damage). Office: Fed Res Plz 600 Atlantic Ave 25th Fl Boston MA 02210-2211 Fax: (617) 523-7743. E-mail: Licata@worldnet.att.net.

LICHT, RICHARD A. lawyer; b. Providence, Mar. 25, 1948; s. Julius M. Licht and Irene (Lash) Olson; m. Roanne Sragow; children: Jordan David, Jeremy Michael, Jaclyn Rose, Jacob Adam. AB cum laude, Harvard U., 1968, JD cum laude, 1972; LLM in Taxation, Boston U., 1975. Law clk. to chief justice R.I. Supreme Ct., Providence, 1973-74; ptnr. Letts, Quinn & Licht, Providence, 1974-84; mem. R.I. Senate, Providence, 1975-84, chmn. judiciary com. and rules com., 1984; lt. gov. State of R.I., Providence, 1985-89; mng. ptnr. Tillinghast, Licht, Perkins, Smith & Cohen LLP, Providence, 1989—. Former chmn. R.I. Commn. on Racial, Religious and Ethnic Harrassment, Dr. Martin Luther King Jr. Holiday Commn., State Energy and Tech. Study Commn. rules com.; chmn. Coun. of State Govt., Intergovtl. Affairs Com., Nat. Focus Team, Bd. Gov. Higher Edn.; bd. regents Elem. and Secondary Edn.; mem. Pub. Telecom. Authority R.I., Univ. R.I. Found., Community Coll. R.I. Found. Bd. dirs., mem. corp. Roger Williams Hosp.; advisor Community Prep. Sch.; corporator Roger Williams Hosp.; trustee Save the Bay, Inc., Emma Pendleton Bradley Hosp.; bd. dirs. Temple Emanuel, Providence, Jewish Fedn. R.I., Samaritans; chmn. Small Bus. Adv. Council, Task Force on Teenage Suicide Prevention, CD Civil Preparedness Adv. Council, Urban League R.I., 1980-82, John Hope Settlement House, 1976-81; chair Am. Cancer Soc. Ball, 1989, Jewish Fedn. R.I. Passage to Freedom, 1989; chair R.I. chpt. Anti-Defamation League; mem. Women and Infants Corp., Dorcas Place, PARI, UNITAM, NCLG task force of Youth Suicide Prevention, Jewish Home for the Aged of R.I., bd. govs. for the handicapped; active YWCA of Greater R.I., Vols. in Action, Inc., Big Sister Assn. of R.I., Big Bros. R.I.; coordinator vols. gubernatorial campaigns Frank Licht, 1968, 70; active Jewish Community Ctr., Providence, 1975-83, East Side Sr. Citizens Ctr., 1975-76, R.I. Youth Guidance Ctr., Inc., 1987, Block Island Conservancy, Inc., Notre Dame Health Care Corp., 1987; Dem. candidate for U.S. Senate, 1988; chmn. ann. campaign Meeting Street Sch., 1990-91, mem. steering com. for capital fund drive, 1989-92; mem. corp. Womens and Infants Hosp.; Dem. candidate U.S. Senate, 2000. Named an Outstanding Young Man of R.I., R.I. Jaycees, 1979; recipient David Ben Gurion award State of Israel Bonds, 1977, Outstanding Pub. Service award Temple Torat Yisrael, 1985, Disting. Services to the Hispanic Community award Casa Puerto Rico, 1985, Hon. Pub. Service award Meeting St. Sch., 1986, Recognition award R.I. Day Care Dirs. Assn., 1986, award of Appreciation Child Care/Human Services, 1986, Govtl. Services award Ocean State Residences for the Retarded, 1987. Mem. R.I. Bar Assn., Hosp. Assn. R.I. (bd. dirs. 1997). Democrat. Office: Tillinghast Licht Perkins Smith & Cohen 10 Weybosset St Providence RI 02903-2818 Fax: 401-456-1210. E-mail: rlicht@tlslaw.com.

LICHTENSTEIN, ELISSA CHARLENE, legal association executive; b. Oct. 23, 1954; d. Mark and Rita (Field) L. AB cum laude, Smith Coll., Northampton, Mass., 1976; JD, George Washington U., 1979. Bar: D.C. 1980, U.S. Dist. Ct. (D.C. dist.) 1980, U.S. Ct. Appeals (D.C. cir.) 1980. Law clk. U.S. EPA, Washington, 1978-79; staff dir. ABA, Washington, 1979—, assoc. dir. pub. svcs. divsn., 1981-85, dir., 1985—. Editor, contbr.: Common Boundary/Common Problems: The Environmental Consequences of Energy Production, 1982, Exit Polls and Early Election Projections, 1984, The Global Environment: Challenges, Choices and Will, 1986, (newsletter) Environ. Law; co-editor, contbr. The Environ. Network; co-editor: Determining Competency in Guardianship Proceedings, 1990, Due Process Protections for Juveniles in Civil Commitment Proceedings, 1991, Environmental Regulation in Pacific Rim Nations, 1993, The Role of Law in the 1992 UN Conference on Environment and Development, 1992, Trade and the Environment in Pacific Rim Nations, 1994, Public Participation in Environmental Decisionmaking, 1995, Endangered Species Act Reauthorization: A Biocentric Approach, 1996, Sustainable Development in the Americas: The Emerging Role of the Private Sector, 1996, Environmental Priorities in Southeast Asian Nations, 1997, Law School Public Interest Law Programs, 1995, 99, numerous others. Named Outstanding Young Woman of Am., 1982. Mem.: NAFE, ABA, Greater Washington Soc. Assn. Execs., D.C. Bar Assn., Met. Washington Environ. Profls. (pres. 1986—96), Assn. Women in Comms., Am. Soc. Assn. Execs., Environ. Law Inst. (assoc.). Democrat. Jewish. Office: ABA Div Pub Svcs 740 15th St NW 9th Fl Washington DC 20005-1019

LICHTENSTEIN, NATALIE G. lawyer; b. N.Y.C., Sept. 17, 1953; d. Abba G. and Cecile (Geffen) L.; m. Willard Ken Tom, June 10, 1979. AB summa cum laude, Radcliffe Coll., 1975; JD, Harvard U., 1978. Bar: D.C. 1978. Atty., advisor U.S. Dept. Treasury, Washington, 1978-80; prin. counsel World Bank, Washington, 1980-94, chief counsel East Asia and Pacific divsn. Legal Dept., 1994-99, adviser to v.p. legal, 1999-2001, chief counsel instnl. affairs, 2001—. Adj. prof. Chinese law Georgetown U., Washington, 1982-86. Contbr. articles on Chinese and Vietnamese law to profl. jours. Public international.

LICHTENSTEIN, NATHAN H. lawyer; b. Chgo., June 12, 1953; s. Henry and Mary (Mayerowicz) L.; m. Aviva Shelly Zackai, Nov. 20, 1977; children— Sarah, Elana, Rachel, Nahum. B.A., Northwestern U., 1974; J.D., DePaul U., 1977; LL.M., John Marshall U., 1981. Bar: Ill. 1977, Fla. 1977, U.S. Dist. Ct. (no. dist.) Ill. 1977. Assoc. Goldgehn, Leonardo, Goldgehn & Isaacson, Chgo., 1977-83; ptnr. Aronberg, Goldgehn, Davis & Garmisa, Chgo., 1984—. Federal civil litigation, State civil litigation, Corporate, general. Office: Aronberg Goldgehn Davi & Garmisa 1 E Ibm Plz Chicago IL 60611-3586

LICHTENSTEIN, ROBERT JAY, lawyer; b. Phila., Jan. 23, 1948; s. Irving M. and Marjorie J. (Weiss) L.; m. Sandra Paley, Aug. 14, 1971; children: David P., Kate. BS in Econs., U. Pa., 1969; JD, U. Pitts., 1973; LLM in Taxation, NYU, 1974. Bar: Pa. 1974, U.S. Tax Ct. 1978, U.S. Dist. Ct. (ea. dist.) Pa. 1979, U.S. Ct. Appeals (3rd cir.) 1982, U.S. Ct. Appeals (4th cir.) 1987. Ptnr. Saul, Ewing, Remick & Saul, 1978-88; assoc. Morgan, Lewis & Bockius, Phila., 1974-78, ptnr., 1988—; dir. Maritrans Inc. Instr. Main Line Paralegal Inst., Wayne, Pa., 1984-87, Paralegal Inst., Phila., 1987-90; adj. prof. law Villanova U. Sch. Law, 1991—, U. Pa. Sch. of Law, 1999—. Trustee Temple Brith Achim, King of Prussia, Pa., 1986-91. Mem. ABA, Pa. Bar Assn., Phila. Assn. Democrat. Avocations: skiing, tennis, reading. Pension, profit-sharing, and employee benefits, Corporate taxation, Taxation, general. Office: Morgan Lewis Bockius LLP 1701 Market St Philadelphia PA 19103-2903 E-mail: rlichtenstein@morganlewis.com.

LICHTENSTEIN, SARAH CAROL, lawyer; b. East Orange, N.J., May 25, 1953; d. Carl and Hilda Ruth (Warshaw) L. BA, Wellesley Coll., 1975; JD, Columbia U., 1978. Bar: N.Y. 1979, U.S. Dist. Ct. (ea. and so. dists.) N.Y. 1979, U.S. Ct. Appeals (2d cir.) 1981. Assoc. Milbank, Tweed, Hadley & McCloy, N.Y.C., 1978-84, Dreyer and Traub, N.Y.C., 1984-87, ptnr., 1987-93, Shea & Gould, N.Y.C., 1993-94; arbitrator small claims ct. Civ. Ct. of the City of New York, 1988-93; ptnr. Morrison Cohen Singer & Weinstein LLP, N.Y.C., 1994-2000; counsel Lamb & Barnosky, LLP, Melville, N.Y., 2000—. Dir. Eleven Riverside Dr. Corp., 1986-89, 98-2000, pres., 1988-89; mem. panel of chpt. 7 trustees So. Dist. of N.Y., 1993-97; mem. mediation panel U.S. Dist. Ct. So. Dist. N.Y., Bankruptcy Ct. So. Dist. N.Y.; mem. faculty N.E. Deposition Program, Nat. Inst. Trial Advocacy. Contbr. articles to profl. jours. Trustee Stephen Wise Free Synagogue, 1987-90, officer, 1990-98. Wellesley scholar, 1975, Stone scholar Columbia U., 1977-78. Mem. ABA, Suffolk County Bar Assn. Bankruptcy, General civil litigation, Probate (including wills, trusts). E-mail: scl@lambbamosky.com.

LICHTY, WARREN DEWEY, JR., lawyer; b. Colorado Springs, Dec. 17, 1930; s. Warren D. and Margaret (White) L.; m. Margaret Louise Grupy, Dec. 8, 1962. Student, Chadron State Coll., 1948-50; BS in Law, U. Nebr., 1952, JD, 1954. Bar: Nebr. 1954, U.S. Dist. Ct. Nebr. 1954, U.S. Ct. Appeals (8th cir.) 1973, U.S. Supreme Ct. 1979. Spl. agt. CIC, 1955-58; county judge Dawes County, Nebr., 1958-61; spl. asst. atty. gen. Nebr. Dept. Justice, Lincoln, 1961-69; mng. asst. atty. gen., chief counsel Nebr. Dept. Roads, Lincoln, 1969-97. Lectr. law Chadron State Coll., 1959-60; mem. com. on eminent domain and land use, transp. rsch. bd. NAS,-NRC, 1973-90. Served with U.S. Army, 1954-58. Decorated grand sovereign United Grand Imperial Coun., Red Cross of Constantine. Mem. Nebr. Bar Assn., Lincoln Bar Assn., Am. Assn. State Hwy. and Transp. Ofcls. (subcom. on legal affairs 1969-97), Scottish Rite Rsch. Soc. (pres. 1990-95, bd. dirs. 1990—), Am. Legion, Internat. Supreme Coun. (hon., Order of DeMolay), Hiram Club (past pres.), Masons (33d degree, grand master Nebr. 1979, vice chmn. conf. Grand Masters N.Am. 1980, bd. dirs. Home Corp. Nebr. 1979-90, pres. George Washington nat. meml. assn.), Shriners, Royal Order Scotland, Scottish Rite (1st Grand Equerry, supreme coun. southern jurisdiction, U.S. and sovereign grand insp. gen. in Nebr. 1991—, bd. dirs. Found. Nebr. 1981-90, pres. bd. dirs. Found. Nebr. 1990—). Republican. Episcopalian. Home: PO Box 22559 Lincoln NE 68542-2559

LICKE, WALLACE JOHN, lawyer; b. Bemidji, Minn., Jan. 23, 1945; s. George John and Lois (Sanford) L.; m. Martha Miriam Eddy, Dec. 19, 1969; children: Loriann, Paul. BA, U. Minn., 1967, MA, 1970, JD cum laude, 1973. Bar: Minn. 1973, U.S. Dist. Ct. Minn. 1973, U.S. Ct. Appeals (8th cir.) 1981, U.S. Supreme Ct. 1981. Instr. Itasca C.C., Grand Rapids, Minn., 1968—; assoc. Helgesen, Peterson, Engberg & Spector Attys. at Law (now Peterson, Engberg & Peterson), Mpls., 1972-75; sec., gen. counsel Blandin Paper Co. and UPM-Kymmene Inc., subs. UPM-Kymmene Corp., a Finnish Co., Helsinki, 1975—2002; pvt. practice, 2002—. Bd. dirs. Vol. Atty. Program Super Bd., Judy Garland Mus. and Children's Discovery Mus.; chmn. bus. retention and expansion strategies program U. Minn.; mem. panel of arbitrators Am. Arbitration Assn. Mem. bd. editors Minn. Law Rev. Area rep. Minn. awareness project Minn. Internat. Ctr./World Affairs Ctr.; Bd. dirs., pres. hon. bd. dirs. Itasca County Family YMCA, Itasca County Family YMCA, Grand Grand Rapids; bd. dirs., v.p., pres. Itasca County unit Am. Cancer Soc.; bd. dirs., pres. Myles Reif Performing Arts Ctr.; chmn., sec. post com. computer-small bus. explorer post Boy Scouts Am.; adult leader 4-H program Agrl. Extension Svc. U. Minn., St. Paul; mem. Bass Brook Twp. (Minn.) Econ. Devel. Com.; mem. promotion and prospecting com. Itasca Devel. Corp.; trustee Grand Rapids area community found; chmn. coop. solutions adv. bd. Grand Rapids, Minn.; trustee Libr. Found., Grand Rapids, Minn., Cmty. Libr. Found.; class rep. U. Minn. Law Sch.; bd. dirs. Judy Garland Mus. and Children's Discovery Mus., Grand Rapids, Minn. Recipient William Spurgeon III award Boy Scouts Am., 1988; NDEA Title IV fellow, 1967, Paul Harris fellow. Mem. ABA (com. mem.), Fed. Bar Assn., Minn. Bar Assn. (del., planning com.), Itasca County Bar Assn. (past sec., pres.), Minn. 15th Dist. Bar Assn. (com. mem.), Am. Corp. Counsel Assn. (charter), Am. Soc. Corp. Secs., Grand Rapids C. of C. (chmn. com., bd. dirs.), Rotary (bd. dirs., pres., sec. Grand Rapids, dist. rep.), Order of Ski U Mah, Phi Beta Kappa. Corporate, general, General practice, Labor (including EEOC, Fair Labor Standards Act, labor-management relations, NLRB, OSHA). E-mail: john_licke@yahoo.com.

LIDE, VINTON DEVANE, lawyer; b. Greenville, S.C., May 4, 1937; s. Theodore Ellis and Mary Elizabeth (DeVane) L.; m. Carol Jean Keisler, July 8, 1979; children: Wade Patrick, Emily Elizabeth. AB, Davidson Coll., 1959; LLB (now JD), U. Va., 1962. Bar: Va. 1962, S.C. 1962, U.S. Ct. Appeals (4th cir.) 1974, U.S. Ct. Appeals (9th cir.) 2001, U.S. Supreme Ct. 1980. Assoc. Shand & Wilmeth, Hartsville, S.C., 1962-64; ptnr. Shand & Lide, Hartsville, S.C., 1964-78; pub. defender Darlington County, S.C., 1969-76; exec. asst./legal advisor to gov. S.C., 1978-79; asst. atty. gen. State of S.C., 1978-79; gen. counsel S.C. Dept. Social Svcs., 1979-81; chief counsel, staff dir. Com. on the Judiciary, U.S. Senate, Washington, 1981-85; adminstrv. asst. to U.S. Senator Strom Thurmond Washington, 1985—. Mcpl. ct. judge, Hartsville, 1963—69; U.S. atty. Dist. of S.C., 1985—89. Recipient cert. of Appreciation, Drug Enforcement Adminstrn., U.S. Dept. Justice, 1980. Mem. ABA (ho. dels. 1978-82), S.C. Bar Assn., Va. Bar Assn. Republican. Lutheran. Office: Vinton D Lide & Assocs LLC 5179 Sunset Blvd Lexington SC 29072 E-mail: dee@lidelaw.com.

LIDSKY, ELLA, retired law librarian; b. Wilno, Poland; came to U.S., 1962; d. Leib and Sheina (Izygzon) Cwik; m. Alexander Lidsky, Feb. 20, 1963 (dec. Mar., 1996); 1 son, David Abraham. BA, Pedagogical Inst. Odessa, USSR; MS, Columbia U., 1966, MA, 1973. Cert. Russian and Hebrew lang. tchr. Tchr. high sch., Poland, 1948-51; elem. sch., 1961-62; asst. cataloger Tchrs. Coll. Columbia U., N.Y.C., 1966-68; cataloger Fairleigh Dickinson U., Teaneck, N.J., 1968-69, asst. dir. tech. services Madison, N.J., 1973-84; head cataloger Ramapo Coll., Mahwah, N.J., 1971-73; asst. libr. U.S. Ct. Internat. Trade Law Libr., N.Y.C., 1985-2000. Mem. Am. Assn. Law Libraries, Law Librarians of Greater N.Y., N.Y. Tech. Services Librarians, N.J. Law Librarians Assn. Democrat. Jewish. Avocations: music, travel. E-mail: Hella_@msn.com.

LIDSTONE, HERRICK KENLEY, JR., lawyer; b. New Rochelle, N.Y., Sept. 10, 1949; s. Herrick Kenley and Marcia Edith (Drake) L.; m. Mary Lynne O'Toole, Aug. 5, 1978; children: Herrick Kevin, James Patrick, John Francis. AB, Cornell U., 1971; JD, U. Colo., 1978. Bar: Colo. 1978, U.S. Dist. Ct. Colo. 1978. Assoc. Roath & Brega, P.C., Denver, 1978-85, Brenman, Epstein, Raskin & Friedlob, P.C., Denver, 1985-86; shareholder Brenman, Raskin & Friedlob, P.C., Denver, 1986-94; mem. Friedlob Sanderson Raskin Paulson & Tourtilott, LLC, Denver, 1995-98, Norton Lidstone, P.C., Greenwood Village, Colo., 1998—2002, Burns, Figa & Will, P.C., Englewood, Colo., 2002—. Adj. prof. U. Denver Coll. Law, 1985-2000; spkr. in field various orgns.; mem. state securities bd. Colo. Dept. Regulatory Agys., 1999—, vice chair, 2000—01, chair, 2001-02. Author: Federal and State Securities Regulation for the General Practitioner in Colorado, 2000; editor U. Colo. Law Rev., 1977-78; co-author: Federal Income Taxation of Corporations, 6th edit.; contbg. author: Legal Opinion Letters Formbook, 1996, supplement, 1999; contbr. articles to profl. jours. Served with USNR, 1971-75, with USNR, 1975-81. Mem. ABA (Am. Law Inst.), Colo. Bar Assn., Arapahoe County Bar Assn., Denver Assn. Oil and Gas Title Lawyers. Avocation: fluent spanish language. Corporate, general, Mergers and acquisitions, Securities. Office: Burns Figa & Will PC Ste 1030 6400 S Fiddlers Green Cir Englewood CO 80111 E-mail: hklidstone@bfw-law.com.

LIEB, L. ROBERT, lawyer; b. Jersey City, July 15, 1941; s. Nathan Philip and Elizabeth (Blum) Lieb; m. Sherry Young, Sept. 11, 1971; children: Elizabeth Ann, Nathan Young. BA, U. Buffalo, 1962; LLB, NYU, 1965. Bar: N.J. 1967, N.Y. 1970, U.S. Dist. Ct. (so. and ea. dists.) N.Y. 1970. Law clk., appellate divsn. Superior Ct. N.J., 1965—66; sr. ptnr. Kimmelman, Lieb, Wolf & Samson, West Orange, NJ, 1972—77; chmn. Mountain Devel. Corp., West Paterson, NJ, 1978—, Bretton Woods Corp., NH, 1980—84. Chmn., bd. dirs. NorCrown Bank of Roseland, 1987. Pres. The Children's Inst., Livingston, NJ; trustee Passaic County 200 Club, YMCA of the Oranges, Livingston Edn. Found.; co-chmn. Bryant Park Mgmt. Corp. Served 1st lt. JAGC USAF, 1966—72. Scholar Harry Rudin, NYU, 1963—65. Mem.: Essex County Bar Assn., Green Brook Country Club (North Caldwell, N.J.). Office: Mountain Devel Corp PO Box 1069 100 Delawanna Ave Ste 100 Clifton NJ 07014-1069

LIEBELER, SUSAN WITTENBERG, lawyer; b. July 3, 1942; d. Sherman K. and Eleanor (Klivans) Levine; m. Wesley J. Liebeler, Oct. 21, 1971; 1 child, Jennifer. BA, U. Mich., 1963, postgrad., 1963-64; LLB, UCLA, 1966. Bar: Calif. 1967, Vt. 1972, D.C. 1988. Law clk. Calif. Ct. of Appeals, 1966-67; assoc. Gang, Tyre & Brown, 1967-68, Greenberg, Bernhard, Weiss & Karma, L.A., 1968-70; assoc. gen. counsel Rep. Corp., 1970-72; gen. counsel Verit Industries, 1972-73; prof. Loyola Law Sch., L.A., 1973—85; spl. counsel, chmn. John S. R. Shad, SEC, Washington, 1981-82; commr. U.S. Internat. Trade Commn., Washington, 1984-88, vice-chmn., 1984-86, chmn., 1986-88; ptnr. Irell & Manella, L.A., 1988-94; pres. Lexpert Rsch. Svcs., L.A., 1995—. Vis. prof. U. Tex., summer 1982; cons. Office of Policy Coordination, Office of Pres.-elect, 1981-82; cons. U.S. Ry. Assn., 1975, U.S. EPA, 1974, U.S. Price Commn., 1972; mem. Adminstrv. Conf. U.S., 1986-88. Mem. editl. adv. bd. Regulation mag. CATO Inst.; sr. editor UCLA Law Rev., 1965-66; contbr. articles to profl. jours. Mem. adv. bd. U. Calif. Orientation in USA Law; bd. govs. Century City Hosp., 1992—2002, vice chair, 1997—99, chair, 1999—2001. Stein scholar UCLA, 1966. Mem. State Bar Calif. (treas., vice chair, chair exec. com. internat. law sect.), Practicing Law Inst. (Calif. adv. com.), Washington Legal Found. (acad. adv. bd.), Order of Coif. Jewish. E-mail: lexpert@lexpertresearch.com.

LIEBEN, THOMAS GEOFFREY, lawyer; b. Omaha; s. Theodore Jack and Eileen (Brooks) L.; m. Anne C., June 26, 1971; children: Elizabeth, Caroline, Andrew. BA, Creighton U., 1968; JD, NYU, 1971. Bar: Nebr. 1971, U.S. Dist. Ct. Nebr. 1971, U.S. Ct. Appeals (8th cir.) 1972, U.S. Tax Ct. 1972. Ptnr. Fitzgerald & Brown, Omaha, 1971-88; prin. Lieben, Whitted, Houghton, Slowiaczek & Cavanagh, P.C., Omaha, 1988—. Dir. Financial Dynamics Inc., Omaha, 1988-99. Contbr. articles to profl. jours. Recipient Order of the Coif award NYU, 1971; fellow Nebr. Bar Found., Lincoln, 1994; named in Best Lawyers in Am., 1983—. Mem. Omaha Bar Assn., Nebr. Bar Assn., ABA, Omaha Estate Planning Coun., Omaha Pension Coun., Employee Benefits Roundtable. Democrat. Avocation: tennis. Estate planning, Labor (including EEOC, Fair Labor Standards Act, labor-management relations, NLRB, OSHA), Probate (including wills, trusts). Office: Lieben Whitted Houghton Slowiaczek & Cavanagh PC 2027 Dodge St Ste 100 Omaha NE 68102-1238 E-mail: jlieben@liebenlaw.com.

LIEBERMAN, JOSEPH I. senator; b. Stamford, Conn., Feb. 24, 1942; s. Henry and Marcia (Manger) L.; m. Hadassah Freilich, Mar. 20, 1983; children: Matthew, Rebecca, Ethan, Hana. BA, Yale U., 1964, JD, 1967. Bar: Conn. 1967. Mem. Conn. Senate, 1971-81, senate majority leader, 1975-81; ptnr. Lieberman, Segaloff & Wolfson, New Haven, 1972-83; atty. gen. State of Conn., Hartford, 1983-89; U.S. senator from Conn., 1989—; chmn. govtl. affairs com. Mem. armed svcs. com., environment and pub. works com., small bus. com.; chmn. Dem. Leadership Coun., 1995-2000. Author: The Power Broker, 1966, The Scorpion and the Tarantula, 1970, The Legacy, 1981, Child Support in America, 1986, In Praise of Public Life, 2000. Candidate for v.p. U.S., 2000 Democrat. Jewish. Office: 706 Hart Senate Office Bldg Washington DC 20510-0001*

LIEBERMAN, MARVIN SAMUEL, lawyer; b. N.Y.C., Apr. 26, 1935; s. Abe and Gertrude (Connelly) L.; m. Kathryn Fuhrer, Aug. 10, 1963; children: Kathryn, Willis. BA, Lafayette Coll., 1955; JD, Rutgers U., 1962. Bar: N.J. 1962, U.S. Ct. Appeals (3d cir.) 1965; cert. civil trial atty., N.J. Assoc. Jacob, Alfred & Richardson Levinson, Perth Amboy, N.J., 1962-69; ptnr. Levinson, Conover, Lieberman & Fink, Perth Amboy, N.J., 1969-71, Lieberman & Ryan, Somerville, N.J., 1971-83, 88-95, Lieberman, Ryan, Richardson, Welaj & Miller, Somerville, N.J., 1983-87, Lieberman, Ryan & Forrest, Somerville, N.J., 1995—. With USAF, 1955-58. Mem. ATLA, N.J. Bar Assn., N.J. Trial Lawyers Assn., Middlesex County Trial Lawyers Assn., N.J. Lawyers Assn., Am. Bd. Trial Advs. Personal injury (including property damage), Product liability, Workers' compensation. Home: 14 Riverview Terr Hillsborough NJ 08844 Office: Lieberman Ryan & Forrest 141 W End Ave Somerville NJ 08876-1809 also: 84 Park Ave Flemington NJ 08822 Business E-Mail: liryfo@aol.com.

LIEBERMAN, NANCY ANN, lawyer; b. N.Y.C., Dec. 30, 1956; d. Elias and Elayne Hildegarde (Fox) L.; m. Mark Ellman, Sept. 6, 1997. BA summa cum laude, U. Rochester, 1977; JD, U. Chgo., 1979; LLM in Taxation, NYU, 1981. Bar: N.Y. 1980. Intern White House, Washington, 1975; law clk. Hon. Henry A. Politz U.S. Ct. Appeals (5th cir.), Shreveport, La., 1979-80; assoc. Skadden Arps Slate Meagher & Flom LLP, N.Y.C., 1981-87; ptnr. Skadden Arps Slate Meagher & Flom, N.Y.C., 1987—. Bd. trustees U. Rochester, 1994—; bd. dirs. Pacific Coun. Internat. Policy. Mem. ABA, Assn. Bar City N.Y., Coun. Fgn. Rels., Phi Beta Kappa. Republican. Jewish. Commercial, contracts (including sales of goods; commercial financing), Corporate, general. Home: 935 Park Ave New York NY 10028-0212 Office: Skadden Arps Slate Meagher & Flom LLP 4 Times Sq New York NY 10036-6595 E-mail: nlieberm@skadden.com.

LIEBMAN, EMMANUEL, lawyer; b. Phila., Mar. 26, 1925; s. Morris and Pearl (Zucker) L.; m. Anita Forman, Dec. 24, 1953; children: Judith H. Winslow, Lawrence H. B.S. in Econs., U. Pa., 1950; J.D., Rutgers U., 1954. Bar: N.J. 1954, U.S. Tax Ct. 1955, U.S. Supreme Ct. 1960, D.C. 1972, U.S. Ct. Appeals (3d cir.) 1977. Sole practice, Camden, N.J., 1954-70; pres. Emmanuel Liebman, P.A., Cherry Hill, N.J., 1970-72; pres., chmn. Liebman & Flaster, P.A., Cherry Hill, 1972-86; pres. Emmanuel Liebman, Chartered, Cherry Hill, 1986—; lectr., moderator Inst. Continuing Legal Edn., 1962-87. Served with USNR, 1943-46, PTO. Mem. Camden County Bar Assn. (chmn. com. on fed. tax 1964, 68-70, chmn. retirement plan com. 1986-93), N.J. State Bar Assn. (chmn. com. on bus. taxes 1967-69, 71-73, chmn. state capitol com. 1973-77, chmn. ad hoc com. on financing legal fees 1976-79, exec. coun. 1974-89, chmn. sub chpt. legis. com. 1990-92, Ann. medal Honor award), ABA (taxation sect., com. personal svc. corps., real property, probate and trust law sect.), D.C. Bar Assn., N.J. State Bar Found. (trustee 1972-87, pres. 1979-83), Am. Judicature Soc., Am. Arbitration Assn. (panelist 1964-88), Camden County Bar Found. (trustee 1986-93, Peter J. Devine award). Clubs: Haddon Field (Haddonfield, N.J.); Woodcrest Country (Cherry Hill), St. Andrews Country Club (Boca Raton Fl). Lodge: B'nai B'rith. Probate (including wills, trusts), Corporate taxation, Taxation, general. Home: 46 Dublin Ln Cherry Hill NJ 08003-2504 Address: 200 Lake Dr E Ste 204 Cherry Hill NJ 08002-1171

LIEBMAN, LANCE MALCOLM, law educator, lawyer; b. Newark, Sept. 11, 1941; s. Roy and Barbara (Trilinsky) L.; m. Carol Bensinger, June 28, 1964; children: Jeffrey, Benjamin. BA, Yale U., 1962; MA, Cambridge U., 1964; LLB, Harvard U., 1967. Bar: D.C. 1968, Mass. 1976, N.Y., 1995. Asst. to Mayor Lindsay, N.Y.C., 1968-70; asst. prof. law Harvard U., 1970-76, prof., 1976-91, assoc. dean, 1981-84; dean, Lucy G. Moses prof. law Columbia U. Sch. Law, N.Y.C., 1991-96, prof., dir. Parker Sch. Fgn. Law, 1996—, Williams S. Beinecke prof. law, 1998—; dir. Am. Law Inst., 1998—. Successor trustee Yale Corp., 1971-83 Office: Columbia U Sch Law 435 W 116th St New York NY 10027-7297

LIEBMANN, GEORGE W(ILLIAM), lawyer; b. N.Y.C., June 20, 1939; s. William Liebmann and Margaret (Hirschman) Cook; m. Anne-Lise Grimstad, Apr. 29, 1967; children: Pamela, George, Franklin. AB, Dartmouth Coll., 1960; JD, U. Chgo., 1963. Bar: Md. 1964, Ill. 1964. With Chaucer Head Book Shop, Inc., N.Y.C., 1958-59; law clk. to chief judge Ct. Appeals Md., 1963-64; with Frank, Bernstein, Conaway and Goldman, Balt., 1964-79; asst. atty. gen. State of Md., Balt., 1967-69; exec. asst. to Gov. Md., Annapolis, 1979-80; prin. Liebmann and Shively, P.A., Balt., 1980—. Lectr. U. Md. Law Sch., 1977—78, Johns Hopkins U., 1991—92; mem. Gov.'s Commn. to Revise Annotated Code Md., 1974—83; alt. mem. State Planning Coun. on Radioactive Waste Mgmt., 1980—82; chmn. Gov.'s Task Force on Local Govt. Antitrust Liability, 1982—83, Gov.'s Commn. Health Care Providers' Profl. Liability Ins., 1983—84; gen. coun. Md. Econ. Devel. Corp., 1985—; vis. fellow U. Salford, England, 1996, Wolfson Coll., Cambridge, 1996, 98, 99, 2002; panelist U.S. Bankruptcy Trustee, 1980—. Author: Maryland District Court Law and Practice, 2 vols., 1976, Maryland Civil Practice Forms, 2 vols., 1984, The Little Platoons: Sub-Local Governments in Modern History, 1995, The Gallows in the Grove: Civil Society in American Law, 1997, Solving Problems Without Large Government, 1999, Six Lost Leaders: Prophets of Civil Society, 2001; mng. editor U. Chgo. Law Rev., 1962-63. Trustee Hist. Annapolis Found., 1991—99; exec. dir. Calvert Inst. Policy Rsch., 2002—; sec. Coalition Against the SST, Washington, 1969; Rep. primary candidate U.S. Senate, 1998. Simon indsl. and profl. fellow U. Manchester, Eng., 1993-94. Mem. Am. Law Inst., Fed. Jud. Conf. 4th Cir., Libr. Co. Balt. Bar (bd. dirs. 1967—, pres. 1975-77), Engring. Soc. Md. (assoc.) Antitrust, Appellate, Bankruptcy. Office: 8 W Hamilton St Baltimore MD 21201-5020

LIEBMANN, THEODOR S. law educator; b. New Haven, Sept. 2, 1968; s. Karl-Otto Noah and Judith Kusinitz Liebmann; m. Barbara Ellen Weinstein, June 7, 1998; children: Allie Joy, Risa Helena, Ruby Isabel. BA, Yale U., 1990; JD, Georgetown U., 1995. Bar: N.Y. 1996. Cmty. worker Neighborhood Defender Svc. of Harlem, N.Y.C., 1990—92; human rights specialist, ct. atty. N.Y.C. Commn. on Human Rights, N.Y.C., 1995—97; staff atty. juvenile rights divsn. The Legal Aid Soc. , N.Y.C., 1997—99; dir. Hofstra Child Advocacy Clinic, Hempstead, NY, 1999—. Mem. editl. bd.: Family Ct. Rev., 2003; contbr. articles to profl. jours. Street law program coord. Andrew Glover Youth Program, N.Y.C., 1997—99. Mem.: Assn. Bar City N.Y. (com. on children and the law 2001—). Office: Hofstra Child Advocacy Clinic 108 Hofstra Univ Hempstead NY 11549

LIEM, EDWIN T.H. lawyer; b. Jakarta, Indonesia, Mar. 16, 1963; M in Med. Sci., U. Amsterdam, The Netherlands, 1986, M in Netherlands Notarial Law, M in Netherlands Pvt. Law, U. Amsterdam, The Netherlands, 1989. Cert. Netherlands law practice, crown appt. civil law notary. Ptnr. Caron & Stevens/Baker & McKenzie, Amsterdam, 1992—96, Wouters Advt. & Notary/Andersen Legal, Amsterdam, 1999—2001, Baker & Mckenzie, Amsterdam, 2001—. Contbr. articles to profl. jours. Mem. Royal Profl. Orgn. Civil Law Notaries. Corporate, general, Finance, Mergers and acquisitions. Office: Baker & McKenzie PO Box 2720 1000 CS Amsterdam Netherlands Fax: 31 20 6267949. E-mail: edwin.liem@bakernet.com.

LIEN, WALLACE WAYNE, lawyer, land use consultant; b. McMinnville, Oreg., Aug. 19, 1949; s. Allen John and Elaine Eulala (Spafford) L.; m. Neala Gorgeen King, Mar. 14, 1966 (div. 1972); children: Stephen Brian, Wallace Wayne Jr.; m. Janet Kathleen MacInnes, Aug. 20, 1977; children: Elizabeth Andrea, Alexis Anne, Michael Allen. AS, Chemeketa Community Coll.; BS with honors, Oreg. Coll. Edn.; JD, Willamette U. Bar: Oreg. 1979, U.S. Supreme Ct. 1985. Ptnr. Lien, Lien & Hobson, Keizer, Oreg., 1979-81; asst. county counsel Marion County, Salem, Oreg., 1981-82; chief legal counsel Polk County, Dallas, Oreg., 1982-83; instr. Chemeketa Community Coll., Salem, 1980-85; ptnr. Paulus, Rhoten & Lien, Salem, 1983-86; sole practice Salem, 1986—. Mem. bd. dirs. Oreg. Econ. Inst., Portland, 1985; pres. Oreg. Community Coll. Student Assn., Salem, 1972-73; mem. Oreg. Bd. Edn., Salem, 1972. Western Interstate Commn. Higher Edn. scholar, U.S. Govt., 1976; recipient Col. Robertson award Willamette U., 1978, first pl. moot ct. award Willamette Law Sch., 1977. Mem. ABA, Oreg. State Bar Assn. (exec. com. real estate and land use sect.), Marion County Bar Assn., Chemeketa Alumni Assn. Lodges: Elks. Republican. Avocations: water skiing, youth sports coaching and adminstrn., theater, writing. E-mail address. Land use and zoning (including planning), Property, real (including real estate development, water). Home: 1004 Crescent Dr NW Salem OR 97304-2702 Office: 1775 32d Pl NE Salem OR 97303 E-mail: manager@lienlaw.com.

LIESENFELD, VINCENT JOSEPH, lawyer; b. St. Paul, 1947; s. Vincent Edward and Agnes Lillian L.; children: Patricia, Peter. BA summa cum laude, U. Minn., 1970; student, U. Reading, Eng., 1973-74; PhD, U. Wis., 1978; JD summa cum laude, Oklahoma City U., 1996. Bar: Colo., D.C., Minn., Okla., Tex., U.S. Supreme Ct., U.S. Tax Ct. Writer Minn. State Employment Svc., St. Paul, 1970, U. Wis. News and Publs., Madison, 1972; asst. prof. English U. Okla., Norman, 1977-83, assoc. prof., 1983-96; of counsel Salem Law Offices, Norman, 1996—2002, Casseb & Pearl, San Antonio, 2003—. Vis. scholar UCLA, 1980; contbg. writer Am. Coll. Testing Program, Iowa City, 1982; rsch. cons. civil rights cases, Norman, 1982—. Author: The Licensing Act of 1737, 1984; editor: The Stage & the Licensing Act, 1981; contbr. articles and revs. to profl. jours. Vol. Spl. Olympics, Norman, 1990. Fulbright scholar, 1973-74; Woodrow Wilson fellow, 1969, W.A. Clark Libr. Mellon fellow, 1980, Rsch. fellow NEH, 1980-81; Rsch. grantee U. Okla., 1978, 79, 81, Coll. of State Bar of Tex., 2001-03, William J. Holloway Jr. Am. Inn. of Ct., 2001-02. Mem. ABA, Am. Intellectual Property Law Assn., Phi Beta Kappa, Phi Delta Phi, Phi Kappa Phi. Avocations: amateur radio, running, computer programming. Office: Casseb & Pearl 127 E Travis San Antonio TX 78205

LIEUWEN, JOHN N. lawyer; b. Berkeley, Calif., Aug. 19, 1951; s. Edwin and Marian R. (Whitehead) L. BA, U. Calif., Berkeley, 1973; JD, Hastings Coll., 1976; LLM in Taxation, NYU, 1977. Bar: Calif. 1977, N.Mex. 1978, U.S. Tax Ct. 1980. Ptnr. John N. Lieuwen & Assoc., Albuquerque, 2002—. Mem. Calif. Bar Assn., N.Mex. State Bar. Independent. Avocations: fishing, skiing. Pension, profit-sharing, and employee benefits, Corporate taxation, Estate taxation. Office: 4101 Indian School Rd NE Ste 310 Albuquerque NM 87110

LIFLAND, WILLIAM THOMAS, lawyer; b. Jersey City, Nov. 15, 1928; s. Charles and Carolyn (Francks) L.; m. Nancy Moffat, May 29, 1954; children— Carol M., Charles C., J. Kerin, David T. BS, Yale U., 1949; JD, Harvard U., 1952. Bar: D.C. 1954, N.Y. 1955, N.J. 1965-2002; Senior Counsel, 2002-. Law clk. to Justice John M. Harlan U.S. Supreme Ct., 1954-55; assoc. Cahill Gordon & Reindel, N.Y.C., 1955-58, Paris, 1958-60, ptnr. N.Y.C., 1965—2002, sr. counsel, 2002—. Adj. prof. Fordham Law Sch., N.Y.C. Served as lt. USAF, 1952-54 Mem.: ABA, Assn. Bar City N.Y., D.C. Bar Assn., N.J. Bar Assn., N.Y. State Bar Assn., Nassau Club (Princeton, NJ), India House Club (N.Y.C.). Administrative and regulatory, Antitrust, Federal civil litigation. Office: Cahill Gordon & Reindel 80 Pine St Fl 17 New York NY 10005-1790 E-mail: wlifland@cahill.com.

LIFSCHITZ, JUDAH, lawyer; b. N.Y.C., Nov. 28, 1952; s. Morris and Edna (Love) L.; m. Marilyn Feder, Dec. 8, 1974; children: Lisa, Ira, Tamar. BA magna cum laude, Yeshiva U., 1974; JD, George Washington U., 1977. Bar: Md. 1977, U.S. Dist. Ct. D.C. 1980, U.S. Claims Ct. 1980, U.S. Ct. Appeals (D.C. cir.) 1980, U.S. Ct. Appeals (4th cir.) 1982, U.S. Ct. Appeals (fed. cir.) 1985, U.S. Supreme Ct. 1985. Assoc. Hudson, Creyke, Koehler & Tacke, Washington, 1980, Epstein, Becker, Borsody & Green, Washington, 1980-83; ptnr., chmn. govt. contracts dept. Washington Perito & Dubuc, Washington, 1983-91; ptnr. Shapiro, Lifschitz and Schram, P.C., Washington, 1991—. Washington counsel Nat. Coun. Young Israel, N.Y.C., 1980—; pres. Yeshiva of Greater Washington, 1985-89; bd. dirs. Jewish Community Coun., Washington, 1980—, United Jewish Appeal Fedn., Washington, 1985. Recipient Schofar award Nat. Council Young Israel, 1980. Mem. ABA. Construction, Government contracts and claims. Office: Shapiro Lifschitz & Schram Ste 1050 1742 N Street NW Washington DC 20036

LIFSCHULTZ, PHILLIP, financial and tax consultant, accountant, lawyer; b. Oak Park, Ill., Mar. 5, 1927; s. Abraham Albert and Frances Rhoda (Siegel) L.; m. Edith Louise Leavitt, June 27, 1948; children: Gregory, Bonnie, Jodie. BS in Acctg., U. Ill., 1949; JD, John Marshall Law Sch., 1956. Bar: Ill. 1956; CPA. Tax mgr. Arthur Andersen & Co., Chgo., 1957-63; v.p. taxes Montgomery Ward & Co., Chgo., 1963-78; fin. v.p., contr. Henry Crown & Co., Chgo., 1978-81; prin. Phillip Lifschultz & Assocs., Chgo., 1981—. Exec. dir. Dodi Orgn., 1987-90; v.p. Altra Travel, Northbrook, Ill., 1975—; v.p. Tax Execs. Inst., Chgo., 1977-78; pres. Great Lakes Shoe Co., Bannockburn, Ill., 1996—. Adv. coun. Coll. Commerce and Bus. Adminstrn., U. Ill., Urbana-Champaign, 1977-78; chmn. Civic Fedn. Chgo., 1980-82; chmn. adv. bd. to Auditor Gen. of Ill., 1965-73; project dir. Exec. Svc. Corps of Chgo., Chgo. Bd. Edn. and State of Ill. projects, 1980-87. With U.S. Army, 1945-46. Mem. AICPA, Am. Arbitration Assn. (comml. panel 1983-94), Ill. Bar Assn., Chgo. Bar Assn., Ill. CPA Soc., Nat. Retail Merchants Assn. (chmn. tax. com. 1975-78), Am. Retail Fedn. (chmn. taxation com. 1971), Standard Club Chgo. Home and Office: 442 Kelburn Rd Apt 123 Deerfield IL 60015-4370 E-mail: papalif@aol.com.

LIFTIN, JOHN MATTHEW, lawyer; b. Washington, June 25, 1943; children: Eric, Hilary. AB, U. Pa., 1964; LLB, Columbia U., 1967. Bar: N.Y. 1967, D.C. 1974, U.S. Dist. Ct. D.C. 1975, U.S. Ct. Appeals (D.C. cir.) 1975, U.S. Supreme Ct. 1980. Assoc. Sullivan & Cromwell, N.Y.C., 1967-71; spl. counsel to chmn. SEC, Washington, 1971-72, assoc. dir. market reg. div., 1972-74; ptnr. Rogers & Wells, Washington, 1974-85; pres. Quadrex Securities Corp., N.Y.C., 1985-87; sr. v.p., gen. counsel Kidder, Peabody Group Inc., N.Y.C., 1987-96, Prudential Fin., Newark, 1998—. Mem. adv. bd. securities regulation and law reports Bur. Nat. Affairs, Inc., Washington, 1979—; mem. N.Y. Stock Exch. Legal Adv. Com., 2000—. Mem. ABA (chmn. com. of corp. gen. counsel), Univ. Club. Corporate, general, Securities. Office: Prudential Fin Inc Prudential Plz 751 Broad St Newark NJ 07102-3714

LIGHT, ALFRED ROBERT, lawyer, political scientist, educator; b. Dec. 14, 1949; s. Alfred M. Jr. and Margaret Francis (Asbury) L.; m. Mollie Sue Hall, May 28, 1977; children: Joseph Robert, Gregory Andrew. Student, Ga. Inst. Tech., 1967-69; BA with highest honors, Johns Hopkins U., 1971; PhD, U. N.C., 1976; JD cum laude, Harvard U., 1981. Bar: D.C. 1981, Va. 1982. Tax clk. IRS, 1967; lab technician Custom Farm Svcs. Soils Testing Lab, 1968; warehouse asst. State of Ga. Mines, Mining and Geology, 1970; clk.-typist systems mgmt. divsn., def. contract adminstrv. Def. Supply Agy., Atlanta, 1971; rsch. and teaching asst. dept. polit. sci. U. N.C., Chapel Hill, 1971-74; rsch. asst. Inst. Rsch. in Social Sci., 1975-77; program analyst Office of Sec. Def., 1974; asst. prf. polit. sci., rsch. scientist Ctr. Energy Rsch. Tex. Tech. U., Lubbock, 1977-78; rsch. asst. grad. sch. edn. Harvard U., 1978-79; assoc. Butler, Binion, Rice, Cook & Knapp, Houston, 1980, Bracewell & Patterson, Washington, 1980; Hunton & Williams, Richmond, Va., 1981-89; of counsel, 1989-93, 95-96; assoc. prof. St. Thomas U. Sch. Law, Miami, Fla., 1989-93, prof., 1993—. Interim dean, 1993-94; bd. advisors Toxics Law reporter, Bur. Nat. Affairs, Washington, 1987—. Contbr. articles to profl. jours. Charter mem. West Broward Cmty. Ch. Capt. USAR, 1971-85. Grantee NSF, Inst. Evaluation Rsch., U. Mass., Ctr. Energy Rsch., Tex. Tech. U., 1977-78; recipient Julius Turner award Am. Polit. Sci. Assn., 1977. Mem. ABA (vice-chmn.) tort and ins. practice sect. 1988-97, nat. res. and environ. sect. 1993-95, chmn. 1995-2000), Fed. Bar. Assn., Va. Bar Assn., Richmond Bar Assn., Phi Beta Kappa, Phi Eta Sigma. Democrat. Home: 1042 Woodfall Ct Fort Lauderdale FL 33326-2832 Office: St Thomas U Sch Law 16400 NW 32nd Ave Opa Locka FL 33054-6459 E-mail: alight@stu.edu.

LIGHTER, LAWRENCE, lawyer; b. Bklyn., Sept. 13, 1935; s. Abe and Frances (Laufer) L.; m. Gloria Rita Stiefel, June 28, 1959; children: Adam, Todd, Eric. BS in Acctg., Bklyn. Coll., 1956; JD, NYU, 1960. Bar: N.Y. 1962. Staff atty. S.E.S.A.C., N.Y.C., 1961-65; house counsel Mills Music Inc., N.Y.C., 1965-68; N.Y. counsel Capitol Records, N.Y.C., 1969-70; pvt. practice N.Y.C., 1970—. Guest lectr. St. John's U., Queens, N.Y., Five Towns Coll., Huntington, N.Y., NYU, N.Y.C., and others. Gen. legal editor: Encyclopedia of The Music Business, 1984. Commercial, contracts (including sales of goods; commercial financing), Entertainment, Intellectual property. Office: 488 Madison Ave Fl 8 New York NY 10022-5702 Fax: 212 753 3630. E-mail: musicilawA1@aol.com.

LIGHTSTONE, RONALD, lawyer; b. N.Y.C., Oct. 4, 1938; s. Charles and Pearl (Weisberg) L.; m. Nancy Lehrer, May 17, 1973; 1 child, Dana. AB, Columbia U., 1959; JD, NYU, 1962. Atty. CBS, N.Y.C., 1967-69; assoc. dir. bus. affairs CBS News, N.Y.C., 1969-70; atty. NBC, N.Y.C., 1970; assoc. gen. counsel Viacom Internat. Inc., N.Y.C., 1970-75, v.p., gen. counsel, sec., 1976-80; v.p. bus. affairs Viacom Entertainment Group, Viacom Internat., Inc., 1980-82, v.p. corp. affairs, 1982-84, sr. v.p., 1984-87; exec. v.p. Spelling Entertainment Inc., L.A., 1988-91, CEO, 1991-93; chmn. Multimedia Labs. Inc., 1994-97; CEO, pres. New Star Media Inc., 1997-99, vice chmn., 1999-2000. Lt. USN, 1962-66. Mem. ABA (chmn. TV, cable and radio com.), Assn. of Bar of City of N.Y., Fed. Comm. Bar Assn. Corporate, general, Entertainment.

LIGHTY, FREDRICK W. lawyer; b. Danville, Pa., Mar. 18, 1967; s. Raymond G. and Geraldine A. (Brill) L. BA, Lycoming Coll., 1989; JD, Widener U., 1992. Bar: Pa. 1992, U.S. Dist. Ct. (mid. dist.) Pa. 1993, U.S. Ct. Appeals (3d cir.) 1993, U.S. Ct. Internat. Trade 1995. Private practice, Harrisburg, Pa., 1995—. Dir. Enviroquest, Inc., Harrisburg, 1995—. Commercial, consumer (including collections, credit), Private international, Personal injury (including property damage). Office: PO Box 60312 Harrisburg PA 17106-0312 E-mail: Fredrick@lighty.net.

LIGON, STARK, lawyer; b. Greenville, N.C., June 19, 1945; s. Robert S. and Betty (Tyson) L.; m. Marianne Wynne, Apr. 9, 1977; children: Sarah, Stark III. BA in History, U. Ark., 1968, JD, 1975. Bar: Ark. 1975, U.S. Dist. Ct. (ea. dist.) Ark. 1975, U.S. Supreme Ct. 1978. Assoc. Smith & Peters, Little Rock, 1975-77; election law study dir. State of Ark., Little Rock, 1977-78; ptnr. Haley, Claycomb, Ligon & Roper, P.A., Warren, Ark., 1978-85; chancery judge 10th Dist./State of Ark., Warren, 1985-86, cir. judge, 1987-94; chief legal counsel Gov. of Ark., Little Rock, 1995-96; gen. counsel Ark. Workers Compensation, Little Rock, 1996-2000; pvt. mediation and arbitration svcs. Little Rock, 1997-2000; chief bar counsel Ark Office Profl. Conduct Ark. Supreme Ct., 2001—. Dep. pros. atty. Bradley County, Warren, 1979-85; asst. city atty, Warren, 1978-85; mem. jud. discipline com. State of Ark., Little Rock, 1989-94. Col. JAG, Army N.G., 1968—. Methodist. Avocations: reading military history, home repair. Home: PO Box 165226 Little Rock AR 72216-5226 Office: Justice Bldg Rm 110 625 Marshall St Little Rock AR 72201 E-mail: stark.ligon@mail.state.ar.us.

LIGORANO, MICHAEL KENNETH, lawyer; b. Morristown, N.J., July 24, 1954; s. Michael Thomas and Virginia J. Ligorano; m. Debra Ann Baumann, Aug. 12, 1978. BA cum laude, Rutgers U., Newark, 1975; JD, Western New Eng. Law Sch., Springfield, Mass., 1978. Bar: N.J. 1978, U.S. Dist. Ct. N.J. 1978, Fla. 1980, U.S. Ct. Appeals (3d cir.) 1980, U.S. Tax Ct. 1980, U.S. Supreme Ct. 1985, N.Y. 1990; lic. real estate sales N.J. Assoc. Charles M. Lee, Washington, N.J., 1978-79, Hogan Folk Mahon & Simms, Flemington, Somerville, N.J., 1979-82, ptnr., 1982-83, Mahon Moeller & Ligorano, Flemington, 1983-84, Schaff Motiuk et al, Flemington, Trenton, 1984-87, Ligorano & Sozansky P.C., Flemington, 1987-98, Archer & Greiner, P.C., Flemington, Princeton, 1998—2001, Norris, McLaughlin & Marcus, Flemington, Princeton, 2001—. Atty. Mine Hill Twp. Bd. Adjustment, 1978-88; asst. Hunterdon County counsel, 1979-82; legal counsel Hunterdon County Bd. Recreation Commrs., 1980-2000; atty. Alexandria Twp. Bd. Adjustment, 1983-84; spl. counsel Solid Waste, Hunterdon County, 1984; atty. Readington Twp. Planning Bd., 1985-91, Readington Twp., 1991-96, Clinton Twp., 1996, Clinton Twp. Planning Bd., 1997-99, Glen Gardner Bd. Edn., 1996-98; spl. title counsel High Bridge Bd. Edn., 1996; mem. Dist. XIII Ethics Com., 1987-91, chair, 1990-91; mem. Dist. XIII Fee Arbitration Com., 1991-2000; mem. N.J. Supreme Ct. Complementary Disput Resolution Project, 1995-98; instr. N.J. Inst. Continuing Legal Edn., 1995-97; adv. bd. Summit Bank, 1990-92, First Cmty. Bank, 1992-94; gen. counsel The Blue Army, U.S.A., World Apostolate of Fatima, 1999—. Environ. commr. Denville Twp., 1973-75; legis. aide N.J. Assembly, 1974-75; mem. N.J. Natural Areas Coun., 1983-84; mem. Glen Gardner Bd. Health, 1993-95; bd. dirs. HHunterdon chpt. ARC, 1982-84, Glen Gardner Youth Ctr., 1988-90; mem. Hunterdon County Rep. Com., 1983-97; mem. Leukemia Soc. of Am. Team in Tng. Alaska Marathon, 1997, San Diego Marathon, 1999; adv. bd. ARC, 1994—. Mem. N.J. State Bar Assn. (gen. coun. 1993-94, sects. on land use, real property, probate and trust, dispute resolution), N.Y. State Bar Assn. (sect. on real property, probate and trust), The Fla. Bar (sect. on land use, real property, probate and trust), Am. Immigration Lawyers Assn., Hunterdon County Bar Assn. (sec. 1991-92, v.p. 1992-93, pres. 1993-94, trustee 1994-97, equity settlement panel 1994—, chair com. on professionalism 1996—), Hunterdon C. of C. (bd. dirs. 1981-86), Hunterdon/Somerset Realtors Assn., Nat. Geneology Soc., Knights of Columbus. Avocations: genealogy, long distance running. Immigration, naturalization, and customs, Municipal (including bonds), Property, real (including real estate development, water). Office: PO Box 1018 Somerville NJ 08876-1018 E-mail: mkligorano@nmmlaw.com.

LIJOI, PETER BRUNO, lawyer; b. Suffern, N.Y., Sept. 2, 1953; s. Salvatore and Josephine (Gentile) L.; m. Christine Louise Confroy, Aug. 19, 1978; children: Jonathan Peter, Christopher Andrew. BA in History and Econs., Montclair State Coll., 1975; postgrad. in urban planning, Rutgers U., 1975-76; JD, Pace U., 1979; postgrad., Harvard U., 1992. Bar: N.J. 1981, N.Y. 1988; cert. tax assessor, N.J., 2002—. Rsch. intern N.J. Dept. Edn., Trenton, 1976; intern Office U.S. Atty., N.Y.C., 1977-78; energy coord. Rockland County, 1979-80; dep. dir., of counsel Pvt. Industry Coun., Pearl River, N.Y., 1980-91; pvt. practice law Summit, N.J., 1981—; dir., counsel County of Rockland Indsl. Devel. Agy., 1981-95; v.p., gen. counsel Rockland Econ. Devel. Corp., Pearl River, 1990-91. Cons. U.S. Dept. Energy, Washington, 1980; mem. program of instrn. for lawyers Law Sch., Harvard U., 1992; legal counsel and land acquisition mgr. K. Hovnanian Cos. North Jersey, Inc., 1993-95, K. Hovnanian Cos. Northeast, Inc., 1995-2001; v.p. land acquisition and legal counsel D.R. Horton Inc., N.J.; legis. counsel to Assemblyman Eric Munoz, N.J. State Legislature. Guest writer The Bond Buyer. Bd. dirs. Rockland County coun. Girl Scouts U.S., 1982-92; pres. Washington Elem. Sch. PTA, Summit, 1986-88; mem. Summit Planning Bd., desegregation grant adv. and facilities coms. Summit Bd. Edn., 1992—; commr. tax bd. Union County, 1999—. Mem. ABA, N.J. Bar Assn., N.Y. Bar Assn., Union County Bar Assn., Assn. Trial Lawyers Am., Nat. Assn. Bond Lawyers, Summit Soccer Club (pres. 2002—). Roman Catholic. Avocations: running, coaching youth soccer. Environmental, Finance, Property, real (including real estate development, water). Home: 124 Canoe Brook Pkwy Summit NJ 07901-1436 Office: 20 Gibson Place Freehold NJ 07728 Home Fax: 908-273-6926; Office Fax: 732-577-1885.

LILES, RUTLEDGE RICHARDSON, lawyer; b. Miami, Fla., Jan. 30, 1942; s. Rutledge Person and Kathryn (Richardson) L.; m. Noel Doepke, Dec. 28, 1963; children: Ashley Faye, Hillary Lynn, Stacey Noel. BA, Fla. State U., 1964; JD, U. Fla., 1966. Bar: Fla. 1966, U.S. Dist. Ct. (mid. dist.) Fla. 1967, U.S. Supreme Ct. 1972, U.S. Dist. Ct. (no. and so. dists.) Fla. 1978; bd. cert. civil trial lawyer. Pres. Liles, Gavin & Costantino, Jacksonville, Fla., 1991—. Bd. of govs. Fla. Bar, 1981-87, pres.-elect 1987-88, pres. 1988-89. Mem. Jacksonville U. Council, 1966-88; trustee Episcopal High Sch. of Jacksonville, 1986-89, U. Fla. Coll. Law Ctr. Assn., 1981-89. Recipient Pres.'s award Fla. Bar, 1986. Fellow ABA (house dels. 1988-91, 93-94), Am. Coll. Trial Lawyers, Internat. Soc. Barristers; mem. ATLA, Acad. Fla. Trial Lawyers, Jacksonville Bar Assn. (pres. 1976-77), Fla. Blue Key, Am. Bd. Trial Advocates, Fla. Jud. Qualifications Commn., Fed. Jud. Nomination Commn. Democrat. General civil litigation, Personal injury (including property damage), Securities. Home: 1013 Maple Ln Jacksonville FL 32207-4010 Office: Liles Gavin & Costantino One Enterprise Ctr 225 Water St Ste 1500 Jacksonville FL 32202-5148

LILLEHAUG, DAVID LEE, lawyer; b. Waverly, Iowa, May 22, 1954; s. Leland Arthur and Ardis Elsie (Scheel) L.; m. Winifred Sarah (Smith), May 29, 1982; one child, Kara Marie. BA, Augustana Coll., Sioux Falls, S.D., 1976; JD, Harvard U., 1979. Bar: Minn., 1979, U.S. Dist. Ct. Minn., 1979, D.C., 1981, U.S. Ct. Appeals (8th cir.), 1981, U.S. Dist. Ct. D.C., 1982. Law clk. to presiding judge U.S. Dist. Ct., Mpls., 1979-81; assoc. Hogan and Hartson, Washington, 1981-83, 84-85; issues aide, exec. asst. to Walter Mondale, Washington, 1983-84; assoc. Leonard, Street, and Deinard, Mpls., 1985-87, ptnr., 1988-93, 98-99; U.S. atty. Dist. of Minn., 1994-98; atty. Fredrikson and Byron, P.A., Mpls., 2002—. Candidate, U.S. Senate, 1999-2000. Mondale Policy Forum Fellow, U. Minn., 1990-91. Mem. ABA, Minn. Bar Assn. (past chair constrn. law sect., Author's Award 1990). Lutheran. Avocations: fishing, golf. Home: 6701 Parkwood Ln Edina MN 55436-1735 Office: Fredrikson & Byron PA 4000 Pillsbury Ctr Minneapolis MN 55402 E-mail: dlillehaug@fredlaw.com.

LILLEY, ALBERT FREDERICK, retired lawyer; b. Harrisburg, Pa., Dec. 21, 1932; s. Frederick Anthony and Jane Sander (Ingham) L.; m. Judith Carter Pennock, Sept. 1, 1956; children: Kirk Anthony, Kristin Sander, James Alexander. AB, Bowdoin Coll., 1954; LLB, U. Va., 1959. Assoc. Milbank, Tweed, Hadley & McCloy, N.Y.C., 1959-67, ptnr., 1967-96; ret., 1997. Trustee No. Highlands Regional H.S., Allendale, N.J., 1964-65; mem. Allendale Bd. Zoning Adjustment, 1965-66; bd. overseers Bowdoin Coll., 1976-88, overseer emeritus, 1988—; trustee Valley Hosp., Ridgewood, N.J., 1978-92, vice chmn. bd., 1985-89, chmn. bd., 1989-92; bd. dirs. Valley Care Corp., 1992-97, Valley Home and Cmty. Health Care, Inc., 1992-97, Chapel Hill-Carrboro Arts Ctr., 2001—; mem. alumni coun. U. Va. Law Sch., 1991-94, U.S. Can. Law Project Adv. Bd., 1990-95. 1st lt. U.S. Army, 1954-56. Mem. ABA, Am. Law Inst., U. Va. Law Sch. Alumni Assn. (class mgr. annual giving campaign), Chapel Hill Rotary Club (vocat. svc. dir. 1998-99, treas. 1999-2000, sec. 2000-01, v.p. 2001-02, pres. 2002-03),. Corporate, general, Mergers and acquisitions, Securities. Home: 204 Laurel Hill Rd Chapel Hill NC 27514-4325 E-mail: afl@nc.rr.com.

LILLIE, CHARISSE RANIELLE, lawyer, educator; b. Houston, Apr. 7, 1952; d. Richard Lysander and Vernell Audrey (Watson) Lillie; m. Thomas L. McGill Jr., Dec. 4, 1982. BA cum laude, Conn. Wesleyan U., 1973; JD, Temple U., 1976; LLM, Yale U., 1982. Bar: Pa. 1976, U.S. Dt. Ct. (ea. dist.) Pa. 1977, U.S. Ct. Appeals (3d cir.) 1980. Law clk. U.S. Dist. Ct. (ea. dist.) Pa., Phila., 1976-78; trial atty., honors program, civil rights divsn. Dept. Justice, Washington, 1978-80; dep. dir. Cmty. Legal Svcs., Phila., 1980-81; asst. prof. law Villanova U. Law Sch., Pa., 1982-83, assoc. prof., 1983-84, prof., 1984-85; asst. U.S. atty. U.S. Dist. Ct. (ea. dist.) Pa., Phila., 1985-88; with Redevel. Authority of Phila., 1988-90; city solicitor law dept. City of Phila., 1990-92; chair litigation dept. Ballard, Spahr, Andrew & Ingersoll, 2002—, exec. com. bd. dirs., 1994—. Mem. 3d Cir. Lawyers Adv. Com., 1982—85; legal counsel Pa. Coalition of 100 Black Women, Phila., 1983—88; bd. dirs. Juvenile Law Ctr., Phila., Pa. Intergovtl. Coop. Authority, Fed. Res. Bank Phila., dep. chmn. bd. dirs., 1998—2000, chmn. bd. dirs., 2001—02; commr. Phila. Ind. City Charter Commn., 1991—94; trustee Women's Law Project, Phila., 1984—90; mem. Mayor's Commn. on May 13 MOVE Incident, 1985—86; mem. com. on racial and gender bias in the justice sys. Supreme Ct. Pa., 1999—. Bd. dirs. Leadership Inc.; mem. adv. com. Women's Way, Phila., 1986—. Named One of Phila.'s Most Influential African Americans, Phila. Tribune, 2002, 2003, One of Top Three Phila. Labor Mgmt. Attys., Phila. Mag., 1994, 1999; named to the Women's Hall of Fame, Southwest Belmont Cmty. Assn., 2002; recipient Equal Justice award, Cmty. Legal Svcs., Inc., 1991, Outstanding Alumna award, Wesleyan U., 1993, Elizabeth Dole Glass Ceiling award, ARC, Phila. chpt., 1994, Whitney Young Leadership award, Phila. Urban League, 1996, Take the Lead award, U.S. Girl Scouts, 2002, Women of Distinction award, Phila. Bus. Jour., 2002, Penn Towne Links Svc. award, 2002, Image award, Black Women in Sport Found., 2002, J. Michael Brown award, DuPont Minority Counsel Conf., 2002, Bd. Dirs. Hall of Fame award, Teenshop, 2002, Mother of Yr., Mary Mason Cmty. Found., 2002, Women of Achievement award, The Barristers' Assn., 2002, Awards of Excellence, The Thurgood Marshall Scholarship Fund, Inc., 2003; fellow Davenport fellow, 1973, Yale Sch. fellow, 1981. Mem.: ABA (vice chmn. commn. on ethnic diversity in the professio 1997—99, chmn. commn. on ethnic diversity in the professio 1999—2002, mem. standing com. on fed. jud. 2002—), Hist. Soc. U.S. Dist. Ct. (ea. dist.) Pa. (dir. 1983—87), Phila. Bar Assn. (vice chair bd. govs. 1994, chair bd. govs. 1995—96), Barristers Assn. (J. Austin Norris award 1983—87), Am. Law Inst., Nat. Conf. Black Lawyers (pres. 1970), Fed. Bar Assn. (1st v.p. Phila. chpt. 1982—84, pres. Phila. chpt. 1984—86, 3d cir. rep. 1991—), Nat. Bar Assn. Federal civil litigation, State civil litigation, Labor (including EEOC, Fair Labor Standards Act, labor-management relations, NLRB, OSHA). Home: 7000 Emlen St Philadelphia PA 19119-2556 Office: Ballard Spahr Andrews Ingersoll 1735 Market St Fl 51 Philadelphia PA 19103-7599

LILLY, JOHN RICHARD, II, lawyer; b. Phila., July 20, 1962; s. John Richard Sr. and Elizabeth Anne (Brown) L.; m. Anne Katherine Crawford; children: John Richard III, Cameron Lewis. BA, Geoge Washington U., 1987; JD, U. Balt., 1991. Bar: Md. 1992, U.S. Dist. Ct. Md. 1995. Law clk. 7th Jud. Cir. Md., Upper Marlboro, 1991-92; asst. state's atty. State's Atty.'s Office Prince George's County Md., Upper Marlboro, 1992-98; asst. atty. gen. Md. Atty. Gen.'s Office, Balt., 1998-2001; pvt. practice Glen Burnie, Md., 2001—. Adj. prof. U. Balt. Sch. Law, 1999-2000. Comments editor U. Balt. Jour. Environ. Law. Chmn. Oakland Mills Village Bd., Columbia, Md., 1990-92; pres. St. Stephen's Area Civic Assn., Crownsville, Md., 1994-95; soccer coach Green Hornets Athletic Assn., 2000—. Lt. USNR, 1988—. Mem. Anne Arundel Bar Assn. Avocations: tennis, sailing, reading, photography. Criminal, Environmental, Military. Home: 133 Idlewild Rd Severna Park MD 21146 Office: 7439 Baltimore-Annapolis Blvd Glen Burnie MD 21061 E-mail: jrlillyesq@aol.com.

LILLY, JOYCE STAMP, lawyer; b. Providence, Apr. 22, 1952; d. Albert Conrad and Bernice Pearson Stamp; m. Ralph B. Lilly, Nov. 27, 1987. BSN, U. R.I., 1975; JD, Boston U., 1989. Bar: Mass. 1989, R.I. 1990, N.Mex. 1990, Tex. 1992. Nurse Miriam Hosp., Providence, 1975—76; nurse, nurse coord. Butler Hosp., 1981—83; clin. nurse coord. elderly svcs. The Providence Ctr. COunseling and Psychiatric Svcs., 1983—85; student legal cons. The Eunice Kennedy Shriver Ctr., Waltham, Mass., 1987; summer assoc. Edwards & Angell, Providence, 1988; assoc. Atwood & Cherny, Boston, 1989—90; atty. pvt. practice, Providence, 1990—91, Piro*Nichols*Lilly, Houston, 1992—93, pvt. practice, 1992—. Bd. dirs. Epilepsy Found. Southeast Tex., mem. exec. bd. Mem.: ANA, Houston Trial Lawyers Found., Am. Assn. Geriatric Nurses, Am. Assn. Neurosci. Nurses, Am. Assn. Managed Care Nurses, Am. Assn. Critical Care Nurses, Wound Ostomy and Continence Nurses Soc., Tex. Med. Dirs. Assn., Am. Med. Dirs. Assn., Tex. Nurses Assn., Nat. Coalition Nursing Home Reform, Case Mgmt. Soc. Am., Tex. Geriatric Soc., Mass. State Bar Assn., State Bar N.Mex., R.I. Bar Assn., Houston Bar Assn., Assn. Trial Lawyers Am. (profl. negligence and nursing home litigation sects.), Tex. Trial Lawyers Assn., Houston Trial Lawyers Assn., State Bar of Tex. (litigation and health law sects.). Avocations: cooking, outdoor activities, Western history. Personal injury (including property damage). Office: 1177 West Loop S Ste 720 Houston TX 77027

LILLY, NOLTE SCOTT AMENT, lawyer; b. Louisville, Aug. 10, 1951; s. Foster Dillard and Amber Helene (Ament) L.; children: Andrea Nicole, Carson Clinard. BA in Telecommunications, U. Ky., 1973; JD, U. Louisville, 1977. Bar: Ky. 1977, U.S. Dist. Ct. (we. dist.) Ky. 1978, U.S. Ct. Appeals (6th cir.) 1979, U.S. Supreme Ct. 1984. Assoc. Carroll, Chauvin, Miller & Conliffe and predecessor firm, Louisville, 1977-82; asst. county atty. Jefferson County, Louisville, 1977-85; ptnr. Conliffe, Sandmann, Gorman & Sullivan and predessor firm, Louisville, 1982-86; first asst. county atty. Jefferson County, Louisville, 1986—99. Lectr. ABA. Chgo.-Kent Coll. Law, 1993-94, other lectures. Bd. dirs. Louisville Sch. Autistic Children, 1985-86, Ky. Ctr. for Spl. Children, Louisville, 1986. Claude Sullivan scholarship U. Ky. Com. of 101, 1969-73. Mem. ABA, Ky. Bar Assn. Democrat. Methodist. Avocations: golf, travel, hunting. Civil rights, Constitutional, Municipal (including bonds). Office: Jefferson County Attys Office 531 Court Pl Ste 1001 Louisville KY 40202-3316

LILLY, THOMAS GERALD, retired lawyer; b. Belzoni, Miss., Sept. 17, 1933; s. Sale Trice and Margaret Evelyn (Butt) L.; m. Constance Ray Holland, Dec. 29, 1962; children: Thomas Gerald Jr., William Holland, Carolyn Ray. BBA, Tulane U., 1955; LLB, U. Miss., 1960, JD, 1968. Bar: Miss. 1960. Assoc. firm Stovall & Price, Corinth, Miss., 1960—62; asst. U.S. atty. No. Dist. Miss., Oxford, 1962—66; assoc. firm Wise Carter Child & Caraway (and predecessor), Jackson, Miss., 1966—67, ptnr., 1967—94, Lilly & Wise, Jackson, 1994—2000, of counsel, 2001—03. Served with USNR, 1955-88; rear adm. Res. ret. Decorated Legion of Merit, Navy Commendation medal. Fellow The Found. of Fed. Bar Assn. (life); mem. FBA (nat. coun. 1972—, rec. sec. 1975-76, gen. sec. 1976-77, 2d v.p. 1977-78, pres.-elect 1978-79, pres. 1979-80), Hinds County Bar Assn., Miss. State Bar, Miss. Bar Found., Democracy Devel. Inst. (bd. dirs. 1995—), Res. Officers Assn. (pres. Miss. dept. 1982-83), Naval Res. Assn., Mil. Officers Assn. Am., Naval Order of U.S., Navy Supply Corps Assn., Navy League (pres. Ctrl. Miss. Coun. 1993), Mil. Order World Wars, Jackson Civil War Roundtable, Miss. Com. Employer Support Guard and Res., Miss. Geneal. Soc., Chester Dist. Geneal. Soc., Lamar Order, Scabbard and Blade, Omicron Delta Kappa, Phi Delta Phi, Sigma Nu. Methodist. General civil litigation, Commercial, contracts (including sales of goods; commercial financing), Private international.

LILLY, THOMAS JOSEPH, lawyer; b. Bklyn., Feb. 17, 1931; s. Frank A. and Mary Ellen (Kelly) L.; m. Margaret Mary Doherty, June 28, 1959; children: Thomas J., Mary Jo, Joseph, Sean. BA, St. John's Coll., 1953; JD, Fordham U., 1961; LLM, NYU, 1967. Bar: N.Y. 1962, U.S. Dist. Ct. (ea. and so. dists.) N.Y. 1963, U.S. Ct. Appeals (2d cir.) 1965. Dir. rsch. Office and Profl. Employees Internat. Union AFL-CIO, N.Y.C., 1960-62; asst. U.S. atty. U.S. Dist. Ct. (ea. dist.) N.Y., Bklyn., 1962-66; ptnr. Doran, Colleran, O'Hara, Pollio & Dunne, N.Y.C., 1966-79, Quinn & Lilly, P.C., N.Y.C. and Garden City, N.Y., 1979-89; pvt. practice Garden City, 1989—. Adj. prof. N.Y. State Indsl. and Labor Rels. Sch., Cornell U., 1980-81; arbitrator U.S. Dist. Ct. (ea. dist.) N.Y.; mem. Nassau County Pub. Employment Rels. Bd., 1994-2002. With USN, 1953-57. Mem. ABA, N.Y. Bar Assn., Nassau County Bar Assn., Sea Cliff Yacht Club, Prestwick Golf Club. Civil rights, Labor (including EEOC, Fair Labor Standards Act, labor-management relations, NLRB, OSHA), Pension, profit-sharing, and employee benefits. Home: 136 8th Ave Sea Cliff NY 11579-1308 Office: 585 Stewart Ave Garden City NY 11530-3302 E-mail: ThomasJLillySr@LillyandAssociates.net.

LIM, MICHAEL HEE KIANG, lawyer; b. Singapore, May 10, 1948; s. Joseph Teck Chong and Elizabeth Sai Choo (Chua) Lim; m. Mei Pieng Gan, 1976; children: Joseph Hock, Jonathan Soon. LLB with honors, LLM with distinction, Victoria U., Wellington, New Zealand, 1973. Bar: New Zealand Supreme Ct. 1973, Sarawak & Brunei 1974, Malaya 1978. Legal asst. EE & Lim, Kuching, 1974; lectr. Faculty of Law, U. of Malaya, Kuala Lumpur, Malaysia, 1975—78; ptnr. Shearn, Delamore & Co., Kuala Lumpur, 1979—. Bd. dirs. Selanger Properties, Diethlem Holdings, Dijaya Corp., Paragon Union, Insas. Avocations: golf, tennis, swimming. Corporate, general, Mergers and acquisitions, Securities. Home: 131 Jalan Ara Bangsar Baru Kuala Lumpur 59100 Malaysia Office Fax: 603 20726503. Business E-Mail: michaellim@shearndelamore.com.

LIMBAUGH, STEPHEN NATHANIEL, JR., state supreme court chief justice; b. Cape Girardeau, Mo., Jan. 25, 1952; s. Stephen N. and Anne (Mesplay) L.; m. Marsha Dee Moore, July 21, 1973; children: Stephen III, Christopher K. BA, So. Meth. U., 1973, JD, 1976; LLM, U. Va., 1998. Bar: Tex. 1977, Mo. 1977. Assoc. Limbaugh, Limbaugh & Russell, Cape Girardeau, 1977-78; pros. atty. Cape Girardeau County, Cape Girardeau, 1979-82; shareholder, ptnr. Limbaugh, Limbaugh, Russell & Syler, Cape Girardeau, 1983-87; cir. judge 32d Jud. Cir., Cape Girardeau, 1987-92; judge Supreme Ct. Mo., Jefferson City, 1992—. Mem. ABA, State Bar Tex., Mo. Bar. Office: Supreme Ct Mo 207 W High St Jefferson City MO 65101-1516

LIMBAUGH, STEPHEN NATHANIEL, federal judge; b. Cape Girardeau, Mo., Nov. 17, 1927; s. Rush Hudson and Bea (Seabaugh) L.; m. DeVaughn Anne Mesplay, Dec. 27, 1950; children— Stephen Nathaniel Jr., James Pennington, Andrew Thomas. BA, S.E. Mo. State U., Cape Girardeau, 1950; JD, U. Mo., Columbia, 1951. Bar: Mo. 1951. Prosecuting atty. Cape Girardeau County, Mo., 1954-58; judge U.S. Dist. Ct. (ea. and we. dists.) Mo., St. Louis, 1983—. With USN, 1945-46. Recipient Citation of Merit for Outstanding Achievement and Meritorious Service in Law, U. Mo., 1982 Fellow Am. Coll. Probate Counsel, Am. Bar Found.; mem. ABA (ho. of dels. 1987-90), Mo. Bar Assn. (pres. 1982-83). Republican. Methodist. Office: US Dist Ct Thomas F Eagleton Cthse 111 S Tenth St Ste 3 125 Saint Louis MO 63102 E-mail: limbaugh@moed.uscourts.gov.

LIMNILI, DUYGU, lawyer; b. Izmir, Turkey, May 13, 1972; LLB, Dokuz Eylul U., Izmir, Turkey, 1996. Bar: Izmir Bar Assn. 1997. Assoc. Kologlu Law Offices, Izmir, Turkey, 1995—98; legal counsel Sabanci Holding AS, Istanbul, Turkey, 1999—2002; assoc. Paksoy & Co, Istanbul, Turkey, 2002—. Scholar, Turkish Culture Assn. / AFS, 1990. Mem.: Istanbul Bar Assn. Mergers and acquisitions, Intellectual property, Corporate, general. Office: Paksoy & Co Beybi Giz Plz Meydan Sk No28 Kat10 Istanbul 34398 Turkey Office Fax: 90 212 290 2355. E-mail: dlimnili@paksoy-law.com.

LINCKE, KARL HEINRICH, lawyer; b. Bonn, Germany, Mar. 21, 1971; arrived in Spain, 1999; s. Dietrich and Annemarie L.; m. Andrea Henning, Aug. 27, 1999. Abitur, Albert-Einstein-Gymnasium, Bonn, 1991. With AA (Fgn. Affairs), Bonn, 1993, 94, 95, T-Mobil, Bonn, 1996, Deutscher Bundestag, Bonn, 1996-97; atty. Mariscal Abogados, Madrid, 1999—. Co-author: Kurswechsel, 1998, Europäische Fallstricke, 2000. Mem. Rechtsanwaltkammer Cologne, Bund der Selbstandigen. Civil rights, Commercial, consumer (including collections, credit), Mergers and acquisitions. Office: Mariscal & Asociados Paseo De La Habana 54, 2 I E-28036 Madrid Spain Fax: (0034) 31564644617. E-mail: klincke@mariscal.abogados.com.

LINCOLN, ALEXANDER, III, financier, lawyer, private investor; b. Boston, Dec. 1, 1943; s. Alexander Jr. and Elizabeth (Kitchel) L.; m. Isabel Fawcett Ross, Dec. 27, 1969. BA, Denver U., 1967; JD, Boston U., 1971. Bar: Colo. 1972, U.S. Ct. Appeals (10th cir.) 1972, U.S. Supreme Ct. 1979. Atty. Dist. Ct. Denver, 1973-78, Colo. Ct. Appeals, Denver, 1978-80; mng. ptnr. Alexander Lincoln & Co., Denver, 1980—. Mem. Colo. Bar Assn. (fin. com. 1975-76), Colo. Soc. Mayflower Descendants (life, bd. dirs. 1975—), Order of Founders and Patriots (life). Republican. Avocations: skiing, mountain climbing, horticulture. Home and Office: 121 S Dexter St Denver CO 80246-1052

LINDBERG, CHARLES DAVID, lawyer; b. Moline, Ill., Sept. 11, 1928; s. Victor Samuel and Alice Christine (Johnson) L.; m. Marian J. Wagner, June 14, 1953; children: Christine, Breta, John, Eric. AB, Augustana Coll., Rock Island, Ill., 1950; JD, Yale U., 1953; DHL, Augustana Coll., 2000. Bar: Ohio 1954. Assoc. Taft, Stettinius & Hollister, Cin., 1953-61, ptnr., 1961-85, mng. ptnr., 1985-98, of counsel, 1999—. Bd. dirs. Cin. Bengals Profl. Football Team, 1982—2003; chmn. bd. dirs. Schonstedt Instrument Co., 1994—97. Editor Nat. Law Jour., 1979-90. Bd. dirs. Taft Broadcasting Co., Cin., 1973-87, Dayton Walther Corp., 1986-87, Gibson Greeting, Inc., 1991-2000; bd. dirs. Augustana Coll., 1978-87, 91-99, 2000—, sec., 1981-82, vice-chmn., 1982-83, chmn., 1983-86; pres. Cin. Bd. Edn., 1971, 74, Zion Luth. Ch., Cin., 1966-69; chmn. policy com. Hamilton County Rep. Com., 1981-90; mem. exec. com. Ohio Rep. Fin. Com., 1989-90; chmn. Tyler Davidson Com., 1999-2000; trustee Greater Cin. Ctr. Econ. Edn., 1976-91, pres., 1987-89, chmn., 1989-91; chmn. law firm divsn. Fine Arts Fund, 1985; trustee Pub. Libr. Cin. and Hamilton County, 1982—, pres., 1989, 96, 01. Mem. Cin. Bar Assn., Greater Cin. C. of C. (trustee 1985, exec. com., vice chmn. govt. and cmty. affairs com. 1989-91), Ohio Libr. Trustees Assn. (bd. dirs. 1986-87), Ohio C. of C. (bd. dirs. 1988-89), Queen City Club (sec. 1989-91), Commonwealth Club, Comml. Club (sec. 1994-96), Optimists. Corporate, general, Mergers and acquisitions. Office: 1800 US Bank Tower 425 Walnut St Cincinnati OH 45202-3923 E-mail: lindberg@taftlaw.com.

LINDE, MAXINE HELEN, lawyer, business executive, private investor; b. Chgo., Sept. 2, 1939; d. Jack and Lottie (Kroll) Stern; m. Ronald K. Linde, June 12, 1960. BA summa cum laude, UCLA, 1961; JD, Stanford U., 1967. Bar: Calif. 1968. Applied mathematician, rsch. engr Jet Propulsion Lab., Pasadena, Calif., 1961—64; law clk. U.S. Dist. Ct. No. Calif., 1967—68; mem. firm Long & Levit, San Francisco, 1968—69, Swerdlow, Glikbarg & Shimer, Beverly Hills, Calif., 1969—72; sec., gen. counsel Envirodyne Industries, Inc., Chgo., 1972—89; pres. The Ronald and Maxine Linde Found., 1989—; vice chmn. bd., gen. counsel Titan Fin. Group, LLC, Chgo., 1994—98. Mem. bd. visitors Stanford Law Sch., 1989—92, law and bus. adv. coun., 1991—94, dean's adv. coun., 1992—94. Mem.: Alpha Lambda Delta, Pi Mu Epsilon, Phi Beta Kappa, Order of Coif. Corporate, general.

LINDEN, TAYLIR K. lawyer; b. Painesville, Ohio; parents James and Sibylla L. BA, Bethany Coll., 1991; JD, Capital Law Sch., 1994. Bar: Ohio 1994. Ind. contractor Ohio Supreme Ct., Columbus, Ohio, 1993-95; adminstrv. asst. OCDRCM, Columbus, Ohio, 1994-95; asst. prosecutor Lake County, Painesville, 1995—. Mem. ABA, Ohio State Bar Assn., Ohio Women's Bar Assn., Lake County Bar Assn. Office: Lake County Prosecutor's Office PO Box 490 Painesville OH 44077-0490

LINDEN, WILLIAM M. lawyer; b. Denison, Tex., Apr. 4, 1932; BSChemE, U. Tex., 1954, JD, 1969; diploma in Theology, Oxford U., 2001. Bar: Tex. 1969. Mem. Vinson & Elkins, L.L.P., Houston. Mem. Order of Coif, Phi Delta Phi, Tau Beta Pi. Probate (including wills, trusts), Taxation, general, Personal income taxation. Office: Vinson & Elkins 2500 First City Tower 1001 Fannin St Ste 3300 Houston TX 77002-6706 Home: 826 Oak Valley Dr Houston TX 77024

LINDENAUER, SUSAN B(ADIAN), lawyer; b. N.Y.C., Mar. 1, 1941; d. Hyman and Rose (Tuchman) Badian; m. Arthur Lindenauer, July 30, 1961. A.B. magna cum laude, Smith Coll., 1961; LL.B. cum laude, Columbia, U., 1964. Bar: N.Y. 1965, U.S. Ct. Appeals (2d cir.) 1965, U.S. Dist. Ct. (ea. dist.) N.Y. 1972, U.S. Dist. Ct. (so. dist.) N.Y. 1972. Assoc. Cleary Gottlieb Steen & Hamilton, 1964-66; staff atty. Legal Aid Soc. N.Y.C., 1966-77, asst. for legal affairs to exec. dir. 1977-79, counsel to exec. dir. 1979—97; coun. to presidency and atty. in chief, 1998-. Bd. dirs. Project Greenhope, N.Y.C. Mem. Assn. Bar City N.Y., N.Y. County Lawyers' Assn., N.Y. State Bar Assn., ABA, Nat. Legal Aid and Defender Assn., Phi Beta Kappa. General civil litigation, Corporate, general, Criminal. Office: Legal Aid Soc One Battery Park Plz 28th Fl New York NY 10004

LINDENBAUM, SAMUEL HARVEY, lawyer; b. N.Y.C., Mar. 29, 1935; s. Abraham M. and Belle (Axelrad) L.; m. Linda Marion Lewis, June 16, 1957; children: Erica Dale Lindenbaum Tishman, Laurie Ellen. BA cum laude, Harvard U., 1956, JD cum laude, 1959; Fulbright fellow, Oslo U., Norway, 1959-60. Bar: N.Y. 1960. Assoc. Fried, Frank, Harris, Shriver & Jacobson, N.Y.C., 1960-62; mem. Lindenbaum & Young, Bklyn., 1962-74; sr. mem. Rosenman & Colin, N.Y.C., 1974-83, of counsel, 1983—2002; counsel Kramer Levin Naftalis & Frankel, N.Y.C., 2002—. Mem. bd. overseers Albert Einstein Coll. Medicine; chmn. exec. com. Jewish Assn. for Svcs. for the Aged; mem. Counsel Assn. for Better NY; bd. govs., mem. exec. com., v.p. Real Estate Bd. NY; bd. dirs., chmn. exec. com. Am. Friends Israel Mus. Mem. Bklyn. Bar Assn., Harmonie Club, Harvard Club, Friars Club. Home: 998 5th Ave New York NY 10028-0102 Office: Kramer Levin Naftalis & Frankel 919 Third Ave New York NY 10022-2511

LINDER, HARVEY RONALD, lawyer, arbitrator, mediator; b. Pitts., July 23, 1949; s. Charles Joseph and Rose (Ruben) Linder; m. Reva Rebecca Vertman, Aug. 14, 1971 (div.); children: Zalman F., Seth A.; m. Gail Lynne Silberman, May 26, 2002. BA, Duquesne U., 1971, JD, 1975. Bar: Pa. 1975, U.S. Dist. Ct. (we. dist.) Pa. 1975, U.S. Supreme Ct. 1979. Legal intern Dist. Atty.'s Office, Pitts., 1974-75; asst. mgr. arbitration U.S. Steel,

Pitts., 1975-80, mgr. labor rels., 1980-81, supt. employee rels. Clairton, Pa., 1981-83; corp. dir. employee rels. U.S. Steel Agri-Chemicals, Atlanta, 1984-86; corp. dir. law and human resources LaRoche Industries Inc., Atlanta, 1986-88, v.p., gen. counsel, 1988-96, Orion Mgmt. Svcs. Inc., 1996-97, SED Internat., Inc., 1997-99; interim rabbi, 2000—01. Arbitrator, mediator, 1996—; pres. A.C.I.R.A., 1987-90. Contbr. poetry and photography to Duquesne Literary Mag., 1968-74. Exec. cons. Jr. Achievement, Pitts., 1978—83; head coach Atlanta Jewish Cmty. Ctr., Dunwoody, Ga., 1984—, bd. dirs., 1991—, v.p., 2001—; pres. Hunter's Woods Homeowners' Assn., Dunwoody, 1986—87; commr. Baseball & Soccer Leagues; bd. dirs. Atlanta Jewish Fedn., 1995—96, Atlanta YAD, 2000—; pres. B'nai Torah Synagogue, 1995—97, interim rabbi, 2000—01. Steel fellow Am. Iron and Steel Inst., 1977-85. Mem. ABA, Allegheny County Bar Assn., Indsl. Rels. Rsch. Assn., Duquesne U. Law Sch. Alumni Assn. (bd. dirs. 1980-84), B'nai B'rith (local v.p. 1975-80), Amer-Israel C. of C. (bd. dirs. 1993-2001). Democrat. Avocations: coaching, collecting books and sports memorabilia. Alternative dispute resolution, Commercial, contracts (including sales of goods; commercial financing), Corporate, general. Home and Office: 7025 Northgreen Dr Atlanta GA 30328-1453

LINDGREN, D(ERBIN) KENNETH, JR., retired lawyer; b. Mpls., Aug. 25, 1932; s. Derbin Kenneth and Margaret (Anderson) L.; m. Patricia Ann Ransier, Dec. 17, 1955; children— Christian Kenneth, Carol Ann, Charles Derbin BS, U. Minn., 1954, JD, 1958. Bar: Minn. 1958, U.S. Supreme Ct. 1968, U.S. Tax Ct. 1959, U.S. Ct. Appeals (D.C. cir.) 1981. Gen. practice law, Mpls., 1958-99; mem. Larkin, Hoffman, Daly & Lindgren, Ltd., Mpls., 1960-95, of counsel, 1995; ret., 1995. Contbr. articles to profl. jours. Active Ind. Sch. Dist. 287 Bd. Edn. (Area Vocat. Tech. Coll.), 1979-83, Ind. Sch. Dist. 274 Bd. Edn., Hopkins, Minn., 1970-76, chmn., 1972-76; trustee Mpls. Soc. Fine Arts, 1982-88; trustee Minn. Landscape Arboretum Found., 1989-99, pres., 1992-95, hon trustee, 2000; bd. overseers Mpls. Inst. Art, 1986-88, Mpls. Coll. Art and Design, 1980-86, vice-chmn., 1982-83, chmn., 1983-86, trustee, 1988-96; active Govs. Commn. on Reform Govt., 1983. Lt. USAF, 1955-57. Fellow Am. Coll. Trust and Estate Counsel; mem. ABA, Minn. Bar Assn., Hennepin County Bar Assn., Interlachen Country Club (bd. dirs. 1981-89, pres. 1987), Troon Golf and Country Club (bd. dirs. 2000-03), Alpha Delta Phi, Phi Delta Phi. Presbyterian. Corporate, general, Estate planning, Corporate taxation. Home: 11003 E Desert Vista Dr Scottsdale AZ 85255-8061 also: 4804 France Ave S # 2 Edina MN 55410-1756 E-mail: dklindgren@earthlink.net.

LINDHOLM, DWIGHT HENRY, lawyer; b. Blackduck, Minn., May 27, 1930; s. Henry Nathanial and Viola Eudora (Gummert) L.; m. Loretta Catherine Brown, Aug. 29, 1958; children: Douglas Dwight, Dionne Louise, Jeanne Marie, Philip Clayton, Kathleen Anne. Student, Macalester Coll., 1948-49; BBA, U. Minn., 1951, LLB, 1954; postgrad., Mexico City Coll. (now U. of Ams.), 1956-57. Bar: Minn. 1954, Calif. 1958. Sole practice, Los Angeles, 1958-65, 72-81, 84—; ptnr. Lindholm & Johnson, Los Angeles, 1965-69, Cotter, Lindholm & Johnson, Los Angeles, 1969-72; sole practice Los Angeles, 1972-81; of counsel Bolton, Dunn & Moore, Los Angeles, 1981-84. Mem. Calif. Republican Central Com., 1962-63, L.A. Republican County Ctrl. Com., 1962-66; bd. dirs. Family Service L.A., 1964-70, v.p., 1968-70; bd. dirs. Wilshire YMCA, 1976-77; trustee Westlake Girls Sch., 1978-81; hon. presenter Nat. Charity League Coronet Debutante Ball, 1984; bd. dirs. Calif. State U.-Northridge Trust Fund, 1989-93; bd. dirs. Queen of Angeles/Hollywood Presbyn. Med. Ctr., 1990-98; chmn., CEO Queen of Angels, Hollywood Presbyn. Found., 1997-2000; bd. dirs., corp. sec. QueensCare, 1998-2001. Served as capt. JAG Corps USAF, 1954-56. Recipient Presdl. award Los Angeles Jr. C. of C., 1959 Mem. Calif. Bar Assn., L.A. County Bar Assn., Wilshire Bar Assn. (bd. govs. 1989-91), Internat. Genealogy Fellowship of Rotarians (founding pres. 1979-86), Calif. Club, Ocean Cruising Club Eng. (Newport Harbor port officer), Rotary (dir. 1975-78), Delta Sigma Pi, Delta Sigma Rho, Delta Theta Phi (state chancellor 1972-73). Presbyterian. Avocations: sailing, offshore cruising. Office: 3580 Wilshire Blvd Fl 17 Los Angeles CA 90010-2501

LINDLEY, F(RANCIS) HAYNES, JR., foundation executive, lawyer; b. L.A., Oct. 15, 1945; s. Francis Haynes and Grace Nelson (McCanne) L.; m. Hollinger McCloud Lindley, Apr. 1, 1977; 1 child, Anne Hollinger Lindley. BA, Claremont (Calif.) Men's Coll., 1967; MFA, Claremont (Calif.) Grad. Sch., 1972; JD, Southwestern U., L.A., 1976. Bar: Calif. 1976, U.S. Supreme Ct. 1980. Deputy pub. defender Office of Pub. Defender, L.A., 1977-79; staff atty., Dept. Trial Counsel The State Bar of Calif., L.A., 1979-81; pvt. practice, 1981-90; pres. John Randolph Haynes and Dora Haynes Found., L.A., 1987-97, pres. emeritus, 1997—. Trustee John Randolph Haynes and Dora Haynes Found., L.A., 1978—. Mem. bd. dirs. TreePeople, L.A., 1985-87, So. Calif. Assn. Philanthropy, L.A., 1985-89; mem. bd. fellows Claremont (Calif.) U. Ctr. and Grad. Sch., 1987—; mem. bd. dirs. Marin Agrl. Land Trust, 1995—. Recipient Disting. Svc. award The Claremont (Calif.) Grad. Sch., 1994. Avocations: sailing, art history, banjo. Home: PO Box 1404 Ross CA 94957-1404 Office: John Randolph Haynes & Dora Haynes Found 888 W 6th St Ste 1150 Los Angeles CA 90017-2737

LINDSAY, GEORGE PETER, lawyer; b. Bklyn., Feb. 22, 1948; s. Charles Joseph and Marie Antionette (Faraone) L.; m. Sharon Winnett, Sept. 8, 1973; children: William Charles, Kimberly Michelle. BA, Columbia U., 1969; JD, Harvard U., 1973. Bar: N.Y. 1974, Mass. 1985, U.S. Dist. Ct. (so. dist.) N.Y. 1974, U.S. Ct. Appeals (2d cir.) 1975. Assoc. White & Case, N.Y.C., 1973-82; ptnr. Miller, Wrubel & Dubroff, N.Y.C., 1982-83, Sullivan & Worcester LLP, N.Y.C., 1983—. Mem. ABA, Assn. Bar City of N.Y., N.Y. State Bar Assn. Banking, Commercial, contracts (including sales of goods; commercial financing), Finance. Office: Sullivan & Worcester LLP 565 5th Ave New York NY 10017-2413 E-mail: gpl@sandw.com.

LINDSAY, REGINALD CARL, judge; b. Birmingham, Ala., Mar. 19, 1945; s. Richard and Louise L.; m. Cheryl E. Hartgrove, Aug. 15, 1970. Cert., U. Valencia, 1966; AB in Polit. Sci. cum laude, Morehouse Coll., 1967; JD, Harvard U., 1970; LLD (hon.) , New Eng. Sch. Law, 2003. Bar: Mass. 1971, U.S. Ct. Appeals (1st cir.) 1971. Assoc. Hill & Barlow, 1970-75, 78-79, ptnr., 1979-93; judge U.S. Dist. Ct. Mass., Boston, 1994—. Arbitrator, mem. comml. arbitration panel Am. Arbitration Assn., 1994—; commr. Mass. Dept. Pub. Utilities, Boston, 1975-77; pres. adv. bd. Mus. of Nat. Center of Afro-Am. Artists, 1975-81, v.p., 1981— ; trustee Thompson Islands Edn. Center, Boston, 1975-81; bd. dirs. United Way of Mass. Bay, 1981-84, Morgan Meml. Goodwill Industries, Boston, 1992—, Ptnrs. for Youth with Disabilities, Boston; mem. Nat. Consumer Law Ctr. (bd. dirs.), Mass. Commn. on Jud. Conduct, 1982-88; trustee Newton (Mass.) - Wellesley Hosp. Recipient Ruffin-Fenwick Trailblazer award Harvard Black Law Students Assn., 1994, Amanda V. Houston cmty. svc. award Boston Coll., 1998, Frederick E. Berry Expanding Ind. award Easter Seals, 1999, Heroes Among Us award Boston Celtics, 2001, Leadership award New Eng. Black Law Students Assn., 2001. Mem. ABA, Nat. Bar Found., Mass. Bar Assn., Boston Bar Assn. (coun. 1977—, citation jud. excellence 1999), Pi Sigma Alpha, Phi Beta Kappa. Office: 1 Courthouse Way Ste 5130 Boston MA 02210-3007

LINDSEY, LORI DAWN, lawyer; b. Dallas, Apr. 12, 1972; d. Marion Glenn and Judy Jo Lindsey. BA summa cum laude, U. Okla., 1994, JD with highest honors, 1997. Bar: Okla. 1997. Law clk., legal intern, atty. Norman, Edem, McNaughton & Wallace, Oklahoma City, 1995-98; assoc. Pray, Walker, Jackman, Williamson & Marlar, Oklahoma City, 1998-99; law clk. for U.S. Dist. judge Vicki Miles-LaGrange Western Dist. Okla., 1999—. Mem. ABA, ATLA, Okla. Trial Lawyers Assn. Avocations: tennis, puzzles. General civil litigation, General practice, Probate (including wills, trusts). Office: US Dist Ct Western Dist of Okla 200 NW 4th St Ste 5011 Oklahoma City OK 73102-3031

LINDSEY, MICHAEL, lawyer; b. Portsmouth, Hampshire, Eng., Dec. 12, 1960; s. John and Joan L.; m. Elizabeth Mary Emmons, Mar. 25, 1988; children: John Gruffydd, Catherine Elena. LLB with honors, U. Birmingham, Eng., 1983. Bar: solicitor Supreme Ct. Articled clk. H.C.L. Hanne & Co. Solicitors, London, 1985-87; solicitor, 1987-88, Morgan Cole, Cardiff, Wales, 1988-99; ptnr., 1999—. Contbr. articles, revs. to profl. jour. Mem. Intellectual Property Inst., Intellectual Property Lawyers Orgn., Chartered Inst. Patent Agents (assoc.). Avocations: cricket, walking, cooking. Intellectual property, Patent, Trademark and copyright. Office: Morgan Cole Bradley Ct Park Pl CF1O 3DP Cardiff CF10 3DP Wales Fax: 029 2038 5409. E-mail: lindsey.emmons@virgin.net., michael.lindsey@morgan-cole.com.

LINDSKOG, DAVID RICHARD, lawyer; b. Aug. 4, 1936; s. Gustaf Elmer and Charlotte (Birely) L.; m. Elisabeth Lagg, Jan. 28, 1978; 1 child, Stefanie. BA, Yale U., 1958; LLB, U. Va., 1965. Bar: N.Y. 1966, conseil juridique France 1978, avocat 1992. Assoc. Curtis, Mallet-Prevost, Colt & Mosle, N.Y.C., 1965-72, ptnr., 1973-99; sr. v.p., gen. counsel Leach Holding Corp., Westport, Conn., 1999—. Lt. USNR, 1958-62. Mem. Internat. Bar Assn. Episcopalian. Banking, Construction, Private international. Home: 22 Shore Acre Dr Old Greenwich CT 06870-2130 Office: Leach Holding Corp 315 Post Road West Westport CT 06880

LINEBERGER, PETER SAALFIELD, lawyer; b. Akron, Ohio, Mar. 9, 1947; s. Walter F. Jr. and Mary Robinson (Saalfield) L.; children: Katherine Ann, Mary Elizabeth; m. Constance Meyers, Mar. 12, 1988. BA in English, Williams Coll., 1969; JD, Gonzaga U., 1976. Bar: Mont. 1976, Wash. 1994, U.S. Dist. Ct. Mont. 1977, U.S. Dist. Ct. (ea. dist.) Wash. 1994. Legal intern Witherspoon, Kelly, Davenport, Toole, Spokane, 1975; law clk. Mont. Supreme Ct., Helena, 1976; assoc. Landoe, Gary, Bozeman, Mont., 1977-78; ptnr. Landoe, Brown, Planalp, Komers & Lineberger, Bozeman, Mont., 1979-83, Lineberger & Davis, Bozeman, Mont., 1984-85, Lineberger & Harris, PC, Bozeman, Mont., 1986-88, Lineberger, Walsh & McKenna, PC, Bozeman, Mont., 1989-94; pvt. practice Peter S. Lineberger, Spokane, 1994—. City atty. Town of West Yellowstone, Mont., 1978-94; chmn. Gallatin County Legal Svcs. Com., Bozeman, 1985-89, chmn. Mont. Child and Family Law Sect., 1993-94. Lt. USNR, 1969-72. Mem. ABA (family law sect. 1987—), Wash. State Bar Assn. (family law sect., exec. com. 1998-2003, chmn, 2001-2002), Am. Acad. Matrimonial Lawyers, Gallatin County Bar Assn., Mont. City Attys. Assn. (pres. 1983), Spokane County Bar Assn. (vol. lawyers program adv. com. 1996-2000, chmn. 1998-99). Avocations: fly fishing, skiing. Family and matrimonial. Office: US Bank Bldg Ste 1407 422 W Riverside Ave Spokane WA 99201-0306 E-mail: psline@hotmail.com.

LINEEN, EDWARD M. lawyer, computer company executive; b. 1941; BS, JD, Fordham U. Bar: N.Y. 1971. Sr. v.p., gen. counsel IBM, Armonk, NY, 2002—. Office: IBM 1 New Orchard Rd Armonk NY 10504 Office Fax: 914-499-6085.*

LINETT, DAVID, lawyer; b. Perth Amboy, N.J., Apr. 9, 1934; s. Jack K. and Anne L.; children: Jon, Peter, Maren. BA, Yale U., 1956; JD, Harvard U., 1959. Bar: D.C. 1959, N.J. 1960. Law sec. to assignment judge Superior Ct. NJ, 1959—60; assoc. Gross, Weissberger & Linett, New Brunswick, N.J., 1960-62, ptnr., 1962-77; prosecutor Somerset County, N.J., 1977-82; of counsel Lowenstein, Sandler, Brochin, Kohl et al and predecessor, Roseland and Somerville, N.J., 1982-85; ptnr. Gindin & Linett, Bridgewater, N.J., 1985—. Chmn. N.J. State Bar Com. on Programs for Law Enforcement Personnel, 1978-80; mem. com. on county dist. cts. N.J. Supreme Ct., 1980-82, mem. Post-Indictment Delay Task Force, 1980, dist. XIII ethics com., 1986-90, chair N.J. Supreme Ct., 1989-90, ethics fin. com., 1990-94, treas., 1992-94; gen. counsel United Heritage Bank, 1997-. Mem. N.J. Dem. State Com., 1973-77; bd. dirs. Somerset County Resource Ctr. for Women and Their Families, 1982-83; chmn. bd. trustees, Assn. for Advancement of Mentally Handicapped, 1987-89; commr. N.J. Election Law Enforcement Commn., 1987-2000, vice chair, 1996-2000; mem. Ct. House study com., Somerset County Bd. Freeholders, 1979-82; gen.chmn. Rotary Internat. Task Force on Edn. and Tng., 2001-02. Mem. ABA (corp., real property law sect.), Nat. Dist. Attys. Assn. (nat. treas., exec. com. 1981-82, Pres.'s award for outstanding svc. as chmn. fin. com. 1982), New Brunswick Bar Assn. (pres. 1974), N.J. Bar Assn. (land use sect., real property sect.), Somerset County Bar Assn., Somerset County C. of C. (bd. dirs. 1984-90, Outstanding Citizen of Yr. 1989), Rotary (pres. 1986-87, dist. gov. 1991-92). Banking, General civil litigation, Property, real (including real estate development, water). Office: PO Box 6135 1170 Rt 22 Bridgewater NJ 08807 E-mail: ginlin@aol.com.

LINETT, HOWARD B. lawyer; b. Derby, Conn., Sept. 5, 1949; s. Morton and Rhoda Linett; m. Varda Z. Linett. BA in Polit. Sci., Lafayette Coll., 1971; MS in Labor Studies, U. Mass., 1973; JD cum laude, U. Bridgeport, 1982. Bar: Conn. 1982, U.S. Dist. Ct. Conn. 1982, U.S. Ct. Appeals (2nd cir.) 1982, U.S. Dist. Ct. D.C. 1990, U.S. Ct. Appeals (D.C. cir.) 1990, Israel 1997. Pvt. practice Linett & Walsh, Bridgeport, Conn., 1983—89; atty./staff counsel Nat. Mail Handers Union, Washington, 1989—90; atty./contract adminstr. Airline Pilots Assn., Washington, 1990—95; legal intern Israeli Gen. Fedn. Labor, Jerusalem, 1995—96; pvt. practice Jerusalem, 1997—2000; of counsel Zell Goldberg, Jerusalem, 2000—. Mediator Jerusalem Inst. Israel Studies, 1998—. Contbr. articles to mags. Mem.: Jerusalem Region Israeli Bar Assn. (ADR subcom.). Office: Zell Goldberg & Co 31 Mishol Hadekalim 97278 Jerusalem Israel

LINK, GEORGE HAMILTON, retired lawyer; b. Sacramento, Calif., Mar. 26, 1939; s. Hoyle and Corrie Elizabeth (Evans) L.; m. Betsy Leland; children— Thomas Hamilton, Christopher Leland. AB, U. Calif., Berkeley, 1961; LLB, Harvard U., 1964. Bar: Calif. 1965, U.S. Dist. Ct. (no., ea., ctrl. and so dists.) Calif. 1965, U.S. Ct. Appeals (9th cir.) 1965. Assoc. Brobeck, Phleger & Harrison, San Francisco, 1964-69, ptnr., 1970—2001, mng. ptnr. L.A., 1973-93, mng. ptnr. firmwide, 1993-96; ret., 2001. Chmn. Pacific Rim Adv. Coun., 1992-95. Bd. regents U. Calif., 1971-74; trustee Berkeley Found., Jr. Statesmen Am.; bd. govs. United Way, 1979-81; trustee, v.p. Calif. Hist. Soc., 1987—; bd. dirs. Ancient Egypt Rsch. Assocs. Fellow Am. Bar Found.; mem. ABA, Calif. Bar Assn., L.A. Bar Assn., U. Calif. Alumni Assn. (pres. 1972-75), Calif. Club, Bohemian Club, Jonathan Club. Republican. Methodist. E-mail: georgehlink@msn.com.

LINK, ROBERT JAMES, lawyer, educator; b. Washington, May 25, 1950; s. Robert Wendell and Barbara Ann (Bullock) L.; m. Cheryl Ann Brillante, Apr. 22, 1978; children: Robert Edward, Holden James. BA, U. Miami, 1972, JD, 1975. Bar: Fla. 1975, U.S. Dist. Ct. (mid. dist.) Fla. 1980, U.S. Ct. Appeals (5th cir.) 1980, U.S. Ct. Appeals (11th cir.) 1981, U.S. Supreme Ct. 1984, U.S. Dist. Ct. (no. dist.) Fla. 1989. Asst. pub. defender City of Miami, Fla., 1975-78, City of Jacksonville, Fla., 1978-82; ptnr. Greenspan, Goodstein & Link, Jacksonville, 1982-84, Goodstein & Link, Jacksonville, 1984-85; pvt. practice, Jacksonville, 1985-88; assoc. Howell, Liles & Milton, Jacksonville, 1988-89; ptnr. Pajcic & Pajcic P.A., 1990—. Guest instr. U. Miami, 1976, U. Fla., 1979-88, Stetson U. Law Sch., 1984, Jacksonville U., 1987-88, U. North Fla., 1991. Atty. legal panel ACLU, Jacksonville, 1982-88. Mem. Fla. Bar Assn. (chmn. com. for representation of indigents criminal law sect. 1980, cert. criminal trial lawyer 1989), Jacksonville Bar Assn. (trial law sect.), Nat. Assn. Criminal Def. Lawyers (vice-chmn. post conviction com. 1990), Fla. Pub. Defender Assn. (death penalty steering com. 1980-82, instr. 1979—), Assn. Fla. Trial Lawyers (seminar spkr. 2000). Democrat. Methodist. Avocations: sailing, fishing, diving, softball. Criminal, Personal injury (including property damage), Product liability. Home: 3535 Carlyon St Jacksonville FL 32207-5836 Office: 1900 Independent Dr Jacksonville FL 32202-5023

LINK, ROBERT O., JR., lawyer; BS in Acctg. with highest honors, U. Tenn., 1977, MBA, JD, 1980. Bar: (N.Y.), (Ga.), (Tenn.). With Cadwalader, Wickersham & Taft, N.Y.C., 1987—90, ptnr., 1990—. Recipient Am. Jurisprudence awards. Mem.: Mortgage Bankers Assn., N.Y. State Bar Assn., Order of Coif. Office: Cadwalader Wickersham & Taft 100 Maiden Ln New York NY 10038

LINKER, ARTHUR S. lawyer; b. N.Y.C., May 20, 1947; s. Jack and Gertrude (Reibeisen) L.; m. Diane Spanier, June 4, 1973; children: Beth, Jennifer, Michael, Anne. AB summa cum laude, Columbia U., 1968, MA, 1970; JD cum laude, Harvard U., 1974. Bar: N.Y., U.S. Dist. Ct. (so. and ea. dists.) N.Y., U.S. Ct. Appeals (2d cir.) 1975; U.S. Supreme Ct. 1979; U.S. Ct. Appeals (4th cir.) 1989, U.S. Ct. Appeals (8th cir.) 1990. Ptnr. Rosenman & Colin LLP, N.Y.C., 1974—2002, Katten Muchin Zavis Rosenman, N.Y.C., 2002—. Mem. ABA, N.Y. State Bar Assn., Assn. Bar City N.Y. Avocations: computers, astronomy. Bankruptcy, General civil litigation, Intellectual property. Office: Katten Muchin Zavis Rosenman 575 Madison Ave Fl 26 New York NY 10022-2585

LINKER, RAYMOND OTHO, JR., lawyer; b. Charlotte, N.C., Jan. 18, 1946; s. Raymond Otho Sr. and Frances (Baucom) L.; m. Nola Grady Jenning, June 24, 1969; 1 child, John Raymond. BS in Chem. Engring., N.C. State U., 1968; JD, Georgetown U., 1972. Bar: N.C. 1972, U.S. Dist. Ct. (we. dist.) N.C. 1972, U.S. Patent Trademark Office 1972. From assoc. to ptnr. Bell, Seltzer, Park & Gibson, Charlotte, 1972—; patent practice group leader Alston & Bird. Mem. N.C. Bar Assn., Am. Intellectual Property Assn., Carolinas Patent, Trademark and Copyright Law Assn. (past pres.). Presbyterian. Computer, Patent, Trademark and copyright. Office: Alston & Bird LLP Bank of Am Plaza 101 S Tryon St Ste 4000 Charlotte NC 28280 E-mail: rlinker@alston.com.

LINKOUS, WILLIAM JOSEPH, JR., lawyer; b. Roanoke, Va., July 17, 1929; s. William Joseph and Mary Virginia (Lester) L.; m. Anita Marie Stedronsky, Oct. 15, 1960; children— William Joseph III, Brian Keith BA, Roanoke Coll., Salem, Va., 1951; MA in Econs., U. Va., 1954, JD, 1956. Bar: Va. 1956, Ga. 1957. Assoc. Powell, Goldstein, Frazer & Murphy, Atlanta, 1956-62, ptnr., 1962-79, 85—, mng. ptnr., 1979-85. Trustee Holy Innocents Episcopal Sch., Atlanta, 1974-80, Roanoke Coll., 1980-95, emeritus 1995—. Fellow Am. Coll. Trust and Estate Counsel, Am. Bar Found.; mem. State Bar Ga. (past chmn. fiduciary sect., chmn. Ga. trust law revision com. 1988-91, 2003—, chmn. Ga. probate code revision com. 1991-97, chmn. Ga. guardianship code revision com.1997-2003), Va. State Bar, Am. Law Inst., Internat. Acad. Estate and Trust Law, Atlanta Estate Planning Coun. (pres. 1983-84). Avocation: tennis. Estate planning, Probate (including wills, trusts), Estate taxation. Office: Powell Goldstein Frazer & Murphy 191 Peachtree St NE Ste 1600 Atlanta GA 30303-1700 E-mail: wlinkous@pgfm.com.

LINNAN, JAMES DANIEL, lawyer; b. Olean, N.Y., Nov. 29, 1946; s. William Martine and Genevieve (Toohey) L.; married, June 5, 1971; 1 child, Brigid Mary. BS, Northeastern U., Boston, 1969; JD, Albany Law Sch., 1972. BAr: N.Y. 1973, U.S. Dist. Ct. (no. dist.) N.Y., 1973, U.S. Dist. Ct. Vt. 1976, U.S. Ct. Appeals (2d cir.), 1976, U.S. Supreme Ct. 1978, Fla. 1986. Spl. litigation counsel City of Albany, N.Y., 1976-85; assoc. Garry, Cahill & Edmunds, Albany, 1973-76; sole pratice Albany, 1976-84; ptnr. Linnan, Shea & Flannery, Albany, 1987-89, Linnan Bacon & Meyer, 1989-92, Linnan & Fallon, 1992—. Founder, pres., v.p. Northeastern Family and Children's House, Inc., 1981; mem. Albany County Dem. County, 1976-93. Mem. Assn. Trial Lawyers Am., Am. Bd. Trial Advocates (nat. bd. dirs., past pres. Albany chpt.), N.Y. State Bar Assn., N.Y. Trial Lawyers, Capital Dist. Trial Lawyers. Democrat. Roman Catholic. Federal civil litigation, State civil litigation, Personal injury (including property damage). Home and Office: Linnan & Fallon LLP 61 Columbia St Albany NY 12210-2736 E-mail: jdlinnan@linnan-fallon.com.

LINSENMEYER, JOHN MICHAEL, lawyer; b. Columbus, Ohio, June 20, 1940; s. John Cyril and Ruth Theresa (Motz) L.; m. Barbara Panish, Aug. 12, 1961; children: Ann Elizabeth Linsenmeyer Nelson, Thomas More, Barbara Mary Linsenmeyer Malone. AB, Georgetown U., 1961, JD, 1964. Bar: Va. 1964, N.Y. 1965, U.S. Supreme Ct.1967, D.C. 1975. Assoc. Cravath, Swaine & Moore, N.Y.C., 1966-75; ptnr. Forsyth, Decker, Murray & Broderick, N.Y.C., 1975-80, Morgan, Lewis & Bockius, N.Y.C., 1980—. Columnist Southern Conn. Newspapers, Greenwich, 1984—; contbr. articles to profl. jours. Police officer, sgt. Greenwich Police Dept. Special Div., 1966-87; cons. firearms Presdl. Commn. on the Causes and Prevention of Violence, 1968-69; bd. dirs. Fairfield County Fish and Game Agy., Newtown, Conn., 1973-77. Mem. N.Y. State Bar Assn., N.Y.C. Fed. Bar Coun., Univ. Club (N.Y.C.), Squadron A (N.Y.C.), Rocky Point Club (Old Greenwich, Conn.), Royal Can. Mil. Inst. (Toronto.). Republican. Roman Catholic. Avocations: hunting, shooting, horses, military history. Federal civil litigation, General civil litigation, Private international. Home: 9 Hendrie Ave Riverside CT 06878-1808 Office: Morgan Lewis & Bockius 101 Park Ave Fl 43 New York NY 10178-0002 E-mail: jlinsenmeyer@morganlewis.com.

LINTON, JACK ARTHUR, lawyer; b. N.Y.C., May 29, 1936; s. Paul Phillip and Helen (Feller) L.; div.; children: Ann Deborah Linton Wilmot, James Paul, John Michael. BA, Albright Coll., 1958; JD, NYU, 1961, LLM in Taxation, 1966. Bar: Pa. 1962, N.Y. 1963, U.S. Tax Ct. 1966, U.S. Dist. Ct. (ea. dist.) Pa. 1978, U.S. Ct. Appeals, 1984. Assoc. DeLong, Dry & Binder, Reading, Pa., 1961-63; asst. ho. counsel Bob Banner Assocs., Inc., N.Y.C., 1963-66; ptnr. DeLong, Dry, Cianci & Linton, Reading, 1967-70, Williamson, Miller, Murray & Linton, Reading, 1970-72, Gerber & Linton, P.C., Reading, 1972-88, Linton, Giannascoli, Barrett & Distasio, P.C., Reading, 1989-97, Linton, Giannascoli, Distasio & Adams, PC, Reading, 1997-98, Linton, Distasio, Adam & Kauffman, PC, Reading, 1998—2001, Linton, Distasio, Adams & Palange, P.C., Reading, 2001—. Solicitor Reading Parking Authority, 1967-76, City of Reading, 1980-96; bd. dirs. The Group, Inc., Small Bus. Coun. Am., Inc., chmn. polit. action com., 1988—, numerous med. profl. corps., Reading area; lectr. nat. seminars on tax problems for small bus.; co-founder, mem. Estate Planning Coun. Berks County, 1978—. Editor Tax Law Rev., 1965-67; contbr. articles to profl. jours. Pres. Berks County Mental Health Assn., 1968-69, Reading Jewish Community Ctr., 1980-82; mem. Mental Health/Mental Retardation Bd. Berks County, 1974-80; treas., bd. dirs. Reading-Berks Youth Soccer League, 1982-85; bd. dirs. Gov. Mifflin Sch. Dist., Shillington, 1985-93, Exeter Township Sch. Dist., 1999-, v.p., 2000-. Kenneson fellow NYU Sch. Law, 1965-67. Mem. ABA (mem. personal svc. orgn. com., tax sect. 1981—, chairperson task force for repeal top-heavy rules 1987-89, vice chmn. personal svc. orgn. com. 1990-92, chmn. personal svc. orgn. com. 1992-94), Pa. Bar Assn., Berks County Bar Assn. (treas. 1969-72), Berks County C. of C. (mem. nat. affairs com.). Democrat. Jewish. Avocations: sports, reading. Estate planning, Pension, profit-sharing, and employee benefits, Estate taxation. Office: Linton Distasio Adams & Palange PC PO Box 461 1720 Mineral Spring Rd Reading PA 19602-2231

LINTON, SARAH, lawyer; b. Maidstone, Eng., May 15, 1957; m. John Witherow; 3 children. BA in Modern Langs., Oxford (Eng.) U., 1979; Law Soc. Final Exam., City Poly. London, 1992. Solicitor: Eng. Journalist, 1981—90; solicitor Stephenson Harwood, London, 1992—2000; counsel, head U.K. Employment Practice Bryan Cave, London, 2000—. Mem.: European Employment Lawyers Assn., Employment Lawyers Assn. Avocations: politics, education, travel. Labor (including EEOC, Fair Labor Standards Act, labor-management relations, NLRB, OSHA), Immigration, naturalization, and customs. Office: Bryan Cave 33 Cannon St London EC4M 5TE England

LINXWILER, JAMES DAVID, lawyer; b. Fresno, Calif., Apr. 9, 1949; s. George Edwin and Stella Ruth (Schmidt) L.; m. Robyn Kenning, July 12, 1986; children: Elizabeth Ann, John Edwin, Jeffrey David. BA, U. Calif., Berkeley, 1971; JD, UCLA, 1974. Bar: D.C. 1976, U.S. Dist. Ct. Alaska 1976, U.S. Dist. Ct. (D.C. cir.) 1976, Alaska 1977, U.S. Ct. Appeals (9th cir.) 1977, U.S. Supreme Ct. 1988. Lawyer U.S. Dept. Interior, Washington, 1974-76, Cook Inlet Region, Inc., Anchorage, 1976-78, Sohio Petroleum Co., Anchorage, 1978-81; shareholder Guess & Rudd, Anchorage, 1981-2000, mng. shareholder, 2000—. Spkr. seminars on environ. and natural resources law. Contbr. chpts. to book, articles to profl. jours. Chmn. Alaska Coalition Am. Energy Security, 1986-87, Alliance Arctic Nat. Wildlife Refuge Com., 1986-87; bd. dirs. Commonwealth North, 1993--20029, pres., 1999-2000. Mem. ABA, FBA, Alaska Bar Assn. (chmn., exec. com. nat. resources sect. 1988-93), D.C. Bar Assn. Democrat. Administrative and regulatory, Oil, gas, and mineral, Environmental. Home: 2407 Loussac Dr Anchorage AK 99517-1272 Office: Guess & Rudd 510 L St Ste 700 Anchorage AK 99501-1959

LIOZ, LAWRENCE STEPHEN, lawyer, accountant; b. N.Y.C., Sept. 24, 1945; s. William and Irma (Berksohn) L.; m. Carol Renee Skolnik, Nov. 20, 1971; children: Adam Russell, Randall Eric. BS, SUNY, Albany, 1967; JD, SUNY, Buffalo, 1970; LLM in Taxation, NYU, 1975. Bar: N.Y. 1970; CPA, N.Y. Mgr. Ernst & Whinney, N.Y.C., 1970-79; dir. tax affairs Azcon Corp., N.Y.C., 1979-82; mgr. Deloitte Haskins & Sells, N.Y.C., 1982-83, ptnr., 1983-84, Woodbury, NY, 1984-87, Margolin, Winer & Evens LLP, Garden City, NY, 1987—. Speaker in field. Contbr. articles to profl. jours. Pres. Rolling Wood Civic Assn., Roslyn, N.Y., 1983—; trustee Flower Hill (N.Y.) Assn., 1985-87, Village of Flower Hill, 1987-92; treas. Roslyn Sch. Dist., 1986-99. Mem. ABA, AICPAs, N.Y. State Bar Assn., N.Y. State Soc. CPAs (chmn. fed. tax com. Nassau chpt. 1989-92, exec. bd. 1992—, pres. 2000-01). Jewish. Avocations: skiing, golf. Home: 84 Knollwood W Roslyn NY 11576-1319 Office: Margolin Winer & Evens LLP 400 Garden City Plz Fl 5 Garden City NY 11530-3317 E-mail: llioz@mwellp.com.

LIPCON, CHARLES ROY, lawyer; b. N.Y.C., Mar. 20, 1946; s. Harry H. and Rose Lipcon; m. Irmgard Adels, Dec. 1, 1974; children: Lauren, Claudia. BA, U. Miami, 1968, JD, 1971. Bar: Fla. 1971, U.S. Dist. Ct. (so. dist.) Fla. 1971, U.S. Ct. Appeals (5th cir.) 1972, U.S. Supreme Ct. 1976, U.S. Ct. Appeals (D.C. cir.) 1980, U.S. Dist. Ct. (so. dist.) Tex. 1982, U.S. Dist. Ct. (middle dist.) Fla. 2000, U.S. Ct. Appeals (11th cir.) 1994, U.S. Dist. Ct. Colo. 1999, U.S. Dist. Ct. (mid. dist.) Fla. 2000, Ct. of Fed. Claims, 2003. Pvt. practice, Miami, Fla., 1971—. Lectr. U. Miami Sch. Law. Author: Help for the Auto Accident Victim, 1984, Seaman's Rights in the United States When Involved in An Accident, 1989; pub., editor The Cruise Line Law Reporter; contbr. articles to profl. jours. Named Commodore of High Seas, Internat. Seaman's Union. Mem. ABA, ATLA, Fla. Bar Assn., Fla. Trial Lawyers Assn., Dade County Bar Assn., Dade County Trial Lawyers, Fla. Admiralty Trial Lawyers Assn., Mensa. Admiralty, Federal civil litigation, Personal injury (including property damage). Office: 2 S Biscayne Blvd Ste 2480 Miami FL 33131-1803 E-mail: sealaw@aol.com.

LIPE, LINDA BON, lawyer; b. Clarksdale, Miss., Jan. 10, 1948; d. William Ray and Gwendolyn (Stickland) Lipe. BBA in Accountancy, U. Miss., 1970, JD, 1971. Bar: Miss. 1971, Ark. 1976, U.S. Dist. Ct. (no. dist.) Miss. 1971, U.S. Dist. Ct. (ea. dist.) Ark. 1976, U.S. Ct. Appeals (8th cir.) 1985. Sr. tax acct. Arthur Young & Co., San Jose, Calif., 1971-74, A.M. Pullen & Co., Knoxville, Tenn., 1975; legal counsel to gov. State of Ark., Little Rock, 1975-79; dept. pros. atty. 6th Jud. Dist. Ark., Little Rock, 1979-80; chief counsel Ark. Pub. Svcs. Commn., Little Rock, 1980-83; asst. U.S. atty. Ea. Dist. Ark., Dept. Justice, Little Rock, 1983—. Founding bd. dirs. Assn. Cert. Cruelty Investigators, Humane Soc. U.S.; bd. dirs., treas. Humane Soc. Pulaski County, 1997-2002. Mem. ABA, Miss. State Bar Assn., Ark. State Bar Assn. Episcopalian. Office: US Attys Office PO Box 1229 Little Rock AR 72203-1229

LIPEZ, KERMIT V. federal judge, former state supreme court justice; Former judge Maine Superior Ct.; assoc. justice Supreme Jud. Ct. of Maine, Portland, 1994—98; judge U.S. Ct. Appeals (1st cir.) Maine, Portland, 1998—. Office: 156 Federal St Portland ME 04101-4152

LIPFORD, ROCQUE EDWARD, lawyer, corporate executive; b. Monroe, Mich., Aug. 16, 1938; s. Frank G. and Mary A. (Mastromarco) L.; m. Marcia A. Griffin, Aug. 5, 1966; children: Lisa, Rocque Edward, Jennifer, Katherine. BS, U. Mich., 1960, MS, 1961, JD with distinction, 1964. Bar: Mich. 1964, Ohio 1964. Instr. mech. engring. U. Mich., 1961-63; atty. Miller, Canfield, Paddock & Stone, Detroit, 1965-66; asst. gen. counsel Monroe Auto Equipment Co., 1966-70, gen. counsel, 1970-72, v.p., gen. counsel, 1973-77, Tenneco Automotive, 1977-78; ptnr. firm Miller, Canfield, Paddock & Stone, Detroit, 1978—, mng. ptnr., 1988-91. Bd. dirs. La-Z-Boy Inc., Monroe Bank & Trust. Mem.: Knights of Malta, Legatus, Mich. Bar Assn., Mariner Sands Golf and Country Club, Monroe Golf and Country Club, North Cape Yacht Club, Otsego Ski Club, Pi Tau Sigma, Tau Beta Pi. Antitrust, Corporate, general, Estate planning. Home: 1065 Hollywood Dr Monroe MI 48162-3045 Office: Miller Canfield Paddock & Stone 214 E Elm Ave Ste 100 Monroe MI 48162-2682 E-mail: lipford@mcps.com.

LIPMAN, FREDERICK D. lawyer, author, educator; b. Phila., Nov. 16, 1935; s. Charles S. and Beatrice (Sanderow) L.; m. Gail Heller, July 25, 1965; children— L. Keith, Darren A. AB, Temple U.; LLB, Harvard Law Sch. Bar: Pa. 1960, N.Y. Practitioner, Phila., 1960-62; corp. counsel AEL Industries, Inc., Colmar, Pa., 1962-69; ptnr. Blank Rome Comisky & McCauley LLP, Phila., 1970—. Lectr. U. Pa. Law Sch., 1989-98, Temple U. Law Sch., 1989-94, Wharton Sch. of Bus., 1998—. Author: Going Public, 1994, How Much Is Your Business Worth, 1996, Venture Capital and Junk Bond Financing, 1998, Financing Your Business with Venture Capital, 1998, The Complete Going Public Handbook, 2000, Audit Committees, 2001, The Complete Guide to Employee Stock Options, 2001, The Complete Guide to Valuing and Selling Your Business, 2001. Bd. dirs. Phila. Ch. of Bezalel, 1989-91, Walnut St. Theatre, 1997-99, Phila. Geriatric Ctr., Penjerdel. Harvard Law Sch. scholar, 1957; Temple U. scholar, 1953. Mem. Phila. Bar Assn. (bd. govs. 1984-85), Greater Phila. C. of C. (bd. dirs., mem. exec. com. 1980-90, chmn. tech. council 1983-85), Harvard Law Sch. Assn. Greater Phila. (pres. 1988-89). Lodges: Masons. Democrat. Jewish. Avocation: tennis. Corporate, general, Securities. Office: Blank Rome Comisky & McCauley LLP 1 Logan Sq Fl 3 Philadelphia PA 19103-6998 E-mail: lipman@blankrome.com.

LIPPE, EMIL, JR., lawyer; b. Waco, Tex., Nov. 4, 1948; s. Johann August Emil and Agnes Natalie (Fenske) L.; m. Stephanie Woodruff, Jan. 13, 1996. BA, Northwestern U., 1970, J.D. cum laude, 1973. Bar: Tex. 1973, U.S. Dist. Ct. (no. dist.) Tex. 1974, U.S. Ct. Appeals (5th cir.) 1974, U.S. Dist. Ct. (ea. dist.) Tex. 1976, U.S. Dist. Ct. (so. and we. dists.) Tex. 1977, U.S. Supreme Ct. 1977, U.S. Ct. Appeals (11th cir.) 1981, D.C. 1996, Colo. 1997. Pvt. practice law, Dallas, 1973—; assoc. Carrington, Coleman, Sloman & Blumenthal, 1973-76; assoc. Akin, Gump, Strauss, Hauer & Feld, 1976-80, ptnr., 1980-83; mem. Barlow & Lippe, 1983-84, Lippe & Lay, 1984-85, Lippe & Assocs., 1985—; lectr. dept. communications arts Loyola U., Chgo., 1972-73; vice chmn. alternate methods of dispute resolution com. State Bar of Tex., 1982-83. Bd. dirs. Save Open Space Orgn., 1974-75; precinct chmn. Dallas County Dems., 1984-88; bd. dirs. Preservation Dallas, 2001-03. Recipient Outstanding Dir. award Tex. Young Lawyers Assn., 1980-81; Outstanding Young Lawyer in Dallas, 1983. Mem. ABA, Tex. Bd. Legal Specialization (cert. civil trial law 1988, civil appellate law 1989), Tex. Bar Assn., Dallas Bar Assn. (chmn. speakers com. 1980, law day com. 1981), Tex. Young Lawyers Assn. (bd. dirs. 1979-81, chmn. pub. service handbook com. 1979-80, chmn. legis. com. 1980-81, co-chmn. 1981-83, Outstanding Dir. 1980-81), Dallas Young Lawyers Assn. (chmn. speakers com. 1976, co-chmn. continuing legal edn. com. 1977, treas. 1979, bd. dirs. 1979-80, Outstanding Young Lawyer award 1983), Order of Coif. Democrat. Lutheran. Contbr. articles to profl. jours. Antitrust, Federal civil litigation, State civil litigation. Home: 6828 Gaston Ave Dallas TX 75214-4030 Office: Lippe & Assocs 2001 Bryan St Ste 1850 Dallas TX 75201-3005 E-mail: texaslaw@airmail.net.

LIPPE, JERRY LEONARD, lawyer; b. Cleve., May 19, 1942; s. Morry and Odes (Wyman) L.; m. Rosalind E. Levin; 1 child, Ryan Scott; m. Christine E. Bobbey, Oct. 7, 1989; 1 child, Megan Michelle. AB, Miami U., Oxford, Ohio, 1964; JD, Ohio State U., 1967. Bar: Ohio 1967, U.S. Dist. Ct. (so. dist.) Ohio 1970, U.S. Supreme Ct. 1973. Pers. officer State of Ohio, Columbus, 1967; asst. city pros. City of Columbus, 1967-68, asst. city atty., 1968-69; ptnr. Weiner, Lippe & Cromley, 1969-79; pvt. practice, 1979—. Bd. trustees Directions for Youth, Columbus, 1975-79; mem., patroller Nat. Ski Patrol, Bellefontaine, Ohio, 1988—. Mem. Ohio Acad. Trial Lawyers, Ohio Bar Assn., Columbus Bar Assn. Avocations: snow skiing, golf, tennis. Criminal, Personal injury (including property damage). Office: 592 S 3rd St Columbus OH 43215-5754

LIPPE, RICHARD ALLEN, lawyer; b. Bklyn., July 24, 1938; s. Al A. and Thelma (Spaeth) L.; children: Wendy, David, Michael. BA, Tufts U., 1960; LLB, U. Pa., 1964. Bar: N.Y. 1965, U.S. Dist. Ct. (ea. and so. dists. N.Y.) 1965, U.S. Supreme Ct. 1975. Dept. county atty. Nassau County, N.Y., 1965-68; ptnr. Lippe, Ruskin, Schlissel & Moscou, Nassau County, 1968-79; ptnr. Meltzer, Lippe & Goldstein, Mineola, N.Y., 1979—; village atty. Inc. Village of Great Neck Plaza, N.Y., 1972-97, Poly Ventures, Ltd. Partnership; bd. dirs. L.I. Venture Capital Group; counsel Manhasset-Great Neck Econ. Opportunity Council, 1965-68; gen. ptnr. Contemporary Art Consortium; pres. Contemporary Art Pub. Consortium; outside counsel Cheyenne Software, 1995-96. Sec. Nassau Law Svcs. Com., Inc., 1966-96; bd. dir. Nassau County Legal Aid Soc., 1978-81, Waldemar Med. Rsch. Found., 1966-68, Stony Brook Found. Realty Corp., LIMSAT; trustee Stony Brook Found., 1989—; gen. counsel Long Is. Venture Fund, 1995—; gen. counsel, bd. dirs. ListNet; mem. bus. adv. com. Nassau County Mus. Art. Mem. ABA, N.Y. Bar Assn., Nassau County Bar Assn., Fed. Bar Council. Jewish. Contbr. articles to profl. jours. Federal civil litigation, Corporate, general. Office: 190 Willis Ave Mineola NY 11501-2693

LIPPES, RICHARD JAMES, lawyer; b. Buffalo, Mar. 18, 1944; s. Thomas and Ruth (Landsman) L.; m. Sharon Richmond, June 4, 1972; children: Amity, Joshua, Kevin. BA, U. Mich., 1966; JD cum laude, SUNY, Buffalo, 1969. Bar: N.Y. 1970, U.S. Dist. Ct. Md. 1970, U.S. Ct. Appeals (4th cir.) 1970, N.Y. 1971, U.S. Dist. Ct. (we. dist.) N.Y. 1971, U.S. Ct. Appeals (2d cir.) 1971, U.S. Dist. Ct. (no. dist.) N.Y. 1973, U.S. Dist. Ct. (so. dist.) N.Y. 1985. Clk. to presiding justice U.S. Ct. Appeals (4th cir.), Balt., 1970; exec. dir. Ctr. for Justice Through Law, Buffalo, 1971; pvt. practice, Buffalo, 1971-77; ptnr. Allen & Lippes, Buffalo, 1979—, Moriarity, Allen, Lippes & Hoffman, Buffalo, 1977-79, Allen & Lippes, Buffalo, 1979—. Lectr. SUNY, Buffalo, 1978, 79; lead counsel and spl. environ. counsel for hazardous waste, mass toxic tort cases. Contbr. articles to profl. jours. Chmn. Atlantic chpt. Sierra Club, 1978-82; chmn. Buffalo chpt. Am. Jewish Com., 1986-88; chmn. lawyers com. Niagara Frontier chpt. N.Y. Civil Liberties Union, 1971, chpt. chmn., 1972-74; chmn. Buffalo Environ. Mgmt. Commn., 1987-96; bd. dirs. N.Y. State Preservation League, also gen. coun.; chmn. Buffalo Task Force, 1986-87; pres. Erie County Preservation Coalition, 1998—; also various others. Urban and Environ. Law fellow, 1969. Mem. ABA, N.Y. State Bar Assn., Erie County Bar Assn. (former chmn. pub. interest law com. and prepaid legal svcs. com.). Democrat. Environmental, Personal injury (including property damage). E-mail: rlippes@concentric.net.

LIPPINCOTT, WALTER EDWARD, law educator; b. Bronxville, N.Y., Aug. 15, 1959; s. Walter Edwin and Helen (Patterson) L.; m. Andrea Pratt, July 30, 1983; children: Brittany Marie, Matthew, Anna. BS, Roger Williams Coll., 1981; JD, Western New Eng. Coll., 1984; MS, Fla. Inst. Tech., 1995. Bar: Conn. 1984, D.C. 1985. Prosecutor State of Conn. Judicial Dept., Hartford, 1990-93; prof. Naugatuck Valley Cmty. Coll., Waterbury, Conn., 1993—, U. Conn., Storrs, 1996-97. Lt. col. U.S. Army, 1985-90, USAR, 1990—. Mem. ABA, Conn. Bar Assn., D.C. Bar Assn. Home: 613 Highland Ave Torrington CT 06790-4410

LIPSEY, HOWARD IRWIN, law educator, justice, lawyer; b. Providence, Jan. 24, 1936; s. Harry David and Anna (Gershman) L.; children: Lewis Robert, Bruce Stephen. BA(hon.) , Providence Coll., 1957; JD, Georgetown U., 1960. Bar: R.I., 1960; U.S. Dist. Ct. R.I., 1961; U.S. Supreme Ct., 1972. Assoc. Edward I. Friedman, 1963-67, Kirshenbaum and Kirshenbaum, 1967-72; ptnr. Abedon, Michaelson, Stanzler, Biener, Skolnik, and Lipsey, 1972-83, Lipsey and Skolnik Esquires, Ltd., Providence, 1983-93; assoc. justice R.I. Family Ct., Providence, 1993—. Lectr. trial tactics Nat. Coll. Adv., 1986, U. Bridgeport, Yale U., U. Denver, Suffolk U.,1987—; adj. prof. U. Houston ., 1994-98; adj. prof. family law Roger Williams U., 1996-2000. Contbg. author: Valuation and Distribution of Marital Property, 1984; bd. editors Georgetown U. Law Jour. Capt. JAGC, USAR, 1960-71. Fellow: Am. Acad. Matrimonial Lawyers, Am. Coll. Trial Lawyers; mem.: ATLA, ABA (chair trial advocacy inst. 1994—97, coun. 1995—2001, sec. family law sect. 2002—03, chmn. family cts. com., bd. edit. Family Advocate, treas.), Family Law Inn of Ct., R.I. Bar Assn., B'nai B'rith. Office: RI Family Ct 1 Dorrance Plz Providence RI 02903-3922 Fax: (401) 458-5180.

LIPSHAW, JEFFREY MARC, lawyer, chemicals executive; b. Detroit, June 16, 1954; s. Harold Melvin Lipshaw and Renata Adele Freed; m. Alene Susan Franklin, Apr. 10, 1959; children: Arielle, Matthew, James. AB, U. Mich., 1975; JD, Stanford U., 1979. Bar: Mich. 1979, U.S. Supreme Ct. 1984, Ind. 2001. Assoc. Dykema Gossett, Detroit, 1979—87, ptnr., 1987—92, of counsel, 1998—99; sr. counsel automotive Allied Signal, Inc., Southfield, Mich., 1992—93, v.p., gen. counsel automotive, 1993—97; sr. v.p., gen. counsel, sec. Gt. Lakes Chem. Corp., Indpls., 1999—. Co-author: (book) Litigating the Commercial Case, 1992. Bd. dirs. New Enterprise Forum, Ann Arbor, 1999. Recipient Disting. Brief award, Thomas M. Cooley Law Sch., 1987. Jewish. Avocations: tennis, running. Corporate, general, Antitrust, Mergers and acquisitions. Office: Gt Lakes Chem Corp 9025 N River Rd Ste 400 Indianapolis IN 46240 Office Fax: 317-705-6414. Business E-Mail: jlipshaw@glcc.com.

LIPSHUTZ, ROBERT JEROME, lawyer, former government official; b. Atlanta, Dec. 27, 1921; s. Allen A. and Edith (Gavronski) L.; m. Barbara Sorelle Levin, Feb. 16, 1950 (dec.); children: Randall M., Judith Ann, Wendy Jean, Debbie Sue; m. Betty Beck Rosenberg, Feb. 10, 1973; stepchildren: Robert, Nancy Fay. JD, U. Ga., 1943. Bar: Ga. 1943, D.C. 1980. Practice in, Atlanta, 1947-77, 79—; ptnr. firm Lipshutz, Greenblatt & King, 1979—. Counsel to Pres. U.S., Washington, 1977-79 Past vice chmn. Ga. Bd. Human Resources; treas., legal counsel Jimmy Carter Presdl. campaign com., 1976; trustee The Carter Ctr.; adv. com. Jimmy Carter Libr. Lt. AUS, 1943-46. Mem. Am., Ga., Atlanta, D.C. bar assns., Atlanta Lawyers Club, Atlanta., B'nai B'rith (past pres., Disting. Svc. award). Jewish (past pres. The Temple). Office: Lipshutz Greenblatt & King Harris Tower 233 Peachtree St Ste 2300 Atlanta GA 30303-1504

LIPSIG, ETHAN, lawyer; b. N.Y.C., Dec. 11, 1948; s. Daniel Allen and Haddassah (Adler) L. BA, Pomona Coll., 1969; postgrad., Oxford U., 1969-70; JD, UCLA, 1974. Bar: U.S. Dist. Ct. (cen. dist.) Calif. 1974, U.S. Ct. Appeals (9th cir.) 1974, U.S Tax Ct. 1978. Author: Individual Retirement Arrangements, 1980, Downsizing, 1996. Mem. ABA (tax and labor rels. sect.), Calif. C. of C., Order of Coif, Soc. Fellows of Huntington Libr., Calif. Club, L.A. Men's Garden Club. Avocations: travel, horticulture, wine, music, art. Labor (including EEOC, Fair Labor Standards Act, labor-management relations, NLRB, OSHA), Pension, profit-sharing, and employee benefits. Home: 280 California Ter Pasadena CA 91105-1515 Office: Paul Hastings Janofsky & Walker LLP 515S Flower St Fl 25 Los Angeles CA 90071-2280

LIPSKY, BURTON G. lawyer; b. Syracuse, N.Y., May 29, 1937; s. Abraham and Pauline (Leichtner); m. Elaine B. Mannheimer, July 27, 1967; 1 child, Erika S., m. Carol S. Samberg, Feb. 4, 1973; 1 child, Andrew H. BBA, U. Mich., 1959; JD summa cum laude, Syracuse U., 1962. Bar: N.Y. 1962, U.S. Supreme Ct. 1967. Trial atty. U.S. Dept. Justice, Washington, 1962-67; assoc. Kaye, Scholer, Fierman, Hays & Handler, N.Y.C., 1967-72; ptnr. Delson & Gordon, N.Y.C., 1972-87, Lipsky & Stout, N.Y.C., 1991-96; pvt. practice, N.Y.C., 1996—. Mem. bd. visitors Syracuse U. Coll. of Law, 1989—; sec.-treas., dir. Robert Mapplethorpe Found., Inc., 1988—. Mem. ABA, N.Y. Bar Assn., Order of Coif, Justinian Soc., Am. Contract Bridge League (life master). Estate planning, Taxation, general, Probate (including wills, trusts). Office: 100 Park Ave 33rd Floor New York NY 10017-5586 E-mail: BurtLip@aol.com.

LIPSMAN, RICHARD MARC, lawyer, educator; b. Bklyn., Aug. 17, 1946; s. Abraham W. and Ruth (Weinstein) L.; m. Geri A. Russo, 1979; children: Eric, Dara Briana. BBA, CCNY, 1968; JD, St. John's U., Jamaica, N.Y., 1972; LLM in Taxation, Boston U., 1976. Bar: N.Y. 1973, Mass. 1975, U.S. Dist. Ct. (ea. and so. dists.) N.Y. 1977, U.S. Supreme Ct. 1978, U.S. Tax Ct. 1979; CPA, N.Y., Mass. Tax atty. Arthur Young & Co., N.Y.C., 1972-74; assoc. Gilman, McLaughlin & Hanrahan, Boston, 1974-76, Lefrak, Fischer & Meyerson, N.Y.C., 1976-77; ptnr. Tarnow, Landsman & Lipsman, N.Y.C., 1978; pvt. practice N.Y.C., 1979—. Adj. faculty Baruch Coll. CUNY, 1984-86, curriculum specialist Rsch. Found. CUNY, 1977-78; adj. faculty Pratt Inst., Bklyn., 1974, Queensboro Coll., Bayside, N.Y., 1978-80. Author, producer book/cassette program Learning Income Taxes, 1978—. Mem. ABA, AICPA, N.Y. State Bar Assn., Assn. of the Bar of the City of N.Y., N.Y. State Soc. CPA's. Jewish. General civil litigation, Private international, Taxation, general.

LIPSON, ROGER RUSSELL, lawyer; b. Lynn, Mass., May 24, 1937; s. Abraham Abel and Sally G. L.; m. Alberta Lois Grossman, Aug. 29, 1965; 1 child: Andrew Barry. AB, Boston U., 1958, LLM, 1990; JD, New Eng. Sch. Law, Boston, 1962. Bar: Mass. 1963, U.S. Dist. Ct. Mass. 1964, U.S. Tax Ct. 1990, U.S. Ct. Appeals (1st cir.) 1990, U.S. Supreme Ct. 1994. Assoc. Law Offices of Solomon Sandler, Gloucester, Mass., 1963-64, Goldman & Goldman, Lynn, Mass., 1964; pvt. practice, Lynn, Mass., 1965-71; atty. Neighborhood Legal Svcs., Lynn, Mass., 1971-72; exec. dir., gen. counsel Town of Brookline (Mass.) Rent Control Bd., 1972-87; assoc. Israel & Goldenberg, Boston, 1987-91; mem. Goldenberg, Walters & Lipson, P.A., Brookline, Mass., 1991—. Mem. Lynn City Dem. Com., 1970-72; assoc. mem. Brookline Town Dem. Com., 1992—; bd. dirs. Neighborhood Legal Svcs., Inc., 1969-71, pres., 1970-71. With USAR, 1960-66. Recipient Disting. Svc. award Lynn Jaycees, 1971, Recognition award New Eng. Realty Lodge, B'nai B'rith, Boston, 1976, 79. Mem. Mass. Bar Assn. (property sect., landlord-tenant subcom.), Mass. Conveyancers Assn., Temple Israel Brotherhood (pres. 1992-96), Rotary (pres. 1997-98, Paul Harris award 1999), Brookline Adv. Com., 1999-. Avocations: cooking, travel, guitar. General practice, Landlord-tenant, Property, real (including real estate development, water). Home: 622 Chestnut Hill Ave Brookline MA 02445-4154 Office: Goldenberg Walters & Lipson PA 7 Harvard St Ste 220 Brookline MA 02445-7979

LIPTON, MARTIN, lawyer; b. N.J., June 22, 1931; s. Samuel D. and Fannie L.; m. Susan Lytle, Feb. 17, 1982; children: James, Margaret, Katherine, Samantha BS in Econs., U. Pa., 1952; LLB, NYU, 1955. Bar: N.Y. 1956. Ptnr. Wachtell Lipton Rosen & Katz, N.Y.C., 1965—. Mem. coun. Am. Law Inst. Chmn. bd. of trustees NYU; bd. trustees NYU Law Sch.; hon. chmn. Jerusalem Found.; chmn. bd. dirs. Prep for Prep; dir. Inst. Jud. Adminstrn. Mem.: Am. Acad. Arts and Scis. Office: Wachtell Lipton Rosen & Katz 51 W 52nd St Fl 29 New York NY 10019-6150

LIPTON, RICHARD M. lawyer; b. Youngstown, Ohio, Feb. 25, 1952; s. Sanford Y. Lipton and Sarah (Kentor) Goldman; m. Jane Brennan, May 24, 1981; children: Thomas, Anne, Martin, Patricia. BA, Amherst Coll., 1974; JD, U. Chgo., 1977. Bar: Ill. 1977, D.C. 1978, U.S. Dist. Ct. (no. dist.) Ill. 1979, U.S. Dist. Ct. Appeals (D.C. and 7th cirs.) 1979, U.S. Tax Ct. 1977, U.S. Ct. Claims 1979. Law clk. to judge Hall U.S. Tax Ct., Washington, 1977—79; assoc. Isham, Lincoln & Beale, Chgo., 1979—83; ptnr. Ross & Hardies, Chgo., 1983—86; v.p. Pegasus Broadcasting, Chgo., 1986—88; ptnr. Sonnenschein Nath & Rosenthal, Chgo., 1988—99, McDermott, Will & Emery, 2000—02, Baker & McKenzie, 2003—. Contbr. articles to profl. jours. Recipient Order of Coif award, U. Chgo. Law Sch., 1977. Fellow: Am. Coll. Tax Counsel (regent 1998—); mem.: ABA (coun. dir. 1990—93, vice chair taxation sect. 1993—96, chair taxation sect. 2001—02), Chgo. Bar Assn. (subcom. chair, chair fed. taxation com. 1991—92), Conway Farms Club, Mich. Shores Club, Union League Club. Republican. Corporate taxation, Personal income taxation, State and local taxation. Office: Baker & McKenzie 130 E Randolph Chicago IL 60601

LIPTON, ROBERT STEVEN, lawyer; b. N.Y.C., May 12, 1946; s. Max and Mildred (Goodman) L.; m. Stephanie F. Kass, Aug. 8, 1971. BA, NYU, 1967, JD, 1971. Bar: N.Y. 1972, U.S. Ct. Appeals (2d cir.) 1972, U.S. Dist. Ct. (so. dist.) N.Y. 1973, U.S. Supreme Ct. 1975. Assoc. Curtis, Mallet-Prevost, Colt & Mosle, N.Y.C., 1971-80, ptnr., 1980-2001, of counsel, 2001—. Editor NYU Law Rev., 1969-71. Mem. ABA, Fed. Bar Council, N.Y. State Bar Assn., Assn. of Bar of City of N.Y., Phi Beta Kappa. Clubs: India House (N.Y.C.). Bankruptcy, General civil litigation, State civil litigation. Office: Curtis Mallet-Prevost Colt & Mosle 101 Park Ave Fl 34 New York NY 10178-0061 E-mail: rlipton@cm-p.com.

LISA, ISABELLE O'NEILL, law firm administrator, mergers and acquisitions executive; b. Phila., Mar. 12, 1934; d. Thomas Daniel and Margaret Marie (Hayes) O'Neill; m. Donald Julius Lisa, June 15, 1957; children: Richard Allan, Steven Gregory. Student, Harper Community Coll., Rolling Meadows, Ill., 1976, Scottsdale Community Coll., 1980, Ariz. State U., 1981-82, Mesa C.C., 1998—2000. Cost control clk. Curtis Pub. Co., Phila., 1952—56; sec. United Ins. Co., Annapolis, Md., 1956—57; firm adminstr., legal sec. Law Offices Donald J. Lisa, Bloomingdale, Ill., 1987; legal sec. Lisa & Kubida, P.C., Phoenix, 1987—88, firm adminstr., 1987—89, Lisa & Assocs., Phoenix, 1989—90, Lisa & Lisa, Phoenix, 1990—91, Lisa & Assocs., Scottsdale, Ariz., 1991—95, Law Offices of Donald J. Lisa, Scottsdale, 1995—98. Den mother Cub Scouts Am., Milburn, N.J., 1965; founder, pres. Pro-Tem Rutgers U. Law Wives Assn. Mem.: Assn. Catechesis of the Good Shepherd. Republican. Roman Catholic. Avocations: painting, drawing, graphic design, photography, videography. Home and Office: 6636 N 48th Street Paradise Valley AZ 85253-4056

LISHER, JAMES RICHARD, lawyer; b. Aug. 28, 1947; s. Leonard B. and Mary Jane (Rafferty) L.; m. Martha Gettelfinger, June 16, 1973; children: Jennifer, James Richard II. AB, Ind. U., 1969, JD, 1975. Bar: Ind. 1975, U.S. Dist. Ct. (so. dist.) Ind. 1975, U.S. Supreme Ct. 2000. Assoc. Rafferty & Wood, Shelbyville, Ind., 1976, Rafferty & Lisher, Shelbyville, Ind., 1976-77; dep. prosecutor Shelby County Prosecutor's Office, Shelbyville, 1976-78; ptnr. Yeager, Lisher & Baldwin, Shelbyville, 1977-96; pvt. practice, Shelbyville, 1996—. Pros. atty. Shelby County, Shelbyville, 1983-95, pub. defender, 1995—, chief pub. defender, 2000—. Speaker, faculty advisor Ind. Pros. Sch., 1986. Editor: (manual) Traffic Case

Defenses, 1982, First Law Office, 1998. Bd. dirs. Girls Club of Shelbyville, 1979-84, Bears of Blue River Festival, Shelbyville, 1982-2002; pres. Shelby County Internat. Rels. Coun., 1997-2003. Recipient Citation of Merit, Young Lawyers Assn. Mem. ATLA, Nat. Assn. Criminal Def. Lawyers, Ind. Pub. Defender Assn., Ind. State Bar Assn. (bd. dirs. young lawyer sect. 1979-83, bd. dirs. gen. practice sect. 1996-98, treas. 1997-98, vice-chmn. 1998-99, chmn. 2000-01), Shelby County Bar Assn. (sec.-treas. 1986, v.p. 1987, pres. 1988), Ind. Prosecuting Attys. Assn. (bd. dirs. 1985-95, sec.-treas. 1987, v.p. 1988, pres. 1990), Masons, Elks, Lions. Criminal, General practice, Personal injury (including property damage). Home: 106 Western Trce Shelbyville IN 46176-9765 Office: 407 S Harrison St Shelbyville IN 46176-2170

LISHER, JOHN LEONARD, lawyer; b. Indpls., Sept. 19, 1950; s. Leonard Boyd and Mary Jane (Rafferty) L.; m. Mary Katherine Sturmon, Aug. 17, 1974. BA in History with honors, JD, Ind. U., 1975. Bar: Ind. 1975. Dep. atty. gen. State of Ind., Indpls., 1975-78; asst. corp. counsel City of Indpls., 1978-81; assoc. Osborn & Hiner, Indpls., 1981-86; ptnr. Osborn, Hiner & Lischer, P.C., 1986—. Vol. Mayflower Classic, Indpls., 1981-86; pres. Brendonwood Common Inc.; asst. vol. coord. Marion County Rep. Com., Indpls., 1979-80; vol. Don. Bogard for Atty. Gen., Indpls., 1980, Steve Goldsmith for Prosecutor, Indpls., 1979-83, Sheila Suess for Congress, Indpls., 1980. Recipient Outstanding Young Man of Am. award Jaycees, 1979, 85, Indpls. Jaycees, 1980. Mem. ABA, Ind. Bar Assn., Indpls. Bar Assn. (membership com.), Assn. Trial Lawyers Am., Ind. U. Alumni Assn., Hoosier Alumni Assn. (charter, founder, pres.), Ind. Trial Lawyers Assn., Ind. Def. Lawyers Assn., Ind. U. Coll. Arts and Scis. (bd. dirs. 1983-92, pres. 1986-87), Wabash Valley Alumni Assn. (charter), Founders Club, Pres. Club, Phi Beta Kappa, Eta Sigma Phi, Phi Eta Sigma, Delta Xi Alumni Assn. (Outstanding Alumnus award 1975, 76, 79, 83), Delta Xi Housing Corp. (pres.), Pi Kappa Alpha (midwest regional pres. 1977-86, parliamentarian nat. conv. 1982, del. convs. 1978-80, 82, 84, 86, trustee Meml. Found. 1986-91. Presbyterian. Avocations: reading, golf, jogging, roman coin collecting. State civil litigation, Insurance, Personal injury (including property damage). Home: 5725 Hunterglen Rd Indianapolis IN 46226-1019 Office: Osborn Hiner & Lisher PC 8500 Keystone Xing Ste 480 Indianapolis IN 46240-2460 E-mail: jlisher@ohllaw.com.

LISI, MARY M. federal judge; BA, U. R.I., 1972; JD, Temple U., 1977. Tchr. history Prout Meml. High Sch., Wakefield, R.I., 1975-76; law clk. U.S. Atty., Providence, R.I., 1976, Phila., 1976-77; asst. pub. defender R.I. Office Pub. Defender, 1977-81; asst. child advocate Office Child Advocate, 1981-82; also. pvt. practice atty. Providence, 1981-82; dir. office ct. appointed spl. advocate R.I. Family Ct., 1982-87; dep. disciplinary counsel office disciplinary counsel R.I. Supreme Ct., 1988-90, chief disciplinary counsel, 1990-94; U.S. Dist. judge Dist. Ct., Providence, Dist. R.I. (1st cir.), Providence, 1994—. Mem. Select Com. to Investigate Failure of R.I. Share and Deposit Indemnity Corp., 1991-92. Recipient Providence 350 award, 1986, Meritorious Svc. to Children of Am. award, 1987. Office: Fed Bldg and US Courthouse 1 Exchange Ter Providence RI 02903-1744

LISONI, JOSEPH LOUIS, lawyer; b. LA, Mar. 13, 1947; s. Joseph Arthur and Frances Genevieve Lisoni; married, 1984. BA in Polit. Sci., St. Mary's Coll., 1969; JD, U. Calif., San Francisco, 1972. Bar: Calif. 1972, D.C. 1975. Founder Lisoni & Lisoni, Pasadena, Calif., 1972—. Gen. counsel Radio and TV Newscasters Assn., Nat. Jockeys Guild. Dem. nominee 27th congl. dist. U.S. Ho. of Reps., Calif., 1980; active James Rogan for U.S. Ho. of Reps. campaign, 1998, 2000. Mem.: Order Sons of Italy in Am., Italian Am. Lawyers Assn. Democrat. Roman Catholic. Achievements include settling largest Firestone Steeltex tire defect case in the world; won 98.5% of all cases during career. Avocations: swimming, weightlifting. Product liability. Home: 1435 Rutherford Dr Pasadena CA 91103 Office: Lisoni & Lisoni 225 S Lake Ave Pasadena CA 91101 Office Fax: 626-564-6004. E-mail: lisoni@earthlink.net.

LISS, MATTHEW M. lawyer; b. Oak Park, Ill., 1966; BS in Acctg., BS in Fin., So. Ill. U., 1991, MS in Acctg., JD, So. Ill. U., 1994. Bar: Ill. 1994, Ga. 1998. Assoc. Phillip G. Neal and Assocs., Chgo., 1994-95; v.p. and gen. counsel Innovative Health Svcs., Inc., Tampa, Fla., 1995-98; ptnr. Swift, Currie, McGhee and Hiers, LLP, Atlanta, 1998—. Commercial, contracts (including sales of goods; commercial financing), Property, real (including real estate development, water), Estate taxation. Home: 4184 Nashoba Dr NE Roswell GA 30075-1667 Office: Swift Currie McGhee & Hiers LLP Ste 300 The Peachtree 1355 Peachtree St NE Atlanta GA 30309 Office Fax: 404-888-6199. E-mail: mml@scmhlaw.com.

LISS, NORMAN, lawyer; b. N.Y.C., May 7, 1932; m. Sandra Hirsch, Feb. 28, 1959. BS, NYU, 1952, LLB, 1955. Bar: N.Y. 1955, U.S. Dist. Ct. (so. dist.) N.Y. 1961, U.S. Dist. Ct (ea. dist.) N.Y. 1962. Assoc. Booth, Lipton & Lipton, New York, 1956-57, Seymour Detsky, New York, 1957-58; pvt. practice New York, 1958—. Cons. to Portugal Re-Cultural Events in U.S.; jour. chair UJA Trial Lawyers USCG Acad. Law Day, 1987, 89, 94, 98. Contbr. articles to profl. jours. Chmn. Bronx County Bar divsn. United Jewish Appeal, Hist. Documents Exhbn., Operation Sail, 1986, USCG Acad. Law Day, 1987, 89; chmn. devel. Ellis Island Restoration Commn.; counsel N.Y. State Statue of Liberty Centennial Com., Mayor's Handicapped Citizens Adv. Bd., N.Y.C., Coun. on Arts; mem. Bronx County 350 Commn., N.Y.C. Commn. for Presdl. Conv.; rep., counsel N.Y.C. Com. on Bicentennial of U.S. Constitution; cons. Soc. Congl. Medal of Honor; commd. lt. col. N.Y. Guard Judge Advocate Gen. Unit; exec. com. Am. Jewish Congress; trustee Am. Jewish Hist. Soc.; co-chmn. 350th Ann. of 1st Jewish Am. Settlement in U.S.; Def. of Liberty 9/11, N.Y. Recipient Disting. Humanitarian award Inst. of Applied Human Dynamics, Meritorious Pub. Svc. award USCG, 1989, 9/11 Def. of Liberty medal N.Y. Guard; named Man of Yr. Am. Jewish Congress, Man of Yr. Kinneret Sch., 1985. Mem. ABA, N.Y. Bar Assn., Bronx County Bar Assn., Am. Arbitration Assn. (panel arbitrators), Assn. Trial Lawyers Am., Law Day Outreach Com., NYU Alumni Assn. (adv. coun.). Personal injury (including property damage), Education and schools, Property, real (including real estate development, water). Home: 2727 Palisade Ave Bronx NY 10463-1018 Office: 200 W 57th St New York NY 10019-3211

LISTER, STEPHANIE JOYCE, lawyer; b. Spokane, Wash., July 5, 1962; d. David L. and Donna J. Johnson; m. James D. Lister, July 19, 1996. BA, Gonzaga U., Spokane, 1984, JD, 1987. Bar: Wash. Dep. prosecutor Kootenai County Prosecutors Office, Coeur d'Alene, Idaho, 1987; asst. U.S. atty. Dept. of Justice, Ea. Dist. Wash., Spokane, 1987—. Office: US Atty's Office PO Box 1494 Spokane WA 99210-1494

LISTON, STEPHANIE W. lawyer; b. Galesburg, Ill., Mar. 15, 1958; d. Thomas Sherwood and Susan Way Liston; m. Edward Anthony Oakden, Dec. 29, 1989 (div. May 1999); 1 child, Genevieve Marianne Liston Oakden. BA, Colo. Coll., 1980; JD, U. San Diego/U. Notre Dame, 1983; LLM in English Law, Cambridge (Eng.) U., 1984. Bar: Tex. 1985, D.C. 1988, Supreme Ct. Eng. and Wales 1994. Assoc. Fulbright & Jaworski, London, 1984, Houston, 1984—87, Washington, 1987—89; sr. atty. MCI Comm. Corp., Washington, 1990—92; mgr. Freshfields, London, 1992—96; ptnr. Baker & McKenzie, London, 1997—9999, McDermott, Will & Emery, London, 1999—. Mem.: European Competitive Telecom. Assn. (dir. 2001—), Internat. Bar Assn. (vice chmn. comm. com. 2001—), Oxford and Cambridge Club. Corporate, general, Communications. Office: McDermott Will and Emery 7 Bishopsgate London EC2N 3AQ England

LITAN, ROBERT ELI, lawyer, economist; b. Wichita, Kans., May 16, 1950; s. David and Shirley Hermine (Krischer) Litan. BS in Econs., U. Pa., 1972; MPhil in Econs., Yale U., 1976, JD, 1977, PhD in Econs., 1987. Bar: (D.C.) 1980. Rsch. asst. Brookings Instn., 1972-73; instr., then lectr. econs. Yale U., 1975-76; energy cons. NAS, 1975-77; regulation and energy specialist Pres.'s Coun. Econ. Advs., 1977-79; assoc. Arnold & Porter, Washington, 1979-82; assoc., then ptnr. and counsel Powell, Goldstein, Frazer & Murphy, Washington, 1982-90; sr. fellow Brookings Instn., Washington, 1984-92, dir. Ctr. for Econ. Progress, 1987-93; dep. asst. atty. gen. Dept. Justice, Washington, 1993-95; assoc. dir. Office of Mgmt. and Budget, Washington, 1995-96; v.p., dir. econ. studies Brookings Inst., Washington, Cabot family chair in econs. Cons. Inst. Liberty and Democracy, Lima, Peru, 1985—88; vis. lectr. Yale U. Law Sch., 1985—86; mem. Presdl. Congl. Commn. Causes of Savs. and Loan Crisis, 1991—92; cons. U.S. Dept. Treasury, 1996—97, 1999—2000. Author: Energy Modeling for an Uncertain Future, 1978, Reforming Federal Regulation, 1983, Saving Free Trade: A Pragmatic Approach, 1986, What Should Banks Do?, 1987, Liability: Perspectives and Policy, 1988, American Living Standards: Threats and Challenges, 1988, Blueprint for Restructuring America's Financial Institutions, 1989, Banking Industry in Turmoil, 1990, The Revolution in U.S. Finance, 1991, The Liability Maze, 1991, Down in the Dumps: Administration of the Unfair Trade Laws, 1991, The Future of American Banking, 1992, Growth With Equity, 1993, Assessing Bank Reform, 1993, Verdict, 1993, Financial Regulation in a Global Economy, 1994, Footing the Bill for Superfund Cleanups, 1995, American Finance for the 21st Century, 1997, Globaphobia: Confronting Fears of Open Trade, 1998, None of Your Business: World Data Flows and the European Privacy Directive, 1998, The GAAP Gap, 2000, Beyond the Dot.Coms, 2001, Sticking Together: The Israeli Experiment in Pluralism, 2002, Protecting the American Homeland, 2002, Following the Money: Corporate Disclosure After Enron, 2003; contbr. articles to profl. jours. Recipient Class of 1964 award, U. Pa., W. Gordon award, 1972, Albert A. Berg award, 1971, 1972, Felix S. Cohen award, Yale U., 1976, Silver medal, Royal Soc. Arts, 1972; fellow Thouron, Eng., 1972. Mem.: ABA, Coun. on Fgn. Rels., Am. Econs. Assn. Democrat. Home: 5801 Nicholson Ln #831 North Bethesda MD 20852 Office: Brookings Instn 1775 Massachusetts Ave NW Washington DC 20036-2103 E-mail: rlitan@brook.edu.

LITCH, JOHN MICHAEL, lawyer; b. Detroit, Oct. 14, 1927; m. June E. Meyers, June 21, 1953; children: Brian M., Nancy A. LLB, Detroit Coll. Law, 1951, JD, 1968. Mng. ptnr. Litch, Gordon & Assocs., Center Line, Mich., 1952—. Cpl. USAF, 1946-48. Mem. Fla. State Bar Assn., Mich. State Bar Assn., Macomb Probate Bar Assn., Macomb Fin. Planning and Probate Assn. Estate planning, Probate (including wills, trusts), Property, real (including real estate development, water). Office: Litch Gordon & Assocs 26224 Van Dyke Ave Center Line MI 48015-1220

LITMAN, RICHARD CURTIS, lawyer; b. Phila., May 2, 1957; s. Benjamin Norman and Bette Etta (Saunders) L.; m. Cheryl Lynn Goldstein, May 28, 1989; children: Amanda Rose, Jessica Brooke, Daniel Grant, Victoria Grace. BS, Union Coll., 1973; JD cum laude, U. Miami, 1979; LLM in Patent and Trade Regulation, George Washington U., 1980; M of Forensic Sci., Antioch Sch. Law, 1981. Bar: D.C. 1979, Fla. 1979, Pa. 1979, Va. 1980, Md. 1984, U. Ct. Appeals (fed. cir.), U.S. Patent and Trademark Office, U.S. Supreme Ct. Pvt. practice, Arlington, Va., 1983—. Instr. continuing legal edn.; organizer, dir. James Monroe Bank. Contbr. articles to profl. jours. Fellow Food and Drug Law Inst., 1979-80; named Small Bus. of Yr. Arlington C. of C., 1995. Mem. ABA, Fed. Bar Assn., Am. Acad. Forensic Scis., Am. Intellectual Property Law Assn.(chair), Arlington County Bar Assn., DC Bar Assn., Econ. Devel. Commn., Masons (32d degree Scottish Rite), Shriners. Intellectual property, Patent, Trademark and copyright. Office: Litman Law Offices Ltd Patent Law Bldg 3717 Columbia Pike Arlington VA 22204-4255 E-mail: litman@4patent.com.

LITMAN, ROSLYN MARGOLIS, lawyer, educator; b. N.Y.C., Sept. 30, 1928; d. Harry and Dorothy (Perlow) Margolis; m. S. David Litman, Nov. 22, 1950; children: Jessica, Hannah, Harry. BA, U. Pitts., 1949, JD, 1952. Bar: Pa. 1952; approved arbitrator for complex comml. litigation and employment law. Practiced in Pitts., 1952—; ptnr. firm Litman Law Firm, 1952—; adj. prof. U. Pitts. Law Sch., 1958—. Permanent del. Conf. U.S. Circuit Ct. Appeals for 3d Circuit; past chair dist. adv. group U.S. Dist. Ct. (we. dist.) Pa., 1991-94, mem. steering com. for dist. adv. group, 1991—; chmn. Pitts. Pub. Parking Authority, 1970-74; mem. curriculum com. Pa. Bar Inst., 1986—, bd. dirs., 1972-82. Bd. dirs. United Jewish Fedn., 1999—, cmty. rels. com., co-chair ch./state com.; bd. dirs. City Theatre, 1999—. Recipient Roscoe Pound Found. award for Excellence in Tchg. Trial Advocacy, 1996, Disting. Alumnus award U. Pitts. Sch. Law, 1996; named Fed. Lawyer of Yr., We. Pa. Chpt. FBA, 1999. Mem. ABA (del., litigation sect., anti-trust health care com.), ACLU (nat. bd. dirs., Marjorie H. Matson Civil Libertarian award Greater Pitts. chpt. 1999), Pa. Bar Assn. (bd. govs. 1976-79), Allegheny County Bar Assn. (bd. govs. 1972-74, pres. 1975, Woman of Yr. 2001), Allegheny County Acad. Trial Lawyers (charter), Order of Coif. Federal civil litigation, State civil litigation, General practice. Home: 5023 Frew St Pittsburgh PA 15213-3829 Office: One Oxford Centre 34th Fl Pittsburgh PA 15219

LITSCHGI, A. BYRNE, lawyer; b. Charleston, S.C., Dec. 31, 1920; s. Albert William and Mary Catherine (Byrne) L.; m. Mary Elaine Herring, Sept. 13, 1952. BBA, U. Fla., 1941; JD, Harvard U., 1948. Bar: Fla. 1948, D.C. 1950. Atty. Office Gen. Counsel, Treasury Dept., Washington, 1949-52; legis. asst. to U.S. senator, 1952; mem. firm Hedrick & Lane, Washington, 1953-60, Coles, Himes & Litschgi, Tampa, Fla., 1960-62, Shackleford, Farrior, Stallings & Evans, 1962-87, Dykema Gossett, Tampa, Fla., 1988-92; chmn. SL Industries, Inc., 1976-92; mem. firm Holland & Knight, Tampa, 1992—. Incorporator, dir. Communications Satellite Corp., 1962-64; mem. Fla. Jud. Council, 1965-68, U.S. Internal Revenue Commn. Adv. Group, 1967-68 Mem. Harvard Law Sch. Assn. (nat. council 1956-61), ABA (chmn. excise and miscellaneous tax com. tax sect. 1956-59), Fla. Bar, Bar Assn. D.C. Office: Holland & Knight PO Box 1288 Tampa FL 33601-1288

LITTELL, RICHARD GREGORY, lawyer; b. Hartford, Conn., Feb. 7, 1931; s. Elliot Manning and Lilyan Ruth (Stiegel) L.; m. Barbara Anne Diggs, Mar. 31, 1962 (div. Dec. 1983); children: John Gregory, Susan Anne. BA, Cornell U., 1953; JD, Harvard U., 1956; MFA, Goucher Coll., 2001. Bar: D.C., Calif., N.Y. Asst. gen. counsel Civil Aeronautics Bd., Washington, 1967-69, assoc. gen. counsel, 1969-71, gen. counsel, 1973-74, Postal Rate Commn., Washington, 1971-73; ptnr. Dickstein, Shapiro & Morin, Washington, 1974-80, Bishop, Cook, Purcell & Reynolds, Washington, 1980-90; pvt. practice Washington, 1990—. Author: Endangered and Threatened Species, 1992; contbr. numerous articles to profl. publs., gen. interest mags. and newspapers. Chmn. Air Pollution Adv. Com., Met. Washington Coun. of Govts., 1965-67. Mem. Cosmos Club, Nat. Press Club, Belle Haven Country Club. Avocations: flyfishing, tennis. Aviation, Environmental, Utilities, public. Home: 613 S Fairfax St Alexandria VA 22314-3833 Office: 1220 19th St NW Ste 400 Washington DC 20036-2438

LITTENBERG, MICHAEL RICHARD, lawyer; b. N.Y.C., Sept. 27, 1965; BS, Ind. U., 1987; JD, Tulane U., 1990. Bar: N.Y. 1991. Ptnr. Schulte Roth & Zabel LLP, N.Y.C., 1996—. Contbr. articles to profl. jours. Mem.: Manhattan C. of C. (bd. dirs. 2001—). Mergers and acquisitions, Securities, Corporate, general, Venture. Office: Schulte Roth & Zabel LLP 919 Third Ave New York NY 10022 Office Fax: 212-593-5955. E-mail: michael.littenberg@srz.com.

LITTERAL, DANIEL PACE, lawyer; b. Washington, Aug. 10, 1955; s. Kelley Litteral and Kathleen Margaret Olson; m. Katherine Hedwig Madson, Jan. 22, 1977 (div. Oct. 1998); 1 child, Jennifer Erin. BA, Wake Forest U., 1976; JD with honors, U. N.D., 1981. Bar: Md. 1981, Ariz. 2000, U.S. Dist. Ct. Md. 1982. Lawyer, prin. Litteral & Litteral Chartered, Silver Spring, Md., 1981-84, Rockville, Md., 1984-88; pvt. practice law Rockville, 1988—2001; lawyer, assoc. gen. counsel U. Phoenix, 2002—. Adj. lectr. U. N.D., Grand Forks, 1980-81; lectr. Coll. Bd., Phila., 1997, Assn. Ind. Md. Schs., Potomac, 1998, lectr. ed. law assoc., 2001. Author (monthly column) Leisure Living, 1996-99, (profl. newsletter) Pvt. Ednl. Newsletter, 1998, 2001. Capt. U.S. Army/USAR, 1976-83. Mem. Md. State Bar Assn., Montgomery County Bar Assn, State Bar of Ariz. Avocation: private pilot. General civil litigation, Education and schools, Estate planning. Office: U Phoenix 4615 E Elmwood Dr Phoenix AZ 85040

LITTLE, KEVIN GERARD, lawyer; b. N.Y.C., Feb. 25, 1966; s. Henry Leroy Little, Jr. and Bertha Marie Little; m. Virna Liza Santos, Aug. 18, 1990; 1 child, Enrique Raymond Santos. BA cum laude, Harvard U., 1987, JD cum laude, 1990. Bar: Calif. 1990, U.S. Supreme Ct. 1994, U.S. Ct. Appeals (all circuits) 1994, U.S. Ct. Fed. Claims 1994, U.S. Dist. Ct. (cent. dist.) Calif. 1990, U.S. Dist. Ct. (ea. dist.) Calif. 1995, U.S. Dist. Ct. (no. dist.) Calif. 1998, U.S. Dist. Ct. P.R., U.S. Dist. Ct. (we. dist.) Tex. Assoc. O'Melveny & Myers, L.A., 1991—92; law clk. Hon. Consuelo B. Marshall, L.A., 1991—92, Hon. Cecil F. Poole, San Francisco, 1992—93; solo practitioner San Juan, PR, 1993—95; atty. Frampton, Williams & Little, Fresno, Calif., 1995—2001; solo practitioner Fresno, Calif., 2001—. Vis. atty. Boalt Hall Sch. Law, Berkeley, Calif., 2001; guest spkr. Ea. Dist. Calif. Law Enforcement Summit, Squaw Valley, 2002, Bay Area Police Watch, San Francisco, 1999—2000. Sponsor Big Bros./Big Sisters, Fresno, 1996—; participant Campaign Against Prop 209, Fresno, 1997. Named one of most tenacious litigators in Calif., Calif. Lawyers Mag.; recipient Svc. award, Helping Our Own Destiny, Fresno, 1997, San Joaquin Coll. Law, 1998—. Democrat. Civil rights, Criminal, Appellate. Office: 1275 E Province Fresno CA 93780 Office Fax: 559-486-4759. E-mail: fwllaw@aol.com.

LITTLEFIELD, ROY EVERETT, III, association executive, legal educator; b. Nashua, N.H., Dec. 6, 1952; s. Roy Everett and Mary Ann (Prestipino) L.; m. Amy Root; children: Leah Marie, Roy Everett IV, Christy Louise. BA, Dickinson Coll., 1975; MA, Catholic U. Am., 1976, PhD, 1979. Aide U.S. Senator Thomas McIntyre, Democrat, N.H., 1975-78, Nordy Hoffman, U.S. Senate Sergeant-at-arms, N.H., 1979; dir. govt. rels. Nat. Tire Dealers and Retreaders Assn., Washington, N.H., 1979-84; exec. dir. Svc. Sta. and Automotive Repair Assn., Washington, NH, 1984—2003; exec. v.p. Svc. Sta. Dealers of Am., 1994—2003, Tire Industry Assn., 2003—. Cons. Internat. Tire and Rubber Assn., 1984, Tire Industry Assn.; mem. faculty Cath. U. Am., Washington, 1979—. Author: William Randolph Hearst: His Role in American Progressivism, 1980, The Economic Recovery Act, 1982, The Surface: Transportation Assistance Act, 1984; editor Nozzle mag.; contbr. numerous articles to legal jours. Mem. Nat. Dem. Club, 1978—. Mem. Am. Soc. Legal History, Md. Hwy. User's Fedn. (pres.), Nat. Hwy. User's Fedn. (sec.), Nat. Capitol Area Transp. Fedn. (v.p.), N.H. Hist. Soc., Kansas City C. of C., Capitol Hill Club, Phi Alpha Theta. Roman Catholic. Home: 1707 Pepper Tree Ct Bowie MD 20721-3021 Office: 9420 Annapolis Rd Ste 307 Lanham Seabrook MD 20706-3061

LITTMAN, DAVID BERNARD, lawyer; b. Plainfield, N.J., Oct. 16, 1949; s. Alexander and Muriel Roslyn (Block) L.; m. Deborah Joy Fields, Nov. 9, 1980; 1 child, Alexandra Ellen Pauline. AB, Lafayette Coll., 1970; JD, Rutgers U., 1973. Bar: N.J. 1974, U.S. Dist. Ct. N.J. 1974, U.S. Supreme Ct. 1983; cert. criminal trial atty. Assoc. Winetsky & Winetsky, Linden, N.J., 1973-76; pvt. practice Linden, N.J., 1976—. Mcpl. pub. defender Scotch Plains Twp., N.J., 1999. Mem. ABA, N.J. Bar Assn., Union County Bar Assn., Linden Bar Assn. (pres. 1977-80), N.J. Trial Lawyers, Masons (sec. Highland Park lodge 1979-86, treas. 1987—, gen. counselor M.W. grand lodge 1991—). Democrat. Jewish. Criminal, Family and matrimonial, General practice. Home: 1557 Ashbrook Dr Scotch Plains NJ 07076-2854 Office: 129 N Wood Ave Linden NJ 07036-4227

LITVACK, SANFORD MARTIN, lawyer; b. Bklyn., Apr. 29, 1936; s. Murray and Lee M. (Korman) L.; m. Judith E. Goldenson, Dec. 30, 1956; children: Mark, Jonathan, Sharon, Daniel. BA, U. Conn., 1956; LLB, Georgetown U., 1959. Bar: N.Y. 1964, D.C. 1979. Trial atty. antitrust div. Dept. Justice, Washington, 1959-61, asst. atty. gen., 1980-81; assoc. firm Donovan, Leisure, Newton & Irvine, NYC, 1961-69, ptnr., 1969-80, 81-86, Dewey, Ballantine, Bushby, Palmer & Wood, NYC, 1987-91; vice chmn. bd. The Walt Disney Co., Burbank, Calif., 1991—2001, also bd. dirs.; ptnr. Quinn, Emanuel, Urquhart, Oliver & Hedges, 2001. Bd. dirs. Bet Tzedek. Fellow Am. Coll. Trial Lawyers; mem. ABA, Fed. Bar Coun., N.Y. State Bar Assn. (sec. antitrust sect. 1974-77, chmn. antitrust sect. 1985-86), Va. Bar Assn., Calif. Inst. of Arts (bd. dirs.), Am. Arbitration Assn. (bd. dirs.). Federal civil litigation, General civil litigation. Office: Quinn Emanuel Urquhart Oliver & Hedges 865 S Figueroa St Los Angeles CA 90017*

LITVIN, WILLIAM JOSEPH, lawyer; b. West Chester, Pa., Feb. 14, 1948; s. Milton and Margaret Rose (Becker) L. B.B.A., Temple U., 1970; J.D., Dickinson Sch. Law, 1973. Bar: Pa. 1973, U.S. Dist. Ct. (ea. dist.) Pa. 1977, U.S. Supreme Ct. 1977, U.S. Ct. Appeals (3d cir.) 1980. Sole practice, West Chester, 1973-83; ptnr. firm Saling & Litvin, West Chester, 1983— ; spl. master in divorce for Chester County, Pa., 1980—86. Served to capt. U.S. Army, 1973. Mem. Pa. Bar Assn., Chester County Bar Assn. Republican. Family and matrimonial, General practice. Office: Saling & Litvin 442 N High St West Chester PA 19380-2405

LITWIN, BURTON HOWARD, lawyer; b. Chgo., July 26, 1944; s. Manuel and Rose (Boehm) L.; m. Nancy I. Stein, Aug. 25, 1968; children: Robin Litwin Levine, Keith Harris, Jill Stacy. BBA with honors, Roosevelt U., 1966; JD cum laude, Northwestern U., 1970. Bar: Ill. 1970, U.S. Dist. Ct. (no. dist.) Ill. 1970, U.S. Tax Ct. 1971, U.S. Ct. Fed. Claims 1983; CPA, Ill. Sr. counsel Neal, Gerber & Eisenberg, Chgo., 2002—. Author chpts. of books; contbr. articles to profl. jours. Recipient Gold Watch award Fin. Execs. Inst., Chgo., 1965. Mem. ABA (chmn. nonfiler task force for No. Ill. 1992-94), Chgo. Bar Assn. (chmn. adminstrv. practice subcom., fed. taxation subcom. 1982-83) Avocations: roses, painting, photography. Corporate taxation, Taxation, general, Personal income taxation. Office: Neal Gerber & Eisenberg Two N LaSalle St Ste 2200 Chicago IL 60602-3801 E-mail: blitwin@ngelaw.com.

LITWIN, PAUL JEFFREY, lawyer; b. Boston, May 4, 1955; s. Robert I. and Tamara D. L.; m. Robin Gile, June 28, 1986; children: Peter Hill, Alexander James. BA with honors, U. Wis., 1977; JD cum laude, Suffolk U., 1983. Paralegal Hale and Dorr, Boston, 1979-80; clk. to presiding justice Mass. Superior Ct., Boston, 1983-84; staff atty. Mass. Supreme Ct., Boston, 1984-85; sports, entertainment atty. Bob Woolf Assocs., Boston, 1985-86; ptnr. entertainment law practice Shames & Litwin, Boston, 1986—; asst. prof. entertainment law Berklee Coll. Music, Boston, 1990-97, Emerson Coll., Boston, 1995-96. Comml. arbitrator Am. Arbitration Assn., Boston, 1991-97. Co-chmn. Brookline, Mass. Dem. Com., 1984-86; mem. Concord, Mass. Dem. Com., 1986—. Mem. ABA, Mass. Bar Assn., Boston Bar Assn. (founder, chmn. sports and entertainment com. 1987-89). Democrat. Avocations: skiing, sailing, tennis, travel. Entertainment, Intellectual property, Property, real (including real estate development, water). Home: 23 Wright Farm Concord MA 01742-1528 Office: Shames & Litwin 10 St James Ave Boston MA 02116 E-mail: PLitwin@Shames-Litwin.com.

LIU, GE, lawyer, arbitrator; b. Beijing, Dec. 18, 1957; s. Yibin Liang and Yuncai Liu; m. Lynn Z. Lin, Feb. 1, 1992; children: George J.B., Louis Y.S. LLB, Peking U., Beijing, 1982; LLM, U. Fla., 1988. Bar: China 1984. Asst. prof. Peking U. Law Sch., Beijing, 1982—86; China law counsel Jenner & Block, Chgo., 1988—97; ptnr. Jun He Law Offices, Beijing, 1997—, mng.

ptnr., 1999—. Arbitrator China Internat. Econ. and Trade Arbitration Commn., Beijing, 2000—. Mem. bd. advisors Peking U. Legal Sys. Rsch. Ctr., Beijing, 0199—2002. Recipient Silver medal, China Nat. Volleyball League U. and Colls., Qingdao City, China, 1980. Mem.: Beijing Bar Assn. (bd. dirs. 2000—), China Bar Assn. (internat. practice com. 1998—), Pine Valley Golf Club (founder), Beijing Links Golf Club (founder), Beijing Am. Club (founder). Avocations: golf, reading. Corporate, general, Mergers and acquisitions, Entertainment. Office: Jun He Law Offices 8 N Jianguoman Ave Beijing 100005 China Fax: 86-10 8519-1350. E-mail: liug@junhe.com.

LIVAUDAIS, MARCEL, JR., federal judge; b. New Orleans, Mar. 3, 1925; m. Carol Black (dec.); children: Julie, Marc, Durel. BA, Tulane U., 1945, JD, 1949. Bar: La. 1949. Assoc. Boswell & Loeb, New Orleans, 1949-50, 52-56; ptnr. Boswell Loeb & Livaudais, New Orleans, 1956-60, Loeb & Livaudais, 1960-67, 71-77, Loeb Dillon & Livaudais, 1967-71; U.S. magistrate, 1977-84; judge U.S. Dist. Ct. (ea. dist.) La., New Orleans, 1984-96, sr. judge, 1996—. Mem. Am. Judicature Soc. Office: US Dist Ct C-405 US Courthouse 500 Camp St New Orleans LA 70130-3313

LIVELY, PIERCE, federal judge; b. Louisville, Aug. 17, 1921; s. Henry Thad and Ruby Durrett (Keating) L.; m. Amelia Harrington, May 25, 1946; children: Susan, Katherine, Thad. AB, Centre Coll., Ky., 1943; LL.B., U. Va., 1948. Bar: Ky. 1948. Individual practice law, Danville, Ky., 1949—57; mem. firm Lively and Rodes, Danville, 1957—72; judge U.S. Ct. Appeals (6th cir.), Cin., 1972—, chief judge, 1983—88, sr. judge, 1988—97, ret., 1997. Mem. Ky. Commn. on Economy and Efficiency in Govt., 1963—65, Ky. Jud. Advisory Com., 1972. Trustee Centre Coll. With USNR, 1943—46. Mem.: ABA, Am. Judicature Soc., Raven Soc., Order of Coif, Omicron Delta Kappa, Phi Beta Kappa. Presbyterian.

LIVINGSTON, BOB (ROBERT LINLITHGOW LIVINGSTON JR.), lawyer, former congressman; b. Colorado Springs, Colo., Apr. 30, 1943; s. Robert L. and Dorothy (Godwin) Livingston; m. Bonnie Robichaux, Sept. 13, 1965; children: Robert Linlithgow III, Richard Godwin, David Barkley, SuShan Alida. BA in Econs., Tulane U., 1967, JD, 1968; postgrad., Loyola Inst. Politics, 1973. Bar: La. 1968. Ptnr. Livingston & Powers, New Orleans, 1976—77; asst. U.S. atty., dep. chief criminals divsn. U.S. Attys. Office, 1970—73; chief spl. prosecutor, chief armed robbery divsn. Orleans Parish Dist. Atty.'s Office, 1974—75; chief prosecutor organized crime unit La. Atty. Gen.'s Office, 1975—76; mem. 95th-106th Congresses from 1st La. Dist., 1977—99; chair appropriations com., 1996—98; founder The Livingston Group, Washington, 1999—. Bd. dirs. Holcim, Inc., 2000—. Co-chmn. ctr. democracy Am. Univ. Kyrgzstan; bd. suprs. Smithsonian Inst., 1995—98; bd. dirs. Internat. Rep. Inst. Ctr. for Democracy, 1996—; bd. dir. Medal of Honor Found. Named Outstanding Asst. U.S. Atty., 1973. Mem.: ABA, New Orleans Bar Assn., La. Bar Assn., Fed. Bar Assn., Am. Legion, Navy League. Roman Catholic. Office: The Livingston Group 499 S Capitol St SW Ste 600 Washington DC 20003

LIVOLSI, FRANK WILLIAM, JR., lawyer; b. Stamford, Conn., June 6, 1938; s. Frank Sr. and Rose M. Livolsi. BA, Pa. Mil. Coll., 1962; JD, Fordham U., 1965. Bar: Ct. 1968. Ptnr. Plotkin & Livolsi, Stamford, 1970—. Served to capt. U.S. Army, 1965-67, Vietnam. State civil litigation, General practice. Home: 155 Thornwood Rd Stamford CT 06903-2616 Office: Plotkin & Livolsi 1035 Washington Blvd Stamford CT 06901-2294

LIVSEY, ROBERT CALLISTER, lawyer; b. Salt Lake City, Aug. 7, 1936; s. Robert Frances and Rosezella Ann (Callister) L.; m. Renate Karla Guertler, Sept. 10, 1962; children: Scott, Rachel, Daniel, Benjamin. BS, U. Utah, 1962, JD, 1965; LLM, NYU, 1967. Bar: Utah 1965, Calif. 1967. Prof. Haile Selassie U., Addis Ababa, Ethiopia, 1965-66; spl. asst. to chief counsel IRS, Washington, 1977-79; assoc., then ptnr. Brobeck, Phleger & Harrison, San Francisco, 1967—2003; of counsel Morgan, Lewis & Bockius, San Francisco, 2003—. Adj. prof. U. San Francisco Law Sch., 1970-77; mem. adv. com. IRS Dist. Dirs., 1986-89; mem. western region liason com IRS (chmn. 1989). Research editor U. Utah Law Rev., 1964-65; editor Tax Law Rev., 1966-67; contbr. articles to profl. jours. Bd. dirs. Gilead Group, 1986-88, East Bay Habitat for Humanity, 1987-88, Morning Song, 1992-94. Mem. ABA (chmn. subcom. real estate syndications 1981-84), State Bar Calif. (chmn. taxation sect. 1984-85), San Francisco Bar Assn. (chmn. taxation sect. 1982), Am. Coll. Tax Counsel, Am. Law Inst., Tax Litigation Club (pres. 1986-87), Order of Coif, Beta Gamma Sigma. Democrat. Mem. Evangelical Covenant Ch. Club: Commonwealth (San Francisco). Corporate taxation, Personal income taxation. Home: 128 La Salle Ave Piedmont CA 94610-1233 Office: Morgan Lewis & Bockius 1 Market Plz Fl 31 San Francisco CA 94105-1100 E-mail: rlivsey@brobeck.com.

LLOYD, ALEX, lawyer; b. Atlantic, Iowa, Aug. 13, 1942; s. Norman and Ruth (R.) L.; m. Jacqueline Roe, Aug. 24, 1963 (widowed); children: Erin, Andrea, John, Peter. BA in Econs., Colby Coll., 1964; LLB, Law Sch., Yale U., 1967. Bar: Conn., U.S. Dist. Ct. Conn., U.S. Ct. Appeals (2d cir.), U.S. Tax Ct., U.S. Supreme Ct. Assoc. Shipman & Goodwin, 1967-72, ptnr., 1972—, chmn. mgmt. com., 1985-96. Bd. dirs. Hartford Hosp., Conn. Health Sys., Inc., Conn. Bar Found. Recipient Dist. Svc. award, Conn. Legal Svcs. Fellow Am. Bar Found., Conn. Bar Found.; mem. ABA, Am. Soc. of Hosp. Attys., Conn. Bar Assn. (Charles J. Parker award). Avocations: golf, boating, fishing, raquet sports, piano. Corporate, general, Health, Corporate taxation. Office: Shipman & Goodwin 1 American Row Hartford CT 06103-2833 E-mail: alloyd@goodwin.com.

LLOYD, DAVID LIVINGSTONE, JR., lawyer; b. Butler, Pa., Aug. 28, 1952; s. David Livingstone and Jean Marie (Basher) L.; m. Dana L. Kadison, June 26, 1983; children: John Gabriel, Margaret Kadison. BS, AB, U. Pa., 1974, JD, 1977. Bar: N.Y. 1977. Assoc. Dewey Ballantine, N.Y.C., 1977-85, ptnr., 1986-93; sr. counsel Financing and transactions GE Aircraft Engines, Cin., 1993—. Aviation, Finance, Private international. Office: GE Aircraft Engines 1 Neumann Way # F17 Cincinnati OH 45215-1915

LLOYD, FRANCIS LEON, JR., lawyer; b. Winchester, Va., Dec. 1, 1955; s. Francis Leon Sr. and Jeannette Marie (Dove) L.; m. Myra Denise DuBose, Sept. 18, 1982. BA in English and French, U. Richmond, 1978; JD, U. Va., 1981. Bar: Va. 1981, Tenn. 1982, U.S. Dist. Ct. (ea. dist.) Tenn. 1982, U.S. Ct. Appeals (6th cir.) 1984. Assoc. Herndon, Coleman, Brading & McKee, Johnson City, Tenn., 1981-86, ptnr., 1987-88; of counsel The Taylor Group, Ltd., Johnson City, 1983; law clk. to judge U.S. Dist. Ct. (ea. dist.) Tenn., Knoxville, 1988-98; assoc. London & Amburn, PC, Knoxville, 1998-99, mem., 1999—2002; mem. firm London, Amburn & Lloyd, P.C. , Knoxville, 2003—. Bd. dirs. Assn. Retarded Citizens Washington County, Inc., Johnson City, 1982-88. Avocations: literature, music, hiking. General civil litigation, Health, Alternative dispute resolution. Home: 8804 Regent Ln Knoxville TN 37923-1640 Office: London Amburn & Lloyd PC 1716 W Clinch Ave Knoxville TN 37916-2408 E-mail: fllmail@latlaw.com.

LLOYD, HUGH ADAMS, lawyer; b. Pine Apple, Ala., Oct. 5, 1918; s. James Adams and Kate (Compton) L.; m. Lydia Douglas, Sept. 18, 1942; children: Kathryn Lloyd Allen, Sally Douglas (Mrs. Charles Proctor), Elizabeth Anne (Mrs. Thomas Goodman), Hugh Adams Jr. Student, Oglethorpe U., 1936-37, AB, U. Ala., 1941, LL.B., 1942. Bar: Ala. 1942, U.S. Supreme Ct 1958. Adjudicator VA, Montgomery, Ala., 1946-47; ptnr. Lloyd, Dinning, Boggs & Dinning, Demopolis, Ala., 1947—2000; mem. Lloyd & Dinning LLC, Demopolis, 2001—. Active Boy Scouts Am.; chmn. Demopolis Indsl. Devel. Com., 1970; mem. Regional Com. Juvenile Delinquency, 1970; chmn. Marengo County Devel. Bd., 1972-73; mem. Demopolis City Coun., 1974; chmn. Indsl. Devel. Bd. Marengo County, 1980; pres. Marengo County Port Authority, 1987—, Demopolis City Schs. Found., 1995—; trustee Judson Coll., Marion, Ala., 1981, vice-chmn. bd., 1989, chmn., 1991; bd. dirs. Judson Coll.-Merion Inst. Joint Found.; Sunday sch. tchr. Bapt. Ch., 1950—; past chmn. ch. bd. deacons bylaws com. Ala. State Bapt. Conv., 1997. With AUS, 1943-45. Decorated Bronze Star; recipient Silver Beaver award Boy Scouts Am., 1972, Paul Harris Fellow award Rotary Found., 1998, award for cmty. svc. West Ala. Mental Health Bd., 1998, Demopolis Citizen of Yr. award, 1998. Mem. ABA, Am. Judicature Soc., Ala. Bar Assn., 17th Jud. Circuit Bar Assn. (pres.), Marengo County Hist. Soc. (v.p. 1980), Demopolis C. of C. (pres., Citizen of Yr. 1998, Lifetime Achievement award 2002), Ala. Law Inst. (coun.), Bus. Coun. Ala. (dir. 1995), Ala. Safety Coun. (past bd. dirs.), Demopolis Country Club (pres. 1967-68), Kiwanis (dist. gov. 1967, chmn. internat. com. Key clubs 1969, internat. com. on boys and girls work 1972, dist. chmn. laws and regulations com. Ala. dist. 1979). Home: 1408 Colony Dr Demopolis AL 36732-3443 Office: PO Drawer 740 501 N Walnut Ave Demopolis AL 36732-2037

LOAKE, JONATHAN DAVID, lawyer; b. Northampton, England, Mar. 21, 1951; Grad., Coll. Law, England, 1979; MA with honors, Trinity Coll., 1993. Assoc. Denton, Hall & Burgin, London, 1977—83; ptnr. Dallas Brett, Oxford, 1983—97, Morgan Cole, 1997—2000, Brobeck Hale and Dorr, 2000—. Avocations: music, literature, sports. Corporate, general, Entertainment, Mergers and acquisitions. Office: Brobeck Hale & Dorr Park Gate 25 Milton Park Oxford OX14 4SH England E-mail: loake@bhd.com.

LOBEL, MARTIN, lawyer; b. Cambridge, Mass., June 19, 1941; s. I. Alan and Dorothy W. l.; m. Geralyn Krupp, Mar. 15, 1981; children: Devra Sarah, Rachel Melissa, Hannah Krupp. AB, Boston U., 1962; JD, 1965; LLM, Harvard U., 1966. Bar: Mass. 1965, D.C. 1968, U.S. Supreme Ct. 1968. Ptnr. Lobel & Lobel, Boston, 1965-66; asst. prof. law U. Okla., Norman, 1967; congl. fellow Washington, 1968; legis. asst. to Senator William Proxmire, 1968-72; ptnr. Lobel, Novins & Lamont, Washington, 1972—. Lectr. Law Sch. Am. U., Washington, 1972—; resellers referee, U.S. Dist. Ct., Wichita; chmn. Tax Analysts, 1972—. Contbr. articles to legal jours. Chmn. tax notes/tax analysis. Mem. ABA, Mass. Bar Assn., D.C. Bar Assn. (ch,m. consumer affairs com. 1976-77, chmn. steering com. on antitrust and consumer affairs sect.), Order of Coif, Harvard Club (Washington), Boston U. Club (Washington). Administrative and regulatory, Federal civil litigation, Legislative. Home: 4525 31st St NW Washington DC 20008-2130 Office: Lobel Novins & Lamont 1275 K St NW Ste 770 Washington DC 20005-4048 E-mail: lobel@lnllaw.com.

LOBENHERZ, WILLIAM ERNEST, container company/association executive, lawyer; b. Muskegon, Mich., June 22, 1949; s. Ernest Pomeroy and Emajean (Krautheim) L.; m. Carla Rae Krieger; children: Jessica Anne, Rebecca Jean, Christopher William, Andrew William. BBA, U. Mich., 1971; JD cum laude, Wayne State U., 1974. Bar: Mich. 1974. Legal counsel Mich. Legis. Services Bur., Lansing, Mich., 1974-77; legal legis. cons. Mich. Assn. of Sch. Bds., Lansing, 1977, asst. exec. dir. for legal legis. affairs, 1977-79; asst. v.p. state and congl. relations Wayne State U., Detroit, 1979-81, assoc. v.p. state relations, 1981-82, v.p. govtl. affairs, 1982-87; assoc. Dykema Gossett, Lansing, Mich., 1987-89; pres., CEO, Mich. Soft Drink Assn., Lansing, 1989—, MSDA Svc. Corp., Lansing, 1997—. Guest lectr. in govtl. affairs, Wayne State U., U. Mich., U. Detroit; referee Mich. Tax Tribunal, 1993-97. Contbr. chpt. Mich. Handbook for School Business Officials, 1979, 2nd edit., 1980; also articles to profl. jours. and mags. Mem. govtl. affairs com. New Detroit Inc., 1984-87, chmn. state subcom. of govtl. affairs com., 1986-87; chmn. ind. schs. campaign Greater Metro Detroit United Fund Torch Dr., 1979, chmn. Colls. and Univs. campaign, 1980; bd. dirs. Mich. Epilepsy Ctr., 1991-97, Coun. for Mich. Pub. Univs., 1991—, Tourism Industry Coalition of Mich., vice-chair, 1998—; mem. Mich. Recycling Partnership, 1997—. Recipient Book award Lawyer's Coop. Pub. Co., 1973, Outstanding Svc. award Mich. Assn. for Marriage and Family Therapy, 1992, 95, Silver scholar key Wayne State U. Law Sch., 1974; named among Top 10 Single Interest Lobbyists, Inside Mich. Politics, 2001. Mem. Mich. Bar Assn., NAACP, Coun. for Advancement and Support of Edn. (Mindpower citation 1982), Mich. Delta Found. (bd. dirs. 1977-97, sec. 1981-84, v.p. 1987-88), Greater Metro Detroit C. of C. (contact interviewer bus. attraction and expansion coun. 1984-86), City Club. Home: 430 Leland Pl Lansing MI 48917 Office: Mich Soft Drink Assn 634 Michigan National Tower Lansing MI 48933-1707 E-mail: msda@voyager.net.

LOBL, HERBERT MAX, lawyer, writer; b. Vienna, Jan. 10, 1932; s. Walter Leo and Minnie (Neumann) L.; m. Dorothy Fullerton Hubbard, Sept. 12, 1960; children: Peter Walter, Michelle Alexandra. AB magna cum laude, Harvard U., 1953, LLB cum laude, 1959, Avocat honoraire, 1993. Bar: N.Y. 1960, U.S. Tax Ct. 1963, French Conseil Juridique 1973; French avocat. mem. Paris bar, 1992, avocat hon., 1993. Assoc. Davis, Polk & Wardwell, N.Y.C., 1959-90, N.Y.C. and Paris, 1963-69, ptnr., 1969-92, sr. counsel, 1993—; assoc. counsel to Gov. Nelson Rockefeller Albany, N.Y., 1960-62. Lectr. law Columbia U., N.Y.C., 1993-95; supervisory bd. mem. CII-HB Internationale, Amsterdam, The Netherlands, 1977-82. Author: Welcome to West Berlin, 2002. Gov. Am. Hosp. Paris, 1981-83, 88-93; bd. trustees Am. Libr., Paris, 1969-81, Nantucket (Mass.) Cottage Hosp., 1996-99, dir. Nantucket Arts Coun., 2000-02. Served to 1st lt. UASF, 1954-56. Fulbright scholar U. Bonn, Germany, 1954. Mem. Am. C. of C. (bd. dirs. France 1988-90), Univ. Club, Harvard Club. Address: PO Box 2488 Nantucket MA 02584-2488 also: PO Box 118 Rye NY 10580-0118 also: Davis Polk & Wardwell 450 Lexington Ave New York NY 10017-3911 E-mail: hlobl@earthlink.net.

LOCHHEAD, ROBERT BRUCE, lawyer; b. St. Louis, June 20, 1952; s. Angus Tulloch and Matilda Evangeline (Thurman) L.; m. KLynn Walker, June 21, 1974; children: Robert, Richard, Cynthia, Melinda, Rebekah, Elizabeth. BA, Brigham Young U., 1975; JD, Columbia U., 1978. Bar: D.C. 1979, Utah 1980, U.S. Dist. Ct. Utah 1980, U.S. Ct. Appeals (10th cir.) 1980, U.S. Supreme Ct. 1986. Law clk. to judge U.S. Ct. Appeals (10th cir.), Salt Lake City, 1978-79; assoc. Hogan & Hartson, Washington, 1979-80, Larsen, Kimball, Parr & Crockett, Salt Lake City, 1980-82; shareholder Parr, Waddoups Brown, Gee & Loveless, Salt Lake City, 1982—. Judge pro tem Small Claims Ct., Salt Lake City, 1985-88; mem. panel of arbitrators U.S. Bankruptcy Ct., Dist. Utah, 1995—. Harlan Fiske Stone scholar, 1976-78. Mem. ABA, Am. Bankruptcy Inst. Mem. Lds Ch. Bankruptcy, Federal civil litigation, Commercial, contracts (including sales of goods; commercial financing). Home: 492 N Flint St Kaysville UT 84037-9777 Office: Parr Waddoups Brown Gee & Loveless 185 S State St Ste 1300 Salt Lake City UT 84111-1537

LOCHRIDGE, LLOYD PAMPELL, JR., lawyer; b. Austin, Tex., Feb. 3, 1918; s. Lloyd Pampell and Franklyn (Blocker) L.; m. Frances Potter, Jan. 23, 1943; children: Anne, Georgia, Lloyd P. III, Patton G., Hope N., Frances P. AB, Princeton U., 1938; LLB, Harvard U., 1941. Bar: D.C. 1942, Tex. 1945, U.S. Ct. Appeals (5th cir.), U.S. Supreme Ct. Assoc. Law Office Vernon Hill, Mission, Tex., 1945-46; ptnr. Hill & Lochridge, Mission, Tex., 1946-49, Hill, Lochridge & King, Mission, Tex., 1949-59, McGinnis, Lochridge & Kilgore, Austin, 1959—. Mem. adv. bd. Salvation Army, Austin, 1962—; mem. vestry Ch. Good Shepherd, Austin, 1968-73; trustee Austin Lyric Opera, 1986—. Comdr. USNR, 1941-46, ETO. Mem. ABA (bd. govs. 1989-92), State Bar Tex. (pres. 1974-75), Travis County Bar Assn. (pres. 1970-71), Hidalgo County Bar Assn. (pres. 1954-55). Episcopalian. Avocations: tennis, squash, sailing. Federal civil litigation, General civil litigation, Oil, gas, and mineral. Office: McGinnis Lochridge & Kilgore Capitol Ctr 919 Congress Ave Ste 1300 Austin TX 78701-2499 E-mail: llochridge@mcginnislaw.com.

LOCKE, JOHN HOWARD, retired lawyer; b. Berryville, Va., Sept. 4, 1920; s. James Howard and Mary Elizabeth (Hart) L.; m. Frances Rebecca Cook, Feb. 23, 1946; children: Anne Locke Evans, Nancy Locke Curlee, Rebecca Locke Leonard. BS, U. Richmond, 1941; LLB, U. Va., 1948. Bar: Va. 1948. Ptnr. Gentry, Locke, Rakes & Moore, Roanoke, Va., ret., 1985. Apptd. Hearing Officer Supreme Ct. Va., 1987; founder, pres. Big Bros., Roanoke, 1960. With USN, 1942-46. Fellow Am. Coll. Trial Lawyers, Internat. Soc. Barristers (pres. 1970); mem. ABA, Va. State Bar, Va. Bar Assn., Roanoke City Bar Assn. (pres. 1970-71), Internat. Assn. Ins. Counsel, 4th Cir. Jud. Conf., Omicron Delta Kappa, Raven Soc., Shenandoah Club (Roanoke, Va.). Presbyterian.

LOCKE, WILLIAM HENRY, lawyer; b. Eagle Pass, Tex., Nov. 14, 1947; s. William Henry and Genevieve (Moss) L.; children: William Henry III, Elizabeth Madeleine. AA with honors, Del Mar Coll., 1967; BA, U. Tex., 1969, JD with honors, 1972. Bar: Tex. 1972; cert. in real estate law. Exec. dir. The Kleberg Law Firm, Corpus Christi, Tex., 1972-99, Graves, Dougherty, Hearon & Moody, Austin, Tex., 2000—. Co-dir. advanced real estate law course State Bar of Tex., 1986-87. Author: Seizure of Lender's Collateral Under Drug Enforcement Laws, 1990, Contractual Indemnity in Texas, 1991, Civil Forfeiture Actions, 1993, Shifting of Risk: Contractual Provisions for Indemnity, Additional Insureds, Wavier of Subrogation and Exculpation, 1995, Texas Foreclosure Manual, 1995, Risk Management: Through Contractual Provisions for Indemnity, Additional Insureds Waiver of Subrogation, Releases and Exculpation, 1997, 2002, Sales Contracts: A Framework for Risk Allocation, 1998, Due Diligence in the Acquisition of Income Producing Properties, 2000, Annotated Risk Management Forms, 2003, Landlord and Tenant: Risk Management Issues, 2003; contbg. author: Texas Construction Law, 1988. Chmn. Corpus Christi Planning Commn., 1984-85, Corpus Christi Airport Zoning Commn., 1985; bd. dirs., sec. Leadership Corpus Christi, 1984-85; pres. Palmer Drug Abuse Program, Corpus Christi, 1985-87, pres., 2002; treas. St. James Episcopal Elem. Sch., 1987-91. Fellow Tex. Bar Found. (life), Tex. Coll. Real Estate Law (dir. 1990-2001), Coll. Law of State Bar Tex.; mem. ABA, Corpus Christi Bar Assn. (pres. 1987-88), Rotary (bd. dirs. Corpus Christi 1987-88, sec. 1989, Disting. Svc. Above Self award 1985, Corpus Christi merit award 1987), Beta Theta Pi. Democrat. Episcopalian. Commercial, contracts (including sales of goods; commercial financing), Finance, Property, real (including real estate development, water). Fax: 512-478-1976. E-mail: blocke@gdhm.com.

LOCKHART, GREGORY GORDON, prosecutor; b. Dayton, Ohio, Sept. 2, 1946; s. Lloyd Douglas and Evelyn (Gordon) L.; m. Paula Louise Jewett, May 20, 1978; children: David H., Sarah L. BS, Wright State U., 1973; JD, Ohio State U., 1976. Bar: Ohio 1976, U.S. Dist. Ct. (so. dist.) Ohio 1977, U.S. Ct. Appeals (6th cir.) 1988, U.S. Supreme Ct. 1993. Legal advisor Xenia and Fairborn (Ohio) Police Dept., 1977-78; asst. pros. atty. Greene County Prosecutor, Xenia, 1978-87; ptnr. DeWine & Schenck, Xenia, 1978-82, Schenck, Schmidt & Lockhart, Xenia, 1982-85, Ried & Lockhart, Beavercreek, Ohio, 1985-87; asst. U.S. atty. So. Dist. of Ohio, Columbus, 1987-2001, U.S. atty., 2001—. Adj. prof. Coll. Law U. Dayton, 1990—, Wright State U., Dayton, 1979—. Co-author: Federal Grand Jury Practice, 1996. Pres. Greene County Young reps., Xenia, 1977-79. With USAF, 1966-70; Vietnam. Mem. Fed. Bar Assn. (chpt. pres. 1994-95), Dayton Bar Assn., Kiwanis (pres. 1983-84, lt. gov. 1986-87), Jaycees (pres. 1976-79), Am. Inns of Ct. (master of bench emeritus). Methodist. Avocations: golf, tennis, hiking, camping. Office: US Attorney Federal Bldg 200 W 2d St Rm 602 Dayton OH 45402 E-mail: gregory.lockhart@usdoj.gov.

LOCKWOOD, GARY LEE, lawyer; b. Woodstock, Ill., Dec. 3, 1946; s. Howard and Luella Mae (Behrens) L.; m. Cheryl Lynn Wittrock, Jan. 5, 1967; children: Jennifer, Lee, Cynthia. BA magna cum laude, Iowa Wesleyan Coll., 1969; student, Albert Ludwig U., Freiburg in Breisgau, Fed. Republic Germany, 1968-69; JD, Northwestern U., 1976. Bar: Ill. 1976, U.S. Dist. Ct. (no. dist.) Ill. 1976, U.S. Ct. Appeals (7th cir.) 2000, U.S. Ct. Appeals (9th cir.) 2002. Assoc. Lord, Bissell & Brook, Chgo., 1976-85, ptnr., 1985—. Bd. dirs. McHenry Sch. Dist. 15, Ill., 1974-85, pres., 1979-80. Served to sgt. U.S. Army, 1970-72. Mem. ABA (bus. and ins. com. 1985—). Methodist. Avocation: sports. Environmental, Insurance. Home: 333 N Canal St Chicago IL 60606 Office: Lord Bissel & Brook 115 S La Salle St Fl 3600 Chicago IL 60603-3902 E-mail: glockwoo@lordbissell.com.

LOCKYER, BILL, state attorney general; b. Oakland, Calif., May 8, 1941; 1 child, Lisa. BA in Polit. Sci., U. Calif., Berkeley; cert. in sec. tchg., Calif. State U., Hayward; JD, U. of the Pacific. Past tchr., San Leandro, Calif.; Mem. Calif. State Assembly, 1973; state senator State of Calif., 1982; pres. pro tem, chmn. senate rules com., chmn. senate jud. com. Calif. State Senate, 1994—98; atty. gen. State of Calif., 1999—. Active San Leandro Sch. Bd., 1968—73. Past chair Alameda County Dem. Ctrl. Com. Named Legislator of Yr., Planning and Conservation League, 1996, Calif. Jour., 1997. Democrat. Office: Office Atty Gen Dept Justice PO Box 944255 Sacramento CA 94244-2550

LODGE, STEVEN JOHN, lawyer; b. Omaha, Nebr., Nov. 29, 1965; s. James Erwin and Lenore Anne Lodge; m. Tamara Lynn Lodge. BA, U. of Iowa, 1989; JD, U. of Akron, 1994. Bar: Minn. 1995, U.S. Dist. Ct. Minn. 1997, Ohio 1994. Law clk. Sherburne County Dist. Ct., Elk River, Minn., 1994—95; assoc. Ogurak Law Offices, Mpls., 1995—96, Babcock, Locher, Nielsen & Mannella, Anoka, Minn., 1996—99; ptnr. Nash & Lodge, PLLP, Andover, Minn., 1999—. Asst. staff judge advc. USAR, Mpls., 2000—02; asst. staff judge advocate Minn. Army N.G., Rosemount, Minn., 1998—2000. Capt. USAR, 2001—02. Mem.: Hennepin County Bar Assn., Anoka County Bar Assn. Property, real (including real estate development, water), Corporate, general, Land use and zoning (including planning), Commercial, contracts (including sales of goods; commercial financing). Office: Nash & Lodge PLLP 2705 Bunker Lake Blvd NW Ste 107 Andover MN 55304 Office Fax: 763-862-0033. E-mail: lodge@nashandlodge.com.

LOEB, RONALD MARVIN, lawyer; b. Denver, Sept. 24, 1932; s. Ellis and Lillian (Mosko) L.; m. Shirley Ross; children: Joshua Ross, Gabriel Ross, Daniel Seth, Jennifer Miriam, Rachel Sarah.. AB with highest honors, UCLA, 1954; LLB cum laude, Harvard U., 1959. Bar: Calif. 1960. Assoc. Irell & Manella, L.L.P, L.A., 1959-64, ptnr., 1964-97, of counsel, 1997-99; acting CEO Mattel, 2000; sr. v.p., gen. counsel Williams Sonoma, Inc., 1999—. Instr. Stanford Law Sch. Director's Coll., 2001-02, bd. dirs. Mattel, Inc.; course presenter The Esalen Inst., 1994; instr. corp. governance and social responsibility KVK Raju Internat. Leadership Acad., Hyderabad, India; task force on social cohesion sponsored by Danish Min. Pub. Affairs; presenter Fortune Boardroom Forum 2003, Stanford Graduate Sch. Bus. Leadership From Within Program, 2003. Co-editor: Duties and Responsibilities of Outside Directors, 1978. Trustee Crossroads Sch. Arts and Scis., Santa Monica, Calif., 1987-99; past chmn. Pacific Crest Outward Bound Sch.; past founding trustee, dir. World Bus. Acad., 2003; panelist Fortune Boardroom Forum. Mem. ABA, State Bar Assn. Calif., Corporate, general, Mergers and acquisitions, Securities. Office: Williams Sonoma Inc 3250 Van Ness Ave San Francisco CA 94109 E-mail: rloeb@wsgc.com.

LOEFFLER, JAMES JOSEPH, lawyer; b. Evanston, Ill., Mar. 7, 1931; s. Charles Adolph and Margaret Bowe L.; m. Margo M. Loeffler, May 26, 1962; children— Charlotte Bowe, James J. BS, Loyola U.; JD, Northwestern U. Bar: Ill. 1956, Tex. 1956. Assoc. Fulbright & Jaworski, Houston, 1956-69, ptnr., 1969-86, sr. ptnr., 1986, Chamberlain, Hrdlicka, White, Johnson & Williams, Houston, 1986-90; pvt. practice law Houston, 1990-2000. Mem. Ill. Bar Assn., Tex. Bar Assn., Houston County Club. Administrative and regulatory, Labor (including EEOC, Fair Labor Standards Act, labor-management relations, NLRB, OSHA).

LOENGARD, RICHARD OTTO, JR., lawyer; b. N.Y.C, Jan. 28, 1932; s. Richard Otto and Margery (Borg) L.; m. Janet Sara Senderowitz, Apr. 11, 1964; children: Maranda C., Philippa S.M. AB, Harvard U., 1953, LLB, 1956. Bar: N.Y. 1956, U.S. Dist. Ct. (so. dist.) N.Y. 1958. Assoc. Fried, Frank, Harris, Shriver & Jacobson, predecessor firms, N.Y.C., 1956-64, ptnr., 1967-97; of counsel Fried, Frank, Harris, Shriver & Jacobson, N.Y.C., 1997—; dep. tax legis. counsel, spl. asst. internat. tax affairs U.S. Dept. Treasury, Washington, 1964-67. Mem. Commerce Clearing House, Riverwoods, Ill. Editl. bd. Tax Transaction Libr., 1982-94; contbr. articles to profl. publs. Fellow Am. Coll. Tax Counsel; mem. ABA, N.Y. State Bar Assn. (exec. com. tax sect. 1984—, sec. 1994-95, vice chair 1995-97, chair 1997-98), Assn. Bar City N.Y. Taxation, general. Office: Fried Frank Harris Shriver & Jacobson 1 New York Plz New York NY 10004-1980 E-mail: loengri@ffhsj.com.

LOEVINGER, LEE, lawyer, science writer; b. St. Paul, Apr. 24, 1913; s. Gustavus and Millie (Strouse) L.; m. Ruth Howe, Mar. 4, 1950; children: Barbara L., Eric H., Peter H. BA summa cum laude, U. Minn., 1933, JD, 1936. Bar: Minn. 1936, Mo. 1937, D.C. 1966, U.S. Supreme Ct., 1941. Assoc. Watson, Ess, Groner, Barnett & Whittaker, Kansas City, Mo., 1936-37; atty., regional atty. NLRB, 1937-41; with antitrust div. Dept. Justice, 1941-46; ptnr. Larson, Loevinger, Lindquist & Fraser, Mpls., 1946-60; assoc. justice Minn. Supreme Ct., 1960-61; asst. U.S. atty. gen. charge antitrust div. Dept. Justice, 1961-63; commr. FCC, 1963-68; ptnr. Hogan & Hartson, Washington, 1968-85, of counsel, 1986—; v.p., dir. Craig-Hallum Corp., Mpls., 1968-73. Dir. Petrolite Corp., St. Louis, 1978-83; U.S. rep. com. on restrictive bus. practices Orgn. for Econ. Coop. and Devel., 1961-64; spl. asst. to U.S. atty. gen., 1963-64; spl. counsel com. small bus. U.S. Senate, 1951-52; lectr. U. Minn., 1953-60; vis. prof. jurisprudence U. Minn. (Law Sch.), 1961; professorial lectr. Am. U., 1968-70; chmn. Minn. Atomic Devel. Problems Com., 1957-59; mem. Adminstrv. Conf. U.S., 1972-74; del. White House Conf. on Inflation, 1974; U.S. del. UNESCO Conf. on Mass Media, 1975, Internat. Telecomms. Conf. on Radio Frequencies, 1964, 66. Author: The Law of Free Enterprise, 1949, An Introduction to Legal Logic, 1952, Defending Antitrust Lawsuits, 1977, Science As Evidence, 1995; author first article to use term: jurimetrics, 1949; contbr. articles to profl. and sci. jours.; editor, contbr.: Basic Data on Atomic Devel. Problems in Minnesota, 1958; adv. bd. Antitrust Bull., Jurimetrics Jour. Served to lt. comdr. USNR, 1942-45. Recipient Outstanding Achievement award U. Minn., 1968; Freedoms Found. award, 1977, 84. Fellow Am. Acad. Appellate Lawyers; mem. ABA (del. of sci. and tech. sect. to Ho. of Dels. 1974-80, del. to joint conf. with AAAS 1974-76, co-chair 1990-93, liaison 1984-90, 93-98, chmn. sci. and tech. sect. 1982-83, coun. 1986-89, standing com. on nat. conf. groups 1984-90), AAAS, Minn. Bar Assn., Hennepin County Bar Assn., N.Y. Acad. Sci., D.C. Bar Assn., FCC Bar Assn., Broadcast Pioneers, U.S. C. of C. (antitrust coun. 1980-94), Am. Arbitration Assn. (comml. panel), Atlantic Legal Found. (adv. coun.), Cosmos Club (pres. 1990), City Club (Washington), Phi Beta Kappa, Sigma Xi, Delta Sigma Rho, Sigma Delta Chi, Phi Delta Gamma, Tau Kappa Alpha, Alpha Epsilon Rho. Home: 5600 Wisconsin Ave Apt 17D Chevy Chase MD 20815-4414 Office: Hogan & Hartson 555 13th St NW Washington DC 20004-1109 Fax: 202-637-5910. E-mail: loevil@hhlaw.com.

LOEWENTHAL, STEVEN RICHARD, lawyer; b. Beverly Hills, Calif., July 11, 1973; s. William Julius and Martha Rotler Loewenthal. BS in Criminology, U. Tampa, 1996; JD, Stetson U., 1999. Intern Fed. Pub. Defenders Office, Tampa, 1998, Hillsborough County States Atty., 1998; assoc. Moye, O'Brien, O'Rourke, Orlando, 1999—2000; atty pvt. practice, Tampa, 2000—. Criminal, Family and matrimonial, Personal injury (including property damage). Office: 209 S Howard Tampa FL 33606 Fax: 813-576-4400. E-mail: attorney@tampabay.rr.com.

LO FASO, GIOVANNI, lawyer; b. Rome, June 1, 1971; s. Stefano Lo Faso and Maria Vittoria Visconti. Degree in law, U. La Sapienza, 1995. Bar: Italy 1998. With Studio Legale Visconti, Rome, 1995—99; sr. assoc. Puopolo, Sistilli, Geffers & Luise, 1999—2003. Rschr. La Spaienza U., Rome, 1996—; legal svc. dept. Sace Italian Export Credit Agy., 2003—. Avocations: wine expert, basketball, golf. Commercial, contracts (including sales of goods; commercial financing), Corporate, general, Mergers and acquisitions. Office: Sace Plazza Poli 37/42 00186 Rome Italy Fax: 0039 06 6786629. E-mail: g.lofaso@isace.it.

LOFTON, THOMAS MILTON, lawyer; b. Indpls., May 12, 1929; s. Milton Alexander and Jane (Routzong) L.; m. Betty Louise Blades, June 20, 1954; children: Stephanie Louise, Melissa Jane. BS, Ind. U., 1951, JD, 1954, LLD (hon.), 2000, Wabash Coll., 2001. Bar: Ind. 1954, U.S. Ct. Appeals (7th cir.) 1959, U.S. Supreme Ct. 1958. Law clk. to justice U.S. Supreme Ct., Washington, 1954-55; ptnr. Baker & Daniels, Indpls., 1958-91. Dir. Ind. U. Found., Bloomington, 1978-91, Clowes Fund, 1980-2001; chmn. bd. Lilly Endowment, Indpls., 1991—; mem. bd. visitors Ind. U. Law, Bloomington, 1976—. Editor-in-chief Ind. Law Jour., 1953. Trustee Earlham Coll., 1988—91; dir. Allen Whitehill Clowes Charitable Found., 1990—. 1st lt. U.S. Army, 1955—58. Recipient Peck award Wabash Coll., 1982, Disting. Alumni Svc. award Ind. U., 1997. Mem.: Ind. Acad., Masons, Order of Coif, Sigma Nu, Beta Gamma Sigma. Republican. Presbyterian. Probate (including wills, trusts), Corporate taxation, Estate taxation. Home: 9060 Pickwick Dr Indianapolis IN 46260-1714 Office: Lilly Endowment 2800 N Meridian St Indianapolis IN 46208-4713

LOFTUS, THOMAS DANIEL, lawyer; b. Nov. 8, 1930; s. Glendon Francis and Martha Helen (Wall) L. BA, U. Wash., 1952, JD, 1957. Bar: Wash. 1958, U.S. Ct. Appeals (9th cir.) 1958, U.S. Dist. Ct. Wash. 1958, U.S. Ct. Mil. Appeals 1964, U.S. Supreme Ct. 1964. Trial atty. Northwestern Mut. Ins. Co., Seattle, 1958—62; sr. trial atty. Unigard Security Ins. Co., Seattle, 1962—68, asst. gen. counsel, 1969—83, govt. rels. counsel, 1983—89; of counsel Groshong, LeHet & Thornton, 1990—98; mem. Wash. Commn. on Jud. Conduct (formerly Jud. Qualifications), 1982—88, vice-chmn., 1987—88; judge pro tem Seattle Mcpl. Ct., 1973—81; mem. nat. panel of mediators Arbitration Forums, Inc., 1990—. Sec., trustee Seattle Opera Assn., 1980-91; pres., bd. dirs. Vis. Nurse Svcs., 1979-88; pres., v.p. Salvation Army Adult Rehab. Ctr., 1979-86; nat. committeeman Wash. Young Rep. Fedn., 1961-63, vice-chmn, 1963-65; pres. Young Reps. King County, 1962-63; bd. dirs. Seattle Seafair, Inc., 1975; bd. dirs., gen. counsel Wash. Ins. Coun., 1984-86, sec., 1986-88, v.p., 1988-90, Am. Mediation Panel of Mediators, 1990-96; bd. dirs. Arson Alarm Found., 1987-90; bd. visitors Law Sch. U. Wash., 1993—. 1st lt. U.S. Army, 1952-54, col. Res., 1954-85. Fellow Am. Bar Found.; mem. Am. Arbitration Assn. (nat. panel arbitrators 1965—, nat. panel mediators 2000—), Am. Arbitration Forums, Inc. (nat. panel arbitrators 1992), Nat. Assn. Security Dealers (nat. bd. arbitrators 1997—), Am. Mediation Panel, Wash. Bar Assn. (gov. 1981-84), Seattle King County Bar Assn. (sec., trustee 1977-82), ABA (ho. of dels. 1984-90), Internat. Assn. Ins. Counsel, U.S. People to People (del. Moscow internat. law-econ. conf. 1990), Def. Rsch. Inst., Wash. Def. Trial Lawyers Assn., Wash. State Trial Lawyers Assn., Am. Judicature Soc., Res. Officers Assn., Judge Advocate Gen.'s Assn., Assn. Wash. Gens., U. Wash. Alumni Assn., Coll. Club Seattle, Wash. Athletic Club, Masons, Shriners, English Spkg. Union, Ranier Club, Pi Sigma Alpha, Delta Sigma Rho, Phi Delta Phi, Theta Delta Chi. Republican. Presbyterian. Alternative dispute resolution, Insurance, Personal injury (including property damage). Home: 3515 Magnolia Blvd W Seattle WA 98199-1841 Office: Coll Club Bldg 505 Madison St Ste 300 Seattle WA 98104-1123

LOGAN, FRANCIS DUMMER, retired lawyer; b. Evanston, Ill., May 23, 1931; s. Simon Rae and Frances (Dummer) Logan; m. Claude Riviere, Apr. 13, 1957; children: Carolyn Gisele, Francis Dummer. BA, U. Chgo., 1950; BA Juris, Oxford U., 1954; LLB, Harvard U., 1955. Bar: N.Y. 1956, Calif. 1989. Assoc. Milbank, Tweed, Hadley & McCloy, N.Y.C., 1955-64, ptnr. N.Y.C. and L.A., 1965-96, chmn., 1992-96; retired, 1996. Bd. dirs. Pasadena Symphony Orch. Mem.: N.Y. State Bar, Pacific Coun. Internat. Policy, Am. Law Inst., Coun. Fgn. Rels., Calif. State Bar. Banking. Home: 1726 Linda Vista Ave Pasadena CA 91103-1132

LOGAN, JAMES KENNETH, lawyer, former federal judge; b. Quenemo, Kans., Aug. 21, 1929; s. John Lysle and Esther Maurine (Price) Logan; m. Beverly Jo Jennings, June 8, 1952; children: Daniel Jennings, Amy Logan Sliva, Sarah Logan Sherard, Samuel Price. AB, U. Kans., 1952; LLB magna cum laude, Harvard U., 1955. Bar: Kans. 1955, Calif. 1956. Law clk. U.S. Cir. Judge Huxman, 1955—56; with firm Gibson, Dunn & Crutcher, LA, 1956—57; asst. prof. law U. Kans., 1957—61, prof., dean Law Sch., 1961—68; ptnr. Payne and Jones, Olathe, Kans., 1968—77; judge U.S. Ct. Appeals (10th cir.), 1977—98; pvt. practice Logan Law Firm LLC, Olathe, 1998—2001, Foulston Siefkin LLP, Overland Park, Kans., 2002—. Ezra Ripley Thayer tchg. fellow Harvard Law Sch., 1961—62; vis. prof. U. Tex., 1964, Stanford U., 1969, U. Mich., 1976; sr. lectr. Duke U., 1987, 91, 93; commr. U.S. Dist. Ct., 1964—67; mem. U.S. Jud. Conf. Adv. Com. Fed. Rules of Appellate Procedure, 1990—97, chair, 1993—97. Author (with W.B. Leach): Future Interests and Estate Planning, 1961; author: Kansas Estate Administration, 5th edit., 1986; author: (with A.R. Martin) Kansas Corporate Law and Practice, 2d edit., 1979; author: The Federal Courts of the Tenth Circuit: A History, 1992, also articles. Candidate for U.S. Senate, 1968. Served with U.S. Army, 1947—48. Recipient Disting. Svc. citation, U. Kans., 1986, Francis Rawle award, ABA-ALI, 1990; scholar Rhodes Scholarship, 1952. Mem.: ABA, Kans. Bar Assn., Order of Coif, Phi Delta Phi, Alpha Kappa Psi, Pi Sigma Alpha, Omicron Delta Kappa, Beta Gamma Sigma, Phi Beta Kappa. Democrat. Presbyterian. Appellate, Corporate, general, Estate planning.

LOGAN, KENNETH RICHARD, lawyer; b. N.Y.C., Dec. 26, 1944; s. John S. and Hazel (Mathias) L.; m. Grace Winter-Durennel, Aug. 12, 1967; children: Finlay, Emily. BA, Princeton U., 1967; JD, U. Pa., 1972. Bar: N.Y., U.S. Dist. Ct. (so. dist.) N.Y., U.S. Ct. Appeals (2nd cir.). Assoc. Simpson Thacher & Bartlett, N.Y.C., 1972-79; ptnr. Simpson, Thacher & Bartlett, N.Y.C., 1979—. Served with U.S. Army, 1969-70. Antitrust, General civil litigation, Private international. Office: Simpson Thacher & Bartlett 425 Lexington Ave Fl 15 New York NY 10017-3954

LOGAN, SHARON BROOKS, lawyer; b. Nov. 19, 1945; d. Blake Elmer and Esther N. (Statum) Brooks; children: John W. III, Troy Blake. BS in Econs., U. Md., 1967, MBA in Mktg., 1969; JD, U. Fla., 1979. Bar: Fla. 1979. Ptnr. Raymond Wilson, Esq., Ormond Beach, Fla., 1980, Landis, Graham & French, Daytona Beach, Fla., 1981, Watson & Assocs., Daytona Beach, 1982—84; prin. Sharon B. Logan, Esq., Ormond Beach, 1984—. Legal adv. to paralegal program Daytona Beach CC, 1984—. Sponsor Ea. Surfing Assn., Daytona Beach, 1983—, Nat. Scholastic Surfing Assn., 1987—; bd. dir. Ctr. for Visually Impaired, 1991—. Recipient Citizenship award, Rotary Club, 1962—63; fellow Woodrow Wilson, U. md., 1967. Mem.: ABA, Daytona Beach Area Bd. Realtors, Volusia county Estate Planning Coun., Fla. Supreme Ct. Hist. Soc., Volusia County Real Property Coun., Inc. (bd. dirs. 1987—, sec. 1987—88, v.p. 1988—89, pres. 1989—90, sec. 1990—91, 1991—97, pres. 1997—98, 1998—), Volusia County Bar Assn. (bd. dir.), Fla. Bar Assn. (real property and probate sect., cert. real estate atty. 1996), Beech Mountain Country Club, Univ. Ctr. Club (Tallahassee), Daytona Boat Club, Ducks Unlimited, Mus. Arts and Scis., Ormond Beach C. of C., Gator Club, Halifax Club, Tomoka Oaks Country Club, Md. Club, Sigma Alpha Epsilon, Delta Delta Delta (Scholarship award 1964), Omicron Delta Epsilon, Phi Kappa Phi, Alpha Lamba Delta, Beta Gamma Sigma. Democrat. Episcopalian. Avocations: golf, cooking, sewing, tennis, aerobics. Probate (including wills, trusts), Estate planning, Property, real (including real estate development, water). Office: Sharon B Logan Esq 180 Vining Ct PO Box 4258 Ormond Beach FL 32175-4258

LOHEST, THIERRY, lawyer; b. Brussels, Oct. 17, 1966; s. Robert Andre Lohest and Marie Victoire Michiels. Licence en Droit, PhB, U. Cath. de Louvain, Louvain-La-Neuve, Belgium, 1989; LLM, Duke U., 1991. Bar: Brussels 1991. Ptnr. De Bandt, Van Hecke, Lagae & Loesch, London, 1998—2000, White & Case, Brussels, 2001—. Fellow: Cercle Gaulois, Royal Anglo-Belgian Club; mem.: Belgian Jockey Club (dir.). Corporate, general, Banking, Mergers and acquisitions. Office: White & Case 62 rue De La Loi 1040 Brussels Belgium

LOHR, WALTER GEORGE, JR., lawyer; b. Balt., Mar. 3, 1944; s. Walter George and Janet Louise (Carter) L.; children: Lila Meredith, Walter George III, Frederick Boyce. AB, Princeton U., 1966; LLB, Yale U., 1969. Bar: Md. 1969. Law clk.to Hon. Harrison L. Winter U.S. Cir. Ct., Richmond, Va., 1969-70; assoc. Piper & Marbury, Balt., 1970-74, ptnr., 1977-88, Hogan & Hartson, Washington, 1992—; asst. atty. gen. State of Md., Balt., 1974-76; prin. Walter G. Lohr Jr., Balt., 1988-92. Bd. dirs. Danaher Corp., Washington, Cmty. of Sci., Inc., Balt., iSky, Inc., Laurel, Md., chmn.; mem. adv. bd. Prudential Venture Ptnrs., N.Y.C., 1985-93. Trustee Balt. Mus. Art, 1985-1998, 2000-. Office: Hogan & Hartson 111 S Calvert St Ste 1600 Baltimore MD 21202-6191 E-mail: wglohr@hhlaw.com.

LOKDAM, LARS, lawyer; b. Aarhus, Denmark, Mar. 13, 1961; s. Orla and Mary Lokdam; m. Lara Meisen Grut, May 24, 1996; children: Nikolaj, Mik, Malou. LLM, U. Aarhus, 1987. Bar: Copenhagen Bar 1990, High Ct. Assoc. Lokdam Law Firm, Aarhus, 1987—89; lawyer Philips Danmark A/S, Copenhagen, 1990—91, Nyborg & Rordam Law Firm, Copenhagen, 1992—94; ptnr. Qvist Stanbrook A/S, Copenhagen, 1995—2002, Magnusson Wahlin Qvist Stanbrook A/S, Copenhagen, 2002—. Lectr. U. Aarhus, 1987—88; chmn. bd. dirs. Philips Danmark A/S, Copenhagen, 1995—, Intellix A/S, Copenhagen, 2000—; bd. dirs. Oce Danmark A/S, Copenhagen. Avocations: sailing, diving, skiing, tennis. Mergers and acquisitions, Computer, Antitrust. Home: Margrethevej 24 DK 2900 Hellerup Denmark Office: Magnusson Wahlin Qvist Stanbrook Pilestraede 58 Copenhagen Denmark Office Fax: 45 33936023. E-mail: lars.lokdam@dk.maqs.com.

LOKEN, JAMES BURTON, federal judge; b. Madison, Wis., May 21, 1940; s. Burton Dwight and Anita (Nelson) Loken; m. Caroline Brevard Hester, July 30, 1966; children: Kathryn Brevard, Kristina Ayres. BS, U. Wis., 1962; LLB magna cum laude, Harvard U., 1965. Law clk. to chief judge J. Edward Lumbard U.S. Ct. Appeals (2d Cir.), N.Y.C., 1965—66; law clk. to assoc. justice Byron White U.S. Supreme Ct., Washington, 1966—67; assoc. atty. Faegre & Benson, Mpls., 1967—70, ptnr., 1973—90; gen. counsel Pres.'s Com. on Consumer Interests, Office of Pres. of U.S., Washington, 1970; staff asst. Office of Pres. of U.S., Washington, 1970—72; judge U.S. Ct. Appeals (8th cir.), St. Paul, 1990—2003, chief judge, 2003—. Editor: Harvard Law Rev., 1964—65. Mem.: Minn. State Bar Assn., Phi Kappa Phi, Phi Beta Kappa. Avocations: golf, running. Office: US Courthouse 300 S 4th St Ste 11W Minneapolis MN 55415-0848 also: US Ct Appeals 8th Cir 111S 10th St Rm 24-32 Saint Louis MO 63102

LOLLI, DON R(AY), lawyer; b. Macon, Mo., Aug. 9, 1949; s. Tony and Erma Naomi (Gerlich) L.; m. Deborah Jo Mrosek, May 29, 1976; children: Christina Terese, Joanna Elyse, Anthony Justin. BA in Econs., U. Mo., 1971, JD, 1974. Bar: Mo. 1974, U.S. Dist. Ct. (we. dist.) Mo. 1974, U.S. Dist. Ct. (ea. dist) Mo. 1996, U.S. Dist. Ct. Kans. 1998, U.S. Ct. Appeals (8th cir.) 1976, U.S. Ct. Appeals (10th cir.) 1979, U.S. Ct. Appeals (3rd cir.) 1992, U.S. Supreme Ct. 1979, U.S. Tax Ct. 1981. Assoc. Beckett & Steinkamp, Kansas City, Mo., 1974-79; mem. Beckett, Lolli and Bartunek, Kansas City, 1980-96, Swanson, Midgley, LLC, Kansas City, 1997—. Lectr. CLE seminar U. Mo. Sch. Law, Kansas City, 1984, 89. Vol. coach Visitation Sch.; co-chair St. Teresa's Acad. Fundraising. Mem. ABA, Mo. Bar Assn., Kansas City Bar Assn., Lawyers Assn. Kansas City, U. Mo. Alumni Assn., Rotary, Beta Theta Pi (asst. gen. sec. 1997—, Tiedman Inn 1973-74, Merit cert. 1974), Phi Delta Phi (pres.). Roman Catholic. Federal civil litigation, State civil litigation, Family and matrimonial. Home: 645 W 62nd St Kansas City MO 64113-1501 Office: Swanson Midgley LLC Crown Ctr 2420 Pershing Rd Ste 400 Kansas City MO 64108-2505 E-mail: dlolli@swansonmidgley.com.

LOMAX, ROSS DONALD, lawyer; b. Bolton, U.K., May 28, 1969; s. Donald and Annie Ferris Lomax; m. Lindsay Mexer, Dec. 13, 1999; 1 child, Kieran Donald. BA, U of Capetown, 1990, BA honors, 1991; LLB, U of Witwatersrand, 1996; MJ, U of Oxford, U.K., 1999. Bar: South Africa (atty. high ct.) 1997. Dir. Deneys Reitz Attys., Johannesburg, 1999—. Commercial, contracts (including sales of goods; commercial financing), Insurance, Product liability. Office: Deneys Reitz Attnys 82 Maude St Johannesburg Sandton 2196 South Africa

LOMBARD, JOHN JAMES, JR., lawyer, writer; b. Phila., Dec. 27, 1934; s. John James and Mary R. (O'Donnell) L.; m. Barbara Mallon, May 9, 1964; children: John James, William M., James G., Laura K., Barbara E. BA cum laude, LaSalle Coll., 1956; JD, U. Pa., 1959. Bar: Pa. 1960. Ptnr. Obermayer, Rebmann, Maxwell & Hippel, Phila., 1959-84; mgr. personal law sect. Morgan Lewis & Bockius LLP, Phila., 1985-90, vice-chair personal law sect., 1990-92, chair, 1992-99; spl. counsel McCarter & English LLP, Phila., 2000—. Sec., dir. Airline Hydraulics Corp., Phila., 1969-2000; adv. com. on decedents estates laws Joint State Govt. Commn., 1992—, mem. subcom. on powers of atty., 1993—; co-chair So. Jersey Ethics Alliance, 1993-97. Co-author: Durable Powers of Attorney and Health Care Directives, 1984, 3d edit. 1994; contbr. articles to profl. jours. Bd. dirs. Redevel. Authority Montgomery County, Pa., 1980-87, Gwynedd-Mercy Coll., Gwynedd Valley, Pa., 1980-89, LaSalle Coll. H.S., Wyndmoor, Pa., 1991-97. Recipient Treat award Nat. Coll. Probate Judges, 1992, Disting. Estate Planner award Phila. Estate Planning Coun., 2002. Mem. ABA (chmn. com. simplification security transfers 1972-76, chmn. mem. com. 1972-82, mem. coun. real property, probate and trust law sect. 1979-85, sec. 1985-87, divsn. dir. probate div. 1987-89, chair elect 1989-90, chair 1990-91, co-chair Nat. Conf. Lawyers & Corp. Fiduciaries), Pa. Bar Assn. (ho. of dels. 1979-81), Phila. Bar Assn. (chmn. probate sect. 1972), Am. Coll. Trust and Estate Counsel (editor Probate Notes 1983, bd. regents 1986-91, mem. exec. com. 1988-91, elder law com. 1993—), internat. Acad. Estate and Trust Law (exec. com. 1984-88, 90-94), Am. Bar Found., Internat. Fish and Game Assn., Union League Club (Phila.), Ocean City Club (N.J.), Marlin and Tuna Club, Ocean City Yacht Club. Estate planning, Probate (including wills, trusts), Estate taxation. Office: McCarter & English LLP Mellon Bank Ctr Ste 700 1735 Market St Philadelphia PA 19103

LOMBARDI, CORNELIUS ENNIS, JR., lawyer; b. Portland, Oreg., Feb. 12, 1926; s. Cornelius Ennis and Adele (Volk) L.; m. Ann Vivian Foster, Nov. 24, 1954; children— Cornelius Ennis, Gregg Foster, Matthew Volk. BA, Yale, 1949; JD, U. Mich., 1952. Bar: Mo. Since practiced in, Kansas City, Mo.; mem. firm Blackwell, Sanders, Peper, Martin, 1957-92, of counsel. Former pres. Kansas City Mus. Assn., Estate Planning Coun. of Kansas City; trustee Pembroke Country Day Sch.; chmn. soc. of fellows Nelson Gallery Found.; bd. dirs., Mo. Parks Assn. Mem.: Kansas City Country Club, Order of Coif, Phi Alpha Delta. Corporate, general, Estate planning, Property, real (including real estate development, water). Home: 5049 Wornall Rd Kansas City MO 64112-2423 Office: 2 Pershing Sq 2300 Main St Ste 1100 Kansas City MO 64108-2416

LOMBARDI, DAVID RICHARD, lawyer; b. Bremerton, Wash., Mar. 27, 1949; s. Richard Caesar and Virginia Elizabeth (Smallridge) L.; m. Judith Ann Rummell, June 1, 1974; children: Rebecca, Katherine. BA, Stanford U., 1971; JD, U. Santa Clara, 1976. Bar: Idaho 1976, U.S. Dist. Ct. Idaho 1976, U.S. Ct. Appeals (9th cir.) 1985; cert. civil trial specialist. Ptnr. Langroise, Sullivan & Smylie, Boise, Idaho, 1976-84; of counsel Holland & Hart, Langroise & Sullivan, Boise, 1984-85; ptnr. Imhoff & Lynch, Boise, 1985-90, Givens Pursley, LLP, Boise, 1990—. Mem. Am. Health Lawyers Assn., Def. Rsch. Inst., Am. Inns of Ct., Am. Soc. Healthcare Risk Mgmt. Roman Catholic. Avocations: fly fishing, performing and visual arts. General civil litigation, Health, Personal injury (including property damage). Office: Givens Pursley LLP Ste 200 277 N 6th St Boise ID 83702-7720

LOMBARDI, DENNIS M. lawyer; b. L.A., May 15, 1951; s. Peter Joseph and Jean (Nelson) L.; m. Suan Choo Lim, Jan. 9, 1993; children: Alexis Jeanne, Erin Kalani. BA, U. Hawaii, 1974; JD summa cum laude, U. Santa Clara, 1977. Bar: Calif. 1977, U.S. Dist. Ct. Hawaii, 1981. Assoc. Frandzel & Share, Beverly Hills, Calif., 1977-79; pvt. practice Capistrano Beach, Calif., 1979-81; ptnr. Case, Bigelow & Lombardi, Honolulu, 1982—. Environmental, Land use and zoning (including planning), Property, real (including real estate development, water). Office: Case Bigelow & Lombardi 737 Bishop St Fl 26 Honolulu HI 96813-3201

LOMBARDI, FREDERICK MCKEAN, lawyer; b. Akron, Ohio, Apr. 1, 1937; s. Leonard Anthony and Dorothy (McKean) L.; m. Margaret J. Gessler, Mar. 31, 1962; children: Marcus M., David G., John A., Joseph F. BA, U. Akron, 1960; LLB, Case Western Res., 1962. Bar: Ohio 1962, U.S. Dist. Ct. (no. and so. dists.) Ohio 1964, U.S. Ct. Appeals (6th cir.) 1966. Prin., shareholder Buckingham, Doolittle & Burroughs, Akron, 1962—, chmn. comml. law and litigation dept., 1989-99. Bd. editors Western Res. Law Rev., 1961-62. Trustee, mem. exec. com., v.p. Ohio Ballet, 1985-93; trustee Walsh Jesuit H.S., 1987-90; life trustee Akron Golf Charities, NEC World Series of Golf; bd. mem. Summa Health Sys. Found., Downtown Akron Partnership, St. Hilary Parish Found. Mem. Ohio Bar Assn. (coun. of dels. 1995-97), Akron Bar Assn. (trustee 1991-94, 97-2000, v.p., pres.-elect 1997-98, pres. 1998-99), Case Western Res. U. Law Alumni Assn. (bd. govs. 1995-98), Case Western Res. Soc. Benchers, Fairlawn Swim and Tennis Club (past pres.), Portage Country Club, Pi Sigma Alpha. Democrat. Roman Catholic. General civil litigation, Commercial, contracts (including sales of goods; commercial financing), Construction. Office: Buckingham Doolittle & Burroughs 50 S Main St Akron OH 44308-1828 E-mail: flombardi@bdblaw.com.

LOMBARDI, VALENTINO DENNIS, lawyer; b. Providence, Feb. 5, 1943; s. Joseph and Angelina (DiDonato) L.; m. Linda Ann Dardeen, Sept. 5, 1966; children: Valerie Lynn, Nicole Maria, Joseph Thomas. AB, Providence Coll., 1966; JD, Suffolk U., 1971. Bar: R.I. 1971, U.S. Dist. Ct. R.I. 1971. Sole practice, North Providence, 1971—. Legal counsel dept. labor and tng. State of R.I., 1978—, dept. social and rehabilitative services, 1972-73, dept. corrections, 1973-76, chief legal counsel, 1976-78; assoc. judge mcpl. ct. Town of North Providence, R.I., 1986—. Chmn. businessman's athletic club YMCA, Providence, 1976-80; bd. dirs. and sec. Iannotiti Scholarship Fund. Mem. Providence Coll. Alumni Assn. (class agt. 1981—), Sons of Italy (treas. 1995—, 1st v.p. 1997, pres. 2001—). Democrat. Roman Catholic. Avocations: golf, running, sports spectating. Property, real (including real estate development, water), Administrative and regulatory, Probate (including wills, trusts). Home: 11 Stephanie Dr Providence RI 02904-2913 Office: 959 Mineral Spring Ave North Providence RI 02904-4934 E-mail: VnL66@aol.com.

LOMHOFF, PETER GEORGE, lawyer; b. N.Y.C., Jan. 21, 1945; BA, Reed Coll., 1966; MA, U. Chgo., 1970; postgrad., Harvard U., 1970-71; JD, U. Calif. at Berkeley, 1974. Bar: Calif. 1974, U.S. Dist. Ct. (no. dist.) Calif. 1974, U.S. Ct. Appeals (9th cir.) 1974. Law clk. Judge William T. Sweigert,

U.S. Dist. Ct. (no. dist.) Calif., San Francisco, 1975-77; assoc. Law Office John Diaz Coker, Pittsburg, Calif., 1974-75; instr. Lincoln U. Sch. Law, San Francisco, 1977-80; atty. pvt. practice, Oakland, Calif., 1977—. Speaker in field. Contbr. to profl. handbooks. Democrat. Civil rights, Personal injury (including property damage), Elder. Office: 1 Kaiser Plz Ste 1725 Oakland CA 94612-3681

LONDON, MARTIN, lawyer; b. Glen Cove, N.Y., Apr. 4, 1934; s. Abraham and Rebecca (Lasker) L.; m. Mellanie Bell, May, 1958 (div. 1973); children: Jesse, Lizbeth; m. Doris Wilke, July 28, 1983. AB, Cornell U., 1955; LLB, NYU, 1957. Bar: N.Y. 1958, U.S. Dist. Ct. (so. dist.) N.Y. 1962, U.S. Tax Ct. 1968, U.S. Dist. Ct. (ea. dist.) N.Y. 1969, U.S. Ct. Appeals (2d cir.) 1969, U.S. Dist. Ct. D.C. 1970, U.S. Supreme Ct. 1971, U.S. Ct. Appeals (6th and 7th cirs.) 1982, U.S. Ct. Appeals (4th cir.) 1990. Assoc. Gallop, Climenko & Gould, N.Y.C., 1958-61, Paul, Weiss, Rifkind, Wharton & Garrison, N.Y.C., 1962-68, ptnr., 1969—. Spl. counsel judiciary relations com. First Judicial Dept., 1973-74, counsel gov.'s judicial nomination com., 1975-82, chmn. deptl. disciplinary com., 1980-85; spl. trial counsel Ct. on the Judiciary, 1977. Served as sgt. U.S. Army, 1957-58, 61-62. Mem. Am. Coll. Trial Lawyers, Assn. of Bar of City of N.Y., Fed. Bar Council, Am. Arbitration Assn. (nat. panel arbitrators). Avocations: deep sea fishing, skiing. Antitrust, General civil litigation, Criminal. Office: Paul Weiss Rifkind Wharton & Garrison LLP Ste 2613 1285 Avenue Of The Americas New York NY 10019-6028 E-mail: mlondon@paulweiss.com

LONERGAN, KEVIN, lawyer; b. Racine, Wis., Oct. 2, 1954; s. Ralph and M. Janet L.; m. Elizabeth Ison, Oct. 10, 1981; children: Lindsey, Kristen, Emily, Marc. BS, USAF Acad., 1976; JD, U. Wis., 1979. Bar: Wis. 1979, U.S. Dist. Ct. (we. dist.), Wis. 1979; cert. Nat. Bd. Trial Advocates. Commd. 2nd lt. USAF, 1976, med. retirement, 1977; asst. dist. atty. Eau Claire County, Eau Claire, Wis., 1979-81; assoc. Thompson, Parke & Heim, Ltd., LaCrosse, Wis., 1981-82; ptnr., v.p. Herrling, Clark, Hartzheim & Siddall, Ltd., Appleton, Wis., 1982—. Apptd. ct. commr. Outagamie County, 1994—; host (TV program) You and the Law, 1988—; regular guest WHBY "Open Line" Radio show, 1995—. Bd. dirs. Eau Claire Kinship Program, 1981; bd dirs., v.p., pres. Casa Clare Half-Way House, Appleton, 1984-87; mem. United Way Cabinet, 1988, 90. Mem. ATLA, Wis. Acad. Trial Lawyers (bd. dirs. 1991—, treas. 1996, sec. 1997, v.p. 1998, pres.-elect 1999, pres. 2000, past pres. 2001), Outagamie County Bar Assn. (sec. 1992-93, v.p. 1993-94, pres. 1994-95). Roman Catholic. Avocations: family, physical fitness. Insurance, Personal injury (including property damage), Product liability. Home: 44 N Crestway Ct Appleton WI 54913-9510 Office: Herrling Clark Hartzheim & Siddall 800 N Lynndale Dr Appleton WI 54914-3017 E-mail: LKonergan@HerrlingClark.com.

LONERGAN, LAUREN ELIZABETH, lawyer; b. New Milford, Conn., Apr. 2, 1957; d. Leo Edward and Yvonne Althea (Gero) Reap; m. David Paul Lonergan, July 12, 1977. Student, Carleton Coll., 1975-77; BA, Macalester Coll., 1979; JD, U. Minn., 1982. Atty. O'Connor & Hannan, Mpls., 1982-87, Hart, Bruner, O'Brien & Thornton, Mpls., 1987-88; atty., shareholder Briggs & Morgan, P.A., Mpls., 1988—. Mem. ABA, Minn. State Bar Assn. Federal civil litigation, Insurance, Labor (including EEOC, Fair Labor Standards Act, labor-management relations, NLRB, OSHA). Office: Briggs & Morgan 2400 IDS Tower Minneapolis MN 55402

LONG, ANDRE EDWIN, law educator, lawyer; b. San Francisco, Dec. 28, 1957; s. Edwin John and Anna (Suss) L.; m. Michele Jean Dubinsky, Oct. 4, 1986; children: Christian Andre, Katrina Marie. BA, U. Pacific, 1979; MBA, Golden Gate U., 1981; JD, Southwestern U., 1982. Bar: Hawaii 1984, D.C. 1990, Wash. 2001, U.S. Ct. Appeals (9th cir.) 1984. Legal counsel Pure Water, Ltd., Manama, Bahrain, 1982-84; pvt. practice Honolulu, 1984-85; sr. contracts negotiator Litton Data Systems Corp., Van Nuys, Calif., 1985-87; contracts mgr. Eaton, Am. Nucleonics Corp., Westlake Village, Calif., 1987-92; owner, broker A. Long Realty, Ridgecrest, Calif., 1989—; asst. prof. contract law Air Force Inst. Tech., Dayton, 1992-99; assoc. counsel Navy Office of Gen. Counsel, China Lake, 1999—. Lectr. Tech. Tng. Corp., 1991-92; instr. Oxnard Coll., 1990-92, George Washington U. Law Sch./ESI Govt. Contract Law Program; asst. adj. prof. Embry-Riddle U. Author: U.S. Immigration and Visa Laws Made Simple, 1985, 2d edit., 1991, Government Contract Law, 1995, 96, 98, 99, Negotiating Government Contracts, 1996; editor The Clause, 1995-2000, Contract Mgmt. Jour., 1998-2000, Jour. Pub. Procurement.. Fellow Nat. Contract Mgmt. Assn. (pres. China Lake chpt. 2001-02, bd. dirs.); mem. Hawaii Bar Assn., D.C. Bar Assn., Aircraft Owners and Pilots Assn., Bd. Contracts Appeals Bar Assn. (chmn. publs. com. 1995-2000, bd. govs. 1997-2000), Canyon Ranch Assn. (chmn. 2000—). Avocations: scuba diving, snow skiing, sailing, flying. Office: NAWCWD Code 111000D 1 Adminstration Cir Ridgecrest CA 93555 E-mail: andre.long@navy.mil.

LONG, BEVERLY GLENN, retired lawyer; b. Omaha, Mar. 1, 1923; d. Max Edgar and Allise Katherine Dorothea (Nielsen) Glenn; m. Jacob Emery Long, May 6, 1950 AB in Econs., U. Chgo., 1944; LLB, Columbia U., 1947. Bar: N.Y. 1948, R.I. 1951, U.S. Dist. Ct. (so. dist.) N.Y. 1949, U.S. Tax Ct. 1949, U.S. Dist. Ct. R.I. 1951, U.S. Ct. Appeals (2d cir.) 1949, U.S. Ct. Appeals (1st cir.) 1958, U.S. Ct. Claims 1960, U.S. Supreme Ct. 1960. Assoc. Edwards & Angell LLP, Providence, 1950-59, ptnr., 1959-86, of counsel, 1986—. Adv. com. child welfare svcs. R.I. Dept. Social Welfare, 1959-66; pers. com. Big Bros. R.I., 1964-67; mem. Gov.'s Com. on Status of Women, 1965; chmn. R.I. Children's Code Commn., 1967-74; fundraiser Columbia U. Sch. Law, 1947-88, R.I. area for U. Chgo., 1951—; bd. dirs. Child Welfare League of Am., Inc., 1975-80, Children's Friend and Svc., Inc., 1966-75, 77-79, Providence chpt. ARC, 1967-72; bd. dirs. St. Mary's Home for Children, 1966-80, v.p., 1978-80; bd. dirs. R.I. Conf. Social Work, 1961-66, Coun. Cmty. Svcs., Inc., 1957-64; task force evaluation of criminal justice program LEAA, 1974-78; active United Way Southeastern New Eng., Inc., 1951-81, ad hoc adv. com., exec. budget com., 1971-78, bd. dirs., 1973-74, ABA sr. lawyers divsn. coun., 1986-91, sec., 1991-95. Recipient citation for pub. service U. Chgo., 1959 Fellow Am. Bar Found., R.I. Bar Found.; mem. ABA (Outstanding State Membership Chmn. award 1984), R.I. Bar Assn. (ho. dels., exec. com., pres., Merit award 1990), New Eng. Bar Assn. (bd. dirs. 1982-85), Fed. Bar Assn., Am. Law Inst., Am. Judicature Soc. (bd. dirs. 1988-90), U.S. Supreme Ct. Hist. Soc., U. Club R.I. Republican. Home: 200 Elmgrove Ave Providence RI 02906-4233

LONG, CHARLES THOMAS, lawyer, history educator; b. Denver, Dec. 19, 1942; s. Charles Joseph and Jessie Elizabeth (Squire) L.; m. Susan Rae Kircheis, Aug. 9, 1967; children: Brian Christopher, Lara Elizabeth, Kevin Charles. BA, Dartmouth Coll., 1965; JD cum laude, Harvard U., 1970. Bar: Calif. 1971, U.S. Dist. Ct. (cen. dist.) Calif. 1971, U.S. Ct. Appeals (9th cir.) 1975, D.C. 1980, U.S. Dist. Ct. D.C. 1981, U.S. Ct. Claims 1995. Assoc. Gibson, Dunn & Crutcher, Los Angeles, 1970-77, ptnr., 1977-79, Washington, 1979-83; dep. gen. counsel Fed. Home Loan Bank Bd., Washington, 1984-85; ptnr. Jones, Day, Reavis & Pogue, Washington, 1985-98; grad. tchg. asst. hist. dept. George Washington U., 1998—. Bar: Calif. 1971, U.S. Dist. Ct. (ctrl. dist.) Calif. 1971, U.S. Ct. Appeals (9th cir.) 1975, D.C. 1980, U.S. Dist. Ct. 1981, U.S. Ct. Fed. Claims 1995. Contbr. articles to profl. jours. Mem. Chesapeake Bay Maritime Mus., Friends of the Nat. Maritime Mus., Greenwich, Eng.; pres. Leigh Mill Meadows Assn., Great Falls, Va., 1980. Served to lt. USNR, 1965-67. Mem. ABA, Calif. Bar Assn., D.C. Bar Assn., Coun. for Excellence in Govt., Women in Housing and Fin., Dartmouth Lawyers Assn., Herrington Harbour Sailing Assn. (sec.-treas. 1996), Soc. for Mil. History, N.Am. Conf. on Brit. Studies, Navy Records Soc. (London), U.S. Naval Inst. Am. Hist. Assn., Orgn. Am. Historians, Omohundro Inst. Early Am. History and Culture, Chesapeake Bay Maritime Mus., Friends of the Nat. Maritime Mus. (Greenwich, Eng.), Westwood Country Club (Vienna, Va.), Am. Hist. Assn.. Republican. Methodist. Avocations: sailing, photography, computers, naval history.

LONG, DAVID CARTER, lawyer; b. Cleve., July 2, 1947; s. Robert Barr and Helen Beach Long; m. Nina Anne Packard, Sept. 19, 1970 (div. Mar. 1982); children: Edward C., Nora E.; m. Kare Lynne Smigel, May 2, 1992. BSEE, Cleve. State U., 1970, JD, 1974. Bar: Ohio 1975, U.S. Dist. Ct (no. dist.) Ohio 1975. Engr. Addressograph-Multigraph, Euclid, Ohio, 1970—71; sr. engr. Warner & Swasey, Cleve., 1973—75, asst. patent atty., 1975—76; pvt. practice Elyria, Ohio, 1976—88, 1992—2001; gen. counsel Freeman Environ. Corp., Vermilion, Ohio, 1988—92; atty. Rothgery & Assoc., Elyria, 2001—. Mem.: Lorain County Bar Assn., Ohio Acad. Trial Lawyers, Ohio State Bar Assn. Avocation: restoring antique motorcycles. Personal injury (including property damage), Product liability. Office: Rothgery and Assocs 230 Third St Avon Lake OH 44012 Office Fax: 440-323-1213. Business E-Mail: dlong@attylong.com.

LONG, ELIZABETH TERRY, law librarian; b. Richmond, Va., Dec. 30, 1952; d. William Gray and Mildred Edmunds Long. BA, Stetson U., 1974; MSLS, Cath. U. Am., 1989; AA, Sullins Coll., 1972. Asst. law libr. State Law Libr. Supreme Ct. Va., Richmond, Va., 1980—; libr. asst. Archives Br. Va. State Libr., Richmond, Va., 1977—80, libr. asst. Rec. Br., 1974—77. Pres. Southeastern Chpt., Am. Assn. of Law Libraries, 2002—03, Va. Assn. of Law Libraries, 1995—96; ann. meeting program selection com. Am. Assn. of Law Libraries, 1997—98, profl. devel. com., 1998—2000, membership & retention com., 2002—. Contbr. monograph; author: (article) Commercial Electronic Products for Virginia Legal Research, 48 (Feb 2000) Virginia Lawyer 18-19., Bibliography of Virginia Practice Materials 23 (Summer 1998) Southeastern Law Librarian 23. Bd. trustees Richmond Pub. Libr., Richmond, Va., 1995—98; vestry Ch. of the Holy Comforter, Richmond, Va., 1999—2002; sec. Jr. League of Richmond, Richmond, Va., 1994—95; dir. Mt. Vernon Homeowners Assn., Richmond, Va., 1991—93, 2002—; chair, bd. of recognition Jr. League of Richmond, Richmond, Va., 1998—99, sustainer advisor, diversity task force, 2002—03. Mem.: Am. Assn. Law Libraries (ann. meeting program selection com. 1997—98, pres. southeastern chpt. 2002—03, membership and retention com. 2002—), Va. Assn. Law Libraries (pres. 1995—96), Jr. League of Richmond (sec. 1994—95, chair bd. recognition 1998—99, sustainer advisor Diversity Task Force 2002—03). Episcopalian. Avocation: volunteer work. Office: Law Library Supreme Court of Virginia 100 N Ninth St 2d Floor Richmond VA 23219 Office Fax: 804-786-4542. E-mail: tlong@courts.state.va.us.

LONG, GREGORY ALAN, lawyer; b. San Francisco, Aug. 28, 1948; s. William F. and Ellen L. (Webber) L.; m. Jane H. Barrett, Sept. 30, 1983; children: Matthew, Brian, Michael, Gregory. BA magna cum laude, Claremont Men's Coll., 1970; JD cum laude, Harvard U., 1973. Bar: Calif. 1973, U.S. Dist. Ct. (ctrl. dist.) Calif. 1973, U.S. Ct. Appeals (9th cir.) 1976, U.S. Supreme Ct. 1977, U.S. Ct. Appeals (fed. cir.) 1984. Assoc. Overton, Lyman & Prince, L.A., 1973-78, ptnr., 1978-87, Sheppard, Mullin, Richter & Hampton, L.A., 1987—. Arbitrator L.A. Superior Ct. Fellow Am. Bar Found.; mem. ABA (young lawyers divsn. exec. coun. 1974-88, chmn. 1984-85, ho. of dels. 1983-89, exec. coun. litigation sect. 1981-83), Calif. Bar Assn. (del. 1976-82, 87-88), L.A. County Bar Assn. (exec. com. 1979-82, trustee 1979-82, barristers sect. exc. coun. 1976-82, pres. 1981-82, exec. coun. trial lawyers sect. 1984-88, chair amicus briefs com. 1989-92). Federal civil litigation, State civil litigation. Office: Sheppard Mullin Richter & Hampton 333 S Hope St Los Angeles CA 90071-1406 E-mail: glong@smrh.com.

LONG, JAMES JAY, lawyer; b. Pitts., Jan. 23, 1959; s. James E. and Barbara E. (Holsberg) L.; m. Tamara Rae Beer, Sept. 7, 1985. AB, U. Chgo., 1981; JD magna cum laude, U. Minn., 1984. Bar: Ill. 1984, U.S. Dist. Ct. (no. dist.) Ill. 1984, Minn. 1988, U.S. Dist. Ct. Minn. 1989. Atty. Winston & Strawn, Chgo., 1984-87; assoc. Briggs & Morgan, St. Paul, 1987-91, shareholder, 1991—. Contbr. articles to profl. jours. Mem. St. Paul Jaycees (v.p. 1989-90, pres. 1993-94), Order of Coif. Democrat. Avocations: travel, sports, horse racing. Antitrust, General civil litigation, Franchising. Office: Briggs & Morgan 2400 IDS Center 80 S 8th St Ste 2400 Minneapolis MN 55402-2157

LONG, LARRY, state attorney general; b. Martin, S.D. m. Jan Long; 2 children. Grad., S.D. State U., 1969; JD, U. S.D., 1972. Pvt. practice, Martin, 1972—73; state's atty. Bennett County, 1973—90; chief dep. atty. gen. SD, 1991—2002; atty. gen. State of S.D., 2003—. With U.S. Army. Republican. Office: 500 E Capitol Pierre SD 57501-5070*

LONG, MARTIN EDWARD, lawyer; b. Parsons, Kans., Dec. 29, 1955; s. Richard Harvey Long and Francie Ann (Westhoff) Molliconi; m. Joann Rose Ficker, Sept. 17, 1988. BA in Polit. Sci., Western State Coll., Gunnison, Colo., 1976; JD, U. Denver, 1980. Bar: Colo. 1983, U.S. Dist. Ct. Colo. 1983. Landman Fairway Energy Corp., Denver, 1981-83; pvt. practice Denver, 1984—. Mem. Kiwanis, Denver, 1987-89. Republican. Presbyterian. Avocations: skiing, hunting, biking. Bankruptcy, General civil litigation, Property, real (including real estate development, water). Office: 303 E 17th Ave Ste 800 Denver CO 80203-1299 E-mail: longandlongpc@att.net.

LONG, MAXINE MASTER, lawyer; b. Pensacola, Fla., Oct. 20, 1943; d. Maxwell L. and Claudine E. (Smith) M.; m. Anthony Byrd Long, Aug. 27, 1966; children: Deborah E., David M. AB, Bryn Mawr Coll., 1965; MS, Georgetown U., 1971; JD, U. Miami, 1979. Bar: Fla. 1979, U.S. Ct. Appeals (5th cir.) 1980, U.S. Dist. Ct. (so. dist.) Fla. 1980, U.S. Ct. Appeals (11th cir.) 1981, U.S. Dist. Ct. (mid. and no. dists.) Fla. 1987. Law clk. to U.S. dist. judge U.S. Dist. Ct. (so. dist.) Fla., Miami, 1979-80; assoc. Shutts & Bowen, Miami, 1980-90, of counsel, 1990-92, ptnr., 1992—. Mem. Fla. Bar Assn. (cert. bus. litigator, mem. bus. litigation cert. com. 1995-99, vice chair, 1996-97, past chair bus. litigation com., chair-elect bus. law sect. 2003—) Dade County Bar Assn. (mem. fed. cts. com., recipient pro bono award/Vol. Lawyers for the Arts 1989). General civil litigation, Commercial, contracts (including sales of goods; commercial financing), Insurance. Office: Shutts & Bowen 201 S Biscayne Blvd Ste 1500 Miami FL 33131-4308 E-mail: mlong@shutts-law.com.

LONG, NICHOLAS TROTT, lawyer; b. Bethlehem, Pa., Jan. 24, 1947; s. John Cuthbert and Mary Catherine (Parsons) L.; m. Abigail Brooks, Oct. 11, 1981; 1 child, Gabriel Parsons Brooks Long. BA, Cornell U., 1968; JD, Columbia U., 1972. Bar: Pa., R.I. Asst. dist. atty., Phila., 1972-73; pvt. practice, 1973-77, 92—; asst. pub. defender State of R.I., Providence, 1977-79; gen. counsel U. R.I., Kingston, 1979-86; chief asst. A.G. civil divsn. State of R.I., 1987-90, spl. prosecutor and counsel to the atty. gen., 1987-91, counsel to commn. of higher edn., 1992-2000; gen. counsel R.I. Coll., Providence, 2000—. Ednl. cons. Co-author: The Legal Deskbook for Administrators of Independent Colleges and Universities, 1993, rev., 1999, Managing Liability and Overseas Programs, 1999; author: Strategic Legal Planning: The College and University Legal Audit, 1998. Bd. dirs. Internat. Inst. R.I., Providence, 1990—, 1st v.p., 1997-99; pres. Sakonnet Preservation Assn., Little Compton, R.I., 1994-98, bd. dirs., 1985—. Mem. Nat. Assn. Coll. and Univ. Attys. Avocations: sailing, theatre. Education and schools, General practice, Labor (including EEOC, Fair Labor Standards Act, labor-management relations, NLRB, OSHA). Office: 101 Dyer St Ste 400 Providence RI 02903 E-mail: nicholas@ntlong.com.

LONG, REY, lawyer; b. Phila., Feb. 4, 1936; children: Jane, Brian. LLM, Concord U., 1964. Ptnr. Meriks Law Firm, Phila., 2000—03. Gen. counsel Ruger & Harris, PC. Civil rights. Office: Meriks Law Firm 15237 Count Fleet Ct Carmel IN 46032

LONG, STEPHEN CARREL MIKE, lawyer; b. Roswell, N.Mex., Sept. 22, 1951; s. R.E. (Mike) and Evelyn Marie (Row) Long; m. Barbara I. Lowe, July 19, 1980; children: Jennifer Lynn, Joel Raymond Matthew. BBA with honors, N.Mex. State U., 1973; JD, U. N.Mex., 1977; MDiv, Golden Gate Theol. Sem., 2003. Bar: N.Mex. 1977, U.S. Dist. Ct. N.Mex. 1977, U.S. Tax Ct. 1977, U.S. Ct. Appeals (10th cir.) 1977, U.S. Supreme Ct. 1982, U.S. Ct. Mil. Appeals 1982. Pvt. practice, Albuquerque, 1977-82, 85-87; assoc. Wheeler, Nye, McElwee & Martone, Albuquerque, 1982-84; v.p. Wheeler, McElwee, Sprague & Long, P.C., Albuquerque, 1984-85; pres. Long Law Firm, P.A., Albuquerque, 1987-90; dir. Long & Thomas, P.A., Albuquerque, 1990-91; pvt. practice Placitas, N.Mex., 1992-94; assoc. Ron Koch, P.A., Albuquerque, 1994-2001, Bill Gordon & Assocs., Albuquerque, 2001—. Staff judge adv. N.Mex. Dept. Mil. Affairs, 1980—92; adj. prof. Wayland Bapt. U., 1999—2000. Author: Consumer Bankruptcy Law in New Mexico, 3d edit., 1991; editor Nat. Resources Jour., 1976-77; staff N.Mex. Law Rev., 1975-76; contbr. articles to profl. jours. Trial coach N.Mex. Law Related Edn. Project, 1983-88, 99-2000; bd. dirs., Christian Legal Aid & Referral Svcs., Inc., Albuquerque, 1982-88; chmn., bd. dirs., Hosanna, Inc., Albuquerque, 1986-94; assoc. pastor Sierra Vista Bapt. Ch., 1995-99; tchg. pastor First Bapt. Ch., Bosque Farms, N.Mex., 2000-01, Mission Valley Ch., 2001--; clk., mem. exec. com. Ctrl. Bapt. Assn., 1996--. Served to col., N.Mex. Dept. Mil. Affairs. Mem.: N.Mex. Criminal Def. Lawyers Assn., N.Mex. State Bar Assn. (bd. dirs. bankruptcy sect. 1990—94, chmn. 1994), Nat. Assn. Criminal Def. Lawyers, Sigma Pi, Delta Theta Phi. Republican. Baptist. Avocations: cowboy, team roper. Office: 2501 Yale SE Ste 204 Albuquerque NM 87106 E-mail: steve@billgordon.com.

LONG, THAD GLADDEN, lawyer; b. Dothan, Ala., Mar. 9, 1938; s. Lindon Alexander and Della Gladys (Pilcher) L.; m. Carolyn Frances Wilson, Aug. 13, 1966; children: Louisa Frances Stockman, Wilson Alexander. AB, Columbia U., 1960; JD, U. Va., 1963. Bar: Ala. 1963, U.S. Dist. Ct. (no. dist., so. dist., mid. dist.) Ala., U.S. Ct. Appeals (11th cir., 5th cir.), U.S. Supreme Ct. Assoc. atty. Bradley, Arant, Rose & White, Birmingham, Ala., 1963-70, ptnr., 1970—. Adj. prof. U. Ala., Tuscaloosa, 1988—2002, Samford U., Birmingham, Cumberland Law Sch., 1999—2002. Co-author: Unfair Competition Under Alabama Law, 1990, Protecting Intellectual Property, 1990; mem. editl. bd. The Trademark Reporter; contbr. articles to profl. jours. Chmn. Columbia U. Secondary Schs. Com. Ala. Area, 1975—, pres., chmn., Greater Birmingham Arts Alliance, 1977-79; trustee, pres. Birmingham Music Club, 2000-03; trustee Oscar Wells Trust for Mus. Art, Birmingham, 1983—, Canterbury Meth. Found., 1993-2002, sec., 1993—; chmn. Entrepreneurship Inst. Birmingham, 1989; vice chmn., trustee Sons Revolution Found., Ala., 1994-2002; pres. Birmingham-Jefferson Hist. Soc., 1995-97; trustee Birmingham Music Club Endowment, 1995—; mem. Birmingham Com. Fgn. Rels. Mem. U.S. Patent Bar, Internat. Trademark Assn., Am. Law Inst., Ala. Law Inst., Birmingham Legal Aid Soc., Ala. Bar Assn. (chmn., founder bus. torts and antitrust sect.), Biotechnology Assn. of Ala., Inc. (sec. 1998-2001), U. Va. Law Alumni (chmn. Birmingham chpt. 1984-89), S.R. (pres. 1994-95), Gen. Soc. S.R. (gen. solicitor 1994-2000), Am. Arbitration Assn., Order of the Coif, Omicron Delta Kappa. Republican. Methodist. Avocations: travel, writing, table tennis. Antitrust, General civil litigation, Intellectual property. Home: 2880 Balmoral Rd Birmingham AL 35223-1236 Office: One Federal Place Birmingham AL 35203 E-mail: thadlong@aol.com.

LONG, THOMAS LESLIE, lawyer; b. Mansfield, Ohio, May 30, 1951; s. Ralph Waldo and Rose Ann (Cloud) L.; m. Peggy L. Bryant, Apr. 24, 1982. AB in Govt., U. Notre Dame, 1973; JD, Ohio State U., 1976. Bar: Ohio 1976, U.S. Dist. Ct. (so. dist.) Ohio 1976, U.S. Dist. Ct. (no. dist.) Ohio 1977, U.S. Ct. Appeals (6th cir.) 1978. Assoc. Alexander, Ebinger, Fisher, McAlister & Lawrence, Columbus, Ohio, 1976-82, ptnr., 1982-85, Baker & Hostetler, Columbus, 1985—. Mem. ABA, Ohio Bar Assn., Columbus Bar Assn., Fed. Bar Assn., Assn. Trial Lawyer Am. Clubs: Capitol (Columbus). Democrat. Roman Catholic. Federal civil litigation, State civil litigation, Legislative. Home: 2565 Leeds Rd Columbus OH 43221-3613 Office: Baker & Hostetler 65 E State St Ste 2100 Columbus OH 43215-4260

LONG, VIRGINIA, state supreme court justice; m. Jonathan D. Weiner; 3 children. Grad., Dunbarton Coll. of Holy Cross; JD, Rutgers U., 1966. Dep. atty. gen. State of N.J.; assoc. Pitney, Hardin, Kipp and Szuch; dir. N.J. Divsn. Consumer Affairs, 1975; commr. N.J. Dept. Banking, 1977-78; judge N.J. Superior Ct., 1978-84, Appellate Divsn. N.J. Superior Ct., 1984-95, presiding judge, 1995-99; assoc. justice Supreme Ct. N.J., 1999—. Office: Supreme Ct NJ PO Box 023 Trenton NJ 08625-0970

LONGETEIG, IVER J. lawyer; b. Potlatch, Idaho, Apr. 7, 1941; s. Iver J. and Margaret Nell (Waters) L.; m. Jody Kay Wiegand, July 26, 1964 (div. 1978); children: Halle J., Andrew W.; m. Linda Chase, Apr. 15, 1995. BA, U. Idaho, 1962, JD, 1965. Bar: Idaho 1965, Nev. 1982, U.S. Dist. Ct. Idaho 1965, U.S. Supreme Ct. 1970. Assoc. Hawley Troxell, Boise, Idaho, 1965-69; ptnr. Ambrose Fitzgerald & Longeteig, Meridian, Idaho, 1969-74, Runft & Longeteig, Boise, Idaho, 1974-81; house counsel Renaissance Devel., Las Vegas, 1981-83; prin. Longeteig Law Towers, Boise, Idaho, 1983—. Contbr. article to law jour. Lt. comdr. USNR, 1967-74. Recipient Pro-Bono award Idaho State Bar, 1990. Mem. Masons. Avocations: theater, cooking. Home: 5304 N Turret Way Boise ID 83703-3241 Office: Longeteig Law Towers 817 W Franklin St Boise ID 83702-5553 E-mail: ilongeteig@earthlink.net.

LONGFELDER, LAWRENCE LEE, lawyer; b. Seattle, Feb. 23, 1944; s. Harlow J. and Nancy Jane (Nicholson) L.; m. Christine Doucet, Mar. 25, 1978. BA in Polit. Sci., Whitman Coll., 1966; JD, U. Wash., 1970. Bar: Wash. 1971, U.S. Dist. Ct. (we. dist.) Wash. 1971, U.S. Dist. Ct. (ea. dist.) Wash. 1974, U.S. Dist. Ct. (so. dist.) Calif. 1983, Idaho 1994, U.S. Dist. Ct. Idaho 1994. Assoc. Miracle & Pruzan, Seattle, 1971-73; ptnr. Sullivan, Morrow & Longfelder, Seattle, 1973-79; prin., ptnr. Morrow, Longfelder, Tinker & Kidman, Seattle, 1979-83; pres., prin. Longfelder Tinker Kidman Inc., P.S., Seattle, 1983—2002; prin. Longfelder Law L.L.C., Seattle, 2003—. Pres. Forgotten Children's Fund, Seattle, 1984—; mem. bd. adjustment City of Seattle, 1978-81. Mem. ABA, Seattle-King County Bar Assn., Wash. State Bar Assn., Idaho Bar Assn., Wash. Trial Lawyers Assn., Assn. Trial Lawyers Am., Columbia Tower, Seattle Club, Idaho State Bar Assn. General civil litigation, Personal injury (including property damage), Professional liability. Office: Longfelder Law LLC 2505 2nd Ave Ste 610 Seattle WA 98121

LONGHOFER, RONALD STEPHEN, lawyer; b. Junction City, Kans., Aug. 30, 1946; s. Oscar William and Anna Mathilda (Krause) L.; m. Elizabeth Norma McKenna; children: Adam, Nathan, Stefanie. BMus, U. Mich., 1968, JD, 1975. Bar: Mich. 1975, U.S. Dist. Ct. (ea. dist.) Mich., U.S. Ct. Appeals (6th cir.), U.S. Supreme Ct.; cert. chartered fin. analyst, fraud examiner. Law clk. to judge U.S. Dist. Ct. (ea. dist.) Mich., Detroit, 1975-76; ptnr. Honigman, Miller, Schwartz & Cohn, Detroit, 1976—, chmn. litigation dept., 1993-96. Co-author: Courtroom Handbook on Michigan Evidence, 2002, Michigan Court Rules Practice, 1998, Mich. Court Rules Practice-Evidence, 2002, Introducing Evidence at Trial, 2003; author: Courtroom Handbook on Michigan Civil Procedure, 2002; editor Mich. Law Rev., 1974-75. Served with U.S. Army, 1968-72. Mem. ABA, Detroit Bar Assn., Fed. Bar Assn., Investment Analysts Soc. Detroit, Assn. for Investment Mgmt. and Rsch., Assn. Cert. Fraud Examiners, Inst. Bus. Appraisers, U. Mich. Pres.' Club, Order of Coif, Phi Beta Kappa, Phi Kappa Phi, Pi Kappa Lambda. Federal civil litigation, State civil litigation. Home: 974 Penniman Ave Plymouth MI 48170 Office: Honigman Miller Schwartz & Cohn 2290 1st National Bldg Detroit MI 48226. E-mail: rsl@honigman.com.

LONGO, MELLISSA LAYLA, lawyer; b. Elizabeth, N.J., July 16, 1972; d. Joseph Michael Longo Jr. and Linda Ann Longo. BA in English Lit., N.J. City U.; JD, N.Y. Law Sch.; postgrad., St. Peter's Coll. Bar: N.J. 2002. With Merrill Lynch, N.Y.C., par loan trading closer; assoc. Deutsche Bank, Jersey City. Pro bono counsel L&G Immigration Rights Task Force, N.Y.C., 2001—. Mem.: ABA (Silver Key award). Roman Catholic. Avocation: painting. Corporate, general, Immigration, naturalization, and customs, Intellectual property. Home: 100 Warren St Ste 1509 Jersey City NJ 07302 Office: Deutsche Bank 90 Hudson St 5th Fl Jersey City NJ 07302

LONGO, RONALD ANTHONY, lawyer; b. Schenectady, N.Y., Nov. 17, 1952; s. Vito Frank and Frances (Scardamaglia) L.; m. Susan Fraioli, Nov. 15, 1980; children: Kristen, John Michael. BS, Cornell U., 1974; JD, Pace U., 1980. Bar: N.Y. 1981, U.S. Dist. Ct. (so. dist.) N.Y. 1984, U.S Supreme Ct. 1984. Asst. dir. labor rels. Onondaga County, Syracuse, N.Y., 1974-75; dir. employee rels. Ardsley (N.Y.) Sch. Dist., 1975-80; assoc. Plunkett & Jaffe, White Plains, N.Y., 1980-86, ptnr., 1986-93, Keane & Beane, P.C., White Plains, N.Y., 1993—. Dep. town atty. Town of Clarkstown, New City, N.Y., 1985—; adj. assoc. prof. Iona Coll., New Rochelle, N.Y., 1982-90; adj. prof. L.I. U., Brookville, N.Y., 1986-88; instr. labor rels. studies program Cornell U., 1991-92. Author: (with others) Public Sector Labor and Employment Law, 1988, 98. Mem. ABA, N.Y. State Bar Assn., N.Y. State Pub. Employer Labor Rels. Assn. (sec., treas. 1979-81, pres. 1982-83, Disting. Svc. award 1983). Education and schools, Labor (including EEOC, Fair Labor Standards Act, labor-management relations, NLRB, OSHA). Office: Keane & Beane PC 1 N Broadway Ste 700 White Plains NY 10601-2319

LONGSTRETH, ROBERT CHRISTY, lawyer; b. Phoenix, Oct. 11, 1956; s. Robert Daniel and Marion (Petrovich) L.; m. Veronica Marie Platt, May 7, 1988. BA, Haverford Coll., 1978; JD, Yale U., 1981. Bar: N.Y. 1982, U.S. Ct. Appeals (3d cir.) 1982, U.S. Ct. Appeals (9th and 10th cirs.) 1985, U.S. Ct. Appeals (2d and 11th cirs.) 1986, U.S. Ct. Appeals (D.C. cir.) 1988, D.C. 1988, Calif. 1989, U.S. Dist. Ct. (so. dist.) Calif. 1989, U.S. Supreme Ct. 1989. Law clk. U.S. Dist. Ct., N.J., 1981-83; trial atty. U.S. Dept. Justice, Washington, 1983-87; assoc. Wilmer, Cutler & Pickering, Washington, 1987-88, Office of Ind. Counsel Lawrence E. Walsh, Washington, 1988-89, Gray, Cary, Ware & Freidenrich, San Diego, 1989—. Judge pro tem San Diego Superior Ct. Author (with Matthew Bender) Handling Federal Tort Claims, 1988—. Mem. ABA, FBA (past pres. San Diego chpt.), Amnesty Internat., Yale Club San Diego (treas., past pres.), Phi Beta Kappa. Democrat. Episcopalian. Federal civil litigation, Environmental, Insurance. Home: 2225 Pine St San Diego CA 92103-1140 Office: Gray Cary Ware & Freidenrich 401 B St Ste 2000 San Diego CA 92101-4240 E-mail: rlongstreth@graycary.com.

LONNQUIST, GEORGE ERIC, lawyer; b. Lincoln, Nebr., Mar. 29, 1946; s. John Hall and Elizabeth Claire (Hanson) L.; m. Wendi Ann McDonough; children: Alethea, Courtenay, Barrett. BS, U. Tenn., 1968; JD, U. Nebr., 1971; LLM, NYU, 1974. Bar: Calif. 1983, Oreg. 1972, Nebr. 1971. Law clerk Oreg. Supreme Ct., Salem, 1971-72; dep. legis. counsel Oreg. Legislature, Salem, 1972-73; ptnr. Meysing & Lonnquist, Portland, 1974-78; v.p., assoc. gen. counsel Amfac, Inc., Portland and San Francisco, 1978-84; sr. v.p., gen. counsel Homestead Fin. Corp., Millbrae, Calif., 1984-91, Homestead Savs., Millbrae, 1984-93; pvt. practice, San Francisco, 1993—. Democrat. Roman Catholic. Avocation: woodcarving. Corporate, general, Finance, Property, real (including real estate development, water). Home: 1945 Beach Park Blvd Foster City CA 94404-1326 Office: 4000 E 3rd Ave Foster City CA 94404-4805 E-mail: lonn@legacypartners.com.

LOOMAN, JAMES R. lawyer; b. Vallejo, Calif., June 5, 1952; s. Alfred R. and Jane M. (Halter) L.; m. Donna G. Craven, Dec. 18, 1976; children: Alison Marie, Mark Andrew, Zachary Michael. BA, Valparaiso U., 1974; JD, U. Chgo., 1978. Bar: Ill, 1978, U.S. Dist. Ct. (no dist.) Ill. 1978, U.S. Claims Ct. 1979. Ptnr. Sidley Austin Brown & Wood, Chgo., 1986—. Fellow Am. Coll. Comml. Fin. Lawyers; mem. ABA, Chgo. Bar Assn. (chmn. comml. and fin. transaction com. 1996-97, 2002-03), Chgo. Athletic Assn., Skokie Country Club, Mid-Day Club. Lutheran. Corporate, general, Commercial, contracts (including sales of goods; commercial financing), Finance. Office: Sidley Austin Brown & Wood Bank One Plz Chicago IL 60603-2003 E-mail: jlooman@sidley.com.

LOONEY, CULLEN ROGERS, lawyer; b. Edinburg, Tex., July 22, 1946; s. James Cullen and Margaret (Montgomery) L.; m. Carol Lynn Smith, June 22, 1969; children: Lorin Connor, William Kelley, Courtney Lynn. BBA, U. Tex., 1968, JD, 1973. Bar: Tex. 1973. Lawyer Kelley, Looney, Alexander & Sawyer, Edinburg, 1973-87; pvt. practice Edinburg, 1987—; mgr. Edinburg Improvement Assn., 1988—; pres., chmn. bd. Security State Bank, Pharr, Tex., 1989-96. Bd. dirs. Rio Grande Valley Sports Authority, South Tex. Higher Edn. Authority, Edinburg Indsl. Found.; mem. Tex. A&M Kingsville Citrus Adv. Bd., Tijerina Found.; mem. chancellor's coun. U. Tex.; pres. Looney-Montgomery Found. Mem. Tex. House Reps., Austin, 1977-81. 1st lt. U.S. Army. Named Exec. of Yr. Profl. Secs. Internat., 1983. Mem. Tex. State Bar Assn., Hidalgo County Bar Assn., Tex. Bar Found., Edinburg Rotary, Tex. Cowboys, Phi Delta Phi, Sigma Chi. Democrat. Episcopalian. Oil, gas, and mineral, Probate (including wills, trusts). Office: PO Box 118 Edinburg TX 78540-0118 E-mail: CullenRL@aol.com.

LOONEY, WILLIAM FRANCIS, JR., lawyer; b. Boston, Sept. 20, 1931; s. William Francis Sr. and Ursula Mary (Ryan) L.; m. Constance Mary O'Callaghan, Dec. 28, 1957; children: Willam F. III, Thomas M., Karen D., Martha A. AB, JD, Harvard U. Bar: Mass. 1958, D.C. 1972, U.S. Supreme Ct. 1972, U.S. Dist. Ct. (ea. dist.) Mich. 1986. Law clk. to presiding justice Mass. Supreme Jud. Ct., 1958-59; assoc. Goodwin, Procter & Hoar, Boston, 1959-62; chief civil divsn. U.S. Attys. Office, 1964-65; ptnr. Looney & Grossman, Boston, 1965-94, sr. counsel, 1995—. Asst. U.S. atty. Dist. Mass., 1962-65; spl. hearing officer U.S. Dept. Justice, 1965-68; mem. Mass. Bd. Bar Overseers, 1985-91, vice-chmn., 1990-91; corp. mem. Greater Boston Legal Svcs., Inc., 1994—. Mem. Zoning Bd. of Appeals, Dedham, Mass., 1971-74; bd. dirs. Boston Latin Sch. Found., 1981-85, pres. 1981-84, chmn. bd. dirs., 1984-86; trustee Social Law Libr., 1994-97; chmn. ADR adv. com. U.S. Dist. Ct., 1998—. Fellow Am. Coll. Trial Lawyers (state com. 1996-2001); mem. Mass. Bar Assn. (co-chmn. standing com. lawyers responsibility for pub. svc. 1987-88, chmn. fed. ct. adv. com. Alternative Dispute Resolution 1998—), Boston Bar Assn. (pres. 1984-85, coun. 1985-90, chmn. sr. lawyers sect. 1992-94, Maguire award for professionalism 1995), Nat. Assn. Bar Pres.'s, Boston Latin Sch. Assn. (pres. 1980-82, life trustee 1982—, Man of Yr. 1985), USCG Found. (bd. dirs. 1987-2000, dir. emeritus 2000—), Norfolk Golf Club, Harvard Club, Harvard U. Alumni Assn. (bd. dirs.). Democrat. Roman Catholic. Home: 43 Coronation Dr Dedham MA 02026-6230 Office: 101 Arch St Fl 9 Boston MA 02110-1112 E-mail: wlooney@lgllp.com., h.wlooney@socialaw.com.

LOOS, PETRA, lawyer; b. Hessen, Germany, Sept. 27, 1968; Diploma, U. Frankfurt, Germany, 1992. Bar: Regional Ct. Frankfurt/Main, Ct. Appeals Franfurt/Main. Lawyer Feddersen Laule Scherzberg Ohle Hansen Ewerwahn, Frankfurt/Main, Germany, 1995—2000, jr. ptnr., 2000; ptnr. Schulte Lawyers, Frankfurt/Main, 2000—. Labor (including EEOC, Fair Labor Standards Act, labor-management relations, NLRB, OSHA). Office: Schulte Lawyers Hochstraße 49 60313 Frankfurt Germany Office Fax: (069) 900 26999. Business E-Mail: schulte@schulte-lawyers.de.

LOPACKI, EDWARD JOSEPH, JR., lawyer; b. Bklyn., June 4, 1947; s. Edward Joseph and Lillian Jane (Wallace) L.; m. Crystal May Miller, June 21, 1969; children: Edward Joseph III, Elizabeth Jane. BA in sociology, Villanova U., 1971; JD, Vt. Law Sch., 1980. Bar: Fla. 1981, U.S. Dist. Ct. (mid. dist.) Fla. 1983, U.S. Ct. Appeals (11th cir.) 1986. Mgmt. trainee Bankers Trust Co., N.Y.C., 1968-72; counselor N.J. State Employment Svcs., Red Bank, 1972-77; pvt. practice Bradenton, Fla., 1981—. Adj. prof. of law Nova U., Ft. Lauderdale, Fla., 1981, Manatee C.C., Bradenton, Fla., 1994-96; cons. Suncoast Ctr. for Ind. Living, 1999-2001. Mem. Fla. Ind. Living Coun., 1996-2000, dist. VI adv. coun. Fla. Dept. Health and Rehabilitative Svcs., 1988-92, Manatee County Health Care Adv. Bd., 1993—, Manatee County Coun. on Access for the Disabled, 1994—, Suncoast Ctr. for Ind. Living, 1995-99; pres. Cen. Soccer Assn., 1981-82; mem. De Soto Boys Club, 1982-87, sec., 1986-87; chmn. edn. com. Manatee Area c. of C., 1983; mem. Manatee Area Youth Soccer Assn., 1981-82, Manatee Coun. on Aging, 1986-87, Boys' Club Manatee County, 1986-87; bd. dirs. Manatee County G.T. Bray Little League East, 1988-89. Mem. Nat. Orgn. Social Security Claimants Reps., Manatee County Bar Assn. (bd. dirs. 1988-89), KC (advocate 1984-85, 88-91), Lions (pres. Manatee River 1985-86, treas. 1987-88, 90-91, sec. 1988-89, Lion of Yr. award 1988, 94). Democrat. Roman Catholic. Avocations: reading, advocacy for civil rights of people with disabilities. Estate planning, Pension, profit-sharing, and employee benefits, Probate (including wills, trusts). Home: 6612 27th Avenue Dr W Bradenton FL 34209-7405 Office: PO Box 14604 Bradenton FL 34280 E-mail: LopackiLaw@aol.com.

LOPATIN, ALAN G. lawyer; b. New Haven, Conn., May 25, 1956; s. Paul and Ruth (Rosen) L.; m. Debra Jo Engler, May 17, 1981; children: Jonah Adam, Asa Louis. BA, Yale U., 1978; JD, Am. U., 1981. Bar: D.C. 1981, U.S. Supreme Ct. 1985. Law clk. FMC, Washington, 1980-81; counsel com. on post office and civil svc. U.S. Ho. of Reps., Washington, 1981-82, counsel com. on budget, 1982-86, dep. chief counsel, 1986-87, counsel temp. joint com. on deficit reduction, 1986, dep. gen. counsel com. on post office and civil svc., 1987-90, gen. counsel com. on edn. and labor, 1991-94; pres. Ledge Counsel, Inc., Washington, 1995—; exec. dir. Nat. and Cmty. Svc. Coalition, 1995-99; ptnr. Valente Lopatin & Schulze, Washington, 1998—2002; of counsel Valente and Assoc., Washington, 2003—. Mem. presdl. task force Health Care Reform, Washington, 1993. Mem. ABA, D.C. Bar Assn., Nat. Assn. Thrift Savs. Plan Participants (pres. 1999—), Nat. Dem. Club, Yale Club (Washington). Democratic. Jewish. Labor (including EEOC, Fair Labor Standards Act, labor-management relations, NLRB, OSHA), Legislative, Pension, profit-sharing, and employee benefits. Home: 4958 Butterworth Pl NW Washington DC 20016-4354 Office: Ledge Counsel Inc 4958 Butterworth Pl NW Washington DC 20016-4354 E-mail: ledgecnsl@aol.com.

LOPES, BEATRIZ, lawyer; b. Rio de Janeiro, June 22, 1969; d. Pedro and Maria Helena Lopes; m. Marcos Coelho da Rocha, Aug. 27, 1999; 1 child, Manuela Lopes Coelho Da Rocha. JD, U.E.R.J., Rio de Janeiro, 1992; LLM, Northwestern U., Chgo., 1998. Bar: Brazil. Ptnr. Bastos-Tigre Coelho Da Rocha E Lopes Advorados, Rio de Janeiro, 1995—97, 1999—; assoc. White & Case LLP, N.Y.C., 1998—99. Corporate, general, Commercial, contracts (including sales of goods; commercial financing), Alternative dispute resolution. Office: Bastos-Tigire Coelho da Rochea E Lopes Av Rio Branco 99/9 0 Andar 20040-004 Rio de Janeiro Brazil

LOPEZ, DAVID, lawyer; b. N.Y.C., May 9, 1942; s. Damaso and Carmen (Gonzalez) L.; m. Nancy Mary Cea, Aug. 29, 1964; children: David, Jonathan. AB, Cornell U., 1963; JD, Columbia U., 1966. Bar: N.Y. 1966. Assoc. firm Leon, Weill & Mahoney, N.Y.C., 1966-67, Bressler & Meislen, N.Y.C., 1967-70; individual practice law N.Y.C., 1970—. Chmn. bd. A.T.I. Adv. Svcs., Inc., 1979—; dir. Nancy Lopez, Inc., Southampton, N.Y. Mem. ABA, N.Y. State Bar Assn., Suffolk County Bar Assn. Federal civil litigation, Corporate, general, Securities. Office: 171 Edge of Woods Rd PO Box 323 Southampton NY 11969-0323 E-mail: davidlopezesq.com@aol.com.

LOPEZ, DAVID TIBURCIO, lawyer, educator, arbitrator, mediator; b. Laredo, Tex., July 17, 1939; s. Tiburcio and Dora (Davila) L.; m. Romelia G. Guerra, Nov. 20, 1965; 1 child, Vianei López Robinson. Student, Laredo Jr. Coll., 1956-58; BJ, U. Tex., 1962; JD summa cum laude, South Tex. Coll. Law, 1971. Bar: Tex. 1971, U.S. Dist. Ct. (so. dist.) Tex. 1972, U.S. Ct. Appeals (5th cir.) 1973, U.S. Dist. Ct. (we. dist.) Tex. 1975, U.S. Ct. Claims 1975, U.S. Ct. Appeals (fed. cir.) 1975, U.S. Supreme Ct. 1976, U.S. Dist. Ct. (ea. dist.) Tex. 1978, U.S. Dist. Ct. N.Mex. 2000, U.S. Ct. Appeals (11th cir.) 1981, U.S. Ct. Appeals (9th cir.) 1984; cert. internat. com. arbitrator Internat. Ctr. for Arbitration; mediator tng. Atty.-Mediator Inst. Reporter Laredo Times, 1958-59; cons. Mexican Nat. Coll. Mag., Mexico City, 1961-62; reporter Corpus Christi (Tex.) Caller-Times, 1962-64; state capitol corr. Long News Svc., Austin, Tex., 1964-65; publs. dir. Interam. Regional Orgn. of Workers, Mexico City, 1965-67; nat. field rep. AFL-CIO, Washington, 1967-71, publs. dir. Tex. chpt. Austin, 1971-72; pvt. practice Houston, 1971—. Adj. prof. U. Houston, 1972-74, Thurgood Marshall Sch. Law, Houston, 1975-76; mem. adv. com. nat. Hispanic ednl. rsch. project One Million and Counting Tomas Rivera Ctr., 1989-91; mem. adv. bd. Inst. Transnat. Arbitration; charter mem. Resolution Forum Inc.; mem. adv. bd. South Tex. Ctr. Profl. Responsibility; mem. nat. panel of neutrals JAMS/ENDISPUTE, 1996-2000. Bd. dirs. Pacifica Found., N.Y.C., 1970-72, Houston Community Coll., 1972-75; mem. bd. edn. Houston Ind. Sch. Dist., 1972-75. With U.S. Army. Mem. ABA, FBA, Tex. Bar Assn. (com. on pattern jury changes), Houston Bar Assn. (com. on alternative dispute resolution), Internat. Bar Assn., Interam. Bar Assn., Bar of U.S. Fed. Cir., Mex.-Am. Bar Assn., Inter-Pacific Bar Assn., Tex.-Mex. Bar Assn., Hispanic Bar Assn., World Assn. Lawyers (chair internat. lab. sect.), Am. Judicature Soc., Indsl. Rels. Rsch. Assn., Sigma Delta Chi, Phi Alpha Delta. Democrat. Roman Catholic. Federal civil litigation, Private international, Labor (including EEOC, Fair Labor Standards Act, labor-management relations, NLRB, OSHA). Home: 28 Farnham Ct Houston TX 77024 Office: 3900 Montrose Blvd Houston TX 77006-4959 E-mail: dtlopez@lopezlawfirm.com.

LOPEZ, FLOYD WILLIAM, lawyer; b. Albuquerque, Sept. 7, 1952; s. J. Joseph and Eleanor (Marron) L.; m. Susan Templeton, Dec. 27, 1980; children: Kathleen, Melinda, Michael, Carolyn, Owen. BA in English and Spanish, Amherst Coll., 1974; JD, U. N.Mex., 1982. Bar: N.Mex. 1982, U.S. Dist. Ct. N.Mex. 1983, U.S. Ct. Appeals (10th cir.) 1983, U.S. Supreme Ct., 1999. Senate intern N.Mex. Legis., Santa Fe, 1979; messenger Modrall, Sperling, Roehl, Harris & Sisk, Albuquerque, 1979; pvt. practice in constn. Albuquerque, 1979; legal extern Marron & McKinnon, Albuquerque, 1979-81; law clk. to judge Edwin L. Mechem U.S. Dist. Ct., Albuquerque, 1982-84; counsel Gov.'s Organized Crime Prevention Commn., Albuquerque, 1984-86; asst. county atty. County of Bernalillo, Albuquerque, 1991-95; pvt. practice Albuquerque, 1985—. Mem. ethics com. Bernalillo County; analyst N.Mex. Senate, 1993. Mem. Albuquerque Bar Assn. (bd. dirs. 1990-93), Legal Aid Soc. (bd. dirs. 1990-94, Pro Bono award 1986-89). Democrat. Roman Catholic. Avocations: skiing, golf. General civil litigation, Criminal, General practice. Office: PO Box 10285 Albuquerque NM 87184-0285

LOPEZ, JORGE LUIS, lawyer; b. Havana, Cuba, Apr. 21, 1961; s. Luis and Sarah Lopez; m. Mercedes L Rodriguez, Oct. 26, 1996. BA magna cum laude in Polit. Sci., St. Thomas U., 1983, MBA, 1985; JD cum laude, U. Miami, 1987. Bar: Fla. 1987, U.S. Supreme Ct. Fla. 1987. Dir. intergovernmental affairs Miami-Dade County, Fla., 1982—84; of counsel Shutts & Bowen, LLP, Miami, 1996—98; mng. shareholder Verner Liipfert, Bernhard, McPherson and Hand, Miami, 1998—2001; ptnr. Steel Hector & Davis LLP, Miami, 2001—. Mem. exec. com. Beacon Coun., Miami, 2002—. Contbr. articles to profl. jours. including U. Miami Internat. Am Law Rev. Fundraiser Nat. Rep. Fin. Com., Washington, 2000, Pres. George W. Bush Fin. and Inaugural Coms., Austin, Tex., 2000, Gov. Jeb Bush Fin. and Inaugural Coms., Tallahassee, 1998; mem. president's adv. coun. St. Thomas U., Miami, 2001; mem. cabinet United Way, Miami, 2002; mem. Vizcaya and Gardens Trust, Miami, 1998; dir. Carlos Albizu U., Miami, 2002. Mem.: Soc. Bar and Gavel (life), Soc. Wig and Robe (life), Omicron Delta Kappa (life). Catholic. Avocations: golf, reading, racquetball, basketball, reading. Office: Steel Hector & Davis LLP 200 S Biscayne Blvd Ste 4000 Miami FL 33131-2398 E-mail: jlopez@steelhector.com.

LOPEZ, MARTIN, III, lawyer; b. Las Cruces, N.Mex., June 20, 1954; s. Abenicio Rafael and Angelina Cordelia (Griego) L.; m. Elizabeth Crawford, Aug. 5, 1978; children: Alisa Angelina Maria, Martin IV. BA, U. N.Mex., 1976; JD, George Washington U., 1979; MPA, U. N.Mex., 1982, MBA, 1989. Bar: N.Mex. 1979, U.S. Dist. Ct. N.Mex. 1980, U.S. Ct. Appeals (10th cir.) 1981, U.S. Supreme Ct. 1982, U.S. Ct. Claims 1983, U.S. Tax Ct. 1984, D.C. 1985, U.S. Ct. Appeals (4th and 9th cirs.) 1996. Legal intern State of N.Mex. Property Tax Dept., Santa Fe, 1977, Pub. Defender Svc., Washington, 1977-78, EEOC, Washington, 1978-79; asst. pub. defender State of N.Mex., Albuquerque, 1979-82, asst. atty. gen., 1982-84; ptnr., dir. firm Lopez & Lopez, P.C., Albuquerque, 1984-86; prse. Lopez, Lopez & Jaffe, P.C., Albuquerque, 1986-87, Martin Lopez III, P.C., Albuquerque, 1988—. Mem. N.Mex. Bar Examiners, 1998—. Past pres. Alternative House, Inc.; past pres., St. Mary's Sch. Bd., 1990-97; v.p., pres. St. Pius X H.S. adv. sch. bd., 1999—; mem. coun. Holy Rosary Parish, 1991-98; mem. citizens' adv. group City of Albuquerque, 1992-94; mem. Leadership Albuquerque, 1994. Recipient Alumni award U. N.Mex., 1972. Mem. ABA, N.Mex. State Bar Assn., N.Mex. Hispanic Bar Assn., N.Mex. Trial Lawyers Assn., Assn. Trial Lawyers Am., Albuquerque Hispano C. of C., Greater Albuqerque C. of C., Albuquerque Jaycees, Socorro County C. of C., Phi Alpha Theta, Pi Alpha Alpha, Phi Alpha Delta. Democrat. Roman Catholic. General civil litigation, Commercial, contracts (including sales of goods; commercial financing), Criminal. Home: 6124 Carousal Ave NW Albuquerque NM 87120-2171 Office: 1500 Mountain Rd NW Albuquerque NM 87104-1359 E-mail: ML3law@aol.com.

LOPEZ ESCARCENA, R. SEBASTIAN, lawyer, law educator; b. Lima, Peru, Feb. 3, 1972; arrived in Chile, 1974; s. Luis López Cordovez and Patricia Escarcena Burnett. BA, LLB, Pontificia U. Católica Chile, Santiago, 1997; LLM, U. Leiden, The Netherlands, 2001. Bar: Chile 1998. Law clk. Figueroa, Vakuzuela y Cia, Santiago, 1994, Ministerio de Justicia, Santiago, 1996; in-counsel Entel PCS, Santiago, 1998—2000; off-counsel Chilena Consolidada Seguros, Santiago, 2002; assoc. Guerrero, Olivos, Novoa y Errazuriz, Santiago, 2002. Asst. prof. Pontificia Univ. Catolica de Chile, Santiago, 2002. Mem.: Sociedad Chilena de Derecho Internat., Colegio de Abogados de Chile A.G. Roman Catholic. Public international, Private international, General practice. Home: Mónaco 5482 Vitacora Santiago Chile Office: Guerrero Olivos Novoa y Errazuriz Miraflores 178 Piso 12 Santiago Chile

LOPEZ-PINA, ANTONIO, state counsel, legal educator; b. Murcia, Spain, June 4, 1937; s. Antonio and Dolores López-Pina; m. Annegret Pietsch, July 28, 1964; children: Ricardo, Pablo. PhD in Law, U. Complutense, Madrid, 1963; postgrad., U. Munich, 1960-61, Free U. Berlin, 1961-63, U. Paris, 1963-64, U. Mich., U. Harvard, 1964-66. Prof. polit. law Santiago de Compostela U., 1977-79, Valladolid U., 1979-82; prof. constl. law Complutense U., Madrid, 1982—; state counselor Madrid, 1982—; Jean Monnet chair Legal European Culture Complutense U., Madrid, 1998—. Senator Constituent Assembly; mem. Constitutional and Fgn. Affairs Commns., 1977-79, founding father of 1978 Constitution; Democracia representativa y Parlamentarismo, 1994. Author: Derechos y deberes fundamentales en la Constitución española, 1989, La garantía constitucional de los derechos fundamentales: Alemania, España, Francia e Italia, 1991; author, editor: Manual de Derecho Constitucional, 1996, 2d edit., 2001; editor, co-author: Spanisches Verfassungsrecht, 1993, División de Poderes e Interpretación, 1987, Elementos de Derecho público, 2002. Decorated great cross German Fed. Republic; recipient Alexander V. Humboldt award, 1980, Constl. Merit award Spanish govt., 1988; Joint Spanish-Am. Com. Cultural Affairs and Sci. Rsch. grantee, 1978, 79, 84, 90. Mem. Spanish Assn. Polit. Sci. and Constl. Law, Spanish Assn. Human Rights. Mem. Spanish Worker Socialist Party. Office: Consejero de Estado Peña Santa 14 28034 Madrid Spain

LOPRETE, JAMES HUGH, lawyer; b. Detroit, Sept. 17, 1929; s. James Victor and Effie Hannah (Brown) LoP.; m. Marion Ann Garrison, Sept. 11, 1952; children: James Scott, Kimberly Anne, Kent Garrison, Robert Drew. AB, U. Mich., 1951, JD with Distinction, 1953. Bar: Mich. 1954. Practiced law, Detroit, 1954—; atty. Chrysler Corp., Detroit, 1953; assoc. firm Monaghan, LoPrete, McDonald, Yakima, Grenke & McCarthy, P.C. and predecessor firms, Detroit, from 1954; mem. firm Monaghan, LoPrete, McDonald, Yakima & Grenke, P.C. and predecessor firms, 1966—, pres., 1979—2001. Bd. dirs. Drake's Batter Mix Co.; instr. legal writing Wayne State U., Detroit, 1955-57 Trustee U. Mich. Club of Detroit Scholarship Fund, 1967, pres., 1982—; trustee Samuel Westerman Found., 1971—, pres., 1984; trustee John R. & M. Margrite Davis Found.; pres., dir. Louis & Nellie Sieg Found., 2000—, Frank G. and Gertrude Dunlap Found., 2001—. Fellow Am. Coll. Trust and Estate Counsel (litig. com. 1997—), Internat. Acad. Estate and Trust Law; mem. ABA, Oakland County Bar Assn., State Bar Mich. (chmn. probate and estate planning sect. 1977), Detroit Athletic Club (dir. 1983-88, sec. 1986-88), Orchard Lake Country Club, U. Mich. of Greater Detroit (pres. 1966). Corporate, general, Probate (including wills, trusts), Estate taxation. Home: 2829 Warner Dr Orchard Lake MI 48324-2449 Office: Monaghan LoPrete McDonald et al 40700 Woodward Ave Ste A Bloomfield Hills MI 48304-5110 E-mail: mfreeman@managhanpc.com.

LORD, BARBARA JOANNI, lawyer; b. Bay Shore, N.Y., Aug. 7, 1939; d. Theodore and Doris Aileen (Smith) Joanni; m. Robert Wilder Lord, June 24, 1967. BA, U. Miami, 1961; JD, NYU, 1966. Bar: N.Y. 1967, Fla. 1978, U.S. Supreme Ct. 1991. Asst. editor A.M. Best Co., N.Y.C., 1961-64; contract analyst Guardian Life Ins. Co., N.Y.C., 1964-66; legal trainee N.Y. State Liquor Auth., N.Y.C., 1966-67, atty., 1967-70, sr. atty., 1970-80, assoc. atty., 1980—. Mem. ABA, N.Y. State Bar Assn., Fla. Bar Assn., Order Ea. Star. Administrative and regulatory. Office: N Y State Liquor Authority 11 Park Pl New York NY 10007-2801

LORDI, KATHERINE MARY, lawyer; b. Jersey City, Mar. 24, 1949; d. Peter G. and Hilde E. (Illy) Lordi. AB, Trinity Coll., Washington, 1971; JD, Fordham U., 1975. Bar: N.J. 1975, U.S. Dist. Ct. N.J. 1975, U.S. Supreme Ct. 1983, U.S. Ct. Appeals (3d cir.) 1989. Clk. Friedman & D'Allessandro, East Orange, NJ, 1974-75, assoc., 1975-76; pvt. practice Bloomfield, NJ, 1976—. Adj. instr. Coll. St. Elizabeth, Convent Station, NJ, 1978—86, adj. prof., 1986—; legal adviser Mcpl. Ct. Clks. Assn., 1977—84. Notes editor: Fordham Urban Law Jour., 1974—75. Trustee Cath. Family and Cmty. Svcs., 1980—, v.p., 1986—; mem. adv. bd. Acad. St. Elizabeth, Convent Station, 1980—84; mem. Essex County Adv. Bd. Status Women, 1983—92, chmn., 1985—88, co-chair, 1990—92; trustee New Sch. Arts, 1988—89, Family Svc. League, Inc., 1986—2000, pres., 1991—94; trustee Bloomfield C. of C., 1986—94, v.p. legis., 1990—94. Fellow: Royal Soc. Encouragement Arts, Manufactures and Commerce; mem.: ATLA, ABA, Essex County Bar Assn., N.J. Bar Assn., Bloomfield Lawyers Club. Roman Catholic. General practice. Office: 54 Fremont St Bloomfield NJ 07003-3428 E-mail: k.lordi@worldnet.att.net.

LORGE, ROBERT GERALD AUGUSTINE, lawyer, real estate broker; b. New London, Wis., Aug. 18, 1959; s. Gerald David and Christina Cordelia (Ziegler) L.; m. Charn Teresa Maria Kaur Singh Lotay, Nov. 6, 1982. Student, Goeth Inst., U. Freiburg, 1979, Lancaster U., Lancashire, Eng., 1982; BA, U. Wis., 1982; JD, Marquette U., 1985. Bar: Wis. 1986, U.S. Dist. Ct. (ea. and we. dists.) Wis. 1986, U.S. Tax Ct. 1989. Legis. asst.

Wis. Senate, Madison, 1977-82; assoc. Gerald D. Lorge, Bear Creek, Wis., 1985-86; mng. ptnr. Lorge & Lorge Law Firm, Madison, Appleton, Wis., Bear Creek, Wis., 1986—; real estate broker Fortune Real Estate Investments, Appleton, 1987—; pvt. mediator, arbitrator Appleton, 1987—; of counsel James D. Thebo Corp., 1986—; pres. Welcome Co., 1996—; counsel No. Am. Linemans Assn., Inc., 2000—. Corp. counsel Helene Altergott Family Corp., 1986—, Altergott, Inc., 1986—; mcpl. corp. counsel Village of Nichols, Outagamie County, Wis., 1991-92; arbitrator candidate, mediator Wis. Employment Rels. Commn., Madison, 1987—; farmer Capital Hill Farms, Bear Creek, Wis., 1996—; chmn. WYOU Cmty. TV Inc., 2000-2002; mediator Lawfirm.net, 2000—.; rep. candidate and nominee Wis. Sec. State. 2002; hon. chmn. Wis. Business Advisory Coun., 2003—. Mem. Nat. Arbor Day Found., 1989—; chmn. Class of 79-80 Jr. Yr. in Freiburg, Germany Reunion Alumni Com., 1980—; bd. dirs. Innovative Prodn. Fund, 1995—, WYOU Cmty. TV Inc., 1993—; mem. Waupaca County Reps., 2000—. Mem. ABA, Wis. Bar Assn., Assn. Trial Lawyers Am., Outagamie County Bar Assn., Wis. Real Estate Brokers Assn., U. Wis. Alumni Assn., Wis. Meml. Union, Madison Area Reading Counsel, India Music Soc. (life), Hoofers Sailing Club, Princeton Club. Roman Catholic. Avocations: skiing, sailing, equestrian, foreign languages, aviation. Estate planning, Private international, Personal injury (including property damage). Office: Lorge & Lorge PO Box 2606 Appleton WI 54912-2606 also: Lorge & Lorge Law Firm PO Box 14704 Madison WI 53714-0704

LORIA, MARTIN A. lawyer; b. N.Y.C., Apr. 11, 1951; s. Daniel Bernard and Estelle Miriam (Barasch) L.; m. Carol Berkowitz, June 3, 1973; children: Alyson, Marissa. BA, SUNY, Albany, 1972; JD, Suffolk U., 1975. Bar: Mass. 1975, U.S. Dist. Ct. Mass. 1976, U.S. Supreme Ct. 1979. Atty. New Eng. states counsel Lawyers Title Ins. Corp., Boston, 1979-82; ptnr. Adelson, Golden & Loria, P.C., Boston, 1983-2000, Cherwin Theise Adelson & Loria LLP, Boston, 2001—02, Adelson Loria Rizzo & Weisman PC, Boston, 2003—. Lectr. Mass Conveyances Assn. Contbg. author Massachusetts Continuing Legal Education Crocker's Notes. Named Best Real Estate Lawyer in Boston, Boston Mag., 2002. Mem. ABA, Mass. Bar Assn., Boston Bar Assn., Mass. Conveyancers Assn. (pres. 1991, bd. dirs. 1988-2000), Abstract Club (bd. dirs., pres.). Banking, Property, real (including real estate development, water). Office: Adelson Loria Rizzo & Weisman PC One Internat Place Boston MA 02110 E-mail: mloria@ctallaw.com.

LORING, EMILIE, lawyer; b. Bklyn., May 29, 1923; d. Henry L. and Helen K. Smith; m. Len Loring, Mar. 24, 1948 (dec. Apr. 1991); children: Wendy Rightmire, Judith A. BA with high honors, Swarthmore Coll., 1944; MA with honors, U. Mont., 1963, JD with high honors, 1973. Bar: Mont., U.S. Dist. Ct. Mont., U.S. Ct. Appeals (D.C., 9th and 10th cirs.), U.S. Supreme Ct.; also Blackfeet Tribal Ct., Confederated Salish and Kootenai Tribal Ct., Tribal Ct. of Ft. Belknap Indian Cmty., Tribal Ct. of Chippewa Cree Tribe. Instr. U. Mont., Missoula, 1966-67, 69-70; legal intern NLRB, Seattle, 1972; ptnr. Hilley & Loring, Great Falls, Mont., 1973-92; sole practitioner Missoula, 1992—. Mem. state bd. dirs ACLU of Mont., 1988-94; mem. Mont. state adv. com. U.S. Commn. on Civil Rights, 1988-91; pub. mem. State Bd. Cosmetology, 1987-88. Mem. State Bar Mont., Western Mont. Bar Assn. (Disting. Atty. award 1995), Cascade County Bar Assn., Mont. Legal Svcs. Assn. (bd. dirs., pres. 1991-92). Administrative and regulatory, Education and schools, Labor (including EEOC, Fair Labor Standards Act, labor-management relations, NLRB, OSHA). Office: 500 Daly Ave Missoula MT 59801-4413

LOSCALZO, ANTHONY JOSEPH, lawyer; b. Bklyn., May 13, 1946; s. Frank Anthony and Frances (Puliatti) L.; m. Kathryn Mary Pica, Aug. 4, 1973. BBA, St. John's U., 1967, JD, 1969. Bar: N.Y. 1969, Fla. 1971, U.S. Dist. Ct. (so. and ea. dists.) N.Y. 1973, U.S. Ct. Appeals (2d cir.) 1975, U.S. Supreme Ct. 1975. Ptnr. Loscalzo & Loscalzo, P.C., N.Y.C., 1981—. Mem. ABA, Assn. Trial Lawyers Am., Fla. Bar Assn., N.Y. State Trial Lawyers Assn., N.Y. State Bar Assn. State civil litigation, Personal injury (including property damage), Workers' compensation. Office: Loscalzo & Loscalzo PC Ste 408 14 E 4th St Apt 408 New York NY 10012-1141 E-mail: aloscalzo@loscalzolaw.com.

LOSER, JOSEPH CARLTON, JR., dean, retired judge; b. Nashville, June 16, 1932; s. Joseph Carlton and Pearl Dean (Gupton) L.; m. Mildred Louise Nichols, May 25, 1972; 1 child, Joseph Carlton III. Student, U. Tenn., 1950-51, Vanderbilt U., 1952-55; LLB, Nashville YMCA Night Law Sch., 1959. Bar: Tenn. 1959. Pvt. practice, 1959-66; judge Gen. Sessions Ct., Davidson County, Tenn., 1966-69, Cir. Ct. 20th Jud. Dist. Tenn., 1969-86; dean Nashville Sch. Law, 1986—. Mem. ABA, Tenn. Bar Assn., Nashville Bar Assn., Am. Legion, Masons, Shriners, Sigma Delta Kappa, Kappa Sigma. E-mail: jcloser@prodigy.net.

LOSEY, BEVERLEY BROWN, lawyer, nurse; b. Seattle, July 25, 1948; d. Frederick Sherwood and M. Doris (Grimes) Brown; m. Robert F. Losey, Jr., Feb. 12, 1982. BS in Nursing, U. Md., 1970; JD, U. Puget Sound (Seattle U.), 1984. Bar: Wash. 1984, U.S. Dist. Ct. (we. dist.) Wash. 1984. Community health nurse Dept. Army, Tex., S.C., Fed. Rep. Germany, 1970-77; dist. nursing supr. Wyo. Nursing Svcs., Buffalo, 1977-81; pvt. practice Seattle and Tacoma, Wash., 1984—. Mem. ABA, Wash. State Bar Assn., Res. Officers Assn. (v.p. Tacoma chpt. 1986), Zeta Tau Alpha (bd. dirs., treas. Psi chpt. 1986-87). Episcopalian. General civil litigation, Health, Personal injury (including property damage). Office: 1001 4th Ave Ste 3200 Seattle WA 98154

LOSEY, RALPH COLBY, lawyer; b. Daytona Beach, Fla., May 26, 1951; s. George Spar and Alix (Colby) L.; m. Molly Isa Friedman, July 7, 1973; children: Eva Merlinda, Adam Colby. Student, Inst. European Studies, Vienna, Austria, 1971; BA, Vanderbilt U., 1973; JD cum laude, U. Fla., 1979. Bar: Fla. 1980, U.S. Dist. Ct. (mid. dist.) Fla. 1980. Assoc. Subin, Shams, Rosenbluth & Moran, Orlando, Fla., 1980-84; ptnr. Katz, Kutter, Alderman, Bryant & Yon, P.A., Orlando, Fla., 1984—. Author: Laws of Wisdom, 1994, Your Cyber Rights and Responsibilities: Using the Internet, 1996; contbr. articles to profl. jours. Pres. Sch. of Wisdom, Fla. Mem. Fla. Bar Assn., Orange County Bar Assn., Computer Law Assn. Democrat. Avocations: computers, golf, music, philosophy, reading. Federal civil litigation, State civil litigation, Computer. Home: 1661 Woodland Ave Winter Park FL 32789-2774 Office: Katz Kutter Alderman & Bryant PA PO Box 4950 Orlando FL 32802-4950 E-mail: ralphl@katzlaw.com.

LOTHERT, RALF W. lawyer; b. Tuebingen, Germany, Feb. 23, 1965; Grad., U. Tuebingen and Freiburg, 1997. Bar: Tuebingen 1997. Head dept. contract mgmt. Truehandanstalt, 1994—96; v.p. law dept. Koch, Nelt & Oettingen & Co. GmbH, 1996—98; sr. counsel Daimler Chrysler Rail Sys. GmbH, 1998—2000, Philip Morris GmbH, 2000—.

LOTITO, NICHOLAS ANTHONY, lawyer; b. Neptune, N.J., June 19, 1949; s. Nicholas and Grace (Pascazio) L. BA, Emory U., 1971; JD, U. Va., 1975. Bar: Ga. 1975, U.S. Dist. Ct. (no. dist.) Ga., U.S. Ct. Appeals (4th, 5th, 11 cirs.), U.S. Supreme Ct., 2001. Atty. FTC, Atlanta, 1975-76; trial atty. Antitrust Div. U.S. Dept. Justice, Atlanta, 1976-82; of counsel Fierer & Westby, Atlanta, 1983-89; ptnr. Davis, Zipperman, Kirschenbaum & Lotito, Atlanta, 1989—. Contbr. articles to profl. jours. Mem. NACDL, ABA (criminal and antitrust sects.), Atlanta Bar Assn. (task force mcpl. ct. reform 1986), Ga. Assn. Criminal Def. Lawyers (past pres., exec. com., chmn. amicus com.), Lamar Inn of Ct. Democrat. Avocations: sports, writing. Antitrust, Criminal. Home: 1055 Alta Ave NE Atlanta GA 30307-2512 Office: Davis Zipperman Kirschenbaum & Lotito 918 Ponce De Leon Ave NE Atlanta GA 30306-4212 E-mail: nick@dzkl.com.

LOTMAN, ARLINE JOLLES, lawyer; b. Phila., Feb. 5, 1937; d. Samuel Clearsfeld and Sarah (Shiffrin) Jolles; married, Sept. 27, 1959 (deceased); 1 child, Maurice. BA, Temple U., 1960, JD, 1977, MA in Comm., 1984. Bar: Pa. 1977, D.C. 1980, U.S. Dist. Ct. (ea. dist.) Pa. 1983, U.S. Ct. Appeals (3d cir.) 1987, U.S. Supreme Ct. 1997. Exec. dir. gov.'s office Commonwealth of Pa., Harrisburg, Pa., 1972-74; assoc. Adler Barish Levin & Creskoff, Phila., 1978-80; pvt. practice pvt. practice, 1980—. Lectr. in field; spl. counsel Greitzer and Locks, 1998-2000. Commr. Home Rule Charter Commn., Phila., 1993-95. Mem. ABA (ho. of dels. 1992-94, standing com. on election law 1997-2000), Phila. Bar Assn. (chair judicial commn. 1991-92), Pa. Bar Assn., DC Bar Assn., Nat. Assn. Bond Lawyers (nat. bond opinion com.), Jewish Nat. Fund Bd., Temple Law Alumni Assn. (pres. 1993-95). Alternative dispute resolution, Labor (including EEOC, Fair Labor Standards Act, labor-management relations, NLRB, OSHA), Municipal (including bonds). Home: 2210 Independence Pl 233 S 6th St Philadelphia PA 19106-3749 Office: Ste 2210 233 S 6th St Philadelphia PA 19106-3756

LOTTER, CHARLES ROBERT, corporate lawyer, retail company legal executive; b. 1937; married. BA, St. Johns U., 1959, JD, 1962; LLM, NYU, 1969. With anti-trust div. U.S. Dept. Justice, 1962-65; with Revere Copper & Brass, Inc., 1965-69, Del E. Webb Corp., 1969-70, Louis O. Kelso, 1970-71, J.C. Penney, Dallas, 1971—, sr. v.p., 1987—; sec., gen. counsel, 1987-93; exec. v.p., 1993. V.p., sec. JCP Realty, Inc.; sec. J.C. Penney Properties, Inc., J.C. Penney Funding Corp. With USAFR, 1962-64, lt. USNR, 1964-70. Office: J C Penney Co Inc 6501 Legacy Dr Plano TX 75024-3698*

LOTVEN, HOWARD LEE, lawyer; b. Springfield, Mo., Apr. 8, 1959; s. Isadore and Gytel (Tuchmeier) L.; m. Charlotte Lotven. BA, Drake U., 1981; JD, U. Mo., Kansas City, 1984. Bar: Mo. 1984, U.S. Dist. Ct. (we. dist.) Mo. 1984. Pvt. practice, Kansas City, 1984—; asst. prosecutor City of Kansas City, 1985. Prosecutor City of Harrisonville (Mo.), 1989-91, atty., 1989-91; prosecutor City of Napoleon, Mo., 2001—, City of Lake Lafayette, 2001- . Mem. Hyde Park Crime Patrol, 1985—91, Hyde Park Assn. Zoning and Planning Commn., 1993—97; vol. Heartland United Way, 1995; trustee Pilgrim Chapel, 2001—, Heart of Am. Stand Down, 1995—2001; judge Mo. Sta H.S. Moot Ct. Competition, 1992. Named CASA Vol. Atty. of Yr., 2002. Mem. ABA, Mo. Bar Assn. (young lawyers coun. 1986-88, lectr. 1987-90, criminal law com. 1989—, gen. practice law com. 1990—, co-chair criminal law com. 1991-92, exec. coun. gen. practice law com. 1993-99, Law Day spkr. 1986, 96, lectr. 1987-90, 92, 97), Kansas City Bar Assn. (chmn. mcpl. cts. com. 2002, Vol. Atty. Project, 1992—, Vol. Atty. Project award winner 1994, continuing edn. spkr. 2000—), House Rabbit Soc., Delta Theta Phi, Omicron Delta Kappa, others. Democrat. Jewish. Avocation: sports. General civil litigation, Criminal, Family and matrimonial. Office: 1125 Grand Blvd Ste 915 Kansas City MO 64106

LOTWIN, STANFORD GERALD, lawyer; b. N.Y.C., June 23, 1930; s. Herman and Rita (Saltzman) L.; m. Judy Scott, Oct. 15, 1994; children: Lori Hope, David. BS, Bklyn. Coll., 1951, LLB, 1954, LLM, 1957. Bar: N.Y. 1954, U.S. Supreme Ct. 1961, Pa. 1986. Ptnr. Blank Rome LLP, N.Y.C., 1987—; of counsel Frankfurt, Garbus, Klein & Selz, N.Y.C., 1983-87. Served with U.S. Army, 1954-56. Fellow Am. Acad. Matrimonial Lawyers (bd. of mgrs. 1984—); mem. N.Y. State Bar Assn. (family law sect.), N.Y. County Trial Lawyers (lectr. 1980—), Internat. Acad. Matrimonial Attys. Family and matrimonial. Office: 405 Lexington Ave New York NY 10174-0002

LOUDEN, THOMAS EDWARD, judge; b. Urbana, Ohio, Mar. 21, 1942; s. Charles Edward and Mary Elizabeth Louden; m. Shelly Sue Holzhauer, July 11, 1970; children: Lesley Ann, Zachary Thomas. BS in Edn., Ohio No. U., 1965, JD, 1968. Bar: Ohio 1968, Fla. 1968. Pvt. practice, Marysville, Ohio, 1969—71, 1971—79; judge Probate and Juvenile Delaware County, Delaware, Ohio, 1979—; ret., 2003. Asst. prosecutor Union County, Marysville, 1969—70; asst. prosecutor, asst. atty. gen. Delaware County, Delaware, 1971—79; mem. adv. bd. Ohio Dept. Youth Svcs., Columbus, 1982—90, Delaware Mental Health Bd., Delaware, 1979—91. Recipient Rep. C.L. McLin award, Ohio Cmty. Corrections Orgn., 2002. Mem.: Fla. State Bar Assn., Ohio State Bar Assn., Ohio Assn. Juvenile Ct. Judges. Avocations: golf, skiing, running. Home: PO Box 701 Delaware OH 43015 Office: Delaware County Probate and Juvenile Court 88 N Sandusky St Delaware OH 43015

LOUGEE, DAVID LOUIS, lawyer; b. Worcester, Mass., Mar. 20, 1940; s. Laurence H. and Erma Virginia (MacAllister) L.; m. Mary Anne Strebb, July 15, 1979; children: Adam, Sara, Barbara, Laurence. AB, Bates Coll., 1962; LLB, Duke U., 1965. Bar: Mass. 1965. Ptnr. Mirick O'Connell, DeMallie & Lougee, Worcester, 1965—, mng. ptnr., 1985—2001. Bd. dirs. Commonwealth Bio Ventures, Inc., Meridian Med. Techs., Inc. Named Woodward White, The Best Lawyers in Am. Corporate, general, Mergers and acquisitions, Securities. Home: 78 Ridge Rd Hardwick MA 01037 Office: 100 Front St Worcester MA 01608-1425

LOUGHEED, PETER, lawyer, former Canadian premier; b. Calgary, Alta., Can., July 26, 1928; s. Edgar Donald and Edna (Bauld) L.; m. Jeanne Estelle Rogers, June 21, 1952; children— Stephen, Andrea, Pamela, Joseph. BA, U. Alta., 1950, LL.B., 1952; MBA, Harvard U., 1954. Bar: Alta 1955. With firm Fenerty, Fenerty, McGillivray & Robertson, Calgary, 1955-56; sec. Mannix Co., Ltd., 1956-58, gen. counsel, 1958-62, v.p., 1959-62, dir., 1960-62; individual practice law, from 1962; formerly mem. Alta. Legislature for Calgary West; formerly leader Progressive Conservative Party of Alta., 1965-85; premier of Alta., 1971-85; ptnr. Bennett Jones, Calgary, 1986-99, counsel, 1999—. Office: Bennett Jones LLP 855 2nd St SW 4500 Bankers Hall Calgary AB Canada T2P 4K7

LOUGHRIDGE, JOHN HALSTED, JR., lawyer; b. Chestnut Hill, Pa., Oct. 30, 1945; s. John Halsted Sr. and Martha Margaret (Boyd) L.; m. Amy Claire Booe, Aug. 3, 1980 (div. Apr. 1995); 1 child, Emily Halsted. AB, Davidson Coll., 1967; JD, Wake Forest U., 1970. Bar: N.C. 1970, U.S. Dist. Ct. 1970, U.S. Ct. Mil. Appeals 1986, U.S. Supreme Ct. 2002. Divsn. head, v.p., counsel Wachovia Mortgage Co., Winston-Salem, N.C., 1971-79; sr. v.p., counsel Wachovia Bank, Winston-Salem, N.C., 1980—. Mem. UC article 5 drafting com. N.C. Gen. Statues Commn., 1999. Mem. cabinet, chair profl. divsn. United Way Forsyth County, 1994. Col. JAGC, USAR, 1970-2000. Mem.: ABA (corp. banking and bus. law sect. 1970—, internat. law and practice sect. 1999—2002), N.C. Bar Found. (continuing legal edn. program planner 2000—01), Mortgage Bankers Assn. Am. (legal issues com. 1982—92, fin. affiliates com. 1988—92), Am. Corp. Counsel Assn. (bd. dirs. N.C. chpt. 1988—98, 2001—, v.p.), Forsyth County Bar Assn., N.C. Coll. Advocacy, N.C. State Bar, N.C. Bar Assn. (bus. law sect. 1971—, real property sect. 1971—, internat. law sect. 1984—, fin. instns. com. 1985—, governing coun. 1988—91, corp. counsel sect. 1989—, real property curriculum com. 1990—93, governing coun. 1992—98, treas. 1999—2000, bus. law curriculum com. 1999—2001, sec. 2000—01, vice chair 2001—02, chmn. 2002—03), Res. Officers Assn. (chpt. pres. 1996—97, sec. 1997—), Davidson Coll. Alumni Assn. (bd. dirs. 2001—), Rotary, Forsyth Country Club, Twin City Club (sec. 1990—97, gov. 1994—, pres. 1997—2001), Union League Phila., Phi Delta Theta, Phi Delta Phi. Republican. Presbyterian. Avocations: golf, tennis. Banking, Corporate, general, Private international. Home: 615 Arbor Rd Winston Salem NC 27104 Office: Wachovia Bank 301 S College St Charlotte NC 28288-0630 E-mail: john.loughridge@wachovia.com.

LOUIE, DAVID MARK, lawyer; b. Oakland, Calif., Oct. 8, 1951; s. Paul and Emma (Woo) L.; m. Johanna C. Chuan, Sept. 6, 1986; children: Ryan David, Jenna Rachel. AB cum laude, Occidental Coll., 1973; JD, U. Calif., Berkeley, 1977. Bar: Calif. 1977, U.S. Dist. Ct. (no. Dist.) Calif. 1977, U.S. Ct. Appeals (9th cir.) 1977, Hawaii 1978, U.S. Dist. Ct. Hawaii 1978. Ptnr. Case & Lynch, Honolulu, 1977-88; sr. ptnr. Roeca, Louie & Hiraoka, Honolulu, 1988—. Faculty mem. Profl. Edn. Systems, Inc. (PESI) Seminars: Hawaii Ins. & Tort Update, 1995, 1996, Depositions (Strategies, Tactics & Mechanics), 1990, Nat. Bus. Inst. (NBI) Seminars: Arbitrating and Trying the Automobile Injury Case in Hawaii, 1993, Ins. Litigation in Hawaii, 1992, Pacific Law Inst. (PLI) Seminars: Premises Liability, 1995, Hawaii State Bar Assn. Depositions, 1997, Mediation Techniques, 2001, miscellaneous seminars: Hawaiian Bitumuls & Paving Co., Job Site Accidents, 1994, Hawaiian Dredging Construction Co., Job Site Accidents, 1993; mem. Def. Rsch. Inst., 1990—. Contbg. author: Going Back, 1972, Hawaii Tort Liability Issues in Work Site Accident Cases, 1989, Trying the Automobile Accident Case, 1991, Hawaii Tort Law Update, 1992, 94. Bd. dirs. Jr. Achievement Hawaii, Honolulu, Aloha Tower Devel. Corp., 1998—, chmn., 1999—; Sec., v.p., dir. Ohana Ins. Co. Hawaii, Inc., 1994-95. Mem. ABA (sects. on tort and ins. practice litigation 1978—, minority couns. demonstration program 1994), Hawaii State Bar Assn. (bd. dirs. 1994-98, v.p. 2000, pres. 2001), Calif. State Bar Assn., Hawaii Def. Lawyers Assn. (bd. dirs. 1990—, sec.-treas. 1994-99), Nat. Asian Pacific ABA (Hawaii chpt. pres. 1992-95, bd. dirs. 1996—), Mensa, Pacific Club. State civil litigation, Insurance, Personal injury (including property damage). Home: 4122 Pakolu Pl Honolulu HI 96816-3930 Office: Roeca Louie & Hiraoka 841 Bishop St Ste 900 Honolulu HI 96813-3917

LOUIT, CHRISTIAN GEORGES, law educator, solicitor; b. Saint Cyprien Les Attafs, Algeria, Nov. 19, 1943; s. Gaston Marcel Louit and Clotilde Bouer; m. Christiane Pheline; children: Jean François, Jerome. BS, Inst. Polit. Studies, 1963; LLM, Aix en Provence U., 1964, PhD, 1971; DHC (hon.) , La. State U., Chuo U., Lasal U. Prof. Reunion U., 1974-78, Aix Marseille III U., France, 1978—. Dir. Tax Studies Ctr., Aix en Provence, 1979—, European Asian Rsch. Ctr., 1999; lectr. Montreal U., York U., Peking U. Author: Finances of Public Enterprises, 1976; contbr. articles to profl. jours. Recipient Chevalier award Palmes Academiques, 1987, Order of Merit France, 1997, Legion d'honneur, France, 1998; cmdr. Order of Merit Italy, 1990. Mem. Internat. Fiscal Assn., Internat. Bus. Law Assn. (v.p.), Nat. Coun. Univs. Avocations: cycling, photography. Home: L'Eperon Saint Jacques 13100 Le Tholonet France Office: Aix Marseille Univ 3 Avenue R Shuman 13100 Aix-en-Provence France also: 15 rue d'hozier 13002 Marseille France Office: Institut de Recherches Europe-Asie Pavillon de Lanfant 346 Route de Sisteron 13100 Aix-en-Provence France E-mail: clouit@a2a.fr.

LOUNSBURY, STEVEN RICHARD, lawyer; b. Evanston, Ill., July 26, 1950; s. James Richard and Reba Jeanette (Smith) L.; m. Dianne Louise Daley, Apr. 16, 1983; children: Jimson, Cody Summer, Richard. BA, U. Calif., Santa Barbara, 1973; JD, U. West L.A., 1977. Bar: Calif. 1979, Oreg. 1997, U.S. Dist. Ct. (cen. dist.) Calif. 1979, U.S. Dist. Ct. Oreg. 1999. Pvt. practice, L.A., 1979-83; contract atty. FAA, L.A., 1981; trial atty. Hertz Corp., L.A., 1983-86; mng. counsel 20th Century Ins. Co., Woodland Hills, Calif., 1986-94; mng. atty. Lounsbury and Assocs., Brea, Calif., 1986-94; sr. trial atty. Bollington, Lounsbury and Chase, Brea, 1994-99; asst. Coos County counsel, Coquille, Oreg., 1999—2002; county counsel Coos County, 2002—. Arbitrator Orange County Superior Ct., Santa Ana, Calif., 1992-99. Dir. internat. rels. Rotary Internat., Venice-Marina Club, Calif., 1980-81; dir. L.A. Jr. C. of C., 1981-82, chmn. westside com. 1980-81. Mem. ABA, Calif. Bar Assn., Oreg. Bar Assn., Calif. House Counsel (bd. dirs., chmn. membership 1993-94). Avocations: music, flute, saxophone, travel. Government contracts and claims, Land use and zoning (including planning), State and local taxation, Municipal (including bonds). Office: Coos County Office Legal Counsel 250 N Baxter St Coquille OR 97423-1852 E-mail: steven@co.coos.or.us.

LOURIE, ALAN DAVID, federal judge; b. Boston, Mass., Jan. 13, 1935; AB, Harvard U., 1956; MS, U. Wis., 1958; PhD, U. Pa., 1965; JD, Temple U., 1970. Bar: Pa. 1970. Chemist Monsanto Co., St. Louis, 1957-59; lit. scientist, chemist, patent agt. Wyeth Labs., Radnor, Pa., 1959-64; counsel Smith Kline Beecham Corp., Phila., 1964-90; successively as patent agt., atty., dir. corp. patents, asst. gen. counsel, v.p. corp. patents Smith Kline Beechum Corp., Phila.; cir. judge U.S. Ct. Appeals (fed. cir.), Washington, 1990—. Mem. Judicial Conf. Com. on Financial Disclosure, 1990-98; mem. U.S. del. to Diplomatic Conf. on Revision of Paris Conv. for Protection of Indsl. Property, 1982, 84; vice chmn. industry functional adv. com. to U.S. Trade Rep. and Dept. Commerce, 1987-90; chmn. U.S. group of U.S.-Japan Bus. Coun. Task Force on Patents. Bd. visitors Law Sch., Temple U. Mem. ABA, Phila. Patent Law Assn. (pres. 1984-85), Am. Intellectual Property Law Assn. (bd. dirs. 1982-85), Assn. Corp. Patent Counsel (treas. 1987-89), Pharm. Mfrs. Assn. (chmn. patent com. 1981-86), Am. Chem. Soc., Cosmos Club, Harvard Club Washington. Office: US Ct Appeals Fed Cir 717 Madison Pl NW Washington DC 20439-0002

LOVE, GEORGE H., JR., lawyer; b. Latrobe, Pa., Dec. 30, 1943; m. Joann A. Love, Aug. 16, 1969; children: George H. III, Jennifer A. BA, Wabash Coll., 1966; JD, Duquesne U., 1973. Bar: Pa. 1973, U.S. Dist. Ct. (we. dist.) Pa. 1973, U.S. Supreme Ct. 1976. Various positions VA, Pitts., 1970-76, atty. Dist. Counsel's Office, 1977-81, asst. dist. counsel, 1981-95, prin. sr. atty. Regional Counsel's Office, 1995-98, asst. regional counsel, 1998-2001; ret.; mng. ptnr. Love Law Firm, LLC, Youngstown, Pa., 2002—. Cpl. USMC, 1967-68, Viet Nam; lt. JAG, U.S. Navy. Home: RR 4 Box 105B Latrobe PA 15650-9217 Office: PO Box 594 Youngstown PA 15696-0594 E-mail: glovelaw@adelphia.net.

LOVE, MICHAEL JOSEPH, lawyer; b. Chicopee, Mass., Mar. 1, 1958; BA, U. Mass., 1984; student, Vanderbilt U., 1991-92; JD, U. Denver, 1992. Bar: Tenn., U.S. Dist. Ct. (mid. dist.) Tenn. 1992. Ptnr. Zellar, Cartwright & Love, PLLC, Clarksville, Tenn., 1994-96, Cartwright & Love, PLLC, Clarksville, Tenn., 1996—. Gen. editor U. Denver Law Rev. With U.S. Army, 1975-78. Mem. Nat. Assn. Criminal Def. Lawyers (life). Civil rights, Constitutional, Criminal. Office: Cartwright & Love PLLC 215 S 2nd St Clarksville TN 37040-3629 E-mail: MichaelJLove@msn.com.

LOVEJOY, PAUL ROBERT, lawyer; b. Rochester, N.Y., Jan. 30, 1955; s. V. Paul and Jean M. Lovejoy; m. Susan Seyfarth, Dec. 30, 1978; 1 child, Kate Hightower. BA summa cum laude, New Eng. Coll., 1977; JD, Case Western Reserve U., 1981. Bar: N.Y., Ohio. Assoc. Squire, Sanders & Dempsey, Cleve., 1981—89, ptnr., 1989—90; asst. gen. counsel Texaco Internat., White Plains, NY, 1990—99; ptnr. Weil, Gotshal & Manges, N.Y.C., 1999—. Trustee New Eng. Coll., Henniker, N.H., 1993—2002; bd. dirs. Southwest Legal Found., Dallas, 1990—. Corporate, general, Private international, Mergers and acquisitions. Office: Weil Gotshal & Manges 767 Fifth Ave New York NY 10153

LOVELACE, BYRON KEITH, lawyer, management consultant; b. Vernon, Tex., Feb. 15, 1935; s. Joseph Edward and Hattie Pearl (Brians) L.; m. Sandra Alene Daniel, June 17, 1961; children: Kirk Daniel, Bethany Alene, Amy Kathleen. BSChemE, U. Tex., 1958, MS, 1961, PhD, 1973; JD, South Tex. Coll., 1978. Bar: Tex. 1978. R & D engr. Core Labs., Dallas, 1960-61; with Tex. Instruments, Inc., Dallas and Houston, 1961-78, mgr. process control for advanced tech., 1969-70, reliability mgr. metal oxide semicondr. (MOS) divsn., 1971-75, MOS reliability dir., 1975-78; pres. P-V-T Inc., Houston, 1978-80, Mgmt. Resources Internat., Houston, 1980—; pvt. practice Law Offices of Keith Lovelace, Houston, 1980—. Contbr. articles to profl. jours.; patentee in field. Mem. Houston Clean City Commn., 1991-94, Greater Southwest Houston C. of C., bd. dirs., 1996-01, vice-chmn., 1996-97, chmn.-elect, 1998, chmn., 1999. With U.S. Army, 1953. Tex. Instruments fellow, 1965-68, FMC Corp. fellow, 1958-60; Eastern States Petroleum and Chem. scholar, 1957-58, Ethyl Corp. scholar, 1956-57. Mem. ABA, AIChE, Am. Chem. Soc. (award 1958), Soc. Petroleum Engrs. (vice-chmn. reservior group 1979-80), State Bar Tex., Trial Lawyers Am., Tex. Trial Lawyers Assn., S.W. Houston C. of C. (bd. dirs. 1988-91, pres. 1990-91), Bellaire/S.W. Houston Rotary (bd. dirs. 2001—, pres. 2002-), Tau Beta Pi (chpt. v.p. 1958-59), Omega Chi Epsilon (chpt. pres. 1959). State civil litigation. Office: 8303 SW Fwy Ste 975 Houston TX 77074-1607

LOVELESS, GEORGE GROUP, retired lawyer; b. Baldwinsville, N.Y., Sept. 16, 1940; s. Frank Donald and Mayme (Lont) L.; m. Shirley Morrison, Nov. 27, 1965; children: Michael, Peter. BS, Cornell U., 1962, MBA, 1963; JD, U. Md., 1968. Bar: Pa. 1969, U.S. Dist. Ct. (ea. dist.) Pa., U.S. Ct. Appeals (3d cir.). Ptnr. Morgan, Lewis & Bockius LLP, Phila., 1968-2000; ret., 2000. With USAFR, 1963-68. Republican. Presbyterian. Banking, Bankruptcy, Corporate, general. Home: 11 Rose Valley Rd Media PA 19063-4217 Office: Morgan Lewis & Bockius LLP 1701 Market St Philadelphia PA 19103-2921 E-mail: GGL1@cornell.edu.

LOVELL, CARL ERWIN, JR., lawyer; b. Riverside, Calif., Apr. 12, 1945; s. Carl Erwin and Hazel (Brown) L.; mchildren: Carl Erwin III, Timothy C., Tishia R., Ashley P., Garrett T., Christopher C. BA, Vanderbilt U., 1966, JD, 1969. Bar: Nev. 1969, D.C. 1971, U.S. Supreme Ct. 1973. Jr. editor Land and Water Law Rev., 1973-89; instr. bus. law U. Nev., Las Vegas, Clark County C.C.; city atty. City of N. Las Vegas, 1970-73; elected city atty. City of Las Vegas, 1973-77; v.p., sec.-treas., legal counsel Circus Circus Hotels, Inc., Las Vegas, 1977-83; sr. ptnr. Lovell, Bilbray & Potter, Las Vegas, 1984-89; pvt. practice Las Vegas, 1989—; v.p., dir. Air Nev. Airlines, Inc. Chmn. Nat. Inst. Mcpl. Law Officers Consumer Protection Adv. Com., 1973-77, Nev. Crime Commn. Bd., 1974-77; U.S. rep. to China-U.S. Internat. Trade and Law Talks, Beijing, 1987; arbitrator, AAA, 1989—. Bd. dirs., v.p. BBB, 1983-91; chmn. NCCJ; pres. Clark County Young Dems., 1971-72; bd. dirs. Nat. Kidney Found.; pres., trustee Nev. Donor Network, Inc., 1992-96. With USAF, 1966-68. Mem. ABA, ATLA, Nev. State Bar, Nev. Trial Lawyers Assn., Elks (justice Las Vegas chpt. 1985-88). General civil litigation, Estate planning, Family and matrimonial. Office: 2801 S Valley View Blvd Ste 1B Las Vegas NV 89102-0116 E-mail: dcarl@wealthprotectionconcepts.com., lovellachieve4u@earthlink.net.

LOVETT, ROBERT G. lawyer; b. York, Pa., Aug. 17, 1944; BA, U. Pitts., 1966; JD, Duquesne U., 1969. Bar: Pa. 1970. Office: Reed Smith Shaw & McClay 435 6th Ave Ste 2 Pittsburgh PA 15219-1886

LOVING, SUSAN BRIMER, lawyer, former state official; m. Dan Loving; children: Lindsay, Andrew, Kendall. BA with distinction, U. Okla., 1972, JD, 1979. Asst. atty. gen. Office of Atty. Gen., 1983-87, 1st asst. atty. gen., 1987-91; atty. gen. State of Okla., Oklahoma City, 1991-94; ptnr. Lester, Loving & Davies, Edmond, Okla., 1995—. Master Ruth Bader Ginsburg Inn of Ct., 1995-97. Mem. Pardon and Parole Bd., 1995—96, 2003—, vice-chmn., 1995; mem. Gov.'s Commn. on Tobacco and Youth, 1995—97; mem. med. steering com. Partnership for Drug Free Okla., Inst. for Child Advocacy, 1996—97; bd. dirs. Bd. for Freedom of Info., Okla. Inc., 1995—2001, Legal Aid Svcs. of Okla., 2002—, Legal Aid of West Okla., 1995—2001. Recipient Nat. Red Ribbon Leadership award Nat. Fedn. Parents, Headliner award, By-liner award Okla. City and Tulsa Women in Comm., First Friend of Freedom award, Freedom of Info., Okla., Dir. award Okla. Dist. Attys. Assn. Mem.: Oklahoma County Bar Assn. (bd. dirs. 2001—), Okla. Bar Assn. (mem. ho. dels. 1996—97, task force on professionalism and civility 1999—, past chmn. adminstrv. law sect., chmn. adminstrn. of justice com., chmn. profl. responsibility commn., mem. ho. dels. 2001—, Spotlight award 1997), Phi Beta Kappa. Administrative and regulatory, Civil rights, General practice. Office: Lester Loving & Davies PLLC 1505 Renaissance Blvd Edmond OK 73013-3018 E-mail: sloving@lldlaw.com.

LOW, JOHN WAYLAND, lawyer; b. Denver, Aug. 7, 1923; s. Oscar Wayland and Rachel E. (Stander) L.; m. Merry C. Mullan, July 8, 1979; children: Lucinda A., Jan W. BA, Nebr. Wesleyan U., 1947; JD cum laude, U. Denver, 1951. Bar: Colo. 1951, U.S. Dist. Ct. (Colo. dist.) 1951, U.S. Ct. Appeals (10th cir.), U.S. Supreme Ct. 1960. Ptnr. Sherman & Howard LLC, Denver, 1951-93, counsel, 1993—. Trustee U. Denver, 1987—; chmn. bd. Denver Symphony Assn., 1989-90; vice chmn. Colo. Symphony Assn., 1990-96; pres. Colo. Symphony Found., 1995—, Mesa Verde Found., 1997—; chmn. Colo. Alliance of Bus., Denver, 1983-87. 1st lt. U.S. Army, 1942-46, CBI. Recipient Learned Hand award Am. Jewish Com., 1989, Outstanding Alumni award U. Denver, 1994, Evans Disting. Svc. award U. Denver, 2001.. Mem. ABA, Colo. Bar Assn., Denver Bar Assn., University Club of Denver, Garden of Gods Club (Colorado Springs). Republican. Mem. United Ch. of Christ. Office: Sherman & Howard 633 17th St Ste 3000 Denver CO 80202-3665

LOW, TERRENCE ALLEN, lawyer, sole practice, woodworker; b. Calif., Jan. 24, 1950; s. William H. Low and Elisabeth Ann Steiger; m. Jean Simanitis, 1982; children: Alexandra E. Low and Tucker A.J. Low. BA, U. Pa., 1981; JD, Vt. Law Sch., 1984. Bar: Mass. 1985, U.S. Dist. Ct. Mass. 1985, U.S. Ct. Appeals (1st cir.) 1996. Assoc. Pellegrini & Selly, P.C., Springfield, Mass., 1984-92; pvt. practice, Springfield, 1992—. Tchr. Mass. Cont. Legal Edn., Mass. 1996—. Chmn. Hist. Dist. Commn., Longmeadow, 1995—. Mem. ATLA (adv. 1997), Mass. Acad. Trial Lawyers, Hampden County Bar Assn. Avocations: rare book collecting, woodworking. General civil litigation, Personal injury (including property damage), Workers' compensation. Office: Rosen Greenhut Catuogno & Low 244 Bridge St Springfield MA 01103-1410 E-mail: terryalow@aol.com.

LOWE, JAMES ALLISON, lawyer, educator; b. Cleve., July 15, 1945; s. Allison S. and Betty B. (Bernstein) L.; m. Jacalyn S. Scholss, June 24, 1967 (div.); children: David, Joseph, Jeremiah; m. Teresa L. DiPuccio, Aug. 13, 1989; 1 child, Alison. BA, U. Pa., 1967; JD cum laude, Cleve. State U., 1972. Bar: Ohio 1972, U.S. Dist. Ct. (no. dist.) Ohio 1973, U.S. Ct. Appeals (6th cir.) 1981, U.S. Supreme Ct. 1979; cert. civic trial adv. Nat. Bd. Trial Advocacy. Assoc. Berkman, Gordon & Kancelbaum, Cleve., 1972—74; sole practice Cleve., 1974—76; ptnr. Sindell, Lowe & Guidubaldi Co., L.P.A., Cleve., 1976—96, Lowe Eklund Wakefield Co., LPA, Cleve., 1996—2000, Lowe Eklund Wakefield & Mulvihill Co., LPA, Cleve., 2000—. Instr. law Cleve. State U., 1974-77, Case Western Res. U., 1979-92. Author: Products Liability Litigation: Pretrial Practice, 1988, Product Liability in Ohio After Tort Reform, 1988. Active Jewish Cmty. Fedn.; fellow Roscoe Pound Found. Fellow Internat. Soc. Barristers, Am. Bd. Trial Advs., Am. Coll. Trial Lawyers; mem. ABA, ATLA (chmn. products liability adv. com., chmn. products liability sect., dir. products liability sect.), Ohio Acad. Trial Attys. (chmn. products liability sect. 1987-89, trustee 1990—), Ohio Bar Assn., Cleve. Acad. Trial Attys. (bd. dirs. 1988—, v.p. 1990—), Greater Cleve. Bar Assn., Attys. Info. Exch. Group, Am. Bd. Trial Advocates. Federal civil litigation, Personal injury (including property damage), Product liability. Office: Lowe Eklund Wakefield & Mulvihill Co LPA 610 Skylight Office Tower 1660 W 2nd St #610 Cleveland OH 44113-1454 Office Fax: 216-781-2610. Business E-Mail: Jlowe@lewm.com.

LOWE, JOHN STANLEY, lawyer, educator; b. Marion, Ohio, May 11, 1941; s. John Floyd and Florence (Andrews) L.; m. Jacquelyn Taft, Jan. 15, 1968; children: Sarah Staley, John Taft. BA, Denison U., 1963; LLB, Harvard U., 1966. Bar: Ohio 1966, Okla. 1980, U.S. Supreme Ct. 1972, Tex. 1989. Adminstrv. officer Govt. of Malawi, Limbe, 1966-69; assoc. Emens, Hurd, Kegler & Ritter, Columbus, Ohio, 1970-75; asst. and assoc. prof. law U. Toledo, Ohio, 1975—78; prof. law U. Tulsa, 1978-87, So. Meth. U., Dallas, 1987—. Vis. prof. U. Tex., Austin, 1983; disting. vis. prof. natural resources law U. Denver, 1987; disting. vis. prof. U. N.Mex., 1996; vis. lectr. U. Dundee, Scotland, 2001- . Author: Oil and Gas Law in a Nutshell, 1983, 4th edit., 2003; editor: Cases and Materials on Oil and Gas Law, 1986, 4th edit., 2002; editor Internat. Petroleum Transactions, 1993, 2d edit., 2000, others. Pres., trustee Rocky Mountain Mineral Law Found., 2003—. Recipient Outstanding Law Rev. Article award Tex. Bar Found., 1988, 96. Mem. ABA (chair natural resources, energy and environ. law 1992-93), Ctr. Am. and Internat. Law (vice chair, mem. exec. com. adv. bd. Energy Law Inst.), Am. Arbitration Assn., CPR Inst. for Dispute Resolution. Episcopalian. Avocation: sailing. Home: 3526 Greenbrier Dr Dallas TX 75225-5003 Office: So Meth U 3315 Daniel Ave Dallas TX 75275-0001 E-mail: jlowe@mail.smu.edu.

LOWE, LOUIS ROBERT, JR., lawyer; b. Indpls., May 30, 1937; BSCE, Purdue U., 1959; LLD, Ind. U., 1967. Bar: U.S. Dist. Ct. (so. dist.) Ind. 1967, U.S. Tax Ct. 1977; lic. profl. engr. Engr. various cons. engring. cos., Indpls., 1960-64, Ind. Hwy Needs Study, Indpls., 1966-67; ptnr. Lowe, Gray, Steele & Darko, Indpls., 1967—2002, Bose McKinney & Evans, LLP, Indpls., 2003—. Contbr. articles to profl. jours. Sec. English Speaking Union, Indpls., 1967—; trustee Hanover Coll.; elder and tristee Second Presbyn. Ch., Indpls. Fellow Indpls. Bar Found.; mem. Ind. Bar Assn., Purdue U. Alumni Assn., Indpls. Purdue Assn. (pres. 1968-69), Contemporary Club (pres. 1986-87), Columbia Club (bd. dirs. 1993-96), Columbia Club Found. (pres. 1995-97), Gyro Club (bd. dirs. 1982-85). Construction, Probate (including wills, trusts), Securities. Home: 535 Pine Dr Indianapolis IN 46260-1452 Office: 2700 First Ind Plz 135 N Pennsylbania St Indianapolis IN 46204

LOWE, RALPH EDWARD, lawyer; b. Hinsdale, Ill., Nov. 24, 1931; s. Charles Russell and Eva Eleanor (Schroeder) L.; m. Patricia E. Eichhorst, Aug. 23, 1952; children: John Stuart, Michael Kevin, Timothy Edward. BA, Depauw U., 1953; LLB, U. Ill., 1956. Bar: Ill. 1956, U.S. Dist. Ct. (no. dist.) Ill. 1957, Ga. 1974, U.S. Dist. Ct. (no. dist.) Ga. 1980, S.C. 1990. Assoc. Ruddy & Brown, Aurora, Ill., 1956-58; ptnr. Lowe & Richards, Aurora, 1959-62, Vincent, Lowe & Richards, Aurora, 1963-71; pvt. practice, Aurora and Atlanta, 1974-85; prin. Lowe & Steinmetz, Ltd., Aurora and Atlanta, 1985-91; pvt. practice, Aurora, Ill., 1972-74, 92—. Chmn. Inter-Am. Devel. Corp., Ill., 1965-67. Administrative and regulatory, Probate (including wills, trusts), Property, real (including real estate development, water). Office: 407 W Galena Blvd Aurora IL 60506-3946

LOWE, RANDALL BRIAN, lawyer; b. Englewood, N.J., Nov. 20, 1948; BA, U. R.I., 1970; JD, Washington U., 1973. Bar: Ill. 1973, Conn. 1975, D.C. 1976, U.S. Ct. Appeals (2d and D.C. cirs.) 1976, N.J. 1977, U.S. Dist. Ct. N.J. 1977, U.S. Ct. Appeals (3d cir.) 1977, U.S. Ct. Appeals (9th cir.) 1979, N.Y. 1980, U.S. Dist. Ct. (ea. and so. dists.) N.Y. 1980. Atty. Callis & Filcoff, Granite City, Ill., 1973-75, AT&T, Washington and N.Y.C., 1975-78, ITT Corp, 1978-83, Surrey & Morse, Washington, 1983-86; ptnr. Jones, Day, Reavis & Pogue, Washington, 1986-94, Piper & Marbury, Washington, 1994-99, of counsel, 1999-2000; exec. v.p./CLO Prism Comms. Svcs., 1999-2001; ptnr. Davis Wright Tremaine, Washington, 2001—. Administrative and regulatory, Communications, Private international. Office: 1500 K St NW Ste 450 Washington DC 20005-1272

LOWE, ROBERT CHARLES, lawyer; b. New Orleans, July 3, 1949; s. Carl Randall and Antonia (Morgan) L.; m. Theresa Louise Acree, Feb. 4, 1978; 1 child, Nicholas Strafford. BA, U. New Orleans, 1971; JD, La. State U., 1975. Bar: La. 1975, U.S. Dist. Ct. (ea. dist.) La. 1975, U.S. Ct. Appeals (5th cir.) 1980, U.S. Dist. Ct. (we. dist.) La. 1978, U.S. Supreme Ct. 1982. Assoc. Sessions, Fishman, Rosenson, Boisfontaine, and Nathan, New Orleans, 1975-80, ptnr., 1980-87, Lowe, Stein, Hoffman, Allweiss and Hauver, New Orleans, 1987—. Author: Louisiana Divorce, West Pub. Co., 1984; mem. La. Law Rev., 1974-75; contbr. articles to profl. jours. Named one of Best Lawyers in Am. ann., 1983—. Mem. ABA, La. State Bar Assn. (chmn. family law sect. 1984-85), La. Assn. Def. Counsel, New Orleans Bar Assn. (chmn. family law sect. 1991-92), La. State Law Inst., La. Trial Lawyers Assn., Order of Coif, Phi Kappa Phi. Republican. State civil litigation, Family and matrimonial, General practice. Home: 9625 Garden Oak Ln New Orleans LA 70123-2005 Office: 701 Poydras St Ste 3600 New Orleans LA 70139-7735

LOWE, ROBERT STANLEY, lawyer; b. Herman, Nebr., Apr. 23, 1923; s. Stanley Robert and Ann Marguerite (Feese) L.; m. Anne Kirtland Selden, Dec. 19, 1959; children: Robert James, Margaret Anne. AB, U. Nebr., 1947, JD, 1949. Bar: Wyo. 1949. Ptnr. McAvoy & Lowe, Newcastle, 1949—51, Hickey & Lowe, Rawlins, 1951—55; county and pros. atty. Rawlins, 1955—59; pvt. practice, 1959—67; assoc. dir. Am. Judicature Soc., Chgo., 1967—74; gen. counsel True Oil Co. and affiliates, 1974—98, of counsel, 1998—99. Bd. dirs. Hilltop Nat. Bank, Casper, sec., 1981—; legal adv. divsn. Nat. Ski Patrol Sys., 1975-88; city atty. City of Rawlins, 1963-65; atty., asst. sec. Casper Mountain Ski Patrol, 1988—. Chmn. Casper C. of C. Military Affairs Com., 1995-2000; mem. Wyo. Ho. of Reps., 1952-54; bd. dirs. Vols. in Probation, 1969-82; leader lawyer del. to China, People to People, 1986; mem. Wyo. Vets. Affairs Commn., 1994—, chmn., 1996—; mem. legis. com. United Vets. Coun. Wyo., 1993—; trustee Troopers Found., Inc., 1994—, pres., 1994-99; pres. Casper WWII Commemorative Assn., 1995-96, Navy League Wyo. Coun. (pres. 1997-00); state pres. Wyo., 2000-03. Recipient Dedicated Community Worker award Rawlins Jr. C. of C., 1967, Yellow merit star award Nat. Ski Patrol System, 1982, 85, 87, 88, Small Bus. Administrate Vet. Advocate award, 1998, Disting. Svc. award Disabled Am. Vets. Dept., 1994. Fellow Am. Bar Found. (life); mem. VFW (life mem.; post adv. 1991-96, nat. aide-de-camp 1993-94, 98-99, judge adv. dist. 3 Dept. Wyo., 1994—, mil. order of cootie grand judge adv. 1994—), ABA (sec. jud. adminstrn. divsn. lawyers conf., exec. com. 1975-76, chmn. 1977-78, chmn. judicial qualification and selection com. 1986-93, coun. jud. adminstrn. divsn. 1977-78, mem. com. to implement jud. adminstrn. stds. 1978-83, Ho. of Dels. state bar del. 1978-80, 86-87, state del. 1987-93, Assembly del. 1980-83, mem. standing com. on the fed. judiciary 1997-99, ad hoc com. state justice initiatives 1997-99), Am. Judicature Soc. (dir. 1961-67, 85-89, bd. editors 1975-77, Herbert Harley award 1974), Wyo. State Bar (chmn. com. on cts. 1961-67, 77-87), Nebr. State Bar Assn., Ill. State Bar Assn., D.C. Bar, Inter-Am. Bar Assn., Selden Soc., Inst. Jud. Adminstrn., Rocky Mountain Oil and Gas Assn. (legal com. 1976-99, chmn. 1979-82, 90-91), Rocky Mountain Mineral Law Found. (trustee 1980-94), Am. Law Inst. (life), Order of Coif, Delta Theta Phi (dist. chancellor 1982-83, chief justice 1983-93, assoc. justice 1993—; Percy J. Power Meml. award 1983, Gold Medallion award 1990), Casper Rotary Club (pres. 1985-86), Casper Rotary Found. (dir. 1990—, sec. 1990-00). Mem. Ch. of Christ, Scientist. Banking, Corporate, general, Oil, gas, and mineral. Home and Office: 97 Primrose Casper WY 82604-4018 Office: 5905 Cy Ave Casper WY 82604-4101

LOWELL, ROLAND M. lawyer; b. Three Rivers, Mich. m. Ruby Ellon Lowell. BA, Kalamazoo Coll., 1969; JD, Vanderbilt U., 1972. Bar: Tenn. 1972, U.S. Ct. Appeals (6th cir.) 1975, U.S. Supreme Ct. 1976, U.S. Dist. Ct. (mid. dist.) Tenn. 1984, U.S. Dist. Ct. (we. dist.) Tenn. 1992. Ptnr. Ludwick & Lowell, Nashville, 1984-87, Lowell & Bradley, Nashville, 1987-91; atty., of counsel Leitner Warner Moffitt Dooley Carpender & Napolitan, Nashville, 1991-95; atty. Bruce Weathers Corley Dughman & Lyle, Nashville, 1995—. Mem. Am. Moving and Storage Assn. (agt.), Am. Process Agts. (agt.). General civil litigation, Corporate, general, Transportation. Office: Bruce Weathers Corley et al Am South Ctr Ste 2075 315 Deaderick St Nashville TN 37238

LOWENBERG, MICHAEL, lawyer; b. Bklyn., Mar. 6, 1943; s. Leo and Edna (Hanft) L.; m. Julie Goldberg, June 13, 1965; children: Daniel, Frances, Anthony. BA, Bklyn. Coll., 1963; LLB, Harvard U., 1966. Bar: Tex. 1966, U.S. Dist. Ct. (no. dist.) Tex. 1966, U.S. Ct. Appeals (5th cir.) 1967. Assoc. Akin, Gump, Strauss, Hauer & Feld, L.L.P., Dallas, 1966-71; ptnr. Akin, Gump, Strauss, Hauer & Feld, Dallas, 1972—2002; of counsel Gardere Wynne Sewell LLP, Dallas, 2003—. Pres. Dallas Legal Services Found., 1972; chmn. Dallas chpt. Am. Jewish Com., 1973-74. Mem. ABA, Tex. Bar Assn., Bar Assn. of 5th Cir. (past. pres., bd. dirs.), Dallas Bar Assn., Dallas Bar Found., Tex. Bar Found., Coll. of State Bar Tex., Def. Rsch. Inst., Tex. Appleseed (bd. dirs.). Democrat. Federal civil litigation, State civil litigation, Commercial, contracts (including sales of goods; commercial financing). Home: 5321 Drane Dr Dallas TX 75209-5501 Office: Gardere Wynne Sewell LLP 3000 Thanksgiving Twr 1601 Elm St Dallas TX 75201-4761 Fax: 214-999-3135. E-mail: mlowenberg@gardere.com.

LOWENBRAUN, SOLOMON MORTIMER, lawyer; b. N.Y.C., Feb. 1, 1921; s. Harry and Mary L.; m. Florence M. Grossman, Aug. 7, 1945; children: Dale Lowenbraun Boyle, Cathy Lowenbraun McKeon, Leslie Lowenbraun Weitzman. BS in Social Sci., CCNY, 1941; JD, Fordham U., 1949. Bar: N.Y. 1950, U.S. Dist. Ct. (so. dist.) N.Y. 1950, U.S. Dist. Ct. (ea. dist.) N.Y. 1953, U.S. Supreme Ct. 1978. Atty. pvt. practice, N.Y.C., 1950—. Lt. comdr. USNR, 1942-45. Mem. N.Y. State Bar Assn., Queens County Bar Assn. Jewish. General civil litigation, General practice, Personal injury (including property damage). Home: 16625 Powells Cove Blvd Beechhurst NY 11357-1545 Office: 425 Northern Blvd Ste 27 Great Neck NY 11021

LOWENFELS, LEWIS DAVID, lawyer; b. N.Y.C., June 9, 1935; s. Seymour and Jane (Phillips) L.; m. Fern Gelford, Aug. 15, 1965; children: Joshua, Jacqueline. BA magna cum laude, Harvard U., 1957, LLB, 1961. Bar: N.Y. 1961; lic. corp. and securities atty. Ptnr. Tolins & Lowenfels, N.Y.C., 1967—. Adj. prof. Seton Hall U. Law Sch; lectr. Practicing Law Inst., Southwestern Legal Found., U. Minn. Fed. Bar Assn., 1972; pub. gov. Am. Stock Exch., 1993-96. Co-author: Bromberg and Lowenfels on Securities Fraud and Commodities Fraud, 6 vols., 1999; contbr. articles to profl. jours. With USAR, 1957-63. Mem. ABA (fed. regulation of securities com. 1978—, lectr.), N.Y. County Lawyers Assn. (securities and exchanges com. 1974—), Phi Beta Kappa, Harvard Club. Avocations: reading, writing, athletics. Corporate, general, Securities, Administrative and regulatory. Office: Tolins & Lowenfels 747 3d Ave 19th Fl New York NY 10017-1028 E-mail: Lew@TolinsLowenfels.com.

LOWENKRON, RUTH, lawyer; b. Patchogue, NY, Feb. 27, 1960; d. Hans and Irene (Markwald) Lowenkron. BA, Cornell U., 1981; JD, CUNY, 1986. Bar: N.J. 1986, U.S. Dist. Ct. N.J. 1986, N.Y. 1987, U.S. Dist. Ct. (so. and ea. dists.) N.Y. 1991, U.S. Ct. Appeals (2nd cir.) 1993, U.S. Ct. Appeals (3d cir.) 1999, U.S. Supreme Ct. 1993. Staff atty. Community Health Law Project, East Orange, N.J., 1986-90, N.Y. Lawyers for the Pub. Interest, Inc., N.Y.C., 1990-95, dir. Disability Law Ctr., 1995-99; sr. staff atty. Edn. Law Ctr., Newark, 1999—. Adj. assoc. prof. social work and law, disability law Seton Hall U., 1989—; adj. assoc. prof. disability law Sch. CUNY, N.Y.C. Mem. Essex County Bar Assn. (com. on rights of persons with disabilities), ACLU (vol. atty. N.J. chpt.), N.Y. State Bar Assn. (com. on mental and phys. disability). Home: 430 Richmond Ave Maplewood NJ 07040 Office: Edn Law Ctr 60 Park Pl Ste 300 Newark NJ 07102 E-mail: rlowenkron@edlawcenter.org.

LOWENSTEIN, ANTHONY, lawyer, consultant; b. Montreal, Que., Canada, Jan. 9, 1971; s. Aubrey and Betty Lowenstein. LLB, Osgoode Hall Law Sch., Toronto, Ont., Can., 1995. Bar: Calif. 1999. Legal tech. cons. Dept. of Justice / Baker Robbins, San Francisco, 1997—99; assoc. atty. Law Offices, San Mateo, Calif., 1999—2001; pres., CEO Lowenstein Law Office, Burlingame, Calif., 2001—. Legal template developer Lowenstein Law Office, Burlingame, 2002. Bd. mem. Svc. League of San Mateo County, Redwood City, Calif., 2002—. Mem.: Calif. Pub. Defender Assn. (assoc.; mem. 1999, Trial Advocacy 2002). Jewish. Achievements include development of Legal Document Automation. Avocation: aviation - faa certified pilot. General practice, Computer, Criminal. Home: 163 Chenery St Burlingame CA 94010 Office: Lowenstein Law Office 345 Lorton Ave Ste 303 Burlingame CA 94010 Home Fax: 650-745-1010; Office Fax: 650-745-1010. E-mail: anthony@lowensteinlaw.com.

LOWENSTEIN, LOUIS, legal educator; b. N.Y.C., June 13, 1925; s. Louis and Ralphina (Steinhardt) L.; m. Helen Libby Udell, Feb. 12, 1953; children: Roger Spector, Jane Ruth, Barbara Ann. BS, Columbia, 1947, LL.B., 1953; M.F.S., U. Md., 1951. Bar: N.Y. 1953. Pvt. practice law, N.Y.C., 1954-78; Assoc. Judge Stanley H. Fuld, N.Y. Ct. Appeals, 1953-54; assoc., then partner Hays, Sklar & Herzberg, 1954-68; partner Nickerson, Kramer, Lowenstein, Nessen, Kamin & Soll, 1968-78; Simon H. Rifkind prof. emeritus law and fin. Columbia U. Law Sch., 1980—, project dir. Instl. Investor Project, 1988-94; pres. Supermarkets Gen. Corp., Woodbridge, N.J., 1978-79. Bd. dirs. Liz Claiborne, Inc. 1988-96; mem. pub. oversight bd. Panel on Audit Effectiveness, 1998-2000. Author: What's Wrong with Wall Street, 1988, Sense and Nonsense in Corporate Finance, 1991; contbr., co-editor: Knights, Raiders and Targets, 1988; editor in chief Columbia Law Rev., 1951-53. V.p., mem. exec. com. Fedn. Jewish Philanthropies N.Y.; pres. Jewish Bd. Family and Children's Svcs. N.Y., 1974—78; trustee Beth Israel Med. Ctr., N.Y.C., 1975—81; dir. Goddard-Riverside Cmty. Ctr., 1996—2002; chmn. bd. dirs. Coalition for the Homeless, 1997—. Mem. ABA, Assn. of Bar of City of N.Y., Am. Law Inst. Home: 5 Oak Ln Larchmont NY 10538-3917 Office: Columbia U Law Sch 435 W 116th St New York NY 10027-7297

LOWENSTEIN, PETER DAVID, lawyer; b. N.Y.C., Dec. 31, 1935; s. Melvyn Gordon and Katherine Price (Goldsmith) L.; m. Constance Cohen; children from previous marriage: Anthony, Kate E., Christopher. BA, Trinity Coll., 1958; LLB, Georgetown U., 1961. Bar: Conn. 1962, N.Y. 1963. With SEC, Washington, 1961-63; assoc. Whitman & Ransom, N.Y.C., 1963-70, ptnr., 1970-83; sec., gen. counsel Value Line, Inc., N.Y.C., 1983-87; v.p., sec., gen. counsel Service Am. Corp., Stamford, Conn., 1988-90; ptnr. O'Connor, Morris & Jones, Greenwich, Conn., 1990-92; pvt. practice, Greenwich, 1992—. Legal counsel Value Line Mutual Funds. Bd. dirs. Grand St. Settlement, N.Y.C., 1970-92, Greenwich Health Assn., Conn., 1978-85; bd. dirs. Greenwich chpt. ARC, 1989-94, vice chmn., 1991-93. Mem.: Yale Club of N.Y., Greenwich Field Club, Nantucket Yacht Club. Corporate, general, Securities. Home: 496 Valley Rd Cos Cob CT 06807-1627 Office: Two Sound View Dr Ste 100 Greenwich CT 06830-5436 E-mail: PDLOW@aol.com.

LOWERY, TIMOTHY J. lawyer; s. Martin B. and Rita Lowery. BA in English Lit., U. Ill., 1982; JD, Ill. Inst. Tech., 1985. Bar: Ill., U.S. Dist. Ct. (no. dist.) Ill., U.S. Ct. Appeals (7th cir.). Owner Lowery & Assocs., LLC, Chgo.; pvt. practice Chgo. Mem. ABA (transp. sect.), Ill. State Bar Assn., Ill. Assn. Def. Trial Counsel, Def. Rsch. Inst. (trucking law subcom.), Trucking Industry Def. Assn. Personal injury (including property damage), Transportation. Office: Lowery & Assocs 333 W Wacker Dr Ste 420 Chicago IL 60606-1225

LOWERY, W. WILSON, JR., federal agency administrator; BS in Fin., MBA, U. N.C. Fin. analyst IBM, 1968, dir. fin. planning and analysis Info. Sys. and Comm. Group, 1982—84, v.p. plans and controls and bus. devel. Svc. Divsn., 1984—89, asst. gen. mgr. fin. and planning Applications Solutions and Software, 1989—91, v.p., sr. mng. dir. fin. and planning, 1991—94, v.p. quality and reengring., 1994—95, chmn. Credit Corp., gen.

mgr. global fin., 1995—98, ret., 1998; pres. WLLP Capital, 1998—2002; exec. asst. dir. adminstrn. FBI, Washington, 2002—. Office: FBI J Edgar Hoover Bldg 935 Pennsylvania Ave NW Washington DC 20535*

LOWERY, WILLIAM HERBERT, lawyer; b. Toledo, June 8, 1925; s. Kenneth Alden and Drusilla (Pfanner) L.; m. Carolyn Broadwell, June 27, 1947; children: Kenneth Latham, Marcia Mitchell; m. Janice Gamble Gerrie, Dec. 28, 2002. PhB, U. Chgo., 1947; JD, U. Mich., 1950. Bar: Pa. 1951, U.S. Supreme Ct. 1955. Assoc. Dechert Price & Rhoads, Phila., 1950-58, ptnr., 1958-89, mng. ptnr., 1970-72; mem. policy com., chmn. litigation dept., 1962-68, 81-84; of counsel Dechert, Phila., 1989—; counsel S.S. Huebner Found. Ins. Edn., Phila., 1970-89. Faculty Am. Conf. of Legal Execs., Pa. Bar Inst.; permanent mem. com. of visitors U. Mich. Law Sch. Author: Insurance Litigation Problems, 1972, Insurance Litigation Disputes, 1977. Pres. Strafford Civic Assn., 1958; chmn. Tredyffrin Twp. Zoning Bd., Chester County, Pa., 1959—75; bd. dirs. Paoli Meml. Hosp., 1964—89, chmn., 1972—75; bd. dirs. Main Line Health, Radnor, 1984—89; permanent mem. Jud. Conf. 3d Cir. Ct. 2n lt. USAF, 1943—46. Mem. ABA (chmn. life ins. com. 1984-85, chmn. Nat. Conf. Lawyers and Life Ins. Cos. 1984-88), Order of the Coif, Royal Poinciana Golf Club (bd. dirs. 1997-2003, sec. 1997-2000, v.p. 2000-03), Phi Gamma Delta, Phi Delta Phi. Federal civil litigation, Health, Insurance. Home: 122 Moorings Park Dr Apt G-302 Naples FL 34105 Office: Dechert 4000 Bell Atlantic Tower 1717 Arch St Lbby 3 Philadelphia PA 19103-2793

LOWES, ALBERT CHARLES, lawyer; b. Oak Ridge, Mo., Dec. 1, 1932; s. Guy Everett and Lillian Bertina (Tuschhoff) L.; m. Peggy Rae Watson, Aug. 27, 1960; children: Danita Rae, Albert Charles II, Kurt Brandon. Student, Cape State Coll., 1954-56; JD, U. Mo., 1959. Bar: Mo. 1959, U.S. Dist. Ct. (ea. dist.) Mo. 1959, U.S. Ct. Appeals (8th cir.) 1971. With Buerkle, Lowes, Beeson & Ludwig, Jackson, Mo., 1959-84; ptnr. Lowes & Drusch, Cape Girardeau, 1984—. Atty. City of Jackson, 1960-62. Staff sgt. USMC, 1950-54, Korea. Mem. Mo. Bar Assn., VFW (judge adv. dept. Mo.1962-64, 67-68, state judge adv. 1997-98), Masons, Shriners, Elks. Democrat. Lutheran. Avocations: reading, history, legal fields. Criminal, Insurance, Personal injury (including property damage). Office: Lowes & Drusch 2913 Independence St Cape Girardeau MO 63703-8320

LOWINGER, LAZAR, lawyer; b. Antwerp, Berchem, Belgium, Nov. 7, 1934; came to U.S., 1954; s. Julius and Maria (Gilburd) L.; m. Audrey Schwelling, Aug. 15, 1965; children— Jeffrey Paul, Brian Marc. Student Boston U., 1956-57, Sir Geo. Williams Coll., 1957-59; J.D., New England Sch. Law, 1962. Bar: Mass. 1964, U.S. Dist. Ct. Mass. 1965. Sole practice, Newton, Mass., 1964—. Served with U.S. Army, 1954-56. Recipient Mem. of Honour award Cuban Bar in Exile, Miami, Fla., 1971. Mem. Mass. Bar Assn. (chmn.), Assn. Trial Lawyers Am., Mass. Acad. Trial Attys. Clubs: Hazel Hotchkiss Wightman Tennis Ctr. (Weston, Mass.). Fluent in Romanian, Spanish, Italian, Jewish, French. Criminal, General practice, Personal injury (including property damage). Home: 305 Woodcliff Rd Newton MA 02461-2127 Office: 313 Washington St Ste 203 Newton MA 02458-1626

LOWNDES, JOHN FOY, lawyer; b. Jan. 1, 1931; s. Charles L. B. and Dorothy (Foy) L.; m. Rita Davies, Aug. 18, 1983; children: Elizabeth Anne, Amy Scott, John Patrick, Joseph Edward, Jennifer Susanne. BA, Duke U., 1953, LLB, 1958. Bar: Fla. 1958. Pvt. practice, Daytona Beach, Fla., 1958, Orlando, Fla., 1959-69; sr. ptnr., chmn. bd. dirs. Lowndes, Drosdick, Doster, Kantor & Reed, P.A., Orlando, 1969—. Chmn. U. Ctrl. Fla. Found.; mem. Fla. Constl. Rev. Commn., 1998. Former chmn. bd. trustees Orlando Mus. Art, Winter Park Meml. Hosp.; bd. visitors Duke U. Law Sch. Capt. USMCR, 1953-61. Republican. Corporate, general, Property, real (including real estate development, water). Home: 1308 Green Cove Rd Winter Park FL 32789-2549 Office: Lowndes Drosdick Doster Kantor & Reed 215 N Eola Dr Orlando FL 32801-2095

LOWNDES MARQUES, FILIPE, lawyer; b. Lisbon, Portugal, July 30, 1972; s. Paulo and Isabel Lowndes Marques; m. Ulrica Oom Lowndes Marques, Oct. 25, 1997; children: Ulrica, Frederico. Lic., Cath. U., Lisbon, 1994; MJur, U. Oxford, Eng., 1995. Bar: Portugal 1997, England & Wales 2000. Jr. assoc. Abreu & Marques, Lisbon, 1995—2001; assoc. Miguel Galvao Teles Joao Soares Da Silva, 2001—. Author: Foreign Investment in Mozambique, 1998; co-author: Financial Times Capital Taxes, 2002, Tolley's International Succession Law, 2002. Scholar, Brit. Coun., Portugal, 1994, Portuguese Bar Assn., 1996. Mem.: Brit. Portguese C. of C. (bd. dirs. 2001—). Roman Catholic. Securities, Banking, Finance. Office: MGT--JSS Rua Castilho 75-6 1250-068 Lisbon Portugal Fax: +351 213826628. E-mail: flmarques@mgt-jss.pt.

LOWNEY, TIMOTHY JAY, lawyer; b. Boston, Nov. 27, 1973; s. Charles William and Irene (Medieros) Lowney. BA, Boston Coll., 1996; JD, Suffolk U., 1999. Bar: Mass. 99. Law clk. Karol & Karol, Milton, Mass., 1996—99, assoc., 1999—2000, Roberson & Assocs., Hyde Park, Mass., 2000—01, Lawyers Unltd., Hyde Park, 2001—. Mem. warrant com. Town of Milton, Milton, 2001—02, mem. town meeting, 1999—; v.p. Mass. Recreation and Park Assn., 2000—01. Mem.: ATLA, ABA, Mass. Assn. Trial Attys. Personal injury (including property damage), Criminal, Commercial, consumer (including collections, credit). Office: Lawyers Unltd 1234 Hyde Park Ave Ste 102 Boston MA 02136 Fax: 617-364-1400. E-mail: atty.lowney@verizon.net.

LOWRY, EDWARD FRANCIS, JR., lawyer; b. L.A., Aug. 13, 1930; s. Edward Francis and Mary Anita (Woodcock) L.; m. Patricia Ann Palmer, Feb. 16, 1963; children: Edward Palmer, Rachael Louise. Student, Ohio State U., 1948—50; AB, Stanford U., 1952, JD, 1954. Bar: Ariz. 1955, D.C. 1970, U.S. Supreme Ct. 1969. Camp dir. Quarter Circle V Bar Ranch, 1954; tchr. Orme Sch., Mayer, Ariz., 1954—56; trust rep. Valley Nat. Bank Ariz., 1958—60; pvt. practice Phoenix, 1960—; assoc. atty. Cunningham, Carson & Messinger, 1960—64; ptnr. Carson, Messinger, Elliott, Laughlin & Ragan, 1964—69, 1970—80, Gray, Plant, Mooty, Mooty & Bennett, 1981—84, Eaton, Lazarus, Dodge & Lowry Ltd., 1985—86; exec. v.p., gen. counsel Bus. Realty Ariz., 1986—93; pvt. practice, Scottsdale, Ariz., 1986—88; ptnr. Lowry & Froeb, Scottsdale, 1988—89, Lowry, Froeb & Clements, P.C., Scottsdale, 1989—90, Lowry & Clements P.C., Scottsdale, 1990, Lowry, Clements & Powell, P.C., Scottsdale, 1991—. Asst. legis. counsel Dept. Interior, Washington, 1969-70; mem. Ariz. Commn. Uniform Laws, 1972—, chmn., 1976-88; judge pro tem Ariz. Ct. Appeals, 1986, 92-94; mem. Nat. Conf. Commrs. on Uniform State Laws, 1972-97, life mem., 1997—. Chmn. Coun. of Stanford Law Socs., 1968; bd. dirs. Scottsdale Prevention Inst., 1999—; vice chmn. bd. trustees Orme Sch., 1972-74, treas., 1981-83; trustee Heard Mus., 1965-91, life trustee, 1991—, pres., 1974-75; bd. visitors Stanford Sch. Law; magistrate Town of Paradise Valley, Ariz., 1976-83, town councilman, 1998—, mayor, 1998—; juvenile ct. referee Maricopa County, 1978-83. Capt. USAF, 1956-58. Fellow Ariz. Bar Found. (founder); mem. ABA, Maricopa County Bar Assn., State Bar Ariz. (chmn. com. uniform laws 1979-85), Stanford Law Soc. Ariz. (past pres.), Scottsdale Bar Assn. (bd. dirs. 1991—, v.p. 1991, pres. 1992-95), Ariz. State U. Law Soc. (bd. dirs.), Delta Sigma Rho, Alpha Tau Omega, Phi Delta Phi. Estate planning, Probate (including wills, trusts), Property, real (including real estate development, water). Home: 7600 N Moonlight Ln Paradise Valley AZ 85253-2938 Office: Lowry Clements & Powell PC 4200 N 82d St Ste 2001 Scottsdale AZ 85251-2771 also: 6900 E Camelback Rd Ste 1040 Scottsdale AZ 85251-2444

LOWRY, HOUSTON PUTNAM, lawyer; b. N.Y.C., Apr. 1, 1955; s. Thomas Clinton Falls and Jean Allen (Day) L.; m. Kathryn Santoro Curtiss. BA, Pitzer Coll., 1976; MBA, U. Conn., 1980; JD cum laude, Gonzaga U., 1980; LLM in Internat. Law, U. Cambridge, Eng., 1981. Bar: Conn. 1980, U.S. Dist. Ct. Conn. 1981, U.S. Tax Ct. 1982, U.S. Ct. Mil. Appeals 1982, U.S. Ct. Appeals (1st, 2d, 5th, 11th cirs.) 1982, U.S. Ct. Claims 1984, D.C. 1985, U.S. Ct. Appeals (4th, 6th, 7th, 9th, fed., D.C. cirs.) 1985, U.S. Ct. Appeals (3d, 8th, 10th cirs.) 1986, U.S. Supreme Ct., N.Y. 1989. Law clk. to Judge William M. Acker, Jr. U.S. Dist. Ct., Birmingham, Ala., 1982-83; assoc. Tarlow, Levy & Droney, Farmington, Conn., 1983-88; prin. Tarlow, Levy & Droney, P.C., Farmington, Conn., 1989-93, Brown & Welsh P.C., Meriden, Conn., 1993—. Mem. adj. faculty internat. trade law and internat. comml. arbitration U. Conn. Law Sch., 1990-95, 99—. Mem. adv. com. on pvt. internat. law Sec. of State, 1996—. Fellow Chartered Inst. Arbitrators; mem. ABA (various coms.), Conn. Bar Assn. (various coms.), Am. Soc. Internat. Law, Internat. Law Assn., Am. Law Inst., Hon. Soc. Gray's Inn, Hartford Club. General civil litigation, Commercial, contracts (including sales of goods; commercial financing), Private international. Office: Brown & Welsh PC PO Box 183 530 Preston Ave Meriden CT 06450-4893 E-mail: hplowry@brownwelsh.com.

LOWRY, ROBERT DUDLEY, lawyer; b. Washington, Apr. 12, 1949; s. Robert Newton and Mary (Dudley) L.; m. Becky Jo Kangas, Aug. 3, 1974; children: Samuel Robert, Joseph Houston. BA in Biology, U. Oreg., 1971, postgrad., 1971-73, JD, 1980. Bar: Oreg. 1980, U.S. Dist. Ct. Oreg. 1980, U.S. Claims Ct. 1987, U.S. Supreme Ct. 1991, U.S. Ct. Appeals (9th cir.) 1991, U.S. Ct. Appeals (fed. cir.) 1992. Law clk. Oreg. Supreme Ct., Salem, 1980-81; ptnr. Jaqua & Wheatley, Eugene, 1981-91; prin. Robert D. Lowry, Atty. at Law, Eugene. Past chmn. Regional Trauma Adv. Bd., Oreg.; legal counsel Boy Scouts Am., Eugene, 1984—, March of Dimes; past chair Lawyer Reps. to 9th Cir. Jud. Conf., U.S. Cts. Dist. Oreg.; chair Lawyers Reps. Jud. Conf. U.S. Cts. for 9th Cir. Mem. ABA (chmn. joint state med.-legal com. 1988-89), ATLA, Lane County Bar Assn. (chmn. fed. ct. com. 1985-88, med. legal com. 1986-87), Oreg. Assn. Def. Counsel, Def. Rsch. Inst., Nat. Health Lawyers Assn., Phi Delta Phi. Democrat. Episcopalian. Federal civil litigation, Health, Insurance. Home: 2875 Emerald St Eugene OR 97403-2504 Office: PO Box 12010 975 Oak St Ste 790 Eugene OR 97401-3121

LOWRY, STEPHEN GLENN, lawyer; b. Dayton, Ohio, July 10, 1972; s. Robert E. and Joyce Ann Lowry; m. K. Leilani, Jan. 3, 1999. BA in Econs. magna cum laude, BA in History magna cum laude, U. Md. Balt., 1995; JD cum laude, Lewis and Clark Coll., 1998. Bar: Ga. 1998, U.S. Dist. Ct. (no., mid., so. dists.) Ga. 1999, U.S. Ct. Appeals 1999, U.S. Supreme Ct. 1999. Assoc. Freeman, Wright and Herman, Atlanta, 1998—99, Middleton, Mathis, Adams and Tate, Savannah, Ga., 1999—2001, Carter and Tate PC, Savannah, 2001—. Bd. dirs. New Legacy Cmty. Devel. Corp., Savannah; rep. Chatham County Dem. Com., Savannah; judge, adv. Navy League, Savannah, 2000—01. Mem.: Ga. Trial Lawyers Assn. (chairperson Young Lawyers divsn.), Ga. Bar Assn. (bd. dirs. Young Lawyers divsn.). Avocations: running, kayaking, fishing, golf, reading. Personal injury (including property damage), Product liability. Office: Carter and Tate PC PO Box 9060 18 E Bay St Savannah GA 31412

LOWTHER, GERALD HALBERT, lawyer; b. Slagle, La., Feb. 18, 1924; s. Fred B. and Beatrice (Halbert) L.; children by previous marriage: Teresa, Craig, Natalie, Lisa. AB, Pepperdine Coll., 1951; JD, U. Mo., 1951. Bar: Mo. 1951. Since practiced in, Springfield; ptnr. firm Lowther, Johnson, Joyner, Lowther, Cully & Housley. Mem. Savs. and Loan Commn. Mo., 1965-68, Commerce and Indsl. Commn. Mo., 1967-73; lectr. U. Tex., 1955-57, Crested Butte, Colo., 1958-59 Contbr. articles law jours. Past pres. Ozarks Regional Heart Assn.; Del., mem. rules com. Democratic Nat. Conv., 1968; treas. Dem. Party Mo., 1968-72, mem. platform com., 1965, 66, mem. bi-partisan commn. to reapportion Mo. senate, 1966; Bd. dirs. Greene County Guidance Clinic, Ozark Christian Counseling Service, Greene County, Mo.; past pres. Cox Med. Center. Served with AUS, 1946-47; Col. staff of Gov. Hearnes 1964, 68, Mo. Mem. ABA, Mo. Bar Assn., Greene County Bar Assn., Def. Orientation Conf. Assn., Internat. Assn. Ins. Counsel, Def. Rsch. Inst., Springfield C. of C. Clubs: Kiwanian (pres. 1962), Quarterback (pres. 1958), Tip Off (pres. 1960). General civil litigation, Personal injury (including property damage). Office: 901 E Saint Louis St Fl 20 Springfield MO 65806-2540 Home: 350 S John Q Hammons Pkwy Springfield MO 65806-2505

LOWTHER, THOMAS EDWARD, lawyer; b. St. Louis, Aug. 14, 1936; s. Noel Edward and Catherine Virginia (Polliham) L.; m. Lois Duggins, Dec. 28, 1963; children: Nancy, Sandra, Patricia, Susan. LLB, Washington U., St. Louis, 1962, MLA, 1999. Bar: Mo. 1962. Assoc. The Stolar Partnership, St. Louis, 1962, ptnr., 1967—, exec. com., 1985—. Mem. Wash. U. Sch. Law Natl. Coun., 1994—, natl. vice chair campaign cabinet 2001—, co-chair 125th anniversary com.; co-chair 125th Anniversary Comm; alumni bd. govs. Washington U., 1995-, vice chair, 1999, chair, 2000, bd. trustees; pres., St. Joseph's Home for Boys, 1997—, Marion Hall for Girls, 1997-2002, sec., 2002—; co-tee Suzanne Feld Zalk Charitable Trust. Recipient Disting. Alumnus award Washington U. Sch. Law, 1997. 2002. Mem.: Nat. Assn. Bond Lawyers, St. Louis Bar Assn., Mo. Bar Assn., ABA. Avocations: archaeology, travel, trout fishing. Commercial, contracts (including sales of goods; commercial financing), Corporate, general, Finance. Office: The Stolar Partnership 911 Washington Ave Ste 7 Saint Louis MO 63101-1243 E-mail: tel@stolarlaw.com.

LOWY, GEORGE THEODORE, lawyer; b. N.Y.C., Oct. 6, 1931; s. Eugene and Elizabeth Lowy; m. Pier M. Foucault, Sept. 7, 1957. BA cum laude, LLB cum laude, NYU. Bar: N.Y. 1955, U.S. Dist. Ct. (so. dist.) N.Y. 1958, U.S. Supreme Ct. 1972, U.S. Ct Appeals (2d cir.) 1975. Assoc. Cravath, Swaine and Moore, N.Y.C., 1957-65, ptnr., 1965—. Trustee NYU Law Ctr. Found.; bd. dirs. Equitable Life Assurance Soc. U.S., Eramet, Paris, Axa Fin., U.S.; adj. prof. NYU Law Sch., 1983—88; bd. overseers Brandeis U. Grad. Sch. Internat. Econs. and Fin. Fellow ABA; mem. Am. Law Inst., Assn. of Bar of City of N.Y. (chmn. com. on corp. law), Internat. Bar Assn., Union Internat. des Avocats, Cercle Interallie Paris. Private international, Mergers and acquisitions, Securities. Home: 580 Park Ave New York NY 10021-7313 Office: Cravath Swaine & Moore World Wide Pla 825 8th Ave Fl 43 New York NY 10019-7416 E-mail: glowy@cravath.com.

LOWY, PETER ANDREW, lawyer; b. New York, N.Y., Nov. 27, 1969; s. Martin Eric and Pam Mara (Gold) Lowy. LLM, NY U. Sch. of Law, 1997. Bar: U.S. Tax Ct. 1998. Jud. clk. U.S. Dist. Ct., Alexandria, La., 1995—96; attorney-advisor U.S. Tax Ct., Washington, 1997—98; sr. tax atty. Exxon Mobil Corp., Houston, 1998—2001, Shell Oil Co., Houston, 2001—02. Contbr. articles to profl. jours. Co- organizer Low-Income Taxpayer Clinic, Houston, 2000—02. Recipient Young Lawyer of the Year-Nominated, Houston Vol. Lawyer's Program, 2002. Corporate taxation, Tax Litigation. Office: Shell Oil Company 910 Louisiana Ste 4396 Houston TX 77002 Personal E-mail: palowy@justice.com. E-mail: peter.lowy@shell.com.

LOZANO-MERINO, RAUL SANTIAGO, lawyer, consultant; b. Callao, Peru, Mar. 4, 1955; s. Hector Manuel Lozano and Carmen Merino; m. Lauretty Andrea Huerta-Ganoza, May 3, 2000; 1 child, Santiago;1 child, Andrea Giuliana. M in econ. internat. law, Colegio de Abgogados de Lima, 1990. Assoc. Cantuarias, Garrido-Lecca & Mulanovich Assoc. Lawyers, 1977—89; ptnr. Peña, Lozano, Faura & Associated Lawyers, Lima, 1989—; legal adv. Peruvian State Enterprises. Prof. U. Lima, U. Inca Garcilazo de la Vega, Academia Internat. de la Magistrature. Sponsor Peruvian Art and Culture Mus., 1997. Recipient Internat. Lawyer Honors, Ordem Dos Advogados do Brazil, Sao Paulo, Argentinian Bar Assn., Buenos Aires. Mem.: Union Internat. des Advocats, Internat. Econ. Law Iberoamerican Inst. (pres.), Inter-Am. Bar Assn. (pres. 2002—03, Internat. Lawyer Honors). Avocations: reading, art. Corporate, general, Aviation, Commercial, contracts (including sales of goods; commercial financing). Office: Peña Lozano Faura & Associated Lawyers Jiron Junin 165 Lima 18 Peru

LUBAR, CHARLES GORDON, lawyer; b. Washington, May 20, 1941; s. Nathan Marvin and Lenora (Abrams) L.; m. Nancy Kaplan, Apr. 23, 1966 (div. 1977); 1 child, Katherine Nicole; m. Dominique Grierson, Oct. 2, 1977; 1 child, Alexander Nathan. BA magna cum laude, Yale U., 1963; JD, Harvard U., 1966; LLM in Taxation, Georgetown U., 1967. Bar: D.C., Md. Atty.-advisor Chief Counsel's Office IRS, Washington, 1967-69; legal counsel East African Devel. Bank, Kampala, Uganda, 1970; ptnr. Margulies & Sterling, London, 1971-74; founder, ptnr. Lubar & Youngstein, London, 1974-81; ptnr. Morgan Lewis & Bockius, London, 1981—, mng. ptnr., 1981-96, chmn. internat. sect., 1995-98, vice chmn tax sect., 1998—99. Speaker on internat. tax issues at numerous confs. Contbr. articles to profl. jours. Am. sec. Prince of Wales Youth Bus. Trust, London, 1989-90; mem. devel. bd. Am. sect. Nat. Gallery, London, 1990-92; mem., chair several coms. Fulbright Commn. U.K., London, 1986-96, mem. Royal Acad. Art (exec. comm.- Benjamin West Grp.). Mem. ABA, Internat. Fiscal Assn., Yale Alumni Assn. (treas., bd. govs. 1986-90), Yale Club of London (pres. 1990-2002). Avocations: guitar, tennis, running, golf. Estate taxation, Corporate taxation, Taxation, general. Office: Morgan Lewis & Bockius 2 Gresham St London EC2V 7PE England

LUBBEN, CRAIG HENRY, lawyer; b. Fort Lee, Va., Aug. 10, 1956; s. George and Dorothy Marion (Vree) L.; m. Lois Beth Zylstra, June 9, 1979; children: Christina Anne, Brian Craig, Eric George, Kaitlin Louise. BA, Calvin Coll., 1978; JD cum laude, Northwestern U., 1981. Bar: Mich. 1981, U.S. Dist. Ct. (we. dist.) Mich. 1981, U.S. Ct. Appeals (6th cir.) 1984. Ptnr. Miller, Johnson, Snell & Cummiskey, Grand Rapids, Mich., 1981-86, Kalamazoo, 1986—. Pres., Alternative Directions, Grand Rapids, 1985; trustee Grand Rapids Pub. Mus. Assn., 1984-86; pres. Kalamazoo Christian Schs. Devel. Assn., 1988-91, Family and Children's Svcs. Kalamazoo, 1993-96; trustee Kalamazoo Symphony, 2002—. Mem. State Bar Mich. (rep. assemblyperson 1990-92, bd. commrs. 2001—), Kalamazoo County Bar Assn. (pres.-elect 1997-98, pres. 1998-99), Order of Coif. Mem. Christian Reformed Ch. Federal civil litigation, State civil litigation, Commercial, contracts (including sales of goods; commercial financing). Office: Miller Johnson Snell & Cummiskey Rose St Market Bldg 303 N Rose St Ste 600 Kalamazoo MI 49007-3850 E-mail: lubbenc@mjsc.com.

LUBBEN, DAVID J. lawyer; b. Cedar Rapids, Iowa, 1951; BA, Luther Coll., 1974; JD, U. Iowa, 1977. Bar: Minn. 1977. Ptnr. Dorsey & Whitney, Mpls., to 1993; gen. counsel UnitedHealth Group, Minnetonka, Minn., 1993—. Corporate, general, Securities. Office: UnitedHealth Group 9900 Bren Rd E Minnetonka MN 55343-9664*

LUBBEN, RICK RONALD, lawyer; b. Waterloo, Iowa, Apr. 12, 1959; s. Ronald Harry and Joyce Arlene (Williams) L.; m. Kristine Andrea Corbin, June 30, 1984; 2 children. BA, U. Iowa, 1980; JD, Drake U., 1983. Bar: Iowa 1983. Pvt. practice, LaPorte City, Iowa, 1983--. Mem. LaPorte City Coun., 1987-97; mayor LaPorte City, Iowa, 2000—. Mem.: Masons, Phi Alpha Delta. Lutheran. Avocations: military history, personal computers, baseball cards. General practice, Probate (including wills, trusts), Property, real (including real estate development, water). Office: 304 Main St PO Box 153 La Porte City IA 50651-0153

LUBERDA, GEORGE JOSEPH, lawyer, educator; b. N.Y.C., Apr. 27, 1930; s. Joseph George and Mary Loretta (Koslowski) L. Bar: D.C. 1959, U.S. Ct. Appeals (D.C. cir.) 1959, Mich. 1970, Mo. 1973. Washington rep. Ford Motor Co., Washington, 1955-59; atty. FTC, Washington, 1960-64; trial atty. Antitrust Div. Dept. Justice, Washington, 1965-69; sr. atty. Bendix Corp., Mich., 1970-71; assoc. Butzel, Long, Gust, Klein & Van Zile, Detroit, 1972; antitrust counsel Monsanto Co., St. Louis, 1973-88; assoc. Herzog, Crebs and McGhee, 1988-93; ptnr. Luberda & Carp, St. Louis, 1993—2002, Luberda, Gusdorf & Weir, LLC, St. Louis, 2002—. Adj. prof. St. Louis U., 1985-96. Mem. Mo. Bar Assn., Bar Assn. Met. St. Louis. Republican. Roman Catholic. Antitrust, General civil litigation, Corporate, general. Home: 716 Ridgeview Circle Ln Ballwin MO 63021-7810 Office: Luberda Gusdorf & Weir LLC Ste 1220 225 S Meramec Ave Saint Louis MO 63105-3511

LUBET, MARC LESLIE, lawyer; b. Atlanta, Sept. 13, 1946; s. Louis Lubet and Sylvia (Hirsch) Hoppes; m. Carla J Rossi, Mar. 5, 1988. BS in Journalism, U. Fla., 1969; JD, U. Miss., 1974. Bar: Miss. 1974, Fla. 1974, U.S. Dist. Ct. (mid. dist.) Fla. 1974, U.S. Dist. Ct. (no. dist.) Miss. 1974, U.S. Ct. Appeals (5th cir.) 1974, U.S. Supreme Ct. 1977, U.S. Ct. Appeals (11th cir.) 1981. Assoc. Pitts & Eubanks Law Firm, Orlando, Fla., 1974-75, Levine & Cohen, Orlando, 1975-76; sr. ptnr. Lubet & Woodard, Orlando, 1975-88, Lubet & Blechman, Orlando, 1988-99; prin. Marc L. Lubet, P.A., Orlando, 1999—. Mediator Citizens Dispute, Orlando, 1980—; arbitrater SEC, 1995-96. Active Margarita Soc., Orlando, 1983—. Fellow Am. Bd. Criminal Lawyers; mem. Orange County Bar (mem. speakers bur. 1980-82, crim. law commn. 1983—), ABA, Fla. Bar Assn., Miss. Bar Assn., Nat. Assn. Criminal Def. Lawyers. Democrat. Jewish. Avocations: racquetball, fishing. Criminal, Family and matrimonial. Office: Marc L Lubet Esq 209 E Ridgewood St Orlando FL 32801-1926 E-mail: lubetlaw@aol.com.

LUBICK, DONALD CYRIL, lawyer; b. Buffalo, Apr. 29, 1926; s. Louis and Minna D. (Nabith) L.; m. Susan F. Cohen, June 5, 1960; children: Jonathan, Caroline, Lisa. BA summa cum laude, U. Buffalo, 1945; JD magna cum laude, Harvard U., 1949. Bar: N.Y. 1950, Fla. 1974, D.C. 1981; lic. fgn. law cons. Ont., 1989. Teaching fellow Harvard U. Law Sch., 1949-50; lectr. law U. Buffalo, 1950-61; assoc., then ptnr. Hodgson, Russ, Andrews, Woods & Goodyear, Buffalo and Washington, 1950-61, 64-77, 81-94; tax legis. counsel Treasury Dept., Washington, 1961-64, asst. sec. for tax policy, 1977-81, dir. tax adv. program for countries of Ctrl. and Ea. Europe and former Soviet Union, 1994-96, from acting to asst. sec. for tax policy, 1996-99. Adj. prof. of law Washington Coll. Law, Am. U., 2002—. Author: (with Hussey) Basic World Tax Code and Commentary, 1992, 95. Chmn. Tax Revision Com., City of Buffalo, 1958; mem. adv. com. to select Com. on Election Reform, N.Y. State Legislature, 1974, mem. adv. group to commr. internal revenue, 1976. Served with USAAF, 1945-46. Harvard Internat. Tax Program sr. fellow, 1991—. Mem. ABA, Am. Law Inst., Am. Bar Found., N.Y. State Bar Assn., Fla. Bar Assn., Erie County Bar Assn. Democrat. Jewish. Taxation, general. E-mail: donaldlubick@msn.com.

LUBIN, DONALD G. lawyer; b. N.Y.C., Jan. 10, 1934; s. Harry and Edith (Tannenbaum) L.; m. Amy Schwartz, Feb. 2, 1956; children: Peter, Richard, Thomas, Alice Lubin Spahr. BS in Econs., U. Pa., 1954; LLB, Harvard U., 1957. Bar: Ill. 1957. Ptnr. Sonnenschein Nath & Rosenthal, Chgo., 1957—, chmn. exec. com., 1991-96. Bd. dirs., mem. exec. com., fin. com., nominating and corp. governance com. McDonald's Corp., Molex, Inc.; bd. dir. Daubert Industries Inc., Charles Levy Co., Tennis Corp. Am.; founding bd. dirs. Lake County Cmty. Trust. Former mem. Navy Pier Redevel. Corp., Highland Park Cultural Arts Commn., Chgo. (Ill.) Bicentennial Commn.; life trustee, former chmn. bd. Highland Park Hosp., Ravinia Festival Assn.; chmn. Chgo. Metropolis 2020, Anchor Cross Soc.; trustee, mem. exec. com. Rush-Presbyn.-St. Luke's Med. Ctr.; life trustee Chgo. Symphony Orch.; bd. dirs., v.p. Ronald McDonald House Charities, Inc., Chgo. Found. for Edn.; mem. founding bd. Lake County Cmty. Trust; former dir. Smithsonian Inst., Washington; pres., bd. dir. The Barr Fund; former bd. dirs., v.p., sec. Ragdale Found.; bd. govs. Art Inst. Chgo.; former mem. Chgo. Lighthouse for the Blind; mem. citizens bd. U. Chgo.; mem. coun. Children's Meml. Hosp.; former bd. overseers Coll. Arts and Sci., U. Pa.; former dir. Nat. Mus. Am. History, Washington. Woodrow Wilson vis. fellow Fellow Am.

Bar Found., Ill. Bar Found., Chgo. Bar Found.; mem. Chgo. Bar Assn., Civic Com. (mem. steering com.), Lawyers Club Chgo., Chgo. Hort. Soc. (past bd. dirs.), Comml. Club (mem. exec. com.), Std. Club, Lakeshore Club, Beta Gamma Sigma. Corporate, general. Home: 2269 Egandale Rd Highland Park IL 60035-2501 Office: Sonnenschein Nath & Rosenthal 233 S Wacker Dr Ste 8000 Chicago IL 60606-6491 E-mail: dlubin@sonnenschein.com.

LUBIN, STANLEY, lawyer; b. May 7, 1941; children: David Christopher, Jessica Nicole; m. Barbara Ann Lubin. AB, U. Mich., 1963, JD with honors, 1966. Bar: D.C. 1967, U.S. Ct. Appeals (D.C. cir.) 1967, U.S. Ct. Appeals (4th cir.) 1967, Mich. 1968, U.S. Ct. Appeals (6th cir.) 1968, U.S. Supreme Ct. 1970, Ariz. 1972, U.S. Ct. Appeals (9th cir.) 1976, U.S. Ct. Appeals (fed. cir.) 1985, Tex. 2002, U.S. Ct. Appeals (5th cir.) 2002, U.S. Dist. Ct. (ctrl. and so. dist.) Tex. Atty. NLRB, Washington, 1966-68; asst. gen. counsel UAW, Detroit, 1968-72; assoc. Harrison, Myers & Singer, Phoenix, 1972-74, McKendree & Tountas, Phoenix, 1975; ptnr. McKendree & Lubin, Phoenix and Denver, 1975-84; shareholder Treon, Warnicke & Roush, P.A., 1984-86; pvt. practice Law Offices Stanley Lubin, Phoenix, 1986-95, The Law Offices of Stanley Lubin, P.C., 1996-98, Lubin & Enoch, P.C., 1999—. Mem. Ariz. Employment Security Adv. Coun., 1975—77. Co-author: Union Fines and Union Discipline Under the National Labor Relations Act, 1971. Active ACLU, dir. Ariz. chpt., 1974-81; vice chair Ariz. State Cen. Com. Dem. Party, 1986-91, 93-99, sec., 1991-92, mem. state exec. com., 1986-99, Ariz. Dem. Coun., 1987-99, chmn., 1988-93, Thomas Jefferson Forum, 1987-99, chmn., 1988-93. Mem.: ABA (mem. 1968—2002), Ariz. Indsl. Rels. Assn. (exec. bd. 1973—, pres. 1979—80, 1984), Indsl. Rels. Rsch. Assn., Maricopa County Bar Assn., State Bar Ariz. Administrative and regulatory, Entertainment, Labor (including EEOC, Fair Labor Standards Act, labor-management relations, NLRB, OSHA). Home: 7520 N 9th Pl Phoenix AZ 85020-4138 Office: 349 N 4th Ave Phoenix AZ 85003- E-mail: stanley.lubin@azbar.org.

LUBIS, TODUNG MULYA, lawyer; b. Medan, Indonesia, July 4, 1949; s. Maas and Halimah (Nasution) Lubis; m. Damiyati Soendoro, June 5, 1983; children: Tondi Nirita, Oriza Sativa. SH, Indonesia U, Jakosta, Indonesia, 1974; LLM, Harvard, Cambridge, Mass., 1988; SJD, Calif. U, Berkely, CA, 1990. Bar: Indonesian Bar Assoc. 1975. Chmn. Indonesian Legal Aid Inst., Jararta, Indonesia, 1979—81; v.p. Indonesia Election Supervision Com., Jararta, Indonesia, 1999—2000, Indonesian Bar Assoc., Jararta, Indonesia, 2000—03. Founding ptnr. Lubis, Santosa & Maulana, Jararta, Indonesia, 1991—. Author: (novels) In Search of Human Rights, 1999, This the Time to Read Poetries, 1999. Bd. mem. Internat. Crisis Group, Brussels, 2000—, Transparang Internat., Tararta, 2002—. Recipient Adam Malik, Adam Malik Found.,Jararta, 1986, Star of Asia, Bus. Wk., Hong Kong, 2002. Mem.: Mercantile club, Am. club. Avocations: travel, music, tennis, opera, cooking. Home: JL Maribaya G7 NO 3 Pur Cinere Jakarta 16514 Indonesia Office: Lubis Santosa & Maulana Jl Sudirman 28 Jakarta Indonesia

LUBLINSKI, MICHAEL, lawyer; b. Eskilstuna, Sweden, Sept. 11, 1951; came to U.S., 1956; s. Walter and Dora L. BA magna cum laude, CCNY, 1972; JD, Georgetown U., 1975. Bar: N.Y. 1976, Calif. 1980, D.C. 2001, Va. 2002, Ct. Internat. Trade 1981, U.S. Dist. Ct. (cen. dist.) Calif. 1981, U.S. Dist. Ct. (so. dist.) N.Y. 1981, U.S. Ct. Appeals (D.C. cir.) 1982. Atty. U.S. Customs Service, Washington, 1975-79, U.S. Dept. Commerce, Washington, 1980; assoc. Mori & Ota, L.A., 1980-84, Kelley Drye & Warren LLP, L.A., 1984-85, ptnr., mem. intellectual property practice group, 1986—. Panel moderator Calif. continuing edn. of bar Competitive Bus. Practices Inst., Los Angeles and San Francisco, 1984. Mem. ABA, Calif. Bar Assn., Los Angeles County Bar Assn. (arbitrator 1981-82, chmn. customs law sect. 1986), N.Y. State Bar Assn., D.C. Bar Assn., Phi Beta Kappa. Avocations: travel, movies. Immigration, naturalization, and customs, Trademark and copyright. Office: Kelley Drye & Warren LLP 8000 Towers Crescent Drive Ste 1200 Vienna VA 22182 E-mail: mlublinski@kelleydrye.com.

LUBNAU, THOMAS EDWIN, II, lawyer; b. Laramie, Wyo., Dec. 12, 1958; s. Thomas Edwin and Cynthia L'Vere (Kirkland) L. BS in Fin., U. Wyo., 1981, JD, 1984. Bar: Wyo. 1984, U.S. Dist. Ct. Wyo. 1984, U.S. Ct. Appeals (10th cir.) 1984, U.S. Supreme Ct. 1995. Mem. Lubnau, Bailey & Dumbrill, P.C., Gillette, Wyo., 2000—. Chmn. Wyo. Bd. CLE, Cheyenne, 1990-92; trustee Rocky Mountain Mineral Law, Denver, 1992-95; legal counsel Wyo. Jaycees, Gillette, 1986-94, Campbell County Rep. Party, Gillette, 1989—. Contbr. to Land and Water Law rev., 1984. Bd. dirs. Campbell County Libr. Found.; chalice bearer, lay reader Holy Trinity Episcopal Ch., Campbell County Rep. Party (state committeeman 1988-89), Campbell County C. of C. (chmn. 1993-94). Mem. ABA, Assn. Trial Lawyers Am., Campbell County C. of C. (bd. dirs.), Gillette Rotary (bd. dirs.), Wyo. State Bar (commnr. 1998-2001, v.p. 2001-02, pres.-elect 2002-03), Cambell County Bar Assn. (pres. 2000-01), Gov.'s Probate Com. (1984-90), Bd. Continuing Ed. (chmn. 1988-91), Rocky Mtn. Mineral Law Found. (trustee 1992-95), Atty.'s Assistance Com. (co-chair, 1995-96). Republican. Avocations: woodworking, photography, writing. Commercial, contracts (including sales of goods; commercial financing), Oil, gas, and mineral, Probate (including wills, trusts). Office: Lubnau Bailey & Dumbrill PC PO Box 1028 Gillette WY 82717-1028*

LUBY, THOMAS STEWART, lawyer; b. Meriden, Conn., Jan. 12, 1952; s. Robert M. and Ruth (McGee) L.; m. Paula P. Falcigno, July 19, 1985; children: Elizabeth, Caroline, Katherine. BA, Yale U., 1974; JD, U. Conn., 1977. Bar: Conn., U.S. Dist. Ct. Conn., U.S. Ct. Appeals (2d cir.) Law clk. to Hon. T. F. Gilroy Daly U.S. Dist. Ct., Bridgeport, Conn., 1977-78; asst. U.S. atty. New Haven, 1978-81; ptnr. Luby, Olson P.C., Meriden, 1981—. Mem. grievance com. U.S. Dist. Ct. Conn., 1985-90, chmn., 1990-91; mem. U.S. Magistrate SelectionCom., 1996. Rep. Conn. Gen. Assembly, 1987-92, house majority leader, 1993-94; co-chair Conn. Task Force on Groundwater Strategy, 1987-89, chmn. commerce com., 1991-92. Recipient Spl. Achievement award U.S. Dept. Justice, 1980, Outstanding Pub. Service award United Way, 1986; named Legis. Leader of Yr., Greater Hartford C. of C., 1990, Person of Yr., Gov.'s Tourism Council, 1991, team Conn. award Conn. Dept. Econ. and Cmty. Devel., 1996, legis. advocacy award Coalition for Children, 1993. Mem. Conn. Bar Assn., dir. Castle Bank & Trust Co., 1999-; mem. Yale Alumni Schs. Com., 1985-. Democrat. Roman Catholic. General civil litigation, Personal injury (including property damage), Professional liability. Home: 32 Westfield Rd Meriden CT 06450-2426

LUCAS, CRAIG JOHN, lawyer; b. Ogden, Utah, Mar. 15, 1962; s. Frank James and Joan (Christensen) L. BS, Weber State U., 1985; JD, U. Idaho, 1988. Bar: Nev. 1989, D.C. 1992, U.S. Dist. Ct. Nev. 1990, U.S. Ct. Appeals (9th cir.) 1990. Legis. intern Utah House Majority Leader, Salt Lake City, 1984; Congl. intern U.S. Senate, Washington, 1984; legal intern Idaho Prosocuting Atty. Assn., Boise, 1987; law clk. to Hon. Miriam Shearing 8th Dist. Ct., Las Vegas, 1988-90; from assoc. gen. counsel to chief assoc. counsel State Indsl. Ins. System, Las Vegas, 1990-91; pvt. practice Las Vegas, 1992—. Ctrl. com. mem. Rep. Party, Clark County, Nev., 1990-92, conv. del., 1990. Mem. Federalist Soc., Nev. Trial Lawyers Assn. Church of Jesus Christ of Latter-day Saints. Avocations: travel, hiking, skiing. Personal injury (including property damage), Workers' compensation. Office: 3634 N Rancho Dr Las Vegas NV 89130 E-mail: clucas@lv.rmci.net.

LUCAS, JOHN ALLEN, lawyer; b. Washington, Aug. 1, 1943; s. George Luther and Opal (McCollum) L.; m. Carol Kaine, June 7, 1969; children: John Christian, Helen Elizabeth, David Marshall, Kerri Christine. BS, U.S. Mil. Acad., 1969; JD, U. Tex., 1977. Bar: Va. 1978, Tenn. 1984, N.Y. 1986. Assoc. Hunton & Williams, Richmond, Va., 1977-83, ptnr. Knoxville, Tenn., 1984—. Prof. law U. Richmond, 1979-80; lectr. various legal seminars, 1979—. Contbr. articles to profl. jours. Bd. dirs. Knoxville Boys Club, 1984-88; bd. dirs. Tenn. Juvenile Diabetes Assn., 1989-92; pres. West Point Soc. of E. Tenn., 1999--. Capt. U.S. Army, 1969-74. Fellow Tenn. Bar Found.; mem. ABA, Va. Bar Assn., Tenn. Bar Assn. Roman Catholic. Avocations: mountain climbing, sport parachuting, white-water kayaking, triathlons, motorcycling. Bankruptcy, Federal civil litigation, General civil litigation. Office: Hunton & Williams PO Box 951 Knoxville TN 37901-0951

LUCAS, ROBERT FRANK, lawyer; b. Beacon Falls, Conn., Nov. 11, 1935; s. Otto F. and A. Helen (Schuster) L.; m. Regina Abbiati, July 16, 1960; children: Robert Frank Jr., David R., Jennifer J. AB, Bates Coll., Lewiston, Maine, 1956; JD, Boston U., 1959. Bar: Mass. 1960, U.S. Dist. Ct. Mass. 1962, U.S. Supreme Ct. 1973. Trial atty. Boston Legal Aid Soc., 1960-63; prin. Nigro, Pettepit & Lucas, Wakefield, Mass., 1963—. Mem. standing list of masters Mass. Superior Ct., Cambridge, 1979—. Chmn. bd. appeals City of Melrose, Mass., 1982—2003, city solicitor, 2003—; trustee Melrose H.S. Permanent Scholarship Fund, 1979—; mem. Rep. City Com., Melrose, 1980—84; lay leader 1st United Meth. Ch., Melrose, 1979—82. With USAR, 1959—65. Mem. ABA, Mass. Bar Assn. (bd. dels. 1980-83, exec. com. 1993, chmn. fee arbitration bd. 1983-84, 20th Century Club 1985, Cert. of Appreciation 1988, Community Svc. award 1989), Middlesex County Bar Assn. (bd. dirs. 1986-99), 1st Dist. Ea. Middlesex Bar Assn. (pres. 1987-88), Bellevue Golf Club, Masons (dist. dep. grand master 1982-83). Avocations: music, choral singing, youth sports. General civil litigation, Personal injury (including property damage), Probate (including wills, trusts). Home: 20 Pilgrim Rd Melrose MA 02176-3019 Office: Nigro Pettepit & Lucas 649 Main St Wakefield MA 01880-5216

LUCAS, STEVEN MITCHELL, lawyer; b. Ada, Okla., Jan. 19, 1948; s. John Dalton and Cherrye (Smith) Lucas; m. Lori E. Seeberger; children: Steven Turner, Brooke Elizabeth, Sarah Grace. BA, Yale U., 1970; JD, Vanderbilt U., 1973. Bar: DC 1973, U.S. Ct. Mil. Appeals 1974, U.S. Dist. Ct. DC 1979, U.S. Ct. Appeals (DC cir.) 1979, U.S. Supreme Ct. 1979. Assoc. Shaw, Pittman, Potts & Trowbridge, Washington, 1978-82, ptnr., 1983-92; ptnr., head fin. instns. practice Wiley, Rein & Fielding, Washington, 1992-93, Winston & Strawn, Washington, 1993-97; pvt. practice Washington, 1997—. Cons. internat. rels. Rockefeller Found., N.Y.C., 1978; mem. negotiating team Panama Canal Treaty, Washington, 1975—77; legal advisor Dept. Def. Panama Canal negotiations working group; presdl. apptd. U.S. panelist Internat. Ctr. Settlement Investment Disputes, ICSID-World Bank, 2002—. Editor-in-chief: Vanderbilt U. Jour. Transnational Law, 1972—73. Capt. JAGC U.S. Army, 1974—77. Republican. Episcopalian. Banking, Private international, Securities. Home and Office: 1001 Jigger Ct Annapolis MD 21401 E-mail: smlucas@comcast.net.

LUCCHESI, LIONEL LOUIS, lawyer; b. St. Louis, Sept. 17, 1939; s. Lionel Louis and Theresa Lucchesi; m. Mary Ann Wheeler, July 30, 1966; children: Lionel Louis III, Marisa Pilar. BSEE, Ill. Inst. Tech., 1961; JD, St. Louis U., 1969. Bar: Mo. 1969. With Emerson Electric Co., 1965-69; assoc. Polster, Polster & Lucchesi, St. Louis, 1969-74, ptnr., 1974—. City atty. City of Ballwin, Mo., 1979—85, 1992—. Mem. Zoning Commn., 1971—77; alderman City of Ballwin, 1977—79. Recipient Am. Jurisprudence award, St. Louis U., 1968—69; scholar NROTC, 1957—61. Mem.: ATLA, ABA, Newcomen Soc. N.Am., St. Louis Met. Bar Assn. (exec. com., pres.-elect 1984, pres. 1985—86), Am. Patent Law Assn., Forest Hills Club, Rotary (pres.-elect St. Louis 1991—92, pres. 1992—93). Republican. Roman Catholic. Federal civil litigation, Patent, Trademark and copyright. Office: 763 S New Ballas Rd Saint Louis MO 63141-8704 E-mail: llucchesi@patpro.com.

LUCCI, MICHAEL T. judge; b. Milw., Dec. 30, 1942; s. Daniel and Stella (Ranzo) L.; m. Deborah Louise Gibson, Aug. 21, 1970; children: Maxwell Ryan, Carmen Marie. BA in History, U. Wis., Milw., 1966; JD, Marquette U., 1973. Bar: Wis. 1973, U.S. Dist. Ct. (ea. and we. dist.) Wis. 1973. Assoc. Witkin, Johnson & Till, Ltd., Superior, Wis., 1973-75; ptnr. Witkin, Till & Lucci, Ltd., Superior, 1975-85; judge Cir. Ct. Douglas County, Wis., 1985—. Pres. Superior Jaycees, 1978; pres. bd. dirs. Human Resource Ctr. Douglas County, Superior, 1981-83. With U.S. Army, 1967-69. Recipient Disting. Svc. award Superior Jaycees, 1979. Mem. State Bar Wis., Douglas County Bar Assn. (pres. 1981), Rotary (Superior), Elks (Superior). Roman Catholic. Avocations: reading history, racqutball. Home: 2431 Wyoming Ave Superior WI 54880-4528 Office: Douglas County Courthouse 1313 Belknap St Superior WI 54880-2779

LUCIDO, PETER J. lawyer, educator; b. Detroit, July 31, 1960; s. Peter J. and Anne J. Lucido; m. Ann Marie Franzone; children: Briana, Nina, Peter. AA, Macomb C.C., Warren, Mich., 1980; BABS Oakland U., Rochester, Mich., 1982; MBA, Ctrl. Mich. U., 1984; JD, Detroit Coll. Law, 1988. Lic. ins. agt.; bar: Mich.; lic. securities broker, lic. real estate broker. Sole practitioner law, Clinton Twp., Mich., 1990—; instr. Macomb C.C., Clinton Twp., Mich., 1994—. Mem.: Macomb County Bar Assn., State Bar Mich., Italian Am. C. of C. Criminal, Personal injury (including property damage), Family and matrimonial. Office: 39999 Garfield Rd Clinton Township MI 48038-4098

LUCKERT, MARLA JO, judge; b. Goodland, Kans., July 20, 1955; d. William Gottleib and Gladys Iona (Rohr) L.; m. Steven. K. Morse, May 25, 1980; children: Sarah, Alisa. BA, Washburn U., 1977, JD, 1980. Bar: Kans. 1980, U.S. Dist. Ct. Kans. 1980, U.S. Ct. Appeals (10th cir.) 1980. Assoc. Goodell, Stratoon, Edmond & Palmer, Topeka, 1980—; chair Criminal Law Adv. Comm., Kans. Jud. Coun., Kans., 1992; chief judge Third Jud. Dist., Kans. Supreme Ct., Kans.; judge Kans. Supreme Ct., Kans., 2003—. Adj. prof. Washburn Univ. Sch. Law, Topeka, 1980-81, 1990—; pres. Women Attys. Assn. Kans., Topeka, 1988-89. Author: Kansas Consent Manual, 1988, Record Relations Guide, 1988, Kansas Law for Physicians, 1989. Pres. Mobile Meals of Topeka (Kans.), Inc., 1987-89, Mobile Meals of Topeka (Kans.) Found., 1989—; co-chair YWCA Nominating Com., Topeka, 1988-89. Recipient Woman of Excellence Award, YWCA/Topeka, Kans. Mem. ABA (co-chair young lawyers health law com. 1988-90), Am. Acad. Hosp. Attys., Kans. Assn. Hosp. Attys., Kans. Assn. Def. Counsel (bd. dirs. 1988—, disting. svc. award 1990), Kans. Bar Assn. (pres. young lawyers 1989-90, outstanding svc. award 1990), Topeka Bar Assn. (chair law day pubs. com.). Office: Kansas Judicial Ctr 301 SW 10th Ave Topeka KS 66612-1507*

LUCKEY, ALWYN HALL, lawyer; b. Biloxi, Miss., Oct. 3, 1960; s. Toxie Hall and Joy Evelyn (Smith) L.; m. Jeanne Elaine Carter, Aug. 4, 1984; children: Laurel McKay, Taylor Leah. BA in Zoology, U. Miss., 1982, JD, 1985. Bar: Miss. 1985, U.S. Dist. Ct. (so. and no. dist.) Miss. 1985, U.S. Ct. Appeals (5th cir.) 1985. Assoc. Richard F. Scruggs, Pascagoula, Miss., 1985-88, shareholder, 1988—, Asbestos Group PA, 1988-93; prin. Alwyn H. Luckey, Atty. at Law, Ocean Springs, Miss., 1993—. V.p., bd. dirs. Marine Mgmt., Inc., Ocean Springs, Miss., 1987—. Author: Mississippi Landlord Tenant Law, 1985. Deacon First Presbyn. Ch., Ocean Springs, 1989; chmn. Dole for Pres. com., Jackson County, 1988. Mem. Am. Trial Lawyers Assn., Miss. Bar Assn., Miss. Trial Lawyers Assn., Jackson County Bar Assn., Jackson County Young Lawyers Assn. (v.p.), Ocean Springs Yacht Club, Bienville Club, Treasure Oak Country Club. Avocations: tennis, boating, traveling. Personal injury (including property damage), Product liability. Office: PO Box 724 Ocean Springs MS 39566-0724

LUCY, ROBERT MEREDITH, lawyer; b. Poplar Bluff, Mo., Apr. 16, 1926; s. James Raymond and Lucile Hargrove (Meredith) L.; m. Mary White George, June 10, 1947; children— Meredith Lucy Knight, Celia Lucy Denton, John Rackley, Robert Meredith Jr. BS, U.S. Naval Acad., 1947; JD, George Washington U., 1954, MS in Internat. Affairs, 1968. Bar: Mo. 1954, D.C. 1954. Commd. 2d lt. USMC, 1947; advanced through grades to col.; student Air War Coll. Maxwell AFB, Montgomery, Ala., 1967-68; staff judge adv. 1st Marine Div., Danang, Vietnam, 1969-70; asst. for legal affairs Office Asst. Sec. Navy for Manpower and Res. Affairs, Washington, 1970-71; legal advisor, legis. asst. to chmn. Joint Chiefs of Staff, Washington, 1971-74; ret., 1974; ptnr. Bryan Cave, St. Louis, 1974-96; of counsel, 1997-98; chmn. litigation dept. Bryan Cave, St. Louis, 1992-94, vice chmn., 1994-95; ret., 1998. Dir. St. Andrew's Episcopal Presbyn. Found., 1995-2001. Decorated Bronze Star, Legion of Merit (3) Mem. ABA (litigation sect.), TechLaw Group, Inc. (pres. 1994-95), Childrens Home Soc. of Mo. (trustee 1989-98). Presbyterian. Home: 38 Picardy Ln Saint Louis MO 63124-1628 E-mail: rmlu@aol.com.

LUDEMANN, CATHIE JANE, lawyer; b. Glen Ridge, N.J., Jan. 30, 1948; d. Blair Edward and Marie Elizabeth (Blum) L. BA in Econs., Douglass Coll., 1970; MBA in Fin., Fairleigh Dickinson U., 1975; JD, Seton Hall Law Sch., 1986. Bar: N.J. 1986. Mgmt. positions Prudential Ins. Co., Newark, 1970-83; rsch. asst. Seton Hall Law Sch., Newark, 1983-84; atty. Barry D. Berman, Esq., West Orange, N.J., 1984-87, Sala & Caposela, Esqs., Clifton, N.J., 1987-89; sole practitioner Pompton Plains, N.J., 1989—. Editor Law Sch. Newspaper, 1985-86. Commr., planning bd., City of Clifton, 1982-86; commr. bd. of adjustment, Twp. of Pequannock, N.J., 1993; v.p., treas. Richfield Village Tenants Assn., Clifton, 1979-82. Mem. N.J. State Bar Assn. Avocations: antiques and collectibles, book collecting, old movies, big band music. Probate (including wills, trusts), Property, real (including real estate development, water), Elder. Home: 105 Newark Pompton Tpke Bldg C Unit 14 D Pequannock NJ 07440-1638 Office: 287 Boulevard Pompton Plains NJ 07444-1726

LUDINGTON, THOMAS LAMSON, judge; b. Midland, Mich., Dec. 28, 1953; s. John S. and Dorothy (Lamson) L.; m. Katrina McGuire, Sept. 20, 1986. BA, Albion Coll., 1976; JD, U. San Diego, 1979. Bar: Calif. 1980, Mich. 1981. Assoc. Currie & Kendall, P.C., Midland, 1979-2000; cir. ct. judge Midland (Mich.) County Ct. House, 2000—. Mem. hearing panel Atty. Discipline Bd., Detroit, 1987—. Bd. dirs. Jr. Achievement of Midland County, Gerstacker Found.; mem. Midland Found.; bd. trustees Saginaw Valley State U. Found., Albion Coll. Mem. ABA, State Bar Mich., State Bar Calif., Midland County Bar Assn., Assn. Trial Lawyers Am., Nat. Order Barristers. Methodist. Avocation: snow and water skiing. Office: Midland County Ct House 301 Main St Midland MI 48640

LUDWIG, EDMUND VINCENT, federal judge; b. Phila., May 20, 1928; s. Henry and Ruth (Viner) L.; children: Edmund Jr., John, Sarah, David. AB, Harvard U., 1949, LLB, 1952. Assoc. Duane, Morris & Heckscher, Phila., 1956-59; ptnr. Barnes, Biester & Ludwig, Doylestown, Pa., 1959-68; judge Common Pleas Ct., Bucks County, Pa., 1968-85, U.S. Dist. Ct. (ea. dist.), Phila., 1985—. Faculty Pa. Coll. of the Judiciary, 1974-85; presenter Villanova (Pa.) U. Law Sch., 1975-80, lectr., 1984-97; vis. lectr. Temple Law Sch., 1977-80; clin. assoc. prof. Hahnemann U., Phila., 1977-85; mem. Pa. Juvenile Ct. Judge's Commn., 1978-85; chmn. Pa. Chief Justice's Ednl. Com., 1984-85; pres. Pa. Conf. State Trial Judges, 1981-82; co-chmn. 3d cir. task force on counsel for ind. litigants in civil cases, 1998. Contbr. articles to profl. jours. Chmn. Children and Youth Adv. Com., Bucks County, 1978-83; mem. Pa. Adv. Com. on Mental Health and Mental Retardation, 1980-85; founder, bd. dirs. Today, Inc., Newtown, Pa., 1971-85, Probation Vols., Bucks County, 1971-81; bd. dirs. New Directions for Women, Del. Valley, 1988—; mem. Pa. Joint Coun. Criminal Justice, Inc., 1979-80; mem. Joint Family Law Council Pa., 1979-85; vice chmn. Human Services Council Bucks County, 1979-81; mem. Com. to Study Unified Jud. System Pa., 1980-82, Pa. Legislative Task Force on Mental Health Laws, 1986-87; chmn. Juvenile Justice Alliance, Phila., 1992—; co-chmn. Doylestown (Pa.) Revitalization Bd., 1993-96; mem. 3d cir. task force on equal treatment in the cts., 1995-97; chmn. Doylestown (Pa.) Hist. Soc., 1995—. Recipient Disting. Svc. award Bucks County Corrections Assn., 1978, Spl. Svc. award Big. Bros., 1989, Humanitarian award United Way Bucks County, 1980, Founder's award Vol. Svcs., 1982, Spl. award Bucks County Juvenile Ct., 1985, Humanitarian award Ctrl. Bucks County C. of C., 1994, Disting. Jurist award John Peter Zenger Soc., 2000; Wasserstein Pub. Interest fellow Harvard Law Sch., 1996-97. Mem. ABA, Pa. Bar Assn. (chmn. com. legal svcs. to disabled 1990-92), Phila. Bar Assn. (pro bono pub. award 1998, Pub. Interest Disting. Svc. award 1998), Fed. Bar Assn. (hon.), Harvard Club (N.Y.C. and Phila., v.p. 1979-80), Harvard Law Sch. Assn. (exec. com. 1993—), Fed. Judges Assn. (bd. dirs. 1998—, mem. chmn. 1999—), U.S. Jud. Conf. (com. on ct. adminstrn. and case mgmt.), Am. Law Inst. Office: US Dist E Dist PA US Cthse 601 Market St # 12614 Philadelphia PA 19106-1775 Business E-Mail: Chambers_of_Judge__Edmund_V._Ludwig@paed.uscourts.gov.*

LUER, HANS-JOCHEM, lawyer; b. Stuttgart, Germany, Mar. 20, 1938; s. Hanns and Christine Luer; m. Brigitte Ehret, Mar. 13, 1970; children: Thomas, Beatrix. Degree, U. Tübingen, 1961; LLM, U. Calif., 1964; LLD, U. Cologne, 1968. Asst. Inst. for Internat. Pvt. Law and Fgn. Law U. Cologne, Germany, 1967—69; mgr. German Mutual Fund Co., Cologne, 1970—73; ptnr. Gurland, Schlutter & Luer now known as Heuking Kuhn Luer Woitek, Cologne, 1973—. Mem. supervisory bd. Volksfursorge AG, Hamburg, Germany, Stahl Wille GmbH, Wuppertal, Germany, Quarzwerke GmbH, Frechen, Germany; mem. Fedn. Fgn. Policy, Berlin, 1984—. Chmn. insolvency com. DAV, Bonn, Germany, 1990—. Mem.: German Bar Assn. (corp. counsel, mem. fedn. of def.), Am. Coll. Bankruptcy, Internat. Bar Assn. (vice chmn. bus. law com. 1982—). Roman Catholic. Avocations: art, music, jazz, political literature, golf. Corporate, general, Insurance, Mergers and acquisitions. Home: Robert Heuser Str 18 D 50968 Cologne Germany Office: Heuking Kuhn Luer Wojtek Magnusstrasse 13 D 50672 Cologne Germany Fax: +49 221 20 521. E-mail: h.lueer@hklw-cologne.com.

LUFKIN, MARTHA B.G. lawyer, legal writer; b. Boston, May 7, 1954; d. Nathaniel C. and Sareen R. (Epstein) Gerson. Grad., Phillips Exeter Acad., 1972; BA in Polit. Sci. magna cum laude, Yale U., 1976; MLitt in Politics, Oxford (Eng.) U., 1979; JD, Columbia U., 1982. Bar: N.Y. 1983, Mass. 1987. Collaborateur juridique Law Offices of S.G. Archibald, Paris, summer 1981, 82; assoc. Shearman & Sterling, N.Y.C., 1982-87, Bingham, Dana & Gould, Boston, 1987-92; pvt. practice Lincoln, Mass., 1992—; legal writer, 1995—. Author humor column Lincoln Jour., 1992— (Humor prize New Eng. Press Assn. 1996, 97), Alfred Hitchcock Mystery Mag., 1995, 97; U.S. legal corr. The Art Newspaper, 1997—; contbr. Art Antiquity and Law. Sr. Scholar Hertford Coll., Oxford U., 1978-79; Harlan Fiske Stone Scholar Columbia Law Sch., 1982. Probate (including wills, trusts), Estate taxation, Art. Home: 127 Trapelo Rd Lincoln MA 01773-2802

LUGINBUHL, JURG ALEXANDER, atty. b. Zürich, Switzerland, June 9, 1963; s. Karl Hermann and Liselotte Luginbuhl; m. Tanja Hossmann, June 24, 2000. ML, U of Zurich, Zurich, Switzerland, 1988, PhD, 1993. Bar: Zurich, Switzerland 1992. Law clk. Dist. Ct., Zurich, Switzerland, 1991; assoc. atty. Lenz & Staehelin, Zurich, Switzerland, 1993—94, Gibson, Dunn & Crutcher, Hong Kong, China, 1995—96, Lenz & Staehelin, Zurich, Switzerland, 1997—99; ptnr. Vischer Attorneys at Law, Zurich, Switzerland, 2000—. Bd. mem. Author: (thesis) Representations and Warrenties in M&A transactions, 1993 (summa cum laude, 1993). Officer Swiss Army, Switzerland, 1983—. Officer Artillery Platoon Swiss army, 1986—89, Switzerland. Mem.: Zunftzurwaag, Heraldika (chairman 1985—89). Office: Vischer Attys Law Arterstrasse 24 8032 Zürich Switzerland

LUMPKIN, GARY LEONARD, judge; b. Sentinel, Okla. m. Barbara Lumpkin; 1 child. Student, Northwestern State Coll., Alva, Okla., 1964-65;

BS, Southwestern State Coll., Weatherford, Okla., 1968; JD, U. Okla., 1974. Bar: Okla. 1974. Staff atty. Okla. Dept. Consumer Affairs, 1974-75; asst. dist. atty. to 1st asst. dist. atty. Marshall County, Okla., 1976-82, assoc. dist. judge, 1982-85; dist. judge 20th Jud. Dist., Divsn. II, Marshall County, Okla., 1985-89; judge Okla. Ct. Criminal Appeals, Oklahoma City, 1989—, vice-presiding judge, 1991-92, 99-00, presiding judge, 1993—94, 2001—02; USMC res. judge Navy-Marine Ct. Criminal Appeals, 1994-98. Pres. Okla. Jud. Conf., 1989; past mem. sentencing and release policy com. created by Senate Bill 432 of 42d legislature; rep. Ct. Criminal Appeals on Truth in Sentencing Policy Adv. Commn.; mem. Okla. Supreme Ct. com. on uniform civil jury instrns. and ct. liaison to Ct. of Criminal Appeals uniform criminal jury instrn. com.; bd. dir. Nat. Ctr. for State Cts., Williamsburg, Va. With USMC, 1968-98; col. USMCR, Vietnam, ret. Mem. Okla. Bar Assn. (past chair criminal law com., mem. law related edn. com.), Okla. Bar Found., Okla. County Bar Assn., Marshall County Bar Assn., William J. Holloway Jr. Am. Inns of Ct. (pres.-elect, chair program com. 1992, pres. 1993, William J. Holloway Jr. Professionalism award 1999), VFW, Marine Corps Res. Officers Assn. Baptist. Office: Okla Court Criminal Appeals State Capitol Bldg Rm 230 Oklahoma City OK 73105 Fax: 405-521-4980. E-mail: glumpkin@okcca.net.

LUMSDEN, IAN GEORGE, solicitor; b. Glasgow, Scotland, Mar. 19, 1951; s. James Alexander and Sheila Lumsden; m. Mary Ann Welbon, Apr. 22, 1978; children: Richard Alexander, Sarah Henrietta, Louise Mary. BA with honors, Cambridge (Eng.) U., 1971; LLB, Edinburgh U., 1973. Bar: (Scotland) 1975. Trainee solicitor & asst. Maclay Murray & Spens, Glasgow, Scotland, 1973—78; asst. solicitor Slaughter & May, London, 1978—80; ptnr. Maclay Murray & Spens, Glasgow, 1980—. Mem.: Internat. Bae Assn., Royal Faculty Procurators, Law Soc. Scotland. Avocations: golf, shooting. Corporate, general, Securities. Office: Maclay Murray & Spens 3 Glenfinlas St Edinburgh EH3 6AQ Scotland Fax: 0131 226-3174.

LUNA, BARBARA CAROLE, financial analyst, accountant, appraiser; b. N.Y.C., July 23, 1950; d. Edwin A. and Irma S. (Schub) Schlang; m. Dennis Rex Luna, Sept. 1, 1974; children: John S., Katherine E. BA, Wellesley Coll., 1971; MS in Applied Math., Harvard U., 1973, PhD in Applied Math., 1975. CPA; cert. gen. real estate appraiser Calif. Office Real Estate Appraisers; cert. valuation analyst Nat. Assn. Cert. Valuation Analysts; cert. fraud examiner Assn. Cert. Fraud Examiners, mgmt. cons. Inst. Mgmt. Consultants; accredited sr. appraiser Am. Soc. Appraisers; accredited bus. valuation Am. Inst. CPAs. Investment banker Warburg Paribas Becker, L.A., 1975-77; cons., sr. mgr. Price Waterhouse, L.A., 1977-83; sr. mgr. litigation Pannell Kerr Forster, L.A., 1983-86; nat. dir. litigation cons. Kenneth Leventhal & Co., L.A., 1986-88; ptnr. litigation svcs. Coopers & Lybrand, L.A., 1988-93; sr. ptnr. litigation svcs. White, Zuckerman, Warsavsky, Luna & Wolf, Sherman Oaks, Calif., 1993—. Expert witness. Wellesley scholar, 1971. Mem. AICPA, Assn. Bus. Trial Lawyers (com. on experts), Am. Soc. Appraisers, Assn. Cert. Valuation Analysts, Calif. Office Real Estate Appraisers, Assn. Cert. Real Estate Appraisers, Appraisal Inst., Assn. Cert. Fraud Examiners, Inst. Mgmt. Cons., Calif. Soc. CPAs (econ. damages common interest mem. svcs. com., fraud common interest mem. svcs. com., bus. valuation common interest mem. svcs. com.), Am. Bd. Forensic Accts. and Examiners, Harvard-Radcliffe Club So. Calif. (bd. dirs., chair programs), Harvard Grad. Sch. Alumni Coun.. Avocations: golf, swimming. Home: 18026 Rodarte Way Encino CA 91316-4370 E-mail: bluna@lunala.com., bluna@wzwlw.com.

LUNA-ARENA, ALEJANDRO, lawyer; b. Mex. City, Mex., Feb. 15, 1971; s. Eduardo Luna-Arellano and Elia Guadalupe Arena-Arellano; m. Anasol Munoz Puente-Arnaiz, Sept. 28, 2002. Degree, Inst. Tech. Automomo de Mex., 1993; LLM, King's Coll. London, 1996. Bar: ITAM 1995. Paralegal Notary Pub. No. 6, Tijuana, Mexico, 1990; legal clk. Noriega Y Escobedo, A.C., Mex. City, 1991—92; legal clk. and assoc. Santamarina Y Steta, S.C., Mex. City, 1992—. Pro-bono gen. counsel Found. Pro Niños de la Calle, J.A.P., Mex. City, 1997—. Scholar, The Brit. Coun., 1995—96. Mem.: Phi Delta Phi (chpt. chmn. 1992—93). Corporate, general, Mergers and acquisitions, Immigration, naturalization, and customs. Office: Santamarina Y Steta SC Campos Eliseos No 345 Piso 3 11560 Mexico City Mexico Fax: 5255 5280-7614. E-mail: aluna@s-s.com.mx.

LUND, JAMES LOUIS, lawyer; b. Long Beach, Calif., Oct. 4, 1926; s. G. Louis and Hazel Eunice (Cochran) L.; m. Jo Alvarez, Aug. 5, 1950; 1 son, Eric James. Student, Stanford U., 1943; BA in Math., U. So. Calif., 1946; postgrad., Grad. Sch. Annapolis, 1949; JD, Southwestern U., 1955; postgrad. Sch. Law, U. So. Calif., 1956. Bar: Calif. 1955, U.S. Dist. Ct. (cen. dist.) Calif. 1955, U.S. Ct. Appeals (9th cir.) 1955, U.S. Tax Ct. 1955, U.S. Supreme Ct. Spl. agt. U.S. Govt., 1950-52; gen. mgr. Pacific ops., gen. counsel Holmes & Narver, Inc., L.A., 1952-66; exec. v.p. Calif. Fabricators, Oakland and Honolulu, 1966-67; sr. ptnr. James Lund Law Firm, Beverly Hills, Tehran, London and Tokyo, 1967-83; pres., founder Fortres Mgmt. Co.; ptnr. Lund & Lund, 1983—. Chmn. bd. Envirotire, 1998—; dir. Superior Vision Svcs., Inc. Lt. comdr. USNR, 1943-46, 48-50. Mem. ABA, SAR, L.A. County Bar Assn., Internat. Bar Assn., Inter-Am. Bar Assn., Asia Pacific Lawyers Assn., Les Ambassadeurs Club (London). Construction, Private international, Property, real (including real estate development, water). Office: Ste 1555 1901 Avenue Of The Stars Los Angeles CA 90067-6052 Fax: 310-286-2686. E-mail: jlundesq@pacbell.net.

LUNDE, ASBJORN RUDOLPH, lawyer; b. S.I., N.Y., July 17, 1927; s. Karl and Elisa (Andenes) L. AB, Columbia U., 1947, LLB, 1949. Bar: N.Y. 1949. Pvt. practice, N.Y.C., 1950-91; with Kramer, Marx, Greenlee & Backus and predecessors, 1950-68, mem., 1958-68; pvt. practice Columbia County, NY, 1991—. Bd. dirs., v.p. Orch. da Camera, Inc., 1964—, Sara Roby Found., 1971—; bd. dirs. Clarion Concerts in Columbia County, 1999—; mem. vis. com. dept. European paintings Met. Mus. Art. Fellow Met. Mus. Art (life); mem. ABA, N.Y. State Bar Assn., Assn. Bar City N.Y., Met. Opera Club, East India Club (London). Avocation: art collecting (donor paintings and sculptures to Met. Mus. Art, N.Y.C., Nat. Gallery Art, Washington, Mus. Fine Arts, Boston).. Commercial, contracts (including sales of goods; commercial financing), Corporate, general, Private international. Home and Office: 135 LaBranche Rd Hillsdale NY 12529-5713

LUNDEEN, BRADLEY CURTIS, lawyer; b. Karlstad, MN, Nov. 16, 1958; s. Curtis W. and LaVonne M. (Oistad) L.; m. Kristina Ogland, May 18, 1984 (div. Dec. 1991); 1 child, Jonathan B. BA, Moorhead State U, 1980; JD cum laude, William Mitchell Coll. Law, 1984. Bar: Minn. 1984, Wis. 1984, Ariz., 2002. Assoc. Gwin, Gilbert, Gwin, Mudge & Porter, Hudson, Wis., 1984, Gilbert, Mudge & Porter, Hudson, 1985; ptnr. Gilbert, Mudge, Porter & Lundeen, Hudson, 1986-92; lawyer, shareholder Mudge, Porter & Lundeen S.C., Hudson, 1992-94, Mudge, Porter, Lundeen & Seguin S.C., Hudson, 1995-99, Lundeen Law Ltd., 2000—02, Bell O'Connor & Campbell, Phoenix, 2002—. Bd. dirs. Hudson Rotary, 1990-91; chmn. bd. dirs. Bank St. Croix, Hudson, Wis., 1987-94, St. Croix Valley Employers Assn., 1996—; pres. St. Croix Valley Employers Assn., 1999-01. Mem. Def. Rsch. Inst., Ariz. Assn. Def. Counsel, State Bar Ariz., State Bar Minn., State Bar Wis., Masons, Shriners. Lutheran. Avocations: golf, skiing, travel, computers and cooking. Labor (including EEOC, Fair Labor Standards Act, labor-management relations, NLRB, OSHA), Pension, profit-sharing, and employee benefits, Workers' compensation. Home: 19475 N Grayhawk Dr Unit 2126 Scottsdale AZ 85255 Office: Bell O'Connor & Campbell 3838 N Central Ave Phoenix AZ 85012 E-mail: brad.lundeen@boclaw.com.

LUNDERGAN, BARBARA KEOUGH, lawyer; b. Chgo., Nov. 6, 1938; d. Edward E. and Eleanor A. (Erickson) Keough; children: Matthew K., Mary Alice BA, U. Ill., 1960; JD, Loyola U., Chgo., 1964. Bar: Ill. 1964, Ga. 1997, U.S. Dist. Ct. (no. dist.) Ill. 1964, U.S. Tax Ct. 1974. With Seyfarth Shaw, Chgo., 1964—, ptnr., 1971-98, of counsel, 1998—. Fellow Am. Coll. Trust and Estate Counsel; mem. ABA (com. on fed. taxation), Ill. Bar Assn. (coun. sect. on fed. taxation 1983-91, chair 1989, coun. sect. on trusts and estates sect. coun. 1992-97, sec. 1996-97, editl. bd. Ill. Bar Jour. 1993-96), Chgo. Bar Assn. (chmn. trust law com. 1982-83, com. on fed. taxation). Office: Seyfarth Shaw 55 E Monroe St Ste 4200 Chicago IL 60603-5863

LUNDGREN, GAIL M. lawyer; b. Tacoma, Wash., June 14, 1955; d. Arthur Dean and Vera Martha (Grimm) L. AB cum laude, Vassar Coll., 1977; JD cum laude, U. Puget Sound (now Seattle U. Law Sch.), 1980. Bar: Wash. 1981. Legal intern Reed, McClure, Moceri & Thonn, Seattle, 1979, Burges & Kennedy, Tacoma, 1979-80, Lee, Smart, Cook, Martin & Patterson, P.S., Inc., Seattle, 1980-81, assoc., 1981-92; prin. Law Offices Gail L. Weber, Bothell, Wash., 1992-95, Tom Chambers & Assocs., 1995-99; lawyer Law Offices of Kirk Bernard, Seattle, 1999; ptnr. Bernard, Lundgren & Assocs., Seattle, 1999—. Vestry com. Queen Anne Luth. Ch., 1983-86, v.p. congregation, 1988, 89, mem. worship and music com., 1982-83, 84-86, parish edn. com., 1983-84. Recipient Am. Jurisprudence Book award in Criminal Procedure, Corps. and Bus. Planning, 1980. Mem.: ABA, Order of Barristers, Wash. State Trial Lawyers Assn., Fed. Bar Assn., Wash. State Vassar Club (chmn. alumni admissions 1983—85, rep. 1986—92, 2001—, chmn. alumni admissions 2001—). Democrat. Avocations: scuba diving, tennis, classical music, needlepoint, stitchery. General civil litigation, Personal injury (including property damage), Product liability. Office: Bernard, Lundgren & Assocs PLLC Ste 100 900 Aurora Ave N Ste 100 Seattle WA 98109

LUNDING, CHRISTOPHER HANNA, lawyer; b. Evanston, Ill., June 15, 1946; s. Franklin J. and Virginia (Hanna) L.; children: Elizabeth, Nelson, Alexander, Andrew, Kirsten; m. Barbara J. Fontana, Aug. 19, 1989. BA, Harvard U., 1968; JD, Yale U., 1971. Bar: N.Y. 1972, Fla. 1972, U.S. Supreme Ct. 1975. Law clk. to judge 2d Cir. U.S. Ct. Appeals, N.Y.C., 1971-72; assoc. Cleary, Gottlieb, Steen & Hamilton, N.Y.C., 1973-79, ptnr., 1980—. Chmn. Legal Svcs. N.Y.C., 1987—94. Chmn. Belle Haven Tax Dist., Greenwich, Conn., 1986-96, 2001—. Fellow Am. Bar Found. (life); mem. N.Y. County Lawyers Assn. (bd. dirs. 1988-94). General civil litigation, Commercial, contracts (including sales of goods; commercial financing), Mergers and acquisitions. Office: Cleary Gottlieb Steen & Hamilton One Liberty Plz Ste 3800 New York NY 10006 E-mail: CLunding@cgsh.com.

LUNDMAN, ULF PETER MICHAEL, lawyer, composer, writer; b. Helsingborg, Sweden, Sept. 1, 1953; s. Bruno Gottfried and Carla Helena Theresa (Olsson) L.; m. Marion Bast, May 25, 1985; children: Isabella, Mariella. Grad., U. Lund, Sweden, 1978, diploma cum laude, 1979. Notary Alingsas Ct., Sweden, 1978, Sjuharadsbygdens Ct., Boras, Sweden, 1979-80, Lansratten, Gothenburg, 1980-81; atty. Dist. Atty. Gothenburg, Sweden, 1979—; pvt. practice Gothenburg, 1982—; with SKF, Gothenburg, 1971-75. Author, composer: (record album) I Farsens drömmar, 1987. Elected controller City Gothenburg, 1982-90. With spl. svcs. Swedish Airforce, 1973-74. Mem. Swedish Bar Assn. Folkpartiet. Commercial, consumer (including collections, credit). Office: Advokathusl Box 20016 400 50 Gothenburg Sweden E-mail: info@advokathusl.biz., Ulf.Lundman@advokathusl.biz.

LUNDQUIST, WEYMAN IVAN, lawyer; b. Worcester, Mass., July 27, 1930; s. Hilding Ivan and Florence Cecilia (Westerholm) L.; m. Joan Durrell, Sept. 15, 1956 (div. July 1977); children— Weyman, Erica, Jettora, Kirk; m. Kathryn E. Taylor, Dec. 28, 1978; 1 child, Derek. BA magna cum laude, Dartmouth Coll., 1952; LLB, Harvard U., 1955. Bar: Mass. 1955, Alaska 1961, Calif. 1963, Vt. 1994. Assoc. Thayer, Smith & Gaskill, Worcester, 1957-60; atty. U.S. Attys. Office, Mass. and Alaska, 1960-62; assoc. Heller, Ehrman, White & McAuliffe, San Francisco, 1963-65, ptnr., 1967—; counsel, v.p. State Mut. Life Ins. Co., Worcester, 1965-67. Vis. prof. environ. studies Dartmouth Coll., Hanover, N.H., 1980, 84, bus. sch., 1997, vis. scholar, 1994-97, adj. prof. Amos Tuck Bus. Sch., Dartmouth Coll., 1997-99; program chmn. 1990 Moscow Conf. on Law and Bilateral Econs. Rels.; mem. U.S. adv. com. Alaska/Can./Soviet No. Justice Conf., 1993-94, N.Y., San Francisco Cutting Edge Lawyer Liability Programs, 1989; assoc. dir. Inst. Arctic Studies, Dartmouth Coll., 1999—; bd. dirs. U. Press New Eng., 1997, West Coast Magnetics, Stockton, Calif.; chmn. Environmental Careers Orgn.; chmn. ECO, Boston, 2001. Author: (fiction) The Promised Land, 1987, (nonfiction) The Art of Shaping the Case, 1999; contbr. articles to profl. jours. Trustee Natural Resources Def. Coun., 1982-91. Recipient CPR Significant Achievement award, 1987. Fellow ABA (founder and chmn. litigation sect. 1978-79, chmn. Soviet Bar Assn. liaison com. 1986, co-chmn. spl. com. for study discovery abuse 1976-83, spl. com. on tort liability sys. 1981-84, superfund 301e study group advisor to U.S. Congress, 1983), Am. Coll. Trial Lawyers; mem. Dartmouth Lawyer's Assn. (founding mem.), Am. Antiquarian Soc. (councillor), Assn. Life Ins. Coun., U.S. Supreme Ct. Hist. Soc., No. Dist. Hist. Soc., Dartmouth Lawyers Assn., Swedish Am. C. of C. (pres., bd. dirs. western U.S. 1982-89). Avocations: squash, skiing, writing. Federal civil litigation, State civil litigation, Environmental. Home: 16 Occum Rdg Hanover NH 03755-1410 Office: PO Box 5527 53 S Main St Ste 313 Hanover NH 03755-2022 E-mail: wey@dart.edu.

LUNDSTROM, GILBERT GENE, banker, lawyer; b. Sept. 27, 1941; s. Vernon G. and Imogene (Jackett) L.; m. Joyce Elaine Ronin, June 26, 1965; children: Trevor A., Gregory G. BS, U. Nebr., 1964, JD, 1969; MBA, Wayne State U., 1966. Bar: U.S. Dist. Ct. (1st dist.) Nebr. 1969, Nebr. 1969, U.S. Ct. Appeals (5th cir.) 1970, U.S. Ct. Appeals (10th cir.) 1971, U.S. Ct. Appeals (8th cir.) 1974, U.S. Ct. Appeals (3d cir.) 1986. Ptnr. Woods & Aitken Law Firm, Lincoln, Nebr., 1969-93; CEO, chmn. bd. Tier One Bank, 1994—. Chmn., CEO Tier One Corp., a Wis. Corp.; faculty law sch. U. Nebr., Lincoln, 1970-74; bd. dirs. Tier One Bank, TMS Corp. of Ams., Sahara Enterprises, Inc., Sahara Coal Co., Chgo., SMCO, Inc.; dir., vice-chmn. Fed. Home Loan Bank Topeka, 1996-2002 Bd. dirs. Folsom Children's Zoo, Lincoln, 1979-83, St. Elizabeth Hosp. Found., 1998-2002, Tier One Charitable Found. Fellow Nebr. State Bar Assn.; mem. ABA, ATLA, Lincoln Bar Assn., Nebr. Bankers Assn. (bd. dirs.), Newcomer Soc. US, Nebr. Bankers Assn. (bd. dirs.), Country Club of Lincoln, Firethorn County Club, Masons (33 degree), Lincoln C. of C. (bd. dirs.) Republican. Methodist. Home: 9519 Firethorn Ln Lincoln NE 68520-1459 Office: Tier One Bank 1235 N St Lincoln NE 68508-2083

LUNG, HENRY, lawyer; b. Taipei, Taiwan, May 25, 1972; arrived in U.S., 1975; BA in Spanish, BA in Polit. Sci., NYU, 1994; JD, St. John's U., Jamaica, N.Y., 1999. Bar: N.Y. 2000, U.S. Dist. Ct. (ea. and so. dists.) N.Y. 2001. Pvt. practice, Mineola, NY, 2000—. Mem. com. Nassau County Dems., Mineola, 2001—. Baptist. Avocations: collecting antique furniture, basketball. Commercial, consumer (including collections, credit), Landlord-tenant, Criminal. Office: 94 Willis Ave Mineola NY 11501 Office Fax: 516-739-8225. Business E-Mail: tien_syng_l@hotmail.com.

LUNGSTRUM, JOHN W. federal judge; b. Topeka, Kans., Nov. 2, 1945; s. Jack Edward and Helen Alice (Watson) L.; m. Linda Eileen Ewing, June 21, 1969; children: Justin Matthew, Jordan Elizabeth, Alison Paige. BA magna cum laude, Yale Coll., 1967; JD, U. Kans., 1970. Bar: Kans. 1970, Calif. 1970, U.S. Dist. Ct. (ctrl. dist.) Calif., U.S. Ct. Appeals (10th crct.). Assoc. Latham & Watkins, L.A., 1970-71; ptnr. Stevens, Brand, Lungstrum, Golden & Winter, Lawrence, Kans., 1972-91; U.S. Dist. judge Dist. of Kans., Kansas City, Kans., 1991—, chief judge, 2001—. Lectr. law U. Kans. Law Sch., 1973—; mem. faculty Kans. Bar Assn. Coll. Advocacy, Trial Tactics and Techniques Inst., 1983-86; chmn. Douglas County Rep. Ctrl. Com., 1975-81; mem. Rep. State Com.; del. State Rep. Convention, 1968, 76, 80; chair com. on ct. adminstrn. and case mgmt. Jud. Conf. of the U.S., 2000—. Chmn. bd. dirs. Lawrence C. of C., 1990-91; pres. Lawrence United Fund, 1979; pres. Independence Days Lawrence, Inc., 1984, 85, Seem-to-be-Players, Inc., Lawrence Rotary Club, 1978-79; bd. dirs. Lawrence Soc. Chamber Music, Swarthout Soc. (corp. fund-raising chmn.); mem. Lawrence Art Commn., Williams Scholarship Fund, Lawrence League Women Voters, Douglas County Hist. Soc.; bd. trustees, stewardship chmn. Plymouth Congl. Ch.; pres. Lawrence Round Ball Club; coach Lawrence Summertime Basketball; Vice chmn. U. Kans. Disciplinary Bd.; bd. govs. Kans Sch. Religion; bd. dirs. Kans. Day Club, 1980, 81. National Merit scholar, Yale Nat. scholar. Fellow Am. Bar Found.; mem. ABA (past mem. litigation and ins. sect.), Douglas County Bar Assn., Johnson County Bar Assn., Wyandotte County Bar Assn., Kans. Bar Assn. (vice chair legislative com., subcom. litigation, mem. continuing legal edn. com.), U Kans. Alumni Assn. (life), Phi Beta Kappa, Phi Gamma Delta, Phi Delta Phi. Avocations: basketball, hiking, skiing. Office: Robt J Dole US Courthouse Ste 517 500 State Ave Rm 517 Kansas City KS 66101-2400

LUONGO, STEPHEN EARLE, lawyer; b. Phila., June 15, 1947; s. Alfred Leopold and Dorothy West L.; m. Louise Anne Cipriani, Aug. 12, 1972; children: Peter James, Richard Stephen, Michael Paul. BS, U. Pa.; JD, Temple U. Bar: Pa. 1972, U.S. Dist. Ct. (ea. dist.) Pa. 1972. Assoc. atty. Blank, Rome, Comisky & McCauley, Phila., 1972-79, ptnr., 1979—, co.-chmn. corp. dept., 1988-93, mem. ptnr. bd., 1995—. Bd. dirs. Genesis Health Ventures, Inc., Kennett Suare, Pa., 1985-2000. Solicitor Merion Pk. Civic Assn., 1990-93. Mem. ABA, Am. Acad. Hosp. Attys., Pa. Bar Assn., Phila. Bar Assn., Nat. Assn. Coll. and Univ. Attys. Lodges: Order of Sons of Italy. Corporate, general, Health. Home: 215 Winding Way Merion Station PA 19066-1217 Office: Blank Rome Comisky & McCauley One Logan Sq Philadelphia PA 19103-6998

LUPERT, LESLIE ALLAN, lawyer; b. Syracuse, N.Y., May 24, 1946; s. Reuben and Miriam (Kaufman) L.; m. Roberta Gail Fellner, May 19, 1968; children: Jocelyn, Rachel, Susannah. BA, U. Buffalo, 1967; JD, Columbia U., 1971. Bar: N.Y. 1971. Ptnr. Orans Elsen & Lupert, N.Y.C., 1971—. Contbr. articles to profl. jours. Mem. ABA, N.Y. State Bar Assn. (trial lawyers sect.), Assn. of Bar of City of N.Y. (com. fed. legislation 1977-80, profl. and jud. ethics com. 1983-86, com. on fed. cts. 1986-89, 95-96), Phi Beta Kappa. Federal civil litigation, State civil litigation, Criminal. Office: Orans Elsen & Lupert 1 Rockefeller Plz New York NY 10020-2102 E-mail: llupert@oelaw.com.

LUPKIN, STANLEY NEIL, lawyer; b. Bklyn., Mar. 27, 1941; s. David B. and Sylvia (Strassman) L.; m. Anne Rachel Fischler, June 3, 1962; children: Jonathan Daniel, Deborah Eve. BA, Columbia Coll., 1962; LLB, NYU, 1966. Bar: N.Y. 1966, U.S. Dist. Ct. (so. and ea. dists.) N.Y. 1970, U.S. Ct. Appeals (2d cir.) 1970, U.S. Supreme Ct. 1971. Asst. dist. atty., sr. trial atty., chief indictment bur. N.Y. County Dist. Atty.'s Office, N.Y.C., 1966-71; asst. commr. City of N.Y., 1966-71; 1st dep. commr., commr. Dept. Investigation, N.Y.C., 1978-82; ptnr. Litman, Asche, Lupkin, Gioiella & Bassin, N.Y.C., 1982-96; sr. v.p., office pres. Decision Strategies LLC, N.Y.C., 1996—. Mem. faculty Nat. Coll. Dist. Attys., Houston, 1974—75, FBI Nat. Acad., Quantico, Va., 1980—82. Co-author book: Anatomy of A Municipal Franchise: N.Y.C. Bus Shelter Program, 1973-79, 4 vols., 1981. Trustee, counsel Solomon Schechter Sch. of Queens, Flushing, N.Y., 1974—; mem. secondary schs. com. admissions office Columbia Coll., N.Y.C., 1987-99. With USAR, 1963-69. Fellow: N.Y. State Bar Found.; mem.: NACDL, Internat. Assn. Ind. Pvt. Sector Insps. Gen., Am. Corp. Counsel Assn., N.Y. Criminal Bar Assn., N.Y. State Assn. Criminal Def. Lawyers, Assn. Bar City N.Y. (chmn. com. on criminal justice ops. 1982—85, com. on criminal cts. 2001—), N.Y. State Bar Assn. (chmn. com. on def. 1985—2000, chmn. com. on prosecution 1977—85, exec. com. criminal justice sect. 1977—2000, Prosecutor of Yr. award 1981), Soc. Columbia Grads. (v.p. 1989—98, dir. 1989—). Avocations: classical music, talmudic law. Administrative and regulatory, General civil litigation, Criminal. Office: Decision Strategies LLC 33 E 33d St New York NY 10016

LUPO, ANTONELLO, lawyer; b. Nettuno, Italy, June 13, 1968; s. Rocco and Rosa (Di Cesare) Lupo. JD, U.Rome, 1993. Bar: Rome 1996. Trainee Studio Fantozzi e Assocs.i, Rome, 1993—94; prof's. asst. U. of Rome La Sapienza, 1993—97; officer Tax Police, Rome, 1994—95; assoc. Studio Trivoli, Rome, 1995—97, Macchi di Cellere e Gangemi, Rome, 1997—2002; rsch. assoc. Internat. Bur. of Fiscal Documentation, Amsterdam, Netherlands, 1999—2000; sr. assoc. Gianni, Origoni, Grippo & Ptnrs., Rome, 2002—. Mem.: Rome Tax Lawyers Chamber, Internat. Fiscal Assn. (nat. treas., mem. of the exec. com. 2002), Internat. Tax Planning Assn., Internat. Bar Assn., Alumni Assn. Internat. Bur. of Fiscal Documentation. Corporate taxation, Taxation, general, Corporate, general. Office: Gianni Origoni Grippo & Ptnrs via delle Quattro Fontane 20 Rome Italy Office Fax: +39 06 4871101. E-mail: alupo@gop.it.

LURENSKY, MARCIA ADELE, lawyer; b. Newton, Mass., May 4, 1948; BA magna cum laude, Wheaton Coll., 1970; JD, Boston Coll. Law Sch., 1973. Bar: Mass. 1973, D.C. 1990, U.S. Dist. Ct. (we. dist.) Wis. 1978, U.S. Dist. Ct. Mass. 1974, U.S. Ct. Appeals (1st cir.) 1974, U.S. Ct. Appeals (3d cir.) 1982, U.S. Ct. Appeals (4th cir.) 1984, U.S. Ct. Appeals (5th cir.) 1995, U.S. Ct. Appeals (8th cir.) 1985, U.S. Ct. Appeals (9th cir.) 1976, U.S. Ct. Appeals (10th cir.) 1995, U.S. Ct. Appeals (11th cir.) 1982, U.S. Ct. Appeals (fed. cir.) 1989, U.S. Claims Ct. 1989, U.S. Supreme Ct. 1979. Atty. U.S. Dept. Labor, Washington, 1974-90, Fed. Energy Regulatory Commn., U.S. Dept. Energy, Washington, 1990—. Mem. Phi Beta Kappa. Office: Fed Energy Regulatory Commn 888 1st St NE Washington DC 20426-0002

LURIA, MARY MERCER, lawyer; b. Boston, Dec. 29, 1942; d. Albert and Mabel (Jacomb) Mercer; m. Nelson J. Luria, June 19, 1967. AB, Radcliffe Coll., 1964; LLB, Yale U., 1967. Bar: N.Y. 1968. Assoc. Simpson, Thacher & Bartlett, N.Y.C., 1967-68, Hale & Dorr, Boston, 1968-69, Satterlee & Stephens, N.Y.C., 1969-74, ptnr., 1974-86, Patterson, Belknap, Webb & Tyler, N.Y.C., 1986-97, Davis & Gilbert, N.Y.C., 1997—. Mem. ABA, N.Y. State Bar Assn., Assn. Bar City N.Y. Avocations: gardening, photography. Antitrust, Intellectual property, Trademark and copyright. Office: Davis & Gilbert 1740 Broadway Fl 20 New York NY 10019-4379 E-mail: mluria@dglaw.com.

LURIE, ALVIN DAVID, lawyer; b. N.Y.C., Apr. 16, 1923; s. Samuel and Rose L.; m. Marian Weinberg, Aug. 21, 1944; children: James, Jeanne, Margery, Jonathan. AB, Cornell U., 1943, LLB, 1944. Bar: N.Y. 1944, D.C. 1978. Ptnr. Lurie & Rubin, N.Y.C., 1961—68, Aranow, Brodsky, Bohlinger & Einhorn, N.Y.C., 1968—74; asst. commr. for employee plans and exempt orgns. IRS, Washington, 1974—78; ptnr. Chadbourne, Parke, Whiteside & Wolff, N.Y.C., 1978—84, Meyers, Tersigni, Lurie, Feldman & Gray, N.Y.C., 1984—94; atty. Alvin D. Lurie, N.Y.C., 1994—96; pres. Alvin D. Lurie, PC, New Rochelle, NY, 1996—; dir. N.Y. Ctr. Fin. Studies, 1980—. Mem. adv. bd. NYU Tax Inst., 1978-90; mem. adv. bd.Tax Mgmt., 1978—; mem. adv. bd. Tax Analysts and Advocates, 1995-2002; spl. counsel Small Bus. Coun. Am., 1978—; counsel N.Y. Soc. Fin. Svcs. Profls., 1978—. Author: Lurie's Commentaries on Pension Design, 1980, Lurie's Guide to VEBAs, 1983, Collected Commentaries on Pensions, 1984, ESOPs Made Easy, 1985; chair, editor NYU Rev. of Employee Benefits and Executive Compensation, 1998—; contbr. articles to profl. jours.; co-editor-in-chief Cornell Law Quar., 1943-44; pub. Pension & Benefit Power, 2002—. Fellow Am. Coll. Tax Counsel; mem. ABA, N.Y. State Bar Assn. (chmn. spl. com. pension simplification 1986—), Assn. Bar City N.Y., Am. Coll. Employee Benefits Counsel (charter), N.Y. Bar Found. Pension, profit-sharing, and employee benefits, Corporate taxation, Personal income taxation. Office: 145 Huguenot St New Rochelle NY 10801-5200

LURVEY, IRA HAROLD, lawyer; b. Chgo., Apr. 6, 1935; s. Louis and Faye (Grey) L.; m. Barbara Ann Sirvint, June 24, 1962; children: Nathana, Lawrence, Jennifer, Jonathan, David, Robert. BS, U. Ill., 1956; MS, Northwestern U., 1961; JD, U. Calif., Berkeley, 1965. Bar: Calif. 1965, Nev. 1966, U.S. Dist. Ct. (cen. dist.) Calif. 1966, U.S. Tax Ct. 1966, U.S. Ct. Appeals (9th cir.) 1966, U.S. Supreme Ct. 1975. Law clk. to hon. justices Nev. Supreme Ct., Carson City, 1965-66; from assoc. to ptnr. Pacht, Ross, Warne, Bernhard & Sears, Inc., 1966-84; predecessor firm Shea & Gould, L.A.; founding ptnr. Lurvey & Shapiro, L.A., 1984—. Lectr. legal edn. programs; mem. Chief Justice's Commns. on Ct. Reform, Weighted Caseloads; mediator family law L.A. Superior Ct. Editor Community Property Jour., 1979-80, Primary Consultant CFL 2d, 1994; columnist Calif. Family Law Monthly; contbr. articles to profl. jours. Former chmn. L.A. Jr. Arts Ctr.; past pres. Cheviot Hills Homeowners Assn.; exec. v.p., counsel Hillel Acad. Sch., Beverly Hills, Calif., 1977—. With U.S. Army, 1957-58. Fellow Am. Acad. Matrimonial Lawyers (pres. So. Calif. chpt. 1991-92, mem. nat. bd. govs. 1992-94), Internat. Acad. Matrimonial Lawyers; mem. ABA (chair family law sect. 1996-97, liaison family law to sr. lawyers' divsn. 1998—, exec. com. 1991-97, governing coun. 1986—, fin. officer 1991-92, chmn. support com., chmn. CLE, chmn. policy and issues com., vice chmn. com. arbitration and mediation, bd. of editors Family Adv. mag., chmn. issues com. sr. lawyer divsn. 2001—), Calif. Bar Assn. (editor jour. 1982-85, chmn. family law sect. 1986-87, exec. com. family law sect. 1982-88, specialization adv. bd. family law 1979-82), L.A. County Bar Assn. (chmn. family law sect. 1981-82, exec. com. family law 1989-92), Beverly Hills Bar Assn. (chmn. family law sect. 1976-77,). State civil litigation, Entertainment, Family and matrimonial. Home: 2729 Motor Ave Los Angeles CA 90064-3441 Office: Lurvey & Shapiro Ste 1550 1333 Beverly Green Drive Los Angeles CA 90035-1018 E-mail: lurvshap@aol.com.

LUSCOMBE, GEORGE A. II, lawyer; b. Jefferson, Iowa, Oct. 22, 1944; BS, U. Ill., 1966, JD, 1969; LLM, George Washington U., 1972. Bar: Ill. 1969, U.S. Supreme Ct. 1972, U.S. Claims Ct. 1972, D.C. 1972. Asst. br. chief legislation and regulations divsn. IRS Office Chief Counsel, 1972-73; ptnr. Mayer, Brown, Rowe & Maw, Chgo. Adj. prof. law IIT, 1987-93; speaker in field. Mem. ABA (chmn. com. depreciation and investment tax credit, sect. taxation 1980-82), Ill. State Bar Assn. (chmn. fed. tax sect. coun. 1991-92), Chgo. Bar Assn. (chmn. gen. income tax divsn., fed. tax com. 1977-79), D.C. Bar. Office: Mayer Brown Rowe & Maw 190 S La Salle St Ste 3100 Chicago IL 60603-3441

LUSHBAUGH, BRAD, lawyer; b. Fayetteville, Ark., Jan. 31, 1966; s. Harmon Edward and Carolyn Kay (Carter) Lushbaugh; m. Whitnie Robinson, Feb. 1, 1997; 1 child, William Quinn. BBA, U. Tex., 1988; JD, U. Ark., 1993; LLM, U. Denver, 1995. Bar: Ark. 94, U.S. Dist. Ct. (we. dist.) Ark. 94, U.S. Tax Ct. 96. Ptnr. Jones, Jones & Lushbaugh, PLC, Fayetteville, 1995—99; pvt. practice Lushbaugh Law Firm, Ltd., Fayetteville, 2000—. Chmn. Comml. Cons., Ltd., Fayetteville, 2001—. Mem. profl. adv. com. Ark. Children's Hosp., Little Rock, 2000—. Mem.: ABA (mem. asset protection com. 2001—02), Ark. Bar Assn. Estate planning, Mergers and acquisitions, Probate (including wills, trusts). Office: Lushbaugh Law Firm Ltd 5 N West Ave PO Box 1464 Fayetteville AR 72702-1464 Fax: 479-521-2375. E-mail: taxlaw@lushbaugh.com.

LUSKIN, MICHAEL, lawyer; b. N.Y.C., Dec. 29, 1951; s. Bernard and Bernice (Spikol) L.; m. Judith Levine, June 30, 1974; children: Sarah, Rachel. BA, Harvard U., 1973, JD, 1977. Bar: N.Y. 1978, U.S. Dist. Ct. (so. dist.) N.Y. 1978, (ea. dist.) N.Y. 1978, U.S. Ct. Appeals (2nd cir.) 1983. Assoc. Rogers & Wells, N.Y.C., 1977-80, Gelberg & Abrams, N.Y.C., 1980-85, ptnr., 1985-87, Moses & Singer, 1987-89, Luskin, Stern & Eisler LLP, N.Y.C., 1989—. Mem. ABA, N.Y. State Bar Assn., Fed. Bar Coun., Am. Bankruptcy Inst. Bankruptcy, General civil litigation, Commercial, contracts (including sales of goods; commercial financing). Office: Luskin Stern & Eisler LLP 330 Madison Ave New York NY 10017-5001 E-mail: mluskin@lse-law.com.

LUSKIN, ROBERT DAVID, lawyer; b. Chgo., Jan. 21, 1950; s. Bert L. and S. Ruth (Katz) L.; m. Fairlea A. Sheehy, Aug. 23, 1975 (div. Mar. 2000); children: Peter Duncan, Charles Cassimer. BA magna cum laude, Harvard U., 1972, JD magna cum laude, 1979; postgrad., Oxford (Eng.) U., 1972-75. Bar: D.C. 1979, U.S. Ct. Appeals (1st, 2nd, 4th, 5th, 6th, 7th, 8th, 9th, 11th, D.C. and fed. cirs.) 1979, U.S. Supreme Ct., 1983. Law clk. to Hon. Louis F. Oberdorfer U.S. Dist. Ct. for D.C., Washington, 1979-80; spl. counsel organized crime racketeering sect. U.S. Dept. Justice, Washington, 1980-82; ptnr. Onek, Klein & Farr, Washington, 1982-89, Powell, Goldstein, Frazer & Murphy, Washington, 1989-93, Comey, Boyd & Luskin, Washington, 1993-99, Patton Boggs, LLP, 2000—. Lectr. in law U. Va. Sch. Law, 1992—. Rhodes scholar, 1972-75. Mem. ABA (chmn. RICO Forfeitures and Civil Remedies com. 1986-94, vice chmn. task force on forfeitures), Harvard Law Sch. Assn. Washignton (pres.). Federal civil litigation, Criminal. Home: 3415 Prospect St NW Washington DC 20007-3219 Office: Patton Boggs LLP 2550 M St NW Washington DC 20037 E-mail: rluskin@pattonboggs.com.

LUSTIG, DOUGLAS JAMES, lawyer; b. Rochester, N.Y., July 19, 1949; s. Abraham and Ilene (Liberman) L.; m. Karen Ann Schiff, Aug. 17, 1975; children: Benjamin, JoEllen, Lindsay. BS, Syracuse (N.Y.) U., 1971; JD, Bklyn. Law Sch., 1974. Bar: N.Y. 1975, U.S. Dist. Ct. (we. dist.) N.Y. 1975, U.S. Supreme Ct. 1984. Assoc. Laverne, Sortino & Hanks, Rochester, 1975-79; ptnr. Laverne, Sortino, Hanks & Lustig, Rochester, 1979-84; pvt. practice Rochester, 1984—97; ptnr. Saperston & Day PC, 1997—2001, Chamberlain, D'Amanda, Oppenheimer & Greenfield, 2001—. Mem. U.S. panel of trustees We. Dist. N.Y., Bankruptcy Ct., 1983—; lectr. N.Y. State Bar Assn., Monroe County Bar Assn., Nat. Bus. Inst. Past pres. Jewish Family Svc. of Rochester, Inc.; v.p. Helping People With AIDS. Mem. ABA, N.Y. State Bar Assn., Monroe County Bar Assn., Yates County Bar Assn., Nat. Assn. Bankruptcy Trustees, Comml. Law League, Am. Bankruptcy Inst. (pres.), Irondequoit Country Club. Republican. Jewish. Bankruptcy, Commercial, consumer (including collections, credit), Property, real (including real estate development, water). Home: 17 S Pittsford Hill Ln Pittsford NY 14534-2896 Office: 1600 Crossroads Bldg 2 State St Rochester NY 14614-1397 also: 100 E Main St Penn Yan NY 14527-1668 Fax: 585-232-3882. E-mail: djl@cdog.com.

LUTH, THOMAS EDWARD, lawyer; b. Celina, Ohio, June 28, 1952; s. Ralph Edward and Eleanora Jean (Stetler) L.; m. Norma G. Weitzel, Feb. 3, 1979; children: Dylan R., Zebulun L. BA, Wright State U., 1974; JD, Ohio No. U., 1977. Bar: Ohio 1977. Assoc., Meikle & Tesno, 1977-81; ptnr. Meikle, Tesno & Luth, Celina, 1982—. Trustee Allen County Legal Svcs., Lima, Ohio, 1980. Mem. VFW, Ohio State Bar Assn. Lodges: Moose. Avocation: music, boating, cycling. Banking, Bankruptcy, General practice. Office: Meikle Tesno & Luth 100 N Main St Celina OH 45822-1729

LUTHEY, GRAYDON DEAN, JR., lawyer, educator; b. Topeka, Sept. 18, 1955; s. Graydon Dean Sr. and S. Anne (Murphy) L.; m. Deborah Denise McCullough, May 26, 1979; children: Sarah Elizabeth, Katherine Alexandra. BA in Letters with highest honors, U. Okla., 1976, JD, 1979; Fellow in Theology, Oxford (Eng.) U., 1976. Bar: Okla. 1979, U.S. Ct. Appeals (10th cir.) 1979, U.S. Dist. Ct. (no., we. and ea. dists.) Okla. 1980, U.S. Supreme Ct. 1982. Assoc. Jones, Givens, Gotcher, Bogan & Hilborne, Tulsa, 1979-84, ptnr., 1984-92, also bd. dirs.; ptnr. Hall, Estill, Hardwick, Gable, Golden & Nelson, Tulsa, 1992—, also bd. dirs. Adj. assoc. prof. U. Tulsa, 1985-87, adj. prof., 1987—; vis. fellow in theology Keble Coll., Oxford (Eng.) U., 1976; presiding judge Okla. Temporary Ct. Appeals, 1992-93; mem. Okla. Supreme Ct. Rules Com., 1992—. Bd. dirs. Tulsa Ballet, 1987-2000; chmn. Tulsa Pub. facilties Authority, 1990-93; tustee Episcopal Theol. Sem. of S.W., 1991-99, exec. com., 1992-99; vice chmn. Univ. Hosps. Authority, 1993-94, chmn. 1994-98, sec., 1998-99; chancellor Episcopal Diocese Okla., 1986-99; mem. bd. visitors U. Okla. Coll. Arts and Scis., 1997—; mem. State of Okla. Futures Auth., 1998-2002, chmn., 1999-2002. Nat. Merit scholar U. Okla., 1973. Life Fellow Am. Bar Found.; mem. ABA, Okla. Bar Assn. (chmn. continuing legal edn. com. 1989-91), Tulsa County Bar Assn. (bd. dirs. 1983-89, Disting. Svc. award 1988), Am. Law Inst., Am. Inns of Ct., Summit Club, So. Hills Country Club, Beta Theta Pi, Phi Beta Kappa, Omicron Delta Kappa. Federal civil litigation, State civil litigation, Securities. Office: Hall Estill Hardwick Gable Golden & Nelson 320 S Boston Ave Ste 400 Tulsa OK 74103-3704 E-mail: dluthey@hallestill.com.

LUTRINGER, RICHARD EMIL, lawyer; b. N.Y.C., Feb. 4, 1943; s. Emil Vincent Lutringer and Alice Hamilton Rich; m. Dagmar Bonitz, May 1, 1970 (div. 1980); m. Clarinda Higgins, Oct. 11, 1980 (div. 1999); children: Emily, Eric. AB, Coll. of William and Mary, 1964; JD in Internat. Affairs, Cornell U., 1967; MCL, U. Chgo., 1969. Bar: N.Y. 1972, U.S. Dist. Ct. (so. dist.) N.Y. 1972. Assoc. Whitman & Ransom, N.Y.C., 1971-80, ptnr., 1980-94, Morgan, Lewis & Bockius LLP, N.Y.C., 1994—. V.p. N.Y.-N.J. Trail Conf., N.Y.C., 1976-80; pres. German-Am. Roundtable, Inc., 1998—. Mem. ABA, Internat. Bar Assn., Assn. of Bar of City of N.Y. (chmn. com. fgn. and comparative law 1990-93), Am. Fgn. Law Assn. (pres. 1989-93, treas. 1986-89), European-Am. C. of C. (vice-chair trade com. 1992-98), German-Amer. C of C, Inc., Philadelphia (bd. dirs., 1999—, v.p., sec. 2001—), German Am. Law Assn. (bd. dirs. 2001—). Avocations: sailing, hiking, skiing. Commercial, contracts (including sales of goods; commercial financing), Corporate, general, Private international. Home: 32 Bridge St Westport CT 06880-6033 Office: Morgan Lewis & Bockius LLP 101 Park Ave New York NY 10178-0060 E-mail: rlutringer@morganlewis.com.

LUTTER, CHARLES WILLIAM, JR., lawyer; b. Kenosha, Wis., July 12, 1944; s. Charles William and Eva (Kuyawa) L.; m. Carol Hamilton Ewing, July 13, 1974; children: Charles William III, Scott. BS, U. Wis., 1966; postgrad., U. Tex., 1972; JD, St. Mary's U., 1976. Bar: Tex. 1976, U.S. Dist. Ct. (no. dist.) 1977, U.S. Dist. Ct. (so. dist.) 1981, U.S. Dist. Ct. (we. dist.) 1985, U.S. Ct. Appeals (5th and 11th cir.) 1981. Gen. atty. fin. SEC, Atlanta, 1976-80, chief regulations br. Houston, 1980-83; ptnr. Byrnes & Martin, Houston, 1983-84, Martin, Shannon & Drought, Inc., San Antonio, 1984-87; sr. corp. atty. LaQuinta Motor Inns, Inc., San Antonio, 1987-90; v.p., assoc. gen. counsel, sec. United Svcs. Advisors, Inc., 1991-93, v.p., spl. counsel, sec., 1993-95, legal/operational cons., 1995—; counsel to trust and ind. trustees ICON Funds, 1996—, Lindbergh Funds, 1999—, Meml. Funds, 2002—; of counsel MGL Cons. Corp., Houston, 2000—. Mem. planning com. Ann. Securities Regulation Conf., SEC, Tex. Securities Bd., State Bar Tex., U. Tex. Law Sch., 1986—; mem. initial exec. com. San Antonio Tech. Adv. Group, 1985-87; mem. target '90 Goals for San Antonio Sci. and Tech. Venture Task Force, 1985-90, exec. com. for forum on entrepreneurship, 1985-87; mem. estate planning coun. Southwest Found. Biomed. Rsch., San Antonio, 1987—; mem. U. Tex. Health Sci. Ctr. Estate Planning Coun., 1998—; arbitrator Nat. Assn. Securities Dealers, N.Y. Stock Exch., Mcpl. Securities Rulemaking Bd. Contbr. articles to profl. jours. Bd. dirs. Boysville, San Antonio, 1989—, mem. exec. com., 1995-99, pres., 1999; scout leader Alamo Area coun. Boy Scouts Am., 1988—. Capt. USAF, 1966-71. Decorated Air medal (6). Mem. ABA, State Bar Tex. (securities and investment banking com. 1984—, ad hoc subcom. on securities activities of banks 1987-89, subcom. on rules of fair practce for Tex. broker-dealers 1990), Internat. Assn. for Fin. Planning (bd. dirs. and regulatory coord. San Antonio chpt. 1987-98), Investment Co. Inst. (SEC rules com. 1993-95), San Antonio Bar Assn., San Antonio Bar Found., U. Wis. Alumni Assn., Air Force Assn., John M. Harlan Soc., Kiwanis, Phi Delta Phi. Administrative and regulatory, Corporate, general, Securities. Office: 103 Canyon Oaks Dr San Antonio TX 78232-1305 also: care MGL Cons Ste 10077 100 Grogan's Mill Rd The Woodlands TX 77380

LUTTER, PAUL ALLEN, lawyer; b. Chgo., Feb. 28, 1946; s. Herbert W. and Lois (Muller) L. BA, Carleton Coll., 1968; JD, Yale U., 1971. Bar: Ill. 1971, U.S. Tax Ct. 1986. Assoc. Ross & Hardies, Chgo., 1971-77, ptnr., 1978—. Co-author: Illinois Estate Administration, 1993. Dir. Howard Brown Health Ctr. Mem. ABA, Chgo. Bar Assn. Estate planning, Probate (including wills, trusts), Personal income taxation. Home: 2214 N Magnolia Ave Chicago IL 60614-3104 Office: Ross & Hardies 150 N Michigan Ave Ste 2500 Chicago IL 60601-7567

LUTZ, JAMES GURNEY, lawyer; b. Cin., Sept. 18, 1933; s. Arthur Harold and Frances (Gurney) L.; children: Monica, Susan. JD, Duke U Law Sch, U. Cin., 1960. Bar: Ohio 1960, U.S. Dist. Ct. (so. dist.) Ohio 1961, U.S. Ct. Appeals (6th cir.) 1961, U.S. Tax Ct. 1975, U.S. Supreme Ct. 1975. Ptnr. Barbour, Kinpel & Allen, Cin., 1960-68; chief counsel E.C. Industries Inc., Cin., 1968-71; sr. ptnr. Lutz Cornetet & Meyer, Cin., 1971—. Pres., mem. bd. dirs. Motivation Dynamics Inc., Cin., 1978-85. Advisor, staff Hamilton County Vocat. Schs., Cin., 1968; advisor U. Cin. Coll., 1970-75; mem. adv. counsel Wyoming (Ohio) Bd. Edn., 1972-75; mem. bd. Ohio Pvt. Industry Coun., Columbus, 1975; gen. counsel S.W. Ohio Autistic Assn., Cin., 1980—. Mem. ABA, ATLA, Ohio Acad. Trial Lawyers, Ohio State Bar Assn., Cin. Bar Assn. Avocations: psychology, computer science. General civil litigation, Franchising, Personal injury (including property damage). Office: Lutz Cornetet & Meyer 130 Tri County Pkwy Cincinnati OH 45246-3289 E-mail: jlutz@lcalaw.com.

LUTZ, MARTIN J. lawyer; b. Zurich, Switzerland, June 20, 1939; s. Robert Hermann Lutz and Dorothea Helene (Nabholz) Lutz-Nabholz; m. Barbara Ursula Kaufmann; m. Therese Charlotte Bertschinger, Mar. 27, 1969; children: Christoph, Corinne. Lic. iur., U. Zurich, 1963, Dr. iur., 1964; MCL, U. Mich., 1967. Bar: Zurich 1964. Legal adv. Swiss Performing Right Soc., Zurich, 1962—66; with Lenz & Staehelin, Zurich, 1967—73, ptnr., 1973—. Contbr. articles to profl. jours. Pres. Liberal Party, Zumikon, Switzerland, 1985—90; hon. pres. Internat. Assn. Protection Intellectual Property, 2000. Col., Swiss mil. Mem.: AIPPI, Swiss Arbitration Assn., Swiss Bar Assn., Zurich Bar Assn., Licensing Execs. Soc. Avocations: golf, hunting, bridge. Intellectual property, Commercial, contracts (including sales of goods; commercial financing). Office: Lenz & Staehelin Bleicherweg 58 8027 Zürich Switzerland Office Fax: 41 1 204 12 00. Business E-Mail: martin.lutz@lenzstaehelin.com.

LUTZKER, ELLIOT HOWARD, lawyer; b. Flushing, N.Y., Feb. 22, 1953; s. Stanley Lawrence and Mildred Lutzker; m. Jill Leslie Simon, Aug. 24, 1975; children: Stacey, Amanda. BA, SUNY, Stony Brook, 1974; JD, N.Y. Law Sch., 1978. Bar: N.Y. 1979, Fla. 1979, U.S. Dist. Ct. (so. and ea. dists.) N.Y. 1979. Atty. SEC, N.Y.C., 1978-81; assoc. Bachner, Tally, Polevoy, Misher & Brinberg, N.Y.C., 1981-85; ptnr. Snow Becker Krauss P.C., N.Y.C., 1985—. Mem. ABA (corp., banking law div.). Jewish. Avocations: reading, sports. Corporate, general, Securities. Home: 15 Kevin Ct Jericho NY 11753-1308 Office: Snow Becker Krauss PC 605 3rd Ave Fl 25 New York NY 10158-0125 E-mail: elutzker@sbklaw.com.

LUX, JONATHAN, lawyer; b. London, Oct. 30, 1951; arrived in Germany, 2001; s. Martin and Ruth Lux; m. Simone Lux, Sept. 3, 1979; children: Ruth, Dannielle, Adam. Diplome d'Etudes Superieures, U. Aix-Marseilles, France, 1974; LLB with honors, U. Nottingham, Eng., 1973. Solicitor: Eng. and Wales 1977, Hong Kong 1986. Trainee solicitor Ince & Co., London, 1975—77, solicitor, 1977—83, ptnr., 1983—2001, mng. ptnr. Hamburg, Germany, 2001—. Accredited mem. CEDR-The Acad. Experts and ADR Net, England, 1992—; mem. steering group London Shipping Law Ctr. Co-author: The Law of Tug, Tow and Pilotage, 1994, Bunkers, 1994, The Law and Practice of Marine Insurance and Average, 1996; editor: Classification Societies, 1993; contbr. articles to profl. jours. Freeman City of London. Fellow: Chartered Inst. Arbitrators; mem.: Internat. Bar Assn. (chmn. human rights insts. com. on legal sys, coun. mem. sect. on bus. law, vice chmn. standing com. on the UN and other world orgns.), Brit. Brazilian and Portuguese Law Assn. (vice chmn.), Assn. Average Adjusters, Brit. Acad. Experts, London Maritime Arbitrators' Assn. (mem. supporting mem. liaison com.). Avocation: classic car rallies. Office: Ince & Co Grosse Elbstrasse 145B 22767 Hamburg Germany

LYBECKER, MARTIN EARL, lawyer; b. Lincoln, Nebr., Feb. 11, 1945; s. Earl Edward and Jeanette Frances (Kiefer) L.; m. Andrea Kristine Tollefson, Dec. 27, 1969; children: Carl Martin, Neil Anders. BBA, U. Wash., 1967, JD, 1970; LLM in Taxation, NYU, 1971; LLM, U. Pa., 1973. Bar: Wash. 1970, D.C. 1972, Pa. 1982. Atty. investment mgmt. div. SEC, Washington, 1972-75, assoc. dir. div., 1978-81; assoc. prof. SUNY, Buffalo, 1975-78; ptnr. Drinker Biddle & Reath, Washington, 1981-87, Ropes & Gray, Washington, 1987—2002, Wilmer, Cutler & Pickering, Washington, 2002—. Adj. prof. Georgetown U., Washington, 1974-75, 80-81; vis. assoc. prof. Duke U., Durham, N.C., 1977-78, sr. lecturing fellow in law, 2000—. Contbr. articles to law revs. Fellow U. Pa. Ctr. for Study of Fin. Instns., 1971-72. Mem.: ABA (mem. subcom. on investment cos. and investment advisers, mem. com. on fed. regulation of securities bus. law sect., former chairperson com. on devels. in investment svcs. bus. law sect., chair com. on banking law), Am. Law Inst., Univ. Club. Washington. Banking, Corporate, general, Securities. Home: 2806 Daniel Rd Bethesda MD 20815-3149 Office: Wilmer Cutler & Pickering 2445 M St NW Washington DC 20037-1420 E-mail: martin.lybecker@wilmer.com.

LYDDANE, JOHN LAWRENCE ASHTON, lawyer; b. Aug. 22, 1947; s. Russell Hancock and Lucy Barnes (Ashton) L.; m. Virginia Ciurleo, Jan. 14, 1983; children: Ashley Elizabeth, Alexandra Marie, Ariel Ashton, Amanda Scott. AB, U. Rochester, 1969; JD, Syracuse U., 1972. Bar: N.Y. 1973, U.S. Dist. Ct. (no. dist.) N.Y. 1973, U.S. Dist. Ct. (so. and ea. dists.) N.Y. 1975, U.S. Ct. Appeals (2d cir.) 1975, U.S. Supreme Ct. 1976. Asst. atty. gen. N.Y. State, Albany, 1972—73; assoc. Harry H. Lipsig, N.Y.C., 1973—75, Martin, Clearwater & Bell, N.Y.C., 1975—78, ptnr., 1978—. Panelist Supreme Ct. Malpractice Panel, Bronx, 1979—87; commodore Belle Haven Club. Mem. U. Rochester Trustees Coun. Fellow: Am. Coll. Trial Lawyers; mem.: Belle Haven Club (commodore), Univ. Club (N.Y.C.). Republican. Episcopalian. General civil litigation, Product liability, Professional liability. Home: 29 Meadow Wood Dr Greenwich CT 06830-7023 Office: Martin Clearwater & Bell LLP 220 E 42nd St New York NY 10017-5806 E-mail: lyddaj@mcblaw.com.

LYERLA, BRADFORD PETER, lawyer; b. Savanna, Ill., Aug. 2, 1954; s. Ralph Herbert and Nancy Lee (Nelson) L.; m. Marilyn Wyse, Aug. 18, 1979; 3 children. BA, U. Ill., 1976, JD, 1980. Bar: Ill. 1980, U.S. Dist. Ct. (no. dist.) Ill. 1980, U.S. Dist. Ct. (no. dist.) Ind. 1982, U.S. Dist. Ct. (no. dist.) Calif. 1991, U.S. Dist. Ct. (ctrl. dist.) Ill. 1991, U.S. Dist. Ct. (ea. dist.) Wis. 2000, U.S. Dist. Ct. Nebr. 1998, U.S. Ct. Appeals (7th cir.) 1983, U.S. Ct. Appeals (fed. cir.) 1991, U.S. Ct. Appeals (2d cir.) 2002, U.S. Supreme Ct. 1995. Former ptnr. Jenner & Block, Chgo.; trial lawyer Chgo.; ptnr. Marshall, Gustein & Borun, Chgo. Lectr. on litigation and intellectual property law. Author publications in field; editor U. Ill. Law Rev., 1978-80. Bd. dirs. North Suburban Bd. of the Heartland Alliance, Wilmette, Ill., 1987-96, pres. 1993-94; bd. dirs. Traveler's and Immigrant's Aid, Chgo., 1991-95; bd. dirs., sec. Youth Svcs. Project, Inc., Chgo., 1987-91; mem. U. Ill. Pres.'s Coun.; founding mem. Cribbett Soc., U. Ill. Coll. Law; mem. Saints Faith Hope and Charity, Winnetka, Ill. Recipient John Powers Crowley Justice award People's Uptown Law Ctr., 1989. Fellow Am. Bar Found.; mem. ABA (editor litigation sect. intellectual properties litigation quar. 1990—, intellectual property sect. com. on unfair competition litigation), Ill. Bar Assn. (sect. coun. gen. practice sect. 1984-85, intellectual property sect. 1989—, co-editor intellectual property newsletter 1989-95, chair 1996-97), Chgo. Bar Assn. (legal ethics), Am. Intellectual Property Law Assn. (antitrust and fed. lit. com.), Intellectual Property Law Assn. Chgo. (patent litigation), Michigan Shores Club, Phi Beta Kappa, Phi Kappa Phi. Federal civil litigation, Computer, Patent. Office: Marshall Gustein & Borun 233 S Wacker Dr 6300 Sears Tower Chicago IL 60606

LYMAN, DAVID, lawyer; b. Washington, Sept. 25, 1936; s. Albert Moses and Freda (Ring) L. BSEE, Duke U., 1958; cert., US Naval Officers Submarine, Sch., 1960; JD, U. Calif., San Francisco, 1965; postgrad. in fgn./comparative law, Columbia U., 1974. Bar: Calif. 1966. Active minesweepers and submarine force USN, 1958-62; assoc. Fitzsimmons & Petris, Oakland, Calif., 1965-66, Lempres & Seyranian, Oakland, 1966-67, Tilleke & Gibbins, Internat. Ltd., Advocates and Solicitors, Bangkok, assoc. ptnr., 1967-84, chmn. and sr. ptnr., 1984—. Dir. Goodyear (Thailand) Ltd., Triumph Internat. (Thailand) Ltd.; founding mem. Prime Min. Thailand's Fgn. Investment Adv. Coun., 1975, chmn. Fgn. C. of C. in Thailand Law Change lProj. for the Prime Min., 1992; mem. USAID Adv. Com. on US - Thai Trade and Investment, 1988; founder, mem. steering com. tech. cooperation office US Asian Environ. Partnership Program, 1994. Contbr. articles to profl. publ. Chmn. King Bhumiphol Rama IX Park US Geodesic Dome Pavillion Com., 1987; founding mem. Thailand Bus. Coun. Sustainable Devel., 1993—; founder Davos Group World Econ. Forum on Anti-Corruption Std. for Global Bus., 1995-97, co-founder, advisor Cmty. Svc. Bangkok, 1985-1988; mem. Internat. C. of C. Commn. on Corruption, 1997; founder, mem. exec. bd. nat. chpt. Thailand, 1999; sec.-gen. Thailand Soc. Prevention of Cruelty to Animals, 1996-2000. With USN, 1958-1976; lt. comdr. Res. Named Boss of Yr., Women Secs. Assn. Thailand, 1997; recipient U.S. Navel Inst. prize, 1958, Am. Jurisprudence prize, 1965, U.S. Dept. Commerce cert., 1987, Thai Prime Minister's Cert. of Achievement, 1990, 1992, Am. C. of C. Disting. Svc. award, 1990, Honoree Beta Gamma Sigma, Drexel U., 1995; Paul Harris fellow, 1987. Mem. Am. C. of C. in Thailand (bd. gov. 1973—, v.p. 1974, 83-85, pres. 1975, 86), Asia-Pacific Coun. of Am. C. of C. (vice-chmn. 1975-77, 85-89, 92-93, bd. dir. 1975, 86), AmCham Environ. Coun. (founder 1992), Environ. Bus. Exch. (creator 1993), Thai Bd. Trade (bd. dir. 1975, 86), Fgn. Chambers of Commerce Working Group (sec. 1982-87, chmn. 1987-90), Thailand bd. of Investment Environ. Study Adv. Com., 1993, World Econ. Forum (program fellow Europe/East Asia Econ. Forum 1992-94, gov. profl. svc. 2003--), Lex Mundi (bd. dir. 1989-91), ABA, Calif. Bar Assn., Chartered Inst. Arbitrators (UK), Thai Inst. Dir., LAWAISA, US Naval Inst. (life), Naval Submarine League (life), Internat. Oceanographic Found. (life), Thailand Bus. Coalition AIDS Assn. (founder 1994), 1999 Wildlife Trust, Wildlife Fund Thailand, Chaines Des Rotisseurs (chaine de mission 1987-2000), Jewish Assn., Thailand, Tau Epsilon Phi, Fraternity (pres, 1956-1958) Phi Alpha Delta, 1962, Beta Gamma Sigma (hon.), Royal Bangkok Sports Club, Heritage Club (founder Gov. 1985-98), Fgn. Corr. of Thailand (life), Siam Soc. (life), Rotary (1969-89, sec. 1982-83, v.p. Bangkok 1984-85), Cmty Svc. of Bangkok (founder, acting pres. 1986, v.p. 1986-87, bd. dir. 1985-88), Thai Institute of Dir. (grad. mem.) 2002, the Chartered fInst. of Arbitrators (Assoc. mem.), 2002. Home: 39/221 Moo 3 Nichada Thani Soi 11 Tambol Bangtalad Amphur Pakkred Nonthaburi 11120 Thailand Office: Tilleke & Gibbins Internat Ltd 64/1 Soi Tonson Ploenchit Bangkok 10330 Thailand E-mail: dlyman@tillekeandgibbins.com.

LYNCH, JOHN JAMES, lawyer; b. Evergreen Park, Ill., Aug. 22, 1945; s. John J. and Agnes (Daly) L.; m. Kathleen Russell, Aug. 15, 1970; children: Kerry, Elizabeth, Erin. BA, St. Mary of the Lake Sem., 1967; MA in Philosophy, DePaul U., 1970, JD, 1973. Bar: Ill. 1973, U.S. Dist. Ct. (no. dist.) Ill. 1973, U.S. Ct. Appeals (7th cir.) 1976. Assoc. McKenna, Storer, Rowe, White & Haskell, Chgo., 1973-75, Haskell & Perrin, Chgo., 1975-77, ptnr., 1977-2000, Figliulo & Silverman, Chgo., 2000—. Mem.

ABA, Ill. State Bar Assn., Chgo. Bar Assn., Fedn. Def. and Corp. Counsel. General civil litigation, Insurance, Professional liability. Office: Figliulo & Silverman Ten S LaSalle St Ste 3600 Chicago IL 60603 E-mail: jlynch@fslegal.com.

LYNCH, KAREN RENZULLI, lawyer; b. Bridgeport, Conn., Feb. 4, 1946; d. Lidizio Amerigo and Cynthia Maria (Scott) Renzulli; m. Eugene Patrick Lynch Jr., Apr. 12, 1969; children: Tracy Regina, Kevin Anthony. BA, Manhattanville Coll., Purchase, N.Y., 1967; MPA, U. Hartford, West Hartford, Conn., 1975; JD, Western New Eng. Coll., Springfield, Mass., 1981. Bar: Conn. 1981, U.S. Dist. Ct. Conn. 1981. Mgmt. intern U.S. Army Chief of Staff, Washington, 1967-68; intelligence analyst U.S. Army for Sci. and Tech. Ctr., Washington, 1968-69; adminstr. N.Y. State Bd. Equalization, Albany, N.Y., 1969-70, U. Conn. Health Ctr., Farmington, 1971-76; pvt. practice West Hartford, 1981—. Law clk. U.S. Dist. Ct., Hartford, 1980; law intern Conn. Superior Ct., Hartford, 1981. Editor Constabar News of Gen. Practice, 1985-88; mem. editl. bd. The Complete Lawyer, 1996—. Mem. Jewish Family Svc. Greater Hartford Task Force on Conservatorship, West Hartford, 1988; mem. legacy and planned giving com. Greater Hartford chpt. Am. Cancer Soc., 1992-98, bd. dirs., 1993-98, treas., 1993-97. Mem. ABA (coun. sect. gen. practice div. 1987-91, bd. dirs. 1990-91, vice chmn. sole practitioners and small firms com. 1989-99, elder law com. 1991—, chmn. 2002-2003), Conn. Bar Assn. (exec. com. gen. practice sect. 1982—, vice chmn. 1990-91), Hartford County Bar Assn. (chmn. legal svcs. com. Old Am. Day 1986), Hartford Assn. Women Attys. (bd. dirs. 1984-86). Estate planning, General practice, Probate (including wills, trusts). Office: 45 S Main St PO Box 270715 West Hartford CT 06127-0715 E-mail: lynchlaw@juno.com.

LYNCH, LORETTA E. lawyer, former prosecutor; b. Durham, N.C., May 21, 1959; d. Lorenzo Lynch. Grad., Harvard Coll., 1981; JD, Harvard U., 1984. Bar: N.Y., U.S. Dist. Ct. (ea. dist. NY), U.S. Dist. Ct. (so. dist. NY), U.S. Ct. Appeals (2nd cir.). Litigation assoc. Cahill, Gordon & Reindel, 1984-90; with Office of U.S. Atty. for Ea. Dist. of N.Y., 1990—2001; chief L.I. offices, 1994-98; chief asst. U.S. States Atty., 1998—99; U.S. atty. ea. dist. N.Y. U.S. Dept. Justice, Bklyn., 2000—01; ptnr. Hogan & Hartson LLP, 2002—. Instr. Dept. Justice Criminal Trial Advocacy Prog.; adj. prof. St. John's Univ. Sch. Law; bd. dir. Fed. Reserve Bank N.Y., Office of the Appellate Defender; trustee Nat. Inst. Trial Advocacy; mem. Magistrate Judge Selection Panel Ea. Dist. N.Y., Judicial Screening Panel of Sen. Charles Schumer, NYC Charter Revision Commn. Bd. dirs. Nat. Inst. Law and Equity. Mem.: Ea. Dist Com. on Civil Litigation, Fed. Bar. Coun., Assn. Bar N.Y.C. Criminal Law Com. (chair). Avocations: reading, tennis. Office: Hogan & Hartson 875 Third Ave New York NY 10022*

LYNCH, LUKE DANIEL, JR., lawyer; b. Bklyn., Mar. 28, 1945; s. Luke Daniel and Marjorie Carol (Thien) L.; m. Nancy G. Ott, Sept. 19, 1970; children: Luke D. III, Bettina Anne. BA cum laude, Yale U., 1966; JD, Harvard U., 1969. Bar: N.Y. 1969, U.S. Dist. Ct. (so. dist.) N.Y. 1970. Assoc. Shearman & Sterling, N.Y.C., 1969-78; spl. asst. U.S. Treasury Dept., Washington, 1978-79, assoc. gen. counsel 1979-82; gen. counsel Chrysler Corp Loan Guaranty Bd., Washington, 1981-82; ptnr. D'Amato & Lynch, P.C., N.Y.C., 1983—. Mem. ABA. Avocation: golf. Banking, Corporate, general, Insurance. Office: D'Amato & Lynch 70 Pine St Fl 41 New York NY 10270-0110

LYNCH, MARIA REGINA MANGABEIRA ALBERNAZ, lawyer; b. Campinas, Sao Paulo, Brazil, Nov. 20, 1953; d. Paulo Mangabeira Albernaz Filho and Sylvia Stevenson Mangabeira Albernaz. LLB, U. Sao Paulo, 1976; LLM, Columbia U., 1978. Ptnr. Xavier, Bernardes, Braganca, Soc., Advs., Sao Paulo, Brazil, 1995—. Contbr. book. Mem.: ABA, Internat. Bar Assn., Brazilian Bar Assn. Aviation, Commercial, contracts (including sales of goods; commercial financing), Corporate, general. Office: Xavier Bernardes Braganca Soc de Advogados Av Brasil 1008 01430-0000 São Paulo Brazil Office Fax: 55 11 3069 4301. E-mail: reginalynch@xbb.com.br.

LYNCH, PATRICK, lawyer; b. Pitts., Nov. 11, 1941; s. Thomas Patrick and Helen Mary (Grimes) L.; m. M. Linda Maturo, June 20, 1964; children: Megan, Kevin, Colin, Brendan, Erin, Brian, Liam, Eamonn, Kilian, Caitlin, Ryan, Declan, Cristin, Mairin, Sean. BA in Philosophy, Loyola U., L.A., 1964, LLB, 1966. Bar: Calif. 1967, U.S. Dist. Ct. (cen., so., no. and ea. dists.) Calif., U.S. Ct. Appeals (9th cir.), U.S. Supreme Ct. Ptnr. O'Melveny & Myers, Los Angeles, 1966—. Panelist PLI Annual Antitrust Law Inst., 1982-2000. Bd. editors Matthew Bender Fed. Litigation Guide Reporter. Fellow Am. Coll. Trial Lawyers; mem. L.A. County Bar Assn. Office: OMelveny & Myers 400 S Hope St Los Angeles CA 90071-2899

LYNCH, PATRICK C. state attorney general; b. Providence, Feb. 4, 1965; s. Dennis and Irene Lynch; m. Christin Lynch; children: Kelsy, Graham. BA, Brown U., 1987; JD, Suffolk U., 1992. Bar: R.I. 1992, U.S. Dist. Ct. R.I. 1993. Clk. R.I. Superior Ct., 1993—94; pros., mem. Narcotics and Organized Crime Unit Atty. Gens. Office; spl. asst. Atty. Gen. State R.I.; assoc. Tillinghast Licht Perkins Smith and Cohen, LLP, Providence, 1999. Sec., bd. dirs. Advent House; bd. mem. Camp St. Cmty. Ministries, Brown Club, RI; mem. Brown Hall of Fame Com.; former pres. bd. St. Raphael. Mem.: R.I. Bar Assn. Democrat. Office: 150 S Main St Providence RI 02903*

LYNCH, ROBERT BERGER, retired lawyer; b. LaCrosse, Wis., June 10, 1931; s. Jan P. and Eve (Berger) Lynch; m. Iris D. Healy; 1 child, Jan Fredrick. BS, U.S. Merchant Marine Acad., 1955; JD, U. of the Pacific, 1967. Bar: Calif. 1969, US Supreme Ct. 1972. Engr. AeroJet-Gen. Corp., Sacramento, 1955-61, proposal mgr., 1961-63, asst. contract adminstrn. mgr., 1963-66, contract adminstrn. mgr., 1967-70; pvt. practice Rancho Cordova, Calif., 1969—2003; ret., 2003. Instr. bus. law Solano C.C., 1977—79, San Joaquin Delta Coll., 1978—79; mediator family law panel Sacramento Superior Ct.; traffic and small claims pro tem judge Sacramento, 1997—2001; appointed presiding judge Mcpl. Ct., Bisbee, Ariz., 2001—02. Active various charity fund-raising campaigns in Sacramento, 1966-68; mem. mission com. St. Clements Episcopal Ch., Rancho Cordova, Calif., 1967-68; trustee Los Rios C.C. Dist., Calif., 1971-79; vestryman, reader St. Mark's Anglican Ch., Loomis, Calif., 2000-01, St. John the Divine Ch., Hereford, Ariz., 2002-. With USCG, 1949-51, USNR, 1951-80, N.G., 1988-91, maj. AUS, ret. Mem. IEEE, Calif. Wildlife Fedn., Internat. Turtle Club, Marines Meml. Assn., Am. Legion, Mensa. Family and matrimonial, General practice, Probate (including wills, trusts). E-mail: rblynch@starband.net.

LYNCH, SANDRA LEA, federal judge; b. Oak Park, Ill., July 31, 1946; d. Bernard Francis and Eugenia Tyus Lynch; married; 1 child. AB in Philosophy, Wellesley Coll., 1968; JD cum laude, Boston U., 1971. Bar: Mass. 1971, U.S. Supreme Ct. 1974. Law clk. to Hon. Raymond J. Pettine U.S. Dist. Ct., Providence; asst. atty. gen. Commonwealth of Mass., Boston, 1974; gen. counsel Mass. Dept. Edn., Boston, 1974—78; ptnr. Foley, Hoag & Eliot, Boston, 1978—95; judge 1st cir. U.S. Ct. Appeals, Boston, 1995—. Contbr. articles to profl. jours. Past co-chair leading industries com. Greater Boston C. of C. Recipient Disting. Alumnae award, Boston U. Law Sch., 1993, Wellesley Coll., 1997, Disting. Svc. award, Planned Parenthood, 1991. Mem.: ABA, Boston Bar Assn. (pres. 1992—93, Jud. Excellence award 2001), Mass. Bar Assn., Nat. Assn. Women Judges, Women's Forum. Office: US Ct Appeals One Courthouse Way Ste 8710 Boston MA 02210-3010

LYNCH, THOMAS WIMP, lawyer; b. Monmouth, Ill., Mar. 5, 1930; s. William Brennan and Mildred Maurine (Wimp) L.; m. Elizabeth J. McDonald, July 30, 1952; children: Deborah, Michael, Maureen, Karen, Kathleen. BS in Geology, U. Ill., 1955, MS in Geology, 1958, JD, 1959. Bar: Ill. 1960, Okla. 1960, U.S. Supreme Ct. 1971, Tex. 1978. Staff atty. Amerada Hess Corp., Tulsa, 1959-72, asst. gen. counsel, 1972-75; mem. Hall, Estill, Hardwick, Gable, Collingsworth & Nelson, Tulsa, 1975; v.p., gen. counsel Tex. Pacific Oil Co., Inc., Dallas, 1975-80, Oryx Energy Co., Dallas, 1980-94; ret., 1994. Adj. prof. law U. Tulsa, 1974; trustee Southwestern Legal Found., chmn., lectr. ann. Oil and Gas Short course, 1976-92; adv. bd. Oil and Gas Edn. Ctr.; chmn. Oil, Gas and Mineral Law Coun. of State Bar of Tex., 1995-96. Served with USN, 1948-49, U.S. Army, 1951-53. Mem. ABA, Okla. Bar Assn., Tex. Bar Assn., Dallas County Bar Assn. Roman Catholic. Corporate, general, Oil, gas, and mineral.

LYNCH, TIMOTHY CRONIN, lawyer; b. Washington, Mar. 14, 1969; BA cum laude, Loyola Coll., Balt., 1991; JD, U. Md., 1995. Bar: Md. 1995, Va. 1996, DC 1999, U.S. Dist. Ct. (ea. and we. dists.) Va., U.S. Dist. Ct. Md., U.S. Ct. Appeals (4th cir.). Law clk. to hon. J. James McKenna Cir. Ct. for Montgomery County Md., Rockville, 1995-96; ptnr. Shar, Rosen & Warshaw, Balt., 1997—. General civil litigation, Personal injury (including property damage), Securities. Office: Shar Rosen & Warshaw LLC 26 South St Baltimore MD 21202-3215 E-mail: TLynch@triallaw.com.

LYNCH, VICTOR K. lawyer; b. Latrobe, Pa., Sept. 9, 1929; s. Victor E. and Helen (Kamerer) L.; m. Jane Louise Sutherland, June 11, 1951 (div. 1970); children: G. Michael, Janet L. Mutschler, Steven J., David J., Thomas S., Victoria A. BS in Sanitary Engring., Pa. State U., 1951; LLD, Duquesne U., 1958. Bar: Pa. 1959. Design engr., constrn. insp. The Chester Engrs., Pitts., 1953-54, project engr., 1954-58; assoc. Burgwin, Ruffin, Perry & Pohl, Pitts., 1958-62; ptnr. Ruffin, Perry, Springer, Hazlett & Lynch, Pitts., 1962-70; assoc. Litman, Litman, Harris & Specter, P.A., Pitts., 1971-74, Lynch, Lynch, Carr & Kabala, Pitts., 1974-78; ptnr. Lynch and Lynch, Pitts., 1978—. 1st lt. USAF, 1951-53. Recipient Bedell award Water Pollution Control Fedn., 1973. Mem. Water Pollution Control Assn. of Pa. (pres. 1972-73, Sludge Shoveler's award 1970, Johnny Clearwater award 1971), Pa. Soc. Profl. Engrs. Municipal (including bonds). Home: 1000 Grandview Ave Pittsburgh PA 15211-1362 Office: 403 Times Bldg 336 4th Ave Pittsburgh PA 15222-2004

LYNCH, WILLIAM REDINGTON, lawyer; b. N.Y.C., Nov. 17, 1928; s. Francis Russell Vincent and Helen Adams (Barrett) L.; m. Mary Pomeroy Grant, Aug. 22, 1958; children: Melissa L. Woolford, Elizabeth Barrett, Cynthia Pomeroy, Kimberly Townsend, Sarah Phillips. Student, Phillips Exeter Acad., 1944-47; BA, Yale U., 1951; JD, Columbia U., 1958. Bar: N.Y. 1959, Conn. 1963. Assoc. Milbank Tweed Hadley & McCloy, N.Y.C., 1958-62, Cummings & Lockwood, Stamford, Conn., 1962-66, ptnr., 1966—, ptnr. in charge Greenwich office, 1978-88. Bd. dirs. Greenwich Plaza Inc., 1970-74, Harrison & Ellis Inc., Cairo, Ga., 1985-87, Greenwich News Inc., 1986-90; chmn. ADM Mgmt. Corp., 1989-91. Chmn. Pub. Works Com., Greenwich, 1974-77, Greenwich United Way Campaign, 1975-76; vice chmn. Greenwich Bd. Edn., 1977-81, Rep. Town Meeting, 1967-77, dir., sec. Forum World Affairs, 1992-95. Lt. USNR, 1952-56. Mem. ABA, Conn. Bar Assn., Greenwich Bar Assn. (pres. 1979-80), Greenwich Field Club (pres. 1973-75), Round Hill Club (dir., sec. 1993-96). Congregationalist. Home: 100 Bedford Rd Greenwich CT 06831-2535 Office: Cummings & Lockwood 2 Greenwich Plz Ste 5 Greenwich CT 06830-6390

LYNCHESKI, JOHN E. lawyer; b. Throop, Pa., Sept. 10, 1945; s. John W. and Laura B. (Oshetski) L.; m. Kathy D. Penhale, Aug. 26, 1967; children: John H., Marc E., Kristin E. BA in Econs., Cornell U., 1967; JD, U. Pitts., 1970. Bar: Pa. 1970, Fla. 1974, U.S. Supreme Ct. 1982, U.S. Ct. Appeals (3d cir.) 1970, U.S. Dist. Ct. (we. and mid. dists.) Pa. 1970. Assoc. Reed Smith Shaw & McClay, Pitts., 1970-71, 74-81; USN judge advocate Gen. Corps, Pensacola, Fla., 1971-74; dir. Manion Alder & Cohen, Pitts., 1981-84, Alder Cohen & Grigsby, Pitts., 1984-89; dir., chmn. labor and employment group Cohen & Grigsby, PC, Pitts., 1989-99, healthcare group, 1989, exec. com., 1989—. Bd. vis. Robert Morris Coll. Sch. Mgmt., 1997-98; health adv. bd. U. Pitts. Sch. Law, 1996—; steering com. Law Fellows Sch. Law, 1992-98. Pres. Allegheny Beaver United Soccer, Pitts., 1986-94; bd. dirs., legal coun. Jaycees, Pa., 1977-78, pres., Upper St. Clair, 1976-77. Lt. USNR. Mem. Am. Arbitration Assn. (nat. panel), Pa. Bar Assn. (fed.), Fla. Bar Assn. (fed.), Pa. Bar Assn. (labor law com., health care law com.), Fla. Bar Assn. (labor law sect.), Allegheny County Bar Assn. (labor and employment law sect., health law sect.) Am. Health Lawyers Assn. (chmn. labor and employment practice group), Soc. Hosp. Attys. of Western Pa., Pa. Soc. Healthcare Attys., Health Exec. Forum S.W. Pa., Soc. for Human Resource Mgmt., Am. Soc. on Aging, Am. Hosp. Assn. Am. Soc. for Healthcare Risk Mgmt., Am. Coll. Healthcare Administrs., Assisted Living Fedn. Am., Am. Coll. Healthcare Adminstrs. (pres. Pa. chpt.), Am. Soc. for Healthcare Human Resources Adminstrn. (nat. spkrs. bur.), W.Va. Healthcare Human Resources Assn., Federalist Soc., Indsl. Rels. Rsch. Assn., West Pa. chpt. bd. dirs. Pitts. Human Resources Assn., West Pa. Working Together Consortium Health Initiative, Am. Health Lawyers Assn., Alternative Dispute Resolution Svc. (dispute resolver), Bus. Dispute Resolution Alliance, Pa. Govs. Sportsmen's Adv. Coun., Charities Valley Adv. Bd., Western Pa. Soccer Coaches Assn. (sec., bd. dirs. 1987-95), Pa. Soccer Coaches Assn., Nat. Soccer Coaches Assn., Pa. West Soccer Assn. (bd. dirs., exec. com., dir. classic league), Tri-State Referees Assn, Chartiers County Club (bd. dirs., pres., sec., legal adv., greens chmn.), Sewickley Heights Golf Club. Roman Catholic. Avocations: soccer, golf, hunting, fishing, outdoors. Civil rights, Health, Labor (including EEOC, Fair Labor Standards Act, labor-management relations, NLRB, OSHA). Office: Cohen & Grigsby PC 11 Stanwix St 15th Flr Pittsburgh PA 15222-1312 also: Ste 309 27200 Riverview Ctr Blvd Bonita Springs FL 34134

LYNE-ROWAN, DIONNE, law librarian; b. N.Y.C., June 26, 1971; d. David and Johanna Lyne; m. John Rowan, July 27, 2002. BA, Spelman Coll., Atlanta, 1995; MS in Libr. Sci., Clark-Atlanta U., 1997. Law libr. Schreeder, Wheeler & Flint, LLP, Atlanta, 1998—. Co-chair - scholarship com. Atlanta Law Librs. Assn., Atlanta, 2001—02. First v.p. Zeta Phi Beta Sorority, Inc, Kennesaw, Ga., 2000—02. Mem.: Spl. Librs. Assn., Am. Assn. of Law Librs. Office: Schreeder Wheeler & Flint LLP 127 Peachtree St Ste 1600 Atlanta GA 30303

LYNN, THEODORE STANLEY, lawyer; b. N.Y.C., Aug. 2, 1937; s. Irving and Sydell Lynn; m. Linda Isabel Freeman, July 21, 1968; children: Jessica, Douglas. AB, Columbia U., 1958; LLB, Harvard U., 1961; LLM, NYU, 1962; SJD, George Washington U., 1972. Law clk. to Hon. Bruce M. Forrester U.S. Tax Ct., Washington, 1962-64; tchg. fellow in law George Washington U., Washington, 1963-64; ptnr. Webster & Sheffield, N.Y.C., 1964-90, Stroock & Stroock & Lavan, N.Y.C., 1991—. Consult Admin Conf US, Washington, 1974—75; founding counsel Pension Real Estate Asn, Washington, 1981—84. Author: Real Estate Limited Partnerships, 3d ed, 1991, Real Estate Investment Trusts (supplemented annually), 1994; contbr. articles to profl jours. Secy Manhattan Sch Dance, 1974—93; trustee Birch Wathen Lenox Sch, New York, NY, 1975—93; bd dirs Citizens Union, 1991—, vice-chair, 2001—; dir Sutton Area Community Inc, 1995—; treas, trustee Citizens Union Found, 2000—; spec asst Mayor John V Lindsay, New York, NY, 1966—69; bd dirs Manhattan Community Bd # 6, New York, NY, 1977—. Mem.: Asn Bar City NY, Fed Bar Coun, Harvard Club, Univ Club. Alternative dispute resolution, Landlord-tenant, Property, real (including real estate development, water). Office: Stroock & Stroock & Lavan 180 Maiden Ln Fl 17 New York NY 10038-4937 E-mail: tlynn@stroock.com.

LYNTON, HAROLD STEPHEN, lawyer; b. N.Y.C., Nov. 2, 1909; widowed, Mar. 12, 1990; children: Stephen Jonathan, Richard David, Andrew Edward; m. Hattie Gruenstein Kalish, Jan. 27, 1991. AB magna cum laude, Yale U., 1929; JD cum laude, Harvard U., 1932. Bar: N.Y. 1933, U.S. Supreme Ct. 1947. Ptnr. Kaufman, Gallop, Gould, Climenko & Lynton, N.Y.C., 1934-51, Lynton & Klein and predecessors, N.Y.C., 1951-80, Shea & Gould, N.Y.C., 1980-91, counsel, 1992-94, Dornbush Mensch Mandelstam & Schaeffer, N.Y.C., 1994—; gen. counsel, trustee, mem. adv. bd. Barron Collier Cos., Naples, Fla., 1945—; also bd. dirs. Barron Collier Cos. and predecessors, Naples, Fla. Capt. AUS, 1943-45. Mem. ABA, N.Y. State Bar Assn., Assn. of Bar of City of N.Y., N.Y. County Lawyers Assn., Yale Club N.Y., Sunningdale Country Club, Phi Beta Kappa. Avocations: travel, theatre, tennis, swimming. General civil litigation, Corporate, general, Property, real (including real estate development, water). Home: 870 UN Plz New York NY 10017-1807 Office: Dornbush Mensch et al 747 3rd Ave Fl 11 New York NY 10017-2863

LYON, BRUCE ARNOLD, lawyer, educator; b. Sacramento, Sept. 24, 1951; s. Arnold E. and Arlene R. (Cox) L.; m. Patricia J. Gibson, Dec. 14, 1974; children: Barrett, Andrew. AB with honors, U. Pacific, 1974; JD, U. Calif.-Hastings Coll. Law, 1977. Bar: Calif. 1977, U.S. Dist. Ct. (ea. and no. dists.) Calif. 1977. Ptnr. Ingoglia, Marskey, Kearney & Lyon, Sacramento, 1977-84; sole practice Auburn, Calif., 1984-91; ptnr. Robinson, Robinson & Lyon, Auburn, 1991-98, Robinson, Lyon & Springford LLP, Auburn, 1999—. Instr. in law Sierra Coll., Rocklin, Calif., 1983-98. Mng. editor Comment, A Jour. of Comm. and Entertainment Law, 1974; contbr. articles to trade publs. Bd. dirs. Auburn Cmty. Found., Gold Country Sci. and Tech. Found.; pres. Calif. Tule Elk Found. Mem.: ABA, Thurston Soc., Placer County Bar Assn., State Bar Calif., Native Sons of the Golden West, Mensa, Order of Coif. State civil litigation, Commercial, contracts (including sales of goods; commercial financing), Property, real (including real estate development, water). Office: Robinson Lyon & Springford LLP One California St Auburn CA 95603

LYON, CARL FRANCIS, JR., lawyer; b. Sumter, S.C., May 9, 1943; s. Carl Francis and Sophie (Goldstrum) L.; m. Maryann Mercier; children—Barbara Ruth, Sarah Frances, Carl Francis, III. AB, Duke U., 1965, JD with honors, 1968. Bar: N.Y. 1969, D.C. 1977. Assoc., then ptnr. Mudge Rose Guthrie Alexander & Ferdon, N.Y.C., 1968-95, mem. exec. com., 1986-87, 94-95; ptnr. Orrick Herrington & Sutcliffe, N.Y.C., 1995—, mem. exec. com., 1998-2000. Contbr. articles to profl. publs. Mem. ABA (vice-chmn. spl. com. on energy fin. 1988-91), N.Y. State Bar Assn., D.C. Bar Assns., Am. Pub. Power Assn., Duke U. Law Alumni Coun., Order of Coif, Phi Alpha Delta. Corporate, general, Utilities, public. Office: Orrick Herrington Sutcliffe 666 5th Ave Rm 203 New York NY 10103-1798

LYON, DANIEL FRANK SOUTHWORTH, lawyer; b. N.Y., July 4, 1936; s. Daniel R. and Leta B. (Southworth) L.; m. Ida M. Hanson-Lyon, July 6, 1954 (dec. 1996); children: Daniel, Sherry, Dennis, Mary, Tom; m. Yvonne C. Hudson-Lyon, Mar. 15, 1997. BS, Milton Coll., 1963; LLB, Blackstone Sch. Law, 1965; JD, U. N.Mex., 1968. Bar: N.Mex. 1968. Dep. sheriff Rock County Sheriff's Dept., Beloit, Wis., 1958; probation and parole officer New Mex. Probation and Parole Bd., Albuquerque, 1964-68; pvt. practice, Albuquerque, 1968-71; lawyer U.S. West Comm., Albuquerque, 1971-91; cons., counselor Bernalillo County Valuation Bd., Albuquerque, 1991-95; dir. N.Mex. Adult Parole Bd., Santa Fe, 1995-99; asst. to mgr. U.S. Census Bur., Albuquerque, 1999—. Arbitrator State Bar N.Mex., 1980—; commn. Nat. Com. on Uniform State Laws, 1972-78. State rep. N.Mex., 1970-78; chmn. State Employment Security Commn., 1978-81; d el. New Mex. Constitutional Conv., 1989. Mem. ABA, N.Mex. Bar Assn., Wis. Bar Assn., Fed. Bar Assn., Indian Bar Assn., State Bar New Mex. (com. mem.), State Real Estate Com., Internat. Right of Way Assn. (dir. 1978). Avocations: travel, athletic events, watching tv. Home: 9216 Camino Viejo NW Albuquerque NM 87114-5398

LYON, JAMES BURROUGHS, lawyer; b. N.Y.C., May 11, 1930; s. Francis Murray and Edith May (Strong) L. BA, Amherst Coll., 1952; LLB, Yale U., 1955. Bar: Conn. 1955, U.S. Tax Ct. 1970. Asst. football coach Yale U., 1953-55; assoc. Murtha, Cullina LLP (and predecessor), Hartford, Conn., 1956-61, ptnr., 1961-96, counsel, 1996—. Adv. com., lectr. and session leader NYU Inst. on Fed. Taxation, 1973-86; mem. IRS Northeast Key Dist.'s Exempt Orgns. Liaison Group, Bklyn., 1993—. Mem. editl. bd. Conn. Law Tribune, 1988—. Chmn. 13th Conf. Charitable Orgn. N.Y.U. Inst. on Fed. Taxation, 1982; trustee Kingswood-Oxford Sch., West Hartford, Conn., 1961—91, hon. trustee, 1991—, chmn. bd. trustees, 1975—78; exec. com., chmn. Amherst Coll. Alumni Coun., 1963—69; chmn. bd. trustees Old Sturbridge Village, 1991—93; trustee Ella Burr McManus Trust, Hartford, 1987—98, Ellen Battell Stoeckel Trust, Norfolk, Conn., 1994, Hartford YMCA, 1985—, St. Francis Hosp. Found., 1991—, Watkinson Libr., 1990—, pres., 2001—; trustee Wadsworth Atheneum, Hartford, 1968—93, pres., 1981—84, hon. trustee, 1993—; trustee Horace Bushnell Meml. Hall, Hartford, 1993—, sec., 1996—; corporator Inst. Living, 1981—, Hartford Hosp., 1975—, St. Francis Hosp., Hartford, 1976—, Hartford Pub. Libr., 1979—; bd. dirs. Conn. Policy and Econ. Com., Inc., 1991—98; mem. Conn. adv. com. New Eng. Legal Found., 1991—; mem. adv. com. Florence Griswold Mus., Old Lyme, Conn., 1991—; bd. vis. Hartford Art Sch., 1995—; trustee Conn. Hist. Soc., 2000—, sec., 2003—; trustee Conn. Jr. Republic, Litchfield, 2000—; mem. N.E. regional coun. Nat. Club Assn., 1998—. Recipient Eminent Svc. medal Amherst Coll., 1967, Nathan Hale award Yale Club Hartford, 1982, Disting. Am. award No. Conn. chpt. Nat. Football Found. Hall of Fame, 1983, Community Svc. award United Way of the Capital Area, 1986, Thomas Hooker award Ancient Burying Ground Assn., 2003; honored as a direct descendant of its founder Mary Lyon, Mt. Holyoke Coll., South Hadley, Mass. 1997. Fellow: ABA (exempt orgn. com., co-chmn. subcom. on mus. and other cultural orgns. sect. of taxation 1988—), Am. Coll. Tax Counsel, Phi Beta Kappa; mem.: Am. Law Inst., Conn. State Srs. Golf Assn., Univ. Club Hartford (pres. 1976—77), Limestone Trout Club (East Canaan, Conn.), Yale Golf Club, Mory's Assn. (New Haven), Wianno Club (Osterville, Mass.), Dauntless Club (Essex, Conn.), Union Club N.Y.C., Yale Club, Hartford Golf Club. Corporate taxation, Personal income taxation, State and local taxation. Office: 185 Asylum St Hartford CT 06103-3408 E-mail: jlyon@murthalaw.com.

LYON, PHILIP K(IRKLAND), lawyer; b. Warren, Ark., Jan. 19, 1944; s. Leroy and Maxine (Campbell) L.; children by previous marriage: Bradford F., Lucinda H., Bruce P., Suzette P., John P., Martin K., Meredith J.; m. Jayne Carol Jack, Aug. 12, 1982. JD with honors, U. Ark., 1967. Bar: ARk, 1967, U.S. Supreme Ct. 1970, Tenn. 1989. Sr. ptnr., dir. ops. House, Wallace, Nelson & Jewell, P.A., Little Rock, 1967-86; pres. Jack, Lyon & Jones, P.A., Little Rock and Nashville, 1986—. Instr. bus. law, labor law, govt. bus. and collective bargaining U. Ark., Little Rock, 1969-72; lectr. practice skills and labor law, U. Ark. Law Sch., 1979-80; bd. dirs. Southwestern Legal Found., 1978—, Ctr. Am. and Internat. Law; host Straightlyonlaw.com, also radio talk show on entertainment and employment law, 2000-2002; editl. bd. dirs. Entertainment Law and Fin., 1993—; counsel, Acad of Country Music, Capitol Club. Author: Ark. Employment Law Desk Book, 1997; co-author: Schlei and Grossman Employment Discrimination Law, 2d edit., 1982; editor-in-chief: Ark. Law Rev., 1966-67, bd. dirs., 1978-93, v.p., 1990-92; editor: Ark. Employment Law Letter, 1995-97, Ark. Employment Law Ctr., 1998—. Mem. Ark. State C. of C. (bd. dirs. 1984-88), Greater Little Rock C. of C. (chmn. cmty. affairs com. 1982-84, minority bus. affairs 1985-89). Inaugural fellow Coll. Labor and Employment Lawyers, 1996; recipient Golden Gavel award Ark. Bar. Assn., 1978, Writing Excellence award Ark. Bar Found., 1980. Mem. ABA (select com. liaison office fed. contract compliance programs 1982—, select com. liaison EEOC 1984—, select com. immigration law, co-chair ethics & professionlism com. 2000—, forum com. entertainment and sports industries), Ark. Bar Assn. (chmn. labor law com. 1977-78, chmn. labor law sect.

1978-79, chmn. lawyers helping lawyers com. 1988-94), Tenn. Bar Assn. (labor sect., lawyers helping lawyers com. 1989—), Nashville Bar Assn. (entertainment law com., lawyers concerned for lawyers com., employment law com.), Pulaski County Bar Assn., Country Music Assn., Nashville Songwriters Assn. Internat., Internat. Entertainment Buyers Assoc. Civil rights, Entertainment, Labor (including EEOC, Fair Labor Standards Act, labor-management relations, NLRB, OSHA). Home: 350 Ardsley Pl Nashville TN 37215-3247 also: 17 Heritage Park Cir North Little Rock AR 72116-8528 also: Owl Lyon Ranch HC 70 Box 478 Jasper AR 72641-9744 Office: Jack Lyon & Jones PA 11 Music Cir S Ste 202 Nashville TN 37203-4335 also: Jack Lyon & Jones PA 425 W Capitol 3400 TCBY Tower Little Rock AR 72201 E-mail: pklyon@jljnash.com.

LYONS, CHAMP, JR., state supreme court justice; b. Boston, Dec. 6, 1940; m. Emily Lee Oswalt, 1967; children— Emily Olive, Champ III. AB, Harvard U., 1962; LL.B., U. Ala., 1965. Bar: Ala. 1965, U.S. Supreme Ct. 1973. Law clk. U.S. Dist. Ct., Mobile, Ala., 1965-67; assoc. Capell, Howard, Knabe & Cobbs, Montgomery, Ala., 1967-70, ptnr., 1970-76, Helmsing, Lyons, Sims & Leach, Mobile, 1976-98; legal advisor Hon. Fob James, Jr. Gov. State Ala., 1998; assoc. justice Supreme Ct. of Ala., Montgomery, 1998—. Mem. adv. commn. on civil procedure Ala. Supreme Ct., 1971-98, chmn., 1985-98. Author: Alabama Practice, 1973, 3d edit., 1996; contbr. articles to law jours. Mem. ABA, Ala. Bar Assn., Mobile Bar Assn. (pres. 1991), Am. Law Inst., Ala. Law Inst., Farrah Law Soc., Harvard U. Alumni Assn. (S.E. regional dir. 1988-91, v.p.-at-large 1992-94, 1st v.p. 1994-95, pres. 1995-96). Home: PO Box 1033 Point Clear AL 36564-1033 Office: Supreme Ct of Ala 300 Dexter Ave Montgomery AL 36104-3741

LYONS, DENNIS GERALD, lawyer; b. Passaic, N.J., Nov. 20, 1931; s. Denis A.G. and Agnes C. (Dyt) L.; m. Anna Maria Nuñez, 1983; 1 child, Alexandra; children by previous marriage: Andrew, Sarah, Tessa. AB, Holy Cross Coll., 1952; JD, Harvard U., 1955. Bar: D.C. 1955, N.Y. 1956, U.S. Supreme Ct 1960. Law clk. U.S. Supreme Ct., Washington, 1958-60; assoc. firm Arnold & Porter, Washington, 1960-62, ptnr., 1963—; v.p., gen. counsel, dir. Gulf United Corp., Jacksonville, Fla., 1968-80; asst. sec. Braniff Airways, Dallas, 1966-77; trustee GMR Properties, Boston, 1971-81; dir. Gulf Broadcast Co., Dallas, 1983-86; vis. prof. law U. Va., Charlottesville, 1982-83. Pres. Harvard Law Rev., 1954-55 Served with USAF, 1955-58. Mem. ABA, Am. Law Inst. Federal civil litigation, Corporate, general, Transportation. Office: Arnold & Porter 555 12th St NW Washington DC 20004-1206 E-mail: lyonsden@erols.com., dennis_lyons@aporter.com.

LYONS, GEORGE HARRIS, lawyer; b. Garrett, Ind., Mar. 6, 1947; s. Raymond Edward and Josephine Aquinas (Hoeffel) L.; m. Phyllis, Dec. 28, 1968 (div.); children: Douglas, Keegan; m. Veronica Pasko, July 2, 1988. BA cum laude, St. Francis Coll., Loretto, Pa., 1969; JD, U. Notre Dame, 1972. Bar: Ariz. 1973, U.S. Dist. Ct. Ariz. 1973, U.S. Ct. Appeals (9th cir.), U.S. Supreme Ct. 1979. Ptnr. Snell & Wilmer, Phoenix, 1972—2000, Charles M. Brewer, Ltd., 2000—. Mem. disciplinary com. Supreme Ct. Ariz., 1982-90. Editor Notre Dame Law Rev., 1971-72. With USAR, 1971. Mem. ABA, State Bar Ariz. (com. on rules profl. conduct 1983-89), Ariz. Bar Found., Maricopa County Bar Assn., Phoenix Area Def. Coun., Ariz. Trial Lawyers Assn., Def. Rsch. Inst., Trial Lawyers for Pub. Justice, Atty.'s Info. Exch. Group. Republican. Avocations: sailing, skiing. Federal civil litigation, Construction, Utilities, public. Mailing: 5500 N 24th St Phoenix AZ 85016

LYONS, NANCE, lawyer; BA, Boston Coll. (Newton), Chestnut Hill, Mass., 1964; JD cum laude, Suffolk U., 1977. Bar: Mass. 1977, U.S. Dist. Ct. Mass. 1977, cert. mediator 2002. Legis. and adminstrv. asst. to Sen. Edward M. Kennedy, Washington, 1967-70; sole practice Boston, 1977-86; atty. Comras & Jackman, Boston, 1986-90; sole practice Boston, 1990—. With Bar Overseers Disciplinary Hearing Panel, 1987-93; active Joint Bar Com. on Jud. Appts., 1991-93; adj. prof. law Mass. Sch. Law, 1994, 95; lectr. in field. Contbr. articles to profl. jours. Spl. corp. counsel City of Boston, 1977-82; asst. commr. Addiction Svcs. Agy., N.Y.C., 1972-73. Mem. Am. Trial Lawyers Assn., Mass. Acad. Trial Attys. (gov. 1987—, legislation com. 1990-96, mem. exec. com. 1994-2000, chair employment rights com. 1994-2000, women's com. 1994—), Mass. Assn. Women Lawyers (dir. 1983-89, 91-94, chair legis. com. 1984-89), Mass. Bar Assn. (legis. subcom. civil litigation sect. 1985-87, alt. dispute resolution com. 1988), Boston Bar Assn. (vol. lawyers project 1977—). Democrat. General civil litigation, General practice, Labor (including EEOC, Fair Labor Standards Act, labor-management relations, NLRB, OSHA). Office: 5th Fl 132 Boylston St Boston MA 02116

LYONS, PAUL VINCENT, lawyer; b. Boston, July 19, 1939; s. Joseph Vincent and Doris Irene (Griffin) L.; m. Elaine Marie Hurley, July 13, 1968; children: Judith Marie, Maureen Patricia, Paula Anne, Joseph Hurley BS cum laude, Boston Coll., 1960; MBA, NYU, 1962; JD, Suffolk U., Boston, 1968. Bar: Mass. 1968, U.S. Dist. Ct. Mass. 1969, U.S. Cir. Ct. (1st cir.) 1969, U.S. Supreme Ct. 1991. Div. adminstrn. mgr. Pepsi-Cola Co., N.Y.C., 1962-64; mem. bus. faculty Burdett Coll., Boston, 1964-68; atty. NLRB, Boston, 1968-73; assoc. Foley, Hoag & Eliot, Boston, 1973-77, ptnr., 1978—. Mem. faculty Boston U., 1972-74. Mem. Town Meeting, Milton, Mass., 1986—2002, Pers. Bd., Milton, 1994—. Lt. U.S. Army, 1960—62. Mem. ABA, Mass. Bar Assn., Boston Bar Assn. Education and schools, Labor (including EEOC, Fair Labor Standards Act, labor-management relations, NLRB, OSHA). Office: Foley Hoag LLP 155 Seaport Blvd Boston MA 02210-2175 E-mail: plyons@foleyhoag.com.

LYSLE, RICHARD SCOTT, lawyer; b. Pasadena, Calif., Oct. 22, 1947; s. Joseph Archer and Barbara (Blumberg) L.; children: Lily Rae, Joseph David, Maxwell Archer. AB, Cornell U., 1969; JD, U. So. Calif., 1972. Bar: Calif. 1972, U.S. Dist. Ct. (cen. dist.) Calif. 1974. Pvt. practice, Marina del Rey, Calif., 1972—. Judge pro tem L.A. Superior Ct., Santa Monica Superior Ct.; arbitrator Santa Monica Superior Arbitration Panel, Los Angeles Superior Ct. (we. dist.) Arbitration Panel. Mem. E. Clampus Vitus, Lawyers Club of LA County, Town Hall of Calif, LA World Affairs Coun., Culver Marina Bar Assn. Democrat. Avocations: rescue diver, scuba diver. State civil litigation, General practice, Personal injury (including property damage). Office: 7th Fl 5757 W Century Blvd Los Angeles CA 90045 E-mail: lyslelaw@aol.com.

LYTTON, WILLIAM BRYAN, lawyer; b. St. Louis, Mo., Aug. 22, 1948; s. William Bryan and Josephine (Lamy) L.; m. Christine Mary Miller; children— William Bryan IV, Laura Miller. AB, Georgetown U., 1970; JD, Am. U., Washington, 1973. Bar: D.C. 1973, U.S. Ct. Appeals (7th cir.) 1975, U.S. Supreme Ct. 1978, Pa. 1979, U.S. Dist. Ct. (ea. dist.) Pa. 1979, U.S. Ct. Appeals (3d cir.) 1979. Legal counsel, legis. asst. US Senator Charles H. Percy, 1973-75; asst. U.S. atty. US Dist. Ct., Chgo., 1975-78, US Dist. Ct. (ea. dist.), Pa., 1978-83, dep. chief spl. prosecutions div., 1980, dep. chief criminal div., 1980, chief criminal div., 1980-81, 1st asst. U.S. atty., 1981-83; ptnr. Kohn, Savett, Klein & Graf, P.C., Phila., 1983-87, 87-89; chief counsel, staff dir. Spl. Investigation Commn., Phila., 1985-86; dep. spl. counsellor to Pres. of U.S., Washington, 1987; v.p., gen. counsel GE Aerospace, King of Prussia, Pa., 1989-93; v.p., assoc. gen. counsel Martin Marietta & Lockheed Martin, 1993-95; v.p and gen. coun. Internat. Paper, Purchase, NY, 1996—99, sr. v.p., gen. counsel, 1999—2002; exec. v.p and gen. coun. Tyco Internat. Ltd., 2002. Contbr. articles to profl. jours. Committeeman Republican Party, Chester County, Pa.; mem. Easttown Twp. Bd. Suprs., 1990-95. Mem. ABA, Am. Corp. Counsel Assn. (bd. dirs. 1997—). Criminal, Libel. Office: Tyco Internat Ltd One Tyco Pk Exeter NH 03833 Home: 252 Silvermine Rd New Canaan CT 06840-4910*

MAAS, FRANK, judge; b. N.Y.C., June 10, 1950; s. Herbert N. and Vera (Neu) M.; m. Sidney L. Maas, June 22, 1980; children: Edward, Arthur. BA, Harpur Coll./SUNY, Binghamton, 1972; JD, NYU, 1976. Assoc. Curtis, Mallet-Prevost, Coit & Mosle, N.Y.C., 1976-78; asst. U.S. atty. So. Dist. N.Y., N.Y.C., 1980-86; ptnr. Phillips, Lytle, Hitchcock, Blaine & Huber, N.Y.C., 1986-95; 1st dep. commr. N.Y.C. Dept. Investigation, 1995-99; U.S. magistrate judge So. Dist. N.Y., N.Y.C., 1999—. Dep. commr., spl. counsel N.Y.C. Dept. Bus. Svcs., 1995-99. Mem. Coun. on Jud. Admisntrn. (assoc. of the bar 1997—), N.Y. State Bar Assn. (comml. and fed. litigation sect. 1984—), Fed. Bar Coun. Office: US Courthouse 500 Pearl St Rm 740 New York NY 10007-1502

MABEY, RALPH R. lawyer; b. Salt Lake City, May 20, 1944; s. Rendell Noel and Rachel (Wilson) M.; m. Sylvia States, June 5, 1968; children: Kathryn, Rachel, Elizabeth, Emily, Sara. BA, U. Utah, 1968; JD, Columbia U., 1972. Bar: Utah 1972, U.S. Dist. Ct. Utah 1972, U.S. Ct. Appeals (10th cir.) 1976, N.Y. 1985, U.S. Supreme Ct. 1988, U.S. Ct. Appeals (4th cir.) 1988, U.S. Ct. Appeals (3d cir.) 1993. Law clk. Atty. Gen., Salt Lake City, 1970, U.S. Dist. Ct., Salt Lake City, 1972-73; ptnr. Irvine, Smith & Mabey, Salt Lake City, 1973-79; U.S. bankruptcy judge U.S. Ct., Salt Lake City, 1979-83; ptnr. LeBoeuf, Lamb, Greene & MacRae, Salt Lake City and N.Y.C., 1983—. Sr. lectr. Brigham Young U. Sch. Law, Provo, Utah, 1983—, U. Utah Coll. Law, Salt Lake City, 1983-85. Mng. editor Norton Bankruptcy Law Adviser, 1983-85; contbg. author: Collier Bankruptcy Manual, 1986—, Collier on Bankruptcy, 15th Edition. With USAR, 1968-74. Mem. ABA (bus. bankruptcy com., select adv. com. on bus. reorgns.), Nat. Bankruptcy Conf., Am. Law Inst., Am. Bankruptcy Inst., Am. Coll. Bankruptcy (chmn.). Republican. Mem. Lds Ch. Avocations: running, fly fishing. Bankruptcy, General civil litigation, Corporate, general. Home: 253 S 1550 E Bountiful UT 84010-1350 Office: LeBoeuf Lamb Greene & MacRae 1000 Kearns Bldg 136 S Main St Salt Lake City UT 84101-1601 also: 125 W 55th St New York NY 10019-5369 E-mail: mabey@LLGM.com.

MACAN, WILLIAM ALEXANDER, IV, lawyer; b. Boston, Nov. 21, 1942; s. William A. and Carol (Whitten) M.; m. Jane Mitchell Ahern, Sept. 3, 1965; children: Sandi, Andrew. BS, Haverford Coll., 1964; LLB, U. Pa., 1967. Bar: Pa. 1968, U.S. Tax Ct. 1970, N.Y. 1999. Law clk. to judge U.S. Tax Ct., Washington, 1967-69; assoc. firm Morgan, Lewis & Bockius, Phila., 1969-76; ptnr. Morgan, Lewis & Bockius L.L.P., 1976-2000, Allen & Overy, N.Y.C., 2000—. Lectr. legal instns., seminars. Author publs. on tax-oriented equipment leasing, other tax subjects. Mem. ABA. Presbyterian. Finance, Corporate taxation, Personal income taxation. Office: Allen & Overy 1221 Ave of the Americas New York NY 10020 E-mail: william.macan@newyork.allenovery.com.

MACAULEY, WILLIAM FRANCIS, lawyer; b. Boston, Sept. 12, 1943; s. Bernard Joseph and Mary Louise (Dolan) M.; m. Sheila Rose Hubbard, June 29, 1968; children: Jennifer, Douglas, Leiha, Brian. AB, U. Wash., 1966; JD, Boston U., 1969. Bar: Mass. 1969, U.S. Dist. Ct. Mass. 1970, U.S. Ct. Appeals (1st cir.) 1977, U.S. Dist. Ct. R.I. 1979, U.S. Tax Ct. 1982, U.S. Dist. Ct. Conn. 1983. Assoc. Craig & Craig, Boston, 1970-74; prin. Tyler, Reynolds & Craig, Boston, 1975-78; pres. Craig and Macauley, Boston, 1979—. Contbr. articles to profl. jours. Trustee Boston U., The Raymond Found., Boston; bd. dirs. YMCA Greater Boston. Mem. ABA, Mass. Bar Assn., Boston Bar Assn. Bankruptcy, Federal civil litigation, State civil litigation. Home: 55 Buttricks Hill Rd Concord MA 01742-5314 Office: Craig and Macauley Profl Corp 600 Atlantic Ave Ste 2900 Boston MA 02210-2215 E-mail: macauley@craigmacauley.com.

MACBETH, ANGUS, lawyer; b. L.A., May 9, 1942; BA, Yale U., 1964, LLB, 1969. Bar: N.Y. 1970, D.C. 1981. Law clk. to Hon. Harold R. Tyler, Jr. U.S. Dist. Ct. (so. dist.) N.Y., 1969-70, asst. U.S. atty. criminal divsn., 1975-77; chief pollution control sect. Land and Natural Resources Divsn., U.S. Dept. Justice, 1977-79, dep. asst. atty. gen., 1979-81; ptnr. Sidley, Austin, Brown & Wood, Washington. Adj. prof. law N.Y. Law Sch., 1985—; spl. counsel Wartime Relocation and Internment Civilians Commn., 1981-83. Mem. D.C. Bar (steering com. energy and natural resources divsn. 1982-84), N.Y. State Bar Assn., Phi Beta Kappa. Office: Sidley Austin Brown & Wood 1501 K St Washington DC 20005

MACCHIA, VINCENT MICHAEL, lawyer; b. Bklyn., Dec. 30, 1933; s. Vincent and Lina Rose (Cewli) M.; m. Irene Janet Audino, Feb. 27, 1965; children: Lauren, Michele, Michael. BS, Fordham U., 1955, LLB, 1958; LLM, NYU, 1967. Bar: N.Y. 1958. Assoc. Bernard Remsen Millham & Bowdish, N.Y.C., 1959-60; atty. Equity Corp., N.Y.C., 1961-63, Pfizer Inc., N.Y.C., 1964, TWA, N.Y.C., 1964-66; mem. Gifford, Woody, Palmer & Serles, N.Y.C., 1966-85, Townley & Updike, N.Y.C., 1985-90; of counsel Smith, Don, Alampi, Scala & D'Argenio, Ft. Lee, N.J., 1990-91; counsel Tenzer, Greenblatt, LLP, N.Y.C., 1991-2000, Diamant, Katz Kahn & Co. LLP, N.Y.C., 2000—02, Amper, Politziner & Mattia, P.C., N.Y.C., 2002—. Dir. Hudson Rev., Inc. Mem. editl. staff Fordham Law Rev., 1956-58. With USAR, 1958-64. Mem. ABA, N.Y. State Bar Assn. Republican. Roman Catholic. Home: 4 Greentree Dr Scarsdale NY 10583-7014

MACCOLL, J. A. lawyer; b. Evanston, Ill., July 29, 1948; BA, Princeton U., 1970; JD, Georgetown U., 1973. Bar: Md. 1974, U.S. Dist. Ct. Md. 1974, U.S. Ct. Appeals (4th cir.) 1974. Asst. U.S. atty. Dist. Md., 1978—81; ptnr. Piper & Marbury; v.p., gen. counsel U.S. Fidelity & Guaranty Corp., Balt., 1987—91, sr. v.p., gen. counsel, 1991—95, exec. v.p. dept. human resource, gen. counsel, 1995—98; exec. v.p. gen. counsel The St. Paul Cos., Inc., 1998—2002, vice chmn., gen. counsel, 2002—. Editor-in-chief Georgetown Law Jour., 1972-73. Office: The St Paul Cos Inc 5801 Smith Ave Baltimore MD 21209-3611

MACDONALD, KIRK STEWART, lawyer; b. Glendale, Calif., Oct. 24, 1948; s. Bruce Mace and Phyllis Jeanne MacDonald. BSCE, U. So. Calif., 1970; JD, Western State U., 1982. Bar: Calif. 1982, U.S. Dist. Ct. (cen. dist.) Calif. 1982, U.S. Ct. Appeals (9th cir.) 1982, U.S. Dist. Ct. (no. dist.) Calif. 1984, U.S. Dist. Ct. (so. dist.) Calif. 1985, U.S. Dist. Ct. (ea. dist.) Calif. 1987. Dist. engr. Pacific Clay Products, Corona, Calif., 1971-76, Nat. Clay Pipe Inst., La Mirada, Calif., 1976-82; ptnr. Gill and Baldwin, Glendale, Calif., 1982—. Mem. ABA, L.A. County Bar Assn., Water Environ. Assn., Calif. Water Environ. Assn. Avocations: travel, woodworking. General civil litigation, Commercial, contracts (including sales of goods; commercial financing), Construction. Office: Gill & Baldwin Ste 405 130 N Brand Blvd Glendale CA 91203-2646 E-mail: kirk@gillandbaldwin.com.

MACDONALD, LELAND LLOYD, lawyer; b. Mar. 19, 1931; s. John Edward and Nannye Myrtle (Barnett) M.; m. Juanice L. Koen, Nov. 22, 1958; children: David Allen, Kathryn Ann. BBA, Baylor U., 1952, LLB, 1957. Bar: Tex. 1957, U.S. Dist. Ct. (we. dist.) Tex. 1960, U.S. Ct. Appeals (5th cir.). Title analyst Shell Oil Co., Midland, Tex., 1957—60; pvt. practice Midland, 1960—64; ptnr. Kerr, Fitz-Gerald & Kerr, Midland, 1964—73, Turpin, Smith, Dyer & Saxe, MacDonald, 1973—. Mem. admissions com. Tex. State Bar, 1978—80, grievance com., 1976—78. Past chmn. adv. bd. Salvation Army, 1962—. Fellow: Tex. Bar Found. (life); mem.: Midland County Bar Assn. (pres. 1973—74), Baylor Law Alumni Assn. (bd. dirs. 1980—86), Tex. Assn. Def. Counsel, Tex. State Bar Assn., Midland County Jr. Bar Assn. (pres. 1964—65), Midland Jaycees (v.p. 1960), Green Tree Country Club (bd. dirs. 1983), Rotary (pres. 1972—78), Masons. General civil litigation, Insurance, Personal injury (including property damage). Home: 1515 Community Ln Midland TX 79701-4011 Office: 303 W Wall St Ste 700 Midland TX 79701-5122

MACDONALD, THOMAS COOK, JR., lawyer, mediator; b. Atlanta, Oct. 11, 1929; s. Thomas Cook and Mary (Morgan) MacD.; m. Gay Anne Everiss, June 30, 1956; children: Margaret Anne, Thomas William. BS with high honors, U. Fla., 1951, LL.B. with high honors, 1953. Bar: Fla. 1953. Practice law, Tampa, 1953—; mem. firm Shackleford, Farrior, Stallings & Evans, 1953-97; mem. Cook & MacDonald, Tampa, 1997—2002; pvt. practice law Tampa, 2003—. Spl. counsel Gov. of Fla., 1963, U. Fla., 1972-98; del. 5th cir. Jud. Conf., 1970-81; mem. adv. com. U.S. Ct. Appeals (5th cir.), 1975-78, (11th cir.), 1988-93; mem. Fla. Jud. Qualifications Commn., 1983-88, vice chmn., 1987, chmn., 1988, gen. counsel, 1997—; mem. judicial nominating com. Fla. Supreme Ct., 1995-99. Mem. Fla. Student Scholarship and Loan Commn., 1963-67; bd. dirs. Univ. Cmty. Hosp., Tampa, 1968-78, Fla. West Coast Sports Assn., 1965-80, Hall of Fame Bowl (now Outback Bowl) Assn., 1989-93, Jim Walter Corp., 1979-87; mem. Hillsborough County Pub. Edn. Study Commn., 1965; lic. lay eucharistic min. Episcopal Ch., 1961—; chancellor Episcopal Diocese of S.W. Fla., 1990-93, 2000—, ch. atty. for ecclesiastical ct., 1998-2000; bd. dirs. U. Fla. Found., 1978-86, Shands Tchg. Hosp., U. Fla., 1981-95; counsel Tampa Sports Authority, 1983-94. Recipient George Carr award FBA, 1991, Herbert Goldburg award Hillsborough County Bar Assn., 1995. Fellow Am. Coll. Trial Lawyers (chmn. state com. 1990-91), Am. Bar Found., Fla. Bar (chmn. com. profl. ethics 1966-70, bd. govs. 1970-74, bar mem. Supreme Ct. com. on stds. conduct governing judges 1976, Presdl. award of merit 1995); mem. ABA (com. on ethics and profl. responsibility 1970-76), Am. Law Inst. (life), 11th Cir. Hist. Soc. (trustee 1982-95, pres. 1989-95), U. Fla. Nat. Alumni Assn. (pres. 1973), Phi Kappa Phi, Phi Delta Phi, Fla. Blue Key, Kappa Alpha. Episcopalian. Alternative dispute resolution, General civil litigation, Education and schools. Home: 1904 S Holly Ln Tampa FL 33629-7004

MACDOUGALL, GORDON PIER, lawyer; b. Bethlehem, Pa., May 31, 1930; s. Curtis Daniel and Elizabeth (Pier) MacD. AB, U. Mich., 1952; postgrad., Columbia U., 1952-55. Bar: Wis. 1955, N.Y. 1958, D.C. 1960. Atty. N.Y. Cen. R.R. Co., N.Y.C., 1957-59; assoc. LaRoe, Winn & Moerman, Washington, 1959-66; pvt. practice, Washington, 1966—. Spl. asst. atty. gen. Commonwealth Pa., Washington, 1971-78; asst. counsel Pa. Pub. Utility Commn., Washington, 1975-80. Named Disting. Hoosier Gov. Edgar D. Whitcomb, Inpls., 1972. Mem. Assn. Transp. Law, Logistics and Policy, Transp. Lawyers Assn., Maritime Adminstrv. Bar Assn., Transp. Research Forum (gen. counsel). Administrative and regulatory, Utilities, public, Transportation. Office: 1025 Connecticut Ave NW Washington DC 20036-5423 Home: 2000 N St NW Washington DC 20036-2349

MACDOUGALL, MALCOLM EDWARD, lawyer; b. Denver, Jan. 26, 1938; s. Malcolm W. and Helen (Harlow) MacD.; m. Phyllis R. Pomrenke, Dec. 20, 1959; children: Barry Malcolm, Christopher Scott (dec.). BS, Colo. State U., 1959; LLD, U. Colo., 1962. Bar: Colo. 1962, U.S. Dist. Ct. Colo. 1962. Law clk. to judge U.S. Ct. Appeals (10th cir.), Denver, 1962-63; atty. Denver Water Bd., 1963-65; assoc. Saunders, Snyder and Ross, Denver, 1965-68; gen. counsel Golden Cycle Corp., Colorado Springs, Colo., 1968-71; ptnr. Geddes, MacDougall and Worley, P.C., Colorado Springs, 1971-91; sole practitioner MacDougall Law Office, Colorado Springs, 1991-99; shareholder MacDougall, Woldridge & Worley, PC, Colorado Springs, 1999—. Bd. dirs. Park State Bank. Mem. Colo. Bar Assn. Republican. Natural resources, Property, real (including real estate development, water), Oil, gas, and mineral. Office: Ste 204 530 Communication Cir Colorado Springs CO 80905 E-mail: sandy@waterlaw.tv.

MACDOUGALL, PETER, lawyer; b. Boston, Sept. 22, 1937; s. Duncan Peck and Hildegard (Moebius) MacD. AB, Harvard U., 1958, LLB, 1963. Assoc. Ropes & Gray, Boston, 1964-73, ptnr., 1973-97, ret., 1997—. Sheldon fellow Harvard U., 1963-64. Mem.: Harvard (Boston). Avocations: concert and opera going, gardening, reading, travel. Home: 1720 Washington St Key West FL 33040-4916 also: 542 River Rd Westport MA 02790-5161 E-mail: pmacdougall@earthlink.net.

MACDOUGALL, PRISCILLA RUTH, lawyer; b. Evanston, Ill., Jan. 20, 1944; d. Curtis Daniel and Genevieve Maurine (Rockwood) MacDougall; m. Lester H. Brownlee, July 5, 1987. BA, Barnard Coll., 1965; grad. with honors, U. Paris, 1967; JD, U. Mich., 1970. Bar: Wis. 1970, Ill. 1970. Asst. atty. gen. State of Wis., 1970-74; instr. Law Sch. and undergrad. campuses U. Wis., 1973-75; staff counsel Wis. Edn. Assn. Council, Madison, 1975—; instr. Columbia Coll., Chgo., 1988—; litigator, writer, speaker, educator women's and children's names and women's rights and employment issues. Mem. ABA, Wis. State Bar (co-founder sect. on individual rights and responsibilities, chairperson, 1973-75, 78-79), Legal Assn. Women Wis. (co-founder). Author: Married Women's Common Law Right to Their Own Surnames, 1972; co-author: Booklet for Women Who Wish to Determine Their Own Names After Marriage, 1974, supplement, 1975; The Right of Women to Name Their Children, 1985; contbr. articles to profl. jours. Home: 502 Engelhart Dr Madison WI 53713-4742 Office: 33 Nob Hill Dr Madison WI 53713-2198

MACHIN, PETER WILLIAM, lawyer; b. Halifax, Yorkshire, England, Apr. 30, 1949; s. Albert William and Elizabeth Evelyn (Foster) M.; m. Catherine Lorina Salmon, Nov. 10, 1979. BA in Jurisprudence, Oxford U., 1970; MA, 1974, BCL, 1975. Bar: solicitor High Ct. Eng. and Wales, Supreme Ct. New South Wales, Victoria, Australian Capital Ter., We. Australia. Atty. Ashursts, London, 1971-74; assoc. Underwood & Co., London, 1975-77, Gasters, London, 1977-79, Mallesons Stephen Jaques, Perth, Australia, 1979-81; ptnr., 1982-89, 1989-91, 1991-2001, Minter Ellison, 2001—. Contbr. articles to profl. jours. Mem. Internat. Bar Assn., Rocky Mountain Mineral Law Found., Australian Mining and Petroleum Law Assn., Law Coun. Avocations: travel, food and wine, languages, golf, tennis. Commercial, contracts (including sales of goods; commercial financing), Nuclear power, Oil, gas, and mineral. Home: 3209/70 Market St Sydney NSW 2000 Australia Office: Minter Ellison 88 Phillip St Sydney NSW 2000 Australia E-mail: peter.machin@minterellison.com.

MACINTOSH, JAY W. lawyer, realtor, actress; b. Gainesville, Ga., Mar. 30, 1937; d. Jesse Dickson Jewell and Anna Louise Dorough Jewell; m. Darrell William MacIntyre, Aug. 17, 1957 (div. Dec. 1972); children: Tracey Lee, Craig Dickson, Blake William. Student, U. Wis., 1955—57; BFA in Speech and Drama, U. Ga., 1961, MA in Drama, 1962; JD, Whittier Law Sch., Costa Mesa, Calif., 1999. Bar: Calif. 2000, U.S. Dist. Ct. (cen. dist.) Calif. 2000, U.S. Ct. Appeals (9th cir.) 2000. Real estate broker Merrill Lynch Realty, 1976—85, MacIntosh Realtors, 1985—; jud. extern Calif. Ctrl. Dist., 1998, U.S. Bankruptcy Ct.; pvt. practice L.A., 2000—. Prof., head dept. speech and drama Brenau U., Gainesville, Ga., 1962—65; prof., chmn. divsn. humanities Gainesville Coll., 1966—68. Actor: (films) My Science Project, Sgt. Pepper's Lonely Hearts Club Band, The Quest, Like It Is, Hostages, J.W. Coop, Joni, Time Step, Wild Rovers, After Arthur Minsky Died; (TV films) Liz: The Elizabeth Taylor Story, Murder of Innocence, Beverly Hills Madame, Mark, I Love You, Pomeroy's People, The Blue Knight, Incident on a Dark Street, Studs Lonigan, Ishy, The Last of His Tribe, Auto Da Fe, The Haunting of Seacliff Inn, Secret Sins of the Father, Hollywood Wives, Senior Year, The Healers, Pollyanna, Centennial, Elvis and the Beauty Queen, Where Have All The People Gone; (TV series) Picket Fences, Eight is Enough, Cannon, Barnaby Jones, Simon & Simon, The Waltons, many others. Mem.: ABA, FBA, Nat. Assn. Realtors, Calif. Assn. Realtors, Greater L.A. Assn. Realtors, Consumer Attys. Calif., Consumer Attys. Assn. L.A., Women Lawyers Assn. L.A., Century City Bar Assn., Beverly Hills Bar Assn., L.A. County Bar Assn., Acad. TV Arts and Scis. (mem. blue ribbon panels), Women in Film (bd. dirs.), Actors Studio (chmn. members com.), Phi Kappa Phi, Phi Beta Kappa. Democrat. Episcopalian. Avocations: hiking, swimming, theater , reading, skiing.

Entertainment, Intellectual property, Labor (including EEOC, Fair Labor Standards Act, labor-management relations, NLRB, OSHA). Office: Ste 500 1925 Century Park East Los Angeles CA 90067

MACIOCE, FRANK MICHAEL, lawyer, financial services company executive; b. N.Y.C., Oct. 3, 1945; s. Frank Michael and Sylvia Maria (Morea) M.; children: Michael Peter, Lauren Decker, Theodore Kenneth; m. Helen Latourette Duffin, July 9, 1988. BS, Purdue U., 1967; JD, Vanderbilt U., 1972. Bar: N.Y. 1973, U.S. Dist. Ct. (so. dist.) N.Y. 1973, U.S. Ct. Appeals (2d cir.) 1975, U.S. Supreme Ct. 1976. Mem. law dept. Merrill Lynch, Pierce, Fenner & Smith Inc., N.Y.C., 1972-80, v.p., 1978-88, 1st v.p., 1988-2000, Merrill Lynch Investment Mgrs., Plainsboro, NJ, 2000—03. Mgr. corp. law dept. Merrill Lynch & Co., Inc., N.Y.C., 1980-93, asst. gen. counsel, 1982-2000; gen. counsel investment banking group, 1993-95, ops., svcs. and tech. counsel, 1995-2000, sec. of audit, compensation and nominating coms. bd. dirs., 1978-83, sec. exec. com., 1981-83; mng. dir. Merrill Lynch Overseas Capital, N.V., Netherlands Antilles, 1980-85; sec., dir. Merrill Lynch Employees Fed. Credit Union, N.Y.C., 1978-82; dir. Merrill Lynch Pvt. Capital Inc., N.Y.C., 1981-87, Teleport Comm. Group Inc., N.Y.C., 1987-92, Enhance Fin. Services Inc, N.Y.C., 1988-92; fin. planning adv. bd. Purdue U., 1996-2000. Served with U.S. Army, 1969-70. Mem. ABA, Assn. of Bar of City of N.Y. Computer, Corporate, general, Securities. Home: 22 Essex Rd Summit NJ 07901-2802 E-mail: fmacioce@comcast.net.

MACIONE, KYLE PRITCHETT, pharmaceutical company executive, lawyer; b. Jackson, Miss., Dec. 28, 1963; s. Joe and Annette (Pritchett) M.; m. Beatriz Huarte, Sept. 17, 1993; children: Robert Huarte Macione, Alexandra Huarte Macione, Christina Huarte Macione. BA in Accountancy, U. Miss., 1986; MA in Accountancy, U. Ala., 1987; JD, Washington & Lee U., 1991. Bar: Tenn., 1991, Va., 1992, U.S. Dist. Ct. (we. dist.) Va., U.S. Dist. Ct. (ea. dist.) Tenn., 1992, U.S. Dist. Ct. Appeals (6th cir.), 1992; CPA, Miss. CPA tax dept. KPMG Peat Marwick, Jackson, 1988; assoc. atty. Elliott Lawson & Pomrenke, Bristol, Va., 1992—96; pres. King Pharm., Inc., Bristol, Tenn., 1996—. Bd. dirs. Bristol Ballet Company Bristol Va.-Tenn., 1993-99, treas., 1994-95; bd. dirs. Main St. Bristol, 1997-98, Wellmont Found., 2001—; bd. trustees Barter Theatre, 2001—. Mem. Va. State Bar, Va. Bar Assn., Tenn. Bar Assn., Miss. Soc. CPAs, Bristol Va. Bar Assn. (sec., treas. 1993-94), Beta Alpha Psi, Beta Gamma Sigma. Home: 142 E Main St Abingdon VA 24210-2835 Office: King Pharm Inc 501 5th St Bristol TN 37620-2304

MACK, JULIA COOPER, retired judge; b. Fayetteville, N.C., July 17, 1920; d. Dallas L. and Emily (McKay) Perry; m. Jerry S. Cooper, July 30, 1943; 1 dau., Cheryl; m. Clifford S. Mack, Nov. 21, 1957. BS, Hampton Inst., 1940; LL.B., Howard U., 1951; JD (hon.), U. D.C., 1999. Bar: D.C. 1952. Legal cons. OPS, Washington, 1952-53; atty.-advisor office gen. counsel Gen. Svcs. Adminstrn., Washington, 1953-54; trial appellate atty. criminal div. Dept. Justice, Washington, 1954-68; civil rights atty. Office Gen. Counsel, Equal Employment Opportunity Commn., Washington, 1968-75; assoc. judge Ct. Appeals, Washington, 1975-89; sr. judge DC Ct. of Appeals, Washington, 1989—2001. Mem. Am., Fed., Washington, Nat. Bar Assns., Nat. Assn. Women Judges. Home: 1610 Varnum St NW Washington DC 20011-4206

MACK, ROBERT E. lawyer; B, Havard U., 1972; JD, Harvard U., 1975. Prin. Smith Alling Lane, P.S., Tacoma. Instr. U. Wash., U. Puget Sound (name now Seattle U.). Government contracts and claims, Environmental, Utilities, public. Office: 1102 Broadway Ste 403 Tacoma WA 98402-3526 Office Fax: 253-627-0123. Business E-Mail: rmack@smithallinglane.com.*

MACK, SUSAN ELIZABETH, lawyer; b. Beverly, Mass., Nov. 20, 1957; d. Armando and Antonia Astolfi; m. Bruce Bromley Mack, Aug. 30, 1980; children: Andrew, Alicia, Rebecca. BA, Dartmouth Coll., 1979; JD, Boston Coll., 1982. Bar: S.C. 1982, Calif. 1983, Conn. 1986. Assoc. Gassitt Perry and Frank, San Jose, Calif., 1983—85; sr. trial counsel Reins. Office Aetna Life and Casualty, Hartford, Conn., 1988—96; v.p. claims, gen. counsel St. Paul Re, Inc., N.Y.C., 1996—98; v.p., gen. coun. Transamerica Reinsurance, Charlotte, NC, 1998—. Contbr. Mem.: ABA (chair reins. com. 2000—02), Assn. Profl. Ins. Women, Reins. Assn. Am. (chair life com. 2000—02), Women's Execs. of Charlotte, Tournament Players Club. Avocations: golf, travel, gourmet cooking. Alternative dispute resolution, Insurance, Private international. Office: Transamerica Reinsurance 401 N Tryon St Charlotte NC 28202

MACK, THEODORE, lawyer; b. Ft. Worth, Mar. 5, 1936; s. Henry and Norma (Harris) M.; m. Ellen Feinknopf, June 19, 1960; children: Katherine Norma, Elizabeth Ellen, Alexandra. AB cum laude, Harvard U., 1958, JD, 1961. Bar: Tex. 1961, U.S. Supreme Ct. 1971, U.S. Ct. Appeals (5th cir.) 1967, U.S. Ct. Appeals (11th cir.) 1981, U.S. Dist. Ct. (no. dist.) Tex. 1961, U.S. Dist. Ct. (we. dist.) Tex. 1968, U.S. Dist. Ct. (so. dist.) Tex. 1968, U.S. Dist. Ct. (ea. dist.) Tex. 1999. Assoc. Mack & Mack, Ft. Worth, 1961-62, ptnr., 1963-70; dir., pres., v.p., treas., ptnr. Renfro, Mack and Hudman, P.C. and predecessors, Ft. Worth, 1970-93; spl. counsel Brackett & Ellis, P.C. and predecessors, Ft. Worth, 1993—. Trustee Ft. Worth Country Day Sch., 1976-82; bd. dirs. Beth-El Congregation, 1964-73, 75-78, pres. 1975-77; bd. dirs. Jewish Fedn. Ft. Worth, 1965-72; mem. Leadership Ft. Worth, 1973-74; bd. dirs. Sr. Citizens Ctrs., Inc., 1969-81, Family and Individual Svcs., 1981-84, Presbyn. Night Shelter Tarrant County, Inc., 1992-97; pres. Harvard Law Sch. Assn. Tex., 1976-77. Fellow Tex. Bar Found. (life); mem. Tex. Bar Assn., ABA, Am. Inn Ct. (master of the bench John C. Ford Inn), Tarrant County Bar Assn., Bar Assn. 5th Cir. Ct., Colonial County Club, Ft. Worth Club, City Club, Harvard Club (N.Y.C., Boston). Democrat. Jewish. Antitrust, Bankruptcy, Federal civil litigation. Home: 2817 Harlanwood Dr Fort Worth TX 76109-1226 Office: Spl Counsel Brackett & Ellis PC 100 Main St Fort Worth TX 76102-3090 Office Fax: 817-870-2265. E-mail: tmack@belaw.com.

MACKALL, LAIDLER BOWIE, lawyer; b. Washington, Aug. 8, 1916; s. Laidler and Evelyn (Bowie) M.; m. Nancy M. Taylor, Aug. 28, 1942; children: Nancy Taylor Mackall Lurton (dec.), Christie Beall Mackall Connard, Susan Somervell Mackall Smythe, Bruce Bowie Mackall McConihe; m. Prudence Robertson Colbert, July 26, 1978. AB, Princeton U., 1938; postgrad., Georgetown U., 1938-40, JD, 1947. Bar: D.C. bar 1947, ICC bar 1951, U.S. Supreme Ct. bar 1958. Law clk. to chief judge of predecessor to D.C. Ct. Appeals, 1946-47; assoc. Minor, Gatley & Drury, Washington, 1947-49, Steptoe & Johnson, Washington, 1949-51, ptnr., 1952-86, of counsel, 1986-98. Mem. D.C. Ct. Appeals Com. on Admissions, 1974-78, D.C. Circuit Jud. Conf., 1983, 85, 86; bd. mgrs. Nat. Conf. Bar Examiners, 1974-77 Served to col. USAAF, 1940-46, 51. Decorated Silver Star, 2 D.F.C.s, 5 Air medals, 3 Presdl. unit citations. Fellow Am. Coll. Trial Lawyers (emeritus); mem. ABA (past vice chmn. standing com. aviation ins. law), D.C. Bar, Bar Assn. D.C. (past chmn. com. on negligence, motor vehicle and compensation law), Barristers Club (v.p. 1964), Chevy Chase Country Club, Met. Club (Washington), Hawk's Nest Golf Club of Fla. Episcopalian. Federal civil litigation, Insurance, Personal injury (including property damage). Home (Summer): 3809 Village Park Dr Chevy Chase MD 20815-5746 Home: 151 Passage Island Vero Beach FL 32963-4265 E-mail: lbmackall@webtv.net.

MACKAY, HAROLD HUGH, lawyer; b. Regina, Sask., Can., Aug. 1, 1940; s. John Royden and Grace Madeliene (Irwin) MacK.; m. Jean Elizabeth Hutchison, Dec. 27, 1963; children: Carol, Donald. BA, U. Sask., 1960; LLB, Dalhousie U., Halifax, N.S., 1963. Bar: Sask. 1964, Queen's Counsel 1981. Assoc. MacPherson Leslie & Tyerman, Regina, 1963-69, ptnr., 1969-75, 76—, mng. ptnr., 1989-96, chmn., 1997—2003. Bd. dirs. IMC Global Inc.; chmn. task force Future of the Can. Fin. Svcs. Sector, 1997-98; chair Saskatchewan Inst. Pub. Policy; Clifford Clark vis. economist Dept. of Finance, Gov't. of Canada, 2002-03. Trustee Found. for Legal Rsch. Recipient Officer Order of Can., 2002. Mem. Internat. Bar Assn., Can. Bar Assn., Law Soc. Sask. Mem. United Ch. Office: 1500 1874 Scarth St Regina SK Canada S4P 4E9

MACKENZIE, CHARLES ALFRED, lawyer; b. Houston, Sept. 20, 1965; s. Charles Lester and Glenda Faye M.; m. Gretchen Hartberg, Aug. 5, 1989; children: Katherine Ann, James Andrew. BA, Baylor U., 1987, MA, 1988, JD, 1991. Bar: Tex. 1991, 5th Cir. 1994, U.S. Supreme Ct. 1995; bd. cert. civil appellate law Tex. Bd. Legal Specialization. Atty. 10th Ct. Appeals, Waco, Tex., 1991-94; assoc. Haley & Davis, Waco, Tex., 1994—. Grader Tex. Bd. Law Examiners, Waco, 1996-99; lectr. law Baylor U., Waco, 1991-92, 2000, mem. civil appellate law adv. commn. Tex. Bd. Legal Specialization. Recipient Outstanding Young Lawyer award, Waco-McLennan County Young Lawyers Assn., 1999. Mem.: Young Lawyers Assn. (pres. 2000—01), Abner V. McCall Am. Inn of Ct. (sec.-treas. 2000—02), State Bar Tex. (appellate sect. coun. 2001—). Baptist. Avocation: photography. Appellate, General civil litigation. Office: Haley & Davis 510 N Valley Mills Dr Ste 600 Waco TX 76710-6078 Fax: 254-776-6823. E-mail: AMackenzie@HaleyDavis.com.

MACKENZIE, CHARLES RUDD, lawyer; b. Boston, Dec. 19, 1964; s. Alan Eno Mackenzie and Susan Taylor Menges; m. Jessica Stretton, Sept. 2, 2000. BA, Bowdoin Coll., 1987; JD, Western New Eng. Coll., 1993; M of Studies in Environ. Law cum laude, Vt. Law Sch., 1994. Rsch. dir. Senator Chafee Com., Cranston, R.I., 1988; fgn. policy aide U.S. Senator John Chafee, Washington, 1989-90; pvt. practice law Hastings on Hudson, N.Y., 1995—. Bd. dirs. Vols. for Peace Internat. Vol. Svc., Belmont, Vt. Pres. Gitt-Moul Historic Properties, Inc., Hanover, Pa. Mem. N.Y. State Bar Assn., 1995, U.S. Dist. Court (so. and ea. dist. of N.Y. 1995), Westchester County Bar Assn., Yonkers Lawyers Assn., Estate Planning Coun. Westchester, Delta Kappa Epsilon (v.p. chpt. 1985, 86), Yale Club N.Y.C. Office: 230 Park Ave 10th Fl New York NY 10169

MACKENZIE, JANET LYNNE, lawyer; b. Johannesburg, Gauteng, South Africa, Apr. 14, 1965; d. Angus James and Denise Harrison Mackenzie; m. Henri Ludolph Neethling, Oct. 6, 2001. BA, U. Witwatersrand, Johannesburg, 1986; LLB, U. Witwatersrand, 1989, LLM, 2002. Bar: High Ct. South Africa 1992; cert. notary pub. Candidate atty. Van Hulsteyns, Johannesburg, 1989, Cliffe Dekker & Todd Inc., Johannesburg, 1989—91, profl. asst., 1992—93, assoc., 1993—94, dir., 1994—. Mem.: Johannesburg Attys. Assn., Law Soc. No. Provincens. Avocations: literature, gardening, gym. Administrative and regulatory, Communications, Commercial, contracts (including sales of goods; commercial financing). Office: Cliffe Dekker Inc 1 Protea Pl Johannesburg 2010 South Africa

MACKEY, TERRENCE WAYNE, lawyer; b. Denver, Nov. 20, 1942; s. Harold E. Mackey and Dorothy E. (Newville) Brand; m. Catherine Marie Long, Sept. 4, 1966; children: Shawna, Brian, Kristin. AA, Casper (Wyo.) Coll., 1966; BA, U. Wyo., 1968, JD, 1970. Bar: Wyo. 1970, Colo. 1993, U.S. Dist. Ct. Wyo. 1970, U.S. Ct. Appeals (10th cir.) 1970, U.S. Ct. Appeals (9th cir.) 1992, U.S. Supreme Ct. 1973. Mem. firm King & Mackey, Jackson, Wyo., 1970-73, Urbigkit, Mackey & Whitehead, Cheyenne, Wyo., 1973-79; pvt. practice Cheyenne, 1979-82; pres. Terry W. Mackey P.C., Cheyenne, 1982-94, Hickey, Mackey, Evans & Walker, Cheyenne, 1994—. Mem. Drafting Com. Fed. Local Rules, Cheyenne, 1991, Standing Com. Local Rule, Cheyenne, 1992; appellate counsel most significant constl. cases, 1977. Mem. grounds com. Cheyenne Frontier Days, 1986—; mem. coun. Ascension Luth. Ch., Cheyenne, 1989-91; mem. adv. coun. Foster Grandparents, Cheyenne, 1987-89. With USN, 1960-63. Fellow Internat. Soc. Barristers, Am. Coll. Trial Lawyers; mem. ABA, Am. Trial Lawyers Assn. (judge student trial competition 1991), Wyo. State Bar, Wyo. Trial Lawyers (pres. bd. 1977, dir. 1971—), Laramie County Bar. Avocations: hunting, fishing, golf, reading. General civil litigation, Criminal, Personal injury (including property damage). Office: PO Box 467 1712 Carey Ave Cheyenne WY 82001-4420

MACKIE, DAVID LINDSAY, lawyer; b. Eng., Feb. 15, 1946; s. Alastair and Rachel (Goodson) M.; m. Phyllis M. Gershon; children: James, Edward, Bella. MA, Oxford U., 1967. Bar: solicitor 1971; Queen's counsel 1998; accredited mediator Ctr. Dispute Resolution. Assoc. Allen & Overy, London, 1971-75; ptnr., 1975—; head of litigation, 1988—. Recorder Crown Ct., 1989—; dep. High Ct. judge, 1998—; dep. chair Royal Cts. Justice Advice Bur., 1997. Fellow Chartered Inst. Arbitrators; mem. Internat. Bar Assn. (chmn. com. product liability, advtsg. and consumer protection 1987-91). Avocation: climbing. Alternative dispute resolution, Public international. Office: Allen & Overy One New Change London EC4M 9QQ England Fax: 0207-330-9999. E-mail: david.mackie@allenovery.com.

MACKIEWICZ, EDWARD ROBERT, lawyer; b. Jersey City, July 2, 1951; s. Edward John and Irene Helen (Rakowicz) H. BA, Yale U., 1973; JD, Columbia U., 1976. Bar: N.J. 1976, U.S. Dist. Ct. N.J. 1976, N.Y. 1977, U.S. Dist. Ct. (so. and ea. dist.) N.Y. 1977, D.C. 1978, U.S. Dist. Ct. D.C. 1978, U.S. Ct. Appeals (D.C. cir.) 1978, U.S. Ct. Appeals (3d cir.) 1980, U.S. Supreme Ct. 1980, Md. 1984, U.S. Ct. Claims 1984, U.S. Ct. Appeals (4th cir.) 1986, U.S. Dist. Ct. Md. 1990. Assoc. Carter, Ledyard & Milburn, N.Y.C., 1976-77, Covington & Burling, Washington, 1977-82; counsel for civil rights litigation solicitor's office U.S. Dept. Labor, Washington, 1982-83; sr. assoc. Jones, Day, Reavis & Pogue, Washington, 1983-85; gen. counsel Pension Benefit Guaranty Corp., Washington, 1985-87; of counsel Pierson, Ball & Dowd, Washington, 1987-89; ptnr. Reed Smith Shaw & McClay, Washington, 1989; gen. counsel Masters, Mates & Pilots Benefit Plans, Linthicum Heights, Md., 1989-92; of counsel Steptoe & Johnson, L.L.P., Washington, 1992-98, ptnr., 1999—. Mem. adv. coun. Sec. of Labor's ERISA, 1991-93; profl. lectr. in law Nat. Law Ctr., George Washington U., 1993—. Mem. Am. Coun. Young Polit. Leaders (del. to Australia 1985), Univ. Club, Yale Club. Bankruptcy, Labor (including EEOC, Fair Labor Standards Act, labor-management relations, NLRB, OSHA), Pension, profit-sharing, and employee benefits. Home: 3001 Veazey Ter NW Apt 1032 Washington DC 20008-5406 Office: 1330 Connecticut Ave NW Washington DC 20036-1704 E-mail: emackiew@steptoe.com.

MACKINNON, CATHARINE ALICE, lawyer, law educator, legal scholar, writer; d. George E. and Elizabeth V. (Davis) MacKinnon. BA in Govt. magna cum laude with distinction, Smith Coll., 1969; JD, Yale U., 1977, PhD in Polit. Sci., 1987. Vis. prof. Harvard U., Stanford U., Yale U., others, Osgoode Hall, York U., Canada, U. Basel, Switzerland; prof. of law U. Mich., 1990—. Long term vis. prof. U. Chgo., 1997—. Author: Sexual Harassment of Working Women, 1979, Feminism Unmodified, 1987, Toward a Feminist Theory of the State, 1989, Only Words, 1993, Sex Equality, 2001; co-author: In Harm's Way, 1997. Office: U Michigan Law School Ann Arbor MI 48109-1215

MACKO, JOHN, lawyer, farmer; b. Franklin, N.J., Apr. 2, 1947; s. John S. and Dorothy (Kruppa) M.; m. Anna Elin Kjartansson, July 12, 1975; 1 child, John H. BSEE, BS in Mgmt., MIT, 1965-70, MS in Mgmt., 1970; MS in Acctg., JD summa cum laude, Syracuse U., 1978. Bar: N.Y. 1979, Fla. 1979, D.C. 1980. Fin. analyst Xerox Corp., Rochester, N.Y., 1970-72, mkt. planning mgr., 1972-74, fin. mgr., 1974-76; assoc. Harris, Beach, Wilcox, Rubin & Levey, Rochester, 1978-82; ptnr. Githler, Samloff, Rochester, 1982-86, Githler, Samloff, Macko & Githler, Rochester, 1986-87; mng. ptnr. Githler, Macko, Reichert & Clawson, Rochester, 1987-91; owner Barrister Farms, Geneseo, N.Y., 1983—, Macko Apartments, Rochester, 1972—; pvt. practice Rochester, 1992—. Vice-pres., treas bd. Southeast Area Coalition, Rochester, 1978-82; treas. bd. Rochester Housing Coun., 1978-82; chmn. Rochester Sch. Budget Com., 1981, 12th Ward Rep. Com.; scoutmaster Troop 70 and 75 Boy Scouts Am., Geneseo, N.Y., 1991-97, commr. Iroquois Trail Coun., 1997—. Mem. Jaycees (chmn. Xerox chpt.), Order of Coif, Law Rev., Justinian Soc., MIT Club, Beta Alpha Psi. Bankruptcy, Commercial, contracts (including sales of goods; commercial financing), Property, real (including real estate development, water). Home: 42 Second St Geneseo NY 14454-1223 Office: 42 2nd St Geneseo NY 14454-1223

MACLAREN, ROBERT IAN, II, lawyer; b. West Palm Beach, Fla., Aug. 5, 1947; s. Robert Ian and Gertrude Lilly (Carson) MacL.; m. Linda Carl Olson, Dec. 19, 1970; children: Eleonora Olson, Robert Ian III, Carson Hunt, Marylinda Pierce-Mills. BA, U. Fla., 1969, JD, 1972. Assoc. Gunster, Yoakley, Criser, Stewart & Hersey P.A., Palm Beach, Fla., 1973-76; ptnr. Osborne, Hankins & MacLaren, Boca Raton, Fla., 1977—. Adminstrv. asst. to Ho. minority leader Fla. Ho. of Reps., Tallahassee, 1970; bd. dirs. Hospice By The Sea, Inc. Chmn. bd. dirs. Boca Raton Hist. Soc., 1980, 82, YMCA of Boca Raton, Inc., 1981. Served with USMC, 1966-68. Mem. ABA, Fla. Bar Assn., Palm Beach County Bar Assn., South County Bar Assn., Assn. Trial Lawyers Am. Republican. Episcopalian. State civil litigation, Commercial, consumer (including collections, credit), Property, real (including real estate development, water).

MACLAUGHLIN, FRANCIS JOSEPH, lawyer; b. Davenport, Iowa, Oct. 5, 1933; s. Francis Joseph and Sylvia (Boone) MacL.; m. Joan Elizabeth Pfeiffer, Oct. 17, 1959; children: Lisa Ann, Christine Ann, Francis Joseph BA, Yale U., 1955; JD, U. Mich., 1958. Bar: Ill. 1958, Calif. 1963. Assoc. Graham, Califf, Harper & Benson, Moline, Ill., 1958-59, Lillick, McHose & Charles, Los Angeles, 1963-70, ptnr. L.A., 1970-90, White and Case, 1990—. Lt. USN, 1959-63 Mem. ABA, Calif. Bar Assn., Los Angeles County Bar Assn., Maritime Law Assn. U.S. Republican. Banking, General civil litigation, Insurance. Office: White & Case 633 W 5th St Ste 1900 Los Angeles CA 90071-2087

MACLAUGHLIN, HARRY HUNTER, federal judge; b. Breckenridge, Minn., Aug. 9, 1927; s. Harry Hunter and Grace (Swank) MacL.; m. Mary Jean Shaffer, June 25, 1958; children: David, Douglas. BBA with distinction, U. Minn., 1949, JD, 1956. Bar: Minn. 1956. Law clk. to justice Minn. Supreme Ct.; ptnr. MacLaughlin & Mondale, MacLaughlin & Harstad, Mpls., 1956-72; assoc. justice Minn. Supreme Ct., 1972-77; U.S. sr. dist. judge Dist. of Minn., Mpls., 1977—. Part-time instr. William Mitchell Coll. Law, St. Paul, 1958-63; lectr. U. Minn. Law Sch., 1973-86; mem. 8th Cir. Jud. Council, 1981-83. Bd. editors: Minn. Law Rev, 1954-55. Mem. Mpls. Charter Commn., 1967-72, Minn. State Coll. Bd., 1971-72, Minn. Jud. Council, 1972; mem. nat. adv. council Small Bus. Adminstrn., 1967-69. Served with USNR, 1945-46. Recipient U. Minn. Outstanding Achievement award, 1995; named Best Fed. Dist. Ct. Judge in 8th Cir., Am. Lawyer mag., 1983. Mem. ABA, Minn. Bar Assn., Hennepin County Bar Assn., Beta Gamma Sigma, Phi Delta Phi. Congregationalist. Office: US Dist Ct 8E US Courthouse 300 S Fourth St Minneapolis MN 55415*

MACLAY, DONALD MERLE, retired lawyer; b. Belleville, Pa., Feb. 16, 1934; s. Robert Barr and Grace Virginia (Royer) M.; m. Nancy Margaret Hixenbaugh, Sept. 13, 1958; children: Susan Jo (dec.), Timothy Dean. AB magna cum laude, Grove City Coll., 1956; LLB, U. Pa., 1961. Bar: D.C. 1968, Pa. 1970. Commd. fgn. svc. officer U.S. Dept. State, 1961; assigned Am. embassy, Cotonou, Dahomey (Benin), 1962-64, Am. Consulate Gen., Frankfurt, Fed. Republic Germany, 1964-66, U.S. Dept. State, Washington, 1966-69; dir. courses of study Am. Law Inst.-ABA Com. on Continuing Profl. Edn., Phila., 1969-87, dep. exec. dir., 1987-99, ret., 1999. Served with U.S. Army, 1956-58. Mem. Am. Law Inst. Democrat. Presbyterian. Home: 936 Church Rd Springfield PA 19064-3935

MACLEAN, ANDREW BISHOP, lawyer; b. Portland, Maine, Mar. 9, 1962; s. Philip Eugene and Barbara Ann MacLean; m. Erin Cooperrider, Dec. 31, 1988 (div. Dec. 1995); m. Michele Ann Robbins, July 24, 1999; children: Hannah Ryan Fossett, Cameron Burr. AB, Duke U., 1984; JD, U. Maine, Portland, 1991. Bar: Maine 1991, U.S. Dist. Ct. Maine 1991, Ariz. 1992, U.S. Dist. Ct. Ariz. 1993. Atty. Law Offices James A. Hopkinson, Portland, Maine, 1991—92; asst. legal counsel Office of the Gov., State of Maine, Augusta, 1992—94; atty. Law Offices Doyle & Nelson, Augusta, 1994—96; sr. atty. Blue Cross Blue Shield of Maine, South Portland, 1996—98; gen. counsel, divsn. govtl. affairs Maine Med. Assn., Manchester, 1999—. Dir. Am. Cancer Soc., New Eng. Divsn., Inc., Framingham, Mass., 2001—, Cerebral Palsy Assn. Greater Portland, Inc., Portland, Maine, 1995—. Capt. USMC, 1984—88, Hawaii. Mem.: Am. Soc. Assn. Execs., State Bar of Ariz., Main State Bar Assn. Republican. Episcopalian. Avocations: running, skiing, golf, motorcycling, cooking. Administrative and regulatory, Health. Home: 72 Kingsbury St Gardiner ME 04343 Office: Maine Med Assn 30 Association Dr Manchester ME 04351

MACLEAN, BABCOCK, lawyer; b. N.Y.C., Jan. 26, 1946; s. Charles Chalmers and Lee Selden (Howe) MacL.; m. Cynthia Gannon, Feb. 15, 1983. BA, Yale U., 1967; MA, Columbia U., 1970; JD, Case Western Res. U., 1975; LLM in Taxation, NYU, 1987. Bar: Ohio 1975, N.Y. 1983. Assoc. Hadley, Matia, Mills & MacLean, Cleve., 1976-77, mem., 1977-83; tax editor Rsch. Inst. Am., N.Y.C., 1983-85; assoc. Robinson Brog, N.Y.C., 1985-86, mem., 1987—. Adj. asst. prof. taxation Pace U., N.Y.C., 1983-84; adv. bd. Rsch. Inst. Am., 1992-97. Mem. ABA (sect. taxation), N.Y. State Bar Assn. (sect. taxation), Assn. Bar City N.Y., Yale Club, St. Anthony Club, N.Y. Yacht Club, Seawanhaka Corinthian Yacht Club, St. Andrew's Soc. N.Y., Pilgrims of the U.S., Soc. for Preservation of L.I. Antiquities (trustee 2003—). Republican. Episcopalian. Corporate taxation, Taxation, general, Personal income taxation. Home: 77 W 55th St New York NY 10019-4910 Office: Robinson Brog 1345 Avenue Of The Americas New York NY 10105-0144

MACLEAN, JOHN RONALD, lawyer; b. Pueblo, Colo., Jan. 19, 1938; s. John Ronald and Mary Victoria (Curlin) MacL.; m. Carol Jean Turner, Aug. 18, 1962; children— Leslie Carol, John Ronald. Student, U. Okla., 1956; BS, U.S. Mil. Acad., 1961; JD, Vanderbilt U., 1967. Bar: Tex. 1967; cert. in personal injury trial law Tex. Bd. Legal Splzn. Practicing atty. Turner & MacLean, Cleburne, Tex., 1967-68; county atty. Johnson County, Tex., 1968-76; dist. atty. 18th Jud. Dist. Tex., 1976-84; dist. judge 249th Jud. Dist. Tex., 1984-91; pvt. practice MacLean & Boulware, 1992—. Pres. Johnson County United Fund, 1976. Served with AUS, 1961-64. Fellow Tex. Bar Found.; mem. Tex. Bar Assn., Johnson County Bar Assn. (pres. 1969), Am. Bd. Trial Advocates (past nat. dir.), Tex. Trial Lawyers Assn., Vanderbilt U. Law Sch. Bar Assn. (past pres.), Elks. Democrat. Methodist. Criminal, Personal injury (including property damage), Workers' compensation. Home: 1216 W Westhill Dr Cleburne TX 76033-6021 Office: 11 N Main St Cleburne TX 76033-5543

MACLEAN, MERRILEE ANN, lawyer; b. Seattle, Sept. 20, 1952; d. Andrew Kenyon and Cornelia Marie (Mohn) MacL. BS magna cum laude, Lewis and Clark Coll., 1974; JD, U. Calif., San Francisco, 1982. Bar: Wash. 1982, U.S. Dist. Ct. (we. dist.) Wash. 1982, U.S. Dist. Ct. (ea. dist.) Wash. 1989, Hawaii 1990. Assoc. Shidler, McBroom, Gates & Lucas, Seattle, 1982-89; of counsel Bullivant, Houser, Bailey, Pendergrass & Hoffman, Seattle, 1989-91; ptnr. Barnett MacLean, Seattle, 1991-96; mem. BDL MacLean, 1997-2000. Mem. exec. com. Ninth Cir. Jud. Conf., 2002—. Bd. dirs., sec. Bellevue (Wash.) Philharm. Orch., 1985-87; del., mem. exec. com. 48th Dist. Dem. Com., Redmond, Wash., 1984-87; mem. nat. bd. alumni Lewis and Clark Coll., Portland, Oreg., pres., 1994-96. Mem. Fed.

Bar Assn. Western Dist. Wash. (chmn. bankruptcy sect. 1994-96, pres. 1999-2000), Comml. Law League, Am. Bankruptcy Inst., Turnaround Mgmt. Assn. (bd. dirs. 1997-99), Nat. Assn. Credit Mgmt., Nat. Assn. Bankruptcy Trustees. Bankruptcy, Commercial, contracts (including sales of goods; commercial financing). Office: MacLean Reif Nuxoll PLLC 1601 1st Ave # 860 Seattle WA 98101-1524

MACLEOD, JOHN AMEND, lawyer; b. Manila, June 5, 1942; s. Anthony Macaulay and Dorothy Lillian (Amend) M.; m. Ann Klee; children: Kerry, Jack. BBA, U. Notre Dame, 1963, JD, 1969. Bar: D.C. 1969, U.S. Supreme Ct. 1980. Assoc. Jones, Day, Reavis & Pogue, Washington, 1969-73, ptnr., 1974-79, Crowell & Moring, Washington, 1979—. Mem. mgmt. com., 1979-82, 83-86, 91-94, 99-2000, chmn., 1984-85, 93-94. mem. mgmt. bd. and exec. com., 2000—, chmn. of the firm, 2000—. Editor-in-chief Notre Dame Law Rev., 1968-69; contbr. articles to profl. jours. Trustee Energy Mineral and Law Found., 1979—; bd. dirs. St. Francis Ctr., 1982—91; C&M Internat., 1991—94, 1999—. Served to lt. U.S. Army, 1963—65. Recipient disting. mining lawyer award Nat. Mining Assn., 1995, forest industry victory of yr. award Am. Forest and Paper Assn., 1994. Mem. ABA, D.C. Bar Assn., Notre Dame Law Assn. (dir., exec. bd.), Ptnrs. Leadership Forum, Metro. Club (Washington). Administrative and regulatory, Environmental, Natural resources. Home: 4040 Swartz Rd Maurertown VA 22644-2320 Office: Crowell & Moring 1000 Pennsylvania Ave NW Washington DC 20004-2595

MACLIN, ALAN HALL, lawyer; b. DuQuoin, Ill., Dec. 22, 1949; s. John E. and Nora (Hall) M.; m. Joan Davidson (div. Dec. 1981); children: Molly, Tess, Anne; m. Jeanne Sittlow, Nov. 17, 1984. BA magna cum laude, Vanderbilt U., 1971; JD, U. Chgo., 1974. Bar: Minn. 1974, U.S. Dist. Ct. Minn. 1974, U.S. Ct. Appeals (8th cir.) 1974, U.S. Ct. Appeals (5th cir.) 1975. U.S. Supreme Ct. 1978. Asst. atty. gen. Minn. Atty. Gen., St. Paul, 1974-80; chief anti-trust divsn. Briggs & Morgan, St. Paul, 1980—, mem. bd. dirs., 1993-96. Mem. Minn. State Bar Assn. (treas. anti-trust sect. 1978-80, 96-98, chair 1998—), Ramsey County Bar Assn. (sec. jud. com. 1980-82), Phi Beta Kappa. Unitarian Universalist. Antitrust, Federal civil litigation, Insurance. Office: Briggs & Morgan 2200 1st St N Saint Paul MN 55109-3210 E-mail: amaclin@briggs.com.

MACMILLAN, HOKE, former state attorney general; m. Becky Klemt; children: Ryan Klemt, Christopher Klemt. BA, U. Wyo., 1967, JD, 1970. Bar: Wyo., Colo., Nebr., U.S. Ct. Appeals (10th cir.), U.S. Ct. Mil. Appeals, U.S. Supreme Ct. Capt. U.S. Army JAG, 1970—74; mem. Pence and Millett, Laramie, Wyo., 1974—2001, sr. ptnr., 1982—2001; atty. gen. State of Wyo., 2001—02. Fellow: Am. Bar Found.; mem.: Albany County Bar Assn., Nebr. State Bar, Wyo. State Bar (pres. 1996—97).

MACMURREN, HAROLD HENRY, JR., psychologist, lawyer; b. Jersey City, Sept. 18, 1942; s. Harold Sr. and Evelyn (Almone) MacM.; m. Margaret Bartro, Nov. 21, 1970. BA, William Paterson Coll., Wayne, N.J., 1965; MA, Jersey City Coll., 1973; EdD, St. Johns U., N.Y.C., 1985; JD, Rutgers U., 1989. Cert. secondary tchr., N.J.; Bar: N.J. 1989. Instr. Wanaque (N.J.) Bd. Edn., 1965-66, cons. psychologist, 1983-84; instr. Elmwood Park (N.J.) Bd. Edn., 1967-70; coll. faculty mem., psychologist Assoc. Clinic, Jersey City, 1971-72; cons. psychologist Rockaway (N.J.) Bd. Edn., 1972-83; intern lawyer Environ. Law Clinic, Newark, N.J., 1988-89; cons. psychologist Pequannock (N.J.) Bd. Edn., 1984—; pvt. practice law, 2000—. Coord. child study team Sandyston Walpack Sch. Sys.; adj. prof. William Paterson U.; spkr., writer in field. Mem. ABA, NEA, N.J. Edn. Assn., N.J. Psychologist Assn., N.J. Bar Assn., Sierra Club, Phi Delta Kappa. Avocations: reading, travel, skiing, hiking. Home: 4 Systema Pl Sussex NJ 07461-2833

MACNAUGHTON, ANN L. lawyer; b. Lansing, Mich., Sept. 25, 1948; d. John Frederick and Elizabeth Ann (Hackett) MacNaughton. BA, U. Houston, 1972, JD, 1976, MBA, 1980. Bar: Tex. 1977, Colo. 1985. Atty. Aminoil U.S.A., Inc., Houston, 1977-79; assoc. Sowell, Ogg & Hinton, Houston, 1980-81; counsel Superior Oil Co. and Mobil Oil Corp., Houston, Tex., Denver and Richmond, Va., 1981-88; sr. assoc. Vinson & Elkins, Houston, 1988-92; prin. Law Offices of Ann L. MacNaughton, Houston, 1992—; pres. Paragon Dispute Resolution, Inc., Houston, 1993—; v.p., gen. counsel Sustainable Resolutions, Inc., Houston, 2001—; dir. dispute resolution strategies Arthur Andersen LLP, Houston, 1998—2003. Cons. Mobil Oil Corp., Dallas, 1992-98, State of Alaska, Juneau, 1994-95, Exxon USA, 1995-98, UN and Kingdom of Nepal, 2002—. Sr. editor: Environmental Dispute Resolution: An Anthology of Practical Solutions, 2002. Bd. dirs. Houston Repertory Theatre, 1994-95, Cmty. Ptnrs., 1988-91, Tex. Accts. and Lawyers for the Arts, 1996—, U. Houston Law Alumni, 1989-93, U. Houston Alumni Orgn., 1980-84, 90-94, U. Houston Exec. MBA Alumni Orgn., 1999-2001. Mem. ABA (mem. standing com. on environ. law, co-chair subcom. litig. sect. ADR subcom. of environ. com. 1994—, chair internat. law sect., cross-cultural dispute resolution task force 1997—, mem. coun. chair law practice mgmt. sect. 1998—, LPMS mediation task force 1996-98, vice chair LPMS mgmt. divsn. 1993-95, 99—, vice chair ADR coordinating group on ABA sect. on energy, environment and resources), State Bar of Tex. (chair environ. law sect. ADR task force 1993—, chair corp. counsel sect. 1996-97), mem. coun. ADR sect., 2001-, chair MDP/MJP comm., 2001-. Avocations: walking, cooking, dancing, writing. Office: 4545 Bissonet Ste 200 Houston TX 77056

MACNEIL, IAN RODERICK, lawyer, educator; b. N.Y.C., June 20, 1929; s. Robert Lister and Kathleen Gertrude (Metcalf) Macneil; m. Nancy Carol Wilson, Mar. 29, 1952; children: Roderick, Jennifer, Duncan (dec.), Andrew. BA magna cum laude, U. Vt., 1950; LLB magna cum laude, Harvard U., 1955. Bar: N.H. 1956-02. Law clk. Hon. Peter Woodbury, 1955-56; asso. Sulloway Hollis Godfrey & Soden, Concord, N.H., 1956-59; mem. faculty Cornell U. Law Sch., Ithaca, N.Y., 1959-72, 74-80, Ingersoll prof. law, 1976-80; Wigmore prof. law Northwestern U. Sch. Law, Chgo., 1980-99, prof. emeritus, 1999—. Vis. prof. U. East Africa, 1965-67, Duke U., 1971-72; prof. law, mem. Inst. Advanced Studies, U. Va., 1972-74; vis. fellow Centre for Socio-legal Studies and Wolfson Coll., Oxford U., 1979; hon. vis. fellow faculty law U. Edinburgh, 1979, 87; Rosenthal lectr. Northwestern U. Sch. Law, 1979; Braucher vis. prof. Harvard U., 1988-89. Author: Bankruptcy Law in East Africa, 1966, Contracts: Exchange Transactions and Relations, 3d edit., with Paul J. Gudel, 2001. The New Social Contract, 1980, American Arbitration Law: Reformation Nationalization Internationalization, 1992; co-author: Federal Arbitration Law, 1994. Served with U.S. Army, 1951-53. Guggenheim fellow, 1978-79. Fellow Royal Soc. Antiquaries (Scotland); mem. ABA, Am. Law Inst., Am. Acad. Arts and Scis., Standing Coun. Scottish Chiefs, Scottish Soc. No. Studies, The Scottish Medievalists. Home: 95/6 Grange Loan Edinburgh EH9 2ED Scotland

MACRAE, CAMERON FARQUHAR, III, lawyer; b. N.Y.C., Mar. 21, 1942; s. Cameron F. and Jane B. (Miller) MacR.; m. Ann Wooster Bedell, Nov. 30, 1974; children: Catherine Fairfax, Ann Cameron. AB, Princeton U., 1963; LLB, Yale U., 1966. Bar: N.Y. 1966, D.C. 1967, U.S. Dist. Ct. (so. dist.) N.Y. 1975. Atty.-advisor Office of Gen. Counsel to Sec. Air Force, Washington, 1966-69; assoc. Davis, Polk & Wardell, N.Y.C., 1970-72; dep. supt. and counsel N.Y. State Banking Dept., N.Y.C., 1972-74; sr. ptnr. LeBeouf, Lamb, Greene & MacRae, N.Y.C., 1975—. Dir. Nat. Integrity Life Ins. Co., 2000—. Note and comment editor Yale Law Jour., 1965-66. Trustee, sec. St. Andrew's Dune Ch., 1982—; hon. chmn. Clear Pool Inc., 1990-94. Capt. USAF, 1966-69. Mem. Assn. of Bar of City of N.Y. (past mem. securities regulation com., banking law com.), D.C. Bar Assn., Racquet and Tennis Club, Union Club (N.Y.C.), Meadow Club (v.p., bd. govs.), Bathing Corp. Southampton, Shinnecock Hills Golf Club (Southampton), Cottage Club (Princeton, N.J.), Jupiter Island Club. Republican. Episcopalian. Banking, Mergers and acquisitions, Securities. Office: LeBoeuf Lamb Greene & MacRae 125 W 55th St New York NY 10019-5369 E-mail: cfmacrae@llgm.com.

MACRIS, MICHAEL, lawyer; b. Jackson Heights, N.Y., July 12, 1949; Student, Cornell U.; BA with distinction, Stanford U., 1971; JD, Columbia U., 1974. Bar: N.Y. 1975, Conn. 1976. Mem. Cahill Gordon & Reindel, N.Y.C. Bd. editors Columbia Law Rev., 1973-74; co-editor ERISA & Benefits Law Jour., 1992-99. Harlan Fiske Stone scholar. Fellow Am. Coll. Employee Benefits Counsel (charter); mem. ABA (chmn. com. on fiduciary responsibility, real property, probate and trust law sect. 1993—), Phi Beta Kappa. Pension, profit-sharing, and employee benefits. Office: Cahill Gordon & Reindel 80 Pine St Fl 19 New York NY 10005-1790

MACY, JOHN PATRICK, lawyer; b. Menomonee Falls, Wis., June 26, 1955; s. Leland Francis and Joan Marie (LaValle) M. BA, Carroll Coll., 1977; JD, Marquette U., 1980. Bar: Wis. 1980, U.S. Dist. Ct. (we. and ea. dists.) Wis. 1980, U. S. Ct. Appeals (7th cir.) 1980. Assoc. Hippenmeyer Reilly Arenz Molter Bode & Gross, Waukesha, Wis., 1980-83; ptnr. Arenz Molter Macy & Riffle, S.C., Waukesha, 1983--. Lectr. in field. Mem. ABA, Waukesha County Bar Assn. (chair 1995-96). Republican. Roman Catholic. Land use and zoning (including planning), Municipal (including bonds), State and local taxation. Home: 4839 Hewitts Point Rd Oconomowoc WI 53066-3320 Office: Arenz Molter Macy & Riffle SC 720 N East Ave Waukesha WI 53186-4800

MADDEN, EDWARD GEORGE, JR., lawyer; b. Newark, Feb. 21, 1924; s. Edward and Catherine (Mahon) M.; m. Mary B. Haveron, June 20, 1959; children: Maurica, Margaret, Thomas, Mary, Jane. BS, St. Peter's Coll., 1950; JD, U. Mich., 1953. Bar: N.J. 1954, U.S. Dist. Ct. N.J. 1954, U.S. Ct. Appeals (3d cir.) 1981, U.S. Supreme Ct. 1959. Assoc. McCarter & English, Newark, 1954-56, Donohue & Donohue, Nutley, N.J., 1956-61; ptnr. Troast, Mattson & Madden, Newark, 1961-65, Mattson & Madden, Newark, 1965—. Mem. N.J. State Legislature, 1960-62. With USN 1943-46. Fellow Am. Bar Found.; mem. ABA, N.J. Bar Assn. (trustee, treas. 1972-78), Essex County Bar Assn. (trustee 1971-75), Internat. Assn. Def. Counsel, Transp. Lawyers Assn. Democrat. Roman Catholic. State civil litigation, Insurance, Transportation. Office: 33 Bleeker St Millburn NJ 07041-1414

MADDEN, JEROME ANTHONY, lawyer; b. Memphis, Aug. 24, 1948; s. Bernard Clark and Virginia Ann (Golas) M.; m. Cynthia S. Madden, June 27, 1992; 1 child, Clark John. BA, The Franciscan U. Steubenville, Ohio, 1971; JD summa cum laude, U. Dayton, 1978. Bar: Ohio 1978, D.C. 1979, U.S. Dist. Ct. D.C. 1979, U.S. Ct. Appeals (D.C. cir.) 1980, U.S. Ct. Claims 1984, U.S. Ct. Appeals (Fed. cir.) 1984, U.S. Supreme Ct. 1984, U.S. Ct. Appeals (7th and 11th cirs.) 1987, U.S. Ct. Appeals (4th and 5th cirs.) 1988, U.S. Ct. Appeals (9th cir.) 1991, U.S. Ct. Appeals (2d & 10th cirs.) 1992, U.S. Ct. Appeals (1st cir.) 1993. Law clk. to chief justices O'Neill and Leach Ohio Supreme Ct., Columbus, 1978-79; assoc. Cadwalader, Wickersham & Taft, Washington, 1979-85; sr. trial counsel U.S. Dept. Justice, Washington, 1985-91; counsel, then acting sr. counsel, then supervisory counsel FDIC Appellate Litigation Sect., Comml. Litigation Unit, Washington, 1991-98; trial atty. U.S. Dept. Justice, Comml. Litigation Br., Washington, 1998—. Adj. prof. George Washington U. Sch. Law, Washington, 2000—. Editor-in-chief U. Dayton Law Rev., 1977-78. Served with USMCR, 1970-76. Mem. D.C. Bar Assn. Roman Catholic. Avocations: golf, senior baseball. Home: 1502 Powells Tavern Pl Herndon VA 20170-2831 Office: US Dept of Justice 1100 L St NW Washington DC 20005-4035 E-mail: Jerome.Madden@usdoj.gov.

MADDEN, JOHN J. lawyer; b. N.Y.C., May 27, 1946; s. John L. and Bertha M. (Antonades) M.; m. Mary A. O'Neill, June 19, 1976; children: Elisabeth, Samuel. BA, U. Pa., 1968; JD, Fordham U., 1975. Bar: N.Y. 1976, U.S. Dist. Ct. (so. dist.) N.Y. 1976; avocat a la cour de Paris 1994. Assoc. Shearman & Sterling, N.Y.C., 1975-83, ptnr., 1983—, mng. ptnr. European offices Paris, 1991-95; head Shearman & Sterling Mergers and Acquisitions Group, 1986—91, 1995—2001, also mem. firm's policy com. Trustee St. David's Sch., N.Y.C., 1981-91. Served to 1st lt. U.S. Army, 1969-71, Vietnam. Mem. ABA, N.Y. Bar Assn., Assn. of Bar of City of N.Y., Internat. Bar Assn., Cercle de l'Union Interalliee (Paris). Corporate, general, Mergers and acquisitions, Securities. E-mail: jmadden@shearman.com.

MADDEN, MURDAUGH STUART, lawyer; b. Morgantown, W.Va., Feb. 26, 1922; s. Joseph Warren and Margaret (Liddell) M.; m. Constance Viens McKenna, May 12, 1999; children by previous marriage: Liddell Louise, Murdaugh Stuart Jr., Michael Mann. Student, Oberlin Coll., 1939-40; BA, George Washington U., 1942; JD, Harvard U., 1948. Bar: D.C. 1948, Va. 1948, U.S. Supreme Ct. 1953. Asst. counsel Bur. Aero., Washington, 1948-50; sole practice Washington, 1950-61, 71—; sr. ptnr. Shaw, Pittman, Potts, Trowbridge & Madden, Washington, 1961-71. Sr. counsel Humane Soc. U.S., Atlantic Devel. Co. and related corps. Author: (with Sherman L. Cohn) The Legal Status and Problems of the American Abroad, 1966. Trustee Inst. for Study Nat. Behavior, Princeton, N.J., Friends of India Com., Washington; pres. World Fedn. for Protection Animals, The Netherlands; v.p. World Soc. forProtection Animals, London. With USAAF, 1942-45, ETO. Mem. ABA (past chmn. internat. and comparative law com. internat. transp., chmn. subcom. on charitable orgns. internat. law sect. 1985—), D.C. Bar Assn., (past dir., past chmn. com. bar ethics), Va. Bar Assn., The Barristers, Am. Soc. Internat. Law, Harvard Law Sch. Assn., Oberlin Alumni Assn., Metropolitan Club, Harvard Club N.Y., Internat. Lawn Tennis Club U.S., Chevy Chase Club, Phi Sigma Kappa. Episcopalian. Home: 2530 Queen Annes Ln NW Washington DC 20037-2148 Office: 2100 L St NW Washington DC 20037-1525

MADDEN, PALMER BROWN, lawyer; b. Milw., Sept. 19, 1945; m. Susan L. Paulus, Mar. 31, 1984. BA, Stanford U., 1968; JD, U. Calif., Berkeley, 1973. Bar: Calif. 1973, U.S. Dist. Ct. (no. dist.) Calif. 1973, U.S. Supreme Ct. 1982. Ptnr. McCutchen, Doyle Brown & Enersen, Walnut Creek, 1985-98; prin. ADR Svcs., Alamo, Calif., 1999—. Pres. State Bar Bd. Govs., 2000-2001. Chair bd. govs. Continuing Edn. of the Bar, 1997; judge pro tem Contra Costa Superior Ct., 1991-98; pres. Contra Costa Coun., 1995, Kennedy-King Found., 1994; bd. dirs. Episcopal Homes Found., 2001. Mem. Contra Costa County Bar Assn. (pres. 1996-97). Democrat. Episcopalian. General civil litigation. Office: ADR Svcs 3000 Danville Blvd # 543 Alamo CA 94507

MADDEN, PAUL ROBERT, lawyer, director; b. St. Paul, Nov. 13, 1926; s. Ray Joseph and Margaret (Meyer) Madden; m. Rosemary R. Sorel, Aug. 7, 1974; children: Margaret Jane, James Patrick, Derek R. Sorel, Lisa T. Schoutsen. Student, St. Thomas Coll., 1944; AB, U. Minn., 1948; JD, Georgetown U., 1951. Bar: Ariz. 1957, Minn. 1951, D.C. 1951. Assoc. Hamilton & Hamilton, Washington, 1951-55; legal asst. to commr. SEC, Washington, 1955-56; assoc. Lewis and Roca, Phoenix, 1957-59, ptnr., 1959-90, Beus, Gilbert & Morrill, Phoenix, 1991-94, Chapman and Cutler, Phoenix, 1994-97; of counsel Gallagher & Kennedy, Phoenix, 1997—. Mem. nat. bd. visitors U. Ariz. Law Sch.; mem. adv. bd. Cath. Cmty. Found., Cath. Social Svcs. No. Ariz., 2002—; bd. dirs. Ind. Devel. Authority of City of Prescott, 2002—, Yavapai Coll. Dist. Governing Bd., Prescott, 2003—, Found. Jr. Achievement Ctr. Ariz., Phoenix, St. Joseph the Worker, Phoenix, 1984—, Prescott People Who Care, 2001—, Hidden Valley Homeowners Assn., Prescott, 2003—; past bd. dirs., past chmn. Mesa Air Group, Inc., Camelback Charitable Trust, Found. for Sr. Living; past bd. dirs. The Samaritan Found., Phoenix, Ariz. Club, Phoenix, 1990—93; past bd. dirs., vice chmn. Ctrl. Ariz. chpt. ARC; past bd. dirs., past pres. Jr. Achievement Ctrl. Ariz., Inc.; bd. visitors Embry Riddle Aero. U., Prescott, 2002—; Prescott Ambs., 2002—; nat. co-chmn. Youth for Eisenhower, 1951—52; sec. Minn. Fedn. Coll. Rep. Clubs, 1947—48; chmn. 4th dist. Minn. Young Rep. Club, 1948; mem. Ariz. Rep. Com., 1960—62. Served with USNR, 1946—48. Mem. ABA, Ariz. Bar Assn., Maricopa County Bar Assn., Yauapai County Bar Assn., The Barristers Club (Washington), Phi Delta Phi. Corporate, general, Insurance, Securities. Home: 1565 Range Rd Prescott AZ 86303 Office: Gallagher & Kennedy PA 101 E Gurley Ste 214 Prescott AZ 86301 Office Fax: 928-445-5804. E-mail: prm@gknet.com.

MADDEN, WALES HENDRIX, JR., lawyer, director; b. Amarillo, Tex., Sept. 1, 1927; s. Wales Hendrix and Kathryn (Nash) M.; m. Alma Faye Cowden, Nov. 8, 1952; children: Wales Hendrix III, Straughn. BA, U. Tex., 1950, LL.B., 1952. Bar: Tex. 1952. Practiced in Amarillo. Mem. Tex. Constnl. Revision Commn., 1973. Mem. Tex. Coll. and Univ. System Coord. Bd., 1964—69, Amarillo Area Found.; Cal Farley's Boys Ranch; Pres.'s Export Coun., 1981; mem. Select Com. Higher Edn., 1985, 1987; chmn. SWST Regional Panel, Pres.'s Commn. on White House Fellowships, 1989—90, Tex. Water Devel. Bd., 2002; mem. Gov.'s Com. on Ad Valorem Taxes, 1996; bd. regents Amarillo Coll., 1958—59, U. Tex., 1959—65; trustee Trinity U., San Antonio; chmn. bd. Internat. Food and Agrl. Devel., 1990—94. Served with USNR. Named Outstanding Man of Amarillo, 1972; Disting. Alumnus U. Tex., 1979, U. Tex. Law Sch., 1986. Mem. ABA, Amarillo Bar Assn. (pres. 1956), Tex. Philos. Soc., Amarillo C. of C. (pres. 1968), State Bar Tex., State Jr. Bar Tex. (pres. 1956), Friar Soc., Phi Alpha Delta, Phi Delta Theta, Phi Eta Sigma, Pi Sigma Alpha. Presbyterian (elder). Home and Office: PO Box 15288 Amarillo TX 79105-5288

MADDOX, ALVA HUGH, retired state supreme court justice; b. Andalusia, Ala., Apr. 17, 1930; s. Christopher Columbus and Audie Lodella Maddox; m. Virginia Roberts, June 14, 1958; children: Robert Hugh, Jane Maddox. AB in Journalism, U. Ala., Tuscaloosa, 1952, JD, 1957. Bar: Ala. 1957. Law clk. to Judge Aubrey Cates, Ala. Ct. Appeals, Montgomery, 1957-58; field examiner Chief Atty.'s Office, VA, Montgomery, 1958-59; law clk. to Judge Frank M. Johnson, U.S. Dist. Ct., Montgomery, 1959-61; pvt. practice Montgomery, 1961-65; cir. judge, spl. cir. judge Montgomery Cir. Ct., 1963, asst. dist. atty., 1964; legal advisor to govs. including George C. Wallace, Lurleen B. Wallace, Albert P. Brewer, State of Ala., Montgomery, 1965-69; assoc. justice Supreme Ct. Ala., Montgomery, 1969-2001; ret., 2001. Author: Alabama Rules of Criminal Procedure, 1991, supplements, 1992—. Founder youth jud. program YMCA, Montgomery, 1979, also mem. metro. bd. dirs. 2d lt. USAF, 1952-54, col. USAF Res. ret. Recipient Man of Yr. award YMCA, 1988, Disting. Program Svc. award, 1989, Srs. of Achievement award Montgomery Coun. on Aging, 1999. Mem. ABA, Ala. Bar Assn. (Jud. award of merit 1997), Inst. Jud. Adminstrn., Christian Legal Soc. (bd. dirs.), Federalist Soc. (bd. dirs.), Hugh Maddox Inn of Ct. Montgomery (charter, founding mem.), Kiwanis (bd. dirs. Montgomery), Am. Inns of Ct. (trustee), Order of Samaritan/U. Ala. Law Sch. Baptist. Office: Supreme Ct Ala 300 Dexter Ave Montgomery AL 36104-3741

MADERER, WILLIAM F. lawyer; b. N.Y.C., Apr. 16, 1947; s. Paul S. and Miriam (Flexner) M.; m. Marlene D. Richer, Dec. 28, 1969; children: Jill, Paige. AB, Washington U., St. Louis, 1969; JD, N.Y. U., 1973. Bar: N.Y. 1973, N.J. 1977, U.S. Ct. Appeals (2d cir.) 1974, U.S. Ct. Appeals (3rd cir.) 1977, U.S. Supreme Ct. 1985. Assoc. Weil, Gotshal & Manges, N.Y.C., 1973-74; asst. U.S. atty. U.S. Atty.'s Office, Newark, 1974-80, chief spl. prosecutions div., 1978-80; ptnr. Saiber Schlesinger Satz & Goldstein LLC, Newark, 1980—. Federal civil litigation, General civil litigation, Criminal. Office: Saiber Schlesinger Satz & Goldstein LLC 1 Gateway Ctr Ste 1300 Newark NJ 07102-5315

MADIAN, FERRY PAULIANSYAH, lawyer; b. Hong Kong, China, Dec. 13, 1962; m. Henny Pingkan Matindas, May 23, 1994; children: Rosy Karina, Reza Aldo, Rico Dharma. LLM, U. Indonesia, Jakarta, 1985, U. Wash., 1993. Cert.: Jakarta Dist. Cts. and Ct. Appeals 1998. Assoc. Ali Budiardjo, Nugroho, Reksodiputro, Jakarta, 1986—94, ptnr., 1994—99; mng. ptnr. Ali Budiardjo, Nugroho, Reksodiputro (Singapore Office), Singapore, 1999—. Vis. lawyer Loeff & Van de Ploeg, Amsterdam, 1992; co-founder, sec. gen. Indonesian Receivers and Adminstrs. Assn., Jakarta, 1998—2002. Mem.: Indonesian Receivers and Adminstrs. Assn., Indonesian Legal Cons. Capital Market Assn., Indonesian Legal Cons. Assn. Finance, Corporate, general, Mergers and acquisitions. Office: Ali Budiardjo Nugroho Reksodiputro Jakarta Jalan Jenderal Sudirman Kav 58 Jakarta 12190 Indonesia also: Ocean Bldg # 11-04 10 Collyer Quay Singapore 049315 China Office Fax: 62.21-250.5121. E-mail: fmadian@abnrlaw.com.

MADIGAN, LISA, state attorney general; Asst. dean adult, continuing edn. Wilbur Wright Coll.; mem. Ill. Senate, Springfield, 1999—, mem. appropriations, local govt. coms.; atty. gen. State of Ill., 2003—. Bd. dirs. AIDS Living Rememberance Com. Mem. Ill. Bar Assn., Women's Bar Assn. Ill., Chgo. Bar Assn. Democrat. Office: Atty Gen James R Thompson Ctr 100 W Randolph St Chicago IL 60601*

MADISON, JAMES RAYMOND, lawyer; b. White Plains, N.Y., Apr. 27, 1931; s. Raymond S. and Katherine (Sherwin) M.; m. Mary Massey, Sept. 19, 1953; children: Michael, Matthew, Molly. BS, Stanford U., 1953, LLB, 1959. Bar: Calif. 1960, U.S. Dist. Ct. (no. dist.) Calif. 1960, U.S. Ct. Appeals (9th cir.) 1960, U.S. Dist. Ct. (ctrl. dist.) Calif. 1970, U.S. Supreme Ct. 1973, U.S. Dist. Ct. (ea. dist.) Calif. 1981, U.S. Dist. Ct. (so. dist.) Calif. 1988. Assoc. Orrick, Herrington & Sutcliffe, San Francisco, 1959-67, ptnr., 1968-95; pvt. practice Menlo Park, Calif., 1996—. Trustee Antioch U., Yellow Springs, Ohio, 1980-87; bd. dirs. Planned Parenthood Alameda/San Francisco, 1984-89; pres. Calif. Dispute Resolution Coun., 2001. Lt. (j.g.) USN, 1953-56. Mem. ABA, ASCE, State Bar Calif., Bar Assn. San Francisco, San Mateo County Bar Assn., Am. Arbitration Assn. (large complex case panel arbitrators and mediators, No. Calif. regional adv. coun.), Coll. Comml. Arbitrators, Mediation Soc. Coll. Comml. Arbitrators, Calif. Dispute Resolution Coun., Dispute Rev. Bd. Found.g Democrat. Episcopalian. Avocation: soccer. Alternative dispute resolution. Office: 750 Menlo Ave Ste 250 Menlo Park CA 94025-4758 E-mail: jrmcoach@aol.com.

MADORY, RICHARD EUGENE, lawyer; b. Kenton, Ohio, May 14, 1931; s. Harold Richard and Hilda (Strictland) M.; m. Barbara Jean Madory, Sept. 25, 1955; children— Richard Eugene, Terry Dean, Michael Wesly. B.S. in Edn., Ohio State U., 1952; J.D., Southwestern U., 1961. Bar: Calif., 1961, U.S. Ct. Mil. Appeals, U.S. Supreme Ct., U.S. Dist. Ct. (cen. dist.) Calif. With firm Madory, Booth, Zell & Pleiss, Santa Ana, Calif., 1962— , now pres., v.p., sec.-treas. lectr. Continuing Edn. of Bar State of Calif. Served to col. USMC. Fellow Am. Coll. Trial Lawyers; mem. ABA, Orange County Bar Assn., Los Angeles County Bar Assn., So. Calif. Def. Counsel Assn., Am. Bd. Trial Advs., Nat. Bd. Trial Advocacy. State civil litigation, Insurance, Personal injury (including property damage). Office: 17822 17th St Ste 205 Tustin CA 92780-2152

MADRID, PATRICIA A. state attorney general; BA in English and Philosophy, U. N.Mex., 1969, JD, 1973; cert., Nat. Jud. Coll., U. Nev., 1978. Bar: N.Mex. Dist. judge N.Mex. State Dist. Judge, 1978—84; atty. gen. State of N.Mex., 1999—. Named Latina Atty. of Yr., Nat. Hispanic Bar Assn., 2001. Democrat. Office: Atty Gens Office PO Drawer 1508 Santa Fe NM 87504-1508

MADSEN, BARBARA A, state supreme court justice; BA, U. Wash., 1974; JD, Gonzaga U., 1977. Pub. defender King and Snohomish Counties, 1977—82; staff atty. Seattle City Atty.'s Office, 1982—84, spl. prosecutor, 1984—88; judge Seattle Mcpl. Ct., 1988—92; justice Washington Supreme Ct., Olympia, 1993—. Office: Wash Supreme Ct PO Box 40929 Olympia WA 98504-0929

MADSEN, GEORGE FRANK, lawyer; b. Sioux City, Iowa, Mar. 24, 1933; s. Frank O. and Agnes (Cuhel) M.; m. Magnhild Norstog; 1 child, Michelle Marie. BA, St. Olaf Coll., 1954; LLB, Harvard U., 1959. Bar: Ohio 1960, Iowa 1961, U.S. Dist. Ct. (no. and so. dists.) Iowa, U.S. Ct. Appeals (8th cir.), U.S. Supreme Ct. 1991. Trainee Cargill, Inc., Mpls., 1954; assoc. Durfey, Martin, Browne & Hull, Springfield, Ohio, 1959-61; assoc., then ptnr. Shull, Marshall & Marks, Sioux City, 1961-85; ptnr. Marks & Madsen, Sioux City, 1985-97, Marks, Madsen & Hirschbach, Sioux City, 1998-99, Mayne, Marks, Madsen & Hirschbach, LLP, Sioux City, 1999-2001. Author, editor: Iowa Title Opinions and Standards, 1978; contbg. author: The American Law of Real Property, 1991. Sec., bd.dirs. Sioux City Boys Club, 1969-76; mem. Sioux City Zoning Bd. Adjustment, 1963-65; active Iowa Mo. River Preservation and Land Use Authority, 1992-2001, pres., 1997-2001. Lt. USAF, 1954-56. Fellow Iowa State Bar Found.; mem. ABA, Iowa Bar Assn., Woodbury County Bar Assn., Nat. Wildlife Assn., Mont. Wildlife Assn., Pheasants Forever, Phi Beta Kappa (past pres. Siouxland chpt.), Rotary Internat. Avocations: skiing, hunting, swimming, reading. Commercial, contracts (including sales of goods; commercial financing), Corporate, general, Property, real (including real estate development, water). Office: PO Box 3661 Sioux City IA 51102-3661

MADSEN, H(ENRY) STEPHEN, retired lawyer; b. Momence, Ill., Feb. 5, 1924; s. Frederick and Christine (Landgren) Madsen; m. Carol Ruth Olmstead, Dec. 30, 1967; children: Stephen Stewart, Christie Morgan, Kelly Ann. MBA, U. Chgo., 1948; LLB, Yale U., 1951. Bar: Wash. 1951, Ohio 1953, U.S. Supreme Ct. 1975. Rsch. asst. Wash. Water Power Co., Spokane, 1951; assoc. Baker, Hostetler & Paterson, Cleve., 1952-59, ptnr., 1960-88, sr. ptnr., 1989-92; ret., 1992. Danish consul for Ohio, 1973—98. Active Bus. Advisers Cleve.; trustee Ohio Presbyn. Ret. Svcs. With AC U.S. Army, 1943—46. Decorated Knight Queen of Denmark. Fellow: ABA (life); mem.: Cleve. Bar Assn., Am. Law Inst., Am. Coll. Trial Lawyers (life), Country Club Cleve. Federal civil litigation, State civil litigation.

MADU, LEONARD EKWUGHA, lawyer, human rights officer, newspaper columnist, politician, business executive; b. Ibadan, Nigeria, Mar. 17, 1953; came to U.S., 1977; s. Luke E. and Grace (Dureke) M.; m. Jaculine Stephanie Turner, June 4, 1980; children: Christine, Oscar. BA, Marshall U., 1980; JD, U. Tenn., 1988; MA, Am. U. Rsch. assoc. Lamberts Publs., Washington, 1980-82; data specialist Govt. Employees Ins. Co., Washington, 1982-85; law intern Knoxville (Tenn.) Urban League, 1986-88; cons. Morris Brown Coll., Atlanta, 1988; staff atty. East Carolina Legal Svc., Wilson, N.C., 1989-90; cons. youth devel. Nat. Crime Prevention Coun., Washington, 1990; contract compliance officer Walters State C.C., Morristown, Tenn., 1990; examiner Dept. of Human Svc., Nashville, 1990-93; human rights officer Human Rights Commn., Nashville, 1993—; pres. Panafrica, Nashville, 1994—; CEO Madu and Assoc. Internat. Bus. Cons., 1996—; with Bus. Forum & Banquet, 1994—; 1st v.p. Nashville Multicultural Partnership, Inc., 2000—. Polit. cons. Embassy of Nigeria, Washington, 1995; cons. Embassy of Sierra Leone, Washington, 1995, Healthcare Internat. Mgmt. Co., 1996-2001, Embassy of Mozambique, 2000-01, Embassy of Togo, 2001—; bd. dirs. Peace and Justice Ctr., Nashville; pres. African Conglomerates Internat., Inc. Editor: African Nations Handbook, 1994, Directory of African Universities and Colleges, 1994; editor-in-chief Panafrican Digest, 1994, Panafrican Jour. of World Affairs, 1994; columnist Met. Times, Nashville, 1991—, The African Herald, Dallas, 1995—, U.S./African Voice, Balt., 1995—, African Sun Times, 1995—, The Nigerian and African, 1995—, The African Press, N.Y. Co-chmn. Clergy and Laity Concerned, Nashville, 1992-95; mem. curriculum and character com. Met. Sch. Bd., Nashville, 1994-97; co-coordinator The Haitian Project, 1991-94; vice-chmn. Nigerian Network Leadership awards N.Y., 1996; chmn. Internat. Women's Expo, Knoxville, 1996; co-chair Miss Nigeria Internat. Beauty Pageant, Washington, 1995, Miss Africa Internat. Beauty Pageant, Nashville, 1996, Igbo Union Chieftaincy Coronation Ceremony, Nashville, 1995; chmn. Nigerian Patriotic Front, 1997—; coord. United Nigeria Congress Party, 1997-98, Southeast U.S.; recruiter internat. students Tenn. State U., 1998-99; chmn. bd. dirs. Africa Found., Washington, 2001—2002. Recipient World Hunger Devel. Program award Marshall U., 1978-79, Hall of Nations scholar Am. U., 1980, 82, Mary Strohbel award United Way, 1994-95, Non-profit Vol. award Nat. Conf. of Christians and Jews, 1994. Mem. NAACP, U.S. Com. on Fgn. Rels., Soc. Profl. Journalists, UN Assn., Orgn. African Natonals (pres. 1994), African C. of C. (pres. 2000—). Avocations: reading, travel, soccer, ping-pong, tennis. Office: Panafrica 1016 18th Ave S Nashville TN 37212-2105

MADVA, STEPHEN ALAN, lawyer; b. Pitts., July 27, 1948; s. Joseph Edward and Mary (Zulick) M.; m. Bernadette A. McKeon; children: Alexander, Elizabeth. BA cum laude, Yale U., 1970; JD, U. Pa., 1973. Bar: Pa. 1973, U.S. Dist. Ct. (ea. dist.) Pa. 1975, U.S. Ct. Appeals (3d cir.) 1976, U.S. Ct. Appeals (11th cir.) 1987, U.S. Supreme Ct. 1985, N.Y. 1990. Asst. defender Defender Assn. Phila., 1973-75, fed. defender, 1975-77, also bd. dirs., 1985—; assoc. Montgomery, McCracken, Walker & Rhoads, Phila., 1977-81, ptnr., 1981—, mem. mgmt. com., 1993—, chmn. litigation sect., 1993—2002, vice chmn., 2002—03, chmn., 2003—. Bd. dirs. Ferag-Ams., LLC, WRH Mktg. Ams., LLC. Bd. dirs. Ctrl. Phila. Devel. Corp., 1995—, St. Christopher's Hosp. for Children, 2000—; bd. dirs. Opera Co. of Phila., 2000—, v.p., 2002—; bd. dirs. Police Athletic League, 2003—. Fellow Internat. Soc. Barristers, Am. Coll. Trial Lawyers; mem. ABA, Internat. Assn. Def. Counsel, Pa. Bar Assn. (mem. ho. of dels.), Phila. Bar Assn. (bd. govs. 2002--, fed. cts. com., chmn. commn. on jud. selection and retention,), Def. Rsch. Inst., Hist. Soc. Pa., Phila. C. of C. (bd. dirs.), Yale Alumni Assn. (schs. com.), Yale Rowing Assn., Union League of Phila., Sunday Breakfast Club. Democrat. Avocations: tennis, distance running, opera, classical music. Federal civil litigation, Product liability, Toxic tort. Home: 2055 Lombard St Philadelphia PA 19146-1314 Office: Montgomery McCracken Walker & Rhoads LLP 123 S Broad St Fl 24 Philadelphia PA 19109-1099 E-mail: smadva@mmwr.com.

MAECHLING, CHARLES, JR., lawyer, diplomat, educator, writer; b. N.Y.C., Apr. 18, 1920; s. Charles and Eugenie H. M.; m. Janet Leighton, Sept. 2, 1944; children: Philip Leighton and Eugenie Elisabeth (Mrs. David Buchan). Attended, Birch Wathen Sch., N.Y.C., 1924-37; BA with honors, Yale U., 1941; JD, U. Va., 1949. Bar: N.Y. 1949, D.C. 1957. Assoc. Sullivan & Cromwell, N.Y.C., 1949-51; atty. Office Sec. Air Force, 1951-52; counsel Electronics Industries Assn., Washington, 1953-56; founding ptnr. Shaw, Pittman, Potts & Maechling, 1956-61; dir. for internal def. Dept. State, Washington, 1961-63; staff dir. cabinet level spl. group and spl. asst. to undersec. of Averell Harriman, 1963-66; dep. and acting gen. counsel NSF, 1966-71, spl. asst. to dir., 1972-74; prof. law U. Va., 1974-76; spl. counsel N.Y. law firms, 1976-81; sr. assoc. Carnegie Endowment for Internat. Peace, 1981-85; vis. fellow, mem. law faculty Cambridge U. (Wolfson Coll.), Eng., 1985-88; guest scholar internat. law Brookings Inst., Washington, 1989-93; internat. cons., 1993—. Legal adviser internat. matters NAS, 1970-73, mem. ocean policy com.; mem. law-of-sea and other adv. coms. Dept. State; gen. counsel Fairways Corp., 1959-61; adj. prof. Georgetown Univ. Law Sch., Sch. Internat. Svc., Am. U.; mem. adv. bd. Internat. Peace Acad.; lectr. U.S. Def. Schs., also Hague Acad. Internat. Law; arbitrator complex internat. cases; chair U.S.-IIASA Planning Group, 1981-83. Editor-in-chief Va. Law Rev., 1948-49; contbr. articles to N.Y. Times, Internat. Herald Tribune, Boston Globe, L.A. Times, Miami Herald, profl. and lit. jours. Bd. dirs. Coun. for Ocean Law, Washington Inst. Fgn. Affairs; mem. U.S. Com. for IIASA; outside counsel to CIA, 1957-60. From ensign to lt. comdr. USNR, 1941-47, at sea and secretariat Joint Chiefs Staff, 1943-44, del. 1943 Cairo Conf., UN Law of Sea Conf., 1971-82; asst. naval attache Peru, 1945-47. Mem.: ABA (Ross Essay award 1969), Am. Soc. Internat. Law, Yale Club (Washington), Cosmos Club (Washington), City Tavern Club (Washington). Avocation: languages. Home: 3403 Lowell St NW Washington DC 20016-5024 Home (Summer): 367 Bar Rd Saint Andrews NB Canada E5B 2P7

MAEDER, GARY WILLIAM, lawyer; b. L.A., Dec. 21, 1949; s. Clarence Wilbur and Norma Jean (Buckbee) M.; m. Sue Ellen; children: Stephen Gregory, Charlene Michelle. BA, UCLA, 1971, JD, 1975; student, Fuller Seminary, 1971-72. Bar: Calif. 1975. Assoc. Kindel & Anderson, L.A., 1975-82, ptnr., 1982-96; shareholder Heller Ehrman White & McAuliffe LLP, L.A., 1996—. Author: God's Will for Your Life, 1973, 76, 91. Elder adult edn. St. John's Presbyn. Ch., L.A., 1981—86, 1994—96; bd. dirs. Christian Legal Soc. L.A., 1975—, Christian Conciliation Svc. L.A., 1983—88. Mem. Los Angeles County Bar Assn. (state and local tax com.), Christian Legal Soc. (bd. dirs. 1989-92), Order of Coif, Phi Beta Kappa. Corporate taxation, Personal income taxation, State and local taxation. Office: 601 S Figueroa St 40th Fl Los Angeles CA 90017 E-mail: gmaeder@hewm.com.

MAES, PETRA JIMENEZ, state supreme court justice; widowed; 4 children. BA, U. N.Mex., 1970, JD, 1973. Bar: N.Mex. 1973. Pvt. pratice law, Albuquerque, 1973-75; rep., then office mgr. No. N.Mex. Legal Svcs., 1975-81; dist. judge 1st Jud. Dist. Ct., Santa Fe, Los Alamos, 1981-98; chief judge, 1984-87, 92-95; chief justice Supreme Ct. N.Mex., 1998—. Active S.W. coun. Boy Scouts Am., mem. dist. coms.; presenter pre cana St. John's Cath. Ch.; bd. dirs. Nat. Ctr. on Women and Family Law; chairperson Tri-County Gang Task Force; mem. Gov.'s Task Force on Children and Families, 1991-92; mem. adv. com. Santa Fe County Jail, 1996. Mem. N.Mex. Bar Assn. (elderly law com. 1980-81, alternative dispute resolution com. 1987-92, code of jud. conduct com. 1992—, juvenile cmty. corrections svcs. com. chairperson), Hispanic Women's Coun. (charter). Office: Supreme Court NMex PO Box 848 Santa Fe NM 87504-0848

MAFFEO, VINCENT ANTHONY, lawyer, executive; b. Jan. 22, 1951; s. Michael Anthony and Marie Maffeo; m. Debra Maffeo, Dec. 16, 1972. BA summa cum laude, Bklyn. Coll., 1971; JD, Harvard U., 1974. Bar: NY 1975, Calif. 1982, Va. 1988, DC 1988, Mich. 1994. Assoc. Simpson Thacher & Bartlett, N.Y.C., NY, 1974—77; legal counsel Comms. Sys. divsn. ITT, Hartford, Conn., 1977—79; v.p., gen. counsel Bus. Comms. divsn. ITT, Des Plaines, Ill., 1979—80; asst. counsel western region ITT, 1980—83; group counsel ITT Europe, Inc., 1983—86; v.p. gen. coun. ITT Defense Inc., 1987—91; v.p., gen. coun. ITT Automotive, Inc., 1992—95; sr. v.p., gen. counsel ITT Industries, Inc., 1995—. Lt. Judge Adv. Gen. Corps. USNR, 1975. Mem.: ABA, N.Y.State Bar Assn., Calif. State Bar, Phi Beta Kappa. Office: ITT Industries Inc 4 W Red Oak Ln Ste 2 White Plains NY 10604-3617

MAFFITT, JAMES STRAWBRIDGE, lawyer; b. Raleigh, N.C., Oct. 29, 1942; s. James Strawbridge III and Lois (Handy) M.; children: Amy Maffitt Barkley, Margaret Maffitt Kramer; m. Frances Holton, Aug. 15, 1981. BA, Washington and Lee U., 1964, LLB, 1966. Bar: Va. 1966, Md. 1969. Assoc. Apostolou, Place & Thomas, Roanoke, Va., 1966-67; trust officer Mercantile-Safe Deposit & Trust Co., Balt., 1967-71; from assoc. to ptnr. Cable, McDaniel, Bowie & Bond, Balt., 1971-82; ptnr. Maffit & Rothschild, Balt., 1982-85, Anderson, Coe & King, Balt., 1986-90, Miles & Stockbridge , Easton, Balt., 1990—. Chmn. Acad. Art Mus., 1994—97, bd. dirs., 1993—99; trustee Grayce B. Kerr Fund, Inc., 1998—; bd. dirs. Chesapeake Coll., 2002—, Leadership Md., 2002—, United Fund of Talbot County, 1994—98, pres., 1997—98. Fellow Md. Bar Found.; mem. ABA (ho. dels. 1986-88), Md. Bar Assn. (bd. govs. 1989-91), Va. Bar. Assn., Balt. City Bar Assn. (pres. 1985-86), Wednesday Law Club, Talbot Country Club, Harbourtowne Country Club. Republican. Episcopal. Avocations: waterfowl hunting, golf. Commercial, contracts (including sales of goods; commercial financing), Corporate, general, Property, real (including real estate development, water). Home: 9498 Martingham Cir Saint Michaels MD 21663-2238 Office: Miles & Stockbridge 101 Bay St Easton MD 21601-2748 also: Miles & Stockbridge 10 Light St Baltimore MD 21202-1407 E-mail: jmaffitt@milesstockbridge.com.

MAGARGEE, W(ILLIAM) SCOTT, III, lawyer; b. Abington, Pa., Sept. 3, 1940; m. Annette Bruno, July 6, 1963; children: Scott, Todd, Ashley. AB, Princeton U., 1962; LLB, Yale U., 1966. Bar: Pa. 1966, U.S. Dist. Ct. (ea. dist.) Pa. 1966, U.S. Tax Ct. 1973. Assoc. Dechert Price & Rhoads, Phila., 1966-75, ptnr., 1975—. Mem. citizens adv. com. Southeastern Pa. Transp. Authority, 1988—; bd. dirs. United Way Southeastern Pa., 1994—, C.C. Phila. Found., pres., 2000—. Fellow Am. Coll. Employee Benefits Counsel; mem. ABA (sect. taxation, real estate, probate, trust law, bus. law), Phila. Bar Assn., Princeton Club Phila., Princeton Univ. Alumni Coun. (chmn. 1985-87). Pension, profit-sharing, and employee benefits, Probate (including wills, trusts). Office: Dechert LLP 4000 Bell Atlantic Tower 1717 Arch St Philadelphia PA 19103-2793

MAGARIAN, GREGORY P. law educator; b. Milw., Oct. 12, 1967; s. Donald Eldredge and Jean (Schoch) Magarian; m. Melissa Leigh Posten, June 8, 2002. BA, Yale U., 1989; M in Pub. Policy, U. M in Pub. Policy, JD, U. Mich., 1993. Bar: Md. 1994, DC 1995, U.S. Ct. Appeals (DC cir.) 1997, U.S. Supreme Ct. 1999. Law clk. to Hon. Louis F. Oberdorfer U.S. Dist. Ct. DC, Washington, 1993—94; law clk. to Hon. John Paul Stevens U.S. Supreme Ct., Washington, 1994—95; assoc. Jenner & Block, Washington, 1995—99; asst. prof. Sch. Law Villanova (Pa.) U., 1999—2002, assoc. prof., 2002—. Contbr. articles to profl. jours. Office: Villanova U Sch Law 299 N Spring Mill Rd Villanova PA 19085 Office Fax: 610-519-6282. Business E-Mail: margarian@law.villanova.edu.

MAGARIEL, DALE L. law librarian; b. St. Louis, Dec. 4, 1951; d. David Lee and Carol Hart; m. Larry K. Magariel, Jan. 8, 1972. BS in Libr. Mgmt., Park U., 1977. Law libr. Morrison, Hecker, Curtis, Kuder & Parrish, Kansas City, Mo., 1977—81; dir. libr. svcs. Stonson Morrison Hecker LLP, Kansas City, Mo., 1983—. Office: Stinson Morrison Hecker LLP 1201 Walnut Ste 2900 Kansas City MO 64106 Fax: 816-691-3496.

MAGAVERN, JAMES L. lawyer; b. Buffalo, Feb. 1, 1933; s. Samuel D. and Gertrude (Lewis) M.; m. 1955; children: David, William, Margaret, Samuel. Student, Dartmouth Coll., 1951-54; LLB, U. Buffalo, 1959. Bar: N.Y. 1969, U.S. Dist. Ct. (we. and so. dists.) N.Y., U.S. Ct. Appeals (2nd cir.), U.S. Supreme Ct. Dep. asst., then asst. atty. gen. State of N.Y., Albany, 1959-62; ptnr. Magavern, Magavern & Grimm, LLP, Buffalo, 1962-66, 77-78, 80—. Asst. and assoc. prof. law SUNY, Buffalo, 1966-71, adj. prof. law, 1972—; county atty. Erie County, Buffalo, 1972-76; counsel to state comptroller State of N.Y., 1979-80; legal cons. planning and devel. Collaborative Internat.-USAID, South Korea, 1974; co-counsel Commn. on Eminent Domain, State of N.Y., 1971. Contbr. articles to profl. jours. Past bd. dirs. Friendship House, Lackawanna, Community Music Sch., Legal Aid Buffalo, Buffalo and Erie County YMCA, Buffalo Hearing and Speech Ctr.; mem. N.Y. Commn. on Govt. Integrity, 1987-90; chmn. panel to rev. Code of Ethics City of Buffalo, 1986-87; mem. Erie County Fiscal Adv. Commn.; m. Citizens Adv. Coun. to Pub. Svc. Commn., 1976-79; chmn. Buffalo Stadium Design Adv. Com., 1984; former co-chmn. Citizens Coun. Human Rels.; bd. dirs. Excellas Health Care Plan, chair we. N.Y. regional bd., Buffalo Zool. Soc., N.Y. Fair Election Project, Inc., Legal Aid Soc. Buffalo, Inc.; chair City of Buffalo Charter Revision Commn., 1998-99; mem. bd. of ethics City of Buffalo; dean's adv. coun. State U. at Buffalo Law. With U.S. Army, 1954-56. Mem. ABA, N.Y. State Bar Assn., Erie County Bar Assn. (pres. 1982-83), Assn. Asian Studies (chmn. com. on Asian law 1978-80). Republican. Unitarian Universalist. General civil litigation, Health, Municipal (including bonds). Office: Magavern & Magavern 1100 Rand Bldg Buffalo NY 14203-1911

MAGEE, JOHN BENJAMIN, lawyer; b. Seattle, Aug. 4, 1944; s. John B. and Kathryn Rose (Allan) M.; m. Susan Beilby, Dec. 23, 1969; 1 child, Elizabeth. BA, Pomona Coll., 1966; JD, U. Wash., 1972; LLM, Georgetown U., 1977. Bar: Wash. 1972, D.C. 1977. With Miller & Chevalier, Chartered, Washington, 1977-2000, McKee Nelson, LLP, Washington, 2000—. Mem. U. Wash. Law Rev., 1972. Mem. ABA, Am. Law Inst., Columbia Country Club, Washington Athletic Club, Met. Club of Washington D.C., Order of Coif. Corporate taxation. Office: McKee Nelson LLP 1919 M St NW Ste 800 Washington DC 20036 E-mail: jmagee@mckeenelson.com.

MAGEE, THOMAS HUGH, lawyer; b. Rochester, N.Y., Aug. 15, 1943; s. Edward Charles and Jane Kathleen (Cranmer) M.; m. Judith Joy Stone, Oct. 2, 1982; 1 child, Michael Julian. BSME, U. Rochester, N.Y., 1965; JD, Syracuse U., 1973. Bar: N.J. 1974, U.S. Dist. Ct. N.J. 1974, U.S. Ct. Appeals (D.C. cir.) 1975, N.Y. 1981, U.S. Supreme Ct. 1978, U.S. Patent and Trademark Office. Sr. patent counsel RCA Corp., Princeton, N.J., 1973-86, GE/RCA Licensing Operation, Princeton, 1986-88; corp. counsel E.I. duPont de Nemours & Co., Wilmington, Del., 1988—. Lt. USN, 1965-70, Capt. USNR (ret.), 1991. Navy commendation medal with combat V, Vietnam, 1969. Mem. Am. Intellectual Property Law Assn. (com. chair 1974—), Phila. Intellectual Property Law Assn. (com. chmn. 1974—), N.J. Patent Law Assn., Justinian hon. law soc., Phi Alpha Delta. Republican. Presbyterian. Avocations: tennis, handball, coin-collecting. Antitrust, Intellectual property, Patent. Home: 721 Severn Rd Wilmington DE 19803-1724 Office: E I duPont de Nemours & Co Barley Mill Plz BMP 25-1372 Wilmington DE 19880 E-mail: thomas.h.magee@usa.dupont.com.

MAGGIOLO, ALLISON JOSEPH, lawyer; b. New River, N.C., Aug. 29, 1943; s. Allison and Florence Celeste (Vago) M. Cert., U. Paris-Sorbonne, 1965; AB, Brown U., 1966; JD, U. Louisville, 1975. Bar: Ky. 1976, U.S. Dist. Ct. (we. dist.) Ky. 1981. Ops. mgr., stockbroker Bache & Co., Louisville, 1970-73; ptnr. Reisz, Blackburn, Manly & Treitz, Louisville, 1976-78, Greenebaum Boone Treitz Maggiolo & Brown, Louisville, 1978-91, Wyatt, Tarrant & Combs, Louisville, 1991—. Workshop panelist Fin. Adv. Coun., 1994; panelist Seminar on Defaulted Bond Issues, 1987-89, Bond Counsel and the Corp. Trustee, 1990-92, Defaults and Workouts, 1993. Author: Indenture Trustee Liability and Defaulted Bond Issues, 1987, Minimizing Indenture Trustee Liability and Defaulted Bond Issues, 1991, Bond Default Resolution, 1993; co-author: The legal Aspects of Doing International Business in Kentucky, 1990. Mem. exec. com. St. Louis Com. Fgn. Rels., 1979—, chmn., 1991—96; bd. dirs. Ky. Show, Louisville, 1978—91, Ky. Opera, Louisville, 1978—91, mem. hon. coun., 1991—; bd. dirs. Glassworks Found., 2002—. Decorated Bronze Star. Mem. Internat. Bar Assn., Nat. Assn. Bond Lawyers, Bond Attys. Workshop (planning com. 1991-93), Pendennis Club, Wynn Stay Club, Jefferson Club. Banking, Finance, Municipal (including bonds). Office: Wyatt Tarrant & Combs LLP PNC Plz Louisville KY 40202-2823

MAGGIPINTO, V. ANTHONY, lawyer; b. Tucson, Apr. 15, 1943; s. William Vito and Elizabeth Maria (Rice) M.; m. Maria Teresa Zequeira, Aug. 31, 1976; children: Marshall Albert Nicholas, Spencer William Jonathan. AB cum laude, Southampton Coll., 1970; JD, Fordham U., 1976. Bar: Fla. 1977, N.Y. 1978, U.S. Dist. Ct. (ea. and so. dists.) N.Y. 1979, U.S. Ct. Appeals (2d cir.) 1980. Asst. to pres. Interpub. Group of Cos., N.Y.C., 1965-66; asst. dean of admission Southampton (N.Y.) Coll., 1971-73; investigative aide N.Y. State Com. on Jud. Conduct, N.Y.C., 1974-76; asst. state atty. Dade County State Atty., Miami, Fla., 1977-78; asst. dist. atty. Suffolk Dist. Atty., Hauppage, N.Y., 1978-80; asst. county atty. Suffolk County Atty., Hauppauge, 1980-84; sole practice Riverhead and St. James, N.Y., 1982—. Mem. spl. coms. on discovery, civil litigation U.S. Dist. Ct. (ea. dist.) N.Y., Bklyn., 1983-90, 95—, arbitrator, 1986—, Civil Justice Reform Act adv. group, 1990-95, chair jury task force, 1993—, commendation U.S. Dist. Ct., 1997. Mem. appeals bd. SSS, 1982—2001, vice chmn., 1986—97, chmn., 1997—2001. Served with submarine svc. USN, 1961—65. Recipient Disting. Alumni award L.I. U., 1990. Mem.: Nissequogue, Southampton Coll. Alumni Assn. (exec. com. 1997, pres. 2001—02, bd. dirs.), Navy League (judge adv. L.I. coun. 1992—), U.S. Naval Inst., Fla. Bar Assn., Suffolk County Bar Assn., N.Y. State Bar Assn. (exec. com. real property sect. 1997—2002), Golf Club (counsel 1980—, bd. govs.). Republican. Roman Catholic. Avocations: hiking, horseback riding. General civil litigation, Corporate, general, Probate (including wills, trusts). Office: 1212 Roanoke Ave Riverhead NY 11901-2740

MAGIDSOHN, HERMAN EDWARD, lawyer; b. Detroit, Dec. 7, 1936; s. Harry and Barbara M.; m. Leslie Marcia Krimton, July 12, 1970; children: Blair H., Heather B., Allison A. BA, U. Mich., 1959; BBA, U. Miami, 1961; JD, Southwestern U., 1970. Bar: U.S. Dist. Ct. (ctrl. dist.) Calif. 1971, U.S. Ct. Appeals (9th cir.) 1971. Assoc. Mansell & Giddens, L.A., 1971-73, Coleman & Coleman, L.A., 1973-75; pvt. practice Encino, Calif., 1975—. General civil litigation, Commercial, contracts (including sales of goods; commercial financing), Workers' compensation. Office: Law Offices of Herman E Magdsohn 15720 Ventura Blvd Ste 418 Encino CA 91436-4709

MAGILL, FRANK JOHN, federal judge; b. Verona, N.D., June 3, 1927; s. Thomas Charles and Viola Magill; m. Mary Louise Timlin, Nov. 22, 1955; children: Frank Jr., Marguerite Connolly, R. Daniel, Mary Elizabeth, Robert, John. BS in Fgn. Svc., Georgetown U., 1951, LLB, 1955; MA, Columbia U., 1952. Ptnr. Nilles, Hansen, Magill & Davies, Ltd., Fargo, ND, 1955—86; judge U.S. Ct. Appeals (8th cir.), Fargo, 1986—. Chmn. fin. disclosure com. U.S. Jud. Conf., 1993—98. Fellow: Am. Coll. Trial Lawyers; mem.: Cass County Bar Assn. (Pres. 1970). Republican. Avocations: tennis, sailing, skiing. Home: 501 7th St S Apt 301 Fargo ND 58103-2761 Office: Quentin N Burdick US Courthouse 655 1st Ave N Ste 320 Fargo ND 58102-4932 Fax: 701 297-7255. E-mail: frank_magill@ca8.uscourts.gov.

MAGINNIS, JOHN C., III, lawyer; b. Balt., Aug. 24, 1948; BBA, U. Mich., 1970, JD, 1973. Bar: DC 1974, Va. 1978, Md. 1984. Pvt. practice, Washington. Mem.: Md. State Bar Assn., Va. State Bar Assn., DC Bar Assn. Family and matrimonial, Probate (including wills, trusts), Personal injury (including property damage). Office: 1350 Connecticut Ave NW Ste 301 Washington DC 20036

MAGNUSON, PAUL ARTHUR, federal judge; b. Carthage, S.D., Feb. 9, 1937; s. Arthur and Emma Elleda (Paulson) Magnuson; m. Sharon Schultz Magnuson, Dec. 21, 1959; children: Marlene Peterson, Margaret(dec.) , Kevin, Kara Berger. BA, Gustavus Adolphus Coll., 1959; JD honors causa, William Mitchell Coll., 1963; DLL (hon.), Wm. Mitchell Coll., 1991; DLL (hon.) , Gustavus Adolphus Coll., 1982. Bar: Minn. 1963, U.S. Dist. Ct. Minn. 1968. Asst. registrar William Mitchell Coll. of Law, 1959-60; claim adjuster Agrl. Ins. Co., 1960-62; clk. Bertie & Bettenberg, 1962-63; ptnr. LeVander, Gillen, Miller & Magnuson, South St. Paul, Minn., 1963-81; judge U.S. Dist. Ct. Minn., St. Paul, 1981—, chief judge, 1994—2001. Jurist-in-residence Hamline U., 1985, Augsberg Coll., 1986, Bethel Coll., 1986, Concordia Coll., St. Paul, 1987, U. Minn., Morris, 1987; instr. William Mitchell Coll. Law, 1984-92, Corcordia Coll., Moorhead, 1988, St. John's U., 1988, Coll. of St. Benedict, 1988; mem. jud. conf. com. on adminstrn. of Bankruptcy Sys., 1987-96; mem. Eighth Cir. Edn. Com., 1992-97, chmn. 1994-97; mem. jud. conf. com. on Internat. Jud. Rels.,

1996—, chair, 1999—; mem. com. on dist. judges edn. Fed. Jud. Ctr., 1998—; mem 8th cir. Edn. com., 1992-97, chmn. 1994-97. Mem. Met. Health Bd., St. Paul, 1970-72; legal counsel Ind. Rep. Party Minn., St. Paul, 1979-81. Recipient Disting. Alumnus award Gustavus Adolphus Coll., 1982; First Disting. Svc. award William Mitchell Coll. Law, 1999, Dr. of Laws Honors Causa, William Mitchell Coll. of Law, 1991. Mem. Minn. State Bar Assn., 1st Dist. Bar Assn. (pres. 1974-75), Dakota County Bar Assn., 10th Jud. Dist. Bar Assn., Am. Judicature Soc., Fed. Bar Assn., Fed. Cir. Bar Assn., Fed. Judges Assn. (bd. dirs., treas. 1997-2001, v.p. 2001-). E-mail: PAMagnuson@mnd.uscourts.gov.

MAGNUSON, ROGER JAMES, lawyer; b. St. Paul, Jan. 25, 1945; s. Roy Gustaf and Ruth Lily (Edlund) M.; m. Elizabeth Cunningham Shaw, Sept. 11, 1982; children: James Roger, Peter Cunningham, Mary Kerstin, Sarah Ruth, Elizabeth Camilla, Anna Clara, John Edlund, Britta Kristina. BA, Stanford U., 1967; JD, Harvard U., 1971; BCL, Oxford U., 1972. Bar: Minn. 1973, U.S. Dist. Ct. Minn. 1973, U.S Ct. Appeals (8th, 9th, 10th cirs.) 1974, U.S. Supreme Ct. 1978. Chief pub. defender Hennepin County Pub. Defender's Office, Mpls., 1973; ptnr. Dorsey & Whitney, Mpls., 1972—. Dean Oak Brook Coll. of Law and Govt. Policy, 1995—; chancellor Magdalen Coll., 1999—. Author: Shareholder Litigation, 1981, Are Gay Rights Right, The White-Collar Crime Explosion, 1992, Informed Answers to Gay Rights Questions, 1994; Internat. Judicial Asst. in Civil Matters (1999), contbr. articles to profl. jours. Elder, Straitgate Ch., Mpls., 1980—. Fellow, Ctr. of Internat. Legal Studies, Mem. Christian Legal Soc., The Am. Soc. Writers of Legal Subjects, Mpls. Club, White Bear Yacht Club. Republican. Federal civil litigation, Criminal, Libel. Home: 625 Park Ave Saint Paul MN 55115-1663 Office: Dorsey & Whitney LLP 50 S 6th St Ste 1500 Minneapolis MN 55402-1498 Business E-Mail: magnuson.roger@dorseylaw.com.

MAHAN, JAMES CAMERON, judge; b. El Paso, Tex., Dec. 16, 1943; m. Eileen Agnes Casale, Jan. 13, 1968; 1 child, James Cameron Jr. BA, U. Charleston, 1965; JD, Vanderbilt U., 1973. Bar: Nev. 1974, U.S. Dist. Ct. Nev. 1974, U.S. Ct. Appeals (9th cir.) 1975, U.S. Tax Ct. 1980, U.S. Supreme Ct. 1980. Assoc. Lee & Beasey, Las Vegas, Nev., 1974-75; mem. firm John Peter Lee Ltd., Las Vegas, 1975-82; sr. ptnr. Mahan & Ellis, Chartered, Las Vegas, 1982-99; dist. ct. judge 8th Jud. Dist. Nev., Las Vegas, 1999—2002; U.S. dist. judge, 2002—. With USN, 1966-69. Office: 333 Las Vegas Blvd S Las Vegas NV 89101 E-mail: james_mahan@nvd.uscourts.gov.

MAHAR, ELLEN PATRICIA, law librarian; b. Washington, Jan. 15, 1938; d. Richard A. and Lina Mahar. BA, St. Joseph Coll., Emmitsburg, Md., 1959; MLS, U. Md., 1968. Asst. librarian Covington & Burling, Washington, 1971-73, libr. dir., 1978-92; librarian Shea & Gardner, Washington, 1974-78; mgr. info. ctr. Assn. Comml. Real Estate, Herndon, Va., 1992-94; head libr. Caplin & Drysdale Chtd., Washington, 1994—. Co-editor: Legislative History of the Securities Act of 1933 and the Securities Act of 1934, 11 vols., 1973. Mem. Am. Assn. Law Libraries, Spl. Libraries Assn., Law Librarians' Soc. Washington. Office: Caplin & Drysdale Chtd 1 Thomas Cir NW Fl 11 Washington DC 20005-5802

MAHER, DAVID WILLARD, lawyer; b. Chgo., Aug. 14, 1934; s. Chauncey Carter and Martha (Peppers) M.; m. Jill Waid Armagnac, Dec. 20, 1954; children: Philip Armagnac, Julia Armagnac. BA, Harvard, 1955, LLB, 1959. Bar: N.Y. 1960, Ill. 1961, Wis. 1996, U.S. Patent Office 1961. Pvt. practice, Boston, N.Y.C., 1958-60; assoc. Kirkland & Ellis, and predecessor firm, 1960-65, ptnr., 1966-78, Reuben & Proctor, 1978-86, Isham, Lincoln and Beale, 1986-88, Sonnenschein, Nath & Rosenthal, Chgo., 1988—; chmn. bd. dirs. Publ. Interest Registry. Gen. counsel BBB Chgo. and No. Ill.; lectr. DePaul U. Sch. Law, 1973—79, Loyola U. Law Sch., Chgo., 1980—84; chmn. bd. dirs. Pub. Interest Registry. Vis. com. U. Chgo. Div. Sch., 1986—. 2d lt. USAF, 1955-56. Fellow Am. Bar Found. (life); mem. ABA, Am. Law Inst., Ill. Bar Assn., Wis. State Bar, Chgo. Bar Assn., Chgo. Lit. Club, Union League Club. Roman Catholic. Computer, Patent, Intellectual property. Home: 501 N Clinton St Apt 1503 Chicago IL 60610-8886 Office: Sonnenschein Nath & Rosenthal 233 S Wacker Dr Ste 8000 Chicago IL 60606-6491 E-mail: dmaher@sonnenschein.com.

MAHER, EDWARD JOSEPH, lawyer; b. Cleve., Sept. 18, 1939; s. Richard Leo and Lucile (Thompson) M.; m. Marilyn K. Maher, Oct. 8, 1966; children: Richard A., David C., Michael E, Colleen Therese. B.S., Georgetown U., 1961, LL.B., 1964; student U. Fribourg, Switzerland, 1959-61. Bar: Ohio 1964, U.S. dist. ct. (no. dist.) Ohio 1964. Assoc., Sweeney, Maher & Vlad, Cleve., 1964-71; sole practice, Cleve., 1971— . Pres. parish council St. Raphael's Ch., Bay Village, Ohio, 1983-84; former adv. bd. Catholic Family and Children's Services; adv. bd. Cath. Youth Orgn., 1973-79, pres., 1975-76; chmn. Elyria Cursillo Ctr., 1974-75; lay del. to Ohio Cath. Conf., Diocese of Cleve., 1973-75; chmn. adv. bd. Cath. Social Services of Cuyahoga County, 1978-79; trustee Cath. Charities Corp., 1977—2001 , hon. trustee, 2002-, treas., 1979, sec., 1981, 1st v.p., 1983, gen. chmn. campaign, 1983, 84, pres., 1985-86; pres. Diocesan adv. bd. Cath. Youth Orgn., 1980-82; team capt. United Way Services Agy. Team Group, 1981, nominating com., 1983; mem. Tabor House, The Consultation Ctr. of the Diocese of Cleve., pres., 1992-94; mem. bd. regents St. Ignotuis High Sch., 1997—. Recipient Cardinal Robert Bellarmine S.J. award St. Ignatius High Sch., 1990, Cath. Man of the Year award, 1995. Mem. ABA, Ohio Bar Assn., Cuyahoga County Bar Assn., Cleve. Bar Assn., Cath. Lawyers Guild Cleve. (pres. 1970). Clubs: Irish Good Fellowship (pres.), First Friday of Cleve. (pres. 1990). Insurance, Personal injury (including property damage), Probate (including wills, trusts). Office: 1548 Standard Bldg Cleveland OH 44113

MAHER, GARY LAURENCE, lawyer; b. Summit, N.J., Dec. 19, 1965; s. William J. and Eileen B. (Galen) M.; m. Dana V. Dombroski, Nov. 11, 1994; 2 children. BA in Psychology, U. Pa., 1988; JD, Rutgers U., Camden, 1992. Bar: N.J. 1992, Pa. 1992, U.S. Dist. Ct. N.J. 1992. Law clk. to Hon. Ross R. Anzaldi and Hon. Edward J. Toy, Superior Ct. of N.J., Elizabeth, 1993—94; assoc. Mandell & Selesner P.C., Red Bank, NJ, 1994—95; sr. litigation assoc. Shain, Schaffer & Rafanello, P.C., Bernardsville, NJ, 1995—2001; ptnr. Maher & Maher LLC, Garwood, NJ, 2001—. Elected mem. Borough of Garwood Bd. Edn., 2002—. Mem. Geneal. Soc. N.J. (trustee 1995—), Geneal. Soc. West Fields, The Play Trains. Avocations: music, inline skating, genealogy. Banking, General civil litigation, Property, real (including real estate development, water). Office: Maher & Maher LLC 106 Center St PO Box 293 Garwood NJ 07027-0293 E-mail: maherlaw@juno.com.

MAHER, STEPHEN TRIVETT, lawyer, educator; b. N.Y.C., Nov. 21, 1949; s. William John and Jean Dorothy (Trivett) M.; m. Sharon Leslie Wolfe, Nov. 22, 1981 (dec.); children: Meaghan Wolfe, Caitlin Wolfe. BA, NYU, 1971; JD, U. Miami, Coral Gables, Fla., 1975. Bar: Fla. 1975, U.S. Dist. Ct. (so. dist.) Fla. 1976, D.C. 1979, U.S. Dist. Ct. (no. dist.) Fla. 1979, U.S. Supreme Ct. 1980, U.S. Ct. Appeals (5th and 11th cirs.) 1981, U.S. Dist. Ct. (so. dist.) Fla. 1982, U.S. Dist. Ct. (mid. dist.) Fla. 1983. Assoc. Chonin & Levey, Miami, 1975; staff atty. Legal Svcs. of Greater Miami, Inc., 1975-81; assoc. Finley, Kumble, Wagner et al, Miami, 1981-84; dir. clin. program Sch. of Law U. Miami, Coral Gables, 1984-90, assoc. prof. law Sch. of Law, 1984-92; pvt. practice Stephen T. Maher, P.A., Miami, Fla., 1992—2003; ptnr. Shutts & Bowen, 2003—. Mem. Fla. Bar/Fla. Bar Found. Joint Commn. on Delivery Legal Svcs. to the Indigent, Tallahassee, 1990-91, chair, organizer Seventh Adminstrv. Law Conf., Tallahassee, 1990, Conf. on the Fla. Constn., 1995; cons. on in-house legal edn. Contbr. articles to profl. jours. Fellow Fla. Bar Found. (life, bd. dirs. 1984-91); mem. ABA, Fla. Bar (chair adminstrv. law sect. 1993-94, chair coun. of sects. 1996-97), Dade County Bar Assn. Administrative and regulatory, Civil rights, General civil litigation. Home: 1015 Sevilla Ave Miami FL 33134-6328 Office: 1500 Miami Ctr 201 S Biscayne Blvd Miami FL 33131-4332

MAHON, ARTHUR J. lawyer; b. N.Y.C., Jan. 13, 1934; s. Arthur Logan and Mary Agnes (Craine) M.; m. Myra E. Murphy, Aug. 10, 1957; children: Maura, Madonna, Arthur, Nancy. BA, Manhattan Coll., 1955; JD, NYU, 1958. Bar: N.Y., Fla., D.C. Adj. prof. law NYU Sch. of Law, N.Y.C., 1964-78; ptnr. Mudge, Rose, Guthrie, Alexander & Ferdon, N.Y.C., 1970-94; counsel Donovan Leisure Newton & Irvine, N.Y.C., 1994-98, McDermott, Will & Emery, 1998—. Trustee Manhattan Coll., N.Y.C., 1988—, Adrian and Jesse Archbold Charitable Trust, N.Y.C., 1976—, N.Y. Presbyn. Hosp., N.Y.C., 1994—; mem. joint bd. N.Y. Hosp.-Cornell Med. Ctr., N.Y.C., 1990-98; com. on trust and estate gift plans Rockefeller U., N.Y.C., 1984—; bd. dirs. United Way Internat., 1988-94, Alexandria, Va., chmn. planned giving and endowments com. Archdiocese, N.Y.C., 1982-97; bd. overseers Cornell Med. Coll., N.Y.C., 1986—, chmn., 1992-95, vice chmn., 1990-91, 96—; dir. Am. Skin Assn., N.Y.C., 1989—; v.p., dir. Cath. Communal Fund, Archdiocese of N.Y., 1997—, trustee Inner City Scholarship Fund, 1998—. Served to capt. USAF, 1958-60. Root-Tilden scholar NYU. Mem. N.Y. State Bar Assn., Bar Assn. City of N.Y., Fla. Bar Assn., D.C. Bar Assn. Home: 16 Cambridge Dr Madison CT 06443-3016 Office: McDermott Will & Emery 50 Rockefeller Plz Fl 12 New York NY 10020-1600 E-mail: amahon@mwe.com.

MAHON, ELDON BROOKS, former federal judge; b. Loraine, Tex., Apr. 9, 1918; s. John Bryan and Nola May (Muns) M.; m. Nova Lee Groom, June 1, 1941; children: Jana, Martha, Brad. BA, McMurry U., 1939; LLB, U. Tex., 1942; LLD (hon.), McMurry U., 1974; HHD (hon.), Tex. Wesleyan U., 1990. Bar: Tex. 1942. Law clk. Tex. Supreme Ct., 1945-46; county atty. Mitchell County, Tex., 1947; dist. atty. 32d Jud. Dist. Tex., 1948-60, dist. judge, 1960-63; v.p. Tex. Electric Service Co., Ft. Worth, 1963-64; mem. firm Mahon Pope & Gladden, Abilene, Tex., 1964-68; U.S. atty. U.S. Dist. Ct. (no. dist.) Tex., Ft. Worth, 1968-72, judge, 1972-89, sr. judge, 1989—2002. Com. on the budget Judicial Conf. the U.S., 1975-83, 5th cir. judicial coun., 1984-89. Pres. W. Tex. council Girl Scouts U.S.A., 1966-68; former trustee McMurry U.; past bd. dirs. Harris Meth. Hosp. With USAAF, 1942-45. Named an Outstanding Tex. Prosecutor, Tex. Law Enforcement Found., 1957; recipient Disting. Alumnus award McMurry U., 1987. Em. ABA, FBA, Ft.-Worth-Tarrant County Bar Assn. (Silver Gavel award 1998), Am. Judicature Soc., Dist. and County Attys. Assn. Tex. (pres. 1954-55), Tex. Bar Found. (life, Samuel Pessarra outstanding jurist award 1998). Methodist.*

MAHONEY, MARY DENISE, librarian, consultant; b. Ft. Worth, Dec. 18, 1953; d. Albert Joseph and Patsy (Mills) Lepinski; m. Michael T. Mahoney, Feb. 1, 1985; children: Jeremy, Sheila, Molly. BS in Edn., U. N.D., 1976, JD, 1985; MLibr, U. Wash., 1986. Head pub. svcs. Law Libr. Marquette U., Milw., 1986-92, dep. dir. Law Libr., 1992-95; dir. Law Libr. Miss. Coll. Sch. Law, Jackson, 1995—99. Adj. asst. prof. Marquette U. Law Sch., 1990-95; asst. instr. U. Wis., Milw., 1990-95. Burtness scholar U. N.D. Sch. Law, 1982. Mem. Am. Assn. Law Librs. (Little Brown fellow 1986, chair placement com. 1993-94), Law Libr. Assn. Wis. (pres. 1993). Roman Catholic. Office: Peterson Johnson & Murray SC 733 N Van Buren St Fl 6 Milwaukee WI 53202

MAHOOD, JAMES EDWARD, lawyer; b. Sewickley, Pa., Feb. 2, 1948; s. James Calvin and Pauline (DeShields) M.; m. Beth Ann Leuenberger, July 12, 1985. BA, Bard Coll., 1971; JD, U. Pitts., 1974. Bar: Pa. 1974. Atty. Neighborhood Legal Svcs., Pitts., 1974-76, mng. atty., 1976-80; assoc. Wilder & Miller, P.C., Pitts., 1980-83, ptnr., 1983-87, Wilder & Mahood, P.C., Pitts., 1987-92, Wilder, Mahood & Crenney, Pitts., 1992-99, Wilder & Mahood, Pitts., 2000—. Co-author: Pennsylvania Family Law Practice and Procedure Handbook, 1986, 2nd edit., 1989. Named one of Best Lawyers in Am., 2003—. Fellow Am. Acad. Matrimonial Lawyers (cert. matrimonial arbitrator and mediator, 2nd v.p. Pa. chpt. 2002-); mem. ABA, Pa. Bar Assn. (coun., family law sect. 1989-92, treas. 1993-94, sec. 1994-95, 2d vice chair 1995-96, chair elect 1997-98, chair 1998-99, code of evidence com. 1997—), Allegheny County Bar Assn. (coun., family law sect. 1986-97, civil rules com., pub. svc. com.), Joint Family Law Coun. Pa. (adv. com. to jt. state gov. commn. on adoption law 1997—), Neighborhood Legal Svcs. Assn. (bd. dirs. 1993—, treas. 1994-95, pres. 1996-98, equal justice campaign com. 1993-2000, co-chair 2000—). Avocation: american and world history. Family and matrimonial. Office: Wilder & Mahood 10th Fl Koppers Bldg 436 7th Ave Pittsburgh PA 15219-1826 E-mail: jmahood@wildermahood.com.

MAI, HAROLD LEVERNE, retired judge; b. Casper, Wyo., Apr. 5, 1928. BA, U. Wyo., 1950, JD, 1952. Bar: Wyo. 1952, U.S. Supreme Ct. 1963. Sole practice, Cheyenne, Wyo., 1953-62, 67-71; judge Juvenile Ct., Cheyenne, 1962-67; U.S. bankruptcy judge, Cheyenne, 1971-93, ret., 1993. Mem. ABA, Wyo. Bar Assn., Laramie County Bar Assn., Nat. Conf. Bankruptcy Judges.

MAIDMAN, STEPHEN PAUL, lawyer; b. Hartford, Conn., Feb. 8, 1954; s. Harry and Roslyn (Mandell) M.; m. Mari Rosenberg, Oct. 13, 1996. AB summa cum laude, Bowdoin Coll., 1976; MBA, U. Pa., 1979, JD, 1980. Bar: Pa. 1980, Mass. 1996, U.S. Dist. Ct. (ea. dist.) Pa. 1980, U.S. Ct. Appeals (3d cir.) 1980, U.S. Dist. Ct. Mass. 1996, U.S. Ct. Appeals (1st cir.) 1996, U.S. Supreme Ct. 1997. Assoc. Drinker, Biddle & Reath, Phila., 1980-81; atty. IBM, Boca Raton, Fla., 1981-84, N.Y.C., 1984-85, staff atty., 1985-87, Rye Brook, N.Y., 1987-88, lab. counsel Poughkeepsie, N.Y., 1988-92, site counsel Hopewell Junction, N.Y., 1992-95; pvt. practice, Springfield, Mass., 1996—. Adj. faculty U. Conn Law Sch., 2001—. Co-class agt. Bowdoin Coll. Alumni Fund. Mem. Nat. Assn. Criminal Def. Lawyers, Mass. Bar Assn., Mass. Assn. Criminal Def. Lawyers, Hampden County Bar Assn. Avocations: running, black Labradors. E-mail: maidman@prodigy.net. Criminal, General practice. Office: 1145 Main St Ste 417 Springfield MA 01103-2123

MAILAENDER, KARL PETER, lawyer; b. Stuttgart, Federal Republic of Germany, Oct. 23, 1936; s. Karl Robert and Margarete Marianne M.; m. Eva Maria Runde-Wagner, Sept. 5, 1964; children: Daniela, Peter-Oliver. M in Comparative Jurisprudence, NYU, 1961; JD, Tuebingen U., 1961. Bar: Stuttgart 1965. Asst. prof. Law Sch. Tuebingen U., 1962-63, Munich U., 1963-64; practicing atty. Stuttgart, 1965; ptnr. Haver & Mailander, Attys.-at-Law, Stuttgart, 1967—. Chmn. bd. Citibank Germany, Frankfurt, 1967—, MTD Products AG Saarbrücken, 1989—. Author books; contbr. articles to profl. jours. Chmn. German Commn. on Control of Concentration in the Media, Potsdam, Constl. Ct. of State of Baden-Württemberg, Stuttgart. Mem. Am. Bar Orgn., German Bar Orgn., Tax Payers Assn. (chmn. bd.). Avocations: golfing, skiing, history in politics. Antitrust, Banking, Mergers and acquisitions. Home: Lenbachstr 53 70192 Stuttgart Baden-Wuerttemberg Germany Office: Haver & Mailaender Attys Lenzhalde 83-85 70192 Stuttgart Baden-Wuerttemberg Germany Fax: 0049 711 22744 55. E-mail: kpm@haver-mailaender.de.

MAILLE, BRENDA PATRICIA, lawyer; b. Lowell, Mass., Oct. 1, 1956; BS, U. Lowell, 1978; JD, New Eng. Sch. Law, 1982. Bar: Mass. Atty. Zaroulis & Maille, Lowell, 1983-95; pvt. practice Lowell, 1995—. Bd. dirs. Big Bros./Big Sisters Greater Lowell, 1988-97, 2000-, former pres.; coach, advisor City Magnet Sch. Mock Trial Team, Lowell, 1996. Mem. Mass. Bar Assn., Greater Lowell Bar Assn. (dir. 1990-93, Lawyer Yr. award 1994). Avocations: skiing, travel. Family and matrimonial, Probate (including wills, trusts), Property, real (including real estate development, water). Office: 9 Middlesex St Lowell MA 01852-2110

MAINE, MICHAEL ROLAND, lawyer; b. Anderson, Ind., Feb. 22, 1940; s. Roland Dwight and Vivian Louise (Browning) M.; m. Suzanne Bauman, Aug. 25, 1962; children: Christopher Michael (dec.), Melinda Louise. AB with high distinction, DePauw U.; JD with distinction, U. Mich. Bar: Ind., D.C., U.S. Dist. Ct. (so. dist.) Ind., U.S. Ct. Appeals (7th cir.), U.S. Supreme Ct. Assoc. Baker & Daniels, Indpls., 1964-71, ptnr., 1972—. Contbr. articles to profl. jours. Bd. dirs. Ind. Repertory Theatre, Indpls., 1986—, Cmty. Hosp. N., 1988—91; Japan-Am. Soc. of Ind. Inc., 1988—; pres. Mental Health Assn. Ind., Indpls., 1985; bd. visitors Sch. Law Ind. U., Indpls.; trustee De Pauw U., Greencastle, Ind., 1990—; bd. dirs. U.S.-China Bus. Coun. Legal Cooperation Fund, 2002—. Capt. USAF, 1965—68. Named Sagamore of Wabash, Gov. Ind., 1986. Fellow: Indpls. Bar Found., Ind. Bar Found.; mem.: Indpls. Bar Assn. (sec. 1983, pres. 1985, extraordinary svc. award 1985), Ind. Bar Assn. (chmn. fed. judiciary com. 1986—88), Kiwanis (lt. gov. Ind. club 1972, pres. Indpls. club 1969), Masons, Kiwanis (lt. gov. Ind. club 1972, pres. Indpls. club 1969), Masons, Phi Beta Kappa, Order of Coif. Avocation: golf. Corporate, general, Labor (including EEOC, Fair Labor Standards Act, labor-management relations, NLRB, OSHA). Home: 13100 Joseffa Ct Placida FL 33946 Office: Baker & Daniels 300 N Meridian St Ste 2700 Indianapolis IN 46204-1782

MAIOCCHI, CHRISTINE, lawyer; b. N.Y.C., Dec. 24, 1949; d. George and Andreina (Toneatto) M.; m. John Charles Kerecz, Aug. 16, 1980; children: Charles George, Joan Christine. BA in Polit. Sci., MA in Polit. Sci., Fordham U., 1971, JD, 1974; postgrad., NYU, 1977—. Bar: N.Y. 1975, U.S. Dist. Ct. (so. and ea. dists.), N.Y. 1975, U.S. Ct. Appeals (2nd cir) 1975. Law clk. to magistrate U.S. Dist. Ct. (so. dist.) N.Y., N.Y.C., 1973-74; atty. corp. legal dept. The Home Ins. Co., N.Y.C., 1974-76; asst. house counsel corp. legal dept. Allied Maintenance Corp., N.Y.C., 1976; atty. corp. legal dept. Getty Oil Co., N.Y.C., 1976-77; v.p., mgr. real estate Paine, Webber, Jackson & Curtis, Inc., N.Y.C., 1977-81; real estate mgr. GK Techs., Inc., Greenwich, Conn., 1981-85; real estate mgr., sr. atty. MCI Telecom. Corp., Rye Brook, N.Y., 1985-93; real estate and legal cons. Wallace Law Registry, 1994-96; sr. assoc. counsel Met. Transp. Authority, 1996-99, dep. gen. counsel, 1999—. Lectr. Practicing Law Inst., N.Y.C., NY, 1999—. Mem.: ABA, Indsl. Devel. Rsch. Coun. (program v.p. 1985, Profl. award 1987), Nat. Assn. Corp. Real Estate Execs. (pres. 1983—84, treas. 1984—86, bd. dirs. 1995—, exec. v.p. N.Y. chpt. 2000—01), The Corp. Bar (sec. real estate divsn. 1987—89, chmn. 1990—92), Women's Bar Assn. Manhattan, NY. Bar Assn., Dobbs Ferry Women's Club (program dir. 1981—92, 1994—96, publicity dir. 1992—94), Jr. League Club. Avocations: sports, theatre, gardening. Property, real (including real estate development, water). Home: 84 Clinton Ave Dobbs Ferry NY 10522-3004 E-mail: cmaiocch@mtahq.org.

MAIWURM, JAMES JOHN, lawyer; b. Wooster, Ohio, Dec. 5, 1948; s. James Frederick and Virginia Anne (Jones) M.; m. Wendy S. Leeper, July 31, 1971; children: James G., Michelle K. BA, Coll. Wooster, 1971; JD, U. Mich., 1974. Bar: Ohio 1974, D.C. 1986, Md. 1987, N.Y., 1987. Ptnr. Squire, Sanders & Dempsey, Cleve. and Washington, 1974-90; ptnr., group head Crowell & Moring, Washington, 1990-98; ptnr. Squire, Sanders & Dempsey, Washington, 1998-99; chmn., CEO Kaiser Group Internat., Inc., Fairfax, Va., 1999-2000; mng. ptnr. Squire, Sanders & Dempsey, Washington, 2001—03; firmwide mng. ptnr. Squine, Sanders & Dempsey, 2003—. Bd. dirs. Workflow Mgmt., Inc., Kaiser-Hill Co., LLC, Kaiser Group Holdings Inc., George Mason U. Coll. Visual and Performing Arts, Cortez, Inc. Contbr. articles to profl. jours. Bd. trustees Davis Meml. Goodwill Industries, 1996—; bd. govs. Tower Club, 2003—; bd. dirs. Coll. Visual and Performing Arts George Mason U., 2003—. Mem. ABA, D.C. Bar Assn., Leadership Washington, Tu Tower Club (bd. govs. 2003—). Corporate, general, Mergers and acquisitions, Securities. Home: 9419 Brian Jac Ln Great Falls VA 22066-2002 Office: Squire Sanders & Dempsey LLP 14th fl 8000 Towers Crescent Vienna VA 22182

MAJEV, HOWARD RUDOLPH, lawyer; b. N.Y.C., Dec. 10, 1952; s. Benny and Hela (Wolnowicz) M.; m. Janet Brandt; children: Brendan Joshua, Collin Campbell. BA, Johns Hopkins U., 1973; JD, U. Md., 1976. Bar: Md. 1978, D.C. 1995. Exec. asst. to city coun. pres. City of Balt., Balt., 1976-79; assoc. Weinberg and Green, Balt., 1979-84; ptnr. Weinberg & Green, Balt., 1985-94, Piper Rudnick LLP (formerly Rudnick & Wolfe), Washington, 1994—2001, Winston & Strawn, Washington, 2001—. Author: (with K.S. Koenig) How to be a Legal Eagle: A Checklist for Remodelers, 1988; dir. Lex Mundi, 1992-94. Dir. Citizens Planning and Housing Assn., Balt., 1985-95, pres., 1990-92; bd. dirs. Md. Food Bank, Inc., 1988-92, Florence Crittenton Svcs. Balt., 1986-87, Sinai Hosp. Balt., 1990-92, Levindale Hebrew Geriat. Home and Hosp., 1991; devel. coun. The Kennedy Krieger Inst., 1988-92; participant Leadership-Greater Balt. Com., 1986. Mem. ABA, D.C. Bar Assn., Md. State Bar Assn. Avocations: tennis, reading. Land use and zoning (including planning), Landlord-tenant, Property, real (including real estate development, water). Office: Winston & Strawn 1400 L St NW Washington DC 20005 E-mail: hmajev@winston.com.

MAJOR, ALICE JEAN, lawyer; b. Denver; m. Kent H. Major, Feb. 16, 1997; children: David, Thomas, Kassie, Samantha, Cameron, Eve, Zoë, Emma. BS in Bus., U. Colo., 1984, MBA, 1986; JD, U. Kans., 1987. Bar: Mo. 1987, Kans. 1988, U.S. Dist. Ct. Kans. 1988, Colo. 1990, U.S. Dist. Ct. Colo. 1991, U.S. Ct. Appeals (3d cir.) 1993, U.S. Supreme Ct. 1994. Atty. Legal Aid of Western Mo., Kansas City, 1987-88, Spencer, Fane, Britt & Browne, Kansas City, 1988-91; mcpl. and county atty. City and County of Denver, 1991—. Spkr. Colorado Springs mtg. Colo. County Attys. Assn., 1992. Vol. Denver Dumb Friends League, Denver, 1996—. Recipient ribbons and awards for paintings. Mem. Alfred A. Arraj Inn of Ct. (barrister mem.). Avocations: art, skiing, fishing. Office: City Attys Office City and County of Denver 1437 Bannock St Rm 353 Denver CO 80202-5375

MALANY, LE GRAND LYNN, lawyer, engineer, bank executive; b. May 14, 1941; s. LeGrand Franklin and Marion (Jaynes) M.; m. Barbara Bumgarner, June 26, 1965; children: LeGrand Karl, Siobhan, Carleen. BS in Engring. Physics, U. Ill., 1964, JD, 1970. Registered profl. engr., Ill.; bar: Ill. 1970, U.S. Dist. Ct. (cen. dist.) Ill. 1970, Ill. Supreme Ct. 1970, U.S. Ct. Mil. Appeals 1971, U.S. Ct. Appeals (7th cir.) 1972, U.S. Dist. Ct. (so. dist.) Ill. 1974, U.S. Supreme Ct. 1975, U.S. Dist. Ct. (no. dist.) Ill. 1982; lic. real estate broker, bldg. inspector, mgmt. planner, and asbestos project designer Ill. Asst. astonomer Adler Planetarium, Chgo., 1960-63; rsch. asst. Portland Cement Rsch. Assn., Skokie, Ill., 1964; instr. dept. gen. engring. U. Ill., 1965-70; instr. Office Instrn. Resources, 1967-68; lectr. Police Tng. Inst., Urbana, Ill., 1969-70; project dir. driver control program U.S. Dept. Transp., 1971-73, project dir., author driver license examiner tng. curriculum, 1973; assoc. drivers license adminstr. State of Ill., Springfield, 1973-74, asst. auditor gen., 1977-83, asst. atty. gen., dir. policy, planning and tech., 1983-85, chief internal auditor office of atty. gen., 1985-86, spl. asst. atty. gen., 1986—, spl. asst. auditor gen. and gen. counsel office auditor gen., 1986-92, gen. counsel state comptroller Cusas II project, 1986-88; ptnr. Kabumoto and Malany, Springfield, 1986—97. Commr. Williamsville-Sherman Water Commn., 1997—; pres. Microgeneral Ltd., 1983—, assoc. ptnr. Johnson & Assoc., 1990-93, Mgmt. Control Sys., Inc., 1986; chmn. bd. Flowers LaGrand Ltd., 1985—; founder, dir. Foster Bank, Chgo., 1988-90; expert U.S. Fed. Energy Adminstrn., 1974; counsel juvenile divsn. Cir. Ct., Sangamon County, Ill., 1973-75; chief counsel Ill. Dept. Motor Vehicles, Springfield, 1974; trustee Meret Ctr., Inc., 1973-75; internat. dir. construction Shelter Now Internat., HQ Oshkosh, Wis., 1999—. Dem. candidate for States Atty., Sangamon County, Ill., 1980; program dir. sch. renovation projects, Macedonia, 2000, Housing Renovations for Refugees, Macedonia, 1999; bd. dirs. J. Keil Braid Leadership Found., Villagrove, Colo., 1997—, Home Ownership Program for Equity, Springfield, Ill., 1998-2001, Springfield Heritage Found., 1999—; country dir. Macedonia for Shelter Now

Internat., 2000—. Recipient Midwest Intergovtl. Audit Forum Recognition award, 1981. Mem. ABA, Am. Phys. Soc., Nat. Soc. Profl. Engrs., Ill. Socs. Profl. Engrs., Ill. Farm Bur., Ill. Christmas Tree Growers Assn., Ill. Foster parents Assn., Rotary (Springfield chpt. sec. 1983-85, pres. 1986-87, trustee Rotary South Found. 1986-93), Habitat for Humanity-Sangamon County (bd. dirs. 1996-2001, dir. constr. 1998-2000). Achievements include development statewide motorcycle driver licensing program. Home: 600 S Rose Hill Ave Springfield IL 62704-1560 Office: 631 E Adams St Springfield IL 62701-1947

MALATESTA, MARY ANNE, lawyer; b. Wapakoneta, Ohio, Aug. 7, 1954; d. Leo J. Jr. and Ellen E. Malatesta. BA in English, Ohio State U., 1976; JD, U. Colo., 1979. Bar: Colo. 1979, U.S. Dist. Ct. Colo. 1979, U.S. Ct. Appeals (9th cir.) 1989, U.S. Ct. Appeals (10th cir.) 1990, U.S. Dist. Ct. Ariz. 1992. Dep. dist. atty. 1st Jud. Dist., Golden, Colo., 1979-84; assoc. Tilly & Graves, P.C., Denver, 1985-88, shareholder, 1988-93; asst. atty. gen. Office Atty. Gen. State of Colo., Denver, 1994—. Mem. faculty Nat. Inst. Trial Advocacy, South Bend, Ind., 1989-90, asst. team leader, 1990-93, team leader, 1994—; lectr. U. Denver, 1990, 91, 97—; guest faculty U. Colo., 1992—; organizer Victims of Violence seminar; mem. faculty Am. Bd. Trial Advocates seminar, 1992, Domestic Violence Prosecution Tng. Course, 1994, Child Advocates Tng. Course, 1996; master Am. Inns of Ct. Judge William E. Doyle Inn, 1994—, Women's Leadership Forum, 1996-2000. Founder, mem. Facio ut Des, Denver, 1987-94. Mem. Colo. Bar Assn., Denver Bar Assn. (professionalism com. 1990—, co-chair professionalism com. 1994-99, professionalism conciliation panel mem. 1999—), Colo. Women's Bar Assn. Avocations: hiking, horseback riding, spectator sports. General civil litigation, Criminal, Product liability. Office: Office of Atty Gen 1525 Sherman St Fl 5 Denver CO 80203-1700

MALAYIL, THOMAS CONNOLLY, real estate developer; b. Oak Park, Ill., Aug. 18, 1971; s. George Kurian Malayil and Ann Connolly. BS, Ariz. State U., 1993; JD, U. Oreg., 1997. Bar: Wash. 1997. Devel. coord. Dial Cos., Moline, Ill., 1993—94; assoc. Lane Powell Spears Lubersky, Seattle, 1997—98; asst. v.p. The Macerich Co., Santa Monica, Calif., 1998—. Mng. dir. Malabar Properties, Santa Monica, Calif., 1993—. Parishioner, vol. St. Monica's Cath. Ch., 1999—. Named to, Order of Omega, Lubbock, Tex., 1993; recipient GM Vol. Spirit award, Ariz. State U., Tempe, 1993. Mem.: ABA, Wash. State Bar Assn., Internat. Coun. Shopping Ctrs., Delta Tau Delta (pres. 1992—93, resident grad. advisor 1995—97, advisor 2002—, Brother of Yr. 1993). Roman Catholic. Avocations: travel, wine, college football, world affairs. Home: 915 Ocean Ave #206 Santa Monica CA 90403 Office: The Macerich Co 401 Wilshire Blvd #700 Santa Monica CA 90401

MALDONADO, KIRK FRANCIS, lawyer; b. Omaha, Mar. 7, 1950; s. Manuel and Orpha Mae (Kovar) Maldonado. B.A., U. Nebr.-Omaha, 1975; J.D., Creighton U., 1978; M.L.T., Georgetown U., 1981. Bar: Nebr. 1978, Calif. 1982. Atty., Employee Plans and Exempt Orgns. Divsn. Office of Chief Counsel, IRS, Washington, 1978-81; assoc. Gibson, Dunn & Crutcher, Newport Beach, Calif., 1982-85; prin. Stradling, Yocca, Carlson & Rauth, Newport Beach, 1985-89, prin. Riordan & McKinzie, Costa Mesa, Calif., 1989-2001. Mem. ABA (employee benefits com.), State Bar Calif. Contbr. articles to profl. jours. Fax: 949-790-6301. E-mail: kmaldonado@brobeck.com. Pension, profit-sharing, and employee benefits. Office: Brobeck Phleger & Harrison LLP 38 Technology Dr Irvine CA 92618

MALEE, THOMAS MICHAEL, lawyer; b. Omaha, May 25, 1947; BA, Carroll Coll., 1970; JD, U. Mont., 1975. Bar: Mont. 1975, U.S. Dist. Ct. Mont. 1975, U.S. Ct. Appeals (9th cir.) 1986, U.S. Supreme Ct. 1988. Staff atty. State of Mont. Legis. Counsel, Helena, Mont., 1975-76; asst. atty. gen. State of Mont., Helena, 1976; pvt. practice Seattle, Tacoma area, Wash., 1977-78, Helena, 1979-82, Billings, Mont., 1982—. Mem. State Bar of Mont. (ins. com. 1988—). Roman Catholic. Avocations: skiing, fitness. Federal civil litigation, General civil litigation, Personal injury (including property damage). Office: 1109 N 22nd St Ste 103A Billings MT 59101-0253

MALEK, HODGE MEHDI, lawyer; b. London, July 11, 1959; s. Ali A. and Irene Elizabeth (Johnson) M.; m. Inez Dies Vegelin Van Claebergen, 1986; children: Yousef, Cyrus, Leila. Diplome, U. Sorbonne, Paris, 1978; MA in Jurisprudence, Oxford U., 1981; B in Civil Law, 1982. Bar: Gray's Inn 1983; Queen's Counsel 1999. Barrister, London, 1983—; customs and excise prosecution list, 1992-99; supplementary treasury panel, 1999; mem. panel Bar Disciplinary Tribunal, 2000—. Co-author: Discovery, 1992, Disclosure, 2001; gen. editor: Phipson on Evidence, 2002. Atkin scholar Gray's Inn, 1982, Birkenhead scholar Gray's Inn, 1983, Band scholar Gray's Inn, 1984; recipient Lee Essay prize Gray's Inn, 1984. Mem. Comml. Bar assn., Adminstrv. Law Bar Assn., Franco-Brit. Lawyers Soc., Bar Sports Group. Avocations: history, swimming, skiing. Office: 4/5 Gray's Inn Sq Gray's Inn WC1R 5AH London England Fax: 020 7242 7803. E-mail: cyrus.malek@ukgateway.net., hmalek@4-5graysinnsquare.co.uk.

MALESKI, CYNTHIA MARIA, lawyer; b. Natrona Heights, Pa., July 4, 1951; d. Richard Anthony and Helen Elizabeth (Palovcak) M.; m. Andrzej G. Groch, Aug. 7, 1982; 1 child, Elizabeth Maria. BA summa cum laude, U. Pitts., 1973; student U. Rouen (France), 1970; JD, Duquesne U., 1976. Bar: Pa. 1976, U.S. dist. ct. (we. dist.) Pa. 1976, U.S. Supreme Ct. 1980, U.S. Ct. Appeals (3d cir.) 1984. Indsl. rels. adminstr. Allegheny Ludlum Industries, Inc., Brackenridge, Pa., 1972-74; law clk. Conte, Courtney, Tarasi & Price, Pitts., 1974, Paul Hammer, Pitts., 1974-76; sole practice Natrona Heights, Pa., 1978-92, 95—; ins. commnr. Penna, 1992—; mem. Gov.'s cabinet, 1992—; v.p., regulatory coun. Highmak Blue Cross/Blue Shield, 1995—; assoc. dir. pers. Mercy Hosp., Pitts., 1976-77, dir. legal affairs, 1977-81, gen. counsel, 1981-92; spl. master Allegheny County Ct. Common Pleas, 1989; bd. dirs. legal adv. bd. Cath. Health Assn., 1980-82; gen. counsel, vice chmn. nat. assembly of reps. Nat. Confedn. Am. Ethnic Groups, 1980— ; health law cons. and lectr. Co-author: The Legal Dimensions of Nursing Practice (Nurses' Book of Month Club award 1982), 1982; contbr. articles to publs. Corp. sec., pres. Duquesne U. Tamburitzans, Pitts.; vice chmn. Czechoslovak room com. Nationality Rooms Program, U. Pitts., 1983; bd. dirs. S.W. Penn. chpt. ARC, 1996-2002; elected mem. Allegheny County Dem. Com., 1986-89; candidate for del. Dem. Nat. Conv. 20th Pa. Congl. Dist., 1984; v.p. Slovak League Am., 1990—; mem. adv. bd. Children's and Youth Services, Allegheny County, 1984—; mem. Allegheny-Keshi Hist. Soc., 1995—; soloist, speaker various groups, Pitts. Slovakians. Scholar U. Rouen, 1970; Allegheny Ludlum Industries scholar, 1969-73; Andrew Mellon scholar, 1969; tuition scholar U. Pitts., 1969-73; tuition remission grantee Duquesne U., 1975, 76; recipient acad. excellence award Duquesne U., 1976, Disting. Alumnus, 1993; Mem. ABA, Am. Soc. Hosp. Attys., Nat. Health Lawyers Assn., Women Execs. in State Govt. (mem. nat. bd. 1994), Soc. Hosp. Attys. of Hosp. Assn. Pa. (v.p.), Soc. Hosp. Attys. Western Pa., Pa. Bar Assn. (commn. on women, 1996—, exec. women's coun.), Allegheny County Bar Assn., Slavic Edn. Assn. (nat. treas. 1981-86), St. Thomas More Soc. (bd. govs. 1980—), First Cath. Slovak Union, 1st Cath. Slovak Women's Assn., Phi Beta Kappa. Roman Catholic. State civil litigation, General practice, Health. Home: 137 Oak Manor Dr Natrona Heights PA 15065-1949 Office: 2413b Freeport Rd Box 263 Natrona Heights PA 15065-0046

MALHOTRA, ANIL, lawyer; b. Calcutta, India, Aug. 29, 1960; s. Tilak Raj and Raj Malhotra; m. Simmi Khanna, Oct. 7, 1995; children: Ankit, Aastha. BS, Panjab U., Chandigarh, India, 1980, LLB, 1983; LLM, U. London, 1985. Lic.: Bar Coun. India. Pvt. practice adv., Chandigarh, 1986—. Legal advisor in field. Contbr. articles to profl. jours. Mem.: Internat. Lawyers Assn., Immigration Law Practitioners Assn., Internat. Bar Assn., Chandigarh Golf Range, Chandigarh Club. Avocations: reading, writing, travel. Home and Office: 584 Sector 16D Chandigarh India

MALIK, JOHN STEPHEN, lawyer; b. Bryn Mawr, Pa., Sept. 15, 1958; s. John and Mary M. (Pisko) M. BA, St. Joseph's U., 1980; JD, Del. Law Sch., 1983. Bar: Del. 1984, Pa. 1984, U.S. Dist. Ct. Del. 1984, N.J. 1985, U.S. Ct. Appeals (3d cir.) 1990, U.S. Supreme Ct. 1989. Adj. faculty Widener U., Wilmington, 1984-86; sole practice Wilmington, 1985—. Mem. ATLA, Am. Judicature Soc., Nat. Assn. Criminal Def. Lawyers, Del. Assn. Criminal Def. Lawyers, Del. Bar Asns. Democrat. Roman Catholic. Criminal. Office: 100 E 14th St Wilmington DE 19801-3210

MALIK, THOMAS WARREN, lawyer; b. Chgo., Mar. 2, 1948; s. Russell R. and Virginia L. M.; m. Karen L. Coy, June 21, 1975. BA, Northwestern U., 1970; JD, Duke U., 1973. Bar: Ill. 1973, U.S. Dist. Ct. (no. dist.) Ill. 1973, U.S. Ct. Appeals (7th cir.) 1976, U.S. Supreme Ct. 1976. Gen. counsel, asst. gen. counsel, atty. Sun Elec. Corp., Chgo., 1973-78; atty. Trans Union Corp., Lincolnshire, Ill., 1978-79; pvt. practice, Barrington and Wauconda, Ill., 1979—. Arbitrator Cir. Ct. Cook County, Chgo., 1990—, Cir. Ct. 19th Jud. Cir., Waukegan, Ill., 1990—. Mem. Ill. Bar Assn., Lake County Bar Assn., Chgo. Bar Assn. General civil litigation, Probate (including wills, trusts), Property, real (including real estate development, water). Office: 211 S Main St Wauconda IL 60084-1868 E-mail: thomas@malik.lawoffice.com.

MALKIN, CARY JAY, lawyer; b. Chgo., Oct. 6, 1949; s. Arthur D. and Perle (Slavin) M.; m. Lisa Klimley, Oct. 27, 1976; children: Dorothy R., Victoria S., Lydia R. BA, George Washington U., 1971; JD, Northwestern U., 1974. Bar: Ill. 1974, U.S. Dist. Ct. (no. dist.) Ill. 1974, N.Y. 2001. Assoc. Mayer, Brown & Platt, Chgo., 1974-80, ptnr., 1991—2002; ptnr. Mayer, Brown, Rowe & Maw, Chgo., 2002—. Chmn. spl. events com. Mental Health Assn., 1984-85; mem. steering com. Endowment Campaign of the Latin Sch. of Chgo., 1990-91, trustee, 1991-2000, v.p., 1992-98, chmn. capital campaign, 1995-98, nat. trustee, 2000-2002, sr. trustee, 2002—; mem. exec. com. Friends of Prentice Women's Hosp., 1991-92; bd. dirs. SOS Children's Village Ill., 1992-96; mem. M.S. Weiss fund bd. Children's Meml. Hosp., 1989-93; mem. Graziano Fund bd. Children's Meml. Hosp., 1993-96; mem. steering com. Founder's Coun. Field Mus., 1995—, chmn. steering com., 1999-2003, trustee, 1999—. Mem. Chgo. Club, Saddle and Cycle Club, Arts Club, Standard Club, Order of the Coif, Phi Beta Kappa. Banking, Corporate, general, Finance. Home: 23 E Walton St Chicago IL 60611-1526 Office: Mayer Brown Rowe & Maw 190 S La Salle St Ste 3100 Chicago IL 60603-3441

MALKIN, PETER LAURENCE, lawyer, real estate investor; b. N.Y.C., Jan. 14, 1934; s. Samuel and Gertrude (Greenberger) Malkin; m. Isabel L. Wien, July 10, 1955. Grad. cum laude, Poly. Prep. Country Day Sch., 1951; AB summa cum laude, Harvard Coll., 1955; LLB magna cum laude, Harvard U. Law Sch., 1958. Bar: N.Y. 1958, Conn. 1976, Fla. 1977. Sr. ptnr., chmn. Wien & Malkin LLP, N.Y.C., 1958—; mng. Empire State Bldg. Assocs. L.L.C., 1961—; chmn. W & M Properties, Inc., N.Y.C., 1965—. Bd. dirs. U.S. Trust Corp.; ptnr. N.Y.C. Partnership and C. of C., 2001—; founding chmn. Grand Ctrl. Partnership Inc. & 34th Street Partnership, Inc.; dir., sec. Fashion Ctr. Bus. Improvement Dist.; dir. Realty Found. N.Y., 1981—, v.p., 1995—; mem. adv. com. Greenwich (Conn.) Japanese Sch., 1992—; mem. N.Y.C. Mayor's Bus. Adv. Coun., 1997—2002; gov. Real Estate Bd., N.Y.C., 1993—2000, N.Y.C., 2001—; co-founder, hon. co-chmn. Com. to Encourage Corp. Philanthropy, 1998—. Nat. vice-chmn. Harvard Law Sch. Fund, 1967-71, chmn. nat. scholarship com., 1975-76, chmn. N.Y.C. com., 1981-83; founder, bd. dirs. Urban League Southwestern Fairfield County, 1969-73, treas., 1969-71; bd. dirs., mem. exec. com. Lincoln Ctr. for Performing Arts, 1979—; bd. dirs. Inst. Internat. Edn., 1983-89, hon. 1994—; trustee Nat. Trust for Hist. Preservation, 1988-91, mem. adv. coun., 1997—; founding chmn. Greenwich (Conn.) Green & Clean, Inc., 1986—, Greenwich Adopt-A-Road, 1996-; v.p., mem. exec. com. Greenwich chpt. NAACP, 1967-69; trustee Citizens Budget Commn., N.Y.C., 1971-91, Jewish Communal Fund, N.Y., 1976-81; dean's coun., Harvard U., 1987-95; chmn. capital campaign and chmn. dean's coun. Kennedy Sch. Govt., 1995—, mem. overseers com. to visit Kennedy Sch. Govt., 1976-82, 83-89, 90—, to visit Harvard Law Sch. 1977-83; exec. com. Program for Ctr. for Jewish Studies, 1974-80; bd. overseers Harvard Coll., 1989-95, overseers com. univ resources, 1972—, exec. com., 1985—; dean's adv. com., Harvard Law Sch., 1988-90; elected dir. Harvard Alumni Assn., 1981-83; chmn. schs. and scholarship com. Harvard U., Greenwich, 1973-79; exec. com. Assn. Better N.Y., 1972—. Recipient Nat. Preservation Honor award Nat. Trust Hist. Preservation, 1987, President's award Grad. Sch. and Univ. Ctr. CCNY, 1989, Crain's All-Star award, 1994, Nacore Disting. Man of Yr. award, 1995; named Outstanding Young Man, N.Y.C. Jaycees, 1969, fellow Brandeis U., 1970—, Man of Yr., Hist. Soc. Greenwich, Conn., 1993. Mem. Harvard Law Sch. Assn. N.Y.C. (trustee 1968-70, v.p. 1973-74), Assn. Bar City N.Y., Century Assn., The Links N.Y., The Hasty Pudding Inst. 1770, AD Hon., Harvard Varsity Club (Cambridge), Harvard Club N.Y.C. (bd. mgrs. 1979-81), Harvard Club (Fairfield County, Conn., v.p. 1974-75, bd. dirs. 1976-80), Bailwick Club (hon. life mem., founding pres.), Blind Brook Club, Conn. Golf Club, Phi Beta Kappa. Estate planning, Property, real (including real estate development, water), Personal income taxation. Office: 60 E 42d St New York NY 10165-0015 Office Fax: 212-850-2780. E-mail: plmalkin@wienmalkinllp.com.

MALL, JAMES RICHARD, lawyer; b. Pitts., Nov. 15, 1952; s. William John and Margaret (Henry) M.; m. Cathy Jane Conrad, Aug. 14, 1976; children: Jennifer Kathleen, Benjamin James Conrad. BBA, Notre Dame, 1974; MBA, JD, U. Notre Dame, 1978. Bar: Pa. 1978, U.S. Dist. Ct. (ea. dist.) Pa. 1979, U.S. Dist. Ct. (we. dist.) Pa. 1980, U.S. Ct. Appeals (3d cir. 1982), U.S. Supreme ct. 1991. Law clk. to pres. judge Commonwealth Ct. of Pa., Phila., 1978-80; assoc. Meyer, Unkovic & Scott, Pitts., 1980-86, ptnr., 1987—. Fellow Acad. Trial Lawyers Allegheny County; mem. ABA, Pa. Bar Assn., Allegheny County Bar Assn., ATLA, Western Pa. Trial Lawyers Assn., Rivers Club, Sewickley Heights Golf Club (bd. dirs. 1990-98, pres. 1996-98), Notre Dame Club Pitts. (exec. com. 1980—). General civil litigation, Land use and zoning (including planning), Construction. Office: Meyer Unkovic & Scott Oliver Building Ste 1300 Pittsburgh PA 15222-2393 E-mail: jrm@muslaw.com.

MALLAM, PAUL RODERICK, solicitor; b. Australia, Oct. 13, 1957; BA, U of Sydney, 1980; LLB, Australian National U, 1986. Solicitor Blake, Dawson, Waldron, Sydney, Australia, 1988—93, ptnr., 1993—2002. Author: (looseleaf svc.) Media Law and Practice, 1991—; editor: (jour.) Media Law, Jour. and Policy, 1995—99; contbg. editor (cons.): Telecommunications Law & Policy, 1997—2000. Mem.: NSW Soc. Office: Blake Dawson Waldron 225 George St Sydney NSW 2000 Australia

MALLARD, HEATHER K. lawyer; b. New Kensington, Pa., Sept. 23, 1963; d. William and Shirley B. King; m. S. Craig Mallard, Jan. 10, 1998. BA, Grove City Coll., 1985; JD, Washington and Lee U., 1988. Bar: N.C. 1988, U.S. Dist. Ct. (mid. dist.) N.C. 1988. Assoc. Womble Carlyle Sandridge & Rice, PLLC, Winston-Salem, NC, 1988—95, mem., 1995—, Raleigh, NC, 1996—. Mem. econ. devel. com. N.C. Citizens for Bus. and Industry, Raleigh, 2002—03. Participant Lunch with a Lawyer summer program Wake County Bar Assn., Raleigh, 2002—; mem. fin. com. Angier (N.C.) United Meth. Ch., 2002—. Mem.: Washington and Lee U. Law Alumni Assn. (emeritus, pres. 1999—2000). Republican. Avocations: reading, camping, cooking. Corporate, general, Mergers and acquisitions, Securities. Office: Womble Carlyle Sandridge & Rice PLLC Ste 2100 150 Fayetteville St Mall Raleigh NC 27601

MALLAS, KOSTANTINOS, lawyer; b. Bklyn., N.Y., Feb. 11, 1973; s. James and Eugenia Mallas; m. Maria Countouroudas, May 2, 1999; children: Evgenia, Dmitrios. BS, St. John's U., 1995, JD, 1998. Bar: N.Y. 1998, U.S. Dist. Ct. (ea. dist.) N.Y. 1998, U.S. Dist. Ct. (so. dist.) N.Y. 2001. Counsel Crasto & Assocs., Howard Beach, NY, 1998—2000; trial counsel Sullivan Papain Block McGrath & Cannavo, N.Y.C., 2000—. Mem. Cmty. Bd. 10, Bklyn., 2000—. Mem.: ATLA, N.Y. State Trial Lawyers, N.Y. State Bar Assn. Personal injury (including property damage).

MALLIA, MICHAEL PATRICK, lawyer; b. Galveston, Tex., Aug. 1, 1946; s. Simon A. Mallia, Jr. and Aleta Jo (Wooten) Benson; 1 child, Lindsay. BS, Lamar State Coll. Tech., 1968; JD, South Tex. Coll., 1973. Bar: Tex. 1973; bd. cert. Nat. Bd. Trial Advocacy, Personal Injury Trial Law, Civil Trial Law. Atty. Law Offices of Dan Ryan, Houston, 1973-75, Law Office of Michael P. Mallia, Houston, 1975-80; atty., ptnr. Barnhart, Mallia & Cochran, Houston, 1981-89, Mallia & Jacobs, Houston, 1989-99; ptnr. The Mallia Law Firm, Houston, 1999—. Chmn. dist. 4H23 grievance com. State Bar Tex., 1997-2002. With U.S. Army, 1969-71. Fellow ABA, Houston Bar Found.; mem. Trial Lawyers for Pub. Justice (sustaining founder), Tex. Trial Lawyers, Assn. Trial Lawyers Am., Houston Trial Lawyers Assn. (bd. dirs. 1991-93, pres.-elect 1993-94, pres. 1994-95), Tex. Assn. Civil Trial Specialists, Am. Bd. Profl. Liability Attys., Houston Assn. Civil Trial Specialists, Houston Trial Lawyers Found. (Vol. of Yr. 1997-98, bd. dirs. 1992—, pres. 1995-96), Am. Bd. Trial Advocates, Delta Theta Phi (dean 1972-73). Avocations: sailing, snow skiing, running. General civil litigation, Product liability, Personal injury (including property damage). Office: Mallia Law Firm One Riverway Ste 610 Houston TX 77056 E-mail: mike@mallia.com.

MALLORY, CHARLES KING, III, lawyer; b. Norfolk, Va., Nov. 16, 1936; s. Charles King Mallory Jr. and Dorothy Pratt (Williams) Swanke; m. Florence Beale Marshall; children: King, Raburn, Anne, Richard. BA, Yale U., 1958; JD, Tulane U., 1961. Bar: La. 1961, Calif. 1965, D.C. 1972. Ptnr. Monroe & Lemann, New Orleans, 1965-72; acting exec. dir. SEC, Washington, 1972; dep. asst. sec. U.S. Dept. Interior, Washington, 1973, acting asst. sec., 1974; v.p., gen. counsel Middle South Svcs., Inc., New Orleans, 1975-79; ptnr. Hunton & Williams, Washington, 1979—. Gen. counsel Com. on the Present Danger, 1987-91. Mem. Reagan-Bush Transition Team, Washington, 1980-81, Grace Commn. on Pvt. Sector Survey Cost in the Fed. Govt., Washington, 1983-84. Served to lt. USNR, 1961-65. Mem. ABA, La. Bar Assn., Calif. Bar Assn., D.C. Bar Assn., Fed. Energy Bar Assn., Nat. Assn. Bond Lawyers. Republican. Episcopalian. FERC practice, Legislative, Utilities, public. Office: Hunton & Williams 1900 K St NW # 12 Washington DC 20006-1110 E-mail: kmallory@hunton.com.

MALLORY, FRANK LINUS, lawyer; b. Calgary, Alberta, Canada, May 5, 1920; s. Frank Louis and Anna Amy (Allstrum) M.; m. Jean Ellen (Lindsey), Jan. 29, 1944; children: Susan Mallory Remund, Ann, Bruce R. AB, Stanford U., 1941, LLB, 1947. Bar: Calif., 1948. Assoc. Gibson, Dunn, and Crutcher, L.A., 1947-54; ptnr. L.A. and Orange County, 1955-88. Cert. specialist taxation law Calif. Bd. Legal Splty., 1973-89. Pres. town hall of L.A., 1970; Boys Republic, Chino, Calif., 1962-64; pres. Braille Inst. Am., L.A., 1988-92; Lt.(j.g.), USNR, 1942-46. Mem. ABA; Los Angeles County Bar Assn.; Orange County Bar Assn.; Newport Harbor Yacht Club; Big Canyon Country Club; Transpacific Yacht Club (staff commodore); Order of the Coif; Phi Beta Kappa. Republican. Private international, Probate (including wills, trusts). Home: 633 Bayside Dr Newport Beach CA 92660-7213 E-mail: flmallory@cs.com.

MALLOY, MICHAEL PATRICK, law educator, writer, consultant; b. Haddon Heights, N.J., Sept. 23, 1951; s. Francis Edward and Marie Grace (Nardi) M.; divorced; 1 child, Elizabeth; m. Susie Pieratos, Jan., 1992; children: Michael Emil, Nicholas Charles, Edward Francis, Theodora Marie. BA magna cum laude (scholar), Georgetown U., 1973, PhD, 1983; JD (scholar), U. Pa., 1976. Bar: N.J. 1976, U.S. Supreme Ct. 1991. Rsch. assoc. Inst. Internat. Law and Econ. Devel., Washington, 1976—77; atty. advisor Office Fgn. Assets Control Dept. Treasury, Washington, 1977—80, Office of Comptroller of Currency, Washington, 1981; spl. counsel SEC Washington, 1981—82; asst. prof. N.Y. Law Sch., N.Y.C., 1982—83; spl. asst. Office of Gen. Counsel U.S. Dept. Treasury, Washington, 1985; assoc. prof. Seton Hall U. Sch. Law, Newark, 1983—86, prof., assoc. dean, 1986—87; prof. Fordham U. Sch. Law, N.Y.C., 1987—96, dir. grad. studies, 1990—94; prof. U. of Pacific McGeorge Law Sch., 1996—2002, disting. prof. and scholar, 2003—. Law lectr. Morin Ctr. Banking and Fin. Law Studies Boston U. Sch. Law, 1986-90, 95-96, 2001; vis. prof. U. Salzburg, Austria, 2000, Suffolk U. Sch. Law, 2001-2002; cons. bank regulation and pvt. internat. law matters. Author: Corporate Law of Banks, 2 vols., 1988, Economic Sanctions and U.S. Trade, 1990, The Regulation of Banking, 1992, Banking Law and Regulation, 3 vols., 1994, Fundamentals of Banking Regulation, 1998, International Banking, 1998, Banking and Financial Services Law, 1999, Hornbook on Bank Regulation, 1999, 2d edit., 2003, U.S. Economic Sanctions: Theory and Practice, 2001; contbr. articles and revs. and comments to profl. jours. Recipient Spl. Achievement award Dept. Treasury, 1982. Mem.: L'Association des Auditeurs et Anciens Auditeurs de l'Academie de Droit International de la Haye, Hegel Soc. Am., Assn. Am. Law Schs. (chair-elect and program chair 2001—02, chair sect. fin. insts. and consumer fin. svcs. 2002—03), Internat. Law Assn. (com. chair Am. br. 1995—97), Am. Soc. Internat. Law (exec. coun. 1986—89), Phi Beta Kappa. Office: U of Pacific McGeorge Sch Law 3200 5th Ave Sacramento CA 95817-2705 E-mail: malloympm@aol.com.

MALM, ROGER CHARLES, lawyer; b. Hot Springs, S.D., July 8, 1949; s. Harry Milton and Angeline Mae (Johnson) M.; m. Sandra M. Metz, July 15, 1972; children: Andrew, Elliott, Nicholas. BA, St. Olaf Coll., 1971; JD, U. N.D., 1974. Bar: N.D. 1974, Ariz. 1975, Minn. 1980, U.S. Dist. Ct. N.D. 1974, U.S. Dist. Ct. Ariz. 1976, U.S. Ct. Appeals (9th cir.) 1981, U.S. Supreme Ct. 1981, U.S. Ct. Appeals (8th cir) 1982, U.S. Dist. Ct. Minn. 1985, U.S. Claims Ct. 1985, U.S. Tax Ct. 1988. Ptnr. Brink, Sobolik, Severson, Malm & Albrecht, P.A., Hallock, Minn., 1980—; county atty. Kittson County, Minn., 1995—. Pres. N.W. Minn. County Atty.'s Coun. Hospice dir. Kittson County Hospice, Inc., 1984—; bd. dirs. Cmty. Theatre, Hallock, 1987—, Greater Grand Forks Cmty. Theater, 1991-95. Mem. ABA, Ariz. Bar Assn., N.D. Bar Assn., Minn. Bar Assn. (mem. bd. govs. 1993-2000), Am. Acad. Hosp. Attys., Norwest Minn. Atty.'s Coun. (pres.). Lutheran. Avocations: skiing, sailing. General civil litigation, General practice, Health. Office: Brink Sobolik Severson Malm & Albrecht PO Box 790 Hallock MN 56728-0790

MALM, SCOTT, lawyer; BA magna cum laude, Brigham Young U., 1975, JD, 1978. Bar: Calif. 1978, U.S. Dist. Ct. (ea. dist.) Calif. 1978, U.S. Claims Ct. 1991, U.S. Supreme Ct., 1994, U.S. Dist. Ct. (no. dist.) Calif. 1998; cert. Nev. 2d Jud. Dist. 1986. Assoc. Steinheimer, Riggio, Haydel & Mordaunt, Stockton, Calif., 1978-84, prin., 1984-99, Cassel Malm Fagundes, Stockton, Calif., 2000—. Judge pro tem San Joaquin County Mcpl. Ct.; arbitrator San Joaquin County Superior Ct.; spkr. and presenter in field. Contbr. articles to profl. jours. Mem. San Joaquin County Bar Assn. (chair mandatory fee arbitration com. 1983-87, 2001—, chair client rels. com. 1988-89, mem. bus. litig. sect. 1997—). General civil litigation, Commercial, contracts (including sales of goods; commercial financing), Labor (including EEOC, Fair Labor Standards Act, labor-management relations, NLRB, OSHA). Office: 6 S El Dorado Ste 601 Stockton CA 95202 Fax: 209-870-7922. E-mail: scottm@cmf-law.com.

MALME, JANE HAMLETT, lawyer, educator, advisor; b. N.Y.C., Dec. 2, 1934; d. Robert T. and Minnie (Means) Hamlett; m. Charles I. Malme, June 17, 1961; children: Robert H., Karen I. AB, Brown U., 1956; cert., U. Kobenhavn, Copenhagen, Denmark, 1959; JD, Northeastern U., 1977. Bar:

Mass., 1977. Counsel Mass. Tax Commn., Boston, 1978-79; chief bur. local assessment Mass. Dept. Revenue, Boston, 1978-90; prin. Mcpl. Mgmt. and Taxation Cons. Svcs., Hingham, Mass., 1990—; fellow Lincoln Inst. Land Policy, Inc., Cambridge, Mass., 1993—. Faculty Lincoln Inst. Land Policy, Inc., Cambridge, 1989—; adv. property tax OECD, Paris, 1993-97; legal adv. property tax USAID, Russia, 1995-99, Korea Tax Inst., 1995-96, Poland, 1998-99, Slovenia, 2001-03, Lithuania, 2002-03. Author: (with Joan Youngman) Internat. Survey of Taxes on Land and Buildings, 1994, Development of Property Taxation in Countries in Transition, 2001; contbr. articles profl. jours. Trustee Old Ship Ch., Hingham, 1992-97; treas. Betty Taymor Scholarship Fund, Boston, 1992—; pres. Network for Women in Politics and Govt., McCormack Inst., Boston, 1992-94, mem. adv. com. Ctr. for Women in Politics and Pub. Policy, U. Mass., Boston, 1998—. chmn. Friends of Old Ship Meeting House Trust, 2002—. Mem. Internat Assn. Assessing Officers (founder, state and prov. adminstrv. sec., legal com. 1997-, Presidential citation 1983), Mass. Assn. Assessing Officers (hon. lifetime), Mass. Bar Assn., Nat. Tax Assn. (program com. 1998-99), Nat. Assn. Tax Adminstrs. (chair property tax sect. 1988). Unitarian Universalist. Avocations: community service, women in politics, travel.

MALONE, DAVID ROY, educational association administrator; b. Beebe, Ark., Nov. 4, 1943; s. James Roy and Ila Mae (Griffin) M.; m. Judith Kaye Huff, June 20, 1965 (div. Feb. 1990); 1 child, Michael David. BSBA, U. Ark., 1965, JD, 1969, MBA, 1982. Bar: Ark. 1969, U.S. Dist. Ct. (we. dist.) Ark. 1969, U.S. Tax Ct. 1972, U.S. Ct. Appeals (8th cir.) 1972, U.S. Supreme Ct. 1972. Pvt. practice, Fayetteville, Ark., 1969-72; atty. City of Fayetteville, 1969-72; asst. prof. bus. U. Ark., Fayetteville, 1972-76, asst. dean law, 1976-91; mem. Ark. Ho. of Reps., 1980-84, Ark. Senate, 1984—2002; exec. dir. U. Ark. Found., 1991—2002, Ark. Tchr. Ret. Sys., 2003—. Chair Senate edn. com., 1997-2002, co-chair legis. coun., 1999-2000; bd. dirs. Bank of Elkins, 1976-98, S.W. Edn. Devel. Lab., Austin, Tex., 1988-94; legal adv. coun. So. Regional Edn. Bd., Atlanta, 1991-2002. Contbr. articles to profl. jours.; bd. dirs. Ark. Law Rev., 1978-92; contbg. author U. Ark. Press, 1989. Mayor City of Fayetteville, 1979-80; mem. Jud. Article Task Force, Little Rock, 1989-91; chair Motor Voter task force, 1994-95; bd. dirs. Music Festival Ark., 1989-91, Washington County Hist. Soc., 1993-96; bd. dirs. Walton Arts Ctr. Found., 1994-2000, chmn., 1994-98; chmn. bd. dirs. Washington County Law Libr., 1970-84; chmn. Ark. Tuition Trust Authority, 1997-99. Recipient Svc. award Ark. Mcpl. League, 1980, Disting. Service award U. Ark., 1988, Lucas Svc. award, Ark. Alumni Assn., 1998. Mem. Ark. Bar Assn. (ho. of dels. 1977-81, award of merit 1980, exec. 1981-82, Outstanding Lawyer-Citizen award 1990), Washington County Bar Assn., Ark. Inst. Continuing Legal Edn. (bd. dirs. 1979-88), Fayetteville C. of C. (bd. dirs. 1984-99), Ark. Genealogy Soc. (bd. dirs. 1990-99). Democrat. Methodist. Avocations: genealogy, stamp collecting. Home: 804 N Arthur St Little Rock AR 72205-2902 Office: 1400 W Third St Little Rock AR 72201-1048

MALONE, THOMAS WILLIAM, lawyer; b. Seattle, Sept. 16, 1946; s. James Edward and Marie Cecilia (Anderson) M.; m. Drexel Cox, June 19, 1978; children: Jason, Cary, Jane Marie. BA, U. Wash., 1968, JD, 1972; MBA, Golden Gate U., 1982. Bar: Wash. 1972, U.S. Ct. Appeals (9th cir.) 1972, U.S. Tax Ct. 1980, U.S. Ct. Claims 1981, U.S. Supreme Ct. 1980. Prin. Treece Richale Malone PS, Seattle, 1973-2000, Malone, Galvin & Spicer PS, Seattle, 2001—. Pres. Seattle Marine Bus. Coalition, 1983-86; bd. dirs. Ballard Cmty. Hosp., 1982-91, North Seattle C.C. Found., 1989-97, chmn. 1992-93; bd. dirs. Swedish Med. Ctr.-Ballard Found., 1991-95; chmn. bd. dirs. Ballard Cmty. Hosp., 1986-88; bd. dirs. Swedish Health Systems, 1992-; gov. Swedish Found., 2001-; vice-chmn. Swedish Health Systems, 1995, chair 1996-99; chmn. City of Seattle Fair Campaign Practices Commn., 1986-92; bd. ethics City of Seattle, 1986-92; chmn. City of Seattle Ethics and Elections Com., 1992; trustee Seattle C.C. Dist., 1997—, chmn. 1998-2000. Mem. ABA, Wash. Bar Assn., Seattle-King County Bar Assn., Ballard C. of C. (pres. 1981-84). Corporate, general, Estate planning, Taxation, general. Office: Malone Galvin Spicer PS 10202 5th NE #201 Seattle WA 98125

MALONE, WILLIAM GRADY, retired lawyer; b. Minden, La., Feb. 19, 1915; s. William Gordon and Minnie Lucie (Hortman) M.; m. Marion Rowe Whitfield, Sept. 26, 1943; children: William Grady, Gordon Whitfield, Marion Elizabeth, Helen Ann, Margaret Catherine. BS, La. State U., 1941; JD, George Washington U., 1952. Bar: Va. 1952, U.S. Supreme Ct 1971. Statis. analyst Dept. Agr., Baton Rouge, 1941; investigator VA, Washington, 1946-59, legal officer, dep., gen. counsel, asst. gen. counsel, 1959-79; pvt. practice law Arlington, Va., 1979-97. Editor: Fed. Bar News, 1972-73. Pres. Aurora Hills Civic Assn., 1948-49; spl. asst. to treas. Com. of 100, 1979-81, chmn., 1982-83; pres. Children's Theater, 1968-69; trustee St. George's Episc. Ch., 1979— ; chmn. Arlington County Fair Assn., 1979-83. Lt. col. AUS, 1941-46, ETO. Decorated Legion of Merit; recipient Disting. Svc. award, 1979, 3 Superior Performance awards, 1952-72, Outstanding Alumni award George Washington Law Sch., 1978 Mem. Fed. Bar Assn. (pres. D.C. chpt. 1970-71, nat. pres. 1978-79), Va. Bar Assn., Arlington County Bar Assn., Nat. Lawyers Club (dir.), Arlington Host Lions, Ft. Myer Officers Club. Family and matrimonial, Personal injury (including property damage), Probate (including wills, trusts). Home: 900 N Taylor St Apt 1523 Arlington VA 22203 E-mail: wgmalone@juno.com.

MALONE, WILLIAM ROBERT, lawyer; b. Terre Haute, Ind., Apr. 15, 1936; s. Leander Alonso and Dorothy Alice (Reveal) M.; m. Jane H. Foulkes, June 25, 1959 (dec.); children: Elizabeth, David, Christina. AB, Harvard U., 1958, JD, 1962. Bar: Ind. 1962, D.C. 1963, Conn. 1981. Law clk. to presiding justice U.S. Ct. Appeals, D.C., 1962-63; assoc. Covington & Burling, Washington, 1963-70; atty. Gen. Tel. & Electronics Corp., Washington, 1970-72; v.p., assoc. gen. counsel GTE Corp., Stamford, Conn., 1981-86; of counsel Miller & Holbrooke, Washington, 1989-94, Miller, Canfield, Paddock & Stone, Washington, 1994—96; ptnr. Miller & Van Eaton, PLLC, Washington, 1996—. Author: Broadcast Regulation in Can., 1962. Served with signal corps U.S. Army, 1959 Mem. ABA, Fed. Bar Assn., Fed. Communications Bar Assn., Computer Law Assn. (bd. dirs.). Republican. Presbyterian. Appellate, Communications, Trademark and copyright. Home: 9117 Vendome Dr Bethesda MD 20817-4022 Office: Miller & Van Eaton PLLC 1155 Connecticut Ave NW Ste 1000 Washington DC 20036-4306

MALONEY, MARILYN C. lawyer; b. New Orleans, Nov. 24, 1950; BA, La. State U., 1972, JD, 1975. Bar: La. 1975, U.S. Dist. Ct. (ea. dist.) La. Ptnr. Liskow & Lewis, New Orleans, 1975—. Contbr. articles to profl. jours. Fellow Am. Coll. Real Estate Lawyers; mem. La. State Law Inst. (v.p.), La. Bar Found. (bd. dirs.), Order of Coif, Omicron Delta Kappa. Banking, Property, real (including real estate development, water). Office: Liskow & Lewis 1 Shell Sq Fl 50 New Orleans LA 70139

MALONEY, MARYNELL, lawyer; b. Hutchinson, Kans., Jan. 14, 1955; d. Robert Edgar and Marian Ellen (Benson) Baker; m. Michael D. Maloney, Nov. 30, 1977; children: Michelle M., Erica O., Dennis Jr. BA, Oberlin Coll., 1975; MA, Trinity U., San Antonio, 1978; JD, St. Mary's U., San Antonio, 1980. Cert. by Tex. bd. of legal specialization. Assoc. Law Offices Pat Maloney, P.C., San Antonio, 1981-82; ptnr., owner Maloney & Maloney, San Antonio, 1982—. Bd. dirs. San Antonio Internat. Keyboard Competition, 1988-90; bd. govs. St. Peters/St. Joseph's Children's Home, San Antonio, 1989-92. Mem. ACLU of Tex. (bd. dirs. 1990—, v.p. 1995-96, SACLU 1990—), Am. Trial Lawyers Assn., State Bar Tex., Tex. Trial Lawyers Assn. (assoc. bd. dirs. 1989-90, bd. dirs. 1991-2002, dir. emeritus 2002—, cert. personal injury trial law), San Antonio Bar Assn., San Antonio Trial Lawyers Assn. (pres. 1991-92). Democrat. Avocations: reading, writing, film. Civil rights, State civil litigation, Personal injury (including property damage). Office: Maloney & Maloney PC 2000 Milam 115 E Travis San Antonio TX 78205

MALONEY, PAT, SR., lawyer; b. Dallas, Tex., Aug. 9, 1924; s. James Edward and Flora Agnes (Kessler) M.; m. Olive Boger, May 20, 1950; children: Patricia, Pat Jr., Michael, Janice, Tim. BJ, U. Tex., 1948, LLB, 1950. Bar: Tex. 1950, U.S. Dist. Ct. (we. dist.) Tex. 1955, U.S. Supreme Ct. 1951; cert. civil law and personal injury trial law, Tex. Bd. Legal Specialization, civil trial advocacy Nat. Bd. Trial Advocacy. 1st asst. trial chief Dist. Atty.'s Office, San Antonio, Tex., 1950-53; pvt. practice Law Offices of Pat Maloney P.C., San Antonio, 1953—. Moderator, founder annual seminar Anatomy of a Lawsuit, St. Mary's U., San Antonio; frequent lectr. throughout U.S. in areas of product liability and personal injury law. Author: Winning the Million Dollar Law Suit, 1980; co-author: Trials and Deliberations: Inside the Jury Room, 1992. With USMC, 1942-45, PTO. Recipient Warhorse award So. Trial Lawyers Assn., 1992. Fellow Law Sci. Acad. Am., Am. Bd. Trial Advocates (pres. Inner Circle of Trial Advocates) mem. ATLA, Internat. Soc. Barristers, Internat. Acad. Trial Lawyers, San Antonio Trial Lawyers Assn. (co-founder, pres. 1967, 72, bd. dirs. 1967-73,) San Antonio Bar Assn., State Bar of Tex., Tex. Trial Lawyers Assn. (director emeritus) Democrat. Roman Catholic. Achievements include 1977 personal injury verdict awarding his client $26,510,800.00. At that time the largest personal injury verdict in the history of the U.S. He has obtained verdicts and settlements in excess of a million dollars more than fifty times. General civil litigation, Product liability, Personal injury (including property damage). Office: 239 E Commerce St San Antonio TX 78205-2931

MALONEY, ROBERT E., JR., lawyer; b. San Francisco, Sept. 17, 1942; s. Robert E. and Mara A. (Murphy) M.; children: Michael, Sarah, Paul. BA magna cum laude, U. Portland, 1964; JD summa cum laude, Willamette U., Salem, Oreg., 1967. Bar: Oreg., Wash., U.S. Dist. Ct. Oreg., U.S. Dist. Ct. (we. dist.) Wash., U.S. Dist. Ct. (ea. dist.) Wash., U.S. Ct. Appeals (9th cir.). Ptnr. Lane Powell Spears Lubersky, LLP, Portland, 1967—. Bd. dirs., sec. Norm Thompson Outfitters, Inc., Portland; chmn. bd. visitors Willamette U. Law Sch., 1993-95, bd. dirs. emeritus, 1998—; past chair, mem. exec. com. Portland Trial Dept.; lawyers del. 9th Cir. Jud. Conf., 1995-97; pres. adv. coun. U. Portland, 2001—. Bd. dirs., Oreg. chpt. Multiple Sclerosis Soc., 19905-2002, Children's Cancer Assn., Oreg. Independent Coll. Found., Oreg. Lawyers Against Hunger, 1997-99; judge pro tem Multnomah County Cir. Ct., 1994-99. Mem. ABA (co-chair products liability com., trial practice com. 1990-94), Nat. Assn. R.R. Trial Counsel, Fedn. Ins. Corp. Counsel, Oreg. Assn. Def. Counsel (bd. dirs. 1987-94, sec. 1991-92, v.p. 1993-94, pres. 1994), Fed. Bar Assn. (exec. com. Oreg. divsn. 1988-96, pres. 1994-95), Multnomah Athletic Club. Republican. Roman Catholic. General civil litigation, Condemnation (eminent domain), Product liability. Office: Lane Powell Spears Lubersky LLP 601 SW Second Ave Ste 2100 Portland OR 97204-3158 Fax: 503-778-2200.

MALOOF, FARAHE PAUL, lawyer; b. Boston, Feb. 10, 1950; s. Farahe and Emily Suzanna (Puchy) M.; divorced; children: Alexandre F., Melissa F. BS, Georgetown U., 1975, JD, 1978. Bar: D.C. 1978, Va. 1981, Md. 1990. Assoc. Corcoran & Rowe, Washington, 1978-82; ptnr. Berliner & Maloney, Washington, 1982-84; internat. legal counsel Advocacia Oliveira Ribeiro, Sao Paulo, Brazil, 1984-85; sole practice Washington, 1985-86; prin. Maloof & Assocs., Washington, 1986-97; of counsel Haas & Anderson, P.C., McLean, Va., 1997-99; mem. Brincefield Hartnett Maloof & Paleos, P.C., Alexandria, Va., 2000—02; prin. Maloof & Assocs., Alexandria, 2003—. Lectr. Am. U., Washington, 1984-85, Internat. Law Inst., Washington, 1986-87. Active Reagan-Bush campaign, Washington, 1984, Frank Wolf re-election campaign, Arlington, Va., 1986, Bush-Quayle campaign, Washington, 1988. Served to cpl. USMC, 1968-70, Vietnam. Mem. ABA, Va. Bar Assn., D.C. Bar Assn. (litigation and corps. sects.), Fed. Bar Assn. (immigration law sect.), Georgetown U. Alumni Assn. (co-chmn. 1983-84). Republican. Roman Catholic. Avocations: tennis, water skiing. Corporate, general, Immigration, naturalization, and customs, Property, real (including real estate development, water). Home: 1506 Dewberry Ct Mc Lean VA 22101-5629 Office: Maloof & Assocs 526 King St Ste 423 Alexandria VA 22314-3143 E-mail: FPMaloof@aol.com.

MALOON, JERRY L. trial lawyer, physician, medico legal consultant; b. Union City, Ind., June 23, 1938; s. Charles Elias and Bertha Lucille (Creviston) M.; children: Jeffrey Lee, Jerry Lee II. BS, Ohio State U., 1960, MD, 1964; JD, Capital U. Law Sch., 1974. Intern Santa Monica (Calif.) Hosp., 1964-65; tng. psychiatry Ctrl. Ohio Psychiat. HOsp., 1969, Menninger Clinic, Topeka, 1970; clin. dir. Orient (Ohio) Devel. Ctr., 1967-69, med. dir., 1971-83; assoc. med. dir. Western Electric, Inc., Columbus, 1969-71; cons. State Med. Bd. Ohio, 1974-80; pvt. practice law Columbus, 1978—; pres. Jerry L. Maloon Co., L.P.A., 1981—. Medicolegal cons., 1972—; pres. Maloon, Maloon & Barclay Co., L.P.A., 1990-95; guest lectr. law and medicine Orient Devel. Ctr. and Columbus Devel. Ctr., 1969-71; dep. coroner Franklin County (Ohio), 1978-84. Dean's coun. Capitol U. Law Sch. Capt. M.C., AUS, 1965-67. Fellow: Columbus Bar Found., Am. Coll. Legal Medicine; mem.: ATLA, AMA, ABA, Am. Profl. Practice Assn., Columbus Trial Lawyers Assn., Ohio Trial Lawyers Assn., Columbus Bar Assn., Ohio Bar Assn., Ohio State U. Alumni Assn., U.S. Trotting Assn., The Country Club at Muirfield Village, Ohio State U. Pres.'s Buckeye Club. Health, Personal injury (including property damage), Professional liability. Home: 2140 Cambridge Blvd Upper Arlington OH 43221-4104 Office: 9155 Moors Pl North Dublin OH 43017 Office Fax: 614-798-8747.

MALORZO, THOMAS VINCENT, lawyer; b. Rome, N.Y., Jan. 10, 1947; s. Vincent T. and Helen Adeline Malorzo; m. Catherine Marie Malorzo, Dec. 28, 1968; children: Amy, Craig, Mary, Thomas Jr. BA, Walsh U., Canton, Ohio, 1969; JD, Cleve. State U., 1979. Bar: Ohio 1979, U.S. Dist. Ct. (no. dist.) Ohio 1980, U.S. Patent Office 1980, Tex. 1981, U.S. Dist. Ct. (no. dist.) Tex. 1981, U.S. Ct. Appeals (7th cir.) 1994, U.S. Dist. Ct. (ea. dist.) Tex., 1998, U.S. Dist. Ct. (so. dist.) Tex., 2000. Environ. regulations analyst Diamond Shamrock Corp., Dallas, 1979-81; ind. counsel, agt. Southwestern Life Ins. Co., Dallas, 1981-83; staff atty. NCH Corp., Irving, Tex., 1983-89; gen. counsel Wormald US, Inc., Dallas, 1989-90; patent atty. Otis Engring. Corp., Carrollton, Tex., 1990-93; pvt. practice Addison, Tex., 1993-95; ptnr. Falk, Vestal & Fish LLP, 1995; pvt. practice Dallas, 1996-97; of counsel Bennett & Weston P.C., 1997—2002; prin. atty. Malorzo & Tapscott, 2002; sole practitioner Dallas, 2002—. Asst. prof. law Dallas/Ft. Worth Sch. Law, Irving, Tex., 1990-92. Dist. com. Circle 10 Boy Scouts Am., Dallas, 1985—; first aid team ARC, Cleve., 1972-80. Recipient Dist. Award of Merit, Boy Scouts Am., 1990, Silver Beaver award Boy Scouts Am., 1997. Mem. State Bar Tex. (chmn. trademark com. intellectual property sect. 1989). General civil litigation, Corporate, general, Intellectual property. Office: Law Office of Thomas V Malorzo PO Box 59283 Dallas TX 75229-1287 E-mail: patents@prodigy.net.

MALOUF, STEPHEN FERRIS, lawyer; b. Dallas, Nov. 14, 1953; s. Edward Junior and Marie (Moossy) M. BA, U. Dallas, 1977; JD, St. Mary's U., San Antonio, 1982. Bar: Tex., U.S. Dist. Ct. (no. dist.) Tex., U.S. Ct. Appeals (5th cir.). Atty. Tex. Ct. Appeals, Dallas, 1982; assoc. Windle Turley Law Office, Dallas, 1983-84, Boyd Waggoner Law Office, Dallas, 1984-85, Windle, Turley Law Office, Dallas, 1985-87; pvt. practice Dallas, 1987-88; with Milgrim, Thomajan & Lee, Dallas, 1988—90. Mem. ABA, Assn. Trial Lawyers Am., Dallas Trial Lawyers Assn., Tex. Trial Lawyers Assn. (new membership com. 1986-87), Tex. Bar Assn. Roman Catholic. Avocations: painting, music. Personal injury (including property damage). Office: Law Offices of Stephen F Malouf 3506 Cedar Springs Dallas TX 75219

MALTZ, GERALD STUART, lawyer; b. N.Y.C., Jan. 21, 1944. B.A., U. Denver, 1965; J.D. cum laude, N.Y.U., 1968, Bar: N.Y. 1970, U.S. Ct. Appeals (2d cir.) 1971, U.S. Supreme Ct. 1976, Ariz. 1977, U.S. Dist. Ct. Ariz. 1977, U.S. Ct. Appeals (9th cir.) 1978. Assoc. Baer & Marks, N.Y.C., 1970-76, Miller Pitt & Feldman, Tucson, 1977-78; mem. Miller, Pitt, P.C., Tucson, 1978— , dir.; instr. Nat. Inst. Trial Advocacy, Tucson, 1980. Mem. Ariz. State Boxing Commn. Recipient Am. Jurisprudence book awards (9) 1965-68. Mem. N.Y. Bar Assn., State Bar of Ariz., ABA, Pima County Bar Assn. Assoc. editor N.Y. Law Forum. Antitrust, Federal civil litigation, State civil litigation. Office: 1 S Church Ave Ste 900 Tucson AZ 85701-1629

MALZ, HANS-BERNHARD, lawyer; b. Annaberg, Germany, Sept. 19, 1944; s. Johann and Irmgard (Kampf) M.; m. Rosemarie Malz, Aug. 16, 1969; children: Kerstin, Simone, Phillipp. 1 Jurist Staatsprüfung, U. Erlangen, Bayern, Germany, 1972; 2 Jurist Staatsprüfung, Landesprüfungsamt, Bayern, 1974. Lic. volljurist. Pvt. practice, Sulzbach Rosenberg, Germany, 1976—. Syndicus ADAC Sulzbach-Rosenberg, Bayern, 1980—; voustand Auwaltsveueiu Auberg, 1998—. Oberleutnant German mil., 1965-67. Home: An der Reitschule 4 Sulzbach-Rosenberg Bayern Germany Office: Rechtsanwälte Taubmann u Malz Rosenberger St 5 Sulzbach-Rosenberg Bayern Germany

MALZAHN, MARK WILLIAM, lawyer; b. Milw., Nov. 26, 1956; s. Henry William and Rose Ann M.; m. Barbara Jayne Malzahn, Sept. 22, 1979; children: Anna, Joseph, Andrew. BA, St. Cloud State U., 1979; JD, Hamline U., 1983. Bar: Minn. 1983, Wis. 1992, U.S. Dist. Ct. Minn. 1984, U.S. Ct. Appeals (8th cir.) 1984, U.S. Tax Ct. 1984. Atty. Malzahn & Assocs., Ltd. Arbitrator Am. Arbitration Assn. Host, prodr., dir. (pub. access show) Legal Look, 1988—. Mem. Assn. Trial Lawyers Am., Minn. Trial Lawyers Assn. Personal injury (including property damage). Office: Malzahn & Assocs Ltd 229 Jackson St Ste 105 Anoka MN 55303-2254

MAMAT, FRANK TRUSTICK, lawyer; b. Syracuse, N.Y., Sept. 4, 1949; s. Harvey Sanford and Annette (Trustick) M.; m. Kathy Lou Winters, June 23, 1975; children: Jonathan Adam, Steven Kenneth. BA, U. Rochester, 1971; JD, Syracuse U., 1974. Bar: D.C. 1976, U.S. Ct. Appeals (D.C. cir.) 1976, Fla. 1977, U.S. Supreme Ct. 1979, US. Dist. Ct. (ea. dist.) 1983, U.S. Ct. Appeals (6th cir.) 1983, Mich. 1984, U.S. Dist. Ct. (no. dist.) Ind. 1984. Atty. NLRB, Washington, 1975—79; assoc. Proskauer, Rose, Goetz & Mendelsohn, Washington, N.Y.C. and L.A., 1979—83, Fishman Group, Bloomfield Hills, Mich., 1983—85, ptnr., 1985—87; sr. ptnr. Honigman, Miller, Schwartz and Cohn, 1987—94; pres., CEO Morgan Daniels Co., Inc., West Bloomfield, Mich., 1994—; ptnr. Clark Klein & Beaumont, P.L.C., Detroit, 1995—96, Clark Hill, P.L.C., Detroit, 1996—2003, mem. exec. com., 1999—2001; ptnr. Dickinson Wright PLLC, 2003—. Bd. dirs. Mich. Food and Beverage Assn., Air Conditioning Contractors of Am., Air Conditioning Contractors of Mich., Am. Subcontractors Assn., Mich. Mfrs. Assn. Labor Counsel, Jewish Vocat. Svcs., Constrn. Fin. Mgmt. Assn., Mich. Assn. Home Bldg. Gen. counsel Rep. Com. of Oakland County, 1986—; chmn. Constrn. Code Commn. Mich., 1993—; bd. dirs. 300 Club, Mich., 1984-90; pres. 400 Club, 1990-93, chmn., 1993—, chmn. bd., Am. Soc. of Employers, 2003-; mem. Associated Gen. Contractors Labor Lawyers Coun.; mem. Rep. Nat. Com. Nat. Rep. Senatorial Com., Presdl. Task Force, Rep. Labor Coun., Washington; city dir. West Bloomfield, 1985-87; pres. West Bloomfield Rep. CLub, 1985-87; fin. com. Rep. Com. of Oakland County, 1984-93; pres. Oakland County Lincoln Rep. Club, 1989-90; bd. dirs. camping svcs. and human resources com. YMCA, 1989-93, Anti-Defamation League, 1989—; vice chmn. Lawyers for Reagan-Bush, 1984; v.p. Fruehauf Farms, West Bloomfield, Mich., 1985-88; mem. staff Exec. Office of Pres. of U.S. Inquiries/Comments, Washington, 1981-83. Fellow Coll. Labor and Employment Attys.; mem. ABA, FBA, Mich. Bar Assn., Fla. Bar Assn. (labor com. 1977—), Rep. Nat. Lawyers Assn., Mich. Bus. and Profl. Assn., Am. Acad. Constrn. and Labor Attys. (exec. dir. 1998—), Am. Subcontractors Assn. (Southeastern Mich., bd. dirs.), Founders Soc. Detroit Bar Assn., Oakland County Bar Assn., B'nai B'rith (v.p. 1982-83, trustee 1987-88, bd. dirs. Detroit Barristers unit 1983-91, pres. 1985-87), Am. Soc. Employers (chmn. 2003-), Oakpointe Country Club, Detroit Soc. Clubs, Skyline Club, Fairlane Club, Detroit Athletic Club, Renaissance Club, Econ. Club Detroit. Administrative and regulatory, General civil litigation, Labor (including EEOC, Fair Labor Standards Act, labor-management relations, NLRB, OSHA). Office: Dickinson Wright PLLC 500 Woodward Ave Ste 4000 Detroit MI 48226 also: Morgan Daniels Co Inc 5484 Crispin Way Rd West Bloomfield MI 48323-3402 E-mail: fmamat@aol.com., fmamat@dickinsonwright.com.

MAMER, STUART MIES, lawyer; b. East Hardin, Ill., Feb. 23, 1921; s. Louis H. and Anna (Mies) M.; m. Donna E. Jordan, Sept. 10, 1944; children: Richard A., John S., Bruce J. AB, U. Ill., 1942, JD, 1947. Bar: Ill. bar 1947. Assoc. Thomas & Mulliken, Champaign, 1947-55; partner firm Thomas, Mamer & Haughey, Champaign, 1955—. Lectr. U. Ill. Coll. Law, Urbana, 1965-85; Mem. Atty. Registration and Disciplinary Commn. Ill., 1976-82 Chmn. fund drive Champaign County Community Chest, 1955; 1st pres. Champaign County United Fund, 1957; Pres., dir. U. Ill. McKinley Found., Champaign, 1957-69; trustee Children's Home and Aid Soc. of Ill., v.p., 1977-96. Served as pilot USAAF, 1943-45. Mem. Am. Coll. Trust and Estate Counsel (bd. regents 1984-90), Phi Beta Kappa, Phi Gamma Delta. Republican. Presbyterian. Probate (including wills, trusts), Property, real (including real estate development, water), Estate taxation. Home: 101 W Windsor Rd # 3105 Urbana IL 61802-6663 Office: Thomas Mamer & Haughey 30 E Main St Fl 5 Champaign IL 61820-3629 E-mail: smamer@tmh-law.com.

MAMURIC, JOSE ROBERTO LOTA, lawyer; b. Manila, Philippines, Feb. 20, 1966; s. Amado Calangan and Normita Lota M.; m. Jocelyn Bautista, Aug. 28, 1993; children: Carlos Miguel, Amanda Jessica, Antonio Luis, Jose Antonio, Bettina Alessandra. BBA, Loyola Coll., Balt., 1988; JD, Ateneo de Manila Coll. Law, Philippines, 1992. Jr. assoc. Ponce Enrile Reyes & Manalastas, Manila, Philippines, 1993—97, sr. assoc., 1997—2000, jr. ptnr., 2001—. Corp. sec. Air Liquide Philippines, Inc., Manila, 1999—; asst. corp. sec. Sun Microsystems Philippines, Inc., Manila, 1999—. Commercial, contracts (including sales of goods; commercial financing), Corporate, general, Mergers and acquisitions. Office: Ponce Enrile Reyes & Manalas 3/F Vernida IV Bldg Leviste Makati City Philippines Office Fax: 632 8187355. E-mail: jobetmamuric@pecabar.ph.

MANAHAN, JAMES HINCHON, lawyer; b. Madelia, Minn., Aug. 27, 1936; s. Cecil James and Ruth Pearl (Hinchon) M.; m. Suzanne Colette Laurendeau, June 14, 1958 (div. 1975); children: Theodore, Corinne, Matthew, Anne; m. Vanda Botts Hedges, Jan. 30, 1989. AB, Harvard U., 1958, JD, 1961; BA in Spanish, Minn. State U., Mankato, 2001. Bar: Minn. 1961, U.S. Dist. Ct. Minn. 1961, U.S. Ct. Appeals (8th cir.) 1962, U.S. Supreme Ct. 1971, Hawaii 1989, Colo. 1990. Ptnr. Farrish, Zimmerman, Johnson & Manahan, Mankato, Minn., 1962-72, Manahan, Bluth and Kohlmeyer, Mankato, 1972—. Asst. prof. mass comm. law and law enforcement Mankato State U., 1970-82; pub. defender Blue Earth County, 1980-2000; apptd. by Minn. Supreme Ct. to Lawyers Trust Account Bd., 1983-91, Bd. Legal Certification, 1996-99, Jud. Selection Commn., 2001-03; Fulbright schlar U. Austral, Chile, tchg. US criminal law and procedure, 2002. Chair Common Cause in Minn., 1974-75; sec. Mankato Police CSC, 1971-76; pres. Mankato LWV, 2000-2001; sec.-treas. Mankato Area NOW, 1977-79; precinct chair Democratic Farm Labor Party, Mankato, 1976-78, conv. del., 1976, 78, 82, 84, 88, 98. Fellow Am. Bar Found. (life); mem. Minn. Bar Assn. (CLE lectr., 1966, 78, 82, 89, 90, 91, 92, 93, 2000, pres. 6th dist. Bar Assn. 1974-75, chair Criminal Law Sect. 1977-78, chair com. human rights 1981-83), ABA (exec. coun. Sect. Individual Rights and Responsibilities 1978-84, chair com. freedom of speech and press 1980-82, news editor Human Rights mag. 1976-92), Acad. Cert. Trial Lawyers of Minn. (dean 1987-88), ACLU (nat. bd. dirs. 2000—), Minn. Civil Liberties Union (pres. 1998-2000), Nat. Bd. Trial Advocacy (cert. civil and criminal trial specialists 1982—). Criminal, Family and matrimonial, Personal injury (including property damage). Home: 1200 W River Dr Mankato MN 56001-1735 Office: Manahan Bluth and Kohlmeyer PO Box 287 Mankato MN 56002-0287 E-mail: vandajim@mnic.net.

MANCINO, DOUGLAS MICHAEL, lawyer; b. May 8, 1949; s. Paul and Adele (Brazaitis) M.; m. Carol Keith, June 16, 1973. BA, Kent State U., 1971; JD, Ohio State U., 1974. Bar: Ohio 1974, U.S. Tax Ct. 1977, Calif. 1981, D.C. 1981. Assoc. Baker & Hostetler, Cleve., 1974-80; ptnr. Memel & Ellsworth, L.A., 1980-87, McDermott, Will & Emery, L.A., 1987—. Bd. dirs. Health Net of Calif. Inc. Author: Taxation of Hospitals and Health Care Organizations, 2000, (with others) Hospital Survival Guide, 1984, Navigating the Federal Physician Self-Referral Law, 1998; (with F. Hill) Taxation of Exempt Organizations, 2002; co-author quar. tax column Am. Hosp. Assn. publ. Health Law Vigil, (with L. Burns) Joint Ventures Between Hosps. and Physicians, 1987; contbr. articles to profl. jours. Chmn. bd. dirs. The Children's Burn Found. Mem. ABA (tax, bus., real property, probate and trust sects., chair exempt orgns. com. 1995-97, coun. dir. 1999—), Calif. State Bar Assn. (tax, bus. law sects.), Ohio Bar Assn., Calif. State Bar, D.C. Bar Assn., Am. Health Lawyers Assn. (bd. dirs. 1986-95, pres. 1993-94), Calif. Soc. for Healthcare Attys., Bel Air Country Club, The Regency Club, Calif. Yacht Club. Health, Corporate taxation. Office: McDermott Will & Emery 2049 Century Park E Fl 34 Los Angeles CA 90067-3101 E-mail: dmancino@mwe.com.

MANCOFF, NEAL ALAN, lawyer; b. Chgo., May 7, 1939; s. Isadore and Sarah (Leviton) M.; m. Alys Belofsky, June 26, 1966; children: Wesley, Frederick, Daniel. BBA, U. Wis., 1961; JD, Northwestern U., 1965. Bar: Ill. 1965, U.S. Dist. Ct. (no. dist.) Ill. 1965. Assoc. Aaron Aaron Schimberg & Hess, Chgo., 1965-72, ptnr., 1972-80, Schiff Hardin & Waite, Chgo., 1980—. Author: Qualified Deferred Compensation Plans, 1983, Nonqualified Deferred Compensation Agreements, 1987. Lst lt. U.S. Army, 1961-62. Mem. Chgo. Bar Assn. (chmn. employee benefits com. 1984). General practice. Office: Schiff Hardin & Waite 7500 Sears Tower Chicago IL 60606

MANDEL, JOSEPH DAVID, academic administrator, lawyer; b. N.Y.C., Mar. 26, 1940; s. Max and Charlotte Lee (Goodman) M.; m. Jean Carol Westerman, Aug. 18, 1963; children: Jonathan Scott, Eric David. AB, Dartmouth Coll., 1960, MBA with distinction, 1961; JD, Yale U., 1964. Bar: Calif. 1965. Law clk. U.S. Ct. Appeals, 9th cir., L.A., 1964-65; lectr. law U. So. Calif. Law Ctr., L.A., 1965-68; assoc. atty. Tuttle & Taylor, L.A., 1965-69, mem., 1970-82, 90-91, of counsel, 1984-90; vice chancellor UCLA, 1991—, lectr. in law, 1993, 2001—02; v.p., gen. counsel, sec. Natomas Co., San Francisco, 1983. Bd. dirs. LRN, The Legal Knowledge Co., 1994—. Mem. bd. editors Yale Law Jour., 1962-64. Pres. Legal Aid Found., L.A., 1978-79; trustee Southwestern U. Sch. Law, 1982, UCLA Pub. Interest Law Found., 1981-82, L.A. County Bar Found., 1974-79, 82, Coro Found., 1989-92, UCLA Armand Hammer Mus. Art and Cultural Ctr., 1995—, Geffen Playhouse, Inc., 1995-98, Coro So. Calif. Ctr., 1985-92; bd. dirs. pub. coun., 1989-94, cmty. v.p., 1992-94; mem. L.A. Bd. Zoning Appeals, 1984-90, vice-chmn., 1985-86, 89-90, chmn., 1986-87; mem. L.A. City Charter Reform Commn., 1996-99; bd. dirs. Western Justice Ctr. Found., 1989—, v.p., 1992-95, 1st v.p., 1995-97, sr. v.p., 1997-99, pres., 1999—; bd. dirs. Harvard Water Polo Found., 1990-96; bd. govs. Inner City Law Ctr., 1991—; chair Blue Ribbon Screening Com. to Select Insp. Gen., L.A. Police Commn., 1999; mem. bd. overseers Inst. for Civil Justice, RAND, 1999—, bd. dirs. Children's Law Ctr. L.A., 2003-. Recipient Maynard Toll award Legal Aid Found. of L.A., 1991, Shattuck-Price award L.A. County Bar Assn., 1993, West Coast Liberty award Lambda Legal Def. and Edn. Fund, 1994, Cmty. Achievement award Pub. Coun., 1996, Stanley Mosk Liberty Through Justice award ADL, 2003-; named One of Calif.'s 100 Most Influential Attys. by Calif. Bus. Jour., 2000. Mem. State Bar Calif. (legal svcs. trust fund commn. 1985-87, chmn. 1985-86), Yale U. Law Sch. Assn. (exec. com. 1983-88, 90-96, v.p. 1986-88, chmn. planning com. 1990-92, pres. 1992-94, chmn. exec. com. 1994-96), mem. alumni Coun. Dartmouth Coll., 1992-95, Dartmouth Coll. Assn. Alumni (exec. com. 1997-2002, v.p. 2001-02), L.A. Co. Bar Assn. (trustee 1974-74, 1975-81, pres.-elect 1979-80, pres. 1980-81, v.p. 1977-78, sr. v.p. 1978-79, chair pro bono council 1986-87), Order of Coif. Democrat. Jewish. Home: 15478 Longbow Dr Sherman Oaks CA 91403-4910 Office: UCLA Office Chancellor 2135 Murphy Hl Los Angeles CA 90095-1405 E-mail: jmandel@conet.ucla.edu.

MANDEL, MARTIN LOUIS, lawyer; b. L.A., May 17, 1944; s. Maurice S. and Florence (Byer) M.; m. Duree Dunn, Oct. 16, 1982; 1 child, Max Andrew. BA, U. So. Calif., 1965, JD, 1968; LLM, George Washington U., 1971. Bar: Calif. 1969, U.S. Dist. Ct. (cen. dist.) Calif. 1972, U.S. Ct. Claims 1971, U.S. Tax Ct. 1971, U.S. Supreme Ct. 1972. With office of gen. csl. IRS, Washington, 1968-72; ptnr. Stephens, Jones, LaFever & Smith, L.A., 1972-77, Stephens, Martin & Mandel, 1977-79, Fields, Fehn, Feinstein & Mandel, 1979-83; sr. v.p., gen. counsel Investment Mortgage Internat., Inc., 1983-84; ptnr. Feinstein, Gourley & Mandel, 1984-85, Mandel & Handin, San Francisco, 1985—; gen. counsel L.A. Express Football Club, 1983-85. Instr. corps. U. West L.A., 1973-83. Mem. ABA, L.A. County Bar Assn., L.A. Athletic Club, Phi Delta Phi. Corporate, general, Entertainment. Office: 652 Bair Island Rd #210 Redwood City CA 94063 E-mail: martin@tmgtalent.com.

MANDEL, REID ALAN, lawyer; b. Mpls., Mar. 31, 1954; s. Irwin A. and Sandra Harriet (Fink) M.; m. Jeanne Claire Smith, Aug. 29, 1981. BA, Yale U., 1977; JD, NYU, 1980. Bar: Minn. 1981, Ill. 1981, U.S. Dist. Ct. (no. dist.) Ill. 1981, U. S. Tax Ct. 1981. Law clk. to justice Supreme Ct. Minn., St. Paul, 1980-81; assoc. Katten, Muchin Zavis Rosenman, Chgo., 1981-87, ptnr., 1987-. Adj. prof. LLM program John Marshall Sch. Law. Contbr. articles to profl. jours. Mem. Chgo. Vol. Legal Svcs.; bd. dirs., past chmn. Chgo. Lawyers Com. for Civil Rights Under Law, 1985—. Mem. ABA, Chgo. Bar Assn. Jewish. Commercial, contracts (including sales of goods; commercial financing), Taxation, general, Personal income taxation. Office: Katten Muchin Zavis Rosenman 525 W Monroe St Ste 1600 Chicago IL 60661-3693 E-mail: reid.mandel@kmzr.com.

MANDELKER, LAWRENCE ARTHUR, lawyer; b. N.Y.C., Dec. 2, 1943; s. Murray and Sally (Levine) M.; m. Carolyn Anne Bareish, Oct. 4, 1970; children: Daniel H., Benjamin E. BA, Queens Coll., CUNY, 1964; JD, NYU, 1968. Bar: N.Y. 1968, Pa. 1981, U.S. Dist. Ct. (so. and ea. dists.) N.Y. 1973, U.S. Dist. Ct. (ea. dist.) Wis. 1980, (no. dist.) N.Y., 1995, U.S. Ct. Appeals (2d cir.) 1979, U.S. Ct. Appeals (9th cir.) 1989. Law sec. N.Y.C. Civil Ct., 1970-71, N.Y. State Supreme Ct., 1972; mem. Kantor, Davidoff, Wolfe, Mandelker & Kass, P.C.; mem. com. character and fitness 9th Jud. Dist., Coun., N.Y. State Athletic Commn., 1995—2001. Mem. Lewisboro Bd. Assessment Rev., N.Y., 1979—, chmn., 1984—; chmn. Lewisboro Bd. Ethics. Former mem. bd. editors: NY Law Jour.; contbr. articles. Served as staff sgt. USAR, 1968-74. Mem. Assn. Bar City N.Y. (mem. coun. on jud. adminstrn., past mem. com. on state cts. superior jurisdiction civil ct. com., former chmn. spl. com. on election law), NYU Law Alumni Assn. (v.p.). Federal civil litigation, State civil litigation, Legislative. Home: 206 Todd Rd Katonah NY 10536-2410 Office: Kantor Davidoff Wolfe Mandelker & Kass PC 51 E 42nd St New York NY 10017-5404

MANDELL, JOEL, lawyer; b. Hartford, Conn., July 1, 1939; s. Max Edward and Harriet (Shafer) M.; m. Ellen Solomon, Aug. 23, 1964; children: Peter, Ross, Jason. BA, U. Conn., 1961, JD, 1966. Bar: Conn. 1966, U.S. Dist. Ct. Conn. 1967, U.S. Supreme Ct. 1971. Ptnr. Rosenthal, Clayman & Mandell, Hartford, 1966-72; prin. Levy & Droney, Farmington & West Hartford, Conn., 1972—. Mem. adv. bd. First Am. Title Ins. Co., Hartford, 1984—. Bd. dirs. Farmington Valley Jewish Congregation, Simsbury, Conn., 1980-83; mem. State of Conn. Title Ins. Task Force, 1989-90; selectman Town of Simsbury, 1993—, dept. first selectman, 1999—; mem. Town of Simsbury Charter Revision Commn., 1990-92, Simsbury Housing Authority, 1992-93. Mem.: Real Estate Exch., Conn. Assn. Real Estate Profls. (panel mem. 1991, real estate exch. panel moderator 1996, 2000, real estate exchange panel moderator 2002), New Eng. Land Title Assn. (panel mem. 1991, bd dirs. 1996—, panel mem. 2000, panel me. 2000—01), Conn. Bar Assn. (real estate exec. com. 1978—2001, ho. of dels. 1983—86, chmn. 1995—97, emeritus 2001—), Am. Legion Simsbury, KP (chancellor comdr. 1981—82). Property, real (including real estate development, water). Office: Levy & Droney PC 74 Batterson Park Rd Farmington CT 06032-2565 E-mail: joelmandell@attbi.com., jmandell@ldlaw.com.

MANDELSTAMM, JEROME ROBERT, lawyer; b. St. Louis, Apr. 3, 1932; s. Henry and Estelle (London) M.; m. Carolyn A. White; stepchildren: John M. Gagliardi, Maria A. Amundson, Amy E. Gagliardi. AB, U. Pa., 1954; LL.B., Harvard U., 1957. Bar: Mo. 1957. Since practiced in, St. Louis; ptnr. Greenfield, Davidson, Mandelstamm & Voorhees, 1969—81, Schmitz, Mandelstamm, Hawker & Fischer, 1981—82; pvt. practice St. Louis, 1982—. Bd. dirs. Legal Aid Soc. City and County St. Louis, 1967-75, pres., 1969-70; bd. dirs. Lawyers Reference Service Met. St. Louis, 1976-83, chmn., 1978-83; bd. dirs. Mo. Legal Aid Soc., 1977-82; mem. 22d Jud. Cir. Bar Com., 1983-85, gen. chmn., 1984-85 Mem. St. Louis County Bd. Election Commrs., 1973-77. Served with AUS, 1957. Mem. ABA, Mo. Bar Assn., Am. Arbitration Assn. (panel of arbitrators 1984—), Bar Assn. Met. St. Louis (v.p. 1974-75, treas. 1975-76). Corporate, general, Property, real (including real estate development, water), Corporate taxation. Home: 7217 Princeton Saint Louis MO 63130-3000 Office: 1010 Market St Ste 1600 Saint Louis MO 63101-2082

MANEKER, MORTON M. lawyer; b. N.Y.C., Nov. 14, 1932; s. Arthur and Estelle (Hochberg) M.; m. Roberta S. Wexler, 1985; children: Meryl Colle, Amy Jill, Marion Kenneth. AB, Harvard U., 1954, LL.B., 1957. Bar: N.Y. State 1957. Assoc. Shearman & Sterling, N.Y.C., 1957—62; trial atty. antitrust divsn. Dept. Justice, 1962—63; ptnr. Proskauer Rose LLP, N.Y.C., 1963—94; ret., 1994. Trustee Beth Israel Hosp., N.Y.C., 1977—2001. Mem. Am. Law Inst., N.Y. State Bar Assn., Harmonie Club. Jewish. Home: 30 E 65th St New York NY 10021-7013 E-mail: maneker@aol.com.

MANETTA, RICHARD, chemicals executive; b. 1945; BA, U. Mich.; JD, Wayne State U. Legal advisor Detroit City Coun., 1973—74; chief supervising asst./corp. counsel City of Detroit Law Dept., 1974—78; asst. gen. counsel for automotive safety and product litigation Ford Motor Co., 1989—94, asst. gen. counsel for discovery, 1994—99, assoc. gen. counsel for litigation, 1999—2000, dep. gen. counsel, dir. regulatory compliance, 2000—01; corp. v.p., gen. counsel The Dow Chem. Co., Midland, Mich., 2001—. Spkr. in field. Recipient Pres. award, Nat. Bar Assn., 2001, award, Wolverine Bar Assn., 2001. Fellow: Mich. State Bar Found. (life); mem.: ABA, Mich. Gen. Counsel Assn., Mich. State Bar. Office: The Dow Chem Co 2030 Dow Center Midland MI 48674*

MANEY, MICHAEL MASON, lawyer; b. Taihoku, Japan, Aug. 13, 1936; s. Edward Strait and Helen M. M.; m. Suzanne Cochran, Oct. 22, 1960; 1 child, Michele. BA, Yale U., 1956; MA, Fletcher Sch. Law and Diplomacy, Tufts U., 1957; LL.B., U. Pa., 1964. Bar: N.Y. 1966, D.C. 1977. Case officer CIA, 1957-61; law clk. Justice John Harlan, Supreme Ct. U.S., Washington, 1964-65; asso. Sullivan & Cromwell, N.Y.C., 1965-70, ptnr., 1971-77, 81—, mng. ptnr. Washington, 1977-81. Law fellow Salzburg Seminar in Am. Studies, 1967; mem. bd. overseers Fletcher Sch. Law and Diplomacy. Mem. bd. overseers U. Pa. Law Sch. 1st lt. USAF, 1957-61. Mem. ABA, Am. Law Inst., Am. Coll. Trial Lawyers, N.Y. State Bar Assn., Union Club, Down Town Assn., Madison Beach Club, Madison Country Club, Met. Opera Club, New Haven Country Club. Commercial, contracts (including sales of goods; commercial financing), Corporate, general, Private international. Home: 1220 Park Ave New York NY 10128-1733 also: 48 Neptune Ave Madison CT 06443-3210 Office: Sullivan & Cromwell LLP 125 Broad St New York NY 10004-2498 E-mail: maneym@sullcrom.com.

MANG, DOUGLAS ARTHUR, lawyer; b. Little Falls, N.Y., Mar. 25, 1942; s. Willard D. and Mary L. (Murray) M.; m. Nora Ladeane Geren; 1 child, Brittany Nandeana. BS, Cornell U., 1964; LLB, Syracuse U., 1967. Bar: N.Y. 1971, Fla. 1971, U.S. Dist. Ct. (no. dist.) Fla. 1977, U.S. Ct. Appeals (5th and 11th cirs.) 1981, U.S. Dist. Ct. (mid. dist.) Fla. 1982, U.S. Supreme Ct. 1988. Atty. Mut. Life Ins. Co., N.Y.C., 1971-73; asst. gen. counsel Am. Gen. Capital Mgmt., N.Y.C., 1973-77; gen. counsel Fla. Dept. of Ins., Tallahassee, 1977-79; ptnr. Mang & Stowell PA, Tallahassee, 1979-86, Mang Law Firm PA, Tallahassee, 1986—. Served to 1st lt. U.S. Army, 1968-70, Vietnam. Mem. Fla. Def. Lawyers Assn., Tiger Bay Club, Fla. Econs. Club, Rotary, Fedn. Regulatory Counsel (regional dir.). Methodist. Avocations: sailing, golf. Administrative and regulatory, Federal civil litigation, Insurance. Office: Mang Law Firm PA 660 E Jefferson St Tallahassee FL 32301-2582 E-mail: dmang@manglaw.com.

MANGANO, LOUIS, lawyer; b. Passaic, N.J., Sept. 19, 1939; s. Salvatore and Mary Mangano; m. Arlene M. Triolo, Sept. 20, 1964; children: Kenneth L., Eileen M., Louis M., Michael S. BS in Bus. Adminstrn., Seton Hall U., 1970; MA in Criminal Justice, John Jay Coll., 1973; JD, Seton Hall U., 1979. Bar: N.J. 1981, U.S. Dist. Ct. N.J. 1981, U.S. Supreme Ct. 1985. With Elmwood Park (N.J.) Police Dept., 1966-83; pvt. practice atty. Elmwood Park, 1981—. Adj. prof. Fairleigh Dickinson U., Rutherford, N.J., 1973-75, Jersey City (N.J.) State Coll., 1973-75; asst. prof. William Paterson Coll., Wayne, N.J., 1983-84. Trustee, pres. Elmwood Park (N.J.) Bd. Edn., 1980-83, 89-93. With U.S. Army, 1959-61. Mem. Bergen County Bar Assn. General practice. Office: PO Box 305 395 River Dr Elmwood Park NJ 07407-1622

MANGIA, ANGELO JAMES, lawyer; b. Bklyn., Mar. 12, 1954; AB in Govt. cum laude, Georgetown U., 1975; JD, St. John's U., 1978. Bar: N.Y. 1979, U.S. Dist. Ct. (so. and ea. dists.) N.Y. 1979, U.S. Ct. Appeals (2d cir.) 1985. Asst. atty. Town of North Hempstead, N.Y., 1979-81; assoc. Ain, Libert & Weinstein, Garden City, N.Y., 1981; atty. Town of North Hempstead, N.Y., 1982; counsel senate com. on crime State of N.Y., 1983-85, counsel senate com. on banks, 1985-88; chief counsel to majority N.Y. State Senate, 1989-94; mng. dir. Sandler, O'Neill & Ptnrs., L.P., N.Y.C., 1995-2001; pres., CEO Std. Funding Corp., Woodbury, NY, 2001—. Mem. bd. editors N.Y. Law Jour., 1994-96. Recipient Outstanding Work in Field of Criminal Justice Legis. award N.Y. State Bar Assn., 1985, Disting. Svc. award Civil Trial Inst./St. John's Law Sch., 1987, Luther Gulick award for Outstanding Achievement in Pub. Svc. Long Island U., 1992; Toll fellow, 1991. Mem.: Nassau County Bar Assn. Office: 335 Crossways Park Dr Woodbury NY 11797

MANGLER, ROBERT JAMES, lawyer, judge; b. Chgo., Aug. 15, 1930; s. Robert H. and Agnes E. (Sugrue) M.; m. Geraldine M. Delich, May 2, 1959; children: Robert Jr., Paul, John, Barbara. BS, Loyola U., Chgo., 1952, MA, 1983; JD, Northwestern U., 1955. Bar: Ill. 1958, U.S. Dist. Ct. (no. dist.) Ill. 1959, U.S. Supreme Ct. 1976, U.S. Ct. Appeals (7th cir.) 1980. Author: (with others) Illinois Land Use Law, Illinois Municipal Law. Village atty., prosecutor Village of Wilmette, 1965-93; mcpl. prosecutor City of Evanston, 1963-65, adminstrv. law judge, 2000—; chmn. Ill. Traffic Ct. Conf., 1977—; pres. Ill. Inst. Local Govt. Law; mem. home rule attys. com. Ill. Mcpl. League. Mem. ABA (chmn. adv. com. traffic ct. program), Nat. Inst. Mcpl. Law Officers (past pres.), Ill. Bar Assn. (former chmn. traffic laws and ct. com.), Chgo. Bar Assn. (former chmn. traffic ct. seminar, former chmn. traffic laws com.), Caxton Club, Phi Alpha Delta. General practice, Municipal (including bonds).

MANGLONA, JOHN A. judge; b. Rota, Northern Marianas, June 12, 1959; m. Mona V. Monglona; 2 children. BA in Polit. Econ., U. Calif., Berkeley, 1981; JD, Creighton U., 1984; LLM in Taxation, U. Pacific, 1988. Pvt. practice; assoc. judge Commonwealth Superior Ct., 1998—2000; justice Commonwealth Supreme Ct., 2000—. Designated justice Guam Supreme Ct., 2000—. Office: Ho Justice Guma Hustisia, Imwaal Aweewe PO Box 502179 Saipan MP 96950-2179 Office Fax: 670-236-9897. Business E-Mail: cnmilaw@itecnmi.com.*

MANGLONA, RAMONA V. state attorney general; b. 1967; BA, U. Calif.; JD, U. N.Mex. Asst. atty. gen.; atty. gen. No. Mariana Islands, Saipan, 2002—. Office: Capitol Hill 2nd Fl Hon Juan A Sablan Meml Bldg Saipan MP 96950*

MANGUM, JOHN K. lawyer; b. Phoenix, Mar. 7, 1942; s. Otto K. and Catherine F. Mangum; m. Deidre Jansen, Jan. 10, 1969; children: John Jansen, Jeffery Jansen. Student, Phoenix Coll., 1960-62; BS, U. Ariz., 1965, JD, 1969. Bar: Ariz. 1969. Sr. trial atty. criminal divsn. Maricopa County Atty.'s Office, Phoenix, 1969-71; ptnr. Carmichael, McClue and Stephens, P.C., Phoenix, 1972-74; ct. commr., jdge pro tem Maricopa County Superior Ct., Phoenix, 1974-78, spl. commr., 1979-82; legal cousnel to spkr. Ariz. Ho. of Reps., Phoenix, 1975-86; mem. John K. Mangum and Assocs., P.C., Phoenix, 1974-92; ptnr. O'Connor & Cavanaugh, 1992-94; pvt. practice, 1994—. Bd. dirs. Goldwater Inst., 2000—. Mem. Maricopa County Bd. Health, 1974-79, Ariz. State Commn. on Elected Ofcls. Salafies, 1987-93; chmn. curriculum com., mem. legal asst. adv. com. Phoenix Coll., 1973-75; legal counsel Maricopa County Rep. Com., 1986-90; mem. task force com. on career edn. Phoenix Mayor's Youth Commn., 1972-73; v.p. The Samaritans, 1984-87. Mem. State Bar Ariz. (exec. bd. young lawyers sect. 1974-76), Maricopa County Bar Assn. (pres. young lawyers sect. 1974-75, dir. 1973-75), Ariz. C. of C. (dir. 1974-79), Phoenix Country Club, Ariz., Club, Rotary. Corporate, general, Legislative, Property, real (including real estate development, water). Office: 318 W Roosevelt St Phoenix AZ 85003

MANIGAULT, EDWARD MIDDLETON, lawyer; b. stet, Mar. 8, 1970; s. Edward Lining and Dolores Manigault; m. Renee Marion Manigault, Sept. 16, 1995; children: Isabella Kay, Joseph Drayton. BS in Fin. Mgmt., Clemson U., 1992; JD, Emory U., 1995. Bar: Ga. 1995. Assoc. Chamberlain, Hrdlicka, White, Williams & Martin, Atlanta, 1998—99, Jones Day, Atlanta, 1999—. Contbr. articles to profl. jours. Mem.: ABA, Atlanta Bar Assn. Personal income taxation, Estate planning, Taxation, general. Office: Jones Day 1420 Peachtree St Ste 800 Atlanta GA 30309 Office Fax: 404-581-8330. Personal E-mail: edm@mindspring.com. Business E-Mail: emmanigault@jonesday.com.

MANION, PAUL THOMAS, lawyer; b. Decatur, Ill., Apr. 7, 1940; s. Charles F. and Jeannette (Kaufman) M.; m. Bonnie J. Rivard, Aug. 12, 1961; children: Christine, Sheila, Tessy, Michael, Brian, Daniel. BBA in Fin., Notre Dame U., 1961; JD, DePaul U., 1964. Bar: Ill 1964, U.S. Ct. Appeals (7th cir.) 1975. Ins. investigator Hooper Holmes Bur., South Bend, Ind., 1958-61; supr. U.S. Dist. Ct., Chgo., 1961-64; asst. states atty. Iroquois County, Watseka, Ill., 1964-67; sr. ptnr. Manion, Devens & McFetridge, Ltd., Hoopeston, Ill., 1967—. Author: With Friends Like These, 1985. Mem. exec. com. Vermilion County Dem. Party, Danville, Ill., 1974—, county chmn. 1983-87; pres. Vermilion Mental Health Ctr., Danville, 1975-78. Mem. ATLA, Ill. Bar Assn., Ill. Trial Lawyers Assn. (bd. mgrs. 1997—). Democrat. Roman Catholic. General practice, Personal injury (including property damage), Workers' compensation. Home: RR 2 Box 80 Hoopeston IL 60942-9706 Office: Manion Devens & McFetridge 216 S Market St Hoopeston IL 60942-1508

MANKA, RONALD EUGENE, lawyer; b. Wichita, Kans., Dec. 12, 1944; s. James Ashford and Jane Bunn (Meeks) M.; m. Frances Ann Patterson, Aug. 7, 1965 (dec. Dec. 1985); children: Kimberly Ann, Lora Christine; m. Linda I. Bailey, Mar. 11, 1995. BBA cum laude, U. Kans., 1967; JD cum laude, U. Mich., 1970. Bar: Conn. 1970, Mo. 1974, Kans. 1985, Colo. 2001. Assoc. Day, Barry & Howard, Hartford, Conn., 1970-73, Lathrop & Gage L.C., Kansas City, Mo., 1973-78, mem., 1979-82, 85—; group counsel Butler Mfg. Co., Kansas City, 1982-83, div. gen. mgr., 1983-84. Legal com. Boulder County Cmty. Found., Colo., 2002—. Trustee, clk., elder Village Presbyn. Ch., Prairie Village, Kans.; dir., treas. Lyric Opera of Kansas City, 1995—; pres. Genesis Sch., Kansas City, 1987-89; devel. chmn. Kansas City Friends of Alvin Ailey, 1987-89; chmn. Kansas City Mus., 1988-92, gen. counsel, 1994—; gen. counsel Spirit Festival, Kansas City, 1985-87, Kansas City C. of C., 1989-96; pres. Ctr. for Mgmt. Assistance, Kansas City, 1991-93; dir. Colo. Music Festival, 2002-. Mem. ABA, Mo. Bar Assn. (alt. dispute resolution com. 1986—), Lawyers Assn. Kansas City, Silicon Prairie Tech. Assn. (bd. dirs. 1990-92), Homestead Country Club (pres. 1984-85). Democrat. Avocations: bicycling, swimming. Corporate, general, Private international, Mergers and acquisitions. Home: 875 11th St Boulder CO 80302 Office: 4845 Pearl East Cir Ste 300 Boulder CO 80301 Fax: 720-931-3001. E-mail: RManka@LathropGage.com.

MANKO, JOSEPH MARTIN, SR., lawyer; b. Phila., Oct. 7, 1939; s. Horace David and Vivian (Greenberg) M.; m. Lynn Kimmelman, June 17, 1962; children: Joseph Jr., Glenn, Wendy. BA magna cum laude, Yale U., 1961; JD cum laude, Harvard U., 1964. Bar: Pa. 1964. Regional counsel EPA, Phila., 1973-75; assoc. Wolf, Block, Schorr & Solis-Cohen, Phila., 1964-72, ptnr., 1972-73, 75-89, chmn. environ. law, 1978-89; founding ptnr. Manko, Gold, Katcher, Fox, LLP, Bala Cynwyd, Pa., 1989—. Adj. prof. U. Pa. Law Sch., 1988—, Grant Irey lectr., 1989-90, Thomas A. O'Boyle lectr., 2000-01; lectr. in law Vt. Law Sch., 1988—; dir. Pa. Environ. Council, Phila., 1978-85, 99-2001, treas., 1986-87, pres., 1987-89, chmn. 1989-98, dir. emeritus, 2001—, 10,000 Friends of Pa.; chair or co-chair numerous environ. bar assn. coms. Commr. Lower Merion Twp., Ardmore, Pa., 1980-91, 94—, v.p., 1992, pres. 1993; mem. Com. of 70, Phila., 1978-88; pres. Beth David Reform Congregation, Gladwyne, Pa., 1983-86, trustee, 1978-83, 86—; trustee Fedn. Jewish Agys., Phila., 1982-86; bd. dirs. Golden Slipper Camp, 1981-84, 88—, Jewish Cmty. Rels. Coun., 1983-88, Lower Merion Conservancy, 1976-2002, hon. dir., 2002—; bd. dirs. Abramson Ctr. for Jewish Life, 1990-98, hon. dir. 1999—; bd. dirs. Delaware River Basin Water Resources Assn., 1993-96; mem. Dem. State Com., 1986-90; bd. dirs. 21st Century Environ. Commn., 1997-98; chair Pa. Infrastructural Investment Authority, 2003—. Recipient Outstanding Conservation Profl. award Pa. Wildlife Fedn., 2000; named Disting. Environ. Neutral, CPR Inst. for Dispute Resolution, 1996—, Montgomery County (Pa.) Dem. of Yr., 2000. Mem.: ABA, Pa. Bar Inst. (bd. dirs. 1997—2000, 2001—), Phila. Bar Assn., Pa. Bar Assn. (Outstanding Environ. Atty. 2001), Vesper Club, Hamilton Bridge Club, Germantown Cricket Club, Bala Golf Club (Phila.), Lambda Alpha, Phi Beta Kappa, Phi Gamma Delta. Avocations: tennis, golf, jogging, bridge, classical music. Environmental, Land use and zoning (including planning). Home: 96 E Levering Mill Rd Bala Cynwyd PA 19004-2611 Office: Manko Gold Katcher & Fox LLP 401 E City Ave Ste 500 Bala Cynwyd PA 19004-1167 E-mail: Jmanko@mgkflaw.com.

MANKOFF, RONALD MORTON, retired lawyer; b. Gettysburg, S.D., Oct. 13, 1931; s. Harry B. and Sarah (Frank) M.; m. Joy Faith Shechtman, Nov. 3, 1959; children: Jeffrey Walker, Douglas Frank. BSL, U. Minn., JD, 1954; LLM in Taxation, NYU, 1959. Bar: Minn. 1954, Tex. 1959. With Leonard, Street & Deinard, Mpls., 1957-58; research analyst Inst. Jud. Adminstrn., N.Y.C., 1958-59; assoc. Lyne, Blanchette, Smith & Shelton,

Dallas, 1959-60; ptnr. Durant and Mankoff, Dallas, 1960-85; pres. Brice & Mankoff P.C., Dallas, 1985-89, Mankoff, Hill, Held & Metzger, L.L.P., Dallas, 1989-95; chmn./gen. counsel RAC Fin. Group, Inc. (now 1st Plus Fin Group, Inc.), 1994-96. Lectr. law So. Meth. U., 1974-77; speaker in field. Contbr. articles to profl. jours. Chmn. bd. Dallas chpt. Am. Cancer Soc., 1976-77, bd. dirs. Tex. divsn., 1981-94; chmn. Dallas Crusade, 1974-75, bd. dirs., mem. exec. com., 1963-88; mem. Dallas Mcpl. Libr., 1973-75; exec. com. Dallas Citizens Charter Assn., 1971-75; pres. Dallas Arts Found., Inc., 1973-75; mem. exec. com. Nat. Pooled Income Fund, Coun. Jewish Welfare Fedns. and Funds, 1975-77; adv. dir. Dallas Cmty. Chest Trust Fund, 1976-78; chmn. Found. Dallas Jewish Fedn., 1976-77; pres. Temple Emanu-el, Dallas, 1977-79; bd. dirs. Jewish Fedn. Greater Dallas, 1977-79, 99-2002, Dallas Civic Opera, 1981-83, World Union Progressive Judaism, 1981-90; mem. S.W. regional liaison com. IRS, 1980-83; exec. com. Union Am. Hebrew Congregations, 1979-89, trustee, 1979-97, chmn. nat. coll. com., 1983-87, vice chmn. bd. dirs., 1984-88, vice chmn. devel. commn., 1997-99; sec. Dallas Assembly, 1979-84; exec. com. Jewish Cmty. Rels. Coun., 1982-83, Com. for Qualified Judiciary, 1982—; sec. Child Care Partnership, 1984-86, bd. dirs., 1986-88; bd. dirs. Dallas Women's Found., 1985-89, adv. coun., 1989—, chair adv. coun., 1997-99; bd. dirs. Am. Jewish Com., 1982-88, pres. Dallas chpt. 1986-90; bd. dirs. Tex. coun. Girl Scouts U.S., 1982-85, Goodwill Industries of Greater Dallas, 1979-83, Title One Home Improvement Lender's Assn., 1994-96; mem. Mayor's Task Force on Child Care, 1984; bd. govs. Dallas Symphony Assn., 1988-92, 98—; chmn. Temple Emanu El Found., 1988-95; bd. dirs. Dallas Inst. Humanities and Culture, 1998—, Ctr. for Interreligious Understanding, 2001—, Cardio-Pulmonary Rsch. Inst., 2002—, Jane's Due Process, Inc., 2002—, Cmty. Home for Adults Found., 2001—. Lt. (j.g.) USN, 1954-57. Mem. ABA, State Bar Tex., Dallas Bar Assn., Columbian Country Club (bd. dirs. 1967-73), LaJolla Country Club, Crescent Club, Zeta Beta Tau, Delta Sigma Rho. Democrat. Jewish. Estate planning, Taxation, general, State and local taxation. Home: 22 Lakeside Pk Dallas TX 75225

MANLEY, DAVID BOTT, III, lawyer; b. Jacksonville, Fla., June 19, 1953; s. David Bott and Bernadette Claire Manley; m. Gayle Aileen Whitney, Nov. 1, 1978; children: David Jeremiah, Alexandra Ina Claire. BA with honors magna cum laude, U. Ga., 1975, JD, 1982. Bar: Ga. 1983, U.S. Dist. Ct. (no. dist.) Ga. 1983, U.S. Ct. Appeals (11th cir.) 1986. Auditor So. Hostess Sys., Inc., Augusta, Ga., 1975-76; prosecutorial asst. fraud investigator State Ga., Atlanta, 1976-79; assoc. Gadrix & Green, P.C., Atlanta, 1982-83, Lowe, Barham, Eubanks & Lowe, Atlanta, 1983-85; mem. Barham & Manley, Atlanta, 1985-89; dir., ptnr. Campbell Martin & Manley, LLP, Atlanta, 1989—. Corp. counsel Highland Homes, Inc., Dallas and Atlanta, 1990—, Mast Advt. and Pub. Inc., Houston and Nashville, 1991—; corp. sec., counsel Agrisel USA, Inc., Atlanta and Hong Kong, 1998—; mem. Ga. Law Related Edn. Constorium of Carl Vinson Inst. Govt., U. Ga., 2000—. Pres. U.S. Jaycees, Mt. Park/Lilburn, 1985; cert. coach Lucky Shoals Youth Athletic Assn., Norcross, Ga., 1992-98; bd. dirs Fulton County, Ga. Dept. Family and Children's Svcs. (commendation, bd. resolution for bravery, 1978); svc. provider Parent to Parent of Ga.; mem. Dekalb Vol. Lawyers Found., Lawyers Found. Ga. Named Jaycee of Yr., U.S. Jaycees-Mt. Park/Lilburn, Ga., 1984. Mem. ABA, State Bar Ga. (legis. com. corp. and banking law sect. 1987-88, mem. corp. and banking law sect. 1987—, adv. mem. law revision com. 1989-90, mem. trial sect. 1984—, mem. real property sect. 1996—, advocate for spl. needs children 1996—), Nat. Youth Sports Coaches Assn. (continuing mem. 1996—), Sandy Springs Bar Assn. (treas. 1987-88, pres. 1988-89, dir. 1989-90), Omicron Delta Kappa. Avocations: coaching youth sports, model railroading, photography, collecting, travel. General civil litigation, Corporate, general, Property, real (including real estate development, water). Home: 4390 Flippen Trl Norcross GA 30092-3902 Office: Campbell Martin & Manley LLP 990 Hammond Dr NE Ste 800 Atlanta GA 30328-5510 E-mail: dbmanley@chb-cmm.com.

MANLEY, ROBERT EDWARD, lawyer, economist; b. Cin., Nov. 24, 1935; s. John M. and Helen Catherine (McCarthy) M.; m. Roberta L. Anzinger, Oct. 21, 1971 (div. 1980); 1 child, Robert Edward. ScB in Econs, Xavier U., 1956; AM in Econ. Theory, U. Cin., 1957; JD, Harvard U., 1960; postgrad., London Sch. Econs. and Polit. Sci., 1960, MIT, 1972. Bar: Ohio 1960, U.S. Supreme Ct. 1970. Pvt. practice law, Cin., 1960—; chmn. Manley Burke, 1977. Taft teaching fellow econs. U. Cin., 1956-57, vis. lectr. community planning law Coll. Design, Architecture and Art, 1967-73, adj. assoc. prof. urban planning Coll. Design, Architecture, Art and Planning, 1972-81, adj. prof., 1981—, adj. prof. law, 1980—. Author: Metropolitan School Desegregation, 1978, (with Robert N. Cook) Management of Land and Environment, 1981, others; chmn. editl. adv. bd. Urban Lawyer, 1986-95. Mem. Hamilton County Pub. Defender Commn., 1976-79; trustee HOPE, Cin., Albert J. Ryan Found.; counsel, co-founder Action Housing for Greater Cin.; mem. Spl. Commn. on Formation U. Cin. Health Maintenance Orgn., Mayor Cin. Spl. Com. on Housing; chmn. Cin. Environ. Adv. Coun., 1975-76; trustee The Americas Fund for Ind. Univs., 1987-2000; trustee Ohio Planning Conf., 1982-91, pres., 1987-89, trustee, 1987-90; sec. Cin. Mounted Patrol Com., 1993—; active Bd. Cin. Downtown Coun., 1991-98. Mem. ABA (coun. sect. local govt. law 1976-80, 81-85, 88-92), Ohio Bar Assn., Cin. Bar Assn., Am. Judicature Soc., Law and Soc. Assn., Nat. Coun. Crime and Delinquency, Harvard U. Law Sch. Assn. Cin. (pres. 1970-71), Am. Econ. Assn., Am. Acad. Polit. and Social Sci., Queen City Club, Explorers Club (N.Y.C.) (trustee, sec. Clark chpt. 1992—), Athenaeum Club (Phila.), S.Am. Explorers (Lima, Peru). Republican. Roman Catholic. Federal civil litigation, State civil litigation, Property, real (including real estate development, water). Office: Manley Burke 225 W Court St Cincinnati OH 45202-1052 E-mail: info@manleyburke.com.

MANLEY, WALTER WILSON, II, lawyer, business educator; b. Gainesville, Fla., Mar. 16, 1947; s. Walter Wilson and Marjorie Iley (Watkins) M.; children: Marjorie, Benjamin. BA, Fla. So. Coll., 1969; JD, Duke U., 1972; MBA, Harvard U., 1975. Assoc. Blackwell, Walker & Gray, Miami, Fla., 1972-75; pvt. practice, Lakeland, Fla., 1975-84; prof. bus. adminstrn. Fla. State U., Tallahassee, 1985—; ptnr. MacFarlane, Ferguson, Allison & Kelly, Tallahassee, 1991-94. Vis. prof. bus. adminstrn. Ridley Hall Coll. and Cambridge Fedn. Theol. Colls., Eng., 1988-90, Cambridge U. Faculties of Mgmt. Studies, Philosophy, Law, Social and Polit. Scis. and Divinity, 1989-90; pres. Exeter Leadership Cos. Inst., Inc., Tallahassee, 1989-94, Fla. North Shore Tech. Ctrs., Inc., 1995-97. Author: Critical Issues in Business Conduct, 1990, Executive's Handbook of Model Business Conduct Codes, 1991, Handbook of Good Business Practice, 1992, What Florida Thinks, 1997, The History of the Supreme Court of Florida and Its Predecessor Courts, 1821-1917, 1997 (nominated Littleton Griswold prize in Am. Law & Soc. 1998) Chmn. Fla. Endowment Found. for Vocat. Rehab., 1991-93; bd. dirs. Fla. Real Property and Casualty Joint Underwriters Assn., 1987-91, Consumer Coun. Fla., 1992-99; bd. visitors Duke U. Sch. Law, 1991-98; trustee The Webb Sch., BellBuckle, Tenn., 1983-92, nat. fund chmn., 1982; trustee Ctr. for Fla. History; pres. Polk County Legal Aid Soc.; legal editor Harbus, ofcl. Class of 1975 rep. 350th anniversary Harvard U. Recipient Outstanding Alumnus award Fla. So. Coll., 1999. Fellow Fla. Supreme Ct. Hist. Soc. (disting. historian); mem. ABA, Fla. Bar Assn. (Pres.' Pro Bono Svc. award 1985), Lakeland Bar Assn. (pres.), Capital Duke Club (founder, past pres.), Tallahassee Quarterback Club Found. (past chmn., Biletnikoff award), Psi Chi, Omicron Delta Kappa, Sigma Alpha Epsilon (Nation's Outstanding Educator award 1998), Phi Delta Phi. Episcopalian. Avocations: hot air balloons, gliders, fly fishing, wing shooting. Home: 2804 Rabbit Hills Rd Tallahassee FL 32308-0837

MANLY, SAMUEL, lawyer; b. Louisville, Aug. 8, 1945; s. Samuel III and Nell Thornton (Montgomery) M.; m. Tacie Jarrett Bond, Aug. 8, 1970 (div. 1978); children: Julie Elder, Elizabeth Meriwether. BA cum laude, Yale U., 1967; JD, U. Va., 1970. Bar: Ky. 1971, U.S. Dist. Ct. (we. and ea. dists.) Ky. 1972, U.S. Dist. Ct. (so. dist.) Ind. 1972, U.S. Dist. Ct. (we. dist.) Mich. 1995, U.S. Ct. Appeals (6th cir.) 1972, U.S. Ct. Appeals (10th cir.) 1997, U.S. Supreme Ct. 1997. Pres. Madison House, U. Va., Charlottesville, 1968-70; assoc. Greenebaum Doll & McDonald, Louisville, 1970-76; ptnr. Reisz Blackburn Manly & Treitz, Louisville, 1976-78; sr. ptnr. Manly & Sears, Louisville, 1978-81, Manly & Heleringer, Louisville, 1981-84; pvt. practice Law Offices of Samuel Manly, Louisville, 1984—. Sec., gen. counsel Gibbs-Inman Co., Louisville, 1972-78; contract atty. FDIC, Washington, 1976-84; counsel Winston Products Co., 1988—; dir. defender svcs. U.S. Dist. Ct. (we. dist.) Ky., 1992-94; mem. Ky. Criminal Justice Coun., 2002—. Contract atty. Jefferson County, 1977-78, City of Louisville, 1978-83. Capt. USAR, 1967-86. Fellow: Ky. Bar Found. (life); mem.: ATLA, ABA (com. on products liability, subcom uninsured mfrs. sect. ligitation, com. on self-insurers and risk mgrs. sect. tort and ins. law practice), Am. Bankruptcy Inst., Assn. Fed. Def. Attys., Am. Judicature Soc., Comml. Law League of Am., Fed. Bar Assn., Ky. Acad. Trial Lawyers, Nat. Assn. Criminal Def. Lawyers, Ky. Assn. Criminal Def. Lawyers (pres. 2001—, bd. dirs., exec. com. 1986—), Louisville Bar Assn., Ky. Bar Assn. (com. on legal ethics 1978—84, 1996—98), Louisville Boat Club. Republican. Avocations: classical music, fishing, golf. General civil litigation, Probate (including wills, trusts), Criminal. Home: 407 S Sherrin Ave Louisville KY 40207-3817 Office: Law Offices of Samuel Manly 239 S 5th St Ste 1606 Louisville KY 40202-3208

MANN, BRUCE ALAN, lawyer, investment banker; b. Chgo., Nov. 28, 1934; s. David I. and Lillian (Segal) M.; m. Naomi Cooks, Aug. 31, 1980; children: Sally Mann Stull, Jonathan Hugh, Andrew Ross. BBA, U. Wis., 1955, SJD, 1957. Bar: Wis. 1957, N.Y. 1958, Calif. 1961. Assoc. Davis, Polk & Wardwell, N.Y.C., 1957-60, Pillsbury, Madison & Sutro, San Francisco, 1960-66, ptnr., 1967-83; adminstrv. mng. dir. L.F. Rothschild Unterberg Towbin, San Francisco, 1983-87; ptnr. Morrison & Foerster, San Francisco, 1987—; sr. mng. dir. W.R. Hambrecht & Co., San Francisco, 1999—2003. Cons. SEC, 1978; vis. prof. law Georgetown U., 1978; lectr. in field. Author: (with Mattson) California Corporate Practice and Forms, 1999; contbr. articles to profl. jours. Served with USAR, 1957. Mem.: NASD (gov.-at-large 1981—83), ABA (chmn. fed. regulation of securities com. 1981—83, mem. bus. law sect. coun. 1996—99, standing com. on ethics and profl. responsibility 1997—, chmn. com. on venture capital 2000—), Bar Assn. San Francisco (bd. dirs. 1974—75), State Bar Calif., Am. Law Inst., The Family Club. Corporate, general, Mergers and acquisitions, Securities. Office: Morrison & Foerster 425 Market St Ste 3100 San Francisco CA 94105-2482 E-mail: bmann@mofo.com.

MANN, DAVID SCOTT, lawyer; b. Cin., Ohio, Sept. 25, 1939; s. Henry M. and Helen Faye M.; m. Elizabeth Taliaferro, Oct. 5, 1963; children: Michael, Deborah, Marshall. AB cum laude, Harvard Coll., 1961, LLB magna cum laude, 1968. Bar: Ohio 1968. Assoc. Dinsmore & Shohl, Cin., 1968-74, ptnr., 1974-83, Taliaferro and Mann, Cin., 1983-92; councilman City of Cin., 1974-92, mayor, 1980-82, 91; mem. 103d Congress 1st Ohio dist., Washington, 1993-94; mem. armed svcs. com., mem. jud. com. Washington; of counsel Thompson, Hine and Flory, Cin., 1995-96; pvt. practice Mann & Mann, LLC, Cin., 1997—. Adj. prof. Coll. Law U. Cin., 1995—2002. Editor Harvard Law Rev., 1966-68, notes editor, 1967-68; contbr. articles to profl. jours. Mem., chmn. Cin. Bd. Health, 1972-74. With USN, 1961-65. Mem. Cin. Bar Assn. Democrat. Methodist. Civil rights, Labor (including EEOC, Fair Labor Standards Act, labor-management relations, NLRB, OSHA), Personal injury (including property damage). Home: 568 Evanswood Pl Cincinnati OH 45220-1527

MANN, DONEGAN, lawyer; b. Birmingham, Ala., Mar. 6, 1922; s. Ephriam DeValse and Edna Atkins (Donegan) M.; m. Frances Virginia Hindman, Apr. 6, 1957 (dec. May 1993); m. Frances M. Jenkins, Jan. 7, 1995 (dec. Dec. 1997). Student, Birmingham-So., 1940-41; AB, George Washington U., 1947, JD, 1950. Bar: U.S. Dist. Ct. D.C. 1950, U.S. Ct. Appeals (D.C. cir.) 1950, U.S. Ct. Claims 1957, U.S. Supreme Ct. 1961, U.S. Ct. Appeals (fed. cir.) 1982. Acting bur. counsel Civil Aeronautics Bd., Washington, 1953-55; gen. rates atty. GAO, Washington, 1955-57; spl. rate counsel Gen. Svcs. Adminstrn., Washington, 1957-60; assoc. Wolf & Case, Washington, 1960-66; sr. atty., office gen. counsel. U.S. Dept. Treasury, Washington, 1966-79; of counsel Shands & Stupar, Washington, 1979-82; pvt. practice Washington, 1984—. Pres. Friends of Historic Great Falls Tavern, Inc., Potomac, Md., 1977-80, bd. dirs., 1980-83. With USN, 1943-46, PTO. Mem. ABA (treas. pub. contracts sect. 1965-66, chmn. awards com. 1975-76, svc. award sr. lawyers' divsn. 1991, counsel sr. lawyers divsn., 1995-97, chmn. guardianship and conservatorship com. 1989-95, sr. lawyers' divsn. task force to reform guardianship laws 1992-94, vice chmn., wills probate and trust com., 1995—, chmn. citizenship com. 1996-97, vice chmn. Law Day and citizenship com. 1997—), FBA, Fed. Energy Bar Assn., D.C. Bar Assn., Montgomery County Hist. Soc. (exec. v.p. 1980-83, bd. dirs. 1984-86). Democrat. Episcopalian. Avocations: fishing, hunting, golf, tennis, gardening. Administrative and regulatory, Government contracts and claims, Utilities, public. Office: 1000 Connecticut Ave NW Ste 204 Washington DC 20036-5337

MANN, J. KEITH, retired law educator, arbitrator; b. May 28, 1924; s. William Young and Lillian Myrle (Bailey) M.; m. Virginia McKinnon, July 7, 1950; children: William Christopher, Marilyn Keith, John Kevin, Susan Bailey, Andrew Curry. BS, Ind. U., 1948, LLB, 1949; LLD, Monmouth Coll., 1989. Bar: Ind. 1949, D.C. 1951. Law clk. Justice Wiley Rutledge and Justice Sherman Minton, 1949-50; pvt. practice Washington, 1950; with Wage Stblzn. Bd., 1951; asst. prof. U. Wis., 1952, Stanford U. Law Sch., 1952-54, assoc. prof., 1954-58, prof., 1958-88, prof. emeritus, 1988—, assoc. dean, 1961-85, acting dean, 1976, 81-82, cons. to provost, 1986-87. Vis. prof. U. Chgo., 1953; mem. Sec. of Labor's Adv. Com., 1955-57; mem. Pres.'s Commn. Airlines Controversy, 1961; mem. COLC Aerospace Spl. Panel, 1973-74; chmn., mem. Presdl. Emergency Bds. or Bds. of Inquiry, 1962-63, 67, 71-72; spl. master U.S. vs. Alaska, U.S. Supreme Ct., 1980-97. Editor book rev. and articles Ind. U. Law Jour., 1948-49. Ensign USNR, 1944-46. Sunderland fellow U. Mich., 1959-60; scholar in residence Duke U., 1972. Mem. ABA, AAUP, Nat. Acad. Arbitrators, Indsl. Rels. Rsch. Assn., Acad. Law Alumni Fellows Ind. U., Order of Coif, Tau Kappa Epsilon, Phi Delta Phi. Democrat. Presbyterian. Home: 872 Lathrop Dr Stanford CA 94305-1053 Office: Stanford U Sch Law Stanford CA 94305-8610 E-mail: jkmann@leland.stanford.edu.

MANN, LAWRENCE MOSES, lawyer; b. Wilmington, N.C., Jan. 30, 1940; s. Irving Murray and Ada (Frohm) M.; m. Susan Beth Bernstein, Dec. 1, 1961 (div. Nov. 1994); children: Rachel (dec.), Michael, Debra; m. Pat Rosenthal, Mar. 3, 1996. BA, U. N.C., 1962; LLB, Georgetown U., 1966. Bar: D.C. 1967, U.S. Dist. Ct. D.C. 1967, U.S. Ct. Appeals (D.C. and 7th cirs.), 1967, U.S. Ct. Claims, 1970, U.S. Tax Ct. 1970, U.S. Supreme Ct. 1972, U.S. Ct. Appeals (9th, 8th and 4th cirs.) 1975, U.S. Ct. Appeals (10th cir.) 1978, U.S. Ct. Appeals (11th and 5th cirs.) 1981, U.S. Dist. Ct. (ea. dist.) Ky. 1983, U.S. Ct. Appeals (3d cir.) 1987, U.S. Ct. Appeals (2d cir.) 1988, U.S. Ct. Appeals (6th cir.) 1990. Spl. asst. to Sen. Vance Hartke, U.S. Senate, Washington, 1964-65; legal asst. post office and civil svc. com. U.S. Ho. of Reps., Washington, 1965-66; counsel Commn. on Polit. Activity of Govt. Pers., Washington, 1967; ptnr. Alper & Mann , Washington, 1968—. Author: What Every Railroad Worker Should Know About Federal Railroad Safety Laws, 1988. Former mem. bd. dirs. Washington Hebrew Congregation. Mem. ABA, ATLA, Acad. Rail Labor Attys., D.C. Bar Assn. Avocations: art, collecting shells. General practice, Personal injury (including property damage), Transportation. Office: Alper & Mann 1667 K St NW 11th Fl Washington DC 20006

MANN, NATHAN HUGUENOR, lawyer; b. Louisville, Feb. 9, 1948; s. Samuel O. and Catherine (Huguenor) M.; m. Cynthia Morrissey, June 13, 1970; children: Ryan G., Jonathan C. BA, U. Va., 1970; JD, Columbia U., 1973. Bar: D.C. 1974, N.Mex. 1979, U.S. Dist. Ct. N.Mex. 1979, U.S. Ct. Appeals (10th cir.) 1980. Assoc. Roehl & Assocs., Albuquerque, 1979—82; mem. Gallagher & Casados PC, Albuquerque, 1982—85; mng. atty. Gallagher, Casados & Mann PC, Albuquerque, 1985—. Contbr. articles to profl. jours. Bd. dirs. Albuquerque unit Am. Cancer Soc., 1982—, pres., 1985-86, 91-92, 1999-2000. Capt. JAGC, U.S. Army, 1973-79, ETO. Mem. ABA, N.Mex. Bar Assn. Bankruptcy, General civil litigation, Corporate, general. Home: 4137 Hannett Ave NE Albuquerque NM 87110-4940

MANN, ROBERT PAUL, retired lawyer; b. Pitts., July 24, 1929; s. O. Paul and Floy Melinda (Foster) M.; m. Dorothy Neeld, Sept. 4, 1953; children: Robin Duvall Francik, Stewart Neeld Mann. BS, U. Md., College Park, 1951; JD, U. Md., Balt., 1953. Bar: Md. 1954, U.S. Dist. Md. 1965, U.S. Tax Ct. 1976. Pvt. practice, Ruxton, Md., 1956-96; ret., 1996. Trial magistrate, 1957-59. Past pres. Artists Equity, Timonium Rotary, Towson Libr.; active wildlife orgns.; art donor to numerous major mus. Mem. Omicron Delta Kappa, Delta Theta Phi, Sigma Chi. Episcopalian. Probate (including wills, trusts).

MANN, SAM HENRY, JR., lawyer; b. St. Petersburg, Fla., Aug. 2, 1925; s. Sam Henry and Vivian (Moore) M.; m. Mary Joan Bishop, Sept. 7, 1948; children: Vivian Louise, Sam Henry III, Wallace Bishop. BA, Yale U., 1948; LLB, Fla. U., 1951, JD, 1967. Bar: Fla. 1951, U.S. Dist. Ct. (mid. and so. dists.) Fla. 1951, U.S. Ct. Appeals (5th cir.) 1955, U.S. Ct. Appeals (11th cir.) 1996, U.S. Supreme Ct. 1971. Ptnr. Greene, Mann, Rowe, Stanton, Mastry & Burton, St. Petersburg, 1951-84, Harris, Barrett, Mann & Dew, St. Petersburg, 1984—. Trustee, v.p. Mus. Fine Arts, St. Petersburg, 1980-94, Eckerd Coll., St. Petersburg, 1976-79, Webb Sch., Bell Buckle, Tenn., 1966-75; bd. dirs. Regional Cmty. Blood Ctr., St. Petersburg, 1966-93, Fla. Blood Svcs., 1993-94, mem. emeritus 1996—; mem. Disting. Alumni Soc. Webb Sch.; mem., chmn. H. Milton Rogers Heart Found.; bd. dirs., pres. Family and Children's Svc., Inc., 1956-61. Lt. (j.g.) USNR, 1943-48. Fellow Am. Coll. Trial Lawyers, Am. Bar Found., Fla. Bar Found.; mem. ABA, Fla. Bar Assn., Fla. Supreme Ct. Hist. Soc., Am. Counsel Assn., Def. Rsch. Inst., Internat. Assn. Def. Counsel, Pinellas County Trial Lawyers Assn., Nat. Assn. Railroad Trial Counsel, Fla. Def. Lawyers Assn., Assn. Hostp. Attys., Bay Area Vanderbilt, St. Petersburg Bar Assn., Yale and U. Fla. Alumni Assns., Phi Alpha Delta, Delta Kappa Epsilon. Republican. Presbyterian. Avocations: rv travel, boating, gardening, workshop. General civil litigation, Personal injury (including property damage), Probate (including wills, trusts). Home: 531 Brightwaters Blvd NE Saint Petersburg FL 33704-3713 Office: Harris Barrett Mann & Dew Southtrust Bank Bldg 150 Second Ave N Saint Petersburg FL 33731-1441

MANN, THEODORE R. lawyer; b. Czechoslovakia, Jan. 31, 1928; came to U.S., 1929, naturalized, 1930; s. Aaron and Bertha (Schreiber) M.; m. Rowena Joan Weiss, 1954; children: Julie Ellen, Rachel Beth, Marcus Eliyahu. Pvt. practice, Phila., 1953—; ptnr. Wolf, Block, Schorr, Solis-Cohen; advocate in civil liberties, anti-trust and securities fraud cases. Chmn., pres. Nat. Jewish Cmty. Rels. Adv. Coun., 1976-80; Conf. Pres. Major Am. Jewish Orgns., 1978-80; Nat. Conf. Soviet Jewry, 1981-83; Am. Jewish Congress, 1984-88; Mazon-A Jewish Response to Hunger, 1985-90; Project Nishma, 1988-97; exec. com. chair Israel Policy Forum, 1997-2001; trustee internat. coun. New Israel Fund, 2002—. Fellow Temple U. Alumni. Office: 1650 Arch St Fl 22 Philadelphia PA 19103-2097

MANNE, HENRY GIRARD, lawyer, educator; b. New Orleans, May 10, 1928; s. Geoffrey and Eva (Shainberg) M.; m. Bobbette Lee Taxer, Aug. 19, 1968; children: Emily Kay, Geoffrey Adam. BA, Vanderbilt U., 1950; JD, U. Chgo., 1952; LL.M., Yale U., 1953, J.S.D., 1966; LLD, U. Seattle, 1987, U. Francisco Marroquin, Guatemala, 1987, George Mason U., 2000. Bar: Ill. 1952, N.Y. 1969. Practice in, Chgo., 1953-54; assoc. prof. St. Louis U. Law Sch., 1956-57, 59-62; vis. prof. law U. Wis., Madison, 1957-59; prof. George Washington U. Law Sch., 1962-68; Kenan prof. law and polit. sci. U. Rochester, 1968-74; vis. prof. law Stanford (Calif.) Law Sch., 1971-72; disting. prof. law, dir. Law and Econs. Center, U. Miami Law Sch., 1974-80; prof. law Emory U. Law and Econs. Ctr., Atlanta, 1980-86; dean Law Sch., chmn. Law and Econs. Ctr. George Mason U., 1986-96, univ. prof., 1986-99, dean emeritus, 2000—. Vis. prof. law U. Wis., Madison, 1957-59, Stanford (Calif.) Law Sch., 1971-72, U. Chgo. Law Sch., 2000—; dir. Econs. Insts. Fed. Judges, 1976-89. Author: Insider Trading and the Stock Market, 1966, (with H. Wallich) The Modern Corporation and Social Responsibility, 1973, (with E. Solomon) Wall Street in Transition, 1974, Med. Malpractice Guidebook: Law and Economics, 1985; editor: (with Roger LeRoy Miller) Gold, Money and the Law, 1975, Auto Safety Regulation: The Cure or the Problem, 1976; editor: Economic Policy and the Regulation of Corporate Securities, 1968, The Economics of Legal Relationships, 1975; editor: (with James Dorn) Econ. Liberties and the Judiciary, 1987. Served to 1st lt. USAF, 1954-56. Recipient Salvatori award Excellence in Acad. Leadership, 1994; named Cultural Laureate of Va., 1992. Adj. scholar CATO Inst.; fellow Am. Law and Econs. Assn. (hon. life), Mont Pelerin Soc., Order of Coif, Phi Beta Kappa. E-mail: Henry@themannes.com.

MANNING, BRENT V. lawyer; b. Preston, Idaho, Jan. 18, 1950; s. Leon W. and Gwen (Briscoe) M.; m. J. Christine Coffin, Oct. 25, 1969; children: Justin, Britten, John. BA, Idaho State U., 1972; JD, Harvard U., 1975. Bar: Colo. 1975, Utah 1981, U.S. Ct. Appeals (10th cir.) 1978. Assoc. Holme Roberts & Owen, Denver, 1975-80, ptnr., 1980-97, Salt Lake City, 1981-97; founding ptnr. Manning Curtis Bradshaw & Bednar, LLC, Salt Lake City, 1997—. Mem. panel mediators and arbitrators U.S. Dist. Ct. Utah, 1993—; mediation & settlement judge pro tempore 3rd Jud. Dist. State of Utah, 1996—; mem. jud. nominating commn., 2d Jud. Dist. Ct. Utah. Trustee Bountiful (Utah) Davis Art Found., 1985-91, Utah Tibetan Resettlement Project. Mem. ABA, Utah Bar Assn. (chmn. continuing legal edn. com. 1988, mem. disciplinary com. 1991-93, cts. and judges com. 1993—, chmn. 1996-97, chmn. And Justice for All campaign, 2001—), Am. Inns of Ct. (pres. 1997-98, master of bench 1988—), Am. Alpine Club (N.Y.C.) Democrat. Avocations: climbing, bicycling, running. Bankruptcy, General civil litigation, Environmental. Home: 2079 Maple Grove Way Bountiful UT 84010-1005 Office: Manning Curtis 3d Fl Newhouse Bldg 10 Exchange Pl Salt Lake City UT 84111-2714 E-mail: BManning@mc2b.com.

MANNING, J. RICHARD, lawyer; b. Seattle, Nov. 2, 1932; BA, Seattle U., 1954; LLB, Gonzaga U., 1960. Bar: Wash. 1960. Pvt. practice, Seattle. Chmn. Seattle adv. coun. Am. Arbitration Assn., 1985—96, Bd. Govs., 1997—2000; Mem. Law Adv. Bd. Gonzaga U., 1988—; pres. Wash. State Bar Assn., 2002—03. Recipient Nat. Outstanding Svc. award, Am. Arbitration Assn., 1988, Wash. Law and Politics Super Lawyer award, Top 100 Lawyers award, 2002. Mem.: ABA, Assn. Trial Lawyers Am., King County Bar Found. (pres. 1991—93), Am. Judicature Soc., King County Bar Assn. (pres. 1995—96). General civil litigation, Corporate, general, Probate (including wills, trusts). Office: 925 Logan Bldg 500 Union St Seattle WA 98101

MANNING, JEROME ALAN, retired lawyer; b. Bklyn., Dec. 31, 1929; s. Emanuel J. and Dorothy (Levine) M.; m. Naomi Jacobs, Oct. 31, 1954; children: Joy, Stephen, Susan. BA, NYU, 1950, LLB, 1952; LLM, Yale U.,

1953. Bar: N.Y. 1953, Fla. 1977. Assoc. Joseph Trachtman, N.Y.C., 1956-61; ptnr. Stroock & Stroock & Lavan, N.Y.C., 1961-96; prof. NYU Sch. Law, 1956-96. Editor: NYU Law Rev.; author: Estate Planning, 1980, rev. edit., 1995, Estate Planning for Laymen, 1992. Trustee N.Y.U. Sch. Law. Capt. USAF, 1953-56. Estate planning, Probate (including wills, trusts), Estate taxation. Home: 1835 Franklin St San Francisco CA 94109-3483 E-mail: jmanning@stroock.com.

MANNING, KENNETH ALAN, lawyer; b. Buffalo, July 22, 1951; s. Jack Edwin and Dorothea Ann (Ruhland) Manning; children: Michael John, Kathyrn Ann. BS in Engring. Sci., SUNY, Buffalo, 1974, JD, 1977. Bar: N.Y. 1978, U.S. Dist. Ct. (we. dist.) N.Y. 1978, U.S. Dist. Ct. (no. dist.) N.Y. 1980, U.S. Ct. Appeals (2d cir.) 1983, U.S. Ct. Appeals (3d cir.) 1988. Confidential law asst. to assoc. justice Appellate Div. 4th Dept., Buffalo, 1977-79; assoc. Phillips, Lytle, Hitchcock, Blaine & Huber, Buffalo, 1979-84, ptnr., 1985—. Vol. Lawyers Project, Erie County, 1985-2002, Criminal Appeals Program, Erie County, 1988-89; mem. Western N.Y. region NCCJ. Woodburn fellow SUNY, Buffalo, 1973-76. Mem. ABA (TIP sect.), N.Y. State Bar Assn. (ins. negligence sect.), Erie County Bar Assn., Gyro Club (pres. 1988), Park Club. Avocations: sports, hunting. Federal civil litigation, General civil litigation. Office: Phillips Lytle Hitchcock Blaine & Huber 3400 HSBC Ctr Buffalo NY 14203-2887

MANNING, MICHAEL J. lawyer; b. Wichita, Kans., July 18, 1944; BA, U. Kans., 1966; JD, Washburn U., 1969. Bar: Kans. 1969, D.C. 1970. Mem. Fulbright & Jaworski LLP, Washington. Mem. ABA, Fed. Energy Assn., D.C. Bar, Phi Alpha Delta. FERC practice, Oil, gas, and mineral, Natural resources. Office: Fulbright & Jaworski Market Sq 801 Pennsylvania Ave NW Fl 3-5 Washington DC 20004-2623

MANNING, WILLIAM HENRY, lawyer; b. Dallas, Feb. 5, 1951; BA, Creighton U., 1973; JD, Hamline U., 1978. Bar: Minn. 1978, U.S. Dist. Ct. Minn. 1978, U.S. Ct. Appeals (8th cir.) 1979; cert. civil trial specialist. Spl. asst. atty. gen. Minn. Atty. Gen.'s Office, St. Paul, 1980-83, dir. tort litigation div., 1984-86; ptnr. Robins, Kaplan, Miller & Ciresi, Mpls., 1986—. General civil litigation, Personal injury (including property damage), Product liability. Office: Robins Kaplan Miller & Ciresi 800 Lasalle Ave Ste 2800 Minneapolis MN 55402-2015

MANNINO, EDWARD FRANCIS, lawyer, educator; b. Abington, Pa., Dec. 5, 1941; s. Sante Francis and Martha Anne (Hines) M.; m. Mary Ann Vigilante, July 17, 1965 (div. 1990); m. Antoinette K. O'Connell, June 25, 1993; children: Robert John, Jennifer Elaine. BA with distinction, U. Pa., 1963, LLB magna cum laude, 1966. Bar: Pa. 1967. Law clk. 3d cir. U.S. Ct. Appeals, 1966-67; assoc. Dilworth, Paxson, Kalish & Kauffman, Phila., 1967-71, ptnr., 1972-86, co-chmn. litigation dept., 1980-86, sr. ptnr., 1982-86; sr. prin. Elliott, Mannino & Flaherty, PC, Phila., 1986-90; chmn. Mannino Griffith PC, Phila., 1990-95; sr. ptnr. Wolf, Block, Schorr & Solis-Cohen, Phila., 1995-98; ptnr. Akin, Gump, Strauss, Hauer & Feld LLP, Phila., 1998—. Hearing examiner disciplinary bd. Supreme Ct. Pa., 1986—89, mem. adv. com. on appellate ct. rules, 1989—95; lectr. Temple U. Law Sch., 1968—69, 1971—72; mem. Phila. Mayor's Sci. and Tech. Adv. Com., 1976—79; project mgr. Pa. Environ. Master Plan, 1973; chmn. Pa. Land Use Policy Study Adv. Com., 1973—75; chmn. adv. com., hon. faculty history dept. U. Pa., 1980—85, lectr. Am. history, 2001—. Author: Lender Liability and Banking Litigation, 1989, Business and Commercial Litigation: A Trial Lawyer's Handbook, 1995, The Civil RICO Primer, 1996; mem. editl. bd. Litigation mag., 1985-87, Comm. Lending Litigation News, 1988-2001, Bank Bailout Litigation News, 1989-93, Bus. Torts Reporter, 1988-99, Practical Litigator, 1989—, Civil RICO Report, 1991-2001; contbr. articles to profl. jours. Pres. parish coun. Our Mother of Consolation Ch., 1977-79; bd. overseers U. Pa. Sch. Arts and Scis., 1985-89, chmn. recruitment and retention of faculty com.; commonwealth trustee Temple U., 1987-90, audit, bus. and fin. coms. Named one of Nation's Top Litigators Nat. Law Jour., 1990, Pa.'s Top Ten Trial Lawyers, 1999, listed in The Best Lawyers in Am., Am.'s Leading Bus. Lawyers. Fellow Am. Bar Found., ABA (chmn. various coms.), Am. Law Inst., Hist. Soc. U.S. Dist. Ct. Ea. Dist. Pa. (bd. dirs.), Pa. Bar Assn., Phila. Bar Assn. (gov. 1975), Pa. Soc., Order of Coif, Phi Beta Kappa, Phi Beta Kappa Assocs. Democrat. Antitrust, General civil litigation, Professional liability. Office: Akin Gump Strauss Hauer Et Al 2005 Market St Fl 22 Philadelphia PA 19103-7014 E-mail: emannino@akingump.com.

MANNIX, KEVIN LEESE, lawyer; b. Queens, N.Y., Nov. 26, 1949; s. John Warren Sr. and Editta Gorrell M.; m. Susanna Bernadette Chiocca, June 1, 1974; children: Nicholas Chiocca, Gabriel Leese, Emily Kemper. BA, U. Va., 1971, JD, 1974. Bar: Oreg. 1974, U.S. Ct. Appeals (9th cir.) 1976, U.S. Supreme Ct. 1978, Guam 1979. Law clk. to judge Oreg. Ct. Appeals, Salem, 1974-75; asst. atty. gen. Oreg. Dept. Justice, Salem, 1975-77, Govt. of Guam, Agana, 1977-79; judge adminstrv. law Oreg. Workers' Compensation Bd., Salem, 1980-83; assoc. Lindsay, Hart, Neil & Weigler, Portland, Oreg., 1983-86; pres. Kevin L. Mannix Profl. Corp., Salem, 1986—. Chmn. St. Joseph Sch. Bd., Salem, 1981-86; pres. Salem Cath. Schs. Corp., 1985; v.p. Salem Cath. Schs. Found., 1985-88, pres., 1988-90, 91-94, 2000—; pres. bd. dirs. Blanchet Sch., 1995--; vice chair Oreg. Rep. Party, 1998-2000, chair 2003--; state rep., 1989-97, 99-2001; State Senator, 1998-99. Mem. Marion Bar Assn., Rotary (bd. dirs. East Salem 1985-89, pres. 1987-88), KC. Republican. Avocations: photography, scuba diving, travel. State civil litigation, Insurance, Corporate, general. Home: 375 18th St NE Salem OR 97301-4307 Office: 2003 State St Salem OR 97301-4349

MANOLIS, JAMES WILLIAM, lawyer; b. New Castle, Pa., Feb. 19, 1960; s. William and Rose Marie (Moses) M.; m. Rosemary Ritchie, June 24, 1984; children: William James, Nicholas James, Macy Rose. BA, U. Pitts., 1982; JD, U. Dayton, 1986. Bar: Pa. 1986. Assoc. Gamble, Verterano, Mojock, Piccione and Green, New Castle, 1986-91; ptnr. Verterano & Manolis, New Castle, 1991—; solicitor City of New Castle, Pa., 1996—. Dist. and County reporter, Lawrence County Reporter. Mem. ABA, Pa. Bar Assn., Lawrence County Bar Assn. (treas. 1988—, opinion editor jour. 1988—), Am. Trial Lawyers Assn., Pa. Trial Lawyers Assn. Democrat. Mem. Eastern Orthodox Ch. General civil litigation, General practice, Personal injury (including property damage). Home: 301 E Euclid Ave New Castle PA 16105-2622 Office: Verterano & Manolis 2622 Wilmington Rd New Castle PA 16105-1530

MANOS, CHRISTOPHER LAWRENCE, lawyer, mediator; b. Ft. Bragg, N.C., July 1, 1952; m. B.J. Osmon, June 14, 1974; children: Monica, Kelly. BS, U.S. Mil. Acad., 1974; JD, U. N.D., 1982. Bar: Mont. 1983, U.S. Dist. Ct. (Mont.) 1983, U.S. Ct. Appeals (9th cir.) 1983. Assoc. to ptrn. Moore, O'Connell, Refling & Manos, Bozeman, Mont., 1982-92; ptnr. Biglen & Manos, Big Timber, Mont., 1992—97, Manos law firm; part-time dep. county atty. Sweet Grass county, 1992—98; county atty, 1998—. Trainer for mediators The Settlement Ctr. and Alternative Dispute Resolution Assocs., Bozeman and Palo Alto, Calif., 1990—. Contbr. articles to profl. jours. Bd. dirs. Mont. Pub. TV, Bozeman, 1985-92, Mont. Coun. for Internat. Visitors, Bozeman, 1992; mem. Mont. Stat Bar Dispute Resolution Com., Helena, Mont., 1989—. Capt. U.S. Army, 1974-79. Mem. ABA, State Bar of Mont. (pres. 2001-02), Soc. of Profls. in Dispute Resolution. Federal civil litigation, State civil litigation.

MANOS, JOHN M. federal judge; b. Cleve., Dec. 8, 1922; m. Viola Manos; 4 children. BS, Case Inst. Tech., 1944; JD, Cleve.-Marshall Coll. Law, 1950. Bar: Ohio 1950. Asst. plant mgr. Lake City Malleable Iron Co., Cleve., 1946-50; atty. Manos & Manos, 1950-63; law dir. City of Bay Village, 1954-56; industries rep. Cleve. Regional Bd. of Rev., 1957-59; judge Ohio Ct. Common Pleas, Cuyahoga County, 1963-69, Ohio Ct. Appeals, Cuyahoga County, 1969-76; sr. judge U.S. Dist. Ct. (no. dist.) Ohio, Cleve., 1976-91, 1991—. With USN, 1942-45. Named Phi Alpha Delta Man of Yr., 1972, Outstanding Alumnus Cleve.- Marshall Law Alumni Assn., 1976. Mem. ABA, Fed. Bar Assn., Ohio State Bar Assn., Nat. Lawyers Club (hon.), Bar Assn. Greater Cleve., Cuyahoga County Bar Assn., Delta Theta Phi (Man of Yr. 1970). Office: US Dist Ct 801 W Superior # 168 Cleveland OH 44113-1841

MANSFIELD, CHRISTOPHER CHARLES, insurance company legal executive; b. 1950; married. BA, Boston Coll., 1972, JD, 1975. With Liberty Mut. Ins. Co., Boston, 1975—, v.p., 1983, sr. v.p., gen. counsel, 1983—; underwriter Liberty Lloyds of Tex. Ins. Co., 1984-94; v.p., dir. Liberty Ins. Corp., 1985—; v.p. Liberty Mut. Fire Ins. Co., 1985—; v.p., gen. counsel LEXCO Ltd., 1986—; sr. v.p., gen. counsel Liberty Mut. Capital Corp., 1986—. Bd. dirs. Liberty Mut. Ins. Co., Liberty Fin. Cos., Liberty Mut. Bermuda, Liberty Internat., Employers Ins. Wausau, Golden Eagle Ins. Corp., Wausau Gen. Ins. Co., Pine Street Inn; bd. overseers Rand Inst. Civil Justice, 2002--. Office: Liberty Mut Ins Co PO Box 140 175 Berkeley St Boston MA 02117-5066

MANSFIELD, JAMES NORMAN, III, lawyer; b. Chattanooga, Feb. 15, 1951; s. James Norman and Doris June (Hilliard) M.; m. Terry Ann Thomas, Dec. 28, 1975; children: Seth Thomas, James Norman, Scott Michael. BA, U. Tenn., Chattanooga, 1973; MA, La. State U., 1976, JD, 1979. Bar: La. 1979, U.S. Dist. Ct. (we. dist.), La. 1979. Shareholder Liskow and Lewis, Lafayette and New Orleans, La., 1979—. Pres. Raven Soc., Chattanooga, 1973; pres. sch. bd. St. Thomas More H.S. Mem. ABA, La. Bar Assn., La. Min. Law Inst. (adv. coun. mem.), Am. Assn. Profl. Landmen, Lafayette Assn. Petroleum Landmen, Order of Coif. Roman Catholic. Avocations: photography, jogging, fishing. Oil, gas, and mineral, Probate (including wills, trusts), Property, real (including real estate development, water). Home: 103 Asbury Cir Lafayette LA 70503-3632 Office: Liskow & Lewis PO Box 52008 Lafayette LA 70505-2008

MANSFIELD, KAREN LEE, lawyer; b. Chgo., Mar. 17, 1942; d. Ralph and Hilda (Blum) Mansfield; children: Nicole Rafaela, Lori Michele. BA in Polit. Sci., Roosevelt U., 1963; JD, DePaul U., 1971; student U. Chgo., 1959-60. Bar: Ill. 1972, U.S. Dist. Ct. (no. dist.) Ill. 1972. Legis. intern Ill. State Senate, Springfield, 1966-67; tchr. Chgo. Pub. Schs., 1967-70; atty. CNA Ins., Chgo., 1971-73; law clk. Ill. Apellate Ct., Chgo., 1973-75; sr. trial atty. U.S. Dept. Labor, Chgo., 1975—, mentor Adopt-a-Sch. Program, 1992-95. Contbr. articles to profl. jours. Vol. Big Sister, 1975-81; bd. dirs. Altgeld Nursery Sch., 1963-66, Ill. div. UN Assn., 1966-72, Hull House Jane Addams Ctr., 1977-82, Broadway Children's Ctr., 1986-90, Acorn Family Entertainment, 1993-95; mem. Oak Park Farmers' Market Commn., 1996-2002; rsch. asst. Citizens for Gov. Otto Kerner, Chgo., 1964; com. mem. Ill. Commn. on Status of Women, Chgo., 1964-70; del. Nat. Conf. on Status of Women, 1968; candidate for del. Ill. Constl. Conv., 1969. Mem. Chgo. Council Lawyers, Women's Bar Assn. Ill., Lawyer Pilots Bar Assn., Fed. Bar Assn. Unitarian. Clubs: Friends of Gamelan (performer), 99's Internat. Orgn. Women Pilots (legis. chmn. Chgo. area chpt. 1983-86, legis. chmn. North Cen. sect. 1986-88, legis. award 1983, 85). Home: 204 S Taylor Ave Oak Park IL 60302-3307 Office: US Dept Labor Office Solicitor 230 S Dearborn St Fl 8 Chicago IL 60604-1505

MANSFIELD, LORRAINE J. lawyer; JD, U. Wyo., 1979. Bar: Wyo. 1979, Nev. 1981, U.S. Ct. Appeals (10th cir.) 1980, U.S. Ct. Appeals (9th cir.) 1983, U.S. Ct. of Claims, 1990, U.S. Supreme Ct. 1985. Law clk. Wyo. Supreme Ct., Laramie, 1980; sole practitioner law Las Vegas, 1981—. Arbitrator 8th Jud. Cir., Las Vegas, 1992—. Contbr. articles to profl. jours. Avocation: sailing. General civil litigation. Office: Mansfield Law Office 6655 W Sahara Ave # B 200 Las Vegas NV 89146

MANSOLILLO, CHARLES RONALD, lawyer; b. Providence, R.I., Mar. 8, 1949; s. Nicholas William and Adeline Ann Marie (Marcello) M. BA, St. Michael's Coll., 1971; postgrad. Weston Jesuit Sch. Theology, 1997-99; JD, Suffolk U., 1985. Mem. Ho. of Reps., State of R.I., Providence, 1973-75; mem. city coun. City of Providence, 1975-83; chief of staff Mayor's office City of Providence, 1983-84; exec. bd. R.I. league Cities and Towns, 1979-84; mem. Providence Home Rule Charter Commn., 1979-80m Narragansett Bay Commn., 1980-83; bd. dirs. Providence Indsl. Devel. Corp. Trustee Providence Pub. Libr., 1979-87; chmn. bd. dirs. Providence Community Action Program, Inc., 1975-84; Rep. nominee Mayor of Providence, 1986; legal counsel dept. children & families State of R.I., 1987-88, dir. govs. office energy assistance, 1988-89, dir. govs. office Housing, Energy & Intergovtl. Rels., 1989-90, dir. govs. policy office, 1990-91; dep. city solicitor City of Providence, 1991-92, city solicitor, 1992-2003, city solicitor emeritus. Republican. Roman Catholic. Home: 6 Rockland Ave Cranston RI 02910

MANSOUR, JANA WILLIAMSON, lawyer; b. Montreal, Que., Can. Diploma, Coll. Jean-de-Brebeuf, Montreal, 1992; LLB, U. Montreal, 1995; LLM, Columbia U., 1999. Bar: Que. 1996, NY 2000. Assoc. McCarthy Tetrault, Montreal, 1996—98, Hunton & Williams, N.Y.C., 1999—. Harlan Fiske Stone scholar, Columbia Law Sch., 1999. Mem.: Assn. Bar City of NY. Commercial, contracts (including sales of goods; commercial financing), Corporate, general, Finance. Office: Hunton & Williams 200 Park Ave New York NY 10166 Office Fax: 212-309-1100. Business E-Mail: jmansour@hunton.com.

MANTEL, ALLAN DAVID, lawyer; b. N.Y.C., June 27, 1951; s. Bernard and Ruth (Weichman) M.; m. Janet Mantel, June 17, 1985; children: Bernard, Elizabeth. BA, NYU, 1973; JD, SUNY, Buffalo, 1976. Bar: N.Y. 1977, U.S. Dist. Ct. (so. and ea. dists.) N.Y. 1977. Assoc. Rosenthal & Herman P.C., N.Y.C., 1977-82; ptnr. Rosenthal, Herman & Mantel, N.Y.C., 1983-94, Hofheimer, Gartlir & Gross, LLP, N.Y.C., 1995-98, Stein Riso Mantel LLP, N.Y.C., 1999—. Fellow Am. Acad. Matrimonial Lawyers (bd. mgrs. 1998-2000, N.Y. chpt. treas. 2001—); mem. ABA (family law sect.), N.Y. State Bar Assn. (equitable distbn. com.), Assn. Bar City N.Y. (matrimonial law com. 1985-88), N.Y. County Lawyers Assn. (matrimonial law and comml. law). Jewish. State civil litigation, Family and matrimonial. Office: Stein Riso Mantel LLP 405 Lexington Ave New York NY 10174-0002 E-mail: allan.mantel@steinrisomantel.com.

MANTHEI, RICHARD DALE, retired lawyer, health care company executive; b. Olivia, Minn., Dec. 23, 1935; s. Alvin R. and Sidonia (Klatt) M.; m. Karen J. Peterson, Sept. 6, 1959 (dec. Mar. 1985); children: Steven, Jana, Kari, John, Rebecca; m. Lynn E. Graham, Aug. 9, 1986. BS in Pharmacy (Rexall award 1960), S.D. State U., 1960; JD, U. Minn., 1967. Bar: Ind. 1967, Ill. 1970, D.C. 1987, U.S. Supreme Ct. 1987. Sales rep. Eli Lilly & Co., Indpls., 1962-64, atty., 1967-70; atty., then asst. corp. sec., dir. regulatory affairs Am. Hosp. Supply Corp., Evanston, Ill., 1970-79, corp. sec., dep. gen. counsel, 1979-85; assoc. gen. counsel Baxter Travenol Labs., Deerfield, Ill., 1986-87; ptnr. Burditt, Bowles & Radzius, Washington, 1987-90, McKenna & Cuneo, Washington, 1990-96; sr. v.p. regulatory scis. C.R. Bard, Inc., Murray Hill, N.J., 1996-2000. Author articles in field.; Editorial adv. staff: Med. Devices and Diagnostic Industry, 1979. Mem. bd. edn. Libertyville H.S., 1984-87; mem. governing bd. Spl. Edn. Dist. of Lake County, Ill., 1985-87; trustee N.J. Ctr. for Visual Arts. With AUS, 1954-56. Mem. ABA, Health Industry Mfrs. Assn. (chmn. law sect. 1976), Health Industry Assn. (chmn. legal com. 1973), Am. Soc. Corp. Secs. (corp. practices com. 1983-88, group pres. 1985-86, Chgo. regional group 1986-87), Ill. Bar Assn., Ind. Bar Assn., D.C. Bar Assn., Univ. Club (Evanston, Ill., bd. dirs. 1984-86). Administrative and regulatory, Corporate, general, Health. Home: 11608 Stonewall Jackson Dr Spotsylvania VA 22553

MANTILLA-SERRANO, FERNANDO, lawyer; b. Bucaramanga, Colombia, Mar. 22, 1963; s. Arturo Mantilla-Gomez and Alicia Serrano-Becerra; m. Anne Cambournac, Sept. 26, 1998; children: Francisco-Fernando Mantilla-Cambournac, Diego-Arturo Mantilla-Cambournac, Juan-Felipe Mantilla-Cambournac. JD, Pontificia Universidad Javeriana, Bogotá, Colombia, 1985; MCJ (LLM), NYU, 1988; DEA in Internat. Law and Trade Law, DSU in European Law, U. Paris II, 1991. Bar: Colombia 1986, (N.Y.) 1989, Cour d'Appel de Paris 2001, Madrid 2002. Legal asst. Colombian Banking Assn., Bogotá, 1982—84; in-house counsel Acerías Paz del Río (Steel Mill), Bogotá, 1984—87; fgn. assoc. Bracken & Margolin, N.Y.C., 1988—90; legal counsel ICC-International Ct. Arbitration, Paris, 1991—98; ptnr., head internat. arbitration practice GARRIGUES Law Firm, Madrid, 1999—. Fulbright Scholar, 1987—89. Fellow: Chartered Inst. Arbitrators; mem.: Internat. Law Assn., Internat. Bar Assn. Alternative dispute resolution, Private international, Construction. Office: Garrigues Jose Abascal 45 28003 Madrid Spain Office Fax: +34-91-3992408.

MANTLE, RAYMOND ALLAN, lawyer; b. Painesville, Ohio, Oct. 15, 1937; s. Junius Dow and Ada Louise (Stinchcomb) M.; m. Judith Ann LaGrange, Nov. 26, 1967; children: Amanda Lee, Rachel Ann, Leah Amy. BSBA summa cum laude, BA summa cum laude, Kent State U., 1961; LLB cum laude, NYU, 1964. Bar: N.Y. 1964, N.J. 1976, U.S. Supreme Ct. Asst. counsel Gov. Nelson A. Rockefeller, N.Y., 1964-65; assoc. Paul Weiss Rifkind Wharton & Garrison, 1967-69; mem. Varet & Fink P.C. (formerly Milgrim Thomajan & Lee, P.C.), N.Y.C., 1969-95; ptnr. Piper & Marbury L.L.P., N.Y.C., 1995-98; mem. Reitler Brown LLC (formerly Brock Silverstein, LLC), 1998—. Lectr. in computer law field. Contbr. author: Doing Business in China and Intellectual Property China, 1990—. Capt. U.S. Army, 1965-67. Mem.: N.J. Bar Assn., N.Y. State Bar Assn. (co-chmn. ann. meeting seminar on intellectual property 2000—03, co-chair internet com., mem. exec. com. intellectual property sect., treas.). Republican. Methodist. Commercial, contracts (including sales of goods; commercial financing), Corporate, general, Intellectual property. Office: Reitler Brown LLC 800 3rd Ave Fl 21 New York NY 10022-7604 E-mail: rmantle@reitlerbrown.com.

MANTONYA, JOHN BUTCHER, lawyer; b. Columbus, Ohio, May 26, 1922; s. Elroy Letts and Blanche (Butcher) M.; m. Mary E. Reynolds, June 14, 1947 (dec. 1987); children: Elizabeth Claire, Mary Kay, Lee Ann; m. Carole L. Lugar, Sept. 28, 1989. AB cum laude, Washington and Jefferson Coll., 1943; postgrad., U. Mich. Law Sch., 1946-47; JD, Ohio State U., 1949. Bar: Ohio 1949. Assoc. A.S. Mitchell (Atty.), Newark, Ohio, 1949-50, C.D. Lindrooth, Newark, 1950-57; partner firm Lindrooth & Mantonya, Newark, 1957-74; firm John B. Mantonya, 1974-81, John B. Mantonya, L.P.A., 1981—. Mem. North Fork Local Bd. Edn., 1962-69; adv. com. Salvation Army, Licking County, 1965— , Mayor of, Utica, Ohio, 1953-59. Served with AUS, 1943-45. Mem. ABA, Ohio Bar Assn., Licking County Bar Assn. (pres. 1967), Phi Delta Phi, Beta Theta Pi. Probate (including wills, trusts), Property, real (including real estate development, water). Home: 11055 Reynolds Rd Utica OH 43080-9549 Office: 3 N 3rd St Newark OH 43055-5506

MANZONI, CHARLES R., JR., lawyer; b. San Francisco, Jan. 23, 1947; s. Charles R. and Vivian M.; m. Deborah Ann Manzoni, May 27, 1989; children: Charles III, Nicholas. BA in History, U. Santa Clara, Calif., 1969, JD, 1972. Bar: Calif. 1973, Ill. 1975. Staff atty., market regulation SEC, Washington, 1972-73, legal asst. to chmn., 1973-75; asst. v.p., atty. A.G. Becker & Co., Chgo., 1975-77; assoc. Gardner Carton & Douglas, Chgo., 1977-80, ptnr., 1980-96, 98—; exec. v.p., gen. counsel Zurich Kemper Investments, Chgo., 1996-98. Adj. prof. IIT-Kent Sch. Law, 1993-95. 1st lt. U.S. Army Res. Mem. ABA. Avocations: skiing, running. Corporate, general, Securities. Office: Gardner Carton & Douglas 191 N Wacker Dr Ste 3700 Chicago IL 60606-1698

MAPES, WILLIAM RODGERS, JR., lawyer; b. Cleve., Nov. 29, 1952; s. William R. and Marian (Atkins) M.; m. Patricia Soochan, Sept. 3, 1984. BS in Bus. Adminstrn., Miami U., Oxford, Ohio, 1974; JD, Am. U., 1977. Bar: D.C. 1978, U.S. Ct. Appeals (D.C. cir.) 1979, U.S. Ct. Appeals (fed. cir.) 1980, U.S. Ct. Appeals (5th cir.) 1981, U.S. Supreme Ct. 1982, U.S. Ct. Appeals (3d cir.) 1985, U.S. Ct. Appeals (4th cir.) 1987, U.S. Ct. Appeals (6th cir.) 1988. Ptnr. Ross, Marsh & Foster, Washington, 1984—2000, Duane Morris, Washington, 2000—. Treas., bd. dirs. Holy Land Christian Ecumenical Found. Mem. ABA (editor nat. resources sect. newsletter 1984-89), Fed. Energy Bar Assn. Avocations: boating, tennis, cycling. Administrative and regulatory, FERC practice. Home: 11430 Hollowstone Drive Rockville MD 20852 Office: Duane Morris 1667 K St NW #700 Washington DC 20006-1608 E-mail: wrmapes@duanemorris.com.

MAPLE, JOHANNA PHILHOWER, lawyer; b. Cin., July 10, 1972; d. Steven David and Aleen (Creamer) Philhower; m. Theodore Lincoln Maple, May 17, 1997; 1 child, Samuel Theodore. BA summa cum laude, U. Indpls., 1994; JD cum laude, Ind. U., 1997. Bar: Ind. 1997. Law clk. to U.S. Magistrate Judge U.S. Dit. Ct., So. Dist. Ind., Indpls., 1997—99; trial atty. Equal Employment Opportunity Commn., 1999—. Adj. prof. U. Indpls., 1998. Pres. Cir. K Club, U. Indpls., 1993—94, treas., 1992—93; vol. Salvation Army, Indpls., 1992—94, 1998—; active North United Meth. Ch., 2002—. Recipient GM award Excellence in Liberal Arts, U. Indpls., 1992; scholar Presdl. scholar, 1990—94. Democrat. Avocations: travel, jogging, family time.

MAR, EUGENE, lawyer; b. Hong Kong, July 5, 1940; s. Timothy T. and Shuh Yin Lu Mar; children: Christopher E., Jonathan M. BS in Metall. Engring., U. Md., 1964; JD, Cath. U. Am., 1969. Bar: Va. 1970, U.S. Ct. Mil. Appeals, U.S. Supreme Ct., U.S. Tax Ct., U.S. Ct. Appeals D.C. Assoc. Philpitt, Steininger & Priddy, 1964-65; examiner U.S. Patent Office, 1965-68; assoc. Arthur Schwartz, Arlington, Va., 1968-72; ptnr. Bacon & Thomas PLLC, Arlington, 1972—, mng. ptnr., 1981—. Mem. ABA, Am. Intellectual Property Law Assn., Phi Alpha Delta, Phi Kappa Sigma. Patent. Office: 625 Slaters Ln Fl 4 Alexandria VA 22314-1176 E-mail: gmar@baconthomas.com.

MARA, TIMOTHY GERALD, lawyer; b. Cin., July 30, 1949; s. Thomas James and Rose Marie (Sansone) M. B in Community Planning, U. Cin., 1972; JD, No. Ky. U., 1978. Bar: Ohio 1978, U.S. Dist. Ct. Cin. 1979, U.S. Ct. Appeals (6th cir.) 1983. Regional planner Ohio-Ky.-Ind. Regional Coun. of Govts., Cin., 1972-77; spl. asst. U.S. Rep. Thomas A. Luken, Cin., 1977-78; pvt. practice Cin., 1979—. Trustee Green Twp., Hamilton County, Ohio, 1982-86. Mem. Ohio State Bar Assn., Cin. Bar Assn., Hamilton County Dem. Steering Com. Roman Catholic. Avocations: nature walks, biking. Land use and zoning (including planning), Personal injury (including property damage), Probate (including wills, trusts). Office: 1500 Chiquita Ctr 250 E 5th St Cincinnati OH 45202-4119

MARANDAS, JOHN STEVE, lawyer; b. Portland, Oreg., June 3, 1940; s. Steve George and Vasiliki (Paravantis) M.; m. Louise Fay Johnson, Sept. 28, 1996; children— Stephanie Anne, John Steve John, Jason John, Lauren Marie, Sara Louise Julia. B.S., Lewis and Clark Coll., 1962; J.D., Willamette U., 1965. Bar: Oreg. 1966, U.S. Dist. Ct. Oreg. 1966, U.S. Ct. Appeals (9th cir.) 1968, U.S. Supreme Ct. 1972. Hearings referee Oreg. Dept. Motor Vehicles, Salem, 1965-66; asst. atty. gen. Dept. Justice,

1966-69; assoc. Lekas, Dicey & Sherwood, Portland, 1969-72; ptnr. Lekas, Dicey & Marandas, Portland, 1972-75, Bloom, Chaivoe, Ruben, Marandas, Berg, Sly & Barnett, Portland, 1975-79; ptnr. Bloom, Marandas and Sly, Portland, 1979-87; judge pro tem Circuit Ct., 1984-95. Bd. dirs. Oreg. NCCJ, 1975-82, 86-92, chmn., 1980-81, nat. bd. dirs., 1979-85, regional chair, 2002—; pres. Greek Civic Club Oreg., 1975-76, World Affairs Coun., 1977-2000; regional v.p. United Hellenic Am. Congress, 1977-91; trustee Northwestern Sch. Law Lewis & Clark Coll., 1971-73; chmn. bd. dirs. Project Stop, Alcohol Rehab. Clinic, 1976-84; bd. dirs. Oreg. Spl. Olympics, 1983-93, Lewis & Clark Coll. Alumni Bd., 1969-73, 86-90. Served to capt. JAGC, Army N.G., 1965-76. Mem. ABA (family law sect.), Oreg. Bar Assn. (com. fgn. and internat. law, bar trial counsel), Am. Judicature Soc., Am. Immigration Lawyers Assn., Multnomah County Bar Assn. (com. dist. ct. liaison), Am. Hellenic C. of C., Delta Theta Phi. Democrat. Greek Orthodox. Clubs: Portland City, Am. Hellenic Ednl. and Progressive Assn. (Portland). Lodge: Kiwanis. Author: Miscellaneous Opinions of the Attorney General, 1966-69; Tort Liability of Government Officials, 1969; Duties, Tariffs and Import Controls, 1982. State civil litigation, General practice, Immigration, naturalization, and customs. Home: 17950 Royce Way Lake Oswego OR 97034-7321 Office: 1500 SW 1st Ave Ste 840 Portland OR 97201 E-mail: jsmpclaw@aol.com.

MARANO, RICHARD MICHAEL, lawyer; b. Waterbury, Conn., June 22, 1960; s. Albert Nicholas and Angeline Domenica (Viotti) M.; m. Eileen N. Barry. BA, Fairfield U., 1982; JD, Seton Hall U., 1985. Bar: Conn. 1985, U.S. Dist. Ct. Conn. 1985, U.S. Tax Ct. 1986, U.S. Supreme Ct. 1990, U.S. Ct. Appeals (2d cir.) 1991; cert. criminal trial advocate. Assoc. Moynahan, Ruskin, Mascolo & Mariani, Waterbury, 1985-87; ptnr. Marano & Diamond, Waterbury, 1987—2001, Marano Law Offices, 2001—. Bd. of examiners Nat. Bd. Trial Advocacy, 1999—. Author: History of the Order Sons of Italy of Waterbury, Connecticut, 1995, Connecticut Criminal Legal Forms, 1999, Vote Your Conscience: The Last Campaign of George McGovern, 2003; co-author: Growing Up Italian and American in Waterbury, 1997; co-editor: Counsel for the Defense, 1991-93, editor, 1993-98; contbr. law articles to Conn. Bar Jour. Bd. dirs. Italian-Am. Dem. Club, Waterbury, 1988—, Ctrl. Naugatuck Valley HELP, 1992—, Anderson Boys Club, 1989-2002, pres. 1996-98, Waterbury Housing Police Fund, 1992-94, Waterbury Crime Stoppers Inc., 1994-97; pres. Conn. Young Dems., 1981-82; state coord. McGovern for U.S. Presdl. campaign, 1983-84; campaign mgr. Orman for Congress, 1984; active Oxford Dem. Town Com., 2002-; commr. Waterbury Pub. Assistance, 1986-88, Waterbury Fire Bd., 1996-98; justice of the peace, Waterbury, 1989-99; gen. counsel Waterbury Dem. Town Com., 1990-96; trustee Our Lady of Lourdes Ch., 1993—; alderman City of Waterbury, 1988-90. Mem. ABA, ATLA, KC, Conn. Bar Assn., Nat. Assn. Criminal Def. Lawyers (life), Conn. Criminal Def. Lawyers Assn. (pres.-elect 1997-98, pres. 1998-99), Conn. Italian-Am. Bar Assn. (pres. 1993-95), Conn. Trial Lawyers Assn., Waterbury Bar Assn. (bd. dirs. 1993-2002, pres. 1996-98), New Haven County Bar Assn., Nat. Italian-Am. Bar Assn. (Conn. delegate 1993—), Sons of Italy (pres. lodge #66 1994-96), Unico Club (pres. Waterbury chpt. 1997-99), Cath. Lawyers Guild, Conn. Acad. Cert. Trial Lawyers, Nat. Eagle Scout Assn. (life), Elks, Alpha Mu Gamma, Pi Sigma Alpha. Roman Catholic. Criminal, General practice, Personal injury (including property damage). Home: 24 Lake Dr Oxford CT 06478-1172 Office: Marano Law Offices 61 Field St Waterbury CT 06702-1907 E-mail: RichardMarano@aol.com.

MARBURG-GOODMAN, JEFFREY EMIL, lawyer; b. Taipei, Taiwan, Feb. 20, 1957; s. Samuel and Lisl (Marburg) G. BA, Amherst Coll., 1979; JD, Harvard U., 1983; postgrad., U. Aix-Marseille, France, 1983-84. Bar: N.Y. 1986, U.S. Dist. Ct. (so. and ea. dists.) N.Y. 1988. Assoc. Shearman & Sterling, Paris, 1984, N.Y.C., 1985-89, Patton & Boggs, Washington, 1989-91; legal counsel U.S. AID, U.S. Dept. State, Washington, 1991-2000, asst. gen. counsel, 2000—. Mem. nat. steering com. Clinton-Gore '96, Gore 2000, Washington; cons. Gore 2000, Washington. Rotary fellow, 1984. Mem. Harvard Club, Phi Beta Kappa. Avocations: running, weight training, music, theatre, travel. Home: 1401 17th St NW Ph Apt1008 Washington DC 20036-6400 Office: US AID Office Gen Counsel Ronald Reagan Bldg & Interna C Washington DC 20523-0001 E-mail: jmarburg-goodman@usaid.gov.

MARCKS, RONALD HENRY, lawyer, abrasives and diversified products manufacturing company executive; b. New Haven, Dec. 4, 1931; s. Henry John and Mildred Josephine (Perinchief) M.; A.B., Dartmouth Coll., 1952; LL.B., Harvard U., 1960; m. Barbara Ann Wye, Aug. 17, 1968. Bar: Mass. 1960. Assoc., then ptnr. Goodwin, Procter & Hoar, Boston, 1960-74; chief legal counsel Norton Co., Worcester, Mass., 1974-79, v.p., gen. counsel, sec., 1979— . Served with USNR, 1952-56. Mem. Phi Beta Kappa. Author: (under pseudonym Jens O. Parsson) Dying of Money: Lessons of the Great German and American Inflations, 1974.

MARCUS, BERNARD, lawyer, consultant; b. Wilkes-Barre, Pa., Mar. 10, 1924; m. Frances Frank; children: Kate, Aaron, Charles, Mary. Student, U. Pa., 1941-43, Carnegie-Mellon U., 1943-44; LL.B., Harvard U., 1948; postgrad., Loyola U. of South, New Orleans, 1958. Bar: D.C. 1949, La. 1958. Atty. legis. reference service Library of Congress, 1949-50; acting counsel small bus. com. Ho. of Reps., 1950; atty. NLRB, Washington, Cin., Buffalo and New Orleans, 1950-57; assoc. Deutsch, Kerrigan & Stiles, New Orleans, 1957-58, ptnr., 1958-95, mng. ptnr., 1985-89, emeritus ptnr., 1995—. Cons. Dept. State, 1965-69; labor arbitrator Am. Arbitration Assn., Fed. Mediation and Conciliation Svc., NASD, Arbitration Forum, USDA, U.S. Dept. Def., U.S. Dept. Transp., U.S. Dept. Justice, U.S. Dept. Labor, U.S. Dept. Interior, U.S. Dept. Treasury, City of Houston, Houston Met. Transit Authority, Sanyo Mfg. Co., TU Elec., Internat. Paper Co., Inland Paper, ADM Corp., Ingalls Shipbldg., PPG Industries, Ga. Pacific Corp., Westvaco, Hertz, Schering Plough, Chevron, Bryan Foods, Savannah Elec. & Power, Citgo, SBC Corp., Verizon, GTE, GAF, Citgo, Conoco Phillips Petroleum Co., others. Author: Congress and the Monopoly Problem, 1950; contbr. to casebooks. Pres. New Orleans Jewish Community Center, 1973-75; mem. Nat. Jewish Welfare Bd., 1974-83; bd. dirs. New Orleans Jewish Welfare Bd., Jewish Family and Children's Service, New Orleans, Communal Hebrew Sch.; v.p. New Orleans Home for Jewish Aged, 1978-80, Florence Heller Rsch. Found. Served U.S Army, 1943-46. Mem. ABA, Fed. Bar Assn., La. Bar Assn., New Orleans Bar Assn. (exec. com. 1971-74), D.C. Bar Assn. Antitrust, Corporate, general, Labor (including EEOC, Fair Labor Standards Act, labor-management relations, NLRB, OSHA). Home: 630 Burdette St New Orleans LA 70118-3937 Office: 755 Magazine St New Orleans LA 70130-3698 E-mail: bmarcus@dks.com.

MARCUS, ERIC PETER, lawyer; b. Newark, Aug. 31, 1950; s. John J. and Alice M. (Zeldin) M.; m. Terry R. Toll, Oct. 9, 1983. BA, Brown U., 1972; JD, Stanford U., 1976. Bar: N.Y. 1977, N.J. 1977. Assoc. Kaye, Scholer, Fierman, Hays & Handler LLP, N.Y.C., 1976-84, ptnr., 1985—. Contbr. articles to profl. jours. Mem. Phi Beta Kappa. Banking, Commercial, contracts (including sales of goods; commercial financing). Office: Kaye Scholer LLP 425 Park Ave New York NY 10022-3506

MARCUS, MARIA LENHOFF, lawyer, law educator; b. Vienna, June 23, 1933; came to U.S., 1938, naturalized, 1944; d. Arthur and Clara (Gruber) Lenhoff; m. Norman Marcus, Dec. 23, 1956; children: Valerie, Nicole, Eric. BA, Oberlin Coll., 1954; JD, Yale Law Sch., 1957. Bar: N.Y. 1961, U.S. Dist. Ct. (so. and ea. dists.) N.Y. 1962, U.S. Ct. Appeals (2d cir.) 1962, U.S. Supreme Ct. 1964. Assoc. counsel NAACP, N.Y.C., 1961-67; asst. atty. gen. N.Y. State, N.Y.C., 1967-78; chief litigation bur. Atty. Gen. N.Y. State, 1976-78; adj. assoc. prof. NYU Law Sch., 1976-78; assoc. prof. Fordham U. Law Sch., N.Y.C., 1978-86, prof., 1986—, Joseph M. McLaughlin prof., 1997—. Arbitrator Nat. Assn. Securities Dealers; chair subcom. interrogatories U.S. Dist. Ct. (so. dist.) N.Y., 1983-85. Contbr. articles to profl. jours. Recipient Teacher of Year award, Fordham Law School Students, 2001. Fellow N.Y. Bar Found.; mem. Assn. Bar City of N.Y. (v.p. 1995-96, long range planning com. 1996-2000, exec. com. 1976-80, com. audit 1988-95, labor com. 1981-84, judiciary com. 1975-76, chmn. civil rights com. 1972-75), N.Y. State Bar Assn. (exec. com. 1979-81, ho. dels. 1978-81, com. constitution and by-laws 1984-93), N.Y. Women's Bar Assn. (Pres.'s award 1999). Office: Fordham U Law Sch 140 W 62nd St New York NY 10023-7485

MARCUS, PAUL, law educator; b. N.Y.C., Dec. 8, 1946; s. Edward and Lillian (Rubin) M.; m. Rebecca Nimmer, Dec. 22, 1968; children: Emily, Beth, Daniel. AB, UCLA, 1968, JD, 1971. Bar: Calif. 1971, U.S. Dist. Ct. (cen. dist.) Calif. 1972, U.S. Ct. Appeals (D.C. cir.) 1972, U.S. Ct. Appeals (7th cir.) 1976. Law clk. U.S. Ct. Appeals (D.C. cir.), 1971-72; assoc. Loeb & Loeb, L.A., 1972-74; prof. law U. Ill., Urbana, 1974-83; dean Coll. Law U. Ariz., Tucson, 1983-88, prof., 1988-92; Haynes prof. law Coll. William and Mary, Williamsburg, Va., 1992—, interim dean, 1993-94, 97-98. Reporter, cons. Fed. Jud. Ctr. Commn. Author: The Entrapment Defense, 1989, 3d edit., 2003, The Prosecution and Defense of Criminal Conspiracy, 1978, 5th edit., 2002, Gilbert Law Summary, 1982, 7th edit., 2001, Criminal Law: Cases and Materials, 1982, 5th edit., 2003, Criminal Procedure in Practice, 2001, 2d edit., 2003; nat. reporter on criminal law Internat. of Comparative Law, 1978—. Nat. reporter on criminal law Internat. of Comparative Law, 1978—. Office: Coll William & Mary Law Sch PO Box 8795 Williamsburg VA 23187-8795 E-mail: pxmarc@wm.edu.

MARCUS, STEPHEN HOWARD, lawyer; b. N.Y.C., June 30, 1945; s. Jacob and Mildren (Cohen) M.; m. Carol Sylvia Beatrice, June 11, 1967; children: Joshua David, Rebecca Lynn, Daniel Benjamin. BME, MIT, 1967; JD, Harvard U., 1970. Bar: Calif. 1971, U.S. Dist. Ct. (cen. dist.) Calif. 1971, U.S. Dist. Ct. (so. dist.) Calif. 1974, U.S. Dist. Ct. (so. dist.) Calif. 1975, U.S. Ct. Appeals (9th cir.) 1980. Assoc. Mitchell, Silberberg & Knupp, L.A., 1971-72, Greenberg, Bernhard, Weis & Karma, L.A., 1972-76; ptnr. Greenberg, Bernhard, Weiss & Rosin, L.A., 1976-85; assoc. Frandzel & Share, L.A., 1985-87, ptnr., 1987-97, Gittler & Bradford, L.A., 1997—; dir. Cerriton Valley Bancorp., 2001—02. Bd. dirs. Cerritos Valley Bancorp; judge pro tem L.A. Mcpl. Ct., 1976-83. Editor Harvard Law Rev., 1970. Dir. legal com. Temple B'Nai Hayim, 1999-2003, bd. dirs., 1999-2003. Mem. Los Angeles County Bar Assn. (client rels. com. arbitrator 1982—, vice chair, 1996—), Century City Bar Assn. (bd. govs. 1984-90), MIT Club So. Calif. (pres. 1978-79, bd. govs. 1979—), Sigma Xi, Tau Beta Pi. Democrat. Jewish. Avocations: senior soccer, square dancing. Banking, General civil litigation, Commercial, consumer (including collections, credit). Office: Gittler & Bradford 10537 Santa Monica Blvd 3d Fl Los Angeles CA 90025-1793 E-mail: csmarcus@aol.com., smarcus@gblaw.net.

MARCUSA, FRED HAYE, lawyer; b. Paterson, N.J., Jan. 31, 1946; s. Harry and Alice Marcusa; m. Andrea Disario, June 28, 1986; children; Michael, Daniel. AB, Dartmouth Coll., 1967; JD, U. Pa., 1970. Bar: N.Y. 1971. Assoc. Davis, Polk & Wardwell, N.Y.C., 1970-79; v.p., gen. counsel The Coca-Cola Bottling Co. of N.Y., Inc., N.Y.C., 1979-81; ptnr. Kaye Scholer LLP, N.Y.C., 1981—. Corporate, general, Private international, Securities. Office: Kaye Scholer LLP 425 Park Ave New York NY 10022-3506 E-mail: fmarcusa@kayescholer.com.

MARCUSS, STANLEY JOSEPH, lawyer; b. Hartford, Conn., Jan. 24, 1942; s. Stanley Joseph and Anne Sutton (Leone) M.; m. Rosemary Daly, July 6, 1968; children: Elena Daly, Aidan Stanley. BA, Trinity Coll., 1963, Cambridge U., 1965, MA, 1968; JD, Harvard U., 1968. Bar: D.C., N.Y., Conn., U.S. Supreme Ct. Staff atty. office of gen. counsel HUD, Washington, 1968; atty. firm Hogan and Hartson, Washington, 1968-73; counsel to internat. fin. subcom. U.S. Senate Com. on Banking, Housing and Urban Affairs, 1973-77; dep. asst. sec. for trade regulation Dept. Commerce, Washington, 1977-78, sr. dep. asst. sec. for industry and trade, 1978-79, acting asst. sec. for industry and trade, 1979-80, acting asst. sec. for trade regulation, 1980; mem. firm Milbank, Tweed, Hadley & McCloy, Washington, 1980-93, Bryan Cave, 1993—. Former adj. prof. Am. U. Law Sch. Author: Effective Washington Representation, 1983; mem. bd. overseers U. Calif. Berkeley Law Jour.; contbr. articles to profl. jours. Former trustee Trinity Coll., Hartford. Marshall scholar. Mem. ABA, D.C. Bar (former chmn., steering com. internat. law div.), Phi Beta Kappa. Home: 4616 29th Pl NW Washington DC 20008-2105

MARDEN, JACK MORTIMER, lawyer; b. N.Y.C., Jan. 29, 1933; BA in Polit. Sci., NYU, Washington Sq. Coll., 1953; JD, NYU, 1956; LLM, Judge Advocate Gen.'s Sch. U.S. Army, Charlottesville, Va., 1964. U.S. Dist. Ct. (so. dist.) W.Va., U.S. Dist. Ct. (so., ea. dist.) N.Y., (Bar: N.Y. 1956, W.Va. 1986, Pa. 1994-, U.S. Ct. Mil. Appeals, U.S. Army Ct. Mil. Review, U.S. Ct. Appeals (4th cir.), U.S. Supreme Ct. Pa., U.S. Supreme Ct., 1964; cert. U.S. Army mil. judge, appellate judge, NASD arbitrator, U.S. arbitration and mediation svc. mediator, nat. arbitration forum arbitrator. Commd. 1st lt. U.S. Army, 1957; advanced through grades to col. 1st U.S. Army, 1977; asst. staff judge adv. Hdqrs. U.S. Army Inf. Ctr., Ft. Benning, Ga., 1958-59, U.S. Army, Carribbean, Ft. Amador, C.Z., 1959-63; project officer plans div., plans and publs. dept. Judge Adv. Gen.'s Sch., Charlottesville, 1964, chief plans div., 1964-65; post judge adv. U.S. Army Intelligence Command, Ft. Holabird, Md., 1965, command staff judge adv., 1965-68; corps. judge adv. XXIV Corps, Phu Bai, Republic Vietnam, 1968-69, asst. staff judge adv., comdr.-in-chief Pacific, 1969-71, dep. staff judge adv., comdr.-in-chief Pacific, 1971-72; dep. staff judge adv. 1st U.S. Army, Ft. Meade, Md., 1972-74, staff judge adv., 1974-78, supervisory cir. judge Ft. Dix, NJ, 1978-81; legal advisor AF South (NATO), Naples, Italy, 1981-82; supervisory cir. judge U.S. Army, Mannheim, Fed. Republic Germany, 1982-84, sr. appellate judge, ct. mil. rev. Falls Church, Va., 1984-86, ret., 1986; bar counsel The W.Va. State Bar, Charleston, 1986-89; counsel W.Va. Workers Compensation Fund, Charleston, 1989—91; adminstrv. law judge W.Va. Worker's Compensation, 1991—94; pvt. practice, 1994—; assoc. dir. litig. strategies group (formerly med.-legal strategies group) Med. Horizons Unltd., San Antonio, 1996—; assoc. (part time) Mayerson Law Offices, 1999. Instr. bus. law Chaminade Coll., Honolulu, 1971-72, Howard Community Coll., Columbia, Md., 1972-78; nat. judge adv. Nat. Sojourners, 1973-78, nat. pres., 1985-86; tchr. 6th dept. labor adminstrv. law judge conf., nat. assn. adminstrv. law judge conf., 2000, various other courses on legal issues, mil. law, and legal ethics. Contbr. articles to profl. jours. including Sojourner Mag., Ten Year Report, The New Age, 1971, 20 Mil. Law Rev. 139. Past pres. Ner Torah Congregation, Columbia; mem. Sr. Adult Activities Ctr. Indian Valley, 1997-. Decorated Meritorious Svc. medal with Oak Leaf Cluster, Army Commendation medal with Oak Leaf Cluster, Good Conduct medal, Nat. Def. Svc. medal, Vietnam Svc. medal with 4 Battle Stars, Republic of Vietnam Campaign medal, Republic of Vietnam Cross of Galantry with Palm, Meritorious Unit Commendation, Overseas Svc. Ribbon, Army Svc. Ribbon. Mem. ABA (past pres., tchr. presdl. showcase meeting 2000), Ret. Officers Assn. W.Va., Pa. County Bar Assn., Mont. County Bar Assn., Souderton Bar Zoning Bd. (chmn.), Assn. Conflict Resolution, Nat. Sojourner's (past nat. pres. 1985-86, past pres. Panama chpt. #35, Charleston, Va. #440, Saigon #444, past mem., chmn. com. 33, past nat. trustee, past chmn.), Heroes of '76 (past nat. comdr. 1995-96), Ret. Officer's Assn. (Willow Grove chpt., past pres. Mountaineer chpt. 1988-90), Congreg. Tiferes B'nai Israel, Jewish War Vets. U.S. (Post 98), Souderton Borough Zoning Hearing Bd. (chmn. 1999), Valley of Charleston (so. jurisdiction), A.F. & A.M., Ft. Benning Lodge, Shiloh Lodge, Scottish Rite, Legion of Merit (hon.). Military, Workers' compensation. Office: 347 Madison Ave Souderton PA 18964-1863

MAREADY, WILLIAM FRANK, lawyer; b. Mullins, S.C., Sept. 13, 1932; s. Jesse Frank and Vera (Sellers) M.; m. Brenda McCanless, Nov. 3, 1979. AB, U. N.C., 1955, JD with honors, 1958. Bar: N.C. 1958, U.S. Dist. Ct. N.C. 1960, U.S. Ct. Appeals (4th cir.) 1962, U.S. Supreme Ct. 1968. Assoc. Mudge, Stern, Baldwin & Todd, N.Y.C., 1958-60, Hudson, Ferrell, Carter, Petree & Stockton, Winston-Salem, N.C., 1960-65; ptnr. Petree, Stockton & Robinson, Winston-Salem, 1965-92, Robinson, Maready, Lawing & Comerford, 1992-97, Maready, Comerford & Britt, 1997-99; prin. Law Offices of William F. Maready, 1999—. N.C. chmn. Winston-Salem/Forsyth County Bd. Edn., 1968-70, chmn., bd. dirs. and mem. exec. com., N.C. State Port Authority, 1984-97. With Green Berets, U.S. Army, 1952-54. Recipient Disting. Svc. award N.C. Sch. Bds. Assn., Freedom award John Locke Soc., 2000. Fellow Am. Coll. Trial Lawyers, Am. Bar Found.; mem. ABA (chmn. standing com. on aero. law 1979-82, chmn. forum com. on air and space law 1982-86), N.C. Bar Assn. (chmn. litigation sect. 1981-82, adminstrn. of justice com. 1981-82), Nat. Parent Tchr. Assn. (life), Forsyth Country Club, Rotary (Winston-Salem), Order of Coif, Phi Delta Phi, Phi Beta Kappa. Republican. Methodist. Product liability, Professional liability, Toxic tort. Office: 1076 W 4th St Ste 100 Winston Salem NC 27101-2411 E-mail: billmaready@mareadylaw.com.

MAREK, PREMYSL, lawyer; b. Novy Jicin, Czech Republic, Apr. 19, 1974; s. Petr Marek and Vera Markova. DMI, U of Toulouse, Toulouse, France, 1996; ML, Charles U of Prague, Prague, Czech Republic, 1998. Bar: Czech Bar 2001, Slovak Bar 2002. Jr. atty. law Ondrej Peterka, Prague, Czech Republic, 1998—2000, Peterka & Leuchterova vos, Prague, Czech Republic, 2000—01; ptnr. Peterka, Leuchterova & ptnrs. vos, Prague, Czech Republic, 2001—; head Slovak office Peterka, Leuchterova & ptnrs. sro, Bratislava, Slovakia, 2001—. Recipient Leopold Heyrovsky award, Charles U, 1997, Bolzan award, 1998. Avocations: sports, travel. Property, real (including real estate development, water), Commercial, contracts (including sales of goods; commercial financing), Mergers and acquisitions. Office: Peterka, Leuchterova & Partners sro Kapitulska 18/A 811 01 Bratislva Slovakia

MARGER, EDWIN, lawyer; b. N.Y.C., Mar. 18, 1928; s. William and Fannie (Cohen) M.; m. Kaye Sanderson, Oct. 1, 1951; children: Shari Ann, Diane Elaine, Sandy Ben; m. L. Suzanne Smyth, July 5, 1968; 1 child, George Phinney; m. Mary Susan Hamel, May 6, 1987; 1 child, Charleston Faye. BA, U. Miami, 1951, JD, 1953. Bar: Fla. 1953, Ga. 1971, D.C. 1978. Pvt. practice, Miami Beach, Fla., 1953-67, Atlanta, 1971—. Gen. counsel Physicians Nat. Risk Retention Group, 1988-91, Physicians Reliance Assn., 1988-91, Physicians Nat. Legal Def. Corp., 1988-91; spl. asst. atty. gen. Fla., 1960-61; atty., agt. Republic of Haiti, 1962-67, City of Port-au-Prince for Transp. and Housing, 1962, Dominican Republic for Trade and Industry, 1964-65; of counsel Richard Burns, Miami, 1967—. Contbr. articles to profl. jours. Tchr. Nat. Inst. Trial Advocacy; mem. Miami Beach Social Svc. Commn., 1957; chmn. Fulton County Aviation Adv. Com., 1980—; trustee Forensic Scis. Found., 1984-88; v.p., 1986-88; lt. col., a.d.c. Gov. Ga., 1971-74, 80-84; col., a.d.c. Gov. La., 1977-87; Khan Bahador and mem. exiled King of Afghanistan Privy Council, 1980—. With USAAF, 1946-47. Fellow Am. Acad. Forensic Scis. (chmn. jurisprudence sect. 1977-78, sec. 1976-77, bd. dirs. 1978-79, exec. com. 1983-86); mem. ATLA, ABA, Fla. Bar Assn. (aerospace com. 1971-83, bd. govs. 1983-87, 90-94, exec. com. 1993-94), State Bar Ga. (chmn. sect. environ. law 1974-75, aviation law sect. 1978, bd. govs. 1999—, stds. of the profession com.), Ga. Trial Lawyers Assn., Nat. Assn. Criminal Def. Lawyers, Ga. Assn. Criminal Def. Lawyers, Am. Judicature Soc., Am. Arbitration Assn. (commn. panel 1978), Inter-Am. Bar Assn. (sr.), World Assn. Lawyers (founding), Lawyer-Pilots Bar Assn. (founding, v.p. 1959-62), VFW, Rotary, Lions, Advocates Club. Criminal, Family and matrimonial, Personal injury (including property damage). Office: 44 N Main St Jasper GA 30143-1501

MARGETON, STEPHEN GEORGE, law librarian; b. Elizabeth, N.J., Mar. 22, 1945; s. Louis George and Josephine A. (Bednarik) M.; m. Margaret Mary Salter, May 14, 1977; children: Catherine Ann, Elizabeth Ann. AB, Mt. St. Mary's Coll., 1967; JD, George Washington U., 1970; MSLS, Cath. U., 1973. Reference librarian Am.-Brit. law div. Library of Congress, Washington, 1968-72; law libr. Steptoe & Johnson, Washington, 1972-85; librarian Supreme Ct. of U.S., Washington, 1985-88; dir. Judge Kathryn J. DuFour Law Libr. The Cath. Univ. Am., 1988—. Instr. George Mason Law Sch., Arlington, Va., 1977-80. Mem. Am. Assn. Law Libraries, Internat. Assn. Law Libraries. Office: Cath U Am Judge Kathryn J DuFour Law Libr 3600 John Mccormack Rd NE Washington DC 20064-0001

MARGO, ROD DAVID, lawyer; b. Johannesburg, Republic of South Africa, Feb. 14, 1950; came to U.S., 1978; s. Cecil Stanley and Marguerite Giselle (Polné) M. BCom, U. Witwatersrand, 1970, LLB cum laude, 1973; D.Civil Laws, McGill U., 1979. Bar: Ga. 1979, Calif. 1981, DC 1996. From assoc. to ptnr. Condon & Forsyth, L.A., 1980—. Lectr. aviation law UCLA, 1981—. Author: Aviation Ins. 3d edit., 2000; co-author: Shawcross & Beaumont on Air Law, 4th rev. edit., 2003. Fellow Royal Aero Soc.; mem. L.A. County Bar Assn. Democrat. Jewish. Avocations: music, travel, reading. Aviation, Insurance, Private international. Office: Condon & Forsyth Ste 1450 1801 Avenue Of The Stars Los Angeles CA 90067-5899 E-mail: rmargo@cfla.com.

MARGOLIN, STEPHEN M. lawyer; b. Chgo., Dec. 23, 1935; s. Albert and Mae Dorothy (Kaufman) M.; m. Pamela B. Miles, March 28, 1998; children: Jocelyn, Holly, Jonathan. BS, U. Ill., 1957; JD, John Marshall Law Sch., 1964. Bar: Ill. 1964, U.S. Dist. Ct. (no. dist.) Ill. 1964. Field agt., lectr. IRS, 1957-62; ptnr. Brainerd, Brydges and Margolin, Chgo., 1965-68; pvt. practice Chgo., 1968-77; sr. ptnr. Margolin, Zeitlin & Aronson, Chgo., 1977—. Contbr. articles to profl. jours. Co-chmn. lawyers divsn. Jewish United Fund, 1982—. Served to 1st lt. U.S. Army, 1958. Mem. ABA (employee benefit com., tax com.), Ill. State Bar Assn. (employee benefit sect.), Midwest Pension Conf., Chgo. Assn. Commerce and Industry (employee benefit subcom. 1981—). Pension, profit-sharing, and employee benefits, Corporate taxation. Office: Chuhak & Tecson PC 30 S Wacker Dr Ste 2600 Chicago IL 60606-3516 E-mail: smargolin@chuhak.com.

MARGOLIS, ANITA JOY, lawyer; b. Mpls., May 29, 1959; d. Herbert A. and Ursula (Ries) M. BA, U. Wis., 1981; JD, Calif. Western Sch. of Law, 1985. Bar: Calif. 1985, U.S. Dist. Ct. (so. dist.) Calif. 1985, U.S. Dist. Ct. (ctrl. dist.) Calif. 1993. Assoc. Phillips, Campbell, Haskett, Noone & Ingwalson, San Diego, 1986-93; pvt. practice The Law Offices of Anita J. Margolis, San Diego, 1993—; judge pro tem San Diego Superior Court, 2001—, arbitrator, 2001—. Bd. dirs. Tom Homann Law Assoc., 2001—. Mem. task force Women's Resource Fair, 1989—; vol. San Diego Vol. Lawyers Program, 1993-97; gender equity adv. bd. San Diego C.C. Dist., 1990—, chair, 1994—; single parent/displaced homemakers adv. bd. San Diego C.C. Dist., 1990—; judge mock trial Calif. Sch. Law, 1991-95; mem. Citizens Adv. Coun. to Bd. Trustees S.D. City Sch. Dist., 1997-2001; alumni bd. Calif. Western Sch. Law, 1996-98. Mem. San Diego County Bar Assn. (bd. dirs. 2000-03, sec. 2001, v.p. 2002-03), Consumer Attys. San Diego, Lawyers Club San Diego (bd. dirs. 1989-93, sec. 1991-92, asst. sec. 1992-93, chmn. cmty. rels. com. 1989-91, chmn. continuing edn. com. 1992-93). Avocations: soccer, golf, skiing. General civil litigation, Family and matrimonial, Personal injury (including property damage). Office: 600 B St Ste 2400 San Diego CA 92101-4520 E-mail: anitau2@pacbell.net.

MARGOLIS, BENJAMIN ROBERT, lawyer, pharmacist; b. Phila., Jan. 15, 1945; s. Daniel and Sylvia (Rubin) M.; m. Lia Ordaz, Dec. 27, 1971; 1 child, Jonathan Daniel. BSc, U. of the Scis. in Phila., 1967; PharmD, U. So. Calif., 1969; JD, Southwestern U. Sch. Law, 1984. Bar: Calif. 1986, D.C. 1987, U.S. Dist. Ct. (cen. dist.) Calif. 1986, U.S. Tax Ct. 1986, U.S. Ct. Appeals (9th cir.) 1987, U.S. Supreme Ct. 1989. Dir. pharmacy Rancho Los Amigos Nat. Rehabilitation Ctr., Downey, Calif., 1993-2000; pvt. practice Pacific Palisades, Calif., 1986—. Expert witness pharmacy and med. malpractice; adj. asst. prof. pharmacy practice U. So. Calif. Mem. ABA,

ATLA, Los Angeles County Bar Assn., L.A. Trial Lawyers Assn. General practice. E-mail: benmar12001@yahoo.com.

MARGOLIS, DANIEL HERBERT, lawyer; b. Feb. 11, 1926; s. Morris Abraham and Miriam M.; m. Anabel Tendler, Dec. 23, 1951 (dec.); children: Peter, Beth, Laura, James; m. Sidney Millman Moore, Feb. 5, 1983. BA, Johns Hopkins U., 1948; LLB, Harvard U., 1951. Bar: D.C. 1951, U.S. Supreme Ct. 1959. Atty. adv. Office Price Stablzn., Washington, 1951-52; trial atty. Antitrust divsn. Dept. Justice, Washington, 1952-56; sr. ptnr. Bergson, Borkland, Margolis & Adler, Washington, 1962—86, McGuire, Woods, Battle & Boothe, Washington, 1986-89, Patton, Boggs LLP, Washington, 1989—2001; sr. counsel DC Office of Corp. Counsel, 2001—03. With USN, 1945—46. Fellow ABA. Avocations: sailing, skiing, cooking.

MARGOLIS, EMANUEL, lawyer, educator; b. Bklyn., Mar. 18, 1926; s. Abraham and Esther (Levin) M.; m. Edith Cushing; m. Estelle Thompson, Mar. 1, 1959; children: Elizabeth Margolis-Pineo, Catherine, Abby Margolis Newman, Joshua, Sarah. BA, U. N.C., 1947; MA, Harvard U., 1948, PhD, 1951; JD, Yale U., 1956. Bar: Conn. 1957, U.S. Dist. Ct. Conn. 1958, U.S. Supreme Ct. 1969. Instr. dept. govt. U. Conn., 1951-53; assoc. Silberberg & Silverstein, Ansonia, Conn., 1956-60, Wofsey Rosen Kweskin & Kuriansky, Stamford, Conn., 1960-66, ptnr., 1966-96, of counsel, 1996—. Arbitrator State of Conn., 1984-85; adj. prof. Quinnipiac U. Sch. Law, 1986—. Sr. editor Conn. Bar Jour., 1971-80, 83—, editor-in-chief, 1980-83; contbr. to profl. jours. Mem. nat. bd. ACLU, 1975-79; mem. Westport (Conn.) Planning and Zoning Commn., 1971-75; chmn. Conn. CLU, 1988-95, legal advisor, 1995—; exec. com. Yale Law Sch., 2000—. With U.S. Army, 1944-46. Decorated Purple Heart; recipient First Award for Disting. Svc. to Conn. Bar, Conn. Law Tribune, 1987. Fellow Conn. Bar Found. (James W. Cooper fellow 1996); mem. ABA, Conn. Bar Assn. (chmn. human rights sect. 1970-73), Nat. Assn. Criminal Def. Lawyers, Am. Arbitration Assn. (arbitrator 1998—, trial referee 1985—). Civil rights, Federal civil litigation, Criminal. Office: 600 Summer St Stamford CT 06901-1990 Home: 72 Myrtle Ave Westport CT 06880-3512 E-mail: emesq@optonline.net.

MARGOLIS, LAWRENCE STANLEY, federal judge; b. Phila., Mar. 13, 1935; m. Doris May Rosenberg, Jan. 30, 1960; children: Mary Aleta, Paul Oliver. BSME, Drexel U., 1957; JD, George Washington U., 1961. Bar: D.C. 1963. Patent examiner U. S. Patent Office, Washington, 1957-62; patent counsel Naval Ordnance Lab., White Oak, Md., 1962-63; asst. corp. counsel D.C., 1963-66; atty. criminal div., spl. asst. U.S. atty. Dept. of Justice, Washington, 1966-68; asst. U.S. atty. for D.C., 1968-71; U.S. magistrate judge U.S. Dist. Ct., Washington, 1971-82; judge U.S. Ct. Fed. Claims, Washington, 1982—; chmn. task force on discovery reform U.S. Claims Ct., Washington, chmn. alt. dispute resolution. Chmn. Space and Bldg. com., chmn. Ct. Security Com., mem. faculty Fed. Jud. Ctr. Editor-in-chief The Young Lawyer, 1965-66, D.C. Bar Jour., 1967-73; bd. editors The Dist. Lawyer, 1978-82. Trustee Drexel U., 1983-89; bd. govs. George Washington U. Alumni Assn., 1978-85, 93-96 Recipient Contbn. award D.C. Jaycees, 1966, Svc. award Boy Scouts Am., 1970, Alumni Svc. award George Washington U., 1976, Disting. Alumni Achievement award George Washington U., 1985, Disting. Alumni Achievement award Drexel U., 1988, Drexel 100 award, 1992, Alternative Dispute Resolution award Ctr. for Pub. Resources, 1988, Alternative Dispute Resolution Svc. award Ct. of Fed. Claims, 1996, Alumni Recognition award George Washington U., 1996. Fellow Inst. Jud. Adminstrn., Am. Bar Found.; mem. ABA (chmn. jud. adminstrn. divsn., Disting. Svc. award 1981), ABA Nat. Conf. Spl. Ct. Judges (chmn., Disting. Svc. award 1978), D.C. Jud. Conf., Bar Assn. D.C. (bd. dirs. 1970-72, jour. editor-in-chief, Contbn. award young lawyers sect. 1983), Fed. Bar Assn., George Washington U. Nat. Law Assn. (pres. D.C. chpt. 1974-76, pres. 1983-84), Univ. Club., Rotary (bd. dirs. Washington 1984-90, pres. 1988-89, dist. gov. 1991-92, Rotarian of Yr. 1984, Rotary Internat. Rep. to the World Bank and Orgn. of Am. States, 1998-99, pres. Rotary Found. 1999-2000), Charles Fahy Am. Inn of Ct. (Nat. Program award, 1997), Phila. Cen. High Sch. Alumni (bd. mgrs. 2001—). Office: US Ct Fed Claims 717 Madison Pl NW Ste 703 Washington DC 20439-0002 E-mail: lawrence_margolis@ao.uscourts.gov.

MARGULIES, BETH ZELDES, assistant attorney general; b. Hartford, Conn., Apr. 24, 1954; d. Benjamin and Edith Rose (Herrmann) Zeldes; m. Martin B. Margulies, July 26, 1981; children: Max, Adam. BA in Anthropology, McGill U., Montreal, 1976; JD summa cum laude, U. Bridgeport, 1983; LLM, Yale U., 1985. Bar: Conn. 1983, U.S. Dist. Ct. Conn. 1983, U.S. Ct. Appeals (D.C. cir.) 1988, U.S. Supreme Ct., 1989, U.S. Ct. Appeals (2d cir.) 1992. Asst. atty. gen. Atty. Gen.'s Office State of Conn., Hartford, 1985—. Contbr. articles to profl. jours. Home: 79 High Rock Rd Sandy Hook CT 06482-1623 Office: Atty Gen Office State of Conn 55 Elm St Hartford CT 06106-1746 E-mail: beth.margulies@po.state.ct.us.

MARGULIES, MARTIN B. lawyer, educator; b. N.Y.C., Oct. 6, 1940; s. Max N. and Mae (Cohen) M.; m. Beth Ellen Zeldes, July 26, 1981; children: Max Zeldes, Adam Zeldes. AB, Columbia Coll., 1961; LLB, Harvard U., 1964; LLM, NYU, 1966. Bar: N.D. 1968, N.Y. 1974, Mass. 1977, Conn. 1988, U.S. Dist. Ct. Mass. 1977, U.S. Ct. Appeals (2d cir.) 1984, U.S. Supreme Ct. 1995. Asst. prof. law U. N.D., Grand Forks, 1966-69; editor-in-chief Columbia Coll. Today, Columbia U., N.Y.C., 1969-71; assoc. editor Parade Mag., N.Y.C., 1971-72; assoc. prof. law Western New Eng. Law Sch., Springfield, Mass., 1973-76; Bernard Hersher prof. law U. Bridgeport, Conn., 1977-92; prof. law Quinnipiac U., 1992—, Neil H. Cogan Pub. Svc. prof. law, 1997-99. Author: The Early Life of Sean O'Casey, 1970; contbr. articles to profl. jours. Cooperating atty. Conn. Civil Liberties Union, Hartford, 1979—, bd. dirs., 1982-94; bd. dirs. Conn. Attys. for Progressive Legislature, New Haven, 1982: bd. dirs. ACLU, 1987-94, mem. free speech-assn. and poverty constl. rights com., 1988-94; chmn. bd. dirs. Fairfield County Civil Liberties Union, 1982-87, Hampden County Civil Liberties Union, 1976-78; bd. dirs. Civil Liberties Union Mass., Boston, 1975-78, Greater Springfield Urban League, 1976-78, Conn. Civil Liberties Union, 1982-94, ACLU, 1987-94, Ctr. for First Amendment Rights, Inc., 1993—. Recipient Media award N.Y. State Bar Assn., 1972, Gavel award ABA, 1973, Outstanding Tchr. award U. Bridgeport Law Sch., 1986, 87. Mem. Mass. Bar Assn., N.Y. State Bar Assn. Jewish. Home: 79 High Rock Rd Sandy Hook CT 06482-1623 Office: Quinnipiac Univ Sch Law 275 Mt Carmel Ave Hamden CT 06518-1947

MARICK, MICHAEL MIRON, lawyer; b. Chgo., Nov. 20, 1957; s. Miron Michael and Geraldyne Marilyn (Lid) M.; m. LIsa Amy Gelman, May 17, 1986. BA, Denison U., 1979; JD, Ill. Inst. Tech., 1982. Bar: Ill. 1982, US Dist. Ct. (no. dist.) Ill. 1982, Fla. 1983, US Ct. Appeals (3rd cir.) 1987, US Ct. Appeals (6th cir.) 1992, US Supreme Ct., 1992 US Ct. Appeals (5th cir.) 1998, US Ct. Appeals (10th & 11th cirs.) 2002. Assoc. Hinshaw, Culbertson, Moelmann, Hoban & Fuller, Chgo., 1982-85, Phelan, Pope & John, Chgo., 1985-90; ptnr. Pope & John, Chgo., 1990-94, Meckler Bulger & Tilson, Chgo., 1994—. Adj. prof. Ill. Inst. Tech./Chgo.-Kent Coll. Law, 1983-84, 87-99; comml. arbitrator Am. Arbitration Assn., Chgo., 1983—. Mem. Ill. Inst. Tech./Chgo.-Kent Law Rev., 1980-82; contbr. articles on ins. law and litigation to profl. jours. Treas., mem. exec. com. 42d Ward Rep. Orgn., 1984-87. Denison U. Econs. fellow, 1978, State of Ill. Gov.'s fellow, 1978; recipient Disting. Svc. award Ill. Inst. Tech./Chgo. Kent Coll. Law, 1996. Mem. ABA (mem. exec. com., com. on legis. action young lawyers divsn. 1983-84, vice chmn. TIPS excess surplus lines and reins. com. 1990-92), Ill. Bar Assn. (ins. law sect. coun. 1991-96, chair 1994-95, assembly rep. 1993-96), Fla. Bar Assn., Chgo. Bar Assn., Def. Rsch. Inst., Internat. Assn. Def. Counsel, Ill. Inst. Tech./Chgo.-Kent Coll. Law Alumni Assn. (v.p. 1990-94, pres. 1994-95), Trial Lawyers Club, Omicron Delta Upsilon, Pi Sigma Alpha, Alpha Tau Omega. Presbyterian. Federal civil litigation, State civil litigation, Insurance. Home: 3605 Pebble Beach Rd Northbrook IL 60062-3109 Office: Meckler Bulger & Tilson 123 North Wacker Dr Ste 1800 Chicago IL 60606-6339 E-mail: michael.marick@mbtlaw.com.

MARICLE, R. CLETUS, judge; b. Oneida, Ky., July 26, 1943; s. Harvey and Thelma Maricle; m. Judy Carol Maricle, Dec. 26, 1970; children: Donna, Russell Jr., Meredith, Linsey. BA, Georgetown Coll., 1964; JD, U. Ky., 1966. Bar: Ky. 1966, U.S. Dist. Ct. (ea. dist.) Ky. 1967, U.S. Ct. Appeals (6th cir.) 1968. Assoc. Neal and Neal, Owensboro, Ky., 1966; counsel Dept. Natural Resources, Frankford, Ky., 1967; pvt. practice Manchester, Ky., 1967—90; cir. judge Commonwealth Ky., Manchester, 1990—. Asst. counsel 41st Cir. Commonwealth Ky., Manchester, 1981—82. Named Man of Yr., Manchester-Clay County C. of C., 1998, Outstanding Young Dem., Ky. Young Dem., 1968. Democrat. Baptist. Avocations: fishing, camping, boating. Home: 393 Circle Dr Manchester KY 40962 Office: 79 Highway 80 Ste 1 Manchester KY 40962

MARIN, DANIEL, lawyer; b. Barcelona; B of Law, LLM, ESADE. Bar: Barcelona 1999, England & Wales 2001. Assoc. Gomez-Acebo & Pombo, Barcelona. Mergers and acquisitions, Corporate, general, Commercial, contracts (including sales of goods; commercial financing). Office: Gomez-Acebo & Pombo Av Diagonal 442 08037 Barcelona Spain Fax: +34 934158400. E-mail: dmarin@gomezacebo-pombo.com.

MARINACCIO, CHARLES LINDBERGH, lawyer, consultant; b. Stratford, Conn., Dec. 10, 1933; BA, U. Conn., 1957; JD with honors, George Washington U., 1962. Bar: Conn. 1962, D.C. 1982. Trial lawyer U.S. Dept. Justice, Washington, 1963-69; advisor supervisory and regulation div. Fed. Res. Bd., Washington, 1969-73; dir., exec. sec. law enforcement asstistance adminstrn. U.S. Dept. Justice, Washington, 1973-75; gen. counsel banking housing and urban affairs com. U.S. Senate, Washington, 1975-84; commr. SEC, Washington, 1984-85; ptnr. Kelley, Drye & Warren, Washington, 1985-94; ind. cons. Washington, 1995—. Apptd. by Pres. Clinton to bd. dirs. Securities Investor Protection Corp. Home and Office: 4911 Massachusetts Ave NW Washington DC 20016-4310

MARINE, ANDREW CRAIG, lawyer; b. Norman, Okla., Nov. 3, 1960; s. I. Wendell and Helen R. (Landsman) M. BA in Polit. Sci., BS in Gen. Bus., Va. Poly. Inst. and State U., l982; JD, U. S.C., l985. Bar: S.C. l986, U.S. Dist. Ct. S.C. 1988. Assoc. Huguenin, Trueblood & Floyd, Martinez, Ga., l986-87; ptnr. Floyd & Marine, Aiken, S.C., l987-93; pvt. practice Aiken, S.C., 1993—. Chmn. Aiken County Young Republican Com., 1986-89; treas. Aiken County Rep. Party, 1989-95, chmn., 1995-97; mem. City of Aiken Election Commn., 1988-98, S.C. State Ethics Commn., 1998-2003, vice chmn., 2000-01, chmn., 2001-03; bd. dirs. Golden Harvest Food Bank, 1995—, chmn., 2003—; dist. chmn. Boy Scouts Am., 1997-2000. Mem. ABA, S.C. Bar Assn., Aiken C. of C., Sunrise Rotary (pres. 2000-01), Phi Alpha Delta. Republican. Bankruptcy, General practice, Property, real (including real estate development, water). Home: 1010 Williams Dr Aiken SC 29803-5372 Office: 106 Trafalgar St Aiken SC 29801

MARING, MARY MUEHLEN, state supreme court justice; b. Devils Lake, N.D., July 27, 1951; d. Joseph Edward and Charlotte Rose (Schorr) Muehlen: m. David Scott Maring, Aug. 30, 1975; children: Christopher David, Andrew Joseph. BA in Polit. Sci. summa cum laude, Moorhead State U., 1972; JD, U. N.D., 1975. Bar: Minn., N.D. Law clk. Hon. Bruce Stone, Mpls, 1975-76; assoc. Stefanson, Landberg & Alm, Ltd., Moorhead, Minn., 1976-82, Ohnstad, Twichell, Breitling, Rosenvold, Wanner, Nelson, Neugebauer & Maring, P.C., West Fargo, N.D., 1982-88, Lee Hagan Law Office, Fargo, 1988-91; pvt. practice Maring Law Office, Fargo, 1991-96; justice N.D. State Supreme Ct., Bismarck, ND, 1996—. Women's bd. mem. 1st Nat. Bank, Fargo, 1977-82; career day speaker Moorhead Rotarians, 1980-83. Contbr. note to legal rev.; note editor N.D. Law Rev., 1975. Mem. ABA (del. ann. conv. young lawyers sect. 1981-82, bd. govs. 1982-83), Minn. Women Lawyers, N.D. State Bar Assn. (bd. govs. 1991-93), Minn. Trial Lawyers Assn., Clay County Bar Assn. (v.p. 1983-84), N.D. Trial Lawyers Assn. (pres. 1992-93), Roman Catholic. Office: ND Supreme Ct 600 E Boulevard Ave Dept 180 Bismarck ND 58505-0530

MARINIS, THOMAS PAUL, JR., lawyer; b. Jacksonville, Tex., May 31, 1943; s. Thomas Paul and Betty Sue (Garner) M.; m. Lucinda Cruse, June 25, 1969; children: Courtney, Kathryn, Megan. BA, Yale U., 1965; LLB, U. Tex., 1968. Bar: Tex. 1968. Assoc. Vinson & Elkins, Houston, 1969-76, ptnr., 1977—. Bd. dirs. Phoenix House of Tex., Inc., Covenant House Tex. Fellow Tex. Bar Found.; mem. ABA (sec. taxation sect. 1986-87), Houston Country Club, Houston Ctr. Club, Coronado Club. Corporate taxation, Personal income taxation. E-mail: tmarinis@velaw.com.

MARINO, THOMAS A. lawyer; AA, Williamsport Area C.C., 1983; BA, Lycoming Coll.; JD, Dickinson U. Assoc. McNemey, Page, Vanderlin & Hall, Williamsport, Pa., 1988—96; dist. atty. Lycoming County, Pa., 1996—2002; U.S. atty. Mid. Dist. Pa., 2002—. Office: PO Box 309 Scranton PA 18501*

MARINSTEIN, ELLIOTT FRED, lawyer; b. N.Y.C., June 15, 1928; s. Joseph and Rose (Zessman) M.; m. Leita A. Adeson, Dec. 1, 1957; children: Edward Ross, Jay Drew. BA, Bklyn. Coll., 1950; JD, NYU, 1953. Bar: N.Y. 1955, U.S. Dist. Ct. (no. dist.) N.Y. 1956, U.S. Supreme Ct. 1970, U.S. Dist. Ct. (so. and ea. dists.) N.Y. 1986. Sole practice, Troy, N.Y., 1956-86; asst. dist. atty. County of Rensselaer, Troy, 1965-67; ptnr. Marinstein & Marinstein, Troy, 1986-2000, Marinstein & Marinstein, Esqs., PLLC, Troy, 2000—. Counsel charter rev. com. City of Troy, 1972-73; mem. com. on profl. standards Third Jud. Dept., 1988-94. Committeeman Rensselaer County Dem. Com., Troy, 1960-65; del. jud. convention Dem. State Com., Troy, 1978-88; chmn. housing bd. rev. City of Troy, 1979-90. Served to cpl. U.S. Army, 1953-55. Mem. ABA (corp., banking and bus. law sect.,), N.Y. State Bar Assn. (count county courts com., lectr. 1978-83), Rensselaer County Bar Assn. (chmn. grievance com. 1972-75, pres. 1979-80), N.Y. State Dist. Attys. Assn., Comml. Law League Am. (practice com.). Lodges: Knights of Pythias (past chancellor), Masons. Avocation: tennis. Bankruptcy, Commercial, consumer (including collections, credit), Probate (including wills, trusts). Home: 2354 Burdett Ave Troy NY 12180-2409 Office: Marinstein & Marinstein PLLC 200 Broadway Troy NY 12180-3289 Fax: (518) 274-5039. E-mail: mmlaw@capital.net.

MARION, ROGER K. lawyer; BA, Rutgers Coll., New Brunswick, New Jersey, 1990—91; JD, St. John's U. Sch. of Law, Queens, New York, 1991—93. Bar: NY 1994, NJ 1996, US Dist. Ct. 1996, US Dist. Ct. (ea. dist.) 1998, US Dist. Ct. (so. dist.) 1998, US Ct. of Appeals (3rd cir.) 1998, US Supreme Ct. 1999. Trial lawyer (complex civil and white collar criminal) Stein Riso Mantel, LLP, New York, NY, 1999—; trial lawyer Thatcher & Lanza, Flemington, NJ, 1996—99; asst. dist. atty. Kings County Dist. Attorney's Office, Brooklyn, NY, 1994—95. Dir. of law Vertical Evolution, LLC, McLean, Virginia, 2002—. Recipient Young Lawyer of the Yr., Hunterdon County Bar Assn. (New Jersey), 1999. Federal civil litigation, State civil litigation, Criminal. Office: Stein Riso Mantel LLP 405 Lexington Avenue 42nd Floor New York NY 10174 Office Fax: 212-599-6155. Business E-Mail: roger.marion@steinrisomantel.com.

MARIS, STEPHEN S. lawyer, educator; b. Dallas, Dec. 19, 1949; children: Shane, Kara. BS, Stephen F. Austin State, 1971; JD, So. Meth. U., 1975. Bar: U.S. Dist. Ct. (no. dist.) Tex. 1975, U.S. Dist. Ct. (ea. dist.) Tex. 1986, U.S. Dist. Ct. (so. dist.) Tex. 1992, U.S. Ct. Appeals (5th cir.) 1980, U.S. Ct. Appeals (11th cir.) 1981, U.S. Supreme Ct. Tex. 1975. Assoc. Passman & Jones, Dallas, 1975-80, ptnr., 1980-87, Fulbright & Jaworski, Dallas, 1987-97, Jenkens & Gilchrist, Dallas, 1997—. Prof. So. Ill. U., 1979-80, So. Meth. U., Dallas, 1980—; mem. faculty Nat. Inst. Trial Advocacy, 1980—. Editor: Southwest Law Journal, 1973-75. Mem. ABA, State Bar Tex., Dallas Bar Assn., Barristers, Order Coif, Phi Delta Phi. Federal civil litigation, General civil litigation, Professional liability. Office: Jenkens & Gilchrist 1445 Ross Ave Ste 3200 Dallas TX 75202-2785

MARJERISON, THOMAS SYDNEY, lawyer; b. Brunswick, Maine, May 20, 1967; s. Thomas Sydney and Jerilyn Faye Majerison; m. Kirsten Schultz, Sept. 7, 1996. BA, Conn. Coll., 1989; JD, U. Maine, 1993. Bar: Maine 1993, U.S. Dist. Ct. Maine 1993, U.S. Ct. Appeals (1st cir.) 1999, U.S. Supreme Ct. 1999. Asst. atty. gen. Dept. of Atty. Gen., Portland, Maine, 1993-96; atty. Norman, Hanson & DeTroy, Portland, 1996—. Legal specialist Internat. Criminal Tribunal for Former Yugoslavia, The Hague, The Netherlands, 1998; instr. Maine Criminal Justice Acad., Waterville, 1993-96. Author: (manual) Drafting Effective Search Warrants, 1996. Recipient Cert. of Achievement, U.S. Drug Enforcement Adminstrn., 1996, Citation of Merit, City of Portland, 1996. Mem. Maine Assn. Criminal Def. Attys., Maine State Bar Assn. Federal civil litigation, State civil litigation, Criminal. Office: Norman Hanson & DeTroy 415 Congress St Ste 500 Portland ME 04101-3530 E-mail: TMarjerison@NHDLaw.com.

MARK, JONATHAN I. lawyer; b. N.Y.C., Oct. 18, 1947; s. Sandor and Ruth (Weiss) M.; m. B. Kathleen Munguia, May 25, 1986; children: Ramona G., Sandor A. AB, Dartmouth Coll., 1969; JD, Columbia U., 1974. Bar: N.Y., Calif., U.S. Dist. Ct. (so. and ea. dists.) N.Y., U.S. Ct. Appeals (2d cir.). Law clk. to presiding justice U.S. Dist. Ct. (so. dist.) N.Y., N.Y.C., 1974-75; assoc. Cahill Gordon & Reindel, N.Y.C., 1975-82, ptnr., 1982—. Corporate, general, Securities. Office: Cahill Gordon & Reindel 80 Pine St Fl 17 New York NY 10005-1790

MARK, LANCE JOSEPH, lawyer; b. N.Y.C., Feb. 11, 1950; s. Alfred V. and Edith S. (Schulman) M.; m. Patricia E. Maynard, July 3, 1999; children: Adam T., Erin R., Andrew R., Elisa J. BA, Miami U., Oxford, Ohio, 1971; JD, SUNY, Buffalo, 1974. Bar: N.Y. 1974, U.S. Tax Ct. 1985, U.S. Dist. Ct. (we. dist.) N.Y. 1989. Ptnr. Mack, Mark & Assocs., Medina, N.Y., 1978-91; pvt. practice, Medina, 1991—. Asst. dist. atty. Orleans County, N.Y., 1996; mem. grievance com. 8th Jud. Dist., Buffalo, 1981-87; town atty. Town of Barre, N.Y., 1988—; sch. atty. Medina Ctrl. Schs.; gen. counsel Medina Meml. Health Care Sys. Pres., bd. dirs. Medina Meml. Hosp., 1988—, Medina Area C. of C., 1982-88. Lt. comdr. USNR, 1974-77. Decorated Navy Commendation medal; recipient Philanthropy award/Outstanding Mem. Nat. Fund Raising Execs., 1996. Mem. N.Y. State Bar Assn., Orleans County Bar Assn. (past pres.), Phi Beta Kappa. Avocations: sailing, skiing. General civil litigation, Health. Office: 539A Main St Medina NY 14103-1420

MARK, MICHAEL DAVID, lawyer; b. Bklyn., Sept. 16, 1944; s. Irving and Mildred Mark; children: Dana Lynne, Stephanie Lauren. BA, Rutgers U., 1966; JD, U. Tenn., 1969. Bar: Tenn. 1969, N.J. 1970, U.S. Dist. Ct. N.J. 1970, U.S. Supreme Ct. 1973; cert. civil trial atty., N.J. Supreme Ct. 1992. House counsel Liberty Mut. Ins. Co., East Orange, N.J., 1969-71; assoc. Skoloff & Wolfe, Newark, 1971-73; pvt. practice, Union, N.J., 1973—. Past assoc. bd. dirs. United Jersey Bank, Union; Police Benevolent Assn. lawyer City of Linden, N.J., 1980—, Clark Twp., Clark, N.J., 1986; mem. Union-Essex County Early Settlement Panels, Elizabeth and Newark. Mem. Am. Acad. Matrimonial Lawyers (bd. mgrs. 1982—), N.J. Bar Assn., Union County Bar Assn., Union Lawyers Club (past pub. defender). Republican. Avocation: private pilot. General civil litigation, Family and matrimonial, Property, real (including real estate development, water). Office: 2444 Morris Ave Union NJ 07083-5711

MARKE, JULIUS JAY, law librarian, educator; b. N.Y.C., Jan. 12, 1913; s. Isidore and Anna (Taylor) M.; m. Sylvia Bolotin, Dec. 15, 1946; 1 child, Elisa Hope. BS, CCNY, 1934; LLB, NYU, 1937; BS in Libr. Sci., Columbia U., 1942. Bar: N.Y. 1938. Ref. asst. N.Y. Pub. Libr., 1937—42; pvt. practice law N.Y.C., 1939—41; prof. law, law libr. NYU, 1949—83, prof. law emeritus, 1983—, interim dean of librs., 1975—77; Disting. Prof., dir. Law Libr. St. John's U. Sch. Law, 1983—95, disting. rsch. prof. law, 1995—. Lectr. Columbia Sch. Library Service, 1962-78, adj. prof., 1978-85; cons. Orientation Program Am. Law, 1965-68, Found. Overseas Law Libraries Am. Law, 1968-79, copyright Ford Found., law libraries, Coun. Fgn. Rels., 1990—, Shubert Archives, 1991, others. Author: Vignettes of Legal History, 1965, 2d series, 1977, rev. edit., 2000, Copyright and Intellectual Property, 1967 (with R. Sloane) Legal Research and Law Library Management, rev. edit., 1990, 2003; editor: Modern Legal Forms, 1953, The Holmes Reader, 1955, The Docket Series, 1955—, Bender's Legal Business Forms, 4 vols., 1962; compiler, editor: A Catalogue of the Law Collection at NYU with Selected Annotations, 1953, Dean's List of Recommended Reading for Pre-Law and Law Students, 1958, 84, and others; chmn. editl. bd. Oceana Group, 1977—, Index to Legal Periodicals and Books, 1978—; columnist N.Y. Law Jour., 1970—; contbr. articles to profl. jours. Mem. publs. coun. N.Y.U., 1964-80. Sgt. AUS, 1943-45. Decorated Bronze Star. Mem. ABA, Am. Assn. Law Librs. (pres. 1962-63, Disting. Svc. award 1986, Presdl. cert. of merit 2002), Assn. Am. Law Schs., Coun. of Nat. Libr. Assns. (exec. bd., v.p. 1959, 60), Law Libr. Assn. Greater N.Y. (pres. 1949, 50, chmn. joint com. on libr. edn. 1950-52, 60-61), NYU Law Alumni Assn. (Judge Edward Weinfeld award 1987, mem. exec. bd. 1988—), Columbia Sch. Libr. Svc. Alumni Assn. (pres. 1973-75), Order of Coif (pres. NYU Law Sch. br. 1970-83), NYU Faculty Club (pres. 1966-68), Field Inn, Phi Delta Phi. Home: 4 Peter Cooper Rd Apt 8F New York NY 10010-6746

MARKELLO, JEFFREY PHILIP, lawyer; b. Buffalo, Dec. 14, 1964; s. Anthony Philip and Nancy Hammond Markello BA, U. Rochester, 1987; JD, SUNY, Buffalo, 1990. Bar: N.Y. 1991, Mass. 1991. Atty. pvt. practice, Elma, N.Y., 1991-97; ptnr. Sakowski & Markello, Elma, N.Y., 1998—. Dep. town atty. and town prosecutor Town of Aurora, 2002—; bd. trustees East Aurora (N.Y.) Bd. Edn., 1993—2002. Family and matrimonial, General practice, Personal injury (including property damage). Office: Sakowski & Markello PO Box 200 6890 Seneca St Elma NY 14059-0200

MARKER, MARC LINTHACUM, lawyer, investor; b. Los Angeles, July 19, 1941; s. Clifford Harry and Voris (Linthacum) M.; m. Sandra Vocom, Aug. 29, 1965; children: Victor, Gwendolyn. BA in Econs. and Geography, U. Calif.-Riverside, 1964; JD, U. So. Calif., 1967. Asst. v.p., asst. sec. Security Pacific Nat. Bank, L.A., 1970-73; sr. v.p., chief counsel, sec. Security Pacific Leasing Corp., San Francisco, 1973-92; pres. Security Pacific Leasing Svcs. Corp., San Francisco, 1977-85, dir., 1977-92. Bd. dirs., sec. Voris, Inc., 1973-86; bd. dirs. Refiners Petroleum Corp., 1977-81, Security Pacific Leasing Singapore Ltd., 1983-85, Security Pacific Leasing Can. Ltd., 1989-92; lectr. in field. Served to comdr., USCGR. Mem. ABA, D.C. Bar Assn; Club: Army and Navy. Republican. Lutheran. Banking, Commercial, contracts (including sales of goods; commercial financing).

MARKESBERY, MARIA SABA, lawyer; b. Cin., June 2, 1961; d. Khamis Alexander and Judith Diehl Saba; m. Glenn Alan Markesbery, Aug. 29, 1987; children: Michael, Katherine, Emily. BS, Xavier U., 1983; JD, U. Cin., 1986. Bar: Ohio. Dir. risk mgmt., legal svcs. Franciscan Health System, Cin., 1988-98, gen. counsel, 1998-99; assoc. counsel Mercy Health Ptnrs. S.W. Ohio, Cin., 1999—. Mem. Cin. Bar Assn. Health. Office: Mercy Health Ptnrs 2446 Kipling Ave Cincinnati OH 45239-6621

MARKEY, BRIAN MICHAEL, lawyer; b. Teaneck, N.J., Feb. 10, 1956; s. Raymond Joseph and Sheila (Barry) M.; m. Virginia M. Lincoln, Oct. 26, 1986. BA cum laude, Rider Coll., 1978; JD, Suffolk U., 1985. Bar: N.J. 1985, U.S. Dist. Ct. N.J. 1985, N.Y. 1988. Assoc. Kohler & Clinch,

Hackensack, NJ, 1985—90, Law Office J. Dennis Kohler, Hackensack, NJ, 1990—91; pvt. practice law Glen Rock, NJ, 1991—94; ptnr. Lincoln & Markey, Glen Rock, 1995—. Dir. Glen Rock Savs. Bank. Chmn. Glen Rock Planning Bd. Mem. ABA, N.J. Bar Assn., Glen Rock Independence Day Assn. General civil litigation, General practice, Property, real (including real estate development, water). Office: 126 Valley Rd Glen Rock NJ 07452-1796

MARKEY, JAMES KEVIN, lawyer; b. Springfield, Ill., July 15, 1956; s. James Owen and Marjorie Jean (Diesness) M.; m. Allison Markey; children: Lauren, Katherine. BBA with highest honors, U. Notre Dame, 1977; JD cum laude, U. Mich., 1980; MBA, U. Chgo., 1987; LLM in Taxation, DePaul U., 1993. Bar: Ill. 1980; CPA, Ill. Assoc. Chapman & Cutler, Chgo., 1980-81; atty. Quaker Oats Co., Chgo., 1981-84; corp. counsel Baxter Healthcare Corp., Deerfield, Ill., 1984-90; v.p. law and other positions Motorola, Inc., Schaumburg, Ill., 1990-2000; v.p., chief counsel-securities and internat. Kellogg Co., Battle Creek, Mich., 2000—. Mem. ABA, Beta Alpha Psi, Beta Gamma Sigma. Avocations: racquetball, running, bridge. Securities, Intellectual property, Private international. Home: 3541 Sandhill Ln Portage MI 49024 Office: 1 Kellogg Sq Battle Creek MI 49017-3534 E-mail: jim.markey@kellogg.com.

MARKEY, ROBERT GUY, lawyer; b. Cleveland, Ohio, Feb. 25, 1939; s. Nate and Rhoda (Gross) Markey; m. Nanci Louise Brooks, Aug. 25, 1990; children: Robert Guy, Randolph. AB, Brown U., 1961; JD, Case Western Res., 1964. Bar: Ohio 1964. Ptnr. Baker & Hostetler, Cleve., 1983—. Corporate, general, Mergers and acquisitions, Securities. Office: Baker & Hostetler 3200 National City Ctr 1900 E 9th St Ste 3200 Cleveland OH 44114-3475

MARKHAM, CHARLES BUCHANAN, retired lawyer; b. Durham, N.C., Sept. 15, 1926; s. Charles Blackwell and Sadie Helen (Hackney) M. AB, Duke U., 1945; postgrad., U. N.C., 1945-46; LL.B., George Washington U., 1951. Bar: D.C. 1951, N.Y. 1961, N.C. 1980, U.S. Ct. Appeals (2d cir.) 1962, U.S. Ct. Appeals (D.C. cir.) 1955, U.S. Supreme Ct. 1964. Reporter Durham Sun, 1945; asst. state editor, editorial writer Charlotte (N.C.) News, 1947-48; dir. publicity and rsch. Young Dem. Clubs Am., Washington, 1948-49, exec. sec., 1949-50; polit. analyst Dem. Senatorial Campaign Com., Washington, 1950-51; spl. atty. IRS, Washington and N.Y.C., 1952-60; assoc. Battle, Fowler, Stokes and Kheel, N.Y.C., 1960-65; dir. rsch. U.S. Equal Employment Opportunity Commn., Washington, 1965-68; dep. asst. sec. U.S. Dept. HUD, Washington, 1969-72; asst. dean Rutgers U. Law Sch., Newark, 1974-76; assoc. prof. law N.C. Central U., Durham, 1976-81, prof. law, 1981-83; mayor City of Durham, 1981-85; ptnr. Markham and Wickham, Durham, 1984-86. Trustee Hist. Preservation Soc. Durham, 1982-86; bd. dirs. Stagville Ctr., 1984-86; mem. Gov.'s Crime Commn., Raleigh, 1985; dep. commr. N.C. Indsl. Commn., Raleigh, 1986-93. Editor: Jobs, Men and Machines: The Problems of Automation, 1964 Mem. Carolina Club, Phi Beta Kappa, Omicron Delta Kappa, Phi Delta Phi, Phi Delta Theta. Republican. Episcopalian. Administrative and regulatory, Personal injury (including property damage), Workers' compensation. Home: 204 N Dillard St Durham NC 27701-3404

MARKHAM, ROSEMARY, lawyer; b. Pitts., June 12, 1946; d. Chester James and Elizabeth Helen (Seger) M.; m. Wayne Joseph Pfrimmer, Sept. 11, 1965 (div. 1975); 1 child, Adriene. BA, U. Pitts, 1968; JD, Duquesne U., 1978. Bar: Pa. 1978. Adminstrv. asst. West Pa. Conservancy, Pitts., 1968-70; law clk. Girman & DelSole, 1975-76, Watzman & DeAngelis, 1975-78; serious injury rep. Travelors Inc., 1978-79; assoc. Manifesto & Doherty, 1979-81; pvt. practice, 1981—. Adj. prof. Pa. State U., 1981—95. Mem. ABA, Assn. Trial Lawyers Am., Pa. Bar Assn., Pa. Trial Lawyers Assn., Allegheny County Bar Assn., Mensa. Democrat. Roman Catholic. Family and matrimonial, Property, real (including real estate development, water).

MARKLE, JOHN, JR., lawyer; b. Allentown, Pa., July 20, 1931; s. John Markle II and Pauline (Powers) Mulligan; m. Mary B. McLean, Apr. 19, 1952 (div. Apr. 1990); children: Ellen, John III, Patricia, Stephen, Mary; m. Kathryn E. Wheeler, July 14, 1990. Grad., The Hill Sch., Pottstown, Pa., 1949; BA, Yale U., 1953; LLB, Harvard Law Sch., 1958. Bar: Pa. 1959, U.S. Dist. Ct. (ea. dist.) Pa. 1959, U.S. Supreme Ct. 1980, U.S. Ct. Appeals (3d cir.) 1973. Assoc. Drinker Biddle & Reath, Phila., 1958-64, ptnr., 1964-97, counsel, 1997-2000. Chmn. Pa. Labor Rels. Bd., 1996—; bd. dirs. Main Line Health. Contbg. editor: The Developing Labor Law, 1976—. Bd. dirs. Paoli (Pa.) Meml. Hosp. Found., 1982—, chmn., 1995—2000; bd. dirs. The Hill Sch., Pottstown, Pa., 1970—, chmn., 1985—93. Lt. col. USMC, 1950—73. Named Most Outstanding Young Rep. (Pa.), 1966. Mem. ABA, Pa. Bar Assn., Am. Arbitration Assn., Coll. Labor and Employment Lawyers, Yale Club (Phila.), Merion Golf Club, Ekwanok Country Club. Republican. Avocations: golf, photography. Labor (including EEOC, Fair Labor Standards Act, labor-management relations, NLRB, OSHA). Home: 205 Cambridge Chase Exton PA 19341-3137 Office: Drinker Biddle & Reath 1000 Westlakes Dr Ste 300 Berwyn PA 19312-2409 E-mail: jackmarkle@prodigy.net., marklej@dbr.com.

MARKMAN, STEPHEN J. state supreme court justice; b. Detroit, June 4, 1949; s. Julius and Pauline Markman; m. Mary Kathleen Sites, Aug. 25, 1974; children: James, Charles. BA, Duke U., 1971; JD, U. Cin., 1974. Asst. to Rep. Edward Hutchinson, Mich., 1975; legis. asst. to Rep. Tom Hagedorn, Minn., 1976-78; chief counsel, staff dir. subcom. on constn. Senate Com. on Judiciary, 1978-85, dep. chief counsel, 1983; asst. atty. gen. Office Legal Policy, Dept. Justice, Washington, 1985-89; U.S. atty. U.S. Dept. Justice, Detroit, 1989-93; mem. Miller, Canfield, Paddock & Stone, Detroit, 1993-99; justice Mich. Supreme Ct., Lansing, Mich., 1999—. Office: Mich Supreme Ct Hall of Justice 925 W Ottawa St Fl 6 Lansing MI 48915

MARKS, ANDREW H. lawyer; b. N.Y.C., May 5, 1951; s. Theodore and Rosalie Ruth (Goldman) M.; m. Susan G. Esserman, Aug. 3, 1975; children: Stephen Matthew, Clifford Michael, Michael David. AB, Harvard U., 1973; JD, U. Mich., 1976. Bar: Fla. 1976, D.C., 1977, Md. 1984, U.S. Ct. Appeals (D.C. cir.). Law clerk for Hon. Charles R. Richey U.S. Dist. Ct. D.C., Washington, 1976-78; exec. asst. to personal rep. of Pres. to Middle East Peace negotiations, Washington, 1979-81; assoc. Shea & Gardner, Washington, 1978-79, 81-84, ptnr., 1984-86, Crowell & Moring L.L.P., Washington, 1986—. Mem. D.C. Bar (pres. 1998-99, bd. govs. 1989-95, chmn. task force civility in the profession 1993-96), Harvard Club Washington (pres. 1994-96). Insurance, Professional liability. Office: Crowell & Moring LLP 1001 Pennsylvania Ave NW Fl 10 Washington DC 20004-2505

MARKS, BERNARD BAILIN, lawyer, director; b. Sioux City, Iowa, Sept. 6, 1917; s. Meyer A. and Beulah (Bailin) M.;m. Betty L. Marks; 1 child, Susan E. BA, Harvard U., 1939, JD, 1942. Bar: Iowa 1942. With firm Shull, Marshall & Marks, Sioux City, 1946-85, ptnr., 1949-85, Marks & Madsen, Sioux City, 1985-97, of counsel, 1998-99, ret., 2000, sec., asst. treas., dir., 1962-81; sec., dir. KTIV-TV Co., Sioux City, 1965-74; bd. dirs. First Nat. Bank, Firstar Bank, Sioux City, 1963-91; with Flavorland Industries, Inc. Bd. dirs. Iowa Heart Assn., 1960, Woodbury County chpt., 1958-64, pres., 1962-64; bd. dirs. Sioux City Art Center, 1952-54, Sioux City United Fund, 1965-71, Sioux City Community Appeals Bd., 1965-68; trustee Briar Cliff Coll., Sioux City, 1968-74. Served with USAAF, 1942-46. Fellow Iowa Bar Assn. Found.; mem. ABA, Iowa Bar Assn., Woodbury County Bar Assn. (pres. 1958), Am. Coll. Trust and Estate Counsel, Sioux City C. of C. (bd. dirs. 1964-67, treas. 1965-66), Sioux City Lawyers Club (pres. 1951), Sioux City Country Club (bd. dirs. 1963-64). Corporate, general, Probate (including wills, trusts), Taxation, general.

MARKS, HERBERT EDWARD, lawyer; b. Dayton, Ohio, Nov. 3, 1935; s. I.M. and Sarah S. M.; m. Marcia Frager; children: Jennifer L., Susan E. AB with high distinction, U. Mich., 1957; JD, Yale U., 1960; postgrad., George Washington U. Law Sch., 1965-67. Bar: Ohio 1960, D.C. 1964, U.S. Supreme Ct. 1965. Law clk. to chief judge U.S. Ct. Claims, 1964-65; assoc. Wilkinson, Cragun & Barker, Washington, 1965-69, ptnr., 1969-82, Squire, Sanders & Dempsey, Washington, 1982—. Assoc. gen. counsel Presdl. Inaugural Coms., 1969, 73, 81; chmn. U.S. State Dept. Adv. Panel on Internat. Telecom. Law, 1987—91; mem. adv. com. on internat. comm. and info. policy U.S. State Dept., 1988—91, 2002—; mem. U.S. del. ITU European Telecom. Devel. Conf., 1991, ITU Plenipotentiary Conf., 1998, ITU Coun., 2000; mem. ITU Sec. Gen.'s Expert Group, 1999—2002. Contbr. articles to legal jours. Served to capt. JAG USAF, 1960-64. Mem. ABA (chair sci. and tech. sect. 1990-91, chmn. communications div. 1986-88), D.C. Bar Assn., Computer Law Assn. (pres. 1975-77, bd. dirs. 1972-85, adv. bd. 1985—), Fed. Communications Bar Assn., Cosmos Club, Kenwood Golf & Country Club, Phi Beta Kappa. Antitrust, Communications, Public international. Office: Squire Sanders & Dempsey 1201 Pennsylvania Ave NW PO Box 407 Washington DC 20044-0407 also: 5317 Cardinal Ct Bethesda MD 20816-2908

MARKS, JULIE ANN, lawyer; b. Birmingham, Ala., Sept. 30, 1960; d. Morton Jerome and Beverly (Levy) M. Student, U. Ala., Tuscaloosa, 1978-81; BS, U. Ala., Birmingham, 1982; JD, Samford U., 1986. Bar: Ala. 1986. Staff atty. Legal Aid Soc. Birmingham, 1986-94; mng. atty., 1994—. Spkr. to civic orgns.; bd. dirs. Interfaith Hospitality House, Birmingham, 1990-93. Recipient Unsung Hero award, Children's Aid Soc. Birmingham, 2003. Mem. Ala. Bar Assn., Birmingham Bar Assn. Jewish. Avocations: travel, volleyball, reading, working with children. Office: Legal Aid Soc Birmingham 120 2nd Ct N Birmingham AL 35204-4718

MARKS, LAWRENCE J. lawyer; b. Cleve., May 9, 1942; s. Max Lewis Marks and Ruth M. (Getzov) Rosen; m. Jane Marshall Straka, Nov. 29, 1943; children: Risa K. Jacobson, Dara R. BA, U. Colo., 1964; JD, U. Ariz., 1967. Bar: Ariz. 1967, U.S. Dist. Ct. Ariz. 1967, U.S. Ct. Appeals (9th cir.) 1973, U.S. Supreme Ct. 1973. Baliff Maricopa County Superior Ct., Phoenix, 1967-68; pvt. practice Phoenix, 1968—. Part-time instr. Phoenix Coll., 1978-82. Democrat. Jewish. Avocations: hiking, carpentry and repair work. Commercial, contracts (including sales of goods; commercial financing), Family and matrimonial, Personal injury (including property damage). Home: 11601 N 50th Pl Scottsdale AZ 85254-4608 Office: 1708 E Thomas Rd Phoenix AZ 85016-7604 E-mail: Lawrence.Marks@Azbar.org.

MARKS, LEE ROBERT, lawyer; b. N.Y.C., Oct. 22, 1935; s. George L. and Shirley (Chassy) M.; m. Lisl Zach; children: Jan Philip, Benjamin Eli. BA with honors, U. MIch., 1957; LLB cum laude, Harvard U., 1960. Bar: N.Y. 1960, D.C. 1964, U.S. Supreme Ct. 1980, Va 1999. Lectr. law George Washington U., Washington, 1961-68; atty. Office Legal Adviser, Dept. State, Washington, 1961-65, sr. dep. legal advisor, 1977-79, mem. adv. com. on internat. investment, tech. and devel., 1983; ptnr. Ginsburg, Feldman & Bress, Washington, 1965-77, 79-98, Greenberg, Traurig, McLean, Va., 1998—. Past mem. bd. dirs. Washington Opera. Mem. ABA (chmn. com. on fgn. claims 1983). Office: Greenberg Traurig 1750 Tysons Blvd Ste 1200 Mc Lean VA 22102-4211 E-mail: marksl@gtlaw.com.

MARKS, LEONARD HAROLD, lawyer; b. Pitts., Mar. 5, 1916; s. Samuel and Ida (Levine) M.; m. Dorothy Ames, June 3, 1948; children: Stephen Ames, Robert Evan. BA, U. Pitts., 1935, LL.B., 1938. Bar: Pa. 1938, D.C. 1946. Asst. prof. law U. Pitts. Law Sch., 1938-42; prof. law Nat. U., 1943-55; asst. to gen. counsel FCC, 1942-46, ops. counsel, 1986—; ptnr. Cohn & Marks, Washington, 1946-65, 69-86. Chmn. exec. com. Nat. Savs. and Trust Co., 1977-85; chmn. Internat. Conf. on Comm. Satellites, 1968-69; Am. del. Internat. Broadcasting Confs., 1948-69; pres. Internat. Rescue Com., 1973-79, Honor Am. Com., 1977-86; chmn. U.S. Adv. Commn. on Internat. Ednl. and Cultural Affairs, 1973-78; chmn. Fgn. Policy Assn., 1981-87, exec. com., 1987-96; head U.S. del. Internat. Telecom. Union, 1983, 87; chmn. U.S. del. to London Info. Forum, Commn. on Security and Cooperation in Europe, 1989. Mem. ABA (ho. of dels. 1962-64), Fed. Comm. Bar Assn. (pres. 1959-60), Bar Assn. D.C., Acad. Diplmacy (chmn. exec. com. 2000—), World Affairs Council Washington (chmn.), Cosmos Club, Metropolitan Club (v.p., gov.), Federal City Club, Broadcasters Club (pres. 1957-59), Alfalfa Club (Washington), Order of Coif, Phi Beta Kappa, Omicron Delta Kappa, Sigma Delta Chi. Clubs: Cosmos, Metropolitan, Federal City, Broadcasters, (pres. 1957-59), Alfalfa (Washington). Home: 2700 Calvert St NW Washington DC 20008-2621 Office: 1920 N St NW Washington DC 20036-1601

MARKS, MERTON ELEAZER, lawyer, international arbitrator, mediator, consultant; b. Chgo., Oct. 16, 1932; s. Alfred Tobias and Helene Fannie (Rosner) M.; m. Radee Maiden Feiler, May 20, 1966; children: Sheldon, Elise Marks Vazelakis, Alan, Elaine Marks Ianchiou. BS, Northwestern U., 1954, JD, 1956. Bar: Ill. 1956, U.S. Ct. Mil. Appeals 1957, Ariz. 1958, U.S. Dist. Ct. Ariz. 1960, U.S. Ct. Appeals (9th cir.) 1962, U.S. Supreme Ct. 1970; cert. arbitrator U.S. Dist. Ct. Ariz. Assoc. Moser, Compere & Emerson, Chgo., 1956-57; ptnr. Morgan, Marks & Rogers, Tucson, 1960-62; asst. atty. gen. State of Ariz., Phoenix, 1962-64, counsel indsl. commn., 1964-65; from assoc. to ptnr. Shimmel, Hill, Bishop & Greunder, Phoenix, 1965-74; ptnr. Lewis & Roca, Phoenix, 1974—2001. Lectr. on arbitration and mediation, product liability and ins. subjects; Judge Pro Tempore Ariz. Ct. Appeals, 1994; legal columnist Exec. Golfer mag.; comml. complex case panelist, reinsurance panelist Am. Arbitration Assn.; spl. master Ariz. Superior Ct., 2001—; U.S. and internat. alternative dispute resolution cons. Contbr. articles to profl. jours. Past trustee Ariz. Opera Co., past chmn. endowment commn.; past mem. U.S. Olympic Com. for Ariz. Capt. JAGC, USAR, 1957-64. Fellow Chartered Inst. Arbitrators (London); mem. ABA (tort and ins. practice sect., chmn. spl. com. on fed. asbestos legis. 1987-89, chmn. workers compensation and employers liability law com. 1983-84, dispute resolution sect., business law sect., internat. law and practice sect.), Am. Bd. Trial Advocates, Am. Coll. Legal Medicine, Internat. Bar Assn. (sect. on bus. law, product liability, advt., unfair competition and consumer affairs com., internat. litigation com., ins. com., arbitration and alt. dispute resolution com.), State Bar Ariz. (chmn. workers compensation sect. 1969-73), Fedn. Def. and Corp. Counsel (chmn. pharm. litig. sect. 1989-91, chmn. workers compensation sect. 1977-79, v.p. 1978-79, 81, bd. dirs. 1981-89, mem. products liability sect., mem. reinsurance sect., vice chmn. alternative dispute resolution sect.), Internat. Assn. Def. Counsel, Ariz. Assn. Def. Counsel (pres. 1976-77), Maricopa County Bar Assn., Pima County Bar Assn., Def. Rsch. Inst. (drug and device com., chmn. workers compensation com. 1977-78), Assn. Internat. de Droit des Assurances (cert. arbitrator), Reinsurance and Ins. Arbitration Soc., Union Internat. des Avocats, London Ct. of Internat. Arbitration., Nat. Assn. Securities Dealers Dispute Resolution (bd. arbitrators), Internat. C. of C.. Alternative dispute resolution, Insurance, Commercial, contracts (including sales of goods; commercial financing). Office: Scottsdale Exec Office Pk Ste G-223 8655 E Via De Ventura Scottsdale AZ 85258-3363

MARKS, MICHAEL J. lawyer, corporate executive; b. 1938. AB, Cornell U., 1960; JD, U. Chgo., 1963. Assoc. Stroock & Stroock & Lavan, 1964-70, Chun, Kerr & Dodd, 1970-72; counsel Kelso, Spencer, Snyder & Stirling, 1972-75; asst. gen. counsel Alexander & Baldwin Inc., Honolulu, 1975-80, v.p., gen. counsel, 1980-84, v.p., gen. counsel, sec., 1984-85, sr. v.p., gen. counsel, sec., 1985—. Corporate, general. Office: Alexander & Baldwin Inc 822 Bishop St Honolulu HI 96813-3925

MARKS, MURRY AARON, lawyer; b. Carbondale, Ill., July 14, 1933; Student, Northwestern U., 1951-52; BA, Washington U., 1954; attended, U. So. Calif., 1956; JD, Washington U., 1963. Bar: Mo. 1963, U.S. Dist. Ct. (ea. and we. dists.) Mo. 1969, U.S. Ct. Appeals (8th cir.) 1969, U.S. Supreme Ct. 1972, U.S. Tax Ct. 1984. Asst. county counsellor County of St. Louis, 1963-67; ptnr. Elliott, Marks & Freeman, St. Louis, 1967-1971; pvt. practice St. Louis, 1971—. With U.S. Army, 1954-56. Fellow St. Louis Bar Found.; mem. ABA, ATLA, Nat. Assn. Criminal Def. Lawyers (life), St. Louis County Bar Assn., Mo. Bar Assn., Am. Coll. Legal Medicine, Mo. Assn. Trial Attys., Mo. Assn. Criminal Def. Attys. (bd. dirs. 1986-90), First Amendment Lawyers Assn., Met. Bar Assn. St. Louis, Lawyers Assn. St. Louis, Trial Lawyers for Pub. Justice, The Roscoe Pound Found. Federal civil litigation, Criminal, Personal injury (including property damage). Office: 7700 Clayton Rd Ste 307 Saint Louis MO 63117-1347

MARKS, RICHARD DANIEL, lawyer; b. N.Y.C., June 21, 1944; s. Morris Andrew and Dorothy (Schill) M.; m. Cheryl L. Hoffman, Nov. 13, 1971. BA, U. Va., 1966; JD, Yale U., 1969. Bar: D.C., U.S. Ct. Appeals (3rd, 4th, 8th, 11th and D.C. cir.), U.S. Supreme Ct. Assoc. Dow, Lohnes & Albertson, Washington, 1972-78, ptnr., 1978-97, Vinson & Elkins, Washington, 1997-2000, Davis Wright Tremaine, Washington, 2000—. Coauthor: Legal Problems in Broadcasting, 1974. Trustee U. Va. Coll. Found., 2001-03. Capt. U.S. Army, 1970-72. Mem. ABA (chmn. contracting for computer com., sect. for sci. and tech., computer law div., chmn. computer law divsn. 1994-2002, chmn. HIPAA task force 2002—), Fed. Comms. Bar Assn., Am. Law Inst., Computer Law Assn. (dir. 1999-2002), Capital Area Assn. Flight Instrs. (pres. 1989-90), UVA Club of Washington (pres. 1991-92). Avocations: aviation, skiing. Communications, Computer, Trademark and copyright. Office: Davis Wright Tremaine LLP 1500 K St NW Ste 450 Washington DC 20005-1272 Business E-Mail: richardmarks@dwt.com.

MARKS, SCOTT CHARLES, lawyer; b. Gloucester, Mass., Nov. 19, 1956; s. Wilfred Elliot and Marjorie Marks; m. Rhonda Ann Levine, Aug. 22, 1982; children: Eric Ian, Jesse Robert. BS, Boston U., 1978; JD, New Eng. Sch. Law, 1982. Bar: Mass. 1982, U.S. Dist. Ct. Mass. 1983. Assoc. Kline & Gardner, PC, Gloucester, Mass., 1982-87; ptnr. Channell & Marks, Beverly, Mass., 1987-90; assoc. Peter C. DiGangi, Salem, Mass., 1990-97, DiGangi & Legasey P.C., Salem, Mass., 1997—2002; pres. Law Office of Scott C. Marks, Salem, Mass., 2002—. Mem. ABA, Mass. Bar Assn., Salem Bar Assn., Essex County Bar Assn. Family and matrimonial, General practice, Personal injury (including property damage). Office: Law Office of Scott C Marks 70 Washington St Ste 405 Salem MA 01970-3733

MARKS, THEODORE LEE, lawyer; b. N.Y.C., Oct. 18, 1935; s. Irving Edward and Isabel (Goodman) M.; m. Benita Cooper, July 13, 1958; children: Eric, Robert, Jennifer BS, NYU, 1956, LL.B., 1958. Bar: N.Y. 1959, U.S. Dist. Ct. (so. dist.) N.Y. 1963, U.S. Supreme Ct. 1964, U.S. Ct. Appeals (2d cir.) 1975, U.S. Dist. Ct. (ea. dist.) N.Y. 1978. Assoc. Silver, Bernstein, Seawell & Kaplan, N.Y.C., 1959-65; sole practice N.Y.C., 1965-70; ptnr. Lee, Cash & Marks, N.Y.C., 1970-76, Vogel, Marks & Rosenberg, N.Y.C., 1976-79, Bromberg, Gloger, Lifschultz & Marks, N.Y.C., 1979-85, Epstein Becker Borsody & Green, P.C., N.Y.C., 1985-86, Gelberg & Abrams, 1986-87, Morrison Cohen Singer & Weinstein, 1987—. Speaker at meetings of profl. assns. Contbr. articles to profl. jours. Served with Army N.G., 1958-61. Mem. N.Y. State Bar Assn. (mem. real property, banking, corp. and bus. law sects.), N.Y. County Lawyers Assn., Fed. Bar Coun., T&M. Corporate, general, General practice, Property, real (including real estate development, water). Office: Morrison Cohen Singer & Weinstein LLP 750 Lexington Ave New York NY 10022-1200

MARKUS, ALLAN LEWIS, lawyer; b. Newark, Nov. 8, 1948; s. Seymour Bernard and Pearl (Weiss) M.; m. Debra J. Ross, Jan. 6, 1973; children—Dara, Lindsey. B.A. Monmouth Coll., 1970; J.D., Western New Eng. Sch. Law, 1975. Bar: N.J. 1976, U.S. Dist. Ct. N.J. 1976, U.S. Supreme Ct. 1985. Assoc. Miller & Platt, Paterson, N.J., 1976-78; sr. ptnr. Markus & Cohen, Parsippany, N.J., 1978— ; asst. atty. Pub. Defender Essex County, Newark, 1978-81, asst. pub. defender Morris County, Morristown, N.J., 1979-82; mcpl. prosecutor Twp. of Parsippany Troy-Hills, 1980-82. Committeeman Parsippany-Troy Hills Democratic Com., 1977-80, mayoral campaign treas., 1979-80; leader organizing rent control Tenants Assn., Parsippany-Troy Hills, 1977-80; gen. counsel Hoffman Floor Covering Co. Inc., Paul Miller, Inc. Recipient Bancroft-Whitney award Lawyers Coop. Pub. Co., 1974, 75. Mem. N.J. Bar Assn., Morris County Bar Assn., Zeta Beta Tau. Republican. Jewish. General civil litigation, Corporate, general, Property, real (including real estate development, water). Home: 6 Normandy Rd Pine Brook NJ 07058-9750 Office: Markus & Cohen 322 Rt 46 Suite 210 Parsippany NJ 07054

MARLAND, MELISSA KAYE, judge; b. Beckley, W.Va., Feb. 16, 1955; d. James Robert and Fannie Evelyn (Cook) M. BA in Polit. Sci., W.Va U., 1976, JD, 1979. Bar: W.Va. 1979, U.S. Dist. Ct. (so. dist.) W.Va. 1979, U.S. Supreme Ct. 1983. Law clk. Pub. Svc. Commn. W.Va., Charleston, 1979-82, hearing examiner, 1982-87, dep. chief adminstrv. law judge, 1987-89, chief adminstrv. law judge, 1989—. Faculty mem. ann. regulatory studies program Nat. Assn. Regulatory Commrs./Inst. Pub. Utilities, Mich. State U., 1994—. Assoc. editor: West Virginia Digest of Public Utility Decisions, vols. 1-7, 1986-91; contbr. articles to profl. jours. Mem. ABA, NAFE, W.Va. State Bar (com. on corp., banking and bus. law 1987—, adminstrv. law com. 1995—), Nat. Assn. Regulatory Commrs. (chmn. subcom. on adminstrv. law judges 1991-95), Phi Beta Kappa, Phi Alpha Delta, Pi Sigma Alpha. Democrat. Avocations: music, reading. Office: Pub Svc Commn WVa 201 Brooks St Charleston WV 25301-1803 E-mail: mmarland@worldnet.att.net.

MARLATT, MICHAEL JAMES, lawyer; b. L.A., Jan. 15, 1957; s. James Raymond and Norma Jean (Greenfield) M.; m. Donna Marie Healey, Apr. 13, 1985. BA, U. So. Calif., Calif. Poly., Pomona, 1981; JD, Pepperdine U., 1984. Bar: Calif. 1984, U.S. Dist. Ct. (ctrl. dist.) Calif. 1985, U.S. Supreme Ct. 1990. Project liaison U. So. Calif., Sch. Medicine, L.A., 1975-78; documentation rschr. NASA-Jet Propulsion Lab., Pasadena, Calif., 1978-81; ptnr. Thompson & Colegate, Riverside, Calif., 1984—. Bd. dirs. Assn. So. Calif. Def. Counsel, L.A., U. Calif., Riverside; lectr. Calif. Trial Lawyers Assn., 1991-94, Princeton U., 1993, U. Amsterdam Law Sch., 1994, Loma Linda (Calif.) U. Sch. Medicine, 1991-94, 99, 2001-02, Boston Coll. Law Sch., 1997, U. London, 1998; chair Am. Legal Sys. Internat. Law Program Civil Litigation U. of Calif., 1997; lectr., spkr. to ins. cos. on health care, 1988—; radio commentator Stas. KCKC, KCAL, KMEN and KPRO. Pres. U. Calif., Riverside, 1996—99, mem. steering com. We. Conf. Athletic Assn., 2003; v.p. Mission Inn Found., 1996—98, pres., 1999—2001; mem. bioethics com. Riverside Cmty. Hosp., 1999—2002; bd. dirs. Humane Soc.; Mem. ctr. com. Calif. Rep. Party, Sacramento, 1990—93; bd. dirs. U. Calif., Riverside, Mission Inn Found., Riverside County Regional Med. Ctr., ARC. Mem. Am. Bd. Trial Advocates, So. Calif. Assn. Hosp. Risk Mgrs. (bylaws com. 1996-99), Victoria Country Club, Lincoln Club Riverside County, Phi Alpha Delta. Roman Catholic. Avocations: rare book collecting, collegiate athletics, traveling. General civil litigation, Personal injury (including property damage), Professional liability. Office: Thompson & Colegate PO Box 1299 3610 14th St Riverside CA 92501-3843 E-mail: mmarlatt@thompson-Colegate.com.

MARLIN, RICHARD, lawyer; b. N.Y.C., June 1, 1933; s. Edward and Lillian (Milstein) M.; m. Merrel Pincus, June 12, 1955 (div. 1972); children: John F., Elizabeth; m. Jenesta Rutherford, July 29, 1974 (div. 1981); m. Caroline Mary Hirsch Magnus, Nov. 1, 1981. BA magna cum laude, Yale U., 1955, LLB, 1958; LLM, NYU, 1964. Bar: N.Y. 1959, Fla. 1978. Law clk. to presiding justice U.S. Dist. Ct. Conn., New Haven, 1958-59; assoc. Cleary, Gottlieb, Steen & Hamilton, N.Y.C., 1959-62, Wien Lane & Klein, N.Y.C., 1962-64; ptnr. Mnuchin Moss & Marlin, N.Y.C., 1964-66, Marshall, Bratter, Greene, Allison & Tucker, N.Y.C., 1966-79; sr. ptnr. Kramer,

Levin, Naftalis & Frankel LLP, N.Y.C., 1979—. Bd. dirs. FAB Industries, Inc., N.Y.C. Bd. editors Yale Law Jour. Mem. ABA, Assn. Bar City N.Y., N.Y. County Lawyers' Assn. (corp. law com., chmn. subcom.), Glen Oaks Club (Old Westbury, N.Y.) (bd. govs. 1979-85, 92-94), Phi Beta Kappa. Office: Kramer Levin Naftalis & Frankel LLP 919 3rd Ave New York NY 10022-3902

MARLOW, JAMES ALLEN, lawyer; b. Crossville, Tenn., May 23, 1955; s. Dewey Harold and Anna Marie (Hinch) M.; m. Sabine Klein, June 9, 1987; children: Lucas Allen, Eric Justin. BA, U. Tenn., 1976, JD, 1979; postgrad., Air War Coll., Maxwell AFB, Ala., 1990-91, Internat. Studienzentrum, Heidelberg, Germany, 1985-86. Bar: Ga. 1979, D.C. 1980, Tenn. 1980, U.S. Dist. Ct. (mid. dist.) Tenn. 1984, U.S. Ct. Fed. Claims 1987, U.S. Ct. Internat. Trade 1988, U.S. Tax Ct. 1987, U.S. Ct. Mil. Appeals 1980, U.S. Ct. Appeals (fed. cir.) 1987, U.S. Supreme Ct. 1987. Assoc. Carter & Assocs., Frankfurt, Fed. Republic Germany, 1984-85; chief internat. law USAF, Sembach AFB, Germany, 1986-96; pvt. practice Crossville, 1997—. Instr. Ctrl. Tex. Coll., 1997—; asst. prof. Embry-Riddle Aero. U., Kaiserslauten, Fed. Republic Germany, 1985-1999. Capt. USAF, 1980-84, Col. USAFR. Mem. Phi Beta Kappa. Avocations: genealogy, basketball, chess, german and spanish languages. Home and Office: 5746 Highway 127 S Crossville TN 38572

MARLOW, ORVAL LEE, II, lawyer; b. Denver, May 1, 1956; s. Jack Conger and Barbara A. (Stolzenburg) M.; m. Paige Wood, June 8, 1985; children: Lorri Wood, Orval Lee III. BA, U. Nebr., 1978, JD, 1981. Bar: Tex. 1981, U.S. Dist. Ct. (so. dist.) Tex. 1984, U.S. Ct. Appeals (5th cir.) 1984. Assoc. Krist & Scott, Houston, 1981-82; prin. Marlow & Assocs., Houston, 1982-83; ptnr. Lendais & Assocs., Houston, 1983-91; dir. Morris, Lendais, Hollrah & Snowden, 1992—. Mem. ABA, Internat. Bar Assn., Tex. Bar Assn., Houston Bar Assn., Phi Delta Phi. Lutheran. Avocations: golf, snow skiing, chess. Corporate, general, Private international, Property, real (including real estate development, water). Office: Morris Lendais Hollrah & Snowden 1980 Post Oak Blvd Ste 700 Houston TX 77056-3881 E-mail: omarlow@mlhs.net.

MARMET, GOTTLIEB JOHN, lawyer; b. Chgo., Mar. 24, 1946; s. Gottlieb John and Margaret Ann (Saylor) M.; m. Jane Marie Borkowski, Sept. 12, 1970; children: Gottlieb John, Philip Stanley, Thomas Jacob. BS with distinction in Acctg., San Diego State U., 1967; JD, Northwestern U., 1970. Bar: Ill. 1970, U.S. Dist. Ct. (no. dist.) Ill. 1970, U.S. Tax Ct. 1981; CPA, Calif., Ill., Minn. Tax acct. Touche Ross & Co., Chgo., 1970-75; assoc. atty. Howington, Elworth, Osswald & Hough, Chgo., 1975-79; tax mgr. Peat, Marwick, Mitchell & Co., Mpls., 1979-81; assoc. Shefsky, Saitlin & Froelich, Ltd., Chgo., 1981-83; prin. G. John Marmet, Glenview, Ill., 1983—. Lectr. corp. law William Rainey Harper Coll., Arlington Heights, Ill., 1984; instr. Ill. Soc. CPAs, 1976, 77, Minn. Soc. CPAs, 1980. Author: Farm Corporations and Their Income Tax Treatment, 1970, 74; contbr. articles to jours., pubs. Active Northeast Ill. Coun. Boy Scouts Am., 1984—, dist. chmn. Skokie Valley, 1988, mem. exec. bd., 1989-91, 99—; bd. dirs. North Shore Sr. Ctr., 1995-99. Recipient Hon. Mention Chgo. Bar Assn. Art Show, 1972, Boy Scouts Am. Dist. award of merit, 1990, Silver Beaver award, 1997. Mem. AICPA, ABA, Ill. Bar Assn., Chgo. Bar Assn., Rotary (Service Above Self award 1986, 96, bd. dirs. 1988-90, v.p. 1990-91, pres. 1991-92), Beta Gamma Sigma, Beta Alpha Psi, Phi Alpha Delta. Probate (including wills, trusts), Corporate taxation, Personal income taxation. Office: 950 Milwaukee Ave Ste 318 Glenview IL 60025-3779 E-mail: gmarmet@aol.com.

MARQUAND, BRENT RICHARD, lawyer; b. Tulsa, Jan. 1, 1951; s. Harold D. and Adelaide A. Marquand; m. Karen S. Lester, Mar. 30, 1979; children: Zachary B., Chelsea L., Trevor H. BA magna cum laude, Drury Coll., 1973; JD summa cum laude, Washington U., St. Louis, 1976. Bar: Tenn. 1976, U.S. Dist. Ct. (ea. dist.) Tenn. 1979, U.S. Ct. Appeals (5th and 11th cirs.) 1981, U.S. Ct. Appeals (10th and 6th cirs.) 1982, U.S. Supreme Ct. 1987, U.S. Dist. Ct. (we. dist.) Tenn. 1996. Staff atty. TVA, Knoxville, 1976-86, sr. litigation atty., 1986—. Erna Arndt scholar Washington U., 1976. Mem. ABA, Knoxville Bar Assn., Order of Coif. Office: TVA Office Gen Counsel 400 E Summit Hill Dr Knoxville TN 37915-1027

MARQUARDT, CHRISTEL ELISABETH, judge; b. Chgo., Aug. 26, 1935; d. Herman Albert and Christine Marie (Geringer) Trolenberg; children: Eric, Philip, Andrew, Joel. BS in Edn., Mo. Western Coll., 1970; JD with honors, Washburn U., 1974. Bar: Kans. 1974, Mo. 1992, U.S. Dist. Ct. Kans. 1974, U.S. Dist. Ct. (we. dist.) Mo. 1992. Tchr. St. John's Ch., Tigerton, Wis., 1955-56; pers. asst. Columbia Records, L.A., 1958-59; ptnr. Cosgrove, Webb & Oman, Topeka, 1974-86, Palmer & Marquardt, Topeka, 1986-91, Levy and Craig P.C., Overland Park, Kans., 1991-94; sr. ptnr. Marquardt and Assocs., L.L.C., Fairway, Kans., 1994-95; judge Kans. Ct. Appeals, 1995—. Mem. atty. bd. discipline Kans. Supreme Ct., 1984—86. Mem. editorial adv. bd. Kans. Lawyers Weekly, 1992-96; contbr. articles to legal jours. Bd. dirs. Topeka Symphony, 1983-92, 95-2002, Arts and Humanities Assn. Johnson County, 1992-95, Brown Found., 1988-90; hearing examiner Human Rels. Com., Topeka, 1974-76; local advisor Boy Scouts Am., 1973-74; bd. dirs., mem. nominating com. YWCA, Topeka, 1979-81; bd. govs. Washburn U. Law Sch., 1987-2002, v.p., 1996-98, pres., 1998-2000; mem. dist. bd. adjudication Mo. Synod Luth. Ch., Kans., 1982-88. Named Woman of Yr., Mayor, City of Topeka, 1982; Obee scholar Washburn U., 1972-74; recipient Jennie Mitchell Kellogg Atty. of Achievement award, 1999, Phil Lewis medal of Distinction, 2000, Atty. of Achievement award Kans. Women Attys. Assn., Disting. Svc. award Washburn U. Law Sch., 2002. Fellow: Kans. Bar Found. (trustee 1987—89), Am. Bar Found.; mem.: ABA (specialization com. 1987—93, mem. ho. dels. 1988—, chmn. 1989—93, lawyer referral com. 1993—95, state del. 1995—99, bar svcs. and activities 1995—99, bd. govs., program and planning com. 1999—2002, bd. govs. 1999—2002, ctrl. and ea. European law initiative 2001—02, del-at-large ho. of dels. 2002—, African law coun. 2002—, scope & correlation com. 2003—), Law and Organizational Econ. Ctr. (bd. dirs. 2000—02), Am. Bus. Women's Assn. (lectr., corr. sec. 1983—84, pres. career chpt. 1986—87, named one of Top 10 Bus. Women of Yr. 1985), Topeka Bar Assn., Kans. Trial Lawyers Assn. (bd. govs. 1982—86, lectr.), Kans. Bar Assn. (sec., treas. 1981—85, bd. dirs. 1983—, v.p. 1985—86, pres. 1987—88). Home: 3408 SW Alameda Dr Topeka KS 66614-5108 Office: 301 SW 10th Ave Topeka KS 66612-1502 E-mail: marquardt@kscourts.org.

MARQUEZ, ALFREDO C. federal judge; b. 1922; m. Linda Nowobilsky. BS, U. Ariz., 1948, JD, 1950. Bar: Ariz. Practice law Mesch Marquez & Rothschild, 1957-80; asst. atty. gen. State of Ariz., 1951-52; asst. county atty. Pima County, Ariz., 1953-54; adminstrv. asst. to Congressman Stewart Udall, 1955; judge U.S. Dist. Ct. Ariz., Tucson, 1980-91, sr. judge, 1991—. Served with USN, 1942-45 Office: US Dist Ct US Courthouse Rm 327 405 W Congress Ste 6180 Tucson AZ 85701-5060

MARR, DAVID E. lawyer; BA, Colby Coll.; MA, Wesleyan U.; JD with honors, U. Conn. Bar: Conn. 1970, Mass. 1974, U.S. Dist. Ct. Conn. 1971, U.S. Dist. Ct. Mass. 1975, U.S. Ct. Appeals (2d cir.) 1971, U.S. Supreme Ct. 1974, U.S. Tax Ct. 1992. Assoc. Day, Berry & Howard, Hartford, Conn., 1970-73; counsel Honeywell Info. Sys., Inc., Waltham, Mass., 1973-75; pvt. practice Boston, 1975—79, Natick, Mass., 1980—. Editor-in-Chief Law Review, 1970. Author: Employment Law in Connecticut; opinion editor Mass. Lawyers Weekly, 1976-86. Rep. Regional Vocat. Sch.; chmn. Hist. Dist. Com.; bd. dirs. Hist. Soc. and Mus. Mem. ATLA, Mass. Bar Assn. Family and matrimonial, Land use and zoning (including planning), Personal injury (including property damage). Office: 199 Union St Natick MA 01760-4759

MARRERO, VICTOR, lawyer, judge; b. Santurce, P.R., Sept. 1, 1941; s. Ezequiel Marrero and Josefina (Sanabria) Santos M.; m. Veronica M. White, Dec. 1987. BA, NYU, 1964; LLB, Yale U., 1968; postgrad. (Fulbright scholar), U. Sheffield, Eng., 1966-67. Bar: N.Y. 1982. Exec. dir. N.Y.C. Dept. City Planning, 1973-74; spl. counsel to comptroller City of N.Y., 1974-75; 1st asst. counsel to gov. State of N.Y., Albany, 1975-76; chmn. N.Y.C. City Planning Commn., 1976-77; commr. N.Y. State Divsn. Housing and Cmty. Renewal, N.Y.C., 1977-79; under-sec. HUD, Washington, 1979-81; ptnr. Tufo & Zuccotti, N.Y.C., 1982-85, Brown & Wood, N.Y.C., 1986-93; amb., U.S. rep. UN Econ. and Social Coun., N.Y.C., 1993-97; amb., permanent U.S. rep. OAS, Dept. State, Washington, 1998-99; judge U.S. Dist. Ct., N.Y.C., 1999—. Vis. lectr. Yale U. Law Sch., New Haven, 1986, Columbia U. Law Sch., 1991-93. Trustee N.Y. Pub. Libr., 1989—, SUNY, Albany, 1985-93, Cooper Union, 1989-93, Consolidated Edison Co., 1988-93; bd. dirs. P.R. Legal Def. and Edn. Fund., N.Y.C., 1972-86, N.Y. Telephone Co., 1987-93; chmn. N.Y. State Chief Judge's Com. to Improve Availability of Legal Svcs., 1988-90. Mem. ABA (Pro Bono Publico award 1993), N.Y. State Bar Assn. (Root/Stimson Pub. Svc. .award 1992), Assn. Bar City N.Y. (mem. com. modern cts. 1980-93, exec. com. 1986-89, judiciary com. 1991-92, v.p. 1992-93). Office: US Dist Court of NY 40 Centre St New York NY 10007-1502

MARRS, BRUCE F. judge; b. Calif. BA, Pacific U., 1965; JD, Calif. Western U., 1976. Bar: Calif. 1976, U.S. Dist. Ct. (fed. ct.) Calif. 1976. Commr. Santa Anita Mcpl. Ct., Monrovia, Calif., 1986—91; judge L.A. Mcpl. Ct., 1991—2000, L.A. Superior Ct., 2000—. Capt. USMC, 1961—75. Office: LA Superior Ct 111 N Hill St Los Angeles CA 90012

MARS, TOM, lawyer; BA criminology, Ark. State Univ., 1980; law degree, Univ. of Ark. Sch. of Law, Fayetteville, NC, 1985. Pvt. practice Little Rock's Rose Law Firm, Little Rock, Springdale, Kutak Rock LLP, Fayetteville, Nebr., 2001; dir. Ark. State Police, Ark.; gen. coun. Wal-Mart, Bentonville, Ark., 2002—. Mars, while working at his law office of Kutak Rock LLP, used to represent clients who sued companies was hire by Wal-Mart in 2002 as its litigation chief. Office: Wal-Mart 702 SW 8th St Bentonville AR 72712*

MARSH, BENJAMIN FRANKLIN, lawyer; b. Toledo, Apr. 30, 1927; s. Lester Randall and Alice (Smith) M.; m. Martha Kirkpatrick, July 12, 1952; children: Samuel, Elizabeth. BA, Ohio Wesleyan U., 1950; JD, George Washington U., 1954. Bar: Ohio 1955. Pvt. practice law, Toledo, 1955-88; assoc., ptnr. Doyle, Lewis & Warner, Toledo, 1955-71; ptnr. Ritter, Boesel, Robinson & Marsh, Toledo, 1971-88, Marsh & McAdams, Maumee, 1988-98; personnel officer AEC, 1950-54; asst. atty. gen. State of Ohio, 1969-71; asst. solicitor City of Maumee, 1959-63, solicitor, 1963-92; ptnr. Marsh McAdams Scharrly Brogan & Schaefer, Ltd., 1999—. Mem. U.S. Fgn. Claims Settlement Commn., Washington, 1990-94; counsel N.W. Ohio Mayors and Mgrs. Assn., 1990-2000; mem. regional bd. rev. Indsl. Commn. Ohio, Toledo, 1993-94; mem. Ohio Dental Bd., 1995-2000; trustee Corp. for Effective Govt., 1998—; mem. Ohio Elections Commn., 2001—. U.S. rep. with rank spl. amb. to 10th Anniversary Independence of Botswana, 1976; past pres. Toledo and Lucas County Tb Soc., citizens for metro pks.; past mem. Judges Com. Notaries Pub.; formerly mem. Lucas County Bd. Elections; former chmn. bldg. commn. Riverside Hosp., Toledo; past trustee Com. on Rels. with Toledo, Spain; past chmn. bd. trustee Med. Coll., Ohio; past treas. Coglin Meml. Inst.; chmn. Lucas County Rep. Exec. Com., 1973-74; precinct commiteeman, Maumee, 1959-73; legal counsel, bd. dirs. Nat. Coun. Rep. Workshops, 1960-65; pres. Rep. Workshops, Ohio, 1960-64; alt. del. Rep. Nat. Conv., 1964; candidate 9th dist. U.S. Ho. of Reps., 1968; adminstrv. asst. to Rep. state chmn. Ray C. Bliss, 1954; chmn. Lucas County Bush for Pres., 1980; co-chmn. Reagan-Bush Com. for Northwestern Ohio, 1980, vice chmn. fin. com. Bush-Quayle, 1992; co-chmn. Ohio steering com. Bush for Pres., mem. nat. steering com., 1988; del. Rep. Nat. Conv., 1988; past bd. dirs. Ohio Tb and Respiratory Disease Assn.; apptd. Ohio chmn. UN Day, 1980, 81, 82; adminstrv. asst. Legis. Svc. Commn., Columbus, 1954-55; mem. Lucas County Charter Commn., Toledo, 1959-60; vice-chmn. U.S. Nat. Commn. for UNESCO, mem. legal com., del. 17th gen. conf., Paris, 1972, U.S. observer meeting of nat. commns., Africa, 1974, Addis Ababa, Ethiopia; past mem. industry functional adv. com. on standards trade policy matters; mem. nat. def. exec. res. Dept. Commerce; active Am. Bicentennial Presdl. Inauguration, Diplomatic Adv. Com. With USNR, 1945-46. Named Outstanding Young Man of Toledo, 1962. Mem. ABA, Maumee C. of C. (past pres.), Ohio State Bar Assn., Toledo Bar Assn., Ohio Mpcl. League (past pres.), Am. Legion, Lucas County Maumee Valley Hist. Soc. (trustee, past pres.), Internat. Inst. Toledo, Ohio Mcpl. Attys. Assn. (past pres.), Orgn. Security and Cooperation in Europe (registration supr., adjudicator, elections supr. in Bosnia), Ohio Hist. Soc., Canal Soc. Ohio, Toledo Mus. Art, Ohio Wesleyan U. Alumni Assn. (past pres.), Toledo C. of C., Ohio State Bar Found., Toledo Bar Found., Rotary, Toledo Country Club, Capitol Club (Columbus), Omicron Delta Kappa, Delta Sigma Rho, Theta Alpha Phi, Phi Delta Phi. Presbyterian. General practice, Probate (including wills, trusts). Home: 124 W Harrison St Maumee OH 43537-2119 Office: 204 W Wayne St Maumee OH 43537-2125 E-mail: bmarsh124@aol.com.

MARSH, MALCOLM F. federal judge; b. Portland, Oreg., Sept. 24, 1928; m. Shari Marsh. BS, U. Oreg., 1952, LLB, 1954, JD, 1971. Bar: Oreg. 1954, U.S. Dist. Ct. Oreg. 1955, U.S. Ct. Appeals (9th cir.) 1968. Ptnr. Clark & Marsh, Lindauer & McClinton (and predecessors), Salem, Oreg., 1954-87; judge U.S. Dist. Ct. Oreg., Portland, 1987—98, sr. judge, 1998—. With U.S. Army, 1946-47. Fellow Am. Coll. Trial Lawyers; mem. ABA, Oreg. Bar Assn. Office: US Dist Ct 1507 US Courthouse 1000 SW 3d Ave Portland OR 97204*

MARSHALL, CONSUELO BLAND, federal judge; b. Knoxville, Tenn., Sept. 28, 1936; d. Clyde Theodore and Annie (Brown) Arnold; m. George Edward Marshall, Aug. 30, 1959; children: Michael Edward, Laurie Ann. AA, L.A. City Coll., 1956; BA, Howard U., 1958, LLB, 1961. Bar: Calif. 1962. Dep. atty., City of L.A., 1962-67; assoc. Cochran & Atkins, L.A., 1968-70; commr. L.A. Superior Ct., 1971-76; judge Inglewood Mcpl. Ct., 1976-77, L.A. Superior Ct., 1977-80, U.S. Dist. Ct. Central Dist. Calif., L.A., 1980—. Lectr. U.S. Information Agy. in Yugoslavia, Greece and Italy, 1984, in Nigera and Ghana, 1991, in Ghana, 1992. Contbr. articles to profl. jours.; notes editor Law Jour. Howard U. Mem. adv. bd. Richstone Child Abuse Center. Recipient Judicial Excellence award Criminal Cts. Bar Assn., 1992, Ernestine Stalhut award; named Criminal Ct. Judge of Yr., U.S. Dist. Ct., 1997; inducted into Langston Hall of Fame, 2000; rsch. fellow Howard U. Law Sch., 1959-60. Mem. State Bar Calif., Century City Bar Assn., Calif. Women Lawyers Assn., Calif. Assn. Black Lawyers, Calif. Judges Assn., Black Women Lawyers Assn., Los Angeles County Bar Assn., Nat. Assn. Women Judges, NAACP, Urban League, Beta Phi Sigma. Office: US Dist Ct 312 N Spring St Los Angeles CA 90012-4701

MARSHALL, ELLEN RUTH, lawyer; b. N.Y.C., Apr. 23, 1949; d. Louis and Faith (Gladstone) M. AB, Yale U., 1971; JD, Harvard U., 1974. Bar: Calif. 1975, D.C. 1981, N.Y. 1989. Assoc. McKenna & Fitting, Los Angeles, 1975-80; ptnr. McKenna, Conner & Cuneo, Los Angeles and Orange County, Calif., 1980-88, Morrison & Foerster, LLP, Orange County, 1988—2003, Manatt, Phelps & Phillips LLP, Orange County, 2003—. Mem. ABA (bus. law sect., mem. savs. inst. com., mem. asset securitization com., tax sect., mem. employee benefits com.), Orange County Bar Assn. Clubs: Center (Costa Mesa, Calif.). Banking, Corporate, general, Pension, profit-sharing, and employee benefits. Office: Manatt Phelps & Phillips LLP 650 Town Ctr Dr Costa Mesa CA 92626

MARSHALL, ENID ANN, law educator; b. Boyndie, Scotland, July 10, 1932; d. John and Lizzie (Gilchrist) M. MA with 1st class honors, U. St. Andrews, Scotland, 1955, LLB with distinction, 1958, PhD, 1966. Law apprentice Pagan & Osborne, Cupar, Scotland, 1956-59; lectr. law Dundee Coll. Tech., 1959-72; lectr. bus. law U. Stirling, Scotland, 1972-74, sr. lectr. bus. law, 1974-77, reader in bus. law, 1977-94, reader in Scots law rsch., 1994-99. External examiner U. Scotland, 1973-79, Colls. in Scotland, 1974-83; moderator Scotvec, Scotland, 1972-90; external lectr. Coll. Estate Mgmt., Reading, Eng., 1989-94. Author: General Principles of Scots Law, 7 edits., 1971-99, Scots Mercantile Law, 3 edits., 1983-97, Scottish Cases on Contract, 2 edits., 1978-93, Oliver and Marshall's Company Law, 10th to 12th edits., 1987-94, Gill on Arbitration, 4th edit., 2001; editor Scottish Law Gazette, 1983-2001. Chmn. Social Security Appeal Tribunals, Stirling & Falkirk, Scotland. Fellow Royal Soc. Arts; mem. Chartered Inst. Arbitrators (assoc.), Royal Instn. Chartered Surveyors (hon. assoc.), Law Soc. Scotland (solicitor). Avocations: animal welfare, veganism. Home: 3 Ballater Dr Stirling FK9 5JH Scotland

MARSHALL, J. STEPHEN, lawyer; b. Grand Rapids, Mich., Mar. 19, 1948; s. Harry D. and Judy (Corrigan) M.; m. Pamela K. Bergmans, June 17, 1972; children: Sarah Aubrey, Heather Elizabeth. BBA, U. Mich., 1970; JD, Ind. U., Indpls., 1975. Bar: Mich. 1975, U.S. Dist. Ct. (we. dist.) Mich. 1975. Assoc. Norris & Keyser, Grand Rapids, 1975-80; pvt. practice Grand Rapids, 1980—. Dir. Med. Pers. Pool, Grand Rapids, 1980-96. Vol. Big Brothers/Big Sisters, 2000—; trustee Westminster Presbyn. Ch., Grand Rapids, 1989—92, 1994—97, U. Mich. Club of Grand Rapids Scholarship Fund, 1986—. Recipient Disting. Svc. award, U. Mich. Alumni Assn., 1999. Mem. Grand Rapids Bar Assn., U. Mich. Alumni Assn. (dir. 1989-92, 94—, accolade 1994), U. Mich. Club of Grand Rapids (pres., v.p., sec., dir. Grand Rapids chpt. 1975—). General civil litigation, Probate (including wills, trusts), Property, real (including real estate development, water). Home: 2634 Beechwood Dr SE Grand Rapids MI 49506-4207 Office: 40 Pearl St NW Grand Rapids MI 49503-3028

MARSHALL, JOHN DAVID, lawyer; b. Chgo., May 19, 1940; s. John Howard and Sophie (Brezenk) M.; m. Marcia A. Podlasinski, Aug. 26, 1961; children: Jacquelyn, David, Jason, Patricia, Brian, Denise, Michael, Catherine. BS in Acctg., U. Ill., 1961; JD, Ill. Inst. Tech., 1965. Bar: Ill. 1965, U.S. Tax Ct. 1968, U.S. Dist. Ct. (no. dist.) Ill. 1971; CPA, Ill. Ptnr. Mayer, Brown & Platt, Chgo., 1961—. Bd. dirs. Levinson Ctr. for Handicapped Children, Chgo., 1970-75. Fellow Am. Coll. Probate Counsel; mem. Ill. Bar Assn., Chgo. Bar Assn. (agribus. com. 1978—, trust law com. 1969-95, probate practice com. 1969—, com. on coms. 1983-00, vice chmn. 1988-89, chmn. 1989-90, legis. com. of probate practice com. 1983—, chmn. and vice chmn. legis. com. of probate practice com. 1983-84, rules and forms com., 1996—, chmn. exec. com. probate practice com. 1982-83, vice chmn. exec. com. 1981-82, sec. exec. com. 1980-81, div. chmn. 78-79, div. vice chmn. 1977-78, div. sec. 1976-77, Appreciation award 1982-83), Chgo. Estate Planning Council. Clubs: Union League (Chgo.). Roman Catholic. Estate planning, Probate (including wills, trusts), Estate taxation. Office: Mayer Brown & Platt 190 S La Salle St Ste 3100 Chicago IL 60603-3441 Home: 429 N Willow Wood Dr Palatine IL 60074-3831

MARSHALL, JOHN PATRICK, lawyer; b. Bklyn., July 3, 1950; s. Harry W. and Mary Margaret (Kelly) M.; m. Cheryl J. Garvey, Aug. 10, 1975; children: Kelly Blake, Logan Brooke. BA, Rutgers U., 1972; JD cum laude, N.Y. Law Sch., 1976. Bar: N.Y. 1977, N.J. 1977, U.S. Dist. Ct. N.J. 1977, U.S. Dist. Ct. (so. and ea. dists.) N.Y. 1978, U.S. Ct. Appeals (3rd cir.) 1982, U.S. Dist Ct. (no. dist.) N.Y. 1991. Assoc. Kelley Drye & Warren, N.Y.C., 1976-84, ptnr., 1985-98; pres., CEO Metro Ventures, Inc., Short Hills, NJ, 1997—. Pres., CEO Metro Ventures, Inc. Mem. editl. bd. N.Y. Law Sch. Law Rev., 1975-76, staff mem., 1974-75; contbr. articles to profl. jours. Jud. screening com. N.Y. Dem. Com., N.Y. New Dem. Coalition, 1988; exec. v.p. Humanitarian Found. for Nicaragua, 1991; sec. Respect for Law Found., 1996; active So. Dist. N.Y. Mediation Panel, 1994—, Coun. on Jud. Adminstrn., 1996-98. Fellow Am. Bar Found.; mem. ABA, N.Y. County Lawyers' Assn. (sec. 1984-87, mem. com. on Supreme Ct. 1984-94, mem. legal edn., admission to bar and lawyer placement com. 1983-93), Am. Arbitration Assn. (mem. nat. panel arbitrators N.Y. and N.J. regions 1991—, mem. corp. counsel com. 1993-98), Assn. of Bar of City of N.Y. (sec. judiciary com. 1989-92, mem. com. on arbitration 1994-96, sec. coun. on judical adminstrn. 1996-98). Federal civil litigation, State civil litigation, Private international. Home and Office: 50 Highland Ave Short Hills NJ 07078-2812 E-mail: marshall.highland@prodigy.net.

MARSHALL, JOHN TREUTLEN, lawyer, educator; b. Macon, Ga., Nov. 1, 1934; s. Hubert and Gladys (Lucas) M.; m. Katrine White, May 1, 1959; children: Allison, Rebecca, Paul, Mary Anne. BA, Vanderbilt U., 1956; LLB, Yale U., 1962. Bar: Ga. 1962, U.S. Dist. Ct. (no., mid. and so. dists.) Ga. 1962, U.S. Ct. Appeals (5th cir.) 1962, U.S. Supreme Ct. 1978, U.S. Ct. Appeals (11th cir.) 1982. Ptnr. Powell, Goldstein, Frazer & Murphy, Atlanta, 1962—. Adj. prof. law Emory U. Sch. Law, 1968-86, mem. coun.; chmn. No. Dist. Ga. Bar Coun., 1989; chmn. Ga. State Commn. on Continuing Lawyer Competency, 1991-93, Ga. State Commn. on Standards of Profession, 1996-. Bd. editors: Yale Law Jour. Bd dirs. Atlanta Legal Aid, 1972-73; trustee Ga. Inst. Continuing Legal Edn., 1983-90; chmn. adv. bd. Atlanta Vol. Lawyers Found. Recipient S. Phillip Heiner award Atlanta Vol. Lawyers Assn., 1992, A. Gus cleveland award Ga. Commn. on Continuing Edn., Tradition of Excellence award State Bar Ga., 1995. Fellow Am. Coll. Trial Lawyers (state chmn. 1985-86), Am. Acad. Appellate Lawyers, Am. Bar Found., Ga. Bar Found.; mem. ABA (ho. of dels. 1976-86, Harrison Tweed award 1986), Am. Arbitration Assn., State Bar Ga. (chair stds. of profession com.), Atlanta Bar Assn. (pres. 1974-75, Charles E. Watkins Jr. award 1988, Leadership award 1996), Ga. Inst. Trial Advocacy (chmn. 1982-830, Cherokee Town and Country Club, 191 Club, Lawyers Club. Federal civil litigation, State civil litigation. Office: Powell Goldstein Frazer & Murphy 191 Peachtree St NE Fl 16 Atlanta GA 30303-1740

MARSHALL, KATHRYN SUE, lawyer; b. Decatur, Ill., Sept. 12, 1942; d. Edward Elda and Frances M. (Minor) Lahniers; m. Robert S. Marshall, Sept. 5, 1964 (div. Apr. 1984); m. Robert J. Arndt, June 25, 1988; children: Stephen Edward, Christine Elizabeth. BA, Lake Forest Coll., 1964; JD, John Marshall Law Sch., Chgo., 1976. Intern U.S. Atty.'s Office, Chgo., 1974-76; mng. ptnr. Marshall and Marshall Ltd., Waukegan, Ill., 1976-84; pvt. practice Waukegan, 1984-93, Preemptive Solutions, Wash. Contbr. articles to profl. jours. Cert. jud. candidate Dem. party, Lake County, Ill.; bd. mem. Camerata Soc., Lake Forest; bd. mem., v.p. Lake Forest (Ill.) Fine Arts Ensemble; bd. dirs. Island Hosp. Health Found.; mem. steering com. Equal Justice Coalition. Fellow: ABA (gov. 1993—96), Coll. Law Practice Mgmt., Ill. Bar Assn.; mem.: Navy League (life). Avocations: boating, reading, travel. Family and matrimonial, Military.

MARSHALL, MARGARET HILARY, state supreme court chief justice; b. Newcastle, Natal, South Africa, Sept. 1, 1944; came to U.S., 1968; d. Bernard Charles and Hilary A.D. (Anderton) M; m. Samuel Shapiro, Dec. 14, 1968 (div. Apr. 1982); m. Anthony Lewis, Sept. 23, 1984. BA, Witwatersrand U., Johannesburg, 1966; MEd, Harvard U., 1969; JD, Yale U., 1976; LHD (hon.), Regis Coll., 1993. Bar: Mass. 1977, U.S. Dist. Ct. Mass., U.S. Dist. Ct. N.H., U.S. Dist. Ct. D.C., U.S. Dist. Ct. (ea. dist.) Mich., U.S. Tax Ct., U.S. Ct. Appeals (1st, 11th and D.C. cirs.), U.S. Supreme Ct. Assoc. Csaplar & Bok, Boston, 1976-83, ptnr., 1983-89, Choate, Hall & Stewart, Boston, 1989-92; v.p., gen. counsel Harvard U., Cambridge, Mass., 1992-96; justice Supreme Jud. Ct. Commonwealth Mass., 1996-99, chief justice, 1999—. Mem. jud. nominating coun., 1987-90, 92; chairperson ct. rules subcom. Alternative Dispute Resolution Working Group, 1985-87; mem. fed. appts. commn., 1993; mem. adv. com. Supreme Judicial Ct., 1989-92, mem. gender equality com., 1989-94; mem. civil justice adv. group U.S. Dist. Ct. Mass., 1991-93; spl. counsel Jud.

Conduct Commn., 1988-92; trustee Mass. Continuing Legal Edn., Inc., 1990-92. Trustee Regis Coll., 1993-95; bd. dirs. Internat. Design Conf., Aspen, 1986-92, Boston Mcpl. Res. Bur., 1990-94, Supreme Judicial Ct. Hist. Soc., 1990-94, sec., 1990-94. Fellow Am. Bar Found. (Mass. state chair); mem. Boston Bar Assn. (treas. 1988-89, v.p. 1989-90, pres.-elect 1990-91, pres. 1991-92), Internat. Women's Forum, Mass. Women's Forum, Boston Club, Phi Beta Kappa (hon.). Office: Supreme Jud Ct Pemberton Sq 1300 New Courthouse Boston MA 02108-1701

MARSHALL, MARILYN JOSEPHINE, lawyer; b. Dayton, Ohio, May 31, 1945; d. Foy Wylie and Inez Virginia (Smith) Gard; m. Alan George Marshall, June 13, 1965; children: Gwendolyn Scott, Brian George. Student, Northwestern U., 1963-65; BA, Stanford U., 1967; cert. in teaching, U. B.C., Vancouver, 1977; JD, Capital Law Sch., Columbus, Ohio, 1985. Bar: Ohio 1985, Fla. 1993, U.S Dist. Ct. (so. dist.) Ohio 1986, U.S. Dist. Ct. (no. dist., mid. dist. and so. dist.) Fla. 1994, U.S. Ct. Appeals (6th cir.) 1986, U.S. Ct. Appeals (11th cir.) 1994. Tchr. Sutherland Secondary Sch., North Vancouver, B.C., 1977-79; instr. Brit. Coll. Inst. Tech., Burnaby, B.C., 1979-80; assoc. Crabbe, Brown, Jones, Potts & Schmidt, Columbus, Ohio, 1985-86; clk. to judge U.S. Dist. Ct. (so. dist.) Ohio, Columbus, 1986-88; clk. to justice Ohio Supreme Ct., 1988-89; assoc. Squire, Sanders & Dempsey, 1989-92; with Columbus City Atty.'s Office, Columbus, Ohio, 1992-93; asst. atty. gen. civil divsn. State of Fla., Tallahassee, 1994-96; pvt. practice Tallahassee, 1996—. Bd. dirs. Tallahassee Symphony. Mem. ABA, Ohio Bar Assn., Fla. Bar Assn., Tallahassee Bar Assn., Tallahassee Women Lawyers Assn., Capitol U. Law Sch. Alumni Assn. Republican. Avocations: tennis, gardening, music. Office: 254 E 6th Ave Tallahassee FL 32303-6208 E-mail: mjmarshall@aol.com.

MARSHALL, RAYMOND CHARLES, lawyer; b. Aquadilia, Puerto Rico, July 23, 1953; m. Piper Kent-Marshall; 1 child, Kyle. BA summa cum laude, Coll. Idaho, 1975; JD, Harvard U., 1978. Bar: Calif. 1978, D.C. 1989. Ptnr. Bingham McCutchen , San Francisco. Chmn. Calif. Supreme Ct. Adv. Multi-Jurisdictional Practice. Co-author: Environmental Crimes, 1992; contbr. chpt. to manual; contbr. articles to profl. jours. Bd. dirs. Nat. Multiple Sclerosis Soc. Northern Calif. chpt., 1992—; adv. bd. United Negro Coll. Fund Northern Bay Area Chpt., 1992—; bd. trustees Alta Bates Found., 1994—; mem. San Francisco leadership bd. Am. Red Cross Bay Area; adv. coun. mem. San Francisco Sports Coun. Recipient San Francisco Neighborhood Legal Assistance Found. award, 1989, Earl Warren Legal Svcs. award NAACP Legal Def. & Ednl. Found., 1990, Unity award Minority Bar Coalition, 1992, Cmty. Svc. award Wiley Manuel Law Found., 1994, Disting. Jesuit award Anti-Defemation League, 2001. Mem. ABA (met. bar caucus exec. com. 1992-94, vice-chmn. natural resources & energy litigation com. 1989-93, environmental crimes com. 1990-92, nominating com. conf. of minority ptnrs. in maj. corp. law firms 1991, commn. on women in the profession 1994-95, co-chmn. environmental crimes subcom. of white collar crime com. 1994-95), Nat. Bar Assn., Calif. State Bar (bd. govs. 1995—, pres. 1998-99), Charles Houston Bar Assn. Avocations: travel, recreational sports. Office: Bingham McCutchen Three Embarcadero Ctr San Francisco CA 94111

MARSHALL, RICHARD TREEGER, lawyer; b. N.Y.C., May 17, 1925; s. Edward and Sydney (Treeger) M.; m. Dorothy M. Goodman, June 4, 1950; children: Abigail Ruth Marshall Bergerson, Daniel Brooks; m. 2d Sylvia J. Kelley, June 10, 1979. BS, Cornell U., 1948; JD, Yale U., 1951. Bar: Tex. 1952, U.S. Ct.. Appeals (5th cir.) 1966, U.S. Ct. Appeals (10th cir.) 1980, U.S. Supreme Ct. 1959; lic. Tex. Dept. Ins. Pvt. practice, El Paso, Tex., 1952-59, 61-79; assoc. Fryer & Milstead, El Paso, 1952; sr. ptnr. Marshall & Wendorf, El Paso, 1959-61, Marshall & Volk, El Paso, 1979-81; sr. atty. Richard T. Marshall & Assocs., PC, El Paso, 1981-85; sr. ptnr. Marshall, Thomas & Winters, El Paso, 1985-87; sr. atty. Marshall & Winters, 1987-88, Marshall, Sherrod & Winters, 1988-90; pvt. practice El Paso, 1990—. Instr. polit. sci. U. Tex., El Paso, 1961-62; instr. ins. law C.L.U. tng. course Am. Coll.; officer, dir. Advance Funding, Inc., El Paso. Editor El Paso Trial Lawyers Rev., 1973-80; contbr. articles to profl. jours. Mem. ATLA (sec. personal injury law sect. 1967-68, nat. sec. 1969-70, sec.-treas. environ. law sect. 1970-71, vice chmn. family law litigation sec. 1971-72), El Paso Bar Assn., El Paso Trial Lawyers Assn. (pres. 1965-66), Tex. Trial Lawyers Assn.,, Roscoe Pound-Am. Trial Lawyers Found. (commn. on profl. responsibility 1979-82), Nat. Acad. Elder Law Attys., Soc. Cert. Sr. Advisors, Nat. Assn. Charitable Estate Counselors. Estate planning, Personal injury (including property damage), Probate (including wills, trusts). Office: 5959 Gateway Blvd W El Paso TX 79925-3331 E-mail: marshall@texseniorlaw.com.

MARSHALL, ROBERT WILLIAM, lawyer, rancher; b. L.A., Apr. 12, 1933; s. Kenneth I. and Helen (Putnam) M.; m. Nanette Hollenbeck, June 10, 1965; children: Thomas, Victoria, Rebecca, Kathleen. AB in Pre Law, Stanford U., 1955, JD, 1957. Bar: Calif. 1958, Nev. 1958, U.S. Dist. Ct. (so. dist.) Calif. 1958, U.S. Dist. Ct. Nev. 1958. Assoc. Vargas & Bartlett, Reno, Nev., 1958-64, ptnr., 1964-85, sr. ptnr., 1985-94; chmn. of bd. Marshall, Hill, Cassas & de Lipkau, 1994—. Owner Intermountain Cattle Co.; founder Intermountain Pipeline Ltd. Advisor Explorer Boy Scouts Am., Reno, 1971-76, 87-89, scoutmaster Troop 444 Boy Scouts Am., Reno, 1981-85; state chmn. Nev. Young Reps., 1962-64. Mem. ABA, Nat. Cattlemen's Assn., Calif. Bar Assn., Nev. Bar Assn., Washoe County Bar Assn., No. Nev. Large Power Users (organizer), So. Nev. Large Power Users (organizer), Nev. Cattlemen's Assn., Reno Stanford Club (pres. Reno chpt. 1974). Republican. Utilities, public, Property, real (including real estate development, water). Office: Marshall Hill Cassas & deLipkau 333 Holcomb Ave Ste 300 Reno NV 89502-1665

MARSHALL, SHEILA HERMES, lawyer; b. N.Y.C., Jan. 17, 1934; d. Paul Milton and Julia Angela (Meagher) Hermes; m. James Josiah Marshall, Sept. 30, 1967; 1 child, James J.H. BA, St. John's U., N.Y.C., 1959; JD, NYU, 1963. Bar: N.Y. 1964, U.S. Ct. Appeals (2d, 3d, 5th and D.C. cirs.), U.S. Supreme Ct. 1970. Assoc. LeBoeuf, Lamb, Greene & MacRae, N.Y.C., 1963-72, ptnr., 1973—95, of counsel, 1996—. Specialist in field. Mem. ABA, N.Y. State Bar Assn., Assn. of Bar of City of N.Y. Republican. Administrative and regulatory, Insurance, Product liability. Home: 325 E 72nd St New York NY 10021 Office: LeBoeuf Lamb Greene & MacRae 125 W 55th St New York NY 10019-5369

MARSHALL, SIRI SWENSON, corporate lawyer; BA, Harvard U., 1970; JD, Yale U., 1974. Bar: N.Y. 1975. Assoc. Debevoise & Plimpton, 1974-79; atty., sr. atty., asst. gen. counsel Avon Products, Inc., N.Y.C., 1979-85, v.p. legal affairs, 1985-89, sr. v.p., gen. counsel, 1990-94, Gen. Mills, Inc., Mpls., 1994-99, sr. v.p. corp. affairs, gen. counsel, sec., 1999—. Bd. dirs. Jafra Cosmetics, Am. Arbitration Assn. Administrative and regulatory, Corporate, general. Office: Gen Mills Inc Number One Gen Mills Blvd Minneapolis MN 55426

MARSHALL, SUSAN, lawyer; b. Ellsworth, Kans., July 8, 1950; d. Daniel Benjamin and Elizabeth Jean (Bailey) M. BA, U. Kans., 1972; JD with honors, Washburn U., 1976. Bar: Kans. 1976. Summer legal intern Campbell, Erickson, Cottingham, Morgan & Gibson, Kansas City, Mo., 1975; rsch. asst., lobbyist Kans. County and Dist. Attys. Assn., Topeka, 1975-76; assoc. Metz & Metz, Lincoln, Kans., 1977-83; county atty. Lincoln County, Kans., 1980-85, 89-97; pvt practice Lincoln, 1983—. Atty. position Kans. Commn. on Civil Rights, Topeka, 1978-86. Pres. Lincoln Carnegie Libr., 1982-88; bd. dirs. Lincoln Housing Authority, 1998—. Mem. ABA, Kans. Bar Assn., Kans. County and Dist. Attys. Assn., Nat. Dist. Attys. Assn., Kans. Assn. County Commrs. (bd. dirs. 1995-97), Nat. History Soc. Republican. General practice, Probate (including wills, trusts), Taxation, general. Office: PO Box 389 117 S 4th St Lincoln KS 67455-2325

MARSHALL, THOMAS OLIVER, JR., lawyer; b. Americus, Ga., June 24, 1920; s. Thomas Oliver and Mattie Louise (Hunter) M.; m. Angie Ellen Fitts, Dec. 20, 1946; children: Ellen Irwin Marshall Beard, Anne Hunter Marshall Peagler, Mary Olivia Marshall Hodges. BS in Engring., U.S. Naval Acad., 1941; JD, U. Ga., 1948. Bar: Ga. 1947. Pvt. practice law, Americus, Ga., 1948-60; judge S.W. Judicial Circuit, Americus, 1960-74, Ga. Ct. Appeals, Atlanta, 1974-77; justice Ga. Supreme Ct., Atlanta, 1977-86, chief justice, 1986-89; pvt. practice Atlanta, 1989—. Chmn. bd. visitors U. Ga. Law Sch., 1970. Trustee Andrew Coll., So. Ga. Meth. Home for Aged; active ARC, 1948-60, United Givers Fund, 1948-54. Served with USN, World War II, Korean War. Decorated Bronze Star; named Young Man of Yr. Americus, 1953. Mem. ABA, Ga. Bar Assn. (bd. govs. 1958-60), Atlanta Bar Assn., State Bar Ga., Am. Judicature Soc., Nat. Jud. Coll., Jud. Coll. Ga., VFW, Am. Legion. Lodges: Kiwanis, Masons, Shriners. Methodist. General civil litigation, General practice. Home: 238 15th St NE Apt 3 Atlanta GA 30309-3594 Office: 1 Atlantic Ctr 1201 W Peachtree St NW Atlanta GA 30309-3449

MARSHALL, WILLIAM TAYLOR, lawyer; b. Dallas; s. Willis A. and Jane T. Marshall; m. Peggy Taylor, May 18, 1973; 1 child, Taylor. BSPA with honors, U. Ark., 1973, MBA with honors, 1975; JD with honors, U. Ark., Little Rock, 1981. Bar: Ark. 1981, U.S. Dist. Ct. (fed. dist.) 1982, U.S. Ct. Appeals (8th cir.) 1982, U.S. Supreme Ct. 1984; CPA, Ark. Fin. analyst Hosp. Affiliates Internat., Nashville, 1975-76, sr. fin. analyst, 1976-78; CFO Hosp. Affiliates Internat./Doctor's Hosp., Little Rock, 1978-81; assoc. House Holmes & Jewell, Little Rock, 1981-83, ptnr., 1983-85, Robinson, Staley, Marshall & Duke, Little Rock, 1985—. Lectr. in field. Contbr. articles to profl. jours. Mem. ABA, AICPAs, Ark. Bar Assn. (cert. tax specialist, health law sect. 1985—), Am. Health Lawyers Assn. Corporate, general, Health, Corporate taxation. Home: 1900 Beechwood St Little Rock AR 72207-2004 Office: Robinson Staley Marshall & Duke PA 400 W Capitol Ave Ste 2891 Little Rock AR 72201-3463 E-mail: bmarshall@rsmd.com.

MARSTERS, LADAWN MARIE, lawyer; b. Boise, Idaho, Nov. 14, 1965; d. Dean Russell Schouten and Donna Marie Richards; m. Gregory Alvan Marsters, Nov. 18, 1990 (div. Sept. 1993). BS, in Psychology, Boise State U., 1994; JD, U. Idaho, 1997. Bar: Idaho 1997. Assoc. Hamilton & Michaelson LLP, Nampa, Idaho, 1997—98; asst. city atty. Boise City Attys. Office, 1998—2000; sr. assoc. Cosho Humphrey Greenert Welsh P.A., Boise, 2000—. Youth ct. vol. YMCA, Boise, 1999—. Mem.: Idaho State Bar (bar exam grader 1998—, fee arbitrator 2000—, Annual Pro Bono award 2000). Democrat. Product liability, Personal injury (including property damage), Criminal. Office: Cosho Humphrey Greener & Welsh PA 815 W Washington Boise ID 83702

MARSTON, EDGAR JEAN, III, lawyer; b. Houston, July 5, 1939; s. Edgar Jr. and Jean (White) M.; m. Graeme Meyers, June 21, 1961; children: Christopher Graham, Jonathan Andrew. BA, Brown U., 1961; JD, U. Tex., 1964. Bar: Tex. 1964. Law clk. to presiding justice Supreme Ct. Tex., Austin, 1964-65; assoc. Baker & Botts, Houston, 1965-71; ptnr. Bracewell & Patterson, L.L.P., Houston, 1971-89, 96—, of counsel, 1990-96; exec. v.p., gen. counsel Southdown, Inc., Houston, 1987-95, also bd. dirs. Mem. ABA, Tex. Bar Assn., Tex. Bar Found., Houston Bar Assn., Houston Country Club, Coronado Club. Episcopalian. Avocations: hunting, fishing, philately, reading. Office: Bracewell & Patterson LLP 711 Louisiana St Ste 2900 Houston TX 77002-2781 E-mail: emarston@bracepatt.com.

MARTEL, JEAN-PIERRE CLAUDE MARCEL, lawyer; b. St. Max, Neurthe et Moselle, France, Jan. 6, 1944; s. Leon Martel and Lucienne Voirin; m. Delphine Deschamps. Grad., U. Paris, 1967. Registered: Paris Bar (lawyer) 1967. Lawyer, Paris, 1967; founding ptnr. Rambaud Martel, Paris, 1977—. Mem.: Cercle Foch, Club de Tir de Paris et de la Police Nat., Yacht Club France, Automobile Club France. Avocations: swimming, tennis, bicycling. Office: Rambaud Martel 25 Blvd de L Amiral Bruiz 75782 Paris France

MARTEL, JOHN SHELDON, lawyer, writer; b. Stockton, Calif., Jan. 1, 1931; s. Henry T. and Alice L. M.; m. Bonnie Martel; children: John Sheldon, Melissa Ann. BS, U. Calif.-Berkeley, 1956, JD, 1959. Bar: Calif. 1959. Dep. dist. atty., Alameda County, 1960-61; assoc. trial atty. firm Bronson, Bronson & McKinnon, San Francisco, 1961-64; ptnr. firm Farella, Braun & Martel, San Francisco, 1964—. Lectr., mem. adv. bd. Hastings Ctr. for Trial and Appellate Adv., 1983—. Author: (novels) Partners, 1988, Conflicts of Interest, 1994, The Alternate, 1999, Billy Strobe, 2001; author, editor legal pubs.; composer-writer popular songs; profl. musician. Pilot USAF, 1951-54. Winner Am. Song Festival awards, 1978-80, 82, 85, 87. Fellow Am. Coll. Trial Lawyers (state chmn. 1985-87, bd. regents 1993-98); mem. ABA (litigation, antitrust, tort and ins. sects.), Calif. Bar Assn., San Francisco Bar Assn. (former chair litigation sect.), Am. Bd. Trial Advocates (bd. dirs. 1991-93), Am. Fedn. Musicians, Phi Delta Phi, Kappa Sigma. Federal civil litigation, State civil litigation. Office: Farella Braun & Martel 235 Montgomery St Ste 3100 San Francisco CA 94104-2902

MARTENS, DON WALTER, lawyer; b. Darlington, Wis., Mar. 25, 1934; s. Walter W. and Geraldine A. (McWilliams) M.; children: Kim Martens Cooper, Diane Martens Reed. BS in Engring. with hons., U. Wis., 1957; JD with honors, George Washington U., 1963. Bar: Supreme Ct. Calif. 1964, U.S. Ct. Appeals (9th cir.) 1964, U.S. Dist. Ct. (no. and cen. dists.) Calif. 1964, U.S. Supreme Ct. 1973, U.S. Dist. Ct. (so. dist.) Calif. 1977, U.S. Ct. Appeals (fed. cir.) 1982, U.S. Dist. Ct. (ea. dist.) Calif. 1984. Examiner U.S. Patent and Trademark Office, Washington, 1960-63; patent lawyer Standard Oil of Calif., San Francisco, 1963-65; ptnr. Knobbe, Martens, Olson & Bear, Newport Beach, Calif., 1965—. Mem. adv. comm. Fed. Cir. Ct. Appeals, 1991-96, 2000—. Lt. USN, 1957-60. Mem. Orange County Bar Assn. (pres. 1975), Orange County Legal Aid Soc. (pres. 1969), Orange County Patent Law Assn. (pres. 1984), L.A. Patent Law Assn. (pres. 1989), State Bar Calif. (bd. govs. 1984-87, v.p. 1986-87), Am. Intellectual Property Law Assn. (pres. 1995-96), State Bar Intellectual Property Assn. (chmn. 1977), 9th Cir. Jud. Conf. (del. 1985-88, 1995-98), Nat. Inventors Hall of Fame Found. (pres. 1998-99), Nat. Coun. Intellectual Property Law Assn. (chmn. 1998-99), Big Canyon Country Club, Santa Ana Country Club, Rancho La Quinta Country Club. Republican. Roman Catholic. Federal civil litigation, Patent, Trademark and copyright. Office: 2040 Main St 14th Fl Irvine CA 92614 E-mail: dmartens@kmob.com.

MARTIN, ALICE HOWZE, prosecutor; b. Memphis, Apr. 25, 1956; BSN, Vanderbilt U., 1978; JD, U. Miss., 1981. Bar: Tenn. 1981, Miss. 1981, Ala. 1989. Asst. U.S. atty. U.S. Attys. Office , Memphis, 1983-89; ptnr. Harris Harris & Martin , Florence, Ala., 1992—94; dist. mcpl. judge City of Florence, Ala., 1993—97; judge Cir. Ct. State of Ala., 1997—99; U.S. Atty. No. Dist. Ala., 2001—. Avocations: travel, skeet shooting.

MARTIN, ARTHUR LEE, JR., lawyer; b. Montgomery, Ala., Jan. 13, 1949; s. Arthur Lee and Blanche (Bush) M.; children by previous marriage: Elizabeth Leah, Rachel Blanche; m. Diane S. Lamon, Mar. 23, 1993. BA cum laude, Vanderbilt U., 1971; JD, U. Chgo., 1974. Bar: U.S. Dist. Ct. (no. dist.) Ill. 1972, U.S. Ct. Appeals (7th cir.) 1972, Ill. 1975, Ala. 1979, U.S. Dist. Ct. (no. dist.) Ala. 1979, U.S. Ct. Appeals (5th cir.) 1979. Law clk. to sr. judge U.S. Ct. Appeals (5th cir.), Montgomery, 1974-75; assoc. D'Ancona & Pflaum, Chgo., 1975-78; ptnr. Haskell, Slaughter & Young, Birmingham, Ala., 1978-89, Dominick, Fletcher & Yeilding, Birmingham, 1989-95, Berkowitz, Lefkovitz, Isom & Kushner, Birmingham, 1995-98, Johnston & Conwell, Birmingham, 1998—2001, Miller Hamilton Sailer & Odom, Birmingham, 2001—. Gov. Ala. ctrl. dist. Civitan Internat., internat. judge adv. Mem. ABA, Nat. Assn. Bond Lawyers, Ala. State Bar, Birmingham Bar Assn., Am. Acad. Hosp. Lawyers, Downtown Dem. Club, Phi Delta Phi. Democrat. Methodist. Corporate, general, Native American, Property, real (including real estate development, water). Home: 2463 Chuchura Rd Birmingham AL 35244-3254 Office: Miller Hamilton Sailer & Odom 2501 20th Place S Birmingham AL 35223 E-mail: alm@johnstonconwell.com.

MARTIN, ARTHUR MEAD, lawyer; b. Cleveland Heights, Ohio, Mar. 29, 1942; s. Bernard P. and Winifred (Mead) M. AB, Princeton U., 1963; LLB, Harvard U., 1966. Bar: Ill. 1966, U.S. Dist. Ct. (no. dist.) Ill. 1969, U.S. Ct. Appeals (7th cir.) 1970, U.S. Supreme Ct. 1980, U.S. Ct. Appeals (fed. cir.) 2000. Instr. law U. Wis., Madison, 1966-68; assoc. Jenner & Block, Chgo., 1968-74, ptnr., 1975—. Co-trustee Dille Family Trust, 1982—; bd. dirs. Sleepeck Printing Co. Author: Historical and Practice Notes to the Illinois Civil Practice Act and Illinois Supreme Court Rules, 1968-88. Trustee 4th Presbyn. Ch., Chgo., sec. 1997-99, exec. com. 1997-99; bd. dirs. Stop Colon/Rectal Cancer Found., 1998—. Mem. ABA, Am. Law Inst., Ill. Bar Assn., Chgo. Bar Assn. (bd. editors 1972-86), Ill. State Hist. Soc. (adv. bd. 1998-99, bd. dirs. 1999—, exec. com. 1999—, fin. com. 1999—, treas. 2002—), Ill. Centennial Bus. Com., Lake Mich. Fedn. (bd. dirs. 1993-2002, exec. com. 1994-2002, treas. 1994-99, 2001-2002, sec. 1999-2001), Law Club Chgo., Legal Club Chgo. Commercial, contracts (including sales of goods; commercial financing), Corporate, general, Mergers and acquisitions. Office: Jenner & Block 1 IBM Plz Fl 4400 Chicago IL 60611-7603 E-mail: amartin@jenner.com.

MARTIN, CATHLEEN A. lawyer; b. St. Charles, Mo., Apr. 26, 1971; d. David and Bonnie Arnold; m. Jeffrey S. Martin, June 4, 1994. BA in Bus. Adminstrn., BA in Journalism, Truman State U., 1993; JD, U. Mo., 1996. Bar: Mo. 1996, U.S. Dist. Ct. (we. dist.) Mo. 1996, U.S. Ct. Appeals (8th cir.) 1996. Asst. atty. gen. Mo. Atty. Gen.'s Office, Jefferson City, 1996—97; shareholder Newman, Comley & Ruth P.C., Jefferson City, 1997—. Active Grace Evang. Free Ch., Jefferson City, 1996—; bd. dirs. Jefferson City Rape and Abuse Crisis Svc., 1999—, vice chair, 2000, chair, 2001; com. mem. Jefferson City Young Life, 1996—. Mem.: ABA, Jefferson City C. of C., Cole County Bar Assn., Soc. for Human Resource Mgrs., Mo. Bar Assn. (chair labor and employment law com. 2001—), Jefferson City Breakfast Rotary (club svc. chair 1997—98, cmty. svc. chair 1998—2001, sgt.-at-arms 2001—02, treas. 2002—03), Order of Barristers. Avocations: gardening, running, church activities. Administrative and regulatory, General civil litigation, Labor (including EEOC, Fair Labor Standards Act, labor-management relations, NLRB, OSHA). Office: Newman Comley & Ruth PC PO Box 537 Jefferson City MO 65102-0537

MARTIN, CLARENCE EUGENE, III, lawyer; b. Martinsburg, W.Va., Mar. 24, 1946; s. Clarence Eugene Jr. and Catherine Dubois (Silver) M.; m. Judith Anne Gray; 2 children: McKenna Gray Martin, Morgan Elizabeth Martin. AB in English, U. Ariz., 1968; JD, Cath. U., Washington, 1974. Bar: W. Va. 1974, D.C. 1974, Md. 1987, Pa., 1992, U.S. Dist. Ct. D.C. 1975, U.S. Ct. Appeals (D.C. cir.) 1975, U.S. Dist. Ct. (no. dist.) W.Va. 1976, U.S. Dist. Ct. (so. dist.) W.Va., U.S. Dist. Ct. Md. 1986, U.S. Ct. Appeals (4th cir.) 1976, U.S. Supreme Ct. 1979, U.S. Dist. Ct. (no. and ea. dists.) Pa. 1984, U.S. Ct. Appeals (3d cir.) 1984. Asst. couonsel U.S. Ho. Reps., Washington, 1974-75; trial atty. U.S. Dept. Justice, 1975-76; assoc. Martin & Seibert, L.C., Martinsburg, 1976-79, ptnr., 1979—. Bd. dirs. Mchts. & Farmers Bank, Martinsburg, W.Va. Legal Svcs. Plan. Author: (seminar) Impeachment of Witnesses, 1984; co-author ABA publ. Emerging Problems Under the Federal Rules of Evidence, 2d edit., Bad Faith Litigation, The Ethics of Surveillance. Mem. W.Va. Ho. Dels., Charleston, 1976-82; trustee Nat. Parks and Conservation Assn., Washington, 1980-85; bd. govs. Def. Trial Counsel W.Va., 1984-92; commr. Interstate Commn. Potomac River Basin, 1980-86, U.S. Commn. on Agrl. Workers, 1988-94; bd. advs. Shepherd Coll., 1989-93, 95-99, chmn. 1990-93, 95-97; mem. bd. visitors Cath. U. Sch. Law; mem. W.Va. Coun. Cmty. and Econ. Devel.; chmn. W.Va. Devel. Found., W.Va. Devel. Corp.; pres. Discover the Real W.Va. Found.; mem. Greater Ea. Panhandle Ch. Com., 1988—, chmn. 1988—; chmn. St. Joseph's Parish Coun., 1997-99; pres. Washington-Balt. chpt. Patrons of the Arts in the Vatican Mus. Recipient Am. Jurisprudence Scholastic Achievement award, 1972, Assn. Govt. Employees award, 1980. Fellow W.Va. Bar Found.; mem. ABA, W.Va. Bar Assn. (pres. 1990-91), W.Va. State Bar, D.C. Bar Assn., Berkeley County Bar Assn. (pres. 1984), Nat. Assn. R.R. Trial Counsel, Am. Legis. Exch. Coun., Am. Judicature Soc., Def. Rsch. Inst., D.C. Bar Assn., Md. Bar Assn., Pa. Bar Assn., Am. Bd. Trial Advocates (bd. dirs. 1986-94), Internat. Assn. Def. Counsel, Def. Trial Counsel of W.Va. (founding mem., bd. dirs. 1984-92), Md. Def. Trial Counsel, W.Va. Law Inst., Berkeley County Roundhouse Authority (chmn. 1999—), John Carroll Soc., KC, Univ. Club, Order of Malta. Commercial, contracts (including sales of goods; commercial financing), Corporate, general, Personal injury (including property damage). Home: Pendleton House 6393 Arden Nollville Rd Martinsburg WV 25401-8866 Office: Martin & Seibert LC PO Box 1286 Martinsburg WV 25402-1286 E-mail: cemartin@martinandseibert.com.

MARTIN, CONNIE RUTH, retired lawyer; b. Clovis, N.Mex., Sept. 9, 1955; d. Lynn Latimer and Marian Ruth (Pierce) M.; m. Daniel A. Patterson, Nov. 21, 1987; step-children: David Patterson, Dana Patterson. B in Univ. Studies, Ea. N.Mex. U., 1976, MEd, 1977; JD, U. Mo., Kansas City, 1981. Bar: N.Mex. 1981, U.S. Dist. Ct. N.Mex. 1981, Colo. 2002. Asst. dist. atty. State of N.Mex., Farmington, 1981-84; ptnr. Tansey, Rosebrough, Gerding & Strother, PC, Farmington, 1984-93; pvt. practice Connie R. Martin, P.C., Farmington, 1993-94; domestic violence commr. 11th Judicial Dist. Ct., State of N.Mex., 1993-94; with Jeffrey B. Diamond Law Firm, Carlsbad, N. Mex., 1994-96; assoc. Sager, Curran, Sturges and Tepper PC, Las Cruces, N. Mex., 1996-97, Holt & Babington PC, Las Cruces, 1997-2000; ret., 2000. Dep. med. investigator State of N.Mex., Farmington, 1981-84; instr. San Juan Coll., 1987, N.Mex. State U., 1995; spkr. N.Mex. Jud. Edn. Ctr., 1993-94; chair paralegal program adv. com., 1988, Adv Com., St Francis Clin., Presbyn. Med. Svs., 1994-96; bd. Bar Examiners State of N.Mex., 1989—, vice-chair, 1995-97, chair, 1997-99; asst. bar counsel Disciplinary Bd.; mem. profl. adv. com. Meml. Med. Ctr. Found., 1997-2000, trustee, 1997-2000; mem. So. N.Mex. Estate Planning Coun., 1997-2000; mem. character and fitness com. Nat. Conf. Bar Examiners, 2002—. Bd. dirs., exec. com. San Juan County Econ. Opportunity Coun., Farmington, 1982-83; bd. dirs. Four Corners Substance Abuse Coun., Farmington, 1984, N.Mex. Newspapers, Inc.; chmn. Cmty. Corrections-Intensive Supervision Panel, Farmington, 1987-88; jud. selection com. mem. San Juan County, 1991, Chavez County, 1995; nominating com. Supreme Ct./Ct of Appeals, 1991-96; treas. Ft. Morgan United Meth. Ch., 2001—, chmn. fin. com., 2002—. Recipient Distinguished Svcs. award for Outstanding Young Woman San Juan County Jaycees, 1984. Mem. N.Mex. Bar. Assn. (bd. dirs. elder law sect. 1993-96, peer rev. task force 1994-95, asst. to new lawyers com. 1986-87, local bar com. 1988, bd. dirs. young lawyers divsn. 1989-91, bd. dirs. real property probate and trust sect. 1994-97), San Juan County Bar Assn. (treas. 1985-87, v.p. 1987, pres. 1988), Farmington C. of C. (bd. dirs. 1991-93), Rocky Mountain Keehond Club, Northeastern Colo. Kennel Club (v.p. 2003—), Keeshond Club of Am. Methodist. Avocations: health, fitness, reading, dog show and therapy dog vol.. Probate (including wills, trusts), Property, real (including real estate development, water).

MARTIN, DAVID ALAN, law educator; b. Indpls., July 23, 1948; s. C. Wendell and Elizabeth Bowman (Meeker) M.; m. Cynthia Jo Lorman, June 13, 1970; children: Amy Lynn, Jeffrey David. BA, DePauw U., 1970; JD, Yale U., 1975. Bar: D.C. Law clk. to Hon. J. Skelly Wright U.S. Ct. Appeals (D.C. cir.), 1975-76; law clk. to Hon. Lewis F. Powell U.S. Supreme Ct., Washington, 1976-77; assoc. Rogovin, Stern & Huge, Washington, 1977-78; spl. asst. bur. human rights and humanitarian affairs U.S. State Dept.,

Washington, 1978-80; from asst. prof. to assoc. prof. U. Va. Sch. Law, Charlottesville, 1980-86, prof., 1986-91, Henry L. & Grace Doherty prof. law, 1991—2003, F. Palmer Weber Rsch. prof. civil liberties and human rights, 1992—95, 2000—03, Warner-Booker disting. prof. internat. law, 2003—. Cons. Adminstrv. Conf. U.S., Washington, 1988-89, 91-92, U.S. Dept. Justice, 1993-95; gen. counsel U.S. Immigration and Naturalization Svc., 1995-98. Author: Immigration: Process and Policy, 1985, 5th edit., 2003, Asylum Case Law Sourcebook, 1994, 4th edit., 2003, The Endless Quest: Helping America's Farm Workers, 1994; editor: The New Asylum Seekers, 1988, Immigration Admissions, 1998, Immigration Controls, 1998, Rights and Duties of Dual Nationals: Evolution and Prospects, 2002; contbr. articles to profl. jours. Nat. governing bd. Common Cause, Washington, 1972-75; elder Westminster Presbyn. Ch., Charlottesville, 1982-84, 89-92; bd. dirs. Internat. Rescue Com., 2000—. German Marshall Fund Rsch. fellow, Geneva, 1984-85. Mem. Am. Soc. Internat. Law (v.p. 2003—, Book award 1986), Internat. Law Assn. Democrat. Office: U Va Sch Law 580 Massie Rd Charlottesville VA 22903-1738 E-mail: dam3r@virginia.edu.

MARTIN, GARY DUNCAN, lawyer; b. Montgomery, Ala., June 9, 1954; s. Andrew Franklin Jr. and Mary Alice (Duncan) M.; children: Jessica Ruth, Jennifer Helen. BA, Okla. State U., 1976; JD, U. Okla., 1979. Bar: Okla. 1979, Tex. 2000, U.S. Dist. Ct. (we. dist.) Okla. 1980, U.S. Dist. Ct. (no. dist.) Okla. 1981, U.S. Ct. Appeals (10th cir.) 1983, U.S. Supreme Ct., 1984. Assoc. McKnight & Gasaway, Enid, Okla., 1979-81; ptnr. Mitchell & DeClerck, P.C., Enid, 1981-96; atty. in pvt. practice, 1996—2001; asst. county atty. Travis County, Tex., 2002—. Bd. dirs. Cimarron Sch., Inc., 1983-88, Leadership Okla., Inc., 1987-91, Enid Pub. Sch. Found., Inc., 1988—; pres. Downtown Enid, Inc., 1984-88, vice chmn. adminstrv. bd.; lay leader First United Meth. Ch., 1984-85; v.p. exec. com. Okla. Acad. for State Goals, 1989, bd. dirs., 1989-97; trustee Enid Higher Edn. Program, Okla., 1989-97; bd. dirs. United Way of Enid, 1989-91; various community activities; city commr. City of Enid, 1991-95; trustee Enid Mcpl. Authority, Enid Econ. Devel. Authority, Enid Pub. Higher Edn. Trust Authority; elder Presbyn. Ch. U.S.A., 1996; trustee Mission Presbytery. Mem. ABA, Okla. Bar Assn., State Bar Tex., Greater Enid C. of C. (bd. dirs. 1986-89), Rotary (bd. dirs. Enid club 1988-91). Republican. Avocations: travel, reading. Condemnation (eminent domain), Government contracts and claims, Land use and zoning (including planning). E-mail: gdmtexas@yahoo.com.

MARTIN, GARY WAYNE, lawyer; b. Cin., Feb. 14, 1946; s. Elmer DeForrest and Nellie May (Hughes) M.; m. Debra Lynn Goldsmith, June 25, 1982; children: Christopher, Jeremy, Joie, Casey. BA, Wilmington Coll., 1967; JD, U. Cin., 1974. Bar: Fla. 1974. Bd. dirs. Fowler White Gillen Boggs Villareal & Banker, Tampa, Fla., 1974—. Lt. USNR, 1967-71. Mem. Harbour Island Athletic Club. Republican. Presbyterian. Avocation: tennis. Office: Fowler White Gillen Boggs Villareal & Banker 501 E Kennedy Blvd Ste 1600 Tampa FL 33602-5240 E-mail: gmartin@fowlerwhite.com.

MARTIN, GEORGE J., JR., lawyer; b. Port Chester, N.Y., June 7, 1942; s. George J. and Eileen Ann (Buckley) M.; m. Joanne L. Frost, Aug. 21, 1965 (div. May 1986); children: Amy Anne, Ryan Frost; m. Anna Marie Cipriati, June 21, 1986; children: Marissa McCreay, Jill McCreay. BA, Georgetown U., 1964, JD, 1967. Bar: N.Y. 1969; conseil juridique, France, 1977-82. From assoc. to ptnr. Mudge Rose Guthrie Alexander & Ferdon, N.Y.C., 1967-95; ptnr. Coudert Bros., N.Y.C., 1995—. Mem. French Heritage Soc. (gen. counsel, dir.). Roman Catholic. Corporate, general, FERC practice, Finance. Home: 163 Congress St Brooklyn NY 11201-6103 Office: Coudert Bros 1114 Ave of The Americas New York NY 10036-7710 E-mail: george0607@nyc.rr.com., marting@coudert.com.

MARTIN, GREGORY KEITH, lawyer, mayor; b. Conway, S.C., Nov. 7, 1956; s. George Henry Martin and Julia Ann (Johnson) M. Land. BS in Fin. Mgmt., Clemson U., 1979; JD, U. S.C., 1983. Bar: S.C. 1983. Intern U.S. Senate, 1980; law clk. to presiding judge 15th Jud. Cir. Ct., Conway, 1983; assoc. Johnson & Martin, Conway, 1983-88, ptnr., 1988-93, Martin & Smith, Conway, 1993-98; mayor City of Conway, 1995—; pvt. practice, Conway, 1998—. Mem. Conway Planning Commn., 1986-89, chmn., 1989; bd. dirs. Conway-Main St. U.S.A., 1986-90, chmn., 1988; mem. Conway Bd. Appeals, 1987-89, Horry County Bd. Archtl. Rev., 1987-90; mem. Conway City Coun., 1991-94; pres., Horry County Hist. Soc., 1988, 90, mayor pro tem, 1994; mem. adv. bd. Pee Dee Heritage Ctr., 1988—. Mem. ABA, S.C. Bar Assn., Horry County Bar Assn., Sigma Nu, Phi Delta Phi. Methodist. Avocations: tennis, coin collecting. Corporate, general, Probate (including wills, trusts), Property, real (including real estate development, water). Home: 706 Elm St Conway SC 29526-4373 Office: PO Box 736 Conway SC 29528-0736

MARTIN, GUY, lawyer; b. Los Angeles, Jan. 22, 1911; s. I.G. and Mary Pearl (Howe) M.; m. Edith Kingdon Gould, Oct. 12, 1946; children— Guy III, Jason Gould, Christopher Kingdon, Edith Maria Theodosia Burr. AB, Occidental Coll., 1931; BA (1st class hons.), Oxford U., 1934, MA, 1944; LL.B., Yale, 1937. Bar: N.Y. 1938, D.C. 1947. Practiced with Donovan, Leisure, Newton & Lumbard, N.Y.C., 1938-41; gen. counsel All Am. Aviation, Inc., 1942, Am. Mexican Claims Commn., U.S. Dept. State, 1945-47; ptnr. Martin, Whitfield, Smith & Bebchick (and predecessors), Washington, 1952-80; counsel Martin and Smith (and predecessors), 1981-86; pres., vice chmn. bd., dep. chief exec. officer Internat. Bank, 1981-86; with Law Office of Saltzstein & Martin, 1988-99. Served with USN; sea duty 1942-45. Mem. ABA, Assn. of Bar of City of N.Y., Bar Assn. D.C, Phi Beta Kappa, Sigma Alpha Epsilon. Clubs: Yale, Brook, Knickerbocker (N.Y.C.); Metropolitan, City Tavern (Washington). Episcopalian. Home: 3300 O St NW Washington DC 20007-2813

MARTIN, HARRY CORPENING, lawyer, retired state supreme court justice; b. Lenoir, N.C., Jan. 13, 1920; s. Hal C. and Johnsie Harshaw (Nelson) M.; m. Nancy Robiou Dallam, Apr. 16, 1955; children: John, Matthew, Mary. AB, U. N.C., 1942; LLB, Harvard U., 1948; LLM, U. Va., 1982. Bar: N.C. 1948. Pvt. practice, Asheville, N.C., 1948-62; judge N.C. Superior Ct., Asheville, 1962-78, N.C. Ct. Appeals, Raleigh, 1978-82; justice N.C. Supreme Ct., 1982-92; ptnr. Martin & Martin, Attys., Hillsborough, N.C., 1992—. Adj. prof. U. N.C. Law Sch., 1983-92, Duke U., 1990-91, Dan K. Moore disting. vis. prof., U. N.C. Law Sch., 1992-94; sr. conf. atty. U.S. Ct. Appeals for 4th Cir., 1994-99; chief justice Supreme Ct. ea. bd. of Cherokee Indians, 2000—. With U.S. Army, 1942-45, South Pacific. Mem. U.S. Supreme Ct. Hist. Soc., N.C. Supreme Ct. Hist. Soc. (pres.). Democrat. Episcopalian. Education and schools. Home: 1 Hilltop Rd Asheville NC 28803-3017 Office: Cherokee Supreme Ct PO Box 455 Cherokee NC 28719 Fax: 828-497-5705. E-mail: judgemartin@charter.net.

MARTIN, HARRY S., III, law educator, law librarian; AB in History, Harvard U., 1965; JD, U. Minn., 1968; MLS, U. Pitts., 1971. Libr., prof. Harvard Law Sch., Cambridge, Mass., 1981—2002, Henry N. Ess II libr., prof., 2002—. Contbr. articles to profl. jours. Office: Harvard Law Sch Areeda 511 1563 Massachusetts Ave Cambridge MA 02138 Office Fax: 617-495-4449. Business E-Mail: martin@law.harvard.edu.*

MARTIN, HENRY ALAN, public defender; b. Nashville, Sept. 5, 1949; s. James Alvin and Mary Elizabeth (Long) M.; m. Gloria B. Ballard, May 9, 1975; children: Nathan Daniel, Anna Elizabeth. BA, Vanderbilt U., 1971, JD, 1974. Bar: Tenn. 1975, U.S. Dist. Ct. (mid. dist.) Tenn. 1975, U.S. Ct. Appeals (6th cir.) 1976, U.S. Supreme Ct. 1979. Pvt. practice, Nashville, 1975-76; ptnr. Haile & Martin, P.A., Nashville, 1976-82; assoc. firm Barrett & Ray, P.C., Nashville, 1982-85; fed. pub. defender U.S. Dist. Ct. (mid. dist.) Tenn., Nashville, 1985—. Mem. adv. com. on rules criminal procedure U.S. Judicial Conf., 1994-99. CO-author, co-editor trial manual, Tools for the Ultimate Trial, 1985, 2d edit., 1988; contbr. articles to profl. jours. Del., Witness for Peace, Managua, Nicaragua, 1987. Mem. ABA (coun. criminal justice sect. 1993-96), NACDL, Assn. Fed. Defenders (pres. 1995-98), Nashville Bar Assn., Napier Looby Bar Assn., Tenn. Assn. Criminal Def. Lawyers (bd. dirs. 1978-94, pres. 1984-85, Pres.'s award 1984). Democrat. Avocations: jogging, swimming. Home: 3802 Whitland Ave Nashville TN 37205-2432 Office: Fed Pub Defender 810 Broadway Ste 200 Nashville TN 37203-3861 E-mail: henry_martin@fd.org.

MARTIN, JAMES WILLIAM, lawyer; b. Turlock, Calif., Dec. 20, 1949; Student, Ga. Inst. Tech., 1967-69; BS, Stetson U., 1971, JD, 1974. Bar: Fla. 1974, U.S. Dist. Ct. (mid. dist.) Fla. 1974, U.S. Ct. Appeals (5th cir.) 1974, U.S. Ct. Appeals (11th cir.) 1987, U.S. Supreme Ct. 1978. Ptnr. Brickley & Martin, St. Petersburg, Fla., 1974-79; pres. James W. Martin, P.A., St. Petersburg, 1979—. Presenter in field. Author: West's Florida Corporation System, 1984, West's Legal Forms, 3d edit., Non-Profit Corporations, 1991, 92, 93, 94, 96, 97, 98, 99, 2000, 01, 02, 03, West's Florida Legal Forms, Business Organizations, Real Estate, Specialized Forms, 1990, 91, 92, 93, 94, 95; supplement editor Fla. Jur. Forms, Legal and Bus., 1998, 99; contbr. articles to profl. jours. including Word Perfect mag., ALI-ABA Practical Lawyer, Fla. Bar News, Fla. Bar Jour. City councilman, St. Petersburg, 1982-83; active Leadership St. Petersburg; active charter class Leadership Tampa Bay; founding trustee, sec., counsel Salvador Dali Mus., 1980-2003; founding dir., sec., counsel Fla. Internat. Mus., 1992-94. Recipient Outstanding Young Man award Jaycees, 1982, Outstanding Contbn. to City award St. Petersburg C. of C., 1980. Mem.: St. Petersburg C. of C. (arts task force 1987, gen. counsel 1991—92, chmn. urban solutions com. 1992—93, chmn. downtown com. 1993—94, chmn. parking com.), St. Petersburg Bar Assn. (chair probate sect. 1999—2000, chair tech. sect. 2003—), Fla. Bar (chmn. coordinating com. tech. 1992—93, probate rules com. 1994—2000), Fla. Trust for Historic Preservation (bd. dirs. 2002—03), Pinellas County Arts Coun. (councilman 1997—2001), Pres. Club (hon. bd. dirs. 1985—91, founder). Corporate, general, Probate (including wills, trusts), Property, real (including real estate development, water). Fax: 727-823-3479. E-mail: jim@jamesmartinpa.com.

MARTIN, JAY GRIFFITH, lawyer; b. Washington, Oct. 13, 1951; s. Drexel Reese and Joyce (Towne) M.; 1 child, Trevor. BBA, So. Meth. U., 1973, MPA, JD, So. Meth. U., 1976. Bar: Tex., D.C., U.S. Ct. Appeals (5th cir.), U.S. Dist. Ct. (so. dist.) Tex., U.S. Dist. Ct. D.C., U.S. Supreme Ct. Counsel Pennzoil Co., Houston, 1976-78, sr. counsel, 1978-81; divsn. counsel The Superior Oil Co., Houston, 1981-85; sr. counsel Mobil Natural Gas, Houston, 1985-87, gen. counsel, 1987-91; asst. gen. counsel Mobil Oil Corp., Fairfax, Va., 1991-96; ptnr. Andrews & Kurth LLP, Washington, 1996-2000, Phelps Dunbar LLP, Houston, 2000—01, Winstead Sechrest & Minick, Houston, 2001—. Mem. sr. adv. bd. Bus. Laws Inc., Chesterland, Ohio, 1997—; mem. adv. bd. Inst. Transnat. Arbitration, Southwestern Legal Found., 1996—. Author: (books) Environmental Management Systems, 1998, Dispute Resolution for Oil and Gas Practitioners, 2000, Environmental Dispute Resolution, 2002; contbr. articles; mem. adv. bd.: jour. Natural Gas Contracts, 1991—. Chmn. fundraising com. So. Meth. U., Washington, 1996—97, mem. dean's adv. coun. Sch. Law, 1995—; bd. trustees Rocky Mountain Mineral Law Found. Named one of World's Outstanding Energy Lawyers, Euromoney, 1997, 1999, 2001. Fellow: State Bar Coll. of Tex., Tex. Bar Found., State Bar Tex. (life; adv. bd. 1985—, chmn. corp. counsel sect. 1990—91, coun. oil and gas); mem.: Fed. Bar Assn. (chmn. 1986—87, bd. dirs. 1990—92, antitrust sect. 1991—98, chmn. internat. energy com. 1997—), Delta Theta Phi, Rocky Mountain Law Inst. (trustee 1991—), Am. Soc. Internat. Law, Assn. Internat. Petroleum Negotiators, Houston Bar Assn., ABA (litig. sect. rep. on ABA coord. com. on energy law 1991—97, sect. pub. utility law 1991—, chmn. natural resources, energy and environ law internat. energy com. 1996—98, exec. coun., budget chmn. sect. on environment, energy and law 1996—, liaison to Fed. Energy Bar Assn. 1997—, ad hoc mem. of com. 1997—, sr. liaison oversight responsibility for all energy and resource coms. 1998—, vice chmn. sect. on environment, energy and resources' natural gas and), Energy Bar Assn. (chmn. antitrust sect. 1986—87, chmn. internat. energy com. 1998—99, chmn. internat. com.), Internat. Bar Assn. (sect. energy and natural resources 1994—), D.C. Bar Assn. (internat.sect.), Tex. Bar Assn. (dir. Tex.). Avocations: history, current events and politics, tennis, golf, jogging. FERC practice, Oil, gas, and mineral, Environmental. Home: 3133 Buffalo Speedway Apt 7207 Houston TX 77098-1828 Office: Winstead Sechrest & Minick 910 Travis St Ste 2400 Houston TX 77002 E-mail: jmartin@winstead.com.

MARTIN, JOHN CHARLES, judge; b. Durham, N.C., Nov. 9, 1943; s. Chester Barton and Mary Blackwell (Pridgen) M.; m. Margaret Rand; children: Lauren Blackwell, Sarah Conant, Mary Susan; step-children: Louise Short, Carl (Trip) Short. BA, Wake Forest U., 1965, JD, 1967; postgrad., Nat. Judicial Coll., Reno, 1979; cert. justice execs. program, U. N.C. Bar: N.C. 1967, U.S. Dist. Ct. (mid. dist.) N.C. 1967, U.S. Dist. Ct. (ea. dist.) N.C. 1972, U.S. Dist. Ct. (we. dist.) N.C. 1975, U.S. Ct. Appeals (4th cir.) 1976, U.S. Supreme Ct. 2002. Assoc. Haywood, Denny & Miller, Durham, N.C., 1969-72, ptnr., 1973-77; resident judge Superior Ct. 14th Jud. Dist. N.C., Durham, 1977-84; judge N.C. Ct. Appeals, Raleigh, 1985-88, 93—; ptrn. Maxwell & Hutson, P.A., Durham, 1988-92; arbitrator U.S. Dist. Ct. (mid. dist.) N.C., 1988-92. Study com. rules of evidence and comparative negligence N.C. Legis. Research Commn., 1980; mem. N.C. Pattern Jury Instrn. drafting com., 1978-84, N.C. Trial Judge's Bench Book Drafting Com., 1984-87, N.C. News Media-Adminstrn. of Justice Coun., 1987, Appellate Judges' Conf., state/fed. Jud. Coun. N.C., 1985-87, chmn., 1987; bd. visitors Wake Forest U. Sch. Law, 1986—; mem. alumni coun. Wake Forest U., 1993-96, 2001—; mem. N.C. State Jud. Edn. Study Com., 2000—; chmn. N.C. Jud. Stds. Commn., 2001—. Mem. Durham City Coun., 1975—77, chair pub. works com.; panel of arbitrators Duke U. Pvt. Adjudication Ctr., 1988—92. With Mil. Police Corps USAR, 1967—69. Recipient Disting. Svc. award Durham Jaycees, 1976. Mem. ABA, N.C. Bar Assn. (chmn. adminstrn. of justice study com. 1990-92, bench, bar and law sch. com. 1987-91, jud. campaign oversight com. 1990, Lit. Sect. Coun. 1991-94, conv. planning com. 1995—, adminstrn. justice task force 1996-98, appellate rules study com. 1999-2001, strategic planning/emergency trends com. 2002—, v.p. 1997-98), Durham County Bar Assn. (bd. dirs. 1991-92), Wake County Bar Assn., 10th Jud. Dist. Bar Assn., N.C. Jud. Conf. (v.p. 1999-2000), Hope Valley Country Club, Appalachian State U. Parents Assn. (bd. dirs. 1997-2001), Phi Delta Phi. Democrat. Methodist. Office: PO Box 888 Raleigh NC 27602-0888 E-mail: mnj@coa.state.nc.us.

MARTIN, JOHN RANDOLPH, judge; b. Lexington, Ky., May 26, 1948; s. Harry and Geraldine (Gray) M.; m. Jacqueline Lauren Snyder, Apr. 24, 1976; 1 child, Lauren Elizabeth. BA, U. Okla., 1973, MA, 1976, JD, 1980. Bar: Okla. 1981, U.S. Ct. Mil. Appeals 1981, U.S. Dist. Ct. (we. dist.) Okla. 1982, S.C. 1983, U.S. Ct. Appeals (10th cir.) 1983, U.S. Dist. Ct. S.C. 1984, U.S. Ct. Appeals (4th cir.) 1984, U.S. Supreme Ct. 1995. Assoc. Finkel, Georgaklis et al, Columbia, S.C., 1984-86; ptnr. Mumford, Wishart & Martin, North Myrtle Beach, S.C., 1986-87, Gertz, Kastanes, Moore & Martin, North Myrtle Beach, S.C., 1987-91; with Office of Hearings and Appeals, Social Security Adminstrn., Houston, 1991—. Lt. col. U.S. Army, 1967-70, Vietnam, with Res. 1975-78, 84-97, Desert Storm, JAGC, 1981-84. Mem. NRA, Masons, Shriners, Elks, Phi Delta Phi, Pi Kappa Alpha. Republican. Episcopalian. Avocations: singing, shooting. Office: Office of Hearing and Appeals 6800 West Loop S Ste 300 Bellaire TX 77401-4522

MARTIN, JOHN SHERWOOD, JR., federal judge; b. Bklyn., May 31, 1935; BA, Manhattan Coll., 1957; LLB, Columbia U., 1961. Bar: N.Y. 1961, U.S. Dist. Ct. (so. dist.) N.Y. 1963, U.S. Supreme Ct. 1966, U.S. Ct. Appeals (2d cir.) 1983. Law clk. to Hon. Leonard P. Moore U.S. Ct. Appeals (2d cir.), 1961-62; asst. U.S. atty. U.S. Dist. Ct. (so. dist.) N.Y., 1962-66; ptnr. Johnson, Hekker & Martin, Nyack, N.Y., 1966-67; asst. to solicitor gen., 1967-69; sole practitioner, 1969-72; ptnr. Martin, Obermaier & Morvillo, 1972-79, Schulte, Roth & Zabel, 1979-80; U.S. atty. U.S. Dist. Ct. for So. Dist. N.Y., N.Y.C., 1980-83; ptnr. Schulte, Roth & Zabel, 1983-90; judge U.S. Dist. Ct. for So. Dist. N.Y., N.Y.C., 1990—. Cons. Nat. Commn. Law Enforcement and the Adminstrn. of Criminal Justice, 1966-67; counsel to commn. to investigate disturbances Columbia U., 1968. Fellow Am. Coll. Trial Lawyers; mem. Assn. Bar City N.Y. Office: US Dist Ct So Dist NY 500 Pearl St New York NY 10007-1316

MARTIN, JOHN WILLIAM, JR., retired lawyer, automotive industry executive; b. Evergreen Park, Ill., Sept. 1, 1936; s. John William and Frances (Hayes) M.; m. Joanne Cross, July 2, 1966; children: Amanda Hayes, Bartholomew McGuire. AB in History, DePaul U., 1958, JD, 1961. Bar: Ill. 1961, D.C. 1962, N.Y. 1964, Mich. 1970. Antitrust trial atty. Dept. Justice, Washington, 1961-62; assoc. Donovan, Leisure, Newton & Irvine, N.Y.C., 1962-70; sr. atty. Ford Motor Co., Dearborn, Mich., 1970-72, assoc. counsel, 1972-74, counsel, 1974-76, asst. gen. counsel, 1976-77, assoc. gen. counsel, 1977-89, v.p., gen. counsel, 1989-99; ret., 1999. Contbr. articles to profl. jours. Trustee DePaul U., 1998—; bd. dirs. Ctr. Social Gerontology, Inc., Nat. Women's Law Ctr., Friends of Legal Svcs. Corp. Mem.: Am. Law Inst., Assn. Gen. Counsel, Little Traverse Yacht Club. Republican. Roman Catholic. E-mail: jwmartinjrsail@netscape.net.

MARTIN, LAWRENCE M. lawyer; b. N.Y.C., Aug. 23, 1950; BA, Yale U., 1973, JD, 1981; MA, U. Chgo., 1978. Bar: N.Y. 1982, U.S. Dist. Ct. (so. and ea. dist.) N.Y. 1982, U.S. Ct. Appeals (2d. cir.) 1985. Assoc. Debevoise & Plimpton, N.Y.C., 1981-87, Shereff Friedman Hoffman & Goodman, N.Y.C., 1987-90; asst. chief, affirmative litigation divsn. N.Y.C. Law Dept., 1990-97, spl. ins. counsel, 1997—. Mem. Assn. of the Bar of the City of N.Y. (ins. com. 1995-98). Office: New York City Law Dept 100 Church St New York NY 10007-2601 E-mail: lmartin@law.nyc.gov.

MARTIN, MALCOLM ELLIOT, lawyer; b. Buffalo, Dec. 11, 1935; s. Carl Edward and Pearl Maude (Elliot) M.; m. Judith Hill Harley, June 27, 1964; children; Jennifer, Elizabeth, Christina, Katherine. AB, U. Mich., Ann Arbor, 1958, JD, 1962. Bar: N.Y. 1963, U.S. Ct. Appeals (2d cir.) 1966, U.S. Supreme Ct. 1967. Assoc. Chadbourne Parke Whiteside & Wolff (now Chadbourne & Parke LLP), N.Y.C., 1962-73, ptnr., 1974—. Dir., sec. Carl and Dorothy Bennett Found., Inc.; sec., counsel Copper Devel. Assn., Inc. With U.S. Army, 1958-60. Mem. ABA, N.Y. State Bar Assn., Assn. Bar City of N.Y., St. Andrew's Soc. of N.Y., Met. Opera Guild, Oratamin Club (Blauvelt, N.Y.), Nyack Boat Club, Rockefeller Ctr. Club, Copper Club (N.Y.C.). Estate planning, Probate (including wills, trusts), Estate taxation. Home: 74 S Highland Ave Nyack NY 10960-3609 Office: Chadbourne & Parke LLP 30 Rockefeller Plz Fl 31 New York NY 10112-0129 E-mail: mmartin@chadbourne.com.

MARTIN, MARK D. state supreme court justice; b. Apr. 29, 1963; s. M. Dean and Ann M. BS summa cum laude, Western Carolina U., 1985; JD (hon.) , U. N.C., 1988; grad., Nat. Jud. Coll., 1993; LLM, U. Va., 1998; attended, Ohio U., Dayton, 1981. Bar: N.C., U.S. Dist. Ct. (ea. and mid. dists.); N.C. U.S. Ct. Appeals (4th cir.); U.S. Supreme Ct. Law clk. to Hon. Clyde H. Hamilton U.S. Dist. Ct., Columbia, SC, 1988-90; pvt. practice McNair Law Firm, Raleigh, NC, 1990-91; legal counsel to gov. Office of Gov., Raleigh, NC, 1991-92; superior ct. judge Jud. Dist. 3A, Greenville, NC, 1992-94; judge N.C. Ct. Appeals, 1994-99; assoc. justice N.C. Supreme Ct., 1999—. Mem. N.C. Dept. Correction Master Plan Adv. Com., 1992; mem. N.C. Coun. for Women, 1992; legis. and law reform com. Conf. Superior Ct. Judges, 1993-94; co-chair legis liason com. N.C. Jud. Conf., 1995-97; mem. computer com. N.C. Appellate Ct., 1995—; sec. N.C. Jud. Conf., 1997-99; adj. prof. law U. N.C., Chapel Hill; adj. faculty N.C. Ctrl. U. Sch. Law, 2000-2002. Editor-in-chief: Jour Internat. Law and Comml. Regulation. Office coord., United Way Ann. Combined Campaign, 1991, 92. Recipient, Order of Long Leaf Pine, 1992, Disting. Alumnus award We. Carolina U., 1995, Svc. Award City of Raleigh Cmty. Svc. Dept.; Lloyd C. Balfour Fellow, N.C. Inst. Polit. Leadership Fellow, 1992, Coun. of State Govt. Toll Fellow, 2001. Mem., ABA (jud. adminstrv. divsn., coalition for justice com.); N.C. Bar Assn. (minorities in profession com. 1995-2001, multidisciplinary practice task force 1999-01, litigation sect. coun. 2000-, v.p. 2000-01, strategic planning emerging trends com. 2001-, litigation sect. coun. 2000-); N.C. Assn. Black Lawyers, N.C. Coun. for Women, Wake County Bar Assn.; selected for inclusion, 2000, Outstanding Intellectuals of the Twenty First Century, 2d edit., Internat. Biog. Ctr. Cambridge, Eng., UNC Law Davis Soc.; Mortar Board, Carolina Law Alumni Assn. (bd. dirs.), Internat. Hon. Soc., Alpha Lambda Delta, Phi Kappa Phi, Pi Gamma Mu, Omicron Delta Epsilon, Phi Alpha Delta, Delta Sigma Phi (scholar 1986), Beta Gamma Sigma (hon.). Office: North Carolina Supreme Court PO Box 2170 Raleigh NC 27602

MARTIN, MICHAEL DAVID, lawyer; b. Lakeland, Fla., Jan. 4, 1944; s. E. Snow and Mary Y. (Yelvington) M.; m. Joy Lynn Jackson; children: Michael David, Mallory Thomas, Katherine Cecelia, Rachel Lynn. BA, U. of South, 1964; JD, U. Fla., 1967. Bar: Fla. 1968, U.S. Dist. Ct. Fla. 1968, U.S. Ct. Appeals (5th cir.) 1975, U.S. Supreme Ct. 1974, U.S. Ct. Appeals (11th cir.) 1982. Mem. Martin & Martin, Lakeland, Fla., 1968— ; lectr. on estate planning and trial practice, pub. seminars, 1974-83. Bd. dirs. Boys Clubs of Lakeland, 1972-73; mem. Tampa Bay area Com. on Fgn. Relations; pres. Lakeland Spl. Events Inc., 1982-85; trustee John Marshall House. Named Outstanding Young Man of Yr., Lakeland Jaycees, 1969. Mem. ABA, Fla. Bar, Acad. Fla. Trial Lawyers, Assn. Trial Lawyers Am., Am. Judicature Soc., Polk County Trial Lawyers Assn. (pres. 1976-77), Lakeland C. of C. (v.p. 1980, pres. 1982, chmn. bd. 1983—), Polk County Am. Inns of Ct. (master). Clubs: Rotary (dir. club 1972-73), Lakeland Yacht and Country (pres. 1978-79). State civil litigation, Environmental, Estate planning. Office: 200 Lake Morton Dr Ste 202 Lakeland FL 33801-5318

MARTIN, MICHAEL KEITH, lawyer; b. Portland, Maine, Nov. 6, 1957; s. Rupert Keith and Beverly Jo Martin; m. Celeste J. Dougherty, Feb. 4, 1995; children: Mikayla Jean, Cole Dougherty. BA magna cum laude, U. So. Maine, 1985; JD cum laude, U. Maine, 1989. Bar: Maine 1989, U.S. Dist. Ct. Maine 1989. Asst. mgr. A&M Inc., Portland, Maine, 1976-79, gen. mgr., 1980-86; dist. atty. intern State of Maine, Biddeford, 1988; assoc. Petruccelli & Martin, Portland, 1989-95, ptnr., 1995—. Aid to Congressman David Emery, Washington, 1979-80. MEm. ABA, ATLA, Maine State Bar Assn. General civil litigation, Commercial, contracts (including sales of goods; commercial financing), Personal injury (including property damage). Home: 232 Foreside Rd Cumberland Foreside ME 04110-1117 Office: Petruccelli Martin & Haddow LLP 50 Monument Sq Portland ME 04101-4039

MARTIN, PAUL EDWARD, lawyer; b. Atchison, Kans., Feb. 5, 1928; s. Harres Crawford and Thelma Fay (Wilson) M.; m. Betty Lou Crawford, Aug. 28, 1954; children: Cherry Gayle Martin Luna, Paul Alexander, Mary Lou Martin Brieger. BBA, Baylor U., 1955, LLB, JD, 1956; LLM, Harvard U., 1957. Bar: Tex. 1956, Pa. 1958; cert. in estate planning and probate law Tex. Bd. Legal Specialization. Assoc. Ballard, Spahr, Andrews & Ingersoll, Phila., 1957-59; ptnr. Fulbright & Jaworski, Houston, 1959-77, Chamberlain, Hardlicka, White, Williams & Martin, Houston, 1977—2002, shareholder. Former instr. estate planning U. Houston. Co-author: How To Live and Die with Texas Probate, 1968, 7th edit., 1995. Pres. devel. coun. Baylor U., Waco, Tex., 1973-74; past chmn. bd. deacons West Meml. Bapt. Ch., Houston; past trustee fgn. missions bd. So. Bapt. Conv.; past trustee Baylor U., Meml. Hosp. Sys., Houston. Lt. comdr. USN, 1947-53, Korea. Fellow Am. Coll. Trust and Estate Counsel; mem. State Bar Tex., Houston Bar Assn., Houston Estate and Fin. Forum (pres. 1965-66), Houston Bus. and

Estate Planning Coun. Republican. Estate planning, Probate (including wills, trusts), Estate taxation. Home: 126 Lakeside Dr Montgomery TX 77356 Office: Chamberlin Hrdlicka Et Al 1200 Smith St Ste 1400 Houston TX 77002-4401 Fax: (713) 658-2553. E-mail: paul.martin@chamberlainlaw.com.

MARTIN, PHILLIP HAMMOND, lawyer; b. Tucson, Jan. 4, 1940; s. William P. and Harriet (Hammond) M.; m. Sandra S. Chandler, June 17, 1961 (div. Mar. 1989); children: Lisa, Craig, Wade, Ryan; m. Erika Zetty, May 9, 1990. BA, U. Minn., 1961, JD, 1964. Bar: Minn. 1964, U.S. Tax Ct. 1967, U.S. Dist. Ct. Minn. 1968, U.S. Ct. Appeals (8th cir.) 1973, U.S. Supreme Ct. 1981, U.S. Claims Ct. 1983, U.S. Ct. Appeals (fed. cir.) 1988, U.S. Ct. Appeals (7th cir.) 1989. Assoc. Dorsey & Whitney, Mpls., 1964-69, ptnr., 1970—. Mergers and acquisitions, Estate taxation, Taxation, general. Home: 487 Portland Ave Saint Paul MN 55102-2216 Office: Dorsey & Whitney LLP Ste 1500 50 S 6th St Minneapolis MN 55402-1498 E-mail: martin.phil@dorseylaw.com.

MARTIN, QUINN WILLIAM, lawyer; b. Fond du Lac, Wis., Mar. 12, 1948; s. Quinn W. and Marcia E. Martin; m. Jane E. ; children: Quinn W., William J. BSME, Purdue U., 1969; postgrad., U. Santa Clara, 1969-70; JD, U. Mich., 1973. Bar: Wis. 1973, U.S. Dist. Ct. (ea. dist.) Wis. 1973, U.S. Ct. Appeals (7th cir.) 1973. Sales support mgr. Hewlett-Packard, Palo Alto, Calif., 1969-70; assoc. Quarles & Brady, Milw., 1973-80, ptnr., 1980—. Bd. dirs. Associated Bank Milw., U-Line Corp., Gen. Timber and Land, Inc., Fond du Lac. Chmn. Gov. McCallum Trans Com., Wis., U. Mich. Law Sch. Fund; bd. dirs. Milw. Zool. Soc., Found. for Wildlife Conservation. Mem. ABA, Wis. Bar Assn., Milw. Club, Ozaukee Country Club, Chaine des Rottiseurs, Delta Upsilon (sec.), Milw. Club, Rotary. Antitrust, Commercial, contracts (including sales of goods; commercial financing), Corporate, general. Office: Quarles & Brady 411 E Wisconsin Ave Ste 2550 Milwaukee WI 53202-4497

MARTIN, RICHARD KELLEY, lawyer; b. Tulsa, June 30, 1952; s. Richard Loye and Maxine (Kelley) M.; m. Reba Lawson, June 12, 1993; children from previous marriage: R. Kyle, Andrew J. BA, Westminster Coll., 1974; JD, So. Meth. U., 1977. Bar: Tex. 1977, U.S. Tax Ct. 1979. Ptnr. Akin, Gump, Strauss, Hauer & Feld, LLP, Dallas, 1977-95, Haynes and Boone LLP, Dallas, 1995—. Bd. dirs. Goodwill Industries, Dallas, 1986-2000, v.p., 1986-91; bd. dirs. Greater Dallas Youth Orchs., 1987-90; bd. dirs., v.p., pres. Big Bros. and Sisters Met. Dallas, 1988-91; bd. dirs. Tejas coun. Girl Scouts U.S., 1997-2001. Mem. Tex. Bar Assn., Salesmanship Club Dallas. Republican. Methodist. Commercial, contracts (including sales of goods; commercial financing), Property, real (including real estate development, water). Office: Haynes and Boone LLP 1505 N Plano Rd Ste 4000 Richardson TX 75082-4101 E-mail: rick.martin@haynesboone.com.

MARTIN, ROBERT DALE, lawyer; b. Canton, Ohio, Oct. 1, 1937; s. Charles Leroy and Edith Ruby (Turnbull) M.; m. Carla Jean Kibler, Dec. 27, 1966; 1 child, Kendall Dalene. BA, Ohio U., 1960; JD, U. Akron, 1969, M in Taxation, 1979; MBA, Ashland U., 1995; postgrad., Kent State U., 1998. Bar: Ohio 1969, U.S. Dist. Ct. (no. dist.) 1984, U.S. Ct. Appeals (6th cir.) 1984. Pers. adminstr. Hoover Co., North Canton, Ohio, 1966-67; atty. Allmon and Benson, Carrollton, Ohio, 1967-69; legal staff asst. Republic Steel Corp., Canton, 1969-71, indsl. rels. counsel, 1971-73, supr. labor rels., 1973-78, asst. supt. indsl. rels., 1978-85; mgr. human resources Republic Engineered Steel Corp., Canton, 1985-91; gen. counsel, dir. adminstrn. Office of Summit County Engr., Akron, Ohio, 1991-95; adminstr. bus. and human svcs. Ohio Dept. Transp., New Philadelphia, Ohio, 1995—. Adj. prof. bus. law Ashland (Ohio) U., 1988; gen. counsel mgmt. consulting Labor Rels. Assocs., Dayton, Ohio, 1991-93; gen. counsel human resource consulting Human Resources Assocs., Dayton, 1993-95. Sgt. U.S. Army, 1960. Mem. Ohio State Bar Assn. (gen. sect. 1970-97, labor/employment law sect. 1995-99, probate/trust sect. 1996-99, corp. law 1996-99), Nat. Assn. Cert. Govt. Fin. Mgmt. Avocations: walking, fishing, reading, fitness. Home and Office: 850 Mcdaniel Ave Minerva OH 44657-1240 Fax: (330) 868-6161.

MARTIN, ROBERT DAVID, judge, educator; b. Iowa City, Oct. 7, 1944; s. Murray and G'Ann (Holmgren) M.; m. Ruth A. Haberman, Aug. 21, 1966; children: Jacob, Matthew, David. AB, Cornell Coll., Mt. Vernon, Iowa, 1966; JD, U. Chgo., 1969. Bar: Wis. 1969, U.S. Dist. Ct. (we. dist.) Wis. 1969, U.S. Dist. Ct. (ea. dist.) Wis. 1974, U.S. Supreme Ct. 1973. Assoc. Ross & Stevens, S.C., Madison, Wis., 1969-72, ptnr., 1973-78; chief judge U.S. Bankruptcy Ct. We. Dist. Wis., 1978—. Instr. gen. practice course U. Wis. Law Sch., 1974, 76, 77, 80, lectr. debtor/creditor course, 1981-82, 83, 85, 87, 2001, farm credit seminar, 1985, advanced bankruptcy problems, 1989, 91, 96; co-chmn. faculty Am. Law Inst.-ABA Fin. and Bus. Planning for Agr., Stanford U., 1979; faculty mem. Fed. Jud. Ctr. Schs. for New Bankruptcy Judges, 1985-96; chmn. Ann. Continuing Legal Edn. Wis. Debtor Creditor Conf., 1981—. Author: Bankruptcy: Annotated Forms, 1989; co-author: Secured Transactions Handbook for Wisconsin Lawyers and Lenders, Bankruptcy-Text Statutes Rules and Forms, 1992, Ginsberg and Martin on Bankruptcy, 4th edit., 1996. Chmn., bd. dirs., mem. exec. com. Luth. Social Svc. Wis. and Upper Mich.; bd. dirs., mem. exec. com. Turnaround Mgmt. Assn., 1997—. Mem. Wis. State Bar, Am. Coll. Bankruptcy, Am. Judicature Soc., Nat. Conf. Bankruptcy Judges (bd. govs. 1989-91, sec. 1993-94, v.p. 1994-95, pres. 1995-96), Nat. Bankruptcy Conf. Office: 120 N Henry Rm 340 PO Box 548 Madison WI 53701-0548

MARTIN, ROBERT JAMES, lawyer; b. York, Pa. s. Jane Ann (Denham) Cornish; 1 child, Danny Robert. BS in Health Care Services, So. Ill. U., 1979; JD, Thomas Jefferson Sch. Law, 1984. Bar: Calif. 1985, U.S. Dist. Ct. (so., cen, no. and ea. dists.) Calif. 1985, U.S. Dist. Ct. Hawaii 1985, U.S. Ct. Appeals (9th cir.) 1985, U.S. Ct. Claims 1985, U.S. Tax Ct. 1985, U.S. Ct. Mil. Appeals 1985, U.S. Ct. Internat. Trade 1985. Mgr. Nat. TV Rentals, Washington, 1980, regional mgr. Washington, Va. and Md. area, 1981; maintenance engr., housekeeping supr. Rockville (Md.) Nursing Home, 1980-81; assoc. Cornish & Cornish, Hemet, Calif., 1986-87; sole practice Hemet, 1987—. With U.S. Army, 1977-80. Avocations: gardening, fishing, motorcycling, swimming, softball. State civil litigation, Commercial, consumer (including collections, credit), Family and matrimonial. E-mail: rjmartin@lasercom.net.

MARTIN, RONALD ALLEN, lawyer; b. Richmond, Va., Sept. 29, 1952; s. George Thomas Martin and Thelma May (Stanley) Moore; m. Debra Elaine Bodsford, May 27, 1978; 1 child, Kristin Adele. BA in Polit. Sci. and Sociology, U. Richmond, 1974; JD, T.C. Williams Sch. Law, 1977. Bar: Va. 1977, U.S. Dist. Ct. (ea. dist.) Va. 1977, U.S. Ct. Appeals (4th cir.) 1977. Sole practice, Mechanicsville, Va., 1977-82; ptnr. McCaul, Martin, Evans & Cook, P.C. and predecessor firm Martin & Evans, P.C., Mechanicsville, 1982—. Active Hanover Dem. Com., Hanover County, Va., 1983-1999; Hanover Youth Basketball Assn., Mechanicsville, 1980-92, Atlee Youth League, 1989-92. Named One of Outstanding Young Men Am., Jaycees, 1982. Mem. ABA, Hanover Bar Assn. (past pres., v.p., sec. treas. 1978—), Va. Trial Lawyers Assn., Fifteenth Jud. Cir. Bar Assn. (sec., treas. 1985, v.p. 1986, pres. 1987—, past pres., v.p., sec. treas. 1978—), Mechanicsville Businessmen's Assn. (bd. dirs. 1985-86), Hanover Assn. Businesses and C. of C. (bd. dirs. 2002—), Phi Delta Phi, Pi Sigma Alpha. United Methodist. Clubs: Spider (Richmond) (bd. dirs. 1981-82). State civil litigation, Personal injury (including property damage), Property, real (including real estate development, water). Office: McCaul Martin Evans & Cook PC 8122 Mechanicsville Pike Mechanicsville VA 23111-0279

MARTIN, STEPHEN CLARKE, lawyer, mediator; b. N.Y.C., Nov. 14, 1942; s. Walter Henry and Clare Hix Martin; m. Mary Porter Johns, Dec. 21, 1968; children: Meredith Page, Alice Phinizy. BSME, Princeton U., 1964; JD, NYU, 1974. Bar: N.Y. 1975, D.C. 1975, Va. 1978, U.S. Dist. Ct. Va. 1980, U.S. Supreme Ct. 1986. Math. and physics tchr. Thessaloniki (Greece) Internat. H.S., 1964-65; clk. to Sr. Judge Luther W. Youngdahl, motions clk. U.S. Ct. Appeals (D.C. cir.), 1974-75; atty. Bur. Competition FTC, 1975-77; acting dir. Office Competition U.S. Dept. Energy, Washington, 1977-78; founding ptnr. Martin & Nicks, Amherst, Va., 1980-88; ptnr. Pendleton, Martin, Henderson and Garrett, Amherst, 1989-95; pvt. practice Amherst, 1996—. Gen. and family mediator, 1996—; co-commr. accts. Amherst County, 1996—; former substitute judge, commr. in chancery, spl. justice 24th Jud. Dist. Assoc. editor Rev. Law and Social Change, NYU. Treas., counsel Amherst/Nelson Christmas in April; counsel Habitat for Humanity of Amherst County, Va., Peace Through Edn., Bedford, Va., ReSource Coalition, Lynchburg; former bd. dirs. Sweet Briar Coll. Friends of Libr.; bd. dirs. Amherst County Pub. Schs. Edn. Found., former pres., bd. dirs. Amherst/Nelson Alliance for Arts; former bd. dirs. Lime Kiln Theatre, Lexington, Va., Winton Country Club, Amherst, Amherst County Bur.; former mem. exec. com. Blue Ridge Group Sierra Club; former mem. Amherst County Litter Commn. Mem. Va. State Bar (criminal law sect.), Va. Coll. Criminal Def. Attys., Ctrl. Va. Plaintiff Atty. Assn. (treas.), Amherst/Nelson Bar Assn. (past pres.), pub. rels/edn. com.), Va. Mediation Network, Lynchburg Bar Assn. (past pres. exec. bd., past mem. jud. nomination com., family law sect.). Criminal, General practice, Pension, profit-sharing, and employee benefits. Office: 220 South Main ST PO Box 910 Amherst VA 24521-0910 E-mail: stormyscm@aol.com.

MARTIN, STEPHEN DAVID, lawyer; b. Paducah, Ky., May 14, 1947; s. Guy Francis and Hazel (Davis) M.; m. Deborah Sue Brown, Aug. 2, 1974; 1 child, Gary C. BA, Rutgers U., 1969; JD, Capital U., 1973. Bar: Ohio 1974, U.S. Dist. Ct. (so. and no. dists.) Ohio 1977, U.S. Supreme Ct. 1978, U.S. Ct. Appeals (6th cir.) 1982, U.S. Tax Ct. 1991, U.S. Dist. Ct. Ariz. 1992, U.S. Ct. Appeals (9th cir.) 1993. Pers. supr. Janitrol div. Andro Corp., Columbus, Ohio, 1969-72; labor rels. mgr. Celanese Plastics, Hilliard, Ohio, 1972-74; atty. govt. rels. Ohio Edn. Assn., Columbus, 1974-76; prin. Manos, Martin, Pergram & Dietz Co., LPA, Columbus, Delaware, Ohio, 1976—. Adv. bd. dirs. First Merit Bank of Columbus. Committeeman Delaware County Democratic Party, Delaware, Ohio, 1988; trustee Main Street Delaware, Inc., Cmty. Found. Del. County. Fellow Columbus Bar Found.; mem. Ohio Coun. Sch. Bd. Attys., Nat. Coun. Sch. Bd. Attys., Ohio State Bar Assn., Columbus Bar Assn., Delaware County Bar Assn., Worthington C. of C., Delaware C. of C., Ohio State U. Pres.'s Club, Rotary. General civil litigation, Business. Office: Manos Martin Pergram & Dietz Co LPA 50 N Sandusky St Delaware OH 43015-1926

MARTIN, STEPHEN JAMES, retired lawyer; b. Montclair, NJ, Mar. 20, 1930; s. Willis Elwin and Katherine Elizabeth M.; m. Kathleen Ellen Lyons, May 10, 1958; children: Christopher John, Therese Marie. Ph.B., U. Notre Dame, 1951; JD, U. Mich., 1954; LL.M., NYU, 1959. Bar: Mich. 1954, Calif. 1960; CPA, Calif. Mem. pub. acctg. staff Touche, Ross, Bailey & Smart, Detroit, 1954-58; assoc. Pillsbury, Madison & Sutro, San Francisco, 1959-66; ptnr. Pillsbury Winthrop LLP, San Francisco, 1965—91; ret., 1991. Contbr. articles to profl. jours. Mem. ABA (sect. taxation council 1981-83, vice-chmn. 1986-88), AICPA, State Bar Calif., Am. Bar Found., Am. Coll. Tax Counsel, Calif. Soc. CPAs, San Francisco Tax Club (sec.-treas. 1982-83, pres. 1983-84), World Trade Club (San Francisco), Bankers Club (San Francisco). Corporate taxation, Personal income taxation, State and local taxation. Home: 60 Denise Dr Burlingame CA 94010-7150 Office: Pillsbury Winthrop LLP 50 Fremont St San Francisco CA 94120

MARTIN, THOMAS MACDONALD, lawyer; b. Huntington, N.Y., Dec. 17, 1947; s. Raleigh Lloyd and Elizebeth Battle (Gutwein) M.; m. Sheila Lynn Wilkens, July 13, 1968. AAS in Bus. Adminstrn., SUNY, Selden, 1967; BS in Criminal Justice, SUNY, Westbury, 1976; JD, Touro Coll., 1986. Bar: Va. 1988, U.S. Ct. Appeals (4th cir.) 1988, U.S. Supreme Ct. 1993, U.S. Ct. Fed. Claims 1993, U.S. Ct. Appeals (fed. cir.) 1993, U.S. Ct. Mil. Appeals 1993; U.S. Dist Ct. (ea. dist.) Va. 2002; cert. fraud examiner. Customs officer, sky marshall U.S. Customs Agy. Svc., N.Y.C., 1971-75; spl. agt. U.S. Dept. Agr., N.Y.C., 1975-78; supervisory spl. agt. Office of Insp. Gen., N.Y.C., 1978-81, asst. regional insp. gen. then regional insp. gen., 1981-86, dep. div. dir. Washington, 1986-88, chief internal affairs, 1988-91, sr. spl. agt. gen. investigations divsn., 1991-93, sr. spl. agt. program investigation divsn., 1993-98; ret. Fairfax, Va., 1998; pvt. practice law, 1998—; magistrate 19th Jud. Dist., Fairfax County, Va., 1999—2001. With USN, 1967-71. Mem. ABA (litigation sect. 1989—), Fed. Bar Assn., Fairfax Bar Assn., Va. Trial Lawyers Assn., Assn. Trial Lawyers Am., Va. Magistrates Assn., Nat. Geog. Soc., Fed. Law Enforcement Officers Assn., Nat. Assn. Fraud Examiners. Methodist. Avocations: Karate, marksmanship, golf, fishing, reading. General civil litigation, Criminal, General practice. E-mail: MARTINLAW1@excite.com.

MARTIN, WILLARD GORDON, JR., lawyer; b. Boston, Dec. 12, 1937; children: Yves, Sylvie, Melissa, Helen, Abigail, Galya. AB, Bates Coll., 1959; LLB, Harvard U., 1962; LLM, Boston U., 1984. Bar: N.H. 1962, U.S. Dist. Ct. N.H. 1962. Ptnr. Martin, Lord & Osman, P.A., Laconia, N.H., 1962—. City solicitor, Laconia, 1963-66; Belknap County atty., N.H., 1967-68; rep. to gen. ct., N.H., 1969-70; mem. N.H. Jud. Coun., 1971-75; N.H. bar examiner, 1972— ; Spl. justice Laconia Dist. Ct., 1973—; judge N.H. family divsn., 1998—; mem. com. on character and fitness N.H. Supreme Ct., 1975—. Mem. Am. Judicature Soc. (bd. dirs. 1980-84), N.H. Bar Assn. (bd. govs. 1980-82), Belknap County Bar Assn., Phi Beta Kappa. Corporate, general, Probate (including wills, trusts), Personal income taxation. Office: 1 Mill Plz Laconia NH 03246-3438

MARTINA, CARLO JACK, lawyer; b. Wyandotte, Mich., Jan. 1, 1954; s. Carlo and Matilda M.; m. Marie A. Pulte; children: Raphael, Ariel. BS with high distinction, U. Mich., 1976; JD, Wayne State U., 1979. Bar: Mich. 1979, U.S. Dist. Ct. (ea. dist.) Mich. 1980. Assoc. Provisor, Eisenberg et al, Southfield, Mich., 1979-81, Auslander, Babcock & Weiss, Southfield, Mich., 1981-83; atty. pvt. practice, Southfield, Mich., 1983—. Mem. adv. bd. Legal Alternatives for Women, Southfield, 1985-87; co-founder Mich. br. Justice for Children, 1995-97; co-founder, co-publisher, co-owner MetroParent Mag., Southfield, 1987-95; ; mem. task force Oakland County Family Ct., 2001—; lectr. in field. Legal expert (video) Latchkey Kids: Home Alone & Safe, 1994; author: Effective Discovery in Domestic Violence Litigation, 2002. Mem. adv. bd. Gov.'s Internat. Yr. of Family Coun., Lansing, Mich., 1994-95, Roundtable of Christians, Muslims & Jews, Detroit, 1989-91, Anti-Defamation League, Southfield, 1988-90, Coalition Against Domestic Violence; scoutmaster Cub Scout Pack 1016, Birmingham, Mich., 1993-97. James P. Angel scholar U. Mich., 1977-79. Mem. Mich. Trial Lawyers Assn., Mich. Bar Assn. (bd. dirs., family law coun. 2001—, chmn. child support, alimony and friend of ct. com. 2002—, lectr.), Oakland County Bar Assn. (co-chair family court com., friend of ct. subcom.), Wayne County Bar Assn. (family law divsn., liaison to Mich. Bar Assn., family law coun. 2001—). Avocations: reading, fishing, furniture refinishing and home remodeling, model building. Family and matrimonial, Personal injury (including property damage). Office: 19111 W 10 Mile Rd Ste 104 Southfield MI 48075-2449 also: 1158 Main St Plymouth MI 48170 E-mail: MartinaLawOffice@aol.com.

MARTINEAU, ROBERT JOHN, law educator; b. May 18, 1934; s. Francis Joseph and Gertrude (Schauer) M.; m. Constance Ann Zimmerman, Dec. 21, 1957; children: Robert John, Renee, Anne, Jeanne. BS, Coll. Holy Cross, 1956; JD, U. Chgo., 1959. Bar: Md. 1960, U.S. Supreme Ct. 1964, Iowa 1969, Mo. 1974, Wis. 1974. Law clk. to chief judge Md. Ct. Appeals, 1959-60; pvt. practice Md., 1960-68; asst. atty. gen., 1964-65; assoc. prof. U. Iowa, 1968-71; prof., 1971-72; cir. exec. U.S. Ct. Appeals (8th cir.), Mo., 1972-74; exec. officer Wis. Supreme Ct., 1974-78; prof. U. Dayton (Ohio), 1978-80; assoc. dean U. Cin., 1980-82; prof. law, 1980-88; disting. rsch. prof., 1988-93; emeritus, 1994—. Acting dean, 1985-86; spl. prof. alw U. Birmingham, Eng., 1987; cons. Fed. Jud. Ctr., 1978, Nat. Ctr. State Cts., 1978-79, 87, UN Devel. Program, 1999. Author: Wisconsin Appellate Practice, 1978, Judicial Reform in Wisconsin, in Court Reform in Seven States, 1980, Modern Appellate Practice-Federal and State Civil Appeals, 1983, Fundamentals of Modern Appellate Advocacy, 1985, Apellat Practice and Procedure, 1987, Cases and Materials on Appellate Justice in England and the United States: A Comparative Analysis, 1990, Drafting Legislation and Rules in Plain English, 1991. Sec. Md. Constnl. Conv. 1967-68; reporter Wis. Supreme Ct. Com. on Discipline of Attys., 1975-77, Wis. Jud. Coun. Com. Appelate Practice and Procedure, 1976-78. Mem. Assn. Am. Law Schs. (mem. Ho. of Reps. 1981-86), ABA (appellate judges conf. com. on appellate skills tng. 1984-85, co-chair, appellate judges conf. com. on appellate practice 1984-86, mem. Ohio Supreme Ct. adv. com. on rules 1988-91), Md. bar Assn. (v.p. 1967), Am. Jud. Soc. (bd. dirs. 1966-68). Democrat. Roman Catholic. Office: U Cin Coll Law Cincinnati OH 45221-0001 E-mail: r.j.maritneau@netzero.net.

MARTINETTI, RONALD ANTHONY, lawyer; b. N.Y.C., Aug. 13, 1945; s. Alfred Nathan and Frances Ann (Battipaglia) M. Student, The Hotchkiss Sch., 1963, U. Chgo., 1981-82; JD, U. So. Calif., 1982. Bar: Calif. 1982; U.S. Dist. Ct. (cen. and no. dists.) Calif. 1982, U.S. Dist. Ct. Ariz., 1992; U.S. Ct. Appeals (9th cir.) 1982. Ptnr. Kazanjian & Martinetti, Glendale, Calif., 1986—. Co-founder Am. Legends Website, 1995, Am. Legends Pub., 1996. Author: James Dean Story, 1995, Nine Easy Ways to Strengthen Your Bad Faith Care in Discovery, 1991; co-author: Rights of Owners of Lost, Stolen or Destroyed Instruments Under UCC Section3-804: Can They Be Holders in Due Course, 1993; contbr. to Wall St. Jour., Washington Post, The Harvard Conservative, Newsday, Balt. Sun, The New Leader, Columbia U. Forum, 1968-76; pub. James Dean Scrapbook, 1996. Vol. trial lawyer Bet Tzedek Legal Svcs., 1987—; vol. arbitrator L.A. Sup. Ct., 1987—; judge pro tem L.A. Superior Ct., 1994—. Mem. Calif. Bar Assn. Roman Catholic. State civil litigation, Labor (including EEOC, Fair Labor Standards Act, labor-management relations, NLRB, OSHA), Personal injury (including property damage). Office: Kazanjian & Martinetti 520 E Wilson Ave Glendale CA 91206-4374 Fax: 818-241-2193. E-mail: amlegends@aol.com.

MARTINEZ, ALEX J. state supreme court justice; b. Denver, Apr. 1, 1951; m. Kathy Carter; children: Julia, Maggie. Diploma, Phillips Exeter Acad., N.H., 1969; student, Reed Coll., 1969-72; BA, U. Colo., 1973, JD, 1976. Bar: Colo. 1976. Dep. state pub. defender, Pueblo and Denver, 1976-83; county ct. judge Pueblo, 1983-88; dist. ct. judge, 1988-97; justice Colo. Supreme Ct., Denver, 1997—. Supreme Ct. liaison Colo. Criminal Rules Com., Colo. Criminal Jury Instrns.; chmn. Child Welfare Appeals Workgroup, 1997; mem. standing com. Integrated Info. Svcs. Chmn. Pueblo adv. bd. Packard Found., 1993-96; chmn. site-based governing coun. Pueblo Sch. Arts and Scis., 1994-95; mem. site-based governing coun. Roncalli Mid. Sch., 1993-94; bd. dirs. Colo. U. Law Alumni. Mem. Colo. Bar Assn. (regional v.p. 1995-96), Colo. Hispanic Bar Assn., Pueblo Bar Assn. (mem. exec. coun. 1994-96), Pueblo Hispanic Bar Assn. Office: Colo Supreme Ct 2 E 14th Ave Denver CO 80203-2115 E-mail: AJMarti@aol.com.

MARTINEZ, EDUARDO VIDAL, lawyer; b. Travis AFB, Calif., Sept. 27, 1955; s. Vidal and Isidora (Lee) M.; m. Mary Kim Sullivan, Apr. 7, 1984; children: Anthony Michael, Linda Michelle. BA, U. Tex., 1978; MA, Antioch Ctr. for Legal Studies, Washington, 1983; JD, Miss. Coll., 1990; MA, U.S. Army War Coll., 2003. Bar: Miss. 1991, U.S. Dist. Ct. (no. and so. dist.) Miss. 1991, U.S. Ct. Mil. Appeals 1991, U.S. Ct. Appeals (5th cir.) 1991, U.S. Supreme Ct. 1994. Gen. counsel Home-Land Title & Abstract Co. Inc., Jackson, Miss., 1991; pvt. practice Jackson, 1991-92; spl. asst. atty. gen. Office of the Atty. Gen., Jackson, 1992-97; legal counsel, site adminstr. SkyTel Corp., 1997—98, corp. counsel, 1999—; dir. site leasing and acquisition WorldCom Broadband Solutions, Inc., 2001. Editor Legal Eye, 1989-90, 2000-02. Comdr. USNR, 1983-. Comdr. USNR, 2000—03. Scholar Miss. Bar Found., 1988, scholar in environ. law Am. Law Inst., 1990. Mem. ABA, Miss. Bar Assn., Naval Res. Assn. (chpt. pres.), Navy League, Res. Officer Assn. (chpt. pres., nat. naval sect. committeeman 2000-2002), Sea Svs. (nat. v.p. 2000-02, 2002-2003), Nat. Jr. Officer (co-chmn., 1996-97.). Roman Catholic. Administrative and regulatory, Communications, Corporate, general. Office: 515 E Amite St Jackson MS 39201 E-mail: evmart@juno.com.

MARTINEZ, JUDY PERRY, lawyer; b. New Orleans, La., Aug. 15, 1957; BS, La. State U., 1979; JD cum laude, Tulane U., 1982. Bar: La. 1982. Atty., chair Simon, Peragine, Smith & Redfearn, LLP, New Orleans, 1982—. Mem. Elmo B. Hunter Ctr. for Jud. Excellence, 1994—97; chairperson New Orleans Pro Bono Project, 1989. Fellow: Am. Bar Found., La. Bar Found. (life); mem.: ABA (commn. on women in the profession 1991—94, spl. advisor standing com. on fed. jud. 1994—95, bd. govs. 1996—99, exec. com. 1998—99, del.-at-large 1999—, gen. mem. sect. on litigation ABA Ho. of Dels. 2000—, nominating com. 1993—96, chair young lawyers divsn. 1990—91, chair commn. on domestic violence 1999—2001, young lawyers divsn. liaison to sect. litigation 1991—93, mem. exec. coun. young lawyers divsn. 1986—96, divsn. del. 1991—96), Am. Judicature Soc., Assn. for Women Attys., La. State Bar Assn. (chairperson minority involvement com. 1984—87, long range planning com. 1987—92, chairperson professionalism and quality of life com. 1992—93, chairperson post-conviction representation com. 1997—99), New Orleans Bar Assn. (chairperson young lawyers sect. 1986—87). Office: Simon Peragine Smith & Redfearn LLP 30th Fl Energy Ctr 1100 Poydras St New Orleans LA 70163-3000

MARTINEZ, NERI L. lawyer; b. Tampa, Fla., Dec. 15, 1959; s. Edward Robert Martinez and Diana P. Pizzo-Martinez; m. Susan T. Del Valle, June 15, 1990; 1 child, Emily Jean. MD, Spartan Health Sci. Sch. Medicine, 1986; JD, Thomas M. Cooley Law Sch., 1990; BA in Fin., U. South Fla., 1991. Bar: Fla. 1990. Assoc. Bruce L. Schrener & Assocs. P.A., Ft. Myer, Fla., 1990, Epperson & Assocs. P.A., Tampa, 1992, James Guarnieri P.A., Tampa, 1993; ptnr. Guarnier & Martinez, P.A., Tampa, 1994, Guarnieri, Martinez & Odom P.A., Tampa, 2001. Big brother Big Brothers Ybor City, Tampa, 1992—95. Mem.: Optimist Club. Roman Catholic. Personal injury (including property damage). Office: 2314 Dr MLK Jr Blvd Tampa FL 33606

MARTINEZ SAENZ, IVETTE ELISA, lawyer; b. Panama City, Panama, Jan. 25, 1969; d. Rafael Martínez and Fredesvinda Sáenz de Martínez; children: Luis Arturo Castro, Diego Antonio Castro. JD, U. Panama, Panama City, 1993; LLM cum laude, Fordham U., 1996. Legal advisor Privatization Unit- Min. Fin. and Treasury, Panama, 1993—95, Dept. State Land Legal-Min. Fin. and Treasury, Panama, 1993—93; assoc. Pardini & Assocs., Panama, 1995—2001, Sucre, Arias & Reyes, Panama, 2001—. Translator English to Spanish legal docs. Contbr. articles to profl. jours. Recipient Juanita Oller de Mulford award, Sociedad de Esposas de Abogados, 1994, Ricardo J. Alfaro acad. award, Family of Prof. Ricardo J. Alfaro, 1994; fellow World Fellowship Award to Women Educators, Delta Kappa Gamma Soc. Internat., 1995; scholar Fulbright, 1995—96, Instituto para la Formación y Aprovechamiento de Recursos Humanos, 1995. Mem.: Am. C of C and Industries Panama (sec., treas. 2000—02, bd. dirs. 2000—, pres. 2003), ABA, Internat. Union of Lawyers, Panama Bar Assn. (life). Catholic. Avocations: reading, travel. Administrative and regulatory, Banking, Finance. Office: Sucre Arias & Reyes PO Box 0816-01832 Panama 5 Bella Vista 48th East St Panama Panama Office Fax: (507) 264-1355. E-mail: ivette@sucre.net.

MARTINS, BELARMINO GONÇALVES, lawyer, auditor; b. Lisbon, Portugal, Feb. 28, 1938; s. Luís and Autília Gonçalves Martins; m. Maria da Luz Moiteiro, Aug. 4, 1962 (div. July 1975); children: Ana Luís Moiteiro Martins, Marina Moiteiro Martins; m. Maria Júlia Fialho, Dec. 29, 1975 (dec. Aug. 28, 2001); m. Maria Clara Lopes, Dec. 28, 2002. Law Degree, Faculdade de Direito, Coimbra, Portugal, 1966. Bar: Ordem Dos Advogados, Lisbon 1968, Supremo Tribunal de Justica, Portugal 1980. Clk., cost acct. Recauchutagem Triunfo, Lisbon, 1959—65; chief acct. Fabrica Automóveis Portugueses, SA, Lisbon, 1965—69; fin. dir. Autofina-Soc. Distribuidora Automóveis, SA, Lisbon, 1967—69; mgmt. cons., tax cons. Price Waterhouse, Lisbon, 1970—89; ptnr. Belarmino Martins Eugénio Ferreira & Assocs.-SROC, Lisbon, 1985, Belarmino Martins & Assocs.-Soc. Advogados, Lisbon, 1990—99, Oliveira, Martins, Moura, Esteves & Assocs.-Soc. Advogados, Lisbon, 1999—. Prof. postgrad. advanced fin. Inst. Superior de Contabilidade & Adminstrn. de Lisbon-Acctg. and Adminstrn. Inst., 1979—80; mem. working party on co. law European Fedn. Accts., Brussels, 1988—90. Contbr. articles to profl. jours. Named Rough Collie European winner, Internat. Cynological Fedn., Vienna, Austria, 1999. Mem.: Internat. Collie Soc. (founding mem., com. mem.), Ordem Dos Revisores Oficiais de Contas (registered auditor), Ministry Fin. (registered acct.). Avocations: bridge, dog breeding. Mergers and acquisitions, Corporate, general, Commercial, contracts (including sales of goods; commercial financing). Home: Praceta dos Cedros 24 Casal Da Carregueira 2605 Belas Portugal Office: Oliveira Martins Moura Esteves & Asscs Rua Dr Eduardo Neves 9-7o 1050-077 Lisbon Portugal

MARTONE, FREDERICK J. judge; b. Fall River, Mass., Nov. 8, 1943; BS, Coll. Holy Cross, 1965; JD, U. Notre Dame, 1972; LLM, Harvard U., 1975. Bar: Mass. 1972, Ariz. 1974, U.S. Dist. Ct. Mass. 1973, U.S. Dist. Ct. Ariz. 1974, U.S. Ct. Appeals (1st cir.) 1973, U.S. Ct. Appeals (9th cir.) 1974, U.S. Supreme Ct. 1977. Law clk. to Hon. Edward F. Hennessey Mass. Supreme Judicial Ct., 1972-73; pvt. practice Phoenix, 1973-85; assoc. presiding judge Superior Ct. Ariz., Maricopa County, judge, 1985-92; justice Supreme Ct. Ariz., Phoenix, 1992—2002; U.S. dist. judge Dist. of Ariz., 2002—. Editor notes and comments Notre Dame Law Rev., 1970-72; contbr. articles to profl. jours. Capt. USAF, 1965-69. Mem. ABA, Fed. Judges Assn., Maricopa County Bar Assn., Am. Judicature Soc., State Bar Ariz., Horace Rumpole Inn of Ct. Office: US Dist Ct Sandra Day O'Conner US Courthouse 401 W Washington St Spc 62 Ste 526 Phoenix AZ 85003-2158 E-mail: Frederick_Martone@azd.uscourts.gov.

MARTONE, PATRICIA ANN, lawyer; b. Bklyn., Apr. 28, 1947; d. David Andrew and Rita Mary (Dullmeyer) Martone. BA in Chemistry, NYU, 1968, JD, 1973; MA in Phys. Chemistry, Johns Hopkins U., 1969. Bar: N.Y. 1974, U.S. Dist. Ct. (so. and ea. dists.) N.Y. 1975, U.S. Ct. Appeals (2d cir.) 1975, U.S. Ct. Appeals (1st cir.) 1981, U.S. Patent and Trademark Office 1983, U.S. Ct. Appeals (fed. cir.) 1984, U.S. Supreme Ct. 1984, U.S. Dist. Ct. (ea. dist.) Mich. 1985, U.S. Dist. Ct. (no. dist.) Calif. 1995. Tech. rep. computer timesharing On-Line Sys., Inc., N.Y.C., 1969-70; assoc. Kelley Drye & Warren, N.Y.C., 1973-77, Fish & Neave, N.Y.C., 1977-82, ptnr., 1983—. Adj. prof. NYU Sch. Law, 1990—; mem. adv. coun. Engelberg Ctr. Innovation Law & Policy, 1996—; participating atty. Cmty. Law Offices, N.Y.C., 1974—78; atty. Pro Bono Panel U.S. Dist. Ct. (so. dist.) N.Y., 1982—84; lectr. Practising Law Inst., N.Y.C., 1995—, Aspen Law & Bus., 1990—95, Franklin Pierce Law Sch., 1992—97, Lic. Exec. Soc.; chair, bd. dirs. N.Y. Lawyers for the Pub. Interest, 1996—98, vice chair, 1998—2000, 2002—, Legal Svcs., N.Y.C., 1991—95. Mng. editor NYU Law Sch. Rev. Law and Social Change, 1972-73; contbr. articles to profl. jours. Recipient Founder's Day award NYU Sch. Law, 1973; NSF grad. trainee Johns Hopkins U., 1968-69; NYU scholar, 1964-68. Mem. ABA, Assn. Bar City N.Y. (mem. environ. law com. 1978-83, trademarks, unfair competition com. 1983-86), Fed. Bar Coun., Fed. Cir. Bar Assn., Copyright Soc., Am. Chem. Soc., Licensing Execs. Soc., N.Y. Intellectual Property Law Assn., Univ. Club. Federal civil litigation, Patent, Trademark and copyright. Office: Fish & Neave Fl 49 1251 Ave of the Americas New York NY 10020-1105 E-mail: pmartone@fishneave.com.

MARTORI, JOSEPH PETER, lawyer; b. N.Y.C., Aug. 19, 1941; s. Joseph and Teresa Susan (Fezza) M. BS summa cum laude, NYU, 1964, MBA, 1968; JD cum laude, U. Notre Dame, 1967. Bar: D.C. 1968, U.S. Dist. Ct. D.C. 1968, U.S. Dist. Ct. Ariz. 1968, U.S. Ct. Appeals (9th cir.) 1969, U.S. Supreme Ct. 1977. Assoc. Sullivan & Cromwell, N.Y.C., 1967-68, Snell & Wilmer, Phoenix, 1968-69; pres. Goldmar Inc., Phoenix, 1969-71; ptnr. Martori, Meyer, Hendricks & Victor, P.A., Phoenix, 1971-85, Brown & Bain, P.A., Phoenix, 1985-94, chmn. corp. banking & real estate dept., 1994—; chmn. bd. ILX Resorts, Inc., Phoenix. Chmn. ILX Inc., Varsity Clubs Am. Inc. Author: Street Fights, 1987; also articles, 1966-70. Trustee Boys' Clubs Met. Phoenix, 1974-99; consul for Govt. of Italy, State of Ariz., 1987-97. Mem. ABA, State Bar Ariz., Maricopa County Bar Assn., Lawyers Com.for Civil Rights Under Law (trustee 1976—), Phoenix Country Club, Plaza Club (founding bd. govs. 1979-90). Republican. Roman Catholic. Property, real (including real estate development, water), Corporate taxation, Corporate, general. Office: ILX Resorts Inc 2111 E Highland Ave Ste 210 Phoenix AZ 85016-4786 E-mail: jmartori@ILXresorts.com.

MARTZ, CLYDE OLLEN, lawyer, educator; b. Lincoln, Nebr., Aug. 14, 1920; s. Clyde O. and Elizabeth Mary (Anderson) M.; m. Ann Spieker, May 29, 1947; children: Robert Graham, Nancy. AB, U. Nebr., 1941; LLB, Harvard U., 1947. Bar: Colo. 1948, U.S. Ct. Appeals (D.C. cir.) 1968, U.S. Supreme Ct. 1969. Prof. U. Colo., Boulder, 1947-58, 60-62; jud. adminstr. State of Colo., Denver, 1959-60; ptnr. Davis, Graham & Stubbs, Denver, 1962-67, 69-80, 81-87, of counsel, 1988—; asst. atty. gen. U.S. Dept. Justice, Washington, 1967-69; solicitor U.S Dept. Interior, Washington, 1980-81; exec. dir. dept. natural resources State of Colo., 1987. Adj. prof. U. Denver, 1961-79, U. Colo., Boulder, 1988-96; cons. Pres. Materials Policy Commn., 1951; mem. Colo. Adv. Bd. Bur. Land Mgmt., 1967-69; bd. dirs., adv. bd. Natural Resources Law Ctr., 1982-2003. Author: Cases and Materials on Natural Resources Law, 1951, Water for Mushrooming Populations, 1954; co-author: American Law of Property, 1953, Water and Water Rights, 1963; editor, co-author: American Law of Mining, 1960. Co-chmn. Jud. Reorganization Commn., 1961-63; elder Presbyn. Ch., Boulder; pres. Rocky Mountain Mineral Law Found., 1961-62, others. Comdr. USN, 1942-58, PTO, with Res. Decorated Silver Star, Bronze Star, Letter of Commendation, Disting. Svc. award; honored by creation of Clyde O. Martz Natural Resources Scholarship Fund, 2002. Mem. ABA (chmn. natural resources sect. 1985-86), Fed. Bar Assn., Am. Health Lawyers Assn., Colo. Bar Assn. (chmn. water sect. 1957, chmn. mineral sect. 1961, award of merit 1962), Nat. Mining Assn. (Disting. Svc. award 1997), Order of Coif, Phi Beta Kappa. Democrat. Avocations: horticulture, woodworking, mountaineering, skiing. Home: 970 Aurora Ave Apt 205F Boulder CO 80302-7299 Office: Davis Graham & Stubbs PO Box 185 Denver CO 80201-0185

MARVEL, L. PAIGE, federal judge; b. Easton, Md., Dec. 6, 1949; d. E. Warner Marvel and Louise Harrington Harrison; m. Robert H. Dyer, Jr., Aug. 9, 1975; children: Alex W. Dyer, Kelly E. Dyer. BA magna cum laude, Notre Dame Coll., 1971; JD with honors, U. Md., 1974. Bar: Md. 1974, U.S. Dist. Ct. Md. 1974, U.S. Tax Ct. 1975, U.S. Ct. Appeals (4th cir.) 1977, U.S. Supreme Ct. 1980, U.S. Ct. Claims 1981, D.C. 1985. Assoc. Garbis & Schwait, P.A., Balt., 1974-76, shareholder, 1976-85, Garbis, Marvel & Junghans, P.A., Balt., 1985-86; mem. Melnicove, Kaufman, Weiner, Smouse & Garbis, P.A., Balt., 1986-88; ptnr. Venable, Baetjer and Howard LLP, Balt., 1988-98; judge U.S. Tax Ct., Washington, 1998—. Bd. dirs. Loyola/Notre Dame Libr., Inc.; mem. U. Md. Law Sch. Bd. Vis., 1995—2001; mem. adv. com. U.S. Dist. Ct. Md., 1991—93. Co-editor procedure dept. Jour. Taxation, 1989-98; contbr. chpts. to books, articles to profl. jours. Active Women's Law Ctr., 1974-85, Md. Dept. Econ. and Community Devel. Adv. Comm., 1978-80. Recipient recognition award Balt. Is Best Program, 1981; named One of Md.'s Top 100 Women, The Daily Record, 1998; recipient MSBA Taxation section's Tax Excellence award, 2002. Fellow Am. Bar Found., Am. Coll. Tax Counsel (regent 1995-98); mem. ABA (sect. taxation coun. dir. 1989-92, vice-chair com. ops. 1993-95, Disting. Svc. award), Am. Law Inst. (advisor Ali restatement of law third, law governing lawyers), Md. Bar Assn. (chmn. taxation sect. 1982-83, bd. dirs. 1988-90, 96-98, Disting. Svc. award), Md. Bar Found., Balt. Bar Assn. (at-large exec. coun.), Am. Tax Policy Inst. (trustee 1997-98), Serjeant's Inn, Rule Day Club. Avocations: golf, music, travel. Home: 7109 Sheffield Rd Baltimore MD 21212-1628 Office: US Tax Ct 400 2d St NW Washington DC 20217-0001

MARVIN, CHARLES ARTHUR, law educator; b. July 14, 1942; s. Burton Wright and Margaret Fiske (Medlar) M.; m. Elizabeth Maureen Woodrow, July 4, 1970 (div. July 1987); m. Elizabeth Dale Wilson, Mar. 20, 1999; children: Colin, Kristin. BA, U. Kans., 1964; postgrad., U. Toulouse, France, 1964-65; JD, U. Chgo., 1968, M of Comparative Law, 1970. Bar: Ill. 1969. Legal intern EEC, Brussels, 1970; lectr. law U. Kent, Canterbury, Eng., 1970-71; asst. prof. law Laval U., Quebec City, Que., Can., 1971-73; legal adv. constnl., internat. and adminstrv. law sect. Can. Dept. Justice, Ottawa, Ont., 1973-76; assoc. prof. law U. Man., Winnipeg, Can., 1976-77; dir. adminstrv. law project Law Reform Commn., Ottawa, 1977-80; prof. law Villanova (Pa.) U., 1980-83; dir. Adminstrv. Law Reform Project Can. Dept. Justice, 1983-85; prof. law Ga. State U., 1985—, assoc. dean, 1987-89. Legal advisor on adminstrv. code revision to Govt. of Kazakhstan, 1993; law faculty devel. adviser to Bulgaria, 1993; dir. internat. human rights law summer program Regent U. Sch. Law, 1998; lectr., Ivory Coast, 1998; Fulbright prof. Riga Grad. Sch. Law, Latvia, 2000-2002; Fulbright Sr. Specialist, 2003. Acad. mem. Ctr. Am. and Internat. Law. Fulbright scholar U. Toulouse, 1964-65, Summerfield scholar U. Kansas, 1961-64, U. Chgo. scholar, 1965-68; Ford Found. Comparative Law fellow, 1968-70. Mem. ABA, Ill. Bar Assn., Chgo. Bar Assn., Am. Soc. Internat. Law, Am. Fgn. Law Assn., Internat. Bar Assn., Internat. Law Assn., Can. Bar Assn., Can. Coun. on Internat. Law, Phi Beta Kappa, Omicron Delta Kappa, Phi Beta Delta, Phi Delta Phi. Office: Ga State U Coll Law PO Box 4037 Atlanta GA 30302-4037 E-mail: cmarvin@gsu.edu.

MARVIN, DAVID EDWARD SHREVE, lawyer; b. Jan. 6, 1950; s. George Charles Marvin and Shirley Mae (Martin) Schaible; m. Mary Anne Kennedy, Sept. 16, 1972; 1 child, John. BS cum laude, Mich. State U., 1972; JD cum laude, Wayne State U., 1976. Bar: Mich. 1976, U.S. Dist. Ct. (ea. dist.) Mich. 1976, U.S. Dist. Ct. (we. dist.) Mich. 1978, U.S. Ct. Appeals (7th cir.) 1977, U.S. Ct. Appeals (6th cir.) 1979, U.S. Supreme Ct. 1979, U.S. Ct. Appeals (D.C. cir.) 1982, D.C. 1982. Asst. mgr. Alta Supply Co., Lansing, 1972-73; rsch. asst. Wayne State U., Detroit, fall 1975; jud. intern U.S. Dist. Ct., Detroit, summer 1975; shareholder Fraser Trebilcock Davis & Dunlap, P.C., Lansing, 1976—, chair Govt. Law dept., 1992—, v.p., 1997—, also bd. dirs. Pres. Red Rock Prodns., Inc., 1990-94; lectr. Inst. CLE, 1989; mem. qualifications rev. com. U.S. Dist. Ct. (we. dist.) Mich., 2001—. Exec. editor Wayne Law Rev., 1975-76; contbr. articles to law jours. Commr. Mich. Solar Resource Adv. Panel, Lansing, 1978-81, Mich. Commn. Profl. and Occupl. Licensure, 1981-83; chmn. Ingham County Energy Commn., Mason, Mich., 1978-80 (state bar rep. assembly 1985-88); dir., corp. sec. Friends Mich. Hist. Ctr., Inc., 1988-92; treas. Lansing Lawyer Referral Svc., 1981; state del. Nat. Solar Congress, Washington, 1978; hearing officer City of East Lansing, 1985; Tri-County Coun. of Bar Leaders (chmn. 1986); bd. dirs. East Lansing Edn. Found., 1990-92, Impression Five Sci. Mus., 1991-97; regional fin. chmn. Abraham for U.S. Senate, 1993-94, Abraham Senate 2000, 1995-2000; mem. transition team, Gov. Engler, 2000—03, Atty. Gen. Cox, 2002-03; exec. bd. chief Okemos coun. Boy Scouts Am., 1996—, pres., 2001-03. Recipient Disting. Vol. award Tri-County Voluntary Action Ctr., 1990, Gov.'s Minuteman award, 1990, John W. Cummiskey award State Bar Mich., 1990, George Washington Honor medal Freedoms Found., 1990; named Outstandin Young Man Am., 1984, The Outstanding Young Lawyer in Mich., 1985-86, Small Bus. Adv. Yr., C. of C., 1991, Silver Beaver award Boy Scouts Am., 2003; Wm. D. Traitel scholar, 1975. Fellow ABA, Am. Bar Found., Mich. State Bar Found. (life); mem. ABA, State Bar Mich. (com. chmn., sect. coun. 1982—, state chmn. 1988-89), Mich. Soc. Assoc. Execs., Ingham County Bar Assn. (pres. 1985-86), Pro Bono Lawyers Svc. (pres. 1982-83), Lansing Regional C. of C. (v.p. 1987), Mich. Audubon Soc. (bd. dirs. 1991-93), Mich. State Univ. Alumni Assn. (nat. bd. dirs. 1992—), State Capital Law Firm Group (nat. bd. dirs. 1989—, chmn. com. Can. 1990-93, chair pub. utility, energy and comm. sect. 1994—, nat. sec. 1996-97, vice-chmn. 1997-98, chmn. 1998-99), Downtown Coaches Club (bd. dirs., pres. 1987), Nat. Resource Ctr. on State Laws and Regulations (nat. bd. dirs. 1993—, chmn. 1998-99), Mich. State U. Pres.'s Club, Rotary (bd. dirs. 1995-97, Paul Harris fellow), Phi Alpha Delta, Phi Eta Sigma, Theta Delta Chi (pres. 1972). Republican. Administrative and regulatory, Communications, Utilities, public. Home: 1959 Groton Way East Lansing MI 48823-1347 Office: Fraser Trebilcock Davis & Dunlap PC Michigan Nat Towers Fl 10 Lansing MI 48933

MARVIN, MONICA LOUISE WOLF, lawyer; b. San Francisco, Feb. 3, 1947; d. Andrew John and Hazel Louise Wolf; children: Brett Lewis, Elizabeth Louise. Student, Pacific U., Forest Grove, Oreg., 1964-66, Sonoma State U., Rohnert Park, Calif., 1966-67; BA in Psychology, Chico (Calif.) State U., 1969; JD, Empire Coll., Santa Rosa, Calif., 1982. Bar: Calif. 1982, U.S. Dist. Ct. Calif. 1982. Assoc. Fitzgerald Fitzgerald and Gowen, Santa Rosa, Calif., 1982-83, Gowen and Marvin, Santa Rosa, 1983-85, Rodeno Robertson & Assocs., Napa, Calif., 1985-86; pvt. practice St Helena, Calif., 1986—; of counsel Hardell & Yost, LLP, 2000—; gen. ptnr. Bridges, a mediation svc. provider. Judge pro tempore Napa County Consol. Cts., Small Claims Divsn., 1991—. Bd. dirs., v.p. Cmty. Resources for Children, Napa, 1991-94; mem. Napa County Commn. on Children, Youth and Family, 1994-97; mem. Napa County Dem. Ctrl. Com., 1994-98; mem. adv. bd. Napa County Vol. Ctr. Ombudsman Program, 1994-95; founder, chair St. Helena C. of C. Jumelage Com., Sister Chamber affiliation with Libourne C. of C. and Industry, France. Mem. State Bar Calif., Napa County Bar Assn. (bd. dirs. 1994), Napa Women Lawyers (past pres., sec. 1987-92). Corporate, general, Estate planning, General practice. Office: PO Box 271 Saint Helena CA 94574-0271 E-mail: mwmarvin@napanet.net.

MARX, PETER A. lawyer; b. N.Y.C., June 14, 1942; s. Robert L. and Helen (Sohn) M.; m. Barbara K. Marx, Dec. 21, 1974; children: Laura, Lisa. BA, Cornell U., 1965, MBA, JD, 1968. Bar: N.Y. 1969, D.C. 1970, Mass. 1980. Atty., advisor U.S. Securites & Exch. Commn., Washington, 1968-71; assoc. Shaw Pittman, Washington, 1971-74; v.p., gen. counsel Interactive Data Corp., Waltham, Mass., 1975-85; ptnr. Goulston & Storrs, Boston, 1985-87; prin. The Marx Group, Wellesley, Mass., 1987—. Dir. Info. Industry Assn., Washington, 1980-84, hon. counsel to bd., 1993—; chmn. Electronic Bus. Forum, 2002—, N.E. Computer Law Forum, 1982-89; adv. bd. CNC Interactive, 1998, LifetecNet.com, 1999-2001, ForPower.com, 1999-2002, Eye on Interactive, 1999, WebMediate.com, 2000—, Protegent, Inc., 2001-02; host Venture Capital Quest, 1998-2000; vice-chmn. bd. dirs. Internet Alliance, 1999-2000; exec.-in-residence Babson Coll., 2002—; chmn. Electronic Bus. Form, 2002—, Wellesley Cable Access Corp., 2002—. Editor: Contracts in the Information Industry, 1988, II, 1990, III, 1995; mem. bd. advisors Computer Law Strategist, 1987-99; info. law editor Info. Mgmt. Rev., 1987-90; host program Bus. Insight, Sta. WCAB-TV, 1991—; coord. editor The Info. Industry Deal Making Directory, 1994. Mem. ALI-ABA Computer Law Inst. (chmn. 1980-88), New Eng. Corp. Counsel Assn. (chmn. 1981-82), Cornell Club Boston (dir. 2002—). Commercial, contracts (including sales of goods; commercial financing), Computer, Corporate, general. Office: The Marx Group 60 Valley Rd Wellesley MA 02481-1448 E-mail: peter@marxgroup.com.

MARZOTTO CAOTORTA, ANTONIO, lawyer, business executive; b. Florence, Italy, Mar. 20, 1917; s. Alessandro and Marcella (Specher) M.C.; m. Giulia Valdettaro, May 12, 1941; children: Alessandro, Damiano, Tomaso, Costanza, Luigi, Domenico, Matteo. Law degree, U. Florence, 1939, degree in polit. sci., 1940. Cert. lawyer, journalist. Dir. trading firm A. Marzotto, Florence, 1948-56; mgr. OSRAM, Milan, 1957-58, C.G.E., Milan, 1959-61, Breda Holding Co., Milan, 1962-82; pres. AIART-TV, Rome, 1983-90. Author: Visite, 1997; contbr. articles to profl. jours. Mem. Chamber of Deputys., Rome, 1972-83; pres. Transp. Commn., 1979-81; mem. Cons. Coun. TV Users in Rome, 1991-97. 2d lt. Alpini, Italian Army, Albania, 1940. Decorated Silver medal (Italy). Fellow Journalist Order; mem. Federtrasporti Rome (pres. 1970-92), Internat. Union Pub. Transport Brussels (bd. dirs. 1974-92, v.p. 1979-85), Touring Club. Mem. Italian Popular Party. Roman Catholic. Home: Via Gesù 3 20121 Milan Italy

MASERITZ, GUY B. lawyer; b. Balt., June 5, 1937; m. Sally Jane Sugar, Mar. 30, 1961; children: Marjorie Ellen, Michael Louis. BA, Johns Hopkins U., 1959, MA in Econs., 1961; LLB, U. Md., 1966. Bar: Md. 1966, D.C. 1968, U.S. Supreme Ct. 1975, U.S. Dist. Ct. Md. 1979. Atty. SEC, Washington, 1966-70; asst. gen. counsel securities Am. Life Ins. Assn., Washington, 1971-74; atty. eval. sect., chief legis. unit antitrust divsn. U.S. Dept. Justice, Washington, 1974-78, spl. asst. U.S. atty. Alexandria, Va., 1978; pvt. practice Columbia, Md., 1978—. Author: U.S. Department of Justice Antitrust Report on Property-Liability Insurance Industry, 1977; contbr. articles to profl. jours. Mem. Howard County (Md.) Charter Revision Commn., 1979; bd. dirs. Howard County YMCA, 1997-99, disting. bd. mem. 1999. With USAR, 1960-66. Mem. Md. Bar Assn., D.C. Bar Assn., Howard County Bar Assn., Greater Howard County C. of C. (dir., gen. counsel 1981-84). Corporate, general, Trademark and copyright, Securities. Office: Hobbits Glen 5040 Rushlight Path Columbia MD 21044-1295 E-mail: consult@maseritzlaw.com.

MASHRUWALA, ANISH SUBHASH, lawyer; b. Mysore, Karnataka, India; arrived in U.S., 2000; s. Subhash Chandrakant Mashruwala and Sita Subhash Mushruwala. BS, Pune U., 1997, LLB, 1999; LLM, U. Mich., 2001. Bar: N.Y. 2002, Indian Coun. Gujarat 1999. Mem.: ABA, N.Y. State Bar Assn., South Asian Bar Assn. Hindu. Avocations: racquetball, painting, classical Indian dance form of Kathak. Private international, Mergers and acquisitions, Securities. Office: Thompson Hine LLP 1920 N St NW Washington DC 20036

MASI, JOHN ROGER, lawyer; b. Bklyn., Jan. 18, 1954; s. John Roger and Evelyn (Teagno) M.; m. Sherrill Alaine Schlett, June 29, 1985; children: Roger C., Christopher J., Nicholas J. BA, Franklin & Marshall Coll., 1978; JD, Temple U., 1980. Bar: N.J. 1981, Pa. 1981, U.S. Dist. Ct. N.J. 1981. Assoc. Klinger, Nicolette, Mavroudis & Honig, Oradell, NJ, 1982—86, Gern, Dunetz, Roseland, NJ, 1986—87; ptnr. J. Roger Masi, Esq., Hackensack, NJ, 1987—2002; sr. ptnr. Fischer, Porter, Masi and Thomas, 2002—. Committeeman County Rep., Ridgewood, N.J., 1982-84; mem. Ridgewood Zoning Bd. Adjustment, 1990-94; mem. Ridgewood Edn. Found. Mem. Bergen County Bar Assn. Roman Catholic. State civil litigation, Corporate, general, Personal injury (including property damage). Office: Fischer Porter Masi & Thomas 440 Sylvan Ave Ste 130 Englewood Cliffs NJ 07632

MASIELLO, THOMAS PHILIP, JR., lawyer, risk manager; b. Medford, Mass., Oct. 13, 1961; s. Thomas Philip and Diane Marie (Traina) M.; m. Stephanie Hope Sadwin, Sept. 24, 1994; 1 child, Andrew Joseph. BA, Johnson State Coll., Vt., 1982, BFA, 1983; ARM, Bentley Coll., Waltham, Mass., 1986; JD, New Eng. Sch. Law, Boston, 1992. Bar: Mass. 1993, U.S. Supreme Ct. 1998. With Parker, Colter, Daley & White, 1986-88, Am. Internat. Group Ins. Com., 1988-91, McDonald & Wallace, 1991-92, Boston Housing Authority, 1992-95, Cumberland Farms-Gulf Oil, Canton, Mass., 1995—. Exec. dir. Mass. Mcpl. Workers Compensation Group. Author Workers Comp Bull., 1996. Mem. ABA, ATLA, Internat. Risk Mgmt. Inst. (self-insurers and risk mgr. law com.), Boston Bar Assn., Norfolk County Bar Assn., Risk Ins. Mgmt. Soc. (nat. governance com., nat. nominating com.), Mass. Acad. Trial Atty., Quality Ins. Congress, Nat. Assoc. of Convenence Sues (NACS), Mass Acad. Trial Atty.,(MATA). Avocation: adventure travel. Insurance, Personal injury (including property damage), Workers' compensation. Home: 3 Grantland Rd Wellesley Hills MA 02481-7606 Office: Cumberland Farms/Gulf Oil 777 Dedham St Canton MA 02021-1402

MASINTER, PAUL JAMES, lawyer; b. New Orleans, June 28, 1961; s. Milton Paul Masinter and Shirley Mae (Rabé) Bradley; m. Audrey Renee Williams, Oct. 10, 1992. BA in Polit. Sci., La. State U., 1984, JD, 1987. Bar: La. 1987, U.S. Dist. Ct. (ea., mid. and we. dists.) La. 1987, U.S. Ct. Appeals (5th cir.) 1990, U.S. Supreme Ct. 1994. Law clk. to assoc. justice Hon. James L. Dennis La. Supreme Ct., New Orleans, 1987-88; assoc. McGlinchey, Stafford, New Orleans, 1988-90, Stone Pigman Walther Wittmann LLC, New Orleans, 1990-95; ptnr. Stone Pigman Walther Wittmann, LLC, New Orleans, 1996—. Assoc. editor La. Law Rev., 1986-87. Bd. dirs. Save Our Cemeteries, New Orleans, 1993—, treas., 1998, pres., 1999. Mem. ABA (chair newsletter subcom., bus. and corp. litigation com., bus. law sect.), La. State Bar Assn., New Orleans Bar Assn. Democrat. Roman Catholic. Antitrust, Professional liability, Product liability. Home: 1820 Octavia St New Orleans LA 70115-5660 Office: Stone Pigman Walther & Wittmann LLC 546 Carondelet St Ste 100 New Orleans LA 70130-3588 E-mail: PMasinter@stonepigman.com.

MASLOW, LINDA S. law librarian; b. N.Y.C., Oct. 25, 1955; d. Irving and Frances Maslow. BA, Queens Coll., CUNY, 1977; JD, Harvard U., 1980; MLS, U. Mich., 1984. Bar: NY 81, U.S. Supreme Ct. 96. Assoc. Webster & Sheffield, N.Y.C., 1980—82; reference libr. U. Mich. Law Libr., Ann Arbor, 1984, chief reference libr., 1984—88; asst. libr. rsch. svcs. U.S. Supreme Ct. Libr., Washington, 1988—. Author: A Guide to Legal Research in the University of Michigan Law Library, 4th edit., 1987 (Publ. award Am. Assn. Law Librs., 88). Fellow acad. rsch. librarianship, Coun. Libr. Resources, 1982. Mem.: Law Librs. Soc. Washington DC, Am. Assn. Law Librs., Phi Beta Kappa. Office: Supreme Ct US Libr 1 1st St NE Washington DC 20543

MASON, J. WILLIAM L. lawyer; b. Kittery, Maine, Apr. 14, 1940; s. Murray Lawrence and Dolores Elizabeth (Laird) M.; m. Mary Elizabeth Jordan; children: Joseph Patrick, Catherine Shannon, Brendan Michael. BA, U. N.H., 1973, MBA, 1979; JD, New Eng. Sch. Law, 1987. Molder Portsmouth (N.H.) Naval Shipyard, 1958-71, with labor rels., 1973-91; rehab. technician State of N.H., Concord, 1971-73; pvt. practice Portsmouth, 1991—. Staff sgt. N.H. Air Nat. Guard, 1974-81. Mem. ABA, Am. Trial Lawyers Assn., N.H. Bar Assn. Congregationalist. Avocation: coins. Family and matrimonial, Pension, profit-sharing, and employee benefits, Personal injury (including property damage). Home: 27 Old Concord Tpke Lee NH 03824-6729 Office: 5 Greenleaf Woods Dr Ste 301 Portsmouth NH 03801-5442 E-mail: jwlmason@hotmail.com.

MASON, THOMAS ALBERT, lawyer; b. Cleve., May 4, 1936; s. Victor Lewis and Frances (Speidel) M.; m. Elisabeth Gun Sward, Sept. 25, 1965; children: Thomas Lewis, Robert Albert. AB, Kenyon Coll., 1958; LLB, Case-Western Res. U., 1961. Bar: Ohio 1961. Assoc. Thompson, Hine and Flory, Cleve., 1965-73, ptnr., 1973—. Trustee Cleve. YMCA, 1975-94. Capt. USMCR, 1962-65. Mem. Am. Coll. Real Estate Lawyers, Am. Land

Title Assn. (lender's counsel group), Mortgage Bankers Assn. of Met. Cleve., Ohio Bar Assn., Cleve. Bar Assn., The Country Club. Republican. Episcopalian. Avocations: tennis, golf. Property, real (including real estate development, water). Home: 23375 Duffield Rd Cleveland OH 44122-3101 Office: Thompson Hine LLP 3900 Key Ctr 127 Public Sq Cleveland OH 44114-1291 E-mail: tom.mason@thompsonhine.com.

MASON, THOMAS OWEN, lawyer; b. Winthrop, Mass., Nov. 16, 1963; s. Robert Joseph and Carol Ann (St. Croix) M. BA, Salem State Coll., 1987; JD, New England Sch. Law, 1991. Bar: Mass. 1991, U.S. Dist. Ct. Mass. 1992, U.S. Ct. Appeals (1st cir.) 1992. Atty. Law Offices Robert A. Costantino, East Boston, 1992-95; sole practitioner Law Office Thomas O. Mason, East Boston, 1995—. Notary pub. Commonwealth Mass., 1992—. Editor law rev. publs. New England Jour. on Criminal and Civil Confinement, 1988-89, 90-91. Charles F. Kiefer meml. scholar, 1985-86, New England Sch. Law scholar, 1989-91. Mem. ABA, Essex County Bar Assn., Boston Bar Assn., Lynn Bar Assn., Phi Alpha Theta. Republican. Roman Catholic. Avocations: reading, weight training, sports. General practice, Personal injury (including property damage), Property, real (including real estate development, water). Home: 19 Wells Pl Lynn MA 01902-1623 Office: Law Office Thomas O Mason 19 Meridian St East Boston MA 02128-1928 Fax: (781) 599-6237. E-mail: TM715@aol.com.

MASRY, EDWARD L. lawyer; b. Patterson, N.J., July 29, 1932; m. Jacqueline Wilson; children: Louanne, Louis, Nichole; m. Joette Levinson, 1992; children: Chris, Tim. Student, Valley Jr. Coll., 1950—52, U. Calif., Santa Barbara, UCLA, U. So. Calif.; JD, Loyola U., L.A., 1960. Bar: Calif., U.S. Dist. Ct. Calif., U.S. Ct. Appeals (9th cir.), U.S. Supreme Ct. Pvt. practice, L.A., 1961—75, San Fernando Valley, Calif., 1975—82; ptnr. Masry & Vititoe, San Fernando Valley, 1982—97, Westlake Village, Calif., 1997—. Pres., CEO Save World Air, Inc.; mem. adv. bd. Boys & Girls Club, Conejo, Calif., Las Virgenes, Calif.; mem. Thousand Oaks City Coun., Calif., 2000; mayor pro tem City of Thousand Oaks, mayor, 2003—. With U.S. Army, 1952—54, Korea. Recipient U.S. Congl. award Outstanding Lawyer of the Yr., 1982, 1988, 1990, cert. of appreciation, Las Virgenes Unified Sch. Dist., 2002, cert. spl. congl. recognition, Def. Ctr. Commitment Environment Justice, 2002, Environ. Hero award, 2002, award, Nat. Jewish Fund, 2002, Santa Monica Mountains Recreational Area, Calif. Dept. Pks. and Recreation Angeles Dist., Mountains Restoration Trust, others. Mem.: ATLA, ABA, Consumer Attys. Assn. L.A., Los Angeles County Bar Assn., Ventura County Bar Assn., Consumer Attys. Calif., Trial Lawyers Pub. Justice (Acad. Justice award 2001), Phi Alpha Delta (justice, L.A. alumni justice). Office: Masry and Vititoe 5707 Corsa Ave Westlake Village CA 91362 Office Fax: 818-991-6200.*

MASSAD, STEPHEN ALBERT, lawyer; b. Wewoka, Okla., Dec. 20, 1950; s. Alexander Hamilton and Delores Jean (Razook) Massad; children: Caroline, Sarah, Margaret. AB, Princeton U., 1972; JD, Harvard U., 1975. Bar: Tex. 1975. Assoc. Baker Botts L.L.P., Houston, 1975-82, ptnr., 1983—. Corporate, general, Mergers and acquisitions, Securities. Office: Baker Botts LLP 3000 One Shell Plz 910 Louisiana St Houston TX 77002 E-mail: stephen.massad@bakerbotts.com.

MASSARO, TONI MARIE, dean, law educator; BS, Northwestern U., 1977; JD, Coll. William and Mary, 1980. With Vedder, Price, Kaufman and Kammholz; tchr. law Washington and Lee U., U. Fla.; former prof. law U. Ariz., Tucson, dean, Milton O. Riepe chair constl. law, 1999—. Vis. prof. law Stanford U., U. N.C., Johann Goethe U., Frankfurt, West Germany. Author: Constitutional Literacy: A Core Curriculum for a Multi-Cultural Nation; contbr. numerous articles to law revs. Office: U Ariz Coll Law Bldg 204a PO Box 210176 Tucson AZ 85721-0176 Fax: 520-621-9140. E-mail: massaro@nt.law.arizona.edu.

MASSEL, ELIHU SAUL, lawyer; b. Bklyn., May 3, 1940; s. Ezekiel and Sadie (Sutta) M.; m. Matilda Montefiore, May 15, 1968; children: Morris, Richard, Tracy. BA, Alfred U., 1962; JD, NYU, 1965. Bar: N.Y. 1966, U.S. Dist. Ct. (ea. dist.) N.Y. 1967, (so. dist.) N.Y. 1967, (no. dist.) N.Y. 1970, (we. dist.) N.Y. 1970, U.S. Ct. Appeals (2d cir.), 1967, U.S. Supreme Ct. 1970. Law guardian Legal Aid Soc., Bklyn., 1966-67; assoc. Law Offices of Henry Abrams, N.Y.C., 1967-69; asst. atty. gen. N.Y. State Dept. Law, N.Y.C., 1969-72; pvt. practice, N.Y.C., 1972—. Lectr. N.Y. County Lawyers Assn., N.Y.C., 1982-96. Vice-pres. Am. Youth Hostels, Inc., Washington, 1970-79; bd. dirs., past pres. Met. N.Y. Coun. Am. Youth Hostels, Inc., 1969-90; trustee N.Y.C. chpt. Leukemia Soc. Am., 1976-96. Recipient Pro Bono award U.S. Dept. Justice, 1997, 98, Pro Bono award Am. Immigration Lawyers Assn., 1998. Mem. ABA, N.Y. State Bar Assn. (Pro Bono award 1996), Assn. Bar City N.Y., Queens County Bar Assn., Am. Immigration Lawyers Assn. (chmn. N.Y.C. chpt. 1976-77, N.Y.C. chpt. Pro Bono award 1996). Jewish. Avocations: hosteling, bicycling, photography, numismatics. Immigration, naturalization, and customs. Office: 122 E 42nd St New York NY 10168-0002

MASSENGALE, ROGER LEE, lawyer; b. Somerset, Ky., Mar. 23, 1953; s. Wendell Howard and Norma Jean (Neely) M.; m. Debra Kaye Marcum, Mar. 19, 1978; children: Sarah Anne, Jessica Claire. BA, U. Ky., 1975; JD, Capitol U., 1979. Bar: Ky. 1979, U.S. Dist. Ct. (ea. dist.) Ky. 1980, U.S. Ct. Appeals (6th cir.) 1986. Assoc. Lovelace, Carroll & Peck, Monticello, Ky., 1979-80; asst. county atty. Wayne County, Monticello, 1979-80; region counsel Ashland (Ky.) Exploration, Inc., 1980-83; atty. Ashland Oil, Inc., 1983-85; assoc. Wells, Porter & Schmitt, Paintsville, Ky., 1985-88, ptnr., 1988-94; pvt. practice Law Offices Roger L. Massengale, Paintsville, 1994—. Bd. dirs. Parents Anonymous Ea. Ky., Ashland, 1984, Tri-State Fair and Regatta, Ashland, 1983-85; past chmn. adminstrv. bd. First United Meth. Ch., Paintsville, lay del. to Ky. Ann. Conf. Mem. ABA, Ky. Bar Assn. (mem. ho. dels. 1991-98), Ky. Acad. Trial Attys., Johnson County Bar Assn., Def. Rsch. Inst. Avocations: fly fishing, backpacking, wood working. General civil litigation, Insurance, Personal injury (including property damage). Home: 208 4th St Paintsville KY 41240-1150

MASSEY, RAYMOND DAVID, lawyer; b. Goldsboro, N.C., Oct. 13, 1946; s. Raymond L. and Dorris L. (Grant) Massey; m. Barbara A. Warner, Aug. 16, 1967; children: Suzanne, Christine. BA, Wofford Coll., Spartanburg, S.C., 1968; JD, U. S.C., 1971; LLM in Taxation, Emory U., 1985. Bar: S.C. 1971, U.S. Dist. Ct. S.C. 1971. Assoc. Perrin, Perrin & Mann, Spartanburg, Spartanburg, 1971—74; trust officer Bankers Trust of S.C., Columbia, SC, 1974—78; shareholder Brown, Massey, Evans, McLeod & Haynsworth, PA, Greenville, SC, 1978—. Pres. Greenville Estate Planning Coun., 1982; chair Cmty. Found. of Greater Greenville, 2001—02; dir. Greenville Hosp. Sys. Found., 2002—. Mem.: S.C. Bar Assn. (chmn. probate, estate planning and trust sect. 1983), Greenville Bar Assn. (pres. tax sect. 1980—81), Poinsett Club, Greenville Country Club. Presbyterian. State civil litigation, Probate (including wills, trusts), Estate taxation. Office: PO Box 2464 Greenville SC 29602-2464

MASSEY, RAYMOND LEE, lawyer; b. Macon, Ga., Sept. 25, 1948; s. Ford B. and Juanita (Sapp) M.; m. Lynn Ann Thielmeier, Aug. 23, 1967; children: Daniel, Caroline. BA, U. Mo., St. Louis, 1971; JD, U. Louisville, 1974. Bar: Mo. 1974, Ill. 1976, U.S. Dist. Ct. (ea. and we. dists.) Mo. 1974, U.S. Dist. Ct. (so. dist.) Ill. 1976. Assoc. Thompson & Mitchell, St. Louis, 1974-79; ptnr. Thompson & Mitchell (now Thompson & Coburn), St. Louis, 1979—. Mem. Maritime Law Assn. of U.S. (bd. dirs., chmn. ocean and river towing). Admiralty, General civil litigation, Environmental. Home: 3 Wild Rose Dr Saint Louis MO 63124-1465 Office: Thompson Coburn US Bank Ste 3400 Saint Louis MO 63101-1643

MASSLER, HOWARD ARNOLD, lawyer, corporate executive; b. Newark, July 22, 1946; s. Abraham I. and Sylvia (Botwin) M.; children: Justin Scott, Jeremy Ross. BA, U. Pa., 1969; JD, Rutgers U., 1973; LLM in Taxation, NYU, 1977. Bar: N.J. 1974, U.S. Dist. Ct. N.J. 1974, D.C. 1975, U.S. Ct. Appeals (D.C. cir.) 1975, N.Y. 1977, U.S. Dist. Ct. (we. dist.) N.Y. 1977, U.S. Tax Ct. 1977. Counsel house banking, currency and housing com., chmn. sub-com. U.S. Ho. Reps., Washington, 1974-76; tax atty. Lipsitz, Green, Fahringer, Roll, Schuller & James, N.Y.C. and Buffalo, 1977-79; pvt. practice Mountainside, N.J., 1979-89; pres. Bestway Products Inc., A.A. Records Inc., Servor Corp., 1979-85; pres., chief exec. officer, chmn. bd. Bestway Group Inc., Dover, Del., 1985-91; gen. ptnr. 26/27 Law Drive Assocs., 1988—; ptnr. Shonageri, Pearce & Massler, Hackensack, N.J., 1989-90, Mott, Pearce, Williams & Lee, Hackensack and Washington, 1990-91, Pearce & Massler, Hackensack, N.J., 1991-97. Prodn. staff asst. DECCA House Ltd., London, 1968; chief exec. officer Basura Pub., Inc. (affiliated with BMI), 1974-80; arbitrator U.S. Dist. Ct. N.J., 1985—; adj. prof. law Seton Hall U., Newark, N.J., 1988-89, N.J. Inst. for Continuing Legal Edn., 1986; lectr. N.J. Inst. for Continuing Legal Edn., 1986—; assoc. dir. United Jersey Bank/Franklin State Bank, 1987—; del. adv. com. on indsl. trade and econ. devel. U.S./China Joint Sessions, Beijing, People's Republic of China, 1988. Author: QDROs (Tax and Drafting Considerations), 1986, 2nd. ed., 1987; contbr. West's Legal Forms, Vol. 7., 2d edit., 1987, 3d edit., Domestic Relations with Tax Analysis, Contemporary Matrimonial Law Issues: A Guide to Divorce Economics and Practice; tax author: Matthew Bender, NYCP-Matrimonial Actions and Equitable Distribution Actions, 1988; tax author, tax editor: Matthew Bender, Alimony, Child Support & Counsel Fees-Award, Modification and Enforcement, 1988, 2d edit., 1989, 3d edit., 1991, Matthew Bender, Valuation & Distribution of Marital Property, 1988, 89, 91, 92, 94, 95; contbg. author: How to Make Legal Fees Tax Deductible, 1988, Closely Held Corporations, Forms and Checklists, Buy-Sell Agreement Forms with Tax Analysis, 1988, The Encyclopedia of Matrimonial Practice, 1991, 4th edit., 1995; author: New York Practice Guide: Negligence, Tax Law of Compensation for Sickness and Injury, 2d edit., 1992; contbg. editor Pensions and Ins. Problems, 1984—, Taxation, 1984—, Fair$hare, 1984—, Law & Bus., Inc., 1984—; staff contbr., N.J. Law Jour., 1986—; contbr. articles to law revs. and profl. jours. Bd. dirs., legal counsel western N.Y. chpt. Nat. Handicapped Sports and Recreation Assn., 1977-79; counsel Union County, N.J., 1984-85; candidate Springfield (N.J.) Twp. Commn., 1986. Mem. ABA, N.J. Bar Assn. (vice chmn. taxation comm. family law section 1987—), N.Y. Bar Assn. (taxation com., subcom. on criminal and civil penalties), D.C. Bar Assn., Erie County Bar Assn. (sec. taxation com. 1977-79, continuing edn. lectr. taxation 1977—), Essex County Bar Assn. (tax com. 1981—), Union County Bar Assn. (chmn. tax com. 1984—) Republican. Avocation: Sports Car Club Am. formula Ford racing. Corporate taxation, Estate taxation, Personal income taxation. Home: 508 Main St PO Box 399 Boonton NJ 07005-0399 Office: 508 Main St Boonton NJ 07005-1716

MASSMAN, RICHARD ALLAN, lawyer; b. Beaumont, Tex., Aug. 19, 1943; s. Irwin Massman and Sylvia (Schmidt) Schwartz; m. Barbara Elaine Kessler; children: Jason Todd, Karen Faye. BS cum laude, U. Pa., 1965; JD cum laude, Harvard U., 1968. Bar: Tex. 1968; cert. in taxation, Tex. Bd. Legal Specialization. Assoc. Coke & Coke, Dallas, 1968-70, Johnson & Wortley, P.C. (formerly Johnson & Gibbs, P.C.), Dallas, 1970-71, ptnr., 1971-88, shareholder, 1988-94; of counsel Johnson & Wortley P.C., Dallas, 1994-95; sr. v.p., gen. counsel Hunt Consolidated, Inc., Dallas, 1994—. Lectr. So. Meth. U., Dallas, 1973. Bd. dirs. Martin Luther King Jr. Community Ctr., Dallas, 1979-81, Jewish Fedn. Greater Dallas, 1980-83, 89—, The Dallas Opera, 1999—; mem. exec. com. Dallas regional bd. Anti-Defamation League, 1979—, chmn., 1990-92; chmn. Dallas Civil Svc. Bd., 1983; trustee Greenhill Sch., Dallas, 1985-92, vice chmn., 1990-92. Recipient Jurisprudence award Anti-Defamation League, 2000. Mem. Am. Coll. Tax Coun., Tex. State Bar (chmn., sec. taxation 1983-84), Dallas Bar Assn. (chmn., sec. taxation 1978), Dallas Petroleum Club, Columbian Club. Estate planning, Property, real (including real estate development, water), Corporate taxation. Office: Hunt Consolidated Inc Fountain Pl 20th Fl 1445 Ross at Field Dallas TX 75202-2785

MASSONG, JUDY IRENE, lawyer; b. Yakima, Wash., June 23, 1950; d. George E. and Florence N. (Estabrook) Massong; m. Arthur A. Butler, July 30, 1994. BSN, U. Wash., 1973; MSN, U. Calif., San Francisco, 1974; JD, Golden Gate U., 1980. Bar: Wash., U.S. Dist. Ct. Wash. Bd. dirs. N.W. Hort. Assn., Seattle. Mem.: Wash. State Trial Lawyers Assn. (pres.-elect), Wash. State Bar Assn. (pres. litigation sect.). General civil litigation. Office: Peterson Young Putra 1501 4th Ave Ste 2800 Seattle WA 98101-3677

MASTANDREA, LINDA LEE, lawyer; b. Chgo., June 10, 1964; d. Robert Anthony and Dorothy Jean (Kilpatrick) M. BA in Speech Comm., U. Ill., 1986; JD, IIT, 1994. Bar: Ill. 1995. Account rep. Health Chgo. HMO, Lisle, Ill., 1986-87; peer counselor Peninsula Ctr. Ind. Living, Newport News, Va., 1988-89; program mgr. Progress Ctr. Ind. Living, Oak Park, Ill., 1990-91; atty. pvt. practice, Ill., 1995—. Pub. spkr., Ill., 1991—; sec. assoc. bd. Rehab. Inst. of Chgo. Athlete rep. Atlanta Paralympics, 1993-96; v.p. athlete's adv. com., assoc. bd. Rehab. Inst. Chgo., 1992—, sec., assoc. bd., 1997—, pub. policy com., vocat. action com.; athlete rep. on exec. com. Cerebral Palsy Internat. Sport and Recreation Assn. Named Athlete of Yr. Colo. Sports Coun., Denver, 1994, Outstanding Woman in Sports YWCA DuPage Dist., DuPage County, Ill., 1995, Outstanding Chgo. Women in Sports Crohn's and Colitis Found., 1997; recipient IOC Pres. Disabled Athlete award U.S. Sports Acad., Mobile, Ala., 1995, USCPAA Female Athlete of Yr., 1995; paralympics gold medalist 200m, 1996, silver medalist 100m, 1996. Mem. U.S. Cerebral Palsy Athletic Assn. (v.p. 1994—), Nat. Italian Bar Assn., Justinian Soc. Lawyers, Chgo. Bar Assn., ISBA. Avocation: wheelchair track world-record holder 100, 200, 400, 800 and 1500 meters. Civil rights, Education and schools, Labor (including EEOC, Fair Labor Standards Act, labor-management relations, NLRB, OSHA).

MASTERS, BARBARA J. lawyer; b. Denver, July 17, 1933; d. Richard P. and Ruth Ann (Savage) Johnson; children: Eliot, Joan. BA, Middlebury Coll., 1955; JD, U. Conn., 1976. Bar: Conn. 1976, U.S. Dist. Ct. Conn. 1976. Assoc. Maruzo & Lucas, Norwich, Conn., 1976-80; pvt. practice Norwich, Conn., 1980—; prin. Masters and Benson, Norwich, Conn., 1994—2001, Masters and Puhlick, Norwich, Conn., 2001—. Mem. Conn. Coun. for Divorce Mediation. Bd. dirs. United Comty. Svcs., Norwich, 1980-87, Women's Ctr. Southeastern Conn., New London, 1983-89, Madonna Pl., Norwich, 1989-93; vice-chmn. Lebanon (Conn.) Bd. Fin., 1984-88; mem. People to People del. women lawyers to China, 1986, Norwich Arts Coun., 1989-93; alt. Old Lyme Zoning Bd. Appeals, 1993-97, Old Lyme Dem. Town Com., 1994-2001; mem. People to People Family Lawyer's Del., Cuba, 2001. Mem. Conn. Bar Assn., New London County Bar Assn. (pres. 1998-99). Unitarian Universalist. Avocations: sailing, walking, third world travel. State civil litigation, Family and matrimonial, Property, real (including real estate development, water). Home: 2 Point Rd Old Saybrook CT 06475 Office: 199 W Town St Norwich CT 06360-2106 E-mail: norwichlaw@aol.com.

MASTERS, JON JOSEPH, corporate governance consultant, arbitrator, management consultant; b. N.Y.C., June 20, 1937; s. Arthur Edward and Esther (Shady) M.; m. Rosemary Dunaway Cox, June 16, 1962; children: Brooke Alison, Blake Edward. BA, Princeton U., 1958; JD, Harvard U., 1964. Bar: N.Y. 1965, U.S. Dist. Ct. (so. dist.) N.Y. 1965, U.S. Ct. Appeals (2d cir.) 1965. Cons. asst. to under sec. Dept. Army, 1961; mem. policy planning staff asst. sec. for internat. security affairs Dept. Def., 1962; mem. Pres. Johnson's Spl. Polit. Research Staff, Washington, 1964; assoc. Shearman & Sterling, N.Y.C., 1965-68, 69; mem. staff Bedford-Stuyvesant D & S Corp., Bklyn., 1968-69; v.p., sec., gen. counsel, dir. Baker, Weeks & Co., Inc., N.Y.C., 1969-76; ptnr. Christy & Viener, N.Y.C., 1976-96; Vice-chmn. Robb, Peck, McCooey Specialist Corp., N.Y.C., 1996—98; prin. Lear, Yavitz & Assocs., N.Y.C., 1996-2001, mng. prin., 1998—2001; prin. Mercer Delta Cons., N.Y.C., 2001—02; chmn. Masters Governance Cons., LLC, N.Y.C., 2002—. SEC adv. com. broker-dealer compliance, 1972-74; legal advisor NACD Blue Ribbon Commn. on CEO and Dir. Performance Evaluation, 1994; chmn. bd. Clear and Present Prodns., 1992-93. Mem. implementation com. Econ. Devel. Task Force of N.Y. Urban Coalition, 1968; mem. bd. Internat. Social Service, Am. Br., Inc., 1978-83, pres., 1979-83; bd. dirs. The Arts Connection, 1979-85; mem. steering com. N.Y. Lawyers Alliance for Nuclear Arms Control, 1983-96. Served with USN, 1958-61. Mem. ABA, Assn. Bar City N.Y. (com. mcpl. affairs 1977-80), N.Y. State Bar Assn. Corporate, general, General practice, Securities. Office: 350 E 82 NA New York NY 10028 E-mail: mastersjj@aol.com.

MASTERSON, KENNETH RHODES, lawyer; b. Kennett, M.O., Feb. 22, 1944; s. H. Byron and Mary (Rhodes) M.; children— Michael K., Elizabeth Megel, Grace Megel BA, Westminster Coll., 1966; JD, Vanderbilt U., 1970. Bar: Mo. 1970, Tenn. 1976. Ptnr. Thomason, Crawford & Hendrix, Memphis, 1976-79; v.p. legal Fed. Express Corp., Memphis, 1980-81, sr. v.p., gen. counsel, 1981-93, sr. v.p., gen. counsel and sec., 1993-96, exec. v.p., gen. counsel and sec., 1996-98, FedEx Corp., Memphis, 1998—. Mem. ABA, Mo. Bar Assn., Am. Corp. Counsel Assn. Corporate, general. Home: 8679 Classic Dr Memphis TN 38125-8824 Office: FedEx Corp 942 S Shady Grove Rd Memphis TN 38120-4117 Fax: 901-818-7590.*

MASTERSON, WILLIAM A. retired judge; b. N.Y.C., June 25, 1931; s. John Patrick and Helen Audrey (O'Hara) M.; m. Julie Dohrmann Cosgrove; children: Mark, Mary, Timothy, Barbara. BA, UCLA, 1953, JD, 1958. Bar: Calif. 1959, U.S. Supreme Ct. 1965.. Assoc. Sheppard, Mullin, Richter & Hampton, L.A., 1952-62, pntr., 1962-79; ptnr. Rogers & Wells, 1979-83, Skadden, Arps, Slate, Meagher & Flom, 1983-87; judge L.A. Superior Ct., 1987-92; justice Ct. Appeal, 1993-2000; ret., 2000. Author, editor: Civil Trial Practice: Strategies and Techniques, 1986. With inf. U.S. Army, 1953-55. Fellow Am. Coll. Trial Lawyers; mem. Order of Coif. Office: PO Box 190 Mendocino CA 95460

MASTERTON, LUCINDA CRONIN, lawyer; b. Proctor, Vt., May 18, 1950; d. John Donald and Elsie Lipstein M.; m. Lindsay Morris, Mar. 16, 1998; 1 child: Rachael Leigh. BA, Northwestern U., 1972; JD, W. Va. U., 1981. Bar: Ky. 1982. Law clerk to Hon. K.K. Hall, Charleston, W. Va., 1981-82; law clerk to Hon. Edwin Flowers, 1982; assoc. Goodwin & Goodwin, Charleston, W. Va., 1982-83, Lexington, Ky., 1989-93; ptnr., assoc. Vimont & Wills, Lexington, Ky., 1983-89; pvt. practice Lexington, Ky., 1993—. Trustee Chpt. 7 Bankruptcy, Ea. Dist. Ky., Lexington, 1989—. Mem. Jr. League, Parkersburg, Charleston, W. Va., Lexington, Ky., 1978-90. Mem. Fayette County Bar Assn. Avocations: horseback riding, gardening. Bankruptcy, Personal injury (including property damage), Toxic tort. Office: 4857 Paynes Mill Rd Lexington KY 40510-9695

MASTROMARCO, DAN RALPH, lawyer, consultant; b. Saginaw, Mich., Jan. 18, 1958; s. Victor and Helen (Finkbeiner) M. Student, London Sch. of Econs., Eng., 1982; JD, U. Toledo, 1983; LLM, Georgetown U., 1985. Bar: Mich. 1983, D.C. 1984. Counsel U.S. Senate, Permanent Subcom. on Investigations, Washington, 1983-85; trial atty. Tax div. U.S. Dept. of Justice, Washington, 1985-86; asst. chief counsel for tax policy U.S. SBA, Washington, 1986-92; dir. tax and fiscal policy Jefferson Group, Washington, 1992-94; pres., CEO The Argus Group, Washington, 1994—. Coord. Nat. Adv. Coun. for Small Bus., Tax Com., 1986-88; hon. mem. tax com. Small Bus. Legis. Coun., 1986-90; adj. prof. internat. mgmt. program U. Md.; exec. dir. Travel Coun. for Fair Competition; pres. The Prosperity Inst.; exec. dir. Small Bus. Regulators Coun. Author: The Art of Lobbying in Poland, 1995, Out by Its Roots, 1999; contbr. author, editor profl. jours., reports. Mem. Nat. Italian Am. Bar Assn. (trustee scholarship fund, counsel, v.p.), U.S. C. of C. (tax policy com.). Roman Catholic. Office: TAG 333 N Fairfax St Alexandria VA 22314-2632 E-mail: argusgroupdrm@aol.com.

MASUDA, SUSUMU, lawyer; b. Tokyo, June 8, 1955; s. Atsushi Maeda and Sumiko M.; m. Yoshiko Fujii, Sept. 23, 1983; children: Ayako, Shingo. LLB, Tokyo U., 1980; LLM, U. Wash., 1986. Bar: Japan 1982, Calif. 1987. Legal intern Legal Rsch. and Tng. Inst. Supreme Ct., Tokyo, 1980-82; assoc. Mori Hamada & Matsumoto, Tokyo, 1982-85, ptnr., 1988—; assoc. Pillsbury Winthrop, LLP (formerly Lillick, McHose & Charles), L.A., 1986-87. Expert Japanese del. UNIDROIT Conv. on Internat. Interests in Mobile Equipments, 1999-2001. Author: Recent Developments in American Law Regulating Lock-Ups, 1988, Legal Issues Concerning Electronic Money, 1998, Whether Does the Proposal to Reschedule Loans Constitute the Suspension of Payments Under the Insolvency Laws, 1999, Law Regarding Digital Signature and Digital Certification, 2000, Adoption of Unidroit Convention on International Interests in Mobile Equipment, 2002; co-author: Legal Problems in Conditional Sale, 1985, Handbook of How to Deal with Shareholders, 1989, Legal Issues Involved in Electronic Money, 1996-97, Electronic Money in Japan, 1997, prac. analysis on Electronic Money, 1998, International Lawyers' Practice Data-File, 2000, Adoption of Unidroit Convention on International Interests in Mobile Equipments, 2002. Mem.: Internat. C. of C. (fin. svc. com. 1994—, others), Daini-Tokyo Bar Assn. (vice chmn. com. fgn. legal cons. 1994), State Bar Calif. Avocations: reading novels, classical music, golf. Office: Mori Hamada & Matsumoto JFE Bldg 1-1-2 Marunouchi Chiyoda-ku Tokyo 100-0005 Japan Personal E-mail: susumu.masuda@mhmjapan.com.

MATARAZZO, HARRIS STARR, lawyer; b. Portland, Oreg., July 24, 1957; s. Joseph Dominic and Ruth Wood (Gadbois) M.; m. Judith Grace Hudson, Jan. 2, 1988. AB in Polit. Sci., Brown U., 1979; JD, Northwestern Sch. Law, Portland, 1983. Bar: Oreg. 1986, U.S. Dist. Ct. Oreg. 1986, U.S. Ct. Appeals (9th cir.) 1986, U.S. Supreme Ct. 1992. With Aitchison, Imperati, Paull, Barnett and Sherwood, Portland, 1986; assoc. Parks & Bauer, Salem, Oreg., 1987-88; pvt. practice Portland, 1988—. Sprk. Mental Health and the Law conf. Med. Ednl. Svcs., Inc., 1995, 96. Contbr. to Criminal Law Handbook, 1994, 98. Mem. Hist. Preservation League Oreg., Portland, 1984—, Oreg. State Pub. Interest Rsch. Group, Portland, 1985—, The Old Ch. Soc., Portland, 1986; bd. dirs. Bosco Milligan Found., 1992—, Rape Survivors Inc., 1994, Lincoln H.S. Alumni Assn., 1995—, Morrison Ctr., 1996-2001, Network Housing, Inc., 1998—, Oreg. Advocacy Ctr., 1998, 2000—, Italian Businessmen's Club, 1998—, InAct, Inc., 1998—, Rosemont Treatment Ctr. and Sch., 1998-99, Friends of Simon Benson House, 1998-2002, Parents Anonymous, 2001-02; mem. vestry Trinity Episcopal Ch., 1992-95, 2001—; mem. Oreg. Advocacy Ctr. Mental Health Adv. Coun., 1996-2000; mem. planned giving com. Multnomah County Libr., 1997—. Mem. ABA, Fed. Bar Assn., Oreg. State Bar Assn., Oreg. Criminal Def. Lawyers Assn. (spkr. State of Mind. conf. 1990, Property Crimes conf. 1999), Multnomah County Bar Assn. Administrative and regulatory, General practice, Landlord-tenant. Office: Bank Am Fin Ctr 121 SW Morrison St Ste 1020 Portland OR 97204-3140

MATARESE, LAUREN A. police officer, lawyer; b. Framingham, Mass., Dec. 15, 1960; BS summa cum laude, Roger Williams Coll., 1991; JD cum laude, New England Sch. Law, 1995. Bar: RI 1996, Conn. 1997, U.S. Dist. Ct. R.I. 1997, U.S. Supreme Ct. 2002. Police officer Westerly (R.I.) Police Dept. Mem. Internat. Brotherhood Police Officers, R.I. Bar Assn., Conn. Bar Assn., Delta Theta Phi. Avocations: softball, bicycling. Office: Westerly Police Dept 5 Union St Westerly RI 02891-2158

MATAYOSHI, CORALIE CHUN, lawyer, bar association executive; b. Honolulu, June 2, 1956; d. Peter J. and Daisy (Look) Chun; m. Ronald F. Matayoshi, Aug. 8, 1981; children: Scot, Kelly, Alana. BA, U. Calif., Berkeley, 1978; JD, U. Calif., San Francisco, 1981. Bar: Hawaii 1981, U.S. Dist. Ct. Hawaii 1981. Trial atty. U.S. Dept. Justice Antitrust, Washington, 1981-84; assoc. Chun, Kerr, & Dodd, Honolulu, 1984-86; exec. dir. Hawaii Inst. of CLE, Honolulu, 1987-90, Hawaii State Bar Assn., Honolulu, 1990—. Arbitrator Ct. Annexed Arbitration Program, Honolulu, 1992—; adv. bd. Channel 2 TV Action Line, Honolulu, 1993-96. Contbr. chapters to books. Bd. dirs. Neighborhood Justice Ctr., 1994-97, mediator, 1997—. Office: Hawaii State Bar Assn 1132 Bishop St Ste 906 Honolulu HI 96813-2814

MATEAS, KENNETH EDWARD, lawyer; b. Aurora, Ill., May 7, 1949; s. Victor Joseph and Lois Rose (Carder) M. BA, U. Ill., 1971; JD, John Marshall Sch. of Law, 1982. Bar: Ill. 1982, D.C. 1982. Assoc. Law Offices of J. Timothy Loats, Aurora, 1982-83, Law Offices of Michael Marsh, Aurora, 1983-84; atty. Kane County States Atty.'s Office, Geneva, Ill., 1985; assoc. Law Offices of Gerard Kepple, St. Charles, Ill., 1985-89; pvt. practice, Aurora, 1989—. Mem. ABA, Ill. Bar Assn., Nat. Assn. Criminal Def. Lawyers. Lodges: KC. Republican. Roman Catholic. Bankruptcy, Criminal, Family and matrimonial. Office: 408 N Lake St Aurora IL 60506-4106

MATEER, DON M. lawyer; b. Evanston, Ill., July 29, 1945; s. Bruce DeLoss and Ann M.; m. Dawn Rebecca Hallsten, Oct. 4, 1981; children: Andrew, Alexandra; m. Jacquelyn Susan Henkin, June 7, 1969 (div. Apr. 1981); children: Kristin, Julie. BA, U. Mich., 1967; JD, U. Ill., 1971. Bar: Ill. 1971, U.S. Dist. Ct. (no. dist.) Ill. 1972, U.S. Ct. Appeals (7th cir.) 1974, U.S. Supreme Ct. 1981. Assoc. Gilbert & Powers, Rockford, Ill., 1971-74; ptnr. Gilbert, Powers & Mateer, Rockford, 1975, Gilbert, Powers, Mateer & Erickson, Rockford, 1976, Mateer & Erickson, Rockford, 1978-90, Mateer & Assocs., Rockford, 1990—. Arbitrator 17th Jud. Cir. State of Ill., 1988—, mediator, 1992—. Precinct and ward coord. mayoral campaign, Rockford, 1980-84; campaign chmn. Rockford Park Dist. Commr., 1989; bd. dirs. Covenant Children's Home, 1987-93, v.p. 1990-91, pres. 1991-93, chair 100 Hole Golf Marathon fundraiser, 1994-98, mem. fund devel. com., 1994-99, investment adv. com., 1996-2001; mem. Protestant Cmty. Svcs., 1986-92, chmn. pers. com. 1987-89, v.p. 1989-90, pres. 1990-92; mem. Bethesda Covenant Ch., chmn. bd. Christian edn., 1986-88, v.p. 1997-99, pres. 1999-2001, chmn. futures task force, 2001-02. Fellow: Am. Coll. Trial Lawyers; mem.: ABA (vice-chair trial techniques com. tort and ins. practice sect., judge for final rounds of nat. appellate adv. competition 1991), Ill. Def. Counsel, Am. Def. Rsch. Inst., Assn. Trial Lawyers, Ill. Bar Assn. (assembly 1988—94), Winnebago County Bar Assn. (chmn. jud. liaison com. 1986—87), Am. Arbitration Assn. (arbitrator), Union League Club of Chgo., U. Mich. Club (bd. dirs. 1986—92, 1998—, v.p. 1989—90, 1998—99, pres. 1990—91, 1999—2000), Forest Hills Country Club. Democrat. Federal civil litigation, State civil litigation, Personal injury (including property damage). Home: 2006 Oxford St Rockford IL 61103-4833 Office: Mateer & Assocs 401 W State St Ste 400 Rockford IL 61101-1240

MATER, MAUD, lawyer; BA in English, Case Western Reserve U., 1969, JD, 1972. Asst. gen. counsel Freddie Mac, McLean, Va., 1976-78, assoc. gen. counsel, 1978-79, v.p., dep. gen. counsel, 1979-82, v.p., gen. counsel, 1982-84, sr. v.p., gen. counsel, sec., 1984-98, exec. v.p., gen. counsel, sec., 1998—. Mem.: FBA, ABA (com. corp. gen. counsel), Washington Met. Corp. Counsel Assn., Conf. Bd. Coun. of Chief Legal Officers, DC Bar, Ohio Bar, Am. Arbitration Assn. (dir.), Am. Corp. Counsel Assn. Office: Freddie Mac MS # 200 8200 Jones Branch Dr Mc Lean VA 22102-3110

MATERNA, JOSEPH ANTHONY, lawyer; b. Passaic, N.J., June 13, 1947; s. Anthony E. and Peggy Ann Materna; m. Dolores Corio, Dec. 14, 1975; children: Jodi, Jennifer, Janine. BA, Columbia U., 1969, JD, 1973. Bar: N.Y. 1975, Fla. 1977, U.S. Dist. Ct. (ea. and so. dists.) N.Y. 1977, U.S. Supreme Ct. 1977, U.S. Tax Ct. 1978, U.S. Ct. of Claims 1978. Trusts and estates atty. Chadbourne Parke Whiteside & Wolff, N.Y.C., 1973-76, Dreyer & Traub, N.Y.C., 1976-80, Finley Kumble Wagner Heine Underberg & Casey, N.Y.C., 1980-85; ptnr., head trusts and estates dept. Newman Tannenbaum Helpern Syracuse & Hirschtritt, N.Y.C., 1985-90, Shapiro Beilly Rosenberg Aronowitz Levy & Fox LLP, N.Y.C., 1990—. Lectr. in field; expert witness in trusts and estate field ct. litigations, N.Y., 1999—. Contbr. articles to profl. jours. Chmn. planned giving com., mem. bd. govs. Arthritis Found. N.Y. Chpt., N.Y.C., 1980—; mem. bd. trustees, corp. treas. Cath. Interracial Coun., N.Y.C., 1992—; mem. bequests and planned gifts com. Cath. Archdiocese of N.Y., N.Y.C., 1988—; corp. sec. Arthritis Found. N.Y. chpt., N.Y.C., 1997—, mem. budget and fin. com., 2001—; mem. Meml. Sloan-Kettering Nat. Trusts and Estates Assocs. Recipient Planned Giving award Arthritis Found.-N.Y. Chpt., N.Y.C., 1994, Discovery Alliance award Arthritis Found.-N.Y. Chpt., N.Y.C., 1995; named Accredited Estate Planner, Nat. Assn. Estate Planners, Marietta, Ga., 1995. Mem. ABA, Fla. Bar (trusts and estate com.), N.Y. State Bar Assn. (com. on estates and trusts, com. on surrogate's ct.), Bar Assn. of the City of N.Y. (com. on surrogate's ct.), N.Y.C. Estate Planning Coun. (lectr., author), N.Y. County Lawyers Assn. (mem. com. on trusts and estates 1979—, com. on profl. ethics, com. on taxation 2000—, com. on surrogate's ct.), Queen County Bar Assn. (mem. com. trusts and estates 1990—, mem. com. on taxation, mem. com. on profl. ethics, com. on surrogate's ct.), Am. Judges Assn. (civil ct. arbitrator N.Y.C.), Am. Arbitration Assn. (panel of arbitrators), N.Y. State Trial Lawyers Assn., Richmond County Bar Assn. (com. on surrogates ct., com. on estate taxation), Columbia Coll. Alumni Assn. of Columbia U. (class pres. 1969—), Columbia Law Sch. Assn. Republican. Roman Catholic. Avocations: travel, lecturing. Estate planning, Probate (including wills, trusts), Estate taxation. Home: 155 Johanna Ln Staten Island NY 10309-3604 Office: Shapiro Beilly Rosenberg Aronowitz Levy & Fox LLP 225 Broadway New York NY 10007-3001

MATHENY, EDWARD TAYLOR, JR., lawyer; b. Chgo., July 15, 1923; s. Edward Taylor and Lina (Pinnell) Matheny; m. Marion Elizabeth Shields, Sept. 10, 1947; children: Nancy Elizabeth, Edward Taylor III; m. Ann Spears, Jan. 14, 1984. BA, U. Mo., 1944; JD, Harvard, 1949. Bar: Mo. 1949. Pvt. practice, Kansas City, 1949-91; ptnr. firm Blackwell, Sanders, Matheny, Weary & Lombardi, 1954-91. Pres. St. Luke's Hosp., Kansas City, 1980-95; bd. dirs. Dunn Industries, Inc., Tnemec Co., Inc. Author: The Presence of Care (History of St. Luke's Hospital, Kansas City), 1997, A Long and Constant Courtship (The History of a Law Firm), 1998, The Rise and Fall of Excellence, 2000, The Pursuit of a Ruptured Duck (When Kansas Citians Went to War), 2001. Pres. Cmty. Svc. Broadcasting of Mid-Am., Inc., 1971-72; chmn. Citizens Assn. Kansas City, 1958; chmn. bd. dirs. St. Luke's Found., Kansas City, 1980-95; trustee U. Kansas City, 1980-96, Kansas City Cmty. Found., 1983-94, Eye Found., Kansas City, 1990-2000, H&R Block Found., Kansas City, 1996—, Jacob L. and Ella C. Loose Found., Kansas City, 1996—. Mem. Kansas City Bar Assn., Mo. Bar, River Club, Mo. Acad. Squires, Mission Hills Country Club, Phi Beta Kappa, Sigma Chi (Balfour Nat. award 1944) Episcopalian (chancellor emeritus Diocese West Mo.). Home: 2510 Grand Blvd Kansas City MO 64108-2678 Office: 2300 Main St Kansas City MO 64108-2416

MATHERS, WILLIAM HARRIS, lawyer; b. Newport, R.I., Aug. 27, 1914; s. Howard and Margaret I. (Harris) M.; m. Myra T. Martin, Jan. 17, 1942; children: William Martin, Michael Harris, John Grinnell, Myra Tutt, Ursula Fraser. AB, Dartmouth Coll., 1935; JD, Yale U., 1938. Bar: N.Y. 1940. With Milbank, Tweed & Hope, 1938-48; mem. Milbank, Tweed, Hope & Hadley, 1948-57; v.p., sec., dir. Yale & Towne Mfg. Co., Stamford, Conn., 1957-60; ptnr. Chadbourne & Parke, 1960-75, counsel, 1983—; exec. v.p., gen. counsel, sec., dir. United Brands Co., 1975-82. Mayor, trustee Village of Cove Neck, N.Y., 1950-82; trustee Barnard Coll., 1958-69. Served as pvt. to maj. U.S. Army, 1942-46. Mem. ABA, N.Y. State Bar Assn., Nassau County Bar Assn., Assn. of Bar of City of N.Y., New Eng. Soc. in City of N.Y., Casque and Gauntlet, Corbey Court, Piping Rock Club, Seminole Golf Club, N.Y. Yacht Club, Cold Spring Harbor Beach Club, Phi Beta Kappa, Psi Upsilon. Home: 1460 King George Farm Rd Sutton VT 05867 Office: 30 Rockefeller Plz New York NY 10112-0127

MATHES, STEPHEN JON, lawyer; b. N.Y.C., Mar. 18, 1945; s. Joseph and Beatrice M.; m. Michele Marshall, Oct. 22, 1972 (div. 1992); children: Aaron, Benjamin; m. Maria McGarry, Dec. 19, 1992; 1 child, Sara. BA, U. Pa., 1967, JD, 1970. Bar: N.Y. 1971, Pa. 1972, U.S. Dist. Ct. (ea. dist.) Pa. 1971. U.S. Ct. Appeals (3d cir.) 1972, U.S. Ct. Appeals (5th cir.) 1985, U.S. Ct. Appeals (4th cir.) 1985, U.S. Ct. Appeals (9th cir.) 2000, U.S. Supreme Ct. 1978. Law clk. U.S. Ct. Appeals (3d cir.), Phila., 1970-71; asst. dist. atty. major felony unit, spl. investigation unit Office of Phil. Dist. Atty., Phila., 1975; assoc. Dilworth, Paxson, Kalish & Kauffman, Phila., 1971-74, 76-77, sr. ptnr., 1977-91, mem. exec. com., 1987-90, co-chmn. litigation dept., 1987-91; ptnr. Hoyle, Fickler, Herschel & Mathes (formerly Hoyle, Morris & Kerr), Phila., 1992—; bd. dirs. The Levitt Found., 1990—, sec., 1991—. Mgmt. com. Hoyle, Morris & Kerr, Phila., 1992-97, 2001—. Bd. dirs., exec. com. Acad. Vocal Arts, 1993-2000, mem. exec. com., chmn. student aid com.; mem. legal and compliance divsn. Securities Industry Assn., 1998—. Mem. ABA, Am. Law Inst., Securities Industries Assn., Pa. Bar Assn., Phila. Bar Assn. (mem. litigation divsn.), Thanatopsis Soc., Racquet Club, Germantown Cricket Club. Federal civil litigation, State civil litigation. Home: 199 Lynnebrook Ln Philadelphia PA 19118-2706 Office: Holye Morris & Kerr One Liberty Pl Ste 4900 Philadelphia PA 19103 E-mail: smathes@hoylemk.com.

MATHESON, ALAN ADAMS, law educator; b. Cedar City, Utah, Feb. 2, 1932; s. Scott Milne and Adele (Adams) M.; m. Milicent Holbrook, Aug. 15, 1960; children— Alan, David Scott, John Robert. BA, U. Utah, 1953, MS, 1957, JD, 1959; postgrad. asso. in law, Columbia U. Bar: Utah 1960, Ariz. 1975. Asst. to pres. Utah State U., 1961-67; mem. faculty Ariz. State U., Tempe, 1967—, prof. law, 1970—, dean, 1978-84, 89, 97-98. Bd. dirs. Ariz. Ctr. Law in Pub. Interest, 1979-81, DNA Navajo Legal Svcs., 1984-97, Ariz. Found. for Legal Svcs. and Edn., 2002—. Pres. Tri-City Mental Health Citizens Bd., 1973-74; bd. dirs. Ariz. Found. LEgal Svcs. and Edn. Served with AUS, 1953-55. Mem. Utah Bar Assn., Ariz. Bar Assn., Maricopa County Bar Assn., Phi Beta Kappa, Order of Coif. Democrat. Mem. Lds Ch. Home: 720 E Geneva Dr Tempe AZ 85282-3737 Office: Ariz State U Coll Law Tempe AZ 85287

MATHESON, SCOTT MILNE, JR., dean, law educator; b. Salt Lake City, July 18, 1953; s. Scott Milne and Norma (Warenski) M.; m. Robyn Kuida, Aug. 12, 1978; children: Heather Blair, Briggs James. AB, Stanford U., 1975; MA, Oxford U., Eng.; JD, Yale U., 1980. Bar: D.C., 1981, Utah 1986. Assoc. Williams & Connolly, Washington, 1981-85; assoc. prof. law U. Utah, 1985-91; dep. atty. Salt Lake County Attys. Office, 1988-89; vis. assoc. prof. JFK Sch. Govt. Harvard U., Cambridge, Mass., 1989-90; assoc. dean law U. Utah, 1990-93, prof. law, 1991—, dean, 1998—; U.S. atty. Dist. Utah, 1993-97. Adv. com. on rules of evidence Utah Supreme Ct., 1987-93, Utah Constitutional Revision Commn., 1987-93, adv. com. on the local rules of practice, U.S. Dist. Ct. Utah, 1993-97. Contbr. articles to profl. jours. Chmn. U.N. Day for State of Utah, 1991; mem. Univ. Com. on Tanner Lectures on Human Values U. Utah, 1993-2000, Honors Program Adv. Com. U. Utah, 1986-88, Adv. Bd. Hinckley Inst. Politics U. Utah, 1990-93; trustee Legal Aid Soc. of Salt Lake, 1986-93, pres., 1987; trustee TreeUtah, 1992-93; campaign mgr. Matheson for Gov., 1976, 1980; vol. state dir. Clinton/Gore '92. Recipient Up'n Comers award Zions Bank, 1991, Faculty Achievement award Burlington Resources Found., 1993, Disting. Svc. to Fed. Bar award Fed. Bar Assn., Utah chpt., 1998, spl. recognition award Utah Minority Bar Assn., 1999; named one of Outstanding Young Men of Am., 1987, 1988; Rhodes scholar. Mem. ABA, Assn. Am. Law Schs. (chair sect. on mass com. law 1993), Utah State Bar, Salt Lake County Bar Assn. (exec. com. 1986-92), Golden Key Nat. Honor Soc. (hon. 1990), Phi Beta Kappa.

MATHEWS, STANTON TERRY, lawyer; b. May 28, 1952; m. Lisa Diane Earls, Jan. 15, 1977; children: Amy Marie, Adriane Rene, Britton Lafe, Garret Tyler. BA, Brigham Young U., 1976; JD, Western State U. Coll. Law, 1981; cert. in aviation litig., Nat. Jud. Coll., Reno, Nev. Cert. ob-gyn. pediatric malpractice. Pvt. practice law, Laguna Hills, Calif., 1981—. Judge pro tem Orange County Superior Ct. Contbr. articles to profl. jours. Mem. ATLA, Orange County Bar Assn. (lectr. 1990—), Consumer Attys. of Calif., Diplomate Million Dollar Advocates Forum, Western Trial Lawyers Assn., Orange County Trial Lawyers. Libel, Personal injury (including property damage). Office: 24012 Calle De La Plata Ste 320 Laguna Hills CA 92653-7624 E-mail: tortlaw@pacbell.net.

MATHEWSON, GEORGE ATTERBURY, lawyer; b. Paterson, N.J., Mar. 31, 1935; s. Joseph B. and Christina A. (Atterbury) M.; m. Ann Elizabeth, July 31, 1975' 1 child, James Lemuel. AB cum laude, Amherst Coll., 1957; LLB, Cornell U., 1960; LLM, U. Mich., 1961. Bar: N.Y. 1963. Atty office spl. legal assts., trial atty. FTC, Washington, 1963-65; regional atty. N.Y. State Dept. Environ. Conservation, Liverpool, 1972-73; pvt. practice Syracuse, N.Y., 1967-72, 73—; of counsel Banac and Mathewson, Manlius, NY, 2003—. Adj. instr. bus. law Onondaga Community Coll., Syracuse, 1979-84. Bd. dirs. South Side Businessmen, 1971-72, 88-91, v.p., 1992, pres. 1993; elder Onondaga Hill Presbyn. Ch., 1979, 82-85; dir. Manlius C. of C., 1995, v.p., 1997; bd. trustees Steuben County Hist. Soc., 2002—; bd. dirs. Yates County Arts Ctr., 2003—. Mem. ABA, Fed. Bar Assn., N.Y. State Bar Assn. (former mem. state and county bar assn. coms.), Kiwanis (bd. dirs. Onondaga club 1988-89, v.p. 1989, pres. 1989-91). Patentee safety device for disabled airplanes. General civil litigation, General practice, Property, real (including real estate development, water). Office: Banac and Mathewson Attys 224 Fayette St Manlius NY 13104-1804

MATHEWSON, MARK STUART, lawyer, editor; b. Pana, Ill., Mar. 6, 1955; s. Raymond Glenn and Frances (King) M.; m. Barbara Jean Siegert, Oct. 30, 1980; children: Margie, Molly. BA, U. Wis., Madison, 1978; JD, U. Ill., 1984; MA, U. Iowa, 1985. Bar: Ill. 1985. Reporter Ill. Times, Springfield, 1985; asst. prof. Culver Stockton Coll., Canton, Mo., 1986—87; pvt. practice Pana, Ill., 1987—2000; mng. editor Ill. Bar Jour., Ill. State Bar Assn., Springfield, dir. legal pub., 2000—. Home: RR 1 Box 2 Athens IL 62613-9787 Office: Ill State Bar Assn Ill Bar Journal Ill Bar Ctr Springfield IL 62701

MATHIAS, JOSEPH MARSHALL, lawyer, judge; b. Frankfort, Ky., Jan. 23, 1914; s. Harry L. and Catherine Snead (Marshall) M.; children: Mark Wellington, Marcia Ann Mathias Wilson, Marilyn Roberta. AB, U. Md., 1935; JD, Southeastern U., 1942. Bar: Md. 1942, U.S. Supreme Ct. 1949, U.S. Dist. Ct. Md. 1963. Ptnr. Moorman and Mathias, 1946-50, Jones, Mathias and O'Brien and predecessor firms, 1950-65; judge Md. Tax Ct., 1959-65; assoc. judge Circuit Ct. of Montgomery County (Md.), 1965-80; chief judge 6th Jud. Circuit of Md., 1980-81; spl. assignments, 1981-83; spl. counsel Beckett, Cromwell & Myers, P.A., 1983-88; of counsel Frank, Bernstein, Conaway and Goldman, 1988-92. Past dir. Nat. Bank Md., Bank So. Md.; former mem. adv. bd. Citizens Bank and Trust Co. Chmn. Bd. Property Rev., Montgomery, Md., 1992—. Served with USN, 1942-46. Recipient cert. of disting. citizenship Gov. of Md., 1981. Mem. ABA, Md. State Bar Assn., Md. Bar Found., Montgomery County Bar Assn., Am. Judicature Soc. Democrat. Roman Catholic. Home: 10011 Summit Ave Kensington MD 20895-3835 E-mail: rwmjmm@erols.com.

MATHIES, JORDON DEAN, lawyer; b. Dallas, Mar. 15, 1954; 1 child from previous marriage, Michael Aaron Matthies. BS with honors, U. Oreg., 1976; MPA with honors, Portland State U., 1986; JD, Vanderbilt U., 1989. Bar: Tenn. 1999, Wash. D.C. 2000. Staff writer United Fund Oreg., Portland, 1990—91; exec. dir. Nonprofit Rsch., Inc., Portland, 1992—94, Spl. Projects Applied Rsch., Nashville, 1999—; asst. to v.p. Tenn. State U., Nashville, 1998—99; pvt. practice Nashville, 1999—. Issue cons. Dem. Nat. Com., Washington, 1992, 1996, 2000. Mem.: ATLA, Vanderbilt Found. Entertainment Law and Practice, Am. Antitrust Inst., Napier Loopey Bar Assn., Fed. Bar Assn., Nat. Bar Assn. Baptist. Avocations: digital filmmaking, desktop publishing, screenplay writing. Antitrust, Civil rights, Labor (including EEOC, Fair Labor Standards Act, labor-management relations, NLRB, OSHA). Office: 3866 Dickerson Pike Ste 4 Nashville TN 37207 Office Fax: 615-612-5585. Business E-Mail: jmathlaw@access-4-free.com.

MATHIS, PATRICK BISCHOF, lawyer; b. Pinckneyville, Ill., Feb. 1, 1952; s. John Archibald and Theresa Ann (Bischof) M.; m. Rosanne Azar; children: Daniel P., Adrienne C. BA in Chemistry, St. Louis U., 1973; MBA, JD, Washington U., St. Louis, 1978, LL.M. in Taxation, 1979. Bar: Mo. 1978, Ill. 1979, U.S. Tax Ct. 1979, U.S. Dist. Ct. (so. dist.) Ill. 1980, U.S. Ct. Appeals (7th cir.) 1980, U.S. Ct. Claims 1980, U.S. Supreme Ct. 1982. Assoc. John J. Vassen, P.C., Belleville, Ill., 1979-84; ptnr. Mathis, Marifian, Richter & Grandy, Ltd., Belleville, 1984—. Spkr. in field. Contbr. articles to profl. jours. Mem. fin. com. Special Children, Inc. Mamie O. Stookey Sch., 1987-90; parish coun. Blessed Sacrament Parish, 1992-98, pres., 1993-98; chmn. annual fund drive Big Brothers/Big Sisters, St. Clair County, 1994; bd. dirs. Signal Hill Neighborhood Assn., 1989-92, St. Clair County Greenspace Found., 1990-2000, Signal Hill Sch. Edn. Found., 1997-99; mem. Signal Hill Sch. Dist. Bd. Edn., 1999—. Mem. ABA (tax sect. civil and criminal penalties com., domestic rels. tax problems com., vice chmn. subcom. alimony issues, gen. practice sect. chmn. taxation com.), Ill. Bar Assn. (fed. taxation sect. council 1984-85, 89-93, chmn. 1992-93), St. Clair County Bar Assn., Bar Assn. Met. St. Louis, Ill. Inst. Continuing Legal Edn. (chmn. 1996-97, bd. dirs. 1990-98), Am. Coll. Trust and Estate Counsel. Roman Catholic. Mo. Athletic Club, Alpha Sigma Nu, Eta Sigma Phi. Corporate, general, Estate planning, Taxation, general. Home: 33 Oak Knoll Pl Belleville IL 62223-1880 Office: Mathis Marifian Et Al 720 W Main St Ste 100 Belleville IL 62220-1541 Fax: 618-234-9786. E-mail: pmathis@mmrg.com.

MATHY, PAMELA ANN, lawyer; b. Green Bay, Wis., Jan. 11, 1952; d. Bernard George and Inez Claire Mathy. AB, Marquette U., Milw., 1973; MA, U. Tex., 1976; JD, U. Wis., 1978; LLM, Georgetown U., Washington, 1982. Bar: Wis. 1978, D.C. 1979, U.S. Dist. ct. (no. dist.) Ill. 1979, U.S. Ct. Appeals (7th cir.) 1978, Ill. 1979, U.S. Dist. Ct. (we. dist.) Tex. 1983, U.S. Ct. Appeals (5th cir.) 1984, Tex. 1985. Law clk. Chief Judge Walter Cummings, U.S. Ct. Appeals, 7th Cir., Chgo., 1978-80; pvt. practice law Washington, 1980-81; sr. staff atty. U.S. Ct. Appeals (7th cir.), Chgo., 1981-83; asst. U.S. Atty. U.S. Dist. Ct. (we. dist.) Tex., San Antonio, 1983—, 1st asst. criminal divsn., 1996—98; U.S. magistrate judge U.S. Dist. Ct., San Antonio, 1998—. Contbr. articles to profl. jours. Named Prosecutor of Yr., Tex. Narcotics Officers Assn., 1989; recipient Outstanding Arson Prosecution award Tex. Adv. Coun. on Arson, 1991, Dir.'s award U.S. Dept. Justice, 1994. Mem. ABA, Wis. Bar Assn., Tex. Bar Assn., San Antonio Bar Assn., Fed. Bar Assn., Bexar County Women's Bar Assn. Office: US Dist Ct 655 E Durango Blvd San Antonio TX 78206

MATIA, PAUL RAMON, federal judge; b. Cleve., Oct. 2, 1937; s. Leo Clemens and Irene Elizabeth (Linkert) M.; m. Nancy Arch Van Meter, Jan. 2, 1993. BA, Case Western Res. U., 1959; JD, Harvard U., 1962. Bar: Ohio 1962, U.S. Dist. Ct. (no. dist.) Ohio 1969. Law clk. Common Pleas Ct. of Cuyahoga County, Cleve., 1963-66, judge, 1985-91; asst. atty. gen. State of Ohio, Cleve., 1966-69, adminstrv. ast. to atty. gen. Columbus, 1969-70; senator Ohio State Senate, Columbus, 1971-75, 79-83; ptnr. Hadley, Matia, Mills & MacLean Co., L.P.A., Cleve., 1975-84; judge U.S. Dist. Ct. (no. dist.) Ohio, 1991-99, chief dist. judge, 1999—; mem. 6th Cir. Jud. Coun., 1999—. Candidate Lt. Gov. Rep. Primary, 1982, Ohio Supreme Ct., 1988. Named Outstanding Legislator, Ohio Assn. for Retarded Citizens, 1974, Watchdog of Ohio Treasury, United Conservatives of Ohio, 1979; recipient Heritage award Polonia Found., 1988. Mem. Fed. Bar Assn., Club at Key Ctr. Avocations: skiing, gardening, travel. Office: US Dist Ct 801 W Superior Ave Cleveland OH 44113-1834

MATISIK, EDWARD NEWTON, lawyer; b. Johnstown, Pa., July 18, 1962; s. Robert John Matisik and Betty Louise Moore. BS, Boston U., 1984; MA, Am. U., 1991, JD, 1997. Bar: D.C. 1999. Devel. officer The John F. Kennedy Ctr. for Performing Arts, Washington, 1987—99; atty. pvt. practice, 1999—. Author: The ADA and OCD, 1997, The Legal Guide for Pennnsylvania School Teachers, 2001. Bd. dirs. Honor Our Heroes, Lafayette, Calif., 2002—03; gen. counsel Boston U. Alumni of Washington, 2002—03. Mem.: ABA, Assn. Trial Lawyers Am. Republican. Roman Catholic. Avocations: sports, performing arts, reading. Other, Education and schools, Administrative and regulatory. Home and Office: 4201 Mass Ave NW #5047 Washington DC 20016 Fax: 202-246-3544. E-mail: wnmatisik@hotmail.com.

MATL, LOIS TUDOR, lawyer; b. Madison County, Ky., Feb. 19, 1939; d. Humphrey Hill Jr. and Mary Elizabeth (Noland) Tudor; m. Gerry L. Calvert Sr., Sept. 25, 1960 (div. Apr. 1981); children: Catherine Deloach, Gerry L. II, Stephanie Calvert. Grad., Good Samaritan Hosp., 1960; BSN, U. Ky., 1966, JD, 1980. Bar: Ky. 1981. Assoc. Greenbaum Doll & McDonald, Lexington, Ky., 1981-85; atty. pvt. practice primarily family law and workers compensation, Lexington, Ky., 1985—. Bd. trustees Lexington United Meth. Ch., 1982-84, adminstrv. bd., 1991-93; pres. PTA Beaumont Jr. High Sch., Lexington, 1982-83. Methodist. General civil litigation, Family and matrimonial, Workers' compensation. Office: 125 Church St Lexington KY 40507-1102

MATSUKAGE, FAY MARIKO, lawyer; b. Honolulu, Sept. 1, 1955; d. Daniel Ryuzo and Nobuko M. BA summa cum laude, Colo. Coll., 1976; JD, U. Denver, 1979. Bar: Colo. 1980. Assoc. firm McKie and Assocs., Denver, 1980-81, Olsen & Guardi, Denver, 1981-83; ptnr. Olsen & Matsukage, Denver, 1984-86; pvt. practice, Denver, 1986—97, officer, shareholder Dill Dill Carr Stonbraker and Hutchings, Denver, 1997-. Mem. ABA, Denver Bar Assn., Colo. Bar Assn., Phi Beta Kappa. Corporate, general, Securities. Office: Ste 300 455 Sherman St Denver CO 80203-4404

MATSUNAGA, GEOFFREY DEAN, lawyer; b. L.A., Sept. 30, 1949; s. Hideo Arthur and Yuri M.; m. Masako Inoue, Aug. 20, 1981; children: Ayako, Hideko, Lisa Fumi. BS, USAF Acad., 1971; MBA, UCLA, 1972; postgrad., Inter U. Ctr. Japanese Lang. Studies, 1979-80; JD, U. Calif., Berkeley, 1982. Bar: Calif. 1982, U.S. Dist. Ct. (cen. dist.) Calif. 1982, N.Y. 1983, U.S. Dist. Ct. (so. dist.) N.Y. 1983. Jud. extern U.S. Dist. Ct. (cen. dist.), L.A., 1981; assoc. Milbank, Tweed, Hadley & McCloy, N.Y.C., 1982-84, Tokyo, 1984-87, Sidley & Austin, Tokyo, 1987-88, L.A., 1988-91; counsel Sheppard, Mullin, Richter & Hampton, L.A., 1991-94; ptnr. Kagei & Matsunaga, L.A., 1995—2001; sole practice L.A., 2002—. Founding bd. dirs. Futures Industry Assn., Japan, 1987; counsel East West Players, 1992-95. Lt. USN, 1972-78. Japan Found. fellow, Tokyo, 1979-80. Mem. Los Angeles County Bar Assn., Japan Bus. Assn. So. Calif., Japan Am. Soc. So. Calif. (adv. bd. South Bay 1992-95), Sabre Soc. Episcopalian. Corporate, general, Property, real (including real estate development, water), Finance. Office: Law Offices of Geoffrey D Matsunaga 19191 S Vermont Ave Ste 420 Torrance CA 90502-1051

MATTAR, LAWRENCE JOSEPH, lawyer; b. Buffalo, Apr. 17, 1934; s. Joseph and Anne (Abraham) M.; m. Elaine Kolbe, Aug. 1, 1959; children: Lorraine, Brenda, Anne, Deborah. Grad., Canisius Coll., 1956; JD, SUNY, Buffalo, 1959. Bar: N.Y. 1959, Fla. 1977, U.S. Supreme Ct. 1972. Sole practice, Buffalo, 1959-62; sr. ptnr. Mattar & D'Agostino and predecessors, Buffalo, 1962—. Asst. to county ct. judge, 1961-66; counsel N.Y. State Senate Pub. Utilties Com., 1969-71. Bd. dirs. Better Bus. Bur. Western N.Y.; mem. exec. com. pres.'s coun. Canisius Coll.; mem. ho. of dels. United Way of Buffalo and Erie County; mem. Nat. Maronite Bishops' Adv. Coun., U.s. Congl. Adv. Bd.; Selective Svc. Bd., Western N.Y. Rep.Presdl. Task Force; del. Rep. Jud. Conv. 8th Dist., 1985. Decorated Knight of St. Charbiel, highest honor available to a Maronite Cath.; recipient award for outstanding svc. Buffalo Eye Bank, 1962, Leadership award Lions Club Buffalo, 1963, Citizen's award Erie C.C., 1982, Nat. Tree of Life award Bd. dirs. Jewish Nat. Fund Am., 1987. Mem. Erie County Bar Assn., Erie County Trial Lawyers Assn., N.Y. State Bar Assn., Fla. Bar Assn., N.Y. State Trial Lawyers Assn., Buffalo C. of C., NFL Players Alumni Assn. (assoc.), Di Gamma (life), Rotary Club (sec. 1978-79, dir. 1978-80, trustee, sec., mem. exec. com. Buffalo Rotary Found.), Buffalo Club (Buffalo), Transit Valley Country Club (East Amherst, N.Y.). Roman Catholic. Avocations: golf, skiing. Federal civil litigation, State civil litigation, Corporate, general. Home: 386 Woodbridge Ave Buffalo NY 14214-1530 Office: Mattar & D'Agostino LLP 17 Court St Ste 600 Buffalo NY 14202-3294

MATTESON, WILLIAM BLEECKER, lawyer; b. N.Y.C., Oct. 20, 1928; s. Leonard Jerome and Mary Jo (Harwell) M.; m. Marilee Brill, Aug. 26, 1950; children: Lynn, Sandra, Holly. BA, Yale U., 1950; JD, Harvard U., 1953. Bar: N.Y. 1954. Clk. to judge Augustus N. Hand U.S. Ct. Appeals, 1953-54; clk. to U.S. Supreme Ct. Justice Harold H. Burton, 1954-55; assoc. firm Debevoise & Plimpton (and predecessors), N.Y.C., 1955-61, ptnr., 1961—98, Debevoise & Plimpton (European office), Paris, 1973-78; presiding ptnr. Debevoise & Plimpton, 1988-93. Lectr. Columbia U. Law Sch., 1972-73, 78-80. Trustee Peddie Sch., Hightstown, N.J., 1968-73, Kalamazoo Coll., 1972-77, Miss Porter's Sch., Farmington, Conn., 1977-83, N.Y. Inst. Spl. Edn., 1981—, Salk Inst., La Jolla, Calif., 1993-96, vice-chair, 1994-96, Statue of Liberty Ellis Island Found., 1996—, Hartford Found., 1996—; active USA Bus. and Industry Adv. Com. to the Orgn. for Econ. Coop. and Devel., Paris, 1986-2000; chmn. Worldwide Bus. and Industry Adv. Com., 1994-96; vice chmn. U.S. Coun. for Internat. Bus., 1990-2000, hon. trustee. Mem. ABA, FBA, Internat. Bar Assn., N.Y. State Bar Assn., Assn. of Bar of City of N.Y. (chmn. securities regulation com. 1968-71), Harvard U. Law Sch. Assn. N.Y.C. (trustee 1968-73), Coun. Fgn. Rels., Union Club, Sky Club, Sankaty Head Club, John's Island Redstick, and Windsor Clubs, N.Y. Yacht Club. Corporate, general, Private international. Office: Debevoise & Plimpton 919 3d Ave 47th Fl New York NY 10022 E-mail: wbmatteson@debevoise.com.

MATTHEWS, BARBARA CARIDAD, lawyer; d. Frederick Lawrence and Caridad Ofelia Matthews; m. Andrew Michael Danas, Nov. 6, 1999; 1 child, Lydia Marguerite Danas. B.Sc.F.S., Georgetown U., 1986; JD, LLM, Duke U., 1991. Bar: N.Y. 1992. Assoc. banking advisor Inst. Internat. Fin., Washington, 1992—94, banking advisor, regulatory counsel, 1996—; assoc. Morrison & Foerster, Washington, 1994—96. Mem. editl. bd. Jour. Derivatives Use, Trading and Regulation, 1997—; contbr. articles to profl. jours., chapters to books. Pres. Friends Assisting the Nat. Symphony, Washington, 1998—99; bd. dirs. Young Audiences, Washington, 2000—; mem. exec. com. women's leadership group Boys & Girls Clubs Greater Washington, 2000. Fellow internat. law, Ford Found., 1991—92. Mem.: ABA, N.Y. State Bar Assn., Internat. Assn. Fin. Engrs., Pi Sigma Alpha, Alpha Sigma Nu. Avocations: photography, tennis, travel. Office: Inst Internat Fin 2000 Pennsylvania Ave NW Washington DC 20006-1812 Office Fax: 202-463-0993. Business E-Mail: bmatthews@iif.com.

MATTHEWS, CHARLES W. lawyer; b. Houston, Tex., 1945; Grad., U. Tex., 1967, U. Houston, 1970. Trial atty. law dept. Exxon Corp., 1971-78, region atty. southeastern and southern region mktg. offices, 1978-81, assoc. gen. atty. litigation sect., gen. counsel & dir. Petroleum Casualty Co. and Exxon Risk Mgmt. Svcs., 1981-92; from assoc. gen. counsel law dept. to gen. counsel law dept. Exxon U.S.A., 1992; v.p., gen. counsel Exxon Corp., 1995—. Adv. dir. U. Houston Law Found. Nat. trustee Southwest Region Boys & Girls Clubs of Am.; trustee Nat. Jud. Coll.; trustee Am. Inns Ct. Found. Recipient Alumnus of the Yr., Univ. of Houston, 2000. Fellow Am. Bar Found., Tex. Bar Found., Houston Bar Found.; mem. ABA (mem. com. of corp. gen. counsel), Houston Bar Assn., Dallas Bar Assn., Dallas Bar Found., Assn. Gen. Counsel, Internat. Assn. of Def. Counsel Found. (bd. dirs.), Southwestern Legal Found. (trustee). Office: Exxon Corp 5959 Las Colinas Blvd Irving TX 75039-2298*

MATTHEWS, DOUGLAS EUGENE, lawyer, educator, consultant; b. Highland Park, Mich., July 28, 1953; s. Max and Mary Elizabeth (Crane) Matthews. BA with high distinction, Judson Coll., Elgin, Ill., 1982; JD cum laude, U. Wis., 1985, MS in Legal Instns., 1988; LLM, Harvard U., 1991. Bar: Fla. 1986, Ill. 1987, D.C. 1989. Assoc. Gunster, Yoakley, Criser & Stewart, West Palm Beach, Fla., 1986, Zukowski, Rogers, Flood & McArdle, Crystal Lake, Fla., 1987; asst. pub. defender McHenry County, Woodstock, Ill., 1988—89; law lectr. No. Ill. U., De Kalb, 1990; asst. prof. St. Thomas U. Sch. Law, Miami, Fla., 1991—94, assoc. prof., 1994—96, adj. prof. law, 1996—2002; co-founder, v.p. The Grifo Group, Inc., Miami, Fla., 1997—. Past v.p., bd. dirs. Youth Svc. Bur., Woodstock. Mem.: Ind. Computer Cons. Assn., Dade County Bar assn., Ill. Bar Assn., Fla. Bar Assn., Harvard Club Miami. Democrat. Unitarian Universalist. Avocations: gardening, historic preservation. Office: 686 NE 74th St Miami FL 33138-5114 E-mail: matthews@post.harvard.edu.

MATTHEWS, ELIZABETH WOODFIN, law librarian, law educator; b. Ashland, Va., July 30, 1927; d. Edwin Clifton and Elizabeth Frances (Luck) Woodfin; m. Sidney E. Matthews, Dec. 20, 1947; 1 child, Sarah Elizabeth Matthews Wiley. BA, Randolph-Macon Coll., 1948, LLD (hon.), 1989; MS in Libr. Sci., U. Ill., 1952; PhD, So. Ill. U., 1972; LLD, Randolph-Macon Coll., 1989. Cert. law libr., med. libr., med. libr. III. Libr. Ohio State U., Columbus, 1952-59; libr., instr. U. Ill., Urbana, 1962-63; lectr. U. Ill. Grad. Sch. Libr. Sci., Urbana, 1964; libr., instr. Morris Libr. So. Ill. U., Carbondale, 1964-67; classroom instr. So. Ill. U. Coll Edn., Carbondale, 1967-70; med. libr., asst. prof. Morris Libr. So. Ill. U., Carbondale, 1972-74, law libr., asst. prof., 1974-79, law libr., assoc. prof., 1979-85, law libr., prof., 1985-92, prof. emerita, 1993—. Author: Access Points to Law Libraries, 1984, 17th Century English Law Reports, 1986, Law Library Reference Shelf, 1988, 5th edit., 2003, Pages and Missing Pages, 1983, 2d edit., 1989, Lincoln as a Lawyer: An Annotated Bibliography, 1991. Mem. AAUW (pres. 1976-78, corp. rep. 1978-88), Am. Assn. Law Librs., Postdoctoral Acad. Higher Edn., Beta Phi Mu, Phi Kappa Phi. Methodist. Home: 811 S Skyline Dr Carbondale IL 62901-2405 Office: So Ill U Law Libr Carbondale IL 62901

MATTHEWS, PAUL AARON, lawyer; b. Memphis, May 7, 1952; s. Joseph Curtis and Sarah Rebecca (Barret) M.; m. Roberta Bartow, July 29, 1978; children: Sarah Pierrepont, Elizabeth Barret. AB, Duke U., 1974; JD, Vanderbilt U., 1977. Bar: Tenn. 1977, U.S. Dist. Ct. (we. dist.) Tenn. 1977, U.S. Dist. Ct. (ea. dist.) Mich. 1987, U.S. Dist. Ct. (ea. dist.) Tenn. 1991, U.S. Ct. Appeals (6th cir.) 1991, U.S. Dist. Ct. (ea. and we. dists.) Ark. 1995, U.S. Dist. Ct. (mid. dist.) Tenn. 1998, U.S. Dist. Ct. (no. and so. dists.) Miss. 2000, U.S. Supreme Ct. 1998; cert. in bus. bankruptcy law and consumer bankruptcy law, Am. Bd. Certification and Tenn. Comm. on Cont. Legal Edn. and Specialization. Assoc. Armstrong Allen, PLLC, Memphis, 1977-82, mem., 1982—. Chief justice Vanderbilt Law Sch. Moot Ct. Bd., Nashville, 1976-77. Co-author: Passport to Tennessee History, 1996; contbg. editor: Martindale-Hubbell Tenn. Law Digest, 1994—99; contbr. articles to profl. publs. Com. chmn. Memphis-in-May Internat. Festival, 1977-79, Tenn. Hist. Commn., 1987-97; bd. dirs. Davies Manor Assn., Brunswick, Tenn., 1994-99, pres. 1996-97; mem. Leadership Memphis Class of 1987, alumni adv. coun., 2000—; trustee Tenn. Hist. Commn. Found., 1998—, Shelby County Hist. Commn., 1997—, vice-chmn. 1999, chmn., 2000-01; commr. Tenn. Wars Commn., 1994-97; vestry Episcopal Ch. of the Holy Communion, 1995-98; trustee St. Mary's Episcopal Sch., 2001—. Recipient Newman award Memphis Heritage, Inc., 1992. Fellow, Tenn. Bar Found.; mem. ABA, SAR (Isaac Shelby chpt.), Am. Bankruptcy Inst., Tenn. Bar Assn., Memphis Bar Assn. (publs. coun. 1990-98, bd. dirs. 1999-2001, jud. practice and procedures com. 2000-02, vice chmn. professionalism com. 2003—), Memphis and Shelby County Mental Health Assn. (pres. 1984-85), Duke U. Alumni Assn. (pres. Memphis chpt. 1986-88), Descendants of Early Settlers of Shelby County (v.p. 1999—), Sigma Alpha Epsilon. Episcopalian. Bankruptcy, Corporate, general, Commercial, contracts (including sales of goods; commercial financing). Home: 4271 Heatherwood Ln Memphis TN 38117-2302

MATTHEWS, PHILIP RICHARD, lawyer; b. San Francisco, Aug. 27, 1952; s. Richard Thomas and Marjorie Hilda (Dean) M.; m. Dana Lynn Meier, Aug. 8, 1981; children: Lauren Alison, Lyndsey Ann. BA in Polit. Sci., George Washington U., 1974; JD, U. Calif.-San Francisco, 1977. Bar: Calif. 1978, U.S. Ct. Appeals (9th cir.) 1978, U.S. Dist. Ct. (no. and so. dists.) Calif. 1978, U.S. Dist. Ct. (ea. dist.) Calif. 1980. Assoc. Dinkelspiel, Pelavin, San Francisco, 1978—80, Hancock, Rothert & Bunshoft, San Francisco, 1980—85, ptnr., 1985—, mgmt. com. mem., 1989—94, 1996—99, mng. ptnr., 1992—94, 1997—99. Mem. ABA, State Bar Assn. of Calif., Bar Assn. of San Francisco, Commonwealth Club. Democrat. Episcopalian. Avocations: sports, outdoors, genealogy, travel, hiking. State civil litigation, Environmental, Insurance. Office: Hancock Rothert & Bunshoft Ste 300 4 Embarcadero Ctr San Francisco CA 94111-4168

MATTHEWS, WARREN WAYNE, state supreme court justice; b. Santa Cruz, Calif., Apr. 5, 1939; s. Warren Wayne and Ruth Ann (Maginnis) M.; m. Donna Stearns, Aug. 17, 1963; children: Holly Maginnis, Meredith Sample. AB, Stanford U., 1961; LL.B., Harvard U., 1964. Bar: Alaska 1965. Assoc. firm Burr, Boney & Pease, Anchorage, 1964-69, Matthews & Dunn, Matthews, Dunn and Baily, Anchorage, 1969-77; assoc. justice Alaska Supreme Ct., Anchorage, 1977—, justice, chief justice. Bd. dirs. Alaska Legal Services Corp., 1969-70. Mem. Alaska Bar Assn. (bd. govs. 1974-77), ABA, Anchorage Bar Assn.

MATTHIES, MARY CONSTANCE T. lawyer; b. Baton Rouge, Mar. 22, 1948; d. Allen Douglas and Mazie (Poche) Tillman. B.S., Okla. State U., 1969; J.D., U. Tulsa, 1972. Bar: Okla. 1973, U.S. Ct. Appeals (10th cir.) 1974, U.S. Ct. Appeals (8th and D.C. cirs.) 1975, U.S. Supreme Ct. 1976. Assoc., ptnr. Kothe, Nichols & Wolfe, Inc., Tulsa, 1972-78; pres. sr. prin. Matthies Law Firm, P.C., Tulsa, 1978—; guest lectr. U. Tulsa Coll. Law, U. Okla. Sch. Law, Oral Roberts U. Sch. Contbr. articles to profl. jours; mem. staff Tulsa Law Jour., 1971-72. Fellow Am. Coll. of Labor and Employment Lawyers; mem. ABA (mem. spl. subcom. for liaison with EEOC, 1974—, spl. subcom. for liaison with OFCCP, 1979—, mgmt. co-chmn. equal employment law subcoms. on nat. origin discrimination 1974-75, class actions and remedies 1975-80), Okla. Bar Assn. (coun. mem. labor law sect. 1974-80, chmn. 1978-79), Women's Law Caucus, Phi Delta Phi. Presbyterian. Civil rights, Federal civil litigation, Labor (including EEOC, Fair Labor Standards Act, labor-management relations, NLRB, OSHA). Office: Thompson Bldg 20 E 5th St Ste 310 Tulsa OK 74103-4435 Business E-Mail: mattlawfrm@aol.com.

MATTICE, HARRY SANDLIN, JR., prosecutor; b. Chattanooga, Mar. 10, 1954; s. Harry Sandlin Sr. and Kathryn (McCoy) M.; m. Janet Lynn LeVan, Jan 4, 1975; children: Harry Sandlin III, Bryan Christopher, Keven LeVan. BS, U. Tenn., Chattanooga, 1976; JD, U. Tenn., 1981. Bar: Tenn. 1982, U.S. Dist. Ct. (ea. dist.) Tenn. 1982, U.S. Ct. Appeals (6th cir.) 1984, U.S. Tax Ct. 1984, U.S. Claims Ct. 1984, U.S. Ct. Appeals (11th cir.) 1987, U.S. Dist. Ct. (we. dist.) Tenn. 1989. Staff acct. Deloitte, Haskins & Sells, Chattanooga, 1976-78; from assoc. to ptnr. Miller & Martin, Chattanooga, 1981—2000; of counsel Baker, Donelson, Bearman & Caldwell, Chattanooga, 2000—01; U.S. atty. ea. dist. U.S. Dept. of Justice, Tenn., 2001—. Pres. Chattanooga Tax Practitioners. Asst. to pres. Chattanooga Goodwill Industries, 1988—; precinct chmn. Hamilton County Rep. Party Coun., Signal Mountain, Tenn., 1989—, treas., 1991—. Mem. Order of Coif, Mountain City Club, Signal Mountain Golf and Country Club, Phi Kappa Phi. Episcopalian. Home: 609 Marr Dr Signal Mountain TN 37377-2280 Office: US Atty 800 Market St Ste 211 Knoxville TN 37902*

MATTOON, PETER MILLS, lawyer; b. Bryn Mawr, Pa., Oct. 22, 1931; s. Harold Gleason and Marguerite Jeanette (Mills) M.; m. Mary Joan Henley, June 27, 1953; children: Pamela M. Zisselman, R. Stephen, Peter H., Philip P. AB, Dartmouth Coll., 1953; LLB, Harvard U., 1959; LLD (hon.), Widener U., 2001. Bar: Pa. 1960. Assoc. Ballard Spahr Andrews & Ingersoll, Phila., 1959-67; ptnr. Ballard Spahr Andrews & Ingersoll, LLP, Phila., 1967—2001, sr. counsel, 2002—. Emeritus trustee The Episcopal Acad., Merion, Pa., 1970—, former chmn.; trustee, v.p. Widener Meml. Found., Lafayette Hill, Pa., 1972—; trustee Thomas Jefferson U., Phila., 1989—; overseer Widener U. Law Sch., Wilmington, 1979—. Served to lt. USN, 1953-56. Office: Ballard Spahr Andrews & Ingersoll LLP 1735 Market St Fl 51 Philadelphia PA 19103-7599

MATTSON, JAMES STEWART, lawyer, environmental scientist, educator; b. Providence, July 22, 1945; s. Irving Carl and Virginia (Lutey) M.; m. Carol Sandry, Aug. 15, 1964 (div. 1979); children: James, Birgitta; m. Rana A. Fine, Jan. 5, 1983. BS in Chemistry, U. Mich., 1966, MS, 1969, PhD, 1970; JD, George Washington U., 1979. Bar: D.C. 1979, Fla. 1983, U.S. Dist. Ct. D.C. 1979, U.S. Dist. Ct. (so. dist.) Fla. 1984, U.S. Ct. Appeals (D.C. cir.) 1979, U.S. Ct. Claims 1985, U.S. Supreme Ct. 1985, U.S. Ct. Appeals (11th cir.) 1985, U.S. Ct. Appeals (5th cir.) 1987, U.S. Ct. Appeals (fed. cir.) 1990. Staff scientist Gulf Gen. Atomic Co., San Diego, 1970-71; dir. R & D Ouachita Industries, Inc., Monroe, La., 1971-72; asst. prof. chem. oceanography Rosenstiel Sch. Marine & Atmospheric Sci., U. Miami, Fla., 1972-76; phys. scientist NOAA, Washington, 1976-78; mem. profl. staff & congl. liaison Nat. Adv. Commn. on Oceans and Atmosphere, 1978-80; ptnr. Mattson & Pave, Washington, Miami, Key Largo, 1980-86, Mattson & Tobin, Key Largo, 1987-2000; founder/CEO Great House of Wine, Inc, Ft. Lauderdale, Fla., 1997—, Napa, Calif., 1997—; sole practitioner Key Largo, Fla., 2000—. Adj. prof. law U. Miami, 1983-93; cons. Alaska Dept. Environ. Conservation, 1981-91. Author: (with H.B. Mark) Activated Carbon: Surface Chemistry and Adsorption from Solution, 1971; editor (with others): Computers in Chemistry and Instrumentation, 8 vols., 1972-76; The Argo Merchant Oil Spill: A Preliminary Scientific Report, 1977, (with H.B. Mark) Water Quality Measurement: Modern Analytical Techniques, 1981; contbr. articles to profl. jours. Candidate dist. 120 Fla. Ho. of Reps., 1994. Fellow Fed. Water Pollution Control Adminstrn., 1967-68; recipient Spl. Achievement award U.S. Dept. Commerce, 1976-77; Regents Alumni scholar U. Mich., 1963. Mem. ABA, Am. Chem. Soc. (chmn. Symposium on Oil Spill Indentification 1971), Order of Coif. Administrative and regulatory, Environmental, Land use and zoning (including planning). Address: PO Box 586 Key Largo FL 33037-0586 E-mail: jmattson@mattsonlaw.com.

MATUNE, FRANK JOSEPH, lawyer; b. Youngstown, Ohio, Jan. 11, 1948; s. Walter John and Eve (Skiljo) M.; m. Doreen Mary Dolan, June 1, 1974; children: Molly Catherine, John Walter, Kelly Dolan. BA, Ill. Benedictine Coll., 1970; JD, Thomas M. Cooley Law Sch., Lansing, Mich., 1979; LLM, Georgetown U., 1980. Bar: Pa. 1979, Ohio, 1998, U.S. Dist. Ct. (western dist.) Pa. 1982, U.S. Tax Ct. 1980. Tax clk. Bd. Tax Appeals State Mich. Dept. Revenue, Lansing, 1978-79; ptnr. Routman, Moore, Goldstone & Valentino, Sharon, Pa., 1981-98, Nadler, Nadler & Burdman Co., LPA, Youngstown, Ohio, 1998—. Author: Pennsylvania Tax Service, 1987, Federal Tax Service, 1988. Mem. ABA, Ohio Ba Assn., Pa. Bar Assn., Mercer County Bar Assn. (treas. 1983-86). Republican. Roman Catholic. Avocations: sports, classical music. Corporate taxation, Taxation, general, State and local taxation. Home: 798 Lillian Dr Hermitage PA 16148-1571 Office: Nadler Nadler & Burdman Co 20 Federal Plz W Ste 600 Youngstown OH 44503-1424

MAULDIN, JOHN INGLIS, public defender; b. Atlanta, Nov. 6, 1947; s. Earle and Isabel (Inglis) M.; m. Cynthia Ann Balchin, Apr. 15, 1967 (div. Dec. 1985); children: Tracy Rutherford, Abigail Inglis; m. Linda W. Farmer, Nov. 7, 1998. BA, Wofford Coll., 1970; JD, Emory U., 1973. Bar: S.C. 1974, U.S. Ct. Appeals (4th cir.) 1974, U.S. Dist. Ct. S.C. 1975, U.S. Supreme Ct. 1978. Asst. pub. def. Defender Corp. Greenville County, S.C., 1974-76; ptnr. Mauldin & Allison, Greenville, 1977-92; pub. defender Greenville County, S.C., 1992—. Chair S.C. Commn. on Indigent Def., 1993-96; adj. prof. Greenville Tech. Coll., 1975-80; sec., treas. Def. Corp. Greenville County, 1979-92, bd. dirs. Bd. dirs. Speech Hearing & Learning Ctr., Greenville, 1977-90, pres., 1982; bd. dirs. Save Our Sons, 1995—. Named S.C. Atty. Yr. ACLU, S.C., 1986. Mem.: SC Pub. Defender Assn. (bd. dirs. 1992—), SC Assn. Criminal Def. Lawyers (bd. dirs. 1997—99), SC Trial Lawyers Assn., Nat. Legal Aid and Defender Assn. (defender policy group 1999—, bd. dirs. 2002—), Nat. Assn. Criminal Def. Attys., Rotary, Sigma Delta Phi. Democrat. Methodist. Office: PO Box 10264fs Greenville SC 29603

MAULE, JAMES EDWARD, law educator, lawyer; b. Phila., Nov. 26, 1951; s. Edward Randolph George and Jennie Elisabeth (Zappone) M.; m. Susan Margaret Noonan, June 26, 1982 (div. May 1988); children: Charles Edward, Sarah Margaret; m. Susan K. Garrison, Apr. 7, 1990 (div. 1991). BS cum laude, U. Pa. Wharton Sch., 1973; JD cum laude, Villanova U., 1976; LLM with highest honors, George Washington U., 1979. Bar: Pa. 1976, U.S. Tax Ct. 1986. Atty.-adv. Office Chief Counsel to IRS Legis. and Regulations Divsn., Washington, 1976-78; atty.-adv. judge U.S. Tax Ct., Washington, 1978-80; asst. prof. law Dickinson Sch. Law, 1981-83, lectr. and tax program chmn. continuing legal edn., 1981-83; assoc. prof. Villanova Sch. Law, 1983-86, prof., 1986—. Lectr. continuing legal edn. Pa. Bar Inst. , Harrisburg, Continuing Legal Edn. Satellite Network, Inc., 1988; lectr. state and local taxes Georgetown U. Law Ctr. Inst., 1992; sr. tax and tech. ptnr. Ctr. Info. Law and Policy, 1993—99; owner JEMBook Pub. Co.; owner TaxJEM Inc.; co-owner Starjem LLC ; lectr. continuing legal edn. Phila. Tax Conf., 1996, 2001. Author: Cases and Materials in Federal Income Taxation, 1981, (22d edit.) , 2003, Materials in Partnership Law and Taxation, 1985, (6th edit.) , 1991, Materials in Partnership Taxation, 1987, (22d edit.) , 2003, Materials in Introduction to Taxation, 1987, (2d edit.) , 1988, Cases and Materials in Introduction to the Taxation of Business Entities, 1992, (11th edit.) , 2003, Materials in Taxation of Fundamental Wealth Transfers, 1986, (2d edit.) , 1988, Materials in Tax Consequences of Disposition of Property, 1983, (3d edit) , 1985, Materials and Problems in Taxation of Property Disposition I, 1987, Materials in Tax Planning for Real Estate, 1986, Materials in Estate and Gift Tax, 1983, (3d edit) , 1985, Materials in Taxation of Real Estate Transactions, 1986, (3d edit.) , 1992, Taxation of Residence Transactions, 1985, S Corporations: State Law and Taxation, 1989, (supp.edits) , 1989, 1990, 1991, 1992, 1993, Materials and Problems in Computer Applications in the Law, 1990, (6th edit.) , 1995, Materials in Tax Policy, 1990, Materials in Digital Legal Practice Skills, 1996, Materials and Problems in Computer Applications in Tax Law, 1991, (8th edit.) , 1998, Better That 100 Witches Should Live, 1995, Materials in Decedents Estates and Trusts, 1997, (6th edit.) , 2002; author: (with A. Clay) Preparing the 1065 Return, 1992, 1993; author: Continuing Legal Edn. Publs., 1981—; contbg. author: Federal Tax Service, 1989, Tax Practice Series, 1989—; contbr. articles, chapters to books, monographs; author, developer: Computer Assisted Legal Edn. Programs in Taxation, owner, author, editor: computer assisted tax law instruction TaxJEM Inc., cons., prin. author: ABA Section of Taxation Model S Corporation Income Tax Act and Commentary, 1989, author, editor: Report of the Subcommittee on Comparison of S Corporations and Partnerships, 1990, 1991, case and comment editor: Villanova Law Rev., 1975—76, columnist, mem. editl. bd.: S Corps. Jour., 1987—91, Jour. of Ltd. Liability Cos., 1994—98, BNA Tax Mgmt., 1994—. Recipient Dist. Author award, BNA Tax Mgmt., 1993; scholar Nat. Merit, 1969—73. Mem. ABA (chair and reporter phaseout Elimination Project, Tax Simplification and Restructuring Com., sect. of taxation, cons., ex-officio mem. subcom. on state law, S Corp. com., chmn. subcom. on comparison of partnerships, mem. task force on pass-through entities, tax sect., former chmn. subcom. manuscripts and unpub. tchg. material, com. tchg. tax), Phila. Bar Assn. (lectr. tax sect. state and local tax CLE program 1991, fed. income taxes 1992—), Ctr. Info. Law and Policy, Order of Coif, Friars Sr. Soc. (Phila), Beta Alpha Psi. Home: 219 Comrie Dr Villanova PA 19085-1402 Office: Villanova U Sch Law Villanova PA 19085 E-mail: maule@law.villanova.edu.

MAULSBY, ALLEN FARISH, lawyer; b. Balt., May 21, 1922; AB, Williams Coll., Williamstown, Mass., 1944; LL.B., U. Va., 1946. Bar: Md. 1947, N.Y. 1950. Law clk. to judge U.S. Circuit Ct. Appeals 4th Circuit, 1946-47; assoc. firm Cravath Swaine & Moore, N.Y.C., 1947-57, ptnr., 1958-95. Vestryman St. James' Episcopal Ch., N.Y.C., 1962-68, 80-85, warden, 1986-87; trustee Greer-Woodycrest Child Care, 1961-82; bd. dirs. Episc. Ch. Found., 1973-86. Mem. Am. Bar Found., N.Y. Bar Found., Am. Coll. Trial Lawyers, Am. Bar Assn., N.Y. State Bar Assn., Fed. Bar Assn., Assn. Bar City N.Y., N.Y. County Lawyers Assn. Antitrust, General civil litigation, Mergers and acquisitions. Office: Cravath Swaine & Moore 825 8th Ave New York NY 10019-7475 E-mail: amaulsby@cravath.com.

MAUPIN, A. WILLIAM, state supreme court justice; children: Allison, Michael. BA, U. Nev., 1968; JD, U. Ariz., 1971. Atty., ptnr. Thorndal, Backus, Maupin and Armstrong, Las Vegas, 1976—93; judge 8th Jud. Dist. Clark County, 1993—97; assoc. justice Supreme Ct. Nev., 1997—. Bd. govs. Nev. State Bar, 1991—95. Mem.: Nev. Supreme Ct (study com. to review jud. elections, chmn. 1995, alternate dispute resolution implementation com. chmn. 1992—96). Office: Nev Supreme Ct 201 S Carson St Carson City NV 89701-4702

MAUPIN, ARMISTEAD JONES, lawyer; b. Raleigh, N.C., Nov. 10, 1914; s. Alfred McGhee and Mary Armistead (Jones) M.; m. Diana Jane Barton, May 16, 1942 (dec.); children: Armistead Jones, Anthony Westwood, Jane Stuart; m. Cheryl Leigh Erhard, July 31, 1982. AB, U. N.C., 1936; JD, George Washington U., 1940. Bar: N.C. 1939. Ptnr. Maupin, Taylor & Ellis., Raleigh. Pres. Occoneechee coun. Boy Scouts Am., 1962-64; pres. Carolina Charter Corp., 1976-80, 93—; former chancellor Episcopal Diocese of N.C.; former sr. warden Christ Ch. Parish; vice chmn. Am. Battle Monuments Commn., 1981-90. Comdr. USNR, WWII, PTO. Decorated chevalier French Legion of Honor. Fellow: Am. Bar Found.; mem.: ABA (ho. of dels. 1960—72), Soc. of Cin. (v.p. gen. 1968—70, pres. gen. 1971—74, pres. N.C. soc. 1964—67), N.C. State Bar (coun. 1955—60, pres. 1959—60), Triangle Fox Hounds, Cir. Club, Carolina Country Club. Republican. Episcopalian. Administrative and regulatory, Federal civil litigation, State civil litigation. Home: 2005 Banbury Rd Raleigh NC 27608-1121 Office: Highwoods Tower One 3200 Beech Leaf Ct Raleigh NC 27604-1085

MAURENBRECHER, BENEDIKT, lawyer; b. St. Gallen, Switzerland, Feb. 1, 1964; s. Karl and Dolores (Karrer) M.; m. Karin Bischof, Aug. 25, 1995; children: Thomas, Jonathan. ML summa cum laude, U. Bern, Switzerland, 1989, PhD summa cum laude, 1994; MBA, INSEAD, Fontainebleau, France, 1999. Bar: Zurich, 1992. Clk. Dist. Ct. Affoltern, Zurich, Switzerland, 1990; atty. Homburger, Zurich, 1994-98, 2000—; assoc. UBS Warburg, Zurich, 1999-2000. Author: Loans at Interest in Swiss Law, 1994; editor (Swiss sect.) Securities Transactions in Europe, 1998; contbg. author: Basle Commentary on the Swiss Code of Obligations and The International Practice of Law. Pres. Zofinger Fellowship, Bern, 1989. Private 1st class Divisional Ct. 11, 1994—, Zurich. Mem. Zurich Bar Assn., Swiss Bar Assn. Avocations: traveling, english literature. Banking, Securities, Corporate, general. Office: Homburger Weinbergstrasse 56/58 CH-8006 Zürich Switzerland

MAURO, RICHARD FRANK, lawyer, investment manager; b. Hawthorne, Nev., July 21, 1945; s. Frank Joseph and Dolores D. (Kreimeyer) M.; m. LaVonne M. Madden, Aug. 28, 1965; 1 child, Lindsay Anne. AB, Brown U., 1967; JD summa cum laude, U. Denver, 1970. Bar: Colo. 1970. Assoc. Dawson, Nagel, Sherman & Howard, Denver, 1970-72, Van Cise, Freeman, Tooley & McClearn, Denver, 1972-73, ptnr., 1973-74, Hall & Evans, Denver, 1974-81, Morrison & Forester, Denver, 1981-84; of counsel Parcel & Mauro, P.C., Denver, 1984—; pres. Parcel, Mauro & Hultin, P.C., Denver, 1988-90; of counsel Parcel, Mauro P.C., Denver, 1992-99; pres. Sundance Oil Exploration Co., 1985-88; exec. v.p. Castle Group, Inc., 1992-97, pres., 1998—, Richard F. Mauro, P.C., 1999—; ptnr. Moye, Giles, O'Keefe, Vermeire & Gorrell, 1999—. Adj. prof. U. Denver Coll. Law, 1981-84. Symposium editor: Denver Law Jour., 1969-70; editor: Colorado Corporation Manual; contbr. articles to legal jours. Pres. Colo. Open Space Coun., 1974; mem. law alumni coun. U. Denver Coll. Law, 1988-91. Francis Wayland scholar, 1967; recipient various Am. jurisprudence awards Mem. ABA, Colo. Bar Assn., Denver Bar Assn., Colo. Assn. Corp. Counsel. (pres. 1974-75), Am. Arbitration Assn. (comml. arbitrator), Order St. Ives, Denver Athletic Club (bd. dirs. 1986-89). Commercial, contracts (including sales of goods; commercial financing), Corporate, general, Securities. Home: 2552 E Alameda Ave Unit 128 Denver CO 80209-3330 Office: 1225 17th St Fl 29 Denver CO 80202-5534 E-mail: dick.mauro@moyelaw.com.

MAUSKOPF, ROSLYNN R. prosecutor; b. Washington, 1957; BA, Brandeis U., 1979; JD, Georgetown U., 1982. Asst. dist. atty. N.Y. County Dist. Atty.'s Office, 1982—95, dep. chief spl. prosecution bur., 1992, chief frauds bur., 1993; insp. gen. State of N.Y., 1995—2002; U.S. atty. U.S. Dept. Justice, Ea. Dist. N.Y., Bklyn., 2002—. Chair Moreland Commn. N.Y.C. Schs., 1999. Office: Ea Dist NY 147 Pierrepont St Brooklyn NY 11201 Office Fax: 718-254-6479.*

MAXEY, DAVID WALKER, lawyer; b. Scranton, Pa., May 17, 1934; s. Paul Harold and Margaret (Walker) M.; m. Catharine Eglin, June 6, 1968; children: Paul Eglin, Margaret Wilson. AB, Harvard U., 1956, LLB cum laude, 1960. Bar: Pa. 1961, U. S. Dist. Ct. (ea. dist.) Pa. 1961, U.S. Ct. Appeals (3d cir.) 1963. Assoc. Drinker Biddle and Reath LLP, Phila., 1960-66, ptnr., 1967-2000, chmn. real estate dept., 1970-88, mng. ptnr., 1977-91, co-chmn., 1988-91, of counsel, 2000—. Vis. faculty Villanova (Pa.) U. Law Sch., 1987-95. Contbr. articles to profl. jours. Sec., bd. dirs. Greater Phila. Internat. Network, 1981-94; bd. dirs. Young Audiences Ea. Pa., Phila., 1985-95, Libr. Co., Phila., 1993-2000, sec., 1997-2000; chmn. bd. dirs. Hist. Soc. Pa., Phila., 1991-93; chmn. internat. adv. com. Greater Phila. First, 1994-98; bd. dirs. Gladwyne (Pa.) Libr., 1991-98, pres., 1996-98; bd. dirs. Phila. Soc. Preservation Landmarks, 2002-. Recipient Hughes-Gossett award U.S. Supreme Ct. Hist. Soc., Washington, 1991. Mem. ABA, Pa. Bar Assn., Phila. Bar Assn., Am. Coll. Real Estate Lawyers, Harvard Club Phila. (pres. 1970-72), Merion Cricket Club. Avocation: historical research and publication. Banking, Environmental, Property, real (including real estate development, water). Home: 829 Black Road Rd Gladwyne PA 19035 Office: One Logan Sq 18th and Cherry Streets Philadelphia PA 19103-6996 E-mail: cdmmax@aol.com., maxeydw@dbr.com.

MAXFIELD, GUY BUDD, lawyer, educator; b. Galesburg, Ill., May 4, 1933; s. Guy W. and Isabelle B. Maxfield; m. Carol Tunick, Dec. 27, 1970; children: Susan, Stephen, Karen. AB summa cum laude, Augustana Coll., 1955; JD, U. Mich., 1958. Bar: N.Y. 1959. Assoc. White & Case, N.Y.C., 1958-63; prof. law NYU, N.Y.C., 1963—; of counsel August & Kulunas, P.A. Author: Tennessee Will and Trust Manual, 1982, Federal Estate and Gift Taxation, 8th edit., 2002, Florida Will and Trust Manual, 1984, Tax Planning for Professionals, 1986; contbr. articles to law jours. Trustee Acomb Found., Newark, 1974—. With U.S. Army, 1958-64. Fellow Am. Coll. Tax Counsel; mem. ABA, Am. Law Inst., N.Y. State Bar Assn., Order of Coif, Phi Beta Kappa. Office: NYU Sch Law 40 Washington Sq S New York NY 10012-1099

MAXWELL, JOE EDWIN, lieutenant governor; b. Kirksville, Mo., Mar. 17, 1957; s. Robert E. and Molly B. Maxwell; m. Sarah Baker; children: Megan, Shannen. BS in Secondary Edn., Social Studies, U. Mo., 1986, JD, 1990. Farmer, Rush Hill, Mo., 1976-78; ptnr., operator Maxwell Svc., Laddonia, Mo., 1978-84; rural mail carrier U.S. Postal Svc., Rush Hill, 1980-84; outstate field coord. Travis Morrison's Campaign for State Auditor, Mo., 1986; Mo. state field coord. Richard Gephardt for Pres., 1986-87; atty. Mexico, Mo., 1992—; mem. Mo. House, 1990-94, Mo. Senate, 1995—. Mem. Senate Appropriations, Judiciary, Labor and Indsl. Rels., Pub. Health and Welfare coms.; vice chair Elections, Corrections, and Vet.'s Affairs coms.; chair Commerce and Environment Com. Assoc. editor-in-chief Mo. Jour. of Dispute Resolution, 1989. Mem. Am. Legion, 1982—, adj. Post 510, 1982-84; mem. Young Dem. Clubs Mo., 1982—, jud. coun. Young Dems. Am., 1985, pres., 1984-87, 9th Congl. Dist. chmn., 1982; mem. Laddonia Bapt. Ch., 1975—, Sunday Sch. tchr., 1990-91, pulpit com.; bd. dirs. Handi-Shop Inc., Mexico, 1981-84, chmn. mfg. and mktg. com., 1982-84; bd. dirs. Boy Scouts Am. Troop 94, 1980-82. Recipient St. Louis Globe Dem. award for outstanding achievement, 1979, Cert. of Appreciation, Troop 94, Boy Scouts Am., 1982, Mo.'s Outstanding Male Young Dem. award, 1987, George B. Freeman award for outstanding svc., 1987, Appreciation award Mo. Bar, 1992, Mo. Ho. of Reps. Resolution # 624 for exceptional svc. Mo., 1987, Mo. State Senate Resolution # 382 for exceptional svc. Mo., 1987; named one of Outstanding Young Men of Am., 1983, 85. Mem. Moose, Jaycees (Laddonia chpt. pres. 1978-79, coord. Laddonia Area Blood Drive, coord. Laddonia City Clean-up Day, chmn. Mexico Soybean Festival 1989, chmn. Lenten Breakfast 1990, Presdl. award of honor 1979), Kappa Delta Pi, Golden Key Nat. Honor Soc. Democrat. Office: Office of Lt Gov Rm 121 Capitol Bldg Jefferson City MO 65101

MAXWELL, ROBERT EARL, federal judge; b. Elkins, W.Va., Mar. 15, 1924; s. Earl L. and Nellie E. (Rexstrew) M.; m. Ann Marie Grabowski, Mar. 29, 1948; children— Mary Ann, Carol Lynn, Ellen Lindsay, Earl Wilson. LLD (hon.), Davis and Elkins Coll., 1984; LLB, W.Va. U., 1949; LLD (hon.), Davis and Elkins Coll., 1984. Bar: W.Va. 1949. Practiced in, Randolph County, 1949; pros. atty., 1952-61; U.S. atty. for No. Dist. W.Va., 1961-64; judge, then sr. judge U.S. Dist. Ct. (no. dist.) W.Va., Elkins, 1965—; judge Temp. Emergency Ct. of Appeals, 1980-89. Past chmn. budget com. Jud. Conf. U.S.; former mem. exec. com. Nat. Conf. Fed. Trial Judges; former mem. adv. bd. W.Va. U. Mem. bd. advisors W.Va. U., past chmn.; bd. advisors Mary Babb Randolph Cancer Ctr. Recipient Alumni Disting. Svc. award Davis and Elkins Coll., 1969, Religious Heritage Am. award, 1979, Outstanding Trial Judge award W.Va. Trail Lawyers Assn., 1988, Order of Vandalia award W.Va. U., Outstaning Alumnus award, 1992, Tenured Faculty Mem. Recognition award Bd. Govs., Def. Trail Coun., W.Va., 1992, Cert. of Merit, W.Va. State Bar, 1994, Justitia Officium award Coll. of Law, W.Va. U., 1994; fellow W.Va. Bar Found., 1999; Melvin Jones fellow Lions Internat. Found., 2001. Mem. Nat. Conf. Federal Trial Judges, Dist. Judges Assn. 4th Cir. (past pres.), Moose (life), Lions (life), Beta Alpha Beta (merit award), Elkins-Randolph County C. of C. (citizen of yr. 1994). Office: US Dist Ct No Dist PO Box 1275 Elkins WV 26241-1275 E-mail: rmaxwell@neumedia.net.

MAXWELL, WILLIAM STIRLING, retired lawyer; b. Chgo., May 2, 1922; s. W. Stirling and Ethel (Bowes) Maxwell Reineke. AB with distinction, U. Mich., 1947, postgrad., 1946-49, JD, 1949. Bar: Ill. 1949, U.S. Ct. Mil. Appeals 1951, U.S. Supreme Ct. 1952. Assoc. Sidley & Austin, Chgo., 1949-60, 61, ptnr., 1962-84; now ret.; sr. legis. counsel U.S. Treasury, Washington, 1960-61. Trustee Mid-North Animal Shelter Found., Chgo., 1971— . Mem. Order of Coif, Phi Beta Kappa Clubs: Lawyers Club. Republican. Episcopalian. Home: PO Box 1839 Brookings OR 97415-0048

MAY, ALAN ALFRED, lawyer; b. Detroit, Apr. 7, 1942; s. Alfred Albert and Sylvia (Sheer) M.; m. Elizabeth Miller; children: Stacy Ann, Julie Beth. BA, U. Mich., 1963, JD cum laude, 1966. Bar: Mich. 1967, D.C. 1976; former reg. nursing home adminstr., Mich. Ptnr. May and Mapy PC, Detroit, 1979—2001, Kemp Klein, Umphrey and May, P.C., Troy, 2001—. Spl. asst. atty. gen. State of Mich., 1970—; pres., instr. Med-Leg Seminars, Inc., 1978; lectr. Wayne State U., 1974; instr. Oakland U., 1969. Chmn. Rep. 18th Congressional Dist. Com., 1983-87, now chmn. emeritus; chmn. 19th Congressional Dist. Com., 1981-83; mem. Mich. Rep. Com., 1976-84; del. Rep. Nat. Conv., 1984, rules com., 1984; del. Rep. Nat. Conv., 1988, platform com., 1988; former chmn. Mich. Civil Rights Commn.; former mem. Mich. Civil Svc. Commn., 1984-88; former trustee, mem. exec. bd., vice chmn. nat conf. for cmty. and justice NCCJ; trustee Temple Beth El Birmingham, Mich., past pres. exec. bd.; mem. Electoral Coll.; former bd. dirs. ADL, Mich.; bd. dirs. exec. bd., past pres. Detroit Region/Nat. Conf. Cmty. and Justice, Charfoos Charitable Found. Mem. Nat. Conf. Cmty. and Justice (exec. bd., vice chmn.), Detroit Bar Assn., Oakland County Bar Assn., Victors Club, Franklin Hills Country Club (past pres., bd. dirs.), President's Club (trustee). State civil litigation, Probate (including wills, trusts), Workers' compensation. Home: 4140 Echo Rd Bloomfield Hills MI 48302-1941 Office: Kemp Klein Umphrey Endelman & May PC 201 W Big Beaver Rd Ste 600 Troy MI 48084

MAY, APRIL MICHELLE, lawyer; b. Ft. Worth, Tex., June 27, 1968; d. Charles Richard and Sandra (Crouch) M. BBA, Baylor U., 1989, JD, 1991. Bar: Tex. 1992, U.S. Supreme Ct. 1999, cert.: Tex. (bd. cert. family law) 1997. Pvt. practice, Belton, Tex., 1992—97; assoc. Erwin A, Cain, P.C., Dallas, 1997-98, McCurley, Kinser, McCurley Nelson Orsinger, LLP, Dallas, 1998—2000, Downs Stanford PC, Dallas, 2000—02, McCurley, Kinser, McCurley, Nelson Orsinger LLP, Dallas, 2002—. Mem. ABA, Tex. Bar Assn., Dallas Bar Assn. (dir. family law sect. 2003—), Bell County Bar Assn. (dir.), Bell County Young Lawyers Assn. (pres.), Dallas Young Lawyers Assn., Tex. Assn. Family Law Specialists. Appellate, State civil litigation, Family and matrimonial. Office: 5950 Sherry Ln Ste 800 Dallas TX 75225 E-mail: michelle@mkmn.com.

MAY, FRANK BRENDAN, JR., lawyer; b. Bronx, N.Y., Oct. 17, 1945; s. Frank Brendan and Margaret May; m. Mary Frances Fitzsimmons, June 19, 1976; children: David Brendan, Brian Christopher. BA in Econs., NYU, 1973, postgrad., 1973-75; JD, John Marshall Law Sch., Chgo., 1978. Bar: Ill. 1979, U.S. Dist. Ct. (no. dist.) Ill. 1979, U.S. Ct. Appeals (7th cir.), 1979, U.S. Supreme Ct. 1995, lic. Ill. real estate broker 1994. Legal intern criminal div. Cook County State's Atty.'s Office, Chgo., 1977-78; legal intern juvenile div. DuPage County State's Atty.'s Office, Wheaton, Ill., 1978; sr. assoc. atty. Lillig, Kemp & Thorness, Ltd., Oak Brook, Ill., 1978-81; v.p., gen. counsel Coldwell Banker, Oak Brook, 1981-90, Prudential Preferred Properties, Des Plaines, Ill., 1991-98, Law Offices, Frank B. May, Jr., Wheaton, Ill., 1999-2001; sr. corp. atty., asst. sec. Budget Rent a Car Corp., Lisle, Ill., 2001—03; sr. v.p., asst. sec., gen. coun. Coldwell Banker Primus Reality, Oswego, Ill., 2003—. Arbitrator 18th Jud. Cir. Ct., Dupage County, Ill., 1993—. Dir. Ray Graham Found. for People with Disabilities, 1999—. Sgt. USAF, 1963-67. NYU Coun. scholar, 1971-73; David Davis Meml. scholar, 1970-71. Mem. DuPage County Bar Assn. (real estate law com.), Medinah Country Club (mem. legal/bylaws com. 1998-2000, membership com. 1997—, chmn. PGA credentials com. 1999), Ill. Assn. Realtors (mem. large brokers coun. 1996-98, exec. com., fin. com. 1998-1999, lic. law rewrite task force, nominating com. 1998-99), Realtor Assn. Western Suburbs (legal counsel 1999-2000). Avocations: golf, music, gourmet cooking, wine collector. General civil litigation, Corporate, general, Property, real (including real estate development, water). Home: 2064 Stonebridge Ct Wheaton IL 60187-7177 Office: Coldwell Banker Primus Realty 15 W Merchants Dr Oswego IL 60543 Fax: 630-897-4913. Business E-Mail: fmay@cbprimus.com.

MAY, JOSEPH LESERMAN (JACK MAY), lawyer; b. Nashville, May 27, 1929; s. Daniel and Dorothy (Fishel) M.; m. Natalie McCuaig, Apr. 12, 1957 (dec. May 1990); children: Benjamin, Andrew, Joshua, Maria; m. Lynn Hewes Lance, June 10, 1994. BA, Yale U., 1951; JD, NYU, 1958; postgrad., Harvard Bus. Sch., 1969. Bar: Tenn. 1959. Prodr. Candied Yam Jackson Show, 1947-51; with CIA, 1951-55; pres. Nuweave Socks, Inc., N.Y.C., 1955-59, May Hosiery Mills, Nashville, 1960-83, Athens Hosiery Mills, Tenn., 1966-83; v.p. Wayne-Gossard Corp., Chattanooga, 1972-83; pvt. practice law Nashville, 1984—. Mem. adv. bd. Asian Strategies Group, 1994. Bd. dirs. Vanderbilt Cancer Ctr., 1994-99; pres. Jewish Cmty. Ctr., 1969; chmn. Guardianship and Trust Corp., 1994-96, Campus for Human Devel., 2000-02; mem. AAA panel of neutrals. With USN, 1947-53, U.S. Army, 1954. Mem. Tenn. Bar Assn., Nashville Bar Assn., Am. Arbitration Assn. Panel of Neutrals, Tenn. Hist. Soc. (trustee, pres. 2000-02), Eagle Scout Assn., Belle Meade Country Club, Shamus Club, Old Oak Club, Yale Club N.Y., Rotary (pres. Nashville 1971). Republican. Jewish. Home: 13 Abbottsford Nashville TN 37215-2442 Office: PO Box 190628 424 Church St Ste 2000 Nashville TN 37219-3304

MAY, LAWRENCE EDWARD, lawyer; b. N.Y.C., Aug. 7, 1947; s. Jack and Ann Marie (Schnell) M.; m. Rosalind Marsha Israel, Feb. 3, 1979; children: Jeremy, Lindsey. BA, UCLA, 1969, JD, 1972. Bar: Calif. 1972, N.Y. 1973. Assoc. Paul, Weiss, Rifkind, Wharton & Garrison, N.Y.C., 1972-76, Levine, Krom & Unger, Beverly Hills, Calif., 1976-79, Weissburg & Aronson, L.A., 1979-81, Valensi & Rose, L.A., 1981-83; prin. Lawrence E. May, P. C., L.A., 1983—. Bd. dirs. Pub. Counsel, 1989-97; pres., 1995-96. Mem. editorial adv. bd. L.A. Jewish Jour., 1985-91, exec. com. Pacific S.W. Region Anti-Defamation League, 1985—; bd. dirs. L.A. Youth, 1997-2002. Mem. State Bar Calif., Los Angeles County Bar Assn. (trustee 1987-88, pro bono coun. 1995-98), Beverly Hills Bar Assn. (bd. govs. 1981-90, pres. 1988-89, chmn. bus. law sect. 1984-85). Democrat. Avocations: current events, golf, family activities. Corporate, general, Estate planning, Property, real (including real estate development, water). Office: Ste 350 10350 Santa Monica Blvd Los Angeles CA 90025-5075 E-mail: lmay@maylaw.com.

MAY, RANDOLPH JOSEPH, lawyer; b. Wilmington, N.C., Aug. 11, 1946; s. Aaron and Norma (Eisen) M.; m. Laurie Eisenberg, Mar. 28, 1971; children: Joshua, Brooke. A.B., Duke U., 1968, J.D., 1971. Bar: D.C. 1973: U.S. Dist. Ct. D.C. 1973, U.S. Ct. Appeals (D.C. cir.) 1973, U.S. Supreme Ct. 1980. Law clk. U.S. Ct. Appeals (D.C. cir.), Washington, 1972-73; assoc. Steptoe and Johnson, Washington, 1973-78; assoc. gen. counsel FCC, Washington, 1978-81; ptnr. McKenna, Wilkinson & Kittner, Washington, 1981-86; ptnr., Bishop, Cook, Purcell & Reynolds, Washington, 1986-91; ptnr., Sutherland, Asbill & Brennan, Washington, 1991-96; sr. fellow, dir. comms. policy studies, 1999—. Pres. Chancellor Farms Civic Assn., Springfield, Va., 1975, Voluntary Action Ctr., Fairfax, Va., 1976; chmn. ann. fund Duke Law Sch., 1993—, mem. bd. vis., 1994—. Named Outstanding Sr. Exec. FCC, 1980. Mem. D.C. Bar Assn., Fed. Bar Assn. (communications com. 1979-81), Fed. Communications Bar Assn. (jud. rev. com. 1981-83), ABA (chair ratemaking section adminstrv. law 1993-94, chair ratemaking com. 1993—, adminstrv. conf. of the U.S. 1994—). Jewish. Administrative and regulatory, Entertainment, Utilities, public. Home: 10701 Stapleford Hall Dr Rockville MD 20854-4448 Office: The Progress and Freedom Found 1401 H StNW Washington DC 20005 E-mail: may@pff.org.

MAY, RONALD ALAN, lawyer; b. Waterloo, Iowa, Sept. 8, 1928; s. John W. and Elsie (Finlayson) M.; m. Naomi Gray, Aug. 18, 1950 (div. Feb. 1974); children: Sarah, Jonathan, Andrew, Rachel; m. Susan East Gray, May 9, 1975. BA, U. Iowa, 1950; LL.B., Vanderbilt U., 1953. Bar: Ark. 1953. Atty. Daggett & Daggett, Marianna, 1953-57, Wright, Lindsey & Jennings, Little Rock, 1957-84, sr. ptnr., 1984-96, of counsel, 1996—. Editor: Automated Law Research, 1972, Sense and Systems in Automated Law Research, 1975; contbg. editor Fifty State Construction Lien and Bond Law, 1992, Fifty State Public Construction Contracting, 1996; assoc. editor Jour. Irreproducible Results. Pres. Spl. Com. on Pub. Edn., Ark. Assn. for Mental Health, Friends of Library, Central Ark. Radiation Therapy Inst.; chmn. Ark. Cancer Research Ctr., 1990-92; bd. dirs. Nat. Assn. for Mental Health, Ark. State Hosp., Gaines House, State Bd. Architects; bd. dirs. State Bd. Bar Examiners, chmn. 1987-88, Ark. ethics com., 1991-93; trustee Mus. Sci. and Natural History, Little Rock, chmn., 1973; mem. profl. adv. bd. sch. architecture U. Ark., 1990-96, mem. profl. adv. bd. sch. urban studies and design, 1993—; mem. human rsch. adv. com. U. Ark. for Med. Scis., 2000—. Served with AUS, 1946-47. Mem. ABA (chmn. sci. and tech. sect. 1975-76), Ark., Pulaski County Bar Assns., Internat. Assn. Def. Counsel, Am. Inns of Ct. (Master of the Bench), Assn. for Computing Machinery, Order of Coif, Phi Beta Kappa. Republican. Episcopalian. General civil litigation. Home: 821 Ash St Little Rock AR 72205-2051 Office: Wright Lindsey & Jennings 200 W Capitol Ave Ste 2200 Little Rock AR 72201-3699 E-mail: rmay@wlj.com.

MAY, TIMOTHY JAMES, lawyer; b. Denver, Aug. 3, 1932; s. Thomas Henry and Helen Frances (O'Conner) M.; m. Monica Anita Gross, Aug. 24, 1957; children: Stephanie, Maureen, Cynthia, Timothy, Anthony. BA, Cath. U. Am., 1954; LLB, Georgetown U., 1957, LLM, 1960. Bar: D.C. 1957, U.S. Supreme Ct. 1961. Law clk. to judge U.S. Ct. Appeals, D.C. Cir., 1957-58; assoc. Covington & Burling, Washington, 1958-61; cons. Exec. Office of Pres. U.S., Washington, 1961-62; chief counsel subcom. on stockpile Armed Svcs. Com., U.S. Senate, Washington, 1962-63; mng. dir. Fed. Maritime Commn., Washington, 1963-66; gen. counsel U.S. Post Office Dept., Washington, 1966-69; sr. ptnr. Patton Boggs, L.L.P., Washington, 1969—. Bd. dirs. Legal Aid Soc. D.C., 1984—; pres. Coun. for Ct. Excellence, Washington, 1999—, Marine Corps Law Enforcement Found., 1996—; chmn. bd. regents Cath. U. Am., 1988-93, trustee, 1993—; pres. Holy Family of Bethlehem Found., 1997-99. Recipient Servant of Justice award Legal Aid Soc. D.C., 1997, St. Elizabeth Ann Seton award SOAR!, 1998, Caritas award Archdiocese D.C., 1998. Fellow Am. Bar Found. (life); mem. ABA (House of Dels.), Fed. Bar Assn., Bar Assn. of D.C. (pres. 1991-92, Lawyer of the Yr. award 1999), Congl. Country Club (bd. govs. 1992-98, sec. 1994-97), Nat. Christian Leadership Conf. for Israel (mem. exec. com.), Met. Club, Indian Creek Country Club (bd. dirs. 1999—, v.p. 2001—), Fed. City Coun., Econ. Club D.C. (bd. dirs. 2001—), Knight of Malta, Constantinian Order St. George (knight). Democrat. Roman Catholic. Administrative and regulatory, Federal civil litigation, Corporate, general. Home: 3828 52nd St NW Washington DC 20016-1924 Office: Patton Boggs LLP 2550 M St NW Washington DC 20037-1350 Home (Winter): 286 Bal Bay Dr Miami FL 33154 E-mail: tmay@pattonboggs.com.

MAYDEN, BARBARA MENDEL, lawyer; b. Chattanooga, Sept. 18, 1951; d. Eugene Lester Mendel and Blanche (Krugman) Rosenberg; m. Martin Ted Mayden, Sept. 14, 1986. AB, Ind. U., 1973; JD, U. Ga., 1976. Bar: Ga. 1976, N.Y. 1980. Assoc. King & Spalding, Atlanta, 1976-79, Willkie Farr & Gallagher, N.Y.C., 1980, Morgan Lewis & Bockius, N.Y.C., 1980-82, White & Case, N.Y.C., 1982-89; spl. counsel Skadden, Arps, Slate, Meagher & Flom, N.Y.C., 1989-95; mem. Bass, Berry & Sims PLC, Nashville, 1996—; lectr. Vanderbilt U. Sch. Law, Nashville, 1995-97. Mem. bd. visitors U. Ga. Sch. Law, Athens, 1986—89; mem. Leadership Nashville, 1999—2000; mem. adv. bd. Women's Fund of the Cmty. Found. of Mid. Tenn., 2001—; bd. dirs. YWCA, 2001—, Jewish Cmty. Ctr., 2001—02. Fellow Am. Bar Found. (life); mem. ABA (sec. 2001-2002, vice chmn. 2002-, bus. law sect., chair young lawyers div. 1985-86, house of dels. 1986—, commr. commn. on women 1987-91, commr. commn. opportunities for minorities in profession 1986-87, chmn. assembly resolutions com. 1990-91, select com. of the house 1989-91, membership com. of the house 1991-92, chair com. on rules and calendar 1996-98, bd. govs. 1991-94, chair bd. govs. ops. com., exec. com. 1993-94, mem. task force long range fin. planning 1993-94, com. scope correlation of work 1998—, chair 2001-2002), Nat. Assn. Bond Lawyers (bd. dirs. 1985-86), Bond Attys.' Workshop (chmn. 1986), N.Y. State Bar Assn. (mem. ho. of dels. 1993-95), Assn. of Bar of City of N.Y. (internat. human rights com. 1986-89, 2d century com. 1986-90, com. women in the profession, 1989-92), N.Y. County Lawyers Assn. (com. spl. projects, chair com. rels with other bars), Am. Law Inst. Democrat. Jewish. Corporate, general, Mergers and acquisitions, Securities. Home: 4414 Herbert Pl Nashville TN 37215-4544 Office: Bass Berry & Sims PLC 315 Deaderick St Ste 2700 Nashville TN 37238-0002 E-mail: bmayden@bassberry.com.

MAYER, CARL JOSEPH, prosecutor, lawyer; b. Boston, Apr. 23, 1959; s. Arno Joseph and Nancy Sue (Grant) M. AB magna cum laude, Princeton U., 1981; JD, U. of Chgo., 1986; LLM, Harvard U., 1988. Bar: N.J. 1986, Mass. 1988, N.Y. 1989, D.C. 1989. Writer for Ralph Nader, Washington, 1981-83; law clk. to presiding justice U.S. Dist. Ct., Wilmington, Del., 1986-87; law assoc., prof. Hofstra Law Sch., Hempstead, N.Y., 1989-94; atty. Milberg, Weiss, Bershad, Hynes and Lerach, N.Y.C., 1995-96; spl. counsel N.Y. State Atty. Gen.'s Office, N.Y.C., 1999—. Cons. U.S. Senate Com., Washington, 1988-89. Author: Shakedown, 1998; co-author: Public Domain, Private Dominion, 1985; contbr. articles to profl. jours. Town committeeman, Princeton, N.J., 1995-98. NYU fellow, 1988-89. Mem. ABA, N.Y. Bar Assn., N.J. Bar Assn., Mass. Bar Assn. Avocations: marathon running, squash, tennis. Home: 58 Battle Rd Princeton NJ 08540-4902 Office: NY State Atty Gen Office 120 Broadway New York NY 10271-0002 E-mail: carlmayer@aol.com.

MAYER, HALDANE ROBERT, federal chief judge; b. Buffalo, N.Y., Feb. 21, 1941; s. Haldane Rupert and Myrtle Kathleen (Gaude) Mayer; m. Mary Anne McCurdy, Aug. 13, 1966; children: Anne Christian, Rebecca Paige. BS, U.S. Mil. Acad., 1963; JD, Coll. William and Mary, 1971. Bar: Va. 1971, D.C. 1980, U.S. Ct. Appeals (4th cir.) 1972, U.S. Dist. Ct. (ea. dist.) Va. 1972, U.S. Ct. Mil. Appeals 1973, U.S. Supreme Ct. 1977, U.S. Ct. Claims 1984. Law clk. U.S. Ct. Appeals (4th cir.), Richmond, Va., 1971—72; atty. McGuire Woods & Battle, Charlottesville, Va., 1975—77; spl. asst. to chief justice U.S. Supreme Ct., Washington, 1977—80; atty. Baker & McKenzie, Washington, 1980—81; acting spl. counsel U.S. Merit Systems Protection Bd., Washington, 1981—82; judge U.S. Claims Ct., Washington, 1982—87, U.S. Ct. Appeals (fed. cir.), Washington, 1987—97, chief judge, 1997—. Adj. prof. U. Va. Sch. Law, 1975—77, 1992—94, George Washington U. Law Sch., 1992—96. Bd. dirs. William and Mary Law Sch. Assn., 1979—85. Maj. U.S. Army, 1963—75, ret. lt. col. USAR. Decorated Bronze Star. Mem.: West Point Soc. D.C., Army Athletic Assn., West Point Assn. Grads., Omicron Delta Kappa. Office: US Ct Appeals for Fed Cir 717 Madison Pl NW Washington DC 20439-0002

MAYER, JAMES HOCK, mediator, lawyer; b. Neptune City, N.J., Nov. 1, 1935; s. J. Kenneth and Marie Ruth (Hock) M.; m. Carol I. Keating, Sept. 20, 1958 (div. Feb. 1981); children: Craig, Jeffrey; m. Patrisha Renk, Mar. 28, 1981 (div. July 2001). AB with distinction, Dartmouth Coll., 1957; JD, Harvard U., 1964. Bar: Calif. 1965, U.S. Dist. Ct (no. dist., so. dist.) Calif. 1965, U.S. Ct. Appeals (9th cir.) 1965, U.S. Supreme Ct. 1974. Assoc. Pillsbury, Madison & Sutro, San Francisco, 1964-72, ptnr., 1973—; ind. mediator, 1992—. Rear adm. USNR, 1957-93. Rufus Choate scholar Dartmouth Coll., 1956-57. Mem. Newcomen Soc., Navy League, Naval Order of U.S., Harvard Club. Alternative dispute resolution, Commercial, contracts (including sales of goods; commercial financing), Corporate, general. Home and Office: Mayer Mediation Svcs 1476 Sierra Linda Dr Escondido CA 92025 E-mail: just-results@msn.com.

MAYER, JAMES JOSEPH, retired corporate lawyer; b. Cin., Nov. 27, 1938; s. Cletus Joseph and Berna Mae (Schroeder) M.; m. Margaret Ann Hobbs, Oct. 24, 1964; children: Kimberly, Susanne, Terri. BEE, U. Cin., 1961; JD, No. Ky. U., 1969. Registered profl. engr., Ohio. Bar: Ohio 1969, Ky. 1975. Engr. Cin. Gas & Electric Co., 1961-69, atty., 1969-85, gen. counsel, 1986-91, v.p., gen. counsel, 1991-95, ret., 1995; of counsel Taft, Stetinius & Hollister, Cin., 1995—. With USAFR, 1961-64. Mem. Ohio Bar Assn., Ky. Bar Assn., Cin. Bar Assn., Bankers Club. Republican. Roman Catholic. Avocations: home remodeling, sports, golf. Administrative and regulatory, Corporate, general, Utilities, public. E-mail: mayer@taftlaw.com.

MAYER, NEAL MICHAEL, lawyer; b. N.Y.C., Dec. 4, 1941; s. Joseph Henry and Cele (Brodsky) M.; m. Jane Ellen Greenberg, Aug. 24, 1963; children: Andrew Warren, Amy Lynn, Rebecca Ann, Jenny Leigh. BA in History with honors, Kenyon Coll., 1963; JD, Georgetown U., 1966. Bar: D.C. 1967, U.S. Dist. Ct. D.C. 1967, U.S. Ct. Appeals (D.C. cir.) 1967, U.S. Customs Ct. 1967, U.S. Supreme Ct. 1970, U.S. Ct. Appeals (5th cir.) 1975. Assoc. Coles & Goertner, Washington, 1966-71, ptnr., 1971-82; sr. ptnr. Hoppel, Mayer & Coleman, Washington, 1982—. Trustee Kenyon Coll., 1995-2002. Mem. ABA, D.C. Bar Assn., Maritime Adminstrv. Bar Assn. (pres. 1979), Assn. for Transp. Law, Logistics and Policy, Propeller Club of U.S. (Washington), Kenyon Coll. Alumni Assn. (pres. 1993-94). Administrative and regulatory, Admiralty, Transportation. Office: Hoppel Mayer & Coleman 1000 Connecticut Ave NW Washington DC 20036-5302 E-mail: nmayer@hmc-law.com.

MAYER, RENEE G. lawyer; b. Elizabeth, N.J., Apr. 17, 1933; d. Harry and Bertha Sheinblatt Miller; m. Joseph C. Mayer, June 19, 1955; children: Douglas, Julia, Amy, Andrew. BS, Cornell U., 1955; JD, Hofstra U., 1978. Bar: N.Y. 1979, U.S. Dist. Ct. (ea. dist.) N.Y. 1979, U.S. Ct. Appeals (2d cir.) 1983, U.S. Supreme Ct. 1982. Assoc. atty. Meyer, English & Cianciulli, Mineola, N.Y., 1978-79; pvt. practice Mineola, N.Y., 1979-89; ptnr. Riebesehl, Mayer, Keegan & Horowitz, Garden City, N.Y., 1989-97; pvt. practice law Mineola, N.Y., 1997-2001, Port Washington, N.Y., 2001—. Mem. N.Y. State Bar Assn., Nassau Lawyers Assn. Long Island, Inc. (pres. 1996-97, first vice chancellor conf. of continuing legal edn.), Nassau County Women's Bar Assn. (pres. 1985-86), Nassau County Bar Assn. (dir. 1984-87, asst. dean acad. law 1987-91), Cornell Club (bd. govs. 1980-90), Democratic Com. (zone leader, Port. Washington, N.Y., 1980-93). Avocations: reading, theatre, travel. Family and matrimonial. Home and Office: 7 Leeds Dr Port Washington NY 11050-4116

MAYERS, DANIEL KRIEGSMAN, lawyer; b. Scarsdale, N.Y., July 10, 1934; s. Chauncey Maurice and Helen P. (Kriegsman) M.; m. Karen E. Silverman, Sept. 30, 1956, children: Peter D., Leslie H. Shroyer. AB, Harvard U., 1955, LLB, 1960. Bar: D.C. 1961, U.S. Supreme Ct. 1961. Law clk. to Justice Felix Frankfurter, U.S. Supreme Ct., Washington, 1960-61; spl. asst. U.S. Dept. Justice, Washington, 1961-62; assoc. Wilmer Cutler & Pickering, Washington, 1962-65, ptnr., 1967-99, of counsel, 2000—; exec. asst. to undersec. U.S. State Dept., Washington, 1965-66. Vis. com. Harvard Law Sch., Cambridge, Mass., 1982-89, chmn., 1986-89; chmn. Legal Action Ctr., N.Y.C., 1998—, Washington Ednl. TV Assn., 1993-97, Survivors Fund for Pentagon Victims, 2001-; bd. dirs. Hypres Corp., Netscan, Inc. Pres. Nat. Symphony Orch., Washington, 1987-89; chmn. Sidwell Friends Sch., Washington, 1979-81; mem. Ams. for Peace Now, 1991—, Fed. City Coun., Washington, 1981—; trustee Cmty. Found. for Nat. Capital Area, 1997—; counsel, dir. Ctr. for Nat. Policy, Washington, 1984-93. With U.S. Army, 1955-57. Recipient Sears prize Harvard Law Sch., 1959 Mem. ABA, Met. Club, Burning Tree Woodstock Country Club. Democrat. Jewish. Avocations: tennis; fishing. Home: 3222 Woodland Dr NW Washington DC 20008-3547 Office: Wilmer Cutler & Pickering 2445 M St NW Washington DC 20037-1487

MAYERSON, SANDRA ELAINE, lawyer; b. Dayton, Ohio, Feb. 8, 1952; d. Manuel David and Florence Louise (Tepper) M.; m. Scott Burns, May 29, 1977 (div. Oct. 1978); 1 child, Katy Joy. BA cum laude, Yale U., 1973; JD, Northwestern U., 1976. Bar: Ill. 1976, N.Y. 1997, U.S. Ct. Appeals (7th cir.) 1976, U.S. Dist. Ct. (no. dist.) Ill. 1977, U.S. Dist. Ct. Md. 1989, U.S. Ct. Appeals (5th cir.) 1994, U.S. Dist. Ct. (so. and ea. dists.) N.Y. 1997, U.S. Ct. Appeals (2nd Cir.) 1997, U.S. Dist. Ct. (ea. dist.) Mich. 2000. Assoc. gen. counsel JMB Realty Corp., Chgo., 1979-80; assoc. Chatz, Sugarman, Abrams et al, Chgo., 1980-81; ptnr. Pollack, Mayerson & Berman, Chgo., 1981-83; dep. gen. counsel AM Internat., Inc., Chgo., 1983-85; ptnr. Kirkland & Ellis, Chgo., 1985-87; ptnr., chmn. bankruptcy group Kelley Drye & Warren, N.Y.C., 1987-93; ptnr., chmn. N.Y. bankruptcy group McDermott, Will & Emery, N.Y.C., 1993-99; ptnr., bankruptcy nat. practice group leader Holland and Knight, N.Y.C., 1999—. Examiner Interco chpt. 11, 1991. Contbr. articles to profl. jours. Bd. dirs. Jr. Med. Rsch. Inst. coun. Michael Reese Hosp., Chgo., 1981-86, Self Help Inc., 2000-; met. divsn. Jewish Guild for Blind, 1990-92; nat. legal afffairs com. Anti-Defamation League, 1990-; lawyers' exec. com. United Jewish Appeal; chair Holland & Knight Nat. Bankruptcy & Creditors Rights Group, 2001-. Named one of Top 50 Women Litigators, Nat. Law Jour., 2001; assoc. fellow, Branford Coll., Yale U., 1993—. Mem. ABA (bus. bankruptcy com. 1976—, sec. 1990-93, chair avoiding powers subcom. 1993-96, chair claims trading subcom. 1997-2000, chair strategic planning subcom., 2000-), Ill. State Bar Assn. (governing council corp. and securities sect. 1983-86), Chgo. Bar Assn. (current events chmn. corp. sect. 1980-81), 7th Cir. Bar Assn., Yale Club (N.Y.C.). Democrat. Jewish. Bankruptcy, Corporate, general. Office: Holland and Knight 195 Broadway Fl 24 New York NY 10007-3100

MAYFIELD, RICHARD HEVERIN, lawyer; b. Washington, Sept. 29, 1921; s. Robert Edwin and Helen May (Benton) M.; m. Caroline C. Mayfield; children: Elinor D., Nancy L., Anne W. AB, Swarthmore Coll., 1943; LLB, Harvard U., 1948. Bar: D.C. 1948, Md. 1954. Assoc. Craighill, Mayfield, Fenwick, Cromelin & Cobb, Washington, 1948-54, ptnr., 1954—. Editor: Will Forms and Clauses, 1969, Trust Forms and Clauses, 1975. Bd. govs. Beauvoir Sch., 1961-67, chmn., 1967. Served with AUS, 1943-46. Fellow Am. Coll. Trust and Estates Counsel; mem. Washington Estate Planning Coun., Barrister Club (sec. 1959), Lawyers Club, Columbia Country Club, Masons, Shriners. Estate planning, Probate (including wills, trusts), Estate taxation. Home: 5 E Kirke St Bethesda MD 20815-4216 Office: Craighill Mayfield Fenwick Cromelin & Cobb 4910 Massachusetts Ave NW Washington DC 20016-4300

MAYNARD, ELLIOTT, state supreme court justice; b. Williamson, W.Va., Dec. 8, 1942; BS in Psychology, Fla. So. Coll., 1967; JD, W.Va. U., 1974. Judge W.Va. Cir. Ct. 30th Jud. Cir., 1982-97; justice W.Va. Supreme Ct. Appeals, Charleston, 1997—, chief justice, 2000. Prosecuting atty., Mingo County, 1976, 80. Mng. dir. Tug Valley C. of C., 1968-70; active Boy Scouts Am.; dist. chmn. Mingo-Pike Dist., Chief Cornstalk Dist.; bd. dirs. Buckskin Coun. With USAF, 1961-66. Recipient Silver Beaver award Boy Scouts Am. Office: State Capital State Ct Appeals Bldg 1 Rm E306 Charleston WV 25305

MAYNARD, JOHN RALPH, lawyer; b. Mar. 5, 1942; s. John R. and Frances Jane (Mitchell) Maynard Kendryk; m. Meridee J. Sagadin, Sept. 10, 1995; children: Bryce James, Pamela Ann. BA, U. Wash., 1964; JD, Calif. Western U., San Diego, 1972; LLM, Harvard U., 1973. Bar: Calif. 1972, Wis. 1973. Assoc. Whyte & Hirschboeck, Milw., 1973-78, Minahan & Peterson, Milw., 1979-91, Quarles & Brady, Milw., 1991-2000, Davis & Kuelthau, Milw., 2000—. Bd. dirs. Am. Heart Assn., 1979—82, Transitional Living Svcs., Inc., 1999—2003; pres. Milw. Chamber Orch., 2000—02; mem. Wis. Adv. Coun. to U.S. SBA, 1987—89. Mem.: ABA, Milw. Yacht Club, Harvard Club (Wis.). Commercial, contracts (including sales of goods; commercial financing), Corporate, general, Estate planning. Home: 809 E Lake Forest Ave Milwaukee WI 53217-5377 Office: Davis & Kuelthau 111 E Kilbourn Ste 1400 Milwaukee WI 53202

MAYNARD, PETER DAVID, lawyer; b. Phila., Sept. 16, 1950; s. Albert Thomas Jr. and Mary E. (Leonard) M.; m. Kathryn L. Curley, Aug. 16, 1975; children: Agibail, Andrew. BA, Mercyhurst Coll., Erie, Pa., 1974; JD, Widener U., 1977. Bar: Pa. 1978, U.S. Dist. Ct. (ea. dist.) Pa. 1980, U.S. Ct. Appeals (3d cir.) 1981, U.S. Supreme Ct., 1991. Asst. dist. atty. Berks County, Reading, Pa., 1978-80, asst. pub. defender, 1981-83; pvt. practice, Reading, 1980—. Editor Berks County Law Jour., 1983-85. Mem. Ceol Neamh Pipe Band. Mem. Ea. U.S.Pipe Band Assn., Pa. Bar Assn., Berks County Bar Assn., Mensa, Nat. Welsh-Am. Found. Republican. Episcopalian. Avocation: bagpipes. Criminal, Family and matrimonial, General practice.

MAYNARD, ROBERT HOWELL, retired lawyer; b. San Antonio, Feb. 15, 1938; s. William Simpson Sr. and Lillian Isabel (Tappan) M.; m. Joan Marie Pearson, Jan. 6, 1962; children: Gregory Scott, Patricia Kathryn, Alicia Joan, Elizabeth Simms. BA, Baylor U., 1959, LLB, 1961; LLM, Georgetown U., 1965. Bar: Tex. 1961, D.C. 1969, Ohio 1973. Trial atty. gen. litigation sect. lands div. U.S. Dept. Justice, Washington, 1964-65; spl. asst. to solicitor U.S. Dept. Interior, Washington, 1965-69; legis. asst. U.S. Senate, Washington, 1969-73; ptnr., dept. head Smith & Schnacke, Dayton, Ohio, 1973-83; dir. Ohio EPA, Columbus, Ohio, 1983-85; ptnr., environ. policy and strategy devel., tech. law Vorys, Sater, Seymour and Pease, Columbus, 1985-2000; ret., 2000; pres. Tappan Woods LLC, 2001—. Trustee Ohio Found. for Entrepreneurial Edn., Bus. Tech. Ctr., 1994-2000, Episcopal Cmty. Svcs. Found., 1990-96, Columbus Technology Coun., 1992-2001, Johnson's Island Preservation Soc. USNR, 1962-65. Episcopalian. Administrative and regulatory, Environmental, Natural resources. Office: Vorys Sater Seymour & Pease PO Box 1008 52 E Gay St Columbus OH 43215-1008

MAYNE, WILEY EDWARD, lawyer; b. Sanborn, Iowa, Jan. 19, 1917; s. Earl W. and Gladys (Wiley) M.; m. Elizabeth Dodson, Jan. 5, 1942; children— Martha (Mrs. F.K. Smith), Wiley Edward, John. S.B. cum laude, Harvard, 1938; JD, State U. Iowa, 1941. Bar: Iowa 1941, US Supreme Ct. 1950. Practiced in, Sioux City, 1946-66, 75—; mem. Shull, Marshall, Mayne, Marks & Vizintos, 1946-66, Mayne and Berenstein, 1975-87, Mayne & Mayne, 1988-99, Mayne, Marks and Madsen, Sioux City, 1999—. Spl. agt. FBI, 1941-43; Mem. 90th-93d Congresses, 6th Dist. Iowa; mem. judiciary com., agr. com. Commr. from Iowa Nat. Conf. Commrs. Uniform State Laws, 1956-60; chmn. grievance commn. Iowa Supreme Ct., 1964-66; del. FAO, 1973; chmn. Woodbury County Compensation Bd., 1975-80 Chmn. Midwest Rhodes Scholar Selection Com., 1964-66; pres. Sioux City Symphony Orch. Assn., 1947-54, Sioux City Concert Course, 1947-54; vice chmn. Young Republican Nat. Fedn., 1948-50; bd. dirs. Iowa Bar Found., 1962-68. Served to lt. (j.g.) USNR, 1943-46. Fellow Am. Coll. Trial Lawyers; mem. ABA (ho. of dels. 1966-68), Iowa Bar Assn. (pres. 1963-64), Sioux City Bar Assn., Internat. Assn. Def. Counsel (exec. com. 1961-64), Harvard Club (N.Y.C.), Sioux City Country Club, Masons (Scottish Rite/33 deg.). Federal civil litigation, State civil litigation, Insurance. Home: 2728 Jackson St Sioux City IA 51104 Office: Pioneer Bank Bldg 701 Pierce St Ste 300 Sioux City IA 51101 Fax: 712-252-1535. E-mail: maynelaw@pionet.net.

MAYORKAS, ALEJANDRO, lawyer, former prosecutor; b. Cuba; With Patterson, Belknap, Webb & Tyler, L.A., 1986-89; asst. U.S. atty., 1989-99; chief office's gen. crimes sect., 1996-98; U.S. atty. cen. dist. Calif. U.S. Dept. Justice, 1999—2001; ptnr. O'Melveny & Myers, L.A., 2001—. Tchr. trial advocacy Loyola Law Sch., 1997-98. Office: O'Melveny & Myers 400 S Hope St Los Angeles CA 90071-2899

MAYS, JANICE ANN, lawyer; b. Waycross, Ga., Nov. 21, 1951; d. William H. and Jean (Bagley) M. AB (hon.), Wesleyan Coll., Macon, Ga., 1973; JD, U. Ga., 1975; LLM in Taxation, U. Georgetown, 1980. Bar: Ga. 1976. Tax counsel com. on ways and means U.S. Ho. Reps., Washington, 1975-88, chief tax counsel com. on ways and means, staff dir. subcom. select revenue measures, 1988-93, chief counsel, staff dir. com. on ways and means, 1993-95, minority chief counsel, staff dir. com. on ways and means, 1995—. Recipient Disting. Achievement in Profession Alumnae award Wesleyan Coll., 1998. Mem. Tax Coalition (past chair). Office: Ways & Means Com 1106 Longworth Office Bldg Washington DC 20515-0001

MAZER, JASON S. lawyer; b. Ft. Leonard Wood, Mo., Nov. 4, 1972; s. Alan L. and Lois R. Mazer; m. Jodi A. Hirschfield, May 5, 2001. BA, Tufts U., 1994; JD, Washington U., 1998. Bar: Fla. 1998, U.S. Dist. Ct. (so., mid. and no. dists.) Fla. 1998, U.S. Ct. Appeals (11th cir.) 1999. Assoc. Morgan, Lewis & Bockins, Miami, Fla., 1998—99; sr. assoc. Ver, Ploeg & Lumpkin, P.A., Miami, 1999—. Mem.: Order of Coif (sec. 1998). Insurance, Labor (including EEOC, Fair Labor Standards Act, labor-management relations, NLRB, OSHA), Appellate. Office: Ver Ploeg and Lumpkin PA 100 SE 2d St Ste 2150 Miami FL 33131 Office Fax: 305-577-3558. Business E-mail: jmazer@vpl-law.com.

MAZO, MARK ELLIOTT, lawyer; b. Phila., Jan. 12, 1950; s. Earl and Rita (Vane) M.; m. Fern Rosalyn Litman, Aug. 19, 1973; children: Samantha Lauren, Dana Suzanne, Ross Elliott, Courtney Litman. AB, Princeton U., 1971; JD, Harvard U., 1974. Bar: D.C. 1975, U.S. Dist. Ct. D.C. 1975, U.S. Claims Ct. 1975, U.S. Ct. Appeals (D.C. cir.) 1976, U.S. Supreme Ct. 1979. Ptnr. Hogan & Hartson, L.L.P., Washington and Paris, 1990—. Contbr. articles to profl. jours. White House intern Exec. Office of Pres., Washington, 1972. Capt. USAR, 1971-79. Mem. ABA, Harvard Law Sch. Assn., D.C. Bar Assn., Columbia Country Club, Princeton Club (N.Y.C.), Colonial Club, City Club, Phi Beta Kappa. Republican. Commercial, contracts (including sales of goods; commercial financing), Private international, Mergers and acquisitions. Home: 3719 Cardiff Rd Chevy Chase MD 20815-5943 Office: Hogan & Hartson LLP 555 13th St NW Washington DC 20004-1161 also: Hogan & Hartson Cariddi Mee Rue 12 rue de la Paix 75002 Paris France E-mail: memazo@hhlaw.com.

MCADAMS, JOHN POPE, lawyer; b. Phila., June 5, 1949; s. Eugene P. and Mary (Miller) McA.; m. Anne Christina Connelly, Sept. 5, 1970; children: Emily Lane, Anne Connelly. BA, U. N.C., 1971; JD, Wake Forest U., 1976. Bar: Fla. 1976, N.C. 1976, U.S. Dist. Ct. (mid. dist.) Fla. 1977. Assoc. Carlton Fields, Tampa, Fla., 1976-82, ptnr., 1982—. Contbg. editor: The Developing Labor Law, 1983, Employee Duty of Loyalty, 1995; contbr. articles to profl. jours. Pres. Hillsborough Cmty. Mental Health Ctr., Tampa, 1983; trustee City of Temple Terrace (Fla.) Pension Plan, 1985-89; pres. Hyde Park Preservation, Inc., Tampa, 1993; bd. dirs., pres. Child Abuse Coun., Inc., Tampa Lighthouse for the Blind. Mem. ABA, ABA Equal Rights & Responsibilities Com., Fla. Bar Assn. (exec. coun. labor sect. 1987-89). Republican. Episcopalian. Labor (including EEOC, Fair Labor Standards Act, labor-management relations, NLRB, OSHA). Home: 820 S Delaware Ave Tampa FL 33606-2915 Office: Carlton Fields PO Box 3239 Tampa FL 33601-3239 E-mail: jmcadams@carltonfields.com.

MCAFEE, CHESNEY FALK, lawyer; b. 1969; m. Marty McAfee. JD, U. Memphis, 1996. Bar: Tenn. 1996, U.S. Dist. Ct. (we. dist.) Tenn. 1998, U.S. Supreme Ct. 2001. Asst. dist. atty. gen. Shelby County Dist. Attys. Office, Memphis, 1996—98; assoc. Harris, Shelton, Dunlap & Cobb, Memphis, 1998—2000; ptnr. McAfee & McAfee, Memphis, 2000—. Mentor Big Bros./Big Sisters, Memphis, 1998—2003; mem. St. John's United Meth. Ch., Memphis. Mem.: ABA, Am. Inns Ct., Memphis Bar Assn. General civil litigation, Appellate, Criminal. Office: McAfee & McAfee 246 Adams Ave Memphis TN 38103

MCAFEE, WILLIAM GAGE, lawyer; b. NYC, Mar. 23, 1943; arrived in Hong Kong, 1976; s. Horace J. and Kathryn (Gage) McA.; m. Linda Ho, June 3, 1978; children: Zachary, Dallas, Matthew. AB, Harvard U., 1965; JD, Columbia U., 1968. Bar: NY 1969, US Supreme Ct. 1973, DC 1979. Legal adviser AID Dept. State, Saigon, Vietnam, 1969-71; adj. prof. Saigon U. Faculty Law, Vietnam, 1970-71; assoc. Davis Polk Wardwell, NYC, 1971-73; with Coudert Bros., Singapore, Hong Kong, China, 1973-76, ptnr., 1976-94. Advisor consultative com. for the basic law of Hong Kong, 1986-89, pres., 1985-86; v.p. AmCham, 1992, chmn. govt. rels. com., 1987-90, trustee Charitable Found.; mng. dir. The GE Asia Pacific Capital Tech. Fund, Asia Pacific Capital Ltd. and APC Asset Mgmt. (HK) Ltd.; dir. Internet Tech. Group Ltd., Chinney Alliance Group Ltd.; mem. Hong Kong Gen. C. of C., legal com., dep. chmn. exec. com.; mem. campaign com. Cmty. Chest of Hong Kong, coun. mem. Coun. Fgn. Rels.; sec. Law Assn. for Asia and the Western Pacific Energy Sect.; mem. Law Reform Commn., 1993-99; mem. Andover Devel. Bd. Andover Phillips Acad., The Fairbank Ctr. com. Harvard U.; assoc. Urban Land Inst.; comml. panel arbd Inst.; comml. panel arbitrators Am. Arbitration Assn. Editor Energy Law and Policy in Asia and the Western Pacific, 1985, Introduction to the Energy Laws of Asia, 1984; contbg. editor Oil & Gas Law & Taxation Rev.; hon. cons. Econ. & Law Rev.; adv. com. China Oil mag. Mem. ABA, Internat. Bar Assn., DC Bar Assn., NY Bar Assn., Internat. Inst. Strategic Studies, Chartered Inst. Arbitrators (legal panel Hong Kong br.), Porcellian Club (Cambridge), Harvard U. (NYC, Hong Kong), Pacific Club (bd. govs.), Fgn. Correspondents' Club. Episcopalian. Home: House D 7 Peel Rise, The Peak Hong Kong China Office: APC Mgmt (HK) Ltd 15/F 3A Chater Rd Hong Kong China

MCAFEE, WILLIAM JAMES, lawyer; b. Bronx, N.Y., June 18, 1962; s. James J. and Marie A. (Theyson) McA.; m. Helen W. Wagner, Oct. 12, 1962; children: Rebecca A., Ryan P. BA, AA, U.C.F., 1984; JD, Stetson U., St. Petersburg, Fla., 1987. Bar: Fla. 1987, U.S. Dist. Ct. (so. dist.) Fla. 1988, U.S. Dist. Ct. (mid. dist.) Fla. 1989. Asst. states atty. County of Palm Beach, West Palm Beach, Fla., 1987-88; assoc. Schuler & Wilkerson, West Palm Beach, 1988-89, Slawson & Burman, West Palm Beach, 1989-90; ptnr. Wagner, Johnson & McAfee, West Palm Beach, 1990—2000, Ricci Hubaro Leopolo Frankel Farmer & McAfee, West Palm Beach, 2000—02, McAfee & Russo, 2002—. Contbr. articles to profl. jours. Mem. Fla. Acad. Trial Lawyers (pres. young lawyers sect. 1989-92, frequent lectr.). Avocations: family, fishing, exercise, yard work, Karate. Insurance, Personal injury (including property damage). Office: McAfee Russo 701 Northpoint Pkwy Ste 415 West Palm Beach FL 33407

MCALHANY, TONI ANNE, lawyer; b. Decatur, Ind., May 1, 1951; d. Robert Keith and Evelyn L. (Fisher) McA. BA, Ind. U., 1973; JD, Valparaiso U., 1976. Bar: Mich. 1976, Ind. 1982, Ill. 1986, U.S. Dist. Ct. (no. dist.) Ind. 1989. Asst. prosecutor Ottawa County Prosecutor's Office, Grand Haven, Mich., 1976-81; assoc. Hann, Doss & Persinger, Holland, Mich., 1981-82, Romero & Thonert, Auburn, Ind., 1982-85; ptnr. Dahlgren & McAlhany, Berwyn, Ill., 1985-88, Colbeck, McAlhany & Stewart, Angola, Ind. & Coldwater, Mich., 1988-98; friend of the ct. for Branch County, domestic rels. referee, 1999—. Atty. Angola Housing Authority, 1989-98. Bd. dirs. Child and Family Svcs., Ft. Wayne, Ind., 1983, Fillmore Ctr., Berwyn, 1986-88, Altrusa, Coldwater, 1989-92. Mem. ATLA, State Bar Mich., State Bar Ind., State Bar Ill., Mich. Friend of the Ct. Assn., Referees Assn. Mich., Branch County Bar Assn., Steuben County Bar Assn. Avocations: traveling, horseback riding. Family and matrimonial, General practice, Personal injury (including property damage). E-mail: tmcalhany@hotmail.com.

MCALILEY, GARY LEX, judge, prosecutor, educator; b. Dothan, Ala., Jan. 1, 1948; s. Lex and Alice (Brackin) McA.; m. Janet Ann Roach, Nov. 29, 1974; children: Lee Ann, Megan. BS in Bus. Adminstrn. instrn., Samford U., 1970; JD, Cumberland Sch. Law, 1974; postgrad. U. Nev., summers 1977-82, Harvard U., summer 1978, Yale Law, 1994, Kans. Law Sch., 2001. Bar: Ala. 1974, admitted U.S. Dist. Ct. Ala. 1974. Sole practice, Enterprise, Ala., 1974-76; dist. judge State of Ala., Coffee County, Enterprise, 1976-86; judge 12th jud cir. State of Ala., 1986-2003, dist. atty., 2003-; instr. law Enterprise State Jr. Coll., 1975-87, Troy State U., Ft. Rucker, Ala., 1978-87; mem. Ala. Probate Code Revision Com., 1978—. Mem. Ala. Child Support Commn., 1985—; pres. Coll. St. Sch. P.T.O., 1987, 88. Named Ala. Judge of Yr., Ala. Child Support Assn., 1984, Man of Yr., City of Enterprise, 1987. Mem. Ala. Bar Assn., Coffee County Bar Assn., chmn. bd., Coffee County Vol. of Am., Ala. Dist. Judges Assn., Ala Dist. Attorney's Assn., Ala. Cir. Judge's Assn., Ala. Juvenile Judges Assn. Democrat. Baptist. Home: 609 W College St Enterprise AL 36330-2840 Office: 12th Cir Dist Atty PO Box 311102 Enterprise AL 36330

MCALPIN, KIRK MARTIN, lawyer; b. Newark, Sept. 14, 1923; s. Aaron Champion and Margaret (Martin) McA.; m. Sarah Frances Morgan, Dec. 14, 1951; children: Kirk Martin Jr., Philip Morgan, Margaret Champion Margeson. LLB, U. Ga., 1948; postgrad., Columbia U., 1949. Bar: Ga. 1949. Asst. solicitor gen. Ea. Jud. Cir. Ct. Ga., 1951; assoc. Bouhan, Lawrence, Williams, Levy & McAlpin, Savannah, Ga., 1952-53, ptnr., 1954-63; sr. ptnr. King & Spalding, Atlanta, 1963-86; pvt. practice Savannah, 1987-97, Atlanta, 1998—. Chmn. Inst. Continuing Legal Edn., 1980-81, Inst. Continuing Jud. Edn. in Ga., 1981-84, Jud. Council Ga., 1979-82. Pres. Atlanta Legal Aid Soc., 1971. Fellow Am. Bar Found., Am. Law Inst., Am. Coll. Trial Lawyers, Internat. Acad. Trial Lawyers, Internat. Soc. Barristers; mem. ABA (Jr. Bar Conf. chmn. 1958-59, chmn. gen. practice sect. 1972-73, chmn. sr. lawyers div. 1986-87, ho. of dels. 1960-90, state del. 1970-90, bd. govs. 1973-76), State Bar Ga. Assn. (chmn. Young Lawyers 1953-54, bd. govs. 1953-63, pres. 1979-80), Atlanta Bar Assn., Savannah Bar Assn. (v.p. 1960-61), Nat. Conf. Bar Pres. (exec. com. 1981-83), Ga. Def. Lawyers Assn., Ga. Trial Lawyers Assn., Am. Trial Lawyers Assn., Fed. Bar Assn., Am. Judicature Soc., Assn. R.R. Trial Counsel, Soc. of Cin., Sons Colonial Wars, St. Andrews Soc., Capital City Club, Piedmont Driving Club, Oglethorpe Club, Phi Delta Phi, Sigma Alpha Epsilon. Episcopalian. Administrative and regulatory, General civil litigation, Personal injury (including property damage). Office: 77 E Andrews Dr NW Apt 352 Atlanta GA 30305-1392 Fax: 404-467-0619. E-mail: kmcasraty@mindspring.com.

MCAMIS, EDWIN EARL, lawyer; b. Cape Girardeau, Mo., Aug. 8, 1934; s. Zenas Earl and Anna Louise (Miller) McAmis; m. Malin Eklof, May 31, 1959 (div. 1979); 1 child, Andrew Bruce; life ptnr. Gerson Gonzalez. AB magna cum laude, Harvard U., 1956, LLB, 1959. Bar: N.Y. 1960, U.S. Dist. Ct. (so. dist.) N.Y. 1962, U.S. Supreme Ct. 1965, U.S. Ct. Appeals (2d and 3d cirs.) 1964, U.S. Ct. Appeals (D.C. cir.) 1981. Assoc. law firm Webster, Sheffield & Chrystie, N.Y.C., 1959-61, Regan Goldfarb Powell & Quinn,

N.Y.C., 1962-65, Lovejoy, Wasson, Lundgren & Ashton, N.Y.C., 1965-69, ptnr., 1969-77, Skadden, Arps, Slate, Meagher & Flom, N.Y.C., 1977-90, spl. ptnr., pro bono, 1990-93; adj. prof. law Fordham U., 1984-85, Benjamin N. Cardozo Sch. Law, N.Y.C., 1985-90. Mem. Lambda Legal and Edn. Fund, 1991—95; bd. dirs. Aston Magna Found. Music, Inc., 1982—93, Cmty. Rsch. Initiative N.Y., 1988—89. With U.S. Army, 1961—62. Mem.: ABA, Selden Soc. Federal civil litigation, State civil litigation. Home: 4110 Kiaora St Coconut Grove FL 33133-6350

MCANANEY, KEVIN GEORGE, lawyer; b. Yonkers, N.Y., Mar. 22, 1949; s. Francis A. and Katherine A. (McClatchy) McA.; m. Catherine R. McCabe, Sept. 9, 1978; children: Sheila, Cara, Patrick. BA, U. N.C., 1971; JD, Columbia U., 1977. Bar: N.Y. 1979, U.S. Dist. Ct. (so. dist.) N.Y. 1979, DC 1990. Assoc. Kelley Drye & Warren, N.Y.C., 1977-80; asst. counsel to Gov. Hugh Carey State of N.Y., Albany, N.Y., 1980-83; assoc. Dewey Ballantine, Washington, 1983-86, ptnr., 1986-97; chief industry guidance br., Office of Counsel to Insp. Gen. U.S. Dept. HHS, Washington, 1997—2003; atty. Law Offices of Kevin G. McAnaney, Washington, 2003—. Bd. dirs. Hosp. Sick Children, Washington, 1992-96. Mem. Am. Health Lawyers Assn. (bd. dirs. 2001—), Peter and Adeline Ruffin Found. (trustee 1980—), Phi Beta Kappa. Health. Office: 1800 K St NW Ste 720 Washington DC 20006

MCANDREW, PAUL JOSEPH, JR., lawyer; b. Kalona, Iowa, Mar. 8, 1957; s. Paul Joseph and Virginia (Krowka) McA.; m. Lola Maxine Miller, Mar. 1, 1975; children: Stephanie, Susan, Rose, Paul Joseph III, Bridget. BA with honors, U. Iowa, 1979, JD with high distinction, 1983. Bar: Iowa 1983, U.S. Dist. Ct. Iowa 1985, U.S. Claim Ct. 1985, U.S. Ct. Appeals (8th cir.) 1999, U.S. Supreme Ct. 2000. Law clk. to chief judge U.S. Dist. Ct. (so. dist.) Iowa, Des Moines, 1983-85; ptnr. Meardon, Sueppel, Downer & Hayes, Iowa City, 1985-99, Paul J. McAndrew Law Firm, Coralville, 1999—. Claimant's counsel rep. Iowa Workers' Compensation Adv. Com., 2000—. Recipient Hancher-Finkbine award, 1979. Mem. ABA, ATLA (chair workers' compensation sect. 2003), Iowa Bar Assn. (chair workers' compensation sect. 1993-95), Iowa Trial Lawyers Assn. (rep. bd. govs. 1993—, workers' compensation sect. 1997—), Johnson County Bar Assn., Iowa Assn. Workers Compensation Attys. (rep. bd. govs. 1993—), Work Injury Litigation Group (Iowa rep. to nat. bd. govs. 1997—). Democrat. Roman Catholic. Avocations: jogging, biking, golf, travel. Personal injury (including property damage), Workers' compensation. Home: 620 Scott Park Dr Iowa City IA 52245-5140 Office: Paul McAndrew Law Firm 2590 Holiday Rd Ste 100 Coralville IA 52241 Fax: 319 887 1693.

MCANDREW, THOMAS JOSEPH, lawyer; b. Providence, Oct. 19, 1945; s. Joseph L. and Amelia L. (Bonhotel) McA.; m. Luise Mary Fogarty, June 13, 1970; children: John Maxwell, Mercedes, Hope, Marya, Cornelia. BA, Providence Coll., 1968; JD, Georgetown U.-Am. U.-George Washington U., 1971; LLM, Georgetown U., 1973. Bar: R.I., 1971, U.S. Dist. Ct. R.I., 1972, D.C. 1972, U.S. Ct. Claims, 1972, U.S. Tax Ct., 1971, U.S. Custom and Patent Ct., 1971, U.S. Ct. Mil. Appeals, 1971, U.S. Ct. Appeals (1st cir.), 1971, U.S. Ct. Appeals (D.C.), 1971, U.S. Supreme Ct., 1974, Comm. of Mass., 1985. Trial atty. Civil Aeros. Bd., Washington, 1971-72; legal asst. to John H. Fanning NLRB, Washington, 1972-73; labor rels. officer dept. edn. State of R.I., Providence, 1973-74, dep. asst. commr. edn., 1974-79, adminstr. labor rels., 1979-80; counsel Powers & McAndrew, Inc., Providence, 1980-87; pvt. practice Providence, 1987—. Adj. prof. law U. R.I., Kingston, 1976; lectr. in field. Contbr. articles to profl. jours. Treas., trustee John E. Fogarty Found., Providence, 1974—; mem. Providence Com. on Fgn. Rels., Providence. Mem. ABA (com. on labor law) FBA, ATLA, Am. Arbitration Assn. (adv. coun.). Avocations: golf, tennis, walking. Civil rights, Education and schools, Labor (including EEOC, Fair Labor Standards Act, labor-management relations, NLRB, OSHA). Home: 6 Wingate Rd Providence RI 02906-4910 Office: Ste 205 One Turks Head Place Providence RI 02903 Fax: 401-455-0882. E-mail: mcalaw@hotmail.com.

MCANDREWS, JAMES PATRICK, lawyer; b. Carbondale, Pa., May 11, 1929; s. James Patrick and Mary Agnes (Walsh) McA.; m. Mona Marie Steinke, Sept. 4, 1954; children: James P., George A., Catherine McAndrews Hazel, Joseph M., Anne Marie, Michael P., Edward R., Daniel P. BS, U. Scranton, 1949; LL.B., Fordham U., 1952; grad., Real Estate Inst., NYU, 1972. Bar: N.Y. 1953, Ohio 1974. Assoc. James F. McManus, Levittown, N.Y., 1955; atty. Emigrant Savs. Bank, N.Y.C., 1955-68; counsel Tchrs. Ins. and Annuity Assn., 1968-73; assoc. Thompson, Hine & Flory, 1973-74, ptnr., 1974-84, Benesch, Friedlander, Coplan & Aronoff, Cleve., 1984-94. Mem. law faculty Am. Inst. Banking, N.Y.C., 1968-69; mem. faculty Lakeland C.C., 1995-97. Author: Commercial Real Estate Law Practice Manual with Forms, 2001. 1st lt. USAF, 1952-54. Fellow Am. Bar Found. (life); mem. Am. Coll. Real Estate Lawyers (gov. 1983-86, treas. 1986-88, chmn. membership devel. com. 1985-87), Ohio Land Title Assn. (life, trustee 1985-88), Bar Assn. Greater Cleve. (past chmn. real estate sect.), Ohio State Bar Assn. Roman Catholic. Construction, Landlord-tenant, Property, real (including real estate development, water). Home: 6638 Duneden Ave Cleveland OH 44139-4048

MCARDLE, ERIN DOUGHERTY, lawyer; b. Dec. 22, 1969; JD, U. Memphis, 1994. Bar: Tenn. Atty. D. Ragsdale Law Offices, Memphis, 1993—96, Moffatt & McArdle, Bristol, 1996—2001, State of Tenn., Johnson City, 2001—. Mem.: N.E. Tenn. Young Lawyers Assn. (pres. 1999—2001), Tenn. Bar Assn. (young lawyers divsn. 1998—, sec. bd. 2002—). Office: Tenn Dept Children's Svcs 2514 1/2 Wesley St Ste 5 Johnson City TN 37601

MCATEE, DAVID RAY, lawyer; b. Rosebud, Tex., Nov. 20, 1941; s. Lee Ray and Florine (Davis) McA.; m. Carole Kay Pendergraft, Jan. 28, 1967; children— David Ray, Kristin Carole. B.B.A. with honors, Baylor U., 1964; LL.B., U. Tex., 1967. Bar: Tex. 1967; U.S. Dist. Ct. (no. dist.) Tex. 1968, (so. dist.) Tex., 1994; U.S. Ct. Appeals (5th cir.) 1969, (11th cir.) 1981; U.S. Tax Ct., 1993. Briefing atty. Supreme Ct. Tex., Austin, 1967-68; ptnr. Thompson & Knight, Dallas, 1968-90; ptnr. Gibson Dunn & Crutcher, Dallas, 1990-95; with Akin, Gump, Strauss, Hauer & Feld, L.L.P., Dallas, 1995—. Founder, bd. dirs. No. Hills Neighborhood Assocs., Inc., 1974-76; pres., bd. dirs. Montessori Sch. of Park Cities, 1975-78; mem. Goals for Dallas Com., City of Dallas Citizens Safety Adv. Com., 1975-77; chmn. City of Dallas Thoroughfare Com., 1979-81; mem. City of Dallas Plan Commn., 1979-83, vice-chmn., 1981-83. Mem. Dallas Bar Assn. (legal ethics com. 1979-81), Tex. Bar Assn. (legal ethics com. 1975-81), ABA (antitrust sect.). Democrat. Methodist. Antitrust, Federal civil litigation, State civil litigation. Office: Akin Gump Strauss Hauer & Feld 1700 Pacific Ave Ste 4100 Dallas TX 75201-4675

MCAULIFFE, ROSEMARY, lawyer; b. New Rochelle, N.Y., May 24, 1927; d. William J. and Rose B. (Payne) McA. BA, Regis Coll., 1949; JD, New Eng. Sch. Law, 1954; MEd, Boston State Coll., 1971, Cert. advanced grad studies, 1981; LLD (hon.) , New Eng. Sch. Law, Boston, 2002. Bar: Mass. 1956, U.S. Dist. Ct. Mass. 1957, U.S. Supreme Ct. 1961. Pvt. practice law, Boston, 1956—. Tchr. City of Boston, 1965-93. Prodr. (weekly TV show) The Legal Line, Boston Pub. Access Answer Channel. Active World Affairs Coun., Boston, 1980-95; sec. Italian Hist. Assn. Mass., 1988—. Mem. Mass. Bar Assn., Am. Acad. Trial Lawyers, Mass. Assn. Women Lawyers. General practice. Home and Office: 61 Prince St Boston MA 02113-1829

MCAULIFFE, STEVEN JAMES, federal judge; b. 1948; BA, Va. Mil. Inst., 1970; JD, Georgetown U., 1973. Capt. appellate coun. U.S. Army Judge Advocate Gens. Corps, 1973-77; asst. atty. gen. Office N.H. Atty. Gen., 1977-80; ptnr. Gallagher, Callahan, Gartrell, P.A., Concord, N.H., 1980-92; fed. judge U.S. Dist. Ct. (N.H. dist.), Concord, 1992—. Trustee Univ. System of N.H., 1986-94; bd. dirs. N.H. Med. Malpractice Stabilization Res. Fund Trust, 1987-92, Office Pub. Guardian, 1980-92, Challenger Ctr. for Space Sci. Edn.; active N.H. Dem. Leadership Coun., 1988-92. Capt. U.S. Army, 1970-77, USAR, 1977-80, N.H. Army NG, 1980-88. Fellow N.H. Bar Found.; mem. ABA, N.H. Bar Assn. (pres. 1991-92, pres.-elect 1990-91, v.p. 1989-90, mem. ex-officio N.H. Supreme Ct. com. profl. conduct 1989-90, mem. ethics com. 1984-86), Nat. Conf. Bar Pres., Merrimack County Bar Assn., D.C. Bar Assn., U.S. Supreme Ct. Hist. Soc., N.H. Jud. Coun. (vice-chmn. 1991-92), Aircraft Owners and Pilots Assn., Concord Country Club. Office: US Dist Ct 55 Pleasant St Room 416 Concord NH 03301-3904

MCAVOY, JOHN JOSEPH, lawyer; b. Worley, Idaho, June 28, 1933; s. Earl Francis and Florence Jewel (Mitchell) McA.; m. Joan Marjorie Zeldon, Sept. 20, 1964; children: Jason, Jon. BA, U. Idaho, 1954, LLB, 1958; LLM, Yale U., 1959. Bar: Idaho 1958, U.S. Supreme Ct. 1962, N.Y. 1963, U.S. Tax Ct. 1969, D.C. 1976. Asst. prof. law George Washington U., Washington, 1959-62; staff atty. stockpile investigating subcom. Armed Forces Com. U.S. Senate, Washington, 1962; assoc. White & Case, N.Y.C., 1963-71, ptnr., 1972-95; of counsel Lukas, Nace, Gutierrez & Sachs, Washington, 1995—. Adj. prof. Washington Coll. Law, Am. U., Washington, 1990. Bd. dirs. N.Y. Civil Liberties Union, 1975-77, commr. Uniform State Laws, 2001—; chmn. due process com. ACLU, 1971-75. With U.S. Army, 1954-56. Mem. D.C. Bar Assn. (ethics com. 1982-88, vice chmn. 1986-87, chmn. 1987-88), Phi Beta Kappa, Phi Alpha Delta. Democrat. Avocations: swimming, bicycling, fgn. travel. Federal civil litigation, Communications, Professional liability. Office: Lukas Nace Gutierrez & Sachs 1111 19th St NW Washington DC 20036-3603

MCBARNETTE, BRUCE OLVIN, lawyer, corporate executive; b. N.Y.C., Oct. 7, 1957; s. Olvin R. and Yvette Fay (Francis) McB. BA, Princeton U., 1980; JD, NYU, 1983. Bar: N.Y. 1985, Hawaii 1987, D.C. 1989. Atty. Natural Resources Def. Coun., N.Y.C., 1984, U.S. Judge Adv.Gen.'s Corp., Aberdeen Proving Grand, Md., 1988-89, Schofield, Hawaii, 1985-88; legis. asst. U.S. Ho. of Reps., Washington, 1989; counsel impeachment trial com. U.S. Senate, Washington, 1989-90; sr. counsel Fed. Nat. Mortgage Assn., Washington, 1990-93; pres. Summit Connections, Inc., Washington, 1993—. Faculty George Washington U.; dir. devel. Charlies Pl., 1998—. Coord. Achieve Speakers Bur., Washington, 1990. Capt. U.S. Army, 1985-88. Mem. ABA (contbg. author newsletter for mil. pers.), SAG, D.C. Bar Assn., N.Y. Bar Assn., Hawaii Bar Assn. Democrat. Episcopalian. Avocation: track and field. Banking, Military, Securities. Home: 248 Willow Ter Sterling VA 20164-1628 Office: Summit Connections Inc 248 Willow Ter Sterling VA 20164-1628

MCBRIDE, BEVERLY JEAN, lawyer; b. Greenville, Ohio, Apr. 5, 1941; d. Kenneth Birt and Glenna Louise (Ashman) Whited; m. Benjamin Gary McBride, Nov. 28, 1964; children: John David, Elizabeth Ann. BA magna cum laude, Wittenberg U., 1963; JD cum laude, U. Toledo, 1966. Bar: Ohio 1966. Intern Ohio Gov.'s Office, Columbus, 1962; asst. dean women U. Toledo, 1963-65; assoc. Title Guarantee and Trust Co., Toledo, 1966-69; spl. counsel Ohio Atty. Gen.'s Office, Toledo, 1975; assoc. Cobourn, Smith, Rohrbacher and Gibson, Toledo, 1969-76; v.p., gen. counsel, sec. The Andersons, Maumee, Ohio, 1976—. Exec. trustee, bd. dirs. Wittenberg U., Springfield, Ohio, 1980-83; trustee Anderson Found., Maumee, 1981-93; mem. Ohio Supreme Ct. Task Force on Gender Fairness, 1991-94, Regional Growth Partnership, 1994—; chmn. Sylvania Twp. Zoning Commn., Ohio, 1970-80; candidate for judge Sylvania Mcpl. Ct., 1975; trustee Goodwill Industries, Toledo, 1976-82, Sylvania Cmty. Svcs. Ctr., 1976-78, Toledo-Lucas County Port Authority, 1992-99, vice chair Fla. CPA; chair St. Vincent Med. Ctr., 1992-99; founder Sylvania YWCA Program, 1973; active membership drives Toledo Mus. Art, 1977-87. Recipient Toledo Women in Industry award YWCA, 1979, Outstanding Alumnus award Wittenberg U., 1981. Fellow Am. Bar Found.; mem. ABA, AAUW, Ohio Bar Assn., Toledo Bar Assn. (pres., treas., chmn., sec. various coms.), Toledo Women Attys. Forum (exec. com. 1978-82), Pres. Club (U. Toledo exec. com.). Home: 5274 Cambrian Rd Toledo OH 43623-2626 Office: The Andersons 480 W Dussel Dr Maumee OH 43537-1690

MCBRIDE, JUDITH BLISS, lawyer, educator, writer; b. East Cleveland, Ohio, Nov. 11, 1959; d. Jack Clarence and Gene Marie (Dowd) Bliss; m. James Dominick McBride; children: Jean Marie, Madelyn Ann. BA cum laude, John Carroll U., 1982; JD, Case Western U., 1985. Bar: Ohio 1986, U.S. Dist. Ct. (no. dist.) Ohio 1988. Sole practice, Cleve., 1986—; staff instr. Mead Data Cen., Inc., Cleve., 1986-88, account rep., 1988, sr. account rep., 1989-91; atty. editor product devel. Banks-Baldwin Law Pub. Co., Cleve., 1991-93, product mgr. electronic svcs., 1992-93; rep. Primerica Fin. Svcs., Cleve., 1991-95; atty.-editor, cons., 1993—. Deacon Lyndhurst (Ohio) Bapt. Ch., 1986-88, bd. stewardship and missions, 1989-91, moderator, 1991-92, vice moderator, 1993-94; bd. Christian edn. Brecksville United Ch. of Christ, Christian Edn. Cmty., 1997-99, chair 1999, Christian Edn. Sch. tchr., 1999—, mem. bldg. land task force, 1997-01; mem. Our Ch.'s Wider Mission Cmty., 2000—, co-chair, 2001—. Mem.: Ohio State Bar Assn., Ohio Bar, Lambda Iota Tau (v.p. 1981—82), Alpha Sigma Nu. Republican. General practice. Home: 7886 Cambridge Dr Brecksville OH 44141-1063

MCBRIDE, MICHAEL FLYNN, lawyer; b. Milwaukee, Mar. 27, 1951; s. Raymond Edward and Marian Dunne (McBride); m. Kerin Ann (O'Brien), Mar. 23, 1991; children: Raymond Erin, Barbara Marian. BS in chem. and biology, U. Wis., 1972, JD, 1976; MS in environ. engr. sci., Calif. Inst. Tech., 1973. Bar: Wis., 1976; D.C. , 1976. Assoc. LeBoeuf, Lamb, Greene, and MacRae, Washington, 1976-84, ptnr., 1985—. Mem. Assn. for Transp. Law, Logistics and Policy (v.p., energy tranp.); law inst. com. 1990, co-chmn. 1991—, pres. 1994-95, editor ATLLP Jour.; Chantilly Nat. Golf and Country Club. Avocations: golf, reading, travel. Federal civil litigation, FERC practice, Nuclear power. Home: 6648 Byrns Pl Mc Lean VA 22101-4419 Office: LeBoeuf Lamb Greene & MacRae LLP 1875 Connecticut Ave NW Washington DC 20009-5728 E-mail: MICHAEL.McBRIDE@llgm.com.

MCBRIDE, MILFORD LAWRENCE, JR., lawyer; b. Grove City, Pa., July 16, 1923; s. Milford Lawrence and Elizabeth B. (Douthett) McB.; m. Madeleine Coulter, Aug. 6, 1947; children: Marta, Brenda, Trip, Randy, Barry. AB, Grove City Coll., 1944; BS, N.Y.U., 1944; JD, U. Pa., 1949. Bar: Pa. 1949, U.S. Dist. Ct. (we. dist.) Pa. U.S. Supreme Ct. Ptnr., McBride & McBride, Grove City, 1949-77, sr. ptnr., 1992—; ptnr. McBride and McNickle, Grove City, 1977-92; dir. Integra Fin. Corp., 1988-93; trustee Grove City Coll., 1995—. Served to 1st lt. USAAF, 1943-46. Mem. Mercer County Bar Assn. (state treas. 1970-77), ABA, Am. Bar Found. Republican. Clubs: Oakmont Country, University (Pitts.). Corporate, general, Probate (including wills, trusts), Property, real (including real estate development, water). Office: 211 S Center St Grove City PA 16127-1508

MCBRIDE, TERRY H. judge; b. Tulsa, Okla., Oct. 5, 1950; s. Hayden and Betty J. McBride; m. Candace Gay Monger; children: Jefferson Elliott, Taylor Chase. BS, Okla. State U., 1975; JD, U. Tulsa, 1979. Bar: Okla. 1979, U.S. Dist. Ct. (no. dist.) Okla. 1980, U.S. Ct. Appeals (10th cir.) 1999. Mailing: PO Box 989 Pryor OK 74362-0989

MCBRYDE, JOHN HENRY, federal judge; b. Jackson, Oct. 9, 1931; m. Betty Vinson; children: Rebecca McBryde Dippold, Jennifer, John Blake. BS in Commerce, Tex. Christian U., 1953; LLB, U. Tex., 1956. Bar: Tex. 1956, U.S. Ct. Appeals (5th cir.) 1958, U.S. Dist. Ct. (no. dist.) 1958, U.S. Dist. Ct. (ea. dist.) 1989, U.S. Supreme Ct. 1972. Assoc. Cantey, Hanger, Johnson, Scarborough & Gooch, Ft. Worth, 1956-62; ptnr. Cantey & Hanger and predecessor firm, Ft. Worth, 1962-69, McBryde, Bennett and predecessor firms, Ft. Worth, 1969-90; judge U.S. Dist. Ct. (no. dist.) Tex., Ft. Worth, 1990—. Fellow Am. Bar Found. (life), Tex. Bar Found. (life), Am. Coll. Trial Lawyers. Office: US Dist Ct US Courthouse 501 W 10th St Ste 401 Fort Worth TX 76102-3642

MCBRYDE, NEILL GREGORY, lawyer; b. Durham, N.C., Jan. 11, 1944; s. Angus M. and Priscilla (Gregory) McBryde; m. Margaret McPherson, Aug. 1, 1970; children: Margaret Courtauld NcBryde Young, Neill Gregory Jr. AB cum laude, Davidson Coll., 1966; JD with high honors, U. N.C., 1969. Bar: N.C. 1969., Ga. 1972. Assoc. King & Spalding, Atlanta, 1971-76; ptnr. Fleming, Robinson, Bradshaw & Hinson, Charlotte, N.C., 1977-81, Helms, Mulliss & Johnston, Charlotte, 1981-86, Smith Helms Mulliss & Moore, Charlotte, 1986-90, Moore & Van Allen PLLC, Charlotte, 1990—. Lectr. in field, conducter workshops in field. Author, editor: First Union National Bank of North Carolina Will Book, 1986; contbr. to profl. jours. Elder and Deacon Myers Park Presbyn. Ch., Charlotte, 1980-86, 92-95, 2001-04; dir. sec. Presbyn. Home for Aged, Charlotte, 1978-82; trustee Charlotte Latins Schs., Inc., 1980-86, 87-93; past chmn., past trustee Mint Mus. Charlotte. Fellow Am. Coll. Trust and Estate Counsel (past mem. bd. regents, past pres.), Am. Coll. Tax Counsel; mem. ABA, Ga. Bar Assn., N.C. Bar Assn. (probate and fiduciary law sect.), Order of Coif, Phi Beta Kappa, Omicron Delta Kappa. Republican. Avocations: tennis, golf, fishing. Corporate, general, Estate planning, Mergers and acquisitions. Office: Moore & Van Allen PLLC Bank of Am Corp Ctr 100 N Tryon St Fl 47 Charlotte NC 28202-4003

MCBRYDE, THOMAS HENRY, lawyer; b. New Albany, Miss., Oct. 26, 1925; s. Henry Thornton and Mary Catherine (Davis) McB.; m. Barbara White, Dec. 28, 1946; children: Elise, William Henry, John Thomas. BS, U.S. Mil. Acad., 1946; LLB, U. Va., 1952. Bar: Va. 1952, N.Y. 1959. Commd. 2d lt. U.S. Army, 1946, advanced through grades to capt., 1950; assigned to Japan, ETO and U.S.; instr. law U.S. Mil. Acad., 1956-57; resigned, 1957; asst. counsel N.Y. State Banking Dept., 1960-61; assoc. Rogers & Wells and predecessors, N.Y.C., 1957-60, 61-65, ptnr., 1965-93, sr. counsel, 1993—; chief counsel N.Y. State Joint Legis. Com. to Revise Banking Law, 1962-65, minority counsel, 1965-66. Mem. comml. panel Am. Arbitration Assn., 1976— ; mem. adv. com. supervision mut. instns. Office N.Y. Banking Supt., 1966-67 Mem. Assn. Grads. U.S. Mil. Acad., Order of Coif, Am. Yacht Club, Heritage Club. Republican. Episcopalian. Banking, Corporate, general, Insurance. Home: 4912 NW 62d St Gainesville FL 32653 Office: Clifford Chance Rogers & Wells 200 Park Ave Ste 5200 New York NY 10166-0005

MCBURNEY, CHARLES WALKER, JR., lawyer; b. Orlando, Fla., June 6, 1957; s. Charles Walker McBurney and Jeane (Brown) Chappell. BA, U. Fla., 1979, JD, 1982. Bar: Fla. 1982, U.S. Dist. Ct. (mid. dist.) Fla. 1983, U.S. Ct. Appeals (11th cir.) 1984. Assoc. Mathews, Osborne, McNatt, Gobelman & Cobb, Jacksonville, Fla., 1982-84; asst. state's atty. State's Atty.'s Office, Jacksonville, 1984-90, civil atty., 1987-88, sr. trial atty., 1988-90; ptnr. Fischette, Owen, Held & McBurney, Jacksonville, 1990—. Dir. Serious or Habitual Juvenile Offender Program, 1986. Bd. dirs. Civic Round Table, 1988-92, treas., 1988-89, pres. 1989-90; chmn. com. congl. campaigns, Jacksonville, 1982, 84, 88; mem. Mayor's Bicentennial Constnl. Commn., 1989-91; dir. Internat. Devel. Commn. for Jacksonville, 1993—, treas., 1995-97; bd. dirs. Am. Heart Assn. N.E. Fla., 1990-92. Mem. ABA, Jacksonville Bar Assn. (chmn. bankruptcy sect. 1998-2000, 2002—), Jacksonville Bankruptcy Bar Assn. (bd. dirs. 1999—), Nat. Dist. Attys. Assn., Comml. Law League (So. region exec. coun. 1998—, treas. 2000—), Fla. Jaycees (legal counsel 1987-88, most outstanding local pres. award 1987), Jacksonville Jaycees (pres. 1986, Jaycee of yr. 1984), Jacksonville C. of C. (bd. govs. 1987, govtl. affairs com. 1998—), Summit Civitan (judge adv. 1991-93, 2001-), Masons, Bull Snort Club (pres. 1995-96, 99-2000, chmn. bd. 1996-97, 1998-99), First Coast Tiger Bay Forum (bd. dirs. 2001—), C. of C. (trustee 1996-98, govtl. affairs com. 1998—), N.E. Fla. Phi Beta Kappa Alumni Assn. (v.p. 1998-2000), James Madison Inst., Jacksonville Hist. Soc., S.E. CPAC (environ. sub-chmn. 2001-), Southside Bus. Men's Club (v.p. 2003—), Duval County Rep. Club (treas. 2002—). Republican. Presbyterian. Commercial, contracts (including sales of goods; commercial financing), Bankruptcy, General civil litigation. Home: 6326 Christopher Creek Rd E Jacksonville FL 32217-2485 Office: Fishette Owen Held & McBurney Riverplace Tower Ste 1916 Jacksonville FL 32207

MCCAA, JAMES CURETON, III, lawyer; b. Memphis, Jan. 31, 1949; s. James Cureton McCaa Jr. and Madeleine Perkins Jehl; m. Betty Driver, Aug. 23, 1969; children: Hunter D., Margaret C. BSBA, U. Ark., 1971; JD, U. Memphis, 1974. Bar: Ark. 1974, Tenn. 1974, Va. 1985. Assoc. Skillman & Durrett, West Memphis, Ark., 1974-76; ptnr. Hightower & McCaa, West Memphis, 1977-85; asst. city atty. City of West Memphis, 1978-85; instr. East Ark. C.C., West Memphis, 1983-85; assoc. Preston Wilson & Crandley, Virginia Beach, Va., 1985-89, Vandeventer Black Meredith & Martin, Norfolk, Va., 1989-90; ptnr. Taylor & Walker, Norfolk, 1990—. Mem. Va. Assn. Def. Attys. Episcopalian. Avocations: golf, home. General civil litigation, Insurance, Personal injury (including property damage). Office: Taylor & Walker PC 555 E Main St Ste 1300 Norfolk VA 23510-2235 E-mail: jmccaa@taywal.com.

MCCABE, JOHN L. lawyer; b. Chgo., Oct. 17, 1941; BA, U. Notre Dame, 1963; LLB, Harvard U., 1966. Bar: Ill. 1967, Colo. 1967. Ptnr. Davis, Graham & Stubbs, Denver. Corporate, general, Finance, Entertainment. Office: Davis Graham & Stubbs 1550 Seventeenth St Ste 500 Denver CO 80202 E-mail: john.mccabe@dgslaw.com.

MCCABE, MICHAEL J. insurance executive; b. Denver, June 19, 1945; s. Joseph J. and Mary J. (Kane) McC.; m. Catherine Corrine Marquette, July 21, 1978; children: Brian Michael, Shannon Marquette. BS, U. No. Colo., 1967; JD, Cath. U. Am., 1971. Bar: D.C. Air transport econ. analyst U.S. Civil Aeronautics Bd., Washington, 1967-71; Washington counsel Allstate Ins. Co., 1971-74, of counsel, 1974-82, asst. v.p. bus. planning, 1982-84, v.p. corp. planning, 1984-89, group v.p., gen. atty., 1989-95; v.p., gen. counsel Allstate Corp.; sr. v.p., gen. counsel Allstate Ins. Co., 1999—. Bd. advisors No. Ill. U. Sch. Bus., DeKalb, 1986—. Chmn. Gateway Found. Mem. ABA, Fed. Bar Assn., D.C. Bar Assn., Planning Forum, Sigma Chi, Pi Alpha Delta. Democrat. Roman Catholic. Office: Allstate Ins Co 2775 Sanders Rd Northbrook IL 60062*

MCCABE, THOMAS EDWARD, lawyer, business executive; b. Washington, Jan. 22, 1955; s. Edward Aeneas and Janet Isabel McCabe; m. Kelly Marie McCarthy; children: Edward Charles, Benjamin Patrick, Adrienne Marie, Therese Eileen, Luke Stevens, Nicholas Joseph, Maximilian Karol, Eva Christina. AB, Georgetown U., 1977; MBA, JD, U. Notre Dame, 1981. Bar: D.C. 1982, U.S. Dist. Ct. D.C. 1983, U.S. Ct. Appeals (D.C. cir.) 1983, Va. 1989, U.S. Supreme Ct. 1990. Law clk. U.S. Dist. Ct. Judge Hon. Charles R. Richey, Washington, 1981-82; assoc. Reavis & McGrath, Washington, 1982-84, Venable Baetjer Howard & Civiletti, Washington, 1984-85, McCarthy & Durrette, Washington, 1985-88; ptnr. McCarthy & Burke, Washington, 1988-91; sr. v.p., dir. corp. devel., gen. counsel, sec. GRC Internat., Inc., Vienna, Va., 1992—2000; pres., CEO MicroBanx Sys., LLC, Great Falls, Va., 2001—. Republican. Roman Catholic. Corporate, general, Government contracts and claims, Securities. E-mail: tmccabe@microbanx.com.

MCCAFFREY, CARLYN SUNDBERG, lawyer; b. N.Y.C., Jan. 7, 1942; d. Carl Andrew Lawrence and Evelyn (Back) Sundberg; m. John P. McCaffrey, May 24, 1967; children: John C., Patrick, Jennifer, Kathleen. Student, Barnard Coll., 1963; AB in Econs., George Washington U., 1963; LLB cum laude, NYU, 1967, LLM in Taxation, 1970. Bar: N.Y. 1974. Law clk. to presiding justice Calif. Supreme Ct., 1967-68; teaching fellow law NYU, N.Y.C., 1968-70, asst. prof. law, 1970-74; assoc. Weil, Gotshal & Manges, N.Y.C., 1974-80, ptnr., 1980—. Prof. in residence Rubin Hall NYU, 1971-75; adj. prof. law NYU, 1975—, U. Miami, 1979-81; lectr. in field. Contbr. articles to profl. jours. Mem. ABA (chmn. generation-skipping transfer tax 1979-81, 93—, real property pro ate and trust law sect.), N.Y. State Bar Assn. (exec. com. tax sect. 1979-80, chmn. estate and gift tax com. 1976-78, 95—, life ins. com. 1983-85, trusts and estates sect.), Assn. of Bar of City of N.Y. (matrimonial law com., chmn. tax subcom. 1984-86, Am. College Trusts & Estates Counsel (bd. regents 1992—, mem. exec. com. 1995—, pres. 2002--). Family and matrimonial, Probate (including wills, trusts). Home: PO Box 232 Waccabuc NY 10597-0232 Office: Weil Gotshal & Manges 767 5th Ave Fl Concl New York NY 10153-0119 E-mail: Carlyn.mccaffrey@weil.com.

MCCAGUE, JOHN JOSEPH, III, lawyer; b. Pitts., Apr. 30, 1954; s. John Joseph McCague, Jr., M.D. and Eileen (Mulvihill) McCague; m. Kathleen Muldoon, Sept. 21, 1991; 1 child, Ian Joseph. BA, Washington and Jefferson Coll., 1976; MA, U. London, Eng., 1978; MBA, Am. Grad. Sch. Thunderbird, Glendale, Ariz., 1979; JD, Duquesne U., 1989. Bar: Allegheny County, Pa. 1989, U.S. Dist. Ct. (We. Dist.) Pa. 1989, U.S. Ct. Appeals (3d cir.) 1989. Assoc. Kirkpatrick & Lockhart, Pitts., 1989—95; shareholder, mem. DKW Law Group PC, Pitts., 1995—. Bd. dirs. DKW Law Group, PC. Contbr. articles to publs. Legal advisor, mem. Bach Choir of Pitts., 1984—; major gifts com. March of Dimes, Pitts., 1999—; adv. com. Ireland Inst. Pitts., 1998—; vol. Am. Cancer Soc., Pitts., 2003—. Mem.: Longue Vue Club, Duquesne Club. Republican. Roman Catholic. Avocations: golf, tennis, choral singing. Securities, Corporate, general, Corporate governance. Home: 405 Jefferson Dr Pittsburgh PA 15528 Office: DKW Law Group PC 58th Fl US Steel Tower 600 Grant St Pittsburgh PA 15219 Office Fax: 412-355-2609. E-mail: jmccague@dklaw.com.

MCCALEB, JOE WALLACE, lawyer; b. Nashville, Dec. 9, 1941; s. J.W. McCaleb and Majorie June (Hudson) DePriest; m. Glenda Jean Queen, June 26, 1965. BA, Union U., 1964; JD, Memphis State U., 1970; MSEL cum laude, Vt. Law Sch., 1995. Bar: Tenn. 1971, U.S. Dist. Ct. (mid. dist.), Tenn., 1977, U.S. Ct. Appeals (6th cir.) 1984, U.S. Supreme Ct. 1978, U.S. Dist. Ct. (ea. dist.) Tenn. 2001. Law clk. to presiding justice Tenn. Supreme Ct., Memphis, 1970-71; staff atty. Tenn. Dept. of Pub. Health Bur. Environ. Svcs., Nashville, 1971-77; pvt. practice Hendersonville, Tenn., 1977-94, 96—. Chmn. Hendersonville Recycling Com., 1990-91. Mem. Tenn. Bar Assn., Sierra Club (chmn. local chpt. 1980-81, chmn. mid.-Tenn. group 1989-90, 93-94, chmn. water quality com., co-chmn. forestry com.), Tenn. Environ. Coun. (v.p. 1987-88, conservation adv. 1991-92), Tenn. Clean Water Network (pres. 2001-03), Defenders of Wildlife, Save Our Cumberland Mountains. Democrat. Avocations: wilderness backpacking, photography, forestry, environmental protection. Administrative and regulatory, Federal civil litigation, Environmental. Home: 100 Colonial Dr Hendersonville TN 37075-3205 Office: 315 W Main St Ste 112 Hendersonville TN 37075 E-mail: jeremyah@bellsouth.net.

MCCALL, JACK HUMPHREYS, JR., lawyer; b. Nashville, Jan. 10, 1961; s. Jack Humphreys Sr. and Patricia Jean (Holmes) McC.; m. Jennifer Lynn Ashley, Oct. 4, 1992; 1 child, Margaret Ashley. BA, Vanderbilt U., 1983; JD, U. Tenn., 1991. Bar: Tenn. 1992, US Ct. Appeals (6th cir.) 1993. Clk. Hon. Gilbert S. Merritt, Chief Judge US Ct. Appeals 6th Cir., Nashville, 1991-92; assoc. Farris, Warfield & Kanaday, Nashville, 1992-94; counsel Hunton & Williams, Knoxville, Tenn., 1994—2003; assoc. gen. counsel CTI Molecular Imaging, Inc., Knoxville, 2003—. Adj. prof. U. Tenn. Coll. Law, Knoxville, 1997—; bd. dir. Legal Aid of East Tenn., 2001-03. Author: Pogiebait's War, 2001; contbr. chpt. to book and articles to profl. jour. Mem. alumni adv. coun. U. Tenn. Coll. Law, Knoxville, 1992-95. Capt. US Army, 1983-88. Recipient Loevinger prize ABA Sect. of Sci. and Tech., 1992, Bruno Bittker award ABA Standing Com. World Order Law, 1993, Pro Bono Lawyer award Knoxville Legal Aid Soc., 1999, 2000. Mem. Tenn. Bar Assn., Nashville Bar Assn. (elder law com. chair young lawyers divsn. 1993-94, vice-chair internat. law and practice com. 1993-94), Knoxville Bar Assn.(com. chair young lawyers sect. 1995-97, bd. gov. 2001--), Nat. Assn. Real Estate Investment Trusts. Meth. Avocations: history, writing, genealogy, languages, travel. Corporate, general, Finance, Securities. Office: CTI Molecular Imaging, Inc. 810 Innovation Dr Knoxville TN 37932

MC CALLUM, CHARLES EDWARD, lawyer; b. Memphis, Mar. 13, 1939; s. Edward Payson and India Raimelle (Musick) McC.; m. Lois Ann Gowell Temple, Nov. 30, 1985; children: Florence Andrea, Printha Kyle, Chandler Ward, Sabra Nicole Temple. BS, MIT, 1960; JD, Vanderbilt U., 1964. Bar: Mich., Tenn. 1964. Assoc. Warner Norcross & Judd LLP, Grand Rapids, Mich., 1964-69, ptnr., 1969—, mng. ptnr., 1992-97. Rep. assemblyman State Bar Mich., 1973-78; chmn. Rsch. and Tech. Inst. West Mich., 1989-91; lectr. continuing legal edn. programs; chmn., bd. dirs. Butterworth Ventures, 1987-96; mem. West Mich. World Trade Week Com., 1988-99, chmn., 1990-91; mem. Mich. Dist. Export Coun., 1990-99, chmn., 1992-97; vice-chmn. TerraLex, 2002—. Chmn. Grand Rapids Area Transit Authority, 1976-79, mem., 1972-79; regional v.p. Nat. Mcpl. League, 1978-86, mem. coun., 1971-78; pres. Grand Rapids Art Mus., 1979-81, 96-98, trustee, 1976-83, 94-99; chmn. Butterworth Hosp., 1979-87, trustee, 1977-87; chmn. Butterworth Health Corp., 1982-89, dir., 1982-97, vice chmn., 1989-91, sec., 1991-97; vice chmn. Citizens Com. for Consolidation of Govt. Svcs., 1981-82; mem. nat. alumni bd. Vanderbilt U. Sch. Law, 1998-2001; chmn. Priority Health, 1995—, bd. dirs., 1995—. Woodrow Wilson fellow, 1960-61; Fulbright scholar U. Manchester, Eng., 1960-61. Fellow Coll. Law Practice Mgmt.; mem. ABA (com. on law firms 1994-98, coun. mem. bus. law sect. 1998-2002, com. on multijurisdictional practice, chair com. on multidisciplinary practice 2000-02, com. on corp. structure 2000-02, chmn. bus. law sect. com. on profl. conduct, standing com. on ethics and profl. responsibility, task force on corp. responsibility, editl. bd. 2002—), Am. Bar Found., Am. Law Inst., Tenn. Bar Assn., Mich. Bar Assn. (mem. coun. bus. law sect. 1983-89, sect. chmn. 1988-89, ex-officio coun. bus. law sect. 1989—, chmn. takeover laws subcom. 1986-88, co-chmn. internat. bus. law com., internat. law sect. 1988-89), Grand Rapids Bar Assn., Internat. Bar Assn., Grand Rapids C. of C. (pres. 1975, bd. dirs. 1970-76), Univ. Club, Order of Coif, Sigma Xi. Corporate, general, Private international, Mergers and acquisitions. Home: 110 Bittersweet Ln NE Ada MI 49301-9552 E-mail: mccallce@wnj.com.

MCCAMPBELL, ROBERT GARNER, prosecutor; b. Oklahoma City, Nov. 23, 1957; s. Stanley Reid and Joan Fontaine (Garner) McC. BA in History with honors, Vanderbilt U., 1980; JD, Yale U., 1983. Bar: Okla. 1983. Assoc. Crowe & Dunlevy, Oklahoma City, 1983-87; asst. U.S. atty. Western Dist. Okla., 1987-94, chief fin. fraud unit, 1990-94; dir. Crowe & Dunlevy, 1994—2001; U.S. atty. We. Dist. Okla., 2001—. Dir. Ctr. for Advancement of Sci. and Tech., 1995, chmn., 1999—. Mem. ABA, Phi Beta Kappa. Republican. Episcopalian. Office: US Atty 210 W Park Ave Ste 400 Oklahoma City OK 73102

MCCANN, BRADLEY, lawyer; b. Rockford, Ill., July 8, 1971; s. Terrance Richard and Donna Kay McCann; m. Ginger Ann Freund, Oct. 17, 1998. BS in Acctg., No. Ill. U., 1993; JD, Quinnipiac Coll., 98; JD DePaul U. Bar: Ill., U.S. Tax Ct. CPA Clifton, Gunderson & Co., Joliet, Ill., 1993—96; tax/corp. atty. Nisen-Elliott, Chgo., 1998—. Mem.: AICPA, ABA, Univ. Club Chgo., Delta Sigma Pi. Republican. Presbyterian. Avocations: running, swimming, sports. Taxation, general, Corporate, general, Estate planning. Office: Nisen & Elliott 200 W Adams St Ste 2500 Chicago IL 60606 Fax: 312-346-2414. E-mail: bmcann@nisen.com.

MCCANN, CLIFTON EVERETT, lawyer; b. Des Moines, July 11, 1950; s. George Lockhart and Evelyn Elizabeth (Miller) McC.; m. Marcia Ellen Morrow, Feb. 19, 1984; children: Gregory Lockhart, Jeanna Lauren. BA in Psychology, No. Ill. U., 1972; JD, Columbus Sch. Law, 1977; LLM in Intellectual Property, George Washington U., 1985. Bar: Va. 1978, U.S. Patent Office 1980, U.S. Ct. Appeals (fed. cir.) 1982, U.S. Supreme Ct. 1983, D.C. 1984. Assoc. Beveridge, DeGrandi & Kline, Washington, 1978-83; ptnr. Lane, Aitken & McCann, Washington, 1983-2000, Venable, Baetjer, Howard & Civiletti, LLP, Washington, 2000—. Counsel intellectual property Am. Mensa, Ltd., Fort Worth, 1984—. Mem.: Am. Intellectual Prperty Law Assn., Bar Assn. D.C. (chair steering com. patent, trademark, copyright sect. 1984—, chair 1996—97), D.C. Bar Assn. (chmn. trademark com. of the patent, trademark and copyright sect. 1985—89), Va. Bar Assn., ABA (chair fed. litigation sub-com. on patent claim interpretation 1996—99, chair com. on intellectual property litigation 1999—2001), Patent Lawyers Club (Washington), Delta Theta Phi. Federal civil litigation, Patent, Trademark and copyright. Home: 5508 Grove St Chevy Chase MD 20815-3410 Office: Venable Baetjer Howard & Civiletti 1201 New York Ave NW Ste 1000 Washington DC 20005-6197

MCCANN, JOHN JOSEPH, lawyer; b. N.Y.C., Feb. 4, 1937; s. John and Katherine (McKeon) Mc C.; m. June M. Evangelist, Oct. 16, 1965; children: Catherine Anne, John Bernard, Robert Joseph, James Patrick. AB, Fordham U., 1958; LLB, Columbia U., 1961. Bar: N.Y. 1962, N.J. 1974, Fla. 1994. Exec. v.p., chief legal officer Orion Capital Corp., Farmington, Conn. Mem. legal adv. com. N.Y. Stock Exch., 1989-92. Mem. ABA (chair bus. law sect. 1992-93), Am. Law Inst., Am. Coll. Investment Counsel (pres. 1984-85), Am. Arbitration Assn. (bd. govs. 1985-96), Canoe Brook Golf and Country Club. Roman Catholic. Corporate, general, Insurance, Mergers and acquisitions. Office: Orion Capital Corp 9 Farm Springs Rd Farmington CT 06032-2526

MCCANN, JOSEPH LEO, lawyer, former government official; b. Phila., Aug. 27, 1948; s. Joseph John and Christina Mary (Kirwan) McC.; m. Aida Laico Kabigting, Dec. 6, 1986; 1 child, Angela Kathleen. BA, St. Charles Sem., Phila., 1970, postgrad., 1970-71; MA, Temple U., 1975, JD, 1977. Bar: Pa. 1977, U.S. Dist. Ct. (ea. dist.) Pa. 1977, U.S. Dist. Ct. (mid. dist.) Pa. 1978, U.S. Ct. Appeals (3d cir.) 1978, D.C. 1986, U.S. Supreme Ct. 1986, Md. 1987, U.S. Ct. Appeals (Fed. cir.) 1988, U.S. Ct. Internat. Trade 1988. Law clk. to chief justice Pa. Supreme Ct., Phila., 1977-78; dep. atty. gen. Pa. Dept. Justice, Harrisburg, 1978-80; sr. atty. U.S. GAO, Washington, 1980-96; sr. asst. gen. counsel GSA, Washington, 1996-99; pres., counsel, headmaster The Kabigting-Kirwan Meml. Nonprofit Corp., 1997-2000; atty., 2001—. Mem. Pa. Bar Assn., Phila. Bar Assn., Md. State Bar Assn. Roman Catholic. Home and Office: 204 Bookham Ln Gaithersburg MD 20877-3789 E-mail: ajmccann1@msn.com.

MCCANN, MAURICE JOSEPH, lawyer; b. St. Louis, July 26, 1950; s. James M. and Marie V. (Del Commune) M.; m. Suzanne Marie Grob, Dec. 29, 1990; 1 child, Mathew Maurice. BS, So. Ill. U., 1972, MA, 1974, PhD, 1976, JD, 1986. Bar: Ill. 1986, Mo. 1987, U.S. Dist. Ct. (ea. dist.) Mo. 1987, U.S. Dist. Ct. (so. dist.) Ill. 1988, U.S. Ct. Appeals (7th cir.) 1998. Teaching asst. So. Ill. U., Carbondale, 1972-76; asst. dir. Vermillion County Comprehensive Employment and Tng. Act, Danville, Ill., 1976; prof. John A. Logan Coll., Carterville, Ill., 1977; adj. prof. St. Louis U., 1977-78; exec. dir. Jackson County Comprehensive Employment and Tng. Act, Murphysboro, Ill., 1978-81, Jackson County YMCA, Carbondale, 1982-83; ptnr. McCann & Foley, Murphysboro, 1986-88; pvt. practice law Murphysboro, 1988—. Atty. Murphysboro Fire Protection Dist., Jackson County, 1988—; instr. dept. fin. So. Ill. U., 1988—, instr. dept. higher edn., 1994-96. Author: A Prelude to McCarthyism, 1974, Truman Administration and Federal Aid to Education, 1976, The Black Sox Scandal, 1986. Mem. Found. for Restoration of Ste. Genevieve, Mo., 1984; bd. dirs. So. Ill. Spl. Olympics, Carbondale, 1983-86; commr. Murphysboro Pk. Dist., 1990-92. Harry S. Truman scholar Truman Libr., Independence, Mo., 1975. Mem. ABA, Ill. Bar Assn., St. Louis Bar Assn., Mo. Bar Assn., Jackson County Bar Assn. Roman Catholic. Probate (including wills, trusts), Criminal, Property, real (including real estate development, water). Home: 42 Brian Ave Murphysboro IL 62966-6189 Office: 1331 Walnut St Murphysboro IL 62966-2026

MCCANN, RICHARD EUGENE, retired lawyer; b. Billings, Mont., Aug. 14, 1939; s. Oakey O. and Edith May (Miller) McC.; m. Mona N. Miyagishima, Apr. 27, 1964; children: Tami, Todd (dec.), Jennifer. BA magna cum laude, Rocky Mountain Coll., 1965; JD with highest honors, U. Mont., 1972. Bar: Mont. 1972, Washington 1977, Alaska 1982. Law clk. to Judge W. Jameson U.S. Dist. Ct., Billings, 1972-73; assoc. Crowley, Haughey, Hansen, Toole & Dietrich, Billings, 1973-77, Perkins Coie, Seattle, 1977-80, ptnr., 1981—2002, counsel, 2003—. Contbr. articles to profl. jours. Trustee Rocky Mountain Coll., Billings., 1973-77. Served with USMC, 1957-61. Mem. ABA, Mont. Bar Assn., Wash. Bar Assn., Alaska Bar Assn. Environmental, Land use and zoning (including planning), Property, real (including real estate development, water). Office: Perkins Coie 1201 3rd Ave Fl 40 Seattle WA 98101-3029 E-mail: mccar@perkinscoie.com.

MCCANN, RICHARD STEPHEN, lawyer; b. Wilmington, Del., Dec. 26, 1938; s. Francis E.B. and Naomi H. (Riley) McC.; m. Gloria M. Baum (div. 1973); 1 child, Heather Marie; m. Sharon R. Cannon. BA, Georgetown U., 1960, JD, 1963; MA in City Planning, U. Pa., 1965. Bar: Del. 1964. Alderman City of Newark, Newark, 1964-66, pvt. practice law, 1970—; city planner Dover, Del., 1966-70. Atty. Del. Police Chief's Coun., Dover, 1971—, Del. Police Chief's Found., Dover, 1983—. Atty. Aetna Hose, Hook & Ladder Co., Newark, 1975—. Mem. ABA, Del. Bar Assn. Avocations: skiing, gardening, cannons. Land use and zoning (including planning), Probate (including wills, trusts), Property, real (including real estate development, water). Home: PO Box 4706 Newark DE 19715-4076 Office: 125 E Delaware Ave Newark DE 19711-4644 E-mail: rsmccannesq@aol.com.

MCCARRON, JEFFREY BALDWIN, lawyer; b. Bryn Mawr, Pa., Mar. 7, 1961; s. John R. and Bette R. McC.; m. Kathryn Gilmour, Oct. 18, 1982; children: Sarah Jane, Jacqueline Lillian. BA, Hampshire Coll., 1983; JD, Temple U., 1987. Bar: Pa. 1987, N.J. 1987, U.S. Dist. Ct. N.J. 1987, U.S. Dist. Ct. (ea. dist.) Pa. 1989, U.S. Ct. Appeals (3d cir.) 1990; bd. cert. profl. liability atty. Am. Bd. Profl. Liability Attys., bd. cert. civil trial advocate Nat. Bd. Trial Advocacy. Atty. maj. trial divsn. Defender Assn. Phila., 1987-90; ptnr. Swartz, Campbell & Detweiler, Phila., 1990—. Mem.: ABA, Phila. Bar Assn., Pa. Bar Assn. (vice chmn. profl. liability com. 1997—98). Professional liability. Office: Swartz Campbell LLC 1601 Market St Fl 34 Philadelphia PA 19103-2397 E-mail: jmccarron@swartzcampbell.com.

MC CARTAN, PATRICK FRANCIS, lawyer; b. Cleve., Aug. 3, 1934; s. Patrick Francis and Stella Mercedes (Ashton) Mc Cartan; m. Lois Ann Buchman, Aug. 30, 1958; children: M. Karen, Patrick Francis III. AB magna cum laude, U. Notre Dame, 1956, JD, 1959. Bar: Ohio 1960, U.S. Ct. Appeals (6th cir.) 1961, U.S. Ct. Appeals (3rd cir.) 1965, U.S. Ct. Appeals (DC cir.) 1980, U.S. Ct. Appeals (5th cir.) 1981, U.S. Ct. Appeals (4th cir.) 1989, U.S. Ct. Appeals (7th cir.) 1992, U.S. Supreme Ct. 1970. Law clk. to Hon. Charles Evans Whittaker, U.S. Supreme Ct., 1959; assoc. Jones, Day, Reavis & Pogue, Cleve., 1961—65, ptnr., 1966—93, mng. ptnr., 1993—2002, sr. ptnr., 2003—. Trustee U. Notre Dame, 1989—, chair, 2000—; trustee Cleve. Clinic Found.; chair Greater Cleve. Roundtable; mem. standing com. on rules of practice and procedure Jud. Conf. of U.S. Fellow: Internat. Acad. Trial Lawyers, Am. Coll. Trial Lawyers; mem.: ABA, Bar Assn. Greater Cleve. (pres. 1977—78), Ohio Bar Assn., 6th Cir. Jud. Conf. (life), U.S.-Japan Bus. Coun., Coun. on Fgn. Rels., Greater Cleve. Growth Assn. (chmn. 1997—2000), Musical Arts Assn. (trustee). Roman Catholic. Federal civil litigation, State civil litigation, Corporate, general. Office: Jones Day Reavis & Pogue North Point 901 Lakeside Ave E Cleveland OH 44114-1190 E-mail: pmccartan@jonesday.com.

MCCARTER, CHARLES CHASE, lawyer; b. Pleasanton, Kans., Mar. 17, 1926; s. Charles Nelson and Donna (Chase) McC.; m. Clarice Blanchard, June 25, 1950; children— Charles Kevin, Cheryl Ann. BA, Principia Coll., 1950; JD, Washburn U., 1953; LLM, Yale U., 1954. Bar: Kans. 1953, U.S. Supreme Ct. 1962, Mo. 1968. Asst. atty. gen. State of Kans., 1954-57; lectr. law sch. Washburn U., 1956-57; appellate counsel FCC, Washington, 1957-58; assoc. Weigand, Curfman, Brainerd, Harris & Kaufman, Wichita, 1958-61; gen. counsel Kans. Corp. Commn., 1961-63; ptnr. McCarter, Frizzel & Wettig, Wichita, 1963-68, McCarter & Badger, Wichita, 1968-73; pvt. practice law St. Louis, 1968-76; ptnr. McCarter & Greenley, St. Louis, 1976-85; mng. ptnr. Gage & Tucker, St. Louis, 1985-87, Husch and Eppenberger, St. Louis, 1987-89, McCarter & Greenley, LLC, St. Louis, 1990—. Prof. law, assoc. dir. law sch. Nat. Energy Law and Policy Inst. Tulsa U., 1977-79; prof. law, coach nat. moot ct. coll. of law Stetson U. Coll., St. Petersburg, Fla., 1980-84; mem. govtl. adv. coun. Gulf Oil Corp., 1977-81 ; legal com. Interstate Oil Compact Commn.; mem. adv. bd. Allegiant Bank, 1997—. Co-author: Missouri Lawyers Guide; assoc. editor Washburn U. Law Rev., 1952-53; contbr. articles to profl. jours. Chmn. Wichita Human Rels. Devel. Adv. Bd., 1967-68; bd. dirs. Peace Haven Assn.; active St. Louis estate planning coun., 1987—, bequests and endowment com. Salvation Army, 1995—, YMCA endowment com., 1996—. With USNR, 1944-46. Recipient Excellent Prof. award U. Tulsa , 1979; vis. scholar Yale U., 1980 Mem. ABA (sect. real property, probate and trust law, bus. law sect.), Kans. Bar Assn., Mo. Bar Assn. (probate and trust com., tax com.), Am. Legion, VFW, Native Sons and Daus. Kans (pres. 1957-58), Kappa Sigma, Delta Theta Phi, Principia Dads Club (bd. dirs.) Republican. Corporate, general, Estate planning, Property, real (including real estate development, water). Office: One Metropolitan Sq Ste 2100 Saint Louis MO 63102-2797 E-mail: cmccarter@mccartergreenley.com.

MCCARTHY, CHARLES FRANCIS, JR., lawyer; b. Springfield, Mass., Dec. 9, 1926; s. Charles Francis and Maude Veronica (Clayton) McC.; m. Dorothy B. Sadosky, June 14, 1952 (dec. June 1987); children: Richard J., Linda A. Moylan, Robert P. AB, St. Michael's Coll., 1949; JD, Boston Coll., 1951. Bar: Mass. 1952, U.S. Dist. Ct. Mass. 1953. Assoc. Ganley, Crook & Smith, Springfield, Mass., 1954-67, Laming, Smith & Auchter, Springfield, 1967-80; of counsel Bacon & Wilson, P.C. and predecessor firms, Springfield, 1980-94; ret., 1994. Clk. Ellis Title Co., Inc., Springfield, 1988-94. Democrat. Roman Catholic. Home: 48 Palmyra St Springfield MA 01118-2027

MCCARTHY, DANIEL J. lawyer; b. Yonkers, N.Y., May 5, 1971; s. Justin Joseph and Jane Susan McCarthy; m. Sherry Lynn McCarthy, Apr. 27, 1999. BBA in Mktg., Western Conn. State U., 1993; JD, Thomas M. Cooley Law Sch., 1999. Bar: Mich. 1999, U.S. Dist. Ct. (ea. dist.) Mich. 1999. Law clk. Mich. Supreme Ct., Detroit, 1999—2000; prehearing atty. Mich. Ct. Appeals, Southfield, Mich., 2000; litig. assoc. Hyman Lippitt, P.C., Birmingham, Mich., 2000—. Mem.: ATLA, Oakland County Bar Assn., Fed. Bar Assn. Avocations: piano, music. Appellate, Commercial, contracts (including sales of goods; commercial financing), Construction. Office: Hyman Lippit PC 322 N Old Woodward Birmingham MI 48009 Office Fax: 248-646-8375. Business E-Mail: dmccarthy@hymanlippit.com.

MCCARTHY, KEVIN BART, lawyer; b. Washington, May 7, 1948; s. Frank Jeremiah and Frances Patricia (Bilderback) McC.; m. Patrice Borders, Apr. 3, 1971; children: Kevin Patrick, Charles Ryan, Molly Virginia, Bridget Louise, Moira Patrice. BBA, U. Notre Dame, 1970; JD, Ind. U., Indpls., 1973. Bar: Ind. 1973, U.S. Dist. Ct. (so. dist.) Ind. 1973, U.S. Ct. Appeals (7th cir.) 1974, Ill 1976, U.S. Dist. Ct. (cen. dist.) Ill. 1985, U.S. Ct. Appeals (6th cir.) 1985. Bail commr. Mcpl. Ct. Marion County, Indpls., 1972-73; asst. regional counsel Fed. Hwy. Adminstrn., Homewood, Ill., 1973-75; 1st asst., chief counsel Ill. Dept. Transp., Springfield, 1975-77; counsel com. on interstate and fgn. commerce, subcom. on transp. and commerce Ho. Reps., Washington, 1977-79, asst. counsel com. on pub. works and transp., 1979-82, counsel com. on pub. works and transp., 1982; pvt. practice law Springfield, 1982-87; acting U.S. trustee Dept. Justice, Springfield, 1987-88, U.S. trustee Indpls., 1988—. Pvt. practice Indpls. and Springfield. Mem. Ill. State Bd. Agrl. Advisors, 1987-88. Home: 5619 Surrey Hill Rd Indianapolis IN 46226-1561

MCCARTHY, KEVIN JOHN, lawyer; b. N.Y.C., Apr. 8, 1941; s. Vincent Patrick and Mary (H.) McC.; m. Marianne Pitts, Nov. 5, 1966; children: Mary Rita, Kevin, Colin. BS, U. Md., 1963; JD, U. Md., Balt., 1966. Bar: Md. 1966, U.S. Dist. Ct. Md. 1966, U.S. Ct. Appeals (4th cir.) 1966, U.S. Supreme Ct. 1972, D.C. 1976, U.S. Dist. Ct. D.C. 1976, U.S. Ct. Appeals (D.C. cir.) 1976, Fla. 1998. Law clk. Cir. Ct. for P.G. County, Upper Marlboro, Md., 1964-66; assoc., ptnr. Sasscer, Clagett & Channing, Upper Marlboro, Md., 1966-76; ptnr. O'Malley, Miles & McCarthy, Upper Marlboro, Md., 1976-86, McCarthy, Bacon & Costello, Landover, Md., 1986—. Arbitrator Am. Arbitration Assn., Washington, 1972—. Contbg. author: Maryland Civil Patter Jury Instructions, 1975, 2d edit., 1984, 3d edit., 1993. Named The Best Lawyers in Am., Woodward/White. Fellow Am. Bar Found., Md. Bar Found.; mem. Internat. Assn. Ins. Counsel, Fedn. Ins. and Corp. Counsel, Def. Rsch. Inst., Am. Trial Lawyers Assn., Md. Trial Lawyers Assn., Assn. Def. Trial Attys., Million Dollar Advocates Forum, Trial Lawyers for Pub. Justice. Avocations: golf, racquetball, coaching soccer and lacrosse. General civil litigation, Personal injury (including property damage), Product liability. Office: One Town Center 4201 Northview Dr Ste 410 Bowie MD 20716-2668 E-mail: Kevin@McCarthyCostello.com.

MCCARTHY, ROBERT EMMETT, lawyer; b. Bklyn., May 26, 1951; s. John Joseph and Leona Mary (Hart) McC.; m. Elizabeth Anne Naumoff, May 20, 1978; children: John Philip, Emily Jane. BS in Fgn. Studies, Georgetown U., 1973, MS in Fgn. Studies, JD, 1978. Bar: N.J. 1978, U.S. Dist. Ct. (ea. and so. dists.) N.Y. 1979. Assoc. Patterson, Belknap et al, N.Y.C., 1978-84; gen. counsel MTV Networks Inc., N.Y.C., 1984-86; v.p., counsel/communications Viacom Internat., N.Y.C., 1986-87; exec. v.p. Nelson Vending Tech., Ltd., N.Y.C., 1987-89; exec. v.p., gen. counsel Cateret Savs. Bank FA, Morristown, N.J., 1989-91; cons. McCarthy Comms., Elizabeth, N.J., 1991-95; sr. v.p., gen. counsel Time, Inc., N.Y.C., 1996—. Cons. UN Ctr. on Transnat. Corps., N.Y.C., 1979; exec. dir. Spl. Master Reapportionment of N.Y., 1982; term mem. Council Fgn. Relations, N.Y.C., 1980-84. Founder, pres. Elizabeth (N.J.) Dem. Assn., 1980; coordinator Florio for Gov., Union County, N.J., 1981. Mem. ABA, N.Y. State Bar Assn., N.J. State Bar Assn., Assn. Bar City N.Y. Roman Catholic. Communications, Corporate, general, Entertainment. Home: 3 Woods Ln Chatham NJ 07928-1760 Office: Time Inc 33rd Fl 1271 Avenue Of The Americas New York NY 10020-1300 E-mail: RobertMcCarthy1@aol.com.

MCCARTHY, THOMAS JAMES, JR., lawyer; b. Pulaski, Va., Nov. 24, 1943; s. Thomas James and Jane (Osborne) McC.; m. Sally Stockdale, July 25, 1987. BA in Econs., Washington and Lee U., 1967; JD, U. Va., 1970. Bar: Va. 1970, U.S. Dist. Ct. (we. dist.) Va. 1974, U.S. Supreme Ct. 2000. Asoc. Gilmer, Sadler, Ingram Sutherland & Hutton, Pulaski, 1970-75, ptnr., 1975—; county atty. Pulaski County, Pulaski, 1983—. Adminstrv. hearings officer Commonwealth of Va., 1983—; commr. of accts. Pulaski County, 1989—. Bd. dirs. New River C.C., 1980-88, 96—, vice-chair, 1981-88,

2000-02, chair 2002—, found. bd., 1989-91. Col. JAGC, U.S. Army Res., ret., 1997. Decorated Legion of Merit, Meritorious Svc. medal, Army Commendation medal. Mem. Va. Bar Assn., 27th Jud. Cir. Bar Assn. (pres. 1978-81), Pulaski County Bar Assn., Sigma Chi, Phi Alpha Delta. Democrat. Episcopalian. Home: PO Box 818 Pulaski VA 24301-0818 Office: Gilmer Sadler et al 65 E Main St Pulaski VA 24301-5013

MCCARTNEY, FRANK HOWARD, III, lawyer; b. Maysville, Ky., Sept. 30, 1949; s. Frank Howard and Gladys E. (Evans) McC.; m. Marsha Jane McNeill, Aug. 14, 1971; children: Rachael Evans, Laura Anne. BA, U. Ky., 1971, JD, 1973. Bar: Ky. 1974, U.S. Dist. Ct. (ea. dist.) Ky. 1975, U.S. Ct. Appeals (6th cir.) 1983, U.S. Supreme Ct. 1994. Ptnr. Suit, McCartney & Price, PLLC, Flemingsburg, Ky., 1974—. Atty. County of Fleming, Flemingsburg, 1977-90. Contbg. author: Kentucky Health Law Handbook, also 2d and 3d edits; mem. staff Ky. Law Jour., 1973-74 (Cite and Substance award 1974). Mem. Ky. Child Support Commn., 1987-91; bd. dirs. Lime Stone YMCA, 1991-99, pres., 1997-99. Recipient Disting. Svc. award Ky. Atty. Gen., 4th Ann. Kentuckians Involved with Dependent Support award. Mem. ABA (health law sect.), Ky. Bar Assn., Am. Acad. Hosp. Attys., Nat. Dist. Attys. Assn., Ky. Acad. Hosp. Attys. (pres. 1986-87, co-editor Jour., headnote editor 1980-90), Ky. County Attys. Assn. (bd. dirs. 1977-90), Flemingsburg Jaycees (State Speak-up award 1975, past pres.), Lions, Order of Coif. Democrat. Banking, General civil litigation, Health. Office: Suit McCartney & Price 207 Court Sq Flemingsburg KY 41041-1364

MC CARTNEY, RALPH FARNHAM, lawyer; b. Charles City, Iowa, Dec. 11, 1924; s. Ralph C. and Helen (Farnham) McC.; m. Rhoda Mae Huxsol, June 25, 1950; children: Ralph, Julia, David. JD, U. Mich., 1950; B. Sci., Iowa State U., 1972. Bar: Iowa 1950. Mem. firm Miller, Heuber & Miller, Des Moines, 1950-52, Frye & McCartney, Charles City, 1952-73, McCartney & Erb, Charles City, 1973-78; judge Dist. Ct. Iowa, Charles City, 1978-87; chief judge 2d Judicial Dist., 1987-92; sr. judge Ct. Appeals, 1992—. Mem. jud. coordinating com. Iowa Supreme Ct. Chmn. Supreme Ct. Adv. Com. on Adminstrn. of Clks. Offices; mem. Iowa Ho. of Reps., 1967-70, majority floor leader, 1969-70; mem. Iowa Senate, 1973-74. Bd. regents U. Iowa, Iowa State U., U. No. Iowa, Iowa Sch. for Deaf, Iowa Braille and Sight Saving Sch. Served with AUS, 1942-45. Mem. Iowa Judges Assn. Appellate. Home: 1828 Cedar View Dr Charles City IA 50616-9129

MCCARTNEY, ROBERT CHARLES, retired lawyer; b. Pitts., May 3, 1934; s. Nathaniel Hugh and Esther Mary (Smith) McC.; m. Janet Carolyn Moore, June 16, 1956; children: Ronald K., Sharon S., Carole J. AB, Princeton U., 1956; JD, Harvard U., 1959. Bar: D.C. 1959, Pa. 1960, U.S. Dist. Ct. (we. dist.) Pa. 1960, U.S. Ct. Appeals (3d dist.) 1960, U.S. Supreme Ct. 1966. Assoc. Eckert Seamans Cherin & Mellott, LLC, Pitts., 1959-64, ptnr., 1965-93, mem. exec. com., 1991-93, of counsel, 1993—. Sec., gen. counsel Ryan Homes, Inc., 1969-93; bd. dirs. United Meth. Found. of Western Pa., 1971— v.p., 1981-85, chmn., 1985-86; sec., gen. counsel Rimoldi of Am., Inc., 1989-99. Solicitor North Pitts. Cmty. Devel. Corp., 1968-76, alt. dir., 1968-80; mem. McCandless Twp. Govt. Study Commn., 1973-74, Princeton U. Leadership Devel. Coun., 2002—; solicitor, asst. sec. McCandless Indsl. Devel. Authority, 1972-98; mem. exec. com. Princeton U. Alumni Coun., 1966-70, 76-85, vice chmn., 1981-83, chmn., 1983-85, co-chair Spl. Com. for 250th Anniversary of Princeton U., 1994-97; nat chmn., class planned giving chair program, 2002—; trustee Otterbein Coll., 1975-83, Pa. S.W. Assn., 1992-96, Pitts. Cultural Trust, 1992-99; chmn. conf.-wide endowment program United Meth. Conf. We. Pa., 1985-87; bd. dirs. Pitts. Civic Light Opera Assn., 1984—, v.p., 1987-92, pres., 1992-99; dir. The Ireland Inst. Pitts., 1991—, vice chmn., 1996—; mem. No. Ireland Partnership, 1991—; bd. dirs. Pitts. Irish and Classical Theater. Princeton fellow Harvard U., 1956-59. Mem. Princeton U. Alumni Assn. West Pa. (pres. 1976-78), Duquesne Club, Nassau Club. Republican. Home: 9843 Woodland Rd N Pittsburgh PA 15237-4347 Office: Eckert Seamans Cherin Et Al 600 Grant St Ste 42D Pittsburgh PA 15219-2703

MCCAULEY, CLEYBURN LYCURGUS, lawyer; b. Houston, Feb. 8, 1929; s. Reese Stephens and Elizabeth Ann (Burleson) McC.; m. Elizabeth Kelton McKoy, June 7, 1950; children: Stephens Francis, Lillian Elizabeth, Cleyburn, Lucy Annette. BS, U.S. Mil. Acad., 1950; MS in Engring. Econ., Statistical Quality Control and Indsl. Engring., Stanford U., 1959; JD, Coll. William and Mary, 1970. Bar: D.C. 1971, Va. 1970, Tex. 1970, U.S. Ct. Claims 1971, U.S. Tax Ct. 1971, U.S. Supreme Ct. 1973. Commd. 2d lt. U.S. Air Force, 1950, advanced through grades to lt. col., 1971, ret., 1971; pvt. practice law, Washington, 1975—. Mem. Fed. Bar Assn., Va. Bar Assn., Tex. Bar Assn., D.C. Bar Assn., IEEE, AIAA, Am. Soc. Quality Control, Phi Alpha Delta. Banking, Corporate, general, Corporate taxation. Home: 402 S 3rd St Wilmington NC 28401-5102

MCCAUSLAND, MARGARET A. lawyer, educator; b. Bryn Mawr, Pa., Feb. 2, 1950; d. Joseph Edward and Margaret Mary O'Donnell; m. Paul Joseph McCausland, June 22, 1968; children: Patricia, Joseph. BS summa cum laude, St. Joseph's U., Phila., 1984; JD cum laude, Villanova U., 1987. Bar: Pa. 1987, U.S. Dist. Ct. (ea. dist.) Pa. 1987, U.S. Dist. Ct. (we. dist.) Mich. 1995, U.S. Ct. Appeals (3d cir.) 1997, U.S. Supreme Ct. 2002. Sec. Bankers Life, Bala Cynwyd, Pa., 1968—70, 1975—77, Frederick Brown & Assoc., Newton Square, Pa., 1977—84; assoc. Dechert LLP, Phila., 1987—93, Blank, Rome, Comisky & McCauley, Phila., 1993—97; ptnr. Blank Rome LLP, 1997—. Adj. faculty Villanova (Pa.) U. Law Sch., 1999—, mem. bd. advisors, 2001—. Vol. atty. Support Ctr. Child Advs., Phila., 1987—; tutor Phila. Reads, 2001—; mem. bd. advisors Archbishop Prendergast HS Girls, Phila., 2001—; bd. dirs. Robin's Nest, Inc., Glassboro, NJ, 1995—; pres., bd. dirs. CeaseFire Pa., Phila., 2002—. Named Disting. Adv., Support Ctr. Child Advs., 1996, Woman of Distinction, Phila. Bus. Jour., 2001. Mem.: AAUW, Pa. Bar Assn., ABA, J. Willard O'Brien Inn Ct., Phila. Bar Assn., Forum Exec. Women, Nawbo, Order of the Coif. Labor (including EEOC, Fair Labor Standards Act, labor-management relations, NLRB, OSHA), General civil litigation. Office: Blank Rome LLP One Logan Sq Philadelphia PA 19103 Office Fax: 215-832-5548. Business E-Mail: mccausland@blankrome.com.

MCCLAIN, RICHARD DOUGLAS, lawyer; b. Lincoln, Nebr., June 28, 1927; s. Leo LeRoy and Laura Thelma McC.; s. Donna J. Burbach, July 25, 1949; children: Daniel Douglas, Laurie Lynn. BA, U. Nebr., 1951; JD, U. So. Calif., 1959. Bar: Calif. 1960, Nebr. 1970, Oreg. 1991, U.S. Dist. Ct. Nebr. 1970, U.S. Supreme Ct. 1978. Atty. Union Pacific R.R., L.A., 1960-64, Hindin, Sterling, McKittrick & Powsner, Beverly Hills, Calif., 1964-67, Carnation Co., L.A., 1967-68, Atlantic Richfield Co., L.A., 1968-69; dep. county atty. County Atty., Lincoln, 1970-74; pvt. practice Lincoln, 1974—. Pres. Exec. Toastmasters 412, L.A., 1967, Res. Officers Assn., Lincoln, 1990—, pres. Nebr. dept. 1993; counsellor Footprinters, Lincoln, 1990—. Lt. USNR, 1951-55. Republican. Avocations: sailing, skating, shooting. General practice, Probate (including wills, trusts), Property, real (including real estate development, water). Home: 3235 W Pershing Rd Lincoln NE 68502-4844 Office: 1919 S 40th St Ste 111 Lincoln NE 68506-5247

MCCLAIN, WILLIAM ANDREW, lawyer; b. Sanford, N.C., Jan. 11, 1913; s. Frank and Blanche (Leslie) McC.; m. Roberta White, Nov. 11, 1944. AB, Wittenberg U., 1934; JD, U. Mich., 1937; LLD (hon.), Wilberforce U., 1963, U. Cin., 1971; LHD, Wittenberg U., 1972. Bar: Ohio 1938, U.S. Dist. Ct. (so. dist.) Ohio 1940, U.S. Ct. Appeals (6th cir.) 1946, U.S. Supreme Ct. 1946. Mem. Berry, McClain & White, 1937-58; dep. solicitor, City of Cin., 1957-63, city solicitor, 1963-72; mem. Keating, Muething & Klekamp, Cin., 1972-73; gen. counsel Cin. br. SBA, 1973-75; judge Hamilton County Common Pleas Ct., 1975-76; judge Mcpl. Ct., 1976-80; of counsel Manley, Burke, Lipton & Cook, Cin., 1980—; adj. prof. U. Cin., 1963-72, Salmon P. Chase Law Sch., 1965-72. Mem. exec. com. ARC, Cin., 1978—; bd. dirs. NCCJ, 1975—. Served to 1st lt. JAG, U.S. Army, 1943-46. Decorated Army Commendation award; recipient Nat. Layman award, A.M.E. Ch., 1963; Alumni award Wittenberg U., 1966; Nat. Inst. Mcpl. Law Officers award, 1971, Ellis Island Medal of Honor, 1997. Fellow Am. Bar Found.; mem. ABA, FBA, Am. Judicature Soc., Cin. Bar Assn., Ohio Bar Assn., Nat. Bar Assn., Friendly Sons St. Patrick, Bankers Club, Masons (33d degree), Alpha Phi Alpha, Sigma Pi Phi. Republican. Methodist. Home: 2101 Grandin Rd Apt 904 Cincinnati OH 45208-3346

MCCLARY, PATRICIA ANN, lawyer; b. Rockville Centre, N.Y., Apr. 20, 1957; d. Francis Griffith and Edna Margaret (Maher) McC. AB, Princeton (N.J.) U., 1979; JD, Harvard U., 1982. Bar: N.Y. 1983, D.C. 1984, U.S. Dist. Ct. (no. dist.) N.Y. 1987, U.S. Ct. Appeals (D.C. cir.) 1985, U.S. Ct. Appeals (3d cir.) 1986, U.S. Ct. Appeals (2d cir.) 1992. Jud. clk. to presiding justice Alaska Supreme Ct., Anchorage, 1982-83; assoc. Chadborne & Parke, Washington, 1983-86; asst. counsel Cornell U., Ithaca, N.Y., 1986-88, assoc. counsel, 1988—. Mem. Nat. Assn. Coll. and Univ. Attys. Avocation: sports. Home: 414 Elm St Ithaca NY 14850-3021 Office: Cornell U 300 CCC Bldg Ithaca NY 14853-2801

MCCLAUGHERTY, JOE L. lawyer, educator; b. June 1, 1951; s. Frank Lee and Elease (Terrell) McC. BBA with honors, U. Tex., 1973, JD with honors, 1976. Bar: Tex. 1976, N.Mex. 1976, U.S. Dist. Ct. N.Mex. 1976, U.S. Ct. Appeals (10th cir.) 1976, U.S. Supreme Ct. 1979, Colo. 1988. Assoc. Rodey, Dickason, Sloan, Akin & Robb, P.A., Albuquerque, 1976-81, ptnr., dir., 1981-87, resident ptnr. Santa Fe, N.Mex., 1983-87, mng. ptnr., 1985-87; ptnr. Kemp, Smith, Duncan & Hammond, P.C., 1987-92, mng. ptnr., 1987-92; ptnr. McClaugherty & Silver, P.C., Santa Fe, 1992—. Adj. prof. law U. N.Mex., Albuquerque, 1983—; faculty Nat. Inst. Trial Advocacy, so. regional, So. Meth. U. Law Sch., 1983—, Rocky Mt. regional, U. Denver Law Sch., 1986—, nat. session U. Colo. Law Sch., 1987; faculty Hastings Ctr. for Trial and Appellate Advocacy, 1985—; bd. dirs. MCM Corp., Raleigh, N.C., Brit.-Am. Ins. Co., Ltd., Nassau, The Bahamas, 1985-91. Mem. N.Mex. Bar Assn. (bd. dirs. trial practice sect. 1976-85, chairperson 1983-84, dir. young lawyers divsn. 1978-80), N.Mex. Assn. Def. Lawyers (pres. 1982-83, bd. dirs. 1982-85). Personal injury (including property damage), Product liability, Private international. Office: McClaugherty & Silver PC PO Box 8680 Santa Fe NM 87504-8680

MCCLELLAN, CRAIG RENE, lawyer; b. Portland, Oreg., June 28, 1947; s. Charles Russell and Annette Irene (Benedict) McC.; m. Susan Armistead Nash, June 7, 1975; children: Ryan Alexander, Shannon Lea. BS in Econs., U. Oreg., 1969; JD magna cum laude, Calif. We. U., 1976. Bar: Calif. 1976, U.S. Dist. Ct. (so. dist.) Calif. 1976, U.S. Dist. Ct. (ea., ctrl., no. dists.) Calif. 1991, U.S. Supreme Ct. 1991. Compliance specialist Cost of Living Coun. and Price Commn., Washington, 1972-73, dir. Oil Policy subcom., 1973; ptnr. Luce, Forward, Hamilton & Scripps, San Diego, 1976-87; owner McClellan & Assocs., San Diego, 1987—. Chmn. annual fundraising auction KPBS, 1984. Capt. USMC, 1969-72. Fellow Am. Coll. Trial Lawyers; mem. Assn. Trial Lawyers Am., Am. Bd. Trial Advocates, Am. Inns of Ct. (master), Calif. State Bar Assn., San Diego County Bar Assn., Calif. Trial Lawyers Assn. (bd. govs. 1985-87), San Diego Trial Lawyers Assn. (bd. dirs. 1983-90), Nat. Forensics League, Phi Gamma Delta, Phi Alpha Delta. Presbyterian. Avocations: reading, running, tennis, chess, civic activities. Personal injury (including property damage), Product liability. Office: McClellan & Assocs 1144 State St San Diego CA 92101-3529 E-mail: craig@mcclellanlaw.com.

MCCLELLAN, JANET ELAINE, law educator; b. Salina, Kans., June 30, 1951; d. William Francis and Ethel Mary (Rinebold) McC. BA in Govt., Adminstrn., Park Coll., Parkville, Mo., 1976; MPA, U. Dayton (Ohio), 1978; postgrad., U. Kans., 1982-86. Police officer City of Leavenworth, Kans., 1970-71; narcotics agt. Kans. Bur. Investigation, Topeka, 1971-73; asst. to chief Police Dept., Ellensberg, Wash., 1973-76, dir. juvenile divsn. Centerville, Ohio, 1976-79, watch comdr. Douglas, Wyo., 1978-79; dir. criminal justice adminstrn. Park Coll., 1979—. Directing advisor Tau Lambda Alpha Epsilon and Alpha Phi Omega, Park Coll., 1980-98; cons. Probation-Parole Dept., Kansas City, Mo., 1979-80, Police Dept., Leavenworth, 1981-82, Sheriff's Dept., Liberty, Mo., 1984-86; corrections adminstr. Kans. Dept. of Correction, 1988-96; police chief Pawnee Rock, Kans., 1996-98; prof. criminal justice, 1998—. Author: mystery book series including K.C. Bomber, 1996, Murder in Cloud City, 2000, Penn Valley Phoenix, 1997, River Quay, 1998, Chimney Rock Blues, 1999, Windrow Garden, 1999; contbr. articles to profl. jours.; reviewer criminal justice textbooks, jours., reviewing editor book Introduction to Criminal Justice, 1984, Modern Police Management, Criminal Justice and Public Policy. Chmn. S.W. Montgomery County Youth Commn., Dayton, Ohio, 1977-79; bd. dirs. Synergy Youth Half-way House, Parkville, 1980-86. Mem. Internat. Assn. Chiefs of Police, Am. Soc. Criminology, Am. Criminal Justice Soc., Am. Correctional Assn., Mo. Polit. Sci. Assn., Am. Soc. Pub. Adminstrn., Mo. Acad. Sci., Pi Gamma Mu, Pi Sigma Alpha, Delta Tau Kappa. Democrat. Office: Southwestern Oreg CC 1988 Newmark Ave Coos Bay OR 97420-2911 E-mail: jmcclellan@socc.edu.

MCCLELLAND, JAMES RAY, lawyer; b. Eunice, La., June 21, 1946; s. Rufus Ray and Homer Florene (Nunn) McC.; m. Sandra Faye Tate, Feb. 6, 1971; children: Joseph Ray, Jeffrey Ross. BS, La. State U., 1969, MBA, 1971, JD, 1975. Bar: La. 1975, U.S. Ct. Appeals (5th cir.) 1976, U.S. Dist. Ct. (ea. dist.) La. 1976, U.S. Dist. Ct. (we. dist.) La. 1976, U.S. Dist. Ct. (mid. dist.) La. 1994. Assoc. Aycock, Horne & Coleman, Franklin, La., 1975-78, ptnr., 1978—; dir. Bayou Bouillon Corp., Cotten Land Corp. Mem. exec. com. Democratic Party, St. Mary Parish, 1980-88; del. La. Dem. Party, 1982, 84. Mem. La. State Bar Assn. (ho. of dels. 1982-95, 98-99, law reform com. 1984-86, bd. govs. 1995-98, 99-2002, sec. 2003-), St. Mary Parish Bar Assn. (pres. 1978-79), Order of Coif, Rotary (pres. 1981-82). State civil litigation, Criminal, Personal injury (including property damage). Home: PO Box 268 Franklin LA 70538-0268 Office: PO Box 592 Franklin LA 70538-0592

MC CLENDON, WILLIAM HUTCHINSON, III, retired lawyer; b. New Orleans, Feb. 19, 1933; s. William H. and Eleanor (Eaton) McC.; m. Eugenia Mills Slaughter, Feb. 6, 1960; children: William Hutchinson, IV, Virginia Morris, Eleanor Eaton, Bryan Slaughter. BA, Tulane U., 1956, LLB, 1958. Bar: La. 1958, U.S. Supreme Ct. 1964. Atty. Humble Oil & Refining Co., 1958-60; with firm Taylor, Porter, Brooks & Phillips, Baton Rouge, 1960—, ptnr., 1966-2001, mem. exec. com., 1987-2001; mediator, assoc. Mediation Arbitration Profl. Sys., Inc., 1999—2001. Instr. comml. law and negotiable instruments Am. Inst. Banking, 1963-74; lectr. movable Property La. Bar Assn. Bridging the Gap Inst., 1965; lectr. La. State U. LAw Sch. and Real Estate Seminar chmn., 1972, 74, 76, 80, 82, 85, 87, 95, La. Soc. of Profl. Surveying, 1989, La. Soc. CPA's, 1991, Banking Seminar, 1995; adj. prof. La. State U. Legal Negotiation, 1983—, U. Tenn., 2003-, Western Carolina U., 2003-; mem. faculty Profl. Edn. Group, Inc., We. Carolina U. Contbr. articles to legal jours. Bd. dirs. Cancer Soc. Baton Rouge, 1968-71; trustee Episcopal High Sch., 1976-78; mem. Dean's council Tulane U. Law Sch., 1984-88. Served to capt. AUS. Recipient Preservation award Found. for Hist. La., 1997. Mem. ABA, Am. Judicature Soc., La. Bar Assn. (chmn. sect. trust estates, probate and immovable property law 1969-70, Meml. award article 1987), Baton Rouge Bar Assn. (chmn. title standards com. 1968-69), Tulane Alumni Assn. Greater Baton Rouge (pres. 1968-69), Baton Rouge Green (bd. dirs. 1991-93), Hilltop Aboretum (bd. dirs. 1993-95), La. Civil Svc. League (pres. 1992-94), La. Tulane Law Alumni (treas., 2d v.p. 1964-65), Baton Rouge Assembly (treas. 1983, ball chmn. 1997, chmn. 1999), Toastmasters (pres. 1970), Baton Rouge Country Club, Camelot Club, Pickwick Club, Rotary (bd. dirs. Baton Rouge club 1972), Kappa Alpha, Baton Rouge Symphony (bd. dirs. 2001-02). Republican. Episcopalian (vestry, sr. warden 1975, 81, 84, diocesan standing com. 1985-89). E-mail: wh.mcclendon@verizon.net.

MCCLINTOCK, GEORGE DUNLAP, retired lawyer; b. Pocatello, Idaho, Nov. 30, 1920; s. George Dunlap and Jessie (McCabe) McC.; m. Aileen McHugh, Sept. 19, 1945 (dec. Jan. 2000); children— Jessie Kelly, Catharine, George, Jane Wyatt, Michael, Anne AB cum laude, Dartmouth Coll., 1942; LLB, Harvard U., 1948. Bar: Minn. 1948. Ptnr. Faegre & Benson, Mpls., 1948-90. Dir. Merchants Bank, Rugby, N.D.; trustee Douglas Rees Trust, 1966—, Paul R. Held Testamentary Trusts, 1980—. Trustee, mayor City of Woodland, Minn., 1970-79; exec. bd., Viking council Boy Scouts Am., Mpls., 1959-74, pres., 1966-67; gen. campaign chmn. United Way of Mpls., 1972, bd. dirs., 1973-81, pres., 1976; trustee Convent of Visitation Sch., St. Paul, 1975-81; trustee North Meml. Med. Ctr., Robbinsdale, Minn., 1959-75; trustee, sec. Minn. Med. Found., Mpls., 1982-90. Served to lt. USNR, 1942-46 Recipient Disting. Eagle Scout award Boy Scouts Am., 1982 Mem. Mpls. Club (governing com. 1983-89, pres. 1987), Woodhill Country Club (trustee 1985-94). Republican. Presbyterian. Avocations: golf, waterfowl hunting.

MCCLOUD, ROBERT OLMSTED, JR., lawyer; b. Chgo., Dec. 7, 1951; s. Robert Olmsted and Suzanne (Eyerly) McC.; m. Kathryn Bartholomees, June 3, 1978; children: Lyle Olmsted, Stewart Wilcox, Kathryn Suzanne. Student, U. Ga., 1970-72; AB, Duke U., 1974; JD, U. Ga., 1977. Bar: Ga. 1977, U.S. Dist. Ct. (no. dist.) Ga. 1977, U.S. Ct. Appeals (5th and 11th cirs.) 1977. Assoc. Webb, Young, Daniel & Murphy, Atlanta, 1977-80, Jones & Van Gerpen, Atlanta, 1980-82, Carter & Ansley, Smith & McLendon, Atlanta, 1982-84; ptnr. Carter & Ansley, Atlanta, 1985-2000, mng. ptnr., 1991-94; shareholder Davis, Matthews & Quigley P.C., Atlanta, 2000—. Bd. dirs. Wildwood Civic Assn., Atlanta, 1984-86. Mem. ABA, Atlanta Bar Assn., Lawyers Club Atlanta (treas. 1988-89, exec. com. 1988-90), Cherokee Town and Country Club. Republican. Presbyterian. Bankruptcy, Communications, Corporate, general. Home: 3137 Rockingham Dr NW Atlanta GA 30327-1234 Office: Davis Matthews & Quigley PC 14th Fl Lenox Towers II 3400 Peachtree Rd NE Atlanta GA 30326 Fax: 404-261-0159. E-mail: rmccloud@dmqlaw.com.

MCCLOUD, SAMUEL ALFRED, lawyer; b. Chgo., Feb. 24, 1943; s. Walter Hall and Jeraldine Mae McCloud; children: Eric, Daniel, Christina, Amber, Samantha, Cassondra, Cheyenne, Rockel, Travis, Johnna. JD, Wm. Mitchell Coll. Law, 1977. Pvt. practice, Shakopee, Minn. With U.S. Air Force, 1962-66. Mem. Nat. Assn. Criminal Def. Lawyers. Office: PO Box 216 Shakopee MN 55379

MCCLOW, ROGER JAMES, labor lawyer; b. St. Johns, Mich., July 23, 1947; s. Jack Gordon and Madalene V. (Mahaffy) McC.; m. Suzanne Terese Posler, July 13, 1978. BA in Polit. Sci. with distinction, U. Mich., 1969; JD magna cum laude, Wayne State U., 1976. Bar: Mich. 1977, U.S. Dist. Ct. (ea. dist.) Mich. 1977, U.S. Ct. Appeals (6th cir.) 1985, U.S. Ct. Appeals (8th cir.) 1987, U.S. Supreme Ct. 1988. Assoc. Miller, Cohen, Martens & Sugerman, Detroit, 1977-81, Klimist, McKnight & Sale, P.C., Southfield, Mich., 1981-83; ptnr. Klimist, McKnight, Sale, McClow & Canzano, P.C., Southfield, 1983—. Bd. dirs. Hemid (Sr. Citizen's Agy.), Detroit, 1982-2002; tutor Children's Ctr., Detroit, 1990-93; vol. Hospice Legal Aid, Detroit, 1991—, Patient Advocate Found., 1998—; mem. gun safety com. Alliance for Greater, Safer Detroit, 1993-95. Recipient Outstanding Vol. Svc. award Children's Ctr. Detroit, 1993. Mem. State Bar Mich. (coun. mem., labor law and employment sect. 1992-96), Detroit Bar Assn., Oakland County Bar Assn., Assn. Trial Lawyers Am., Mich. Trial Lawyers Assn., Indsl. Rels. Rsch. Assn., Phi Sigma Alpha. Democrat. Avocations: antiques, tennis, historic home restoration, landscaping. Labor (including EEOC, Fair Labor Standards Act, labor-management relations, NLRB, OSHA), Pension, profit-sharing, and employee benefits, Personal injury (including property damage). Office: Klimist McKnight Sale McClow & Canzano 400 Galleria Officentre Ste 117 Southfield MI 48034-2161 E-mail: rmcclow@kmsmc.com.

MCCLUNG, J(AMES) DAVID, corporate executive, lawyer, academic administrator; b. Lamesa, Tex., July 16, 1943; s. Jack Weldon Sr. and Ruby (Brown) McC.; m. Linda Nelson, Feb. 12, 1966; children: LeEtta McClung Felter, Dennis, Pamela McClung Frazier, Jennifer McClung Panicker. Student, N.E. La. State Coll., 1961-62, McNeese State Coll., 1963; BSBA cum laude, Bethany Nazarene Coll., 1965; postgrad., U. Okla., 1967-68; JD cum laude, Baylor U., 1973. Bar: Tex. 1973, U.S. Dist. Ct. (no. dist.) Tex. 1975, U.S. Ct. Appeals (5th cir.) 1974. Assoc. Jackson & Walker, Dallas, 1973-76; exec. v.p. Austin Industries, Inc., Dallas, 1976-88; pres., chief exec. officer, chmn. bd. Green Internat., Inc., Denver, 1988—; owner NazNet.Com, 1999—. Arbitrator Am. Arbitration Assn., 1978—; bd. dirs. Green Holdings, Inc., Denver; chmn. bd. Green Construction Co., Green Mining, Inc., Green Alaska, Inc., GEM Investors, Inc., Green Overseas Corp., Northland Maintenance Co., Northland Alaska, Inc., Green Investments, Inc., Denver, 1988—; pres. Triton Marine Cons., 1994-2000; chmn. Triton Marine Cons., 2000—; pres. Ea. Nazarene Coll., 2002—. Contbr. articles to profl. jours. Trustee So. Nazarene U., Bethany, Okla., 1978—; mem. gen. bd. Ch. of the Nazarene, Kansas City, 1985-89, sec. Commn. Report, 1989. Capt. USAF, 1965-71, Vietnam. Decorated 6 Air medals; recipient Young Grads. award of merit Baylor U., 1983, Outstanding Alumni award So. Nazarene U., 1989, Disting. Svc. award Ch. of the Nazarene, 1989. Mem. ABA, Tex. Bar Assn., The Beavers. Republican. Avocations: digital photography, fishing. Home: 3504 C St NW Gig Harbor WA 98335-7801 Office: Ea Nazarene Coll 23 E Elm Ave Quincy MA 02170-1663 E-mail: mcclung@naznet.com.

MCCLURE, ANN CRAWFORD, judge, lawyer; b. Cin., Sept. 5, 1953; d. William Edward and Patricia Ann (Jewett) Crawford; m. David R. McClure, Nov. 12, 1983; children: Kinsey Tristen, Scott Crawford. BFA magna cum laude, Tex. Christian U., 1974; JD, U. Houston, 1979. Bd. cert. in family law and civil appellate law Tex. Bd. Legal Specialization. Assoc. Piro and Lilly, Houston, 1979-83; pvt. practice El Paso, Tex., 1983-92; ptnr. McClure and McClure, El Paso, 1992-94; justice 8th Ct. of Appeals, El Paso, 1995—. Past mem. Tex. Bd. Law Examiners, Bd. Disciplinary Appeals; mem. Family Law Specialization Exam Com., 1989—93; mem. civil appellate law adv. com. Tex. Bd. Legal Specialization; mem. Tex. Jud. Coun. Contbr. articles to profl. jours.; past editor The Family Law Forum; past contbg. editor: Texas Family Law Service; mem. editl. bd. Tex. Family Law Practice Manual, 1982-93; editl. cons. Matthew Bender Tex. Family Law Practice and Procedure. Mem.: Tex. Jud. Coun., El Paso Bar Assn. (sec. 2002—, treas.), Tex. Acad. Family Law Specialists (past dir.), State Bar Tex. (family law sect. chair 1997—98, appellate divsn. jud. sect. chair 2000—01). Democrat. Presbyterian.

MCCLURE, DANIEL M. lawyer; b. Enid, Okla., Feb. 5, 1952; s. Larry M. and Marie Dolores (Sarver) McC.; m. Judy Lynn Pinson, Jan. 3, 1976; children: Andrew Mead, Mark William, Kathleen Claire. BA with highest hons., U. Okla., 1974; JD cum laude, Harvard U., 1978. Bar: Tex. 1978, U.S. Dist. Ct. (so. dist., ea. dist.) Tex. 1979, U.S. Ct. Appeals (5th cir., 11th cir.) 1981. Assoc. Fulbright & Jaworski, LLP, Houston, 1978-86, ptnr., 1986—. Fellow Tex. Bar Found.; mem. ABA, Nat. Health Lawyers Assn., Nat. Assn. R.R. Trial Counsel, Tex. Bar Assn., Houston Bar Assn. (cert. civil trial law), Am. Inns of Ct., Harvard Law Sch. Assn. Avocation: tennis. Antitrust, General civil litigation, Oil, gas, and mineral. Home: 2 Long Timbers Ln Houston TX 77024-5445 Office: Fulbright & Jaworski LLP 1301 McKinney St Houston TX 77010-3031 E-mail: dmcclure@fulbright.com.

MCCLURE, JAMES FOCHT, JR., federal judge; b. Danville, Pa., Apr. 6, 1931; s. James Focht and Florence Kathryn (Fowler) McC.; m. Elizabeth Louise Barber, June 14, 1952; children: Holly McClure Kerwin, Kimberly Ann Pacala, Jamee McClure Sealy, Mary Elizabeth Hudec, Margaret McClure Persing. AB, Amherst Coll., 1952; JD, U. Pa., 1957. Bar: D.C. 1957, Pa. 1958, U.S. Dist. Ct. D.C. 1957, U.S. Dist. Ct. (ea. and mid. dist.) Pa. 1958, U.S. Ct. Appeals (3d cir.) 1959. Atty., advisor Dept. State, Washington, 1957-58; assoc. Morgan, Lewis & Bockius, Phila., 1958-61; atty. Merck & Co., Inc., N.Y.C., 1961-65; ptnr. McClure & McClure, Lewisburg, Pa., 1965-77, McClure & Light, Lewisburg, 1978-84; pres., judge Ct. Common Pleas, 17th Jud. Dist. Pa., Lewisburg, 1984-90; sr. dist. judge U.S. Dist. Ct. (mid. dist.) Pa., Williamsport, Pa., 1990—. Dist. atty. Union County, Lewisburg, 1974-75. Pres. bd. sch. dirs. Lewisburg Area Sch. Dist., 1969-74. Cpl. U.S. Army, 1952-54. Mem. Pa. Bar Assn., Union County Bar Assn., Bucknell U. Golf Club, Susquehanna Valley Chorale, Order of Coif, Phi Beta Kappa. Republican. Presbyterian. Office: US Dist Ct 240 W 3rd St Ste 320 Williamsport PA 17701-6466 E-mail: gary_palmer@unc.edu.

MCCLURE, JAMES JULIUS, JR., lawyer, former city official; b. Oak Park, Ill., Sept. 23, 1920; s. James J. and Ada Leslie (Baker) McC.; m. Margaret Carolyn Phelps, Apr. 9, 1949; children: John Phelps, Julia Jean, Donald Stewart. BA, U. Chgo., 1942, JD, 1949. Bar: Ill. 1950. Ptnr. Gardner, Carton & Douglas, Chgo., 1962-91, of counsel, 1991—; mem. Oak Park Plan Commn., 1966-73, Northeastern Ill. Planning Commn., 1973-77, pres., 1975-77, Village of Oak Park, 1973-81, Oak Park Exch. Congress Inc., 1978—2002. Mem. Bus. Leaders for Transp., 1998—. Pres. United Christian Cmty. Svcs., 1967-69, 71-73, Erie Neighborhood House, 1953-55, Oak Park-River Forest Cmty. Chest, 1967; moderator Presbytery Chgo., 1969; mem. Gov.'s Spl. Com. on MPO, 1978-79; bd. dirs. Leadership Coun. of Met. Open Cmtys., 1981-2002, sec., 1990-98; bd. dirs. Met. Planning Coun., 1982-93, hon. dir., 1993—; bd. dirs. Cmty. Renewal Soc., 1982-91, v.p., 1984-88, treas. 1988-91; bd. dirs. Christian Century Found., 1972—, chmn., 1981—; trustee McCormick Theol. Sem., 1981—, chmn. bd. 1987-90. hon. trustee, 1990—; mem. ch. vocations unit, 1987-92, vice chair 1990; mem. gen. assembly coun. Presbyn. Ch. U.S.A., 1987-90, mem. gen. assembly Permanent Jud. Commn., 1997-2003; bd. dirs. Oak Park Edn. Found., 1991-96, Oak Park River Forest Cmty. Found., 1991-2002; mem. Vision 2000 (Oak Park) Coordinating Com., 1995. With USNR, 1942-46. Recipient Disting. Citizen award Oak Park, 1976; Silver Beaver award; Disting. Eagle Scout award Boy Scouts Am., Carl Winters Cmty. Svc. award Oak Park Rotary Club, 1996, William Staczak award Oak Park Edn. Found., 1997, Rita Johnson award Oak Park Family Svc. and Mental Health Ctr., 1997, Public Svc. award U. Chgo. Alumni Assn., 1997, Tradition of Excellence award Oak Pk. River Forest H.S., 1998, Alumni Service Medal, Alumni Svc. medal, 2003, U. Chgo. Alumni Assn., 2003, Gutenberg Award Chgo. Bible Soc., 2003; named one of 100 disting. Oak Parkers for Millenium, Wed Jour., 2002. Mem. ABA, Am. Coll. Trust and Estate Counsel, Ill. State Bar Assn., Chgo. Bar Assn., Am. Law Inst., Order of the Coif, Lambda Alpha. Clubs: Univ. (Chgo.). Home: One Calvin Cir # C 309 Evanston IL 60201 Office: Gardner Carton & Douglas 191 N Warker Dr Chicago IL 60606-4719

MCCLURE, ROGER JOHN, lawyer; b. Cleve., Nov. 22, 1943; s. Theron R. and Colene (Irwin) McClure. BA, Ohio State U., 1965, JD cum laude, 1972; MA, Northwestern U., 1966. Bar: Va. 1973, Md. 1973, U.S. Ct. Appeals (D.C. cir.) 1974, U.S. Supreme Ct. 1978, Ohio, U.S. Ct. Appeals (4th, 5th & 10th cirs.). Asst. atty. gen. State of Ohio, Columbus, 1972; trial atty. FTC, Washington, 1972-76; sr. assoc. Law Offices of A.D. Berkeley, Washington, 1976-81; pvt. practice Alexandria, Va., 1981—; pres. Roger J. McClure, PC, Alexandria, 1987—; del. Va. Gen. Assembly, 1992—2002, co-chmn. militia and police com., 1998—2002. Adj. prof. Acad. Multidisciplinary Practice Mich. State U., Lansing, 2001—; host talk show Sta. WRC Radio, 1987—93, 1999—2001, Sta. WPGC, 1993—94. Co-author: (book) Winning the Syndication Game, 1988, Advanced Estate Planning in Virginia, 2001, Virginia Elder Law, 1988, Asset Protection in Virginia, 1999, Estate and Wealth Strategies Planning, 2000, Choice of Entity in Virginia, 2000, Business Succession and Sale of Businesses, 2003, (book) Family Limited Partnerships and LLCS, 2003; contbg. reviewer; contbr. articles to profl. jours. Mem. No. Va. Transp. Commn., 2001, commr.; bd. dirs. No. Va. Cmty. Found., 1995—. With U.S. Army, 1967—69. Decorated Bronze Star; fellow Masters, Espertis Peterson Inst., 1996—. Mem.: Dulles Area Transp. Assn. (bd. dirs.), Nat. Network Estate Planning Attys., No. Va. Apt. Assn. (bd. dirs. 1988—92, 1st v.p. 1987—88, pres. 1988—89), D.C. Bar Assn. (real estate steering com. 1982—84, chmn. antitrust divsn. 1975—76), Washington Nat. Cathedral, Wolf Trap Found. (adv. coun.). Avocation: sailing. Estate planning, Property, real (including real estate development, water), Estate taxation. Office: 500 N Washington St Alexandria VA 22314-2314 E-mail: rmcclure@ix.netcom.com.

MCCLURE, THOMAS EDWARD, lawyer; b. Urbana, Ill., Nov. 8, 1954; s. William Leslie McClure and Carolyn Jean (Hovey) McClure Byrnes; m. Karen Leah Zinn, Dec. 14, 1985. BS, Ill. State U., 1976; JD, DePaul U., 1979; MS, Ill. State U., 2001. Bar: Ill. 1979, U.S. Dist. Ct. (no. dist.) Ill. 1979, U.S. Ct. Appeals (7th cir.) 1980, U.S. Dist. Ct. (cen. dist.) Ill. 1983, U.S. Dist. Ct. (no. dist.) Ind. 1991, U.S. Supreme Ct. 1993. Law clk. to presiding justice Ill. Ct. Appeals (1st dist.), Chgo., 1979-81; assoc. Elliott & McClure, Bourbonnais and Momence, Ill., 1981-88; ptnr. Elliott & McClure P.C., Bourbonnais and Momence, Ill., 1988—. Legal counsel Ill. Jaycees, 1985-86, individual devel. v.p., 1987-88, regional dir., 1988-89; atty. Village of Bourbonnais, 1989-93, Village of Chebanse, 1993-97, Village of Manteno, 1999-2001; bd. mem. Bourbonnais Elem. Sch. Dist., 2001-, pres., 2003—. Editor DePaul Law Rev., 1978-79; contbr. articles to profl. jours. Recipient Outstanding Instrn. award Dale Carnegie & Assocs., 1982, 83, Dennis Hamilton Meml. award U.S. Jaycees, 1988. Mem. ABA, Ill. Bar Assn. (cert. of recognition 1983), 7th Cir. Bar Assn. (cert. of recognition 1994), Chgo. Bar Assn., Kankakee County Bar Assn., Appellate Lawyers Assn., Ill. Jaycees (individual devel. v.p. 1987-88, Outstanding Local Pres. 1985, Outstanding Local Dir. East Region 1984, Outstanding Portfolio V.P. 1987-88, Outstanding Regional Dir. 1988-89), Kankakee Jaycees (pres. 1984-85, bd. dirs. 1983-86), Ill. Jaycees Charitable Found., Inc. (bd. dirs., mem. and legal counsel 1986-89), Ill. Jaycees Charitable Camp, Inc. (bd. dirs., legal counsel 1989-91). Civil rights, Federal civil litigation, Personal injury (including property damage). Office: Elliott & McClure 18 Briarcliff Prof Ctr Bourbonnais IL 60914-1775

MCCOBB, JOHN BRADFORD, JR., lawyer; b. Orange, N.J., Oct. 14, 1939; s. John Bradford and Dorothea Joyce (Hoffman) M.; m. Maureen Kelly, Oct. 6, 1973; 1 dau., Carrie Elizabeth. A.B., Princeton U. cum laude, 1961; J.D., Stanford U., 1966; LL.M., NYU, 1973. Bar: Calif. 1967. Assoc., IBM, Armonk, N.Y., 1966-1974, gen. counsel, Tokyo, 1974-77, lab. counsel, Endicott, N.Y., 1977-79, sr. atty., White Plains, N.Y., 1979-81, regional counsel, Dallas, 1981-83; counsel, sec. IBM Instruments, Inc., Danbury, Conn., 1983-87; area counsel European Labs, Hursley, England, 1987-90; counsel govtl. programs IBM, Washington, 1990-97. Trustee Princeton-in-Asia, Inc., 1970-86 . Princeton-in-Asia-teaching fellow at Chinese Univ. of Hong Kong, 1963-65. Mem. ABA, State Bar of Calif., Phi Beta Kappa. Contbr. articles to profl. jours. Antitrust, Computer, Private international.

MCCONKIE, OSCAR WALTER, lawyer; b. Moad, Utah, May 26, 1926; s. Oscar Walter and Margaret Vivian (Redd) M.; m. Judith Stoddard, Mar. 17, 1951; children: Oscar III, Ann, Daniel, Gail, Clair, Pace Jefferson, Roger James, Edward. BS in Polit. Sci., U. Utah, 1949, JD, 1952. Bar: Utah 1952, U.S. Ct. Appeals (10th cir.) 1952, U.S. Supreme Ct. 1981, U.S. Ct. Appeals (8th cir.) 1994. County atty. Summit County (Utah), 1959-63; instr. bus. law Stevens Henager Coll., Salt Lake City, 1952-67; ptnr. Kirton & McConkie, Salt Lake City, 1967—. Author: The Kingdom of God, 1962, God and Man, 1963, The Priest in the Aaronic Priesthood, 1964, Angels, 1975, Aaronic Priesthood, 1977, She Shall Be Called Woman, 1979. Mem. Utah Ho. of Reps., 1955-57; pres. Utah State Senate, 1965-66; chmn. Utah Bd. Edn., 1983-85. With USN, 1944-46. Mem. Utah Bar Assn., Salt Lake City County Bar Assn. Democrat. Mem. Lds Ch. General practice, Legislative. Home: 1954 Laird Dr Salt Lake City UT 84108-1823 Office: 1800 Eagle Gate Tower 60 E South Temple Salt Lake City UT 84111-1004 E-mail: omcconkie@kmclaw.com.

MCCONNAUGHEY, GEORGE CARLTON, JR., retired lawyer; b. Hillsboro, Ohio, Aug. 9, 1925; s. George Carlton and Nelle (Morse) McC.; m. Carolyn Schlieper, June 16, 1951; children: Elizabeth, Susan, Nancy. BA, Denison U., 1949; LL.B., Ohio State U., 1951, JD, 1967. Bar: Ohio 1951. Sole practice, Columbus; ptnr. McConnaughey & McConnaughey, 1954-57, McConnaughey, McConnaughey & Stradley, 1957-62, Laylin, McConnaughey & Stradley, 1962-67, George, Greek, King, McMahon & McConnaughey, 1967-79, McConnaughey, Stradley, Mone & Moul, 1979-81, Thompson, Hine & Flory (merger McConnaughey, Stradley, Mone & Moul with Thompson, Hine & Flory), Cleve., Columbus, Cin., Dayton, Washington, N.Y.C., and Brussels, 1981—93; ret. ptnr. Thompson Hine LLP, Columbus, 1993—. Bd. dirs. N.Am. Broadcasting Co. (Sta. WMNI, WBZX and WEGE Radio); asst. atty. gen. State of Ohio, 1951-54. Pres. Upper Arlington (Ohio) Bd. Edn., 1967-69, Columbus Town Meeting Assn., 1974-76; chmn. Ohio Young Reps., 1956; U.S. presdl. elector, 1956; trustee Buckeye Boys Ranch, Columbus, 1967-73, 75-81, Upper Arlington Edn. Found., 1987-93; elder Covenant Presbyn. Ch., Columbus. With U.S. Army, 1943-45, ETO. Fellow Am. Bar Found., Ohio Bar Found., Columbus Bar Found.; mem. ABA, Ohio State Bar Assn., Columbus Bar Assn., Am. Judicature Soc., Scioto Country Club, Athletic Club, Rotary, Masons. Home: 1993 Collingswood Rd Columbus OH 43221-3741 Office: Thompson Hine LLP One Columbus 10 W Broad St Ste 700 Columbus OH 43215-3435

MCCONNELL, DAVID KELSO, lawyer; b. N.Y.C., July 12, 1932; s. David and Caroline Hanna (Kelso) McC.; m. Alice Schmitt, Dec. 26, 1953; children: Elissa Anne McConnell Henebry, Kathleen Anne, David Willet. BCE, CCNY, 1954; LLB, Yale U., 1962. Bar: Conn. 1962, U.S. Dist. Ct. Conn. 1963, U.S. Ct. Appeals (2d cir.) 1964, U.S. Ct. Appeals (3d cir.) 1966, U.S. Sup. Ct. 1970, U.S. Dist. Ct. (ea. dist.) Pa. 1971, Pa. 1975, N.Y. 1986. Asst. counsel N.Y.N.H. & H. R.R., New Haven, 1962-65, counsel, 1966-68; asst. atty. gen. U.S. V.I., 1965-66; asst. gen. atty. Pa. Cen. Transp. Co., New Haven, 1969-70, asst. gen. counsel Phila., 1970-71, sr. reorganization atty., 1971, adminstrv. officer, spl. counsel to trustees, 1971-76, gen. atty., 1977-78; asst. to chmn., CEO The Penn Cen. Corp., N.Y.C., 1979-80, corp. sec., 1980-82; v.p., gen. counsel Gen. Cable Co., Greenwich, Conn., 1982-85; pvt. practice Stamford, Conn., 1985-86, Pelham, N.Y., 1989-91, Greenwich, Conn., 1991-98. Of counsel McCarthy, Fingar, Donovan, Drazen & Smith, White Plains, N.Y., 1986-89. Dep. supr., councilman Town of Pelham, N.Y., 1986-90, budget officer, 1996; dep. mayor, trustee Village of Pelham, 1992-95, village atty., 1995-96; clk. of session, elder, trustee, deacon Huguenot Meml. Ch., Pelham N.Y. With U.S. Navy, 1954-59, USNR, 1959-79. Mem.: Yale Law Sch. Assn. (exec. com. 1988—91, dir. New Eng. 2001—), Assn. Bar City NY, NY Bar Assn., Conn. Bar Assn., St. Andrews Soc. NY (bd. mgrs. 1986—89, 1996—99, chmn. bd. mgrs. 1988—89), The Corinthians (mem. afterguard, dir. The Corinthians Assn., fleet capt. New Eng. fleet, trustee, pres., treas. The Corinthians Endowment Fund), Rotary Club of Newport RI (dir. 2001—), Rotary Club of The Pelhams NY (pres. 1993—94). Corporate, general, General practice, Municipal (including bonds). Home: 68 1/2 Roseneath Ave Newport RI 02840-3849 E-mail: david.mcconnell.law.62@aya.yale.edu.

MCCONNELL, EDWARD BOSWORTH, legal organization administrator, lawyer; b. Greenwich, Conn., Apr. 3, 1920; s. Raymond Arnott and Anna Bell (Lee) McC.; m. Jeanne M. Rotton (dec. 1984); children: Annalee, Marilyn, Edward, Barbara, William; m. Florence M. Leonard, (dec. 1994); stepchildren: Susan L. Little, William R. Leonard, Molly M. Leonard. AB, U. Nebr., 1941, LLB, 1947; MBA with distinction, Harvard U., 1943. Bar: Nebr. 1947, N.J. 1950. Mem. faculty Rutgers U. Sch. Bus. Adminstrn., Newark, 1947-53; assoc. firm Toner, Speakman and Crowley, Newark, N.J., 1949-50; adminstrv. asst. and law sec. to Chief Justice of N.J., 1950-53; adminstrv. dir. Cts. of N.J., Trenton, 1953-73; also standing master Supreme Ct., 1953-73; pres. Nat. Center for State Cts., Williamsburg, 1973-90, bd. dirs., 1980-90, pres. emeritus, 1990—, cons. on ct. mgmt., 1990—. Mem. U.S. Dept. Justice Coun. on Role of Cts. in Am. Soc., 1978-83; mem. adv. com. Dispute Resolution Policy Study, Social Sci. Rsch. Inst., U. So. Calif., 1975-79, Civil Litigation Rsch. Project, U. Wis. and U. So. Calif., 1979-83, nat. judg. edn. program to promote equality for men and women in the cts., 1980—; mem. Nat. Inst. Criminal Justice Task Force, Urban Consortium, 1979-83; participant Access To Justice Colloquium, European Univ. Inst., Florence, Italy, 1979; nat. adv. coun. Ctr. Adminstrn. Justice, Wayne State U., 1973-77; nat. project com. State Jud. Info. Sys. Project SEARCH Group, 1973-76; lectr. Inst. of Local and State Govt. Wharton Sch. U. Pa., 1955-65, Appellate Judges Seminar, Inst. Jud. Adminstrn., NYU, 1962-75; vis. expert UN Asia and Far East Inst., Tokyo, 1971; mem. Cts. Task Force Nat. Adv. Commn. Criminal Justice Standards and Goals, 1971-73; nat. adv. com. D.C. Ct. Mgmt. Project, 1966-70; trustee Inst. Ct. Mgmt., 1969-73, 84-86; chmn. Nat. Conf. Ct. Adminstrv. Officers, 1956; mem. nat. task force on gender bias in cts. Nat. Assn. Women Judge's 1985-90; mem. adv. bd. Nat. Ctr. for Citizen Participation in Adminstrn. of Justice, 1984-90; mem. Nat. Commn. Trial Ct. Performance Standards, 1991-95. Mem. adv. com. on article III Commn. on the Bicentennial of the Constitution, 1989-91; adv. com. Judicary Leadership Coun., 1990-95. Maj. C.E., AUS, 1943-46. Decorated Bronze Star medal; recipient Warren E. Burger award for greatest contbn. to improvement of ct. adminstrn. Inst. for Ct. Mgmt., 1975, Herbert Lincoln Harley award for efficient adminstrn. justice Am. Judicature Soc., 1973, Glenn R. Winters award for outstanding service in jud. adminstrn. Am. Judges Assn., 1974, Tom C. Clark award for outstanding contbns. to field of ct. adminstrn. Nat. Conf. Met. Cts., 1983, Award of Merit Nat. Assn. Ct. Mgmt., 1987, Spl. award, Nat. Assn. Women Judges, 1989, Paul C. Reardon award for disting. svc. Nat. Ctr. for State Cts., 1991, Alumni Achievement award U. Nebr., 1991, Robert B. Yegge award ABA Jud. Divsn. Lawyers Conf., 1997. Fellow Nat. Acad. Pub. Adminstrn. (mem. panel on evaluation budget decentralization project of fed. cts. 1989-91, chmn. panel long range planning in fed. cts. 1991-92, mem. panel for study of fed. trial ct. adminstrv. structure 1995-96); mem. ABA (fellow-at-large, coun. mem. 1960-66, 71-80, house of dels., 1977-80, chmn. com. on oversight and goals 1975-76, chmn. com. on jud. compensation jud. adminstrn. div. 1984-89, chmn. jud. adminstrn. div. 1976-77, sect. of litigation task force on excess litigiousness in Am. 1986-88, task force on reduction of litigation cost and delay, jud. adminstrn. dir. 1984-94, chmn. 1991-94, mem. long range planning com. 1989-94), N.J. Bar Assn., Nebr. Bar Assn., Fellows of Am. Bar Found. (life), Warren E. Burger Soc., Kingsmill (Va.) Golf Club, Kingsmill Tennis Club (pres. 2001), Kingsmill Yacht Club, Order of Coif (hon.), Delta Upsilon, Sigma Delta Phi, Phi Delta Phi. E-mail: ebm80@aol.com.

MCCONNELL, JOHN JAMES, JR., lawyer; b. Providence, May 9, 1958; s. John James Sr. and Mary Jane (Macioci) McC.; m. Sara Elizabeth Shea, Nov. 1, 1986. AB, Brown U., Providence, 1980; JD, Case Western Reserve U., 1983. Bar: R.I. 1983, Mass. 1984, S.C. 1987, D.C. 2000, U.S. Dist. Ct. R.I. 1984, U.S. Dist. Ct. Mass. 1984, U.S. Dist. Ct. D.C. 2000, U.S. Ct. Appeals (1st cir.) 1986, U.S. Ct. Appeals (3d cir.) 1991, U.S. Ct. Appeals (D.C. cir.) 1999. Law clk. R.I. Supreme Ct., Providence, 1983-84; assoc. Mandell, Goodman, Famiglietti & Schwartz, Ltd., Providence, 1984-86, Ness, Motley, Loadholt, Richardson & Poole, Providence, 1986-89; ptnr., 1989—2003; atty. Motley Rice LLC, 2003—. Instr. Am. Inst. Paralegal Studies, Phila., 1985-90; vis. prof. dept. polit. sci. U. R.I., spring 2000; mem. adv. bd. Providence Mediation Ctr., 2000—. Vol. Big Bros. of R.I., Providence, 1984-89; mem. adv. com. Law Related Edn. Program, Providence, 1985-87; sec. George Wiley Ctr., Pawtucket, R.I., 1985-88, bd. dirs., 1985-88; mem. bd. mgmt. Greater Providence YMCA, 1985-86; co-chair ann. fund Trinity Reperatory Theatre, 1999, trustee, 2000—, co-chair govt. affairs com., 2001—; bd. dirs. Planned Parenthood of R.I., 1997-2001; trustee Nat. Dem. Com., 1996—; treas. R.I. PAC, 1995—; mem. fin. com. York for Gov., 1994; acting exec. dir. R.I. Dem. State Com., 1995-97; R.I. chair Bill Bradley for Pres. campaign, 1999-2000. Recipient Childhood Lead Action Project award, 1998, Pres.'s award Nat. Assn. Attys. Gen., 1998, Dorothy Lohman Pub. svc. award 1998, Silver Bullet award R.I. ARC. Mem. ABA, ATLA, NAACP, R.I. Bar Assn., R.I. Trial Lawyers Assn., Mass. Bar Assn., S.C. Bar Assn., S.C. Trial Lawyers Assn., So. Poverty Law Ctr., Greenpeace, Amnesty Internat., Save The Bay, Clean Water Action, St. Thomas Moore Soc. of R.I. Democrat. Roman Catholic. General civil litigation, Environmental, Personal injury (including property damage). Home: 750 Elmgrove Ave Providence RI 02906-4900

MCCONNELL, JOHN WILLIAM, JR., lawyer; b. Bessemer, Ala., Apr. 17, 1921; s. John W. and Elizabeth (Sheridan) McC.; m. Margaret B. Snider, Jan. 7, 1944; children— Margaret E. (Mrs. John Evans), Rebecca L. (Mrs. A.D. Braden), Catherine L., John W. III. AB, U. Ala., 1942, MA, 1946; LL.B., Yale, 1948. Bar: Ala. 1948, D.C. 1977. Atty. Inge, Twitty, Armbrecht & Jackson, Mobile, Ala., 1948-56, Armbrecht, Jackson, McConnell & DeMouy, 1956-65; dir. U.S. Peace Corps, Nigeria, 1965-68; v.p. legal Sea-Land Service, Inc., Menlo Park, N.J., 1968-76; also dir., of counsel Haight, Gardner, Poor & Havens, Washington, 1977-94. Atty. for Reynolds v. Sims on legislative reapportionment, U.S. Supreme Ct., 1963-64 Mem. Ala. Dem. Exec. Com., 1963-65. Served to capt. AUS, 1943-46, 50-52. Mem. ABA, Ala. Bar Assn., D.C. Bar Assn., Maritime Law Assn. Home: 926 Sea Gull Dr Mount Pleasant SC 29464-4145

MCCONNELL, MICHAEL THEODORE, lawyer; b. San Francisco, June 18, 1954; s. Lawrence V. and Ann McConnell. BS, U. Oreg., 1977; JD, U. Denver, 1980. Bar: Colo., Wyo., U.S. Dist. Ct. Colo., U.S. Ct. Appeals (10th cir.), U.S. Supreme Ct., U.S. Dist. Ct. Wyo. Ptnr. Long & Jaudon, Denver, 1980—2001; founding mem., CEO McConnell Siderius Fleischner Houghtaling & Craigmile, LLC, Denver, 2002—. Fellow Am. Coll. Trial Lawyers; mem. ABA, Colo. Bar Assn., Denver Bar Assn., Colo. Def. Lawyers Assn. Appellate, Professional liability, Personal injury (including property damage). Office: McConnell Siderius et al 2401 15th St Ste 300 Denver CO 80202 E-mail: mmcconnell@msfhc.com.

MC CONNELL, MICHAEL W. judge, law educator; b. 1955; BA, Mich. State U., 1976; JD, U. Chgo., 1979. Bar: D.C. 1981. Law clk. to Hon. J. Skelly Wright U.S. Ct. Appeals (D.C. cir.), 1979-80; law clk. to Hon. William J. Brennan Jr. U.S. Supreme Ct., D.C., 1980-81; asst. gen. counsel U.S. Office of Mgmt. and Budget, D.C., 1981-83; asst. to the sol. gen. U.S. Dept. Justice, D.C., 1983-85; asst. prof. U. Chgo., 1984-89, prof., 1989—. Mem. Pres'. Intelligence Oversight Bd., 1988—. Mem. Supreme Ct. Hist. Soc., bd. editors yearbook, 1988—. Mem. Order of the Coif, Phi Beta Kappa, Phi Kappa Phi. Office: Byron White US Courthouse 1823 Stout St Denver CO 80257*

MCCONNELL, NICHOLAS STILLWELL, lawyer; b. Chgo., May 25, 1946; s. James Millholland and Emily (Robinson) McC.; m. Nancy Haines Fifield, Dec. 14, 1968; children: Abigail Haven, Rebecca Fifield. BA, Bowdoin Coll., 1968; JD, George Wash. U., 1972. Bar: Va. Supreme Ct. 1972, U.S. Supreme Ct. 1973, U.S. Ct. Appeals D.C. 1973, D.C. Ct. Appeals 1973, U.S. Dist. Ct. D.C. 1973, Md. Ct. Appeals 1978. Assoc. Jackson, Gray & Laskey, Washington, 1972-78; prin., Jackson & Campbell, P.C., Washington, 1978—, dir. Mem. faculty Nat. Inst. Trial Advocacy, South Bend, Ind., 1984—; dir. Sauls Lithograph Co., Inc., Washington, 1986—. Pres., dir. Combined Health Appeal Nat. Capital Area, Washington, 1980-93; dir. Combined Health Appeal Am., Atlanta, 1993-94. With U.S. Army, 1969-71. Recipient Young Lawyer of Yr. award Bar Assn. D.C., 1982. Mem. Health Lawyers Assn., D.C. Def. Lawyers, Def. Rsch. Inst., Barristeres, Counsellors, D.C. Bar Assn. (pres.-elect 2002-03). Congregationalist. Avocations: tennis, squash, golf, sailing. General civil litigation, Health, Personal injury (including property damage). Home: 5004 Warren St NW Washington DC 20016-4370 Office: Jackson & Campbell PC 1 Lafayette Ctr 300 S Tower 1120 20th St NW Washington DC 20036-3437*

MCCONNELL, R(OBERT) PERRY, lawyer; b. Sept. 27, 1956; BA in Physics, Rice U., 1979, MA in Physics, 1983; JD, U. Houston, 1993. Bar: Tex. 1993, U.S. Dist. Ct. (so. dist.) Tex. 1993, U.S. Patent Office 1994, U.S. Ct. Appeals (Fed. cir.) 1994, U.S. Ct. Appeals (5th cir.) 1997, U.S. Supreme Ct. 1997. Staff cons. Sys. Application Engring., Inc., Houston, 1987-90; assoc. Rosenblatt & Redano, P.C., Houston, 1993-95; adj. prof., assoc. dir. interscholastic moot ct. U. Houston Law Ctr., 1994-98; pres. R. Perry McConnell, P.C., The Woodlands, Tex., 1995—. Adj. prof. U. Houston Law Ctr., 2000—. Office: 9001 Forest Xing Ste F The Woodlands TX 77381-1132

MCCONNICO, STEPHEN E. lawyer; b. Jacksonville, Tex., Apr. 8, 1950; s. Charles Kit and Ruth (Nettle) McC. BA, U. Tex., 1972; JD, Baylor U., 1976. Bar: Tex. 1976. Briefing atty. Tex. Supreme Ct., Austin, 1976-77; assoc. Andrews & Kurth, Houston, 1977-81; ptnr. Scott, Douglass & Mcconnico, Austin, 1981—. Mem. Tex. Supreme Ct. Adv. Com., Austin, 1982-93. Mem. Austin Dem. Forum, 1984. Fellow Am. Coll. Trial Lawyers, Internat. Acad. Trial Lawyers, Internat. Soc. Barristers, Am. Bar Found., Tex. Bar Found.; mem. ABA, Travis County Bar Assn. (bd. dirs. 1986), Tex. Young Lawyers Assn., Austin Young Lawyers Assn. (outstanding young lawyer 1984), Am. Bd. Trial Advocates (pres. Austin chpt. 1994—, Tex. bd. dirs. 1993-94), Headliners Club, Westwood Club. General civil litigation, Personal injury (including property damage). Home: 1403 Hardouin Ave Austin TX 78703-2516 Office: Scott Douglass & McConnico 600 Congress Ave Ste 1500 Austin TX 78701-2589

MCCORD, GUYTE PIERCE, JR., retired judge; b. Tallahassee, Sept. 23, 1914; s. Guyte Pierce and Jean (Patterson) McC.; m. Laura Elizabeth Mack, Dec. 1, 1939 (dec. Oct. 8, 2000); children: Florence Elizabeth, Guyte Pierce III, Edward LeRoy; m. Elizabeth Rogers Green, May 24, 2002. Student, Davidson Coll., 1933-34; BA, JD, U. Fla., 1940. Bar: Fla. 1940. Summer ranger Yosemite Nat. Park, 1936-39; rsch. aide Fla. Supreme Ct., summer 1940; pvt. practice Tallahassee, 1940-48; dep. commr. Fla. Indsl. Commn., 1946-47; pros. atty. Leon County, 1947-48; asst. gen. counsel Fla. Pub. Svc. Commn., 1949-60; judge 2d Jud. Cir. Fla., Tallahassee, 1960-74, Ct. Appeals 1st Dist. Fla., 1974-83, chief judge, 1977-79. Mem. Fla. Senate Pres.'s Council on Criminal Justice 1972; mem. appellate ct. rules com. Fla. Supreme Ct., 1977-78, mem. appellate ct. structure commn. 1978-79. Pres. Murat House Assn., Inc., 1967-69; bd. dirs. Fla. Heritage Found., 1969-70, mem. exec. com., 1965-69; mem. Andrew Jackson staff of Springtime Tallahassee, 1973-74, 84-86, Andrew Jackson, 1987. Comdr. USNR, 1942-46, 52-53. Mem. ABA, Ret. Officers Assn., Fla. Bar, Fla. Conf. Cir. Judges (sec.-treas. 1970, chmn. 1972), Fla. State U. Pres. Club, Kiwanis (dir. 1958-59). Presbyterian (elder 1960—, ch. trustee 1981-86). Home: 2718 Timbertrail Cir Tallahassee FL 32308-5745

MC CORD, JOHN HARRISON, lawyer, educator; b. Oceanside, N.Y., Dec. 22, 1934; s. John Francis and Elsie (Powers) McC.; m. Maureen Ursula Maclean, Dec. 30, 1961; children: John F.X., Paul V., David G., Maureen E. AB, Fordham Coll., 1957; JD magna cum laude, St. John's U., 1960; LLM, U. Ill., 1965. Bar: N.Y. 1960, Ill. 1964. Atty. U.S. Dept. Justice, Washington, 1960-61; mem. faculty U. Ill. Coll. Law, Champaign, 1964—, prof. law, 1965—, assoc. dean for acad. affairs., 1990-92; of counsel Meyer Capel PC, 1998—; auditor/notary Cath. Diocese of Peoria, 2000—. Acad. cons. Ill. Inst. Continuing Legal Edn., 1968-72; vis. prof. law U. N.C., 1975, U. Hawaii, 1976 Author: (with Keeton and O'Connell) Crisis in Car Insurance, 1967, Buying and Selling Small Businesses, 1969, (with O'Byrne) Deskbook for Illinois Estate Planners, 1969, Closely Held Corporations, 1971, (with O'Neill, Pearlman and Stroud) Buying, Selling and Merging Businesses, 1975, (with Lowndes and Kramer) Estate and Gift Taxes, 3d edit, 1974, (with McKee) Federal Income Taxation-A Summary Analysis, 1975, (with Kramer) Problems for Federal Estate and Gift Taxes, 1976, Estate and Gift Tax Reform, 1977, Estate and Gift Tax Summary, 15th edit. 1993, Estate, Gift and Generation-Skipping Taxes, 1999; editor: Dimensions and Academic Freedom, 1969, With All Deliberate Speed: Civil Rights Theory and Reality, 1969, Ill. Law Forum, 1965-69; contbr. articles to profl. jours.; author computer programs for estate planning, 1984—. Served to capt. JAGC, USAF, 1961-64. St. Thomas More fellow St. John's U., 1960. Fellow Am. Coll. Trust and Estate Counsel; mem. ABA (com. CLE and chief reporter for study outline on buying, selling and merging businesses sect. fed. tax 1969-73, com. estate and gift taxes 1973-84, chmn. subcom. gross estate issues 1976-78, subcom. tax reform 1978-84), Ill. Bar Assn. (exec. coun. fed. tax sect. 1966-73, chmn. sect. 1971-72, exec. coun. bus. planning sect. 86-91), Champaign County Bar Assn., Am. Arbitration Assn. (nat. panel arbitrators 1969-90), Eastern Ill. Estate Planning Coun. (pres. 1970-71), U. Miami Inst. Estate Planning (adv. coun. 1979-87), Assn. Am. Law Schs. (fed. taxation roundtable coun. 1969-72), Ill. Inst. CLE (bd. dirs. 1991-2000, estate planning adv. com. 2000—), U.S. Navy League, Order of Coif. Home: 104 E Sherwin Dr Urbana IL 61802-7133 Office: U Ill Coll Law Champaign IL 61820 E-mail: jmccord@law.uiuc.edu.

MCCORKINDALE, DOUGLAS HAMILTON, lawyer, publishing company executive; b. N.Y.C., June 14, 1939; s. William Douglas and Kathleen (Miles) McC.; m. Nancy Walsh, Dec. 24, 1991; children by previous marriage: Laura Ann, Heather Jean. BA, Columbia U., 1961, LLB cum laude (Harlan Fiske Stone scholar), 1964. Bar: N.Y. 1964. Assoc. Thacher Proffitt & Wood, N.Y.C., 1964-70, ptnr., 1970-71; gen. counsel, sec. Gannett Co., Inc., Arlington, Va., 1971-72, v.p., gen. counsel, sec., 1972-77, sr. v.p. fin. and law, 1977-79, sr. v.p., chief fin. officer, 1979-83, pres. diversified media div., 1980-83, exec. v.p., 1983, vice chmn., CFO, 1984—, chief adminstrv. officer, 1986—, vice chmn., pres., 1997—, CEO, 2000—, chmn., pres., CEO, 2001—. Bd. dirs. AP, Continental Airlines Inc., Lockheed Martin Corp., The Global Govt. Plus Fund Inc., Prudential Global Genesis Fund Inc., Prudential Natural Resources Fund Inc., Prudential Multi-Sector Fund Inc.; trustee Prudential Equity Income Fund, Prudential Allocation Fund, Prudential Mcpl. Bond Fund, Mut. Ins. Co. Ltd. Mem. ABA (chmn. com. Exch. Art of 1934 1971-73), Newspaper Assn. Am., Pine Valley Golf Club, Mid Ocean Club, Burning Tree Club. Corporate, general, Mergers and acquisitions, Securities. Office: Gannett Co Inc 7950 Jones Branch Dr Mc Lean VA 22102

MC CORMACK, FRANCIS XAVIER, lawyer, former oil company executive; b. Bklyn., July 9, 1929; s. Joseph and Blanche V. (Dengel) Mc C.; m. Margaret V. Hynes, Apr. 24, 1954; children: Marguerite, Francis Xavier, Sean Michael, Keith John, Cecelia Blanche, Christopher Thomas. AB cum laude, St. Francis Coll., Bklyn., 1951; LLB, Columbia U., 1954. Bar: N.Y. 1955, Mich. 1963, Calif. 1974, Pa. 1975. Assoc. Cravath, Swaine & Moore, N.Y.C., 1956-62; sr. atty. Ford Motor Co., 1962-64, asst. gen. counsel, 1970-72; v.p., gen. counsel, sec. Philco-Ford Corp., 1964-72; v.p., gen. counsel Atlantic Richfield Co., 1972-73, sr. v.p., gen. counsel, 1973-94. Editor Columbia U. Law Rev., 1954. Decorated commendatore Ordine al Merito (Italy); Stone scholar Columbia U., 1954. Mem. Calif. Club, Chancery Club, Annandale Golf Club. Home and Office: 975 Singingwood Dr Arcadia CA 91006-1924

MCCORMACK, HOWARD MICHAEL, lawyer; b. Bklyn., Aug. 26, 1932; s. Michael Francis and Sarah Catherine (Russell) McC.; m. Patricia Anne Riley, Aug. 24, 1957; children: Sean M., Maureen A. MacDougall. AB cum laude, Coll. Holy Cross, Worcester, Mass., 1954; LLB, Fordham U., N.Y.C., 1961; LLM in Internat. Law, NYU, 1965. Bar: N.Y. 1962, U.S. Dist. Ct. (so. and ea. dists.) N.Y. 1963, U.S. Ct. Appeals (2d cir.) 1964, U.S. Ct. Appeals (4th cir.) 1977, U.S. Ct. Appeals (1st cir.), U.S. Supreme Ct. 1966, U.S. Dist. Ct. Md. 1975, U.S. Dist. Ct. (so. dist) Tex. 1983, U.S. Dist. Ct. Conn. 2001, U.S. Ct. Appeals (5th cir.) 1984, U.S. Ct. Mil. Appeals 1994. Acct. exec. C.R. Black Jr. Corp., N.Y.C., 1958-61; ptnr. Zock, Petrie, et al., N.Y.C., 1961-71; maritime counsel Bethlehem Steel Corp., N.Y.C., 1972-79; ptnr. Healy & Baillie LLP, N.Y.C., 1979—; adj. prof. law Fordham U. Adj. prof. law Touro Law Sch. Contbr. articles to profl. publs. Lt. (j.g.) USN, 1954-57; comdr. JAGC, USNR, ret. Mem.: Average Adjusters Assn. U.S. (chmn. 2001—02), Maritime Law Assn. U.S. (pres. 1998—2000). Avocations: tennis, golf, wine studies. Admiralty, Federal civil litigation, Insurance. Office: Healy & Baillie LLP New York NY 10006 E-mail: hmccormack@healy.com.

MCCORMACK, JOHN ROBERT, lawyer; b. Middletown, Conn., Mar. 30, 1962; s. John Francis and Ann Jane (Monarca) McC.; m. Cristina Dorthea Dwyer, Sept. 27, 1986; children: Kevin, Cara. BS, Univ. Conn., 1984; JD, Stetson Univ., 1990. Assoc. Kelly & McKee, P.A., Tampa, Fla., 1990-92; ptnr. Wiggins & McCormack, Clearwater, Fla., 1992-94; sole practitioner J. Robert McCormack, P.A., Clearwater, Fla., 1994-00; ptnr. Persante & McCormack, P.A., 2000—. Editor: Labor and Employment in Florida, 1990, Critical Issues in Labor and Employment Labor, 1990. Mem. ABA (labor and employment law sect.), Fla. Bar Labor and Employment Law Sect., Barney Masterson Inn of Ct. (treas. 1998-99), Clearwater Bar Employment Law Com. (co-chair 1997-99). Administrative and regulatory, Labor (including EEOC, Fair Labor Standards Act, labor-management relations, NLRB, OSHA). Office: Persante & McCormack P A 2555 Enterprise Rd Bldg 15 Clearwater FL 33763

MCCORMACK, MICHAEL, state supreme court justice; b. Omaha, July 20, 1939; JD, Creighton U., 1963. Asst. pub. defender, Douglas County, Nebr., 1963-66; pvt. practice Omaha, 1966-97; justice Nebr. Supreme Ct., 1997—. Office: State Capitol Bldg Rm 2218 Lincoln NE 68509 also: PO Box 98910 Lincoln NE 68509

MCCORMICK, DAVID ARTHUR, lawyer; b. McKeesport, Pa., Oct. 26, 1946; s. Arthur Paul and Eleanor Irene (Gibson) McC. BA, Westminster Coll., 1967; JD, Duquesne U., 1973; MBA, U. Pa., 1975. Bar: Pa. 1973, D.C. 1978, U.S. Ct. Appeals (3d cir.) 1977, U.S. Ct. Appeals (4th and D.C. cirs.) 1980, U.S. Supreme Ct. 1980. Asst. commerce counsel Penn Cen. R.R., Phila., 1973-76; assoc. labor counsel Consol. Rail Corp., Phila., 1976-78; atty. Dept. Army, Washington, 1978—. Author various geneal. and hist. works; contbr. articles to profl. jours. Mem. ATLA, Pa. Bar Assn., Phila. Bar Assn., D.C. Bar Assn., Assn. Transp. Practitioners, Soc. Cin. (Del. chpt.), SAR (Pitts. chpt.), Am. Legion, Res. Officers Assn., Masons, Phi Alpha Delta, Theta Chi. Presbyterian.

MCCORMICK, HOMER L., JR., lawyer; b. Frederick, Md., Nov. 11, 1928; s. Homer Lee McCormick and Rosebelle Irene Biser; m. Jacquelyn R.; children: Deidre Ann and Thomas Lee. Student, George Washington U., 1946-48; AB, San Jose State U., 1951; JD, U. Calif., San Francisco, 1961. Bar: Calif. 1961, U.S. Dist. Ct. Ctrl. Dist. Calif. 1972, U.S. Dist. No. Calif. 1961, U.S. Dist. Ct., So. Dist. Calif. 1976, U.S. Dist. Ct. of Appeals (9th cir. 1961), U.S. Tax Ct. 1977, U.S. Ct. Claims 1977, U.S. Supreme Ct. 1977. Atty. Holiway Jones State of Calif., 1961-63; atty. assoc. Rutan & Tucker, Santa Ana, Calif., 1963-66, atty. ptnr., 1966-70, atty., sr. ptnr. Costa Mesa, Calif., 1970-88, dept. head pub. law, 1974-88, mng. ptnr., 1984-88; founding ptnr., sr. ptnr. McCormick, Kidman & Behrens, Costa Mesa, 1988—. Arbitrator Am. Arbitration Assn., 1966-88; judge pro tem Orange County Superior Ct., 1975, 81, 84; spkr., lectr. Cal. Continuing Edn. of the Bar, 1976-88; profl. designation Internat. Right of Way Assn.; elected mem. Cal. Condemnation Lawyers, 1994—. Contbg. author: Real Property Remedies, 1982; contbr. articles to profl. jours. Mem. bd. govs. Bus. Com. Arts, Orange County Philharm. Soc. Lt. USMCR, 1951-56; pilot, Korea. Named Alumnus of Year Hastings Law Sch., 1992. Mem. ABA (com. chair 1991), Am. Bd. Trial Adv. (pres. O.C. chpt. 1973), Orange City Atty. Assn. (pres. 1972), Fed. Bar Assoc., Consumer Attys. Calif., Am. Judicature Soc., Orange County Bar Assn. (com. chair 1991-92), Orange County Bus. Trial Lawyers, Order Coif, Thurston Soc., Hastings Alumni Assn. (pres. 1973), Springs Country Club, Delta Theta Pi. Republican. Episcopalian. Avocations: boating, fishing, flying, golf, foreign travel. General civil litigation, Condemnation (eminent domain), Property, real (including real estate development, water).

MCCORMICK, HUGH THOMAS, lawyer; b. McAlester, Okla., Nov. 24, 1944; s. Hugh O. and Lois (McGucken) McC.; m. Suzanna G. Weingarten, Dec. 5, 1975; 1 child, John B. BA, U. Mich., 1968; JD, Rutgers U., 1977; LLM in Taxation, Georgetown U., 1980. Bar: N.Y. 1977, D.C. 1979, Maine 1981. Atty. office chief counsel interpretative divsn. IRS, Washington, 1977-81; assoc. Perkins, Thompson, Hinkley & Keddy, Portland, Maine, 1981-83, LeBoeuf, Lamb, Leiby & MacRae, N.Y.C., 1983-88, counsel, 1989-91; ptnr. LeBoeuf, Lamb, Greene & MacRae, L.L.P., N.Y.C., 1992—. Dir. Ins. Tax. Conf., 1993—, pres., 2002—. Mem. bd. contbrs. and advisors Jour. of Taxation of Investments; contbr. articles to profl. jours. Trustee U.S. Team Handball Found., N.J., 1985-95. Fellow Am. Bar Found.; mem. ABA (chmn. com. on taxation of ins. cos. 1989, chmn. subcom. sect. of taxation 1989-96, mem. torts and ins. practice sect., sect. on taxation), D.C. Bar Assn. Democrat. Insurance, Corporate taxation. Home: 555 Pelham Manor Rd Pelham NY 10803-2525 Office: LeBoeuf Lamb Greene MacRae LLP 125 W 55th St New York NY 10019-5369 E-mail: hmccormi@llgm.com.

MCCORMICK, JOHN HOYLE, lawyer; b. Pensacola, Fla., July 30, 1933; s. Clyde Hoyle and Orrie Brooks (Frink) McC.; m. Patricia McCall, Dec. 27, 1974. BS, U. Fla., 1955; JD, Stetson U., 1958. Bar: Fla. 1958. Ptnr. McCormick, Drury & Scaff, Jasper, Fla., 1958-74; county atty., 1973—; sr. ptnr. McCormick, Drury & Scaff, Jasper, 1974-91; pvt. practice Jasper, 1991—. County judge, Hamilton County, Fla., 1960-72; local counsel So. Ry. System, 1968—, CSX, Ry., 1972—; atty. Hamilton County Devel. Authority, 1970-91; bd. dirs. 1st Fed. Savs. Bank Fla.; bd. dirs., v.p., atty. Hamilton County Bank. Mayor City of White Springs, Fla., 1959; pres. Hamilton County C. of C., Jasper, 1961. Mem. Phi Delta Phi. Lodges: Masons. Democrat. Methodist. Avocations: gardening, motorhome camping, college football. Banking, Government contracts and claims, Probate (including wills, trusts). Home: 403 2nd Ave NW Jasper FL 32052-6687 Office: 215 2nd St NE Jasper FL 32052-6616 Address: PO Drawer O Jasper FL 32052-0695

MCCORMICK, KATHRYN ELLEN, prosecutor; b. Milw., Dec. 27, 1952; d. James Patrick and Kathryn Goss McCormick; 1 child, Joshua Patrick-Edwin Davis. BS cum laude, Ariz. State U., 1989; JD, U. Ariz., 1994. Bar: Ariz. 1994, U.S. Dist. Ct. Ariz. 1994; cert. peace officer Ariz. Police officer Scottsdale Police Dept., Ariz., 1972—77; investigator Maricopa County Atty.'s Office, Phoenix, 1977—80; spl. agt. Ariz. Atty. Gen.'s Office, Phoenix, 1980—91; def. atty. Maricopa County Pub. Defenders Office, Phoenix, 1994—98; prosecutor Securities divsn. Ariz. Corp. Commn., Phoenix, 1998—2002; dep. county atty. Office of County Counsel Govt. Rels., Phoenix, 2002—. Mem. consumer protection com. Ariz. State Bar, Phoenix, 1999—. Mem., pres. Tumbleweed Ctr. for Youth Devel., Phoenix, 1998—; commr. Phoenix Women's Commn., 1999—. Named Police Office of the Yr., Phoenix Exchange Club, 1975. Mem.: Ariz. Alliance for the Mentally Ill, Nat. Alliance for the Mentally Ill, Ariz. Women Lawyers Assn. Avocations: gardening, swimming, hiking, reading. Home: 2034 W Edgemont Phoenix AZ 85009-1944 Office: Office of County Counsel 222 North Central Ste 1100 Phoenix AZ 85004

MCCORMICK, MICHAEL JERRY, retired judge; b. Fort Lewis, Wash., Oct. 17, 1945; s. Thaddeus Charles and Geraldine (Fogle) McC.; m. Katleen Karen Kelley, Sept. 2, 1967; children: Patrick Kelley, Karen Michelle. BA, U. Tex.-Austin, 1967; JD, St. Mary's U., 1970. Bar: Tex. 1970. Briefing atty. Tex. Ct. Criminal Appeals, 1970-71; asst. dist. atty. Travis County, Tex., 1971-72; exec. dir. Tex. Dist. and County Attys. Assn., Austin, 1972-80; judge Tex. Ct. Criminal Appeals, Austin, 1981—2001, chief presiding judge, 1988-2000, sr. judge, 2001—; of counsel Law Office Kelley McCormick, Lockhart, Tex., 2002—. Dir. Tex. Ctr. for Judiciary, 1983; vice-chmn. Tex. Commn. on Sentencing, 1984; mem. Tex. Jud. Budget Bd., 1983; co-chair Tex. Jud. Coun., 1997—. Author: Branch's Annotated Penal Code, 3d edit., Criminal Forms and Trial Manual, 10th edit., Tex. Justice Court Deskbook, Tex. Constables Civil Process Handbook. Pres. Joslin (Tex.) P.T.A., 1981-82. Served with U.S. Army, 1966-72. Named Rosewood Gavel Outstanding Jurist, St. Mary's U. Sch. Law, 1984, Disting. Law Grad., 1992. Mem. State Bar Tex., Tex. Dist. and County Attys. Assn. Office: 119 W San Antonio St Lockhart TX 78644*

MCCORMICK, THOMAS A., JR., city attorney; BBA, U. N.C., 1967, JD, 1973. Asst. to spkr. N.C. House Reps., 1973-74; city atty. Office of the City Atty., Raleigh, N.C., 1976—. Office: Office of City Attorney Raleigh Mcpl Bldg Rm 218 222 W Hargett St Raleigh NC 27601-1316

MCCOTTER, CHARLES KENNEDY, JR., lawyer; b. New Bern, N.C., Oct. 29, 1946; s. Charles Kennedy and Lucy (Dunn) McCotter; m. Patricia Byrum, Aug. 3, 1968; children: Virginia Byrum, Patricia Dunn. BS in Bus., U. N.C., 1968, JD, 1971. Bar: N.C. 1971, U.S. Dist. Ct. (ea. dist.) N.C. 1971, U.S. Ct. Appeals (4th cir.) 1973; lic. mcht. marine master. Law clk. to judge U.S. Dist. Ct. (ea. dist.) N.C., 1971—72; pvt. practice New Bern, 1973, 1995—97; ptnr. McCotter and Mayo, New Bern, 1974—79; U.S. magistrate judge U.S. Dist. Ct. (ea. dist.) N.C., 1979—95; ptnr. McCotter and McAfee, PLLC, New Bern, 1998, McCotter, McAfee & Ashton, New Bern, 1998—2002, McCotter, Ashton & Smith, P.A., New Bern, 2002—. Permanent del. to 4th Cir. Jud. Conf.; chmn. local rules com. for revision of local admiralty rules, 1985; mem. Ea. Dist. N.C. Com. on Arraignment Procedures, 1986; jud. rep. to local adv. com. Implementation of Civil Justice Reform Act, 1991—94; lectr. in field. Bd. visitors U. N.C. Marine Scis. Inst.; mem. law alumni bd. U. N.C. Mem.: ABA, Maritime Law Assn., Craven County Bar Assn., N.C. Bar Assn., N.C. Trial Lawyers Assn., New Bern C. of C., New Bern Hist. Soc., Ea. N.C. Inn of Ct., Rotary. Episcopalian. Federal civil litigation. Office: PO Box 12800 New Bern NC 28561-2800

MCCOURT, JOYCE ELISE, lawyer; b. Framingham, Mass., Jan. 31, 1949; d. Paul Joseph and Joyce Loraine McCourt; m. Ronald Richard Perry, June 29, 1980 (dec. July 1997). BA in Psychology, U. Mass., 1971; JD, Boston Coll., 1976. Bar: Mass. 1977 (1st and 2d cirs.). Asst. regional counsel Dept. HHS, Boston, 1976—. Home: 291 Lions Mouth Rd Amesbury MA 01913-5426 Office: Dept HHS Rm 2250 JFK Bldg Boston MA 02203 E-mail: JMcCourt@os.dhhs.gov.

MCCOWN, FRANK J. judge; b. Ironton, Ohio, Feb. 6, 1940; s. Henry Anderson and Adrienne (Tucker) McC.; m. 2d, Tyna L. Dilley, Mar. 3, 1979; 1 son, Brigham A. B.S. in Bus. Adminstrn., Miami U., 1962; J.D., Ohio State U., 1964. Bar: Ohio 1965. Ptnr., Crowe & McCown, Ironton, 1965— ; atty. City of Ironton, 1966-82; asst. atty. gen. State of Ohio, 1971-81; instr. law Shawnee State Coll., Ohio U.-Ironton, 1974—; judge of the ct. Author (column) It's the Law, Ironton Tribune. Mem. Democratic Exec. Com., Lawrence County, Ohio, 1965— ; former Dem. candidate for Ohio Ho. of Reps.; campaign chmn. United Way of Lawrence County, 1981-82. Recipient Disting. Svc. award Ohio State U., 1967; Lawrence County Assocs. award Lawrence County Bd. Realtors, 1981; named several times Outstanding Lawyer, Lawrence County Legal Secs. Mem. Ohio State Bar Assn., Lawrence County Bar Assn. (past pres.), Ohio Land Title Assn., Masons, Kiwanis (past pres.), Phi Alpha Delta (internat. pres. 1978-80, chmn. bd. 1980-82). Methodist. Home: 111 S 4th St Ironton OH 45638-1522 E-mail: judgemac@hotmail.com.

MCCOY, DOUGLAS LEON, lawyer; b. Atlanta, Mar. 15, 1957; s. Johnny L. and Nell (Wilson) McC.; m. Karen Delchamps, Jan. 3, 1987. BS, U. Tenn., 1979; JD, Duke U., 1982. Bar: Ala. 1982, U.S. Ct. Appeals (2d, 5th and 11th cirs.). Assoc. Hand, Arendall, LLC, Mobile, Ala., 1982—87, ptnr., 1987—. Lectr. in field. Mem. ABA (litig. sect.), Mobile Bar Assn. Methodist. General civil litigation, Commercial, contracts (including sales of goods; commercial financing), Securities. Office: Hand Arendall LLC 107 St Francis St Ste 2600 Mobile AL 36602

MCCOY, JERRY JACK, lawyer; b. Pitts., Aug. 4, 1941; s. Norris and Martha (Jack) McC.; m. Alexandra Armstrong; children: MadeleineRena, Allison Norah, Jonathan Howard. BS, W.Va. U., 1963; LLB, Duke U., 1966; LLM in Taxation, N.Y.U., 1967. Bar: D.C. 1968, N.Y. 1967. Assoc. Silverstein & Mullens, Washington, 1968-72, ptnr., 1973-92; of counsel Reid and Priest, N.Y.C., Washington, 1992-94; sole practitioner Washington, 1994—. Adj. law faculty U. Miami, Fla., 1983—, Law Ctr. Georgetown U., 1996—. Co-author: Family Foundation Handbook, 2001; exec. editor Tax Management, Estates Gifts and Trusts series, Washington, 1972—92, co-founder, co-editor Charitable Gift Planning News, Dallas, 1983—, Family Foundation Advisor, 2002—; contbr. Mem. ABA, Am. Law Inst., Am. Coll. Trust and Estate Counsel (past chair com. on charitable planning and exempt orgns.), Am. Coll. Tax Counsel. Democrat. Jewish. Estate planning, Non-profit and tax-exempt organizations, Estate taxation. Home: 3560 Winfield Ln NW Washington DC 20007-2368 Office: PO Box 66491 Washington DC 20035-6491 E-mail: mccoylaw@aol.com.

MCCOY, JOHN JOSEPH, lawyer; b. Cin., Mar. 15, 1952; s. Raymond F. and Margaret T. (Hohmann) McC. BS in Math. summa cum laude, Xavier U., 1974; JD, U. Chgo., 1977. Bar: Ohio 1977, D.C. 1980. Ptnr. Taft, Stettinius & Hollister, Cin., 1977—. Lectr. Greater Cin. C. of C., 1984. Pro bono rep. Jr. Achievement Greater Cin., 1978; fund raiser Dan Beard coun. Boy Scouts Am., 1983; fund raising team leader Cin. Regatta, Cin. Ctr. Devel. Disorders, 1983; account mgr. United Appeal, Cin., 1984; mem. green areas trust adv. com. Village of Indian Hill, 1994-98. Mem. ABA, Ohio State Bar Assn. (banking, comml. and bankruptcy law com., corp. law com., fed. ct. practice com.), Cin. Bar Assn. (fed. cts., common pleas cts. and negligence law coms., trustee Vol. Lawyers for the Poor Found. 1994—, chmn. 1996-97), Cin. Inn. of Ct. (barrister 1984-86), Cin. Athletic Club (pres. bd. trustees 1986-89, nominating com. 1989—), Rhodesian Ridgeback Club of the U.S. (bd. dirs. 2000—). Federal civil litigation, State civil litigation, Corporate, general.

MCCOY, REAGAN SCOTT, oil company executive, lawyer; b. Port Arthur, Tex., Nov. 25, 1945; s. William Murray and Elizabeth (Gilbert) McC.; m. Pat Kowalski, June 21, 1969; 1 child, Traci. BCE, Ga. Inst. Tech., 1968; JD, Loyola U., 1972. Bar: Tex. 1972, La. 1978; registered profl. engr., Tex., La. Structural engr. McDermott Inc., New Orleans, 1966-72, data processing mgr. London, 1972-76, cons. engr. New Orleans, 1976-79; adminstrv. mgr. Concord Oil Co., San Antonio, 1979-81, v.p., 1981—. Mem. World Affairs Coun., Tex. Luth. U. Bus. Sch. Adv. Com. Treas. Countryside San Pedro Recreation Club, 1981-82; bd. dirs. Countryside San Pedro Homeowners Assn., 1984-86; v.p. Bluffview Homeowners Assn., 1998-99, pres., 1999—; pres. San Antonio Baylor U. Parents League, 1995-96; mem. Tex. State Bd. Pub. Accountancy, 1997-2003, chair CPE com., 2002-03; bd. dirs. Consumer Credit Counseling Svc. Greater San Antonio, 2000—, treas., 2003-, exec. com., 2003-. Fellow Tau Beta Pi; mem. ABA, NSPE, ASCE, Am. Assn. Profl. Landmen (San Antonio chpt. treas. 1990-91, v.p. 1991-93, pres. 1993-94), La. State Bar Assn., Tex. State Bar, San Antonio Bar Assn. (natural resources com. treas. 1986-87, vice chmn. 1987-88, chmn. 1988-89), Tex. Soc. Profl. Engrs., La. Soc. Profl. Engrs., So. Tex. Assn. Divsn. Order Analysts (v.p. 1993, pres. 1994, 98, bd. dirs. 1999—), Fin Execs. Inst. (treas. 1991-92, sec. 1992-93, v.p. 1993-94, pres. 1994-95, bd. dirs. 1995-97), Soc. Mining Engrs., Real Estate Fin. Soc. (bd. dirs. 1986-89, v.p. 1987-88, pres. 1988-89, 98-2000, pres. coun.), Adminstrv. Mgmt. Soc. (pres. 1985-86, 89-90), Plz. Club, Sonterra Club, Tex. Ind. Producers and Royalty Owners Assn., Am. Petroleum Inst. (South Tex. chpt. pres. 1997-2000). Presbyterian. Avocations: water sports, reading, woodworking. Home: 14103 Bluff Manor Dr San Antonio TX 78216-7976 Office: Concord Oil Co 105 S Saint Marys St Ste 1500 San Antonio TX 78205-2898

MCCRACKEN, EUGENE LUKE, lawyer; b. Savannah, Ga., Aug. 9, 1932; s. John and Estelle (Powers) M.; m. Helen Kelly Morekis, May 9, 1964; A.A., Armstrong State Coll., 1952; BA, Mercer U., 1954; LLB, U. Ga., 1957. Bar: Ga. 1958, U.S. Dist. Ct. (so. dist.) Ga. 1959, U.S. Ct. Appeals (11th cir.) 1961, U.S. Supreme Ct. 1978. Assoc. Brannen, Clark & Hester, Savannah, 1958-64; sole practice, Savannah, 1964—; asst. dist. atty. Chatham County, Ga., 1963-64; asst. city atty. City of Savannah, 1970-74; judge pro tem Juvenile Ct. of Chatham County, 1974-80. Bd. dirs. United Way of Savannah, 1973-74; mem. Chatham County Zoning Bd. Appeals, 1967-70; chmn. Chatham County Reps., 1985-87, 1st congl. dist. Ga. Rep. Party, 1987-89. Named Savannah's Outstanding Young Man of Yr., Jaycees, 1966; recipient Sword of Hope award Am. Cancer Soc., 1968. Mem. State Bar of Ga., Armstrong State Coll. Alumni Assn. (pres. 1973, 83), Hibernian Soc. St. Andrews Soc. Savannah, First City Club. Roman Catholic. General practice, Probate (including wills, trusts), Personal injury (including property damage). Home: 16 Brightwater Dr Savannah GA 31410-3301 Office: 223 W York St Savannah GA 31401-3636

MCCRAY, HUBERT TODD, lawyer; b. Beaumont, Tex., Oct. 20, 1962; s. Hubert Winston and Dorothy Maie (Todd) McC. Student, Lamar U., 1981-84; BBA, U. Tex., 1986; JD, St. Mary's U., 1990. Bar: Tex. 1990; bd. cert. in criminal law, Tex. Law clerk Heard, Goggan, Blair, Williams, Houston, 1989; rsch. and writing asst., instr. St. Mary's U. Sch. Law, San Antonio, 1989-90; asst. county atty. Grayson County Atty., Sherman, Tex., 1990-92; asst. criminal dist. atty. Bexar County Criminal Dist. Atty., San Antonio, 1992-94; atty. pvt. practice, San Antonio, 1994—. 1st chair misdemeanor prosecutor Grayson County Atty., Sherman, 1991, 1st chair felony prosecutor, 1991-92. Explorer post advisor Texoma counsel Boy Scouts Am., Sherman, 1991-92, explorer post com. Alamo counsel, San Antonio, 1992. Mem. ABA, Tex. Dist. and County Attys. Assn., San Antonio Bar Assn., Grayson County Bar Assn., Tex. Criminal Def. Lawyers Assn., Bexar County Criminal Def. Lawyers Assn. Home: PO Box 830804 San Antonio TX 78283-0804 Office: 110 E Nueva Stumberg Sq San Antonio TX 78204

MCCREADY, GUY MICHAEL, lawyer; b. Tulsa, Mar. 21, 1960; s. John McCready and Patsy Ann (Xander) Ryman; children: Sean, Loren. BA, Ft. Hays State U., 1984; JD, Washburn Law Sch., 1987; diploma, Nat. Inst. for Trial Advocacy, 1992. Bar: Colo. 1987, U.S. Dist. Ct. Colo. 1989, U.S. Ct. Appeals (10th cir.) 1990. Pvt. practice, Colorado Springs, 1987—. Prof. ethics U. So. Colo., Colorado Springs, 1991; mem. jud. com. to reform juvenile ct. procedure, 2000. Author: Manitou, 2002; author: (asst.) Yearbook of School Law, 1987; contbr. articles to profl. jours. Vol. Pikes Peak Legal Svcs., Colorado Springs, 1987—. Mem. Assn. Trial Lawyers Am., Colo. Trial Lawyers Assn., Colo. Bar Assn., El Paso County Bar Assn., Order of Barristers. Avocations: skiing, hiking, jogging. General civil litigation, Constitutional, Personal injury (including property damage).

Office: Ste 1100 2 N Cascade Ave Colorado Springs CO 80903 Home: 102 Alpine Trl Manitou Springs CO 80829

MCCREEDY, EDWIN JAMES, lawyer; b. Atlanta, Dec. 29, 1939; s. Harold D. McCreedy and Annette Raymond (Denton) Chapman; m. Linda Jandora, Mar. 20, 1965; children: James M., Matthew B. BA, Columbia U., 1961; JD, Fordham U., 1968. Bar: N.J. 1968, U.S. Supreme Ct. 1982, cert. civil trial atty. N.J. Supreme Ct. 1982. Ptnr. McCreedy & Cox, Cranford, NJ, 1984—. Pres. Richard J. Hughes Inn of Court, 1991-92; mem. civil practice com. Supreme Ct. N.J., 1985-96. Fellow ABA, Internat. Soc. Barristers, Internat. Acad. Trial Lawyers, Am. Coll. Trial Lawyers (chair state com, 1995-97); mem. N.J. State Bar Assn. (trustee 1997-2001, chmn. jud. adminstrn. com. 1994-96, treas. 2001, 1st v.p. 2002, pres. elect 2002-03), Trial Attys. N.J. (trustee), Union County Bar Assn. (pres. 1987). Avocations: golf, travel. State civil litigation, Personal injury (including property damage), Professional liability. Office: McCreedy & Cox 6 Commerce Dr Ste 13 Cranford NJ 07016-3551

MCCRIMMON, TERESA NORVELL, lawyer; b. Kerrville, Tex. d. Allen James Hammons and Florence Marie Mills; children: David I. Banyard, Derek A. Banyard; m. James P. McCrimmon, Sept. 7, 1996. AB cum laude, Harvard U., 1976; JD, Regent U., 1988. Bar: Va., 1989. Staff atty. Tidewater Legal Aid, Norfolk, Va., 1989-90; assoc. city atty. City of Virginia Beach, Va., 1990—. Mem. Va. State Bar, Virginia Beach Bar Assn., Va. Assn. Def. Attys. Office: City Atty's Office Ste 260 Municipal Ctr Virginia Beach VA 23456

MCCROHON, CRAIG, lawyer; b. Harvey, Ill., Oct. 17, 1961; s. Maxwell and Nancy McCrohon. BA, Harvard U., 1984; postgrad., London Sch. Econs., 1988; JD, MBA, U. Pa., 1989. Bar: Ill. 1989, U.S. Dist. Ct. (no. dist.) Ill. 1989. Ptnr. Holland & Knight, Chgo., 2001—. Mem. Ill. .Gov.'s Transition Team Venture Capital, 2002. Editor: Let's Go: USA, 1983. Ill. Gov. transition team Venture Capital and Regulated Industries, 2002. Mem.: Tech. Execs. Roundtable (pres. 1996—2001), Ill. C. of C. (working group econ. devel. com. 1992), Chgo. Bar Assn. (chmn. com. on consumer fin. svcs. 1991—92). Banking, Computer, Corporate, general. Home: 2 E 8th St Apt 2708 Chicago IL 60605-2134 Office: 131 S Dearbourn St Chicago IL 60603

MCCRORY, JOHN BROOKS, retired lawyer; b. St. Cloud, Minn., Oct. 23, 1925; s. John Raymond and Mary Lee (Rutter) McC.; m. Margaret Joan Dickson, Sept. 4, 1954 (dec. Apr. 1957); 1 child, William B.; m. Elizabeth Ann Quick, June 27, 1959; children— John B., Ann Elizabeth BA, Swarthmore Coll., 1948; JD, U. Pa., 1951. Bar: N.Y. 1952, D.C. 1985. Assoc. Donovan, Leisure, Newton, Lumbard & Irvine, N.Y.C., 1951-52, Nixon, Hargrave, Devans & Doyle, Rochester, N.Y., 1952-62, ptnr., 1963-92; ret., 1992. Author: Constitutional Privilege in Libel Law, 1977-90. Served to lt. comdr. USNR, 1943-47, PTO Fellow Am. Coll. Trial Lawyers; mem. ABA, Monroe County Bar Assn., N.Y. State Bar Assn., D.C. Bar Assn. Democrat. Quaker. Address: 25 Kendal Dr Kennett Square PA 19348-2321 Office: Nixon Peabody LLP Clinton Sq PO Box 31051 Rochester NY 14603-1051

MCCULLOUGH, EDWARD EUGENE, patent agent, inventor; b. Baldwin, N.D., June 4, 1923; s. Elmer Ellsworth and Emma Izelda (Nixon) McC. BA, U. Minn., 1957; postgrad., Utah State U., 1965. Machine designer Sperry Rand Corp., Mpls., 1952-58; patent adminstr. Thiokol Corp., Brigham City, Utah, 1958-86, patent cons., 1986; pvt. practice, 1986—. Patentee 34 U.S. patents including instruments for making perspective drawings, apparatus for forming ignition surfaces in solid propellant motors, passive communications satellite or similar article, flexible bearings and process for their manufacture, rocket nozzel support and pivoting system, cavity-shaping machine, others. Pianist Aldersgate Meth. Ch., Brigham City, 1959—. Staff Sgt. U.S. Army, 1949-52. Decorated Korean War Svc. medal, two battle stars. Avocations: philosophy, music composition, hiking in the mountains. Patent. E-mail: ed@burgoyne.com.

MCCULLOUGH, RALPH CLAYTON, II, lawyer, educator; b. Daytona Beach, Fla., Mar. 28, 1941; s. Ralph C. and Doris (Johnson) McC.; m. Elizabeth Grier Henderson, Apr. 5, 1986; children from previous marriage: Melissa Wells, Clayton Baldwin. BA, Erskine Coll., 1962; JD, Tulane U., 1965. Bar: La. 1965, S.C. 1974. Assoc. Baldwin, Haspel, Maloney, Rainold and Meyer, New Orleans, 1965-68; asst. prof. law U. S.C., 1968-71, asso. prof., 1971-75, prof., 1975—, chair prof. of advocacy, 1982—, asst. dean Sch. Law, 1970-75, instr. Med. Sch., 1970-79, adj. prof. law and medicine Med. Sch., 1979—; adj. prof. medicine Med. U. S.C., 1984—; of counsel Finkel & Altman, 1978—. Adj. prof. pathology Med. U. S.C., 1985—; asst. dean U. S.C. Sch. Law 1970-75, Disting. prof. law, 2001, Disting. prof. law emeritus, 2003—; mem. fourth cir. adv. com. on rules and procedures U.S. Ct. Appeals, 2001—. Author: (with J.L. Underwood) The Civil Trial Manual, 1974, 7th supplement, 1987, The Civil Trial Manual II, 1984, 87, (with Myers and Felix) New Directions in Legal Education, 1970, (with Finkel) S.C. Torts II, 1986, III, 1990, IV, 1995; co-reporter S.C. Criminal Code, 1977, S.C. Study Sentencing, 1977. Trustee S.C. dist. U.S. Bankruptcy Ct., 1979— ; exec. dir. S.C. Continuing Legal Edn. Program.; bd. visitors Erskine Coll.; reporter S.C. Jury Charge Commn., 1991-95. Mem. ATLA, ABA, La. Bar Assn., S.C. Bar (sec. 1975-76, exec. dir. 1972-76, award of service 1978), New Orleans Bar Assn., Am. Law Inst., Am. Coll. Trial Lawyers, Southeastern Assn. Am. Law Schs. (pres.), S.C. Trial Lawyers Assn. (bd. govs. 1984-88), Forest Lake Club, Phi Alpha Delta. Republican. Episcopalian. Home: PO Box 1799 Columbia SC 29202-1799 Office: 1201 Main St Ste 1800 Columbia SC 29201-3294

MC CUNE, BARRON PATTERSON, retired federal judge; b. West Newton, Pa., Feb. 19, 1915; s. James Patterson and Lyda Barron (Hammond) McC.; m. Edna Flannery Markey, Dec. 23, 1943; children: Edward M., James H., Barron Patterson. AB, Washington and Jefferson Coll., 1935; LLB, U. Pa., 1938. Bar: Pa. bar 1939. Practiced in, Washington, Pa., 1939-64; judge 27th Jud. Dist. Ct. Common Pleas, Washington, Pa., 1964-71, U.S. Dist. Ct., Western Dist. Pa., Pitts., 1971-95, sr. fed. judge; ret., 1995. Trustee emeritus Washington and Jefferson Coll.; bd. dirs. emeritus Washington (Pa.) Hosp. Served with USNR, 1942-45. Home: 144 Lemoyne Ave Washington PA 15301-3636

MCCUNE, G. BLAIR, lawyer; b. Columbus, Ohio, May 13, 1946; s. Shannon and Edith (Blair) McCune; m. Sue Lynn McCune, Sept. 9, 1992; 1 child, Brandilyn Elliott. BA, U. Mass., 1973; JD, U. Fla., 1976. Bar: Fla. 1976, Alaska 1979, U.S. Dist. Ct. Alaska 1980, U.S. Ct. Appeals (9th cir.) 1980, U.S. Supreme Ct. 1995. Staff atty. Fla. Rural Legal Svcs., Belle Glade, 1976—77; atty. Cowper & Madson, Fairbanks, Alaska, 1978—80; asst. pub. defender Alaska Pub. Defender Agy., Anchorage, 1981—96, dep. pub. defender, 1997—2001; pvt. practice Anchorage, 2001—. With U.S. Army, 1967—71, Vietnam. Mem.: Alaska Acad. Trial Lawyers. Democrat. Criminal. Home: 4714 Mills Dr Anchorage AK 99508 Office: 425 G St Ste 620 Anchorage AK 99501 Business E-Mail: mccune@gci.net.

MCCUNE, PHILIP SPEAR, lawyer; b. Spokane, Wash., Sept. 14, 1965; s. Calmar A. McCune and Katrina Y. Spear; m. Joey Leigh Hankins, 1993; children: Emma Sophia, Jackson Spear. BA magna cum laude, Dartmouth Coll., 1987; JD cum laude, U. Mich., 1991. Law clk. Hon. John C. Coughenour chief judge U.S. Dist. Ct. (we. dist.) Wash., Seattle, 1991—93; with Heller, Ehrman, White and Maculliffe, Seattle, 1993—97; ptnr., founder Summit Law Group, Seattle, 1997—. Author: The Forest Practices Act, Washington Environmental Law and Practice, 1997; sr. editor U. Mich. Jour. Law Reform, 1989-91; contbr. articles to profl. jours. Bd. dirs. Friends of Ind. Schs. and Better Edn., Seattle Repertory Theater; pres. bd. dirs. Am. Friends St. Michaels U. Sch. Recipient Wash. Law and Politics Rising Star award, 2002, 2003. Mem. ABA, Washington State Bar Assn., King County Bar Assn., Wash. Athletic Club, U. Mich. Law Sch. Barristers. Avocations: hiking, running. General civil litigation, Environmental, Land use and zoning (including planning). Office: Summit Law Group 315 Fifth Ave S Ste 300 Seattle WA 98104-2682 E-mail: philm@summitlaw.com.

MCCURLEY, CARL MICHAEL, lawyer; b. Denton, Tex., July 15, 1946; s. Carl and Geneva McC.; m. Mary Jo Trice, June 5, 1983; 1 child, Melissa Renee. BA, N. Tex. State U., 1968; JD, So. Meth. U., 1972. Bar: Tex. 1972, U.S. Dist. Ct. (no. dist.) Tex. 1972, U.S. Dist. Ct. (ea. dist.) Tex. 1974, U.S. Supreme Ct. 1977. Ptnr. McGuire, Levy & McCurley , Irving, Tex., 1972-82, Koons, Fuller, McCurley & Vanden Eykel, Dallas, 1982-92, McCurley, Orsinger, McCurley, & Nelson, 1992—. Contbr. articles to profl. jours. Mem. Family Law Coun. (chmn. 1991-93), Dallas Bar Assn., Am. Acad. Matrimonial Lawyers (treas. 1990-93, v.p. 1993-96, pres.-elect 1997, pres. 1998), Internat. Acad. Matrimonial Lawyers. Family and matrimonial. Home: 4076 Hanover Ave Dallas TX 75225-7009 Office: McCurley Orsinger McCurley & Nelson 5950 Sherry Ln Ste 800 Dallas TX 75225-6533

MCCURLEY, MARY JOHANNA, lawyer; b. Baton Rouge, La., Oct. 3, 1953; d. William Edward and Leora Elizabeth (Block) Trice; m. Carl Michael McCurley, June 6, 1983; 1 stepchild, Melissa Reneé Rockenbach. BA, Centenary Coll., 1975; JD, St. Mary's U., 1979. Bar: Tex. 1979; cert. family law. Assoc. Martin, Withers & Box, Dallas, 1979-82, Raggio & Raggio, Inc., Dallas, 1982-83; ptnr. Bruner, McColl, McColloch & McCurley, Dallas, 1983-87; assoc., ptnr. Selligson & Douglass, Dallas, 1987-90; jr. ptnr. Koons, Fuller, McCurley & VanderEykel, Dallas, 1990-92; ptnr. McCurley, Kinser, McCurley Nelson & Orsinger, Dallas, 1992—. Contbr. articles to profl. jours. Adv. Women's Service League, Dallas, 1993—. Mem.: Dallas Bar Assn., Tex. Acad. Family Law Specialist, Tex. State Bar Assn. (sec. 2001, vice-chair 2001, treas. 2001, chair 2003—, family law coun.), Dallas Bar Assn. (chair family law sect. 1985), Am. Acad. Matrimonial Lawyers (treas. Tex. chpt. 1993—95, sec. 1995—96, pres. 1997, pres. Tex. chpt. 1997—98, bd. govs. 2000, nat. sec. 2000—01, nat. v.p. 2003, nat. bd. dirs.). Methodist. Avocations: golf, travel, jogging, horseback riding. Family and matrimonial. Home: 4076 Hanover Ave Dallas TX 75225-7009 Office: McCurley Kinser McCurley & Nelson LLP 5950 Sherry Ln Ste 800 Dallas TX 75225-6533 Fax: 214-273-2470. E-mail: maryjo@mkmn.com.

MCCURLEY, ROBERT LEE, JR., lawyer, educator; b. Gadsden, Ala., Sept. 7, 1941; s. Robert Lee and Nellie Ruth McC.; m. Barbara; 1 child, Allison Leah. BS, U. Ala., 1963, JD, 1966. Bar: Ala. 1966, D.C. 1973, U.S. Ct. Mil. Appeals 1966, U.S. Supreme Ct. 1970, U.S. Ct. Appeals (5th cir.) 1972, U.S. Ct. Appeals (11th cir.) 1973, U.S. Ct. Appeals (fed. cir.) 1981. Asst. to dir. Fed. Savs. & Loan Ins. Corp., Washington, 1966-67; partner firm Rains, Rains, McCurley & Wilson, Gadsden, Ala., 1967-75; city judge Southside, Ala., 1970-75; dir. Ala. Law Inst., 1975—; assoc. dir. U. Ala. Center Public Law and Service, 1981-82; asst. dean Sch. Law U. Ala., 1978-81. Panelist White House Conf. on Volunteerism; pres. Gadsden Jaycees, 1972; mem. White House Fifty States Project; Henry Toll fellow Coun. State Govt., 1992. Editor: Divorce, Alimony and Child Support Custody, 3d edit., 1993, Land Laws of Alabama, 7th edit. rev., 2001, The Legislative Process, 8th edit., 2003, Alabama Law Office Practice Deskbook, 9th edit., 2001, Federally Mandated State Legislation, 1990, Alabama Legislation, Cases and Statutes, 4th edit., 1998, Alabama Election Handbook, 10th edit., 2002. Pres. Gadsden Boys Club, 1971, Kiwanis Internat. Found., 1998—2000; mem. Nat. Dem. Charter Commn., 1974. Fellow ABA, Ala. Bar Assn., mem. Am. Law Inst. (life), Order of Coif, Scribes, Farrah Law Soc., Commn. Uniform State Laws, Kiwanis (pres. Tuscaloosa club 1976, gov. Ala. dist. 1984, internat. found. v.p. 1991-92, pres. 1998-2000), Indian Hills County Club, Univ. Club. Baptist. Legislative, Property, real (including real estate development, water).

MCCURN, NEAL PETERS, federal judge; b. Syracuse, N.Y., Apr. 6, 1926; LL.B., Syracuse U., 1952, JD, 1960. Bar: N.Y. 1952. Ptnr. Mackenzie Smith Lewis Mitchell & Hughes, Syracuse, 1957-79; judge U.S. Dist. Ct. (no. dist.) N.Y., 1979-88; chief judge U.S. Dist. Ct. (no. dist.), N.Y., 1988-93; sr. judge, 1993—. Del. N.Y. State Constl. Conv., 1976; mem. 2d Cir. Jud. Council, 1987-93. Pres. Syracuse Common Coun., 1970-78. Mem. ABA, N.Y. State Bar Assn. (chmn. state constn. com.), Onondaga County Bar Assn. (past pres.), Am. Coll. Trial Lawyers, Am. Judicature Soc. (bd. dirs. 1980-84). Office: US Dist Ct 100 S Clinton St Rm 344 Syracuse NY 13261-6100

MCCUSKEY, JOHN F. lawyer; b. Clarksburg, W.Va., Nov. 7, 1947; BS, W.Va. Wesleyan Coll., 1969; BSEE, U. Pa., 1970; JD, W.Va. U., 1973. Bar: W.Va. 1974, U.S. Dist. Ct. (no. dist.) W.Va., U.S. Dist. Ct. (so. dist.) W.Va., U.S. Ct. Appeals (4th cir.). Mem. W.Va. Ho. of Dels., 1972—76, 1978—82; justice Supreme Ct. Appeals W.Va., 1998; atty. Shuman, McCuskey & Slicea, Charleston, W.Va. Capt. USAR, 1974—80. Recipient Disting. Faculty award, Def. Trial Counsel of W.Va. Mem.: ABA, W.Va. State Bar, Kanawha County Bar Assn., W.Va. Bar Assn. (pres.-elect), Omicron Delta Kappa. Appellate, Commercial, consumer (including collections, credit), Product liability. Office: Shuman McCuskey and Slicea PO Box 3953 405 Capitol St Ste 1007 Charleston WV 25301*

MCCUTCHAN, GORDON EUGENE, retired lawyer, insurance company executive; b. Buffalo, Sept. 30, 1935; s. George Lawrence and Mary Esther (De Puy) McC.; m. Linda Brown; children: Lindsey, Elizabeth. BA, Cornell U., 1956, MBA, 1958, LLB, 1959. Bar: N.Y. 1959, Ohio 1964. Pvt. practice, Rome, N.Y., 1959-61; atty., advisor SEC, Washington, 1961-64; ptnr. McCutchan, Druen, Maynard, Rath & Dietrich, 1964-94; mem. office of gen. counsel Nationwide Mut. Ins. Co., Columbus, Ohio, 1964-94, sr. v.p., gen. counsel, 1982-89, exec. v.p., gen. counsel, 1989-94; exec. v.p. Law and Corp. Svcs., Nationwide Ins. Enterprise, 1994-98; ret., 1998. Trustee, bd. govs. Franklin U., 1992-97; trustee Ohio Tuition Trust Authority, 1992-97. Mem. Columbus Bar Assn., Ohio Bar Assn., Am. Corp. Counsel Assn., Assn. Life Inst. Counsel (bd. govs. 1990-94), Fedn. Ins. and Corp. Counsel, Am. Coun. Life Ins. (chair legal sect. 1992-93). Home: 2376 Oxford Rd Columbus OH 43221-4011 E-mail: tunkpa@columbus.rr.com.

MCCUTCHEON, JAMES EDWARD, III, lawyer; b. San Antonio, Aug. 7, 1968; s. James Edward McCutcheon Jr. and Barbara Letitia Rogers; m. Elizabeth Jean Cooper, Aug. 21, 1992; children: Davis, Ashley Grace. BA in Econs., Dartmouth Coll., 1990; JD, U. Tex., 1994. Bar: Tex. 1994, U.S. Tax Ct. 1995, Wash. 1998, U.S. Ct. Appeals (5th cir.) 1999, U.S. Dist. Ct. (we. dist.) Wash. 2002. Assoc. Gresham, Davis Gregory, Worthy & Moore, San Antonio, 1994—97, of counsel, 1997—2001, Vander Wel, Jacobson and Bishop, Bellevue, Wash., 1999—. Chmn., exec. dir. N.W. Christian Legal Found. Mem.: Wash. Bar Assn., Tex. Bar Assn., Rotary, Chancellors, Order of the Coif, Phi Beta Kappa. General practice, Probate (including wills, trusts). Office: 10500 NE 8th St Ste 1900 Bellevue WA 98004-4358 E-mail: INFO@mccutcheonlaw.com.

MCDADE, THOMAS RAMBAUT, lawyer, rancher; b. Shreveport, La., Jan. 15, 1933; s. Ross Elias Jr. and Maybelle (Williams) McD.; m. Dorothy Burgess, Sept. 15, 1956; children: Kellye Marie McDade Pyle, Melinda Anne Schearer, Mallory Rambaut McDade Bakkenist. BBA in pers. mgmt., U. Tex., 1956, JD, 1962; student, Tex. A&M Coll., 1951-54. Bar: Tex. 1962, U.S. Supreme Ct. 1976, U.S. Dist. Ct. (so., we. and ea. dists.) Tex., U.S. Ct. Appeals (5th and 11th cirs.). Atty. Fulbright, Crooker, Freeman, Bates & Jaworski, Houston, 1962-71, ptnr., 1971-91; sr. ptnr. Fulbright & Jaworski, Houston, 1991, McDade Fogler Maines, L.L.P., Houston, 1992—. Bd. dirs. various state and nat. banks and pub. and pvt. cos., including The Coastal Corp., Houston, El Paso Corp. Bd. dirs. Tex. Bd. Corrections, 1983-87. Capt. USAF, 1956-59. Fellow Am. Bar Found., Am. Coll. Trial Lawyers, Tex. Bar Found., Houston Bar Found. Episcopalian. Federal civil litigation, General civil litigation, Criminal. Office: McDade Fogler Maines LLP 909 Fannin St Ste 1200 Houston TX 77010-1007

MCDANIEL, DONALD HAMILTON, lawyer; b. Washington, Apr. 26, 1948; s. Roy Hamilton and Mildred Dean (Borden) McD.; m. Eva Styron, Dec. 29, 1973; children: Sharon, Michelle. BS, La. State U., 1970; JD, U. Miss., 1973. Bar: Miss. 1973; bd. cert. tax atty., 1987—; bd. cert. estate planning & adminstrn. atty. Atty. IRS, Washington, 1974-77; tax law specialist Bourgeois Bennett Thokey, New Orleans, 1977-81; ptnr. McCloskey Dennery Page, New Orleans, 1981-85, Lemle & Kelleher, New Orleans, 1985—. Author: Estate Planning in Louisiana, 1991. Trustee St. Martins Episcopal Sch., New Orleans, 1993, East Jefferson Hosp. Found., New Orleans, 1995, United Meth. Found., New Orleans, 1995. Mem. ABA, La. State Bar Assn. (chmn. com. on trusts, estates and immovable property 1997—), Miss. State Bar Assn., New Orleans Estate Planning Coun. Avocations: golf, fishing. Estate planning, Estate taxation, Taxation, general. Office: Lemle & Kelleher LLP 601 Poydras St Ste 2100 New Orleans LA 70130-6021

MCDANIEL, JAMES EDWIN, lawyer; b. Dexter, Mo., Nov. 22, 1931; s. William H. and Gertie M. (Woods) McD.; m. Mary Jane Crawford, Jan. 22, 1955; children: John William, Barbara Anne. AB, Washington U., St. Louis, 1957, JD, 1959. Bar: Mo. 1959. Assoc. firm Walther, Barnard, Cloyd & Timm, 1959-60, McDonald, Barnard, Wright & Timm, 1960-63, ptnr., 1963-65; ptnr. firm Barnard, Timm & McDaniel, St. Louis, 1965-73, Barnard & Baer, St. Louis, 1973-82; ptnr. Lashly & Baer, St. Louis, 1982—2002, of counsel, 2002—; pros. atty. St. Louis, 1968—. City atty. City of Glendale, Mo., 1996—; bd. dirs. Eden. Theol. Sem.; lectr. Latvian U., Riga, Inst. Fgn. Rels., Banking in Am., 1992-93. Leader legal del. Chinese-Am. Comparative Law Study, People's Republic China, 1988, Russian-Am. Comparative Law Study, USSR, 1990; trustee, past chmn., past treas. 1st Congl. Ch. St. Louis. With USAF, 1951-55. Fellow Am. Bar Found. (life), St. Louis Bar Found. (life); mem. ABA (bd. govs. 1997-2000, ho. of dels. 1976-80, 84-92, 97-2000, state del. 1986-92, chmn. lawyers conf., jud. adminstrn. divsn. 1992-95, 8th cir. rep. standing com. on fed. jud. 1995-98, mem. standing com. on jud. qualification, tenure and compensation 1996-97), The Mo. Bar (pres. 1981-82, bd. govs. 1974-83), Mo. Assn. Def. Counsel, Bar Assn. Met. St. Louis (pres. 1972), Internat. Assn. Ins. Counsel, Assn. Def. Counsel St. Louis (past pres.), Phi Delta Phi. General civil litigation, Insurance, Labor (including EEOC, Fair Labor Standards Act, labor-management relations, NLRB, OSHA). Home: 767 Elmwood Ave Saint Louis MO 63122-3216 Office: Lashly & Baer 714 Locust St Saint Louis MO 63101-1699

MCDANIEL, JARREL DAVE, lawyer; b. Clovis, N. Mex., Oct. 17, 1930; s. Raymond Lee and Blanch (Booth) McD.; m. Anne Louise McAllister; children: Jarrel Dave Jr., Julia Anne. AA, Riverside Coll., 1951; BA, U. Tex., 1956, LL.B., 1957. Bar: Tex. 1957. Assoc. Vinson & Elkins, Houston, 1957-69, ptnr., 1969-96; of counsel Sheinfeld, Maley & Kay, Houston, 1997-2001; sr. counsel Akin, Gump, Strauss, Hauer & Feld, L.L.P., Houston, 2001—. Author, lectr. in field. Served with USAF, 1950-54. Mem.: ABA, Am. Bankruptcy Inst., State Bar Tex., Am. Coll. Bankruptcy, Houston Club. Roman Catholic. Bankruptcy. Home: 1217 Potomac Dr Houston TX 77057-1919 Office: Akin Gump Strauss Hauer & Feld LLP 711 Louisiana St Ste 1900 Houston TX 77002 E-mail: jmcdaniel@akingump.com.

MCDANIELS, WILLIAM E. lawyer; b. Needham, Mass., July 1, 1941; BA, Williams Coll., 1963; JD, Georgetown U., 1966. Bar: D.C. 1967, Md. 1983. Grad. fellow criminal law, litigation U. Pa., Phila., 1966-68; pub. defender Phila. Pub. Defender's Office, 1966-68; adj. prof. evidence, criminal law, advanced criminal procedure Georgetown U. Law Ctr., Washington, 1970-87; mem. Williams & Connolly, Washington, 1968—. Instr. Nat. Inst. Trial Advocacy, 1975—. Fellow Am. Coll. Trial Lawyers; mem. ABA, Md. State Bar Assn, D.C. Bar. General civil litigation, Criminal, Intellectual property. Office: Williams & Connolly 725 12th St NW Washington DC 20005-5901

MCDAVID, JANET LOUISE, lawyer; b. Mpls., Jan. 24, 1950; d. Robert Matthew and Lois May (Bratt) Kurzeka; m. John Gary McDavid, June 9, 1973; 1 child, Matthew Collins McDavid. BA, Northwestern U., 1971; JD, Georgetown U., 1974. Bar D.C. 1975, U.S. Ct. Appeals (fed. cir.) 1975 (D.C. cir. 1976), U.S. Supreme Ct. 1980, U.S. Ct. Appeals (5th cir.) 1983, (9th cir.) 1986. Assoc. Hogan & Harston, Washington, 1974-83, ptnr., 1984—. Gen. counsel ERAmerica, 1977-83; mem. antitrust task force Dept. Defense, 1993-94, 96-97; mem. antitrust coun. U.S. C. of C., 1994—; advisor Bush adminstrn. transition team, 2001. Contbr. articles to profl. jours. Participant Clinton and Bush adminstrn. transition team FTC. Mem. ABA (antitrust sect., vice chmn. civil practice com. 1986-89, sect. 2 com. 1989-90, chmn. franchising com. 1990-91, coun. mem. 1991-94, program officer 1994-97, vice chair 1997-98, chair-elect 1998-99, chair 1999-2000, immediate past chair, governing com. of forum on franchising 1991-97), ACLU, U.S. C. of C. (antitrust coun. 1995—), Washington Coun. Lawyers, D.C. Bar Assn., Fed. Bar Assn., Womens Legal Def. fund. Democrat. Antitrust, Federal civil litigation, Franchising. Office: Hogan & Hartson 555 13th St NW Washington DC 20004-1109

MCDAVID, WILLIAM HENRY, lawyer; b. NYC, May 10, 1946; m. Sylvia Noin, Dec. 21, 1984; children: Andrew, Madeline, William, Flora. AB, Columbia Coll., N.Y.C., 1968; JD, Yale U., 1972. Assoc. Debevoise & Plimpton, NYC, 1972-81; asst. gen. counsel Bankers Trust Co., NYC, 1981-83, assoc. gen. counsel, 1983-84, v.p., 1984-85, v.p., counsel, 1986-88; gen. counsel JP Morgan & Co., NYC, 1988—. Banking, Corporate, general, Finance. Office: JP Morgan & Co Office Gen Coun 270 Park Ave Fl 8 New York NY 10017-2014*

MCDERMOTT, FRANCIS OWEN, retired lawyer; b. Denver, Feb. 25, 1933; s. Paul Harkins and Agnes (Clark) McD.; divorced; children: Diana, Daniel, Christopher, Anthony, Justine; m. Estella Marina Idiaquez, June 6, 1986; stepchildren: Bernard, Michael, Nicole, Marie, Steven. JD, Am. U., 1960. Bar: D.C. 1960, U.S. Dist. Ct. D.C., 1960, U.S. Ct. Appeals (D.C. cir.) 1960, u.S. Tax Ct. 1961, U.S. Supreme Ct. 1964. Trial atty. office regional counsel IRS, Washington, 1961-65; mem. profl. staff com. on fin. U.S. Senate, Washington, 1965-68; tax counsel Assn. Am. R.R.s, Washington, 1968-73; assoc. Hopkins & Sutter, Washington, 1973-76, ptnr., 1976-98, ret., 1999; ret. ptnr. Foley & Lardner, Washington, 2001—02. Gen. counsel Inst. Ill., Washington, 1987-96. Mem. ABA, Fed. Bar Assn., Nat. Def. Transp. Assn. (v.p., gen. counsel 1974—). Roman Catholic. Avocation: tennis. Home: 1 S Montague St Arlington VA 22204-1007 E-mail: fmcdermott@foleylaw.com.

MCDERMOTT, JOHN ARTHUR, lawyer; b. Rochester, N.Y., Nov. 23, 1944; s. David E. and Doris L. McDermott; m. Gail Ann Van Putte, Sept. 24, 1965; children: Shawn, Ashley, Wendy. BA, U. Fla., 1966, JD with honors, 1968. Bar: Fla. 1969, U.S. Ct. Mil. Appeals 1969, Colo. 1973, U.S. Dist. Ct. Colo. 1973, U.S. Ct. Appeals (10th cir.) 1981. Rsch. asst. to chief judge Fla. Ct. Appeals, Lakeland, 1969; pvt. practice, Canon City, Colo., 1973—; county atty. Fremont County, Canon City, 1987-89. City atty. Canon City, Colo., 1989—90; bd. dirs. Fremont Cmty. Found., 2000—01, chmn., 2001. Pres. Fremont Rel Sch. Bd., 1977-81, mem. 1975-81; bd. dirs. West Cen. Mental Health Clinic, Canon City, 1973-75. Capt. U.S. Army, 1969-73. Mem. Colo. Bar Assn. (v.p. 1984-85), Colo. Trial Lawyers Assn.

(bd. dirs. 1987-89, 91-97, exec. com. 1988-89), Colo. Bar Found., 11th Jud. Dist. Bar Assn. (pres. 1980-82, mem. jud. nominating com. 1980-81, 2003-), Assn. Trial Lawyers Am., Lions (prs. 1985-86), Elks. Democrat. Avocations: skiing, motorcycling, amateur radio. General civil litigation, Federal civil litigation, Personal injury (including property damage). Home: 715 Pisgah St Canon City CO 81212-4340 Office: PO Box 1040 Canon City CO 81215-1040

MCDERMOTT, JOHN H(ENRY), lawyer; b. Evanston, Ill., June 23, 1931; s. Edward Henry and Goldie Lucile (Boso) McD.; m. Ann Elizabeth Pickard, Feb. 19, 1966; children: Elizabeth A., Mary L., Edward H. BA, Williams Coll., 1953; JD, U. Mich., 1956. Bar: Mich. 1955, Ill. 1956. Assoc. McDermott, Will & Emery, Chgo., 1958-64, ptnr., 1964-99, of counsel, 2000—. Bd. dirs. Patrick Industries Inc. 1st lt. USAF, 1956-58. Mem. ABA, Chgo. Bar Assn. Clubs: Commerical of Chgo., Econ. of Chgo., Legal Chgo. (pres. 1981-82), Law Chgo. (pres. 1986-87). Banking, Corporate, general, Securities. Home: 330 Willow Rd Winnetka IL 60093-4130 Office: McDermott Will & Emery 227 W Monroe St Ste 3100 Chicago IL 60606-5096 E-mail: mcdermott330@cs.com.

MCDERMOTT, KEVIN R. lawyer; b. Youngstown, Ohio, Jan. 26, 1952; s. Robert J. and Marion D. (McKeown) McD.; m. Cindy J. Darling, Dec. 11, 1976; children: Ciara, Kelly. AB, Miami U., Oxford, Ohio, 1974; JD, Ohio State U., 1977. Bar: Ohio 1977, U.S. Dist. Ct. (so. dist.) Ohio 1978, U.S. Dist. Ct. (no. dist.) Ohio 1988, U.S. Dist. Ct. (we. dist.) Mich. 1993, U.S. Supreme Ct. 1990, U.S. Ct. Appeals (3rd cir.) 1996, U.S. Ct. Appeals (6th cir.) 1988. Assoc. ptnr. Murphey Young & Smith, Columbus, Ohio, 1977-88; ptnr. Squire Sanders & Dempsey, Columbus, Ohio, 1988-90, Schottenstein Zox & Dunn, Columbus, Ohio, 1990—. Adv. bd. mem. Capital U. Legal Asst. Program, Columbus, Ohio, 1988—. Bd. pres. Easter Seal Soc. Ctrl. Ohio, Columbus, 1992-94, bd. mem. 1988-92; pres. Upper Arlington Civic Svc. Commn., Columbus, Ohio, 1988-93. General civil litigation, Constitutional, Securities. Office: Schottenstein Zox & Dunn 41 S High St Ste 2600 Columbus OH 43215-6109

MCDERMOTT, RICHARD FRANCIS, judge; b. Seattle, Feb. 18, 1948; s. Richard F. Sr. and Madeline (Frison) McD.; m. Susan Lynn Brandt, Feb. 19, 1977; children: Kelsey Anne, Megan Marie, Michael Brandt. BA in Polit. Sci., Seattle U., 1970; JD, U. Wash., 1973; grad., Nat. Jud. Coll., 2002. Bar: Wash. 1973, U.S. Dist. Ct. (we. dist.) Wash. 1973, U.S. Ct. Appeals (9th cir.) 1973, U.S. Supreme Ct. 1981. Atty. King County, Seattle, 1973-76; assoc. Parks, Johnson & East, Bellevue, Wash., 1976-78; ptnr. Revelle, Ries & McDermott, Bellevue, 1978-86, McDermott & Jones, Bellevue, 1986—93, Richard F. McDermott, Jr. P.S., 1993—2000; King County Superior Ct. judge, 2000—. Mem. Minorities and Justice Commn., 1993—; adj. prof. law Seattle U. Sch. Law, 1999—; mem. Bd. Ct. Edn., 2003. Author: (with others) Best of CLE Seminar, 1986, Auto Accident Deskbook, 1988. Served to 1st lt. USAR, 1970-78. Named Wash. Super Lawyer, Wash. Law and Politics, 1999. Mem. Wash. State Bar Assn. (spl. disciplinary counsel 1993-99), Seattle King County Bar Assn., East King County Bar Assn., Assn. Trial Lawyers Am., Wash. State Trial Lawyers Assn. (bd. dirs. 1982-90), Superior Ct. Judge's Assn. (spring conf. chair 2002). Lodges: Rotary. Roman Catholic. Avocations: golf, baseball. Office: King County Superior Ct 401 4th Ave No Kent WA 98032

MCDERMOTT, ROBERT B. lawyer; b. Washington, June 16, 1927; s. Edward H. and Goldie Lucile (Boso) McD.; m. Julia Wood, Nov. 16, 1950; children: John, Jeanne, Charles; m. Jane S. Whitman, July 31, 1973; m. Sarah Jaicks, Jan. 6, 1996. AB, Princeton U., 1948; LL.B., Harvard U., 1951. Bar: D.C. 1951, Ill. 1955. Atty. Office Gen. Counsel, Navy Dept., Washington, 1951-52; assoc McDermott, Will & Emery, Chgo., 1954-60, ptnr., 1961-92, chmn., 1986-91, of counsel, 1992—. Trustee Ill. Inst. Tech., Chgo., 1985—, The Mather Found., Evanston, Ill., 1988—; bd. dirs. Ct. Theatre. Lt. USNR, 1945-46, 52-54. Mem. Chgo. Bar Assn. Clubs: Chicago, Economic, University (Chgo.). Corporate, general, Corporate taxation. Home: 990 N Lake Shore Dr Apt 31E Chicago IL 60611-1386 E-mail: bobmcder61@aol.com.

MCDERMOTT, ROBERT J. lawyer; b. Bklyn., Sept. 5, 1944; AB, Georgetown U., 1966; JD cum laude, NYU, 1970, LLM in Taxation, 1974. Bar: N.Y. 1971. Ptnr. Dewey Ballantine, N.Y.C. Mem. ABA, N.Y. State Bar Assn. (exec. com., tax sect. 1980-91), Assn. of Bar of City of N.Y., Order Coif. Office: Dewey Ballantine 1301 Avenue Of The Americas New York NY 10019-6022

MCDERMOTT, THOMAS JOHN, JR., lawyer; b. Santa Monica, Calif., Mar. 23, 1931; s. Thomas J. Sr. and Etha Irene (Cook) McD.; m. Yolanda Amante Jatap; children: Jodi Friedman, Kimberly E., Kish S. BA, UCLA, 1953, JD, 1958. Bar: Calif. 1959. Ptnr. Gray, Binkley and Pfaelzer, L.A., 1964-67, Kadison, Pfaelzer, Woodward, Quinn and Rossi, L.A., 1967-87, Rogers & Wells, L.A., 1987-93, Bryan Cave, L.A., 1993-95, Manatt, Phelps & Phillips, LLP, L.A., 1995-99, Shanks and Herbert, San Diego. Served with U.S. Army, 1953-56, Korea. Fellow Am. Coll. Trial Lawyers; mem. ABA, Assn. Bus. Trial Lawyers (pres. 1980-81, mem. exec. com. 9th cir. jud. conf. 1993—, chair 1997), State Bar Calif. (chair litigation sect. 1993-94), UCLA Law Alumni Assn. (pres. 1961-62), Order of Coif. Federal civil litigation, General civil litigation, State civil litigation. Office: Shanks & Herbert Ste 330 4350 La Jolla Village Dr San Diego CA 92122

MCDEVITT, CHARLES FRANCIS, retired state supreme court justice, lawyer; b. Pocatello, Idaho, Jan. 5, 1932; s. Bernard A. and Margaret (Hermann) McD.; m. Virginia L. Heller, Aug. 14, 1954; children: Eileen A., Kathryn A., Brian A., Sheila A., Terrence A., Neil A., Kendal A. LLB, U. Idaho, 1956. Bar: Idaho 1956. Ptnr. Richards, Haga & Eberle, Boise, 1956-62; gen. counsel, asst. sec. Boise Cascade Corp., 1962-65; mem. Idaho State Legislature, 1963-66; sec., gen. counsel Boise Cascade Corp., 1965-67, v.p. sec., 1967-68; pres. Beck Industries, 1968-70; group v.p. Singer Co., N.Y.C., 1970-72, exec. v.p., 1973-76; pub. defender Ada County, Boise, 1976-78; co-founder Givens, McDevitt, Pursley & Webb, Boise, 1978-89; justice Idaho Supreme Ct., Boise, 1989-97, chief justice, 1993-97; ptnr., founder McDevitt & Miller, LLP, Boise, 1997—. Served on Gov.'s Select Com. on Taxation, Boise, 1988-89; mem. State Select Com. on Campaign Ethics and Campaign Finances, State Select Com. on Legis. Compensation. Chair Idaho Jud. Coun., 1993-97, Cts. Advisors Coun., 1994-98; mem. Multi-State Tax Com. Home: 4940 Boise River Ln Boise ID 83716-8816 Office: McDevitt & Miller LLP 537 W Bannock St Ste 215 Boise ID 83702-5759 E-mail: chas@McDevitt.org.

MCDEVITT, JAMES A. lawyer; b. July 1943; Bachelor, U. Wash.; MBA, JD, Gonzaga U. Asst. atty. gen. State of Wash., Office of Atty. Gen., 1975—77; from sr. ptnr. to mng. ptnr. Reed & Geisa, Spokane, Wash., 1977—94; ptnr. Preston, Gates & Ellis, Spokane, Wash., 1994—2002; U.S. atty. Ea. Dist. Wash., 2002—. With USAF, 1965—71, brig. gen. Wash. Air Nat. Guard, ret. Office: PO Box 1494 Spokane WA 99210*

MCDIARMID, ROBERT CAMPBELL, lawyer; b. N.Y.C., July 13, 1937; s. Norman Hugh and Dorothy (Shoemaker) McD.; m. Ruth Sussman, 1963 (div. 1996); children: Jennifer, Alexander Samuel; m. Frances Enseki Francis, 1996. BS in Mech. Engring., Swarthmore Coll., 1958; MS in Engring. Physics, Cornell U., 1960; LLB, Harvard U., 1963. Bar: D.C. 1964, Va. 1964, U.S. Supreme Ct. 1967, U.S. Ct. Appeals (4th, 6th and 9th cirs.) 1965, U.S. Ct. Appeals (3d, 5th and 10th cirs.) 1966, U.S. Ct. Appeals (7th, 8th and D.C. cirs.) 1967, U.S. Ct. Appeals (2d cir.) 1970, U.S. Ct. Appeals (1st cir.) 1979, U.S. Ct. Appeals (11th cir.) 1981. Assoc. Weaver & Glassie, Washington, 1963-64; trial atty. civil divsn. appellate sect. Dept. Justice, Washington, 1964-68; asst. to gen. counsel Fed. Power Commn., Washington, 1968-70; assoc. Law Office of George Spiegel, Washington, 1970-73; ptnr. Spiegel & McDiarmid, Washington, 1973—. Mem. alumni coun. Swarthmore Coll., 1986-89. Mem. ABA, Va. State Bar, Bar Assn. D.C., D.C. Bar, Energy Bar Assn. (exec. com. 1982-83, bd. dirs. 1997-2000). Democrat. Mem. Soc. Of Friends. Antitrust, Federal civil litigation, FERC practice. Home: 3625 Fulton St NW Washington DC 20007-1452 Office: Spiegel & McDiarmid 1333 New Hampshire Ave NW Washington DC 20036 E-mail: robert.mcdiarmid@spiegelmcd.com.

MCDONALD, ALAN ANGUS, federal judge; b. Harrah, Wash., Dec. 13, 1927; s. Angus and Nell (Britt) McD.; m. Ruby K., Aug. 22, 1949; children: Janelle Jo, Saralee Sue, Stacy. BS, U. Wash., 1950, LLB, 1952. Dep. pros. atty. Yakima County, Wash., 1952-54; ptnr. Halverson, Applegate & McDonald, Yakima, 1954—85; judge U.S. Dist. Ct. (ea. dist.) Wash., Yakima, 1985-95, sr. judge, 1995—. Fellow Am. Coll. Trial Lawyers; Yakima C. of C. (bd. dirs.). Clubs: Yakima Country, Royal Duck (Yakima). Office: US Dist Ct PO Box 2706 Yakima WA 98907-2706

MCDONALD, BRADLEY G. lawyer; m. Ann Gilbert, Sept. 2, 1964; 1 child, Perry. BA, U. Okla.; JD, Georgetown U., 1961. Bar: D.C. 1961, U.S. Ct. Appeals (D.C., 11th and 4th cirs.), U.S. Supreme Ct. With McDonald & Karl, Washington. Lawyer; b. Okla.; m. Ann Gilbert, Sept. 3, 1964; 1 child, Perry. BA, U. Okla.; JD, Georgetown U., 1961. Bar: D.C. 1961, U.S. Ct. Appeals (D.C. cir.), U.S. Ct. Appeals (11th cir., 4th cir.) U.S. Supreme Ct. Nat. Alumni Adv. Coun. U. Okla.; mem. Arlington Com. of 100; bd. dirs. McLean Montessori, , Sigma Nu Ednl. Found.; trustee, treas. Randolph-Macon Acad. Served to 1st lt. USMC, 1956-58. Named to Legion of Honor, Delta Epsilon, Sigma Nu; recipient 1st Regent's Alumni award U. Okla. Mem. nat. alumni adv. coun. U. Okla; mem. Arlington Com. of 100; bd. dirs. McLen Montessori; trustee, treas. Randolph-Macon Acad. 1st lt. USMC, 1956-58. Recipient 1st Regent's Alumni award U. Okla. Mem. Sigma Nu (mem. Ednl. Found.), Delta Epsilon. General practice, Civil rights, Estate planning.

MCDONALD, CHARLES EDWARD, lawyer; b. El Paso, Tex., Nov. 13, 1957; s. Carlos and Armida (Adauto) McD.; 1 child, Miranda Lee. BA in Philosophy, U. St. Thomas, Houston, 1980; JD, South Tex. Coll. Law, 1985. Bar: Tex. 1985, U.S. Ct. Appeals. (5th cir.) 1991, U.S. Supreme Ct. 1992. Prin. Law Office Charles E. McDonald, El Paso, 1985-2000, McDonald and Assocs, El Paso, 2000—. Comms. liaison Coleman Re-election Congl. Campaign, El Paso, 1984, 86. Mem. ATLA, Tex. Trial Lawyers Assn., State Bar Tex., El Paso County Bar Assn. (ethics com. 1997-98, rules com. 1997-98, clin. law coun. 1997-98), Nat. Assn. Cave Divers. Roman Catholic. Avocations: cave diving, chess, traveling, foreign language (spanish). Personal injury (including property damage), Product liability, Labor (including EEOC, Fair Labor Standards Act, labor-management relations, NLRB, OSHA). Office: 4150 Rio Bravo St Ste 136 El Paso TX 79902-1013 E-mail: cemassoc@yahoo.com.

MC DONALD, JOHN RICHARD, lawyer; b. Connersville, Ind., Aug. 8, 1933; s. Vernon Louis and Thelma (Venham) McD.; m. Mary Alice Boyd, Aug. 17, 1957; children: Anne Elizabeth, John Richard, Colleen Lynn. BA, U. Ariz., 1957, LL.B., 1960. Bar: Ariz. 1960. Since practiced in, Tucson; assoc. Richard N. Roylston, 1961-62; pvt. practice, 1963-65; ptnr. McDonald & Rykken, 1965-68, DeConcini & McDonald (now DeConcini, McDonald, Yetwin, Lacy, P.C.), 1968—. Mem. adv. bd. Dependable Nurses, Inc., 1994—. Mem. Ariz. Law Rev. Pres., bd. dirs. emeritus Comstock Children's Hosp. Found.; v.p. Ariz. Sch. Bds. Assn., 1979, pres., 1981; v.p. All Ariz. Sch. Bd., 1981; v.p., bd. dirs. Tucson Assn. for Blind, 1966-86; trustee Catalina Foothills Sch. Dist., 1976-82; bd. dirs. Tucson Unified Sch. Dist. Ednl. Enrichment Found., 1994—, Ariz. Acad., 1981-89, Tucson Symphony Soc., 1997—, Catalina Foothills Sch. Dist. Found., Grand Canyon Music Festival, 1993—. Mem. Ariz. Bar Assn., Ariz. Law Rev. Assn. (pres. 1994), Pima County Bar Assn. (dir. 1978-86, pres. 1984-85), Nat. Coun. Sch. Attys. (dir. 1992-96), Delta Chi. Independent. Presbyterian. Civil rights, Federal civil litigation, State civil litigation. Home: 6151 N Camino Almonte Tucson AZ 85718-3729 Office: 2525 E Broadway Blvd Tucson AZ 85716-5398 E-mail: jmcdonald@dmyl.com., mjr44@qwest.net.

MCDONALD, JOSEPH F., III, lawyer; b. Rockville Centre, N.Y., Feb. 6, 1956; s. Joseph F. Jr. and Rita M. McD.; m. Laurie Hurd, Nov. 24, 1978; children: Geoffrey, Ryan, Molly. BA, St. Anselm's Coll., 1978; JD, Suffolk U., 1983; LLM, Boston U., 1987. Bar: N.H., U.S. Dist. Ct., U.S. Tax Ct. Dir., shareholder Cleveland, Waters & Bass, Concord, N.H., 1988-92, 94-98; v.p. trust New London (N.H.) Trust Co., 1992-94; ptnr. McDonald & Kanyuk, PLLC, Concord, 1998—. Dir. AAA No. New England, Portland, Maine, 1997—. Fellow Am. Coll. Trust and Estate Counsel. Estate planning, Probate (including wills, trusts), Estate taxation. Office: McDonald & Kanyuk PLLC 7 Hills Ave Concord NH 03301-4804

MCDONALD, MICHAEL EUGENE, lawyer, educator, clergyman; b. Buffalo, N.Y., Aug. 13, 1956; s. Ned and Margaret (Hereford) McD.; m. Darlene Carver, July 1, 1989; 1 child, Miranda Danielle. AA, BS, Middle Tenn. State U., 1979; MPA, So. Ill. U., 1984; JD, John Marshall Sch. Law, Chgo., 1987; MDiv, Vanderbilt U., 1989—91. Bar: Ill. 1986, Tenn. 1990; cert. adminstr. elections, Tenn., 1994; cert. civil mediator; ordained to ministry United Meth. Ch., 1996. Legis. intern Office of the Speaker, Ill. Ho. of Reps., Springfield, 1982-83; fellow Exec. Office of the Gov., State of Ill., Springfield, 1983-84; law clk. intern U.S. Dist. Ct. No. Dist. Ill., Chgo., 1984-85; adminstrv. asst. to dir. Ill. Dept. State Police, Chgo., 1984-87; asst. atty. gen. Ill. Atty. Gen.'s Office, Chgo., 1986-87; spl. asst. to mayor Exec. Office of the Mayor, Nashville, 1987-90; assoc. King & Ballow, Nashville, 1991-93; election adminstr. Davidson County Election Commn., Nashville, 1993—. Adj. prof. polit. sci., bus. law and paralegal studies program Middle Tenn. State U., Murfreesboro, 1987—; gen. counsel Gov.'s Alliance for a Drug Free Tenn., Davidson County, 1987—; asst. prof. The Honors Program, Tenn. State U., 1996—; instr. U. Tenn. Ctr. for Govt. Tng., 1995—' instr. Ptnrs. in Policymaking, Tex., Kans., Mo., Tenn., N.J., Ga.; mediator U.S. EEOC, 1998-99. Vol. Buddies of Nashville, 1988—; loaned exec. United Way Mid. Tenn., 1990; mem. Leadership Nashville, 1990-91, Citizens Police Acd., 1997; ordained deacon Bethlehem Ctrs. of Nashville, 2000—; mem. design com. Internat. Convocation of Deacons and Diaconate Mins., Dalals, 2003. Recipient Disting. Young Alumni Achievement award Middle Tenn. State U., 1987, Disting. African Am. Alumni Achievement award; Coun. on Legal Edn. Opportunity fellow, Thurgood Marshall scholar, 1984-87. Mem. ABA (del. ho. of dels.), Nat. Bar Assn., Ill. State Bar, Alpha Phi Alpha, Phi Alpha Delta. Avocations: basketball, running, Karate, sport card collecting, playing guitar. Home: 1603 Benjamin St Nashville TN 37206-2511 Office: Election Commn Met Govt of Nashville Howard Sch Bldg Rm 153 2d Ave S Nashville TN 37210-0650

MCDONALD, MICHAEL SCOTT, lawyer; b. Ft. Stockton, Tex., Feb. 6, 1962; s. Roland R. and Harriett L. McD.; m. Sara; children: Matthew, Michael. BA, U. Tex., El Paso, 1984; JD, U. Tex., Austin, 1987. Bar: Tex. 1987, U.S. Ct. Appeals (5th and 10th cirs.), U.S. Dist. Ct. (all dists.) Tex. With Littler Mendelson, Dallas; mng. shareholder Littler, Mendelson, Dallas. Co-author, editor: Chapter 9, The 1999 National Employer; The Texas Employer; contbg. editor Covenents Not to Compete-A State by State Survey, 1995—, Employee Duty of Loyalty, 1995—, Trade Secrets - A State by State Survey, 1998—; contbr. articles to profl. jours. Mem. ABA (litigation sect., labor and employment law sect.), Tex. Bar Assn. (labor and employment law sect.), Tex. Assn. Bus., Dallas Bar Assn. (employment law sect., chmn. 2000, exec. com. 1994-2001). General civil litigation, Labor (including EEOC, Fair Labor Standards Act, labor-management relations, NLRB, OSHA). Office: Littler Mendelson 2001 Ross Ave Ste 2600 Dallas TX 75201-2931

MCDONALD, PATRICK ALLEN, lawyer, arbitrator, educator; b. Detroit, May 11, 1936; s. Lawrence John and Estelle (Maks) Mc D.; m. Margaret Mercier, Aug. 10, 1963; children: Michael Lawrence, Colleen Marie, Patrick Joseph, Timothy, Margaret, Thomas, Maureen. PhB cum laude, U. Detroit, 1958, JD magna cum laude, 1961; LLM (E. Barrett Prettyman Trial scholar, Hugh J. Fegan fellow), Georgetown U., 1962. Bar: D.C. 1961, Mich. 1961, Colo. 1993. Case worker Dept. Pub. Welfare, Detroit, 1958; field examiner NLRB, Detroit, 1961; practiced in Washington, 1961-62; trial cons. NIH, Bethesda, Md., 1962; staff judge adv. USAF, France, 1962-65; ptnr. Monagham, LoPrete, Mc Donald, Yakima & Grenke, Detroit, 1965—. Bd. dirs., past chmn. Delta Dental Plan Mich.; past chmn. Delta Dental Plan Ohio; bd. dirs., v.p. Guest House, Lake Orion, Mich., Rochester, Minn., Detroit Athletic Club, Brighton Hosp.; instr. polit. sci. and law U. Md., 1963-65, U. Detroit Law Sch., adj. prof., 1965—; adj. prof. Ave Maria Law Sch., 2003—. Co-author: Law and Tactics in Federal Criminal Cases, 1963. Mem. Detroit Bd. Edn., 1966-76, pres.; sec., trustee Mt. Elliott Cemetary Assn.; mem. U. Detroit Sports Hall of Fame; mem. adv. bd. Providence Hosp., Southfield, Mich.; exec. bd. U. Detroit Pres.'s Cabinet. Named one of Five Outstanding Young Men of Mich., Outstanding Young Man of Detroit. Mem. ABA, Detroit Bar Assn., State Bar Mich. (commr.), U. Detroit Alumni Assn. (bd. dirs.), Mensa, Blue Key, Alpha Phi Omega (pres. Eta Pi chpt. 1955), Alpha Sigma Nu (v.p. 1960). Labor (including EEOC, Fair Labor Standards Act, labor-management relations, NLRB, OSHA). Home: 13066 Lashbrook Ln E Brighton MI 48114-6002 Office: 40700 Woodward Ave Bloomfield Hills MI 48304-2211

MCDONALD, PAUL KIMBALL, lawyer, investment executive; b. Worcester, Mass., June 8, 1932; s. Irving Thomas McDonald and Marie Agnes Haggerty; m. Sally Lou Kirkendall, Oct. 26, 1957; children: Katrina Louise Greenly, Linda Marie Bennett, Heidi Ann Bishop. AB, Harvard U., 1953, LLB, 1956, JD, 1957. Asst. to pres. W.R. Grace & Co., N.Y.C., 1956-65; pres. Paul McDonald & Co., N.Y.C., 1965-89. Bd. dirs. several corps. Trustee St. Vincent's Hosp., N.Y.C., 1967-74, N.Y. Foundling Hosp., 1967-74, others. Home: 128 Cutler Rd Greenwich CT 06831-2511

MCDONALD, WILLIAM HENRY, lawyer; b. Niangua, Mo., Feb. 27, 1946; s. Milburn and Fannie M. McDonald; m. Janice E. Robinson, July 13, 1968; children: Melissa L., Meghan M. BS in Pub. Adminstrn., Southwest Mo. State U., 1968; JD, U. Mo., 1971. Bar: Mo. 1971, U.S. Dist. Ct. (we. dist.) Mo. 1973, U.S. Supreme Ct. 1978, U.S. Ct. Appeals (8th cir.) 1982. Ptnr., pres. Woolsey, Fisher, Whiteaker & McDonald, PC, 1973-95; pres. William H. McDonald & Assocs., PC, Springfield, Mo., 1995—. Chmn. blue ribbon task force on Delivery of Mental Health Services to Southwest Mo., Mo. Commn. Continuing Legal Edn.; pres. Tan Oaks Homeowners Assn.; mem. fin. com. Child Adv. Council, Rep. Nat. Com., Mo. Rep. Com., Greene County Nat. Com.; active various Southwest Mo. State U. Clubs; bd. dirs. Greene County div. Am. Heart Assn., Ozarks regional Am. Athletic Union Jr. Olympics; pres., bd. dirs. Springfield Little Theatre; v.p. pub. affairs Springfield Area C. of C., bd. dirs., 1995-98. Capt. U.S. Army, 1971-73. Named one of Outstanding Young Men Am., 1978, 81, Outstanding Young Men Springfield, 1980. Fellow ABA (life, antitrust and litigation and torts and ins. sects.); mem. ATLA, Fed. Bar Assn., Mo. Bar Assn. (chmn. spol. com. on mandatory continuing edn., various coms., Pres.'s award 1986), Mo. Assn. Trial Attys. (bd. govs. 1998-2001), Springfield Met. Bar Assn. (bd. dirs., chmn. pub. edn. speakers bur.), Met. Bar Assn. St. Louis, Def. Rsch. Inst., Am. Judicature Soc., Am. Bd. Trial Advs. (state coord.), Nat. Bd. Trial Advs., Am. Coll. Barristers, Million Dollar Forum, 31st Jud. Cir. Bar Com. (chmn.), Supreme Ct. Hist. Soc., U. Mo.-Kansas City Sch. Law Found., Springfield Claims Assn. (pres.), U.S. Cavalry Assn. (life), Am. Legion, 1st Inf. Divsn. Soc., K.T., Beta Omega Tau, Kappa Epsilon. Presbyterian. Federal civil litigation, State civil litigation, Personal injury (including property damage). Home: 4857 E Royal Dr Springfield MO 65809-2425

MCDONNELL, JOHN L., JR., lawyer; JD, U. San Francisco. Bar: Calif. 1964. With Crosby Heafey Roach & May; counsel Reed Smith, Oakland, Calif., 2003—. Lectr. in field; cons. in field. Contbr. articles to profl. jours. Trustee East Bay Cmty. Found., Holy Names Coll.; chair bd. trustees Oakland Mus. Calif. Found.; founder, bd. mem., sec. Calif. Patrons of the Arts in the Vatican Mus.; bd. counselors U. San Francisco Sch. Law. Fellow: Am. Coll. Trust and Estate Counsel (Calif. state chair, bd. regents); mem.: ABA (bd. govs. 14th dist. 2000—03, mem. drug adv. task force, chair estate planning, trust and probate law sect., chair probate com., advisor standing com. on lawyer competence), Internat. Acad. Estate and Trust Law (acaemician), State Bar Calif. (bd. govs., v.p., chair estate planning, trust and probate law sect. legal svcs. com., com. on profl. stds. and admissions, consortium on competence), Alameda County Bar Assn. Avocations: choral music, reading, foreign languages, fishing. Estate planning. Office: Reed Smith 26th Fl 1999 Harrison St Oakland CA 94612-3573*

MC DONOUGH, JOHN RICHARD, lawyer; b. St. Paul, May 16, 1919; s. John Richard and Gena (Olson) McD.; m. Margaret Poot, Sept. 10, 1944; children— Jana Margaret, John Jacobus. Student, U. Wash., 1937-40; LLB, Columbia U., 1946. Bar: Calif. 1949. Asst. prof. law Stanford U., 1946-49, prof., 1952-69; assoc. firm Brobeck, Phleger & Harrison, San Francisco, 1949-52; asst. dep. atty. gen. U.S. Dept. Justice, Washington, 1967-68, assoc. dep. atty. gen., 1968; of counsel and ptnr. firm Keatinge & Sterling, L.A., 1969-70; ptnr. Ball, Hunt, Hart, Brown and Baerwitz, L.A., 1970-90, Carlsmith Ball Wichman Case & Ichiki, L.A., 1990-96, of counsel, 1996-98, Carlsmith Ball, L.A., 1998—2002. Exec. sec. Calif. Law Revision Commn., 1954-59, mem. commn., 1959-67, vice chmn., 1960-64, chmn., 1964-65. Served with U.S. Army, 1942—46. Mem.: Am. Coll. Trial Lawyers. Democrat. Federal civil litigation, State civil litigation.

MCDONOUGH, RUSSELL CHARLES, retired state supreme court justice; b. Glendive, Mont., Dec. 7, 1924; s. Roy James and Elsie Marie (Johnson) McD.; m. Dora Jean Bidwell, Mar. 17, 1946; children: Ann Remmich, Michael, Kay Jensen, Kevin, Daniel, Mary Garfield. JD, George Washington U., 1949. Bar: Mont. 1950. Pvt. practice, Glendive, Mont., 1950-83; judge Gen. Jurisdiction State of Montana, Glendive, 1983-87; justice Mont. Supreme Ct., Helena, 1987-93, ret., 1993. City atty. City of Glendive, 1953-57; county atty. Dawson County, Mon., 1957-63; del. Mont. Constl. Conv., Helena, 1972. 1st lt. AC, U.S. Army, 1943-45, ETO. Decorated DFC. Mem. Mont. Bar Assn. Roman Catholic. Home: 441 W Paseo Solana Green Valley AZ 85614-2727

MC DOUGALL, DUGALD STEWART, retired lawyer; b. Indpls., May 15, 1916; s. George and Effie (Barclay) McD.; m. Carol Brueggeman, Aug. 1938; children: George, Duncan, Walter, Robert; m. Judith Stephen, Dec. 1967. AB, U. Chgo., 1935, JD, 1937. Bar: Ill. 1937. Since practiced in, Chgo.; sr. ptnr. McDougall, Hersh & Scott, 1961-87. Sec., dir. Aladdin Industries, Inc. Served with USNR, 1942-46. Fellow Am. Coll. Trial Lawyers; mem. ABA, Am. Patent Law Assn., Patent Law Assn. Chgo., Law Club Chgo., Union League (Chgo.). Clubs: Union League (Chgo.); Olympia Fields (Ill.) Country. Office: 25 Pine Forest Ln Haines City FL 33844-9675

MCDOUGALL, GERALD DUANE, lawyer; b. Hammond, Ind., Sept. 18, 1931; s. John and Carol Maxine (Lind) McD.; m. Ingrid Rosina Kempf, Jan. 26, 1960 (dec. 2000); children: Manfred, James. JD, Mercer U., 1971. Bar: U.S.V.I. 1972, Colo. 1973, Germany 1973, Tex. 1985. Atty. US V.I. Dept. Labor, St. Thomas, 1971-72; pvt. practice, Denver, 1972-74, 76-84, Heilbronn, Neckar, Germany, 1974-76, Amarillo, Tex., 1985—. Precinct committeeman Rep. Ctrl. Com., Denver, 1978-84. Sgt. U.S. Army, 1951-54,

ETO, 61-67, Vietnam. Mem. Tex. Bar Assn., Tex. Criminal Defense Lawyers Assn., Amarillo Bar Assn., State Bar Coll. Admiralty, Appellate. Home: 7910 Merchant Dr Amarillo TX 79121-1028 Office: PO Box 50898 Amarillo TX 79159-0898

MCDOUGALL, RODERICK GREGORY, lawyer; BBA in Econs., JD, U. Ariz. Bar: Ariz. 1965, U.S. Ct. Claims 1965, U.S. Supreme Ct. 1970, U.S. Dist. Ct. Ariz. 1972, U.S. Ct. Appeals (9th cir.) 1972. Law clk. Ariz. Supreme Ct., 1964, Ariz. Ct. Appeals, 1965; dep. county atty. Maricopa County, 1965-67; staff atty. Ariz. State Senate, 1967; asst. atty. gen., 1967-74; chief asst. Atty. Gen., Ariz., 1974-84; city atty. City of Phoenix, 1984-2000. Advisor Ariz. Supreme Ct. Mem. ABA, Internat. Mcpl. Lawyers Assn. (bd. dirs. 1994-2000), Ariz. Bar Assn., Maricopa County Bar Assn.

MCDOWELL, CHARLES EAGER, lawyer, retired military officer; b. Manchester, N.H., Sept. 9, 1923; s. Joseph Curry and Mildred (Eager) McD.; m. Carolyn A. Gibbons, June 21, 1947; children— Robin, Patricia. AB, Dartmouth Coll., 1947; JD, U. Va., 1950. Bar: Tex. 1950, Va. 1981, D.C. 1981. With land div. Shell Oil Co., Houston, 1950; commd. lt. (j.g.) USN, 1951, advanced through grades to rear adm., 1976; staff legal officer Comdr. Service Force, U.S. Pacific Fleet; staff judge adv., head internat. law div. Naval War Coll., 1963-66; staff legal officer, comdr. 7th Fleet, 1966-68; sr. Navy mem. ad hoc com., dep. asst. judge adv. gen. Office Judge Adv. Gen. Dept. Def., Washington, 1968-72; staff judge adv. on staff comdr. in chief U.S. Naval Forces, Europe, London, 1972-75; comdg. officer Naval Justice Sch., Newport, R.I., 1975-76; dep. judge adv. gen. Navy Dept., Washington, 1976-78, judge adv. gen., 1978-80; pvt. practice Dumfries, Va., 1981-96. Served to 2d lt. AUS, 1943-46. Decorated D.S.M., Bronze Star, Joint Service Commendation medal, Navy Commendation medal with Combat V, Purple Heart, Combat Inf. badge. Mem. FBA, Tex. Bar Assn., Va. Bar Assn., Judge Advs. Assn., Order of Coif, Chi Phi, Square Dancer Club. Methodist. Home: 1106 Croton Dr Alexandria VA 22308-2008

MCDOWELL, CHARLES S. lawyer; b. Norfolk, Va., June 20, 1945; AB cum laude, Princeton U., 1967; JD, U. Va., 1974. Bar: Del. 1975. Ptnr. Potter Anderson & Corroon LLP, Wilmington, Del. Counsel Del. Health Facilities Authority. Dir. WHYY, Inc. (Delaware Valley Pub. TV and Radio); mem. com. LPGA Urban Youth Golf Program. Mem.: ABA, Nat. Assn. Bond Lawyers, Del. State Bar Assn. (pres. 2003—). Finance, Municipal (including bonds). Office: Potter Anderson and Corroon LLP Hercules Plz PO Box 951 1313 N Market St Wilmington DE 19899-0951*

MCDOWELL, KAREN ANN, lawyer; b. Ruston, La., Oct. 4, 1945; d. Paul and Opal Elizabeth (Davis) Bauer; m. Gary Lee McDowell, Dec. 22, 1979. BA, U. La., Monroe, 1967; JD, U. Mich., 1971; diploma, John Robert Powers Sch., Chgo., 1976, Nat. Inst. Trial Advocacy, 1990. Bar: Ill. 1973, Colo. 1977, U.S. Dist. Ct. (so. dist.) Ill. 1973, U.S. Dist. Ct. Colo. 1977. Reference libr. assoc. Ill. State Library, Springfield, 1972-73; asst. atty. gen. State of Ill., Springfield, 1973-75; pvt. practice Boulder, Colo., 1978-79, Denver, 1979—. Mem. So. Poverty Law Ctr.; mem. hate violence task force, Colo. Lawyers Com.; bd. dirs., foster mom for young kittens Recycled Critter Rescue. Mem.: DAR, ABA, Colo. Women's Bar Assn. (editor newsletter 1982—84), Denver Bar Assn., Colo. Bar Assn. (legal fee arbitration com.), Am. Assn. Retired Persons, Survivors United Network (legal coord. 1992—93), Ams. of Royal Descent, Toastmasters Internat. (Able Toastmaster Bronze 1992), Colonial Dames, Survivors United Network Profls. (exec. com. 1992), Mensa (local sect. Ann Arbor, Mich. 1968), Nat. Soc. Magna Carta Dames, Colonial Order of Crown, Sovereign Colonial Soc., Alpha Lambda Delta, Sigma Tau Delta, Phi Alpha Theta. Avocations: philately, chess, needlework, dinosaurs, horatio alger stories. Family and matrimonial. Office: 1525 Josephine St Denver CO 80206-1406 E-mail: kamcdowell@qwest.net.

MCDUFFY, ADITYA, lawyer; d. Louis and Brenda McDuffy. LLM in Corp. Law and Fin., Widener U., 1998; JD, Tex. So. U., 1995; BA, Howard U., 1990. Bar: Pa. 1996, cert.: mediator Justice Ctr., Atlanta 2000. Asst. counsel dept. def. Def. Logistics Agy., Phila., Def. Supply Ctr., Phila., 1998—. Presenter, organizer in field at seminars, tng. sessions, presentations. Creator, editor (legal edn. website) Blacks In Government's Online Legal Resources Center; editor (creator): (newsletter) EEO Flash. Vol. atty. Consumer Bankruptcy Advocacy Program, Phila., 1997—98; chair, nat. legal rev. com. Nat. Orgn. Blacks in Govt., Wash., 2000—; mem. Met. Wilmington Urban League, 2003; asst. chaplain Hillside Ch. Christ, Wilmington, Del., 1998—2003. Recipient Vol. award, Girls Inc., 1998, Cert. of Achievement, Fed. Exec. Bd., Ptnrs. In Equality, 2001, Achiever's award, Def. Supply Ctr., Phila., 2001, Spl. Act award, 2001. Mem.: Am. Constn. Soc., Am. Comm. Assn., Zeta Phi Beta Sorority, Inc. (chpt. v.p., chpt. sec. 2000—03, coord. state com. 2003—). Federal civil litigation, Labor (including EEOC, Fair Labor Standards Act, labor-management relations, NLRB, OSHA), Government contracts and claims. Home Fax: 1-800-430-7848. Personal E-mail: asmcduffy@yahoo.com.

MC ELHANEY, JOHN HESS, lawyer; b. Milw., Apr. 16, 1934; s. Lewis Keck and Sara Jane (Hess) McE.; m. Jacquelyn Masur, Aug. 4, 1962; children— Scott, Victoria. BBA, So. Meth. U., 1956, JD, 1958. Bar: Tex. bar 1958. Pvt. practice law, Dallas, 1958—; pntr. Locke, Liddell & Sapp, L.L.C., Dallas, 1976—. Lectr. law So. Meth. U., 1967-76 Contbr. articles to legal jours. Trustee St. Mark's Sch. Tex., 1980-86. Fellow Am. Coll. Trial Lawyers; mem. Am. Bd. Trial Advs., ABA, Tex. Bar Assn., So. Meth. U. Law Alumni Assn. (pres. 1972-73, dir. 1970-73), Town and Gown Club (pres. 1981-82). Presbyterian. Federal civil litigation, General civil litigation, Libel. Home: 5340 Tanbark Dr Dallas TX 75229-5555 Office: Locke Liddell & Sapp 2200 Ross Ave Ste 2200 Dallas TX 75201-6776

MCELHINNY, HAROLD JOHN, lawyer; b. San Francisco, Jan. 5, 1947; s. Harold James and Margaret I. (Mahoney) McE.; m. Mary Ellen McElhinny, June 22, 1968; children: Hannah, Jennifer, William. BA in Polit. Sci., U. Santa Clara, 1970; JD, U. Calif., Berkeley, 1975. Bar: Calif. 1976, U.S. Supreme Ct. 1983. Vol. Peace Corps., Tripoli, Libya, 1968-69; juvenile counselor Santa Clara County (Calif.) Juvenile Hall, 1969-72; law clk. U.S. Dist. Ct., Hartford, Conn., 1975-76; ptnr. Morrison & Foerster, San Francisco, 1976—. Mem. ABA, Calif. Bar Assn., State Bar Calif. (rev. dept. 1986-89, chmn. 1988), San Francisco Bar Assn., Am. Intellectual Property Law Assn., Assn. Bus. Trial Lawyers (bd. govs. 1992-97, pres. 1997). Democrat. Roman Catholic. Office: Morrison & Foerster 425 Market St Fl 30 San Francisco CA 94105-2482 E-mail: hmcelhinny@mofo.com.

MCELROY, HOWARD CHOWNING, lawyer; b. Shreveport, La., Mar. 26, 1946; s. Charles Imogene and Verna Mae (Snow) McE.; m. Heidi Margot Hansen, June 17, 1970; children: Andrew, Christopher, Karen. BS, U.S. Mil. Acad., 1968; JD, Georgetown U., 1977. Bar: Va. 1977, U.S. Dist. Ct. (we. dist.) Va. 1977, U.S. Ct. Appeals (4th cir.) 1977. Ptnr. Bundy McElroy Hodges, Abingdon, Va., 1995—. Mem. mandatory continuing legal edn. bd. Va. State Bar 1986-89, professionalism course faculty, 1991-94. Capt. M.I. U.S. Army, 1968-72, Vietnam. Fellow Am. Bar Found., Va. Law Found.; mem. ABA, Am. Bd. Trial Advocates (Va. chpt.), Def. Rsch. Inst., Va. Bar Assn. (exec. com. 1991-95, sec. 1993-95), Va. Assn. Def. Attys. (pres. 1995-96), Internat. Assn. Def. Counsel, Assn. Def. Trial Attys., Rotary (pres. local club 1983-84, Paul Harris fellow). Episcopalian. Federal civil litigation, State civil litigation, Insurance. Home: 160 Crestview Dr NE Abingdon VA 24210-2010 Office: Bundy McElroy Hodges 330 Cummings St Abingdon VA 24210-3208 E-mail: hmcelroybmhlaw@naxs.net.

MCELROY, MICHAEL ROBERT, lawyer; b. Providence, Feb. 7, 1951; s. Gerald Robert and Jeannette (Belanger) McE.; m. Christine Anne O'Donnell, June 5, 1976; children: Brian Robert, Dianne Elizabeth, Erin Christine. BA with highest distinction, U. R.I., 1973; JD cum laude, Boston U., 1976; MS in Taxation cum laude, Bryant Coll., 1987. Bar: Tenn. 1976, Mass. 1985, U.S. Dist. Ct. (ea. dist.) Tenn. 1977, U.S. Ct. Appeals (5th cir.) 1977, U.S. Supreme Ct. 1979, U.S. Ct. Appeals (6th cir.) 1980, R.I. 1981, U.S. Dist. Ct. R.I. 1981, U.S. Ct. Appeals (1st cir.) 1981, U.S. Dist. Ct. Mass. 2000. Trial atty. TVA, Knoxville, 1976-81; counsel R.I. Pub. Utilities Commn., Providence, 1982-83; spl. asst. atty. gen. Office Atty. Gen., Providence, 1982-83; ptnr. O'Leary & McElroy, Providence, 1981-85; sole practice Providence, 1985-87; ptnr. Schacht & McElroy, Providence, 1987—. Pres. Utility Cons., Inc., Providence, 1983; ptnr. McElroy, Lawrence, Edge & Assocs., Providence, 1983-85. Legal counsel for candidate Congl. campaign, Providence, 1982; legal counsel Pawtuxet Valley Preservation and Hist. Soc., West Warwick, R.I., 1983—; chief speech writer for candidate gubernatorial campaign, R.I., 1984; chief legal counsel for candidate gubernatorial campaign, R.I., 1988, Gov. Bruce Sundlun's successful gubernatorial campaign, 1990; legal counsel to R.I. Pers. Appeal Bd., 1991—; arbitrator Superior Ct. R.I., 1992—; spl. master/commr., 1993—; mediator Superior Ct., 1999—; spl. legal counsel to R.I. Ethics Commn., 2000-02. Danforth Found. hon. fellow, 1973; Rhodes scholar nominee, 1973; honoree for life-saving CPR, TVA, 1980; nominated for judgeship Jud. Nom. Commn. Superior Ct., 1994. Mem.: ATLA, Million Dollar Advs. Forum, Assn. Trial Lawyers R.I., R.I. Bar Assn. Roman Catholic. General civil litigation, General practice, Utilities, public. Home: 345 Sharon St Providence RI 02908-2220 Office: PO Box 6721 Providence RI 02940-6721 E-mail: mcelroymik@aol.com.

MCELVEEN, JUNIUS CARLISLE, JR., lawyer; b. Rogersville, Tenn., Feb. 17, 1947; s. Junius Carlisle and Martha Kathleen (Harrison) McE.; m. Mary Wallace Pyles, Sept. 22, 1973; children: Kathryn Carlisle, Sarah Elizabeth. BA cum laude, U. Va., 1969, JD, 1972. Bar: Va. 1972, Calif. 1975, U.S. Dist. Ct. (ea. dist.) Va. 1976, D.C. 1978, U.S. Ct. Appeals (4th cir.) 1978, U.S. Ct. Appeals (Fed. cir.) 1986, U.S. Ct. Appeals (11th cir.) 1990. Rsch. assoc. Atlantic Richfield, Washington, 1972; assoc. Pender & Coward, Norfolk, Va., 1976-77; from assoc. to ptnr. Seyfarth, Shaw, Washington, 1977—83; ptnr. Jones Day, Washington, 1983—. Mem. adv. com., reproductive hazards in the workplace Office of Tech. Assessment, Washington, 1984-86; mem. adv. council Ctr. Environ. Health, U. Conn., 1986-95; mem. editorial bd. The Occupational and Environ. Medicine Report, 1986—, Human and Ecol. Risk Assessment, 1998—. Contbr. articles to legal jours. Elder Kirkwood Presbyn. Ch., Springfield, Va., 1984-86. Served as lt. USN, 1972-75. Mem. ABA, Va. State Bar, State Bar Calif., Phi Beta Kappa, Phi Delta Phi (sec. local chpt. 1971-72, Outstanding Grad. award 1972). Federal civil litigation, Environmental, Labor (including EEOC, Fair Labor Standards Act, labor-management relations, NLRB, OSHA). Home: 318 S Pitt St Alexandria VA 22314-3712 Office: Jones Day 51 Louisana Ave NW Washington DC 20001 E-mail: jcmcelveen@jonesday.com.

MCELVEIN, THOMAS IRVING, JR., lawyer; b. Buffalo, N.Y., Apr. 19, 1936; s. Thomas I. and Edith Marian (Bowen) McE.; m. Ernesta F. McElvein, June 26, 1965; children: Christopher, Andrew, Kathryn. BA, Antioch Coll., 1959; JD, Yale U., 1962. Bar: N.Y. 1962, U.S. Dist. Ct. (we. dist.) N.Y. 1969. Atty. Village Akron, N.Y., 1963-99, spl. project atty., 2000—. Bd. dirs. Meals on Wheels of Buffalo and Erie County, Inc. Mem. N.Y. State Bar Assn., Erie County Bar Assn. General practice. Home: 295 Nottingham Ter Buffalo NY 14216-3125 Office: 1500 Liberty Bldg Buffalo NY 14202-3612

MCELWEE, DENNIS JOHN, lawyer, former pharmaceutical company executive; b. New Orleans, July 30, 1947; s. John Joseph and Audrey (Nunez) McE. BS, Tulane U., 1970; JD, U. Denver, 1992. Clean room and quality control analyst Sci. Enterprises Inc., Broomfield, Colo., 1975-76; analytical chemist in toxicology Poisonlab. Inc., Denver, 1977; analytical chemist, then dir. quality control program Colo. Sch. Mines Rsch. Inst., 1977-79; dir. quality control, then dir. compliance Benedict Nuclear Pharms. Co., Golden, Colo., 1979-84; pres. MC Projections Inc., Morrison, Colo., 1985-86; dir. regulatory affairs Electromedics Inc., Englewood, Colo., 1986-89; pvt. practice, 1992—. Author: Mineral Research Chemicals, Toxic Properties and Proper Handling, 2d edit., 1979; mem. editl. bd. CF Network Mag.; contbr. articles to profl. jours. Bd. dirs. Denver chpt. Cystic Fibrosis Found., 1996, Assn. of Vols. for Children's Hosp., Denver, 1999. Recipient Sutton prize in internat. law U. Denver Sch. Law, 1991, Finest award Denver Charities, 1999. Mem. Colo. Bar Assn., Colo. Criminal Def. Bar, Denver Bar Assn., 1st Jud. Dist. Bar Assn. E-mail: dionysius@prodigy.net.

MCELYEA, MONICA SERGENT, lawyer; b. Pennington Gap, Va., Jan. 15, 1967; d. Birg Eugene and Lana Kay (Turner) Sergent; m. Jeffrey Earl McElyea, Dec. 16, 1994. BA, Randolph-Macon Woman's Coll., Lynchburg, Va., 1988; JD, Mercer U., 1991. Bar: Ga. and Va. 1991, Tenn. 1993, U.S. Dist. Ct. (no. dist.) Ga. 1991, U.S. Dist. Ct. (we. dist.) Va. 1992, U.S. Dist. Ct. (ea. dist.) Va. 1995, U.S. Dist. Ct. Colo. 1998, U.S. Ct. Appeals (4th cir.) 1992, U.S. Supreme Ct. 1995, Colo. 1997, U.S. Dist. Ct. Colo., 1998. Law clerk U.S. Magistrate Judge Cynthia D. Kinser, Abingdon, Va., 1991-92; assoc. atty. Birg E. Sergent Atty. at Law, Pennington Gap, Va., 1992-93; asst. Commonwealth's atty. Lee County, Jonesville, Va., 1993-94; pvt. practice Pennington Gap, Va., 1993-94; asst. atty. gen. Office of Atty. Gen., Richmond, Va., 1994-97; assoc. Law Offices David A. Helmer, Frisco, Colo., 1997—. Methodist. General civil litigation, Criminal, Personal injury (including property damage). Office: Law Offices David A Helmer PO Box 868 611 Main St Frisco CO 80443 E-mail: monica@helmerlaw.com.

MCEVERS, DUFF STEVEN, lawyer; b. L.A., Apr. 21, 1954; s. Milton Stoddard and Virginia Mary (Tongue) McE.; m. Jeannine Marie Matthews, July 14, 1984; children: Tay Colleen, Reily Maureen. BA, U. So. Calif., 1976; JD, Western State U., 1980. Bar: Calif. 1981, U.S. Dist. Ct. (so. dist.) Calif. 1993, U.S. Dist. Ct. (ctrl. dist.) Calif. 1982, U.S. Ct. Appeals (9th cir.) 1988. Assoc. Donald B. Black Inc., Laguna Beach, Calif., 1981-85; pvt. practice Laguna Beach and Newport Beach, Calif., 1985-88, Assoc. Law Office of Terry J. Coniglio, Inc., Long Beach, Calif., 1988-89; with Barclay Law Corp., 1989-91; pvt. practice Newport Beach and Sonoma, Calif., 1992-2000; of counsel Walker Law Firm, P.C., Newport Beach, 1992-2000; assoc. Cooksey, Toolen, Gage Duffy & Woog, Costa Mesa, Calif., 2000—02; atty. Law Office of Duff S. McEvers, Laguna Nicuel, 2002—. Editor: Law Review, 1979. Mem. Calif. Bar Assn., Assn. Bus. Trial Lawyers. State civil litigation, Private international, Property, real (including real estate development, water). Office: 27881 LaPaz Rd Ste G Laguna Niguel CA 92677

MCEVILLY, JAMES PATRICK, JR., lawyer; b. Phila., July 30, 1943; s. James P. and Virginia Frances (Madden) McE.; m. Joan Elizabeth O'Connor; children: James III, Christopher (dec.), Sara, Michael. BS, St. Joseph's U., 1965; JD, Temple U., 1971. Bar: Pa. 1971, U.S. Dist. Ct. (ea. dist.) Pa. 1972, U.S. Ct. Appeals (3d cir.) 1975, U.S. Supreme Ct. 1982. Law clk to pres. judge Phila. Mcpl. Ct., 1971-73; assoc. Galfand, Berger, Lurie & March, Phila., 1973-76; asst. dist. atty. Phila. Dist. Atty., 1976-79; prin. McEvilly Law Office, Feasterville, Pa., 1979—. Editor Temple U. Law Rev., 1971. Mem. Pa. Trial Lawyers Assn., Phila. Bar Assn., Phila. Trial Lawyers. Criminal, General practice, Personal injury (including property damage). Home: 1401 Silo Rd Yardley PA 19067-4240 Office: 1200 Bustleton Pike Ste 1B Trevose PA 19053-4108

MCEVOY, SHARLENE ANN, law educator; b. Derby, Conn., July 6, 1950; d. Peter Henry Jr. and Madaline Elizabeth (McCabe) McE. BA magna cum laude, Albertus Magnus Coll., 1972; JD, U. Conn., West Hartford, 1975; MA, Trinity Coll., Hartford, 1980, UCLA, 1982, PhD, 1985. Bar: Conn., 1975. Pvt. practice, Derby, 1984—; asst. prof. bus. law Fairfield (Conn.) U. Sch. Bus., 1986—92; adj. prof. bus. law, polit. sci. Albertus Magnus Coll., New Haven, 1978-80, U. Conn., Stamford, 1984-86; acting chmn. polit. sci. dept. Albertus Magnus Coll., 1980; assoc. prof. law Fairfield U., 1992-98, prof. bus. law, 1998—. Chmn. Women's Resource Ctr., Fairfield U., 1989-91. Staff editor Jour. Legal Studies Edn., 1989-94; reviewer Am. Bus. Law Assn. jour., 1988—, staff editor, 1995—; sr. articles editor N.E. Jour. of Legal Studies in Bus., 1995-96. Mem. Derby Tercentennial Commn., 1973—74; justice of the peace City of Derby, 1975—83; alt. mem. Parks and Recreation Commn., Woodbury, 1995—99; v.p. N.E. Acad. Legal Studies in Bus., 2001—02, 2001—02, pres. and program chair, 2003—; editor-in-chief N.E. Jour. of Legal Studies, 2003—04; mem., treas. Woodbury Dem. Town Com., 1995—96, corr. sec., 1996—98; bd. dirs. Valley Transit Dist., Derby, 1975—77. Recipient Best Paper award N.E. Regional Bus. Law Assn., 1990, Best Paper award Tri-State Regional Bus. Law Assn., 1991; Fairfield U. Sch. Bus. rsch. grantee 1989, 91, 92, Fairfield U. rsch. grantee, 1994. Mem. ABA, Conn. Bar Assn., Acad. Legal Studies in Bus., Mensa (coord. SINISTRAL spl. interest group 1977—). Democrat. Roman Catholic. Avocations: running, chess, tennis, swimming. Office: 198 Emmett Ave Derby CT 06418-1258 E-mail: samcevoy@mail.fairfield.edu.

MCEWEN, WILLARD WINFIELD, JR., lawyer, judge; b. Evanston, Ill., Dec. 26, 1934; s. Willard Winfield Sr. and Esther (Sprenger) McE.; children: Michael, Elizabeth, Allison. BS, Claremont Men's Coll., 1956; LLB, U. Calif., San Francisco, 1959. Bar: Calif. 1960, U.S. Dist. Ct. (no. and so. dists.) Calif. 1960, U.S. Supreme Ct. 1974. Commd. U.S. Army, 1956, advanced through grades to capt., 1965, resigned, 1968; dep. legis. counsel. City of Sacramento, Calif., 1960-61; asst. city atty. City of Santa Barbara, Calif., 1961-62; sole practice Santa Barbara, 1962—; judge U.S. Magistrate Ct., Santa Barbara County, 1973—; atty. Goleta Water Dist., 1986-87. Lectr. Santa Barbara Adult Edn. Program. Founder, bd. dirs., officer, gen. legal coun. Santa Barbara Coun. for Retarded, 1962-72; active WORK Workshop for Handicapped, Assn. Retarded Citizens, Santa Barbara City Landmarks Adv. Com., 1967-73; v.p. Santa Barbara Harbor Pageants and Exhibits Com., 1964; chmn. Citizens Save our Shoreline Com., 1964, Citizens Cmty. Master Plan Com., 1964, YMCA Membership Drive, 1964, Citizens Adv. Com. on Sch. Dist. Tax Needs, 1965; commr. Santa Barbara City Water Commn., 1965, City of Santa Barbara Recreation Commn., 1970-73; elected to founding bd. dirs. City Commerce Bank. Recipient Disting Svc. award Santa Barbara Jaycees, 1965; named Santa Barbara's Young Man of Yr. Sanata Barbara C. of C. 1983. Mem. Am. Heart Assn. (pres. Santa Barbara County chpt. 1981-82), Santa Barbara Heart Assn. (bd. dirs., pres. bd. dirs. 1981-82, chmn. Heart Sunday 1973, 75), Santa Barbara Malacological Soc., Santa Barbara Kiwanis (pres. 1967), C. of C. (com. on local govt., state legisaltion com., bd. dirs., past v.p. bd. dirs., pres. bd. dirs. 1981-82, chmn. several coms.). Republican. Roman Catholic. Avocations: golf, skiing. Corporate, general, Estate planning, Property, real (including real estate development, water). Office: US Courthouse 8 E Figueroa St Ste 210 Santa Barbara CA 93101-2745 E-mail: imannieo@aol.com.

MCFADDEN, FRANK HAMPTON, lawyer, business executive, former judge; b. Oxford, Miss., Nov. 20, 1925; s. John Angus and Ruby (Roy) McF.; m. Jane Porter Nabers, Sept. 30, 1960; children— Frank Hampton, Angus Nabers, Jane Porter. BA, U. Miss., 1950; LL.B., Yale U., 1955. Bar: N.Y. 1956, Ala. 1959. Assoc. firm Lord, Day & Lord, N.Y.C., 1955-58, Bradley, Arant, Rose & White, Birmingham, Ala., 1958-63, partner, 1963-69; judge U.S. Dist. Ct. No. Dist. Ala., Birmingham, 1969-73, chief judge, 1973-81; sr. v.p., gen. counsel Blount, Inc., Montgomery, Ala., 1982-91, exec. v.p. adminstrn. and govt. affairs, 1991, exec. v.p. legal affairs, 1991-93, exec. v.p., gen. counsel, 1993-95; mem. Capell & Howard, P.C., Montgomery, 1995—. Chmn. Blount Energy Resource Corp., Montgomery, 1983-88. Mem. jud. panel CPR Inst. for Dispute Resolution, 1985—. Served from ensign to lt. USNR, 1944-49, 51-53. Fellow Am. Coll. Constrn. Lawyers; mem. Am. Corp. Counsel Assn. (bd. dirs. 1984-93, chmn. 1989). Alternative dispute resolution, General civil litigation, Construction. Office: Capell & Howard PC 150 S Perry St Montgomery AL 36104-4227

MCFADDEN, MONICA ELIZABETH, lawyer; BS, Cornell U., 1973; MA, Mich. State U., 1976; JD, U. Chgo., 1993. Bar: Ill. 1993, U.S. Dist. Ct. (no. dist.) Ill. 1993. Campaign mgr. Iowa ERA, Des Moines, 1979-80; dep. campaign mgr. Conlin for Gov., Des Moines, 1980-82; message coord. Cranston for Pres., Washington, 1982-84; dir. polit. programs Nat. Women's Polit. Caucus, Washington, 1984-86; dir. govt. rels. Bus. and Profl. Women USA, Washington, 1987-89; sr. staff U.S. Bipartisan Com. on Health Care, Washington, 1989-90; clk. Hofeld & Schaffner, Chgo., 1990-93, assoc., 1993-96; prin. McFadden Law Offices, Chgo., 1996—. Prin. McFadden Consulting, Washington and Chgo., 1984—. Contbr. articles to profl. jours. Fellow AAUW, Washington, 1992; named Outstanding Young Woman of Am. Mem. ATLA (com. chair 1993—, sect. officer employment sect. 1997—), Ill. Trial Lawyers Assn., Ill. State Bar Assn. (sect. rep. 1996—), Women's Bar Assn. Civil rights, General civil litigation, Personal injury (including property damage). Office: McFadden Law Offices 100 N La Salle St Ste 2115 Chicago IL 60602-2409

MCFADDEN, ROSEMARY THERESA, lawyer, financial services executive; b. Oct. 1, 1948; came to U.S., 1951, naturalized, 1967; d. John and Winifred (Quinn) McFadden; m. Brian Doherty, May 26, 1973. BA, Rutgers U., 1970, MBA, 1974; JD, Seton Hall U., 1978; hon. doctorate, St. Elizabeth's Coll., Convent Station, N.J., 1985. Bar: N.J. 1978, U.S. Dist. Ct. N.J. 1978. Spl. asst. Office of the Mayor, Jersey City, 1973-76; exec. dir. Hudson Health Sys., Jersey City, 1976-81; assoc. legal counsel N.Y. Merc. Exch., N.Y.C., 1981-82, exec. v.p., 1982-84, pres., 1984-89, spl. policy advisor to bd. dirs., 1989-91; of counsel Shulman, Hanlon and Doherty, Jersey City and N.Y.C., 1989-97; sr. mgr. Price Waterhouse Internat. Practice Group, 1993-97; sr. v.p. Donaldson Lufkin & Jenrette/Pershing, Jersey City, 1997-98; mng. dir. global devel. CSFBdirect, Jersey City, 1999—. Mem. deans adv. coun. Rutgers U. Grad Sch. Mgmt., Newark, 1985. Bd. dirs. Jersey City Med. Ctr., 1985-87, UNICEF, 1989-92, Futures Industry Assn., 1989-90. Named Alumna of Yr., Rutgers U., 1985, Seton Hall U. Mem. ABA, N.J. Bar Assn., Futures Industry Assn., Securities Industry Assn., Rutgers U. Alumni Assn. Roman Catholic. Avocations: travel, antiques. Office: CSFBdirect Harborside Plz II 5th Fl Jersey City NJ 07311 E-mail: RMcFadden@CSFBdirect.com.

MCFADYEN, DOUGLAS ROBERT ANDREW, lawyer; b. Toronto, Ont., Can., Nov. 28, 1961; s. John E. and Sandra J. McFadyen; m. Rosa Testani, Aug. 13, 1999. BA, U. Toronto, 1983, LLB, 1986; LLM, NYU, 1995. Bar: NY 1996. Clk. to chief judge Tax Ct. Can., Ottawa, 1988—89; tax policy advisor Dept. Fin., Ottawa, 1989—93; sr. mgr. Ernst & Young, N.Y.C., 1994—95; assoc. Sherman & Sterling, N.Y.C., 1995—98, ptnr., 1999—. Contbr. articles to profl. jours. Corporate taxation. Office: Shearman & Sterling 599 Lexington Ave New York NY 10022 Office Fax: 212-848-4554. E-mail: dmcfadyen@shearman.com.

MCFALL, DONALD BEURY, lawyer; b. Charleston, W.Va., Aug. 2, 1941; s. Henry Tucker and Elizabeth Katharine (Beury) McF.; m. Donna Glenn Binion, May 27, 1972; children: Katharine Atkinson, Mary Crawford. BA, Washington and Lee U., 1964, JD, 1969. Bar: Va. 1969, Tex. 1969, U.S. Supreme Ct. 1979, U.S. Dist. Ct. (we., no., so. and ea. dists.) Tex. 1969. Asst. U.S. atty. U.S. Dept. Justice, Houston, 1970-71; assoc. Butler & Binion, Houston, 1971-77, ptnr., 1977-85, McFall, Sherwood & Sheeny, Houston, 1985-2000; shareholder McFall, Martinez, Sherwood, Breitbeil & Sullivan and predecessor firm, Houston, 2000—. Trustee

Humana Hosp.-Sharpstown, Houston, 1984—85, Southmore Med. Ctr., 1994—98; bd. dirs. Planned Parenthood Houston and S.E. Tex., 1978—88; trustee Woodberry Forest Sch., Orange, Va., 1984—90, Washington and Lee U., 1997—. 1st lt. U.S. Army, 1964—66. Fellow: Internat. Soc. Barristers, Am. Coll. Trial Lawyers, Houston Bar Found., Tex. Bar Found.; mem.: Am. Bd. Trial Advocates (adv.), Fedn. Ins. and Corp. Counsel, Tex. State Bar Assn., Va. State Bar Assn., Internat. Assn. Def. Counsel. Federal civil litigation, State civil litigation, Personal injury (including property damage). Office: McFall Martinez Sherwood Breitbeil & Sullivan 4800 ChevronTexaco Plz 1111 Bagby St Houston TX 77002 Fax: 713-590-9399; Office Fax: 713-590-9300. Personal E-mail: dbmcf@aol.com. Business E-Mail: dmcfall@mcfall-law.com.

MCFARLAND, CAROL ANNE, lawyer; b. Eugene, Oreg., Aug. 25, 1951; d. Harvey John and Muriel Anne (Walker) McF.; children: Annette Catherine, Miles Patrick. BS, Oreg. State U., 1973; JD, Western State U., 1977. Bar: Calif. 1977, U.S. Dist. Ct. (so. dist.) Calif. 1977. Assoc. Sankary & Sankary, San Diego, 1977-81; pvt. practice San Diego, 1981-88; dep. dist. atty. Family Support divsn., Clackamas County, Oreg., 1990—. Vol. atty. Supervision Ctr. Women's Studies-Clinic Domestic Violence Restraining Orders, 1983-88, San Diego Vol. Lawyers Assn., 1986-88. Mem. ABA, Calif. Bar Assn., Oreg. State Bar Assn., Clackamas County Bar Assn., Oreg. Women Lawyers, Rotary Internat., Delta Theta Phi. Commercial, consumer (including collections, credit), Criminal, Family and matrimonial. Office: 619 Madison St # 106 Oregon City OR 97045

MCFARLAND, KAY ELEANOR, state supreme court chief justice; b. Coffeyville, Kans., July 20, 1935; d. Kenneth W. and Margaret E. (Thrall) McF. BA magna cum laude, Washburn U., Topeka, 1957, JD, 1964. Bar: Kans. 1964. Sole practice, Topeka, 1964-71; probate and juvenile judge Shawnee County, Topeka, 1971-73; dist. judge Topeka, 1973-77; assoc. justice Kans. Supreme Ct., 1977-95, chief justice, 1995—. Mem. Kans. Bar Assn., Women Attys. Assn. Topeka., Topeka Bar Assn. Office: Kans Supreme Ct Kans Jud Ctr 301 SW 10th Ave Topeka KS 66612-1507 Fax: (785) 291-3274.

MCFARLANE, WALTER ALEXANDER, lawyer, educator; b. Richlands, Va., May 4, 1940; s. James Albert and Frances Mae (Padbury) McF.; m. Judith Louise Copenhaver, Aug. 31, 1962. BA, Emory and Henry Coll., 1962; JD, U. Richmond, 1966. Bar: Ba. 1966, U.S. Supreme Ct. 1970, U.S. Ct. Appeals (4th cir.) 1973, U.S. Ct. Appeals (D.C. cir.) 1977, U.S. Dist. ct. (ea. dist.) Va. 1973. Asst. atty. gen. Office Va. Atty. Gen., Richmond, 1969-73, dep. atty. gen., 1973-90; exec. asst., chief counsel, dir. policy Gov.'s Office Commonwealth of Va., 1990-94, supt. Dept. Correctional Edn., 1994—. Acting dir. Dept. Juvenile Justice, 1997, State Bd. Dept. Criminal Justice Svcs., 1994-; prof. adj. staff U. Richmond, 1978-2003, A.L.Philpott disting. prof. T.C. Williams Sch. Law, 2003; chmn. transp. law com. Transp. Rsch. Bd., Nat. Rsch. Bd. Nat. Acads. Sci. and Engring., Washington, 1977-85, 88-94, chmn. legal affairs com., 1978-85, chmn. environ., archeol. and hist. com., 1985-90; mem. State Water Commn., 1994-96, mem., Coun. of State Govts. Henry Toll Fell., 1988, Legal Task Force, 1988-2002. Contbr. articles to profl. jours. Mem. exec. com., bd. govs. Emory and Henry Coll., 1985-98; pres. Windsor Forest Civic Assn., Midlothian, Va., 1975-76; bd. dirs. Greater Midlothian Civic League, 1980-86, v.p., 1980; instr. water safety ARC, 1962-87; chmn. bldg. com. Mt. Pisgah United Meth. Ch., 1980-85, pres. men's club, 1980-81; bd. dirs. cen. Va. chpt. Epilepsy Assn. Va., 1988-91. Capt. JAGC, USAF, 1966-69. Recipient J.D. Buscher Disting. Atty. award Am. Assn. State Hwy. and Transp. Ofcls., 1983, John C. Vance legal writing award Nat. Acads. Sci. and Engring., 4th ann. outstanding evening lectr. award Student Body, U. Richmond, 1980. Mem. Chesterfield Bar Assn., Richmond Bar Assn. (bd. dirs. 1989-93), Richmond Scottish Soc. (bd. dirs. 1980-82), Emory and Henry Coll. Alumni Assn. (chpt. pres. 1971-73, regional v.p. 1974-77, pres. 1981-83), Meadowbrook Country Club (bd. dir. 2001-). Home: 9001 Widgeon Way Chesterfield VA 23838-5274 Office: 101 N 14th St Richmond VA 23219-3684

MCGAFFEY, JERE D. lawyer; b. Lincoln, Nebr., Oct. 6, 1935; s. Don Larsen and Doris McG.; m. Ruth S. Michelsen, Aug. 19, 1956; children: Beth, Karen. BA, BSc with high distinction, U. Nebr., 1957; LLB magna cum laude, Harvard U., 1961. Bar: Wis. 1961. Mem. firm Foley & Lardner, Milw., 1961—, ptnr., 1968—. Dir. Smith Investment Co., Northwestern Mut. Trust Co., Lord Balt. Corp., Wis. Gas Co., 1978-2000. Author works in field. Chmn. bd. dirs. Helen Bader Found.; vice chmn. legis. Milw. Met. Assn. Commerce; former chmn. Wis. Taxpayers Alliance, sec.-treas., 1994—; former chmn. bd. dirs. Aurora Health Care, 1986—; chmn. bd. advisors U. Wis. Nursing Sch., Milw. Mem. ABA (chmn. tax sect. 1990-91, ho. dels. 1995-2000), AICPA, Wis. Bar Assn., Wis. Inst. CPAs, Am. Coll. Tax Counsel (chmn. 1996-98), Am. Coll. Trust and Estate Counsel (chmn. bus. planning com. 1994-97, regent 2000—), Am. Law Inst., Univ. Club (Milw.), Milw. Club, Milw. Country Club, Harvard Club N.Y.C., Univ. Club Washington, Phi Beta Kappa, Beta Gamma Sigma, Delta Sigma Rho. Corporate, general, Corporate taxation, Estate taxation. Home: 12852 NW Shoreland Dr Mequon WI 53097-2304 Office: Foley & Lardner 777 E Wisconsin Ave Ste 3600 Milwaukee WI 53202-5302 E-mail: jmcgaffey@foleylaw.com.

MCGARRY, CHARLES WILLIAM, lawyer; b. Mt. Kisco, N.Y., June 23, 1957; m. Lori J. Voss. BA in Philosophy, SUNY, Binghamton, 1979; JD, U. Tex., 1982. Bar: Tex. 1983. Law clk. Atty. Gen. of Tex., Austin, 1980-82; briefing atty. Tex. Ct. of Appeals, Dallas, 1982-83; pvt. practice Dallas, 1984-93, 95—; chief justice Tex. Ct. Appeals, Dallas, 1993-94. Mediator Dallas County Juvenile Dept., 1984-93; arbitrator Better Bus. Bur., Dallas, 1985-93. Editor: Aviation Litigation, 1986. Chmn. Irving (Tex.) Dems., 1987-91; pres. Dallas Jazz Orch., 1990-92. Mem. Tex. Bar Assn., Dallas Bar Assn., Irving Bar Assn. Democrat. Roman Catholic. Appellate, Entertainment, General civil litigation. Home: 4324 Twin Post Rd Dallas TX 75244-6743 Office: 701 Commerce St Ste 400 Dallas TX 75202 E-mail: cmcgarry@ix.netcom.com.

MCGARRY, RICHARD LAWRENCE, lawyer; b. Flushing, N.Y., Jan. 12, 1960; s. Richard J. and Loretta (McCarthy) McG.; m. Lynda R. Jones, Dec. 21, 1987; children: Abraham A. Eichelberger, Chelsea Eichelberger St. Clair, David B. Eichelberger. BS, Hampden Sydney Coll., 1982; JD, Washington and Lee U., 1989. Bar: Va. 1989, U.S. Dist. Ct. (we. dist.) Va., U.S. Supreme Ct., 1993. Assoc. Jeffrey H. Krasnow and Assocs., Roanoke, Va., 1989-93; ptnr. Johnson & McGarry, P.C., Charlottesville, Va., 1993-94; pvt. practice Roanoke, 1994—. Bd. dirs. Roanoke Valley SPCA. Mem. Va. Trial Lawyers Assn., Assn. Trial Lawyers Am., Roanoke Bar Assn., Va. Bar Assn. General civil litigation, Personal injury (including property damage), Product liability. Office: PO Box 21565 2320 Electric Rd SW Roanoke VA 24018 E-mail: rick.mcgarry@att.net.

MCGEACHIE, JEFFREY STUART, lawyer; b. Glasgow, Scotland, Aug. 24, 1963; s. Douglas Stuart and Isabelle McGeachie; m. Sally Anne Burlton; children: Robert, Laura, Ross. LLB, Edinburgh U., 1985; LLM, U. Coll. London, 2001. Assoc. Stephnson Harwood, London, 1957—93, Travers Smith Braitwaite, 1993—95; assoc., ptnr. Anderson Legal, 1995—2002; ptnr. Bird & Bird, 2002—. Corporate, general, Commercial, contracts (including sales of goods; commercial financing). Office: Bird & Bird 90 Fetter Ln London EC4A 1SP England E-mail: jeff.mcgeachie@twobirds.com.

MCGEOUGH, ROBERT SAUNDERS, lawyer; b. Aug. 30, 1930; s. Edward James and Florence Isabelle (Saunders) McG.; m. Janet James, Nov. 24, 1961; children: Maureen, Michael, Molly. AB, Duke U., 1952; JD, U. Mich., 1959. Assoc. Hoppe, Frey, Hewitt & Milligan, Warren, Ohio, 1965-70, ptnr., 1970-98; of counsel Harrington, Hoppe & Mitchell, Warren, Ohio, 1999—. Dir. First Pl. Bank, 1973-2003; state trustee Jaycees, Warren, 1963; pres. Warren Exchange Club, 1965; pres. Children's Rehab. Ctr. Found., Warren, 1979, trustee, 1983-97; trustee First Fed. Cmty. Found., 1999—. Editor Lawyer's Desk Book, 1978, 98. Recipient award of merit Ohio Legal Ctr. Inst., 1978. Mem. Ohio State Bar Assn., Trumbull County Bar Assn. Republican. Avocation: golf. Banking, Commercial, contracts (including sales of goods; commercial financing), Corporate, general. Home: 3264 Crescent Dr NE Warren OH 44483-6306 Office: Harrington Hoppe & Mitchel Ltd 108 Main Ave SW Ste 500 Warren OH 44481-1010 E-mail: BobMcGeo@webtv.com.

MC GIFFERT, DAVID ELIOT, lawyer, former government official; b. Boston, June 27, 1926; s. Arthur Cushman and Elizabeth (Eliot) McG.; m. Enud De Kibedi-Varga, Jan. 21, 1966; children: Laura, Carola.; m. Nelse Greenway, Apr. 9, 1983. Student, U. Calif.-Berkeley, 1944; BA, Harvard U., 1949, LL.B., 1953; postgrad., Cambridge (Eng.) U., 1950. Bar: D.C. 1954. With firm Covington & Burling, Washington, 1953-55, 57-61, ptnr., 1969-77, 81—. Lectr. law U. Wis., 1956; asst. to sec. def. for legis. affairs Dept. Def., 1962-65, undersec. army, 1965-69, asst. sec. for internat. security affairs, 1977-81 Served with USNR, 1944-46. Mem. Am. Bar Assn., Council Fgn. Relations, Alpha Delta Phi. Clubs: Metropolitan (Washington). Home: 3819 Veazey St NW Washington DC 20016-2230 Office: Covington & Burling PO Box 7566 1201 Pensylvania Ave NW Washington DC 20044-7566

MCGILL, GILBERT WILLIAM, lawyer; b. Glen Cove, N.Y., Mar. 28, 1947; BS, L.I. U., 1972; JD, Hofstra U., 1975. Bar: N.Y. 1975, U.S. Dist. Ct. 1976, U.S. Supreme Ct. 1979. Pvt. practice, Huntington, N.Y., 1975-76; ptnr. Dunne & McGill, Huntington and Sea Cliff, N.Y., 1976-81; pvt. practice Sea Cliff, N.Y., 1981—. Citizens adv. com. North Shore Schs., Glen Head, N.Y., 1977-79, mem. local waterfront revitalization com. Town of Oyster Bay, 1988—; chmn. legal adv. com. Sea Cliff Civic Assn., 1978-79; adv. com. North Shore Republican Club, Glen Head, 1979-81; trsutee Sea Cliff Village Libr., 1980-86; trustee Angelo J. Melillo Ctr. for Mental Health, 1986—, pres., 1986—. Mem. ABA, N.Y. State Bar Assn., Nassau County Bar Assn., Nassau County Lawyers Assn., North Shore Lawyers Assn. (chmn. 1977-78), Sea Cliff Bus. Assn. (pres. 1979-85), Rotary (pres. Glen Head 1983-84, 97-99). General practice. Office: 203 Glen Cove Ave Sea Cliff NY 11579-1437

MCGINLEY, JOHN REGIS, JR., lawyer; b. Pitts., Nov. 26, 1943; s. John R. and Marie E. (Rooney) McGinley. BS, St. Bonaventure U., 1965; JD, Duquesne U., 1968. Bar: Pa. 1968, U.S. Dist. Ct. (we. dist.) Pa. 1968, U.S. Ct. Appeals (3d cir.) 1973, U.S. Supreme Ct. 1983. Asst. dist. atty. Allegheny County, Pa., 1968-70; ptnr. Eckert Seamans Cherin & Mellott; assoc. Duff Grogan & Doyle & Duff, Grogan Graffam, Pitts., 1970—71; chmn. Grogan, Graffam, McGinley, 1971—2002; ptnr. Eckert Seaman Cherin & Mellott, 2002—. Mem. disciplinary bd. Pa. Supreme Ct.; mem., chmn. Pa. Ind. Regulatory Rev. Commn.; adj. prof. law Duquesne U. Sch. Law. Contbr. Duquesne U. Law Rev., 1968, articles to legal jours. Chmn. trustee Mercy Hosp. Found.; former trustee St. Bonaventure U., mem. exec. com. Fellow: Am. Coll. Trial Lawyers; mem.: ABA, Duquesne U. Law Alumni (pres. 1998), Acad. Trial Lawyers, Allegheny County Bar Assn., Pa. Bar Assn. Federal civil litigation, State civil litigation. Office: 4th Fl US Steel Tower 600 Grant St Pittsburgh PA 15219

MCGINLEY, PAUL ANTHONY, JR., lawyer; b. Allentown, Pa., Apr. 24, 1948; s. Paul A. Sr. and Mary (McGurl) McG.; m. Deborah C. Reinhart; children: Paige, Laura, Paul Anthony III, Jonathan. AB, Princeton U., 1970; JD, Georgetown U., 1974. Bar: Pa. 1974, U.S. Dist. Ct. (ea. dist.) Pa. 1974, U.S. Supreme Ct. 1987. Assoc. Gross & Brown, Allentown, 1974-76; asst. pub. defender Lehigh County, Allentown, 1976-77, asst. county solicitor, 1977-78; ptnr. Gross, McGinley & McGinley, Allentown, 1976-83, Gross, McGinley, McGinley & LaBarre, Allentown, 1983-86, Gross, McGinley & LaBarre, Allentown, 1986-87, Gross, McGinley, LaBarre & Eaton, Allentown, 1987—. Mem. legal affairs com. Mag. Pubs. Am., 1994—; chmn. hearing com. disciplinary bd. Supreme Ct. of Pa., 1986-90, 97—. Bd. dirs. Swain Sch., Allentown, 1984-89, Cedar Crest Coll. Bd. Assocs., Allentown, 1986-88; trustee Allentown YWCA, 1985-88. Mem. ABA, Pa. Bar Assn., Lehigh County Bar Assn. (bd. dirs. 1978-84, pres. 1987), Pa. Trial Lawyers Assn., Allentown-Lehigh County C. of C., Princeton Quadrangle Club (bd. dirs.), Velodrome Fund (dir., sec. 1995—), Rodale Inst. (dir. 1998—), Rodale Inc. (asst. sec. 1999—). Democrat. Roman Catholic. Avocations: skiing, tennis. Federal civil litigation, Corporate, general, Property, real (including real estate development, water). Office: Gross McGinley LaBarre & Eaton 33 S 7th St Allentown PA 18101-2436

MCGINNIS, MARY MARGARET, lawyer; b. Ft. Meade, Md., June 3, 1960; d. Bernard Carmen and Mary Margaret Pfeiffer; m. Wayne Thomas McGinnis, Feb. 14, 1996. BA, Western Md. Coll., 1982; JD, U. Memphis, 2000. Bar: Tenn. 2000. Law clk. Shelby County Govt. Divsn. 4 Cir. Ct., Memphis, 1999—2001; assoc. Pounders Coleman , Memphis, 2001—. Commr. Memphis City Beautiful Commn., 2002—. Mem.: Assn. for Women Attys. (sec. 1998—), Leo Bearman, Sr. Am. Inns Ct. (assoc.). Family and matrimonial. Home: 3764 Rhea Ave Memphis TN 38122 Office: Pounder & Coleman Ste 102 1770 Kirby Pkwy Memphis TN 38138

MCGINTY, BRIAN DONALD, lawyer, author; b. June 22, 1937; s. Donald Bruce and Natalia Vallejo (Haraszthy) M. AB, U. Calif., Berkeley, 1959, JD, 1962. Bar: Calif. 1963. Assoc. Twohig, Weingarten & Haas, Seaside, Calif., 1962-63; ptnr. Weingarten & McGinty, Seaside, Calif., 1963-70; sole practice Monterey, Calif., 1970-73, San Francisco, 1973-83; writer, editor Matthew Bender & Co., San Francisco, Oakland, Calif., 1984-93. Author: Haraszthy at the Mint (Famous Calif. Trials Series), 1975, The Palace Inns, 1978, We the People, 1987, Strong Wine: The Life and Legend of Agoston Haraszthy, 1998; contbg. author: The Craft of the Essay, Historical Times Illustrated Encyclopedia of the Civil War, Portrait of America, 5th edit., 1990, California Real Estate Law and Practice, California Forms of Pleading and Practice, California Legal Forms, California Insurance Law, California Probate Law and Practice, California Public Agency Law and Practice, California Wills and Trusts; editor: Napa Wine (Rounce and Coffin Club award 1975), 1974; contbr. numerous articles to profl. jours. Recipient Excellence in Writing award Nat. Hist. Soc., 1976, Editor's award for Hist. Scholarship, Sonoma County Hist. Soc., 1999. Estate planning, Property, real (including real estate development, water).

MCGLAMRY, MAX REGINALD, lawyer; b. Wilcox County, Ga., Sept. 12, 1928; s. Edgar Lee and Allie Bea (Faircloth) McG.; m. Jean Louise Hilyer, Dec. 28, 1950; children: Sharon Kay McGlamry Hendrix, Michael Lee. BS, Auburn U., 1948; LLB cum laude, Mercer U., 1952, JD cum laude, 1970. Bar: Ga. 1953, U.S. Dist. Ct. (mid. dist.) Ga. 1954, U.S. Ct. Appeals (5th cir.) 1964, U.S. Supreme Ct. 1972, U.S. Ct. Appeals (11th cir.) 1981, U.S. Ct. Appeals (4th cir.) 1985, U.S. Dist. Ct. (no. dist.) Calif. 1988, U.S. Dist. Ct. (no. dist.) Ga. 1989. Pvt. practice, Columbus, Ga., 1953-64; from ptnr. to officer Swift, Pease, Davidson & Chapman (name changed to Page, Scrantom, Harris, McGlamry, & Chapman, P.C.), Columbus, 1964-85; ptnr. Pope, Kellogg, McGlamry, Kilpatrick & Morrison, Columbus, 1985-90, Pope, McGlamry, Kilpatrick & Morrison, LLP, Columbus, 1990-2000; pres. Max R. McGlamry, P.C., Columbus, 2000—. Exec. com. Muscogee County Dem. Orgn., Columbus, 1956-60; bd. dirs. Columbus Jr. C. of C. Ens. USN, 1948-49. Am. Coll. Trust & Estate Counsel fellow, 1973, Lawyers Found. Ga. fellow, 1983. Mem. ABA, ATLA, State Bar Ga., Ga. Trial Lawyers Assn., Assn. U.S. Army, Ga. Golfers Sr. Assn., Valley Sr.'s Golf Assn. (pres. 2003), Urban League of Greater Columbus, Inc., Columbus Lawyers Club (pres. 1964-65), Lions (Columbus chpt. pres. 1967-68), Chattahoochee River Club, Green Island Country Club, Phi Kappa Phi, Alpha Epsilon Delta, Phi Alpha Delta, Pi Kappa Alpha. Democrat. Methodist. Avocations: golf, fishing. Personal injury (including property damage), Product liability. Home: 6941 Wethersfield Rd Columbus GA 31904-3317 Office: Max R McGlamry PC PO Box 4481 Columbus GA 31904-0481

MCGLONE, MICHAEL ANTHONY, lawyer; b. New Orleans, Jan. 6, 1951; s. James Godfrey and Dorothy (Barta) McG.; m. Suzanne Blanchard, Nov. 27, 1976; children: Kevin, Kathleen, Meghan. BBA cum laude, Loyola U., New Orleans, 1972, JD, 1975. Bar: La. 1975, U.S. Dist. Ct. (ea. dist.) La. 1975, U.S. Ct. Appeals (5th and 11 cirs.) 1975, U.S. Dist. Ct. (we. dist.) La. 1978, U.S. Dist. Ct. (mid. dist.) La. 1979, U.S. Supreme Ct. 1981. Law clk. to Hon. Herbert W. Christenberry U.S. Dist. Ct., New Orleans, 1975-76; ptnr. Lemle and Kelleher, New Orleans, 1976—. Mem. ABA, ALA, FBA (bd. dirs. New Orleans chpt. 1986—, pres. 1995-96), La. Bar Assn., Southeastern Admiralty Law Inst., New Orleans Bar Assn., Maritime Law Assn., St. Thomas More Inn of Ct. (master barrister), Alpha Sigma Nu, Beta Gamma Sigma. Democrat. Roman Catholic. Admiralty, Federal civil litigation, Personal injury (including property damage). Home: 4708 N Turnbull Dr Metairie LA 70002-1447 Office: Lemle and Kelleher 601 Poydras St New Orleans LA 70130-6029 E-mail: MMcGlone@lemle.com.

MCGOLDRICK, JOHN LEWIS, lawyer; b. Plainfield, N.J., Mar. 2, 1941; s. John Leslie and Sarah (Walker) McG.; m. Ann Chapman Puffer, Oct. 1, 1966; children: Scott Runyon, Jennifer Winslow. BA cum laude, Harvard U., 1963, LLB, 1966. Bar: N.J. 1966, N.Y. 1985. Assoc. McCarter & English, Newark, 1966-73, ptnr., 1974-95; exec. v.p. Bristol-Myers Squibb Co., N.Y.C., 1995—. Vice-chmn., bd. dirs. N.J. Transit Corp., Newark; bd. dirs. Bristol-Myers Squibb Found., Zimmer Holdings, Inc., HealthCare Inst. N.J., Regional Plan Assn., bd. mem. N.J. Network, Trustee Essex-Newark Found. Legal Svcs. N.J.; mem. com. to visit The Coll., mem. com. to visit Sch. Pub. Health, Harvard Bd. Overseers. Fellow Am. Coll. Trial Lawyers, Am. Bar Found., Am. Acad. Appellate Lawyers; mem. ABA, World Econ. Forum, Legal Svcs. N.J. (bd. dirs.), N.J. Bar Assn., N.Y. Bar Assn., Assn. Bar City of N.Y., Assn. Fed. Bar N.J. (former pres., mem. adv. bd.), Am. Law Inst., Assn. Gen. Counsel, Chief Legal Officers Roundtable, Coun. of Chief Legal Officers (The Conf. Bd. Inc.), CPR Inst. for Dispute Resolution (mem. exec. com.), Aspen Inst. on the World Economy, Coun. on Fgn. Rels., Harvard Law Sch. Assn. N.J. (former pres.), mem. Coun. for the U.S. and Italy, Mem. Nat. Panel of Arbitrators, Am. Arbitration Assn.. Home: 25 Vandeventer Ave Princeton NJ 08542-6937 Office: Bristol-Myers Squibb Co 345 Park Ave New York NY 10154-0004

MCGOUGH, WALTER THOMAS, JR., lawyer; b. Pitts., Nov. 7, 1953; s. Walter Thomas and Jane (Fitzpatrick) McG.; m. Rebecca Gai Frazier, June 24, 1978; children: Emily Ann, Walter Thomas III. BA, Princeton U., 1975; JD, U. Va., 1978. Bar: Pa., D.C., U.S. Dist. Ct. (we. dist.) Pa. 1980, U.S. Ct. Appeals (3d cir.) 1983, U.S. Ct. Appeals (6th cir.) 1984, Pa. Supreme Ct. 1978, U.S. Supreme Ct. 1983. Law clk. to judge U.S. Ct. Appeals 3d Cir., Wilmington, Del., 1978-79; law clk. to Hon. William H. Rehnquist U.S. Supreme Ct., Washington, 1979-80; asst. U.S. atty. We. Dist. Pa., 1980-82; assoc. Reed Smith LLP, Pitts., 1982-86, ptnr., 1987—, head of litigation dept., 1999—. Assoc. counsel Sen. Select Com. on Secret Mil. Asst. to Iran and the Nicaraguan Opposition, Washington, 1987; mem. lawyers adv. com. U.S. Ct. Appeals (3d cir.), 1987-89, chmn., 1989; atty. Fed. Criminal Justice Def. Panel West Dist. Pa., 1983—; mem. appellate rules com. U.S. Jud. Conf., 1998—. Co-author: federal Appellate Procedure, 3rd Circuit, 1996; contbr. articles to profl. jours. Trustee Sta. WQED, Pitts., 1996-2001, vice chmn,, 1997-99, chmn., 1999-2002; mem. 3d Cir. Task Force on Rule 11, 1987-89. Mem. Am. Coll. Trial Lawyers, Am. Acad. Appellate Lawyers, Allegheny County Bar Assn. (ethics com. 1983-86, bd. govs. 1994-2001, pres. 1999-2000), Allegheny County Acad. Trial Lawyers, Duquesne Club, Ross Mountain Club, World Affairs Coun. General civil litigation, Criminal, Libel. Office: Reed Smith LLP 435 6th Ave Ste 2 Pittsburgh PA 15219-1886

MCGOVERN, PETER JOHN, law educator; b. N.Y.C., Dec. 6, 1938; s. John Phillip and Helen Marie (Gaisser) McG.; m. Catherine Bigley, Aug. 31, 1963; children: Brian Peter, Sean Daniel. AB, Notre Dame U., 1961; JD, Fordham U., 1964; EdD, U. S.D., 1980. Bar: N.Y. 1964, S.D. 1972, Ind. 1983, Ill. 1990, U.S. Supreme Ct. 1968. Atty. criminal divsn. Dept. Justice, 1971-72; prof. law U. S.D., Vermillion, 1972-83; from asst. dean to assoc. dean U. S.D. Sch. Law, Vermillion, 1972-77, dir. programs and planning, 1979-83; dean Valparaiso (Ind.) U. Sch. Law, 1983-85, St. Thomas U. Sch. Law, Fla., 1985-87, John Marshall Law Sch., Chgo., 1987-90, prof. law, 1990—. Dir. Ctr. for Internat. Bus. and Trade Law, 2000; dir. continuing legal edn. State Bar S.D., 1972-83; past chmn. S.D. Family Law Com.; bd. dirs. Legal Svcs. of Greater Gary Inc. Past pres. Vermillion Area Arts Coun., Nat. Anti-Vivisection Soc.; bd. dirs. Lawyer for Creative Arts, 1990-92. Lt. comdr. JAGC, USN, 1965-71. Recipient Legal Writing award Fed. Bar Assn., 1969. Fellow Ind. Bar Found.; mem. ABA, bd. dirs., mediator, arbitrator, Internat. Acad. Dispute Resolution Democrat. Roman Catholic. Home: 2 East Erie St Apt 2705 Chicago IL 60611-7679 Office: John Marshall Law Sch 315 S Plymouth Ct Chicago IL 60604-3968 E-mail: mcgover@jmls.edu.

MC GOVERN, WALTER T. federal judge; b. Seattle, May 24, 1922; s. C. Arthur and Anne Marie (Thies) McG.; m. Rita Marie Olsen, June 29, 1946; children: Katrina M., Shawn E., A. Renee. BA, U. Wash., 1949, LL.B., 1950. Bar: Wash. 1950. Practiced law in Seattle, 1950-59; mem. firm Kerr, McCord, Greenleaf & Moen; judge Municipal Ct., Seattle, 1959-65, Superior Ct., Wash., 1965-68, Wash. Supreme Ct., 1968-71, U.S. Dist. Ct. (we. dist.) Wash., 1971-87, chief judge, 1975-87, sr. judge, 1987—. Mem. subcom. on supporting personnel Jud. Conf. U.S., 1981-87, chmn. subcom., 1983, mem. adminstrn. com., 1983-87, chmn. jud. resources com., 1987-91. Mem. Am. Judicature Soc., Wash. State Superior Ct. Judges Assn., Seattle King County Bar Assn. (treas.), Phi Delta Phi. Clubs: Seattle Tennis (pres. 1968). Office: US Dist Ct US Courthouse 5th Fl 1010 5th Ave Ste 215 Seattle WA 98104-1189

MCGOWAN, PATRICK FRANCIS, lawyer; b. N.Y.C., July 23, 1940; s. Francis Patrick and Sonia Veronica (Koslow) M.; m. Patricia Neil, June 6, 1964; children: Susan Claire, Kathleen Anne. BA, Rice U., 1962; JD, U. Tex., Austin, 1965. Bar: Tex. 1965, U.S. Ct. Appeals (5th cir.) 1969, U.S. Tax Ct. 1972, U.S. Supreme Ct. 1970, U.S. Ct. Appeals (11th cir.) 1981, U.S. Ct. Appeals (fed. cir.) 1993. Briefing atty. Tex. Supreme Ct., Austin, 1965-66; ptnr. Strasburger & Price, Dallas, 1966-98, Akin, Gump, Strauss, Hauer & Feld, Dallas, 1998—. Pres., chmn. bd. Tex Lex, Inc., 1991-98; faculty I.P. Law Instit. Ctr. Am. and Internat. Law, 2001. Contbr. numerous articles on internet trademark, copyright and franchise law. Bd. advisors Dallas Ft. Worth Sch. Law. Fellow Coll. State Bar Tex. (faculty Franchising Inst. 1987, Intellectual Property Inst. 1992, S.W. Legal Found. Patent Law Inst. 1992, Practising Law Inst. 1996, Ctr. for Am. and Internat. Law I.P. Inst. 2001); mem. ABA (alt. dispute resolution, forum com. on franchising, trademark and unfair competition com., patent, trademark and copyright law sect.), State Bar Tex. (alt. dispute resolution, intellectual property sect., com. continuing legal edn.), Dallas Bar Assn. (dir. intellectual property law sect. 1994—, chmn. I.P. Basics seminar 1999, sect. vice chmn. 2001, chmn. 2002), ALFA Internat. Tel. Symposium, Internat. Anti-Counterfeiting Assn., Tex. Law Rev. Editors Assn., Phi Delta Phi. Patent, Trademark and copyright, Alternative dispute resolution. Office: Akin Gump 1700 Pacific Ave Ste 4100 Dallas TX 75201-4675 E-mail: pmcgowan@akingump.com.

MCGRANE, MILES A., III, lawyer; b. Oct. 3, 1947; m. Patricia Lea McGrane; children: Miles IV, Ashley, Blake. AS in Bus. Adminstrn., Jr. Coll. Broward County, 1968; BS in Bus. Adminstrn., Fla. Atlantic U., 1970; JD, Samford U., 1975. Bar: Fla. 1975, D.C. 1982, U.S. Dist. Ct. (so. dist.)

Fla. 1976, U.S. Dist. Ct. (so. dist. trial bar) Fla. 1976, U.S. Ct. Appeals (5th cir.) 1976, U.S. Tax Ct. 1977, U.S. Supreme Ct. 1979. Assoc. Adams, George, Wood, Lee & Schulte, 1975—78, George & Thompson, P.A., 1978—80; ptnr. Kubicki, Draper, Gallagher & McGrane PA, 1980—93, McGrane & Nosick, P.A., Miami, Fla., 1993—. Adj. prof. trial program sch. law U. Miami, 1980—; mem. Judicial Nominating Comsn., 11th Cir., 1990-1994. Bd. govs. Fla. Med. Malpractice Joint Underwriting Assn., 1982-85, 88-90, 90-92, 1992-2002; bd. dirs. Legal Svcs. Greater Miami, Inc., 1984-90, v.p., 1987-88, pres., 1988-90; mem. bldg. com. U. Miami Law Sch., com. of 100; bldg. com. St. Thomas Episcopal Parish Sch. Recipient Leadership Award, Legal Svcs. Greater Miami Inc., 2001, Dist. Alumni Award, Broward Community Coll., 2002. Mem. Am. Coll. Legal Medicine, Am. Soc. Law and Medicine, Am. Acad. Hospital Attys., Internat. Assn. Def. Counsel (legal malpractice com. 1994-96, med. malpractice com. 1994-96, casualty insurance com. 1994-96), Fla. Def. Lawyers Assn., The Fla. Bar (pres. 2002-03, various coms. and positions), D.C. Bar, Dade County Bar Assn. (various coms. and positions), Dade County Def. Bar Assn.; diplomate Am. Bd. Trial Advocates (exec. com. Miami chpt. 1994-2000, treas. 1999, sec. 2000, v.p. 2001, pres. 2002, Nat. Bd. mem 1994-96.) Civil rights, General civil litigation, Insurance. Office: McGrane & Nosich PA 2801 Ponce de Leon Blvd 12th Fl Coral Gables FL 33134

MCGRATH, CHRISTOPHER THOMAS, lawyer; b. Inwood, N.Y., Nov. 25, 1958; s. John J. and Dolores Marie McG.; m. Monica Jean DiPalma, Sept. 15, 1984; children: Kristin Marie, Kelli Anne, Katelynn. BS cum laude, St. John's U., Jamaica, N.Y., 1980; JD, U. Dayton, 1983. Bar: N.Y. 1984, U.S. Dist. Ct. (so. and ea. dists.) N.Y. 1984, U.S. Supreme Ct. 1987; bd. cert. civil trial advocacy Nat. Bd. Trial Advocacy. Assoc. Sullivan & Liapakis, N.Y.C., 1983-89, ptnr., 1989-99, Sullivan, Papain, Block, McGrath & Cannavo P.C., N.Y.C., 1999—. Lectr. N.Y. State Bar Assn., N.Y. State Trial Lawyers Assn., Assn. Trial Lawyers Am. Chmn. humanitarian award Nassau County 4th Precinct Police, 1985—. Mem. ATLA, N.Y. State Trail Lawyers Assn., Nassau County Bar Assn. (bd. dirs., chair med. legal com. 1997-98, chair jud. com. 1999—, mem. exec. com. 2000—), N.Y. State Bar Assn., Kiwanis (disting. past pres. Peninsula chpt. 1988-89). Republican. General civil litigation, State civil litigation, Personal injury (including property damage). Home: 1348 Hewlett Ln Hewlett NY 11557-2208 Office: Sullivan Papain Block McGrath Cannavo PC 120 Broadway New York NY 10271-0002 also: 55 Mineola Blvd Mineola NY 11501-4220 E-mail: cmcgrath@traillaw1.com.

MCGRATH, MIKE, attorney general, lawyer; b. Aug. 22, 1947; BS, U. Mont., 1970; JD, Gonzaga U., 1975. Bar: Wash. 75, Mont. 77, U.S. Ct. Appeals (9th cir.) 80, U.S. Supreme Ct. 80. Reginald Heber Smith cmty. lawyer fellow; atty. Washoe County Legal Svcs., Reno, 1975—76; asst. atty. gen. State of Mont., Helena, 1977—82, atty. gen., 2001—; county atty. Lewis and Clark County, Helena, 1983—2001. Pres. Mont. Legal Svcs. Assn., 1984—85, 1995—96, bd. dirs., 1980—; bd. dirs. Mountain chpt. Nat. Com. for Prevention of Child Abuse, 1985—90, Big Bros. Sisters, Helena, 1977—83, Friendship Ctr. Helena, 1989—, pres., 1995—97, Conf. We. Attys. Gen., 2003—. With USAF, 1970—72. Mem.: Mont. County Attys. Assn. (pres. 1996—97), Nat. Dist. Attys. Assn., Mont. Bar Assn. Democrat. Home: 514 Hayes Ave Helena MT 59601-6106 Office: 215 N Sanders PO Box 201401 Helena MT 59620

MCGRATH, THOMAS J. lawyer, writer, film producer; b. N.Y.C., Oct. 8, 1932; m. Mary Lee McGrath, Aug. 4, 1956 (dec.); children: Maura Lee, J. Connell; m. Diahn Williams, Sept. 28, 1974; 1 child, Courtney C. BA, NYU, 1956, JD, 1960. Bar: N.Y. 1960. Assoc. Milbank, Tweed, Hadley & McCloy, N.Y.C., 1960-69; ptnr. Simpson, Thacher & Bartlett, N.Y.C., 1970-95; retired, 1995. Lectr., writer Practicing Law Inst., 1976—, Am. Law Inst. ABA, 1976-81. Author: Carryover Basis Under Tax Reform Act, 1977; contbg. author: Estate and Gift Tax After ERTA, 1982; producer: feature film Deadly Hero, 1977. Bd. dirs. N.Y. Philharm.; pres. Am. Austrian Found. With U.S. Army, 1953-54, Korea. Fellow Am. Coll. Trust and Estate Coun.; mem. ABA, N.Y. State Bar Assn., Assn. Bar City N.Y. Estate planning, Probate (including wills, trusts), Estate taxation. Home: 988 5th Ave New York NY 10021-0143 Office: Simpson Thacher & Bartlett 425 Lexington Ave New York NY 10017-3954 E-mail: mcgrathtwf@aol.com, mcgraththomasj@aol.com.

MCGRATH, WILLIAM ARTHUR, arbitrator, mediator; b. Hackensack, NJ, Jan. 31, 1941; s. Donald Marble and Elinor (Peck) McGrath; m. Diane Gurley, Apr. 25, 1965 (div. Nov. 1976); children: Philip M., Christian P.; m. Jackie Wynne, Aug. 10, 2002. BS, Calif. U., Long Beach, 1963; JD, U. Pacific, 1972. Bar: Colo. 1972, U.S. Dist. Ct. Colo. 1972. Pvt. practice, Breckenridge, Colo., 1972—82, Aurora, Colo., 1982—84; ptnr. McGrath & Callan, P.C., Breckenridge, 1975—80, McGrath & Lavenhar, Esq., Denver, 1984—85; prin. William A. McGrath & Assocs., Denver, 1985—88; pvt. practice San Diego, 1988—, Sacramento, 1993—. Vocat. instr. Colo. Mountain Coll., 1972—80. Mem.: ABA, Colo. Assn. Realtors, Colo. Trial Lawyers Assn. Republican. Episcopalian. State civil litigation, General practice, Property, real (including real estate development, water). Home: 1916 Bidwell Way Sacramento CA 95818 E-mail: wmcgrathppl@aol.com.

MC GRAW, DARRELL VIVIAN, JR., state attorney general; b. Mullens, W.Va., Nov. 8, 1936; s. Darrell Vivian and Julia (ZeKany) Mc Graw; m. Jorea Marple; children: Elizabeth, Sarah, Darrell, Elliott. AB, W.Va. U., 1961, JD, 1964, MA, 1977. Bar: W.Va. 1964. Gen. atty. Fgn. Claims Settlement Commn., U.S. Dept. State, 1964; counsel to gov. State of W.Va., 1965—68; pvt. practice Charleston, Shepherdstown and Morgantown, 1968—76; judge W.Va. Supreme Ct. Appeals, Charleston, 1977—88, chief justice, 1982—83; atty. gen. State of W.Va., Charleston, 1993—. With U.S. Army, 1954—57. Fellow, W.Va. U., Nat. Ctr. Edn. in Politics/Ford Found. Fellow: Am. Polit. Sci. Assn., Rotary. Democrat. Office: Office of Atty Gen 1900 Kanawha Blvd E Rm E-26 Charleston WV 25305-0009

MCGRAW, PATRICK JOHN, judge; b. Detroit, Feb. 3, 1956; s. John William and Elizabeth Kay (Foley) McG.; m. Susan Elaine Borowiak, Jan. 14, 1978; children: Kelly Elizabeth, Ryan Patrick, Brandon David, Kyle Elaine. BS, Cen. Mich. U., 1979; JD, Cooley Law Sch., 1982. Bar: Mich. 1982. Ptnr. McGraw, Martin & Heyn, P.C., Saginaw, Mich., 1982-99; judge Probate Ct. 10th Jud. Cir., Saginaw, Mich., 1999—. Instr. Ctrl. Mich. U., Mt. Pleasant, Mich., 1986-90. Atty. Sch. Program, Saginaw, 1986—; mem. YMCA; bd. trustees Saginaw Twp., 1988-1999; sch. coun. mem. Saginaw Nouvel Cath. Ctrl. H.S., 1988—; apptd. Mich. Bd. of Counseling, 1994—, apptd. probate judge by Gov. Engler, 1999; elected probate judge, 2000. Mem. ABA, ATLA, Nat. Coll. Probate and Juvenile Judges, Mich. Bar Assn., Saginaw County Bar Assn., Mich. Probate Judges Assn., Phi Alpha Delta. Avocations: black belt karate, hunting, fishing, racquetball. E-mial. Home: 5220 Overhill Dr Saginaw MI 48603-1727 Office: Saginaw County Govtl Bldg 111 S Michigan Ave Saginaw MI 48602-2019 E-mail: pmcgraw@saginawcounty.com.

MCGRAW, WARREN RANDOLPH, state supreme court justice; b. Wyoming County, W.Va., May 10, 1939; m. Peggy Shufflebarger; children: W. Randolph, H. Suzanne, Rebecca L. AB, U. Charleston, 1960; postgrad., W.Va. U.; JD, Wake Forest U., 1963. Bar: W.Va. 1963. Trial atty. U.S. Dept. Justice, Washington; legal svc. atty.; elected W.Va. Ho. of Dels., 1968, 70, W.Va. Senate, 1972, 76, 80; elected prosecuting atty. Wyoming County, 1996; justice W.Va. Supreme Ct. Appeals, 1998—, chief justice, 2001—. Instr. W.Va. U. Ext. Agy.; W.Va. del. Dem. Nat. Conv., 1972, 74; mem. Del. and Senatorial Dist. Exec. Coms.; del. State Dem. Jud. Conv. and State Dem. Conv.; elected pres. W.Va. Senate, 1980, 82; co-chmn. Crime Commn.; mem. Nat. Conf. Lt. Govs. Featured on Nat. Pub. TV series Bill Moyers Journal. Trustee 1st United Meth. Ch., Pineville; participant Marshall U.'s Taft Lectr. Series; elected W.Va. del. Dem. Nat. Conv., 1972, 74, Wyo. County Bd. Edn., 1986, 44th pres. W.Va. Sen., 1980, 82; del. State Dem. Jud. Conv., State Dem. Conv.; past pres. Jaycees; mem. Nat. Conf. Lt. Govs., Heart Fund, Wyoming County Cancer Fund, Del. and Sen. Dist. Exec. Coms.; past chmn. Wyoming County Dem. Exec. Com.; co-chmn. Crime Commn. Named one of nation's Outstanding Legislators, Rutgers U.; recipient Friend of Edn., Margaret Baldwin award W.Va. Edn. Assn. Mem. Wyo. Bar Assn., Raleigh County Bar Assn., Rotary Internat. Office: Bldg 1 Rm E-302 Capitol Complex Charleston WV 25305

MCGUANE, FRANK L., JR., lawyer; b. White Plains, N.Y., July 10, 1939; s. Frank L. and Dorothy P. (McGrath) McG.; m. Carla L. Miller, June 26, 1993; children: Lauri Elizabeth, Molly Elizabeth. BA, U. Notre Dame, 1961; JD, U. Cin., 1968. Bar: Colo. 1968, U.S. Dist. Ct. Colo. 1968, U.S. Ct. Appeals (10th cir.) 1970, U.S. Supreme Ct. 1971. Shareholder McGuane and Malone, P.C., Denver, 1981-95; pres. Frank McGuane & Assocs., P.C., Denver, 1995—; ptnr. McGuane & Hogan, LLP, Denver, 1997—. Mem. faculty Nat. Inst. for Trial Advocacy, 1987—; lectr. in field. Author: Domestic Relations-Colorado Methods of Practice, 1983; co-author: Colorado Family Law and Practice, 1999; contbr. articles to profl. jours. Chmn. Denver area chpt. Nat. Eagle Scout Assn. Boy Scouts Am,. 1980-82. With USMC, 1961-63. Fellow Am. Acad. Matrimonial Lawyers (jour. editor 1990-95, 2000-01, bd. govs. 1988-95, pres. Colo. chpt. 1988-89), Internat. Acad. Matrimonial Lawyers (founding fellow, bd. govs. 1997—); mem. ABA, Colo. Bar Assn. (chmn. family law sect. 1977-78), Denver Bar Assn., Arapahoe County Bar Assn., Douglas-Elbert County Bar Assn., Pitkin County Bar Assn., Am. Coll. Family Trial Lawyers (diplomate), Cath. Lawyers Guild. Family and matrimonial. Office: The Galleria 720 S Colorado Blvd Ste 910N Denver CO 80246-1935 E-mail: flm@mcguanehogan.com.

MCGUCKIN, JOHN HUGH, JR., lawyer; b. Bryn Mawr, Pa., Nov. 8, 1946; AB magna cum laude, Harvard Coll., 1968, JD, 1971. Bar: Mass. 1971, Calif. 1973. Assoc. Orrick, Herrington, Rowley & Sutcliffe, 1972-79; sr. counsel legal divsn. Bank Am., 1979-81; exec. v.p., gen. counsel, corp. sec. UnionBanCal Corp./Union Bank Calif., N.A., San Francisco, 1981—. Adj. instr. Hastings Coll. Law U. Calif., 1980-82; judge pro tem San Francisco Superior Ct. Contbr. articles to profl. jours. Mem. ABA, State Bar Calif. (v.p., treas., bd. govs., chmn. subcom. duties and liabilities trustees probate and trust law sect. 1985-86, legal svcs. trust fund commn. 1989-90, minimum CLE com.), Calif. Bankers Assn. (legal affairs com. 1988-90), Bar Assn. San Francisco (chmn. probate and trust law sect. 1985, exec. com., vice chmn. corp. law dept. sect. 1985-87), Phi Beta Kappa. Corporate, general. Office: Union Bank Calif NA 16th Fl 400 California St San Francisco CA 94104-1320

MCGUIRE, JEANNE MARIE, lawyer; b. Kalamazoo, Mich., Nov. 2, 1956; d. Donald Joseph and Dorothy Anne (Mattimore) McG.; m. David Stanley Rollins, Aug. 15, 1986. BA in Psychology cum laude, Aquinas Coll., 1978; JD, Wayne State U., 1983. Bar: Mich. 1983, U.S. Dist. Ct. (ea. dist.) Mich. 1983, U.S. Ct. Appeals (6th cir.) 1985, U.S. Dist. Ct. (we. dist.) Mich. 1995. Law clk. Sachs, Nunn & Kates, Detroit, 1983-84; staff atty. Wayne County Neighborhood Legal Svcs., Detroit, 1984-85, UAW Legal Svcs. Plans, Detroit, 1985-90, John G. Mooney, P.C., Detroit, 1990-92; mng. atty. Wayne County Neighborhood Legal Svcs., 1992-95; exec. dir. Legal Svcs. Orgn. of Southcentral Mich., 1995-99, Camden (N.J.) Regional Legal Svcs., 1999—2001; interim exec. dir. PA Low Income Housing Coalition, 2001—02; exec. dir. Nationalities Svc. Ctr., Phila., 2002—. Mem. State Bar Mich. (chair legal aid com. 1995—99, access to justice task force 1996-99), Women's Lawyers' Assn. Mich. (pres. S.W. region 1996-97, regional dir. 1997-98). Democrat. Roman Catholic. Avocation: travel.

MCGUIRE, TIMOTHY JAMES, lawyer, editor; b. Mount Pleasant, Mich., Mar. 24, 1949; s. James Edward and Anita Matilda (Starr) McGuire; m. T. Jean Fannin, May 10, 1975; children: Tracy, Jason, Jeffrey. BA, Aquinas Coll., Grand Rapids, Mich., 1971; JD cum laude, William Mitchell Coll. Law, St. Paul, 1987. Bar: Minn. 1987. Mng. editor Ypsilanti Press, Mich., 1973—75, Corpus Christi Caller, Tex., 1975—77, Lakeland Ledger, Fla., 1977—79, Mpls. Star, 1979—82; mng. editor features and sports Mpls. Star and Tribune, 1982—84, mng. editor, 1984—91, exec. editor, 1991—93, editor, sr. v.p., 1993—2002; syndicated columnist and spkr. in field. Pulitzer Prize juror, 1988—89, 1995—2002. Lay preacher at St. Joseph Roman Cath. Ch., Mpls., 1995—. Mem.: Minn. State Bar Assn., Am. Soc. Newspaper Editors (bd. dirs. 1992—, chmn. change com. 1994—95, chmn. program com. 1996—97, treas. 1998—99, sec. 1999—2000, v.p. 2000—01, pres. 2001—02). Roman Catholic. Home: 3645 Rosewood Ln N Minneapolis MN 55441-1127

MCGUIRE, WILLIAM B(ENEDICT), lawyer; b. Newark, Feb. 14, 1929; children: Joan Ellen, Ralph R., James C., Keith P., Grant W. BS, Fordham U., 1950; JD, Seton Hall U., 1958; LLM in Taxation, NYU, 1963. Bar: N.J. 1958, U.S. Dist. Ct. N.J. 1958, U.S. Supreme Ct. 1971, U.S. Ct. Appeals (3d cir.) 1980, N.Y. 1982. Chief acct. Hanover Fire Ins. Co., N.Y.C., 1950-58; sr. ptnr. Lum, Blunno & Tompkins, Newark, 1958-83, Tompkins McGuire Wachenfeld & Barry LLP, Newark, 1984—, mng. ptnr. Asst. prosecutor Essex County, N.J., 1964-65; bd. dirs. Ind. Coll. Fund of N.J.; trustee St. Barnabas Corp., St. Barnabas Med. Ctr. and Irvington Gen. Hosp.; mem. Essex County Ethics Com., 1974-77; mem. com. to review State Commn. of Investigation, 1982. Fellow Am. Coll. Trial Lawyers, Am. Bar Found. (state chmn.), Am. Bd. Trial Advocates, Internat. Acad. Trial Lawyers, Internat. Soc. Barristers; mem. ABA, N.J. State Bar Assn. (trustee 1982-89, sec. 1989-90, treas. 1990-91, 2d v.p. 1991-92, 1st v.p. 1992-93, pres.-elect 1993-94, pres. 1994-95), N.J. State Bar Found. (pres. 1988-89), Essex County Bar Assn. (pres. 1975-76), Internat. Assn. Ins. Counsel, Fedn. Ins. Counsel, Def. Rsch. Inst., Maritime Law Assn., U.S. Am. Arbitration Assn., Trial Attys. N.J., Assn. Fed. Bar N.J. (pres. 1985-88), Essex County Country Club (pres. 1983), Newark Club. Roman Catholic. Federal civil litigation, State civil litigation, Professional liability. Office: Tompkins McGuire Wachenfeld & Barry LLP 4 Gateway Ctr 100 Mulberry St Newark NJ 07102-4007 E-mail: WMcGuire@tompkinsmcguire.com.

MCGUIRL, MARLENE DANA CALLIS, law librarian, educator; b. Hammond, Ind., Mar. 22, 1938; d. Daniel David and Helen Elizabeth (Baludis) Callis; m. James Franklin McGuirl, Apr. 24, 1965. AB, Ind. U., 1959; JD, DePaul U., 1963; MALS, Rosary Coll., 1965; LLM, George Washington U., 1978; postgrad., Harvard U., 1985. Bar: Ill. 1963, Ind. 1964, D.C. 1972. Asst. DePaul Coll. of Law Libr., 1961-62, asst. law libr., 1962-65; ref. law librarian Boston Coll. Sch. Law, 1965-66; libr. dir. D.C. Bar Libr., 1966-70; asst. chief Am.-Brit. Law Divsn. Libr. of Congress, Washington, 1970, chief, 1970-90, environ. cons., 1990—; counsel Cooter & Gell, 1992-93; adminstr. Washington Met. Transit Authority, 1994—. Libr. cons. Nat. Clearinghouse on Poverty Law, OEO, Washington, 1967-69, Northwestern U. Nat. Inst. Edn. in Law and Poverty, 1969, D.C. Office of Corp. Counsel, 1969-70; instr. law librarianship Grad. Sch. of U.S. Dept. of Agr., 1968-72; lectr. legal lit. Cath. U., 1972; adj. asst. prof., 1973-91; lectr. environ. law George Washington U., 1979—; judge Nat. and Internat. Law Moot Ct. Competition, 1976-78, 90—; pres. Hamburger Heaven, Inc., Palm Beach, Fla., 1981-91, L'Image de Marlene Ltd., 1986-92, Clinique de Beautè Inc., 1987-92, Heads & Hands Inc., 1987-92, Horizon Design & Mfg. Co., Inc., 1987—; dir. Stoneridge Farm Inc., Gt. Falls, Va., 1984—. Contbr. articles to profl. jours. Mem. Georgetown Citizens Assn.; trustee D.C. Law Students in Ct.; del. Ind. Democratic Conv., 1964. Recipient Meritorious Svc. award Libr. on Congress, 1974, letter of commendation Dirs. of Pers., 1976, cert. of appreciation, 1981-84. Mem. ABA (facilities law libr. Congress com. 1976-89), Fed. Bar Assn. (chpt. council 1972-76), Ill. Bar Assn., Women's Bar Assn. (pres. 1972-73, exec. bd. 1973-77, Outstanding Contbn. to Human Rights award 1975), D.C. Bar Assn., Am. Bar Found., Nat. Assn. Women Lawyers, Am. Assn. Law Libraries (exec. bd. 1973-77), Law Librarians Soc. of Washington (pres. 1971-73), Exec. Women in Govt. Home: 3416 P St NW Washington DC 20007-2705 E-mail: mmcguirl@wmata.com.

MCGUIRL, ROBERT JOSEPH, lawyer; b. Jersey City, June 16, 1952; s. Joseph Francis and Edna Louise (Davis) McG.; m. Gloria Pauline Clemente, Oct. 10, 1981; children: Brian, Jennifer. BA cum laude, Coll. Holy Cross, Worcester, Mass., 1974; JD, Georgetown U., 1977. Bar: N.Y. 1978, U.S. dist. Ct. (so. and ea. dists.) N.Y. 1979, N.J. 1981, U.S. Dist. Ct. N.J. 1981, U.S. Supreme Ct. 1987, U.S. Ct. Appeals (3d cir.) 1988; cert. civil trial atty. Asst. dist. atty. Office of Dist. Atty. New York County, N.Y.C., 1977-81; ptnr. Priestley, McGuirl & Wachenfeld, Newark, 1981-92; pvt. practice law Westwood, N.J., 1992—. Mem. ABA (vice-chmn., com. profl. officers' and dir.'s liability 1987-89, contbg. editor self-insurers, risk mgrs. com. newsletter 1990), N.J. State Bar Assn. (chair products liability and toxic tort com. 1992—), Trial Attys. N.J., Bergen County Bar Assn. (vice-chmn. med. legal com. 1986-87), Def. Rsch. Inst. Roman Catholic. General civil litigation, Personal injury (including property damage), Product liability. Office: 345 Kinderkamack Rd Ste B Westwood NJ 07675-1600 E-mail: rjmcguirl@att.net.

MCGURK, EUGENE DAVID, JR., lawyer; b. Phila., Feb. 27, 1951; s. Eugene David and Mary Rose (O'Donnell) McG.; m. Kathleen Mary Murphy, Dec. 28, 1973 (dec. Aug. 1978). BA, LaSalle Coll., 1973; JD summa cum laude, Widener U., 1978. Bar: Pa. 1978, N.J. 1978, U.S. Dist. Ct. (ea. dist.) Pa. 1978, U.S. Dist. Ct. N.J. 1978, U.S. Ct. Appeals (3rd cir.) 1981, U.S. Supreme Ct. 1982. Mgmt. analyst Mng. Dirs. Office, Phila., 1974-76; adminstr. Dept. Commerce, Phila., 1976-78; asst. city solicitor law, sr. trial atty. City of Phila., 1978-81; with Raynes, McCarty, Binder, Ross & Mundy, Phila., 1981-87, ptnr., 1987—. Guest lectr. Thomas Jefferson U. Med. Sch., 1083, 1984, Del. Law Sch., 1980, U. Pa. Dental Sch., 1985—90, Med. Coll. Pa., Phila.; vis. instr. Dept. Comty. and Preventive Medicine, 1983—91, Am. Soc. Law and Medicine, 1987—; lectr. internat. law studies program (summer) U. Nairobi, Kenya, 1990; adj. faculty Widener U. Sch. Law, 1993—; mem. disciplinary bd. hearing commn. Pa. Supreme Ct., Harrisburg, 1993—98, chmn.disciplinary bd. hearing commn., 1995—97, alt. mem. disciplinary bd. hearing commn., 1999—. Articles editor Del. Jour. Corp. Law, 1977-78. Mem. Camden County Bd. Elections, 1970; bd. of overseers Widener U. Sch. Law, Wilmington, Del., 1985—; bd. trustees, 2001—. Recipient award Fed. Bar Assn., 1978, Mayoral award City of Phila., Am. Judisprudence award, 1978. Mem. ABA, Assn. Trial Lawyers Am., Pa. Bar Assn., N.J. Bar Assn., Camden County Bar Assn., Phila. Bar Assn. (bench bar com. 1982, profl. responsibility com. 1982), Widener U. Sch. Law Alumni Assn. (bd. dirs. 1980—, v.p. 1982-85, pres. 1985-92), Phila. Ctr. City Proprietors Assn., Phi Kapp Phi, Phi Alpha Delta (scholastic award Read chpt. 1978); trustee Widener U., 2001-. Federal civil litigation, General civil litigation, State civil litigation. Office: Raynes McCarty Binder Ross & Mundy PA 1845 Walnut St Ste 2000 Philadelphia PA 19103-4767 also: NJ Mng Atty 116 White Horse Pike Haddon Heights NJ 08035-1928

MCHALE, EDWARD ROBERTSON, retired lawyer; b. Chgo., Jan. 24, 1921; s. Edward F. and Martha (Robertson) McH.; m. Helen Louise Lindgren, Aug. 28, 1953; children: Nancy Ellen McHale Kaufman, Sally Jane McHale Cutler, John Robertson. BSS., Northwestern U., 1942; LL.B., Harvard U., 1948. Bar: Calif. 1949. Asst. U.S. atty. U.S. atty. So. Dist. Calif., 1949—61, chief tax div., 1954—61; assoc. Mitchell, Silberberg & Knupp, Los Angeles, 1961—64, ptnr., 1965—86, mgr. litigation dept, 1978—82; pres. Edward R. McHale, P.C., 1979—86; ret., 1986. Lectr. U. So. Calif. Law Center, 1958-61 Co-author: Handling Federal Tax Litigation, 1961. Served to lt. USNR, 1943-46. Mem. Fed. Bar Assn. (past pres. Los Angeles chpt., past nat. v.p. for 9th Circuit), Assn. Bus. Trial Lawyers (bd. govs. 1981-83), State Bar Calif., Delta Sigma Rho. Clubs: South Hills Country (West Covina); Clan Donnachaidh Soc. Lutheran. Home: 1116 S Serena Dr West Covina CA 91791-3754 E-mail: casu8@earthlink.net.

MCHALE, MICHAEL JOHN, lawyer; b. N.Y.C., Apr. 14, 1960; s. Michael Joseph and Mary Beatrice (Graddy) McH. BA, U. of the South, 1982; JD, Samford U., 1985. Bar: Ala. 1986, U.S. Dist. Ct. (no., mid. and so. dists.) Ala. 1986, U.S. Ct. Appeals (11th cir.) 1986, Fla. (cert. admiralty and maritime law) 1991, U.S. Dist. Ct. (mid. and so. dists.) Fla. 1991, U.S. Dist. Ct. (no. dist.) Fla. 1997, U.S. Supreme Ct. 1991; cert. admiralty and maritime lawyer Fla. Bar Bd. of Legal Specialization, mediator, arbitrator Fla. Supreme Ct. Assoc. Wagner, Nugent, Johnson, Roth, Romano, Eriksen & Kupfer, West Palm Beach, Fla., 1989-92; ptnr. Whalen & McHale, West Palm Beach, Fla., 1992-95, Daves, Whalen, McHale & Considine, West Palm Beach, Fla., 1995-98; sole practitioner Jensen Beach, Fla., 1998—; of counsel Deorchis, Corsa & Hillenbrand LLP, Miami, Fla., 1998—. Author: Strategic Use of Circumstantial Evidence, 2nd edit., 1991, Evaluating and Settling Personal Injury Claims, 1992, supplement through present, Making Trial Objections, 1993, supplement through present, Expert Witnesses: Direct and Cross Examination, 1993, supplement through present; editor, author: Litigating TMJ Cases, 1993 and yearly supplements. Named one of Outstanding Young Men of Am., 1988. Mem. ABA (mem. admiralty com.), ATLA, Am. Acad. Fla. Trial Lawyers, Maritime Law Assn. U.S. (procter), Southeastern Admiralty Law Inst., Fla. Bar (admiralty law com. editl. bd., admiralty and maritime cert. com.), Palm. Beach Bar Assn., Martin County Bar Assn., Sigma Nu Phi. Avocation: vessel building. Admiralty, Federal civil litigation, Commercial, contracts (including sales of goods; commercial financing). Home: 1905 NE River Ct Jensen Beach FL 34957-6423 Office: 1925 NE Ricou Terr Jensen Beach FL 34957 Office Fax: 772-225-2077.

MCHENRY, BARNABAS, lawyer; b. Harrisburg, Pa., Oct. 30, 1929; s. William Cecil and Louise (Perkins) McH.; m. Marie Bannon Jones, Dec. 13, 1952; children: Thomas J.P., W.H. Davis, John W.H. AB, Princeton U., 1952; LLB, Columbia U., 1957. Bar: N.Y. 1957. Assoc. Lord, Day, & Lord, N.Y.C., 1957-62; gen. counsel The Reader's Digest Assn., Inc., N.Y.C., 1962-85; exec. dir. Wallace Funds, N.Y.C., 1985-86; chmn. N.Y. state orgns., 1986—. Trustee, pres. Boscobel Restoration, Inc., 1964; trustee Am. Conservation Assn., 1977, Saratoga Performing Arts Ctr., 1984, Aperture Found., 1986; trustee emeritus Met. Mus. Art, 1980; coun. mem. Villa I Tatti, Harvard Sch. Renaissance Studies, 1982; regent emeritus Smithsonian Instn., 1985; commr. Palisades Interstate Park Commn., 1987; chmn. Hudson River Valley Greenway Coun., 1989. Home: 164 E 72nd St New York NY 10021-4363 Fax: 212-681-4552.

MCHOLD, SHARON LAWRENCE, lawyer, mediator; b. Albion, Mich., Mar. 26, 1941; d. Ted E. and Ruth M. (Whelan) McH.; m. Frank H. Lawrence (div. July 1987); children: Christopher, Brian, Kimberly. BS, U. Del., 1963; MS, Tufts U., 1965; JD, U. Maine, 1983. Rschr. U. Ind. Med. Sch., Indpls., 1966-67; instr. Marian Coll., Indpls., 1967-70, Westbrook Coll., Portland, Maine, 1973-79; law clk. Curtis Thaxter, Portland, 1982—84, assoc., 1985-91; law clk. Superior Ct., 1983—84; pvt. practice Yarmouth, Maine, 1991-93; mediator Conflict Solutions, Portland, 1993—. Trustee Maine Audubon Soc., Falmouth, Maine, 1977-80; clk. Island Inst., Rockland, Maine, 1985-92; trustee Maine Island Trail Assn., Portland, 1993-94, Oceanside Conservation Trust, 1993-2002; pres. Yarmouth Land Trust, 2002-, Friends Royal River Land Trust, 2002-. Nat. Def. fellow, 1963-65. Mem.: Assn. Conflict Resolution, Maine Bar Assn. Alternative dispute resolution, Property, real (including real estate development, water), Land use and zoning (including planning). Home: 30 Riverbend Dr Yarmouth ME 04096-5337 Office: Conflict Solutions 75 Pearl St Portland ME 04101-1102

MCHUGH, JAMES JOSEPH, lawyer; b. Phila., Sept. 15, 1961; s. James Joseph and Helene Anne (Kiernan) McHugh; m. Colette Marie McHugh, May 20, 1989; children: Albert Taylor, James Joseph III, Cole Michael, Sophia Kiernan. BSME, Drexel U., 1985; JD magna cum laude, Villanova (Pa.) Law Sch., 1992. Bar: Pa. 1992, N.J. 1992, U.S. Dist. Ct. (ea. dist.) Pa., U.S. Dist. Ct. N.J. Ptnr. McHugh Plumbing & Heating, Phila., 1984-89; project mgr. Fluidics Mech Contractors, Phila., 1989-92; assoc. Pepper, Hamilton & Scheetz, Phila., 1992-94, Beasley, Casey & Erbstein, Phila., 1994—. Author, editor case notes. Mem. adv. com. Penn Pub. Svc. Program, Sch. Law, U. Pa. Named to Order of the Coif, Villanova Law Sch., 1992. Mem. ATLA, Pa. Bar Assn., Phila. Bar Assn. Civil rights, Libel, Personal injury (including property damage). Home: 65 Brooks Rd Moorestown NJ 08057-3855 Office: The Beasley Firm 1125 Walnut St Philadelphia PA 19107-4918 E-mail: jjm@tortlaw.com.

MCHUGH, JAMES LENAHAN, JR., lawyer; b. Pitts., June 28, 1937; s. James Lenahan and Annette (Dalton) McH.; m. Mary-Ann Curto, Feb. 16, 1963 (div. 1988); children: Angela Dalton Sherrill, Hillary Lenahan Clagett; m. Rosa Lamoreaux, Sept. 8, 1991. BA, Duquesne U., 1959; LLB, Villanova U., 1962. Bar: D.C. 1963. Law clk. U.S. Dist. Ct. (ea. dist.) Pa., Phila., 1962-63; law clk. to Assoc. Justice Tom C. Clark, U.S. Supreme Ct., Washington, 1963-64; assoc. Steptoe & Johnson, Washington, 1967-70, ptnr., 1970-94; gen. counsel APA, Washington, 1994—2001, sr. counsel, 2001—. Mem. bd. consultors Law Sch., Villanova (Pa.) U., 1973—; dir. Higher Achievement Program, Washington, 1984-87; coord. Washington Lawyers' Project, Robert F. Kennedy Meml. Found., Washington, 1972-75. Editor-in-chief Villanova Law Rev., Vol. VII, 1961-62; chmn. editl. adv. bd. Fed. Comm. Law Jour., 1981-84. Bd. dirs. Columbia Hosp. for Women's Found., Washington, 1985-96, Children's Radio Theatre, Washington, 1983-86; chmn. exec. giving Archbishop's Appeal, Archdiocese of Washington, 1982-84; mem. bd. visitors Ctr. for Study of Orgns. and Mgmt., U. Md. Univ. Coll., 1987-92; bd. dirs. Human Resources Rsch. Orgn., Inc., 1978—; chmn. bd. dirs., 1991—; mem. adv. bd. Inst. for Conflict Analysis and Resolution, George Mason U., 1990-94. Capt. U.S. Army, 1964-67. Mem. ABA (sect. on health law, tax, antitrust, intellectual property and legal edn.), D.C. Bar Assn., Am. Soc. Assn. Execs. (chmn. Washington Legal Symposium 2003, mem. legal sect. coun.), Choral Arts Soc., Villanova Law Alumni Assn. (pres. Greater Balt./Washington area chpt. 2002—), Order of Coif, Confrerie des Chevaliers du Tastevin. Corporate, general, Health, Non-profit and tax-exempt organizations. Home: 4112 Fessenden St NW Washington DC 20016-4227 Office: APA 750 1st St NE Washington DC 20002-4242 E-mail: jmchugh@apa.org.

MCILVAINE, JAMES ROSS, lawyer; b. Youngstown, Ohio, July 22, 1944; s. Earl Eugene and Caroline E. (Clawson) McI.; m. Carol Beth Boyer, June 24, 1967; children: Andrew S., Katherine Erin. BA, Muskingum Coll., 1966; JD cum laude, Ohio State Coll., 1969. Bar: Ohio 1969, U.S. Dist. Ct. (no. dist.) Ohio 1971. Assoc. Oestricher, Seamon, Newman & Knoll, Akron, Ohio, 1969-70; asst. prosecuting atty. Summit County Prosecutor's Office, Akron, Ohio, 1970-71; ptnr. Palecek, McIlvaine, Paul & Hoffman, Co., Wadsworth, Ohio, 1971—. Mem. citizen's adv. bd. Medina County Correctional Facility Study, 1983; founding trustee Wedsworth City Schs. Performing Arts Found., 1994—; mem. bd. edn. Wadsworth City Sch., 1988—; trustee Wadsworth-Rittmann Hosp., 1999—; bd. dirs. Medina County Law Libr., 1979—83, Wadsworth chpt. ARC, 1981—94. Mem. ATLA (state del. 1985-87, bd. govs. 1987-88), Ohio Acad. Trial lawyers (Editor profl. newsletter 1982-84, chair regional trial sems. 1980-81, sec. 1981-83, lectr. criminal law sem. 1981, ins. law sem. 1980, 84, 86, negligence law sem. 1984, 86, 88, chair student advocacy divsn. 1976-78, pres. 1984-85, trustee, bd. dirs. 1976-83), Medina County Bar Assn. (pres. 1983, dir., chmn. common pleas ct. rules com., lectr. sms. 1986, 87), Ohio State Bar Assn., Wadsworth Area C. of C. (bd. dirs. 1995—, v.p. 1997-98, pres. 1998-99), Lions. Corporate, general, Family and matrimonial, Personal injury (including property damage). Office: 200 Smokerise Dr Ste 200 Wadsworth OH 44281-9460

MCILWRATH, MICHAEL J. lawyer; b. Columbia, Mo., Aug. 26, 1962; s. James J. and Rolleen K. McIlwrath; m. Mariane A. Grin, Feb. 18, 1997; 1 child, Samuel. AB, U. Calif., Berkeley, 1985; JD, Cornell U., 1994. Assoc. Willkie Farr and Gallagher, N.Y.C., 1994—99. Dir. Nat. Ctr. for Sci. Edn., Berkeley, 1998—; sec. com. on product liability City Bar of N.Y., N.Y.C., 1996-1999. Office: GE Oil & Gas/Nuovo Pignone Via F Matteucci 2 Florence 50127 Italy

MC INERNEY, DENIS, lawyer; b. N.Y.C., May 31, 1925; s. Denis and Anne (Keane) McI.; m. Mary Irene Murphy, Nov. 14, 1953; children: Kathleen Mc Inerney O'Hare, Denis J., Maura Mc Inerney Romano. BSS, Fordham U., 1948, JD cum laude, 1951, LLD (hon.), 1996. Bar: N.Y. 1951, D.C. 1961. Instr. philosophy Fordham U., 1948-51; assoc. Cahill Gordon & Reindel, N.Y.C., 1951-61, ptnr., 1961-90, sr. counsel, 1991—. Vice chmn. Com. Character and Fitness Admission State Bar N.Y., 1st Jud. Dept., 1979-97, chmn. Departmental Disciplinary Com., 1st Jud. Dept., 1997—; lectr. in field. Co-author: Practitioners Handbooks for Appeals to the Appellate Divisions of the State of New York, 1979, and to the Court of Appeals of the State of New York, 1981. Bd. dirs. Vols. of Legal Svc., Inc., 1985-2001, Cath. Youth Orgn., 1975—; mem. adv. bd. St. Vincent's Hosp., Westchester, N.Y., 1988—; chmn. bd. visitors Fordham Law Sch., 1989—; trustee Fordham U., 1988-94. Sgt. 82d Airborne Divsn. U.S. Army, 1943-46, ETO. Decorated Knight of Malta, Knight of the Holy Sepulcher; recipient Achievement in Law award Fordham U., 1977; St. Thomas More award Archdiocese NY Cardinal's Com. of Laity Lawyers' Divsn., 2001 Fellow Am. Coll. Trial Lawyers (state chmn. 1980-82); mem. ABA, N.Y. State Bar Assn., Bar Assn. City N.Y., New York County Lawyers Assn. (pres. 1982-84), N.Y. County Lawyers Assn. Inn of Ct. (pres. 1996-2002), Fordham U. Law Alumni Assn. (pres. 1968-72, medal of achievement 1975). Clubs: Westchester Country, Univ. Roman Catholic. Antitrust, General civil litigation, Corporate, general. Office: Cahill Gordon & Reindel 80 Pine St Fl 20 New York NY 10005-1790 E-mail: d.mcinerney@cahill.com.

MCINERNEY, NOREEN LINDA, lawyer; b. Evergreen Park, Ill., Sept. 27, 1971; d. Patrick Joseph and Florence Murphy; m. Michael Joseph McInerney, June 4, 1995; 1 child, Cortney Marie. BAS in Econs., U. Ill., 1993; JD, Ill. Inst. Tech., 1996. Bar: 1996. With First Chgo., Chgo., 1997; atty. Griffin & Gallagher, Palos Hills, Ill., 1997—. Mem.: ABA, Clare Assn., Ill. State Bar Assn. Roman Catholic. Avocations: running, bicycling, reading. Office: Griffin & Gallagher 10001 S Roberts Rd Palos Hills IL 60465 Business E-Mail: linda@griffingallagher.com.

MCINTOSH, CAROLYN LEIGH, lawyer; b. Boulder, Colo., Dec. 10, 1955; d. Glen Elvis and Alice Joy McIntosh; m. Roger Alan Bucholz, Oct. 4, 1980 (div. Dec. 1998); m. Leland Kioshi Marable, Dec. 11, 1998. BA cum laude, Middlebury Coll., 1978; JD, U. Colo., 1981. Bar: Colo. 1981, U.S. Dist. Ct. Colo. 1981, Mon. 1988 (specially admitted), U.S. Dist. Ct. Mont. 1989, U.S. Ct. Appeals 2000. Rsch. asst. Rocky Mountain Mineral Law Found., Boulder, 1979-80; assoc. Sisk, Foley, Hultin & Driver, Denver, 1981-83, Hultin, Driver & Spaanstra, Denver, 1983-85; asst. atty. gen. Colo. Dept. of Law, Denver, 1986-88; assoc. Cogswell & Wehrle, Denver, 1988-89, shareholder, 1989-90; spl. asst. atty. gen. State of Mont., 1988-90; sr. assoc. Patton, Boggs & Blow, Denver, 1990-92; ptnr. Patton Boggs, LLP, Denver, 1992—, mng. ptnr. Denver office, 1993—2002. Assoc. adj. prof. Colorado Sch. Mines, 1991-2000; mem., atty. program to provide legal svcs. to indigent, Denver, 1982-86. Mem. procedural rules subcom. Colo. Air Quality Control Commn., 1983-84; mem. Lafayette Planning Commn., 1986-87, 95-99, Lafayette City Coun., 1987-99, mayor pro tem, 1989-91, mayor, 1995-99; mem. bd. Denver Regional Coun. Govts., 1990-99; mem. Regional Air Quality Coun., 1992-99, mem. exec. com., 1996-99; mem. Colo. Water Conservation Bd., 2001—, Urban Drainage and Flood Control Bd., 1995-99. Mem. ABA (natural resources sect.), Colo. Bar Assn., Denver Bar Assn. (legal fees arbitration com. 1983-84, 86-87), Alliance Profl. Women (bd. dirs. 1986-90), Internat. Inst. Environ. Risk Mgmt. (bd. govs. 1996—). General civil litigation, Environmental. Office: Patton Boggs 1660 Lincoln St Ste 1900 Denver CO 80264-1901 E-mail: cmcintosh@pattonboggs.com.

MCINTYRE, ANITA GRACE JORDAN, lawyer; b. Louisville, Ky., Jan. 29, 1947; d. Blakely Gordan and Shirley Evans (Grubbs) Jordan; m. Kenneth James McIntyre, Oct. 11, 1969; children: Abigail, Jordan Kenneth. BA, Smith Coll., 1969; JD, U. Detroit, 1975. Bar: Mich. 1975, U.S. Dist. Ct. (ea. dist.) Mich. 1975, U.S. Dist. Ct. (we. dist.) Mich. 1979, U.S. Ct. Appeals (6th cir.) 1979. Ptnr. Rollins White & Rollins, Detroit, 1975-79; vis. assoc. prof. Detroit Coll. Law, 1979-81; assoc. Tyler & Canham, Detroit, 1981-82; prin. Anita G. McIntyre, P.C., Grosse Pointe, Mich., 1982-87, 91—; of counsel Nederlander Dodge & Rollins, Detroit, 1987-90; assoc. Damm & Smith, P.C., Detroit, 1990-91. Hearing panel chmn. Atty. Discipline Bd., 1985—. Editor, author (case notes) U. Detroit Jour. Urban Law, 1975; contrbr. articles to profl. jours. Sec. Berry Subdivsn. Assn., Detroit, 1975-77; pres. Smith Coll. Club Detroit, 1982-86; mem. parents bd. U. Liggett Sch., Grosse Pointe, Mich., 1991,95; vice chair state pub. affairs com. Mich. State Coun. Jr. Leagues, 1998-2000, chair, 2001-. Mem.: Wayne County Juvenile Trial Lawyers Assn., Wayne County (Mich.) Probate Bar Assn., State Bar Mich., Edgemont Park Assn. (sec.), Jr. League Detroit (chair pub.affairs com. 1998—2001, vice chair Mich. state pub. affairs com. 1999—2001, chair 2001—02). Episcopalian. Avocations: skiing, swimming, needle point. General civil litigation, Family and matrimonial, Property, real (including real estate development, water). Office: 15324 Mack Ave Ste 201 Grosse Pointe Park MI 48230 E-mail: agmcintyr@cs.com.

MCINTYRE, CARL HENRY, JR., lawyer; b. Washington, May 9, 1958; s. Carl Henry and Joyce Lee (Booker) McI. BA cum laude, Am. U., 1980; JD, Howard U., 1984. Bar: Pa. 1985, U.S. Ct. Appeals (D.C. cir.) 1986, U.S. Ct. Appeals (9th cir.) 1987, U.S. Ct. Appeals (5th cir.) 1988, U.S. Ct. Appeals (10th cir.) 1989, U.S. Ct. Appeals (7th, 1st, 3d and 4th cirs.) 1991, U.S. Supreme Ct. 1990, D.C. 1991. Motions atty. Ct. Appeals (D.C.), 1984-85; atty., advisor U.S. Labor Dept., Washington, 1985-86; clk. to presiding justice Ct. Appeals (D.C.), 1986-87; trial atty. civil div. U.S. Dept. Justice, Washington, 1987-95, sr. litigation counsel, 1995—. Voting del. Jud. Conf. D.C., 1988-2002; profl. musician trumpet, toured with Gladys Knight and the Pips; performed with Temptations, Four Tops, Dells, Manhattans, O'Jays, Thad Jones and Mel Lewis Big Band, Melba Moore, Dave Brubeck, Jerry Butler; prin. trumpet Internat. Festival Orch., Internat. Festival of Youth Orch., under the direction of Aaron Copeland, London, 1974. Assoc. editor Howard Law Jour., 1983-84. Active Friends of the Kennedy Ctr., Washington, 1988-92, Washington Area Tennis Patrons Found., 1988-90; bd. dirs. Takoma Park Symphony Orch., 1990-97. D.C. Youth Orch. Trumpet scholar, 1974; recipient Civil Divsn. Quality Step Increase U.S. Dept. Justice, 1989, 93, 95, 97, 99, Spl. Achievement award, 1990, 91, 92, 94, 96, 98, 2000, 02. Mem. ABA, Nat. Bar Assn. Democrat. Roman Catholic. Home: 3900 16th St NW Apt 631 Washington DC 20011-8314

MCINTYRE, MONTY ALAN, lawyer; b. Kittery, Maine, Sept. 18, 1955; s. James Gaylord and Paula Carol McIntyre; m. Lann G. Gottesman, Mar. 13, 1982; children: Erin Lindsay, Jessica Anne. BA in History with honors, U. Calif., San Diego, 1977; JD, U. San Diego, 1980. Bar: Calif. 1980, U.S. Dist. Ct. (so. dist.) Calif. 1980, U.S. Ct. Appeals (9th cir.) 1987, U.S. Supreme Ct. 1988. Assoc. Sparber, Haas & Ferguson, San Diego, 1980-82, McGinnis, Fitzgerald, Rees, San Diego, 1982-84; pvt. practice, San Diego, 1984-85; sr. atty. Lowell, Robbin & McIntyre, San Diego, 1985-90; shareholder Thompson & McIntyre, San Diego, 1990-94; pres. McIntyre & McIntyre, San Diego, 1994—2001; of counsel Seltzer Caplan McMahon Vitek, San Diego, 2001—. Evidence law editor San Diego Trial Bar News, 1988—; contbr. articles to legal publs. Bd. dirs., chmn. San Diego Sch. Christian Studies, 1985-91. Mem. San Diego County Bar Assn. (pres. 2002), Am. Bd. Trial Advocates, Enright Am. Inn of Ct. (master), San Diego Trial Lawyers Assn. (Outstanding Trial Lawyer awards 1992, 94), Calif. State Bar (com. on rules 1989-91), San Diego Inn of Ct. (instr.), San Diego County Barristers Club (bd. dirs. 1982-84), Lawyers Club, Barristers. Avocations: music, golf, reading. Insurance, Personal injury (including property damage), Professional liability. Office: Seltzer Caplan McMahon Vitek 750 B St Ste 2100 San Diego CA 92101

MCKAY, DONALD ROSS, lawyer; b. Sharon, Pa., Nov. 29, 1928; s. Leo H. and Ruth (Ellis) McK.; m. Martha Van de Walle, Aug. 23, 1950; children— Jean, Thomas. B.A., Allegheny Coll., 1950; LL.B., U. Pa., 1953. Bar: Pa. 1954, U.S. Dist. Ct. (we. dist.) Pa. 1958, U.S. Ct. Appeals (3d cir.) 1979. Ptnr. Cusick Madden Joyce McKay, Sharon, Pa., 1956-95. Fellow Am. Coll. Trial Lawyers; mem. Fedn. Ins. Counsel. Republican. Methodist. Banking, State civil litigation, Insurance. Office: 701 N Hermitage Rd Hermitage PA 16148-3234

MCKAY, DONNA, legal association administrator; V.p. devel. U.S. Fund for UNICEF; dir. program funding Planned Parenthood, N.Y.C., devel. dir., v.p. for external affairs Chgo.; dir. devel. ACLU, N.Y.C. Office: ACLU 18th Fl 125 Broad St New York NY 10004*

MCKAY, JOHN, lawyer; b. Seattle, June 19, 1956; s. John Larkin and Kathleen (Tierney) M. BA, U. Wash., 1978; JD, Creighton U., 1982. Bar: Wash. 1982, U.S. Dist. Ct. (we. dist.) Wash. 1982, U.S. Supreme Ct. 1990, U.S. Ct. Appeals (9th cir.) 1990, D.C. 1999. Ptnr. Lane Powell Spears Lubersky, Seattle, 1982-92, Cairncross & Hempelmann, Seattle, 1992-97; pres. Legal Svcs. Corp., Washington, 1997—2001; U.S. atty. We. dist. Wash. U.S. Dept. Justice, 2001—. White House fellow, Washington, 1989-90. Mem. ABA (bd. govs. 1991-94), Wash. State Bar Assn. (pres. young lawyers divsn. 1988-89). Republican. Roman Catholic. Avocations: soccer, golf. General civil litigation. Office: US Atty 601 Union St Ste 5100 Seattle WA 98101-3903

MCKAY, JOHN DOUGLAS, lawyer; b. Wheeling, W.Va., Feb. 27, 1960; s. Douglas and Margaret Ann McK.; m. Jennifer Hall, June 13, 1987; children: John Wallace, Megan Diane, Hannah Nadine, Katherine Lorraine. BA with distinction, U. Va., 1982; JD, U. Maine, 1985. Bar: W.Va. 1985, Maine 1985, U.S. Dist. Ct. (so. dist.) W.Va. 1985, U.S. Dist. Ct. Maine 1985, U.S. Ct. Appeals (1st cir.) 1986, Va. 1988, U.S. Ct. Appeals (4th cir.) 1988, U.S. Dist. Ct. (we. dist.) Va. 1988, Colo. 1997, Fla. 1999, N.Y. 2002, Calif. 2002. Assoc. Petruccelli, Cohen, Erler & Cox, Portland, Maine, 1985-88, Taylor & Zunka, Ltd., Charlottesville, Va., 1988-91; ptnr. McKay & Cattano PLC, Charlottesville, 1991-97; prin. McKay Law Offices, Charlottesville, 1997—. Founder, editor (legal newsletter) Equine Law & Bus. Letter, 1990-95; contbr. articles to profl. jours. Elder Presbyn. Ch. Recipient Best Adv. award U. Maine Sch. of Law, 1988. Mem. Va. State Bar (7th dist. disciplinary com. 1994-2000), W.Va. State Bar, Charlottesville-Albemarle Bar Assn. (bd. dirs. 1994-96), Thomas Jefferson Inn of Ct. (past pres). General civil litigation, Commercial, contracts (including sales of goods; commercial financing), Communications. Office: McKay Law Offices 1 Boars Head Ln Charlottesville VA 22903-4610

MCKAY, JOHN JUDSON, JR., lawyer; b. Anderson, S.C., Aug. 13, 1939; s. John Judson and Polly (Plowden) McK.; m. Jill Hall Ryon, Aug. 3, 1961 (div. Dec. 1980); children: Julia Plowden, Katherine Henry, William Ryon, Elizabeth Hall; m. Jane Leahey, Feb. 18, 1982; children: Andrew Leahey, Jennifer McFaddin. AB in History, U. S.C., 1960, JD cum laude, 1966. Bar: S.C. 1966, U.S. Dist. Ct. S.C. 1966, U.S. Ct. Appeals (4th cir.) 1974, U.S. Supreme Ct. 1981, U.S. Dist. Ct. (so. dist.) Ga. 1988, U.S. Ct. Appeals (11th cist.) 1990. Assoc. Haynsworth, Perry, Bryant, Marion & Johnstone, Greenville, S.C., 1966-70; ptnr. Rainey, McKay, Britton, Gibbes & Clarkson, P.A. predecessor, Greenville, 1970-78; sole practice Hilton Head Island, S.C., 1978-80; ptnr. McKay & Gertz, P.A., Hilton Head Island, 1980-81, McKay & Mullen, P.A., Hilton Head Island, 1981-88, McKay & Taylor, Hilton Head Island, 1988-91; pvt. practice, 1991—. Editor-in-chief U. S.C. Law Rev., 1966; contbr. articles to legal jours. E-mail: jmckay@mckaylawfirm.com. Served to lt. (j.g.) USNR, 1961-64; lt. comdr. Res. (ret.). Mem. ABA, S.C. Bar Assn. (pres. young lawyers sect. 1970, exec. com. 1971-72, assoc. mem. grievance and disciplinary com. 1983-87), S.C. Bar, Beaufort County Bar Assn., Hilton Head Bar Assn., Assn. Trial Lawyers Am., S.C. Trial Lawyers Assn., S.C. Bar Found. (pres. 1977), Blue Key, Wig and Robe, Phi Delta Phi. Clubs: Poinsett (Greenville). Episcopalian. Federal civil litigation, State civil litigation, Personal injury (including property damage). Home: 17 Foxbriar Ln Hilton Head Island SC 29926 Office: 203 Watersedge Hilton Head Island SC 29928-3541 E-mail: jmckay@mckaylawfirm.com.

MCKAY, MICHAEL DENNIS, lawyer; b. Omaha, May 12, 1951; s. John Larkin and Kathleen (Tierney) McK.; children: Kevin Tierney, Kathleen Lindsay, John Larkin. BA in Polit. Sci. with distinction, U. Wash., 1973; JD, Creighton U., 1976. Bar: Wash. 1976, U.S. Dist. Ct. (we. dist.) Wash. 1978, U.S. Dist. Ct. (ea. dist.) Wash. 1982, U.S. Ct. Appeals (9th cir.) 1982, U.S. Supreme Ct. 1993. Sr. dep. pros. atty. King County, Seattle, 1976-81; ptnr. McKay & Gaitan, Seattle, 1981-89; U.S. atty. we. dist. Wash. Seattle, 1989-93; ptnr. Lane Powell Spears Lubersky, Seattle, 1993-95, McKay Chadwell PLLC, Seattle, 1995—. Bd. dirs. Mental Health North, Seattle, 1982-85, St. Joseph Sch. Bd., 1984-87, Our Lady of Fatima Sch. Commn., 1994-97, Creighton U., 1988-90; mem. stadium adv. bd. Seattle Kingdome, 1987-89; mem. U.S. Atty. Gen. Adv. Com., 1991-93, vice chmn., 1992; mem. Washington Citizens' Commn. on Salaries for Elected Officials, 1997—; vice chmn., 1999—; vice chmn. Seattle Expert Rev. Panel, 1999; co-chair Washington State George W. Bush Campaign, 2000. Mem. Creighton U. Alumni Assn. (pres. 1988-90, nat. alumni bd. 1988-92), Wash. Athletic Club, Columbia Tower Club. Republican. Roman Catholic. Avocations: swimming, golf. Federal civil litigation, State civil litigation, Criminal. Office: McKay Chadwell PLLC 600 University St Ste 1601 Seattle WA 98101 E-mail: mdm@mckay-chadwell.com.

MCKAY, MONROE GUNN, federal judge; b. Huntsville, Utah, May 30, 1928; s. James Gunn and Elizabeth (Peterson) McK.; m. Lucile A. Kinnison, Aug. 6, 1954; children: Michele, Valanne, Margaret, James, Melanie, Nathan, Bruce, Lisa, Monroe. BS, Brigham Young U., 1957; JD, U. Chgo., 1960. Bar: Ariz. 1961. Law clk. Ariz. Supreme Ct., 1960-61; assoc. firm Lewis & Roca, Phoenix, 1961-66, ptnr., 1968-74; assoc. prof. Brigham Young U., 1974-76, prof., 1976-77; judge U.S. Ct. Appeals for 10th Cir., Denver, 1977-91, chief judge, 1991-94, sr. judge, 1994—. Mem. Phoenix Community Council Juvenile Problems, 1968-74; pres. Ariz. Assn. for Health and Welfare, 1970-72; dir. Peace Corps, Malawi, Africa, 1966-68; bd. dirs., pres. Maricopa county Legal Aid Soc., 1972-74. Served with USMCR, 1946-48. Mem. Ariz. Bar Assn. Mem. Lds Ch. Office: US Ct Appeals 10th Cir Fed Bldg 125 S State St Ste 6012 Salt Lake City UT 84138-1181

MCKAY, ROBERT CONNALLY, lawyer; b. Tyler, Tex., Apr. 28, 1950; s. Connally and Glee (McCrary) McK.; m. Bonnie Swain, Mar. 31, 1979; children: Robert Connally, Sarah Catherine, Caroline Swain. BA, Baylor U., 1972, J.D., 1975. Bar: Tex., U.S. Dist. Ct. (so. dist.) Tex.; cert. in Oil, Gas and Mineral Law Tex. Bd. Legal Specializaiton. Asst. counsel com. on pub. works and transp. U.S. Ho. of Reps., Washington, 1975-77; dir. Scott, Robins, McKay, Smith & Rigsby, Victoria, Tex., 1977-85; chmn., chief exec. officer McKay, Smith, Robins, Russell & Rigsby, 1986-87; chmn., chief exec. officer McKay & Russell, P.C., 1987-92, McKay & Crain, P.C., 1992-96, Stephenson & McKay, L.L.P., 1996-2001, Cole, Cole & Easley, P.C., 2001——; pres. Victoria Savs. Assn., 1985; mem. Tex. State Ethics Adv. Commn., 1983-88. Bd. dirs. Victoria Regional Mus. Assn., 1981-84, Victoria Econ. Devel. Corp., 1983-89; mem. Mayor's Image Com., Victoria, 1983-84. Mem. Coll. of State Bar of Tex., Tex. Bar Found., Victoria County Bar Assn. (pres. 1989-90), Rotary. Presbyterian. Banking, Oil, gas, and mineral, Property, real (including real estate development, water). Home: 303 Leisure Ln Victoria TX 77904-1670 Office: 5606 Hallettsville Hwy Victoria TX 77904-1700

MCKEAGUE, DAVID WILLIAM, judge; b. Pitts., Nov. 5, 1946; s. Herbert William and Phyllis (Forsyth) McK.; m. Nancy L. Palmer, May 20, 1989; children: Mike, Melissa, Sarah, Laura, Elizabeth, Adam. BBA, U. Mich., 1968, JD, 1971. Bar: Mich. 1971, U.S. Dist. Ct. (we. dist.) Mich. 1972, U.S. Dist. Ct. (ea. dist.) 1978, U.S. Ct. Appeals (6th cir.) 1988. Assoc. Foster, Swift, Collins & Smith, Lansing, Mich., 1971-76, ptnr., 1976-92, sec.-treas., 1990-92; adj. prof. Thomas M. Colley Law Sch., 1995—96; judge U.S. Dist. Ct., Western Dist. Mich., Lansing, 1992—. Adj. prof. TDetroit Coll. of Law, Mich State U., 1998—. Nat. com. U. Mich. Law Sch. Fund, 1980-92; gen. counsel Mich. Rep. Com., 1989-92; adv. coun. Wharton Ctr., Mich. State U., 1996—; adv. bd. Corp. for Supportive Housing, 2002—. Mem. FBA (bd. dirs. Western Mich. chpt. 1991—), Mich. Bar Assn., Am. Inns of Ct. (pres. Mich. State U. Detroit Coll. of Law chpt. 1999-01), Country Club Lansing (bd. govs. 1988-92, 96—), The Federalist Soc. for Law and Pub. Studies (lawyers divsn. Mich. chpt. 1996—). Roman Catholic. Office: US Dist Ct 315 W Allegan St Lansing MI 48933-1500

MCKEAN, ROBERT JACKSON, JR., retired lawyer; b. N.Y.C., Dec. 21, 1925; s. Robert Jackson and Isabel (Murphy) McK.; m. Sally H. Ament; children from previous marriage: Katherine, Douglas, Lauren, Andrew. BA, Amherst Coll., 1950; LL.B., Harvard U., 1953. Bar: N.Y. 1954. Assoc. Simpson Thacher & Bartlett, N.Y.C., 1953-62, ptnr., 1962-85. Trustee Amherst Coll., Mass., Folger Shakespeare Library, Washington. Served with U.S. Army, 1944-46, ETO. Recipient medal for eminent service Amherst Coll., 1968 Mem. Phi Beta Kappa. Democrat.

MCKEE, CATHERINE LYNCH, law educator, lawyer; b. Boston, June 7, 1962; d. Robert Emmett and Anne Gayle (Tanner) Lynch; m. Bert K. McKee Jr., Dec. 25, 1990; children: Timothy Kingston, Shannon Lancaster. BA in Biol. Sci., U. Calif. Berkeley, 1984; JD, U. San Diego, 1988. Bar: Calif. 1988, U.S. Dist. Ct. (cen., so. and ea. dists.) Calif. 1989, U.S. Ct. Appeals (9th cir.) 1989. Assoc. Parkinson, Wolf, Lazar & Leo, L.A., 1988-89, McCormick & Mitchell, San Diego, 1989-91; prof. Mt. San Antonio Coll., Walnut, Calif., 1994—, mock trial coach, 1994—2000, dir. paralegal program, 1999—2003. Cert. rev. hearing officer, Orange County, 1994—; legal counsel Imperial Valley Lumber Co., Valley Lumber and Truss Co., 1998—; coach nat. champion C.C. mock trial team, 2000; mem. acad. senate exec. coun. Mt. San Antonio Coll., 1996-2000, chmn. campus equivalency com., 1999. Contbr. weekly newspaper column, 1993-99; prodr., star videos An Attorney's Guide to Legal Research on the Internet, 1998, 99; co-author: Jeff and Catherine's World's Best List of Legal (and Law-related) Internet Sites. Chair scholarship com. U. Calif. Alumni Assn., Ea. San Gabriel Valley area, 1995—; capt. auction team SCATS Gymnastics, 2000—02. Named Cmty. Person of Yr. Diamond Bar C. of C., 1995. Mem. State Bar Calif. (probation monitor 1993—), Ea. Bar Assn. L.A. (trustee 2000—), Am. Inns of Ct., Calif. Assn. Lanterman-Petris-Short Hearing Officers. Avocations: weight lifting, photography, reading. Office: Mount San Antonio Coll 1100 N Grand Ave Walnut CA 91789-1341 E-mail: cmckee@mtsac.edu.

MCKEE, FRANCIS JOHN, medical association consultant, lawyer; b. Bklyn., Aug. 31, 1943; s. Francis Joseph and Catherine (Giles) McK.; m.

Antoinette Mary Sancis; children: Lisa Ann, Francis Dominic, Michael Christopher, Thomas Joseph. AB, Stonehill Coll., 1965; JD, St. John's U., 1970. Bar: N.Y. 1971. Assoc. Samuel Weinberg, Esquire, Bklyn., 1970-71, Finch & Finch, Esquire, Long Island City, N.Y., 1971-72; staff atty. Med. Soc. of State of N.Y., Lake Success, N.Y., 1972-77; prin. Francis J. McKee Assocs., Clinton, NY, 1984—2001; exec. dir. Suffolk Physicians Rev. Orgn., East Islip, N.Y., 1977-81, N.Y. State Soc. Surgeons, Inc., Clinton, N.Y., 1981-2000, N.Y. State Soc. Orthopaedic Surgeons, Inc., Clinton, NY, 1981—2000, Upstate N.Y. chpt. ACS, Inc., Clinton, N.Y., 1981-2000, N.Y. State Ophthalmol. Soc., 1984-92, N.Y. State Soc. Obstetricians and Gynecologists, 1985-2001, Orthopac of N.Y., 1986-2000, Nat. Com. for the Preservation Orthopaedic Practice, New Hartford, N.Y., 1989-2000; L.I. Ophthalmological Soc., 1994-2000. Coun. Suffolk County Med. Soc., Hauppauge, N.Y., 1977-81. With U.S. Army, 1966-68. Mem.: Oneida County Bar Assn., N.Y. State Bar Assn., Am. Legion, Skenandoa Club. Conservative. Roman Catholic. Home and Office: 19 Mulberry St Clinton NY 13323-1532 Fax: (315) 859-1137. E-mail: Frank4Mets@aol.com.

MCKEE, ROGER A. lawyer; b. L.A., Aug. 24, 1943; s. Jerome F. and Florence A. McKee; 1 child, Andrew. BS, UCLA, 1965; JD, U. San Diego, 1969; diploma, Northwestern U., 1970. Bar: Colo. 1970, Calif. 1970, Ariz. 1971, U.S. Ct. Appeals (9th cir.) 1974, U.S. Supreme Ct. 1974. Legal advisor Ariz. Dept. Pub. Safety, Phoenix, 1970—71; dep. county atty. Maricopa County Atty., Phoenix, 1971—74; town atty. Town of Paradise Valley, Ariz., 1974—78; pvt. practice Phoenix, 1978—. Mem.: State Bar Ariz. (chmn. sole practitioners sect. 1991—92, bd. govs. 1993—95). Labor (including EEOC, Fair Labor Standards Act, labor-management relations, NLRB, OSHA), Civil rights. Office: 6554 N 7th Ave Unit 12 Phoenix AZ 85013-1155 Office Fax: 602-864-3389.

MCKEE, ROGER CURTIS, retired federal judge; b. Waterloo, Iowa, Feb. 11, 1931; s. James A. and Leonace (Burrell) McK.; m. Roberta Jeanne Orvis, Sept. 3, 1954; children: Andrea Jane, Brian Curtis, Paul Robert. BA, State Coll. of Iowa, 1955; MA, U. Ill., 1960; JD, U. San Diego, 1968. Bar: Calif. 1970, U.S. Dist. Ct. (so. dist.) Calif. 1969, U.S. Ct. Appeals (9th cir.) 1971. Telegrapher, agt. Ill. Cen. R.R., 1950-55; tng. asst. No. Ill. Gas Co., Aurora, 1959-60; with indsl. rels. dept. Convair div. Gen. Dynamics Corp., San Diego, 1960-68; contract adminstr. and supr. Datagraphix div. Gen. Dynamics Corp., San Diego, 1968-69, asst. counsel, 1969-70; ptnr. Powell & McKee, San Diego, 1970-75, Millsberg, Dickstein & McKee, San Diego, 1975-83; magistrate judge U.S. Dist. Ct. for So. Dist. Calif., San Diego, 1983-97; presiding magistrate judge, 1993-97. Bd. trustees So. Calif. Presbyn. Homes, L.A., 1979-81; moderator Presbytery of San Diego, 1980. Capt. USNR, 1949-85. Mem. Calif. Bar Assn., Fed. Magistrate Judges Assn., Navy League U.S., Naval Res. Officers Assn., Res. Officers Assn., Dixieland Jazz Soc. (bd. dirs. San Diego chpt. 1984—). Republican. Fax: (858) 277-0444. E-mail: rcmckee10@cs.com.

MCKEEVER, JOHN EUGENE, lawyer; b. Phila., Oct. 24, 1947; s. John James and Marie Julia (Supper) McK.; m. Kathleen Marie Wynne, Dec. 9, 1995; children: John Joseph, Jeannine Marie. BA magna cum laude with distinction, U. Pa., 1969, JD magna cum laude, 1972. Bar: Pa. 1972, U.S. Dist. Ct. (ea. dist.) Pa. 1972, U.S. Dist. Ct. (mid. dist.) Pa. 1977, U.S. Ct. Appeals (3rd cir.) 1979, U.S. Ct. Appeals (D.C. cir.) 1981, U.S. Supreme Ct. 1981. Assoc. Schnader, Harrison, Segal & Lewis, Phila., 1972-80, ptnr., 1980-98, Piper Rudnick LLP, Phila., 1998—. Trustee Lawyers Com. for Civil Rights Under Law, Washington, 2003—. Mem. pres.'s coun. De Sales U., Center Valley, Pa., 1980—; mem. Bus. Leadership Organized for Cath. Schs., Phila., 1984—; mem. adv. com. De Sales Sch. Theology, Washington, trustee, 1988-91; capt. spl. gifts com. Cath. Charities Appeal, Phila., 1986-91; bd. dirs. Jr. Achievement, Phila., 1986—; co-chair Oblates of St. Francis De Sales Capital Campaign, 1998-99. Mem. Phila. Bar Assn., Pro-Life Lawyers' Guild (bd. dirs. 1983-84, chancellor 1984-86), St. Thomas More Soc. (gov. 1979-91, pres. 1981-82), Order of Coif, Phi Beta Kappa, Pi Gamma Mu. Republican. Roman Catholic. Administrative and regulatory, Federal civil litigation, Postal. Office: Piper Rudnick LLP 3400 Two Logan Sq 18th and Arch Sts Philadelphia PA 19103-2762 E-mail: john.mckeever@piperrudnick.com.

MCKEEVER, KENT, library director, law librarian; b. Southampton, N.Y., Sept. 6, 1952; BA, SUNY, Oswego, 1974; JD, La. State U., 1980. Bar: La. 1980. Ref. libr. Fordham U. Sch. Law Libr., 1981—82; internat., fgn. and comparative law libr. Columbia U. Law Sch. Libr., N.Y.C., 1982—83, assoc. law libr., head collection devel. and tech. svcs., 1983—93, acting law libr., 1994—95, dir. Diamond Law Libr., 1996—. Lectr. Fudan U., Shanghai, 1986, Columbia U. Sch. Libr. Svc., N.Y.C., 1986—91, Columbia Summer Program, Leiden, Netherlands, 1998—2000; cons. Beijing U., Dept. of Treaty and Law, China, MetaMetrics, Inc.; grant application evaluator NEH. Class of 1950 scholar, La. State U., Supr.'s scholar, Tullis-Herget scholar. Office: Diamond Law Libr 435 W 116th St New York NY 10027 Home: 456 Riverside Dr # 10B New York NY 10027 Office Fax: 212-854-3295. Business E-Mail: mckeever@law.columbia.edu.*

MCKELVEY, JUDITH GRANT, lawyer, educator, university dean; b. Milw., July 19, 1935; d. Lionel Alexander and Bernadine R. (Verdun) Grant. BS in Philosophy, U. Wis., 1957, JD, 1959. Bar: Wis. 1959, Calif. 1968. Atty. FCC, Washington, 1959-62; adj. prof. U. Md., Europe, 1965; prof. law Golden Gate U. Sch. Law, San Francisco, 1968-99, dean, 1974-81. Mem. State Jud. Nominees Evaluation Commn., 1981-82. Contbr. to: Damages Book, 1975, 76. Bd. dirs. San Francisco Neighborhood Legal Assistance Found. Fellow Am. Bar Found.; mem. ABA, Wis. Bar Assn., Calif. Bar Assn., San Francisco Bar Assn. (dir. 1975-77, chmn. legis. com., sec.-treas., pres.-elect 1980-83, pres. 1984), Calif. Women Lawyers (1st pres.), Law in a Free Soc. (exec. com.), Continuing Edn. of Bar (chmn. real estate subcom., mem. joint adv. com.), Legal Svcs. to Children Inc. (pres. 1987-89), San Francisco Neighborhood Legal Assistance Found. (dir. and exec. com. 1985-87), Lawyers Com. for Urban Affairs (dir. and exec. com. 1985-87, co-chairperson 1988-90). Office: Golden Gate U Sch Law 536 Mission St San Francisco CA 94105-2921

MCKENDRY, JOHN H., JR., lawyer, educator; b. Grand Rapids, Mich., Mar. 24, 1950; s. John H. and Lois R. (Brandel) McK.; m. Linda A. Schmalzer, Aug. 11, 1973; children: Heather Lynn, Shannon Dawn, Sean William. BA cum laude, Albion Coll., 1972; JD cum laude, U. Mich., 1975. Bar: Mich. 1975. Assoc., then ptnr. Landman, Latimer, Clink & Robb, Muskegon, Mich., 1976-85; ptnr. Warner, Norcross & Judd, Muskegon, 1985—. Dir. debate Mona Shores High Sch., Muskegon, 1979-90; adj. prof. of taxation (employee benefits), Grand Valley State U., 1988—; debate instr. Muskegon C.C., 1999-2001. Pres. local chpt. Am. Cancer Soc., 1979; bd. dirs. West Shore Symphony, 1993-2000, v.p. 1995-97, pres., 1997-99; bd. dirs. Cath. Social Svcs., 1998—; chair profl. divsn. United Way, 1994, 98. Recipient Disting. Service award Muskegon Jaycees, 1981; named 1 of 5 Outstanding Young Men in Mich., Mich. Jaycees. 1982; named to Hall of Fame, Mich. Speech Coaches, 1986, Diamond Key Coach Nat. Forensic League, 1987. Mem. ABA, Mich. Bar Assn., Muskegon County Bar Assn. (dir. 1992-98, pres. 1996-97), Muskegon C. of C. (bd. dirs. 1982-88), Mich. Interscholastic Forensic Assn. (treas. 1979-86), Optimists (pres. 1992). Republican. Roman Catholic. Pension, profit-sharing, and employee benefits. Home: 1575 Brookwood Dr Muskegon MI 49441-5276 Office: Warner Norcross & Judd LLP PO Box 900 400 Terrace Pla Muskegon MI 49443-0900 E-mail: mckendjh@wnj.com.

MCKENNA, ALVIN JAMES, lawyer; b. New Orleans, Aug. 17, 1943; s. Dixon N. Sr. and Mabel (Duplantier) McK.; m. Carol Jean Windheim, 1963; children: Sara, Alvin James Jr., Martha, Andrea, Erin, Rebecca. AB, Canisius Coll., 1963; JD, Notre Dame U., 1966. Bar: N.Y. 1966, Ohio 1967, U.S. Dist. Ct. (so. dist.) Ohio 1968, U.S. Dist. Ct. (no. dist.) Ohio 1978, U.S. Ct. Appeals (6th cir.) 1969, U.S. Supreme Ct. 1977. Law clk. to judge of U.S. Dist. Ct. (so. dist.), Columbus, Ohio, 1966-68; asst. U.S. atty., 1968-70; ptnr. Porter, Wright, Morris & Arthur, 1970—. Mem. Gahanna (Ohio) City Council, 1972-80, 82-84; chmn. Gahanna Charter Rev. Commn., 1981; pres. Community Urban Redevel. Corp., Gahanna, 1984—. Named one of Ten Outstanding Young Persons in Columbus, Jaycees, 1974. Mem. ABA, Ohio Bar Assn., Fed. Bar Assn. (pres. Columbus chpt. 1973-74), Columbus Bar Assn. (chair fed. cts. com. 1972-74). Administrative and regulatory, Federal civil litigation, Labor (including EEOC, Fair Labor Standards Act, labor-management relations, NLRB, OSHA). Home: 202 Academy Ct Columbus OH 43230-2104 Office: Porter Wright Morris & Arthur 41 S High St Ste 2800 Columbus OH 43215-6194 E-mail: amckenna@porterwright.com.

MCKENNA, FRANK JOSEPH, lawyer; b. Apohaqui, N.B., Can., Jan. 19, 1948; s. Durward and Olive (Moody) McK.; m. Julie Friel; children: Tobias John, Christine Alice, James Durward. BA with honors, St. Francis Xavier U., 1970; postgrad., Queen's U., 1970-71; LLB, U. N.B., 1974; DSc (hon.), Université de Moncton, Can., 1988; LLD (hon.), University of N.B., Can., 1988, Mt. Allison U., 1991. Spl. asst. to pres. Privy Council, 1971; rsch. asst. Constl. Law Unit, 1973-74; v.p. U. N.B. Faculty of Law Liberal Assn., Fredericton, 1974; ptnr. Martin, Lordon, McKenna & Bowes, Chatham, 1974-87; mem. N.B. Liberal Party, 1982, leader, 1985; premier Province of N.B., Fredericton, 1987-97; with McInnes Cooper, Moncton, NB, Can. Dir. Bank of Montreal, Noranda Inc., Zenon Environ., Acier LeRoux, various provincial, nat. and internat. cos. Recipient Vanier award, 1988, Distinction award Can. Advanced Tech. Assn., 1994; named Econ. Developer of Yr., Econ. Developers' Assn. Can., 1993, Chair, Can. Quality Month, 1994. Mem. Can. Bar Assn., N.B. Bar Assn. Liberal. Avocations: jogging, baseball, hockey. Office: McInnes Cooper PO Box 1368 Moncton NB Canada E1C 8T6

MCKENNA, KAREN L. lawyer; b. Weymouth, Mass., July 4, 1963; d. James M. and Beryl S. Denker; m. Brian K. McKenna, Dec. 30, 1995. BS, U. of Mass., 1985; JD, Duke U., 1997. Bookkeeper/purchasing agt. Union Gear & Sprocket Corp., Quincy, Mass., 1985—88; text editor Cornell U., Ithaca, NY, 1986—88; asst. acctg. mgr. Solco Basle, Inc., Hingham, Mass., 1988—90; acctg. mgr. Eldred Wheeler, Inc., Hingham, Mass., 1990—91; adminstrv. mgr. Pub. Svc. Computer Software, Inc., Cambridge, Mass., 1991—92; treas. Vertical Tech. & Info. Co., Inc., Scituate, Mass., 1992—; ops. & acctg. mgr. JEM Computers Inc., Brighton, Mass., 1993—94; pres. Boston Computer Consignment Inc., Boston, 1993; assoc. atty. Kirkpatrick & Lockhart LLP, Pitts., 1997—2000, Boston, 2001—, Choate, Hall & Stewart, Boston, 2000—01. Contbr. Mem.: Pa. Bar Assn., Mass. Bar Assn., Boston Bar Assn. Republican. Methodist. Avocations: origami, interior decorating, animals. Environmental, Estate taxation. Home: 50 Sylvester Rd Scituate MA 02066 Office: Kirkpatrick & Lockhart LLP 75 State St Boston MA 02109 Home Fax: 781-545-6425; Office Fax: 617-261-3175. Personal E-mail: klmckenna@attbi.com. E-mail: kmckenna@kl.com.

MCKENNA, MATTHEW MORGAN, lawyer; b. Apr. 29, 1950; s. James Aloysius and Rebecca (Rial) McK.; m. Nancy Fitzpatrick, Sept. 11, 1976; children: Matthew, James, Christine, Connor. BA, Hamilton Coll., 1972; JD, Georgetown U., 1975, LLM, 1978. Bar: N.Y. 1977. Clk. to Hon. Fred B. Ugast Superior Ct., Washington, 1975—76; assoc. Winthrop, Stimson, Putnam & Roberts, N.Y.C., 1979—83, ptnr., 1984—93, sr. v.p., treas., 1998—2001, sr. v.p. fin., 2001—02. Adj. prof. Sch. Law Fordham U., N.Y.C., 1983—94, N.Y.C., 2002—. Trustee Merrill Lynch Found., 1986—95, Mt. St. Mary's Coll., Emmitsburg, Md., 1994—2002; bd. trustees SUNY, Purchase, NY, 2003—, Hamilton Coll., 2003—. Mem.: ABA (tax sect.), Assn. Bar of City of N.Y., N.Y. State Bar Assn. (chmn. com. on fgn. activities of U.S. taxpayers). Corporate taxation. Home: 35 Valley Rd Bronxville NY 10708-2226 Office: PepsiCo 700 Anderson Hill Rd Purchase NY 10577-1444

MCKENNAN, JOHN T. lawyer; b. New Hartford, N.Y., Nov. 25, 1918; s. John Patrick and Rena C. (Dowd) McK.; m. Marguerite Gallagher, May 7, 1955; children: John, Timothy. BS, Utica Acad., 1938, Scarborough Sch., 1939; postgrad., Syracuse U., 1939-41; LLB, Union U., 1945. Bar: N.Y. 1945. Assoc. Hawkins, Delafield & Longfellow, N.Y.C., 1945; pvt. practice Utica, N.Y., 1946—. Judge N.Y. State Supreme Ct. for 5th Jud. Dist., 1982. Mem. N.Y. State Senate, 1949-51; mayor City of Utica, 1956-60; sec. N.Y. State Constl. Conv., Albany, 1967. Mem. Yahnundasis Golf Club. Democrat. Roman Catholic. Avocation: golf. General practice, Personal injury (including property damage), Probate (including wills, trusts). Home: 15 Foxcroft Rd New Hartford NY 13413-2734

MCKENZIE, COLIN JOHN, mediator, consultant; b. Christchurch, New Zealand, Jan. 9, 1955; s. John Alexander and Muriel Edna McKenzie. BSc in Geography, Otago U., New Zealand, 1978; MSc in Resource Mgmt., U. Canterbury, New Zealand, 1982; diploma in dispute resolution, Program on Negotiation, Boston, 1994; MES in Conflict Resolution, York U., Toronto, Can., 1996. Project mgr. Liquie Fuels Trust Bd., Wellington, New Zealand, 1983—87; program mgr. N.Z. Planning Coun., Wellington, 1987—89; cons. Conflict Mgmt. Group, Boston, 1993—97; dir. Conflict Mgmt. N.Z. Ltd., Wellington, 1997—. Guest editor: quar. Culture, Resources and Conflict: Challenging our Assumptions, 1995; contbr. articles to profl. jours. Recipient Bertrand Gerstein scholarship, 1990, Howlett scholarship, 1990, 1992; scholar, York U., 1990—93. Mem.: Soc. for Conflict Resolution in Ont., Soc. Profls. in Dispute Resolution (affiliate), Arbitrators and Mediators Inst. New Zealand. (assoc.). Avocations: climbing, boating. Office: CMNZ Ltd Level 13 114 The Terrace Wellington 6005 New Zealand Fax: 04 4997301. E-mail: colin@cmnz.co.nz.

MCKENZIE, ELIZABETH MCDANIEL, law librarian; b. Lexington, Ky., June 27, 1954; d. William E. and JoAnn E. (Harris) McDaniel; m. James A. McKenzie, May 20, 1978; children: Joseph D., E. Alexa. BA with distinction, Transylvania U., 1975; JD, U. Ky., 1981, MLS with distinction, 1984. Bar: Ky. 1981, U.S. Dist. Ct. (ea. dist.) Ky. 1981. Reginald Heber Smith community lawyer fellow Cen. Ky. Legal Svcs., Lexington, 1981-83; info. specialist Ky. Dept. for Environ. Protection, Frankfort, Ky., 1984-85; readers svcs. librarian St. Louis U. Law Library, 1986-96; dir. Suffolk U. Law Libr., Boston, 1996—. Owner, mgr. Juris Data Legal Rsch. Co., Lexington, 1985-86. Contbg. author: Libraries, Erotica and Pornography. Recipient Article of Yr. award Law Libr. Jour., 1999; Nat. Merit scholar Transylvania U., 1972-75. Mem. ABA, Ky. Bar Assn., Am. Assn. Law Libraries, Law Libraries New England, New England Law Library Consortium, Assn. Boston Law Libraries. Democrat. Roman Catholic. Office: Suffolk U Law Sch 120 Tremont St Boston MA 02108-4977

MCKENZIE, FRANKLIN COOPER, JR., lawyer; b. Laurel, Miss., Dec. 19, 1946; s. Franklin Cooper and O.Z. McKenzie; m. Joann Cheeks, June l, 1968; children: Elizabeth Allyn, Jonathan Adam, Sarah Jo. AA, Jones Jr. Coll., 1966; BA, U. So. Miss., 1968; JD, U. Miss., 1972. Bar: Miss. 1972, U.S. Dist. Ct. (no. and so. dists.) Miss. 1972, U.S. Ct. Appeals (5th cir.). Assoc. Law Office Charles W. Pickering, Laurel, 1972-74; ptnr. Pickering, Walters & McKenzie, Laurel, 1975-77, Pickering & McKenzie, Laurel, 1977-80; sr. ptnr. McKenzie & Pickering, Laurel, 1980-83, Franklin C. McKenzie, Jr., P.A., Laurel, 1983-94; Chancery judge 19th Dist. Miss., 1995—. City atty. City of Laurel, 1973-85, 89-94; mem. adv. bd. dirs. Sunburst Bank, Laurel. Mem. Miss. Bar Assn., Jones County Bar Assn. (pres. 1976-77). Methodist. Avocations: gardening, hunting, coaching youth sports. Corporate, general, General practice, Personal injury (including property damage). Office: PO Box 1961 Laurel MS 39441-1961

MCKENZIE, JAMES FRANKLIN, lawyer; b. Mobile, Ala., May 3, 1948; s. Frank L. McKenzie and Mary K. (Crow) McKenzie O'Neal; m. Randy Jo Jones, June 25, 1977; children: Katherine J., J. Alistair. BA magna cum laude, U. W. Fla., 1970; JD with honors, U. Fla., 1973. Bar: Fla. 1973, U.S. Dist. Ct. (no. dist.) Fla. 1973, U.S. Ct. Appeals (5th cir.) 1975, U.S. Ct. Appeals (11th cir.) 1982, U.S. Supreme Ct. 1988. Lectr. bus. law U. Fla., Gainesville, 1972-73; assoc. Levin, Warfield et al, Pensacola, Fla., 1973-76; ptnr. Myrick & McKenzie, PA, Pensacola, Fla., 1976-82, McKenzie, Taylor & Zarzaur, P.A., Pensacola, Fla., 1982—. Contbr. chpts. to books, articles to profl. jours. Pres. N.W. Fla. Easter Seal Soc., Pensacola, 1975; bd. dirs. Five Flags Sertoma Club, 1977; trustee Fla. Lawyers Action Group, Tallahassee, 1996-97; adv. bd. Lupus Soc., N.W. Fla., 1992. Mem.: 1st Cir. Acad. Trial Lawyers (founding mem., pres. 1984), ATLA (bd. govs. 2001—, pres. club), ABA, Million Dollar Advocates Forum, Civil Justice Found. (founding sponsor), Nat. Bd. Trial Advocacy (cert. civil trial advocacy), Escambia-Santa Rosa Bar Assn., Fla. Bar Assn. (cert. in civil trial law), Acad. Fla. Trial Lawyers (bd. dirs. 1986—93, exec. com. 1990—91, bd. dirs. 2000—, coll. diplomates, Silver Eagle award 1989, 2002, ABCD award 1991), Pensacola Country Club, Order of Coif, Phi Delta Phi, Omicron Delta Kappa, Phi Kappa Phi. Republican. Methodist. General civil litigation, Insurance, Personal injury (including property damage). Home: 12 Tristan Way Pensacola Beach FL 32561-5121 Office: McKenzie Taylor & Zarzaur PA 905 E Hatton St Pensacola FL 32503-3931 E-mail: jfm01@bellsouth.net.

MCKENZIE, JOHN F. lawyer; b. Chgo., Sept. 28, 1947; s. John Cummings and Mary Jane (Manny) McK.; m. Lucy A. Roman, Jan. 14, 1978; children: Melissa Ann, Sean Cummings. BA, Williams Coll., 1969; JD, Harvard U., 1976. Bar: Calif. 1976, U.S. Dist. Ct. (no. dist.) Calif. 1976, U.S. Ct. Appeals (10th cir.) 1985, Ct. Internat. Trade. Assoc. Baker & McKenzie, San Francisco, 1976-83, ptnr., 1983—. Articles editor Harvard Law Review, 1974—76. Contbg. author, editor Computers & Software, 4th edit., 1989; contbr. articles on export controls, anti-boycott regulations and software licensing to profl. publs. Mem. ABA (internat. sect.), State Bar of Calif. (internat. sect.), Bar Assn. San Francisco, Santa Clara Valley World Trade Assn., Am. Electronics Assn. (lawyers com.), Calif. Coun. on Internat. Trade, U.S. Dept. Commerce (no. Calif. dist. export coun.); Phi Beta Kappa (Magna Cum Laude) Commercial, contracts (including sales of goods; commercial financing), Computer, Private international. Home: 10 Mann Dr Kentfield CA 94904-1034 Office: Baker & McKenzie 2 Embarcadero Ctr Ste 2400 San Francisco CA 94111-3909 also: Baker & McKenzie 1 Prudential Pla 130 E Randolph St Ste 3700 Chicago IL 60601-6316

MCKENZIE, ROBERT ERNEST, lawyer; b. Cheboygan, Mich., Dec. 7, 1947; s. Alexander Orlando and Edna Jean (Burt) McK.; m. Theresia Wolf, Apr. 26, 1975; 1 child, Robert A. BA in Personnel Adminstrn., Mich. State U., 1970; JD with high honors, Ill. Inst. Tech., 1979. Bar: Ill. 1979, U.S. Dist. Ct. (no. dist.) Ill. 1979, U.S. Tax Ct. 1979, U.S. Ct. Appeals (7th cir.) 1979, U.S. Supreme Ct. 1984; lic. pvt. pilot. Revenue officer IRS, Chgo., 1972-78; ptnr. McKenzie & McKenzie, Chgo., 1979-2000, Arnstein & Lehr, 2000—. Lectr. Tax Seminars Inst., Chgo., 1984—. Author: Representation Before the Collection Divison of the IRS, 1989; co-author: Representing the Audited Taxpayer Before the IRS, 1990; contbr. articles to profl. jours. Mem. tax adv. com. Nat. Bankruptcy Rev. Commn., 1997; del. Rep. Nat. Conv., Detroit, 1980, Ill. State Rep. Conv., Peoria, 1980. Served with U.S. Army, 1970. Recipient scholarship Mich. State U., 1966-70, State of Mich., 1966-70, Silas Strawn scholarship ITT, 1977. Fellow Am. Bar Found., N.W. Suburban Bar Assn; mem. ABA (chmn. employment tax com. tax sect. 1992-94, co-chmn. bankruptcy task force 1997-98, coun. tax sect. 1998-2001, vice chmn. tax sect. 2003—), Chgo. Bar Assn. (chmn. com. devel. tax com. 1996-97), Fed. Bar Assn. (tax com.), Rotary (pres. Norridge club 1985-86). Corporate taxation, Personal income taxation. Office: Ste 1200 120 S Riverside Plz Chicago IL 60606 E-mail: remckenzie@arnstein.com.

MCKEON, THOMAS JOSEPH, lawyer; b. Feb. 3, 1955; s. Thomas Michael and Mary Rose (Luzar) McKeon. BA, Ind. U., 1974; JD cum laude, U. Ind., Indpls., 1977. Bar: Ind. 1977, U.S. Dist. Ct. (so. dist.) Ind. 1977, U.S. Supreme Ct. 1979. Assoc. Nisenbaum & Brown, Inpls., 1977, Osborn & Hiner, Inpls., 1977; counsel Am. Family Ins., Inpls., 1982—; asst. counsel Radio Earth Internat., Inc., Radio Earth Curacao, Netherlands Antilles, 1985—. Author: (book) Post Traumatic Stress Disorder: Real or Imagined, 1986, Repetition Strain as a Compensable Injury, 1987; contbr. articles to profl. jours. Mem.: ABA, ATLA (assoc.), Ind. Arson and Crime Assn., Ind. Assn. Pvt. Detectives, Am. Corp. Counsel Assn., Def. Rsch. & Trial Lawyers Assn., Indpls. Bar Assn., Ind. Trial Lawyers Assn., Ind. Def. Lawyers Assn., Ind. Bar Assn., San Diego Turtle and Tortoise Soc. Communications, Insurance, Arson, fraud. Office: 7330 Shadeland Sta Indianapolis IN 46256-3919

MCKEOWN, H. MARY, lawyer, educator; b. West Palm Beach, Fla., Sept. 17, 1952; d. Honore Stephen McKeown and Margaret Berg McKeown Growney; m. Jon Henry Barber, Sept. 18, 1981; children: Sean Patrick, Mary Kathleen. AA, St. Petersburg Jr. Coll., Fla., 1970; BA in Polit. Sci. and Sociology, U. South Fla., 1972; JD cum laude, Samford U., 1976. Bar: Fla. 1976, U.S. Dist. Ct. (mid. dist.) Fla. 1977, U.S. Ct. Appeals (5th and 11th cirs.) 1981, U.S. Supreme Ct. 1992. Asst. state atty. 6th Jud. Ct., Clearwater, Fla., 1976-90; ptnr. Growney, McKeown & Barber, St. Petersburg, 1976—. Adj. prof. Stetson Coll. of Law, St. Petersburg, 1990—. Chairperson Child Welfare Std. and Tng. Coun., 1995—98; mem. nominee qualifications rev. com. Health and Human Svcs. Bd. Dist. 5, 1992—2000; mem. Study Commn. Child Welfare, 1990—91; leader Girl Scouts U.S., 1991—2001. Recipient Victim Advocacy award Pinellas County Victims Rights Coalition, 1984, Law and Order award Elks, Pinellas County, 1991. Mem.: St. Petersburg Bar Assn., Fla. Bar Assn., Acad. Fla. Trial Lawyers, Phi Alpha Delta. Personal injury (including property damage). Office: 7455 38th Ave N Saint Petersburg FL 33710-1228

MCKEOWN, MARY MARGARET, federal judge; b. Casper, Wyo., May 11, 1951; d. Robert Mark and Evelyn Margaret (Lipsack) McKeown; m. Peter Francis Cowhey, June 29, 1985; 1 child, Megan Margaret. BA in Internat. Affairs and Spanish, U. Wyo., 1972; JD, Georgetown U., 1975. Bar: Wash. 1975, D.C. 1982. Assoc. Perkins Coie, Seattle, 1975—79, Washington, 1979—80; White House fellow U.S. Dept. Interior and White House, Washington, 1980—81; ptnr., mem. exec. com. Perkins Coie, Seattle, 1981—98, mng. dir. strategic planning and client rels., 1990—95; judge U.S. Ct. Appeals for 9th Cir., Seattle, 1998—2001, San Diego, 2001—. Trustee The Pub. Defender, Seattle, 1982—85; rep. 9th Cir. Judicial Conf., San Francisco, 1985—89; mem. gender bias task force, 1992—93; jud. conf. Com. on Codes of Conduct, 2001—; exec. com. 9th Cir., 2001—. Author: Girl Scout's Guide to New York, 1990; contbr. chpt. to book and articles to profl. jours. Nat. bd. dirs. Girl Scouts U.S., N.Y.C., 1976—87; mem. exec. com. Corp. Coun. for the Arts, Seattle, 1988—98; bd. gen. counsel Downtown Seattle Assn., 1986—89; mem. exec. com. Wash. Coun. Internat. Trade, 1994—; bd. mem. YMCA Greater Seattle, 1998—; bd. dirs. Family Svcs., Seattle, 1982—84. Named one of 100 Young Women of Promise, Good Housekeeping, 1985, Washington's Winningest Trial Lawyers, Washington Jour., 1992, Top 50 Women Lawyers, Nat. Law Jour., 1998; recipient Rising Stars of the 80's award, Legal Times Washington, 1983; fellow Japan leadership, 1992—93. Fellow: ABA (ho. of dels. 1990—); mem.: Nat. Assn. Iolta Programs (bd. dirs. 1989—91), Wash. Women Lawyers (bd. dirs., pres. 1978—79), Legal Found. Wash. (trustee, pres. 1989—90), Seattle-King County Bar Assn. (trustee, sec. 1984—85, Outstanding Lawyer award 1992), Wash. Bar Assn. (chmn. jud. recommendations 1989—90), Fed. Bar Assn. (trustee western dist. Wash. 1980—90), White House Fellows Found. (bd. dirs. 1998—, pres. 2000—01). Avocations: travel, classical piano, hiking, gourmet cooking, tennis. Office: US Ct Appeals 401 West A St Ste 2000 San Diego CA 92101-7908 E-mail: Judge_McKeown@ca9.uscourts.gov.

MCKERNS, CHARLES JOSEPH, lawyer; b. Shenandoah, Pa., July 17, 1935; s. Charles Francis and Bridgett Ann (Barrett) McK.; m. Helen Patricia Nott, Feb. 13, 1960; children: Charles J. Jr., Michael H., Patricia B. BS, Georgetown U., 1957, JD, 1960. Bar: D.C. 1960, U.S. Ct. Appeals (D.C. cir.) 1961, U.S. Supreme Ct. 1971, Va. 1992. Law clk. to assoc. judge U.S. Ct. Appeals (D.C. cir), Washington, 1960—61; assoc. Dow, Lohnes & Albertson, Washington, 1961—65, ptnr., 1965—91, of counsel, 1991—95; ptnr. McKerns and McKerns, Heathsville, Va., 1991-96, of counsel, 1996—98. 1st lt. U.S. Army, 1957—59. Mem. ABA, University Club (Washington), Belle Haven Country Club (Alexandria, Va.), Indian Creek Yacht and Country Club (Kilmarnock, Va.). Republican. Roman Catholic. Avocations: hiking, reading, swimming. Communications, Corporate, general, Mergers and acquisitions. Home: Windy Blue PO Box 248 Ophelia VA 22530 Office: McKerns & Hill PO Box 220 Heathsville VA 22473-0220 also: Dow Lohnes & Albertson 1200 New Hampshire Ave NW Washington DC 20036-6802

MCKEY, THOMAS J. retired lawyer; b. Detroit, Jan. 9, 1934; s. Thomas J. and Pauline H. (Feys) McK.; m. Lila W. Webber, Sept. 3, 1960; children: Tim, Christopher, Heather, Brenda. BS, USCG Acad., 1955; JD, U. Mich., 1962; MA in Psychology, Antioch U., 1995. Bar: Wash. 1962. With Bogle & Gates, Seattle, 1962-94, ptnr., 1970-94; arbitrator/mediator, pres., bd. dirs. North Pacific Dispute Resolution Svc., 1996—2001. Former chmn. N.W. Admiralty Law Inst., Seattle; mem. permanent adv. bd. Tulane Admiralty Law Inst., New Orleans, 1981—. Former bd. dirs. Bellvue (Wash.) Area Self-Improvement Coun., N.W. Seaport, Seattle, Coast Guard Mus. N.W., Seattle, Friends of Youth, Seattle, Resource Inst., Seattle. Comdr. USCGR, ret. USCGR. Mem. Maritime Law Assn. U.S. (exec. com. 1979-82), Seattle C. of C. (former chmn. maritime steering com.). Admiralty.

MCKIBBEN, HOWARD D. federal judge; b. Apr. 1, 1940; s. James D. and Bernice McKibben; m. Mary Ann McKibben, July 2, 1966; children: Mark, Susan. BS, Bradley U., 1962; MPA, U. Pitts., 1964; JD, U. Mich., 1967. Assoc. George W. Abbott Law Office, 1967-71; dep. dist. atty. Douglas County, Nev., 1969-71, dist. atty., 1971-77; dist. ct. judge State of Nev., 1977-84; judge U.S. Dist. Ct. Nev., Reno, 1984—. Mem. Nev. Bar Assn., Am. Inns of Ct. (pres. Nev. chpt. 1986-88). Methodist. Avocations: tennis, golf, racquetball. Home: PO Box 588 Verdi NV 89439-0588 Office: US Dist Ct 400 S Virginia St Ste 804 Reno NV 89501-2197

MCKIM, SAMUEL JOHN, III, lawyer; b. Pitts., Dec. 31, 1938; s. Samuel John and Harriet Frieda (Roehl) McK; children: David Hunt, Andrew John; m. Eugenia A. Leverich. AA cum laude, Port Huron Jr. Coll., 1959; BA cum laude, U. Mich., 1961, JD cum laude, 1964. Bar: Mich. 1965, U.S. Dist. Ct. (so. dist.) Mich. 1965, U.S. Ct. Appeals (6th cir.) 1969, U.S. Supreme Ct. 1994. Assoc. Miller, Canfield, Paddock and Stone, PLC, Detroit, Bloomfield Hills, 1964-71, sr. mem., 1971—, head state and local tax sect., 1985—, chmn. tax dept., 1989-94, mng. ptnr., 1979-85, chmn., mng. ptnr., 1984-85. Mem. tax coun. State Bar Mich., 1981-94, chmn. state and local tax com. real property sect., 1982-90; adj. prof. law sch. Wayne State U., 1993-. Assoc. editor Mich. Law Rev. Bd. dirs., past chmn. Goodwill Industries of Greater Detroit, 1970-2000; dir. Goodwill Industries Found., 1982-95; tchg. elder Presbyn. Ch., Stevens min. Fellow: Am. Tax Counsel; mem.: ABA, Barrister's Soc., Detroit Bar Assn., Mich. Bar Assn., Mariner Sands Country Club, Port Huron Golf Club, Nomads Club, Order of Coif, Phi Delta Phi. Corporate, general, State and local taxation. Home (Summer): 8351 Lakeshore Rd Lexington MI 48450 Home: 6403 SE Brandywine Ct # 124 Stuart FL 34994 Office: Miller Canfield Paddock & Stone 150 W Jefferson Ave Ste 2500 Detroit MI 48226-4416

MCKINNEY, JAMES DEVAINE, JR., lawyer; b. Muscatine, Iowa, Dec. 13, 1931; s. James D. and Jeffie Lillian (Eblen) McK.; m. Betty A. Guy, June 10, 1966; children: James D. III, Cynthia Dee, Jennifer Jean. BA, U. Iowa, 1956, LLB, 1958. Bar: Iowa 1958, D.C. 1960, U.S. Ct. Appeals (D.C. cir.) 1961, U.S. Supreme Ct. 1962. Trial atty. FPC, Washington, 1958-60; assoc. Law Offices Charles E. McGee, Washington, 1960-65, Ross, Marsh & Foster, Washington, 1965-68, ptnr., 1968—. Mem. ABA, D.C. Bar Assn., Energy Bar Assn. (exec. com. 1979-82), Met. Club, Washington Golf and Country Club. Administrative and regulatory, Appellate, FERC practice. Home: 6105 Lee Hwy Arlington VA 22205-2110 Office: Ross Marsh & Foster 2001 L St NW Washington DC 20036-4910 E-mail: jmckinney@rossmarshfoster.com.

MCKINNEY, JANET KAY, law librarian; b. Kansas City, Mo., Feb. 15, 1959; d. Charles Durward and Helen Jean (Bost) Freeman; m. Larry Emmett McKinney, July 11, 1981. BA, Avila Coll., 1981; MA in Libr. Sci., U. Mo., 1989; MA in Religious Studies, Ctrl. Bapt. Theol. Sem., 1997. Circulation libr. Midwestern Bapt. Theol. Sem., Kansas City, 1981-84, acquisitions libr., 1984-85, reference libr., 1985-90; environ. divsn. libr. Black & Veatch, Kansas City, 1990-91; dir. collection resources U. Mo. Leon E. Bloch Law Libr., Kansas City, 1991-2000; computer svcs. libr. Shook, Hardy & Bacon, Kansas City, 2000—. Mem. ALA, Am. Assn. Law Librs. (com. on rels. with info. vendors 1994-96, editl bd. Tech. Svcs. Law Libr. 1994-96, tech. svcs. spl. interest sect. chair 1999-2000, treas pvt. law librs. spl. interest sect. 2001—, index to fgn. legal periodicals adv. com. 2001—, cataloging and intranet access to electronic resources spl. com. 2002-03, program com. 2003—), Mid-Am. Assn. Law Librs. (newsletter adv. mgr. 1993-94, treas. 1997-99, 2002-2003), Southwestern Assn. Law Librs., N.Am. Serials Interest Group, Spl. Librs. Assn. (chpt. employment com. chmn. 1990-91, chpt. treas. 1991-94, chpt. pres. 1995-96, program selection com., 2003—), Kansas City Assn. Law Librs. (v.p., pres. 2000). Office: Shook Hardy & Bacon LLP 1200 Main St Kansas City MO 64105 E-mail: jmckinney@shb.com.

MCKINNEY, LARRY J. federal judge; b. South Bend, Ind., July 4, 1944; s. Lawrence E. and Helen (Byers) McK.; m. Carole Jean Marie Lyon, Aug. 19, 1966; children: Joshua E., Andrew G. BA, MacMurray Coll., Jacksonville, Ill., 1966; JD, Ind. U., 1969. Bar: Ind. 1970, U.S. Dist. Ct. (so. dist.) Ind. 1970. Law clk. to atty. gen. State of Ind., Indpls., 1969-70, dep. atty. gen., 1970-71; ptnr. Rodgers and McKinney, Edinburgh, Ind., 1971-75, James F.T. Sargent, Greenwood, Ind., 1975-79; judge Johnson County Cir. Ct., Franklin, Ind., 1979-87, U.S. Dist. Ct. (so. dist.) Ind., Indpls., 1987—, chief judge, 2001—. Presbyterian. Avocations: reading, jogging. Office: US Dist Ct 204 US Courthouse 46 E Ohio St Indianapolis IN 46204-1903

MCKINNEY, LINDA OTANI, prosecutor; b. Manhattan, N.Y., July 29, 1959; d. Raymond Yoshiteru and Michi Otani; m. Jim McKinney, Apr. 15, 1988; children: Jimmy, Mark, Matthew. BA, Brigham Young U., 1981; JD, Georgetown U., 1987. Bar: D.C., D.C. Superior Ct., Pa., U.S. Dist. Ct. D.C., U.S. Ct. Appeals (D.C. cir.). Law clk. D.C. Superior Courthouse, Washington, 1987-90; asst. U.S. atty. U.S. Attys. Office for D.C., Washington, 1990—. Office: US Attys Office for DC 555 4th St NW Washington DC 20001-2733

MCKINNEY, RONALD W. lawyer; b. Greenville, S.C., Mar. 23, 1948; s. William R. and Doris (Chadwick) McK.; m. Kathleen Crum, Jan. 13, 1979; children: William, Kathleen. BA, Furman U., 1970; MA, U. N.C., 1973; JD, U. S.C., 1978. Bar: S.C. 1978. Atty. S.C. Consumer Advocate's Office, Columbia, 1978-81; ptnr. Duggan, Reese & McKinney, Greer, S.C., 1981-95; city atty. City of Greenville, S.C., 1995—, interim city mgr., 2000. Chair Greenville County Transportation Com., 1994-95. Mem. ABA, S.C. Bar Assn., Internat. Mcpl. Lawyers Assn., S.C. Mcpl. Attys. Assn. (pres. 1997). Methodist. Avocations: travel, reading. Office: City of Greenville PO Box 2207 Greenville SC 29602-2207 E-mail: mckinnr@greatergreenville.com.

MCKINSTRY, RONALD E. lawyer; b. Bakersfield, Calif., Aug. 11, 1926; s. Melville Jack and Lillian Agatha (Saner) McK.; m. Shirley Danner, June 19, 1948; children: Michael R., Jill I. McKinstry Epperson, Jeffrey A., Carol A. McKinstry Sundquist. BS, U. Wash., 1950, JD, 1951. Bar: Wash. 1951, U.S. Ct. Claims 1970, U.S. Ct. Appeals (D.C. cir.) 1981, U.S. Supreme Ct. 1982. Assoc. Evans, McLaren, Lane, Powell & Beeks, Seattle, 1951-55, Bogle, Bogle & Gates, Seattle, 1955-61; ptnr. Bogle & Gates, Seattle, 1962-91, chmn. litigation dept., 1970-91; sr. trial ptnr. Ellis Li & McKinstry, Seattle, 1992—. Apptd. spl. master by U.S. Dist. Ct. (we. dist.) Wash., 1976-81, apptd. settlement mediator, 1980— Editor-in-chief Washington Civil Procedure Before Trial Deskbook, 1981, Supplement to Deskbook, 1986; contbr. articles to profl. jours. Attends Christ Meml. Ch., Poulsbo, Wash. With USN, 1944-46, PTO. Recipient Svc. award Western Ctr. for Law and Religious Freedom, 1990. Fellow Am. Coll. Trial Lawyers (regent 1978-82); mem. ABA, Internat. Assn. Def. Counsel (mem. exec. com. 1974-78), CPR Panels of Disting. Legal Neutrals, AAA Club Wash. (mem. exec. com. 1983-98). Avocations: golf, travel. Federal civil litigation, General civil litigation, Environmental. Office: Ellis Li & McKinstry Two Union Square 601 Union St Ste 4900 Seattle WA 98101-3906 E-mail: rmckinstry@elmlaw.com.

MCKINZIE, CARL WAYNE, lawyer; b. Lubbock, Tex., Dec. 3, 1939; s. J. Clyde and Flora (Cates) McK.; m. Rowena Ann Williams; children: Wayne, Clinton, Morgan (dec.). BBA, Tex. Tech U., 1962, MBA, 1963; JD, So. Meth. U., 1966. From assoc. to ptnr. Nossaman, Guthner, Knox & Elliot, L.A., 1966-80; prin. Riordan & McKinzie, L.A., 1980—. Bd. dirs., vice chair, exec. com., Saint John's Health Ctr., Santa Monica, Calif., 2001—, vice chmn., 2002—. Contbr. articles to law jours. Trustee Jaquish Found., Raymond Marshall Found., 1993-; bd. visitors Sch. Law So. Meth. U., Dallas, 1979-82, 90—, bd. dirs., 1970-73, 84-89, chmn. exec. com., 1996-98; bd. visitors Ariz State U. Coll. Law, 1990-98; bd. dirs. Riordan Found., 1992—; bd. dirs. Rx for Reading, 1992—; v.p., bd. dirs. Libr. Found. L.A., 2002—, Pub. Counsel, 1996-99, Calif. Cmty. Found., 1994-98; bd. advisors Coll Law, U. Wyo., 1987-91, 2001—. Recipient disting. alumni award So. Meth. U., Dallas, 1994. Mem. ABA (chmn. current devel. subcom., com. tax problems 1978-80), Nat. Assn. Real Estate Investment Trusts (bd. govs. 1986-89), Calif. Bar Assn., Los Angeles County Bar Assn., Jonathan Club, City Club on Bunker Hill, L.A. Country Club. Republican. Corporate, general, Mergers and acquisitions, Securities. Home: 527 21st Pl Santa Monica CA 90402-3047 Office: Riordan & McKinzie 29th Fl 300 S Grand Ave Ste 29 Los Angeles CA 90071-3110

MCKITTRICK, NEIL VINCENT, lawyer; b. Framingham, Mass., June 21, 1961; s. Harold Vincent and Dorothy Frances (Alexander) McK.; m. Karen Beth Hoffman, May 30, 1987; children: Kerry Alexandra, Brian Hoffman, Robert Hoffman. AB magna cum laude, Brown U., 1983; JD, U. Va., 1987. Bar: Mass. 1988, U.S. Dist. Ct. Mass. 1989, U.S. Ct. Appeals (1st cir.) 1989, U.S. Supreme Ct. 1999. Law clk. to Hon. Frank M. Johnson Jr. U.S. Ct. Appeals (11th cir.), Montgomery, Ala., 1987-88; assoc. Hill & Barlow, Boston, 1988-95, mem., 1995—2002; pub. defender Suffolk County (Mass.) Bar Advocate, 1990-91; asst. dir. White House sec. rev. U.S. Dept. Treasury, 1994-95; case conf./mediator Boston Mcpl. Ct. Alternative Dispute Resolution Program, 1997—; dir. Goulston & Storrs, Boston, 2002—. Editor U. Va. Law Rev., 1985-87. Bd. dirs. Lawyers' Com. for Civil Rights Under Law, 1998—, Bd. trustees, 2001—. Recipient Disting. Citizens award, Mass. Assn. for Retarded Citizens, 1996, Charles River Gala Benefit award, 2001; fellow Dillard fellow, U. Va., 1985—86. Mem.: FBA (Mass. chpt.exec. com. 1997—, treas. 2000—01, sec. 2001—02, v.p. 2002—03), ABA (Pro Bono Publico award 2001), Boston Bar Assn., Mass. Bar Assn. (coun. mem. Access to Justice Sect. Coun. 2001—, Access to Justice Pro Bono Publico award 2001), Order of the Coif, Theta Delta Chi, Phi Beta Kappa. General civil litigation, Criminal, Personal injury (including property damage). Office: Goulston & Storrs 400 Atlantic Ave Boston MA 02110 E-mail: nmckittrick@goulsonstorrs.com.

MCKITTRICK, WILLIAM WOOD, lawyer; b. Mt. Carmel, Ill., July 11, 1915; s. Lafe E. and Mary Lynn (Wood) McK.; m. Carolyn Lenne Davis, Dec. 19, 1942; children: Lynn McKittrick Pond, Bruce W. AB, DePauw U., 1936; JD, Northwestern U., 1939. Bar: Ill. Assoc. Pope & Ballard, Chgo., 1939-48, ptnr., 1948-52; atty. Office Gen. Counsel, Panama C.Z., 1942; ptnr. Vedder, Price, Kaufman & Kammholz, Chgo., 1952-95; lectr. on labor law Northwestern U. Sch. Law, Chgo., 1961-62. Case note editor, mem. editorial bd. Ill. Law Rev., 1938-39. Life trustee Orchestral Assn. of Chgo. Symphony Orch., 1980—, Chgo. Symphony Musicians Pension Trust, 1987-98; bd. dirs. Am. Symphony Orch. League, 1986-93, mem. exec. com., 1988-91; trustee Newberry Libr., Chgo., 1984-98, life trustee, 1998—, exec. com., 1989-98; vice chmn. exec. bd. Libr. Coun., Northwestern U., 1984-96; chmn. Friends of Ryerson & Burnham Librs., Art Inst. Chgo., 1988-90, mem. com. on librs., 1982—. Lt. USNR, 1943-45, PTO. Recipient Svc. award Northwestern U., 1968. Mem. ABA, Ill. Bar Assn., Chgo. Bar Assn. (lectr. various programs 1940-70, bd. mgrs. 1961-63), Lawyers Club of Chgo., Univ. Club (Chgo.), Michigan Shores Club, Skokie Country Club, Caxton Club of Chgo. (v.p. 1982-83, pres. 1983-85). Labor (including EEOC, Fair Labor Standards Act, labor-management relations, NLRB, OSHA), Pension, profit-sharing, and employee benefits, Corporate taxation. Home: 232 Essex Rd Kenilworth IL 60043-1122

MCKUSICK, VINCENT LEE, former state supreme court chief justice, lawyer, arbitrator, mediator; b. Parkman, Maine, Oct. 21, 1921; s. Carroll Lee and Ethel (Buzzell) McK.; m. Nancy Elizabeth Green, June 23, 1951; children: Barbara Jane McKusick Liscord, James Emory, Katherine McKusick Ralston, Anne Elizabeth. AB, Bates Coll., 1943; SB, SM, MIT, 1947; LLB, Harvard U., 1950; LLD, Colby Coll., 1976, Nasson Coll., 1978, Bates Coll., 1979, Bowdoin Coll., 1979, Suffolk U., 1983; LHD, U. So. Maine, 1978, Thomas Coll., 1981. Bar: Maine 1952. Law clk. to Chief Judge Learned Hand, 1950-51; to Justice Felix Frankfurter, 1951-52; partner Pierce, Atwood, Scribner, Allen & McKusick and predecessors, Portland, Maine, 1953-77; chief justice Maine Supreme Jud. Ct., 1977-92; of counsel to Pierce Atwood (formerly Pierce, Atwood, Scribner, Allen, Smith, & Lancaster), Portland, Maine, 1992—. Mem. adv. com. rules civil procedure Maine Supreme Jud. Ct., 1957-59, chmn., 1966-75, commr. uniform state laws, 1968-76, sec. nat. conf., 1975-77; mem. Conf. Chief Justices, 1977-92, bd. dirs., 1980-82, 91-92, pres.-elect, 1989-90, pres., 1990-91. standing com. past pres., 1992—; dir. Nat. Ctr. for State Ctrs., 1988-89, chmn.-elect, 1989-90, chmn., 1990-91; spl. master U.S. Supreme Ct. Conn. v. N.H., 1992-93, La. v. Miss., 1994-96, Kans. v. Nebr., 1999—; master Mass. S.J.C. Liquidation Am. Mutual Liability Ins. Co., 1995-96; leader Am. Judges Del. to China, 1983, USSR, 1988, U.S. State Dept. Rule of Law Del. to Republic of Ga., 1992; mem. permanent com. Oliver Wendell Holmes Devise, 1993-2001. Author: Patent Policy of Educational Institutions, 1947, (with Richard H. Field) Maine Civil Practice, 1959, supplements, 1962, 67, (with Richard H. Field and L. Kinvin Wroth) 2d edit., 1970, supplements, 1972, 74, 77; also articles in legal publs. Trustee emeritus Bates Coll.; mem. adv. com. on pvt. internat. law U.S. State Dept., 1980-85, Fed.-State Jurisdiction com., Jud. Conf. of U.S., 1987-89. With AUS, 1943-46. Recipient The Maine prize U. Maine Sys., 1993, Benjamin E. Mays award Bates Coll., 1994, Big M award Maine State Soc. Washington, 1995, Paul C. Reardon award Nat. Ctr. for State Ctrs., 1999. Fellow Am. Bar Found. (bd. dirs. 1977-87), Am. Philos. Soc. (coun. 1990-96, 97-02, v.p. 2002—); mem. ABA (chmn. fed. rules com. 1966-71, bd. editors jour. 1971-80, chmn. 1976-77, mem. study group to China 1978, ho. dels. 1983-87, coun. sr. lawyers divsn. 1997-01), Maine Bar Assn., Cumberland County Bar Assn., Am. Arbitration Assn. (bd. dirs. 1994—), Am. Judicature Soc. (dir. 1976-78, 92-98), Am. Law Inst. (coun. 1968—), Maine Jud. Coun. (chmn. 1977-92), Inst. Jud. Adminstrn., Supreme Ct. Hist. Soc. (trustee 1994—), Rotary Club (hon., past pres. Portland club), Phi Beta Kappa, Sigma Xi, Tau Beta Pi. Republican. Unitarian Universalist. Home: 1152 Shore Rd Cape Elizabeth ME 04107-2115 Office: 1 Monument Sq Portland ME 04101-1110 E-mail: judgemac@aol.com., vmckusick@pierceatwood.com.

MCLAIN, DENNIS O. lawyer; b. Detroit, Aug. 11, 1945; s. Francis William McLain and Hazel Joyce (Owen) Hortop. BA, U. Mich., 1971; JD, Detroit Coll. Law, 1975. Bar: Mich. 1975. Assoc. Collins & McCormick, Ypsilanti, Mich., 1972—77; gen. ptnr. McLain & Winters, Ypsilanti, Mich., 1977—. Mem.: Ypsilanti C. of C., Ypsilanti Bar Assn., Wastenau County Bar Assn., Mich. Bar Assn., Fed. Bar Assn. Democrat. Roman Catholic. General practice, Personal injury (including property damage), Land use and zoning (including planning). Office: McLain & Winters 61 N Huron St Ypsilanti MI 48197-2675

MCLAIN, LYNN, law educator; b. Chestertown, Md., May 6, 1949; d. Joseph Howard McLain and Margaret Ann Hollingsworth; m. Bryson Leitch Cook, May 21, 1977 (div. Apr. 1993); 1 child, Joseph Bryson Cook. BA, U. Pa., Phila., 1971; JD, Duke U., 1974. Bar: Md. 1974, U.S. Supreme Ct. 1990. Assoc. Piper & Marbury, Balt., 1974—76; Bradway fellow Duke U. Law Sch., Durham, NC, 1976—77; asst. prof. law U. Balt. Law Sch., 1977—80, assoc. prof. law, 1980—83, prof. law, 1983—. Spl. reporter on codification of rules of evidence Rules Com., Ct. Appeals of Md., Crownsville, 1989—94. Author: Maryland Evidence: State and Federal, 3 vols., 2d edit., 2001, Maryland Rules of Evidence, 2d edit., 2002. Bd. dirs. Prevent Child Abuse Md., Annapolis, 2002—. Office: U Balt Law Sch 1420 N Charles St Baltimore MD 21201

MCLAIN, WILLIAM ALLEN, lawyer; b. Chgo., Oct. 19, 1942; s. William Rex and Wilma L. (Raschka) McL.; divorced; children: William A., David M., Heather A.; m. Kristine R. Zierk. BS, So. Ill. U., 1966; JD, Loyola U., Chgo., 1971. Bar: Ill. 1971, U.S. Dist. Ct. (no. dist) Ill. 1971, U.S. Ct. Appeals (7th cir.) 1971, Colo. 1975, U.S. Dist. Ct. Colo. 1975, U.S. Ct. Appeals (10th cir.) 1975. Law clk. U.S. Dist. Ct. (no. dist.) Ill., Chgo., 1971-72; assoc. Sidley & Austin, Chgo., 1972-75; ptnr. Welborn, Dufford, Brown & Tooley, Denver, 1975-86; pres. William. A. McLain PC, 1986—; ptnr. McLain & Singer, Denver, 1990—. Mem. Dist. 10 Legis. Vacancy Commn., Denver, 1984-86. Served with U.S. Army, 1966-68. Recipient Leadership and Scholastic Achievement award Loyola U. Alumni Assn., 1971. Mem. Colo. Bar Assn. (lobbyist 1983-85), Denver Bar Assn., Colo. Assn. Commerce and Industry (legis. policy coun. 1983-88), Colo. Mining Assn. (state and local affairs com. 1978-88), Inst. Property Taxation, Roundup Riders of the Rockies Club, Masons, Shriners, Scottish Rite, York Rite. Republican. Legislative, State and local taxation. Home and Office: 3962 S Olive St Denver CO 80237-2038

MCLANE, FREDERICK BERG, lawyer; b. Long Beach, Calif., July 24, 1941; s. Adrian B. and Arlie K. (Burrell) McL.; m. Lois C. Roberts, Jan. 28, 1967; children: Willard, Anita. BA, Stanford U., 1963; LLB, Yale U., 1966. Bar: Calif. 1967, U.S. Dist. Ct. (cen. dist.) Calif. 1967. Assoc. prof. law U. Miss., Oxford, 1966-68; assoc. O'Melveny & Myers LLP, L.A., 1968-74, ptnr., 1975—. Com. of counsel HUD, Los Angeles, 1979-84; lectr. in field. Pres., bd. dirs. Legal Aid Found., L.A., 1974-83; deacon Congl. Ch., Sherman Oaks, Calif., 1979-83; vice-chair L.A. Music Ctr., Unified Fund, 1992-94; bd. dirs. Calif. Sci. Ctr. Found., 1991-2000. Mem. ABA (banking com., fed. regulation of securities com.), Calif. Bar Assn. (fin. insts. com., uniform comml. codes), L.A. Bar Assn., Order of Coif, Calif. Club (L.A.), L.A. Country Club (bd. dirs.), Lakeside Golf Club (L.A.). Democrat. Avocations: golf, walking, reading. Corporate, general, Mergers and acquisitions, Securities. Office: O'Melveny & Myers 400 S Hope St Los Angeles CA 90071-2899 E-mail: fmclane@omm.com.

MCLAREN, RICHARD WELLINGTON, JR., lawyer; b. Cin., May 15, 1945; s. Richard Wellington and Edith (Gillett) McL.; m. Ann Lynn Zachrich, Sept. 4, 1971; children: Christine, Richard, Charles. BA, Yale U., 1967; JD, Northwestern U., 1973. Bar: Ohio 1973, Ill. 1997, U.S. Dist. Ct. (no. dist.) Ohio 1973, U.S. Dist. Ct. (no. dist.) Ill. 1997, U.S. Ct. Appeals (6th cir.) 1978, U.S. Ct. Appeals (7th cir.) 1997, U.S. Ct. Appeals (fed. cir.) 1997, U.S. Supreme Ct. 1981. Assoc. Squire, Sanders & Dempsey, Cleve., 1973-82, ptnr., 1983-87; prin., counsel Ernst & Whinney, Cleve., 1988-89; assoc. gen. counsel Ernst & Young, Cleve., 1989-93; prin. counsel Centerior Energy Corp., Cleve., 1994-96; prin. Welsh & Katz, Ltd., Chgo., 1997—. 1st lt. U.S. Army, 1967-70. Mem. ABA (litigation, intellectual property and corp. law), FBA, Am. Judicature Soc., Ohio Bar Assn., Ill. Bar Assn. Federal civil litigation, General civil litigation, Corporate, general. Home: 638 S Monroe St Hinsdale IL 60521-3926 Office: 120 S Riverside Plz Fl 22D Chicago IL 60606-3913 E-mail: rwmclaren@welshkatz.com.

MCLAUGHLIN, JAMES PATRICK, lawyer, educator; b. Jamesport, Mo., June 2, 1953; s. Robert Lee and Doris Ruth (Cox) McL.; m. Lana Gale Linville, June 10, 1978; children: Jamie Megan, Erin Brianne. BSBA, Cen. Mo. State U., 1975; JD, U. Mo., Kansas City, 1978. Bar: Mo., U.S. Dist. Ct. Mo. Assoc. prof. N.W. Mo. State U., Maryville, 1978—, chmn. dept. acctg., econs. and fin., 1988—; pvt. practice Maryville, 1979—. Pros. atty. City of Maryville, 1979—; asst. pros. atty. County of Nodaway, Maryville, 1980—; judge Mcpl. Ct., City of Rock Port and Tarkio, Mo., 1985—; atty. City of Burlington Junction, Mo., 1988, Bolckow, Barnard and Ravenwood, Mo., Clyde and Skidmore, 1998, Rosendale, Clearmont, Arkoe. Avocation: golf. Environmental, General practice, Personal injury (including property damage). Office: 1250 Chick Ave Maryville MO 64468-2741 also: NW Mo State U 2120 Colden Hall Maryville MO 64468

MCLAUGHLIN, JEFFREY REX, lawyer; b. Decatur, Ala., May 2, 1960; s. Francis Joseph and Pat Fitzpatrick McLaughlin; m. Stacy Deason, June 3, 1995; children: John Francis Lynne, William Fitzpatrick. BA, Birmingham-So. Coll., 1982; postgrad., Trinity Coll., Dublin, Ireland, 1985-86; JD, Harvard U., 1990. Bar: Ala. 1991, U.S. Dist. Ct. (no. dist.) Ala. 1991, U.S. Ct. Appeals (11th cir.) 1998. History and civics tchr. John Carroll H.S., Birmingham, Ala., 1982-87; law clk. to presiding judge Seybourn Lynne U.S. Dist. Ct. (no. dist.) Ala., 1990-91, U.S. Ct. Appeals (11th cir.), 1998; assoc. Maynard Cooper & Gale, P.C., Birmingham, 1991-94; ptnr. McLaughlin & Edmondson, LLC, Guntersville, Ala., 1995—. Mem. Marshall County chpg. ARC, Guntersville, 1995-97, mem. Alabama House of Reps., 2001, 2002. Rotary Found. scholar, 1985-86. Mem. Marshall County Bar Assn. (pres. 1998-99), Civitan, Phi Beta Kappa. Roman Catholic. Avocations: home restoration, woodworking, bicycling, hiking, fishing. General civil litigation, Corporate, general, Probate (including wills, trusts). Office: McLaughlin & Marshall LLC 321 Blount Ave PO Box 1037 Guntersville AL 35976-7037

MCLAUGHLIN, JOHN SHERMAN, lawyer; b. Pitts., Apr. 1, 1932; s. John H. and Dorothy I. (Schrecongost) McL.; m. Suzanne Shaver, June 5, 1971; children— Dorothy, Sarah, Martha. AB, Harvard U., 1954, LLB, 1957. Bar: Pa. 1958, U.S. Supreme Ct. 1967. Assoc. Reed, Smith, Shaw & McClay, Pitts., 1957-71, ptnr., 1971—2002, of counsel, 2002—. Trustee Harmarville Rehab. Ctr., Inc., 1980-87; pres., trustee Western Pa. Sch. for the Deaf, 1985—; pres. Pa. NG Assn., 1976-78; justice of peace Borough of Edgewood, 1963-73; trustee Winchester Thurston Sch., 1987-94, emeritus trustee, 1994—; life trustee Carnegie Libr. of Pitts., Carnegie Inst., 1994—, Carnegie Mus. Art, 1997—; dir. Pitts. Symphony, 1985-95, adv. 1996-99. Lt. col. Air NG, 1957-79. Mem.: Allegheny County Bar Assn., Am. Law

Inst., Rolling Rock Club (Ligonier, Pa.), Duquesne Club. General practice, Probate (including wills, trusts). Office: Reed Smith LLP 435 6th Ave Ste 2 Pittsburgh PA 15219-1886 E-mail: jmclaughlin@reedsmith.com.

MCLAUGHLIN, JOSEPH MICHAEL, federal judge, law educator; b. Brooklyn, N.Y., Mar. 20, 1933; s. Joseph Michael and Mary Catherine (Flanagan) McLaughlin; m. Frances Elizabeth Lynch, Oct. 10, 1959; children: Joseph, Mary Jo, Matthew, Andrew. AB, Fordham Coll., 1954, LL.B., 1959; LL.M., NYU, 1964; LL.D., Mercy Coll., White Plains, N.Y., 1981; LLD, Fordham U., 1998. Bar: N.Y. 1959. Assoc. Cahill, Gordon, N.Y.C., 1959—61; prof. law Fordham U., N.Y.C., 1961—71, dean Sch. of Law, 1971—81, adj. prof., 1981—; judge U.S. Dist. Ct. Eastern Dist. N.Y., Bklyn., 1981—90; judge U.S. Ct. Appeals (2nd Cir.), N.Y.C., 1990—98; sr. judge, 1998—. Adj. prof. St. John's Law Sch., N.Y.C., 1982—97; chmn. N.Y. Law Revision Commn., Albany, 1975—82. Author (with Peterfreund): New York Practice, 1964; author: Evidence, 1979, also articles. Capt. Corps of Engineers U.S. Army, 1955—57, Korea. Mem.: ABA, N.Y. State Bar Assn., Assn. of Bar of City of N.Y., Lotos Club. Roman Catholic. Office: US Courthouse US Ct Appeals 40 Foley Sq Rm 2402 New York NY 10007-1502

MCLAUGHLIN, JOSEPH THOMAS, lawyer; b. Boston, Mar. 30, 1944; s. James Francis and Madeline Louise (Hickman) McL.; m. Christine E. Mullen, Sept. 2, 1967; children: Amy Melissa, Caitlin Christine, Ian Michael. BA magna cum laude, Boston Coll., 1965; JD, Cornell U., 1968. Bar: Mass. 1969, N.Y. State 1968, U.S. Supreme Ct. 1974. Research asst. Brit. Council of Archaeology, Winchester, Eng., 1964, site supr., 1966; legis. asst. Rep. Thomas P. O'Neill, Washington, 1967; research asst. Cornell U., 1967-68; law clk. to chief justice Mass. Superior Ct., 1968-69; assoc. Shearman & Sterling, N.Y.C., 1969-76, ptnr., 1976-97; exec. v.p., legal and regulatory affaais Credit Suisse First Boston, 1997—2001; chmn. Credit Suisse First Boston Found. Trust, 2001—02; ptnr., chmn. Heller, Ehrman, White & McCauliffe, N.Y.C., 2002—. Adj. prof. Fordham Law Sch., 1981-88; vis. prof. Cornell Law Sch., 1995-96. Author: Federal Class Action Digests, 1974, 1976; contbr. articles to profl. jours. Exec. dir. Brooklyn Heights Draft Counseling Svc., 1970-74, Presbyn. Task Force for Justice Counseling Svc., 1973-75; v.p., bd. dirs. Brooklyn Heights Assn., 1973-77; bd. dirs. Willoughby Settlement House, Inc., Ingersoll-Willoughby Cmty. Ctr., Inc., 1970-75, United Neighborhood Houses, 1976-78, Good Shepherd Svcs., Resources for Children with Spl. Needs, Inc., Internat. House, Bklyn. Mus. Art. Mem. ABA, Assn. of Bar of City of N.Y. (mem. com. on profl. discord 1986—, chmn. com. to promote diversity in the legal profession), N.Y. State Bar Assn. (chmn. com. on marijuana and drug abuse 1972-75), Am. Law Inst., Am. Arbitration Assn., N.Y. Lawyers for Pub. Interest (chmn. bd. dirs.) ABAC (com. on promoting settlements), Heights Casino Club. Banking, Federal civil litigation, Private international. Home: 174 State St Brooklyn NY 11201 Office: 120 W 45th St New York NY 10036 E-mail: jmclaughlin@hewm.com.

MCLAUGHLIN, MICHAEL JOHN, retired insurance company executive; b. Cambridge, Mass., Feb. 14, 1944; s. Michael John and Evelyn Katherine (Quinn) McL. AB, Boston Coll., 1965; JD, N.Y. U., 1968. Bar: N.Y., Mass. With N.Y. Life Ins. Co., 1968—, sr. v.p. info. systems and services dept., 1982-88, sr. v.p., 1988-91, sr. v.p., dep. gen. counsel, 1991-95, sr. v.p., gen. counsel, 1995-2000. Mem. ABA, N.Y. State Bar Assn., Assn. Bar City N.Y. E-mail: mmclau2260@aol.com.

MCLAUGHLIN, PATRICK MICHAEL, lawyer; b. Monahans, Tex., July 23, 1946; s. Patrick John and Ann (Donnelly) M.; m. Christine Manos, Aug. 21, 1970; children— Brian Patrick, Christopher Michael, Conor Andrew B.Gen. Studies, Ohio U., 1972; JD, Case Western Res. U., 1976. Bar: Ohio 1976, U.S. Dist. Ct. (no. dist.) Ohio 1978, U.S. Ct. Appeals (6th cir.) 1979, U.S. Supreme Ct. 1980; U.S. Dist. Ct. (so. dist.) Ohio 1989, U.S. Ct. Appeals (5th cir.). Dir. vets. edn. project. Am. Assn. Community and Jr. Colls., Washington, 1972-73; law clk. Common Pleas Ct., Cleve., 1976-77; law clk. to judge 8th Jud. Dist. Ct. of Appeals, Cleve., 1977-78; asst. U.S. atty. No. Dist. Ohio, Cleve., 1978-82, chief civil div., 1982-84, U.S. atty., 1984-88; ptnr. Janik & McLaughlin, Cleve., 1988-89, Mansour, Gavin, Gerlack & Manos Co., L.P.A., Cleve., 1989-97; apptd ind. spl. prosecutor Ohio Attorneys General, 1993-96; mng. ptnr. McLaughlin & McCaffrey, LLP, Cleve., 1997—. Cons. Nat. League of Cities, U.S. Conf. Mayors, 1971-72; co-creator Opportunity Fair for Veterans Concept, 1971 Editor-in-chief Case Western Res. Jour. Internat. Law, 1975-76 Chmn. North Ohio Drug Abuse Task Force, 1986-88; chmn. Law Enforcement Coordinating Commn., North Ohio, 1985-88; chmn. civil issues subcom. Atty. Gen.'s Adv. Com., 1986-88; exec. v.p. Greater Cleve. Vets. Meml., Inc., 1993, pres., 1994—. Decorated Silver Star, Bronze Star, Purple Heart, Army Commendation medal, Vietnamese Cross of Gallantry with Silver and Bronze Stars Mem. ABA, FBA, Ohio Bar Assn., Cleve. Bar Assn., Nat. Assn. Former U.S. Attys., Soc. 1st Divsn., 18th Inf. Regiment Assn., Order of Ahepa, Vietnam Vets. Am., Nat. Vietnam Vets. Network (Disting. Vietnam Vet. award 1985), Nat. Assn. Concerned Vets. (nat. v.p. external affairs 1971-72, exec. dir. 1972-73), Cuyahoga County Vets. (award 1985), Nat. Soc. SAR (law enforcement commendation medal 1989). Republican. Roman Catholic. General civil litigation, Product liability, Professional liability. Office: McLaughlin & McCaffrey LLP Eaton Ctr 1111 Superior Ave Ste 1350 Cleveland OH 44114-2500

MCLAUGHLIN, PHILIP T. lawyer, former state attorney general; b. Nashua, N.H., Jan. 23, 1945; s. Philip J. and Pauline (Reilly) McLaughlin; m. Janice Livingston, 1968; children: Matthew, Timothy, Emily, Katherine, Philip. AB in History, Holy Cross coll., 1967; MPA, U. R.I., 1971; JD, Boston Coll., 1974. Bar: N.H. 1974. Atty. Belknap County, NH, 1979—81; ptnr. McLaughlin, Hemeon & Lahey, P.A., Laconia, NH, 1981—97; atty. gen. State of N.H., 1997—2002; pvt. practice law, 2002—. Past pres. Lakes Region Mental Health Ctr., Laconia; mem. Laconia City Coun., 1976—80, Laconia Sch. Bd., 1985—94, also chair; mem. prof. conduct com. N.H. Supreme Ct., 1983—92, 1994—97; del. N.H. Constl. Conv., 1984. Lt. USN, 1969—71. Democrat. Office: Atty Gen Office 33 Capitol St Concord NH 03301-6397

MCLEAN, CHRISTOPHER ANTHONY, lawyer, former government official; b. Chgo., Mar. 21, 1958; s. Earl James and Joan A. (Wolski) McL.; m. Hae Kyung Oh. BSBA, Creighton U., 1980, JD, 1982; LLM, Georgetown U., 1985. Bar: Nebr. 1982, U.S. Dist. Ct. Nebr. 1982, D.C. 1983, U.S. Ct. Appeals (D.C. cir.) 1985, U.S. Supreme Ct. 1990. Sales clk. J.L. Brandeis Co., Omaha, 1975-82; legal counsel, legis. asst. Senator J.J. Exxon, Washington, 1982—96; legis. counsel Senator Bob Kerrey, Washington, 1997; dep. adminstr. Rural Utilities Svc., Washington, 1989—2000, adminstr., 2000; pvt. practice Washington, 2001—; counsel ComCare Alliance, 2001—; v.p. Nat. Strategies, Inc., Wash., DC, 2001; prin. e-Copernicus, Wash., DC, 2003. Vol. Dem. campaigns, Nebr., 1973—. Mem. ABA, Nebr. Bar Assn., D.C. Bar Assn., Alpha Sigma Nu. Roman Catholic. Avocations: politics, photography, travel. Home: 4701 Davenport St NW Washington DC 20016-4405 also: 1620 S 138th St Omaha NE 68144-1135 Office: Ste 800 101 Constitution Ave Washington DC 20001

MCLEAN, DENNIS EDGAR, lawyer; b. Portland, Oreg., July 11, 1954; s. Dennis A. and Wauneta M. (Jones) McLean; m. Bonnie Berk, Oct. 10, 1981. BA, U. Calif., Berkeley, 1976; JD, U. Calif., San Francisco, 1980. Bar: Wash. 1980, U.S. Dist. Ct. (we. dist.) Wash. 1980. Ptnr. Davis Wright Tremaine, LLP, Seattle, 1980—. Trustee, vice chmn. western Wash. chpt. Multiple Sclerosis Soc., Seattle, 1987—95; dir., sec. Seattle Habitat for Humanity, 1996—2001; trustee Bertschi Sch., 1999—2001. Mem.: ABA, Seattle-King County Bar Assn., Wash. State Bar Assn. Commercial, contracts (including sales of goods; commercial financing), Landlord-tenant, Property, real (including real estate development, water). Office: Davis Wright Tremaine LLP 2600 Century Sq 1501 4th Ave Ste 2600 Seattle WA 98101-1688 E-mail: dennismclean@dwt.com.

MCLEAN, R. BRUCE, lawyer; b. N.Y.C., Nov. 15, 1946; BS with honors, Ind. U., 1968, JD cum laude, 1971. Bar: Ind. 1971, DC 1974. Atty. appellate ct. br. Nat. Labor Rels. Bd., 1971—73; chmn. Akin, Gump, Strauss, Hauer & Feld L.L.P., Washington. Bd. visitors Ind. U. Sch. Law, 1989—, vice chair, 1998—; bd. visitors Georgetown Law Ctr., 2003—. Mem.: ABA, DC Bar, Fed. Bar Assn., Order of Coif, Phi Alpha Delta. Federal civil litigation. Office: Akin Gump Strauss Hauer & Feld LLP 1333 New Hampshire Ave NW Washington DC 20036-1564 E-mail: bmclean@akingump.com.

MCLEAN, ROBERT ALEXANDER, lawyer; b. Memphis, Oct. 24, 1943; s. Albert A and Harriet Spencer (Pond) McLean; m. Sydney Ross, July 16, 1977; children: Robert Alexander, Ross Andrew. BA with honors, Rhodes Coll., 1965; MA, Princeton U., 1968, PhD, 1974; JD, U. Memphis, 1978. Bar: Tenn 1979, US Dist Ct (we dist) Tenn 1979, US Dist Ct (ea dist) Wis 1985, US Ct Appeals (5th cir) 1986, US Dist Ct (ea and we dists) Ark 1990, US Ct Appeals (8th cir) 1990, US Ct Appeals (10th cir) 1991, US Ct Appeals (6th cir) 1998, US Supreme Ct 1998. Asst. prof. Russian lit. U. Calif., Santa Cruz, 1971-76; staff atty. FCA, Washington, 1979-81; assoc. Wildman, Harrold, Allen, Dixon & McDonnell, Memphis, 1981-88, ptnr., 1988-89; ptnr. McDonnell Boyd, Memphis, 1989-94; mem. McDonnell Dyer, PLC, Memphis, 1994-95; spl. counsel Wolff Ardis, P.C., Memphis, 1995-96, shareholder, 1997; mem. Farris Mathews Branan Bobango & Hellen, PLC, 1997—; asst. city atty. Germantown, Tenn., 1981—. Adj asst prof Russian lang Rhodes Col, Memphis, 1982—86. Translator: (book) Mozart and Salieri, 1973; mem: journal Univ Memphis Law Rev, 1977—78. Mem session Germantown Presbyn. Ch, Tenn., 1988—, chmn fin comm., 1989—94. Fellow Charlotte Elizabeth Procter, Princeton Univ, 1968, Fulbright, USSR, 1969, Regents, Univ Calif, Santa Cruz, 1975. Mem.: ABA, Memphis Bar Assoc., Tenn Bar Assoc. Republican. Avocations: golf, quail hunting. General civil litigation, Environmental, Private international. Home: 8820 Somerset Ln Germantown TN 38138-7375 Office: Farris Matthews et al Ste 2000 One Commerce Sq Memphis TN 38103 E-mail: envtlatty@aol.com.

MCLEAN, STEPHEN M. lawyer; b. Minot, N.D., May 19, 1948; s. Robert M. and Louise M. McLean; m. Susan J. Sheldon, May 29, 1971; 3 children. BA, N.D. State U., 1970; JD, U. N.D., 1973. Bar: N.D. Pvt. practice law, Oakes, N.D., 1974—; states atty. Dickey County, N.D., 1998—. City atty. City of Oakes, 1974—; Dickey County State's atty., 1998-2003, Oakes-Ellendale, 1998-2002; indigent def. atty. barnes, Dickey and LaMoure Counties, N.C., 1989-98. Adv. bd. Oakes Good Samaritan Ctr., 1976-94; pres. ch. coun. Grace Luth. Ch., 1997-98. Capt. USAF, 1973. Mem. S.E. N.D. Bar Assn. (sec.-treas. 1998—, pres. elect, pres.), N.D. Mcpl. Attys. Assn. (pres. bd. dirs. 1995-97), N.D. State Bar Assn. (bd. govs.), Oakes C. of C. (sec.-treas. 1974-86), Lions (pres. 1992), Oakes Country Club (pres. 1975). Republican. Office: 606 Main Ave Oakes ND 58474-1639

MCLEES, JOHN ALAN, lawyer; b. Mpls., Jan. 19, 1948; s. Alan L. and Marian G. (Melby) McL.; m. Bozena Nowicka, June 25, 1993; children: Alexandra, Thomas. BA, U. Chgo., 1970, MBA, 1973, JD, 1974; MS in Econs., London Sch. Econs., 1971. Bar: D.C. 1974, Ill. 1975. Assoc. Keck Mahin & Cate, Chgo., 1975-79; atty. advisor office of sec. U.S. Dept. Energy, Washington, 1979-81; mng. atty. Sidley & Austin, Muscat, Oman, 1981-83, assoc. Chgo., 1983-88, Morgan Lewis & Bockius, Washington, 1988-91; dir. Latin Am. tax svc. Coopers & Lybrand, Chgo., 1991-97; ptnr. Baker & McKenzie, Chgo., 1997—. Organizer, chmn. confs. on Mex. and Latin Am. tax laws, 1992—. Editor (loose leaf treatise) CCH Latin Am. Tax Guide, 2000; contbr. articles to profl. jours. Adv. bd. Com. for Pub. Autonomous Schs., Washington, 1989—; chmn. of bd. dirs. Mid Am. Chpt., U.S. Mex. C. of C., 1993-97. Named Leading Tax Advisor, Euromoney Guide to Leading U.S. Tax Lawyers, 1997, Euromoney Guide to the World's Leading Tax Advisors, 1999, Leading Advisor on Latin Am. Tax, Internat. Tax. Review, 1996-2003. Mem. ACLU, ABA, Internat. Fiscal Assn. Episcopalian. Private international, Mergers and acquisitions, Corporate taxation. Home: 1434 S Plymouth Ct Chicago IL 60605-2729 Office: Baker & McKenzie 130 E Randolph Dr Ste 3700 Chicago IL 60601-6342 E-mail: john.a.mclees@bakernet.com.

MCLEMORE, GILBERT CARMICHAEL, JR., lawyer; b. Savannah, Ga., Dec. 15, 1942; s. Gilbert Carmichael and Jeannie Elizabeth (Gulley) McL.; m. Susan Ellen Hair, Nov. 21, 1965; children: Kimberly Bates, Gilbert Carmichael, Erin Frances. AB in Polit. Sci., U. N.C., 1965; JD, U. Ga., 1970. Bar: Ga. 1970, U.S. Dist. Ct. (so. dist.) Ga. 1970. Assoc. Fendig, Dickey, Fendig & Whelchel, Brunswick, Ga., 1970-74, ptnr., 1974-77, Fendig, McLemore, Taylor, Whitworth & Durham, P.C., Brunswick, 1977—2001; pvt. practice Brunswick, 2001—. Bd. dirs. Glyn County chpt. ARC; bd. dirs. Humane Soc. South Coastal Ga. Served to lt. USNR, 1965-67. Mem. Glynn County Bar Assn. (treas. 1072-73, v.p. 1973-74, pres. 1974-75), Brunswick-Golden Isles Estate Planning Coun. (pres. 1980-81), Brunswick-Golden Isles C. of C. (chmn. com. 1975), Rotary. Democrat. Methodist. Banking, Probate (including wills, trusts), Property, real (including real estate development, water). Home: 545 Old Plantation Rd Jekyll Island GA 31527-0718 Office: PO Box 1985 Brunswick GA 31521-1985 E-mail: gmclemore@mclemorelaw.com., gcmjr@bellsouth.net.

MCLEMORE, JAMES LATINUS, III, lawyer; b. Norfolk, Va., Feb. 4, 1945; s. James L. Jr. and Jane Warren (Coulbourn) McL.; m. Marjorie Jane Rebentisch, Sept. 30, 1972; children: James L. IV, Thomas B., Sarah Elizabeth. BA in Polit. Sci., Randolph-Macon Coll., 1967; JD, Coll. William and Mary, 1970. Chief dep. clk. Nansemond County Cir. Ct., Va., 1973; clk. cir. ct. City of Suffolk, Va., 1974; sole practitioner Suffolk. Author: A History of the McLemore Family of Virginia and The Carolinas, 1988, B.F. McLemore, His Ancestors and Descendants, 1991. Bd. dirs. various civic orgns., Suffolk, active Boy Scouts Am., 1971-2001; active Main St. Meth. Ch., Suffolk. Mem. Suffolk Bar Assn. (past pres.), various other bar assns., Suffolk Rotary Club (pres. 1996-97). Avocations: model railroading, genealogy, history. Family and matrimonial, Probate (including wills, trusts), Property, real (including real estate development, water). Office: PO Box 1085 129 N Saratoga St Suffolk VA 23434-5230

MCLENDON, MELBURNE DEKALB, lawyer, arbitrator; b. Atlanta, Apr. 21, 1921; s. Jesse Martin and Elizabeth Lee (Sartain) McL.; m. Loyce Jacqueline Kirkland, Dec. 31, 1949; children: James Kirkland, Loyce Eloise McLendon Snyder. LLB, U. Ga., 1948. Bar: Ga. 1949, U.S. Dist. Ct. (no. dist.) Ga. 1949, U.S. Ct. Appeals (5th cir.) 1965, U.S. Supreme Ct. 1973, U.S. Dist. Ct. (mid. dist.) Ga. 1985. Law clk. Fulton County Superior Ct., Atlanta, 1949-50; ptnr. Carter Ansley Smith & McLendon, Atlanta, 1950-86; dir. Amica Mutual Ins. Co., 1976-96; cons. U.S. VA Hosp., Decatur, Ga., 1996—; pro bono. Arbitrator N.Y. Stock Exch., 1980-88, U.S. Dist. Ct. (mid. dist.) Ga., Macon, 1988—. Scout master Boy Scouts Am., Atlanta, 1959-70; active pro bono work for war vets., 1998—. Staff sgt. USAAF, 1942-45, ETO. Recipient Disting. Svc. award U. Ga., 1996, Exceptional Performance citation def. Rsch. Inst., 1985. Mem. Ga. Def. Lawyers Assn. (pres. 1984), Atlanta Bar Assn., Lawyers Club of Atlanta, Univ. Yacht Club, Buckhead Men's Garden Club (pres. 2002), Masons (32 deg.). Republican. Methodist. Avocations: gardening, woodwork, travel, fishing, spectator sports. E-mail: melburnem@aol.com.

MCLEOD, SIMON NICHOLAS, lawyer; b. Eng., Sept. 16, 1957; s. John and Nanette McLeod. LLB, Bristol (Eng.) U., 1979. Trainee Slaughter & May, London, 1980—82; sr. lawyer Sinclair Roche, London, 1982—83, McKenna & Co., London, 1985—91; ptnr. S.J. Berwin, London, 1991—. Mem.: Law Soc. Avocations: scuba diving, theater , movies, golf. Corporate, general, Government contracts and claims. Office: SJ Berwin 222 Grays Inn Rd London WC1X 8XF England

MCLOUGHLIN, JAMES PATRICK, JR., lawyer; b. Jersey City, Aug. 2, 1956; s. James Patrick McLoughlin, Sr. and Mary P. McLoughlin; m. Jill Hickey; children: Margaret Rose, Brendan Patrick. BA cum laude, Holy Cross , Worcester, Mass., 1978; JD, Duke U., 1982. Bar: N.Y. 1984, U.S. Dist. Ct. (ea., we., no. and so. dists.) N.Y. 1985, U.S. Ct. Appeals (5th cir.) 1985, N.C. 1986, U.S. Dist. Ct. (we. dist.) N.C. 1986, U.S. Ct. (ea. dist.) N.C. 1987, U.S. Dist. Ct. (mid. dist.) N.C. 1989, U.S. Tax Ct. 1989, U.S. Supreme Ct. 1993, U.S. Ct. Appeals (fed. cir.) 2001. Law clk. to hon. Eugene Gordon Sr. Judge U.S. Dist. Ct. (mid. dist.) N.C., Greensboro; assoc. Paul Weiss Rifkind & Wharton, N.Y.C., 1983—86, Moore & Van Allen PLLC, Charlotte, 1986—91, ptnr., 1991—. Vol. counsel Better Bus. Bur. So. Piedmont, Charlotte. Mem.: ABA, N.Y. Bar Assn., N.C. Bar Assn., Nat. Assn. Criminal Def. Lawyers. Avocation: coaching children's soccer. General civil litigation, Criminal. Office: Moore & Van Allen PLLC Ste 4700 100 N Tryon St Charlotte NC 28202-4003

MCLURKIN, THOMAS CORNELIUS, JR., lawyer; b. L.A., July 28, 1954; s. Thomas Cornelius and Willie Mae (O'Connor) McL.; m. Charmaine Bobo. BA, U. So. Calif., 1976, MPA, 1980, postgrad., 1998; JD, U. LaVerne, 1982. Bar: Calif. 1984, U.S. Dist. Ct. (ctrl. dist.) Calif. 1984, U.S. Dist. Ct. Hawaii 1984, U.S. Ct. Appeals (9th cir.) 1984, U.S. Dist. Ct. (ea., no. and so. dists.) Calif. 1985, U.S. Tax Ct. 1988, U.S. Ct. Mil. Appeals 1989, U.S. Army Ct. Mil. Rev. 1993, U.S. Supreme Ct., 1995. Law clk. dept. water and power City of L.A., 1979-82; jud. clk. cen. dist. U.S. Dist. Ct., L.A., 1982-83; law clk. Office City Atty., L.A., 1983-84, dep. city atty., 1984—. Author (with others): Facts in American History, 1968, 2nd edit. 1989, Eagle Scout, 1970. Mem. L.A. World Affairs Coun., 1980—, Smithsonian Assocs.; bd. dirs. L.A. Area coun. Boy Scouts Am., Hillsides Homes for Children; provisional patron Tournament of Roses Assn., Pasadena, 1994—; mem. Verdugo Hills Area coun. Boy Scouts Am. Mem. ABA, ALA, ASPA, Los Angeles County Bar Assn., Assn. Trial Lawyers Am., Langston Law Assn. L.A., U. So. Calif. Gen. Alumni Assn. (bd. govs. exec. bd. 1986-90), U. So. Calif. Black Alumni Assn.-Ebonics (pres. 1988-89), U. So. Calif. Pres.'s Cir., Elks, Am. Legion, Phi Alpha Delta, Kappa Alpha Psi. Republican. United Methodist. Avocations: sailing, tennis, volunteer work, american and world history. Office: LA City Atty Office 200 N Main St Ste 600 Los Angeles CA 90012-4110 E-mail: tmclurk@atty.lacity.org.

MCMAHON, DENNIS C. lawyer, writer; b. Bklyn., Aug. 4, 1950; s. John Thomas and Ruth Mildred McMahon. BA summa cum laude, Fordham U., 1972; JD, Bklyn. Law Sch., 1977. Bar: N.Y. 1978, U.S. Dist. Ct. (so. and ea. dists.) N.Y. 1978, U.s. Dist. Ct. (no. dist.) N.Y. 1984, U.S. Ct. Appeals (3d cir.) 1992, U.S. Ct. Appeals (1st cir.) 2003. Reporter, news editor Home Reporter and Sunset News, Bklyn., 1970—77; weekly press coord. Speaker's Office, N.Y. State Assembly, N.Y.C., 1977; atty. McHugh & O'Conor, N.Y.C., 1978-87, Peter F. Broderick, N.Y.C., 1987-93; pvt. practice N.Y.C., 1993—. Arbitrator N.Y.C. Small Claims Ct., Bklyn., 1985—; cons. law firms in Republic of Ireland. Author column Bklyn. Spectator, 1983—. Bd. dirs. N.Y.C. Econ. Devel. Corp., 1987-97; mem. Sch. Bd. Dist. 20, Bklyn., 1977-93, pres., 1989-90. Recipient local civic awards. Mem. Am. Arbitration Assn. (arbitrator N.Y. civil ct.), Commodore Barry Club, Downtown Athletic Club (bd. dirs., Heisman Trophy award com., 1993-96), Lake Champlain Maritime Mus., Green Mountain Hist. Soc., Sons of Norway. Democrat. Roman Catholic. Avocations: Ireland, music, travel, politics, human rights. General civil litigation, Commercial, contracts (including sales of goods; commercial financing), Personal injury (including property damage). Office: 70 South Winooski Ave Burlington VT 05401 Home: 72 Murray Street Burlington VT 05401 E-mail: dennislaw9@canada.com.

MCMAHON, EDWARD RICHARD, lawyer; b. Jersey City, June 7, 1949; s. Edward Barnawall and Jean (Sullivan) McM.; m. Ellen Mary Bosek; children: Meghan Jean, Kerry Eileen, Ryan Edward. AB, Colgate U., 1972; JD, Seton Hall U., 1975. Bar: N.J. 1975, U.S. Dist. Ct. N.J. 1975, U.S. Ct. of Appeals (3rd circ.) 1980. Law clk. to judge U.S. Dist. Ct., Newark, 1975-77; assoc. Lum, Biunno & Tompkins, Newark, 1977-83; ptnr. Lum, Danzis, Drasco, Positan & Kleinberg, Roseland, 1983—. Mem. Morris County Rep. Com., N.J., 1982-94; mem. Chatham (N.J.) Boro Rep. com., 1982-94, chmn., 1986-94; bd. dirs. Madison area YMCA, 1989-95; bd. trustees Richard J. Hughes Found., 2001-; mem. N.J. State Rep. Com., 1994-. Mem. ABA (litigation and banking sects.), N.J. Bar Assn., Assn. Fed. Bar N.J., Am. Judicature Soc., Morris County Bar Assn., Essex County Bar Assn., Delbarton Sch. Alumni Assn. (class rep. 1984—), 200 Club Morris County, Delta Upsilon, Phi Alpha Delta . Clubs: Colgate (No. N.J.). Republican. Roman Catholic. Banking, Federal civil litigation, State civil litigation. Home: 150 Van Houton Ave Chatham NJ 07928-1239 Office: Lum Danzis Drasco Positan & Kleinberg LLC 103 Eisenhower Pkwy Roseland NJ 07068-1029

MCMAHON, JAMES CHARLES, lawyer; b. Bklyn., Dec. 4, 1951; s. James Charles and Rosemary Margaret (Gilroy) McM.; m. Nancy M. Neble, Oct. 30, 1984; children: Deirdre Kathleen Wright, Laura Elizabeth, Elizabeth Jane. BA, Boston Coll., 1973; JD, Fordham U., 1977. Bar: N.Y. 1978, Mass. 1996, U.S. Supreme Ct. 1996. Assoc. Winthrop Stimson Putnam & Roberts, N.Y.C., 1977-78, Brodsky, Linett, Altman, Schechter & Reicher, N.Y.C., 1978-82; ptnr. Brodsky, Altman & McMahon, LLP, N.Y.C., 1982—, mng. ptnr., 1988—. Exec. sec., counsel N.Y. Movers Tariff Bur., Inc., N.Y.C., 1984-99; gen. counsel Mass. Movers Assn., Woburn, 1986—, Movers and Warehousemen's Assn. Greater N.Y., 1984-98, Met. Moving & Storage Assn., 1979-1998, Commonwealth Transp. Compensation Corp., Andover, Mass., 1992—, Transport Health Plan, Woburn, 1994—, N.Y. State Movers and Warehousemen's Assn., N.Y.C., 1984-2002, Nat. Moving and Storage Assn., Fairfax, Va., 1988-98, Am. Moving & Storage Tech. Found., Alexandria, Va., 1988—. Mem. editl. bd. Fordham Urban Law Jour., 1976. Recipient Disting. Svc. award Mass. Movers Assn., 1992. Mem. N.Y. State Bar Assn. (labor and employment law sect.), Assn. Bar City N.Y. (transp. com. 1997-99), Assn. Comml. Fin. Attys., Transp. Lawyers Assn., Assn. for Transp. Law, Logistics and Policy, N.Y. Athletic Club. Democrat. Roman Catholic. Antitrust, Labor (including EEOC, Fair Labor Standards Act, labor-management relations, NLRB, OSHA), Transportation. Home: 196 Pinesbridge Rd Ossining NY 10562-1428 Office: Brodsky Altman & McMahon LLP 60 E 42d St Ste 1540 New York NY 10165-1544 also: 10 State St Woburn MA 01801-6820 E-mail: jmcmahon@mcmahonlaw.com.

MCMAHON, JAMES E. lawyer; b. 1951; m. Kathy McMahon; 3 children. BS, Morningside U.; JD, U. S.D., 1977. Asst. atty. gen. S.D. Atty. Gen.'s Office, 1978—81; ptnr. Boyce, Murphy, McDowell & Greenfield, 1981—2002; pvt. practice Sioux Falls, SD, 2002—; U.S. atty. Dist. S.D., 2002—. Recipient Trial Lawyer of Yr. award, S.D. Trial Lawyers Assn., 2000. Office: PO Box 5073 4600 S Deerfield Cir Sioux Falls SD 57117*

MCMAHON, JOHN PATRICK, lawyer; b. Monroeville, Ohio, Feb. 8, 1919; s. George James and Eleanor Helene (Ruffing) McM.; m. Patricia Patterson McDanel, May 6, 1950 (dec. July 1983); children: Colleen, Kevin, Patricia, Brian, Barry, Michael; m. Mary Echard, Mar. 7, 1987. BA cum laude, Ohio State U., 1940, JD summa cum laude, 1942. Bar: Ohio 1942, U.S. Supreme Ct. 1949, U.S. Dist. Ct. Ohio 1949, U.S. Ct. Appeals (6th cir.) 1959, U.S. Ct. Appeals (D.C. cir.) 1975. Ptnr. George, Greek, King, McMahon, Columbus, Ohio, 1954-79, Baker & Hostetler, Columbus, 1979-85; with nat. coun. Ohio State U. Coll. Law, 1980—. Capt. USAAF, 1943-46, PTO. Mem. ABA, Ohio Bar Assn., Columbus Bar Assn., Transp. Lawyers Assn., Pres.' Club of Ohio State U. (Columbus), Athletic Club

(Columbus), Home: 2880 Halstead Rd Columbus OH 43221-2916 Office: Baker & Hostetler 65 E State St Ste 2100 Columbus OH 43215-4260 E-mail: jmemahon@columbus.rr.com.

MCMAHON, JOSEPH EINAR, lawyer, consultant; b. Chgo., Aug. 26, 1940; s. Reynold Bernard and Dorothy Marie (Oftedahl) McM. BA cum laude, Denison U., 1962; JD, U. Mich., 1965. Bar: Mass. 1968, D.C. 1980. Asst. to Atty. Gen. and Senator Edward Brooke, Boston and Washington, 1965-67; exec. asst. Lt. Gov. Sargent of Mass., Boston, 1967-69; v.p. BedStuy D&S Corp. Restoration, Bklyn., 1969-74; dir. govt. regulations Westinghouse Electric Corp., Washington, 1974-78; v.p. corp. affairs Federated Dept. Stores, Cin., 1978-80; atty., cons. McMahon and Assocs., Washington, 1980—; v.p. pub. policy Covenant House, 2001—. Exec. dir. (part time), bd. dirs. The Get Ahead Found./USA, 1991-99. Life trustee Denison U.; visitor U. Mich. Law Sch.; 1st v.p. Boston Rep. Com., 1968-69; presdl. appointee Nat. Coun. Econ. Opportunity, 1975-76; exec. dir. Nat. Bus. for Reagan-Bush Com., 1980; dir. emeritus Luther Inst., Washington, Rodale Inst., Emmaus, Pa.; dir. Luth. Lesbian and Gay Min., San Francisco, 1994-2003; mem. outreach bd. Evang. Luth. Ch. in Am., 1995-2001. Mem. Capitol Hill Club, Phi Delta Phi, Pi Sigma Alpha, Omicron Delta Kappa. Lutheran. Nuclear power, Environmental, Legislative. Office: McMahon & Assocs 2031 Q St NW Washington DC 20009 E-mail: McMahon@aol.com.

MCMAHON, ROBERT ALBERT, JR., lawyer; b. New Orleans, July 23, 1950; s. Robert Albert and Marie Rose (Kennedy) McM.; m. Cynthia Ann Steffan, June 29, 1979; children: Angela, Jennifer, Robyn. BA cum laude, U. Southwestern La., 1972; JD, Loyola U., 1975. Bar: La. 1975, U.S. Dist. Ct. (ea. dist.) La. 1977, U.S. Ct. Appeals (5th cir.) 1978, U.S. Dist. Ct. (mid. dist.) La. 1985, U.S. Dist. Ct. (ea. dist.) Tex. 2000, U.S. Supreme Ct. 1989, U.S. Dist. Ct. (we. dist.) La. 1991. Atty. Brown & Hull, Metairie, La., 1975-76, Stewart Title La., New Orleans, 1976, Duplechin & Assocs., Gretna, La., 1977-80, Zelden & Zelden, New Orleans, 1980-81; ptnr. Bernard, Cassisa, Elliott & Davis, Metairie, La., 1982—. Vol. New Orleans Pro Bono Project, 1991—. NRA-Inst. for Legis. Action, Washington, 1991—. Recipient scholarship U. New Orleans, 1968, U. Southwestern La., 1968. Mem. Def. Rsch. Inst., La. Assn. Def. Counsel, Jefferson Bar Assn., La. State Bar Assn.(ho. dels. 1993—), Hibernians, Phi Kappa Theta. Republican. Roman Catholic. Avocations: military history, hunting, tennis, golf. Transportation, Insurance, Product liability. Office: Bernard Cassisa Elliott & Davis 1615 Metairie Rd Metairie LA 70005-3926 E-mail: mcmahonr@bernard-assisa.com.

MCMAHON, TERI LYNN, lawyer; b. Gainesville, Fla., Feb. 28, 1962; d. Edward F. and Suzann (Tope) Threadgill; m. Kevin Michael McMahon, Jan. 2, 1988; children: Kelly Marie, Rebecca Suzanne. BA, Duke U., 1984; JD, U. Mich., 1987. Bar: Ga. 1987. Assoc. Powell, Goldstein, Frazer & Murphy, Atlanta, 1987-94, Alston & Bird, Atlanta, 1994-95, ptnr., 1995—. Mem. DeKalb Med. Ctr. Found., Decatur, Ga., 1992-96, Ga. 100 Program, Atlanta, 1995; elder Decatur Presbyn. Ch., mem. class 1998, Leadership Atlanta. Mem. Druid Hills Golf Club. Democrat. Avocations: tennis, sporting clays. Corporate, general, Mergers and acquisitions. Office: Alston & Bird 1 Atlantic Center 1201 W Peachtree St Atlanta GA 30309-3400 E-mail: tmcmahon@alston.com.

MCMAHON, THOMAS MICHAEL, lawyer; b. Evanston, Ill., May 11, 1941; s. Robert C. and Kathryn D. McM.; m. M. Ann Kaufman, July 11, 1964; children— Michael, Patrick. Student, U. Notre Dame, 1959-61; BA, Marquette U., 1963; JD magna cum laude, Northwestern U., 1970. Bar: Ill. 1970. Mgr. legal adv. sect. Ill. EPA, Springfield, 1970-72; assoc. Sidley & Austin, Chgo., 1972-75, ptnr., founder nat. environ. group, 1975-2000, sr. counsel, 2001—. Lectr. in field; mem. City of Evanston Environ. Control Bd., 1981-83. Author: The Superfund Handbook, 1989, International Environmental Law and Regulation, 1992, Legal Guide to Working with Environmental Consultants, 1992, The Environmental Manual, 1992. Lt. USN, 1963-67. Decorated Republic of Vietnam Campaign medal. Mem. ABA (vice-chmn. alternative dispute resolution com., past vice-chmn. environ. quality com., environ. aspects of bus. trans. com., internat. environ. law com., lectr. confs., teleconfs. and satellite seminars), Order of Coif. Alternative dispute resolution, Corporate, general, Environmental. Office: Sidley Austin Brown & Wood Bank One Plz Chicago IL 60603-2000 E-mail: tmcmahon@sidley.com.

MCMANAMAN, KENNETH CHARLES, lawyer; b. Fairfield, Calif., Jan. 25, 1950; s. Charles James and Frances J. (Holys) McM.; m. Carol Ann Wilson, Apr. 15, 1972; children: Evan John, Kinsey Bridget, Klerin Rose. BA cum laude, S.E. Mo. State U., 1972; JD, U. Mo., Kansas City, 1974; grad., Naval Justice Sch., Newport, R.I., 1975; MS in Bus. Mgmt. summa cum laude, Troy State U., Montgomery, Ala., 1978; LLM in Advanced Litigation, Nottingham-Trent U., 2003. Bar: Mo. 1975, U.S. Dist. Ct. (we. dist.) Mo. 1975, Fla. 1976, U.S. Dist. Ct. (No. and mid. dists.) Fla. 1976, U.S. Dist. Ct. Mil. Appeals 1977, U.S. Ct. Appeals (5th and 8th cirs.) 1977, U.S. Dist. Ct. (ea. dist.) Mo. 1978, U.S. Supreme Ct. 1978, D.C. 1991; cert. mil. judge spl. and gen. ct. martials; diplomate Am. Bd. Forensic Examiners. Prof. bus. law Troy (Ala.) State U., 1976-78; pvt. practice Cape Girardeau, Mo., 2002—; ptnr. O'Loughlin, O'Loughlin & McManaman, Cape Girardeau, Mo., 1978—2002; prof. bus. law S.E. Mo. State U., Cape Girardeau, 1978-84, prof. criminal justice, 1998—; prof. leadership Sch. Law William Woods U., 1998—; prof. bus. mgmt. Sch. Law Nat. Inst. Trial Advocacy. Mem. Cape Girardeau County Coun. on Child Abuse, 1980—89; membership dir. S.E. Mo. scouting coun. Boy Scouts Am., 1980—82; mem. Cape Girardeau County Mental Health Assn., 1982—92; sponsor drug edn./prevention program in schs.; sec., pres. Jackson Area Soccer Assn., 1987—93; mem. Jackson R-2 Alt. Sch. ADv. Bd., 1999—; mem. dept. acctg. and fin. adv. bd. S.E. Mo. State U., 2001—; active local and state Dem. Party, del. Dem. Nat. Conv., San Francisco, 1984; chmn. County Dem. Com., 1984—96; mem. 8th Congl. Dist. Dem. Com. , 1984—86; mem. 27th State Dem. Senatorial Com., 1980—90; ward committeeman Dem. Party, 1984—94; bd. dirs. Area-wide Task Force on Drug and Alcohol Abuse , 1984—87, Cape County chpt. Nat. Kidney Found. , 1988—93. Capt. JAGC USNR, 1994—. Recipient Robert Chilton award City of Jackson for Leadership, Integrity and Responsibility, 1995-97; named One of Outstanding Young Men Am., 1981, 82, 84, 85, Outstanding Pub. Svc. award Cape Girardeau Police Dept. Mem. ABA (Mo. del. young lawyers divsn. 1982-83), Mo. Bar Assn. (chmn. trial advicacy task force 1983), Mo. Bar (young lawyers sect. coun. rep. dist. 13 1980-85), Fla. Bar Assn., Kansas City Bar Assn., Assn. Trial Lawyers Am., Fed. Bar Assn., Nat. Coll. Dist. Attys., Cape Girardeau County Bar Assn. (founder, pres. young lawyers sect. 1981-82), Cape County Bar Assn. (sec. 1999, treas. 2000, v.p. 2001), Naval Res. Assn. (v.p. Southeast Mo/So. Ill. chpt. 1980-85), S.E. Mo. State Alumni Coun., Sigma Chi (numerous awards), Sigma Tau Delta, Pi Delta Epsilon. Roman Catholic. General practice, Workers' compensation. Home: 1162 Trail Ridge Dr Jackson MO 63755-3507 Office: Blattner Bldg Ste One 1028A N Kings Hwy Cape Girardeau MO 63701 Office Fax: 573-335-0105. E-mail: kenmcm@sbcglobal.net., kmcmanaman@charter.net.

MCMANIS, JAMES, lawyer; b. Haverhill, Mass., May 28, 1943; s. Charles and Yvonne (Zinn) McM.; m. Sara Wigh, Mar. 30, 1968. BA, Stanford U., Palo Alto, Calif., 1964; JD, U. Calif., Berkeley, 1967. Bar: Calif. 1967, U.S. Dist. Ct. (no. dist.) Calif. 1967, U.S. Ct. Appeals (9th cir.) 1967, U.S. Supreme Ct. 1971. Dep. dist. atty. Santa Clara County Dist. Atty., 1968-71; mem. McManis, Faulkner & Morgan, San Jose, Calif., 1971—. Spl. master tech. equities litigation, 1987-98; spl. examiner State Bar Calif., 1995-98; prof. law Lincoln U. Law Sch., San Jose, 1972-82; lectr. Calif. Continuing Edn. of Bar, 1989-90; instr. U. Calif. Law Sch., 1992-96, Stanford U. Sch. Law, 1994-99. Pres. Santa Clara County Bar Assn. Law Found., 1996, dir., 1987—. Fellow Am. Coll. Trial Lawyers, Internat. Acad. Trial Lawyers; mem. ABA, State Bar Calif., Calif. Trial Lawyers Assn., Santa Clara County Bar Assn., Boalt Hall Alumni Assn. Avocations: history, books, travel, running. General civil litigation, Criminal, Intellectual property. Office: McManis Faulkner & Morgan 50 W San Fernando St Ste 1999 10th flr San Jose CA 95113 Fax: 408-279-3244. E-mail: jmcmanis@mfmlaw.com.

MCMANUS, CONSTANCE, lawyer; b. Savannah, Ga. d. Joseph John McManus and Lucy Youngquist; (div.); 1 child, Kristen Marie. BS in Edn., U. Ga., 1972; postgrad., Coll. of William & Mary, 1972; JD, Woodrow Wilson Coll. Law, 1980. Bar: Ga. 1980, U.S. Dist. Ct. (no. dist.) Ga. 1981, U.S. Supreme Ct. 1985. Tchr., West Point, Va., 1973; claims supr. Home Ins. Co., Atlanta, 1974-77; pvt. practice Marietta, Ga., 1980—. Editor Law Rev., Woodrow Wilson Coll. of Law, 1979-80. Former bd. dirs., officer Horseshoe Bend Civic Club, Marietta; bd. dirs., officer Anna L. Haas Humane Soc., Marietta, 1985-92; bd. dirs. Stingrays, Inc.,1989-93, Marietta Civitan Club, Ga. N.G. Youth Challenge Acad.; chmn. Ga. AAU, 1991-93; pres. bd. dirs. Oaks Homeowners Assn., Club Office Park; bd. dirs. Youth Challenge Acad., Ga. Nat. Guard. Mem. ATLA, Ga. Bar Assn. (juvenile com.), Cobb Bar Assn. (Law Day com. 1993-94, cir. defender panel 1993-99), Atlanta Bar Assn., Ga. Criminal Def. Lawyers, Atlanta Track Club, Chattahoochee Road Runners Club (v.p. 1992-94, pres. 1994-95), Cobb C. of C. Baptist. Avocations: running, tennis, aerobics. Office: 540 Powder Springs St SE Marietta GA 30064-3549

MC MANUS, EDWARD JOSEPH, federal judge; b. Keokuk, Iowa, Feb. 9, 1920; s. Edward W. and Kathleen (O'Connor) McM.; m. Sally A. Hassett, June 30, 1948 (dec.); children: David P., Edward W., John N., Thomas J., Dennis Q.; m. Esther Y. Kanealy, Sept. 15, 1987. Student, St. Ambrose Coll., 1936-38; BA, U. Iowa, 1940, JD, 1942. Bar: Iowa 1941. Gen. practice of law, Keokuk, 1946-62; city atty., 1946-55; mem. Iowa Senate, 1955-59; lt. gov. Iowa, 1959-61; chief U.S. judge No. Dist. Iowa, 1962-85, sr. U.S. judge, 1985—. Del Democratic Nat. Conv., 1956, 60. Served as lt. AC USNR, 1942-46. Office: US Dist Ct 329 US Courthouse 101 1st St SE Cedar Rapids IA 52401-1202

MCMANUS, F. SHIELDS, lawyer; b. Phila., 1947; s. Frank A. McManus, Jr. and Sara Ann Shields; m. Bertha M. McManus, Sept. 21, 1968; children: Barry, Justin. AA, St. John Vianney Coll., Miami, 1967; BA in Govt., Fla. State U., 1969, JD cum laude, 1972. Bar: Fla. 1972, U.S. Trial Bar (so. dist.) Fla. 1984, U.S. Supreme Ct. 1978, Ga. 2002, U.S. Dist. Ct. (no. dist.) Ga.; bd. cert. civil trial law, Fla. Local bills aide Martin/St. Lucie/Indian River/Brevard County Fla. Legislator, 1970; pvt. practice Stuart, Fla., 1972-75; mem. McManus, Stewart, Ferraro & Sewell PA and predecessor firms, Stuart, Fla., 1976-89, Kohl, Bobko, McKey, McManus, Higgins PA, Stuart, Fla., 1990-93; ptnr. Gary, Williams, Parenti, Finney, Lewis, McManus, Watson & Sperando, Stuart, Fla., 1993—. Bd. govs. young lawyers sect. Fla. Bar, 1977-81, chmn. legal forms com. young lawyers sect., 1980-81; pres. Martin County Bar Assn., 1982-83; chmn. 19th Cir. Jud. Nominating Commn., 1982-84; mem. 19th Cir. Grievance Com., 1983-85; chmn. fla. Bar Jud. Nominating Procedures Com., 1984-85; mem. Supreme Ct. Com. on Standards of conduct Governing Judges, 1987, others. Contbr. articles to profl. jours. Mem. adv. bd. Cath. Charities for Martin and St. Lucie Counties, 1988-96; active Martin County United Way Campaign, 1993; legal advisor Holy Redeemer Cath. Ch., Palm City, Fla., 1983-99, others. Capt. USAR, 1969-81. Mem. Fla. Bar Found. (dir. 1989-92), Stuart-Martin County C. of C. (pres. 1983-84). Office: Gary Williams Parenti Finney Lewis McManus Watson & Sperando Waterside Profl Bldg 221 SE Osceola St Stuart FL 34994-2289

MCMANUS, JAMES WILLIAM, lawyer; b. Kansas City, Mo., Aug. 1, 1945; s. Gerald B. and Mary M. McManus. BA, Rockhurst Coll., 1967; JD, St. Louis U., 1971. Bar: Mo. 1971, U.S. Dist. Ct. (we. dist.) Mo. 1972, U.S. Ct. Appeals (8th cir.) 1974, U.S. Supreme Ct. 1979, U.S. Ct. Appeals (10th cir.) 1984, U.S. Dist. Ct. Kans., 1995. Law clk. to presiding justice U.S. Dist. Ct. (we. dist.) Mo., 1971-73; assoc. Shughart, Thomson & Kilroy, P.C., Kansas City, 1973-76, dir., 1977-94; counsel Dysart, Taylor, Lay, Cotter & McMonigle, P.C., Kansas City, 1994—2002, DeWitt & Zeldin, L.L.C., Kansas City, 2002—. Course lectr. med. jurisprudence U. Health Scis., Coll. Osteo. Medicine, Kansas City, 1994. Mem. adv. coun. St. Joseph Health Ctr., 1989-2002. Mem. ABA, ATLA (membership com. 2003-), Mo. Bar Assn., Kansas City Lawyers Assn., Kansas City Met. Bar Assn. (chmn. alternate dispute resolution com. 1996-97, vice chmn. 1994-95, chmn. med. malpractice com. 1989, Congenial Counselor award 2003), Nat. Lawyers Assn., St. Louis Alumni Assn. (pres. 1984-92), St. Louis U. Law Sch. Alumni Assn. Appellate, General civil litigation, Personal injury (including property damage). Home: 6824 Valley Rd Kansas City MO 64113-1929 Office: DeWitt & Zeldin LLC Harzfeld Bldg Ste 700 Town Pavilion 1111 Main St Kansas City MO 64105 E-mail: jamesmcmanus@justice.com.

MCMANUS, RICHARD GRISWOLD, JR., lawyer; b. Rockville Centre, NY, May 12, 1943; s. Richard Griswold and Ruth Mary (Frost) McM. BBA, U. Notre Dame, 1965; JD, U. Denver, 1970. Bar: Colo. 1970, U.S. Dist. Ct. Colo. 1970, U.S. Ct. Appeals (10th cir.) 1971, U.S. Supreme Ct. 1974. Law clk. Office Atty. Gen., State of Colo., Denver, 1969-70, asst. atty. gen., 1970-78; pvt. practice Denver, 1978-80, 88—; ptnr. Miles & McManus, Denver, 1980-86, Miles, McManus & Epstein, Denver, 1986-88; judge Mcpl. Ct., Aurora, Colo., 1993—, Edgewater, Colo., 2003—. Rep. candidate for Colo. Atty. Gen., 1990. 1st lt. U.S. Army, 1965-67. Fellow Colo. Bar Found.; mem. Colo. Bar Assn. (bd. govs. 1984-86, v.p. 1986-87), Denver Bar Assn., Aurora Bar Assn., Catholic Lawyers Guild, Colo. Bd. of Examiners of Psychologists, Assn. State and Provincial Psychology Bds. (mobility com.). Administrative and regulatory, Health, Labor (including EEOC, Fair Labor Standards Act, labor-management relations, NLRB, OSHA). Home: 1521 Central St Unit 3F Denver CO 80211-3945 Office: Ste 1100 1801 Broadway Denver CO 80202-3839

MCMASTER, HENRY DARGAN, state attorney general; b. Columbia, S.C., May 27, 1947; s. John Gregg and Ida Bacot (Dargan) McM.; m. Peggy Jean McAbee, Mar. 18, 1978 BA, U. S.C., 1969, JD, 1973. Bar: S.C., U.S. Dist. Ct. S.C., U.S. Ct. Claims, U.S. Ct. Appeals (4th cir.), U.S. Supreme Ct. Atty., legis. asst. U.S. Senator Strom Thurmond, Washington, 1973-74; ptnr. Tompkins & McMaster, Columbia, SC, 1974—81, 1985, 2003; U.S. atty. Dist. S.C., Columbia, 1981-85; atty. gen. State of SC, 2003—. Mem. U.S. Atty. Gen.'s adv. com. of U.S. Attys., Washington, 1981-83; chmn. Com. on Ct. Rules and Legislation, Washington, 1983-85. Contbr. articles to legal publs. Mem. region IV youth adv. bd. EPA, Atlanta, 1972; mem. S.C. Commn. on Higher Edcn., 1991-94; chmn. S.C. Rep. Party, 1993-2002; bd. dirs. S.C. Policy Coun., 1991-2003; atty. gen. S.C., 2003-. Mem. Richland County Bar Assn. (program com. 1978), S.C. Bar, ABA, Nat. Assn. R.R. Trial Counsel, Def. Rsch. Inst., Forest Lake Club, Centurian Soc., Caroliniana Ball Club, St. Andrew's Soc. (Columbia), Phi Delta Phi, Blue Key, Kappa Alpha (dep. province comdr. 1974-75, province comdr. 1975-91). Republican. Presbyterian. Office: 1731 Senate St Columbia SC 29201 also: Atty Gen Rembert C Dennis Office Bldg PO Box 11549 Columbia SC 29211

MCMENAMIN, JOHN ROBERT, lawyer; b. Evanston, Ill., Sept. 30, 1946; BA, U. Notre Dame, 1968, JD, 1971. Bar: Ill. 1971. Law clk. to presiding judge U.S. Ct. Appeals (7th cir.), 1971-72; ptnr. Mayer, Brown & Platt, Chgo., 1978-89, McDermott, Will & Emery, Chgo., 1989—. Chmn. adv. bd. Holy Trinity High Sch., Chgo., 1986-88. Mem. ABA, Mid-Am. Com. Clubs: Law, Legal, University (Chgo.), Econ. (Chgo.). Roman Catholic. Banking, Corporate, general. Office: McDermott Will & Emery 227 W Monroe St Ste 3100 Chicago IL 60606-5096

MCMENAMIN, RICHARD F. lawyer; b. Nov. 23, 1946; BA, St. Joseph's Coll., 1968; MA, Boston U., 1971; JD, Temple U., 1977. Bar: Pa. 1977. Ptnr. Morgan, Lewis & Bockius, Phila. Office: Morgan Lewis & Bockius 1701 Market St Philadelphia PA 19103-2903

MCMICHAEL, DONALD EARL, lawyer; b. Denver, Aug. 8, 1931; s. Earl L. and Charlotte F. McM.; m. Zeta Hammond, July 6, 1955; children: Lauren A. McMichael Burnett, Thomas D., Susan E. McMichael Markle. AB, Dartmouth Coll., 1953; LLB, U. Colo., 1956. Bar: Colo. 1956, U.S. Dist. Ct. Colo. 1956, U.S. Ct. Appeals (10th cir.) 1956. Assoc. Holme Roberts & Owen, 1956-58; pres. Corp. Ins. Assocs., 1958-70; dir. trust devel. Ctrl. Bank Denver, 1970-72; ptnr. Brenman, Sobol & Baum, Denver, 1972-74, McMichael, Benedict, Multz & Lipton, Denver, 1974—99; of counsel Schmidt & Horen, Denver, 2000—02; pvt. practice, 2002—. Chmn. Denver Ctrl. YMCA, 1971-73. Capt. USAR, 1956-64. Named Layman of Yr. Denver Ctrl. YMCA, 1973, named to Denver Metro YMCA Hall of Fame, 1989. Mem. Colo. Bar Assn., Denver Bar Assn., Denver Estate Planning Coun. (sec. 1971-73). Republican. Methodist. Corporate, general, Estate planning, Probate (including wills, trusts). Office: 6325 W Mansfield Ave Unit 234 Denver CO 80235-3015 E-mail: dmcmic@aol.com.

MCMICHAEL, LAWRENCE GROVER, lawyer; b. West Orange, N.J., Aug. 18, 1953; s. Robert Gerard McMichael and Mary C. (Bragg) Lewis; children: Elizabeth Joan, David Stern; m. Virginia Lee Hinrichs, Nov. 12, 1994; children: John Lawrence, Mary Christine. AB, Duke U., 1975, JD, 1978. Bar: Pa. 1978, U.S. Ct. Appeals (3d cir.) 1979, U.S. Dist. Ct. (ea. dist.) Pa. 1980, U.S. Supreme Ct. 1984. Ptnr. Dilworth Paxson LLP, Phila., 1978—. Bd. Dir. Wynnewood Civic. Assn., 1986-88. Mem. ABA, Pa. Bar Assn., Phila. Bar Assn., Pa. Bar Inst. (mem. faculty, 1984—). Bankruptcy, Federal civil litigation. Office: Dilworth Paxson LLP 3200 The Mellon Bank Ctr 1735 Market St Philadelphia PA 19103-7501

MC MILLAN, GEORGE DUNCAN HASTIE, JR., lawyer, former state official; b. Greenville, Ala., Oct. 11, 1943; s. George Duncan Hastie and Jean (Autrey) McM.; m. Ann Louise Dial, Nov. 20, 1971; children: George Duncan Hastie, III, Ann Dial. BA magna cum laude, Auburn U., 1966; LL.B. (Southeastern Regional scholar), U. Va., 1969. Bar: Ala. bar 1969. Research asst. dept. agronomy Auburn U., summers 1963-65; law clk. firm Lange, Simpson, Robinson & Somerville, Birmingham, Ala., summers 1967-68; law clk. to judge U.S. Dist. Ct. No. Dist. Ala., 1969-70; instr. U. Ala. Law Sch., 1969-70; individual practice law Birmingham, 1970-71; ptnr. firm McMillan & Spratling, Birmingham, 1971-86; of counsel Haskell, Slaughter, Young and Lewis, 1986; ptnr. McMillan, Jones and Assocs., 1987-90; pres. McMillan Assocs., 1990—; mem. Ala. Ho. of Reps., 1973, Ala. Senate, 1974-78; lt. gov. Ala., 1979-83. Vice-chmn. Nat. Conf. Lt. Govs., 1980-82; mem. Permanent Study Commn. on Ala.'s Jud. System, 1975-79 Chmn. Ala. Film Commn., 1976-83; mem. Arts Task Force, Nat. Conf. State Legislatures, 1978-80, Multi-State Transp. Adv. Bd., 1974-79; mem. exec. com. So. Growth Policies Bd., 1974-83, vice chmn., 1981-83; bd. dirs. Campfire, Inc., 1975-82, Met. YMCA, Birmingham, Boys and Girls Ranches, Ala., Positive Maturity, 1987—; chmn. bd., pres. Birmingham Cultural and Heritage Found., 1988—; pres., bd. dirs. Birmingham Repertory Theatre, 1989—; exec. producer City Stages; Served to lt. USAR, 1969. Recipient award Ala. Nurses Assn., 1975; named Legislator of Yr. Ala. Forestry Assn., 1978; Hardest Working Senator Capitol Press Corps, 1976; 1 of 4 Outstanding Young Men Ala. Jaycees, 1977; 1 of 10 Most Outstanding State Legislators Assn. Govtl. Employees, 1978; award Birmingham Emancipation Assn., 1977; award Ala. Hist. Commn., 1978; James Tingle award, 1979, Citizen of Yr. award City of Birmingham, 1990. Mem. Birmingham Bar Assn., Ala. Bar Assn., Am. Bar Assn., Birmingham Jaycees, Ala. Jaycees (dir. 1970-72), Birmingham Urban League, United Negro Coll. Fund. Democrat. Mem. Ch. of Christ. Club: Rotary (Birmingham). Office: Mc Millan Assocs PO Box 11311 Birmingham AL 35202-1311

MCMILLAN, LEE RICHARDS, II, lawyer; b. New Orleans, Aug. 26, 1947; s. John H. and Phoebe (Skillman) McM.; m. Lynne Clark Pottharst, June 27, 1970; children: Leslie Clark, Hillary Anne, Lee Richards III. BS in Commerce, Washington and Lee U., 1969; JD, Tulane U., 1972; LLM in Taxation, NYU, 1976. Bar: La. 1972. Assoc. Jones, Walker, Waechter, Poitevent, Carrere & Denegre, New Orleans, 1976-79, ptnr., 1979—, sect. head, corp. and securities sect., 1987—90, 1994—2002, exec. com., 1990—94, 1996—99, 2001—02, chmn. exec. com., 1991—94, 1996—98, 2001—02. Vice-chmn. Mech. Equipment Co., Inc., New Orleans, 1980-86, chmn. bd., 1986—, pres. 1989-99; mem. The Bus. Coun. Greater New Orleans, 1998—, exec. com., 1999—; bd. dirs. The Chamber/New Orleans and the River Region, 1996-98; bd. trustees Alton Ochsner Med. Found., 1995—. Trustee New Orleans Mus. Art., 1989-95; bd. dirs. Bur. Govt. Rsch. New Orleans, 1987-93, Louise S. McGehee Sch., New Orleans, 1982-88, co-chmn. capital fund dr., 1984-86, pres. bd. dirs., 1986-88; bd. govs. Isidore Newman Sch., New Orleans, 1991-95. Lt. JACG USNR, 1972-75. Mem. ABA (com. on negotiated acquisitions 1986-94), La. State Bar Assn. (chmn. corp. and bus. law sect. 1985-86, mem. com. on bar admissions 1986-87), Young Pres. Orgn., Washington and Lee U. Alumni Assn. (bd. dirs. 1995-99). Republican. Episcopalian. Avocation: sailing. Banking, Mergers and acquisitions, Securities. Office: Jones Walker Waechter Poitevent Carrere & Denegre 201 Saint Charles Ave Ste 5100 New Orleans LA 70170-5101

MCMILLAN, ROBERT RALPH, lawyer; b. N.Y.C., May 21, 1932; s. Harry and Vivian (Beatty) McM.; m. Phoebe Parker Bunn, Nov. 2, 1996; children: Robin, Karen, Kenneth. Student, Adelphi U., 1951-52, 55-56; JD, Bklyn. Law Sch., 1960. Bar: N.Y. 1960. Spl. asst. staff of Richard M. Nixon, N.Y., Washington, 1960, 64-65; counsel Senator Kenneth B. Keating, Washington, 1960-62; govt. rels. advisor Mobil Oil Co., N.Y.C., 1962-63, 65-68; v.p. Avon Products, N.Y.C., 1973-78, 79-85; sr. v.p. A&S Dept. Stores, N.Y.C., 1978-79; counsel Rivkin, Radler, Bayh, Hart & Kremer, Uniondale, N.Y., 1986-91; ptnr. McMillan, Rather, Bennett & Farinoci, P.C., Melville, NY, 1991—2003, Fischbein Badillo Wagner Harding, Melville, 2003—. Bd. dirs. Empire Blue Cross Blue Shield, Panama Canal Commn., 1989-94, chmn., 1993-94; mem. nat. adv. coun. FannieMae, 1998-2000. News commentator Sta. WLIW-TV, 1993—. Trustee Adelphi U., 1984-89; bd. dirs. L.I. (N.Y.) Assn.; chmn. L.I. Housing Parntership, 1988-2002. 1st lt. U.S. Army, 1952-54. Decorated Bronze Star. Mem.: AMA (bd. trustees), Suffolk County Bar Assn., Nassau County Bar Assn. Republican. Avocations: golf, fishing. Office: Fischbein Badillo Wagner Harding 48 S Service Rd Melville NY 11747-2335 E-mail: mcmillan@aol.com.

MCMILLEN, ROBERT STEWART, lawyer; b. Yonkers, N.Y., Feb. 25, 1943; s. David Harry and Blodwyn Elizabeth (Evans) McM; m. Dorothea Anne Murray, July 2, 1966; children: Elissa London (Mrs. Elliott Aten), Tara Evans. BS, U. Rochester, 1964; JD cum laude, Albany Law Sch. Union U., 1969. Bar: N.Y. 1969, U.S. Dist. Ct. (no. dist.) N.Y. 1969. Assoc. Clark, Bartlett & Caffry, Glens Falls, N.Y., 1969-73; ptnr. Caffry, Pontiff, Stewart, Rhodes & Judge, Glens Falls, 1974-80; prin. Bartlett, Pontiff, Stewart & Rhodes, P.C., Glens Falls, 1981—. Sr. law examiner N.Y. State Bd. Law Examiners, Albany, 1986-2001, bd. mem. 2001—; bd. dirs. Cmty. Title Agy., Inc., Glens Falls, 1984—, pres., 1984-99, v.p., sec., 1999—. Editor-in-chief Albany Law Rev., 1968-69. Bd. dirs., officer Voluntary Action Ctr. of Glens Falls Area, Inc., 1970-97; bd. dirs., treas. Arts and Crafts Ctr. of Warren County, Inc., Glens Falls, 1984-94; mem. Warren County Rep. Com., Queensbury, N.Y., 1979-2001; alt. or del. Rep. Jud. Nomination Com. 4th Jud. Dist. N.Y., 1977—. Recipient Disting. Svc. award Voluntary Action Ctr. of Glens Falls Area, Inc., 1990. Mem. ABA, Nat. Conf. Bar Examiners (mem. multistate performance test com. 2001—), N.Y. State Bar Assn. (mem. com. profl. ethics 1990-99, 2000—), Warren County Bar Assn.

(bd. dirs. 1979-82, treas. 2001—), Adirondack Regional C. of C. (bd. dirs. 1997-2000, vice chmn. 1999-2000, counsel 2000—), Rotary. Avocations: travel, downhill skiing, boating. Corporate, general, Property, real (including real estate development, water), Probate (including wills, trusts). Home: 147 Assembly Point Rd Lake George NY 12845-5201 Office: 1 Washington St Glens Falls NY 12801-2963

MCMILLIAN, THEODORE, federal judge; b. St. Louis, Jan. 28, 1919; m. Minnie E. Foster, Dec. 8, 1941. BS, Lincoln U., 1941, HHD (hon.), 1981; LLD, St. Louis U., 1949; HHD (hon.), U. Mo., St. Louis, 1978. Mem. firm Lynch & McMillian, St. Louis, 1949-53; asst. circuit atty. City of St. Louis, 1953-56; judge U.S. Ct. Appeals (8th cir.), 1978—. Judge Circuit Ct. for City St. Louis, 1956-72, Mo. Ct. Appeals eastern div., 1972-78; asso. prof. adminstrn. justice U. Mo., St. Louis, 1970— ; asso. prof. Webster Coll. Grad. Program, 1977; mem. faculty Nat. Coll. Juvenile Justice, U. Nev., 1972— Served to 1st lt. Signal Corps U.S. Army, 1942-46. Recipient Alumni Merit award St. Louis U., 1965, ACLU Civil Liberties award, 1995, Disting. Lawyer award Bar Assn. Met. St. Louis, 1996, Salute to Excellence Civil Rights award St. Louis Am., 1997, Spirit of Excellence award ABA, 2003; named Disting. Non-Alumnus U. Mo.-Columbia Law Sch., 1999. Mem. Am. Judicature Soc., Am. Bd. Trial Advs. (hon. diplomate), Lawyers Assn. Mo., Mound City Bar Assn., Phi Beta Kappa, Alpha Sigma Nu. Office: Thomas F Eagleton Court House Ste 25 162 111 S 10th St Saint Louis MO 63102

MCMORROW, MARY ANN G. state supreme court chief justice; b. Chgo., Jan. 16, 1930; m. Emmett J. McMorrow, May 5, 1962; 1 dau., Mary Ann. Student, Rosary Coll., 1948-50; JD, Loyola U., 1953. Bar: Ill. 1953, U.S. Dist. Ct. (7th dist.) Ill. 1960, U.S. Supreme Ct. 1976. Atty. Riordan & Linklater Law Offices, Chgo., 1954-56; asst. state's atty. Cook County, Chgo., 1956-63; sole practice Chgo., 1963-76; judge Cir. Ct. Cook County, 1976-85, Ill. Appellate Ct., 1985-92, Supreme Ct. Ill., 1992—. Faculty adv. Nat. Jud. Coll., U. Nev., 1984. Contbr. articles to profl. jours. Mem. Chgo. Bar Assn., Ill. State Bar Assn., Women's Bar Assn. of Ill. (pres. 1975-76, bd. dirs. 1970-78), Am. Judicature Soc., Northwestern U. Assocs., Ill. Judges Assn., Nat. Assn. Women Judges, Advocates Soc., Northwest Suburban Bar Assn., West Suburban Bar Assn., Loyola Law Alumni Assn. (bd. govs. 1985—), Ill. Judges Assn. (bd. dirs.), Cath. Lawyers Guild (v.p.), The Law Club of the City of Chgo., Inns of Ct. Office: Supreme Ct of Ill 160 N La Salle St Chicago IL 60601-3103

MCNAIR, RUSSELL ARTHUR, JR., lawyer; b. Detroit, Dec. 2, 1934; s. Russell Arthur and Virla (Standish) McN.; m. Rosemary M. Chesbrough, Apr. 6, 1957; children: Julie McNair Schwerin, Russell Arthur III, Douglas S. AB in Econs. cum laude, Princeton U., 1956; JD with distinction, U. Mich., 1960. Bar: Mich. 1960, Fla. 2001. Assoc. Dickinson, Wright, Moon, Van Dusen & Freeman (now Dickinson Wright PLLC), Detroit, 1960-67, ptnr., 1968-98, chmn., 1994-98. Cons. Evans & Luptak, Boca Raton, 2000-; adj. prof. U. Detroit Sch. Law, 1968-72; mem. adv. bd. Fin. Transactions Inst., 1984-94; adj. prof. Wayne State U. Law Sch., 1994-96; spkr. in field. Trustee Children's Home, Detroit, 1975-95, pres. 1986-87, hon. trustee 1995—; mem. community leaders coun., United Way, 1994-98; dir. Mich. Jobs Commn., 1995-98. Mem. Mich. Bar Assn., Detroit Bar Assn., Am. Law Inst., Am. Coll. Real Estate Lawyers. Republican. Presbyterian. Avocations: golf, tennis, platform tennis. Banking, Corporate, general, Property, real (including real estate development, water). Home: 4383 Gleneagles Dr Boynton Beach FL 33436-4802 Office: Evans & Luptak 4th Fl 4700 NW Boca Raton Blvd Boca Raton FL 33431 E-mail: ramcnair@aol.com., ramcnair@bellsouth.net.

MCNAIR, TIMOTHY DEAN, lawyer; b. Richfield, Ohio, Aug. 21, 1954; s. Fred Denman and Marjorie Faye (Gynn) McN.; m. Karin P. Sarner Loucy, Oct. 22, 1988; 1 child, Peter Michael; stepchildren: James Sarner Loucy, Gregory Sarner Loucy, Brianne Patrice Loucy. BA, Allegheny Coll., 1977; JD, U. Pitts., 1981. Bar: Pa. 1981. Jud. clk. to Hon. Jess S. Jiuliante Ct. Common Pleas, Erie, Pa., 1982-84; assoc. Schroeck & Segel, Erie, 1984-87, Bifulco, Scarpitti et al, Erie, 1987-90; ptnr. Vendetti Talarico & McNair, Erie, 1990-94, Talarico & McNair, Erie, 1994-97; pvt. practice, Erie, 1997—. Mem. exec. com. Erie County Dem. Party, 2000—, parliamentarian, 2001—. Owens fellow U. Pitts., 1979-81. Mem. ATLA, Pa. Trial Lawyers Assn. (bd. govs. 1996—, chair workers compensation sect. 2003—), Erie County Bar Assn. Presbyterian. Avocations: computer technology, boating. Federal civil litigation, Personal injury (including property damage), Workers' compensation. Office: 821 State St Erie PA 16501-1316 E-mail: tmcnair@velocity.net.

MCNALLY, GERALD, JR., lawyer; b. Kalamazoo, Dec. 28, 1947; s. Gerald and Elizabeth Louise (Lake) McN.; m. Barbara Frances Robinson, Mar. 17, 1979 (div.); children: Charles Patrick Ritchie, Fiona Kathleen. Student, Mich. State U., 1965-67; JD, Whittier Coll., 1984. Bar: Calif., 1984. Treas. Ch. of Scientology, San Diego, 1971-74; customer svc. rep. Xerox Corp., L.A., 1974-78; acct., enrolled agt. L.A., 1981—84; pvt. practice Glendale, Calif., 1984—; ptnr. McNally & Moore LLP, Glendale, Calif., 2001—. Served with USN, 1967-71. Mem. Assn. for Childbirth at Home Internat. (bd. dirs. 1980). Republican. Avocations: computers, golf, swing dancing. E-mail address. Bankruptcy, Corporate, general, Taxation, general. Home: 7590 N Glen Oaks Blvd #103 PO Box 3189 Burbank CA 91508-3189 E-mail: mcnallylaw@relaypoint.net.

MCNALLY, JOHN JOSEPH, retired lawyer; b. N.Y.C., July 1, 1927; s. Edward E. and Virginia L. (O'Brien) McNally; m. Sally Vose Greeley, Jan. 25, 1958; children: Martha, Sarah, Elizabeth, Julie, Thomas. AB, Coll. Holy Cross, 1950; LLB, Harvard U., 1953. Bar: N.Y. 1953. Assoc. White & Case, N.Y.C., 1953-63, ptnr., 1964-94; ret., 1994. Bd. dirs. Mohawk Paper Mills, Inc. Pres. Lavelle Fund for the Blind, 1999—; bd. govs. Lawrence Hosp., Bronxville, NY, 1990—95; trustee Caedmon Sch., N.Y.C., 1968—, Lavelle Sch. for Blind, N.Y.C., 1997—99, All Hallows Found., 2000—, All Hallows H.S., N.Y.C., 2001. Fellow: Am. Bar Found.; mem.: Assn. Bar of City of N.Y., N.Y. County Lawyers Assn., N.Y. State Bar Assn. Home: 58 Avon Rd Bronxville NY 10708-1723 Office: White & Case 1155 Ave of Americas New York NY 10036-2711

MCNALLY, SEAN PATRICK, prosecutor; b. Scranton, Pa., Aug. 5, 1953; s. John Patrick and Elizabeth Jane McNally; m. Diane Maureen Campanaro, June 29, 1985; 1 child, Brigid S. AA, Citrus Coll., 1973; BA, UCLA, 1975; JD, Western State U., 1979; postgrad., U. So. Calif., 1981, 82. Bar: U.S. Tax Ct. 1980, U.S. Dist. Ct. (ctrl. dist.) Calif. 1980, U.S. Dist. Ct. (so. dist.) Calif. 1981, U.S. Ct. Appeals (8th cir.) 1981. Law libr. Orange County Law Libr., Santa Ana, Calif., 1975-80; intern Orange County Dist. Atty., Santa Ana, 1978; assoc. Law Offices of Leon Najman, Costa Mesa, Calif., 1980-81; dep. dist. atty. San Bernardino County, Calif., 1981—. Mem. ABA, Calif. Trial Lawyers Assn., Assn. of Trial Lawyers of Am., Calif. Dist. Atty. Assn., L.A. Police Dept. Emerald Soc., L.A. Trial Lawyers Assn., Riverside County Bar Assn., San Bernardino County Bar Assn., Los Angeles County Bar Assn., Orange County Bar Assn., Western State U. Alumni Assn., Calif. Narcotics Officers Assn., B.P.O.Elks, Delta Tau Delta, Delta Theta Phi. Republican. Roman Catholic. Avocations: boating, running, collegiate sporting events. Home: 6007 E Brighton Ln Anaheim CA 92807-4702 Office: 316 N Mountain View Ave San Bernardino CA 92415-1016

MCNAMARA, ANNE H. lawyer, corporate executive; b. Shanghai, Republic of China, Oct. 18, 1947; came to U.S. 1949; d. John M. and Marion P. (Murphy) H. AB, Vassar Coll., 1969; JD, Cornell U., 1973. Bar: N.Y. 1973, Tex. 1981. Assoc. Shea, Gould, Climenko & Casey, N.Y.C., 1972-76; from asst. corp. sec. to corp. sec. Am. Airlines, Inc., Dallas, 1976-88, v.p. pers. resources, 1988; sr. v.p., gen. counsel Am. Airlines (AMR Corp.), Dallas, 1988—. Bd. dirs. Louisville Gas & Electric Co., LG&E Energy Corp., Sabre Group Holdings, Inc. Antitrust, Corporate, general, Securities. Office: Am Airlines Inc Dallas/Fort Worth Airport PO Box 619616 Dallas TX 75261-9616

MCNAMARA, MICHAEL JOHN, lawyer; b. Hutchinson, Minn., July 1, 1948; s. John Oliver and Lucille Violet (Wedell) M.; m. Kathleen Elizabeth Dahl; children: Jennifer, Kelly. BA, U. Utah, 1976; JD, U. Minn., 1980. Bar: Minn. 1981, U.S. Dist. Ct. Minn. 1981, U.S. Ct. Appeals (8th cir.) 1982, U.S. Supreme Ct. 1988, Wis. 1992. Pvt. practice, Mpls., 1981—. Panel arbitrator Hennepin County Dist. Ct. Contbr. articles to profl. jours. Sgt. U.S. Army, 1968-71, Vietnam. Nat. Merit scholar. Mem. Fed. Bar Assn., ATLA, The Federalist Soc., Internat. Platform Assn., Minn. State Bar Assn., Hennepin County Bar Assn. (mem. spkrs. bur.). Avocations: jogging, biking, hiking. General civil litigation, Corporate, general, Criminal. Office: Henderson Howard et al 6200 Shingle Creek Pkwy Ste 385 Minneapolis MN 55430-2176

MCNAMARA, PATRICK JAMES, lawyer; b. Bethpage, N.Y., Mar. 27, 1959; s. James Francis and Kathleen (Marrinan) McN.; m. Kimberly McNamara, Dec. 7, 1991; children: James Patrick, Emma Kathleen. BA in History, Rutgers U., New Brunswick, N.J., 1981, MA in Polit. Sci., 1985; JD, Rutgers U., Camden, N.J., 1987. Bar: N.J. 1987, U.S. Dist. Ct. N.J. 1987, Pa. 1987. Legal sec. to Hon. Neil F. Deighan Jr., Appellate Divsn. N.J. Superior Ct., 1987-88; with Giordano, Halleran & Ciesla, Middletown, N.J., 1988-91; ptnr. Carpenter, Bennett and Morrissey, Newark, 1991-94, Scarinci & Hollenbeck, Secaucus, N.J., 1994—. Gen. counsel Nat. Assn. Flavor and Food Ingredient Systems, Inc., 1995—, Chem. Sources Assn., 1998—, Soc. of Flavor Chemists, 2001-. Assoc. editor Food Exec. mag., 1997, Food Product Design mag., 1999; contbr. author to profl. jours. Mcpl. atty. Township of Aberdeen, 1992-95; spl. counsel Twp. of Aberdeen, 1996-97, Fredon Twp. Zoning Bd. of Adj., 1999-, Borough of S. River, 2001-; lead counsel City of Elizabeth Planning Bd., 1999—. Rutgers U. Grad. fellow Eagleton Inst. Politics, 1984-85. Mem. N.J. State Bar Assn. (environ. law sect.), Environ. Law Inst., N.J. Group Small Chem. Businesses, Rutgers Alumni Assn. (bd. dirs.). Avocations: sports, travel, golf, politics. Land use and zoning (including planning), Environmental, Property, real (including real estate development, water). Office: 1100 Valley Brook Ave PO Box 790 Lyndhurst NJ 07071 Fax: 201-348-3877. E-mail: patrick@njlegalink.com.

MCNAMARA, PATRICK ROBERT, lawyer; b. Conneaut, Ohio, Dec. 16, 1950; s. Robert John and Retagene (Bailey) McN.; m. Sue Brozina, July 12, 1975; children: Brian, Meghan, Erin, Robert. BS in Edn., Northwestern U., 1973; JD, U. Ariz., 1976. Bar: Ariz. 1976, U.S. Dist. Ct. Ariz. 1976, U.S. Ct. Appeals (9th cir.) 1981; cert. specialist workers' compensation law Ariz. Bd. Legal Specialization. Assoc. Davis, Eppstein & Tretschok, Tucson, 1976-79; adminstrv. law judge Indsl. Commn. Ariz., Tucson, 1979-81; ptnr. Tretschok & McNamara, P.C., Tucson, 1981—. Mem. Pima County Bar Assn., Assn. Trial Lawyers Am., Ariz. Trial Lawyers Assn., Ariz. State Bar (past pres. worker's compensation law sect.), So. Ariz. Workers Compensation Claims Assn., Nat. Orgn. Social Security Claimants Reps. Democrat. Roman Catholic. Workers' compensation. Office: Tretschok & McNamara PC PO Box 42887 Tucson AZ 85733-2887 Fax: 520 792 2417. E-mail: mcnamara@tmpllaw.com.

MCNAMEE, STEPHEN M. federal judge; b. 1942; BA, U. Cinn., 1964; MA, U. Ariz., 1967, JD, 1969. U.S. atty. Dist. of Ariz., Phoenix, 1985-90; U.S. Dist. judge, 1990—99; chief judge U.S. Dist. Ct. Ariz., Phoenix, 1999—. Office: US Dist Judge Sandra Day O'Connor US Ct 401 W Washington St SPC 60 Phoenix AZ 85003-2158

MCNEELY, JAMES LEE, lawyer; b. Shelbyville, Ind., May 4, 1940; s. Carl R. and Elizabeth J. (Orebaugh) McN.; m. Rose M. Wisker, Sept. 5, 1977; children: Angela, Susan, Meg, Matt. AB, Wabash Coll., 1962; JD, Ind. U., 1965. Bar: Ind. 1965, U.S. Dist. Ct. (so. dist.) Ind. 1965, U.S. Ct. Appeals (7th cir.) 1970. Assoc. Pell & Matchett, Shelbyville, 1965-70; ptnr. Matchett & McNeely, Shelbyville, 1970-74; sole practice Shelbyville, 1974-76; sr. ptnr. McNeely & Sanders, Shelbyville, 1976-86, McNeely, Sanders & Stephenson, Shelbyville, 1986-89, McNeely, Sanders, Stephenson & Thopy, Shelbyville, 1989-96, McNeely, Stephenson, Thopy & Harrold, Shelbyville, 1997—. Guest lectr. Franklin Coll., Ind., 1965-72; judge Shelbyville City Ct., 1967-71. Chmn. Shelbyville County Rep. Cen. Com., 1968-88; bd. dirs. Ind. Lung Assn., 1972-75, Crossroads Council Boy Scouts Am., 1982; bd. dirs., pres. Shelbyville Girls Club. Named Sagamore of the Wabash, Gov. Ed Whitcomb, 1971, Gov. Otis Bowen, 1977, Gov. Robert Orr, 1986, 88, Gov. Evan Bayh, 1996, Gov. Frank O'Bannon, 1999. Fellow Ind. Bar Found. (patron, sec. 1999-2000, chair elect 2000-01, chmn. 2002-03); mem. ABA, Ind. Bar Assn. (sec. 1985-87, bd. dirs. 1976-78, chair-elect Ho. Dels. 1994-95, chair 1995-96, v.p. 1996-97, pres.-elect 1997-98, pres. 1998-99), Shelby County Bar Assn. (pres. 1975), Ind. Lawyers Commn. (pres., dir.), Fed. Merit Selection Commn. (adv. mem. 1988-92, chmn. 2001—), Shelbyville Jaycees (Distinguished Service award 1969, Good Govt. award 1970), Wabash Coll. Nat. Assn. Wabash Men (dir. 1983-89, sec. 1989-91, v.p. 1991-93, pres. 1993-95, Man of Yr. 1995), Kappa Sigma Alpha Pi chpt. (Hall of Fame 1995). Lodges: Lions, Elks, Eagles. Methodist. Avocations: golf, travel. State civil litigation, Insurance, Labor (including EEOC, Fair Labor Standards Act, labor-management relations, NLRB, OSHA). Home: 1902 E Old Rushville Rd Shelbyville IN 46176-9569

MCNEIL, CHRISTOPHER BLACK, lawyer, educator; b. Bad Godesburg, Germany, Nov. 26, 1955; arrived in U.S., 1956; s. Thomas John and Janet Elisabeth McNeil; m. L. Camille Hebert, July 30, 1983; children: Amanda R., Caitlin E., Ian C. AA in Bus., L.A. City Coll., 1975; B in Gen. Studies, U. Kans., Lawrence, 1978, JD, 1981. Bar: Kans. 1981, Ohio 1989, (U.S. Supreme Ct.) 1991, (U.S. Ct. Appeals (6th cir.)) 1991, (U.S. Ct. Appeals (3d cir.)) 1994, (U.S. Dist. Ct. (no. and so. dists.) Ohio) 1991. Dep. pub. defender 8th Jud. Dist. Kans., Junction City, 1981—83; pvt. practice Kansas City, Kans., 1983—85; with child support enforcement divsn. State of Kans. Dept. Social and Rehab. Svcs., Kansas City, 1985—88; asst. Ohio atty. gen. bus. and govt. regulation sect., lead counsel and supervising atty. Bur. Motor Vehicles Office of Ohio Atty. Gen., Columbus, 1988—94; adminstrv. hearing examiner State of Ohio, Columbus, 1994—; legal rsch. and writing faculty Capital U. Law Sch., Columbus, 1995—. Subject matter specialist in writing for adminstrv. law judges USDA, Washington, 1998—2000, Ohio Dept. Job and Family Svcs., Columbus, 1999—2002, Mich. Dept. Consumer and Industry Svcs., 2001; mem. bd. advisors Jour. Nat. Assn. Adminstrv. Law Judges, 1999—2000. Author: (book) Preventing and Responding to Workplace Sexual Harassment, 2d edit.; contbg. author: book Ohio Administrative Law Guide and Directory, 1994—95; author: Kansas Statutes of Limitation and Time Standards, 1988; contbr. articles to profl. jours. Sgt. U.S. Army, 1974—76, Korea. Recipient Nat. Hwy. Traffic Safety Adminstrn. Adminstrv. Law Judge fellow, 2001—03. Fellow: Ohio State Bar Found.; mem.: ABA (jud. divsn., chair cts. and cmty. com. 1998—99, vice chair edn. com. 1998—99), Am. Inns of Ct. (master lawyer Robert M. Duncan chpt. 1995), Nat. Assn. Adminstrv. Law Judges (vice-chair ednl. stds. com. 1997—99, nat. fellowship in adminstrv. law 1997—98), Ohio State Bar Assn. (chair adminstrv. law com. 1996—98). Democrat. Roman Catholic. Avocation: Cajun cooking. Office: PO Box 595 Worthington OH 43085 Office Fax: 614-888-2687. E-mail: cmcneil@iwaynet.net.

MCNEIL, MARK SANFORD, lawyer; b. Shawnee, Okla., Feb. 4, 1950; s. Irving Jr. and Sylvia Louise (Sanford) McN.; m. Cathy Marleen Yandell, Sept. 7, 1974; children: Elizabeth, Laura. Assoc. Lillick McHose & Charles, San Francisco, 1974-76; rsch. asst. Kyoto (Japan) U., 1976-77; internat. law cons. Amita & Hirokawa, Osaka, Japan, 1976-77, Ono Law Office, Osaka, 1976-77; internat. counsel Medtronic, Inc., Mpls., 1978-84; mgr. contract adminstrn. Cray Rsch., Inc., Mpls., 1985, internat. counsel, 1986-88, dir. internat. contracts, 1988-91, dir. corp. contacts, 1991; assoc. Briggs and Morgan, P.A., Mpls., 1995-97. Adj. prof. William Mitchell Coll. Law, St. Paul, 1989-91. Bd. dirs. Midwest China Ctr. Mem. ABA, Minn. Bar Assn. (chmn. internat. bus. law sect. 1986-87), Hennepin County Bar Assn., Corp. Counsel Assn., Minn. World Trade Assn. (bd. dirs. 1996—, pres. 1998-99). Avocations: photography, music, fiction writing, rafting. Computer, Corporate, general, Private international. Home: 514 5th St E Northfield MN 55057-2220 Office: Lindquist and Vennum PLLP 4200 IDS Ctr Minneapolis MN 55402 E-mail: mmcneil@lindquist.com.

MCNEILL, PAUL DEANE, lawyer; b. Little Rock, Aug. 31, 1954; s. Charles Adrian and Erma (Rife) McN.; 1 child, Hallie Susanne. BBA, U. Ark., 1976; JD with high honors, 1979. Bar: Ark. 1979, U.S. Dist. Ct. (ea. dist.) Ark. 1979, U.S. Ct. Appeals (8th cir.) 1987. Ptnr. Barrett, Wheatley, Smith & Deacon, Jonesboro, Ark., 1979-92, Womack, Landis, Phelps, McNeill & McDaniel, Jonesboro, 1992—. Bd. dirs. N.E. Ark. Legal Svcs. Bd. dirs. United Way Jonesboro, 1986-90, Jonesboro Area Softball Assn., 1987-90, Ark. State U. Sigma Chi House Corp., 1986—; telethon v.i.p. United Cerebral Palsy, Jonesboro, 1986-90; deacon First Bapt. Ch. Mem. ABA (litigation sect.), Am. Bd. Trial Advocates (pres. Ark. chpt. 2001), Am. Coll. Trial Lawyers, Def. Rsch. Inst., Fedn. Ins. Corp. Counsel, Ark. Ba r Assn. (exec. coun., ho. of dels., civil procedure com. 1997-2000, chmn. legal aid com.), Ark. Def. Lawyers Assn. (program chmn. 1994, pres. 1997-98), Craighead County Bar Assn. (sec. 1984-85, pres. 2001, 1st jud. trial practice com.). Baptist. Avocations: golf, softball, snow skiing. Insurance, Personal injury (including property damage). Office: Womack Landis Phelps McNeill & McDaniel Century Ctr Madison at Washington Jonesboro AR 72401

MCNEILL, THOMAS B. retired lawyer; b. Chgo., Oct. 28, 1934; s. Donald T. and Katherine M. (Bennett) McN.; m. Ingrid Sieder, May 11, 1963; children: Christine, Thomas, Stephanie. BA, U. Notre Dame, 1956, JD, 1958. Ptnr. Mayer, Brown, Rowe & Maw, Chgo., 1962—99. Dir. Deltona Corp., Ocala, Fla. Served to capt. JAGC USAF, 1959-62. Fellow Am. Coll. Trial Lawyers; mem. Chgo. Bar Assn., Chgo. Council Lawyers, The Lawyers Club (Chgo. chpt.). Clubs: Indian Hill (Winnetka, Ill.). General civil litigation, Commercial, contracts (including sales of goods; commercial financing). Home: 2418 Iroquois Rd Wilmette IL 60091-1335 E-mail: tomingrid@aol.com.

MCNEILL, THOMAS RAY, lawyer; b. Pitts., June 2, 1952; s. Thomas William McNeill and Mary (Shiveley) Hiss; m. Patsy Lynch, June 25, 1977; children: Elizabeth, Kathleen, Thomas. BSBA, U. Fla., 1974; JD, Emory U., 1977. Bar: Ga. 1977, U.S. Dist. Ct. (no. dist.) Ga. 1977. Assoc. Powell, Goldstein, Frazer & Murphy, LLP, Atlanta, 1977-84, ptnr., 1984—, mgr. corp. dept., 1993-95, bd. ptnrs., 1998—. Mem. Ga. Bar Assn., Emory U. Alumni Assn. (pres. exec. com. Atlanta chpt. 1988-89, Law Sch. coun. 1990-2000), Soc. of Internat. Bus. Fellows, Beta Gamma Sigma. Finance, Private international, Mergers and acquisitions. Office: Powell Goldstein Frazer & Murphy 191 Peachtree St NE Ste 1600 Atlanta GA 30303-1700 E-mail: tmcneill@pgfm.com.

MCNEIL STAUDENMAIER, HEIDI LORETTA, lawyer; b. Preston, Iowa, Apr. 7, 1959; d. Archie Hugo and Heidi (Waltert) McN.; m. L. William Staudenmaier III; children: Kathleen Louise McNeil Staudenmaier, Jacob William Staudenmaier. BA in Journalism and Broadcasting with distinction, U. Iowa, 1981, JD with distinction, 1985. Bar: Ariz. 1985, U.S. Dist. Ct. Ariz. 1985, U.S. Ct. Appeals (9th cir.) 1985, U.S. Ct. Appeals (10th cir.) 1990. Sports journalist The Daily Iowan, Iowa City, 1977-81, Quad City Times, Davenport, Iowa, 1981-82; ptnr. Snell & Wilmer, Phoenix, 1985—. Judge pro tem, Maricopa County, Phoenix, 1992—, Ariz. Ct. Appeals, 1998—. Mem. ABA (mem. domestic violence commn. 1995-98, Ho. of Dels. 1995-98, 2001—, chair young lawyers career issues com. 1992-93, mem. affiliate assistance program com. 1992-93, dir. 1993-94, spl. projects coord. 1994-95, bus. law sect., editor-in-chief Bus. Law Today, co-chair fellows program), Internat. Assn. Gaming Attys., Internat. Masters of Gaming Law (prs. 2003), Ariz. Bar Assn. (Indian law sect. exec. coun. and chair, 1995-99, young lawyers exec. coun. 1991-94), Maricopa County Bar Assn. (bd. dirs. 1991—, young lawyers divsn. 1987-93, pres. 1991-92, 99-2000), Ariz. Women Lawyers, Phoenix Assn. Def. Counsel, Native Am. Bar Assocs., Phi Beta Kappa, Phi Eta Sigma. Lutheran. Avocations: running, golf, skiing, hiking, bicycling. General civil litigation, Native American.

MCNIDER, JAMES SMALL, III, lawyer; b. Richmond, Va., Aug. 23, 1956; s. James Small Jr. and Phoebe Warwick (Johnston) McNider; m. Anna Mary Van Buren, Apr. 30, 1983; children: Anna Lee, Mary Tyler, James S. IV, Ellen Page. BS, Washington & Lee U., 1978, JD, 1981. Bar: Va. 1981, U.S. Tax Ct. 1981, U.S. Dist. Ct. (ea. dist.) Va. 1986. Assoc. Kaufman & Canoles, Norfolk, Va., 1981-85, Willcox & Savage, Norfolk, 1985-87, ptnr., 1987-95, James S. McNider, III P.L.C., Hampton, Va., 1995—. Author (with others): (book) ABA Sales and Use Tax handbook, 1988. Mem.: ABA, Va. Bar Assn. (chmn. tax sect. 1993—94), Princess Anne Country Club, Omicron Delta Kappa. Episcopalian. Avocations: private pilot, tennis, golf. Corporate, general, Corporate taxation, State and local taxation. Home: 808 Park Pl Hampton VA 23669-4152 Office: PO Box I Hampton VA 23669-0256 E-mail: jmcnider@valaw.com.

MCNULTY, PAUL J. prosecutor; BA, Grove City Coll.; JD, Capital U. Counsel U.S. House Com. on Standards of Official Conduct, Washington, 1983—85; dir. legal svcs. Legal Svcs. Corp., Washington, 1985—87; minority counsel House Judiciary Subcom. Crime, 1987—90; dep. dir. Office Policy Devel., dir. Office Policy and Comms. U.S. Dept. Justice, Washington, 1990—93; counsel Shaw, Pittman, Potts and Trowbridge, 1993—95, U.S. Ho. Reps. Com. on Judiciary, Washington, 1995—99; prin. assoc. dep. atty. gen. U.S. Dept Justice, 2001; chief counsel, dir. legis. ops. Office of Majority Leader U.S. Ho. Reps., Washington, 1999—2001; U.S. atty. ea. dist. U.S. Dept. Justice, Va., 2001—. Office: 2100 Jamieson Ave Alexandria VA 22314*

MC PHEE, HENRY ROEMER, lawyer; b. Ames, Iowa, Jan. 11, 1925; s. Harry Roemer and Mary (Ziegler) McP.; m. Joanne Lambert, May 19, 1956 (div. Dec. 1991); children: Henry Roemer III, Joanne, Larkin, Charles; m. Selby Fleming, Jan. 27, 1999. AB cum laude, Princeton U., 1947; LLB, Harvard U., 1950. Bar: N.J. 1951, Ill. 1961, D.C. 1966. Exec. asst. to gov. State of N.J., Trenton, 1950-52; assoc. R.E. & A.D. Watson, New Brunswick, N.J., 1952-54; asst. to gen. counsel FTC, Washington, 1954; exec. asst. White House, Washington, 1954-57; asst. spl. counsel Pres. U.S., Washington, 1957-58, assoc. spl. counsel, pres., 1958-61; ptnr. Hamel & Park, Washington, 1961-88, mem. mgmt. com., 1975-85, mng. ptnr., 1980-83; ptrnr. Hopkins & Sutter, 1988-93, of counsel, 1994—2002, Foley & Lardner, 2002—. Sec. N.J. Commn. on Interstate Cooperation, 1952-54; gen. counsel Rep. Nat. Fin. Com., 1968-73, Rep. Nat. Com., Washington, 1968. Chmn. bldg. com. Potomac (Md.) Presbyn. Ch., 1965-67; v.p. Rep. Club, Princeton, 1952-54; bd. dirs. Eisenhower Inst., 1983—, treas., 1991-93, mem. exec. com., 1991—. Mem. ABA, D.C. Bar Assn., N.J. Bar Assn., Lincoln's Inn Soc. Harvard Law Sch. Clubs: Tower (Princeton U.); Princeton (Washington) (pres. 1970-72), Metropolitan (Washington), Capitol Hill (Washington). Republican. Presbyterian. Avocation: tennis. Administrative and regulatory, Corporate, general, Private international. Office: Hopkins & Sutter 888 16th St NW Ste 600 Washington DC 20006-4105 Address: 915 15th St NW Washington DC 20005 Office: Foley & Lardner 3000 K St NW Ste 500 Washington DC 20007

MCPHERSON, DONALD PAXTON, III, lawyer; b. Balt., Aug. 9, 1941; s. Donald Paxton Jr. and Janet Lewis Russell McPherson; m. Anna Mary Teaff; children: David Russell, Cynthia Quandt. AB, Princeton U., 1963; LLB, Columbia U., 1966. Bar: Md. 1966, U.S. Dist. Ct. Md. 1967, U.S. Ct. Appeals (4th cir.) 1967. Assoc. Piper & Marbury, Balt., 1966-74, ptnr., 1974-98, head real estate dept., 1980-94, of counsel, 1998—. Mem. ABA, Md. Bar Assn. Democrat. Presbyterian. Avocations: swimming, bicycling, hiking. Finance, Property, real (including real estate development, water). Office: Piper Rudnick LLP 6225 Smith Ave Baltimore MD 21209-3600

MC PHERSON, HARRY CUMMINGS, JR., lawyer; b. Tyler, Tex., Aug. 22, 1929; s. Harry Cummings and Nan (Hight) McP.; m. Clayton Read, Aug. 30, 1952 (div.); children: Courtenay, Peter B.; m. Mary Patricia DeGroot, Oct. 17, 1981; 1 child, Sam B. BA, U. South, 1949, DCL, 1965; student, Columbia U., 1949-50; LLB, U. Tex., 1956. Bar: Tex. 1955, D.C. 1969. Asst. gen. counsel Democratic policy com. U.S. Senate, 1956-59, asso. counsel, 1959-61, gen. counsel, 1961-63; dep. under sec. internat. affairs Dept. Army, 1963-64; asst. sec. ednl. and cultural affairs Dept. State, 1964-65; spl. asst. and counsel to Pres. Johnson, 1965-66, spl. counsel, 1966-69; pvt. practice law Washington, 1969—. Chmn. task force on domestic policy Dem. Adv. Coun. Elected Ofcls., 1974-76; mem. Pres.'s Commn. on Accident at Three Mile Island, 1979; vice chmn. John F. Kennedy Ctr. for Performing Arts, 1969-76, gen. counsel, 1977-91; bd. dirs. Woodrow Wilson Internat. Ctr. for Scholars, 1969-74; pres. Fed. City Coun., 1983-88; apptd. vice chmn. U.S. Internat. Cultural and Trade Ctr. Commn., 1988-93. Author: A Political Education, 1972, 88, 95. Mem. U.S. Base Closure and Realignment Commn., 1993. 2d lt. USAF, 1950-53. Recipient Disting. Civilian Svc. award Dept. Army, 1964, Arthur S. Flemming award, 1968, Judge Learned Hand Human Rels. award Am. Jewish Com., 1994. Mem. D.C. Bar Assn., N.Y. Council on Fgn. Relations (dir. 1974-77), Econ. Club. of Washington (pres. 1992-99). Democrat. Episcopalian. Entertainment, Legislative, Transportation. Home: 10213 Montgomery Ave Kensington MD 20895-3325 Office: 901 15th St NW Washington DC 20005-2327 E-mail: harry.mcpherson@piperrudnick.com.

MC QUADE, LAWRENCE CARROLL, lawyer, corporate executive; b. Yonkers, N.Y., Aug. 12, 1927; s. Edward A. and Thelma (Keefe) McQ.; m. de Rosset Parker Morrissey, Aug. 3, 1968 (dec. Oct. 1978); 1 child, Andrew Parker; m. Margaret Osmer, Mar. 15, 1980. BA with distinction, Yale U., 1950; BA, Oxford (Eng.) U., 1952, MA, 1956; LLB cum laude, Harvard U., 1954; MA (hon.), Colby Coll., 1981. Bar: N.Y. 1955, D.C. 1968. Assoc. Sullivan & Cromwell, N.Y.C., 1954-60; spl. asst. to asst. sec. for internat. security affairs U.S. Dept. Def., Washington, 1961-63; dep. asst. sec. U.S. Dept. Commerce, Washington, 1963-64, asst. to sec., 1965-67, asst. sec., 1967-69; pres. Procon Inc., Des Plaines, Ill., 1969-75, CEO, dir., 1969-75; v.p. Universal Oil Products Co., 1972-75, W.R. Grace & Co., N.Y.C., 1975-78, sr. v.p., 1978-83, exec. v.p., 1983-87, also bd. dirs.; vice chmn. Prudential Mut. Fund Mgmt., N.Y.C., 1988-95; mng. dir. Prudential Securities Inc., 1988-92; chmn. Qualitas Internat., 1994—. Chmn., CEO Universal Money Ctrs., 1987—88; co-chmn. River Capital Internat., 1997—; expert advisor commn. on transnat. corps. UN, 1989—93; bd. dirs. BUNZL, Quixote Corp., Oxford Analytica, Solar Outdoor Lighting, Laredo Nat. Bancshares. Author: (with others) The Ghana Report, 1959; contbr. (with others) articles to profl. jours. Bd. dirs. Fgn. Bondholders Protective Coun., N.Y.C., 1978--, The Am. Forum, 1985-96, Am. Coun. on Germany, 1985-94; trustee Colby Coll., 1981-89, trustee emeritus, 1989—; dir. Czech and Slovak Am. Enterprise Funds, 1994-96; chmn. Czech and Slovak AE Fund, 1995-96; dir. Paul and Daisy Soros Fellowships for New Ams., 1998—. Rhodes scholar Oxford U., 1952. Mem. Coun. Fgn. Rels. N.Y., Chgo. Coun. Fgn. Rels. (bd. dirs. 1969-75), Nat. Fgn. Trade Coun. (bd. dirs. 1979-87), Atlantic Coun. U.S. (bd. dirs. 1969-99), Mgmt. and Devel. Inst. (bd. dirs. 1970-99), Overseas Devel. Coun. (bd. dirs. 1974-87), Pres.'s Cir. of NAS, Harvard Club, Century Club, Met. Club (Washington), Phi Beta Kappa. E-mail: lmcquade@rivercapital.com.

MCQUARRIE, CLAUDE MONROE, III, lawyer; b. Ft. Benning, Ga., Oct. 15, 1950; s. Claude Monroe Jr. and Rosanne (Sprinkle) McQ.; children: Kevin Andrew, Ryan Christopher, Erin Elizabeth. BS, U.S. Mil. Acad., 1972; JD with distinction, St. Mary's U., San Antonio, 1978. Bar: Tex. 1978, U.S. Dist. Ct. (so. dist.) Tex. 1982, U.S. Ct. Mil. Appeals 1979. Commd. 2d lt. U.S. Army, 1972, advanced through grades to capt., 1976, resigned, 1982; assoc. Fulbright & Jaworski, Houston, 1982-89, ptnr., 1989—. Editor Law Rev., 1977-78. Mem. ABA, Houston Bar Assn., John M. Harlan Soc., Phi Delta Phi. Avocations: golf, skiing. State civil litigation, Health, Personal injury (including property damage). Home: 5610 Orchard Valley Ct Kingwood TX 77345-1920 Office: Fulbright & JaworskiLLP 1301 Mckinney St Ste 5100 Houston TX 77010-3031

MCQUISTON, JOHN WARD, II, lawyer; b. Memphis, Sept. 19, 1943; s. John Ward and Anna Vance (Hall) McQ.; m. Robbie Walker, Aug. 20, 1966; children— Anna Stewart, Katherine Walker. B.A., Rhodes Coll., Memphis, 1965; J.D., Vanderbilt U., 1968; hon. grad. U.S. Naval Justice Sch., 1969. Bar: Tenn. 1968. Ptnr., Goodman, Glazer, Greener, Schneider & McQuiston, Memphis, 1972-91, Evans & Petree, 1991-2001, Stokes, Bartholomew Evans & Petree, Memphis, 2001—; instr. constrn. contract law Memphis State U., 1982. Author: Always We Begin--The Benedictine Way of Living, 1996. Pres., Les Passes Rehab. Ctr., 1982; pres. St. Mary's Episcopal Sch., 1986, chmn. 1986-88, bd. dirs. NCCJ. Lt. comdr. USCG, 1968-72. Mem. ABA, Tenn. Bar Assn. (chmn. sect. on antitrust 1983-84) Memphis and Shelby County Bar Assn. (dir. 1987), Forum Com. on Constrn. Law, Order of Coif, Univ. Club (Memphis). Episcopalian. Avocations: golf, hiking. Federal civil litigation, Corporate, general, General. Office: Evans & Petree 81 Monroe Ave Ste 600 Memphis TN 38103-2400

MCQUISTON, ROBERT EARL, lawyer; b. Pitts., Feb. 4, 1936; s. Theodore O. and Bertha L. (Kegley) McQ.; m. Mary Hope Missimer, June 30, 1962; children: Mary Hope, Elizabeth Ann. BA magna cum laude, Yale U., 1958; JD cum laude, Harvard U., 1961. Bar: Pa. 1962. Assoc. Ballard, Spahr, Andrews & Ingersoll, LLP, Phila., Balt., Denver, Washington, Salt Lake City, 1962—69, ptnr., 1969—2001, sr. counsel, 2001—. Mem. nat. adv. group to Commr. IRS, Washington, 1985-87; lectr. in law Temple U., 1968-69, also various tax insts.; bd. dirs. Macromedia Inc., Hackensack, N.J., Gateway Communications, Inc., Binghamton, N.Y. Contbr. articles to profl. jours. Mem. Rep. Fin. Com., Harrisburg, Pa., 1983-86; trustee Am. Soc. Hypertension, 1992-98. Mem. ABA (active numerous coms. sect. taxation 1969—, including coun. mem. 1979-85, vice chmn., sec. 1982-85), Phila. Bar Assn. (bd. govs. 1978-80, mem. coun. 1969-84, sec. treas sect. on taxation 1973-75, vice chmn. 1976-78, chmn. 1978-80), Am. Coll. Tax Counsel (charter, regent 1990-98, vice chmn. 1993-94, chmn. 1994-96), Am. Tax Policy Inst. (trustee 1996-2003, pres. 2001-03), Nat. Conf. Lawyers and CPAs, Merion Cricket Club. Episcopalian. Corporate taxation, Taxation, general, Personal income taxation. Home: 1218 Round Hill Rd Bryn Mawr PA 19010-1938 Office: Ballard Spahr Andrews et al 1735 Market St Ste 5100 Philadelphia PA 19103-7599 E-mail: mcquiston@ballardspahr.com.

MCRAE, CHARLES R. (CHUCK MCCRAE), state supreme court presiding justice; BA, Marietta Coll., 1962; JD cum laude, Miss. Coll. Sch. Law, 1970. Trial atty., Pascagoula, Miss., 1970—90; spl. chancellor, cir. ct. judge Jackson, Forrest and Lincoln Counties, Miss., 1990; justice Miss. Supreme Ct, Jackson, 1991—. Mem.: ABA, Magnolia Bar Assn., Fed. Bar Assn., Am. Judicature Soc., ATLA, Miss. Trial Lawyer's Assn. (life). Office: Supreme Court Gartin Bldg PO Box 249 Jackson MS 39205

MCRAE, HAMILTON EUGENE, III, lawyer; b. Midland, Tex., Oct. 29, 1937; s. Hamilton Eugene and Adrian (Hagaman) McR.; m. Betty Hawkins, Aug. 27, 1960; children: Elizabeth Ann, Stephanie Adrian, Scott Hawkins BSEE, U. Ariz., 1961; student, USAF Electronics Sch., 1961-62; postgrad., U. Redlands, Calif., 1962-63; JD with honors and distinction, U. Ariz., 1967; LHD (hon.), Sterling Coll., 1992; vis. fellow, Darwin Coll. and Martin Ctr., Cambridge (Eng.) U., 1996-97. Bar: Ariz. 1967, U.S. Supreme Ct. 1979; cert. real estate specialist, Ariz. Elec. engr. Salt River Project, Phoenix, 1961; assoc. Jennings, Strouss & Salmon, Phoenix, 1967-71, ptnr., 1971-85, chmn. real estate dept., 1980-85, mem. policy com., 1982-85, mem. fin. com., 1981-85, chmn. bus. devel. com., 1982-85; ptnr. and co-founder Stuckey & McRae, Phoenix, 1985—; co-founder, chmn. bd. Republic Cos., Phoenix, 1985—. Magistrate Paradise Valley, Ariz., 1983-85; juvenile referee Superior Ct., 1983-85; pres., dir. Phoenix Realty & Trust Co., 1970—; officer Indsl. Devel. Corp. Maricopa County, 1972-86; instr. and lectr. in real estate; officer, bd. dirs. other corps.; adj. prof. Frank Lloyd Wright Sch. Architecture, Scottsdale, Ariz., 1989—; instr. Ariz. State U. Coll. Architecture and Environ. Design; lead instr. ten-state-bar seminar on Advanced Real Estate Transactions, 1992; evaluation com. for cert. real estate specialist Ariz. Bar, 1994-96; mem. real estate adv. commn. Ariz. Bar, 1996—. Author: Development in Third World Countries, 2002; exec. prodr. film documentary on relief and devel. in Africa, 1990; contbr. articles to profl. jours. Elder Valley Presbyn. Ch., Scottsdale, Ariz., 1973-75, 82-85, 96-98, chair evangelism com. 1973-74, corp. pres., 1974-75, 84-85, trustee, 1973-75, 82-85, chmn. exec. com., 1984, mem. mission com. 1993—, chmn. 1998; trustee Upward Found., Phoenix, 1977-80, trustee, Valley Presbyn. Found., 1982-83, Ariz. Acad., 1971—; trustee, mem. exec. com. Phi Gamma Delta Ednl. Found., Washington, 1974-84; trustee Phi Gamma Delta Internat., 1984-86; bd. dirs. Archon, 1986-87, Hall of Fame Ariz., 1999; founder, trustee, pres. McRae Found., 1980—; bd. dirs. Food for Hungry Inc. (Internat. Relief), 1985-95, exec. com., 1986-95, chmn. bd. dirs., 1987-92; chmn. bd. dirs. Food for Hungry Internat., 1993-95, pres. adv. coun., 1995—, mem. building com., 1999—; trustee, mem. exec. com. Ariz. Mus. Sci. and Tech., 1984—, 1st v.p., 1985-86, pres., 1986-88, chmn. bd. dirs., 1988-90, exec. com. 1984-90, exhibits com. 1990—, strategic planning com., 1999—, svc. recognition 1999; Lambda Alpha Internat. Hon. Land Econs. Soc, 1988-98; sec.-treas. Ariz. State U. Coun. for Design Excellence, 1989-90, bd. dirs. 1988-99, pres. 1990-91, trustee 1999—; mem. Crisis Nursery Office of the Chair, 1988-89, Maricopa Community Colls. Found., 1988—, sec. 1990-91, 2d v.p. 1993-94, 1st v.p. and pres. elect 1994-95, pres. 1995-96, mem. Elsner scholarship com., 1999—, web site com., 1999, capital campaign cabinet, 1995-96, 98-99, mem. of chair, 1998-99, mem. nominating com., 1997—, deferred gifts com., 1999—, strategic planning com., 2000—, mem. adv. bd., 2002--; mem. Phoenix Cmty. Alliance, 1988-90, Interchurch Ctr. Corp., 1987-90, Western Art Assocs., bd. dirs., 1989-91, Phoenix Com. on Fgn. Rels., 1988-99, U. Ariz. Pres.'s Club, 1984—, chmn., 1991-92; bd. dirs. Econ. Club of Phoenix, 1987— , sec.-treas., 1991-92, v.p., 1992-93, pres. 1993-94; bd. dirs. Ctrl. Ariz. Shelter Svcs., 1995—, bd. dir., Ariz. Community Found., 1996—, invest. com., 1996—, chair, 2000-, exec. com. 1997—, treas. 1997—, chair nominating com. 1997-98, vice chair bd. dirs., 1999—, chair devel. com., 1999—, advancement com., 1999-2000, chair, 1999—, fin. and adminstrn. com. 1999—; founding mem. Alliance linking poverty and homelessness, 1996-98, bd. dirs., 1996-98, mem. exec. com., 1996-98, co-chair long range planning com., 1997-98; mem. adv. bd. Help Wanted USA, 1990-92; vol. fund raiser YMCA, Salvation Army, others; bd. dirs. Frank Lloyd Wright Found., 1992—, chair fin. com. 1997-98, chmn. bd. dirs., 1998—; mem. Taliesin Coun., 1985—; bd. dirs. Taliesin Arch., 1992-98, Taliesin Conservation Com. (Wis.), 1992—; founding mem. Frank Lloyd Wright Soc., 1993—; mem. fin. com. Kyl for Congress, 1985-92, bd. dir. campaign bd. Kyl for U.S. Senate, 1993-94, 99—; Senator Kyl Council, 1995-98; campaign com. Symington for Gov. '90, 1989-90, mem. gubernatorial adv. bd., 1990-91; mem. Gov.'s Selection Com. for State Revenue Dir., 1993; mem. bond com. City of Phoenix, 1987-88; mem. Ariz. State U. Coun. of 100, 1985-89, investment com., 1985-89; bd. govs. Twelve Who Care Hon Kachina, 1991; mem. adv. coun. Maricopa County Sports Authority, 1989-93; mem. Ariz. Coalition for Tomorrow, 1990-92; founding mem., bd. dirs. Waste Not Inc., 1990-94, pres., 1990-92, chmn., 1992-94, adv. bd. 1996—; bd. dirs. Garden Homes at Teton Pines Home Owners Assn., 1996—; selected as bearer for the Olympic Torch Relay Team, 1996; adv. bd. KAET TV PBS (Channel 8) 1999-2000. 1st lt. USAF, 1961-64. Recipient various mil. awards; 1st place award Ariz. Bar exam, 1967; named to Ariz. Hall of Fame, 1999. Mem. ABA, AIEE, AIME, Ariz. Bar Assn., Maricopa County Bar Assn., U. Ariz. Alumni Assn., Nat. Soc. Fund Raising Execs. (Philanthropy award Ariz. chpt. 1991, 97), Clan McRae Soc. N.Am. Phoenix Exec. Club, Internat. Platform Assn., Am. Friends of the U. Cambridge (Eng.), Jackson Hole Racquet Club, Teton Pines Country Club, Tau Beta Pi. Republican. General civil litigation, Corporate, general, Taxation, general. Address: Republic Cos 11811 N Tatum Blvd Ste 1005 Phoenix AZ 85028-1617 E-mail: repcos@aol.com.

MCRAE, ROBERT MALCOLM, JR., federal judge; b. Memphis, Dec. 31, 1921; s. Robert Malcolm and Irene (Pontius) McR.; m. Louise Howry, July 31, 1943; children: Susan Campbell, Robert Malcolm III, Duncan Farquhar, Thomas Alexander Todd. BA, Vanderbilt U., 1943; LLB, U. Va., 1948. Bar: Tenn. 1948. Practice in, Memphis, 1948-64; judge Tenn. Circuit Ct., 1964-66, U.S. Dist. Ct. (we. dist.) Tenn., Memphis, 1966-94, chief judge, 1979-86, sr. judge, 1987-94, inactive sr. judge, 1995—; mem. Jud. Council 6th Cir., 1982-85, Jud. Conf. Commn. Adminstrn. Criminal Law, 1979-86, Jud. Conf. U.S., 1984-87; ret. (sr. status), 2001—. Pub.: Oral History of the Desegregation of the Memphis City Schools (1954-74), 1997. Pres. Episcopal Ch. men of Tenn., 1964-65. Mem. Dist. Judges Assn. 6th Circuit (pres.). Home: 1914 Poplar Ave Apt 10/06 Memphis TN 38104

MCRAE, STEPHANIE A. lawyer; d. Hamilton E. and Betty McRae; m. Todd W. Campbell. BA magna cum laude, hons. in psychology, Vanderbilt U., Nashville, Tenn., 1989; JD cum laude, Ariz. State U., Tempe, Ariz., 1993. Bar: Ariz., Calif. Assoc. systems engr. Bridgestone Software USA, Torrance, Calif., 1989—90; assoc. Jennings, Strouss & Salmon, P.L.C., Phoenix, 1993—2000, ptnr., 2002—; spl. counsel Heller Ehrman White & McAuliffe, Menlo Park, CA, Calif., 2000—02. Chmn. biotech and life sci. practice group Jennings, Strouss & Salmon PLSC, Phoenix. Corporate, general, Securities, Mergers and acquisitions, Licensing. Office: Jennings Strouss & Salmon PLC 201 E Washington St 11th Fl Phoenix AZ 85004 E-mail: smcrae@jsslaw.com.

MCREYNOLDS, MARY ARMILDA, lawyer; b. Carthage, Mo., Sept. 2, 1946; d. Allen and Virginia Madeliene (Hensley) McR. BA, Mt. Holyoke Coll., 1968; JD, Georgetown U., 1971; LLM, Harvard U., 1973. Bar: D.C. 1971, U.S. Ct. Appeals (D.C. cir.) 1971, U.S. Ct. Appeals (2d cir.) 1975, U.S. Ct. Appeals (4th cir.) 1979, U.S. Ct. Appeals (1st, 5th, 6th, 9th 10th cirs.) 1980, U.S. Supreme Ct. 1980, U.S. Ct. Appeals (11th cir.) 1981, U.S. Ct. Appeals (3rd, 7th, 8th cirs.) 1983, U.S. Ct. Appeals (fed. cir.) 1988. Law clk. U.S. Ct. Appeals for D.C. cir., 1971-72; assoc. Wilmer, Cutler & Pickering, Washington, 1973-77; sr. trial atty. civil divsn. fed. program br. U.S. Dept. Justice, 1977-79, mem. appellate staff, 1979-81; ptnr. McReynolds & Mutterperl, Washington, 1981-83, Wilner & Scheiner, Washington, 1983-89, Haley, Bader & Potts, 1989-92; prin. Law Offices of Mary A. McReynolds, P.C., 1992—. Gen. counsel Anchor Ednl. Found., 2002-; bd. dirs., gen. counsel Washington Bach Consort, 1977-81, 1985-92, pres. 1981-82, 89-90; pres. bd. dirs., ArtsAm., 1993—. Contbr. articles to profl. jours. Mem. ABA, Kenwood Club, City Tavern Club. Episcopalian. Administrative and regulatory, Federal civil litigation, Communications. Home: 2101 Connecticut Ave NW Apt 26 Washington DC 20008-1754 Office: Ste 300 1701 Pennsylvania Ave NW Washington DC 20006 E-mail: marymcreynolds@aol.com.

MCREYNOLDS, STEPHEN PAUL, lawyer; b. Sacramento, Oct. 16, 1938; s. Leslie N. and Mary C. McR.; m. Chodi D. Greeno, Sept. 29, 1970. AB, U. Calif., Davis, 1969; JD, U. Calif., 1972. Bar: Calif. 1972. Sole practice, Sunnyvale, Calif., 1972—. Served with U.S. Navy, 1956-62. Mem. Mensa Internat. General practice. Office: 1111 W El Camino Real # 329 Sunnyvale CA 94087-1056

MCSLOY, STEVEN PAUL, lawyer; b. Syosset, N.Y., June 12, 1964; s. Paul Thomas and Emilie Helen (Winter) McS.; m. Alison Jane Rooney, Oct. 26, 1991; 1 child, Maeve Rooney. BA magna cum laude, NYU, 1985; JD cum laude, Harvard U., 1988. Bar: N.Y. 1989. Atty. Cravath, Swaine & Moore, LLP, N.Y.C., 1988-91, 98—; prof. St. John's Law Sch., Queens, N.Y., 1991-95; gen. counsel Oneida Indian Nation, Oneida, N.Y., 1995-98. Lectr. BAR/BRI Bar Rev., N.Y.C., 1991-97; adj. prof. law Syracuse (N.Y.) Law Sch., 1995-98, NYU Law Sch., 1993-95, Cardozo Law Sch., N.Y.C., 1990, 93-95. Contbr. articles to law revs. Corporate, general, Finance, Native American. Office: Cravath Swaine & Moore LLP Worldwide Plz 825 8th Ave New York NY 10019-7475

MC SWAIN, ANGUS STEWART, JR., retired law educator; b. Bryan, Tex., Nov. 26, 1923; s. Angus Stewart and Lois (Pipkin) McS.; m. Betty Ann McCartney, June 3, 1956; 1 child, Angus Earl. BS in Civil Engring., Tex. A. and M. U., 1947; LLB, Baylor U., 1949; LL.M., U. Mich., 1951. Bar: Tex. 1949. Mem. faculty Baylor U. Law Sch., 1949—, prof. law, 1956—, dean, 1965-84, ret., 1994. Mem. panel arbitrators Fe. Mediation and Conciliation Service. Author: (with Wendorf) Cases and Materials on Texas Trusts and Probate, 1965, Supplementary Cases and Materials on Property, 1965, 78, (with Norvell and Simpkins) Cases and Materials for Texas Land Practice, 1968. Served to 1st lt., C.E. AUS, 1943-46. Mem. ABA, Tex.Bar Assn. (chmn. family law sect. 1967-69, chmn. com. on standards of admission 1972-73, 77-79), Tau Beta Pi, Phi Alpha Delta Home: 4600 Kenny Ln Waco TX 76710-2059

MCTURNAN, LEE BOWES, lawyer; b. N.Y.C., Sept. 13, 1937; s. Lee M. and Alice (Light) McT.; m. Susan Cassady, Aug. 2, 1969; children: John M., Sarah D. AB magna cum laude, Harvard U., 1959; diploma in law, Oxford (Eng.) U., 1961; JD, U. Chgo., 1963. Bar: Ill. 1965, U.S. Dist. Ct. (no. dist.) Ill. 1965, U.S. Ct. Appeals (7th cir.) 1966, U.S. Supreme Ct. 1969, Ind. 1978, U.S. Dist. Ct. (so. dist.) Ind. 1978, U.S. Dist. Ct. (no. dist.) Ind. 1987. Law clk. to hon. justice U.S. Supreme Ct., Washington, 1963-64; assoc. Sidley & Austin, Chgo., 1964-69, ptnr., 1970-78, Hackman, McClarnon & McTurnan, Indpls., 1978-88, McTurnan & Turner, Indpls., 1989—. Assoc. spl. counsel procs. on chief justice R.I. Commn. Jud. Tenure and Discipline, Providence, 1985; mem. Local Rules Adv. Com. for So. Dist. Ind., 1995-2000. Adminstrv. bd. Meridian St. United Meth. Ch., 1987-90. Mem. ABA, Ind. Bar Assn., Ill. Bar Assn., Indpls. Bar Assn., 7th Cir. Bar Assn., Law Club of Indpls. (pres. 1988-90), Legal Club of Chgo., Columbia Club, Woodstock Club, Lit. Club, Rotary. Republican. Avocations: running, reading, gardening. Antitrust, Federal civil litigation, General civil litigation. Home: 9907 Summerlakes Dr Carmel IN 46032 Office: McTurnan & Turner 2400 Market Tower 10 W Market St Indianapolis IN 46204-2954

MCVEY, HENRY HANNA, III, retired lawyer; b. Richmond, Va., Aug. 12, 1935; s. Henry Hanna Jr. and Eva Lawson (Jennings) McVey; m. Reba Jean Robinson, Dec. 12, 1964; children: Margaret Anne McVey Singleton, Lewis Lawson, Ian Douglas. BS, BA magna cum laude, Hampden-Sydney Coll., 1957; LLB, U. Va., 1960. Bar: Va. 1960, U.S. Dist. Ct. (ea. dist.) Va. 1960, U.S. Ct. Appeals (4th cir.) 1965, U.S. Supreme Ct. 1970. Assoc. Battle, Neal, Harris, Minor & Williams, Richmond, 1960-66; ptnr. McGuireWoods LLP and predecessor firms, Richmond, 1966-99; ret., 1999. Mem. adv. group under Civil Justice Reform Act of 1990 U.S. Dist. Ct. (ea. dist.) Va. Trustee Hampden-Sydney Coll., 1989—94, 1995—, vice chair, 2001—03, chair bd. trustees, 2003—; mem. Commn. on Archtl. Rev. City of Richmond, 1985—95; mem. Planning Commn. Gloucester County, 2001—; bd. dirs. Richmond Symphony, 1977—78, 1987—99, v.p., 1979—81, exec. v.p., 1981—83, pres., 1983—85, chmn. bd. dirs., 1985—87, pres. Symphony Coun., 1999—; bd. dirs. Carpenter Ctr. for Performing Arts, 1982—89, Rosewell Found., 1999—, pres., 2001—02, v.p., 2002—03. Recipient Algernon Sydney Sullivan medallion for svc. to coll., Hampden Sydney Coll., 2001. Fellow: Am. Bar Found., Am. Coll. Trial Lawyers; mem.: ABA, Va. Bar Assn., Bar Assn. City of Richmond, Fedn. Defense and Corp. Counsel, Def. Rsch. and Trial Lawyers Assn. (past state chmn., regional v.p. 1985—87, bd. dirs. 1987—90), Va. Assn. Def. Attys. (v.p. 1981—83, treas. 1983—84, pres.-elect 1984—85, pres. 1985—86), Ware River Yacht Club (bd. dirs. 2000—). Presbyterian. General civil litigation, Insurance, Legislative. Home: PO Box 43 Schley VA 23154-0043 E-mail: mcvey@rivnet.net.

MCVISK, WILLIAM KILBURN, lawyer; b. Chgo., Oct. 8, 1953; s. Felix Kilburn and June (DePear) Visk; m. Marlaine Joyce McDonough, June 20, 1975. BA, U. Ill, 1974; JD, Northwestern U., 1977. Bar: Ill. 1977, Ind. 1999, U.S. Dist. Ct. (no. dist.) Ill. 1977, U.S. Ct. Appeals (7th cir.) 1978, U.S. Dist. Ct. (no. and so. dists.) Ind. 1999, U.S. Ct. Appeals (10th cir.) 2001. Assoc. Jerome H. Torshen, Ltd., Chgo., 1977-80, Silets & Martin, Chgo., 1980-81, Peterson & Ross, Chgo., 1981-85, ptnr., 1985-95, Johnson & Bell Ltd., Chgo., 1995—. Contbr. articles to profl. jours. Mem.: ABA, Ill. Assn. Def. Trial Lawyers (chmn. ins. coverage com.), Ill. Assn. Hosp. Attys. (pres., bd. dirs.), Am. Health Lawyers Assn., Def. Rsch. Inst., Chgo. Bar Assn. Health, Insurance, General civil litigation. Office: Johnson & Bell 55 E Monroe St Fl 41 Chicago IL 60603-5713 E-mail: mcviskw@jbltd.com.

MCWHERTER, LOUIS ALFRED, lawyer; b. East St. Louis, Ill., Nov. 17, 1943; s. James Washington and Artie Marie (Johnson) McW.; divorced; 1 child: JeTaime. BS, So. Ill. U., 1969; JD, Tex. So. U., 1976. Bar: Tex. 1976, Ill. 1991, U.S. Supreme Ct. 1980. Tchr. Sch. Dist. 189, East St. Louis, 1970-71; relocation agt. Ill. Dept. Transp., East St. Louis, 1970-73; instr. Tex. So. U., Houston, 1974-76; case worker Tex. Dept. Human Resources, Houston, 1976-80; instr. Houston C.C., 1978-81; atty. in pvt. practice Houston, 1976—, 1991—. Mem. adv. bd. Houston C.C., 1981-83. With U.S. Army, 1966-68. Mem. Phi Alpha Delta. Democrat. Baptist. Avocation: music. Criminal, Personal injury (including property damage), Probate (including wills, trusts). Office: 723 Main St Ste 510 Houston TX 77002-3308 Home: 3015 S Braeswood Houston TX 77025

MCWHIRTER, BRUCE J. lawyer; b. Chgo., Sept. 11, 1931; s. Sydney and Martha McWhirter; m. Judith Hallett, Apr. 14, 1960; children: Cameron, Andrew. BS, Northwestern U., 1952; LLB, Harvard U., 1955. Bar: DC 1955, Ill 1955, US Ct Appeals (7th cir) 1963, US Supreme Ct. Assoc. Lord, Bissell & Brook, Chgo., 1958-62; from assoc. to sr. ptnr. Ross & Hardies, Chgo., 1962-95, of counsel, 1996—. Editor: Donnelley SEC Handbook, 1972—87; contbr. articles to profl jours. With U.S. Army, 1955—57. Mem.: ABA, Harvard Law Soc Ill., Chgo. Bar Assn., Harvard Club (N.Y.C.), Lawyers Club Chgo., Phi Beta Kappa. Democrat. Home: 111 Sheridan Rd Winnetka IL 60093-4223 Office: Ross & Hardies 150 N Michigan Ave Ste 2500 Chicago IL 60601-7567 E-mail: jbmcw@aol.com.

MCWHORTER, HOBART AMORY, JR., lawyer; b. Birmingham, Ala., Dec. 24, 1931; s. Hobart Amory and Marjorie (Westgate) McW.; remarried Feb. 1, 1997; children: Margaret G., Marjorie W. BA, Yale U., 1953; LLB, U. Va., 1958. Bar: Ala. 1958. Ptnr. Bradley Arant Rose & White, Birmingham, 1958—. 1st lt. U.S. Army, 1953-55. Fellow Am. Coll. Trial Lawyers; mem. Internat. Assn. Ins. Counsel, Nat. Assn. r.R. Counsel. Republican. Presbyterian. General civil litigation, Personal injury (including property damage), Securities. Office: Bradley Arant Rose & White One Federal Pl 1819 Fifth Ave N Birmingham AL 35203-2104

MCWILLIAMS, JOHN MICHAEL, lawyer; b. Annapolis, Md., Aug. 17, 1939; s. William J. and Helen (Disharon) McW.; m. Frances Edelen McCabe, May 30, 1970; children: M. Edelen, J. Michael Jr., James McC. BS, Georgetown U., 1964; LL.B., U. Md., 1967; LLD (hon.), U. Balt., 1993. Bar: Md. 1967, U.S. Supreme Ct. 1970, U.S. Ct. Internat. Trade 1991, U.S. Ct. Mil. Appeals 1992; cert. mediator NASD. Law clk. Chief Judge Roszel C. Thomsen, U.S. Dist. Ct. Md., 1967-68; assoc. Piper and Marbury, Balt., 1968-69; asst. atty. gen. State of Md., 1969-76; gen. counsel Md. Dept. Transp., 1971-76; sr. ptnr. Tydings and Rosenberg, Balt., 1977-97; pres. McWilliams Dispute Resolution, Balt., 1997—. Permanent mem. 4th Jud. Conf.; mem. panel of disting. neutrals CPR Inst. for Dispute Resolution, 1994—2001; mem. Md. Alt. Dispute Resolution Commn., 1994—2002. Asst. editor Law Rev., U. Md., 1967; mem. nat. bd. advisors Ohio State Jour. Dispute Resolution. Chmn. Md. adv. coun. to Nat. Legal Svcs. Corp., 1975-78; mem. Gov.'s Commn. to Revise Annotated Code of Md., 1973-78; transition dir. Md. Gov.-Elect Harry Hughes, 1978-79; mem. Md. Indsl. Devel. Financing Authority, 1980; mem. Greater Balt. Com., 1979-94; mem. exec. com. Econ. Devel. Coun. Greater Balt., 1979-83; vice chmn. bd. Washington/Balt. Regional Assn., 1980-83; mem. Md. Econ. and Cmty. Devel. Adv. Commn., 1983-87; chmn. bd. Md. Econ. Devel. Corp., 1984-89. Served to 1st lt. U.S. Army, 1958-60. Fellow Am. Bar Found. (bd. dirs. 1986-88, 91-93), Internat. Acad. Mediators (v.p. 1998—), Coll. Comml. Arbitrators (sec. 2000, v.p. 2002—), Md. Bar Found. (dir. 1980-82); mem. ABA (pres. 1992-93, mem. ho. of dels. 1976—, chmn. 1986-88, chmn. Md. del. 1976-86, bd. editors jour. 1986-88, 91-93) Md. Bar Assn. (pres. 1981-82), Nat. Conf. Bar Pres. (exec. council 1982-85), Bar Assn. Balt. City, Am. Law Inst., Am. Judicature Soc. (dir. 1974-81, exec. com. 1975-77), Am. Acad. Judicature Edn. (dir. 1977), Md. Law Rev. (trustee 1980-83), Md. Inst. Continuing Edn. Lawyers (trustee 1980-83), Inst. Internat. Bus. Law and Practice (corr.), Md. Club, Rule Day Club. Democrat. Roman Catholic. Alternative dispute resolution. Home: 3 Merryman Ct Baltimore MD 21210-2815 Office: 1106 N Charles St Ste 300 Baltimore MD 21201

MCWILLIAMS, MIKE C. lawyer; b. Dallas, Nov. 10, 1948; s. Earl Dewitt and Mary Louise (Campbell) McW.; m. Sally Swatzell, Sept. 1, 1973; children: Michael, Matthew. BBA in Fin., U. Tex., 1969, JD, 1973. Bar: Tex. 1973. Assoc. Elliott, Meer, Vetter, Denton & Bates, Dallas, 1973-78; ptnr. Denton & Generis, Dallas, 1978-80, Moore & Peterson, P.C., Dallas, 1980-89, Winstead, Sechrest & Minick, Dallas, 1989—. Editor: Texas International Law Journal, 1972-73. Mem. Tex. State Bar Assn., Dallas Bar Assn., Phi Delta Phi, Beta Gamma Sigma. Property, real (including real estate development, water). Office: Winstead Sechrest & Minick 5400 Renaissance Tower 1201 Elm St Ste 5400 Dallas TX 75270-2199

MCWILLIAMS, ROBERT HUGH, federal judge; b. Salina, Kans., Apr. 27, 1916; s. Robert Hugh and Laura (Nicholson) McW.; m. Catherine Ann Cooper, Nov. 4, 1942 (dec.); 1 son, Edward Cooper; m. Joan Harcourt, Mar. 8, 1986. AB, U. Denver, 1938, LL.B., 1941. Bar: Colo. bar 1941. Colo. dist. judge, Denver, 1952-60; justice Colo. Supreme Ct., 1961-68, chief justice, 1969-70; judge U.S. Ct. Appeals (10th cir.), Denver, 1970—, now sr. judge. Served with AUS, World War II. Mem. Phi Beta Kappa, Omicron Delta Kappa, Phi Delta Phi, Kappa Sigma. Republican. Episcopalian. Home: 137 Jersey St Denver CO 80220-5918 Office: Byron White US Courthouse 1823 Stout St Rm 216 Denver CO 80257-1823

MEAD, MATTHEW HANSEN, prosecutor; Graduate, Trinity U., U. Wyo. Sch. Law. Deputy Co. Atty. Cambell Co. Atty Office , Wyo., 1987—90; Asst. US Atty. and Special Asst. US Atty. Dist. of Wyo., 1991—95; ind. practice, 1995—97; ptnr. Mead and Phillips, 1997—2001; US Atty. Dist. of Wyo., 2001—. Office: US Attorney 2120 Capitol Rm 4002 Cheyenne WY 82001

MEADER, JOHN DANIEL, judge; b. Ballston Spa, N.Y., Oct. 22, 1931; s. Jerome Clement and Doris Luella (Conner) M.; m. Joyce Margaret Cowin, Mar. 2, 1963; children: John Daniel Jr., Julia Rae, Keith Alan. BA, Yale U., 1954; JD, Cornell U., 1962. Bar: N.Y. 1963, U.S. Dist. Ct. (no. dist.) N.Y. 1963, U.S. Ct. Appeals (2d cir.) 1966, U.S. Supreme Ct. 1967, U.S. Ct. Mil. Appeals 1973, Ohio 1978, U.S. Dist. Ct. (no. dist.) Ohio 1979, Fla. 1983, U.S. Ct. Appeals (4th cir.) 1992, U.S. Ct. Appeals (fed. cir.) 1993. Sales engr. Albany (N.Y.) Internat. Corp., 1954-59; asst. track coach Cornell U., 1959-62; asst. sec., asst. to pres. Albany Internat. Corp., 1962-65; asst. atty. gen. State of N.Y., Albany, 1965-68; ops. counsel, attesting sec. GE, Schenectady, 1968-77; gen. counsel, asst. sec. Glidden div. SCM Corp., Cleve., 1977-81; chmn. bd., pres. Applied Power Tech. Co., Fernandina Beach, Fla., 1981-84; pres. Applied Energy, Inc., Ballston Spa, 1984-88; judge N.Y. State Workers Compensation Bd., Albany, 1988—. Dir. Saratoga Mut. Fire Ins. Co. Author: Labor Law Manual, 1972, Contract Law Manual, 1974, Patent Law Manual, 1978. Candidate U.S. Ho. of Reps., 29th Dist. N.Y., 1964, N.Y. Supreme Ct., 1975, 87, 93. Brig. gen. JAGC, USAR, 1968-1984, dep. staff judge adv. 3d U.S. Army & Ctrl. Command, 1984, col. JAGC and Fin. Corps, N.Y. Guard, 1984-2002, state staff judge adv. and state comptr. Nat. AAU High Sch. 1000 Yard Indoor Track Champion, 1949, Nat. AAU Prep. Sch. 440 and 880 Yard Indoor Track Champion, 1950, Nat. AAU Outstanding Performer award, Melrose Games Assn., 1950, Heptagonal Track 880-Yard Champion 1954. Mem. ABA, N.Y. State Bar Assn., Fla. Bar, Amelia Island Plantation Club, Cyprus Temple Club, Yale Club Jacksonville (pres.), Masons. Republican. Presbyterian. Home: 271 Round Lake Rd Ballston Lake NY 12019-1714 Office: NY State Workers Compensation Bd 100 Broadway Albany NY 12241-0001 E-mail: john.meader@wcb.state.ny.us.

MEADOR, DANIEL JOHN, law educator; b. Selma, Ala., Dec. 7, 1926; s. Daniel John and Mabel (Kirkpatrick) M.; m. Janet Caroline Heilmann, Nov. 19, 1955; children: Janet Barrie, Anna Kirkpatrick, Daniel John. BS, Auburn U., 1949; JD, U. Ala., 1951; LLM, Harvard U., 1954; LLD (hon.), U. S.C., 1998. Bar: Ala. 1951, Va. 1961. Law clk. to Justice Hugo L. Black U.S. Supreme Ct., 1954-55; assoc. firm Lange, Simpson, Robinson & Somerville, Birmingham, Ala., 1955-57; faculty U. Va. Law Sch., Charlottesville, 1957-66, prof. law, 1961-66; prof., dean U. Ala. Law Sch., 1966-70; James Monroe prof. law U. Va., Charlottesville, 1970-94, prof. emeritus, 1994—; asst. atty. gen. U.S., 1977-79; dir. grad. program for judges, 1979-95. Fulbright lectr., U.K., 1965-66; vis. prof. U.S. Mil. Acad., 1984; chmn. Southeastern Conf. Assn. Am. Law Schs., 1964-65; chmn. Cts. Task Force Nat. Adv. Commn. on Criminal Justice, 1971-72; dir. appellate justice project Nat. Ctr. for State Cts., 1972-74; mem. Adv. Coun. on Appellate Justice, 1971-75, Coun. on Role of Cts., 1978-84; bd. dirs. State Justice Inst., 1986-92; exec. dir. commn. on structural alternatives Fed. Ct. Appeals, 1998-99. Author: Preludes to Gideon, 1967, Criminal Appeals-English Practices and American Reforms, 1973, Mr. Justice Black and His Books, 1974, Appellate Courts: Staff and Process in the Crisis of Volume, 1974, (with Carrington and Rosenberg) Justice on Appeal, 1976, Impressions of Law in East Germany, 1986, American Courts, 1991, 2000 (with J. Bernstein) Appellate Courts in the United States, 1994, His Father's House, 1994, Unforgotten, 1999, (with Rosenberg and Carrington) Appellate Courts: Structures, Functions, Processes, and Personnel, 1994; editor: Hardy Cross Dillard: Writings and Speeches, 1995; editor Va. Bar News, 1962-65; contbr. articles to profl. jours. 1st lt. U.S. Army, 1951-53; col. JAGC, USAR ret. Decorated Bronze Star.; IREX fellow German Dem. Republic, 1983 Mem. ABA (chmn. standing com. on fed. jud. improvements 1987-90), Ala. Bar Assn., Va. Bar Assn. (exec. com. 1983-86), Am. Law Inst., Am. Judicature Soc. (bd. dirs. 1975-77, 80-83), Soc. Pub. Tchrs. Law, Am. Soc. Legal History (bd. dirs. 1968-71), Order of Coif, Raven Soc., Phi Delta Phi, Omicron Delta Kappa, Kappa Alpha. Presbyterian. Office: U Va Sch Law 580 Massie Rd Charlottesville VA 22903-1738

MEADOWS, JOHN FREDERICK, lawyer; b. Manila, Mar. 7, 1926; s. Grover Cleveland and Millie M.; m. Karen Lee Morris, Nov. 17, 1962; children: Ian Joseph, Marie Irene. AA, U. Mich., 1944; BA (Freshman Alumni Scholar, 1943), U. Calif., Berkeley, 1948; LLB, Boalt Hall, 1951. Bar: Calif 1952, U.S. Dist. Ct. (no. dist.) Calif. 1952, U.S. Ct. Apls. (9th cir.) 1952, U.S. Sup. Ct. 1958. Assoc. Wallace, Garrison, Norton & Ray, San Francisco, 1952-56; atty. advisor Maritime Adminstrn, U.S. Dept. Commerce, Washington, 1956; trial atty., Admiralty and Shipping Sect. U.S. Dept Justice, West Coast Office, San Francisco, 1956-64, atty. in charge, 1964-72; sr. resident ptnr. Acret & Perrochet, San Francisco, 1972-76; sr. ptnr. Meadows, Smith, Lenker, Sterling & Davis, San Francisco, 1976-93, Long Beach, Calif., 1976-93, Seattle, 1976-93; mng. ptnr. west coast Kirlin, Campbell, Meadows & Keating, N.Y.C., 1993; ptnr. Jedeikin Meadows & Schneider, San Francisco, 1994. Cons. maritime law, UN; lectr. seminar Taipei, Taiwan, 1968. Author: Preparing a Ship Collision Case for Trial, 1970, Ship Collision Cases: Technical and Legal Aspects; Investigation and Preparation for Suit, 1997, contbr. articles to legal publs.; assoc. editor: Am. Maritime Cases. Lt. M.I. AUS, 1944-46. Mem. ABA, Maritime Law Assn., San Francisco Bar Assn. Republican. Roman Catholic. Admiralty, Federal civil litigation, Insurance. Home: 205 The Uplands Berkeley CA 94705-2818 Office: 333 Pine St 5th Floor San Francisco CA 94104-1958 Fax: 415-421-5658. E-mail: jmeadows@jmslex.com.

MEADOWS, JUDITH ADAMS, law librarian, educator; b. Spartanburg, SC, June 5, 1945; d. Thomas Taylor and Virginia (Dayton) Adams; m. Bruce R. Meadows; children: Beth Ann Blackwood, Ted Adams Meadows. BA, Am. U., 1967; MLS, U. Md., 1979. Law libr. Aspen Sys. Corp., Gaithersburg, Md., 1979-81; dir. Fairfax (Va.) Law Libr., 1981-84, State Law Libr., Helena, Mont., 1984—. Vis. prof. U. Wash., Seattle, 1994; adj. prof. U. Great Falls, Mont., 1989-96; presiding ofcl. Gov.'s Conf. on Libr. Info. Svc., Helena, Mont., 1991. Author: (book chpts.) From Yellow Pads to Computers, 1991, Law Librarianship, 1994; contbr. articles to profl. jours. Bd. dirs. Helena Presents, 1986-92, Holter Mus. Art, 1995-2002, Mont. Supreme Ct. Commn. on Tech., Mont. Supreme Ct. Commn. on Self-Represented Litigants, Mont. Equal Justice Task Force, 2001—, Helena Edn. Found., v.p., 2003. Recipient Disting. Svc. award State Bar of Mont., 1991. Mem. Am. Assn. Law Librs. (treas. 1992-95, v.p. 1996—, pres. 1997-98, past pres. 1998—), N.W. Consortium of Law Librs. (pres.), Mont. Libr. Assn. (sec. 1986-88). Avocations: gourmet cooking, cross-country skiing, reading, gardening. Office: State Law Libr Mont PO Box 203004 Helena MT 59620-3004

MEAGLEY, JAMES GORDON, lawyer; b. Cobleskill, N.Y., Oct. 20, 1952; s. Gordon Hugh Meagley and Hilda June Van Dusen; m. Natalie A. Hess, May 30, 1987. BS cum laude, St. Lawrence U., Canton, N.Y., 1974; JD cum laude, U. Miami, 1981. Bar: N.Y. 1982. Import specialist U.S. Customs Svcs., Buffalo, 1974—77, Miami, 1977—79; assoc. Phillips, Lytle, Buffalo, 1981—88, ptnr., 1989—97, spl. counsel, 1998—99; sr. counsel Hodgson, Russ LLP, Buffalo, 1999—2002, ptnr., 2003—. Mem.: World Trade Assn. (dir. Buffalo chpt. 1984—86), Am. Immigration Lawyers Assn. (sec. upstate N.Y. chpt. 1988), Park Country Club. Republican. Methodist. Avocations: golf, baseball memorabilia collecting, genealogy. Immigration, naturalization, and customs. Home: 53 Gaslight Trail Williamsville NY 14221 Office: Hodgson Russ LLP One M&T Plaz Ste 2000 Buffalo NY 14203 E-mail: jmeagley@hodgsonruss.com.

MEANS, ELIZABETH ROSE THAYER, financial consultant, writer, lawyer; b. N.Y.C., Aug. 29, 1960; d. Cyril Chesnut and Rosaline (Limtiuco y Sy) M. Student, Sch. of Am. Ballet-Lincoln Ctr, N.Y.C., 1970-75, Harvard Coll., 1980, Tufts U., 1981, Fletcher Sch. Law/Diplomacy, 1983-84; BS, Chatham Coll., 1983; cert. in comparative law, Heidelberg U., 1988; JD, Samford U., 1989; LLM in Internat. Banking Law, Boston U., 1990. Bar: Mass. 1991, Pa. 1991; cert. for piloting, seamanship and small boat handling USCG Aux. Dancer The N.Y.C. Ballet Co., 1971, Balanchine Cast for PBS The Nutcracker Suite, N.Y.C., 1971; docent The Hammond Castle Mus., Gloucester, Mass., 1982-85; asst. mgr. The Gallery, Rockport, Mass., 1977-83; cons. The Galleries, Ltd., Wellesley, Mass., 1988; legal intern U. Ala. Health Svcs. Found., Birmingham, 1988-89; loan officer UN/UNFCU, N.Y.C., 1984-86; overnight counselor Germaine Lawrence Sch., Arlington, Mass, 1989-90; contracts mgr. for Eastern Region Unisys Corp., Berkeley Heights, N.J., 1990-92; fin. cons. Innovatech, Lexington, Mass., 1992-93, 94-95; contract analyst Guy Carpenter & Co., Inc., N.Y.C., 1994; gen. counsel Mojo Working Prodns., N.Y.C., 1996. Chair Cordell Hull Speakers' Forum, Birmingham, 1988-89; alumnae class sec. Chatham Coll. Class of 1980s, Pitts., 1983-87, 97—. Clk. of vestry The Ch. of the Resurrection, N.Y.C., 1993-95, mem. vestry, 1995-97, accolyte, 1970s, Sunday sch. tchr., 1970s; overnight counselor The Germaine Lawrence Sch., Arlington, Mass., 1989-90. Recipient Cert. of Appreciation 1990 Alumni award Cumberland Sch. Law, 1990; named to Nat. Dean's List, 1989-90. Mem. DAR (Cape Ann chpt. const. week chair 1993-94, Mass. const. week chair 1995-97, N.Y.C. chpt. jr. com. mem. Sons and Daus. Gala Ball 1996), The Federalist Soc. (Cumberland chpt. treas. 1988-89, adv. bd. 1983, sec. 1987-88), Clan Menzies Soc. N.Am., Clan Menzies Soc. Scotland, Princeton Club, Thayer Families Assn., Daus. Union Vets. of Civil War 1861-65: Hudson Valley-N.Y. Metro Tent, Mass. Soc. Mayflower Descs., Baronial Order Magna Charta, Dames of Ct. of Honor, Nat. Soc. Magna Charta Dames and Barons, Nat. Soc. Col. Daus. Seventeenth Century (Rensselaerswyck chpt.), Nat. Soc. First Families of Minn., Soc. of the Friends of St. George's and Descs. of Knights of the Garter, Soc. of Desc. of Knights of the Most Noble Order of the Garter, Hugenot Soc. Am., Order of Wash., N.Y. State Continental Soc. Daus. of Indian Wars 1607-1900, St. Georges Soc. N.Y., First Families Ohio, Colonial Order the Crown, The Sovereign Colonial Soc. Ams. of Royal Descent, The Plantagenet Soc., Nat. Soc. Descs. of Early Quakers, Nat. Soc. Colonial Daus. of the 17th Century. Republican. Episcopalian. Avocations: lobstering, sailing, fishing, swimming, bicycling. Home: Brier Neck 13 Salt Island Rd Gloucester MA 01930-1972 Fax: 516-498-1729. E-mail: meansert@email.msn.com.

MEANS, THOMAS CORNELL, lawyer; b. Charleston, S.C., Oct. 3, 1947; s. Thomas Lucas and Dean (Cornell) M.; m. Judith Faye Perlmutter, Sept. 10, 1977; children: Benjamin, Samuel. AB, Dartmouth Coll., 1969; postgrad., Princeton Theol. Sem., 1970-71; M of Pub. Adminstrn., U. Colo., 1975; JD, George Washington U., 1978. Bar: D.C. 1978, U.S. dist. Ct. (D.C. dist.), U.S. Ct. Appeals (4th and D.C. cirs.) 1979, U.S. Ct. Appeals (10th cir.) 1983, U.S. Ct. Appeals (6th and 11th cirs.) 1989, U.S. Ct. Appeals (9th cir.) 1992, U.S. Ct. Appeals (8th cir.) 1993, U.S. Ct. Appeals (5th cir.) 1996. Social worker Vinyard Childcare, Ann Arbor, Mich., 1969-70; rsch. analyst, registered lobbyist Colo. Counties, Inc., Denver, 1972-75; assoc. Jones, Day, Reavis and Pogue, Washington, 1978-79; assoc. then ptnr. Crowell & Moring LLP, Washington, 1979—. Mem. state adv. coun. on pub. Pers. Mgmt., Colo. State Govt., Denver, 1974-75; lectr. mining law; chmn. coal com. Ea. Mineral Law Found., 1988-89, chmn. spl. insts., ass. sec., 1989-91, sec., 1991-92, v.p., 1992-93, pres., 1993-94, exec. com., 1989-96, trustee, 1989—, mem. bd. editors, 1994—; bd. advisors Nat. Law Ctr., 1993-94, adv. bd. W. Va. Legal Review on Nat. Coal Issues, 2001—, mem. Energy & Mineral Law Found. (pres. award 2002). Contbr. articles to profl. jours. Mem. George Washington Law Alumni Assn. (bd. dirs. 1986-96, exec. com. 1987-96, treas. 1987-88, sec. 1988-90, pres. 1992-94), Order of Coif, Cosmos Club (Washington), Phi Beta Kappa. Administrative and regulatory, Federal civil litigation, Natural resources. Home: 6411 Dahlonega Rd Bethesda MD 20816-2101 Office: Crowell & Moring LLP 1001 Pennsylvania Ave NW Fl 10 Washington DC 20004-2595

MEARS, PATRICK EDWARD, lawyer; b. Oct. 3, 1951; s. Edward Patrick and Estelle Veronica (Mislik) M.; m. Geraldine O'Connor, July 18, 1981. BA, U. Mich., 1973, JD, 1976. Bar: N.Y. 1977, Ill. 1996, Ind. 1997, U.S. Dist Ct. (so. and ea. dists) N.Y. 1977, Mich. 1980, U.S. Dist. Ct. (we. and ea. dists.) Mich. 1980, U.S. Ct. Appeals (6th cir.) 1983, Ill. 1996, Ind. 1997, U.S. Dist. Ct. (no. dist.) Ill. 1998, U.S. Dist. Ct. (no. dist.) Ind. 1998. Assoc. Milbank, Tweed, Hadley & McCloy, N.Y.C., 1976-79; ptnr. Warner, Norcross & Judd, Grand Rapids, Mich., 1980-91; sr. mem. Dykema Gossett PLLC, Grand Rapids, Mich., 1991—2002; equity mem. Dickinson Wright, PLLC, Grand Rapids, 2002—. Adj. prof. Grand Valley State U., Allendale, Mich., 1981-84; dir. Children's Law Ctr., 1994, Grand Rapids Ballet, 1994-99, East Grand Rapids Pub. Sch. Found., 1994-98. Author: Michigan Collection Law, 1981, 2d edit., 1983, Basic Bankruptcy Law, 1986, Bankruptcy Law and Practice in Michigan, 1987, 1995, Revised Article 9 of the UCC in Michigan, 2001; contbg. author Collier Bankruptcy Practice Guide; contbr. articles to profl. jours.; editor: Jour. of the Hist. Soc. of the U.S. Dist. Ct. for the Western Dist. of Mich., 2003—. Chmn. legis. com. East Grand Rapids PTA, 1992-94. Fellow: Mich. State Bar Found. (sec. coun. real property sect. 1993—97, chair Uniform Comml. Code com. bus. law sect. 2000—), Am. Coll. Bankruptcy; mem.: ABA (chmn. com. real property sect. 1997—, chmn. workouts, bankruptcy and foreclosures), Fed. Bar Assn. (chmn. bankruptcy sect. We. Mich. chpt. 1992—94, newsletter editor 1998—2002, pres. 2001—02), Am. Law Inst., Am. Bankruptcy Inst., Mich. State Bar Assn., East Hills Athletic Club. Bankruptcy, Commercial, consumer (including collections, credit), Commercial, contracts (including sales of goods; commercial financing). Office: Dickinson Wright PLLC 200 Ottawa Ave NW Ste 900 Grand Rapids MI 49503 E-mail: pmears@dickinsonwright.com.

MECHAM, GLENN JEFFERSON, lawyer, mayor; b. Logan, Utah, Dec. 11, 1935; s. Everett H. and Lillie (Dunford) M.; m. Mae Parson, June 5, 1957; children: Jeff B., Scott R., Marcia, Suzanne. BS, Utah State U., 1957; JD, U. Utah, 1961; grad., Air Command and Staff Coll., 1984, Air War Coll., 1984. Bar: Utah 1961, Supreme Ct. U.S., U.S. Ct. Appeals (10th cir.), U.S. Dist. Ct. Utah, U.S. Ct. Claims. Gen. practice law, 1961-65; atty. Duchesne County, Utah, 1962, City of Duchesne, 1962; city judge Roy City, Utah, 1963-66; judge City of Ogden, Utah, 1966-69, mayor, 1992-2000. Lectr. law and govt. Stevens-Henager Coll., Ogden, 1963-75; asst. U.S. atty., 1969-72; ptnr. Mecham & Richards, Ogden, Utah, 1972-82; pres. Penn Mountain Mining Co., South Pacific Internat. Bank, Ltd.; mem. Bur. Justice Stats. Adv. Bd., U.S. Dept. Justice, U.S. Conf. Mayors; chmn. Marina Capital Inc. Chmn. Ogden City Housing Authority, Marine Capital, Inc.; chmn. bd. trustees Utah State U., Space Dynamics Lab; mem. adv. coun. Fed. Home Loan Bank; pres. Utah League Cities and Towns, 1981—82; vice chmn. Wasatch Front Reg. Coun. Col. USAF, 1957; No. Utah liaison U.S. Sen. Robert F. Bennett. Recipient Disting. Svcs. award Utah State U., Weber State U. Mem ABA, Weber County Bar Assn. (pres. 1966-68), Utah Bar Assn., Am. Judicature Soc., Weber County Bar Legal Svcs. (chmn. bd. trustees 1966-69), Utah Assn. Mcpl. Judges (sec.), Ogden-Weber C. of C. (Order of the Big Hat), Sigma Chi, Phi Alpha Delta. Corporate, general, Education and schools, Property, real (including real estate development, water). Home: 1715 Darling St Ogden UT 84403-0556

MEDAGLIA, MARY-ELIZABETH, lawyer; b. Suffern, N.Y., Oct. 13, 1947; d. Joseph Mario and Edith Elizabeth (Price) M. BA, Sweet Briar Coll., 1969; JD, U. Va., 1972. Bar: Va. 1972, D.C. 1974, U.S. Ct. Appeals (D.C. cir.) 1974, U.S. Supreme Ct. 1980, U.S. Ct. Appeals (4th, 5th, 9th and 11th cirs.) 1981, U.S. Ct. Appeals (10th cir.) 1982, Md. 1990, U.S. Ct. Appeals (2d cir.) 1998. Law clk. to judge D.C. Ct. Appeals, Washington, 1972-74; asst. atty. U.S. Atty.'s Office, Washington, 1974-79; deputy solicitor Fed. Labor Relations Authority, Washington, 1979-82, acting solicitor, 1982; assoc. Jackson & Campbell P.C., Washington, 1982-84, ptnr., 1984—. Sec. D.C. Bar, 1983-84, bd. govs. 1984-87. Fellow Am. Bar Found.; mem. ABA (chmn. TIPS com. on ins. coverage litigation 1989-91, ho. of dels. 1981-83), D.C. Bar Assn. (bd. dirs. 1980-83, chmn. young lawyers sect. 1980-81), Women's Bar Assn. D.C. (pres. 1982-83), Charles Fahy Am. Inn of Ct. (pres. 1990-92), Fedn. Def. and Corp. Counsel, Am. Soc. Writers on Legal Subjects, Phi Beta Kappa. Federal civil litigation, State civil litigation, Insurance. Office: Jackson & Campbell PC South Tower 1120 20th St NW Ste 300S Washington DC 20036-3437 E-mail: LMedaglia@jackscamp.com.

MEDAK, WALTER HANS, lawyer; b. Vienna, May 10, 1915; came to U.S., 1938; s. Hugo and Grete (Figdor) M.; m. Edith Rhodes, 1944 (div. 1957); 1 child, Ronald Harvard; m. Renée Rasens, 1996. Grad., Acad. of Commerce, Vienna, 1934, U. Vienna, 1938; postgrad., U. Ga., 1939-40; MA in Econs., U. Calif., Berkeley, 1949; JD, Harvard U., 1948. Prodn. mgr. Mabs, Inc., L.A., 1942-43; prodn. engr. Kaiser Co., Richmond, Calif., 1943-45; atty. Belli & Medak, Walnut Creek, Calif., 1957-59; pvt. practice law Walnut Creek and Moraga, Calif., 1950—. Bd. dirs. Snyder/Newell, Inc., San Francisco; bd. dirs. Carnelian Woods, Carnelian Bay, Calif., pres., 1974-80. Mem. ABA, Calif. County Bar Assn., Assn. Trial Lawyers Am., Calif. Trial Lawyers Assn., Harvard Club (chmn. admissions and scholarship com. San Francisco chpt. 1973-74). Avocations: skiing, swimming, music, travel, French and German. State civil litigation, Insurance, Personal injury (including property damage). Home: 2833 Ptarmigan Dr Apt 3 Walnut Creek CA 94595-3135 E-mail: walterhmedak@aol.com.

MEDALIE, RICHARD JAMES, lawyer; b. Duluth, Minn., July 21, 1929; s. William Louis and Mona (Kolad) M.; m. Susan Diane Abrams, June 5, 1960; children: Samuel David, Daniel Alexander. BA summa cum laude, U. Minn., 1952; cert., U. London, 1953; A.M., Harvard U., 1955, JD cum laude, 1958. Bar: D.C. 1958, N.Y. 1963. Law clk. to Hon. George T. Washington U.S. Ct. Appeals, Washington, 1958-59; asst. solicitor gen. U.S., 1960-62; assoc. Kaye, Scholer, Fierman, Hays & Handler, N.Y.C., 1962-65; dep. dir. Ford Found. Inst. Criminal Law and Procedure, Georgetown U. Law Ctr., 1965-68; ptnr. Friedman & Medalie and predecessors, Washington, 1968-98; pres. Pegasus Internat., Washington, 1970—; exec. dir. The Appleseed Found., Washington, 1993-94, chmn. bd., 1993—2002, pres., 1995-98; of counsel Brock Ptnrs. LLC, N.Y.C., 1995—; pvt. practice Washington, 1998—. Adj. prof. adminstrv. and criminal law Georgetown U. Law Center, 1967-70; Mem. D.C. Law Revision Commn., 1975-87, chmn. Criminal Law Task Force, mem. exec. com., 1978-82; panel comml. arbitrators Am. Arbitration Assn., 1964— ; vice chmn. Harvard Law Sch. Fund, 1981-84, chmn. nat. maj. gifts, 1984-86, dep. chmn., 1986-87, chmn. 1987-89; v.p., bd. dirs. Trial Lawyers for Pub. Justice, Washington, 1998—. Author: From Escobedo to Miranda: The Anatomy of a Supreme Court Decision, 1966; co-author: Federal Consumer Safety Legislation, 1970; co-author, editor: Commercial Arbitration for the 1990s, 1991; co-editor: Crime: A Community Responds, 1967; staff: Harvard Law Rev., 1956-58; case editor, 1957-58; contbr. articles to legal jours. Bd. dirs. alumni assn. Expt. in Internat. Living, Brattleboro, Vt., 1961-64, pres., 1962-63. Fulbright scholar, 1952-53; Ford fellow, 1954-55. Mem. ABA (program chair 1984, 90, chair legis. subcom. 1986-89, ADR/arbitration com., rep. on adv. com. nat. conf. Emerging ADR Issues in State and Fed. Cts. 1991, vice chair 1991-94, arbitration com. litigation sect., co-chair nat. conf. Critical Issues in Arbitration 1993), D.C. Unified Bar, Assn. Bar City of N.Y., Am. Law Inst., D.C. Estate Planning Coun.; fellow Am. Bar Found., Harvard Law Sch. Assn. D.C. (pres. 1976-77, nat. v.p. 1977-78), Harvard Alumni Assn. (law sch. dir. 1991-95), Cosmos Club, Harvard Club of Washington, Phi Beta Kappa, Phi Alpha Theta. Home: 3113 Macomb St NW Washington DC 20008-3325 Office: 1750 K St NW Ste 1200 Washington DC 20006-2303 E-mail: rmedalie@att.net.

MEDALIE, SUSAN DIANE, lawyer, management consultant; b. Boston, Oct. 7, 1941; d. Samuel and Matilda (Bortman) Abrams; m. Richard James Medalie, June 5, 1960; children: Samuel David, Daniel Alexander. BA, Sarah Lawrence Coll., 1960; MA, George Washington U., 1962, cert. pubs. spec., 1977; JD, Am. U., 1986. Bar: Pa. 1987, DC 1987. Pres. Medalie Cons., Washington, 1980—; dep. dir. U.S. Holocaust Meml. Coun., Washington, 1980-82; assoc. pub. Campaigns & Elections, Washington,

1983-84; legis. analyst Subcom./House Energy and Commerce, Washington, 1985; ea. regional dir. Josephson Found. for Adv. Ethics, L.A., 1986-88; asst. dean for external affairs George Washington U. Nat. Law Ctr., Washington, 1988-90; exec. dir. Internat. Soc. Global Health Policy, Washington and Paris, 1990-93; pvt. practice Washington, 1993-2000; exec. dir. Women's Campaign Fund, Washington, 2000—. Corp. liaison First Hosp. Corp., Norfolk, Va., 1986—88. Editor, pub.: Getting There mag., 1977—80, sr. editor: Am. U. Law Rev., 1984—86; assoc. prodr., cons. (TV series) Prof. Arthur Miller's "Headlines on Trial", 1987—91. Mem. exec. bd., DC Bar rep. Coalition Against Drugs and Violence, 1997—2000; nat. dep. fin. dir. Edward M. Kennedy for Pres. Com., Washington, 1979—80; del. DC Ward 3 Dem. Ctrl. Com., 1996—2000; bd. dirs., mem. exec. com. Women's Campaign Fund, 1999—2000. Mem.: ABA, DC Unified Bar. Family and matrimonial, General practice. Office: 734 15th St NW Washington DC 20005 E-mail: susanmedalie@wcfonline.org.

MEDEARIS, MILLER, lawyer; b. Liberty, Mo., Jan. 19, 1921; s. Thomas Whittier and Mara (Miller) M.; children: Christy Crochet, Kellee Reed. LLB, Cumberland U., 1948; JD, Stamford U., 1969. Bar: Okla. 1948, Calif. 1957. Claims adjustor Transit Casualty Co., L.A., 1950-56, atty., trial counsel, 1956-58; ptnr. Hagenbaugh, Murphy & Medearis, L.A., 1958-69, Medearis and Grimm, L.A., 1969—. Sec., Bd. Med. Quality Assurance, Sacramento, 1979-84, v.p., 1984-86; bd. dirs. Pico Rivera Cmty. Hosp., 1975-85; mem. Dem. Bus. Council, L.A., 1980; commr. L.A. Bd. Transp., 1986-92. With USN, 1945-46. Mem. ABA, State Bar Calif., Calif. Trial Lawyers Assn., Okla. Bar Assn., Lawyers Club L.A. Democrat. Baptist. Avocations: boating, water skiing, downhill skiing. Antitrust, Criminal, Personal injury (including property damage). Home: 2175 Ridge Dr Los Angeles CA 90049-1153 Office: Medearis and Grimm 1331 W Sunset Blvd Los Angeles CA 90026-4499

MEDEIROS, MATTHEW FRANCIS, lawyer; b. Little Compton, R.I., Apr. 30, 1945; s. Manuel S. and Marie F. (Goulart) M.; m. Sarah Judith Medjuck, July 26, 1970. AB, Brown U., 1967; JD, NYU, 1970. Bar: R.I. 1970, Mass. 1985, U.S. Dist. Ct. R.I. 1971, D.C. 1971, U.S. Dist. Ct. D.C. 1971, U.S. Ct. Appeals (1st cir.) 1972, U.S. Ct. Appeals (D.C. cir.) 1972, U.S. Supreme Ct. 1974. Summer assoc. Lewis & Roca, Phoenix, 1969; law clk. to chief judge U.S. Dist. Ct. R.I., 1970-71; assoc. Covington & Burling, Washington, 1971-76; on leave with Neighborhood Legal Svcs. Program, Washington, 1973; ptnr. Edwards & Angell, Providence, 1977-87, Flanders & Medeiros Inc., Providence, 1987-2000, Little, Bulman, Medeiros & Whitney, P.C., 2000—. Chmn. planning com. 1st Cir. Jud. Conf., 1980-81; mem. jud. screening coms. U.S. Bankruptcy Judge and U.S. Magistrate, 1981-82; mem. adv. com. for U.S. Ct. Appeals (1st cir.), 1983-88; adj. prof. fed. trial practice So. New Eng. Sch. Law, 1986-88; editor: NYU Law Rev., 1969-70; bd. dirs. Associated Alumni Brown U., 1969-71; bd. dirs. R.I. br. ACLU, 1977-79. Mem. ABA, Am. Bd. Trial Advocates, Fed. Bar Assn. (pres. R.I. chpt. 1978-80), R.I. Bar Assn. Antitrust, Federal civil litigation, General civil litigation. Office: Little Bulman Medeiros & Whitney 72 Pine St Providence RI 02903

MEDINA, J. MICHAEL, lawyer, educator; b. N.Y.C., June 28, 1950; s. Abel and Renee Medina. BA summa cum laude, Southwestern Coll., Winfield, Kan., 1972; JD with special distinction, U. Okla., 1975. Bar: Okla. 1975, U.S. Ct. Appeals (10th cir.) 1977, U.S. Ct. Appeals (5th cir.) 1978, U.S. Ct. Appeals (fed. cir.) 1982, U.S. Ct. Appeals (2d cir.) 1990, U.S. Ct. Appeals (D.C. cir.) 1994, U.S. Ct. Appeals (7th and 8th cirs.) 2002, U.S. Supreme Ct. 1979. Assoc. Holiman, Langhoz, Runnels & Dorwart, Tulsa, 1975-80, ptnr., 1980-86, shareholder, 1986-94; pvt. practice Tulsa, 1994—. Judge Okla. Ct. Appeals Temporary Divsn. # 14, 1992-93; adj. prof. law U. Tulsa Law Sch., 1988, 92-2003; mem. Supreme Ct. Appellate Rules Revision Com. Contbr. articles to profl. jours.; editor U. Okla. Law Review, 1973-75. Mem. Am. Acad. Appellate Lawyers, Order of the Coif (sec.), Assn. Bar U.S. Ct. Appeals Tenth Cir. Republican. Roman Catholic. Avocations: bridge, reading, travel. Appellate, General civil litigation, Oil, gas, and mineral. Office: 124 E 4th St Ste 100 Tulsa OK 74103-5005

MEDLOCK, DONALD LARSON, lawyer; b. Port Chester, N.Y., Mar. 8, 1927; s. J. Harold and Emma Adelaide (MacLennan) M.; m. Katharine Smedes Nicholson, May 21, 1955; children: Katharine Baird, Margaret MacLennan, William Nicholson. BA with honors, Yale U., 1947, LLB, 1950. Bar: N.Y. 1950, U.S. Dist. Ct. (so. dist.) N.Y. 1951, U.S. Dist. Ct. (ea. dist.) N.Y. 1952, U.S. Tax Ct. 1952, U.S. Ct. Custom and Patent Appeals, U.S. Ct. Appeals (2d cir.) 1951. Assoc. Putnam & Roberts, N.Y.C., 1950-56, ptnr., 1957-94, sr. counsel, 1995—. Bd. dirs. Bancard Sys. of N.Y. Inc., Port Washington. Editor Yale Law Jour., New Haven, 1948-50. Sec., bd. dirs. Port Washington Community Chest, 1959-61; bd. dirs. Port Washington Estates Assn., 1958-61; mem. ann. fund parents com. Taft Sch., 1979-81; bd. mgrs., exec. com. William Sloane Ho. YMCA of Greater N.Y., 1979-84; chmn. univ. coun. com. on Law Sch. Yale U., 1979-86; chmn. Yale Alumni Fund, 1984-86, bd. dirs., 1955—, exec. com., 1980-88; chmn. Yale Law Sch. Fund, 1974-76; mem. devel. bd. Yale U., 1984-88, exec. com., 1984-86; exec. com. Yale Law Sch., 1975-79, hon., 1979—; bd. dirs. Assn. Yale Alumni, 1984-86, rep.-at-large, 1979-82, com. on undergrad. admissions, 1979-82, com. on Yale medal, 1981; exec. com. Assn. Families U. Denver, 1982-84. Recipient citation Yale Law Sch., 1977, Yale Alumni Fund Chmn.'s award, 1979, 87, Yale medal, 1994. Mem. Fed. Power Bar Assn., Assn. of Bar of City of N.Y. (com. on profl. ethics 1958-61), Corbey Ct. Yale Law Sch., Tuscarora Club (Margaretville, N.Y., bd. dirs. 1963-95, sec. 1970-86, v.p. 1984-86), Country Club of Landfall, Manhasset Bay Yacht Club, Mory's Assn., India House, Scroll and Key Soc., Yale Club N.Y.C., Phi Beta Kappa, Phi Delta Phi. Avocations: trout fishing, tennis, reading, crossword puzzles, golf. Home: Landfall 800 Oyster Lndg Wilmington NC 28405-5292

MEDNICOFF, DAVID MICHAEL, lawyer, educator; b. Bangor, Maine, Oct. 25, 1959; s. Irma Mednicoff; m. Joya Misra, Mar. 24, 1996; 1 child, Amina Mednicoff-Misra. AB, Princeton (N.J.) U., 1982; JD, Harvard U., 1989, AM, 1988, postgrad. Cons. Amnesty Internat., Washington, 1994-98; asst. prof. U. Mass., Amherst, 1999—. Pres., bd. dirs. U. Georgia Hillel Found., Athens, 1996-99; exec. com., bd. dirs. Atlanta Jewish Young Adult Agy., 1996-99; cons., advisor Nat. Conf. of Christians and Jews, Boston, 1987-88; mem. Congregation B'nai Israel. Fulbright scholar Coun. for Internat. Exch. of Scholars, 1990, 92-93. Democrat. Avocations: choral performance, piano, travel, cooking. Public international, Private international. Office: U Mass 221 Hampshire House 131 County Cir Amherst MA 01003-9257 Fax: 413-545-1640. E-mail: mednic@legal.umass.edu.

MEDOF, CAROL J. lawyer; BA, UCLA; JD, Southwestern U., 1979; postgrad., UCLA, U. So. Calif. Lic. life and health ins. agt. Calif.; bar: Calif., U.S. Dist. Ct. Calif., U.S. Ct. Appeals (9th cir.); lic. real estate broker Calif., registered rep. series 6 and 63 NASD. Pvt. practice dispute resolution Carol J. Medof, Esq., Encino, Calif., 1979—. Mem.: Soc. of Profls. in Dispute Resolution, So. Calif. Mediation Assn. Office: Carol Medof Esq 15900 Woodvale Rd Encino CA 91436

MEDRANO, ROBERTO M. lawyer; b. Hermosillo, Sonora, Mexico, May 20, 1969; s. Roberto C. Medrano and Ana S. Martinez. LLM, U. of Ariz., Tucson, 1996—97. Sr. ptnr. Mex. Legal Group Hermosillo, S.C., Hermosillo, Mexico, 2001—; litig. assoc. Bryan, Gonzalez Vargas y Gonzalez Baz, S.C., Mexico, Mexico, 1999—2001; litigant assoc. Lizarraga, Robles, Tapia y Cabrera, S.C., Hermosillo, Mexico, 1993—99. Recipient The Best Student of Mex., 1992, Diario de Mex., Mex. City, 1992. Mem.: Mex. Legal Group. Commercial, consumer (including collections, credit), General civil litigation, Corporate, general. Office: Mexico Legal Group Hermosillo SC Vasco de Gama no 48 Col Los Arcos Hermosillo Sonora 83250 Mexico Office Fax: (662)218-2117. Personal E-mail: robertomedrano@mexico.com. E-mail: rmedrano@mexicolegalgroup.com.

MEDVECKY, ROBERT STEPHEN, lawyer; b. Bridgeport, Conn., Feb. 12, 1931; s. Stephen and Elizabeth (Petro) M.; m. Ellen R. Munt, Nov. 11, 1966; children— Allison L., Beth A., Craig R. AB, Dartmouth, 1952; JD, Harvard, 1955. Bar: Ill. bar 1955, Conn. bar 1958, D.C. bar 1972, Fla. bar 1989. Asso. firm Lord, Bissell & Brook, Chgo., 1955-57; gen. atty. So. New Eng. Telephone Co., New Haven, 1957-71; v.p., gen. counsel, sec. Amtrak, Washington, 1971-75; partner firm Lord, Bissell & Brook, Washington, 1975-78, Reid & Priest, N.Y.C., 1978-87. Clubs: Harvard (N.Y.C.), Fiddlesticks Country (Ft. Meyers, Fla.), Saphire Valley Country (Cashlers, N.C.). Home: 15491 Kilbirnie Dr Fort Myers FL 33912-2424 also: 457 Round Hill Rd Sapphire NC 28774-7608 E-mail: bmedvecky@yahoo.com.

MEDVECKY, THOMAS EDWARD, lawyer; b. Bridgeport, Conn., Apr. 22, 1937; s. Stephen and Elizabeth P. Medvecky; m. Patricia Conneally, Aug. 25, 1967; 1 son, Thomas Edward, II. A.B., Bowdoin Coll., 1959; LL.B., St. John's U., 1962. Bar: Conn. 1962. Assoc., Louis Katz, Danbury, Conn., 1963-68; sole practice, Bethel, Conn., 1968— ; asst. town counsel Town of Bethel, 1963-67; assoc. dir. State Nat. Bank Conn. Mem. budget com. Danbury (Conn.) Community Chest, 1966-68. Served with USAR, 1962-68. Recipient Am. Jurisprudence award 1962. Mem. ABA, Conn. Bar Assn., Danbury Bar Assn. Democrat. Lutheran. General practice, Probate (including wills, trusts), Property, real (including real estate development, water). Office: 99 Greenwood Ave PO Box 272 Bethel CT 06801-0272

MEDVED, PAUL STANLEY, lawyer; b. Milw., May 6, 1956; s. Frank F. and Evelyn F. (Poplawski) M.; m. Danita C. Cole, Aug. 27, 1988. BA with honors, Marquette U., 1978; JD, Columbia U., 1981. Bar: Wis. 1981, U.S. Dist. Ct. (ea. dist.) Wis. 1981, U.S. Dist. Ct. (we. dist.) Wis. 1984, U.S. Ct. Appeals (7th cir.) 1984. Assoc. Michael, Best & Friedrich, Milw., 1981-88, ptnr., 1988-97; shareholder Mallery & Zimmerman, S.C., Milw., 1997—. Bankruptcy, Commercial, contracts (including sales of goods; commercial financing), Corporate, general. Office: Mallery & Zimmerman SC 731 N Jackson St Ste 900 Milwaukee WI 53202-4697 E-mail: pmedved@mzmilw.com.

MEDVED, ROBERT ALLEN, lawyer; b. Cleve., July 22, 1945; s. Joseph Jack and Mary (Blasko) Medved. BBA, Kent State U., 1968; JD cum laude, Seattle U., 1975. Bar: Wash. 1976, U. S. Ct. Appeals (9th cir.) 1976, U.S. Dist. Ct. (we. dist.) Wash. 1976, U.S. Dist. Ct. (ea. dist.) Wash. 1979, U.S. Supreme Ct. 1981, U.S. Ct. Appeals (D.C. cir.) 1989. Fin. analyst Ford Motor Co., Sandusky, Ohio, 1972; rsch. asst. Seattle U., 1973—75; law clk Judge U.S. Ct. Appeals (9th cir.), 1974; asst. to labor arbitrator Tacoma, 1975; law clk. to Judge U. S. Dist. Ct. (ctrl. dist.) Calif., 1976; assoc. Graham & Dunn, Seattle, 1986—92, ptnr., 1982—83, Drake and Whiteley, Bellevue, Wash., 1983—86, Foster, Pepper & Shefelman, Seattle, 1986—97; owner Law Offices Robert A. Medved, Bellvue, 1997—. Spl. dist. counsel 8th Congl. Dist., W.Va., 1983—86. Editor (in-chief): Seattle U. Law Rev. Bd. dirs. Bellevue C.C. found., 1986—98. Lt. USN, 1968—71. Scholar, Seattle U., 1974. Mem.: ABA, Wash. State Bar Assn. Roman Catholic. General civil litigation, Environmental, Property, real (including real estate development, water). Office: 212 108th Ave SE Bellevue WA 98004-6209 E-mail: bob@ramedved.com.

MEEHAN, MICHAEL JOSEPH, lawyer; b. St. Louis, Aug. 28, 1942; s. Joseph Michael and Frances (Taylor) M.; m. Sharon Kay McHenry (div. 1988); m. Patricia Ann Shive, July 8, 1989 (dec. 1999); m. Shelley Fujiko Lee, 2002. BS in Engring., U.S. Coast Guard Acad., 1964; JD with high distinction, U. Ariz., 1971. Bar: Ariz. 1971, U.S. Ct. Appeals (6th, 8th, 9th and 10th cirs.), U.S. Supreme Ct. 1975. Law clk. Assoc. Justice William H. Rehnquist, U.S. Supreme Ct., 1972; assoc. Molloy, Jones & Donahue, P.C., Tucson, 1971-75, shareholder, 1975-93; chmn. exec. com., head trial dept., 1986-93; founder Meehan & Assocs., Tucson, 1993-2001; ptnr. Quarles & Brady/Striech Long, Tucson, 2001—. Mem. fed. appellate rules adv. com. Jud. Conf. U.S., 1994-99. Author chpt. on appellate advocacy: State Bar of Arizona Appellate Practice Handbook. Fellow Am. Acad. Appellate Lawyers (pres.-elect); mem. Ariz. Bar Assn. (past chair appellate practice sect. 1995-99). Republican. Lutheran. Avocation: golf. Federal civil litigation, Communications, Securities. Office: Quarles & Brady 1 S Church Ave Ste 1700 Tucson AZ 85701-1621 E-mail: mmeehan@quarles.com.

MEEHAN, PATRICK L. prosecutor; BA, Bowdoin Coll., 1978; JD, Temple U., 1986. Assoc. Dilworth, Paxon, Kalish and Kauffman; sr. counsel, exec. dir. U.S. Sen. Arlen Specter; dist. atty. Delaware County, Pa., 1986—2001; U.S. atty. Ea. Dist. Pa. U.S. Dept. Justice, 2001—. Office: 615 Chestnut St Philadelphia PA 19106*

MEEKS, WILLIAM HERMAN, III, lawyer; b. Ft. Lauderdale, Fla., Dec. 30, 1939; s. Walter Herman Jr. and Elise Walker (McGuire) M.; m. Patricia Ann Rayburn, July 30, 1965; 1 son, William Herman IV; m. 2d, Miriam Andrea Bedsole, Dec. 28, 1971; 1 child, Julie Marie. AB, Princeton U., 1961; LLB, U. Fla., 1964; LLM in Tax, NYU, 1965. Bar: Fla 1964, U.S. Dist. Ct. (so. dist.) Fla. 1965, U.S. Tax Ct. 1966, U.S. Ct. Appeals (11th cir.) 1981, U.S. Supreme Ct. 1985. Ptnr. McCune, Hiaasen, Crum, Ferris & Gardner, Ft. Lauderdale, 1964-89, Fleming, O'Bryan & Fleming, Ft. Lauderdale, 1990-95, Niles, Dobbins, Meeks, Raleigh & Dover, Ft. Lauderdale, 1995—. Dir. Attys. Title Svcs., Inc., 1978-79, Attys. Title Svcs. of Broward County, Inc., 1971—, chmn., 1976-77; mem. Attys. Real Estate Coun. Broward County. Mem. ABA, Fla. Bar Assn., Broward County Bar Assn., Attys. Title Ins. Fund, Ft. Lauderdale Hist. Soc., Ft. Lauderdale Mus., Kiwanis, Lauderdale Yacht Club, Tower Club (Ft. Lauderdale), Phi Delta Phi. Democrat. Presbyterian. Corporate, general, Probate (including wills, trusts), Property, real (including real estate development, water). Office: Niles Dobbins Meeks Raleigh & Dover 4th Fl 2601 E Oakland Park Blvd Fl 4 Fort Lauderdale FL 33306-1606 E-mail: whmeeks@ndmrd.com.

MEFFORD, R. DOUGLAS, lawyer; b. 1963; BS, Western Ky. U., 1985; JD, U. Ky., 1991. Bar: Tenn. 1991, U.S. Dist. Ct. (mid. dist.) tenn. 1991, Ky. 1992. Acctg. officer Trans Fin. Inc., Bowling Green, Ky., 1985-88; assoc. Bass, Berry & Sims, Nashville, 1991-96; v.p., assoc. gen. counsel PhyCor Inc., Nashville, 1996-2001; v.p., divsn. counsel Gambro Healthcare Inc., Brentwood, Tenn., 2001—. Corporate, general, Health, Securities. E-mail: doug.mefford@us.gambro.com.

MEGALLY, NAZIH HABIEB, lawyer; b. Cairo, Dec. 2, 1944; s. Habieb Megally and Hakima (Guirges) To'orom. LLB, Cairo U., 1973. Bar: 1974. Editor, teletypist AP Cairo Bur., 1969—74; assoc. Hashem Ibrahim, Cairo, 1975—79; pvt. practice Cairo, 1980—82, 1985—; ptnr. Nazih & Wahid, Cairo, 1982—. Mem. Christian Orthodox Ch. Mem.: Internat. Bar Assn., Egyptian Bar Assn. Home: 139 El-Tahrir St Cairo Egypt Office: Nazih H Megalley Lawyer & Patent Atty 26 Adly St Cairo Egypt

MEGYERI, LESLIE LASZLO, lawyer, govt. ofcl.; b. Rozsnyo, Hungary, Apr. 2, 1941; came to U.S., 1959, naturalized, 1964; s. Laszlo and Ilona (Polgar) M.; BA, George Washington U., 1963, JD, 1968, MBA, 1980; ABA, Benjamin Franklin U., 1973; grad. U.S. Army Command and Gen. Staff Coll., 1979, U.S. Army War Coll., 1986; m. Kathryn Ann Wilker, Dec. 18, 1970. Admitted to D.C. bar, 1969; atty. FAA, 1969-74; staff mem. ways and means com. and appropriations com. U.S. Congress, 1975-77; with GAO, Washington, 1977-82, audit mgr., 1982; counsel Com. on Govt. Ops., U.S. Congress, 1982— . Bd. govs. Benjamin Franklin U., 1978— . Served to lt. col. D.C. N.G., 1963-88. CPA, Md. Mem. Am. Bar Assn., Am. Inst. CPAs, D.C. Bar Assn., Aircraft Owners and Pilots Assn. Roman Catholic. Home: 1618 A Belmont St NW Washington DC 20009 Office: 1762 Church St NW Washington DC 20036-0001 E-mail: Megyeri@juno.com.

MEHLMAN, MARK FRANKLIN, lawyer; b. L.A., Dec. 18, 1947; s. Jack and Elaine Pearl (Lopater) M.; m. Barbara Ann Novak, Aug. 20, 1972; children: David, Jennifer, Ilyse. BA, U. Ill., 1969; LLB, U. Mich., 1973. Bar: Ill. 1973; U.S. Dist. Ct. (no. dist.) Ill. 1973. Assoc. Sonnenschein, Nath & Rosenthal, Chgo., 1973-80, mem. policy and planning com., 1989—. Trustee Groveland Health Svcs., Highland Park (Ill.) Hosp., 1991-97; trustee, treas., exec. com. Spertus Inst. Jewish Studies, Chgo., 1992-97, vice chmn. bd. trustees, 1996—; vice-chmn. regional bd. Anti-Defamation League, 1987-89, hon. life mem. nat. commn., 1993—. Fellow Am. Bar Found.; mem. ABA (chmn. mortgages and other debt financing subcom. 1991-95, supervisory coun. 1997—), Am. Coll. Real Estate Lawyers (bd. govs. 2000—, chmn. MDP com. 2000—, chmn. mem. selection com. 2000-01), Nat. Conf. Lawyers and CPAs, Ango-Am. Real Property Inst., Legal Club of Chgo., Lake Shore Country Club, Standard Club, Exec. Club of Chgo. Commercial, contracts (including sales of goods; commercial financing), Finance, Property, real (including real estate development, water). Office: Sonnenschein Nath & Rosenthal 233 S Wacker Dr Ste 8000 Chicago IL 60606-6491

MEHTA, EILEEN ROSE, lawyer; b. Colver, Pa., Apr. 1, 1953; d. Richard Glenn and Helen (Wahna) Ball; m. Abdul Rashid Mehta, Aug. 31, 1973. Student, Miami U., 1971-73; BA with distinction, Fla. Internat. U., 1974; JD cum laude, U. Miami, 1977. Bar: Fla. 1977, U.S. Dist. Ct. (so. dist.) Fla. 1977, U.S. Ct. Appeals (11th cir.) 1981. Law clk. to presiding judge U.S. Dist. Ct. (so. dist.) Fla., Miami, 1977-79; asst. atty. County of Dade, Miami, 1979-89; shareholder Fine Jacobson Schwartz Nash Block & England, Miami, Fla., 1989-94; ptnr. Eckert Seamans Cherin & Mellott, Miami, 1994-98, Bilzin Sumberg Baena Price & Axelrod, Miami, 1998—. Lectr. in field; v.p., bd. dirs. Mehtatron Enterprises, Inc., Miami, Shalimar Homes Inc., Anderson, S.C. Miami U. scholar, 1971-73. Mem. Fla. Bar Assn., Dade County Bar Assn. Appellate, Government contracts and claims, Land use and zoning (including planning). Office: Sumberg Baena Price & Axelrod 2500 First Union Fin Ctr Miami FL 33131

MEIERHENRY, JUDITH KNITTEL, judge, lawyer; b. Burke, S.D., Jan. 20, 1944; d. Adolph John and Anna Elizabeth (Voos) Knittel; m. Mark Vernon Meierhenry, May 14, 1961; children: Todd, Mary. BA in English, U. S.D., 1966, MA, 1968, JD, 1977. Bar: S.D. 1977. H.S. tchr. English Plattsmouth (Nebr.) Pub. Schs., 1966-67; instr. U. S.D., 1968-70, Hiram Scott Coll., Scottbluff, Nebr., 1970; tchr. Todd County Pub. Schs., Mission, S.D., 1971-74; ptnr. Meierhenry, DeVaney, Krueger & Meierhenry, Vermillion, S.D., 1977-79; cabinet sec. S.D. Dept. Labor, Pierre, 1980-84; cabinet sec. edn. and cultural affairs State S.D., 1983-84; sr. mgr., asst. gen. counsel Citibank S.D., 1985-88; cir. ct. judge State S.D., 1988—2002; justice S.Dak. Supreme Ct., 2002—. Mem. ABA, S.D. Bar Assn. (civil pattern jury instrn. com.), S.D. Trial Lawyers Assn. Office: South Dakota Supreme Ct 425 N Dakota Ave Sioux Falls SD 57104-2400 E-mail: jmeierh@aol.com.

MEIJER, JEAN YVONNE, lawyer; b. Johannesburg, May 8, 1969; d. Philipus Jacobus and Yvonne Hilda Meijer; m. Rupert Frederick Nanni, Apr. 18, 1998. BA, LLB, Rhodes U., South Africa, 1992; LLM, U. South Africa, 1997. Bar: South Africa 1994, cert.: High Ct. South Africa (notary) 1994. Profl. asst. Garlicke & Bousfield, Inc., Durban, South Africa, 1994—96, dir., 1996—99, Cliffe Dekker Inc., Johannesburg, 1999—. Mem.: Inst. Dirs. Antitrust. Office: Cliffe Dekker Inc 1 Protea Pl 4th Fl Sandown Gauteng South Africa

MEIRA, FERNANDO ALVES, lawyer; b. Sao Paulo, May 3, 1968; m. Fernanda Chamma Alves, June 9, 2000; 1 child, Gustavo Alves; m. Monica De Mello, Oct. 13, 1993 (div. July 1998). JD, U. Sao Paulo, 1991. Bar: Brazil 1994. With Sao Paulo Exec. Exch.; fgn. assoc. Cravath, Swaine & Moore, N.Y.C., 1995—97; assoc. then ptnr. Pinheiro Neto Advogados, Sao Paulo, 1991—. Bd. dirs. Suk Anerios S.A., Rio de Janeiro. Mergers and acquisitions, Corporate, general, Commercial, contracts (including sales of goods; commercial financing). Office: Pinheiro Neto Advogados Rua Boa Vista 9 Andar 254 01014-907 São Paulo Brazil Fax: 55 11 3247-8600. E-mail: fmeira@pinheironeto.com.br.

MEISEL, GEORGE VINCENT, lawyer; b. St. Louis, Sept. 24, 1933; s. Leo Otto and Margaret (Duggan) M.; m. Joy C. Cassin, May 18, 1963 BS summa cum laude, St. Louis U., 1956, JD cum laude, 1958. Bar: Mo. 1958. Assoc. Grand Peper & Martin, St. Louis, 1961-64, ptnr., 1965; jr. ptnr. Bryan Cave McPheeters & McRoberts, St. Louis, 1966-69; ptnr. Bryan Cave, LLP, St. Louis, 1970-2000, of counsel, 2000—. Served to 1st lt. USAF, 1958-61 Mem. ABA, Bar Assn. Met. St. Louis, Mo. Bar Assn. Clubs: Saint Louis, Mo. Athletic (St. Louis). Roman Catholic. Property, real (including real estate development, water). Home: 2029 S Warson Rd Saint Louis MO 63124-1151 E-mail: gvmeisel@bryancavellp.com.

MEISELMAN, ALYSON, lawyer, mediator/arbitrator; b. Washington, Jan. 24, 1951; BA, U. Md., 1973; JD, Potomac Sch. Law, Washington, 1979. Bar: U.S. Dist. Ct. Md. 1981, Md. 1981, U.S. Supreme Ct. 1993, U.S. Ct. Appeals (4th cir.) 1994. Pvt. practice, Frederick, Md., 1981-84, Rockville, Md., 1986—87, 1992—2002; assoc. Alan D. Massengill, PA, Gaithersburg, Md., 1984-86; prin. Haspel & Meiselman, Chartered, Rockville, 1987-92. Mem. ABA, Md. Bar Assn., Bar Assn. Montgomery County, Nat. Assn. Women Lawyers, Harry Benjamin Internat. Gender Dysphoria Assn., Nat. Lesbian and Gay Law Assn., Women's Bar Assn., Harry Benjamin Internat. Gender Dysphoria Assn., Inc. Appellate, Family and matrimonial, Gender & Sexuality. Office: Law Offices Scurti & Gulling PA 1511 Court Sq Bldg 200 E Lexington St Baltimore MD 21202-3530 Office Fax: 410-244-0775. E-mail: ameiselman@scurtiandgulling.com.

MEISINGER, LOUIS M. lawyer; b. NYC, Dec. 12, 1942; BA, UCLA, 1964, JD, 1967. Bar: Calif. 1968. Atty. Hill Wynne Troop & Meisinger, LA; exec. v.p., gen. coun. Walt Disney Co., Burbank, Calif., 1997—2003; sr. advisor Sheppard, Mullin, Richter & Hampton, LLP, Los Angeles, Calif., 2003—. Editor: UCLA Law Rev., 1965-67. Recipient Entertainment Lawyer of the Yr., Beverly Hills Bar Assoc./ Calif., 1999. Mem. State Bar Calif., L.A. County Bar Assn., Century City Bar Assn., Order of Coif, Phi Beta Kappa, Sigma Delta Pi, Phi Delta Phi. Commercial, contracts (including sales of goods; commercial financing), Entertainment, Intellectual property. Office: Sheppard Mullin Richter & Hampton 333 S Hope St Los Angeles CA 90071 Office Fax: 213-620-1398.*

MEISTER, ROBERT ALLEN, lawyer; b. N.Y.C., July 17, 1936; s. Milton and Sheba M.; m. Margaret A. Lewiston Goodman, July 15, 1962 (div. Oct. 15, 1969); 1 child, Deborah A.; m. Jeanne Cioffi, June 15, 1986; 1 child, Danielle M. AB, N.Y.U., 1959; LLB, Columbia U., 1962. Bar: N.Y. 1963, U.S. Dist. Ct. (so. dist.) N.Y., U.S. Dist. Ct. (no. dist.) N.Y., U.S. Dist. Ct. (ea. dist.) N.Y., U.S. Dist. Ct. (we. dist.) N.Y., U.S. Ct. Appeals (2d, 3rd, 5th, 9th, 11th, D.C. and fed. cirs.), U.S. Ct. Claims, U.S. Supreme Ct. Assoc. Dewey, Ballantine, Bushby, Palmer & Wood, N.Y.C., 1962-72; mem. Varet & Fink, P.C., aka Milgrim, Thomajan & Lee, P.C., N.Y.C., 1972-95; ptnr. Piper Rudnick LLP, N.Y.C., 1995—. Adj. prof. law Cardozo Sch. Law, N.Y.C., 1999—; arbitrator civil ct. City of N.Y., 1971—. Inspector Office of Equal Opportunity, Washington, 1966; coord. rules and credentials McCarthy for Pres., 1968; coord. Kennedy for Pres. com., N.Y.C., 1972. Joseph P. Chamberlain fellow Columbia U. Sch. Law, 1961-62. Mem. ABA, N.Y. State Bar Assn., Assn. of the Bar of the City of N.Y. (mem. fed. cts. com.

1970-73). Democrat. Avocations: classical music, skiing, tennis. General civil litigation, Intellectual property, Securities. Office: Piper Rudnick LLP 1251 Avenue the Americas New York NY 10020-1104

MEKEEL, ROBERT K. lawyer; b. Ossining, N.Y., Mar. 21, 1950; s. Ira III and Carmen E. (Munson) M.; m. Martha J. Keller, Sept. 29, 1979; 1 child, Meryl Fox. BA, Wesleyan U., Middletown, Conn., 1972; JD, U. Puget Sound, 1978. Bar: N.H. 1978, N.Y. 1979, U.S. Dist. Ct. (so. dist.) N.Y. 1980, U.S. Ct. Appeals (2d cir.) 1981, U.S. Dist. Ct. N.H. 1983, U.S. Ct. Appeals (1st cir.) 1983. Asst. dist. atty. Westchester County N.Y. Dist. Atty., White Plains, N.Y., 1979-82; assoc. Craig Wenners & McDowell, Manchester, N.H., 1983-84; clk. ct. Coos County Superior Ct., Lancaster, N.H., 1985; ptnr. McKible & Mekeel, P.A., Concord, N.H., 1986-89, Cullity Kelley & McDowell, Manchester, 1989-93, McDowell & Mekeel P.A., Manchester, 1994-96; prin. Robert K. Mekeel, P.A., Concord, 1996—. Mem. mentor program Franklin Pierce Law Sch., Concord, 1992; lectr. Nat. Bus. Inst., Eau Claire, Wis., 1993-95; mem. Million Dollar Advocates forum; mediator N.H. Superior Cts.; pvt. mediator, arbitrator disputes involving personal injury claims, pvt. mediation svcs. Fellow N.H. Bar Found.; mem. ATLA (N.H. rep.), N.H. Trial Lawyers Assn. (amicus com. 1994-96), N.H. Bar Assn. (com. on cooperation with cts., lectr. evidence seminar 1994). Democrat. Avocations: running, biking, swimming, drawing, wood working. Personal injury (including property damage), Product liability, Workers' compensation. Home and Office: 73 Main St Contoocook NH 03229-2628

MEKLER, ARLEN B. lawyer, chemist; b. N.Y.C., May 4, 1943; s. Lev A. and Ethel (Fox) M.; children from previous marriage: Jeffrey Arlen, Rebecca Ann, Ann-Marie Laura, Victoria Arlene, Lamar Adam, Lars Arlen; m. Molly L. Malone, Feb. 3, 1995. BS in Chemistry, Reed Coll.-San Jose State U., 1953; MS in Organic Chemistry, Iowa State U., 1955; PhD, Ohio State U., 1958; JD, Temple U., 1972. Bar: Del. 1972, Pa. 1972, U.S. Supreme Ct. 1976. Sr. rsch. chemist E.I. du Pont de Nemours & Co., Wilmington, Del., 1958-69; ptnr. Mekler and Maurer, Wilmington, 1972—. Chief appellate div. Office Pub. Defender, State of Del., 1973-77; pres. Del. Law Ctr., Wilmington, 1973— ; instr. constl. law Wilmington Coll., 1976-80; dir. Bar Rev. Del., 1972— ; mem. 3d Circuit Ct. Appeal Jud. Nominating Commn., 1977-81, 3d Circuit Ct. Appeals Jud. Conf. Contbr. monographs to legal publs. Pres. Mental Health Aux. for Gov. Bacon Health Ctr., 1964-66; mem. Citizens Conf. for Modernization of State Legislatures, 1964-68; state chmn., Reform Commn. for Modernization Polit. Party Rules, 1965-68; pres. Del. Citizens for Fair Housing, 1965-69; state commr. Nat. Conf. on Uniform State Laws, 1972— ; pres. Democratic Forum Del., 1966-70; mem. Del. Dem. Platform Com., 1966, 68, 72, 76; research dir. Del. Citizens for Humphrey-Muskie, 1968, Citizens for Biden, 1972, 78, 84, Citizens for McDowell, 1986—, Biden for Pres., 1986—; del. Dem. Nat. Conv., 1980; mem. social action com. Unitarian Ch., Wilmington, 1962-68. Recipient Keyman award, 1964, 65; State Govtl. Affairs award, 1964, 65 Mem. ABA, Del. Bar Assn. (com. on rules of criminal procedure 1973-74, supreme ct. com. on revision of criminal law 1973— , supreme ct. com. on rules of evidence 1976— , com. on revised rules of evidence 1976— , com. on revised rules of Del. Supreme Ct. 1974— , family law com. 1979— , continuing legal edn. com. 1981—), Pa. Bar Assn., Am. Chem. Soc., N.Y. Acad. Scis., Chem. Soc. (London), AAAS, Catalyst Club Phila., Wilmington Organic Chemists Club, ACLU (bd. dirs.), Sigma Xi, Phi Alpha Delta Constitutional, Criminal, Family and matrimonial. Home: Brandywine Hills 714 W Matson Run Pky Wilmington DE 19802-1912 Office: PO Box 2285 Wilmington DE 19899-2285 E-mail: drlaw@mac.com.

MELAMED, ARTHUR DOUGLAS, lawyer; b. Mpls., Dec. 3, 1945; s. Arthur Charles and Helen Beatrix (Rosenberg) M.: m. Carol Drescher Weisman, May 26, 1983; children: Kathryn Henrie, Elizabeth Allyn. BA, Yale U., 1967; JD, Harvard U., 1970. Bar: D.C. 1970, U.S. Ct. Internat. Trade 1985, U.S. Ct. Appeals (9th cir.) 1971, U.S. Ct. Appeals (2d cir.) 1975, U.S. Ct. Appeals (D.C. cir.) 1978, U.S. Ct. Appeals (8th cir.) 1981, U.S. Ct. Appeals (fed. cir.) 1985, U.S. Ct. Appeals (4th cir.) 1989, U.S. Ct. Appeals (10th cir.) 1993, U.S. Supreme Ct. 1981. Law clk. U.S. Ct. Appeals for 9th Circuit, 1970-71; assoc. Wilmer, Cutler & Pickering, Washington, 1971-77, ptnr., 1978-96, 2001—; prin. dep. asst. atty. gen. U.S. Dept. Justice, 1996-2000, acting asst. atty. gen. antitrust divsn., 2000-2001. Vis. prof. Georgetown U. Law Ctr., 1992-93, adj. prof., 1993-94. Contbr. articles to profl. jours. D.C. area chair Yale campaign, 1993-97; mem. social scis. coun. com. Yale U., 1989-94; trustee Nat. Child Rsch. Ctr., 1990-93, Sidwell Friends Sch., 2000—. Mem. ABA, Am. Law Inst., Yale Club (N.Y.C.), Kenwood Country Club. Antitrust, Federal civil litigation. Home: 6405 Shadow Rd Bethesda MD 20815-6613 Office: Wilmer Cutler & Pickering 2445 M St NW Washington DC 20037 Business E-Mail: doug.melamed@wilmer.com.

MELDMAN, CLIFFORD KAY, lawyer; b. Milw., July 27, 1931; s. Edward H. and Rose (Bortin) M.; children: Mindy, David, Linda, James, Noah. JD, Marquette U., 1956. Bar: Wis. 1956. Ptnr. Meldman & Meldman, Milw., 1956-73; pres. Meldman & Meldman S.C., Milw., 1973-98; pvt. practice Milw., 1956—. Contbr. articles to profl. jours., also editor. Mem.: Wis. Bar Assn. (chmn. family law sect.), Milw. Bar Assn. (bd. dirs. 1984—86, pres. 1986—87, chmn. family law sect.), Am. Acad. Matrimonial Lawyers (Wis. chpt., pres. 1982). Family and matrimonial. Home and Office: 170 W Cherokee Cir Milwaukee WI 53217-2716

MELDMAN, ROBERT EDWARD, lawyer; b. Milw., Aug. 5, 1937; s. Louis Leo and Lillian (Gollusch) M.; m. Sandra Jane Setlick, July 24, 1960; children: Saree Beth, Richard Samuel. BS, U. Wis., 1959; LL.B., Marquette U., 1962; LL.M. in Taxation, NYU, 1963. Bar: Wis. 1962, Fla. 1987, Colo. 1990, U.S. Ct. Fed. Claims, U.S. Tax Ct. 1963, U.S. Supreme Ct. 1970. Practice tax law, Milw., 1963—; pres. Meldman, Case & Weine, Ltd., Milw., 1975-85; dir. tax div. Mulcahy & Wherry, S.C., Milw., 1985-90; shareholder Reinhart, Boerner, Van Deuren, S.C., 1991—. Adj. prof. taxation U. Wis., Milw., 1970—2000, mem. tax adv. coun., 1978—2000; adj. prof. Marquette U. Sch. Law, Milw., 2001—02, The U. of Queensland T.C. Beirne Sch. Law, 2002; mem. Internat. Revenue Svc. Taxpayer Adv. Panel, 2001—; sec. Profl. Inst. Tax Study, Inc., 1978—; bd. dirs. Wis. Bar Found., 1988—94; exec. in residence Deloitte & Touche Ctr. for Multistate Taxation, U. Wis., Milw., 1996—2000. Co-author: Federal Taxation Practice and Procedure, 1983, 1986, 1988, 1992, 1998, Practical Tactics for Dealing with the IRS, 1994, A Practical Guide to U.S. Taxation of International Transactions, 1996, 1997, 2000, Federal Taxation Practice and Procedure Study Guide/Quizzes, 1998; editor: Jour. Property Taxation, 1996—2002; mem. editl. bd.: Tax Litigation Alert, 1995—2000; contbr. articles to legal jours. Recipient Adj. Taxation Faculty award UWM Tax Assn., 1987; named Outstanding Tax Profl. 1992 Corp. Reports Wis. Mag. and UWM Tax Assn. Fellow Am. Coll. Tax Coun.; mem. ABA, Fed. Bar Assn. (pres. Milw. chpt. 1966-67), Milw. Bar Assn. (chmn. tax sect. 1970-71), Wis. Bar Assn. (bd. dirs. tax sect. 1964-78, chmn. 1973-74), Internat. Bar Assn., The Law Assn. for Asia and the Pacific (chair tax sect. 2000—, dep. chair bus. law sect.), Friends of Gold Meir Libr. (bd. dirs.), Marquette U. Law Alumni Assn. (bd. dirs. 1972-77), Milw. Athletic Club, Wis. Club, B'nai B'rith (trustee, Ralph Harris Meml. award Century Lodge 1969-70), Phi Delta Phi, Tau Epsilon Rho (chancellor Milw. chpt. 1969-71, supreme nat. chancellor 1975-76, v.p. Wis. chpt., tech. 1992-2000). Jewish (trustee congregation 1972-77). Private international, Corporate taxation, Personal income taxation. Home: 7455 N Skyline Ln Milwaukee WI 53217-3327 Office: 1000 N Water St Ste 2100 Milwaukee WI 53202-3197 E-mail: rmeldman@reinhartlaw.com.

MELE, GREGG CHARLES, lawyer; b. Hackensack, N.J., May 4, 1965; s. Charles Archangelo and Jennie (Johobowska) M. BS cum laude, Montclair State Coll., 1986; MS, Steven Inst. Tech., 1988; MBA, Baruch Coll., 1998; JD cum laude, N.Y. Law Sch., 1998; LLM, NYU, 2000. Bar: N.J. 1998, N.Y. 1999. Lab. asst. Montclair (N.J.) State Coll., 1984-86; computer programmer Bac Data Med. Info. Systems, Wayne, N.J., 1985-86; computer programmer/analyst corp. hdqrs. AT&T, Somerset, N.J., 1986-90; computer systems analyst, project leader The Bank of N.Y., N.Y.C., 1990-94; project leader Andersen Consulting, N.Y.C., 1994-96; project mgr. Mutual Benefit Life, Newark, N.J., 1996; acct. mgt. IMI Systems, N.Y.C., 1996-97; asst. treas. Bankers Trust Co., N.Y.C., 1997-98; atty. asst. v.p. Merrill Lynch, N.Y.C., 1998-2000; v.p., dir. Deutsche Bank, N.Y.C., 2000—02; atty. in pvt. practice Summit, NJ, 2002—; dir. State St. Bank, 2002—. Author: The Best in the Business, 1983, Baker's Dozen, 1987. Garden State scholar Montclair State Coll., 1984, 85; finisher in N.Y.C. Marathon, 1991. Roman Catholic. Home: 40 Sulfrian Rd New Providence NJ 07974-1227 Office: 34 Maple St Summit NJ 07901

MELGREN, ERIC FRANKLIN, lawyer; b. Minneola, Kans., Dec. 16, 1956; s. Carl James and Louise C. (Loechnor) M.; m. Denise Melgren, June 16, 1979; children: David W., Susan C., Peter J., Abigail J. B, Wichita State U., 1979; JD, Washburn Sch. Law, Topeka, 1985. Bar: Kans. 1985, U.S. Dist. Ct. Kans. 1985, U.S. Ct. Appeals (10th cir.) 1987, U.S. Tax Ct. 1988, U.S. Supreme Ct. 1995. Law clk. U.S. Dist. Ct. Kans., Wichita, 1985-87; assoc. Foulston, Siefkin, Powers & Eberhardt, Wichita, 1987-92; ptnr. Foulston & Siefkin, Wichita, 1992—2002; US atty. U.S. Dept. of Justice, Kans., 2002—. Trustee Leadership Wichita, 1994—. Mem. Christian Legal Soc. (state dir. 1989-94), Wichita State Alumni Assn. (exec. com. 1993—), West Wichita Rotary Club. Republican. Administrative and regulatory, Taxation, general, State and local taxation. Office: 1200 Epic Ctr 301 N Main Wichita KS 67202*

MELI, SALVATORE ANDREW, lawyer; b. N.Y.C., Sept. 18, 1947; s. Andrew and Marie (Ruggiero) M.; m. Barbara Ann Chiesa, Aug. 16, 1970. BA, St. John's U., Jamaica, N.Y., 1969, JD, 1975. Bar: N.Y. 1976, Fla. 1976, U.S. Dist. Ct. (ea. and so. dist.) N.Y. 1976. Sole practice, Flushing, N.Y., 1976-78; ptnr. Muratori & Meli, Flushing and Lake Worth, Fla., 1978-97; sole practice Flushing and Lake Worth, Fla., 1997—. Lectr. Lawyers in the Classroom program, N.Y.C., 1977-81; mem. adv. bd. Title Ins. Co., Queens, N.Y., 1985—. Recipient Regents Scholarship, N.Y. State Bd. Regents, 1965. Mem. ABA, N.Y. State Bar Assn., Fla. Bar Assn., Queens County Bar Assn. Probate (including wills, trusts), Property, real (including real estate development, water).

MELIN, ROBERT ARTHUR, lawyer; b. Milw., Sept. 13, 1940; s. Arthur John and Frances Magdalena (Lanser) M.; m. Mary Magdalen Melin, July 8, 1967; children: Arthur Walden, Robert Dismas, Nicholas O'Brien, Madalyn Mary. BA summa cum laude, Marquette U., 1962, JD, 1967. Bar: Wis. 1966, U.S. Dist. Ct. (ea. dist.) Wis. 1966, U.S. Ct. Appeals (7th cir.) 1966, U.S. Ct. Mil. Appeals 1967, U.S. Supreme Ct. 1975. Law clk. U.S. Dist. Ct. Eastern Dist., Wis., 1966; instr. bus. law U. Ga., Hinesville, 1968; lectr. bus. law U. Md., Asmara, 1970; lectr. law Haile Salassie I. U. Law Faculty, Addis Ababa, Ethiopia, 1971-72; with Walther & Halling, Milw., 1973-74, Schroeder, Gedlen, Riester & Moerke, Milw., 1974-82; ptnr. Schroeder, Gedlen, Riester & Melin, Milw., 1982-84, Schroeder, Riester, Melin & Smith, Milw., 1984—. Author: Evidence in Ethiopia, 1972; contbg. author Ann. Survey African Law, 1974; contbr. numerous articles to legal jours. Rep. Class of 2000, West Point Parent Assn. Wis., 1996-99, 99—, exec. bd., 1997-98, 98—; lectr. charitable solicitations and contracts Philanthropy Monthly 9th Ann. Policy Conf., N.Y.C., 1985; chmn. Milw. Young Dems., 1963-64. Capt. JAGC, AUS, 1967-70. Mem. ABA, Wis. Acad. Trial Lawyers, Wis. Bar Assn., Milw. Bar Assn., Am. Legion, Friends Ethiopia, Delta Theta Phi, Phi Alpha Theta, Pi Gamma Mu. Roman Catholic. Federal civil litigation, State civil litigation, Non-profit and tax-exempt organizations. Home: 8108 N Whitney Rd Milwaukee WI 53217-2752 Office: 135 W Wells St Milwaukee WI 53203-1807

MELLEN, FRANCIS JOSEPH, JR., lawyer; b. Williamsport, Pa., Dec. 19, 1945; s. Francis Joseph and Mary Emma (Oberst) M.; m. Mary Wilder Davison, Aug. 2, 1975 (div. 1987); m. Beverly Joan Glascock, Sept. 2, 2000; children: Elizabeth, Catherine, Robert, Christine. BA, U. Ky., 1967, MA, 1971; JD, Harvard U., 1973. Bar: N.Y. 1974, Ky. 1975, U.S. Dist. Ct. (so. dist.) N.Y. 1974, U.S. Dist. Ct. (ea. dist.) Ky. 1977, U.S. Dist. Ct. (we. dist.) Ky. 1978, U.S. Ct. Appeals (2d cir.) 1975, U.S. Ct. Appeals (6th cir.) 1982. Assoc. atty. Rogers & Wells, N.Y.C., 1973-75, Wyatt, Grafton & Sloss, Louisville, 1975-80; ptnr. Wyatt, Tarrant & Combs, Louisville, 1980—. Panelist Nat. Arbitration Forum. Co-author: Kentucky Mineral Law, 1986, Kentucky Forms and Transactions, 1991. Contbr. articles to profl. jours. Mem. spl. study com. for Uniform Commercial Code, Ky. Legis. Rsch. Comsn., Frankfort, 1984-91; bd. dirs. Leadership Louisville Found., 1995-2002, counsel, 1996-98, 2000-02; bd. dirs. Stage One: The Louisville Children's Theatre, 1995-2001, v.p., 1997-98, pres., 1998-2000; bd. dirs. Louisville-Jefferson County A.W.A.R.E. Coalition, 1994-98. Mem. ABA, Am. Arbitration Assn. (panel), Nat. Arbitration Forum (panel), Ky. Bar Assn. (ho. dels. 1986-92), Louisville Bar Assn. (chmn. com. profl. responsibility 1992-94), Jefferson Club, Filson Club, Am. Mensa, Hon. Order of Ky. Cols. Republican. Corporate, general, Mergers and acquisitions. Home: 2944 Lexington Rd Louisville KY 40206-2934 Office: Wyatt Tarrant & Combs LLP 2800 PNC Plz Louisville KY 40202 E-mail: fmellen@wyattfirm.com.

MELLEY, STEVEN MICHAEL, lawyer; b. Rhinebeck, N.Y., Jan. 3, 1950; s. James Christopher and Virginia (Madonna) M.; children: Aliza, Steven Jonathan, Olivia, Bennett; m. Phoebe Kirwood. BA in Russian Studies with honors, Colgate U., 1972; JD, Tulane U., 1975. Bar: N.Y. 1976, U.S. Dist. Ct. 1976, U.S. Supreme Ct. 1980. Law clk. to hon. Matthew Braniff Criminal Dist. Judge, Orleans Parish, New Orleans; assoc. Woody N. Klose Law Offices, Red Hook, N.Y., 1975-78; ptnr. Klose & Melley, Rhinebeck, 1978-83; pvt. practice Rhinebeck, 1983—. Atty. Village of Tivoli, N.Y., 1977-78. Contbg. editor: New York Motor Vehicle Accidents, 1999; assoc. editor Tulane Forum, 1974-75. Mem. ABA, ATLA (sustaining), N.Y. State Bar Assn. (past com. mem. on specialization), Dutchess County Bar Assn. (sustaining), N.Y. State Trial Lawyers Assn., Million Dollar Advocates Forum, Phi Alpha Delta, Kappa Delta Rho. Personal injury (including property damage). Office: 24 Closs Dr Rhinebeck NY 12572 Fax: (914) 876-5745. E-mail: melleyinjurylaw@aol.com.

MELLINGER, LOUIS PHILIP, lawyer; b. Newark, Sept. 12, 1950; s. Leonard and Clarice Helen Mellinger; m. Rebecca Ann Thompson, Nov. 17; children: William Leonard, Robert Jon. BS with high honors, U. Md., 1972; JD, Widener U., Wilmington, Del., 1976; Cert. in Internat. Law, Institut Catholique, Paris, 1974. Bar: N.J. 1976, U.S. Dist. Ct. N.J. 1976, U.S. Supreme Ct. 1997. Sr. ptnr. Mellinger Sanders & Kartzman, LLC, Morris Plains, NJ, 1977—. Asst. city atty. City of Orange, NJ, 1978—80; exec. v.p. Anthem World Transport, Jersey City, 1987—; mcpl. ct. judge Allamuchy Twp., NJ, 1990—, Raritan Twp., NJ, 1997—; adv. counsel mem. Fleet Bank N.J., 1994—. Committeeman Rep. Party Warren County, NJ, 1989; chmn. com. for formation and implementation of cmty. dispute resolution program for Warren County Adminstrv. Offices of the Ct., 1993. Nominee Humanitarian of the Yr., Martial Arts Hall of Fame, Orlando, Fla., 2002; named to Cir. of Masters, Inst. of Sci. Martial Arts Angelic System, Hillside, N.J., 1996; recipient Disting. Svc. award in recognition of outstanding contbns. and dedicated svc. to Italian Am. Cmty., Consul Gen. on Behalf of the Italian Govt., 1996, Honor for dedicated svcs. to children of Allamuchy Elem. Sch., Allamuchy Bd. of Edn., 2002. Mem.: ATLA, ABA, Soc. of Children's Book Writers and Illustrators, Order of Ky. Cols., Kappa Tau Alpha. Avocations: running, writing children's stories, golf, martial arts, coaching youth basketball. Banking, Commercial, consumer (including collections, credit), Personal injury (including property damage). Office: Mellinger Sanders & Kartzman LLC 101 Gibraltar Dr Ste 2F Morris Plains NJ 07950

MELLO, FABIANA PEIXORO DE, lawyer; b. Rio de Janeiro, Oct. 14, 1969; LLB, U. Brasilia, Brazil; corp. mgmt. specialization course, Found. Dom Carral, Belo Horizonte, Brazil, 1992. Bar: OAB-DF 1992, OAB-RJ, OAB-SP. Lawyer Companhia Vale do Rio Doce, Brasilia, 1992—97; assoc. Veirando e Advogados Associados, Rio de Janeiro, 1997—2002; ptnr. Barbosa, Mussnich & Aracao Advogados, São Paulo, Brazil, 2002—. Private international, Mergers and acquisitions. Office: Barbosa Müssnich & Aracao Advogados Av Pres Juscenino Kubitsca 04543 São Paulo Brazil

MELLON, HOWARD JAY, lawyer; b. N.Y.C., Mar. 2, 1952; s. Aaron and Judith (Gersh) M BBA, Pace U., 1973; JD, Ohio State U., 1977. Bar: Ohio; CPA, N.Y., Ohio. Tax mgr. Arthur Andersen & Co., Columbus, Ohio, 1980-82; sole practice Columbus, 1982—; ptnr. Mellon & Mellon CPA's, Columbus, 1982—96; Law Enforcement Instr. Eastland Police Acad., 1999—; Magistrate Village of Ashville Mayor's Court, 2000—. Bd. dirs., sec.-treas. First Americable Corp., Columbus, 1983-91. Mem. Ohio Bar Assn., Columbus Bar Assn., Ohio Soc. CPA's. Home: 4823 Wynwood Ct Columbus OH 43220-3140 Office: 4823 Wynwood Ct Columbus OH 43220-3140

MELLUM, GALE ROBERT, lawyer; b. Duluth, Minn., July 5, 1942; s. Lester Andrew and Doris Esther (Smith) M.; m. Julie Murdoch Swanstrom, July 23, 1966; children: Eric Scott, Wendy Jane. BA summa cum laude, U. Minn., 1964, JD magna cum laude, 1968. Bar: Minn. 1968. Assoc. Faegre & Benson, Mpls., 1968-75, ptnr., 1976—, mem. mgmt. com., 1986-98. Planning com. Garret Corp. and Securities Law Inst., Northwestern U. Law Sch., 1984—; adv. bd. Quali Tech Inc., Chaska, Minn., 1985-98, bd. dirs.; bd. dirs. The Tesseract Group, Inc., Mpls.; corp. sec. Excelsior-Henderson Motorcycle Mfg. Co., Belle Plaine, Minn., 1997-2000. Hockey chmn. LARC Bd., Mpls., 1980—85. Mem. ABA (fed. securities regulation com.), Minn. Bar Assn., Hennepin County Bar Assn. (securities regulation com.). Republican. Lutheran. Avocations: tennis, golf, snow and water skiing, handball, boating. Corporate, general, Mergers and acquisitions, Securities. Home: 3833 Thomas Ave S Minneapolis MN 55410 Office: Faegre & Benson 2200 Wells Fargo Ctr 90 S 7th St Ste 2200 Minneapolis MN 55402-3901 E-mail: gmellum@faegre.com.

MELNIK, SELINDA A. lawyer; b. Ft. Worth, Aug. 22, 1951; d. Mitchell Mandel Melnik and Sylvia (Hoffman) Goldberg. BA, Temple U., 1972; M of City and Regional Planning, Rutgers U., 1974; JD summa cum laude, N.Y. Law Sch., 1984. Bar: N.Y. 1985, Del 2001, U.S. Dist. Ct. (so. and ea. dists.) N.Y. 1985, U.S. Dist. Ct. Del. 2001, U.S. Ct. Appeals (D.C. cir.) 1993, Ct. Internat. Trade 1993. Program assoc. to John D. Rockefeller III, 1974-78; cons. to various orgns. U.S., internat., 1975—; sr. policy analyst Planned Parenthood, 1978-79; dir. Ms. and Free to Be Founds., 1979-81; assoc. Milbank, Tweed, Hadley & McCloy, N.Y.C., 1984-87, LeBoeuf, Lamb, Leiby, MacRae, N.Y.C., 1987-90; ptnr. Dechert, Price & Rhoads, N.Y.C., 1991-93; internat. counsel Rogers & Wells, N.Y.C., 1993-96; pres. Internat. Counsel, NYC, 1996-2000; ptnr. Smith, Katzenstein & Furlow LLP, Wilmington, Del., 2000—02; shareholder Buchanan Ingersoll P.C., Wilmington, 2002—. Founder, 1st pres. Internat. Women's Insolvency and Restructring Confederation, cons. internat. law, trade Cross Border Insolvency and Bankruptcy Prevention Planning, 1987—; cons. fgn. govts. internat. trade and insolvency law; writer, lectr. internat. trade and insolvency law. Mem. ABA, Internat. Bar Assn. (chair membership, chair com. on creditors rights and insolvency 2000--, rep. to UN Commn. on Status of Women), Internat. Lawyers Club, N.Y. State Bar Assn., Order of Coif. Bankruptcy, Commercial, contracts (including sales of goods; commercial financing), Private international. Office: Buchanan Ingersoll PC 1201 N Market St Ste 1501 Wilmington DE 19801 E-mail: samelnik@aol.com.

MELO, PEDRO, lawyer; b. Lisbon, Feb. 29, 1972; s. António José Nunes de and Maria Eduarda (Coelho Nunes de) Melo; m. Leonor Lopes de, Mar. 20, 1999. Degree in law, Lisbon Faculty Law, 1995, postgrad. in adminstrv. law, 1998; postgrad. in energy law, Inst. Français Pétrole, 2002. Trainee Pena, Machete and Assocs., Lisbon, 1995—97; assoc. Pena, Machete, Botelho Moniz, Nobre Guedes, Ruiz and Assocs., 1997—2001; ptnr. Rui Pena, Arnaut and Assocs., 2002—. Author: Construction - Legal Frame Work, 2000. Mem.: Portuguese Fencing Fedn. (pres. disciplinary bd. 2000—). Avocations: fencing, horseback riding. Administrative and regulatory, Construction, Nuclear power. Office: Rui Pena Arnaut & Assocs Av Conselheiro Fernando de Sousa N 19 17 1070-072 Lisbon Portugal Home: Rua da Cruz dos Poiais N 111 1200-136 Lisboa Portugal Fax: 00351 21 3828155.

MELTON, BARRY, lawyer, musician; b. N.Y.C., June 14, 1947; s. James Gerald and Terry Melton; m. Barbara Joy Langer; children: Kingsley, Kyle. Bar: Calif. 1982, U.S. Dist. Ct. (no. dist.) Calif. 1982, U.S. Dist. Ct. (cen. dist.) Calif. 1983, U.S. Ct. Appeals (9th cir.) 1983, U.S. Dist. Ct. (ea. dist.) Calif. 1985, U.S. Supreme Ct. 1988. Pvt. practice, San Francisco, 1982-94; pub. defender Yolo County, Calif., 2000—. Musician, pub. Seafood Music, San Francisco, 1965—; pro-tem judge San Francisco Mcpl. Ct., 1987-94. Musician, composer various mus. recs., 1965—. Mem. State Bar Calif. (cert. criminal law specialist 1993—, vol. legal svc. awards 1983-87), Calif. Attys. Criminal Justice, Calif. Pub. Defenders Assn. (bd. dirs. 1999—). Criminal, Juvenile. Office: Yolo County Pub Defender 814 North St Woodland CA 95695-3538 E-mail: melton@counterculture.net., thefish@counterculture.net.

MELTON, EMORY LEON, lawyer, state legislator, publisher; b. McDowell, Mo., June 20, 1923; s. Columbus Right and Pearly Susan (Wise) M; m. Jean Sanders, June 19, 1949; children: Stanley Emory, John Russell. Student, Monett Jr. Coll., 1940-41, S.W. Mo. State U., 1941-42; LLB, U. Mo., 1945. Bar: Mo. 1944. Pvt. practice, Cassville, Mo., 1947—; pres. Melton Publs., Inc., 1959—; pros. atty. Barry County (Mo.), 1947-51; mem. Mo. Senate, 1973-97. Chmn. Barry County republican Com., 1964-68. Served with AUS, 1945-46. Recipient Meritorious Pub. Svc. award St. Lousi Globe-Democrat, 1976. Mem. Mo. Bar Assn., Lions, Masons. Office: PO Box 488 Cassville MO 65625-0488

MELTON, HOWELL WEBSTER, SR., federal judge; b. Atlanta, Dec. 15, 1923; s. Holmes and Alma (Combee) M.; m. Margaret Catherine Wolfe, Mar. 4, 1950; children— Howell Webster, Carol Anne. JD, U. Fla., 1948. Bar: Fla. 1948. With Upchurch, Melton & Upchurch, St. Augustine, 1948-61; judge 7th Jud. Circuit of Fla., St. Augustine, 1961-77, U.S. Dist. Ct. (mid. dist.) Fla., Jacksonville, 1977-91, sr. judge, 1991—. Past chmn. Fla. Conf. Cir. Judges, 1974; past chmn. coun. bar pres.'s Fla. Bar. Trustee Flagler Coll., St. Augustine. Served with U.S. Army, 1943-46. Recipient Disting. Service award St. Augustine Jaycees, 1953 Mem. ABA, St. Johns County Bar Assn., Jacksonville Bar Assn., Fed. Bar Assn., Fla. Blue Key, Officers Club, Masons, Phi Delta Theta, Phi Delta Phi. Methodist. Office: US Dist Ct 300 N Hogan St Ste 11-300 Jacksonville FL 32202

MELTZER, BERNARD DAVID, law educator; b. Phila., Nov. 21, 1914; s. Julius and Rose (Welkov) M.; m. Jean Sulzberger, Jan. 17, 1947; children: Joan, Daniel, Susan. AB, U. Chgo., 1935, JD, 1937; LL.M., Harvard U., 1938. Bar: Ill. 1938. Atty., spl. asst. to chmn. SEC, 1938-40; assoc. firm Mayer, Meyer, Austrian & Platt, Chgo., 1940; spl. asst. to asst. sec. state, also acting chief fgn. funds control div. State, 1941—43; asst. trial counsel U.S. prosecution Internat. Nuremberg War Trials, 1945-46; from professorial lectr. to disting. svc. prof. law emeritus U. Chgo. Law Sch., 1946—;

counsel Vedder, Price, Kaufman & Kamnholz, Chgo., 1954-55, Sidley and Austin, Chgo., 1987-89. Hearing commr. NPA, 1952-53; labor arbitrator; spl. master U.S. Ct. Appeals for D.C., 1963-64; bd. publs. U. Chgo., 1965-67, chmn., 1967-68; mem. Gov. Ill. Adv. Commn. Labor-Mgmt. Policy for Pub. Employees in Ill., 1966-67, Ill. Civil Service Commn., 1968-69; cons. U.S. Dept. Labor, 1969-70 Author: Supplementary Materials on International Organizations, 1948, (with W.G. Katz) Cases and Materials on Business Corporations, 1949, Labor Law Cases, Materials and Problems, 1970, supplement, 1972, 75, 2d edit., 1977, supplements, 1980, 82 (with S. Henderson), 3d edit. (with S. Henderson), 1985, supplement, 1988; also articles. Bd. dirs. Hyde Park Community Conf., 1954-56, S.E. Chgo. Commn., 1956-57. Served to lt. (j.g.) USNR, 1943-46. Mem. ABA (co-chmn. com. devel. law under NLRA 1959-60, mem. spl. com. transp. strikes), Ill. Bar Assn., Chgo. Bar Assn. (bd. mgrs. 1972-73), Am. Law Inst., Coll. Labor and Employment Lawyers, Am. Acad. Arts and Scis., Order of Coif, Phi Beta Kappa Home: 1219 E 50th St Chicago IL 60615-2908 Office: U Chgo Law Sch 1111 E 60th St Chicago IL 60637-2776

MELTZER, JAY H. lawyer, retail company executive; b. Bklyn., Mar. 30, 1944; s. Solomon G. and Ethel L. (Kraft) M.; m. Bonnie R. Rosenberg, June 27, 1965; children: Wendy, Elizabeth, Jonathan. AB, Dartmouth Coll., 1964; JD, Harvard U., 1967. Bar: N.Y. 1968, Mass. 1978, U.S. Dist. Ct. Mass. 1979. Law clk. to U.S. dist. judge, 1967-68; assoc. firm Shearman & Sterling, N.Y.C., 1968-72; with Damon Corp., Needham Heights, Mass., 1972-84, gen. counsel, sec., 1973-84, v.p., 1979-84; v.p., corp. counsel The TJX Cos., Inc., Framingham, Mass., 1984-87, v.p., gen. counsel, sec., 1987-89, sr. v.p., gen. counsel, sec., 1989—. Dir. coun. Better Bus. Bur., 1990-93. Mem. ABA, Am. Soc. Corp. Secs., Am. Corp. Counsel Assn. (bd. dirs. N.E. chpt. 1991-2000), Retailers Assn. Mass. (bd. dirs., exec. com., sec.), New Eng. Corp. Counsel Assn. (bd. dirs.). Commercial, contracts (including sales of goods; commercial financing), Corporate, general, Securities. Office: TJX Cos Inc 770 Cochituate Rd Framingham MA 01701-4672 E-mail: jay_meltzer@tjx.com.

MELTZER, ROBERT CRAIG, lawyer, educator; b. Chgo., July 31, 1958; s. Franklyn Richard and Zelma (Cohen) M. BA, U. Colo., 1980; cert., Inst. de Internat., Strasbourg, France, 1984; JD, No. Ill. U., DeKalb, 1985; postgrad., U. Salzburg, Austria, 1985. Bar: Ill. 1985, U.S. Dist. Ct. (no. dist.) Ill. 1985, U.S. Ct. Appeals (7th cir.) 1988, U.S. Supreme Ct. 1989. Law clk. Hurwitz & Abramson, Washington, 1980, Mayer, Brown & Platt, Chgo., 1983; lawyer UN WHO, Geneva, Switzerland, 1985; assoc. Robert C. Meltzer & Assocs., Chgo., 1986-91, Katz, Randall & Weinberg, Chgo., 1991-93, Arnstein & Lehr, Chgo., 1993-98, Grotefeld & Denenberg, Chgo., 1998-99; pres. Visanow.com., Inc., Chgo., 1999—. Adj. prof. internat. law Ill. Inst. Tech/Chgo.-Kent Coll. Law, 1994-98; creator online immigration processing. Contbr. articles to profl. jours.; editor The Globe, Springfield, Ill., 1984-99. Pro bono lawyer Fed. Bar Assn., Chgo., 1985-98. Recipient Medal of Appreciation, Ministry of Justice, Beijing, 1996. Mem. Ill. State Bar Assn. (internat. and immigration law sect. 1985—, chair internat. law sect. 1990-91, Editor's award 1989, 94, 99), Am. Immigration Law Assn. Avocations: history, racquet sports, golf, arts, music. Immigration, naturalization, and customs, Private international. Home: 71 E Division St Chicago IL 60610 Office: Visanow com Inc 350 N La Salle St 1400 Chicago IL 60610 E-mail: meltzer@visanow.com.

MELTZER, ROGER, lawyer; b. N.Y.C., Jan. 31, 1951; s. Irwin Samuel and Beula (Jacobs) M.; m. Robin Hirtz, July 20, 1975; children: Justin, Martin, Elizabeth. BA cum laude, Harvard U., 1973; postgrad., Tulane U., 1974-75; JD cum laude, NYU, 1977. Bar: N.Y. 1978, D.C. 1979. Assoc. Cahill, Gordon & Reindel, N.Y.C., 1977-84, ptnr., 1984—, mem. exec. com., 2000—. Mem. ABA, Order of the Coif. Corporate, general, Securities. Office: Cahill Gordon & Reindel 80 Pine St Fl 17 New York NY 10005-1790

MELVIN, NORMAN CECIL, lawyer; b. Balt., Aug. 21, 1916; s. Norman Cecil and Anna H. (Holzworth) M.; m. Louise A. Gillen, Feb. 10, 1945 (dec. Oct. 1958); children: Leigh G., Norman Cecil III; m. Virginia Brown Lester, Nov. 2, 1959; 1 dau., Susan A. AB, Johns Hopkins U., 1939; LL.B., Harvard U., 1942. Bar: Md. 1942. Practice law, Balt., 1946—; mem. firm Brown & Brune, 1946-52; gen. atty. Western Md. Ry. Co., Balt., 1952-66, gen. solicitor, 1966-68, v.p., gen. counsel, 1968-75, dir., 1970-75. Asst. peoples counsel Pub. Service Commn. Md., 1951-52; instr. U. Balt., 1957-66 Served to capt. AUS, 1942-46. Recipient Erskine M. Ross essay award ABA, 1950 Mem. ABA, Md. Bar Assn., Balt. Bar Assn., Soc. Colonial Wars (coun. 1966-69), SAR, Johns Hopkins Alumni Assn. (pres. 1968-70, Disting. Alumni award 1970, Heritage award 1980), Harvard Club, Johns Hopkins Club. Home: 4202 Wickford Rd Baltimore MD 21210-2930

MELVIN, R. BAILEY, lawyer; b. Asheville, N.C., Nov. 5, 1966; s. Robert Alfred and Ann Roberts Melvin; m. Connie Godwin, Dec. 29, 1990; children: Wesley, Willy Stephen, Kelli. BA, U. N.C., 1989, JD, 1992. Bar: N.C. 1992, U.S. Dist. Ct. (ea. dist.) N.C. 1992. Atty. Duffus & Melvin, Greenville, NC, 1992—. Deacon Trinity Free Will Bapt. Ch., Greenville, 1999—2001; chmn. bd. dirs. Trinity Christian Sch., Greenville, 1997—2000, Caroline Pregnancy Ctr., Greenville, 1999—; fellow Boscoe Pane Found. Mem.: Eastern N.C. Inn Ct. Avocation: golf. Personal injury (including property damage). Office: Duffus and Melvin 3001 Stantonsburg Rd Greenville NC 27834 Office Fax: 252-551-3080. Personal E-mail: baileymelvin@netscape.com.

MEMEL, SHERWIN LEONARD, lawyer; b. Buffalo, Mar. 28, 1930; s. Maurice and Nellie (Munshen) M.; m. Iris C. Gittleman, Aug. 17, 1952 (dec. 2002); children: Jana Sue, Steven Keith, David Scott, Mara Jean. BA, UCLA, 1951, JD with honors, 1954. Bar: Calif. 1955, U.S. Ct. Appeals (9th cir.) 1955, U.S. Dist. Ct. (cen. dist.) Calif. 1959, U.S. Supreme Ct. 1963, D.C. 1979. Sr. ptnr. healthcare industry practice group Manatt, Phelps & Phillips, LA, 1987—. Bd. dirs., former chmn. bd. Pac. Pub. Radio Sta. KKJZ; mem. adv. bd., adj. prof. health law U. So. Calif. Sch. Policy, Planning and Devel.; cons. and lectr. in field. Co-author: (with R. Barak) Real Estate Issues in the Health Care Industry, 1996; contbr. articles to profl. jours. Chmn. L.A. Arts Coun., 1986-87; chmn. bd. Jazz Bakery non-profit pub. performance space; vice-chmn. Dem. Bus. Coun., Washington, 1985-86; past pres. Calif. Bd. Med. Quality Assurance. Recipient Disting. Service award Fedn. Am. Hosps., 1970. Mem. ABA (com. health law), Am. Hosp. Assn. (life, Award of Honor 1971), Am. Soc. Law and Medicine, Am. Health Lawyers Assn., Calif. Soc. for Healthcare Attys. (life, pres. 1983), Calif. Bar Assn., D.C. Bar Assn., L.A. County Bar Assn. Administrative and regulatory, Health, Legislative. Office: Manatt Phelps & Phillips 11355 W Olympic Blvd Los Angeles CA 90064-1614

MENAKER, FRANK H., JR., lawyer; b. Harrisburg, Pa., Aug. 23, 1940; s. Frank H. and Romaine (Sadler) M.; m. Sharon Ann Lynch, Feb. 21, 1981; children: Denise L., Jamie E.; children by previous marriage: David C., Michelle R. BA, Wilkes Coll., 1962; JD, Am. U., 1965. Bar: D.C. 1966, Md. 1975, U.S. Supreme Ct. 1975. Formerly staff counsel Office Gen. Counsel, GAO, Washington; v.p., gen. counsel Martin Marietta Corp., 1981-95, Lockheed Martin, 1995-96, sr. v.p., gen. counsel, 1996—. Spl. counsel U.S. Commn. on Govt. Procurement, 1971. Mem. ABA (mem. sect. pub. contract law, former chair), Md. Bar Assn., Wash. Met. Corp. Counsel Assn. (bd. dirs. 1988-95). Corporate, general, Government contracts and claims, Mergers and acquisitions. Office: Lockheed Martin 6801 Rockledge Dr Bethesda MD 20817-1877*

MENAKER, PAMELA SAKOWICZ, lawyer; BSJ, Northwestern U., 1975, MSJ, 1976; LLD, Loyola U., 1984. Bar: Ill. 1984, U.S. Ct. Appeals (7th cir.) 1987. With Clifford Law Offices, Chgo. Mem. adv. bd. Ctr. Elder and Disability Law, Chgo., 2003—. Prodr.: ABC, WLS-TV news, 1976—84; reporter Chgo. Tribune, 1974—76. Mem.: ATLA, ABA (unpublished references com. chair 2002—), Chgo. Bar Assn. (book rev. editor 1999—), Ill. Trial Lawyers Assn. Avocation: improvisational comedy. Personal injury (including property damage), Toxic tort. Home: Elmwood Ave Wilmette IL 60091 Office: Clifford Law Offices 120 N LaSalle St Chicago IL 60602

MENCER, GLENN EVERELL, federal judge; b. Smethport, Pa., May 18, 1925; s. Glenn Hezekiah and Ruth Leona (Rice) M.; m. Hannah Jane Freyer, June 24, 1950; children— Ruth Ann, Cora Jane, Glenn John BBA, U. Mich., 1949, JD, 1952. Bar: Pa. 1953, U.S. Dist. Ct. (we. dist.) Pa. 1953, U.S. Supreme Ct. 1958. Sole practice, Eldred, Pa., 1953-64; dist. atty. McKean County, Pa., 1956-64; judge 48th Jud. Dist. Ct., Smethport, 1964-70, Commonwealth Ct. of Pa., Harrisburg, 1970-82, U.S. Dist. Ct., Erie, Pa., 1982—. Served with U.S. Army, 1943-45, ETO Mem. Fed. Judges Assn., Pa. Bar Assn., McKean County Bar Assn. Lodges: Masons (33 degree). Republican. Methodist. Home: 30 W Willow St Smethport PA 16749-1524 Office: US Dist Ct Fed Courthouse PO Box 1820 Erie PA 16507-0820

MENCHETTI, DAVID BARRY, lawyer; b. Chgo., Dec. 13, 1959; s. Leo and Diane M.; m. Lorraine C. Dorff, June 2, 1984; children, Cecilia, Quinn. BA, Stanford U., 1981; JD, Loyola U., Chgo., 1984. Bar: Ill. 1984. Staff atty. Ill. State Senate, Sprinfield, 1984-86; ptnr. Cullen, Haskins, Nicholson & Menchetti P.C., Chgo., 1986—. Author: (notebook) Penalties in Workers' Compensation Illinois Trial Lawyers WC Notebook, 1990—. Mem. Ill. State Bar Assn. (chair workers compensation com. 1996-97), Chgo. Bar Assn. (chair workers' compensation com., 1993-94), Workers Compensation Lawyers Assn. (pres. Chgo. 1999, bd. dirs. 1997—), Workplace Injury Litigation Group. Democrat. Roman Catholic. Workers' compensation. Office: Cullen Haskins Nicholson & Menchetti 35 E Wacker Dr Ste 1760 Chicago IL 60601-2271

MENDELOWITZ, MICHAEL SYDNEY, solicitor; b. Liverpool, Eng., June 8, 1952; s. Arnold and Rachel (Levinsohn) M.; m. Kim Merle Momberg, July 20, 1980; children: Jonathan, Alice. BA, U. Witwatersrand, Johannesburg, South Africa, 1974, LLB, 1976; BCL, Oxford U., Eng., 1979. Advocate of Supreme Ct. of South Africa, 1977, barrister of Mid. Temple, 1981, solicitor Supreme Ct. of Eng. and Wales, 1989. Barrister, Johannesburg, 1983-87; asst. Barlow Lyde & Gilbert, London, 1987-90, ptnr., 1990—. Co-author: Insurance Disputes, 1999, Insurance Handbook, 2000; editor, co-author: Reinsurance Practice and the Law, 1993; contbr. articles to profl. jours. Mem. Internat. Assn. for Ins. Law (asst. sec., gen. adminstrn.), British Ins. Law Assn., U.K. Environtl. Law Assn., Chartered Ins. Inst. Avocations: family, music, skiing. General civil litigation, Insurance, Toxic tort. Office: Barlow Lyde & Gilbert Beaufort Ho 15 Saint Botolph St London EC3A 7NJ England Fax: 44-20-7071-9000. E-mail: mmendelowitz@blg.co.uk.

MENDELSOHN, MARTIN, lawyer; b. Bkyln., Sept. 6, 1942; s. Hyman and Gertrude M.; m. Syma Barbara Rossman, Aug. 15, 1964; children: Alice S., James D. BA, Bklyn. Coll., 1963; LLB, George Washington U., 1966. Bar D.C. 1967, U.S. Ct. Appeals (D.C. cir.) 1967, U.S. Supreme Ct. 1970, U.S. Ct. Appeals (3d cir.) 1971, U.S. Ct. Appeals (7th cir.) 1973, Ill. 1973, U.S. Ct. Appeals (9th cir.) 1987, U.S. Tax Ct. 1988, U.S. Ct. Appeals (2d cir.) 1988, U.S. Ct. of Appeals (5th cir.) 2000, U.S. Ct. Appeals (4th cir.) 2002. With Gen. Counsel's Office, HEW, Washington, 1966—67; legal svcs. Washington, 1967—70, 1971—72, 1973—75; counsel Legal Svcs. Corp., Washington, 1976; adminstrv. asst. U.S. Congress, Washington, 1977; chief spl. litigation U.S. Dept. Justice, Washington, 1977—79, dep. dir. office spl. investigations, 1979—80; counsel House Judiciary Com., 1980; pvt. practice Washington, 1980—88; ptnr. Dilworth, Paxon, Kalish & Kauffman, 1989—91, Verner, Liipfert, Bernhard, McPherson & Hand, 1991—2002, Schnader, Harrison, Segal and Lewis, Washington, 2002—. Author: (with Aaron Freiwald) The Last Nazi, 1994. Named officer, Order of Merit, Poland, 2000; recipient Grand Order Merit, Austria, 2002. Mem.: ABA, D.C. Bar Assn., Cosmos Club. Jewish. Private international, Public international, Legislative. Home: 5705 Mckinley St Bethesda MD 20817-3638 Office: 1300 I St NW Ste 1200 E Washington DC 20005-2327 E-mail: mmendelsohn@schnader.com.

MENDELSON, STEVEN EARLE, lawyer; b. Los Angeles, Mar. 24, 1948; s. Robert Alexander and Nell Earle (Jacobs) M.; children: Carolyn, Laurel. BA, U. Calif., Santa Cruz, 1971; JD, Golden Gate U., 1975. Bar: Calif. 1975, U.S. Dist. Ct. (no. dist.) Calif. 1975. Assoc. Law Offices Robert A. Mendelson, Los Angeles, 1975-76, Law Offices Paul A. Eisler, San Francisco, 1976-77; sole practice Oakland, Calif., 1977-84; owner Mendelson & Mendelson, Oakland, 1985—. Founding sponsor Civil Justice Found., 1986. Mem. Assn. Trial Lawyers Am., Calif. Trial Lawyers Assn. (speaker), Alameda Contra Costa Trial Lawyers Assn., Calif. Applicant Atty's Assn., Am. Back Soc. (workshop dir., speaker, bd. dirs. com. on programs and interprofl. relations, incorporator, legal counsel 1981—). Personal injury (including property damage), Toxic tort. Office: Mendelson & Mendelson 120 11th St Oakland CA 94607-4806 E-mail: semendel@lawyer.com.

MENDENHALL, HARRY BARTON, lawyer; b. Oct. 31, 1946; BA, Colo. Coll., 1968; JD, U. Colo., 1971. Bar: Colo. 1971. Ptnr. Mendenhall & Malouff, R.L.L.P., Rocky Ford, Colo., 1971—. Mem. nominating com. Colo. Supreme Ct., Denver, 1986-91; pres. Colo. Lawyer Trust Account Found., Denver, 1995-97. Mem. Colo. Bar Assn. (pres. 1999-2000). Estate planning, Probate (including wills, trusts), Property, real (including real estate development, water). Office: Mendenhall & Malouff 805 Chestnut Ave Rocky Ford CO 81067-1224 E-mail: bmendenhall@centurytel.org.

MENDES, ROBERT JOSEPH, lawyer; b. Chgo., Sept. 15, 1966; s. Anthony J. Mendes and Elinor Coleman. BA, U. Ill., 1988; JD, U. Chgo., 1991. Bar: Ill. 91, U.S. Dist. Ct. (no. dist.) Ill. 91, Tenn. 95, U.S. Dist. Ct. (mid. dist.) Tenn. 96, U.S. Ct. Appeals (6th cir.) 97. Assoc. Altheimer & Gray, Chgo., 1991—95; pvt. practice Nashville, 1995—96; ptnr. Stanton & Mendes, PLLC, Nashville, 1996—98, Mendes & Gonzales, PLLC, Nashville, 1998—. Commercial, contracts (including sales of goods; commercial financing), Bankruptcy. Office: Mendes & Gonzales PLLC 120 30th Ave N Nashville TN 37203

MENDOLA, JOSEPH VINCENT, lawyer, chemical engineer; b. Bklyn., Sept. 25, 1953; s. Vincent and Gloria Mendola. BEng, Cooper Union; MEng, Manhattan Coll.; MBA, Adelphi U.; JD, Fordham U. Bar: N.Y. 1986; registered profl. engr. N.Y. Design engr. Lummus Co., Bloomfield, NJ; adminstr. mgr. Ravenswood sta. 74th Street Sta., Consolidated Edison Co., N.Y.C.; pvt. practice law N.Y.C.; constrn. mgr. N.Y.C. Transit. Mem. ASME, Nassau County Bar Assn. Property, real (including real estate development, water). Office: 24 Rhoda St West Hempstead NY 11552-2820

MENEFEE, SAMUEL PYEATT, lawyer, anthropologist; b. Denver, June 8, 1950; s. George Hardiman and Martha Elizabeth (Pyeatt) M. BA in Anthropology and Scholar of Ho. summa cum laude, Yale U., 1972; diploma in Social Anthropology, Oxford (Eng.) U., 1973, BLitt, 1975; JD, Harvard U., 1981; LLM in Oceans, U. Va., 1982, SJD, 1993; MPhil in Internat. Rels., U. Cambridge, Eng., 1995. Bar: Ga. 1981, U.S. Ct. Appeals (11th cir.) 1982, Va. 1983, La. 1983, U.S. Ct. Mil. Appeals 1983, U.S. Ct. Internat. Trade 1983, U.S. Ct. Claims 1983, U.S. Ct. Appeals (10th cir.) 1983, U.S. Ct. Appeals (fed., 1st, 3d, 4th, 5th, 6th, 7th, 8th and 9th cirs.) 1984, D.C. 1985, Nebr. 1985, Fla. 1985, U.S. Supreme Ct. 1985, U.S. Ct. Appeals (D.C. cir.) 1986, Maine 1986, Pa. 1986. Assoc. Phelps, Dunbar, Marks, Claverie & Sims, New Orleans, 1983-85; of counsel Barham & Churchill PC, New Orleans, 1985-88; sr. assoc. Ctr. for Nat. Security Law U. Va. Sch. Law, 1985—, fellow Ctr. for Oceans Law and Policy, 1982-83, sr. fellow, 1985-89, Maury fellow, 1989—, adv. bd., 1997—. Vis. lectr. U. Cape Town, 1987; vis. asst. prof. U. Mo.-Kansas City, 1990; law clk. Hon. Pasco M. Bowman, U.S. Ct. Appeals (8th cir.), 1994-95; vis. prof. Regent U., 1996-97, scholar-at-large, 1997—, prof., 1998—; adv. The Am. Maritime Forum/The Mariners' Mus., 1997-98; lectr. various nat. and internat. orgns.; mem. ICC Consultative Task Force on Comml. Crime, 1996—. Author: Wives for Sale: An Ethnographic Study of British Popular Divorce, 1981, Contemporary Piracy and International Law, 1995, Trends in Maritime Violence, 1996; co-editor: Materials on Ocean Law, 1982; contbr. numerous articles to profl. jours. Recipient Katharine Briggs prize Folklore Soc., 1992; Bates traveling fellow Yale U., 1971, Rhodes scholar, 1972; Cosmos fellow Sch. Scottish Studies U. Edinburgh, 1991-92, IMB fellow, ICC Internat. Maritime Bur., 1991—, Piracy Reporting Ctr. fellow, Kuala Lampur, 1993—, Huntington fellow The Mariners Mus., 1997. Fellow Royal Anthrop. Inst., Am. Anthrop. Assn., Royal Asiatic Soc., Royal Soc. Antiquaries of Ireland, Soc. Antiquaries (Scotland), Royal Geog. Soc., Soc. Antiquaries; mem. ABA (vice-chmn. marine resources com. 1987-90, chmn. law of the sea com. subcom. naval warfare, maritime terrorism and piracy 1989—, mem. law of the sea com. steering com. 1996—, mem. working group on terrorism), Southeastern Admiralty Law Inst. (com. mem.), Maritime Law Assn. (proctor, com. mem., chmn. subcom. law of the sea 1988-91, vice chmn. com. internat. law of the sea 1991— , chair working group piracy 1992—, UNESCO study group, 1998—), Marine Tech. Soc. (co-chmn. marine security com. 1991—), Selden Soc., Am. Soc. Internat. Law, Internat. Law Assn. (com. mem., rapporteur Am. br. com. EEZ 1988-90, rapporteur Am. br. com. Maritime Neutrality 1992, observer UN conv. on Law of the Sea meeting of States Parties 1996, chmn. Am. br. com. on Law of the Sea 1996—), rapporteur joint internat. working group on uniformity of the law of piracy 1998—, (Com. Maritime Internat.), Am. Soc. Indsl. Security (com. mem.), U.S. Naval Inst., USN League, Folklore Soc., Royal Celtic Soc., Internat. Studies Assn., Royal Scottish Geog. Soc., Royal African Soc., Egypt Exploration Soc., Arctic Inst. N.Am., Internat. Studies Assn., Am. Hist. Soc., Internat. Assn. Rsch. on Peasant Diaries (nat. editor 1996—), Nat. Eagle Scout Assn., Raven Soc., Jefferson Soc., Fence Club, Mory's Assn., Elizabethan Club, Yale Polit. Union, Leander Club, Cambridge Union, United Oxford and Cambridge Univ. Club, Yale Club (N.Y.C.), Paul Morphy Chess Club, Pendennis Club, Round Table Club (New Orleans), Phi Beta Kappa, Omicron Delta Kappa. Republican. Episcopalian. Avocations: anthropology, archaeology, social history, crew, hill walking. Office: U Va Ctr Nat Sec Law 580 Massie Rd Charlottesville VA 22903-1738

MENES, PAUL IRA, lawyer; b. Chgo., Jan. 10, 1955; s. Herbert and Leona (Lustig) M.; m. Sheryl Renee Jakofsky, Mar. 19, 1988. Student, Calif. State U., Northridge, 1973-74; AB, UCLA, 1976; JD, Southwestern U., 1980. Bar: Calif. 1981, U.S. Dist. Ct. (cen. dist.) Calif. 1981. Assoc. Menes & Turtle, L.A., 1981-82; assoc. Barry A. Menes & Assoc., P.C., L.A., 1982—; ptnr. Menes Law Corp., L.A., 1982—. Judge pro tem Mcpl. Ct., L.A. Jud. Dist., 1986—; spkr., lectr. South by Southwest Music Conf., North by Northwest Music Conf., Founds. Forum, Showbiz Expo, Calif. Lawyers for the Arts, others. Mem. ABA, Century City Bar Assn. (spl. award 1987), Assn. Trial Lawyers Am., Calif. Lawyers for the Arts, Nat. Acad. Rec. Arts and Scis. Entertainment, Intellectual property, Trademark and copyright. Office: 1801 Century Park E Ste 1560 Los Angeles CA 90067-2317 E-mail: paulm@meneslaw.com.

MENGEL, CHRISTOPHER EMILE, lawyer, educator; b. Holyoke, Mass., Sept. 11, 1952; s. Emile Oscar and Rose Ann (O'Donnell) M.; m. Ellen Christine Creager, Dec. 6, 1991; children: Meredith Anne, Celia Claire; step-children: Cara Elizabeth Creager, Kristen Michele Creager. Student, U. Notre Dame, 1970-71; BA, Holy Cross Coll., 1974; JD, Detroit Coll. Law, 1979. Bar: Mich. 1979, U.S. Dist. Ct. (ea. dist.) Mich. 1989, U.S. Ct. Appeals (6th cir.) 1990. Tchr. Holyoke Pub. Schs., 1974-76; assoc. Fried & Sniokaitis P.C., Detroit, 1980-82; prof. Detroit Coll. Law, 1982-85; pvt. practice Detroit, 1982-91; mng. ptnr. Berkley, Mengel & Vining, PC, 1992—. Mem. coun. St. Ambrose Parish, Grosse Pointe Park, Mich., 1985-88, pres. 1986-87. Matthew J. Ryan scholar, 1970; recipient Disting. Brief award Thomas M. Cooley Law Rev., 1996. Mem. ABA, Mich. Bar Assn., Detroit Bar Assn. Democrat. Roman Catholic. Avocations: baseball, sailing, photography. Appellate, State civil litigation, General practice. Home: 1281 N Oxford Rd Grosse Pointe MI 48236-1857 Office: Berkley Mengel & Vining PC 3100 Penobscot Bldg Detroit MI 48226 E-mail: cmengel@flash.net.

MENGLER, THOMAS M. dean; b. May 18, 1953; BA in Philosophy magna cum laude, Carleton Coll., 1975; MA in Philosophy, U. Tex., 1977, JD, 1981. Bar: Ill., Tex., D.C., U.S. Ct. Appeals (5th, 7th and 10th cirs.), U.S. Dist. Ct. (we. dist.) Tex. Law clk. to Hon. James K. Logan U.S. Ct. Appeals for 10thCir., Olathe, Kans., 1980-81; assoc. atty. Arnold & Porter, Washington, 1982-83; asst. atty. gen. Office of Atty. Gen. of Tex., Austin, 1983-85; asst. prof. law U. Ill. Coll. Law, Champaign, 1985-89, assoc. prof., 1989-91, prof. law, 1991—, assoc. dean for acad. affairs, 1992-93, dean, 1993—2002; dean, prof. law U. St. Thomas Sch. Law, Mpls., 2002—. Contbr. numerous articles to profl. jours. Mem. ABA, Ill. State Bar Assn., Order of Coif, Phi Beta Kappa. Office: Univ St Thomas Sch Law Mail TMH 440 1000 LaSalle Ave Minneapolis MN 55403-2005

MENOYO, ERIC FELIX, lawyer; b. N.Y.C., May 9, 1944; s. Enrique and Frances (Villela) M.; m. Deirdre Caitlin Ryan, Aug. 12, 1967; children: Eric Edward, Sarah Micela. AB in English, Georgetown U., 1966, JD, 1969; LLM in Taxation, NYU, 1975. Bar: N.Y. 1969, Mass. 1976, U.S. Dist. Ct. (ea. dist.) Mass. 1976, U.S. Ct. Appeals (1st cir.) 1976. Assoc. Barrett Smith Schapiro & Simon, N.Y.C., 1969-76, Palmer & Dodge, Boston, 1976-77, ptnr., 1978—. Lectr. law Northeastern U., 1986-87, Mass. Continuing Legal Edn., Boston, 1978—; trustee, Cora du Bois Charitable Trust, 1995-. Trustee Nashoba-Brooks Sch. Concord (Mass.), Inc., 1984-90, 1st Parish Sudbury, 1979-82, Sudbury Valley Trustees, Inc., 1991—, pres., 1994-96. Fellow Am. Coll. Trust and Estate Counsel; mem. ABA, Boston Bar Assn., Am. Law Inst., Larchmont Yacht Club. Unitarian Universalist. Avocations: sailing, hiking. Private international, Probate (including wills, trusts), Estate taxation. Home: 388 Willis Rd Sudbury MA 01776-1332 Office: Palmer & Dodge LLP 111 Huntington Ave Boston MA 02199-7613 E-mail: emenoyo@palmerdodge.com.

MENTON, TANYA LIA, lawyer, educator; b. Chgo., Sept. 13, 1964; d. Joseph Bernard and Rosalind Marie (Macey) M. BA magna cum laude, Northwestern U., 1986, JD, 1989. Bar: Calif. 1989, N.Y. 1993. Atty. O'Melveny and Myers, L.A., 1989-91, Townley and Updike, N.Y.C., 1991-96; exec. counsel ABC, Inc., N.Y.C., 1996—. Adj. prof. Mercy Coll., Dobbs Ferry, N.Y., 1993-2000; lectr. on sexual harassment various orgns. including Def. Rsch. Inst. programs, N.Y.C., 1995-96. Editor: (legal publ.) California Employment Law Letter, 1989-91. Nat. Harry S. Truman scholar, 1982-86. Mem. ABA, Calif. Bar Assn. (labor and employment sect.), N.Y. State Bar Assn. (labor and employment sect.). Democrat. Avocations: horseback riding, softball, cooking. Home: # 17P 301 E 79th St Apt 17P New York NY 10021-0940 Office: ABC Inc 77 W 66th St New York NY 10023-6201

MENTULA, ARTTU, lawyer; b. Helsinki, Finland, Aug. 9, 1965; s. Perttu Mentula and Ann-Mari Grandell; m. Kirsi-Marjut Hintikka Mentula; children: Sara-Sofia, Lari Artturi. LLM, U. Helsinki, 1992. Assoc. Kari Kuitunen Atty. at Law, Helsinki, 1990—94; trained on bench Dist. Ct. Vantaa, Finland, 1994—95; legal counsel Valio Ltd., Helsinki, 1995—98, joint gen. counsel, 1998—99; atty. Castrén & Shellman, Attys. at Law,

Helsinki, 1999—2002; ptnr. Merilampi Marttila Laitasalo, Atty. at Law, Helsinki, 2002—. Author: Cartels in Finnish and in EC Competition Law, 2002; co-author: Abuse of a Dominant Position in Competition Law, 1997. Mem.: Finnish Competition Law Assn. (chmn. 2000—02, editor 2002—), Finnish Bar Assn., Assn. for European Law, Internat. Bar Assn. Avocations: golf, skiing, hunting, squash. Antitrust. Office: Merilampi Marttila Laitasalo Atty Law Eteläesplanadi 22A 00130 Helsinki Finland

MENTZ, HENRY ALVAN, JR., federal judge; b. New Orleans, Nov. 10, 1920; s. Henry Alvan and Lulla (Bridewell) M.; m. Ann Lamantia, June 23, 1956; children: Ann, Carli, Hal, Frederick, George BA, Tulane U., 1941; JD, La. State U., 1943. Bar: La. 1943, U.S. Dist. Ct. (ea. dist.) La. 1944. With legal dept. Shell Oil, New Orleans, 1947-48; pvt. practice Hammond, 1948-82; judge U.S. Dist. Ct. (ea. dist.) La., New Orleans, 1982—, sr. judge, 1992—. Editor: Combined Gospels, 1976 Pres. La. Soc. Music and Performing Arts, 1994-97, L.A. Civil Svc. League, 1979-81; bd. dirs. Southea. La. U. Found., Salvation Army; chmn. Tulane U. 50th Anniversary Reunion for 1991. Decorated 2 Battle Stars, Bronze Star; recipient Disting. Svc. award AMVETS, 1950. Mem. SAR, Royal Soc. St. George (pres.), Boston Club New Orleans, Delta Tau Delta. Republican. Episcopalian. Home: 2105 State St New Orleans LA 70118-6255 Office: US Dist Ct C-114 US Courthouse 500 Camp St New Orleans LA 70130-3313*

MENTZ, LAWRENCE, lawyer; b. N.Y.C., Nov. 5, 1946; s. Joseph Walter and Audrey Cecilia (Armstrong) M.; m. Barbara Antonello, Nov. 10, 1973; children: Kathleen Elizabeth, Lawrence Goodwin. BS in Physics, Rensselaer Poly. Inst., 1968; JD, U. Notre Dame, 1973. Bar: N.Y. 1973, DC 1974. Assoc. Condon & Forsyth, N.Y.C., 1973-80, ptnr., 1981-89, Biedermann, Hoenig, Massamillo & Ruff, N.Y.C., 1990—; counsellor at law. Speaker Worldwide Airlines Customer Rels. Assn. Conf., Singapore, 1983, 2d Cir. Speakers Bur., Com. on BiCentennial of U.S. Constn., 1987; arbitrator U.S. Dist. Ct. (ea. dist.) Bklyn., 1986—; bd. dirs. Black Mountain Mgmt. Inc. With USNR, 1969-70. Mem. ABA, Fed. Bar Coun., N.Y. State Bar Assn. (exec. com. sect. on comml. and fed. litigation, fed. judiciary com., 1993, com. Supreme Cts.), Assn. of Bar of City of N.Y. (com. on aeronautics law, task force on N.Y. Constl. Conv., com. on state legis.), Wings Club. Roman Catholic. Avocations: swimming, running, philately. Aviation, Federal civil litigation, Insurance. Office: Biedermann Hoenig Massamillo & Ruff 90 Park Ave New York NY 10016-1301 E-mail: lmentz@bhmr.com.

MERANUS, LEONARD STANLEY, lawyer; b. Newark, Jan. 7, 1928; s. Norman and Ada (Binstock) M.; m. Jane B. Holzman, Sept. 20, 1989; children: Norman, James M., David. LittB, Rutgers U., 1948; LLB, Harvard U., 1954. Bar: Ohio 1954. Assoc. Paxton & Seasongood, cin., 1954-59, ptnr., 1959-85, pres., 1985-89; ptnr. Thompson, Hine and Flory, 1989-96, ptnr.-in-charge Cin. office, 1989-91, mem. firm mgmt. com., 1991-93, of counsel, 1998—; adj. prof. law U. Cin. Coll. Law, 1998-2000. Bd. dirs. Jewish Hosp., 1976-86, chmn. of the bd., 1983-86; trustee Andrew Jergens Found., 1962-97. Mem. ABA, Ohio Bar Assn., Cin. Bar Assn., Am. Arbitration Assn. (chmn. comml. arbitration adv. com., Ohio panel large, complex arbitration cases). Corporate, general, Mergers and acquisitions, Property, real (including real estate development, water). Office: Thompson Hine LLP 312 Walnut St Ste 14 Cincinnati OH 45202-4089

MERAZ, SALVADOR ADRIAN, lawyer; b. Juarez, Chihuahua, Mexico, Mar. 16, 1973; s. Salvador Meraz and Hortensia Ferreyra. LLM in Corp. Law, U. Juarez, Chihuahua, 2002. Of counsel Chihuahua Ministry Of Urban Devel. And Eco, Juarez, Mexico, 1992—93; govt. atty. Gen. Attorney's Office For Chihuahua, Juarez, 1993—94; of counsel Bryan, Gonzalez Vargas y Gonzalez Baz, 1994—95; associated atty. LexCorp Abogados, 1995—. Mem.: Tex.-Mex. Bar Assn. Avocations: bicycling, reading. Environmental, Corporate, general, Administrative and regulatory. Office Fax: (01152656)618-3001. E-mail: ameraz@lexcorpabogados.com.

MERCER, EDWIN WAYNE, lawyer; b. Kingsport, Tenn., July 19, 1940; s. Ernest LaFayette and Geneva (Frye) M. BBA, Tex. Tech U., 1963; JD, S. Tex. Coll. Law, 1971. Bar: Tex. 1971, U.S. Dist. Ct. (no. dist.) Tex 1975, U.S. Supreme Ct. 1976, U.S. Ct. Appeals (5th Cir.) 1979. Pvt. practice, Houston, 1971-73; gen. counsel, corp. sec. Alcon Labs., Inc., Ft. Worth, 1973-81; ptnr. Gandy Michener Swindle Whitaker Pratt & Mercer, Ft. Worth, 1981-84; v.p., gen. counsel, corp. sec. Pengo Industries, Inc., Ft. Worth, 1984-90, also bd. dirs.; pvt. law practice, 1990—. Bd. dirs. Soc. for Prevention Blindness, 1979—. Mem. ABA, State Bar Tex., Coll. State Bar Tex., South Tex. Coll. Law Alumni Assn., Tex. Tech U. Ex-Assn., Ft. Worth Club, Delta Theta Phi, Phi Delta Theta. Methodist. Corporate, general, Public international. Mailing: PO Box 148 Fort Worth TX 76101-0148

MERCER, WILLIAM W. prosecutor; BA, U. Mont.; MPA, Harvard U.; JD, George Mason U. Counselor to asst. atty. gen., sr. policy analyst Office of Policy Devel. U.S. Dept. Justice, 1989—94, asst. U.S. atty. Dist. Mont., 1994—2001, U.S. atty., 2001—. Office: PO Box 1478 Billings MT 59103*

MERCORELLA, ANTHONY J. lawyer, former state supreme court justice; b. N.Y.C., Mar. 6, 1927; s. Sante and Josephine (Bozzuti) M.; m. Maria G. Delucia, June 16, 1956; children: Anne Mercorella Flynn, Susan Mercorella Creavin, Robert, Carole Crinieri. BA, L.I. U., 1949; LLD, Fordham U., 1952. Bar: N.Y. Law asst. City Ct., City of N.Y., 1955-62; chief law asst. Civil Ct., City of N.Y., 1962-65; mem. N.Y. State Assembly, 1965-72; councilman City Coun., City of N.Y., 1973-75; judge Civil Ct., City of N.Y., 1975-79; justice Supreme Ct., N.Y.C., 1980-84; ptnr. Wilson, Elser, Moskowitz, Edelman & Dicker, N.Y.C., 1984—. Currently arbitrator and mediator in various dispute resolution systems. With USN, 1945-46, Europe, Pacific. Mem. ABA (del. N.Y. State Bar Assn.), N.Y. State Bar Assn., Assn. of Bar of City of N.Y., Bronx County Bar Assn. (pres. 1971), Columbian Lawyers Westchester County (pres. 1984). Office: Wilson Elser Moskowitz Edelman & Dicker 150 E 42nd St New York NY 10017-5612 E-mail: mercorellaa@wemed.com., ajmmediate@aol.com.

MERDEK, ANDREW AUSTIN, publishing/media executive, lawyer; b. Portland, Maine, Oct. 11, 1950; s. Philip and Eleanor (Weiss) M.; m. Jeanne Mullen, July 22, 1983; children: David, Jonathan. AB, Middlebury Coll., 1972; JD, U. Va., 1978. Bar: D.C. 1978, U.S. Dist. Ct. D.C. 1979, U.S. Ct. Appeals (D.C. cir.) 1979, U.S. Supreme Ct. 1982. Reporter, editor Portland Press Herald, 1973-75; assoc. Dow, Lohnes & Albertson, Washington, 1978-86, ptnr., 1986-87; v.p., gen. mgr. Atlanta Constitution and Journal, 1987-92; v.p. legal affairs Cox Enterprises, Inc., Atlanta, 1993—, gen. counsel, 1993—, corp. sec., 1993—. Mem. Newspaper Assn. of Am. (chmn. legal affairs com.), Order of Coif, Phi Beta Kappa. Home: 445 Mount Vernon Hwy NW Atlanta GA 30327-4313 Office: Cox Enterprises Inc 6205 Peachtree Dunwoody Rd Atlanta GA 30328- E-mail: andy.merdek@cox.com.

MERHIGE, ROBERT REYNOLD, JR., lawyer; b. NYC, Feb. 5, 1919; s. Robert Reynold and Eleanor (Donovan) Merhige; m. Shirley Galleher, Apr. 24, 1957; children: Robert Reynold III, Mark Reynold. LLB, U. Richmond, 1942, LLD (hon.), 1976; LLM, U. Va., 1982; LLD (hon.), Washington and Lee U., 1990, Wake Forest U., 1994. Bar: Va. 1942. Ptnr. Bremner Merhige Montgomery & Baber, Richmond, 1945-67; judge U.S. Dist. Ct., Richmond, 1967—; resigned, 1998; counsel Hunton & Williams, Richmond, 1998—. Guest lectr. trial tactics Law Sch. U. Va., Edwald Disting. prof. law, 1987—88; adj. prof. Law Sch. U. Richmond, 1973—87; appeal agt. Henrico County Draft Bd., 1954—67; mem. NCAA spl. com. discipline rules; profl.-in-residence, Zambia, 1994. Co-author: Virginia Jury Instructions. Mem. Richmond Citizens Assn. With USAF, World War II. Decorated Air medal with four oak leaf clusters; named Citizen of the Yr., 3d Dist. Omega Psi Phi, 1972, Richmond Urban League, 1977, Style Mag., 1986, Richmonder of the Yr., 1984, 1987; named one of 100 Most Influential Richmonders of Last Century, Style Mag. and Valentine Mus., 2000; recipient Amara Civic Club award, 1968, Spl. award, City of Richmond, 1967, Disting. Alumni award, U. Richmond, 1979, Disting. Svc. award, Nat. Alumni Coun. U. Richmond, 1979, Herbert T. Harley award, Am. Judicature Soc., 1982, Athenian Citizen medal, 1979, Torch of Liberty award, Anti-Defamation League of B'nai B'rith, 1982, T.C. Williams Sch. of Law Disting. Svc. award, 1983, Pres.'s award, Old Dominion Bar Assn., 1986, William J. Brennan award, 1986, Merit Citation award, NCCJ, 1987, William B. Green award for professionalism, U. Richmond, 1989, Marshal-Wythe medallion (William & Mary Faculty award), 1989, Lewis F. Powell, Jr. award, Am. Inns of Ct., 1999. Fellow: Va. Law Found.; mem.: Nat. Arbitration Forum (arbitrator), Nat. Patents Bd. (cert. panelist), FedNet (dispute resolution), John Marshall Inns of Ct. (founding mem.), Jud. Conf. U.S., Va. Trial Lawyers Assn. (chmn. membership com. 1964—65, Disting. Svc. award 1977), Am. Law Inst. (faculty), Richmond Bar Assn. (pres. 1963—64, multi-dist. lit. panel 1990—, Hill-Tucker award 1991), Va. Bar Assn., Omicron Delta Kappa (Hunter W. Martin Profl. award 1998). Alternative dispute resolution, General civil litigation, Intellectual property. Office: Hunton & Williams Riverfront Plz East Tower 951 E Byrd St Richmond VA 23219-4074 E-mail: MerhigeR@Hunton.com.

MERLY, MIRIAM NAVEIRA, state supreme court justice; b. Santurce, P.R., July 28, 1934; married; 2 children. BA, Mount St. Vincent Coll., N.Y., 1956; JD, U. P.R. Law Sch., 1960; LLM, Columbia U., 1969; postgrad., Leiden U., Holland, 1971-72; LLD, U. Georgetown Sch. Law, 1990. Law clerk P.R. Supreme Ct., 1963-71, asst. atty. gen. Dept. Justice, 1966-73, asst. solicitor gen. Dept. Justice, 1973-76, assoc. justice, 1985—, pres. judicial commn. on gender bias, 1992—; tchr. Law Sch. U. P.R., 1971-72; atty. pvt. practice, 1976-85; prof. Sch. Law Inter-Am. U. Office: Supreme Ct PO Box 2392 San Juan PR 00902-2392

MERMELSTEIN, JULES JOSHUA, lawyer, township commissioner; b. Phila., Apr. 25, 1955; s. Harry and Ellen Jane (Greenberg) M.; m. Ruth Susan Applebaum, Aug. 18, 1974; children: Hannah Leona, Benjamin Isaac. BA, Temple U., 1977; JD, Am. U., 1979; MEd, Beaver Coll., 1994. Bar: Pa. 1980, U.S. Dist. Ct. (ea. dist.) Pa. 1980, U.S. Ct. Appeals (3d cir.) 1982, U.S. Supreme Ct. 1983. Ptnr. Mermelstein & Light, Norristown and Hatboro, Pa., 1980-83; v.p., gen. counsel Am. Ins. Cons., Feasterville, Pa., 1983; staff atty. Hyatt Legal Svcs., Phila., 1983-84, mng. atty., 1984-85; pvt. practice Phila./Montgomery County, 1985-93; tchr., social studies coord. The Bridge, 1997-99; ednl. cons. Interim House, 1998-2000. Prof. law, St. Matthew Sch. Law, Phila., 1985-87; adj. prof. criminal justice Glassboro State U., N.J., 1988; faculty polit. sci. dept. Temple U., 1989; atty. Levin & Assocs., Wyncote, Pa., 1998-2001; mng. atty. Levin & Assocs., Wyncote, 2002—; title agt. Forward Abstract, LLC, Wyncote, 2002—. Editor: The Montco Democrat, 1990-92. Vol. atty. ACLU, Phila., 1980-93; chmn. Tikkun Olam (Repair the World) Com., 1989-92, 98-2000; area rep. Montgomery County Dem. Exec. Com., 1982-85, 88-94; treas., 1994-98, candidate coord., 1982, nominee for dist. atty., 1983, committeeman, 1973-77, 82-85, 88-92, campaign mgr. Talbot for state legis., 1988; Upper Dublin chmn. Dukakis-Bentsen, 1988, chair Upper Dublin Dem. Com., 1990-91, commr. Upper Dublin Twp., 1992—; Dem. candidate Pa. State Legis., 2000; bd. dirs. Reconstructionist Congregation Or Hadash, Ft. Washington, Pa., 1988-92, 96-2000, 2001-2003, confirmation tchr., 1994—. Jewish. Appellate, State civil litigation, Constitutional. Home: 18 Northview Dr Glenside PA 19038-1318 E-mail: JulesMermelstein@hotmail.com.

MEROW, JOHN, lawyer; b. Little Valley, N.Y., Dec. 20, 1929; s. Luin George and Mildred Elizabeth Merow; m. Mary Alyce Smith, June 19, 1957; 1 child, Alison. Student, UCLA, 1947-48; BS in Engring., U. Mich., 1952; JD, Harvard U., 1958. Bar: N.Y. 1958, U.S. Supreme Ct. 1971. Assoc. Sullivan & Cromwell, N.Y.C., 1958-64, ptnr., 1965-96, vice chmn., 1986-87, chmn., sr. ptnr., 1987-94, sr. counsel, 1997—. Bd. dirs. Seligman Group Investment Cos., Commonwealth Industries, Inc.; trustee, vice chmn. N.Y. Presbyn. Healthcare Sys., Inc.; trustee N.Y. Presbyn. Hosp.; trustee Friends of the Archbishop of Canterbury's Anglican Communion Fund. Chmn. bd. dirs. Am.-Australian Assn., 1986—89; vice chmn. bd. dirs. U.S.-New Zealand Coun.; bd. dirs. Mcpl. Art Soc. N.Y.; trustee Am. Friends of Nat. Gallery of Australia; trustee, mem. exec. com., sec. U.S. Coun. Internat. Bus.; bd. dirs., sec. Met. Opera Club, 1986—94; trustee Anglican Investment Agy. Trust. Lt. USN, 1952—55. Named hon. officer Order of Australia. Mem. Am. Law Inst. (advisor corp. governance project 1978-92), Coun. on Fgn. Rels., Fgn. Policy Assn. (bd. dirs., treas.), Soc. Mayflower Desc., Links Club, Pilgrims, Piping Rock Club, Down Town Assn., Union Club, Griffis Faculty Club, River Club. Home: 435 E 52d St New York NY 10022 also: 51 Fruitledge Rd Glen Head NY 11545-3316 Office: Sullivan & Cromwell LLP 125 Broad St New York NY 10004-2498 E-mail: merowj@sullcrom.com.

MERRIAM, DWIGHT HAINES, lawyer, land use planner; b. Norwood, Mass., Apr. 20, 1946; s. Austin Luther and Lillian Diana (Olsen) M.; m. Cynthia Ann Hayes, May 21, 1966 (div. June 1992); children: Sarah Ann Leilani, Jonathan Hayes; m. Susan Manning Standish, May 6, 1995; children: Alexander Harlan, Lucy Caroline. BA cum laude, U. Mass., 1968; M in Regional Planning, U. N.C., 1974; JD, Yale U., 1978. Bar: Conn. 1978, Mass. 1980, U.S. Dist. Ct. Conn. 1981, U.S. Dist. Ct. Hawaii 1984, U.S. Supreme Ct. 1990, U.S. Ct. Appeals (4th cir.) 1993. Land use planner Charles E. Downe, Newton, Mass., 1968; assoc. Byrne, Buck & Steiner, Farmington, Conn., 1978, Robinson, Robinson & Cole, Hartford, Conn., 1979-83; ptnr. Robinson & Cole LLP, Hartford, 1984—. Adj. prof. law Western New Eng. Coll., 1978-86, U. Conn., 1982, 84-87, Vt. Law Sch., 1994—; instr. planning U. Bridgeport, 1981-83, U. Conn., 1986-92; mem. faculty Nat. Coll. Dist. Attys., 1983-87, Nat. Jud. Coll., 1994; mem. faculty Am. Law Inst.-ABA Land Use Inst., 1988—; instr. city and regional planning Memphis State U., 1989, 94; speaker in field. Co-author: The Takings Issue, 1999; co-editor: Inclusionary Zoning Moves Downtown, 1985; contbr. Bd. dirs. Conn. chpt. Appleseed Found., 1997-2000, Am. Boat Builders and Repairers Assn., 1995-1999, Growth Mgmt. Inst., Washington, 1992—, Housing Edn. Resource Ctr., 1984-88, Housing Coalition for Capitol Region, Inc., 1984-86; bd. dirs. Conn. Fund for Environment, 1981-85, legal adv. com., 1985-88, legal adv. bd., 1978-81; mem. Environment 2000 environ. plan adv. bd. Conn. Dept. Environ. Protection, 1987-91; assoc. Environ. Law Inst., 1987—; mem. housing task force Conn. Dept. on Aging, 1981; mem. Gov.'s Housing Task Force, Conn., 1980-81. With USN, 1968-75, Vietnam; capt. USNR, 1975-99. Fellow: Am. Inst. Cert. Planners (pres. 1988—90); mem.: ABA, Am. Coll. Real Estate Lawyers, Assn. State Floodplain Mgrs., Internat. Mcpl. Law Assn. (chmn. sect. on zoning, planning and land devel. 1988—89), Am. Planning Assn. (bd. dirs. 1988—90, chmn. planning and law divsn. 1984—86, exec. com. planning and law divsn. 1978—88, chmn. legis. com. Conn. chpt. 1978—80, editl. adv. bd. 1984—92), Conn. Bar Assn. (exec. com. zoning and planning sect. 1985—87, 1991—). Democrat. Unitarian Universalist. Avocations: sailing, skiing. Environmental, Land use and zoning (including planning), Property, real (including real estate development, water). Home: 80 Latimer Ln Weatogue CT 06089 Office: Robinson & Cole LLP 280 Trumbull St 27th Fl Hartford CT 06103-3597

MERRIFIELD, LEROY SORENSON, law educator; b. Mpls., Nov. 18, 1917; s. Edgar Eugene and Alice Sorenson M.; m. Marian Grace Hansen, Apr. 25, 1943; children: Lois, Eric, Randall, Karen. BA, U. Minn., 1938, JD, 1941; MPA, Harvard U., 1942, SJD, 1956. Bar: Minn. 1941, D.C. 1979, U.S. Supreme Ct. 1957. Atty. U.S. Office Price Adminstrn., Boston, 1942, U.S. Dept. Justice, Washington, 1946; prof. law George Washington U., Washington, 1947-87; prof. emeritus, 1987—. Lt. USN, 1943-45. Mem. ABA, Am. Arbitration Assn., Internat. Indsl. Rels. Assn., Order of Coif, Phi Beta Kappa. Democrat. Unitarian Universalist. Avocations: singing, tennis, golf.

MERRILL, ABEL JAY, lawyer; b. Balt., Mar. 25, 1938; s. Yale and Evelyn (Cordish) M.; m. Susan Stein, June 15, 1963; children: Adam L., Julie F. BA, Colgate U., 1959; LLB, U. Md., 1964. Bar: Md. 1964. Law clk. U.S. Ct. Appeals, Balt., 1964-65; assoc. Gordon, Feinblatt & Rothman, Balt., 1965-70; atty. pvt. practice, Annapolis, Md., 1970-78, 83—; prin. Blumenthal, May, Downs & Merrill, Annapolis, Md., 1979-83; mem. firm Merrill & Cruttenden, P.A. Mem. inquiry com. Atty. Grievance Commn. Md., 1975-85, character com. Ct. of Appeals, 1987-88; mem. pension oversight bd. Anne Arundel County, Md. Fellow Am. Coll. Probate Counsel; mem. ABA, Md. Bar Assn., Anne Arundel County Bar Assn. Estate planning, Probate (including wills, trusts), Estate taxation. E-mail: abelj@merillaw.com.

MERRILL, GEORGE VANDERNETH, lawyer, investment executive; b. N.Y.C., July 2, 1947; s. James Edward and Claire (Leness) M.; m. Janice Anne Humes, May 11, 1985; children: Claire Georgina, Anne Stewart. Student, Phillips Exeter Acad., 1960-64; AB magna cum laude, Harvard U., 1968, JD, 1972; MBA, Columbia U., 1973. Bar: N.Y. 1973, U.S. Dist. Ct. (so. and ea. dists.) N.Y. 1974, U.S. Ct. Appeals (2d cir.) 1974. Assoc. Cleary, Gottlieb, Steen & Hamilton, N.Y.C., 1974-77, Hawkins, Delafield & Wood, N.Y.C., 1977-79; v.p. Irving Trust Co., N.Y.C., 1980-82, Listowel, Inc., N.Y.C., 1982-84, bd. dirs., exec. v.p., 1984-93; v.p. instl. portfolio mgmt. Shawmut Investment Advisors, 1993-95; also co-mgr. Shawmut Growth & Income Equity Mut. Fund; v.p. instl. portfolio mgmt. Fleet Investment Advisors, 1995-96, also co-mgr. Galaxy Growth & Income Equity Mut. Fund.; v.p. trust and instl. portfolio mgmt., mem. Fla. equity com. No. Trust Corp., Chgo., 1996-2000; v.p., sr. personal investment officer, sector head Bank of N.Y., N.Y.C., 2000—. Bd. dirs. Pres. Arell Found., N.Y.C., 1985-93, also bd. dirs., pres. Northfield Charitable Corp., N.Y.C., 1986-93; v.p., sec. Brougham Prodn. Co., N.Y.C., 1986-89, bd. dirs., sr. v.p., sec., 1990-93; v.p., sec. Marinetics Inc., N.Y.C., 1988-90, sr. v.p., sec., 1991-93, also bd. dirs., 1989-93; v.p. Sci. Design and Engring. Co., Inc., N.Y.C., 1987-88, bd. dirs., exec. v.p., 1989-93. John Harvard scholar; recipient Detur award Harvard U., 1968. Mem. ABA, Am. Mgmt. Assn., Nat. Cum Laude Soc., The Brook, Union Club (N.Y.C.), Down Town Assn., Racquet and Tennis Club, Somerset Club (Boston), Signet Soc. (Cambridge), Pilgrims of U.S. Corporate, general, Estate planning, Finance. Home: 2 Pierce Rd Riverside CT 06878 Office: The Bank of NY 5th Fl 1290 Ave of the Americas New York NY 10104 E-mail: gmerrill@bankofny.com.

MERRILL, RICHARD AUSTIN, lawyer; b. Logan, Utah, May 20, 1937; s. Milton Rees and Bessie (Austin) M.; m. Elizabeth Duvall, Aug. 26, 1961; children— Patricia, John. AB, Columbia U., 1959, LLB, 1964; BA (Rhodes scholar), Oxford (Eng.) U., 1961, MA, 1965. Bar: N.Y. 1964, D.C. 1965, Va. 1980. Law clk. to Hon. Carl McGowan, U.S. Ct. Appeals for D.C., 1964-65, Va. bar, 1980; assoc. firm Covington & Burling, Washington, 1965-69, spl. counsel, 1991—; assoc. prof. law U. Va., 1969-72, prof., 1972-75, Daniel Caplin prof. law, 1977—, Arnold Leon prof., 1985-88, dean sch. law, 1980-88, Albert C. Tate Jr. rsch. prof., 1989-91. Gen. counsel FDA, Washington, 1975-77; cons. in field. Mem. Inst. Medicine (council) 1985-88, Nat. Acad. Scis., 1977—, Bd. on Toxicology and Environ. Health Hazards, 1979-85; bd. dirs. Immunex Corp. Author: (with Jerry L. Mashaw and Peter Shane) American Administrative Law, 2d edit., 1985, (with Peter B. Hutt) Food and Drug Law, 1980. Bd. trustees Thomas Jefferson Meml. Found. Mem. Am. Bar Found., Va. Bar Found., Am. Law Inst., Food and Drug Inst. (trustee). Administrative and regulatory, Environmental, Health. Office: U Va Sch Law 580 Massie Rd Charlottesville VA 22903-1738

MERRILL, THOMAS WENDELL, lawyer, law educator; b. Bartlesville, Okla., May 3, 1949; s. William McGill and Dorothy (Glasener) M.; m. Kimberly Ann Evans, Sept. 8, 1973; children: Jessica, Margaret, Elizabeth. BA, Grinnell Coll., 1971, Oxford U., 1973; JD, U. Chgo., 1977. Bar: Ill. 1980, U.S. Dist Ct. (no. dist.) Ill. 1980, U.S. Ct. Appeals (5th cir.) 1982, U.S. Ct. Appeals (7th cir.) 1983, U.S. Ct. Appeals (9th and D.C. cirs.) 1984, U.S. Supreme Ct. 1985. Clk. U.S. Ct. Appeals (D.C. cir.), Washington, 1977-78, U.S. Supreme Ct., Washington, 1978-79; assoc. Sidley & Austin, Chgo., 1979-81, counsel, 1981-87, 90—; dep. solicitor gen. US Dept. Justice, 1987-90; prof. law Northwestern U., Chgo., 1981—2003, John Paul Stevens prof., 1993—2003; prof. law Columbia U., 2003—. Contbr. articles to profl. jours. Rhodes scholar Oxford U., 1971; Danforth fellow, 1971. Home: 2828 Broadway Apt 7C New York NY 10025 Address: 435 W 116th St New York NY 10027

MERRILL, WILLIAM H., JR., lawyer, corporate professional; b. Indpls., Apr. 11, 1942; s. William H. and Jane (Robinson) M.; m. Winifred Jane Baur, July 25, 1964; children: Michele Jane, Betsy Diane. BS, Butler U., 1965; JD, Ind. U., 1967. Bar: Ind. 1967. Trust officer Mchts. Nat. Bank, Indpls., 1965—69; gen. counsel Everett I. Brown Co., Indpls., 1969—85; v.p., gen. counsel Landeco, Inc., Indpls., 1970—85; pres. Bash Seed Co., Indpls., 1975—97; gen. ptnr. Meta Ptnrs., 1984—90. Pres. Meta Investment Co., 1988-90, Meta Mgmt. Co., 1988-90, Northwest Develop. Corp., 1975—, Scotts Garden Ctr., Inc., 1977-97; bd. dirs. Custom Molded Products, Inc. Mem. Carmel (Ind.) City Plan Commn., 1975-85, pres. 1982-85. Mem. ABA, Ind. Bar Assn., Indpls. Bar Assn., Crooked Stick Golf Club. Corporate, general, Property, real (including real estate development, water). Home: 3725 W 106th St Carmel IN 46032-7719 Office: 3205 W 71st St Indianapolis IN 46268-2244

MERRIMAN, WILLIAM OTTO, JR., lawyer; b. Parkersburg, W.Va., Sept. 11, 1969; s. William Otto and Anna Ruth Merriman; m. Erica Lynn Merriman, May 25; 1 child, Savannah Sloane. JD, Capital U., 1996. Bar: W.Va. 96, U.S. Dist. Ct. (so. dist.) W.Va. 96. Assoc. Law Offices of William Jacobs, Parkersburg, W.Va., 1996—98; asst. city atty. City of Parkersburg, 1998—2001; ptnr. Cosenza Underwood and Merriman, Parkersburg, 1998—. Mem.: ATLA, W.Va. Trial Lawyers Assn. Personal injury (including property damage), Product liability, Professional liability. Office: Cosenza Underwood and Merriman 515 Market St Parkersburg WV 26101 Fax: 304-485-1090.

MERRITT, BRUCE GORDON, lawyer; b. Iowa City, Oct. 4, 1946; s. William Olney and Gretchen Louise (Kuever) M.; m. Valerie Sue Jorgensen, Dec. 28, 1969; children: Benjamin Carlyle, Alicia Marie. AB magna cum laude, Occidental Coll., 1968; JD magna cum laude, Harvard U., 1972. Bar: Calif. 1973, D.C., 1996, N.Y. 1996. Assoc. Markbys, London, 1972-73, Nossman, Krueger & Marsh, L.A., 1973-79, ptnr., 1979-81; asst. U.S. Atty., L.A., 1981-85; ptnr. Hennigan & Mercer, L.A., 1986-88, Debevoise & Plimpton, L.A., 1989-95, N.Y., 1996—2001. Fellow Am. Coll. Trial Lawyers; mem. Calif. State Bar Assn. (exec. com. litigation sect. 1992-95), L.A. County Bar Assn. (del. state bar conf. 1984-86), Phi Beta Kappa, Harvard Club (N.Y.C.). Federal civil litigation, State civil litigation. E-mail: BruceGMerritt@aol.com.

MERRITT, JAMES EDWARD, lawyer; b. Hickory, N.C., June 10, 1938; s. Eddy Schmidt and Dorothy (Hunt) M.; m. Joan L. Hiscock, June 14, 1960 (div. 1983); children: James Edward Jr., Catherine Hunt; m. Kristine McFadden, May 4, 1983. AB, Duke U., 1959; LLB, Harvard U., 1962. Bar: D.C. 1962, Calif. 1968; cert. tax specialist, Calif. Assoc. Pogue & Neal, Washington, 1962-64; trial atty. regional counsel IRS, San Francisco, 1964-68; assoc. Morrison & Foerster, LLP, San Francisco and Washington, 1968-72, ptnr., 1972—98, sr. counsel, 1998—. Lectr. Golden Gate U., San Francisco, 1970-74; cons. chief counsel IRS, Washington, 1983; mem. adv.

bd. Tax Mgmt. Inc., N.Y.C., 1987—. Contbr. articles to profl. jours. Mem. Am. Coll. Tax Counsel (regent, chair 1997-2000), ABA (coun., dir., sect. taxation 1990-93, mem. commn. on legal problems of elderly 1993-96), Bar Assn. D.C., Bar Assn. San Francisco (Outstanding Tax Lawyer 1983), J. Edgar Murdock Inn of Ct. Avocations: travel, gardening, sports. Corporate taxation, Taxation, general, Personal income taxation. Office: Morrison & Foerster LLP 30 Winster Fax Williamsburg VA 23185-5542

MERRITT, JERALYN E. lawyer; b. N.Y.C., N.Y., Sept. 28, 1949; BA, Case Western Res. U., 1971; JD, U. Denver, 1973. Bar: Colo. 1974, (U.S. Dist. Ct. Colo.), U.S. Ct. Appeals (10th cir.) 1981, (N.Y.) 1990, U.S. Supreme Ct. 1990, (Ariz.) 1999, U.S. Ct. Appeals (9th cir.). Mem. legal adv. bd. Martindale-Hubbell LexisNexis, 1996—; mem. editl. bd. Matthew Bender Criminal Publs., 1999—; lectr. law U. Denver Coll. Law, 2001—. Fellow: Am. Bd. Criminal Lawyers (mem. bd. govs. 1994—); mem.: ABA (criminal justice sect. coun. 2000—), Colo. Criminal Def. Bar, Denver Bar Assn., Colo. Bar Assn., Nat. Assn. Criminal Def. Lawyers (bd. dirs. 1995—2001, sec. 2002—, co-chair/vice-chair legis., Internet, and innocence project coms. 1995—, 1st Ann. Marshall Stern award for outstanding legis. achievement 1995). Office: Ste 1700 950 17th St Denver CO 80202

MERRITT, NANCY-JO, lawyer; b. Phoenix, Sept. 24, 1942; d. Robert Nelson Meeker and Violet Adele Gibson; children: Sidney Kathryn, Kurt, Douglas. BA, Ariz. State U., 1964, MA, 1974, JD, 1978. Bar: Ariz. 1978, U.S. Dist. Ct. Ariz. 1978, U.S. Ct. Appeals (9th cir.) 1984. Shareholder Fennemore Craig, P.C., Phoenix. Author: Understanding Immigration Law, 1993; sr. editor: Immigration and National Law Handbook, 1993—; contbr. articles to profl. jours. Chair bd. dirs. TERROS, 1995-97. Fellow Ariz. Bar Found.; mem. ABA, Am. Immigration Lawyers Assn. (chairperson Ariz. chpt. 1985-87, several coms., Pro Bono award), Am. Immigration Law Found. (trustee), Ariz. Bar Assn. (immigration sect.), Nucleus Club. Democrat. Avocations: modern literature, south american literature, hiking, gardening. Immigration, naturalization, and customs. Office: Fennemore Craig PC 3003 N Central Ave Ste 2600 Phoenix AZ 85012 E-mail: njmerritt@fclaw.com.

MERRITT, THOMAS BUTLER, lawyer; b. Toledo, Apr. 3, 1939; s. George Robert and Bernice (Gerwin) M.; m. Mary Jane Bothfeld, July 23, 1966; children— Thomas Butler, Haidee Soule, Theodore Bothfeld AB magna cum laude, Harvard U., 1961, LLB cum laude, 1966. Bar: Mass. 1966, U.S. Supreme Ct. 1974, N.H. 1994. With N.Y. State Dept. Civil Svc., Albany, 1961-62; intern Office of Legal Advisr U.S. Dept. State, Washington, 1965; law clk. to assoc. justice Arthur E. Whittemore Supreme Jud. Ct. Mass., Boston, 1966-67; assoc. Nutter, McClennen & Fish, Boston, 1967-69, Palmer & Dodge, Boston, 1969-73; asst. counsel to Gov. Mass., 1973; reporter of decisions Supreme Jud. Ct. Mass., Boston, 1974-94; pvt. practice Hollis, N.H., 1994—. Contbr. articles to profl. jours. Mem. Conservation Commn. Town of Sherborn, Mass., 1969-74, chmn., 1972-74; mem. corp. Tenacre Country Day Sch., Wellesley, Mass., 1972-84, trustee, 1973-78; planning bd. Town of Hollis, N.H., 1995-98. 1st lt. U.S. Army, 1962-63, capt. USAR, 1963-69. Mem.: Assn. Reporters of Jud. Decisions (pres. 1983—84), Internat. Law Assn. (Am. br.), Am. Soc. Internat. Law, Fed. Bar Assn., N.H. Bar Assn., Mass. Bar Assn., Am. Law Inst. (life), Harvard Faculty Club (Cambridge), Harvard Club of Boston, Union Club. Episcopalian. Public international. Office: 5 Hutchings Dr PO Box 1646 Hollis NH 03049-1646

MERRITTS, JACK MICHAEL, lawyer; b. Denver, Oct. 1, 1948; m. Victoria Ann Neils, Aug. 24, 1974; children: Karl, Daniel, Andrew. BS in Mining Engring., Pa. State U., 1970; JD, Harvard U., 1973. Bar: Colo., U.S. Dist. Ct. Colo. 1973, U.S. Ct. Appeals (10th cir.) 1989. Assoc. Sherman & Howard, Denver, 1973-78; assoc., ptnr. Hall and Evans, Denver, 1978-81; ptnr. Montgomery, Little and McGrew, Englewood, Colo., 1981-92, McKenna & Cuneo, Denver, 1992-94; spl. counsel Burns, Wall, Smith & Mueller, Denver, 1994—. Contbr. articles to profl. jours. Trustee Rocky Mountain Mineral Law Found., Denver, 1990-95; boy scout leader Boy Scouts Am., Lakewood, 1984-96. Mem. Soc. of Mining Engring., Denver Coal Club, Ind. Petroleum Assn. of Mountain States (exec. com., bd. dirs. 1986-95), Phi Kappa Phi, Tau Beta Pi, Sigma Tau, Phi Delta Kappa. Avocations: hunting, fishing, trap shooting. General civil litigation, Oil, gas, and mineral, Environmental. Home: 470 Cody Dr Lakewood CO 80226-1146 Office: Burns Wall Smith & Mueller 303 E 17th Ave Ste 800 Denver CO 80203-1299

MERSKY, ROY MARTIN, law educator, librarian; b. N.Y.C., Sept. 1, 1925; s. Irving and Rose (Mendelson) Mirsky; m. Rosemary Bunnage; children: Deborah, Lisa, Ruth. BS, U. Wis., 1948, JD, 1952, MALS, 1953. Bar: Wis. 1952, U.S. Supreme Ct. 1970, Tex. 1972, U.S. Ct. Appeals (5th cir.) 1981, N.Y. 1983. U.S. govt. documents cataloger U. Wis. Law Libr., 1951-52; reference asst. Madison (Wis.) Free Libr., 1952; pvt. practice law Wis., 1952-54; readers adv., reference and catalog libr., mcpl. reference libr. at City Hall, Milw. Pub. Libr., 1953-54; chief readers and reference svc. Yale Law Libr., 1954-59; dir. Wash. State Law Libr., 1959-63; exec. sec. Jud. Coun. Commn. Wash. Court Report, State of Wash., 1959-63; prof. law, law libr. U. Colo., Boulder, 1963-65; prof. law, dir. rsch. U. Tex., Austin, 1965—, William Stamps Farish Centennial prof. law, 1996—2001, Harry M. Reasoner Regents chair in law, 2001—, adj. prof. Grad. Sch. Libr. and Info. Sci., 1976—. Vis. prof. law, dir. law libr. N.Y. Law Sch., N.Y.C., 1982-84; M.D. Anderson Found. vis. prof. law Queen Mary and Westfield Coll., U. London, 1994; interim dir. Jewish Nat. and Univ. Libr., Hebrew U., 1972-73; vis. fellow Australian Nat. U. Fac. of Law, Canberra, 1999; cons. to legal pubs. and law schs.; panelist various confs.; lectr. in field. Author: A Treasure in Jerusalem, 1974, (with J. Myron Jacobstein) Fundamentals of Legal Research, 7th edit., 1998, 8th, edit., 2002, (with Dunn) Legal Research Illustrated, An Abridgement of Fundamentals of Legal Research, 8th edit., 2002, (with Dunn), (with Albert P. Blaustein) The First One Hundred Justices: Statistical Studies on the Supreme Court of the United States, 1978, (with Gary R. Hartman, Suzanne F. Young and Jill Duffy) A Documentary History of the Legal Aspects of Abortion in the United States, 1990, 96, 2001 (with Jacobstein Hartman and Bonnie Koneski-White) Reports on Successful and Unsuccessful Nominations, 1992, 95, 96; contbr. articles to profl. jours., chpts. to books; editor numerous books in field. Bd. dirs. Ctrl. Tex. chpt. ACLU, pres., 1968; bd. dirs. Human Rights Documentation Exch., 1997-2001; mem. bd. advisors Anti-Defamation League, Austin, 1974-78, Tex. Book Festival, 2001—; bd. dirs. Hillel Found., 1980-83; bd. dirs. Tex. Com. for Humanities, 1978-80, chair, 1980-82, conf. facilitator, 1982. With U.S. Army, 1944-46, ETO. Decorated Bronze Star. Fellow Am. Bar Found. (life), Coll. Law Practice Mgmt., Tex. Bar Found.; mem. ABA (various coms.), AAUP (chmn. nominating com. 1979-80), Am. Law Inst., Assn. Am. Law Schs. (various coms.), Internat. Assn. Lawyers and Jurists (bd. govs. Am. sect. 1980-95), Nat. Bar Assn., Am. Assn. Law Librs. (chair various coms.), Am. Soc. Info. Sci. (pres. Tex./Okla. chpt. 1992-94), Scribes (bd. dirs. 1974-94, book awards com. 1978-96, pres. 1991-93, chair Scribes Law Review Competition award com. 1993—), Soc. Am. Law Tchrs. (bd. govs. 1979-88, nominations com. 1984), ALA (rsch. librs. group 1987, libr. edn. divsn.), Am. Soc. Indexers, Internat. Assn. Law Librs. (U.S. adv. coun.), Internat. Fedn. Libr. Assns., Nat. Librs. Assn. (pres. 1980-81), Spl. Libr. Assn., State Bar Tex. (com. Tex. Bar Jour. 1983-90), State Bar Wis. (bd. mem. nonresident lawyers divsn. 1992-98), Nat. Assn. Coll. and Univ. Attys., Tex. Assn. Coll. Tchrs., Tex. Humanities Alliance (bd. dirs. 1986-88), Tex. Supreme Ct. Hist. Soc. (bd. trustees 1988-94), Order of Coif (mem. triennial book award com.). Home: 6412 Cascada Dr Austin TX 78750-8157 Office: U Tex Sch Law Tarlton Law Libr 727 E Dean Kelton St Austin TX 78705-3224

MERZ, MICHAEL, federal judge; b. Dayton, Ohio, Mar. 29, 1945; s. Robert Louis and Hazel (Appleton) M.; m. Marguerite Logan LeBreton, Sept. 7, 1968; children: Peter Henry, Nicholas George. AB cum laude, Harvard U., 1967, JD, 1970. Bar: Ohio 1970, U.S. Dist. Ct. (so. dist.) Ohio 1971, U.S Supreme Ct. 1974, U.S. Ct. Appeals (6th cir.) 1975. Assoc. Smith & Schnacke, Dayton, Ohio, 1970-75, ptnr., 1976-77; judge Dayton Mcpl. Ct., 1977-84; magistrate judge U.S. Dist. Ct. (so. dist.) Ohio, 1984—. Adj. prof. U. Dayton Law Sch., 1979—; mem. rules adv. com. Ohio Supreme Ct., 1989-96. Bd. dirs. United Way, Dayton, 1981-95; trustee Dayton Metro Libr., 1991—, Montgomery County Hist. Soc., 1995—, Ohio Libr. Coun., 1997-2000; pastoral coun., Cincinnati Archdiocese. Fellow Am. Bar Found.; mem. ABA, Fed. Bar Assn., Am. Judicature Soc., Fed. Magistrate Judges Assn. (trustee 1997-2000), Ohio State Bar Assn. (chair Fed. Cts. Com., 2003-), Dayton Bar Assn. Republican. Roman Catholic. Office: US Dist Ct 902 Federal Bldg 200 W 2nd St Dayton OH 45402-1430

MESCHKOW, JORDAN M. lawyer; b. Bklyn., Mar. 25, 1957; s. Gerald Meschkow and Florence Y. (Katz) Silverman; m. Susan G. Scher, Aug. 10, 1980; children: Sasha Hayley, Alisha Sadie. BS in Biology, SUNY, Stony Brook, 1979; JD, Chgo. Kent Coll. Law, 1982. Bar: Ariz. 1982, Fla. 1983; registered U.S. Patent and Trademark Office 1983. Assoc. James F. Duffy, Patent Atty., Phoenix, Ariz., 1982; ptnr. Duffy & Meschkow, Phoenix, 1983-84; sole practice Phoenix, 1984-92; sr. ptnr. Meschkow & Gresham, P.L.C., Phoenix, 1992—. Frequent talk radio guest and spkr. at seminars on patent, trademark and copyright law. Contbr. article series to profl. jours.; patentee in field. Exec. bd. City of Phoenix Fire Pub. Awareness League, 1996—. Mem. Am. Intellectual Property Law Assn., State Bar Ariz. (intellectual property sect. 1982—), State Bar Fla. Avocations: gardening, motorcycling, bicycling, skating, swimming. Intellectual property, Patent, Trademark and copyright. Office: 5727 N 7th St Ste 409 Phoenix AZ 85014-5818 E-mail: MG@patentmg.com.

MESERVE, RICHARD ANDREW, lawyer; b. Medford, Mass., Nov. 20, 1944; s. Robert William and Gladys Evangeline (Swenson) M.; m. Martha Ann Richards, Sept. 20, 1966; children: Amy, Lauren. BA, Tufts U., 1966; JD, Harvard U., 1975; PhD in Applied Physics, Stanford U., 1976. Bar: Mass. 1975, D.C. 1980, U.S. Supreme Ct. 1982. Law clk. Mass. Supreme Jud. Ct., Boston, 1975-76; law clk. to presiding justice U.S. Supreme Ct., Washington, 1976-77; legal counsel Pres. Sci. Adviser, Washington, 1977-81; ptnr. Covington & Burling, Washington, 1981-99; chmn. U.S. Nuc. Regulatory Commn., Washington, 1999—2003; pres. Carnegie Instn. Washington, 2003—, also bd. dirs. Chmn. com. to assess safety and tech. issues at Dept. Energy reactors, NAS, 1987-88, chmn. com. on fuel economy of automobiles and light trucks, 1991-92, chmn. com. on declassification of info. for Dept. Energy's environ. programs, 1994-95; co-chmn. AAAS-ABA Nat. Conf. Lawyers and Scientists, 1988-94; mem. adv. bd. Sec. Energy, 1996-99; mem. bd. overseers for arts and scis. Tufts U. Fellow: AAAS, Am. Acad. Arts and Scis., Am. Phys. Soc.; mem.: NAE, Am. Philos. Soc., Sigma Xi, Phi Beta Kappa. Democrat. Administrative and regulatory, General civil litigation, Environmental. Home: 708 Berry St Falls Church VA 22042-2402

MESERVE, WILLIAM GEORGE, lawyer; b. Medford, Mass., June 14, 1940; s. Robert William and Gladys Evangeline (Swenson) M.; m. Susan Mary Rycroft, Oct. 21, 1967; children: Daniel Scott, Susan Elizabeth, Jonathan Robert. BA, Tufts U., 1962; LLB, Harvard U., 1965; MSc, London Sch. Econs., 1966. Bar: Mass. 1966, U.S. Dist. Ct. Mass. 1970, U.S. Ct. Appeals (1st cir.) 1973. Legal asst. to commr. FTC, Washington, 1966-67; staff counsel com. on commerce U.S. Senate, Washington, 1967-69; assoc. Ropes & Gray, Boston, 1970-76, ptnr., 1976—2002, sr. counsel, 2002—. Geology field asst. McMurdo Sound, Antarctica, 1959-60, Inglefield Land, Greenland, summer 1965. Trustee Tufts U., Medford, 1977—97, AFS Intercultural Programs Inc., N.Y.C., 1979—92, 1993—96, New Eng. Med. Ctr., Inc., Boston, 1988—97, Lifespan of Mass., Inc., 1997—2002; bd. visitors Fletcher Sch. Law and Diplomacy Tufts U., Medford, 1971—; bd. dirs. United South End Settlements, Boston, 1979—, Earthwatch Expdns., Inc., The Ctr. for Field Rsch., Maynard, 1996—; bd. govs. New Eng. Med. Ctr. Hosps., Boston, 1982—94, 1995—97. Fellow Am. Coll. Trial Lawyers; mem. ABA, Boston Bar Assn., Phi Beta Kappa. Clubs: Appalachian Mountain (Boston) (rec. sec. 1977-78). Democrat. General civil litigation, Construction. Office: Ropes & Gray 1 International Pl Fl 41 Boston MA 02110-2624

MESKILL, THOMAS J. federal judge; b. New Britain, Conn., Jan. 30, 1928; s. Thomas J.M. Meskill; m. Mary T. Grady; children: Maureen Meskill Heneghan, John Peter, Eileen Meskill Gallupe, Thomas. BS, Trinity Coll., Hartford, Conn., 1950, LL.D., 1972; JD, U. Conn., 1956; postgrad., Sch. Law, NYU; LL.D., U. Bridgeport, 1971, U. New Haven, 1974. Bar: Conn. 1956, Fla. 1957, D.C. 1957, U.S. Ct. Appeals (2d cir.) 1975, U.S. Supreme Ct. 1971. Former mem. firm Meskill, Dorsey, Sledzik and Walsh, New Britain; mem. 90th-91st Congresses 6th Conn. Dist.; gov. Conn., 1971-75; judge U.S. Ct. Appeals (2d cir.), New Britain, Conn., 1975—, chief judge, 1992-93, sr. judge, 1993—. Pres. New Britain Council Social Agys.; Asst. corp. council City of New Britain, 1960-62, mayor, 1962-64, corp. counsel, 1965-67; mem. Constl. Conv., Hartford, 1965. Served to 1st lt. USAF, 1950-53. Recipient Disting. Svc. award Jr. C. of C., 1964, Jud. Achievement award ATLA, 1983, Learned Hand medal for Excellence in Fed. Juridprudence, Fed. Bar Coun., 1994. Mem. Fla. Bar Assn., Con. Bar Assn. (Henry J. Naruk Jud. award 1994), Hartford County Bar Assn., New Britain Bar Assn., KC. Republican. Office: US Ct Appeals 114 W Main St New Britain CT 06051-4223

MESSEMER, GLENN MATTHEW, lawyer; b. Hartford, Conn., Jan. 7, 1947; s. Joseph M. and Mary S. Messemer. BSBA, Georgetown U., 1968; JD, U. Conn., 1971. Bar: Conn. 1972. Staff atty. Kaman Corp., Bloomfield, Conn., 1972-74; asst. sec., 1974-79; asst. v.p., 1979-81; v.p., gen. counsel, 1981—. Prof. bus. law Sch. Bus. Adminstrn., U. Hartford (Conn., 1974-80; legal counsel Am. Helicopter Soc.; arbitrator Am. Arbitration Assn., 1978-82. Bd. dirs., trustee, regent U. hartford, 1993—. Served with M.I., U.S. Army, 1969-75. Mem. ABA, Conn. Bar Assn. (founding; exec. com., sec.), Hartford County Bar Assn. Clubs: Hartford Golf, Hartford, Masons. Commercial, contracts (including sales of goods; commercial financing), Private international, Labor (including EEOC, Fair Labor Standards Act, labor-management relations, NLRB, OSHA). Office: Kaman Corp 1332 Blue Hills Ave Bloomfield CT 06002

MESSERSMITH, LANNY DEE, lawyer; b. Laverne, Okla., Oct. 3, 1942; s. Harry D. and Vivian D. (Bowers) M.; m. Christine Diane Smith, Sept. 28, 1974; 1 child, Nicholas Ryan. BA, U. N.Mex., 1966, JD, 1969; DCL (hon.), Holy Cath. Apostolic Ch., 1975. Bar: N.Mex. 1969, U.S. Ct. Claims 1978, U.S. Supreme Ct. 1981. Asst. dist. atty. 1st Dist. State of N.Mex., Santa Fe, 1969-70, asst. atty. gen., 1974-76; assoc. Rhodes & McCallister, Albuquerque, 1970-72; ptnr. McCallister, Messersmith & Wiseman, Albuquerque, 1972-74, Lanny D. Messersmith, PA, Albuquerque, 1974-85, Messersmith, Eaton & Keenan, Albuquerque, 1985-89, Schuler, Messersmith, Daley & Lansdowne, Albuquerque, 1989—. Cons., hon. consul Govt. of Fed. Republic of Germany, 1981—. Mem. Albuquerque Com. on Fgn. Rels., 1988—, Sister Cities, 1988—. Mem. N.Mex. Bar Assn. (bd. dirs. internat. com.), Albuquerque Bar Assn., N.Mex. Retail Assn. (pres. 1987), Albuquerque UN Assn. (bd. dirs. 1985), Albuquerque Country Club, Masons (scholarship chmn. Albuquerque chpt. 1984-87), Shriners, Rotary Internat. Avocations: sailing, reading. Federal civil litigation, Private international, Probate (including wills, trusts). Home: 7904 Woodridge Dr NE Albuquerque NM 87109-5258 Office: Schuler Messersmith Daly & Lansdowne 4300 San Mateo Blvd NE Ste B380 Albuquerque NM 87110-8401 E-mail: mesersmith@aol.com .

MESSINA, BONNIE LYNN, lawyer; b. Lima, Ohio, Mar. 17, 1961; m. Dominick Messina. BA, We. Md. Coll., 1983; JD magna cum laude, U. Balt., 1991. Bar: Md. 1991. Claim adjuster The Hartford, Hunt Valley, Md., 1983-86, claim supr., 1986-88; assoc. Venable, Baetjer & Howard, Balt., 1991-94; sr. counsel U.S. Fidelity & Guaranty Co., Balt., 1994-98, St. Paul Fire & Marine Ins. Co., Balt., 1999, group claims counsel, 1999—. Assoc. editor U. Balt. Law Rev., 1990-91. Mem. jud. selection com. Women's Law Ctr., Balt., 1993-2000; mentor U. Balt. Sch. of law, Balt., 1993-97. Recipient Am. Jurisprudence award Balt., 1989, 90 (2). Mem. ABA, Md. State Bar Assn., Balt. County Bar Assn., Md. Assn. Def. Trial Counsel, Def. Rsch. Inst., Inc. General civil litigation, Insurance. Office: St Paul Fire & Marine Ins Co Ins Co 5801 Smith Ave Baltimore MD 21209-3652

MESSING, ARNOLD PHILIP, lawyer; b. N.Y.C., Sept. 2, 1941; s. Louis Messing and Ruth Aaron; m. Esther S. Buchman, Oct. 1, 1967; 1 child, Noah. BA magna cum laude, NYU, 1962; JD, Yale U., 1965. Bar: N.Y. 1966, Mass. 1976, Pa. 1985, U.S. Dist. Ct. (so. and ea. dists.) N.Y., U.S. Dist. Ct. Mass. 1976, U.S. Ct. Internat. Trade 1977, U.S. Ct. Appeals (1st, 2d, 6th, D.C. and fed. cirs.), U.S. Supreme Ct. 1977, U.S. Tax Ct. 1984. Assoc. Cravath, Swaine & Moore, N.Y.C., 1967-76; ptnr. Gaston & Snow and predecessor firm, Boston, 1976-91, Choate, Hall & Stewart, Boston, 1991—2001. Bd. dirs. law alumni mentoring program NYU. Bd. dirs. Union Am. Hebrew Congregations; trustee nat. bd. N.E. Coun.; Boston adv. coun. Internat. Refugee Com. Boston Chpt.; co-chmn. Boston chpt. Ashoka. Served to sgt. USAFR, 1965-71. Mem. ABA, Boston Bar Assn., Yale Law Sch. Assn. (exec. com.), NYU Alumni Assn. (bd. dirs.) Antitrust, Federal civil litigation, State civil litigation. Home: 271 Mill St Newton MA 02460-2438 E-mail: amessing@choate.com.

MESSINGER, DONALD HATHAWAY, lawyer; b. Lyons, N.Y., July 1, 1943; s. Donald H. and Thelma (Hubbard) M.; m. Sara L. Stock, June 3, 1967; children— Michael David, Robert Stephen, Daniel Mark BA, Colgate U., 1965; JD, Duke U., 1968. Bar: Ohio 1968. Assoc. Thompson Hine LLP, Cleve., 1968-76, ptnr., 1976—, vice chair corp. practice group, 1989-92, ptnr.-in-charge Cleve. office, 1991-96, mem. exec. com., 1996-2000. Sec., bd. dirs. Am. Steel and Wire Corp., 1986-93; bd. dirs. Cedar Fair Mgmt. Co., 1993-2002. Trustee Community Info.-Vol. Action Ctr., 1981-88, pres. 1981-84; trustee Free Med. Clinic Greater Cleve., 1970—, sec., 1970-82, v.p. 1982-86, 96-2002, pres. 2002-; trustee Cleve. Hearing and Speech Ctr., 1980—, v.p. 1984-86, 92-93, pres., 1986-88, 98-2000; trustee U. for Young Ams., 1982-95, sec., 1982-86, pres., 1986-88, chmn. 1991-95; mem. exec. bd. Boy Scouts Am., 1983-88; Leadership Cleve., 1984—; trustee, sec. Bus. Vols. Unltd., 1992—; sec. Buckeye Area Devel. Corp., 1970-90; mem. adv. bd. Greater Cleve. New Stadium. Recipient Community Svc. award Fedn. for Community Planning, 1981-82; named one of Outstanding Young Citizens of Greater Cleve., 1971-75. Mem. ABA, Ohio Bar Assn., Cleve. Bar Assn. (trustee 1975-79, chmn. securities law inst. 1983), Nat. Assn. Bond Lawyers Corporate, general, Securities, Public. Home: 21550 Shelburne Rd Shaker Heights OH 44122

MESSITTE, PETER JO, judge; b. Washington, July 17, 1941; s. Jesse B. and Edith (Wechsler) M.; m. Susan P. Messitte, Sept. 5, 1965: children: Zachariah, Abigail. BA cum laude, Amherst Coll., 1963; JD, U. Chgo., 1966. Bar: Md. 1969, D.C. 1969, U.S. Ct. Appeals (4th cir.) 1977, U.S. Supreme Ct. 1973, U.S. Ct. Appeals (DC cir.) 1982, U.S. Ct. Appeals (5th cir.) 1983. Assoc. Zuckert, Scoutt & Rasenberger, Washington, 1968-71; solo practice Chevy Chase, Md., 1971-75; mem. Messitte & Rosenberg, P.A., Chevy Chase, 1975-81; prin. Peter J. Messitte, P.A., Chevy Chase, 1981-85; assoc. judge Cir. Ct. for Montgomery County Rockville, Md., 1985-93; judge U.S. Dist. Ct. Md., Greenbelt, 1993—. Mem. Internat. Jud. Rels. Com. Jud. Conf. U.S., 1997—. Bd. dirs. Cmty. Psychiat. Clinic, Montgomery County, Md., 1974-85, v.p. 1980-85; Peace Corps vol. , Sao Paulo, Brazil, 1966-68; Md. del. Dem. Nat. Conv., N.Y.C., 1980. Recipient teaching citations Fed. Deposit Ins. Corp. Bank Exam. Sch., 1975, 79, Am. Inst. Banking, 1978, Elizabeth Scull award for Outstanding Svc. to Montgomery County, Md., 1993, Spl. citation Divorce Roundtable Montgomery County, 1993, Gran Cruz da Ordem São José Operário-Brazilian Labor Tribunal, Mato Grosso, 2001, Medalha de Mérito Académico, Academia Paulista de Magistrados, 2002, Contbn. Mental Health Cmty. Psychiat. Clinic, 1986, Leadership in Law award, Md. Daily Record, 2002. Fellow: Md. Bar Found. (H. Vernon Eney award for contbn. to adminstrn. of justice 2001); mem.: Jud. Inst. Md. (bd. dirs. 1989—93), Montgomery County Inn of Ct. (pres. 1988—90, Leadership in Law award 2002), Charles Fahy Inn of Ct. (master 1987—88), Fed. Judges Assn. (4th jud. cir.), Am. Law Inst., Montgomery County Bar Assn. (Century of Svc. award 1999), Instituto Paulista de Advogados (hon.), Md. Bar Assn., D.C. Bar Assn., Inter-Am. Bar Assn., FBA, ABA. Jewish. Office: US Courthouse 6500 Cherrywood Ln Greenbelt MD 20770-1249

MESTEL, MARK DAVID, lawyer; b. May 15, 1951; s. Oscar L. and Katherine (Waldner) M.; m. Linda Antonik, Jan. 6, 1984; children: Brenton V., Spenser Andrew. BA, Northwestern U., 1973; JD, U. Mich., 1976. Bar: Mich. 1976, D.C. 1977, Wash. 1978, U.S. Dist. Ct. (we. dist.) Wash. 1979, U.S. Ct. Appeals (9th cir.) 1984, U.S. Dist. Ct. (ea. dist.) Wash. 1986, U.S. Supreme Ct. 1991; cert. criminal trial specialist Nat. Bd. Trial Advocacy, 1982, 86, 91. Atty. EPA, Washington, 1976-77; pvt. practice Washington, 1977-78, Everett, Wash., 1981-84; staff atty. Snohomish County Pub. Defender, Everett, 1978-80, dir., atty., 1980-81; ptnr. Mestel & Muenster, Everett, 1984-94; pvt. practice, 1994—. Mem. ATLA, Nat. Assn. Criminal Def. Lawyers, Wash. Trial Lawyers Assn., Wash. Assn. Criminal Def. Lawyers. Civil rights, Criminal, Personal injury (including property damage). Office: Mark D Mestel Inc PS 3221 Oakes Ave Everett WA 98201-4407 E-mail: markmestel@bigfoot.com.

MESTRES, RICARDO ANGELO, JR., lawyer; b. N.Y.C., Aug. 12, 1933; s. Ricardo Angelo and Anita (Gwynne) M.; m. Ann Farnsworth, June 18, 1955; children: Laura, Ricardo III, Lynn, Anthony. AB, Princeton U., 1955; LLB, Harvard U., 1961. Bar: N.Y. 1962, U.S. Supreme Ct. 1970. Assoc. Sullivan & Cromwell, N.Y.C., 1961-67, ptnr., 1968-2000, chmn., sr. ptnr., 1995-2000, sr. counsel, 2001—. Trustee Unitarian Ch. All Souls, N.Y.C., 1973-79, 84-87; trustee Phillips Exeter Acad., 1989-99, pres. bd. trustees, 1993-99. Served to lt. USN, 1955-58. Mem.: ABA, Coun. Fgn. Rels., Am. Law Inst., Assn. Bar City N.Y. (corp. law, securities regulation law and state legis. coms.), N.Y. State Bar Assn., Mill Reef Club (Antigua), Links Club, Phi Beta Kappa. Corporate, general, Mergers and acquisitions, Securities. Office: Sullivan & Cromwell 125 Broad St Fl 32 New York NY 10004-2498

METCALFE, WALTER LEE, JR., lawyer; b. St. Louis, Dec. 19, 1938; s. Walter Lee and Carol (Crowe) Metcalfe; m. Cynthia Williamson, Aug. 26, 1965; children: Carol, Edward. AB, Washington U., St. Louis, 1960; JD, U. Va., 1964. Bar: Mo. 1964. Ptnr. Armstrong, Teasdale, Kramer & Vaughan, St. Louis, 1964—81; sr. ptnr. Bryan Cave LLP, St. Louis, 1982—, now chmn. Dep. chmn. Fed. Res. Bd. St. Louis; bd. dirs. Washington U., Danforth Found., St. Louis RCGA, Pulitzer Found. for Arts, St. Louis Children's Hosp. Mem.: ABA, St. Louis Bar Assn., Mo. Bar Assn., Noonday Club, Bogey Club (pres.). Episcopalian. Corporate, general. Home: 26 Upper Ladue Rd Saint Louis MO 63124-1675 Office: Bryan Cave 211 N Broadway 1 Metropolitan Sq Ste 3600 Saint Louis MO 63102-2750

METHVIN, THOMAS JAMES, lawyer; b. Eufaula, Ala., Feb. 19, 1963; s. Robert Gordon and Claudia Slade (Lindsey) Methvin; m. Amy Agee, Apr. 13, 1991; children: Thomas Rucker, William Slade. BSBA in Commerce, U. Ala. Tuscaloosa; JD, Samford U., 1988. Bar: Supreme Ct. Ala. 1988, U.S. Dist. Ct. (mid. and no. dists.) Ala. 1988. Assoc. Beasley Wilson, Montgomery, Ala., 1988—94; ptnr. Beasley Allen Crow Methvin Portis & Miles P.C., Montgomery, Ala., 1994—98, mng. shareholder, 1998—. Exec. coun. mem.

Ala. State Bar, Montgomery, 2001; pres. Montgomery County Bar Assn., Montgomery, Ala., 1996, Montgomery County Trial Lawyers Assn., Montgomery, Ala., 1996; bd. of bar commissions Ala. State Bar, Montgomery, Ala. Recipient Top 40 Under 40, Montgomery Advertiser, 2001, Top 40 Litigators Under 40, Nat. Law Jour., 2002. Mem.: ABA, Ala. Trial Lawyers Assn., Montgomery County Trial Lawyers Assn. (pres. 1996), Ala. State Bar Assn. (exec. coun. 2001, bd. bar commns. 2002—), Montgomery County Bar Assn. (pres. 1996), Nat. Assn. Consumer Advocates, Trial Lawyers for Pub. Justice, Christian Legal Soc. Avocations: hunting, fishing, travel. Office: Beasley Allen Etal 218 Commerce St Montgomery AL 36104 Office Fax: 334-954-7555.

METZ, CRAIG HUSEMAN, business executive; b. Columbia, S.C., Aug. 26, 1955; s. Leonard Huseman and Annette (Worthington) M.; m. Karen Angela McCleary, Aug. 11, 1984; 1 child, Preston Worthington. BA, U. Tenn., 1977; JD, U. Memphis, 1986; cert., U.S. Ho. of Reps. Rep. Leadership Parliamentary Law Sch., 1987. Bar: S.C., D.C., U.S. Ct. Claims, U.S. Supreme Ct., U.S. Ct. Appeals (4th cir.). Canvass coord., liaison Campaign to Re-elect Congressman Floyd Spence, 1978; del., chmn. Shelby County Del. to 1983 Tenn. Young Rep. Fedn. Conv.; vice chmn. Shelby County Young Reps., 1983-84, chmn., 1984-85; Shelby County adminstr., asst. to Tenn. state exec. dir. Reagan-Bush Campaign, 1984; field rep. Campaign to Re-elect Congressman Floyd Spence, 1986; spl. asst. to Congressman Floyd Spence, 1986-88; counsel com. on labor and human resources U.S. Senate, 1988-90; commr.'s counsel U.S. Occupl. Safety and Health Rev. Commn., Washington, 1990-91; spl. asst. to asst. sec. for legis. and congl. affairs, dep. asst. sec. for congl. liaison US Dept. Edn., 1991—93; asst. dir. Divsn. Congl. Affairs AMA, Washington, 1993; chief of staff Congressman Floyd Spence, Washington, 1993—2001; adminstr. Office of the Second Congl. Dist. of S.C., U.S. Ho. of Reps., Washington, 2001; govt. rels. mgr. EMC Corp., Arlington, Va., 2001—. Judge nat. writing competition U.S. Constn. Bicentennial, S.C. 1987-88; mem. Ch. of the Ascension and Saint Agnes, Washington. Recipient award of merit Rep. Party of Shelby County, 1985; Outstanding Leadership award Shelby County Young Reps., 1985; Meritorious Svc. medal Mil. Dept. S.C.; Legis. award Res. Officers Assn. U.S.; Order of the Palmetto; Hon. Washington Fellow, The Univ. of S.C. Washington Fellows Program; Palmetto Patriot Award; Pres.'s Award of the Nat. Guard Assoc. of S.C. Mem. Rep. Nat. Lawyers Assn. (state chmn. S.C. chpt. 1987-90), Freedoms Found. Valley Forge, Va. Hist. Soc., Assn. for Preservation Va. Antiquities, Land Trust of Va., Preservation Alliance of Va., Geneal. Soc., U. South Caroliniana Soc., Palmetto Trust for Historic Preservation, Lowcountry Heritage Soc., Orangeburg County (S.C.) Hist. Soc., Savannah River Valley Geneal. Soc., Hist. Soc. of Washington County Va., The Oyster Bay Hist. Soc., Hist. Soc. of Washington County, Va., Nat. Trust for Hist. Preservation (assoc. Capital region), SAR, St. David's Soc., St. Andrew's Soc. Washington, Royal Soc. St. George/St. George's Soc. Balt., Mil. Soc. War of 1812, Vet. Corps Arty. State of N.Y., Gen. Soc. War of 1812, Mil. Order Loyal Legion of U.S., Order of St. John (Hospitaller), SCV, Mil. Order Stars and Bars, Sons and Daus. Colonial and Antebellum Bench and Bar 1565-1861, Sons of the Revolution, Soc. King Charles the Martyr, Clan Lockhart, Friend of Scouting, Boy Scouts of Am., Ky. Col., Nat. Cathedral Assn., Washington D.C. Area Alumni Assn. of Sigma Alpha Epsilon Fraternity, U. Tenn. Nat. Alumni Assn., Sigma Alpha Epsilon, Phi Alpha Delta (v.p. McKellar chpt., Outstanding Svc. award 1983). Republican. Episcopalian. Home: 8505 Westown Way Vienna VA 22182-2513 Office: Crystal Park One Ste 907 2011 Crystal Dr Arlington VA 22202

METZ, ERIC BENNETT, lawyer; b. Wichita, Kans., Sept. 30, 1955; s. Carl Bennett and Peggy Ann (Lane) M. BA with highest honors, Friends U., 1977; JD, U. Kans., 1980. Bar: Kans. 1980. Assoc. Martin, Pringle, Fair, Davis & Oliver, Wichita, 1980-84; ptnr. Martin, Pringle, Oliver, Triplett & Wallace, Wichita, 1984-85, Triplett, Woolf & Garretson, LLC, Wichita, 1985—, mng. mem., 1999—. Mem. bd. trustees Friends U., Wichita, 1988-2001, mem. exec. com., 1988-01, treas., 1991-93, vice-chmn., 1993-97; bd. dirs. Rainbows United, Inc., Wichita, 1987-91. Mem. ABA, Kans. Bar Assn., Wichita Bar Assn., Def. Rsch. Inst., Kans. Assn. Def. Counsel, Order of Coif, Phi Kappa Phi. Civil rights, General civil litigation, Labor (including EEOC, Fair Labor Standards Act, labor-management relations, NLRB, OSHA). E-mail: ebmetz@twgfirm.com.

METZ, LARRY EDWARD, lawyer; b. Phila., Mar. 20, 1955; s. Harry Franz and Joan (Nye) Metz; m. Mariko Tomisato, Mar. 26, 1980; children: Marla Jo, Christina Jill. BA, U. Fla., 1976; JD with high honors, Fla. State U., 1983. Bar: Fla. 1983, U.S. Dist. Ct. (so., mid. and no. dists.) Fla. 1984, U.S. Ct. Appeals (11th cir.) 1984, U.S. Supreme Ct. 1987. Assoc. Fleming, O'Bryan & Fleming, Ft. Lauderdale, Fla., 1983-86; atty. Westinghouse Electric Corp., Coral Springs, Fla., 1986-88; pvt. practice Ft. Lauderdale, 1988-91, Coral Springs, 1991-93; assoc. Herzfeld & Rubin, Miami, Fla., 1993-96, ptnr. Ft. Lauderdale, 1996-99; assoc. Unger, Acree, Weinstein, Marcus, Merrill, Kast & Metz, P.L., Orlando, Fla., 1999-2000; ptnr. Unger, Acree, Weinstein, Marcus, Merrill, Kast & Metz, PL, Orlando, Fla., 2000—. Rep. nominee U.S. Ho. Reps. 195th dist. Fla., 1992; area leader, sign co-chmn., spkr. George Bush for Pres. Broward County (Fla.) Victory Com., 1988; pres. Broward County Regional Rep. Club, 1991, 1995; mem. exec. com. Broward County Reps., 1988—91, 1993—96, Lake County Reps., 1999—; mem. Cmty. Ch. Howey-in-the-Hills, Fla., 1999—, chmn. stewardship and fin. com., 2000—02; mem. Fla. Guardian Ad Litem Program, 1991—97. Capt. USMC, 1976—82. Recipient Outstanding Mem. of the Yr. award, Broward Lawyers Care, 1989, 1990, Disting. Svc. Award, Marine Corps League, N. Lake Detachment, Fl., 2002. Mem.: ABA, Order of Coif, Lake County Bar Assn., Marine Corps League (judge adv. North Lake detachment, Fla. 2000—03, trustee 2003—). General civil litigation, Personal injury (including property damage), Product liability. Office: Unger, Acree Weinstein et al 701 Peachtree Rd Orlando FL 32804-6847 E-mail: lmetz@ungerlawfirm.com.

METZER, PATRICIA ANN, lawyer; b. Phila., Mar. 10, 1941; d. Freeman Weeks and Evelyn (Heap) M.; m. Karl Hormann, June 30, 1980. BA with distinction, U. Pa., 1963, LLB cum laude, 1966. Bar: Mass. 1966, D.C. 1972, U.S. Tax Ct. 1988. Assoc., then ptnr. Mintz, Levin, Cohn, Glovsky and Popeo, Boston, 1966-75; assoc. tax legis. counsel U.S. Treasury Dept., Washington, 1975-78; shareholder, dir. Goulston & Storrs, P.C., Boston, 1978-98; stockholder Hutchins, Wheeler & Dittmar, P.C., Boston, 1998—2002; of counsel Vacovec, Mayotte & Singer LLP, Newton, Mass., 2003—. Lectr. program continuing legal edn. Boston Coll. Law Sch., Chestnut Hill, Mass., spring, 1974; lectr. grad. tax program Boston U. Law Sch., 2001—03; mem. adv. com. NYU Inst. Fed. Taxation, N.Y.C., 1981—87; mem. practitioner liaison com. Mass. Dept. Revenue, 1985—90; spkr. in field. Author: Federal Income Taxation of Individuals, 1984; mem. adv. bd. Corp. Tax and Bus. Planning Review, 1996—; mem. author's panel Jour. Passthrough Entities, 2003-; mem. editl. bd. Am. Jour. Tax Policy, 1995-98; contbr. articles to profl. jours., chpts. to books. Bd. mgrs. Barrington Ct. Condominium, Cambridge, Mass., 1985-86; bd. dirs. University Road Parking Assn., Cambridge, 1988—; trustee Social Law Libr., Boston, 1989-93. Mem. ABA (tax sect., vice-chair publs. 2000-2002, mem. coun. 1996-99, chmn. subcom. allocations and distbns. partnership com. 1978-82, vice chmn. legis. 1991-93, chmn. 1993-95, com. govt. submissions, vice liaison 1993-94, liaison 1994-95, North Atlantic region, co-liaison 1995-96, N.E. region, regional liaison meetings com.), FBA (coun. on taxation, chmn. corp. taxation com. 1977-81, chmn. com. partnership taxation 1981-87), Mass. Bar Assn. (coun. tax sect. 2001-), Boston Bar Assn. (coun. 1987-89, chmn. tax sect. 1989-91), Am. Coll. Tax Counsel (bd. regents 1999—), Boston Estate Planning Coun. (exec. com. 1975, 79-82). Avocation: vocal performances (as soloist and with choral groups). Corporate taxation, Estate taxation, Taxation, general. Office: Vacovec Mayotte & Singer LLP Two Newton Pl Ste 340 255 Washington St Newton MA 02458-1634

METZGER, JEFFREY PAUL, lawyer; b. Oct. 13, 1950; s. John E. and Ellen J. M; m. Stephanie Ann Stahr, Dec. 27, 1977. BA magna cum laude, Amherst Coll., 1973; JD, Georgetown U., 1976. Bar: D.C. 1977. Legis. asst. U.S. Senator Joseph Biden, Jr., Del., 1973; assoc. Collier, Shannon, Rill and Scott, Washington, 1976-79, Cole and Groner PC, Washington, 1979-82; trial atty. comml. litigation br. civil divsn. U.S. Dept. Justice, Washington, 1982-85; mem. prof. staff Pres.'s Blue Ribbon Commn. on Def. Mgmt., Washington, 1985-86; asst. gen. counsel Unisys Corp., McLean, Va., 1986-88, v.p., assoc. gen. counsel, 1989—. Mem. ABA. E-mail: jmetz10771@aol.com.

METZGER, JOHN MACKAY, lawyer; b. Princeton, N.J., Mar. 8, 1948; s. Bruce Manning and Isobel Elizabeth (Mackay) M.; m. Sandra Kay Wellington, May 8, 1999. BA cum laude, Harvard U., 1970; JD, NYU, 1973; postgrad., London Sch. Econs., 1973-74. Bar: Pa. 1976, N.J. 1976, U.S. Dist. Ct. N.J. 1976, U.S. Tax Ct. 1977, D.C. 1978, U.S. Ct. Appeals (fed. cir.) 1982. Tax adminstr. N.J. Div. Taxation, Trenton, 1976-86, 88—; atty. McCarthy & Schatzman PA, Princeton, 1986-88. Mem. N.J. Econ. Devel. Coun., 1987-90. Contbr. articles to profl. jours. Pres., trustee Friends of N.J. State Libr., 2000—. Mem. ABA, Am. Soc. Internat. Law, Harvard Club of N.Y.C., N.J. Hist. Soc., Supreme Ct. Historical Soc. Republican. Home: 52 Coriander Dr Princeton NJ 08540-9434 Office: 50 Barrack St Trenton NJ 08695-0269 E-mail: MetzgerEsq@aol.com.

METZGER, PAUL THOMAS, lawyer; b. Trenton, Mich., May 26, 1950; s. Roland Arthur and A. Doreen (Bloomer) M.; children: Timothy, Andrew, Christopher. AB, Harvard U., 1971, JD, 1976. Bar: Ill. 1976, U.S. Tax. Ct. 1977. Assoc. Bell, Boyd & Lloyd, Chgo., 1976-83, ptnr., 1984—, chmn. tax dept., 1988—. Spkr. Am. Mgmt. Assn., Chgo., 1987-95. Bd. dirs. Assn. House, Chgo., 1984—, treas., 1986-88, pres., 1990-92; bd. dirs. Ounce of Prevention Fund, Chgo., 1983—, chmn., 1995-98; mem. adv. bd. Cabrini Green Legal Aid Clinic, Chgo., 1985-96. Recipient Vol award Assn. House Chgo., 1986, Leadership citation United Way Crusade of Mercy, 1987. Mem. ABA (cert. appreciation Young Lawyers sect. Chgo. 1986-87), Chgo. Coun. Lawyers, Chgo. Fed. Tax Forum, Mid-Day Club. Democrat. Corporate, general, Mergers and acquisitions, Corporate taxation. Home: 1956 W Evergreen Ave Chicago IL 60622-1932 Office: 70 W Madison St Ste 3200 Chicago IL 60602-4244 E-mail: pmetzger@bellboyd.com.

METZGER, ROBERT STREICHER, lawyer; b. St. Louis, Sept. 27, 1950; s. Robert Stanley and Jean Harriet (Streicher) M.; m. Stephanie Joy Morgan, Nov. 16, 1980; children: Michael, Kristen, Marisa. BA, Middlebury Coll., 1974; JD, Georgetown U., 1977. Bar: Calif. 1978, D.C. 1978. Legis. aide U.S. Rep. Robert F. Drinan, Washington, 1972-73; legis. asst. U.S. Rep. Michael J. Harrington, Washington, 1973-75; rsch. fellow Ctr. for Sci. and Internat. Affairs Harvard U., Cambridge, Mass., 1977-78; assoc. Latham & Watkins, L.A., 1978-84, ptnr., 1984-90, Kirkland & Ellis, L.A., 1990-93, Troop, Meisinger, Steuber & Pasich and predecessor, L.A., 1993-97, Gibson, Dunn & Crutcher LLP, L.A., 1997—. Chmn. Aerospace and Govt. Practice Group, 1997—, Telecomms. Practice Group, 2000--; cons. Congl. Rsch. Svc., Washington, 1977-78. Contbr. articles to profl. jours. Mem. ABA (litigation pub. contracts sect.), Internat. Inst. for Strategic Studies, Jonathan Club. Federal civil litigation, Computer, Government contracts and claims. Office: Gibson Dunn & Crutcher LLP 333 S Grand Ave Los Angeles CA 90071-3197

METZINGER, TIMOTHY EDWARD, lawyer; b. L.A., Aug. 21, 1961; s. Robert Cole and Mary Jean (Cusick) M.; m. Cynthia Lee Stanworth, Nov. 16, 1991. BA, UCLA, 1986; JD, U. San Francisco, 1989. Bar: Calif. 1989, U.S. Dist. Ct. (ctrl., so., ea. and no. dists.) Calif. 1989, U.S. Ct. Appeals (9th cir.) 1989, U.S. Supreme Ct. 1994. Assoc. Bronson, Bronson & McKinnon, L.A., 1989-93; ptnr. Price, Postel & Parma, Santa Barbara, Calif., 1993—. Editor Santa Barbara Lawyer, 1999—. Pres. Santa Barbara County Bar Assn. Mem. Santa Barbara Mus. Natural History (bd. advisors), Santa Barbara Barristers Club (pres.), Order of Barristers, Am. Inns. Ct. Santa Barbara Club. Avocations: diving, moutaineering, sailing. General civil litigation, Commercial, contracts (including sales of goods; commercial financing), Environmental. Office: Price Postel & Parma 200 E Carrillo St Ste 400 Santa Barbara CA 93101-2190

METZNER, CHARLES MILLER, federal judge; b. N.Y.C., Mar. 13, 1912; s. Emanuel and Gertrude (Miller) M.; m. Jeanne Gottlieb, Oct. 6, 1966. AB, Columbia U., 1931, LL.B., 1933. Bar: N.Y. 1933. Pvt. practice, 1934; mem. Jud. Council State N.Y., 1935-41; law clk. to N.Y. supreme ct. justice, 1942-52; exec. asst. to U.S. atty. Gen. Herbert Brownell, Jr., 1953-54; mem. firm Chapman, Walsh & O'Connell, 1954-59; judge U.S. Dist Ct. (so. dist.) N.Y., 1959—. Mem. Law Revision Commn. N.Y. State, 1959; chmn. com. adminstrn. magistrates system U.S. Jud. Conf., 1970-81; chmn. Columbia Coll. Coun., 1965-66. Pres. N.Y. Young Republican Club, 1941; Trustee Columbia U., 1972-84, trustee emeritus, 1984—; bd. dirs. N.Y.C. Ctr. Music and Drama, 1969-74. Recipient Lawyer Div. of Joint Def. Appeal award, 1961, Columbia U. Alumni medal, 1966, Founders award Nat. Coun. U.S. Magistrates, 1989. Mem. ABA, Am. Law Inst., Fed. Bar Coun. (cert. Disting. Jud. Svc. 1989).

MEYER, CARL BEAT, chemical consultant, mediator, arbitrator, lawyer; b. Zurich, Switzerland, May 5, 1934; came to U.S., 1960; s. Karl and Alice (Wegenstein) M.; m. Elizabeth Anne Cousins, Feb. 26, 1960; 1 child, Birgit Franziska. Matura, Kantonsschule, Zuerich, Switzerland; PhD in Chemistry, U. Zurich, 1960; JD, Calif. Western Sch. Law, 1988. Bar: Nev. 1988, Calif. 1989. Postdoctoral fellow U. Calif., Berkeley, 1961-64; from asst. prof. to prof. chemistry U. Wash., Seattle, 1964-86; cons. San Diego, 1986—; pvt. practice, 1988—. Cons. Lawrence Berkeley Lab., U. Calif., Berkeley, 1964-88, U.S. Consumer Product Safety Commn., Washington, 1980-83. Author: Sulfur, Energy and Environment, 1976, Urea-Formaldehyde Resins, 1978, Indoor Air Quality, 1984; contbr. 118 articles to profl. jours. Recipient Nathan Burkan Meml. Competition award ASCAP, 1988. Fellow Am. Inst. Chemists; mem. ASTM (vice chair com. D-22.05 1986-96), ABA, Am. Chem. Soc. (chmn.-elect divsn. chemistry and law 2001, chmn., 2002), Am. Phys. Soc., Calif. Bar Assn., Nev. Bar Assn. Achievements include 2 patents in field. Home and Office: 704 Rand Ave Oakland CA 94610-2269 E-mail: cbmeyer@msu.com.

MEYER, CHRISTOPHER HAWKINS, lawyer; b. Springfield, Mo., Sept. 29, 1952; s. Richard DeWitt and Nancy (Hawkins) M.; m. Karen Anne Adams, Aug. 8, 1987; 1 child, C. Andrew Meyer. BA in Econs. magna cum laude, U. Mich., 1977, JD cum laude, 1981. Bar: D.C. 1981, U.S. Ct. Appeals (D.C. cir.) 1982, U.S. Ct. Appeals (9th cir.) 1983, Colo. 1985, U.S. Ct. Appeals (10th cir.) 1985, Idaho, U.S. Ct. Appeals (8th cir.). Counsel water resources program Nat. Wildlife Fedn., Washington, 1981-84, assoc. prof. adjoint, counsel Rocky Mountain Natural Resources Clinic Boulder, Colo., 1984-91; ptnr. Givens Pursley, Boise, 1991—. Contbr. articles to profl. publs. Mem. steering com. Idaho Environ. Forum. Recipient Lawyer of Yr. award Environ. Policy Inst., 1984, Water Conservationist of Yr. Nebr. Wildlife Fedn., 1989. Mem. Phi Beta Kappa. Democrat. Roman Catholic. FERC practice, Environmental, Natural resources. Home: 3443 S Millspur Way Boise ID 83716-8648 Office: Givens Pursley LLP 277 N 6th St Boise ID 83702-7720

MEYER, DAVID DOUGLAS, lawyer, educator; b. Grinnell, Iowa, Nov. 4, 1961; s. Richard DeWitt and Nancy Meyer; m. Amy Gajda, Aug. 29, 1986; children: Michael, Matthew. BA, U. Mich., 1984, JD, 1990. Bar: Mich. 1992, Ill. 1995, U.S. Ct. Appeals (7th cir.) 1995. Spl. asst. U.S. Senator Chas McC. Mathias, Washington, 1984-87; judicial law clk. D.C. Cir. Ct., 1990-91, U.S. Supreme Ct., Washington, 1992-93; assoc. Sidley & Austin, Chgo., Washington, 1991-92, 94-96; legal advisor Iran-U.S. Claims Tribunal, The Hague, The Netherlands, 1993-94; asst. prof. law U. Ill., Champaign, 1996-2000, assoc. prof. law, 2000—02, prof. law, 2002—. Editor-in-chief Mich. Law Rev., Ann Arbor, 1989-90. Mem. ABA. Office: U Ill Coll Law 504 E Pennsylvania Ave Champaign IL 61820-6909 E-mail: dmeyer@law.uiuc.edu.

MEYER, G. CHRISTOPHER, lawyer; b. Fremont, Nebr., Mar. 27, 1948; s. Gerald William and Mildred Ruth (Clausen) M.; m. Linda Haines, Dec. 27, 1969; children: Kate, Stacy, Jon, Robert. Student, Grinnell (Iowa) Coll., 1966-69; BA, U. Kans., 1970; JD, U. Pa., 1973. Bar: Ohio 1973, U.S. Dist. Ct. (no. dist.) Ohio 1975, U.S. Ct. Appeals (6th cir.) 1982. Assoc. Squire, Sanders & Dempsey, L.L.P., Cleve., 1973-82, ptnr., 1982—. Mem., Greater Cleve. Bar Assn., Am. Coll. Bankruptcy. Bankruptcy, Commercial, contracts (including sales of goods; commercial financing), Corporate, general. Office: Squire Sanders & Dempsey LLP 4900 Key Tower 127 Public Sq Cleveland OH 44114-1304 E-mail: cmeyer@ssd.com.

MEYER, GEORGE HERBERT, lawyer; b. Detroit, Feb. 19, 1928; s. Herbert M. and Agnes F. (Eaton) M.; m. Carol Ann Jones, 1958 (div. 1981) children: Karen Ann, George Herbert Jr.; m. Katherine Palmer White, Nov. 12, 1988. BA, U. Mich., 1949; JD, Harvard U., 1952; cert., Oxford (Eng.) U., 1955; LLM in Taxation and Labor Law, Wayne U., 1962. Bar: D.C. 1952, Mich. 1953. Assoc. firm Fischer, Franklin & Ford, Detroit, 1956-63, mem. firm, 1963-74; established firm George H. Meyer, 1974-78; sr. mem. firm Meyer and Kirk, 1978-85; sr. mem. Meyer, Kirk, Snyder & Safford PLLC, Bloomfield Hills and Detroit, Mich., 1985-99; mng. mem. Meyer, Kirk, Snyder & Lynch PLLC, Bloomfield Hills, Mich., 2000—. Curator Step Lively exhibit Mus. Am. Folk Art, N.Y.C., 1992; lectr. Am. Folk Art. Author: Equalization in Michigan and Its Effect on Local Assessments, 1963, Folk Artists Biographical Index, 1986, American Folk Art Canes: Personal Sculpture, 1992. Chmn. Birmingham (Mich.) Bd. Housing Appeals, 1964-68; vice chmn. Birmingham Bd. Zoning Appeals, 1966-69; mem. Birmingham Planning Bd., 1968-70; trustee, Bloomfield Village, Mich., 1976-80, pres., 1979-80; trustee Am. Mus. Folk Art, N.Y.C., 1987—; mem. exec. bd. Detroit Area coun. Boy Scouts Am., 1976—, counsel, 1986-95,v.p., 1996—; mem. nat. adv. bd. Folk Art Soc. Am., 1994—; trustee Detroit Sci. Ctr., 1985-99. 1st lt. JAG, USAF, 1952-55, maj. Res. ret. Recipient Silver Beaver award Detroit Area coun. Boy Scouts Am., 1989. Mem. ABA, Detroit Bar Assn., Oakland County Bar Assn., State Bar Mich., Harvard Law Sch. Assn. Mich. (dir. 1959—, pres. 1970-78), Detroit Sci. Mus. Soc. (pres. 1961-74, chmn. 1974-76), Am. Folk Art Soc. (pres. 2000—), Cranbrook Writers Guild (pres. 2002—), Prismatic Club,(pres. 2002—), Scarab Club, Harvard Club (N.Y.C.), Detroit Athletic Club, Masons, Rotary, Phi Beta Kappa, Alpha Phi Omega, Pi Sigma Alpha. Republican. Unitarian. Corporate, general, Property, real (including real estate development, water), Trademark and copyright. Office: Meyer Kirk Snyder & Lynch PLLC 100 W Long Lake Rd Ste 100 Bloomfield Hills MI 48304-2773 E-mail: gmeyer@meyerkirk.com.

MEYER, HELEN M. judge; BSW, U. Minn.; JD, William Mitchell Coll. Law. Cert.: Nat. Bd. Trial Advocacy (civil trial specialist). Ptnr. Pritzker & Meyer, 1987—96, Meyer and Assocs., 1996—2002; assoc. justice Minn. Supreme Ct., St. Paul, 2002—. Mem. Jud. Merit Selection Commn., Minn. Mem.: Acad. Cert. Trial Lawyers, Minn. Trial Lawyers Assn. (bd. dirs.), Minn. State Bd. Legal Cert. (bd. dirs.), Minn. State Bar Assn. (cert. civil trial specialist). Office: Minn Jud Ctr 25 Reverend Dr Martin Luther King Jr Blv Saint Paul MN 55155 Office Fax: 651-297-5636.*

MEYER, IRWIN STEPHAN, lawyer, accountant; b. Monticello, N.Y., Nov. 14, 1941; s. Ralph and Janice (Cohen) M.; children: Kimberly B., Joshua A. BS, Rider Coll., 1963; JD, Cornell U., 1966. CPA NJ; bar: NY 1966. Tax mgr. Lybrand Ross Bros. & Montgomery, N.Y.C., 1966-71; mem. Ehrenkranz, Ehrenkranz & Schultz, N.Y.C., 1971-74; prin. Irwin S. Meyer, 1974-77, 82-96; mem. Levine, Honig, Eisenberg & Meyer, 1977-78, Eisenberg, Honig & Meyer, 1978-81, Eisenberg, Honig, Meyer & Fogler, 1981-82, Janow & Meyer, LLC., 1997—. With U.S. Army, 1966—71. Mem. ABA, N.Y. Bar Assn., Am. Assn. Atty.-CPA, N.Y. Assn. Atty.-CPA, N.J. Soc. CPA. Estate taxation, Taxation, general, Personal income taxation. Office: 1 Blue Hill Plz Ste 1006 Pearl River NY 10965-3100 E-mail: irwin@janow-meyer.com.

MEYER, JOHN ALBERT, lawyer; b. Sioux Falls, S.D., Dec. 6, 1946; s. John Richard Meyer and Beryl Geneva (Birkland) Ritz; m. Donna Rae Finch, Jan. 21, 1983; 1 child, Elizabeth Ann. BS, Iowa State U., 1969; JD, U. Iowa, 1972. Bar: Iowa 1972, Ill. 1972, U.S. Dist. Ct. (no. dist.) Ill. 1972, U.S. Supreme Ct. 1977, U.S. Tax Ct. 1981. Asst. U.S. atty. U.S. Atty's Office U.S. Dist. Ct. (no. dist.) Ill., Chgo., 1972-77; ptnr. Johnson & Colmar, Chgo., 1977-83, Bortman, Meyer & Barasa, Chgo., 1983—. Recipient Disting. Svc. award FBI, 1975. Mem. Chgo. Bar Assn., Ill. State Bar Assn., ABA. Federal civil litigation, State civil litigation, Criminal. Office: 20 S Clark St Ste 2210 Chicago IL 60603-1805 E-mail: chgolegal@aol.com.

MEYER, LAWRENCE GEORGE, lawyer; b. East Grand Rapids, Mich., Oct. 2, 1940; s. George and Evangeline (Boerma) M.; children from previous marriage: David Lawrence, Jenifer Lynne; m. Linda Elizabeth Buck, May 31, 1980; children: Elizabeth Tilden, Travis Henley. BA with honors, Mich. State U., 1961; JD with distinction, U. Mich., 1964. Bar: Wis., 1965, Ill. 1965, U.S. Supreme Ct. 1968, D.C. 1972. Assoc. Whyte, Hirschboeck, Minahan, Hardin & Harland, Milw., 1964-66; atty. antitrust div. U.S. Dept. Justice, Washington, 1966-68; legal counsel U.S. Senator Robert P. Griffin, Mich., 1968-70; dir. policy planning FTC, 1970-72; ptnr. Patton, Boggs & Blow, Washington, 1972-85, Arent, Fox, Kintner, Plotkin & Kahn, Washington, 1985-96, Gadsby & Hannah, 1996-2001; pvt. practice Washington, 2001—. Contbr. articles on antitrust and trial practice to law jours.; asst. editor. U. Mich. Law Rev., 1960-61. Bd. dirs. Hockey Hall of Fame, Toronto, 1993-99, Woodrow Wilson House, 1997—. Recipient Disting. Svc. award FTC, 1972. Mem. ABA, D.C. Bar Assn., Wis. Bar Assn., Ill. Bar Assn., US Senate Ex S.O.B.s Club, City Tavern Club, Sulgrave Club, Congl. Country Club. Administrative and regulatory, Antitrust, Federal civil litigation. Home: 8777 Belmart Rd Potomac MD 20854-1610

MEYER, MARTIN ARTHUR, lawyer; b. Saratoga Springs, N.Y., Mar. 17, 1934; s. Edward and Ann Rita (Mintzer) M.; m. Lynn Greenberg, Apr. 16, 1961; 1 child, Steven. BA, Union Coll., 1955; LLB, Columbia U., 1958. Bar: N.Y. 1959, U.S. Dist. Ct. (no. dist.) N.Y. 1959, U.S. Ct. Appeals (2d cir.) 1978, U.S. Tax Ct. 1966. Assoc. McPhillips, Fitzgerald & McCarthy, Glens Falls, N.Y., 1958-60; ptnr. McPhillips, Fitzgerald & Meyer, Glens Falls, 1961-70, McPhillips, Fitzgerald, Meyer & McLenithan, Glens Falls, 1971-88, McPhillips, Fitzgerald & Meyer, Glens Falls, 1989-96, of counsel, 1997-98. Atty. City of Glens Falls, 1970-74. Bd. govs. Glens Falls Hosp., 1976-88; mem. Glens Falls Civic Ctr. Commn., 1977-79; mem. bd. edn. City of Glens Falls, 1984-89; past mem., pres. and trustee Congregation Shaaray Tefila, Glens Falls, 1961-81; pres. Glens Falls Area Coun. Chs.; N.Y. State Dem. committeeman, 1969-70. Mem. ABA, N.Y. State Bar Assn. (trial lawyers sect. mem. exec. com. 1986-96, chmn. 1995-96), B'nai B'rith. State civil litigation, Personal injury (including property damage), Probate (including wills, trusts). Home: 22 Roosevelt Ave Glens Falls NY 12801-2532

MEYER, MARTIN JAY, lawyer; b. Wilkes-Barre, Pa., Aug. 1, 1932; s. Max and Rose (Wruble) M.; m. Joan Rosenthal, Aug. 24, 1954; children: Leah, Gary. BA, Wilkes Coll., 1954; postgrad., U. Miami, 1956-57; LLB, Temple U., 1959. Bar: Pa. 1960, U.S. Dist. Ct. (mid. dist.) Pa. 1961, U.S. Ct. Appeals (3d cir.) 1966, U.S. Supreme Ct. 1978. Assoc. Mack, Kasper & Meyer, Wilkes-Barre, 1961-66; ptnr. Mack & Meyer, Wilkes-Barre, 1966—80; sr. ptnr. Meyer & Swatkoski, Kingston, Pa., 1980—. Chmn. disciplinary hearing com. Pa. Supreme Ct.; apptd. spl. trial master State Ct., 1995; apptd. cert. mediator U.S. Dist. Ct. (mid. dist.) Pa., 2000. Legal columnist to local newspapers; creator TV program Call The Lawyer. Chmn. Muscular Dystrophy Assn., 1960; co-chmn. March of Dimes, 1962; trustee Temple Israel Wilkes-Barre; bd. dirs. Jewish Home Scranton, Family Svc. Assn.; arbitrator U.S. Arbitration and Mediation of N.E., Inc., Am. Arbitration Assn., Million Dollar Advocates Forum. With U.S. Army, 1955-56. Fellow Pa. Bar Found.; mem. DAV, ATLA, Am. Arbitration Assn., Pa. Soc., Pa. Bar Assn. (former co-chmn., adoption com. family law sect., alt. dispute resolution com.), Nat. Conf. Bar Pres.'s, Pa. Trial Lawyers Assn. (lectr.), Luzerne County Bar Assn. (pres. 1984-85, chmn. Ct. Rules Com. 1994-2000), NE Pa. Lawyers Assn., Elks (trustee), Masons (32 degree), B'nai Brith (pres. 1967), Tau Epsilon Rho. Republican. Family and matrimonial, General practice, Personal injury (including property damage). Office: 405 3rd Ave Kingston PA 18704-5802 Fax: 570-288-1003. E-mail: mslawyers@earthlink.net.

MEYER, MAX EARL, lawyer; b. Hampton, Va., Oct. 31, 1918; s. Earl Luther and Winifred Katherine (Spacht) M.; m. Betty Maxwell Dodds, Sept. 22, 1945; children— Scott Maxwell, Ann Culliford. AB, U. Nebr., 1940, JD, 1942. Bar: Nebr. 1942, Ill. 1946. Assoc. firm Lord, Bissell & Brook, Chgo., 1945-53, ptnr., 1953-85; chmn. Chgo. Fed. Tax Forum, 1965, U. Chgo. Ann. Fed. Tax Conf., 1972; mem. Adv. Group to Commr. of IRS, 1967. Lectr. in field. Bd. dirs. Music Acad. of the West, chmn. 1993-94. Mem. ABA (mem. council tax sec. 1969-72), Ill. Bar Assn. (mem. council tax sect. 1973-76), Nebr. Bar Assn., Chgo. Bar Assn. (chmn. taxation com. 1959-61), Am. Coll. Tax Counsel Clubs: Legal, Law (Chgo.); Valley Club of Montecito, Birnam Wood Golf. Lodges: Masons. Republican. Presbyterian. Corporate, general, Mergers and acquisitions, Taxation, general.

MEYER, MICHAEL EDWIN, lawyer; b. Chgo., Oct. 23, 1942; s. Leon S. and Janet (Gorden) M.; m. Catherine Dieffenbach, Nov. 21, 1982; children: Linda, Mollie, Patrick, Kellie. BS, U. Wis., 1964; JD, U. Chgo., 1967. Bar: Calif. 1968, U.S. Supreme Ct. 1973. Assoc. Lillick & McHose, L.A., 1967-73, ptnr., 1974-90, mng. ptnr., 1986-87; ptnr. Pillsbury Madison Sutro, 1990—, mem. mgmt. com., 1990-92, chmn., 1999—. Judge pro tem Beverly Hills Mcpl. Ct., Calif., 1976-79, Los Angeles Mcpl. Ct., 1980-86; lectr. in field. Bd. dirs. Bldg. Owners and Mgrs. Assn. Greater L.A., L.A. coun. Boy Scouts Am., L.A. Sports and Entertainment Commn., L.A. Econ. Devel. Corp.; pub. counsel United Way Greater L.A., Los Angeles County Bar Found., trustee, 1997—, Reviving Baseball in Inner Cities; mem. L.A. County Sheriff Youth Found. Recipient Good Scout award L.A. coun. Boy Scouts Am., 1992, Man of Yr. award United Way, 1996, NACORE Real Estate Profl. of the Yr., 2002. Mem. ABA, Am. Arbitration Assn. (arbitrator), Calif. Bar Assn., Los Angeles County Bar Assn. (trustee 1997—), L.A. Bar Assn., Am. Coll. of Real Estate Lawyers, U. Chgo. Alumni Assn. So. Calif. (pres. 1980-82), Calif. Club, U. L.A. Club (dir. 1979-85, pres. 1984-85), L.A. Country Club. Jewish. Home: 759 31st St Manhattan Beach CA 90266-3456 Office: Pillsbury Winthrop 725 S Figueroa St Los Angeles CA 90017-5524 E-mail: mmeyer@pillsburywinthrop.com.

MEYER, MICHEL, lawyer; b. Paris, Apr. 5, 1946; Lic., U. Panthéon-Assas, Paris, 1968. Bar: Paris. Assoc. Cohen & Meyohas, Paris, 1970—78; ptnr. Meyohas Cohen Meyer, Paris, 1978—92, Cohen Meyer Chouchana Meilichzon, Paris, 1993—96, Caubet Chouchana Meyer, Paris, 1997—. Property, real (including real estate development, water), Mergers and acquisitions. Home: 22 ave de la Grande Armée 75017 Paris France Office: Caubet Chouchana Meyer 49 Champs Elysées 75008 Paris France Office Fax: (33-1) 40754040. E-mail: mmeyer@lexforce.com.

MEYER, MILTON EDWARD, JR., lawyer, artist; b. St. Louis, Nov. 26, 1922; s. Milton Edward and Jessie Marie (Hurley) M.; m. Mary C. Kramer, Nov. 5, 1949 (dec. Dec. 1999); children: Milton E. III, Melanie M. Meyer Francis, Daniel K., Gregory N.; m. Mildred R. Emrick, Nov. 18, 2003. BS in Bus. Adminstrn, Washington U., 1943; LL.B., St. Louis, U., 1950; LL.M., N.Y. U., 1953. Bar: Mo. 1950, Colo. 1956. Trust adminstr. Mississippi Valley Trust Co., St. Louis, 1946-50; asso. firm Burnett, Stern & Liberman, St. Louis, 1953-56; founding partner firm Hindry & Meyer, Denver, 1956-79, chmn. bd., 1970-79; spl. counsel Schmidt, Elrod & Wills, and predecessors, 1979-83, pres., 1980-82; sec. C.A. Norgren Co., Littleton, Colo., 1960-78, dir., 1971-78. Contbr. articles to profl. jours. Chmn. Denver Rotary's Artists of Am. Exhbn., 1990—92; bd. dirs. Nat. Club Assn., 1971—91, pres., 1976—78; bd. dirs. Denver Cmty. Concert Assn., 1960—64, Sewall Rehab. Ctr., Denver, 1965—68, Carl A. Norgren Found., 1960—70; Denver Leadership Found., 1983—93, Found. Colo. Women's Coll., 1982—86, chmn., bd. dirs., 1984—86; bd. dirs. Conf. Pvt. Orgns., 1982—89, chmn., bd. dirs., 1984—88. Officer, U.S. Airborne Infantry U.S. Army, 1943—46, World War II, officer, U.S. Airborne Infantry U.S. Army, 1950—52, Korean War. Recipient Wisdom Soc. award of honor. Mem. ABA, Colo. Bar Assn., Denver Bar Assn., Greater Denver Tax Counsels Assn. (founder, chmn. 1957, Denver Estate Planning Coun. (founder, pres. 1958), Am. Coll. Probate Counsel, Knickerbocker Artists, Pastel Soc. Am., Pastel Soc. West Coast (Disting. Pastellist award), Internat. Assn. Pastel Socs. (founder, dir. 1994—), Salmagundi Club, Cherry Hills Country Club, Pinehurst Country Club (pres. 1979-80), Denver Execs. Club, Hundred Club Denver, Rotary (bd. dirs. 1991-93), Phi Eta Sigma, Beta Gamma Sigma, Omicron Delta Kappa, Beta Theta Pi. Republican. Roman Catholic. Home: 7123 W Belmont Dr Littleton CO 80123 E-mail: miltonmeyer@comcast.net.

MEYER, PAUL RICHARD, lawyer; b. St. Louis, Apr. 12, 1925; s. Abraham Paul and Adele (Rosenfeld) M.; m. Alice Turtledove, Mar. 16, 1958; David Paul, Sarah Elizabeth, Andrea Ruth. BA, Columbia U., 1949; JD, Yale U., 1952. Bar: Oreg. 1953, Calif. 1953, N.Y. 1953, U.S. Dist.Ct. Oreg. 1953, U.S. Dist. Ct. (no. dist.) Calif. 1953, U.S. Ct. Appeals (9th cir.) 1953, U.S. Supreme Ct. 1958, U.S. Ct. Claims 1958, U.S. Tax Ct. 1958, U.S. Ct. Appeals (fed. cir.) 1958. Assoc. law sch. U. Calif., Berkeley, 1952-53; assoc. King, Miller et al, Portland, Oreg., 1953-60; ptnr. Kobin & Meyer, Portland, 1960-85; pvt. practice law Portland, 1985—2002; mediation & arbitration, 2003—. Mem. Bd. of Mediators and Arbitrators, Am. Arbitration Assn., NASD. Mem. nat. bd., exec. com. ACLU, N.Y.C., 1971-93, ACLU nat. adv. coun., 1993—. With U.S. Army, 1943-46, ETO. Decorated Purple Heart, Bronze Star. Alternative dispute resolution. Home and Office: 1325 SW Myrtle Dr Portland OR 97201-2274 Fax: (503) 295-1884. E-mail: paulalice@aol.com.

MEYER, PHILIP GILBERT, lawyer; b. Louisville, June 26, 1945; s. Henry Gilbert and Adele (Gutermuth) M.; m. Jackie Darlene Watson, Jan. 30, 1971 (div. Apr. 1976); m. Sylvia Saunders, Oct. 9, 1976. BBA, U. Mich., 1967; JD, U. Tex., 1970. Bar: Tex. 1970, Mich. 1971, U.S. Tax Ct. 1972, U.S. Dist. Ct. (ea. dist.) Mich. 1971, U.S. Ct. Appeals (6th cir.), 1972, U.S. Dist. Ct. (no. dist.) Ohio 1976, U.S. Dist. Ct. (we. dist.) Mich. 1993, U.S. Dist. Ct. (no. dist.) Ill. 1998. Law clk. Wayne County Cir. Ct., Detroit, 1970-72; atty. Leonard C. Jaques, Detroit, 1972; assoc. Christy & Robbins, Dearborn, Mich., 1972-73; ptnr. Foster, Meadows & Ballard, Detroit, 1973-79; of counsel Christy, Rogers & Gantz, Dearborn, 1979-81, Rogers & Gantz, Dearborn, 1981-86; prin. Philip G. Meyer and Assocs., Farmington Hills, 1986—. Adj. prof. U. Detroit Sch. Law, 1979. Mem. ABA (com. vice chmn. rules and procedure 1982-88), Maritime Law Assn. U.S., Mich. Bar Assn. (vice chmn. admiralty sect. 1978), Tex. Bar Assn., Detroit Bar Assn. (vice chmn. admiralty com. 1991-93, chmn. admiralty sect. 1993-95), Propeller-Port of Detroit Club (pres. 1984-85). Republican. Home: 5905 Independence Ln West Bloomfield MI 48322-1854 Office: Ste 113 30300 Northwestern Hwy Farmington Hills MI 48334-3212

MEYER, RAYMOND GEORGE, II, lawyer; b. Racine, Wis., Dec. 12, 1947; s. Raymond George and Marie Johanna (Heusdens) M.; m. Elaine Ann Pulvermacher, Aug. 18, 1973; children: Raymond George III, Amaliya R. BA, U. Wis., 1969, JD, 1974. Bar: Wis. 1974, U.S. Dist. Ct. (ea. and we. dists.) Wis. 1974. Assoc. Koenen Law Office, Port Washington, Wis., 1974-77; ptnr. Koenen & Meyer, Port Washington, 1978—. Contbr. articles to Railroad Model Craftsman, Railmodel Jour. With USMC, 1969-71. Recipient legal svcs. grant Wis. Trust Account Found., Madison, 1987, 89, 91. Mem.ABA, Wis. Bar Assn., Ozaukee County Bar Assn. (pres. 1986-87), Saukville C. of C. (pres. 1980-82), Port Washington C. of C., Port Washington-Saukville Jaycees (pres. 1977-78) (senator 1983). Avocations: cycling, model shipbuilding, model trains. General practice. Home: 616 S Garfield Ave Port Washington WI 53074-2317 Office: Koenen & Meyer 110 E Main St Port Washington WI 53074-1914 E-mail: ray2@execpc.com.

MEYER-FABRE, NATHALIE, lawyer; b. Neuilly sur Seine, France, Apr. 26, 1964; Diploma of the Course of Lectures in Internat. Law, U. Vienna, Austria, 1986; LLM, U. Paris II, 1986; postgrad. diploma in pvt. internat. law and internat. trade, U. Paris I, 1987. Cert.: Paris Bar Sch. 1988. Assoc. Jeantet & Associes, Paris, 1988—99, Salans, Paris, 1999—2000, ptnr., 2001—. Drafting sec. Hague Conf. Pvt. Internat. Lawo, The Hague, Netherlands, 1990—96; tchr. U. Paris I, 1987—88, U. Paris XI, 1990, U. Cergy-Pontoise, France, 1993. Mem.: Internat. Law Assn., French Com. on Arbitration, French Com. on Pvt. Internat. Law. Private international, Public international, Arbitration. Office: Salans 9 rue Boissy d'Anglas Paris 75008 France Office Fax: 33 1 4268 1545. E-mail: nmeyer-fabre@salans.com.

MEYERS, ALAN HOGE, lawyer; b. Brookfield, Mo., Nov. 2, 1949; s. Francis E. and Dorothy K. (Hoge) Meyers; m. Nancy Blaker Mitchell, July 31, 1976; children: Meredith Blaker, Courtney Alyson, Mitchell Cutler. BA with honors, U. Tex., 1973, JD, 1976. Bar: Tex. 1977, U.S. Tax Ct. 1978. Assoc. J.C. Blazier, Austin, 1976—78, Cotton, Bledsoe, Tighe & Dawson, Midland, Tex., 1978—82, ptnr., 1983—96, Morgan, Leecton & Meyers, P.C., Midland, 1996—. Participant Leadership Midland, 1981—82. Served to 1st lt. U.S. Army N.G., 1971—78. Mem.: Tex. State Bar Assn., Midland County Bar Assn. (pres.-elect). Banking, Probate (including wills, trusts), Property, real (including real estate development, water). Home: 1704 Normandy Ln Midland TX 79705-1701 Office: Morgan Leeton & Meyers PC 306 W Wall St Ste 700 Midland TX 79701 Personal E-mail: meyers@mo.quik.com. Business E-Mail: mlm700@aol.com.

MEYERS, DAVID W. lawyer, writer, educator; b. Hobart, Tasmania, Australia, July 19, 1942; came to U.S., 1946; s. Philip T. and Margaret M. Meyers; m. Jane Arthur Meyers, Dec. 27, 1969; children: Duncan, Vanessa. BA magna cum laude, U. Redlands, 1964; JD, U. Calif., Berkeley, 1967; LLM, U. Edinburgh, Scotland, 1968. Bar: Calif. 1968, U.S. Dist. Ct. (no. dist.) Calif. 1971, U.S. Ct. Appeals (10th cir.) 1994, U.S. Supreme Ct. 1976. Tutor dept. comparative law U. Edinburgh, Scotland, 1967-68; assoc. Rutan & Tucker, Santa Ana, Calif., 1968-71; ptnr. Dickenson, Peatman, Fogarty, Napa, Calif., 1972—. Adj. lectr. U. Calif. Med. Sch., San Francisco, 1985-87; vis. fellow U. Edinburgh, Scotland, 1999, U. Tasmania, 2000-03. Author: Human Body and the Law, 1972, rev. edit., 1990, Medical-Legal Implications of Death & Dying, 1981; contbr. chpts. to books, articles to profl. jours. Pres. Napa Valley Coll. Found., 1997-99; trustee Queen of the Valley Hosp., 1987-93, pres., 1990-93. Mem. State Bar Calif., Napa County Bar Assn. (pres. 1986). Democrat. Avocations: writing, bicycling, skiing, sailing, travel. General civil litigation, Municipal (including bonds), Property, real (including real estate development, water). Office: Dickenson Peatman & Fogarty 809 Coombs St Napa CA 94559-2994

MEYERS, DONAL ALEXANDER, lawyer, accountant; b. Queens, N.Y., Feb. 7, 1952; s. Alexander B. and Julia M. Meyers; children: Matthew, Sydney, Alyson. BS, St. Johns U., Jamaica, N.Y., 1975; JD, Fordham U., 1988. Bar: N.Y. 1989, U.S. Dist. Ct. (so. and ea. dists.) N.Y. 1990, U.S. Tax Ct. 1991; CPA, 1980. Acct., N.Y., 1979-88; sole practitioner atty., acct., 1988—. Mem. AICPA, N.Y. State Soc. CPAs (web site forum moderator, state and local taxation, 1997). Taxation, general. Office: 1040 Ave of the Americas 24th Fl New York NY 10018

MEYERS, HOWARD CRAIG, lawyer; b. Chgo., Nov. 15, 1951; s. Spencer M. and Joyce L. (Dresdner) M. BA in English, Ariz. State U., 1973, JD, 1977. Bar: Ariz. 1977, N.Mex. 2000; cert. bus. bankruptcy specialist, cert. creditors rights specialist Am. Bd. Cert.; cert. bankruptcy specialist State Bar Ariz. Of counsel Burch & Cracchiolo, P.A., Phoenix, Ariz. Mem. ABA, Comml. Law League of Am., Am. Bankruptcy Inst., State Bar Ariz. (debtor-creditor com.), Maricopa County Bar Assn.(profl. devel. com., alternative dispute resolution com.), Internat. Council of Shopping Ctrs. Bankruptcy, Commercial, contracts (including sales of goods; commercial financing). Home: 6711 E Camelback Rd Unit 65 Scottsdale AZ 85251-2067 Office: Burch & Cracchiolo PA 702 E Osborn Rd Ste 200 Phoenix AZ 85014-5234 E-mail: hmeyers@bcattorneys.com.

MEYERS, JERRY IVAN, lawyer; b. McKeesport, Pa., Mar. 26, 1946; s. Eugene J. and Gladys Claire (Rubenstein) M.; m. Judith Drake Aughenbaugh, June, 26, 1971; 1 child, Lindsey Drake. BA in Philosophy and Rhetoric, U. Pitts., 1972; JD cum laude, U. Miami, 1975. Bar: Pa. 1975, U.S. Dist. Ct. (we. dist.) Pa. 1975. Assoc. Berger & Kapetan, Pitts., 1975-78; ptnr. Meyers, Rosen, Louik & Perry P.C., Pitts., 1978—. Mem. Assn. Trial Lawyers Am., Pa. Trial Lawyers Assn. (past pres. western Pa. chpt., bd. govs. legis. policy com., med.-legis. com.), Acad. Trial Lawyers Allegheny County. Personal injury (including property damage). Office: Meyers Rosen Louik & Perry PC The Frick Building Ste 200 Pittsburgh PA 15219-6002 E-mail: meyers@meyersmedmal.com.

MEYERS, KAREN DIANE, lawyer, educator, corporate officer; b. Cin., July 8, 1950; d. Willard Paul and Camille Jeannette (Schutte) M.; m. William J. Jones, Mar. 27, 1978. BA summa cum laude, Thomas More Coll., 1974; MBA, MEd, Xavier U., 1978; JD, U. Ky., Covington, 1978. Bar: Ohio 1978, Ky. 1978; CLU; CPCU. Clk. to mgr. Baldwin Co., Cin., 1970-78; adj. prof. bus. Thomas More Coll., Crestview Hill, Ky., 1978—, CSSC-U. Notre Dame, 1994, CSSC, 1994; asst. sec., asst. v.p., sr. counsel The Ohio Life Ins. Co., Hamilton, 1978-91; prin. KD Meyers & Assocs., 1991; v.p. Benefit Designs, Inc., 1991-96, Little, Meyers, Garretson & Assocs., Ltd., Cin., 1996—; adj. prof. Miami U., 1998—. Bd. dirs. ARC, Hamilton, 1978-83, vol., 1978—; bd. dirs. YWCA, Hamilton, 1985-91. Gardner Found. fellow, 1968-71; recipient Ind. Progress award Bus. & Profl. Women, 1990. Fellow Life Mgmt. Inst. Atlanta; mem. ABA, Soc. Chartered Property Casualty Underwriters (instr. 1987—), Cin. Bar Assn., Butler County Bar Assn., Ohio Bar Assn., Ky. Bar Assn. Roman Catholic. Avocations: aerobics, jogging, crafts. Corporate, general, Insurance. Home: 7903 Hickory Hill Ln Cincinnati OH 45241-1363

MEYERS, PAMELA SUE, lawyer; b. Lakewood, N.J., June 13, 1951; d. Morris Leon and Isabel (Leibowitz) M.; m. Gerald Stephen Greenberg, Aug. 24, 1975; children: David Stuart Greenberg, Allison Brooke Greenberg. AB with distinction, Cornell U., 1973; JD cum laude, Harvard U., 1976. Bar: N.Y. 1977, Ohio 1990. Assoc. Stroock & Stroock & Lavan, N.Y.C., 1976-80; staff v.p., asst. gen. counsel Am. Premier Underwriters, Inc., Cin., 1980-96; legal counsel Citizens Fed. Bank, Dayton, Ohio, 1997-98; gen. counsel, sec. Mosler Inc., Hamilton, Ohio, 1998—2001. Bd. dirs. Hamilton County Alcohol and Drug Addiction Svc. Bd., 1996-2000, Adath Israel Synagogue, 1999—. Mem. Cin. Bar Assn., Harvard Club of Cin. (pres. 1998-99, bd. dirs. 1993-2000), Phi Beta Kappa. Jewish. Avocations: piano, reading, golf. Commercial, contracts (including sales of goods; commercial financing), Corporate, general, Mergers and acquisitions. Home: 3633 Carpenters Creek Dr Cincinnati OH 45241-3824 E-mail: psmeyers@fuse.net.

MEYERS, TEDSON JAY, lawyer; b. Bayonne, N.J., May 6, 1928; s. Irving and Norma Miriam (Anson) M.; m. Patricia Elizabeth Sullivan, Apr. 10, 1965 (div. Apr. 1978); children: Mary, John, Katherine; m. Lynn Scholz, Aug. 6, 1978 (div. Oct. 1992); m. Arden Schell, Dec. 27, 2000. Student, Ohio State U., 1945-47; BA, NYU, 1949, MA, 1950; JD, Harvard U., 1953. Bar: D.C. 1953, N.Y. 1957, U.S. Supreme Ct. 1971. Asst. counsel Office Gen. Counsel, Dept. Navy, Washington, 1955-56; assoc. Liebman, Eulau & Robinson, N.Y.C., 1956-58; staff counsel for govt. regulations ABC, N.Y.C., 1958-61; adminstrv. asst. to chmn. FCC, Washington, 1961-62; asst. to dir., dir. overseas ednl. TV projects Peace Corps, Washington, 1962-68; pvt. practice Washington, 1968-70; ptnr. Sullivan Beauregard Meyers & Clarkson, Washington, 1970-74, Peabody Lambert & Meyers, Washington, 1974—84, Reid & Priest, Washington, 1984-96, Coudert Brothers, Washington, 1996—. Adj. prof. comm. San Diego State U., 1993—; founding pres. Harvard Legis. Rsch. Bur., 1952—53; mem. White House Task Force on Ednl. TV Overseas, 1966—68; trustee, pres. Global Legal Info. Network Found., 2001—; mem. adv. panel on internat. telecomm. law U.S. State Dept., 1987—; bd. govs. Internat. Coun. for Computer Comm., 1986—, pres., 2000—; bd. dirs. Cyber Century Forum. Contbr. conf. papers and articles to profl. publs. Mem. City Coun. Washington, 1972-75; bd. govs. Met. Washington Coun. Govts., 1973-75; chmn. Bicycle Fedn. of Am., 1977—; bd. dirs. U.S. Coun. for World Comm. Yr. 83, 1982-84; dir. The Arthur C. Clarke Found. of the U.S. Inc., 1987—. Lt. USMC, 1953-55, Korea. Rsch. fellow Carnegie Found., 1949. Fellow: Am. Bar Found.; mem.: ABA (co-founder and chmn. internat. telecomm. com., sect. sci. and tech. 1982—85, coun. mem. sect. sci. and tech. 1983—87, chmn. standing com. law libr. congress 2000), Soc. Satellite Profls., Pacific Telecomm. Coun., Royal TV Soc., Internat. Inst. Comm., Fed. Comm. Bar Assn., Potomac Boat Club, Cosmos Club Found. (trustee, chmn. 1985—88, 1990—), Cosmos Club (pres. 1988—90), Alpha Epsilon Pi. Avocations: bicycling, motorcycling, computers, sculling, military music. Office: Coudert Brothers Ste 1200 1627 I St NW Washington DC 20006-4007 E-mail: tmeyers@tedson.com.

MEYERSON, CHRISTOPHER CORTLANDT, lawyer; b. Princeton, N.J., July 7, 1962; s. Dean and Beatrice Meyerson; m. Megumi Kawaguchi; children: Kenneth, David. BA in Govt. magna cum laude, cert. in L.Am. studies, MA in History, Harvard U., 1985; MPhil in Polit. Sci., Columbia U., 1993; LLM, Kyoto (Japan) U., 1994; JD, Columbia U., 2001. Bar: D.C. 2001. Intern Bur. Inter-Am. Affairs, Office Policy Planning/Coord. U.S. State Dept., Washington, summer 1982; rsch. asst. Harvard U., 1982-83; intern, rschr. macro econ. rsch. dept. Banco Itau, São Paulo, 1983-84; human rights intern Coalition for Homeless, N.Y.C., summer 1988; legal intern gen. counsel Mus. Modern Art, N.Y.C., summer 1989; law clk. Office of Chief Counsel for Internat. Commerce U.S. Commerce Dept., Washington, summer 1991; editl. asst. Kyoto Comparative Law Ctr., summer 1994, 95; vis. scholar Associated Kyoto Program, 1996. Summer assoc. Venable, Baetjer, Howard & Civiletti, Washington, 1998; law clk. Office of Chief Counsel for Import Adminstrn., U.S. Commerce Dept., Washington, 1999-2000. Contbr. articles to profl. jours. Recipient scholarship, Japanese Govt., 1991—97, Jr. Scholar award, Internat. Studies Assn. Internat. Polit. Economy, 2000. Mem. ABA. Episcopalian. Home: 7306 Summit Ave Chevy Chase MD 20815-4030

MEYERSON, IVAN D. lawyer, holding company executive; AB, U. Calif., Berkeley, 1966; JD, Stanford U., 1969. Bar: Calif. 1970. Assoc. Herzstein & Maier, San Francisco, 1970-75, ptnr., 1976-78; atty. SEC, 1975-76; assoc. gen. counsel McKesson Corp, San Francisco, 1984-87; v.p., gen. counsel McKesson Corp., San Francisco, 1987-98; sr. v.p., gen. counsel McKesson - HBOC Inc., San Francisco, 1998—. Corporate, general. Office: McKesson Corp 1 Post St Ste 3275 San Francisco CA 94104-5292*

MEYERSON, STANLEY PHILLIP, lawyer; b. Apr. 13, 1916; s. Louis A. and Ella Meyerson; m. Sherry Maxwell, Nov. 30, 1996; children: Marianne Martin, Camilla, Margot Ellis, Stanley P. AB, Duke U., 1937, JD, 1939. Bar: S.C. 1939, N.Y. 1940, Ga. 1945, U.S. Supreme Ct. Ptnr. Johnson Hatcher & Meyerson, Atlanta, 1945-55, Hatcher, Meyerson, Oxford & Irvin, Atlanta, 1955-78, Westmoreland, Hall, McGee, Oxford & Meyerson, Atlanta, 1978-88, McGee & Oxford, Atlanta, 1988—. Former adj. prof. Ga. State U.; dir., officer various corps. Contbr. Co-founder West Paces Ferry Hosp., Atlanta, Annandale at Suwanee for the Handicapped; trustee Hudson Libr., Inc., Highlands, NC, MetroGroup, Atlanta; del. Moscow Conf., Law and Bilateral Econ. Rels., 1990. Lt. comdr. USNR, 1943—45. Mem.: ABA (former professionalism com.), Atlanta Bar Assn. (former sec.), Ga. Bar Assn. (former chmn. tax com.), Duke U. Alumni Assn. (former pres. Atlanta chpt.). Corporate, general, Entertainment, Estate planning.

MEZGRAVIS, ANDRÉS A. lawyer; b. Caracas, Venezuela, Dec. 4, 1965; s. Andrés and Praxila (Hatgi) Mezgravis. Degree in law, U. Católica Andrés Bello, Caracas, 1983—88; specialist in procedural law, U. C.V., Caracas, 1996—98. Bar: Caracas 1988. Assoc. Baker & McKenzie, Caracas, 1988—93; ptnr. Travieso, Evans, Arria Rengel and Paz, Caracas, 1993. Pres. Arbitration Com. VenAmchan, Caracas, 1998—2000. Contbr. several articles to pubs. including Revista de Derecho. Achievements include coordinator of the commission in charge of writing the Rules of Business Center of Concilation any Arbitration. Alternative dispute resolution, General civil litigation. Office: Travieso Evans Ave Principal Caracas La Castellana 1060 Venezuela Office Fax: 58212 2773334. Business E-Mail: amh@traviesoevans.com.

MEZZULLO, LOUIS ALBERT, lawyer; b. Balt., Sept. 20, 1944; m. Judith Scales, Jan. 2, 1970. BA, U. Md., 1967, MA, 1976; JD, T.C. Williams Law Sch., 1976. Bar: Va. 1976. Sales rep. Humble Oil (name now Exxon), Richmond, Va., 1970-72; acctg. Marcoin, Inc., Richmond, 1972-73; pvt. practice bookkeeping, tax preparation, Richmond, 1973-76; assoc. McGuire, Woods, Battle and Boothe, Richmond, 1976-79; dir. Mezzullo & McCandlish, Richmond, 1979-2000; mem. Mezzullo & Guare, PLC, Richmond, 2000—. Contbr. articles to profl. jours. Former bd. dirs. Richmond Symphony; bd. dirs. Va. Mus. Fine Arts Found.; former pres. Southampton Citizens Assn., Richmond, 1986. Served with USAR, 1969-75. Mem. ABA (tax sect.), Internat. Acad. Estate and Trust Law, Am. Coll. Trust and Estate Counsel, Am. Coll. Tax Counsel, Va. State Bar (tax sect.), Am. Coll. EMployee Benefit Counsel, Va. Bar Assn., Am. Bar Found., Va. Law Found., Estate Planning Coun. Richmond, Trust Adminstrs. Coun., Am. Coll. Employee Benefits Counsel, Willow Oaks Country Club. Corporate, general, Estate planning, Corporate taxation. Home: 2961 Westchester Rd Richmond VA 23225-1842 Office: Mezzullo & Guare PLC 6802 Paragon Pl Ste 100 Richmond VA 23230 E-mail: lmezzullo@mezzulloguare.com.

MICHAEL, DOUGLAS CHARLES, law educator; b. Omaha, Dec. 8, 1957; s. B.B. and Arleen M. (Heinz) M.; m. Susan Lindsey, Jan. 11, 1986; children: Stuart Douglas, Amanda Lindsey. AB, Stanford U., 1979; MBA, U. Calif., Berkeley, 1982, JD, 1983. Bar: Calif. 1984, D.C. 1988. Staff atty. SEC, Washington, 1983-85, commr.'s counsel, 1985-87; assoc. Arnold and Porter, Washington, 1987-89; asst. prof. U. Ky. Coll. Law, Lexington, 1989-93, assoc. prof., 1993-97, prof., 1997—. Vis. prof. law U. Fla., 2000.

Contbr. articles to legal jours.; author: Legal Accounting: Principles and Applications, 1997. Mem. ABA, Order of Coif. Office: U Ky Coll Law Lexington KY 40506-0048 Home: 1224 Sebring Ln Lexington KY 40513 E-mail: michaeld@uky.edu.

MICHAEL, JAMES HARRY, JR., federal judge; b. Charlottesville, Va., Oct. 17, 1918; s. James Harry and Reuben (Shelton) m. Barbara E. Puryear, Dec. 18, 1946; children: Jarrett Michael Stephens, Victoria von der Au. BS, U. Va., 1940, LLB, 1942. Bar: Va. 1942. Sole practice, Charlottesville; ptnr. Michael & Musselman, 1946-54, J.H. Michael, Jr., 1954-59, Michael & Dent, 1959-72, Michael, Dent & Brooks Ltd., 1972-74, Michael & Dent, Ltd., 1974-80; assoc. judge Juvenile and Domestic Rels. Ct., Charlottesville, 1954-68; judge U.S. Dist. Ct., Charlottesville, 1980-95, sr. judge, 1996—; mem. Va. Senate, 1968-80. Exec. dir. Inst. Pub. Affairs, U. Va., 1952; chmn. Council State Govts., 1975-76, also mem. exec. com.; chmn. So. Legis. Conf., 1974-75. Mem. Charlottesville Sch. Bd., 1951-62; bd. govs. St. Anne-Belfield Sch., 1952-76. Served with USNR, 1942-46; comdr. Res. ret. Wilton Park fellow Wilton Park Conf., Sussex, Eng., 1971 Fellow Am. Bar Found.; mem. ABA, Va. Bar Assn. (v.p. 1956-57), Charlottesville-Albermarle Bar Assn. (pres. 1966-67), Am. Judicature Soc., 4th Jud. Conf., Va. Trial Lawyers Assn. (Va. disting. svc. award 1993), Assn. Trial Lawyers Am., Raven Soc., Sigma Nu Phi, Omicron Delta Kappa. Episcopalian (lay reader). Office: US Dist Ct 255 W Main St Rm 320 Charlottesville VA 22902-5058*

MICHAEL, M. BLANE, federal judge; b. Charleston, S.C., Feb. 17, 1943; AB, W.Va. U., 1965; JD, NYU, 1968. Bar: N.Y. 1968, U.S. Dist. Ct. (so. and ea. dists.) N.Y. 1968, W.Va. 1973, U.S. Ct. Appeals (4th cir.) 1974, U.S. Dist. Ct. (so. dist.) W.Va. 1981. Counsel to Gov. W.Va. John D. Rockefeller IV, 1977—80; atty. Jackson & Kelly, Charleston, W.Va., 1981—93; fed. judge U.S. Ct. Appeals (4th cir.), Charleston, W.Va., 1993—. Mem.: ABA, Kanawha County Bar Assn., W.Va. Bar Assn., Phi Beta Kappa. Office: US Circuit Judge Robert C Byrd US Courthouse 300 Virginia St E Rm 7404 Charleston WV 25301-2504

MICHAEL, ROBERT ROY, lawyer; b. Washington, Dec. 28, 1946; s. Colin Lamar and Mary Elva (Wilson) M.; m. Carolyn Ann Sandberg, Dec. 20, 1975; children: Shawn Robert, Erika Rae, Andrew Jon. BA, George Washington U., 1968, JD, 1971. Bar: Md. 1972, D.C. 1972, U.S. Dist. Ct. Md. 1972, U.S. Dist. Ct. D.C. 1972, U.S. Ct. Appeals (4th cir.) 1972, U.S. Supreme Ct. 1973. Assoc. A.D. Massengill, Esq., Gaithersburg, Md., 1972-73, Massengill & Jersin, Gaithersburg, 1973-74; ptnr. Massengill, Jersin & Michael, Gaithersburg, 1974-77; pres. Robert R. Michael, Chartered, Bethesda, Md., 1977-84; ptnr. Shadoan & Michael L.L.P., Rockville, Md., 1984—. Lectr. continued profl. edn. of lawyers Md. Inst., Balt., 1984—, continuing legal edn., Rockville, 1984—, continuing legal edn. of Montgomery and Prince George's Counties; lectr. various schs. and bar assns., 1983—. Author: Videotape Depositions, 1987, Comparative Liability; co-author: Automobile Accident Deskbook; co-editor: The Annual Review of Maryland Case Law, 1983; contbr. Product Liability in Maryland, articles to profl. jours. Mem. legis. taskforce product liability, Annapolis, 1980; trustee Redland Bapt. Ch.; founder Trial Lawyers for Pub. Justice, 1982. Named Sect. Chmn. of Yr., Montgomery County, 1986-87. Mem. ABA, ATLA (gov. 1984-86, del. 1982-83), Md. Trial Lawyers Assn. (pres. 1982-83, lectr.), Montgomery County Bar Assn. (jud. selections com. chmn. 1990-91, exec. com. 1991-93, trial cts. jud. nominating commn., 1992-94, adminstrn. of Justice Comm., 1993-94, pres. 1995), Montgomery County Bar Assn. Found. (pres. bar leaders 1996-97), Am. Bar Assn. Found., Assn. Plaintiffs Trial Lawyers Met. Washington, Civil Justice Found. (trustee 1987-89), Md. State Bar (jud. selections com. 1988-94, litigation sect. coun. 1989—, chair 1997—), Am. Inns Ct. (exec. com. 1988—, chpt. LXI program chmn. 1988-89, organizer, pres. 1990, bd. govs., founder Montgomery chpt. program chair 1989-90, pres. 1990-91), Nat. Inst. Advocacy (lectr.), Am. Bd. Trial Advocates, Am. Coll. Trial Lawyers, Internat. Acad. Trial Lawyers, Inner Cir. Advs. Democrat. Baptist. Personal injury (including property damage), Product liability, Professional liability. Home: 8921 Brink Rd Gaithersburg MD 20882-1013 Office: Shadoan & Michael LLP 108 Park Ave Rockville MD 20850-2694

MICHAELIS, KAREN LAUREE, law educator; b. Milw., Mar. 30, 1950; d. Donald Lee and Ethel Catherine (Stevens) M.; m. Larry Severtson, Aug. 2, 1980 (div. Aug. 1982); 1 child, Quinn Alexandra Michaelis. BA, U. Wis., 1972, BS, 1974; MA, Calif. State U., L.A., 1979; MS, U. Wis., 1985, PhD, 1988, JD, 1989. Bar: Wis., U.S. Dist. Ct. (we. dist.) Wis. Asst. prof. law Hofstra U., Hempstead, N.Y., 1990-93; assoc. prof. law Ill. State U., Normal, 1993-95, Wash. State U., Pullman, 1995—2002; atty. pvt. practice, Madison, Wis., 2002—. Author: Reporting Child Abuse: A Guide to Mandatory Requirements for School Personnel, 1993, Theories of Liability for Teacher Sexual Misconduct, 1996, Postmodern Perspectives and Shifting Legal Paradigms: Searching For A Critical Theory of Juvenile Justice, 1998; Student As Enemy: A Legal Construct of the Other, 1999; editor Ill. Sch. Law Quarterly, 1993-95; mem. editl. bd. Nat. Assn. Profs. of Edn1. Adminstrn., 1994-95, Planning and Changing, 1993-95, Jour. Sch. Leadership, 1991-99, People & Education: The Human Side of Edn., 1991-96. Mem. ABA, State Bar of Wis., Nat. Coun. Profs. Ednl. Adminstrn. (program com. 1994-95, morphet fund com. 1993-2000), Nat. Orgn. Legal Problems in Edn. (publs. com. 1993-2001, program com. 1995, exec. bd.), Edn. Law Assn. (bd. dirs. 1998-2000, co-chair publs. com. 1998—).

MICHAELS, GARY DAVID, lawyer; b. Pitts., Apr. 27, 1955; s. Edgar Wolfe and Norma Flora (Barker) M.; m. Joan Marie Kelly, June 9, 1984; children: Jeffrey Thomas, Abbey Rose. BA, U. Pa., 1977; JD, George Washington U., 1980. Bar: D.C. 1980, U.S. Dist. Ct. D.C. 1981, U.S. Ct. Appeals (D.C. cir.) 1981, U.S. Ct. Appeals (4th cir.) 1985, U.S. Supreme Ct. 1985, U.S. Ct. Appeals (1st cir.) 1987. Assoc. Troy, Malin & Pottinger, Washington, 1981-82, Ballard, Spahr, Andrews & Ingersoll, Washington, 1982-84, Krivit & Krivit P.C., Washington, 1984-98, Fed. Comm. Commn., Washington, 1998—. Bd. dirs. Hinkel-Hofmann Supply Co. Inc., Pitts., 1976—. Mem. The George Washington Law Rev., 1978-80. Vol. legal staff Gary Hart Presdl. Campaign, Washington, 1983, field coord. N.H. and Pa., 1984; bd. dirs. Van Ness South Tenants Assn., Inc., 1986-88, v.p., 1987, pres., 1988, of counsel, 1989-90. Mem. ABA, D.C. Bar Assn. Democrat. Jewish. Administrative and regulatory, Federal civil litigation, Communications. Home: 11922 Coldstream Dr Potomac MD 20854-3602 Office: Fed Comm Commn 445 12th St SW Washington DC 20554-0001 E-mail: gmichael@fcc.gov.

MICHAELS, RICHARD EDWARD, lawyer; b. Chgo., June 10, 1952; s. Benjamin and Lillian (Borawski) Mikolajczewski; m. Karen Lynn Belau Michaels, May 17, 1980; children: Jonathan R., Timothy R., Matthew R. BS in Commerce summa cum laude, DePaul U., 1973; JD, Northwestern U., 1977. Bar: Ill. 1977, U.S. Dist. Ct. (no. dist.) Ill. 1977, U.S. Ct. Appeals (7th cir.) 1977; CPA, Ill. Acct. Touche Ross & Co., Chgo., 1973-74; assoc. Schuyler, Roche & Zwirner and predecessor firm Hubachek & Kelly Ltd., Chgo., 1977-83; ptnr. Schuyler, Roche & Zwirner, Chgo., 1983—, pres., 1994—. Mem. adv. bd. Thrivent Fin., 2002—. Mem. Northwestern U. Law Rev., 1976-77. Mem. adv. bd. Greater Chgo. agy. Luth. Brotherhood, 1999—2002; chmn. Hawks swimming Main South H.S., 2001—02; vice chmn. congregation St. Andrew's Luth. Ch., Park Ridge, Ill., 1990—92, chmn. congregation, 1992—94. Mem. ABA, Internat. Bar Assn., Ill. Bar Assn., Chgo. Bar Assn., DePaul U. Alumni Assn., DePaul U. Boosters, Chgo. Athletic Assn., Northwestern Club, C.A.A. Club, Beta Gamma Sigma, Pi Gamma Mu, Beta Alpha Psi. Lutheran. Avocations: photography, golf. Antitrust, Corporate, general, Private international. Home: 808 Elm St Park Ridge IL 60068-3312 Office: Schuyler Roche & Zwirner 130 E Randolph St Ste 3800 Chicago IL 60601-6342 E-mail: rmichaels@srzlaw.com.

MICHAELSEN, HOWARD KENNETH, lawyer; b. Odessa, Wash., May 1, 1927; s. Henry Emil and Marie (Ropte) Michaelsen; m. Fayetta Mable Moulton, May 27, 1929; children: Barbara Ann, Howard David, Steven Hardy, Angelia Jean. BA in Social Studies, Wash. State U., 1952; JD, Gonzaga U., 1958. Bar: Wash. 1959, U.S. Dist. Ct. (ea. dist.) Wash. 1959. Tchr. Spokane (Wash.) Sch. Dist. 81, 1954-60; pvt. practice law Spokane, 1960—. Dir. Spokane Lilac Festival Assn., 1974. With U.S. Army, 1945—47, with U.S. Army, 1950—52. Mem.: ABA, Wash. Trial Lawyers Assn., Wash. Bar Assn. (arbitrator), Shriner, Masons, Lions. Democrat. Mem. United Ch. Christ. Avocations: fishing, hiking, swimming. Commercial, consumer (including collections, credit), Estate planning, Property, real (including real estate development, water). Home: 8004 N Fox Point Dr Spokane WA 99208-6430 Office: 320 W Spofford Ave Spokane WA 99205-4750 E-mail: corfin@icehouse.net.

MICHAELSON, BENJAMIN, JR., lawyer, director; b. Annapolis, Md., May 30, 1936; s. Benjamin and Naomi Madora (Dill) M.; m. Frances Means Blackwell, Apr. 12, 1986; children: Benjamin, Robert Wendell. BA, U. Va., 1957; JD, U. Md., 1962. Bar: Md. 1962, U.S. Dist. Ct. Md. 1976. Assoc. Goodman, Bloom & Michaelson, Annapolis, Md., 1962-63; atty. pvt. practice, Annapolis, 1963-73, 77-81; sr. ptnr. Michaelson & Christhilf, Annapolis, 1973-77; ptnr. Michaelson & Simmons, Annapolis, 1982-86, Michaelson & Newell, Annapolis, 1987-88, Michaelson, Krause & Ferris, Annapolis, 1988-91; atty. pvt. practice, Annapolis, 1991-2000; of counsel McNamee, Hosea, Jernigan & Kim, 2000—. Pres. Michaelson Title & Escrow Co., 1993-2001; gen. counsel, dir. Annapolis Fed. Savs., 1965-94 Counsel Anne Arundel County (Md.) Bd. Edn., 1966-76; mem. vestry St. Anne's Episcopal Ch., Annapolis, 1997-2003, sr. warden, 1999-2003. Lt. U.S. Army, 1957-59. Fellow: Am. Coll. Mortgage Attys.; mem.: Anne Arundel County Bar Assn., Md. Bar Assn. (chmn. real property, planning and zoning sect. coun. 1982—84, grievances commn. inquiry panel 1976—85, vice chmn. 1983—85, grievance commn. rev. bd. 1985—88), Jaycees (Md. state legal counsel 1964—65, nat. dir. 1965—66, Outstanding Young Men Am. 1995), Rotary (pres. 1975—76, Paul Harris fellow), Sailing Club Chesapeake (commodore 1982), Delta Theta Phi. Republican. Episcopalian. Banking, Probate (including wills, trusts), Property, real (including real estate development, water). Home: 1612 Winchester Rd Annapolis MD 21401 Office: 705 Melvin Ave Ste 102 Annapolis MD 21401-1534

MICHALAK, EDWARD FRANCIS, lawyer; b. Evanston, Ill., Sept. 6, 1937; s. Leo Francis Michalak and Helen Sophie (Wolinski) Krakowski. BSBA, Northwestern U., 1959; LLB, Harvard U., 1962. Bar: Ill. 1962. Assoc. McDermott, Will & Emery, Chgo., 1963-69, ptnr., 1969—. Served to sgt. USAR, 1962-68. Mem. Ill. Bar Assn., Chgo. Bar Assn., Beta Gamma Sigma, Beta Alpha Psi. Roman Catholic. Avocations: golf, opera. Corporate taxation, Personal income taxation, Pension, profit-sharing, and employee benefits. Home: 3455 Harrison St Evanston IL 60201-4953 Office: McDermott Will & Emery 227 W Monroe St 47th Fl Chicago IL 60606-5096 E-mail: emichalak@mwe.com.

MICHALIK, JOHN JAMES, legal educational association executive; b. Bemidji, Minn., Aug. 1, 1945; m. Diane Marie Olson, Dec. 21, 1968; children: Matthew John, Nicole, Shane. BA, U. Minn., 1967, JD, 1970. Legal editor Lawyers Coop. Pub. Co., Rochester, NY, 1970—75; dir. continuing legal edn. Wash. State Bar Assn., Seattle, 1975—81, exec. dir., 1981—91; asst. dean devel. and cmty. rels. Sch. Law U. Wash., 1991—95; dir., CEO Assn. Legal Adminstrs., Vernon Hills, Ill., 1995—. Fellow: Coll. Law Practice Mgmt.; mem.: Nat. Trust Hist. Preservation, Am. Mgmt. Assn., Am. Soc. Assn. Execs. Lutheran. Office: Assn Legal Adminstrs #325 175 E Hawthorn Pkwy Ste 325 Vernon Hills IL 60061-1460 E-mail: jmichalik@alanet.org.

MICHAUD, NORMA ALICE PALMER, paralegal, real estate investor; b. Concord, N.H., May 6, 1946; d. Leon Charles and Goldie May (Maxfield) Palmer (both dec.); m. Bob Michaud, July 21, 1973; 1 child, Derrick Charles. AAS in Bus. Mgmt., Mississippi County C.C., 1994; student, State Tech., Memphis, 1994-99. With United Life & Accident Ins. Co., Concord, N.H., 1965-68, 71-74; data processor Blue Cross/Blue Shield, Concord, 1968-71; with Daniel Law Firm, 1994—95, Walter Lee Bailey & Assocs., 1996—98, Shuttleworth, Williams, Harper, Waring & Derrick, 1999; adminstr. U.S. Govt., 1972—2003; house renovator, real estate owner Blytheville, Ark., 1986—. Mem. FPCC, Nat. Wildlife Assn., Nat. Geog. Soc., Bus. Profls. Am. (chpt. v.p. 1994), Phi Theta Kappa. Methodist. Avocations: reading, painting, travel.

MICHEL, CLIFFORD LLOYD, lawyer, investment executive; b. N.Y.C., Aug. 9, 1939; s. Clifford William and Barbara Lloyd (Richards) M.; m. Betsy Shirley, June 6, 1964; children: Clifford Fredrick, Jason Lloyd, Katherine Beinecke. AB cum laude, Princeton U., 1961; JD, Yale U., 1964. Bar: N.Y. 1964, U.S. Dist. Ct. (so. dist.) N.Y. 1968, U.S. Ct. Appeals (2d cir.) 1967, U.S. Supreme Ct. 1972. Assoc. Cahill Gordon & Reindel, N.Y.C., 1964-67, Paris, 1967-69, N.Y.C., 1969-71, ptnr. Paris, 1972-76, N.Y.C., 1976-2001, sr. counsel, 2001—; pres., CEO, Wenonah Devel. Co., 1976—. Bd. dirs. Alliance Capital Mgmt. Mut. Funds, Placer Dome Inc. Bd. dirs. Jockey Hollow Found., Michel Found., St. Mark's Sch., Morristown Meml. Hosp., Meml. Health Found., Atlantic Health Sys. Mem. ABA, FBA, N.Y. State Bar Assn., New York County Lawyers Assn., Am. Soc. Internat. Law, Racquet and Tennis Club, River Club, The Links, Shinnecock Hills Golf Club, Somerset Hills Country Club, Essex Hunt Club, Sankaty Head Golf Club (Mass.), Golf de Morfontaine (France), Travellers Club (Paris), Loch Lomond Club (Scotland), Nantucket Golf Club, Mayacama Golf Club, Tarratine Club. Republican. Corporate, general, Private international, Securities.

MICHEL, JEAN-PAUL, lawyer; b. Virton, Belgium, May 21, 1959; s. Joseph and Christiane (Adam) M. Degree in law, U. Louvain la Neuve, Louvain la Neuve, Belgium, 1982; degree in econs., U. Louvain la Neuve, 1985; degree in bus. adminstrn., London Sch. Fgn. Trade, 1984. Pvt. practice law, Virton, Belgium, 1985—. Active City Coun. Mem. Jaycees, Rotary, Jr. Chamber Internat. (world v.p.). Avocations: jogging, tennis, sailing, reading. Home and Office: Rue Des Combattants 30 B 6760 Virton Belgium E-mail: jpaul.michel@pi.be.

MICHEL, PAUL REDMOND, federal judge; b. Philadelphia, Pa., Feb. 3, 1941; s. Lincoln M. and Dorothy (Kelley) Michel; m. Sally Ann Clark, 1965 (div. 1987); children: Sarah Elizabeth, Margaret Kelley; m. Elizabeth Morgan, 1989. BA, Williams Coll., 1963; JD, U. Va., 1966. Bar: Pa. 1967, U.S. Supreme Ct. 1970. Asst. dist. atty. Dist. Atty.'s Office, Phila., 1967—71, dep. dist. atty. for investigations, 1972—74; asst. spl. prosecutor Watergate investigation Dept. Justice, Washington, 1974—75, dep. chief pub. integrity sect., Criminal div. and prosecutor "Koreagate" investigation, 1976—78, assoc. dep. atty. gen., 1978—81, acting dep. atty. gen., 1979—80; asst. counsel intelligence com. U.S. Senate, 1975—76, counsel and adminstrv. asst. to Sen. Arlen Specter, 1981—88; judge U.S. Ct. Appeals (Fed. cir.), Washington, 1988—. Instr. appellate practice and procedure George Washington U. Nat. Law Ctr., 1991—; instr. appellate advocacy John Marshall Law Sch., Chgo., 1991—. 2d lt. USAR, 1966—72. Office: US Ct Appeals Fed Cir 717 Madison Pl NW Washington DC 20439

MICHELI, FRANK JAMES, lawyer; b. Zanesville, Ohio, Mar. 23, 1930; s. John and Theresa (Carlini) M.; m. Doris Joan Clum, Jan. 9, 1954; children: Michael John, James Carl, Lisa Ann, Matthew Charles. Student, John Carroll U., Cleve., 1947-48, Xavier U., Cin., 1949-50; LL.D., Ohio No. U., Ada., 1953. Bar: Ohio 1953. Since practiced in, Zanesville; partner Leasure & Micheli, 1953-65, Kincaid, Micheli, Geyer & Ormond, 1965-75, Kincaid, Cultice, Micheli & Geyer (and predecessor), 1982-92; ptnr. Micheli, Baldwin, Bopeley & Northrup, 1992—. Instr. bus. law Meredith Bus. Coll., Zanesville, 1956; lectr. on med. malpractice, hosp. and nurse liability. Dir. Public Service for, City of Zanesville, 1954. Mem. Internat. Assn. Ins. Counsel, Def. Rsch. Inst., Ohio Def. Assn., Am. Ohio bar assns., Am. Judicature Soc., Am. Arbitration Assn. (mem. nat. panel), Am. Bd. Trial Advs. (bd. dirs. Ohio chpt. 1991-95, pres. 1997). Clubs: Elk. General civil litigation, Personal injury (including property damage), Product liability. Home: 160 E Willow Dr Zanesville OH 43701-1249 Office: PO Box 788 3808 James Ct Ste 2 Zanesville OH 43702-0788 E-mail: micheli@cyberzane.net.

MICHELS, HERMAN D. lawyer; b. Weehawkin, NJ, Oct. 16, 1927; s. Herman Christian and Grace Englehardt Michels; m. Ann Harrison Michels; children: Sarah Sigmund, Stephen H., Christian;children: Martha, Linda Carchia. AB, Muhlonberg Coll., 1950; LLB, Rutgers U., 1953. Bar: N.J. 1953, U.S. Dist. Ct. N.J. 1953, U.S. Ct. Appeals (3d. cir.) 1956, U.S. Supreme Ct. 1956, cert.: counsellor-at-law 1955. Assoc. to ptnr. Toner, Crowley, Woelper and Vanderbilt, Newark, 1953—67; sr. ptnr. Michels, Schwartz and Maher, Newark, 1968—72; judge law divsn. Superior Ct., Newark, 1972—74, judge to presiding judge to adminstr. appellate divsn., 1974—97; of counsel Ravin Sarasohn, Roseland, 1997—99, Gibbons, Del Der, Doland, Griffinger and Veccione, Newark, 1999—. Contbr. articles to profl. jours.; mem. Rutgers Law Rev., 1951—53. With USN, 1945—46, Hawaii. Recipient Milton Unger Meml. award, 1953, Mcpl. Corp. Law prize, 1953. Mem.: ABA, Coun. Chief Judges State Cts. Appeals (former pres.), Am. Coll. Trial Lawyers, Am. Judicature Soc., N.J. Bar Assn., N.J. Supreme Ct. Com. Drug Abuse, N.J. Supreme Ct. Com. Ct. Reporting, N.J. Ethics Commn., Am. Inn of Ct. Alt. Dispute Resolution. Episcopalian. Alternative dispute resolution, General civil litigation. Home: 6 Benson Ct Short Hills NJ 07078 Office: Gibbons DelDeo Dolan Griffinger & Vecchi Newark NJ 07102-5497 Office Fax: 973-639-8323. Business E-Mail: hmichels@gibbonslaw.com.

MICHELS, KEVIN HOWARD, lawyer; b. Newark, Dec. 30, 1960; s. Herbert Phillip and Alice Barbara Michels; m. Kathryn Ann Hockenjos, Oct. 6, 1990. BA with honors, Rutgers U., 1983, JD, 1986. Bar: N.J. 1986, U.S. Dist. Ct. N.J. 1986, U.S. Ct. Appeals (3rd cir.) 1996, U.S. Tax Ct. 1990. Law clk. N.J. Supreme Ct., Morristown, 1986-87; assoc. Pitney, Hardin, Kipp & Szuch, Morristown, 1987-88, Herold and Haines, Liberty Corner, N.J., 1988-90; pvt. practice Flemington, NJ, 1990—2002; ptnr. Michels & Hockenjos, P.C., Stirling. Mem. commn. on rules of prof. conduct N.J. Supreme Ct., 2001—02. Author: New Jersey Attorney Ethics, 2003; rsch. editor Rutgers Law Rev., 1985—86. Mem. ABA, N.J. Bar Assn., Phi Beta Kappa. General civil litigation, Corporate, general, Professional liability. Office: 70 Church St Flemington NJ 08822

MICHELSTETTER, STANLEY HUBERT, lawyer; b. Milw., July 8, 1946; s. Donald Lee and Gloria (Menke) M.; m. Joyce Bladow, Apr. 29, 1972; children: Chad S., Chris E. BA in Math., U. Wis., 1968, JD, 1972. Bar: Wis. 1972, U.S. Dist. Ct. (we. dist.) Wis. 1972. Staff atty. Wis. Employment Rels. Commn., Milw., 1972-80; pvt. practice, Milw., 1980—; adminstrv. law judge, equal rights div. adminstrat. Wis. Dept Industry, Labor & Human Rels., Milw., 1992-93. Chmn. North Shore Rep. Club, Milw., 1984-86; bd. dirs. Jewish Family Svcs., 2002—. Served to 2d lt. Wis. N.G., 1968-74; dir. Jewish Family Svcs. 2002-. Mem. Wis. Bar Assn. (chmn. 1993), Milw. Bar Assn., Nat. Acad. Arbitrators, Indsl. Rels. Rsch. Assn. (bd. dirs. 1987—), Rotary. Republican. Jewish. Alternative dispute resolution, General practice, Labor (including EEOC, Fair Labor Standards Act, labor-management relations, NLRB, OSHA). Home: 1500 W Green Brook Rd Milwaukee WI 53217-1515 Office: 1749 N Prospect Ave Milwaukee WI 53202-1966 also: PMB 37 5185 Broadway Gary IN 46409-2708 E-mail: stan@expcpc.com.

MICHENFELDER, ALBERT A. lawyer; b. St. Louis, July 21, 1926; s. Albert A. and Ruth Josephine (Donahue) M.; m. Lois Barbara Sullivan, Sept. 03, 1949 (div. May 2, 1967); children: Michael J., Ann C. Michenfelder Yancey, Elizabeth D. Michenfelder Brown; m. Ramona Jo Dysart, July 12, 1968 (dec. Jan. 2, 1998); 1 child, Julie D. Michenfelder Wolfe. B of Naval Sci., Marquette U., 1946; LLB, St. Louis U., 1950. Bar: Mo. 1950, U.S. Dist. Ct. (ea. dist.) Mo. 1950, U.S. Supreme Ct. 1975. Assoc. Flynn & Challis, St. Louis, 1950-54; pvt. practice St. Louis, 1954-55; of counsel Husch & Eppenberger LLC, St. Louis. Mem. 21st Cir. Jud. Commn., St. Louis, 1981-87. Contbr. articles to profl. jours. City atty. City of Webster Groves, Mo., 1966-79; mem. John Marshall Club, St. Louis. Lt. (j.g.) USNR, 1944-47. Mem. Mo. Bar Assn., Bar. Assn. Met. St. Louis, St. Louis County Bar Assn. (pres. 1966), Westborough Country Club. Republican. Avocations: golf, tennis. Appellate, General civil litigation, Land use and zoning (including planning). Office: Husch & Eppenberger LLC 190 Carondelet Plz Ste 600 Saint Louis MO 63105-3441 Office Fax: 314-480-1505. E-mail: al.michenfelder@husch.com.

MICHOD, CHARLES LOUIS, JR., lawyer; b. Champaign, Ill., July 19, 1943; s. Charles Louis Sr. and Florence Wise Michod; m. Susan Alexander, Aug. 16, 1969; children: Alexander, Richard, Michael. AB, Princeton U., 1995; JD, U. Mich., 1968. Bar: N.Y. 1968, Ill. 1969. Assoc. Shearman & Sterling, N.Y.C., 1968-69, Hopkins & Sutter, Chgo., 1969-72; ptnr. Martin, Craig, Chester & Sonnenschein, Chgo., 1972-94, Kelly, Olson, Michod, De Haan & Richter, Chgo., 1995—. Ptnr. DePaul Devels., Chgo., 1986—, Carpenter Ventures, Chgo., 1989—; bd. dirs. Bouquet Assocs., Chgo. and St. Gallen, Switzerland. Bd. govs. Sch. Art Inst., Chgo., 1990—; chmn. Oxbow, Inc., Saugatuck, Mich., 1995-2001. Recipient Cert. of Appreciation, Law Club of the City of Chgo., 1997, Cert. of Merit, Ill. Dept. Conservation, 1980. Mem. ABA, Chgo. Bar Assn., Univ. Club Chgo., Law Club (pres. 1996-97), Lawyers Club, Coral Creek Club, Point O'Woods Country Club. Avocations: golf, squash, art, jazz. Corporate, general, Property, real (including real estate development, water), State and local taxation. Office: Kelly Olson Michod De Haan Richter 30 S Wacker Dr Ste 2300 Chicago IL 60606 E-mail: cmichod@komdr.com.

MICKEL, JOSEPH THOMAS, lawyer; b. Monroe, La., Nov. 12, 1951; s. Toufick and Ruth Ella (Phelps) M.; m. Carlene Elise Nickens, Dec. 10, 1981 (div.); children: Thomas, Matthew. BA, La. State U., 1975; postgrad., Tulane U., 1977-78; JD, So. U., 1979. Bar: La. 1979, U.S. Dist. Ct. (mid. dist.) La. 1981, U.S. Ct. Appeals (5th cir.) 1981, U.S. Dist. Ct. (we. dist.) La. 1983, U.S. Ct. Mil. Appeals 1985, U.S. Supreme Ct. 1985. Staff atty. Pub. Defenders Office, Baton Rouge, La., 1979-80; assoc. Law Offices of Michael Fugler, Baton Rouge, 1981; asst. dist. atty. La. 4th Jud. Dist. Atty.'s Office, Monroe, 1982-89; ptnr. Bruscato, Loomis & Street, Monroe, 1984-85; Asst. U.S. Atty. Western Dist., U.S. Atty.'s Office, Lafayette, 1989—. Adj. prof. Northeast La. U., Monroe, 1988; mem. U.S. Dept. Justice Organized Crime Drug Task Force, 1992-93; instr. Acadiana Law Enforcement Tng. Acad., U. La.., Lafayette, 1995—; asst. bar examiner, com. on bar admissions Supreme Ct. State of La. Elder Presbyn. Ch., 1995—. Republican. Avocations: trapshooting, skeetshooting, bird hunting, fishing. Home: PO Box 91961 Lafayette LA 70509-1961 Office: US Atty Office 800 Lafayette St Ste 2200 Lafayette LA 70501-6865 E-mail: joseph.mickel@usdoj.gov.

MIDDLEDITCH, LEIGH BENJAMIN, JR., lawyer, educator; b. Detroit, Sept. 30, 1929; s. Leigh Benjamin and Hope Tiffin (Noble) M.; m. Betty Lou Givens, June 27, 1953; children: Leigh III, Katherine Middleditch McDonald, Andrew B. BA, U. Va., 1951, LLB, 1957. Bar: Va. 1957. Assoc. James H. Michael, Jr., Charlottesville, Va., 1957-59; ptnr. Battle, Neal, Harris, Minor & Williams, Charlottesville, 1959-68; legal adviser U. Va., Charlottesville, 1968-72; ptnr. McGuire, Woods, Battle & Boothe (now McGuire Woods LLP), Charlottesville, 1972-99, of counsel, 2000—; v.p.

McGuire Woods Cons. LLC, Charlottesville, 2001—. Lectr. Grad. Bus. Sch., U. Va., Charlottesville, 1958-94, lectr. Law Sch., 1970-90. Co-author: Virginia Civil Procedure, 1978, 2d edition, 1992; contbr. articles to profl. jours. Chmn. U. Va. Health Svcs. Found., 1988-97; bd. mgrs. U. Va. Alumni, 1994-2001, pres., 2000-01; bd. dirs., chmn. Va. Health Care Found., 1997-98; trustee Claude Moore Found., 1991—; mem. Va. Health Planning Bd., 1989—; bd. visitors U. Va., 1990-94; trustee Thomas Jefferson Meml. Found., Monticello, 1994-2002. Fellow Am. Bar Found., Va. Bar Found.; mem. ABA (bd. govs. 1999-2002), Va. State Bar (coun., chmn. bd. govs. various sects.), Charlottesville-Albemarle Bar Assn. (pres. 1979-80), U. Va. Law Sch. Alumni Assn. (pres. 1979-81), U.S. C. of C. (bd. dirs. 1998—), Va. C. of C. (pres. 1988-90), Omicron Delta Kappa. Episcopalian. Non-profit and tax-exempt organizations, Probate (including wills, trusts). Office: McGuire Woods LLP PO Box 1288 Charlottesville VA 22902-1288

MIDDLETON, J. HOWARD, JR., lawyer; b. Camden, N.J., Mar. 1, 1939; s. J. Howard and Helen Marie (Casper) M.; m. Betty Jo Bittinger, Aug. 22, 1965; children: J. Howard III, Lucia Katherine. BA, Haverford Coll., 1962; MDiv., Union Theol. Sem., 1965; JD, Georgetown U., 1972. Bar: Va. 1972, U.S. Dist. Ct. (ea. dist.) Va. 1973, U.S. Ct. Appeals (D.C. cir.) 1974, U.S. Supreme Ct. 1976, U.S. Ct. Claims 1978; ordained minister. Manpower analyst U.S. Dept. Labor, Washington, 1971-72; asst. atty. City of Alexandria, Va., 1972-76, dep. atty., 1976-78; sole practice Alexandria, Va., 1978-81; ptnr. Thomas & Fiske P.C., Alexandria, Va., 1981—. Chmn. Alexandria mcpl. liaison com. Northern Va. Builders, 1986; active Va. legis. com. Washington Bd. Trade, Alexandria, 1986; v.p. sr. svs. Alexandria. Bd. dirs. Circle Terr. Hosp., Alexandria, 1986. Mem. Lambda Alpha, Areal Estate Econs. Hon. Soc., Va. Assn. Comml. Real Estate, Va. Commerce Bank, No. Va. NAIOP (mem. adv. com.). Democrat. Environmental, Property, real (including real estate development, water). Office: Reed Smith LLP PO Box 12001 Falls Church VA 22042-0681

MIDDLETON, JACK BAER, lawyer; b. Phila., Jan. 13, 1929; s. Harry C. and Mildred Cornell (Baer) M.; m. Ann Dodge, Aug. 22, 1953; children: Susan D., Jack B. Jr., Peter C. AB, Lafayette Coll., 1950; JD cum laude, Boston U., 1956. Bar: N.H. 1956, U.S. Dist. Ct. Vt. 1988, U.S. Ct. Appeals (1st cir.) 1957, U.S. Supreme Ct. 1972. Assoc. McLane, Graf, Raulerson & Middleton, Manchester, NH, 1956—62, ptnr., dir., 1962—. Spl. justice Merrimack (N.H.) Dist. Ct., 1964-87; bd. dirs. Greater Manchester Devel. Corp., 1983-95; commr. Uniform State Laws, 1971-74; trustee New Eng. Law Inst., 1977-80. Author: (with others) Summary of New Hampshire Law, 1964, Compendium of New Hampshire Law, 1969, Trial of a Wrongful Death Action in New Hampshire, 1977; editor Boston U. Law Rev., 1954-56; contbr. articles to legal jours. Mem. Mt. Washington Commn., 1969—, Bedford (N.H.) Sch. Bd., 1960-66; mem. adv. bd. Merrimack Valley Coll.; trustee, sec. Mt. Washington Obs., 1957—; chmn. bd. trustees White Mountain Sch., 1976-79; campaign chmn. United Way Greater Manchester, 1987, bd. dirs., 1986-92, chmn., 1990-91; bd. dirs. N.H. Pub. Radio, 1988-91; bd. govs. N.H. Pub. TV, 1994—, chmn., 1997-99. Sgt. USMCR, 1950-52. Fellow Am. Coll. Trial Lawyers (chmn. N.H. sect. 1988-90), Am. Bar Found. (life); mem. ABA (ho. dels. 1984—, bd. govs. 1996-2002, sec.-elect 1998-99, sec. 1999-2002), New Eng. Bar Assn. (bd. dirs. 1977-88, pres. 1982-83), N.H. Bar Assn. (pres. 1979-80), N.H. Bar Found. (bd. dirs. 1979-92, chair 1983-90), Nat. Ctr. State Cts. (dir. 1999—), Nat. Conf. Bar Found. (trustee 1985-92, pres. 1989-90), Nat. Conf. Bar Pres. (exec. coun. 1987-95, pres. 1993-94), N.H. Bus. and Industry Assn. (bd. dirs. 1988—, sec. 1990—), Manchester C. of C. (bd. dirs. 1967-89, chmn. 1984-85), New Eng. Coun. (bd. dirs. 1991—), New Eng. Legal Found. (bd. dir. 2001-). Appellate, General civil litigation, Personal injury (including property damage). Office: McLane Graf Raulerson & Middleton 900 Elm St Ste 1001 Manchester NH 03101-2029

MIDDLETON, JAMES BOLAND, retired lawyer; b. Columbus, Ga., Aug. 19, 1934; s. Riley Kimbrough and Annie Ruth (Boland) M.; 1 child, Cynthia. BA in Psychology, Ga. State U., 1964; JD, Woodrow Wilson Coll. Law, 1972. Bar: Ga. 1972, U.S. Patent Office. Draftsman, paralegal and office mgr. to patent atty., Atlanta, 1955-68; draftsman, paralegal and office mgr. Jones & Thomas, Atlanta, 1968-72, assoc., 1972-76; pvt. practice intellectual property Decatur, Ga., 1976-98; ret., 1998. Mem. editl. bd. Atlanta Lawyer, 1973-82, assoc. editor, 1978-81, editor-in-chief, 1981-82. Dir. arts coun. Unitarian-Universalist Congregation Atlanta, 1989-91; bd.d irs. Unitarian-Universalist Endowment Fund, 1993-96, vice chair, 1994-95, sec., 1995-96; bd. dirs., sec. Decatur Arts Alliance, 1990-94; bd. dirs. Life Enrichment Svcs., Inc., 2002-. With U.S. Army, 1957-59. Mem. ABA, Am. Intellectual Property Law Assn., Am. Arbitration Assn. (comml. panel 1983-94), DeKalb Bar Assn., State Bar Ga. (editl. bd. jour. 1985-92, patent trademark and copyright sect. 1972-2000, chmn. 1982-83, pub. rels. com. 1982-88), Fed. Cir. Bar Assn. Intellectual property. E-mail: jimbmid@yahoo.com.

MIERZEWSKI, MICHAEL BRIAN, lawyer; b. Holyoke, Mass., Sept. 14, 1951; s. Edward Frank and Alice Marie (Lynch) Mierzewski; m. Kathleen Denise Kozlowski, July 10, 1976. BA, Cath. U. Am., 1973; JD magna cum laude, valedictorian, Howard U., 1980. Bar: DC 80, U.S. Ct. Appeals (DC cir.) 83, U.S. Dist. Ct. DC 83, U.S. Supreme Ct. 84. Assoc. Arnold & Porter, Washington, 1980—87, ptnr., 1988—98, sr. ptnr., 1999—. Contbg. author: Antitrust Law Developments Ann. Update, 1998—. Mem.: ABA (vice chmn. fin. mkarets and instns. 1998—). Avocations: travel, reading, wine, theater . Banking, Administrative and regulatory, Antitrust. Office: Arnold & Porter 55 12th St NW Washington DC 20004 Fax: 202-942-5999. E-mail: michael_mierzewski@aporter.com.

MIERZWA, JOSEPH WILLIAM, lawyer, legal communications consultant; b. Chgo., Nov. 21, 1951; s. Joseph Valentine and Betty Ann (Ray) M.; m. Rolana Conley, May 18, 1974. BA, U. Kans., 1981, JD, 1985. Bar: Kans. 1985, U.S. Dist. Ct. Kans. 1985. Pvt. practice, Prairie Village, Kans., 1985-86; gen. counsel Hyatt Legal Svcs., Kansas City, Mo., 1986-87; corp. counsel NLS Corp., Inc., Lakewood, Colo., 1988; owner, mgr. Joseph W. Mierzwa Cons., Lakewood, 1988-92; pres. Prose Assocs., Inc., Highlands Ranch, Colo., 1991—. Cons. Nat. Legal Shield, Lakewood, 1988-92, Reader's Digest Assn., Pleasantville, N.Y., 1988—, Hyatt Legal Svcs., Cleve., 1988-94, USLaw.com, 2000-02, ComPsych, 2001—, BestEver.com, 2003—, others; editor OverDrive Sys., Inc., Cleve., 1990-95. Author: The 21st Century Family Legal Guide, 1994. Mem. ABA, Kans. Bar Assn. Avocations: cooking, travel, creative writing. General practice. Office: 9889 S Spring Hill Dr Highlands Ranch CO 80129-4349 E-mail: paibooks@aol.com.

MIGHELL, KENNETH JOHN, lawyer; b. Schenectady, N.Y., Mar. 17, 1931; s. Richard Henry and Ruth Aline (Simon) M.; m. Julia Anne Carstarphen, Aug. 24, 1961; children: Thomas Lowry, Elizabeth Anne. BBA, U. Tex., 1952, JD, 1957. Bar: Tex. 1957. Assoc. Scurry, Scurry, Pace & Wood, Dallas, 1957-61; asst. U.S. Atty. Justice Dept., Dallas, 1961-77; 1st asst. No. Dist. Tex., 1972-77; U.S. Atty. No. Dist., Tex., 1977-81; ptnr. Cowles & Thompson, Dallas, 1981-96, of counsel, 1996—. Chmn. bd. mgmt. Downtown Dallas YMCA, 1974-76; pres. Dallas Area Am. Lung Assn., 1985-87; bd. dirs. YMCA Met. Dallas, 1987—; chmn. adv. bd. Southwestern Law Enforcement Inst., 1994-98; mem. SW Legal Found. (CLE adv. com. 1999—). With USN, 1952-54; capt. USNR, 1954-78. Mem.: FBA, Nat. Assn. Former U.S. Attys. (pres. 1995), State Bar Tex. (bd. dirs. 1994—95), Dallas Bar Found. (trustee 1994—, vice chmn. 1999—2000, chmn. 2001—02), Dallas Bar Assn. (bd. dirs. 1984—89, chmn. 1989, v.p. 1990—91, pres. 1993). Democrat. Methodist. Alternative dispute resolution, General civil litigation, Personal injury (including property damage). Office: Cowles & Thompson 901 Main St Ste 4000 Dallas TX 75202-3793 E-mail: kmighell@cowlesthompson.com.

MIHM, MICHAEL MARTIN, federal judge; b. Amboy, Ill., May 18, 1943; s. Martin Clarence and Frances Johannah (Morrissey) M.; m. Judith Ann Zosky, May 6, 1967; children— Molly Elizabeth, Sarah Ann, Jacob Michael, Jennifer Leah BA, Loras Coll., 1964; JD, St. Louis U., 1967. Asst. prosecuting atty. St. Louis County, Clayton, Mo., 1967-68; asst. state's atty. Peoria County, Peoria, Ill., 1968-69; asst. city atty. City of Peoria, Ill., 1969-72; state's atty. Peoria County, Peoria, Ill., 1972-80; sole practice Peoria, Ill., 1980-82; U.S. dist. judge U.S. Govt., Peoria, Ill., 1982—; chief U.S. dist. judge U.S. Dist. Ct. (ctrl. dist.) Ill., 1991-98. Chmn. com. internat. jud. rels. U.S. Jud. Conf., 1994—96, mem. exec. com., 1995—97, mem. com. jud. br., 1987—93, mem. com. internat. jud. rels., 1998—2002; mem. Supreme Ct. Fellows Commn., 2000—; adj. prof. law John Marshall Law Sch., 1990—. Past mem. adv. bd. Big Brothers-Big Sisters, Crisis Nursery, Peoria; past bd. dirs. Salvation Army, Peoria, W.D. Boyce council Boy Scouts Am., State of Ill. Treatment Alternatives to Street Crime, Gov.'s Criminal Justice Info. Council; past vice-chmn. Ill. Dangerous Drugs Adv. Council; trustee Proctor Health Care Found., 1991-2002. Recipient Good Govt. award Peoria Jaycees, 1978, Vincent C. Immel Alumni Merit award St. Louis U. Sch. Law, 1997, Disting. Alumnus in Pub. Svc. award Loras Coll., 2000. Mem. Peoria County Bar Assn. Roman Catholic. Office: US Dist Ct 204 Federal Bldg 100 NE Monroe St Peoria IL 61602-1003

MIHOV, JULIAN, lawyer; b. Rousse, Bulgaria, May 31, 1969; married. ML, Sofia U." St. K.Ohridski", Sofia, 1995. Bar: Ministry of Justice 1995. Legal cons. Deloitte & Touche, Sofia, Bulgaria, 1994—98, asst. mgr. The Hague, Netherlands, 1999—2000, sr. cons. Sofia, Bulgaria, 2000—. Scholar, Open Soc. Found., 1993. Immigration, naturalization, and customs, Sports, Personal income taxation. E-mail: jmihov@deloittece.com.

MIKELS, RICHARD ELIOT, lawyer; b. Cambridge, Mass., July 14, 1947; s. Albert Louis and Charlotte Betty (Shapiro) M.; m. Deborah Gwen Katz, Aug. 29, 1970; children: Allison Brooke, Robert Jarrett. BS in Bus. Adminstrn., Boston U., 1969, JD cum laude, 1972. Bar: Mass. 1972, U.S. Dist. Ct. Mass. 1974, U.S. Ct. Appeals (1st cir.) 1978. Legal examiner ICC, Washington, 1972-74; ptnr. Riemer & Braunstein, Boston, 1974-80; ptnr., chmn. comml. law sect. Peabody & Brown, Boston, 1980-88; mem., chmn. comml. law sect. Mintz, Levin, Cohn, Ferris, Glovsky and Popeo, P.C., Boston, 1988—. Contbr. articles to profl. jours. Tng. adv. com. Jewish Vocat. Svc., Boston, 1991, 95, 96, bd. dirs., 1995-99, vice chair microenterprise adv. com. 1997; vice-chair lawyers com. Combined Jewish Philanthropies, 1994, 95. Fellow Am. Coll. Bankruptcy; mem. ABA, Am. Bankruptcy Inst. (bd. dirs. 2000—), Assn. Comml. Fin. Attys., Comml. Law League Am., Mass. Bar Assn., Boston Bar Assn., Boston U. Law Alumni Assn. (mem. exec. com., pres. exec. com. 2000-01). Office: Mintz Levin Cohn Ferris Glovsky & Popeo PC 1 Financial Ctr Fl 39 Boston MA 02111-2657

MIKESELL, RICHARD LYON, lawyer, financial counselor; b. Corning, N.Y., Jan. 29, 1941; s. Walter Ray and Clara Ellen (Lyon) M.; m. Anna May Creese, Mar. 16, 1973; 1 child, Joel. BSChemE, U. Calif., Berkeley, 1962; LLB, Duke U., 1965; BA in Liberal Studies, UCLA, 1977. Bar: U.S. Supreme Ct. 1971, Ohio 1965, Calif. 1967, U.S. Ct. Appeals (9th cir.) 1982, U.S. Ct. Appeals (2d cir.) 1993, U.S. Patent Office 1967. Patent atty. Procter & Gamble, Cin., 1965-66, Rocketdyne divsn. N.Am. Aviation, L.A., 1966-69; pvt. practice law L.A., 1969-81; prin. Law Offices of R.L. Mikesell, L.A., 1981—. Fin. counselor L.A. Police Dept., 1986—; arbitrator Am. Arbitration Assn., L.A., 1980—. Pres. San Fernando Valley Fair Housing Coun., L.A., 1969-72, Valley Women's Ctr., L.A., 1990; line res. officer L.A. Police Dept., 1969-72. Named Res. Officer of Yr. L.A. Police Dept., 1990, 98; recipient 1st Place award Nat. SPAM Recipe Contest, 1998. Avocation: high power rifle shooting. General civil litigation, Patent, Property, real (including real estate development, water). Office: 14540 Hamlin St Ste B Van Nuys CA 91411-4147 E-mail: richlyon@worldnet.att.com.

MIKVA, ABNER JOSEPH, lawyer, retired federal judge; b. Milw., Jan. 21, 1926; s. Henry Abraham and Ida (Fishman) M.; m. Zoe Wise, Sept. 19, 1948; children: Mary, Laurie, Rachel. JD cum laude, U. Chgo., 1951; DL (hon.) , U. Ill., 1980, Am. U., 1991, Northwestern U., 1991, Tulane U., 1993, Ill. Inst. Tech., 1997, Santa Clara U., 2000, Wm. Mitchell Coll. Law, 2001; DHL (hon.) , Hebrew U., 1989, U. Wis., 1995, De Paul U. Law Sch., 2002. Bar: Ill. 1951, D.C. 1978. Law clk. to Hon. Sherman Minton U.S. Supreme Ct., 1951; ptnr. Devoe, Shadur, Mikva & Plotkin, Chgo., 1952-68, D'Ancona, Pflaum, Wyatt & Riskind, 1973-74; lectr. Northwestern U. Law Sch., Chgo., 1973-75, U. Pa. Law Sch., 1983-85, Georgetown Law Sch., 1986-88, Duke U. Law Sch., Durham, N.C., 1990-91, U. Chgo. Law Sch., 1992-93; mem. Ill. Gen. Assembly from 23d Dist., 1956-66, 91st-92d Congresses from 2d Dist. Ill., 94th-96th Congresses from 10th Dist. Ill.; mem. ways and means com., judiciary com. ways and means com., judiciary com.; chmn. Dem. Study Group; resigned, 1979; from judge to chief judge U.S. Circuit Ct. Appeals D.C., 1979-94, chief judge, 1991-94; counsel to the President The White House, Washington, 1994-96; arbitrator JAMS, Inc., 1997—. Vis. prof., Walter Schaefer chair in pub. policy U. Chgo., 1996-98; vis. prof. U. Ill. Coll. Law, 1998-2000, U. Chgo., 2000—. Author: The American Congress: The First Branch, 1983, The Legislative Process, 1995, An Introduction to Statutory Interpretation, 1997. With USAAF, WWII. Sr. fellow Inst. Govt. & Pub. Affairs U. Ill., 1998-2000; recipient Page One award Chgo. Newspaper Guild, 1964, Best Legislator award Ind. Voters Ill., 1956-66, Alumni medal U. Chgo., 1996, Paul Douglas Ethics in Govt. award, 1998; named one of ten Outstanding Young Men in Chgo., Jr. Assn. Commerce and Industry, 1961. Fellow Am. Acad. Arts and Scis.; mem. ABA, Chgo. Bar Assn. (bd. mgrs. 1962-64), D.C. Bar Assn., Am. Law Inst., U.S. Assn. Former Mems. Congress, Order of Coif, Phi Beta Kappa. Home: Ph 6 5020 S Lake Shore Dr Chicago IL 60615-3253 E-mail: amikva@law.uchicago.edu.

MILAM, JOSEPH WALTON, JR., judge; b. Danville, Va., June 3, 1956; s. Joseph Walton and Calvine (Pegram) M.; m. Katherine Warfield, Aug. 15, 1981; children: Joseph III, Wallis Warfield. BS, Emory U., 1978; JD, U. Richmond, 1983. Bar: Va. 1983. Prin. Woods, Rogers & Hazlegrove, Plc (and predecessor firms), Roanoke, Va., 1983—2001; cir. judge 22d Cir. of Va., 2001—. Assoc. editor U. Richmond Law Rev., 1982-83. Bd. dirs., sec. Roanoke Vocat. Edn. Found., Inc., 1986-89; bd. dirs. Leadership Danville, 1990-94; bd. dirs. Goodwill Industries, Danville, 1996-2001, pres., 1999-2000; bd. dirs. Danville Mus. History and Fine Arts, 1997-2000, United Way Danville, Pittsylvania County, 1997-2000; treas. Leadership Southside, 1993-94; pres. Danville Estate Planning Coun., 1997-98. Mem. ABA, Va. State Bar Assn., Va. Bar Assn., Danville Bar Assn. (past pres.), Danville Area C. of C. (bd. dirs., vice-chmn. 1992-94, chmn. 1995). Office: Cts and Jail Bldg 401 Patton St PO Box 1401 Danville VA 24543-1401 E-mail: milamjw@ci.danville.va.us.

MILBOURNE, WALTER ROBERTSON, lawyer; b. Phila., Aug. 27, 1933; s. Charles Gordon and Florie Henderson (Robertson) M.; m. Georgena Sue Dyer, June 19, 1965; children: Gregory Broughton, Karen Elizabeth, Walter Robertson, Margaret Henderson. AB, Princeton U., 1955; LL.B., Harvard U., 1958. Bar: Pa. 1959. Assoc. firm Pepper, Hamilton & Sheetz, Phila., 1959-65, Obermayer, Rebmann, Maxwell & Hippel, Phila., 1965-67, ptnr., 1968-84, Saul, Ewing, Remick & Saul, 1984-2000, of counsel, 2001—. Bd. dirs. Pa. Lumbermen's Mut. Ins. Co., Phila. Reins. Corp.; co-chmn. Nat. Conf. Lawyers and Collection Agys., 1979-90; chmn. bus. litigation com. Def. Rsch. Inst., 1986-89, mem. law instsn. com., 1989-95. Chmn. mental health budget sect. Phila. United Fund, 1967—70; pres. Found. Internat. Assn. Def. Counsel, 1997—2001. Fellow: Am. Coll. Trial Lawyers (mem. internat. com. 1992—96); mem.: ABA, Phila. Bar Assn., Pa. Bar Assn., Phila. Lawn Tennis Assn. (pres. 1969—70), Merion Cricket Club. Republican. Federal civil litigation, State civil litigation, Alternative dispute resolution. Home: 689 Fernfield Cir Wayne PA 19087-2002 Office: Saul Ewing Remick & Saul 3800 Centre Sq W Philadelphia PA 19102 E-mail: Waltermilb@aol.com.

MILDER, FORREST DAVID, lawyer; b. Oceanside, N.Y., Sept. 28, 1953; s. Arthur Aaron and Helen Claire M.; m. Sara Packard, June 15, 1975; children: Stephen, Elinor. SB in Math., MIT, 1973, SM in Econs., 1974; JD, Harvard U., 1977; LLM in Taxation, Boston U., 1983. Bar: Mass. 1977, U.S. Dist. Ct. Mass. 1978, U.S. Supreme Ct. 1985, U.S. Ct. Appeals (1st cir.) 1978, U.S. Tax Ct. 1981, U.S. Claims Ct. 1985. Assoc. Goodwin Procter & Hoar, Boston, 1977-81, Brown, Rudnick, Berlack Israels, Boston, 1981-85, ptnr., 1985—. Lectr. law Boston U., 1990-95; mem. exec. bd. MIT Enterprise Forum, Cambridge, Mass., 1998—, chmn., 2001-03. Author: Rehabilitation Tax Credit and Low Income Housing Tax Credit, 1996; mem. bd. editors Matrimonial Strategist. Mem. ABA (bd. govs., chair internet and tech. Forum on Affordable Housing and Cmty. Devel. 2000—), Boston Bar Assn., Phi Beta Kappa. Corporate, general, Corporate taxation, Personal income taxation. Home: 122 Hoover Rd Needham MA 02494-1548 Office: Brown Rudnick Berlack Israels 1 Fin Ctr Boston MA 02111 Business E-Mail: fmilder@brbilaw.com. E-mail: milder@attbi.com.

MILES, DAVID MICHAEL, lawyer; b. Jackson, Mich., Aug. 5, 1954; s. Richard George and Joann Marie (Stefanoff) M.; m. Noelle Suzanne McHugh, Sept. 6, 1986; children: Amy Elizabeth, Margaret Noelle, Lane McHugh. Student, U. Mich., 1972-74; BA cum laude, Clark U., 1976; JD magna cum laude, George Washington U., 1979. Bar: D.C. 1979, U.S. Ct. Appeals (4th cir.) 1980, U.S. Dist. Ct. Md. 1980, U.S. Dist. Ct. D.C. 1983, U.S. Supreme Ct. 1983, U.S. Ct. Appeals (D.C. cir.) 1981, U.S Ct. Appeals (9th cir.) 1984, U.S. Ct. Appeals (2d cir.) 1986. Law clk. to Chief Judge Edward Northrop, U.S Dist. Ct. Md., 1979-80; law clk. to Cir. Judge George MacKinnon U.S. Ct. Appeals, Washington, 1980-81; assoc. Fried, Frank, Harris, Shriver & Jacoboson, Washington, 1981-86, ptnr., 1986-92, Sidley & Austin, Washington, 1992—. Co-author: The Law of Financial Services, 1988; contbr. articles to profl. jours. Democrat. Roman Catholic. Banking, Finance, Securities. Home: 5229 Westpath Way Bethesda MD 20816 Office: Sidley, Austin, Brown & Wood 1501 K St NW Washington DC 20005 E-mail: DavidM9876@aol.com., dmiles@sidley.com.

MILES, DAVID R. lawyer; b. Richmond, Ind., Apr. 13, 1955; s. John R. and Joyce L. M.; m. Mary E. McMorrow, Apr. 17, 1982; children: Julie, Kathleen. BA in Polit. Sci., Wittenberg U., 1977; JD, U. Toledo, 1980. Bar: Ohio 1981, U.S. Dist. Ct. (so. dist.) Ohio 1981. Pvt. practice, Fairborn, Ohio, 1981—. Editor Dayton Bar Assn. Mem. S.W. Ohio Assn. Businessmen, Phi Gamma Delta. Avocation: sports. General civil litigation, Criminal, Family and matrimonial. Office: 125 W Main St Ste 201 Fairborn OH 45324-4749

MILES, GAVIN WENTWORTH, lawyer; b. Cambridge, Mass., Sept. 10, 1960; s. Perry Ambrose and Kathleen (McCartney) B.; m. Sarah Jane Berger, Jan. 16, 1995; 1 child: Benjamin. BA in Pol. Sci., Columbia Coll., 1982; JD, Emory U., 1989. Bar: N.Y. 1990. Asst. dist. atty. King's County (N.Y.) Dist. Atty's. Office, Bklyn., 1989-94, sr. asst. dist. atty., 1994-96, spl. counsel, rackets, 1996-2000, dep. bur. chief, rackets, 2000-01, 1st dep. bur. chief, rackets, 2001—. Mem. N.Y.C. Bar Assn. (criminal cts. com. 1996-98). Avocation: history. Office: Kings County DA'S Office 350 Jay St Brooklyn NY 11201-2900

MILES, HARRY LEHMAN, lawyer, educator; b. May 4, 1944; s. Sidney and Beatrice (Lehman) M. AB, Dartmouth Coll., 1965; JD, Bklyn. Law Sch., 1969; MA in Comms., U. Mass., Amherst, 1972. Tchr. James Madison H.S., Bklyn., 1966-70; instr. U. Mass., Amherst, 1970-72; practice law Amherst, 1971-75; asst. dist. atty. Northwestern Dist., Mass., 1975-79, 1st asst. dist. atty., 1979-80; ptnr. Growhoski, Callahan & Miles, Northampton, Mass., 1980-94, Green, Miles, Lipton, White & Fitz-Gibbon, Northampton, Mass., 1994—. Past adj. prof. law Western New Eng. Coll. Sch. Law; v.p., dir. Western Mass. Legal Services Corp. Mem. Shutesbury (Mass.) Bd. Health, 1972-74, Shutesbury Fin. Com., 1973-74. Fellow Am. Acad. Forensic Scis. (jurisprudence sect.), Am. Coll. Trial Lawyers, Mass. Bar Found.; mem. ABA, Mass. Bar Assn., Hampshire County Bar Assn., Mass. Assn. Criminal Defense Lawyers, Dartmouth Lawyers Assn. Democrat. Civil rights, State civil litigation, Personal injury (including property damage). Office: Green Miles Lipton White Fitz-Gibbon 77 Pleasant St PO Box 210 Northampton MA 01061-0210 E-mail: harrymiles@aol.com.

MILES, WENDELL A. federal judge; b. Holland, Mich., Apr. 17, 1916; s. Fred T. and Dena Del (Alverson) M.; m. Mariette Bruckert, June 8, 1946; children: Lorraine Miles, Michelle Miles Kopinski, Thomas Paul. AB, Hope Coll., 1938, LLD (hon.), 1980; MA, U. Wyo., 1939; JD, U. Mich., 1942; LLD (hon.), Detroit Coll. Law, 1979. Bar: Mich. Ptnr. Miles & Miles, Holland, 1948-53, Miles, Mika, Meyers, Beckett & Jones, Grand Rapids, Mich., 1961-70; pros. atty. County of Ottawa, Mich., 1949-53; U.S. dist. atty. Western Dist. Mich., Grand Rapids, 1953-60, U.S. dist. judge, 1974—, chief judge, 1979-86, sr. judge, 1986—. Cir. judge 20th Jud. Cir. Ct. Mich., 1970-74; instr. Hope Coll., 1948-53, Am. Inst. Banking, 1953-60; adj. prof. Am. constl. history Hope Coll., Holland, Mich., 1979— ; mem. Mich. Higher Edn. Commn.; apptd. Fgn. Intelligence Surveillance Count, Washington, 1989—. Pres. Holland Bd. Edn., 1952-63. Served to capt. U.S. Army, 1942-47. Recipient Liberty Bell award, 1986. Fellow Am. Bar Found.; mem. ABA, Mich. Bar Assn., Fed. Bar Assn., Ottawa County Bar Assn., Grand Rapids Bar (Inns of Ct. 1995—), Am. Judicature Soc., Torch Club, Rotary Club, Masons. Office: US Dist Ct 236 Fed Bldg 110 Michigan St NW Ste 452 Grand Rapids MI 49503-2363 E-mail: miles@miwd.uscourts.gov.

MILGRIM, ROGER MICHAEL, lawyer; b. N.Y.C., Mar. 22, 1937; s. Isreal and Iola (Lash) M.; m. Patricia Conway, July 10, 1971; children: Justin. BA, U. Pa., 1958; LLB, NYU, 1961, LLM, 1962. Bar: N.Y., U.S. Supreme Ct. Assoc. Baker & McKenzie, Paris, 1963-65, Nixon Mudge et al, N.Y.C., 1965-68; mem. Milgrim Thomajan & Lee P.C., N.Y.C., 1968-92; ptnr., chmn. intellectual property group Paul, Hastings, Janofsky & Walker LLP, N.Y.C., 1992—, chmn. litigation dept., 1999-2000. Adj. prof. sch. law NYU, N.Y.C., 1974—; bd. suprs. Technip Coflexip S.A., 2001—03, bd. dirs., 2003—. Author: Milgrim on Trade Secrets, 1968, supplement, 2003, Milgrim on Licensing, 1990, supplement, 2003. Trustee Coll. Wooster, 1994-97, Bklyn. Hosp., 1982-91; bd. dirs. Fulbright Assn., 1998—, chmn. Fulbright Prize com., 1999-01; bd. advs. UniStates LLC. Mem. Knickerbocker Club, Phila. Cricket Club. Republican. Corporate, general, Intellectual property, Private international. Home: 301 E 52nd St New York NY 10022-6319 Office: Paul Hastings Janofsky & Walker LLP 75 E 55th New York NY 10022-3205 E-mail: rogermilgrim@paulhastings.com.

MILHAM, JULEE LYNN, lawyer, mediator, arbitrator; b. Chapel Hill, N.C., May 24, 1963; d. Richard Joseph and Peggy Joyce Milham. BA, Stetson U., DeLand, Fla., 1983; JD, Stetson U., St. Petersburg, Fla., 1986. Bar: Fla. 1986, Calif. 1987, D.C. 1989, U.S. Dist. Ct. (mid. dist.) Fla. 1991, U.S. Ct. Appeals (11th cir.) 1994; cert. mediator, Fla. Atty. at law sole propr., St. Petersburg, 1986—. Traffic ct. hearing officer Pinellas County Ct., Fla., 1994—, small claims hearing officer, 1997—; mediator/arbitrator, 1994—. Author: The Practice of Music Law in Florida, 2003. Mem. Fla. Bar (chair emeritus entertainment sect., chair small claims rules com.); bd. govs. NARAS. Criminal, Family and matrimonial, General practice. Office: 505 76th Ave St Petersburg Beach FL 33706-1805 Fax: 727-363-1925. E-mail: julee@eMusiclaw.com.

MILIAN, DAVID PHILIP, lawyer; b. Chgo., Sept. 7, 1965; s. Daniel Osvaldo Milian and Janice Lee Reed; m. Ivy Surloff-Milian, Sept. 9, 1995; 3 children. BA, U. Fla., 1986, JD with honors, 1989. Bar: Fla. 1990, U.S. Dist. Ct. (so. and ctrl. dists.) Fla. 1990, U.S. Ct. Appeals (11th cir.) 1994. Assoc. Morgan Lewis & Bockius LLP, Miami, 1990—93, Kozyak Tropin & Throckmorton, Miami, 1993, shareholder, 1997—. Mentor Midnight Basketball League, Overtown/Miami, Fla., 1992—95. Mem.: Dade County Bar Assn. (bd. dirs. 1997—2001), Fla. Bar Young Lawyers Divsn. (bd. govs. 1998—, spl. commn. on multijurisdictional practices 2002—, Diversity award 2001). Presbyterian. Commercial, contracts (including sales of goods; commercial financing), Intellectual property, Professional liability. Office: Kozyak Tropin & Throckmorton PA 200 S Biscayne Blvd Ste 2800 Miami FL 33131 Office Fax: 305-372-3508 . E-mail: dmilian@kttlaw.com.

MILITA, MARTIN JOSEPH, lawyer; b. Vineland, N.J., May 14, 1953; s.Martin Joseph and Mary Elizabeth (Gavigan) M.; m. Janet D. Milita, Oct. 3, 1981; 1 child, Samantha Anne. BA, Kings Coll., 1976; JD, Temple U., 1979. Bar: Pa. 1979, N.J. 1979, U.S. Dist. Ct. N.J. 1979. Tchg. fellow Temple U., Phila., 1978; asst. dist. atty. Bucks County Dist. Atty.'s Office, Doylestown, Pa., 1979-81; asst. prosecutor Hunterdon County Prosecutor's Office, Flemington, N.J., 1981-84; dep. atty. gen. State of N.J., Trenton, 1984-90; assoc. Sills Cummis et al, Newark, 1990-94; counsel Riker, Danzig, Scherer, Hyland & Perretti, LLP, Morristown, N.J., 1994—. Contbr. articles to law jours. Mem. adv. bd. Rep. Nat. Com., Washington, 1994—. Mem. N.J. Bar Assn. Roman Catholic. Avocations: civil war history, collecting civil war art and artifacts. Office: A Fiore & Sons 1230 McCarter Hwy Newark NJ 07104-3710

MILLAR, RICHARD WILLIAM, JR., lawyer; b. LA, May 11, 1938; LLB, U. San Francisco, 1966. Bar: Calif. 1967, U.S. Dist. Ct. (cen. dist.) Calif. 1967, U.S. Dist. Ct. (no. dist.) Calif. 1969, U.S. Dist. Ct. (so. dist.) Calif. 1973, U.S. Supreme Ct. Assoc. Iverson & Hogoboom, Los Angeles, 1967-72; ptnr. Eilers, Stewart, Pangman & Millar, Newport Beach, Calif., 1973-75, Millar & Heckman, Newport Beach, 1975-77, Millar, Hodges & Bemis, Newport Beach, 1979—. Fellow: Am. Bar Found.; mem.: Orange County Bar Assn. (chmn. bus. litig. sect. 1981, chmn. judiciary com. 1988—90, sec. 1999, treas., dir. charitable fund 2000, pres.-elect 2001, pres. 2002), Calif. Bar Assn. (lectr. CLE), ABA (litigation sect. trial practice com., ho. of dels. 1990—), Palm Valley Country Club (Palm Desert, Calif.), Pacific Club, Bohemian Club (San Francisco). Federal civil litigation, State civil litigation. Home: 71 Hillsdale Newport Beach CA 92660 Office: Millar Hodges & Bemis One Newport Pl Ste # 900 Newport Beach CA 92660 E-mail: millar@mhblaw.net.

MILLARD, NEAL STEVEN, lawyer; b. Dallas, June 6, 1947; s. Bernard and Adele (Marks) M.; m. Janet Keast, Mar. 12, 1994; 1 child, Kendall Lynn. BA cum laude, UCLA, 1969; JD, U. Chgo., 1972. Bar: Calif. 1972, U.S. Dist. Ct. (cen. dist.) Calif. 1973, U.S. Tax Ct. 1973, U.S. Ct. Appeals (9th cir.) 1987, N.Y. 1990. Assoc. Willis, Butler & Schiefly, Los Angeles, 1972-75; ptnr. Morrison & Foerster, Los Angeles, 1975-84, Jones, Day, Reavis & Pogue, Los Angeles, 1984-93, White & Case, L.A., 1993—. Instr. Calif. State Coll., San Bernardino, 1975-76; lectr. Practising Law Inst., N.Y.C., 1983-90, Calif. Edn. of Bar, 1987-90; adj. prof. USC Law Ctr., 1994—. Citizens adv. com. L.A. Olympics, 1982-84; trustee Altadena (Calif.) Libr. Dist., 1985-86; bd. dirs. Woodcraft Rangers, L.A., 1982-90, pres., 1986-88; bd. dirs. L.A. County Bar Found., 1990-2000, pres., 1997-98; mem. Energy Commn. of County and Cities of L.A., 1995-99; bd. dirs. Inner City Law Ctr., 1996-99; mem. jud. procedures commn. L.A. County, 1999—, chair, 2000-02. Mem. ABA, Calif. Bar Assn., N.Y. State Bar Assn., L.A. County Bar Assn. (trustee 1985-87), Pub. Counsel (bd. dirs. 1984-87, 90-93), U. Chgo. Law Alumni Assn. (pres. 1998-2001), USC Inst. for Corporate Counsel (advisory bd. 1998—), Calif. Club, Phi Beta Kappa, Pi Gamma Mu, Phi Delta Phi. Banking, Private international, Property, real (including real estate development, water). Office: White & Case 633 W 5th St Ste 1900 Los Angeles CA 90071-2087 E-mail: nmillard@whitecase.com.

MILLARD, RICHARD STEVEN, lawyer; b. Pasadena, Calif., Feb. 6, 1952; s. Kenneth A. and Kathryn Mary (Paden) M.; m. Jessica Ann Edwards, May 15, 1977; children: Victoria, Elizabeth, Andrew. AB, Stanford U., 1974; JD magna cum laude, U. Mich., 1977. Bar: Calif. 1977, Ill. 1985. Assoc. Heller, Ehrman, White & McAuliff, San Francisco, 1977-81, Mayer, Brown & Platt, Chgo., 1982-83, ptnr., 1984-99, Weil, Gotshal & Manges, Redwood Shores, Calif., 1999—. Mem. ABA, Order of Coif. Mergers and acquisitions, Securities, Finance. Office: Weil Gotshal & Manges 201 Redwood Shores Pkwy Redwood City CA 94065 E-mail: richard.millard@weil.com.

MILLBERG, JOHN C. lawyer; b. New London, Conn., Jan. 4, 1956; s. Melvin Roy and Dorothy (Van Zandt) M.; m. Lori Bruce, Oct. 18, 1981; children: Kathryn Faye, Rebecca Ann, Melvin Roy III. BA, Bowling Green State U., 1977; JD, Wake Forest U., 1980. Bar: Tex. 1980, N.C. 1986, S.C. 2000, U.S. Dist. Ct. (so. dist.) Tex. 1981, U.S. Ct. Appeals (5th and 11th cirs.) 1981, U.S. Dist. Ct. (ea., mid. and we. dists.) N.C. 1986, U.S. Ct. Appeals (4th cir.) 1986, U.S. Dist. Ct. S.C. 2002. Assoc. Crain Caton James & Womble, Houston, 1981—85; assoc., dir. Maupin, Taylor, Ellis & Adams, Raleigh, NC, 1985—94; mng. ptnr. Millberg, Gordon & Stewart, PLLC, Raleigh, NC, 1994—. Mem. bar candidate com. N.C. Bd. Law Examiners, 1988-90. Scholar Wake Forest U. Sch. Law, 1977-80. Mem. N.C. Assn. Def. Attys. (exec. com., v.p. southeastern region), Nat. Assn. R.R. Trial Counsel. General civil litigation, Insurance, Personal injury (including property damage). Office: Millberg Gordon & Stewart PLLC S 104 1101 Haynes St Raleigh NC 27604-1455

MILLER, ALFRED MONTAGUE, lawyer; b. Augusta, Ga., Jan. 5, 1940; s. Dessie Ford and May Belle (Power) M.; m. Lynthia Wofford, Aug. 25, 1962 (div. 1979); children— William Montague, Stephen Mathews; m. Peggy Elaine Mays, July 26, 1980. B.B.A., U. Ga., 1961, J.D., 1963. Bar: Ga. 1962, Superior Ct. Ga. 1962, U.S. Dist. Ct. (so. dist.) Ga. 1963, U.S. Ct. Appeal (11th cir.) 1981, U.S. Supreme Ct. 1978. Ptnr. Fulcher, Fulcher, Hagler, Harper and Reed, Augusta, 1963-71, Dye, Miller, Tucker and Everitt, P.A., Augusta, 1971—90, of counsel 1990-; pres. Club Car, Inc., 1990-2001; dir. First Bank of Ga., 2001-. Fellow Ga. Bar Found., Am. Coll. Trial Lawyers; mem. Am. Judicature Soc., ABA, Lawyers-Pilot Bar Assn., State Bar Ga. (bd. govs. 1977-85), Augusta Bar Assn. (pres. 1985), Internat. Assn. Def. Counsel, Beta Gamma Sigma, Chi Phi (pres. 1960-61), Phi Delta Phi. Presbyterian. Federal civil litigation, State civil litigation, Personal injury (including property damage). Home: 4384 Deer Run Evans GA 30809-4440 Office: Tucker Everitt Long Brewton & Lanier PO Box 2426 Augusta GA 30903-2426 E-mail: mill4384@aol.com.

MILLER, ALLAN JOHN, lawyer; b. Beachwood, Ohio, Oct. 17, 1921; s. Carl Frederick and Rhoda (Warren) M.; m. Marjorie Hewitt Pirtle, Aug. 10, 1946; children: James W., Patricia Anne. BBA, Fenn Coll., 1946; LL.B., Western Res. U., 1948; D. (hon.), Dyke Coll., Cleve., 1986. Bar: Ohio 1948. With Standard Oil Co., Ohio, 1948-77, treas., 1967-77; mem. firm Kiefer, Knecht, Rees, Meyer & Miller, Cleve., 1977-81. Dir. United Screw & Bolt Corp., 1977-97. Chmn. bd. dirs. Luth. Med. Ctr., Cleve., 1967-82; pres. Luth. Med. Ctr. Med. Staff Found., 1979-85; bd. dirs. Christian Residencies Found., 1972-77, St. Luke's Hosp. Assn., 1973-84; chmn. bd. trustees Dyke Coll., Cleve., 1971-86. With AUS, 1943-46, PTO. Mem. Cleve. Treas.'s Club. Clubs: Capri Isles Golf Club (Venice, Fla.). Presbyterian. Home: Apt 531 900 Tamiami Trl S Venice FL 34285-3627 E-mail: ajmvenice@cs.com.

MILLER, ALLEN TERRY, JR., lawyer; b. Alexandria, Va., Sept. 19, 1954; s. Allen Terry and Eleanor Jane (Thompson) M.; m. Maureen Ann Callaghan, June 22, 1985; children: Brendan Allen, Patrick Joseph, Brigit Eleanor. BA, U. Va., 1977; JD, Seattle U., 1982. Bar: Wash. 1982, U.S. Dist. Ct. (we. dist.) Wash. 1982, U.S. Ct. Appeals (9th cir.) 1985, U.S. Dist. Ct. (ea. dist.) Wash. 1986, U.S. Dist. Ct. (no. dist.) N.Y. 1990, U.S. Dist. Ct. (we. dist.) Mich. 1990, U.S. Supreme Ct. 1990, U.S. Ct. Appeals (2d and 6th cirs.) 1991. Legis. asst. Congressman Paul N. McCloskey Jr., Washington, 1978-79; asst. atty. gen. State of Washington, Olympia, 1982-92; prin. Connolly, Tacon & Meserve, Olympia, 1992—. Adj. prof. environ. law Seattle U., 1991—2001. Commr. Olympia Planning Commn., 1987-92, vice-chair, 1991, chair, 1992; sec. North Capitol Campus Heritage Pk. Devel. Assn., 1989-90, pres., 1991—; pres. Olympia Chorale and Light Opera Co., 1984-85; mem. St. Michael's Sch. Bd., 1993-96, chair, 1994-96; bd. dirs. South Sound YMCA, 1996—, Olympia Symphony, 1999-2001, Olympia Sch. Dist. Found., 1998-2002; pres. bd. dirs. United Way Thurston County, 1998-2003, pres. 2000-02, campaign chair, 2002—; pres. Olympia Yashiro Sister City Assn., 2001-02. Recipient Merit award Am. Planning Assn., 1989, 92, Citizen of Yr. award Thurston County, 1998. Mem. ABA, Wash. Bar Assn. (mem. environ. law sect. 1984—, ct. rules com. 1985-89, jud. recommendation com. 1991-94, legis. com. 1994-97, ct. improvement com. 1997-2000, character and fitness com. 2002—), Thurston County Bar Assn., Leadership Thurston County, Olympic-Thurston C. of C. (trustee 1996-00, pres.-elect 1997, pres. 1998), Rotary (Olympia, bd. dirs. 2002—). Democrat. Roman Catholic. Avocations: mountaineering, kayaking, tennis, piano. Environmental, Land use and zoning (including planning), Property, real (including real estate development, water). Home: 1617 Sylvester St SW Olympia WA 98501-2228 Office: Heritage Bldg 5th and Columbia Olympia WA 98501-1114

MILLER, ANDREW PICKENS, lawyer; b. Fairfax, Va., Dec. 21, 1932; s. Francis Pickens and Helen (Hill) M.; m. Penelope Farthing, Nov. 18, 1990; children: Julia Lane, Andrew Pickens, Elise Givhan, Winfield Scott, Lucia Holcombe. AB magna cum laude, Princeton U., 1954; postgrad., New Coll., Oxford (Eng.) U., 1954-55; LLB, U. Va., 1960. Bar: Va. 1960, U.S. Supreme Ct. 1967, D.C. 1979. Assoc. Penn, Stuart & Stuart, 1960-62; ptnr. Penn, Stuart & Miller, Abingdon, Va., 1963-69; atty. gen. State of Va., 1970-77; ptnr. Mays, Valentine, Davenport & Moore, Richmond, Va., 1977-78, Dickstein, Shapiro, Morin & Oshinsky, LLP, Washington, 1979—2002, Powell Goldstein Frazer & Murphy LLP, Washington, 2003—. Pres., Young Democratic Clubs Va., 1966-67; chmn. Washington County Dem. Com., 1967-69; Dem. nominee for U.S. Senate from Va., 1978; bd. dirs. Barter Found., 1962-69; trustee King Coll., 1966-74; mem. adv. bd. Ams. for Effective Law Enforcement, 1973-77, Center for Oceans Law and Policy, 1975-79; vice-chmn. Va. Bd. Corrections, 1983-86. Served to 1st lt. AUS, 1955-57. Fellow Am. Bar Found.; mem. ABA (ho. dels. 1971-76, action commn. to reduce ct. costs and delay 1979-84, commn. on pub. understanding about the law 1992-95), So. Conf. Attys. Gen. (vice chmn. 1972-73, chmn. 1973-74), Nat. Assn. Attys. Gen. (exec. com. 1973-74, chmn. antitrust com. 1971-76, Wyman Meml. award 1976), Va. Bar Assn. (chmn. young lawyers sect. 1967-68, exec. com. 1985-88), Am. Judicature Soc. (bd. dirs. 1973-76, exec. com. 1974-76), Soc. of Cin. (Va. standing com. 1986-89, 93-96, asst. sec., 1992-95, sec. gen. 1995-98), The John Marshall Found. (pres. 1987-89), Phi Beta Kappa, Omicron Delta Kappa. Presbyterian. Legislative, Antitrust, General civil litigation. Home: 1503 35th St NW Washington DC 20007-2729 Office: Powell Goldstein Frazer & Murphy LLP 1001 Pennsylvania Ave 6th Fl Washington DC 20004-2582

MILLER, ANNE BURKE, lawyer; b. Kansas City, Kans., Sept. 18, 1956; d. Paul and Patricia Ann (Pierson) Burke; children: Emily, Kathleen, Erin. BA in Liberal Arts, U. Kans., 1978, JD, 1981. Bar: Kans. 1981, U.S. Dist. Ct. Kans. 1981. Assoc. Miller, Ball & Miller, Manhattan, Kans., 1981-86; ptnr. Everett, Seaton, Miller & Bell, Manhattan, 1986—. Mem. Leadership Kans., 1986; bd. dirs. United Way, Manhattan, 1987. Veta B. Lear and Watkins-Berger scholar Kans. U., 1975-78. Fellow Am. Acad. Matrimonial Lawyers, Am. Bar Found., Kans. Bar Found. (bd. dirs., sec.-treas. 1999, pres.-elect 2000); mem. ABA, Kans. Bar Assn. (chmn. domestic violence task force 1985, pres. family law sect., pres. young lawyers divsn. 1987-88, bd. govs. 1988-94, Outstanding Svc. award 1996), Riley County Bar Assn. (pres. 1988—), Jr. League, Phi Beta Kappa, Phi Kappa Phi. Republican. Presbyterian. Avocations: skiing, traveling, reading, swimming. General civil litigation, Commercial, contracts (including sales of goods; commercial financing), Family and matrimonial. Home: 3130 Amherst Ave Manhattan KS 66503-3008 Office: Seaton Miller Bell & Seaton LLP 410 Humboldt St Manhattan KS 66502-6031

MILLER, ARTHUR MADDEN, lawyer, investment banker; b. Greenville, S.C., Apr. 10, 1953; s. Charles Frederick and Kathryn Irene (Madden) M.; m. Roberta Beck Connolly, Apr. 17, 1993; children: Isabella McIntyre Madden, Roberta Beck Connolly. AB in History, Princeton U., 1973; MA in History, U. N.C., 1976; JD with distinction, Duke U., 1978; LLM in Taxation, NYU, 1982. Bar: N.Y. 1979, U.S. Dist. Ct. (so. dist.) N.Y. 1979. Assoc. Mudge Rose Guthrie Alexander & Ferdon, N.Y.C., 1978-85; v.p. pub. fin. Goldman, Sachs & Co., N.Y.C., 1985—. Trustee Convent Sacred Heart, N.Y., 2003-, St. Andrew's Sch., Del., 2003-; mem. adv. bd. Mary Baldwin Coll., Staunton, Va., 1982-86; trustee Princeton U. Rowing Assn., N.J., 1980—, pres., 1986-95; trustee Rebecca Kelly Dance Co., N.Y.C., 1984-86; mem. Power Ten, N.Y., steward, 1992-95. Mem. ABA (tax sect. com. on tax exempt financing 1985—), Nat. Assn. Bond Lawyers (lectr. 1985—), Pub. Securities Assn. (cons. 1985—), Practising Law Inst. (lectr. 1980, editor/author course materials 1980—), Bond Attys. Workshop (editor/author course material 1983—, lectr. 1983—), Princeton Club. Municipal (including bonds), Securities, Personal income taxation. Office: Goldman Sachs & Co 85 Broad St New York NY 10004-2456 E-mail: arthur.miller@gs.com.

MILLER, BENJAMIN K. retired state supreme court justice; b. Springfield, Ill., Nov. 5, 1936; s. Clifford and Mary (Luthyens) M. BA, So. Ill. U., 1958; JD, Vanderbilt U., 1961. Bar: Ill. 1961. Ptnr. Olsen, Cantrill & Miller, Springfield, 1964-70; prin. Ben Miller-Law Office, Springfield, 1970-76; judge 7th jud. cir. Ill. Cir. Ct., Springfield, 1976-82, presiding judge Criminal div., 1977-81, chief judge, 1981-82; justice Ill. Appellate Ct., 4th Jud. Dist., 1982-84, Ill. Supreme Ct., Springfield, 1984-2001, chief justice, 1991-93, ret., 2001. Adj. prof. So. Ill. U., Springfield, 1974—; chmn. Ill. Cts. Commn., 1988-90; mem. Ill. Gov.'s Adv. Coun. on Criminal Justice Legis., 1977-84, Ad Hoc Com. on Tech. in Cts., 1985—. Mem. editorial rev. bd. Illinois Civil Practice Before Trial, Illinois Civil Trial Practice Pres. Cen. Ill. Mental Health Assn., 1969-71; bd. govs. Aid to Retarded Citizens, 1977-80; mem. Lincoln Legals Adv. Bd., 1988—. Lt. USNR, 1964-67. Mem. ABA (bar admissions com. sect. of legal edn. and admissions to bar 1992—), Ill. State Bar Assn. (bd. govs. 1970-76, treas. 1975-76), Sangamon County Bar Assn., Ctrl. Ill. Women's Bar Assn., Am. Judicature Soc. (bd. dirs. 1990-95), Abraham Lincoln Assn. (bd. dirs. 1988-98). Address: 1918 Jeanette Ln Springfield IL 62702

MILLER, CARROLL GERARD, JR., (GERRY MILLER), lawyer; b. San Antonio, Tex., Dec. 12, 1944; s. Carroll Gerard Sr. and Glyn (Roddy) M.; m. Sylvia Louise Mertins, Mar. 7 1971 (dec. 1982); children: Glyn Marie Bennett, Roddy Gerard, Gina Louise. AS, Del Mar Coll., 1965; BS, U. Houston, 1967; JD, Tex. Tech. U., 1970. Bar: Tex. 1970, Colo. 1987, D.C. 1989, U.S. Dist. Ct. (so. dist.) Tex. 1971, U.S. Ct. Appeals (5th cir.) Tex. 1973, U.S. Supreme Ct. 1974, U.S. Ct. Appeals (D.C. 1976); bd. cert. in criminal law. Assoc. Allison, Madden, White & Brin, Corpus Christi, Tex., 1970-71; asst. city atty. City of Corpus Christi, 1971; asst. dist. atty. Nueces County Dist. Attys. Office, Corpus Christi, 1971-73; asst. city atty. civil div. City of Corpus Christi, 1973-74; atty. Corpus Christi Police Dept.-City of Corpus Christi, 1974-77; pvt. practice Corpus Christi, 1973—. Adj. prof. Bee County Coll., Beeville, Tex., 1973-74, Tex. A & I U., Corpus Christi, 1975-76. Past treas. and diaconate First Presbyn. Ch., Corpus Christi; bd. dirs., incorporator Iron Curtain Outreach; 20/20 coun. Open Doors. Mem. SAR, SCV, Assn. Trial Lawyers Am., Tex. Criminal Def. Lawyers Assn., Nat. Criminal Def. Lawyers Assn., Coll. State Bar Tex., Sons of Republic Tex., Crime Stoppers, Inc. (past dir.), Bay Yacht Club (dir.). Republican. Avocations: sailing, scuba diving, photography, astronomy. Criminal, Personal injury (including property damage). Home: 1209 Sandpiper Dr Corpus Christi TX 78412-3821 Office: 1007 Kinney St Corpus Christi TX 78401-3009 E-mail: lawgmiller@aol.com.

MILLER, CHARLES A. lawyer; b. Oakland, Calif., Feb. 7, 1935; s. Frank and Janice (Greene) M.; m. Jeanette Segal, Sept. 27, 1964; children: Jennifer Fay Haight, Charlotte Irene Marvin, Ira David. AB, U. Calif., Berkeley, 1955, LLB, 1958. Law clk. to assoc. justice U.S. Supreme Ct., Washington, 1958-59; assoc. Covington & Burling, Washington, 1959-67, ptnr., 1967—, chmn. mgmt. com., 1991-95. Mem. criminal justice coordinating bd., Washington, 1977-78; chmn. hearing com. Bd. on Profl. Responsibility, Washington, 1980-86. Pres. U. Calif. Alumni Club, Washington, 1962-70; mem. various coms. and adv. bds. Washington Pub. Sch. System, 1972-79; chmn. lawyers com. Washington Performing Arts Soc., 1984-86; bd. dirs. Dumbarton Concert Series, Washington, 1986—, chmn., 1990—; trustee U. Calif. Berkeley Found., 2001—, Fed. City Coun.; chair D.C. Citizens Welfare Transformation Com., 1996-97; co-chair Task Force on D.C. Governance, 1996-98; mem. Mayor's Commn. on Juvenile Justice, Washington, 2001-02. Fellow Am. Coll. Trial Lawyers; mem. ABA, D.C. Bar Assn., U. Calif. Alumni Assn. (trustee 1989-92). Clubs: Burning Tree (Bethesda, Md.). Democrat. Jewish. Administrative and regulatory, Appellate, Health. Office: Covington & Burling 1201 Pennsylvania Ave NW PO Box 7566 Washington DC 20044-7566 E-mail: cmiller@cov.com.

MILLER, CHARLES E. (CHUCK MILLER), judge; b. Washington, Sept. 26, 1944; s. Charles Edward Miller and Mary (Cox) M.; divorced; 1 child, Samantha Mcgill Cox. BA, So. Meth. U., 1971, JD, 1972. Bar: Tex. 1972. Assoc. Roseborough & Curlee, Dallas, 1972-77; judge County Criminal Ct. #7, Dallas, 1977-82, Ct. Criminal Appeals, Austin, Tex., 1983-94; state judge at large State of Tex., 1995—. Arbitrator comml., employment and labor panels Am. Arbitration Assn., 1995—; adj. prof. criminal law So. Meth. U. Law Sch., Dallas, 1980—82; labor abitrator Fed. Mediation and Conciliation Svc., 2002—, arbitrator, labor roster, 2003—. Author and lectr. in field. Mem. nat. adv. coun. Nat. victim Ctr., N.Y.C. and Washington; mem. nat. steeringcom. Victims Constitutional Amendment Network; mem. adv. bd. victims Organized to Ensure Rights and Safety; mem. victim assistancecom. Tex. Young Lawyers Assn.; parliamentarian state exec. bd. People Against Violent Crime. With U.S. Army, 1966-70. Named Disting. Mil. Grad., Officer Candidate Sch., Ft. Sill, Okla., 1968, Best Dallas Misdemeanor Ct. Judge, Dallas Bar Assn., 1982, Best Dallas Criminal Ct. Judge, Dallas County Criminal Bar Assn., 1982; decorated Army Commendational medal, 1970; recipient Sunny von Bulow Nat. Victim Advocacy Ctr. Appreciation cert., 1987, U.S. Dept. Justice Victims of Crime Appreciation cert., 1992, Victims Organized to Ensure Rights and Safety Advocate for Justice award, 1993, People Against Violent Crime Appreciation cert., 1993. Mem. SAR, State Bar Tex. (chmn. criminal law sect. 1981-82, course dir. advanced criminal law course 1990, chmn. crime victim com. 1992-94, crime victim & witness, 1994, cert. specialist in criminal law), Coll. State Bar Tex., Tex. Bar Found. Republican. Home and Office: 1701 Foggy Glen Cv Austin TX 78733-1541 E-mail: judgechuckmiller@att.net.

MILLER, CHARLES MAURICE, lawyer; b. L.A., Sept. 7, 1948; BA cum laude, UCLA, 1970; postgrad., U. So. Calif., L.A., 1970-71; JD, U. Akron, 1975. Bar: Ohio 1975, Calif. 1978, U.S. Dist. Ct. (cen. dist.) Calif. 1978, U.S. Ct. Appeals (9th cir.) 1978, U.S. Supreme Ct. 1981. Gen. atty. U.S. Immigration & Naturalization Svc., U.S. Dept. Justice, L.A., 1976-79; ptnr. Miller Law Offices, L.A., 1979—. Adj. prof. law U. West L.A., 1989-90. Co-editor: The Visa Processing Guide: Process and Procedures at U.S. Consulates and Embassies, 10th edit., 2003; articles editor U. Akron Law Rev., 1974-75. Mem. Calif. Bd. Legal Specialization, San Francisco, 1988-89. Mem. Bar of Calif. (chmn. immigration splty. 1988-89, commr. immigration splty. 1987-90), Am. Immigration Law Found. (bd. trustees 1995-98), Am. Immigration Lawyers Assn. (bd. dirs. 1998-2001, mem. bd. govs., chair So. Calif. chpt. 1993-94, INS headquarters liaison com. 1997-98, co-chair mentor program 1990-91, co-chair visa office liaison 1991-92, vice chair 1994-95, co-chair consular rev. task force 1993-95, Jack Wasserman Meml. award for excellence in immigration litigation 1995). Immigration, naturalization, and customs. Office: Miller Law Offices 12441 Ventura Blvd Studio City CA 91604-2407

MILLER, CHARLES T. lawyer; b. Winslow, Wash., June 27, 1948; s. Charles Wilbur and Pharoeba H. (Good) M.; m. Rebecca Louise Campbell, Aug. 17, 1974; chidren: Angela Dawn, Emily Grace, Kathryn Louise. BS in Criminal Justice, W.Va. State Coll., 1973; JD, W.Va. U., 1977. Bar: W.Va. 1977, U.S. Ct. Appeals (4th cir.) 1977. Asst. prosecuting atty., Kanawha County, W.Va., 1977-82; assoc. and prnr. E. F. Thaxton Attys., Charleston, 1982-84; 1st asst. U.S. atty. so. dist. W.Va. Dept. Justice, Charleston, 1984-93, 94—, former U.S. atty. so. dist. W.Va. With USN, 1966-69, Vietnam; maj. W.Va. Army Nat. Guard; lt. col. W.Va. Air Nat. Guard. Decorated Navy Achievement medal, Rep. of Vietnam Svc. medal, Rep. of Vietnam Campaign ribbon, Rep. of Vietnam Cross of Gallantry, Combat Action ribbon, Presdl. Unit citation. Presbyterian. Avocation: carpentry.*

MILLER, CHRISTINE ODELL COOK, judge; b. Oakland, Calif., Aug. 26, 1944; m. Dennis F. Miller; 2 children. BA in Polit. Sci., Stanford U., 1966; JD, U. Utah, 1969. Bar: D.C., Calif. Law clk. to Hon. David T. Lewis U.S. Ct. Appeals (10th cir.), Salt Lake City; trial atty. Dept. Justice, U.S. Ct. Claims; team leader atty. FTC; atty. Hogan & Hartson, Washington; spl. counsel Pension Benefit Guaranty Corp.; dep. gen. counsel U.S. Ry. Assn.; ptnr. Shack & Kimball, Washington; judge U.S. Ct. Fed. Claims, Washington, 1982—. Comment editor Utah law Rev. Scholar U. Utah Coll. Law. Mem. D.C. Bar Assn., Calif. State Bar, Order of Coif, Univ. Club (bd. govs.), Cosmos Club. Avocation: geneology. Office: US Ct Fed Claims 717 Madison Pl NW Ste 617 Washington DC 20439-0002

MILLER, CLAIRE CODY, lawyer, mediator; BA, SUNY, Albany, 1983; JD, N.Y. Law Sch., 1986. Assoc. Bruce G. Behrins & Assoc., Staten Island, 1987-90; pvt. practice Claire Cody Miller, Esq., Staten Island, 1990—. Mediator Edgewater Mediation, Staten Island, 1995; com. mem. character and fitness com. appellate divsn. 2nd dept. Supreme Ct. N.Y., 1997. Del. to jud. nominations Richmond County Dem., Bklyn., 1992, 94, 95, 96, 97, 98. Mem. Staten Island Women's Bar (pres. 1991-93), Women's Bar Assn. N.Y. (del. 1992, 94, co-chair working mother's com. 1995—), Richmond County Bar Assn. (mem. grievance com. 1993—), Assn. Bar City of N.Y. (mem. matrimonial com.). Family and matrimonial, General practice, Property, real (including real estate development, water). Office: Claire Cody Miller Esq 1 Edgewater Plz Ste 201 Staten Island NY 10305-4900

MILLER, CLIFFORD JOEL, lawyer; b. L.A., Oct. 31, 1947; s. Eugene and Marian (Millman) M. BA, U. Calif., Irvine, 1969; JD, Pepperdine U., 1973. Bar: Calif. 1974, Hawaii 1974, U.S. Dist. Ct. Hawaii 1974. Ptnr. Rice, Lee & Wong, Honolulu, 1974-80, Goodsill Anderson Quinn & Stifel, Honolulu, 1980-89, McCorriston Miller Mukai MacKinnon, Honolulu, 1989—. Mem. ABA, Calif. Bar Assn., Hawaii Bar Assn., Am. Coll. Real Estate Lawyers. Avocations: sailing, volleyball, swimming, history. Corporate, general, Private international, Property, real (including real estate development, water). Office: McCorriston Miller Mukai MacKinnon 5 Waterfront Plz 500 Ala Moana Blvd Ste 400 Honolulu HI 96813-4920 E-mail: cmiller@m4law.com.

MILLER, DANIEL RAYMOND, prosecutor; b. Evansville, Ind., Sept. 20, 1963; s. Daniel Edgar and Virginia Sue (Baumgart) M. BA magna cum laude, DePauw U., 1985; JD cum laude, Ind. U., 1989. Bar: Ind. 1989. Clk. to Hon. William I. Garrard, Ind. Ct. of Appeals, Indpls., 1989-90; dep. pros. atty. Vanderburgh County Pros.'s Office, Evansville, 1990—, dir. gun violence program, 2003—. Pres. Substance Abuse Coun. Vanderburgh County, 1997-98; chmn. pastoral coun. St. John Cath. Ch., Evansville, 1995-98; mem. Diocese of Evansville Pastoral Coun., 1997-2000; pres. 4-H Coun., 1999-2003. Meml. Ind. Bar Assn., Ind. Drug Enforcement Assn., Nat. Dist. Attys. Assn., 4-H Club Assn. (bd. dirs. 1995-2001, leader Energetics club 1991—, treas. 2000-2001, pres. Vanderburgh County 4-H Leaders 2001-02), St. Vincent DePaul Soc. (pres. 1994, sec. conf. 1995—) Vanderburgh County Coop. Ext. Svc. (bd. dirs. 2000—). Republican. Roman Catholic. Avocations: gardening, church choir. Home: 13521 N Green River Rd Evansville IN 47725-9769 Office: Vanderburgh Co Pros Office Rm 108 City County Adm Bldg Evansville IN 47708 E-mail: drmprosec@aol.com.

MILLER, DAVID A. lawyer; b. Charleroi, Pa., Dec. 7, 1952; s. Francis E. and Betty L. Miller. A. in Specialized Tech., Pa. Tech. Inst., Pitts., 1975; BA, George Mason U., 1982; JD, U. Va., 1985. Bar: Va. 1985, Pa. 1987. Svc. engr. Compugraphic Corp., 1975-80; assoc. Roeder, Durrette & Davenport, Fairfax, Va., 1985-86; law clk. Hon. David L. Gilmore, Washington, Pa., 1986-87; assoc. Karlowitz, Hoffman, McCall & Kane, Pitts., 1987-89, Amatangelo, Baisley & Rega, Donora, 1989—2001, Raphael, Ramsden & Behers, Pitts., 2001—. Mem. Pa. Bar Assn., Va. State Bar (assoc.), Washington County Bar Assn., Westmoreland County Bar Assn., Allegheny County Bar Assn. Avocations: golf, skiing, computers. Bankruptcy, Family and matrimonial, Personal injury (including property damage). Office: 437 Grant St Ste 1200 Pittsburgh PA 15219

MILLER, DAVID ANTHONY, lawyer; b. Linton, Ind., Oct. 6, 1946; s. Edward I. and Jane M. (O'Hern) M.; m. Carol E. Martin, Aug. 9, 1970; 1 child, Jennifer Rose. Student, Murray State U., 1965; BS, Ind. State U., 1969; JD, Ind. U., Indpls., 1973. Bar: Ind. 1973, U.S. Dist. Ct. (so. dist.) Ind. 1973, U.S. Supreme Ct. 1981, U.S. Ct. Appeals (7th cir.) 1982. Dep. atty. gen. State of Ind., Indpls., 1973-76, dir. consumer protection divsn. office atty. gen., 1976-93, asst. atty. gen., 1977-80, chief counsel office atty. gen., 1981-93; prin. Hollingsworth, Meek, Miller and Minglin, Indpls., 1993—. Youth dir. Emmanuel Luth. Ch., Indpls., 1981-85, exec. dir., 1988-90; chmn. bd. Chambers Found., 1994—; pres. bd. Lutheran H.S., 1996-2002; bd. dirs., vice chmn. Greater Indpls. Rep. Fin. Com.; pres. Perry Twp. Firefighter Found., Inc. Mem. ABA, Ind. State Bar. Assn., Indpls. Bar Assn., Ind. State U. Alumni Assn., Columbia Club, Lambda Chi Alpha. Republican. Avocations: numismatics, golfing. Administrative and regulatory, Commercial, contracts (including sales of goods; commercial financing), Legislative. Home: 6454 Forrest Commons Blvd Indianapolis IN 46227-7105 Office: 7550 S Meridian St Ste A Indianapolis IN 46217

MILLER, DEBORAH SLYE, lawyer; b. Navasota, Tex., July 13, 1949; d. Bennie F. and Peggy Slye Miller; children: Brian M. Rollings, Terry Brett Rollings. BA magna cum laude, U. Tex.-Dallas, Richardson, 1990; JD, U. Houston, 1993. Bar: Tex., U.S. Dist. Ct. (no. dist.) Tex. Ptnr. Miller, Shelton & Pace, Dallas, 1993—. Bd. dirs. Internat. Alliance Holistic Lawyers. Bd. dirs. Dallas O.K., 1996—. Mem. Coll. of State Bar Tex., Inst. Bd. Dirs. Collaborative Law Inst. Tex. Criminal, Family and matrimonial, Personal injury (including property damage). Office: Miller Shelton & Pace 4514 Cole Ave Ste 525 Dallas TX 75205-4172 E-mail: dsmiller@millersheltonpace.com.

MILLER, DECATUR HOWARD, lawyer; b. Balt., June 29, 1932; s. Lawrence Vernon and Katharine Louise (Baum) M.; m. Sally Burnam Smith, Nov. 23, 1963; 1 dau., Clemence Mary Katherine. BA, Yale U., 1954; LL.B., Harvard U., 1959. Bar: Md. 1959. Assoc. Piper & Marbury, Balt., 1959-62, 1963-66, ptnr., 1967-94, ptnr. emeritus, 1995—, mng. ptnr., 1974-87, chmn., 1987-94; Md. Securities commr., 1962-63. Bd. dirs. Mercantile Funds. Trustee Enoch Pratt Free Libr., 1975—, v.p., 1977—85, pres., 1985—89; trustee Calvert Sch., Balt., 1976—89, pres., 1982—87; trustee Walters Art Gallery, Balt., 1987—91; mem. bd. sponsors Sellinger Sch. Bus. and Mgmt. Loyola Coll., 1990—98; mem. Mayor's Bus. Adv. Coun., 1993—99; mem. bd. visitors U. Md. Balt. County, 1994—2000; mem. bus. sch. adv. coun. Morgan State U., 1994—96; chmn. Equal Justice Coun., 1999—; bd. dirs. Balt. Symphony Orch., 1970—; v.p., 1978—86, Balt. Symphony Orch., 1988—90; pres., Balt. Symphony Orch., 1990-92, life dir., 2002-; bd. dirs. United Way Ctrl. Md., 1988—91, The Leadership, 1990—93, Empower Balt. Mgmt. Corp., 1995—, Coll. Bound Found., 1990—2001, chmn., 1994—96; bd.dirs. Greater Balt. Com., 1988—96, chmn., 1992—94; bd. dirs. U. Md. Found., 2000—; life dir. Balt. Symphony Orch., 2002—. With U.S. Army, 1954—56. Mem. Md. Bar Assn., Am. Law Inst., Am. Bar Found., Md. Bar Found., Elkridge Club, Ctr. Club, Elizabethan Club, Lawyers Round Table. Home: 3704 N Charles St Apt 1305 Baltimore MD 21218 Office: Piper Rudnick LLP 6225 Smith Ave Baltimore MD 21209-3600

MILLER, DOUGLAS L. lawyer; b. Reading, Pa., Nov. 17, 1950; BA, MA, Yale U., 1972; JD, Harvard U., 1975. Bar: Ga. 1975. Lawyer Troutman Sanders, Atlanta, 1975—99, mng. ptnr. having oversight of the Project Develop. and Fin. Practice Group Hong Kong, China, 1997—99. Miller acted as lead counsel in state regulatory rate case proceedings, as well as fuel cost recovery and demandside cost recovery riders, prudence reviews of nuclear power plant construction, nuclear power plant ops., fossil plant construction, and coal procurement practices. Mem. ABA, State Bar Ga. As a ptnr. responsible for troutman Sanders' independent power and internat. privatization practice, Miller fparticipated in independent power projects throughout the US and in numerous fgn. countries, including Mexico, China, Indonesia, Pakistan, the Philippines, and Turkey. He also participated in privatization projects in the Bahamas, Trinidad and Tobago, Argentina, Brazil, Chile, Venezuela, and Australia. Private international, Utilities, public. Address: Troutman Sanders Corp Hdqs 1155 Perimeter Ctr W Atlanta GA 30338*

MILLER, EDWARD BOONE, lawyer; b. Milw., Mar. 26, 1922; s. Edward A. and Myra (Munsert) M.; m. Anne Harmon Chase Phillips, Feb. 14, 1969 (dec. Dec. 2001); children by previous marriage: Barbara Miller Anderson, Ellen Miller Gerkens, Elizabeth Miller Lawhun, Thomas; stepchildren: T. Christopher Phillips, Sarah Phillips Parkhill. BA, U. Wis., 1942, LL.B., 1947; student, Harvard Bus. Sch., 1942-43. Bar: Wis. 1947, Ill. 1948. With firm Pope, Ballard, Shepard & Fowle, Chgo., 1947-51, 52-70, ptnr., 1953-70, 75-93, mng. partner, 1979-82, chmn. labor and employment law dept., 1975-76, 87-88, 90-91; of counsel Seyfarth Shaw, Chgo., 1994—. Mem. adv. com. Ctr. for Labor Mgmt. Dispute Resolution, Stetson U., 1984—, Inst. Indsl. Rels., Loyola U., 1987-91, Kent Pub. Employee Labor Rels. Conf., 1988—, Ill. Ednl. Labor Rels. Bd., 1988—; exec. asst. to industry mems. Regional Wage Stblzn. Bd., Chgo., 1951-52, industry mem., 1952; chmn. NLRB, Washington, 1970-74; mem. panel of labor law experts Commerce Clearing House, 1987—; dir. Chgo. Wheel & Mfg. Co., 1965-70, 75-88, Andes Candies, Inc., 1965-68, 75-80 Mem. Gov. Ill. Commn. Labor-Mgmt. Policies for Pub. Employees, 1966-67; chmn. Midwest Pension Conf., 1960-61; mem. labor relations com. Ill. C. of C., 1953-70; bd. dirs. Am. Found. Continuing Edn., 1960-69. Served to lt. USNR, 1943-46. Mem. ABA (NLRB practice and procedures com., internat. labor law com.), Ill. Bar Assn., Wis. Bar Assn., Chgo. Assn. Commerce and Industry (chmn. labor relations com. 1980-86, bd. dirs. 1987-97), Am. Employment Law Coun. (mem. adv. bd. 1995—), Coll. Labor and Employment Lawyers (emeritus mem.), Order of Coif. Clubs: Legal (Chgo.), Law (Chgo.), Cliff Dwellers (Chgo.). Republican. Congregationalist. Home: 632 Chatham Rd Glenview IL 60025-4402 Office: 55 E Monroe St Chicago IL 60603-5713 E-mail: milleed@seyfarth.com.

MILLER, ELIZABETH H. lawyer, educator; b. Pomona, Calif., Oct. 3, 1970; d. John M. and Diane E. Hawkins; m. Eric S. Miller, May 28, 1995. BA, UCLA, 1992; JD, Yale U., 1995. Bar: Calif. 1996, U.S. Dist. Ct. Calif (no. dist.) 1997, Vt. 1998, U.S. Dist. Ct. Vt. 1998, U.S. Ct. Appeals (2d cir.) 1999. Jud. clk. U.S. Ct. Appeals (2d cir.), Brattleboro, Vt., 1995—96; atty. Mornson & Foerster, San Francisco, 1996—98, Dinse, Knapp & McAndrew, Burlington, Vt., 1998—2000; tchr. C.C. of Vt., Burlington, 1999—; mem., mgr. Spink & Miller, PLC, Burlington, 2000—. Mem. Leadership Champlain, 2001; dir. Vt. Alliance for Arts Edn., 2001—. Mem.: ABA, Vt. Bar Assn. Office: Spink & Miller PLC One Lawson Ln Burlington VT 05401

MILLER, EVAN, lawyer; b. Bklyn., Sept. 18, 1956; s. Richard and Lois Pearl (Hirsch) M. BA, Columbia U., 1978; JD, Georgetown U., 1981. Bar: N.Y. 1982, D.C. 1983, U.S. Dist. Ct. D.C. 1984, U.S. Ct. Appeals (D.C. and 11th cirs.) 1985. Law clk. to presiding justice U.S. Dist. Ct. (so. dist.) Ga., Brunswick, 1981-82; assoc. Pepper, Hamilton & Scheetz, Washington, 1982-88; ptnr. Johnson & Gibbs, Washington, 1988-94, Hogan & Hartson, Washington, 1994—. Sr. editor Employee Benefits Law (BNA) 2d edit., 1999. Mem. ABA (employee benefits com. labor sect., employee benefits com. labor sect. and corp. and bus sect.) Pension, profit-sharing, and employee benefits. Office: Hogan & Hartson LLP 555 13th St NW Ste 800E Washington DC 20004-1161

MILLER, FRANK LOUIS, lawyer; b. N.Y.C., July 15, 1967; s. Theodore Norman and Margaret (L'Engle) M.; m. Felicity Rosalind Toube, June 13, 1999. BS, U. Ill., 1989; MBA, JD, NYU, 1995. Bar: N.Y. 1996; solicitor Eng. and Wales, 2000. Fin. analyst IBM Corp., Mt. Pleasant, N.Y., 1989-92; law clk. to Hon. John G. Koeltl N.Y.C., 1995-96; assoc. Wachtell Lipton Rosen & Katz, N.Y.C., 1996-98, Freshfields Bruckhaus Deringer, London, 1999—2003, ptnr., 2003—. Office: Freshfields Bruckhaus Deringer 65 Fleet St London EC4Y 1HS England

MILLER, GALE TIMOTHY, lawyer; b. Kalamazoo, Sept. 15, 1946; s. Arthur H. and Eleanor (Johnson) M.; m. Janice Lindvall, June 1, 1968; children: Jeremy L., Amanda E., Timothy W. AB, Augustana Coll., 1968; JD, U. Mich., 1971. Bar: Mich. 1971, Colo. 1973, U.S. Dist. Ct. Colo. 1973, U.S. Ct. Appeals (10th cir.) 1979, U.S. Supreme Ct. 1997. Trial atty. FTC, Washington, 1971-73; assoc. Davis Graham & Stubbs LLP, Denver, 1973-77, ptnr., 1978—, chmn. exec. com., 1998—2001. Bd. dirs. Sr. Housing Options, Inc., 1980-93, Colo. Jud. Inst., 1999—; chair Colo. Lawyers Com., 1989-91, bd. dirs., 1987—, Individual Lawyer of Yr., 1994. Recipient Cmty. Svc. award Colo. Hispanic Bar Assn., 1996. Mem. ABA (antitrust sect. task force on model civil antitrust jury instrns. 1985-87), Colo. Bar Assn. (chair antitrust sect. 1996-98), Denver Bar Assn. Democrat. Lutheran. Antitrust, Federal civil litigation, State civil litigation. Office: Davis Graham & Stubbs LLP 1550 17th St Ste 500 Denver CO 80202

MILLER, GARY C. lawyer; b. Little Rock, Ark., May 23, 1955; s. William Scott, Jr. and Margaret Imogene (Puckett) M.; m. Mary Catherine Miller, Oct. 23, 2000; children: Daniel, Sarah. BA in Econs. and Managerial Studies, Rice U., 1977; JD, U. Tex., 1980. Bar: Tex. 1980, U.S. Dist. Ct. (so. dist.) Tex. 1981, U.S. Dist. Ct. (no. and we. dists.) Tex. 1991, U.S. Dist. Ct. (ea. dist.) Tex. 1993, U.S. Ct. Appeals (5th cir) 1980, U.S. Supreme Ct. 1995. Atty. Wood, Campbell, Moody & Gibbs, Houston, 1980-83, Gibbs & Ratliff, Houston, 1983-85, Andrews & Kurth LLP, Houston, 1985—. Contbr. articles to profl. jours. Chmn. Westminster Weekday Sch., Houston, 1993-96; chmn., bd. trustees Westminster United Methodist Ch., Houston, 1996-98. Mem. ABA (bus. in bankruptcy com., bus. & corp. litigation com.), Houston Bar Assn., Phi Beta Kappa, Order of the Coif. Bankruptcy, Federal civil litigation, General civil litigation. Office: Andrews & Kurth LLP 600 Travis Ste 4200 Houston TX 77002 E-mail: gmiller@akllp.com.

MILLER, GAY DAVIS, lawyer; b. Florence, Ariz., Dec. 20, 1947; d. Franklin Theodore and Mary (Belshaw) Davis; 1 child, Katherine Alexandra. BA, U. Colo., 1969; JD, Am. U., 1975. Bar: D.C. 1975. Atty., spl. asst. to gen. counsel, sr. counsel corp. affairs Inter Am. Devel. Bank, Washington, 1975-78, 83—; atty. Intelsat, Washington, 1978-80. Articles editor: Am. U. Law Rev., 1974—75, contbg. author: The Inspection Panel of the World Bank: A Different Complaints Procedure, 2001. Bd. dirs. Hist. Mt. Pleasant, Inc., Washington, 1985-86, Washington Bridle Trails Assn., 1992—. Mem.: ABA, Am. Soc. Internat. Law, Inter Am. Bar Assn. Corporate, general, Public international, Labor (including EEOC, Fair Labor Standards Act, labor-management relations, NLRB, OSHA). Office: Inter Am Devel Bank 1300 New York Ave NW Washington DC 20577-0001 E-mail: gaym@iadb.org.

MILLER, GEORGE DEWITT, JR., lawyer; b. Detroit, Aug. 20, 1928; s. George DeWitt and Eleanor Mary Miller; m. Prudence Brewster Saunders, Dec. 28, 1951; children: Margaret DeWitt, Joy Saunders. BA magna cum laude, Amherst Coll., 1950; JD with distinction, U. Mich., 1953. Bar: Mich. 1953, U.S. Dist. Ct. (so. dist.) Mich. 1953, U.S. Ct. Appeals (6th cir.) 1960, U.S. Tax Ct. 1960. Assoc. Bodman, Longley & Dahling, Detroit, 1957-61, ptnr., 1962—. Trustee, mem. Matilda R. Wilson Fund, 1993—, pres., 1998—; trustee Maplegrove Ctr./Kingswood Hosp., Henry Ford Health Sys., 1995—. Capt. USAF, 1953-56. Recipient Commendation medal. Fellow Mich. State Bar Found.; mem. ABA, State Bar Mich., Detroit Bar Assn., Detroit Athletic Club, Orchard Lake Country Club, Order of Coif, Phi Beta Kappa. Episcopalian. Avocations: yacht racing, shooting, gardening. Estate planning, Probate (including wills, trusts), Estate taxation. Home: 320 Dunston Rd Bloomfield Hills MI 48304-3415 Office: Bodman Longley & Dahling 100 Renaissance Ctr Ste 34 Detroit MI 48243-1001

MILLER, GREGORY R. lawyer; Chief asst. U.S. atty. Dept. Justice, Tallahassee, U.S. atty., 1993-98; asst. U.S. atty. Dept Justice, Tallahassee, 2000—02, U.S. atty, 2002—; assoc. Fowler, White, Gillen, Boggs, Villareal and Banker, PA, Tallahassee, 1998-2000. Office: US Atty's Office 111 N Adams St Tallahassee FL 32301

MILLER, HAROLD ARTHUR, lawyer; b. St. Marie, Ill., Aug. 18, 1922; s. Arthur E. and Luletta (Noé) M.; m. Michele H. Rogivue, Nov. 21, 1947; children: Maurice H., Jan Leland, Marc Richard. BS in Acctg., U. Ill., 1942, JD, 1950. Bar: Ill. 1950, U.S. Dist. Ct. Ill. 1950, U.S. Tax Ct. 1950. Fgn. svc. officer U.S. State Dept., Paris, France, 1945-48; ptnr. Filson, Williamson & Miller, Champaign, Ill., 1950-60, Williamson & Miller, Champaign, 1960-72, Miller & Hendren, Champaign, 1972—. Atty. Christie Clinic Found., Champaign, 1960—; atty. pub. schs. dists., Champaign & Vermilion Counties, Ill., 1960—; atty. for municipalities in Champaign County, Ill., 1970—. Author: Estate Planning for Doctors, 1961, Intervivos Trusts Alternative to Probate, 1996. Bd. dirs., officer Urbana Ill. Sch. Dist., 1957-69; chmn., trustee Parkland Coll., Champaign, 1971-91; founding bd. mem. CCDC Found., Champaign-Urbana Ednl. Found., Moore Heart Found., Christie Clinic Found.; life mem. PTA. With Spl. Svcs., U.S. Army, 1942-45, ETO. Mem. ABA, Am. Judicature Soc., Ill. and Local Bar Assns., Ill. Trial Lawyers Assn., Alpha Kappa Psi. Presbyterian. Education and schools, Estate planning. Office: Miller & Hendren Attys 30 E Main St #200 Champaign IL 61820-3629 E-mail: ham@mhlawoffice.com.

MILLER, HAROLD O. lawyer; b. Locust Dale, Pa., July 29, 1937; s. Harold O.N. and Margaret (Ramsdale) M.; m. Jeanine W. Waddel, Feb. 2, 1963; children— Mason, Garner. A.B., Lebanon Valley Coll., 1960; J.D., George Washington U., 1965. Bar: Va. 1965, D.C. 1973. Assoc. law firm Harrell & Mutchler, Baileys Crossroads, Va., 1965-68; ptnr. Harrell & Mutcheler, 1968-69; ptnr. Miller, Gattsek, Tavenner & Rosenfeld, 1969-74; sr. ptnr. Miller, O'Connor & Bucholtz, Reston, Va., 1974— . Mem. Fairfax County (Va.) Bd. of County Suprs., 1968-72; chmn. Fairfax County Dem. Com., 1972-74. Served with U.S. Army, 1961-62. Mem. Va. Bar Assn., D.C. Bar Assn., Fla. Bar Assn., Phi Alpha Delta. Democrat. Unitarian. Club: Rotary. Commercial, contracts (including sales of goods; commercial financing), Probate (including wills, trusts), Property, real (including real estate development, water). Office: 7350 S Tamiami Tr #210 Sarasota FL 34231 Home: 218 Woodland Dr Osprey FL 34229-9552

MILLER, HARVEY ALLAN, lawyer; b. Paterson, N.J., May 5, 1946; s. David and Rose Miller; m. Naomi Calka, Mar. 22, 1970; children: Philip, Joshua. BA cum laude, Rutgers U., 1967, JD, 1970. Bar: N.J. 1970, U.S. Dist. Ct. N.J. 1970. Law clk. to judges Passaic County Ct, Paterson, 1970-71; ptnr. Cole, Schotz, Meisel, Forman & Leonard, P.A., Hackensack, N.J., 1971—. Founder and pres. Parents for Deaf Awareness, Inc., 1979-83, trustee, 1979—, editor newsletter, 1980-87; mem. adv. coun. Union County Coll., 1980-84, N.J. Adv. Coun. on Edn. of Hearing Impaired, 1984-85; trustee, exec. v.p., prin. of adult edn. sch.; mem. edn. and pers. com. Shomrei Torah, Wayne, N.J., 1987—; trustee North Jersey Regional Hebrew High Sch., 1989-95, The Fair Lawn Deaf Program, 1994-99; mem., publicity dir. Ephrayis Prodns., LLC.; mem. of edn. com. Jewish Fed. of North Jersey, 2000—. Recipient Man of Yr. awrd Shomrei Torah, 1999, award N.J. Assn. of the Deaf, 1986, Man of the Yr. award, Parents for Deaf Awareness, 1983. Mem. N.J. Bar Assn., Bergen County Bar Assn., Passaic County Bar Assn. (program chmn. young lawyers div. 1971-73), N.J. Mortgage Bankers Assn., Am. Soc. for Deaf Children, N.J. Assn. of the Deaf, Nat. Assn. of the Deaf, C.A.M.E.R.A., Jewish Deaf and Hearing Impaired Coun., Phi Beta Kappa. Jewish. Commercial, contracts (including sales of goods; commercial financing), Franchising, Property, real (including real estate development, water). Office: Cole Schotz Meisel Forman & Leonard PO Box 800 Hackensack NJ 07602-0800

MILLER, HENRY FRANKLIN, lawyer; b. Phila., May 19, 1938; s. Lester and Bessie (Posner) M.; m. Barbara Ann Gendel, June 20, 1964; children: Andrew, Alexa. AB, Lafayette Coll., 1959; LLB, U. Pa., 1964. Bar: Pa. 1965. Law clk. U.S. Dist. Ct. Del., Wilmington, 1964-65; assoc. Wolf, Block, Schorr & Solis-Cohen, Phila., 1965-71, ptnr., 1971—. Pres. Soc. Hill Synagogue, Phila., 1978-79, Big Brothers/Big Sisters Assn. of Phila., 1980-81, Jewish Family & Children's Agy., Phila., 1986-88. 1st lt. U.S. Army, 1959-60. Mem. Am. Coll. Real Estate Lawyers. Avocations: swimming, hiking, cycling, reading. Construction, Property, real (including real estate development, water). Office: Wolf Block Schorr & Solis-Cohen 1650 Arch St Fl 21 Philadelphia PA 19103-2029 E-mail: hmiller@wolfblock.com.

MILLER, HERBERT H. lawyer; b. Balt., May 24, 1921; s. Louis Miller and Rebecca Platt; m. Irene R. Rosen, Aug. 27, 1944; children: Rose, Marjorie, Fran. JD cum laude, U. Balt., 1942; ABA in Acctg., Balt. Coll. of Commerce, 1947. Bar: Md. 1943, U.S. Dist. Ct. Md. 1944, U.S. Supreme Ct. 1986; notary pub., Md. Law clk. Rubenstein and Rubenstein, Balt., 1938-39, Joel J. Hochman, Balt., 1939-40, Feikin & Talkin, Balt., 1940-42; atty. Sherbow, Harris & Medwedeff, Balt., 1942-43, Harris & Medwedeff, Balt., 1943-45; pvt. practice Balt. and Towson, Md., 1946—. Mem. inquiry panel Atty. Grievance Com. Md., Balt. County, 1985—; panel chmn. Health Claims Arbitration, Balt., 1994—. Bd. trustees Balt. Coll. Commerce, 1948-52, Beth El Congregation, Balt. County, 1990-94; youth advisor B'nai B'rith, Balt., 1943-88, mem. B'nai B'rith Youth Orgn., pres., 1940-42. Mem. Md. State Bar Assn., Balt. City Bar Assn., Balt. County Bar Assn., Mensa Internat. (arbitrator Md.). Avocations: reading, handyman work, walking. Corporate, general, Probate (including wills, trusts), Property, real (including real estate development, water). Office: 200 E Joppa Rd Ste 205 Towson MD 21286-3107

MILLER, JAMES ANTHONY, lawyer; b. Alexandria, La., Jan. 18, 1957; s. James Walter and LeMaude (Lazarus) M.; m. Avis Lynn Swander, Dec. 17, 1983; children: Margaret Grace, Mary Elizabeth, Samuel William, John Carlile, Paige Catherine. BS in Ecology and Evolutionary Biology, U. Ariz., 1979; JD, Oral Roberts U., 1983. Bar: Okla. 1983, U.S. Dist. Ct. (no. dist.) Okla. 1983, U.S. Dist. Ct. (we. dist.) Okla. 1992, U.S. Dist. Ct. (ea. dist.) Okla. 1997, U.S. Dist. Ct. (no. dist.) Tex. 1995, U.S. Ct. Appeals (10th cir.) 1984. Atty. McBride & Miller, 1983-85, Studenny & Assocs., 1985-90; atty., shareholder Pickard, Miller & Gray, P.C., 1990-92, Pickard & Miller, P.C., 1992; atty., sole practitioner, 1992—. Town atty. Town of Kiefer, Okla., 1996—, Town of Mounds, Okla., 1999—; instr. U. Tulsa, 1992-93; mem. legal asst. adv. com. Met. Coll. Legal Studies, Tulsa, 1996-99, mem. ct. reporting adv. com., 1996-99. Author: Texas v. Johnson, The Flag Burning Case, 1997; contbr. articles to mags. Deacon, Christ Presbyn. Ch., Tulsa, 1989-95, elder, 1995—; bd. dirs. Sheltered Workshop of Tulsa, 1994. Mem.: Am. Trial Lawyers Assn., Okla. Bar Assn. Republican. Municipal (including bonds), Personal injury (including property damage), General civil litigation. Home: 1709 S Carson Ave Tulsa OK 74119-4609 Office: 1722 S Carson Ave Ste 3101 Tulsa OK 74119-4643

MILLER, JAMES M. lawyer; b. Berwyn, Ill., Apr. 25, 1950; m. Luz Angela Aristizabal, July 13, 1991; children: Hillary Daniela, Maxwell James. BA magna cum laude, U. Miami, 1972; JD, U. Chgo., 1975. Bar: Fla. 1975. Shareholder Akerman, Senterfitt & Eidson P.A., Miami, Fla. Bd. dirs. Miami Mus. Sci., pres. 1989-91. Mem. ABA (litigation sect., corp., banking and bus. law sect.), Fla. Bar (vice-chmn. 11th jud. cir. grievance com. B 1982-84), Dade County Bar Assn. Banking, General civil litigation, Securities. Office: Akerman Senterfitt SunTrust International Center One SE 3d Ave 28th Fl Miami FL 33131

MILLER, JAMES MONROE, lawyer; b. Owensboro, Ky., Apr. 20, 1948; s. James Rufus and Tommie (Melton) M.; m. Patricia Kirkpatrick, Nov. 28, 1975; children: Marian Elizabeth, James Graham. Student, George Washington U., 1966-67; BE, U. Ky., 1970, JD, 1973. Bar: Ky. 1973, U.S. Dist. Ct. Ky. 1973, U.S. Ct. Appeals (6th cir.) 1976, U.S. Supreme Ct. 1976. Law clk. to chief judge U.S. Dist. Ct. (we. dist.) Ky., Louisville and Owensboro, 1973-74; mng. ptnr. Sullivan, Mountjoy, Stainback & Miller, P.S.C., Owensboro, 1974—80, 2000—. Mem. Leadership Ky., 1988, Leadership Owensboro, 1986; bd. dirs. Leadership Ky. Found., 2002—; sec., bd. dirs. Wendell Foster Ctr. Endowment Found., Inc., Owensboro; sec. Owensboro-Daviess County Indsl. Found., Inc. Mem. ABA, Ky. Bar Assn. (chmn. Law Day/Spkrs. Bur. com. 1989-91), Daviess County Bar Assn., Ky. Coun. on Higher Edn. (chmn. programs com. 1991-93, chmn. 1993-96), Coun. Postsecondary Edn., Gov.'s Higher Edn. Rev. Commn. (chmn. 1993), Gov.'s Task Force on Tchr. Edn. Democrat. Methodist. Avocations: fishing, hunting, hiking, golf, skiing. Corporate, general, General practice, Utilities, public. Home: 1920 Sheridan Pl Owensboro KY 42301-4525 Office: Sullivan Mountjoy Stainback & Miller PSC PO Box 727 100 Saint Ann St Owensboro KY 42303-4144

MILLER, JAN PAUL, lawyer; b. Md. married; 2 children. Bachelor, U. N.C., 1982; grad. cum laude, Harvard U., 1985. Adj. prof. George Washington U., Washington; asst. U.S. atty. Dist. Md., 1989—2002; U.S. atty. Ctrl. Dist. Ill., 2002—. Chief narcotics prosecution unit Dist. Md., 1992; pros. atty. So. Divsn. Dist. Md., 1995, sr. litigation counsel, 2000. Recipient numerous commendations from law enforcement agencies, including FBI, U.S. Customs Svc., Drug Enforcement Adminstrn., U.S. Secret Svc., U.S. Postal Ins. Office: Ctrl Dist Ill 600 E Monroe St Ste 312 Springfield IL 62701*

MILLER, J(OHN) WESLEY, III, lawyer; b. Springfield, Mass., Oct. 3, 1941; s. John Wesley Jr. and Blanche Ethel Miller. AB, Colby Coll., 1963; AM, Harvard U., 1964, JD, 1981. Bar: Mass. 1984, U.S. Dist. Ct. Mass. 1984, U.S. Supreme Ct. 1993. Instr. English Heidelberg Coll., Tiffin, Ohio, 1964-69, U. Wis., 1969-77; real estate broker, 1977-84. Founder Miller-Wilson Family Papers, U. Vt., Madison (Wis.) People's Poster and Propaganda Collection, St. Hist. Soc. Wis. Author: History of Buckingham Junior High School, 1956, The Millers of Roxham, 1958, Symphonic Heritage, 1959, Community Guide to Madison Murals, 1977, Aunt Jennie's Poems, 1986, Blanche and John's Fernbank: A Wilbraham Camping Experience, 2001; founding editor: Hein's Poetry and the Law Series, 1985—; editor: Curiosities and Law of Wills, 1989, Lawyers Alcove, 1990, Famous Divorces, 1991, Legal Laughs, 1993, Coke in Verse, 1999, Law and Lawyers Laid Open, 2002; founding editor: Law Libr. Microform Consortium Arts Law Letters Collection, 1991—; exhibitor A Salute to Street Art, State Hist. Soc. Wis., 1974; contbr. Poems of Ambrose Philips, 1969, Oxford English Dictionary, 1995—. Recipient Cmty. Activism award Bay State Objectivist, 1993, 94, 95; fellow Wisdom Hall of Fame, 2000, Samuel Victor Constant fellow, 2001. Mem. MLA, Am. Philol. Assn., Milton Soc., New Eng. Historic Geneal. Soc., Vt. Hist. Soc., Wis. Acad. Scis., Arts and Letters, Pilgrim Soc., Ancient and Hon. Arty. Co., Mayflower Soc., Soc. Colonial Wars, Sons and Daus. of the Victims of Colonial Witch Trials, Mensa, Springfield Renaissance Group. Office: 5 Birchland Ave Springfield MA 01119-2708

MILLER, JOHN EDDIE, lawyer; b. Wayne, Mich., Nov. 14, 1945; s. George Hayden and Georgia Irene (Stevenson) M.; m. Nancy Carol Sanders, Jan. 7, 1968; children: Andrea Christine, Matthew Kit. BA, Baylor U., 1967; JD, U. Memphis, 1973; LLM, U. Mo., 1980. Bar: Mo. 1974, U.S. Dist. Ct. (we. dist.) Mo. 1974, Tex. 1982. Asst. prof. Central Mo. State U., Warrensburg, 1973-74; sole practice Sedalia, Mo., 1974-79; sr. contract adminstr. Midwest Research Inst., Kansas City, Mo., 1979-81, Tracor Inc., Austin, Tex., 1981-84; contract negotiator Tex. Instruments, Austin, 1984-86; sr. contract adminstr. Tracor Aerospace Inc., Austin, 1986-87, Radian Corp., Austin, 1987-96; counsel., asst. co. sec. Radian Internat. LLC, Austin, 1996—. Corp. sec. Radian Southeast Asia (SEA) Ltd., Bangkok, 1995—, dir. Radian Southeast Asia (SEA) Ltd., Bangkok, 1996—; corp. sec. Radian Internat. Overseas Mgmt. Co., 1996—; instr. bus. law State Fair Community Coll., Sedalia, 1974-79, Austin Community Coll., 1983-84. Bd. dirs. Legal Aid Western Mo., 1977—79, Boy's Club, Sedalia, 1974—79. Served with U.S. Army, 1968—71. Mem.: U.S. Tennis Assn., Tex. Bar Assn. (intellectual property law sect., internat. law sect., computer law sect.), Mo. Bar Assn. (internat. law com., patent, trademark and copyright law com., tech. law com.), Phi Alpha Delta. Computer, Intellectual property, Private international. E-mail: johnemiller@excite.com.

MILLER, JOHN LEED, lawyer; b. Geneva, Ill., May 7, 1949; s. John Axel and Martha Mary (Masilunis) M.; m. Roosy Yanti, Jan. 2, 2001. BA, Northwestern U., 1971; JD, U. Chgo., 1975. Bar: Ill. 1975, U.S. Dist. Ct. (no. dist.) Ill., U.S. Ct. Appeals (7th and 8th cirs.). Assoc. counsel Profl. Ind. Mass-Mktg. Adminstrs., Chgo., 1975-76; legis. counsel to minority leader Ill. Ho. of Reps., Chgo. and Springfield, Ill., 1977-80, chief legal counsel, 1980, chief counsel to spkr., 1981-83; ptnr. Shaw and Miller, Chgo., 1981-84, Theodore A. Woerthwein, Chgo., 1984-85, Woerthwein & Miller, Chgo., 1985—. Statewide chmn. Ill. Young Voters for the Pres., 1972; dir. Ill. Ho. Rep. campaign com., 1976, 78, cons., 1982; pres. Newberry Pla. Condominium Assn., 1989-94. With ISNG, 1969-75. James scholar, 1970. Mem. Lawyers for the Creative Arts, Primitive Art Soc. Chgo. (treas. 1984-86, v.p. 1987, pres. 1988-89), Indonesia-Am. Assn. Ill. (bd. dirs.), Adventurers Club (participant first descent of Boh River, Borneo), Phi Eta Sigma, Phi Beta Kappa. Moslem. Corporate, general, Legislative. Home: 1030 N State St Apt 9D Chicago IL 60610-5484 Office: Woerthwein & Miller PO Box A 3612 Chicago IL 60690-3612

MILLER, JOHN T., JR., lawyer, educator; b. Waterbury, Conn., Aug. 10, 1922; s. John T. and Anna (Purdy) M.; children: Kent, Lauren, Clare, Miriam, Michael, Sheila, Lisa, Colin, Margaret. AB with high honors, Clark U., 1944; JD, Georgetown U., 1948; Docteur en Droit, U. Geneva, 1951; postgrad., U. Paris, 1951. Bar: Conn. 1949 (inactive), D.C. 1950, U.S. Ct. Appeals (2d, 3d, 5th, 10th, 11th and D.C. cirs.), U.S. Supreme Ct. 1952. With Econ. Cooperation Adminstn. Am. Embassy, London, 1950-51; assoc. Covington & Burling, 1952-53, Gallagher, Connor & Boland, 1953-62; pvt. practice Washington, 1962—. Adj. prof. law Georgetown U. Law Ctr., Washington, 1959—; mem. Panel on Future of Internat. Ct. Justice. Co-author: Regulation of Trade, 1953, Modern American Antitrust Law, 1958, Major American Antitrust Laws, 1965; author: Foreign Trade in Gas and Electricity in North America: A Legal and Historical Study, 1970, Energy Problems and the Federal Government: Cases and Material, 8th edit., 1996; contbr. articles, book revs. to legal pubs. Trustee Clark U., 1970-76, De Sales Sch. of Theology, 1993-97; mem. bd. advisors Georgetown Visitation Prep. Sch., 1978-94, trustee, 1994-96, emeritus trustee, 1996—; former fin. chmn. troop 46 Nat. Capital Area coun. Boy Scouts Am.; pres. Thomas More Soc. Am., 1996-97. 1st lt. U.S. Army, 1943-46, 48-49. Decorated Bronze Star; recipient 10 yr. teaching award Nat. Jud. Coll., 1983. Mem. ABA (coun., chmn. adminstrv. law sect. 1972-73, ho. dels. 1991-93), AAUP, D.C. Bar Assn., Energy Bar Assn. (pres. 1990-91), Congl. Country Club, Army and Navy Club (bd. govs. 2000—), DACOR, Prettyman-Leventhal Am. Inn of Ct. (master 1988-99, pres. 1995-96), Sovereign Mil. Order of Malta (knight). Republican. Roman Catholic. Administrative and regulatory, FERC practice, Appellate. Home: 4721 Rodman St NW Washington DC 20016-3234 Office: 1001 Connecticut Ave NW Washington DC 20036-5504 E-mail: jtmillerjr@erols.com.

MILLER, KERRY LEE, lawyer; b. West Palm Beach, Sept. 11, 1955; s. Clyde Howard and Alice (Hummel) M.; m. Myrna Patricia Garza, June 9, 1979; children: Alexander James, Eric Anthony. BA, George Mason U., 1977; JD, Cath. U., 1981. Bar: D.C. 1981, Va. 1982, U.S. Dist. Ct. (D.C. dist.) 1982, U.S. Ct. Appeals (D.C. and 4th cirs.) 1982, U.S. Ct. Appeals (fed. cir.) 1989, U.S. Ct. Claims 1989, U.S. Supreme Ct. 1989, U.S. Dist. Ct. (ea. and we. dists.) Va. 1993. Asst. gen. counsel Office Gen. Counsel U.S. Govt. Printing Office, Washington, 1981-87, assoc. gen. counsel contracts and procurement, 1987-99; adminstrv. law judge Bd. Contract Appeals U.S. Govt. Printing Office, Washington, 1999—. Mem. Fed. Bar Assn. (mem. chpt. coun. Capitol Hill chpt.), Bd. Contract Appeals Judges Assn., Computer Law Assn., Contract Appeals Bar Assn. Office: US Govt Printing Office Office Bd Contract Appeals 732 N Capitol St NW Washington DC 20401-0001 E-mail: kmiller@gpo.gov.

MILLER, KIRK EDWARD, lawyer, health foundation executive; b. San Jose, Calif., June 9, 1951; BA in Polit. Sci., U. Calif., Riverside, 1973; JD, Syracuse U., 1976. Bar: Colo. 1976, Calif. 1980, Tex. 1993. Assoc. Hughes & Dorsey, Denver, 1977-78; v.p., assoc. gen. counsel Am. Med. Internat., Inc., Dallas, 1979-88, v.p., sec., gen. counsel, 1988-91; with McGlinchey Stafford Lang, Dallas, 1991-94; sr. v.p., sec., gen. counsel Kaiser Found. Health Plan, Inc., Kaiser Found. Hosps., Inc., Oakland, Calif., 1994—2002, sr. v.p., legal svcs., 2002—. Instr. Syracuse U., 1975-76. Mem. ABA (co-vice chair com. health care fraud and abuse 1995-96). Office: Kaiser Found Health Plan 1 Kaiser Plz Oakland CA 94612-3610*

MILLER, LESLIE ANNE, lawyer; b. Franlin, Ind., Nov. 4, 1951; d. G. Thomas and Anne (Gaines) Miller; m. Richard B. Worley, Feb. 14, 1987. AB cum laude, Mt. Holyoke Coll., South Hadley, Pa., 1973; MA in Polit. Sci., Eagle Inst. Politics Rutgers U., New Brunswick, N.J., 1974; JD, Dickinson Sch. of Law, Carlisle, Pa., 1977; LLM with honors, Temple U., 1994. Bar: Pa. 1977, U.S. Dist. Ct. (ea. dist.) Pa. 1977, U.S. Ct. Appeals (3d cir.) 1980, U.S. Dist. Ct. (ea. dist.) Pa. 1987. Assoc. LaBrum & Doak, Phila., 1977-81, ptnr., 1982-86, Goldfein & Joseph, Phila., 1986-95, McKissock & Hoffman, P.C., Phila., 1995—2003; gen. counsel Gov. Pa., 2003—. Bd. dirs. WHYY-TV, 1996—; del. Third Circuit Jud. Conf., 1981, 82, 85; mem. Jud. Inquiry and Rev. Bd., 1990-94, chair, 1993-94; mem. faculty trial advocacy program Dickinson Sch. Law, 1992, 94; mem. hearing com., disciplinary bd. Supreme Ct. Pa., 1996—; mem. faculty Acad. Advocacy Temple U., 1994—; judge pro tem Ct. of Common Pleas. Mem. acad. ball com. Phila. Orch., 1986-87, 89-91, 95-96, mem. acad. music com. 1998—; mem. Open Space Task Force Com., Lower Merion Twp., Pa., 1990, bd. dirs., 1990-94, mem. counsel, 1990, Lower Merion Conservancy, 1995-97, 2000—, others; bd. dirs. Med. Coll. Pa., 1985-96, sec., 1987-92, chair presdl. search com., 1993, chair presdl. inauguration, 1987, chair com. on acad. affairs, 1989-95, chair dean's search com., 1994-95, chair nomenclature com., 1996; bd. dirs. Med. Coll. Hosps., 1991-96, Allegheny Health Edn. and Rsch. Found., 1993-96, Hahnemann U. Med. Sch., 1994-96, Pa. Ballet, 1994—, St. Christopher's Hosp. for Children, 1991-94, vice chair, 1990-94; bd. dirs. Phila. Free Libr., 1997—, bd. dirs. Kimmel Center for the Performing Arts, 1999—, interim pres. 2001-2002, co-chair, bd. dirs., 2002—; trustee Mt. Holyoke Coll., 2000—; bd. govs. Dickinson Sch. Law, Pa. State U., 2001—. Recipient Mary Lyon award, Mt. Holyoke Alumni Assn., 1985, Alumnae Medal of Honor, 1988, Hon. Alumnae award, 1989, Pres.'s award Med. Coll. Pa., 1993, Sylvia Rambo award Dickinson Sch. of Law, 1997, Star award Forum of Exec. Women, 1998, Ann Alpern award PBA Women in the Profession, 1999, Sandra Day O'Connor award Phila. Bar Assn., 1999, Outstanding Leadership in Support of Legal Svcs. award Pa. Legal Svcs., 1999; named to Pa. Honor Roll of Women, 1996, Disting. Dau. of Pa., Gov. Tom Ridge, 1999. Fellow Am. Bar Found., Pa. Bar Found.; mem. ABA, Phila. Bar Assn. (mem. exec. com. divsn. young lawyers 1982-85, mem. bicentennial com 1986-87, bd. govs. 1990-93, mem. gender bias task force 1993-97, chair com. on jud. selection and retention 1987-89, vice chair 1985-87, investigative divsn. 1982-85, chair Andrew Hamilton Ball 1989, trustee Phila. Bar Found. 1990-97, co-chair century three commn. 1995-97, others), Pa. Bar Assn. (found. ho. dels. life fellow, bd. govs. 1980-83, 84-87, 91-93, chair young lawyers divsn. 1982-83, mem. long range planning com. 1985-87, mem. com. on professionalism, 1987-91, vice chmn. jud. inquiry and rev. bd. study com. 1989-91, sec. 1984-87, chair ho. dels. 1991-93, chair commn. on women in the profession 1993-95, v.p. 1996-97, pres. 1998-99, immediate past pres. 1999—, apptd. mem. ct. jud. discipline 1999), Pa. Bar Inst. (mem. faculty, course planner), Phila. Assn. Def. Counsel (mem. exec. coun. 1987-90, 94, mem. joint trial demonstration with Phila. Trial Lawyers Assn. 1993), Def. Rsch. Inst. (spkr. toxic torts seminar 1983), Phila. Bar Edn. Advocacy Women Litigators (course planner, mem. faculty 1995), Women's Assn. Women's Alternatives (bd. dirs. 1983-94, vice chair 1985-94), Phila. Forum Exec. Women, Pa. Women's Forum, Com. of Seventy, Mt. Holyoke Alumnae Assn. (bd. dirs. 1986-89, 1999—). Democrat. Lutheran. Avocations: collecting Am. antiques, gardening, running. General civil litigation, Personal injury (including property damage), Alternative dispute resolution. Office: Governors Office of Gen Counsel 225 Main Capitol Bldg Harrisburg PA 17120 E-mail: millesq@aol.com.

MILLER, LOUIS H. lawyer; b. Lampeter, U.K., Apr. 22, 1945; m. Diane Matuszewski, Dec. 31, 1973; children: Margaret, Anthony. BA in History, Rutgers Coll., 1967; JD, Temple U., 1970. Bar: N.J. 1970, U.S. Dist. Ct. N.J. 1970, U.S. Supreme Ct. 1996. Law clk. to Judge Thomas Beetel Hunterdon County Ct., Flemington, N.J., 1970-71; law clk. to Judge Baruch Seidman Superior Ct. N.J. Chancery, Trenton, N.J., 1971-72; assoc. Jefferson, Jefferson & Vaida, Flemington, 1972-75; ptnr. Vaida & Miller, Flemington, 1975-78; pvt. practice Flemington, 1978-81, 88—; judge Superior Ct. N.J., Flemington, 1981-88; of counsel Levinson Axelrod Wheaton & Grayzel, Flemington, 1990-97. Spl. dep. atty. gen. N.J. Hunterdon County Prosecutor Office, Flemington, 1972-73; condemnation commr. Appt. Superior Ct. N.J., Flemington, 1988—, N.J. Assembly spkrs. commr.; commr. N.J. State Commn. Investigation, Trenton, 1993-97; arbitrator U.S. Fed. Dist. Ct. N.J., 1989—. Twp. committeeman Alexandria Twp. Com., R.D. Milford, N.J., 1978-81. Mem. Am. Judges Assn., Am. Judicature Soc., N.J. State Bar Assn. (mem. dist. ethics com. 1980-81, mem. mcpl. ct. practice com. 1996—), Hunterdon County Bar Assn., Consular Law Soc., Welsh Am. Geneal. Soc., Welsh North Am. C. of C. (bd. dirs.), USF Constellation Mus. Republican. Avocations: paleontology, traveling, hiking. Criminal, Family and matrimonial, Personal injury (including property damage). Office: PO Box 850 40 Main St Flemington NJ 08822-1411 E-mail: millerlh@earthlink.net.

MILLER, MAX DUNHAM, JR., lawyer; b. Des Moines, Oct. 17, 1946; s. Max Dunham and Beulah (Head) M.; m. Melissa Ann Dart, Jan. 10, 1969 (div. July 1975); 1 child, Ann Marie Victoria; m. Caroline Jean Armendt, Sept. 19, 1981 (div. Dec. 2001); children: Alexander Bradshaw, Benjamin Everrett. BS with high honors, Mich. State U., 1968; postgrad., George Washington U., 1970-71; JD, U. Md., 1975. Bar: Md. 1976, U.S. Dist. Ct. Md. 1976, U.S. Ct. Appeals (4th cir.) 1981, U.S. Supreme Ct. 1982. Engr. U.S. Dept. of Def., Aberdeen Proving Ground, Md., 1968-72; law clk. to presiding judge Md. Cir. Ct., Higinbothom in Bel Air, Md., 1975-76; asst. county atty. Harford County, Bel Air, 1976-79; assoc. Lentz & Hooper P.A., Balt., 1979-81; ptnr. Miller, Olszewski & Moore, P.A., Bel Air, 1981-94; prin. Law Offices of Max D. Miller, P.A., 1994—. County atty. Harford County, Md., 1983-88. Mem. Md. Bar Assn., Assn. Trial Lawyers Am., Md. Trial Lawyers Assn., Harford County Bar Assn., Phi Kappa Phi, Phi Eta Sigma. Avocations: golf, sailing, canoeing, bicycling, ice and roller hockey. General civil litigation, Corporate, general, Property, real (including real estate development, water). Home: 308 Whetstone Rd Forest Hill MD 21050-1332 Office: 5 S Hickory Ave Bel Air MD 21014-3732

MILLER, MICHAEL PATIKY, lawyer; b. Huntington, N.Y., Apr. 16, 1944; s. George J. and Alida (Patiky) Miller; m. Dorothy Denn, Dec. 25, 1966; children: Lauren M. Golubtchik, Jonathan M., Rachel Miller Lazarus. AB, Rutgers U., 1965; JD, NYU, 1968. Bar: N.J. 1968, U.S. Dist. Ct. N.J. 1968, Calif. 1975, U.S. Dist. Ct. (no. dist.) Calif. 1975, U.S. Tax Ct. 1977, U.S. Ct. Appeals (9th cir.) 1977, U.S. Ct. Appeals (fed. cir.) 1984, U.S. Dist. Ct. (cen. dist.) Calif. 1982, U.S. Supreme Ct. 1983, U.S. Claims Ct. 1986. Atty. Electric Power Research Inst., Palo Alto, Calif., 1974-77; assoc. Weinberg, Ziff & Kaye, Palo Alto, 1977-78; ptnr. Weinberg, Ziff & Miller, Palo Alto, 1978—, mng. ptnr., 1990-98; lectr. on tax and estate planning U. Calif. Extension, 1980—. Author: Creditor Rights in Proceedings Outside Estate Adminstrn., 1995, rev., 1999, Estate Planning for Foreign Nationals in Silicon Valley, 2000, Death, Debts and Taxes 2000, rev. 2002; co-author: Decedents Estate Practice, 2001, rev. 2002, Trust Administration, 2d edit., 2001-03; contbg. author: California Wills and Trusts, 1991, Estate Planning for Unmarried Couples, 1998, California Trust Administration, 1999; contbr. chpts. in books and articles to profl. jours. Treas. No. Calif. region United Synagogue Am., 1985-89, pres., 1992-95. Capt. U.S. Army, 1969-74, Vietnam, Ethiopia. Recipient Lion of Judah award, 1984, Cert. Merit U. Judaism, 1992. Mem. ABA (chmn. region VI pub. contract law sect. 1975-78, commn. tax practice in small law firms, com. on taxation of trusts, estates, taxation sect. 1986—), N.J. State Bar, State Bar of Calif. (commr. tax law adv. commn. 1989-92, 93-95, chair 1994-95, mem. bd. legal specialization 1994-95), Silicon Valley Bar Assn. (pres. 2000-02, trustee 2002-). Probate (including wills, trusts), Estate taxation, Personal income taxation. Office: Weinberg Ziff & Miller 400 Cambridge Ave Palo Alto CA 94306-1507 Fax: 650-324-2822.

MILLER, MICHAEL THOMAS, lawyer; b. Mpls., Jan. 22, 1959; BA, U. Minn., 1981, JD, 1985. Bar: Minn. 1985, U.S. Dist. Ct. Minn. 1985, U.S. Ct. Appeals (8th cir.) 1987, U.S. Ct. Appeals (10th cir.) 1996, U.S. Supreme Ct. 1989. Law clk. Hon. Peter S. Popovich Minn. Ct. Appeals, St. Paul, 1985-87; assoc. Briggs & Morgan, P.A., Mpls., 1987-92, shareholder, 1992—. Contbr. articles to profl. jours. Appellate, Labor (including EEOC, Fair Labor Standards Act, labor-management relations, NLRB, OSHA). Office: Briggs & Morgan 2200 IDS Ctr Minneapolis MN 55402

MILLER, MILTON ALLEN, lawyer; b. L.A., Jan. 15, 1954; s. Samuel C. and Sylvia Mary Jane (Silver) Miller; m. Mary Ann Toman, Sept. 10, 1988; 1 child, Mary Ann. AB With distinction and honors in Econs., Stanford U., 1976; JD with honors, Harvard U., 1979. Bar: Calif. 1979, U.S. Ct. Appeals 9th cir.) 1979, U.S. Supreme Ct. 1989, Calif. (U.S. Dist. Ct. (cen., no. and so. dists.)) 1981. Law clk. U.S. Ct. Appeals (9th cir.), Sacramento, 1979—80; assoc. Latham & Watkins, L.A., Calif., 1979—87, ptnr., 1987—. Chmn. ethics com. Latham & Watkins, L.A., 1986—. Author: (non fiction) Attorney Ethics, 1993; editor: (articles) Harvard Law Rev., 1978—79; contbr. articles to profl. jours. Mem.: ATLA, ABA, L.A. County Bar Assn. (chmn. profl. responsibility and ethics com.), Calif. State Bar Assn. (mem. com. on profl. responsibility), Phi Beta Kappa (Named to Best Lawyers in Am. 2003). Federal civil litigation, General civil litigation, Insurance. Office: Latham & Watkins 633 W 5th St Ste 4000 Los Angeles CA 90071-2005 E-mail: milt.miller@lw.com.

MILLER, MORRIS HENRY, lawyer; b. Thomasville, Ga., June 14, 1954; s. Gibbes Ulmer and Marianne (Morris) M.; m. Anita Carol Payne, Mar. 23, 1985; children: Morris Payne, Rose Elizabeth, David Gibbes, Paul Louis Henry, John Henry. BS in Acctg. summa cum laude, Fla. State U., 1976; JD, U. Va., 1979. Bar: Fla. 1979. Assoc. Holland & Knight, Tampa, Fla., 1979-84, ptnr. Tallahassee, 1984—, chmn. health law practice, 1989—, knowledge mgmt. ptnr., 2001—. Founder, chair PENmd.com. Dist. fin. chmn. Gulf Ridge coun. Boy Scouts Am., 1988-89, mem. pack com., cubmaster Pack 23, Suwannee River Area coun., 1995-98, scoutmaster Troop 182, 1997-99, scoutmaster Troop 10, 2000-01, asst. scoutmaster, 2002—, dist. nominating com.; mem. Leadership Tampa, 1986, Leadership Tampa Bay, 1989; bd. dirs. John G. Riley House Mus. Ctr. for African-Am. History and Culture, 1998-99, Tallahassee YMCA, 1994-2002, chmn. long range planning com., 1997; founder, chmn. Tampa Bus. Com. for Arts, Inc., 1988-89; elder Presbyn. Ch. Mem. ABA (health law sect.), Fla. Bar (chmn., vice chmn. computer law com. 1983-89, Fla. corp. law revision com. 1986-89, health law sect.), Tallahassee Bar Assn. Computer, Corporate, general, Health. Office: Holland & Knight 315 S Calhoun St Ste 600 Tallahassee FL 32301-1897

MILLER, NODINE, judge; b. Dayton, Ohio, Dec. 13, 1938; d. Joseph Frederick and Nellie Naomi (Balzer) Cook; 1 child, Jessica Inez; m. Donald Alan Antrim, Jan. 2, 1998. Student, U. Vienna, Austria, 1961, Georgetown U., 1959; BA, Miami U., 1960; JD, Capital U., 1976. Bar: Ohio 1976, U.S. Dist. Ct. (so. and ea. dists.) Ohio 1981. Legal asst. Mayer, Tingley, Hurd & Emens, Columbus, Ohio, 1971-72; law clk. Brownfield, Kosydar, Bowen, Bally & Sturtz, Columbus, Ohio, 1975; atty. assigned to commr. Divsn. Securities, Ohio Dept. Commerce, Columbus, 1976-79, atty. inspector securities, 1977-79, deputy commr. securities, 1978-81; atty. Luper, Wolinetz, Sheriff & Niedenthal, Columbus, 1981-92; judge Franklin County Mcpl. Ct., Columbus, 1982-92. Mem. ABA, Am. Inn of Ct., Ohio State Bar Ass., Columbus Bar Assn., Avocations: quilting, hiking, fly fishing, skiing, reading. Office: Common Pleas Ct Hall of Justice 369 S High St Fl 6B Columbus OH 43215-4516

MILLER, PAUL J. lawyer; b. Boston, Mar. 27, 1929; s. Edward and Esther M.; children— Robin, Jonathan; m. Michal Davis, Sept. 1, 1965; children— Anthony, Douglas BA, Yale U., 1950; LL.B., Harvard U., 1953. Bar: Mass. 1953, Ill. 1957. Assoc. Miller & Miller, Boston, 1953-54; assoc. Sonnenschein Nath & Rosenthal, Chgo., 1957-63, ptnr., 1963—. Bd. dirs. Oil-Dri Corp. Am., Chgo. Trustee Latin Sch. of Chgo., 1985-91. 1st lt. JAGC, U.S. Army, 1954-57. Fellow Am. Bar Found.; mem. Tavern Club, Saddle and Cycle Club, Law Club, Phi Beta Kappa. Avocation: gardening. Commercial, contracts (including sales of goods; commercial financing), Corporate, general, Securities. Office: Sonnenschein Nath & Rosenthal 233 S Wacker Dr Ste 8000 Chicago IL 60606-6491 E-mail: pjm@sonnenschein.com.

MILLER, PAUL S(AMUEL), lawyer; b. Paterson, N.J., Apr. 8, 1939; s. Louis and Etta (Wolff) M.; m. Carol Plesser, Mar. 26, 1961; children: Nicole F., Margo H., Jason E. BA, Rutgers U., 1960, JD magna cum laude, 1962. Bar: N.Y. 1963. Assoc. Kaye, Scholer, Fierman, Hayes & Handler, N.Y.C., 1962-63, Rubin, Baum & Levin, N.Y.C., 1964; ptnr. Fishman, Miller & Zimet, N.Y.C., 1964-70; counsel Leasing Cons., Inc., Rosyln, N.Y., 1970-71; with Pfizer Inc., N.Y.C., 1971—2002, assoc. gen. counsel, v.p., gen. counsel, 1986-92, sr. v.p., gen. counsel, 1992-99, exec. v.p., gen. counsel, 1999—2002; spl. counsel Kaye Scholer LLP, N.Y.C., 2002—. Ofcl. corr. Pharm. Mfrs. Assn., mem., chmn. exec. com. law sect., 1989-90. Mem. United Jewish Appeal Com., Essex County, 1981-83, co-chmn. Livingston sect., 1982; chmn. bd. dirs. Citizens Crime Commn. of N.Y.C., Inc.; bd. dirs. Am. Israel Pub. Affairs Com., Am. Jewish Congress, Jewish Theol. Sem., U.S. C. of C., chmn. Nat. Chamber Litigation Coun.; mem. bus. adv. coun. Touro Law Sch.; mem. bd. overseers Inst. Civil Justice, RAND. Albert Einstein Coll. Medicine, Jaffee Inst. Strategic Studies at Tel Aviv U. Mem. ABA (antitrust law sect., corp. banking and bus. law sect., natural resources law sect., sci. and tech. sect., mem. health law forum com.), N.Y. State Bar Assn. (antitrust law sect., food and drug law sect.). Corporate, general, Environmental. Office: Kaye Scholer LLP 425 Park Ave New York NY 10022

MILLER, RAYMOND VINCENT, JR., lawyer; b. Providence, July 1, 1954; s. Raymond Vincent and Mary Eunice (Mullen) M.; m. Elizabeth Ann White, May 31, 1980; children: Travis, Charles. BA, U. R.I., 1976; JD cum laude, U. Miami, 1981. Bar: Fla. 1981, U.S. Dist. Ct. (so. dist.) Fla. 1981, U.S. Ct. Appeals (11th cir.) 1986, U.S. Dist. Ct. (mid. dist.) Fla. 1987. Area supr. job devel. and tng. div. R.I. Dept. Econ. Devel., Providence, 1977-78; assoc. Thornton & Herndon, Miami, Fla., 1981-83, Britton, Cohen et al, Miami, 1983-85, Edward A. Kaufman, P.A., Miami, 1985-88; ptnr. Kaufman, Miller, Dickstein & Grunspan, Miami, 1988-2000; shareholder Gunster, Yoakley & Stewart, P.A., 2000—. Mem. ABA, Fla. Bar Assn., Nat Order Barristers, Soc. Bar and Gavel. Federal civil litigation, Bankruptcy, State civil litigation. Office: Gunster Yoakley & Stewart PA 2 S Biscayne Blvd Ste 3400 Miami FL 33131 E-mail: RMiller@gunster.com.

MILLER, REBECCA ANNE, lawyer, mediator; b. Las Vegas, Nev., Mar. 21, 1961; d. Vincent and Roxanne Hopkins; m. Michael C. Miller, Nov. 3, 1991. BA, U. Nev., Las Vegas, 1983; JD, Pepperdine U., 1986. Bar: Nev. 1986, U.S. Dist. Ct. (so. dist.) Nev. 1986. Jud. law clk. to Hon. Michael Wendell Dist. Ct. Nev., Las Vegas, 1986—87; atty. Law Offices Paul Schofield, Las Vegas, 1987—92, McCullough & Assocs., Las Vegas, 1992—95; atty., of counsel Alverson, Taylor, Mortensen et. al., Las Vegas, 1995—. Mem., sec. bench bar com. Family Ct., Las Vegas, 1993—98. Scholar, L.A. Family Law, 1986. Mem.: State Bar Nev. (mem. exec. coun. family law sect. 1993—), Social Register Las Vegas, Las Vegas C. of C. Avocations: travel, cooking, decorating. Family and matrimonial, Probate (including wills, trusts), Bankruptcy. Office: Alverson Taylor Law Firm 7401 W Charleston Blvd Las Vegas NV 89117 Office Fax: 702-385-7000.

MILLER, RICHARD ALLAN, lawyer; b. N.Y.C., Oct. 28, 1947; s. Harold B. and Helen (Schwartz) M.; m. Karen R. Mangold, July, 5, 1970; children: David, Matthew. BA, SUNY, Buffalo, 1969; MA, Ohio State U., 1970; JD, NYU, 1973. Bar: N.Y. 1974, U.S. Dist. Ct. (so. and ea. dists.) N.Y. 1974, U.S. Ct. Appeals (2d cir.) 1977, U.S. Supreme Ct. 1980. Assoc. Paul Weiss et al, N.Y.C., 1973-75; asst. dist. atty. N.Y. County, N.Y.C., 1975-77; ptnr. Newman, Tannenbaum et al, N.Y.C., 1980-91, Katten Muchin & Zavis, N.Y.C., 1992-96, White & Case, 1996—2002; v.p., corp. counsel Prudential Fin., 2002—. Staff counsel Presdl. Task Force on Market

Mechanisms, 1987-88; speaker Internat. Conf. Futures Money Mgmt., 1990-92; adj. prof. law, Columbia U. Sch. Law, 2002-. Editor Futures & Derivatives L. Rpt., 1981—, Securities Arbitration Commentator, 1988—. Mem. Assn. of the Bar of the City of N.Y. (chair futures regulations com.). Jewish. Avocation: golf. Administrative and regulatory, Federal civil litigation, Securities. Home: 22 Roosevelt Rd Maplewood NJ 07040-2116 Office: Prudential Fin 751 Broad St Newark NJ E-mail: richard.a.miller@prudential.com.

MILLER, RICHARD ALLEN, lawyer; b. East Chicago, Ind., Nov. 22, 1945; s. Ernest R. and Sophie D. (Kurmis) M.; m. Patricia Annette Bratton, July 26, 1969 (div. May 1974); 1 child, Jason Todd; m. Kathleen Patrice Sills, Jan. 3, 1976; children: Andrew Christian, Caroline Grace. BS, Ind. U., 1967; JD, Valparaiso U., 1973. Bar: Ind. 1974, U.S. Dist. Ct. (no. dist.) Ind. 1974, U.S. Supreme Ct. 1985, U.S. Ct. Appeals (7th cir.) 1987, U.S. Claims Ct. 1990. Assoc. Owen W. Crumpacker & Assocs., Hammond, Ind., 1974-76, Benjamin, Greco & Gouveia, Gary, Ind., 1976-77; ptnr. Greco, Gouveia, Miller & Pera, Gary, 1978-79, Greco, Gouveia, Miller, Pera & Bishop, Merrillville, Ind., 1979-85, Gouveia & Miller, Merrillville, 1985—. Spl. counsel City of Hammond, 1974-76; trial counsel Ind. Toll Rd. Com., South Bend, 1981-82, Ind. Dept. Highways Toll Rd. Div., Granger, 1982-87; spl. asst. U.S. Rep. Peter J. Visclosky, Gary and Washington, 1985-86. Author: Indiana Rules of Evidence Applying to Expert Testimony, 1991. Campaign mgr. Visclosky for U.S. Congress, 1st Congl. Dist., Ind., 1983-88; dist. coordinator Nat. Bicentennial Competition on U.S. Constitution and Bill of Rights, 1st Congl. Dist., Ind., 1987-88. Mem. Ind. Bar Assn., Assn. Trial Lawyers Am., Ind. Trial Lawyers Assn. Democrat. Lutheran. Avocations: fly fishing, walking dog. General civil litigation, Condemnation (eminent domain), Personal injury (including property damage). Home: 10313 Marlou Dr Munster IN 46321-4339 Office: Gouveia & Miller 433 W 84th Dr Merrillville IN 46410-6173 E-mail: rambeaulaw@aol.com.

MILLER, RICHARD JOSEPH, lawyer; b. San Diego, Jan. 20, 1941; s. Daniel Preston and June (Beissel) M.; divorced, 1972; 1 child, Shelli Renee; m. Paula Anne English, May 29, 1982. BA, U. Tex., Arlington, 1970; M of Pub. Adminstrn., So. Meth. U., Dallas, 1974; JD, Baylor U., 1983. Bar: U.S. Dist. Ct. (we. dist.) Tex. 1988. Officer, supr. Dallas Police Dept., 1963-75; program coord. Tex. Organized Crime Prevention Council, Austin, 1975-76; chief of police Killeen (Tex.) Police Dept., 1976-79; tng. cons. Tex. Commn. on Law Enforcement Officer Standards and Edn., Austin, 1979-80; chief of police Denton (Tex.) Police Dept., 1980; sole practice Killeen, 1983-88; ptnr. Kleff, Lewis, Miller & Assocs., Killeen, 1989; pvt. practice Killeen, Tex., 1989-92; elected county atty. Bell County (Tex.), Bell County, 1993—. Author: The Train Robbing Bunch, 1981, Texas Firemen's and Policemen's Civil Service Law, 1987, Bounty Hunter, 1988, Bloody Bill Longley, 1996, Sam Bass & Gang, 1999. Vice chmn. Leon Valley dist. Boy Scouts Am., 1987-88; bd. dirs. Killeen Crimestoppers, Inc., 1986-91, Killeen Literacy Coun., 1987-90; mem. Bell County Hist. Commn., 1988-91. With U.S. Army, 1958-61. Fellow Tex. Bar Found.; mem. Bell-Lampasas-Mills Counties Bar Assn., Tex. Dist. and County Attys. Assn., Nat. Assn. Outlaw and Lawman History (bd. dirs. 1986—), Western Writers of Am., Rotary. Avocations: old west research, jogging, cartooning. Office: PO Box 1127 Belton TX 76513-5127 Home: 1917 Sutton Pl Trl Harker Heights TX 76548-6043

MILLER, RICHARD MARK, lawyer; b. Feb. 12, 1952; s. Abraham and Phyllis (Isaacson) M.; m. Beverly Elaine Sparks, Aug. 7, 1976 (div. 1992); m. Cathryn Alexandra Mitchell, Oct. 3, 1993; children: Jeffrey Brian, David Gregory, Scott Alan, Jenifer Marlena. BA, Bklyn. Coll., 1973; JD, SUNY, Buffalo, 1976. Bar: N.Y. 1977, N.J. 1977, U.S. Dist. Ct. (so. and ea. dists.) N.Y. 1977, U.S. Dist. Ct. N.J. 1977. Gen. counsel Amswiss Internat. Corp., Jersey City, 1976-78; assoc. gen. counsel Loeb Rhoades, Hornblower, N.Y.C., 1978-79, Shearson Loeb Rhoades, 1979-80; assoc. counsel Bausch & Lomb Inc., Rochester, N.Y., 1980-83, counsel, 1983-85; sr. atty. Cheseborough Pond's Inc., 1985-87; corp. counsel Prince Sports Group, Inc. (formerly Prince Mfg., Inc.), Princeton, N.J., 1987-90, gen. counsel, 1990-93; cons. Proskauer Rose Goetz & Mendelsohn, N.Y.C., 1993-94; counsel Stark & Stark, Princeton, 1994-96; prin. Miller & Mitchell, Princeton, 1996—. Chmn. Internat. Trade Network; mem. Internat. Trade Adv. Commn., Mercer County C.C. Mem.: Rotary Club. Commercial, contracts (including sales of goods; commercial financing), Corporate, general, Mergers and acquisitions. Home: 29 Crusher Rd Hopewell NJ 08525-2201 Office: MillerMitchell PC 863 State Rd Princeton NJ 08540 E-mail: rmiller@millermitchell.com.

MILLER, RICHARD SHERWIN, law educator; b. Boston, Dec. 11, 1930; s. Max and Mollie Miller; m. Doris Sheila Lunchick, May 24, 1956; children: Andrea Jayne Armitage, Matthew Harlan. BSBA, Boston U., 1951, JD magna cum laude, 1956; LLM, Yale U., 1959. Bar: Mass. 1956, Mich. 1961, Hawaii 1977. Pvt. practice law, Boston, 1956-58; assoc. prof. law Wayne State U., Detroit, 1959-62, prof., 1962-65, Ohio State U., Columbus, 1965-73, dir. clin. and interdisciplinary program, 1971-73; prof. U. Hawaii, Honolulu, 1973-95, prof. emeritus, 1995—, dean, 1981-84. Vis. prof. law USIA/U. Hawaii, Hiroshima U. Affiliation Program, Japan, 1986, Victoria U., Wellington, N.Z., 1987; del. Hawaii State Jud. Conf., 1989-92; cons. Hawaii Coalition for Health, 1997—. Author: Courts and the Law: An Introduction to our Legal System, 1980; editor: (with Roland Stanger) Essays on Expropriations, 1967; editor-in-chief: Boston U. Law Rev., 1955-56; contbr. articles to profl. jours. Mem. Hawaii Substance Abuse Task Force, 1994-95; arbitrator Hawaii Ct. Annexed Arbitration Program, 1995-99; bd. dirs. Drug Policy Forum Hawaii, 1996—; mem. Save our Star-Bulletin Com., 1999-2001; mem. Citizens for Competitive Air Travel, 2002. 1st lt. USAF, 1951-53. Sterling-Ford fellow Yale U., 1958-59; named Lawyer of Yr. Japan-Hawaii Lawyers Assn., 1990; recipient Cmty. Svc. award Hawaii Med. Assn. Alliance, 1999. Mem. ABA, Hawaii State Bar Assn., Hawaii ACLU, Am. Inn of Ct. IV (emeritus founding mem., master of the bench), Am. Law Inst., Honolulu Cmty.-Media Coun. (chair 1994-89, treas. 2000-02, vice chair 1998-2000, 02—), Yale Club of Hawaii. Office: U Hawaii Richardson Sch Law 2515 Dole St Honolulu HI 96822-2328

MILLER, RICHARD STEVEN, lawyer; b. Mt. Vernon, N.Y., Dec. 5, 1951; s. Norman and Mildred (Curtis) M. BA, U. Pa., 1974; JD, NYU, 1977. Bar: N.Y. 1978, U.S. Dist. Ct. (so. and ea. dists.) N.Y. 1978, U.S. Ct. Appeals (2d cir.) 1978. Asst. dist. atty. Kings County, N.Y., 1977-79; with Hahn & Hessen, N.Y.C., 1979-82, Levin & Weintraub & Crames, N.Y.C., 1982-87; counsel, then ptnr. Rogers & Wells, N.Y.C., 1987-91; ptnr. Dewey Ballantine LLP, N.Y.C., 1991-2001; prin. shareholder Greenburg Traurig LLP, N.Y.C., 2001—, co-chmn. nat. reorgn., bankruptcy and restructuring practice, 2001—. Mem. ABA, Internat. Bar Assn., Am. Bankruptcy Inst. Bankruptcy, Mergers and acquisitions, Property, real (including real estate development, water). Office: Greenberg Traurig 200 Park Avenue 15th Fl New York NY 10166 Office Fax: 212-801-6400. E-mail: millerrs@gtlaw.com.

MILLER, ROBERT JOSEPH, lawyer, former governor; b. Evanston, Ill., Mar. 30, 1945; s. Ross Wendell and Coletta Jane (Doyle) Miller; m. Sandra Ann Searles, Oct. 17, 1949; children: Ross, Corrine, Megan. BA in Polit. Sci., U. Santa Clara, 1967; JD, Loyola U., 1971. First legal advisor Las Vegas (Nev.) Met. Police Dept., 1973—75; justice of the peace Las Vegas Twp., 1975—78; dep. dist. atty. Clark County, Las Vegas, 1971—73, dist. atty., 1979—86; lt. gov. State of Nev., 1987—89, gov., 1989—98, 1991—98; sr. ptnr. Jones Vargas, Las Vegas, 1999—. Chmn. Nev. Commn. on Econ. Devel., Carson City, 1987—91, Nev. Commn. on Tourism, Carson City, 1987—91; mem. Pres. Reagan's Task Force on Victims of Crime, 1982; chmn. Nev. divsn. Am. Cancer Soc., 1988—90. Mem.: Nev. Dist. Attys. Assn. (pres. 1979, 1983), Nat. Govs. Assn. (vice chmn. exec. com. 1995—96, chmn. 1996—97, past chmn. com. on justice and pub. safety, chmn. legal affairs com. 1992—94, lead gov. on transp. 1992—), Western Govs. Assn. (chmn. 1993—94), Nat. Dist. Attys. Assn. (pres. 1984—85). Democrat. Roman Catholic. Office: Jones Vargas 3rd Fl S 3773 Howard Hughes Pkwy Las Vegas NV 89109-0949

MILLER, RODNEY CRAIG, lawyer; b. London, July 19, 1971; s. Jonathan Henry and Susan Sherrer Miller; m. Dana Ellen Hester, July 22, 1995; 1 child, Hannah Grace. BS, U. Ga., 1994; JD, U. Memphis, 1997. Bar: Tenn. 1998, U.S. Dist. Ct. (ea. dist.) Tenn. 1999. Solo practitioner, Cleveland, Tenn., 1999—. Mem.: ABA, Bradley County Bar Assn. (sec., treas.), Tenn. Bar Assn., Am. Bankruptcy Inst. Republican. Southern Baptist. Bankruptcy, Family and matrimonial, Personal injury (including property damage). Home: 755 Samples Chapel Rd SE Cleveland TN 37323 Office: 481 Second St NW Cleveland TN 37364-0906 E-mail: rodlaw@bellsouth.net.

MILLER, RUTH LOYD, lawyer, author; b. Ida, La., May 29, 1922; d. Cecil A. and Gladys (Means) Loyd; m. Minos D. Miller, Jr., Dec. 22, 1942; children: Bonner M. Cutting, Minos D. III, James Valcour. BA in Speech, La. State U., 1942; MA in English, U. La., 1987. Bar: La. 1957. Sole practice, Jennings, La., 1957—; sec. Jennings Gas Co., 1959—. Author, editor: Shakespeare Identified, 3rd edit., 1975, Hidden Allusions in Shakespeare's Plays, 3rd edit., 1975, A Hundreth Sundrie Flowers, 2d edit., 1975. First v.p. La. Constnl. Conv., 1973; mem. La. Mineral Bd., 1972-73; mem. bd. suprs. La. State Univ. Sys., 1974-88, chmn., 1983-84; active polit. campaigns, La. Named Nat. Woman of Yr., Delta Zeta, 1983; selected as one of La.'s Women of Distinction La. Women in the Mainstream for Women's Pavilion, World's Fair, New Orleans, 1984; honoree La. interfaith conf., 1985; inducted into Hall of Fame La. State U. Alumni Assn., 1995; recipient Lifetime Achievement award Shakespeare Oxford Soc., 1993. Mem. ABA, La. State Bar Assn., Brit. Marlowe Soc. (Hon. Lifetime award 1980). Democrat. Methodist. Education and schools, Oil, gas, and mineral, Intellectual property. Home: PO Box 1309 Jennings LA 70546-1309

MILLER, STANTON BERNETT, lawyer; b. Chgo., Mar. 5, 1944; s. Nathan and Isabel P. (Edelman) M.; m. Peggy G. Goodkind, Dec. 11, 1971; 1 dau., Margaret Katherine. A.B., Miami U., Oxford, Ohio, 1965; J.D., U. Ill., 1968; LL.M. in Taxation, John Marshall Law Sch., 1979. Bar: Ill. 1969, U.S. Dist. Ct. (no. dist.) Ill. 1969, U.S. Ct. Mil. Appeals 1972. Assoc., Edelman & Rappaport, Chgo., 1969-76; ptnr. Michael, Best, & Friedrich, Chgo., 2001— ; instr. IIT, 1980-82. Pres. Chgo. chpt. Dysautonomia Found., 1980-81; active Chgo. Estate Planning Council, 1979— . Served with USAR, 1968-74. Mem. Chgo. Bar Assn., Ill. Bar Assn., ABA. Contbr. articles to profl. jours. Corporate, general, Probate (including wills, trusts). Office: Michael Best & Friedrich 401 N Michigan Ave Chicago IL 60611

MILLER, STEPHEN RALPH, lawyer; b. Chgo., Nov. 28, 1950; s. Ralph and Karin Ann (Olson) M.; children: David Williams, Lindsay Christine. m. Sheila L. Krysiak, Feb. 2, 1998. BA cum laude, Yale U., 1972; JD, Cornell U., 1975. Bar: Ill. 1975. Assoc. McDermott, Will & Emery, Chgo., 1975-80, income ptnr., 1981-85, equity ptnr., 1986—, mgmt. com. mem., 1992-95. Mem. spl. task force on post-employment benefits Fin. Acctg. Standards Bd., Norwalk, Conn., 1987—91. Contbr. articles to profl. jours. Mem. Chgo. Coun. on Fgn. Rels., 1978—, devel. com., 1997-2002, chair devel. subcom., 1999-2002, external rels. com., 2002—; trustee police pension bd., Wilmette, Ill., 1992-98; trustee Seabury We. Theol. Sem., Evanston, Ill., 1994-2002, chancellor, 1996-97, chair trusteeship com., 2000-02. Mem.: ABA, Lawyers' Club of Chgo., Yale Club Chgo. Avocations: sailing, water-skiing, cross country skiing. Pension, profit-sharing, and employee benefits. Office: McDermott Will & Emery 227 W Monroe St Ste 4700 Chicago IL 60606-5096 E-mail: smiller@mwe.com.

MILLER, STEVEN JEFFREY, lawyer; b. Chgo., Feb. 13, 1954; s. Hadley Allan and Carol Joan (Prince) M.; m. Mona Joy Deutsch, Aug. 21, 1977. BA magna cum laude, U. Pa., 1974; JD, Stanford U., 1977. Bar: Calif. 1977, U.S. Dist. Ct. (cen. dist.) Calif. 1978, U.S. Dist. Ct. (so. dist.) Calif. 1982, U.S. Dist. Ct. (no. and ea. dists.) Calif. 1987, U.S. Dist. Ct. Ariz. 1990, U.S. Ct. Appeals (9th cir.) 1978, U.S. Ct. Appeals (10th cir.) 1981, U.S. Supreme Ct. 1982. Assoc. Lawler, Felix & Hall, L.A., 1977-84, Wyman, Bautzer, Kuchel & Silbert, L.A., 1984-86; sole practitioner Bel Air, Calif., 1987-89; assoc. gen. counsel Ernst & Young, L.A., 1989-94; v.p., dir. legal rsch. Legal Rsch. Network, L.A., 1996-99; gen. counsel, sec. InterPacket Networks, Inc., 1999-2001; atty. The Quisenberry Law Firm, 2001—02. Judge pro tem L.A. County Mcpl. Ct., 1987-89. Trustee U. Synagogue, L.A., 1984—, sec., 1985-89, pres., 1989-91, exec. com., 1985-94. Mem. ABA, Calif. Bar Assn., L.A. County Bar Assn. Democrat. Avocations: softball, racquetball, bowling, bridge, rotisserie league baseball.

MILLER, SUZANNE MARIE, state librarian; b. Feb. 25, 1954; d. John Gordon and Dorothy Margaret (Sabatka) M.; 1 child, Altinay Marie. BA in English, U. S.D., 1975; MA in Library Sci., U. Denver, 1976, postgrad. in law, 1984. Librarian II U. S.D. Sch. of Law, Vermillion, 1977-78; law libr. U. LaVerne, Calif., 1978-85, instr. in law, 1980-85; asst. libr. tech. svcs. McGeorge Sch. Law, Calif., 1985-99, prof. advanced legal rsch., 1994-99; state librarian S.D. State Library, Pierre, S.D., 1999—. Co-author (with Elizabeth J. Pokorny) U.S. Government Documents: A Practical Guide for Library Assistants in Academic and Public Libraries, 1988; contbr. chpt. to book, articles to profl. jours. Pres. Short Grass Arts Coun., 2001—03; bd. dirs. Black Hills Playhouse Bd., 1999—, S.D. Ctr. for the Book Bd., 2002—. Recipient A. Jurisprudence award Bancroft Whitney Pub. Co., 1983. Mem.: ALA, Western Coun. State Librs. (sec. 2001—02), Chief Officers of State Libr. Agys. (sec. 2002—), Western Pacific Assn. Law Librs. (sec. 1990—94, pres. elect 1994—95, pres. 1995—96, local arrangements chair 1997), No. Calif. Assn. Law Librs. (mem. program com., inst. 1988), Mt. Plains Libr. Assn. (S.D. rep. to exec. bd. 2001—), So. Calif. Assn. Law Librs. (arrangements com. 1981—82), Am. Assn. Law Librs., S.D. Libr. Assn. Roman Catholic. Home: 505 N Grand Ave Pierre SD 57501-2014 Office: SD State Library 800 Governors Dr Pierre SD 57501-2235 E-mail: suzanne.miller@state.sd.us.

MILLER, THOMAS EUGENE, lawyer, writer; b. Bryan, Tex., Jan. 4, 1929; s. Eugene Adam and Ella Lucille (Schroeder) M. BA, BS, Tex. A&M U., 1950; MA, U. Tex., 1956, JD, 1966; postgrad., U. Houston, 1956-58, U. Calif., 1983. Bar: Tex. 1966. Rsch. technician M.D. Anderson Hosp., Houston, 1956-58; claims examiner trainee Social Security Adminstrn., New Orleans, 1964; trademark examiner U.S. Patent and Trademark Office, Washington, 1966; editor Bancroft-Whitney Co., San Francisco, 1966-92. Author: (under pseudonym Millard Thomas) Home From 7-North, 1984; contbr. to numerous legal publs. Contbg. mem. Dem. Nat. Com., 1981—; mem. Celebrate Bryan Com., chmn. Bryan Med. Heritage Com. Mem. ABA, World Lit. Assn., World Inst. Achievement, United Writers Assn. India, Nat. Trust for Hist. Preservation, Tex. Bar Assn., U. Tex. Sch. of Law, Non-practicing Alumni Adv. Coun., African Wildlife Found., World Wildlife Fund, Internat. Platform Assn., Nat. Writers Assn., Scribes, Acad. Polit. Sci., Press Club, Commonwealth Club, Rotary Club (Paul Harris fellow, Found. fellow), Menninger Soc., Tex. A&M U. Faculty Club, Phi Kappa Phi, Psi Chi, Phi Eta Sigma. Methodist. Home: 101 N Haswell Dr Bryan TX 77803-4848

MILLER, THOMAS J. state attorney general; b. Dubuque, Iowa, Aug. 11, 1944; s. Elmer John and Betty Maude (Kross) Miller; m. Linda Cottington, Jan. 10, 1981; 1 child, Matthew. BA, Loras Coll., Dubuque, 1966; JD, Harvard U., 1969. Bar: Iowa 1969. With VISTA, Balt., 1969—70; legis. asst. to U.S. rep. John C. Culver, 1970—71; legal edn. dir. Balt. Legal Aid Bur., part-time faculty U. Md. Sch. Law, 1971—73; pvt. practice McGregor, Iowa, 1973—78; city atty., 1973—79, Marquette, Iowa; atty. gen. of Iowa, 1978—90, 1994—; ptnr. Faegre & Benson, Des Moines, 1991—95. Chmn. Microsoft case exec. com.; co-chmn. Airline Competition Working Group; pres. 2d Dist. New Dem. Club , Balt., 1972. Mem.: NAAG (pres. 1989—90, chmn. consumer protection, ins., budget, and antitrust coms., Wyman award 1990), ABA, Iowa Bar Assn., Common Cause. Democrat. Roman Catholic. Office: Office of the Atty Gen Hoover State Office Bldg 1305 E Walnut St Des Moines IA 50319-0112*

MILLER, THOMAS ROBBINS, lawyer, publisher; b. Chgo., Mar. 8, 1938; s. William Whipple and Helen (Robbins) M.; m. Tran Tuong Nhu, July 3, 1974; children: Toby, Teddy, Nathalie, Gabriella. BA, Yale U., 1960; LLB, Stanford U., 1965; cert., Parker Sch. Fgn. and Comparative Law, Columbia U., 1966. Bar: N.Y. 1966, Calif. 1974. Assoc. Webster & Sheffield, N.Y.C., 1965-68; sole practice N.Y.C., 1968-74, Berkeley, 1974-89; pub. Lancaster Miller Pubs., Berkeley, 1974-89; sr. ptnr. Miller & Ngo, PLC, Oakland, Calif., 1989—. Founder, pres. Internat. Children's Fund, Berkeley, 1974—; cons. Peace Corps, Washington, 1961, Ctr. for Constl. Rights, UNICEF, N.Y.C., 1973-76; dep. dir. Calif. Rural Legal Assistance, San Francisco, 1977-79; gen. counsel Global Exch.; co-founder Afghan Women's Microlending Fund. Named 1 of 10 Outstanding Young Men in U.S., U.S. Jaycees, 1974 Democrat. Office: 725 Washington St Oakland CA 94607-3924 E-mail: viasco@aol.com.

MILLER, THORMUND AUBREY, lawyer; b. Pocatello, Idaho, July 14, 1919; s. Roy Edmund and Lillian (Thordarson) Miller; m. Hannah A. Flansburgh, Feb. 10, 1946 (dec. Jan. 2003); children: Karen Lynette Van Gerpen, Christine Alison Westall. BA, Reed Coll., 1941; LLB, Columbia U., 1948; grad., Advanced Mgmt. Program, Harvard Bus. Sch., 1961. Bar: Calif. 1949, D.C. 1951, U.S. Supreme Ct. 1960. Assoc. McCutchen, Thomas, Matthews, Griffiths & Greene, San Francisco, 1948-50; atty. So. Pacific Transp. Co., Washington, 1950-56, asst. gen. atty., 1956-59, gen. atty., 1959-66, sr. gen. atty., 1966-75, gen. solicitor, 1975-79, gen. commerce counsel, 1979-83, dir., mem. exec. com., 1983-87, v.p., gen. counsel, 1983-89; gen. counsel So. Pacific Communications Co., San Francisco, 1970-79, dir., 1970-81; pvt. practice law Atherton, Calif., 1989-96. Pres. Wood Acres Citizens Assn., Bethesda, Md., 1955-56; exec. com. Holbrook Palmer Recreation Park Found., 1979—, pres., 1982-84; bd. dirs. Atherton Civic Interest League, 1981—, pres., 1992-94; mem. Atherton Park and Recreation Commn., 1991-95, San Mateo Civil Grand Jury, 1997; alumni bd. Reed Coll., 1971-72, trustee, 1987-2002, campaign com., 1995-2000; joint donor Thormund A. Miller/Walter Mintz chair in econ. history; bd. dirs. Assocs. U. Calif. Press, 1994—. Lt. USNR, 1942-46. Mem.: ABA, Calif. Bar Assn. Presbyterian.

MILLER, WARREN LLOYD, lawyer; b. Bklyn., July 18, 1944; s. Allan and Ella Miller; m. Jana Lee Morris, May 13, 1978; children: Lindsey Beth, Alan Gregory, William Brett. BA with high honor, Am. U., 1966; JD with honors, George Washington U., 1969. Bar: Va., 1969, D.C., 1969, U.S. Supreme Ct., 1981. Law clk. to Hon. Edward A. Beard Superior Ct. D.C., 1968-69; asst. U.S. atty. for D.C., 1969-74; ptnr. Stein, Miller & Brodsky, 1974-85; pres. Warren L. Miller, P.C., 1986—; of counsel Reed, Smith, Shaw & McClay, 1986-93. Lectr. Georgetown U. Law Sch., 1970-71, Am. U., 1971-72; guest spkr. various radio & TV programs and legal forums; mem. Jud. Conf. D.C. Cir., 1984—; pres. Asst. U.S. Attys. Assn. of D.C., 1983-84. Contbr. articles to profl. jours. Parliamentarian credentials and rules coms. Rep. Nat. Conv., 1984; mem. D.C. Law Revision Commn., 1987-91 (apptd. by Pres. Reagan), mem. U.S. Commn. for Preservation of Am.'s Heritage Abroad, 1992— (apptd. by Pres. Bush, reapptd. by Pres. Clinton 1996, 99), now chmn. (apptd. by Pres. Bush) 2001—; bd. dirs. Found. for Buchenwald and Mittelbau-Dora Memls., 1994—; spkr. ceremonies commemorating 50th anniversary of liberation of Buchenwald Concentration Camp, Buchenwald, Germany, 1995, Ceremony Dedicating Little Camp Meml., Buchenwald, Germany, 2002; spkr. U.S. Holocaust Meml. Mus., 1995, 2002; fundraiser for Rep. Nat. Com. and Pres. Bush, 1988-92; co-chmn. dinner for V.P. Bush, 1988; vice-chmn. Pres.'s Dinner, 1989; co-chmn. Pres.'s Club, Washington, 1990-92; chmn. fundraiser for U.S. Senator Christopher Bond, 1992, 97; chmn., fundraiser U.S. Senator John Warner, 1996; vice-chmn., fundraiser Senator Bob Dole, 1996; co-chmn., fundraiser Gov. George W. Bush Presdl. Exploratory Com., 1999, mem. host com., fundraiser for Gov. George W. Bush, 2000, U.S. Sen. John Warner, 2001, Gov. Jeb Bush, 2002. Mem. Congl. Country Club (Bethesda, Md.), Phi Delta Phi, Omicron Delta Kappa, Pi Gamma Mu. Office: 2300 N St NW Washington DC 20037-1122

MILLER, WILLIAM NAPIER CRIPPS, lawyer; b. Long Branch, N.J., June 7, 1930; adopted s. Julia (Erwin) M.; m. Carolyn Anderson, Jan. 19, 1951 (div. 1963); children: Bruce Douglass, Jennifer Erwin; m. Hannelore Steinbeck, Dec. 4, 1970 AA, Coll. Marin, 1949; student, U. Calif.-Berkeley, 1949-51, JD, 1955. Bar: N.Y., Calif. 1956, U.S. Supreme Ct. 1983. Assoc. Mudge, Stern, Baldwin & Todd, N.Y.C., 1955-58, Pillsbury, Madison & Sutro, San Francisco, 1959-65, ptnr., 1966—; staff NYU Law Sch., 1957-58; ct. adv. com. Calif. State Assembly Judiciary Com., 1979-80. Author: Long Pig, 2002. Bd. dirs. Laguna Honda Hosp., San Francisco, 1966— ; bd. visitors U. Calif.-Hastings Law Sch. Served with USAF, 1951-52. Recipient Bur. Nat. Affairs award U. Calif.-Hastings, 1955; recipient Thurston Soc. award, 1953. Fellow Am. Coll. Trial Lawyers; mem. ABA, San Francisco Bar Assn., Order of Coif, St. Francis Yacht Club, Silverado Country Club. Antitrust, Federal civil litigation, General civil litigation. Home: 16 George Ln Sausalito CA 94965-1890 Office: Pillsbury Winthrop LLP PO Box 7880 San Francisco CA 94120-7880

MILLER, YVETTE, lawyer, publishing executive; BA, Adelphi U.; JD, St. John's U., N.Y. Litig. assoc. Weil, Gotshal & Manges; gen. atty. pub. sect. CBS; v.p., dep. gen. counsel Hachette Filipacchi; with G + J USA, N.Y.C., 1993—2000, v.p., gen. counsel, 2000—. Office: G + J USA Pub Legal Dept 375 Lexington Ave New York NY 10017-5514*

MILLER-LERMAN, LINDSEY, state supreme court justice; b. L.A., July 30, 1947; BA, Wellesley Coll., 1968; JD, Columbia U., 1973; LHD (hon.), Coll. of St. Mary, Omaha, 1993. Bar: N.Y. 1974, U.S. Dist. Ct. (so. dist.) N.Y. 1974, U.S. Ct. Appeals (2d cir.) 1974, Nebr. 1976, U.S. Dist. Ct. (ea. dist.) N.Y. 1975, U.S. Dist. Ct. Nebr. 1976, U.S. Ct. Appeals (8th cir.) 1979, U.S. Supreme Ct. 1982, U.S. Ct. Appeals (6th cir.) 1984, U.S. Ct. Appeals (10th cir.) 1987. Law clk. U.S. Dist. Ct., N.Y.C., 1973-75; from assoc. to ptnr. Kutak Rock, Omaha, 1975-92; judge Nebr. Ct. Appeals, Lincoln, 1992-98, chief judge, 1996-98; justice Nebr. Supreme Ct., 1998—. Contbr. articles to profl. jours. Bd. dirs. Tuesday Musical, Omaha, 1985—. Office: Nebr Supreme Ct State Capitol Rm 2222 Lincoln NE 68509

MILLER UDELL, BRONWYN, lawyer; b. Danbury, Conn., Aug. 7, 1972; BA, Barnard Coll., Columbia U., 1994; JD, U. Miami, 1997. Bar: (Fla.) 1997. Asst. state atty. State of Fla., 1997—; adj. prof. Fla. Internat. U., Miami, 2001—02. Mem. Witness Justice Adv. Bd. With Comtys. in Schs. Miami Mentoring Program, Coral Gables Sr. H.S. Parent Tchr. Assn. Mem.: Ednl. Com., Fla. Prosecuting Attys. Assn., Federalist Soc. Lawyer's Divsn., Elephant Forum, Phi Delta Phi. Office: Office of the State Atty 1350 NW 12th Ave Miami FL 33136

MILLHISER, THOMAS MCNALLY, lawyer; b. Richmond, Va., Mar. 30, 1949; s. Ross Randolph and Eleanor Katherine (McGue) M.; m. Rochelle Diane DeCovny, May 19, 1971; children: Ian R., Neil McG., James McN. BS, Georgetown U., 1971; JD summa cum laude, Washington and Lee U., 1981. Bar: Va. 1981, U.S. Tax Ct. 1984, U.S. Ct. Appeals (4th cir.) 1984,

U.S. Supreme Ct. 2003. Data processing mktg. rep. IBM Corp., Arlington, Va., 1971-73; v.p. Hill-n-Dale Meat Co., Downingtown, Pa., 1973-78; ptnr. Hunton & Williams, Richmond, Va., 1981—. Note and comment editor Washington and Lee U. Law Rev., 1981; contbr. articles to profl. jours. Bd. dirs. ARC, Greater Richmond chpt., 1986-92, chmn., 1991-92, Sch. of Performing Arts in Richmond Cmty., 1986-92, Washington and Lee U. La. Coun., 1990-99, pres., 1994-95, Riverside Sch., 1995—, v.p. 1997—; bd. dirs. Family and Children's Svcs., 1995-2001; trustee The Hill Sch., 2001—, Valentine Mus., Richmond History Ctr., 1999—. Mem. Va. State Bar, Am. Coll. Trust and Estate Counsel, Richmond Estate Planning Coun., Commonwealth Club, Country Club Va., The Hill Sch. Alumni Assn. (pres. 1997-2001), Order of Coif. Avocations: tennis, bridge, swimming, automobiles. Estate planning, Probate (including wills, trusts), State and local taxation. Home: 8703 Berwickshire Dr Richmond VA 23229-7832 Office: Hunton & Williams Riverfront Plz East Twr/951 East Byrd St Richmond VA 23219

MILLIGRAM, STEVEN IRWIN, lawyer; b. N.Y.C., July 16, 1953; s. Harry William and Judith Edith (Soffen) M.; m. Evan L. Greenberg; children: David Michael, Brian Harry; stepchildren: Caitlin Anderson, Kyle Smith. BA, SUNY, Buffalo, 1976; JD, Pace U., 1981. Bar: N.Y. 1982, U.S. Dist. Ct. (ea. and so. dists.) N.Y. 1982, N.J. 1982, U.S. Dist. Ct. N.J. 1982, U.S. Dist. Ct. (no. dist.) N.Y. 1993. Asst. dist. atty. County of Bronx, N.Y., 1982-86; assoc. Meiselman, Farber, Packman & Eberz, Poughkeepsie, N.Y., 1986-91, Drake, Sommers, Loeb, Tarshis and Catania, P.C., Newburgh, N.Y., 1991-96, ptnr., 1996—. Founding atty. Bedford (N.Y.) Mt. Kisco Youth Ct., 1984-85; lectr. Nat. Bus. Inst., 1991, 92, Practising Law Inst., 1993. Contbg. author: Trial Advocacy in New York, 1991, Civil Trial Procedures in New York, 1991, Winning the Slip and Fall Case, 1993. Mem. ABA, ATLA, N.Y. State Trial Lawyers Assn., N.Y. State Bar Assn., Fed. Bar Council, Pace U. Alumni Assn., Orange County Bar Assn. (bd. dirs. 2000—, chmn. law day com.). Jewish. State civil litigation, Insurance, Personal injury (including property damage). Home: 178 Rye Hill Rd Monroe NY 10950-3023 Office: Drake Sommers Loeb Tarshis and Catania One Corwin Ct Newburgh NY 12550 E-mail: smilligram@dsltc.com.

MILLIKEN, CHARLES BUCKLAND, lawyer; b. New Haven, June 2, 1931; s. Arthur and Susan Lord (Buckland) M.; m. Sandra Stewart, July 6, 1957; children: Susan S., Andrew S. BA, Yale U., 1952; JD, Harvard U., 1957. Bar: Conn. 1957. Assoc. Shipman & Goodwin, Hartford, Conn., 1957-60, ptnr., 1961-92, counsel, 1993—. Lectr. law corp. taxation U. Conn. Contbr. articles to profl. jours. Trustee Westminster Sch., Simsbury, Conn., 1969—, sec., 1970-74, chmn., 1974-80; bd. dirs. Hartford Symphony, 1959-74, 1980—, sec., 1960-62, pres., 1962-64; bd. dirs. Greater Hartford Arts Council, 1971-90; trustee Hartt Sch. Music, 1980-94, 95—, chmn., 1988-90; regent U. Hartford, 1988-94. With U.S. Army, 1952-54. Fellow Am. Coll. Trust and Estate Counsel., Am. Coll. Tax Counsel; mem. ABA, Conn. Bar Assn. (chmn. tax sect. 1979-82), Hartford County Bar Assn. Corporate, general, Probate (including wills, trusts), Taxation, general. Home: 56 Ely Rd Farmington CT 06032-1707 Office: 1 American Row Hartford CT 06103-2819

MILLIMET, ERWIN, lawyer; b. N.Y.C., Oct. 7, 1925; s. Maurice and Henrietta (Cohen) Millimet; children: Robert, James, Rachel, Sarah. BA magna cum laude, Amherst Coll., 1948; LLB cum laude, Harvard U., 1951. Bar: N.Y. 1952. Formerly sr. ptnr., chmn. exec. com. Stroock & Stroock & Lavan, N.Y.C.; ret., 1991. Mem. faculty Grad. Sch. Mgmt., U. Mass. Mem. bd. visitors U. San Diego Law Sch.; mem. Five Coll. LIR, Northhampton, Mass.; active Nat. Support Group for Africa; founder Citizens for Am., Washington, 1984; mem. Rep. Presdl. Task Force. Mem. N.Y. State Bar Assn., Assn. of Bar of City of N.Y., Fed. Bar Assn., Rep. Club (N.Y.C. and Washington), Phi Beta Kappa. Corporate, general, Mergers and acquisitions, Securities. E-mail: emill@gis.net.

MILLMAN, BRUCE RUSSELL, lawyer; b. Bronx, N.Y., June 4, 1948; s. Meyer and Garie (Solomon) M.; m. Lorrie Jan Liss, Aug. 12, 1973; children: Noemi, Avi. AB, Princeton U., 1970; JD, Columbia U., 1973. Bar: N.Y. 1974, U.S. Dist. Ct. (ea. and so. dists.) N.Y. 1975, U.S. Ct. Appeals (2d dir.) 1978, U.S. Supreme Ct. 1978. Assoc. Rains & Pogrebin and predecessors Rains, Pogrebin & Scher, Mineola, N.Y., 1973-79, ptnr., 1980—. Arbitrator Nassau County Dist. Ct., Mineola, 1981-83. Contbr. New York Employment Law, 1995, Labor and Employment Law for the Corporate Counselor and General Practitioner, 1994, Updating Issues in Employment Law, 1986, Public Sector Labor and Employment Law, 1988. Bd. dirs. West Side Montessori Sch., N.Y.C., 1984-90, sec., 1985-87, pres., 1987-90. Harlan Fiske Stone scholar Columbia U. Law Sch., N.Y.C., 1971, 73. Mem. ABA, N.Y. State Bar Assn. (chair labor and employment law sect. 1997-98), Nassau County Bar Assn., Indsl. Rels. Rsch. Assn. (bd. dirs. L.I. chpt. 1984—, pres. 1995-96). Civil rights, Education and schools, Labor (including EEOC, Fair Labor Standards Act, labor-management relations, NLRB, OSHA). Home: 60 Riverside Dr New York NY 10024-6108 Office: Rains & Pogrebin PC 210 Old Country Rd Ste 12 Mineola NY 11501-4288 also: 375 Park Ave New York NY 10152-0002 E-mail: bmillman@rainslaw.com.

MILLMAN, JODE SUSAN, lawyer, writer; b. Poughkeepsie, N.Y., Dec. 28, 1954; d. Samuel Keith and Ellin Sadenberg (Bainder) M.; m. Michael James Harris, June 20, 1982; children: Maxwell, Benjamin. BA, Syracuse U., 1976, JD, 1979. Bar: N.Y. 1980, Mich. 2001, U.S. Dist. Ct. (so. and ea. dists.) N.Y. 1982, U.S. Supreme Ct. 1983. Asst. corp. counsel City of Poughkeepsie, 1979-81; assoc. Law Office of Lou Lewis, Poughkeepsie, 1981-85; pvt. practice Poughkeepsie, 1985—; pres. Seats Pub. Co., 2001—. Staff counsel City of Poughkeepsie Office of Property Devel., 1990—; gen. mgr. WCZX-Comms. Corp. Author: (novels) (children's books) Birthday Wishes and Rock'n Roll Dreams, The Firebird Ballet, Goldie Lox and the Three Behrs, (non-fiction) SEATS: New York (150 Seating Plans to Metro N.Y. Theatres, Conceert Halls and Stadiums); contbg. author: Kaminstein Legislative History of the Copyright Law, 1979. Pres. Dutchess County (N.Y.) Vis. Bur., 1980—82; mem. assigned counsel program Dutchess County Family Ct.1985, 1985—; trustee Greater Poughkeepsie Libr. Dist., 1991—94, Poughkeepsie Day Sch., 1995—2002; bd. dirs. Poughkeepsie Ballet Theater, 1982, Jewish Cmty. Ctr., 1988. Mem.: Washtenaw County Bar Assn., Mich. Bar Assn., Dutchess County Bar Assn. (grievance com. 1994—2001), N.Y. State Bar Assn. Democrat. Jewish. Corporate, general, Entertainment, Family and matrimonial. Office: 3997 Preserve Dr Dexter MI 48130 E-mail: jodem54@aol.com.

MILLS, BARRY, lawyer; b. Sept. 8, 1950; BA, Bowdoin, 1972; PhD, Syracuse, 1976; JD, Columbia, 1979. Bar: N.Y. 1980. Mem. Debevoise & Plimpton, N.Y.C. Mem. Assn. of Bar of City of N.Y. Property, real (including real estate development, water). Office: Debevoise & Plimpton 875 3rd Ave Fl 23 New York NY 10022-6225

MILLS, CHARLES GARDNER, lawyer; b. Griffin, Ga., Feb. 29, 1940; s. Charles G. and Marguerite (Powell) M. AB, Yale U., 1962; JD, Boston Coll., 1967; LLM, Touro Coll., 2002. Bar: N.Y. 67, U.S. Dist. Ct. (so. and ea. dists.) 72, U.S. Ct. Appeals (2d cir.) 75, U.S. Supreme Ct. 77, U.S. Ct. Fed. Claims 91, U.S. Ct. Appeals for Vets. Claims 96, U.S. Dist. Ct. (no. dist.) N.Y. 99. Assoc. Smart & McKay, N.Y.C., 1967-68, Smart & Mills, N.Y.C., 1969-71, Eaton & VanWinkle, N.Y.C., 1971-82, Payne, Wood & Littlejohn, Glen Cove and Melville, N.Y., 1982-91; pvt. practice, Glen Cove, 1991—. With U.S. Army, 1962-64, ETO. Mem. Assn. Bar City N.Y., Nassau County Bar Assn., Rotary (pres. Glen Cove Club 1989-90), Am. Legion (comdr. Locust Valley, N.Y. post 1988-90, comdr. Nassau County com. 1995-96, N.Y. Judge Advocate, 1998—), Soc. Colonial Wars, SCV, Order of the Arrow. Republican. Roman Catholic. Civil rights, Federal civil litigation, Libel. Office: 56 School St Glen Cove NY 11542-2512

MILLS, DON HARPER, pathology and psychiatry educator, lawyer; b. Peking, China, July 29, 1927; came to U.S., 1928; s. Clarence Alonzo and Edith Clarissa (Parrett) M.; m. Lillian Frances Snyder, June 11, 1949; children: Frances Jo, Jon Snyder. BS, U. Cin., 1950, MD, 1953; JD, U. So. Calif., 1958. Diplomate Am. Bd. Law in Medicine. Intern L.A. County Gen. Hosp., 1953-54, admitting physician, 1954-57, attending staff pathologist, 1959—; pathology fellow U. So. Calif., L.A., 1954-55, instr. pathology, 1958-62, asst. clin. prof., 1962-65, assoc. clin. prof., 1965-69, clin. prof., 1969—, clin. prof. psychiatry and behavioral sci., 1986—. Asst. in pathology Hosp. Good Samaritan, LA, 1956-65, cons. staff, 1962-72, affiliating staff, 1972-91; dep. med. examiner Office of LA County Med. Examiner, 1957-61; instr. legal medicine Loma Linda (Calif.) U. Sch. Medicine, 1960-66, assoc. clin. prof. humanities, 1966-95; cons. HEW, 1972-73, 75-76, Dept. of Def., 1975-80; bd. dirs. Am. Bd. Legal Medicine, Inc., Chgo.; med. dir. Profl. Risk Mgmt. Group, 1989-2001; med. dir., Octagon Risk Svcs., Inc., 2001—. Column editor Newsletter of the Long Beach Med. Assn., 1960-75, Jour. Am. Osteopathic Assn., 1965-77, Ortho Panel, 1970-78; exec. editor Trauma, 1964-88, mem. editl. bd., 1988—; mem. editl. bd. Legal Aspects of Med. Practice, 1972-90, Med. Alert Comms., 1973-75, Am. Jour. Forensic Medicine and Pathology, 1979-87, Hosp. Risk Control, 1981-96; contbr. numerous articles to profl. jours. Bd. dirs. Inst. for Med. Risk Studies, 1988—; mem. adv. bd. Pacific Ctr. for Health Policy and Ethics, 1997—, chmn., 1999—. Recipient Ritz Heerman award Calif. Hosp. Assn., 1986, Disting. fellow Am. Acad. Forensic Scis., 1993, Genesis award Pacific Ctr. for Health Policy and Ethics, 1993, Founder's award Am. Coll. Med. Quality, 1994. Fellow Am. Coll. Legal Medicine (pres. 1974-76, bd. govs. 1970-78, v.p. 1972-74, chmn. malpractice com. 1973-74, jour. editl. bd. 1984—, gold medal 1999), Am. Acad. Forensic Sci. (gen. program chmn. 1966-67, chmn. jurisprudence sect. 1966-67, 73-74, exec. com. 1971-74, 84-88, v.p. 1984-85, pres. 1986-87, ethics com. 1976-86, 91-2001, chmn. ethics com. 1994-2001, long-term planning com. 1990—, jour. editl. bd. 1965-79); mem. AMA (jour. editl. bd. 1973-77), AAAS, ABA, Am. Coll. Med. Quality (hon. life), Calif. Med. Assn., L.A. County Med. Assn., L.A. County Bar Assn., Am. Health Lawyers Assn., Calif. Soc. Hosp. Attys. Home: 700 E Ocean Blvd Unit 2606 Long Beach CA 90802-5039 Office: 5000 Airport Plaza Dr Ste 250 Long Beach CA 90815-4959 Office Fax: 562-420-5999. E-mail: Don.Mills@octagonrs.com.

MILLS, JERRY WOODROW, lawyer; b. Springfield, Mo., July 17, 1940; s. Woodrow Wilson and Billie Louise M.; m. Marion Cargile, Mar. 27, 1964; children: Eric E., Brendon W. BSEE, Tex. A&M U., 1963; JD, Georgetown U., 1967. Bar: Tex. 1967, U.S. Patent Office 1967. Ptnr. Richards, Harris & Hubbard, Dallas, 1970-82, Baker, Mills & Glast, Dallas, 1982-90; sr. ptnr. BakerBotts LLP, Dallas, 1990—. Adj. prof. So. Meth. U. Law Sch., 1994-97. Bd. dirs. Dallas Legal Svcs. Project, 1972-75, Dallas Theater Ctr., 1999—. Fellow Tex. Bar, Dallas Bar; mem. ABA, Tex. State Jr. Bar Assn. (treas. 1975, dir.), Dallas Jr. Bar Assn. (pres. 1971, Outstanding Young Lawyer award 1975), Dallas Bar Assn. (bd. dirs. 1983-85). Methodist. Patent, Trademark and copyright. Office: BakerBotts LLP 800 Trammell Crow Ctr 2001 Ross Ave Ste 900 Dallas TX 75201-2917 E-mail: jmills@bakerbotts.com.

MILLS, JON, dean, law educator; b. Miami, Fla., July 24, 1947; s. Herb J. and Marguerite (Sweat) M.; m. Beth Bechard; children: Marguerite, Elizabeth. BA, Stetson U., 1969, LLD, 1986; JD, U. Fla., 1972. Mem. Fla. Ho. of Reps., 1978-88, majority leader, 1986-87, speaker, 1987-88; ptnr. McGalliard, Mills, DeMontomollin, Smith, Monaco & Sieg; mem. faculty U. Fla., Gainesville, 1973—80, prof. law, 1988—, interim dean, 1999—2001, dean, 2001—. Bar U.S. Ct Appeals (11th Cir.); mem. Fla. Constitution Revision Commn., 1997—98. Co-author: Voting Rights and Democracy, 1996; contbr. articles to profl. jours. 1st lt. USAR. Decorated Order of Coif; recipient Allen Morris award, 1979-80, 1985-86, Outstanding Legis. award Fla. Health Care Assn., 1982; named Rep. of Yr. Assn. Retarded Citizens Fla., 1981. Mem. ABA, Fla. Bar Assn., Pi Kappa Alpha, Fla. Blue Key. Methodist. Home: 2727 NW 58th Blvd Gainesville FL 32606-8516 Office: U Fla Coll Law 230 Bruton-Geer Hall Gainesville FL 32611 also: PO Box 117625 Gainesville FL 32611

MILLS, KAREN, lawyer; b. N.Y.C., May 5, 1942; arrived in Indonesia, 1984; d. Saul and Agnes Karlin Mills. JD, NYU, 1968. Bar: N.Y. 1969, U.S. Dist. Ct. (ea. and so. dists.) N.Y. 1970, chartered arbitrator: London 2000. Law clk. Messrs, Rubin, Wachtel, Baum & Levin, N.Y.C., 1967; assoc. Messrs, Haight, Gardner, Poor & Havens, N.Y.C., 1968—72; legal and bus. cons. ind. internat. practice L.A., 1973—84, Sydney, Australia, 1973—84; sr. cons. PT. Dharma Raksa, Jakarta, 1984—. Legal advisor tax divsn. Gunawan Prijohandojo Utomo/Arthur Andersen, Jakarta, 1986—93; of counsel Albert Hasibuan & Rekan, Jakarta, 1992—97; lectr. faculty law Tarumanegara U., Jakarta, 1993, Lembaga Pengkajiandan Studi Hukum, Jakarta, Indonesia, 2001—; founder, internat. legal advisor Karim Sani Law Firm, Jakarta, 1997—; arbitrator BANI Singapore Internat. Arbitration Ctr., Asian Domain Name Dispute Resolution Ctr., Hong Kong Internat. Arbitration Ctr., CIETAC, China, PDRCI, Philippines; hon. fellow Ctr. for Internat. Legal Studies; mem. ADR adv. bd. Lloyd's of London Press; legal advisor Lembaga Pengkajian dan Studi Hukum, Jakarta, 2001—. Contbr. chapters to books, articles to profl. jours. Fellow: Singapore Inst. Arbitrators, Hong Kong Inst. Arbitrators, Chartered Inst. Arbitrators (chartered arbitrator); mem.: Internat. Fiscal Assn. (vice chmn. 1995—2002), Maritime Law Assn. Singapore, Asian Pacific Tax and Investment Rsch. Coun., Inter-Pacific Bar Assn. (alt. dispute resolution com.), N.Y. State Bar Assn. (internat. law and practice sect., taxation com.), Internat. Bar Assn. (sect. on bus. law, com. on alt. resolution of disputes, com. on maritime and transp. law, com. on tax law, sect. on energy and natural resources law, Asia Pacific forum, organising com. for seminar on econ. law reform), Am. C. of C. Indonesia (chair legal svcs. com., co-chair taxation com., power, energy and mining and services coms.). Alternative dispute resolution, Finance, Oil, gas, and mineral. Office: Karim Sani Law Firm Jl Jend Sudirman Kav 45-46 Level 11 Jakarta 12930 Indonesia Office Fax: 62 21 577 1947.

MILLS, KEVIN PAUL, lawyer; b. Detroit, Oct. 1, 1961; s. Raymond Eugene and Helene Audrey M.; m. Holly Beth Fechner, June 15, 1986. BA, Oberlin Coll., 1983; JD, U. Mich., 1987. Bar: Mich. 1988. High sch. tchr., asst. dir. summer environ. inst. The Storm King Sch., Cornwall-on-Hudson, N.Y., 1983-84; staff atty. E. Mich. Environ. Action Coun., Birmingham, Mich., 1987-90; assoc. Tucker & Rolf, Southfield, Mich., 1988-89; sr. atty., pollution prevention program dir. Environ. Def., Washington, 1990—. Low-level radioactive waste cons. State Mich., Lansing, 1988; founder Pollution Prevention Alliance, 1991, co-founder Great Printer's Project, 1992, co-founder Clean Car Campaign, 1999, staff to co-chair ecoefficiency Pres. Coun. Sustainable Devel., 1993-95, Auto Pollution Prevention adv. group, 1994-98, EPA Auto Mfr. CSI, 1994-97; mem. adv. bd. Nat. Pollution Prevention Roundtable, 1996-2003; mem. adv. com. Working Group on Cmty. Right-to-Know, 1997—; mem. Nat. Adv. Coun. on Environ. Policy and Tech., 1997-2002; bd. mem. Inst. Market Tranformation to Sustainability, 2001-, Senate Employees Child Care Ctr., 2003-. Bd. dirs., v.p. Ea. Mich. Environ. Action Coun., Birmingham, 1985-87; pres. Environ. Law Soc., Ann Arbor, Mich., 1986-87. Recipient Outstanding Achievement award Environ. Def., 2000, Nominating Com. Soc. Auto Engrs. environ. Excellence in Transp. award, 2000-. Mem.: State Bar Mich. Environmental, Transportation. Office: Environ Def 1875 Connecticut Ave NW Washington DC 20009-5728

MILLS, LAWRENCE, lawyer, business and transportation consultant; b. Salt Lake City, Aug. 15, 1932; s. Samuel L. and Beth (Neilson) M. BS, U. Utah, 1955, JD, 1956. Bar: Utah 1956, ICC 1961, U.S. Supreme Ct. 1963. With W.S. Hatch Co. Inc., Woods Cross, Utah, 1947-89, gen. mgr., 1963-89, v.p., 1970-89, also dir. Bd. dirs. Nat. Tank Truck Carriers, Inc., Washington, 1963—, pres., 1974-75, chmn. bd., 1975-76; mem. motor carrier adv. com. Utah State Dept. Transp., 1979—; keynote speaker Rocky Mountain Safety Suprs. Conf., 1976; mem. expedition to Antartica, 1996, Titanic Expedition, 1996. Contbr. articles to legal and profl. jours. and transp. publs. Del. to County and State Convs., Utah, 1970-72; v.p. Utah Safety Coun., 1979-82, bd. dirs., 1979—, pres., 1983-84; mem. Utah Gov's Adv. Com. on Small Bus.; capt. Easter Seal Telethon, 1989, 90; state vice chmn. High Frontier, 1987—; mem. adv. com. Utah State Indsl. Commn., 1988—, chmn. com. studying health care cost containment and reporting requirements 1990—; mem. expdn. to Antarctica, 1996, Titanic '96 expedition, Iceland expedition, 2001, Greenland expedition, 2001. Recipient Safety Dir. award Nat. Tank Carriers Co., 1967, Outstanding Svc. and Contbn. award, 1995, Trophy award W.S. Hatch Co., 1975, Disting. Svc. award Utah State Indsl. Commn., 1992, Outstanding Svc. award Utah Safety Coun., 1994. Mem. Salt Lake County Bar Assn., Utah Motor Transport Assn. (dir. 1967—, pres. 1974-76, Outstanding Achievement Award 1989), Utah Hwy. Users Assn. (dir. 1981—), Indsl. Rels. Coun. (dir. 1974—), Salt Lake City C. of C., U.S. Jaycees (life Senator 1969—, ambassador 1977—, pres. Utah Senate 1979-80, Henry Giessenbier fellow 1989), Nat. Petroleum Coun., Utah Associated Gen. Contractors (assoc. 1975-77, 88—), Silver Tank Club, Hillsdale Coll. President's Club, Traveler's Century Club. Administrative and regulatory, Transportation. Home: HC 11 Box 329 Kamiah ID 83536-9410 Office: PO Box 1495 Kamiah ID 83536-1495

MILLS, MICHAEL PAUL, judge; b. Charleston, South Carolina, Aug. 25, 1956; s. Paul H. and Shirley (Dulaney) M.; m. Mona (Robinson), Aug. 2, 1976; children: Alysson, Chip, Rebekah, Penn. AA, Itawamba Cmty. Coll., Fulton, Miss., 1976; BA, U. Miss., 1978, JD, 1980; LLM, U. Va., 2001. Bar: Miss., 1980; U.S. Ct. Appeals (Fed. Cir.), 1986; U.S. Ct. Appeals (5th cir.), 1980; U.S. Supreme Ct., 1990. Pvt. practice, Miss., 1980-95; legis. Miss. Ho. of Reps., Jackson, Miss., 1983-95; mem. Nat. Conf. Commr. on Uniform State Laws, 1993—; justice Miss. Supreme Ct., Jackson, Miss., 1995—2001; judge US Dist. Ct. (no. dist.), Miss., Oxford, 2001—. Adj. prof. law U. Miss. Office: Fed Bldg Rm 335 911 Jackson Ave Oxford MS 38655

MILLS, REESE FERRIS, lawyer; b. Oct. 28, 1946; s. Reese and Charlotte Gorman (Ferris) M.; m. Victoria M. Voegele, Aug. 5, 1978. BA, Denison U., 1968; JD, U. Mich., 1974. Bar: Ohio 1975. Tchr. pub. schs., Mansfield, Ohio, 1980—87, City of Galion, 1988—. Trustee Mansfield Meml. Park, 2002—, Mansfield Area Y., 1977—, pres. bd. trustees, 1987—89; trustee YMCA-YWCA Bldg. Corp., 1985—86, pres., bd. trustees, 1988—89. Mem.: Richland County Bar Assn., Ohio State Bar Assn., Univ. Club, Kiwanis. Presbyterian. Home: 1815 Westover Ln Mansfield OH 44906-3344 Office: Mabee & Mills 24 W 3d St Suite 300 Mansfield OH 44902

MILLS, RICHARD HENRY, federal judge; b. Beardstown, Ill., July 19, 1929; s. Myron Epler and Helen Christine (Greve) M.; m. Rachel Ann Keagle, June 16, 1962; children: Jonathan K., Daniel Cass. BA, Ill. Coll., 1951; JD, Mercer U., 1957; LLM, U. Va., 1982. Bar: Ill. 1957, U.S. Dist. Ct. Ill. 1958, U.S. Ct. Appeals 1959, U.S. Ct. Mil. Appeals 1963, U.S. Supreme Ct. 1963. Legal advisor Ill. Youth Commn., 1958-60; state's atty. Cass County, Virginia, Ill., 1960-64; judge Ill. 8th Jud. Cir., Virginia, 1966-76, Ill. 4th Dist. Appellate Ct., Springfield, Ill., 1976-85, U.S. Dist. Ct. (cen. dist.) Ill., Springfield, 1985—. Adj. prof. So. Ill. U. Sch. Medicine, 1985—; mem. adv. bd. Nat. Inst. Corrections, Washington, 1984-88, Ill. Supreme Ct. Rules Com., Chgo., 1963-85. Contbr. articles to profl. jours. Pres. Abraham Lincoln coun. Boy Scouts Am., 1978-80. With U.S. Army, 1952-54, Korea, col. res.; maj. gen. Ill. Militia. Recipient George Washington Honor medal Freedoms Found., 1969, 73, 75, 82, Disting. Eagle Scout Boy Scouts Am., 1985. Fellow Am. Bar Found.; mem. ABA, Nat. Conf. Fed. Trial Judges (chmn. 1999-00), Ill. Bar Assn., Chgo. Bar Assn., Cass County Bar Assn. (pres. 1962-64, 75-76), Sangamon County Bar Assn., 7th Cir. Bar Assn., Am. Law Inst., Fed. Judges Assn., Army and Navy Club (Washington), Sangamo Club, Masons (33 degree), Lincoln-Douglas Am. Inn of Ct. 150 (founding, pres. 1991-93). Republican. Office: US Dist Ct 600 E Monroe St Ste 117 Springfield IL 62701-1659

MILLS, WILLIAM HAYES, lawyer; b. Gordo, Ala., Mar. 30, 1931; s. Early S. and Bama (Cameron) M. LL.B., U. Ala., 1956. Bar: Ala. 1956. Since practiced in Birmingham; partner Rogers, Howard, Redden & Mills, 1961-79, Redden, Mills & Clark, 1979—. Arbitrator Fed. Mediation and Conciliation Service, Am. Arbitration Assn. Served with AUS, 1948-50, 50-51. Mem. ABA, Ala., Birmingham bar assns., Am., ATLA. Baptist. Appellate, General civil litigation, Product liability. Home: 2105 Williamsburg Way Birmingham AL 35223-1740 Office: Redden Mills & Clark 940 Financial Ctr Birmingham AL 35203 E-mail: whm@rmclaw.com.

MILLSTEIN, IRA M. lawyer, lecturer; b. N.Y.C., Nov. 8, 1926; s. Harry M. and Birdie E. (Rosenbaum) M.; m. Diane G. Greenberg, July 3, 1949; children: James Eliot, Elizabeth Jane. BS, Columbia U., 1947, LL.B., 1949. Bar: N.Y. 1949, U.S. Supreme Ct. 1973. Atty. antitrust div. Dept. Justice, Washington, 1949-51; assoc. firm Weil Gotshal & Manges, N.Y.C., 1951-57, ptnr., 1957—. Fellow faculty govt. John F. Kennedy Sch. Govt., Harvard U., 1983-87; Eugene F. Williams Jr. vis. prof. in competetive enterprise and strategy, mem. adv. bd. Yale Sch. Mgmt., 1996—; chmn. pvt. sector adv. group on corp. governance World Bank/OECD-Paris, Washington, 1999—; counsel, bd. dirs. Lower Manhattan Devel. Corp., 2002--; sponsor Global Corp. Governance Forum. Author: (with Katsh) The Limits of Corporate Power, 1981; contbr. articles to profl. jours. Mem. Nat. Commn. on Consumer Fin., 1969-72, chmn., 1971-72; chmn. exec. com. bd. overseers Albert Einstein Coll. Medicine, Yeshiva U., Bronx, N.Y., 1981—; former chmn. bd. trustees Cen. Pk. Conservancy, 1990-99; co-chair NYSE, NASD Blue Ribbon com. on improving audit coms., 1999. Decorated chevalier Nat. Order of Merit, France. Mem. Am. Acad. Arts and Scis. (elected), ABA (chmn. antitrust law sect. 1977-78), N.Y. State Bar Assn. (chmn. antitrust law sect. 1967-68), Nat. Assn. Corp. Dirs. (bd. dirs. 1994—), Met. Club, Quaker Ridge Golf Club. Antitrust, Federal civil litigation. Home: 1240 Flagler Dr Mamaroneck NY 10543-4601 Office: Weil Gotshal & Manges 767 5th Ave Ste 3201 New York NY 10153-0023 E-mail: ira.millstein@weil.com.

MILLSTONE, DAVID JEFFREY, lawyer; b. Morgantown, W.Va., 1946; AB, Johns Hopkins U., 1968; JD, W.Va. U., 1971. Bar: Ohio 1971. Ptnr. Squire, Sanders & Dempsey LLP, Cleve. Co-author: Wage Hour Law--How to Comply, 2001; editor: Ohio and Fed. Employment Law Manual, 2001. Chair regional bd., nat commr. Anti-Defamation League. Mem.: ABA. Labor (including EEOC, Fair Labor Standards Act, labor-management relations, NLRB, OSHA), Administrative and regulatory. Office: Squire Sanders & Dempsey 4900 Key Tower 127 Public Sq Ste 4900 Cleveland OH 44114-1304 E-mail: dmillstone@ssd.com.

MILME, PATRICK JOSEPH, retired lawyer; b. Oct. 2, 1939; s. Hugh A. Milmoe and Mary Francis (O'Connell) Steenken; m. Carolyn Mann, Nov. 30, 1963; children: Mary Kaye Chryssicas, Caroline Pugh, Hugh. BA, Coll. William and Mary, 1959; JD, U. Va., 1962. Bar: N.Y. 1962, Va. 1962, Fla. 1989. With Davis & Polk, N.Y.C., 1965-72; ptnr. Hunton & Williams, Richmond, Va., 1972-2001, ret., 2001—. Chmn. DARE Marina, Inc., Grafton, Va., 1992—, States Roofing Corp., Norfolk, Va., 1994—, Virginia Beach Marlin Club, Inc., Sterling Eagle, 1980—. Trustee Village of Atlantic Beach, N.Y., 1965-72; bd. dirs. St. Joseph's Villa, Richmond, Va., 1985-91, Hanover Tavern Found., 1998-2001. Capt. U.S. Army, 1963-65. Mem. Am. Coll. Real Estate Lawyers. Avocations: boating, fishing. Office: Hunton & Williams Riverfront Plz East Tower 951 E Byrd St Richmond VA 23219-4074 E-mail: pmilmoe@hunton.com.

MILMED, PAUL KUSSY, lawyer; b. Newark, Oct. 15, 1944; s. Leon Sidney and Bella (Kussy) M.; m. Debra R. Anisman, Oct. 23, 1988; children: Laura, Julia. AB, Amherst Coll., 1966; MSc, U. London, 1968; EdM, Harvard U., 1969; JD, NYU, 1975. Bar: N.J. 1975, N.Y. 1976, U.S. Ct. Appeals (2d cir.) 1975, U.S. Dist. Ct. N.J. 1975, U.S. Dist. Ct. (so. dist.) N.Y. 1976, U.S. Dist. Ct. (ea. dist.) N.Y. 1994. Law clk. Hon. Alan B. Handler N.J. Superior Ct. Appellate Divsn., Newark, 1975-76; assoc. Weil, Gotshal & Manges, N.Y.C., 1976-83; asst. U.S. atty. U.S. Atty.'s Office, So. Dist. N.Y., N.Y.C., 1983-93, chief environ. protection unit, 1990-93; of counsel White & Case, N.Y.C., 1993—. Ct.-apptd. mediator U.S. Dist. Ct., So. Dist. N.Y., 1996—. Rsch. editor NYU Rev. of Law and Social Change, 1974-75; editl. adv. bd. Fordham Environ. Law Jour., 1993—; contbr. articles to profl. jours. Mem. bd. trustees The Town Sch., N.Y.C. Mem. ABA, Assn. Bar City of N.Y. Avocation: photography. Alternative dispute resolution, General civil litigation, Environmental. Home: One Gracie Terr New York NY 10028 Office: White & Case 1155 Avenue Of The Americas New York NY 10036-2787 E-mail: pkm@post.harvard.edu.

MILNER, IRVIN MYRON, lawyer; b. Cleve., Feb. 5, 1916; s. Nathan and Rose (Spector) M.; m. Zelda Winograd., Aug. 15, 1943 AB cum laude, Western Res. U. (now Case Western Res. U.), 1937, JD, 1940, LL.M., 1970. Bar: Ohio 1940, U.S. Dist. Ct. (no. dist.) Ohio 1946. Pvt. practice, Cleve., 1946—. Exec. sec., counsel Men's Apparel Club Ohio, Cleve., 1947-48; adj. instr. Sch. Law, Case Western Res. U., 1965-66; spl. counsel Ohio Office Atty. Gen., 1960-70; legal counsel Korean Am. Assn. Greater Cleve., 1973-95. Mem. Cleve. Fgn. Consular Corps., 1970-96, hon. consul Rep. of Korea for Cleve., 1970-96; bd. dirs. Internat. Human Assistance Programs, Inc., 1973-79, voting corp. mem., 1980-88; mem. Republican Nat. Com. Served with U.S. Army, 1941-45, ETO. Decorated Order Diplomatic Svc. Merit-Heung-in medal (Republic of Korea), 1975; named to Disting. Alumni Hall of Fame, Cleveland Heights (Ohio) High Sch., 1983. Fellow Internat. Consular Coll., Ohio Bar Found.; mem. ABA (small bus. com., corp. bus. law sect. 1971-74), Greater Cleve. Bar Assn., Cuyahoga County Bar Assn. (pres. 1975-76, co-chmn. jud. standards com. 1987-88, life trustee, award of Special Merit 1976, Pres.' award 1988), Ohio State Bar Assn. (coun. dels., 1976-86, com. on legal ethics and profl. conduct 1984-97), Cuyahoga County Bar Found. (sec.-treas. 1980-84, bd. dirs. 1984—), Cuyahoga County Coun. Ohio VFW (comdr. 1958, Merit award 1958), Am. Security Coun. (nat. adv. bd.), Cleve. Coun. on World Affairs, Western Res. Coll. Alumni Assn. (bd. dirs. 1982-88), Cleve. City Club, Masons (32 deg.), Tau Epsilon Rho (chancellor Cleve. Grad. chpt. 1987-88), Delta Phi Alpha. Jewish.

MILNER, KENNETH PAUL, lawyer; b. Phila., June 2, 1951; s. Stanley O. and Marcia Elva Milner; m. Ruth Marie Kosonovich, June 16, 1973; children: Zachary Stanton, Adrienne Nicole. BA, U. Pa., 1973; JD, Boston U., 1976. Bar: Pa. 1976, U.S. Dist. Ct. (ea. dist.) Pa. 1976, U.S. Supreme Ct., 2000. Assoc. Law Office of Donald Joel, Phila., 1976-77; assoc. counsel, gen. counsel Cottman Transmission System, Inc., Ft. Washington, Pa., 1977-82; owner Law Office of Kenneth P. Milner, Phila., 1982-88; ptnr. Gold & Bowman, Phila., 1988-90, Starfield & Payne, P.C., Ft. Washington, 1990-94; dir., shareholder McTighe, Weiss, O'Rourke & Milner, P.C., Norristown, Pa., 1994-00; ptnr. Masterson, Braunfeld & Milner LLP, Norristown, Pa., 2000—. Sec., vice chair, chair Montgomery County Realtor/Atty. Joint Liaison Com., 1996—. Pres., counsel, mem. exec. bd., pres. Montgomery County Literacy Network, 1996—; co-chair diversity Upper Dublin (Pa.) Strategic Planning Com., 1993-96. Recipient Chmn.'s award Am. Heart Assn., Eastern Montgomery, Pa., 1996. Mem. ABA, Pa. Bar Assn., Montgomery Bar Assn. (chair franchise law com. 1994-98, 2003, mem. long range planning com. 1998-00, bd. dirs. 1999-2001, mem. exec. com. 1999), Upper Dublin Soccer club (bd. dirs., sec. 1990-96). Corporate, general, Franchising, Property, real (including real estate development, water). Office: Masterson Braunfeld & Milner LLP 702 One Montgomery Plz Norristown PA 19401 E-mail: kmilner@masterbraun.com.

MILONE, FRANCIS MICHAEL, lawyer; b. Phila., June 18, 1947; s. Michael Nicholas and Frances Theresa (Fair) Milone; m. Maida R. Crane, Nov. 25, 1991; children: Michael, Matthew. BA, LaSalle Coll., 1969; MS, Pa. State U., 1971; JD, U. Pa., 1974. Bar: Pa. 1974, U.S. Dist. Ct. (ea. dist.) Pa. 1974, U.S. Dist. Ct. (mid. dist.) Pa. 1979, U.S. Dist. Ct. (ea. dist.) Mich. 1983, U.S. Ct. Appeals (3d cir.) 1978, U.S. Ct. Appeals (4th and 5th cirs.) 1979, U.S. Supreme Ct. 1979. Assoc. Montgomery, McCracken, Walker & Rhoads, Phila., 1974—77; ptnr. Morgan, Lewis & Bockius, Phila., 1981—. Mem.: ABA (labor and litig. sects.), Phila. Bar Assn., Pa. Bar Assn. Federal civil litigation, State civil litigation, Labor (including EEOC, Fair Labor Standards Act, labor-management relations, NLRB, OSHA). Home: 912 Field Ln Villanova PA 19085-2003 Office: Morgan Lewis & Bockius 1701 Market St Philadelphia PA 19103-2903 E-mail: fmilone@morganlewis.com.

MILSTEIN, ELLIOTT STEVEN, law educator, academic administrator; b. Oct. 19, 1944; s. Samuel M. and Mildred K. Milstein; m. Bonnie Myrun, Oct. 1, 1967 (div. Oct. 1992); 1 child, Jacob. BA, U. Hartford, 1966, LLD (hon.) , 1997; JD, U. Conn., 1969; LLM, Yale U., 1971; LLD (hon.) , Nova Southeastern U., 2001. Bar: conn. 1969, D.C. 1972, U.S. Dist. Ct. Conn. 1969, U.S. Ct. Appeals (D.C.) 1972. Lectr. law U. Conn. Clin. Program, 1969-70; staff counsel New Haven Legal Assistance Assn., 1971-72; asst. prof. law, dir. clin. programs Washington Coll. Law Am. U., 1972-74, assoc. prof., dir. clin. programs, 1974-77, prof., dir. clin. programs, 1977-88, interim dean, 1988-90, dean, 1990—. Prof. law, Washington Coll. Law Am. U., 1995—; co-dir. Nat. Vets. law Ctr., 1978-84; cons. Calif. Bar Bd. of Bar Admissions, Nat. Conf. Bar Examiners, law tng. Practising Law Inst., N.Y.C.; chmn. D.C. Law Students in Ct. Program, 1982-83; mem. Law Tchrs. for Legal Svcs. Bd. dirs. Alliance for Justice, 1996-97. Ford Urban Law fellow, 1971-72. Mem. ABA (skills tng. com. 1983-85, govt. rels. com. 1992—), ACLU, Soc. Am. Law Tchrs., Assn. Am. Law Schs. (chmn. sect clin. edn. 1982, accreditation com. 1984-86, chmn. standing com. clin. edn. 1993—, exec. com. 1996-2001, pres.-elect 1999, pres. 2000, William Pincus award for outstanding contbns. to clin. legal edn. 1992). Democrat. Home: 3216 Brooklawn Ct Bethesda MD 20815-3941 Office: Am U Washington Coll Law 4801 Massachusetts Ave NW Washington DC 20016-8196

MILSTEIN, RACHELLE H. (SHELLY MILSTEIN), lawyer; b. Livingston, N.J., Oct. 6, 1968; m. Jed M. Milstein, Sept. 17, 1994. AB in English with honors, U. Mich., 1990; JD, Georgetown U., 1993. Bar: N.J. 1993, U.S. Dist. Ct. N.J. 1993, U.S. Dist. Ct. N.Y. 1994, U.S. Ct. Appeals (3d cir.) 1998. Law clk. Superior Ct. N.J., Union County, Elizabeth, 1993-94; assoc. Fishman & Callahan, East Hanover, N.J., 1994-98, Shanley & Fisher, Morristown, NJ, 1998—2001, Braff Harris & Sukoneck, Livingston, NJ, 2001. General civil litigation. Office: Braff Harris & Sukoneck 570 W Mount Pleasant Ave Livingston NJ 07039

MILSTEIN, RICHARD SHERMAN, lawyer; b. Westfield, Mass., May 9, 1926; s. Abraham and Sarah (Yudman) M. BA, Harvard U., 1948; JD, Boston U., 1952. Bar: Mass. 1952, U.S. Supreme Ct. 1959. Ptnr. Ely & King, Springfield, Mass., 1954-95, Chaplin & Milstein, Boston, 1984-91; sr. counsel Robinson, Donovan, Madden & Barry P.C., Springfield, 1995-98. Dir. Mass. Continuing Legal Edn., 1969-80; cons. dir., 1980—. Commr. Springfield Parking Authority, 1984—90; trustee Cmty. Music Sch., Springfield, 1994—96, Springfield Symphony Orch., 1995—99, Springfield Libr. Mus. Assn., Baystate Hosp. Found., 2001—; overseer Mass. Supreme Jud. Ct. Hist. Soc., 1995—, Boston Lyric Opera, 1999—; trustee Baystate Hosp., v.p., 1995—97; vice chmn. Westfield Acad., 1980—99; chmn. Horace Smith Fund, 1977—93; bd. dirs., v.p. Boston Ctr. for Adult Edn., 1998—; bd. overseers Huntington Theater, Boston, 1999—; mem. vis. com. Mus. Fine Arts, Boston, 2002—. Lt. comdr. USCGR, 1952—64. Recipient Am. Law Inst.-ABA Harrison Tweed Spl. Merit award for contbn. to CLE, 1997, Mass. Bar Cmty. Svc. award, 1998, William Pynchon award for Cmty. Svc. City of Springfield, 1999. Fellow Am. Coll. Trust and Estate Counsel, Mass. Bar Found. (life); mem. Am. Law Inst. (life), Am. Bar Found. (life). Estate planning, General practice, Probate (including wills, trusts), Education and schools. Home: 300 Boylston St Boston MA 02116-3923 also: Mass Continuing Legal Edn 10 Winter Pl Boston MA 02108-4751 Home (Winter): 330 S Ocean Blvd Apt 2E Palm Beach FL 33480 E-mail: rsmilstein@aol.com.

MILSTEN, ROBERT B. lawyer; b. Tulsa, Nov. 6, 1932; s. Travis I. and Regina (Jankowsky) M.; m. Jane Herskowitz, June 24, 1956; children: Stuart Paul, Leslie Jane. BS, Ind. U., 1954; LL.B., U. Okla., 1956; postgrad., So. Meth. U., 1959. Bar: Okla. 1956, U.S. Ct. of Appeals 1956, U.S. Tax Ct 1956. Practiced in, Oklahoma City, 1962—; govt. atty. Office Chief Counsel, IRS, 1958-62; atty. Fuller, Smith, Mosburg & Davis, 1962-63; sr. counsel Andrews, Davis, Legg, Bixler, Milsten & Price, Inc., 1964—, mem. firm, 1966—, dir., 1977-82, 96-98. Mem. S.W. region IRS/Bar Liaison Com., 1994-97. Past pres., trustee Temple B'nai Israel. Served as lt., JAGC USAF, 1956-58. Mem. ABA (com. civil and criminal tax penalties sect. taxation 1962—98), Okla. Bar Assn., Fed. Bar Assn. (2d v.p. local chpt. 1976), Econ. Club Okla., Quail Creek Golf and Country Club, Men's Dinner Club , Phi Delta Phi (treas. 1955-56) Probate (including wills, trusts), Estate taxation, Taxation, general.

MILTENBERGER, HENRY JAMES, JR., lawyer; b. New Orleans, Aug. 24, 1952; s. Henry James and Barbara Douglas (Ellis) M.; m. Cheryl Graddy, June 1, 1974; 1 child, Catherine. BA, So. Meth. U., 1974; JD, La. State U., 1977, CEBS, 1990. Bar: La. 1977; registered profl. liability underwriter. Assoc. Hudson, Potts & Bernstein, Monroe, La., 1977-80; v.p. Gilsbar, Inc., Covington, La., 1980-84, pres., 1984—; ptnr. Miltenberger & Ziegler, Covington, 1980—. Contbr. articles to jours. and mags. Chmn. Christian Businessmen's Com., Covington, 1982-83, 90-91, 91—, nat. bd. dir s., 1995-98; bd. dirs. S.E. La. Youth for Christ, 1983-84; bd. dirs. La. Health Plans. Named to Order of Coif, 1977, La. State U. Hall of Fame, 1987. Mem. ABA, La. Bar Assn., Internat. Soc. Cert. Employee Benefit Specialists, Soc. Profl. Benefit Adminstrs., Profl. Liability Underwriting Soc. Avocations: jogging, running marathons and triathlons. State civil litigation, Health, Insurance. Home: 105 Blackburn Pl Covington LA 70433-9019 Office: Gilsbar Inc 2100 Covington Ctr Covington LA 70433 E-mail: hmiltenberger@gilsbar.com.

MILTON, CHAD EARL, lawyer; b. Brevard County, Fla., Jan. 29, 1947; s. Rex Dale and Mary Margaret (Peacock) M.; m. Ann Mitchell Bunting, Mar. 30, 1972; children: Samuel, Kathleen, Kelsey. BA, Colo. Coll., 1969; JD, U. Colo., 1974; postgrad., U. Mo., 1976-77. Bar: Colo. 1974, Mo. 1977, U.S. Dist. Ct. Colo. 1974, U.S. Dist. Ct. (we. dist.) Mo. 1977. Counsel Office of Colo. State Pub. Defender, Colo. Springs, 1974-76; pub. info. officer, counsel Mid-Am. Arts Alliance, Kansas City, Mo., 1977-78; claims counsel Employers Reinsurance Corp., Kansas City, Mo., 1978-80; sr. v.p. Media/Profl. Ins., Kansas City, Mo., 1981-2000; sr. v.p. nat. practice leader, intellectual property & media Marsh, Kansas City, Mo., 2000—. Reporter, photographer, editor Golden (Colo.) Daily Transcript, 1970; investigator, law clk. Office of Colo. State Pub. Defender, Denver, Golden, 1970-74; participant Annenberg Project on the Reform of Libel Laws, Washington, 1987-88; adj. prof., comm. and advt. law Webster U., 1989-93; lectr. in field. Pres. bd. dirs. Folly Theater, 1992-94. Mem. ABA (chair intellectual property law com. of the torts and ins. practice sect., forum com. on comm. law, ctrl. and Ea. European law initiative), Mo. Bar Assn., Kansas City Met. Bar Assn., Libel Def. Resource Ctr. (editorial bd., exec. com.). Avocations: tennis, golf, skiing, sailing, antique maps. Insurance, Libel, Trademark and copyright. Home: 8821 Alhambra St Shawnee Mission KS 66207-2357 Office: Marsh 2405 Grand Blvd Kansas City MO 64108-2510 E-mail: chad.e.milton@marsh.com.

MIMMS, THOMAS BOWMAN, JR., lawyer; b. Atlanta, Oct. 11, 1944; s. Thomas Bowman and Alice Buehl Mimms; m. Alison Hayward, July 22, 1967; children: Karen Mimms Swift, Christina Mimms Couret. BA, U. N.C., 1965; JD, Columbia U., 1969. Bar: Fla. 1969, Ga., 1999, U.S. Dist. Ct. (mid. dist.) Fla. 1972, U.S. Supreme Ct. 1973, U.S. Ct. Appeals (11th cir.) 1981 Ga. Supreme Ct., 2000. Assoc. atty. Fleming O'Bryan, Fort Lauderdale, Fla., 1969-72; shareholder Macfarlane Ferguson & McMullen, Tampa, Fla., 1972-99. Fellow Am. Bar Found.; mem. Fla. Bar Assn. (exec. coun. bus. law sect. 1987-99, chair bus. law legislation com. 1995-99, chair bus. law bankruptcy/UCC com. 1988-89, chair fin. instns. com. 1993-94), Tampa Bay Bankruptcy Bar Assn. (pres. 1992-93), Columbia U. Alumni Club (dir. 1991-99). Democrat. Episcopalian. Bankruptcy, Commercial, contracts (including sales of goods; commercial financing), Property, real (including real estate development, water). Office: Mimms Enterprises 85A Mill St Ste 100 Roswell GA 30075-4952 E-mail: legal@mimms.org.

MINAHAN, DANIEL FRANCIS, lawyer, retired manufacturing executive; b. Orange, N.J., Dec. 3, 1929; s. Alfred A. and Katherine (Kelly) M.; m. Mary Jean Gaffney, May 2, 1953; children: Daniel F. Jr., John A. AB magna cum laude, U. Notre Dame, 1951; JD magna cum laude, U. Conn., 1964; grad., Advanced Mgmt. Program, Harvard, 1975. Bar: Conn. 1964, U.S. Supreme Ct 1969, U.S. Ct. of Appeals (2d cir.), U.S. Dist. Ct. Conn. 1971. Mgr. indsl. engring. Uniroyal, Inc., Naugatuck, Conn., 1952-59, mgr. indsl. relations, 1959-64, dir. labor relations N.Y.C., 1964-66; v.p. indsl. relations and labor counsel Phillips Van Heusen Corp., N.Y.C., 1966-69; v.p. personnel-adminstrn. Broadway-Hale Stores, Inc., L.A., 1969-70; v.p. employee relations, sec. Magnavox-N.Am., Philips Corp., 1970-73, v.p. ops., group exec., 1973-83, sr. v.p. adminstrn., 1984-89, exec. v.p., 1989-93, vice-chmn., 1991-93; vice-chmn. nat. found. bd. Robert Anderson Sch. Mgmt., U. N.Mex., 1993-98; pvt. practice, 1998—. Trustees adv. coun., Fairfield U., mem. dean's coun. Grad. Sch. Bus. Co-author: The Developing Labor Law, 1971. Chmn. bd. Internat. Fedn. Keystone Youth Orgns., London and Chgo., 1984-88; vice-chmn. nat. found. bd. Anderson Sch. Mgmt., U. N.Mex., 1993-98. With USMC. Mem. The Forum for World Affairs, Conn. Bar Assn., Harvard Club, Club Internat. (Chgo.). Corporate, general, Environmental, Labor (including EEOC, Fair Labor Standards Act, labor-management relations, NLRB, OSHA).

MINARDI, RICHARD A., JR., lawyer; b. Mobile, Ala., Aug. 15, 1943; s. Richard A. and Martha F. (Beck) Minardi; m. Frances Archer Guy, Oct. 21, 1989. BA, Yale U., 1965, LLB, 1968. Bar: Va. 1969. Assoc. McGuire Woods & Battle, Richmond, Va., 1968-71; ptnr. Staples, Greenberg Minardi & Kessler, Richmond, 1971-86, Mays & Valentine, Richmond, 1986-2000, Troutman Sanders LLP, Richmond, 2001—. Mem.: ABA, Richmond Bar Assn., Va. Bar Assn. Corporate, general, Securities, Corporate taxation. Home: 211 Santa Clara Dr Richmond VA 23229-7152 Office: Troutman Sanders LLP PO Box 1122 Richmond VA 23218-1122 E-mail: rick.minardi@troutmansanders.com.

MINER, ROGER JEFFREY, judge; b. Apr. 14, 1934; s. Abram and Anne M. Miner; m. Jacqueline Mariani; 4 children. BS, SUNY; LLB cum laude, N.Y. Law Sch., 1956; postgrad., Bklyn. Law Sch., Judge Advocate Gen.'s Sch., U. Va.; LLD (hon.), N.Y. Law Sch., 1989, Syracuse U., 1990, Albany Law Sch./Union U., 1996; attended, Emory U. Bar: N.Y. 1956, U.S. Ct. Mil. Appeals 1956, Republic of Korea 1958, U.S. Dist. Ct. (so. and ea. dists.) N.Y. 1959. Ptnr. Miner & Miner, Hudson, NY, 1959—75; corp. counsel City of Hudson, 1961—64; asst. dist. atty. Columbia County, 1964, dist. atty., 1968—75; justice N.Y. State Supreme Ct., 1976—81; judge U.S. Dist. Ct. (no. dist.) N.Y., 1981—85, U.S. Ct. Appeals (2d cir.), Albany, NY, 1985—, now sr. judge. Adj. assoc. prof. criminal law State U. Sys., NY, 1974—79; adj. prof. law N.Y. Law Sch., 1986—96, Albany Law Sch. Union U., 1997—; lectr. state and local bar assns.; lectr. SUNY, Albany, 1985; with N.Y. Law Sch. Bd. Trustees, 1991—96; hon. trustee N.Y. Law Sch. bd. trustees, 1996—; mem. jud. coun. 2d Cir., 1992—96; chmn. 2d Cir. Com. on Hist. and Commemorative Events, 1989—94; with Cameras in the Courtoom Com., 1993—96, No. Dist. Hist. Com., 1981—85, State, Fed. Jud. Coun. of N.Y., 1986—91, chmn., 1990—91, Jud. Conf. on U.S. com. on fed.-state jurisdiction, 1987—92; trustee Practicing Law Inst., 1995—2002. Mng. editor: N.Y. Law Sch. Law Rev.; contbr. articles to law jours. 1st lt. JAGC U.S. Army, 1956—59, capt. USAR, ret. Named Columbia County Man of Yr., 1984; recipient Dean's medal for disting. profl. svc., N.Y. Law Sch., Disting. Alumnus award, Charles W. Froessel award for Valuable Contbn. to Law, Albany Jewish Fedn. award, Abraham Lincoln award, Cmty. Svc. award, Kiwanis, others, Ellis Island medal of honor. Mem.: ATLA, ABA, Columbia County Magistrates Assn., Am. Soc. Writers on Legal Subjects, Fed. Bar Coun., Fed. Judges Assn., Am. Judicature Soc., Am. Law Inst., Columbia County Bar Assn., Assn. of Bar of City of N.Y., N.Y. State Bar Assn., B'nai Brith, N.Y. Law Sch. Alumni Assn. (hon.; bd. dirs.), Supreme Ct. Hist. Soc., Columbia County Hist. Soc., Elks (past exalted ruler). Jewish. Office: US Ct Appeals 445 Broadway Ste 414 Albany NY 12207-2926

MINES, MICHAEL, lawyer; b. Seattle, May 4, 1929; s. Henry Walker and Dorothy Elizabeth (Bressler) M.; m. Phyllis Eastham, Aug. 24, 1957; children: Linda Mines Elliott, Sandra, Diane Paull, Michael Lister. BA, U. Wash., 1951, JD, 1954. Bar: Wash. 1954, U.S. Dist. Ct. (we. dist.) Wash. 1957, U.S. Dist. Ct. Mont. 1970, U.S. Ct. Appeals (9th cir.) 1961, U.S. Supreme Ct. Assoc. Skeel, McKelvy, Henke, Evenson & Uhlman, Seattle, 1956-66, ptnr., 1966-68, Hullin, Roberts, Mines, Fite & Riveland, Seattle, 1968-75, Skeel, McKelvy, Henke, Evenson & Betts, Seattle, 1975-79, Betts, Patterson & Mines, 1978—. Moderator Wash.-No. Idaho conf. United Ch. of Christ, 1975-76; trustee Plymouth Housing Group, 1991-97; chair adult edn. bd. Plymouth Congl. Ch., Seattle, 1998-2001. With U.S. Army, 1954-56. Mem. ABA, Wash. State Bar Assn., Seattle-King Bar Assn., Am. Coll. Trial Lawyers (state chair 1984-85), Internat. Acad. Trial Lawyers (bd. dirs. 1991-96), U. Wash. Law Sch. Alumni Assn. (trustee, pres. bd. dirs. 1995-97). Federal civil litigation, State civil litigation, Insurance. Home: 2474 Crestmont Pl W Seattle WA 98199-3714 Office: Betts Patterson Mines PS One Convention Ctr Ste 1400 700 Pike St Seattle WA 98101-3927 E-mail: mpmines@aol.com., mmines@bpmlaw.com.

MINGLE, JAMES JOHN, lawyer; AB in English, St. Joseph's Coll., Phila., 1968; JD, U. Va., 1973. Bar: Md. 1974, Va. 1990, N.Y. 1996. Asst. to pres. Frostburg State Coll., 1973-77, adj. prof. bus. law, 1975-77; asst. atty. gen. State of Md., 1977-89; chief counsel state Md. univ. and coll. sys. U. Md., Md. Pub. TV, 1981-89; gen. counsel U. Va., Charlottesville, 1989-95, lectr. law, 1994-95; gen. counsel, sec. corp., adj. prof. law Cornell U., Ithaca, NY, 1995—. Adj. prof. law U. Md., 1984-88; asst. to bus. mgr. Phila. 76ers NBA Club, 1968-69; city atty. City of Frostburg, Md., 1974-76; joint adv. bd., Cornell Med. Coll., Qatar, 2001—. Mem.: Nat. Assn. Coll. and Univ. Attys.

MINISH, ROBERT ARTHUR, lawyer; b. Mpls., Dec. 25, 1938; s. William Arthur and Agnes Emilia (Olson) M.; m. Marveen Eleanor Allen, Sept. 16, 1961; 1 child, Roberta Ruth. BA, U. Minn., 1960, JD, 1963. Bar: Minn. 1963. Assoc. Popham, Haik, Schnobrich & Kaufman, Ltd., Mpls., 1963-67, 1967-97; ptnr. Hinshaw & Culbertson, Mpls., 1997—. Bd. dirs. Braas Co., Mpls. Mem. ABA, Minn. Bar Assn. Avocations: fishing, traveling. Corporate, general, Mergers and acquisitions, Securities. Home: 331 Pearson Way NE Minneapolis MN 55432-2418 Office: Hinshaw & Culbertson 3100 Piper Jaffray Tower 222 S 9th St Minneapolis MN 55402-3389

MINKEL, HERBERT PHILIP, JR., lawyer; b. Boston, Feb. 11, 1947; s. Herbert Philip and Helen (Sullivan) M. BA, Holy Cross Coll., 1969; JD, NYU, 1972. Bar: Mass. 1973, N.Y. 1976, U.S. Dist. Ct. Mass. 1973, U.S. Dist. Ct. (so. dist.) N.Y. 1976. Law clk. U.S. Dist. Ct. Mass., Boston, 1972-73; assoc. Milbank, Tweed, Hadley & McCloy, N.Y.C., 1973-79; ptnr. Fried, Frank, Harris, Shriver & Jacobson, N.Y.C., 1979-94; mem. adv. com. on bankruptcy rules Jud. Conf. U.S., 1987-93; sr. ptnr. Minkel and Assocs., NYC and Boston, 1994—. Adj. assoc. prof. NYU Law Sch., 1987-94. Contbg. author: American Bankers Assn. Bankruptcy Manual, 1979; contbg. editor: 5 Collier on Bankruptcy, 15th edit., 1979-96; contbr. articles to profl. jours. Bd. advisors Internat. Yacht Restoration Sch., Newport, R.I., Spl. Olympics, Spl. Smiles. Root-Tilden scholar NYU, 1969-72. Mem. ABA, Nat. Bankruptcy Conf., Assn. Bar City of N.Y. Bankruptcy. Home: 68 Bumps River Rd Osterville MA 02655-1525 Office: Minkel and Assocs 131 E 62d St New York NY 10021 also: 112 Revere St Boston MA 02114

MINKOWITZ, MARTIN, lawyer, former state government official; b. Bklyn., 1939; s. Jacob and Marion (Kornblau) M.; m. Carol L. Ziegler; 1 son from previous marriage, Stuart Allan. AA, Bklyn. Coll., 1959, BA, 1961; JD, Bklyn. Law Sch., 1963, LLM, 1965. Bar: N.Y. 1963, U.S. Supreme Ct. 1967, U.S. Tax Ct. 1974, all four U.S. Dist. Cts. N.Y. Ptnr. Minkowitz, Hagen & Rosenbluth, N.Y.C., 1964-76; gen. counsel State of N.Y. Workers' Compensation Bd., N.Y.C., 1976-81; dep. supt. and gen. counsel State of N.Y. Ins. Dept., N.Y.C., 1981-88; instr. CUNY, 1975; ptnr. Stroock & Stroock & Lavan, N.Y.C., 1988—. Adv. bd. Coll. Ins., 1987-90; adj. prof. law N.Y. Law Sch., N.Y.C., 1982—; lectr. ABA, N.Y. C. of C., Practicing Law Inst., N.Y. State Bar Assn., Nat. Assn. Ins. Commrs., Nat. Conf. Ins. Legis.; hearing officer N.Y.C. Transp. Dept., 1970-75; cons. City Coun. N.Y.C. 1969. Author: West's New York Workers' Compensation, 2003, (with others) Rent Stabilization and Control, 1973; (with others) Handling the Basic Workers' Compensation Law Case, 1996, West's New York Worker's Compensation, 2003; co-author: Workers Compensation, Insurance and Law Practice-The Next Generation, 1989; commentaries to McKinney's Consol. Laws, 1982—; mem. editl. bd. Jour. Occupl. Rehab. U. Rochester, 1991—; contbr. articles to profl. jours. Bd. dirs., sec. Kingsbay YM-YWHA, Bklyn., 1978-99, elected dir. emeritus, 1999—; pres. bd. dirs. Shore Terrace Co-op., Bklyn., 1982-83; co-chmn. exec. bd., met. coun., nat. v.p. Am. Jewish Congress, N.Y.C., 1983-91; bd. dirs. Met. Coord. Coun. on Jewish poverty, 1993—, Nat. Conf. for Cmty. and Justice (bd. dir. N.Y. divsn. 1994-2001, nat. bd. trustees 1995-2001, chair N.Y. divsn. 1998-2001). Recipient cert. meritorious svc. Bklyn. Law Sch., Outstanding Pub. Svc. award Ind. Ins. Agt. Assn., citation outstanding performance State of N.Y. Workers' Compensation Bd., Disting. Leadership award N.Y. Claims Assn., City of Peace award State of Israel Bonds, Brotherhood award NCCJ, Man of Yr. award Congregation B'Nai Avraham, Bklyn., 2003. Fellow N.Y. State Bar Found.; mem. N.Y. County Lawyers Assn. (chmn. unlawful practice of law com. 1982-86, mem. profl. ethics com. 1985-91, chair worker's compensation com. 1988-91, bd. dirs. 1997-2001, chair profl. ethics com. 2001—, bd. dirs., exec. bd. 2003—), N.Y. State Bar Assn. (mem. ho. of dels. 1999-2003, chmn. unlawful practice of law com. 1981-83, mem. com. on profl. ethics 1981-84, chmn. com. profl. discipline 1988-92, Sustaining Mem. of Yr. award 1995), Soc. Ins. Receivers, Bklyn. Law Sch. Alumni Assn. (v.p. bd. dirs. 1984-92, pres. elect 1993-94, pres. 1995-96). Office: Stroock Stroock & Lavan 180 Maiden Ln Fl 17 New York NY 10038-4937 E-mail: mminkowitz@stroock.com.

MINNA, ANTHONY JOSEPH, lawyer; b. Toronto, Ont., Can., Aug. 13, 1964; arrived in Switzerland, 1999; s. Antonio and Anne (Capicciotti) M. Student, Johannes-Gutenberg U., Mainz, Germany, 1985-86; BA with honours, U. Toronto, 1987, LLB, 1991; LLM with distinction, U. Brussels, 1992. Bar: N.Y. 1992, Ont. 1994. Articling student Siskind, Cromarty, Ivey & Dowler, London, Ont., 1992-93; lawyer Copeland, McKenna, Toronto, 1995, Walch & Schurti, Vaduz, Liechtenstein, 1996-99; compliance ofcr., company sec. Clariden Trust Mgmt., Zurich, Switzerland, 1999—2002; head adminstrn. UBS Trustees Ltd., Nassau, 2003—. Avocations: cycling, swimming, golf.

MINNEY, MICHAEL JAY, lawyer; b. Lancaster, Pa., Aug. 15, 1948; s. Jay W. and Mary Jane (Erisman) M.; m. Barbara Ann Dunlap, June 28, 1975; 1 child, Michael Jayson. Student, U.S. Mil. Acad., 1967; BA, Ohio Wesleyan U., 1970; JD, Villanova U., 1973. Bar: Pa. 1973, U.S. Dist. Ct. (ea. dist.) Pa. 1974, U.S. Supreme Ct. 1977, U.S. Ct. Appeals (3d cir.) 1979. Ptnr. Minney, Mecum & Kohr, Lancaster, 1975-78, 1978-84; sole practice Lancaster, 1973-75, 84—. Regional council Govs. Justice Commn., Harrisburg, Pa., 1975-78; commr. Pa. Commn. on Sentencing, Harrisburg, 1979-81. Candidate U.S. House of Reps., 16th Dist., Pa., 1974, 76; bd. dirs. United Cerebral Palsy, Lancaster, 1976-84, pres. 1983-84; mem., prin. Bring Back Baseball to Lancaster. Named one of Outstanding Young Men of Am., 1976. Mem. Lancaster County Bar Assn., Pa. Bar Assn., James Buchannan Found. for the Preservation of Wheatland (treas, 1998-99, v.p. 2001, pres. 2002—), Elks, Hamilton Club, Conestoga Country Club (Lancaster). Republican. Lutheran. Avocations: running, golf, photography. Estate planning, Probate (including wills, trusts), Property, real (including real estate development, water). Office: 145 E Chestnut St Lancaster PA 17602-2740

MINOR, JOHN T., IV, lawyer; b. Dalton, Ga., July 6, 1957; s. John T. and Ida (Rogers) M.; children: John T., V, Christopher A. BA, Mercer U., 1978, JD, 1981. Bar: Ga. 1981, U.S. Dist. Ct. (no. dist.) Ga. 1981. Assoc. Smith, Shaw, Maddox, Davidson & Graham, Rome, Ga., 1981-83; ptnr. Minor, Bell & Neal, P.C., Dalton, 1983—. Mem. Kiwanis (bd. dirs. 1984—). Democrat. Episcopalian. Property, real (including real estate development, water). Office: Minor Bell & Neal PC 403 Holiday Dr PO Box 2566 Dalton GA 30722-2566

MINOR, ROBERT ALLEN, lawyer; b. Washington, Oct. 20, 1948; s. Robert Walter and Joan (Allen) M.; m. Sue Ellyn Blose, June 13, 1981; children: Robert Barratt, Sarah Allen. AB in English, Duke U., 1970; JD, Ohio State U., 1975. Bar: Ohio 1975, U.S. Dist. Ct. (so. dist.) Ohio 1976, D.C. 1979. Assoc. Vorys, Sater, Seymour & Pease, LLP, Columbus, Ohio, 1975-82, ptnr., 1982—. Author seminar articles. With U.S. Army, 1970-72. Mem. Ohio Bar Assn., Columbus Bar Assn., Athletic Club Columbus, Scioto Country Club. Republican. Presbyterian. Labor (including EEOC, Fair Labor Standards Act, labor-management relations, NLRB, OSHA), Workers' compensation. Office: Vorys Sater Seymour & Pease LLP PO Box 1008 52 E Gay St Columbus OH 43215-3161

MINOW, NEWTON NORMAN, lawyer, educator; b. Milw., Jan. 17, 1926; s. Jay A. and Doris (Stein) M.; m. Josephine Baskin, May 29, 1949; children: Nell, Martha, Mary. BS, Northwestern U., 1949, JD, 1950, LLD (hon.), 1965, U. Wis., Brandeis U., 1963, Columbia Coll., 1972, Govs. State U., 1984, De Paul U., 1989, RAND Grad. Sch., 1993, U. Notre Dame, 1994, Roosevelt U., 1996, Barat Coll., 1996, Santa Clara U. Sch. Law, 1998. Bar: Wis. 1950, Ill. 1950. With firm Mayer, Brown & Platt, Chgo., 1950-51, 53-55; law clk. to chief justice Fred. M. Vinson, 1951-52; adminstrv. asst. to Ill. Gov. Stevenson, 1952-53; spl. asst. to Adlai E. Stevenson in presdl. campaign, 1952, 56; ptnr. firm Stevenson, Rifkind & Wirtz, Chgo., N.Y.C. and Washington, 1955-61; chmn. FCC, Wash., 1961-63; exec. v.p., gen. counsel, dir. Ency. Brit., Chgo., 1963-65; ptnr. Sidley Austin Brown & Wood, Chgo., 1965-91, counsel, 1991—. Former trustee, past chmn. bd., adv. trustee Rand Corp.; past chmn. Chgo. Ednl. TV; chmn. pub. rev. bd. Arthur Andersen & Co., 1974-83; chmn. bd. trustees Carnegie Corp. of N.Y., 1993-97, trustee, 1987-97; Annenberg U. prof. com. policy and law Northwestern U., 1987—; dir. Annenberg Washington Program, 1987-96. Author: Equal Time: The Private Broadcasters and the Public Interest, 1964; co-author: Presidential Television, 1973, Electronics and the Future, 1977, For Great Debates, 1987, Abandoned in the Wasteland: Children, Television, and the First Amendment, 1995; contbr.: As We Knew Adlai. Trustee Notre Dame U., 1964-77, 83-96, life trustee, 1996, Mayo Found., 1973-81; trustee Northwestern U., 1975-87, life trustee, 1987—; co-chmn. presdl. debates LWV, 1976, 80, presdl. debate commn., 1993—; bd. govs. Pub. Broadcasting Svc., 1973-80, chmn. bd., 1978-80; chmn. bd. overseers Jewish Theol. Sem., 1974-77; trustee Chgo. Orchestral Assn., 1975-87, life trustee, 1987—. With AUS, 1944-46. Named 1 of Am.'s 10 Outstanding Young Men 1961; recipient George Foster Peabody Broadcasting award, 1961; Ralph Lowell award, 1982 Fellow Am. Bar Found., Am. Acad. Arts and Scis.; mem. Northwestern U. Alumni Assn. (medal 1978), Comml. Club (pres. 1987-88), Chgo. Club, Century Club (N.Y.C.). Democrat. Communications, General practice. Office: Sidley Austin Brown & Wood Ste 4800 10 S Dearborn St Chicago IL 60603 E-mail: nminow@sidley.com.

MINSKY, BRUCE WILLIAM, lawyer; b. Queens, N.Y., Sept. 28, 1963; m. Jill R. Heinter, May 1992; children: Aryeh Hanan, Elisheva Yael, Calev Betzalel, Refael Akiva. BA in Polit. Sci., Boston U., 1985; JD, Southwestern U., 1988; LLM in Am. Banking, Boston U., 1989. Bar: Calif. 1988, Conn. 1989, N.Y. 1990, U.S. Dist. Ct. (ea. and so. dist.), U.S. Ct. Appeals. Assoc. Quirk & Bakalor, N.Y.C., 1989-91; house counsel, v.p. Banco Popular N.Am., N.Y.C., 1991—, Banco Poplur N. Am., 1999. Atty. Monday Night Law Pro Bono Svcs., N.Y.C. Mem. Assn. of Bar of City of N.Y. (mem. young lawyers com. 1993-95). Avocations: music, sports, literature. Banking, Corporate, general, General practice. Office: 7 W 51st St New York NY 10019-6910

MINTER, KENDALL ARTHUR, lawyer; b. N.Y.C., May 24, 1952; s. William Arthur and Jerolyn (Johnson) M.; m. Revola Fontaine, Sept. 29, 1954; children: Kamali, Namik, Amani. BA, Cornell U., 1974; JD, 1976; postgrad., U. Pa.Wharton Sch. Fin., 1977. Bar: N.Y. 1977, D.C. 1978, U.S. Dist. Ct. (ea. and so. dists.) N.Y. 1978. Disk jockey, newscaster, salesman, dir. black affairs dept. WKTO and WVBR-FM, 1970-76; founder, chmn. bd. Full Circle Enterprises, Inc., 1972-76; corp. counsel, dir. broadcasting Fairchild Industries, Inc., Germantown, Md., 1976-78, Burns, Jackson, Miller, Summit and Jacoby, N.Y.C., 1978-80; sole practice N.Y.C., 1980-88; ptnr. Minter and Gay, P.C., N.Y.C., 1988-92; of counsel Phillips, Nizer, Benjamin Kirm and Ballon (N.Y.C.), Lewin & Rosenthal (Boston), 1992-95, Golden Goodloe & Assocs., Atlanta, 1995—, Rudolph & Beer, Atlanta, 1997—. Chmn. bd. trustees Rhythym and Blues Found.; bd. dirs. Living Legends Found. Mem.: ABA (forum com on entertainment and sports industry), N.Y. State Bar Assn., Black Entertainment and Sports Lawyers Assn. (founding mem. past exec. dir., gen. counsel), Internat. Bar Assn., Nat. Bar Assn., Order of St. John, Knights of Malta. Avocations: scuba diving, boating, golf. Communications, Corporate, general, Entertainment. Office: Golden and Assocs PC 5398 E Mountain St Stone Mountain GA 30083-3079

MINTON, JERRY DAVIS, lawyer, consultant, retired banker; b. Ft. Worth, Aug. 13, 1928; s. Robert Bruch and Anna Elizabeth (Davis) M.; m. Martha Drew Fields, Nov. 28, 1975; children: Marianne, Martha, John Morgan. BBA, U. Tex., Austin, 1949, JD, 1960; grad. cert., Nat. Trust Sch., Northwestern U., 1960. Of counsel Michener, Larimore, Swindle, Whitaker, Flowers et al., 1991-98; adv. dir. Kanaly Trust Co., Houston, 1992-2000. Vice chmn. 1st Nat. Bank Ft. Worth, 1982-84; chmn., CEO 1st City Bank Ft. Worth, 1986-91. Pilot USAF, 1951-55, pilot Tex. Air N.G., 1955-57; capt. USAFR Ret. Decorated D.F.C., Air medal with 3 oak leaf clusters. Mem. State Bar Tex., Tarrant County Bar Assn., Soc. Descs. of Washington's Army at Valley Forge, SAR, SCV, Mil. Order Stars and Bars, Mil. Order World Wars, D.F.C. Soc., Order Quiet Birdmen, Order of Daedalians, River Crest Country Club, Breakfast Club, Sigma Iota Epsilon, Phi Delta Phi. Episcopalian. Home: 5404 El Dorado Dr Fort Worth TX 76107-3236

MINTON, KENT W. lawyer; b. Independence, Mo., May 16, 1955; s. Roy V. and Donabelle M. Minton; m. Karen S. MacDonald, Oct. 21, 1989; children: Kathy, Megan, Abby. BS, Ctrl. Mo. State U., 1976; postgrad., U. Tulsa, 1979-80; JD, U. Mo., Kansas City, 1982. Bar: Mo. 1982, U.S. Dist. Ct. (we. dist.) Mo. 1982, U.S. Ct. Claims 1986. Assoc. Paxton, Block et al, Independence, 1982-83, Holliday & Holliday, Kansas City, 1983-85; ptnr. Raymond, Raymond & Minton, Kansas City, 1985-96, Stewart, Cook, Constance, Stewart, Minton & Wight LLC, Independence, 1996—. Bd. dirs. Comprehensive Mental Health Svcs. Found., Independence. Contbr. chpt. to book. Mem. Mo. Bar (trust law revision subcom.), Kansas City Metro Bar Assn. (probate com.). State civil litigation, Estate planning, Probate (including wills, trusts). Office: Stewart Cook Constance Stewart Minton & Wight LLC 501 W Lexington Ave Independence MO 64050-3648

MINTZ, ALBERT, lawyer; b. New Orleans, Oct. 19, 1929; s. Morris and Goldie (Goldblum) M.; m. Linda Barnett, Dec. 19, 1954; children— John Morris, Margaret Anne. BBA, Tulane U., 1948, JD, 1951. Bar: La. 1951; cert. tax specialist, estate and adminstrn. specialist. Since practiced in, New Orleans; ptnr. Montgomery, Barnett, Brown, Read, Hammond & Mintz, Hurwitz-Mintz Realty Cos., New Orleans. Bd. dirs. Strauss Distbrs., Avrico, Inc. Mem. editl. bd. Tulane Law Rev. Adv. bd. Law Sch. Tulane U.; chmn., dir. adv. bd. Tulane Summer Lyric Theater; bd. dirs. Tulane Ctr. Stage Talent and Shakespearean Theatre; bd. dirs. Jewish Cmty. Ctr., New Orleans, 1965-72, Jewish Fedn., 1968—, Home for Jewish Aged, 1968-71, Jewish Family Svc., New Orleans, 1968-72; trustee, bd. mgrs. Touro Infirmary Hosp. and Found. chosen as the 1999 recipient of the Judah Touro Society Awd. for his outstanding contribution to the hosp. and its foundation; trustee Jewish Endowment Found.; charter mem. La. Hist. Assn. Recipient Tulane Outstanding Alumnus award, Class of 1951, 2001. Mem. ABA, La. Bar Assn. (lectr., publ. on corp., tax, real estate law), New Orleans Bar Assn. (exec. com. 1971-74), Am. Law Inst., U.S. Hist. Assn., New Orleans C. of C. (chmn. com. civic affairs and state legis. 1968-69), City Energy Club, Tulane Bus. Sch. Emeritus Club, Exec. comm. of the Tulane Emeritus Club; Phi Delta Phi, Omicron Delta Kappa, Zeta Beta Tau. Jewish. Corporate, general, Property, real (including real estate development, water), Estate taxation. Home: 1915 State St New Orleans LA 70118-6251 Office: 3200 Energy Ctr 1100 Poydras St New Orleans LA 70163-1101 E-mail: amintz@monbar.com.

MINTZ, JEFFRY ALAN, lawyer, mediator, consultant; b. N.Y.C., Sept. 15, 1943; s. Aaron Herbert and Lillian Betty (Greenspan) M.; m. Susan Politzer, Aug. 22, 1979; children: Jennifer, Melanie, Jonathan. AB, Tufts U., 1964; LLB, Rutgers U., 1967; postgrad., U. Pa. Law Sch., 1968-70. Bar: D.C. 1968, N.Y. 1970, U.S. Supreme Ct. 1972, N.J. 1973, Pa. 1983; registered mediator, N.J. Law clk. to judge U.S. Ct. Appeals, New Orleans, 1967-68; asst. defender Defender Assn. Phila., 1968-70; asst. counsel NAACP Legal Def. and Ednl. Fund, N.Y.C., 1970-74; dir. Office Inmate Advocacy, N.J. Dept. Pub. Adv., Trenton, 1974-81; pvt. practice Haddonfield and Medford, N.J, 1982; ptnr. Stein & Shapiro, Medford, 1982-83, Cherry Hill, N.J., 1983-84, Mesirov, Gelman, Jaffe, Cramer & Jamieson, Cherry Hill, Phila., 1984-90, Schlesinger, Mintz & Pilles, Mt. Holly, N.J., 1990-92; pvt. practice Mt. Holly, 1992—. Trustee Congregation M'hor Shalom, Cherry Hill, 1990-97; mem. Burlington County and Mt. Laurel Dem. Coun. Com., 1993-95, 2002–; chair Moorestown Dem. Com., 1995-2001. Mem. ATLA, N.J. Bar Assn. (del., gen. coun. 1986-88, 89-91), D.C. Bar Assn., Camden County Bar Assn., Burlington County Bar Assn. (trustee 1989-92), Assn. Trial Lawyers N.J. (bd. govs. 1990-95), Barrister, Burlington Am. Inn of Ct. (founding mem.), Dist. Fee Arbitration Com. (vice chmn. 1999-2000, chmn. 2000-01). Jewish. General civil litigation, Personal injury (including property damage). Home: 22 Lexington Ct Mount Laurel NJ 08054-3701 Office: 129 High St Mount Holly NJ 08060-1401 E-mail: mhlaw@eticomm.net.

MINTZ, JOEL ALAN, law educator; b. N.Y.C., July 24, 1949; s. Samuel Isaiah and Eleanor (Streichler) M.; m. Meri-Jane Rochelson, Aug. 25, 1975; children: Daniel Rochelson, Robert Eli. BA, Columbia U., 1970, LLM, 1982, JSD, 1989; JD, NYU, 1974. Bar: N.Y. 1975, U.S. Dist. Ct. (so. and ea. dists.) N.Y. 1982, U.S. Ct. Appeals (2d cir.) 1982. Atty. enforcement div. EPA, Chgo., 1975-76, chief atty. case devel. unit, 1977-78, policy advisor to regional adminstr., 1979; sr. litigation atty. Office Enforcement, EPA, Washington, 1980-81; asst. prof. environ. law Nova U. Law Ctr., Ft. Lauderdale, Fla., 1982-85, assoc. prof., 1985-87, prof., 1987—. Author: State and Local Government Environmental Liability, 1994, Enforcement At the EPA: High Stakes, 1995; author: (with others) Environmental Law, 4th edit., 2000, State and Local Taxation and Finance In A Nutshell, 2nd edit., 2000; contbr. articles to legal jours. and treatises. Mem. ABA, Environ. Law Inst. Assocs., Fla. Bar (assoc.), Internat. Coun. Environ. Law, Internat. Union for Conservation of Nature (commn. on environ. law), Assn. Am. Law Schs. (exec. com., state and local govt. law sect.), Phi Alpha Delta. Avocations: reading, fitness walking, canoeing. Home: 2060 NE 209th St Miami FL 33179-1628 Office: Nova Southeastern U Law Ctr 3305 College Ave Fort Lauderdale FL 33314-7721 E-mail: mintzj@nsu.law.nova.edu.

MINTZ, RICHARD L. lawyer; b. South Bend, Ind., Jan. 23, 1946; s. Charles and Matilda M.; m. Linda Stern, June 24, 1975; children: Jacob, Brian, David. BA, Antioch Coll., 1969; student, Oxford U., 1996-97; JD, U. Mich., 1971. Ptnr. Ferguson & Mintz, Kalamazoo, 1972; staff atty. Consumers Power Co., Jackson, Mich., 1973-76; mng. ptnr. Roemer & Mintz, South Bend, 1977—. Chmn. endowment investment com. Jewish Fedn. St. Joseph County, South Bend, 1996—, dir., 1998—; dir. Project Future, South Bend, 1998—. Mem. ABA, Ind. Bar Assn. Avocations: golfing, skiing, photography, reading, traveling. Corporate, general, Property, real (including real estate development, water). Office: Barnes & Thornburg 660 1st Source Bank Bldg South Bend IN 46601

MINZNER, PAMELA BURGY, state supreme court justice; b. Meridian, Miss., Nov. 19, 1943; BA cum laude, Miami U., 1965; LLB, Harvard U., 1968. Bar: Mass. 1968, N.Mex. 1972. Pvt. practice, Mass., 1968—71, 1971—73; adj. prof. law U. N.Mex., Albuquerque, 1972—73, asst. prof., 1973—77, assoc. prof., 1977—80, prof. law, 1980—84; judge N.Mex. Ct. Appeals, Albuquerque, 1984—94, chief judge, 1993—94; justice N.Mex. Supreme Ct., Santa Fe, 1994—, chief justice, 1999—2001. Mem. faculty Inst. Preparativo Legal U., N.Mex. Sch. Law, 1975, 79; participant NEH Summer Seminars for Law Tchrs. Stanford Law Sch., 1982, U. Chgo. Law Sch., 1978. Author (with Robert T. Laurence): A Student's Guide to Estates in Land and Future Interests: Text, Examples, Problems & Answers, 1981, 2d edit., 1993. Mem.: ABA, State Bar N.Mex. (co-editor newsletter 1979—83, bd. dirs. 1978—79, 1983—84, sect. on women's legal rights and obligations), Gamma Phi Beta. Democrat. Avocations: reading, bridge, movies. Office: Supreme Ct Bldg 237 Don Gaspar Ave Santa Fe NM 87501-2178

MIQUELON, MIRIAM F. lawyer; b. Elmhurst, Ill. children: Aaron, Rachel. Grad., U. Ariz., 1975, DePaul U., 1978; LLM in Taxation, Chgo.-Kent Coll. Law; postgrad. in Taxation, DePaul U.; postgrad. in History, Northwestern U. Lawyer, Houston, Stone, McGuire, Benjamin & Kocoras, Miquelon and Assocs., 1981—88, Keck, Mahin & Cate, Chgo., 1988—91; asst. U.S. atty. Ea. Dist. N.Y., Bklyn., 1991—93, So. Dist. Ill., 1993—99; asst. spl. counsel to Spl. Counsel John C. Danforth, 1999—2000; asst. U.S. atty. So. Dist. Ill., 2000—02, U.S. atty., 2002—. Adj. prof. law Washington U. Sch. Law, St. Louis; adj. faculty Northwestern U. Coll. Law, Chgo. Recipient Chief Postal Inspector's award, U.S. Postal Inspection Svc., 2001, Spl. commendations, FBI, Drug Enforcement Adminstrn., U.S. Customs Svc., IRS. Avocations: volunteering, sports activities. Office: So Dist Ill 9 Executive Dr Ste 300 Fairview Heights IL 62208

MIRABELLO, FRANCIS JOSEPH, lawyer; b. Ft. Lauderdale, Fla., Mar. 2, 1954; s. Frank Guy and Mary (Sorce) M.; m. Marianna Hay O'Neal, Aug. 5, 1978; childen: Diana H., A. Paul. BS in Civil Engring., Princeton U., 1975; JD, Harvard U., 1978. Bar: Calif. 1978, Pa. 1981, Fla. 1983. Assoc. Irell & Manella, Los Angeles, 1978-81; ptnr. Morgan, Lewis & Bockius, Phila., 1981—. Lectr. law Villanova (Pa.) U. Law Sch., adj. prof. law U. Pa., Phila. Mem. ABA, ACTEC. Clubs: Merion Cricket, Phila. Skating, Commonwealth Nat. Golf. Avocations: tennis, golf. Estate planning, Probate (including wills, trusts), Personal income taxation. Office: Morgan Lewis & Bockius 1701 Market St Philadelphia PA 19103-2903

MIRABILE, THOMAS KEITH, lawyer; b. May 11, 1948; s. Joseph Anthony and Marie Johanna (Reynolds) M.; m. Pamela S. Brogan, Sept. 5, 2002; children: Adrian, Joseph. BA, No. Ill. U., 1972; MA, Northeastern Ill. U., 1974; JD, Oklahoma City U., 1975; postgrad., DePaul U. Bar: Okla. 1976, Ill. 1977, U.S. Dist. Ct. (we. dist.) Okla. 1976, U.S. Dist. Ct. Ariz. 1992, U.S. Dist. Ct. (no. dist.) Ill. 2002, U.S. Ct. Appeals (10th cir.) 1980, U.S. Tax Ct. 1977, U.S. Supreme Ct. 1983, U.S. Ct. of Claims 1985. Prof. sociology Oklahoma City U., 1976-77; prof. bus. Edmond, Okla., 1977-82; ptnr. Mirabile and Assocs. P.C., Oklahoma City, 1977—95; prof. Sch. Law, Grad. Sch. Bus. Oklahoma City U., 1986-95; prof. Grad. Sch. Webster U., 1991—. Vis. faculty DePaul U., Chgo. Mem. Ill. Bar Assn., Okla. Bar Assn. Federal civil litigation, Immigration, naturalization, and customs, Securities. Home: 1902 E Willow Ave Wheaton IL 60187 Office: Mirabile and Assocs PC 1751 S Naperville Rd Wheaton IL 60187-

MIRACLE, DALE NEIL, lawyer; b. Tenino, Wash., Oct. 15, 1936; s. Gordon Tipler and Corine Adriana Miracle; children: Mark, Dawn. BBA, U. Wis., 1958, JD, 1962. Bar: Wis. 1962, U.S. Dist. Ct. (ea. dist.) Wis. 1966, U.S. Dist. Ct. (we. dist.) Wis. 1984. Assoc. Johnson & DeBauffer, Attys., Whitewater, Wis., 1962-64; atty. Travelers Ins. Co., Milw., 1964-67, Wis. Gas Co., Milw., 1967-70, Wausau Ins. Co., Milw., 1970-82, Continental Ins. Co., Milw., 1982-85; prin. Miracle Law Office, Elm Grove, Wis., 1985—. With U.S. Army Res., 1959-64. Mem. State Bar Wis., Waukesha Bar Assn. Insurance, Personal injury (including property damage). Office: Miracle Law Office 13435 Watertown Plank Rd PO Box 5016 Elm Grove WI 53122-5016

MIRMAN, JOEL HARVEY, lawyer; b. Toledo, Dec. 3, 1941; s. Benjamin and Minnie (Krapifko) M.; children: Lisa, Julie, Benjamin. BBA, Ohio U., 1963; JD, Ohio State U., 1966. Bar: Ohio 1966, U.S. Dist. Ct. (so. dist.) Ohio 1966, U.S. Supreme Ct. 1972. Ptnr. Topper, Alloway, Goodman, DeLeone & Duffey, Columbus, Ohio, 1966-85, Benesch, Friedlander, Coplan & Aronoff, 1986-93; shareholder Buckingham, Doolittle & Burroughs, Columbus, Ohio, 1994—. Lectr. Ohio CLE Inst., Columbus, 1972—; mem. Supreme Ct. of Ohio Commn. on Certification of Specialists. Author direct examination CLE materials; contbr. articles to profl. jours. Mem. Ohio Elections Commn., 1976-80, vice-chmn. 1980. Mem. Worthington Hills Country Club, Worthington Hills Civic Assn. (pres. 1992-93). General civil litigation, Family and matrimonial. Office: Buckingham Doolittle & Burroughs 191 W Nationwide Blvd Ste 300 Columbus OH 43215 E-mail: jmirman@bdblaw.com.

MISCHTIAN, JOHN MICHAEL, lawyer; b. Temple, Tex., Oct. 22, 1967; s. Adolf Josef and Joyce Marie (Fiedler) M.; m. Dawna Layne Andel, Nov. 12, 1994; children: Zoe Marie, Nicholas Josef. BA in Music, Tex. Luth. Coll., 1990; JD, Baylor U., 1993. Bar: Tex. 1993. Assoc. Bachus, LePak & Noell, Belton, Tex., 1993-95; pvt. practice Temple, 1995—. Bd. dirs. Ctrl. Tex. Network for Children with Spl. Needs. Grad. leadership Temple, 1996; mem. Cmty. Svc. Adv. Bd., City of Temple. 1996-99, chmn., 1999; bd. govs. Temple Civic Theatre, 1997-2000; pres., 2000; bd. dirs. Temple Symphony Orchestra, 1999—, Central Tex. Network for Children with Special Needs, 2001—. Mem. ABA, Bell County Bar Assn., Bell County Young Lawyers Assn., Bell County Criminal Def. Bar Assn., Lions (bd. dirs. 1999—), Order of DeMolay (past master, Chevalier). Lutheran. Criminal, Family and matrimonial, Probate (including wills, trusts). Home: 1120 N 3d St Temple TX 76501 Office: 204 W Calhoun Ave Temple TX 76501-3127

MISEY, ROBERT J., JR., lawyer; b. Milw., Nov. 1, 1960; s. Robert J. and Catherine C. Misey; m. Monica A. Misey, May 25, 1991; children: Robert J. III, Anne Marie, M. Rose, John Roderick. BA, U. Ky., Lexington, 1983; MBA, JD, Vanderbilt U., Nashville, 1987; LLM in Taxation, Georgetown U., 1991. Internat. tax atty. IRS, San Jose, Calif., 1987—89, internat. tax atty., chief counsel Washington, 1989—96; sr. mgr. in internat. taxation Deloitte & Touche, Nashville, 1996—99; atty. Reinhart Boerner Van Deuren, S.C., Milw., 1999—. Contbr. articles to profl. jours. on internat. taxation. Chair, internat. sect. Music City C. of C., Nashville, 1998—99; dir. Lake Park Friends, Milw., 2002—03. Recipient Man of the Yr., Music City C. of C., Nashville, 1999. Mem.: Wis. Bar Assn. (chair-elect, internat. practice sect. 2002—03). Avocations: sailing, skating. Corporate taxation, Private international, Entertainment. Office: Reinhart Boerner VanDeuren SC 1000 N Water St Ste 2000 Milwaukee WI 53202

MISHKIN, BARBARA FRIEDMAN, lawyer; b. Phila., Feb. 19, 1936; d. Maurice Harold and Gertrude (Sanders) F.; m. Martin S. Thaler, Mar. 22, 1958 (div. 1970); children: Diane Sanders, Paul Sanders, David Emile, Amy Suzanne; m. Mortimer Mishkin, May 27, 1971. AB, Mount Holyoke Coll., 1957; MA, Yale U., 1958; JD, Am. U., 1981. Bar: D.C. 1982, U.S. Supreme Ct. 1989, U.S. Ct. Appeals (4th cir.) 1995. Research psychologist NIMH, Bethesda, Md., 1968-69; spl. asst. to chief judge U.S. Ct. Appeals (D.C. cir.), Washington, 1970-71; spl. asst. to scientific dir. Nat. Inst. Child Health, Bethesda, 1971-74; asst. staff dir. Nat. Commn. for the Protection of Human Subjects, Washington, 1974-78; staff dir. Ethics Adv. Bd. HEW, Washington, 1978-80; dep. dir. Pres.' Commn. on Ethics in Medicine and Research, Washington, 1980-83; assoc. Hogan and Hartson, Washington, 1983-89, counsel, 1990-93; ptnr. Hogan & Hartson, 1994—. Cons. Ctr. for Law and Health Scis., Boston, 1970-73; cons., lectr. Johns Hopkins U. Sch. of Medicine, Balt., 1971-73; bd. dirs. Bon Secours Health Systems, Inc., Columbia, Md., 1984-90. Contbr. numerous articles on health law, med. ethics and biomed. research to jours. in field. Mem. policy bd. Legal Counsel for the Elderly, Washington, 1984-88, vice chair, 1988-90; trustee Mt. Holyoke Coll., 1985-90; mem. Mayor's Adv. Task Force on Hospice Licensure, Washington, 1985-87; bd. dirs. Hebrew Home Greater Washington, 1987-91. Mem. ABA (chair sect. on health and environment 1988-92, chair com. on regulating rsch. 1996-98), D.C. Bar Assn. (subcom. rights of the elderly and the handicapped 1985-92, Pro Bono Atty. Yr. 1988), AAAS (com. on sci. freedom and responsibility 1986-92, AAAS/ABA Nat. Conf. Lawyers and Scientists 1992, ABA co-chair 1993-97), Am. Soc. Law, Medicine and Ethics (bd. dirs. 1995-98). Home: 5610 Wisconsin Ave Apt 402 Chevy Chase MD 20815-4429 Office: Hogan & Hartson Columbia Sq 555 13th St Washington DC 20004 E-mail: bfmishkin@hhlaw.com.

MISSAN, RICHARD SHERMAN, lawyer, educator; b. Oct. 5, 1933; s. Albert and Hannah (Hochberg) Missan; m. Aileen Louise Missan; children: Hliary, Andrew, Wendy. BA, Yale U., 1955, JD, 1958. Bar: NY 59, U.S. Dist. Ct. (so. and ea. dists.) NY 79, U.S. Ct. Appeals (2d cir.) 93. Assoc. Kaye, Scholer, Fierman, Hays & Handler, N.Y.C., 1962—67; ptnr. Schoenfeld & Jacobs, N.Y.C., 1968—78, Walsh & Frisch, N.Y.C., 1979—80, Gersten, Savage & Kaplowitz, N.Y.C., 1980—87; v.p., gen. counsel Avis, Inc., 1987—88; pvt. practice N.Y.C., 1988—. Spl. prof. law Hofstra U., 1988—; mem. panel of mediators U.S. Dist. Ct. (ea. dist.) NY. Revision author: Corporations, New York Practice Guide (Business and Commercial). Mem.: ABA, Assn. Bar City NY (mem. com. on corrections, chmn. subcom. on legis., chmn. subcom. on juveinle facilities, mem. com. on atomic energy, mem. com. on mcpl. affairs, mem. com. on housing and urban devel.), Fed. Bar Coun., NY State Bar Assn., Yale Club. General civil litigation, Corporate, general, Property, real (including real estate development, water).

MITCHELL, ALLAN EDWIN, lawyer; b. Okemah, Okla., May 13, 1944; m. Neva G. Ream; children: Brian E. Mitchell, Amy E. Harrison. BA in Mass. Comm., Northwestern Okla. State U., Alva, 1991; JD, U. Okla., 1994. Bar: Okla. 1994, U.S. dist. ct. (we. and no. dists.) 1994. Asst. state mgr. Oklahomans for Right to Work, Oklahoma City, 1967-68; exec. dir. London Sq. Village, Oklahoma City, 1968-73; dist. mgr. Farmland Ins. Svc., Oklahoma City, 1974-80, Nat. Farmers Union, Oklahoma City, 1980-85; dist. agt. Prudential Ins., Cherokee, Okla., 1985-89; atty. Hughes & Grant, Oklahoma City, 1994-96, Collins & Mitchell, Cherokee, Okla., 1996—2000; asst. dist. atty Woods County, Okla., 1996—. Mem. Cherokee Bd. Edn., 1985-90; mem. fin. com. Rep. Party of Okla., 1995, state com., 1997X; scoutmaster, 1981-86, bd. mem. Great Salt Plains Coun. Boy Scouts Am.; adult advisor Girl Scouts Am.; pres. United Way Cherokee, 1984; mem. Okla. Sch. Bd. Mems. Legis. Network, 1985-90, state com. Okla. Rep. Party, 1997; vol. Okla. Spl. Olympics, 1996, 97; lay min. Ch. of the Nazarene. Avocations: public speaking, politics, civic activities. Corporate, general, Criminal, General practice. Office: Office of Dist Atty Woods County Courthouse Alva OK 73717

MITCHELL, BRIANE NELSON, lawyer; b. Seattle, July 4, 1953; s. Robert Max and Frances Marie (Nelson) M.; m. Suzanne Harmatz; children: Brianne Nelson, Brittany Suzanne. AB, Columbia U., 1975; JD, U. Idaho, 1978. Law clk. U.S. Ct. Appeals (9th cir.), 1978-80; assoc. Debevoise & Plimpton, N.Y.C., 1980-84, Paul, Hastings, Janofsky & Walker, L.A., 1984-86, ptnr., 1986-93; with McCambridge, Deixler & Marmaro, L.A., 1994-95; ptnr. Shapiro, Mitchell & Dupont LLP, Santa Monica, 1996-2000, Manatt, Phelps & Phillips LLP, L.A., 2000—. Mem. adv. bd. U. Idaho Law Sch. Mem. adv. coun. U. Idaho Coll. Law, 2002—. Mem.: ABA, Calif. Bar Assn., N.Y. State Bar Assn., Idaho Bar Assn. General civil litigation, Private international, Securities. Office: Manatt Phelps & Phillips LLP 11355 W Olympic Blvd Los Angeles CA 90064-1614 E-mail: bnmitchell@manatt.com.

MITCHELL, BURLEY BAYARD, JR., lawyer; b. Oxford, N.C., Dec. 15, 1940; s. Burley Bayard and Dorothy Ford (Champion) M.; m. Mary Lou Willett, Aug. 3, 1962; children: David Bayard, Catherine Morris. BA with honors, N.C. State U., 1966, DHL (hon.), 1995; JD, U. N.C., 1969; LLD (hon.), Campbell U., 1998. Bar: N.C. 1969, U.S. Ct. Appeals (4th cir.) 1970, U.S. Ct. Appeals (3d cir.) 2002, U.S. Supreme Ct. 1972. Asst. atty. gen. State of N.C., Raleigh, 1969-72, dist. atty., 1973-77, judge Ct. Appeals, 1977-79, sec. crime control, 1979-82; justice Supreme Ct. N.C., Raleigh, 1982-94; chief justice Supreme Ct. of N.C., Raleigh, 1995-99; ptnr. Womble Carlyle Sandridge and Rice, Raleigh, 1999—; atty. Womble Carlyle Sandridge and Rice, PLLC, 2002—. Served with USN, 1958-62, Asia. Recipient N.C. Nat. Guard Citizen Commendation award, 1982 Mem. ABA, VFW, N.C. Bar Assn., Mensa, Am. Legion, Phi Beta Kappa. Democrat. Methodist. Home: 4301 City of Oaks Wynd Raleigh NC 27612-5316 Office: First Union Cptl Ctr Ste 2100 PO Box 831 Raleigh NC 27602-0831

MITCHELL, CAROL ANN, lawyer; b. New Bedford, Mass., Sept. 2, 1957; d. John E. and Edith A. (Mogensen) M. AB, Vassar Coll., 1979; JD, William and Mary Coll., 1982. Bar: D.C. 1983, U.S. Ct. Appeals (Fed. cir.) 1988, U.S. Ct. Internat. Trade 1986. Atty.-advisor Benefits Rev. Bd., Washington, 1982-83; import compliance specialist Internat. Trade Adminstrn. U.S. Dept. Commerce, Washington, 1983-85; assoc. Collier, Shannon & Scott, Washington, 1985-90, Akin, Gump, Strauss, Hauer & Feld, Washington, 1990-91, Dewey, Ballantine, Washington, 1991-94; of counsel Steptoe & Johnson, Washington, 1994—2002. Mem. Vassar Club. Administrative and regulatory, Immigration, naturalization, and customs, Private international.

MITCHELL, DAVID BENJAMIN, lawyer, mediator, arbitrator; b. Miami Beach, Fla., Nov. 3, 1950; s. Quintus Eugene and Gertrude (Ziegler) M.; m. Lynn Stewart, Dec. 11, 1993. BA, U. Miami, Coral Gables, Fla., 1973; JD, Stetson U., 1978. Bar: Fla. 1979, U.S. Dist. Ct. (so. dist.) Fla. 1979, U.S. Tax Ct. 1987; cert. family mediator; cert. arbitrator; cert. ins. mediator. Assoc., sr. assoc. Semet, Lickstein, Morgenstern & Berger, P.A., Coral Gables, 1987-90; pres. David B. Mitchell, P.A., Coral Gables, 1990—. Pres. South Fla. Mediation Assocs., Inc., Coral Gables, 1990-92. Mem. Coral Gables Cmty. Found., 1996—; grad. Leadership Miami, 1987; bd. dirs. Ponce de Leon Devel. Assn., pres., 1992-93; bd. dirs. Internat. Zen Found. of Fla., 1997—, Coral Gables Citizens Crime Watch, 1998—, pres., 2001-2003. Recipient Key to the City of Coral Gables, 1993. Mem. The Fla. Bar (mem. family law sect.), Dade County Bar Assn. (family law com., county cts. com., Cert. of Appreciation 1994-95), Coral Gables Bar Assn. (law day com. 1996, scholarship com. 1996, bd. dirs. 1997—, pres. 2003-), Cuban-Am. Bar Asssn., Fed. Bar Assn. (appellate arbitrator, prudential class action remediation plan 1999-2001), Acad. Family Mediators, U. Miami Alumni Club of Greater Miami (sec., dir. 1996-98), Coral Gables C. of C. (govt. affairs and legal com. 1995—), Republican Nat. Lawyers Assn., Coral Gables City-Wide Anti-Crime Com. (mayoral appointee, vice-chmn. 2002-), SAR (chpt. v.p. 2002-), Coral Gables Cmty. Found., Rotary Club Coral Gables (dir. 2001-). Republican. Buddhist. Avocations: reading, genealogy, travel. Corporate, general, Family and matrimonial. Office: Gables Internat Plz #1001 Coral Gables FL 33134 E-mail: mitchelaw@aol.com.

MITCHELL, DAVID WALKER, lawyer; b. Oakland, Calif., Nov. 11, 1935; s. Theodore Boyd and Helen Louise (Walker) M.; m. Carolyn Hilliard Graves, July 29, 1961; children: Sarah, Betsy. AB in History, Stanford U., 1957; JD, Harvard U., 1960. Bar: Calif. 1961. Assoc. Kindel & Anderson, L.A., 1961-65, Weir, Hopkins, Donovan, San Jose, Calif., 1965-68; ptnr. Hopkins, Mitchell & Carley, San Jose, 1968-87, McCutchen, Doyle, Brown & Enersen, San Jose, 1987-93, Hoge, Fenton, Jones & Appel, San Jose, 1993-2000, of counsel, 2001—. Bd. dirs. Peninsula Open Space Trust, Menlo Park, Calif., 1982—, pres., 1984-92; bd. dirs. Cmty. Found. Silicon Valley., San Jose, 1977-94, 99-2003; chair bd. trustees United Way Santa Clara County, 1983-85. Fellow Am. Bar Found., Am. Leadership Forum (sr.); mem. Santa Clara County Bar Assn. (trustee 1972-75), San Jose C. of C. (bd. dirs. 1975-80). Mem. United Ch. of Christ. Avocations: music, hiking. Property, real (including real estate development, water), Estate taxation, Taxation, general. Office: Hoge Fenton Jones Appel 60 S Market St Ste 1400 San Jose CA 95113-2396 E-mail: dwm@hogefenton.com.

MITCHELL, GARY COLAS, lawyer; b. Santa Fe, Oct. 27, 1950; s. Arney C. and Flocy Manon (Switzer) M.; m. Sharon Lee Stidley, Sept. 2, 1973 (div. 1982); children— Colter Monroe Stidley Mitchell, Shilo Manon Stidley Mitchell; m. Patricia Anne Tully, Aug. 25, 1983; 1 child, Jessica Tricia Tully Mitchell. B.A., Ill. Wesleyan U., 1973; J.D., U. Puget Sound, 1976. Bar: N.Mex. 1977, U.S. Dist. Ct. N.Mex. 1977, U.S. Ct. Appeals (10th cir.) 1982, U.S. Supreme Ct. 1982. Ptnr. firm Payne & Mitchell, Ruidoso, N.Mex., 1977-83; pres. firm Gary C. Mitchell, P.C., Ruidoso, 1983— ; mng. ptnr. Mitchell Bros. Enterprises, Aragon, N.Mex., 1978— ; pres. Tully-Mitchell, Inc., Ruidoso, 1984— . Bd. dirs. Ruidoso Hondo Valley Hosp., 1981— ; mem. exec. com. N.Mex. Democratic Party, 1982— ; chmn. Lincoln County Dem. Party, 1984-87; bd. dirs. LIncoln County Med. Ctr., 1982—; mem. N.Mex. Bar Found., Am. Assn. Trial Lawyers, N.Mex. State Racing Commn., Albuquerque, 1984-87. Mem. N.Mex. Criminal Lawyers Assn., N.Mex. Trial Lawyers Assn., Nat. Assn. Criminal Def. Lawyers, Assn. Trial Lawyers Am., ABA. Methodist. Avocation: cattle and horse ranching. Criminal, State civil litigation, Constitutional, Civil rights. Home and Office: PO Box 2460 Ruidoso NM 88355-2460

MITCHELL, HENRY ALLEN, JR., lawyer, insurance company executive; b. High Point, NC, Oct. 18, 1935; s. Henry Allen and Connie Estelle (Idol) M.; m. Helen Heck, June 6, 1958; children: Henry Allen III, Michael William, Martha Helen. AB in Econs., Guilford Coll., 1957; JD, Wake Forest U., 1961. Bar: N.C. 1961. Law clk. U.S. Dist. Ct., Greensboro, N.C., 1961-63; assoc. Smith, Leach, Anderson & Dorsett, Raleigh, N.C., 1963-70; dep. gen. counsel Export-Import Bank U.S., Washington, 1970-71; ptnr. Smith, Anderson, Blount & Mitchell, Raleigh, 1971-78, Smith, Anderson, Blount, Dorsett, Mitchell & Jernigan, LLP, Raleigh, 1978—; bd. dirs. Lawyers Mut. Liability Ins. N.C., Raleigh, 1978—, chmn. bd. dirs., 1985—. Bd. dirs., exec. com. Ga. Lawyers Ins. Co., 2002—. Bd. dirs. NC Symphony Soc., Raleigh, 1991—. Mem.: Fellows of Am. Bar Found. (state chair 2003—), N.C. Bar Assn. (v.p. 2003—). Republican. Presbyterian. Avocations: travel, classical music, tennis, hiking. Administrative and regulatory, Corporate, general, Insurance. Home: 3424 Williamsborough Ct Raleigh NC 27609-6367 Office: Smith Anderson Blount Et Al 2500 1st Union Capital Ctr 150 Fayetteville Street Mall Raleigh NC 27601-1395 E-mail: hmitchell@smithlaw.com.

MITCHELL, HUGH ALLEN, JR., lawyer; b. Olney, Md., May 9, 1956; s. Ruth Anne (Waple) M.; m. Denise A. Eldridge, Aug. 19, 1979; children: Jason, Samuel, Timothy, Hugh, Kayla, Josiah, Eben, Evangeline. BA in Econs., U. Md., 1977; JD, U. Va., 1980. Bar: Md. 1980, D.C. 1982. Law clk. to Hon. Ridgely P. Melvin, Jr., Md. Ct. Spl. Appeals, Annapolis, 1980-81; assoc. Glassie, Pewett, Dudley, Beebe & Shanks, Washington, 1981-83, Law Office Ronald R. Holden, Annapolis, Md., 1983-87; dir. devel. Annapolis Area Christian Sch., 1987-91; assoc. Barr & Testa, P.A., Balt., 1991-93; ptnr. Barr & Mitchell, P.A., Balt., 1993-96, Stewart, Plant & Blumenthal, LLC, Balt., 1996—. Spkr., instr. Md. Inst. for Continuing Edn. Lawyers, Balt. and Annapolis, 1992—, Md. Assn. CPAs, Balt. and Gambrills, Md., 1995—. Contbr. articles to law publs. Elder Evang. Presbyn. Ch., Annapolis, 1985-89; founder, pres. Recreational Youth Athletic League, Annapolis, 1993-99; mem. Anne Arundel County Human Rights Adv. Com., Annapolis, 1994-97. Fellow Am. Coll. Trust and Estate Counsel; mem. Md. Bar Assn. (augmented estate com. 1994-2000, coun. elder law sect. 1994-96, coun. estates and trusts sect. 1996-98), Phi Beta Kappa. Avocations: reading, teaching. Estate planning, Probate (including wills, trusts), Estate taxation. Office: 7 Saint Paul St Ste 910 Baltimore MD 21202-1672

MITCHELL, JACK H., III, lawyer; b. Birmingham, Ala., Sept. 9, 1947; BSChE, Clemson U., 1969; JD, Vanderbilt U., 1972. Bar: S.C. Assoc. Horton Law Firm, Greenville, SC, 1973—74, John M. Dillard PA, Greenville, 1974—75; ptnr. Dillard & Mitchell, Greenville, 1975—77, Dillard Mitchell & Ariail, Greenville, 1977—79, Mitchell & Ariail, Greenville, 1979—97; pvt. practice Jack H. Mitchell III, Atty., Greenville, 1997—. Lt. USAF, 1972—73. Mem.: S.C. State Bar Assn., Poinsett Club, Cotillion Club. Episcopalian. Home: 128 Bridgeton Dr Greenville SC 29615-2653 Office: 119 Williams St Greenville SC 29601-3144

MITCHELL, JAMES ALBEE, lawyer; b. Grand Rapids, Mich., Aug. 27, 1943; s. Charles Abram and Helen Eloise (Albee) M.; m. Helen Joan Segard, Dec. 29, 1967; children— Christopher Albee, Andrew Charles. B.S. in Chemistry, Mich. Technol. U., 1965; J.D., U. Mich., 1968. Bar: Mich. 1968, U.S. Ct. Customs and Patent Appeals 1974, U.S. Ct. Appeals (Fed. cir.) 1982, U.S. Ct. Appeals (6th cir.) 1974, U.S. Ct. Appeals (5th cir.) 1975, U.S. Ct. Appeals (8th cir.) 1981, U.S. Dist. Ct. (we. dist.) Mich. 1968, U.S. Supreme Ct. 1981. Assoc., Price, Heneveld, Cooper, Dewitt & Litton, Grand Rapids, Mich., 1968-73, ptnr., 1973— ; speaker patent, trademark, copyright law; instr. seminar in field. Contbr. articles to legal jours. Exec. com. Kent County Reps., 1974-78, 80-82, 86-88; chmn. Fifth Congl. Dist. Conservative Caucus; state co-chmn. Jack Kemp for Pres.; elder Reformed Ch.; trustee Mich. Tech. Fund; mem. jud. selection com. We. Dist. Mich.; chmn. bd. control Mich. Tech. U. Mem. ABA, Mich. Bar Assn. (exec. council for patent and trademark sect.), Grand Rapids Bar Assn., L'Association International pour la Protection de la Propriete Industrial, U.S. Patent Law Assn., Mich. Patent Law Assn., Patent and Trademark Inst. Can., Theta Tau (outstanding achievement award). Private international, Patent, Trademark and copyright. Office: Price Heneveld Cooper DeWitt & Litton 695 Kenmoor Ave SE Grand Rapids MI 49546-2375

MITCHELL, JANET E. mediator; b. Staunton, Va., Mar. 29, 1951; d. Olden Davis and Myrtle Belle Mitchell; children: David Mitchell-Dix, Daniel Mitchell-Dix. BA in Psychology and Polit. Sci., Elmhurst Coll., Ill., 1972; JD, U. Mich. Law Sch., Ann Arbor, 1976. Bar: Ind. 1976, Oreg. 1981. Co-dir. Ft. Wayne Mediation Ctr., Ind., 1988—92; dir. Midwest Mediation Tng., Ft. Wayne, Ind., 1992—. Mem. adv. bd. IPFW, 1989—. Contbr. chapters to books. Practitioner mem. Acad. of Family Mediations, Washington, NC, 1987—99; mem. steering com. Min. of Reconciliation, Elgin, Ill., 1983—88; co-founder Common Ground, Ft. Wayne, Ind., 1993—99; mem. Ch. of the Brethren. Recipient Svc. award, Maltnomah Bar Assn. Young Lawyers, 1984, Peace award, Associated Chs. of Ft. Wayne and Allen County, 1996. Mem.: ABA (homelessness com. mem. 1984—86, standing com. mem., Lawyers Pub. Com. Svc. 1983—87), Assn. for Conflict Resolution (advanced practitioner 1999—). Achievements include mediating more than 600 disputes. Office: Janet E Mitchell Mediator 10431 Octe Valley Rd Fort Wayne IN 46865 Office Fax: 260-483-7660. E-mail: JanetEMitchell@aol.com.

MITCHELL, LYNDA J. lawyer; b. Newburgh, N.Y., June 25, 1959; d. George Balogh and Doris Mae Jurgens. BA, SUNY, New Paltz, 1981; JD, Pace U., 1989. Bar: N.Y., Conn. Probation officer Orange County Probation Dept., Goshen, NY, 1981—86; asst. dist. atty. Orange County Dist. Atty.'s Office, Goshen, 1989—. Office: Orange County Dist Attys Office 255 Main St Walden NY 12586

MITCHELL, MEADE WESTMORELAND, lawyer; b. Pascagoula, Miss., Aug. 20, 1968; s. Melvin U. and Sara (Westmoreland) M.; m. Holly Henderson, Dec. 31, 1995; children: William Westmoreland, Mary Elliot. B in Acctg., U. Miss., 1990, JD, 1993. Bar: Miss. 1993, U.S. Dist. Ct. (so. dist.) Miss. 1993, U.S. Ct. Appeals (5th cir.) 1993. Law clk. U.S. Dist. Ct. So. Dist. Miss., Jackson, 1993-94; assoc. Holcomb, Dunbar P.A., Jackson, 1994-97; ptnr. Butler, Snow, O'Mara, Stevens & Cannada, P.L.L.C., Jackson, 1997—. Contbr. articles and comments to law jours. Mem. ABA, Def. Rsch. Inst., Miss. Def. Lawyers Assn., Jackson Young Lawyers Assn. (pres. 2000-01), Hinds County Bar Assn. (bd. dirs. 1998-2000). Avocations: swimming, golf, jogging. Bankruptcy, State civil litigation, Insurance. Office: PO Box 22567 Jackson MS 39225-2567 E-mail: meademitchell@butlersnow.com.

MITCHELL, RONNIE MONROE, lawyer, educator; b. Clinton, N.C., Nov. 10, 1952; s. Ondus Corneilius and Margaret Ronie (Johnson) M.; m. Martha Cheryl Coble, May 25, 1975; children: Grant Stephen, Mitchell, Meredith Elizabeth Mitchell. BA, Wake Forest U., 1975, JD, 1978. Bar: N.C. 1978, U.S. Dist. Ct. (ea. dist.) N.C. 1978, U.S. Ct. Appeals (4th cir.) 1983, U.S. Supreme Ct. 1984. Assoc. atty. Brown, Fox & Deaver, Fayetteville, N.C., 1978-81; ptnr. Harris, Sweeny & Mitchell, Fayetteville, 1981-91, Harris, Mitchell & Hancox, 1991-96, Harris & Mitchell, 1997-98, Harris, Mitchell, Burns & Brewer, 1998-2000, Mithchell, Brewer, Richardson, Adams, Burns and Boughman, 2000—. Adj. prof. law Norman Adrian Wiggins Sch. of Law, Campbell U.; bd. dirs. Mace, Inc. Contbr. chpts. to books. Chmn. Cumberland County Bd. Adjustment, 1985-92, Cumberland County Rescue Squad, 1986-93; bd. dirs. Cumberland County Rescue Squad, Fayetteville, 1983-91. Recipient U.S. Law Week award Bur. Nat. Affairs, 1978. Mem. ABA, ATLA, Twelfth Judicial Dist. Bar Assn. (pres. 1988-89), N.C. Bar Assn. (councillor Young Lawyers divsn. 1982-85), N.C. Legis. Rsch. Commn. (family law com. 1994), Cumberland County Bar Assn. (mem. family law com., N.C. State Bar Bd. legal specialization), N.C. Acad. Trial Lawyers, Fayetteville Ind. Light Infantry Club, Dem. Men's Club (pres. 1993-94), Moose, Masons. Home: RR 1901 Water Oaks Dr Fayetteville NC 28301-9125 Office: Mitchell Brewer Richardson Adams Burns and Boughman 308 Person St Fayetteville NC 28301-5736

MITCHELL, ROY SHAW, lawyer; b. Sherwood, N.Y., Jan. 16, 1934; s. Malcolm Douglas and Ruth Landon (Holland) M.; m. Nancy Elizabeth Bishop, Aug. 27, 1955; children: Mark E., Jeffrey B., Jennifer R. BS, Cornell U., 1957; JD with honors, George Washington U., Washington, D.C., 1959. Bar: D.C. 1959, Ohio 1960, Va. 1967, U.S. Ct. Fed. Claims 1963, U.S. Supreme Ct. 1965. Atty. Squire, Sanders & Dempsey, Cleve., 1960-61, Hudson & Creyke, Washington, 1961-67, Lewis, Mitchell & Moore, Vienna, Va., 1967-87, Morgan, Lewis & Bockius LLP, Washington, 1987-99; pres., CEO constrn. claims group Hill Internat., Inc., Washington, 1999—. Vice-chmn. Ameribanc Savs. Bank, Annandale, Va., 1980-95; trustee Ameribanc Investors Group, Annandale, 1980-95. Co-author: (with others) Handbook of Construction Law and Claims, 1982, 89; contbr. numerous articles to profl. jours. Fellow ABA (pub. contract law sect.), Am. Coll. Construction Lawyers, Va. Bar Assn., D.C. Bar Assn. Presbyterian. Avocation: boating. Construction, Government contracts and claims, Private international. Home: 5 Jefferson Run Rd Great Falls VA 22066-3200 Office: Constrn Claims Group Hill Internat Inc 1225 Eye St NW Ste 601 Washington DC 20005-5961 E-mail: roymitchell@hillinti.com.

MITCHELL, WILLIAM GRAHAM CHAMPION, lawyer, business executive; b. Raleigh, Dec. 24, 1946; s. Burley Bayard and Dorothy Ford (Champion) M.; children: William Graham, Margaret Scripture. AB, U. N.C., 1969, JD with highest hons., 1975. Bar: N.C. 1975, U.S. Dist. Ct. (ea., mid. and we. dists.) N.C. 1976, U.S. Ct. Appeals (4th cir.) 1978. Ptnr. Womble, Carlyle, Sandridge & Rice, Winston-Salem, 1975-87; sr. v.p. for external affairs RJR Nabisco, Atlanta, 1987-89; exec. v.p. R.J. Reynolds Tobacco Co., Winston-Salem, 1988-89; ptnr. Howrey & Simon, Washington, 1990-94; spl. counselor to chmn. bd. True North Comm., Inc., Chgo., 1996; chmn. bd., CEO Global Exch. Carrier Co., Leesburg, Va., 1997-00; pres., CEO Global Comms. Techs. Inc., Reston, Va., 1999-2000; chmn. bd., CEO Convergence Equipment Co., Manassas, Va., 1999-2000; chmn. bd. Qfactor Inc., Bethesda, Md., 2000-01; exec. v.p., gen. mgr. Verisign Inc., Mountainview, Calif., 2001—; pres. Network Solutions, Inc., Dulles, Va., 2003—. Bd. dirs. Fed. Agrl. Mortgage Corp., Washington. Mem. Pres.'s Adv. Com. on Trade Policy and Negotiations, Indsl. Policy Adv. Com., Washington, 1991—; exec. com. Nat. Assn. Mfrs., Washington, 1988-89, Nat. Fgn. Trade Coun., 1988-89; chmn. Tobacco Inst., Washington, 1988-89; bd. dirs. Washington Performing Arts Soc., 1988-92; bd. advisors Dem. Leadership Coun., 1988—; founding trustee Progressive Policy Inst., 1988—; vice chmn. fin. Bush Campaign. Mem.: ABA (vice chmn. antitrust sect., pvt. litigation com. 1987—89, chmn. FTC com. 1986), Forsyth Country Club, City Club of Washington, Georgetown Club, Order of the Coif. Antitrust, Mergers and acquisitions, Product liability. E-mail: cmitchell@verisign.com., Wgchamp@aol.com.

MITCHELL, WILLIAM P. (BILLY MITCHELL), mediator, arbitrator; b. Fairmont, N.C., Apr. 5, 1930; s. Julius Pender Mitchell and Dolibel Mitchell Caudell; m. Jerry Stevenson Mitchell (div.); children: Sharon Lynne Huggins, Steven Lee, Amy Elizabeth Boyt; m. Rebecca Burroughs, Apr. 2, 1983. AB, Duke U., 1953. Cert.: Va. Supreme Ct., N.C. Dispute Resolution Commn. Exec. v.p. Gainesville (Fla.) Area C. of C., 1961—70, Greater Macon (Ga.) C. of C., 1970—80; pres. Metro Jackson (Miss.) C. of C., 1980—82; mgr. chamber rels. U.S. C. of C., Washington, 1982—95; pres. Arlington Mediation Svc., Hendersonville, NC, 1994—. Bd. dirs. Carolina Forum, Hendersonville, 2002—. Aviation cadet USAF, 1953—55. Mem.: N.C. Bar Assn. (dispute resolution sect.), N.C. Assn. Profl. Family Mediators (pres. 2002), Assn. for Conflict Resolution (advanced practitioner), Am. Arbitration Assn., Bus. Mediation Assocs. Washington (assoc.). Republican. Presbyterian. Office: Arlington Mediation Svc 29 Hunters Ln Hendersonville NC 28791

MITCHEM, ALLEN P. lawyer; b. Burley, Idaho, Oct. 30, 1918; s. James Edgar and Adah Elizabeth (Allen) M.; m. Katherine I. Webber, Aug. 21, 1993; children— Allen P., James E., Lowell E. A.B., Ft. Hays State U., 1940; J.D. magna cum laude, Washburn U., 1947; LL.M., Columbia U., 1948. Bar: Kans. 1947, Colo. 1949. Assoc. prof. Coll. Law U. Denver, 1948-53; practice, Denver, 1953-60; minority counsel interior and insular affairs com. U.S. Senate, Washington, 1961-62; practice, Denver, 1963—; vis. lectr. Sch. Law U. Colo., 1954, 57, 59; lectr. Sch. Law U. Denver, 1953-63; labor arbitrator, Denver, 1965— . Trustee Endowment Assn. Ft. Hays State U., 1968-78; dir. Colo. Christian Home, Denver, 1974-80; pres. Denver Civitan Club, 1955-56; dist. gov. Civitan Internat., 1957-58, judge adv., 1958-59; dir. Denver Area Council of Churches, 1955, 57; pres. Denver Execs. Club, 1986-88; chmn. gen. bd. Central Christian Ch., 1963-65, 75-76. Served to capt. USMC, 1942-45. Recipient alumni achievement award Ft. Hays State U., 1970. Mem. ABA, Colo. Bar Assn., Denver Bar Assn. Contbr. article to legal review. Estate planning, General practice, Probate (including wills, trusts). Home: 420 S Marion Pkwy Apt 2002 Denver CO 80209-5526

MITCHEM, JAMES E. lawyer; b. Denver, July 3, 1949; s. Allen P. and K. Irene (Egan) M.; m. Rose M. Flanigan, Dec. 13, 1975; children: Margaret, Rachael. AB, Brown U., 1971; JD, U. Denver, 1974. Bar: Colo. 1974, U.S. Dist. Ct. Colo. 1974, U.S. Ct. Appeals (10th cir.) 1976, U.S. Supreme Ct. 1986. Ptnr. Mitchem and Mitchem, Denver, 1974-95, Mitchem & Flanigan, Englewood, 1995—. Author: The Lawyer's Duty to Report Ethical Violations, vol. 18, no. 10, Colorado Lawyer, 1989. Mem. ABA, Colo. Bar Assn. (chmn. com. on law and tech. 1984-86), Denver Bar Assn., Am. Arbitration Assn. (panel of arbitrators 1980-2000). Federal civil litigation, General civil litigation, Property, real (including real estate development, water). Home: 5929 S Akron Cir Englewood CO 80111-5215 Office: Ste 150 4610 S Ulster St Denver CO 80237-4326

MITNICK, CRAIG ROBERT, lawyer; b. Phila., Apr. 30, 1965; s. Harvey M. Mitnick and Carol M. Feldman Mitnick; m. Fern B. Miller; children: Oylan Alexander, Cameron Reed. BBA, Emory U., 1984; LLM, George Washington U., 1987. Bar: N.J. 1987, Pa. 1987, U.S. Dist. Ct. N.J. 1987. Asst. prosecutor Burlington County Prosecutor's Office, Mt. Holly, NJ, 1987—89, Camden (N.J.) County Prosecutor's Office, 1989—91; pvt. practice Haddonfield, NJ, 1991—. Criminal, General civil litigation. Office: 35 Kings Hwy E Haddonfield NJ 08033 Office Fax: 856-489-3006. Business E-Mail: craigmitnick@crmtrust.com.

MITROVIC, LAURENCE, lawyer; b. Clichy, France, Nov. 9, 1963; d. Dragoslav Mitrovic and Jacqueline Lhugnot; m. Eric Borysewicz, May 21, 1994; children: Alexandre Borysewicz, Marine Borysewicz. Lic., Paris V U., 1984, maitrise, 1985. Bar: N.Y. 1988, Paris 1988. Assoc. Bernard, Tessler, Mertz, Paris, 1988—90, Monahan & Duhot, Paris, 1990—92, Skadden, Arps, Slate, Meagher & Flom, Paris, 1992—97, European counsel, 1997—. Contbr. articles to profl. jours. Mergers and acquisitions, Corporate, general. Office: Skadden Arps 68 rue du Faubourg 75008 Saint-Honore Paris France

MITSEFF, CARL, lawyer; b. Detroit, Nov. 16, 1928; s. Frank H. and Katherine (Schaffer) M.; m. Phyllis Schlitters, June 28, 1952; children: C. Randall, Bradley Scott, Julie, Emily, Faye. BS, Wayne State U., 1952, LL.B., 1955. Bar: Mich. 1956. Practiced in Detroit, 1956—; staff atty. Burroughs Corp., 1955-60; mem. firm LeVasseur, Mitseff, Egan & Capp, 1960-80, Mitseff & Baril, 1980-85, Fitzgerald, Hodgman, Cox, Cawthoren & McMahon, 1986-90, Cox & Hodgman, 1990—. Spl. asst. atty. gen. State of Mich.; lectr. in field. Named to Mich. Workers Compensation Hall of Fame, 2000. Mem. ABA, State Bar Mich., Internat. Assn. Ins. Counsel, Internat. Assn. Indsl. Accident Bds. and Commns., Detroit Athletic Club (bd. dirs.), Beavers (pres.), Lochmoor Club, Grosse Pointe Yacht Club, Pi Kappa Alpha, Delta Theta Phi. Workers' compensation. Home: 612 N Brys Dr Grosse Pointe Woods MI 48236-1247 Office: 1001 Woodward Ave Ste 1000 Detroit MI 48226-1904

MITTENTHAL, PETER A. lawyer; b. White Plains, N.Y., June 16, 1953; BA, U. Fla., Gainesville, 1975; JD, U. LaVerne, 1978. Bar: Calif. 1979, U.S. Dist. Ct. (ctrl. dist.) Calif. 1980, U.S. Ct. Appeals (9th cir.) Calif. 1982, U.S. Dist. Ct. (no. dist.) Calif. 1998, U.S. Dist. Ct. (so. dist.) Calif. 1999; lic. radio broadcaster, FAA. Assoc. Snyder, Dorenfeld, Calabasas, Calif., 1996—2002, Soltman, Levitt & Flaherty LLP, Westlake Village, Calif., 2002—. Prosecutor discipinary procs. (pro bono) State Bar Calif., L.A., 1988; former disc jockey and comml. voiceover announcer, Fla.; arbitrator L.A. Superior Ct. Former judge pro tem L.A. Mcpl. Ct., 1985-90. Mem. ABA, So. Calif. Fraud Investigator's Assn., Am. Horse Shows Assn. Avocation: equestrian showjumping. General civil litigation, Personal injury (including property damage), Sports. Office: Soltman Levitt & Flaherty 2535 Townsgate Rd # 307 Westlake Village CA 91361

MIXTER, CHRISTIAN JOHN, lawyer; b. Basel, Switzerland, Mar. 13, 1953; s. Keith Eugene and Beatrice Maria (Ruf) M.; m. Linna M. Barnes, Dec. 17, 1977; children: Sara Elizabeth Barnes Mixter, Laura Ellen Barnes Mixter. BA, Ohio State U., 1974; JD, Duke U., 1977. Bar: N.Y. 1978, D.C. 1981. Assoc. Davis Polk & Wardwell, N.Y.C. and Washington, 1977-87; assoc. counsel Office Ind. Counsel (Iran/Contra), Washington, 1987-91; asst. chief litigation counsel Enforcement divsn. SEC, Washington, 1991-97, chief litigation counsel, 1997-2000; ptnr. Morgan, Lewis & Bockius LLP, Washington, 2000—. Mem. ABA (bus. law and litig. sects.), Assn. Bar City N.Y., Phi Beta Kappa, Order of the Coif. Administrative and regulatory, Federal civil litigation, Securities. Office: Morgan Lewis & Bockius LLP 1111 Pennsylvania Ave NW Washington DC 20004 E-mail: cmixter@morganlewis.com.

MIYASHITA, YOSHIYUKI, lawyer; b. Aizuwakamatsu City, Fukushima, Japan, Dec. 1, 1958; s. Takasi and Kazuko (Yamaguchi) M.; m. Takako Suzuki, Nov. 15, 1986; 2 children. LLB, Tohoku U., Miyagi, Japan, 1982; grad., Legal Rsch. and Tng. Inst., Tokyo, 1984; LLM, Cornell U., 1990. Bar: N.Y., 1991, Japan, 1984. Assoc. Yagi Fukushima & Yamanouchi, Tokyo, 1984—85, Showa Law Office, Tokyo, 1985—91, O'Melveny & Myers, N.Y.C., 1990—91; ptnr. Showa Law Office, Tokyo, 1992—2001, Asahi Koma Law Offices, Tokyo, 2002—. Mem. Copyright Coun./Agy. for Cultural Affairs, Japan, 1995—. Mem. ABA, Federation of Bar Assns. Japan (vice-chmn. computer rsch. com. 1994-97), Dai-ni Tokyo Bar Assn. Office: Asahi Koma Law Offices New ATT Bldg 11-7 Akasaka 2-chome Tokyo 107-8485 Japan

MIYOSHI, DAVID MASAO, lawyer, international investment consultant; b. Overton, Nev., Jan. 2, 1944; s. Joseph Masaru and Jean Michiye (Horikiri) M.; m. Teruko Ochiai, July 16, 1977; children: Mark Masahiro, Brandon Kohei. BS, U. So. Calif., 1966; JD, U. Calif., San Francisco, 1973; cert. completion, Waseda U., Tokyo, 1976; MBA, Harvard U., 1978. Bar: Calif. 1973, U.S. Dist. Ct. (cen. dist.) Calif. 1973. Fgr. assoc. atty. Matsuo and Kosugi Law Offices, Tokyo, 1974-76; assoc. atty. Matsuo Law Office, Tokyo, 1976-78; assoc. Mori & Ota, L.A., 1978-80, Morgan, Lewis & Bockius, L.A., 1980-82; pres., chief exec. officer Trans-Continental Investment, L.A., 1982-84; sr. atty. Miyoshi Law Office, L.A., 1983—; pres. Dai-Ichi Mortgage Co., L.A., 1984-86; sr. atty. Law Offices of David Miyoshi, L.A., 1986-93; pres. Global Fin. Corp., L.A., 1988-93, Wallstreet Masters, 2000—; legal counsel Japanese Am. Med. Assn., 2000—. Bd. dirs. Global Masters, Inc., L.A.; gen. counsel Japanese Am. Med. Assn., 1999—, Little Tokyo Coun., Inc., 2003--. Author: U.S. Condominium Regulations, 1976, U.S. Real Property Investment, 1986, Gingrich, America's De Gaulle; editor: U.S. trade Laws newsletter, 1978, U.S. Real Estate Report, 1987-93; contbr. articles to profl. jours. Bd. dirs. Am. Bapt. Soc., Los Angeles, 1986, Palos Verdes (Calif.) Bapt. Ch., 1986; hon. co-chmn. bus. adv. coun. Nat. Rep. Congl. Com., 2003—, mem. adv. coun. Rep. Party, 2002—. Served to capt. USMC, 1966-69, Vietnam. Mem. ABA, Calif. Bar Assn., L.A. County Bar Assn., Japanese Am. Med. Assn. (corp. counsel, 1999—). Republican. Avocations: tennis, golf, flying, skiing. Corporate, general, Private international, Property, real (including real estate development, water). Office: 707 Wilshire Blvd Ste 3260 Los Angeles CA 90017-3514

MLSNA, KATHRYN KIMURA, lawyer; b. Yonkers, N.Y., Apr. 23, 1952; d. Eugene T. and Grace Kimura; m. Timothy Martin Misna; children: Lauren Marie, Matthew Christopher, Michael Timothy. BA, Northwestern U., 1974, JD, 1977. Bar: Ill. 1977, U.S. Dist. Ct. (no. dist.) Ill. 1977. Mng. counsel McDonald's Corp., Oak Brook, Ill., 1977—. Speaker in field. Contbr. author to 2 ABA books. Bd. dirs. Japanese Am. Svc. Com.; mem. adv. bd. intellectual property DePaul U. Sch. Law, 1999—; chair Coun. of One Hundred, 2002—. Mem. ABA, Ill. Bar Assn., Chgo. Bar Assn., Asian Am. Bar Assn. (bd. dirs. 1996-98), Promotion Mktg. Assn. (v.p. 1988-92, chmn., pres. 1992-93, chmn. integrated mktg. com. 1993-94, chmn. assn. alliance com., co-chair legal and govtl. affairs com.), Northwestern U. Alumni Assn. (officer, bd. dirs. 1994-98), Coun. of One Hundred (chmn. 2002—), Girl Scouts DuPage County (bd. dirs. 2003-). Entertainment, Intellectual property. Office: McDonald's Corp 2915 Jorie Blvd Oak Brook IL 60523-1911

MO, CURTIS LUKE, lawyer; b. N.Y.C., Feb. 8, 1963; s. Luke W. and Doris C. Mo; m. Wai T. Ngai; children: Cullen A. Mo., Ryan J. Mo. BA, Columbia U., 1985, JD, 1988. Bar: NY 89, Calif. 97. Ptnr. Dewey Ballantine, N.Y.C., 1988—96, Brobeck, Phleger & Harrison LLP, Palo Alto, Calif., 1997—2003, Weil Gotshal & Manges LLP, Redwood Shores, Calif., 2003—. Co-chmn. PLI Securities Regulation Inst., PLI Venture Capital Conf. Corporate, general, Mergers and acquisitions, Securities. Office: Weil Gotshal & Manges LLP 201 Redwood Shores Pkwy Redwood City CA 94065 Fax: 650-802-3245. E-mail: curtis.mo@weil.com.

MOATES, G. PAUL, lawyer; b. May 26, 1947; s. Guy Hart and Virginia Rose (Mayolett) Moates; m. Constance A. Sadler. BA, Amherst Coll., 1969; JD, U. Chgo., 1975. Bar: Ill. 1975, D.C. 1976, U.S. Ct. Appeals (D.C. cir.) 1976, U.S. Supreme Ct. 1980, U.S. Ct. Appeals (6th cir.) 1984, U.S. Ct. Appeals (3d cir.) 1991, U.S. Ct. Appeals (7th cir.) 1993. Assoc. Sidley & Austin, Washington, 1975—82, ptnr., 1982—. Contbr. articles to profl. jours. Mem.: ABA, D.C. Bar Assn., Ill. Bar Assn. Administrative and regulatory, Antitrust, Transportation. Office: Sidley Austin Brown & Wood 1501 K Street NW Washington DC 20005

MOBLEY, JOHN HOMER, II, lawyer; b. Shreveport, La., Apr. 21, 1930; s. John Hinson and Beulah (Wilson) M.; m. Sue Lawton, Aug. 9, 1958; children: John Lawton, Anne Davant. AB, U. Ga., 1951, JD, 1953. Bar: Ga. 1952, U.S. Dist. Ct. D.C. Ptnr. Kelley & Mobley, Atlanta, 1956-63, Gambrell & Mobley, Atlanta, 1963-83; sr. ptnr. Sutherland, Asbill & Brennan, Atlanta, 1983—. Chmn., Cities in Schs. of Ga.; bd. dirs. Cities in Schs.; mem. bd. visitors Emory U.; trustee Canterbury Ct. Episcopal Retirement Home of Atlanta, Episcopal Diocese of Atlanta Found. Capt. JAGC, USAF, 1953-55. Mem. ABA, D.C. Bar, State Bar Ga., Atlanta Bar Assn., Am. Judicature Soc., Atlanta Lawyers Club, Atlanta Athletic Club, Atlanta Country Club, Commerce Club, Piedmont Driving Club, Georgian Club, N.Y. Athletic Club, Met. Club of Washington, Phi Delta Phi. Municipal (including bonds). Home: 4348 Sentinel Post Rd NW Atlanta GA 30327-3910 Office: Sutherland Asbill & Brennan 999 Peachtree St NE Ste 2300 Atlanta GA 30309-3996 Office Fax: 404-853-8806. E-mail: jhmobley@sablaw.com.

MOBLEY, STACEY J. consumer products company executive; b. Chester, Pa., Nov. 19, 1945; s. James Otis and Retha B. (Hollis) M.; m. Joan Thompson, Aug. 28, 1970; children: Michele. BS in Pharmacy, Howard Univ. Sch. of Pharm., 1968; JD, Howard Univ. Sch. of Law, 1971. Bar: Pa., D.C., U.S. Supreme Ct. Sr. v.p., chief admin. officer and gen. coun. DuPont Co., Wilmington, Del., 1972—83, dir. of Fed. Affairs Wash., DC, 1983—86, v.p. Fed. Affairs, 1986—92, sr. v.p. comm. in External Affairs Wilmington, Del., 1992—99, chief admin. officer and gen. coun., 1999—2001, sr. v.p., 2001—. Mem. Wilmington Club, Carlton Club. Gov. Ruth Ann Minner appointed Mr. Mobley to chair the Delaware Strategic Econ. Coun., 2001. Office: DuPont Co 1007 Market St Wilmington DE 19898-0001*

MOCH, ROBERT GASTON, retired lawyer; b. Montesano, Wash., June 20, 1914; s. Gaston and Fleeta Belle (Metcalf) M.; m. Barbara M. Kent, Sept. 2, 1940 (dec.); children: Marilynn A., Michael K., Robert M.; m. LaVerne I. Miller, May 29, 1968. BA magna cum laude, U. Wash., 1936; JD, Harvard Coll., 1941. Bar: Mass. 1941, Wash. 1945. Asst. crew coach U. Wash., 1936-39; head crew coach Mass. Inst. Tech., 1939-44; asso. Herrick, Smith, Donald, Farley & Ketchum, Boston, 1941-44; assoc. Eggerman, Rosling & Williams, Seattle, 1945-50, Weter, Roberts & Shefelman, Seattle, 1950-53; ptnr. Roberts & Shefelman, Seattle, 1953-87; of counsel Foster, Pepper & Shefelman, 1988—2001; ret., 2001. Del. Nat. Conf. on Law and Poverty, 1965, Nat. Defender Conf., 1969; chmn. King County Pub. Defender Adv. Com., 1970 Mem. U. Wash. Crew, 1933-36. Recipient Olympic Gold medal, 1936; named to Nat. Rowing Found. Hall of Fame, U. Wash. Hall of Fame. Mem. Wash. Bar Assn. (hon.), U. Wash. Alumni Assn. (pres. 1978-79, Disting. Svc. award 1986), Wash. Alumni Advs. (pres. 1985-87), Rainier Club, Rotary, Phi Beta Kappa, Beta Gamma Sigma, Alpha Kappa Psi, Phi Delta Phi, Phi Gamma Delta. Mem. Christian Ch. Corporate, general, General practice, Probate (including wills, trusts). Home: 22975 SE Black Nugget Rd Apt # 459 Issaquah WA 98029-7308

MODEROW, JOSEPH ROBERT, lawyer, package distribution company executive; b. Kenosha, Wis., 1948; Grad., Calif. State U., Fullerton, 1970; JD, Western State U., 1975. Bar: Calif. 1975, U.S. Dist. Ct. (cen. dist.) Calif. 1975, U.S. Supreme Ct. 1982. Sr. v.p. legal and pub affairs, sec., gen. counsel, dir. United Parcel Svc., Inc., Atlanta, 1986—; sorter/ unloader UPS, 1968—70. Mem.: supreme Court Hist. Soc. (trustee), Southern Ctr. for Internat. Studies (vice Chmn.), Shepherd Ctr. Hosp. (Dir. of the Brain Injury Assoc. of Ga.), UPS Bd. of Dir., Legal Group Mgr. (corp. Sec. 1986, public affairs 1989, pub. rels. 2001). Corporate, general. Office: United Parcel Svc Inc 55 Glenlake Pkwy NE Atlanta GA 30328-3498*

MODIN, RICHARD F. lawyer; b. Kansas City, Mo., Feb. 2, 1951; s. C.F. and Helen Majorie M.; m. Jeanne A. Modin, Oct. 31, 1975; children: Rebecca, Andrew, Lindsey, Luke. BA in Polit. Sci., U. Mo., Kansas City, 1977, JD with distinction, 1979. Bars: Mo. 1979, U.S. Dist. Ct. (ea. dist) 1979, Mo. 1979, Kans. 1994, U.S. Dist. Ct. Kans. 1994. Pvt. practice, Kansas City, Mo., 1983—. Mem. sch. bd. Platte County, 1991-; pastor Ch. of Christ, Kansas City, 1995—. Lt. cmdr. USN, 1979-82. Mem. Nat. Lawyers Assn., Lawyers for Life, Mo. Bar Assn., Platte County Bar Assn. General civil litigation, Insurance, Product liability. Office: Dougherty Modin & Holloway 10100 Ambassador Dr Ste 220 Kansas City MO 64153

MODISETT, JEFFREY A. lawyer, state attorney general, business executive; b. Windfall, Ind., Aug. 10, 1954; s. James Richard and Diana T. Modisett; m. Jennifer Ashworth, June 9, 1990; children: Matthew Hunter Ashworth, Haden Nicholas. BA, UCLA, 1976; MA, Oxford (Eng.) U., 1978; JD, Yale U., 1981. Bar: Ind., Calif., D.C. Clk. to Hon. R. Peckham U.S. Dist. Ct. (no. dist.) Calif., San Francisco, 1981—82; asst. U.S. atty. Office U.S. Atty. (ctrl. dist.) Calif., L.A., 1982—88; issues dir. Evan Bayh for Gov., Indpls., 1988; exec. asst. to gov. State of Ind., Indpls., 1988—90; prosecutor Marion County, Indpls., 1991—94; sr. counsel Ice Miller Donadio & Ryan, Indpls., 1995—96; atty. gen. State of Ind., 1997—2000; dep. CEO, gen. counsel Dem. Nat. Conv., 2000; co-CEO TechNet, Palo Alto, Calif., 2000—01; ptnr. Manatt Phelps & Phillips LLP, 2001—02, Bryan Cave LLP, 2002—. Chmn. Gov. Commn. for Drug Free Ind., Indpls., 1989—, Gov. Coun. on Impaired and Dangerous Driving, Indpls., 1989—; pres. Family Advocacy Ctr., Indpls., 1991—94, Hoosier Alliance Against Drugs, Indpls., 1993—96; dir. Cmty. Couns. of Indpls., 1991—93; chmn. Ind. Criminal Justice Inst., Indpls., 1989—90, dir., 1989—; vice chmn. Juvenile Justice and Youth Gang Study Com., Indpls., 1992—94; legal analyst Sta. WTHR-TV, Indpls., 1995—96. Author: Prosecutor's Perspective, 1991—94; editor-in-chief: Yale Jour. Internat. Law, 1980—81. Co-chair Ind. State Dem. Coordinated Campaign, Indpls., 1996. Named Top Lawyer, Indpls. Monthly mag., 1993; named to Sagamore of Wabash, State of Ind., 1995; recipient Spl. Enforcement award, U.S. Customs, 1988, Child Safety Adv. award, Automotive Safety for Children, 1997, STAR Alliance Impact award, 1998, Spirit of Ind. award, Am. Lung Assn., 1999. Mem.: Indpls. Bar Assn., Ind. Bar Assn. Democrat. Avocation: bicycling.

MODLIN, HOWARD S. lawyer; b. N.Y.C., Apr. 10, 1931; s. Martin and Rose Modlin; m. Margot S. Modlin, Oct. 18, 1956; children: James, Laura, Peter. AB, Union Coll., Schenectady, 1952; JD, Columbia U., 1955. Bar: N.Y. 1956, D.C. 1973. Assoc. Weisman, Celler, Spett & Modlin, P.C., N.Y.C., 1956-61, ptnr., 1961-76, mng. ptnr., 1976-95, pres., 1996—. Chmn. bd. dirs., sec. Gen. DataComm Industries, Inc., Naugatuck, Conn.; bd. dirs. Am.-Book-Stratford Press, Inc., N.Y.C., Fedders Corp., Liberty Corner, NJ, Trans-Lux Corp., Norwalk, Conn. Chmn. bd. dirs. Daus. of Jacob Geriat. Ctr., Bronx, N.Y. Mem. ABA, Assn. of Bar of City of N.Y., D.C. Bar Assn. Commercial, contracts (including sales of goods; commercial financing), Corporate, general, Securities. Office: Weisman Celler Spett & Modlin PC 445 Park Ave New York NY 10022-2606

MOE, RICHARD PALMER, lawyer; b. Duluth, Minn., Nov. 27, 1936; s. Russell James and Virginia Mary (Palmer) M.; m. Julia Neimeyer, Dec. 26, 1964; children— Eric Palmer, Andrew Neimeyer, Alexandra Julia. BA, Williams Coll., 1959; LL.B., U. Minn., 1966. Bar: Minn. 1967, D.C. 1979, N.Y. 1991. Adminstrv. asst. to mayor, City of Mpls., 1961-62; to lt. gov., 1963-66; fin. dir. Minn. Democratic Farmer-Labor Party, 1967-69, chmn., 1969-72; adminstrv. asst. to Sen. Walter F. Mondale of Minn., Washington, 1972-76; chief of staff Vice Pres. Walter F. Mondale, 1977-81; counsel Davis Polk & Wardwell, Washington, 1981-85, ptnr., 1985-92; pres. Nat. Trust for Hist. Preservation, Washington, 1992—. Trustee Ford Found., 1998—. Administrative and regulatory, Legislative. Office: Nat Trust for Hist Preservation 1785 Massachusetts Ave NW Washington DC 20036-2117

MOEHLE, CARM ROBERT, lawyer; s. Robert Rudolph Moehle and Catherine Marie Whitcraft. BSCE, U. Mo., Rolla; JD, U. Mo. Bar: Mo., Ariz., Colo., U.S. Dist. Ct. Ariz., U.S. Dist. Ct. (we. dist.) Mo., U.S. Supreme Ct. Law clk. Mo. Ct. Appeals (we. dist.), Kansas City; prosecuting atty. Greene County, Springfield, Mo.; law clk. Ariz. Supreme Ct., Phoenix; staff atty. Ariz. Ct. Appeals, Phoenix; atty. Bosco & DiMatteo, P.C., Phoenix, 1983-91, Scult, Lazarus, French, Zwillinger and Smock, P.A., Phoenix, 1992-93; pvt. practice Phoenix, 1994—. Chmn. bd. dirs. Ariz. Coun. Trout Unlimited, Phoenix, 1989—; trustee Maricopa County Bar Found., Phoenix, 1992-95; mem. cmty. adv. bd. Ariz. Dept. Environ. Quality. Mem. Ariz. Trial Lawyers Assn., Maricopa County Bar Assn. (vol. lawyers program). Avocations: backpacking, hiking, flyfishing, golf, skiing. General civil litigation, Personal injury (including property damage), Property, real (including real estate development, water). E-mail: carm.moehle@azbar.org.

MOEHLMAN, MICHAEL SCOTT, lawyer; b. Columbus, Ohio, Apr. 11, 1938; s. Arthur Henry and Marguerite Caroline M.; m. Carol Jean Shafer, Sept. 28, 1963; 1 son, Matthew. BA, Harvard U., 1960; LLB, U. Tex., 1963. Bar: Tex. 1963. With Strasburger & Price, Houston. Bd. dirs. St. Martin's Episcopal Children's Ctr. Fellow Tex. Bar Found.; mem. ABA (com. bank securities), Internat. Bar Assn., Tex. Bar Assn. (com. revision corp. law), Houston Bar Assn. (judicature com.), Tex.-Mex. Bar Assn., Am. Judicature Soc., Houston Bar Found. (chmn. bd. dirs.), Phi Delta Phi. Clubs: Houston (chmn. fin. com., bd. dirs., pres.), Houston Racquet, Houston Yacht, Harvard (Boston), St. Charles Bay Hunting. Episcopalian. Banking, Corporate, general, Securities. Office: Strasburger & Price 1401 McKinney St Ste 2200 Houston TX 77010-4035 E-mail: michael.moehlman@strasburger.com.

MOELING, WALTER GOOS, IV, lawyer; b. Quantico, Va., Feb. 16, 1943; s. Walter Goos III and Dorothy M.; m. Nell Frances Askew, Aug. 27, 1965; children: Charles H., Christine E. BA, Duke U., 1965, JD, 1968. Bar: Ga. 1968. Assoc. Powell, Goldstein, Frazer & Murphy, Atlanta, 1968-75, ptnr., 1975—. Bd. dirs. So. Banking Law and Policy Conf., 1989-96, Southeastern Conf. for Bank Dirs., 1996—, Children's Rehab. Ctr., Atlanta, 1982—, Gatchell Home, Atlanta, 1983—; bd. dirs. Frazer Ctr., 1989—, chmn. bd. dirs., 1993. Mem. ABA (mem. banking com. 1986—), Ga. C. of C. (bd. dirs. 1998-2000), Ga. Bar Assn., Ga. Bankers Assn. (assoc., chairperson bank counsel sect. 1992-95, bd. dirs. 1998-2000), Cmty. Bankers Assn. (assoc.), Capital City Club, Willow Point Country Club. Democrat. Unitarian Universalist. Avocations: golf, fly-fishing. Banking, Corporate, general, Finance. Office: Powell Goldstein Frazer & Murphy 191 Peachtree St NE Ste 16 Atlanta GA 30303-1740 E-mail: wmoeling@pgfm.com.

MOELLER, FLOYD DOUGLAS, lawyer; b. Safford, Ariz., Aug. 16, 1949; s. Floyd Albert and Helen Lou (Posey) M.; m. Tyra Brown, Dec. 18, 1970; children: Kristin, Sam, John, Susan. BS in Police Sci., Brigham Young U., 1972, JD, 1977; MS in Mgmt., Lesley Coll., 1985, MA in Counseling Psychology, 1987; LLM in Tax, Washington Sch. Law, 1987, D of Juridicial Sci., 2001. Bar: N.Mex. 1978, U.S. Dist. Ct. N.Mex. 1978, U.S. Dist. Ct. Ariz. 1978, U.S. Ct. Appeals (10th cir.) 1979 , U.S. Tax Ct. 1981, U.S. Supreme Ct. 1981, Navajo Nation, Hopi Tribe, Jicarilla Apache Tribe, White Mountain Apache Tribe, So. Ute Tribe, Ute Mountain Tribe, So. Paiute Coun., Ft. Belknap Indian Ct., Gila River Indian Ct., Mescalaro Apache Ct., S.W. Inter Tribal Ct. Appeals, Zuni Tribal Ct. Assoc. Wade Beavers & Assocs., Farmington, N.Mex., 1978-79; ptnr. Nunn & Moeller, Farmington, 1979; sole practice Farmington, 1979-80, 87—; ptnr. Moeller & Burnham, Farmington, 1980-87. Mem. exec. com. Better Bus. Bur. of 4 Corners, 1978, bd. dirs., 1978—; bd. dirs. Farmington Pub. Library Bd., 1979-86, San Juan Med. Found., San Juan Pub. Library Found., Halvorson House; chmn. local troop coms. Boy Scouts Am., Farmington, 1985—. Capt. USMC, 1972-75. Named diplomat Nat. Bd. Trial Advocacy, 1986. Mem. ABA, J. Reuben Clark Law Soc., Nat. Panel Consumer Arbitrators, Am. Arbitration Assn., N.Mex. Trial Lawyers Assn., N.Mex. State Bar Assn. (CLE, fee arbitration coms. 1985, pres. trial practice sect. 1988), Navajo Nat. Bar Assn., San Juan County Bar Assn., 4 Corners Inn of Ct. Republican. Mem. Lds Ch. Avocations: reading, poetry, gardening, knot tying. General civil litigation, General practice, Personal injury (including property damage). Office: PO Box 15249 Farmington NM 87401-5249 Fax: (505) 362-0818. E-mail: dmoeller@acrnet.com.

MOELLER, GALEN ASHLEY, lawyer; b. Ballinger, Tex., Jan. 17, 1950; s. Norbert Edward and Magdaline O. (Kocich) M.; m. Roseann Dominguez, Aug. 12, 1977; children— Tatum Cheree, Taylor Ashley. B.A. in History, St. Mary U., San Antonio, 1972, J.D., 1974. Bar. Tex. 1975, U.S. Dist. Ct. (no. dist.) Tex. 1976. Sole practice, San Angelo, 1975— . Mem. ABA, Tex. Bar Assn., Tom Green County Bar Assn., Tex. Trial Lawyers Assn., Tex. Criminal Def. Lawyers Assn., Sons of Hermann Rowena, Elks, K.C., Lambda Chi Alpha (hon.). Roman Catholic. General practice, Personal injury (including property damage), Probate (including wills, trusts). Office: 331 W Avenue B San Angelo TX 76903-6811 E-mail: Gmoe@justice.com.

MOERBEEK, STANLEY LEONARD, lawyer; b. Toronto, Ont., Can., Nov. 12, 1951; came to U.S., 1953; s. John Jacob and Mary Emily Moerbeek; m. Carol Annette Mordaunt, Apr. 17, 1982; children: Sarah, Noah. BA magna cum laude, Calif. State U., Fullerton, 1974; student, U. San Diego-Sorbonne, Paris, 1977; JD, Loyola U., 1979. Bar: Calif. 1980; cert. in internat. bus. transactions, bankruptcy and bus. rehab., and civil trial practice. From law clk. to assoc. McAlpin Doonan & Seese, Covina, Calif., 1977-81; assoc. Robert L. Baker, Pasadena, Calif., 1981-82, Miller Bush & Minnott, Fullerton, 1982-83; prin. Law Office of Stanley L. Moerbeek, Fullerton, 1984—. Judge pro tem Orange County Superior Ct., Calif., 1984—; notary pub., lt. gov. 9th cir. law student divsn. ABA, 1979. Mem. Heritage Found., Washington, 1989—. Calif. Gov.'s Office scholar, 1970; recipient Plaque of Appreciation, Fullerton Kiwanis, 1983. Mem. Calif. Assn. Realtors (referral panel atty. 1985—), Orange County Bar Assn. (Coll. of Trial Advocacy 1985), Calif. C. of C., Phi Kappa Phi. Roman Catholic. Avocations: history, politics, sports. General civil litigation, Personal injury (including property damage), Property, real (including real estate development, water). Office: 1370 N Brea Blvd Ste 210 Fullerton CA 92835-4128 E-mail: slmlaw@netzero.net.

MOERDLER, CHARLES GERARD, lawyer; b. Paris, Nov. 15, 1934; came to the U.S., 1946, naturalized, 1952; s. Herman and Erna Anna (Brandwein) M.; m. Pearl G. Hecht, Dec. 26, 1955; children: Jeffrey Alan, Mark Laurence, Sharon Michele. BA, L.I.U., 1953; JD, Fordham U., 1956. Bar: NY 1956, U.S. Supreme Ct. 1962. Assoc. Cravath, Swaine & Moore, N.Y.C., 1956-65; spl. counsel coms. City of N.Y. and judiciary N.Y. State Assembly, 1960-61; commr. bldgs. City of N.Y., 1966-67; sr. ptnr., chmn. litigation dept. Stroock & Stroock & Lavan, N.Y.C., 1967—. Bd. dirs., gen. counsel, dir. N.Y. Post Co., Inc., 1987-92; cons. housing, urban devel. and real estate to Mayor of N.Y.C., 1967-73; mem. com. on character and fitness of applicants for admission to Bar, Appellate divsn. 1st Dept., N.Y., 1977—, vice chmn. 1998—; mem. disciplinary com. appellate divsn. 1st Dept., N.Y., 1998—, commr. N.Y. State Ins. Fund, 1978-97, vice chmn., 1986-94, chmn., 1995-97; mem. Mayor's Com. on Judiciary, 1994-2001; mem. N.Y.C. Housing Devel. Corp., 1997—; bd. dirs. N.Y.C. Residential Mortgage Ins. Corp., 1997—; chmn. bd. dirs. Bank Austria Creditanstalt LLC, 1999-2001; mem. N.Y.C. Bd. Collective Bargaining, 2000—. Mem. editorial bd. N.Y. Law Jour., 1985—; assoc. editor Fordham Law Rev., 1956. Asst. dir. Rockefeller nat. presdl. campaign com., 1964; adv. bd. Sch. Internat. Affairs Columbia U., 1977-80; bd. govs. L.I.U., 1966, trustee, 1985-91; chmn. Cmty. Planning Bds. 8 and 14, Bronx County, 1977-78; nat. bd. govs. Am. Jewish Congress, 1966; bd. overseers Jewish Theol. Sem. Am., 1993-95; trustee St. Barnabas Hosp., Bronx, N.Y., 1985—. Recipient Walker Metcalf award L.I. U., 1966. Mem. Am. Bar Assn., N.Y. State Bar Assn., N.Y. County Lawyers Assn., Internat. Bar Assn., Assn. of Bar of City of N.Y., Free Sons of Israel, Metro. Club. Federal civil litigation, Labor (including EEOC, Fair Labor Standards Act, labor-management relations, NLRB, OSHA), Property, real (including real estate development, water). Home: 7 Rivercrest Rd Bronx NY 10471-1236 Office: Stroock Stroock & Lavan 180 Maiden Ln New York NY 10038 E-mail: cmoerdler@stroock.com.

MOFFATT, MICHAEL ALAN, lawyer; b. Indpls., Feb. 22, 1964; s. James L. Kelso and Peggy A. Tackett; m. Nancy Norman, Sept. 23, 1989; children: Patricia Margaret, Michael Alan, Nicole Elizabeth, Michelle Ann. BA in Polit. Sci., Depauw U., 1986; JD, Ind. U., 1989. Bar: Ind. 1989, U.S. Dist. Ct. (so. and no. dists.) Ind. 1989, U.S. Ct. Appeals (7th cir.) 1991, U.S. Supreme Ct., 1999. Law clk., assoc. White & Raub, Indpls., 1987-94; assoc. Wooden McLaughlin & Sterner, Indpls., 1994-95, Barnes & Thornburg,

Indpls., 1995-2000, ptnr., 2001; shareholder Ogletree Deakins, Nash, Smoak and Stewart, P.C., 2001—. Lectr. litigation, paralegal program, Ind. U./Purdue U., Ind. CLE Forum & labor/employment seminars. Contbr. articles to legal jours. Co-chmn. Keep Am. Beautiful, Greencastle, Ind., 1986, bd. dirs., sec., 1990—94; v.p. Fall Creek Little League, 2002—03; mem. devel. control com. Geist Harbors Property Owner's Assn., Indpls., 1993—94, cons., 1994, pres., 1997—99; bd. dirs., tournament chair Fall Creek Little League, 2001—; cons. pediatric ethics com. Meth. Hosp., Indpls., 1990—92; winners cir. mentor U.S. Auto Club. Mem.: ABA (labor and employment sect.), Indpls. Bar Assn. (exec. coun. labor law sect. 1999, vice chmn. 2000, chmn. 2001), Ind. Bar Assn. (mem. exec. coun. labor law sect. 2002—), Fed. Bar Assn., Exch. Club (pres.-elect 1997—98, pres. 1998—99, past pres. 1999—2000). Avocations: golf, basketball, softball. General civil litigation, Labor (including EEOC, Fair Labor Standards Act, labor-management relations, NLRB, OSHA). Office: Ogletree Deakins Nash Smoak & Stewart PC One Indiana Sq Ste 2300 Indianapolis IN 46204 Business E-Mail: mike.moffatt@odnss.com.

MOFFETT, J. DENNY, lawyer; b. Atlanta, Sept. 20, 1947; s. James Denny Moffett Jr. and Dorothy (Mckenzie) McCall; m. Mary F. Ray, June 6, 1987; children: David, Jenny. BA, U. Okla., 1969; JD with honors, George Washington U., 1972, LLM in Taxation, 1974. Bar: Okla. 1972, U.S. Tax Ct. 1973, Wyo. 2001. Legis. asst. U.S. Senate, Washington, 1973-74; ptnr. Conner & Winters, Tulsa, 1974-90, McKenzie, Moffett, Elias & Books, Tulsa, Oklahoma City, 1990-97, Moffett & Assocs., P.C., Tulsa and Jackson, Wyo., 1997—. Adj. faculty U. Tulsa Law Sch., 1978; arbitrator Nat. Assn. Securities Dealers. Commr. Ark.-Okla. River Compact Commn., 1990-94; pres. Nicholas Club Tulsa, 1984; endowment com. Trinity Episcopal Ch., 1990—. 2d lt. U.S. Army, 1972-74; bd. dirs. Am. Cancer Soc., Tulsa, 1991-94. Mem. Am. Arbitration Assn., Tulsa Tax Club (pres. 1981, 94). Republican. Bankruptcy, General civil litigation, Taxation, general. Home: 2132 E 32nd Pl Tulsa OK 74105-2222 Office: Moffett & Assocs PC 1722 S Carson Ave Ste 3203 Tulsa OK 74119

MOGELMOSE, HENRIK, lawyer; b. Kerteminde, Denmark, Mar. 13, 1958; s. Lise-Lotte Mogelmose, June 1989; children: Louise, Julie. Law degree, U. Aarhus, Denmark, 1983; LLM, U. Chgo., 1991. Bar: Denmark 1988, N.Y. 1992. Assoc. Kromann Reumert, Copenhagen, 1988—93, ptnr., 1993—; fgn. assoc. Skadden, Arps, Slate, Meagher & Flom, N.Y.C., 1991—92. Mem. ABA, Danish Bar Assn., Internat. Bar Assn. Corporate, general, Finance, Mergers and acquisitions. Home: Vermehrensvej 3 DK-2930 Klampenborg Denmark Office: Kromann Reumert Sundkrogsgade 5 DK-2100 Copenhagen Denmark Fax: 45-70-12-13-11. E-mail: HM@Kromannreumert.com.

MOGLEN, LELAND LOUIS, lawyer, educator; b. N.Y.C., Apr. 5, 1944; s. Maxwell David and Ruth Leah (Weiss) M.; m. Phyllis Jane Moglen, June 26, 1976; children: David Joseph, Kimberly Hanna, Daniel Justin, Marc Edward. BA, Columbia U., 1966; MSBA, San Francisco State U., 1981, JD, 1982. Bar: Calif. 1989. Tchr. Great Hollow Jr. H.S., Smithtown, N.Y., 1966-68; tchr. English Ecole Nickerson, Paris, 1968-70; owner Nature's Best Health Foods, Kodiak, Alaska, 1970-72; acct. City/County of San Francisco, 1972-76, departmental mgr., 1976-86; assoc. prof. Chapman Coll., Sacramento, 1987-89; pvt. practice Auburn, Calif., 1989—. Pro bono atty. Voluntary Legal Svcs. Program, Auburn, 1990; pro tem judge Placer Mcpl. Ct., 1995. Prin. Nevada City (Calif.) Jewish Cmty. Ctr. Sunday Sch., bd. dirs., 1988-93. Avocations: tennis, racquetball, chess. Corporate, general, Personal injury (including property damage), Property, real (including real estate development, water). Home: 23286 Lone Pine Dr Auburn CA 95602-8027 Fax: 530-268-6828. E-mail: moglen@usamedia.tv.

MOGOL, ALAN JAY, lawyer; b. Balt., July 29, 1946; s. Jesse and Kitty (Stutman) m.; m. Ellen Epstein, June 19, 1969; children: Andrew Stephen, Jonathan David. BA with distinction, U. Va., 1968, JD, 1971. Bar: Md. 1972, U.S. Dist. Ct. Md. 1972, U.S. Ct. Appeals (4th cir.) 1972, U.S. Supreme Ct. 1978. Assoc. Ober, Kaler, Grimes & Shriver, Balt., 1971-77, ptnr., 1978—. Chmn. comml. finance Ober, Kaler, Grimes & Shriver, Balt., 1980-81, 84-85, 91-97, 2002—, chmn. equipment leasing practice group, 1998—; lectr. on continuing edn. Md. Inst. Continuing Profl. Edn. for Lawyers, 1988-92, trustee, 1990-93; spkr. seminars Nat. Health Lawyers Assn., Washington, 1986-87, Rocky Mountain Mgmt., Denver, 1987, Med. Imaging Expo., 1995, Washington, 1995. Co-author: In Structuring the Secured Loan Agreement, 1991, Commercial Finance Guide, 1997, Equipment Leasing, 1999; contbr. articles to profl. jours. and local newspapers. Bd. dirs. Transitional Living Coun., Balt., 1972-92; bd. trustees Md. Inst. of Continuing Profl. Edn. for Lawyers, 1990-93. Fellow Md. Bar Found., Inc., Am. Bar Found., Inc.; mem. ABA, Equipment Leasing Assn. Am. (lawyers com. 1986-89, program com. 1986-91, speaker seminars), Md. Bar Assn. (uniform comml. code com. 1988—, chmn. 1991-93, vice chmn. bus. sect. 1995-96, chmn. bus. sect. 1996-97). Avocation: tennis. Commercial, contracts (including sales of goods; commercial financing), Corporate, general. Office: Ober Kaler Grimes & Shriver 120 E Baltimore St Ste 800 Baltimore MD 21202-1643 E-mail: ajmogol@ober.com.

MOHR, ANTHONY JAMES, judge; b. L.A., May 11, 1947; s. Gerald Leonard and Rita Lenore (Goldstein) M. BA in Govt. cum laude with honors, Wesleyan U., 1969; JD, Columbia U., 1972; diploma with honors, Internat. Faculty for Comparative Law, 1975. Bar: Calif. 1972, U.S. Dist. Ct. (cen. dist.) Calif. 1973, U.S. Ct. Appeals (9th cir.) 1974, D.C. 1976, U.S. Supreme Ct. 1981. Law clk. to judge U.S. Dist. Ct. (cen. dist.) Calif., 1972-73; assoc. Alschuler Grossman, Stein & Kahan, 1973-75; pvt. practice L.A., 1976-94; judge L.A. Mcpl. Ct., 1994-97, L.A. Superior Ct., 1997—. Faculty atty. asst. tng. program UCLA, 1982-97, bd. dirs. internat. student ctr., 1986—, Performing Tree, 1997-2002. Mem. editl. bd. Calif. Bar Jour., 1979-80, L.A. Lawyer Mag., 1989-94; contbr. articles to profl. jours. Del. White House Conf. on Youth, 1971; faculty Ctr. Jud. Edn. and Rsch, 1997—; nat. adv. coun. Ctr. for Study of Presidency, 1974-99; mem. L.A. Dist. Atty.'s Adv. Coun., 1976-82; hearing officer L.A. County Employees Ret. Assn., 1986-94. Mem. ABA, Calif. Judges Assn. Ethics Com. (2001-), C, Beverly Hills Bar Assn. (bd. govs. 1975-80, chmn. litig. sect. 1983-85, chair resolutions com. 1991-92, ex. officio bd. dirs. 1998-99, 2002—, Dist. Svc. award 1992), Assn. of Bus. Trial lawyers (bd. govs. 2001—), Barristers of Beverly Hills Bar Assn. (pres. 1979-80), Am. Judicature Soc. (dir. 1982-83), L.A. County Bar Assn., Phi Beta Kappa, Phi Delta Phi. Office: LA Superior Ct 600 S Commonwealth Ave Los Angeles CA 90005 E-mail: amohr@lasuperiorcourt.org.

MOISE, STEVEN KAHN, lawyer, rancher, merchant banker; b. Lubbock, Tex., July 28, 1944; s. Joseph J. and Marguerite K. M.; m. Beth Maxwell, June 2, 1968; children: Adam, Grant. BA, U. Colo., 1966, JD, 1969. Bar: Colo. 1969, N.Mex. 1971. Assoc. Rothgerber, Appel & Powers, Denver, 1969-71, Sutin, Thayer & Browne, Albuquerque, 1971-74, ptnr., 1974-94, pres., CEO, 1984-88, chmn., 1989-94, of counsel, 1995; pres. Moise & Co., Albuquerque, 1995—; v.p. NB3 Cons. LLC, Albuquerque, 2002—. Bd. dirs. Wells Fargo Bank, N.Mex., N.A. Bd. dirs. U. Colo. Found., Boulder, 1969-79, 87-94, 2002—; bd. dirs. U. Colo. Sch. Law Alumni, 1985-89, N.Mex. Amigos, 1987—; bd. dirs., exec. com. Albuquerque Cmty. Found., 1981-2001, pres. 1984-88, emeritus bd. dirs., 2001—; bd. dirs. Albuquerque Econ. Devel., 1982—, sec., 1984-86, v.p., 1986-88, pres., 1988-90, exec. com., 1984—; mem. Albuquerque Econ. Forum, 1989-98; chmn. Bingaman Circle, 1990-96; trustee Albuquerque Acad., 2001—, advisory dir. sr. discounts.com, 2001—; mem. U. N.Mex. Cancer Coalition Coun., 2002—. Mem. N.Mex. Bar Assn., Colo. Bar Assn. Democrat. Jewish. Oil, gas, and mineral, Finance, Property, real (including real estate development, water). Home: 5001 Snow Goose Ct NW Albuquerque NM 87120 Office: Moise & Co PO Box 1705 Albuquerque NM 87103-1705 E-mail: steve@moiseco.biz.

MOK, BARBARA WAI KUN, lawyer; b. Hong Kong, Nov. 26, 1957; d. Keith K.H. Mok and Louise Y.M. Ho; m. Raymond W.M. Lo, Nov. 24, 1998; 1 child, Audrey S.Y. Lo. LLB, U. Hong Kong, 1980; Postgrad. Cert. Laws, 1981, LLM, 1988. Asst. solicitor Gallant Y.T. Ho & Co., Hong Kong, 1983-86; ptnr., 1986-90; cons. Victor Chu & Co., Hong Kong, 1991-92; ptnr., 1992-99, Jones, Day, Reavis & Pogue, Hong Kong, 1999—. Vis. atty. Pillsbury, Madison & Sutro, LLP, San Francisco, 1986. Mem. Law Soc. Hong Kong, Law Soc. Eng. Home: Apt 12N 28 Scenic Villa Dr Pokfulam Hong Kong Office: Jones Day Reavis & Pogue 31st Flr Edinburgh Tower-The Landmark 15 Queen's Rd Central Hong Kong China Office Fax: (852) 2868-5871. E-mail: bmok@jonesday.com.

MOLER, DONALD LEWIS, JR., lawyer; b. Charleston, Ill., Sept. 9, 1955; s. Donald Lewis Sr. and A. Margaret (Ansdell) M.; m. Judith Lynn Enos, Aug. 9, 1986; 1 child, Seth Ansdell; stepchildren, Eric Philip Anderson, Marc Paul Anderson. BA, Ea. Ill. U., 1976, MA, 1977; MA in Pub. Adminstrn., U. Ill., 1983; JD, U. Kans., 1985. Bar: Kans. 1985, U. S. Dist. Ct. Kans. 1985, U.S. Supreme Ct., 1988. Lobbyist League Kans. Mcpls., Topeka, 1985—, exec. dir., 1999—. Adj. prof. law, Washburn U. Sch. of Law, Topeka.; bd. dirs. Natl. League of Cities. Editor: Standard Traffic Ordinance for Kansas Cities, 1986—, Uniform Public Offense Code for Kansas Cities, 1986—. Mem. ABA, Kans. Bar Assn., Topeka Bar Assn. Methodist. Avocation: restoration jaguar automobiles. Home: 401 SW Danbury Ln Topeka KS 66606-2227 Office: League Kans Mcpls 300 SW 8th Ave Topeka KS 66603-3912

MOLER, EDWARD HAROLD, lawyer; b. Oklahoma City, May 26, 1923; s. Harold Stanley and Rosemary (Callahan) M.; m. Donna Blocksom Cram, Sept. 12, 1964; children: John Frederick, Shelley Elizabeth, Christopher Bryan. BA, U. Okla., 1947, LLB, 1948. Bar: Okla. 1948, U.S. Supreme Ct. 1951. Pvt. practice law, Oklahoma City, 1948-52, 61—; asst. mcpl. counselor, 1952-59; mcpl. counselor, 1959-61; spl. justice Okla. Supreme Ct., 1977. Trustee Oklahoma City Mcpl. Improvement Authority, 1960-61; bd. dirs. Mummers Theatre, Inc., 1969—; bd. dirs. Greater Oklahoma City YMCA, 1981-91. 2d lt. USAAF, 1943-45. Mem. ABA, Okla. Bar Assn., Oklahoma County Bar Assn. (bd. dirs. 1963-67, pres. 1968), Rotary, Phi Delta Phi, Phi Gamma Delta (pres. local chpt. 1946, pres. Nu Omega Housing Assn. 1963-65). Home: 2540 NW Grand Blvd Oklahoma City OK 73116-4110 Office: 204 N Robinson Ste 2800 Oklahoma City OK 73102

MOLHO, ISAAC, lawyer; b. Jerusalem, Jan. 30, 1945; s. Raphael and Rachel Molho; m. Irene Shlomit Shimron, 1967; children: Hadar Valero, Vered. LLB, Hebrew U., Jerusalem, 1969. Apprentice to Erwin S. Shimron, Jerusalem, 1968-70; assoc. Proskauer Rose LLP, N.Y.C., 1971-72, Shimron, Novick, Levitt, Jerusalem, 1972-75; ptnr. Shimron, Novick, Levitt, Molho, Jerusalem, 1975-78; mng. ptnr. E. S. Shimron I. Molho, Persky & Co., Jerusalem, 1978—. Bd. dirs. Triumph Internat., Ltd. Hon. consul Republic of Austria, Jerusalem, 1979—; bd. dirs., dep. chmn. Jerusalem Internat. YMCA, 1980-2001; mem. bd. govs. Hebrew U., Jerusalem, 1990-2001; mem. internat. coun. Jerusalem Found., 1992-2001; mem. Prime Minister's envoy to Palestinian Leadership and Chmn. Yasser Arafat, Jerusalem, 1996-99; chief Israeli negotiator Palestinian Authority Hebron and Wye Agreements, 1996-99; chmn. Israel Mus., 1999-2001. Capt. Israel Def. Forces, 1963-65. Decorated Silbernes Ehrenzeichen (Austria), 1994. Mem. Israel Bar Assn., Internat. Orgn. Jewish Jurists. Avocation: tennis. Communications, Corporate, general, Intellectual property. Office: ES Shimron I Molho Persky & Co Tech Pk Bldg 1 Manahat 91487 Jerusalem Israel Office Fax: 972-2-649-0659. E-mail: officejm1@smplaw.co.il.

MOLINARO, THOMAS J. lawyer; b. Cleve., June 4, 1952; s. Albert J. and Marilyn Molinaro; children: Daniel, Paul, Marisa, Anna. BS, U. Wis., 1976; JD, U. Wis. Law Sch., 1979. Bar: Wis., U.S. Dist. Ct. (we. and ea. dists.) Wis. Law clk. Wis. Ct. Appeals, Waukesha, 1979-80; assoc. Crooks, Law & Connell, Wausau, 1980-83; ptnr. Brady, Hoover & Molinaro, Wausau, 1983-85, Brady & Molinaro, Wausau, 1986-92; sole practice law Wausau, 1993—2002; ptnr. Grischke, Molinaro & Laughlin, LLSC, Wausau, 2003—. Bd. dirs. Marathon Civic Corp., Wausau, 1988-94, Wausau Area Youth Soccer Assn., 1990-94; membership com. YMCA, Wausau, 1988-90. Mem. ATLA, Wis. Bar Assn., Marathon County Bar Assn. Avocations: antique collecting and restoration, skiing, soccer. Family and matrimonial, Personal injury (including property damage), Workers' compensation. Office: 1400 Merrill Ave Wausau WI 54401

MOLINARO, VALERIE ANN, lawyer; b. N.Y.C, Oct. 21, 1956; d. Albert Anthony and Rosemary Rita (Zito) M.; m. Howard Robert Birnbach; 1 child, Michelle Annalise Birnbach. BA with honors, SUNY, 1978; JD, MPA, Syracuse U., 1980. Asst. counsel. New York State Housing Finance Agy., N.Y.C., 1980-82; assoc. counsel, asst. secy. N.Y. State Urban Devel. Corp., N.Y.C., 1982-85; assoc. Mudge Rose Guthrie Alexander & Ferdon, N.Y.C., 1985-87, Bower & Gardner, N.Y.C., 1988, Hawkins, Delafield & Wood, N.Y.C., 1988-91; of counsel McKenzie McGhee, N.Y.C., 1991-98; assoc. Battle Fowler, N.Y.C., 1998-2000, Garfunkel Wild & Travis PC, Gt. Neck, NY, 2000—02; of counsel Emmet, Marvin & Martin, N.Y.C., 2002—. Author: Am. Bar Assn. Jour., 1981-1989 Mem. N.Y.C. Commn. on Status of Women, 1995-99. Mem. ABA, N.Y. State Bar Assn., (tax exempt fin. com.), Assn. Bar City of N.Y., Nat. Assn. Bond Lawyers, N.Y.C. Commn. on the Status of Women (legis. chmn.). E-mail: vmolinaro@emmetmarvin.com.

MOLINEAUX, CHARLES BORROMEO, lawyer, arbitrator, columnist, poet; b. N.Y.C., Sept. 27, 1930; s. Charles Borromeo and Marion Frances (Belter) M.; m. Patricia Leo Devereux, July 2, 1960; children: Charles, Stephen, Christopher, Patricia, Peter, Elizabeth. BS cum laude, Georgetown U., 1950; JD, St. Johns U., 1959. Bar: N.Y. 1959, Mass. 1981, D.C. 1988. From assoc. to ptnr. Nevius, Jarvis & Pilz and successor firms, N.Y.C., 1959-77; ptnr. Gadsby & Hannah, N.Y.C., 1978-80; v.p., gen. counsel Perini Corp., Framingham, Mass., 1980-87; pvt. practice Washington, 1987—. Adj. faculty Internat. Law Inst., Washington, 1989—. Author numerous poems. Mem. adv. bd. Inst. for Transnat. Arbitration; committeeman, Rep. Party, Nassau County , NY, 1965—71, committeeman, mem. exec. com. Fairfax County, Va., 1969. 1st lt. U.S. Army, 1954—56. Fellow Am. Bar Found.; mem. ASCE, Am. Arbitration Assn. (constrn. ADR task force 1994—), Chartered Inst. Arbitrators, Fedn. Internat. Engrs.-Conseils (Assoc. Gen. Contractors del. constrn. contract com., Louis Prangey award for svc. to profession cons. engring. 1996), Del. Hist. Soc., London Ct. Internat. Arbitration, Fellowship Cath. Scholars. Roman Catholic. Construction, Private international. Home: 8321 Weller Ave Mc Lean VA 22102-1717 Office: 1660 International Dr Ste 400 Mc Lean VA 22102 also: 46 Essex St London WC2R 3GH England E-mail: cmlnx@aol.com.

MOLITOR, GRAHAM THOMAS TATE, lawyer; b. Seattle, Apr. 6, 1934; s. Robert Franklin and Louise Margaret (Graham) M.; m. Carlotta Jean Crate, July 30, 1960; children: Graham Thomas Tate, Anne Therese, Christopher Robert. BS, U. Wash., 1955; LLB, Am. U., 1963. Bar: D.C. 1963. Rsch. asst. U. Wash., Seattle, 1957; bailiff U.S. Criminal Ct. D.C., 1958-59; legis. counsel U.S. Ho. of Reps., Washington, 1961-63; dir. candidate rsch. Rockefeller for Pres. Com., 1963-64, 68; D.C. counsel, asst. dir. govt. rels. Nabisco, Inc., Washington, 1964-70; dir. govtl. rels. Gen. Mills, Inc., Washington, 1970-77; pres., CEO Pub. Policy Forecasting, Inc., Potomac, Md., 1977—; prin. ptnr. Pub. Policy Communicators, 1989-91. Prin., ptnr. Pub. Policy Action Inst., Potomac; adv. bd. Creative Bus. Strategies, Inc.; adj. prof. Grad. Sch. Bus. Am. U., Washington, 1969—75, Washington, 1979—85, Montgomer Coll., Rockville, Md., 1987—88; dir. rsch. White House Conf. on Indsl. World Ahead, 1971—72; mem. White House Adv. Com. on Social Indicators, 1975—76; chmn. Commn. on the Future of Montgomery County, 1986—88; guest lectr. numerous univs.; mem. White House Confs. on Food, Nutrition and Health, 1969—71, White House Conf. on Youth, 1970; bd. dirs. First Global Conf. on the Future, Inc., Can., 1980—; organizing com. Found. for the Future, 1997—, bd. advisors, 1999—, mem. scholar adv. bd., 2001—. Contbg. editor Food Tomorrow Newsletter, 1976-77; co-editor, chmn. editl. bd. Ency. of the Future, 1991-96; cons. editor Hist. Guide to Am. Govt., 1995-97, McMillan Compendium of the Twenty-First Century, 1998-99; editor Technol. Forecasting and Social Change, 1999—; chmn. editl. bd. Future Survey, 1995-97, World Ency. of Police Forces and Correctional Systems, 2003—; mem. bd. editors Hudson Inst. Study of World Food Problems, 1975-77; mem. editl. bd. Bus. Tomorrow Newsletter, 1977-79, Jour. of Futures Studies, 2001; mem. bd. advisors New Mktg. Techs. Monitor, 1983-85; polit. editor On the Horizon, 1993-95; contbr. articles to profl. jours. Mem. Food Adv. Bd., N.Y.C., 1980-86. Served to 1st lt. U.S. Army, 1958-61. Recipient Disting. Service award Grocery Mfrs. Am., 1973-74, Disting. Service award Nat. Consumer Info. Center, 1974, Disting. Service award Am. Mgmt. Assn., 1975. Fellow: World Acad. Art and Sci. (mem. bd. trustees); mem.: World Future Soc. (gen. chmn. 2d Gen. Assembly 1975, v.p., dir. 1981—94, v.p., legal counsel 1994—, Disting. Svc. award 1975), E.D. Export Coun., Washington Indsl. Roundtable, Washington Bus.-Govt. Rels. Coun. (mem. exec. com. 2000—, chmn. commn. on Yr. 3000 2001—), Univ. Club, Phi Alpha Delta, Phi Kappa Sigma. Republican. Presbyterian. Home and Office: 9208 Wooden Bridge Rd Rockville MD 20854-2416

MOLJORD, KARE I. lawyer; b. Kristiansand, Norway, Mar. 28, 1953; 2 children. LLB, U. Oslo, 1978. Bar: Norway 1999. Assoc. judge, Oslo, 1982-84; atty. KPMG Audit Co., Norway, 1984-87, Bugge, Arentz-Hansen & Rasmussen, 1987-89; ptnr. Advokatfirmaet de Besche & Co., Oslo, 1989-2001, Arntz3n de Besche, Oslo, 2001—. Chmn. Paintbox AS, Norway, 1999—; bd. dirs. various cos. Author: Pledge of Real Estate, 1982; contbr. articles to profl. jours. Chm. Nat. Acctg. Adv. Bd., Oslo, 1989-92. Served to 2s lt. Norwegian Army, 1978-79. Mem. Internat. Fin. Assn., Norwegian Bar Assn. Avocations: bridge, golf. Corporate, general, Mergers and acquisitions, Corporate taxation. Office: Arntzen de Besche AS PO Box 2734 Solli N-0204 Oslo Norway E-mail: kare.i.moljord@ArntzenDeBesche.no.

MOLLOY, MAUREEN KATHERINE, lawyer, consultant, physician, consultant; b. N.Y.C., Aug. 15, 1932; d. James X. and Helen R. Molloy. BA, Barnard Coll., N.Y.C., 1953; MD, SUNY, 1957; MS in Hygiene, Harvard U., 1964; JD, Cornell U., 1990. Lic. physician, Mass., N.Y., Vt.; Bar: N.Y. 1991, Vt. 1992; diplomate Am. Bd. Orthop. Surgery. Intern, jr. resident surgery Royal Victoria Hosp., Montreal, Que., Can., 1957-59; sr. resident pediatric surgery Montreal Children's Hosp., 1959-60; resident orthop. surgery Harvard Combined Orthop. Program Mass. Gen. Hosp.-Children's Hosp., 1960-63; postdoctoral fellow epidemiology Harvard Sch. Pub. Health, Boston, 1964-66; dir. orthop. Handicapped Children's Svc., Vt. Dept. Health, 1966-87; assoc. True, Walsh & Miller, Ithaca, N.Y., 1990-91; law clk. Vt. Atty. Gen's Office, 1991-92; med.-legal cons. Shelburne, Vt., 1991—. Clin. assoc. prof. orthop. surgery U. Vt. Coll. medicine, 1974-87. Contbr. articles to profl. jours. Recipient Dist. Svc. award, 1996, 2000. Mem. ABA, Am. Acad. Orthop. Surgeons, Pediatric Orthop. Soc., Scoliosis Rsch. Soc. (chair prevalence and natural history com. 1984-95), Vt. Med. Soc. (coun. 1995—, v.p. 1998-99, pres. elect 1999-2000, pres. 2000-01), Vt. State Orthop. Soc., Vt. Bar Assn. (chair interprofl. rels./doctors com. 1993-96, N.Y. State Bar Assn., Franklin and Grand Isle Counties Bar Assn., Chittenden County Bar Assn., Am. Inns of Ct., Nat. Acad. Forensic Engrs. (corr.). Personal injury (including property damage), Product liability, Professional liability. Office: 5935 Dorset St Shelburne VT 05482-7097

MOLO, STEVEN FRANCIS, lawyer; b. Chgo., June 30, 1957; s. Steven and Alice (Babinski) M.; m. Mary Wood, Dec. 31, 1986; children: Alexander, Madeline, Julia, Allison. BS, U. Ill., 1979, JD, 1982. Bar: Ill. 1982. Asst. atty. gen. criminal pros. and trial divsn., Chgo., 1982-86; assoc. Winston & Strawn, Chgo., 1986-89, ptnr., 1989—, mem. exec. com., 2000—. Adj. prof. Loyola U. Law Sch., Chgo., 1988-93,. Northwestern U. Law Sch., Chgo., 1989—; mem. faculty Nat. Inst. Trial Advocacy, Chgo., 1989—; lectr. on trial advocacy, appellate advocacy, and evidence to various orgns. Co-author: Corporate Internal Investigations, 1993, updated annually, 1993—; bd. editors Bus. Crimes Bull: Litigation and Compliance, 1994—; contbr. articles to legal jours. Spl. counsel Ill. Jud. Inquiry Bd., 1986-90; spl. reapportionment counsel Cook County Judiciary, 1988-89, spl. reapportionment counsel to Rep. leadership Ill. Ho. of Reps. and Senate, 1991-92. Named one of World's Leading White Collar Crime Lawyers, Euromoney PLC, 1995, Leading Ill. Attys. Comml. Litigation and Criminal Law, 1996, Crain's Chicago Bus. "40 Under 40" Chicago Leaders, 1997, Best Lawyers in Am., 2000, Disting. Alumnus, U. Ill. Coll. Law, 2003, Am.'s Leading Bus. Litigators, Chamber's Guide, 2003. Fellow: Am. Acad. Appellate Lawyers; mem. ABA, FBA, Ill. Bar Assn., Chgo. Bar Assn., Theodore Roosevelt Assn., Chgo. Athletic Assn., Econ. Club Chgo., Tavern Club, Chgo. Inn of Ct. (master of bench, pres. 1997-98), Saddle & Cycle Club, Gilda's club Chgo. (presdl. gov. bd. 1999—). Federal civil litigation, General civil litigation, Criminal. Office: Winston & Strawn 35 W Wacker Dr Ste 4200 Chicago IL 60601-1695

MOLONEY, STEPHEN MICHAEL, lawyer; b. L.A., July 1, 1949; s. Donald Joseph and Madeline Marie (Sartoris) M.; m. Nancy Paula Barile, Jan. 15, 1972; children: Michael, John, Kathleen. Student, St. John's Sem., Camarillo, Calif., 1967-69; BS, U. Santa Clara, 1971, JD, 1975. Bar: Calif. 1975, U.S. Dist. Ct. (cen. dist.) Calif. 1976, U.S. Supreme Ct. 1990. Assoc. Gilbert, Kelly, Crowley & Jennett, L.A., 1975-80, from ptnr. to sr. ptnr., 1980—. Arbitrator, settlement officer Los Angeles Superior Ct., 1985—. Contbr. articles to profl. jours. Dir. Calif. Def. Polit. Action Com., Sacramento, 1991—. With USAR. Recipient Svc. award to Pres. of So. Calif. Def. Counsel, Def. Rsch. Inst., Chgo., 1992. Mem. Assn. So. Calif. Def. Counsel (pres. 1992-93), Calif. Def. Counsel (dir. 1991—), L.A. County Bar Assn. (vols. in parole, 1976-77, exec. com. alternative dispute resolution com. 1992-96), Oakmont Country Club, La Quinta Resort and Club. Democrat. Roman Catholic. Avocations: politics, golf, reading, travel. Construction, Labor (including EEOC, Fair Labor Standards Act, labor-management relations, NLRB, OSHA), Personal injury (including property damage). Office: Gilbert Kelly Crowley & Jennett 1200 Wilshire Blvd Ste 6 Los Angeles CA 90017-1908 E-mail: smm@gilbertkelly.com.

MOLONEY, THOMAS E. lawyer; b. Rockville Ctr., N.Y., Jan. 9, 1949; BS, U. Dayton, 1971; JD, U. Notre Dame, 1974. Bar: Ohio 1974. Prin. Am. Energy Svcs., Inc., Columbus, Ohio. Office: Am Energy Svcs Inc 1105 Schrock Rd Ste 602 Columbus OH 43229-1174

MOLONEY, THOMAS JOSEPH, lawyer; b. Bklyn., Oct. 14, 1952; s. Thomas J. and Grace (Nelson) M.; m. Molly K. Heines, Dec. 26, 1976. AB, Columbia U., 1973; JD cum laude, NYU, 1976. Bar: N.Y. 1977, U.S. Dist. Ct. (so. dist.) N.Y. 1977, U.S. Dist. Ct. (ea. dist.) N.Y. 1978, U.S. Ct. Appeals (2d cir.) 1981, U.S. Dist. Ct. (no. dist.) N.Y. 1988, U.S. Ct. Appeals (4th cir.) 1989, U.S. Supreme Ct. 1991. Assoc. Cleary, Gottlieb, Steen & Hamilton, N.Y.C., 1976-84, ptnr., 1984—. Bd. dirs. N.Y. Lawyers for Pub. Interest, N.Y.C., 1986-91; mediator U.S. Bankruptcy Ct. for So. Dist. N.Y., 1995. Asst. counsel Gov.'s Jud. Nominating Com., N.Y.C., 1981-85; chmn. bus. adv. coun. Washington Irving H.S., 1994—. Mem. ABA, Am. Bankruptcy Inst., Assn. of Bar of City of N.Y. (bankruptcy, corp. reorganization coms. 1983-86, chair com. legal assistance 1995-97), Order of Coif. Avocations: chess, golf, dance, travel, wine. Bankruptcy, Federal civil litigation, State civil litigation. Office: Cleary Gottlieb Steen & Hamilton 1 Liberty Plz Fl 38 New York NY 10006-1470

MOLONY, MICHAEL JANSSENS, JR., lawyer, arbitrator, mediator; b. New Orleans, Sept. 2, 1922; s. Michael Janssens and Marie (Perret)M.; m. Jane Leslie Waguespack, Oct. 21, 1951; children: Michael Janssens III (dec.), Leslie, Megan, Kevin, Sara, Brian, Ian, Duncan. JD, Tulane U., 1950. Bar: La. 1950, D.C. 1979, U.S. Dist. Ct. (ea. and mid. dists.) La. 1951, U.S. Ct. Appeals (5th cir.) 1953, U.S. Supreme Ct. 1972, U.S. Dist. Ct. (we. dist.) La. 1978, U.S. Ct. Appeals (11th and D.C. cirs.) 1981. Ptnr. Molony & Baldwin, New Orleans, 1950; assoc. Jones, Flanders, Waechter & Walker, New Orleans, 1951-56; ptnr. Jones, Walker, Waechter, Poitevent, Carrere & Denegre, New Orleans, 1956-75, Milling, Benson, Woodward, Hillyer, Pierson & Miller, New Orleans, 1975-91, Chaffe, McCall, Phillips, Toler & Sarpy, New Orleans, 1991-92, Sessions & Fishman, New Orleans, 1993-2000, Molony Law Firm, New Orleans, 2000—. Instr., lectr. Med. Sch. and Univ. Coll. Tulane U., 1953-59; mem. Eisenhower Legal Com., 1952. Mem. bd. commrs. Port of New Orleans, 1976-81, pres., 1978; mem. bd. rev. Assoc. Br. Pilots, 1990—; bd. dirs. La. World Expn. Inc., 1974-84; bd. dirs., exec. com. New Orleans Tourist and Conv. Commn., 1971-74, 78, chmn.; family attractions com. 1973-75; chmn. La. Gov.'s Task Force on Space Industry, 1971-73; chmn. La. Gov.'s Citizens' Adv. Com. Met. New Orleans Transp. and Planning Location of new Miss. River Bridge, 1971-77; mem. La. Gov.'s Task Force Natural Gas Requirements, 1971-72; mem. La. Gov.'s Proaction Commn. for Higher Edn., 1995; mem. Goals Found. Coun. and ex-officio mem. Goals Found., Met. New Orleans, 1969-73; vice chmn. Port of New Orleans Operation Impact, 1969-70, mem. Met. Area Com., New Orleans, 1970-84; trustee Pub. Affairs Rsch. Coun. La., 1970-73, mem. exec. com. Bus./Higher Edn. Coun., U. New Orleans, 1980-94, bd. dirs., 1980-2000, dir. emeritus, 2000—, v.p., 1986-88, pres., 1988-90, chmn. Task Force on Pub. Higher Edn. Funding, 1990-95, chmn. govtl. affairs, 1995-2000, Task Force on Edn./Econ. Devel. Alliances, 1993-95; mem. Mayor's Coun. on Internat. Trade and Econ. Devel., 1978; mem. Mayor's Transition Task Force Econ. Devel., 1994; bd. dirs. La. Partnership for Tech. and Innovation, 1989—, Acad. Sacred Heart, 1975-77, Internat. House, 1985-86, adv. coun., 1985—; bd. dirs. U. New Orleans Found., 1991-2003; mem. vis. com. Sch. Bus. Adminstrn., Loyola U., New Orleans, 1981-2001, trustee Loyola U., 1985-91, vice chmn. bd. trustees, 1990-91; mem. Dean's Coun. Tulane U. Law Sch., 1988-96, vice chmn. bldg. com., 1991-95; bd. dirs., mem. exec. com. Internat. Trade Mart, chmn. internat. bus. com., 1983-85; bd. dirs. World Trade Ctr.-New Orleans, 1983—, mem. port activity com. 1985-91, transp. com. 1991-95, 2000, 2001, 2002, 2003, govt. affairs com. 1996-99; chmn. Task Force on Internat. Banking, 1982; mem. Mayor's Task Force on Drug Abuse, 1989-90. With USAAC, 1942-46, PTO; capt. JAGDR, USAF, 1950-. Recipient Leadership award AIAA, 1971, Yenni award Loyola U., New Orleans, 1979, New Orleans Times Picayune Loving Cup, 1986, First Citizen of the Learning Soc. Dean's award UNO Met. Coll., 1992; also various civic contbn. awards; co-recipient Silver Anvil award New Orleans chpt. Pub. Rels. Soc. Am., 1991. Fellow Coll. Labor and Employment Lawyers; mem. ABA (labor and employment law and litigation sects., com. equal opportunity law, chmn. regional EEO com. liaison with equal opportunity commn., office of fed. contract compliance programs), D.C. Bar Assn., Fed. Bar Assn., La. Bar Assn. (past sec.-treas., bd. govs. 1957-60, editor jour. 1957-59, sec. spl. supreme ct. com. on drafting code jud. ethics), New Orleans Bar Assn. (dir legal aid bur. 1954, chmn. standing com. legis. 1968, vice chmn. standing com. pub. rels. 1970-71), Am. Judicature Soc., La. Law Inst. (asst. sec.-treas. 1958-70), Am. Arbitration Assn. (bd. dirs., 1995-98, chmn. reg. adv. coun., chmn. reg. adv. coun. employment law cases, mem. panels-employment, employee benefits, large complex employment and comml. arbitration/mediation cases, Whitney North Seymour Sr. award 1991), So. Inst. Mgmt. (founder), AIM, U.S. C. of C. (urban and regional affairs com. 1970-73), La. C. of C. (bd. dirs. 1963-66), New Orleans and River Region C. of C. (v.p. met. devel. and urban affairs 1969, past chmn. labor rels. coun., bd. dirs. 1970-78, pres. 1971, dir., exec. com. 1972, ex officio mem., bd. dirs. 1979—), Mil. Order Fgn. Wars (vice comdr. La. Commandery 2000-02, comdr. 2003—), Nat. Arbitration Forum, Panel Arbitrators, Bienville Club, Pickwick Club, Plimsoll Club, Serra Club, So. Yacht Club, Sigma Chi (pres. alumni chpt. 1956). Roman Catholic. Alternative dispute resolution, General civil litigation, Labor (including EEOC, Fair Labor Standards Act, labor-management relations, NLRB, OSHA). Home: 3039 Hudson Pl New Orleans LA 70131-5337 Office: Molony Law Firm 201 Saint Charles Ave Ste 3500 New Orleans LA 70170-3500 Fax: 504-582-1553. E-mail: mjm@mmolony-law.com.

MOLTZ, MARTIN PAUL, lawyer; b. Chgo., Nov. 22, 1944; s. Joseph and Celia Moltz; m. Ann Kaplan, May 26, 1974; 1 child, Benjamin Harold. BA, U. Ill., Chgo., 1966; JD, U. Okla., 1969. Bar: Ill. 1971, Fla. 1976. Asst. states atty. Cook County States Atty.'s Office, Chgo., 1970-72; staff atty. States Atty.'s Appellate Prosecutor's Office, Elgin, Ill., 1972-98, dep. dir., 1997—. Instr. Roosevelt U., Chgo., 1987—. Contbr. articles to profl. jours. Mem. 49th Ward Dems., Chgo., 1970—. With U.S. Army, 1969-75. Mem. Chgo. Bar Assn. (bd. mgrs. 1997—; bd. dirs. pub. interest law initiative 1997—), Decalogue Soc. Lawyers (bd. mgrs. 2001-). Jewish. Avocations: amusement parks, roller coasters, tournament bridge. Home: 7306 N Winchester Ave Chicago IL 60626-5529 Office: States Attys Appellate Prosecutor 2032 Larkin Ave Elgin IL 60123-5845

MONACI NALDINI, JACOPO, lawyer; b. Siena, Italy, Jan. 2, 1969; s. Claudio Naldini and Elisabetta Monaci. B, U. Di Siena, 1994; LLM, U. Coll. London, 1999. Bar: Florence, Italy 2000. Ptnr. Law Firm Olivieri, Florence, Italy, 2000—. Mem.: Assn. Internat. Young Lawyers, Chartered Inst. Arbitrators. Commercial, contracts (including sales of goods; commercial financing), Oil, gas, and mineral, Sports. Home: Strada Del Paradiso 25 53100 Siena Italy Office: Law Firm Olivieri Lungarno Vespucci 58 50123 Tuscany Italy Fax: +39 099 2676050. E-mail: 1@olcilaw.com.

MONACO, DANIEL JOSEPH, lawyer; b. Easton, Pa., May 12, 1922; s. Federico and Maria (Romano) M.; m. Marian P. Monaco, June 26, 1953 (div.); children: Denise E., Mimi D. AB with honors, Lafayette Coll., 1943; postgrad. studies, U. Mich., 1944-45; MA, U. Chgo., 1946; JD, Stanford U., 1950. Bar: Calif. 1951, U.S. Dist. Ct. (no. dist.) Calif. 1951, U.S. Supreme Ct. 1961. Mem. faculty U. Miami, Fla., 1946-47; founder, of counsel Monaco, Anderlini & Finkelstein, San Mateo, Calif., 1953—; probate judge State of Calif., 1963-67. Real estate broker, Calif., 1957-67; judge pro tem Calif. Mcpl and Superior Cts. Chmn. San Mateo County Dem. Ctrl. Com., 1960-61, Citizen World Ct.; mem. Calif. State Dem. Exec. Bd.; founder, pres. Circlon Internat., 1978-81; chmn. World Peace Through Law Ctr. com. to establish a Citizens' World Ct.; pres. peninsula com. UN Ednl. Sci. & Cultural Orgn., 1955-59; mem. No. Calif. Coun. Fgn. Affairs; San Mateo County Hosp. Found. Bd. With U.S. Army, 1943-46, lt. USAR, 1946-50. Mem. ABA, ATLA, UN Assocs.-U.S.A. (pres. San Mateo County chpt. 1958-65), Calif. S ate Bar Assn., Calif. Trial Lawyers Assn. (bd. govs.) San Mateo County Trial Lawyers Assn. (pres.), World Jurist Assn. (pres. Ams., 1991-93, 2d v.p. 1995-97, 1st v.p. 1997-99, pres. 1999-2001, fin. chmn. 1995—), Am. Bd. Trial Advocates, Internat. Law Assn. World Citizens, Gorbachev Found., The Commonwealth Club, Peninsula Golf and Country Club. Democrat. Avocations: travel, internat. law. Public international, Personal injury (including property damage). Home: 295 Darrell Rd Hillsborough CA 94010-7109 Office: 400 S El Camino Real Ste 700 San Mateo CA 94402-1744 Fax: 650-348-0962. E-mail: dukemonaco@aol.com.

MONACO, GRACE POWERS, lawyer; b. Union City, N.J., Sept. 3, 1938; s. Rea John and Grace Elizabeth (FitzGibbons) Powers; m. Lawrence Anthony Monaco, Aug. 10, 1963; children: Kathleen Rae(dec.) , David Gordon, Stephen Michael, Peter Joseph. BA, Coll. Misericordia-Pa., 1960, LittD (hon.) , 1979; JD, Georgetown U., 1963. Bar: D.C. 1964. Honor law grad. program Dept. Justice, Washington, 1963—64; pvt. practice Washington, 1965—66; assoc. Wheatley & Wollesen, Washington, 1967—78; ptnr. Fairman, Frisk & Monaco, Washington, 1978—82, White, Fine & Verville, Washington, 1983—88, of counsel, 1988—90; v.p. Emprise, Inc., 1988—91, Med. Care Mgmt. Corp., 1992—; dir. Med. Care Ombudsman Program, 1990—. Contbr. chpts. to books, articles to profl. jours. Chmn. bd. dirs. Candlelighters Childhood Cancer Found., 1978—90; chmn. bd. Capitol Hill Hosp., 1982—85; vice-chmn. Medlantic Healthcare Group, 1982—88, Medlantic Rsch. Found., 1989—95; adv. com. on oncogic drugs FDA, 1988—92; adv. com. on hematotogic and neoplastic drugs U.S. Pharmacopeia, 1987—90, pub. bd., 1990—2000; pub. mem. data and safety monitoring com. St. Jude's and Children's Oncology Group, 2000—. Named Day of June 28 in her honor, 1987; recipient Nat. award, Am. Cancer Soc., 1978, Achievement award, Capital Hill Cmty., 1985, Lloyd Bentsen Nat. award, 1995, 1997, Lifetime Achievement award, Nat. Coalition for Cancer Survivorship. Mem.: Fed. Energy Regulatory Bar Assn., Am. Health Lawyers Assn., Fed. Bar Assn., D.C. Bar Assn., Women's Bar Assn., Capitol Hill Restoration Soc. Democrat. Roman Catholic. Administrative and regulatory, Health, Insurance. Home: 874 Monument Dr Montross VA 22520

MONAGHAN, PETER GERARD, lawyer; b. Belfast, Ireland, July 12, 1949; came to U.S., 1961; s. William Liam and Elizabeth (Eccles) M.; m. Barbara Marion Farrenkopf, Sept. 24, 1972; children: Brian Patrick, Kevin James, Allison Mary. BS, Fordham U., 1970; JD, St. John's U., Jamaica, N.Y., 1977. Bar: N.Y. 1978, U.S. Dist. Ct. (so. dist.) N.Y. 1978, U.S. Dist. Ct. (ea. dist.) N.Y. 1979, U.S. Supreme Ct. 1986. Claims examiner Royal Ins. Co., N.Y.C., 1970-76; assoc. Kroll, Edelman, Elser and Dicker, N.Y.C., 1976, Bower and Gardner, N.Y.C., 1977-83, ptnr., 1984-91, Bartlett, McDonough, Bastone & Monaghan, LLP, Mineola, N.Y., 1992—. Cubmaster Boy Scouts Am., Bayside, N.Y., 1985-89. Capt. U.S. Army Res., 1970-78. Mem. ATLA, ABA, Queens County Bar Assn., N.Y. State Bar Assn. (trial lawyers sect. com. on med. malpractice 1988—), Assn. Bar City N.Y. (com. on med. malpractice 2002—), Nassau-Suffolk Trial Lawyers Assn., Nassau County Bar Assn. Federal civil litigation, State civil litigation, General practice. Office: Bartlett McDonough Bastone & Monaghan LLP 300 Old Country Rd Mineola NY 11501-4198

MONAGHAN, THOMAS JUSTIN, former prosecutor; JD, U. Nebr. Law School. Adjunct faculty College of St. Mary, Nebr., 1985—91; ptnr. Monaghan, Tiedman & Lynch, Omaha, 1978—93; U.S. atty. Dept. Justice, Omaha, 1993—2001. Office: Monaghan Group 1321 Jones St Omaha NE 68102

MONAHAN, COURTNEY WILSON, lawyer; b. L.A., Sept. 14, 1963; d. Bruce and Joyce Wilson; m. Michael John U. Monahan, Oct. 22, 1994; children: Lauren Marie, Olivia Hannon. BA, U. Colo., 1985; JD, Suffolk U., 1989. Bar: N.Y. 1990, U.S. Dist. Ct. (ea. and so. dist.) N.Y. 1990. Assoc. atty. Colucci & Umans, N.Y.C., 1990-96, prnt., 1997—. Intellectual property. Office: Colucci & Umans 101 E 52nd St New York NY 10022-6018 E-mail: cwilson@colucci-umans.com.

MONAHAN, MARIE TERRY, lawyer; b. Milford, Mass., June 26, 1927; d. Francis V. and Marie I. (Casey) Terry; m. John Henry Monahan, Aug. 25, 1951; children: Thomas F., Kathleen J., Patricia M., John Terry, Moira M., Deirdre M. AB, Radcliffe Coll., 1949; JD, New Eng. Sch. Law, 1975. Bar: Mass. 1977, U.S. Dist. Ct. Mass. 1978, U.S. Supreme Ct. 1982. Tchr. French and Spanish Holliston (Mass.) High Sch., 1949-52; pvt. practice Newton, Mass., 1977—. Mem. Mass. Assn. Women Lawyers (pres. 1986). Avocations: reading, travel. State civil litigation, Family and matrimonial, Probate (including wills, trusts). Home and Office: 34 Foster St Newton MA 02460-1511

MONCREIFF, ROBERT P. lawyer; b. Evanston, Ill., Mar. 26, 1930; s. W. Philip and Maxine E. M.; m. Elisabeth M.; children: Anne, Philip, Jane. BA, Yale U., 1952; MA, Oxford U., Eng., 1954; LLB, Harvard U., 1957. Bar: Mass. 1957. Assoc. Palmer & Dodge, Boston, 1957-62, ptnr., 1963-95, of counsel, 1995—. City councillor, Cambridge, Mass., 1970-74. Office: Palmer & Dodge LLP 111 Huntington at Prudential Ctr Boston MA 02199-7613 E-mail: rmoncreiff@palmerdodge.com.

MONCURE, JOHN LEWIS, lawyer; b. Houston, Nov. 4, 1930; s. Walter Raleigh Daniel and Margaret (Atkins) M.; m. Norma Steed, Dec. 29, 1954 (dec. June 1982); children: John Carter, Michael Lewis, Douglas Lee, Stuart Richard, Mary Margaret; m. Margaret Edmonston, Nov. 12, 1983. BBA, U. Houston, 1953; JD, U. Tex., 1956. Bar: Tex. 1956. Assoc. Butler, Binion, Rice, Cook & Knapp, Houston, 1956-68; ptnr. Prappas, Moncure & Eidman, Houston, 1969-86, John L. Moncure and Assocs., Houston, 1987—. Lectr. bus. law U. Houston, 1958-59, 68-69 Mem. sch. bd. St. Thomas Episcopal Sch., Houston, 1965-78; mem. vestry St. Thomas Episc. Ch., 1975-78. Named Distinguished Alumni Coll. Bus., U. Houston, 1968 Fellow Am. Coll. Probate Counsel; mem. Am., Tex., Houston bar assns., Assn. Christian Schs. (trustee), Coll. Bus. Alumni Assn. U. Houston (pres., dir.), U. Houston Alumni Fedn. (treas., dir.), Sigma Alpha Epsilon. Republican. Probate (including wills, trusts), Property, real (including real estate development, water), Estate taxation. Home: 1220 W Clay Houston TX 77019 Office: 1200 River Oaks Tower 3730 Kirby Dr Houston TX 77098-3905

MONDRAGON, JORGE, lawyer; b. Mexico City, DF, Mexico, May 23, 1969; s. Manuel and Martha (Domínguez) Mondragón; m. Leonora Gomez Tagle, Nov. 20, 1993; children: María, Jorge, Alexa. LLB, U. Nat. Autónomo de México, Mexico City, Mexico, 1993—96; law grad. studies, Inst. Tecnológico Autónomo de México, Mexico, 1996. Bar: Mexican Bar Assoc. Law clk. Solís,Castellanos & Ochoa, Mexico City, 1991; legal mgr. Gonzalez Calvillo & Forastieri, Mexico City, 1991—92; law clk. Xabre Servicios, SA de CV, Mexico City, 1992—94; assoc. Cantú & Rangel, SC, Mexico City, 1994—96, González Calvillo & Forastieri, Mexico City, 1996—98; ptnr. González Calvillo, SC, Mexico City, 1998—2003. Prof. U. Panamericana, Mexico City, 2002—. Mem.: Internat. Franchise Assoc. Avocations: running, reading, music. Office: González Calvillo SC Montes Urales 632 Piso 3 11000 Mexico City Mexico

MONDUL, DONALD DAVID, patent lawyer; b. Miami, Fla., Aug. 24, 1945; s. David Donald and Marian Wright (Heck) M.; children: Alison Marian, Ashley Megan; m. Anna Marie Towle, Oct. 12, 1996. BS in Physics, U.S. Naval Acad., 1967; MBA, Roosevelt U., 1976; JD, John Marshall Law Sch., 1979. Bar: Ill. 1979, Fla. 1980, Tex. 1998; U.S. Patent Office 1980; U.S. Ct. Appeals (fed. cir.) 1982; U.S. Supreme Ct. 1990. Commd. ensign USN, 1967, advanced through grades to comdr., 1977; mktg. rep. Control Data Corp., Chgo., 1977-79; patent atty. Square D Co., Palatine, Ill., 1979-81; group patent counsel Ill. Tool Works Inc., Chgo., 1981-87; assoc. Cook, Wetzel & Egan, Chgo., 1987-89; ptnr. Foley & Lardner, Chgo. and Milw., 1989-95; sr. patent atty. IBM, East Fishkill, N.Y., 1995-96; gen. patent counsel Ericsson, Inc., Richardson, Tex., 1996-99; pvt. practice Dallas, 1999—. Patentee in method and apparatus for multiplying a plurality of numbers, N numbers, and determining the product of two numbers, air baffle apparatus, electrical encoding device, apparatus and method for establishing an operating parameter for a power supply device, and apparatus and method for locating objects in a three-dimensional space. Commander, USNR, 1967-87. Achievements include patents in field of Electrical Encoding Device; Method and Appartus for Determining the Produt of Two Numbers; Apparatus for Providing Power to Selected Portions of a Multiplying Device; Method and Apparatus for Multiplying a Plurality of Numbers; Method and Apparatus for Multiplying a Plurality of Numbers; Method and for Establishing an Operating Parameter for a Power Supply Device; Apparatus and Method for Locating Objects in a Three-Dimensional Space. Patent. Office: 6631 Lovington Dr Dallas TX 75252-2519 E-mail: dmondul@aol.com.

MONE, MICHAEL EDWARD, lawyer; b. Brockton, Mass., May 15, 1942; s. Edward Patrick and June Elizabeth (Kelliher) M.; m. Margaret E. Supple, Sept. 11, 1965; 1 child, Michael Edward. BA, Middlebury Coll., 1964, LLB (hon.), 2000; JD, Boston Coll., 1967; LLB (hon.), Suffolk U., 1999. Bar: Mass. 1967, U.S. Dist. Ct. Mass. 1968, U.S. Ct. Appeals (1st cir.) 1968. Trial atty. Schneider & Reilly, Boston, 1967-73, ptnr., 1969-73; trial lawyer Esdaile, Barrett & Esdaile, Boston, 1973—, ptnr., 1976—. Instr. Boston Coll. Law Sch., 1981. Chmn. Zoning Bd. Appeals, Brockton, 1976-78. Fellow Am. Coll. Trial Lawyers (bd. regents 1995-2001, sec. 1997-98, pres. 1999-2000); mem. ABA, ATLA (bd. govs. 1975-78), Mass. Bar Assn. (pres. 1993-94), Mass. Acad. Trial Lawyers (pres. 1981-84, joint bar com. on jud. nominations 1986-90). Federal civil litigation, State civil litigation, Personal injury (including property damage). Office: Esdaile Barrett & Esdaile 75 Federal St Boston MA 02110-1913 E-mail: Mone@ebelaw.com.

MONE, ROBERT PAUL, lawyer; b. Columbus, Ohio, July 23, 1934; s. Henry P. and Ann E. (Freedlund) M.; m. Lucille L. Willman, May 3, 1960; children: Robert, Maria, Andrew, Richard. BA, U. Dayton, 1956; JD, U. Notre Dame, 1959. Bar: Ohio 1959. Law clk.to presiding judge U.S. Dist. Ct. (no. dist.) Ohio, Cleve., 1960-62; assoc. George, Greek, King, et al, Columbus, 1962-66, ptnr., 1966-79, McConnaughey, Stradley, et al, Columbus, 1979-81, Thompson Hine LLP, Columbus, 1981—. Cpl. U.S. Army, 1959-60. Mem. ABA, Ohio State Bar Assn., Energy Bar Assn., Columbus Bar Assn., Nat. Generation and Transmission Coop. Lawyers Assn. (1st pres.), Rotary. Corporate, general, Utilities, public. Home: 2300 Tremont Rd Columbus OH 43221-3706 Office: Thompson Hine LLP 10 W Broad St Ste 700 Columbus OH 43215-3435

MONGE, JAY PARRY, lawyer; b. N.Y.C., Mar. 15, 1943; s. Joseph Paul and Dorothy Emma (Oschmann) M.; m. Julia T. Burdick, 1966 (div. 1994); children: Justin Parry, Lindsay Newton; m. Elizabeth Ann Tracy, 1994. AB, Harvard U., 1966; LLB, U. Va., 1969. Bar: Ill. 1969, N.Y. 1981, N.C. 2003. Assoc. Mayer, Brown & Platt, Chgo., 1969-75, ptnr., 1976-79, N.Y.C., 1980-99, mng. ptnr., 1981-94, ptnr. Charlotte, NC, 2000—. Contbr. legal commentaries Ill. Inst. Continuing Legal Edn., 1974, 78, 81, 84, 87, 93, 96, 2002. Trustee Wagner Coll., 1996-2002. Mem. ABA, Assn. Bar City N.Y., Chgo. Club, Onwentsia Club, Sky Club, Westchester Country Club, Charlotte City Club, Carmel Country Club. Banking, Corporate, general, Finance. Office: Mayer Brown Rowe & Maw 214 N Tryon St Ste 3800 Charlotte NC 28202 E-mail: jmonge@mayerbrownrowe.com.

MONICA, ANTONIO DE CARVALHO GODINHO, lawyer; b. Lisbon, Portugal, Aug. 2, 1951; s. José António and Maria Margarida (Carvalho) M.; m. Isabel Sacadura, Ju ne 16, 1984; children: Martim, Duarte, Isabel. Lic. by Faculty of Law, Lisbon U., Lisbon, 1976. Mem. legal dept. Supa SA, Lisbon, 1973-77; pvt. practice civil, comml. banking, environ., family, admin. real estate, 1976—; Internat. Bankers Course of Midland Bank, London, 1979—. Mem. internat. and legal dept. Banco Totta & Azores, Lisbon, 1979-84. Advisor to Portuguese State Sec. of Treasury, 1981; chief of staff External Trade Sec. of State, Lisbon, 1988-89; del. to 3d and 4th Portuguese Congress of Lawyers. Decorated Italian Grande Officiale Order of Merit, 1989. Mem. Portuguese Bar Assn. Lisbon County, Ginasio Clube Portuguese, Automovel Clube Portugal, Clube Naval Cascais, Portuguese C. of C. and Industry (sec. gen., Portugal del. to Internat. C. of C. 1991-95). Avocations: water skiing, motorcycles, reading, antiques. Administrative and regulatory, General civil litigation, General practice. Office: Av Alvares Cabral no 84 2 1250 Lisbon Portugal Fax: 3511 213882554.

MONK, CARL COLBURN, lawyer, academic administrator; b. Sept. 11, 1942; BA in Polit. Sci., Okla. State U., 1965; JD, Howard U., 1971. Bar: D.C. 1971, N.Y. 1973. Assoc. Simpson, Thacher & Bartlett, N.Y.C., 1971-74; from asst. prof. to assoc. prof. Washburn U., Topeka, Kans., 1974-78, from assoc. dean to dean, prof., 1976-88, disting. prof. law, 1988—. Dep. dir. Assn. Am. Law Schs., Washington, 1988-90, exec. dir., 1992—; vis. scholar Bklyn. Law Sch., 1985-86; vis. prof. law W.S. Richardson Sch. Law U. Hawaii Manao, 1990-91; lit. cons. Contbr. articles to profl. jours. Bd. dirs. Kans. Civil Liberties Union. Office: Assn Am Law Schs Ste 800 1201 Connecticut Ave NW Washington DC 20036-2605 E-mail: cmonk@aals.org.

MONNICH, JOHN ROBERT, lawyer; b. Detroit, Dec. 9, 1947; s. William Joseph and Sally Jean Monnich; m. Jane Cetrone, June 20, 1970; children: John Robert Jr., Brian William. BBA, U. Notre Dame, 1970; JD, U. Detroit, 1973. Bar: Mich. 1974, U.S. Dist. Ct. (ea. dist.) Mich. 1974, U.S. Ct. Appeals 1976, U.S. Dist. Ct. (we. dist.) Mich. 1987; CLU, CPCU. Assoc. Dinan & Schenden, Troy, Mich., 1974-75, Brian M. Smith, Troy, 1975-76; ptnr. Maybaugh, Wellman & Monnich, Troy, 1976-81, Monnich, Malloy & Delie, Troy, 1981—2001; pvt. practice Royal Oak, 2001—. Roman Catholic. Avocation: sports. Insurance, Personal injury (including property damage). Office: # Secondf 225 S Main St Royal Oak MI 48067-2611

MONROE, CARL DEAN, III, lawyer; b. Birmingham, Ala., Sept. 15, 1960; s. Carl D. and Martha Jo M. BA, Birmingham-So. Coll., 1982; JD, Georgetown U., 1985. Bar: Ala. 1986, U.S. Ct. Appeals (11th cir.) 1988. Scheduler Siegelman for Atty. Gen., Montgomery, 1986; legal rsch. aide Office of Sec. of State State of Ala., Montgomery, 1986; asst. atty. gen., adminstrv. asst. Office of Atty. Gen., Montgomery, 1987-89; atty.-advisor Office Gen. Counsel, U.S. Dept. Energy, Washington, 1989—. Mem. panel of judges Georgetown Law Ctr. Moot Ct., 1991, 92, CIA Environ. Roundtable; lectr. waste mgmt. Johns Hopkins U., natural resources George Washington U. Mem. panel of judges Ala. YMCA Youth Legislature, Montgomery, 1979, 87, 88, 89; office coord. blood dr. ARC, Montgomery, 1987, 88; com. mem. Georgetown Alumni Admissions, Washington, 1986-91; mem. Nat. Trust for Hist. Preservationmem. Beahrs Environ. Leadership Seminar, Greater Smithsonian Devel., U. Calif.-Berkeley, 2001. Mem. ABA (author environ. law sect. newsletter Looking Ahead), Acad. Polit. Sci., Ala. Bar Assn., Birmingham-So. Alumni (alumni leader 1986—), Phi Beta Kappa. Democrat. Presbyterian. Avocations: water skiing, tennis, horseback riding. Home: 901 S 15th St # 622 Arlington VA 22202 E-mail: dean.monroe@hq.doe.gov.

MONROE, KENDYL KURTH, retired lawyer; b. Clayton, N.Mex., Sept. 6, 1936; s. Dottis Donald and Helen (Kurth) M.; m. Barbara Sayre, Sept. 12, 1956; children: Sidney, Dean, Loren. AB, Stanford U., 1958, LLB, 1960. Bar: N.Y. 1961, Calif. 1961. Assoc. Sullivan & Cromwell, N.Y.C., 1960-67, ptnr., 1968-94. Chmn. TEB Charter Svcs., Inc., Teterboro, NJ, El Valle Escondido Ranch Ltd. Co., Seneca, N.Mex., Eklund Assn. Clayton, N.Mex., N.Y. Chamber Soloists, N.Y.C.; bd. dirs. Clan Munro Assn., Great Falls, Va. Chmn. adv. coun. The Mandala Ctr., Des Moines, N.Mex.; mem. adv. com. Cornerstones Cmty Partnerships, Santa Fe; bd. dirs. N.Mex. Water Dialogue, Gallup, Clayton (N.Mex.) Health Sys., Inc.; dir. emeritus Pub. Health Rsch. Inst., Newark; bd. dirs. N.Mex. Heritage Preservation Alliance, Santa Fe. Mem. State Bar Calif., Assn. of Bar of City of N.Y., N.Mex. Amigos, Met. Club (N.Y.C.). Property, real (including real estate development, water), Securities, Corporate taxation. Home: 189 Sayre Rd Seneca NM 88415 E-mail: kkmonroe@ptsi.net.

MONSANTO, RAPHAEL ANGEL, lawyer; b. N.Y.C., Oct. 3, 1946; s. Rafael Monsanto and Margarita Velazquez. BSEE, NYU, 1969, JD, 1975. Bar: N.J. 1975, U.S. Patent Office 1976, N.Y. 1978, Mich. 1998. Atty. Bell Telephone Lab., Murray Hills, N.J., 1975-78; intellectual property counsel J.C. Penney, N.Y.C., 1978-80; atty. Kenyon & Kenyon, N.Y.C., 1980-84, Rohm & Monsanto Plc, Detroit, 1984—. Intellectual property cons. various orgns., Detroit, 1996—; presenter, author seminar course, 1996 Holder patent. Dir., counsel Boys Choir of Detroit, 1998—. Recipient Achievement award Ctr. for Hemispherical Coop., 1996. Mem. ABA, N.Y. Intellectual Property Law Assn., N.J. Trial Lawyers Assn. Avocation: musician. Federal civil litigation, Intellectual property, Patent. Office: Rohm & Monsanto PLC 660 Woodward Ave Ste 1525 Detroit MI 48226-3518 E-mail: ramonsanto@aol.com.

MONSON, JOHN RUDOLPH, lawyer; b. Chgo., Feb. 4, 1941; s. Rudolph Agaton and Ellen Louise (Loeffler) M.; m. Susan Lee Brown, May 22, 1965; children: Elizabeth Louisa, Christina Lee, Donald Rudolph. BA with honors, Northwestern U., 1963; JD with distinction, U. Mich., 1966. Bar: Ill. 1966, N.H. 1970, Mass. 1985. Atty. assoc. Chapman & Cutler, Chgo., 1966-68, Levenfeld, Kanter, Baskes & Lippitz, Chgo., 1968-70, Nighswander, Martin & Mitchell, Laconia, N.H., 1970-71; mem., ptnr. Wiggin & Nourie, P.A., Manchester, N.H., 1972—, pres., 1991-94. Sec., gen. counsel Rock of Ages Corp., 1996-2000. Mem. N.H. Fish and Game Commn., Concord, 1980-94, chmn., 1983-93; sr. bd. dirs. Brown-Monson Found., 1991—; incorporator Cath. Med. Ctr., 1988-95, Optima Health, 1994-99; commr. N.H. Land and Cmty. Heritage Commn., 1998-2000. Fellow Am. Coll. Trust and Estate Counsel, Safari Club Internat. (v.p. 1999-2001, dir.-at-large 1997-99, treas. 2001-02, pres. elect 2002—). Republican. Avocations: skiing, hunting, running. Corporate, general, Estate planning. Home: 24 Wellesley Dr Bedford NH 03110-4531 Office: Wiggin & Nourie PA 20 Market St Manchester NH 03101-1931

MONTAGUE, H. DIXON, lawyer; b. Midland, Tex., Feb. 7, 1952; BA, Tulane U., 1974; JD, U. Miss., 1977. Bar: Miss. 1977, Tex. 1978. Ptnr. Vinson & Elkins L.L.P., Houston. General civil litigation, Condemnation (eminent domain). Office: Vinson & Elkins LLP 2500 First City Tower 1001 Fannin St Ste 3300 Houston TX 77002-6706

MONTAGUE, ROBERT LATANE, III, lawyer; b. Washington, Sept. 18, 1935; s. Robert Latane and Frances Breckinridge (Wilson) M.; m. Prudence Darnell, June 20, 1964; children: Anne Steele Mason Montague, Robert Latane IV. BA, U. Va., 1956, LLB, 1961. Bar: Va. 1961, D.C. 1966, U.S. Supreme Ct. 1966. Asst. atty. gen., Ky., 1961-64; pres. Historic Alexandria Found., 1968-70; chmn. Alexandria Environ. Policy Commn., 1970-74; pres. Conservation Coun. Va., 1978-80; chmn. Alexandria Commn. on Bicentennial of U.S. Constitution, 1987-91, Alexandria Historical Restoration and Preservation Commn., 1988—2001; trustee Assn. for Preservation of Va. Antiquities, 1990-96. Chmn. Bd. of Vis. of Gunston Hall, 1987-92; del. Moscow Conf. on Law and Econ. Coop., 1990. Comdr. USNR, 1956-79. Mem. Va. Bar Assn., Va. State Bar (chmn. environ. law sect. 1973-74), Alexandria Bar Assn. Office: 1007 King St Alexandria VA 22314-2922

MONTEDONICO, JOSEPH, lawyer; b. Washington, May 30, 1937; s. Joseph and Linda (Love) M.; m. Lynne Morrell, Nov. 12, 1979; 1 child, Maria. BA, U. Md., 1962, JD, 1965. Bar: Md. 1965, D.C. 1965, U.S. Dist. Ct. D.C. 1965, U.S. Dist. Ct. Md. 1965. Law clk. to justice, Rockville, Md., 1965-66; assoc. Donahue, Ehrmantraut Mitchell, Rockville, 1966-78; ptnr. Donahue, Ehrmantraut, Montedonico, Washington, 1978-88, Montedonico & Mason, Rockville, 1988-91, Montedonico, Hamilton & Altman, PC, Chevy Chase, Md., 1991—2001, Montedonico, Belcoure & Tazzara, Washington, 2001—. Cons., lectr. in field. Author: Medical Malpractice and Health Care Care, 1987; (with others) Anesthesia Clinics, 1987, Surgical Pathology, 1989. With U.S. Army, 1956-58. Named one of Best Lawyers in Am., Washingtonian Mag., 1989—96, Best 75 Lawyers in Washington, 2002. Mem.: D.C. Bar Assn., Md. Bar Assn., Internat. Acad. Trial Lawyers, Am. Bd. Trial Lawyers (pres. D.C. chpt.), Inns of Ct. Republican. Avocations: scuba, skiing, photography. General civil litigation, Health, Personal injury (including property damage). Office: Montedonico Belcoure & Tazzara 1020 19th St NW Ste 420 Washington DC 20036 E-mail: Joseph.Montedonico@mbt_legal.com.

MONTELLARO, RANDELL, lawyer; b. Forest Hills, N.Y., Oct. 31, 1960; s. Lee and Bernadette (Shenton) M.; m. Lisa McCaffrey, Nov. 29, 1991. BBA, Hofstra U., 1982, JD, 1985. Bar: N.Y. 1986, D.C. 1987. Sr. tax cons. Deloitte, Haskins & Sells, N.Y.C., 1985-87; sr. cons. Price Waterhouse, N.Y.C., 1988-89; assoc. Summit Soloman & Feldesman, N.Y.C., 1989-93; ptnr. Epstein Becker & Green, N.Y.C., 1993—. Mem. Hofstra Law Rev., 1984-85; contbg. author Employee Benefits Law, 1991. Mem. N.Y. State Bar Assn., D.C. Bar Assn. Democrat. Home: 81 N Kings Ave North Massapequa NY 11758-3402 Office: Epstein Becker & Green 250 Park Ave Fl 13 New York NY 10177-1211 E-mail: rmontellaro@ebglaw.com.

MONTERRUBIO ALCANTARA, LUIS MANUEL, lawyer; b. Mexico, Fed. Dist., Mexico, June 21, 1967; s. Luis Manuel Monterrubio and María de Lourdes Alcántara; m. Waleska Marcela Pría, Aug. 3, 1973; 1 child, Emiliano Monterrubio. LLB, Inst. Tech. Méx., Fed. Dist., 1989. Bar: Mex. Coll. Lawyers, Fed. Dist. 1997. Paralegal Noriega y Escobedo, A.C., Mex. City, 1987—89, assoc., 1989—95, ptnr., 1995—. Prof. Law Inst. Tech. Auto. Mex., Mex. City, 1995—2002; arbitrator Mex. Arbitration Ctr., Mex. City, Fed. Dist., 1998—; bd. dirs. Inst. Mediation, Mex., Mex. City, Fed. Dist., 1999—. Avocations: golf, triathlon. Antitrust, Alternative dispute resolution, Mergers and acquisitions, Commercial, consumer (including collections, credit). Office: Noriega y Escobedo AC Sierra Mojada No 626 Mexico City 11010 Mexico Office Fax: (55) 52.84.33.27.. E-mail: lmonterrubio@noriegayescobedo.com.mx.

MONTGOMERIE, BRUCE MITCHELL, lawyer; b. South Bend, Ind., Feb. 9, 1946; s. Ralph H. and Dorothy (Larson) M.; m. Kathleen Ann McIntyre, June 21, 1969 (dissolved); m. Claire Desrosier, Nov. 28, 1985. BA, DePauw U., 1968; JD, MIA, Columbia U., 1972; LLM in Taxation, NYU, 1975. Bar: N.Y. 1973. From assoc. to ptnr. Milbank, Tweed, Hadley & McCloy, N.Y.C., 1972-83; ptnr. Willkie, Farr & Gallagher, N.Y.C., 1983—. Mem. N.Y. State Bar (tax sect. exec. com. 1982-90), Nat. Assn. Real Estate Investment Trusts (bd. govs. 1983-85). Property, real (including real estate development, water), Corporate taxation. Home: 142 Interlaken Rd Lakeville CT 06039 Office: Willkie Farr & Gallagher 787 7th Ave New York NY 10019-6018 E-mail: bmontgomerie@willkie.com.

MONTGOMERY, BETTY DEE, state auditor, former state attorney general, former state legislator; BA, Bowling Green State U.; JD, U. Toledo, 1976. Former criminal clk. Lucas County Common Pleas Ct.; asst. pros. atty. Wood County, Ohio, 1977—78, pros. atty., 1981—88, City of Perrysburg, Ohio, 1978—81; mem. Ohio Senate, 1989—94; atty. gen. State of Ohio, Columbus, 1995—. Mem.: Wood County Bar Assn. Republican. Office: Auditor of State 88 E Broad St 5th Fl Columbus OH 43215

MONTGOMERY, CHARLES HARVEY, lawyer; b. Spartanburg, S.C., Jan. 28, 1949; s. Dan Hugh and Ann Louise (Gasque) M.; m. Renée Jean Gubernot, Mar. 27, 1971; children: Charles Scott, Marie Renée. BA, Duke U., 1971; JD, Vanderbilt U., 1974. Bar: N.C. 1974, U.S. Dist. Ct. (ea. dist.) N.C. 1974, U.S. Supreme Ct. 1979, U.S. Dist. Ct. (mid. dist.) N.C. 1991; cert. family law specialist, N.C., 1995. Assoc. Jordan Morris & Hoke, Raleigh, N.C., 1974-75; atty. Wake County Legal Svcs., Raleigh, 1975-76; pvt. practice, Raleigh, 1977; ptnr. Montgomery & Montgomery, Cary, N.C., 1978-79, Sanford Adams McCullough & Beard, Raleigh, 1979-86, Adams McCullough & Beard, Raleigh, 1986-88, Toms Reagan & Montgomery, Cary, 1989-92, Toms & Montgomery, Cary, 1992-93; pvt. practice, Cary, 1993—. Bd. dirs. Br. Bank and Trust, Cary; pres. Family Law Mediation, Inc. Councilman Town of Cary, 1977-81, 83-87; vice-chmn. Wake County Dem. party, Raleigh, 1991-92; commr. Wake County, Raleigh, 1992; bd. dirs. East Cen. Cmty. Legal Svcs., Inc., 1997—, State Capitol Found., 1994—. Mem.: ABA, N.C. Acad. Trial Lawyers (chair family law sect. 1996—98), Wake County Bar Assn. (bd. dirs. 1999—2001), N.C. Bar Assn. (chmn. pub. info. com. 1994—96, dir. family law coun. 1994—97). Methodist. Avocation: sailing. State civil litigation, Family and matrimonial, Land use and zoning (including planning). Office: PO Box 1325 590 New Waverly Pl Ste 110 Cary NC 27512-1325 E-mail: charles@montylaw.com.

MONTGOMERY, JOHN WARWICK, law educator, theologian; b. Warsaw, N.Y., Oct. 18, 1931; s. Maurice Warwick and Harriet (Smith) M.; m. Joyce Ann Bailer, Aug. 14, 1954; children: Elizabeth Ann, Catherine Ann; m. Lanalee de Kant, Aug. 26, 1988; 1 adopted child, Jean-Marie (Baron of Kiltartan and Lord of Morris, Comte de St. Germain de Montgommery). AB in Philosophy with distinction, Cornell U., 1952; BLS, U. Calif., Berkeley, 1954, MA, 1958; BD, Wittenberg U., 1958, MST, 1960; PhD, U. Chgo., 1962; Docteur de l'Université, mention Théologie Protestante, U. Strasbourg, France, 1964; LLB, LaSalle Extension U., 1977; diplôme cum laude, Internat. Inst. Human Rights, Strasbourg, 1978; MPhil in Law, U. Essex, Eng., 1983; D in Civil and Canon Law (hon.), Inst. Religion and Law, Moscow, 1999; LLM, Cardiff U., Wales, 2000. Bar: Va. 1978, Calif. 1979, D.C. 1985, Wash. 1990, U.S. Supreme Ct. 1981, Eng. 1984; lic. real estate broker Calif.; cert. law librarian; diplomate Med. Library Assn.; ordained to ministry Luth. Ch., 1958. Librarian, gen. reference service U. Calif. Library, Berkeley, 1954-55; instr. Bibl. Hebrew, Hellenistic Greek, Medieval Latin Wittenberg U., Springfield, Ohio, 1956-59; head librarian Swift Libr. div. and Philosophy, mem. federated theol. faculty U. Chgo., 1959-60; assoc. prof., chmn. dept. history Wilfred Laurier U. (formerly Waterloo Luth. U.), Ont., Can., 1960-64; prof., chmn. div. ch. history, history of Christian thought, dir. European Seminar program Trinity Evang. Div. Sch., Deerfield, Ill., 1964-74; prof. law and theology George Mason U. Sch. Law (formerly Internat. Sch. of Law), Arlington, Va., 1974-75; theol. cons. Christian Legal Soc., 1975-76; dir. studies Internat. Inst. Human Rights, Strasbourg, France, 1979-81; founding dean, prof. jurisprudence, dir. European program Simon Greenleaf U. Sch. Law, Anaheim, Calif., 1980-88; lic. disting. prof. theology and law, dir. European program Faith Evang. Luth. Sem., Tacoma, 1989-91; from prin. lectr. to reader in law Luton U., Eng., 1991-93, prof. law and humanities, dir. Ctr. Human Rights, 1993-97, emeritus prof., 1997—; disting. prof. apologetics, law, and history of Christian thought, v.p. acad. affairs U.K. and Europe Trinity Coll. and Theol. Sem., Newburgh, Ind., 1997—; disting. prof. law Regent U., Va., 1997-99; sr. counsel European Ctr. Law and Justice, 1997-2001; founding dir. Internat. Acad. of Apologetics, Evangelism and Human Rights, Strasbourg, France, 1997—. Vis. prof. Concordia Theol. Sem., Springfield, Ill., 1964-67, DePaul U., Chgo., 1967-70; hon. fellow Revelle Coll., U. Calif., San Diego, 1970; rector Freie Fakultaten Hamburg, Fed. Republic Germany, 1981-82; lectr. Rsch. Scientists Christian Fellowship Conf. St. Catherines Coll., Oxford U., 1985, Internat. Anti-Corruption Conf., Beijing, China, 1995; Pascal lectr. on Christianity and the Univ., U. Waterloo, Ont., Can., 1987; A. Kurt Weiss lectr. biomed. ethics U. Okla., 1997; adj. prof. Puget Sound U. Sch. Law, Tacoma, 1990-91; founding dir. Internat. Acad. Apologetics, Evangelism and Human Rights, Strasbourg, France, 1997—; Worldwide Adv. Conf. lectr. Inns of Ct. Sch. Law, London, 1998; law and religion colloquium lectr. U. Coll. London, 2000; numerous other invitational functions. Author: The Writing of Research Papers in Theology, 1959, A Union List of Serial Publications in Chicago Area Protestant Theological Libraries, 1960, A Seventeenth-Century View of European Libraries, 1962, 1962, Chytraeus on Sacrifice: A Reformation Treatise in Biblical Theology, 1962, The Shape of the Past: An Introduction to Philosophical Historiography, 1962; author: (rev. edit.), 1975; author: The Is God Dead Controversy, 1966; author: (with Thomas J.J. Altizer) The Altizer-Montgomery Dialogue, 1967; author: Crisis in Lutheran Theology, 2 vols., 1967; author: (rev. edit.), 1973; author: Es confiable el Christianismo?, 1968, Ecumenicity, Evangelicals, and Rome, 1969, Where is History Going?, 1969, History and Christianity, 1970, Damned Through the Church, 1970, The Suicide of Christian Theology, 1970, Computers, Cultural Change and the Christ, 1970, In Defense of Martin Luther, 1970, La Mort de Dieu, 1971; author: (with Joseph Fletcher) Situation Ethics: True or False?, 1972; author: The Quest for Noah's Ark, 1972; author: (rev. edit.), 1974; author: Verdammt durch die Kirche, 1973, Christianity for the Toughminded, 1973, Cross and Crucible, 2 vols., 1973, Principalities and Powers: The World of the Occult, 1973; author: (rev. edit.), 1975; author: How Do We Know There is a God?, 1973, Myth, Allegory and Gospel, 1974, God's Inerrant Word, 1974, Jurisprudence: A Book of Readings, 1974; author: (4th edit.), 1992; author: The Law Above the Law, 1975, Cómo Sabemos Que Hay un Dios?, 1975, Demon Possession, 1975, The Shaping of America, 1976, Faith Founded on Fact, 1978, Law and Gospel: A Study for Integrating Faith and Practice, 1978; author: (3rd edit.), 1994; author: Slaughter of the Innocents, 1981, The Marxist Approach to Human Rights: Analysis & Critique, 1984, Human Rights and Human Dignity, 1987, Wohin marschiert China?, 1991, Evidence for Faith: Deciding the God Question, 1991, Giant in Chains: China Today and Tomorrow, 1994, Law and Morality: Friends or Foes?, 1994, Jésus: La Raison Rejoint L'Histoire, 1995; author: (with C.E.B. Cranfield and David Kilgour) Christians in the Public Square, 1996; author: Conflicts of Law, 1997, The Transcendent Holmes, 2000, The Repression of Evangelism in Greece, 2001, Tractatus Logico-Theologicus, 2002, Christ Our Advocate, 2002, History, Law and Christianity, 2002; editor: Lippincott's Evangelical Perspectives, 7 vols., 1970-72, 1970—72, International Scholars Directory, 1973, Simon Greenleaf Law Rev., 7 vols., 1981—88, Global Jour. Classical Theology, 1998—; contbg. editor: Christianity Today, 1965—84, New Oxford Review, 1993—95; author: (films) Is Christianity Credible, 1968, In Search of Noah's Ark, 1977, Defending the Biblical Gospel (11 videocassette series), 1985, (TV series) Christianity on Trial, 1987—93; contbr. articles to acad., theol., legal encys. and jours., chapters to books. Nat. Luth. Ednl. Conf. fellow, 1959-60; Can. Council postdoctoral sr. research fellow, 1963-64; Am. Assn. Theol. Schs. faculty fellow, 1967-68; recipient Angel award Nat. Religious Broadcasters, 1989, 90, 92. Fellow Trinity Coll. (Newburgh, Ind.), Royal Soc. Arts (Eng.), Victoria Inst. (London), Soc. for Advanced Legal Studies (U.K.), Acad. Internat. des Gourmets et des Traditions Gastronomiques (Paris), Am. Sci. Affiliation (nat. philosophy sci. and history sci. commn. 1966-70); mem. ALA, European Acad. Arts, Scis. and Humanities (corr. mem., Paris), Acad. Lit. France (titulary mem.), Lawyers' Christian Fellowship (hon. v.p. 1995—), Nat. Conf. U. Profs., Calif. bar Assn. (human rights commn. 1980-83), Internat. Bar Assn., World Assn. Law Profs., Mid. Temple and Lincoln's Inn (barrister mem.), Am. Soc. Internat. Law, Union Internat. des Avocats, Nat. Assn. Realtors, Tolkien Soc. Am., N.Y. C.S. Lewis Soc., Am. Hist. Assn., Soc. Reformation Rsch., Creation Rsch. Soc., Tyndale Fellowship (Eng.), Stair Soc. (Scotland), Presbyn. Hist. Soc. (North Ireland), Heraldry Soc., Soc. of Genealogists, Irish Geneaol. Soc., Am. Theol. Libr. Assn., Bibliog. Soc. U. Va., Evang. Theol. Soc., Internat. Wine and Food Soc., Soc. des Amis des Arts (Strasbourg), Chaîne des Rôtisseurs (commandeur), Athenaeum (London), Wig and Pen (London), Players' Theatre Club (London), Sherlock Holmes Soc. London, Soc. Sherlock Holmes de France (hon.), Club des Casseroles Lasserre (Paris), Ordre des chevaliers du Saint-Sepulcre Byzantin (commandeur), Heraldry Soc., Soc. Genealogists, Irish Geneal. Soc., Freeman of City of London, Freeman and Liveryman of Scrivener's Co., Phi Beta Kappa, Phi Kappa Phi, Beta Phi Mu. Office: Church Lane Cottage 3-5 High St Lidlington Bedfordshire MK43 0RN England also: 2 rue de Rome 67000 Strasbourg France E-mail: 106612.1066@compuserve.com.

MONTGOMERY, JULIE-APRIL, lawyer; b. Chgo., June 17, 1957; d. Constance Louise Montgomery. BS, U. San Francisco, 1978; MBA, Roosevelt U., 1979; JD, NYU, 1983, LLM in Taxation, 1985. Bar: Ill. 1983, U.S. Dist. Ct. (no. dist.) Ill. 1983, N.Y. 1990, U.S. Supreme Ct. 1995. Legis. advisor Ill. State Senator Charles Chew, Chgo., 1983-84; staff atty. Ill. Indsl. Comm., Chgo., 1984; sole practice Chgo., 1985-86; asst. corp. counsel City of Chgo. Office of Corp. Counsel, 1986—. Co-author Ill. Inst. Cont. Legal Edn. States and Local handbook, 1990; contbr. articles to profl. jours. Instr. Minority Legal Edn. Resources Inc., Chgo., 1983—; vol. March of Dimes Chgo., 1995—; shelter vol. children's program Chgo. Christian Indsl League, 1996—. Mem. ABA, Ill. State Bar Assn. (state local tax sect. 1996—), Ill. Cert. Pub. Accts. Soc. (state and local tax sect. 1995—), Chgo. Bar Assn. (state and local tax sect. 1986—, chmn. com. 1994-95), Phi Alpha Delta, Phi Chi Theta, Alpha Sigma Nu. Lutheran. Avocations: cross-stitching, collecting betty boop, puzzles, movies, history. Administrative and regulatory, State civil litigation, State and local taxation. Office: City of Chgo Corp Counsel 30 N La Salle St Ste 1040 Chicago IL 60602-2503

MONTGOMERY, RICHARD C. lawyer; b. Pitts., June 25, 1936; s. Harry M. and Bertha W. M.; m. Elizabeth Elliott; (dec.); m. Kathleen Weber, Sept 29, 1979; 1 child, Mary. AB, Brown U., 1958; LLB, U. Pa., 1964. Bar: Pa., U.S. Dist. Ct. (we. dist) Pa., U.S. Tax Ct. Of counsel Kirkpatrick & Lockhart LLP, Pitts., 1964—. Bd. dirs. PC Solutions, Pitts. Past pres., bd. dirs. Pitts. Dance Coun. Lt. (j.g.) U.S. Navy, 1958-61. Mem. ABA (mem. real estate tax problems com.), Pa. Bar Assn. (mem. judicial reform, ethics and sr. lawyers coms.), Allegheny County Bar Assn. (coun. mem., taxation and fee dispute com.). Taxation, general. Office: Kirkpatrick & Lockhart LLP 1500 Oliver Bldg Pittsburgh PA 15222

MONTGOMERY, ROBERT MOREL, JR., lawyer; b. Birmingham, Ala., June 9, 1930; s. Robert Morel and Ella Bernice (Smith) M.; m. Mary Lemerle McKenzie, Mar. 6, 1953; 1 child, Courtnay Elizabeth. BS, U. Ala., 1952; LL.B., U. Fla., 1957. Bar: Fla. 1957; diplomate Acad. Fla. Trial Lawyers. With Howell & Kirby Attys at Law, Jacksonville, Fla., 1957-59; ptnr. Howell, Kirby, Montgomery, Sands & D'Aiuto, Jacksonville, Fla., 1959-66, Howell, Kirby, Montgomery, D'Aiuto, Dean & Hallowes, West Palm Beach, Fla., 1966-75, Montgomery, Lytal, Reiter, Denny & Searcy, West Palm Beach, Fla., 1976-85, Montgomery Searcy & Denny, West Palm Beach, Fla., 1986-89; sr. ptnr. Montgomery & Larson, LLP, West Palm Beach, Fla., 1989—. Civil trial adv. Nat. Bd. Trial Advocacy; lectr. Princeton U., U. Oxford Law Sch. Chmn. Palm Beach Opera; chmn. emeritus Palm Beach Cultural Coun.; co-chmn. The Children's Place at Home Safe, Inc.; founder Armory Art Ctr., Palm Beach Inst. Contemporary Art; trustee Nat. Pub. Radio. 1st lt. AUS, 1952-54. Named Alumnus of Yr. U. Fla. Law Rev., 1983, Philanthropist of Yr. Nat. Assn. Fund Raising Execs., 1990, Honoree for Yr. City of Hope, 1991, Victim Adv. of Yr., Palm Beach County Sheriff's Office, 1997, Child Advocate of the Yr., 1996; recipient Learned Hand award Am. Jewish Com., 1985, Humanitarian award Albert Einstein Coll., 1990, Pub.'s award honor for contbg. most to improving quality of life in Broward and Palm Beach counties, 1992, Great Am. Traditions award B'nai B'rith, 1996, Humanitarian award Albert Einstein Coll. Medicine, 1999, Haym Solomon award Anti-Defamation League, 2000, Palm Beach C.C. Leadership award, 2002, Man of Yr. award Lake Worth Cultural Spotlight Com., 2002. Mem. ABA, Fla. Bar Assn. (lectr. continuing edn.), Palm Beach County Bar Assn., Trial Lawyers Assn. Am., Inner Circle Advs. Federal civil litigation, State civil litigation, Personal injury (including property damage). Home: 1800 S Ocean Blvd Palm Beach FL 33480-5104 Office: PO Box 3086 West Palm Beach FL 33402-3086 E-mail: rmm@rmmjr.com.

MONTGOMERY, WILLIAM ADAM, lawyer; b. Chgo., May 22, 1933; s. John Rogerson and Helen (Fyke) Montgomery; m. Jane Fauver, July 28, 1956 (div. Dec. 1967); children: Elizabeth, William, Virginia; m. Deborah Stephens, July 29, 1972; children: Alex, Katherine. AB, Williams Coll., 1955; LLB, Harvard U., 1958. Bar: D.C. 1958, Ill. 1959, U.S. Ct. Appeals (7th cir.) 1959, U.S. Supreme Ct. 1977. Atty. civil divsn., appellate sect. Dept. Justice, Washington, 1958—60; assoc. Schiff Hardin & Waite, Chgo., 1960—68, ptnr., 1968—93; v.p., gen. counsel State Farm Ins. Cos., Bloomington, Ill., 1994—97, sr. v.p., gen. counsel, 1997—99; ptnr. Schiff Hardin & Waite, Chgo., 1999—. Author: (39 corp. practice series) Tying Arrangements, 1984; co-author: Insurance Antitrust and Unfair Trade Practices Law, 2002; contbr. articles to profl. jours. Fellow: Am. Coll. Trial Lawyers; mem.: ABA (coun. antitrust sect. 1989—92), Seventh Cir. Bar Assn. (pres. 1988—89), Chgo. Bar Assn., Econ. Club Chgo., Lawyers Club Chgo. Avocations: skiing, woodturning. Antitrust, Federal civil litigation, General civil litigation. Office: Schiff Hardin & Waite 6600 Sears Tower Chicago IL 60606 E-mail: wmontgomery@schiffhardin.com.

MONTON, ANTHONY ALLEN, lawyer; b. Ludington, Mich., Apr. 24, 1951; s. John and Theresa (Appleton) M.; m. Kareen A. Keating, Aug. 18, 1973; 1 child, Brian James Monton. BA in Econ., Mich. State U., 1973; JD, U. Notre Dame, 1976. Ptnr. Urick and Monton Law Firm, Hart, Mich., 1976-88; pros. atty. County Oceana, Hart, Mich., 1981-88; judge 27th Jud. Cir. of Newaygo and Oceana Counties, Hart, 1989—. Rep. Mich. State Bar Rep. Assebly, Lansing 1982-90, hearings officer Atty. Discipline Bd. State Bar, Lansing 1987-94, pres. 27th Jud. Cir. Bar Assn., Hart 1978. Treas. Oceana Co. Republican Group, Hart 1981-85, pres. Hart Pub. Schs. Found., 1988, v.p. Oceana Hosp. Assn., 1982-84. Fellow Mich. State Bar Found., 1987--, mem. ABA, State Bar Mich., Prosecuting Atty. Assn. Mich., Pentwater Yacht Club. Avocations: sailing, jogging, hunting. Home: 6865 Lakeview Pentwater MI 49449-9521 Office: Ocean County Cir Ct PO Box 885 White Cloud MI 49349-0885

MONTOYA, SARAH MARIE, lawyer; b. Springer, N.Mex, Aug. 28, 1958; d. John R. and Elvira (Nolan) Montoya; m. Darwin L. Jensen, Mar. 25, 1974 (div. Apr. 1981); children: Darice Marie Jensen, Matthew Lyle Jensen, Michael Raymond Jensen; m. Richard A. Maddaleni, Sept. 18, 1998; 1 child, Sofia Terese Maddaleni. AA, Trinidad (Colo.) State Jr. Coll., 1988; BS, Western N.Mex. U., 1991; MBA, N.Mex State U., 1992; JD, U. Ariz., 1995. Bar: N.Mex. 1996, U.S. Dist. Ct. N.Mex. 1997. Asst. dist. atty. 7th Jud. Dist. N.Mex, Estancia, 1996, 4th Jud. Dist. N.Mex., Las Vegas, 1996; pvt. practice Raton, N.Mex., 1997—. Mem. N.Mex Legal Svcs. Bd., Santa Fe, 1997—98. Mem.: N.Mex Criminal Def. Lawyers Assn., Beta Sigma Phi. Republican. Roman Catholic. Avocations: flower arranging, bowling, golf, crafts. Criminal, Family and matrimonial, General practice. Office: 210 Cook Ave Ste 210 Raton NM 87740 Office Fax: 505-445-0500. Business E-Mail: montoylaw@bacavalley.com.

MONYA, NOBUO, law educator, arbitrator; b. Minato-ku, Tokyo, Aug. 21, 1936; s. Tohjiro and Hiro (Nakajima) M.; m. Makiko Kubota, Mar. 26, 1968; children: Takatoshi, Masanori. LLB, Tokyo U., 1960, 62, LLM, 1964, JD, 1967. Assoc. prof. law Seikei U., Tokyo, 1967-75, prof. law, 1975—. Lectr. law Tohoku U., Sendai, Japan, 1979-89, Tokyo U., 1977, 79, Hokkaido U., Sapporo, Japan, 1986, 89, Keio U., Tokyo, 1993—. Author: (book) Outline of Intellectual Property Right Laws, 9th edit., 2001; editor: (book) Commentary Patent Law, 1986; co-author: (book) New Technology Development and Law, 1993; co-editor: (book) The Know-how of Copyright Law, 6th edit., 2002. Mem. exam. com. Com. of Patent Attys. Exam. Bd., The Patent Agy., 1978-85, mem. Indsl. Property Coun., The Patent Agy., 1979-87; mem. Agrl. Material Coun., Ministry of Agr., Forestry and Fishery, 1985-93, mem. experts group for environ. safety of genetically modified organisms, 2000-2001; mem. Copyright Coun., Ministry of Edn., 1993—; mem. Legal Deposit Sys. Coun., Nat. Diet Libr., 1997—. Mem. Japan Assn. Econ. Jurisprudence (dir. 1984—), Japan Assn. Indsl. Property Law (dir. 1974—), Copyright Law Assn. Japan (dir. 1987—), Japan Assn. Internat. Econ. Law (dir. 1991—), Brazil Pub. Info. Union (hon.). Avocations: mountain climbing, scuba diving. Home: Honkomagome 3-9-14 113-0021 Bunkyo-ku Tokyo Japan Office: Seikei U Kichijoji Kitamachi 3-3-1 180-8633 Musashino Tokyo Japan

MOODY, WILLARD JAMES, SR., lawyer; b. Franklin, Va., June 16, 1924; s. Willie James and Mary (Bryant) M.; m. Betty Glenn Covert, Aug. 21, 1948; children: Sharon Paige Moody Edwards, Willard J. Jr., Paul Glenn. AB, Old Dominion U., 1946; LLB, U. Richmond, 1952. Bar: Va.

1952. Pres. Moody, Strople Kloeppel & Basilone Inc., Portsmouth, Va., 1952—. Commr. Chancery, Portsmouth, 1960—, Accounts, 1960—. Del. Va. Ho. of Reps., Portsmouth, 1956-68; senator State of Va., 1968-83; chmn. Portsmouth Dems., 1983—. Recipient Friend of Edn. award Portsmouth Edn. Assn., 1981. Mem. ABA, Va. Bar Assn., Portsmouth Bar Assn. (pres. 1960-61, lectr. seminars), Va. Trial Lawyers Assn. (pres. 1968-69), Hampton Roads C. of C. (bd. dirs. 1983-86), Portsmouth C. of C. (bd. dirs. 1960-61), Inner Circle Advs., VFW, Cosmopolitan Club, Moose. General civil litigation, Labor (including EEOC, Fair Labor Standards Act, labor-management relations, NLRB, OSHA), Personal injury (including property damage). Home: 120 River Point Cres Portsmouth VA 23707-1028 Office: Moody Strople Kloeppel & Basilone Inc 500 Crawford St Portsmouth VA 23705

MOOG, MARY ANN PIMLEY, lawyer; b. Havre, Mont., May 29, 1952; d. Orville Leonard and Della Mae (Cole) Pimley; m. Daren Russell Moog, Apr. 15, 1978; children: Eric John, Keith Cole, Trygg Orville. BS, Mont. State U., 1975; JD, U. Mont., 1981; LLM, NYU, 1983. Bar: Mont. Law clk. Mont. Supreme Ct., Helena, 1981-82; assoc., ptnr., staff atty. Bosch, Kuhr, Dugdale, Martin & Kaze, Havre, 1984—. Recipient Am. Jurisprudence Book award Lawyers Coop. Publ. Co., 1980-81, Tax award Prentice Hall, Inc., 1981, Northwestern Union Trust Co. award, 1981. Mem. ABA, Mont. Bar Assn., 12th Jud. Bar Assn. (pres. 1987-88), Phi Delta Phi. Democrat. Roman Catholic. Avocations: sports, arts and crafts, photography. Estate planning, Estate taxation, Personal income taxation. Home: 925 Wilson Ave Havre MT 59501-4331 Office: Bosch Kuhr Dugdale Martin & Kaze PO Box 7152 Havre MT 59501-7152

MOON, RONALD T. Y. state supreme court chief justice; b. Sept. 4, 1940; m. Stella H. Moon. B in Psychology and Sociology, Coe Coll., 1962, LLD, 2001; LLB, U. Iowa, 1965; D Laws (hon.) , Coe Coll., 2001. Bailiff, law clk. to Chief Judge Martin Pence U.S. Dist. Ct., 1965-66; dep. prosecutor City and County of Honolulu, 1966-68; assoc. Libkuman, Ventura, Ayabe, Chong & Nishimoto (predecessor firm Libkuman, Ventura, Moon & Ayabe), Honolulu, 1968-72, ptnr., 1972-82; judge 9th div. 1st cir., Cir. Ct., State of Hawaii, Honolulu, 1982-90; assoc. justice Supreme Ct., State of Hawaii, Honolulu, 1990-93, chief justice, 1993—. Adj. prof. law U. Hawaii, 1986, 87, 88; lectr., guest spkr. numerous events. Recipient Disting. Svc. award, Nat. Ctr. for State Cts., 2003. Mem. ABA, Hawaii Bar Assn., Assn. Trial Lawyers Am., Am. Bd. Trial Advocates (pres. 1986-93, nat. sec. 1989-91), Am. Inns of Cts. IV (bencher 1983—), Am. Judicature Soc., Hawaii Trial Judges' Assn., Conf. Chief Justices (bd. dirs.). Office: Supreme Ct Hawaii 417 S King St Honolulu HI 96813-2902 E-mail: Ronald.T.Moon@courts.state.hi.us.

MOONEY, JEROME HENRI, lawyer; b. Salt Lake City, Aug. 7, 1944; s. Jerome Henri and Bonnie (Shepherd) M.; m. Carolyn Lasrich, Aug. 10, 1965 (div. Dec. 1978); 1 child, Dierdre Nicole; m. Kaitlyn Cardon, Sept. 23, 1995. BS, U. Utah, 1966, JD, 1972. Bar: Utah 1972, Calif. 1998, U.S. Ct. Appeals (10th cir.) 1974, U.S. Supreme 1984, U.S. Ct. Appeals (7th cir.) 1999, U.S. Ct. Appeals (9th cir.) 2001, U.S. Ct. Appeals (4th cir.) 2002. Sole practice, Salt Lake City, 1972-75, 79-83; sr. ptnr. Mooney, Jorgenson & Nakamura, Salt Lake City, 1975-78, Mooney & Smith, Salt Lake City, 1983-87, Mooney & Assoc., Salt Lake City, 1987-94, Mooney Law Firm, Salt Lake City, 1995-98, Larsen & Mooney Law, Salt Lake City, 1999—. Bd. dirs. Mooney Real Estate, Salt Lake City; mem. Active Music, Calif. Copyright Conf. Mem. Gov.'s Coun. on Vet. Affiars, Salt Lake City, 1982-89; trustee Project Realty, Salt Lake City, 1976—, P.E.A.C.E.; SAMHSA sponsor Project Reality, 1994—; vice chair State Mil. Acad. Assoc. Served with U.S. Army N.G., 1992-93. Mem. ABA (criminal justice sect. U.S. Sentencing Commn. com.), Utah Bar Assn. (chmn. criminal bar sect. 1987-88), Beverly Hills Bar Assn., Nat. Assn. Rec. Industry Profls., Utah NG Assn. (trustee 1976), 1st Amendment Lawyers Assn. (v.p. 1986-88, pres. 1988-89), Nat. Assn. Criminal Def. Lawyers, Families Against Mandatory Minimums (adv. coun.), VFW. Democrat. Jewish. Avocations: sailng, computers. Criminal, Entertainment. Home: 128 I St Salt Lake City UT 84103-3418 Office: 50 W Broadway Ste 100 Salt Lake City UT 84101-2066 E-mail: JerryM@MooneyLaw.com.

MOONEY, MICHAEL EDWARD, lawyer; b. Beloit, Wis., Jan. 21, 1945; s. William C. and Edith (Slothower) M. BA in Econs., St. Norbert Coll., 1966; JD, Boston Coll., 1969. Bar: Mass. 1969, Maine 1969, U.S. Tax Ct. 1975, U.S. Ct. Internat. Trade 1986. Assoc. Nutter, McClennen & Fish, LLP, Boston, 1969-77, sr. ptnr., 1978—, now mng. ptnr. V.p., exec. dir. Fed. Tax Inst. New Eng.; spkr., lectr. numerous seminars. Co-editor: Considerations in Buying or Selling a Business, 1985; mem. bd. editors Accounting and Financial Planning for Law Firms, 1988—. Fellow Am. Coll. Tax Counsel; mem. Boston Bar Assn. (chmn. tax highlights com. 1986-95, mem. fin. com. 1990-92), Boston Tax Forum. Corporate, general, Corporate taxation, Personal income taxation. Office: Nutter McClennen & Fish World Trade Ctr West 155 Seaport Blvd Boston MA 02210-2604 E-mail: mmooney@nutter.com.

MOONEY, THOMAS ROBERT, lawyer; b. Montclair, N.J., June 16, 1933; s. Thomas Edward and Ruth Evelyn (Meurling) M.; m. Mary Frances Davis, Aug. 23, 1958; children: Terrance Kevin, Rebecca Lee Poyner, Thomas Edward. BA in Econs., Fla. So. Coll., Lakeland, 1956; LLB, JD, Stetson U., St. Petersburg, Fla., 1961. BAr: Fla. 1961, Ga. 1962, U.S. Dist. Ct. (mid. dist.) 1964, U.S. Supreme Ct. 1965. Claims adjuster State Farm Mut. Ins. Co., Atlanta, 1961-63; atty. Maguire, Voorhis & Wells, P.A., Orlando, Fla., 1963-64, Meyers & Mooney, P.A., Orlando, 1964-94, Meyers, Mooney Stanley & Hollingsworth, Orlando, 1994—. Chair Workers Compensation Ednl. Conf., Fla., 1980-81. Chmn. bd. dirs. Epilepsy Assn. Ctrl. Fla., Orlando, 1964-67; bd. dirs. Children's Home Soc., Orlando, 1970-75, chmn., 1970-72. 1st lt. U.S. Army, 1956-58, Korea. Mem. ATLA, ABA, Fla. Bar Assn., Ga. Bar Assn., Acad. Fla. Trial Lawyers (chair workers compensation sect. 1985), Fla. Workers Advocates (bd. dirs. 1992—). Democrat. Methodist. Avocations: skiing, golf, travel, hiking, rafting. Personal injury (including property damage), Workers' compensation. Office: Meyers Mooney Stanley & Hollingsworth P A 17 Lake Ave Orlando FL 32801-2730

MOORE, ANDREW GIVEN TOBIAS, II, investment banker, law educator; b. New Orleans, Nov. 25, 1935; m. Ann Elizabeth Dawson, June 5, 1965; children— Cecily Elizabeth (dec.), Marianne Dawson. BBA, Tulane U., 1958, JD, 1960. Bar: La. 1960, Del. 1963. Law clk. to chief justice Del., Dover, 1963; assoc. firm Killoran & Van Brunt, Wilmington, Del., 1964-70, partner, 1971-76; partner firm Connolly, Bove & Lodge, Wilmington, 1976-82; justice Del. Supreme Ct., Wilmington, 1982-94; sr. mng. dir. Wasserstein Perella & Co., Inc., N.Y.C., 1994—2001, Drsdner Kleinwort Wasserstein, Inc., N.Y.C., 2001—. Mem. Del. Bar Examiners, 1975-82; mem. Del. Gen. Corp. law com., 1969-83; chmn. joint com. Del. Bar Assn.-Del. Bankers Assn., 1978-79; chmn. Del. Jud. Proprieties Com., 1983-94, Del. Bench and Bar Conf., 1988-94; trustee Del. Bar Found., 1984-94; faculty Tulane Inst. European Legal Studies, Paris Inst., 1990-96, 99; adj. prof. law Georgetown U. Law Ctr., Widener U. Sch. Law, U. Iowa Coll. Law; guest lectr. law Columbia U., Tulane U., U. Toronto, Can., U. Tex., Villanova U., Washington U., St. Louis, U. Iowa, George Mason U., DeVrije U. van Brussel, Cath. U. Louvain La Neuve; mem. pres.'s coun. Tulane U., 1990-96; chmn. Tulane Corp. Law Inst., 1988-95; Lehmann disting. vis. prof. law Washington U., St. Louis, 1994, 96; Mason Ladd disting. vis. prof. U. Iowa, 1995; disting. vis. prof. law St. Louis U., 1995, 96, 99; bd. dirs. Am. Lawyer Media, Inc. Trustee Del. Home and Hosp. for Chronically Ill, Smyrna, 1966-70, chmn., 1966-69; mem. New Castle County Hist. Rev. Bd., Wilmington, 1974-82; mem. Del. Cts. Planning Com., 1982-94; dean's coun. Tulane U. Law Sch., 1988-96; bd. visitors Walter F. George Sch. Law, Mercer U., 1985-91, chmn., 1988-90. With JAGC, USAF, 1960-63. Mem. ABA, La. Bar Assn., Del. Bar Assn. (v.p. 1976-77, exec. com. 1982-83), Am. Judicature Soc. (bd. dirs. 1982-86), Order Barristers, Phi Delta Phi, Delta Theta Phi (hon.), Omicron Delta Kappa Democrat. Presbyterian.

MOORE, CHARLES LOYD, lawyer; b. El Paso, Tex., Aug. 14, 1944; s. Charles McKinney and Alice Adeline (Loyd) M.; m. Peggy Jo ball, Dec. 20, 1969; children: Kirk, Julie. BS in Mil. Engring., U.S. Mil. Acad., West Point, N.Y., 1966; MSME, Calif. Inst. Tech., 1968; JD summa cum laude, So. Meth. U., Dallas, 1975. Bar: N.Mex. 1975, U.S. Dist. Ct. 1975. Commd. 2d. lt. U.S. Army, 1966, advanced through grades to capt., 1968, resigned, 1972; assoc. Keleher & McLeod, P.A., Albuquerque, 1975-79, mem. firm, 1979—. Assisted bd. of bar examiners in writing and grading bar exam questions, Sante Fe, 1990—2000. Contbr. articles to profl. jours. Dist. co-chmn. ann. fund campaign McMurry U., Abilene, Tex., 1988, trustee, 1989—92, Hatton W. Sumners Found., Dallas, 1999—; dir. Robert O. Anderson Schs. Mgmt. Found. Bd., U. N.Mex., 2003—. Decorated Vietnam Svc. Medal, Vietnam Campaign Medal, Joint Svc. Commendation Medal, Bronze Star Medal; named one of Best Lawyers of Am., 1989—90, 1991—92, 1993—94, 1995—96, 1997—98, 1999—2000, 2001—02, 2003—. Mem. ABA, State Bar of N.Mex. (v.p. young lawyers div. 1977-78, chair bus. law sect. 2001), Albuquerque Bar Assn., Phi Delta Phi (Internat. Grad. of Yr. Biennial Conv. 1975), Phi Kappa Phi. Avocations: running, reading. Corporate, general, Utilities, public, Securities. Home: 7929 American Heritage Dr NE Albuquerque NM 87109-3103 Office: Keleher & McLeod PA PO Box Aa Albuquerque NM 87103-1626 E-mail: clm@keleher-law.com.

MOORE, CHRISTOPHER M. lawyer; b. L.A., Oct. 12, 1938; s. Prentiss Elder and Josephine (French) M.; m. Gillian Reed, Sept. 29, 1965; children: Stephanie Kia Conn, Carrie Christine McKay. AB, Stanford U., 1961; JD, Harvard U., 1964. Dep. county counsel L.A. County Counsel, 1965-66; ptnr. Moore & Lindelof, L.A., 1966-69, Burkley & Moore, Torrance, Calif., 1969-74; pvt. practice Law Offices of Christopher Moore, Torrance, 1974-81; ptnr. Burkley, Moore, Greenberg & Lyman, Torrance, 1981-90; prin. Christopher M. Moore & Assoc., Torrance, 1990-2000, Moore, Bryan & Schroff, Torrance, 2000—. Mem. bd. edn. Palos Verdes (Calif.) Peninsula Unified Sch. Dist., 1972-77. Fellow: Am. Acad. Matrimonial Lawyers, Am. Coll. Trust and Estate Counsel; mem.: Palos Verdes Golf Club, L.A. Yacht Club. Avocations: sailing, golf. Estate planning, Family and matrimonial, Probate (including wills, trusts). Office: Moore Bryan & Schroff Ste 490 21515 Hawthorne Blvd Torrance CA 90503-6525 E-mail: chris@mbslawcorp.com.

MOORE, DAVID GREGORY, lawyer; b. Winfield, Kans., Nov. 30, 1946; s. Warren Keith and Mary Margaret (Felt) M.; m. Alice Jane Wiley, Feb. 23, 1974; children: Geoffrey Haven Wiley Moore, Caroline Elizabeth Wiley Moore. BA, Albion Coll., 1968; MA, U. Mich., 1971, JD, 1982. Bar: Mich. 1982. Writer, photographer Albion (Mich.) Evening Recorder, 1962-76, editor, 1976-79; assoc. Tuck & Garrison, Albion, 1982-85; mem. Tuck, Garrison & Moore, P.L.L.C., Albion, 1986—. Pres. Albion Vol. Svc. Orgn., 1987-88, 91-92, bd. dirs., 1987-88, 91-92; trustee Albion Civic Found., pres., 1985, 92; chmn. planned giving adv. coun. Albion Coll., 1989-92; chair mcpl. water study team Greater Albion Alliance 2000, 1991-99; mem. Albion Bd. Edn., 2000—, v.p. 2001—. Named Michigan Minuteman, Greater Mich. Found., Lansing, Mich., 1979. Mem. ABA, Calhoun County Bar Assn. Avocations: cabinetmaking, letterpress printing. General practice. Office: Tuck Garrison & Moore PLLC 403 S Superior St PO Box 660 Albion MI 49224-0660

MOORE, DEBRA, lawyer; Grad., U. Utah, 1983. Shareholder Watkiss & Saperstein; employment sect. chief litigation divsn. Utah Atty. Gen.'s Office, 1991—. Instr. legal writing U. Utah Coll. Law, 1993—96; rep. Utah Jud. Coun. Mem.: Utah State Bar (pres.-elect, commn. 1994—2000). Office: Atty Gens Office PO Box 140856 160 E 300 S Fl Salt Lake City UT 84114-0856*

MOORE, DONALD FRANCIS, lawyer; b. N.Y.C., Dec. 14, 1937; s. John F. and Helen A. (McLoughlin) M.; m. Alice L. Kalmar; children: Christina M., Marianne, Karen L., Alison A. AB, Fordham U., 1959; JD, St. John's U., Bklyn., 1962. Bar: N.Y. 1962, D.C. 1970, U.S. Supreme Ct. 1993. Assoc. Paul, Weiss, Rifkind, Wharton & Garrison, N.Y.C., 1962-70, ptnr., 1970-97, of counsel, 1998—. Editor in chief St. John's U. Law Rev., 1962. Served to 1st lt. U.S. Army, 1962-64. Mem. N.Y. State Bar Assn., Assn. of Bar of City of N.Y. Roman Catholic. Avocation: fishing. Pension, profit-sharing, and employee benefits, Probate (including wills, trusts). Home: 7 Wedgewood Ct Glen Head NY 11545-2229 Office: Paul Weiss Rifkind Wharton & Garrison Ste 4200 1285 Avenue Of The Americas Fl 21 New York NY 10019-6065

MOORE, DWIGHT TERRY, lawyer; b. Nashville, Apr. 22, 1948; s. George Howard and Minnie Laura (Gregory) M.; m. Barbara Franklin, May 7, 1977; 1 child, Marian. BA, Vanderbilt U., 1970; MPA, U. Memphis, 1975, JD, 1983. Bar: Tenn. 1984, U.S. Dist. Ct. (we. dist.) Tenn. 1984, U.S. Ct. Appeals (6th cir.) 1991. With State of Tenn., Nashville, 1970-73, Shelby County, Memphis, 1974-79; asst. prof. U. Memphis, 1983-88; ptnr. Gardner & Moore, Memphis, 1984-91, Olsen, Kuhn & Moore, Memphis, 1991-93, Lowrance & Monypeny, Memphis, 1993-94; pvt. practice Memphis, 1994-99; with Olsen Kuhn & Moore, Memphis, 1999—. Mem.: ABA, Memphis Bar Assn. Libertarian. Unitarian Universalist. Avocations: tae kuk, fitness, reading. Entertainment, General practice, Trademark and copyright. Office: 5100 Stage Rd Ste 4 Memphis TN 38134-3164 E-mail: dwightmoore1@aol.com.

MOORE, EDWARD WARREN, lawyer; b. Odessa, Tex., July 21, 1959; s. Edward Warren and Gloria (Schroeter) M.; m. JoAnne Bisso; children: Peggy, Barbara. BA in Econs., Princeton U., 1981; JD, So. Meth. U., 1984. Bar: Tex. 1984, U.S. Dist. Ct. (no. dist.) Tex. 1984, U.S. Ct. Appeals (5th cir.) 1984, U.S. Ct. Appeals (10th cir.) 1985. Assoc. Ravkind, Kuehne & Biesel, Dallas, 1984-85; ptnr. Kuehne & Moore, Dallas, 1984-96; pvt. practice, 1996-2000; mng. ptnr. Moore & Anderson. Dir. Rsch. Group Tex., Inc., Ascend Student Health Svcs., LLC. Vol. Park Cities YMCA, Ronald McDonald Ho. Mem. AAAS, ABA (litigation sect., trial practice sect. and com., product liability, antitrust, intellectual property sect.), ATLA (toxic, environ. and pharm. litigation sect., comml. litigation sect.), State Bar Tex., Dallas Bar Assn., Tex. Trial Lawyers Assn., Dallas Country Club, Safari Club Internat. (life), Dallas Safari Club, DSC 100 (vol.). Methodist. General civil litigation, Intellectual property, Product liability. Home: 7044 Turtle Creek Blvd Dallas TX 75205-1254 E-mail: eddymoor@sprynet.com.

MOORE, ERNEST CARROLL, III, lawyer; b. Honolulu, Oct. 24, 1944; s. Ernest Carroll Jr. and Frances (Miller) M.; children: Tiffany Meredith, Alyssa Judi. BA, Dartmouth Coll., 1967; JD, So Meth. U., 1974. Bar: Hawaii 1974, U.S. Dist. Ct. Hawaii 1974, U.S. Ct. Appeals (9th cir.) 1974. Ptnr. Torkildson, Katz, Fonseca, Moore & Hetherington, Honolulu, 1974—. Trustee Hawaii Sch. Girls, 1998—. Bd. dirs. Hawaii chpt. ARC, Honolulu, 1979, trustee La Pietra-Hawaii Sch. for Girls, 1998—, Outrigger Duke Kahanamoku Found., 1999-, Bd. of Governors (the Pacific Club). Mem. Am. Acad, Hosp. Attys., Nat. Health Lawyers Assn., Indsl. Relations Research Assn., Soc. for Human Resources Mgmt., Order of Coif, Pacific Club (bd. govs.), Outrigger Canoe Club. Republican. Episcopalian. Avocations: tennis, photography. Labor (including EEOC, Fair Labor Standards Act, labor-management relations, NLRB, OSHA). Office: Torkildson Katz Fonseca Jaffe Moore & Hetherington 700 Bishop St Fl 15 Honolulu HI 96813-4187

MOORE, FRANCIS XAVIER, lawyer; b. Bklyn., May 12, 1933; s. Michael Joseph and Catharine Agnes (Shea) M.; m. Harriet Joan Rogers; children: Christine Mari, Ann-Therese, Francis X. Jr., Tara Louise, Timothy Rogers. BS, Fordham U., 1955, LLB, LLD, 1960. Bar: N.Y. 1961, N.J. 1961, U.S. Dist. Ct. N.J. 1961, U.S. Dist. Ct. N.Y. (so. and ea. dist.)1961, U.S. Supreme Ct. 1976. Cert. chem. breath test experts, DUI def. lawyer, Natl. Coll. of Defense Attys., 2002. Ptnr. Meyer, Ferrara, Moore, N.Y.C., 1960; assoc. Durand, Ivins, Carton, Asbury Park, N.J., 1960-63; dep. atty. gen. State of N.J., Trenton, 1963-64, N.J. spl. rep. to U.S. Senate subcom. organized crime Washington, 1964-65; ptnr. Sorenson and Moore, Atlantic Highlands, N.J., 1965-68, McGowan, Saling, Bolglo, Moore, Eatontown, N.J., 1968-76, Moore, Coogan, Feldman, Red Bank, N.J., 1976-80; prin., sr. ptnr. Francis X. Moore and Assocs., Red Bank, N.J., 1980—. Mem. N.J. Sup. Ct. Improvement, Trenton, 1984-92, N.J. State Bar Mcpl. Comm., New Brunswick, N.J., 1994—, Nat. Coll. Driving Under Influence Defense Regent, Houston, 1992—, Founding mem. Natl. Campaign for Tolerance. Author: Defense of Drunk Driving, 1990, (manual) National College-Defense, 1996; contbr. articles to profl. jours. Anchor Club scholar 1948, Hayden grant, Fordham U., 1951; recipient Honor Legion award N.J. Police Depts., Woodbridge, N.J., 1994. Mem. ABA, N.J. State Bar Assn., N.J. Criminal Defense Lawyers, Monmouth Bar Assn. (trustee 1962—, pres. 1975-76), Kiwanis Internat. (local chpt., past pres.), Friendly Sons St. Patrick (local chpt., past pres.), 200 Club (local chpt., bd. dirs.) Roman Cath. Avocations: card, coin, and stamp collections. Criminal. Office: Francis X Moore PA 211 Maple Ave (Rt 35) Red Bank NJ 07701 E-mail: FXM_LAW1@aol.com., jaymond@absolutelynotguilty.com.

MOORE, GEORGE CRAWFORD JACKSON, lawyer; b. Tenn. BA, U. Fla., 1963; PhB in Soviet Law, U. St. Andrews, Scotland, 1966; MA in English Law with honors, Cambridge U., Eng., 1968, LLM in Internat. Law, 1969. Bar: Eng. (Barrister, Inner Temple) 1970, Jamaica 1971, Fla. 1973, Turks & Caicos Islands 1974, U.S. Supreme Ct. 1976, Antigua and Barbuda, Brit. V.I., Grenada, Montserrat, St. Lucia 1977, Anguilla 1999. Legis. asst. to U.S. sen., Washington, 1970-72; asst. pub. defender Palm Beach County, Fla., 1973; pvt. practice West Palm Beach, Fla., 1973—. Founding pres. World Trade Coun. of Palm Beach County, 1981—; chmn. Fla. Coun. Internat. Devel., 1983—84, 2000—, Fla. Gov.'s Conf. on World Trade and Investment, 1989, Fla. Export Coun. of U.S. Dept. Commerce, 1991—92. Editor spl. issues Fla. Bar Jour., 1982, 87, chmn. editorial bd., 1988-89; mem. editorial bd. The Internat. Lawyer jour. of ABA, 1979-84; contbr. articles to profl. jours. Chmn. Fla. Econ. Growth and Internat. Devel. Commn., 1989-90. Fellow: Ctr. for Internat. Legal Studies, Soc. Internat. Bus. Fellows (v.p.); mem.: ABA, Fla. Bar (chmn. internat. law sect. 1994—95, mem. internat. law certification bd. 1998—, bd. cert. specialist in internat. law 1999—). Private international, British law. Office: 105 S Narcissus Ave Ste 812 West Palm Beach FL 33401-5530

MOORE, HUGH JACOB, JR., lawyer; b. Norfolk, Va., June 29, 1944; s. Hugh Jacob and Ina Ruth (Hall) M.; m. Jean Garnett, June 10, 1972; children: Lela Miller, Sarah Garnett. BA, Vanderbilt U., 1966; LLB, Yale U., 1969. Bar: Tenn. 1970, U.S. Dist. Ct. (mid. dist.) Tenn. 1970, U.S. Dist. Ct. (ea. dist.) Tenn. 1973, U.S. Dist. Ct. (we. dist.) Tenn. 1982, U.S. Ct. Appeals (6th cir.) 1973, U.S. Ct. Appeals (fed. cir.) 1999, U.S. Supreme Ct. 1972. Law clk. U.S. Dist. Ct. (mid. dist.) Tenn., Nashville, 1969-70; trial atty. civil rights divsn. U.S. Dept. Justice, Washington, 1970-73; asst. U.S. atty. Eastern Dist. of Tenn., Chattanooga, 1973-76; assoc. Witt, Gaither & Whitaker, P.C., Chattanooga, 1976-77, shareholder, 1977—2002, also bd. dirs.; shareholder Shumacker, Witt, Gaither & Whitaker, P.C., 2002—. Mem. Commn. Women and Minorities Profession Law, 1995-97; mem. hearing com. Bd. Profl. Responsibility Supreme Ct. Tenn., 1996-2002; mem. mediation and arbitration panel U.S. Dist. Ct. (ea. dist.) Tenn.; cert. arbitrator, cert. mediator Tenn. Rule 31 Nat. Assn. Securities Dealers; cert. artbitrator N.Y. Stock Exch., Nat. Arbitration Forum; mem. adv. commn. on rules of civil and appellate procedure Tenn. Supreme Ct., chmn., 1999—. Contbr. articles to profl. jours. Bd. dirs. Adult Edn. Coun., Chattanooga, 1976-81, pres., 1977-79; bd. dirs. Chattanooga Symphony and Opera Assn., 1981-87, Riverbend Fesitval, 1983-85, 91—, pres., 1995-97, Landmarks Chattanooga, 1983-84, Cornerstones, 1995-98, Orange Grove Sch., 1996—; mem. alumni coun. McCallie Sch., 1980-85; trustee St. Nicholas Sch., 1983-89, chmn., 1986-88. Fellow Am. Coll. Trial Lawyers, Tenn. State Com., Tenn. Bar Found., Chattanooga Bar Found, Am. Bar Found.; mem. ABA (mem. bd. editors jour. Litigation News 1983-90), Tenn. Bar Assn., Chattanooga Bar Assn. (mem. bd. govs. 1985-87), Am. Ins. Ct. (master Brock-Cooper Inn), Mountain City Club, Rotary. Methodist. Federal civil litigation, General civil litigation, Criminal. Home: 101 Ridgeside Rd Chattanooga TN 37411-1830 Office: Schumacker Witt Gaither & Whitaker 110 Sun Trust Bank Bldg 736 Market St Chattanooga TN 37402 E-mail: hmoore@swgwlaw.com.

MOORE, JAMES E. state supreme court justice; b. Laurens, S.C., Mar. 13, 1936; s. Roy Ernest and Marie (Hill) M.; m. Mary Alicia Deadwyler, Jan. 27, 1963; children: Erin Alicia, Travis Warren. BA, Duke U., 1958, JD, 1961; Dr. of Humanities (hon.) , Lander Univ., 1997. Bar: S.C. 1961, U.S. Dist. Ct. S.C. 1961. Pvt. practice, Greenwood, S.C., 1961-76; cir. judge 8th Jud. Cir. S.C., Greenwood, 1976-91; assoc. justice S.C. Supreme Ct., 1992—. Mem. S.C. Ho. of Reps., Columbia, 1968-76. Mem. S.C. Bar Assn., ABA, Am. Judicature Soc., Baptist. Baptist. Home: 148 Amherst Dr Greenwood SC 29649-8901 Office: PO Box 277 Greenwood SC 29648-0277

MOORE, JOHN JOSEPH, lawyer; b. West New York, N.J., Jan. 24, 1933; s. George Thomas and Dorothy (Zimmer) M.; m. Carmela Macrini, Mar. 10, 1957; children: Christine, John Joseph. BS, Jersey City State Coll., 1956; LLB, N.Y. Law Sch., 1961; LLM, NYU, 1970. Bar: N.Y. 1961. Since practiced in, N.Y.C.; assoc. with firm Dwyer & Lawler, after 1961; then mem. firm Reid, Devlin, Grubbs & Moore; chmn. bd. Leber Inc., 1983-93; mem. Barry McTierman and Moore, 1970—. Guest lectr. disclosure Fordham U.; tchr. social studies pub. schs., Union City, N.J.; Sponsor, coach local Biddy Basketball Team, 1972— Author: Discovery and Inspection, 1969, Legal Significance, 1975; editor: Defendant, 1969-73, 1987-92, 97-98. Trustee devel. fund. New Jersey City U., 1973-81; trustee New Jersey City U., 1982, vice chmn. bd. trustees, 1983-87, chmn., 1989—; chmn. governing bds. Assn. State Colls. N.J., 1985-87; chair Civilian Rev. Complaint Bd., Teaneck, N.J., 1992—; mem. Bd. Higher Edn. State N.J., 1985-87, Coun. N.J. State Colls., 1984-85; mem. governing bds. Assn. State Colls. N.J., 1985-89. With AUS, 1956-58. Mem. ABA, Am. Arbitration Assn. (arbiter 1968—), N.Y. State Bar Assn., N.Y. County Bar Assn., Def. Assn. N.Y. (pres. 1973-74, chmn. bd. 1974-75, governing bd.), Assn. State Colls. N.Y. (gov. bd. 1985-93), Cath. Ins. Guild (pres. 1972-73, chmn. bd. 1973-74), Def. Rsch. Inst. (regional v.p. 1983-86). Roman Catholic (dir. mus. group). Home: 573 Standish Rd Teaneck NJ 07666-2605 Office: 2 Rector St New York NY 10006-1010 E-mail: jjm6160@aol.com.

MOORE, KAREN NELSON, judge; b. Washington, Nov. 19, 1948; d. Roger S. and Myrtle Nelson; m. Kenneth Cameron Moore, June 22, 1974; children: Roger C., Kenneth N., Kristin K. AB magna cum laude, Radcliffe Coll., 1970; JD magna cum laude, Harvard U., 1973. Bar: DC 1973, Ohio 1976, U.S. Ct. Appeals (DC cir.) 1974, U.S. Supreme Ct. 1980, U.S. Ct. Appeals (6th cir.) 1984. Law clk. to Hon. Harry A. Blackmun U.S. Supreme Ct., Washington, 1974—75; assoc. Jones, Day, Reavis & Pogue, Cleve., 1975—77; asst. prof. Case Western Res. Law Sch., Cleve., 1977—80, assoc. prof., 1980—82, prof., 1982—95; judge U.S. Ct. Appeals (6th cir.), Cleve., 1995—. Vis. prof. Harvard Law Sch., 1990—91. Mem. Harvard Law Rev., 1971—73; contbr. articles. Trustee Lakewood Hosp., Ohio, 1978—85, Radcliffe Coll., Cambridge, 1980—84. Fellow: Am. Bar Found.;

mem.: Harvard U. Alumni Assn. (bd. dirs. 1984—87), Am. Law Inst., Phi Beta Kappa. Office: US Ct Appeals 6th Cir Carl B Stokes US Courthouse 801 W Superior Ave Cleveland OH 44113-1831

MOORE, KENNETH CAMERON, lawyer; b. Chgo., Oct. 25, 1947; s. Kenneth Edwards and Margaret Elizabeth (Cameron) M.; m. Karen M. Nelson, June 22, 1974; children: Roger Cameron, Kenneth Nelson, Kristin Karen. BA summa cum laude, Hiram Coll., 1969; JD cum laude, Harvard U., 1973. Bar: Ohio 1973, U.S. Dist. Ct. Md. 1974, U.S. Ct. Appeals (4th cir.) 1974, D.C. 1975, U.S. Dist. Ct. (no. dist.) Ohio 1976, U.S. Ct. Appeals (6th cir.) 1977, U.S. Ct. Appeals (D.C. cir.) 1979, U.S. Supreme Ct. 1980. Law clk. to judge Harrison L. Winter U.S. Ct. Appeals (4th cir.), Balt., 1973-74; assoc. Squire, Sanders & Dempsey, Washington, 1974-75, Cleve., 1975-82, ptnr., 1982—, mem. fin. com., 1990—, profl. ethics ptnr., 1996—. Chmn. Ohio Fin. Com. for Jimmy Carter presdl. campaign, 1976; del. Dem. Nat. Conv., 1976; chief legal counsel Ohio Carter-Mondale Campaign, 1976; trustee Hiram Coll., 1997—, mem. exec. com., 1999, chair audit com., 1999, vice chair bd. trustees, 2000—, chair faculty affairs subcom. of ednl. policy com., 2000—. With AUS, 1970-76. Mem. ABA, Fed. Bar Assn., Ohio Bar Assn., Cleve. Bar Assn., Cleve. City Club. Federal civil litigation, State civil litigation, Environmental. Home: 15602 Edgewater Dr Cleveland OH 44107-1212 Office: Squire Sanders & Dempsey 4900 Society Ctr 127 Public Sq Ste 4900 Cleveland OH 44114-1304

MOORE, LLOYD EVANS, retired lawyer; b. Feb. 10, 1931; s. Bascom Sturgill and Julia M. (Martin) M.; m. Marilyn Moore, June 12, 1955; children: William, Erik, Julia. BA, Ohio State U., 1957, JD, 1958. Bar: Ohio 1959, U.S. Dist. Ct. (so. dist.) Ohio 1962, U.S. Dist. Ct. (ea. dist.) Ky. 1965, U.S. Supreme Ct. 1963. County prosecutor Lawrence County, Ohio, 1973-76; assoc. Moore, Wolfe & Bentley, Ironton, Ohio, 1989-95; ret., 1995. Author: The Jury, 1973, rev., 1988. Mem. Ironton Sch. .Bd., 1966-69, pres., 1968-69; bd. dirs. Lawrence County Joint Vocat. Sch., 1966-69. With USMC, 1950-54. Fellow Royal Photog. Soc. Personal injury (including property damage), Criminal, Family and matrimonial.

MOORE, MARILYN, federal agency administrator; b. Md. B in Bus. Mgmt., Pers. and Labor Rels. magna cum laude, U. Md., 1990; M in Applied Mgmt., U. Coll. Md., 1997. Pers. staffing specialist U.S. Office Pers. Mgmt., Washington, 1990; mgmt. analyst U.S. Census Bur., chief corr. mgmt./info. mgmt. staff Policy Office, 1998, chief corr. quality assurance; exec. secretariat records mgmt. divsn. FBI, Washington, 2002—. With D.C. Air Nat. Guard, 1986—95. Office: FBI J Edgar Hoover Bldg 935 Pennsylvania Ave NW Washington DC 20535*

MOORE, MIKE, state attorney general; m. Tisha Moore; 1 child, Kyle. Grad., Jackson County Jr. Coll., 1972; BA, U. Miss., 1974, JD, 1976. Asst. dist. atty. State of Miss., 1977—78, dist. atty., 1979, atty. gen., 1988—. Democrat. Office: Office of Atty Gen PO Box 220 Jackson MS 39205-0220*

MOORE, MITCHELL JAY, lawyer, law educator; b. Lincoln, Nebr., Aug. 29, 1954; s. Earl J. and Betty Marie (Zimmerlin) M.; m. Sharon Lea Campbell, Sept. 5, 1987. BS in Edn., U. Mo., Columbia, 1977, JD, 1981. Bar: Mo. 1981, U.S. Dist. Ct. (we. dist.) Mo. 1981, Tex. 1982, U.S. Ct. Appeals (8th cir.) 1998. Tchr. Clinton Mid. Sch., 1978; sole practice Columbia, Mo., 1981—. Coordinating atty. student legal svcs. ctr. U. Mo., Columbia, 1983-89. Mem. Columbia Substance Abuse Adv. Commn., 1989—; bd. dirs. Planned Parenthood of Ctrl. Mo., Columbia, 1984-86, Opportunities Unltd., Columbia, 1984-86, ACLU of Mid-Mo., 1991-98; Libertarian candidate for Atty. Gen. of Mo., 1992, 2000, for 9th congl. dist. U.S. Ho. of Reps., 1994, 96, for Mo. State Rep. 23d dist., 1998, for Atty. Gen. Mo., 2000; mem. Probation and Parole Citizens Adv. Bd., 1997-99. Mem. Boone County Bar Assn., Assn. Trial Lawyers Am., Phi Delta Phi. Libertarian. Unitarian Universalist. Avocations: softball, camping, Tae Kwon Do. Criminal, Family and matrimonial, Personal injury (including property damage). Office: 1210 W Broadway Columbia MO 65203-2126 E-mail: mmoore259@mchsi.com.

MOORE, ROBERT MADISON, food industry executive, lawyer; b. New Orleans, June 21, 1925; s. Clarence Greer and Anna Omega (Odendahl) M.; m. Evelyn Eileen Varva, Apr. 11, 1953; children: Eileen Alexandria Moore Wynne, John Greer. BBA, Tulane U., 1947; JD, U. Va., 1952; LLM (Food Law Inst. fellow), NYU, 1953. Bar: La. 1956, Calif. 1972. Asst. to pres., gen. counsel Underwear Inst., N.Y.C., 1953-55; pvt. practice law New Orleans, 1955-56; asst. gen. atty., dir. Legal services, sec. and gen. atty. Standard Fruit & Steamship Co., New Orleans, 1957-72; v.p., gen. counsel Castle & Cooke Foods, 1972-81, Castle & Cooke, Inc., 1973-81, sr. v.p. law and govt., 1981-82; pres. Internat. Banana Assn., 1983-98; acting exec. dir. Pan Am. Devel. Found., 1999. Dir. Ferson Optics of Del., Inc., 1958-69, Baltime Securities Corp., Pan American Devel. Found. Asst. atty. gen., La., 1960-66. Served with AUS, 1943-46. Mem. ABA, Calif. Bar Assn., La. Bar Assn., SAR (sec. 1960-61), KM, Cosmos Club, Phi Delta Phi, Alpha Tau Omega. Democrat. Roman Catholic. Home: 3323 R St NW Washington DC 20007-2310 E-mail: rmevmoore@aol.com.

MOORE, ROY S. state supreme court chief justice; m. Kayla Moore; children: Heather, Roy, Caleb, Micah. BS, U.S. Mil. Acad., 1969; JD, U. Ala., 1977. Dep. dist. atty. Etowah County, Ala., 1977—82; pvt. practice Gadsden, Ala., 1982—92; cir. judge 16th Judicial Cir., Gadsden, 1992—2001; chief justice Ala. Supreme Ct., 2001—. Republican. Baptist. Office: Ala Supreme Ct 300 Dexter Ave Montgomery AL 36104-3741

MOORE, STEPHEN JAMES, lawyer; b. Kansas City, Mo., Aug. 9, 1947; s. James Andrew and Frances Clare (Kennedy) M. BSBA, Rockhurst U., 1969, BA, 1975; JD, U. Mo., Kansas City, 1977, LLM, 1997. Bar: Mo. 1978, U.S. Dist. Ct. (we. dist.) Mo. 1978, U.S. Ct. Appeals (8th cir.) 1980, U.S. Ct. Appeals (10th cir.) 1981, U.S. Ct. Fed. Claims 1991, U.S. Ct. Appeals (6th cir.) 1997. Law intern Mo. Atty. Gen.'s Office, Kansas City, 1976-77, asst., 1978; assoc. Popham, Conway, Sweeny, Fremont & Bundschu PC, Kansas City, 1978-84, Freilich, Leitner & Carlisle, PC, Kansas City, 1985, Herrick, Feinstein, Kansas City, 1985-86, Freilich, Leitner, Carlisle & Shortlidge, Kansas City, 1986-90; ptnr. Freilich, Leitner & Carlisle, Kansas City, Dallas, L.A., 1987-2000, Aspen, Colo., 1997-2000, Peters, Moore & Jones, LLC, Kansas City, Mo., 2001—02, Peters & Moore, L.L.C., 2002—. Adj. prof. law U. Mo., Kansas City, 1995—. Mem. Friends of Art, Nelson-Atkins Mus. Art, Kansas City, 1988—, Smithsonian Inst., Washington, 1985—, Nat. Trust for Historic Preservation, Washington, 1988—, Libr. of Congress Assocs., The Federalist Soc., Nat. Audubon Soc. Mem. ABA, Assn. Trial Lawyers Am., Kansas City Metro Bar Assn., Sports Car Club Am., Am. Mus. Nat. History, Porsche Club Am., Lake Ozarks Yacht Assn., Boat Owners Assn. U.S., Ancient Order of Hibernians, Delta Theta Phi, Tau Kappa Epsilon. Roman Catholic. Avocations: vintage sportscars, boating. Land use and zoning (including planning), Municipal (including bonds), Property, real (including real estate development, water). Home: 5840 McGee St Kansas City MO 64113-2132 Office: Peters & Moore LLC 1500 Traders on Grand Bldg 1125 Grand Ave Kansas City MO 64106 E-mail: moore@p-mlaw.com.

MOORE, THELMA WYATT, judge; b. Amarillo, Tex., July 6, 1945; d. James Odis and Annie LaVernia (Lott) Wyatt; m. Luke C. Moore (dec. Nov. 1994); children: Khari Cummings, Ayanna Cummings. BA, UCLA, 1965; JD, Emory U., 1971. Bar: Ga. 1971. Atty. Ward and Wyatt, Atlanta, 1974-77; judge Mcpl. Ct., Atlanta, 1977-80, City Ct., Atlanta, 1980-85, State Ct., Fulton County, Ga., 1985-90; judge, chief judge Superior Ct., Fulton County, 1998—2002; judge Superior Ct. Fulton County, 1998—. Mem. exec. com. Nat. Jud. Coun., 1987—, chmn., 1986-87; spkr. in field. Assoc. editor Jour. Pub. Law, 1969-71; contbr. articles to profl. jours. Former chair adminstrv. bd. Cascade United Meth. Ch.; bd. trustees Emory U.; bd. dirs. Joint Ctr. for Polit. and Econ. Studies. Recipient WSB TV Living Legend award, 1991, 92, Disting. Alumni award Emory U., 1986, Essence award, 1982, Wiley Branton award NBA, 1999, Rehnquist award for Jud. Excellence, 2001, numerous others; John Hay Whitney fellow; Nat. Urban League fellow; Emory Law scholar; State of Ill. fellow. Mem. ABA, Nat. Bar Assn., Ga State Bar Assn., Atlanta Bar Assn., Gate City Bar Assn. (historian 1990-93), World Peace Through Law Ctr., Am. Judges Assn., Ga. Assn. Black Women Attys., Nat. Assn. Women Judges, Mo-So Lit. Circle, Order of Coif, Bryan Soc., Alpha Kappa Alpha, Phi Delta Phi. Office: 185 Central Ave SW Ste T4905 Atlanta GA 30303-3691

MOORE, THOMAS A. lawyer; b. Waterford, Ireland, May 2, 1942; STL, Cath. U., 1968; JD, Fordham U., 1972. Bar: N.Y. 1973, U.S. Dist. Ct. (so. and ea. dists.) N.Y. 1973, U.S. Supreme Ct. 1991. Lawyer Kramer, Dillof, Livingston & Moore, N.Y.C., 1973—. Lectr. in field. Mem.: ATLA (nat. bd. dirs. 1992), Am. Bd. Trial Advs., N.Y. State Trial Lawyers Assn. Personal injury (including property damage), Health, General civil litigation. Office: Kramer Dillof Livingston & Moore 217 Broadway New York NY 10007*

MOORE, THOMAS KAIL, district court judge; b. Idaho Falls, Idaho, Jan. 15, 1938; s. Burton L. and Clara E. (Kail) Moore; m. Judith Diane Gilman, July 30, 1966; children: David T., Jonathan G. AB in Phys. Scis., Harvard U., 1961; JD, Georgetown U., 1967. Bar: D.C., V.I., Va. Law clk. to Hon. John A. Danaher U.S. Ct. Appeals (D.C. Cir.), 1967-68; staff atty. Office Gen. Coun., Office Sec. Dept. Transp., Washington, 1968-69; assoc. Stanford, Reed & Gelenian, Washington, 1969-70; asst. U.S. Atty. U.S. Attys. Office, Washington, 1970-71, U.S. Attys. Office (ea. dist.), Va., 1971-76, prin. asst. Alexandria office, 1974-76; asst. U.S. Atty. U.S. Attys. Office (V.I. dist.), 1976-78; pvt. practive St. Thomas, V.I., 1978-81; shareholder Hoffman & Moore, P.C., St. Thomas, 1981-87; ptnr. Grunert, Stout, Moore & Bruch, St. Thomas, 1987-92; dist. judge U.S. Dist. Ct. (V.I. dist.), 1992—. Editor-in-chief Georgetown Law Journal, 1966-67. Scoutmaster Antilles Sch. Troop; trustee V.I. Montessori Sch. Capt. USAF, 1961-64, USAFR. Mem.: ABA, Va. Bar Assn., V.I. Bar Assn. (judicial), St. Thomas Yacht Club. Avocations: tennis, swimming, sailing. Office: Dist Ct of VI 5500 Veterans Dr Ste 310 St Thomas VI 00802-6424

MOORE, THOMAS RONALD (LORD BRIDESTOWE), lawyer; b. Duluth, Minn., Mar. 27, 1932; s. Ralph Henry and Estelle Marguerite (Hero) M.; m. Margaret C. King, Sept. 10, 1955; children: Willard S., Clarissa, Charles R.H. BA magna cum laude, Yale U., 1954; JD, Harvard U., 1957. Bar: N.Y. 1958, U.S. Supreme Ct. 1965. Instr. Harvard Law Sch., 1956-57; with Dewey Ballantine, N.Y.C.; ptnr. Breed, Abbott & Morgan, N.Y.C., Finley Kumble & Wagner, N.Y.C., Law Offices of Thomas R. Moore, N.Y.C. Lectr. on law Cornell Law Sch., NYU, Practising Law Inst., N.Y.C., Las Vegas, New Orleans; lectr. Oxford, N.Y.C., San Antonio, Tampa, LA, Moscow, Charlottesville, Washington, Kansas City. Author: Plantagenet Descent, 31 Generations from William the Conqueror to Today, 1995; co-author: Estate Planning and the Close Corporation; editor-in-chief: Gastronome, bd. editors: The Tax Lawyer; contbr. articles to profl. jours.; often in popular press and TV commentaries, including 12 media interviews Jan. 24, 2002. Bd. dirs. exec. com. Citymeals on Wheels; pres. bd. dirs. Nat. Soc. to Prevent Blindness, 1973-81, chmn., 1981-83, now hon. pres.; sec.-treas., trustee A.D. Henderson Found., Del.; trustee, Fla.; bd. dirs. Phoenix Theatre Inc., Inst. Aegean Prehistory, Found. Future of Man, Am. and Internat. Friends of Victoria and Albert Mus., London; conservator N.Y. Pub. Libr.; trustee Found. for Renaissance of St. Petersburg (Russia), Malcolm Wiener Found., Lawrence W. Levine Found.; bd. dirs. Gov.'s Commn. on Scholastic Achievement, 2002--; constl. advisor to Pres. George Bush; advisor to King Michael of Romania. Recipient Coat of Arms and created Knight of St. John, Queen Elizabeth II, Order of Crown of Charlemagne, Order of Plantagenet, Order of Barons of Magna Charta, Order of Descendants Knights of the Garter, Thomas R. Moore Disting. Pub. Servant award, Nat. Soc. to Prevent Blindness; scholar of House, Class Marshall, Yale. Mem.: St. Andrews Soc., St. George Soc., Confrerie de la Chaine des Rotisseurs (nat. pres., dir., exec. com. world coun. Paris), Robert Burns Soc., Nat. Wine Coalition (bd. dirs. 1989—), Chevalier du Tastevin, The Pilgrims, Church Club, Univ. Club, Delta Sigma Rho. Republican. Episcopalian. General civil litigation, Estate planning, Taxation, general. Office: 590 Madison Ave Ste 2100 New York NY 10022

MOORE, THURSTON ROACH, lawyer; b. Memphis, Dec. 10, 1946; s. Richard Charlton Moore and Halcyon Hall (Roach) Lynn; m. Corell Luckhardt Halsey, Sept. 26, 1998. BA with distinction, U. Va., 1968, JD, 1974. Bar: Va. 1974. Rsch. analyst Scudder, Stevens & Clark, N.Y.C., 1968—71; ptnr. Hunton & Williams, Richmond, Va., 1974—. Bd. dirs. Met. Advantage Corp., Richmond. Trustee Va. Aerospace Bus. Roundtable, Hampton, 1989—, Va. Ea. Shore Sustainable Devel. Corp., 1995—2000; bd. dirs. Mary Morton Parsons Found., Charlottesville, Va., The Nature Conservancy, Charlottesville, chmn. Va. chpt. Mem.: ABA (bus. law sect., chmn. ptnrs. com. 1992—96, mem. fed. regulation security com., bus. law coun.), Va. State Bar, Va. Bar Assn. Office: Hunton & Williams Riverfront Plz E Tower 951 E Byrd St Richmond VA 23219-4074

MOORE, TOM WHITE, JR., lawyer; b. July 19, 1943; s. Tom White and Barbara Jeanice (Byrne) Moore; m. Linda Kay Blankinship, Aug. 29, 1967; children: Tom White, Heather Lucille. BS, U. Tenn., 1967; JD, Samford U., Birmingham, Ala., 1970. Bar: Tenn. 1970, U.S. dist. Ct. (mid. dist.) Tenn. 1970, U.S. Ct. Appeals (6th cir.) 1977, cert.: Nat. Elder Law Found. and Tenn. Comn. Legal Edn.and Specialization (elder law specialist) 2001. Assoc. Moore, Henry, Henry, Lewis & Cain, Pulaski, Tenn., 1970—71; ptnr. Henry, Lewis, Cain & Moore, Columbia, Tenn., 1971—74, Cain & Moore, Columbia, 1974—82, Cain, Moore & Peden, Columbia, 1982—87, Moore & Peden, Columbia, 1987—. Served with USANG, 1961—67. Mem.: Maury County Bar Assn. (pres. 1979), Nat. Acad. Elder Law Attys., Tenn. Trial Lawyers Assn. (bd. dir. 1971—), Assn. Trial Lawyers Am., Tenn. Bar Assn., Kiwanis. Probate (including wills, trusts), Estate planning, Estate taxation. Home: 1205 Confederate Dr Columbia TN 38401 Office: Moore & Peden PC 700 N Garden St AmSouth Bank 3rd Fl Columbia TN 38401-3355

MOORE, VERNON JOHN, JR., pediatrician, lawyer, medical consultant; b. Chgo., Mar. 18, 1942; s. Vernon John Moore; m. Rutheva deVera Dizon, Feb. 27, 1979; children: Christopher, Joseph. BS, Loyola U., Chgo., 1964, JD, 1986; MD, U. Ill.-Chgo., 1968. Bar: Ill. 1986, U.S. Dist. Ct. (no. dist.) Ill. 1986. Intern St. Joseph Health Care Ctrs. and Hosp., Chgo., 1968-69, resident in pediats., 1971-74, chief resident, 1972-74, mem. med. staff, 1974-76, 78-86; pvt. practice Chgo., 1974-76, 97—; mem. med. staff Naval Hosp. Great Lakes, 1976-78; med. officer Chgo. Mil. Entrance Processing Sta., 1996—2002, Midwest Ctr. for Youth and Families, Kouts, Ind., 1997—; mem. med. staff Ill. Masonic Med. Ctr., Chgo., 1997—, Swedish Covenant Hosp., Chgo., 1998—, Luth. Gen. Hosp., Park Ridge, Ill., 1998—, Alexian Bros. Med. Ctr., Elk Grove Village, Ill., 2000—. Asst. dir. pediat. edn. St. Joseph Health Care Ctrs. and Hosp., 1974-76, co-dir., 1978-86, acting chmn. dept. pediats., 1985-86; clin. assoc. prof. pediat. Loyola U., Maywood, Ill., 1981-87; med. cons. CNA Ins. Cos., Chgo., 1987-94; pediatric med. cons. Hartgrove Hosp., Chgo., 1996—, Alexian Bros. Behavioral Health Hosp., Hoffman Estates, Ill., 1999-2001. Part-time staff Chgo. office Sen. Everett M. Dirksen, 1961-64. Served in med. corps USNR, 1969—2002, ret. as capt., 2002. Fellow Am. Acad. Pediat., 1985-2000; mem. U. Ill. Alumni Assn. (bd. dirs. 1983-89), Alumni Assn. Coll. Medicine U. Ill. (alumni councillor 1989-99), U. Ill. Pres. Coun. Republican. Roman Catholic. Home: 146 Park Ave River Forest IL 60305-2040 Office: 5758 N California Ave Chicago IL 60659-4726

MOORE, VICTORIA GUMBS, lawyer; b. Mineola, NY, July 21, 1970; BS, St. John's U., 1994; JD, Touro Law Ctr., 2000. Bar: N.Y. 2000. Exec. asst. to town atty. Town of Babylon, Lindenhurst, NY; policy analyst N.Y.S. Comptroller's Office, Hauppauge, NY, counsel; prin. law clk. N.Y.S. Supreme Ct., Mineola, NY.

MOORHEAD, THOMAS BURCH, lawyer, corporation and government executive; b. Evanston, Ill., May 3, 1934; s. John William and Jane (Hendrich) M.; m. Christie Barnard, Dec. 31, 1966 (div. June 1992); children: Merrell Hendrich, Hannah Christie, Rachel McGill; m. Elizabeth Howard, May 3, 2002. BA, Yale U, 1956; postgrad., The Hague Acad. Internat. Law, 1958; JD, U. Pa., 1959; LLM, NYU, 1964. Bar: N.Y. 1960, Conn. 1971, U.S. Supreme Ct. 1965. Assoc. Milbank, Tweed, Hadley & McCloy, N.Y.C., 1959-63; assoc. counsel, asst. sec. Hooker Chem. Corp., N.Y.C., 1963-68, dir. indsl. rels., 1968-69, v.p. indsl. rels., 1969-72; v.p. employee rels. Champion Internat. Corp., N.Y.C., 1972-74; v.p. adminstrn. Beker Industries Corp., Greenwich, Conn., 1974-76; v.p. corp. affairs Estée Lauder, Inc., N.Y.C., 1976-84, sr. v.p., 1984-87; v.p. human resources Carter-Wallace, Inc., N.Y.C., 1987—2001; dep. undersec. for internat. affairs U.S. Dept. Labor, Washington, 2001—. Bd. dirs., vice chmn. Transaction Billing Resources, Inc., 1991-97; elected mem. Corp. Culinary Inst. of Am., 1993-2000. Mem. New Canaan (Conn.) Rep. Town Com., 1980-85; elected mem. New Canaan Town Coun., 1985-2001, vice chmn., 1989-98, chmn. 1998-2001; justice of the peace State of Conn., 2001—; bd. dirs. Employment Policy Found., 1993-2001, Les Amis d'Escoffier Soc., 1990-2001, Les Amis d'Escoffier Found., 1990-2001, Yale U. Alumni Fund, 1987-92, Nat. Choral Coun., 1988-93, United Way Tri-State, Inc., 1986-89, United Way New Canaan, 1983-89, pres., 1986-87; mem. Conn. Oversight Commn., Metro-North Commuter R.R., 1985-89; U.S. del. ILO, 1985, 93, 94, 95, 96, 2000, 01, 02, head U.S. employer del., 1994, 95, 96, 2000 and to ILO Asian Regional Meeting, 1997, ILO Ams. regional meeting, 1999, 2002, head U.S. govt. delegation, ILO Assn. Reg. Meeting, 2002, elected v.p. ILO conf., Geneva, 2000, elected mem. governing body ILO, 2001—. Mem. ABA, Assn. of Bar of City of N.Y., Am. Soc. Internat. Law, Met. Club, New Canaan Country Club, Gridiron Club of New Canaan (pres. 1990-2001), Yale Club. Home: 800 25th St NW Apt 501 Washington DC 20037 Office: 200 Constitution Ave NW Washington DC 20210

MOORMAN VAN KAPPEN, OLAV, legal historian, law educator; b. The Hague, The Netherlands, Mar. 11, 1937; s. Karel Sigurd Olaf van Kappen and Johanna Jacoba Moorman; m. Froukje Andrea Bosma, Sept. 12, 1963; children: Olaf Frederik Jacob, Joanne Jacobine Marije. LLM, Utrecht U., 1961, LLD, 1965; LHD (hon.), U. Rene Descartes, Paris, 1996. Asst. faculty law Utrecht U., 1961-64, jr. lectr. law, 1964-68; sr. lectr. law Amsterdam U., 1968-71; asst. prof. legal sci. Leyden U., 1971-72; prof. legal history Nijmegen U., 1971-2000, prof. emeritus, 2000—. Guest prof. U. Munster and Dusseldorf, U. Poitiers, U. Paris, 1982-99. Contbr. numerous books and articles to profl. jours.; mem. editl. bd. legal history jours., including Legal History Rev., 1983—. Mem. curatorium Netherlands Sch. for Archivists, 1979-95, chmn., 1981-95; mem. Netherlands Coun. Archives and State Commn. Archives, 1979-95, v.p., 1986-92, pres., 1993-95; mem. Netherlands Coun. Nat. Heritage, 1990-95. Decorated Cross of Merit, 1st class Order of Merit (Germany), officier Order Palmes Academiques (France), officier Order van Orange-Nassau (Netherlands). Mem. Royal Netherlands Acad. Arts and Scis., Acad. Scis. Gottingen, Learned and Sci. Soc. Holland, Rotary. Office: Inst Legal Scis KUN PO Box 9049 6500 KK Nymegen Netherlands

MOOTY, JOHN WILLIAM, lawyer; b. Adrian, Minn., Nov. 27, 1922; s. John Wilson and Genevieve (Brown) M.; m. Virginia Nelson, June 6, 1952 (dec. 1964); children: David N., Bruce W., Charles W.; m. Jane Nelson, Jan. 15, 1972. BSL, U. Minn., 1943, LLB, 1944. Bar: Minn. 1944. Ptnr. Gray, Plant, Mooty & Bennett, Mpls., 1945—. Bd. dirs. Internat. Dairy Queen, Inc., Bur. of Engraving, Inc., Riverway Co. and subs., Rio Verde Svcs., Inc., Ariz. Author: (with others) Minnesota Practice Methods, 1956. Chmn. Gov.'s Task Force on Edn., 1981; pres. Citizens League Mpls., 1970; acting chmn. Republican Party of Minn., 1958. Mem. ABA, Minn. Bar Assn., Hennepin County Bar Assn., U. Minn. Alumni Assn. (pres. 1982), Tonto Verde Country Club, Minikahda (Mpls.) Club, Mpls. Club. Home: 6601 Dovre Dr Minneapolis MN 55436-1711

MORALES, DEBRA A. lawyer; b. Whittier, Calif., July 27, 1953; B in Social Welfare, U. Wash., 1991, JD, 1994. Bar: Wash., U.S. Dist. Ct. (we. dist.) Wash., U.S. Ct. Appeals (9th cir.). Assoc. Helsell Fetterman LLP, Seattle, 1994—98, Bogle & Gates PLLC, Seattle, 1998—99; ptnr. Marks, Holmes, Foley & Morales, P.S., Seattle, 1999—. Bd. dirs. Downtown Emergency Svc. Ctr., 1999—. Mem.: ABA, King County Bar Assn. (dir. Bilingual Legal Clinic 2001), Washington State Hispanic Bar Assn. (pres. 1997—99), Hispanic Nat. Bar Assn., Am. Immigration Lawyers Assn., U. Wash. Sch. Law Alumni Assn. (bd. dirs. 2001—). Immigration, naturalization, and customs, Family and matrimonial. Office: Marks Holmes Foley and Morales PS 1001 4th Ave # 3130 Gig Harbor WA 98329 Office Fax: 206-621-9478. Business E-Mail: dmorales@mhfmlaw.com.

MORALES, JULIO K. lawyer; b. Havana, Cuba, Jan. 17, 1948; came to U.S., 1960; s. Julio E. and Josephine (Holsters) M.; m. Suzette M. Dussault, May 31, 1970 (div. 1978); children: Julio E., Karel A.; m. Barbara A. Miller, July 14, 1979 (div. 1988); 1 child, Nicolas W. BA, Carroll Coll., 1969; JD, U. Mont., 1972. Bar: Mont. 1972, U.S. Dist. Ct. Mont. 1972, U.S. Ct. Mil. Appeals 1972, U.S. Ct. Appeals (9th cir.) 1980. Law clk. to presiding justice Mont. Supreme Ct., Helena, 1972; sole practice Missoula, Mont., 1973-78, 88—; sr. ptnr. Morales & Volinkaty, Missoula, 1978-88; pvt. practice law Morales Law Office, 1988—. Author: Estate Planning for the Handicapped, 1975. Pres. Rockmont, Inc., Missoula, 1985-2001. Served to 2d lt. U.S. Army, 1972. Named Boss of the Yr., Missoula chpt. Mont. Assn. Legal Secs., 1988. Mem. ABA (dist. rep. 1975-79, exec. coun. young lawyer divsn. 1977-79), Mont. Bar Assn. (chmn. law day 1974, 75, 77), Am. Judicature Soc., Assn. Trial Lawyers Am., World Assn. Lawyers, Missoula Soccer Assn. (pres. 1983-85), Mont. Sailing Assn. (bd. dirs. 1994—), Nat. Exch. Club (bd. dirs. Yellowstone dist. 1987-88, pres. 1990-91), Missoula Exch. Club, Elks (officer 1999-2001, exalted ruler 2001-02), Phi Delta Phi. Roman Catholic. Avocations: sports, coaching youth, boating, skiing, golf. Personal injury (including property damage), Probate (including wills, trusts), Workers' compensation. Office: PO Box 9311 430 Ryman St Missoula MT 59802-4249 E-mail: jmorales@moraleslaw.com.

MORAN, JAMES BYRON, federal judge; b. Evanston, Ill., June 20, 1930; s. James Edward and Kathryn (Horton) M.; children: John, Jennifer, Sarah, Polly; stepchildren: Katie, Cynthia, Laura, Michael. AB, U. Mich., 1952; LLB magna cum laude, Harvard U., 1957. Bar: Ill. 1958. Law clk. to judge U.S. Ct. of Appeals (2d cir.), 1957-58; assoc. Bell, Boyd, Lloyd, Haddad & Burns, Chgo, 1958-66, ptnr., 1966-79; judge U.S. Dist. Ct. (no. dist.) Ill., Chgo., 1979—. Dir. Com. on Ill. Govt., 1960-78, chmn., 1968-70; vice chmn., sec. Ill. Dangerous Drug Adv. Coun., 1967-74; dir. Gateway Found., 1969— ; mem. Ill. Ho. of Reps., 1965-67; mem. Evanston City Council, 1971-75. Served with AUS, 1952-54. Mem. Chgo. Bar Assn., Chgo. Council Lawyers, Lawyers Club, Phi Beta Kappa. Home: 117 Kedzie St Evanston IL 60202-2509 Office: US Dist Ct 219 S Dearborn St Chambers 1846 Chicago IL 60604-1800 E-mail: jbm117@aol.com.

MORAN, KEVIN PAUL, lawyer; BSME, U. Wis., 1986, JD, 1992. Bar: Wis. 1992, Colo. 1992, Minn. 1995. Engr. Trek Bicycle Corp., Waterloo, Wis., 1986—89; assoc. Sheridan, Ross & McIntosh, Denver, 1992—95; assoc./ptnr. Michael Best & Friedrich LLP, Milw., 1995—. Lectr. in field. Contbr. Alternative dispute resolution, Intellectual property, Patent. Office: Michael Best & Friedrich LLP N19 W24133 Riverwood Dr Waukesha WI 53188

MORANDO, MARTA LUCILE HOPE, lawyer; b. Portland, Oreg., June 20, 1952; d. Sil. S. and Jeanne Hope Morando. AB summa cum laude, U. Calif., Berkeley, 1972, JD, 1975. Bar: Calif. 1975. Assoc. Gray, Cary, Ware & Freidenrich and predecessor firm, Palo Alto, Calif., 1975-80, ptnr., 1980—, mem. exec. com., 1983-86. Lectr. on various legal topics. Mem. ABA, Calif. Bar Assn., Calif. Women's Lawyers Assn. Republican. Lutheran. Corporate, general, Securities. Office: Gray Cary Ware & Freidenrich 400 Hamilton Ave Palo Alto CA 94301-1833

MORD, IRVING CONRAD, II, lawyer; b. Mar. 22, 1950; s. Irving Conrad and Lillie Viva (Chapman) M.; m. Julia Ann Russell, Aug. 22, 1970 (div. Apr. 1980); children: Russell Conrad, Emily Ann; m. Kay E. McDaniel, Aug. 31, 1985; children: Kurt August, Clayton Troy. BS, Miss. State U., 1972; JD, U. Miss., 1974. Bar: Miss. 1974, U.S. Dist. Ct. (no. dist.) Miss. 1974, U.S. Dist. Ct. (so. dist.) Miss. 1984. Counsel to bd. suprs. Noxubee County, Miss., 1976-80, Walthall County, Miss., 1980—, Bd. Edn., Walthall County, 1982—. County pros. atty. Noxubee County, Macon, Miss., 1974—80, Walthall County, Tylertown, Miss., 1982—88, Tylertown, 1991—96. Bd. dirs. East Miss. Coun., Meridian, 1978-80, Trustmark Nat. Bank, Tylertown, 1986—, chmn., 2002-; v.p. Macon coun. Boy Scouts Am., 1978, mem. coun., 1979; county crusade chmn. Am. Cancer Soc., Macon, 1976-78, county pres., 1979; chmn. fund dr. fine arts complex Miss. State U., Macon, 1979; Walthall County family master, 1996—, Walthall County Youth referee, 1996—; mem. Local Workforce Investment Bd., 2000—. Recipient Youth Leadership award Miss. Econ. Coun., 1976. Mem. Miss. Assn. Bd. Attys. (v.p. 1985, pres. 1986), Miss. Assn. Sch. Bd. Attys., Miss. State Bar, Am. Judicature Soc. (Torts award 1972), Nat. Fed. Ind. Bus., Miss. State U. Alumni Assn., Walthall County C. of C., Phi Kappa Tau (bd. govs. 1976-80, grad. coun. 1972—, pres. grad. coun. 1977-80, pres. house corp. 1977-80, Alumnus of Yr. Alpha Chi chpt. 1979), Rotary (sec.-treas. 1977, v.p. 1978, pres. Macon 1979, pres. Tylertown club 1986-87), Phi Delta Phi. Office: 729 Beulah Ave Tylertown MS 39667-2709 E-mail: icmord@telapex.com.

MORE, DOUGLAS MCLOCHLAN, lawyer; b. N.Y.C., Apr. 21, 1926; s. Morgan Berkeley and Lucinda (Bateson) M.; m. Pamela Bennett Marr, Aug. 6, 1954; children— Robin Maclachlan More Eddy, Alison Marr More Davies. Grad., Phillips Exeter Acad., 1943; BA, Harvard U., 1947; LL.B., Columbia U., 1950. Bar: N.Y. State bar 1950, Conn. bar 1981, Fla. bar 1983. With N.Y. Trust Co., 1950-51; asso. firm Bigham, Englar, Jones & Houston, N.Y.C., 1951-53; fin. analyst Johns-Manville Corp., 1953-54; assoc. firm Kissam & Halpin, N.Y.C., 1954-59; assoc. counsel Hooker Chem. Corp., 1959-63, gen. counsel, 1963-72, v.p., 1967-72; v.p. law Airco, Inc., 1972-75; gen. counsel Beker Industries Corp., 1975-81, v.p., 1975-78, sr. v.p., 1978-81; ptnr. firm More Phillips & Duncan, P.C., Greenwich, Conn., 1981-88, of counsel, 1988—. Served to lt. (j.g.) USNR, 1943-46. Mem. ABA, Conn. Bar Assn., Greenwich Bar Assn., Phi Delta Phi, Phoenix S-K Club, Hasty Pudding Inst. 1770 (Harvard). Commercial, contracts (including sales of goods; commercial financing), Corporate, general, General practice. Home and Office: 27 Skylark Rd Greenwich CT 06830-4624

MOREL, PAUL, lawyer; b. Sept. 13, 1954; m. Martine Morel; children: Marion, Juliette, Nicolas, Caroline. Licence en Lettres, U. Paris IV, 1978; LLM, George Washington U., 1980; Doctorate, U. Paris I, 1984. Bar: Paris 1992. Assoc., 1984—95; ptnr. Salans Paris, 1995—. Co-author: French Company Law, 1992. Mem.: AFIC (mem. LBO com.). Office: Salans 9 rue Boissy d Anglas 75008 Paris France

MORELLI, CARMEN, lawyer; b. Oct. 30, 1922; s. Joseph and Helen (Carani) Morelli; m. Irene Edna Montminy, June 26, 1943; children: Richard A., Mark D., Carl J. BSBA, Boston U., 1949, JD, 1952. Bar: Conn. 1955, U.S. Dist. Ct. Conn. 1958. Asst. prosecutor Town of Windsor, 1957—58; mem. Conn. Ho. of Reps., 1959—61; atty. Town of Windsor, 1961; rep. Capitol Regional Planning Agy., 1965—72. Mem. Windsor Town Com., 1957—82, chmn., 1964—65, treas., 1960—64, mem. planning and zoning commn., 1965—74, mem. charter revision com., 1963—64; rep. Presdl. Task Force. Served with USN, 1943—45. Mem.: ABA, Am. Arbitration Assn., Windsor Bar Assn. (pres. 1979), Hartford Bar Assn., conn. Bar Assn., Rotary (sgt. arms, sec. 1989—90, pres. 1990—91), Elks, Windsor C. of C. (v.p. 1978). Roman Catholic. General practice, Personal injury (including property damage), Probate (including wills, trusts). Home: 41 Farmstead Ln Windsor CT 06095-1834 Office: 66 Maple Ave Windsor CT 06095-2926

MORENO, CARLOS R. state supreme court justice; b. L.A., Nov. 4, 1948; m. Christine Moreno; children: Keiko, Nicholas. BA in Polit. Sci., Yale U., 1970; JD, Stanford U., 1975. Dep. city atty. L.A. City Atty.'s Office; atty. with Mori & Ota (now known as Kelley, Drye & Warren), 1979; apptd. justice Mncpl. Ct., 1986—93; justice L.A. County Superior Ct., 1993—97, US Dist. Ct. (ctrl. dist.) Calif., 1998—2001; assoc. justice Supreme Ct. Calif., 2001—. Bd. visitors Stanford Law Sch.; bd. govs. Assn. Yale Alumni; dir. Arroyo Vista Family Health Ctr. Recipient Criminal Justice Superior Ct. Judge of Yr. award, L.A. County Bar Assn., 1997, For God, For Country and For Yale award, Yale U., 2001. Avocations: theater , opera, crossword puzzles. Office: Calif Supreme Ct 350 McAllister St San Francisco CA 94102-4783*

MORETTI, JAY DONALD, lawyer; b. Waukesha, Wis., May 20, 1947; s. Orest and Jeanne A. (Charlevoix) M.; m. Joann Senn, Nov. 8, 1975; children: Angela, Rocco, Luciano. BA in History, U. Wis., 1969, JD, 1971. Bar: Wis. 1972, U.S. Dist. Ct. (we. dist.) Wis. 1972, U.S. Dist. Ct. (ea. dist.) Wis. 1973. Atty. Reigel Law Office, Madison, Wis., 1971-72; pvt. practice Madison, 1973-76, Cross Plains, Wis., 1975—. Supr. Dane County, Madison, 1990-96, chmn. pub.protection and judiciary com., chmn. planning structure com., vice chmn. ways and means com., mem. EXPO expansion com.; mem. Bd. Health; mem. exec. bd. Dane County Rep. Com., 1988-90; mem. Wis. Citizens com. AODA, 1987-91. Recipient William Campbell award Wis. Rep. Com., 1989, svc. award, 1991; community svc. award Cross Plains Jaycees, 1980, Columbian of the Yr. award 1999, Excellence award Dane County Dep. Sheriff's Assn., 1995. Mem. State Bar Wis., Dane County Bar Assn., Cross Plains Bus. Assn. (pres. 1979,99, v.p.), Am. Legion, Italian Workmen's Club (pres. 1976), Lions (pres. Cross Plains 1985, dist. parliamentarian 1986-2001, zone chmn. 1988-91). Roman Catholic. Avocations: canoeing, gardening. Estate planning, Family and matrimonial, Property, real (including real estate development, water). Office: 2305 Main St Cross Plains WI 53528-9529 E-mail: moretti@chorus.net.

MORF, DARREL ARLE, lawyer; b. Fredericksburg, Iowa, Dec. 24, 1943; s. Arle Eric and Ruth Dagne (Vaala) M.; m. Mildred Mae Petersen, 1968; children: Paul Petersen, Andrew Thomas, John Alexander. BA, U. Iowa, 1966, JD, 1969. Bar: Iowa, U.S. Dist. Ct. (no. and so. dists.) Iowa 1970, U.S. Tax Ct. 1980, U.S. Ct. Appeals (8th cir.) 1970. Clk. to judge U.S. Ct. Appeals (8th cir.), 1969-70; ptnr. Simmons, Perrine, Albright & Ellwood, Cedar Rapids, Iowa, 1970-91; lectr. U. Iowa Coll. Law, 1973-91; mem. probate & trust law com. Iowa State Bar. Fellow, Am. Coll. Trust and Estate Counsel, Bd. dirs., sec. Hall Found.; trustee Herbert Hoover Presdl. Libr. Assn.; bd. dirs. Am. Bapt. Churches USA, Mercy Hosp., Cedar Rapids. Mem. ABA, Iowa State Bar Assn., Linn County Bar Assn., Order of Coif, Rotary, Lions, Masons. Office: Simmons Perrine Albright & Ellwood Ste 1200 115 3rd St SE Cedar Rapids IA 54201

MORGADO, MILDRED, lawyer; b. Miami, Fla., June 30, 1973; d. Alcides and Anely Morgado. BA in Polit. Sci. and Internat. Affairs, Fla. State U., 1995; JD, Loyola U., New Orleans, 1998. Bar: Fla. 1998. Sr. assoc. Bauwerman Brauwerman and June, P.A., Miami, 1998—. Vol. atty. Put Something Back Project, Miami, 1999—. Mem.: Cuban Am. Bar Assn., Dade County Bar Assn. Immigration, naturalization, and customs. Office: Brauwerman Brauwerman & June PA Ste 1040 1000 Brickell Ave Miami FL 33131

MORGAN, CHARLES OXFORD, JR., lawyer; b. Miami, Fla., Jan. 21, 1940; s. Charles O. and Corabel (Klefeker) M.; m. Marabel Hawk, June 25, 1964; children: Laura M. Horton, Michelle R. Knott. BA, Wheaton (Ill.) Coll., 1962; JD, U. Miami, Fla., 1965; LLM in Taxation, NYU, 1966. Bar: Fla. 1965. Assoc. Peters, Maxey & McDonald, Miami, 1966-68; ptnr. Peters, Maxey, Short & Morgan, Miami, 1969-82; pvt. practice Miami, 1983—. Author: Jesus On Line, 1995. Exec. dir. Don Shula Found., Inc., Miami, 1991—; chmn. bd. dirs. Tyndale Theol. Sem., Amsterdam, Holland, 1989-92; dir. Miami Heart Inst., 1982-84, Billy Graham Evangelistic Assn., Mpls., 1983—. Estate planning, Probate (including wills, trusts). Office: 1300 NW 167th Ste 3 Miami FL 33169-5738

MORGAN, CHARLES RUSSELL, lawyer; b. New Orleans, La., Oct. 15, 1946; s. Charles and Marian E. (Wetzel) M.; children: Charles Bradford, William Russell, Elizabeth Anne. BA, U. N.C., 1968; JD, Columbia U., 1971. Bar: N.Y. 1973, Ill. 1981, Ohio 1994. Law clk. to cir. judge US Ct. Appeals, Washington, 1971-72; atty. Davis Polk & Wardwell, NYC, 1972-80; sr. staff counsel Household Internat., Inc., Prospect Heights, Ill., 1980-83; v.p., asst. gen. counsel Kraft, Inc., Glenview, Ill., 1983-85, v.p., sr. corp. counsel, 1985-88; v.p., gen. counsel, sec. Chiquita Brands Internat., Cin., 1988-95; ptnr. Mayer Brown & Platt, Chgo., 1995-98; exec. v.p., gen. counsel BellSouth Corp., Atlanta, 1998—. V.p., sec., dir. John Morrell & Co., Inc. Contbg. editor The Corp. Counselor, 1986—, The Environmental Corporate Counsel Report. Recipient Spirit of Excellence Award, Am. Bar Assoc., Corp. Legal Diversity Award, Am. Corp. Counsel Assoc., 2000, Nat. Diversity Leadership Award, Coalition of fBar Assoc. of Color, Diversity 2000 Award, Minority Corp. Coun. Assoc. Mem. ABA (chmn. corp. counsel com. 1983-86, chmn. comm. com. 1986—), Am. Law Inst., Am. Corp. Counsel Assn. (bd. dirs.), Am. Arbitration Assn. (bd. dirs.), Legal Club Chgo., Army-Navy Club of Washington. In Nov., 2000, Morgan was appointed by the Chief Justice of the Supreme Court of Ga. as Chair of the Supreme Court's Blue Ribbon Commission on Indigent Defense. Corporate, general, Mergers and acquisitions, Securities. Office: BellSouth Corp 1155 Peachtree St NE Ste A Atlanta GA 30309-3610*

MORGAN, CYNTHIA MAKIE, lawyer; b. Tacoma, Feb. 4, 1970; d. Theodore William and Beverly Jean Bolton; m. John Patrick Morgan, Aug. 6, 1994. BA, U. Wash., 1992; JD, Seattle U. (formerly U. Puget Sound), 1996. Bar: Wash. 1996, U.S. Dist. Ct. (we. dist.) Wash. 1996, Oreg. 2002. Atty. Messina Bulzomi, P.S., Tacoma, 1996—. Author: (book) WSLA Deskbook, 2000, WSBA Deskbook, 2001. Bd. dirs. YWCA, Tacoma, 2002—; fellow Roscoe Pond Foudn., 1997—. Mem.: ATLA (lobbyist 1997—), Wash. State Trial Lawyers Assn. (lobbyist 1996—, chair roundtable 1999, chair women sect. 2000—02). Avocations: running, hiking, reading. Personal injury (including property damage). Office: Messina Bulzomi 5316 Orchard St W Tacoma WA 98467 Office Fax: 253-761-2583. Business E-Mail: morgan@messinalaw.com.

MORGAN, DENNIS KEITH, lawyer; b. St. Louis, Dec. 12, 1947; s. Charles Gustave and Justine Estelle (Picarelli) M.; children: James, Elizabeth, Rebecca. BJ, U. Mo., 1970, JD, 1972; LLM, Washington U., St. Louis, 1978. Bar: Mo. 1972, U.S. Dist. Ct. (we. dist.) Mo. 1972, Ill. 1978, U.S. Dist. Ct. (ea. dist.) Mo. 1978, U.S. Ct. Appeals (8th cir.) 1978, Tex. 1981, U.S. Tax Ct. 1981, U.S. Ct. Mil. Appeals 1981., Pa. 2003. Spl. counsel U.S. Dept. Energy, 1979—80; exec. v.p. adminstrn., gen. counsel, corp. sec. So. Union Co., Wilkes-Barre, Pa., 1981—. Mem. exec. com. Austin Visual Arts Assn.; bd. dirs. Austin Symphony Orch.; trustee Everhart Mus. Maj. JAGC USAR, 1970—86. Mem. ABA, Tex. Bar Assn., Fed. Energy Bar Assn., Internat. Bar Assn., Mo. Bar Assn., Pa. Bar Assn., Am. Gas Assn. (legal com.), Mex. Gas Assn., So. Gas Assn. (legal com.). Lutheran. Avocations: teaching, history, travel. Office: So Union Co One PEI Ctr Wilkes Barre PA 18711 Home: 1104 Tennyson Close Moosic PA 18507

MORGAN, DENNIS RICHARD, lawyer; b. Jan. 3, 1942; s. Benjamin Richard and Gladys Belle (Brown) Morgan. BA, Washington and Lee U., 1964; JD, U. Va., 1967; LLM in Labor Law, NYU, 1971. Bar: Ohio 1967, Va. 1967, U.S. Ct. Appeals (4th cir.) 1968, U.S. Ct. Appeals (6th cir.) 1971, U.S. Supreme Ct. 1972. Law clk. to chief judge U.S. Dist. Ct. (ea. dist.) Va., 1967—68; mem. Marshman, Snyder & Seeley, Cleve., 1971—72; dir. labor rels. Ohio Dept. Adminstrv. Svcs., 1972—75; asst. city atty. Columbus, Ohio, 1975—77; dir. Ohio Legis. Reference Bur., Columbus, 1979—81; assoc. Clemans, Nelson & Assocs., Columbus, 1981; pvt. practice Columbus, 1978—92. Lectr. in field; guest lectr. Cen. Mich. U., 1975; judge moot ct. Ohio State U. Sch. Law, 1981, 83, grad. divsn., 73, 74, 76; guest lectr. Baldwin-Wallace Coll., 1973; legal counsel Dist. IV Comms. Workers Am., 1982—88; pers. dir. Pub. Utilities Commn., Ohio, 1989—91; asst. atty. gen. State of Ohio, 1991—. Negotiator Franklin County United Way, 1977—81; regional chmn. ann. alumni fund-raising program U. Va. Sch. Law; mem. Greater Hilltop Area Commn., 1989—; pres. Woodbrook Village Condominium Assn., 1985—; vice-chmn. Franklin County Dem. Party, 1976—82; dem. com. person Ward 58, Columbus, 1973—95; chmn. rules com. Ohio State Dem. Conv., 1974; co-founder, trustee Greater West Side Dem. Club; bd. dirs. Hilltop Civic Coun., Inc., 1997—99. Capt. U.S. Army, 1968—70. Recipient Am. Jurisprudence award, 1967; scholar Robert E. Lee Rsch., 1965. Mem.: ABA, Am. Judicature Soc., Fed. Bar Assn., Indsl. Rels. Rsch. Assn., Columbus Metropolitan club (charter), Pi Sigma Alpha. Roman Catholic. Administrative and regulatory, Labor (including EEOC, Fair Labor Standards Act, labor-management relations, NLRB, OSHA), Legislative. Home: 1261 Woodbrook Lane G Columbus OH 43223-3243 Office: 30 E Broad St Fl 26 Columbus OH 43215-3400

MORGAN, DONALD CRANE, lawyer; b. Detroit, Sept. 17, 1940; s. Donald Nye and Nancy Morgan; m. Judith Munro, June 23, 1962; children: Wendy, Donald. BA, Ohio Wesleyan U., 1962; JD, U. Mich., 1965. Bar: Mich. 1966, U.S. Dist. Ct. (ea. dist.) Mich. 1966, U.S. Ct. Appeals (6th cir.) 1967, U.S. Supreme Ct. 1971. Ptnr. Kerr, Russell and Weber, Detroit, 1965-87; of counsel Draugelis & Ashton, Plymouth, Mich., 1988-93; pvt. practice Plymouth, Mich., 1993—. Twp. atty. Plymouth Twp., 1970-85, Northville Twp., 1972-85; city atty. City of Plymouth, 1995-98; mediator Wayne County Mediation Tribunal, Detroit, 1981—, Oakland County Mediation Tribunal, Pontiac, Mich., 1992—; hearing panelist Mich. Atty. Discipline Bd., 1981—. Chmn. Wayne County II congl. Dist. Rep. Party, 1979-81; bd. dirs. Growth Works, Inc., 1999—, treas., 1992-95, pres. 1995-99, dir. 2000—; mem. charter rev. com. City of Plymouth, 2002—; ruling elder 1st Presbyn. Ch., Plymouth, 1976-79, 90-93; local bd. 222 mem. U.S. Selective Svc. Sys.; mem. spl. grants and agy. admissions com. United Way Cmty. Svcs.; mem. home rule charter rev. com, City of Plymouth, 2002—; elder commr. Detroit Presbytery. Paul Harris fellow, 1980. Mem. ABA, State Bar of Mich. (rep. assembly 1979-85, 89-95, 2003—, chmn. medicolegal problems com. 1995-96), Oakland County Bar Assn., Detroit Assn. Def. Trial Counsel, Plymouth Rotary (pres. 1985-86), Plymouth Rotary Found., Inc. (sec. 1996-98, dir. 1995, 99-2002), Phi Alpha Delta, Sigma Alpha Epsilon, Pi Sigma Alpha. Republican. Presbyterian. Avocations: reading, travel, sports. General practice, Corporate, general, Property, real (including real estate development, water). Home: 1440 Woodland Pl Plymouth MI 48170-1569 Office: 134 N Main St Plymouth MI 48170-1236 E-mail: morganlaw48170@aol.com.

MORGAN, FRANK EDWARD, II, lawyer; b. Burlington, Vt., May 16, 1952; s. Robert Griggs and Ruth (Jepson) M. First Class Cert. Merit, U. Edinburgh, Scotland, 1973; AB with honors, Brown U., 1974; LLM, Cambridge U., Eng., 1976; JD, U. Va., 1978. Bar: Mass. 1978, N.Y. 1990. Assoc. Gaston & Snow, Boston, 1978—82; v.p., gen. counsel Madison Fund, Inc. and Adobe Resources Corp., N.Y.C., 1982—87; ptnr. Gaston & Snow, N.Y.C., 1987—91, Mayer, Brown & Platt, N.Y.C., 1991—96, Dewey Ballantine, N.Y.C., 1996—2003; pres., CEO Coller Capital, Inc., N.Y.C., 2003—. Mem. ABA, N.Y. State Bar Assn., Am. Soc. Internat. Law. Republican. Congregationalist. Corporate, general, Private international, Securities. Home: 14 Sutton Pl S New York NY 10022-3071 Office: Coller Capital Inc PO Box 1353 FDR Station New York NY 10150-1353 Business E-Mail: morgan@collercapital.com.

MORGAN, GLENN L. lawyer; b. New Orleans, Dec. 1943; m. S.E. and S.T. Morgan. BA, U. La., Lafayette, 1965; JD, Loyola U., 1972. Bar: La. 1972, U.S. Dist. Ct. (all dists.) La. 1972, U.S. Ct. Appeals (5th cir.) 1972, U.S. Supreme Ct. 1975, U.S. Ct. Appeals (fed. cir.) 1982, U.S. Claims Ct. 1982, U.S. Internat. Trade Ct. 1982, U.S. Mil. Appeals Ct. 1986. Adj. faculty U. Phoenix South La. C.C. Republican. Appellate, General civil litigation, Criminal. Home: PO Box 354 Breaux Bridge LA 70517-0354 Office: PO Box 5006 Lafayette LA 70502-5006 Fax: 337-332-0584. E-mail: morgancaw@juno.com.

MORGAN, HENRY COKE, JR., judge; b. Norfolk, Va., Feb. 8, 1935; s. Henry Coke and Dorothy Lea (Pebworth) M.; m. Margaret John McGrail, Aug. 18, 1965; children: A. Robertson Hanckel Jr., Catherine Morgan Stockwell, Coke Morgan Stewart. BS, Washington and Lee U., 1957, JD, 1960; LLM in Jud. Process, U. Va., 1998. Bar: Va. 1960, U.S. Dist. Ct. (ea. dist.) Va. 1961, U.S. Ct. Appeals (4th cir.) 1964. Asst. city atty. City of Norfolk, 1960-63; ptnr. Pender & Coward, Virginia Beach, Va., 1963-92; vice chmn., gen. counsel Princess Anne Bank, 1986-92; judge U.S. Dist. Ct. (ea. dist.) Va., 1992—. Served with U.S. Army, 1958-59. Episcopalian. Office: US Dist Ct Eastern Dist Va Walter E Hoffman US Courthouse 600 Granby St Ste 183 Norfolk VA 23510-1915 E-mail: henry_morgan@vaed.uscourts.gov.

MORGAN, JACK M. lawyer; b. Portales, N.Mex., Jan. 15, 1924; s. George Albert and Mary Rosana (Baker) M.; m. Peggy Flynn Cummings, 1947; children: Marilyn, Rebecca, Claudia, Jack. BBA, U. Tex., 1948, LLB, 1950. Bar: N.Mex. 1950. Sole practice law, Farmington, N.Mex., 1956—. Mem. cmty. bd. dirs. Wells Fargo, Farmington, N.Mex. Mem. N.Mex. State Senate, 1973-88. Served with USN, 1942-46. Mem. N.Mex. Bar Assn., S.W. Regional Energy Coun. (past chmn.), Kiwanis, Elks. Republican. Commercial, consumer (including collections, credit), Corporate, general, Probate (including wills, trusts). Office: PO Box 2151 Farmington NM 87499-2151 E-mail: jmorgansr@fisi.net.

MORGAN, KERMIT JOHNSON, lawyer; b. Henderson, Iowa, Feb. 13, 1914; s. Samuel Jr. and Jennie Amelia Morgan; m. Georgina R. Morgan, Oct. 12, 1940 (dec. 1958); children: Georgina Morgan Street, Wilson S.; m. Ortrud Impol, Dec. 9, 1960. BA, U. Iowa, 1935; JD, U. So. Calif., 1937. Bar: Calif. 1939. Pvt. practice, LA, 1940—45, 1971—80, 1991—, Santa Monica, Calif., 1991—; ptnr. McBain & Morgan, L.A., 1945-65, Kermit Morgan, 1971—80, McBain, Morgan & Roper, L.A., 1965—71, Morgan & Armbrister, L.A., 1980-91. Mem. ABA, Am. Bd. Trial Advs. (diplomate, nat. pres. 1973, pres. L.A. 1972), Assn. Def. Trial Attys. (bd. dirs. 1982-85), Internat. Assn. Ins. Counsel, Hon. Order of Blue Goose, Calif. State Bar, Assn. So. Calif. Def. Counsel (bd. dirs. 1966-67), L.A. Bar Assn. Republican. Congregationalist. Avocation: golf. Insurance, Personal injury (including property damage). Home: 2108 Stradella Rd Los Angeles CA 90077-2325 Office: 3420 Ocean Pk Blvd Santa Monica CA 90405

MORGAN, MARY ANN, lawyer; b. Orlando, Fla., Mar. 12, 1955; d. Charles Clayburn and Eileen Louise (Mutzbauer) M.; m. Patrick Thomas Burke, Dec. 12, 1992. BS in Criminology, Fla. State U., 1978, JD, 1986. Bar: Fla. 1986, U.S. Dist. Ct. (mid. dist.) Fla. 1986, U.S. Supreme Ct. Investigator Auditor Gen.'s Office State of Fla., Orlando, 1979-83; staff analyst criminal justice com. Fla. Ho. of Reps., Tallahassee, 1985-86; ptnr. Billings, Cunningham, Morgan & Boatwright, Orlando, 1986—. Chmn. renovation com. Orange County Hist. Mus., Orlando, 1995—; spkr. Physician/Lawyer Drug Awareness Program, Orange County Schs., Orlando, 1997. Mem. ABA, ATLA, Fla. Bar Assn. (spkrs. bur. 1997, chair grievance com. 1993-96, vice chair 9th jud. cir. fee arbitration com.), Orange County Bar Assn. (exec. coun. 1991—, chmn. renovation com. 1995—, del. ABA 1989, 90, pres. young lawyers sect. 1990-91, pres. 2001—), Acad. Fla. Trial Lawyers, Ctrl. Fla. Assn. for Women Lawyers (bd. dirs. 1990-92), Fla. State U. Alumni Assn. (bd. dirs. 1996—), Orange County Legal Aid Soc. (bd. dirs. 1997—, pres.-elect 1998-99, pres. 1999—), Nat. Assn. Women Lawyers, Am. Inns of Ct., Tiger Bay Club, Million Dollar Advs. Club. Avocations: waterskiing, golf, boating. Personal injury (including property damage). Office: Billings Cunningham Morgan & Boatwright 330 E Central Blvd Orlando FL 32801-1921

MORGAN, MICHAEL VINCENT, lawyer; b. July 31, 1947; s. Stanley William and Alice (Michalski) M.; m. Susan Wanda Staub, Aug. 21, 1970; children: Jason, Allison. BA, U. Detroit, 1969, JD, 1972. Bar: Mich. 1972, U.S. Dist. Ct. (ea. dist.) Mich. 1972. Chmn. Lic. Appeal Bd. Mich. Dept. State, Detroit, 1972-73; pvt. practice Detroit, 1973-75, Troy, Mich., 1975—. Lectr. in field. Editor: Michigan Drunk Driving Law & Practice, 1986, 3rd edit. 1999; contbr. articles to profl. publs. Bd. dirs. U. Detroit Nat. Alumni Bd., 1974-77. Recipient Athletic Dirs. award U. Detroit, 1983. Mem. Mich. Bar Assn., U. Detroit Law Alumni Assn. (bd. dirs. 1996—), Titan Club (bd. dirs. 1982-86), Advocates Club (Detroit). Roman Catholic. Criminal. Office: 3155 W Big Beaver Rd Ste 100 Troy MI 48084-3006

MORGAN, R. GREGORY, lawyer; b. Long Beach, Calif., Jan. 24, 1954; s. Donald M. and Barbara P. Morgan; m. Virginia S. Popper, Apr. 23, 1983; children: Emily, Peter. BA, UCLA, 1976; JD, U. Mich., 1979. Bar: Calif. 1981, U.S. Dist. Ct. (ctrl. dist.) Calif. 1981. Clk. to Judge J. Edward Lumbard U.S. Ct. Appeals, 2d cir., N.Y.C., 1979—80; clk. to Justice Lewis Powell U.S. Supreme Ct., Washington, 1980—81; ptnr. Munger Tolles & Olson LLP, L.A., 1981—. Adj. prof. law U. So. Calif. Law Sch., L.A., 1985—86; vis. prof. law UCLA Law Sch., 1988—89. Trustee New Roads Sch., Santa Monica, Calif., 2001—. Mergers and acquisitions, Securities, Corporate, general. Office: Munger Tolles & Olson LLP 355 S Grand Ave Los Angeles CA 90071

MORGAN, RICHARD GREER, lawyer; b. Houston, Dec. 23, 1943; s. John Benjamin (stepfather) and Audrey Valley (Brickwede) Haus; children: Richard Greer, Jonathan Roberts. AB in History, Princeton U., 1966; JD, U. Tex., 1969. Bar: Tex. 1969, D.C. 1970, Minn. 1976, U.S. Ct. Appeals (D.C. cir.) 1970, U.S. Ct. Appeals (5th and 9th cirs., temporary emergency ct. appeals) 1976. Atty., advisor to commr. Lawrence J. O'Connor, Jr. Fed. Power Commn., Washington, 1969-71; assoc. Morgan, Lewis & Bockius, Washington, 1971-75; ptnr. O'Connor & Hannan, Washington, 1975-89, Lane & Mittendorf, Washington, 1989-97; mng. ptnr. Shook, Hardy & Bacon, L.L.P., Houston, 1997—. Bd. dirs. Hexagon, Inc.; instr. law seminars; lectr. in field. Author: Gas Lease and Royalty Issues, Natural Gas Yearbook, 1989, 90, 91, 92, 2002; contbr. articles on energy law to profl. jours. Bd. dirs. Mighty Spl. Music Makers, U. Tex. Law Sch. Found. Mem. ABA, Fed. Bar Assn., Energy Bar Assn. (bd. dirs.), D.C. Bar Assn., Princeton Alumni Coun., Princeton Alumni Assn. Houston, Energy Law Found. (pres.). Commercial, contracts (including sales of goods; commercial financing), Nuclear power, Oil, gas, and mineral. Office: Shook Hardy and Bacon LLP 600 Travis St Ste 1600 Houston TX 77002-2911

MORGAN, ROBERT HALL, lawyer; b. San Jose, Calif., Oct. 14, 1950; s. William Robert and Willa June (Hall) M.; m. Susan Kay Meyer, June 16, 1972 (div.); children: Robert Scott, Ryan William, Cory Benjamin, Nathan Thomas, Katherine Linn. BA, U. Oreg., 1974; MBA, U. Santa Clara, 1975, JD summa cum laude, 1978. Bar: Calif. 1978, U.S. Dist. Ct. (no. dist.) Calif. 1978. Legal extern Supreme Ct. Calif., San Francisco, 1978; pvt. practice law, 1978—; counsel Better Bus. Bur. Santa Clara Valley, Ltd., San Jose, 1980-86. Bd. dirs. Youth Sci. Inst., 1987-92, pres. 1990-92; bd. dirs. Triton Mus. of Art, 1998-; prin. Morgan Law Offices; bd. dirs. Nat. Mus. of The Morgan House, 2002—. Mem. Santa Clara County Bar Assn., Assn. Trial Lawyers Am. Democrat. Federal civil litigation, State civil litigation, Probate (including wills, trusts). Office: Morgan Law Offices 1501 The Alameda San Jose CA 95126-2311 E-mail: RHM@Morganlawoffices.com.

MORGAN, TIMI SUE, lawyer; b. Parsons, Kans., June 16, 1953; d. James Daniel and Iris Mae (Wilson) Baumgardner; m. Rex Michael Morgan, Oct. 28, 1983; children: Tessa Anne, Camma Elizabeth. BS, U. Kans., 1974; JD, So. Meth. U., 1977. Bar: Tex. 1977, U.S. Dist. Ct. (no. dist.) Tex. 1978, U.S. Ct. Appeals (5th cir.) 1979, U.S. Tax Ct. 1980; cert. tax law specialist. Assoc. Gardere & Wynne, Dallas, 1977-79, Akin, Gump, Strauss, Hauer & Feld, Dallas, 1979-83, ptnr., 1984-86; of counsel Stinson, Mag & Fizzell, Dallas, 1986-88; sole practice Dallas, 1988—. Adj. lectr. law So. Meth. U., 1989-90, 92-98. Bd. dirs. Dallas Urban League Inc., 1987-91. Mem. State Bar Tex. (mem. taxation sect.), Dallas Bar Assn., So. Meth. U. Law Alumni Coun. (sec. 1985-86), Order of Coif, Beta Gamma Sigma. Republican. Episcopalian.

MORGAN, WILLIAM ADAMS, lawyer; b. Detroit, Dec. 5, 1956; s. Thomas Oliver and Katharine (Egerton) M.; m. M. Gwen Herrin, Aug. 29, 1987. BA in Polit. Sci. cum laude, Ill. Wesleyan U., 1979; JD, U. Ill., 1982. Bar: Ill. 1982, U.S. Dist. Ct. (no. dist.) Ill. 1982, U.S. Ct. Appeals (7th cir.) 1996. Atty. Pope Ballard Shepard & Fowle, Chgo., 1982-91; assoc. gen. counsel, personal injury/workers' compensation Bd. of Edn. of the City of Chgo., 1991—. Recipient Recognition of Outstanding Svc. award Intergovtl. Risk Mgmt. Agy., 1996. Mem. ABA, Ill. State Bar Assn., Appellate Lawyers Assn. (bd. dirs. 2000-01, treas. 2001-02, sec. 2002-03). Avocations: gourmet cooking, wine collecting, traveling, photography. Home: 1925 W Bradley Pl Chicago IL 60613-3513 Office: Bd of Edn of City of Chgo 125 S Clark St Ste 700 Chicago IL 60603-5200 E-mail: wmorgan@csc.cps.k12.il.us.

MORGAN-PRAGER, KAROLE, lawyer, publishing executive; Assoc. Morrison & Foerster, L.A., 1987—92; assoc. gen. counsel Times Mirror Co., 1992—95; gen. counsel, corp. sec. McClatchy Co., Sacramento, 1995—, v.p., 1998—. Office: McClatchy Co Legal Dept 2100 Q St Sacramento CA 95818-6899*

MORGANROTH, FRED, lawyer; b. Detroit, Mar. 26, 1938; s. Ben and Grace (Greenfield) M.; m. Janice Marilyn Cohn, June 23, 1963; children: Greg, Candi, Erik. BA, Wayne State U., 1959, JD with distinction, 1961. Bar: Mich. 1961, U.S. Dist. Ct. (ea. dist.) Mich. 1961, U.S. Ct. Claims 1967, U.S. Supreme Ct. 1966; trained matrimonial arbitrator. Ptnr. Greenbaum, Greenbaum & Morganroth, Detroit, 1963-68, Lebenbom, Handler, Brody & Morganroth, Detroit, 1968-70, Lebenbom, Morganroth & Stern, Southfield, Mich., 1971-78; pvt. practice, Southfield, 1979-83; ptnr. Morganroth & Morganroth P.C., Southfield, 1983-94, Morganroth, Morganroth, Alexander & Nye, P.C., Birmingham, Mich., 1994-98, Morganroth, Morganroth, Jackman & Kasody, PC, Bloomfield Hills, Mich., 1999—. Mem. ABA (family law sect. 1987—), Mich. Bar Assn. (hearing panelist grievance bd. 1975—, Oakland County family law com. 1988—, vice chmn. 1992-93, chair 1993—), State Bar Mich. (mem. family law coun. of family law sect. 1990—, treas. 1993-94, chmn.-elect 1994-95, chmn. 1995-96), Detroit Bar Assn., Oakland Bar Assn. (cir. ct. mediator 1984—), Am. Arbitration Assn. (Oakland County family law com. 1985—, vice chmn. 1992-93, chmn. 1993-94, trained matrimonial arbitrator), Detroit Tennis Club (Farmington, Mich., pres. 1978-82), Charlevoix Country Club, Tam-O-Shanter Country Club. Jewish. Avocations: commercial pilot, golfing. Alternative dispute resolution, Family and matrimonial. Home: 30920 Woodcrest Ct Franklin MI 48025-1435 Office: 40701 Woodward Ave Ste 250 Bloomfield Hills MI 48304 E-mail: fmmman1@aol.com.

MORGANROTH, MAYER, lawyer; b. Detroit, Mar. 20, 1931; s. Maurice Jack Morganroth and Sophie (Reisman) Blum; m. Sheila Rubinstein, Aug. 16, 1958; children: Lauri, Jeffrey, Cherie. JD, Detroit Coll. Law, 1954. Bar: Mich. 1955, U.S. Dist. Ct. Mich. 1955, Ohio 1958, U.S. Dist. Ct. (no. dist.) Ohio 1958, U.S. Dist. Ct. D.C. 2002, U.S. Ct. Appeals (6th cir.) 1968, U.S. Supreme Ct. 1971, N.Y. 1983, U.S. Dist. Ct. N.Y. 1985, U.S. Tax Ct. 1985, U.S. Ct. Appeals (4th cir.) 1985, U.S. Ct. Claims 1986, U.S. Ct. Appeals (2d cir.) 1986, U.S. Ct. Appeals (fed. cir.), U.S. Ct. Appeals (8th cir.) 1994. Sole practice, Detroit, 1955—, N.Y.C., 1983—; ptnr. Morganroth & Morganroth, PLLC, 1989—. Cons. to lending instns.; lectr. on real estate NYU, 1980—, bus. entities and structures Wayne State U., 1981—; trial atty. in fed. and state jurisdictions, nationwide. Served with USN, 1948-50. Mem. ATLA, ABA, FBA, N.Y. State Bar Assn., Southfield Bar Assn., Oakland Bar Assn., Assn. Trial Lawyers Mich., Am. Judicature Soc., U.S. Supreme Ct. Hist. Soc., Nat. Assn. Criminal Def. Attys., West Bloomfield (Mich.) Club, Fairlane Club (Dearborn, Mich.), Knollwood Country Club, Edgewood Athletic Club (pres. 1963-65). Democrat. Jewish. Federal civil litigation, General civil litigation, Criminal. Office: 3000 Town Ctr Ste 1500 Southfield MI 48075-1186 also: 156 W 56th St Ste 1101 New York NY 10019-3800

MORGANSTERN, GERALD H. lawyer; b. N.Y.C., Dec. 19, 1942; s. Jack and Mildred M.; m. Karen Gibbs, Apr. 28, 1968; children: Jeffrey, Bradley. BS in Econs., U. Pa., 1963; LLB, Columbia U., 1966. Bar: N.Y. 1967, U.S. Dist. Ct. (ea. dist.) N.Y. 1967. Atty. Hofheimer Gartlir & Gross LLP, N.Y.C., 1967—, mgn. ptnr., 2000—. Mayor Village Hewlett Harbor (N.Y.), 1990-2000, trustee, 1982-90. General practice, Non-profit and tax-exempt organizations, Property, real (including real estate development, water). Home: 207 Richards Ln Hewlett NY 11557-2629 Office: Hofheimer Gartlir & Gross LLP 530 5th Ave New York NY 10036-5101 E-mail: gmorganstern@hgg.com.

MORGAN-WHITE, STEPHANIE LYNN, lawyer; b. Elizabethtown, Ky., Sept. 3, 1970; d. James Carrol and Evelyn Jeanette Morgan. BA cum laude, Wittenberg U., 1992; JD, Samford U., 1995. Bar: Ky. 1995, Ala. 1996, U.S. Dist. Ct. (mid. dist.) Ala. 1996, U.S. Dist. Ct. (we. dist.) Ky. 1997, U.S. Dist. Ct. (ea. dist.) Ky. 1998, U.S. Ct. Appeals (6th cir.) 1998. Staff atty. Ky. Ct. Appeals, Bowling Green, 1995-97; assoc. Goldberg & Simpson, Louisville, 1997—. Mem. Jr. League Louisville, Bus. and Profl. Women, Alpha Delta Pi. Avocation: scuba diving. Appellate, Family and matrimonial. Office: Goldberg & Simpson 3000 National City Tower Louisville KY 40202 E-mail: smorgan-white@gsatty.com.

MORGENSTERN, ROBERT TERENCE, lawyer; b. N.Y.C., Aug. 23, 1944; s. Carl G. and Jean C. (Madden) M.; m. Nancy G. Golden, June 29, 1968; children: Cynthia, John, Kathryn, Brian. BA, Villanova U., 1966, JD, 1969. Bar: N.J. 1969, U.S. Supreme Ct. 1986; cert. civil trial atty. Assoc. Dolan & Dolan, Newton, N.J., 1969-74, officer, dir., 1975—. Mem. ABA, Assn. Trial Lawyers Am., N.J. Fedn. Planning Officials, Sussex County Bar Assn., N.J. State Bar Assn. (trustee), Rotary. Roman Catholic. State civil litigation, Personal injury (including property damage), Probate (including wills, trusts). Home: 44 Deire Dr Sparta NJ 07871-1134 Office: Dolan & Dolan PA 53 Spring St & 1 Legal Ln PO Box D Newton NJ 07860-0605

MORGENTHALER-LEVER, ALISA, lawyer; b. St. Louis, June 3, 1960; d. Gerald Thomas and Mary Louise (Neece) M. BA, S.W. Mo. State U., 1982; JD, Cornell U., 1985. Bar: N.Y. 1986, D.C. 1988, Calif. 1990. Law clk. City of Springfield, Mo., 1981; atty. bd. govs. Fed. Res. Sys., Washington, 1984, staff atty., 1985-86; assoc. Kirkpatrick & Lockhart, Washington, 1986-88, Stroock & Stroock & Lavan, Washington, 1988-89; ptnr. Christensen, Miller, Fink, Jacobs, Glaser, Weil & Shapiro, L.A., 1989—. Sec., bd. dirs. L.A. Retarded Citizens Found. Mem. ABA, Calif. Bar Assn. (del. to com. on adminstrn. justice), D.C. Bar Assn., N.Y. Bar Assn., L.A. County Bar Assn. (jud. appts. com.), Beverly Hills Bar Assn., Century City Bar Assn., Women Lawyers Assn. of L.A. (v.p., bd. dirs.), Malibu Riviera III Homeowners Assn. (v.p., bd. dirs.), 3019 Third St. Owners Assn. (v.p., bd. dirs.), Order of Omega, Phi Alpha Delta, Rho Lambda, Phi Kappa Phi, Pi Sigma Alpha, Gamma Phi Beta. Banking, General civil litigation. Office: Christensen Miller Fink Jacobs Glaser Weil & Shapiro 2121 Ave Of Stars Fl 18 Los Angeles CA 90067-5010 E-mail: amorgenthaler@chrismill.com.

MORGENTHAU, ROBERT MORRIS, prosecutor; b. N.Y.C., July 31, 1919; s. Henry Jr. and Elinor (Fatman) M.; m. Martha Pattridge (dec.); children: Joan, Anne, Elinor, Robert P., Barbara; m. Lucinda Franks, Nov. 19, 1977; children: Joshua, Amy. Grad., Deerfield (Mass.) Acad., 1937; BA, Amherst Coll., 1941, LLD (hon.), 1966; LLB, Yale U., 1948; LLD (hon.), N.Y. Law Sch., 1968, Syracuse Law Sch., 1976, Albany Law Sch., 1982, Colgate U., 1988. Bar: N.Y. 1949. Assoc. firm Patterson Belknap & Webb, N.Y.C., 1948-53, ptnr., 1954-61; U.S. atty. So. Dist. N.Y., 1961-62, 62-70; dist. atty. New York County, 1975—. Former pres. N.Y. State Dist. Attys. Assn.; lectr. London Sch. Econs., 1993. Chmn. Police Athletic League; trustee Baron de Hirsch Fund; chmn. Gov.'s Adv. Com. on Sentencing, 1979; counsel N.Y. State Law Enforcement Coun.; chmn. A Living Meml. to the Holocaust-Mus. of Jewish Heritage; Dem. candidate for Gov. of N.Y., 1962; trustee Temple Emanu-El, N.Y.C.; bd. dirs. P.R. Legal Def. and Edn. Fund. Lt. comdr. USNR, 1940—45. Recipient Emory Buckner award Fed. Bar Coun., 1983, Yale Citation of Merit, 1982, Fordham-Stein prize, 1988, Thomas Jefferson award in law U. Va., 1991, Brandeis medal U. Louisville, 1995, Omanut award Yeshiva U., 1995, Trumpeter award Nat. Consumers League, 1995, Frank S. Hogan award N.Y. State Dist. Atty's. Assn., 2000, Lone Sailor award USN Meml. Found., 2000; Matheson-Morgenthau Disting. Professorship in Law named in his honor, Va. Law Sch. Fellow Am. Bar Found.; mem. ABA, N.Y. State Bar Assn. (award for Excellence in Pub. Svc. 2001), Assn. of the Bar of the City of N.Y., N.Y. County Lawyers Assn. (Disting. Pub. Svc. award 1993), Amherst Alumni Assn. (hon. pres. 2001), Phi Beta Kappa. Office: Office Dist Atty 1 Hogan Pl New York NY 10013-4311

MORIARTY, GEORGE MARSHALL, lawyer; b. Youngstown, Ohio, Sept. 16, 1942; s. George Albert Moriarty and Caroline (Jones) Bass; m. Elizabeth Bradley Moore, Sept. 11, 1965 (div. 1986); children: Bradley Marshall, Caroline Walden, Sarah Cameron; m. Phyllis A.N. Thompson, May 2, 1998. BA magna cum laude, Harvard U., 1964, LLB magna cum laude, 1968. Bar: Mass. 1969, U.S. Dist. Ct. Mass. 1973, U.S. Ct. Appeals (1st cir.) 1976, U.S. Ct. Appeals (D.C. cir.) 1984, U.S. Claims Ct. 1983, U.S. Supreme Ct. 1976, U.S. Ct. Appeals (2d cir.) 1997. Law clk. to Hon. Bailey Aldrich U.S. Ct. Appeals (1st cir.), Boston, 1968-69; law clk. to Hon. Warren Burger, Hon. Hugo Black, Hon. Potter Stewart, Hon. Byron White U.S. Supreme Ct., Washington, 1969-70; spl. asst. to Hon. Elliot L. Richardson, Dept. Health, Edn. & Welfare, Washington, 1970-71, exec. asst., 1971-72; assoc. Ropes & Gray, Boston, 1972-77, ptnr., 1977—. Pres. Boston Athenaeum; chmn. Brigham and Women's Hosp. Mem. ABA, Am. Law Inst., Boston Bar Assn., Somerset Club, Tavern Club, Met. Club. Federal civil litigation, General civil litigation, State civil litigation. Office: Ropes & Gray 1 Internat Pl Boston MA 02110

MORIARTY, PAUL J. lawyer; b. Boston, Oct. 4, 1929; s. Archie and Leanora (Ferreira) M.; children: Mark, Cheryl, Karen, Gail; m. Peggy Sahagian, Oct. 4, 1986. BSBA, Suffolk U., 1954, JD, 1958, MS, 1961. Sr. legal asst., asst. bldg. commr. City of Boston Bldg. Dept., 1962-68; asst. corp. counsel City of Boston Law Dept., 1968-73; chief legal counsel Commonwealth of Mass. Bldg Code Commn., Boston, 1973-81; pres. Paul J. Moriarty & Assocs., Inc., Norwell, Mass., 1981—. Sgt. in USAF, 1952-55. Mem. Norfolk Bar Assn., Mass. Bldg. Inspectors and Commrs. Assn., Southeastern Bldg. Inspectors and Commrs. Assn., Home Builders of Mass. (bd. dirs. 1982—, sec./treas. 1994-95), Builders Assn. Greater Boston (v.p. 1988-89, assoc. gen. counsel 1992—). Avocations: golf, travel, carpentry. Construction. Office: 22 Washington St Norwell MA 02061-1732

MORING, JOHN FREDERICK, lawyer; b. Farmville, Va., Oct. 30, 1935; s. Scott O'Ferrall and Margaret Macon (Mitchell) M.; m. Margaret Ann Clarke, Mar. 30, 1959; children: Martha, Elizabeth, Scott, Lee. BS, Va. Poly. Inst., 1957; JD, George Washington U., 1961. Bar: Va. 1961, D.C. 1962, U.S. Supreme Ct. 1964. Assoc. Morgan, Lewis & Bockius, Washington, 1961-68, ptnr., 1969-78, Jones, Day, Reavis & Pogue, Washington, 1978-79; founding ptnr. Crowell & Moring, Washington, Irvine, N.Y.C., London, Brussels, 1979-2000. Sec. Associated Gas Distbrs., Inc., 1977-2000. Local gas utility columnist: Nat. Gas Jour., 1989—2000; mem. editl. bd. Natural Gas Contracts, 1994—2001. Mem. nat. panel neutrals Am. Arbitration Assn., 2003—; chmn. bd. dirs. Washington Legal Counsel for Elderly, 2000—01; Rep. candidate 23d Dist./Va. Gen. Assembly, Alexandria, 1973; mem. bd. govs. St. Stephen's and St. Agnes Sch., Alexandria, 1989—95; pres. St. Stephen's Found., Inc., 1990—93; sr. warden Immanuel Ch. on the Hill, Alexandria, 1988, 1989; trustee Ch. Schs. of Diocese of Va., 1996—; mem. bd. govs. St. Margaret's Sch., Tappahannock, Va., 2002—. 2d lt. U.S. Army, 1958. Mem.: ABA (natural resources law sect. 1982—86, coun.), Fed. Energy Bar Assn. (sec. 1963—66, pres. 1982—83), Indian Creek Yacht and Country Club (Kilmarnock, Va.). Episcopalian. Avocations: golf, fishing, canoeing. FERC practice, Utilities, public, Federal civil litigation. Home: PO Box 224 White Stone VA 22578 Office: Crowell & Moring 1001 Pennsylvania Ave NW Fl 10 Washington DC 20004-2595 also: 2010 Main St Irvine CA 92614-7203 also: 180 Fleet St London ECAA2 HD England also: 590 Madison Ave Ste 2100 New York NY 10022 also: 27 Ave Des Arts B-1040 Brussels Belgium E-mail: fmoring@cromor.com.

MORONEY, FRANCIS XAVIER, lawyer; b. N.Y.C., July 27, 1949; s. Francis John and Eleanor Marie (Higgins) M.; children: Erin Margaret, Becky Ann. BA in Polit. Sci., St. John's U., 1971, JD, 1976. Bar: N.Y. 1977, U.S. Ct. Appeals (2d cir.) 1977, U.S. Dist. Ct. (ea. and so. dists.) N.Y. 1978, U.S. Tax Ct. 1983. Assoc. N. Michael LoRusso, Queens Village, N.Y., 1977-78, Dalton, Henoch & Kadin, Hempstead, N.Y., 1978-79, Jaspan, Kaplan, Levin & Daniels, Garden City, N.Y., 1979-80; ptnr. Carway, Flipse & Moroney, Williston Park, N.Y., 1981-84; pvt. practice, 1984-90; ptnr. McCarthy & Moroney, Carle Place, NY, 1990—94; pvt. practice, 1994—; chief counsel Senator Michael J. Tully, Jr., 1983—91; counsel Senate Adminstrv. Regulations Rev. Commn., 1992—93; chief counsel N.Y. State Senate Energy and Telecomms. Com., 1997—. Counsel Vet. com. N.Y. State Senate, Albany, 1985-88; councilman North Hempstead, 1991; exec. dir. Nassau County Commn. on Govt. Revision, 1993-96; co-exec. dir. Nassau County Temporary Districting Adv. Commn., 2002-03. Pres. Carle Pl. Civic Assn., 1980-91; mem. Nassau County Rep. Com., 1982—; former mem. Environ. Commn. Village of Westbury, Cablevision Commn. Town of North Hempstead; former bd. dirs. Eastern Queens YMCA. Recipient community svc. award Nassau County Aux. Police, 1984, Carle Place Citizen of Yr. Carle Place Tchr. Assn., 1985, Carle Place Citizen of Yr. Carle Place Am. Legion, 1983, Health Care Execs. Community Svc., 1989. Mem. ABA, Nassau County Bar Assn. (vice-chair health law com. gen. practice sect.). Republican. Roman Catholic. Family and matrimonial, Probate (including wills, trusts), Property, real (including real estate development, water). Office: 497 Westbury Ave Carle Place NY 11514-1401

MORONEY, LINDA L.S. (MUFFIE), lawyer, educator; b. Washington, May 27, 1943; d. Robert Emmet and Jessie (Robinson) M.; m. Clarence Renshaw II, Mar. 28, 1967 (div. 1977); children: Robert Milnor, Justin W.R. BA, Randolph-Macon Woman's Coll., 1965; JD cum laude, U. Houston, 1982. Bar: Tex. 1982, U.S. Ct. Appeals (5th cir.) 1982, U.S. Dist. Ct. (so. dist.) Tex. 1982, U.S. Supreme Ct. 1988. Law clk. to assoc. justice 14th Ct. Appeals, Houston, 1982-83; assoc. Pannill and Reynolds, Houston, 1983-85, Gilpin, Pohl & Bennett, Houston, 1985-89, Vinson & Elkins, Houston, 1989-92. Adj. prof. law U. Houston, 1986-91, dir. legal rsch. and writing, 1992-96, civil trial and appellate litigation and mediation, 1996—. Mem. ABA, State Bar Tex., Houston Bar Assn., Assn. of Women Attys., Tex. Women Lawyers, Order of the Barons, Phi Delta Phi. Episcopalian. Alternative dispute resolution, General civil litigation, Education and schools. Home and Office: 4010 Whitman St Houston TX 77027-6334

MORONEY, MICHAEL JOHN, lawyer; b. Jamaica, N.Y., Nov. 8, 1940; s. Everard Vincent and Margaret Olga (Olson) M.; children: Sean, Megan, Matthew. BS in Polit. Sci., Villanova U., 1962; JD, Fordham U., 1965; Police Sci. (hon.), U. Guam, 1976. Bar: Hawaii 1974, U.S. Dist. Ct. Hawaii 1974, U.S. Ct. Appeals (9th cir.) 1974, Guam 1976, U.S. Dist. Ct. (Guam dist.) 1976, U.S. Ct. Claims 1976, U.S. Tax Ct. 1976, U.S. Ct. Mil. Appeals 1977, U.S. Supreme Ct. 1977, High Ct. Trust Ters. 1977, U.S. Dist. Ct. (No. Mariana Islands) 1983. Spl. agt. FBI, Memphis and Nashville, 1965-67, Cleve. and Elyria, Ohio, 1967-71; spl. agt., prin. legal advisor FBI, U.S. Dept. Justice, Honolulu, 1971-97; v.p. Merrill Corp., Honolulu, 1997-2000; mgr. Investigative Svcs. Worldwide, 2000—; mng. dir. Paradise Meml. Park, LLC, Honolulu, 2000—; pres., mgr. ISW, LLC, 2000—. Bar examiner and applications rev. com. Supreme Ct. Hawaii, 1980—; pres. Hawaii State Law Enforcement Assn., 1985-86; mem. and del. to congress Gov.'s Task Force on Hawaii's Internat. Role, 1988; mem. Charter Commn., City and County of Honolulu, 1998-2000; mem. Consular Corps of Hawaii, 1997-2000; regent Harris Manchester Coll., Oxford U., 2000—. Gov.'s task force, del. gov.'s congress on Hawaii's Internat. Role, 1988—; apptd. hon. consul gen. Republic of Palau; pres. Tommy E. Remongesau, Jr., 2002—, pres. Kunio Nakamura, 1999, 2002—. Recipient Govs. Award for outstanding contbns. to law enforcement Govt. of Guam, 1974, 76, cert. of appreciation Supreme Ct. Hawaii, 1981, Honolulu Police Commn., 1984, 86; named Fed. Law Enforcement Officer of Yr., State of Hawaii, 1992, Outstanding Career award in law enforcement and commitment to Hawaii State Law Enforcement Ofcls. Assn., 1998. Mem. ABA, Hawaii Bar Assn., Guam Bar Assn., Inst. Jud. Adminstrn., Hawaii State Law Enforcement Ofcls. Assn., Hilo Yacht Club, Oahu Country Club, Plaza Club, Rotary Club Honolulu. Address: 7858 Makaaoa Pl Honolulu HI 96825-2848 Office: Paradise Meml Park LLC 1154 Fort Street Mall Ste 300 Honolulu HI 96813-2712 Fax: 808-599-5004. E-mail: mmoro007@aol.com.

MORPHONIOS, DEAN B. lawyer; b. Miami, Fla., Apr. 27, 1956; s. Alexander George and Ellen (James) M.; m. Susan Diana, 2002; children: Kimberly Anne Long, Matthew James, Joy Shalom. BA, Fla. Internat. U., Miami, 1979; JD, Fla. State U., 1983. Bar: Fla. 1983, U.S. Dist. Ct. (so. dist.) Fla. 1985, U.S. Dist. Ct. (mid. and no. dists.) 1988, U.S. Ct. Appeals, U.S. Supreme Ct. 1989. Assoc. gen. counsel Fla. Police Benevolent Assn., Tallahassee, 1983-84; pvt. practice Miami, 1984-86; asst. state atty. State Attys. Office/2d Jud. Cir., Tallahassee, 1986-88; assoc. Kitchen Judkins Simpson & High, Tallahassee, 1988-97; pvt. practice Tallahassee, 1997—. Mem. Bench Bar Com., Tallahassee, 1996—, Conflict Rev. Com., Tallahassee, 1996—. Mem. Fla. Assn. Criminal Defendant Attys. (pres. Tallahassee chpt. 1994-95). Republican. Criminal, Family and matrimonial. Office: 1921 Capital Cir NE Ste E Tallahassee FL 32308

MORPHY, JAMES CALVIN, lawyer; b. Pitts., Jan. 16, 1954; s. Robert Samson and Autumn (Phillips) M.; m. Priscilla Winslow Plimpton, July 11, 1981; children: Calvin, Katherine, Victoria. BA, Harvard U., 1976, JD, 1979. Bar: N.Y. 1980. Assoc. Sullivan & Cromwell, N.Y.C., 1979-86, ptnr., 1986—, mng. ptnr. com., 1992—, mng. ptnr. M&A group, 1995—. Author (contbg.): (treatise) New York and Delaware Business Entities: Choice Formation, Operation, Financing, and Acquisition, 1997, Transactional Lawyer's Deskbook, 2001. Trustee Greenwich Acad. Mem. ABA (com. on fed. securities law 1992—), Assn. Bar of City of N.Y., Wianno Club (bd. govs.), Greenwich Country Club, Harvard Club N.Y., Wianno Yacht Club, Phi Beta Kappa. Mergers and acquisitions, Securities. Office: Sullivan & Cromwell 125 Broad St Fl 28 New York NY 10004-2489

MORRIONE, MELCHIOR S. management consultant, accountant; b. Bklyn., 1937; m. Joan Finnerty; children: Karyn Morrione Frick, Nicole. BBA magna cum laude, St. John's U., 1959. CPA, N.J., N.Y. Tax ptnr. Arthur Andersen, N.Y.C., 1959-91; mng. dir. MSM Consulting LLC, Woodcliff Lake, N.J., 1992—. Lectr. in field. Contbr. articles to profl. jours. With U.S. Army, 1960-61. Mem. CPAs, N.Y. State Soc. CPAs, N.J. Soc. CPAs, Internat. Fiscal Assn., Internat. Tax Assn., Ridgewood Country Club. Republican. Roman Catholic. Avocations: golf, tennis. Office: MSM Consulting LLC 11 Ginny Dr Woodcliff Lake NJ 07677-8115 E-mail: morrione@att.net.

MORRIS, CHRISTOPHER DAVID, lawyer; b. Rochester, Ind., Mar. 25, 1957; s. William Laurence Morris and Maxine (Bailey) Bearss; m. Jeannine Kreiter, June 20, 1986. BA, Kalamazoo (Mich.) Coll., 1979; JD, Cooley Law Sch., Lansing, Mich., 1983. Bar: Mich. 1984, U.S. Dist. Ct. (we. dist.) Mich. 1984, U.S. Ct. Appeals (6th cir.) 1988. Assoc. Ryan, Jamieson and Hubbell, Kalamazoo, 1984-86; ptnr. Ryan, Jamieson, Hubbell and Morris, Kalamazoo, 1986-89; assoc. Varnum, Riddering, Schmidt and Howlett, Kalamazoo, 1989-90; ptnr. Ryan, Jamieson and Morris, Kalamazoo, 1990—. Adj. mem. Mich. Workers' Compensation Appeal Bd., 1991-92; spl. asst. atty. gen., 2003. Mem. ABA, Mich. Bar Assn., Kalamazoo County Bar Assn. Labor (including EEOC, Fair Labor Standards Act, labor-management relations, NLRB, OSHA), Workers' compensation. Home: 9830 E Shore Dr Kalamazoo MI 49002-7477 Office: 121 W Cedar St Kalamazoo MI 49007-6221

MORRIS, DAVID MICHAEL, insurance executive, lawyer; b. San Juan, P.R., Dec. 8, 1948; s. Edwin Thaddeus and Winifred Isabel (Walsh) M.; m. Carol Anderson Worden, Aug. 7, 1971; children: Laura H., John C. BA, U. Md., 1971; JD, U. Balt., 1975. Bar: Md. 1976, U.S. Dist. Ct. Md. 1976; CLU. Owner Franklin/Morris Assocs., LLC, Balt., 1976—. Columnist legal newspaper Daily Record, 1985-87. Pres., trustee 2d Presbyn. Ch., Balt., 1980-86, elder, 1988-98; vice chmn. Balt. div. United Way, 1981-84; fund raiser Johns Hopkins Children's Ctr., Balt., 1984-88; trustee Roland Park Country Sch., 1988-89, 90-98; mem. exec. com. Gilman Sch. Parents Assn., 1989-91; grad. Leadership Md., 1998. Mem. ABA, Md. Bar Assn., Balt. Bar Assn., Assn. Advanced Life Underwriting, Balt. Life Underwriters Assn. (chmn. ethics 1977-80, bd. dirs. 1982-85, bd. dirs. Charitable Found., 1998—), Balt. Soc. CLUs and Chartered Fin. Cons. (chmn. ethical guidance com., bd. dirs.), Million Dollar Round Table (life), Md. Club, Balt. Country Club, Leadership Maryland. Avocations: tennis, golf, wine. Home: 205 Paddington Rd Baltimore MD 21212-3438 Office: Franklin/Morris Assocs LLC One N Charles St Ste 2400 Baltimore MD 21201

MORRIS, EDWARD WILLIAM, JR., lawyer; b. Medford, Oreg., Apr. 12, 1943; s. Edward William and Julia Loretta (Sullivan) M.; m. Margaret Ellen McKenna, 1976; children: John McKenna, Elizabeth Anne. BS, Fordham Coll., 1965, JD, 1971. Bar: N.Y. 1973. Dir. Drug Products Co., Inc., Union City, N.J., 1968-71; asst. arbitration dir. N.Y. Stock Exch.,

N.Y.C., 1971-73, arbitration dir., 1973-74, asst. sec., arbitration dir., 1974-89, v.p. arbitration, 1989-91, chief hearing officer, 1991—. Dir. Stock Clearing Corp., N.Y.C.; mem. Securities Industry Conf. on Arbitration, N.Y.C., 1977— ; lectr. in field. Served to sgt. U.S. Army, 1965-68, Vietnam. Mem. ABA, Am. Arbitration Assn. (comml. law com. 1983—), Assn. Bar City N.Y. (retail fin. svcs. com. 1989—), N.Y. County Lawyers Assn. (sec. com. on arbitration 1983—), High Mountain Golf Club, N.Y. Roadrunners Club. Securities. Home: 67 Arlton Ave Allendale NJ 07401-1331 Office: NY Stock Exch Inc 20 Broad St New York NY 10005-1974 E-mail: emorris@nyse.com.

MORRIS, EUGENE JEROME, retired lawyer; b. N.Y.C., Oct. 14, 1910; s. Max and Regina (Cohn) M.; m. Terry Lesser, Mar. 28, 1934 (dec. Sept. 1993); 1 child, Richard S.; m. Blanche Bier Funke, June 22, 1994. BSS., CCNY, 1931; LL.B., St. John's U., 1934. Bar: N.Y. 1935. Practiced, N.Y.C., 1935-99; sr. and founding partner firm Demov, Morris & Hammerling, 1946-87; v.p., sr. counsel Ea. region Am. Title Ins. Co., N.Y.C., 1990-93; of counsel Spector & Feldman, 1991-99; ret., 1999. Adj. prof. land use regulation NYU Grad. Sch. Pub. Adminstrn., 1978-81; adj. prof. legal issues in real estate, Real Estate Inst. NYU, 1988—; spl. master Supreme Ct. State of N.Y., 1979-99; arbitrator Civil Ct. N.Y., 1994-99. Editor weekly column N.Y. Law Jour., 1965-87, It's the Law, Real Estate Forum, 1982-87; editor-in-chief N.Y. Practice Guide: Real Estate, 4 vols., 1986, Real Estate Development, 4 vols., 1987; contbr. articles to profl. jours. Mem. N.Y. State Tax Revision Commn., 1977-80, N.Y.C. Rent Guidelines Bd., 1983-85. Served with AUS, 1943-45. Recipient Justice award N.Y. sect. Am. Jewish Congress, 1996. Mem. ABA (chmn. spl. com. housing and urban devel. 1970-73, coun. sect. real property, probate and trust law 1971-74, assoc. editor Real Property, Probate and Trust Jour. 1979-86, editor Real Property, Probate and Property mag., articles editor 1986-94), Am. Judges Assn., Assn. Bar City N.Y. (chmn. com. housing and urban devel. 1971-74, com. on lectures and continuing edn. 1980-83, coun. on jud. adminstrn. 1989-92), N.Y. State Bar Assn. (exec. com. 1980-97, chmn. com. meetings and lectrs. 1982-92, CLE com. 1984-90, ho. of dels. 1986-95, co-editor Real Property Jour. 1995-97, Professionalsim award 2002), Citizens Union, Lambda Alpha (bd. dirs. 1990-98, pres. N.Y. chpt. 1990-93, sec. 1993-95, treas. 1996-97). Home: 200 Central Park S New York NY 10019-1415 Fax: 212-983-0874. E-mail: specfeld@aol.com.

MORRIS, JAMES MALACHY, lawyer; b. Champaign, Ill., June 5, 1952; s. Walter Michael and Ellen Frances (Solon) M.; m. Mary Delilah Baker, Oct. 17, 1987; children: James Malachy Jr., Elliot Rice Baker, Walter Michael, Nicholas Aidan. Student, Oxford U. (Eng.), 1972; BA, Brown U., 1974; JD, U. Pa., 1977. Bar: N.Y. 1978, U.S. Dist. Ct. (so. and ea. dists.) N.Y. 1978, Ill. 1980, U.S. Tax Ct. 1982, U.S. Supreme Ct. 1983; admitted to Barristers Chambers, Manchester, Eng., 1987. Assoc. Reid & Priest, N.Y.C., 1977-80; sr. law clk. Supreme Ct. Ill., Springfield, 1980-81; assoc. Carter, Ledyard & Milburn, N.Y.C., 1981-83; sole practice N.Y.C., 1983-87; counsel FCA, Washington, 1987—; acting sec., gen. counsel FCS Ins. Corp., McLean, Va., 1990-98. Cons. Internat. Awards Found., Zurich, 1981-2002, Pritzker Architecture Prize Found., N.Y.C., 1981—, Herbert Oppenheimer, Nathan & VanDyck, London, 1985—. Contbr. articles to profl. jours. Mem. ABA, Ill. Bar Assn., N.Y. State Bar Assn., N.Y. County Lawyers Assn., Assn. Bar City N.Y., Brit. Inst. Internat. and Comparative Law, Am. Inst. Parliamentarians, Lansdowne Club (London), Casanova (Va.) Hunt Club. Corporate, general, General practice, Probate (including wills, trusts). Office: PO Box 1407 Mc Lean VA 22101-1407

MORRIS, LEAH MCGARRY, lawyer; b. Boston, Mar. 27, 1951; d. A. Louis and Shirley L. (Pustilnick) McGarry; m. Justin T. Loughry, May 19, 1990; children: Benjamin, Lindsay, Nora. AB, Bryn Mawr Coll., 1972; JD, Temple U., 1975. Bar: Pa. 1975, N.J. 1976. Staff atty. Camden (N.J.) County Pub. Defender's Office, 1976-96, first asst. dep., 1996—2000; asst. pub. defender N.J. Office Pub. Defender, Trenton, NJ, 2001—, N.J. Supreme Ct. com. on minority concerns, 2001—. Bd. trustees Camden Regional Legal Svcs., 1996-2000; mem. com. on women, N.J. Supreme Ct., 2002—. Mem. Camden County Youth Svcs. Commn., 1984-2000, Camden County Vicinage Com. Minority Concerns, 1997-2000, Camden County Human Rels. Commn., 1997-2000; vice chair Haddonfield (N.J.) Human Rels. Commn., 1994—; chair Haddonfield Neighborhood Disputes Mediation Commn., 1997—; mem. Camden County Citizens Adv. Bd. Named one of the Women Who Have Made a Difference Camden County Bd. Freeholders and Camden County Commn. Women, 1996; fellow Leadership N.J. (Partnership for N.J.), 1998; recipient N.J. 15th Anniv. Leadership Justice award, 2001. Mem. Assn. Criminal Def. Lawyers N.J. (bd. trustees 1994—), N.J. Network Drug Ct. Profls., Camden County Bar Assn. (co-chair criminal practice com. 1997-2000, bd. trustees 1998-2000). Democrat. Avocations: mediation, advocacy for youth, writing. Home: 106 Prospect Rd Haddonfield NJ 08033-1314 Office: Box 850 Hughes Justice Complex Trenton NJ 08625

MORRIS, NANCY B. lawyer; b. Bklyn. m. Craig Morris; children: David, Michael. JD cum laude, Pace U., White Plains, N.Y., 1991. Bar: N.Y., N.J., U.S. Dist. Ct. (so. dist.) N.Y., U.S. Dist. Ct. N.J. Assoc. Law Office of Anne Glickman, New City, N.Y., 1992-96; pvt. practice New City, 1996—. Mem. Rockland County Bar Assn., Rockland County Women's Bar Assn. (treas. 1998—). Family and matrimonial, Probate (including wills, trusts). Office: 2 New Hempstead Rd New City NY 10956-3635 E-mail: nmorris@attorney.com.

MORRIS, NORVAL, criminologist, educator; b. Auckland, New Zealand, Oct. 1, 1923; s. Louis and Vera (Burke) M.; m. Elaine Richardson, Mar. 18, 1947; children: Gareth, Malcolm, Christoper. LLB, U. Melbourne, Australia, 1946, LLM, 1947; PhD in Criminology (Hutchinson Silver medal 1950), London Sch. Econs., 1949. Bar: called to Australian bar 1953. Asst. lectr. London Sch. Econs., 1949-50; sr. lectr. law U. Melbourne, 1950-58, prof. criminology, 1955-58; Ezra Ripley Thayer teaching fellow Harvard Law Sch., 1955-56, vis. prof., 1961-62; Boynthon prof., dean faculty law U. Adelaide, Australia, 1958-62; dir. UN Inst. Prevention Crime and Treatment of Offenders, Tokyo, Japan, 1962-64; Julius Kreeger prof. law and criminology U. Chgo., 1964—, dean Law Sch., 1975-79. Chmn. Commn. Inquiry Capital Punishment in Ceylon, 1958-59; mem. Social Sci. Rsch. Coun. Australia, 1958-59; Australian del. confs. div. human rights and sect. social def. UN, 1955-66; mem. standing adv. com. experts prevention crime and treatment offenders. Author: The Habitual Criminal, 1951, Report of the Commission of Inquiry on Capital Punishment, 1959, (with W. Morison and R. Sharwood) Cases in Torts, 1962, (with Colon Howard) Studies in Criminal Law, 1964, (with G. Hawkins) The Honest Politicians Guide to Crime Control, 1970, The Future of Imprisonment, 1974, Letter to the President on Crime Control, 1977, Madness and the Criminal Law, 1983, Between Prison and Probation, 1990, The Brothel Boy and Other Parables of the Law, 1992, The Oxford History of the Prison, 1995, Maconochie's Gentlemen, 2001. Served with Australian Army, World War II, PTO. Decorated Japanese Order Sacred Treasure 3d Class. Fellow Am. Acad. Arts and Scis. Home: 1207 E 50th St Chicago IL 60615-2908 Office: U Chgo Law Sch 1111 E 60th St Chicago IL 60637-2776 E-mail: norval_morris@law.uchicago.edu.

MORRIS, ROY LESLIE, lawyer, electrical engineer, venture capitalist; b. N.Y.C. BE, SUNY, Stony Brook, 1975; EE, SM, MIT, 1978; JD, George Washington U., 1984; MBA, Wharton U., 1995. Bar: D.C. 1984, U.S. Patent Office. Mem. tech. staff Bell Telephone Labs., Holmdel, N.J., 1978-80; sr. staff engr. FCC, Washington, 1981-83; assoc. regulatory counsel MCI Communications, Washington, 1983-87; dep. gen. counsel Allnet Comms., Washington, 1988-95; dir. pub. policy and regulatory affairs Allnet/Frontier Comms., Washington, 1989-96; mng. ptnr. RoyLyn L.L.C., Arlington, Va., 1996—; v.p. govt. affairs and revenue devel. US ONE Comms., McLean, Va., 1996-97; mng. ptnr. Strategic Tech. Investors LLC, Arlington, Va., 1998—; pres. MIT Enterprise Forum, Washington/Balt., 1998—. Ednl. counselor MIT; adj. prof. Capitol Coll., Laurel, Md., 1998—; advisor VC, 2002. Contbr. Author: Internet Encyclopedia, 2003; contbr. numerous articles to profl. publs. Mem. ABA, IEEE, MIT Enterprise Forum, Sigma Xi, Tau Beta Pi. Administrative and regulatory, Communications, Finance. Address: Strategic Tech Investors LLC 4001 9th St N Ste 306 Arlington VA 22203-1957

MORRIS, SANDRA JOAN, lawyer; b. Chgo., Oct. 13, 1944; d. Bernard and Helene (Davies) Aronson; m. Richard William Morris, May 30, 1965 (div. Jan. 1974); children: Tracy Michelle, Bretton Todd; m. William Mark Bandt, July 12, 1981; 1 child, Victoria Elizabeth. BA, U. Ariz., 1965; JD, Calif. Western U., 1969. Bar: Calif. 1970, U.S. Dist. Ct. (so. dist.) Calif. 1970; diplomate Am. Coll. Family Trial Lawyers. Ptnr. Morris & Morris, APC, San Diego, 1970-74; sole practice San Diego, 1974—. Mem. Adv. Commn. on Family Law, Calif. Senate, 1978-79. Contbr. articles to profl. jours. Pres. San Diego Community Child Abuse Coordinating Coun., 1977; mem. human rsch. rev. bd. Children's Hosp., San Diego, 1977-92. Fellow: Internat. Acad. Matrimonial Lawyers, Am. Acad. Matrimonial Lawyers (chpt. pres. 1987—88, nat. bd. govs. 1987—89, parliamentarian 1989—91, nat. bd. govs. 1993—94, treas. 1994—97, v.p. 1997—2000, 1st v.p. 2000—01, pres. 2002—); mem.: San Diego Cert. Family Law Specialists (chair 1995—96), State Bar Calif. (cert. family law specialist 1980—), ABA (family law sect. exec. com. marital property 1982—83, 1987—94, faculty mem. Trial Advocacy Inst. 2001—), Lawyers Club San Diego (bd. dirs. 1973). Republican. Jewish. Avocations: art, travel, skiing. Family and matrimonial. Office: 3200 4th Ave Ste 101 San Diego CA 92103-5716

MORRISON, ANDREW, lawyer; b. Sydney, NSW, Australia, Oct. 18, 1967; s. Ian Francis and Jan Morrison; m. Fiona Kate Morrison, Apr. 17, 1993; children: Lachlan, Isabel. BA, U. Sydney, 1989, LLB, 1991, LLM, 1999; Diploma in Legal Studies, U. Tech., Sydney, 1991. Admitted as solicitor: High Ct. Australia, Victoria, N.S.W. and Western Australia. Solicitor Clayton Utz, Sydney, 1992—95, sr. assoc., 1996—2001, ptnr. Melbourne, Australia, 2002—. Mem.: Nat. Product Liability Assn. (pres. 2002—03), Australian Ins. Law Assn., Internat. Bar Assn. Product liability, Toxic tort, Product liability. Office: Clayton Utz Level 18 333 Collins St Melbourne VIC 3000 Australia E-mail: amorrison@claytonutz.com.

MORRISON, BRUCE ANDREW, government executive, public affairs consultant; b. N.Y.C., Oct. 8, 1944; s. George and Dorothea A. (Meyer) M.; m. Nancy A. Wanat, Sept. 22, 1991; 1 child, Drew. S.B., MIT, 1965; MS, U. Ill., 1970; JD, Yale U., 1973; Litt.D. (hon.), Quinnipac Coll. Staff atty. New Haven Legal Assistance Assn., 1973-74, mng. atty., 1974-76, exec. dir., 1976-82; mem. 98th-101st Congresses from 3d Conn. dist., 1983-91; chmn. L.I. Sound Caucus, chmn. Third World Debt Caucus. Chmn. judiciary subcom. on immigration, refugees, and internat. law U.S. Ho. of Reps.; chmn. Fed. Housing Fin. Bd., 1995-2000 ; co-chmn. ad hoc com. on Irish affairs; mem. U.S. commn. on immigration reform, 1991-97; chair Irish Ams. for Clinton-Gore, 1992, 96; chair Ams. for a New Irish Agenda, 1993-95; vice chmn. GPC Internat., 2000-2001; chmn. Morrison Pub. Affairs Group, 2001-. Mem. Nat. Dem. Ethnic Coordinating Com.; bd. dirs. Rock Mountain Mut. Housing Assn., Alliance for Responsible Cuba Policy. Mem. ABA, Conn. Bar Assn., New Haven County Bar Assn., Am. Immigration Lawyers Assn. Democrat. Lutheran. Office: 6004 Onondaga Rd Bethesda MD 20816 E-mail: b.a.m@att.net.

MORRISON, DAVID EUGENE, lawyer; b. York, Nebr., May 6, 1952; s. Louis Eugene and Eleanor (Curry) M. BA, U. Nebr., 1974; JD, Duke U., 1977. Bar: Tex. 1977. Sr. ptnr. Thompson & Knight LLP, Dallas, 1977-2000; ptnr. Fulbright & Jaworski LLP, Dallas, 2000—. Mem. bd. govs. Dallas Symphony Assn., Inc., 1990-2001, mem. exec. bd., 1993-2001, sec., 1993-98; trustee Tex. Internat. Festivals, Inc., Dallas, 1997-98, mem. exec. com., 1997-98, sec., 1997-98; mem. bd. mgmt. Town North Family YMCA, Dallas, 1997-2000; mem. garden and grounds com. Dallas Arboretum & Botanical Soc., 2002—. Methodist. Avocations: spectator sports, gardening, woodworking. Corporate, general, Mergers and acquisitions, Securities. Home: 4738 San Gabriel Dr Dallas TX 75229-4233 Office: Fulbright & Jaworski LLP 2200 Ross Ave Ste 2800 Dallas TX 75201 E-mail: dmorrison@fulbright.com.

MORRISON, MICHAEL DEAN, lawyer, law educator; BA with high honors, Okla. U., 1971, JD, 1974. Bar: Okla. 1975, Kans. 1975, Tex. 1981, U.S. Ct. Appeals (5th cir.) 1980, U.S. Dist. Ct. (ea., no. and so. dists.) Tex. 1983, U.S. Dist. Ct. (we. dist.) Tex. 1980, U.S. Dist. Ct. (we. dist.) Okla. 1975, U.S. Supreme Ct. 1979. Pvt. practice, Wichita, Kans., 1974-75; asst. dir. Law Ctr. Okla. U., 1975-77, asst. prof., 1977-80, assoc. prof., 1980-82, prof. law, 1982-90, William J. Boswell chair of law, 1990—. Mayor City of Waco, 1996—2000; ordained elder 1st Presbyn. Ch. Waco, stated clk. of session, 1996—98. Mem. Order of Coif, Phi Beta Kappa. Office: PO Box 97288 Waco TX 76798-7288

MORRISON, PAUL A. lawyer; b. Mo., June 11, 1958; s. John Coulter and Rita (Dickey) Morrison; m. Delmara Faye Bayliss, May 11, 1988 (div. 1995); children: Hunter, Gracie; m. Mary Beth Bradley, Oct. 5, 1996. BA with honors, U. So. Miss., 1984; JD, Washington and Lee U., 1987. Bar: Va. 1987, U.S. Dist. Ct. (ea. dist.) Va. 1989, U.S. Ct. Appeals (4th cir.) 1990, U.S. Supreme Ct. 1998. Mng. ptnr. Morrison & Bayliss, Leesburg, Va., 1987—89, 1992—95, Morrison, Bayliss & Briel, Leesburg, 1989—92, Howard, Morrison & Howard, Warrenton, Va., 1998—; atty. Clark, Scott & Sullivan, Mobile, Ala., 1995—96; pvt. practice Warrenton, 1996—98. Neutral case evaluator Fauquier County Bar, 2000—02. Mem.: ABA, ATLA, Coudoun County Bar Assn. (bd. dirs. 1993), Va. Trial Lawyers Assn. Personal injury (including property damage), Family and matrimonial, Criminal. Home: 5568 Valley Green Dr Broad Run VA 20137 Office: Howard Morrison and Howard 1 Wall St Warrenton VA 20186 Office Fax: 540-349-4422. Business E-Mail: paul.morrison@starband.net.

MORRISSEY, GEORGE MICHAEL, judge; b. Chgo., Aug. 12, 1941; s. Joseph Edward and Mary Bernice (Shields) M.; m. Mary Kay McCarthy, Jan. 3, 1976; children: Meghan Catherine, Colleen Mary. BS, Ill. Inst. Tech., 1963; JD, De Paul U., 1971. Bar: Ill. 1972, U.S. Dist. Ct. (no. dist.) Ill. 1978, U.S. Supreme Ct. 1981. Auditor Touche Ross & Co., Chgo., 1963-68; pvt. practice Evergreen Park and Worth, Ill., 1972-77; chief 5th Mcpl. Dist. Cook County Pub. Defender, Chgo., 1978-90; assoc. judge Cook County Cir. Ct., Chgo., 1991—. Mem. spl. commn. on adminstrn. of justice in Cook County, Chgo., 1984-91. Mem. commn. on future of Ill. Inst. Tech., Chgo., 1976-77; bd. trustees Oak Lawn (Ill.) Library, 1979-85; bd. dirs. Crisis Ctr. for South Suburbia, Worth, 1979—. Served with U.S. Army, 1963-69. Mem. Chgo. Bar Assn. (jud. retention com., bar pres. com.), S.W. Bar Assn. (past pres.), Coalition of Suburban Bar Assn. (past pres.), Alpha Sigma Phi. Clubs: Columbia Yacht (commodore 1976-78) (Chgo.), Chgo. Yachting (commodore 1982). Lodges: Elks. Roman Catholic. Office: Cir Ct of Cook County 2600 Richard J Daley Ctr Chicago IL 60602

MORRISSEY, JOHN CARROLL, SR., lawyer; b. N.Y.C., Sept. 2, 1914; s. Edward Joseph and Estelle (Caine) M.; m. Eileen Colligan, Oct. 14, 1950; children: Jonathan Edward, Ellen (Mrs. James A. Jenkins), Katherine, John, Patricia, Richard, Brian, Peter. BA magna cum laude, Yale U., 1937, LLB, 1940; JSD, N.Y. U., 1951; grad., Command and Gen. Staff Sch., 1944. Bar: N.Y. State 1940, D.C. 1953, Calif. 1954, U.S. Supreme Ct. 1944. Asso. firm Dorsey and Adams, 1940-41, Dorsey, Adams and Walker, 1946-50; counsel Office of Sec. of Def., Dept. Def., Washington, 1950-52; acting gen. counsel def. Electric Power Adminstrn., 1952-53; atty. Pacific Gas and Electric Co., San Francisco, 1953-70, assoc. gen. counsel, 1970-74, v.p., gen. counsel, 1975-80; individual practice law San Francisco, 1980-2000. Dir. Gas Lines, Inc. Bd. dirs. Legal Aid Soc., San Francisco; chmn. Golden Gate dist. Boy Scouts Am., 1973-75; commr. Human Rights Commn. of San Francisco, 1976-89, chmn., 1980-82; chmn. Cath. Social Svc. of San Francisco, 1966-68; adv. com. Archdiocesean Legal Affairs, 1981—; regent Archdiocesan Sch. of Theology, St. Patrick's Sem., 1994-99; dir. Presidio Preservation Assn., 1995-99. Served to col. F.A. U.S. Army, 1941-46. Decorated Bronze star, Army Commendation medal. Mem. NAS, AAAS, ABA, Calif. State Bar Assn., Fed. Power Bar Assn., N.Y. Acad. Scis., Calif. Conf. Pub. Utility Counsel, Pacific Coast Electric Assn., Pacific Coast Gas Assn., Econ. Round Table of San Francisco, World Affairs Council, San Francisco C. of C., Calif. State C. of C., Harold Brunn Soc. Med. Rsch., Electric Club, Serra Club, Commonwealth Club, Yale Club of San Francisco (pres. 1989-90), Pacific-Union Club, Sometimes Tuesday Club, Sovereign Mil. Order Malta, Phi Beta Kappa. Roman Catholic. Corporate, general, Nuclear power, Utilities, public. Home: 2030 Jackson St San Francisco CA 94109-2840 Office: 1661 Pine St # 1135 San Francisco CA 94105 E-mail: dadjcm@aol.com.

MORROW, DORSEY W., JR., lawyer; BS in Computer Sci., Troy State U., 1989, MBA, 2001; JD, Jones Sch. Law, 1993. Bar: Ala. 1994, U.S. Dist. Ct. (mid. dist.) Ala. 1994, Mass. 2002, U.S. Supreme Ct. 1997; cert. info. sys. security profl., 1999. Systems mgr. Ala. Christian Coll., Montgomery, 1984-86; software developer Tangram Systems Corp., Cary, N.C., 1988; systems mgr. Palomar Ins. Corp., Montgomery, 1990-91; ind. cons. pvt. practice, Montgomery, 1991-92; law clk. Addison, Vickers & Howell, Montgomery, 1992-93; atty. pvt. practice, Montgomery, 1994—2000; gen. counsel (ISC)2, Inc., Framingham, Mass., 2000—. Mem. editl. bd. Montgomery County Bar Docket, 1995-96. Dir. Montgomery Humane Shelter, 1995. Mem. Am. Inns. of Ct., Copyright Soc. Am., Computer Law Assn., Computer Profls. for Social Responsibility, Montgomery County Bar Assn. General civil litigation, Computer, Criminal. Office: PO Box 1226 Montgomery AL 36102-1226

MORROW, JOHN E. lawyer; b. L.A., Mar. 17, 1943; s. Charles Henry and Lillian (Harmon) M.; m. Sue C. Taylor, June 28, 1989. BS, U. Southern Calif., 1965; JD, U. Chgo., 1968; postgrad., U. Munich, 1969. Bar: Calif. 1969, Ill. 1971. Law clk. to judge U.S. Dist. Ct. (cen. dist.) Calif., 1969-70; ptnr. Baker & McKenzie, Chgo., 1970-73, 75-76, 83—, Zurich, Switzerland, 1974-75, Hong Kong, 1976-82. Mem. ABA (subcom. on internat. bus. law com. corp. sect.). Finance, Private international, Mergers and acquisitions. Office: Baker & McKenzie One Prudential Plz 130 E Randolph St Fl 32 Chicago IL 60601-6207 E-mail: john.e.morrow@bakernet.com.

MORSCH, THOMAS HARVEY, lawyer; b. Oak Park, Ill., Sept. 5, 1931; s. Harvey William and Gwenodyne (Maun) M.; m. Jacquelyn Casey, Dec. 27, 1954; children: Thomas H. Jr., Margaret, Mary Susan, James, Kathryn, Julia. BA, Notre Dame U., 1953; BSL., Northwestern U., 1953, JD, 1955. Bar: Ill. 1955, D.C. 1955. Assoc. Crowell & Leibman, Chgo., 1955-62; ptnr. Leibman, Williams, Bennett, Baird & Minow, Chgo., 1962-72, Sidley & Austin, Chgo., 1972-97, counsel, 1998-2000. Bd. dirs. Chgo. Lawyers Com. for Civil Rights Under Law, chmn., 1982-83; bd. dirs. Pub. Interest Law Initiative, pres., 1993-95; No. Dist. Ill. Civil Justice Reform Com., 1991-95, Ill. Equal Justice Commn., 1999—; mem. vis. com. Law Sch. Northwestern U., 1989-90, dir. Small Bus. Opportunity Ctr., 1998—, assoc. clin. prof., 1998—. Pres. Republican Workshops of Ill., 1970; gen. counsel Ill. Com. to Re-elect the Pres., 1972; mem. LaGrange Plan Commn., Ill., 1972-80, LaGrange Fire and Police Commn., 1968-72; trustee LaGrange Meml. Hosp., 1983-89; adv. bd. Catholic Charities of Chgo., 1985—; mem. Kellogg Ctr. for Nonprofit Mgmt., 2001—. Fellow Am. Coll. Trial Lawyers; mem. ABA, Ill. State Bar Assn., Chgo. Bar Assn. (bd. mgrs. 1979-81), DC Bar, 7th Cir. Bar Assn., Northwestern Law Sch. Alumni Assn. (pres. 1988-89), Chgo. Bar Found. (bd. dirs., pres. 1995-97), Univ. Club (Chgo.), LaGrange Country Club, Palisades Park Country Club (Mich.), Point O'Woods Country Club (Mich.). Roman Catholic. Home: 301 S Edgewood Ave La Grange IL 60525-2153 Office: Northwestern U Sch Law 357 E Chicago Ave Chicago IL 60611 E-mail: tmorsch@law.northwestern.edu.

MORSE, DUANE D(ALE), lawyer; b. Stevens Point, Wis., Sept. 19, 1950; s. Douglas D. and Rosemary (Adamson) M.; m. Diane C. Crampton, June 23, 1973; children: Jason V., Julia C. BA, Northwestern U., 1972; JD magna cum laude, U. Mich., 1979. Bar: D.C. 1980, U.S. Dist. Ct. D.C. 1981, U.S. Ct. Appeals (D.C. cir.) 1987, U.S. Dist. Ct. Md. 1989, U.S. Ct. Appeals (4th cir.) 1990. Law clk. to judge U.S. Ct. Appeals (6th cir.), Nashville, 1979-80; assoc. Wilmer, Cutler & Pickering, Washington, 1980-86, ptnr., 1987—. Editor Mich. Law Rev., 1977-79; contbr. articles to profl. publs., chpt. to book. Mem. ABA, Am. Bankruptcy Inst., Order of Coif. Bankruptcy, Commercial, contracts (including sales of goods; commercial financing), Corporate, general. Office: Wilmer Cutler & Pickering 1600 Tysons Blvd Fl 10 Mc Lean VA 22102

MORSE, JACK CRAIG, lawyer; b. Evanston, Ill., Aug. 11, 1936; s. Leland Robert and Pauline (Pettibone) M.; children by past marriage: David Leland, Katherine Malia. BA, Beloit Coll., 1958; JD, Northwestern U., 1965. Bar: Hawaii 1967, U.S. Dist. Ct. Hawaii 1969, U.S. Ct. Appeals (9th cir.) 1977. Legal staff Bishop Estate, Honolulu, 1966-68; dep. atty. gen. State of Hawaii, Honolulu, 1968-71; ptnr. Saunders & Morse, Honolulu, 1971-73; assoc. Chuck & Wong, Honolulu, 1974-75; officer, dir. Morse, Nelson & Ross, Honolulu, 1976-85; mem. Hawaii Med. Claim Conciliation Panel, Honolulu, 1977—, chmn., 1980—; mem. panel of arbitrators First Judicial Cir., Hawaii, 1986—. Lt. USN, 1959-62. Hardy scholar Northwestern U., 1962. Mem. Am. Judicature Soc., Assn. Trial Lawyers Am., Omicron Delta Kappa. Federal civil litigation, State civil litigation, Personal injury (including property damage). Office: 700 Richards St Ste 1706 Honolulu HI 96813-4619 E-mail: jmorseesq@aol.com.

MORSE, JOHN HARLEIGH, lawyer, director; b. Estherville, Iowa, Sept. 22, 1910; s. James W. and Winifred E. (Williams) M.; m. Marie A. Forrest, Nov. 11, 1936 (div. June 1962); children: James W. II, Bruce F.; m. Ann U. Stanton, May 23, 1964. BA, State U. Iowa, 1930; MBA, Harvard U., 1932; JD, Yale U., 1935. Bar: N.Y. 1936. Since practiced in, N.Y.C.; with firm Carter, Ledyard & Milburn, 1935, Cravath, Swaine & Moore, 1936-76, ptnr., 1946-76; vice chair Nat. Forge Co., 1977-91. Pres. Forest Property Owners Assn., 1992-94. Mem. ABA (chmn. labor rels. law sect. 1961-62), Phi Beta Kappa, Phi Gamma Delta. Address: Shell Point 5807 Turban Ct Fort Myers FL 33908-1668

MORSE, M. HOWARD, lawyer; b. Louisville, May 30, 1959; s. Marvin Henry and Betty Anne (Hess) M.; m. Laura E. Loeb, Apr. 17, 1988; children: Elizabeth Loeb, Marni Loeb. AB summa cum laude, Dartmouth Coll., 1981; JD cum laude, Harvard U., 1984. Bar: D.C. 1984, U.S. Ct. of Internat. Trade 1985, U.S. Ct. Appeals (fed. cir.) 1985, U.S. Dist. Ct. D.C. 1986, U.S. Ct. Appeals (D.C. cir.) 1986, U.S. Ct. Appeals (4th cir.) 1987. Assoc. Arnold & Porter, Washington, 1984-88; atty. FTC Bur. Competition, Washington, 1988-91, dep. asst. dir. for policy, 1991-93, asst. dir., 1993-97; ptnr. Drinker, Biddle & Reath, Washington, 1998—. Adj. prof. law Georgetown Law Ctr., Washington, 1995—2000. Mem.: ABA (chair computer industry com. 1996—99, chair intellectual property com. 1999—2002, coun. 2002—, mem. antitrust sect.), D.C. Bar Assn., Phi Beta Kappa. Office: Drinker Biddle & Reath 1500 K St NW Ste 1100 Washington DC 20005-1209 E-mail: howard.morse@dbr.com.

MORSE, SAUL JULIAN, lawyer; b. Jan. 17, 1948; s. Leon William and Goldie (Kohn) M.; m. Anne Bruce Morgan, Aug. 21, 1982; children: John Samuel, Elizabeth Miriam. BA, U. Ill., 1969, JD, 1972. Bar: Ill. 1973, U.S. Dist. Ct. (so. dist.) Ill. 1976, U.S. Ct. Appeals (7th cir.) 1983, U.S. Supreme

Ct. 1979, U.S. Tax Ct. 1982. Law clk. State of Ill. EPA, 1971-72, Ill. Commerce Commn., 1972, hearing examiner, 1972-73; trial atty. ICC, 1973-75; asst. minority legal counsel Ill. Senate, 1975, minority legal counsel, 1975-77; mem. Ill. Human Rights Commn., 1985-91; dir., treas., chair grievance com. Ill. Comprehensive Health Ins. Plan, 1987—2002; gen. counsel Ill. Legis. Space Needs Commn., 1978-92; pvt. practice Springfield, Ill., 1977-79; ptnr. Gramlich & Morse, Springfield, 1980-85; prin. Saul J. Morse and Assocs., 1985-87; ptnr. Morse, Giganti and Appleton, 1987-92; v.p., gen. counsel Ill. State Med. Soc., 1992—. Lectr. in continuing med. edn., 1986-90; counsel symposia; adj. asst. prof. med. humanities So. Ill. Sch. Medicine; pres. Springfield Profl. Baseball, LLC. Bd. dirs. Springfield Ctr. for Ind. Living, 1984-89, Ill. Comprehensive Health Ins. Plan Bd., 1987-2002, United Way Ctrl. Ill., Inc., 1991-97, G.I.N.I. Inst., 2002, Hope Sch., Springfield, 1996-2003, Springfield Jewish Fedn., 1992-95; bd. dirs. United Cerebral Palsy Land of Lincoln, v.p., 2002; mem. task force on transp. Rep. Nat. Com., 1979-80; mem. Springfield Jewish Comty. Rels. Coun., 1976-79, 97-2002; bd. dirs. internat. Post Polio Health Internat., 2002, Springfield Jewish Fedn. Endowment; mem. spl. com. on zoning and land use planning Sangamon County Bd., 1978; treas. City of Leland Grove, 1999—; exec. com. AMA and State Med. Socs. Litigation Ctr., 1999—, chmn. 2003; commr. Ill. Guardianship and Advocacy Commn., 2002; mem. chancellor's cmty. adv. coun. U. Ill., Springfield, 2002. Named Disabled Adv. of Yr., Ill. Dept. Rehab. Svcs., 1985; recipient Chmn.'s Spl. award Ill. State Med. Soc., 1987, Susan S. Suter award as outstanding disabled citizen of Ill., 1990. Mem. ABA (vice-chmn. medicine and law com. 1988-90, tort and ins. practice sect., forum com. on health law), Am. Assn. Health Lawyers, Am. Soc. Law and Medicine, Ill. State Bar Assn. (spl. com. on reform of legis. process 1976-82, spl. com. on the disabled lawyer 1978-82, young lawyers sect. com. on role of govt. atty. 1977-80, chmn. 1982, sect. coun. adminstrv. law, vice-chmn. 1981-82), Sangamon County Bar Assn., Am. Soc. Med. Assn. Counsel, Phi Delta Phi. Health, Insurance, Legislative. Home: 1701 S Illini Rd Springfield IL 62704-3301 Office: Ill State Med Soc 600 S 2nd St Ste 200 Springfield IL 62704-2578 E-mail: morse@ismie.com.

MORTENSEN, ARVID LEGRANDE, lawyer; b. July 11, 1941; s. George Andrew and Mary Louise (Myers) M.; m. Elaine Marie Mains, Aug. 2, 1968; children: Marie Louise, Anne Catherine, Joseph Duncan, Susan Kumari. BS in English and Psychology, Brigham Young U., 1965, MBA in Mktg. and Fin., 1967; JD cum laude, Ind. U., 1980. Bar: Ind. 1980, U.S. Supreme Ct. 1983, Mo. 1985, D.C. 1985; CLU; accredited estate planner; cert. dive master Profl. Assn. Diving Instrs.; lic. amateur radio operator FCC, amateur extra class. Agt. Conn. Mut. Life Ins. Co., Salt Lake City, 1967-68, agt., br. mgr. Idaho Falls, Idaho, 1968-74; with Rsch. and Rev. Svc. Am., Inc./Newkirk Assocs., Inc., Indpls, 1974-83, sr. editor, 1975-79, mgr. advanced products and seminars, 1979-80, sr. mktg. exec., 1980-83; tax and fin. planner Indpls., 1980-85, St. Louis and Chesterfied, Mo., 1985-90, Tampa Bay, Fla., 1990-91, Orange County, Calif., 1991—. Mem. sr. mgmt. com., v.p. Allied Fidelity Corp., 1983-85, Allied Fidelity Ins. Co., 1983-85, Tex. Fire and Casualty Ins. Co., 1983-85; v.p., bd. dirs. Gen. Am. Ins. Co., St. Louis, 1985-86, v.p., 1985-90; pvt. practice law, Indpls., 1980-85, St. Louis, Chesterfield and Bridgeton, Mo., 1985-90, Tampa Bay, 1990-91, Orange County, 1991—. Author: Employee Stock Ownership Plans, 1975, Fundamentals of Corporate Qualified Retirement Plans, 1975, 78, 80, Buy-Sell Agreements, 1988, The Key Executive Sale, 1989, (with Norman H. Tarver) The IRA Manual, 1975-87 edits., The Keogh Manual, 1975, 77, 78, 80 edits., The Section 403 (b) Manual, 1975, 77, 78, 80, 84, 85, 87 edits., sole author, 1991, 93, 94, edits., (with Leo C. Hodges) The Life Insurance Trust Handbook, 1980; contbr. articles to profl. jours.; editor-in-chief various tax and fin. planning courses; bd. editors Ind. Law Rev., 1977-78. Active Ch. Jesus Christ of Latter-day Saints, Denver, Idaho Falls, Indpls., St. Louis, Chesterfield, Tampa Bay Area and Orange County, Calif. Mem. Assn. Advanced Life Underwriting, Mo. Bar Assn., Bar Assn. Met. St. Louis, D.C. Bar Assn., Ind. Bar Assn., Am. Soc. CLUs, Nat. Assn. Life Underwriters, Orange County. Corporate, general, Estate planning, Private international. Office: 620 Newport Center Dr Ste 1100 Newport Beach CA 92660-8011 also: PO Box 6362 Laguna Niguel CA 92607-6362

MORTIMER, WENDELL REED, JR., judge; b. Alhambra, Calif., Apr. 7, 1937; s. Wendell Reed and Blanche (Wilson) M.; m. Cecilia Vick, Aug. 11, 1962; children: Michelle Dawn, Kimberly Grace. AB, Occidental Coll., 1958; JD, U. So. Calif., L.A., 1965. Bar: Calif. 1966. Trial atty. Legal div. State of Calif., L.A., 1965-73; assoc. Thelen, Marrin, Johnson & Bridges, L.A., 1973-76, ptnr., 1976-93; pvt. practice San Marino, Calif., 1994-95; judge L.A. Superior Ct., 1995—, mem. complex litigation panel, 2000—. With U.S. Army, 1960-62. Mem. ABA, Internat. Acad. Trial Judges, Los Angeles County Bar Assn., Calif. Judges Assn., Am. Judicature Soc., Am. Judges Assn., Legion Lex., Am. Bd. Trial Advocacy (nat. bd. dirs., exec. com. L.A. chpt.), San Marino City Club (bd. dirs.), Pasadena Bar Assn., Balboa Yacht Club. Home: 1420 San Marino Ave San Marino CA 91108-2042

MORTON, FRED J. lawyer; b. El Paso, Tex., Nov. 13, 1935; s. R.A.D. and Julianne (More) M.; m. Anne Adele Reynolds, July 19, 1960; children: Chris, Anne, John, Robert, Peter, Mary Virginia, Thomas, Mary Katherine. BA, U. Tex., El Paso, 1957; LLB, U. Tex., Austin, 1958. Bar: Tex. 1958. Asst. U.S. atty., El Paso, 1961-65; U.S. commr. cts., 1966-71. Trustee, Southwestern Children's Home Trust, El Paso, 1983—; pres. El Paso County Hist. Soc., 1967. Fellow U. Tex. Law Sch. Ctr. for Pub. Policy Dispute Resolution, 1996. Mem. Tex. Bar Assn., El Paso Trial Lawyers Assn. (pres. 1972), El Paso Bar Assn. (pres. 1985), Sigma Alpha Epsilon, Phi Delta Phi. Democrat. Roman Catholic. Alternative dispute resolution, General practice, Property, real (including real estate development, water). Home: 1101 Montana Ave El Paso TX 79902-5509 E-mail: f.morton@att.net.

MORTON, RICHARD, lawyer, financial consultant; b. Jamaica, N.Y., Sept. 25, 1925; s. Lawrence and Irma (Gross) M.; m. Helen Malone, May 9, 1965; children: Bruce, Greg, Terri L. Sloan. BSBA, U. Denver, 1949; postgrad., Stetson Coll. Law, 1961; JD, U. Miss., 1963; LLM, Yale U., 1964. Bar: Miss. 1963, Fla. 1971. Builder, developer, N.Y., Fla., 1962-60; prof. law U. Ga., Athens, 1965-68; pvt. practice law Miami, 1971—; mng. ptnr. Morton Towers, 1988-97. Pres. S. Fla. Savs. & Loan, Miami, 1980-84; bd. dirs. Bank of Fla., Founders Nat. Mortgage Corp.; of counsel Katz, Barron, Squitero & Faust, 1998—; adv. com. Apt. Investment & Mgmt. Co., Denver. Contbr. articles to profl. jours. Served to 1st. lt. U.S. Army. Decorated Bronze Star. Office: 2699 S Bayshore Dr Fl 7 Miami FL 33133-5408 Home: 17215 Courtland Ln Boca Raton FL 33496 E-mail: richardmorton@msn.com.

MOSCHOS, DEMITRIOS MINA, lawyer; b. Jan. 8, 1941; s. Constantine Mina and Vasiliky (Strates) Moschos; m. Celeste Thomaris, Sept. 28, 1975; children: Kristin M, Thomas W. BA magna cum laude, U. Mass., 1962; JD magna cum laude, Boston U., 1965; grad., U.S. Army JAG Sch., 1966. Bar: Mass 1965, US Dist Ct Mass 1975, US Ct Mil Appeals 1966. Exec. asst. to city mgr., spl. legal counsel City of Worcester, 1968-75, asst. city mgr., spl. legal counsel, 1975-80; assoc. Mirick, O'Connell, Worcester, 1980-81, ptnr., 1982—. Lectr labor relations Worcester State Col, 1975—88, Clark Univ, 1978—; chmn Worcester Housing Comt, 1968—78, Worcester Energy Comt, 1978—80; mem Mass Joint Labor Mgt Comt, 1978—80. Drafter admin codes: ; contbr. articles to profl jours. Past pre.s archiocesan coun. Greek Orthodox Archdiocese Am.; bd. dirs. Worcester Regional Rsch. Bur., Worcester Regional C. of C. Capt JAGC U.S. Army, 1966—68. Decorated Army Commendation Medal; named Outstanding Young Man of Worcester County, Worcester County Jaycees, 1969, in resolution of commendation, Worcester City Coun, 1980; recipient Alumni Acad Achievement Award, Boston Univ Law Sch, 1965. Fellow: Coll. Labor and Employment Lawyers; mem.: ABA, Worcester County Bar Assn. (former chmn labor sect), Mass. Bar Assn. (Comty Serv Award 1987), Tatnuck Country Club. Labor (including EEOC, Fair Labor Standards Act, labor-management relations, NLRB, OSHA), Education and schools, Municipal (including bonds). Office: Mirick O'Connell 100 Front St Ste 1700 Worcester MA 01608-1426

MOSCHOS, MICHAEL CHRISTOS, lawyer; b. Worcester, Mass., Jan. 8, 1941; s. Constantine Mina and Vassiliky (Strates) M.; m. Mary Patricia Dermody, Feb. 20, 1977 (div. Dec. 1991); children: Charles, Michael Patrick; m. Susan Smith Harrington, June 6, 1998; 1 stepchild, Katherine L. BBA cum laude, U. Mass., 1962; JD, Boston U., 1965. Bar: Mass. 1965, N.Y. 1970, U.S. Dist. Ct. Mass. 1982, U.S. Supreme Ct. 1982. Lawyer Investors Group, N.Y.C., 1968-72; assoc., spl. counsel Cabot, Cabot, Forbes, Boston, 1972; pvt. practice Boston, 1973, Worcester, 1979—. Spl. counsel Esso-Pappas, S.A., Athens, Greece, 1969-70; investment banker, counsel Worcester Bancorp., 1974-79; cons. atty. Baskins-Sears Esq., N.Y.C., 1979; counsel Downtown Worcester Bus. Devel. Corp., 1974-76. Legal officer Worcester Heritage Soc., 1975-82; mems. coun. Worcester Art Mus., 1975-83; incorporator Worcester Natural History Soc., 1977-98; spl. counsel, acting mng. dir. Hellenic Bottling Co., S.A., Hellenic Canning Industries, S.A., Internat. Canning Industry, S.A., Athens, Greece, 1973. Capt. U.S. Army, 1965-67. Mem. Worcester County Bar Assn. Greek Orthodox. Construction, Family and matrimonial, Property, real (including real estate development, water). Home: 4004 Brompton Cir Worcester MA 01609-1160 Office: 250 Commercial St Ste 210 Worcester MA 01608

MOSENSON, STEVEN HARRIS, lawyer; b. Phila., Dec. 3, 1956; BS, NYU, 1978, M of Pub. Adminstrn., 1979; JD, Yeshiva U., 1982. Bar: N.Y. 1983, U.S. Ct. Appeals (2d cir.) 1983, U.S. Dist. Ct. (so. and ea. dists.) N.Y. 1983, U.S. Ct. Internat. Trade 1985, U.S. Supreme Ct. 1986. Assoc. Baden Kramer Huffman & Brodsky, N.Y.C., 1982-85; asst. corp. counsel N.Y.C. Law Dept., 1985-89; gen. counsel United Cerebral Palsy Assns. of N.Y. State, Inc., N.Y.C., 1989—. Pres. bd. dirs. Bklyn. Heights Ctr. for Counseling, Inc., 1992—; bd. dirs. Walden, N.Y. Local Devel. Corp., 1998—; mem. Walden Cmty. Coun., 1998—. Mem. N.Y. State Bar Assn. (former chmn. com. on issues affecting people 1997—, treas. corp. counsel sect.), Guardianship Assn. of N.Y. State, Inc. (v.p. 1995—). Office: United Cerebral Palsy Assns of NY 330 W 34th St Fl 13 New York NY 10001-2488 Fax: 212-356-0746. E-mail: mosenson@aol.com.

MOSER, C. THOMAS, lawyer; b. Seattle, Aug. 10, 1947; s. Carl Thomas and Helen Louise (Felton) M.; m. Deborah J. St. Clair, Sept. 25, 1976; children: Nicole, Lauren. BA, Cen. Wash. U., 1972; M in Pub. Adminstrn., George Washington U., 1974; JD, Gonzaga U., 1976. Bar: Wash. 1977; U.S. Dist. Ct. (we. dist.) Wash. 1977, U.S. Dist. Ct. (ea. dist.) Wash. 1980, U.S. Ct. Appeals (9th cir.) 1980, U. S. Supreme Ct. 1981. Dep. pros. atty. Skagit County Pros. Atty., Mount Vernon, Wash., 1976-77, chief civil dep., 1979-80, pros. atty., 1980-86, San Juan County Pros. Atty., Friday Harbor, Wash., 1977-79; pvt. practice Mount Vernon, 1987—. Hearing examiner pro tem Skagit County, 1992—. Author: Gonzaga Law Review, 1975. Bd. dirs. Wash. Environ. Coun., Seattle, 1971-72, Padilla Bay Found., Skagit County, Wash., 1988; bd. trustees Wash. Assn. County Ofcls., Olympia, 1983; exec. bd. North Pacific Conf. Evang. Covenant Ch., vice sec. 1991-96; bd. trustees Skagit Valley Coll., 2000—. Sgt. U.S. Army, 1967-69, Korea. Recipient Silver Key award ABA Student Law Div., 1976, Legion of Honor award Internat. Order DeMolay, Kansas City, Mo., 1982, Chevalier award 1982. Mem. ATLA, Nat. Coll. Advocacy (advocate), Wash. State Trial Lawyers Assn. (bd. govs. 1990-92, 96-97), Wash. Assn. Pros. Attys. (bd. dirs. 1983-85), Skagit County Bar Assn. (pres. 1995-96), Kiwanis Club Mt. Vernon, Affiliated Health Svc. (ethics com.), Christian Legal Soc. Democrat. Evangelical. Avocations: skiing, golf, woodworking. Criminal, Land use and zoning (including planning), Personal injury (including property damage). Office: 411 Main St Mount Vernon WA 98273-3837

MOSER, M(ARTIN) PETER, lawyer; b. Balt., Jan. 16, 1928; s. Herman and Henrietta (Lehmayer) M.; m. Elizabeth Kohn, June 14, 1949; children— Mike, Moriah, Jeremy AB, The Citadel, Charleston, S.C., 1947; LLB, Harvard U., 1950. Bar: Md. 1950, U.S. Supreme Ct., U.S. Ct. Appeals (4th cir.). Asst. states atty. City of Balt., 1951, 53-54; assoc. Blades Rosenfeld, Balt., 1950, 53-54; ptnr. Frank, Bernstein, Conaway & Goldman and predecessor firms, Balt., 1955-90, co-chmn. firm, 1983-86; counsel, 1991-92; of counsel Piper Marbury Rudnick & Wolfe LLP, 1992—. Instr. U. Balt. Law Sch., 1954-56, 86, U. Md. Law Sch., 1986-87. Contbr. articles to profl. jours. Del., chmn. local govt. com. Md. Constl. Conv., 1967-68; mem. Balt. City Planning Commn., 1961-66, Balt. Regional Planning Council, 1963-66, Md. Commn. to Study Narcotics Laws, 1965-67, Mayor's Task Force on EEO, 1966-67, Met. Transit Authority Adv. Council, 1962, Com. to Revise Balt. City Planning Laws, 1962, Com. to Revise Balt. City Charter Provision on Conflicts of Interest, 1969-70; mem. Citizens Adv. Com. on Dist. Ct., chmn., 1971, Dist. Adv. Bd. for Pub. Defender System for Dist. 1, 1973-85; mem. Atty. Grievance Commn. of Md., 1975-78, chmn. 82-86; chmn. Md. State Ethics Commn., 1987-89; bd. dirs. Sinai Hosp., 1983—, Lifebridge Health Sys., 1998—, Ct. of Appeals Comm. to Study the Model Rules, 1983-86, 2002-. Served with JAGC, U.S. Army, 1951-53 Fellow: Balt. Bar Found., Md. Bar Found., Am. Bar Found. (pres. 2002—); mem.: Lawyers' Round Table Club, Wednesday Law Club, Balt. Bar Assn., Md. State Bar Assn. (pres. 1979—80), ABA (ho. of dels. 1978—2002, treas. 1993—96, bd. govs. 1984—87). Democrat. Jewish. Corporate, general, Estate planning, Health. Office: Piper Rudnick LLP 6225 Smith Ave Baltimore MD 21209-3600

MOSER, MICHAEL JOSEPH, lawyer; b. N.Y.C., Aug. 31, 1950; s. Joseph Georg and Patricia Ann (Robertson) M.; m. Yvonne Yi-Feng Wei, Aug. 17, 1973; children: Yeone, Anna-Sieglinde, Christa Isolde. BSFS, Georgetown U., 1972; MA, Columbia U., 1974, Phd, 1981; JD, Harvard U., 1980. Bar: N.Y. 1981, D.C. 1989. Vis. scholar Academia Sinica, Taiwan, Republic of China, 1974-76; rsch. assoc. Kyoto Comparative Law Ctr., Doshisha U., Japan, 1978-79; assoc. Coudert Bros., Hong Kong, 1980-82, Peking, People's Republic of China, 1982-83, Baker and McKenzie, 1983-85, ptnr., 1985-99, Freshfields Bruckhaus Deringer, Hong Kong, 2000—. Prof. law Peking U., City U. Hong Kong; lectr. law U. Zurich. Author: Law and Social Change in a Chinese Community, 1982, Business Strategies in the People's Republic of China, 1986, (with others) China Tax Guide, 1987, 93, 99; editor: (book) Foreign Trade, Investment and the Law in the People's Republic of China, 1984, 87, China Business Law Guide, 1990, Foreigners Within the Gates: The Legations at Peking, 1993, Hong Kong and China Arbitration, 1994, International Arbitration in the People's Republic of China, 1995, 2000, Arbitration in Asia, 2001, Arbitration in Hong Kong, 2003; bd. advisors World Arbitration and Mediation Report. V.p. Am. C. of C., Peking, 1983. Fellow Chartered Inst. Arbitrators London (arbitrator), Hong Kong Inst. Arbitrators Ltd. (arbitrator), Royal Geog. Soc.; mem. ABA, N.Y. State Bar Assn., D.C. Bar Assn., Internat. Bar Assn., Am. Bar Assn. (arbitrator), China Internat. Econ. and Trade Arbitration Commn. (Beijing) (arbitrator), Beijing Arbitration Commn. (arbitrator), Hong Kong Internat. Arbitration Ctr. (arbitrator, governing coun., mgmt.), UN Working Group on Ofcl. Translation of Chinese Fgn. Investment Legislation, Hong Kong Arbitration Ordinance Review Com., China Securities Regulatory Com., Beijing (arbitrator), Singapore Internat. Arbitration Ctr. (arbitrator), Australian Ctr. Internat. Commercial Arbitration (arbitrator), B.C. Internat. Comml. Arbitration Ctr. (arbitrator), The Indian Coun. Arbitration (arbitrator), Internat. Arbitration Ctr. Austrian Fed. Econ. Chamber (arbitrator), C. of C. Industry of Geneva (arbitrator), WIPO Arbitration Ctr. (arbitrator), MCCI Permanent Ct. of Comml. Arbitration (arbitrator), Cairo Regional Ctr. for Internat. Comml. Arbitration (arbitrator), Royal Hong Kong Yacht Club, The Hong Kong Club, Aberdeen Marina Club, Harvard Club N.Y. Roman Catholic. Avocations: opera, poetry, sports. Office: Frshflds Bruck Deringer 11/F 2 Exch Sq 8 Connaught Pl Central Hong Kong Hong Kong also: Freshfields 2 Dong San Huan Bei Lu Chaoyang Beijing 100027 China

MOSES, ALFRED HENRY, lawyer, writer, diplomat; b. Balt., July 24, 1929; s. Leslie William and Helene Amelia (Lobe) Moses; m. Carol Whitehill, Nov. 24, 1955; children: Barbara, Jennifer, David, Amalie. BA, Dartmouth, 1951; postgrad., Woodrow Wilson Sch., Princeton U., 1951-52; JD, Georgetown U., 1956. Bar: D.C. 1956. Assoc. Covington & Burling, Washington, 1956-65, ptnr., 1965-94, 97—; spl. advisor, spl. counsel Pres. Jimmy Carter, Washington, 1980-81; amb. to Romania, 1994-97; Pres. spl. emissary for Cyprus, 1999-2001; gen. counsel Promontory Interfin. Network, LLC, 2003—. Legal advisor minority rights Dem. Nat. Com., Washington, D.C. Commn. Urban Renewal; commr. Pub. Housing, Fairfax County, Va., 1971—72; chmn. UN Watch, Geneva, 2001—; chmn. nat. bd. Hebrew Coll., Newton Ctr., Mass., 2002—; lectr. in field. Contbr. articles to profl. jours. Pres. Am. Jewish Com., 1991—94; bd. dirs. Paralysis Cure Rsch. Found., 1978—81; trustee Phelps Stokes Fund, N.Y.C., 1978—84, Jewish Publ. Soc., 1989—94, Haifa U., 1988—90; co-chmn. legal divsn. United Givers Fund, Washington, 1975—76; mem. Coun. Fgn. Rels., N.Y.C., 1977—; pres. Nat. Children's Island, Washington, 1975—76, Golda Meir Assn., 1986—88, nat. chmn., 1988—93; mem. bd. regents Georgetown U., 1986—92. Mem.: ABA, D.C. Bar Assn., Met. Club. Democrat. Jewish. General civil litigation, Corporate, general, Property, real (including real estate development, water). Home: 7710 Georgetown Pike Mc Lean VA 22102-1431 Office: 1201 Pennsylvania Ave NW Washington DC 20004-2401

MOSES, RAPHAEL JACOB, lawyer; b. Girard, Ala., Nov. 6, 1913; s. William Moultrie and Anna (Green) M.; m. Marian Eva Beck, Aug. 22, 1938 (dec. Feb. 1976); 1 child, Marcia (Mrs. William S. Johnson); m. Fletcher Lee Westgaard, Jan. 20, 1979. AB, U. Colo., 1935, JD, 1937. Bar: Colo. 1938. Practiced in, Alamosa, 1938-62, Boulder, 1962—; pres. Moses, Wittemyer, Harrison & Woodruff (P.C.), from 1970, now of counsel. Spl. asst. atty. gen. Rio Grande Compact, 1957-58; mem. Colo. Water Conservation Bd., 1952-58, chmn., counsel, 1958-76, cons., 1976-77; research asso., faculty law U. Colo., 1962-66, vis. lectr., 1966-76, resident counsel, 1964-66, regent, 1973-74; grad. faculty Colo. State U., 1963-67; mem. Western States Water Council, 1965-77, chmn., 1966-70. Trustee Rocky Mountain Mineral Law Inst., 1964-66; bd. dirs. U. Colo. Found., 1977-97, chmn., 1977-79, mem. chancellor's adv. coun., 1981-97; bd. dirs. Colo. Open Lands, 1983-91, U. Colo. Improvement Corp., 1980-90, Colo. Endowment for Humanities, 1986-89; mem. adv. bd. Natural Resources Ctr., U. Colo. Sch. Law, 1983-92, chmn., 1986-88. Served to lt. (s.g.) USNR, 1942-45. Recipient William E. Knous award U. Colo. Sch. Law, 1971, Norlin award U. Colo., 1972; Raphael J. Moses Disting. Natural Resources professorship established U. Colo., 1994. Fellow Am. Bar Found. (life), Colo. Bar Found. (trustee 1977-90), Am. Coll. Trial Lawyers; mem. ABA (chmn. water rights com. sect. natural resources 1959-60), Colo. Bar Assn. (pres. 1959-60, Award of Merit 1972), San Luis Valley Bar Assn. (pres. 1942), Am. Counsel Assn., Order of Coif (hon.) Presbyterian (elder). Clubs: Boulder Country; Garden of the Gods (Colorado Springs). Home: 4913 Clubhouse Cir Boulder CO 80301-3715 E-mail: RayMoise@aol.com.

MOSICH, NICHOLAS JOSEPH, lawyer; b. San Pedro, Calif., July 2, 1951; s. Nicholas Andrew and Barbara Yvonne (Chutuk) M.; m. Susanne Melinda Wolf, Dec. 18, 1976 (dec. Jan. 1998); m. Jessica V. Schutte, Dec. 22, 2002; children: Nicholas Daniel, Andrea Michelle. BA, Santa Clara U., 1974; JD, Pepperdine U., 1977. Bar: Calif. 1977, U.S. Dist. Ct. (so. dist.) Calif. 1979, U.S. Dist. Ct. (ctrl. dist.) Calif. 1980. Assoc. Forgy & Inadomi, Santa Ana, Calif., 1978-83, ptnr., 1983-92, Mosich & Fotone, 2002. Bd. dirs. Young Men's Christian Assn., Santa Ana, 1980-87. Mem. ABA, Orange County Bar Assn., Assn. Trial Lawyers Am. Republican. Roman Catholic. General civil litigation, General practice, Other. Office: 2204 E 4th St Ste 100 Santa Ana CA 92705-4071

MOSK, RICHARD MITCHELL, judge; b. L.A., May 18, 1939; s. Stanley and Edna M.; m. Sandra Lee Budnitz, Mar. 21, 1964; children: Julie, Matthew. AB with great distinction, Stanford U., 1960; JD cum laude, Harvard U., 1963. Bar: Calif. 1964, U.S. Supreme Ct. 1970, U.S. Ct. Mil. Appeals 1970, U.S. Dist. Ct. (no., so., ea., and cen. dists.) Calif 1964, U.S. Ct. Appeals (9th dist.) 1964. Staff Pres.'s Commn. on Assassination Pres. Kennedy, 1964; rsch. clk. Calif. Supreme Ct., 1964-65; ptnr. Mitchell, Silberberg & Knupp, L.A., 1965-87; prin. Sanders, Barnet, Goldman, Simons & Mosk, PC, L.A., 1987-2000; justice Calif. Ct. Appeal, 2nd Dist., 2001—. Spl. dep. Fed. Pub. Defender , L.A., 1975—76; instr. U. So. Calif. Law Sch., 1978; judge Iran-U.S. Claims Tribunal, 1981—84, 1997—2001, substitute arbitrator, 1984—97; mem. L.A. County Jud. Procedures Commn., 1973—82, chmn., 1978; co-chmn. Motion Picture Assn. Classification and Rating Adminstrn., 1994—2000; mem. panel Ct. Arbitration for Sport-Geneva, 1998—2001. Contbr. articles to profl. jours. Mem. L.A. City-County Inquiry on Brush Fires, 1970; bd. dirs. Calif. Mus. Sci. and Industry, 1979-82, Vista Del Mar Child Ctr., 1979-82; trustee L.A. County Law Libr., 1985-86; bd. govs. Town Hall Calif., 1986-91; mem. Christopher Commn. on L.A. Police Dept., 1991; mem. Stanford U. Athletic Bd., 1991-95. With USNR, 1964-75. Hon. Woodrow Wilson fellow, 1960; recipient Roscoe Pound prize, 1961. Fellow: Am. Bar Found.; mem.: FBA (pres. L.A. chpt. 1972), ABA (coun. internat. law sect. 1986—90), L.A. County Bar Assn., Beverly Hills Bar Assn., Internat. Bar Assn., Phi Beta Kappa. Office: Ct Appeal 300 S Spring St Los Angeles CA 90013

MOSKIN, MORTON, lawyer, director; b. N.Y.C., Mar. 28, 1927; s. Barnett and Sonia (Burr) M.; m. Rita Lee Goldberg, June 15, 1952; children: Tina, Ilene, Jonathan. BA, Pa. State Coll., 1947; LL.B., Cornell U., 1950. Assoc. White & Case, N.Y.C., 1950-61, ptnr., 1962-94, cons., 1995—. Chmn. exec. com. Mallinckrodt, Inc. (formerly IMCERA, previously Internat. Minerals & Chem. Corp.), St. Louis, 1988-91, chmn. corp. governance com., 1993-97; dir. Crum & Forster, 1973-82, sec. BT Mortgage Investors, Garden City, N.Y., 1975-82. Editor (with Field): New York and Delaware Business Entities: Choice, Formation, Operation, Financing, Acquisitions, 1997, Transactional Lawyer's Deskbook: Advising Business Entities, 2001; editor: Commercial Contracts: Strategies for Drafting and Negotiating, 2002. Bd. dirs. Fedn. Employment and Guidance Svcs.; bd. dirs., pres. Henry M. Blackmer Found., N.Y.C.; bd. dirs. Achievement Found., Stamford, Conn., pres., 1988-94; bd. dirs. Jewish Cmty. Svcs. L.I., 1974-93, pres., 1984-87. Fellow Am. Bar Found.; mem. ABA, N.Y. State Bar Assn., N.Y. County Lawyers Assn. (dir. 1981-86, 99-2002), Norfolk (Conn.) Country Club, Cornell Club N.Y. Corporate, general, Mergers and acquisitions, Securities. Home: 1160 Park Ave Apt 15B New York NY 10128-1212 Office: White & Case 1155 Ave of Americas New York NY 10036-2711 E-mail: mmoskin@whitecase.com.

MOSKOWITZ, JOEL STEVEN, lawyer; b. N.Y.C., Jan. 14, 1947; s. Jack I. and Myra (Shor) M.; m. Anna Boucher; children: David, Michael, Ellen. BA, UCLA, 1967, JD, 1970. Bar: Calif. 1971, U.S. Ct. Appeals (9th cir.) 1971, U.S. Ct. Appeals (D.C. cir.) 1975, U.S. Supreme Ct. 1975, U.S. Ct. Appeals (2d cir.) 1979. Dep. atty. gen. Calif. Dept. Justice, Sacramento, 1970-83; dep. dir. Calif. Dept. Health Svcs., Sacramento, 1983-85; of counsel Gibson, Dunn & Crutcher, L.A., 1985-88, ptnr., 1988-96, Moskowitz, Brestoff, Winston & Blinderman LLP, 1996—. Author: Environmental Liability in Real Property Transactions, 1995; contbr. articles to legal pubs. Mem. Phi Beta Kappa. Environmental. Office: 1880 Century Park E Ste 300 Los Angeles CA 90067-1631 E-mail: jsm6@ix.netcom.com.

MOSMAN, MICHAEL W. prosecutor; BA, Utah State U.; JD, Brigham Young U. Assoc. Miller, Nash, Portland, Oreg., 1986—88; asst. U.S. atty. Dist. Oreg. U.S. Dept. Justice, 1988—2001, U.S. atty. Dist. Oreg., 2001—. Office: 1000 SW 3rd Ave Ste 600 Portland OR 97204-2902*

MOSS, AMBLER HOLMES, JR., lawyer, former ambassador; b. Balt., Sept. 1, 1937; s. Ambler Holmes and Dorothea Dandridge (Williams) M.; m. Serena Welles, May 6, 1972; children: Ambler H., Benjamin Sumner, Serena Montserrat, Nicholas George Oliver. BA, Yale U., 1960; JD, George Washington U., 1970. Bar: D.C., Fla. Joined Fgn. Svc., Dept. State, 1964; vice consul Barcelona, 1964-66; adviser U.S. del. to OAS, 1966-69; Spanish desk officer Dept. State, Washington, 1968-70; assoc. Coudert Bros., Washington, 1971-73, resident atty. Brussels, 1973-76; mem. U.S. Negotiating Team for Panama Canal treaties, 1977; dep. asst. Sec. of State, Washington, 1977-78; amb. to Panama, Am. Embassy, Panama City, 1978-82; of counsel Greenberg, Traurig, LLP, Miami, 1982-87, 95—; prof., dir. North-South Ctr. U. Miami, Fla., 1984—, dean Grad. Sch. Internat. Studies, 1984-94. Bd. dirs. Espirito Santo Bank of Fla. Mem. Panama Canal Consultative Com., 1995-2000. With USN, 1960-64. Mem. ABA, Am. Soc. Internat. Law, Inter-Am. Bar Assn., Am. Fgn. Svc. Assn., Coun. Fgn. Rels., Am. Legion, Inter-Am. Dialogue (Washington), Navy League, Greater Miami C. of C. (gov. 1983-86), Royal Inst. Internat. Affairs (London), Internat. Inst. Strategic Studies (London), Army and Navy Club, Order of the Coif. Address: 5711 San Vicente St Coral Gables FL 33146-2724 E-mail: ahmoss@miami.edu.

MOSS, ARTHUR HENSHEY, lawyer; b. Reading, Pa., July 26, 1930; s. John Arthur and Christine Bracken (Henshey) M.; m. E. Leslie Fritz, Feb. 1982; 1 child by previous marriage, John Arthur. AB, Williams Coll., 1952; JD, U. Pa., 1955. Bar: Pa. 1956. Assoc. Montgomery, McCracken, Walker & Rhoads, Phila., 1960-69, ptnr., 1969-2000, of counsel, 2000—. Editor U. Pa. Law Rev., 1953-55; contbr. articles to profl. jours. Pres. Wayne Civic Assn., 1964—65; commr. gen. assembly Presbyn. Ch. (U.S.A.), 1983; steward, deacon Wayne Presbyn. Ch., 1966—72, 1979—84, 1989—95, ruling elder, 1966—72, 1979—84, 1989—95, clk. of session, 1973—74, 1978—89, trustee, 1987—93, Presbytery of Phila., 1994—2001, treas., 1996—2001; chmn,. Radnor-Haverford-Marple Sewer Authority, 1968—83; bd. dir. John Bartram Assn., 1987—2002, treas., 1989—2002, emeritus dir., 2002—; trustee Radnor Twp. Meml. Libr., 2001—. Mem. Radnor Hist. Soc. (dir., sec. 1978-90), Broadacres Trouting Assn., Anglers Club of Phila., Athenaeum of Phila., Merion Golf Club, Edgemere Club. Home: 200 Walnut Ave Wayne PA 19087-3423 Office: Montgomery McCracken Walker & Rhoads 123 S Broad St Philadelphia PA 19109-1099 E-mail: wwww.esq@verizon.net.

MOSS, BILL RALPH, lawyer; b. Amarillo, Tex., Sept. 27, 1950; s. Ralph Voniver and Virginia May (Atkins) M.; 1 child, Brandon Price. BS with honors, West Tex. A&M U., 1972, MA, 1974; JD, Baylor U., 1976; cert. regulatory studies program, Mich. State U., 1981. Bar: Tex. 1976, U.S. Dist. Ct. (no. dist.) 1976, U.S. Tax Ct. 1979, U.S. Ct. Appeals (5th cir.) 1983. Briefing atty. Ct. Appeals 7th Supreme Jud. Dist. Tex., Amarillo, 1976-77; assoc. Culton, Morgan, Britain & White, Amarillo, 1977-80; hearings examiner Pub. Utility Commn. Tex., Austin, 1981-83; asst. gen. counsel State Bar Tex., Austin, 1983-87; founder, owner Price & Co. Publs., Austin, 1987-97; asst. gen. counsel Tex. Ethics Commn., Austin, 1997—. Instr., lectr. West Tex. State U., Canyon, Ea. N.Mex. U., Portales, 1977-80; spkr. in field. Active St. Matthew's Episcopal Ch.; election inspector State of Tex., 1998—. Mem. ABA, Tex. Bar Assn., Nat. Orgn. Bar Counsel, Internat. Platform Assn., Alpha Chi, Lambda Chi Alpha, Omicron Delta Epsilon, Phi Alpha Delta, Sigma Tau Delta, Pi Gamma Mu. Administrative and regulatory, Professional liability, Ethics. Home: 506 Explorer St Lakeway TX 78734-3447 Office: Sam Houston Bldg 201 E 14th St Fl 10 Austin TX 78701 E-mail: bill.moss@ethics.state.tx.us.

MOSS, FRANKLIN KASS, lawyer; b. N.Y.C., Nov. 2, 1947; s. Morris H. and Lillian (Bassen) M.; m. Nancy Sills; 1 child, Joanna. BA, Cornell U., 1968; JD, Harvard U., 1978. Bar: N.Y. 1979, U.S. Dist. Ct. (so. dist.) N.Y. 1980, U.S. Dist. Ct. (ea. dist.) N.Y. 1981, U.S. Ct. Appeals (2d and 3d cirs.) 1981, U.S. Supreme Ct. 1986. Law clk. U.S. Ct. Appeals (2d cir.), N.Y.C., 1978-79; mem. faculty NYU Sch. Law, N.Y.C., 1979-81; assoc., then ptnr. Cohen, Weiss & Simon, N.Y.C., 1981-87; ptnr. Friedman, Levy, Warren & Moss, N.Y.C., 1987-89, Spivak, Lipton, Watanabe, Spivak & Moss, N.Y.C., 1989—; adj. prof. Cornell Law Sch., 2001. Mem. Nat. Lawyers Guild, N.Y. State Bar Assn. Labor (including EEOC, Fair Labor Standards Act, labor-management relations, NLRB, OSHA), Pension, profit-sharing, and employee benefits. Office: Spivak Lipton Watanabe Spivak & Moss 1700 Broadway New York NY 10019-5905 E-mail: FMoss@spivak-Lipton.com.

MOSS, JACK GIBSON, lawyer; b. Jackson, Miss., Sept. 1, 1956; s. Joe G. and Permelia (Williams) M. AA, Hinds Jr. Coll., Raymond, Miss., 1975; BS, Miss. State U., 1977; JD, U. Miss., 1980. Bar: Miss. 1980, U.S. Dist. Ct. (no. and so. dists.) Miss. 1980. Assoc. Keyes, Moss & Piazza, Jackson, 1980-82; pvt. practice Raymond, 1982—. Mem. ABA, Miss. Bar Assn., Hinds County Bar Assn., Hinds Community Coll. Alumni Assn. (pres. Hinds chpt. 1987-88), Ducks Unltd. (regional v.p. 1999-2002, state chmn. 1997-99). Baptist. Avocation: sports. General practice, Probate (including wills, trusts), Property, real (including real estate development, water). Office: PO Box 49 Raymond MS 39154-0049

MOSS, JUDITH DOROTHY, lawyer, consultant, lecturer; b. Indpls., June 2, 1945; d. Frank Maxwell and Dorothy Grace (Wisnofske) M.; A in Computer Sci., Electronic Computer Programming Inst., Columbus, Ohio, 1969; BSBA, Ohio State U., 1975, JD, 1977. Bar: Ohio 1978, U.S. Dist. Ct. (so. dist.) Ohio 1978. Organic chemistry research technician O.M. Scott and Sons, Marysville, Ohio, 1965-68; computer programmer/systems analyst State of Ohio, Columbus, 1969-75; pvt. practice, Columbus, 1978-81; pres. Barrett and Barrett Co., L.P.A., Columbus, 1982-85; pres. Barrett & Moss Co., L.P.A., 1985-86; ptnr. Brownfield, Cramer & Lewis, Columbus, 1986—; cons. to Pres. U.S. and Congress, Nat. Adv. Council on Women's Ednl. Programs, chmn. civil rights com., 1983-84, 86—; pub. speaker and guest lectr. on constl. integrity. Coordinator Ohio Eagle Forum, 1982, gen. counsel, 1978-82, 83—; mem. Ohio Gov.'s Coordinating Commn. for Ohio, White House Conf. on Families, 1980, also nat. task force, 1980; del. Central Regional White House Conf. on Families, 1980; ofcl. observer Internat. Women's Yr. Conf., Houston, 1977; adv. bd. Franklin County (Ohio) Extension Service, Area Soil Conservation Service, 1980—; trustee United Conservatives of Ohio, 1984—, 1st v.p. 1985—; mem. Chmn.'s Club, Franklin County Ohio Republican Com., 1981— ; active leadership program Pvt. Industry Council of Columbus and Franklin County, Inc., 1985-86; adv. commn. Columbus Area Cable TV, 1985—, Ohio Elections Commn., 1986—; past pres., chmn. planning com. Ravine Condominium Unit Owners Assn.; trustee Friends of 4-H, Area Soil Conservation Service, Cen. Ohio Lung Assn., Crossroads Counseling; bd. dirs. Pvt. INdustry Council Columbus and Franklin County; mem. adv. council Columbus Area Cable TV. Recipient Eagle award Phyllis Schlafly and Eagle Forum, 1980, cert. appreciation Pres. Carter, White House Conf. on Families Nat. Task Force, 1980. Mem. Ohio Bar Assn., Columbus Bar Assn., Alpha Xi Delta. Author various positions papers, pamphlets on constl. integrity. Probate (including wills, trusts), Estate planning.

MOSS, STEPHEN B. lawyer; b. Jacksonville, Fla., July 14, 1943; s. Rudy and Betty (Sobel) M.; m. Rhoda Goodman, Nov. 24, 1984; children: Kurt, Shannon. BA, Tulane U., 1964; JD, Samford U., 1968. Bar: Fla. 1968, U.S. Dist. Ct. (so. dist.) Fla., U.S. Tax Ct. From assoc. to ptnr. Heiman & Crary, Miami, Fla., 1971-74; pvt. practice law So. Miami, Fla., 1974-75; ptnr. Glass, Schultz, Weinstein & Moss P.A., Coral Gables, Fla., 1975-78, Ft. Lauderdale, Fla., 1978-80, Holland & Knight, LLP, Ft. Lauderdale, 1980—. Mem. pro bono com. 17th Jud. Cir., 2000; co-founder, co-chair Broward County Child Welfare Initiative, 2001. Capt. U.S. Army, 1968-70, Vietnam. Named Outstanding Kiwanian, Miami, Fla., 1974, Child Advocate of the Yr., Broward County, Fla., 2003; named an Olympic torchbearer, 1996. Fellow ABA, Fla. Bar Found.; mem. Fla. Bar Assn., Legal Aid Svc. of Broward County (bd. dirs. 2000), Greater Ft. Lauderdale C. of C. (gen. counsel 1991-92, chmn. bd. dirs., bd. govs. 1995, Chmn.'s award 1991, 2000, trustee rep. 2003), Tower Club, Tower Forum (pres. 1993-94, bd. dirs. 2001—). Democrat. Jewish. Avocations: running, softball, hiking. Property, real (including real estate development, water). Office: Holland & Knight LLP 1 E Broward Blvd Fl 13 Fort Lauderdale FL 33301-1845 E-mail: smoss@hklaw.com.

MOSS, STEPHEN EDWARD, lawyer; b. Washington, Nov. 22, 1940; s. Morris and Jean (Sober); m. Sharon S. Moss; children: Aubrey, Hilary. BBA, Baldwin-Wallace Coll., 1962; JD with honors, George Washington U., 1965, LLM, 1968. Bar: D.C. 1966, Md. 1971. Assoc. Cole & Groner, Washington, 1965—70; pvt. practice law Bethesda, Md., 1971—80; pres. Stephen E. Moss, P.A., Bethesda, 1981—89, Moss, Strickler & Weaver, Bethesda, 1990—94, Moss, Strickler & Sachitano, P.A., Bethesda, 1995—2003; mem. firm. Deckelbaum Ogens & Raftery, Bethesda, 2003—. Lectr. in family law and trial practice. Fellow Am. Acad. Matrimonial Lawyers (cert.), Internat. Acad. Matrimonial Lawyers; mem. Montgomery County Bar Assn. Inc. (chmn. cmty. rels. com. 1979, family law sect. 1980), Md. Bar Found., Inc. (cert. mediator). General civil litigation, Family and matrimonial, General practice. Office: Deckelbaum Ogens & Raftery 3 Bethesda Metro Ctr Ste 200 Bethesda MD 20814 E-mail: smoss@deckelbaum.com.

MOSS, THOMAS E. prosecutor; Grad., U. Idaho; JD, U. Idaho Coll. Law. Prosecuting atty. Bingham County Dist. Ct., 1967—71, 1979—99; ptnr. Moss, Cannon and Romrell, Blackfoot, Idaho; U.S. atty. U.S. Dept. of Justice, Idaho, 2001—. Mem.: Idaho Ho. of Reps. Office: PO Box 32 Boise ID 83707-0032 Office Fax: 208-334-9375.*

MOSSAWIR, HARVE H., JR., retired lawyer; b. Morton, Miss., Aug. 9, 1942; s. Harve H. and Madeline (Price) M.; children: Anna Christine, Karen Elyse; m. Judy S. Bardugo, Aug. 5, l985; 1 child, Leigh Sarah. BA with honors, U. Ala., l964; MA in Econs., U. Manchester, l965; JD with honors, U. Chgo., l968. Bar: Calif. l970. Asst. prof. U. Ala. Law Sch., Tuscaloosa, l968-69; assoc. Irell & Manella, L.A., l969-74, ptnr., 1974-94, of counsel, 1994-96. Mem. bd. editors U. Chgo. Law Rev., l966-68; contbr. articles to profl. jours. Fulbright scholar, 1964-65, Floyd Russell Mecham scholar, l965-68. Republican. Corporate, general, Corporate taxation, Personal income taxation. E-mail: labard1@yahoo.com.

MOSSINGHOFF, GERALD JOSEPH, lawyer, educator; b. St. Louis, Sept. 30, 1935; m. Jeanne Carole Jack, Dec. 29, 1958; children: Pamela Ann Jennings, Gregory Joseph, Melissa M. Ronayne. BSEE, St. Louis U., 1957; JD with honors, George Washington U., 1961. Bar: Mo. 1961, D.C. 1965, Va. 1981. Project engr. Sachs Electric Corp., 1954-57; dir. congl. liaison NASA, Washington, 1967-73, dep. gen. counsel, 1976-81; asst. Sec. Commerce, commr. patents and trademarks U.S. Patent Office, 1981-85; pres. Pharm. Rsch. and Mfrs. Am., Washington, 1985-96; Cifelli prof. intellectual property law George Washington U., Washington, 1996—; sr. counsel Oblon, Spivak, McClelland, Maier & Neustadt, Arlington, Va., 1997—. Amb. Paris Conv. Diplomatic Conf.; adj. prof. George Mason U. Law Sch. Recipient Exceptional Svc. medal NASA, 1971, Disting. Svc. medal, 1980, Outstanding Leadership medal, 1981, Jefferson medal, 2000; Disting. Alumnus George Washington U., 1996; granted presdl. rank of meritorious exec., 1980; Disting. Pub. Svc. award Sec. of Commerce, 1983 Fellow Am. Acad. Pub. Adminstrn.; mem. Reagan Alumni Assn. (bd. dirs.), Cosmos Club, Knights of Malta, Order of Coif, Eta Kappa Nu, Pi Mu Epsilon. Health, Patent. Home: 1530 Key Blvd Penthouse 28 Arlington VA 22209-1532 Office: Oblon Spivak McClelland Maier & Neustadt 1755 Jefferson Davis Hwy Fl 4 Arlington VA 22202-3509

MOST, CAROL W. lawyer; b. N.Y.C., Apr. 15, 1949; d. Meyer and Bunny Wilen; m. Richard W. Most, Sept. 26, 1971; children: Michael, Lara. BA, CUNY, 1971; MA, Queen's Coll., 1973; JD, Pace U., 1993. Bar: N.Y., U.S. Dist. Ct. (ea. and so. dist.) N.Y., U.S. Supreme Ct. Lawyer, ptnr. Skyer & Most, N.Y.C., 1994—2001; pvt. practice Westchester County, NY, 2002—. Mem.: Womans Bar State N.Y. (co-chair matrimonial com. 1999—2001), West County Womans Bar Assn. (co-chair matrimonial com. 2001—). Family and matrimonial. Office: 120 Bloomingdale Rd White Plains NY 10605

MOST, JACK LAWRENCE, lawyer, consultant; b. N.Y.C., Sept. 24, 1935; s. Meyer Milton and Henrietta (Meyer) M.; children: Jeffrey, Peter; m. Irma Freedman Robbins, Aug. 8, 1968; children: Ann, Jane. BA cum laude, Syracuse U., 1956; JD, Columbia U., 1960. Bar: N.Y. 1960, U.S. Dist. Ct. (so. and ea. dists.) N.Y. 1963. Assoc. Hale, Grant, Meyerson and O'Brien, N.Y.C., 1960-66; dep. assoc. dir. OEO, Exec. Office of The Pres., Washington, 1965-67; asst. to gen. counsel C.I.T. Fin. Corp., N.Y.C., 1968-70; corp. counsel PepsiCo, Inc., Purchase, N.Y., 1970-71; v.p. legal affairs Revlon, Inc., N.Y.C., 1971-76; asst. gen. counsel Norton Simon, Inc., N.Y.C., 1976-79; ptnr. Rogers Hoge and Hills, N.Y.C., 1979-86, Finkelstein Bruckman Wohl Most & Rothman LLP, N.Y.C., 1986-97, mng. ptnr., 1990-93, Ferster Bruckman Wohl Most & Rothman LLP, 1997-98; ptnr. Goetz, Fitzpatrick, Most & Bruckman LLP, 1999—. Corp. sec. Requa, Inc., Flowery Beauty Products, Inc., 1987—. Contbr. articles to profl. jour. and mags. Bd. dirs. Haym Salomon Home for the Aged, 1978-91, pres., 1981-91; bd. dirs. The Jaffa Inst. for Advancement Edn., 1994-95; bd. dirs. Jewish Fellowship of Hemlock Farms, 1995-2001, treas., 1996-98, sec. 1998-99; bd. dirs., 1992—, pres. Haym Salomon Found., 1992-99; mem. bd. advisors Touro Coll. Health Scis., 1989-90. Mem. ABA (food, drug and cosmetic law com., trademark and unfair competition com.), N.Y. State Bar Assn. (food, drug and cosmetics sect.), YRH Owners Corp. (bd. dirs., pres. 1989-92), Lords Valley Country Club (bd. govs. 1984-90, 1st v.p. 1987-88, 2d v.p. 1989-90), Zeta Beta Tau, Omicron (trustee Syracuse chpt. 1988-91). Jewish. Administrative and regulatory, Corporate, general, Trademark and copyright. Home: 429 E 52nd St New York NY 10022-6430 Office: Goetz Fitzpatrick Most & Bruckman LLP One Penn Plz New York NY 10119 E-mail: jmost@goetzfitz.com.

MOSTOFF, ALLAN SAMUEL, lawyer, consultant; b. N.Y.C., Oct. 19, 1932; s. Morris and Ida (Goldman) M.; m. Alice Tamara Popelowskuy, July 31, 1955; children: Peter Alexander, Nina Valerie. BS, Cornell U., 1953; MBA, NYU, 1954; LLB, N.Y. Law Sch., 1957. Bar: N.Y. 1958, D.C. 1964. Assoc. Olwine Connelly Chase O'Donnell & Weyher, N.Y.C., 1958-61; atty. SEC, Washington, 1962-66, asst. dir., 1966-69, assoc. dir., 1969-72, dir. divsn. investment mgmt. regulation, 1972-76; ptnr. Dechert Price & Rhoads, Washington, 1976—2002, Dechert, Washington, 2000—03; ptnr. emeritus, sr. counsel Dechert LLP, Washington, 2002—. Adj. prof. Georgetown U. Law Ctr., 1972-82; mem. Fin. Acctg. Standards Adv. Bd., 1982-86; adv. bd. Investment Lawyer; adv. bd. BNA Securities Regulation and Law Report, 1977-87. Mem. ABA, Assn. of Bar of City of N.Y., Fed. Bar Assn. (past chmn. exec. coun. securities regulation com. 1990-92), Am. Law Inst. Corporate, general, Securities. Home: 6417 Waterway Dr Falls Church VA 22044-1325 Office: Dechert LLP 1775 I St NW Washington DC 20006-2402 E-mail: allan.mostoff@dechert.com.

MOTEJUNAS, GERALD WILLIAM, lawyer; b. Boston, Jan. 18, 1950; s. Peter and Eva C. (Jankus) M.; m. Patricia A. McKeon, June 23, 1984; children: Scott Peterson, Mark Whitney. BA, Northeastern U., 1972; JD, Suffolk U., 1976. Bar: Mass. 1976, U.S. Dist. Ct. Mass., 1977, U.S. Supreme Ct. 1983. Assoc. Lecomte, Emanuelson, Motejunas & Doyle, Boston, 1976-85, ptnr., 1985—2002; shareholder Smith & Brink, 2002—. Author: Suffolk U. Law Rev., 1975; editor, 1976. Mem. ABA (chmn., editor, vice chmn. property ins. law com.), ATLA, Def. Rsch. Inst., Mass. Bar Assn., Boston Bar Assn., Loss Execs. Assn., Boston Athenaeum, Appalachian Mountain Club (exec. com. 1980-81). Avocations: skiing, golf. General civil litigation, General practice, Insurance. Office: Smith & Brink 122 Quincy Shore Dr Quincy MA 02171

MOTES, CARL DALTON, lawyer; b. May 31, 1949; s. Carl Thomas and Orpha Jeanette (McGauley) M.; m. Maria Eugenia Aguirre, Apr. 19, 1975. AA with honors, St. Johns River Jr. Coll., 1969; BA, Fla. State U., 1971, JD with honors, 1974. Bar: Fla. 1974, U.S. Dist. Ct. (cen., no. and so. dists.) Fla. 1975, U.S. Ct. Appeals (11th cir.) 1980. Assoc. Maguire, Voorhis & Wells P.A., Orlando, Fla., 1975-79, ptnr., 1979-97, Motes & Sears P.A., Winter Park, Fla., 1998-99, Motes & Carr, P.A., Orlando, 1999—; asst. to pres. Fla. Bar, Tallahassee, 1974-75. Dir. Legal Aid Soc., Orlando, 1979-83, pres., 1983-84; lectr. at various Bar Assns. and ednl. insts. Mem. editl. bd. Jour. Trial Advocate Quar., 1981-91, chmn., 1989-91; contbr. articles to profl. jours. Active in Planning & Zoning Bd., Altamonte Springs, Fla., 1977-79, Capital Funds Project Rev. Com., Cen. Fla., 1983; bd. dirs. Cen. Fla. coun. Boy Scouts Am., mem. exec. bd., v.p. adminstrn. 1993-94. Mem. Internat. Assn. Def. Counsel, Fla. Def. Lawyer's Assn. (bd. dirs. 1989-94, sec., treas. 1991-92, pres.-elect 1992-93, pres. 1993-94), Fla. Bar, Fed. of Ins. and Corp. Coun., Orange County Bar Assn. (sec. 1979-80, exec. coun. 1980-83, named Outstanding Mem. 1981-82, Outstanding Com. Chmn. 1977), Fla. State U. Coll. Law Alumni Assn. (bd. dirs. 1975-78, pres. 1979), Def. Rsch. Inst. (state chair 1994), Phi Delta Phi. Republican. Federal civil litigation, State civil litigation, Professional liability, General civil litigation, Insurance. Office: Motes & Carr PO Box 149205 Orlando FL 32802-9205 Fax: 407-897-6949. E-mail: carl@moteslaw.com.

MOTHERWAY, NICHOLAS J. lawyer; b. Chgo., Jan. 21, 1940; s. Daniel Lawrence and Margaret Ann Motherway; m. Kathleen Elizabeth Butler, Dec. 23, 1967; children: Daniel, Nicholas, Carolyn, Brian. BSc, Loyola U., 1961; JD, DePaul U., 1965. Bar: Ill. 1965, U.S. Dist. Ct. (no. dist.) Ill. 1965, U.S. Ct. Appeals (7th cir.) 1996. Asst. states atty. Cook County States Atty., Chgo., 1966—73; assoc. Philip H. Corboy, Chgo., 1973—82; prin. Motherway and Napleton, Chgo., 1982—. Lt. USAR, 1961—67. Fellow: Am. Coll. Trial Lawyers; mem.: ATLA (bd. govs. 1990—95), Am. Bd. Trial Adv. (pres. Ill. chpt. 1995—96, nat. bd. dirs. 1996—). Personal injury (including property damage), Product liability, Professional liability. Office: Motherway and Napleton 100 W Monroe St Chicago IL 60603

MOTLEY, CONSTANCE BAKER (MRS. JOEL WILSON MOTLEY), federal judge, former city official; b. New Haven, Sept. 14, 1921; d. Willoughby Alva and Rachel (Huggins) Baker; m. Joel Wilson Motley, Aug. 18, 1946; 1 son, Joel Wilson, III. AB, NYU, 1943; LLB, Columbia U., 1946. Bar: N.Y. 1948. Mem. Legal Def. and Ednl. Fund, NAACP, 1945-65; mem. N.Y. State Senate, 1964-65; pres. Manhattan Borough, 1965-66; U.S. dist. judge So. Dist. N.Y., 1966-82, chief judge, 1982-86, sr. judge, 1986—. Author: Equal Justice Under Law, 1998. Mem. N.Y. State Adv. Council Employment and Unemployment Ins., 1958-64. Mem. Assn. Bar City N.Y. Office: US Dist Ct US Courthouse 500 Pearl St New York NY 10007-1316 E-mail: constance_motley@nysd.uscourts.gov.

MOTT, JOHN C. judge; b. LeRoy Twp., Pa., May 23, 1955; s. Charles S. and H. Grace (Spencer) M.; m. Brenda K. Bailey, Aug. 19, 1972; children: Reeve A., Nicholas H., Adam R. BA with honors, Mansfield U., Pa., 1977; JD, Dickinson Sch. of Law, Carlisle, Pa., 1980. Bar: Pa. 1980, U.S. Dist. Ct. (mid. dist.) Pa. 1983. Assoc. firm Vineski, Brann, Williams and Caldwell, Troy and Canton, Pa., 1980-83; ptnr. firm Vineski, Brann, Williams, Caldwell and Mott, Troy and Canton, 1984-87; judge Ct. of Common Pleas Bradford County, Towanda, Pa., 1988—. Committeeman Bradford County Republican Com., Pa., 1982-87, chmn., 1984-85; deacon Canton Ch. of Christ (Disciples), 1982-88, chmn. steward-ship com. 1983-84, elder 1989—; Bradford County crusade chmn. Am. Cancer Soc., Sayre, Pa., 1983-84; dir. N.Y.-Pa. Health System Agy., Binghamton, N.Y., 1984-85, Troy Community Hosp., Inc., 1983-85. Mem. Bradford County Bar Assn. (sec.-treas. 1980-82), Pa. Bar Assn., Pa. Conf. State Trial Judges (jud. ethics com., exec. com.), Masons, Lions (pres. 1983-84), Elks. Office: Bradford County Courthouse Main St Towanda PA 18848

MOTZ, DIANA GRIBBON, federal judge; b. Washington, July 15, 1943; d. Daniel McNamara and Jane (Retzler) Gribbon; m. John Frederick Motz, Sept. 20, 1968; children: Catherine Jane, Daniel Gribbon. BA, Vassar Coll., 1965; LLB, U. Va., 1968. Bar: U.S. Dist. Ct. Md. 1969, U.S. Ct. Appeals (4th cir.) 1969, U.S. Supreme Ct. 1980. Assoc. Piper & Marbury, Balt., 1968—71; asst. atty. gen. State of Md., Balt., 1972—81, chief of litigation, 1981—86; ptnr. Frank, Bernstein, Conaway & Goldman, Balt., 1986—91; judge Md. Ct. of Special Appeals, 1991—94, U.S. Ct. Appeals (4th Cir.), 1994—. Mem.: ABA, Fed. Cts. Study Com., Lawyers Round Table, Md. Bar Found., Am. Bar Found., Am. Law Inst., Balt. City Bar Assn. (exec. com. 1988), Md. Bar Assn., Wranglers Law Club. Roman Catholic. Office: 920 US Courthouse 101 W Lombard St Ste 920 Baltimore MD 21201-2611

MOTZ, JOHN FREDERICK, federal judge; b. Balt., Dec. 30, 1942; s. John Eldered and Catherine (Grauel) M.; m. Diana Jane Gribbon, Sept. 20, 1968; children: Catherine Jane, Daniel Gribbon AB, Wesleyan U., Conn., 1964; LLB, U. Va., 1967. Bar: Md. 1967, U.S. Ct. Appeals (4th cir.) 1968, U.S. Dist. Ct. Md. 1968. Law clk. to Hon. Harrison L. Winter U.S. Ct. Appeals (4th cir.), 1967-68; Assoc. Venable, Baetjer & Howard, Balt., 1968-69; asst. U.S. atty. U.S. Atty.'s Office, Balt., 1969-71; assoc. Venable, Baetjer & Howard, Balt., 1971-75, ptnr., 1976-81; U.S. atty. U.S. Atty.'s Office, Balt., 1981-85; judge U.S. Dist. Ct. Md., Balt., 1985—, chief judge, 1994—2001. Trustees Friends Sch., Balt., 1970-77, 1981-88, Sheppard Pratt Hosp., 1987-97, 99—. Mem.: ABA, Am. Coll. Trial Lawyers (mem. bd. editors. Manual of Complex Litigation (4th), mem. Judicial Panel on Multidist. Litigation), Am. Law Inst., Am. Bar Found., Md. State Bar Assn. Republican. Mem. Soc. Of Friends. Office: US Dist Ct 101 W Lombard St Rm 510 Baltimore MD 21201-2605

MOUGHAN, PETER RICHARD, JR., lawyer; b. Phila., July 29, 1951; s. Peter Richard and Catherine L. (Gavin) M.; m. Janice Billick, Aug. 3, 1974 (div. Aug. 2000); children: Peter Richard III, Gavin Patrick, Jacob Daniel. BA, Wheeling Coll., 1973; MS, Gonzaga U., 1975, MBA, JD, Gonzaga U., 1977. Bar: Pa. 1973, N.Mex. 1980. Legal rschr. Am. Law Inst.-ABA, Phila., 1977-78; claim rep. Allstate Ins., Phila., 1978-79; assoc. Larry D. Beall, P.A., Albuquerque, 1979-81; pvt. practice law Moughan Law Firm , Albuquerque, 1981—. Mem.: K.C., Albuquerque Aardvarks Rugby Football Club (chmn. 1980—84), Ancient Order of Hibernians (Albuquerque) (pres. 1984—85, 1992—), Phi Alpha Delta. Commercial, contracts (including sales of goods; commercial financing), Personal injury (including property damage), Probate (including wills, trusts). Office: PO Box 715 Albuquerque NM 87103-0715 Home: 623 San Pedro Dr SE Albuquerque NM 87108 E-mail: moughan2@lawyer.com., moughan2@yahoo.com.

MOULDS, JOHN F. federal judge; m. Elizabeth Fry, Aug. 29, 1964; children: Donald B., Gerald B. Student, Stanford U., 1955-58; BA with honors, Calif. State U., Sacramento, 1960; JD, U. Calif, Berkeley, 1963. Bar: U.S. Supreme Ct., U.S. Dist. Ct. (no. dist.) Calif., U.S. Dist. Ct. (ea. dist.) Calif. 1968, U.S. Ct. Claims 1982, U.S. Ct. Appeals (9th cir.) 1967, Calif. Rsch. analyst Calif. State Senate Fact-Finding Com. on Edn., 1960-61; adminstrv. asst. Senator Albert S. Rodda, Calif., 1961-63; staff atty. Calif. Rural Legal Assistance, Marysville, 1966-68, dir. atty. Marysville field office and Sacramento legis. adv. office, 1968-69; staff atty. Sacramento Legal Aid, 1968-69; ptnr. Blackmon, Isenberg & Moulds, 1969-85, Isenberg, Moulds & Hemmer, 1985; magistrate judge U.S. Dist. Ct. (ea. dist.) Calif., 1985—, chief magistrate jduge, 1988-97. Moot ct. and trial practice judge U. Calif. Davis Law Sch., 1975—, U. of Pacific McGeorge Coll. Law, 1985—; part-time U.S. magistrate judge U.S. Dist. Ct. (ea. dist.) Calif., 1983-85; mem. 9th Cir. Capital Case Com., 1992—, U.S. Jud. Conf. Com. on the Magistrate Judge Sys., 1992—, Adv. Com. to the Magistrate Judges' Divsn. Adminstv. Office of U.S. Jud. Conf., 1989—. Author: (with others) Review of California Code Legislation, 1965, Welfare Recipients' Handbook, 1967; editor: Ninth Circuit Capital Punishment Handbook, 1991. Atty. Sacramento Singlemen's Self-Help Ctr., 1969-74; active Sacramento Human Relations Commn., 1969-75, chair, 1974-75; active community support orgn. U. Calif. at Davis Law Sch., 1971—; mem., atty. Sacramento Community Coalition for Media Change, 1972-75; bd. dirs. Sacramento Country Day Sch., 1982-90, Sacramento Pub. Libr. Found., 1985-87; active various polit. orgns. and campaigns, 1960-82. Mem. ABA, Fed. Bar Assn., Nat. Coun. Magistrates (cir. dir. 1986-88, treas. 1988-89, 2d v.p. 1989-90, 1st v.p. 1990-91), Fed. Magistrate Judges Assn. (pres.-elect 1991, pres. 1992-93), Calif. State-Fed. Jud. Coun. Conf. (panelist capital habeas corpus litigation 1992), Fed. Jud. Ctr. Training Conf. for U.S. Magistrate Judges (panel leader 1993), Milton L. Schwartz Inns of Ct. Office: 8240 US Courthouse 501 First St 16th Fl Ste 1640 Sacramento CA 95814-7300

MOULTON, HUGH GEOFFREY, lawyer, retired business executive; b. Boston, Sept. 18, 1933; s. Robert Selden and Florence (Bracq) M.; m. Catherine Anne Clark, Mar. 24, 1956; children: H. Geoffrey, Cynthia C. Moulton Bassett. BA, Amherst Coll., 1955; LL.B., Yale U., 1958; postgrad. Advanced Mgmt. Program, Harvard U., 1984. Bar: Pa. 1959. Assoc. Montgomery, McCracken, Walker-Rhoads, Phila., 1958-66, ptnr., 1967-69; v.p., counsel Dolly Madison Industries, Inc., Phila., 1969-70; sec. Alco Std. Corp., Valley Forge, Pa., 1970-72, v.p. law, 1973-79, v.p., sec., gen. counsel, 1979-83, sr. v.p., gen. counsel, 1983-92, exec. v.p., chief adminstrv. officer, gen. counsel, 1992-94; exec. v.p. Alco Std. Corp. now IKON Office Solutions Inc., Valley Forge, Pa., 1994-96, Unisource Worldwide, Inc., 1997-99; ret., 1999. Pres. Wissahickon Valley Watershed Assn., Ambler, Pa., 1975-78, treas., 1978—; mem. Pa. Coun. for Econ. Edn., bd. dirs., 1985-95; trustee Arcadia U., 1991—, chair, 1998-02; Montgomery Co. Lands Trust (trustee 2000—), Whitemarsh Found. (trustee, pres. 2002—). Mem. Am. Corp. Counsel Assn. (bd. dirs. Delaware Valley chpt. 1984-88, pres. 1986-87), Nature Conservancy (trustee Pa. chpt. 1991—, chmn. 1993-97), Sunnybrook Golf Club (Plymouth Meeting, Pa.), Cape Cod Nat. Golf Club (Harwich, Mass.), Lemon Bay Golf Club (Englewood, Fla.). Home: 300 Williams Rd Fort Washington PA 19034-2015 E-mail: hgmoulton@att.net.

MOUTZOURIDOU, VICTORIA G. lawyer; b. Athens, Greece, May 27, 1972; d. George Moutzourides and Denise Moutzouridou. Diploma, Athens Coll., 1990; Degree, Athens U., 1995. Bar: Athens 1995. Jr. assoc. Spyropoulos Law Office, Athens, 1995—97, assoc., 1997—99; sr. assoc. Kyriakides-Georgopoulos Law Firm, Athens, 1999—2002, Dryllerakis & Assocs. Law Firm, Athens, 2002—. Avocations: internet, writing, collections. Civil rights, Computer, Product liability. Office: Dryllerakis & Assocs Law Firm 25 Voukourestiou St 106 71 Athens Greece

MOW, ROBERT HENRY, JR., lawyer; b. Cape Girardeau, Mo., Dec. 10, 1938; s. Robert H. Sr. and Ann Elise (Beck) M.; m. Jody K. Boggs, Aug. 29, 1987; children: Robert M., Brynn A., W. Brett, Rebecca M., W. Kirk, Allison M. Student, Westminster Coll., 1956-57; AB with distinction, U. Mo., 1960; LLB magna cum laude, So. Meth. U., 1963. Bar: Tex. 1963, U.S. Dist. Ct. (no. dist.) Tex. 1965, U.S. Dist. Ct. (so. dist.) Tex. 1969, U.S. Dist. Ct. (ea. and we. dists.) Tex. 1976, U.S. Ct. Claims 1973, U.S. Ct. Appeals (5th cir.) 1972, U.S. Ct. Appeals (11th cir.) 1981, U.S. Ct. Appeals (fed. cir.) 1994, U.S. Supreme Ct. 1978. Assoc. Carrington, Johnson & Stephens, Dallas, 1963-69; ptnr. Carrington, Coleman, Sloman & Blumenthal, Dallas, 1970-85, Hughes & Luce, LLP, Dallas, 1985, mng. ptnr., 2003—. Editor-in-chief Southwestern Law Jour., 1962-63. Trustee First Bapt. Acad., chair, 1999-2002. Served to 1st lt. U.S. Army, 1963-65. Fellow Am. Coll. Trial Lawyers; mem. Dallas Assn. Def. Counsel (chmn. 1976-77), Tex. Assn. Def. Counsel (v.p. 1981-82), Am. Bd. Trial Advocates (pres. Dallas chpt. 1983-84). Republican. Baptist. Federal civil litigation, State civil litigation, Professional liability. Office: Hughes & Luce LLP 1717 Main St Ste 2800 Dallas TX 75201-4685 E-mail: mowb@hughesluce.com.

MOWELL, GEORGE MITCHELL, lawyer; b. Balt., July 31, 1951; s. George Robert and Polly (Sattler) M.; m. Patricia Edith Forbes, Sept. 23, 1978; children: Rachel Elizabeth, George Robert. BA, Washington Coll., Chestertown, Md., 1973; JD, U. Balt., 1977. Bar: Md. 1978, U.S. Dist. Ct. Md. 1981, U.S. Bankruptcy Ct. 1982. Claims authorizer Social Security Adminstrn., Balt., 1973-79; law clk. to presiding justice Kent County Cir. Ct., Chestertown, 1979-81; ptnr. Boyer & Mowell, Chestertown, 1981-87, Mowell, Nunn & Wadkorsky, Chestertown, 1987-98, Wadkovsky & Mowell, Chestertown, 1998—. Atty. Kent County Planning Commn., Chestertown, 1982—, Betterton Planning Commn., 1987—, Town of Rock Hall, 1987—; panel atty Public Defenders Office, 1981—, Md. Vol. Lawyers, 1981—; mem. adv. bd. Farmers Bank of Md., 1994-99. Bd. dirs. Kent County Heart Assn., Chestertown, 1983-84; atty. Galena Planning Commn., 1997—. Mem. ABA, Md. Bar Assn. (com. on laws 1984-87), Kent County Bar Assn. (sec. 1985-86, treas. 1987-88, v.p. 1988-89, pres. 1990-93), Balt. Bar Assn., Md. Trial Lawyers Assn., Elks. Democrat. Episcopalian. Family and matrimonial, General practice, Land use and zoning (including planning). Home: 140 Deer Field Dr Chestertown MD 21620-2482 Office: Wadkovsky & Mowell 107 Court St Chestertown MD 21620-1507 Fax: 410-778-9325.

MOWRIS, GERALD WILLIAM, lawyer; b. Grand Forks, N.D., Oct. 2, 1948; s. Robert Earl and Lillian Vivian (Zavoral) M.; m. Alice Hulick, Apr. 2, 1970 (div.); m. Susan Leah Sachtjen; children: Danae E., Jeffrey W. Student, Mich. State U., 1966-67; JD, U. Wis., 1973. Bar: Wis. 1973, U.S. Dist. Ct. (we. dist.) Wis. 1973, U.S. Ct. Appeals (7th cir.) 1984, U.S. Ct. Mil. Appeals 1984. Asst. dist. atty. Dane County Dist. Atty.'s Office, Madison, 1973-79; ptnr. Pellino, Rosen, Mowris & Kirkhuff, Madison, 1979—. Bd. dirs. YMCA of Met. Madison, 1991-94; mem. ARC Cmty. Svcs., Madison, 1980—, past pres. Maj. USAR, 1970-92. Mem. State Bar Wis. (co-chmn. com. for local bar leaders 1995-97, bd. govs. 1999-2000, pres. 2001-02), Dane County Bar Assn. (pres. 1994-95), Wis. Assn. Criminal Def. Lawyers (pres. 1995-96), Nat. Assn. Criminal Def. Lawyers, Wis. Acad. Trial Lawyers, Nat. Ski Patrol (patroller 1967—). Avocations: skiing, fishing, hiking, canoeing, golf. Criminal, Family and matrimonial, Personal injury (including property damage). Office: Pellino Rosen Mowris & Kirkhoff SC 131 W Wilson St Ste 1201 Madison WI 53703-3243 Fax: 608-255-4345. E-mail: gmowris@prmk.com.

MOY, MARY ANASTASIA, lawyer; b. Melrose Park, Ill., Aug. 13, 1964; d. Kenneth Kwok and Chuk Ying (Tsang) M. BA cum laude, Wellesley Coll., 1986; JD, U. Pa., 1989. Bar: N.Y. 1991, D.C. 1993, U.S. Dist. Ct. (so. and ea. dists.) N.Y. 1992. Law clk. to Hon. Glenn E. Mencer U.S. Dist. Ct. (we. dist.), Pitts., 1989-90; assoc. Thelen, Reid & Priest, N.Y.C., 1990—93, Ladas & Parry, N.Y.C., 1993—98, 1999—2000, ptnr., 2001—, Bristol-Myers Squibb Co., N.Y.C., 2000—01. Assoc. counsel N.Y. State Gov.'s Jud. Screening Com. for 1st Jud. Dept., 1991-92. Articles editor U. Pa. Jour. of Internat. Bus. Law, 1988-89. Mem. Asian Am. Bar Assn. of N.Y., Internat. Trademark Assn. Republican. Avocations: opera, music, dance, travel. Federal civil litigation, Trademark and copyright. Office: Bristol-Myers Squibb Co 345 Park Ave New York NY 10154

MOYA, OLGA LYDIA, law educator; b. Weslaco, Tex., Dec. 27, 1959; d. Leonel V. and Genoveva (Tamez) M.; children: Leanessa Geneva Byrd, Taylor Moya Byrd. BA, U. Tex., 1981, JD, 1984. Bar: Tex. 1984. Legis. atty. Tex. Ho. of Reps., Austin, 1985; atty. Tex. Dept. Agr., Austin, 1985-90; asst. regional counsel U.S. EPA, Dallas, 1990-91; from asst. prof. to assoc. prof. South Tex. Coll. of Law, Houston, 1992-97; prof. law South Tex. Coll. Law, Houston, 1997—. Author: (with Andrew L. Fono) Federal Environmental Law: The User's Guide, 1997, 2d edit., 2001. Bd. dirs. Hermann Children's Hosp., Houston, 1993-97; mem. Leadership Tex., Austin, 1991—; bd. trustees Meml. Hermann Healthcare Sys. Found., 1997-99; bd. dirs. Tex. Clean Water Coun., Austin, 1992, Met. Transit Authority of Harris County, 1999—; U.S. del. to UN Conf. on the Environ. for Latin Am. and the Caribbean, San Juan, P.R., 1995. Recipient Nat. Top 12 Hispanics in Law, Miller Brewing Co., 1996; Vol. of Yr. award George H. Hermann Soc., 1995, Hispanic Law Prof. of Yr. Hispanic Nat. Bar Assn., 1995. Mem. ABA (environ. law sect.), Hispanic Bar Assn. (bd. dirs. 1992—, Excellence award 1995, 96), Mex.-Am. Bar Assn. Office: South Tex Coll of Law 1303 San Jacinto St Houston TX 77002-7013

MOYA, PATRICK ROBERT, lawyer; b. Belen, N.Mex., Nov. 7, 1944; s. Adelicio E. and Eva (Sanchez) Moya; m. Sara Dreier, May 30, 1966; children: Jeremy Brill, Joshua Dreier. AB, Princeton U., 1966; JD, Stanford U., 1969. Bar: Calif. 1970, Ariz. 1970, D.C. 1970, U.S. Dist. Ct. (no. dist.) Calif. 1970, U.S. Ct. Claims 1970, U.S. Tax Ct. 1970, U.S. Ct. Appeals (D.C. cir.) 1970, U.S. Supreme Ct. 1973. Assoc. Lewis and Roca, Phoenix, 1969—73, ptnr., 1973—83; sr. ptnr. Moya, Bailey, Bowers & Jones, P.C., Phoenix, 1983—84; ptnr., mem. nat. exec. com. Gaston & Snow, Phoenix, 1985—91; ptnr. Quarles & Brady LLP, Phoenix, 1991—2003, mem. nat. exec. com., 2000—02; exec. v.p., gen. counsel, sec. Insight Enterprises, Inc., Tempe, Ariz., 2002—. Instr. sch. of law Ariz. State U., 1972; bd. dirs. homebid.com, inc., 1999-2000; BIGE Real Estate, Inc., 2000-. Mem. Paradise Valley Bd. Adjustment, 1976-80, chmn., 1978-80; mem. Paradise Valley Town Coun., 1980-82; bd. dirs. Phoenix Men's Arts Coun., 1973-81, pres., 1979-80; bd. dirs. The Silent Witness, Inc., 1979-84, pres., 1981-83; bd. dirs. Enterprise Network, Inc., 1989-94, pres., 1991-92; bd. dirs. Phoenix Little Theatre, 1973-75, Interfaith Counseling Svc., 1973-75; precinct committeeman Phoenix Rep. Com., 1975-77; dep. voter registrar Maricopa County, 1975-76; mem. exec. bd. dirs. Gov.'s Strategic Partnership for Econ. Devel.; pres. GSPED, Inc.; mem. of Steering Com. for Sonora-Ariz. Joint Econ. Plan; mem. Gov.'s Adv. Com., Ariz. and Mex., Ariz. Corp. Commn. Stock Exch. Adv. Coun., Ariz. Town Hall. Mem. ABA, Nat. Hispanic Bar Assn., Los Abogados Hispanic Lawyers Assn., Nat. Assn. Bond Lawyers, Ariz. Bar Assn., Maricopa County Bar Assn., Paradise Valley Country Club, Univ. Club. Corporate, general, Mergers and acquisitions, Securities. Office: Insight Enterprises Inc 1305 W Auto Dr Tempe AZ 85284

MOYE, JOHN EDWARD, lawyer; b. Deadwood, S.D., Aug. 15, 1944; s. Francis Joseph and Margaret C. (Roberts) M.; children: Kelly M., Mary S., Megan J. BBA, U. Notre Dame, 1965; JD with distinction, Cornell U., 1968; LLD, U. Denver, 1999. Bar: N.Y. 1968, Colo. 1971. Prof. law U. Denver, 1972-78, assoc. dean Coll. Law, 1974-78; prof. law So. Meth. U., Dallas, 1973; ptnr. Moye, Giles, O'Keefe, Vermeire & Gorrell, Denver, 1976—. Lectr. Harcourt Brace Jovanovich, Chgo., 1972-95, Profl. Edn. Group, Minnetonka, Minn., 1982-95, West Profl. Tng. Program, 1995-98; chmn. Bd. Law Examiners, Denver, 1988-92. Chmn. Denver Urban Renewal Authority, 1988-93, Colo. Hist. Found., Denver, 1987—; pres. Downtown Denver, Inc., 1986-88; mem. Consumer Credit Commn., 1985-99; chmn. Stapleton Devel. Corp., 1995—; bd. dirs. Denver Bot. Gardens, 1996—, Colo. Pub. Radio, 1998-99. Named Prof. of Yr., U. Denver, 1972-74, 76-78, Outstanding Faculty Mem., 1997. Fellow Am. Bar Found.; mem. ABA, Colo. Bar Assn. (chmn. corp., banking and bus. sect. 1982-84, pres. 2002, Young Lawyer of Yr. award 1980), N.Y. State Bar Assn., Denver Bar Assn. (Young Lawyer of Yr. award 1980), Law Club (pres. 1982-84). Republican. Roman Catholic. Banking, Commercial, contracts (including sales of goods; commercial financing), Corporate, general. Office: 1225 17th St Denver CO 80202-5534

MOYER, CRAIG ALAN, lawyer; b. Bethlehem, Pa., Oct. 17, 1955; s. Charles Alvin and Doris Mae (Schantz) M.; m. Candace Darrow Brigham, May 3, 1986; 1 stepchild, Jason; 1 child, Chelsea A. BA, U. So. Calif., 1977; JD, U. Calif., L.A., 1980. Bar: Calif. 1980, U.S. Dist. Ct. (cen. dist.) Calif. 1980. Assoc. Nossaman, Krueger et al, L.A., 1980-83, Finley, Kumble et al, Beverly Hills, Calif., 1983-85; ptnr. Demetriou, Del Guercio, Springer & Moyer, L.A., 1985—, Manatt, Phelps, & Phillips, LLP, L.A. Instr. Air Resources Bd. Symposium, Sacramento, 1985—, U. Calif., Santa Barbara, 1989—; lectr. Hazmat Conf., Long Beach, Calif., 1986—, Pacific Automotive Show, Reno, Nev., 1989—; lectr. hazardous materials, environ. law UCLA; lectr. environ. law U. Calif., Santa Barbara; lectr. hazardous materials regulatory framework U. Calif., Santa Barbara. Co-author: Hazard Communication Handbook: A Right to Know Compliance Guide, 1990, Clean Air Act Handbook, 1991, Brownfields: A Practical Guide to the Cleanup, Transfer and Redevelopment of Contaminated Property, 1997; contbr. articles to profl. jours. Pres. Calif. Pub. Interest Rsch. Group, L.A., 1978-80. Mem. ABA (natural resources sect.), Calif. Bar Assn., L.A. County Bar Assn. (environ. law sect., chmn. legis. rev. com., mem. exec. com.), Tau Kappa Epsilon (pres. L.A. chpt. 1975-76, Outstanding Alumnus 1983). Republican. Avocation: bicycling. Oil, gas, and mineral, Environmental. Fax: 310-312-4224. E-mail: cmoyer@manatt.com.

MOYER, HOMER EDWARD, JR., lawyer; b. Atlanta, Nov. 20, 1942; s. Homer Edward and Mildred Joye (Wilkerson) M.; m. Beret Butter, July 6, 1974; children: Bronwen, Homer, Eli, Kaia Joye. BA, Emory U., 1964; LLB, Yale Law Sch., 1967. Bar: Ga. 1967, D.C. 1973. Assoc. Covington & Burling, Washington, 1973-76; from dep. gen. counsel to gen. counsel U.S. Dept. of Commerce, Washington, 1976-81; ptnr. Miller & Chevalier, Washington, 1981—. Author: The R.A.T. (Real-World Aptitude Test): Preparing Yourself for Leaving Home, 2001; co-author: Export Controls as Instruments of Foreign Policy, 1988, Justice and the Military, 1972. Bd. visitors Emory U., Atlanta, 1987-91; chmn. Friends of CEELI Inst. Mem. ABA (chmn. internat. law and practice sect. 1990-91, chmn. trade com. 1984-86, chmn. Cen. and East European Law Initiative 1990-2002, chmn. Friends of the CEELI Inst., chmn. Moscow conf. on law and bilateral econ. rels. 1990), Coun. on Fgn. Rels. Episcopalian. Administrative and regulatory, Private international, Public international. Office: Miller & Chevalier 655 15th St NW Ste 900 Washington DC 20005-5799

MOYER, MICHAEL EDWARD, lawyer; b. Allentown, Pa., Apr. 3, 1952; s. Howard Charles and Elizabeth (Sherer) M.; 1 child, Kyle. BA, Temple U., 1974, JD, 1977. Bar: Pa. 1977, U.S. Dist. Ct. (ea. dist.) Pa. 1977, U.S. Dist. Ct. (mid. dist.) Pa. 1998, U.S. Ct. Appeals (3d cir.) 1991, U.S. Supreme Ct. 1986. Asst. dist. atty. Lehigh County Dist. Atty., Allentown, 1977-81, 84-88; asst. pub. defender Lehigh County Pub. Defender, Allentown, 1981-84; pvt. practice Allentown, 1981—. Mem. Bar Assn. of Lehigh County (pres. 1997), Nat. Assn. Criminal Def. Lawyers, Pa. Criminal Def. Attys., Pa. Bar Assn., Am. Inn Ct. Criminal. Office: 523 W Linden St Allentown PA 18101-1415

MOYER, THOMAS J. state supreme court chief justice; b. Sandusky, Ohio, Apr. 18, 1939; s. Clarence and Idamae (Hessler) M.; m. Mary Francis Moyer, Dec. 15, 1984; 1 child, Drew; stepchildren: Anne, Jack, Alaine, Elizabeth. BA, Ohio State U., 1961, JD, 1964. Asst. atty. gen. State of Ohio, Columbus, 1964-66; pvt. practice law Columbus, 1966-69; dep. asst. Office Gov. State of Ohio, Columbus, 1969-71, exec. asst., 1975-79; assoc. Crabbe, Brown, Jones, Potts & Schmidt, Columbus, 1972-75; judge U.S. Ct. Appeals (10th cir.), Columbus, 1979-86; chief justice Ohio Supreme Ct., Columbus, 1987—. Sec. bd. trustees Franklin U., Columbus, 1986-87; trustee Univ. Club, Columbus, 1986; mem. nat. council adv. com. Ohio State U. Coll. Law, Columbus. Recipient Award of Merit, Ohio Legal Ctr. Inst.; named Outstanding Young Man of Columbus, Columbus Jaycees, 1969. Mem. Ohio State Bar Assn. (exec. com., council dels.), Columbus Bar Assn. (pres. 1980-81), Critchon Club, Columbus Maennerchor Club. Republican. Avocations: sailing, tennis. Office: Ohio Supreme Ct 30 E Broad St Fl 3 Columbus OH 43215*

MOYLAN, DOUGLAS, state attorney general; b. Guam; m. Deborah Moylan. B in Bus. Admin., U. Notre Dame, 1988; JD, Santa Clara U., 1991. Bar: Guam Bar Admissions 92, Calif. Bar Admissions 1992, cert.: D.C. Ct. of Appeals 1993. Law clk. Judge Alberto C. Lamenora Superior Ct. Guam, 1991, staff atty., 1991—93; atty. with Robert Torres P.C. Legis. Counsel, 24th, 25th, 26th Guam Legis., 1993—96; small claims ct. referee Superior Ct. Guam, 1995—97; pvt. practice Moylan & Van de Veld Law Offices, 2002; atty. gen., 2002—. Bd. mem. Guam Election Commission, 1996—2000. Bd. mem. Guam's Election Commn. Bd. Office: Judicial Ctr Bldg Ste 2-200E 120 W OBrien Dr Hagatna GU 96910

MOYLAN, JAMES HAROLD, lawyer; b. Omaha, Oct. 17, 1930; s. Harold Thomas and Margaret Ellen (Emery) M.; m. Lila Marie Fitzgerald, July 9, 1960; children: James P., Michael T., Patrick W., Jean M., Mary M., Molly C. BS, Creighton U., 1952, JD, 1957. Bar: Nebr. 1957, Iowa 1957, U.S. Dist. Ct. Nebr. 1957, U.S. Dist. Ct. (so. dist.) Iowa 1957. Assoc. Richling, Shrout & Brown, Omaha, 1957-60; dep. atty. Douglas County, Omaha, 1960-67; ptnr. Garvey, Nye, Crawford, Kirchner & Moylan, Omaha, 1967-87, Fellman, Moylan, Omaha, 1987—. Chmn. Douglas County Dem. Com., 1966-68; mem. Christ and King Sch. Bd., Omaha, 1967-71, Archbishop's Com. on Ednl. Devel., Omaha, 1975—; assoc. bd. regents St. Mary's Coll., Omaha, 1968-72; bd. regents U. Nebr., 1971-89. Mem. Nebr. Bar Assn. (exec. coun. 1975-81), Iowa Bar ASsn., Nat. Lawyers Assn., Sokol Club, Regency Lake and Tennis Club, Westroads Racquet Club, Am. Legion. Avocation: politics. Corporate, general, Legislative, Probate (including wills, trusts). Home: 2245 S 86th St Omaha NE 68124-2131 Office: Fellman Moylan Natvig Wilke & Wik 100 Continental Bldg Omaha NE 68102 E-mail: jameshmoylan@aol.com.

MOYLAN, JAMES JOSEPH, lawyer; b. Forest Hills, N.Y., Feb. 3, 1948; s. James Gerard and Jessie Cora (Geary) M.; m. Barbara Chesrow, Aug. 29, 1970; children: James, C., Joseph O., Alicia G. BSBA, U. Denver, 1969, JD, 1971. Bar: Colo. 1972, D.C. 1972, Ill. 1975, U.S. Dist. Ct. Colo. 1972, U.S. Supreme Ct. 1975. Trial atty. SEC, Washington, 1972-75; assoc. gen. counsel Chgo. Bd. Options Exch., Ill., 1975-77; assoc. Abramson & Fox, Chgo., 1977-80; ptnr. Bowen, Knepper & Moylan Ltd., Chgo., 1980-82, Moylan & Early, Ltd., Chgo., 1983-84; prin. James J. Moylan and Assocs., Ltd., Chgo., 1984-95; ptnr. Arnstein & Lehr, Chgo., 1995-2000, Tressler, Soderstrom, Maloney & Priess, Chgo., 2000—. Adj. prof. law IIT Chgo. Kent Coll. Law, 1976—; former pub. dir. MidAm. Commodity Exch. divsn. Chgo. Bd. Trade, Chgo. Contbr. articles to profl. jours. Mem.: ABA (sect. corp., banking and bus. law, sect. litigation), D.C. Bar Assn., Chgo. Bar Assn., Ill. State Bar Assn. (sect. coun. mem.), Theta Chi (grand chpt. 1993—2000, funds bd. 2000—). Republican. Roman Catholic. Corporate, general, Securities, Commodities.

MOYNIHAN, JOHN BIGNELL, retired lawyer; b. N.Y.C., July 25, 1933; s. Jerome J. and Stephanie (Bignell) M.; m. Odilia Marie Jacques, Nov. 13, 1965; children: Blair, Dana. BS, Fordham U., 1955; JD, St. John's U., N.Y.C., 1958. Bar: Tex. 1961, U.S. Supreme Ct. 1965, U.S. Dist. Ct. (we. dist.) Tex. 1968, U.S. Ct. Appeals (5th cir.) 1973. Sole practice, Brownsville, Tex., 1961-62; asst. city atty. City of San Antonio, 1962-63; sole practice San Antonio, 1963-65; estate tax atty. IRS, San Antonio, 1965-73; dist. counsel EEOC, San Antonio, 1974-79; asst. U.S. atty. Office U.S. Atty., San Antonio, 1980-87, sr. litigation counsel, 1987-94; sole practice San Antonio, 1995-98; ret., 1998. Chmn. reform and renewal com., San Antonio Roman Cath. Archdiocese, 1968. Served with U.S. Army, 1958-60; lt. col. USAFR (ret.), 1986. Mem. San Antonio Bar Assn. (chmn. state and nat. legis. com. 1972-73, Meritorious Svc. award 1968), Fed. Bar Assn. (bd. dirs. San Antonio chpt. 1983—, pres. elect 1986, pres. 1987), KC (pres. 1967). Civil rights, Federal civil litigation, Labor (including EEOC, Fair Labor Standards Act, labor-management relations, NLRB, OSHA). Home: 11011 Whispering Wind St San Antonio TX 78230-3746 E-mail: djmoynihan@aol.com.

MRACHEK, LORIN LOUIS, lawyer; b. Fairmont, Minn., Jan. 5, 1946; s. Louis L. and Kathleen (Loring) M.; m. Elizabeth Moss, Aug. 31, 1968; children: Kathleen Elizabeth, Louis Moss. BA with honors, Fla. State U., 1968; MBA, JD, Columbia U., 1974. Bar: Fla. 1974, Va. 1977, U.S. Ct. Mil. Appeals 1977, U.S. Supreme Ct. 1978; cert. in civil trial law and bus. litigation Fla. Bar Bd. Certification; cert. in bus. bankruptcy law Am. Bd. Bankruptcy Certification; cert. in civil trial advocacy Nat. Bd. Trial Advocacy. Commd. 2d lt. USMC, 1969, advanced through grades to capt., 1974, chief def. counsel Marine Corps. Recruit Depoit, 1975-77, resigned, 1977; spl. asst. to gen. counsel U.S. Ry. Assn., Washington, 1977-78; shareholder Gunster, Yoakley, Valdes-Fauli & Stewart, P.A., West Palm Beach, Fla., 1978-2000; founding shareholder Page, Mrachek, Fitzgerald & Rose, West Palm Beach, Fla., 2000—. Mem. leadership coun. Fla. State U. Coll. Arts. and Scis. Editor-in-chief Columbia Jour. Law and Social Problems, 1973-74; contbr. articles to profl. jours. Fellow Am. Coll. Trial Attys.; mem. ABA, Am. Bankruptcy Inst., So. Fla. Bankruptcy Bar Assn. Avocations: running, tennis, golf. Bankruptcy, General civil litigation. Office: 505 S Flagler Dr Ste 600 West Palm Beach FL 33401-5941 E-mail: lmrachek@pm-law.com.

MUCCI, GARY LOUIS, lawyer; b. Buffalo, Nov. 12, 1946; s. Guy Charles and Sally Rose (Battaglia) M.; m. Carolyn Belle Taylor, May 4, 1991. BA cum laude, St. John Fisher Coll., 1968; JD, Cath. U., 1972. Bar: N.Y. 1972. Law clk. to Hon. John T. Curtin U.S. Dist. Ct., Buffalo, 1972-74; assoc. atty. Donovan Leisure Newton & Irvine, N.Y.C., 1974-75, Saperston & Day P.C., Buffalo, 1975-80, sr. ptnr., 1980—2001; ptnr. Hiscock Barclay Saperston & Day, 2001—. Chmn. bd. Buffalo Philharm. Orch., 1985-86; pres. Hospice Buffalo, 1986-87; mem. N.Y. State Coun. on the Arts, 1987-2000; chmn. Citizens Com. on Cultural Aid, Buffalo, 1992-98; trustee St. John Fisher Coll., Hardin Acad.; mem. City of Buffalo Bd. Ethics. Recipient Brotherhood award NCCJ, Buffalo, 1983; named Man of Yr. William Paca Soc., 1984. Mem. Erie County Bar Assn., N.Y. State Bar Assn. Antitrust, Corporate, general, Property, real (including real estate development, water). Home: 27 Tudor Pl Buffalo NY 14222-1615 Office: Hiscock Barclay Saperston & Day PC 3 Fountain Plz Ste 1100 Buffalo NY 14203-1486

MUCCIA, JOSEPH WILLIAM, lawyer; b. N.Y.C., May 31, 1948; s. Joseph Anthony and Charlotte (Mohring) M.; m. Margaret M. Reynolds, June 29, 1985. BA magna cum laude, Fordham U., 1970, JD, 1973. Bar: N.Y. 1974, U.S. Dist. Ct. (so. dist.) N.Y. 1974, U.S. Dist. Ct. (ea. dist.) N.Y. 1980, U.S. Ct. Appeals (2d cir.) 1974, U.S. Ct. Appeals (D.C. cir.) 1980, U.S. Supreme Ct. 1980. Assoc. Cahill Gordon & Reindel, N.Y.C., 1973-82; ptnr. Corbin Silverman & Sanseverino, N.Y.C., 1983—2001, Brown Raysman Millstein Felder & Steiner LLP, N.Y.C., 2002—. Assoc. editor Fordham Law Rev., 1972-73. Mem. ABA (litigation sect.), N.Y. County Lawyers Assn., Fed. Bar Coun., N.Y. State Bar Assn. (com. litigation sect.), Phi Beta Kappa, Pi Sigma Alpha. Federal civil litigation, State civil litigation, Securities. Office: Brown Raysman et al 900 3d Ave New York NY 10022 E-mail: jmuccia@brownraysman.com.

MUCHIN, ALLAN B. lawyer; b. Manitowoc, Wis., Jan. 10, 1936; s. Jacob and Dorothy (Biberfeld) M.; m. Elaine Cort, Jan. 28, 1960; children: Andrea Muchin Leon, Karen, Margery Muchin Goldblatt. BBA, U. Wis., Manitowoc, 1958, JD, 1961. Gen. counsel IRS, Chgo., 1961-65; assoc. Altman, Kurlander & Weiss, Chgo., 1965-68, ptnr., 1968-74; co-mng. ptnr. Katten Muchin Zavis Rosenman, Chgo., 1974-95, chmn. emeritus, 1995—. Bd. dirs. Chgo. Bulls, Chgo. White Sox, Alberto-Culver Co., Acorn Investment Trust; bd. visitors U. Wis. Law Sch.; trustee Noble St. Charter Sch. Pres. Lyric Opera Chgo., 1993—; mem. adv. com. Am. Com. for Weizmann Inst. of Sci., Chgo., 1991—. Mem. Econ. Club Chgo., Comml. Club Chgo. Avocations: travel, tennis, reading. Office: Katten Muchin Zavis Rosenman 525 W Monroe St Ste 1600 Chicago IL 60661-3693

MUCHIN, ARDEN ARCHIE, lawyer, director; b. Manitowoc, Wis., Dec. 9, 1920; s. Alfred and Ida (Golden) M.; m. Bettie Lou Barenbaum, Dec. 19, 1948; children: Ann L., Efrem B., Jay Z. BA, U. Wis., 1942, JD, 1947; IA, Harvard U. Grad. Sch. Bus. Adminstrn., 1943. Bar: Wis. 1947, U.S. Dist. Ct. (ea. dist.) Wis. 1948, U.S. Tax Ct. 1965. Pres. Muchin, Muchin & Brüce, S.C. and predecessors, Manitowoc, 1947-92; ptnr. Nash, Spindler, Dean & Grimstad, 1993—; sec. and/or dir. Foster Needle Co., Inc., Manitowoc, Foster Needle Ltd. (Eng.), Sorenson Industries, Inc., Manitowoc; sec., dir. WaterCare Corp., Water Svcs. Corp.; sec. Schwartz Mfg. Co., Heresite Protective Coatings, Inc.; sec., v.p. CUB Radio, Inc., Manitowoc; gov. State Bar Wis., 1976-80. Bd. dirs. Manitowoc United Way Inc., 1968-92; mem. Wis. adv. com. U.S. Commn. Civil Rights, 1985-89. Mem. ABA, Manitowoc County Bar Assn. (pres. 1972-73), B'nai Brith (nat. commn. anti-defamation league). Corporate, general, Estate planning. Home and Office: 1426 Arden Ln Manitowoc WI 54220-2517

MUDD, JOHN O. lawyer; b. 1943; BA, Cath. U., 1965, MA, 1966; JD, U. Mont., 1973; LLM, Columbia U., 1986; JSD of Law, 1994. Bar: Mont. 1973. Pntr. Mulroney, Delaney, Dalby & Mudd, Missoula, Mont., 1973-79; lectr. U. Mont., Missoula, 1973-74, 75-76, prof. law, dean, 1979-88; ptnr. Garlington, Lohn & Robinson, Missoula, 1988—99; sr. v.p. Providence Svcs., 2000—, also bd. dirs. Pres. Mid-Continent Assn. Law Schs., 1982—83; bd. dirs. Ascension Health. Editor: Mont. Law Rev., 1972—73. Chmn. Mont. Commn. Future of Higher Edn.; elected Dem. candidate U.S. Senate, 1994; bd. dirs. St. Patrick Hosp., 1985—90. With U.S. Army, 1967—73. Mem.: State Bar Mont., Am. Judicature Soc. (bd. dirs. 1985—89). General civil litigation, Labor (including EEOC, Fair Labor Standards Act, labor-management relations, NLRB, OSHA), Legislative.

MUECKE, CHARLES ANDREW (CARL MUECKE), former federal judge; b. N.Y.C., Feb. 20, 1918; s. Charles and Wally (Roeder) M.; m. Claire E. Vasse; children by previous marriage: Carl Marshall, Alfred Jackson, Catherine Calvert. BA, Coll. William and Mary, 1941; LL.B., U. Ariz., 1953. Bar: Ariz. 1953. Rep. AFL, 1947-50; reporter Ariz. Times, Phoenix, 1947-48; since practiced in Phoenix; with firm Parker & Muecke, 1953-59, Muecke, Dushoff & Sacks, 1960-61; U.S. atty. Dist. Ariz., 1961-64, U.S. dist. judge, 1964—97, sr. judge, 1984—97. Mem. Phoenix Planning Commn., 1955-61, chmn., 1960; chmn. Maricopa County Dem. Party, 1961-62. Maj. USMC, 1942-45, USMCR, 1945-60. Mem. Fed. Bar Assn., Ariz. Bar Assn., Maricopa Bar Assn., Dist. Judges Assn. Ninth Circuit, Phi Beta Kappa, Phi Alpha Delta, Omicron Delta Kappa.*

MUELLER, DIANE MAYNE, lawyer; b. Milw., Aug. 8, 1934; d. George and Ann (Matuszewski) Markussen; widowed; 1 child, Paul Wilhite; m. Milton W. Mueller, Jan. 1, 1990. AB, Valparaiso U., 1956; MSW, Fla. State U., 1963; JD summa cum laude, DePaul U., 1974. Bar: Ill. 1974, U.S. Dist. Ct. (no. dist.) Ill. 1974, U.S. Dist. Ct. (ea. dist.) Wis. 1977, N. Mex., 1996. Assoc. Seyfarth, Shaw, Fairweather & Geraldson, Chgo., 1974-82, ptnr., 1982-86; asst. group counsel LTV Steel Co., Cleve., 1986-93, sr. atty., 1993-95. Adj. prof. Northwestern U. Sch. Law, 1984-86. Mem. Exec. Club of Chgo. (chmn. bd. 1984-85, mem. adv. bd. 1986-96), Econ. Club Chgo., Albuquerque Petroleum Club. Corporate, general. Home: 1216 Rock Rose Rd Albuquerque NM 87122-1115

MUELLER, MARK CHRISTOPHER, lawyer; b. Dallas, June 19, 1945; s. Herman August and Hazel Deane (Hatzenbuehler) M.; m. Linda Jane Reed. BA in Econs., So. Meth. U., 1967; MBA in Acctg., 1969, JD, 1971. Bar: Tex. 1971, U.S. Dist. Ct. (no. dist.) Tex. 1974, U.S. Tax Ct. 1974; CPA, Tex. Acct. Arthur Young & Co., Dallas, 1967-68, A.E. Krutilek, Dallas, 1968-71; pvt. practice law Dallas, 1971—; assoc. L. Vance Stanton, Dallas, 1971-72. Instr. legal writing and rsch. So. Meth. U., Dallas, 1970-71, instr. legal acctg., 1975; mem. unauthorized practice of law com. Supreme Ct. Tex. Leading articles editor Southwestern Law Jour., 1970-71. Mem. NRA, Tex. Bar Assn., Tex. State Rifle Assn., Tex. Soc. CPA's, Dallas Bar Assn., SAR, Sons Republic Tex., Sons of Union Vets. of Civil War, Sons Confederate Vets., Mil. Orer Stars and Bars, Order of Coif, Dallas Hist. Soc., Dallas County Pioneer Assn., Rock Creek Barbeque Club, Masons, Shriners, York Rite, Grotto, Scottish Rite (32 degree Knight Commdr. Ct. of Honor), Beta Alpha Psi, Phi Delta Phi, Sigma Chi. State civil litigation, General practice, Property, real (including real estate development, water). Home: 7310 Brennans Dr Dallas TX 75214-2804 Office: 6510 Abrams Rd Ste 565 Dallas TX 75231-7292

MUELLER, VIRGINIA SCHWARTZ, lawyer; b. Palo Alto, Calif., Apr. 27, 1924; d. William Leonard and Anstrice (Bryant) S.; m. Paul F.C. Mueller, Sept. 24, 1945; children: Christian William, Lisa Turcotte. AB in Polit. Sci. and Law, Stanford U., 1944; JD, Cornell U., 1946; LLD, U. Paris, 1950. Bar: Calif. 1946, Wash. 1952, U.S. Supreme Ct. 1966. Research atty. Calif. Dist. Ct. Appeals, San Francisco, 1946-49; atty.-at-law Karr and Combelic, Seattle, 1952-53; dep. pros. atty. King County, Seattle, 1953-56; dep. supr. Inheritance Tax div. Wash. State Tax Commn., Olympia, 1956-58; asst. atty. counsel Calif. Bd. of Equalization, Sacramento, 1959; dep. dist. atty. Sacramento County Dist. Atty., 1959-66; legal counsel Legal Aid Soc. of Sacramento, 1966-71; pvt. practice Sacramento, 1971—. Chmn. Port of Sacramento, 1988-90, commr., 1983-91; adv. bd. Alternative Sentencing Program, Sacramento, 1976—. Contbr. articles to profl. jours. Pres. No. Calif. chpt. Sister Cities Internat., 1990-93, state rep., Va., 1987-89, coord. for No. Calif., 1993-2000; counselor Soc. Mayflower Descs. inCalif., 1981-2001; chmn. bd. visitors spl. com. on status of women in law Stanfrd U., 1973-75; pres. World Affairs Coun. Sacramento, 1971-72, chmn. by-laws com., 1976-77; No. Calif. rep. nat. com. UNICEF, 1972-75. Named Outstanding Woman YMCA Sacramento, 1985, Disting. Businesswoman Sacramento C. of C., 1980. Mem. ABA (standing com. World Order under Law 1979-86, coun. mem. sect. internat. law 1976-80, sr. lawyers divsn. liaison to sect. internat. law, co-chair membership com., sr. lawyers divsn. council 2001—), Sacramento County Bar Assn. (chair sr. lawyers sect. 2000-02, Lawyer of Yr. 1995), Nat. Assn. Women Lawyers (pres. 1985-86, liaison sect. internat. law and practice), Fedn. Internat. des Femmes des Carrieres Juridiques (bd. dirs. 1972-88, 97—, v.p. 2000—), State Bar Calif. (chair standing com. on sr. lawyers, 2003), Union Internat. des Avocats, Women Lawyers of Sacramento (pres. 1964, 65, Frances Newell Carr Achievement award 1995), Internat. Fedn. Women Lawyers (v.p. 2000-02, rep. to UN 2001—), AAUW (pres. 1978-79, Centennial award 1981), Soroptimist (pres. 1975-76). Avocation: travel. Estate planning, Family and matrimonial, Probate (including wills, trusts). Home: 4310 Moss Dr Sacramento CA 95822-1662 Office: 106 L St Sacramento CA 95814-3227 E-mail: vsmueller@webtv.net.

MUENSTER, JOHN ROLFING, lawyer; b. Cleve., 1949; s. William Rolfing and Helen Bush (Brandenburg) M.; m. Kim Diane Koenig, 1982. BA, Yale U., 1971; JD, Harvard U., 1975. Bar: Wash. 1975, Calif. 1980, U.S. Dist. Ct. (we. dist.) Wash. 1976, U.S. Ct. Appeals (9th cir.) 1977, U.S. Dist. Ct. (ea. dist.) Wash. 1990, U.S. Dist. Ct. (no. dist.) Calif. 1996. Staff atty. Seattle-King County Pub. Defender Assn., 1975-81; dir. Snohomish County Pub. Defender Assn., Everett, Wash., 1981-84; ptnr. Mestel and Muenster, Seattle, 1984-94, Muenster & Koenig, Seattle, 1995—. Mem. Wash. Supreme Ct. Task Force on Jury Instrns., Seattle, 1985-86; coord. subcom. civil rights jury instrns. Washington Supreme Ct. Com. Jury Instrns., 1994—. Mem. Wash. State Bar Assn. (chmn. criminal law sect. 1983-84, civil rights com. 1997—). Avocations: photography, travel. Civil rights, Constitutional, Criminal. Office: Muenster & Koenig 1111 3rd Ave Ste 2220 Seattle WA 98104 E-mail: JMKK1613@aol.com.

MUETH, JOSEPH EDWARD, lawyer; b. St. Louis, Aug. 8, 1935; s. Joseph and Marie Clare (Reher) M.; m. Ellen Agnes O'Heron, Dec. 24, 1973; children: Erin R., Patricia A. B.Chem. Engring., U. Dayton, 1957; LL.B., Georgetown U., 1960, LL.M., 1961. Bar: Calif. 1964. Practice law, L.A.; ptnr. Wills, Green & Mueth, L.A., 1974-83; pvt. practice law Calif., 1983-94; of counsel Sheldon & Mak, Pasadena, Calif., 1994—. Adj. prof. law U. Calif. Hastings Coll. Law, San Francisco, 1972-75; lectr. Claremont Grad. Sch., 1982—. Author: Copyrights Patents and Trademarks, 1974. Chmn. bd. Rio Hondo council Camp Fire Girls Inc., 1967-72. Mem. AAAS, Am., Los Angeles County bar assns., State Bar Calif., N.Y. Acad. Scis., L.A. Athletic Club. Home: PO Box 3369 1217 Seal Way Seal Beach CA 90740-6419 Office: 225 S Lake Ave Ste 800 Pasadena CA 91101-4858

MUGRIDGE, DAVID RAYMOND, lawyer, educator, writer; b. Detroit, Aug. 6, 1949; s. Harry Raymond and Elizabeth Lou (Aldrich) M.; m. Sandra Lee Jackson, June 25, 1988; children: James Raymond, Sarah Lorraine. BA, U. of Ams., Puebla, Mex., 1970; MA, Santa Clara U., 1973; JD, San Joaquin Coll. of Law, 1985. Bar: Calif. 1986, U.S. Dist. Ct. (ea. dist.) Calif. 1986, U.S. Ct. Appeals (9th cir.) 1987, U.S. Supreme Ct. 1996; cert. specialist in criminal law. Staff atty. to presiding justice 5th Dist. Ct. Appeals, Fresno, Calif., 1985-87; assoc. Law Office of Nuttall, Berman, Magill, Fresno, 1987-88; pvt. practice Fresno, 1988—. Tchr. Fresno City Coll., 1988-96; tchr. Spanish for legal profession, Fresno, 1994; tchr. Fresno Pacific U., 1997—; arbitrator Fresno County Bar Assn., 1988—; judge pro-tem juvenile, traffic and small claims Fresno County Superior Ct., 1988—. Contbg. author: Practical Real Estate Law, 1995,99, 2003. Mem. Calif. Attys. for Criminal Justice, Calif. State Bar Assn. (cert. specialist in criminal law). Republican. Roman Catholic. Avocations: fishing, travel, photography, hiking. Appellate, Criminal, Personal injury (including property damage).

MUHLBACH, ROBERT ARTHUR, lawyer; b. Los Angeles, Apr. 13, 1946; s. Richard and Jeanette (Marcus) M.; m. Kerry Eldene Mahoney, July 26, 1986. BSME, U. Calif., Berkeley, 1967; JD, U. Calif., San Francisco, 1976; MME, Calif. State U., 1969; M in Pub. Adminstrn., U. So. Calif., 1978. Bar: Calif. 1976. Pub. defender County of Los Angeles, 1977-79; assoc. Kirtland & Packard LLP, Los Angeles, 1979—85, ptnr., 1986—2001, sr. ptnr., 2001—. Chmn. Santa Monica Airport Commn., Calif., 1984-87, chmn., bd. dirs. Hawthorne Airport Cmty. Assn. Inc. Served to capt. USAF, 1969-73. Mem. ABA, AIAA, Internat. Assn. Def. Counsel, Am. Bd. Trial Advs. Construction, Insurance, Product liability. Office: Kirtland & Packard LLP 2361 Rosecrans Ave 4th Fl El Segundo CA 90245 E-mail: ram@kirtland-packard.com.

MUIR, J. DAPRAY, lawyer; b. Washington, Nov. 9, 1936; s. Brockett and Helen Cassin (Dapray) M.; m. Louise Rutherfurd Pierrepont, July 16, 1966. AB, Williams Coll., 1958; JD, U. Va., 1964. Bar: Md., Va., D.C. 1964, U.S. Supreme Ct. 1967. Asst. legal advisor for econ. and bus. affairs U.S. Dept. State, 1971-73; ptnr. Ruddy & Muir, LLP, Washington. Mem. U.S. del. to Joint U.S./USSR Comml. Commn., 1972; chmn. D.C. Securities Adv. Com., 1981-84, mem. 1985-88. Bd. editors Va. Law Rev, 1963-64; contbr. articles to profl. jours. Bd. dirs. Trust Mus. Exhbns., 1997—, Internat. Fedn. Insts. Advanced Study, 1992—97. Lt. (j.g.) USNR, 1958—61. Mem. Am. Arbitration Assn. (panel of comml. arbitrators, 1997—), D.C. Bar (chmn. internat. law div. 1977-78, chmn. environ., energy and natural resources div. 1982-83), Met. Club (Washington), Chevy Chase (Md.) Club. Corporate, general, Securities. Home: 3104 Q St NW Washington DC 20007-3027 Office: 1717 K St NW Ste 600 Washington DC 20036

MUIR, MALCOLM, federal judge; b. Englewood, N.J., Oct. 20, 1914; s. John Merton and Sarah Elizabeth Muir; m. Alma M. Brohard, Sept. 6, 1940 (dec. 1985); children: Malcolm, Thomas, Ann Muir, Barbara (dec.), David Clay. BA, Lehigh U., 1935; LL.B., Harvard U., 1938. Sole practice, Williamsport, Pa., 1938-42, 45-49, 68-70; mem. firm, 1949-68; judge U.S. Dist. Ct. (mid. dist.) Pa., 1970—. Active charitable orgns., Williamsport, 1939-70 Mem. ABA, Pa. Bar Assn. (pres.-elect 1970) Avocation: reading. Office: US Dist Ct Ste 401 240 W 3rd St Williamsport PA 17701-6461

MUIR, ROBERT, JR., retired judge, lawyer; b. Newark, May 22, 1932; s. Robert and Olive Klehm Muir; m. Harriet Ann Coltman, July 18, 1959; children: Alison Lee Muir Helmer, Robert Muir III, Beth Ann Muir McGlothlin. BA, Wesleyan U., 1954; JD, NYU, 1959. Bar: N.J. 1960, U.S. Tax Ct. 1968, U.S. Dist. Ct. N.J. 2000, U.S. Supreme Ct. 1969. Mem. Mills, Doyle & Muir, Morristown, NJ, 1960—71; judge Morris County Ct., Morristown, 1971—73, Superior Ct. N.J., Trenton, 1973, gen. equity judge, 1973—76, assignment judge, 1976—85, appellate divsn. judge, 1986—98, presiding judge, 1998—2000, ret., 2000; of counsel Porzio Bromberg & Newman, Moorristown, 2000—. Mem., chair Supreme Ct. coms. N.J. Superior Ct. Sys., Trenton, 1976—2000; adj. prof. Seton Hall Law Sch., Newark, 1983—84, Nat. Jud. Coll., Reno, 1989, Fairleigh Dickinson U., Madison, NJ, 1993—94. Pres., mem. Morris County Jaycees, Morristown, 1964—68; borough councilman Mendham Boro Governing Body, 1965—67; trustee Vis. Nurses Assn. No. N.J., Morristown, 2000—; elder Presbyn. Ch., Mendham, NJ, 1964—. Lt. j.g. USN, 1954—56. Fellow, Inst. Ct. Mgmt. NCSC, 1986. Fellow: ABA; mem.: FBA, Morris County Bar Assn., N.J. Bar Assn. Avocations: golf, stained glass, reading. Office: Porzio Bromberg & Newman 100 Southgate Pkwy Morristown NJ 07960-1997

MUKASEY, MICHAEL B. federal judge; b. 1941; AB, Columbia U., 1963; LLB, Yale U., 1967. Assoc. Webster Sheffield Fleishchmann Hithcock & Brookfield, 1967-72, Patterson, Belknap, Webb & Tyler, 1976-88; asst. U.S. atty. U.S. Dist. Ct. (so. dist.) N.Y., 1972-76, dist. judge, 1988—. Lectr. in law Columbia Law Sch. Contbr. articles to profl. jours. Office: US Dist Ct US Courthouse 500 Pearl St New York NY 10007-1316

MULCAHY, ROBERT JOSEPH, lawyer; b. Evergreen Park, Ill., Jan. 22, 1942; s. Robert J. and Mary J. Mulcahy. BS, U. Ill., 1964; JD, Calif. Western Law Sch., 1972. Bar: Calif. 1973, Ill. 1973; cert. legal specialist in work compensation, Calif. Pvt. practice, Chgo., 1973-81, San Diego, 1981-85; dep. city atty. criminal divsn. City of San Diego, 1986-91, dep. city atty. civil divsn., 1991—. Capt. USMC, 1964-67, Vietnam. Decorated Purple Heart. Office: City of San Diego 1200 3d Ave Ste 1100 San Diego CA 92101 E-mail: rum@cityatty.sannet.gov.

MULCHINOCK, DAVID STEWARD, lawyer; b. Allentown, Pa., Feb. 10, 1945; s. Daniel F. and May E. (Heffner) M. BA, Georgetown U., 1967; JD, Cornell U., 1970. Bar: N.Y. 1971, N.J. 1974, U.S. Supreme Ct. 1978, Pa. 1994. Assoc. Hale, Grant, Meyerson, O'Brien & McCormick, N.Y.C., 1970-72, ptnr., 1972-77; pvt. practice law Princeton, N.J., 1977—. Corporate, general, Probate (including wills, trusts), Taxation, general. Home: 107 Windy Bush Rd New Hope PA 18938 Office: One Palmer Sq Princeton NJ 08542

MULDDON, PAUL, legal association administrator; B, U. Ottawa, Can.; MA, McMaster U.; ML, McGill U. Staff lawyer Can. Environ. Law Assn., Tortonto, Canada, 1994—2001, exec. dir., 2001—. Author: (book) Law of Intervention; contbr. articles to profl. jours. Mem. Environ. Bill Rights Task Force; mem. sci. adv. bd. Internat. Joint Commn.; mem. adv. bd. MISA, Canada. Office: Can Environ Law Assn 130 Spadina Ave Ste 301 Toronto ON Canada M5V 2L4 Office Fax: 416-960-9392.*

MULDOON, ROBERT JOSEPH, JR., lawyer; b. Somerville, Mass., Nov. 16, 1936; s. Robert Joseph and Catherine Eileen (Hurley) M.; m. Barbara Joyce Mooney, Aug. 24, 1968; children: Andrew Robert, Catherine Lane, Timothy John. AB, Boston Coll., 1960, MA, 1961, LLB, 1965. Bar: Mass. 1965, U.S. Tax Ct. 1966, U.S. Supreme Ct. 1970. Law clk. Supreme Jud. Ct. Mass., 1965-66; assoc. Withington, Cross, Park & Groden, Boston, 1966-71, ptnr., 1972-82, Sherin and Lodgen, LLP, Boston, 1982—. Mem. Bd. Bar Examiners Mass.; chmn. Nat. Conf. Bar Examiners, 1985-86; pres. Mass. Continuing Legal Edn., Inc., 1992-94. Trustee Boston Coll. H.S., 1990-96, chmn. bd. trustees, 1995-96. Fellow Am. Coll. Trial Lawyers; mem. Am. Law Inst., Boston Bar Assn., Curtis Club, Nisi Prius Club, Tavern Club. General civil litigation, Land use and zoning (including planning), Product liability. Office: Sherin and Lodgen LLP 100 Summer St Ste 2800 Boston MA 02110-2109 E-mail: rjmuldoon@sherin.com.

MULHAUSER, FREDERICK VAN NORDEN, lawyer; b. Pomona, Calif., Apr. 16, 1943; s. Frederick Ludwig Jr. and Margaret Marie (Lehman) M.; m. Karen Webber, Aug., 1968; 1 child, Christopher. AB magna cum laude, Harvard Coll., 1964; MA, Yale U., 1966; EdM, Harvard U., 1982; JD, Georgetown U., 2001. Spl. asst. Rep. John Brademas, U.S. Ho. of Reps., Washington, 1973-74; sr. rsch. assoc. U.S. Nat. Inst. Edn., Washington, 1974-83; evaluator, asst. dir. program evaluation divsn. U.S. GAO, Washington, 1983-93; litigation screening cord. Nat. Capital area chpt. ACLU, Washington, 1993—2001, staff atty., 2001—. Adj. lectr. Am. U., Washington, 1981-83; mem. adv. bd. edn. adminstrn. program Tchrs. Coll., N.Y.C., 1977-78; adj. prof. U. DC Law Sch., 2002-03. Bd. editors, co-chair Harvard Ednl. Rev., 1967-69; contbr. articles and revs. to profl. jours, chpts. to books; author GAO evaluation reports to Congress, 1983-93. Mem. neighborhood sch. bd. D.C. Pub. Schs., Washington, 1978. Woodrow Wilson Found. fellow, 1964, Upham scholar Harvard U., 1966, edn. policy fellow Ford Found./Inst. for Ednl. Leadership, Washington, 1973. Mem. DC Bar Assn., Country Music Assn., Washington Area Music Assn. Avocation: music. Home: 319 7th St NE Washington DC 20002-6103 Office: ACLU/NCA 1400 20th St NW Ste 119 Washington DC 20036-5920

MULHEARN, CHRISTOPHER MICHAEL, lawyer; b. Providence, June 14, 1969; s. Michael R. and Judith A. Mulhearn; m. Melissa L. Mulhearn. BA in Polit. Sci., Marquette U., 1991; JD, Cleveland-Marshall Coll. Law, 1994. Bar: R.I. 1994, U.S. Dist. Ct. R.I. 1995, Mass. 1995, U.S. Dist. Ct. Mass. 1996. Assoc. Rodio & Brown, Ltd., Providence, 1994-96, Tate & Elias, Providence, 1996-99, Carroll, Kelly & Murphy, Providence, 1999; prin. Christopher M. Mulhearn, Esq., Counselor at Law, P.C., Providence, 1999—2001; sr. litigation assoc. Ferrucci, Russo, PC, Providence, 2001—. Bd. dirs. Children's Shelter of Blackstone Valley, Inc., Pawtucket, R.I., 1996-2002; mem. alumni bd. dirs. Bishop Hendricken H.S., Warwick, R.I., 1996—, bd. dirs. Bios Care Ocean State 2002-. Mem. ABA, Mass. Bar Assn., R.I. Bar Assn. Avocations: golf, music. General civil litigation, Estate planning, Probate (including wills, trusts). Home: 449 Narragansett Pkwy Warwick RI 02888-4002 Office: Ferrucci Russo PC 49 Weyrosset St 2nd Flr Providence RI 02903 Office Fax: 401-455-7778. E-mail: cmulhearn@frlawri.com., cmulhearn@frlawri.com.

MULHERN, EDWIN JOSEPH, lawyer; b. Bklyn., Mar. 8, 1927; s. Edward Thomas and Jennie (Keenan) M.; m. Maureen P. Purcell, Oct. 2, 1964; children: Edwin T., Deborah J., Kevin T. BBA, St. John's U., 1950, LLB, 1954. Bar: N.Y. 1954, U.S. Dist. Ct. (ea. and so. dists.) N.Y. 1954, U.S. Supreme Ct. 1960. Sr. acct. Susquehanna Mills Inc., N.Y.C., 1947-53; chief acct. Rockwood Chocolate Co., Bklyn., 1953-54; trial atty. Allstate Ins. Co., Freeport, N.Y., 1954-57; claims rep. State Farm Ins. Co., Hempstead, N.Y., 1957-58; sole practice, Bellmore, N.Y., 1958-70, Mineola, N.Y., Carle Place, N.Y., 1970—; mem. joint grievance com. for 10th jud. dist. (N.Y.), 1981-89. Pres. Christian Bros. Boys' Assn., 1975-82; bd. dirs. Legal Aid Soc. of Nassau County, 1980—. Served with USAAF, 1945-46. Mem. ABA, N.Y. State Bar Assn., Nassau Bar Assn. (bd. dirs. 1981-83, chmn. admissions com. 1979, chmn. grievance com. 1980-82), Suffolk County Bar Assn., Nassau Lawyers Assn. (pres. 1975, exec. dir. 1993—, Man of Yr. 1981), Criminal Cts. Bar Assn. of Nassau County (pres. 1976), Criminal Cts. Bar Assn. of Suffolk County, Am. Assn. Trial Lawyers. Clubs: University of L.I. (Hempstead), K.C. (new Hyde Park, N.Y.). Criminal, Family and matrimonial, Personal injury (including property damage). Office: 1 Old Country Rd Ste 145 Carle Place NY 11514-1801

MULL, GALE W. lawyer; b. Hillsdale, Mich., Sept. 8, 1945; s. Wayne E. and Vivian M. (Bavin) M.; m. Holly Ann Allen, Aug. 2, 1969 (div. Nov. 1983); 1 child, Carter B.; m. Jeanne Anne Haughey, Aug. 18, 1985. BA, Mich. State U., 1967; MA in Sociology, Ind. U., 1969; JD, Emory U., 1972. Bar: Ga. 1972, U.S. Dist. Ct. (no. dist.) Ga. 1972, U.S. Ct. Appeals (5th cir.) 1973, U.S. Ct. Appeals (11th cir.) 1981. Instr. sociology Clemson (S.C.) U., 1968-69, Spelman Coll., Atlanta, 1969-70; pvt. practice, Atlanta, 1972-75; ptnr. Mull & Sweet, Atlanta, 1975-81; pres. Gale W. Mull, P.C., Atlanta, 1981—. Bd. dirs. BOND Community Fed. Credit Union, Atlanta, 1975-81; directing atty. Emory Student Legal Services, Atlanta, 1975-91; Sociology instr. Clemson U., Clemson, S.C., 1968-69, Spelman Coll., Atlanta, Ga., 1969-70. Pres. Inman Park Restoration, Inc., Atlanta, 1972—74, BASS Orgn. for Neighborhood Devel., Inc., 1974—78; mem. Housing Appeals Bd., Atlanta, 1982—88, Mayor's Task Force on Prostitution, 1984—86; bd. dirs. Trinity Towers, Inc., 1999—2000; vestry St. John's Episc. Ch., 1992—99, 2003—, sr. warden, 1998—99; bd. dirs. St. John's Episcopal Day Sch., 1992—97, Bethlehem Ministries, 1997—, ACLU Ga., 1981—92, sec. bd. dirs., 1983—85, cooperating atty., 1972—. Mem. ABA, Ga. Bar Assn., Atlanta Bar Assn., Lawyers Club Atlanta. Clubs: Quail Unltd. (bd. dirs., sec. 1984-86). Criminal, Family and matrimonial, General practice. Office: 2149 Rugby Ave Atlanta GA 30337

MULLALLY, DAVID SMART, lawyer; b. Oakland, Calif., Jan. 30, 1948; s. Walter E. and Jeanne S. Mullally; m. Linda B. Baxendale, Oct. 9, 1983; 1 child, Christopher D. BA, UCLA, 1974; JD, Western State U., Fullerton, Calif., 1976; MA, John F. Kennedy U., Orinda, Calif., 1984. Bar: Calif. 1976, Hawaii 1988, D.C. 1988. Assoc. Law Office Robert Kaiser, Oakland, 1976-78; ptnr. Mullally, Cederborg & Mullally, Oakland, 1978-79; pvt. practice, Walnut Creek, Calif., 1980-84, Monterey, Calif., 1984—. Prof. law Monterey Coll. Law, 1984-85. Author: Order in the Court: A Writer's Guide to the Legal System, 2000. Vol. firefighter Carmel Valley (Calif.) Fire Dept., 1992-96; dir. fundraising Carmel chpt. ARC, 1995. Mem. Mensa. Avocations: jogging, scuba diving, travel, photography, painting. General practice. Office: PO Box 369 Carmel Valley CA 93924-0369

MULLANEY, THOMAS JOSEPH, lawyer; b. N.Y.C., Feb. 9, 1946; s. James Joseph and Dorothy Mary (Fulling) M.; m. Christine E. Hampton, Aug. 16, 1969; children: Richard, Jennette. BA, Fordham U., 1967; JD, U. Va., 1970; LLM, NYU, 1977. Bar: Va. 1970, N.Y. 1971, U.S. Dist. Ct. (so. and ea. dists.) N.Y. 1972, U.S. Ct. Appeals (2d cir.) 1972, U.S. Supreme Ct. 1975. Assoc. Brown, Wood, Ivey, Mitchell & Petty, N.Y.C., 1970-79, Law Offices of John M. Kenney, Garden City, N.Y., 1979-84; ptnr. Abrams, Thaw & Mullaney, N.Y.C., Farmingdale, N.Y., 1985-91; dir., sr. counsel law dept. Merrill Lynch & Co., Inc., N.Y.C., 1991—. Capt. JAGC, U.S. Army, 1971-74. Mem. Va. State Bar Assn., N.Y. State Bar Assn. Republican. Roman Catholic. Federal civil litigation, State civil litigation, Securities. Home: 104 Huntington Rd Garden City NY 11530-3122 Office: 222 Broadway Fl 14 New York NY 10038-2510 E-mail: tmullaney@exchange.ml.com.

MULLARE, T(HOMAS) KENWOOD, JR., lawyer; b. Milton, Mass., Jan. 19, 1939; s. Thomas Kenwood and Catherine Marie (Leonard) M.; m. Joan Marie O'Donnell, May 27, 1967; children: Jennifer M. Cedrone, Tracy K., Jill M., Joyce M. AB, Holy Cross Coll., 1961; LLB, Boston Coll., 1964. Bar: Mass. 1964. Atty. New Eng. Electric System, 1964-69; v.p., gen. counsel, sec. AVX Corp., N.Y.C., 1970-73; v.p., gen. counsel, clk. Tyco Labs., Inc., Exeter, N.H., 1974-77; v.p., gen. counsel, sec. SCA Svcs., Inc., Boston, 1978-83; spl. counsel Houghton, Mifflin Co., Boston, 1984-85, v.p., dir. bus. software divsn., 1985-92; pres. North River Capital Co., Inc., Norwell, Mass., 1990—; gen. counsel, sec. Aztec Tech. Ptnrs., Inc., Braintree, Mass., 1999—2002. Bd. dirs. Friendship Home, Inc. Mem. regional adv. bd. Commonwealth of Mass. Dept. Mental Retardation, 1994-97; bd. dirs. Barque Hill Assn., Norwell, 1980-84, pres., 1981-83; pres. Ch. Hillers, Norwell, 1983-84; bd. dirs. South Shore Assn. for Retarded Citizens, Weymouth, Mass., 1993-98, chmn., 1995-97. Mem. Boston Bar Assn. Corporate, general, Intellectual property, Mergers and acquisitions. Home: 31 Barque Hill Dr Norwell MA 02061-2815

MULLARKEY, MARY J. state supreme court chief justice; b. New London, Wis., Sept. 28, 1943; d. John Clifford and Isabelle A. (Steffes) M.; m. Thomas E. Korson, July 24, 1971; 1 child, Andrew Steffes Korson. BA, St. Norbert Coll., 1965; LLB, Harvard U., 1968; LLD (hon.), St. Norbert Coll., 1989. Bar: Wis. 1968, Colo. 1974. Atty.-advisor U.S. Dept. Interior, Washington, 1968-73; asst. regional atty. EEOC, Denver, 1973-75; 1st atty. gen. Colo. Dept. Law, Denver, 1975-79, solicitor gen., 1979-82; legal advisor to Gov. Lamm State of Colo., Denver, 1982-85; ptnr. Mullarkey & Seymour, Denver, 1985-87; justice Colo. Supreme Ct., Denver, 1987—, chief justice, 1998—. Fellow ABA Found., Colo. Bar Found.; mem. ABA, Colo. Bar Assn., Colo. Women's Bar Assn. (Mary Lathrop award 2002), Denver Bar Assn., Thompson G. Marsh Inn of Ct. (pres. 1993-94). Office: Supreme Ct Colo Judicial Bldg 2 E 14th Ave Denver CO 80203-2115

MULLEN, GRAHAM C. federal judge; b. 1940; BA, Duke U., 1962, JD, 1969. Bar: N.C. 1969. Ptnr. Mullen, Holland, Cooper, Morrow, Wilder & Sumner, 1969-90; judge U.S. Dist. Ct. (we. dist.) N.C., Charlotte, 1990—. Lt. USN, 1962-66. Mem. N.C. Bar Assn. (bd. govs. 1983-88), Mecklenburg County Bar Assn. Office: US Courthouse 401 W Trade St Rm 230 Charlotte NC 28202-1619 E-mail: gmullen@ncwd.net.

MULLEN, J. THOMAS, lawyer; b. Evanston, Ill., Aug. 27, 1940; BSE, Princeton U., 1963; JD cum laude, U. Mich., 1967. Bar: Ill. 1967. Ptnr. Mayer, Brown, Rowe & Maw, Chgo.; ptnr.-in-charge London office, 1974-78. Bd. dirs. Legal Assistance Found. Chgo., 1979-85. Mem. ABA, Chgo. Bar Assn., Chgo. Coun. Lawyers. Office: Mayer Brown Rowe & Maw 190 S La Salle St Ste 3100 Chicago IL 60603-3441 E-mail: tmullen@mayerbrownrowe.com.

MULLEN, PETER P. lawyer; b. N.Y.C., Apr. 8, 1928; m. Cecilia Kirby; 5 children. AB cum laude, Georgetown U., 1948; LLB, Columbia U., 1951. Bar: N.Y. 1951. Ptnr. Skadden, Arps, Slate, Meagher & Flom LLP, N.Y.C., 1961-98, exec. ptnr., 1981-94, of counsel, 1998—. Co-chmn. Cardinal's Com. Laity Archdiocese N.Y., 1989-2003; bd. dirs., sec., treas., Eye Surgery, Inc. Formerly mem., pres. Bd. Edn. Pub. Schs., Bronxville, N.Y., 1979-81; chmn. Skadden Fellowship Found., 1988—; bd. dirs., vice-chmn. Lawrence Hosp., Bronxville, 1984-89; bd. dirs., sec. Project Orbis Internat., 1985-, Georgetown U., Washington, 1982-99, chmn., 1985-92; bd. dirs. Legal Aid Soc., 1987-93, Vols. Legal Svcs., Inc., 1988-99, United Way Bronxville, 1985-93, New Milford Hosp. 1997-, Practicing Attys. Law Students, 1988-99; trustee Lawyer's Commn. Civil Rights Under Law, 1984-99; chmn. Gregorian U. Found., 1989—; bd. dirs., exec. com. Vatican Obs. Found., 1993. Named Man of Yr. Cath. Big Bros., 1987; recipient John Carroll award Georgetown U., 1984, John Carroll Medal Merit, 1988, Thomas More award Lawyers Com. Cardinal's Com. of the Laity, 1996, Elizabeth Ann Seton award Nat. Cath. Edn. Assn., 1998; named Stone scholar Columbia U., 1951. Mem. Am. Bar Assn., N.Y. State Bar Assn. (com. securities regulation 1980-83), Assn. Bar City N.Y. (com. corp. law 1964-67, com. admissions 1965-68, com. securities regulation 1970-73), Soc. Friendly Sons St. Patrick (N.Y., pres. 1989-90), Knight Malta. Office: Skadden Arps Slate et al LLP 4 Times Sq New York NY 10036-6522

MULLEN, REGINA MARIE, lawyer; b. Cambridge, Mass., Apr. 22, 1948; d. Robert G. and Elizabeth R. (McHugh) M. BA, Newton Coll. Sacred Heart, 1970; JD, U. Va., 1973. Bar: Pa., Del., U.S. Dist. Ct. Del., U.S. Ct. Appeals (3d cir.), U.S. Supreme Ct. Dep. atty. gen. State Del. Dept. Justice, Wilmington, 1973—79, state solicitor, 1979—83, chief fin. unit, 1983—88; v.p., counsel MBNA Am. Bank, N.A., Wilmington, Del., 1988—91, 1st v.p., sr. v.p., counsel, 1991—98, exec. v.p., sr. counsel, 1998—. Bd. profl. responsibility State of Del., 1996-99. Bd. dirs. Wilmington Music Festival, 1992-98, New Castle Hist. Soc., 1999—, World Affairs Coun. Wilmington, 2002—; fin. com. Chesapeake Bay coun. Girl Scout Am., Wilmington, 1985-94, bd. dirs., 1988-94, v.p., 1990-94, cmty. devel. com., 1994-96, 99—, chair pers. com., 1996-99; bd. dirs. Cmty. Legal Aid Soc., 1994-99, treas., 1995-97. Mem. ABA, Del. State Bar Assn. (chair adminstrv. law sect. 1983-85), U. Va. Law Sch. Alumni Assn. (mem. alumni coun.). Democrat. Roman Catholic. Office: 1100 N King St Wilmington DE 19884-0001

MULLENBACH, LINDA HERMAN, lawyer; b. Sioux City, Iowa, Dec. 25, 1948; d. Verner Wilhelm and Margaretta Victoria (Grant) Herman; m. Hugh James Mullenbach, Aug. 22, 1970; children: Erika Lynn, Linnea Britt. BS in Speech, Northwestern U., 1971, MS in Speech, 1972, JD, 1979. Bar: Ill. 1979, U.S. Dist. Ct. (no. dist.) Ill. 1979, DC 1983, U.S. Dist. Ct. DC 1983, U.S. Ct. Appeals (7th, DC and fed. cirs.) 1983, U.S. Supreme Ct. 1984. Assoc. Jenner & Block, Chgo., 1979-83, Dickstein, Shapiro & Morin, Washington, 1983-85, prin., 1985-87, ptnr., 1988-93; v.p., assoc. gen. counsel Zurich Small Bus. and Zurich Comml. Legal Divsn., Balt., 1994-99; asst. gen. counsel, v.p. Corp. Law Divsn. Zurich U.S., Balt., 1999-2001; asst. gen. counsel, v.p. corp. law divsn. Zurich N.Am., Balt., 2001—02, sr. v.p., assoc. gen. counsel corp. law divsn., 2002—. Mem.: ABA, Women's Legal Def. Fund, Women's Bar Assn., DC Bar Assn., Mortar Bd., Zeta Phi Eta. Federal civil litigation, Criminal, Labor (including EEOC, Fair Labor Standards Act, labor-management relations, NLRB, OSHA). Home: 8201 Killean Way Potomac MD 20854-2728

MULLENDORE, JAMES MYERS, lawyer; b. Charlottesville, Va., Mar. 21, 1946; s. James M. and Elaine (Gregg) M.; m. Kristine B. Mullendore; children: Margaret E., Sean T. BS, W.Va. U., 1968; JD, U. Va., 1975. Bar: Mich. 1975, U.S. Dist. Ct. (we. dist.) Mich. Ptnr. Mullendore, Beach & Thrall, Greenville, Mich., 1975—. Pres., v.p. Greenville Bd. Edn., 1976-82; ofcl. Mid-Am. Football Conf., 1985-86, Big Ten Football Ofcls., 1987-2001,—; bd. dirs. United Way Greenville, 1978-83; chmn. controlled substances adv.com. State Mich.; bd. dirs. Danish Festival Inc, 1997-2000. Mem. ABA, Assn. Trial Lawyers Am., Mich. Trial Lawyers Assn. (pres. 1982-83), U.S. Football League (ofcl. 1983), Greenville Area C. of C. (chmn. bd. dirs.), Rotary (v.p. 1983-84). Congregationalist. Criminal, Family and matrimonial, Personal injury (including property damage). Home: 7678 Greenbrier NE Rockford MI 49341 Office: PO Box 40 Greenville MI 48838

MULLER, KURT ALEXANDER, lawyer; b. Chgo., June 21, 1955; s. Jack and Janet (Kasten) M.; m. Sylvia Saltoon, Apr. 6, 1986; 1 child, Marissa Grace. BS, U. Wis., Parkside, 1977; JD, John Marshall Law Sch., 1986. Bar: Ill. 1986, U.S. Dist. Ct. (no. dist.) Ill. 1986, Ariz. 1987, U.S. Dist. Ct. (ea. dist.) Wis. 1989; approved child rep. Cook County Ct. Creative dir. Brand Advt., Chgo., 1977-80; dep. sheriff Cook County, Chgo., 1978-86; broker Gerstenberg Commodities, Chgo., 1980-83; assoc. Gordon & Glickson, P.C., Chgo., 1986-87, Michael Harry Minton, P.C., Chgo., 1987-90; pvt. practice Chgo., 1990-92; ptnr. Law Offices of Richter-Muller, P.C., Chgo., 1992-95; lawyer, CEO The Muller Firm, Ltd., Chgo., 1995—. Lectr. Nat. Bus. Inst. Author: In Consideration of Divorce: Giving Credit (and Debits) to Dissolution, 1991, 3d edit., 1998; contbr. The Jewish American Prince Handbook, 1986; contbr. articles to profl. jours. and newspapers; host (CBS radio show) Kurt Muller's Uncommon Law; monthly columnist for Chgo. Social: Ask Muller. Mem. ABA, ACLU, Nat. Smoker's Alliance, Chgo. Bar Assn., Masons. Avocations: interior design, films, theater, writing. E-mail: www. mullaw.com. Alternative dispute resolution, Family and matrimonial, Juvenile. Office: The Muller Bldg 110 W Grand Ave Chicago IL 60610-4269 Fax: 312-467-0252.

MULLER, PETER, lawyer, entertainment company executive, retail company executive, consultant; b. Teplitz-Sanov, Czechoslovakia, Mar. 4, 1947; came to U.S., 1949; s. Alexander and Elizabeth Rudolpha (Weingarten) M.; m. Irene Smolarski, Nov. 18, 1971 (div. 1973); children: Chloe, Aurora; m. Esther Unterman Meisler, Jan. 4, 1987 (div. 1995). BA, NYU, 1968, JD cum laude. Entertainment editor Ambience mag., N.Y.C., 1978-79, Women's Life mag., N.Y.C., 1980-81; sole practice N.Y.C., 1984—; entertainment writer Jewish Press; chief exec. officer Producers Releasing Corp., N.Y. and Nev., 1987-88, pres. entertainment div., 1987-88; pres., founder Muller Entertainment Group, N.Y.C. and Calif., 1988—; pres., chief oper. officer ACA Joe, Inc., San Francisco and N.Y.C.; also bd. dirs. ACA Joe Inc., San Francisco and N.Y.C. Expert tech. adv. svc. for attys., Pa., 1987—; lectr. entertainment and comm. bus. to various orgns.; adj. prof. NYU, UCLA. Author: Show Business Law, 1991, The Music Business: A Legal Perspective, 1994. Bd. dirs. NYU Coll. Arts and Sci.; vol. Lawyers for the Arts, N.Y.C., 1987—. Mem. ABA (forum on entertainment and sports industries, forum on copyright, trademark and patent law), N.Y. State Bar Assn., NYU Alumni Assn. (bd. dirs. 1987—, v.p. bd. dirs., coun.), Assn. of Am. Mgmt. Assn. (pres.). Avocations: sports, swimming, history, writing, travel. Communications, Entertainment, Public international.

MULLERAT, RAMON, JR., lawyer; b. Barcelona, Mar. 3, 1966; s. Ramon M. Mullerat and Margarita M. Prat; m. Nuria Domingo de Mullerat, May 18, 1967; children: Julia, Claudia, Nuria. LLB with honors, U. London, 1988; LLM, U. Notre Dame, 1989; ITP, Harvard U., 1992. Legal asst. DePinna, Scorers & John Venn, London, 1986—89; assoc. Hughes, Hubbard & Reed, N.Y.C., 1990; legal asst. Levi Strauss & Co., San Francisco, 1990—92; ptnr. PricewaterhouseCoopers, N.Y.C., 1992—2000, Landwell-PWC, Madrid. Author: Tax Management's BNA Business Operations in Venezuela, 1995, 2003; contbr. articles to profl. jours. Mem.: Brotherhood Monastery of Poblet, Golf Club Costa Dorada. Avocations: tennis, soccer. Taxation, general. Office: PricewaterhouseCoopers Paseo De La Castellana 53 28046 Madrid Spain

MÜLLER FILHO, LUIZ EUGÊNIO ARAÚJO, lawyer; b. Rio de Janeiro, Rio de Janeiro, Brazil, Feb. 16, 1962; s. Luiz Eugênio Araújo Müller and Vera Regina Monteiro de Souza Dantas; m. Maria Illy Clark Fontainha, Dec. 10, 1983; children: Gabriela Clark Fontainha, Nikolau Clark Fontainha, Leo Clark Fontainha. Bar: Rio de Janeiro 1988, São Paulo 1997. Ptnr. Lobo & Ibeas Advogados, Rio de Janeiro, 1990—, São Paulo office ptnr. in charge São Paulo, Brazil, 1999—. Contbr. chapters to books. Corporate, general, Private international, Mergers and acquisitions. Home: Brazil Office: Lobo & Ibeas Advogados Alameda Santos 2224 - 6th fl São Paulo São Paulo 01418200 Brazil Office Fax: 55 11 30613637. E-mail: muller@loboeibeas.com.br.

MULLIGAN, CASEY JOHN, lawyer; b. Denver, Mar. 3, 1967; s. Gene Joseph and Ann Rita Mulligan; m. Mary Claire McLaughlin; children: Emma, Will, Joseph. BA in Polit. Sci., U. Colo., 1989, JD, 1992. Bar: Colo. 92, U.S. Dist. Ct. Colo. 92. Dep. state pub. defender Colo. Pub. Defender, Denver, Greeley, Brighton, 1992—99; pvt. practice Boulder, Colo., 1999—. Source editor : Colo. Jour. Internat. Environ. Law and Policy, 1991—92. Mem.: Colo. Criminal Def. Bar, Nat. Assn. Criminal Def. Lawyers, Boulder Criminal Def. Bar. Avocations: hiking, bicycling, skiing, fishing. Criminal, Appellate, Juvenile. Office: 4450 Arapahoe Ave Ste 100 Boulder CO 80303 Fax: 303-245-8100. E-mail: caseyandmc@aol.com.

MULLIGAN, ELINOR PATTERSON, lawyer; b. Bay City, Mich., Apr. 20, 1929; d. Frank Clark and Agnes (Murphy) P.; m. John C. O'Connor, Oct. 28, 1950; children: Christine Fulena, Valerie Clark, Amy O'Connor, Christopher Criffan O'Connor; m. William G. Mulligan, Dec. 6, 1975. BA, U. Mich., 1950; JD, Seton Hall U., 1970. Bar: N.J. 1970. Assoc., Springfield and Newark, 1970-72; pvt. practice, Hackettstown, N.J., 1972; ptnr. Mulligan & Jacobson, N.Y.C., 1973-91, Mulligan & Mulligan, Hackettstown, 1976—. Atty. Hackettstown Planning Bd., 1973-86, Blairstown Bd. Adjustment, 1973-95; sec. Warren County Ethics Com., 1976-78, sec. Dist. X and XIII Fee Arbitration Com., 1979-87, mem. and chair, 1987-91, mem. dist. ethics com. XIII, 1992—; mem. spl. com. on atty. disciplinary structure N.J. Supreme Ct., 1981—; lectr. Nat. Assn. Women Judges, 1979, N.J. Inst. Continuing Legal Edn., 1988—. Contbr. articles to profl. jours. Named Vol. of Yr., Attys. Vols. in Parole Program, 1978. Fellow Am. Acad. Matrimonial Lawyers (1st woman pres. N.J. chpt. 1995-96); mem. ABA, Warren County Bar Assn. (1st woman pres. 1987-88), N.J. State Bar ASsn., N.J. Women Lawyers Assn. (v.p. 1985—), Am. Mensa Soc., Union League Club (N.Y.C.), Baltusrol Golf Club (Springfield, N.J.), Panther Valley Golf and Country Club (Allamuchy, N.J.), Kappa Alpha Theta. Republican. State civil litigation, Family and matrimonial, Probate (including wills, trusts). Home: 12 Goldfinch Way Hackettstown NJ 07840-3007 Office: 933 County Road 517 Hackettstown NJ 07840-4654 E-mail: llp-nj@mindspring.com

MULLIGAN, MICHAEL DENNIS, lawyer; b. St. Louis, Mar. 9, 1947; s. Leo Virgil and Elizabeth (Leyse) M.; m. Theresa Baker, Aug. 7, 1971; children: Brennan, Colin. BA in Biology, Amherst Coll., 1968; JD, Columbia U., 1971. Bar: Mo. 1971, U.S. Dist. Ct. (ea. dist.) Mo. 1972, U.S. Ct. Appeals (8th cir.) 1982, U.S. Tax Ct. 1985. Law clk. to judge U.S. Dist. Ct. (ea. dist.) Mo., 1971-72; assoc. Lewis, Rice & Fingersh, L.C., St. Louis, 1972-80, ptnr., 1980—. Mem. editl. bd. Estate Planning Mag., 1985—. Served as cpl. USMC, 1968-70. Fellow Am. Coll. Trust and Estate Counsel; mem. ABA (mem. real property, probate and trust, and taxation sects.), Mo. Bar Assn. (mem. probate and trust, taxation sects.). Probate (including wills, trusts), Estate taxation. Office: Lewis Rice & Fingersh LC 500 N Broadway Ste 2000 Saint Louis MO 63102-2147 E-mail: mmulligan@lewisrice.com.

MULLIN, PATRICK ALLEN, lawyer; b. Newark, N.J., Jan. 13, 1950; s. Gerard Vincent and Frances Regina (Magnanti) M. BA, William Paterson U., 1972, MEd, 1974; JD, NYU, 1979, LLM in Taxation, 1990; postgrad., Harvard Law Sch., 1979; Gerry Spence's Trial Lawyers Coll., Duboise, Wyo., 1997. Bar: N.J. 1979, D.C. 1980, N.Y. 1990; cert. criminal trial atty. N.J. Supreme Ct. Law clk. to Hon. Dickinson R. DeBevoise, U.S. Dist. Ct. N.J., Trenton, 1979-80; assoc. Charles Morgan Assocs., Washington, 1980-81; pvt. practice, Hackensack, N.J., 1988—. Mem. Practitioners Adv. Group U.S. Sentencing Commn.; lctr., "Criminal Trial Preparation", Seton Hall Law Sch., 2001, 02, 03, "White Collar Federal Sentencing Guidelines" Assn. of Trial Lawyers of Am., 2003. Contbr. articles to profl. jours. Mem. ABA. Roman Catholic. Avocations: jogging, martial artist. Criminal, Taxation, general. Address: 25 Main St # 200 Hackensack NJ 07601-7015 also: 305 Madison Ave Ste 449 New York NY 10165-0006 Fax: 201-487-2840. E-mail: mullin.law@verizon.net.

MULLINIX, EDWARD WINGATE, lawyer; b. Balt., Feb. 25, 1924; s. Howard Earle and Elsie (Wingate) M.; m. Virginia Lee McGinnes, July 28, 1944; children: Marcia Lee Ladd, Edward Wingate. Student, St. John's Coll., 1941-43; JD summa cum laude, U. Pa., 1949. Bar: Pa. 1950, U.S. Supreme Ct. 1955; cert. BBB Auto Line arbitrator. Assoc. Schnader Harrison Segal & Lewis LLP, Phila., 1950-55, ptnr., 1956-92, now sr. coun. Mem. adv. bds. Antitrust Bull., 1970-81, BNA Antitrust and Trade Regulation Report, 1981-94; mem. Civil Justice adv. group U.S. Dist. Ct. (ea. dist.) Pa., 1998—; mem. Civil Justice Reform Act of 1990 adv. group U.S. Dist. Ct. (ea. dist.) Pa., 1991-98; co-chmn. Joint U.S. Dist. Ct./Phila. Bar Assn. Alternative Dispute Resolution Com., 1990-2002; cons. on revision of local civil rules U.S. Dist. Ct. (ea. dist.) Pa., 1995—; mem. adv. com. U. Pa. Law Sch. Ctr. on Professionalism, 1988-92; judge pro tem Day Forward and Commerce case mgmt. programs, chmn. adv. com. Commerce program Ct. Common Pleas of Phila. County; advocate, mem. steering com. in elderly-victim-assistance program Phila. Dist. Atty.'s Office Elder Justice Project; faculty participant Pa. Bar Inst. and other CLE programs. Trustee Sta. KYW-TV Project Homeless Fund, 1985-86. Served with USMCR, 1943-44; to lt. (j.g.) USNR, 1944-46. Fellow Am. Bar Found. (life), Am. Coll. Trial Lawyers (emeritus, mem. complex litig. com. 1980-91, vice-chmn. com. 1981-83); mem. ABA (spl. com. complex and multidist. litig. 1969-73, co-chmn. com. 1971-73, coun. litig. sect. 1976-80), Pa. Bar Assn., Phila. Bar Assn., Hist. Soc. U.S. Dist. Ct. (ea. dist.) Pa. (bd. dirs. 1984—, pres. 1991-94), Juristic Soc., Order of Coif, Union League (Phila.), Socialegal Club (Phila.), Aronimink Golf Club (Newtown Sq., Pa.). Republican. Presbyterian. Alternative dispute resolution, Federal civil litigation, Professional liability. Home: 251 Chamounix Rd Saint Davids PA 19087-3605 Office: 1600 Market St Ste 3600 Philadelphia PA 19103-7286 Office Fax: 215-972-7262. E-mail: ewm@shsl.com.

MULLMAN, MICHAEL S. lawyer; b. N.Y.C., Sept. 17, 1946; s. Herbert and Harriet (Weissman) M.; m. Ellen Mullman, 1975; children: Jeremy, Cassie. BA in Polit. Sci. cum laude, Union Coll., Schenectady, N.Y., 1968; JD, Columbia U., 1971. Bar: N.Y. 1972, U.S. Ct. Appeals (2d cir.), U.S. Dist. Ct., 1975. Ptnr. Schonwald, Schaffzin & Mullman, N.Y.C., 1980-89, Tenzer Greenblatt LLP, N.Y.C., 1989-99; adminstrv. ptnr. in charge N.Y. Blank Rome LLP, N.Y.C., 2000—, mem. exec. com., distbn. com., ptnr. bd. Bd. editors Columbia Jour. Law and Soc. Problems, articles edition, 1970-71. Nott scholar Union Coll., 1967, Harlan Fiske Stone scholar Sch. Law Columbia U., 1971. Mem. Bar Assn. N.Y.C., Phi Beta Kappa. Avocations: tennis, skiing, reading, gardening. Corporate, general, Mergers and acquisitions, Property, real (including real estate development, water). Office: Blank Rome LLP The Chrysler Bldg 405 Lexington Ave New York NY 10174-0002

MULVANIA, WALTER LOWELL, lawyer; b. Rock Port, Mo., Sept. 20, 1905; s. Jesse L. and Eva Viola (Stewart) Mulvania; m. Eunice Mary Umbarger, Jan. 31, 1945 (dec. May 2002); 1 child, Eva Jo Mulvania Van Meter. BA, William Jewell Coll., Liberty, Mo., 1927; JD, U. Mo., 1931. Pvt. practice law, Rock Port, 1931—. Fellow Am. Coll. of Trust and Estate Counsel; mem. ABA, Mo. Bar Assn. (bd. govs. 1965-71), Rotary (pres. 1951-52). Democrat. Baptist. Estate planning, Probate (including wills, trusts), Property, real (including real estate development, water). Office: 213 S Main St Rock Port MO 64482-1531

MULVIHILL, KEITHLEY D. lawyer; b. Pitts., Oct. 16, 1956; s. Bernard H. and Doris L. M.; m. Donna Colella, 1980; children: Michael, Mary Katherine. BA in History, Ind. U. Pa., 1978; JD, U. Pitts., 1981. Bar: Pa. 1981, U.S. Dist. Ct. (we. dist.) Pa. 1981, U.S. Ct. Appeals (3d cir.) 1982; CPCU. Assoc. Rose, Schmidt, Hasley & DiSalle, Pitts., 1981-88, shareholder, 1988-2001; ptnr., head litigation dept. Leech, Tishman, Fuscaldo & Lampl, Pitts., 2001—03; ptnr. Rawle & Henderson LLP, 2003—. Spl. master Ct. of Common Pleas of Allegheny County, Pa.; commr. Municipality of Mt. Lebanon, Pa., 1999—, v.p. 2002, pres., 2003. Mng. editor U. Pitts. Law Rev., 1980—81. Mem. Allegheny County Dem. Com; rep. Mt. Lebanon South Hills Area Coun. of Govts.; mem. St. Bernard Roman Cath. Ch. (past mem. parish coun.). Mem. ABA, Pa. Bar Assn., Pa. Def. Inst. (treas. 1998—), Allegheny County Bar Assn., Assn. Def. Trial Attys. (Pa. state chair), Def. Rsch. Inst., CPCU Soc. (pub. rels. chmn. Allegheny chpt.). General civil litigation, Insurance, Product liability. Office: Rawle & Henderson LLP Ste 910 Henry W Oliver Bldg 535 Smithfield St Pittsburgh PA 15222 E-mail: kmulvihill@rawle.com.

MUMFORD, MANLY WHITMAN, lawyer; b. Evanston, Ill., Feb. 25, 1925; s. Manly Stearns and Helen (Whitman) M.; m. Luigi Thorne Horne, July 1, 1961; children— Shaw, Dodge. AB, Harvard U., 1947; JD, Northwestern U, Chgo., 1950. Bar: Ill. 1950, U.S. Supreme Ct. 1969. Assoc. Chapman and Cutler, Chgo., 1950-62, ptnr., 1963-90. Author: The Old Family Fire, 1997; contbr. articles to profl. jours. Served with USNR, 1942-46. Fellow Am. Coll. Bond Counsel (hon.); mem. Nat. Assn. Bond Lawyers (Bernard P. Friel medal 1987). Clubs: Cliff Dwellers, University, Chgo. Literary. Democrat. Avocation: computers. Municipal (including bonds). Home: 399 W Fullerton Pky Chicago IL 60614-2810 Office: 22 W Monroe St Ste 1503 Chicago IL 60603-2505 E-mail: manly@mumford.cx.

MUMFORD, WILLIAM PORTER, II, retired lawyer; b. Kewanee, Ill., July 13, 1920; s. Harold E. and Mary K. (Harry) M.; m. Jean N. Hagemann, Nov. 22, 1951; children— William Porter III, James F., Michael E. BS in Accounting, U. Ill., 1943, JD, 1949. Bar: Ill. bar 1949, Oreg. bar 1955; C.P.A., Ill., Oreg. Jr. accountant Price Waterhouse & Co., Chgo., 1949-51; practiced in Chgo., 1951-54, Grants Pass, Ore., 1955-57, Eugene, Oreg., 1957—; mem. firm McAdams & Kirby, 1951-55; sr. accountant B.K. Herndon & Co., 1955-57; partner Thompson, Mumford, Anderson & Fisher, 1957-86, ret., 1986. Eugene campaign mgr. Hatfield for Gov., 1960-62; Chmn. bd. trustees Oreg. State Library. Served to capt. inf. AUS, 1943-46. Mem. Am. Legion, Pi Kappa Alpha, Phi Alpha Delta. Clubs: Elk. Republican. General practice, Personal injury (including property damage), Probate (including wills, trusts). Home: 1960 Alder St Eugene OR 97405-2938

MUMM, CHRISTOPHER ERIC, lawyer, county government official; b. Reno, Dec. 9, 1950; s. Hans Heinrich and Yolanda Victoria (Erickson) M.; m. Stephanie Wasile, Nov. 27, 1984; children: Melody Anishka, Alexander Matthew. AAS in Real Estate, Truckee Meadows C.C., 1976; JD, Nev. Sch. Law, 1985. Bar: Nev. 1987, Calif. 1987; lic. real estate broker, Nev. Dep. appraiser Washoe County, Reno, 1976-80, dep. tax assessor, 1980—2001; ind. real estate broker Reno, 1979—; pvt. practice law, 1987—. Chief tribal ct. judge Pyramid Lake Indian Reservation, 1994-98. Pres. PTA, Sparks Mid. Sch., 1999, Alice Maxwell Elem. Sch., 1998. With U.S. Army, 1970-72. Mem. Calif. Bar Assn., Nev. Bar Assn., Soc. Real Estate Appraisers (v.p. edn. Reno chpt. 1984-86), Internat. Assn. Assessing Ofcls., Nev. Jr. C. of C. (pres. 1986), U.S. Jaycees (exec. bd. dirs. 1986, amb., sen.), Acquarian Toastmasters (pres. 1988), Sertoma. Republican. Roman Catholic. Home: 3815 Moorpark Ct Sun Valley NV 89433-8240

MUMPHREY, J. WAYNE, lawyer; b. New Orleans, July 16, 1947; m. Victoria B. Brown, Dec. 27, 1969; children: Claude S. II, Wayne B., Sarah B. JD, Loyola U., 1971. Bar: La. 1971, U.S. Ct. Appeals (5th cir.) 1983, U.S. Claims Ct. 1990. Atty. pvt. practice, Chalmette, La., 1981—. Mem.: La. Trial Lawyers Assn., Am. Trial Lawyers Assn. Toxic tort, Personal injury (including property damage), General civil litigation. Home: PO Box 90 Chalmette LA 70044 Office: Mumphrey Law Firm LLC 9061 West Judge Perez Dr Chalmette LA 70043 Office Fax: 504-279-0806. E-mail: jwmumphrey@mumphreylaw.com.

MUND, GERALDINE, judge; b. L.A., July 7, 1943; d. Charles J. and Pearl M. BA, Brandeis U., 1965; MS, Smith Coll., 1967; JD, Loyola U., 1977. Bar: Calif. 1977. Bankruptcy judge U.S. Ctrl. Dist. Calif., 1984—, bankruptcy chief judge, 1997—2002. Past pres. Temple Israel, Hollywood, Calif.; past mem. Bd. Jewish Fedn. Coun. of Greater L.A. Mem. ABA, L.A. County Bar Assn. Office: 21041 Burbank Blvd Woodland Hills CA 91367-6606

MUNDEN, GAIL S. legal information administrator; MS in Libr. Sci., La. State U., 1971. Dir. legal info. Mayer, Brown Rowe & Maw, Chgo., 1978—. Office: Mayer Brown Rowe & Maw 190 S LaSalle St Chicago IL 60603 Office Fax: 312-701-7711. E-mail: gmunden@mayerbrownrowe.com.

MUNDHEIM, ROBERT HARRY, law educator; b. Hamburg, Germany, Feb. 24, 1933; m. Guna Smitchens; children: Susan, Peter. BA, Harvard U., 1954, LLB, 1957; MA (hon.), U. Pa., 1971. Bar: N.Y. 1958, Pa. 1979. Assoc. Shearman & Sterling, N.Y.C., 1958-61; spl. counsel to SEC Washington, 1962-63; vis. prof. Duke Law Sch., Durham, N.C., 1964; prof. law U. Pa., Phila., 1965—. Univ. prof. law and fin., 1980-93, dean, 1982-89, Bernard G. Segal prof. law, 1987-89; co-chmn. Fried, Frank, Harris, Shriver & Jacobson, N.Y.C., 1990-92; exec. v.p., gen. counsel Salomon Inc., 1992-97; sr. exec. v.p., gen. counsel Salomon Smith Barney Holdings, Inc., 1997-98; of counsel Shearman & Sterling, 1999—; gen. counsel U.S. Dept. Treasury, Washington, 1977-80, trustee and pres. Am. Acad. in Berlin, 2000—; chmn. legal adv. bd. NASDAQ, chmn. legal adv. bd. NASD; pres. Appleseed Found.; trustee New Sch. U.; bd. dirs. eCollege, Salzburg Seminar, The Kitchen; gen. counsel Chrysler Loan Guarantee Bd., 1980; mng. dir., mem. mgmt. bd. Salomon Bros. Inc., N.Y.C., 1992-97; overseer Curtis Inst. Fin., 2000—. Author: Outside Director of the Publicity Held Corporation, 1976; American Attitudes Toward Foreign Direct Investment in the United States, 1979; Conflict of Interest and the Former Government Employee: Re-thinking the Revolving Door, 1981; chmn. adv. bd. Jour. Internat. Econ. Law, 1996-97. Trustee SEC Hist. Soc. With USAF, 1961-62. Recipient Alexander Hamilton award U.S. Dept. Treasury, 1980, Harold P. Seligson award Practicing Law Inst., 1988, Francis J. Rawle award, ABA-ALI, 1992, Anti-Defamation League Human Rels. award, 1999. Mem. ABA (task force on corp. responsiblity), Am. Law Inst., San Diego Securities Regulation Inst. (exec. com.). Office: Shearman & Sterling 599 Lexington Ave Fl 16 New York NY 10022-6069

MUNDY, GARDNER MARSHALL, lawyer; b. Roanoke, Va., July 19, 1934; s. Gardner Adams and Betty (Marshall) M.; m. Jean Stephens, Nov. 13, 1956 (div. 1979); children: Stephens M., Liza I.; m. Jenice Hamrick, June 21, 1980 (div. 1998); children: G. Marshall Jr., Natalie J.; m. Monika Ferguson, Aug. 28, 1999. BA, Va. Mil. Inst., 1956; LLB, U. Va., 1962. Bar: Va. 1962, U.S. Dist. Ct. (we. dist.) Va. 1962, U.S. Ct. Appeals (4th cir.) 1962. Ptnr. Woods, Rogers & Hazlegrove, Roanoke, 1962-71, Mundy & Garrison, Roanoke, 1973-76, Mundy & Strickland, Roanoke, 1976-82; pvt. practice Roanoke, 1982-86; ptnr. Mundy, Rogers & Frith, Roanoke, 1986—. 1st lt. U.S. Army, 1957-59. Fellow Am. Coll. Trial Lawyers, Am. Bd. Trial Advocates (pres. Western Va. chpt. 1990-91), Am. Bar Found., Va. Bar Found.; mem. ABA, Va. State Bar (chmn. bd. govs. litig. sect. 1985-86, bd. govs. sr. law sect. 2000—), Roanoke Bar Assn. (bd. dirs. 1986-90, pres. 1990-91), Shenandoah Club, Roanoke Country Club, Coral Beach and Tennis Club (Bermuda). Presbyterian. Avocations: tennis, skiing, cooking, growing roses. General civil litigation, Family and matrimonial, Personal injury (including property damage). Home: 1542 Electric Rd Roanoke VA 24018-1106 Office: Mundy Rogers & Frith 1328 3rd St SW Roanoke VA 24016-5219 Fax: 540-982-1362. E-mail: gmundy@mrf-law.com.

MUNGIA, SALVADOR ALEJO, lawyer; b. Tacoma, Feb. 19, 1959; s. Salvador Alejo Sr. and Susie (Tamaki) M. BA, Pacific Luth. U., 1981; JD, Georgetown U., 1984. Bar: Wash. 1984, U.S. Dist. Ct. (we. dist.) Wash. 1985, U.S. Ct. Appeals (9th cir.) 1986, U.S. Supreme Ct. 1992. Law clk. to Justice Fred Dore Wash. State Supreme Ct., Olympia, 1984-85; law clerk to Hon. Carolyn R. Dimmick U.S. Dist. Ct. (we. dist.) Wash., Seattle, 1985-86; assoc. Gordon, Thomas, Honeywell, Malanca, Peterson & Daheim, Tacoma, 1986-91, ptnr., 1991—. Adj. prof. Pacific Luth. U., 1993-94. Vol. atty. ACLU, Tacoma, 1986—, bd. dirs., 1987-92; commr. Tacoma Human Rights Commn., 1990-96; bd. dirs. Legal Aid for Washington, 1992-96, life bd. dirs., 1997—, pres., 2002-2003; dir. bd. dirs. Grand Cinema, Tacoma, 2003. Recipient Am. Leadership Forum fellowship, 2001—02. Mem.: ABA, Pierce County Young Lawyers Assn. (trustee 1988—90), Tacoma-Pierce County Bar Assn. (pres. 1999), Fed. Bar Assn. Western Wash., Wash. State Bar Assn., Tacoma Club, Tacoma Lawn Tennis Club. Avocations: mountain climbing, skiing, tennis, running. Federal civil litigation, State civil litigation. Home: 525 Broadway # 201 Tacoma WA 98402 Office: Gordon Thomas Honeywell Malance Peterson & Daheim PO Box 1157 Tacoma WA 98401-1157 E-mail: mungs@gth-law.com.

MUNIZ, JOAQUIM TAVARES DE PAIVA, lawyer, law educator; b. Rio de Janeiro, Apr. 10, 1974; s. Luiz Gonzaga de Paiva and Maria José (Tavares de Paiva) Muniz. JD, State U. Rio de Janeiro, 1996; LLM, U. Chgo., 1999. Bar: Rio de Janeiro State Bar 1997. Trainee Castro, Barros e Sobral Adv., Rio de Janeiro, 1994—95; atty. Castro, Bardos e Sobral Adv., Rio de Janeiro, 1997—99; trainee Lobo & Ibeas Advogados, Rio de Janeiro, 1996; atty. Baker & McKenzie, Rio de Janeiro, 1999—. Law prof. FGU Bus. Sch., Rio de Janeiro, 2000—, UERJ Law Sch., Rio de Janeiro, 2001—, IBMEC Bus. Sch., Rio de Janeiro, 2001—. Contbr. articles to profl. jours. Mem.: AIDA, Com. Brasileiro de Arbitragen (founding mem.), Am. Arbitration Assn. Corporate, general, Mergers and acquisitions, Oil, gas, and mineral. Office: Trench Rossi & Watanabe-Baker & McKenzie Av Rio Branco 1 19th Fl 20090-003 Rio de Janeiro Brazil Fax: 5521 2206-4949. E-mail: j-muniz-7@alumni.uchicago.edu.

MUNIZ, RENATA MARIA (RENATA NOVOTNY), lawyer; b. Sao Paulo, May 10, 1967; d. Norberto and Therezinha Pereira Novotny; m. Ian De Porto Alegre Muniz, June 27, 1996; 1 child, Mariana Novotny. Degree cum laude in law, Rio de Janeiro Fed. U., 1989. Mgr. Arthur Andersen, Rio de Janeiro, 1988—93; ptnr. Lobo & Ibeas, 1993—. Mem.: Assn. Brazilian Dir. Fin. Roman Catholic. Avocations: orchids, ceramics. Taxation, general, Corporate, general, State and local taxation. Office: Lobo & Ibeas Av Rio Branco 125 12 Andar 20040-006 Rio de Janeiro Brazil Fax: 5521 2221 5070. E-mail: ren@loboeibeas.adv.br.

MUNN, CECIL EDWIN, lawyer; b. Enid, Okla., Aug. 8, 1923; s. Cecil Edwin and Margaret (Kittrell) M.; m. Carolyn Taylor Culver, May 8, 1948; children: Franklin Culver, Charlotte Munn Forswall. BA, U. Okla., 1945; JD cum laude, Harvard U., 1947. Bar: Okla. 1947, Tex. 1955. Practice in, Enid, 1947-54, Ft. Worth, 1954—; partner firm Cantey & Hanger, Ft. Worth, 1960-91, of counsel, 1992—. With Champlin Petroleum Co., 1954-60, v.p., atty., 1958-60, dir., 1962-75. Fellow Am. Coll. Trial Lawyers, Am. Bar Found.; mem. ABA (chmn. natural resources law sect. 1970-71), Southwestern Legal Found. (past dir.), Tex. Bar Found., Phi Delta Theta, Phi Delta Phi. Presbyterian. Office: 2100 Burnett Plz 801 Cherry St Fort Worth TX 76102-6803 Home: 1725 Hulen St Fort Worth TX 76107-3828

MUNOZ, SHANE THOMAS, lawyer; b. New Orleans, Oct. 12, 1955; s. Scott Muni and Frances Isabelle Davis; m. Elizabeth Joan DeDeyn, Aug. 16, 1986; children: Margaret Anne, Sarah Catherine. Student, Northwe. U., 1973-74; BS in Plant Sci., U. N.H., 1977; JD, U. Conn., 1989. Bar: Conn. 1989, U.S. Dist. Ct. Conn. 1990, U.S. Dist. Ct. (no., mid. and so. dists.) Fla. 1995, U.S. Ct. Appeals (11th cir.); cert. expert in labor and employment law Fla. Bar, 2001; AV rating Martindale-Hubbell. Mgr. Tuttle Market Gardens, Inc., Dover, N.H., 1977-86; lawyer Day, Berry & Howard, Hartford, Conn., 1989-95, Brown, Clark & Walters, Sarasota, Fla., 1995-97, Zinober & McCrea, P.A., Tampa, Fla., 1997—. Mem. standing com. on advt. Fla. Bar, 1999—; chmn. standing com. adv. Fla. Bar, 2002-; bd. dirs., 1998, 99, 2002, sec., 1999, v.p., 2000, pres., 2001, v.p., 2003, W. Ctrl. Fla., Indsl. Rels., Rsch. Assn. Recipient Book award Am. Jurisprudence, 1987, 88. Civil rights, Federal civil litigation, Labor (including EEOC, Fair Labor Standards Act, labor-management relations, NLRB, OSHA). Office: Zinober & McCrea PA 201 E Kennedy Blvd Ste 800 Tampa FL 33602-5863 E-mail: smunoz@zmlaw.com.

MUNRO, MEREDITH VANCE, lawyer; b. Natick, Mass., Aug. 4, 1938; s. George Lawrence and Florence Estella (Murphy) Munro; m. Gail Wittekind, June 10, 1960 (div. 1974); children: Susan Heidi, Elizabeth Holly, Meredith Heather. AB, Princeton U., 1960; JD, Harvard U., 1963. Bar: Mass. 1963. Assoc. atty. Gaston Snow & Ely Barlett, Boston, 1963-71, ptnr., 1971-90. Trustee The Tabor Acad., Marion, Mass., 1975—2002. Avocations: antiques, gardening, cooking. Corporate, general, Estate planning, Property, real (including real estate development, water). Home: 5 Patricia Rd Framingham MA 01701-3931

MUNSON, ALEX ROBERT, judge; b. L.A., Sept. 25, 1941; s. Robert Alexander and Lillian Agnus (Hamel) M.; m. Kathleen Rae Abernathey, June 29, 1968. BA, Long Beach (Calif.) State Coll., 1964, MA, 1965; EdD, U. So. Calif., L.A., 1970; JD, Loyola U., L.A., 1975. Atty. Kirtland and Packard, L.A., 1978-82; chief justice High Ct. of The Trust Terr. of The Pacific Islands, Saipan, Commonwealth of the No. Mariana Islands, 1982-88; chief judge U.S. Dist. Ct. of No. Mariana Islands, Saipan, Commonwealth of the No. Mariana Islands, 1988—. Mem. ABA, Calif. Bar Assn. Republican. Home: PO Box 5356 Saipan MP 96950-5356 Office: US Dist Ct NMI PO Box 500687 Saipan MP 96950-0687

MUNSON, HOWARD G. federal judge; b. Claremont, N.H., July 26, 1924; s. Walter N. and Helena (O'Halloran) M.; m. Ruth Jaynes, Sept. 17, 1949; children: Walter N., Richard J., Pamela A. BS in Economics, U. Pa., 1948; LL.B., Syracuse U., 1952. Bar: N.Y. With Employers' Assurance Corp., Ltd., White Plains, N.Y., 1949-50; mem. firm Hiscock, Lee, Rogers, Henley & Barclay, Syracuse, N.Y., 1952-76; judge U.S. Dist. Ct. No. Dist. N.Y., Syracuse, 1976—. Mem., pres. Syracuse Bd. Edn.; bd. dirs. Sta. WCNY-TV; chmn. ethics com. Onondaga County Legislature. Served with U.S. Army, 1943-45, ETO. Decorated Bronze Star, Purple Heart. Mem. Am. Coll. Trial Lawyers, Nat. Assn. R.R. Trial Counsel, Am. Arbitration Assn., Justinian Soc., Alpha Tau Omega, Phi Delta Phi. Office: US Dist Ct US Courthouse P O Box 7376 Syracuse NY 13261-7376

MUNSON, NANCY KAY, lawyer; b. Huntington, N.Y., June 22, 1936; d. Howard H. and Edna M. (Keenan) Munson. Student, Hofstra U., 1959-62; JD, Bklyn. Law Sch., 1965. Bar: N.Y. 1966, U.S. Supreme Ct. 1970, U.S. Ct. Appeals (2d cir.) 1971, U.S. Dist. Ct. (ea. and so. dists.) N.Y. 1968. Law clk. to E. Merritt Weidner, Huntington, 1959-66; sole practice, 1966—. Mem. legal adv. bd. Chgo. Title Ins. Co., Riverhead, N.Y., 1981—; bd. dirs., legal officer Thomas Munson Found. Trustee Huntington Fire Dept. Death Benefit Fund; pres., trustee, chmn. bd. Bklyn. Home Aged Men Found.; bd. dirs. Elderly Day Svcs. on the Sound, Huntington Rural Cemetery Assn., Inc. Mem. ABA, N.Y. State Bar Assn., Suffolk County Bar Assn., Bklyn. Bar Assn., NRA, DAR (trustee, treas. Ketewamoke chpt.), Soroptimists (past pres.). Republican. Christian Scientist. General practice, Probate (including wills, trusts), Property, real (including real estate development, water). Office: 197 New York Ave Huntington NY 11743-2711

MUNSON, PETER KERR, lawyer; b. Sherman, Tex., Dec. 5, 1944; s. William Ben and Martha M. (deGolian) M.; m. Kathleen Cook, Aug. 30, 1969; children— Peter, Brian, Christopher. B.B.A., U. Notre Dame, 1967; J.D., U. Tex., 1970. Bar: Tex. 1970, U.S. Dist. Ct. (ea. dist.) Tex. 1970, U.S. Ct. Appeals (5th cir.) 1970; cert. specialist in family law, Tex. Sr. mem. Munson, Munson & Pierce, Grayson County, Tex. 1970— ; Gov's. appointee Commn. on Uniform State Laws, State of Tex., 1985-91, 97—. Chmn. adv. bd. Sherman-Denison Salvation Army, 1983— ; chmn. parish council St. Mary's Ch., Sherman, 1982-83; scoutmaster, dist. commr. Boy Scouts Am.; adv. bd., past chmn. Salvation Army; bd. dirs. Grayson County United Way, Sherman, 1973— . Ford Found. grantee, 1969. Mem. North Tex. Bar Assn., Tex. Council Sch. Bd. Attys. Roman Catholic. Corporate, general, Family and matrimonial, Property, real (including real estate development, water). Office: Munson Munson Cardwell & Pierce 123 S Travis St Sherman TX 75090-5928

MUNTEANU, VICTOR JOHN, lawyer; b. Ft. Devens, Mass., Jan. 11, 1958; s. Virgil Peter and Ligita (Gutmanis) M.; m. Kathleen Galman, Oct. 10, 1987; children: Sydney Rose, Peter John. BA in Polit. Sci., Lebanon Valley Coll., Annville, Pa., 1979; JD, U. Tenn., 1981. Bar: Colo. 1982, U.S. Dist. Ct. Colo. 1982, U.S. Ct. Appeals (10th cir.) 1982. Assoc. Caskins & Chanzit, Denver, 1982-90; pvt. practice, Denver, 1990—. General civil litigation, Corporate, general, Property, real (including real estate development, water). Office: 1080 Kalamath St Denver CO 80204-3949 E-mail: vjmunteanu@earthlink.net.

MUNZER, STEPHEN IRA, lawyer; b. N.Y.C., Mar. 15, 1939; s. Harry and Edith (Isacowitz) M.; m. Patricia Eve Munzer, Aug. 10, 1965; children: John, Margaret. AB, Brown U., 1960; JD, Cornell U., 1963. Bar: N.Y. 1964, U.S. Supreme Ct. 1974, U.S. Dist. Ct. (so. and eas. dists.) N.Y., U.S. Ct. Appeals (3d cir.). Formerly ptnr. Pincus Munzer Bizar & D'Alessandro, 1978-83; atty., real estate investor Munzer & Saunders, LLP, 1984—. Pres. Simcor Mgmt. Corp., N.Y.C., 1984—. Lt. USNR, 1965-75. Mem. Assn. of Bar of City of N.Y., N.Y. State Bar Assn., Washington Club. Jewish. Avocations: golf, skiing. Federal civil litigation, General civil litigation, Property, real (including real estate development, water). Home: 30 Lincoln Plz New York NY 10023 also: 170 Shearer Rd Washington CT 06793-1013 Office: 609 5th Ave New York NY 10017-1021

MURAI, RENE VICENTE, lawyer; b. Havana, Cuba, Mar. 11, 1945; came to the U.S., 1960; s. Andres and Silvia (Muñiz) M.; m. Luisa Botifoll, June 12, 1970; 1 child, Elisa. BA, Brown U., 1966; JD cum laude, Columbia U., 1969. Bar: Fla. 1970, N.Y. 1972, U.S. Supreme Ct. 1977. Atty. Reginald Heber Smith Fellow Legal Svcs. Greater Miami, Fla., 1969-71; assoc. Willkie, Farr & Gallagher, N.Y.C., 1971-73; ptnr. Paul, Landy & Beiley, Miami, 1973-79; shareholder Murai, Wald, Biondo & Moreno, Miami, 1979—. Vice-chmn. Premier Am. Bank, Miami; dir. Cuban Am. Bar Assn., 1982-96, pres., 1985; vice chmn., lectr. Internat. Conf. for Lawyers of the Ams., 1982, chmn. and lectr., 1984; mem. panel grievance com. Fla. Bar, 1983-86. Mng. editor Columbia Law Rev., 1967-69. Bd. dirs., sec. Archtl. Club of Miami, 1978-86, Dade Heritage Trust, 1979-82, Facts About Cuban Exiles, Inc., 1982—, pres., 1989, Legal Svcs. of Greater Miami, Inc., 1980-90, pres. 1986-88, ARC, 1984-90, exec. com., 1988-90, Mercy Hosp. Found., 1985-91, Dade Cmty. Found., 1988-93, chair grants com., 1991-93, United Way, 1989-95, Miami Chldn.'s Hosp., 2000—; chmn. adminstrn. of justice com. Fla. Bar Found., 1996-98, bd. dirs., 1991-2000, chmn. audit and fin. com., 1993-98, sec., 1997-98, pres. 1999-2000; mem. task force leadership Dade County Ptnrs. for Safe Neighborhoods, 1994-95, Code Enforcement Bd. City of Coral Gables, 1982-86, Bd. Adjustment, 1987-89, city mgr. selection com., 1987, charter rev. commn., 1980; trustee U. Miami, 1994-96; bd. dirs. Miami Children's Hosp., 1999—. Mem. ABA, Cuban-Am. Bar Assn., Dade County Bar Assn. (dir. 1987-88), Greater Miami C. of C., Spain-U.S. C. of C., Miami City Club (bd. dirs. 1997—2001, pres. 2000—01). Democrat. Roman Catholic. Avocation: sports. Banking, Commercial, contracts (including sales of goods; commercial financing), Corporate, general. Home: 3833 Alhambra Ct Coral Gables FL 33134-6229 Office: Murai Wald Biondo & Moreno PA 25 SE 2nd Ave Ste 900 Miami FL 33131-1600 E-mail: rmurai@mwbm.com.

MURANE, WILLIAM EDWARD, lawyer; b. Denver, Mar. 4, 1933; s. Edward E. and Theodora (Wilson) M.; m. Rosemarie Palmerone, Mar. 26, 1960; children: Edward Wheelock, Peter Davenport, Alexander Phelps. AB, Dartmouth Coll., 1954; LLB, Stanford U., 1957. Bar: Wyo. 1957, Colo. 1958, D.C. 1978, U.S. Supreme Ct. 1977. Assoc. then ptnr. Holland & Hart, Denver, 1961-69; dep. gen. counsel U.S. Dept. Commerce, Washington, 1969-71; gen. counsel FDIC, Washington, 1971-72; ptnr. Holland & Hart, Denver, 1972—2000. Pub. mem. Adminstrv. Conf. of the U.S., Washington, 1978-81. Bd. dirs. Ctr. for Law and Rsch., Denver, 1973-76, Acad. in the Wilderness, Denver, 1986—, Colo. Bus. Com. for Arts, 2002—; trustee Colo. Symphony Orch., 1994-2000; mem. bd. visitors Stanford U. Law Sch. Capt. USAF, 1958-61. Fellow Am. Coll. Trial Lawyers; mem. ABA (ho of dels. 1991-96), U. Club, Cactus Club. Republican. Avocations: fishing, classical music. Administrative and regulatory, General civil litigation, Libel. Office: Holland & Hart 555 17th St Ste 2700 Denver CO 80202-3950

MURASE, JIRO, lawyer; b. N.Y.C., May 16, 1928; BBA, CCNY, 1955; JD, Georgetown U., 1958, LL.D. (hon.), 1982. Bar: D.C. 1958, N.Y. 1959. Sr. ptnr. Marks & Murase L.L.P., N.Y.C., 1971-97, Bingham McCutchen Murase , N.Y.C., 1997—. Legal counsel Consulate Gen. of Japan; mem. Pres.'s Adv. Com. Trade Negotiations, 1980-82; mem. Trilateral Commn., 1985—; apptd. mem. World Trade Coun., 1984-94; adv. com. internat. investment, tech. and devel. Dept. State, 1975. Editorial bd.: Law and Policy in Internat. Bus. Trustee Asia Found., 1979-83, Japanese Ednl. Inst. N.Y.; bd. dirs. Japan Soc., Japanese C. of C. in N.Y., Inc.; bd. regents Georgetown U.; bd. visitors Georgetown Law Ctr.; adv. coun. Pace U., Internat. House Japan; pres. Japanese-Am. Assn. N.Y., Inc., 1996-98—, Japan Ctr. Internat. Exch., 2001—. Recipient N.Y. Gov.'s citation for contbns. to internat. trade, 1982; named to Second Order of Sacred Treasure (Japan), 1989. Mem. ABA, Assn. of Bar of City of N.Y., N.Y. State Bar Assn., N.Y. County Lawyers Assn., Maritime Law Assn., Consular Law Soc., Fed. Bar Coun., Am. Soc. Internat. Law, World Assn. Lawyers, Japanese-Am. Soc. Legal Studies, Am. Arbitration Assn., Lic. Execs. Soc., U.S. C. of C. Clubs: Nippon (dir.); Ardsley Country; N.Y. Athletic; Mid-Ocean (Bermuda). Office: Bingham McCutchen Murase 399 Park Ave New York NY 10022-4614

MURASKI, ANTHONY AUGUSTUS, lawyer; b. Cohoes, N.Y., July 28, 1946; s. Adam Joseph and Angeline Mary (Vozzy) M.; m. Jeanne Marie Muraski; children: Adam Peter, Emily Jo, Talia Rose, Lydia Fern, Mariah Willow. BA, MA in Speech/Hearing, Sacramento State Coll., 1970; PhD in Audiology/ Hearing Sci., U. Mich., 1977; JD, Detroit Coll. Law, 1979. Bar: Mich. 1980, U.S. Dist. Ct. (ea. dist.) Mich. 1981, U.S. Ct. Appeals (6th cir.) 1982, U.S. Claims Ct. 1989, U.S. Supreme Ct. 1990, Pa. 1990. Asst. Kresge Hearing Research Inst. U. Mich., Ann Arbor, 1971-77; asst. prof. Wayne State U. Med. Sch., Detroit, 1979-82; assoc. Kitch, Suhrheinrich, Saurbier & Drutchas, Detroit, 1982-83; assoc. prof. Detroit Coll. Law, 1983-85; mng. ptnr. Muraski & Sikorski, Ann Arbor, 1985—. Cons. audiology Ministry of Environment, Ont., Can., 1980-81; trustee Deaf, Speech and Hearing Ctr., Detroit, 1981—; legal adv. on air WWJ Radio, Detroit, 1984—; mem. mental health adv. bd. on deafness Dept. Mental Health, 1984, vis. com. U. Mich. Sch. Edn., 1986—. Author: Legal Aspects of Audiological Practice, 1982, Hearing Conservation in Industry: Licensure, Liability and Forensics, 1985. Mem. ABA, Mich. Bar Assn., Washtenaw County Bar Assn., Am. Speech-Lang.-Hearing Assn. (sci. merit award, 1981), Ann Arbor C. of C. Avocations: photography, writing. Health, Private international, Labor (including EEOC, Fair Labor Standards Act, labor-management relations, NLRB, OSHA). Home: 3830 Warren Ct Ann Arbor MI 48105

MURCHISON, DAVID CLAUDIUS, lawyer; b. N.Y.C., Aug. 19, 1923; s. Claudius Temple and Constance (Waterman) M.; m. June Margaret Guilfoyle, Dec. 19, 1946 (dec. June 2001); children: David Roderick, Brian, Courtney, Bradley, Stacy; m. Janet Miller Paro, Aug. 10, 2002. AA, George Washington U., 1947, BA, JD with honors, George Washington U., 1949. Bar: D.C. 1949, Supreme Ct. 1955. Assoc. Dorr, Hand & Dawson, N.Y.C., 1949-50; founding ptnr. Howrey & Simon, Washington, 1956-90, counsel, 1990—. Legal asst. under sec. army, 1949-51; counsel motor vehicle, textile, aircraft, ordinance and shipbldg. divsns. Nat. Prodn. Authority, 1951-52; assoc. gen. counsel Small Def. Plants Adminstrn., 1952-53; legal adv. and asst. to chmn. FTC, 1953-55 Chmn. So. Africa Wildlife Trust. With AUS, 1943-45, ETO. Mem. ABA (chmn. com. internat. restrictive bus. practices sect. antitrust law 1954-55, sect. adminstrv. law, sect. litigation), FBA, D.C. Bar Assn., N.Y. State Bar Assn., Order of Coif, Met. Club, Chevy Chase Club, Talbot Country Club, Congl. Country Club, Columbia Country Club. Republican.

MURCHISON, DAVID RODERICK, lawyer; b. Washington, May 28, 1948; s. David Claudius and June Margaret (Guilfoyle) M.; m. Kathy Ann Kohn, Mar. 15, 1981; children: David Christopher, Benjamin Michael. BA cum laude, Princeton U., 1970; JD, Georgetown U., 1975. Bar: D.C. 1975, Fla. 1993. Legal asst. to vice chmn. CAB, Washington, 1975-76, enforcement atty., 1976-77; sr. atty. Air Transport Assn., Washington, 1977-80, asst. v.p., sec., 1981-85; sr. assoc. Zuckert, Scoutt and Rasenberger, Washington, 1980-81; v.p., asst. gen. counsel Piedmont Aviation, Inc., Winston-Salem, N.C., 1985-88; v.p., gen. counsel, sec. Braniff, Inc., Dallas, 1988-89, chief exec. officer Orlando, 1990-94; fed. adminstrv. law judge Office of Hearings and Appeals, Charleston, W.Va., 1994-96, chief adminstrv. law judge Mobile, Ala., 1996-99, adminstrv. law judge, 1999—. Lectr. continuing legal edn. program Wake Forest U., Winston-Salem, 1988. Contbr. articles to legal jours. Lt. USNR, 1970-72. Mem. ABA, Met. Club Washington. Republican. Roman Catholic. Administrative and regulatory, Corporate, general, Legislative. Office: Office Hearings and Appeals 3605 Springhill Bus Park Mobile AL 36608-1239

MURDOCH, DAVID ARMOR, lawyer; b. Pitts., May 30, 1942; s. Armor M. and N. Edna (Jones) M.; m. Joan Wilkie, Mar. 9, 1974; children: Christina, Timothy, Deborah. AB magna cum laude, Harvard U., 1964, LLB, 1967. Bar: Pa. 1967, U.S. Dist. Ct. (we. dist.) Pa. 1967, U.S. Ct. Mil. Appeals 1968, U.S. Supreme Ct. 1990, U.S. Ct. Appeals (3d cir.) 1991. Assoc. Kirkpatrick & Lockhart, LLP, Pitts., 1971-78, ptnr., 1978—. Mem. adv. bd. Ctr. for Internat. Legal Edn., U. Pitt., 1997—. Co-author: Business Workouts Manual. V.p., bd. dirs. Avonworth Sch. Dist., 1977-83; mem. bd. dirs. Pitts. Expt., 1988-93, chmn., 1989-90; mem. Pa. Housing Fin. Agy., 1981-88, vice chmn., 1983-87; alt. del. Rep. Nat. Conv., 1980; elder The Presbyn. Ch. of Sewickley, 1986-92; past pres. Harvard Law Sch. Assn. W. Pa.; bd. advisors Geneva Coll., 1993-94, trustee, 1994-97; trustee Sewickley Pub. Libr., 1994-2002, vice chmn., 1997-2002; trustee World Learning, Inc., 1995—, vice chmn., 1998-2000, chmn., 2000—; dir. Allegheny County Libr. Assn., 1994-96; chair Czech Working Group, Presbyn. Ch. USA, 1995-2000; bd. visitors U. Ctr. Internat. Studies, U. Pitts., 1996—; bd. advisors The Ctr. for Bus., Religion, and Pub. Life, Pitts. Theol. Sem., 1997—; bd. dirs. World Affairs Coun. Pitts., 1998—, Am. Coun. Germany, 1998—; hon. consul Fed. Rep. of Germany in Pitts., 2002—. Capt. U.S. Army, 1968-71. Recipient Disting. Svc. award Allegheny County Libr. Assn., 2001. Fellow Am. Coll. Bankruptcy, Am. Bar Found.; mem. ABA (mem. bus. bankruptcy com., chmn. subcom. on bankruptcy coms., trust indentures and claims trading 1991-97), Am. Law Inst. Bankruptcy, Commercial, contracts (including sales of goods; commercial financing), Corporate, general. Office: Kirkpatrick & Lockhart LLP Henry W Oliver Bldg 535 Smithfield St Pittsburgh PA 15222-2312 E-mail: dmurdoch@kl.com.

MURGUIA, RAMON, lawyer; b. Kansas City, Kans., Mar. 13, 1959; s. Alfredo Olivarez and Amalia Fernandez M.; m. Sally Atha, Jan. 20, 1996; children: R. Miguel, Amalia A. BS, U. Kans., 1981; JD, Harvard U., 1984; postgrad., Mex. and Am. Solidarity Found., Mexico City, 1994, Inst. de

Estudios Superiores, 1996. Bar: Mo. 1985, U.S. Dist. Ct. (we. dist.) Mo. 1987. Assoc. Armstrong, Teasdale, Schafly, Davis & Dicus and predecessor, Kansas City, Mo., 1984-91; prin., owner Murguia Law Offices, Kansas City, Mo., 1991—; of counsel Watson & Dameron, LLP, Kansas City, Mo., 1991—. Ptnr., cons. Access Internat., Kansas City, Kans., 1996-2000. Commr. Kans. Citizens Justice Initiative, 1997-2000; del. Pres.'s Summit for Am.'s Future, Phila., 1997; mem. adv. bd. Initiative for Competitive Inner City, Kansas City, Mo., 1998—; mem. Kansas City Tomorrow, Kansas City, Kans. Planning Commn., 1987-90, Kansas City, Kans. Bd. of Edn., 1990-91; chmn. Greater Kansas City Hispanic Devel. Fund, 1987—, Greater Kansas City Empowerment Zone Steering Com., 1994-98, Greater Kansas City Enhanced Enterprise Community Exec. Com.; bd. dirs. KCPT-TV, 1987-91, Hispanics in Philanthropy, San Francisco, 1990-95, Youth Opportunities Unltd., Kansas City, Kans., 1994-98, Learning Exch., Kansas City, Mo., 1994-2000, Greater Kansas City C. of C., 1995-2001, Francis Families Found., Kansas City, Mo., 1997—, Wyandotte Health Found., Kansas City, Kans., 1998—; bd. dirs., Nat. Coun. of La Raza, Washington, 1992-2002, chmn. 1998-2001; bd. dirs. Greater Kansas City Community Found. and Affiliated Trusts, 1990-96, 98—, sec., 1995-96; bd. dirs. Cath. Charities, Kansas City, 2000—, Hosp. Authority U. Kans., 2000-2002, Harry S. Truman Libr. Inst., 2001—; bd. trustees, Union Sta. Kansas City, Inc., 2000—. Recipient Outstanding Svc. to Kansas City Met. Community award, Mid-Am. Regional Coun., 1994, Community Svc. award Greater Kansas City Hispanic Heritage Month Com. Inc., 1995, Piñata Buster award Greater Kansas City Hispanic Scholarship Fund, 1997, Kans. City Spirit award, 1999, Delta award Donnelly Coll., Kans. City, 1999. Mem. Hispanic Nat. Bar Assn. Democrat. Roman Catholic. Avocation: basketball. Corporate, general, Personal injury (including property damage), Probate (including wills, trusts). Home: 2500 Strong Ave Kansas City KS 66106-2138 Office: 2500 Holmes St Kansas City MO 64108-2743 E-mail: rmurguia@kctriallawyers.com.

MURI, ANTHONY FREDERICK, lawyer; b. Providence, Dec. 29, 1948; s. Sam and Jacqueline (Perron) M.; m. Janet Patricia Hufnagel, Oct. 23, 1970; children: Nicole, Benjamin. BA, Coll. Holy Cross, Worcester, Mass., 1970; JD, Boston U., 1973. Bar: R.I. 1973, Mass. 1973, Maine 2002, U.S. Dist. Ct. R.I. 1974, U.S. Ct. Appeals (1st cir.) 1976, U.S. Supreme Ct. 1983. Assoc. Levy, Goodman, Semonoff & Gorin, Providence, 1973-78; ptnr. Licht & Semonoff, Providence, 1978-88, Goldenberg & Muri, Providence, 1988—. Mem. Fed. Bar Assn., ABA (sect. of litig.) R.I. Bar Assn. (mem. fed. bench/bar com. 1985—), Superior Ct. (bench/bar. com. 2002—), Def. Research Inst. Federal civil litigation, State civil litigation, Environmental.

MURPHY, ARTHUR WILLIAM, lawyer, educator; b. Boston, Jan. 25, 1922; s. Arthur W. and Rose (Spillane) M.; m. Jane Marks, Dec. 21, 1948 (dec. Sept. 1951); 1 dau., Lois; m. Jean C. Marks, Sept. 30, 1954; children— Rachel, Paul. AB cum laude, Harvard, 1943; LL.B., Columbia, 1948. Bar: N.Y. State bar 1949. Asso. in law Columbia Sch. Law, N.Y.C., 1948-49; asso. dir. Legislative Drafting Research Fund, 1956, prof. law, 1963—; trial atty. U.S. Dept. Justice, 1950-52; asso. firm Hughes, Hubbard, Blair & Reed, N.Y.C., 1953-56, 57-58; partner firm Baer, Marks, Friedman & Berliner, N.Y.C., 1959-63. Mem. safety and licensing panel AEC, 1962-73; mem. spl. commn. on weather modification NSF, 1964-66; mem. Presdl. Commn. on Catastrophic Nuclear Accidents, 1988-90 Author: Financial Protection against Atomic Hazards, 1957, (with others) Cases on Gratuitous Transfers, 1968, 3d edit., 1985, The Nuclear Power Controversy, 1976. Served with AUS, 1943-46. Decorated Purple Heart. Mem. ABA, Assn. of Bar of City of N.Y. (spl. com. on sci. and law) Office: Columbia Sch of Law 435 W 116th St New York NY 10027-7297

MURPHY, BARRY AMES, lawyer; b. Summit, N.J., Mar. 3, 1938; s. Robert Joseph and Florence C. (Ames) M.; m. Leslie Lynn Smith, June 9, 1962; children— Karen Irene, Sean Patrick, Conor Brendan, Ilana Taraleigh. BA in English, Stanford U., 1960; MBA, Harvard U., 1963; JD, U. So. Calif., 1972. Bar: Calif. bar 1973, U.S. Supreme Ct 1976, U.S. Tax Ct 1976. Fin. analyst Office of Sec. Def., 1963-65; pres. Tech. Industries Inc., Los Angeles, 1966-72; invididual practice law San Mateo, Calif., 1972-74; corp. counsel Falstaff Brewing Co., San Francisco, 1974-77; sr. partner firm Levine & Murphy, San Francisco, 1978-81; v.p. Microvertics, Mountain View, Calif., 1981-86; pres. Murphy Law Corp., San Anselmo, 1987—. Mem. Am., Calif. bar assns., Calif. Trial Lawyers. Address: 28 Fern Ln San Anselmo CA 94960-1807 E-mail: barry@murphy.law.com.

MURPHY, BETTY SOUTHARD (MRS. CORNELIUS F. MURPHY), lawyer; b. East Orange, N.J. d. Floyd Theodore and Thelma (Casto) Southard; m. Cornelius F. Murphy, May 1, 1965; children: Ann Southard, Cornelius Francis Jr. AB, Ohio State U.; student, Alliance Française and U. Sorbonne, Paris; JD, Am. U.; LLD (hon.), Eastern Mich. U., 1975, Capital U., 1976, U. Puget Sound, 1986; LHD, Tusculum coll., 1987. Bar: D.C. Corr., free lance journalist, Europe and Asia, UPI, Washington; practiced in Washington, 1960—74; mem. firm McInnis, Wilson, Munson & Woods (and predecessor firm); dep. asst. sec., adminstr. Wage and Hour Divsn. Dept. Labor, 1974-75; chmn. and mem. NLRB, 1975-79; ptnr. firm Baker & Hostetler, 1980—. Adj. prof. law Am. U., 1972-80, 99—; mem. adv. com. on rights and responsibilities of women to Sec. HHS; mem. panel conciliators Internat. Ctr. Settlement Investment Disputes, 1974-85; mem. Adminstrv. Conf. U.S., 1976-80, Pub. Svc. Adv. Bd., 1976-79; mem. human resouces com. Nat. Ctr. for Productivity and Quality of Working Life, 1976-80; mem. Presdl. Commn. on Exec. Exch., 1981-85. Trustee Mary Baldwin Coll., 1977-85, Am. U., 1980-99, George Mason U. Found., Inc., 1990-2000, 01—, George Mason U. Edn. Found., 1993-2000; nat. bd. dirs. Med. Coll. Pa., bd. corporators, 1976-85; bd. dirs. Ctr. for Women in Medicine, 1980-86; bd. govs. St. Agnes Sch., 1981-87; mem. exec. com. Commn. on Bicentennial of U.S. Constn., chmn. internat. adv. com., 1985-92; vice chmn. James Madison Meml. Fellowship Found., 1989-96; bd. dirs. Meridian Internat. Ctr., 1992-98; trustee Friends of Congl. Law Libr., 1992—, Friends of Dept. of Labor, 1984—; mediator World Intellectual Property Orgn., 1996—. Recipient Ohio Gov.'s award, 1980, fellow award, 1981, Outstanding Pub. Service award U.S. Info. Service, 1987; named Disting. Fellow John Sherman Myers Soc., 1986, 96; fellow Nat. Acad. Human Resources, 1998. Mem.: Am. U. Alumni Assn. (bd. dirs.), Supreme Ct. Hist. Soc. (gov. bd. 2002—), Union Internat. des Advocats (gov. bd. 1997—2000, 2003—), Rep. Nat. Lawyers Assn. (nat. v.p. 1990—95, nat. vice chmn. 1996—2000, 2001—), Am. Arbitration Assn. (bd. dirs. 1985-2000, bd. dirs. 2002-, mem. editl. bd. 1992, mem. exec. com. 1995—2000, mem. internat. arbitration com. 1997—, steering com. lawyers for Bush 2000), Bar Assn. D.C., Inter-Am. Bar Assn. (co-chmn. labor law com. 1975—83, editor newsletter, Silver medal 1967), FBA, ABA (chmn. labor law com. 1980—83, chmn. internat. and comparative law adminstrv. law sect. 1983—88, chmn. customs, tariff and trade com. 1988—90, employment law sect. 1990, chmn. internat. com. dispute resolution sect. 1995—, adminstrv. law sect.), World Peace Through Law Ctr., Mortar Bd., Kappa Beta Pi. Republican. Office: Baker & Hostetler LLP Ste 1100 1050 Connecticut Ave NW Washington DC 20036-5304 E-mail: bsmurphy@bakerlaw.com.

MURPHY, DANIEL IGNATIUS, lawyer; b. Phila., Mar. 14, 1927; s. John Anthony Murphy and Irene Cooper Thorn; m. Jeanne B. Genetti, July 28, 1956 (div. Aug. 1978); children: Jewel A., Daniel I. Jr.; m. Barbara Ann Uncles, Jan. 1, 1979. BS in Econs., U. Pa., 1950; LLB, Yale U., 1953. Bar: Pa. 1954, U.S. Dist Ct. (ea. dist.) Pa. 1954, U.S. Ct. Appeals (3d cir.) 1954, U.S. Tax Ct. 1956, U.S. Supreme Ct. 1959. Assoc. Evans, Bayard & Frick, Phila., 1953-55; asst. city solicitor City of Phila., Pa., 1956-59; ptnr. Cavanaugh, Murphy & Kalodner, Phila., 1958-64, Shapiro, Stalberg, Cook, Murphy & Kalodner, Phila., 1964-66, Takiff, Bolger & Murphy, Phila., 1966-72, Waters, Gallagher, Collins & Masterson, Phila., 1972-80, Stradley, Ronon, Stevens & Young, Phila., 1980-92, ret., of counsel, 1993. Tchr. Am. Soc. CLUs, Villanova, Pa., 1956-57; mem. exec. com. Phila. Estate Planning Coun., 1958-60; lectr. Pa. Bar Inst., Harrisburg, 1974-92, Pa. Coll. Orphans Ct. Judges, Harrisburg, 1978, Pitts., 1991; apptd. spl. master for trial mgmt. of complex litigation Phila. County Ct. Common Pleas, 1994—; judge pro tem Philadelphia County Ct. Common Pleas, 2000—; arbitrator Nat. Assn. Securities Dealers, 2001—. Editor: Phila. Bar Assn. Mag. The Shingle, 1958-67; contbr. chpts. to manuals and articles to profl. jours. Chmn. Phila. Chpt. Am. Cancer Soc., 1956-63; mem. Com. of 70, Phila., 1968-2003, chmn., 1972-74; trustee Hahnemann U., Phila., 1983-86. With USN, 1945-46. Fellow: Pa. Bar Found. (life); mem.: ABA, Colonial Soc. Pa. (bd. dirs. 2001), Phila. Bar Assn. (vice chmn. com. censors 1971), Pa. Bar Assn., Pa. Soc. S.R., Soc. Colonial Wars, Phila. Country Club, Union League Phila. Democrat. Roman Catholic. Avocation: U.S. Civil War history. E-mail: dmurphyesq@prodigy.net.

MURPHY, DEBORAH JANE, lawyer; b. Clinton, Tenn., Dec. 19, 1955; d. Robert C. and Mary R. (Melton) M.; m. Ashley B. Dickson, 2002. BS, U. Tenn., 1977; JD, Nashville Sch. Law, 1987. Bar: Tenn. 1987, U.S. Dist. Ct. (D.C. dist.) 1988, U.S. Dist. Ct. (6th cir.) 1988. Estate tax atty. U.S. Dept. Treasury, Knoxville, Tenn., 1987—2002, Atlanta, 2003—; mcpl. judge Lake City, Tenn., 1997—. Bd. dirs. Tenn. Lawyers Assn. Women, Nashville, 1997-01. Mem. cmty. adv. bd. East Tenn. Children's Hosp., 1998-01. Mem. ABA, Tenn. Bar Assn., Club LeConte. Dem. Methodist. Avocations: reading, golf, travel. Home and Office: 2695 W Sharon Church Rd Loganville GA 30052 E-mail: DMDickson@Bellsouth.net.

MURPHY, DIANA E. federal judge; b. Faribault, Minn., Jan. 4, 1934; d. Albert W. and Adleyne (Heiker) Kuske; m. Joseph Murphy, July 24, 1958; children: Michael, John E. BA magna cum laude, U. Minn., 1954, JD magna cum laude, 1974; postgrad., Johannes Gutenberg U., Mainz, Germany, 1954—55, U. Minn., 1955—58; LLD, St Johns U., 2000. Bar: Minn. 1974, U.S. Supreme Ct. 1980. Assoc. Lindquist & Vennum, 1974—76; mcpl. judge Hennepin County, 1976—78, Minn. State dist. judge, 1978—80; judge U.S. Dist. Ct. for Minn., Mpls., 1980—94, chief judge, 1992—94; judge U.S. Ct. of Appeals (8th cir.), Minneapolis, 1994—. Chair U.S. Sentencing Commn., 1999—. Bd. editors: Minn. Law Rev., Georgetown U. Jour. on Cts., Health Scis. and the Law, 1989—92. Dir. Nat. Assn. Pub. Interest Law Fellowships for Equal Justice, 1992—95; Bd. dirs. Mpls. United Way, 1985—2001, treas., 1990—94, vice-chmn., 1996—97, chmn. bd. dirs., 1997—98; bd. dirs. Bush Found., 1982—, chmn. bd. dirs., 1986—91, also organizer, 1st chmn. adv. coun.; bd. dirs. Amicus, 1976—80; mem. Mpls. Charter Commn., 1973—76; bd. dirs. Ops. De Novo, 1971—76, chmn. bd. dirs., 1974—75; mem., chmn. bill of rights com. Minn. Constl. Study Commn., 1971—73; regent St. Johns U., 1978—87, 1988—98, vice-chmn., chmn. bd., 1985—98, bd. overseers sch. theology, 1998—2001; mem. Minn. Bicentennial Commn., 1987—88; trustee Twin Cities Pub. TV, 1985—94, chmn. bd., 1990—92; trustee, treas. U. Minn. Found., 1990—; bd. dirs. Sci. Mus. Minn., 1988—94, vice-chmn., 1991—94; trustee U. St. Thomas, 1991—; Bd. dirs. Spring Hill Conf. Ctr., 1978—84. Recipient Amicus Founders' award, 1980, Outstanding Achievement award, U. Minn., 1983, YWCA, 1981, Disting. Citizen award, Alpha Gamma Delta, 1985, Devitt Disting. Svc. to Justice award, 2001, Disting. Alumnus award, U. Minn. Law Sch., 2002; scholar Fulbright. Fellow: Am. Bar Found.; mem.: ABA (mem. ethics and profl. responsibility judges adv. com. 1981—88, standing com. on jud. selection, tenure and compensation 1991—94, mem. standing com. on fed. jud. improvements 1994—97, Appellate Judges conf. exec. com. 1996—99, chmn. ethics and profl. responsibility judges adv. com. 1997—2000), Fed. Jud. Ctr. (bd. dirs. 1990—94, 8th cir. jud. coun. 1992—94, convener task force 1993, mem. U.S. jud. conf. com. on ct. adminstrn. and case mgmt. 1994—99, chair gender fairness implementation com. 1997—98, 8th cir. jud. coun. 1997—), Hist. Soc. for 8th Cir. (bd. dirs. 1988—91), Fed. Judges Assn. (bd. dirs. 1982—, v.p. 1984—89, pres. 1989—91), U. Minn. Alumni Assn. (bd. dirs. 1975—83, nat. pres. 1981—82), Minn. Women Lawyers (Myra Bradwell award 1996), Nat. Assn. Women Judges (Leadership Judges Jud. Adminstrn. award 1998, Honoree of Yr. 2002), Nat. Assn. Governing Bds. Univs. Colls. (dir. 1998—), Am. Judicature Soc. (bd. dirs. 1982—93, v.p. 1985—88, treas. 1988—89, chmn. bd. 1989—91), Am. Law Inst., Hennepin County Bar Assn. (gov. coun. 1976—81), Minn. Bar Assn. (bd. govs. 1977—81), Order of Coif, Phi Beta Kappa. Office: 11 E US Courthouse 300 S 4th St Minneapolis MN 55415-1320

MURPHY, EARL FINBAR, legal educator; b. Indpls., Nov. 1, 1928; AB, Butler U., 1949, MA, 1954; JD, Ind. U., 1952; LLM, Yale U., 1955, JSD, 1959. Bar: Ind. 1952. Sole practice Indpls., 1952-54; asst. prof. SUNY-Binghamton, 1955-57; Rockefeller fellow U. Wis. Law Sch., Madison, 1957-58; asst. prof. Temple U., Phila., 1958-60, assoc. prof., 1960-65, prof. law, 1965-69; prof. Ohio State U., Columbus, 1969-81, C. William O'Neill prof. law and jud. adminstrn., 1981-2000, prof. emeritus, 2000—. Vis. prof. U. Ariz., 1980. Author: Water Purity, 1961; Governing Nature, 1967; Man and His Environment: Law, 1971; Nature, Bureaucracy and the Rules of Property, 1977; Energy and Environmental Balance, 1980; Quantitative Groundwater Law, 1991. Chmn. Ohio Environ. Bd. Rev., 1972-74. Mem. ABA, Ind. Bar Assn., Fed. Bar Assn., Am. Soc. Legal History, World Soc. Ekistics (pres. 1982-84). Democrat. Unitarian. Clubs: Masons. Unitarian. Home: 4475 Langport Rd Columbus OH 43220-4257 Office: Ohio State U Moritz Coll Law 55 W 12th Ave Columbus OH 43210-1306 E-mail: Murphy.14@osu.edu.

MURPHY, EWELL EDWARD, JR., lawyer; b. Washington, Feb. 21, 1928; s. Ewell Edward and Lou (Phillips) M.; m. Patricia Bredell Purnell, June 26, 1954 (dec. 1964); children: Michaela, Megan Patricia, Harlan Ewell. BA, U. Tex., 1946, LLB, 1948; DPhil, Oxford U., Eng., 1951. Bar: Tex. 1948. Assoc. Baker & Botts, Houston, 1954-63, ptnr., 1964-93, head internat. dept., 1972-89. Pres. Houston World Trade Assn., 1972-74; trustee Southwestern Legal Found., 1978—; chmn. Houston Com. on Fgn. Rels., 1984-85, Inst. Transnat. Arbitration, 1985-89, Internat. and Comparative Law Ctr., 1986-87; mem. J. William Fulbright Fgn. Scholarship Bd., 1991-96, vice chmn., 1992-93, chmn., 1993-95; vis. prof. U. Tex. Law Sch., 1993-97; Disting. lectr., U. Houston Law Ctr., 1996—. Contbr. articles to profl. jours. Served to lt. USAF, 1952-54. Recipient Carl H. Fulda award U. Tex. Internat. Law Jour., 1980; Rhodes scholar, 1948-51 Mem. ABA (chmn. sect. internat. law 1970-71), Houston Bar Assn. (chmn. internat. law com. 1963-64, 70-71), Houston C. of C. (chmn. internat. bus. com. 1964, 65), Philos. Soc. Tex., Internat. Law Inst. (bd. dirs. 1994—), Fulbright Assn. (bd. dirs. 1999—, v.p. 2002-), Coun. on Fgn. Rels. Corporate, general, Private international. Home and Office: 17 W Oak Dr Houston TX 77056-2117

MURPHY, GREGORY GERARD, lawyer; b. Helena, Mont., Feb. 3, 1954; s. Michael Anthony and Elizabeth (Cooney) M.; m. Katherine Joan Koch, Dec. 30, 1977; children: Megan, Brian, Allison. BA, U. Mont., 1976; JD, U. Notre Dame, 1979. Bar: Oreg. 1979, U.S. Dist. Ct. Oreg. 1979, U.S. Ct. Appeals (9th cir.) 1979, Mont. 1980, U.S. Dist. Ct. Mont. 1980, Crow Tribal Ct., No. Cheyenne Tribal Ct., U.S. Supreme Ct. 1996. Clk. to judge U.S. Ct. Appeals (9th cir.), Portland, 1979-80; assoc. Moulton, Bellingham, Longo & Mather P.C., Billings, Mont., 1980-84; shareholder Moulton, Bellingham, Longo & Mather, P.C., Billings, Mont., 1984—. Trustee Mont. dist. U.S. Bankruptcy Ct., 1982-85; examiner Mont. Bd. Bar Examiners, 1985-95, chmn. 1995-2002; trustee Nat. Conf. Bar Examiners, 1990-2002, chmn., 2000-2001, mem. multistate bar exam. com., 1986-94, chmn. 1994-98; vice chmn. commn. on rules of admission to the bar Mont. Supreme Ct., 1996-97. Assoc. editor Notre Dame Law Rev., 1978-79. Bd. dirs. Billings Symphony Soc., 1982-91, French hornist, 1981—. Thomas and Alberta White scholar U. Notre Dame, 1978-79. Mem. ABA (law sch. accreditation com. 2002-), Mont. Bar Assn., Oreg. Bar Assn., Am. Law Inst., Yellowstone County Bar Assn., Rotary. Roman Catholic. Avocations: French horn, golf, camping. General civil litigation, Environmental, Health. Home: 5533 Gene Sarazen Dr Billings MT 59106-1121 Office: Moulton Bellingham et al PO Box 2559 Billings MT 59103-2559

MURPHY, HAROLD LOYD, federal judge; b. Haralson County, Ga., Mar. 31, 1927; s. James Loyd and Georgia Gladys (McBrayer) M.; m. Jacqueline Marie Ferri, Dec. 20, 1958; children: Mark Harold, Paul Bailey. Student, West Ga. Coll., 1944-45, U. Miss., 1945-46; LL.B., U. Ga., 1949. Bar: Ga. 1949. Pvt. practice, Buchanan, Ga., from 1949; ptnr. Howe & Murphy, Buchanan and Tallapoosa, Ga., 1958-71; judge Superior Cts., Tallapoosa Circuit, 1971-77; U.S. dist. judge No. Dist. of Ga., Rome, 1977—. Rep. Gen. Assembly of Ga., 1951-61; asst. solicitor gen. Tallapoosa Jud. Circuit, 1956; mem. Jud. Qualifications Commn., State of Ga., 1977 With USNR, 1945-46. Fellow Am. Bar Found.; mem. ABA, Ga. Bar Assn., Dist. Judges Assn. for 11th Cir. Bar Assn., Am. Judicature Soc., Tallapoosa Cir. Bar Assn., Old War Horse Lawyers Club, Am. Inns Ct. (past pres. Joseph Henry Lumpkin sect.), Fed. Judges Assn. Methodist. Home: 321 Georgia Highway 120 Tallapoosa GA 30176-3114 Office: US Dist Ct PO Box 53 Rome GA 30162-0053

MURPHY, JAMES BURTON, JR., lawyer; b. Mobile, Ala., July 2, 1954; s. James Burton and Sarah (McKee) M.; m. Jane Marie, June 5, 1982; children: Caroline Elizabeth, Courtney Erin, James Matthew. BA, Fla. Atlantic U., 1976; JD, U. Fla., 1979. Bar: Fla. 1979. Law clerk Hon. Wm. Terrell Hodges, U.S. Dist. Judge, Tampa, Fla., 1979—81; ptnr. Shook, Hardy, & Bacon, LLP, Tampa. Author: (with others) Discovery of Trade Secrets, 1989; contbr. articles to profl. jours. Pres. Westshore Breakfast Sertoma Club, Tampa, 1988-89, Bolesta Oral Tchg. Ctr., Inc., Tampa, 1990-92; bd. trustees, chmn. U. Tampa, 1994-95, 2002-, chmn. bd. counselors, 1994-95, 2002-, chmn. bd. fellows, 2002-03; mem. Leadership Tampa Program, 1991-92. Named Counselor of Yr. U. Tampa Bd. Counselors, 1991-92. Mem. Fla. Bar Assn. (chmn. bus. litig. com., chmn. bus. law sect. 2003—), Hillsborough County Bar Assn. (bd. dirs., trial lawyers sect., chmn. corp. banking, 1992-93), Ferguson-White Inn of Ct. (exec. coun.). Democrat. Methodist. Avocations: reading, golf. Federal civil litigation, State civil litigation, Insurance. Office: Shook Hardy & Bacon LLP 100 N Tampa St Ste 2900 Tampa FL 33602 E-mail: jbmurphy@shb.com.

MURPHY, JAMES PAUL, lawyer; b. Jackson, Tenn., Apr. 29, 1944; s. Paul Joseph and Marjorie Mary (Smyth) Murphy; m. Marcia Mae Gaughan, Sept. 5, 1975. BA cum laude, U. Notre Dame, 1966; JD, U. Mich., 1969. Bar: Ohio 1969, D.C. 1984, Md. 1984, U.S. Dist. Ct. (no. dist.) Ohio 1970, U.S. Ct. Appeals (6th cir.) 1972, U.S. Supreme Ct. 1976, U.S. Dist. Ct. Md. 1984, U.S. Dist. Ct. D.C. 1984, U.S. Dist. Ct. of Appeals (4th cir., D.C. cir.) 1984. Vol. VISTA, 1969—70; assoc. Squire, Sanders & Dempsey, LLP, Cleve., 1970—79, ptnr., 1979—. Mem.: Ohio State Bar Assn. (antitrust sect.), D.C. Bar Assn., Md. Bar Assn., Cleve. Bar Assn. (fed. ct. com.), City Club (Washington), Westwood Country Club (Rocky River, Ohio). Antitrust, Federal civil litigation, State civil litigation. Home: 4512 Wetherill Rd Bethesda MD 20816-1837 Office: Squire Sanders & Dempsey LLP PO Box 407 1201 Pennsylvania Ave NW Washington DC 20044-2401 E-mail: jmurphy@ssd.com.

MURPHY, JAMES TRUDEN, lawyer; b. Cin., Jan. 18, 1949; s. Francis Edward and Virginia Marie Murphy; m. Susan Mary Cooney, June 16, 1973; children: John, Michael, Noel, Katherine, Elizabeth, Caroline. BA cum laude in English, Boston Coll., 1971; JD cum laude, Suffolk U., 1975. Bar: R.I. 1975, Mass. 1975, U.S. Dist. Ct. Mass. 1983, U.S. Dist. Ct. R.I. 1975, U.S. Ct. Appeals (1st cir.) 1983, U.S. Ct. Mil. Appeals 1977. Assoc. Lovett & Linder Ltd., Providence, 1975; ptnr. Hanson Curran, 1979—. Mock trial coach R.I. Legal Edn. Partnership, St. Mary's Acad., 1997—; mem. fin. coun. St. Bernard Parish, Wickford, RI, 1985—. Comdr. USNR, 1976—94. Mem.: Fed. Bar Assn. (pres. elect 2001—03), R.I. Assn. Def. Trial Attys. (pres., state rep. 2003). Avocations: history, travel. Personal injury (including property damage), Environmental, Admiralty. Office: Hanson Curran 146 Westminster Providence RI 02852 Fax: 401-521-7040. E-mail: jtm@hansoncurran.com.

MURPHY, JOHN RICHARD, lawyer; b. Chgo., Oct. 29, 1964; s. Donald R. and Esther Murphy; m. Denice Irene Murphy, June 20, 1997; 1 child, Madison Rey. AB in Polit. Philosophy, AB in Polit. Sci., Syracuse U., 1986; JD, Georgetown U., 1992. Bar: SD 93, U.S. Dist. Ct. SD 93, U.S. Ct. Appeals (8th cir.) 94, U.S. Supreme Ct. 02. Law clk. to judge U.S. Dist. Ct. SD, Pierre, 1992—93; sr. atty., dir. Indian Law Project Black Hills Legal Svc., Rapid City, SD, 1993—96; pvt. practice Law Offices of John R. Murphy, Rapid City, 1996—. Criminal. Office: Law Office of John R Murphy PO Box 5634 Rapid City SD 57709 Fax: 605-343-9760. E-mail: jmurphysd@hotmail.com.

MURPHY, JOHN THOMAS, lawyer; b. Pierre, S.D., July 20, 1932; s. Bernard J. and Gertrude (Loner) M.; m. Rose Marie Cogorno. LLB, U. S.D., 1957. Bar: S.D. 1957, Calif. 1962. Pvt. practice, Stockton, Calif., 1965-75, Modesto, Calif., 1975—; atty. office gen. counsel quartermaster gen. U.S. Army, 1957-58, asst. chief counsel, 1958-63, gen. counsel, 1963-65; assoc. Short, Short, Scott & Murphy (and predecessor firm), 1965-68; ptnr. Hulsey, Beus, Wilson, Scott & Murphy, Stockton, 1968-70. Bd. dirs. Delta-Stockton Humane Soc., 1970-75, bd. dirs. Tuolumne River Preservation Trust; bd. govs. Calif. Trout Inc.; mem. Stanislaus River Task Force, Stanislaus County Water Coord. Com.; chmn. Southwestern Trial Bd. Mem. State Bar Calif., Assn. Trial Lawyers Am., mem. Consumer Atty. of Calif., Beta Theta Pi, Phi Delta Phi, Stockton Beagler's Club (sec., dir.), Am. Kennel Club (Beagle adv. com. 1984-86). Republican. Episcopalian. Office: 1124 11th St Modesto CA 95354-0826 E-mail: bigbad@inreach.com.

MURPHY, KATHLEEN MARY, former law firm executive; b. Bklyn., Dec. 16, 1945; d. Raymond Joseph and Catherine Elizabeth (Kearney) M. BA in Edn., Molloy Coll., 1971; MS in Edn., Bklyn. Coll., 1975. Ordained minister Ch. of the Loving Servant; cert. hypnotherapist; cert. elem. sch. tchr., N.Y. Elem. sch. tchr. various parochial schs., L.I., Bklyn., Queens, N.Y., 1969-80; from asst. prin. to prin. parochial sch. Queens, 1980-82; supr.-trainer Davis, Polk, Wardwell law firm, N.Y.C., 1982-88; mgr. Schulte Roth & Zabel, N.Y.C., 1988-95; Reiki master (alternative healing profl.), 1996—. Trainer program for new employees, 1984; speaker edn. topics, Bklyn., Queens, 1979-81. Mem. NAFE, Reiki Alliance. Democrat. Roman Catholic. Avocations: psychic phenomenon, workings of mind, ancient histories, crossword puzzles, museums.

MURPHY, LAURA, legal association administrator; b. Md. Grad., Wellesley Coll. Devel. dir. ACLU Found. So. Calif.; lobbyist ACLU, Washington, dir. D.C. office, 1993—. Mem.: ABA (mem. adv. commn. to the standing com. on election law 1998). Office: ACLU 122 Maryland Ave NE Washington DC 20002*

MURPHY, LEWIS CURTIS, lawyer, former mayor; b. N.Y.C., Nov. 2, 1933; s. Henry Waldo and Elizabeth Wilcox (Curtis) M.; m. Carol Carney, Mar. 10, 1957; children— Grey, Timothy, Elizabeth. BSBA, U. Ariz., 1955, LLB, 1961. Bar: Ariz. 1961. Pvt. practice, Tucson, 1961-66; trust officer So. Ariz. Bank & Trust Co., 1966-70; atty. City of Tucson, 1970-71; mayor, 1971-87; ret., 1987. Mem. Schroeder & Murphy, Tucson, 1978-88; trustee U.S. Conf. Mayors, 1978-87, chmn. transp. com., 1984-87; pub. safety steering com. Nat. League Cities, 1973-87, transp. steering com., 1973-87; v.p. Ctrl. Ariz. Project Assn., 1978-87. Bd. dirs. Cmty. Food Bank,

1987-2000, United Way Greater Tucson, 1988-90. With USAF, 1955-58. Mem. Ariz. Bar Assn., Pima County Bar Assn., Ariz. Acad., Sigma Chi (Significant Sig award). Republican. Presbyterian.

MURPHY, MAX RAY, lawyer; b. July 18, 1934; s. Loren A. and Lois (Mink) M.; children: Michael Lee, Chad Woodrow. BA, DePauw U., 1956; JD, Yale U., 1959; postgrad., Mich. State U., 1960. Bar: Mich. 1960. Assoc. Glassen, Parr, Rhead & McLean, Lansing, Mich., 1960—67, Lokker, Boter & Dalman, Holland, Mich., 1967—69; ptnr. Dalman, Murphy, Bidol, & Bouwens, P.C., Holland, 1969—91, Cunningham Dalman, P.C., Holland, 1991—. Instr. Lansing Bus. U., 1963-67; asst. pros. atty. Ottawa County, Mich., 1967-69. Dem. candidate for Ingham County (Mich.) Pros. Atty., 1962, 1964. Mem. ABA, Ottawa County Bar Assn. (sec. 1970-71), Mich. Bar Assn. (mem. family law sect.). Family and matrimonial, General practice. Home: 3169 E Crystal Waters 3 Holland MI 49424-8091 Office: 321 Settlers Rd Holland MI 49423-3778 E-mail: mmurphy@sirus.com.

MURPHY, MICHAEL CARY, lawyer; b. Mt. Airy, N.C., Aug. 11, 1951; s. Ralph Bill Murphy and Jamalee (Bartlett) Nickle. BA, Carson-Newman Coll., 1973; JD, U. Memphis, 1980; postgrad., U. Tenn. Coll. Trial Advocacy, 1981. Bar: Tenn. 1980, U.S. Dist. Ct. Tenn. 1981, U.S. Ct. Appeals (6th cir.) 1982. Atty. Legal Svcs. Upper East Tenn., Morristown, 1980-81, EEO Office, TVA, Knoxville, Tenn., 1981-82; pvt. practice Morristown, 1982—. Part-time judge Mcpl. Ct., Morristown, Tenn., 1996-2000. Pres. bd. dirs. Cen. Svcs., Morristown, 1987-89; chmn. legal div. Morristown United Way, 1987, 88. Mem. ABA, Tenn. Bar Assn., Assn. Trial Lawyers Am., Tenn. Trial Lawyers Assn., Lakeway Tennis Assn., Cherokee Lake Sailing Club, Kiwanis (chmn. community svcs. com.), Phi Delta Phi. Methodist. Avocations: tennis, photography, snow skiing, hiking, biking. Family and matrimonial, Labor (including EEOC, Fair Labor Standards Act, labor-management relations, NLRB, OSHA), Personal injury (including property damage). Office: PO Box 1365 Morristown TN 37816-1365

MURPHY, MICHAEL R. federal judge; b. Denver, Aug. 6, 1947; s. Roland and Mary Cecilia (Maloney) M.; m. Maureen Elizabeth Donnelly, Aug. 22, 1970; children: Amy Christina, Michael Donnelly. BA in History, Creighton U., 1969; JD, U. Wyo., 1972. Bar: Wyo. 1972, U.S. Ct. Appeals (10th cir.) 1972, Utah 1973, U.S. Dist. Ct. Utah 1974, U.S. Dist. Ct. Wyo. 1976, U.S. Ct. Appeals (5th cir.) 1976, U.S. Tax Ct. 1980, U.S. Ct. Appeals (9th cir.) 1981, U.S. Ct. Appeals (fed. cir.) 1984. Law clk. to chief judge U.S. Ct. Appeals (10th cir.), Salt Lake City, 1972-73; with Jones, Waldo, Holbrook & McDonough, Salt Lake City, 1973-86; judge 3d Dist. Ct., Salt Lake City, 1986-95, pres. judge, 1990-95; judge U.S. Ct. Appeals (10th cir.), Salt Lake City, 1995—. Mem. adv. com. on rules of civil procedure Utah Supreme Ct., 1985—95, mem. bd. dist. ct. judges, 1989—90; mem. Utah State Sentencing Commn., 1993—95, Utah Adv. Com. on Child Support Guidelines, 1989—95, Utah Child Sexual Abuse Task Force, 1989—93; mem. com. on fed.-state jurisdiction Jud. Conf. of U.S., 2001—. Recipient Freedom of Info. award, Soc. Profl. Journalists, 1989, Utah Minority Bar Assn. award, 1995, alumni Achievement citation, Creighton U., 1997; named Judge of Yr., Utah State Bar, 1992. Fellow Am. Bar Found.; mem. ABA (editl. bd. Judges' Jour. 1997-99), Utah Bar Assn. (chmn. alternative dispute resolution com. 1985-88), Sutherland Inn of Ct. II (past pres.). Office: 5438 Federal Bldg 125 S State St Salt Lake City UT 84138-1102

MURPHY, MICHAEL TERRENCE, lawyer; b. Riverside, Calif., July 25, 1946; s. James Bernard and Opal (Cully) M. BS, Calif. State U., Long Beach, 1973; JD, Pepperdine U., 1976. Bar: Calif. 1976, N.Mex. 1977, U.S. Dist. Ct. N.Mex. 1977, U.S. Claims Ct. 1977, U.S. Tax Ct. 1977, U.S. Ct. Appeals (tenth cir.) 1977, U.S. Supreme Ct. 1980; bd. cert. specialist in family law. Ptnr. Shuler, Murphy & Shuler, Carlsbad, N.Mex., 1976-77, Rosenberg, Shuler & Murphy, Carlsbad, 1978-87; shareholder Weinbrenner, Richards, Paulowsky, Sandenaw & Ramirez, P.A., Las Cruces, N.Mex., 1987-95, Weinbrenner, Richards, Ramirez, McNeill & Murphy, P.A., Las Cruces, 1995, Pickett & Murphy, Las Cruces, 1995—. With USAF, 1967-73. Fellow Am. Acad. Matrimonial Lawyers; mem. ABA (chmn.), N.Mex. Bd. Bar Examiners. Episcopalian. General civil litigation, Family and matrimonial, Probate (including wills, trusts). Office: Pickett & Murphy 500 N Church St Las Cruces NM 88001-3440

MURPHY, PATRICK GUYON, lawyer; b. Lansing, Mich., Aug. 30, 1970; s. Patrick Brian and Mary Jane Murphy; m. Jill Kristine Eytcheson, Aug. 20, 1994. BS in Bus., Ind. U., Ft. Wayne, 1993; JD, Ind. U., Indpls., 1996. Bar: Ind. 1996, U.S. Dist. Ct. (no. and so. divsn.) 1996. Dep. prosecuting atty. Allen County Prosecuting Atty.'s Office, Ft. Wayne, Ind., 1996—99; atty. Barrett & McNagny LLP, Ft. Wayne, Ind., 1999—. Adj. prof. evidence Ind. U., Ft. Wayne, 1999—2001; co-author, presenter manual/conf. Trying the Soft Tissue Injury Case in Ind., 2001. Bd. dirs. Cmty. Harvest Food Bank, Ft. Wayne, 2000—. Mem.: ABA, Def. Rsch. Inst., Def. Trial Counsel Ind., Allen County Bar Assn., Ind. Bar Assn. Personal injury (including property damage), Product liability, Commercial, contracts (including sales of goods; commercial financing), Criminal. Office: Barrett & McNagny LLP 215 E Berry St Fort Wayne IN 46801-Office Fax: 260-423-8920. E-mail: pat@barrettlaw.com.

MURPHY, PATRICK NEIL, lawyer; b. Wahoo, Nebr., Jan. 15, 1946; s. Albert S. and Alice B. (Daley) M.; m. Kathryn Ann Kearns, June 8, 1968; children: Megan, Mia, Michael. BA, U. Nebr., 1968; JD, Creighton U., 1972. Bar: Nebr. 1973, Iowa 1973, U.S. Dsit. Ct. Nebr. 1973, U.S. Dist. Ct. (no. dist.) Iowa 1975, U.S. Supreme Ct. 1992. 1973asst atty. County of Plymouth, Iowa, 1973—92; ptnr. Murphy & Collins, LeMars, Iowa, 1973--. Dist. chmn. Prarie Gold council Boy Scouts Am., 1976-83; central committeeman Plymouth County Dems., 1974-1984; bd. dirs. Plains Area Mental Health Ctr., 1975-82, chmn., dir. Catholic Charities Diocese Sioux City, 1992-1998; charter dir. Plymoth Cnty. Conservation Found., 1993-; pres. LeMars Community Sch. Bd. Dirs., 2000-2002, pres. Plymouth County REAP Congress Plymouth County Civil Service Commn., 1988-2000, post commander, trustee Am. Legion #241, Sgt. U.S. Army, 1969-71. Mem. ABA, Iowa Bar Assn.(mem. Am. Citizenship Comm., 1974-, Grievance Comm., 1997), Nebr. Bar Assn., Assn. Trial Lawyers Am., Iowa Assn. Trial Lawyers (Bd. Govnrs. 1996-2000), Nebr. Assn. Trial Lawyers, LeMars C. of C. (bd. dirs. 1980-83), Sertoma, Elks, KC. Roman Catholic. General civil litigation, Insurance, Personal injury (including property damage). Home: 1517 1st Ave SW Le Mars IA 51031-2707 Office: Murphy and Collins PLC PO Box 526 Le Mars IA 51031-0526

MURPHY, RICHARD PATRICK, lawyer; b. Elizabeth, N.J. AB with distinction, Cornell U., 1976; JD cum laude, AM, U. Mich., 1980. Bar: D.C. 1980, U.S. Dist. Ct. (D.C.) 1981, U.S. Ct. Appeals (D.C. cir.) 1981, U.S. Supreme Ct. 1984, Calif. 1987, U.S. Dist. Ct. (so. dist.) Calif. 1987, U.S. Dist. Ct. (cen. dist.) Calif. 1992, Ga. 1993, U.S. Dist. Ct. (no. dist.) Ga. 1993, U.S. Ct. Appeals (11th cir.) 1993. Assoc. Bergson, Borkland, Margolis & Adler, Washington, 1980-82; atty. enforcement div. SEC, Washington, 1982-84, br. chief enforcement div., 1984-87; assoc. Gray, Cary, Ames & Frye, San Diego, 1987-92; sr. trial counsel SEC, Atlanta, 1993-99, asst. dist. adminstr., 1999—. Mem. ABA, D.C. Bar Assn., Calif. Bar Assn., Ga. Bar Assn. Office: SEC 3475 Lenox Rd NE Ste 1000 Atlanta GA 30326-1239

MURPHY, SANDRA ROBISON, lawyer; b. Detroit, July 28, 1949; m. Richard Robin. BA, Northwestern U., 1971; JD, Loyola U., Chgo., 1976. Bar: U.S. Dist. Ct. (no. dist.) Ill. 1976. Assoc. Notz, Craven, Mead, Maloney & Price, Chgo., 1976-78; ptnr. McDermott, Will & Emery, Chgo., 1978—. Mem. ABA (family law sect.), Ill. Bar Assn. (chair sect. family law coun. 1987-88), Chgo. Bar Assn. (chair matrimonial law com. 1985-86), Am. Acad. Matrimonial Lawyers (sec. 1990-91, v.p. 1991-92, pres. Ill. chpt. 1992-93, pres.-elect 1994-95, pres. 1995-96), Legal Club Chgo. Family and matrimonial.

MURPHY, TIMOTHY JAMES, lawyer; b. Topeka, Sept. 30, 1946; s. Miles J. and Norine D. Murphy; m. Patricia MacKinnon, Apr. 7, 1990. BA, U. Ga., 1968; JD, Washington & Lee U., 1970; LLM, Harvard U., 1976. Bar: Va. 1970, Fla. 1972. Atty. Shutts & Bowen, Miami, Fla., 1976—. Mem. Fla. Ho. of Reps., 1982-84; bd. dirs. Cath. Charities, Inc., 1982-97, Cath. Charities Legal Svcs., Inc., Miami, 2000—; mem. adv. bd. Miami-Dade County Pub. Libr., 1988-2002. Col. JAG Corps USAFR, 1970-95. Mem.: Biscayne Bay Yacht Club, Army and Navy Club (Washington). Democrat. Roman Catholic. Corporate, general, Immigration, naturalization, and customs, Private international. Office: Shutts & Bowen 201 S Biscayne Blvd Ste 1500 Miami FL 33131-4308

MURPHY, TIMOTHY PAUL, lawyer; b. Syracuse, N.Y., Aug. 7, 1964; s. Thomas Joseph and Mary Jane Murphy; m. Mary Ann Young, Aug. 12, 1989; children: Timothy P., Colleen M., Ciara M. BA in History, Le Moyne, 1986; JD, Syracuse U., 1989. Bar: N.Y. 1990, U.S. Ct. Appeals (2d cir.) 1992, U.S. Dist. Ct. (no. dist.) N.Y. 1990. Ptnr. Hancock & Estabrook, Syracuse, NY, 1989—. Mem.: Upstate Trial Lawyers Assn., N.Y. State Trial Lawyers Assn., Assn. Trial Lawyers Am. Avocations: reading, boating, golf. Personal injury (including property damage), Product liability, General civil litigation. Office: Hancock & Estabrook LLP 1500 Mony Tower I Syracuse NY 13221-4976 Fax: 315-471-3167.

MURRAY, BRYAN KENNETH, judge; b. Bakersfield, Calif., Mar. 12, 1956; s. Earl Lamonte and Joan (Adams) Murray; m. Lorie Lindquist; children: Seleta, Nicolette, Benjamin, Tyson. BA in History and Govt., Idaho State U., 1980; JD, U. Idaho, 1982. Pvt. practice, Pocatello, Idaho, 1983—95; judge State of Idaho Cts., Pocatello, 1993—. Recipient Commrs. award, U.S. Dept. Health and Human Svcs., 2001, Silver Beaver, Boy Scouts Am., 1994. Mem.: Gate City Rotary. Mem. Lds Ch. Office: Juvenile Court Bannock County Courthouse Pocatello ID 83201

MURRAY, CLAUDE ROBERT, JR., lawyer; b. Houston, Nov. 8, 1947; s. Claude Robert and Merijjeanne (Swenson) M.; m. Catherine Hume, Sept. 19, 1969 (div. 1973); m. Patricia Ann Barry, July 4, 1976; children: Christopher Robin, Alexandra Hollis, Ronald Patrick. BA, Davidson Coll., 1971; JD, U. Miami, Fla., 1974. Bar: Fla. 1974, U.S. Supreme Ct. 1982. Ptnr. Mitchell, Harris, Canning & Murray, P.A., Miami, Fla., 1974-86, Canning & Murray, P.A., Miami, 1986—2001, George, Hartz, Lundeen, Fulmer, Johnstone, King & Stevens, 2001—. Bd. dirs. Met. Dade County YMCA, Miami, 1973-78. Mem. Fla. Bar Assn., Southeastern Admiralty Law Inst. Republican. Roman Catholic. Admiralty, Insurance, Pension, profit-sharing, and employee benefits. Home: 1907 NW 137th Terrace Pembroke Pines FL 33028 Fax: 305-667-3622. E-mail: crobertmurray@georgehartz.com.

MURRAY, DANIEL CHARLES, trial lawyer; s. John Joseph and Marjorie Ellen M.; m. Martha Jane Gerity; children: Michaela, Tyler, Brian. BA in Econs., Marquette U., 1971; JD, Loyola U., Chgo., 1976. Bar: Ill. 1976, U.S. Ct. Appeals (7th cir.) 1979, U.S. Dist. Ct. (no. dist.) Ill. 1980, U.S. Dist. Ct. (ea. dist.) Mich. 1992, U.S. Dist. Ct. (ea. dist.) Wis. 1994, U.S. Dist. Ct. (so.dist.), Ill. 2003. Jud. law clk. U.S. Ct. Appeals for 7th Cir., Chgo., 1976-78; asst. U.S. atty. Office U.S. Atty. U.S. Dept. Justice (no. dist.) Ill., Chgo., 1978—91; shareholder, chmn. pro bono program Johnson & Bell, Ltd., Chgo., 1991—. Trial instr. U.S. Atty. Gen.'s Advocacy Inst., Washington, 1989; mem. Environ. Crimes Task Force, 1991. Active Chgo. Vol. Legal Svcs. Found., 1977—, Chgo. Legal Advocacy to Incarcerated Mothers, 1995—; participant Chgo. North-of-Howard Task Force. Recipient Disting. Svc. award Chgo. Vol. Legal Svcs. Found., 1983, 87, award for significant contbns. in drug law enforcement U.S. Drug Enforcement Adminstrn., 1988, Insp. Gen.'s nat. award GSA, 1989, Spl. Achievement award U.S. Dept. Justice, 1990. Mem. Fed. Bar Assn. (bd. dirs. Chgo. chpt.), 7th Fed. Cir. Bar Assn. Federal civil litigation, Criminal, Environmental. Office: Johnson & Bell Ltd Ste 4100 55 E Monroe St Chicago IL 60603-5896 E-mail: murrayd@jbltd.com.

MURRAY, DANIEL RICHARD, lawyer; b. Mar. 23, 1946; s. Alfred W. and Gloria D. Murray. AB, U. Notre Dame, 1967; JD, Harvard U., 1970. Bar: Ill. 1970, U.S. Dist. Ct. (no. dist.) Ill. 1970, U.S. Ct. Appeals (7th cir.) 1971, U.S. Supreme Ct. 1974. Ptnr. Jenner & Block, Chgo., 1970—. Trustee Chgo. Mo. and Western Rlwy. Co., 1988-97; adj. prof. U. Notre Dame, 1997—. Co-author: Secured Transactions, 1978, Illinois Practice: Uniform Commercial Code with Illinois Code Comments, 2003, Uniform Laws Annotated—Uniform Commercial Code Forms, 2001, Illinois Practice: Uniform Commercial Code Forms, 2002. Bd. regents Big Shoulders Fund, Archdiocese of Chgo., Bernardin Ctr., Cath. Theol. Union. Mem.: Assn. Transp. Practitioners, Transp. Lawyers Assn., Am. Coll. Comml. Fin. Lawyers, Am. Bankruptcy Coll., Am. Law Inst., Am. Bankruptcy Inst., Cath. Lawyers Guild (bd. dirs.), Lawyers' Club Chgo. Roman Catholic. Bankruptcy, Commercial, contracts (including sales of goods; commercial financing), Transportation. Home: 1307 N Sutton Pl Chicago IL 60610-2007 Office: Jenner & Block One IBM Plz Chicago IL 60611-3605 E-mail: dmurray@jenner.com.

MURRAY, FLORENCE KERINS, retired state supreme court justice; b. Newport, R.I., Oct. 21, 1916; d. John X. and Florence (MacDonald) Kerins; m. Paul F. Murray, Oct. 21, 1943 (dec. June 2, 1995); 1 child, Paul F. AB, Syracuse U., 1938; LLB, Boston U., 1942; EdD, R.I. Coll. Edn., 1956; grad., Nat. Coll. State Trial Judges, 1966; LLD (hon.), Bryant Coll., 1956, U. R.I., 1963, Mt. St. Joseph Coll., 1972, Providence Coll., 1974, Roger Williams Coll., 1976, Salve Regina Coll., 1977, Johnson and Wales Coll., 1977, Suffolk U., 1981, So. New Eng. Law Sch., 1995; D (hon.), New England Inst. Tech., 1998. Bar: Mass. 1942, R.I. 1947, U.S. Dist. Ct. 1948, U.S. Tax Ct. 1948, U.S. Supreme Ct. 1948. Sole practice, Newport, 1947-52; mem. firm Murray & Murray, Newport, 1952-56; assoc. judge R.I. Superior Ct., 1956-78; presiding justice Superior Ct. R.I., 1978-79; assoc. justice (ret.-active) R.I. Supreme Ct., 1979—. Staff, faculty adv. Nat. Jud. Coll., Reno, Nev., 1971-72, dir., 1975-77, chmn., 1979-87, chair emeritus, 1990—; mem. com. Legal Edn. and Practice and Economy of New Eng., 1975—; former instr. Prudence Island Sch.; legal adv. R.I. Girl Scouts; sec. Commn. Jud. Tenure and Discipline, 1975-79; apptd. by Pres. Clinton to bd. dirs. State Justice Inst., 1994-99; participant, leader various legal seminars; presdl. appointment R.I. State Justice Inst. Mem. R.I. Senate, 1948-56; chmn. spl. legis. com.; mem. Newport Sch. Com., 1948-57, chmn., 1951-57; mem. Gov.'s Jud. Coun., 1950-60, White House Conf. Youth and Children, 1950, Ann. Essay Commn., 1952, Nat. Def. Adv. Com. on Women in Service, 1952-58, Gov.'s Adv. Com. Mental Health, 1954, R.I. Alcoholic Adv. Com., 1955-58, R.I. Com. Youth and Children, Gov.'s Adv. Com. on Revision Election Laws, Gov.'s Adv. Com. Social Welfare, Army Adv. Com. for 1st Army Area; mem. civil and polit. rights com. Pres.'s Commn. on Status of Women, 1960-63; mem. R.I. Com. Humanities, 1972—, chmn., 1972-77; mem. Family Ct. Study Com., R.I. com. Nat. Endowment Humanities; bd. dirs. Newport YMCA; sec. Bd. Physicians Service; bd. visitors Law Sch., Boston U.; bd. dirs. NCCJ; mem. edn. policy and devel. com. Roger Williams Jr. Coll.; trustee Syracuse U.; pres. Newport Girls Club, 1974-75, R.I. Supreme Ct. Hist. Soc., 1988—; chair Supreme Ct. Mandatory Continuing Legal Edn. Com., 1993—; apptd. bd. dirs. Touro Synague; apptd. R.I. Found. Served to lt. col. WAC, World War II. Decorated Legion of Merit; named named Judge of Yr., Nat. Assn. Women Judges, 1984, Outstanding Woman, Bus. and Profl. Women, 1972, Citizen of Yr., R.I. Trial Lawyers Assn., Newport courthouse renamed in her honor, 1990; recipient Arents Alumni award, Syracuse U., 1956, Carroll award, R.I. Inst. Instn., 1956, Brotherhood award, NCCJ, 1983, Herbert Harley award, Am. Judicature Soc., 1988, Silver Citizenship award, DAR, R.I., 1980s, Gold Citizenship award, DAR, 1990s, Merit award, R.I. Bar Assn., 1994, John Manson/Carl Robinson award, Nat. Probation Officers Assn., 1996, Longfellow Humanitarian award, ARC, 1997. Mem. ABA (chmn. credentials com. nat. conf. state trial judges 1971-73, chair judges adv. com. on standing com. on ethics and profl. responsibility 1991—, joint com. on jud. discipline of standing com. on profl. discipline 1991-94), R.I. Found. (bd. dirs. 1998—), AAUW (chmn. state edn. com. 1954-56), Am. Arbitration Assn., Nat. Trial Judges Conf. (state chmn. membership com., sec. exec. com.), New Eng. Trial Judges Conf. (com. chmn. 1967), Boston U. Alumni Coun., Am. Legion (judge adv. post 7, mem. nat. exec. com.), Bus. and Profl. Women's Club (past state v.p., past pres. Newport chpt., past pres. Nat. legis. com.), Auota Club (past gov. internat., past pres. Newport chpt.), Alpha Omega, Kappa Beta Pi.

MURRAY, GLENN EDWARD, lawyer; b. Niskayuna, N.Y., Dec. 11, 1955; BA cum laude, Siena Coll., 1977; JD, Union U., Albany, N.Y., 1980. Bar: N.Y. 1981, U.S. Dist. Ct. (no. dist.) N.Y. 1981, U.S. Ct. Mil. Appeals 1981, U.S. Dist. Ct. (we. dist.) N.Y. 1985, U.S. Supreme Ct. 1987, U.S. Bankruptcy Ct. 1989, U.S. Ct. Appeals (2d cir.) 1992. Pvt. practice, Buffalo, 1990—; prosecutor Village of Williamsville, 1992—2002. Adj. prof. Am. constl. law Canisius Coll., 1993-94. Author: Collateral Consequences of Criminal Conduct, 1989, Civil Consequences of Criminal Conduct, 51 Am. Jr. Trials 337, 1994; contbr. articles to profl. jours. Mem. social action com. Temple Beth Am, Amherst, N.Y., 1987—; instr. Jewish Community Ctr. Greater Buffalo, 1988—; instr. police legal survival Operation Tri-Star (SWAT team conf.), Ft. Drum, N.Y., 1989-91. Capt. U.s. Army, 1981-84, mem. N.Y. Army N.G. ret. Decorated Bronze Star. Mem. ABA, N.Y. State Bar Assn. (chmn. spl. com. on mil. and vet. affairs 1991-94), Erie County Bar Assn. (instr., panelist), N.Y. Defenders Assn., N.Y. State Assn. Criminal Def. Lawyers, N.Y. Civil Liberties Union. General civil litigation, Criminal, Family and matrimonial. Home: 84 Highland Dr Buffalo NY 14221-6802 Office: The Cornell Mansion 484 Delaware Ave Buffalo NY 14202-1304

MURRAY, JAMES MICHAEL, librarian, law librarian, legal educator, lawyer; b. Seattle, Nov. 8, 1944; s. Clarence Nicholas and Della May (Snyder) M.; m. Linda Monthy Murray. MLaw Librarianship, U. Wash., 1978; JD, Gonzaga U., 1971. Bar: Wash. 1974, U.S. Dist. Ct. (we. dist.) Wash. 1975, U.S. Dist. Ct. (ea. dist.) Wash. 1985. Reference/reserve libr. U. Tex. Law Libr., Austin, 1978-81; assoc. law libr. Washington U. Law Libr., St. Louis, 1981-84; law libr., asst. prof. Gonzaga U. Sch. Law, Spokane, 1984-91; libr. East Bonner County Libr., 1991-97, U.S. Cts. Libr., Spokane, 1997—. Mem. state adv. bd. Nat. Reporter on Legal Ethics and Profl. Responsibility, 1982-91; cons. in field. Author: (with Reams and McDermott) American Legal Literature: Bibliography of Selected Legal Resources, 1985, (with Gasaway and Johnson) Law Library Administration During Fiscal Austerity, 1992; editor Tex. Bar Jour. (Books Appraisals Column), 1979-82; contbr. numerous articles and revs. to profl. jours., acknowledgements and bibliographies in field. Bd. dirs. ACLU, Spokane chpt., 1987-91, Wash. Vol. Lawyers for the Arts, 1976-78. Mem. ABA, Idaho Libr. Assn., Wash. State Bar Assn. (law sch. liaison com. 1986-88, civil rights com. 1996-97). Home: 921 W 29th Ave Spokane WA 99203-1318 Office: US Cts Libr 920 W Riverside Ave Ste 650 Spokane WA 99201-1008 Office Fax: 509-353-0540. E-mail: james_murray@lb9.uscourts.gov.

MURRAY, JAY J. lawyer; b. Hartford, Conn., July 6, 1970; s. J. W. Murray and Norma Sousa. Student, U. Coll. London, 1992; BA, So. Meth. U., 1992; postgrad., U. Notre Dame, London, 1994; JD, Tex. Wesleyan U., 1995. Assoc. Sommerman, Parham & Mitchell, LLP, Dallas, 1996—97, Burleson, Pate & Gibson, LLP, Dallas, 1997—2000, Parham, Jones & Shiver, LLP, Dallas, 2001—. Co-author: Accident Investigation in the Private Sector: Volume II Guide to Depositions and Trials for Police Officers and Private Sector Reconstructionists, Sex Crimes. Mem.: Dallas Trial Lawyers Assn. (bd. dirs.), Tex. Trial Lawyers Assn. (bd. dirs./advs. 2000—01, bd. dirs. 2002—03), Dallas Bar Assn. (bd. dirs. 2000—03), State Bar Tex. Personal injury (including property damage). Office: Parham Jones & Shiver LLP Ste 800 2626 Cole Ave Dallas TX 75204

MURRAY, JENNIFER SUE, law librarian; b. Salinas, Calif., Mar. 8, 1972; d. William Lee Murray and Sonja Sue Phillips. BS, Ariz. State U., 1994, JD, 1998; MLS, U. Ariz., 2001. Bar: Ariz. 1998. Counsel Wilcox & Wilcox PC, Phoenix, 1998—2000; libr. asst. II U. Ariz., Tucson, 2000—01; sr. law libr. U. So. Calif., L.A., 2001—. Mem.: So. Calif. Assn. Law Librs. (chair union list com. 2001—03), Am. Assn. Law Librs. (mentoring com. 2002—03). Office: Univ So Calif 699 Exposition Blvd Los Angeles CA 90089-0072

MURRAY, JOHN WILLIAM, JR., writer, legal investigator; b. Apr. 8, 1934; s. John William and Frances (Bryan) M.; m. Norma Sousa, Oct. 30, 1959 (div. Apr. 1989); children: John William III, James Patrick, Jeffrey Dean, Jerome Bryan, Jay Joseph. BS, U. Hartford, 1968; MBA, U. Conn., 1971. Cert. fraud examiner, legal investigator, criminal def. investigator. Legal investigator, Dallas, 1974—. Author: Accident Investigation in the Private Sector, 1994 (Best New Investigative Book of Yr., 1994), Accident Investigation in the Private Sector, vol. 2, 1997, Forensic Photography in the Private Sector, 1995, Sex Crimes, 1995, Photographing Vehicles for Litigation, 1995, Guide to Depositions and Trials for Police Officer and Accident Reconstructionists, 1999, Guide to the Internet for Accident Investigators, 2001. 1st lt. USMC, 1957-60. Named One of Top 5 Investigators in Am. PI Mag., 1998, One of Top 25 Investigators of the Century, Nat. Assn. Investigative Specialists. Mem. Nat. Assn. Legal Investigators (cert., chmn. nat. cert. 1987-89, nat. chmn. editor-pub. awards com. 1992-96, regional dir. 1999-2000, Editor-Pub. award Legal Investigator mag. 1989, 91, Nat. Dirs. award 1997, Author of Yr. award 2002), Evidence Photographers Internat. Coun., Nat. Assn. Investigative Specialists (cert. expert in investigative photography, expert in accident investigation, Outstanding Spkr. of Yr. award 1995, Lifetime Achievement award 1996, named Author of Yr. 2002), Nat. Acad. for Continuing Edn. (co-founder), North Tex. Pvt. Investigators Assn. (pres. 2000). Avocations: photography, stamp collecting. Office: 3942 Rochelle Dr Dallas TX 75220-1814 E-mail: jwmpi@aol.com.

MURRAY, KATHLEEN ANNE, lawyer; b. LA, Feb. 14, 1946; d. Francis Albert and Dorothy (Thompson) M.; 1 child, Anne Murray Ladd; m. Arthur T. Perkins Jr., June 29, 1991. BA, U. Mich., 1967; JD, Hastings Coll. of Law, 1973. Bar: Calif. 1973, U.S. Dist. Ct. (no. dist.) Calif. 1973, U.S. Ct. Appeals (9th cir.) 1973. Sr. staff atty Child Care Law Ctr., San Francisco, 1979-84, cons. child day care law and regulation, 1984-86; atty Epstein & Harris, San Francisco, 1985-86; gen. counsel Fisher Friedman Assocs., San Francisco, 1986-89; assoc. gen. counsel Calif. State Automobile Assn., San Francisco, 1989-98; sr. counsel Firemen's Fund Ins. Co., San Francisco, 1998—2002; prin. Mercer HR Cons., San Francisco, 2003—. Exec. dir., editl. adv. bd. Parenting Mag., 1985-87; chair Labor and Employment Law Com., Am. Corp. Coun. Assn., 2001-03. Editor: Child Care Center Legal Handbook; Tax Guide for California Child Care Providers; contbr. articles to profl. jours. Mem. adv. coun. Humanities West, Inc., 1986-96, North of Market Child Devel. Ctr., San Francisco, 1987-90; vestry Episcopal Ch. of St. Mary the Virgin, 1990-92; pres. Parents' Assn., Lick-Wilmerding High Sch., 1993-94; Personnel Practices Com. of Episcopal Diocese of Calif. Democrat. Episcopalian. Business E-Mail: kathleen.murray@mercer.com.

MURRAY, MICHAEL KENT, lawyer; b. Missoula, Mont., Feb. 14, 1948; s. Paul R. and Virginia F. Murray; children: Britton M., Spencer J. BA, U. Calif., Santa Barbara, 1970; JD, U. Santa Clara, 1974. Bar: Wash. 1974, U.S. Ct. Claims 1975, U.S. Tax Ct. 1976, U.S. Dist. Ct. Wash. 1977, U.S.

Ct. Appeals (fed. cir.) 1982. Trial atty. honor law grad. program U.S. Dept. Justice, Washington, 1974-76; atty. Foster Pepper & Riviera, Seattle, 1976-79, ptnr. Seattle and Bellevue, 1980-86, ptnr.-in-charge Bellevue, 1983-86; atty., pres. Michael K. Murray, P.S., Seattle, 1986—. Pres. N.W. Properties Devel. Corp., Seattle, 1986-92; of counsel Lasher Holzapfel Sperry & Ebberson, Seattle, 1992-2001; v.p. and gen. mgr. constrn. defect repair div., BELFOR USA Group, Inc., Seattle, 2001—. Articles editor Santa Clara Lawyer, U. Santa Clara Sch. Law, 1973-74. Trustee Pacific Northwest Ballet, Seattle, 1979-81; dir. Bellevue Downtown Assn., 1984-87. Mem. Wash. State Bar Assn., King County Bar Assn., Seattle Yacht Club, Seattle Tennis Club. Avocations: sailing, fly fishing, biking, boating. Construction, Land use and zoning (including planning), Property, real (including real estate development, water). Home: 1570 9th Ave N Edmonds WA 98020-2627 Office: 3826 Woodland Park Ave N Seattle WA 98103-7926 E-mail: michael.murray@US.belfor.com.

MURRAY, ROBERT FOX, lawyer; b. Burlington, Vt., Feb. 28, 1952; s. Robert and Mary (Fox) Murray; m. Ann Marie Bevilacqua, Aug. 20, 1988. BA, Colgate U., 1974; JD, Boston U., 1978. Bar: Mass. 1978, U.S. Dist. Ct. Mass. 1979. Assoc. Law Offices of George Howard, Dedham, Mass., 1978—80; from assoc. to ptnr. Fairbanks & Silvia Koczera, Fountain, Murray, New Bedford, Mass., 1980—84; pvt. practice New Bedford, 1984—. Bd. dirs., clk. New Bedford, Inc. Mem.: Bristol County Bar Assn., New Bedford Bar Assn., Mass. Bar Assn. Democrat. State civil litigation, Environmental, Personal injury (including property damage). Office: One Johnny Cake Hill New Bedford MA 02740

MURRAY, STEPHEN JAMES, lawyer; b. Phila., Jan. 27, 1943; s. Paul Martin and Hannah (Smith) M.; m. Linda Sanders, June 20, 1970; children: Gordon Joshua, Cara Sanders. AB cum laude, Brown U., 1963; JD, Harvard U., 1966; LLM, George Washington U., 1967. Bar: N.Y. 1968, U.S. Ct. Appeals (2nd cir.) 1971, U.S. Ct. Appeals (fed. cir.) 1998, U.S. Dist. Ct. (so. and ea. dists.) N.Y. 1972, U.S. Ct. Claims 1974, U.S. Supreme Ct. 1975, Conn. 1988, U.S. Dist. Ct. Conn. 1988, U.S. Ct. Internat. Trade 1998. Spl. asst. SEC, Washington, 1966-67, Maritime Adminstrn., Washington, 1967-68; assoc. Hill, Betts & Nash, N.Y.C., 1970-76; transp. atty. Union Carbide Corp., N.Y.C., 1976-78, sr. transp. atty., 1978-85, chief transp. counsel Danbury, Conn., 1985—2001, group counsel, 1986—2001, chief real estate counsel, 1992—2001, comml. counsel, 1993—2001, customs and internat. trade counsel, 1997—2001; of counsel Mahoney & Keane, New York City, 2001—, 2001—. Spkr. in field. Contbr. articles to profl. jours. Lt. JAGC, USN, 1968-70. Mem. ABA, Conn. State Bar Assn., U.S. Naval Inst., Navy League of U.S., Maritime Law Assn., U.S. Transp. Lawyers Assn., N.Y. State Bar Assn., Am. Corp. Counsel Assn. (co-chair real estate com. Westchester-So. Conn. chpt.), Conn. Maritime Assn., Harvard Club, Brown Club (co-pres.), Brown Faculty Club, Brown Alumni Schs. Commn. (chmn. Fairfield County), Brown Alumni Assn. (bd. govs.). Admiralty, Property, real (including real estate development, water), Transportation. Home: 14 Pilgrim Ln Weston CT 06883-2412 Office: Mahoney & Keane 14 Pilgrim Ln Weston CT 06883 E-mail: sjmurray@snet.net.

MURRAY, VIRGINIA, lawyer; b. Harlow, Essex, Eng., Feb. 13, 1968; m. Nikolaos Melanitis, Jan. 4, 1997. BA, Cambridge (Eng.) U., 1989, MA, 1993. Bar: Eng. 1992, Wales 1992, Athens Ct. Appeal 1998. Barrister Chambers of David Farrer, London, 1992-96; ptnr. IKRP Rokas & Ptnrs., Athens, 1997—. Contbg. author: Telcommunications Law in Europe, 1998. Commercial, consumer (including collections, credit), Communications, Insurance. Office: IKRP Rokas & Ptnrs 25 Boukourestiou St Athens 104 44 Greece E-mail: athens@rokas.com.

MURRAY, WILLIAM MICHAEL (MIKE MURRAY), lawyer; b. Ottumwa, Iowa, Dec. 28, 1947; s. William Bernard and Thelma Jean (Hart) M.; m. Ann Elizabeth Wawzonek, Oct. 11, 1973; children: Kathleen Elizabeth, Daniel Webster. BA, U. Iowa, 1970; JD, 1973. Bar: Iowa 1973, U.S. Dist. Ct. (so. dist.) Iowa 1976, U.S. Dist. Ct. (no. dist.) Iowa 1978, U.S. Ct. Appeals (8th cir.) 1978. Staff counsel Iowa Civil Rights Commn., Des Moines, 1973-76; assoc. Bertroche & Hagen, Des Moines, 1976-78; ptnr. Murray, Jankins & Noble, Des Moines, 1978—. Spkr., co-author: Workers' Compensation Claims in Iowa, 1999. Bd. dirs. Iowa Civil Liberties Union, Des Moines, 1978-83, pres., 1982-83; bd. dirs. Polk County Legal Aide Soc., Des Moines, 1984-88. Mem. ABA, Asn. Trial Lawyers Am., Assn. Trial Lawyers Iowa, Iow Assn. Workers' Compensation Lawyers, Iowa State Bar Assn., Polk County Bar Assn., Des Moines Jaycees Club (bd. dirs. legal counsel 1980-81). Democrat. Personal injury (including property damage), Workers' compensation. Home: 600 SW 42nd St Des Moines IA 50312-4605 Office: Murray Jankins & Noble 2903 Ingersoll Ave Des Moines IA 50312-4014 E-mail: murray@iowa-law.com.

MURRAY, WILLIAM MICHAEL, lawyer; b. Buffalo, Dec. 21, 1953; s. William Joseph and Mary Ann (Lichtenthal) M.; m. Suzanne M. Raynor; children: Colleen Elizabeth, William Michael Jr., Caitlin Anne, Matthew Francis Johnson. BA, U. Notre Dame, 1975; JD, U. Detroit, 1978. Bar: N.Y. 1978, U.S. Dist. Ct. (we. dist.) N.Y. 1980. Asst. county atty. Erie County, Buffalo, 1978-79; ptnr. Stamm & Murray, Williamsville, N.Y., 1979-96, Renaldo Myers & Palumbo, Williamsville, N.Y., 1996-98; dep. atty. Town of Amherst, N.Y., 1993-96; gen. counsel Town of Amherst Indsl. Devel. Agy., 1996—. Mem. Amherst (N.Y.) Rep. Com., 1980—; chmn. Amherst Zoning Bd. Appeals, 1986-93. Mem. N.Y. State Bar Assn., Erie County Bar Assn., Williamsville Bus. Assn. (bd. dirs., v.p. 1985-96), Rotary (pres. Williamsville 1989). Roman Catholic. General practice, Land use and zoning (including planning), Municipal (including bonds). Office: 130 John Muir Dr Amherst NY 14228-1148 E-mail: wmurray@amherstida.com.

MURRELL, ROBERT GEORGE, lawyer; b. Jan. 27, 1932; s. Samuel Edwin and Myrtle Josephine (Hailey) M.; m. Bonnie Bird Robinson, Nov. 11, 1961; children: Robert George, Michele Grace, Bonnie Melissa. BA, U. Fla., 1951, JD, 1953. Bar: Fla. 1953, N.Y. 1981, U.S. Dist. Ct. (so. dist.) Fla. 1953, U.S. Dist. Ct. (mid. dist.) Fla. 1980, U.S. Ct. Appeals (5th cir.) 1953, U.S. Ct. Appeals (11th cir.) 1981, U.S. Ct. Mil. Appeals 1958, U.S. Supreme Ct. 1958, U.S. Ct. Claims 1975, U.S. Tax Ct. 1975, U.S. Ct. Customs and Patent Appeals 1975, U.S. Ct. Appelas (D.C. cir.) 1989, U.S. Ct. Appeals (3rd, 4th, 6th, 7th, 8th, 9th, 10th cirs.) 1989, U.S. Ct. Appeals (2nd cir.) 1990, U.S. Ct. Vet. Appeals 1992; arbitrator Am. Arbitration Assn. Atty. Sam E. Murrell & Sons., Orlando, Fla., 1953—. Mem. Ctirus Assocs. of N.Y. Stock Exch.; pres. Colonial Mortgage Co. Fla., Inc.; dir. Weiss Realty Corp., Lake Margaret Co. Sgt. U.S. Army, 1953—55. Mem.: ATLA, ABA, Acad. Fla. Trial Lawyers, Orange County Bar Assn., Univ. Winter Park, Elks (Orlando), Shriners, Masons. Republican. Baptist. General civil litigation, Criminal, Personal injury (including property damage). Home: 415 Raintree Ct Winter Park FL 32789-2561 Office: Sam E Murrell & Sons 1 N Rosalind Ave Orlando FL 32801-1682

MURRIAN, ROBERT PHILLIP, retired state judge, educator; b. Knoxville, Tenn., Apr. 1, 1945; s. Albert Kinzel and Mary Gilbert (Eppes) M.; m. Jerrilyn Sue Boone, Oct. 29, 1983; children: Kimberley Ann, Jennifer Rebecca, Albert Boone, Samuel Robert. BS, U.S. Naval Acad., 1967; JD, U. Tenn., 1974. Bar: Tenn. 1974, U.S. Dist. Ct. (ea. dist.) Tenn. 1975, U.S. Ct. Appeals (6th cir.) 1982. Law clk. to judge U.S. Dist. Ct. (ea. dist.) Tenn., 1974-76; assoc. Butler, Vines, Babb & Threadgill, Knoxville, 1976-78; magistrate, judge U.S. Dist. (ea. dist.) Tenn., Knoxville, 1978—2002; ptnr. Kramer, Rayson, Leake, Rodgers & Morgan, LLP, Knoxville, 2002—. Adj. prof. U. Tenn. Coll. Law, 1990-93, 95-96, 2002. Lt. USN, 1967-71. Green scholar, 1973-74, Nat. Moot Ct. scholar, 1974. Fellow Tenn. Bar Found.; mem. ABA, Tenn. Bar Assn., Knoxville Bar Assn. (bd. govs. 1994), Sixth Cir. Jud. Conf. (life), Order of Coif, Am. Inn of Ct. (master of the bench, pres. 1997-98), Phi Kappa Phi. Presbyterian. Office: Kramer Rayson Leake Rodgers & Morgan LLP PO Box 629 Knoxville TN 37901-0629 Address: First Tennessee Plz 800 S Gay St Ste 2500 Knoxville TN 37929 Fax: 865-522-5723. E-mail: rpmurrian@kramer-rayson.com.

MURRY, HAROLD DAVID, JR., lawyer; b. Holdenville, Okla., June 30, 1943; s. Harold David Sr. and Willie Elizabeth (Dees) M.; m. Ann Moore Earnhardt, Nov. 1, 1975; children: Elizabeth Ann, Sarah Bryant. BA, Okla. U., 1965, JD, 1968. Bar: Okla. 1968, D.C. 1974. Asst. to v.p. U. Okla., Norman, 1968-71, legal counsel Research Inst., 1969-71; atty. U.S. Dept. Justice, Washington, 1971-74; spl. asst. U.S. Atty., Washington, 1972; assoc. Clifford & Warnke, Washington, 1974-78, ptnr., 1978-91, Howrey & Simon, Washington, 1991-98, Baker Botts LLP, Washington, 1998—. Mem. ABA, Okla. Bar Assn., D.C. Bar Assn., Fed. Bar Assn., Met. Club (Washington), Chevy Chase Club (Md.), Phi Alpha Delta. Democrat. Administrative and regulatory, Antitrust, Federal civil litigation. Home: 8931 Bel Air Pl Potomac MD 20854-1606 Office: Baker Botts LLP Ste 1300 1299 Pennsylvania Ave NW Washington DC 20004-2408

MURTAUGH, CHRISTOPHER DAVID, lawyer; b. Darby, Pa., Oct. 25, 1945; s. John Michael and Rita (Sullivan) M.; m. Nancy R. Hanauer, Nov. 30, 1968; children: Jason C., Colin M., Alison M. AB, U. Ill., 1967, JD, 1970. Bar: Ill. 1970, Fla. 1973, U.S. Dist. Ct. (no. dist.) Ill. 1975. Ptnr. Winston & Strawn, Chgo., 1974—, capital ptnr., 1987—, real estate dept. chmn., 1994—. Mem. Glen Ellyn (Ill.) Capital Improvements Com., 1985-89, Glen Ellyn Plan Com., 1989-96, Met. Planning Coun., 1995—; bd. visitors U. Ill. Coll. of Law, 1998-2001. Lt. USNR, 1971-74. Mem. ABA, Am. Coll. Real Estate Lawyers, Fla. Bar Assn., Ill. State Bar Assn., Chgo. Bar Assn., Urban Land Inst., Internat. Coun. Shopping Ctrs., Order of Coif. Property, real (including real estate development, water). Office: Winston & Strawn 35 W Wacker Dr Ste 4200 Chicago IL 60601-1695 E-mail: cmurtaugh@winston.com.

MUSGRAVE, R. KENTON, federal judge; b. 1927; Student, Ga. Inst. Tech., 1945-46, U. Fla., 1946-47; BA, U. Wash., 1948; JD with distinction, Emory U., 1953. Asst. gen. counsel Lockheed Internat., 1953-62; v.p., gen. counsel Mattel, Inc., 1963-71; mem. firm Musgrave, Welbourn and Fertman, 1972-75; asst. gen. counsel Pacific Enterprises, 1975-81; v.p., gen. counsel Vivitar Corp, 1981-85; v.p., dir. Santa Barbara Applied Rsch., 1982-87; judge U.S. Ct. Internat. Trade, N.Y.C., 1987—. Trustee The Dian Fossey Gorilla Fund, Dolphins of Sharks Bay (Australia); hon. trustee Pet Protection Soc.; mem. United Way, Save the Redwoods League; active Palos Verdes Community Assn. Mem. Internat. Bar Assn., Pan Am. Bar Assn., State Bar Calif. (chmn. corp. law sect. 1965-66, del. 1966-67), L.A. County Bar Assn., Fng. Trade Assn. So. Calif. (bd. dirs.). Office: US Ct Internat Trade 1 Federal Plz New York NY 10278-0001

MUSICK, ROBERT LAWRENCE, JR., lawyer; b. Richlands, Va., Oct. 3, 1947; s. Robert Lawrence and Virginia (Brooks) M.; m. Beth Pambianchi, 1996; children: Elizabeth, Robert. BA in History with honors, U. Richmond, 1969; JD, MA in Legal History, U. Va., 1972; LLM, Coll. William and Mary, 1986. Bar: Va. 1972, U.S. Ct. Appeals (4th cir.) 1974. Law clk. Supreme Ct. Va., Richmond, 1972-73; assoc. Williams, Mullen & Christian, Richmond, 1973-78; ptnr. Williams, Mullen, Christian & Dobbins, Richmond, 1978-99, Williams Mullen Clark & Dobb, Richmond, 1999—. Bd. govs. estates and property sect. Va. State Bar, 1977-80, chmn., 1980. Author: RIA Non Qualified Deferred Compensation, 1997, (with others) CCH Federal Tax Service, 1989; contbr. articles to profl. jours. Trustee U. Richmond, 1991-94, Va. Intermont Coll., 2002—; mem. Estate Planning Coun. Richmond, 1981—, U. Richmond Estate Planning Coun., 1984—; bd. dirs. Va. Bapt. Homes, Inc., 1994—. Lt. col. USAR. Fellow Am. Coll. Employment Benefit Counsel; mem. ABA, Va. Bar Assn., Richmond Bar Assn., So. Pension Conf., Va. Assn. Professions (pres. 1980-81), Commonwealth Club, Willow Oaks Country Club (dir. 1999—, pres. 2002). Baptist. Avocations: tennis, golf, scuba. Corporate, general, Estate planning, Pension, profit-sharing, and employee benefits. Office: Williams Mullen Clark & Dobbins 2 James Center PO Box 1320 Richmond VA 23218-1320

MUSKIN, VICTOR PHILIP, lawyer; b. N.Y.C., Mar. 1, 1942; s. Jacob Cecil and Fanya (Solomonoff) M.; m. Odette Cheryl Spreier, June 10, 1979; children: Adam James, Liana Jeanne. BA, Oberlin Coll., 1963; JD, NYU, 1966. Bar: N.Y. 1969, U.S. Dist. Ct. (so. and ea. dists.) N.Y. 1972, U.S. Ct. Appeals (2d cir.) 1974, U.S. Supreme Ct. 1974, U.S. Ct. Appeals (9th and 10th cirs.) 1978, U.S. Ct. Appeals (3d cir.) 1987. Asst. corp. counsel divsn. gen. litigation City of N.Y., 1969-73; assoc. Wolf, Popper, Ross, Wolf & Jones, N.Y.C., 1973-74, Reavis and McGrath, N.Y.C., 1974-78; pvt. practice N.Y.C., 1979; ptnr. Gruen & Muskin, N.Y.C., 1980-81, Gruen, Muskin & Thau, N.Y.C., 1981-89, Munves, Tanenhaus & Storch, N.Y.C., 1989-90, Solin & Breimdel, N.Y.C., 1991-92; pvt. practice N.Y.C., 1992—2003; of counsel Scheichet & Davis, P.C., 2003—. Served with Peace Corps, 1966—68; pres. Brotherhood, Ctrl. Synagogue, N.Y.C., 1998—2002. Mem. N.Y.C. Bar Assn. (com. computer law 1982-84, com. internat. law 1996-99). Federal civil litigation, State civil litigation, Private international. Home: 529 E 84th St New York NY 10028-7330 Office: 800 Third Ave New York NY 10022 E-mail: vp.muskin@verizon.net.

MUSSEHL, ROBERT CLARENCE, lawyer; b. Washington, May 1, 1936; s. Chester Carl and Clara Cecelia (Greenwalt) Mussehl; children: Debra Lee (dec.), David Lee; m. Misook Chung, Mar. 22, 1987; 1 child, Omar. BA, Am. U., 1964, JD, 1966. Bar: Wash. 1967, U.S. Dist. Ct. (we. dist.) Wash. 1967, U.S. Ct. Appeals (9th cir.) 1968, U.S Supreme Ct. 1971. Sr. ptnr. Thom, Mussehl, Navoni, Hoff, Pierson & Ryder, Seattle, 1967-78, Neubauer & Mussehl, Seattle, 1978-80, Mussehl & Rosenberg, Seattle, 1980—2001. Speaker law convs. and other profl. orgns.; moot ct. judge Nat. Appelate Advocacy Competition, San Francisco, 1987; panel mem. ABA Symposium on Compulsory Jurisdiction of World Ct., San Francisco, 1987. chair dispute resolution com., 2001-02; chmn. bd., chief exec. officer The Seattle Smashers profl. volleyball club, 1976-80. Contbr. numerous articles to legal publs. Mem. Wash. Vol. Lawyers for Arts, 1976-80; statewide chair Lawyers for Durning for Gov., 1976; mem. task force on the single adult and ch. Ch. Coun. Greater Seattle, 1976-78; bd. dirs. Wash. State Pub. Interest Law Ctr., 1976-81; founder, past chair Lawyers Helping Hungry Children campaign, bd. dirs., 1991-2003; founder, past chair Wash. State Lawyers Campaign for Hunger Relief, 1991—. Recipient Jefferson award for cmty. and pub. svc. State of Wash., Am. Inst. for Pub. Svc., 1997. Fellow Am. Bar Found. (life), Am. Acad. Matrimonial Lawyers; mem. ABA (ho. of dels. 1979-91, 2003—, spl. adv. com. on internat. activities 1989-91, chair marriage and family counseling and conciliation com. family law sect. 1981-83, world order under law standing com. 1983-89, chair, 1986-89, chair ad hoc com. on the assembly 1986-89, assembly resolutions com. 1979-91, blue ribbon com. for world ct. 1987-88, standing com. on dispute resolution, 1992-93; exec. coun. sect. dispute resolution 1993-95, asst. budget officer, 1995-97, budget officer 1997-99, vice-chair 1999—, chair 2001-02, sect. liaison commn. on racial and ethnic diversity 2002-03), Wash. State Bar Assn. (exec. com. family law sect. 1973-75, chmn. internat. law com. 1974-76, sec.-treas., exec. com. world peace through law sect. 1980—, chair 1981-82, mem. edit. bd. Family Law Deskbook 1987-89), Wash. State Trial Lawyers Assn., Seattle-King County Bar Assn. (family law sect. 1971-90, other coms. 1970—, chmn. young lawyers sect. 1971-72, sec. 1972-73, trustee), Am. Arbitration Assn. (panel arbitrators), World Assn. Lawyers of World Peace Through Law Ctr. (founding mem.), Heritage Club YMCA Greater Seattle (charter 1977—), UN Assn. USA (bd. dirs. Seattle chpt. 1989-91). Avocations: squash, biking, tennis, weight training, painting, religious studies. Personal injury (including property damage), Sports. Home: One Pacific Tower 2000 1st Ave Apt 902 Seattle WA 98121-2167 Office: Ste 3000 1000 2nd Ave Seattle WA 98104-1093 E-mail: bobmussehl@earthlink.net.

MUSSELMAN, ROBERT METCALFE, lawyer; b. N.Y.C., June 12, 1914; s. Joseph Franklin and Susan M. (Metcalfe) Musselman; m. Lucie Carolyn Clarke, Sept. 6, 1958; 1 child, Susan Carole. BS, U. Va., 1934, MA in Polit. Sci., 1940, LLB, 1945. Bar: Va. 1945, U.S. Dist. Ct. (ea. dist.) Va. 1948, U.S. Tax Ct. 1948, U.S. Dist. Ct. (we. dist.) Va. 1951, U.S. Ct. Appeals (4th cir.) 1953, U.S. Supreme Ct. 1964, U.S. Claims Ct. 1986, U.S. Ct. Appeals (11th cir.) 1987, U.S. Ct. Appeals (fed. cir.) 1988, U.S. dist. Ct. (ctrl. dist.) Ill. 1994, U.S. Ct. Appeals (7th cir.) 1994. Instr., lectr. U. Va., Charlottesville, 1936-59, chief acct., 1943-46; law clk. to judge U.S. Ct. Appeals (4th cir.), 1945-46; ptnr. Michael and Musselman, Charlottesville, 1946-53, Musselman and Drysdale, Charlottesville, 1953-56; pvt. practice Charlottesville, 1956—. Lectr. in field. Editor-in-chief: Alexander's Federal Tax Handbook, 1955—61, bd. editors: Jour. Taxation, 1954—73. Pres. Charlottesvill-Albemarle Young Dem. Club, 1940—43; mem. Albemarle County Dem. Com., 1978—. Mem.: AICPA, ABA, Va. Soc. CPAs (bd. dirs.), Charlottesville-Albemarle Bar Assn., Va. Bar Assn., Am. Assn. Atty.-CPAs (charter, bd. dirs.), 4th Cir. Jud. Conf., Phi Sigma Kappa. Episcopalian. Bankruptcy, Probate (including wills, trusts), Personal income taxation. Home: 1438 Lilac Ct Charlottesville VA 22901-6403 Office: 413 7th St NE PO Box 254 Charlottesville VA 22902-0254 E-mail: rmmesquire@aol.com.

MUSSER, SANDRA G. retired lawyer; b. Hollywood, Calif., July 23, 1944; d. Donald Godfrey Gumpertz and Gloria G. (Rosenblatt) King; m. Michael R.V. Whitman, Feb. 19, 1980. BA, UCLA, 1965; JD, Hastings Coll. of Law, 1970. Bar: Calif. 1971, U.S. Dist. Ct. (no. dist.) Calif. 1971, U.S. Ct. Appeals (9th cir.) 1971. Clk. 9th Cir. Ct. of Appeals, 1971-72; lawyer pvt. practice of family law, 1972-86; ptnr. Musser & Ryan, San Francisco, 1986-97; pvt. practice San Francisco, 1997-98; ret., 1998. Judge pro tem San Francisco County Superior Ct., 1988-98; dealer antique Chinese rugs and textiles, 1996—. Contbr. articles to profl. jours. Mem. adv. coun. Textile Mus., Washington, 1996—. Fellow Acad. Matrimonial Lawyers; mem. ABA (chair litig. sect. domestic rels. and family law com. 1993-94), State Bar Calif. (state bar family law sect. 1977—, chair 1982-83, advisor 1983-84), Bar Assn. San Francisco. Family and matrimonial. Office: 361 Oak St San Francisco CA 94102-5615

MUSSMAN, WILLIAM EDWARD, III, lawyer; b. San Francisco, Jan. 31, 1951; s. William Edward and Janet Jonn (Skittone) M.; m. Carol Lynne Johnson, Jan. 9, 1988; children: Katherine Ann, Laura Lynne, Elizabeth Ashley. BS cum laude, Stanford U., 1973; JD, U. Calif.-San Francisco, 1976. Bar: Calif. 1976, U.S. Dist. Ct. (cen. dist.) Calif. 1982, U.S. Dist. Ct. (ea. dist.) Calif. 1998, U.S. Dist. Ct. (no. dist.) Calif. 1976, U.S. Ct. Appeals (9th cir.) 1987, U.S. Supreme Ct. 1985. Assoc. Lasky, Haas, Cohler & Munter, San Francisco, 1980-82, Pillsbury, Madison & Sutro, San Francisco, 1982-84, Carr & Mussman, San Francisco, 1984-91, ptnr., 1991-95, Carr, Mussman & Harvey, LLP, San Francisco, 1996-99, Mussman & Mussman, LLP, Modesto, Calif., 2000—. Contbr. articles to profl. jours. Vol., rep., Ch. Jesus Christ Latter Day Sts., Tokyo, 1977-78. Mem. Calif. State Bar Assn. (litigation sect., law practice mgmt. sect.), Stanislaus County Bar Assn., Stanford Alumni Assn. (life), Tau Beta Phi. Antitrust, Alternative dispute resolution, General civil litigation. Office: Mussman & Mussman LLP 1101 Sylvan Ave Ste C106 Modesto CA 95350-1687 E-mail: wmussman3@mussmanlaw.com.

MUSTAIN, DOUGLAS DEE, lawyer; b. Shreveport, La., Nov. 2, 1945; s. Reginald K. and Dorothy J. (Green) M.; m. Sharon L. Tegarden, Aug. 19, 1967; children: Kristi Kaye, Kari Dee, Kenton Douglas, Kyle Robert, Kirk Stephen, Kali Elizabeth. Student Knox Coll., 1963-64, Murray State U., 1964-66; BS, U. Ill., 1971; JD, U. Iowa, 1974. Bar: Iowa 1974, Ill. 1974; U.S. Dist. Ct. (cen. dist.) Ill. 1974, U.S. Ct. Appeals (7th cir.) 1980, U.S. Supreme Ct. 1986. Law clk. Shulman, Phelan, Tucker, Boyle & Mullin, Iowa City, 1972-74; assoc. Stuart, Neagle & West, Galesburg, Ill., 1974-76; ptnr. West, Neagle & Williamson, Galesburg, 1977-89, Mustain & Lindstrom, Galesburg, 1989—; instr. real estate law Carl Sandburg Coll., Galesburg, 1977-81. Chmn. Citizens Referendum Com., Galesburg, 1983, 1987-88; bd. dirs. YMCA, Galesburg, 1983—, Cottage Hosp. Care Corp., Galesburg, 1984—; trustee 1st Presbyn. Ch., Galesburg, 1984; commr. Galesburg Pub. Transp. Commn., 1985—; pres., founder Galesburg Pub. Sch. Found., 1987-94. Served to SP5 U.S. Army, 1966-69, Vietnam. Decorated Army Commendation with oak leaf cluster. Mem. Knox County Bar Assn. (pres. 1980-82), ABA (comml. litigation com. 1981—), Assn. Trial Lawyers Am., Ill. Trial Lawyers Assn. Republican. State civil litigation, General practice. Home: 1234 N Prairie St Galesburg IL 61401-1852 Office: Mustain Lindstrom & Henson 1865 N Henderson St Ste 11B Galesburg IL 61401-1377

MUSTARD, LEWIS WILLIAMS, management consultant, educator, legal consultant; b. Durham, N.C., Sept. 4, 1942; s. Harry S. and Elizabeth (Williams) M.; divorced; children: Juliana Janice, Lewis Williams Jr. AB in English, U. N.C., 1966; cert. in hosp. adminstrn., Duke U., 1970; LLB, La Salle U., Chgo., 1974; D Bus. Adminstrn., Western Coll. U., 1976; PhD in Health Adminstrn., Union Grad. Sch., Cin., 1992; MA in Humanities, Calif. State U., Dominguez Hills, 1995. Hosp. adminstr. Watts (S.C.) Hosp., 1968-70; exec. dir. AID, Inc., Bryn Mawr, Pa., 1970-73; sr. hosp. cons. Summerour & Assocs., Atlanta, 1975-76; regional adminstr. Qualicare, Inc., New Orleans, 1976-78, Triage Corp., Clearwater, Fla., 1978-80; pres. Healthcare Mgmt. Cons., Atlanta, 1980-88; mem. continuing edn. faculty Duke U., Durham, N.C., 1994—; with Mgmt. Cons., Chapel Hill, N.C., 1993—. Adj. prof. Cen. Mich. U., Mt. Pleasant, 1993—, So. Ill. U., Carbondale, 1993—, Webster U., St. Louis, 1994—; expert witness, solo practitioner, 1992—. Served with USNR Res., 1959-68. Episcopalian.

MUSTO, JOSEPH JOHN, lawyer; b. Pittston, Pa., Nov. 22, 1943; s. James and Rose Musto; m. Fortunata Giudice, July 5, 1969; children: Laura, Joseph Robert. BA, King's Coll., Wilkes-Barre, Pa., 1965; JD, Dickinson Sch. Law, Carlisle, Pa., 1968. Bar: Pa. 1968, U.S. Ct. Appeals (3d cir.) 1968, U.S. Dist. Ct. (mid. dist.) Pa. 1971. Asst. dist. atty. City of Phila., 1968-69; assoc. Bedford, Waller, Griffith, Darling & Mitchell, Wilkes-Barre, 1969-73; ptnr. Griffith, Darling, Mitchell, Aponick & Musto, Wilkes-Barre, 1973-75; prin. Griffith, Aponick & Musto, Wilkes-Barre, 1975-90; ptnr. Rosenn, Jenkins & Greeenwald, Wilkes-Barre, 1990-93; judge Ct. Common Pleas of Luzerne County, 1993-94; mem. Hourigan, Kluger, Spohrer & Quinn, Wilkes-Barre, Pa., 1994-97; prin. Musto & Saunders, PC, Plymouth, Pa., 1997—. Solicitor Yatesville (Pa.) Borough, 1973-80, Duryea (Pa.) Borough, 1975-80, Pittston Area Sch. Dist., 1973-93. Mem. Luzerne County Gov. Study Com., Wilkes-Barre, 1973-74; mem., chmn. No. Luzerne Health Adv. Coun., Wilkes-Barre, 1976-80; pres., mem. Health Sys. Agy. of N.E. Pa., Avoca, 1980-86; pres. Pa. Health Planning Assn., Harrisburg, 1985-86; mem. civil justice reform act adv. com. Fed. Dist. Ct. Pa. Ct., 1991-95. Mem. Fed. Bar Assn. (past pres. Ctrl. Pa. chpt.), Pa. Bar Assn., Wilkes-Barre Law and Libr. Assn. Democrat. Roman Catholic. Alternative dispute resolution, Health. Home: 7 Prospect Pl Pittston PA 18640-2627 Office: Musto & Saunders 117 W Main St Plymouth PA 18651-2926

MÜTZE, MICHAEL W. lawyer; b. Cologne, Germany, May 2, 1952; s. Heinz August and Gisela Charlotte (Brandt) Mütze; m. Susanne von Hippel, Oct. 28, 1987. LLD, U. Cologne, 1981. Bar: Düsseldorf 1981. Assoc. Lauenroth & Ptnrs., Düsseldorf, Germany, 1981—83, sr. ptnr., 1984—96, Mütze & Ptnrs., Düsseldorf, 1997—99; ptnr. PricewaterhouseCoopers, Düsseldorf, 1999—. Mem.: Forum Vergabe e.V., Arge Baurecht im Deutschen Anwaltsverein, Deutsche Gesellschaft für Baurecht. Avocations: hunting, sports, music. Construction, Land use and zoning (including planning), Property, real (including real estate development, water). Office: PwC Veltins Rechtsanwaltsgesellschaft mbH Werdener St 10 40227 Düsseldorf Germany

MYCOCK, FREDERICK CHARLES, lawyer; b. Columbus, Ga., Oct. 3, 1943; s. Edwin S. and Elaine M.M. BSBA, Boston U., 1965, LLB, 1968. Bar: Mass. 1968, U.S. Dist. Ct. Mass. 1974, U.S. Supreme Ct. 1980. Assoc. Roderick E. Smith, Hyannis, Mass., 1968-71; asst. atty. gen. State of Mass., 1972-73; ptnr. Mycock, Kilroy, Green & Mycock, Hyannis, 1972-77, Mycock, Nwewll & Morse, Barnstable, Mass., 1977-86; atty. pvt. practice, Barnstable, Mass., 1987—. Mem. ABA, Assn. Trial Lawyers Assn., Nat. Assn. Criminal Defense Lawyers, Mass. Bar Assn., Mass. Acad. Trial Lawyers, Barnstable County Bar Assn. Republican. Methodist. Criminal, General practice. Home: Santuit Rd Cotuit MA 02635 Office: 3291 Main St Barnstable MA 02630-1105

MYERS, BILL, lawyer; b. Highland Park, Mich., Dec. 3, 1951; s. William Joseph Jr. and Zornicka Mildred Irus (Lukas) M.; m. Cathy Susan Davis, May 23, 1985 (div. 1998); children: Amelia Anne, Abigail Amy. AB with distinction, U. Mich., 1973; JD, U. Denver, 1979; MA, Regis U., 2002. Bar: Colo. 1979, U.S. Dist. Ct. Colo. 1979, U.S. Ct. Appeals (10th cir.) 1979. Atty. in sole practice, Denver, 1979-94; pub. interest lawyer, environ. advocate, pres. Bill Myers, P.C., Denver, 1994—. Exec. dir. Gt. Outdoors-Denver, 1996—. Mem. League Conservation Voters Edn. Fund, 1998; mem. Colo. Environ. Leadership Inst. Program, 1998; bd. dirs. Nat. Campaign to Stop Sprawl, 1998—. Mem. Sierra Club (bd. dirs. Rocky Mountain chpt. 1995-2002, Disting. Svc. award 1995, 98, South Platte Group Activist award 1997). Environmental. Fax: 303-935-6922. E-mail: billmyers@earthlink.net.

MYERS, DANE JACOB, lawyer, podiatrist; b. Murray, Utah, June 20, 1948; s. Lorin LaVar Myers and Irma Lee (Bell) Willette; m. Mary Jo Jackson, June 22, 1970; children: Troy, Chad, Melissa, Apryll, Tristan, Remington. DPM, Pa. Coll. Podiatric Medicine, 1977; BA, U. Utah, 1983; JD, U. Ark., 1986. Bar: Ark 1986. Pres. Tooele (Utah) Foot Clinic, 1977-83; owner N.W. Ark. Foot Clinic, Rogers, Ark., 1983—; pvt. practice law Fayetteville, 1986-97. Served to maj med serv corps USAR, 1977—94. Mem.: APHA, ABA, Ark. Podiatric Medicine Assn., Am. Podiatric Medicine Assn., Am. Soc. Law and Medicine, Ark. Bar Assn., Am. Diabetes Assn., Am. Coll. Foot and Ankle Surgeons (assoc.), Delta Theta Phi. Republican. Mem. Lds Ch. Avocations: golf, computers, history. Health. Home: 2005 Oakhill Dr Springdale AR 72762 Office: NW Ark Foot Clinic 700 N 13th St Rogers AR 72756-3436 E-mail: danejmyers@hotmail.com.

MYERS, DANIEL N. lawyer, association executive; b. Independence, Kans., Sept. 17, 1942; s. James Kenneth and Evalyn Clair Petty (Feather) M.; m. Eileen Carruthers, Dec. 14, 1966; children: Yvette Christine, John Joseph. AA, Coffeyville Coll., 1961; BA, U. Okla., 1963; JD, Georgetown U., 1975. Bar: Va. 1976, U.S. Ct. Customs and Patent Appeals 1977, Ill. 1991. Asst. to pres. J.V. Hurson Assoc., Inc., Washington, 1968-74; mgr. fed. legis. affairs AICPA, Washington, 1974-77; dir. legis. svcs., assoc. counsel Nat. LP-Gas Assn., Arlington, Va., 1977-79; gen. counsel, v.p. govt. relations Nat. Propane Gas Assn., Arlington, Va., 1979-88, exec. v.p. Lisle, Ill., 1989—2003; exec. dir. Churchill Ctr., Washington, 2003—. Contbr. articles on good samaritan laws and genealogy to various publs. Bd. dirs. Washington Area State Rels. Group, 1980-82, mem. energy task force White House Conf. on Small Bus., 1980; chmn. good samaritan coaliton hazardous materials Adv. Coun., Washington, 1982-88; mem. motor carrier adv. com. Fed. Hwy. Adminstrn., Washington, 1982-88. Sgt. U.S. Army, 1964-68. Mem. Am. Soc. Assn. Execs. (legal sect. coun. 1980—, chmn. legal sect. 1991-92, bd. dirs. 1991-92), Spl. Indsl. Radio Svc. Assn. (bd. dirs. 1979-88), Indsl. Telecomm. Assn. (bd. dirs. 1995-97), Chgo. Soc. Assn. Execs., Nat. Vol. Firefighters Coun. Found. (bd. dirs. 1995-97). Avocations: golf, genealogy, racquetball, woodworking. Office: 4901 Forest Ave Downers Grove IL 60515 E-mail: dmyers@winstonchurchill.org.

MYERS, FRANKLIN, oil industry executive; b. Pensacola, Fla., Nov. 2, 1952; m. Elizabeth A. Berner; children: Amanda C., Adam F., Anne Marie M.;1 child, Mary Lauren Miller. BS, Miss. State U., 1974; JD, U. Miss., 1977. Bar: Miss. 1977, Tex. 1978. Ptnr. Fulbright and Jaworski, Houston, 1978-88; sr. v.p., gen. counsel Baker Hughes Inc., Houston, 1988-95; sr. v.p. Cooper Cameron Corp., Houston, 1995—, CFO, 2002. Adj. prof. U. Tex. Sch. Law, 1990—; bd. dirs. InPut Output Inc. Fellow: Houston Bar Assn., Miss. Bar Assn., Tex. Bar Assn., Houston Bar Found.; mem.: Tex. Bar Found. (bd. dirs.). Office: Cooper Cameron Corp 1333 W Loop South Ste 1700 Houston TX 77027

MYERS, HARDY, state attorney general, lawyer; b. Electric Mills, Miss., Oct. 25, 1939; m. Mary Ann Thalhofer, 1962; children: Hardy III, Christopher, Jonathan. AB with distinction, U. Miss., 1961; LLB, U. Oreg., 1964. Bar: Oreg., U.S. Ct. of Appeals (9th cir.), U.S. Dist. Ct. Law clerk U.S. Dist. Judge William G. East, 1964—65; pvt. practice Stoel Rives LLP, 1965—96; atty. gen. State of Oreg., 1997—. Mem. Oreg Ho. of Reps., 1975—85, spkr. of the ho., 1979—83. Pres. Portland City Planning Commn., 1973—74; chair Oreg. Jail Project, 1984—86, Citizen's Task Force on Mass Transit Policy, 1985—86, Oreg. Criminal Justice Coun., 1987—91, Portland Future Focus, 1990—91, Metro Charter com., 1991—92, task force on state employee benefits, 1994; co-chair gov. task force on state employee compensation, 1995. Democrat. Office: Oreg Atty Gen Justice Dept 1162 Court St NE Salem OR 97310-1320

MYERS, JOHN WILLIAM, lawyer; b. Aug. 8, 1941; s. Fred L. and Dossie (Huddleston) Myers; m. Jane Hill, July 29, 1995; children: John William II, James Bryan. BS, U. Tenn., 1963, JD, 1965. Bar: Tenn. 1965. Ptnr. Myers & Bell, Attys., Newport, Tenn., 1966—. Dir. Newport Fed. Bank, 1975—, chmn., 1981—. Mem.: Tenn. Bar Assn. Republican. Episcopalian. General practice. Home: 404 6th St Newport TN 37821-3712 Office: Myers & Bell Attys PO Box 160 Newport TN 37822-0160

MYERS, LAWRENCE JOSEPH, lawyer; b. East Orange, N.J., Nov. 27, 1957; s. Lawrence Edward and V. Gloria Myers; children: Thomas Cunningham, Laura Elizabeth. BA, U. N.C., 1979, JD, 1983. Bar: Ga. 1983, U.S. Ct. Appeals (11th cir.) Ga. 1989, U.S. Dist. Ct. (no. dist.) Ga. 1983, U.S. Dist. Ct. (mid. dist.) Ga. 1990. Ptnr. Smith Helms Mulliss & Moore, L.L.P., Atlanta, 1998—2002, Hawkins & Parnell, L.L.P (f/k/a Freeman & Hawkins), 1990—98; assoc. Freeman & Hawkins, 1983—90; ptnr. Smith Moore LLP, 2002—. Registered neutral (gen. mediation) Ga. Office of Dispute Resolution, Atlanta, 2001—; cert. mediator 7th Jud. Adminstrv. Dist., Cartersville, 2001—; civil mediator Gwinnett County Dispute Resolution Program, Lawrenceville, 2001—. Vol. and mem., bd. of trustees, fin. and risk mgmt. committees Buckhead Christian Ministry, Inc., Atlanta, 1998. Named to Dean's List, U. N.C., Chapel Hill, 1975—79, Academic Honor Roll, Atlantic Coast Conf. (ACC), 1976—79; scholar, Alpha Tau Omega Frat. Found., 1977—78, Atlantic Coast Conf. (ACC), 1979. Mem.: ABA, Def. Rsch. Inst., Atlanta Bar Assn., State Bar of Ga., Druid Hills Golf Club, Lawyers Club of Atlanta. Roman Catholic. Achievements include Holderness Moot Court Bench (Voluntary Competition Finalist); Staff Member, North Carolina Journal of International Law and Commercial Regulation. Avocations: golf, travel, antiques, reading, walking. Product liability, Alternative dispute resolution, Toxic tort. Home: 767 Moores Mill Road NW Atlanta GA 30327-1525 Office: Smith Moore LLP 1355 Peachtree Street NE Suite 750 Atlanta GA 30309 Office Fax: 404-962-1200. E-mail: larry.myers@smithmoorelaw.com.

MYERS, LONN WILLIAM, lawyer; b. Rockford, Ill., Nov. 14, 1946; s. William H. and Leona V. (Janvrin) M.; m. Janet L. Forbes, May 14, 1968; children: Andrew, Hillary, Corwin. BA, Mich. State U., 1968; MBA, Ind. U., 1973; JD, Harvard U., 1976. Bar: Ill. 1976, U.S. Ct. of Fed. Claims 1977, U.S. Tax Ct. 1977, U.S. Ct. Appeals (7th cir.) 1977. Ptnr. McDermott, Will & Emery, Chgo., 1976—. Served to maj. USAR, 1968-80. Mem. ABA (capital recovery and leasing com. tax sect., tax exempt fin. com. tax sect.). Episcopalian. Municipal (including bonds), Corporate taxation, Personal income taxation. Home: 1711 Highland Ter Glenview IL 60025-2284 Office: McDermott Will & Emery 227 W Monroe St Chicago IL 60606-5096

MYERS, R(ALPH) CHANDLER, lawyer; b. L.A., Jan. 9, 1933; s. Ralph Cather and Winifred (Chandler) M.; m. Rebecca Blythe Borkgren, Jan. 11, 1963. BA, Stanford U., 1954, JD, 1958; LLD (hon.), Whittier Coll., 1988. Bar: Calif. 1959, U.S. Dist. Ct. (cen. dist.) Calif. 1959, U.S. Supreme Ct. 1971. Law clk., then assoc. Parker, Stanbury, Reese & McGee, L.A., 1958-63; assoc. Nicholas, Kolliner & Van Tassel, L.A., 1963-65; ptnr. Myers & D'Angelo and predecessors, L.A. and Pasadena, Calif., 1965—. Nat. panelist Am. Arbitration Assn., L.A., 1964— ; bd. visitors Stanfor d U. Law Sch., Calif., 1970-73; mem. judge pro tem panel L.A. Mcpl. Ct., 1971-81; mem. Los Angeles County Dist. Atty.'s Adv. Coun.., 1976-83 Nat. vice chmn. Keystone Gifts, Stanford Centennial Campaign, 1987—92; trustee Whittier Coll., Calif., 1973—2001, chmn. bd. trustees, 1981—87, trustee emeritus, 2001—; trustee Flintridge Prep. Sch., LaCanada-Flintridge, Calif., 1981—88, chmn. bd. trustees, 1985—88; co-founder Whittier Law Sch., 1975, trustee, 1975—2001, chmn. bd. trustees, 1981—87, trustee emeritus, 2001—; bd. dirs. Opera Guild So. Calif., L.A., 1971—83, pres., 1980—82; bd. dirs. Guild Opera Co. L.A., 1974—83, pres., 1975—77; bd. dirs. Western Justice Ctr. Found., 1993—, treas., 1996—99, 2d v.p., 1999—2001, 1st v.p., 2001—; bd. dirs. L.A. Child Guidance Clinic, 1972—83, pres., 1977—79; bd. dirs. Opera Assocs. of the Music Ctr., L.A., 1976—78. Recipient Stanford Assocs. award, 1984, Centennial Medallion award, 1991, Gold Spike award Stanford U., 1989, Disting. Svc. award Whittier Law Sch., 1993, Outstanding Achievement award Stanford Assocs., 1998. Mem. Wilshire Bar Assn. (bd. govs. 1972-81, pres. 1979-80), L.A. County Bar Assn. (trustee 1979-81), Stanford Law Soc. So. Calif. (bd. dirs. 1967-72, pres. 1970-71), Stanford Assocs. (bd. govs. 1992-97, treas. 1995-97), Jonathan Club, University Club (Pasadena), Stanford Club of L.A. (bd. dirs. 1963-70, pres. 1968-69). State civil litigation, Corporate, general, Probate (including wills, trusts). Home: La Canada 5623 Burning Tree Dr La Canada Flintridge CA 91011-2861 Office: Myers & D'Angelo 301 N Lake Ave Ste 800 Pasadena CA 91101-4108

MYERS, RODMAN NATHANIEL, lawyer; b. Detroit, Oct. 27, 1920; s. Isaac Rodman and Fredericka (Hirschman) Myers; m. Jeanette Polisei, Mar. 19, 1957 (dec. 1996); children: Jennifer Myers Grabenstein, Rodman Jay. BA, Wayne State U., 1941; LLB, U. Mich., 1943. Bar: Mich. 1943, U.S. Supreme Ct. 1962. Agt. IRS, Detroit, 1943; from assoc. to ptnr. Butzel, Keidan, Simon, Myers & Graham, Detroit, 1943-90; of counsel Honigman Miller Schwartz and Cohn, Detroit, 1991—. Mem. blue ribbon task force Mich. Dept. Edn., 1988—90; founding mem., trustee Mich. chpt. Leukemia and Lymphoma Soc., founding pres., 1984—86, nat. trustee, 1984—; founding mem., trustee Detroit Sci. Ctr.; commr. Detroit Mcpl. Parking Authority, 1963—71; pres., trustee Bloomfield Twp. Pub. Libr.; trustee Temple Beth El, Bloomfield Hills, Mich.; bd. dirs. United Cmty. Svcs. of Met. Detroit, 1978—85, v.p., 1981—85, chmn. social svcs. divsn., 1982—85; bd. dirs. Children's Ctr. of Wayne County, Mich., 1963—88, pres., 1969—72. Mem. ABA, State Bar Mich. (chmn. atty. discipline panel, past vice chmn. unauthorized practice of law com., past mem. character and fitness com.). Corporate, general. Home: 3833 Lakeland Ln Bloomfield Hills MI 48302-1328 Office: 2290 1st National Bldg Detroit MI 48226

MYERS, RONALD LYNN, lawyer; b. Houston, Jan. 18, 1949; s. E. Carlton and Elizabeth Anne (Boyette) M.; m. Nancy G. Finney, May 20, 1972. BS in History, Kans. State U., 1971; JD, U. Kans., 1974. Bar: Mo. 1974, U.S. Dist. Ct. (we. dist.) Mo. 1974, U.S. Ct. Appeals (8th cir.) 1977, U.S. Supreme Ct. 1978. Assoc. Strop, Watkins et al, St. Joseph, Mo., 1974-76; ptnr. Daniel, Clampett et al, Springfield, Mo., 1976-84; pvt. practice Springfield, 1984—. Author: Exemplifying Punitive Damages, 1976. Mem. com. counsel Springfest '84, Springfield, 1984; dir., counsel Agape House Springfield, 1984; bd. dirs. Coun. of Chs. of the Ozarks, 1990-96. Mem. Mo. Bar Assn., Springfield Met. Bar Assn. Republican. Methodist. Federal civil litigation, Insurance, Personal injury (including property damage). Home: 920 E Northfield Rd Springfield MO 65803-9229 Office: 2045 S Glenstone Ave Ste 201 Springfield MO 65804

MYERS, STEPHEN HAWLEY, lawyer; b. Washington, Mar. 28, 1953; s. Robert Holt and Antoinette (Hawley) M.; children: Stephen, Hampton, Brielle; m. Laura Lee Fuller, Dec. 1, 1989. BA in Polit. Sci. with honors, Union Coll., 1976; JD, Loyola U., 1979. Bar: D.C. 1979, La. 1979, U.S. Dist. Ct. D.C. 1980, U.S. Tax Ct. 1980, U.S. Ct. Claims 1980, U.S. Ct. Appeals (fed. and D.C. cirs.) 1980, U.S. Ct. Appeals (5th cir.) 1985, U.S. Dist. Ct. (we., mid. and ea. dists.) La. 1985, U.S. Supreme Ct. 1989. Atty. advisor to hon. judge Edward S. Smith U.S. Ct. Appeals (Fed. cir.), Washington, 1979-80; assoc. Duncan Allen & Mitchell, Washington, 1980-82; atty. advisor to Judge Jules G. Körner U.S. Tax Ct., Washington, 1982-84; assoc. Davidson Meaux Sonnier & McElligott, Lafayette, La., 1984-85; ptnr. Roy Forrest, Lopresto, DeCourt & Myers and predecessor firms, Lafayette, 1985-97; pvt. practice Stephen Hawley Myers, LLC, Lafayette, La., 1997—. Lectr. for continuing legal edn. seminars on corp., bus. and sales tax litigation; chmn. Nat. Bus. Adv. Coun., Washington, 2002—; mem. La. State Police Commn., 2002—. Vice chmn., bd. dirs. La. Coun. for Fiscal Reform, New Orleans, 1986-96; bd. dirs., treas. Acadiana Youth, Inc., Lafayette, 1986-94; mem. La. State Police Commn., 2002--. Mem. ABA, Am. Platform Assn., Lafayette Bar Assn., La. Counsel Def. Attys., La. Trial Lawyer's Assn., Phi Delta Phi. Avocations: writing, photography, skeet shooting, sports clay shooting, hunting. Private international, Corporate, general, State and local taxation. Office: 600 Jefferson St Ste 401 Lafayette LA 70501-8919 Home: 105 Mill Valley Run Lafayette LA 70508-7027

MYERS, THOMAS EVERETT, lawyer; b. Lubbock, Tex., Aug. 26, 1954; s. Edward Nelson and Mary Elizabeth (Worrell) M.; m. Cynthia Kay Ridlehoover, Aug. 4, 1979; children: Holly Elizabeth, Paige Michelle. BS, Baylor U., 1976, JD, 1979. Bar: Tex. 1979, U.S. Dist. Ct. (no. dist.) Tex. 1979, U.S. Dist. Ct. (we. dist.) Tex. 1988, U.S. Ct. Appeals (5th cir.) 1980, U.S. Supreme Ct. 1983; cert. in consumer law and criminal law, Tex. Bd. Legal Specialization. Asst. dist. atty. Tarrant County, Ft. Worth, 1979—84; shareholder Rohne Hoodenpyle Lobert Myers P.C., Arlington, Tex., 1984—98, Brackett & Ellis, P.C., Arlington, Tex., 1998—. Deacon 1st Bapt. Ch. Arlington, 1985—. Mem. ABA, Tex. Bar Assn., Tarrant County Bar Assn., Tex. Criminal Def. Lawyers Assn., Baylor U. Alumni Assn. (pres. Arlington chpt. 1983-84), Kiwanis (pres. Arlington chpt. 1989-90). Baptist. Avocations: music, movies, golf, reading. State civil litigation, Criminal, Education and schools. Office: 100 Main St Fort Worth TX 76102-3009

MYLONAKIS, STAMATIOS GREGORY, patent agent, polymer science consultant; b. Athens, Aug. 18, 1937; s. Gregory S. and Vassiliki (Charalambopoulos) Mylonakis; m. Pamela H. Morton, May 5, 1965 (dec. Mar. 1978); 1 child, Gregory (dec.). BS, Nat. U. of Athens, 1961; MS, Ill. Inst. of Tech., 1964; PhD, Mich. State U., 1970. Rsch. assoc. Ill. Inst. of Tech., Chgo., 1964-65; rsch. scientist Brookhaven Nat. Lab., Upton, N.Y., 1965-68; instr. U. Calif., Berkeley, 1971-73; group leader Rohm and Haas Co., Springhouse, Pa., 1973-76; supr. DeSoto, Inc., Des Plaines, Ill., 1976-79; staff scientist Borg-Warner Corp., Des Plaines, 1979-82, mgr., 1982-87; dept. head Enichem Am., Monmouth Junction, N.J., 1988-94; tech. advisor, registered patent agt. law firm Oblon, Spivak, Arlington, Va., 1994-2000; cons., patent law practitioner, 2000—; sci. fellow Nuc. Rsch. Ctr. Democritos, Athens, 1960—62. Tech. adv. bd. Ctr. Applied Polymer Rsch. Case Western Res. U., Cleve.; adv. bd. NSF Ctr. Polymer Interfaces Lehigh U. Assoc. editor: Jour. Applied Polymer Sci.; contbr. articles to profl. jours. Lt. Greek Army. Fellow Sci., Nuc. Rsch. Ctr. Democritos, Athens, Greece, 1960—62, NSF, Mich. State U., 1968—70, U. Calif., 1971—73. Mem.: AAAS, Am. Chem. Soc., N.Y. Acad. Scis., Sigma Xi. Greek Orthodox. Achievements include patents in field of polymer sci. tech. Avocations: photography, painting, travel. Home and Office: 7009 Cashell Manor Ct Derwood MD 20855-1201 E-mail: mylonakis@msn.com.

MYTELKA, ARNOLD KRIEGER, lawyer; b. Jersey City, July 24, 1937; s. Herman Donald and Jeannette (Krieger) M.; m. Rosalind Marcia Kaplan, Dec. 17, 1961; children: Andrew Charles, Daniel Sommer. AB, Princeton U., 1958; LLB cum laude, Harvard U., 1961; postgrad., London Sch. Econs., 1961-62. Bar: N.J. 1961, U.S. Dist. Ct. N.J. 1963, U.S. Supreme Ct. 1970, U.S. Ct. Appeals (3d cir.) 1978, U.S. Dist. Ct. (so. and ea. dist.) N.Y. 1983. Law sec. Chief Justice N.J. Supreme Ct., Newark, 1962-63; assoc. Clapp & Eisenberg, Newark, 1963-68, ptnr., 1968-94; prin. Kraemer, Burns, Mytelka, Lovell & Kulka, Springfield, N.J., 1994—. Lectr. Rutgers Law Sch., Newark, 1973; mem. Am. Law Inst., Phila., 1989—; mem. cons. group The Law Governing Lawyers, 1990-99; founding trustee Newark Legal Svcs. Project, 1965-68; trustee Edn. Law Ctr., 1974-75; chmn. dist. V ethics com. Supreme Ct. N.J., 1983-84, mem. 1981-84; trustee Legal Svcs. Found. Essex County, 1982—, pres., 1990-92; lectr. in land use law. Mem. editorial bd. N.J. Law Jour., 1991—; contbr. legal articles to profl. jours. Chmn. bd. trustees Ramapo Coll. N.J., 1979-80, mem. 1975-80; mediator chancery divsn. N.J. Superior Ct., 1990—, trustee, 1998-2000, spl. fiscal agt., 1997, 2003, spl. master, 1999, 2000. Frank Knox Meml. fellow Harvard U., London Sch. Econs. and Polit. Sci., 1961-62. Mem. ABA (mem. litigation sect.), N.J. State Bar Assn. (chmn. appellate practices study com. 1977-79, chmn. land use sect. 1984-85). Appellate, General civil litigation, Land use and zoning (including planning). Home: 56 Hall Rd Chatham NJ 07928-1723 Office: Kraemer Burns Mytelka Lovell & Kulka 675 Morris Ave Springfield NJ 07081-1523 E-mail: amytelka@kraemerburns.com.

NACE, BARRY JOHN, lawyer; b. York, Pa., Nov. 28, 1944; s. John Harrison and Mildred Louise (Orwig) N.; m. Andrea Marcia Giardini. Apr. 28, 1973; children: Christopher Thomas, Jonathan Barry, Matthew Andrew. BS, Dickinson Coll., 1965, JD, 1969, LLD (hon.) , 1994. Bar: Md. 1970, D.C. 1971, Pa. 1972, W.Va. 1997, U.S. Ct. Appeals (3d, 4th and D.C. cirs.), U.S. Supreme Ct. Ptnr. Davis & Nace, Washington, 1972-78, Paulson & Nace, Bethesda, Md., 1978-85, 98—; sr. ptnr. Paulson, Nace & Norwind, Washington, 1986-97. Fellow Roscoe Pound Found. (trustee); mem. Nat. Bd. Trial Advocacy in Civil Litigation (bd. govs. 2001—), D.C. Bar Assn., Montgomery County Bar Assn., Assn. Trial Lawyers Am. (gov. 1976-87, pres. 1993-94), Met. D.C. Trial Attys. (pres. 1977-78, 87-88, Atty. of Yr. 1976), Trial Lawyers for Pub. Justice, Internat. Acad. Trial Lawyers, Lambert Soc., Am. Inns of Ct., Am. Law Inst. Am. Bd. of Profl. Liability Attorneys. Avocations: golf, tennis, reading, racquetball. Federal civil litigation, State civil litigation, Personal injury (including property damage). Home: 6208 Garnett Dr Bethesda MD 20815-6618 Office: Paulson & Nace 1814 N St NW Washington DC 20036-2404 E-mail: BJN@Lawtort.com.

NACHMAN, ERWIN B(EHR), lawyer; b. Newport News, Va., Nov. 22, 1934; s. Max E. and Sadye (Bodner) N.; 1 child, Elizabeth S. BS in Commerce, U. Va., 1956, LLB, 1960. Bar: Va. 1960, U.S. Dist. Ct. (ea. dist.) Va. 1961, U.S. Ct. Appeals (4th cir.) 1966, U.S. Supreme Ct. 1966, U.S. Claims Ct. 1966, U.S. Ct. Mil. Appeals 1966. Assoc. Fine, Fine, Legum & Fine, Norfolk, Va., 1961-67; atty. sole practice Erwin B. Nachman, Newport News, 1967-75, 88—; ptnr. Frank, Nachman & Frank, Newport News, 1975-79, Frank, Poinsett, Nachman & Frank, Newport News, 1979-88. Trustee in bankruptcy U.S. Bankruptcy Ct., Newport News, 1974-99; commr. in chancery Newport News Cir. Ct., 1989-98, asst. commr. accounts, 1993-98, chief commr. accounts, 1998—. Chmn. Newport News Cable TV Adv. Com., 1990-92. 1st lt. U.S. Army Res., 1964-67. Mem. Va. Bar Assn., Newport News Bar Assn., Tidewater Bankruptcy Bar Assn. (treas. 1998-99, sec. 1999-2000), Phi Delta Phi (treas. 1959-60). Bankruptcy, Family and matrimonial, Probate (including wills, trusts). Office: Erwin B Nachman Atty 708 Thimble Shoals Blvd Newport News VA 23606-4547 Fax: 757-873-3028. E-mail: erwincoa@visi.net.

NACHTIGAL, PATRICIA, lawyer; b. 1946; BA, Montclair State U.; JD, Rutgers U.; LLM, NYU. Tax atty. Ingersoll-Rand Co., Ltd., Hamilton, Bermuda , 1979—83, dir. taxes and legal, 1983—88, sec., mng. atty., 1988—91, v.p., gen. counsel, 1991—2000, sr. v.p., gen. counsel, 2000—, bd. dirs., 2002—. Corporate, general. Office: Ingersoll-Rand Co Ltd 200 Chestnut Ridge Rd Woodcliff Lake NJ 07677

NACHWALTER, MICHAEL, lawyer; b. N.Y.C., Aug. 31, 1940; s. Samuel J. Nachwalter; m. Irene, Aug. 15, 1965; children: Helynn, Robert. BS, Bucknell U., 1962; MS, L.I. U., 1967; JD cum laude, U. Miami, 1967; LLM, Yale U., 1968. Bar: Fla. 1967, D.C. 1979, U.S. Dist. Ct. (so. dist.) Fla. 1967, U.S. Dist. Ct. (mid. dist.) Fla. 1982, U.S. Ct. Appeals (5th and 11th cirs.) 1967, U.S. Supreme Ct. 1975. Law clk. to judge U.S. Dist. Ct. (so. dist.) Fla.; shareholder Kelly, Black, Black & Kenny; now shareholder Kenny Nachwalter Seymour Critchlow & Spector, P.A., Miami. Lectr. Law Sch. U. Miami. Editor-in-chief U. Miami Law Rev., 1966-67. Fellow Am. Coll. Trial Lawyers; mem. ABA, FBA, Am. Bd. Trial Advs., Fla. Bar Assn. (bd. govs. 1982-90), Internat. Soc. Barristers (dir.), Dade County Bar Assn., Jud. Qualifications Commn. (vice chmn. 1995-2000), Iron Arrow, Soc. Wig and Robe, Omicron Delta Kappa, Phi Kappa Phi, Phi Delta Phi. Antitrust, Federal civil litigation, State civil litigation. Office: Kenny Nachwalter Seymour Arnold Critchlow & Spector PA 201 S Biscayne Blvd Ste 1100 Miami FL 33131-4327

NACOL, MAE, lawyer; b. Beaumont, Tex., June 15, 1944; d. William Samuel and Ethel (Bowman) N.; children: Shawn Alexander Nacol, Catherine Regina Nacol. BA, Rice U., 1965; postgrad., South Tex. Coll. Law, 1966. Bar: Tex. 1969, U.S. Dist. Ct. (so. dist.) Tex. 1969. Pvt. practice law, Houston, 1969—; escrow officer Commonwealth Land Title Co., Houston; mem. bd. devel. Prosperity Bank, Houston. Author, editor ednl. materials on multiple sclerosis, 1981-85. Nat. dir. A.R.M.S. of Am. Ltd., Houston, 1984-85. Recipient Mayor's Recognition award City of Houston, 1972. Mem. Houston Bar Assn. (chmn. candidate com. 1970, membership com. 1971, chmn. lawyers referral com. 1972), Assn. Trial Lawyers Am., Tex. Trial Lawyers Assn., Am. Judicature Soc. (sustaining), Houston Fin. Coun. Women, Houston Trial Lawyers Assn. Presbyterian. Admiralty, Corporate, general, Personal injury (including property damage). Office: 600 Jefferson St Ste 750 Houston TX 77002 also: 8401 Westheimer Ste 104 Houston TX 77063

NADEAU, JOSEPH P. state supreme court justice; AB, Dartmouth Coll.; LLB, Boston U., 1962. Pvt. practice trial atty., 1962—81; justice Durham Dist. Ct., 1968-81; judge N.H. Superior Ct., 1981-92, chief justice, 1992; assoc. justice N.H. Supreme Ct., 2000—. Mem. Jud. Br. Adminstrv. Coun., Supreme Ct. Jud.Edl. Svcs. Com., Supreme Ct. Accreditation Commn.; pres. Am. Acad. Jud. Edn., 1990-92; participant ct. study program former Soviet Union, facutly jud. edn. program, Latvia, study programs in Russia, Georgia, Armenia; involved in jud. edn. seminars and legis. activities in Albania, Bulgaria, Kazakhstan, Poland. Mem. Gov.'s Commn. on Domestic Violence. Office: Supreme Ct Bldg One Noble Dr Concord NH 03301-6160

NADEAU, ROBERT BERTRAND, JR., lawyer; b. Miami Beach, Fla., July 15, 1950; s. Robert B. and Ernestine Inez (Nicholson) N. BBA magna cum laude, U. Notre Dame, 1972; JD with honors, U. Fla., 1975. Bar: Fla. 1975, U.S. Dist. Ct. (mid. dist.) Fla. 1976, U.S. Dist. Ct. (so. dist.) Fla. 1982, U.S. Ct. Appeals (11th cir.) 1982. Asst. to pres. The Fla. Bar, Tampa,

Fla., 1975-76; ptnr. Akerman, Senterfitt & Eidson, P.A., Orlando, Fla., 1976—. Arbitrator Am. Arbitration Assn., Orlando, 1987—. Mem. ABA, The Fla. Bar (chmn. student edn. and admission to bar com., vice chmn. 9th cir. grievance com.), Notre Dame Club Greater Orlando (pres. 1979-80). Avocations: golf, running. Alternative dispute resolution, General civil litigation, Construction. Office: Akerman Senterfitt & Eidson PA 255 S Orange Ave Orlando FL 32801-3445

NADELMAN, CARY, lawyer; b. N.Y.C., Nov. 30, 1970; s. Sheldon and Rita Nadelman; m. Tisha Garrett, Dec. 5, 1998. BS, Am. U., 1992; JD, Yeshiva U., 1998. Bar: NY 1999, NC 2001. Acct. Anchin, Block & Anchin, N.Y.C., 1992—95; assoc. Olshan Grundman Frome Rosenzweig & Wolosky, N.Y.C., 1998—2000, Moore & Van Allen, Charlotte, NC, 2000—. Securities. Office: Moore & Van Allen 100 N Tryon St Fl 47 Charlotte NC 28202 E-mail: carynadelman@mvlaw.com.

NADLER, MYRON JAY, lawyer, director; b. Youngstown, Ohio, July 22, 1923; s. Murray A. and Jean (Davis) N.; m. Alice Blue, Nov. 4, 1951; children: Jed M., Wendy D., John M.S. Student, N.Mex. State Coll., 1943-44; BS in Econs. Wharton Sch., U. Pa., 1947; JD with distinction, U. Mich., 1949. Bar: Ohio 1950. Pres., shareholder Nadler, Nadler & Burdman Co., L.P.A., Youngstown, 1950-95, pres., 1950-95; ret., 1996. Asst. editor Mich. Law Rev., 1949; instr. Youngstown U. Law Sch., 1952-59. Author: (with Saul Nadler) Nadler on Bankruptcy, 1965, April's Bankruptcy Forms and Practice, 1964; contbr. articles to profl. jours. Chmn. exec. budget com. United Appeal, Youngstown, 1964-66, v.p., 1967-70; co-chmn. Mayor's Commn. Human Rights, 1957; mem. Mahoning County Planning Commn., 1965-71, Nat. Budget and Consultation Com., 1967-70; trustee Cmty. Corp., Youngstown, v.p., 1977-82, chmn. pers. com., 1974-92; bd. dirs. Ctr. for Learning, Villa Maria, Pa., 1969-95, pres., 1981-89, chmn. bd., 1989-94. With AUS, 1943-45. Decorated Purple Heart with oak leaf cluster. Mem. Fellows of Ohio Bar Assn. Found., ABA, Ohio Bar Assn., Mahoning County Bar Assn., Scribes Assn. Legal Writers, Comml. Law League Am., Squaw Creek Country Club (pres. 1966-68), Hamlet Country Club. Home: 601 Pine Lake Dr Delray Beach FL 33445-9042 Office: 20 Federal Plz W Ste 600 Youngstown OH 44503-1423

NAFTALIS, GARY PHILIP, lawyer, educator; b. Newark, Nov. 23, 1941; s. Gilbert and Bertha Beatrice Naftalis; m. Donna Arditi, June 30, 1974; children: Benjamin, Joshua, Daniel, Sarah. AB, Rutgers U., 1963; AM, Brown U., 1965; LLB, Columbia U., 1967. Bar: N.Y. 1967, U.S. Dist. Ct. (so. dist.) N.Y. 1969, U.S. Ct. Appeals (2d cir.) 1968, U.S. Ct. Appeals (3d cir.) 1973, U.S. Ct. Appeals (D.C. cir.) 1993, U.S. Supreme Ct. 1974. Law clk. to judge U.S. Dist. Ct. So. Dist. N.Y., 1967-68; asst. U.S. atty. So. Dist. N.Y., 1968-74, asst. chief criminal divsn., 1972-74; spl. asst. U.S. atty. for V.I., 1972-73; spl. counsel U.S. Senate Subcom. on Long Term Care, 1975, N.Y. State Temp. Commn. on Living Costs and the Economy, 1975; ptnr. Orans, Elsen, Polstein & Naftalis, N.Y.C., 1974-81, Kramer, Levin, Naftalis & Frankel, N.Y.C., 1981—. Lectr. Law Sch. Columbia U., 1976-88; vis. lectr. Law Sch. Harvard U., 1979; mem. deptl. disciplinary com. Appellate div. 1st Dept., 1980-86. Author: (with Marvin E. Frankel) The Grand Jury: An Institution on Trial, 1977, Considerations in Representing Attorneys in Civil and Criminal Enforcement Proceedings, 1981, Sentencing: Helping Judges Do Their Jobs, 1986, SEC Actions Seeking to Bar Securities Professionals, 1995, SEC Cease and Desist Powers Limited, 1997, The Foreign Corrupt Practices Act, 1997, Prosecuting Lawyers Who Defend Clients in SEC Actions, 1998, Obtaining Reports from a Credit Bureau for Litigation May be a Crime, 1999, Encouraging Cooperation by Individual Respondents in SEC Enforcement Investigations, 2002, Navigating the Foreign Corrupt Practices Act, 2002, Fugitive Disentitlement in Civil Forfeiture Proceedings, 2002; editor: White Collar Crimes, 1980. Trustee Boys Brotherhood Rep., 1978—, Blueberry Treatment Ctr., 1981-91, Joseph Haggerty Children's Fund, 1991—; bd. dirs. The Legal Aid Soc., 2000—. Fellow: Am. Coll. Trial Lawyers; mem.: ABA (white collar crime com. criminal justice sect. 1985—, coun. criminal justice sect. 2002—), N.Y. Coun. Def. Lawyers (bd. dirs. 2000—01), Internat. Bar Assn. (bus. crimes com. 1988—), N.Y. Bar Assn. (com. state legis. 1974—76, exec. com. comml. and fed. litigation sect.), Fed. Bar. Coun. (com. cts. 2d cir. 1974—77), Assn. of Bar of City of N.Y. (com. criminal cts. 1980—83, com. judiciary 1984—87, coun. criminal justice 1985—88, com. on criminal law 1987—90, 1997—2001). General civil litigation, Health. Home: 1125 Park Ave Apt 7B New York NY 10128-1243 Office: Kramer Levin Naftalis & Frankel 919 3rd Ave New York NY 10022-3902

NAFZIGER, JAMES ALBERT RICHMOND, lawyer, educator; b. Mpls., Sept. 24, 1940; s. Ralph Otto and Charlotte Monona (Hamilton) N. BA, U. Wis., 1962, MA, 1969; JD, Harvard U., 1967. Bar: Wis. 1967. Law clk. to chief judge U.S. Dist. Ct. (ea. dist.) Wis., 1967-69; fellow Am. Soc. Internat. Law, Washington, 1969-70, adminstrv. dir., 1970-74; exec. sec. Assn. Student Internat. Law Socs., 1969-70; lectr. Sch. Law Cath. U. Am., Washington, 1970-74; assoc. prof. law Coll. Law Willamette U., Salem, Oreg., 1977-80, prof., 1980-95, Thomas B. Stoel prof., 1995—, assoc. dean, 1985-86, dir. internat. programs, 1984—. Scholar-in-residence Rockefeller Found. Ctr., Bellagio, Italy, 1985; vis. assoc. prof. Sch. Law, U. Oreg. 1974-77; vis. prof. Nat. Autonomous U. Mex., 1978; hon. prof. East China U. of Politics and Law, 1999—; lectr. tutor Inst. Pub. Internat. Law and Internat. Rels., Thessaloniki, Greece, 1982; cons. Adminstrv. Conf. U.S., 1988-90, Internat. Com. Migration, 1997—; mem. bd. advisors Denver Jour. Internat. Law and Policy, Am. Jour. Comparative Law (bd. dirs. 1985—). Editor Procs. of Am. Soc. Internat. Law 1977; Am. author: Conflict of Laws: A Northwest Perspective, 1985, International Sports Law, 1988; co-editor: Law and Justice in a Multistate World, 2002; contbr. articles to profl. jours. Bd. dirs. N.W. Regional China Coun., 1987—89. 1st lt. U.S. Army, 1962—64. Recipient Burlington No. Faculty Achievement award, 1988, Willamette U. Pres.'s award for excellence in scholarship, 2000. Mem.: ACLU (pres. chpt. 1980—81, mem. state bd. 1982—88, sec. 1983—87), UNA-USA (pres. Oreg. divsn. 1987—90, v.p. 1990—94, bd. dirs. 1990—, exec. com. coun. chpt. and divsn. prof.), ABA (legal specialist ctrl. and east European law initiative 1992—), Am. Coun. Learned Socs. (exec. com. conf. adminstrv. officers 2002—), Nat. Sports Law Inst. (bd. advisors 2002—), Internat. Sports Law Assn. (v.p. 1992—), Oreg. Internat. Coun., Am. Law Inst., Assn. Am. Law Schs. (chmn. law and arts sect. 1981—83, chmn. internat. law sect. 1984—85, chmn. law and arts sect. 1989—91, chmn. immigration law sect. 1990—91, chmn. internat. law workshop 1995, com. on sects. and ann. meeting 1995—98), Internat. Studies Assn. (exec. bd. 1974—77, internat. law sect.), Washington Fgn. Law Soc. (v.p. 1973—74), Internat. Law Assn. (chmn. human reighs com. 1983—88, Am. br. exec. com. 1986—, rapporteur cultural heritage law com. 1990—, co-dir. studies 1991—95, v.p. 1994—2000, pres. 2000—), Internat. Acad. Comparative Law, Am. Soc. Comparative Law (bd. dirs. 1985—, treas. 1997—), Am. Soc. Internat. Law (exec. coun. 1983—86, chmn. ann. meeting 1988, chmn. nominating com. 1989, exec. coun. 1992—95). Home: 3775 Saxon Dr S Salem OR 97302-6041 Office: Willamette U Coll Law Salem OR 97301

NAGEL, BRUCE H. lawyer; b. Paterson, N.J., Aug. 28, 1952; s. David A. and Norma N.; m. Marla Nagel, July 15, 1978; children: Arielle, Emma, Molly. BS in Indsl. and Labor Rels., Cornell U., 1974; JD, NYU, 1977. Bar: N.J. 1977, U.S. Dist. Ct. N.J. 1977, U.S. Ct. Appeals (3rd cir.) 1977, U.S. Ct. Appeals (3d, 1st and 4th cir.) 1995; cert. civil trial atty. Sr. ptnr. Nagel, Rice & Mazie, Livingston, NJ, 1983—. Adj. prof. Seton Hall Law Sch.; lectr. Inst. Continuing Legal Edn.; chmn. bd. trustees Kairos Inst., Madison, N.J., 1998—; bd. dirs. Teardrop Golf Co., Morton Grove, Ill.; moderator and lectr. in field. Contbr. articles to profl. jours. Mem. ATLA, N.J. Bar Assn., Essex County Bar Assn., Million Dollar Advocate Forum. General civil litigation, Personal injury (including property damage), Product liability. Office: Nagel Rice & Mazie 301 S Livingston Ave Ste 201 Livingston NJ 07039-3991

NAGIN, STEPHEN ELIAS, lawyer, educator; b. Phila., Nov. 7, 1946; s. Harry S. and Dorothy R. (Pearlman) N.; m. Marjorie Riley, Sept. 4, 1983. BBA, U. Miami, 1969; JD, 1974. Bar: Fla. 1974, D.C. 1976, U.S. Supreme Ct. 1978. Asst. atty. gen. State of Fla., Miami, 1974-75; atty. FTC, 1975-80; spl. asst. U.S. Atty., Washington, 1980-81; ptnr. Nagin, Gallop & Figueredo, P.A., 1987—. Adj. prof. St. Thomas U. Sch. Law, 1984-94; instr. Nat. Inst. Trial Advocacy, 1992—. Mem. ABA (editor, trial lawyers sect. 1983-84, mem. spl. antitrust task force 1983—, chmn. editl. bd., Florida Bar Jour. 1982-83, chmn. antitrust com. 1996-98, chmn. intellectual property com. 2001—, chmn. antitrust and trade regulation cert. com. 2000—), Patent Lawyers Assn. South Fla. (sec., 2000), Coral Gables Bar Assn. (bd. dirs. 1983-87), Assn. Trial Lawyers Am., Am. Arbitration Assn., Nat. Health Lawyers Assn. Antitrust, Federal civil litigation, Intellectual property. Office: Nagin Gallop & Figueredo PA 3225 Aviation Ave Fl 3D Miami FL 33133-4741

NAGLE, DAVID EDWARD, lawyer, columnist; b. Natick, Mass., May 31, 1954; s. Edward G. and Eleanor (Fitz) N.; m. Sue Ellen Southard, Oct. 1, 1988. BS in Govt. and Philosophy, Coll. William and Mary, 1976; JD, U. Richmond, 1981; LLM in Labor Law, Georgetown U., 1983. Bar: Va. 1981. Police officer City of Richmond (Va.), 1976-79; atty. Williams, Mullen & Christian, Richmond, Va., 1981-86; sole practice Richmond, Va., 1986-89; ptnr. Hazel & Thomas, Richmond, Va., 1989-93, LeClair Ryan, Richmond, Va., 1993—; columnist Richmond News-Leader, Va., 1986-90; editor Va. Employment Law Letter, 2003—. Lectr. U. Richmond Sch. Law and Sch. Bus., Med. Coll. Va. Sch. Hosp. Adminstrn.; appellate practice before U.S. Supreme Ct. and U.S. Cts. of Appeals. Contbr. articles to law revs. Mem. Va. Polygraph Bd., 1985-89, Richmond Corrections Bd., 1988-92; dir. Fan Dist. Assn., 1995-97, Monument Ave. Preservation Soc., 1994-97, Richmond Area Assn. Retarded Citizens, 1993-99. Mem. ABA, Va. Bar Assn., Bar Assn. City of Richmond, Am. Arbitration Assn. (arbitrator 1982-94). Appellate, Labor (including EEOC, Fair Labor Standards Act, labor-management relations, NLRB, OSHA). Office: LeClair Ryan 707 E Main St Richmond VA 23219-2814

NAGLE, ROBERT OWEN, lawyer; b. Watertown, S.D., Feb. 10, 1929; s. John Raymond and Kathleen Margaret (McQuillen) N.; m. Louise Emerson H'Doubler, Mar. 14, 1954; children— Robert Owen Jr., Charles Francis, Margaret Louise. BS in Econs., U. Wis., 1951; LLB, U. Calif., 1957. Bar: Calif. 1957. Asso. firm Morrison, Foerster, Holloway, Clinton and Clark, San Francisco, 1957-62, ptnr., 1962-64; gen. atty. Spreckels Sugar div. Amstar Corp., San Francisco, 1964-66, v.p., 1966-68, exec. v.p., 1968-71, v.p. parent co., 1971-76; exec. v.p. Am. Sugar div. Amstar Corp., N.Y.C., 1975-76; pres., chief exec. officer Calif. and Hawaiian Sugar Co., San Francisco, 1976-82, also dir.; ptnr. Brobeck, Phleger & Harrison, 1982-86; pvt. investor Piedmont, Calif., 1986—. Bd. dirs. Providence Hosp., Oakland, Calif. Mem. Law Rev. Bd. dirs. San Francisco Bay Area coun. Boy Scouts Am.; trustee U. Calif. Berkeley Found., Wis. Alumni Rsch. Found., Pacific Vascular Rsch. Found., San Francisco. Served to lt. j.g. USN, 1951-54, Korea. Decorated Bronze Star with V, Air medal. Mem. ABA, State Bar Calif., Bar Assn. San Francisco, Order of Coif. Clubs: Claremont Country, Pacific Union.

NAHITCHEVANSKY, GEORGES, lawyer, educator; b. N.Y.C., Dec. 7, 1958; BS in Fgn. Svc., Georgetown U., 1979; MA, Northwestern U., 1981; JD magna cum laude, Bklyn. Law Sch., 1991. Bar: N.Y. 1992, U.S. Dist. Ct. (so. dist.) N.Y. 1993, U.S. Dist. Ct. (ea. dist.) N.Y. 1997, U.S. Ct. Appeals (2d cir.) 1998. Atty. Kramer Levin Naftalis Kamin & Frankel, N.Y.C., 1991-94; mem. firm Fross Zelnick Lehrman & Zissu, PC, N.Y.C., 1994. Adj. prof. Bklyn. Law Sch., 1992-2001. Prodr., dir.: (film) Refugees in Our Backyard, 1991. Bd. dirs. Russian Children's Welfare Soc., Inc., N.Y.C., 1995—. Mem. ABA, Assn. of Bar of City of N.Y. Intellectual property. Office: Fross Zelnick Lehrman & Zissu PC 866 United Nations Plz New York NY 10017-1822

NAKAMURA, HIDEO, law educator; b. Tokyo, Mar. 2, 1926; s. Muneo and Fumiko (Mitani) N.; m. Mitsuko Terai, Feb. 25, 1958; children: Eri, Akiyoshi. LLB, Waseda U., Tokyo, 1947, LLD, 1980; Dr. honoris causa, Athens U., 1995. Assoc. prof. Faculty of Law Waseda U., tokyo, 1955-60, prof., 1960, dean Grad. Sch. Law, 1980-82, dir. Inst. Comparative Law, 1984-88, pres. Law Assn., 1990-94; dir. Inst. Comparative Civil Law, tokyo, 1975—; ret. hon prof. Waseda U., 1996. Author: (in German) The Japanese Criminal Procedure Code, 1970, Japan and German Civil Procedure, 1995, (in Japanese) Collected Works on Civil Procedure, Vols., 1-5, 1975-86; Civil Procedure, 1987; co-author: (in German) The Japanese Civil Procedure Code, 1978; editor: Family Law Litigation, 1984. Recipient Honor of Freedom award City of Athens, 1998. Mem. Japanese Assn. of Law of Civil Procedure (exec. com. 1960-80, hon.), Japanese Assn. of Law of Pub. Notary (coun. 1978—), Japan Fedn. of Bar Assn. (commr. disciplinary com. 1984-87), Acad. Assn. of Law of Internat. Procedure. Avocation: photography. Home: 2-6-6 Kamitakata Nakano-ku Tokyo 164-0002 Japan Office: Inst Comparative Civil Law 43 Waseda-Minamicho Shinjuku-ku Tokyo 162-0043 Japan

NAKATA, GARY KENJI, lawyer; b. Okinawa, Japan, Nov. 13, 1964; came to the U.S., 1971; s. Hiroshi Nakata and Miwako Kin; m. Jo Ann Akiko Tengan, Aug. 22, 1998. BBA in Fin., U. Hawaii, 1988; JD with distinction, U. of the Pacific, 1995. Bar: Hawaii 1996, Calif. 1996, U.S. Dist. Ct. Hawaii, 1996; cert. mgmt. acct.; cert. fin. mgr.; cert. grad. Am. Banker's Assn. Nat. Sch. Regulatory Compliance. Credit analyst Bank of Hawaii, Honolulu, 1988-90, sr. credit analyst, 1990-92; law clk. Hawaii Atty. Gen. Tax Divsn., Honolulu, 1994; sr. assoc. Kobayashi, Sugita & Goda, Honolulu, 1995—. Mem. new product devel. adv. bd. Warren Gorham & Lamont, N.Y.C., 1997-98. Editor-in-chief: The Transnational Lawyer, 1994, 95. Pres., enlisted adv. coun. Hawaii Air Nat. Guard, Honolulu, 1986-92; mem. ex officio alumni coun., mem. membership com., mem. membership benefits subcom. U. Hawaii Alumni Assn., Honolulu, 1990-91; mem. fin. com. and bylaws subcom. Soc. Coll. Bus. Alumni and Friends, U. Hawaii Coll. Bus. Adminstrn. Alumni Affairs, Honolulu, 1990-91, founding mem., treas., 1990-91, mem. steering com. to form alumni orgn., 1997—, pres., 1998—; at-large rep., treas., legis. liaison Neighborhood Bd., Kaneohe, Hawaii, 1991-92. Mem.: ABA (bus. law sect., comml. fin. svcs. com., consumer fin. svcs. com.), Hawaii Fin. Regulatory Compliance Assn. (bd. dirs. 1997—, cahirperson fair credit reporting act regulatory update com. 1998—), Inst. Cert. Mgmt. Accts. (bd. dirs. 1998—2000, dir. mem. acquisition 1998—2000), Calif. State Bar Assn., Hawaii State Bar Assn. (mem. real property and fin. svcs. sect. 1997—), Hawaii Jaycees (legal counsel 2000—01, exec. v.p. 2002, pres. 2003), Hawaii Bus. Jaycees (chater mem., charter pres. 1991—92, chmn. bd. 1992—93). Banking, Corporate, general, Property, real (including real estate development, water). Office: Kobayashi Sugita & Goda 999 Bishop St Ste 2600 Honolulu HI 96813-4430

NAKAYAMA, PAULA AIKO, state supreme court justice; b. Honolulu, Oct. 19, 1953; m. Charles W. Totto; children: Elizabeth Murakami, Alexander Totto. BS, U. Calif., Davis, 1975; JD, U. Calif., 1979. Bar: Hawaii 1979. Dep. pros. atty. City and County of Honolulu, 1979-82; ptnr. Shim, Tam & Kirimitsu, Honolulu, 1982-92; judge 1st Cir. Ct. State of Hawaii, Oahu, 1992-93; justice State of Hawaii Supreme Ct., Honolulu, 1993—. Mem. Am. Judicature Soc., Hawaii Bar Assn., Sons and Daughters of 442. Office: Hawaii Supreme Ct Ali'iolani Hale 417 S King St Honolulu HI 96813-2902

NAMOTO, KIMIKUNI, lawyer; b. Ehime-ken, Japan, July 12, 1929; m. Satomi Inamine, May 13, 1959; children: Mituo, Yosohisa. B in Law, Tokyo U., 1953. Bar: Japan. Mem. policy bd. Bank Japan, Tokyo, 1981—82; v.p., dir. gen. Assn. Regional Banks, Tokyo, 1985—94; pvt. practice Tokyo, 1994—. Author: (book) The Legal Effectivity of Internatinal Contract, 1956. Mem.: 2nd Tokyo Lawyers Assn. Office: K Namoto Law office RANDIC 3rd Ginza Bldg 7-10-5 Ginnza Tokyo Chuuou-ku 104-0061 Japan Business E-Mail: namoto-office@md.neweb.ne.jp.

NANCE, ALLAN TAYLOR, retired lawyer; b. Dallas, Jan. 31, 1933; s. A.Q. and Lois Rebecca (Taylor) N. BA, So. Meth. U., 1954, LLB, 1957; LLM, NYU, 1978. Bar: Tex. 1957, N.Y. 1961. With Simpson Thacher & Bartlett, N.Y.C., 1960-65; asst. counsel J.P. Stevens & Co., Inc., N.Y.C., 1965-70, sec., 1970-78, asst. gen. counsel, 1970-89; counsel J.P. Stevens & Co. Inc. and WestPoint-Pepperell Inc., 1989-93; asst. gen. counsel West-Point Stevens Inc., N.Y.C., 1993-98, ret., 1998. With USNR, 1957-59. Woodrow Wilson fellow Columbia U., 1959-60. Mem. Phi Beta Kappa. Corporate, general, Mergers and acquisitions, Property, real (including real estate development, water). Home: 201 E 66th St New York NY 10021-6451

NANCE, JOHN JOSEPH, lawyer, writer, air safety analyst, broadcaster, consultant; b. Dallas, July 5, 1946; s. Joseph Turner and Margrette (Grubbs) N.; m. Benita Ann Priest, July 26, 1968; children: Dawn Michelle, Bridgitte Cathleen, Christopher Sean. BA, So. Meth. U., 1968, JD, 1969; grad., USAF Undergrad. Pilot Tng., Williams AFB, Ariz., 1971. Bar: Tex. 1970, U.S. Ct. Appeals (fed. cir.) 1994. News reporter, broadcaster, newsman various papers and stas, Honolulu and Dallas, 1957-66; news anchorman Sta. WFAA-AM, Dallas, 1966-70; newsman including on camera Sta. WFAA-TV, Dallas; pvt. practice Dallas, 1970—; news dir. Newscom Network, Dallas, 1970; airline pilot Braniff Internat. Airways, Dallas, 1975-82, Alaska Airlines, Inc., Seattle, 1985—; chmn., pres. Exec. Transport, Inc., Tacoma, 1979-85; chmn., CEO EMEX Corp., Kent, Wash., 1987—; mng. ptnr. Phoenix Ptnrs., Ltd., Tacoma, Wash., 1995—; project devel. assoc. Columbia Tristar TV, 1997—; with Nance & Carmichael, PLLC, Austin, Tex., 1997—. Spkr. Human Mgmt., 1984—, Teamwork and Comms. in the Med. Profession; airline safety, advocate Ind. Cons., earthquake preparedness spokesman Ind. Cons.; dir. steering com. Found. for Issues Resolution in Sci. Tech., Seattle, 1987-89; speaker Northwestern Transp. Ctr. Deregulation and Safety Conf., 1987; cons. NOVA Why Planes Crash, PBS, 1987, ABC World News Tonight Crash of US AIR 427, 1994; aviation analyst ABC-TV and radio, 1995—; aviation editor: ABC Good Morning Am., 1995—; broadcast analyst, 1986—; spkr. in field. Author: Scorpion Strike, 1982, Splash of Colors, 1984, Blind Trust, 1986, On Shaky Ground, 1988, Final Approach, 1990, What Goes Up, 1991, Operating Handbook USAF Air Carrier Safety and Inspection, 1991, Phoenix Rising, 1994, Medusa's Child, 1997, The Last Hostage, 1998, Blackout, 2000, Headwind, 2001, Turbulence, 2002, Skyhook, 2003; contbr. ; actor: appeared in Sheep on the Runway, 1975; (TV series) Pandora's Clock, 1996; tech. advisor (TV series) Pandora's Clock, 1996; actor: (TV series) Medusa's Child, 1997; prodr., prodr.: USAF SOC CRM Program, 1992; author: USF Video Prodns.: ANG Introduction to CRM, 1992, USAF SOC CRM Program, 1992, The Teamwork Connection, 1996; prodr., dir.: USF Video Prodns.: ANG Introduction to CRM, 1996; dir., dir.: The Teamwork Connection, 1992. Pres. Fox Glen Homeowners Assn., Tacoma, 1974-77; cons. Congl. Office Tech. Assessment, Tacoma, 1987; witness air safety hearings U.S. Congress, Washington, 1986-88; bd. dirs. St. Charles Borromeo Sch., Tacoma, 1975-78, Nat. Patient Safety Found. of AMA, 1997—; mem. Mayor's Vets. Task Force, Tacoma, 1991; bd. advisors Jour. Air Law and Commerce So. Meth. Sch. Law, 1995—, exec. bd. Sch. of Law, 1998—; bd. advisors Pacific Northwest Writer's Conf., 1994—; adv. bd. supply and logistics mgmt. program Portland State U., 1997-98. Capt. USAFR, 1975-94; lt. col. Persian Gulf. Decorated Merit Svc. medal; named Airline Safety Man of Year Wash. State Div. of Aeronautics, 1987. Fellow Chartered Inst. Transport (Canberra, Australia); mem. ABA, SAG, Tex. Bar Assn., Author's Guild Am., Res. Officers Assn. (life), Aircraft Owners' and Pilots' Assn., Phi Alpha Delta, Delta Chi. Home and Office: John Nance Prodns 4512 87th Ave W Tacoma WA 98466-1920 Office: Phoenix Ptnrs Ltd PO Box 24465 Federal Way WA 98093-1465

NANGLE, JOHN FRANCIS, federal judge; b. St. Louis, June 8, 1922; s. Sylvester Austin and Thelma (Bank) N.; m. Jane Adams, June 7, 1986; 1 child, John Francis Jr. AA, Harris Tchrs. Coll., 1941; BS, U. Mo., 1943; JD, Washington U., St. Louis, 1948. Bar: Mo. 1948. Pvt. practice law, Clayton, 1948-73; judge U.S. Dist. Ct., 1973—, chief judge, 1983-90, sr. judge, 1990—91, Ga., 1991—. Mem. 8th Cir. Jud. Coun.; mem. exec. com. Jud. Conf. U.S.; chmn. Jud. Panel on Multidist. Litigation, mem. working group on mass torts, mem. jud. resources working group. Mem. Ad Hoc Comm. on Abestos. Mem. Mo. Rep. Com., 1958-73; mem. St. Louis County Rep. Cen. Com., 1958-73, chmn., 1960-61; pres. Mo. Assn. Reps., 1961, Reps. Vets. League, 1960; mem. Rep. Nat. Com., 1972-73; Grand Orator and bd. dirs. Masonic Home Mo. With AUS, 1943-46. First Sgt. USAR. Named Mo. Republican of Year John Marshall Club, 1970, Mo. Republican of Year Mo. Assn. Reps., 1971; recipient Most Disting. Alumnus award Harris-Stowe Coll., Most Disting. Alumnus award Washington U. Sch. Law, 1986. Mem. ABA, Legion of Honor DeMolay, Mo. Bar Assn., St. Louis Bar Assn., St. Louis County Bar Assn. (mem. com.).

NANTS, BRUCE ARLINGTON, lawyer; b. Orlando, Fla., Oct. 26, 1953; s. Jack Arlington and Louise (Hulme) N. BA, U. Fla., 1974, JD, 1977. Bar: Fla. 1977. Asst. state's atty. State Atty.'s Office, Orlando, 1977-78; pvt. practice, Orlando, 1979—. Columnist The Law and You, 1979-80. Auctioneer pub. TV sta., 1979; campaign coord. cen. Fla. steering com. Bob Dole for Pres., 1988; bd. dirs. Cystic Fibrosis Found. Mem. Acad. Fla. Trial Lawyers, Am. Arbitration Assn., Fellowship Christian Athletes (past bd. dirs. Cen. Fla.), Tiger Bay Club Cen. Fla., Orlando Touchdown Club, Fla. Blue Key, Omicron Delta Kappa, Phi Beta Kappa, Phi Delta Theta. Democrat. Baptist. Avocations: tennis, golf, swimming, scuba diving. Home: 1112 Country Ln Orlando FL 32804-6934 Office: PO Box 547871 Orlando FL 32854-7871

NAOR, SAMUEL, lawyer; b. Tarnopol, Poland, Feb. 12, 1925; arrived in Israel, 1937; s. Nachum and Tova (Shapiro) Leiner; m. Malka Ast, Dec. 19, 1950; children: Shalva, Varda, Adi. LLB, U. London, 1950; postgrad., Israel, 1951. Ptnr., Tel Aviv, 1951—2002; pvt. practice, 1956-97. Chmn. Labour Party, Ramat-Gan, Israel, 1965-69; mem. Ramat-Gan coun., 1965-73. Mem. Israel Bar Assn. (mem. disciplinary ct. 1997), Jr. Chamber Internat. (vice world pres. 1964). Home and Office: 11 Daniel St Ramat-Gan Israel

NAPLES, CAESAR JOSEPH, law and public policy educator, lawyer, consultant; b. Buffalo, Sept. 4, 1938; s. Caesar M. and Fannie A. (Occhipinti) N.; children: Jennifer, Caesar; m. Sandra L. Harrison, July 16, 1983. AB, Yale U., 1960; JD, SUNY, 1963. Bar: N.Y. 1963, Fla. 1977, Calif. 1988, U.S. Supreme Ct. 1965. Assoc. Moot & Sprague, Buffalo, 1965-69; asst. dir., employee rels. N.Y. Gov. Office, Albany, 1969-71; asst. v. chancellor SUNY, Albany, 1971-75; vice chancellor and gen. counsel Fla. State U. System, 1975-82; v. chancellor Calif. State U. System, 1983-92; vice chancellor emeritus Calif. State U., 1992—; prof. law and fin. Calif. State U. System, Long Beach, 1983—; bd. dirs., gen. counsel, corp. sec. Open U., Denver and Wilmington, Del., 1999—. Cons. Govt. of Australia, U. Nev. Sys., Assn. Can. Colls. and Univs., Que., also other univs. and colls. Contbr. articles to profl. jours.; co-author: Romanov Succession, 1989 with J.Victor Baldridge. Bd. dirs., gen. counsel Walden U., 1997—; mem. Metlife Resources Adv. Bd., 1986—, chmn., 1992—; mem. Meml. Heart Inst. Long Beach Meml. Hosp., 1993—, bd. dirs., chmn. 1998—, found. bd., 1996—; bd. dirs. Calif. Acad. Math. and Scis., 1995—. Capt. U.S.

Army, 1963-65. Mem. Acad Pers. Adminstrn. (founder), Nat. Ctr. for Study Collective Bargaining Higher Edn. (bd. dirs.). Avocations: opera, tennis. Office: 816 N Juanita Ave Ste B Redondo Beach CA 90277-2200 Fax: 310-798-0065. E-mail: cjnaples@csulb.edu.

NAPLETON, ROBERT JOSEPH, lawyer; b. Evergreen Park, Ill., Jan. 13, 1963; s. Francis Edward and Elizabeth (Raynor) N.; m. Clare Therese McEnery, June 6, 1992; children: Martin Joseph, Nora Elizabeth, Patricia Clare, Francis James, Luke John. BBA, Loyola U., Chgo., 1985, JD, 1988. Bar: Ill. 1988, U.S. Dist. Ct. (no. dist.) Ill. 1988, U.S. Dist. Ct. (ctrl. dist.) Ill. 1995, U.S. Dist. Ct. (we. dist.) Wis. 1998, U.S. Dist. Ct. Colo. 2000, U.S. Supreme Ct. 1999. Law clk. to Chief Judge James E. Murphy Circuit Ct. of Cook County, Chgo., 1985-87; mem. staff State's Atty. Office of Cook County, Markham, Ill., 1987-88; assoc. Motherway & Glenn, Chgo., 1988-98; ptnr. Motherway, Glenn & Napleton, Chgo., 1999—2002, Motherway & Napleton, Chgo., 2003—. Spkr., presenter in field. Treas. campaign Citizens to Elect James Brosnahan State Rep. for 36th Dist., Ill., 1996—. Fellow Roscoe Pound Found.; mem. ATLA (aviation law com.), Ill. Trial Lawyers Assn. (bd. advocates 1993-97, bd. mgrs. 1997—, med. negligence and product liability coms. 1994—, civil practice com. 1995—), Ill. State Bar Assn. (bd. govs. 1994-2000, tort law sect. coun. 1992-95), Southwest Bar Assn., Chgo. Bar Assn. (trial techniques com. 1991-92), Catholic Lawyers Guild, Brother Rice H.S. St. Thomas More Soc. Democrat. Roman Catholic. Avocations: golf, skiing, ice hockey, reading. Personal injury (including property damage), Product liability, Professional liability. Home: 400 Sunset Ave La Grange IL 60525-6115 Office: Motherway & Napleton 100 W Monroe St Ste 200 Chicago IL 60603-1923

NAPOLITANO, JANET ANN, governor; b. N.Y.C., Nov. 29, 1957; d. Leonard Michael and Jane Marie (Winer) Napolitano. BS summa cum laude, U. Santa Clara, Calif., 1979; JD, U. Va., 1983. Bar: Ariz. 1984, U.S. Dist. Ct. Ariz. 1984, U.S. Ct. Appeals (9th cir.) 1984, U.S. Ct. Appeals (10th cir.) 1988, U.S. Ct. Appeals (5th cir.), U.S. Ct. Appeals, U.S. Ct. Appeals (7th cir.), U.S. Ct. Appeals (8th cir.). Law clk. to Hon. Mary Schroeder U.S Ct. Appeals 9th Cir., 1983—84; assoc. Lewis & Roca, Phoenix, 1984—89, ptnr., 1989—93; U.S. atty. Dist. Ariz., Phoenix, 1993—97; atty. Lewis and Roca, Phoenix, 1997—98; atty. gen. State of Ariz., Phoenix, 1999—2002, gov., 2003—. Mem. Atty. Gen.'s Adv. Com., 1983—, chair, 1995—96; chair victims rights subcom. Ariz. Criminal Justice Commn.; chair Ariz. High Intensity Drug Traficking Area; mem. Ariz. Peace Officer Stds. and Tng. Bd., Ariz. Pros. Attys.' Adv. Coun.; past com. to study civil litigation abuse, cost and delay Ariz. Supreme Ct.; past pres. Ariz. Cmty. Legal Svcs. Corp.; past judge pro tem Ariz. Ct. Appeals. Contbr. articles to profl. jours. Chmn. Nucleus, 1989—91; active Phoenix Design Stds. Rev. Com., 1989—91, Ariz. Women's Forum, Charter 100; hon. chmn. Camp Fire Boys and Girls, 1999; 1st vice-chmn. Ariz. Dem. Com., 1990—92; active Dem. Nat. Com., 1990—92; chmn. Ariz. del. Dem. Nat. Conv., 1992, chmn., 2000; active Ariz. Bd. Tech. Registration, 1989—92; bd. dirs. Ariz. Fire Fighters and Emergency Paramedics Meml., Phoenix Children's Hosp., Actors' Lab Ariz., Inc., Ariz. Peace Officers Meml.; bd. regents Santa Clara U., 1992—. Named Ariz. Dem. of Yr., 1989; recipient Leader of Distinction award, Anti-Defamation League, Human Betterment award, Roots and Wings, Golden Apple award, West Valley NOW, Nat. Network To End Domestic Violence award, Woman of Distinction award, Crohns and Colitis Disease Found., Women Making History award, Nat. Mus. Women's History, Tribute to Women award, YWCA; fellow Dillard fellow; scholar, Truman Scholarship Found, 1977. Fellow: Ariz. Bar Found.; mem.: ABA, Raven Soc., Sandra Day O'Connor Inn of Ct. (barrister), Ariz. Women Lawyers Assn., Ariz. State Bar (chmn. civil practice and procedure com. 1991—92), Am. Judicature Soc., Maricopa County Bar Assn. (past long range planning com.), Ariz. Bar Assn. (past com. on minorities in law, past chmn. civil practice and procedure com.), Nat. Assn. Attys. Gen. (exec. com., tobacco bankruptcy working group, health care fraud group, co-chmn. civil rights com., stop underage smoking com., exec. working group on prosecutorial rels.), Am. Law Inst., Alpha Sigma Nu, Phi Beta Kappa. Democrat. Avocations: hiking, walking, travel, reading, film. Office: Office of Gov 1700 W Washington Phoenix AZ 85007

NARANJO, CAROLYN R. lawyer; b. Far Rockaway, N.Y., Nov. 28, 1954; d. Anthony J. and Mary (Lautazi) Spina. BA in Spl., Elem. Edn. summa cum laude, Bklyn. Coll., CUNY, 1976; JD, Temple U., 1981; student, Fordham U., 1980-81. Asst. counsel to head regional counsel First Am. Title Insurance, N.Y.C., 1981-82; legal counsel Creative Abstract Corp., N.Y.C., 1982-84; assoc. firm Friedman & Kornheiser, N.Y.C., 1982-84; assoc. Quinn, Cohen, Shields & Bock, N.Y.C., 1984-86; mng. ptnr. Collier, Cohen, Crystal & Bock, N.Y.C., 1986-94; pvt. practice Baldwin, N.Y., 1994—. Mem. ABA, Columbian Lawyers Assn. of Nassau County, Nassau Bar Assn., N.Y. State Bar Assn. Commercial, consumer (including collections, credit), Estate planning, Finance. Office: Ralph M Verni Bldg 746 Merrick Rd Baldwin NY 11510-3517

NARAYAN, BEVERLY ELAINE, lawyer; b. Berkeley, Calif., June 19, 1961; d. Jagjiwan and Alexandra Mataras Narayan; m. James Dean Schmidt, Jan. 7, 1989 (div. May 2002); children: Sasha Karan Narayan-Schmidt, Kaiya Maria Narayan-Schmidt; m. Corey Kryst Boe, Dec. 28, 2002. Student, San Francisco State U., 1979—80; BA, U. Calif., Berkeley, 1983; JD, U. Calif., San Francisco, 1987. Bar: Calif. 1987, U.S. Dist. Ct. (no. dist.) Calif. 1987, U.S. Dist. Ct. (ctrl. dist.) 1988. Atty. Daniels Barratta & Fine, L.A., 1988-89, Kornblum Ferry & Frye, L.A., 1990-91, Clapp Moroney Bellagamba Davis & Vucinich, Menlo Park, Calif., 1991-93, pvt. practice, Burlingame, Calif., 1993—2002; mng. dir. KarmaTek, Burlingame, Calif., 1999—2000; sr. trial atty. Allstate Ins. Co., San Jose, 2002—; lead counsel; staff counsel Encompass and Allstate Ins. Cos., San Jose, 2003—. Arbitrator Nat. Assn. Securities Dealers, San Francisco, 1987-2003, Pacific Exch., San Francisco, 1994—; mediator Peninsula Conflict Resolution Ctr., San Mateo, Calif., 1995—; appellate mediator First Dist. Ct. Appeals, 2000—; neutral San Mateo County Multi-Option ADR Project. Candidate Sch. Bd. San Mateo (Calif.) Unified Sch. Dist., 1993; mem. San Mateo County Task Force Violence Against Women. Recipient U. Calif. Hastings Coll. Law Achievement award, 1986; named Barrister of Yr., San Mateo County, 1996. Mem. ABA, San Mateo County Bar Assn. (co-chair women lawyers 1995, bd. dirs. 1994-96), South Asian Bar Assn., Nat. Women's Polit. Caucus (bd. dirs., diversity chair 1993-96), San Mateo County Barristers Club (bd. dirs. 1993-99, child watch chair 1995-99). Avocations: baking, cooking, reading, travel, motorcycles, family. General civil litigation, Personal injury (including property damage), Insurance. Office: 1797 Fox Dr #100 San Jose CA 95131

NARDI, STEPHEN J. lawyer; b. Kalispell, Mont., Feb. 11, 1951; s. Micheal Stephen and Grace Elaine N.; m. Darlene R. Nardi, May 26, 1979. BA in History, U. Mont., 1974, BA in Polit. Sci., JD, 1977. Bar: Mont. 1977, U.S. Dist. Ct. Mont. 1977, U.S. Ct. Appeals (9th cir.) 1977. Ptnr. Sherlock & Nardi, Kalispell, 1977—. Instr. Flathead Valley C.C., Kalispell, 1979-84. Mem.: NACDL, Mont. Trial Lawyers Assn., Mont. Assn. Criminal Def. Attys., Mont. State Bar Assn. Avocations: boating, golf, skiing, scuba diving. Criminal, Personal injury (including property damage). Office: Sherlock & Nardi 30 5th St E Ste 101 Kalispell MT 59901-4999 E-mail: stevenardi@centurytel.net.

NARDI RIDDLE, CLARINE, chief of staff; b. Clinton, Ind., Apr. 23, 1949; d. Frank Jr. and Alice (Mattioda) Nardi; children: Carl Nardi, Julia Nardi. AB in Math with honors, Ind. U., 1971, JD, 1974; LHD (hon.), St. Joseph Coll., 1991. Bar: Ind. 1974, U.S. Dist. Ct. (so. dist.) Ind. 1974, Conn. 1979, Fed. Dist. Ct. Conn. 1980, U.S. Supreme Ct. 1980, U.S. Ct. Appeals (2d cir.) 1986, U.S. Ct. Appeals (D.C. cir.) 1994. Staff atty. Ind. Legis. Svc. Agy., Indpls., 1974-78, legal counsel, 1978-79; dep. corp. counsel City of New Haven, 1980-83; counsel to atty. gen. State of Conn., Hartford, 1983-86, dep. atty. gen., 1986-89, acting atty. gen., 1989, atty. gen., 1989-91, judge Superior Ct., 1991-93; assn. exec., sr. v.p., gen. counsel Nat. Multi-Housing Coun., Nat. Apartment Assn., 1995—2003; chief of staff Senator Joseph I. Lieberman, Washington, 2003—. Asst. counsel state majority Conn. Gen. Assembly, Hartford, 1979, legal rsch. asst. to prof. Yale U., New Haven, 1979; legal counsel com. on law revision Indpls. State Bar Assn., 1979; mem. Chief Justice's Task Force on Gender Bias, Hartford, 1988-90; mem. ethics and values com. Ind. Sector, Washington, 1988-90; co-organizer Ind. Continuing Legal Edn. Forum Inst. Legal Drafting Legislature and Pvt. Practice; Internat. Women's Yr. panelist Credit Laws and Their Enforcement; mem. Atty. Gen.'s Blue Ribbon Commn., Chief Justice's Com. Study Publs. Policy Conn. Law. Jour., Law Revision Commn. Adminstrv. Law Study, Chief Justice's Task Force Gender, Justice and Cts., Gov.'s Task Force Fed. Revenue Enhancements; mem. exec. com. Jud. Dept.; mem. panel arbitrators Am. Arbitration Assn., 1994; gen. counsel Nat. Multi Housing Coun.; lectr. in field. Author: (with F.R. Rembusch) Drafting Manual for the Indiana General Assembly, 1976; sr. editor Ind. U. Law Sch. Interdisciplinary Law Jour.; contbr. articles to profl. jours. Bd. visitors Ind. U., Bloomington, 1974-92; mem. Gov.'s Missing Children Com., Hartford, Conn. Child Support Guidelines Com., Gov.'s Task Force on Justice for Abused Children, Hartford, 1988-90; mem. Mayor's City of New Haven Task Force Reorganization Corp. Counsel's Office, Gov.'s Child Support Commn., Mayor of New Haven's Blue Ribbon Commn.; former bd. dirs. New Haven Neighborhood Music Sch.; bd. dirs., mem. youth adv. com. Gov.'s Partnership Prevent Substance Abuse Workforce-Drugs Don't Work. Recipient Women in Leadership Recognition award Hartford Region YWCA, 1986, Award of Merit, Women & Law Sect. Conn. Bar Assn., 1989, Fellowship award South End Ladies Dem. Club, 1989, Woman of Yr. award Greater Hartford Fedn. of Bus. & Profl. Women's Clubs, 1990, Conn. Original award Somers-Mabelle B. Avery Sch., 1990, Cert. of Recognition, Consortium Law-Related Edn., 1990, Citizen award Conn. Task Force Children's Constl. Rights, 1991, Ann. award Hartford Assn. Women Attys., 1993; named Conn. History Maker, U.S. Dept. Labor, Women's Bur. & Permanent Commn. Status Women, 1989, Impact Player, The Conn. Law Tribune, 1992; inductee Ind. U. Sch. Law Alumni Acad. Fellow, 1999. Mem. ABA, Conn. Bar Assn. (chair com. on gender bias, Citation of Merit women and law sect. 1989), Nat. Assn. Attys. Gen. (chair charitable trusts and solicitation 1988-90), New Haven Neighborhood Music Sch. (bd. dirs.), Am. Arbitration Assn. (arbitration panel 1994), Ind. Bar Assn., Conn. Bar Assn. (chair com. gender bias legal profession), Indpls. Bar Assn., Ind. Civil Liberties Union (bd. dirs., mem. exec. com., chair long range planning com., mem. women's rights project, membership v.p., Disting. Svc. award), Conn. Consortium Law and Citizenship Edn., Inc. (bd. dirs.), Conn. Judges Assn. (mem. legislation com.), Ind. U. Law Sch. Alumni Assn. (bd. dirs.), Enomene Hon. Soc., Pleiades Hon. Soc., Mortar Bd. (nat. fellow), Alpha Lambda Delta. Democrat. Presbyterian. Office: Nat Multi Housing Coun 1850 M St NW Ste 450 Washington DC 20036-5803

NARDONE, WILLIAM ANDREW, lawyer; b. Groton, Conn., June 16, 1954; s. Henry Joseph and Mary Frances (Herley) N.; m. Diane Ruth Hall, July 1, 1988; children: Madison Catherine, William Chase. BA, U. R.I., 1976; JD, Suffolk U., 1980. Bar: R.I. 1981, U.S. Dist. Ct. R.I. 1981, U.S. Supreme Ct. 1991. Assoc. Law Office of M.L. Lewiss, Westerly, R. I., 1980-83; ptnr. Orsinger & Nardone Law Offices, Westerly, 1983—. Solicitor Westerly Sch. Dept., 1984-90, 94-96, 98-2000, 02—. Mem. com. Westerly YMCA, 1980, bd. dirs., 1991—, exec. com., 1994—; bd. dirs., pres. Westerly Adult Day Care Ctr., 1985-93; trustee Westerly Hosp., 1993—, sec., asst. treas., 1999-2001, treas. and v.p., 2002—; trustee SNEPHO, 1994—. Mem. Nat. Coun. Sch. Attys., R.I. Bar Assn. (rep. Ho. of Dels. 1984-90), Nat. Assn. Legal Problems in Edn. Republican. Roman Catholic. Commercial, contracts (including sales of goods; commercial financing), Land use and zoning (including planning), Property, real (including real estate development, water). Home: 38 Wicklow Rd Westerly RI 02891-3644 Office: Orsinger & Nardone 53 High St Westerly RI 02891-6001

NARIN, STEPHEN B. lawyer; b. Phila., Nov. 23, 1929; s. Bernard E. and Anne (Lipsius) N.; m. Sandra C. Goldberg, Sept. 29, 1963; children: Howard Glen, Brenda Teri. BS, Temple U., 1951, LL.B., 1953; LL.M. in Taxation, NYU, 1960. Bar: Pa. 1954, U.S. Supreme Ct. 1958; CPA, Pa. Dep. atty. gen. Commonwealth of Pa., Harrisburg, 1955-57; instr. acctg. Temple U., Phila., 1954-55; lectr. in law grad. legal studies div. Temple U. Sch. Law, Phila., 1976-85; lectr. Practicing Law Inst., 1967-69; ptnr. Narin & Chait, Phila., 1970-89, Predecessor Ptnrships., Phila., 1955-70; v.p., gen. counsel Travelco Assocs., Phila., 1989-90; of counsel Krekstein, Wolfson & Krekstein, Phila., 1989-92; v.p., gen. counsel Eagle Nat. Bank, 1990-91; counsel Schachtel, Gerstley, Levine & Koplin, Phila., 1993-98; pvt. practice, Ardmore , Pa., 1998—. Mem. Phila. County Bd. Law Examiners, 1961-65. Mem. nat. governing council Am. Jewish Congress, 1963-84, nat. exec. com., 1978-84, pres. Greater Phila. council, 1965-67; mem. Nat. Commn. on Law and Social Action, 1964-84. Mem. Phila. Bar Assn., Phi Alpha Delta. Corporate, general, General practice, Alternative dispute resolution. Office: 631 Kenilworth Rd Ardmore PA 19003-2914

NASH, GORDON BERNARD, JR., lawyer; b. Evergreen, Ill., Feb. 24, 1944; s. Gordon Bernard and Lilyan (Grafft) N.; m. Roseanne Joan Burke, Aug. 24, 1968; children: Caroline, Brian, Terry, Maureen. BA, Notre Dame U., 1966; JD, Loyola U., Chgo., 1969. Bar: Ill., U.S. Dist. Ct. (no. dist.) Ill. Atty. Office U.S. Atty. No. Dist. Ill., Chgo., 1971-78; prin. Gardner Carton & Douglas, LLC, Chgo., 1978—. Chmn. Ill. Bd. Ethics, Springfield, 1980-85. Served to capt. U.S. Army, 1969-71. Recipient John Marshall award U.S. Dept. Justice, 1978, Spl. Commendation award, 1975, Disting. Achievement award Internat. Acad. Trial Lawyers, 1969. Mem. ABA, Ill. Bar Assn., Chgo. Bar Found. Local Chpt. (bd. dirs. 1983-85, 87-89), Fed. Bar Assn. (bd. govs. 1986-91), Chgo. Bar Assn. (bd. mgrs. 1983-85, pres. 1990-91), Constl. Rights Found. Com. (bd. dirs. 1993—, chmn., 1998-2001), Am. Coll. Trial Lawyers, Ctr. for Conflict Resolution (bd. 1992-2000, v.p. 1995-2000), Chgo. Inn of Ct. (pres. 1996-97), Olympia Fields Country Club. Democrat. Roman Catholic. Federal civil litigation, State civil litigation, Criminal. Home: 5101 Harvey Ave Western Springs IL 60558-2042 Office: Gardner Carton & Douglas LLC 191 N Wacker Dr Ste 3700 Chicago IL 60606-1698 E-mail: gnash@gcd.com.

NASON, LEONARD YOSHIMOTO, lawyer, writer, publisher; b. N.Y.C., Feb. 17, 1954; s. Leonard Hastings and Mary Yukiko (Yoshimoto) N.; m. Linda Thayer, Sept. 26, 1981; children: Victoria, Kelsey, Jennifer. BA, Tufts U., 1975; JD, Northeastern U., Boston, 1979. Bar: Mass. 1979, U.S. Dist. Ct. 1979, U.S. Ct. Appeals (1st cir.) 1985. Assoc. Ricklefs & Uehlein, Natick, Mass., 1979-84; ptnr. Uehlein, Nason & Wall, Natick, 1985-95, Nason, Wall & Wall, P.C., Lexington, Mass., 1995—. Pres. Legal Info. Svcs., Inc., Lexington, 1986—; interviewer admissions Tuft U. Author: (handbook) Mass. Workers' Compensation, 1986, (statute book) Mass. Workers' Compensation, 1987; co-author: Massachusetts Practice Series, Vol. 29, 1989, 95, 2002; contbg. author: A Judicial Guide to Labor and Employment Law, 1990, SBANE HR Guide for 2002. Bd. dirs. Newton Community Service Ctr., 1981; coach soccer, basketball and softball, Little League. Mem. ABA, Mass. Bar Assn., Boston Bar Assn., Assn. Trial Lawyers Am. Avocations: tennis, sailing, softball, music. Personal injury (including property damage), Workers' compensation. Office: Nason Wall & Wall PC 113 The Great Rd Bedford MA 01730 E-mail: Lyn@Legalinfosysinc.com., LNASON1750@aol.com.

NASSAR, WILLIAM MICHAEL, lawyer; b. Methuen, Mass., June 5, 1958; s. William M. and Catherine M. Nassar; m. Ermelinda Amezcua, June 26, 1982; children: Brandon Michael, Elyse Renae. AAS, R.I. C.C., 1978; BSBA, U. Redlands, 1980; JD, Western State Coll. of Law, 1986. Legal adminstr. Bourns Inc., Riverside, Calif., 1988-90, dir. worldwide contracts adminstr., 1990-94, dir. worldwide contracts/legal counsel, 1994-97, sr. legal counsel, 1997-2000; v.p., gen. counsel Standard MEMS, Inc., Burlington, Mass., 1999—2002; ptnr. Law Offices Anton Beck & Nassar, Redlands, Calif., 2002—. Bd. dirs. Advanced Med. Inc., Riverside, Calif., Global Pathways Inc., Riverside; v.p. Bourns Employees Fed. Credit Union, bd. dirs. Adv. bd. Ronald McDonald House, Loma Linda, Calif., 1994-98. Roman Catholic. Avocations: sailing, boating, skiing, reading. Commercial, contracts (including sales of goods; commercial financing), Corporate, general, Intellectual property. Home: 13015 Burns Ln Redlands CA 92373-7415 Office: 300 E State St Ste 200 Redlands CA 92373 Office Fax: 909-798-6189. E-mail: william.nassar@verizon.net.

NASSAU, MICHAEL JAY, lawyer; b. N.Y.C., June 3, 1935; s. Benjamin and Belle (Nassau) N.; m. Roberta Bluma Herzlich, June 26, 1971; children: Stephanie Ellen, William Michael. BA summa cum laude, Yale U., 1956, LLB cum laude, 1960. Bar: N.Y. 1960, U.S. Ct. Appeals (2d cir.) 1963, U.S. Tax Ct. 1963, U.S. Supreme Ct. 1965, U.S. Dist. Ct. (so. dist.) N.Y. 1978. Asst. instr. in constl. law Yale U., 1959-60; law clk. to judge U.S. Ct. Appeals 2d Cir., 1960-61; assoc. tax dept. Paul, Weiss, Rifkind, Wharton & Garrison, N.Y.C., 1961-73; ptnr. Kramer Levin Naftalis & Frankel LLP, and predecessor, N.Y.C., 1974—. Mem. adv. bd. Matthew Bender Fed. Pension Law Service, 1975-76; mem. adv. com. NYU Ann. Inst. Employee Plans and Exec. Compensation, 1976-79; mem. steering com. Am. Pension Conf., 1981-83; lectr. in field; panelist various seminars on employee benefits; panelist Pension Video Seminar, 1983; mem. N.E. region pension liaison group IRS. Mem. editl. bd. Bank and Corp. Governance Law Reporter, 1989—; contbr. chpts. to books and articles to profl. jours. Recipient Excellence in Benefits award for achievement in benefits svc., Worldwide Employee Benefits Network, 2003. Charter fellow Am. Coll. Employee Benefits Counsel; mem. ABA (sect. taxation, employee benefits com. 1993—), N.Y. State Bar Assn. (co-chmn. employee benefits sect. taxation 1976-78, mem. exec. com. sect. taxation 1976-79), Assn. of Bar of City of N.Y. (chmn. subcom. pension legis. of com. taxation 1975-76, employee benefits com. 1987-92), WEB (N.Y. chpt. bd. dirs. 1990—, pres. 1993-94), Phi Beta Kappa. Pension, profit-sharing, and employee benefits. Office: Kramer Levin Naftalis & Frankel LLP 919 3rd Ave New York NY 10022-3902

NAST, DIANNE MARTHA, lawyer; b. Mount Holly, N.J., Jan. 30, 1948; d. Henry Daniel and Anastasia (Lovenduski) N.; m. Joseph Francis Roda, Aug. 23, 1980; children: Michael, Daniel, Joseph, Joshua, Anastasia. BA, Pa. State U.; JD, Rutgers U., 1976. Bar: Pa. 1976, U.S. Dist. Ct. Pa. 1976, N.J. 1976, U.S. Dist. Ct. N.J. 1976, U.S. Ct. Appeals (3d, 5th, 6th, 7th, 8th and 11th cirs.) 1976, U.S. Supreme Ct. 1982, U.S. Dist. Ct. Ariz. 1985. Dir., v.p. Kohn, Nast & Graf, P.C., Phila., 1976-95, Roda & Nast, P.C., Lancaster, Pa., 1995—. Mem. lawyers adv. com. U.S. Ct. Appeals (3d cir.), 1982-84, chmn., 1983-84, mem. com. on revision jud. conf. conduct rules, 1982-84; mem. U.S. Ct. Appeals for the 3d Cir. Jud. Conf. Permanent Planning Com., 1983-90; bd. dirs. 3d Cir. Hist. Soc., 1993—; bd. dirs. Phila. Pub. Def., 1980-89; dir. Fed. Judicial Ctr. Found., 1991—, chair, 1996-2003; chmn. lawyers adv. com. U.S. Dist. Ct. (ea. dist.) Pa., 1982-90. Pres. Hist. Soc., 1988-91. Fellow ABA (coun. litigation sect. 1986-89, co-chmn. anti-trust com. litigation sect. 1984-86, div. dir. 1990-91, practical litigation editl. bd. 1989—, ho. of dels. 1992-94, mem. task force state justice initiatives, mem. task force state of justice system, 1993, mem. task force long range planning com. 1994), Am. Law Inst. (chair internat. professionalism com. 1991-94, civil justice task force 1993-95), Am. Arbitration Assn. (bd. dirs., mem. alt. dispute resolution and mass torts task force), Am. Judicature Soc., Pa. Bar Assn. (bd. of dels. 1983-95), N.J. Bar Assn., Pa. Trial Lawyers Assn., Phila. Bar Assn. (bd. govs. 1985-87, chmn., bicentennial com. 1986-87, chmn. bench bar conf. 1988-89), Lancaster Bar Assn. (co-chair civil litigation and rules com. trial law sect.), Rutgers Law Sch. Alumni Assn. Antitrust, Federal civil litigation, Product liability. Home: 1059 Sylvan Rd Lancaster PA 17601-1923 Office: Roda & Nast PC 801 Estelle Dr Lancaster PA 17601-2130 E-mail: dnast@rodanast.com.

NASU, TAKETO, lawyer; b. Uto, Kumamoto-pref., Japan, Aug. 18, 1968; s. Kenji and Hiroko Nasu. LLB, Sophia U., 1991; LLM, U. Tex., 2000. Bar: Japan 1996, N.Y. 2001. Legal apprentice The Legal Rsch. & Tng. Inst., Saitama, Japan, 1994—96; assoc. Yuasa & Hara, Tokyo, 1996—99; fgn. assoc. intern Porter Wright Morris & Arthur, Columbus, Ohio, 2001—02; sr. assoc. Yuasa & Hara, 2002—. Mem.: ABA, N.Y. State Bar Assn., Dai-ichi Tokyo Bar Assn. Avocation: Shorinji-Kempo (3d degree black belt). Corporate, general, Intellectual property, Private international. Office: Yuasa & Hara Sect 206 New-Ohtemachi Bldg 2-1 Ohtemachi 2-chome Chiyoda-ku Tokyo 100-0004 Japan Fax: +81-3 3246 0233. E-mail: taketon@yuasa-hara.co.jp.

NATALIE, RONALD BRUCE, lawyer; b. Lynn, Mass., Nov. 29, 1935; s. John Richard and Cecelia Lucy (Fish) N.; m. Betty Ann McEnteggart, Aug. 22, 1958; children: Ronald Bruce Jr., Karen Lorraine Walker, Donna Leslie Lee, John Francis. AB, Tufts Coll., 1957; JD with highest honors, George Washington U., 1962. Bar: D.C. 1962, U.S. Ct. Appeals (D.C. cir.) 1964, U.S. Ct. Appeals (2d cir.) 1970, U.S. Ct. Appeals (5th cir.), 1991, U.S. Ct. Appeals (3d cir.) 1992, U.S. Supreme Ct. 2000. Atty. Office of Gen. Counsel, U.S. Commn. on Civil Rights, Washington, 1962-64; assoc. Verner, Liipfert, Bernhard, McPherson and Hand, Washington, 1964-68, ptnr., 1968-81; shareholder Verner Liipfert, Bernhard, McPherson & Hand, Washington, 1981—2002, gen. counsel, dir., 2001—02; ptnr. Piper Rudnick, LLP, Washington, 2002—. Chief counsel Pres.'s Commn. to Investigate the Accident at Three Mile Island, Washington, 1979; vice chmn. Close Up Found., Alexandria, Va., 1971-98, chmn., 1998—. Lt. USN, 1957-62. Mem. ABA, D.C. Bar Assn., Ba Assn. of D.C., Assn. for Transp., Law, Logistics and Policy, Phi Alpha Delta. Democrat. Federal civil litigation, Labor (including EEOC, Fair Labor Standards Act, labor-management relations, NLRB, OSHA), Legislative. Home: 3307 39th St NW Washington DC 20016-3711 Office: Piper Rudnick LLP 901 15th St NW Ste 600 Washington DC 20005-2306 E-mail: ronald.natalie@piperrudnick.com.

NATCHER, STEPHEN DARLINGTON, lawyer, business executive; b. San Francisco, Nov. 19, 1940; s. Stanlus Zoch and Robena Lenore Collie (Goldring) N.; m. Carolyn Anne Bowman, Aug. 23, 1969; children: Tanya Michelle, Stephanie Elizabeth. AB in Polit. Sci., Stanford U., 1962; JD, U. Calif., San Francisco, 1965. Bar: Calif. 1966. Assoc. firm Pillsbury, Madison & Sutro, San Francisco, 1966-68; counsel Douglas Aircraft div. McDonnell Douglas Corp., Long Beach, Calif., 1968-70; v.p., sec. Security Pacific Nat. Bank, 1971-79; asst. gen. counsel Security Pacific Corp., 1979-80; v.p., sec., gen. counsel Lear Siegler, Inc., Santa Monica, Calif., 1980-87; v.p., gen. counsel Computer Sci. Corp., El Segundo, Calif., 1987-88; exec. v.p., gen. counsel, sec. CalFed Inc., 1989-90; sr. v.p. adminstrn., gen. counsel, sec. Wyle Electronics, Irvine, Calif., 1991-98; gen. counsel VEBA Electronics LLC, Santa Clara, Calif., 1998—2002. With USCG, 1965-71. Mem.: St. Francis Yacht Club (San Francisco). Republican. Corporate, general, General practice, Securities. E-mail: snatcher@starstream.net.

NATHAN, FREDERIC SOLIS, lawyer; b. N.Y.C., June 24, 1922; s. Edgar Joshua and Mabel (Unterberg) N.; m. Frances E., Oct. 28, 1956; children: Jean E., Frederic S. Jr., William E. BA, Williams Coll., Williamstown, Mass., 1943; LLD, Yale U., 1948. Bar: N.Y. 1948, U.S. Dist. Ct. (so. and ea. dists) N.Y. 1948, U.S. Ct. Appeals (2d cir.) 1953, U.S. Supreme Ct. 1968. Instr. Williams Coll., Williamstown, 1948; assoc. Rathbone Perry Kelley & Drye, N.Y.C., 1948-53; asst. U.S. atty. U.S. Attys.' Office (so. dist.), N.Y.C., 1953-56; assoc. Greenbaum, Wolff & Ernst, N.Y.C., 1956-58, ptnr., 1959-65, 70-82; 1st asst. corp. counsel N.Y.C. Law Dept., N.Y.C., 1966-69; ptnr. Kelley, Drye & Warren, N.Y.C., 1982—. Mem. N.Y. Rep. County Com.,

N.Y.C., 1948-66; trustee Mt. Sinai Hosp., N.Y.C., 1970—; chmn. bd. FOJP Svc. Corp., N.Y.C., 1977-85, bd. dirs., 1979—; bd. dirs., v.p. Am. Jewish Soc. for Svc., N.Y.C., 1950—; bd. dirs. Everybody Wins Found., Inc., 1992—. With U.S. Army, 1943-45, ETO. Fellow Am. Coll. Trial Lawyers; mem. ABA, Assn. of Bar of City of N.Y. (exec. com. 1979-81), Fed. Bar Council (pres. 1975-76), N.Y. State Bar Assn. Clubs: Century Assn., Yale of N.Y.C.; Sunningdale Country. Republican. Jewish. Estate planning, Probate (including wills, trusts). Home: 180 East End Ave New York NY 10128-7763 Office: Kelley Drye & Warren 101 Park Ave New York NY 10178-0062 E-mail: fnathan@kelleydrye.com.

NATHAN, J(AY) ANDREW, lawyer; b. St. Louis, Aug. 25, 1947; s. Ira L. Nathan and Babette Gross Simon; m. Linda L. Berenbeim, July 27, 1969; children: Joshua, Marni. BA, U. Mo., 1969; JD, U. Colo., 1972. Bar: Colo. 1972, U.S. Dist. Ct. Colo. 1972, U. S. Ct. Appeals (10th cir.) 1972. Assoc. atty. Burnette, Watson, Horan & Hilgers, Denver, 1972-73; shareholder, pres. Watson, Nathan & Bremer, P.C., Denver, 1973-97, Nathan, Bremer, Dumm & Myers, P.C., Denver, 1997—. Mem Colo. Def. Lawyers Assn., Def. Rsch. Inst., Am. Bd. Trial Advs. (pres. Colo. chpt. 1990, nat. bd. dirs. 1990-96). Avocations: scuba diving, golf, oenology. Civil rights, Insurance, Personal injury (including property damage). Office: Nathan Bremer Dumm & Myers PC 3900 E Mexico Ave Ste 1000 Denver CO 80210-3945

NATIONS, HOWARD LYNN, lawyer; b. Dalton, Ga., Jan. 9, 1938; s. Howard Lynn and Eva Earline (Armstrong) Lamb; m. Ella Lois Johnson, June 4, 1960 (div. Nov. 1976); children: Cynthia Lynn Nations Garcia, Angela Jean Gordon. BA, Florida State U., 1963; JD, Fla. State U., 1966. Bar: Tex. 1966; cert. trial atty. Tex. Bd. Legal Specialization. Assoc. Butler, Rice Cook & Knapp, Houston, 1966-71; pres. Nations & Cross, Houston, 1971—; v.p., dir., co-founder Ins. Corp. Am., Houston, 1972—; pres. Caplinger & Nations Galleries, Houston, 1973—, Nations Investment Corp., Houston, 1975—, NCM Trade Corp., Houston, 1975; v.p. Delher Am. Inc., Houston, 1975—; pres. Howard L. Nations, PC, Houston, 1971—, Trial Focus, Inc., 1995—. Founder Nations Found.; adj. prof. So. Tex. Coll. Law, Houston, 1967—; speaker in field. Author: Structuring Settlements, 1987; co-author: Texas Workers' Compensation, 1988, (with others) The Anatomy of a Personal Injury Lawsuit, 3rd rev. edit. 1991; editor: Maximizing Damages in Wrongful Death and Personal Injury Litigation, 1985; contbr. articles to profl. jours. Chmn., trustee Nat. Coll. Advocacy, Washington, 1985-92. With M.I. Corps, U.S. Army, 1957-60. Recipient Gene Cavin Excellence award State Bar Tex., 2000. Fellow Tex. Bar Found., Houston Bar Found. (life); mem. ATLA (exec. com. 1991-95), Nat. Bd. Trial Advocacy (diplomate civil trial advocacy), So. Trial Lawyers Assn. (pres. 1994-95), Tex. Trial Lawyers Assn. (pres. 1992-93). General civil litigation, Personal injury (including property damage), Product liability. Office: The Sterling Mansion 4515 Yoakum Blvd Houston TX 77006-5821

NAUGHTON, JOHN ALEXANDER, lawyer; b. Chgo., Jan. 26, 1947; s. Hugh and Margaret (Durkin) N.; m. Raydeen E. Banfi, Dec. 27, 1969; children: Teryn Alisa, Tysen Anne, Ryan Eric, Justen Aran. BS in Commerce, De Paul U., 1970; JD, John Marshall Law Sch., Chgo., 1977. Bar: Ill. 1977, U.S. Dist. Ct. (no. dist.) Ill. 1978. Assoc. Kusper & Raucci, Chartered, Chgo., 1978-81; city atty. Berwyn, 1981-82; pvt. practice, 1981—. Twp. atty. Berwyn Health Dept., 1982-85. Bd. dirs. Altenheim, Forest Park, Ill., 1977-88; alderman Berwyn City Council, 1977-80, mayor, 1980-81. Mem. Ill. Bar Assn., W. Suburban Bar Assn. Criminal, Family and matrimonial, Property, real (including real estate development, water).

NAUHEIM, MARKUS A. lawyer; b. Limburg, Germany, Aug. 29, 1968; Staatsexamen, U of Mainz, Mainz, Germany, 1995; LLM, Duke U sch. of Law, Durham, NC, 1996; Staatsexamen, State of Hessen, Wiesbaden, Germany, 1999; JD, U of Mainz, Mainz, Germany, 2000. Bar: NY 1997, Munich, Germany 1999. Fgn. intern Mayer, Brown & Platt, Washington, 1996; legal intern Bruckhaus, Westrick, Stegemann, Frankfurt, Germany, 1997, CLT - UFA, Luxemburg, 1998; assoc. BBLP Beiten Burkhardt, Mittl & Wegener, Munich, 1999—2001, Gibson, Dunn & Crutcher, Munich, 2002—. Mem. German-Am. Lawyers Assoc., Bonn, Germany, 1991—; co-pres. Duke Club of Germany, Munich, 2001—; mem. Dajv M&A Practice Group, Frankfurt, Germany, 2000—. Author: Die Rechtmässigkeit des Must-Carry-Prinzips im Bereich des Digitalen Kabelfernsehens in der Bundesrepublick Deutschland. Roman Catholic. Office: Gibson Dunn & Crutcher LLP Widenmayer Str. 10 80538 Munich Germany

NAUHEIM, STEPHEN ALAN, lawyer; b. Washington, Nov. 17, 1942; s. Ferdinand Alan and Beatrice Lillian (Strasburger) N.; children: Terry Beth, David Alan. BS in Acctg., U. N.C., 1964; JD, Georgetown U., 1967; LLM, George Washington U., 1970. Bar: D.C. 1968, U.S. Ct. Claims 1968, U.S. Tax Ct. 1971. Atty. adviser office chief counsel IRS, Washington, 1967-71, asst. br. chief, 1970-71; assoc. Surrey & Morse, Washington, 1971-75, ptnr., 1975-81; prin. Anderson, Hibey, Nauheim & Blair, Washington, 1981-91, Schall, Boudreau & Gore, Washington, 1991-93; pres., gen. counsel CMW Group, Ltd., Washington, 1994-96; dir. Pricewaterhouse Coopers LLP, 1996—. Mem. adv. bd. World Trade Inst., N.Y.C., 1978—, Tax Mgmt. Adv. Bd., Washington, 1980—. Mem. editl. bd. Internat. Tax Jour., N.Y.C., 1982—; contbr. to profl. pubs. Mem. ABA (former com. chmn. taxation sect.), Internat. Fiscal Assn., D.C. Bar Assn. (mem. steering com. tax sect. 1987-92, chmn. tax sect. 1990-92), Am. Coll. of Tax Counsel. Avocations: traveling, sailing. Corporate, general, Property, real (including real estate development, water), Corporate taxation. Office: Pricewaterhouse Coopers 1301 K St NW Ste 800W Washington DC 20005-3317

NAUMAN, SPENCER GILBERT, JR., lawyer; b. Bryn Mawr, Pa., Mar. 4, 1933; s. Spencer Gilbert and Gertrude Howard (Olmsted) N.; m. Helen Gibbon Trimble, Oct. 19, 1963; children— Spencer G., Helen G., John T. A.B., Princeton U., 1955; LL.B., U. Pa., 1961. Bar: Pa. 1962, U.S. dist. ct. (mid. dist.) Pa. 1968. Assoc. Nauman, Smith, Shissler & Hall, Harrisburg, Pa., 1962-66, ptnr, 1966— ; asst. city solicitor City of Harrisburg, 1962-69. Dir. Wagner Bros. Containers, Inc., Balt. Past pres., trustee emeritus Harrisburg Acad.; bd. dirs. Harrisburg chpt. ARC; bd. mgrs. Harrisburg Cemetery Assn., Harrisburg Hosp., 1973-79. Served with U.S. Army, 1955-58. Mem. ABA, Pa. Bar Assn., Dauphin County Bar Assn. Republican. Episcopalian. Clubs: Racquet (Phila.); Princeton (N.Y.C.); W. Shore Country (Camp Hill, Pa.). Insurance, Probate (including wills, trusts), Corporate taxation. Home: Creek Farm Bowmansdale PA 17008 Office: 200 N 3d St 18th Fl Harrisburg PA 17108-0840

NAUMANN, STEFAN, lawyer; b. Geneva, Oct. 10, 1963; s. Hans August and Nannette Deloris (Hall) Naumann; m. Vanessa Belpomme Naumann, Oct. 5, 1995; 1 child, Michael Prince. BA, Harvard U, Cambridge, Mass., 1986; JD, Boalt Hall U of CA, Berkeley, CA, 1990; M CJ, U of Paris II, Paris, France, 1991; CEIPI, Strasbourg U, Strasbourg, France, 1995. Bar: CA 1992, Paris 1993. Summer intern Rosenfeld, Meyer & Susman, Bev. Hills, Calif., 1988; intern ICC Internat. CT of Arbitration, Paris, 1989; assoc. Duclos Thorne Mollet-Vieville, Paris, 1990—94, Sales Vincent & Assocs., Paris, 1994—98, of counsel, 1998—2000; ptnr. Denton Wilde Sapte, Paris, 2000—. Mem.: Harvard Club of France (President 2000—02), Internat. Trademark Assoc., Internat. Assoc. for the Protection of Intellectual Property. Home: 46 Rue la Fayette F-75009 Paris France Office: Denton Wilde Sapte 43 Rue Du Fbg St Honore Fbg F-75008 Paris France

NAVARRO, BRUCE CHARLES, lawyer; b. West Lafayette, Ind., Oct. 30, 1954; s. Joseph Anthony and Dorothy Gloria (Gnazzo) N.; children: Philip Joseph, Joanna Christina. BA, Duke U., 1976; JD, Ind. U., 1980. Bar: D.C. 1980. Asst. counsel U.S. Senate Labor Subcom., Washington, 1981-84; acting dep. undersec. for legis. affairs Dept. Labor, Washington, 1984-85; atty. advisor EEOC, Washington, 1985-86; dir. Office of Congl. Rels. Office of Pers. Mgmt., Washington, 1986-89; prin. dep. asst. atty. gen. for legis. U.S. Dept. of Justice, Washington, 1989-91; spl. asst. to gen. counsel U.S. Dept. HHS, Washington, 1991; expert cons. U.S. Dept. Def., Washington, 1992; counsel to the vice chmn. U.S. Consumer Product Safety Commn., Bethesda, Md., 1992-95; prin. Navarro Regulatory and Legis. Affairs, Washington, 1995—. Mem. Arlington County Republican Com. (Va.), 1983; bd. dirs. Prince William Cmty. Safe Kids Coalition, 1997-99. Mem. D.C. Bar Assn. Roman Catholic. Avocations: music, golf. Administrative and regulatory, Health, Legislative. Office: 2121 K St NW Ste 800 Washington DC 20037 Home: 12580 Cricket Lane Woodbridge VA 22192

NAVARRO-GONZALEZ, ANTONIO J. lawyer, educator; b. Alicante, Spain, June 11, 1968; Licenciate in Law, U. of Murcia, Spain, 1991; LLM, Instituto de Empresa, Madrid, 1992, NYU, 1995. Bar: Madrid 1992, N.Y. 1999. Assoc. Uría & Menéndez, Madrid, Spain, 1992—94; fgn. assoc. Fox, Horan & Camerini, New York, NY, 1995—96; ptnr. Broseta Abogados, Valencia, Spain, 1996—. Recipient Premio Antonio Maura for legal articles, Madrid Bar Assn., 2001; scholar, La Caixa de Barcelona, 1994. Mem.: Internat. Bar Assn. Corporate, general, Finance, Mergers and acquisitions. Office: Broseta Abogados Plaza Tetuán 8 2 Spain Valencia 46003 Spain Office Fax: +34963921088. E-mail: ajnavarro@broseta.com.

NAVATTA, ANNA PAULA, lawyer; b. Hackensack, N.J., Jan. 7, 1956; d. Jack Anthony and Natalie (Pretto) N. BA, Rutgers U., 1978, MA, 1979; JD, Seton Hall U., 1982. Bar: N.J. 1983, U.S. Dist. Ct. N.J. 1983, U.S. Ct. Appeals (3d cir.) 1986. Law clk. to presiding justice Superior Ct. N.J., Hackensack, 1982-83; staff atty. Bergen County Legal Svcs., Hackensack, 1983—. Instr. Am. Inst. Paralegal Studies, Mahwah, N.J., 1986-95; atty. Lyndhurst (N.J.) Planning Bd., 1987-89. Mem. ABA, Fed. Bar Assn., N.J. State Bar Assn., Bergen County Bar Assn., Emblem Club. Democrat. Roman Catholic. Administrative and regulatory, Land use and zoning (including planning), Landlord-tenant. Office: Northeast NJ Legal Svcs 61 Kansas St Hackensack NJ 07601-5351

NAVRAT, CHRISTOPHER TODD, lawyer; b. Oklahoma City, Nov. 7, 1968; s. Robert John Navrat and Harriett Janet Krasuski; m. Stephanie Bess Fite; 1 child, Hallie Katherine. BS in Bus. Adminstrn. and Acctg., U. Kans., 1991, MS in Bus., 1992; JD, Washburn U., 1995. Assoc. atty. Wallaly, Saunders et. al., Overland Park, Kans., 1996—97, Hillix, Brower, et. al., Kansas City, Kans., 1997—98; sr. atty. Layne Christensen Co., Westwood, Kans., 1998—2001, Hallmark Cards, Inc., Kansas City, Mo., 2001—. Reform. Roman Catholic. Office: Hallmark Cards Inc 2501 McGee MD 339 Kansas City MO 64141

NAYLOR, PAUL DONALD, lawyer; b. St. Bernard, Ohio, May 28, 1925; s. David Frederick and Erna Helen (Miller) N.; m. Geraldine L. Lacy, Jan. 20, 1945; children: Linda S., Paul Scott, Todd L. JD, U. Cin., 1948. Bar: Ohio 1948. Ptnr. Pulse & Naylor, Cin., 1949-65; pvt. practice Cin., 1965—. Mem. Nat. Rep. Com. Lt. (j.g.) USN, 1943-46. Recipient Svc. to Mankind award Sertoma Internat. Mem. Cin. Bar Assn. (real property com. 1966-86), Ohio Bar Assn., Cin. Lawyers Club (pres. 1955), Order of the Coif. Property, real (including real estate development, water). Office: 30 E Central Pky Ste 210 Cincinnati OH 45202-1118

NAZETTE, RICHARD FOLLETT, lawyer; b. Eldora, Iowa, July 27, 1919; s. Hilmer H. and Genevieve A. (Follett) N.; m. Joan Chehak, June 20, 1942; children— Ronald D., Randall A. BA, U. Iowa, 1942, JD with distinction, 1946. Bar: Iowa bar 1946. Practiced in, Cedar Rapids, 1946—; partner firm Nazette, Marner, Wendt, Knoll & Usher, 1968—; asst. atty. Linn County, Iowa, 1951-56; county atty., 1957-63. Dir. United States Bank, Cedar Rapids, 1968-91, State Surety Co., Des Moines, 1966-78 Bd. dirs. Linn County Health Center, 1968-73, chmn., 1968-69; mem. Iowa Bd. Parole, 1981-84. Served with AUS, 1942-44. Fellow Am. Bar Found., Iowa Bar Assn. (bd. govs. 1972-76), Iowa State Bar Found.; mem. Linn County Bar Assn. (pres. 1963), Iowa County Attys. Assn. (pres. 1959), Iowa Acad. Trial Lawyers (pres. 1964), Sigma Phi Epsilon. Clubs: Masons, Shriners, Jesters, Elks, Optimists (internat. v.p. 1955), Scottish Rite KCCH. Republican. Presbyterian. General practice, Probate (including wills, trusts), Property, real (including real estate development, water). Home: 100 Thompson Dr SE #124 Cedar Rapids IA 52403 Office: 100 1st St SW Cedar Rapids IA 52404-5701 E-mail: r.nazette@nazmar.com.

NEACSU, E. DANA, law librarian, lawyer; b. Pucioasa, Romania, May 20, 1967; arrived in U.S., 1996; d. Paul Mircea Galopenta and Viorica Neacsu; m. Mickey Davis, June 21, 1996; children: Abby Davis, Zoe Davis. Diploma, U. Bucharest, Romania, 1989; DEA, Caen Faculte de Droit, France, 1991; LLM, Harvard U., 1994; MLS, CCNY, 2000. Bar: NY 1997. Asst. prof. law U. Bucharest, 1991—94; atty. Bickel & Brewer, N.Y.C., 1997—98; asst. corp. counsel Corp. Coun. Office, N.Y.C., 1998—2000; law reference libr. Columbia Law Sch., N.Y.C., 2000—. Contbr. articles to profl. jours. Mem.: N.Y.C. Bar Assn., Harvard Club. Office: Columbia U Law Sch Libr 435 W 116th St New York NY 10027

NEAL, CHARLES D., JR., lawyer; b. McAlester, Okla., Jan. 4, 1949; BSBA, Okla. State U., 1972; JD Okla. City U., 1975. Bar: Okla. 1975, U.S. Dist. Ct. Okla. (ea., we., no. dists.), U.S. Dist. Ct. Ark. (ea. and we. dists.), U.S. Ct. Appeals (10th, 8th and 5th cirs.), U.S. Supreme Ct. Ptnr. Steidley & Neal, McAlester, 1976—; mcpl. judge Kiowa, Okla., 1981—88, Krebs, Okla., 1981—. Fellow: Okla. Bar Found. (trustee 1998—2001), Am. Bar Found.; mem.: Okla. Assn. Def. Counsel, Def. Rsch. Inst., Pittsburg County Bar Assn. (pres. 1980—81), Okla. Bar Assn. (pres. 2001—02), ABA (ho. dels. 2000—01). Insurance. Office: Steidley & Neal 100 E Carl Albert Pkwy PO Box 1165 Mcalester OK 74502

NEAL, EDWARD GARRISON, lawyer; b. Abingdon, Va., Mar. 20, 1940; s. James Wiley Neal and Edna Mae (Felty) Millsap; m. Diane T. Neal, Feb. 16, 2002; children: Jay Garrison, Heather Leigh. BA, Fla. State U., 1962; JD, U. Balt., 1966; LLM, George Washington U., Washington, 1969. Bar: Md. 1966, U.S. Dist. Ct. Md. 1968, U.S. Supreme Ct. 1972. Asst. trust officer Md. Nat. Bank, Balt., 1964-66; gen. counsel Hatch Act Study Commn., Washington, 1967; exec. asst. U.S. Sen. Daniel Brewster, Washington, 1966-68; asst. states atty. Office of States Atty., Balt., 1968-71; chief criminal div. States Atty. Prince George's County, Upper Marlboro, Md., 1971-76; assoc. county atty. Prince George's County Office of Law, Upper Marlboro, 1976-79; pvt. practice College Park, Md., 1979—. Law lectr. Prince Georges County and Md. State Police Acads., 1971—76; law lectr. U.S. Secret Svc. Fed. Law Enforcement Tng. Ctr., 2000—; legal advisor Office Tech. Assistance U.S. Treasury Dept., Moldova, 1999; spl. reporter Md. criminal rules com. Prince Georges County and Md. State Police Acads. Vice chmn. Women's Sexual Assault Commn., Upper Marlboro, Md., 1974—75; pres. PTA Concordia Luth. Sch., Hyattsville, Md., 1976—77; Dem. precinct chmn. University Park, Md., 1972—80; pres. bd. trustees Rossborough Festival, Kapell Internat. Piano Competition, College Park, 1986—89, 1989—. Recipient cert. of Appreciation, Prince George's County Coun., Upper Marlboro, Md., 1975. Mem.: Nat. Dist. Attys. Assn. (scholarship award 1968, 1970, 1975, 1976), Md. State's Attys. Assn. (legislative liaison Md. Gen. Assembly 1972—76), Md. State Bar Assn. (various coms.), George Washington U. Alumni Assn. (bd. dirs. 1980—), Fla. State U. Varsity Club, Kiwanis, Phi Alpha Delta (dist. v.p. 1962—, pres. 1963). Episcopalian. Avocations: music, reading, tennis, basketball, bridge. General civil litigation, Criminal, Personal injury (including property damage). Home: Ste 1613 6100 Westchester Park Dr College Park MD 20740-2847 Office: 7309 Baltimore Ave Ste 117 College Park MD 20740-3200

NEAL, JAMES F. lawyer; b. Sumner County, Tenn., Sept. 7, 1929; s. Robert Gus and Emma Clendenning N.; m. Victoria Jackson , Mar. 21, 1985 (div.); children: James F., Julie Ellen; m. Dianne Ferrell Neal, March 3, 1990. BS, U. Wyo., 1952; LL.B., Vanderbilt U., 1957; L.L.M., Georgetown U., 1960. Bar: Tenn. 1957, D.C. 1958. Asso. firm Turney & Turney, 1957-60; spl. asst. to Atty. Gen. U.S., 1961-64; U.S. atty. for Middle Dist. of Tenn., 1964-66; partner Cornelius Collins Neal & Higgins, Nashville, 1966-70; partner firm Neal & Harwell, Nashville, 1971—. Assoc. spl. prosecutor Watergate prosecuting force, 1973, 74; lectr. law Vanderbilt U., 1966-79; chief counsel U.S. Senate Select Commn. on Undercover Ops., 1982; bd. dirs. Ingram Industries., Inc. Vice chmn. Nashville Human Rights Com., 1968-70; vice chmn. Nashville Urban League, 1969-71; dir. Lawyers Com. for Civil Rights Under Law, 1978— , Am. Bar Assn. Found. Served with USMCR, 1952-54. Mem. Am. Bar Assn., Tenn. Bar Assn., Fed. Bar Assn., Am. Coll. Trial Lawyers, Internat. Acad. Trial Lawyers, Bar Assn. D.C. Clubs: Richland Country, Nashville City. Office: 2000 One Nashville Pl 150 4th Ave N Nashville TN 37219-2415

NEAL, THOMAS FREDERICK, lawyer; b. Orlando, Fla., Jan. 18, 1960; s. Thomas Earl and Nina Delores (Tomarelli) N. BGS, U. Mich., 1982; JD, U. Fla., 1985. Bar: Fla. 1986, U.S. Dist. Ct. (mid. dist.) Fla. 1987, U.S. Ct. Appeals (11th cir.) 1987, U.S. Supreme Ct. 1991. Assoc. Sam E. Murrell & Sons, Orlando, 1986-87, Drage, de Beaubien, Knight & Simmons, Orlando, 1987-90, ptnr., 1990-92, Drage, deBeaubien, Knight Simmons, Mantzaris and Neal, Orlando, 1992—2002, de Beaubien, Knight, Simmons, Mantzaris & Neal, 2002—. Bd. dirs., chmn. govt. rels. com. Lakeside Alternatives, Inc. Mem. ABA, ATLA, Orange County Bar Assn., Touchdown Club (bd. dirs., past pres.). Democrat. Roman Catholic. General civil litigation, Construction, General practice. Home: 4126 Shorecrest Dr Orlando FL 32804-2227 Office: de Beaubien Knight Simmons Mantzaris and Neal 332 N Magnolia Ave Orlando FL 32801-1609 E-mail: tneal@dbksmn.com.

NEALON, WILLIAM JOSEPH, JR., federal judge; b. Scranton, Pa., July 31, 1923; s. William Joseph and Ann Cannon (McNally) N.; m. Jean Sullivan, Nov. 15, 1947; children: Ann, Robert, William, John, Jean, Patricia, Kathleen, Terrence, Thomas, Timothy. Student, U. Miami, Fla., 1942-43; BS in Econs, Villanova U., 1947; LL.B., Cath. U. Am., 1950; LL.D. (hon.), U. Scranton, 1975. Bar: Pa. 1951. With firm Kennedy, O'Brien & O'Brien (and predecessor), Scranton, 1951-60; mem. Lackawanna County Ct. Common Pleas, 1960-62; U.S. dist. judge Middle Dist. Pa., 1962—, chief judge, 1976-88, sr. judge, 1989—. Mem. com. on adminstrn. of criminal law Jud. Conf. U.S., 1979— ; lectr. bus. law and labor law U. Scranton, 1951-59; mem. jud. council 3d Cir. Ct. Appeals, 1984—; dist. judge rep. from 3d Cir. Jud. Conf. of U.S., 1987—. Mem. Scranton Registration Commn., 1953-55; hearing examiner Pa. Liquor Control Bd., 1955-59; campaign dir. Lackawanna County chpt. Nat. Found., 1961-63; mem. Scranton-Lackawanna Health and Welfare Authority, 1963—; assoc. bd. Marywood Coll., Scranton; pres. bd. dirs. Cath. Youth Center; pres. Father's Club Scranton Prep. Sch., 1966; chmn. bd. dirs. Mercy Hosp., 1991-95; chmn. bd. trustees U. Scranton; vice chmn. bd. trustees Lackawanna Jr. Coll., Scranton; bd. dirs. St. Joseph's Children's and Maternity Hosp., 1963-66, Lackawanna County unit Am. Cancer Soc., Lackawanna County Heart Assn., Lackawanna County chpt. Pa. Assn. Retarded Children, Scranton chpt. ARC, Lackawanna United Fund, Mercy Hosp., Scranton, 1975— ; trustee St. Michael's Sch. Boys, Hoban Heights; adv. com. Hosp. Service Assn. Northeastern Pa. Served to 1st lt. USMCR, 1942-45. Recipient Americanism award Amos Lodge B'nai B'rith, 1975; Cyrano award U. Scranton Grad. Sch., 1977; Disting. Service award Pa. Trial Lawyers Assn., 1979; named one of 50 Disting. Pennsylvanians Greater Phila. C. of C., 1980, Outstanding Fed. Trial Judge Assn. Trial Lawyers Am., 1983 Mem. Pa. Bar Assn., Lackawanna County Bar Assn. (Chief Justice Michael J. Eagen award 1987), Friendly Sons St. Patrick (pres. Lackawanna County 1963-64), Pi Sigma Alpha. Clubs: Scranton Country (Clarks Summit, Pa.) (bd. dirs.). Lodges: K.C. Office: US Courthouse PO Box 1146 Scranton PA 18501-1146

NEARING, VIVIENNE W. lawyer; b. N.Y.C. d. Abraham M. and Edith Eunice (Webster) N. BA, Queens Coll.; MA, JD, Columbia U. Bar: N.Y., D.C., U.S. Dist. Ct. (so. and ea. dists.) N.Y., U.S. Ct. Appeals (2d cir.), U.S. Claims Ct. Ptnr. Stroock & Stroock & Lavan, N.Y.C. Mem. editorial bd. Communications and the Law, 1978-82, adv. bd. 1982—; mem. editorial bd. U.S. Trademark Reporter, 1982-86. Bd. dirs. Light Opera of Manhattan, 1981-82, Lyric Opera N.Y., 1984-90, Concert Artists Guild, 1989-91, Plays for Living, 1998—. Mem. ABA, Fed. Bar Coun., N.Y. State Bar Assn., U.S. Trademark Assn., Copyright Soc. U.S.A., N.Y. Lawyers for Pub. Interest (bd. dirs. 1983-87), Am. Arbitration Assn., Commn. for Law and Social Justice, Carnegie Coun., Women's City Club, Respect for Law Alliance. Federal civil litigation, Entertainment, Trademark and copyright. Office: Stroock Stroock & Lavan 180 Maiden Ln New York NY 10038-4982

NEBELONG, HENRIK, barrister; b. Copenhagen, June 22, 1944; s. Bent and Signe Clorius Nebelong; 1 child, Signe. Cand.Jur., U. Copenhagen, 1970. Bar: Denmark 1974. Barrister, Denmark, 1980. Head mission to Kosovo Advocats Sans Frontiers, Pristina, 1999—2000. Home: Fiolstraede 28 DK 1171 Copenhagen Denmark Office: Nebelong & Partnere Oestergade 16 DK 1007 Copenhagen Denmark Fax: +45 33324775. E-mail: hn@nebelong.dk.

NECCO, ALEXANDER DAVID, lawyer, educator; b. Gary, Ind., Jan. 31, 1936; s. Alesandro Necco and Mary Millonovich; m. Caroline Chappel, Apr. 20, 1958 (dec. Mar. 1978); 1 child, Laurie Ann Necco Stansbury; m. Edna Joanne Painter, July 1, 1989. BA in Philosophy, U. Nev., 1958; JD, Oklahoma City U., 1965. Bar: Okla. 1965, U.S. Dist. Ct. (we. dist.) Okla. 1965, U.S. Ct. Appeals (10th cir.) 1987), U.S. Ct. Claims 1989, U.S. Ct. Vets. Appeals 1994. Assoc. Robert Jordan, Oklahoma City, 1965-66, Stuckey & Witcher, Oklahoma City, 1968-69; atty. Okla. Hwy. Dept., Oklahoma City, 1966, Oklahoma City Urban Renewal, 1966-67; ptnr. Stuckey & Necco, Oklahoma City, 1969-71, Necco & Dyer, Oklahoma City, 1978-82, Dyer, Necco & Byrd, Oklahoma City, 1982-88; pvt. practice Oklahoma City, 1965—; ptnr. Necco & Byrd, Oklahoma City, 1988—. Adj. prof. Oklahoma City U. Sch. Bus., 1965—, Webster U., 1995—. Cubmaster Boy Scouts Am., Oklahoma City. With USMC, 1953-82, lt. col. Res. ret. Named Pro-bono Atty. of Month Okla. County. Mem.: ABA, Okla. Trial Lawyers Assn., Assn. Trial Lawyers Assn., Marine Corps Res. Officers Assn. (pres. Oklahoma City chpt. 1984—85), Sigma Nu, Phi Delta Phi. Republican. Roman Catholic. Avocations: golf, swimming, tennis. General civil litigation, Family and matrimonial, Probate (including wills, trusts). Office: Necco & Byrd PC Landmark Towers W 3555 NW 58th St Ste 130 Oklahoma City OK 73112-1662 E-mail: dnecco@neccoandbyrd.com.

NECKERS, BRUCE WARREN, lawyer; b. Jamestown, N.Y., May 13, 1943; s. Carlyle and Doris (Van Lente) N.; m. Susan E. Sonnevelot, June 17, 1967; children: Matthew, Melissa, Allison. BA, Hope Coll., Holland, Mich., 1965; JD, Ohio State U., 1968. Bar: Mich. 1968, Ohio 1968, U.S. Dist. Ct. (we. dist.) Mich. 1968. Assoc., ptnr. Mohey, Goodrich & Titta, Grand Rapids, Mich., 1968-87; ptnr. Rhoades McKee , Grand Rapids, 1987—, chmn. exec. com., 1994—. Chmn. gen. program coun., mem. gen. synod exec. com., mem., officer Exec. Found., Ref. Ch. in Am. Fellow Mich. Bar Found.; mem. Fed. Bar Assn. (pres. Western Mich. chpt. 1980-81), State Bar Mich. (pres. 2001-02), Grand Rapids Bar Assn. (pres. 1991-92). Avocations: all sports, golf, skiing. General civil litigation, Personal injury (including property damage), Product liability. Office: Rhoades McKee 161 Ottawa Ave NW Ste 600 Grand Rapids MI 49503-2766

NEEL, SAMUEL ELLISON, lawyer; b. Kansas City, Mo., Feb. 22, 1914; s. Ellison Adger and Serena (Smith) N.; m. Mary Wilson, Oct. 11, 1941; children: James Adger, Amy Bowen, Wilson (dec. 1947), Wendy Busselle,

Mary Ellison, Sophia Talbot. BA, Westminster Coll., Mo., 1935, LLD, 1995; LLB, Yale U., 1938. Bar: Mo. 1938, D.C. 1946, Va. 1953. Spl. asst. to atty. gen. anti-trust div. U.S. Dept. Justice, Washington, 1938-40, rep. State-War Dept. Mission on Japanese Combines, 1946; legal staff adv. commn. Coun. Nat. Def., OPM, WPB, 1940-42; pvt. practice Washington and McLean, Va., 1946-93. Bd. dirs. emeritus Rouse Co.; v.p., dir. Image Hunter Publ. Co., 1997-99. Mem. Fed. City Coun., Washington, 1954-58; pres. McLean Citizens Assn., 1953-54, Pub. Utilities Commn., Fairfax County, Va., 1956-57, The Squam Lakes Assn., N.H., 1987-89; chmn. Fairfax County Water Authority, 1957-63, Fairfax County Housing Authority, 1970-72; mem. adv. com. mortgage fin. FHA, 1956-66; pres. Neel Found.; trustee Westminster Coll. Comdr. USNR, 1942-46; staff comdr. air forces Pacific Fleet. Mem. Mortgage Bankers Assn. Am. (exec. v.p. 1965-66, gen. counsel 1946-74), Soc. Cin., Beta Theta Pi, Omicron Delta Kappa. Democrat. Episcopalian (past trustee). Clubs: Lawyers (Washington), Metropolitan (Washington); N.Y. Yacht. Home: 1157 Chain Bridge Rd Mc Lean VA 22101 Office: PO Box 385 Mc Lean VA 22101

NEELY, RICHARD, lawyer; b. Aug. 2, 1941; s. John Champ and Elinore (Forlani) N.; m. Carolyn Elaine Elmore, 1979; children: John Champ, Charles Whittaker. AB, Dartmouth Coll., 1964; LLB, Yale U., 1967. Bar: W.Va. 1967. Practiced in, Fairmont, W.Va., 1969-73; chmn. Marion County Bd. Pub. Health, 1971-72; mem. W.Va. Ho. of Dels., 1971-73; justice, chief justice W.Va. Supreme Ct. of Appeals, Charleston, 1973-95; ptnr. Neely & Hunter, Charleston, 1995—. Chmn. bd. Kane & Keyser Co., Belington, W.Va., 1970-88. Author: How Courts Govern America, 1980, Why Courts Don't Work, 1983, The Divorce Decision, 1984, Judicial Jeopardy: When Business Collides with the Courts, 1986, The Product Liability Mess: How Business Can Be Rescued from State Court Politics, 1988, Take Back Your Neighborhood: A Case for Modern-Day Vigilantism, 1990, Tragedies of our Own Making: How Private Choices have Created Public Bankruptcy, 1994; contbr. articles to nat. mags. Mem. bd. advisors BNA Class Action Litigation Report. Capt. U.S. Army, 1967-69. Decorated Bronze Star, Vietnam Honor medal 1st Class. Fellow: Internat. Acad. of Trial Lawyers; mem.: Am. Legion, VFW, Fourth Cir. Jud. Conf. (life), Internat. Brotherhood Elec. Workers, W.Va. Bar Assn., Moose, Phi Sigma Kappa, Phi Delta Phi. Episcopalian. Federal civil litigation, General civil litigation, State civil litigation. Office: Neely & Hunter 159 Summers St Charleston WV 25301-2134

NEELY, SALLY SCHULTZ, lawyer; b. L.A., Mar. 2, 1948; BA, Stanford U., 1970, JD, 1971. Bar: Ariz. 1972, Calif. 1977. Law clk. to judge U.S. Ct. appeals (9th cir.), Phoenix, 1971-72; assoc. Lewis and Roca, Phoenix, 1972-75; asst. prof. Law Sch. Harvard U., Cambridge, Mass., 1975-77; assoc. Shutan & Trost, P.C., L.A., 1977-79; ptnr., sr. counsel Sidley & Austin, L.A., 1980—. Mem. faculty Am. Law Inst.-ABA Chpt. 11 Bus. Reorgns., 1989-95, 97—, Banking and Comml. Lending Law, 1997-99, Nat. Conf. Bankruptcy Judges, 1988, 90, 95, 96, 97, 99, 2002, Fed. Jud. Ctr., 1989, 90, 94-95, Southeast Bankruptcy Law Inst., 2002, Workshop Bankruptcy and Bus. Reorgn. NYU, 1992—; rep. 9th cir. jud. conf., 1989-91; mem. Nat. Bankruptcy Conf., 1993—, co-chair com. on legislation, 2001-. Chair Stanford U. Law Sch. Reunion Giving, 1996; bd. vis. Stanford U. Law Sch., 1990-92. Mem. ABA, Am. Coll. Bankruptcy (regent-at--large 1998-2003, trustee 2003—), Calif. Bar Assn. Bankruptcy. Office: Sidley Austin Brown & Wood LLP 555 W 5th St Ste 4000 Los Angeles CA 90013-3000 E-mail: sneely@sidley.com.

NEELY, WILLIAM F. lawyer; b. Abingdon, Va., Dec. 3, 1951; s. John D. and Ann F. Neely; m. Vickie M. Neely, July 27, 1974; 1 child, Sarah. BA, Emory and Henry Coll., 1974; JD, U. Richmond, 1981. Assoc. Martin, Corboy Hartley, Pearisburg, Va., 1981-82; asst. commonwealth's atty. Spotsylvania (Va.) County C.A., 1982-88, commonwealth atty., 1988—. Mem. Spotsylvania County Dem. Com., 1988—; charter mem., elder Spotsylvania Presbyn. Ch., 1984—; legal advisor Spotsylvania Vol. Rescue Squad, 1986-97. Mem. Lions Club. Democrat. Presbyterian. Office: PO Box 2629 Spotsylvania VA 22553-6816 E-mail: bneely@spotsylvania.va.us.

NEFF, A. GUY, lawyer; b. Calcutta, India, Mar. 24, 1951; BA, Vanderbilt U., 1972; JD, U. Fla., 1975. Bar: Fla. 1975. Lawyer Holland & Knight, LLP, Orlando, Fla. Mem. ABA, Fla. Bar Assn., Phi Delta Phi (magister 1975). Banking, Private international, Property, real (including real estate development, water). Office: Holland & Knight LLP 200 S Orange Ave Ste 2600 Orlando FL 32801-3453

NEFF, CAROLE CUKELL, lawyer; b. Geneva, N.Y., Aug. 3, 1951; d. Samuel and Hannah (Schoenfeld) C.; m. Richard Theodore Neff, Dec. 28, 1976; children: Alex Ryan, Hilary Shayna. BS magna cum laude, SUNY, Buffalo, 1973; JD, Tulane U., 1977. Bar: La. 1977. Law clk. La. State Supreme Ct., New Orleans, 1977—78; assoc. Session & Fishman, New Orleans, 1978—83; ptnr. Session, Fishman & Nathan, LLP, New Orleans, 1983—. Co-author: (with Mas Natzen) Louisiana Estate Planning, Will Drafting and Estate Administration 2nd ed., 2000; mem. bd. editors Tulane U. Law Rev. Bd. dirs., 1st v.p., sec., chmn. devel. com. Jewish Endowment Found., New Orleans, 1983—. Named Achiever, Am. Coun. for Career Women, 1990, Woman of Yr., New Orleans Bus. and Profl. Women, 1991, YWCA Role Model, 1992. Fellow Am. Coll. Trust and Estate Counsel; mem. NCJW, ABA, La. Bar Assn., New Orleans Bar Assn. (CLE chair 1987-89, 3d v.p. 1989-90, probate chair 1991-2000), Women's Profl. Coun. (bd. dirs., 1st v.p. 1989-90, pres. 1990-91), Profl. Fin. Planners of Greater New Orleans (sec. 1982-83, pres. 1983-84), New Orleans Estate Planning Coun. (pres. 2002-03), Order of Coif, Rotary Internat. (bd. dirs. 1994-96), Hadassah. Democrat. Jewish. Avocations: cooking, piano playing, travel. Estate planning, Probate (including wills, trusts). Office: Session Fishman & Nathan LLP 201 Saint Charles Ave Ste 3500 New Orleans LA 70170-3500

NEFF, MICHAEL ALAN, lawyer; b. Springfield, Ill., Sept. 4, 1940; s. Benjamin Ezra and Ann (Alpert) N.; m. Lin Laghi, Mar. 26, 1977; 1 son, Aaron Benjamin. Student, U. Ill., 1958-61; BA, U. Calif., Berkeley, 1963, postgrad., 1963-64; JD, Columbia U., 1967. Bar: N.Y. 1967, U.S. Dist. Ct. (so. and ea. dists.) N.Y. 1969, U.S. Ct. Appeals (2d cir.) 1988, U.S. Supreme Ct. 1988. Congl. intern U.S. Ho. of Reps., 1965; assoc. Sage, Gray, Todd & Sims, N.Y.C., 1967-74, Fellner & Rovins, N.Y.C., 1974-75; ptnr. Poier, Tulin, Clark & Neff, N.Y.C., 1976-77; pvt. practice N.Y.C., 1977-83; pres. private practice, 1983—. Counsel St. Dominic's Home, 1971-74, Louise Wise Services, 1976-77, Edwin Gould Service for Children, 1969-79, 76—, Family Service of Westchester, Inc., 1977-87, The Children's Village, 1977-84, Brookwood Child Care, 1980— , Forestdale, 1988—, Fam. Support Systems Unlimited, 1990—, Educational Assistance Corp., 1990-95, Coalition for Hispanic Family Services, 1992-93, Soc. Children and Families, 1996—, Pius XII Youth and Family Services, 2000—, Child Developmen Support Corp, 2001—, Hale House Ctr., Inc., 2001—; teaching asst. U. Calif., 1963-64; instr. Social Welfare Policy and Law, Marymount Manhattan Coll., 1973; mem. Indigent Defendant's Legal Panel, Appellate Div., First Dept., 1974-84; participant N.Y. State Conf. on Children's Rights, 1974; asst. sec. Edwin Gould Services for Children, 1977—; cons. N.Y. Task Force on Permanency Planning For Children in Foster Care, 1985-90, N.Y. State Foster and Adoptive Parent Assn., Inc., 1988—, N.Y. Spaulding for Children, 1988-90, Ct. Appointed Spl. Advocates, 1988-91; instr. adoption law in N.Y., City Bar Ctr. for CLE, 2001—; mem. Adoption Adv. Com. N.Y. State Dept. Social Svcs., 1997-98; advisor Nat. Resource Ctr. for Foster Care and Permanency Planning, 2000—; trainer Inst. for Families and Children, 1992-95, New York City Adminstrn. for Children's services, 1996-97; facilitator Parenting Journey, 2000—; group leader Model Approach to Partnerships in Parenting, 2001—. Author: Freeing Foster Children for Adoption, A Child's Right to a Plan of Permanency, 1972, Permanent Neglect Proceedings, 1980, Adoption Proceedings, Basic Matrimonial Practice in New York, 1980, Foster Parenting Handbook, 1997 Adopting Foster Children: A Handbook for Foster Parents, 1999, Permanency Planning ASFA,Best Practices: A Handbook for Caseworkers, 2000; Contbr. articles to profl. jours. Mem. Protestant Bd. of Guardians, 2001—. Mem. ABA, Am. Acad. Adoption Attys., Assn. Bar City of N.Y. (mem. com. on children and law, family law sect.). State civil litigation, Family and matrimonial, General practice. Home: 5 W 86th St Apt 6B New York NY 10024-3664 Office: 36 W 44th St Ste 1212 New York NY 10036-8102 E-mail: manpc@aol.com.

NEFF, ROBERT CAREY, lawyer; b. Orange, N.J., Nov. 9, 1935; s. Walter Holt and Nan Carey Neff; m. Shirley Ruth Fitzeram, May 6, 1961; children: Robert C. Jr., Sandra Wilichowski, Carl J., Thomas H. BA, Yale U., 1957; LLB, Georgetown U., 1964. Cert. N.J. 1965, U.S. Dist. Ct. N.J. 1965, U.S. Supreme Ct. 1965. Assoc. Carey & Jardine, Newark, 1965-67; ptnr. Meth, Wood Neff & Cooper, Newark, 1967-76, Shanley & Fisher, Newark, 1976-82, Kraft & Hughes, Newark, 1982-87, Pitney, Hardin, Kipp & Szuch, Morristown, N.J., 1987—. Trustee N.J. Cmty. Found., Morristown, 1990-97, Riverview Hosp. Found., 2002—; commr. N.J. State Racing Commn., 1986-90; mem. Rumson Fair Haven Regional Bd. Edn., 1985-86; councilman Borrough of Shrewsbury, N.J., 1969-71. Capt. USMCR, 1957-61. Fellow Am. Coll. of Trust and Estate Counsel; mem. ABA (chmn. com. legal svcs. for elderly 1989-91), N.J. Bar Assn. Republican. Roman Catholic. Estate planning, Probate (including wills, trusts), Estate taxation. Home: 85 Grange Ave Fair Haven NJ 07704-3039 Office: Pitney Hardin Kipp & Szuch 125 Halfmile Rd Red Bank NJ 07701

NEFF, ROBERT MATTHEW, lawyer, financial services executive; b. Huntington, Ind., Mar. 26, 1955; s. Robert Eugene and Ann (Bash) N.; m. Lee Ann Loving, Aug. 23, 1980; children: Alexandra, Graydon, Philip. BA in English, DePauw U., 1977; JD, Ind. U., Indpls., 1980. Bar: Ind. 1980, U.S. Dist. Ct. (so. dist.) Ind. 1980, U.S. Supreme Ct., 1993. Assoc. Krieg, DeVault, Alexander & Capehart, Indpls., 1980-85, ptnr., 1986-88; ptnr. Baker & Daniels, Indpls., 1988-92; of counsel, 1993-96; dept. to chmn. Fed. Housing Fin. Bd., Washington, 1992-93; pres., CEO Circle Investors, Inc., Indpls., 1993-97, also bd. dirs.; chmn., CEO Senex Fin. Corp., Indpls., 1998—. Mem. faculty Grad. Sch. of Banking of South, 1988—90; chmn. Liberty Bankers Life Ins. Co., 1995—98, Am. Founders Life Ins. Co., Laurel Life Ins. Co., Aztek Life Assurance Co., 1996—97. Exec. editor Ind. Law Rev., 1979-80. Participant Lacy Exec. Leadership Conf., Indpls., 1985-86; trustee DePauw U., 1977-80; bd. govs. Riley Children's Found., 1999—. Mem. ABA (chmn. bus. law com. young lawyers divsn. 1988-90, banking law com. 1990-92), Ind. Bar Assn. (chmn. corps. banking and bus. law sect. 1987-88), DePauw Alumni Assn. (bd. dirs. 1982-88), Phi Kappa Psi, Phi Beta Kappa. Avocations: Tae Kwon Do, golf. Banking, Corporate, general, Securities. Home: 7202 Merriam Rd Indianapolis IN 46240 Office: Senex Fin Corp 3500 DePauw Blvd # 3050 Indianapolis IN 46268 E-mail: neffrm@senexco.com.

NEGRON, FRANCISCO MARIA, JR., lawyer; b. Ancon, Canal Zone, Oct. 1, 1964; s. Francisco Maria Negron-Cadiz and Telva Eneida Negron-Alzamora; life ptnr. James Daniel Scott, Aug. 1, 1992. BA, U. West Fla., 1986; JD, Fla. State U., 1991. Bar: Fla. 1992. Law clk. Eubanks & Barrett, Tallahassee, 1989—91; trial ct. law clk. First Jud. Cir. Ct., Pensacola, Fla., 1991—93; asst. atty. gen. Fla. Office Atty. Gen., Tallahassee, 1993—96; staff counsel Fla. Edn. Assn./United, Tallahassee, 1996—2000; gen. counsel Sch. Bd. Escambia County, Pensacola, Fla., 2000—. Pres., co-founder Hispanic Bar Assn., Tallahassee, 1989—99, bd. dirs., 1999—2000; co-chair Pub. Svc. Fellows Fla. State U. Coll. Law, Tallahassee, 1989—90; vice chair subcom. on the rights of children ABA, Washington, 1999; presenter in field. Contbr. articles to profl. jours. Com. mem. Escambia County Dem. Exec. Com., Pensacola, Fla., 2002; dir. Girl Scout Coun. Of The Appalachee Big Bend, Tallahassee, 1989—2000, Big Bend Cares, Tallahassee, 1989—2000. First lt. USAR, 1986—92. Named Best Report Writer, Guardian At Litem Program-Second Jud. Cir., 1997; recipient Outstanding Work In A Juvenile Case award, 1995, Recognition For Outstanding Support To The Hispanic Heritage Month Commemoration Program, Fed. Prison Camp, Pensacola, 2000, Liberty Bell award, Freedoms Found. Valley Forge, Pensacola Chpt., 2002, George Wash. medal, 2002; Pub. Svc. fellow, Fla. State U. Coll. Law, 1989—91. Mem.: Coun. Sch. Attys., Fla. Sch. Bd. Attys. Assn., Hispanic Bar Assn. of the Second Jud. Cir. (pres., co-founder 1998—99, bd. dirs. 1998—2000, Cert. of Appreciation 1999), Escambia/Santa Rosa Bar Assn. (treas. 2002—03, mem. exec. coun. 2001—, chair law week com. 2002, President's award 2002), Pensacola Am. Inn Ct., Pensacola Rotary Club. Roman Catholic. Avocations: writing, sketching, woodworking, piano. Office: Sch Bd Escambia County Fla 215 West Garden St Pensacola FL 32501 Office Fax: 850-469-6303. E-mail: fnegron@escambia.k12.fl.us.

NEGRON-GARCIA, ANTONIO S. former territory supreme court justice; b. Rio Piedras, P.R., Dec. 31, 1940; s. Luis Negron-Fernandez and Rosa M. Garcia-Saldana; m. Gloria Villardefrancos-Vergara, May 26, 1962; 1 son, Antonio Rogelio. BA, U. P.R., 1962, LL.B., 1964. Bar: P.R. bar 1964. Law aide and lawyer legal div. Water Resources Authority, 1962-64; judge Dist. Ct., 1964-69, Superior Ct., 1969-74; justice P.R. Supreme Ct., San Juan, 1974—; administrating judge, 1969-71; exec. officer Constl. Bd. for Revision Senatorial and Rep. Dists., 1971-72; mem. Jud. Conf., 1974—2000; first exec. sec. Council for Reform of System of Justice in P.R., 1973-74; prof. InterAmerican U. Puerto Rico, 2001—. Chmn. Gov.'s Advisory Com. for Jud. Appointments, 1973-74; lectr. U. P.R. Law Sch., 1973-74 Mem. P.R. Bar Assn., Am. Judicature Soc. Roman Catholic. Office: Univ InterAmericana de Puerto Rico Apartado 70351 San Juan PR 00936-8351*

NEHRBASS, SCOTT C. lawyer; b. Topeka, Kans., Nov. 23, 1966; s. Carl Herbert and Connie Kay Nehrbass; m. Jennifer Ann Nehrbass, Aug. 17, 1991; children: John Carl, Andrew Scott. BA in Econs./Polit. Sci., Kans. U., 1989, JD, 1993. Bar: Kans. 1993, Mo. 1995, U.S. Ct. Appeals (10th cir.), U.S. Supreme Ct. Law clk. to U.S. Dist. judge U.S. Dist. Ct. Kans., Wichita, 1993-95; assoc. Shook, Hardy & Bacon LLP, Overland Park, Kans., 1995—2002, ptnr., 2002—. Co-author: Kansas Federal Practice Handbook; contbr. articles to profl. jours. Precinct committeman Rep. Party, Johnson County, 1998-2000; bd. dirs. Children's Benefits Svcs. for Families, Kansas City, 1998—. Mem. Johnson County Bar Assn., Kans. Bar Assn., Christian Legal Soc., Kans. Assn. of Def. Counsel. Office: Shook Handy and Bacon LLP 84 Mastin Rd Overland Park KS 66225

NEIDELL, MARTIN H. lawyer; b. Bklyn., Apr. 5, 1946; s. Sidney B. and Sophie (Goldstein) N.; m. Suzan C. Rucker, June 23, 1968; children: Michael, Sari. BA magna cum laude, Lehigh U., 1968; JD cum laude, NYU, 1971. Bar: N.Y. 1972, U.S. Dist. Ct. (ea. and so. dists.) N.Y. 1973, U.S. Ct. Appeals (2d cir.) 1973. Law clk. to presiding justice U.S. Dist. Ct. (ea. dist.) N.Y., Bklyn., 1971-73; assoc. Stroock & Stroock & Lavan LLP, N.Y.C., 1973-79; ptnr. Stroock & Stroock & Lavan, N.Y.C., 1980—. Sec. Page Am. Group, Hackensack, N.J., 1983—. Editor NYU Law Rev., 1971. Trustee North Shore Synagogue, Syosset, N.Y., 1984-90. Mem. ABA. Corporate, general, Mergers and acquisitions, Securities. Office: Stroock & Stroock & Lavan LLP 180 Maiden Ln New York NY 10038-4925

NEIDICH, GEORGE ARTHUR, lawyer; b. N.Y.C., Feb. 22, 1950; s. Hyman and Rosalyn N.; m. Alene Wendrow, Jan. 10, 1982; 1 child, Hannah Lauren. BA, SUNY, Binghamton, 1971; JD magna cum laude, SUNY, Buffalo, 1974; MLT, Georgetown U., 1981. Bar: N.Y. 1975, D.C. 1979, Va. 1996, Conn. 1990. Assoc. Runfola & Birzon, Buffalo, 1973-75, Duke, Holzman, Yaeger & Radlin, Buffalo, 1975-77; gen. counsel subcom. on capital, investments and bus. opportunity, com. on small bus. U.S. Ho. of Reps., Washington, 1977-79, subcom. on gen. oversight, 1979-80; sr. legal advisor Task Force Product Liability and Accident Compensation Office of Gen. Counsel, Dept. Commerce, Washington, 1980-81; assoc. Steptoe & Johnson, Washington, 1981-86, of counsel, 1986-89; gen. counsel, sr. v.p. Preferred Health Care, Ltd., Wilton, Conn., 1989-93; COO Value Behavioral Health, Inc., Falls Church, Va., 1993-95; counsellor at law, 1995—; gen. counsel CareAdvantage, Inc., Iselin, NJ, 1999—. Adj. prof. Georgetown U. Law Ctr., 1985-87. Author: Report on Product Liability, 1980; contbr. articles to profl. jours. Corporate, general, Health. Office: 9301 Morison Ln Great Falls VA 22066-4153 E-mail: gneidich@aol.com.

NEILL, JOSEPH VINCENT, lawyer; b. St. Louis, Mar. 19, 1953; s. Thomas Patrick and Agnes J. Neill; m. Elizabeth Gidionsen, Dec. 27, 1986; children: John Francis, Joseph Holland, Thomas Patrick, Clare Elizabeth. Bar: Mo. 1977, U.S. Dist. Ct. (ea. dist.) Mo. 1977, U.S. Dist. Ct. (so. dist.) Ill. 1995, U.S. Ct. Appeals (8th cir.) 1988. Sole proprietor, St. Louis, 1978—. Mem. jud. commn. St. Louis Cir. Ct., 1986-91. Mem. bd. election commrs. City of St. Louis, 1994-2001. Democrat. Roman Catholic. General practice, Personal injury (including property damage), Workers' compensation. Office: 5201 Hampton Ave Saint Louis MO 63109-3102 E-mail: neill5300@aol.com.

NEIMAN, DONALD FLINT, lawyer; b. Hammond, Ind., Oct. 17, 1944; s. John Hammond and Madeline Clare (Flint) N.; m. Susan Maher, July 25, 1969; children: Amy Maher, Donald Flint II. BBA, U. Iowa, 1966; JD, Drake U., 1969. Bar: Iowa 1969, U.S. Dist. Ct. (no. and so. dists.) Iowa, Ct. Appeals (8th cir.). Pres., shareholder Neiman, Neiman, Stone & Spellman, PC, Des Moines, 1972-90, Bradshaw, Fowler, Proctor & Fairgrave PC, Des Moines, 1991—. Trustee U.S. Bankruptcy Ct., Des Moines, 1972—. Chmn. tax assessment com. West Des Moines, 1998-99, chmn. capital planning com., 1990-95. Capt. USAF, 1969-72. Mem.: Natl. Assn. of Bankruptcy Trustees, Federal Bar Assn., Iowa State Bar Assn. Republican. Roman Catholic. Avocations: handball, skiing, hunting. Bankruptcy, Commercial, contracts (including sales of goods; commercial financing). Office: Bradshaw Fowler Proctor et al 801 Grand Ave Ste 3700 Des Moines IA 50309-2727 E-mail: neiman.donald@bradshawlaw.com.

NEIS, JAMES MICHAEL, lawyer; b. Chgo., Mar. 3, 1946; BA, DePaul U., 1969, JD, 1973. Bar: Ill. 1973, U.S. Tax Ct. 1974. Ptnr. Winston & Strawn, Chgo., 1977-93, mng. ptnr., 1993—. Adj. prof. law DePaul U., 1979-86. Mem. ABA, Ill. State Bar Assn., Chgo. Bar Assn. Corporate, general, Taxation, general. Office: Winston & Strawn 35 W Wacker Dr Ste 4200 Chicago IL 60601-1695*

NEITER, GERALD IRVING, lawyer; b. L.A., Nov. 11, 1933; s. Harry and Ida Florence (Alperin) N.; m. Margaret P. Rowe, Mar. 5, 1961; children: David, Karen, Michael. BSL, JD, U. So. Calif., 1957. Bar: Calif. 1958. Judge pro tem Mcpl. Cts., L.A. and Beverly Hills, 1970-94; judge pro tem and mediator Calif. Superior Ct., L.A. County, 1974-94, family law mediator, 1976—; prin. Gerald I. Neiter, P.C., L.A., 1981—. Lectr. State Bar of Calif., 1968, 76, 79, 81; former referee State Bar Ct.; arbitrator Am. Arbitration Assn. Mem. Am., Los Angeles County (arbitrator), Beverly Hills, Century City bar assns., State Bar Calif. Office: 1925 Century Park E Ste 200 Los Angeles CA 90067-2701 E-mail: Neitlaw@aol.com.

NEITZKE, ERIC KARL, lawyer; b. Mobile, Ala., Dec. 10, 1955; s. Howard and Otti S. Neitzke; m. Kathryn Sloan; children: Kyle, Blake, Blaire. BA, U. Fla., 1979, JD, 1982. Bar: Fla. 1982, U.S. Dist. Ct. (mid. dist.) Fla. 1987. Asst. state atty. 7th Jud. Cir., State Atty., Daytona Beach, Fla., 1982; atty. Dunn, Smith & Withers, Daytona Beach, 1982-88, Monaco, Smith, Hood and Perkins, Daytona Beach, 1988—. Adj. faculty family law and criminal law Daytona C.C.; chmn. adv. com. Juvenile Detention Ctr. Contbr. articles to profl. jours. Mem. Fla. Acad. Trial Lawyers, Assn. Trial Lawyers Am., Volusia Bar Assn., Fla. Assn. Criminal Def. Lawyers, Phi Beta Kappa. Avocations: water sports, shooting, travel. Criminal, Family and matrimonial, Personal injury (including property damage). Home: 19 Lost Creek Ln Ormond Beach FL 32174-4840 Office: Eric K Neitzke PA 444 Seabreeze Blvd Ste 900 Daytona Beach FL 32118-3953

NELSON, BARBARA ANNE, judge; b. Mineola, N.Y., Jan. 16, 1951; d. Richard William and Dorothee Helen (Thorne) N. BA, Inter Am. U. P.R., 1972; JD, New Eng. Sch. Law, 1975. Legal editor Prentice Hall Pub. Co., Englewood Cliffs, N.J., 1976-77; assoc. Antonio C. Martinez Law Firm, N.Y.C., 1977-79, Pollack & Kramer, N.Y.C., 1979-83; pvt. practice N.Y.C., 1983-95; immigration judge U.S., N.Y.C., 1995—. Author, spkr., tng. film. Mem. ACLU, Legal Aid Soc. N.Y., Amnesty Internat., Asia Soc., Internat. Assn. Refugee Judges. Avocations: travel, yoga, foreign languages. Home: 324 W 14th St Apt 5A New York NY 10014-5003 Office: 26 Federal Plz New York NY 10278-0004 E-mail: nelsonferrets@yahoo.com.

NELSON, BRYAN MAYNARD, lawyer; b. Mpls., Mar. 28, 1949; BA, U. Minn., 1971; JD, Gonzaga U., 1977. Bar: Nev. 1977, U.S. Dist. Ct. Nev. 1978, U.S. Ct. Appeals (9th cir.) 1980, U.S. Supreme Ct. 1985. Chief dep. atty. gen. Nev., Carson City, 1980-90; pvt. practice, 1990—. Faculty for 20 seminars on AIDS related legal issues Nev. Atty. Gen. Office, 1985-90. Rep. nominee for Office of Atty. Gen., Nev., 1990; Christian conciliator. Mem. Assn. Trial Lawyers Am., Nev. Trial Lawyers Assn. Avocations: competitive cycling, skiing, roller hockey, motorcycling. Personal injury (including property damage). Office: 623 W Washington St Ste 2 Carson City NV 89703-3847

NELSON, CARL ROGER, retired lawyer; b. Gowrie, Ia., Dec. 26, 1915; s. Carl Helge and Inez Olivia (West) N.; m. Elizabeth Boswell Campbell, Apr. 27, 1946; children: Thomas C., Nancy L. AB, Grinnell Coll., 1937; MA, Columbia, 1938, LLB, 1941. Bar: N.Y. 1941, D.C. 1947, U.S. Supreme Ct. 1947. Law clk. to Chief Justice Stone, 1941-42; Washington asso. firm Root, Ballantine, Harlan, Bushby & Palmer, 1946-51; mem. firm Purcell & Nelson, Washington, 1951-80, Reavis & McGrath, 1980-83, Nelson Thurston Jones & Blouch, 1984-86. Mem. Adminstrv. Conf. U.S., 1967-73 Served to capt. AUS, 1942-46. Fellow Am. Bar Found.; mem. ABA (mem. ho. dels. 1964-66, mem. coun. 1960-66, chmn. sect. adminstrv. law 1963-64), Mediation Panel U.S. Ct. Appeals (D.C. cir.), Chevy Chase (Md.) Club, Lawyers Club (Washington), Met. Club (Washington), Phi Beta Kappa. Mem. United Ch. of Christ. Administrative and regulatory, Corporate, general.

NELSON, DAVID ALDRICH, judge; b. Watertown, N.Y., Aug. 14, 1932; s. Carlton Low and Irene Demetria (Aldrich) Nelson; m. Mary Dickson, Aug. 25, 1956; 3 children. AB, Hamilton Coll., 1954; postgrad., Cambridge U., Eng., 1954—55; LLB, Harvard U., 1958. Bar: Ohio 1958, N.Y. 1982. Atty.-advisor Office of the Gen. Counsel, Dept. of the Air Force, 1959—62; assoc. Squire, Sanders & Dempsey, Cleve., 1958—67, ptnr., 1967—69, 1972—85; judge U.S. Ct. Appeals (6th cir.), Cin., 1985—99, sr. judge, 1999—. Gen. counsel U.S. Post Office Dept., Washington, 1969—71; sr. asst. postmaster gen., gen. counsel U.S. Postal Svc., Washington, 1971; nat. coun. Ohio State U. Coll. Law, 1988—98. Trustee Hamilton Coll., 1984—88. Served to maj. USAFR, 1959—69. Recipient Fulbright scholarship, 1954—55, Benjamin Franklin award, U.S. Post Office Dept., 1969. Fellow: Am. Coll. Trial Lawyers; mem.: Cin. Bar Assn., Ohio Bar Assn., Fed. Bar Assn., Emerson Lit. Soc., Ct. of Nisi Prius (sgt. emeritus), Phi Beta Kappa. Office: US Ct Appeals 6th Cir Potter Stewart US Ct House 5th and Walnut St Cincinnati OH 45202-3988

NELSON, DOROTHY WRIGHT (MRS. JAMES F. NELSON), federal judge; b. San Pedro, Calif., Sept. 30, 1928; d. Harry Earl and Lorna Amy Wright; m. James Frank Nelson, Dec. 27, 1950; children: Franklin Wright, Lorna Jean. BA, UCLA, 1950, JD, 1953; LLM, U. So. Calif., 1956; LLD (hon.) , U. San Diego, 1997, U. So. Calif., 1983; LLD (hon.) , Georgetown U., 1988; LLD (hon.) , Whittier U., 1989, U. Santa Clara, 1990, Whittier U., 1989. Bar: Calif. 1954. Rsch. assoc. fellow U. So. Calif., 1953—56, instr., 1957, asst. prof., 1958—61, assoc. prof., 1961—67, prof., 1967—, assoc. dean., 1965—67, dean., 1967—80; judge U.S. Ct. Appeals 9th Cir., 1979—95, sr. judge, 1995—. Com. to consider stds. for admission to practice in fed. cts. Jud. Conf. U.S. , 1976—79; cons. project STAR Law Enforcement Assistance Adminstrn.; select com. on internal procedures Calif. Supreme Ct., 1987—; co-chair Sino-Am. Seminar on Mediation and Arbitration, Beijing, 1992. Contbr. articles to profl. jours.; author: Judicial Adminstration and The Administration of Justice, 1973; author: (with Christopher Goelz and Meredith Watts) Federal Ninth Circuit Civil Appellate Practice, 1995. Co-chair Confronting Myths in Edn. for Pres. Nixon's White House Conf. on Children, Pres. Carter's Commn. for Pension Policy, 1974—80; pres. Reagon's Madison Trust; active Nat. Spiritual Assembly of Bahais of U.S., 1967—; bd. dirs. Dialogue on Transition to a Global Soc., Weinacht, Switzerland, 1992; bd. vis. U.S. Air Force Acad., 1978; bd. dirs. Coun. on Legal Edn. for Profl. Responsibility, 1971—80, Constnl. Right Found., Am. Nat. Inst. for Social Advancement; adv. bd. Nat. Ctr. for State Cts., 1971—76; adv. com. to promote equality for woman and men in cts. Nat. Jud. Edn. Program; bd. dirs. Pacific Oaks Coll., Childrens Sch. & Rsch. Ctr., 1996—98; adv. bd. World Law Inst., 1997—, Tahirih Justice Inst., Washington, 1998—; chmn. bd. Western Justice Ctr., 1986—; chair 9th Cir. Standing Com. on Alternative Dispute Resolution, 1998—. Named Law Alumnus of Yr., UCLA, 1967, Woman of Yr., Times, 1968, Disting. Jurist, Ind. U. Law, 1994; recipient Profl. Achievement award, 1969, AWARE Internat. award, 1970, Humanitarian award, U. Judaism, 1973, Ernestine Stalhut Outstanding Woman Lawyer award, 1972, Pub. Svc. award, Coro Found., 1978, Pax Orbis ex Jure medal, World Peace thru Law Ctr., 1975, Hollzer Human Rights award, Jewish Fedn. Coun., 1988, Medal of Honor, UCLA, 1993, Emil Gumpert Jud. ADR Recognition award, L.A. County Bar Assn., 1996, Julia Morgan award, YWCA, 1997, Samuel E. Gates Litigation award, Am. Coll. Trial Lawyers, 1999, Bernard E. Witkin award, State Bar Assn. Calif., 2000, Judge of the Year award, Pasadena Bar Assn., 2002; fellow Lustman fellow, Yale U., 1977, Davenport Coll. Fellow: Davenport Coll., Am. Bar Found.; mem.: ABA (sect. on jud. adminstrn., chmn. com. on edn. in jud. adminstrn. 1973—89, D'Alemberte/Raven award 2000), Assn. Am. Law Schs. (chmn. com. edn. in jud. adminstrn.), Am. Judicature Soc. (bd. dirs., Justice award 1985), Bar Calif. (bd. dirs. continuing edn. bar commn. 1967—74), Order of Coif (nat. v.p. 1974—76), Phi Beta Kappa. Office: US Ct Appeals Cir 125 S Grand Ave Ste 303 Pasadena CA 91105-1621

NELSON, DOUGLAS CLARENCE, lawyer, consultant; b. Norfolk, Nebr., May 30, 1946; s. Clarence Nels Peter and DeLoris Ella (Kleveland) N. BS, U. Nebr., 1968, JD, 1971, MS, 1973, PhD in Resource Econs., 1981. Bar: Nebr. 1971, Ariz. 1976, U.S. Dist. Ct. Nebr., U.S. Dist. Ct. Ariz. Lectr. U. Nebr., Lincoln, 1971-73; property mgr. Northwestern Mut. Life Ins. Co., Milw., 1973-78; assoc. Rawlins, Ellis, Burris & Kiewit, Phoenix, 1978-81; pres. Douglas C. Nelson PC, Phoenix, 1981—. Mem. Maricopa County Flood Control Adv. bd., Phoenis, 1988-92; mem. adv. bd. Ariz. Water Resources Rsch. Ctr., 1987—; active Valley Leadership Assn., PHoenix; chmn. Ariz. Water Quality Appeals Bd., Phoenix, 1998. Recipient cert. of appreciation Am. Right of Way Assn., 1978, Hohakam Resource Conservation and Defel. Area, 1988, Prescott C. of C., 1990, Ariz. Planning Assn., 1991. Mem. FBA (pres. Ariz. chpt. 1983-84), Am. Water Resources Assn. (chmn. water law sect. 1983-87), Ariz. Agrl. Law Assn. (founder, chmn. 1982-86), Ariz. Rural Water Assn. (exec. v.p. 1984—). Civil rights, Natural resources, Utilities, public. Home: 7525 N 21st Pl Phoenix AZ 85020-4751 Office: PMB 307 7000 N 16th St Ste 120 Phoenix AZ 85020-5547 E-mail: dcn@netwrx.net.

NELSON, EDWARD SHEFFIELD, lawyer, former utility company executive; b. Keevil, Ark., Feb. 23, 1941; s. Robert Ford and Thelma Jo (Mayberry) N.; m. Mary Lynn McCastlain, Oct. 12, 1962; children: Cynthia, Lynn (dec.), Laura. BS, U. Cen. Ark., 1963; LLB, Ark. Law Sch., 1968; JD, U. Ark., 1969. Mgmt. trainee Ark. La. Gas Co., Little Rock, 1963-64, sales engr., 1964-67, sales coordinator, 1967-69, gen. sales mgr., 1969-71, v.p., gen. sales mgr., 1971-73, pres., dir., 1973-79, pres., chmn., chief exec. officer, 1979-85; ptnr., chmn. bd., chief exec. officer House, Wallace, Nelson & Jewel, Little Rock, 1985-86; pvt. practice law Little Rock, 1986—; of counsel Jack, Lyon & Jones, P.A., 1991—. Bd. dirs. Fed. Res. Mem. N.G., 1957-63, Fellowship Bible Ch.; bd. dirs. U. Ark., Little Rock, vice chmn. bd. visitors, 1981; bd. dirs. Philander Smith Coll., 1981; chmn. Ark. Indsl. Devel. Commn., 1987, 88; past chmn. Little Rock br. Fed. Res. Bd. St. Louis; chmn. Econ. Expansion Study Commn., 1987—; bd. dirs. Ark. Ednl. TV Found., Ark. Game and Fish Commn. Found.; founder, 1st pres. Jr. Achievement Ark., 1987-88; Rep. nominee for Gov. of Ark., 1990, 94; co-state chmn. Ark. Reps., 1991-92, nat. committeeman Ark. GOP, 1993-2000; mem. Ark. Higher Edn. Coord. Bd., 1997-99; apptd. commr. Ark. Game and Fish Commn., 2000—. Named Ark.'s Outstanding Young Man Ark. J. C. of C., 1973; One of Am.'s Ten Outstanding Young Men U.S. Jr. C. of C., 1974; Citizen of Yr. Ark. chpt. March of Dimes, 1983; Humanitarian of Yr. NCCJ, 1983; Best Chief Exec. Officer in Natural Gas Industry Wall Street Transcript, 1983; recipient 1st Disting. Alumnus award U. Cen. Ark., 1987. Mem. Am., Ark., Pulaski County bar assns., Ark. C. of C. (dir.), Little Rock C. of C. (dir., pres. 1981), Sales and Mktg. Execs. Assn. (pres. 1975, Top Mgmt. award 1977), U. Ark. Law Sch. Alumni Assn. (pres. 1980), Sigma Tau Gamma (Ben T. Laney Leadership award for leadership and achievment 2000). Fellowship Bible Ch. Corporate, general, Finance. Office: 6th and Broadway 3400 TCBY Bldg Little Rock AR 72201

NELSON, JAMES C, state supreme court justice; b. Idaho, Feb. 20, 1944; m. Chari Werner; 2 children. BS, U. Idaho, 1966; JD cum laude, George Washington U., 1974. Fin. analyst SEC, Washington; pvt. practice Cut Bank; county atty. Glacier County; assoc. judge Mont. Supreme Ct., 1993—. Former mem. State Bd. Oil and Gas Conservation, also chmn.; former mem. State Gaming Adv. Counsel, Gov. Adv. Coun. on Corrections and Criminal Justice Policy; liaison to Commn. of Cts. of Ltd. Jurisdiction, mem. adv. com. Ct. Assessment Program. Served U.S. Army. Office: Supreme Ct PO Box 203001 Helena MT 59620

NELSON, KEITH MILTON, lawyer; b. Ft. Worth, May 10, 1957; s. Paul Milton and Betty Pauline (Martin) N.; m. Terry Gayle Beaver, Apr. 11, 1987; children: Staley, Ashley, Chad, Caroline, Erin, Katelyn. BA, Baylor U., 1979; JD, Baylor U., 1983. Bar: Tex. 1983, U.S. Dist. Ct. (no. dist.) Tex. Ptnr. Ashley, Nelson & Leake, Irving, Tex., 1987-88; assoc. Koons, Fuller, McCurley and Vanden Eykel, Dallas, 1988-92; ptnr. McCurley, Orsinger, McCurley & Nelson, Dallas, 1992—. Speaker in field. Contbr. articles to profl. jours. Cons. Lawyers Against Domestic Violence; mem. visitation subcom. Supreme Ct. Adv. Com. on Child Support and Visitation Guidelines. Mem. ABA (family law sect.), Am. Acad. Matrimonial Lawyers, Tex. Acad. Family Law Specialists, Tex. Trial Lawyers Assn., State Bar Tex., Dallas Bar Assn. (family law sect., bd. dirs.), Irving Bar Assn. (pres. 1991-92), Nat. Assn. Counsel for Children. Baptist. Avocations: racquetball, snow skiing, spectator sports. Family and matrimonial. Office: McCurley Orsinger McCurley & Nelson 5950 Sherry Ln # 800 Dallas TX 75225-6533

NELSON, KEITHE EUGENE, state court administrator, lawyer; b. Grand Forks, N.D. m. Shirley Jeanne Jordahl, June 10, 1955; children: Kirsti Lynn Nelson Hoerauf, Scott David, Kenen Edward, Karen Lee Nelson Strandquist. PhB, U. N.D., 1958, JD, 1959. Bar: N.D. 1959, U.S. Ct. Mil. Appeals 1967., U.S. Supreme Ct. 1967. With Armour & Co., Grand Forks, 1958-59; commd. 2d lt. USAF, 1958, advanced through grades to maj. gen., 1985, judge advocate, 1959-73, chief career mgmt., 1973-77; comdt. USAF JAG Sch., Montgomery, Ala., 1977-81; staff judge adv. Tactical Air Command USAF, Hampton, VA., 1981-82, SAC, Omaha, 1984-85; dir. USAF Judiciary, Washington, 1982-84; dep. JAG USAF, Washington, 1985, JAG, 1988-91, JAG, 1988, ret. JAG, 1991; dir. jud. planning Supreme Ct. N.D.; state ct. administr., from 1992. Chmn. editorial bd. USAF Law Rev., 1977-81. Decorated D.S.M., Legion of Merit with two oak leaf clusters. Mem. ABA. Lutheran. Avocations: skeet shooting, hunting, tennis, theater. Home: Bismarck, ND. Died July 2002.

NELSON, L. BRUCE, lawyer; b. Mpls., Aug. 6, 1946; s. Leo W. and Sylvia E. Nelson; m. Nancy E. Cook, Aug. 23, 1969; 1 child, Andrew C. AB, Hamilton Coll., 1968; JD, U. Colo., 1971. Bar: Colo., D.C., U.S. Ct. Appeals (10th cir.). Assoc./ptnr. Sherman & Howard, Denver, 1972-83; dir., shareholder Isaacson, et al, Denver, 1983-91; counsel Inverness Properties, Denver, 1991-94; dir., shareholder Ducker, Montgomery, et al, Denver, 1994—. Clk. Judge Jean Breitenstein, 10th Cir. Ct. Appeals, Denver, 1971. Mem. ABA, Colo. Bar Assn., Colo. Corp. Counsel. Office: Ducker Montgomery 1560 Broadway Ste 1500 Denver CO 80202-5151

NELSON, LESTER, lawyer; b. N.Y.C., Dec. 23, 1928; s. Samuel and Celia (Plotkin) N.; m. Vita Reiner, Aug. 27, 1961; children: Lee Reiner, Clifford Samuel, Cara Ritchie. BSS, CCNY, 1950; LLM, NYU, 1959; JD, Havard U., 1953. Bar: N.Y. 1953. Ptnr. Gerdes & Montgomery, N.Y.C., 1955-83, Golenbock & Barell, N.Y.C., 1983-85, Rabinovich, Nelson, Gordon & Burstein, N.Y.C., 1985-95, Nelson & Nelson, N.Y.C., 1995—. Adj. prof. N.Y. Law Sch., N.Y.C., 1972-87; internat. adv. bd. Oceana Publs., Inc., 1988-92. Author: Credit Manual of Commercial Laws, 1972-92; editor Digest of Comml. Laws of the World, 1972-98, Digest of Intellectual Property Laws of the World, 1972-98, N.Y. Internat. Law Rev., 1992— Sec. The Spanish Inst., N.Y.C., 1975; bd. dirs. Am. Jewish Com., Westchester Co., 1983-89, 96—, Inst. for Continuing Edn. in Law and Librarianship, 1980-92. With U.S. Army, 1953-55. Mem. ABA, N.Y. Co. Lawyers Assn. (chmn. fgn. and internat. law com. 1985-89), N.Y. State Bar Assn. Jewish. Avocations: tennis, skiing, reading, music. Bankruptcy, Corporate, general, Private international. Home: Pleasant Ridge Rd Harrison NY 10528 Office: Nelson & Nelson 60 E 42nd St Rm 565 New York NY 10165-0565

NELSON, RICHARD ARTHUR, lawyer; b. Fosston, Minn., Apr. 8, 1947; BS in Math., U. Minn., 1969, JD, 1974. Bar: Minn. 1974, U.S. Ct. Appeals (D.C. cir.) 1975, U.S. Dist. Ct. Minn. 1975. Law clk. U.S. Ct. Appeals (D.C. cir.), Washington, 1974-75; ptnr. Faegre and Benson, Mpls., 1975—, group head employee benefits group, 2002—. Seminar lectr. in employee benefits and labor laws, 1983—. Note and articles editor Minn. Law Rev., 1973-74. Active Dem.-Farmer-Labor Party State Cen. Com., Minn., 1976—, del. dist. and local coms. and convs., 1970—, state exec. com., 1990—; student rep. bd. regents U. Minn., Mpls., 1973-74; mem. adv. coun. IRS Mid-States Key Dist. EP/EO, 1996-2000, IRS Ctrl. Mountains Region TE/GE, 2001—; chair Mpls. Pension Coun., 1999-2000. Served with U.S. Army, 1970-72. Mem. ABA, Minn. Bar Assn. (chair employee benefits sect. 1997-98), Order of Coif, Tau Beta Pi. Lutheran. Labor (including EEOC, Fair Labor Standards Act, labor-management relations, NLRB, OSHA), Pension, profit-sharing, and employee benefits. Office: Faegre and Benson 90 S 7th St Ste 2200 Minneapolis MN 55402-3901 E-mail: rnelson@faegre.com.

NELSON, RICHARD DAVID, lawyer; b. Chgo., Jan. 29, 1940; s. Irving E. and Dorothy (Apolsky) N.; m. Davida Distenfield, Dec. 17, 1960; children: Cheryl, Laurel. BS in Acctg., U. Ill., 1961, LLB, 1964. Bar: Ill. 1964. Ptnr. Defrees & Fiske Law Offices, Chgo., 1964-81; ptnr., counsel, chief adminstrv. officer Heidrick & Struggles, Inc., Chgo., 1981—2001; pres. Galrk Sheridan, Inc., Highland Park, Ill., 2001—. Bd. dirs., exec. com. Heidrick & Struggles, Inc., Chgo., 1981-99. Pres. Jewish Cmty. Ctrs. of Chgo., 1987-89; chmn. Sign Graphics Task Force, Highland Park, Ill., 1986-88, Bus. and Econ. Devel. Commn., Highland Park; chmn. Econ. Devel. Commn. Highland Park, 1993-96, Ft. Sheridan Joint Plan Commn., 1997-2000, Bus. and Econ. Devel. Commn., Highland Park, 2000—. Mem. ABA, Ill. State Bar Assn., Chgo. Bar Assn., Standard Club, Northmoor Country Club. Corporate, general, Private international, Taxation, general. Office: Galrk Sheridan Inc 1896 Sheridan Rd Ste 200 Highland Park IL 60035-4635

NELSON, ROBERT LOUIS, lawyer; b. Dover, N.H., Aug. 10, 1931; s. Albert Louis and Alice (Rogers) N.; m. Rita Jean Hutchins, June 11, 1955; children: Karen, Robin Andrea. BA, Bates Coll., Lewiston, Maine, 1956; LLB, Georgetown U., 1959. Bar: D.C. 1960. With U.S. Commn. Civil Rights, 1958-63, AID, 1963-66; program sec. U.S. Mission to Brazil, 1965-66; exec. dir. Lawyers Com. Civil Rights Under Law, 1966-70; dep. campaign mgr. Muskie for Pres., 1970-72; v.p. Perpetual Corp., Houston, 1972-74; sr. v.p., gen. counsel Washington Star, 1974-76; pres. broadcast div. Washington Star Communications, Inc., 1976-77; asst. sec. of army U.S. Dept. Def., 1977-79; spl. advisor to chief N.G. Bur., Dept. Def., 1980-85; pres., dir. Mid-Md. Communications Corp., 1981-85; ptnr. Verner, Liipfert, Bernhard, McPherson and Hand, 1979-87; gen. counsel Paralyzed Vets. Am., 1988-99, sr. counsel, 2000—. Vice chmn. D.C. Redevel. Land Agy., 1976-77; bd. dirs. Friends of Nat. Zoo, 1975—89, pres., 1982-84; bd. dirs. Downtown Progress, 1976-77, Fed. City Coun., 1976-77, 83-87, Pennsylvania Ave. Devel. Corp., 1976-77, Cmty. Found. Greater Washington, 1977-78, Pep Direct, 2003—; trustee Wolfe's Neck Farm Found., 2001—. Served with AUS, 1953-54. Mem. ABA, D.C. Bar Assn., Army Navy Club (Washington). Democrat. Episcopalian. Corporate, general, Non-profit and tax-exempt organizations. Office: 801 18th St NW Washington DC 20006-3517 Home (Winter): 11 Zeitler Farm Rd Brunswick ME 04011

NELSON, ROY HUGH, JR., lawyer, mediator, arbitrator; b. St. Paul, May 13, 1955; s. Roy H. and Helen S. Nelson; m. MaryJean G. Froehlich, Aug. 13, 1994; children: Benjamin, Calla. BS, U. Wis., Milw., 1979, MS, 1985; JD, U. Wis., 1988. Bar: Wis. 1988, U.S. Dist. Ct. (ea. and we. dists.) Wis. 1988, U.S. Dist. Ct. (ea. dist.) Mich. 1991, U.S. Ct. Appeals (7th cir.) 1988, U.S. Ct. Appeals (fed. cir.) 1996, U.S. Supreme Ct. 1999. Police officer City of Brookfield, Wis., 1978-88; assoc. Borgelt, Powell, Peterson & Frauen, Milw., 1988-92; shareholder, dir. Petrie & Stocking SC, Milw., 1992—; mediator, arbitrator, dir. Conflict Resolution Svcs., Milw., 1997—2001. Chair adv. bd. Mediation Ministries, Sun Prairie, Wis., 1998—. Mem. Wis. Bar Assn., Wis. Assn. Mediators. Lutheran. Alternative dispute resolution, General civil litigation, Intellectual property. Office: Petrie & Stocking SC 111 E Wisconsin Ave Ste 1500 Milwaukee WI 53202-4808 E-mail: rnelson@petriestocking.com.

NELSON, STEVEN CRAIG, lawyer; b. Oakland, Calif., May 11, 1944; s. Eskil Manfred and Florence Lucille (Boatman) N.; m. Kathryn Cassel Stoltz, Nov. 30, 1974 (div. Apr. 1997); children: Carleton Philip, Whitney Cassel. BA in Econs. with exceptional distinction, Yale U., 1966, LLB, 1969. Bar: DC 1969, Minn. Supreme Ct. 1975, U.S. Supreme Ct. 1973, Hong Kong 2000. From atty. adviser to asst. legal adviser U.S. Dept. State, Washington, 1969-74; from assoc. to ptnr. Oppenheimer, Wolff, Foster, Shepard & Donnelly, St. Paul and Mpls., 1975-85; ptnr. Dorsey & Whitney LLP, Mpls., 1985—. Mem. bd. appeals NATO, Brussels. 1977—; adj. prof. law U. Minn, 1980-86; spkr. in field. Contbr. articles to profl. jours. Mem. ABA (chmn. internat. law and practice 1988-89), Minn. Bar Assn., Am. Fgn. Law Assn., Am. Soc. Internat. Law, Internat. Bar Assn. (mem. coun. 1996-2000), Union Internat. des Avocats (1st v.p. 1991-94), Minikahda Club. Avocations: golf, tennis, skiing, sailing. Commercial, contracts (including sales of goods; commercial financing), Corporate, general, Private international. Office: Dorsey & Whitney 50 S 6th St Ste 1500 Minneapolis MN 55402-1498

NELSON, STEVEN DWAYNE, lawyer; b. Austin, Minn. m. Vicky L. Staab, July 6, 1990. BA in English, SUNY, Buffalo, 1972; JD, U. Mont., 1978. Bar: Mont. 1978, U.S. Dist. Ct. Mont. 1978. Sole practice, Bozeman, Mont., 1978—; city prosecutor City of Bozeman, 1979-82; city atty. City of Ennis (Mont.), 1980-82; prof. U. Great Falls, Mont., 1990—, mediator, 1998—. Mem. ABA, Mont. State Bar Assn., Phi Delta Phi. Avocations: fishing, skiing, hiking. General civil litigation, Criminal, General practice. Home and Office: 4590 Maiden Rock Rd Bozeman MT 59715-7769 E-mail: Nelsonsvl@cs.com.

NELSON, WALTER GERALD, retired insurance company executive; b. Peoria, Ill., Jan. 2, 1930; s. Walter Dennis and Hazel Marie (Tucker) Nelson; m. Mary Ann Olberding, Jan. 28, 1952 (dec. Nov. 1989); children: Ann Larkin, Michael, Susan Boor, Patrick, Thomas, Timothy, Molly Edwards; m. Mary Jo Sunderland, Apr. 6, 1991. Student, St. Benedict's Coll., Atchison, Kans., 1947-49, Bradley U., Peoria, Ill., 1949; JD, Creighton U., Omaha, 1952. Bar: Nebr 1952, Ill 1955. Practice in, Peoria, 1955-56; with State Farm Life Ins. Co., Bloomington, Ill., 1956—, counsel, 1968—, v.p., 1970-96; adj. prof. Ill. State U., Bloomington, 1996—. Past dir Ill Life Ins Coun; past chmn legal sect Am Coun Life Ins; spkr in field. Contbr. articles to profl jours. Community bd dirs St Joseph Med Ctr, Bloomington, Ill., 1994. Mem.: ABA, Nat. Orgn. Life and Health Ins. Guaranty Assn. (past pres.), Assn. Life Ins. Counsel (past pres.), Nebr. Bar Assn., Ill. Bar Assn., Bloomington Country Club, KofC. Republican. Roman Catholic. E-mail: WGN1930@aol.com.

NELSON, WILLIAM EUGENE, lawyer; b. Roland, Iowa, Sept. 23, 1927; s. Sam J. and Katherine A. (Coffey) N.; m. Sherlee M. Stanford, July 11, 1959; children: Anne, Kristin, William. BA, U. Iowa, 1950; JD, Drake U., 1957. Bar: Iowa 1957, D.C. 1965, Md. 1976. Trial atty. civil divsn. U.S. Dept. Justice, 1957—65, asst. chief tort sect., 1966—70, chief r.r. reorgn. unit, 1970—71; gen. counsel Cost of Living Coun. Phase I, 1971, chief econ. stblzn. sect., 1971—74; ptnr. Nelson and Nelson, LLP, Washington, Bethesda, Md., 1975—. Gen. counsel the Communicators, Inc., Myersville, Md. Assoc. editor Drake Law Rev., 1955-57. With USN, 1945-46. Recipient Atty. Gen.'s Disting. Svc. award, 1972. Mem. Order of Coif, Omicron Delta Kappa. Probate (including wills, trusts), Estate planning, Personal injury (including property damage). Home: 511 Colston Dr Falling Waters WV 25419 Office: Nelson & Nelson LLP 3 Bethesda Metro Ctr Ste 700 Bethesda MD 20814-6300 E-mail: sswen@aol.com.

NELTNER, MICHAEL MARTIN, lawyer; b. Cin., July 31, 1959; s. Harold John and Joyce Ann Neltner; m. Barbara Ann Phair, July 9, 1988; children: Brandon August, Alexandra Nicole. BA, Mercy Coll., 1981; MA, Athenaeum of Ohio, 1987; JD, U. Cin., 1994. Bar: Ohio 1994, U.S. Dist. Ct. (so. dist.) Ohio 1995. Tchr. Elder H.S., Cin., 1985-91; ins. agt. Ky. Ctrl., Cin., 1987-91; mediator City of Cin., 1992-94; tchg. asst. Ohio Gov.'s Inst., Cin., 1992; legal extern to Chief Justice Thomas Moyer Ohio Supreme Ct., 1993; assoc. Eagen, Wykoff & Healy, LPA, Cin., 1994-99, Thompson Hine & Flory, Cin., 1999-2000, Freund, Freeze & Arnold, Cin., 2000—. Editor-in-chief Mercy Coll. Ljt. Mag., 1980-81, U. Cin. Law Rev., 1993-94. Campaign coord. Rep. Orgn. Detroit, 1980. Recipient Merit scholarship Cin. Enquirer, 1977-81, Sage scholarship Mercy Coll., 1980, Am. Jurisprudence award Lawyers Coop. Publishing, 1994. Mem ABA, Ohio Bar Assn., Cin. Bar Assn. (mem. acad. medicine com. 1995—, chair Ct. Appeals com. 1998-2000). Estate planning, Insurance, Personal injury (including property damage). Home: 3344 Milverton Ct Cincinnati OH 45248-2865 Office: Freund Freeze & Arnold LPA 105 E 4th St Cincinnati OH 45202-4006 E-mail: mneltner@ffalaw.com.

NEMEC, MICHAEL LEE, lawyer; b. Tulsa, Aug. 1, 1949; s. Milton L. and Betty D. (Lawrence) N.; m. Vivian Strobel, Dec. 26, 1970; children: Adam, Jennifer, David. BA in Polit. Sci., U. Tulsa, 1971, JD, 1976. Bar: Okla. 1976. Pvt. practice law, Tulsa, 1976-78; dir. deferred giving Okla. State U. Found., Stillwater, 1978-80; asst. v.p., trust officer Bank Okla. N.A., Tulsa, 1980; v.p., trust officer Bank Commerce & Trust Co., Tulsa, 1980-85; pvt. practice law Tulsa, 1985-89; assoc. Hall, Estill, Hardwick, Gable, Golden & Nelson P.C., Tulsa, 1989-93, shareholder, 1993—. Mem. fin. com. Monte Cassino Sch., Inc., Tulsa, 1987; vol. Boy Scouts Am., Tulsa, 1984—86, 1997—2001; founders chorus Tulsa Boy's Home; mem. Planned Giving Coun.; mem. major gifts coun. Am. Heart Assn., 1998—99; participant U.S. Naval Acad. Fgn. Affairs Conf., 1971. Named Family of Yr., LDS Ch., Tulsa, 1985. Mem.: ABA, Tulsa Tax Forum (pres. 1994, 1995), Tulsa Estate Planning Forum (bd. dirs. 2000—03), Tulsa Title and Probate Lawyers (bd. dirs. 2001—, sec. 2003), Tulsa County Bar Assn. (sec. tax sect. 1988), Okla. Bar Assn., U. Tulsa Coll. Law Alumni Assn. (bd. dirs. 2002—), Soc. for Preservation and Encouragement of Barber Shop Quartet Singing in Am. Roman Catholic. Estate planning, Probate (including wills, trusts), Estate taxation. Office: Hall Estill Hardwick Gable Golden & Nelson PC 320 S Boston Ave Ste 400 Tulsa OK 74103-3704

NEMEROFF, DAVID BRIAN, lawyer; b. Chgo., Ill., Dec. 19, 1961; s. Elliot and Ilene Nemeroff; m. Tara Gross, July 5, 1992; 1 child, Andrew Louis. BS in Mktg., U. Md., 1984; JD, SUNY, Buffalo, 1995. Bar: Ill. 1995, U.S. Dist. Ct (no. dist.) Ill. 1995, U.S. Ct. Appeals (7th cir.) 1998. Atty. Raymond P. Concannon, Ltd., Chgo., 1995—97, Birg & Associates, Ltd., Lincolnwood, 1997—99; ptnr. Nemeroff Law Offices, Ltd., Chgo., 2000—. Bd. dirs. Alliance Against Intoxicated Motorists, Schaumburg, Ill., 1999. Mem.: Million Dollar Advocates Forum. Personal injury (including property damage), Workers' compensation. Office: Nemeroff Law Offices Ltd 161 N Clark St Ste 3575 Chicago IL 60601 Office Fax: 312-629-0388. Personal E-mail: juryman1@aol.com. E-mail: juryman1@aol.com.

NEMEROFF, MICHAEL ALAN, lawyer; b. Feb. 16, 1946; s. Bernard Gregor and Frances (Gotleib) N.; m. Sharon Lynn Leininger, Sept. 22, 1974; children: Theodore, Patrick, James. BA, U. Chgo., 1968; JD, Columbia U., 1971. Asst. counsel Subcom. on Juvenile Delinquency of Senate Jud. Com., Washington, 1971-73; assoc. Sidley & Austin, Washington, 1973-78; ptnr. Sidley Austin Brown & Wood, Washington, 1978—. Treas. Friends of Jim Sasser, 1978-96, Andy Ireland Campaign Com., 1984-92. Administrative and regulatory, Government contracts and claims. Office: Sidley Austin Brown & Wood LLP 1501 K St NW Washington DC 20005

NEMETH, PATRICIA MARIE, lawyer; b. Flint, Mich., Sept. 18, 1959; d. Gyula Nemeth and Marie (Glaska) Adkins. BA, U. Mich., 1981; JD, Wayne State U., 1984, LLM, 1990. Bar: Ill. 1987, Mich. 1984, U.S. Ct. Appeals (6th cir.), U.S. Dist. Ct. (ea. dist.) Mich., U.S. Dist. Ct. (we. dist.) Mich. Teaching asst. Wayne State U., Detroit, 1982; intern. U.S. Dist. Ct. (ea. dist.) Mich., Detroit, 1983; assoc. Bloom & Bloom, Birmingham, Mich., 1984-85, Stringari, Fritz, Kreger, Ahearn, Bennett & Hunsinger, Detroit, 1985-92; prin. Law Offices of Patricia Nemeth, P.C., Detroit, 1992-97, Nemeth Burwell, P.C., Detroit, 1998—. Lectr. in field; adj. prof. Walsh Coll., 1992—94. Guest appearance (TV) Straight Talk, 1994, 95, 2002; contbr. articles to profl. jours. Mem. adv. bd. Vista Maria, 2001-02, bd. dirs., 2002—; mem. pers. com. Met. Detroit coun. Girl Scout Am., 2002—. Named one of Top 10 Best Places to Work in Southeastern Mich., Crain's/IRI, 2001, Best and Brightest Cos. to Work For, 2001—02. Mem. ABA (labor sect.), Mich. Bar Assn. (labor sect.), Ill. Bar Assn., Nat. Order Barristers, Nat. Assn. Women Bus. Owners (sec., exec. bd., bd. dirs., named One of Top Ten Women Bus. Owners of Distinction 2002), Women's Econ. Club (strategic com. 2002—), Lawyers Assn. Mich., Detroit Bar Assn., Health Care Assn. of Mich., Small Bus. Assn. Mich. Roman Catholic. Avocations: sailing, golf, rollerblade. Civil rights, Labor (including EEOC, Fair Labor Standards Act, labor-management relations, NLRB, OSHA). Office: 200 Talon Centre Detroit MI 48207- E-mail: nemethburwell@michbar.org.

NEMETH, VALERIE ANN, lawyer; b. Sutton Surrey, Eng., Mar. 23, 1954; d. Gerald Arnold and Louise Marian (Ross) N.; m. Larry Nagelberg, Dec. 28, 1978 (div. Nov. 1979); m. Hyman Joseph Zacks, Oct. 28, 1984 (div. 1997). BA, UCLA, 1976; JD, Whittier Coll., 1979. Assoc. Grayson, Gross, Friedman, L.A., 1979-80; gen. counsel Red Wind Prodns., L.A., 1979-80; sole practice L.A., San Diego, 1980—; gen. counsel, ptnr. MarValUs Entertainment Co., L.A., 1984—; arbitrator Los Angeles County Superior Ct., 1985—, San Diego Superior Ct., 1985—. Legal cons. Centre Devel., San Diego, 1985-87; adj. prof. mgmt. and bus. U. Redlands, 1994—; bd. dirs. Ind. Film Soc. Mem. legal com. Fairbanks Ranch Assn., Rancho Santa Fe, Calif., 1987-92; adminstrv. dir. community svcs. dist. Fairbanks Ranch, 1988-92. Mem. Am. Film Inst., Ind. Film Soc. (bd. dirs. 2000[0097]), State Bar Calif. (mem. intellectual property sect.), Variety Clubs Internat., Hadassah (life), Zool. Soc. San Diego., Republicans for Environmental Protection. Republican. Jewish. Avocations: films, art, outdoors, travel. Entertainment, Intellectual property, Trademark and copyright. Office: 619 S Vulcan Ave Ste 215 Encinitas CA 92024-3654 Fax: 760-942-6043. E-mail: vanemeth@cs.com.

NEMIR, DONALD PHILIP, lawyer; b. Oakland, Calif., Oct. 31, 1931; s. Philip F. and Mary (Shavor) N. AB, U. Calif., Berkeley, 1957, JD, 1960. Bar: Calif. 1961, U.S. Dist. Ct. (no. dist.) Calif. 1961, U.S. Ct. Appeals (9th cir.) 1961, U.S. Dist. Ct. (ctrl. dist.) Calif. 1975, U.S. Supreme Ct. 1980. Pvt. practice, San Francisco, 1961—. Pres. Law Offices of Donald Nemir, A Profl. Corp. Mem. Calif. State Bar Assn. General civil litigation, Corporate, general, Property, real (including real estate development, water). Home: PO Box 1089 Mill Valley CA 94942-1089

NEMO, ANTHONY JAMES, lawyer; b. St. Paul, May 18, 1963; s. Joseph Marino Jr. and Dianne Marie (Wegner) N.; m. Mary Rose Mazzitello, July 17, 1987; children: Anne Marie, Katherine Mary, Anthony James Jr. BA in English Lit., U. St. Thomas, 1986; JD, William Mitchell Coll. Law, 1991. Bar: Minn. 1991, U.S. Dist. Ct. Minn., U.S. Dist. Ct. Ariz., U.S. Dist. Ct. (ea. dist.) Wis., U.S. Ct. Appeals (4th cir.), U.S. Supreme Ct. Account exec. div. info. svcs. TRW, Mpls., 1986-90; ptnr. Meshbesher & Spence, Ltd., St. Paul, 1990—. Assoc. editor William Mitchell Law Rev., 1988-90; author law rev. note. Recipient R. Ross Quaintance award, Douglas K. Amdahl-Mary O'Malley Lyons Trial Advocacy award. Mem. ABA, Minn. Trial Lawyers Assn., Assn. Trial Lawyers Am., Minn. State Bar Assn., Hennepin County Bar Assn., John P. Sheehy Legal History Soc. Roman Catholic. Criminal, Personal injury (including property damage), Product liability. Home: 2125 Heath Ave N Oakdale MN 55128-5207 Office: Meshbesher & Spence Ltd 1616 Park Ave Minneapolis MN 55404

NEMON, NANCY SUSAN SCHECTMAN, lawyer; b. Providence, Jan. 20, 1943; d. Robert and Bessie (Greenberg) Schectman; m. Leonard I. Nemon, Oct. 24, 1971. A.B., Boston U., 1964; J.D., Harvard U., 1967. Bar: Mass. 1967, R.I. 1967, U.S. Dist. Ct. Mass. 1970, U.S. Ct. Appeals (2d cir.) 1987. Atty. John Hancock Mut. Life Ins. Co., Boston, 1967-72; dep. regional atty. HHS, Boston, 1972-86, dep. chief counsel, 1986-95, acting chief counsel, 1995-96, chief counsel, 1996—. Recipient Superior Service award HHS, 1982, Exceptional Service award HHS, 1987, Sec.'s Disting. Svc. award HHS, 1998. Mem. Mass. Bar Assn., R.I. Bar Assn., Boston Bar Assn., Harvard Law Sch. Assn., Phi Beta Kappa. Jewish. Office: HHS Office of Gen Counsel JFK Federal Bldg Rm 2250 Boston MA 02203-0002

NE MOYER, EDGAR CARROLL, judge; b. Buffalo, N.Y., June 5, 1932; s. Edgar Henry and Mary Elizabeth (Carroll) Ne M.; m. Josephine Kiely, July 4, 1954; children: Patricia Catanzaro, Daniel, Michael. Student, Georgetown U., 1950-52; BA, U. Buffalo, 1954, JD, 1961; LLM, U. Wis., 1962. Asst. U.S. atty. U.S. Dept. Justice, Buffalo, 1967-68, acting U.S. atty., 1968-69; dep. corp. counsel City of Buffalo, 1969; assoc. prof. SUNY, Albany, 1969-71; ptnr. Boreanaz, Ne Moyer & Baker, Buffalo, 1971-84; justice N.Y. State Supreme Ct., Buffalo, 1984; judge N.Y. State Ct. Claims, Buffalo, 1985—. Clk. N.Y. State Supreme Ct., Buffalo, 1976-77; part-time instr. SUNY-Buffalo Law Sch., 1979-83. Capt. USAF, 1955-58. Named Citizen of Yr., Detective Sgts., Buffalo Police Dept., 1986. Mem. Am. Legion, Mensa. Office: Webster-Szanyi 1400 Liberty Bldg Buffalo NY 14202

NEPOM, MARVIN S. lawyer; b. Portland, Oreg., Aug. 29, 1926; s. David and Sophie (Garber) N.; m. Leah Tkatch, June 29, 1947; children: Hannah, Gerald, David. BBA, U. Wash., 1948; JD, Northwestern Sch. Law, 1962. Bar: Oreg. 1962, U.S. Dist. Ct. Oreg. 1962, U.S. Ct. Appeals (9th cir.) 1964, U.S. Supreme Ct. 1965. Sole practice law, Portland, 1963—. Mediator U.S. Arbitration & Mediation Oreg., Portland. Mem. Multnomah Bar Assn. (pres.). Office: 3718 SW Condor Ave Ste 100 Portland OR 97239 Office Fax: 503-223-3511.

NEPPLE, JAMES ANTHONY, lawyer; b. Carroll, Iowa, Jan. 5, 1945; s. Herbert J. and Cecilia T. (Irlmeier) N.; m. Jeannine Ann Jennings, Sept. 9, 1967; children: Jeffrey B., Scott G., Carin J., Andrew J. BA, Creighton U., 1967; JD, U. Iowa, 1970; postgrad. in bus., Tex. Christian U., 1971; LLM in Taxation, NYU, 1982. Bar: Iowa 1970, Ill. 1973, U.S. Dist. Ct. (so. dist.) Iowa 1972, U.S. Dist. Ct. (cen. dist.) Ill. 1972, U.S. Dist. Ct.(no. dist.) Iowa 1975, U.S. Ct. Appeals (7th and 8th cirs.) 1975, U.S. Supreme Ct. 1975, U.S. Ct. Claims 1976, U.S. Tax Ct. 1976. Tax acct. Arthur Young & Co., Chgo., 1970; v.p., treas., bd. dirs. Stanley, Rehling, Lande & VanDerKamp, Muscatine, Iowa, 1972-92; pres. Nepple, VanDerKamp & Flynn, P.C., Rock Island, Ill., 1992-98; prin. Nepple Law Offices, P.L.C., 1999—. Scoutmaster Boy Scouts Am., Muscatine, 1982—85; trustee State His. Soc. Iowa, 1986—92, vice-chmn., 1991—92; bd. dirs. Iowa Hist. Found., 1988—95, pres., 1991—93; trustee Musser Pub. Libr., 2000—; pres. Muscatine Hist. Preservation Commn., 2001—. Recipient Gov.'s Vol. award State of Iowa, 1988, 90, Jr. Achievement of the Quad Cities Bronze award, 1996, Silver award, 2000. Fellow: Ill. Bar Found., Iowa Bar Found., Am. Bar Found., Am. Coll. Trust and Estate Counsel; mem.: ABA (tax sect. 1972—, chair agrl. tax com. 2001—03), Quad City Estate Planning Coun. (pres. 1987), Iowa Assn. Bus. and Industry (tax com. 1978—, chmn. 1986—88), Rock Island County Bar Assn., Scott County Bar Assn., Muscatine Bar Assn. (pres. 1982—83), Ill. Bar Assn. (fed. tax. sect. coun. 1993—99, chair 1997—98), Fed Bar Assn., Muscatine C. of C. (pres. 1985), Geneva Golf and Country Club (pres. 1990—91), Elks, Kiwanis (pres. Muscatine chpt. 1978). Republican. Roman Catholic. Estate planning, Pension, profit-sharing, and employee benefits, Taxation, general. Home: 2704 Mulberry Ave Muscatine IA 52761-2746 Fax: 563-264-6844. E-mail: jim@nepplelaw.com.

NEREBERG, ELIOT JOEL, lawyer; b. N.Y.C., May 15, 1949; s. Harry and Muriel (Gravitz) N.; m. Amy V. Jaffe, June 1, 1973; children: Rebecca, Kate. BS, CCNY, 1970; JD, NYU, 1973. Bar: Conn. 1973, U.S. Dist. Ct. Conn. 1973, U.S. Ct. Appeals (2d cir.) 1975. Clin. supr. sch. law. U. Conn., West Hartford, 1973-75; pvt. practice West Hartford, 1975—. Spl. masters Hartford County Family Ct., 1985—. Mem. ABA (bd. dirs. publ. bd. family law sect.), Conn. Bar Assn. (chair family law sect. 1999-2000), Hartford County Bar Assn. (co-chmn. family law sect. 1990-92). Democrat. Jewish. Corporate, general, Family and matrimonial, Property, real (including real estate development, water). Home: 62 Walbridge Rd West Hartford CT 06119-1343 Office: 10 N Main St West Hartford CT 06107-1968 E-mail: enerenberg@rcn.com.

NESBIT, PHYLLIS SCHNEIDER, judge; b. Newkirk, Okla., Sept. 21, 1919; d. Vernon Lee and Irma Mae (Biddle) Schneider; m. Peter Nicholas Nesbit, Sept. 14, 1939. BS in Chemistry, U. Ala., 1948, BS in Law, 1958, JD, 1969. Bar: Ala. 1958. Ptnr. Wilters, Brantley and Nesbit, Robertsdale, Ala., 1958-74; pvt. practice Robertsdale, 1974-76; dist. judge Baldwin County Juvenile Ct., 1977-88; supernumerary dist. judge and juvenile ct. judge Baldwin County, 1989—. Bd. dirs. Baldwin Youth Svcs.; bd. dirs., v.p. women's activities So. Ala. chpt. Nat. Safety Coun., 1978-83; chmn. quality assurance com. The Homestead Retirement Village, 1992-95. Mem. Nat. Assn. Women Lawyers, Nat. Assn. Women Judges, N.Am. Judges Assn., Ala. Dist. Judges Assn., Ala. Coun. Juvenile Judges, Am. Judicature Soc., Baldwin County Bar Assn., Baldwin Sr. Travelers (sec. 1994-98), Spanish Fort, Fairhope Bus. and Profl. Women's, Phi Alpha Delta. Methodist.

NESBITT, CHARLES RUDOLPH, lawyer, energy consultant; b. Miami, Okla., Aug. 30, 1921; s. Charles Rudolph and Irma Louise (Wilhelmi) N.; m. Margot Dorothy Lord, June 6, 1948; children: Nancy Margot Nesbitt Nagle, Douglas Charles, Carolyn Jane Nesbitt Gresham-Fiegel. BA, U. Okla., 1942; JD, Yale U., 1947. Bar: Okla. 1947, U.S. Supreme Ct. 1957. Pvt. practice, Oklahoma City, 1948-62, 67-69, 75-91, 95—; atty. gen., 1963-67; mem. Okla. Corp. Commn., 1968-75, chmn., 1969-75; sec. of energy State of Okla., 1991-95; pvt. practice Oklahoma City, 1995—. Okla. rep., v.p. Interstate Oil and Gas Compact. Trustee endowment fund St. Gregory's Coll.; pres. Hist. Preservation, Inc.; pres. bd. trustees Okla. Mus. Art; v.p., bd. dirs. Western History Collections Assocs., U. Okla. Librs.; mem. panel arbitrators Am. Arbitration Assn., NASD, NYSE. With AUS, 1942-46. Mem. ABA, Okla. Bar Assn., Oklahoma City C. of C., Phi Beta Kappa, Phi Delta Phi. Episcopalian. General civil litigation, Oil, gas, and mineral, General practice. Home: 1703 N Hudson Ave Oklahoma City OK 73103-3428 Office: 125 NW 6th St Oklahoma City OK 73102-6014

NESBITT, SEAN MILO, lawyer; b. Glasgow, Eng., Feb. 25, 1966; BA with honors, Oxford U., England, 1987; Common Profl. Exam., Trent Polytechnic, Nottingham, 1988, Law Society Finals, 1989. Solicitor Slaughter and May, London, 1991-97; ptnr., solicitor Garretts, London, 1997—2002; ptnr., solicitor Taylor Wessing, London, 2002—. Immigration, naturalization, and customs, Labor (including EEOC, Fair Labor Standards Act, labor-management relations, NLRB, OSHA). Office: Taylor Wessing Carmelite 50 Victoria Embankment London EC4Y 0DX England Office Fax: 44 020 7300 7100. E-mail: s.nesbitt@taylorwessing.com.

NESCI, VINCENT PETER, lawyer; b. New Rochelle, N.Y., Feb. 27, 1947; s. Vincent S. and Carmela (DeMasi) N.; m. Donna M. Dahlgren, July 21, 1968; children: Vincent P. Jr., Joseph E., Patricia A. BA, Sacred Heart U., 1969; JD, St. John's U., 1971. Bar: N.Y. 1972, U.S. Dist. Ct. (ea. dist.) N.Y. 1973, U.S. Dist. Ct. (so. dist.) N.Y. 1978), U.S. Supreme Ct. 1976. Assoc. Campbell, Hyman & Lang, New Rochelle, 1972-76; ptnr. Lang & Nesci, P.C., New Rochelle, 1976-79; pvt. practice Yonkers, N.Y., 1980-93. Gen. counsel Liberty Lines, Yonkers, 1979-93; CEO Specialized Risk Mgmt., White Plains, N.Y., 1993—; mgr. ptnr. Nesci Keane Piekarski Keogh & Corrigan, White Plains, 1993—; cons. Summit Investment, Queensland, Australia, 1992—. Avocation: auto racing. State civil litigation, Personal injury (including property damage), Transportation. Home: RR 2 Bedford NY 10506-9802 Office: 245 Main St Ste 600 White Plains NY 10601 E-mail: vpn@aol.com.

NESLAGE, JOHN EDWARD, lawyer; b. Pampa, Tex., Aug. 13, 1946; AA cum laude, N.Mex. Milit. Inst., 1966; BBA magna cum laude, Tex. Tech. U., 1969; JD cum laude, U. Houston, 1972. Bar: Tex. 1972. Mem. Baker & Botts L.L.P., Houston. Mem. ABA, State Bar Tex., Houston Bar Assn., Phi Kappa Phi, Phi Alpha Delta, Order of the Barons. Office: Baker & Botts LLP One Shell Plz 1200 Smith St Ste 1200 Houston TX 77002-4592

NESS, ANDREW DAVID, lawyer; b. San Francisco, Oct. 29, 1952; s. Orville Arne and Muriel Ruth (Trendt) N.; m. Rita M. Kobylenski, May 25, 1980; children: Katherine, Austin, Emily. BS, Stanford U., 1974; JD, Harvard U., 1977. Bar: Calif. 1977, D.C. 1979, Va. 1986, U.S. Dist. Ct. (no. dist.) Calif. 1977, U.S. Dist. Ct. D.C. 1983, U.S. Dist. Ct. (ea. dist.) Va. 1988, U.S. Ct. Appeals (4th cir.) 1989. Law clk. U.S. Dist. Ct., San Francisco, 1977-78; assoc. Lewis, Mitchell & Moore, Vienna, Va., 1979-82, ptnr., 1982-87, Morgan, Lewis & Bockius LLP, Washington, 1987-2000, Thelen Reid & Priest LLP, Washington, 2000—, mng. ptnr. D.C. office, 2001—. Instr. U. Md., College Park, 1987-90; mem. faculty constrn. exec. program Stanford (Calif.) U., 1984-87. Co-editor Fed. Govt. Construction Contracts, 2003; contbr. chpt. to books, articles to profl. jours. Mem. ABA (forum on constrn. industry, pub. contract law sect., editor fed. govt. constrn. contracts). Avocations: hiking, bicycling. Construction, Government contracts and claims. Office: Thelen Reid & Priest LLP 701 Pennsylvania Ave NW Washington DC 20004-2608 E-mail: adness@thelenreid.com.

NETTLES, BERT SHEFFIELD, lawyer; b. Monroeville, Ala., May 6, 1936; s. George Lee and Blanche (Sheffield) N.; m. Elizabeth Duquet, Sept. 16, 1967; children: Jane, Mary Katherine, Susan, Anne. BS, U. Ala., Tuscaloosa, 1958, JD, 1960. Bar: Ala. 1960. Asst. atty. gen. State of Ala., Montgomery, 1961-62; ptnr. Johnston, Johnston & Nettles, Mobile, Ala., 1962-69, Nettles & Cox, Mobile, 1969-81, Nettles, Barker, Janecky & Copeland, Mobile, 1981-89, Spain, Gillon, Grooms, Blan & Nettles, Birmingham, Ala., 1989-94, London & Yancey, Birmingham, 1995—. Contbr. articles to profl. jours. Mem. Ala. Ho. of Reps., 1969-74; bd. dirs. U. South Ala. Med. Sci. Found., Mobile, 1982-89, U. So. Ala. Health Svcs. Found., 1985-89; chancellor Episcopal Diocese of Cen. Gulf Coast, Mobile, 1983-88; asst. chancellor Episcopal Diocese of Ala., 2000-03. 2d lt. inf. U.S. Army, 1960-61, capt., inf. Res., 1960-67. Recipient Exceptional Performance citation Def. Rsch. Inst. and ATLA, 1987. Mem. ABA (chmn. standing com. on legis. 1978), Ala. Bar Assn. (chmn. young lawyers divsn. 1966-67, chair task force on appellate restructuring 1988-91), Am. Right of Way Assn. (sr.), Ala. Def. Lawyers Assn. (pres. 1986-87), Ala. Supreme Ct. (com. on appellate rules 2001—, pattern jury instructions/civil, 1990—). Republican. Avocation: reading. General civil litigation, Insurance, Professional liability. Home: 1416 Windsor Cir Birmingham AL 35213-3434 Office: London & Yancey 2001 Park Pl Birmingham AL 35203-2735

NETZLY, DWIGHT H. lawyer; b. Navarre, Ohio, May 7, 1919; s. Harry E. Netzly and Lillian N. Ramsey; m. Martha L. Emerick, Jan. 29, 1949; children: Duane, Dwight K., Doyle, Derek. BSBA, Kent State U., 1948; LLB, William McKinley Law Sch., 1952. Bar: Ohio 1952. Acct. H.C. Schwitzgebul, Canton, Ohio, 1948-52; pvt. practice law and acctg. Massillon, Ohio, 1952—. Sgt. U.S. Army, 1941-45. Mem. Am. Assn. Atty. CPAs, Ohio State Bar Assn., Ohio Soc. CPAs, Am. Legion (state treas. 1993-94). Republican. Corporate, general, Probate (including wills, trusts), Taxation, general. Home: 6179 Pigeon Run Rd SW Navarre OH 44662-8738 Office: 1237 Lincoln Way E Massillon OH 44646-6954 E-mail: dhnetz@aol.com.

NEUFELD, TIMOTHY LEE, lawyer; b. Glendale, Calif., Apr. 23, 1947; s. Stanley and Marie E. (Scott) N.; m. Naomi Das, Nov. 27, 1971; children: Pamela, Katherine. AB, Brown U., 1969; JD, Boston U., 1975. Bar: Calif. 1975. Assoc. Richards, Watson & Gershon, L.A., 1975—80, ptnr., 1980—2001, Neufeld Jaffe, LLP, L.A., 2001—. Lt. (j.g.) USN, 1969-72. Mem. State Bar Calif., L.A. County Bar Assn. Avocation: competitive running. Federal civil litigation, General civil litigation, State civil litigation. Office: Neufeld Jaffe LLP 30th Fl 555 W Fifth St Los Angeles CA 90013

NEUMAN, LINDA KINNEY, state supreme court justice; b. Chgo., June 18, 1948; d. Harold S. and Mary E. Kinney; m. Henry G. Neuman; children: Emily, Lindsey. BA, U. Colo., 1970, JD, 1973; LLM, U. Va., 1998. Ptnr. Betty, Neuman, McMahon, Hellstrom & Bittner, 1973-79; v.p., trust officer Bettendorf Bank & Trust Co., 1979-80; dist. ct. judge, 1982-86; supreme ct. justice State of Iowa, 1986—. Mem. adj. faculty U. Iowa Grad. Sch. of Social Work, 1981; part-time jud. magistrate Scott County, 1980-82; mem. Supreme Ct. continuing legal edn. commn.; chair Iowa Supreme Ct. commn. planning 21st Century; mem. bd. counselors Drake Law Sch., time on appeal adv. com. Nat. Ctr. State Cts. Trustee St. Ambrose U. Recipient Regents scholarship, U. Colo. award for disting. svc. Fellow ABA (chair appellate judges conf., mem. appellate standards com., JAD exec. coun.); mem. Am. Judicature Soc., Iowa Bar Assn., Iowa Judges Assn., Scott County Bar Assn., Nat. Assn. Women Judges (bd. dirs.), Dillon Am. Inn of Ct., U.S. Assn. Constl. Law. E-mail: linda.k.neuman@jb.state.ia.us.

NEUMAN, ROBERT HENRY, lawyer; b. N.Y.C., Oct. 14, 1936; s. Sydney A. and Ethel (Pekelner) N.; m. Emily Mann, Dec. 30, 1960 (div. 1975); children: David Marshall, Anthony Howard, Amanda Sarah; m. Joyce Thompson, May 5, 1975; 1 child, Nicole Sydney. AB magna cum laude, Harvard U., 1958, JD, 1961. Bar: N.Y. 1962, D.C. 1962. Ford Found. fellow, West Africa, 1961-62; assoc. Meyers & Batzell, Washington, 1962-64; asst. legal adviser U.S. Dept. of State, Washington, 1964-70; ptnr. Arent, Fox, Kintner, Plotkin & Kahn, Washington, 1970-93, Baker & Hostetler, Washington, 1993-98. Adj. prof. The George Washington U., 1998, Elliott Sch. Internat. Affairs, 2001-02. U.S. rep. to UN Conf. on Marine Pollution, 1969. Recipient Superior Honor award Dept. State, 1965. Mem. ABA, FBA, Am. Soc. Internat. Law, Internat. Bar Assn., Phi Beta Kappa. Avocation: sailing. Private international. Home: 334 Catbrier Ct Kiawah Island SC 29455

NEUMAN, TODD HOWARD, lawyer; b. Buffalo, Dec. 1, 1967; s. Melvin M. and Elaine Neuman; m. Lee Anne Stepanick, Aug. 23, 1997; children: Sidney, Jillian, Melanie, Travis. BS in Fin., Ohio State U., 1989; JD, W.Va. U., 1992. Bar: Ohio 1992, Fla. 1993, U.S. Dist. Ct. (so. dist.) Ohio 1993. Assoc. Thompson, Hine & Flory, Columbus, Ohio, 1992-95; ptnr. Swedlow, Butler, Lewis & Dye Co., LPA, Columbus, 1995—. Gen. counsel, mem. exec. bd. Columbus U.S.A. Orgn., 1993-95; mem. Jr. Achievement-Young Profls., Columbus, 1998—. Mem. ABA, Ohio Bar Assn., Columbus Bar Assn. (various coms., bd. dirs. barrister leadership program 1996-97), Inns of Ct., Million Dollar Advs. Forum. Avocations: sports, outdoor activities, family. General civil litigation, Land use and zoning (including planning), Securities. Office: Swedlow Butler Levine Et Al 10 W Broad St Ste 2400 Columbus OH 43215-3469

NEUMANN, GORDON RICHARD, JR., lawyer; b. Des Moines, Sept. 30, 1950; s. Gordon R. Neumann and Mary Jane Gray; m. Elizabeth Montgomery, July 25, 1949; children: Jeannette, Eleanore, Neil. BA in Econs., U. Colo., 1972; JD, Drake U., 1976. Bar: Iowa 1976. Nyemaster, Goode, Voigts, West, Hansell & O'Brien, P.C., Des Moines, 1976-80, shareholder, 1980—. Greensboro C. of C., 2001; pres. Old North State Coun. Boy Scouts Am., 2003; chmn. Greensboro Merchants Assn., 1993; chair Downtown Cmty. Alliance, 2000—, City-County Consolidation Commn., 2002—; bd. mem. Iowa Capital Investment Bd., 2002—. Mem.: Des Moines Club (pres. 1988—89), Des Moines Pioneer Club (pres. 1998, Vol. of Yr. 1997). Corporate, general, Mergers and acquisitions, Securities. Home: 3950 John Lynde Rd Des Moines IA 50312-3036 Office: 700 Walnut St Ste 1600 Des Moines IA 50309-3899 Fax: 515-283-3108. E-mail: grneumann@nyemaster.com.

NEUMANN, RITA NUNEZ, lawyer; b. New Brunswick, N.J., Apr. 23, 1944; d. Arno Otto and Florence (Alligier) N. BA in Math., Trenton State Coll., 1965; MS in Math., Stevens Inst. Tech., 1970; JD, Seton Hall U., 1976; LLM in Tax Law, U. San Diego, 1983. Bar: D.C. 1984, U.S. Tax Ct. 1984, N.Y. 1985, N.J. 1986, U.S. Supreme Ct. 1989, Mont. 1990, U.S. Ct. Appeals (9th cir.) 1991. Instr. math. Middlesex County Coll., Edison, N.J., 1971-74; tax cons. Evan Morris Esq. Offices, Woodland Hills, Calif., 1975-85; asst. to editor Jour. Taxation, N.Y.C., 1985-86; pvt. practice law New Brunswick, 1986-94, Las Cruces, N.Mex., 1994—; mcpl. prosecutor Manville, N.J., 1987. Adj. instr. bus. law and fin. L.A. C.C. Dist., 1976-82; adj. instr. law and bus. calculus Ventura (Calif.) C.C. Dist., 1977-82; adj. prof. bus. calculus Calif. State U., Northridge, 1981-83; adj. instr. internat. law Laverne U. and San Fernando Valley Coll. Law, 1983-85; disting. lectr. in law and mgmt. Troy State U., Holloman AFB/White Sands Missile Range.; atty. Ability Ctr. of Las Cruces; candidate Ct. of Appeals of N.Mex., 2000. Author: Doing Business in North America, 1994, 95, 96, Legal Aspects of Doing Business in North America, 1995-2003; contbr. articles to profl. publs. Vol. to farm workers ctr., Moorpark, Calif., 1979; instr. community extension ctr. for women, Calif., 1980; vol. atty. for N.J. Vietnam Vets., 1986; organizer 10-kilometer run to benefit ill children, Manville, N.J., 1986; guest lectr. taxes Second Ann. Bus. Seminar for Vets. and Non-Vet. Am. Indians of N.W. U.S., Billings, Mont., 1988; candidate for freeholder, Middlesex County, 1988; active with numerous Am. Indian tribes thoughout the U.S. in bus. devel. and Indian rights. Fellow Nat. Sci. Found., 1968-71. Mem. Kappa Delta Phi. Avocation: 10-kilometer runs (recipient several medals). Labor (including EEOC, Fair Labor Standards Act, labor-management relations, NLRB, OSHA). Office: 1850 N Solano Dr Las Cruces NM 88001-1851

NEUMANN, WILLIAM ALLEN, state supreme court justice; b. Minot, N.D., Feb. 11, 1944; s. Albert W. and Opal Olive (Whitlock) N.; m. Jaqueline Denise Buechler, Aug. 9, 1980; children: Andrew, Emily. BSBA, U. N.D., 1965; JD, Stanford U., 1968. Bar: N.D. 1969, U.S. Dist. Ct. N.D. 1969. Pvt. practice law, Williston, N.D., 1969-70, Bottineau, N.D., 1970-79; former judge N.D. Judicial Dist. Ct., N.E. Judicial Dist., Rugby and Bottineau, 1979-92; justice N.D. Supreme Ct., Bismarck, 1993—. Chmn. elect N.D. Jud. Conf., 1985-87, chmn. 1987-89. Mem. ABA, State Bar Assn. N.D., Am. Judicature Soc. (bd. dirs. 1998—). Lutheran. Office: ND Supreme Ct Jud Wing 1st Fl Dept 180 600 E Boulevard Ave Bismarck ND 58505-0530

NEUMARK, MICHAEL HARRY, lawyer; b. Cin., Oct. 28, 1945; s. Jacob H. and Bertha (Zubor) N.; m. Sue Daly, June 5, 1971; children: Julie Rebecca, John Adam. BS in Bus., Ind. U., 1967; JD, U. Cin., 1970. Bar: Ohio 1970, D.C. 1972. Atty. chief counsel's office IRS, Washington, 1970-74, acting br. chief, 1974-75, sr. atty. regional counsel's office, 1975-77; assoc. Paxton & Seasongood Legal Profl. Assn., Cin., 1977-80; ptnr. Thompson, Hine & Flory, 1980—, mem. mgmt. com., 1993—. Chmn. So. Ohio Tax Inst., 1987; mem. IRS and Bar Liaison Com., 1991-93; spkr. at profl. confs. Contbr. articles to profl. jours. Bd. dirs. 1987 World Figure Skating Championship, Cin., 1986-89; precinct exec. Hamilton County Rep. Orgn., 1980-86; vol. referee Hamilton County Juvenile Ct., 1980-86; trustee Cin. Contemporary Arts Ctr., St. Rita Sch. for Deaf, 1991-97, Legal Aid Soc. Cin., 1997—, v.p., 2002—; bd. visitors U. Cin. Coll. Law. Recipient Commendation Resolution Sycamore Twp., 1987. Mem. ABA (ho. of dels. 1998-2002), Ohio State Bar Assn., Cin. Bar Assn. (pres. 1996-97, recognition award 1985, treas., bd. trustees 1988-91, trustee 1992—, chair tax sect., 1990-91), Leadership Cin., Ohio Met. Bar Assn. (pres. 1996-97), Kenwood Country Club, Indian Hill Club, Ohio Met. Bar (pres. 1996-97), Cin. Acad. of Leadership for Lawyers (founder, chair). Republican. Avocations: golf, travel. Corporate, general, Taxation, general. Office: Thompson Hine & Flory 312 Walnut St Ste 1400 Cincinnati OH 45202-4089

NEUMEIER, MATTHEW MICHAEL, lawyer, educator; b. Racine, Wis., Sept. 13, 1954; s. Frank Edward and Ruth Irene (Effenberger) N.; m. Annmarie Prine, Jan. 31, 1987; children: Ruthann Marie, Emilie Irene, Matthew Charles. B in Gen. Studies with distinction, U. Mich., 1981; JD magna cum laude, Harvard U., 1984. Bar: N.Y. 1987, Mich. 1988, Ill. 1991, U.S. Dist. Ct. (ea. dist.) Mich. 1988, U.S. Dist. Ct. (ea., no. dists. and trial bar) Ill. 1991, U.S. Ct. Appeals (7th cir.) 1992, U.S. Ct. Appeals (fed. cir.) 1998, U.S. Supreme Ct. 1991. Sec.-treas. Ind. Roofing & Siding Co., Escanaba, Mich., 1973-78; mng. ptnr. Ind. Roofing Co., Menominee, Mich.,

1977-78; law clk. to presiding justice U.S. Ct. Appeals (9th cir.), San Diego, 1984-85; law clk. to chief justice Warren E. Burger U.S. Supreme Ct., Washington, 1985-86; spl. asst. to chmn. U.S. Constn. Bicentennial Commn., Washington, 1986; assoc. Cravath, Swaine & Moore, N.Y.C., 1986-88; spl. counsel Burnham & Ritchie, Ann Arbor, Mich., 1988; assoc. Schlussel, Lifton, Simon, Rands, Galvin & Jackier, P.C., Ann Arbor, 1988-90, Skadden, Arps, Slate, Meagher & Flom, Chgo., 1990-96; ptnr. Jenner & Block, Chgo., 1996—. Adj. prof. computer law and high tech. litig. John Marshall Law Sch., Chgo., 1999—. Editor Harvard Law Rev., 1982-84. Pres., bd. dirs. Univ. Cellar Inc., Ann Arbor, 1979-81; bd. dirs. Econ. Devel. Corp., Menominee, 1978-79, Midwestern divsn. Am. Suicide Found., sec., 1992-97, Commonwealth Plaza Condominium Assn., dir., 1999—, pres., 2000—, Harvard Law Soc. Ill., 2003-; mem. vestry Ch. of Our Savior, 1997-2000; bd. dirs. Chgo. Children's Mus., 1999—, sec., 2003-; chmn. Harvard Law Sch. 15 Yr. Reunion Gift Fund, 1999. Mem. ABA, State Bar Mich., Assn. of Bar of City of N.Y., Chgo. Bar Assn., Def. Rsch. Inst., The 410 Club, Econ. Club Chgo, City Club of Chgo. Republican. Avocations: classic automobiles, piano, choir. Intellectual property, Commercial, consumer (including collections, credit), Product liability. Office: Jenner & Block Ste 4200 One IBM Plz Chicago IL 60611 E-mail: mneumeier@jenner.com.

NEUMEIER, RICHARD L. lawyer; b. Boston, Nov. 22, 1946; s. Victor L. and Crystal Gladys (Mueller) N.; m. Mary Edna Malcolm, Mar. 15, 1975; children: Hannah Catherine, Edmund Malcolm, Thomas Richard. AB, AM, U. Chgo., 1968; JD, Columbia U., 1971. Bar: N.Y. 1972, U.S. Dist. Ct. (so. dist.) N.Y. 1972, Mass. 1973, U.S. Dist. Ct. Mass. 1973, U.S. Ct. Appeals (1st cir.) 1974, R.I. 1979, U.S. Supreme Ct. 1985. Assoc. Hart & Hume, N.Y.C., 1971-73; from assoc. to ptnr. Parker, Coulter, Daley & White, Boston, 1973-95; ptnr. McDonough, Hacking, Neumeier, & Lavoie LLP, Boston, 1995—. Mem. editl. bd. Def. Counsel Jour., 1989-92, editor, chmn. bd. editors, 1992—; mem. editl. bd. Boston Bar Jour., 1988-94; contbr. articles to profl. jours. Bd. dirs. Common Cause/Mass., Boston, 1980-91, 94-96, chmn., 1990-91; mem. Town Meeting, Lexington, Mass., 1989—. Fellow Am. Bar Found.; mem. ABA, Fed. Bar Assn. (pres. Mass. chpt. 1989-90), Am. Law Inst., Mass. Bar Assn., Boston Bar Assn. (chmn. ethics com. 1991-94, chmn. torts com. 1994-96), Internat. Assn. Def. Counsel (exec. com. 1992-97). Democrat. Civil rights, Insurance, Personal injury (including property damage). Home: 2 Pitcairn Pl Lexington MA 02421-7134 Office: McDonough Hacking Neumeier & Lavoie LLP 6 Beacon St Ste 815 Boston MA 02108-3013 E-mail: rneumeier@mhnattys.com.

NEUMEYER, RICHARD ALBERT, lawyer; b. L.A., Oct. 7, 1944; s. Albert G. and Sally (Wohl) N.; children: Andrew Richard, Kari Elizabeth; m. Carol Boyd. BS, Northwestern U., 1966; JD, UCLA, 1969. Bar: Calif. 1970, U.S. Dist. Ct. (cen. dist.) Calif. 1970, U.S. Ct. Appeals (9th cir.) 1973, U.S. Supreme Ct. 1973, U.S. Dist. Ct. (no., so. and ea. dists.) Calif. 1983. Assoc. Youngman, Hungate & Leopold, Los Angeles, 1970-72, Spray, Gould & Bowers, Los Angeles, 1972-76; ptnr. Grace & Neumeyer, Inc. and predecessor firms, Los Angeles, 1976-87; of counsel Grace & Neumeyer Inc., Los Angeles, 1987—90; ptnr. Neumeyer and Boyd, LLP, 1990—. Former judge pro tem Los Angeles Mcpl. and Superior Cts.; former arbitrator Los Angeles Superior Ct.; officer atty. settlement Ct. Appeals Atty. Appellate Settlement program. Mem. ABA, Calif. Bar Assn., Los Angeles County Bar Assn., Calif. Acad. Appellate Lawyers, Dean's Counsel, UCLA Law Sch., Phi Delta Phi. Office: Neumeyer & Boyd LLP 2029 Century Park E Suite 1100 Los Angeles CA 90067

NEUPERT, WALTER DIETER, lawyer; b. May 5, 1942; m. Katarina Laves; 2 children. ML magna cum laude, U. Zurich, 1969, LLD magna cum laude, 1976; D (hon.) , Tech. U., Azerbaidjan, Baku, 1998. Assoc. Hoffmann, Frick, Widmer & Partners, Zurich, Switzerland, 1974—81, ptnr., 1981—2000; sr. ptnr. Neupert & Ptnrs., Zollikon-Zurich, Switzerland, 2000—. Vice chmn. Aerosuisse; chmn. European Bus. Aviation Assn., Switzerland; mem. Swiss Aviation Arbitration Ct.; legal counsel Swiss Helicopter Assn.; head legal com. Swiss Sailing; mem. constn. com. Internat. Sailing Fedn. Contbr. articles to profl. jours. Mem. organizing com. Olympic Sailing Regatta, Pusan, Republic of Korea, 1998; del. Swiss Liberal Dem. Party. Col. Swiss Air Force. Mem.: ABA, Internat. Fiscal Assn, Zurich Bar Assn., Swiss Bar Assn., Internat. Bar Assn., Spanish C. of C., German C. of C., Am. C. of C., Aircraft Owners and Pilots Assn. Liberal Democrat. Aviation. Office: Neuport and Partner Dufourstrasse 58 CH 8702 Zollikon Zurich Switzerland Home: Buehlstrasse 8a CH 8700 Kuesnacht Zurich Switzerland

NEUWIRTH, GLORIA S. lawyer; b. N.Y.C., Aug. 16, 1934; d. Nathan and Jennie (Leff) Salob; m. Robert S. Neuwirth, June 9, 1957; children: Susan Madeleine Guerra, Jessica Anne, Laura Helaine, Michael Jonathan. BA, Hunter Coll., 1955; JD, Yale U., 1958. Bar: N.Y. 1959, Fla. 1979, U.S. Supreme Ct. 1976, U.S. Dist. Ct. (so. and ea. dists.) N.Y. 1976. Assoc. dir. Joint Rsch. Project on Ct. Calendar Congestion Columbia U., N.Y.C., 1958-61; assoc. Kridel & Friou, N.Y.C., 1974-76; ptnr. Kridel, Slater and Neuwirth, N.Y.C., 1976-82, 87-94; assoc. Kaye, Scholer, Fierman, Hays and Handler, N.Y.C., 1982-84, Graubard Moskovitz McGoldrick Dannett & Horowitz, N.Y.C., 1984-86; ptnr. Davidson, Dawson & Clark, N.Y.C., 1995—. Vol. arbitrator Better Bus. Bur. Author: (with R.B. Hunting) Who Sues in New York City: A Study of Automobile Accident Claims, 1962; contbr. articles to profl. jours. Trustee Blueberry Inc., 1962-70, Riverdale Country Sch., 1981-86; trustee, v.p., sec. Nat. Kidney Found., Inc., N.Y./N.J., 1980-2002, trustee nat. office, 1980-90; dir. Estate Planning Coun. N.Y.C., Riverdale Mental Health Assn., Bronx Opera Co., The Ruth Turner Fund, The Associated Blind; sec. Kidney & Urology Found. Am., 2002-. Recipient C. LaRue Munson prize Yale Law Sch., 1958. Fellow Am. Coll. Trust and Estate Counsel; mem. ABA, N.Y. State Bar Assn. (vice chmn. com. on law of the elderly), Assn. Bar City N.Y., Fin. Women's Assn., Estate Planning Coun. N.Y., Nat. Health Lawyers Assn., Appalachian Mtn. Club. Non-profit and tax-exempt organizations, Probate (including wills, trusts), Estate taxation. Office: Davidson Dawson & Clark LLP 330 Madison Ave Fl 35 New York NY 10017-5094 Fax: 212-286-8513. E-mail: gsneuwirth@davidsondawson.com.

NEVELOFF, JAY A. lawyer; b. Bklyn., Oct. 11, 1950; m. Arlene Sillman, Aug. 26, 1972; children: David, Kevin. BA, Bklyn. Coll., 1971; JD, NYU, 1974. Bar: N.Y. 1975, D.C. 1992, U.S. Dist. Ct. (so. and ea. dists.) N.Y. 1975, U.S. Ct. Appeals (2d cir.) 1975, U.S. Supreme Ct. 1982. Assoc. Marshall, Bratter, Greene, Allison & Tucker, N.Y.C., 1974-82, Rosenman, Colin, Freund, Lewis & Cohen, N.Y.C., 1982-83, ptnr., 1983-88, Kramer, Levin, Naftalis, Nessen, Kamin & Frankel, N.Y.C., 1988—98. Editor N.Y. Real Property Service. Mem. planning bd. Briarcliff Manor, 1995—. Mem. ABA (vice chmn. com. partnerships, joint ventures and other investment vehicles 1988-95), Am. Law Inst., Am. Coll. Real Estate Attys., N.Y. State Bar Assn. (financing com.), Practising Law Inst. (lectr. 1988—, mem. adv. bd. 1991—), N.Y. County Lawyers Assn. (lectr. 1984-94), Assn. Bar City N.Y. (real property law com., lectr. 1984-88), Cmty. Assns. Inst. (lectr. 1986), Law Jours. Seminars (lectr. 1987—), Strategic Resources Inst. (lectr. 1994-98), Internat. Health Network Soc. (vice chmn. 1995-2000), Inst. Internat. Rsch. (lectr. 1994—). Property, real (including real estate development, water). Home: 134 Alder Dr Briarcliff Manor NY 10510-2218 Office: Kramer Levin Naftalis & Frankel LLP 919 3rd Ave New York NY 10022-3902 E-mail: jneveloff@kramerlevin.com.

NEVES, KERRY LANE, lawyer; b. San Angelo, Tex., Dec. 19, 1950; s. Herman Walter and Geraldine (Ball) N.; m. Sharon Lynn Briggs, July 28, 1973; 1 child, Erin Lesli. BBA, U. Tex., 1975, JD, 1978. Bar: Tex. 1978, U.S. Dist. Ct. (so. and ea. dists.) Tex. 1979, U.S. Ct. Appeals (5th cir.) 1979, U.S. Dist. Ct. (we. dist.) 1980; cert. personal injury trial law, Tex. Bd. Legal Specialization, 1994. Ptnr. Mills, Shirley, Eckel & Bassett, Galveston, Tex., 1978—93, Neves & Crowther, Galveston, Tex., 1993—2002; pvt. practice Law Offices of Kerry L. Neves, Galveston, 2002—. Vice-chmn. Bldg. Stnds. Commn., Dickinson, Tex., 1991-98; mem. City Coun. Dickinson, Tex., 1998—. Sgt. USMC, 1969-72. Fellow Tex. Bar Found. (life); mem. ABA, State Bar Tex. (grievance com. 1989-92, disciplinary rules profl. conduct com. 1990-92, dir. dist. 5 1997-2000), Galveston County Bar Assn. (pres. 1989-90), U. Tex. Law Alumni Assn. (pres. 1991-92). Avocations: gardening, wine, reading. General civil litigation, Personal injury (including property damage), Product liability. Home: RR 2 Box 95 Dickinson TX 77539-9204 Office: 1802 Broadway St Ste 206 Galveston TX 77550-4953

NEVIÈRE, EMMANUEL, lawyer; b. Saint-Céré, France, July 20, 1969; s. Jean-François Nevière and Marie-Hélène Pagès; m. Sophie Joubert, May 6, 2000; 1 child, Simon. DEA Droit Social, Paris I Panthèon-Sorbonne, 1992, Institut d'Etudes Judiciaires, 1994; CAPA, Ecole de Formation du Barreau, 1995. Of counsel Price Waterhouse Juridique Fiscal (Landwell), 1995—97, Lefèvre Pelletier and Associés, 1997—. Contbr. articles. Labor (including EEOC, Fair Labor Standards Act, labor-management relations, NLRB, OSHA). Office: Lefèvre Pelletier and Associés 136 avenue des Champs-Elysées 75008 Paris France

NEVILLE, CARA LEE T. judge; JD, William Mitchell Coll. Law, 1975. Lawyer felony divsn. Hennepin County Attys. Office, 1972; asst. pub. defender Hennepin County, 1978; judge Hennepin County Mcpl. Ct., 1983, Hennepin County Dist. Ct., 1986; dist. ct. judge 4th Jud. Dist., Mpls., 1986—. Mem.: ABA (bd. govs. 9th dist. 2000—03). Office: Hennepin County Dist Ct 1859-C Govt Ctr 300 S 6th St Minneapolis MN 55487-0999*

NEVILLE, JAMES MORTON, retired lawyer, consumer products executive; b. Mpls., May 28, 1939; s. Philip and Maurene (Morton) N.; m. Judie Martha Proctor, Sept. 9, 1961; children: Stephen Warren, Martha Maurene Hereford. BA, U. Minn., JD magna cum laude, 1964. Bar: Minn. 1964, Mo. 1984. Assoc. Neville, Johnson & Thompson, Mpls., 1964-69, ptnr., 1969-70; assoc. counsel Gen. Mills, Inc., Mpls., 1970-77, sr. assoc. counsel, 1977-83, corp. sec., 1976-83; v.p., sec., asst. gen. counsel Ralston Purina Co., St. Louis, 1983-84, v.p., gen. counsel, sec., 1984-96, v.p., gen. counsel, 1996-2000, v.p., sr. counsel, 2000-01; ret., 2001; chmn. The Thompson Ctr., 2002. Lectr. bus. law. U. Minn., 1967-71. Named Man of Yr., Edina Jaycees, 1967. Mem. ABA, Mo. Bar Assn., U.S. Supreme Ct. Bar Assn., St. Louis Bar Assn., U. Minn. Law Sch. Alumni Assn., Old Warson Country Club, Ladue Racquet Club, Order of Coif, Phi Delta Phi, Psi Upsilon. Episcopalian. Corporate, general. Home: 9810 Log Cabin Ct Saint Louis MO 63124-1133 E-mail: jnev57@aol.com.

NEVOLA, ROGER, lawyer; b. N.Y.C., Apr. 30, 1947; m. Molly Cagle; children: Adrienne L., Jake F. Student, U. Notre Dame, 1964-66; BSME, Stanford U., 1968; JD, U. Tex., 1974. Bar: Tex. 1974. Assoc. Vinson & Elkins, Houston, 1974-79, Austin, 1979-81, ptnr., 1981-95; pvt. practice Austin, 1995—. Fellow Tex. Bar Found. (life). Administrative and regulatory, Environmental, Property, real (including real estate development, water). Home: 4304 Bennedict Ln Austin TX 78746-1940 Office: PO Box 2103 Austin TX 78768-2103 E-mail: roger@nevola.com.

NEWBERN, WILLIAM DAVID, retired state supreme court justice; b. Oklahoma City, May 28, 1937; s. Charles Banks and Mary Frances (Harding) N.; m. Barbara Lee Rigsby, Aug. 19, 1961 (div. 1968); 1 child, Laura Harding; m. Carolyn Lewis, July 30, 1970; 1 child, Alistair Elizabeth. BA, U. Ark., 1959, JD, 1961; LL.M., George Washington U., 1963; MA, Tufts U., 1967. Bar: Ark. 1961, U.S. Dist. Ct. (we. dist.) Ark. 1961, U.S. Supreme Ct. 1968, U.S. Ct. Appeals (8th cir.) 1983. Commd. 1st lt. advanced to maj. U.S. Army JAGC, 1961-70; Prof. law U. Ark., Fayetteville, 1970-84; adminstr. Ozark Folk Ctr., Mountain View, Ark., 1973; judge Ark. Ct. Appeals, Little Rock, 1979-80; assoc. justice Ark. Supreme Ct., Little Rock, 1985-99. Mem. faculty sr. appellate judges seminar NYU, 1987-91; panel chmn. com. on profl. conduct Ark. Supreme Ct., 2001—. Editor Ark. Law Rev., 1961; author: Arkansas Civil Practice and Procedure, 1985, (with John J. Watkins) 3d edit., 2003. Mem. Fayetteville Bd. Adjustment, 1972-79; bd. dirs. Decision Point, Inc., Springdale, Ark., 1980-85, Hot Springs Music Festival, 2000—; bd. dirs. Little Rock Wind Symphony, 1993-2001, pres. 1993-95. Fellow Ark. Bar Found.; mem. Ark. Bar Assn., Am. Judicature Soc. (bd. dirs. 1985-89), Inst. Jud. Adminstrn., Ark. IOLTA Found. (bd. dirs. 1985-87). Democrat. Avocations: string band-guitar, mandolin, banjo and brass quintet-tuba. E-mail: dnewbern@aristotle.net.

NEWBURG, ANDRE, retired lawyer; b. Berlin, Jan. 9, 1928; s. Hugo and Olga (Cherniak) N.; m. Ellen French Vanderbilt, Dec. 27, 1953 (div. 1996); children: Michael W., Anne C., Daniel F., Thomas H.; m. Susan Renwick Baring, June 26, 1997. AB, Harvard U., 1949, LLB, 1952. Bar: N.Y. 1952. Mem. Cleary, Gottlieb, Steen & Hamilton, N.Y.C., 1952-91, Paris, 1956-59, 74-76, Brussels, 1960-64, Hong Kong, 1980, ptnr., 1963-91, ret., counsel, 1997—; gen. counsel European Bank for Reconstrn. and Devel., London, 1991-95, sr. adv., 1995-97. Coun. Fgn. Rels., 1973—; Sm. Enterprise Assistance Funds, 1999—, SEAF Macedonia; bd. trustees Am. Sch. Classical Studies at Athens, 1965—99, Gennadius Libr., Athens, 2000—. Decorated Order of Leopold II (Belgium). Mem. ABA, Am. Assn. Internat. Commn. Jurists (bd. dirs. 1971—, chmn. 1989-91), Internat. Bar Assn., Internat. Law Assn. (monetary law com.), Assn. Bar City N.Y. chmn. spl. com. on Soviet affairs 1989-91), London Ct. Internat. Arbitration (arbitrator), Royal Inst. Internat. Affairs, Century Assn., Brooks's, Polo Club (Paris). Finance, Public international. Office: Cleary Gottlieb Steen Hamilton 55 Basinghall St London EC2V 5EH England Home: 18 Cleveland Sq London W2 6DG England also: 84 Rue du Cherche Midi Paris 75006 France E-mail: anewburg@aol.com.

NEWCOM, JENNINGS JAY, lawyer; b. St. Joseph, Mo., Oct. 18, 1941; s. Arden Henderson and Loyal Beatrice (Winans) N.; m. Cherry Ann Phelps, Apr. 4, 1964; children: Shandra Karine, J. Derek Arden. BA, Graceland U., Lamoni, Iowa, 1964; JD, Harvard U., 1968; LLD (hon.), Graceland U., 1999. Bar: Ill. 1968, Calif. 1973, Mo. 1979, Kans. 1981, Colo. 1999. Atty. McDermott, Will & Emery, Chgo., 1968-73; ptnr. Rifkind, Sterling & Lockwood, Beverly Hills, Calif., 1973-79, Shook, Hardy & Bacon L.L.P., Kans. City, Mo., 1979-99, Davis, Graham & Stubbs, LLP, Denver, 1999—; gen. counsel Putnam Lovell Capital Ptnr., Inc., LA, 1999—; dir. Skillpath Seminars, Overland Pk., Kans.; bd. dir. Stein Roe Investment Counsel, Chgo., Atlantic Asset Mgmt. LLC, Stamford, Conn., Stanford, Conn., Berkeley Capital Mgmt., LLC, San Francisco. Trustee Hubbard Found., Linde Found., Graceland U. Mem. Denver Bar Assn., State Bar Assn. Calif. Corporate, general, Mergers and acquisitions, Securities. Office: Davis Graham & Stubbs LLP 1550 17th St Ste 500 Denver CO 80202-1500

NEWCOMER, CLARENCE CHARLES, federal judge; b. Mount Joy, Pa., Jan. 18, 1923; s. Clarence S. and Marion Clara (Charles) N.; m. Jane Moyer Martin, Oct. 2, 1948; children: Judy (Mrs. Kenneth N. Birkett Jr.), Nancy Jane Newcomer (Mrs. Edward H. Vick), Peggy Jo Pollack (dec.). AB, Franklin and Marshall Coll., 1944; LL.B., Dickinson Sch. Law, 1948. Bar: Pa. 1950, U.S. Dist. Ct. Pa., U.S. Ct. Appeals (3rd cir.), U.S. Supreme Ct. Pvt. practice, Lancaster, 1950-52; spl. dep. atty. gen. Dept. Justice, Commonwealth of Pa., 1952-54; partner firm Rohrer, Honaman, Newcomer & Musser, Lancaster, 1957-60; with Office of Dist. Atty., Lancaster, 1960-64, 1st asst. dist. atty., 1964-68, dist. atty., 1968-72; partner Newcomer, Roda & Morgan, 1968-72; fed. dist. judge Eastern Dist. Pa., Phila., 1972-88, sr. judge, 1988—. Served to lt. (j.g.) USNR, 1943-46, PTO. Office: US Dist Ct 13614 US Courthouse 601 Market St Philadelphia PA 19106-1713

NEWITT, JOHN GARWOOD, JR., lawyer; b. Charlotte, N.C., Apr. 9, 1941; s. John Garwood and Sarah Elizabeth (Stratford) N.; m. Catherine Elizabeth Hubbard, Aug. 28, 1965; children: Catherine Stratford, Elizabeth Blake. BA, Wake Forest U., 1963, JD, 1965; postgrad., U. Va., 1966-68; CBA in Bus. Mgmt., Ctrl. Piedmont C.C., 2001. Bar: N.C. 1965, U.S. Ct. Mil. Appeals 1965, U.S. Dist. Ct. (we. dist.) N.C. 1968, U.S. Ct. Claims 1968, U.S. Tax. Ct. 1968, U.S. Ct. Appeals (4th cir.) 1984. Ptnr. Newitt & Newitt, Charlotte, 1968-73; sr. ptnr. Newitt & Bruny, Charlotte, 1973—. Lectr. The Judge Advocate Gen.'s Sch., 1965-68, United Way Vol. Leadership Devel. Program, 1986-93. Contbr. articles to profl. jours. Chmn. Bd. Zoning Adjustment, 1971-77; bd. dirs. Carolina Group Homes, 1992-95. Recipient awards ASCAP. Mem. N.C. Bar Assn., Mecklenburg County Bar Assn., N.C. Coll. Advocacy (cert. competency), Charlotte Econs. Club, Myers Park Country Club (past pres., bd. dirs.), Selwyn Men's Fellowship (past pres.), Good Fellows, Phi Delta Phi (past sec.). Republican. Presbyterian. Avocations: jogging, golf. General civil litigation, Corporate, general, Mergers and acquisitions. Home: 3216 Ferncliff Rd Charlotte NC 28211-3259 Office: Newitt & Bruny 417 East Blvd Ste 104 Charlotte NC 28203-5163 E-mail: johnnewitt@cs.com., newittbru@cs.com.

NEWMAN, CAROL L. lawyer; b. Yonkers, N.Y., Aug. 7, 1949; d. Richard J. and Pauline Frances (Stoll) N. AB/MA summa cum laude, Brown U., 1971; postgrad., Harvard U. Law Sch., 1972-73; JD cum laude, George Washington U., 1977. Bar: D.C. 1977, Calif. 1979. With antitrust divsn. U.S. Dept. Justice, Washington and L.A., 1977-80; assoc. Alschuler, Grossman & Pines, L.A., 1980-82, Costello & Walcher, L.A., 1982-85, Rosen, Wachtell & Gilbert, L.A., 1985-88, ptnr., 1988-90, Keck, Mahin & Cate, L.A., 1990-94; pvt. practice L.A., 1994—. Adj. prof. Sch. Bus., Golden Gate U., spring 1982. Commr. L.A. Bd. Transp. Commrs., 1993—98, v.p., 1995—96; pres. Bd. Taxicab Commrs., 1999—2001; candidate for State Atty. Gen., 1986; bd. dirs. Women's Progress Alliance, 1996—98. Mem. ABA, State Bar Calif., L.A. County Bar Assn., Ventura County Bar Assn., L.A. Lawyers for Human Rights (co. pres. 1991-92), Log Cabin (bd. dirs. 1992-97, 2003—, pres. 1996-97), Calif. Women Lawyers (bd. govs. 1991-94), Order of Coif, Phi Beta Kappa. Antitrust, Appellate, General civil litigation. E-mail: cnewman540@aol.com.

NEWMAN, CHARLES A. lawyer; b. L.A., Mar. 18, 1949; s. Arthur and Gladys Newman; children: Anne R., Elyse S. BA magna cum laude, U. Calif., 1970, JD, Washington U., 1973. Bar: Mo. 1973, U.S. Dist. Ct. (ea. dist.) Mo. 1973, U.S. Dist. Ct. (ctrl. dist.) Ill. 1996, U.S. Dist. Ct. (so. dist.) Ill. 2001, U.S. Dist. Ct. (ea. dist.) Mich. 2002, U.S. Ct. Appeals (8th cir.) 1975, U.S. Supreme Ct. 1976, D.C. 1981, U.S. Tax Ct. 1981, U.S. Claims Ct. 1981, U.S. Ct. Appeals (11th cir.) 1994, U.S. Ct. Appeals (9th cir.) 1995, U.S. Dist. Ct. (ctrl. dist.) Ill. 1996, U.S. Ct. Appeals (3d, 5th, 7th and 10th cirs.) 1996, U.S. Ct. Appeals (6th cir.) 1997. From assoc. to ptnr. Thompson & Mitchell, St. Louis, 1973-96; ptnr. Thompson Coburn, St. Louis, 1996-97, Bryan Cave LLP, St. Louis, 1997—. Lectr. law Washington U., St. Louis, 1976-78. Bd. dirs. Hawthorn Found., 1997-2000; trustee Mo. Bar Found., 1990-96, mem. Mo. Bar Bd. Govs, 1980-84; bd. dirs. United Israel Appeal, N.Y.C., 1990-93, Coun. Jewish Fedns., N.Y.C., 1992-95, United Jewish Appeal Young Leadership Cabinet, N.Y.C., 1985-88, Ctr. for Study of Dispute Resolution, 1985-88, Legal Svcs. Ea. Mo., 1985-94, St. Louis Community Found., 1992-2001, vice-chmn. 1997-99, St. Louis chpt. Young Audiences 1993-95, Planned Parenthood St. Louis, 1986-89, Jewish Fedn., St. Louis, 1986-98, asst. treas., 1989-90, v.p. fin. planning, 1990-93, asst. sec., 1994-95; v.p. Repertory Theatre, St. Louis, 1986-89, sr. v.p., 1990-91; pres. St. Louis Opportunity Clearinghouse, 1974-78. Recipient Lon O. Hocker Meml. Trial award Mo. Bar Found., 1984. Mem. Bar Assn. Met. St. Louis (Merit award 1976). Democrat. Avocations: golf, reading, music, sailing. Appellate, General civil litigation, Transportation. Office: Bryan Cave LLP One Metropolitan Square Saint Louis MO 63102-2750

NEWMAN, CHARLES FORREST, lawyer; b. Grenada, Miss., Jan. 15, 1937; s. Wiley Clifford and Lurene (Westbrook) N.; m. Jeannette Kay Bailey, May 26, 1973. BA magna cum laude, Yale U., 1959, JD, 1963; postgrad., U. Bonn, Fed. Republic Germany, 1959-60. Bar: Tenn. 1964, U.S. Supreme Ct. 1981. Law clk. U.S. Dist. Judge Bailey Brown, Western Dist. Tenn., 1963-64; mem. firm Burch Porter & Johnson, Attys., Memphis, 1965—, ptnr., 1966—; bd. dirs./trustees Memphis Pub. Libr. Found., Nat. Civil Rights Mus.; mem. exec. com. Yale U. Law Sch. Assn., 1984-88; chair Pres.'s Coun. Rhodes Coll., 1994-95; commr. Memphis Landmarks commn., 1983-87; mem. class coun. Class of '59, Yale Coll., 1980-90, Memphis Bar Assn.; assoc. Environ. Law Inst.; former bd. dirs./trustees Lemoyne-Owen Coll., Memphis Coll. Art, Tenn. Nature Conservancy. Adenauer fellow U. Bonn, 1959-60; recipient 1990 Disting. Svc. medal Rhodes Coll. Fellow Am. Bar Found., Tenn. Bar Found.; mem. ABA, Tenn. Bar Assn., Memphis Bar Assn. (bd. dirs. 1990-96, pres. 1996), Am. Judicature Soc., Am. Inns Ct. (master of bench), Memphis Downtown Rotary Club, Econ. Club of Memphis, Yale Club of Memphis (past pres.), Phi Beta Kappa. Federal civil litigation, State civil litigation, General practice. Home: 3880 Poplar Ave Memphis TN 38111-7614 Office: Burch Porter & Johnson 130 N Court Ave Memphis TN 38103-2288

NEWMAN, DENNIS NATHAN, lawyer; b. N.Y.C., Aug. 16, 1946; s. Isidor and Dorothy (Siegel) Newman; m. Ronna Susan Smith, July 31, 1971; 1 child, Abigail. BA, Brandeis U., 1969; JD, U. Mich., 1972. Bar: Ill. 1972, U.S. Dist. Ct. (no. dist.) Ill. 1972, U.S. Ct. Appeals (7th cir.) 1973. Assoc. Sonneschein Carlin Nath & Rosenthal, Chgo., 1972-79, ptnr., 1979-88, Sonnenschein Nath & Rosenthal, Chgo., 1989—. Adj. prof. Chgo.-Kent Coll. Law, 2000, 01. Mem.: ABA. Jewish. Corporate, general, Securities. Office: Sonnenschein Nath Rosenthal 8000 Sears Tower 233 S Wacker Dr Ste 8000 Chicago IL 60606-6491

NEWMAN, JAMES MICHAEL, judge, lawyer; b. Bklyn., Apr. 3, 1946; s. Sheldon and Ethel (Silverman) Newman; m. Lee Galen; children: Danielle Cari, Matthew Evan, Merrie Lee, Cindy Joy, Bradley Curtis. BA, Queens Coll., 1966; JD, NYU, 1969, LLM, 1975. Bar: NY 1970, NJ 1977, cert.: NJ. (matrimonial atty.). Assoc. Kramer, Marx, Greenlee & Backus, N.Y.C., 1970-73, Forsyth, Decker, Murray & Broderick, N.Y.C., 1973-74; ptnr. Tommaney & Newman, N.Y.C., 1975-82, Goldzweig, Reilly, Grossman & Newman, Marlboro, N.J., 1978-79, Canarick & Newman, Freehold, N.J., 1979-97, Newman, Scarola & Assocs., Freehold, 1998—2001, Newman Scarola & Schneider, Freehold, 2001—; pub. defender Marlboro Twp. (N.J.), 1984-86; judge Marlboro Twp., 1986—, Englishtown Borough, 1990—, Farmingdale Borough, 1991—, Manalapan Township, 1993—, Borough Fair Haven, 1996—2002. Dep. mayor Marlboro Twp., 1975—79, dir. econ. develop., 1975—79, dir. commuter affairs, 1974; interim commr. Monmouth Utilities Authority, 1977; mem. Ctrl. N.J. Transp. Bd., 1974—76. Mem.: Am. Judges Assn., Monmouth County Judges Assn. (pres 1995), Monmouth County Bar Assn. (co-chairperson family law comt 1996—98, trustee 1999—2002), N.J. Bar Assn., Masons. Jewish. Office: 64 W Main St Freehold NJ 07728-2142 E-mail: jnewman@monmouthlaw.com.

NEWMAN, JOHN M., JR., lawyer; b. Youngstown, Ohio, Aug. 15, 1944; BA, Georgetown U., 1966; JD, Harvard U., 1969. BAr: Ill. 1970, Calif. 1972, Ohio 1976. Law clerk ctrl. dist. U.S. Dist. Ct., Calif., 1969-70, asst. U.S. Atty. ctrl. dist., 1970-75; ptnr. Jones, Day, Cleve. Fellow Am. Coll. Trial Lawyers; mem. Phi Beta Kappa. General civil litigation. Office: Jones Day North Point 901 Lakeside Ave E Cleveland OH 44114-1190 E-mail: jmnewman@jonesday.com.

NEWMAN, JON O. federal judge; b. N.Y.C., May 2, 1932; s. Harold W. Jr. and Estelle L. (Ormond) Newman; m. Martha G. Silberman, June 19, 1953; children: Leigh, Scott, David. Grad., Hotchkiss Sch., 1949; AB magna cum laude, Princeton U., 1953; LLB, Yale U., 1956; LLD (hon.) , U.

Hartford, 1975, U. Bridgeport, 1980, Bklyn. Law Sch., 1995, N.Y. Law Sch., 1996. Bar: Conn. 1956, D.C. 1956. Law clk. to Hon. George T. Washington U.S. Ct. Appeals, 1956—57; sr. law clk. to Hon. Earl Warren U.S. Supreme Ct., 1957—58; ptnr. Ritter, Satter & Newman, Hartford, Conn., 1958—60; counsel to majority Conn. Gen. Assembly, 1959; spl. counsel to gov. Conn., 1959—61; asst. to sec. HEW, 1961—62; adminstrv. asst. to U.S. senator, 1963—64; U.S. atty. Dist. of Conn., 1964—69, U.S. dist. judge, 1972—79; pvt. practice, 1969—71; U.S. cir. judge, 1979—93; chief judge U.S. Ct. of Appeals 2d Cir., Hartford, 1993—97, sr. judge, 1997—. Co-author: Politics: The American Way, 1964, A Genealogical Chart of Greek Mythology, 2003. With USAR, 1954—62. Recipient Learned Hand medal, Fed. Bar Coun., 1987. Fellow: Am. Bar Found.; mem.: ABA, Am. Judicature Soc., Conn. Bar Assn., Am. Law Inst. Democrat. Office: US Ct Appeals 2d Cir 450 Main St Hartford CT 06103-3022

NEWMAN, LAWRENCE, lawyer, educator; b. N.Y.C., May 31, 1931; s. Herman and Sarah (Steinsaltz) N.; m. Helaine J. Glickstein, June 6, 1954; children: Debra, Daniel, Karen. AB, Dartmouth Coll., 1952; LL.B., Yale U., 1955; SJD, N.Y. Law Sch., 1963. Bar: N.Y. 1956. Law clk. to Hon. Lawrence E. Walsh U.S. Dist. Ct., N.Y.C., 1955-57. Adj. prof. U. Pa. Law Sch., Phila., 1969—, Yale U. Law Sch., 1983-85; adj. prof. wills and estate planning Columbia U. Law Sch., N.Y.C., 1994— Author: (with Albert Kalter) Postmortem Estate Planning, 1976, 2nd edit., 1994. Mem. exec. com. Am. Friends of Hebrew U., chmn. bd., 1994-98. Fellow Am. Bar Found., Am. Coll. Trust and Estate Coun.; mem. ABA (chmn. sect. legal edn. 1979-80, chmn. com. estate & gift taxation 1976-78), Estate Planning Council N.Y.C. (pres. 1979-80), N.Y. State Bar Assn. Estate planning, Probate (including wills, trusts). Office: 1633 Broadway 46th Fl New York NY 10019

NEWMAN, LAWRENCE WALKER, lawyer; b. Boston, July 1, 1935; s. Leon Bettoney and Hazel W. (Walker) N.; children: Timothy D., Isabel B., Thomas H. AB, Harvard U., 1957, LL.B., 1960. Bar: D.C. 1961, N.Y. 1965. Atty. U.S. Dept. Justice, 1960-61, Spl. Study of Securities Markets and Office Spl. Counsel on Investment Co. Act Matters, U.S. SEC, 1961-64; asst. U.S. atty. So. Dist. N.Y., 1964-69; assoc. Baker & McKenzie, N.Y.C., 1969-71, ptnr., 1971—. Mem. internat. adv. coun. World Arbitration Inst., 1984-87; mem. adv. com. Asia Pacific Ctr. for Resolution of Internat. Trade Disputes, 1987—; mem. adv. bd. Inst. for Transnational Arbitration, 1988—; chmn. U.S. Iranian Claimants Com., 1982—; mem. adv. bd. World Arbitration and Mediation Report, 1993-2002, chmn., 2002—; mem. bd. adv. to Corporate Counsel's Internat. Adviser, 1995—. Co-author: The Practice of Internat. Litigation, 1992, 93, 2nd edit. 1998, Litigating Internat. Commercial Disputes, 1996; columnist N.Y. Law Jour., 1982—; bd. advisors Corp. Counsel's Internat. Adviser; contbr. articles to profl. jours. and books on litigation and internat. arbitration; editor: Enforcement of Money Judgments, Attachment of Assets; chmn. editl. bd. Juris Pub., Inc.; co-editor: Revolutionary Days: The Iran Hostage Crisis and the Hague Claims Tribunal, A Look Back, 1999. Mem. ABA (internat. litigation com., internat. arbitration com.), Internat. Bar Assn. (com. dispute resolution, com. constrn. litigation), Inter-Am. Bar Assn., Fed. Bar Coun., Am. Fgn. Law Assn., Maritime Law Assn. U.S., Assn. Bar City N.Y. (com. on arbitration and alternative dispute resolution 1991-94), Am. Arbitration Assn. (corp. counsel com. 1987—, panel internat. arbitrators), U.S. Coun. Internat. Bus., Ct. Arbitration of Polish Chamber Fgn. Trade (panel of arbitrators), Brit. Col. Internat. Comml. Arbitration Ctr., Am. Law Inst., Bar Assn. City N.Y. (inaugural mem. com. on internat. dispute resolution). Federal civil litigation, Commercial, contracts (including sales of goods; commercial financing), Private international. Office: Baker & McKenzie 805 3rd Ave New York NY 10022-7513

NEWMAN, MARIE STEFANINI, law librarian, educator; b. Boston, Aug. 30, 1951; d. Mario and Elizabeth (Just) S.; m. Gary Nathaniel Newman, Sept. 30, 1978; children: Alexander, Elizabeth. AB, Smith Coll., 1973; MS, Columbia U., 1974; JD, Rutgers U., 1983. Bar: N.Y. 1984. Jr. librarian Bayonne (N.J.) Pub. Library, 1974-75; editor Microfilming Corp. Am., Glen Rock, N.J., 1975-78; circulation librarian SUNY Downstate Med. Ctr, Bklyn., 1979-80; head reference svcs. N.Y. Law Sch., N.Y.C., 1984-90, adj. assoc. prof. law, 1985-90; assoc. dir. Pub. Svcs., lectr. U. Pa. Law Sch., 1991-93; dep. libr. dir. and adj. prof. law Pace U. Sch. Law, White Plains, N.Y., 1993-99, libr. dir., assoc. prof. law, 1999—. Database mgr. Inst. Internat. Comml. Law, 1994—. Mem. Am. Assn. Law Libraries. Office: Pace Law Libr 78 N Broadway White Plains NY 10603-3710 E-mail: mnewman@law.pace.edu.

NEWMAN, MICHAEL RODNEY, lawyer; b. N.Y.C., Oct. 2, 1945; s. Morris and Helen Gloria (Hendler) N.; m. Cheryl Jeanne Anker, June 11, 1967; children: Hillary Abra, Nicole Brooke. Student NASA Inst. Space Physics, Columbia U., 1964; BA, U. Denver, 1967; JD, U. Chgo., 1970. Bar: Calif. 1971, U.S. Dist. Ct. (cen. dist.) Calif. 1972, U.S. Ct. Appeals (9th cir.) 1974, U.S. Dist. Ct. (no. dist.) Calif. 1975, U.S. Supreme Ct. 1978, U.S. Dist. Ct. (so. dist.) Calif. 1979, U.S. Tax Ct. 1979, U.S. Dist. Ct. (ea. dist.) Calif. 1983. Assoc. David Daar, 1971-76; ptnr. Daar & Newman, 1976-78, Miller & Daar, 1978-88, Miller, Daar & Newman, 1988-89, Daar & Newman, 1989—; judge pro-tem L.A. Mcpl. Ct., 1982—, L.A. Superior Ct., 1988—. Vice chmn., bd. dirs. German-Am. C. of C.; bd. govs. U. Haifa, Israel, mem. fin. and phys. devel. com.; bd. dirs. Consulegis EEIG; mem. bd. dirs. Ctr. Study Emerging Markets (Grad. Coll. Bus. and Econs. Calif. State U. Fullerton); founder, facilitator First, Second and Third Ann. German-Am. Strategic Partnership Conf.; lectr. Ea. Claims Conf., Ea. Life Claims Conf., Nat. Health Care Anti-Fraud Assn., AIA Conf. on Ins. Fraud, Consulegis A.G.M.'s Paris, 1997, Madrid, 1998, Dublin, 1999. Mem. L.A. Citizens Organizing Com. for Olympic Summer Games, 1984, mem. govtl. liaison adv. commn., 1984; mem. So. Calif. Com. for Olympic Summer Games, 1984; cert. ofcl. Athletics Congress of U.S., co-chmn. legal com. S.P.A.-T.A.C., chief finish judge; trustee Massada lodge B'nai Brith; bd. dirs. Ctr. for the Study of Emerging Markets, Calif. State U. Fullerton Grad. Sch. Bus. and Econs. Recipient NYU Bronze medal in Physics, 1962, Maths. award USN Sci., 1963. Mem.: TAC (bd. dirs., Disting. Svc. award 1988), ABA (multi-dist. litigation subcom., com. on class actions), German Am. C. of C. (vice chmn.), So. Pacific Assn., Conf. Ins. Counsel, Los Angeles County Bar Assn. (chmn. attys. errors and omissions prevention com., mem. cts. com., mem. internat. law com., state cts. coord. com. litigation sect.), City Club on Bunker Hill, Breakfast Club, Porter Valley Country Club. Federal civil litigation, State civil litigation, Insurance. Office: 865 S Figueroa St Ste 2300 Los Angeles CA 90017-2567

NEWMAN, PAULINE, judge; b. N.Y.C., N.Y., June 20, 1927; d. Maxwell Henry and Rosella Newman. BA, Vassar Coll., 1947; MA, Columbia U., 1948; PhD, Yale U., 1952; LLB, NYU, 1958. Bar: N.Y. 1958, U.S. Supreme Ct. 1972, U.S. Ct. Customs and Patent Appeals 1978, Pa. 1979, U.S. Ct. Appeals (3d cir.) 1981, U.S. Ct. Appeals (fed. cir.) 1982. Research chemist Am. Cyanamid Co., Bound Brook, NJ, 1951—54; mem. patent staff FMC Corp., N.Y.C., 1954—75, Phila., 1975—84, dir. dept. patent and licensing, 1969—84; judge U.S. Ct. Appeals (fed. cir.), Washington, 1984—; Disting. prof. George Mason Law Sch., 1995—. Program specialist Dept. Natural Scis. UNESCO, Paris, 1961—62; mem. State Dept. Adv. Com. on Internat. Indsl. Property, 1974—84; lectr. in field. Contbr. articles to profl. jours. Trustee Phila. Coll. Pharmacy and Sci., 1983—84; bd. dirs. Med. Coll. Pa., 1975—84, Midgard Found., 1973—84. Mem.: ABA (coun. sect. patent trademark and copyright 1983—84), Coun. Fgn. Rels., U.S. Trademark Assn. (bd. dirs. 1975—79, v.p. 1978—79), Pacific Indsl. Property Assn. (pres. 1979—80), Am. Inst. Chemists (bd. dirs. 1960—66, 1970—76), Am. Chem. Soc. (bd. dirs. 1972—81), Am. Patent Law Assn. (bd. dirs. 1981—84), Yale Club, Vassar Club, Cosmos Club. Office: US Ct Appeals Nat Cts Bldg 717 Madison Pl Washington DC 20439-0002

NEWMAN, SANDRA SCHULTZ, state supreme court justice; BS, Drexel U., 1959; MA, Temple U., 1969; JD, Villanova U., 1972; D (hon.) (hon.) , Gannon U., 1996, Widener U., 1996, Clarion U., 2000. Bar: Pa., U.S. Dist. Ct. (ea. dist.) Pa., U.S. Ct. Appeals (3d cir.), U.S. Supreme Ct. Asst. dist. atty. Montgomery County, Pa.; pvt. practice; judge Commonwealth Ct. of Pa., 1993—95; justice Supreme Ct. of Pa., 1995—. Past chair bd. consultors Villanova U. Law Sch.; mem. jud. coun. Supreme Ct. of Pa., liaison to the 3rd cir. task force on mgmt. of death penalty litigation, liaison to Pa. lawyers fund for client security bd., liaison to domestic rels. procedural rules com.; liaison Pa. Bar Inst.; jud. work group HHS; mem. adv. com. Nat. Ctr. for State Cts., Am. Law Inst.; mem. Drexel U. Coll. Bus. and Adminstrn.; lectr. and spkr. in field. Author: Alimony, Child Support and Counsel Fees, 1988; contbr. Named named Disting. Daughter of Pa.; recipient Phila. award for Super Achiever, Pediatric Juvenile Colitis Found. Jefferson Med. Coll. and Hosp, 1979, award for Dedicated Leadership and Outstanding Contbns. to the Cmty. and Law Employment , Drexel 100 award, Police Chiefs Assn. of Southeastern Pa., 1993, Medallion of Achievement award, Villanova U., 1993, Susan B. Anthony award, Women's Bar Assn. Western Pa., 1996, award, Justinian Soc., 1996, Tau Epsilon Law Soc., 1996, Legion of Honor Gold Medallion award, Chapel of Four Chaplain, 1997, honored by, Women of Greater Phila., 1996. Fellow: Pa. Bar Found., Am. Bar Found.; mem.: Montgomery Bar Assn., Nat. Assn. Women Judges, Am. Law Inst. Office: Supreme Ct Pa Ste 400 100 Four Falls Corporate Ctr West Conshohocken PA 19428-2950

NEWMAN, STEPHEN MICHAEL, lawyer; b. Buffalo, Jan. 12, 1945; s. Howard A. and Mildred (Ballow) N.; m. Gayle Mallon, May 24, 1969; children: Holly, Deborah. AB, Princeton U., 1966; JD, U. Mich., 1969. Bar: N.Y. 1969, Fla. 1976. Assoc. Hodgson, Russ, Andrews, Woods & Goodyear, Buffalo, 1969-73; ptnr. Hodgson Russ, LLP (formerly Hodgson, Russ, Andrews, Woods &, Buffalo, 1973—. Lectr. in field. Bd. dirs. Leukemia Soc., United Jewish Fedn. Buffalo Inc., Jewish Ctr. Greater Buffalo Inc., Temple Beth Zion; bd. dirs., chpt. chmn., exec. com. Am. Jewish Com., Buffalo chpt.; active Vol. Action Ctr. United Way of Buffalo and Erie County. Fellow Am. Coll. Trusts and Estates Coun.; mem. ABA (personal svc. corps. com. tax sect.), N.Y. State Bar Assn. (chair trusts and estates law sect. 2001), Princeton Club of Western N.Y. (sch. com.). Estate planning, Pension, profit-sharing, and employee benefits, Probate (including wills, trusts). Office: Hodgson Russ LLP 2000 1 M&T Plz Buffalo NY 14203 E-mail: snewman@hodgsonruss.com.

NEWMAN, THEODORE ROOSEVELT, JR., judge; b. Birmingham, Ala., July 5, 1934; s. Theodore R. and Ruth L. (Oliver) N. AB, Brown U., 1955, LL.D., 1980; JD, Harvard U., 1958. Bar: D.C. 1958, Ala. 1959. Atty. civil rights div. Dept. Justice, Washington, 1961-62; practiced law in Washington, 1962-70; assoc. judge D.C. Superior Ct., 1970-76; judge D.C. Ct. Appeals, 1976-91, chief judge, 1976-84, sr. judge, 1991—; bd. dirs. Nat. Center for State Cts., v.p., 1980-81, pres., 1981-82. Trustee Brown U. With USAF, 1958-61. Fellow Am. Bar Found.; mem. Nat. Bar Assn. (past pres. jud. coun., C. Francis Stradford award 1984, William H. Hastie award 1988). E-mail: tnewman@dcca.state.dc.us.

NEWMAN, WILLIAM BERNARD, JR., consultant; b. Providence, Nov. 16, 1950; s. William Bernard and Virginia (Crosby) N.; m. Karen O'Connor, Jan. 11, 1951. BA, Ohio Wesleyan U., 1972; JD, George Mason U., Arlington, Va., 1977; postgrad., Harvard U., 1987. Bar: Va. 1977, D.C. 1978. Atty. com. energy Ho. of Reps., Washington, 1978-81; v.p., Washington counsel Consol. Rail Corp. Dept. Govt. Affairs, Washington, 1981-98; cons. Washington, 1999—. Bd. dirs. Nat. Coun. for Adoption, 1994-98. Mem. Va. Bar Assn., D.C. Bar Assn. Home: 1009 Priory Pl Mc Lean VA 22101-2134

NEWSOM, JAMES THOMAS, lawyer; b. Carrollton, Mo., Oct. 6, 1944; s. Thomas Edward and Hazel Love (Mitchell) N.; m. Sherry Elaine Retzloff, Aug. 9, 1986; stepchildren: Benjamin A. Bawden, Holly K. Bawden. AB, U. Mo., 1966, JD, 1968. Bar: Mo. 1968, U.S. Supreme Ct. 1971. Assoc. Shook, Hardy & Bacon, London and Kansas City, Mo., 1972, ptnr., 1976—. Mem. Mo. Law Rev., 1966-68. Lt. comdr. JAGC, USNR, 1968-72. Mem. ABA, Kansas City Met. Bar Assn., U. Mo. Law Sch. Law Soc., U. Mo. Jefferson Club, Order of Coif, Perry (Kans.) Yacht Club, Stone Horse Yacht Club (Harwich Port, Mass.). Avocations: skiing, sailing, car racing. General civil litigation, Product liability. Office: Shook Hardy & Bacon One Kansas City Pl 1200 Main St Ste 3100 Kansas City MO 64105-2139 E-mail: jnewsom@shb.com.

NEWSOME, RANDALL JACKSON, judge; b. Dayton, Ohio, July 13, 1950; s. Harold I. and Sultana S. (Stony) N. BA summa cum laude, Boston U., 1972; JD, U. Cin., 1975. Bar: Ohio 1975, U.S. Dist. Ct. (so. dist.) Ohio 1977, U.S. Ct. Appeals (6th cir.) 1979, U.S. Supreme Ct. 1981. Law clk. to chief judge U.S. Dist. Ct. (so. dist.) Ohio, 1975-77; assoc. Dinsmore & Shohl, Cin., 1978-82; judge U.S. Bankruptcy Ct. (so. dist.) Ohio, 1982-88, U.S. Bankruptcy Ct. (no. dist.) Calif., Oakland, 1988—. Faculty mem. Fed. Jud. Ctr., ALI-ABA, 1987—; mem. Nat. Conf. of Bankruptcy Judges, 1983—, mem. bd. govs., 1987-88, pres., 1998-99. Contbg. author: Chapter 11 Theory and Practice, 1994—, Collier on Bankruptcy, 1997—. Fellow Am. Coll. Bankruptcy; mem. Am. Law Inst., Phi Beta Kappa. Democrat. Office: US Bankruptcy Ct PO Box 2070 Oakland CA 94604-2070

NEWTON, ALEXANDER WORTHY, lawyer; b. Birmingham, Ala., June 19, 1930; s. Jeff H. and Annis Lillian (Kelly) N.; m. Sue Aldridge, Dec. 22, 1952; children: Lamar Aldridge Newton, Kelly McClure Newton Hammond, Jane Worthy Newton, Robins Jeffry Newton. BS, U. Ala., 1952, JD, 1957. Bar: Ala. 1957. Pvt. practice law, Birmingham; assoc. Hare, Wynn & Newell, Birmingham, 1957; ptnr. Hare, Wynn, Newell & Newton, Birmingham, 1961—. Del. U.S. Ct. Appeals (11th cir.) Jud. Conf., 1988, 89, 90, 91; mem. Jefferson County Jud. Nominating Com., 1983-89; mem. Birmingham Airport Authority, 1991—; founding dir. First Comm. Bank. Co-author: (with others) Federal Appellate Procedure, 11th Circuit, 1996. Vice chmn. Birmingham Racing Commn., 1984-87; v.p. U. Ala. Law Sch. Found., 1978-79, pres., 1980-82, exec. com., 1987—; mem. Leadership Ala. Class IV; trustee Ala. Trust Fund, 2002; bd. dirs. St. Vincent Hosp. Found. Capt. inf. U.S. Army, 1952-54. Recipient Disting. Alumnus award Farrah Law Soc. U. Ala., 1982, Sam W. Pipкes Disting. Alumnus award 1982. Fellow Am. Coll. Trial Lawyers (state chmn. 1983-84, regents' nominatin com. 1984-85), Internat. Soc. Barristers (bd. dirs. 1974-75, sec.-treas. 1976-77, v.p. 1977-78, pres. 1979-80), Internat. Acad. Trial Lawyers (bd. dirs. 1998—); mem. ABA, ATLA, Am. Bar Found., Ala. State Bar (chmn. practices and procedures subsect. 1965, governance com. and pres.'s task force 1984-86, pres.'s com. 1987-88), Birmingham Bar Assn. (exec. com. 1967), Ala. Trial Lawyers Assn. (sec.-treas. 1958-65), Am. Judicature Soc., 11th Cir. His. Soc. (trustee 1988—), Sigma Chi. Clubs: Shoal Creek, Birmingham Country (Birmingham); Capital City (Atlanta); Garden of the God (Colorado Springs, Colo.); University Club (New York). Democrat. Presbyterian. Federal civil litigation, State civil litigation, Personal injury (including property damage). Home: 2837 Canoe Brook Ln Birmingham AL 35243-5908 Office: Hare Wynn Newell & Newton 800 Massey Bldg 2025 3d Ave N Birmingham AL 35203-3330

NEWTON, BRENT EVAN, defender; b. Opelika, Ala., Sept. 8, 1967; s. Wesly Phillips and Merlin Owen Newton; m. Tirza Noelle Bartels, May 21, 1994; children: Anna Leone Bartels-Newton, Georgia Lin Bartels-Newton. BA, U. NC, 1989; JD, Columbia U., 1992. Bar: Ga. 92, Tex. 93, Fla. 95. Jud. law clk. U.S. Ct. Appeals (5th cir.), Houston, 1992—93; staff atty. Tex. Capital Def. Resource Ctr., Houston, 1993—95; asst. state pub. defender Dade County Pub. Defender's Office, Miami, Fla., 1995—96; asst. fed. pub. defender Fed. Pub. Defender's Office, Houston, 1996—. Adj. prof. law U. Houston, 2000—. Contbg. editor: Jour. Appellate Practice and Process, 2001—, sr. editor: Columbia Law Rev., 1990—91; contbr. articles to legal jours. Mentor Big Bros., Big Sisters of Houston, 1999—. Avocation: jazz drumming. Office: Fed Pub Defender's Office 440 Louisianna St Ste 310 Houston TX 77002

NEWTON, NELL JESSUP, dean, law educator; b. St. Louis, Apr. 30, 1944; d. Robert Edward and Marcella (Boehm) Mier. BA, U. Calif., Berkeley, 1973; JD, U. Calif., Hastings, 1976. Bar: Calif., Washington, U.S. Ct. Appeals (9th crct.), U.S. Supreme Ct. Prof. Cath. U. Sch. Law , 1976-92; prof. Washington Coll. Law Am. U., Washington, 1992—98; dean U. Denver Law Sch., 1998—2000, U. Conn. Sch. Law, Hartford, 2000—. Lectr. Internat. Law Inst., Washington, 1984-89; prof. Pre-Law Summer Inst. for Native Am. Students, U. N.Mex. Law Sch., Albuquerque, 1990, 91, 93; panelist, speaker NEH, 1981; presenter S.W. Intertribal Ct. of Appeals, 1990; panelist Orgn. Am. Historians, 1991. Co-author: American Indian Law, 3d edit., 1991; contbr. articles to profl. jours. NEH fellow Harvard Law Sch., 1980. Mem. Assn. Am. Law Schs. (Native Am. rights sect., mem. exec. com. 1987—, chair 1987-88, oral argument newsletter editor 1987—, mem. women in legal edn. sect. 1987—, chair profl. devel. workshop com. 1992, sec. 1993), Balt.-Washington-Va. Women Law Tchrs. Group (planning com. Symposium on Scholarship I 1985, II 1986), Thurston Soc., Order of Coif. Office: U Conn Sch Law Hartranft 103 55 Elizabeth St Hartford CT 06105

NEXSEN, JULIAN JACOBS, lawyer; b. Kingstree, S.C., Apr. 14, 1924; s. William Ivey and Barbara (Jacobs) N.; m. Mary Elizabeth McIntosh, Jan. 28, 1948; children: Louise Ivey (Mrs. Heyward Harles Bouknight, Jr.), Julian Jacobs Jr. Student, The Citadel, 1941-43; BS magna cum laude, U. S.C., 1948, JD magna cum laude, 1950. Bar: S.C. 1950, U.S. Supreme Ct. 1960. Partner firm Nexsen Pruet Jacobs & Pollard, Columbia, SC. Trustee Richland County Pub. Libr., chmn., 1976-77; trustee Providence Hosp., chmn., 1984-86; trustee Providence Found., Providence Ministries, Sisters of Charity of St. Augustine Health Sys.; past bd. dirs. Columbia Music Festival Assn., ARC Richland-Lexington Counties, Ctrl. Carolina Cmty. Found.; mem. U.S.C. Law Sch. partnership bd.; elder Presbyn. Ch., trustee Congaree Presbytery, 1967-87, Synod, S.C., 1969-74, mem. Trinity Presbytery Coun., 1991-95. Lt. inf. AUS, 1943-46, ETO, capt., 1950-51, Korea. Decorated Bronze Star with oak leaf cluster; recipient Compleat Lawyer award U. S.C. Sch. Law. Mem. ABA, S.C. Bar (treas., bd. govs. 1974-79, ho. of dels. 1980-92), Richland County Bar Assn. (pres. 1974-75, Disting. Svc. award 1987), Am. Bar Found., S.C. Bar Found. (pres. 1971-72), S.C. Law Inst. (coun., exec. com. 1986—), Am. Law Inst., Am. Coll. Trust and Estate Counsel (regent 1973-82), Am. Judicature Soc., Forest Lake Country Club, Palmetto Club, Kiwanis (bd. dirs. 1972-74, 77-79), Phi Beta Kappa. Corporate, general, Estate planning, Probate (including wills, trusts). Home: 2840 Sheffield Rd Columbia SC 29204-2332 Office: Nexsen Pruet Jacobs & Pollard Drawer 2426 1441 Main St Columbia SC 29202-2848 Fax: 803-253-8277. E-mail: jjn@npjp.com.

NEXSEN, JULIAN JACOBS, JR., lawyer; b. Columbia, S.C., Sept. 22, 1954; s. Julian J. and Mary Elizabeth (McIntosh) N.; m. Christine Spigner Johnston, Feb. 25, 1984; children: Elizabeth Kincaid, Julian J. III, Sarah Ivey. BA, Washington and Lee U., 1976; JD, U. S.C., 1979. Bar: S.C. 1979, U.S. Ct. Appeals (4th cir.) 1982. Assoc. Nexsen, Pruet, Jacobs & Pollard, Columbia, S.C., 1979-84; assoc. in house counsel, asst. sec. Greenwood (S.C.) Mills, Inc., 1984-95, exec. v.p., 1999—2001; exec. v.p., COO Greenwood Devel. Corp., 1995-99, pres., CEO, 1999—. Bd. dirs. County-Bank, Greenwood Devel. Corp., Ctrl. Trust Co., SC Biotech. Incubation Program, Partnership for a Greater Greenwood. Bd. visitors Lander Coll., 1985-87; bd. dirs. Edn. Enrichment Found., 1986-89, Greenwood United Way, 1989-92, Greenwood Community Theatre, 1989-93, Greenwood Uptown Devel. Corp., 1991-93; bd. deacons 1st Presbyn. Ch., 1990-93, session, 1993-96; trustee Self Meml. Hosp., 1992-98, Self Family Found., Self Regional Healthcare Ctr.; bd. dirs. Greenwood County Econ. Alliance, 1999-2001. Mem. ABA, Am. Corp. Counsel Assn., S.C. Bar Assn., Forest Lake Club, Greenwood Country Club, S.C. C. of C. (bd. dirs. 1990-93). Presbyterian. Corporate, general, Land use and zoning (including planning), Property, real (including real estate development, water). Home: 512 E Henrietta Ave Greenwood SC 29649-3142 Office: Greenwood Devel Corp PO Box 1546 Greenwood SC 29648-1546 E-mail: jnexsen@greenwooddevelopment.com.

NEY, JUDY LARSON, lawyer, sociology educator; b. St. Louis, Mar. 4, 1951; d. Robert Israel and Annette (Palan) Larson; m. Leo E. Ney Jr., May 25, 1975; 1 child, Leo E. IV. BA, Bradley U., 1973; MA, MSW, U. Mo., St. Louis, 1975; JD, S. Tex. Coll., 1982. Bar: Tex. 1983, U.S. Dist. Ct. (so. dist.) Tex. 1983. Project controls supr., planner Brown & Root Inc., Houston, 1974—83; pvt. practice Houston, 1983—2001; state govt. atty. Tex. Worker's Compensation Commn., Houston, 2001—. Instr. sociology ITT Tech. Inst., 1993—2000, lectr. on alcohol, drugs and the law, 1984. Info. and referral counselor Mental Health Assn., 1990—95; religious sch. instr. Congregation Emanu El, Houston, Tex., 1990—. Named Vol. of Yr., Mental Health Assn., 1994. Mem.: ABA (Tex. ho. of dels. 1997—98), Houston Bar Assn. (minority opp. com., law day chair 1997, continuing edn. commn., bd. dirs. Houston Lawyer Referral, professionalism com.), Tex. Bar Assn. (disability issues com. 1998—, chair, women and the law sect. 2003—04, bd. dirs. State Bar Coll.), Bradley U. Alumni Assn., South Tex. Coll. Law Alumni, U. Mo.-St Louis Alumni Assn., Phi Alpha Delta. Republican. Jewish. Avocations: travel, politics, reading. Workers' compensation, General practice, Administrative and regulatory. Home: 12242 Brookvalley Dr Houston TX 77071-2722 Office: Tex Worker's Compensation Commn 8485 Gulf Fwy Ste B Houston TX 77017-5001 Fax: 713-723-5380. E-mail: judylneyjd@aol.com.

NG, WING CHIU, accountant, educator, application developer, lawyer, educator, advocate; b. Hong Kong, Oct. 14, 1947; came to U.S., 1966; s. Bing Nuen and Oi Ying (Lee) Ng. BS, MS, Yale U., 1969; PhD, NYU, 1972; JD, U. Hawaii, 2000. Bar: Hawaii 2001; CPA, Hawaii. Rsch. assoc. SUNY, Stony Brook, 1972-74; asst. prof. U. Md., College Park, 1974-76; rsch. physicist U. Bonn, Fed. Republic of Germany, 1976-78; chartered acct. Richter, Usher & Vineberg, Montreal, Can., 1978-80; pvt. practice Honolulu, Hawaii, 1980—; pres. Bowen, Ng & Co., Honolulu, 1983-84, Asia-Am. Investment, Inc., Honolulu, 1983—, Mathematica Pacific, Inc., Honolulu, 1984—. Part-time prof. U. Hawaii, Honolulu, 1982—; ptnr. Advance Realty Investment, Honolulu, 1980—; dir. S & L Internat., Inc., Honolulu, 1987—. Creator: (computer software) Time Billing, 1984, Dbase General Ledger, 1987, Dbase Payroll, 1987, Dbase Accounts Receivable, 1989; co-author: Draft Constitution of the Federal Republic of China, 1994. Dir. Orgn. of Chinese Ams., Honolulu, 1984-86, Fedn. for a Dem. China, Honolulu, 1990—, Hong Kong, 1991—; dir. Alliance Hong Kong Chinese in U.S., 1995—. Included in Prominent People of Hawaii, Delta Pub. Co., 1988. Mem. AICPA, Hong Kong Soc. Accts., Hawaiian Trail & Mountain Club (auditor 1987—). Democrat. Buddhist. Avocations: hiking, the internet. Office: 1149 Bethel St Ste 306 Honolulu HI 96813-2210

NGUYEN, LU TUAN, law librarian; b. Hanoi, Vietnam, Jan. 20, 1954; arrived in U.S., 1975; s. Thang Tuan and Thuan Thi Nguyen. AA in Liberal Arts, El Camino CC, Torrance, Calif., 1979; BA in Polit. Sci., UCLA, 1981; JD, Northrop U., 1985; M in Libr. and Info. Scis., San Jose State U., 2001. Bilingual attendant aide Torrance (Calif.) Unified Sch. Dist., 1977—78; asst. law libr. Northrop U., Inglewood, Calif., 1981—84; legal asst. Roger A. Kander PC, Long Beach, Calif., 1985—87; libr. aid Orange County Pub. Law Libr., Calif., 1991—93, libr. asst. I, 1993—97, libr. asst. II, evening supr., 1997—2001, ref. libr., 2001—. Spkr. in field. Vol. VITAS Hospice program, 1998. Recipient Svc. award, Delta Theta Phi, 1985; Calif. State Libr. grantee, 1999—2000, Calif. State scholar, 1979—81. Mem.: ALA, Chinese Am. Librs. Assn., So. Calif. Assn. Law Libr. (scholar 1996—97),

Calif. Libr. Assn., Am. Assn. Law Libr. Home: 1215 1/2 Seal Way Seal Beach CA 90740-6419 Office: Orange County Pub Law Libr 515 N Flower St Santa Ana CA 92703-2354 Office Fax: 714-834-4375.

NIA, FIROOZEH, lawyer; b. The Haage, Netherlands, May 3, 1969; d. Mahmoud Nia and Faeghe R. Larijani. JD, U. La Verne, L.A., 1998. Bar: Calif. 1999, U.S. Ct. Appeals (9th cir.) 1999. Assoc. atty. Law Offices Of Lawrence Sobel, Woodland Hills, Calif., 1999—2002, Nachshin & Weston, LLP, L.A., 2002—. Contbr. Translator MTO, Burbank, Calif., 2002. Recipient Am. Jurisprudence awards (2), U. of La Verne, 1997. Family and matrimonial, State civil litigation, Private international. Office: Nachshin & Weston LLP 11601 Wilshire Blvd Los Angeles CA 90025 E-mail: faye@nwdivorce.com.

NIBERT, GREGORY JAMES, lawyer; b. Roswell, N.Mex., Jan. 3, 1958; s. James M. and Elaine (LeGrand) N.; m. Carolyn Salazar, Aug. 20, 1983; children: Gregory James Jr., Jeffrey Edward. BA, U. N.Mex., 1980; JD cum laude, Pepperdine U., 1983. Bar: N.Mex. 1983, U.S. Dist. Ct. N.Mex. 1984, U.S. Ct. Appeals (10th cir.) 1984. Assoc. Hinkle, Cox, Eaton, Cofield & Hensley, Roswell, 1983-88, ptnr., 1988—. Trustee Rocky Mountain Min. Law Found.; rsch. fellow Southwestern Legal Fedn. Editor-in-chief Pepperdine U. Law Rev., 1983; rsch. and ann. chpt. supplement author Law of Federal Oil and Gas Leases, 1985—; contbr. articles to profl. publs. Mem. Rocky Mountain Mineral Law Found.; chmn. Rep. Party of Chaves County, 2001-03. Mem. Ind. Petroleum Assn. of N. Mex. (v.p.), Rio Hondo Dist. of Conquistador Coun. BSA (chmn.), Am. Assn. Petroleum Landmen, N.Mex. Landmen's Assn., N.Mex. Bar Assn. (bd. dirs. sect. of natural resources, energy and environ. law 1985—, chair 1990-91), Chaves County Bar Assn., Sand Divers Scuba Club, Kiwanis (bd. dirs. Roswell chpt. 1987, pres. 1993-94). Mem. Ch. of Christ. Avocations: football, basketball, snow skiing, scuba diving, camping. Oil, gas, and mineral, Probate (including wills, trusts), Property, real (including real estate development, water). Office: Hinkle Hensely Shanor and Martin LLP PO Box 10 400 N Pennsylvania St #700 Roswell NM 88202-0010

NICHOL, GENE RAY, JR., dean, department chairman; b. Dallas, May 11, 1951; s. Gene R. and Dolores (Dumas) N.; m. Janet Castle, Aug. 20, 1973 (div. 1978); m. Glenn George, Nov. 25, 1984. BA in Philosophy, Okla. State U., 1973; JD, U. Texas, 1976. Bar: Alaska 1978. Assoc. Ely, Guess and Rudd, Anchorage, 1976-78; asst. prof. W.Va. U., Morgantown, 1978-80, assoc. prof., 1980-82; prof. law U. Fla., Gainesville, 1983-84; Cutler prof. law, dir. Inst. of Bill of Rights Law Coll. William and Mary, Williamsburg, W.Va., 1984-88; dean U. Colo. Law Sch., 1988-95; dean, Burton Craige prof. law U.N.C. Sch. of Law, 1999—. Host Culture Wars, KBDI T.V., Denver, 1995-96. Author: (with M. Redish) Federal Courts; contbr. articles to profl. jours. Posten research grantee U. W.Va., 1980, 81, 82. Mem. Nat. Lawyers Guild (coms. 1978, vice chair Colo. reapportionment commn.), Am. Law Inst., ACLU (coms. 1978—), Am. Bar Found. Fellows, Order of Coif. Roman Catholic. Avocation: back packing. Office: U N C Sch of Law 5011 Van Hecke-Wettach Hall 100 Ridge Rd Chapel Hill NC 27599*

NICHOLAS, FREDERICK M. lawyer; b. N.Y.C., May 30, 1920; s. Benjamin L. and Rose F. (Nechols) N.; m. Eleanore Berman, Sept. 2, 1951 (div. 1963); children: Deborah, Jan, Tony; m. Joan Fields, Jan. 2, 1983. AB, U. So. Calif., 1947; postgrad., U. Chgo., 1949-50; JD, U. So. Calif., 1952. Bar: Calif. 1952, U.S. Dist. Ct. Calif. 1952, U.S. Ct. Appeals (9th cir.) 1952. Assoc. Loeb & Loeb, L.A., 1952-56; ptnr. Swerdlow, Glikbarg & Nicholas, Beverly Hills, Calif., 1956-62; pvt. practice Beverly Hills, 1962-80; pres., atty. Hapsmith Co., Beverly Hills, 1980—. Bd. dirs. Malibu Grand Prix, L.A., 1982-90; gen. counsel Beverly Hills Realty Bd., 1971-79; founder, pres. Pub. Counsel, L.A., 1970-73. Author: Setting Up a Shopping Center, 1960, Commercial Real Property Lease Practice, 1976. Chmn. Mus. Contemporary Art, L.A., 1987—93; chmn. com. Walt Disney Concert Hall, L.A., 1987—95; trustee Music Ctr. Los Angeles County, 1987—95, L.A. Philharm. Assn., 1987—95, Mus. Flying, Santa Monica, Calif., 1991—2002, Frederick R. Weisman Art Found., 2003—, Frederick R. Weisman Philanthropic Found., Pitzer Coll., 1992—95; hon. trustee Art Ctr. Coll. Design, 2001—; chmn. Calif. Pub. Broadcasting Commn., Sacramento, 1972—78; pres. Maple Ctr., 1977—79; co-developer Ronald Reagan Bldg., Washington, 1998; adminstr. Estate of Sam Francis, 1996—. Named Citizen of Yr. Beverly Hills Bd. Realtors, 1978, Man of Yr. Maple Ctr., 1980, Outstanding Founder in Philanthropy, Nat. Philanthropy Day Com., 1990; recipient Pub. Svc. award Coro Found., 1988, Medici award LA C. of C., 1990, Founders award Pub. Counsel, 1990, Trustees award Calif. Inst. Arts, 1993, City of Angels award LA Ctrl. Bus. Assn., Disting. Svc. award U. So. Calif. Law Sch. Class of 1952, 2002. Mem. Beverly Hills Bar Assn. (bd. govs. 1970-76, Disting. Svc. award 1974, 81, Exceptional Svc. award 1986), Beverly Hills C. of C. (Man of Yr. 1983). Property, real (including real estate development, water). Home: 1001 Maybrook Dr Beverly Hills CA 90210-2715 Office: Hapsmith Co 5440 McConnell Ave Los Angeles CA 90066

NICHOLAS, WILLIAM RICHARD, lawyer; b. Pontiac, Mich., June 19, 1934; s. Reginald and Edna Irene (Bartlett) N.; m. Diana Lee Johnson, Aug. 20, 1960; children: Susan Lee, William Richard Jr. BS in Bus., U. Idaho, 1956; JD, U. Mich., 1962. Bar: 1963. Of counsel Latham & Watkins, Los Angeles, 1962-96. Contbr. numerous articles on taxation. Lt. (j.g.) USN, 1956-59. Mem. Calif. Bar Assn., Los Angeles County Bar Assn., Am. Coll. Tax Counsel. Home: 1808 Old Ranch Rd Los Angeles CA 90049-2207 Office: Latham & Watkins 633 W 5th St Ste 4000 Los Angeles CA 90071-2005

NICHOLLS, RICHARD H. lawyer; b. Toronto, Ont., Can., Oct. 27, 1938; s. Richard S. and Roberta T. Nicholls; m. Judy Carter, Apr. 15, 1963; children: Christopher T., Jamie C.; m. Anne Delaney, June 10, 1978. BA cum laude, Amherst Coll., 1960; LLB, Stamford U., 1963; LLM, NYU, 1964. Bar: Calif. 1964, N.Y. 1965, D.C. Assoc. Mudge Rose Guthrie, Alexander & Ferdon and predecessor, N.Y.C., 1964-70, ptnr., 1971-94; of counsel Orrick, Herrington & Sutcliffe, N.Y., 1995—. Mem. ABA, N.Y. State Bar Assn., Nat. Assn. Bond Lawyers, Stamford Yacht Club. Municipal (including bonds), Corporate taxation, Personal income taxation. Home: 159 Ocean Dr W Stamford CT 06902-8004 Office: Orrick Herrington & Sutcliffe 666 5th Ave Rm 203 New York NY 10103-1798 E-mail: rnicholls@orrick.com.

NICHOLS, DAVID E. lawyer; b. Cushing, Okla., Nov. 24, 1952; s. Thomas D. and Ruth (Stephenson) N.; m. Rosemary Davenport, Aug. 30, 1980; children: James Ryan, John Robert. BA, U. Okla., 1975, JD, 1979. Bar: Okla. 1979, U.S. Dist. Ct. (we. dist.) Okla. 1979, U.S. Dist. Ct. (no. dist.) Okla. 1980, U.S. Ct. Appeals (10th cir.) 1980. Assoc. Kerr Irvine & Rhodes, Oklahoma City, 1979-81, Lytle Soule & Curlee, Oklahoma City, 1981-83, ptnr., 1983-94, D'Amour, Jones, Stryker, Duensing & Nichols, St. Thomas, V.I., 1995-97; pvt. practice David E. Nichols, P.C., St. Thomas, 1997—. Mem. ABA, Okla. Bar Assn. (pub. info. com.), Oklahoma County Bar Assn. (bench and bar com.), Quail Creek Country Club. Republican. Presbyterian. Avocations: all sports, travel. Property, real (including real estate development, water). Home: 11-33 Peterborg St Thomas VI 00802 Office: 100 Blackbeards Hill St Thomas VI 00802 E-mail: den2pc@earthlink.net.

NICHOLS, HENRY ELIOT, lawyer, savings and loan executive; b. N.Y.C. m. Frances Griffin Morrison, Aug. 12, 1950 (dec. July 1978); children: Clyde Whitney, Diane Spencer; m. Mary ann Wall, May 31, 1987. BA, Yale U., 1946; JD, U. Va., 1948. Bar: D.C. 1950, U.S. Dist. Ct. 1950, U.S. Ct. Appeals 1952, U.S. Supreme Ct. 1969. Assoc. Frederick W. Berens, Washington, 1950-52; sole practice Washington, 1952—. Real estate columnist Washington Star, 1966-81; pres., gen. counsel Hamilton Fed. Savs. & Loan Assn., 1971-74; vice chmn. bd. Columbia 1st Bank (formerly Columbia 1st Fed. Savs. & Loan Assn.), Washington, 1974-90, bd. dirs.; pres. Century Fin. Corp., 1971-90; regional v.p. Preview, Inc., 1972-78; bd. dirs., exec. com. Columbia Real Estate Title Ins. Co., Washington, 1968-78. Contbr. articles to profl. jours.; patentee med. inventions. Nat. adv. bd. Harker Prep. Sch., 1975-80; exec. com. Father Walter E. Schmitz Meml. Fund, Cath. U., 1982-83; bd. dirs. Vincent T. Lombardi Cancer Rsch. Ctr., 1979-84; del. Pres. Johnson's Conf. LAw and Poverty, 1967; vice chmn. Mayor's Ad Hoc Com. Housing Code Problems, Washington, 1968-71; mem. Commn. Landlord-Tenant Affairs Washington City Coun., 1970-71; vice chmn. Washington Area Realtors Coun., 1970; exec. com., dir. Downtown Progress, 1970; bd. dirs. Washington Mental Health Assn., 1973, Washington Med. Ctr., 1975. Capt. USAAF, 1942-46. Mem. Am. Land Devel. Assn., Nat. Assn. Real Estate Editors, Washington Bd. Realtors (pres. 1970, Realtor of Yr. 1970, Martin Isen award 1981), Greater Met. Washington Bs. Trade (bd. dirs. 1974-80), U.S. League Savs. Assns. (attys. com. 1971-80), Washington Savs. and Loan League, ABA, D.C. Bar Assn., Internat. Real Estate Fedn., Yale Club, Cosmos Club, Rolls Royce Club, Antique Auto Club, St. Elmo Club, Omega Tau Rho. Episcopalian. Property, real (including real estate development, water). Home: Apt 905 4550 N Park Ave Chevy Chase MD 20815 Office: 1112 16th St NW Washington DC 20036-4823

NICHOLS, HENRY LOUIS, lawyer; b. Collin County, Tex., Nov. 7, 1916; s. Jesse Cleveland and Leva (Stiff) N.; m. Elaine Guentherman, May 17, 1949; children: David Michael, Martha Marie. LL.B., So. Meth. U., 1940. Bar: Tex. 1939. Asst. city atty., Dallas, 1946-50; pvt. practice, 1951—. Mem. adv. bd. Ctr. for Legal Mcpl. Studies. Served to lt. col. AUS, 1941-46; col. USAR ret. Rsch. fellow Southwestern Legal Found., 1964. Fellow Am. Bar Found.; mem. ABA, Dallas Bar Assn. (pres. 1963), State Bar Tex., Tex. Bar Found. (charter), Lakewood Country Club. General practice, Land use and zoning (including planning), Municipal (including bonds). Home: 3131 Maple Ave Apt 13H Dallas TX 75201-1206 Office: 1800 Lincoln Plz Dallas TX 75201

NICHOLS, MICHAEL C. food company executive, lawyer; b. Birmingham, Ala., Feb. 4, 1952; s. F.W. and Jeannett (Cooper) N.; m. Marcia Couch, Sept. 23, 1976; children: Joshua, Jessica, Zachary. BA with honors, Brown U., 1974; JD, Emory U., 1977. Bar: Ga., Tex. Mem. Ga. Ho. of Reps., Atlanta, 1977-81; chief adminstrv. officer Appletree Mktg., Houston, 1988-91; gen. counsel SYSCO Corp., Houston, 1981-88, v.p., 1991—. Sec., bd. dirs. Congregation Beth Israel, Houston, 1986—; pres. Houston Food Bank, 1990-92.*

NICHOLS, RALPH ARTHUR, lawyer; b. Clinton, N.Y., Jan. 27, 1919; s. Arthur Britcher and Carrie Lena (Pitcher) N.; m. Pamela Crow Bermingham, May 3, 1947 (dec. Feb. 1980); children: Jeremy Nichols Pierce, Ralph A. Jr., Melinda Nichols Mayer; m. Victoria Requa Lalli, Sept. 5, 1981. AB, Hamilton Coll., 1940; LLB, Yale U., 1947. Bar: Conn. 1949, N.Y. 1947, U.S. Dist. Ct. (so. dist.) N.Y. 1949, U.S. Dist. Ct. Conn. 1950, U.S. Supreme Ct. 1959. Assoc. Burke & Burke, N.Y.C., 1947-49, Maguire, Walker & Middleton, Stamford, Ct., 1949-54; assoc., then ptnr. Cummings & Lockwood, Stamford, 1954—. Founder, former bd. dirs. Stamford Land Conservation Trust; former bd. dirs. Conservationists Stamford, Inc., Stamford YMCA; former bd. dirs., sec. Stamford Area Commerce and Industry; trustee Stamford YMCA. Lt. USNR, 1942-46, ETO, PTO. Fellow Am. Coll. Trust and Estate Counsel; mem. ABA, Woodway Country Club (Darien, Conn.), Yale Club (N.Y.C.), Phi Delta Phi. Republican. Episcopalian. Home: 656 Den Rd Stamford CT 06903-3824 Office: Cummings & Lockwood PO Box 120 4 Stamford Plz Stamford CT 06902-3834 E-mail: rnicho@cl-law.com.

NICHOLS, ROBERT HASTINGS, lawyer; b. Mpls., Aug. 12, 1941; s. James Hastings and Judith (Beach) N.; m. Jean Christy, Nov. 30, 1968; children— Marc O., Seth J., Ethan D., Rebecca J. A.B., Yale U., 1963; cert. in Pub. Affairs, Coro Found., 1964; J.D., U. Chgo., 1967. Bar: Ill. 1967, U.S Dist Ct. (no. dist.) Ill. 1967, U.S. Dist. Ct. (ea. dist.) Wis. 1975; U.S. Ct. Appeals (7th cir.) 1972, U.S. Ct. Appeals (8th cir.) 1975, U.S. Ct. Appeals (D.C. cir.) 1976, U.S. Supreme Ct. 1986. Ptnr. Cotton, Watt, Jones & King, Chgo., 1967—95 ;sr. atty. and MEC coord. United Airlines Master Exec. Coun., Air Line Pilots Assn. Internat., AFL-CIO, 1995—; cons. Govt. of New Zealand, Auckland, 1980; mem. Lawyers Coordinating Com., AFL-CIO. Contbr. articles to legal publs. Democrat. Presbyterian. Club: Columbia Yacht. Federal civil litigation, Labor (including EEOC, Fair Labor Standards Act, labor-management relations, NLRB, OSHA). Home: 1030 E 49th St Chicago IL 60615-1814 Office: Ste 700 6400 Shafer Ct Rosemont IL 60018-6198

NICHOLSON, BRADLEY JAMES, lawyer; b. Montebello, Calif., Sept. 22, 1958; s. Thomas Edwin and Charlotte Elizabeth (Knight) N.; m. Anne Marie Dooley, Oct. 6, 1990. BA, Reed Coll., 1983; JD, U. Pa., 1990. Atty. Wilson, Sonsini, Goodrich & Rosati, Palo Alto, Calif., 1990-91; law clk. to Hon. Morris S. Arnold U.S. Dist. Ct., Ft. Smith, Ark., 1991-92; atty. Coudert Bros., San Jose, Calif., 1992-94; law clerk to Hon. Morris S. Arnold U.S. Cir. Ct., Little Rock, 1994-96; atty. Brown & Bain, Palo Alto, Calif., 1997-98; staff atty. ctrl. legal staff Nev. Supreme Ct., Carson City, 1998-99, prin. staff atty., ctrl. legal staff, 1999-2000; appellate staff atty. Oreg. Supreme Ct., Salem, Oreg., 2000—. Contbr. articles to profl. jours. Mem. Federalist Soc.(vice chmn. publications Litigation practice group, 1997-98, pres. Little Rock lawyers chpt. 1995-96). Avocations: golf, fishing, music. Office: Oreg Supreme Ct 1163 State St Salem OR 97301-2563

NICHOLSON, BRUCE ALLEN, lawyer; b. Phila., Nov. 12, 1949; s. Charles Glanz and Jean (Billman) N.; m. Linda King Barton, Apr. 22, 1972; children: Jessica Ann, James Barton. BA, Cornell U., 1971; JD cum laude, Boston Coll., 1975. Bar: Pa. 1975. Staff asst. Mass Bar Assn., Boston, 1973-75; assoc. Duffy, North, Wilson, Thomas & Nicholson, Hatboro, Pa., 1975-78; ptnr., 1978—. Solicitor Mongomery County (Pa.) Redevel. Authority, 1993—. Pres. Main St. Hatboro Revitalization Com., 1995-98; mem. Hatboro Boro Coun., 1984-88; chmn. Hatboro Hist. Commn., 1981-83; bd. mgrs. Hatboro Area YMCA, 1984-95, bd. chmn., 1990, 91. Named YMCA Vol. of Yr., 1989, 92. Mem. ABA, Pa. Bar Assn., Montgomery Bar Assn., greater Hatboro C. of C. (v.p., bd. dirs.), Rotary, Yacht Club Stone Harbor (N.J.), Riverton Yacht Club (N.J.). General practice, Probate (including wills, trusts), Property, real (including real estate development, water). Office: Duffy North Wilson Thomas & Nicholson PO Box 726 104 N York Rd Hatboro PA 19040-2699 E-mail: banicholson@duffynorth.com.

NICKELS, JOHN L. retired state supreme court justice; m. Merita Nickels; 7 children. Bachelor's degree, No. Ill. U.; law degree, DePaul U. Pvt. practice, 20 yrs; judge Appellate Ct.; cir. judge 16th Jud. Cir.; supreme ct. justice State of Ill., 1992-98; ret., 1998. Bd. dirs. Kane County Bank & Trust Co. Bd. trustees Waubonsee Coll.; mem. adv. coun. and found. Kaneland Sch. Dist.; mem. Kane County Planning Commn., Zoning Bd. Appeals; mem. St. Gall's Parish, Elburn. Home: 17901 Owens Rd Maple Park IL 60151

NICOLAIDES, MARY, lawyer; b. N.Y.C., June 7, 1927; d. George and Dorothy Nicolaides. BCE, CUNY, 1947; MBA with distinction, DePaul U., 1975, JD, 1981. Bar: Ill. 1982, U.S. Dist. Ct. (no. dist.) Ill. 1982, U.S. Patent Office 1983. Sr. design engr. cement subs. U.S. Steel Corp., N.Y.C., then Pitts., 1948-71; sole practice Chgo., 1982—. Republican. Greek Orthodox. Patent, Probate (including wills, trusts), Elder. Address: 233 E Erie St Apt 1804 Chicago IL 60611-2903

NICOLUCCI, JOHN PETER, lawyer; b. Grosse Pointe Park, Mich., Oct. 23, 1964; s. Paul Francis and Suzanne Annette Nicolucci; m. Archana Rano Rajendra, Aug. 8, 1993; children: Chand Rajendra-Nicolucci, Avi Rajendra-Nicolucci, Savera Rajendra-Nicolucci. BS, Purdue U., West Lafayette, Ind., 1986; JD, Ind. U., Indpls., 1993. Bar: Mich. 1993, U.S. Dist. Ct. (we. and ea. dist.) Mich. 1994, U.S. Ct. Appeals (6th cir.) 1994. Assoc. Dilley Dewey Damon & Condon, Grand Rapids, Mich., 1994—96, Jonathan Shove Damon, Grand Rapids, 1996—99, Foster Swift Collins & Smith, Lansing, Mich., 1999—. Rep. assembly State Bar of Mich., Lansing, 2001—02; barrister Am. Inns of Ct., Lansing, 2000—01. Scholar Evans scholar, Western Golf Assn., 1982—86. Mem.: ABA, Ingham County Bar Assn. (chmn. litigation sect. 2000), Par Club of Western Golf Assn. Avocations: golf, basketball, military history. Family and matrimonial, Insurance, Personal injury (including property damage). Office: Foster Swift Collins & Smith 313 S Washington Sq Lansing MI 48933

NIEHOFF, LEONARD MARVIN, lawyer; b. St. Louis, Dec. 2, 1957; s. Leonard Marvin and May (Gordon) Niehoff. BA with high distinction, U. Mich., 1981, JD, postgrad., U. Mich., 1984. Bar: Mich. 1984, U.S. Dist. Ct. (ea. dist.) Mich., 1985, U.S. Dist. Ct. (we. dist.) Mich. 1985, U.S. Ct. Appeals (6th cir.) 1985, U.S. Supreme Ct. 1988. Research asst. U. Mich. Law Sch., Ann Arbor, 1983; shareholder Butzel Long, Detroit, 1984—. Adj. prof. law U. Detroit Law Sch., 1988—, Wayne State U. Law Sch., 1989—, U. Mich. Law Sch., 2002—. Editor U. Mich. Jour. Law Reform, 1983-84. Bd. advisors C.S. Mott Children's Hosp.; bd. dirs. Mich. Theatre Found. Named to 40 Under 40, Crain's Detroit Bus., 1996. Mem. ABA (forum com. on comms. law 1985—), Fed. Bar Assn. (exec. bd. 1995—), State Bar Mich. (chmn. constl. law com., mem. law and media com., bar jour. adv. bd.), Detroit Bar Assn., Washtenaw Bar Assn. (chmn. trial practice sect.), U. Musical Soc. (bd. dirs.), Mich. Theater Found. (bd. dirs.), CS Mott Children's Hosp. (bd. dirs.). Avocations: music, film, art. General civil litigation, Constitutional, Libel. Office: 350 S Main St Ste 300 Ann Arbor MI 48104-2131

NIEHOFF, PHILIP JOHN, lawyer; b. Beaver Dam, Wis., Dec. 31, 1959; s. John Henry and Muriel Jean (Moore) Niehoff. BBA with distinction, U. Wis., 1982, JD cum laude, 1985; LLM in Securities Regulation, Georgetown U., 1988. Bar: Wis. 1985, U.S. Dist. Ct. (we. dist.) Wis. 1985, Ill. 1991. Atty. SEC, Washington, 1985-90; assoc. Mayer, Brown, Rowe & Maw, Chgo., 1990-95, ptnr., 1996—. Co-author: Current Law of Insider Trading, 1990, Public Offerings, securities law handbook, 1997; contbg. author: Securitization of Financial Assets, 1991. Fed. Bar Assn. scholar, 1988. Mem. ABA, State Bar Wis., State Bar Ill., Chgo. Bar Assn., Order of Coif, Golden Key Honor Soc., Beta Gamma Sigma, Phi Kappa Phi, Phi Eta Sigma. Republican. Lutheran. Avocations: fishing, computers, reading, travel. Corporate, general, Securities. Home: 2800 N Lake Shore Dr Apt 2416 Chicago IL 60657-6248 Office: Mayer Brown Rowe & Maw 190 S La Salle St Ste 3100 Chicago IL 60603-3441

NIELSEN, LYNN CAROL, lawyer, educational consultant; b. Perth Amboy, N.J., Jan. 11, 1950; d. Hans and Esther (Pucker) N.; m. Russell F. Baldwin, Nov. 22, 1980; 1 child, Blake Nielsen Baldwin. BS, Millersville U., 1972; MA, NYU, 1979; JD, Rutgers U., 1984. Bar: N.J. 1984; cert. tchr. handicapped, reading specialist, learning disability tchr. cons., elem. edn. supr. Instr. Woodbridge (N.J.) Twp. Bd. Edn., 1972-83; legal intern appellate sect. divsn. criminal justice Atty. Gen. State N.J., Trenton, 1983, dep. atty. gen. divsn. civil law, 1985; assoc. Kantor & Kusic, Keyport, N.J., 1984-86, Kantor & Linderoth, Keyport, N.J., 1986-92. Officer Fords (N.J.) Sch. # 14 PTO, 1974-75; elder First Presbyn. Ch. Avenel, N.J., 1985-88, Flemington (N.J.) Presbyn. Ch., 1997-99; bd. dirs. New Beginnings Nursery Sch., Woodbridge, 1989-90, Flemington Presbyn. Nursery Sch., 1991-93; elder Flemington Presbyn. Ch., 1997-99; bd. mem. Woodside Farms Homeowners Assn., 1996-99. Mem. ABA, N.J. Bar Assn., Monmouth County Bar Assn., Hunterdon County Bar Assn. Avocations: reading, skiing, sailing. Home and Office: 3 Buchannan Way Flemington NJ 08822-3205

NIEMANN, NICHOLAS KENT, lawyer; b. Quincy, Ill., May 2, 1956; s. Ferd E. and Rita M. (Jochem) N.; m. Ann Marie Forbes, June 14, 1980; children: Katie, Becky, Christine, David, Lisa, Trish. BSBA summa cum laude, Creighton U., 1978, JD magna cum laude, 1981. Bar: Nebr. 1981, U.S. Dist. Ct. Nebr. 1981, U.S. Ct. Appeals (8th cir) 1981, U.S Tax Ct. 1981, U.S. Claims Ct. 1985. Assoc. McGill, Koley, Parsonage & Lanphier, P.C., Omaha, 1981-83, McGrath, North, Mullin & Kratz, P.C. LLO, Omaha, 1983-85, ptnr., 1985—. Mem. Nebr. tax rsch. coun., Nebr. tax forum; adj. faculty Creighton Law Sch., Creighton U., 1993-94, 98-2002. Mem. AICPA (taxation sect. 1984—), Nebr. Bar Assn., Omaha Bar Assn., (pub. svc. com. 1983-84, Nebr. Soc. CPAs (taxation com. 1983-90, vice chmn. 1987-88, chmn. 1988-89, small bus. com. 1989-92, vice chmn. 1989-90, chmn. 1990-91)), Omaha C. of C. (pres. club 1986-90, exec. dialogue 1986-93, taxation com. 1988—), Nebr. Tax Forum, Nebr. C. of C. and Industry (taxation coun. 1989—), Kiwanis (membership com. Omaha club 1986), Optimists (bd. dirs. 1987-89), Alpha Sigma Nu (exec. com. 1985—, sec. 1986-87, treas. 1990, pres. 1992), Beta Gamma Sigma. Roman Catholic. Avocations: golf, tennis, riding horses, travel, baseball. Estate planning, Legislative, Corporate taxation. Home: 1537 N 131st Ave Omaha NE 68154-3619 Office: McGrath North Mullin & Kratz First Nat Tower Ste 3700 1601 Dodge St Omaha NE 68102-1627

NIEMETH, CHARLES FREDERICK, lawyer; b. Lorain, Ohio, Nov. 25, 1939; s. Charles Ambrose and Christine Cameron (Mollison) N.; m. Anne Marie Meckes, Oct. 12, 1968. BA, Harvard U., 1962; JD, U. Mich., 1965. Bar: Calif. 1966, N.Y. 1984. Assoc. O'Melveny & Myers, Los Angeles, 1965-72, ptnr., 1973—. Mem. leadership com. Consol. Corp. Fund of Lincoln Ctr. Mem. nat. com. Mich. Law Sch. Fund; trustee Challengers Boys and Girls Club, 1968-83; mem. bus. adv. coun. UCLA, 1979-83; mem. exec. com. Internat. Student Ctr., 1979-83; bd. dirs. Olympic Tower Condominium, 1986-92; bd. visitors Mich. Law Sch., mem. Tri-Bar Opinion Com. Mem. Riviera Tennis Club, Regency Club, N.Y. Athletic Club, Field Club (Greenwich, Conn.), Bel-Air Bay Club. Democrat. Roman Catholic. Corporate, general. Home: 10660 Bellagio Rd Los Angeles CA 90077-3713 also: 70 Oneida Dr Greenwich CT 06830-7131 Office: O'Melveny & Myers 1999 Avenue Of The Stars Los Angeles CA 90067-6035 also: 153 E 53rd St Fl 54 New York NY 10022-4611 E-mail: cniemeth@omm.com.

NIEMEYER, PAUL VICTOR, federal judge; b. Princeton, N.J., Apr. 5, 1941; s. Gerhart and Lucie (Lenzer) Niemeyer; m. Susan Kinley, Aug. 24, 1963; children: Jonathan K., Peter E., Christopher J. AB, Kenyon Coll., 1962; student, U. Munich, Federal Republic of Germany, 1962—63; JD, U. Notre Dame, 1966. Bar: Md. 1966, U.S. Dist. Ct. Md. 1967, U.S. Ct. Appeals (4th cir.) 1968, U.S. Supreme Ct. 1970, U.S. Dist. Ct. (so. dist.) Tex. 1977, U.S. Ct. Appeals (5th cir.) 1978, U.S. Ct. Appeals (3d cir.) 1980. Assoc. Piper & Marbury, Balt., 1966—74, ptnr., 1974—88; U.S. dist. judge U.S. Dist. Ct. Md., Balt., 1988—90; circuit judge U.S. Ct. Appeals (4th cir.), Balt., 1990—. Lectr. advanced bus. law Johns Hopkins U., Balt., 1971—75; lectr. Md. Jud. Conf., Md. Ct. Clks. Assn.; sr. lecturing fellow in appellate advocacy Duke U. Sch. of Law, 1994—; mem. standing com. on rules of practice and procedure cts. appeals, 1973—88; atty. grievance com.-hearing panel, 1978—81; select com.-profl. conduct, 1983—85; adv. com. on Fed. Rules of Civil Procedure, 1993—2000; chmn., 1996—2000. Co-author: Maryland Rules Commentary, 1984, Maryland Rules Commentary supplement, 1988, Maryland Rules Commentary, 2d. edit., 1992; contbr. articles to profl. jours. Recipient Spl. Merit citation, Am. Judicature Soc., 1987. Fellow: Am. Law Inst., Md. Bar Assn. (Disting. Svc. award litigation sect. 1981), Md. Bar Found., Am. Bar Found., Am. Coll. Trial Lawyers; mem.: Lawyers' Round Table, Wednesday Law Club. Republican. Episcopalian. Office: US Cir Ct Md US Courthouse 101 W Lombard St Ste 910 Baltimore MD 21201-2611

NIEMI, ANDREA KAY, lawyer; b. Mpls., Feb. 5, 1951; d. Harry and Edith (Kemp) Greene; m. Kenneth F. Niemi, May 4, 1974; 1 child, Nathaniel. BA, Macalester Coll., 1973; JD, William Mitchell Coll. Law, 1979. Bar: Minn. 1980, U.S. Dist. Ct. Minn. 1985. Asst. atty. Scott Co. Atty.'s Office, Shakopee, Minn., 1980-81; pvt. practice Law Office Andrea Niemi, Mpls., 1981-88; shareholder Niemi Barr & Jerabek P.A., Mpls., 1988—. Dir. Collaborative Law Inst., Minn., 1994—, pres., 1996—. Mem. ABA, Nat. Assn. Counsel for Children, Minn. State Bar Assn., Hennepin County Bar Assn. (co-chair juvenile law com. 1995—), Am. Acad. Matrimonial Lawyers (exec. v.p. 2002-2003), Friends of Children Found. (pres. 2001—). Family and matrimonial, Juvenile. Office: Niemi Barr & Jerabek PA 510 Marquette Ave Ste 200 Minneapolis MN 55402

NIEMI, JANICE, retired lawyer, former state legislator; b. Flint, Mich., Sept. 18, 1928; d. Richard Jesse and Norma (Bell) Bailey; m. Preston Niemi, Feb. 4, 1953 (div. 1987); children: Ries, Patricia. BA, U. Wash., 1950, LLB, 1967; postgrad., U. Mich., 1950-52; cert., Hague Acad. Internat. Law, The Netherlands, 1954. Bar: Wash. 1968. Assoc. firm Powell, Livengood, Dunlap & Silverdale, Kirkland, Wash., 1968; staff atty. Legal Svc. Ctr., Seattle, 1968-70; judge Seattle Dist. Ct., 1971-72, King County Superior Ct., Seattle, 1973-78; acting gen. counsel, dep. gen. counsel SBA, Washington, 1979-81; mem. Wash. State Ho. of Reps., Olympia, 1983-87, chmn. com. on state govt., 1984; mem. Wash. State Senate, 1987-95; sole practice Seattle, 1981-94; superior ct. judge King County, 1995-2000; chief criminal judge, 1997-2000; ret., 2000; mem. Wash. State Gambling Commn., 2002—. Mem. White Ho. Fellows Regional Selection Panel, Seattle, 1974—77, chmn., 1976, 77; incorporator Soudn Savs. & Loan, Seattle, 1975; bd. dirs. Artists Trust; mem. panel Am. Arbitration Assn., 2003—. Bd. visitors dept. psychology U. Wash., Seattle, 1983—87, bd. visitors dept. sociology, 1988—98; mem. adv. bd. Tacoma Art Mus., 1987—; mem. Wash. State Gender and Justice Commn., 1987—89; Bd. dirs. Allied Arts, Seattle, 1971—78, Ctr. Contemporary Art, Seattle, 1981—83, Women's Network, Seattle, 1981—84, Pub. Defender Assn., Seattle, 1982—84, Artist's Trust, 2002—. Named Woman of Yr. in Law, Past Pres.'s Assn., Seattle, 1971, Woman of Yr., Matrix Table, Seattle, 1973, Capitol Hill Bus. and Profl. Women, 1975. Mem. Wash. State Bar Assn., Wash. Women Lawyers, Am. Arbitration Assn. (panel 2003—). Democrat. Home: PO Box 20516 Seattle WA 98102-1516

NIER, HARRY KAUFMAN, lawyer; b. N.Y.C., Aug. 13, 1925; s. Harry K. Sr. and May O. Nier. LLB, U. Colo., 1950. Bar: Colo. 1952, Miss. 1964, U.S. Ct. Appeals 1979, U.S. Supreme Ct. 1959. Pvt. practice, Denver, 1952—. Chmn. Denver-Havana Friendship Cities Project, 1990—. Mem.: Denver Bar Assn., Colo. Bar Assn., Nat. Lawyers Guild. Avocation: mountaineering. Civil rights, Constitutional, Private international. Home: 1470 S Quebec Way Apt 81 Denver CO 80231-2657 Office: 1700 Lincoln St Ste 3850 Denver CO 80203-4539

NIGH, ROBERT RUSSELL, JR., lawyer; b. Enid, Okla., Nov. 1, 1959; s. Robert Russell and Helen Louise Nigh. BA, William Jewell Coll., 1982; JD, U. Okla., 1986. Assoc. Jones, Bryant & Nigh, Enid, 1986-89; asst. pub. defender Tulsa County, Office of Pub. Defender, 1989-92; asst. fed. defender Fed. Pub. Defender's Office, Tulsa, 1992-94, Lincoln, Nebr., 1994-96; pvt. practice Tulsa, 1996-2000; atty. Brewster and De Angelis, Tulsa, 2001—. Mem. Nat. Assn. Criminal Def. Lawyers, Okla. Criminal Def. Lawyers Assn. (bd. dirs. 1991-94), Tulsa County Bar Assn. Avocations: hunting, fishing, basketball. Criminal. Office: 2617 E 21st St Tulsa OK 74114 Business E-Mail: rnigh@brewsterlaw.com.

NIGHTINGALE, TRACY IRENE, lawyer; b. Bloomer, Wis., May 16, 1966; d. Russell L. and Dorothy I. (Bluem) Pederson; m. Brian J. Nightingale, July 16, 1990; children: Austin M., Carson D., Sierra C. BA, U. Wis., Eau Claire, 1988; JD, Hamline U., 1991. Bar: Minn. 1992, U.S. Dist. Minn. 1993, Wis. 1994. Pvt. practice, Mpls., 1992—98; atty. Legal Legacy, Ltd., St. Louis Park, Minn., 1996-98; exec. dir. Nat. Assn. Debt Mgrs., St. Louis Park, 1997-98; atty. Hurwitz Law Firm, 1998-2000; pvt. practice Nightingale Law Office, St. Louis Park, 2000—. Mediator West Suburban Mediation Ctr., Hopkins, Minn., 1992-2001. Author: Trust and Estate Planner, 1996. Mem. ABA, Minn. Bar Assn., Wis. Bar Assn., Hennepin County Bar Assn. Alternative dispute resolution, Estate planning, Personal injury (including property damage). Office: Nightingale Law Office Ste 700 5775 Wayzata Blvd Saint Louis Park MN 55416 E-mail: nightingale-law@justice.com.

NIGRO, RUSSELL M. state supreme court justice; b. Mar. 23, 1946; Justice Pa. Supreme Ct., Phila., 1996—. Office: Pa Supreme Ct 1818 Market St Ste 3205 Philadelphia PA 19103-3639

NIKAS, RICHARD JOHN, lawyer; b. Long Beach, Calif., Sept. 9, 1968; s. John Nikolas and Dorothy (Bernardo) N. BA in Internat. Rels., U. So. Calif., 1991, JD, 1995. Bar: Calif. Spl. projects coord. Vessel Assist Assn. Am., Newport Beach, Calif., 1989-94; ptnr. Samini Naso and Nikas, Costa Mesa, Calif., 2003—. Guest lectr. maritime law U. So. Calif., L.A., 1998—; lectr. admiralty and maritime law Calif. Maritime Acad., Vallejo; chmn. USCG Working Group on Nat. Maritime Incident Reporting Sys., Washington, 1997—. Author: Benedict on Admiralty, 1998, Moore's Federal Practice, 1998, The Last Yankee, 1999, Recreational Boating Law, 2000, Admiralty Practice and Procedure, 2000. Head football coach Ocean View H.S., Long Beach, 1995; mentor Long Beach Unified Sch. Dist., 1997—; pitcher Greek Olympic Baseball Team, Atlantic City Surf Profl. Baseball Club; bd. govs. The Am. Mariner, Loyola U., 1999. Recipient Best Oralist award Spong Nat. Invitational Moot Ct., Williamsburg, Va., 1995, Meritorious Pub. Svc. medal USCG. Mem. Calif. State Bar Assn., Maritime Law Assn., Soc. of Naval Architects and Marine Engrs. (chmn. panel 0-38). Avocation: baseball. Admiralty, Federal civil litigation, Transportation. Address: 17652 Wrightwood Ln Huntington Beach CA 92649-4969 E-mail: rnikas@sumininaso.com.

NIKOLAY, FRANK LAWRENCE, lawyer; b. Marathon County, Wis., Sept. 1, 1922; s. Jacob and Anna Bertha (Illig) N.; m. Mary Elizabeth Gisvold, Aug. 3, 1958. LLB, U. Wis., 1948. Bar: Wis. 1948, U.S. Dist. Ct. (we. dist.) Wis. 1948, U.S. Supreme Ct. 1961. Dist. counsel Office Price Stabilization, Green Bay, Wis., 1951-52; asst. U.S. atty. U.S. Dist. Ct. (we. dist.) Wis., 1952-53, U.S. atty., 1953-54; mem. assembly State of Wis., 1959-70; ptnr. Nikolay Law Offices, Colby, 1970—. Mem. bd. regents U. Wis., Madison, 1983-90; mem. Clark County (Wis.) Bd. Suprs., 1949—. Col. U.S. Army, 1948-74. Mem. ABA, Wis. Bar Assn., Am. Legion (post comdr. 1975—), Lions (sec. 1978). Democrat. Roman Catholic. Administrative and regulatory, Criminal, General practice. Office: Nikolay Law Offices PO Box 465 Colby WI 54421-0465 Office Fax: 715-223-8834.

NILLES, JOHN MICHAEL, lawyer; b. Langdon, N.D., Aug. 20, 1930; s. John Joseph and Isabel Mary (O'Neil) N.; m. Barbara Ann Cook, June 22, 1957; children: Terese M., Daniel J., Marcia L., Thomas M., Margaret J. BA cum laude, St. Johns U., 1955; JD cum laude with distinction, U. N.D., 1958. Bar: N.D. 1958, U.S. Dist. Ct. N.D. 1958, U.S. Ct. Appeals (8th cir.) 1958, Minn. 1991. Shareholder, dir., pres. Nilles, Hansen and Davies, Ltd., Fargo, N.D., 1958-90, of counsel, 1990-95; exec. v.p., gen. counsel Met. Fin. Corp., Mpls., 1990-95, First Bank F.S.B., Mpls., 1995; ret., 1996. Pres., bd. dirs. Legal Aid Soc. N.D., Fargo, 1970-76, Red River Estate Planning Coun., 1980-87; vice-chmn. disciplinary bd. Supreme Ct. N.D., 1984-90. Bd. editors N.D. Law Rev., 1957-58. Mem. exec. bd. Red. River Valley coun. Boy Scouts Am., 1959-70; bd. regents U. Mary, Bismarck, N.D., 1967-77; pres., bd. dirs. Cath. Charities, Fargo, 1959-65, Southeast Mental Health Ctr., Fargo, 1972-80. Staff sgt. USAF, 1951-54. Fellow Am. Coll. Trust and Estate Counsel (state dir. 1979-90); mem. ABA, State Bar Assn. N.D., Minn. Bar Assn., Order of Coif. Republican. Roman Catholic. Avocations: tennis, downhill skiing, cross-country skiing, hunting, gun collecting. Banking, Corporate, general. Home: 10412 Fawns Way Eden Prairie MN 55347-5117

NILSSON, BO GUSTAF HERMAN, lawyer; b. Harnosand, Sweden; s. Sven Ragnar and Ingegard Nilsson; m. Sara Birgitta Lindkvist, Aug. 11, 1979; 1 child, Sofia. BA, Uppsala U., 1973, LLB, 1975. Bar: Sweden 1982. Assoc. Wetter & Wetter, Stockholm, 1979—82; ptnr. Rydincarlsten, 1982—. Mem.: Swedish Bar Assn. (bd. dirs. 1995—2001, chmn. ednl. com. 2001—). Alternative dispute resolution. Office: RydinCarlsten PO Box 1766 Normalmstorg 14 111 87 Stockholm Sweden Fax: +46 8 6114580. E-mail: bo.nilsson@rydincarlsten.se.

NILSSON, OLOF ROBERT, lawyer; b. Nacka, Sweden, Jan. 28, 1949; s. Erik Hugo and Gunborg Louise (Eriksson) N.; m. Eva Antoinetta Gullack, July 30, 1982; children: Maria, Thomas. LLB, U. Stockholm, 1974. Law clk. Dist. Ct. of Solna, Sweden, 1974-76; assoc. Advokatfirman Lagerlof, Stockholm, 1976-80, Advokatfirman Cederquist, Stockholm, 1980-82, ptnr., 1982—. Chmn. bd. dirs. Advokatfirman Cederquist. 1998-2000. Mem. Swedish Bar Assn. Home: Germaniavagen 6B SE-18268 Djursholm Sweden Office: Advokatfirman Cederquist PO Box 1670 SE-11196 Stockholm Sweden E-mail: olof.nilsson@cederquist.se.

NIMETZ, MATTHEW, investment company executive; b. Bklyn., June 17, 1939; s. Joseph L. and Elsie (Botwinik) N.; m. Gloria S. Lorch, June 24, 1975; children: Alexandra Elise, Lloyd. BA, Williams Coll., 1960, LL.D. (hon.), 1979; BA (Rhodes scholar), Balliol Coll., Oxford (Eng.) U., 1962, MA, 1966; LL.B., Harvard U., 1965. Bar: N.Y. 1966, D.C. 1968. Law clk. to Justice John M. Harlan, U.S. Supreme Ct., 1965-67; staff asst. to Pres. Johnson, 1967-69; asso. firm Simpson Thacher & Bartlett, N.Y.C., 1969-74, ptnr., 1974-77; counselor Dept. of State, Washington, 1977-80, acting coord. refugee affairs, 1979-80, under sec. of state for security assistance, sci. and tech., 1980; ptnr. firm Paul, Weiss, Rifkind, Wharton & Garrison, N.Y.C., 1981-2000; ptnr., mng. mem. Gen. Atlantic Ptnrs. LLC, Greenwich, Conn., 2000—. Commr. Port Authority N.Y. and N.J., 1975-77; dir. World Resources Inst., chmn., 1982-94; mem. N.Y. State Adv. Coun. on State Productivity, 1990-92; presdl. envoy Greece-Macedonian Negotiations, 1994-95, spl. rep. UN Sec. Gen., 1999—. Trustee William Coll., 1981-96; chmn. UN Devel. Corp., 1986-94; bd. dirs. Charles H. Revson Found., 1990-98, N.Y. State Nature Conservancy, 1997—; chmn. Carnegie Forum in U.S., Greece and Turkey, 1996-98; chmn. Ctr. for Democracy and Reconciliation in S.E. Europe, 1998—; dir. Inst. Pub. Adminstrn., 1999—; mem. internat. adv. com. Ctrl. European U., Budapest, Hungary, 1998—. Mem. Assn. of Bar of City of N.Y., Coun. on Fgn. Rels. Clubs: Harvard (N.Y.C.). Corporate, general, Private international, Securities. Office: Gen Atlantic Ptnrs LLC 3 Pickwick Plz Greenwich CT 06830-5538 E-mail: mnimetz@gapartners.com.

NIMKIN, BERNARD WILLIAM, retired lawyer; b. N.Y.C., Apr. 15, 1923; s. Myron Benjamin and Anabel (Davidow) N.; m. Jean Horowitz, Feb. 9, 1947; children— David Andrew, Margaret Lee, Katherine. BS cum laude, Harvard U., 1943, LL.B. cum laude, 1949. Bar: N.Y. State bar 1949, U.S. Supreme Ct., 1999. Asso. firm Carter, Ledyard & Milburn, N.Y.C., 1949-58; asso. and partner firm Kaye Scholer, LLP, N.Y.C., 1958-91. Lectr. Practising Law Inst., Banking Law Inst.; Mem. Am. Law Inst.; vis. com. U. Miami Law Sch.; mem. adv. bd. Rev. of Securities Regulation. Contbr. articles to profl. jours. Mem. Conservation Commn., Town of Mamaroneck, N.Y., 1970-74; bd. dirs., sec. United Way of Tri-State, 1985-91. Served to 1st lt. U.S. Army, 1943-46. Mem. ABA (mem. fed. regulation of securities com. 1975—, corp. laws com. 1984-92, legal opinions com. 1989—), N.Y. State Bar Assn. (chmn. sect. banking corp. and bus. law 1979-81, ho. of dels. 1981-84, chmn. corp. law com. 1976-79), Assn. Bar City of N.Y. (chmn. uniform state laws com. 1962-65), Tribar Opinion Com. Democrat. Jewish. Home: 116 E 63rd St New York NY 10021-7325 Office: Kaye Scholer LLP 425 Park Ave New York NY 10022-3506 E-mail: bandjnimkin@earthlink.net.

NINNIS, WILLIAM RAYMOND, JR., lawyer; b. San Francisco, Aug. 23, 1932; s. William Raymond and Oda Marie (Jensen) N.; m. Mary Frances Parker; children: William Bradley, David Raymond. AB, San Francisco State U., 1958; LLB, JD, U. Calif., 1962. Bar: Calif. 1963, U.S. Dist. Ct. (no. dist.) Calif. 1963, U.S. Ct. Appeals (9th cir.) 1963, U.S. Dist. Ct. (ea. dist.) Calif. 1967, U.S. Dist. Ct. (cen. dist.) Calif. 1984. Assoc. house counsel Pacific Gas and Electric Co., San Francisco, 1962-67; trial atty., v.p. and sec. Dawson & Ninnis PLC, Fresno, Calif., 1967-84; ptnr., trial atty. Ninnis & Cribbs, Fresno, 1984—; judge pro tem Workers Compensation Appeals Bd., 1984—, arbitrator, 1994—. Mem. Calif. State Bar Assn., San Francisco County Bar Assn., Fresno County Bar Assn., Clovis Bar Assn. (v.p. , bd. dir. Fresno rape coun. 1988), San Francisco Bar Assn. (chmn. worker's compensation com. 1965-67), No. Calif. Def. Atty.'s Asssn. (bd. dirs. 1973-83). Republican. Methodist. Avocations: hunting, fishing. Civil rights, Personal injury (including property damage), Workers' compensation. Home: 11028 El Capitan Dr Madera CA 93638-7411 Office: Ninnis & Cribbs 3106 Willow Ave Clovis CA 93612-4749 also: PO Box 5314 Fresno CA 93755-5314

NIRO, CHERYL, lawyer; b. Feb. 19, 1950; d. Samuel James and Nancy (Canezaro) Ippolito; m. William Luciano Niro, July 1, 1979; children: Christopher William, Melissa Leigh. BS with highest honors, U. Ill., 1972; JD, No. Ill. U., 1980. Bar: Ill. 1981, U.S. Dist. Ct. (no. dist.) Ill. 1981, U.S. Ct. Appeals (7th cir.) 1990, U.S. Supreme Ct. 1999, cert.: negotiator, mediator, facilitator. Assoc. Pope Ballard Sheppard & Fowle, Chgo., 1980-81; ptnr. Partridge and Niro PC; now ptnr. Quinlan & Carroll, Chgo. Spl. counsel to atty. gen. Office Ill. Atty. Gen., 1996—99; pres. Assocs. in Dispute Resolution Inc.; exec. dir. Com. to Commerorate U.S. Constituion in Ill., 1985—86; creator Bicentennial Law Sch. Program; tchg. asst. program instrn. lawyers mediation and negotiation workshops; guest lectr. Harvard U.; mem. appt. panel U.S. Ct. Appeals (7th cir.); pres. Judicial Dispute Resolution Inc.; found. dir. Nat. Ctr. for Conflict Resolution Edn.; mem. copyright arbitration royalty panel through Libr. of Congress, 2000—03. Chmn of ISBA Task Force on Children; co-chair Ill. Conclave on Legal Edn.; bd dirs Univ Chicago Lying-In Hosp, 1982—. Named one of Ten Most Influential Women Lawyers in Ill, Am Lawyer Media, 2000; named to Today's Chgo. Woman Mag. Hall of Fame, 2002. Mem.: ATLA, ABA (comn multijurisdictional practice, standing comt bar servs, dispute resolution sect coun, house delegs), Internat. Bar Assn., Ill Bar Asn (mem assembly 1993, bd govs 1994—97, treas 1995—96, 2d vpres 1997—98, pres 1999—2000, pres. 1999—2000, standing comt legal-related educ pub), Ill Trial Lawyers Asn. Alternative dispute resolution, Appellate, General civil litigation. Home: 633 N East Ave Oak Park IL 60302-1715 Office: Quinlan & Carroll 30 N Lasalle St Ste 2900 Chicago IL 60602-2590 Business E-Mail: cniro@qclaw.com.

NISHI, MASARU, law educator, lawyer, legal association administrator; b. Wakayama, Japan, July 8, 1928; s. Yoshikazu and Sadako (Yoshimura) N.; m. Emiko Yasuda, Feb. 4, 1957; children: Fumiko, Chikako, Yoko. LLB, Kyoto (Japan) U., 1953, LLD, 1991. Assoc. prof. Kobe (Japan) U., 1957-67, prof., 1967-90, Himeji-Dokkyo (Japan) U., 1990—; counsel Japan Bar Assn., Kobe, 1990—, Inter Pacific Bar Assn., Tokyo, 1991—. Author: Development of Personal Law, 1989. Mem. European Union Studies Assn. (bd. dirs. 1988—, pres. 1994-96), Japan Assn. Internat. Law (bd. dirs. Tokyo chpt. 1976-97), Japan Assn. Pvt. Internat. Law (bd. dirs. Tokyo chpt. 1974—), Internat. Law Assn., Soc. de législation comparée, Brit. Inst. Internat. and Comparative Law. Home: 1-10-21 Akibadai, Nishi-ku Kobe 651-2224 Japan Office: Himeji-Dokkyo U 7-2-1 Kamiono Himeji 670-8524 Japan

NISSMAN, DAVID M. lawyer; b. 1953; m. Carolina Zapata Nissman; 3 children. BA magna cum laude, Emory U., 1975; JD, U. Oreg., 1978. Dep. dist. atty., Eugene, Oreg.; adj. law prof. U. Oreg.; chief asst. U.S. atty. St. Croix, V.I.; pub. Office of Legal Edn., Dept. of Justice; U.S. atty. Author: Proving Federal Crimes, 2001. Recipient Chief Inspector's Award, USPS, 1991, NRC Award, 1994, Environmental Div. Award, U.S. Dept. Justice, 2000, Dir. Awards, Exec. Office U.S. Attys. Office: US Courthouse 5500 Veterans Dr Rm 260 Saint Thomas VI 00802

NITIKMAN, FRANKLIN W. lawyer; b. Davenport, Iowa, Oct. 26, 1940; s. David A. and Janette (Gordon) N.; m. Adrienne C. Drell, Nov. 28, 1972. BA, Northwestern U., 1963; LLB, Yale U., 1966. Bar: Ill. 1966, U.S. Dist. Ct. (no. dist.) Ill. 1967, U.S. Tax Ct. 1972, Fla. 1977, D.C. 1981. Assoc. McDermott, Will & Emery, Chgo., 1966-72, ptnr., 1973—. Co-author: Drafting Wills and Trust Agreements, 1990. Bd. dirs. Jewish United Fund, Owen Coon Found., Glenview, Ill., 1985—, Jewish Fedn. Met. Chgo., 1994—; bd. dirs. Spertus Inst. Jewish Studies, Chgo., 1991—, chmn. bd., 1999—2002. Fellow Am. Coll. Trust and Estate Coun., Am. Bar Found.; mem. Standard Club, Arts Club (Chgo.). Estate planning, Probate (including wills, trusts), Estate taxation. Home: 365 Lakeside Pl Highland Park IL 60035-5371 Office: McDermott Will & Emery 227 W Monroe St Ste 4700 Chicago IL 60606-5096 E-mail: fnitikman@mwe.com.

NITZE, WILLIAM ALBERT, government official, lawyer, not-for-profit developer; b. N.Y.C., Sept. 27, 1942; s. Paul Henry and Phyllis (Pratt) N.; m. Ann Kendall Richards, June 5, 1971; children: Paul Kendall, Charles Richards. BA, Harvard U., 1964, JD, 1969; BA, Oxford U., 1966. Bar: N.Y. 1970, U.S. Supreme Ct. 1987. Assoc. Sullivan and Cromwell, N.Y.C., 1970-72; v.p. London Arts, Inc., N.Y.C., 1972-73; counsel Mobil South, Inc., N.Y.C., 1974-76; gen. counsel Mobil Oil Japan, Tokyo, 1976-80; asst. gen. counsel exploration and producing divsn. Mobil Oil Corp., N.Y.C., 1980-87; dep asst. sec. for environment, health and natural resources U.S. Dept. State, Washington, 1987-90; pres. Alliance to Save Energy, Washington, 1990-94; asst. adminstr. for internat. activities U.S. EPA, Washington, 1994-2001; pres. Gemstar Group, Washington, 2001—. Mem. adv. com. Sch. Advanced Internat. Studies, Washington, 1982-95, professorial lectr., 1993-94, 2001—; vis. scholar Environ. Law Inst., Washington, 1990; bd. dirs. Charles A. Lindbergh Fund, Mpls., 1990-94, Nat. Symphony Orch. Assn., Washington, 1990-2002, Atlantic Coun. U.S., Washington, 2002—; bd. dirs. Charles Darwin Found., Inc., 2001—, Falls Ch., Va., vice chmn. 2002—; bd. dirs. Climate Inst., Washington, 2001-, vice chmn., 2001-02, chmn., 2002-. Trustee Aspen Inst., Queenstown, Md., 1988—, Krasnow Inst., Fairfax, Va., 1996-2001. Mem.: Coun. on Fgn. Rels., Assn. Bar City NY, Links Club, Cosmos Club, Met. Club. Republican. Episcopalian. Avocations: running, piano, collecting art. Home: 1537 28th St NW Washington DC 20007-3059 Office: Gemstar Group 910 17th St NW Ste 1110 Washington DC 20006 E-mail: wanitze@gemstargroup.org.

NIX, EDMUND ALFRED, lawyer; b. Eau Claire, Wis., May 24, 1929; s. Sebastian and Kathryn (Keirnan) N.; m. Mary Kathryn Nagle Daley, Apr. 27, 1968; children: Kim, Mary Kay, Norbert, Edmund Alfred, Michael. BS, Wis. State U., 1951; LL.B., U. Wis., 1954, postgrad. in speech, 1956-57. Bar: Wis. 1954. Practice in, Eau Claire, 1954-65; dist. atty. Eau Claire County, 1958-64; U.S. atty. Western Dist. Wis., Eau Claire, 1965-69, U.S. magistrate, 1969-70; dist. atty. La Crosse County, Wis., 1975-77; mcpl. judge City of La Crosse, 1992—. Co-chmn. United Fund, Eau Claire, 1958; Pres. Young Democrats Wis., 1951-53; mem. adminstrv. bd. Wis. Dem. party, 1953-54; chmn. 10th Congl. dist., 1965; sec. Kennedy for Pres. Club Wis., 1959-60. Served with AUS, 1954-56. Mem. Fed. Bar Assn., Wis. Bar Assn. (state chmn. crime prevention and control com.), La Crosse County Bar Assn. (pres.), Nat. Dist. Attys. Assn., KC. Roman Catholic. Office: 123 4th St N La Crosse WI 54601-3235 E-mail: nixe@ffax.net.

NIXON, JEREMIAH W. (JAY NIXON), state attorney general; b. DeSoto, Mo., Feb. 13, 1956; s. Jeremiah and Betty (Lea) Nixon; m. Georganne Nixon; children: Jeremiah, Will. BS in Polit. Sci., U. Mo., 1978, JD, 1981. Ptnr. Nixon, Nixon, Breeze & Roberts, Jefferson County, Mo., 1981—86; mem. Mo. State Senate from Dist 22, 1986—93; atty. gen. State of Mo., 1992—. Chmn. select com. ins. reform; creator video internat. devel. and edn. opportunity program. Named Outstanding Young Missourian, Jaycees, 1994, Outstanding Young Lawyer, Barrister's Mag., 1993; recipient Conservation Fedn. Mo award, 1992. Mem.: Mo. Assn. Trial Attys., Midwest Assn. Attys. Gen., Nat. Assn. Attys. Gen. Democrat. Methodist. Office: Atty Gen Office PO Box 899 Jefferson City MO 65102-0899*

NIXON, JOHN TRICE, judge; b. New Orleans, La., Jan. 9, 1933; s. H. C. and Anne (Trice) N.; children: Mignon Elizabeth, Anne Trice. AB cum laude, Harvard Coll., 1955; LL.B., Vanderbilt U., 1960. Bar: Ala. bar 1960, Tenn. bar 1972. Individual practice law, Anniston, Ala., 1960-62; city atty., 1962-64; trial atty. Civil Rights Div., Dept. Justice, Washington, 1964-69; staff atty., comptroller of Treasury State of Tenn., 1971-76; pvt. practice law Nashville, 1976-77; cir. judge, 1977-78; gen. sessions judge, 1978-80; judge U.S. Dist. Ct. (mid. dist.) Tenn., Nashville, 1980—, sr. judge, 1998—. Served with U.S. Army, 1958. Mem. Fly Club (Cambridge), Harvard-Radcliffe Club (Nashville). Democrat. Methodist. Office: US Dist Ct 745 US Courthouse Nashville TN 37203

NIXON, SCOTT SHERMAN, lawyer; b. Grosse Pointe, Mich., Feb. 7, 1959; s. Floyd Sherman and Marjorie Jane (Quermann) N.; m. Cathryn Lynn Starnes, Aug. 27, 1983; children: Jeffry Sherman, Kelsy Jane, James Robert. BABA, Mich. State U., 1981; JD, U. Denver, 1984. Bar: Colo. 1984, U.S. Dist. Ct. Colo. 1984, U.S. Ct. Appeals (10th cir.) 1984. Assoc. Pryor, Carney & Johnson, P.C., Englewood, Colo., 1984-89, shareholder, 1990-95; pres., shareholder Pryor, Johnson, Montoya, Carney & Karr, P.C., Englewood, 1995—. Officer, bd. dirs. Luth. Brotherhood Br. 8856, Denver, 1993-99, Mark K. Ulmer Meml. Native Am. Scholarship Found., Denver, 1994—; officer, mem. coun. Bethan Luth Ch., Englewood, 1993-95. Mem.: ABA, Colo. Def. Lawyers Assn., Denver Bar Assn., Colo. Bar Assn. Avocations: music performance, physical fitness, carpentry/construction. Personal injury (including property damage), Product liability, Professional liability. Home: 6984 S Pontiac Ct Englewood CO 80112-1127 Office: Pryor Johnson Montoya Carney & Karr PC Ste 1200 5619 DTC Pky Greenwood Village CO 80111 E-mail: snixon@pjmck.com.

NIZIN, LESLIE STEPHEN, lawyer; b. N.Y.C., Nov. 21, 1939; s. Albert and Bertha D. Nizin; m. Gail L. Gordon. BA, Queens Coll., 1961; LLB, Bklyn. Law Sch., 1964, JD, 1967. Bar: N.Y. 1964. Atty. Sturim & Nizin, Kew Gardens, N.Y., 1969—. Pres. sch. bd. Half Hollow Hills, Huntington, N.Y., 1977-92. Mem.: Network Bar Leaders (pres.), Queens County Bar Assn. (bd. mgrs., v.p., past pres.). Criminal, Family and matrimonial. Office: 12510 Queens Blvd Kew Gardens NY 11415-1519 E-mail: lnasjm@aol.com.

NOACK, HAROLD QUINCY, JR., lawyer; b. San Francisco, May 1, 1931; m. Ann Crosby, Nov. 1952 (div. Sept. 1974); children: Stephen Tracy, Peter Quincy, Andrew Crosby; m. Susan K. Sherwood, Dec. 1975 (div. Jan.

1983); m. Penny Jo Orth, Apr. 2, 1988 (div. May 1989); m. Linda F. Killeen, Mar. 15, 1994 (div. May 1996). BA, U. Calif., Berkeley, 1953; LLB, U. Calif., San Francisco, 1959. Bar: Calif. 1960, Idaho 1969, U.S. Dist. Ct. Idaho 1969. Assoc. Fernoff & Wolfe, Oakland, Calif., 1959-64, Cooley, Crowley, Gaither, Godward, Castro & Huddleson, San Francisco, 1964-65; pvt. practice Oakland, 1965-66; ptnr. Oliphant, Hopper, Stribling & Noack, Oakland, 1966-69; assoc. Eberle, Berlin, Kading & Turnbow, Boise, Idaho, 1969-70; pvt. practice Boise, 1970-83, 85-88; assoc. Anthony Parks, Boise, 1970-75; ptnr. Noack & Korn, Boise, 1970-75, Noack & Hawley, Boise, 1983-85, Lyons & Noack, Boise, 1988-89; pvt. practice law Boise, 1989—. Contbr. articles to profl. jours. Bd. dirs., pres. Idaho Planned Parenthood, Boise, 1970-72; bd. dirs. Idaho Heart Assn., Boise, 1975. 2d lt. U.S. Army, 1954-55. Mem. ABA, Calif. Bar Assn., Idaho Bar Assn. (fee grievance com. 1986—), Boise Bar Assn., Rotary (bd. dirs. Boise club 1980). Avocations: running, walking, fishing, cooking. Bankruptcy, General civil litigation, General practice. Home: PO Box 875 1915 N 24th St Boise ID 83702-0204 Office: 733 N 7th St Boise ID 83702-5500

NOBEL, PETER, lawyer, researcher; b. Stockholm, Dec. 8, 1931; s. Leif Jurij Nobel and Anna Elisabeth (Mellen) Molander; m. Agnes Waldenstrom, Oct. 7, 1961 (div. Dec. 1993); m. Weini Kahsai, Mar. 18, 1994; children: Leif Jakob, Andreas, Jonas. JD (hon.), U. Uppsala, Sweden, 1985. Bar: Sweden 1968-86. Assoc. Advokatfirman, Chrysander, Uppsala, 1963-68, ptnr., 1968-86; assigned expert Swedish Govt. Com. for Reform of Law on Arrest and Custody in Criminal Procs., 1974-80, 83-85, on Law of Asylum, 1985, on Internat. law and disarmement, 1991-95, on Spl. Crisis Support, 1997-98. Del. Swedish Govt. on Children and Youth, 1991-95; lectr. Law Sch., Uppsala, 1964-69; apptd. ombudsman against ethnic discrimination Govt. of Sweden, 1986-91; sec. gen. Swedish Red Cross, 1991-94; commr. for counseling relatives of victims after the shipwreck of Estonia, 1994-96; mem. coun. fgn. affairs peace and security promoting, 1995-97; cons. inf field; mem. com. Ethics of the Press, 1995-2001. Author: (with G. Melander) Invandrarrätt, 1984, Refugee Law in the Sudan, 1982, The Alien Under Swedish Law, 1989, Tankar i Tigertid, 1992, Lag och Ratt och nya religioner, 1999; editor: Refugees and Development in Africa, 1987; (with G. Melander) African Refugees and the Law, 1971, International Legal Instruments on Refugees in Africa, 1979, After Estonia, 1997; editor: Advokaten, Tidskrift for Sveriges Advokatsamfund, 1973-86. Bd. dirs. Uppsala-Gavle Mpcl. Theatre, 1986-80; mem. Social Welfare Com., 1976; hon. treas., trustee European Human Rights Found., Amsterdam/London, 1981-2001; vice-chmn. Swedish NGO Fund for Human Rights, 1991-93; trustee Internat. Alert, London, 1998-2001; pres. Transnational Found. for Peace and Future Rsch., 1994-97; mem. com. elimination racial discrimination UN, 1998-2001. Mem. Swedish Bar Assn. (dep. bd. dirs. 1970-78), Internat. Inst. Humanitarian Law (hon.; coun. mem. San Remo chpt. 1988-97). Home: Vasagatan 1A 3d Fl S-75313 Uppsala Sweden

NOBUMOTO, KAREN S. prosecutor; BA, U. Hartford, 1973; JD Southwestern U., 1989. Dep. dist. atty. County of L.A. Mem.: Assn. Dep. Dist. Attys., Black Women Lawyers L.A., Women Lawyers Assn. L.A., John M. Langston Bar Assn., State Bar Calif. (pres. 2001—02). Office: LA Dist Attys Office 210 W Temple St Ste 18000 Los Angeles CA 90012-3210

NOCAS, ANDREW JAMES, lawyer; b. L.A., Feb. 2, 1941; s. John Richard and Muriel Phyliss (Harvey) N.; m. Cassandra A.; 1 child, Scott Andrew. BS, Stanford U., 1962, JD, 1964. Bar: Calif. 1965. Assoc. Thelen, Marrin, Johnson & Bridges, L.A., 1964-71, ptnr., 1972-91; pvt. practice, L.A., 1992-2000; with Office L.A. City Atty., 2000—. Del. Calif. Bar Conv., 1972-92. Served to capt. JAGC, USAR. Fellow Am. Bar Found.; mem. Los Angeles County Bar Assn. (chmn. sect. law office mgmt. 1980-82, chair errors and ommissions com. 1987-88, chair litigation sect. 1988-89), ABA (chmn. arbitration com. 1981), Am. Bd. Trial Advocates, Los Angeles County Bar Found. (trustee 1992-99). Office: Office LA City Aty 200 No Main St 18th Fl Los Angeles CA 90012 E-mail: anocas@atty.lacity.org.

NOCELLA, RICHARD J. lawyer; b. Roxborough, Pa., Nov. 14, 1969; BSBA cum laude, LaSalle U., Phila., 1992; JD, Widener U., Wilmington, Del., 1997. Bar: N.J. 1997, Pa. 1997, U.S. Dist. Ct. N.J. 1997, U.S. Dist. Ct. (ea. dist.) Pa. 1997, U.S. Tax Ct. 2002. Law clk. The Hon. Irvin J. Snyder, Camden Vicinage, NJ, 1997—98; atty. Parker, McCay & Criscuolo, Marlton, NJ, 1998—2001; tax mgr. PricewaterhouseCoopers LLP, Phila., 2001—. Recipient Outstanding Svc. award, Widener U. Sch. Law, Order of the Barrister, 1997. Mem.: ABA (tax sect.), Pa. Bar Assn., N.J. Bar Assn. Office: PricewaterhouseCoopers LLP 2001 Market St Philadelphia PA 19103

NOCHIMSON, DAVID, lawyer; b. Paterson, N.J., June 19, 1943; s. Samuel S. and Mildred (Singer) N.; m. Roberta Maizel, June 5, 1966 (div. 1972); m. Gail Burgess, May 26, 1978. BA, Yale U., 1965; LLB, Columbia U., 1968; LLM, Australian Nat. U., Canberra, 1969. Bar: N.Y. 1970, Calif. 1977. Assoc. Paul, Weiss, Rifkind, Wharton and Garrison, N.Y.C., 1970-72; sr. v.p. Comprop Equities Corp., N.Y.C., 1972-76; assoc. Mitchell, Silberberg and Knupp, L.A., 1977-80, ptnr., 1980-83, Ziffren, Brittenham, Branca, Fischer, Gilbert-Lurie & Stiffelman, L.A., 1983—. Adv. com. UCLA Entertainment Symposium, 1979-99, co-chmn., 1981-82. Contbr. articles to Encyclopedia of Investments, 1982, profl. jours. Pres. Friends of the L.A. Free Clinic, 1994-96; trustee Santa Monica (Calif.) Mus. of Art, 1995—. Fulbright scholar, Australia, 1968-69. Mem. ABA (forum com. on entertainment and sports industries 1982—, editor The Entertainment and Sports Lawyer 1982-89, chmn. 1989-92), Internat. Bar Assn. (Vice chmn. entertainment com. 1986-90), Am. Bar Found., Beverly Hills Bar Assn. Democrat. Jewish. Avocations: tennis, racquetball, yoga, playing piano, hiking. Office: Ziffren Brittenham Branca & Fischer 1801 Century Park W Los Angeles CA 90067-6406

NOCKELMANN, WOLFGANG, lawyer; b. Schwerte, Germany, Aug. 6, 1957; s. Herbert and Inge Nockelmann; m. Roswitha Parschau, Aug. 29, 1961; children: Linda, Lars, Lea, Lucas. Diplom-Verwaltuugswirt, 1981; 1st Juristisches Staatsexamen, Ruhr-U., Bochum, Germany, 1987; Dr.jur., Ruhr U., Bochum, Germany, 1992; 2nd Juristisches Staatsexamen, Düsseldorf, Germany, 1990. Bar: N.Y. 1990, Germany 1990. Officer German Border Police, Deggendorf/Luebeck, 1976—78; inspector German Postal Bank, Dortmund, Germany, 1978—86; ptnr. Menold and Aulinger, Dortmund, 1990—2002; lawyer Aderhold v. Dalwigk, Dortmund, 2002—. Author: Das Durchsuchungsrecht der EG-Komm, 1992, (loose leaf book) Internationales Erbrecht, 2002. Fellow: Rotary Club Dortmund-Hoerde (bd. mem. 1999); mem.: Can.-German Lawyers Assn. (pres. 1992). Avocations: jogging, skiing, horse riding, model trains. Commercial, contracts (including sales of goods; commercial financing), Private international, Mergers and acquisitions. Office: Aderhold v Dalwigk Knueppel Overbeckstrasse 4 44141 Dortmund Germany

NODDINGS, SARAH ELLEN, lawyer; b. Matawan, N.J. d. William Clayton and Sarah Stephenson (Cox) Noddings; children: Christopher, Aaron. BA in Math., Rutgers U., New Brunswick, N.J., 1965, MSW, 1968; JD cum laude, Seton Hall U., Newark, 1975; postgrad., UCLA, 1979. Bar: Calif. 1976, Nev. 1976, N.J. 1975, U.S. Dist. Ct. (ctrl. dist.) Calif. 1976, U.S. Dist. Ct. N.J. 1975. Social worker Carteret (N.J.) Bd. Edn., 1970-75; law clk. Hon. Howard W. Babcock, 8th Jud. Dist. Ct., Las Vegas, Nev., 1975-76; assoc. O'Melveny & Myers, L.A., 1976-78; atty. Internat. Creative Mgmt., Beverly Hills, Calif., 1978-81, Russell & Glickman, Century City, Calif., 1981-83, Lorimar Prodns., Culver City and Burbank, Calif., 1983-87, v.p., 1987-93; atty. Warner Bros. TV, Burbank, Calif., 1993-2001, v.p., 1993-2001, sr. atty., 1999-2001; pvt. practice , 2001—. Dir. county youth program, rsch. analyst Sonoma County People for Econ. Opportunity, Santa Rosa, Calif., 1968-69; VISTA vol. Kings County Cmty. Action Orgn., Hanford, Calif., 1965-66; officer, PTA bd. West H.S., Casimir Mid. Sch. and Arlington Elem. Sch. Mem. Acad. TV Arts and Scis. (nat. awards com. 1994-96), L.A. Copyright Soc. (trustee 1990-91), Women in Film, L.A. County Bar Assn. (intellectual property sect.), Women Entertainment Lawyers, Media Dist. Intellectual Propr. Bar Assn. (bd. dirs. 1999-2001). Avocations: travel, tennis, skiing, bicycling, swimming. Corporate, general, Entertainment, Intellectual property.

NOE, JAMES ALVA, retired judge; b. Billings, Mont., May 25, 1932; s. James Alva Sr. and Laura Madlen (Parmenter) N.; m. Patricia Arlene Caudill, Aug. 4, 1956; children: Kendra Sue, Jeffrey James, Bradley John, Kirkwood Merle. BA in Polit. Sci., U. Wash., 1954, LLB, 1957; LittD hon., Christian Theol. Sem., 1986. Bar: Wash. 1958, U.S. Dist. Ct. (we. dist.) Wash. 1958, U.S. Ct. Appeals (9th cir.) 1959. Dep. prosecuting atty. King County, Seattle, 1958-61; trial lawyer Williams, Kastner & Gibbs, Seattle, 1961-67; judge Seattle Mcpl. Ct., 1967-71, King County Superior Ct., 1971-96; ret., 1996. Moderator Christian Ch. (Disciples of Christ) in the U.S. and Can., 1977-79. Fellow: Am. Bar Found. (life); mem.: ABA (ho. of dels. 1976—78, 1982—87, 1991—96, 2003—, bd. govs. 1991—94, chmn. jud. divsn. 1988—89, chmn. nat. conf. state trial judges 1981—82, sr. lawyers divsn. coun. 2001—), Nat. Jud. Coll. (trustee 1988—91, 1995—2001, chair 1999—2001), Wash. State Superior Ct. Judges Assn. (pres. 1984—85, Wash. State Jurist of Yr. award 1991). Home: 8250 SE 61st St Mercer Island WA 98040-4902

NOEL, EDWIN LAWRENCE, lawyer; b. St. Louis, July 11, 1946; s. Thomas Currie and Christine (Jones) N.; m. Nancy Carter Simpson, Feb. 7, 1970; children: Caroline, Edwin C. BA, Brown U., 1968; JD cum laude, St. Louis U., 1974. Bar: Mo. 1974, U.S. Dist. Ct. (ea. dist.) Mo. 1974, U.S. Ct. Appeals (8th cir.) 1974, U.S. Ct. Appeals (6th cir.) 1978, U.S. Ct. Appeals (7th cir.) 1994, U.S. Supreme Ct. 1986. Ptnr. Armstrong, Teasdale, Schlafly & Davis, St. Louis, 1974—, mng. ptnr., 1993-97. Bd. dirs. Corley Printing Co., Elcom Industries, St. Louis, Home Fed. Savs. Bank of Mo., 1988-93. Bd. dirs. Edgewood Children's Ctr., St. Louis, 1982-92, St. Louis Assn. for Retarded Citizens, 1984-87, Churchill Sch., 1988-94, Whitfield Sch., 1991-95; chmn. Mo. Clean Water Com., Jefferson City, 1982-86; chmn. environ. com. St. Louis Regional Commerce and Growth Assn., 1982-88. Mem. Mo. Bar Assn., Bar Assn. Met. St. Louis, Attys. Liability Assurance Soc. (bd. dirs. 1995—). Republican. Episcopalian. Federal civil litigation, State civil litigation, Environmental. Home: 301 S Mcknight Rd Saint Louis MO 63124-1884 Office: Armstrong Teasdale LLP 1 Metropolitan Sq Ste 2600 Saint Louis MO 63102-2740 E-mail: enoel@armstrongteasdale.com.

NOEL, NICHOLAS, III, lawyer; b. Pottstown, Pa., June 5, 1952; s. Nicholas Jr. and Elaine (Buckwalter) Noel; m. Karen Bean Schomp, Oct. 28, 1978; children: Carol Elaine, Nicholas IV. BA magna cum laude, Lehigh U., 1974; JD, U. Detroit, 1977. Bar: Pa. 1977, U.S. Dist. Ct. (ea. dist.) Pa. 1979, U.S. Ct. Appeals (3d cir.) 1980, U.S. Supreme Ct. 1986, U.S. Dist. Ct. (mid. dist.) Pa. 1989. Assoc. Hahalis Law Office, Bethlehem, Pa., 1977-84; assoc. Teel, Stettz, Shimer & DiGiacomo, Easton, Pa., 1984-87; ptnr. Teel, Stettz, PC, Easton, 1987-2000, sr. litig. ptnr., 1989-2000, v.p., 1998-2000, pres., 2000, Noel & Kovacs, P.C., Easton, 2000—. Solicitor Chiefs Police Assn. Mid. Ea. Pa., 1977—, Palmer Twp. Zoning Hearing Bd., Easton, 1989—; arbitrator Am. Arbitration Assn., 1986—; adj. prof. Northampton County CC, Bethlehem, 1990, Bethlehem, 97, Bethlehem, 2000; lectr. Pa. Bar Inst., 2001. Contbr. to several books. Mem. Palmer Moravian Day Sch. Bd., 1991—94, 1999—2000, Pa. Ho. Dels., 1998—; trustee Palmer Twp. Moravian Ch., 1985—97, 1999—, pres., 1986—92, sec. bldg. expansion com., 1998—2001; mem. Moravian Ch. No. Province Ch. and Soc. Com., 1990—. Named Outstanding Young Man Am., 1974. Fellow: Pa. Bar Found.; mem.: ABA, Northampton County Bar Assn. (mem. legal ethics and responsibility com. 1987—94, bd. govs. 1991—99, treas. 1995, v.p. 1996, pres.-elect 1997, pres. 1998, past pres. 1999), Pa. Bar Assn. (civil rights chair 1989—92, vice-chmn. legal edn. com. 1992, profl. stds. com. 1983, ho. dels. 1998—). Avocations: sports, swimming, hiking. Civil rights, General civil litigation, Professional liability. Home: 2840 Green Pond Rd Easton PA 18045-2504 Office: 400 S Greenwood Ave Ste 300 Easton PA 18045-3776 E-mail: nn6552@yahoo.com.

NOEL, RANDALL DEANE, lawyer; b. Memphis, Oct. 19, 1953; s. D.A. and Patricia G. Noel; m. Lissa Johns, May 28, 1977; children: Lauren Elizabeth, Randall Walker. BBA with honors, U. Miss., 1975, JD, 1978. Bar: Miss. 1978, U.S. Dist. Ct. (no. and so. dists.) Miss. 1978, Tenn. 1979, U.S. Dist. Ct. (we., mid. and ea. dists.) Tenn. 1979, U.S. Ct. Appeals (5th and 6th cirs.) 1984, U.S. Supreme Ct. 1986. Assoc. Armstrong/Allen, PLLC, Memphis, 1978-85, ptnr., 1985—, mgr. litig. practice group, 1990-94; mgmt. com. Armstrong, Allen, Prewitt, Gentry, Johnston & Holmes, Memphis, 1994-97—; CEO Armstrong/Allen, PLLC, Memphis, 2002—. Fin. com. Memphis in May Internat. Festival, 1980-81; pres. Carnival Memphis, 1996; bd. dirs. Christ United Meth. Ch., Memphis, 1984-87, 89-91, chmn. bd. trustees, 1995; mem. Leadership Memphis, 1994-95. Fellow Am. Bar Found., Tenn. Bar Found., Memphis Bar Found.; mem. ABA (young lawyers divsn., fellow dir. 1988-90, editor The Affiliate newsletter 1987-88, dir. Affiliate Outreach project 1988—, vice-chmn. Award of Achievement com. 1986, ALI-ABA bd. 1992-97, dir. litig. sect. divsn. 2002-, litig. sect. com. chmn., mem. house of dels.), Am. Counsel Assn. (pres. 1997), Tenn. Bar Assn. (pres. young lawyers divsn. 1990, pres. litig. sect. 1988, bd. govs. 1989—, pres., 1999, Pres.'s Disting. Svc. award 1988-89), So. Conf. Bar Pres. (pres. 2000), Memphis and Shelby Bar Assn. (mem. jud, recommendations, law week nominations and membership coms.), Miss. Bar Assn., Def. Rsch. Inst., Tenn. Def. Lawyers Assn., Am. Judicature Soc. (bd. dirs. 1992-96), Tenn. Legal Cmty. Found.(pres. 1999-2001). Federal civil litigation, State civil litigation, Commercial, consumer (including collections, credit). Home: 2938 Tishomingo Ln Memphis TN 38111-2627 Office: Armstrong Allen PLLC 80 Monroe Ave Ste 700 Memphis TN 38103-2467 E-mail: rnoel@armstrongallen.com.

NOFER, GEORGE HANCOCK, lawyer; b. Phila., June 14, 1926; BA, Haverford Coll., 1949; JD, Yale U., 1952. Bar: Pa. 1953. Pvt. practice, Phila., 1953—; ret. ptnr. Schnader, Harrison, Segal & Lewis, Phila., 1961-91, sr. counsel, 1992—. Pres. bd. sch. dirs. Upper Moreland Twp., Pa., 1965—73; trustee Beaver Coll., Glenside, Pa., 1969—76; co-trustee, exec. dir. Oberkotter Found., 1985—; elder, trustee, deacon Abington (Pa.) Presbyn. Ch., 1956—2000; bd. dirs. Fox Chase Cancer Ctr., Phila., 1989—94; bd. dirs. Phila. Presbyn. Homes, Inc., 1983—98, A.G. Bell Assn. for Deaf, Washington, 1992—98. Fellow Am. Coll. Trust and Estate Counsel (regent 1975— , pres. 1983-84, chmn. Pa. 1973-78), Am. Law Inst., Am. Bar Found.; mem. ABA (standing com. on specialization 1980-86, chmn. 1983-86), Pa. Bar Assn., Phila. Bar Assn., Internat. Acad. Estate and Trust Law, Phi Beta Kappa, Phi Delta Phi Home: 108 Quail Ln Radnor PA 19087-2729 Office: Schnader Harrison Segal & Lewis 1600 Market St Ste 3600 Philadelphia PA 19103-7287 E-mail: gnofer@schnader.com.., ghnofer@aol.com.

NOGEE, JEFFREY LAURENCE, lawyer; b. Schenectady, N.Y., Oct. 31, 1952; s. Rodney and Shirley Ruth (Mannes) N.; m. Freda Carolyn Wartel, Aug. 31, 1980; children: Rori Caitlen, Amara Sonia, Jaden Gwynn. BA cum laude, Bucknell U., 1974; JD, Boston U., 1977. Bar: N.Y. 1978, U.S. Dist. Ct. (so. and ea. dists.) N.Y. 1978. Assoc. Hale Russell & Gray, N.Y.C., 1977-83; sr. atty. Ebasco Services Inc., N.Y.C., 1984-88, dir. Countertrade unit, 1985-88; sr. ptnr. Fogh & Nogee Assocs., 1988; ptnr. Brauner, Baron, Rosenzweig, Bauman & Klein, N.Y.C., 1988-90; sr. ptnr. Nogee & Wartel, Westbury, N.Y., 1990—. Pvt. counsellor for internat. bus. firms, 1987—; cert. mediator comml. divsn. N.Y. State Supreme Ct., Nassau County, 2002—. Prin. bassoonist, bd. dirs. The Band of L.I., 1997—, sec., 1997-99, pres., 1999—; prin. bassoonist Rockway-Five Towns Symphony Orch., 1998-99, Lawrence Philharm., 2000—, South Shore Wind and Percussion Ensemble, 2002—; assoc. bassoonist South Shore Symphony, 2002—; pvt. bassoon instr., 2000-. Trustee Temple Emanu-el of East Meadow, 1995-99, v.p., 1996-97. Mem. ABA, Am. Arbitration Assn., Assn. of Bar of City of N.Y., Nassau County Bar Assn., Internat. Platform Assn., N.Y. New Media Assn., Phi Beta Kappa, Pi Sigma Alpha. Avocations: fencing, bassoon and saxophone music, racquet sports, hiking, bicycling. Entertainment, Probate (including wills, trusts), Commercial, contracts (including sales of goods; commercial financing). Office: Ste 211 900 Merchants Concourse Westbury NY 11590-5114 E-mail: jnogee@nogeelaw.com.

NOLAN, ALAN TUCKER, retired lawyer, labor arbitrator, writer; b. Evansville, Ind., Jan. 19, 1923; s. Val and Jeannette (Covert) N.; m. Elizabeth Clare Titsworth, Aug. 26, 1947 (dec. Nov. 1967); children: Patrick A., Thomas C., Mary F., Elizabeth T., John V.; m. Jane Ransel DeVoe, Feb. 7, 1970; adopted children: John C. DeVoe, Ellen R. DeVoe, Thomas R. DeVoe. AB in Govt., Ind. U., 1944, LHD (hon.), 1993; LLB, Harvard U., 1947. Bar: Ind. 1947. Law clk. U.S. Ct. Appeals (7th Cir.), Chgo., 1947-48; assoc. Ice, Miller, Donadio & Ryan, Indpls., 1948-58, ptnr., 1959-93, ret., 1993—. Chmn. Disciplinary Commn. Supreme Ct. Ind., Indpls., 1966-73. Author: The Iron Brigade, 1961, As Sounding Brass, 1964, Lee Considered, 1991; editor (with S. Vipond) Giants in Tall Black Hats, 1998, (with Gary Gallagher) The Myth of the Lost Cause and Civil War History, 2000, Rally Once Again, 2000; contbg. editor The Civil War, 1985-89; contbr. numerous articles to profl. jours. Life mem. NAACP Indpls., v.p., 1950-54; bd. dirs., founder Ind. Civil Liberties Union, Indpls., 1953-60; bd. dirs. Indpls. Art League, 1981-87; chmn., bd. trustees Ind. Hist. Soc., Indpls., 1986-93; trustee Eiteljorg Mus., Indpls., 1987-93. Fellow Co. Mil. Historians, Am. Bar Found., State Hist. Soc. Wis.; mem. ABA, Ind. Bar Assn., Indpls. Bar Assn. (bd. mgrs. 1958-60, chmn. Grievance Com. 1960-64), Indpls. Civil War Round Table, Ensemble Music Soc. (bd. dirs. 1999—). Democrat. Roman Catholic. Avocations: travel, gardening, reading. Home and Office: 4118 N Pennsylvania St Indianapolis IN 46205-2611 E-mail: indynolan@aol.com.

NOLAN, DAVID BRIAN, lawyer; b. Washington, Jan. 1, 1951; s. John Joseph and Mary Jane Nolan; m. Cheryl Ann Cottle, June 30, 1979; children: John Joseph II, David Brian II, Christopher Dalton. BA, Duke U., 1973; MPA, Am. U., 1975; JD, U. La Verne, 1978; postgrad., Georgetown U., 1981-89. Bar: Calif. 1978, U.S. Dist. Ct. (cen. dist.) Calif. 1979, U.S. Ct. Claims 1981, U.S. Tax Ct. 1981, U.S. Ct. Appeals (D.C. cir.) 1984, U.S. Supreme Ct. 2000. Intern Congressman Joel Broyhill, 1971; asst. dir. rsch. Younger-Curb Campaign, L.A., 1978; assoc. L. Rob Werner Law Offices, Encino, Calif., 1979-80; atty. conflicts Office of Pres. Elect, Washington, 1980-81; staff atty. Office of counsel to the Pres. White House, Washington, 1981; staff asst. office of sec. U.S. Dept. Treasury, Washington, 1981-85; spl. asst. office gen. counsel U.S. Dept. Energy, Washington, 1985-90, atty. advisor enforcement div. Office of Nuclear Safety, 1990-91, trial atty. adminstrv. litigation div. Econ. Regulatory Adminstrn., 1991-95, trial atty. Office of Gen. Counsel, 1995-2001; pvt. law practice, 2001—. Bd. dirs., treas. Energy Fed. Credit Union. Mem. editl. bd. New Guard Mag., 1983-85. Steering com. L.A. Reps., 1979-80, Reagan for Pres., L.A., 1980; chmn. 39th Assembly, Rep. Ctrl. Com., 1979-80; alt. del. 1972 Rep. Nat. Conv.; pres. N.C. Coll. Rep. Com., 1972-73; nat. treas., bd. dirs. Young Amers. for Freedom, Sterling, Va., 1983-85; corp. dir. Am. Sovereignty Task Force, Vienna, Va., 1984—, State Dept. Watch Ltd., Vienna, 1984—. Charles Edison Youth Found. scholar, 1971; named one of Outstanding Young Men in Am., Jaycees, 1976-86; recipient Mgr. of Yr. honor Dept. Energy Women's Adv. Coun., 1988, Achievement in Equal Opportunity Deptl. award, 1988. Mem. Fed. Bar Assn., Bar Assn. of D.C. (chmn. ethics com. young lawyers div. 1985-87), D.C. Bar, Calif. Bar, U.S. Supreme Ct. Soc., Federalist Soc., U.S. Justice Found. (co-founder, of counsel 1979-80), Conservative Network Club, Whistle Blowers Ave Patriots (co-founder 1999). Home: 8310 Wagon Wheel Rd Alexandria VA 22309-2175 Office: David B Nolan & Assocs Box 23019 Washington DC 20026-1864 E-mail: dbnesq1@aol.com.

NOLAN, JOHN EDWARD, lawyer; b. Mpls., July 11, 1927; s. John E. and Teresa (Franey) N.; m. Joan Dobbins, June 3, 1950; children: Carol N. Klatt, John Edward III (dec.), Kelly N. Spencer, Richard Clark, Patricia N. McNeill. BS, U.S. Naval Acad., 1950; JD, Georgetown U., 1955. Bar: D.C. 1955, U.S. Supreme Ct. 1959, Md. 1961. Law clk. to Justice Clark U.S. Supreme Ct., 1955-56; adminstrv. asst. to Atty. Gen. Robert F. Kennedy, 1963-64; assoc. Steptoe & Johnson, Washington, 1956-62, ptnr., 1962-63, 65—. Assoc. counsel Cuban families com. Cuban Prisoners Exch., Havana, 1962-63; spl. counsel refugee subcom. Senate Jud. Com., Vietnam, 1967-68; mem. CPR Panel of Disting. Neutrals, Washington, U.S. Ct. Appeals mediator D.C. cir.; mem. exec. com. Lawyers Com. for Civil Rights Under Law; bd. dirs. Hooper Holmes, Inc., Iomega, Inc.; vis. fellow Wolfson Coll., Cambridge (Eng.) U., 1987, 92; counsel U.S. Naval Acad. Alumni Assn. Trustee Robert F. Kennedy Meml., 1969—; bd. dirs. Fund Dem. Majority; moderator Aspen Inst., 1980—; gen. counsel, bd. dirs. U.S. Naval Acad. Found., 1997—; bd. counsel, bd. trustees U.S. Naval Acad. Alumni Assn., 1997—; gen. counsel, bd. dirs. U.S. Naval Acad. Found. 2d. Lt. to Capt. USMC, 1950-54, Korea. Decorated Silver Star, Bronze Star with Combat V, Purple Heart. Mem. ABA, D.C. Bar Assn. (gov.), Am. Law Inst., Met. Club (Washington), Congl. Club, Univ. Club (N.Y.C.). Democrat. Roman Catholic. Administrative and regulatory, Civil rights, Federal civil litigation. Office: 1330 Connecticut Ave NW Washington DC 20036-1704 E-mail: jnolan@steptoe.com.

NOLAN, JOHN MICHAEL, lawyer; b. Conway, Ark., June 21, 1948; s. Paul Thomas and Peggy (Hime) N. BA, U. Tex., 1970, JD, 1973; LLM in Taxation, George Washington U., 1976. Bar: Tex. 1973, D.C. 1975, U.S. Ct. Mil. Appeals 1973, U.S. Ct. Appeals (D.C. cir.) 1975, U.S. Tax Ct. 1975, U.S. Supreme Ct. 1975. Chief counsel to chief judge U.S. Ct. Mil. Appeals, Washington, 1976-77; assoc. Winstead, McGuire, Sechrest & Minick PC, Dallas, 1977-81; shareholder Winstead Sechrest & Minick PC, Dallas, 1981—. Editor in Chief The Advocate, 1973-76. Capt. JAGC, U.S. Army, 1973-76. Named one of Outstanding Young Men in Am., U.S. Jaycess, 1976. Mem. ABA (real property, probate and trust sect., real property com., partnerships, joint ventrues, and other investment vehicles), Tex. Bar Assn. (real property, probate and trust sect.), D.C. Bar Assn., Dallas Bar Assn. (real estate group), Tex. Coll. Real Estate Lawyers, Coll. State Bar Tex., Real Estate Coun., Salesmanship Club Dallas, Royal Oaks Country Club. Presbyterian. Bankruptcy, Property, real (including real estate development, water), Taxation, general. Home: 6681 Crest Way Ct Dallas TX 75230-2868 Office: Winstead Sechrest & Minick 5400 Renaissance Tower 1201 Elm St Ste 5400 Dallas TX 75270-2199

NOLEN, ROY LEMUEL, retired lawyer; b. Montgomery, Ala., Nov. 29, 1937; s. Roy Lemuel Jr. and Elizabeth (Larkin) N.; m. Evelyn McNeill Thomas, Aug. 28, 1965; 1 child, Rives Rutledge. BArch, Rice U., 1961; LLB, Harvard U., 1967. Bar: Tex. 1968, U.S. Ct. Appeals (5th cir.) 1969. Law clk. to sr. judge U.S. Ct. Appeals (5th cir.), 1967-68; assoc. Baker Botts LLP, Houston, 1968-75, ptnr., 1976-2000; co-head Corp. Dept., 1985-90; mem. exec. com., 1988-91; adminstrv. ptnr., 1997-2000; ret., 2000. Cmty. rep. instnl. animal care and use com. M.D. Anderson Cancer Ctr., 2001—. Bd. dirs. Houston Ballet Found., 1980-92, Rice Design Alliance, 1995-96; exec. com. Contemporary Arts Mus., 1990-96, 97-2002; exec. com. Houston Symphony Soc., 1994-99, gen. counsel, 1994-98; trustee Menil Found. (Menil Collection), 1999—, sr. warden Christ Ch. Cathedral, 1991-92; chmn. Houston area devel. initiative Episcopal Diocese of Tex., 1997. 1st lt. USMC, 1961-64. Mem.: State Bar Tex., Briar Club, Paul Jones Dancing Club, Allegro, Coronado Club. Episcopalian. Corporate, general, Securities. Office: Baker Botts LLP One Shell Plz 910 Louisiana St Houston TX 77002-4995

NOLFI, EDWARD ANTHONY, lawyer; b. Warren, Ohio, Sept. 30, 1958; s. Eugene Vincent Sr. and Margaret Joyce (Futey) N.; m. Sheri Ann Loue, June 5, 1982. AB, Brown U., 1980; JD, U. Akron, 1983. Bar: Ohio 1983, N.Y. 1986, U.S. Dist. Ct. (no. dist.) Ohio 1987, U.S. Tax Ct. 1987, U.S. Ct. Appeals (6th cir. 1989), U.S. Supreme Ct. 1989. Juggler Miracle Sta., Warren, 1976; instr. Sch. One, Providence, 1980; tech. writer Doctors' Hosp., Massillon, Ohio, 1982; pvt. practice Warren, 1983-84; assoc. editor Lawyers Coop. Pub. Co., Rochester, N.Y., 1985-87; pvt. practice Akron, Ohio, 1987—. Prof. Acad. Ct. Reporting, Akron, 1988-91; prof. Kent State U., 1993, Mt. Aloysius Coll., Cresson, Pa., 1996; product developer and lead case law editor LexisNexis, Miamisburg, Ohio, 1999—. Author: The Master Juggler, 1980, Basic Legal Research, 1993, Basic Wills, Trusts, and Estates, 1995; articles editor Am. Law Reports, Fed., 1986-87. Roman Catholic. Avocation: juggling. General practice. Home and Office: 4965 State Rte 14 Ravenna OH 44266-9622 E-mail: enolfi@neo.rr.com.

NOLL, STEVEN HARRY, lawyer; b. Jackson, Tenn., June 15, 1952; s. Harry George and Ruth Jane (Armbruster) N. BS with honor, Mich. State U., 1974; JD, Ohio State U., 1977. Bar: Ill. 1978, Ohio 1978, U.S. Patent and Trademark Office 1978, U.S. Dist. Ct. (no. dist.) Ill. 1979, U.S. Ct. Appeals (7th and 8th cirs.) 1979, U.S. Ct. Appeals (fed. cir.) 1980, U.S. Ct. Appeals (6th cir.) 1981, U.S. Supreme Ct. 1982, U.S. Ct. Claims 1985, U.S. Ct. Appeals (11th cir.) 1985. Elec. engr. Magnavox Co., Fort Wayne, Ind., 1974-75; ptnr. Schiff, Hardin & Waite, Chgo., 2000—. Mem. Patent Law Assn. Chgo., Am. Intellectual Property Law Assn., Chgo. Coun. of Lawyers, U.S. Internat. Trade Com., Trial Lawyers Assn. (bd. dirs. 1986-88), Nat. Lawyers Guild, IEEE, ACLU, NOW, Ohio State Alumni Assn., Mich. State Alumni Assn., East Bank Club (Chgo.), Eta Kappa Nu. Office: Schiff Hardin & Waite 6600 Sears Tower Chicago IL 60606

NOLLAU, LEE GORDON, lawyer; b. Balt., Feb. 6, 1950; s. E. Wilson and Carolyn G. (Blass) N.; m. Carol A. Haughney, Aug. 12, 1978; children: Ann G., Catherine E., Margaret C. BA, Juniata Coll., 1972; MAS, Johns Hopkins U., 1975; JD, Dickinson Sch. Law, 1976. Bar: Pa. 1976, U.S. Dist. Ct. (mid. dist.) 1982, U.S. Dist. Ct. (we. dist.) 1988, U.S. Ct. Appeals (3d cir.) 1980, U.S. Supreme Ct. 1982. Instr. Juniata Coll., Huntingdon, Pa., 1976-78; asst. dist. atty. Centre County, Bellefonte, Pa., 1978-80, dist. atty., 1981; assoc. Litke, Lee, Martin, Grine & Green, Bellefonte, 1981-83, Jubelirer & Assocs., State College, Pa., 1983-87; ptnr. Jubelirer, Nollau, Young & Blanarik, Inc., State College, 1988-89, Jubelirer, Rayback, Nollau, Walsh, Young & Blanarik, Inc., State College, 1989-94, Nollau & Young, State Coll., Pa., 1994—. Mental health rev. officer Centre County, Bellefonte, 1982—; instr. Pa. State U. Smeal Coll. Bus. Adminstrn., 1995—; lectr., author Pa. Bar Inst., 1995—. Author: Trial Tactics: Direct Examination of Lay Witnesses. Mem. ABA, Pa. Bar Assn., Centre Co. Bar, Pa. Assn. Criminal Def. Lawyers. Presbyterian. General civil litigation, Criminal, Personal injury (including property damage). Office: Nollau & Young 2153 E College Ave State College PA 16801-7204

NOLTE, HENRY R., JR., lawyer, former automobile company executive; b. N.Y.C., Mar. 3, 1924; s. Henry R. and Emily A. (Eisele) Nolte; m. Frances Messner, May 19, 1951; children: Gwynne Conn, Henry Reed III, Jennifer Stevens, Suzanne Saunders. BA, Duke U., 1947; LLB, U. Pa., 1949. Bar: N.Y. 1950, Mich. 1967. Assoc. Cravath, Swaine & Moore, N.Y.C., 1951-61; assoc. counsel Ford Motor Co., Dearborn, Mich., 1961, asst. gen. counsel, 1964-71, assoc. gen. counsel, 1971-74, v.p., gen. counsel, 1974-89, Philco-Ford Corp., Phila., 1961-64; v.p., gen. counsel, sec. Ford of Europe Inc., Warley, Essex, Eng., 1967-69; gen. counsel fin. and ins. subs. Ford Motor Co., 1974-89; sr. ptnr. Miller, Canfield, Paddock & Stone, Detroit, 1989-93, of counsel, 1993—. Formerly vice chmn. and trustee Cranbrook Ednl. Cmty.; mem. Internat. and Comparative Law Ctr. of Southwestern Legal Found.; trustee Beaumont Hosp. Lt. USNR, 1943-46, PTO. Mem. ABA (past chmn. corp. gen. counsel), Mich. Bar Assn., Assn. Bar City N.Y., Assn. Gen. Counsel, Orchard Lake Country Club, Bloomfield Hills Country Club, Everglades Club (Fla.), Gulfstream Golf Club (Fla.), Ocean Club (Fla.). Episcopalian. Office: Miller Canfield Paddock & Stone 840 W Long Lake Rd Troy MI 48098-6356

NOLTE, JOHN MICHAEL, lawyer, consultant; b. England, Mar. 20, 1941; s. Ernest H. Nolte and Katheryn A. (Reinhart) Robertson; m. S.K. Marren (div. 1979); children: Stephanie Ann, Jennifer Lee, Sarah Sookwang; m. Diane L. Staufenbeil, Apr. 1982. BS, Ariz. State U., Tempe, 1963; MBA in Fin., U. Calif., Berkeley, JD, 1966. Bar: Oreg. 1966, Calif. 1973. Assoc. Keane, Haessler, Bauman & Harper, Portland, Oreg., 1966-71; assoc. gen. counsel Boise Cascade Corp., Palo Alto, Calif., 1972-73, Larwin Group, L.A., 1973-74; mng. ptnr. Leahy, O'Dea & Givens, San Francisco, 1974-81; pvt. practice law and cons. Canterbury and Tunbridge Wells, Eng., 1981-88, Montecito, Calif., 1988-99, Dorset, England, 1999—. Pres. Grand Tour Antiques. Hon. mem. East Sussex/Dorset Conservative Party, Buxted and Wimborne, Eng., 1986—; pres. Glen Oaks Comty. Assn., Montecito, 1990-92; bd. trustees Castaic Union Edn. Found.; program chmn. Nat. Assn. Decorative and Fine Arts Soc. With USMC, 1960-66; lt. comdr. USNR, 1966-70. Mem. ABA, Calif. Bar Assn., Oreg. Bar Assn., Wimborne Civic Soc., Order of Coif, Phi Kappa Phi. Republican. Avocations: skiing, historic automobile racing, cricket, mountaineering, antiques. Home and Office: Pamphill Manor Pamphill Wimborne Dorset BH21 4EE England Fax: 01202 889 762.

NOLTE, MELVIN, JR., lawyer; b. New Braunfels, Tex., Dec. 14, 1947; s. Melvin Sr. and Louise (Beaty) N.; m. Elizabeth C. Tolle, Aug. 26, 1972 (div. June 1980); 1 child, Melvin III; m. Sandra J. Prochazka, Dec. 4, 1984; 1 child, Chad Louis. BA, Southwest Tex. U., 1970; JD, St. Mary's U., San Antonio, 1972. Bar: Tex. 1973. Pvt. practice law, New Braunfels, 1973—. Mem. adv. coun. Cibolo (Tex.) State Bank, 1982-88; chmn. bd. dirs., pres. Garden Villa, Inc., New Braunfels. Mem. New Braunfels Water Adv. Bd., 1987-88, Comal County Water-Oriented REcreation Dist. Bd., New Braunfels, 1987-89, past pres. Mem. ABA, New Braunfels C. of C., Phi Delta Phi, Pi Gamma Mu. Lodges: Lions, Eagles (past pres. local chpt.). Avocations: hunting, fishing. Commercial, contracts (including sales of goods; commercial financing), Probate (including wills, trusts), Property, real (including real estate development, water). Office: 175 N Market St New Braunfels TX 78130-5084

NOME, WILLIAM ANDREAS, lawyer; b. Springfield, Ohio, May 21, 1951; s. Reidar Andreas and Nancy Louisa (Smith) N.; m. Carolyn Ruth Johnson, Feb. 7, 1981. BA, Akron U., 1973; JD, Cleve. State U., 1976. Bar: Ohio 1976, U.S. Dist. Ct. (no. dist.) Ohio 1977, U.S. Ct. Appeals (6th cir.) 1985, U.S. Supreme Ct. 1987. Asst. prosecutor Portage County Prosecutor's Office, Ravenna, Ohio, 1977; pvt. practice Ravenna, 1977-82; assoc. Arthur & Clegg, Kent, Ohio, 1982-85; ptnr. Arthur, Nome & Assocs., Kent, Ohio, 1985-96, Arthur, Nome, Can, Szymanski & Clinard, Kent, Cuyahoga Falls, Ohio, 1996-97, Arthur, Nome, Can & Szymanski, Kent, Cuyahoga Falls, Ohio, 1997-98, Arthur, Nome and Szymanski, Kent, 1998—2002, Arthur, Nome and Assocs., 2002—. Legal advisor Portage Area Regional Transit Authority, Kent, 1986--. Chmn. Highland Home Health Care, Ravenna, 1980, Kent Bd. Bldg. Appeals, 1987, Portage County Mental Health Bd., 1981-88, chmn., 1986-88; trustee Kevin Coleman Mental Health Ctr., 1989-93, pres., 1991-93; pres. Force Investment Club, 1999-2002. Col. Ohio Mil. Res., 1986—. Recipient Cert. of Achievement, Emergency Mgmt. Inst., Fed. Emergency Mgmt. Agy., 1987, 93, 95. Mem. Ohio Bar Assn., Akron Bar Assn., Portage County Bar Assn. (sec.-treas. 1982-85, 98-2000, v.p. 2000-2001, pres. 2001-02), Portage County Estate Planning Coun., Delta Theta Phi. Republican. Lutheran. Avocations: gardening, cooking, target shooting, reading. Bankruptcy, General practice, Probate (including wills, trusts). Office: Arthur Nome & Assocs 1325 S Water St Kent OH 44240-3851 E-mail: anslawyers@aol.com.

NOMER, ERGIN NAMI, law educator, academic administrator, principal; b. Istanbul, Turkey, Jan. 7, 1935; s. Mustafa Resit and Sefika (Gozubuyuk) N.; m. Esin Ayas, Aug. 13, 1962; children: Haluk Nami, Nedret Fusun. Lawyer, Istanbul U., 1957, LLD, 1961. Lectr. Faculty of Law-Istanbul U., 1966-73, prof., 1973—, dean, 1980-82; v.p. Istanbul U., 1974-80, 94-97, pres. civil law, 1998—. Author: Maintenance in International Private Law, 1967, Foreign Law in Civil Proceedings, 1972, International Private Law, 11th edit., 2002, Law of Nationality, 13th edit., 2002. Pres. discipline com. The Green Crescent, 1964—. Lt. Land Force, Turkish Army, 1967-69. Mem.: Turkish Bar Assn. Avocations: bridge, chess, walking. Home: Erenkoy Etemefendi Cad 9 Gokova Apt D5 TR 81060 Istanbul Turkey Office: Istanbul U Faculty of Law Bayazit TR 34452 Istanbul Turkey E-mail: nomer@superonline.com.

NONNA, JOHN MICHAEL, lawyer; b. New York, July 8, 1948; s. Angelo and Josephine (Visconti) N.; m. Jean Wanda (Cleary), June 9, 1973; children: Elizabeth, Caroline, Marianne, Timothy. BA, Princeton U., 1970; JD, N.Y. Univ., 1975. Bar: N.Y., 1976; U.S. Dist. Ct. (so. dist.) N.Y., 1978; U.S. Ct. Appeals (2d cir.), 1978; U.S. Ct. Appeals (9th cir.), 1980; U.S. Ct. Appeals (5th cir.), 1997; U.S. Dist. Ct. Conn., 1988; U.S. Supreme Ct., 1998. Law asst. to Hon. D.L. Gabrielli N.Y. Ct. Appeals, Albany, NY, 1975-77; assoc. Reid and Priest, N.Y.C., 1977-84; ptnr. Werner and Kennedy, N.Y.C., 1984-99, LeBoeuf, Lamb, Greene, and MacRae, N.Y.C., 1999—. Contbr. articles to profl. jour. Dep. mayor, trustee Village of Pleasantville, N.Y., 1990-95; mayor, 1995-2003; acting justice, 1983-89. With USNR, 1970-75. U.S. Olympic Team, Munich, 1972; Moscow, 1980; recipient Paul Harris Award Rotary Internat. Fellow Am. Bar Found. (life); mem. ABA (torts and ins. practice sect. com. chair 1986-87, 92-93); N.Y. State Bar Assn. (chair comml. and fed. litigation sect. 1998-99, co-editor in chief 2000); Assn. Bar City N.Y.; N.Y. Fencers Club (pres. 1990-93),Paul Harris Fellow; Rotary Internat. Avocations: fencing, running, piano. General civil litigation, Insurance. Office: LeBoeuf Lamb Greene & MacRae 125 W 55th St New York NY 10019-5369 E-mail: jnonna@llgm.com.

NOONAN, JAMES C. lawyer, mediator, arbitrator; b. Chgo., July 16, 1928; s. T. Clifford and Ethel (Jennett) N.; m. Carol Colbert, Nov. 24, 1954 (div. June 1975); children: James, Christopher, Mary, Anne, Catherine; m. Ardis Niemann, May 24, 1986. AB, U. Notre Dame, 1953, MA in Criminology, 1954; JD, William Mitchell Coll. Law, St. Paul, 1962. Bar: Minn. 1962, U.S. Dist. Ct. Minn. 1963, U.S. Ct. Appeals (8th cir.) 1971, U.S. Supreme Ct. 1969. Probation officer Ramsey County Juvenile Ct., St. Paul, 1954-57; supt. Woodview Detention Home, St. Paul, 1957-63; assoc. Firestone, Fink, Krawetz, Miley, O'Neill, St. Paul, 1963-67; ptnr. Firestone Fink, Krawetz, Miley, Maas and Noonan, St. Paul, 1967-70, Magistad & Noonan, St. Paul, 1971-75; owner James C. Noonan and Assocs., St. Paul, 1975—. Mem. adv. bd. Home of Good Shepherd, St. Paul, 1958-74; mem. citizen adv. bd. Detention and Corrections Authority, St. Paul, 1966-80. Mem. ABA, Minn. State Bar Assn., Ramsey County Bar Assn., St. Paul Amateur Radio Club, Am. Radio Relay League. Roman Catholic. Avocation: amateur radio (w9osn). Alternative dispute resolution, Estate planning, Probate (including wills, trusts). Home and Office: 339 Summit Ave Saint Paul MN 55102-2176 Fax: (651) 222-3340. E-mail: w9osn@arrl.net.

NOONAN, JOHN T., JR., judge, law educator; b. Boston, Oct. 24, 1926; s. John T. and Marie (Shea) Noonan; m. Mary Lee Bennett, Dec. 27, 1967; children: John Kenneth, Rebecca Lee, Susanna Bain. BA, Harvard U., 1946, LL.B., 1954; student, Cambridge U., 1946—47; MA, Cath. U. Am., 1949, PhD, 1951, LHD, 1980; LL.D., U. Santa Clara, 1974, U. Notre Dame, 1976, Loyola U. South, 1978; LHD, Holy Cross Coll., 1980; LL.D., St. Louis U., 1981, U. San Francisco, 1985; student, Cath. U. Am., 1980, Gonzaga U., 1986, U. San Francisco, 1986; LLD, Duquesne U., 1995, Valparaiso U., 1996, U. San Diego, 1999; LHD, Loyola U., Chgo., 1999. Bar: Mass. 1954, U.S. Supreme Ct. 1971. Mem. spl. staff Nat. Security Council, 1954-55; pvt. practice Herrick & Smith, Boston, 1955-60; prof. law U. Notre Dame, 1961-66, U. Calif., Berkeley, 1967-86, chmn. religious studies, 1970-73, chmn. medieval studies, 1978-79; judge U.S. Ct. Appeals (9th cir.), San Francisco, 1985-96, sr. judge, 1996—. Oliver Wendell Holmes, Jr. lectr. Harvard U. Law Sch., 1972; Pope John XXIII lectr. Cath. U. Law Sch., 1973; Cardinal Bellarmine lectr. St. Louis U. Div. Sch., 1973; Ernest Messenger lectr. Cornell U., 1982; John Dewey Meml. lectr. U. Minn., 1986; Baum lectr. U. Ill., 1988; Strassberger lectr. U. Tex., 1989; chmn. bd. Games Rsch., Inc., 1961—76; overseer Harvard U., 1991—. Author: The Scholastic Analysis of Usury, 1957, Contraception: A History of Its Treatment by the Catholic Theologians and Canonists, 1965, Power to Dissolve, 1972, Persons and Masks of the Law, 1976, The Antelope, 1977, A Private Choice, 1979, Bribes, 1984, The Responsible Judge, 1993, Professional and Personal Responsibilities of the Lawyer, 1997, The Lustre of Our Country, 1998; editor: Natural Law Forum, 1961—70, Am. Jour. Jurisprudence, 1970, The Morality of Abortion, 1970; author: Canons and Canonists in Context, 1997, Narrowing the Nation's Power, 2002. Chmn. Brookline Redevel. Authority , Mass., 1958—62; cons. Papal Commn. on Family, 1965—66, Ford Found., Indonesian Legal Program, 1968, NIH, 1973, 1974; expert Presdl. Commn. on Population and Am. Future, 1971; pres. Thomas More-Jacques Maritain Inst., 1977—; trustee Population Coun., 1969—76, Phi Kappa Found., 1970—76, U. San Francisco, 1971—75; mem. com. theol. edn. Yale U., 1972—77; cons. U.S. Cath. Conf., 1979—86; sec., treas. Inst. for Rsch. in Medieval Canon Law, 1970—88; trustee Grad. Theol. Union, 1970—73; exec. com. Cath. Commn. Intellectual and Cultural Affairs, 1972—75; bd. dirs. Ctr. for Human Values in the Health Scis., 1969—71, S.W. Intergroup Rels. Coun., 1970—72, Inst. for Study Ethical Issues, 1971—73. Recipient St. Thomas More award, U. San Francisco, 1974, Christian Culture medal, 1975, Laetare medal, U. Notre Dame, 1984, Campion medal, Cath. Book Club, 1987, Alemany medal, Western Dominican Province, 1988; fellow Guggenheim fellow, 1965—66, 1979—80, Ctr. for Advanced STudies in Behavioral Scis. fellow, 1973—74, Wilson Ctr. fellow, 1979—80, Kluge chair in Am. law and govt.w, Libr. Congress Ctr. for Scholars, 2002—. Fellow: Am. Acad. Arts and Scis., Am. Soc. Legal Historians (hon.); mem.: Am. Law Inst., Canon Law Soc. Am. (gov. 1970—72), Am. Soc. Polit. and Legal Philosophy (v.p. 1964), Phi Beta Kappa (senator United chpts. 1970—72, pres. Alpha of Calif. chpt. 1972—73). Office: US Ct Appeals 9th Cir PO Box 193939 San Francisco CA 94119-3939

NOONAN, PATRICK MATTHEW, lawyer; b. Bainbridge, Md., Oct. 6, 1952; s. Matthew Aloysius and Alice Jean (Flynn) N.; m. Denise Ann Doyle, Aug. 13, 1977; children: Colleen Doyle, Meghan Doyle, Tara Eileen, Shannon Kelly. BA, Yale U., 1974; JD, U. Va., 1977. Bar: Conn. 1977, U.S. Dist. Ct. Conn. 1977, U.S. Ct. Appeals (2d cir.) 1981. Law clk. to chief judge U.S. Dist. Ct., Hartford, Conn., 1977-79; assoc. Wiggin & Dana, New Haven, 1979-84, ptnr., 1984-90, Delaney, Zemetis, Donahue, Durham & Noonan, Guilford, Conn., 1990—. Mem. Pers. Rev. Bd., Meriden, Conn., 1979-81; v.p. Bd. Edn., Meriden, 1981-85. Fellow Am. Coll. Trial Lawyers; mem. ABA, Conn. Bar Assn., Fed. Practice Com., Meriden Young Lawyers (pres. 1980-82), Ancient Order Hibernians in Am. (treas. 1979-84). Democrat. Roman Catholic. Avocations: softball, racquetball, fishing. Federal civil litigation, Criminal, Personal injury (including property damage). Home: 137 Overshores W Madison CT 06443-2834 Office: Delaney Zemetis Donahue Durham & Noonan 741 Boston Post Rd Ste 306 Guilford CT 06437-2714

NOONAN, WILLIAM DONALD, lawyer, physician; b. Kansas City, Mo., Oct. 18, 1955; s. Robert Owen and Patricia Ruth Noonan. AB, Princeton (N.J.) U., 1977; JD, U. Mo., Kansas City, 1980; postgrad., Tulane U., 1981-83; MD magna cum laude, Oreg. Health Scis. U., 1991. Bar: Mo. 1980, U.S. Ct. Appeals (5th cir.) 1982, U.S. Patent & Trademark Office 1982, U.S. Ct. Appeals (D.C. cir.) 1984, Oreg. 1985, U.S. Ct. Appeals (9th Cir.) 1985. Assoc. Shurgue, Mion, Zinn, Washington, 1983-84, Keaty & Keaty, New Orleans, 1984-85; ptnr. Klarquist, Sparkman, Portland, Oreg., 1985—; intern in internal medicine Portland Providence Med. Ctr., 1993-94; resident in ophthalomology Casey Eye Inst., Portland, 1994-95. Adj. prof. patent law Tulane U., New Orleans, 1984-85, U. Oreg., 1992-93. Casenotes editor U. Mo. Law Rev., 1979. Nat. Merit scholar. Mem. ABA, AMA (Leadership award 1994), Alpha Omega Alpha (pres. Oreg. chpt. 1990-91). Republican. Avocations: raising horses, mountain climbing, hiking. Patent. Office: 1600 World Trade Ctr 121 SW Salmon St Portland OR 97204-2901

NOPAR, ALAN SCOTT, lawyer; b. Myron E. and Evelyn M. Nopar; m. Angela P. Yancey, Aug. 26, 2000. BS, U. Ill., 1976; JD, Stanford U., 1979. Bar: Ariz. 1979, U.S. Dist. Ct. Ariz. 1980, U.S. Ct. Appeals (9th cir.) 1980, U.S. Supreme Ct. 1982, Calif. 1989; CPA, Ill. Assoc. O'Connor, Cavanagh, Anderson, Westover, Killingsworth & Beshears P.A., Phoenix, 1979-85, ptnr., 1985-87; of counsel Tower, Byrne & Beaugureau, Phoenix, 1987-88; ptnr. Minutillo & Gorman, San Jose, Calif., 1989-91, Bosco, Blau, Ward & Nopar, San Jose, 1991-96; exec. v.p., gen. counsel, dir. AmeriNet Fin. Systems, Inc., Ontario, Calif., 1996-97; sole practice law Palo Alto, Calif., 1998-99; ptnr. Bosco, Ward & Nopar, Palo Alto, 2000—. Mem. Ariz. Rep. Caucus, Phoenix, 1984-88. Mem. AICPA, ABA (bus. law and law practice mgmt. sects., mem. forum com. on franchising), Ariz. Bar Assn. (bus. law sect.), Calif. State Bar Assn. (bus. law sect.). Avocations: golf, skiing, tennis. Corporate, general, Property, real (including real estate development, water), Mergers and acquisitions. Office: 425 Sherman Ave Ste 100 Palo Alto CA 94306-1849

NORA, GERALD ERNEST, lawyer; b. Chgo., May 25, 1951; s. Gerald Edwin and Lois (Billingham) N.; m. Patricia Cunniff, June 19, 1976; children: Gerald Joseph, Thomas More, Mary Elizabeth, John Paul. Student, U. Ill., 1970-71; BA, Georgetown U., 1973, JD, 1978. Bar: Ill. 1978, U.S. Supreme Ct. 1983, U.S. Dist. Ct. (no. dist.) Ill. 1983, U.S. Dist. Ct. Ariz. 1993, U.S. Ct. Appeals (7th cir.) 1996. Asst. state's atty. Cook County Office of State's Atty., Chgo. General civil litigation, Criminal, General practice. Office: Office of the Cook County States Atty 69 W Washington St Ste 3200 Chicago IL 60602

NORCOTT, FLEMMING L., JR., state supreme court justice; b. New Haven, Oct. 11, 1943; BA, Columbia U., 1965, JD, 1968. Bar: Conn. 1968. Peace corps vol. U. East Africa, Nairobi, Kenya; legal staff Bedford-Stuyvestant Restoration Corp.; asst. atty. gen. Office Atty. Gen., V.I.; judge Superior Ct., 1979-87, Appellate Ct., 1987-92; assoc. justice Conn. Supreme Ct., Hartford, 1992—. Hearing examiner Conn. Commn. Human Rights and Opportunities; co-founder, exec. dir. Ctr. Advocacy, Rsch. and Planning, Ind., New Haven; lectr. Yale U. Bd. govs. U. New Haven; bd. dirs. Dixwell Community House, Ea. Collegiate Football Ofcls. Assn., New Haven Football Ofcls. Assn., Long Wharf Theatre; assoc. fellow Calhoun Coll., Yale U.; bd. trustees Yale-New Haven Hosp. Mem. Omega Psi Phi Office: PO Box N Hartford CT 06126-1898

NORD, BERYL ANNETTE, judge, educator; b. Frederic, Wis., Oct. 12, 1948; d. Francis Gustaf and Irene Marian N.; 2 children. BA cum laude, U. Minn., 1970, JD cum laude, 1973. Bar: Minn. 1973, U.S. Dist. Ct. Minn. 1973, U.S. Ct. Appeals (8th cir.) 1977. Law clk. to assoc. justice Minn. Supreme Ct., St. Paul, 1973-74; asst. city atty. City of St. Paul, 1974-83; mcpl. judge County of Hennepin, Mpls., 1983-86, dist. ct. judge, 1986—. Adj. prof. U. Minn. Law Sch., Mpls., 1983—87. Big sister St. Paul YWCA Big Sister Program, 1973-76; bd. dirs. 58th Dist. DFL, 1976-80, chairperson, 1980-82; mem. DFL Feminist Caucus, 1974-83, bd. dirs., 1976-78, Criminal Justice Coordinating Coun., 1978-80; mem. DFL Cen. Com., 1980-83; past mem. Minn. Women's Polit. Caucus. Mem. Minn. Judges Assn. (bd. dirs. 1989-96), Nat. Assn. Women Judges (nat. bd. dirs. 10th dist. 1984-87), Hennepin County Bar Assn. (del. state bar convs., governing coun. 1989-91), Minn. Bar Assn. (criminal law sect. 1978-80, 83-88, civil litigation sect. 1982-83, bd. govs. 1989-91), Pi Kappa Delta. Office: 4th Jud Dist Ct 300 S 6th St Minneapolis MN 55487-0001

NORD, ROBERT EAMOR, lawyer; b. Ogden, Utah, Apr. 11, 1945; s. Eamor Carroll and Ella Carol (Winkler) N.; m. Sherryl Anne Smith, May 15, 1969; children: Kimberly, P. Ryan, Debra, Heather, Andrew, Elizabeth. BS, Brigham Young U., 1969; JD, U. Chgo., 1972. Bar: Ill. 1972, U.S. Dist. Ct. (no. dist.) Ill. 1972, U.S. Ct. Appeals (D.C. cir.) 1974, U.S. Dist. Ct. (mid. dist.) Fla. 1976, U.S. Ct. Appeals (7th cir.) 1977, U.S. Dist. Ct. (no. dist.) Ind. 1978, U.S. Dist. Ct. (no. dist.) Fla. 1979, U.S. Supreme Ct. 1981, U.S. Dist. Ct. (ea. dist.) Mich. 1984, U.S. Ct. Appeals (11th cir.) 1985, U.S. Ct. Appeals (3d cir.) 1996, U.S. Ct. Appeals (2nd cir.) 2002. Assoc. Chadwell & Kayser, Chgo., 1972-75; from assoc. to ptnr. Hinshaw & Culbertson, Chgo., 1975—2002, of counsel, 2003—. Republican. Mem. Lds Ch. Antitrust, Federal civil litigation. Home: 481 Woodlawn Ave Glencoe IL 60022-2175 Office: Hinshaw & Culbertson 222 N La Salle St Ste 300 Chicago IL 60601-1081 E-mail: rnord@hinshawlaw.com.

NORDBERG, JOHN ALBERT, federal judge; b. Evanston, Ill., June 18, 1926; s. Carl Albert and Judith Ranghild (Carlson) N.; m. Jane Spaulding, June 18, 1947; children: Carol, Mary, Janet, John. Student, Carleton Coll., 1943—44, student, 1946—47; JD, U. Mich., 1950. Bar: Ill. 1950, U.S. Dist. Ct. (no. dist.) Ill. 1957, U.S. Ct. Appeals (7th cir.) 1961. Assoc. Pope & Ballard, Chgo., 1950-57; ptnr. Pope, Ballard, Shepard & Fowle, Chgo., 1957-76; judge Cir. Ct. of Cook County, Ill., 1976-82, U.S. Dist. Ct. (no. dist.) Ill., Chgo., 1982-95, sr. judge, 1995—. Editor-in-chief, bd. editors Chgo. Bar Record, 1966-74 Magistrate of Cir. Ct. and justice of peace Ill., 1957-65. Served with USN, 1944-46; PTO Mem. ABA, Chgo. Bar Assn., Am. Judicature Soc., Law Club Chgo., Legal Club Chgo., Union League Club of Chgo., Order of Coif. Office: US Dist Ct #1886 219 S Dearborn St Chicago IL 60604-1706

NORDENBERG, MARK ALAN, law educator, academic administrator; b. Duluth, Minn., July 12, 1948; s. John Clemens and Shirley Mae (Tappen) N.; m. Nikki Patricia Pirillo, Dec. 26, 1970; children: Erin, Carl, Michael. BA, Thiel Coll., 1970; JD, U. Wis., 1973. Bar: Wis. 1973, Minn. 1974, U.S. Supreme Ct. 1976, Pa. 1985. Atty. Gray, Plant, Mooty & Anderson, Mpls., 1973-75; prof. law Capital U. Law Ctr., Columbus, Ohio, 1975-77, U. Pitts., 1977—, acting dean Sch. Law, 1985-87, dean Sch. Law, 1987-93, interim univ. sr. vice chancellor and provost, 1993-94, Univ. Disting. Svc. prof., 1994—, interim univ. chancellor, 1995-96, univ. chancellor, 1996—. Mem. U.S. Supreme Ct. Adv. Com. on Civil Rules, Washington, 1988-93, Pa. Supreme Ct. Civil Procedure Rules Com., Phila., 1986-92; reporter civil justice adv. group U.S. Dist. Ct., Pitts., 1991-96; bd. dirs. Mellon Fin. Corp. Author: Modern Pennsylvania Civil Practice, 1985, 2d edit., 1995. Trustee Thiel Coll., Greenville, Pa., 1987-97; bd. dirs. Inst. for Shipboard Edn. Found., Pitts. Regional Alliance, Pitts. Digital Greenhouse, Pitts. Life Scis. Greenhouse, Urban League of Pitts., Pitts. Robotics Foundry, World Affairs Coun. of Pitts., The Carnegie Mus., Pitts., Allegheny Conf. on Cmty. Devel., Pitts., Pitts. Coun. on Higher Edn., Pa. Assn. Colls. and Univs., Coun. on Competitiveness. Named Vectors Pitts. Person of Yr. in Edn., 1996, Person of Yr., 1997, Pitts. Mag. Person of Yr., 2001. Fellow Am. Bar Found.; mem. ABA, Pa. Bar Assn., Allegheny County Bar Assn., Pitts. Athletic Assn., NCAA (bd. dirs.), Law Club Pitts., Assn. Am. U., Nat Collegiate Athletic Assn. (bd. dirs.), Univ. Club, Duquesne Club, Wildwood Golf Club, Pitts. Golf Club. Office: U Pitts Cathedral of Learning Pittsburgh PA 15260

NORDLING, BERNARD ERICK, lawyer; b. Nekoma, Kans., June 14, 1921; s. Carl Ruben Ebben and Edith Elveda (Freeburg) N.; m. Barbara Ann Burkholder, Mar. 26, 1949. Student, George Washington U., 1941-43; AB, McPherson Coll., 1947; JD, U. Kans., 1949. Bar: Kans. 1949, U.S. Dist. Ct.

Kans. 1949, U.S. Ct. Appeals (10th cir.) 1970. Pvt. practice, Hugoton, Kans., 1949—; ptnr. Kramer, Nordling & Nordling, Hugoton, Kans., 1950-99; mem. Kramer, Nordling & Nordling, LLC, Hugoton, Kans., 1999—; city atty. City of Hugoton, 1951-87; county atty. Stevens County, Kans., 1957-63. Kans. mem. legal com. Interstate Oil Compact Commn., 1969-93; mem. supply tech. adv. com. nat. gas survey FPC, 1975-77. Editor U. Kans. Law Rev., 1949. Mem. Hugoton Sch. Bds., 1954-68, pres. grade sch. bd., 1957-63; trustee McPherson Coll., 1971-81, mem. exec. com., 1975-81; mem. Kans. Energy Adv. Coun., 1975-78, mem. exec. com., 1976-78. With AUS, 1944-46. Recipient Citation of Merit, McPherson Coll., 1987, Disting. Alumnus award, Kans. U. Law Sch., 1993, Lifetime Achievement award, Hugoton Kans. Area C. of C., 1994, James Wood Green medallion, Kans. U. Law Sch., 2001. Fellow: Am. Bar Found. (Kans.); mem.: ABA, Am. Inn of Ct., S.W. Kans. Royalty Owners Assn. (exec. sec. 1968—94, asst. exec. sec. 1994—), Nat. Assn. Royalty Owners (bd. govs. 1980—99), City Attys. Assn. Kans. (exec. com. 1975—83, pres. 1982—83), Kans. Bar Assn., Kans. U. Alumni Assn. (bd. dirs. 1992—97, Fred Ellsworth medallion 1997, James Woods Green medallion 2001), Kans. U. Endowment Assn. (trustee 1989—), U. Kans. Law Soc. (bd. govs. 1984—87), Phi Alpha Delta, Order of Coif. Oil, gas, and mineral, General practice, Probate (including wills, trusts). Address: 4404 Nicklaus Dr Lawrence KS 66047 E-mail: benordling@sunflower.com.

NORFOLK, WILLIAM RAY, lawyer; b. Huron, S.D., Mar. 15, 1941; s. James W. and Helen F. (Thompson) N.; m. Marilyn E. Meadors; children: Stephanie G., Allison T., Meredith H. BA, Miami U., Oxford, Ohio, 1963; student, U. London, 1963-64; LLB, Duke U., 1967. Bar: N.Y. 1968, U.S. Dist. Ct. (so. and ea. dists.) N.Y. 1969, U.S. Ct. Appeals (2d cir.) 1969, U.S. Ct. Appeals (9th cir.) 1977, U.S. Ct. Appeals (5th cir.) 1979, U.S. Ct. Appeals (3d and 11th cirs.) 1981, U.S. Dist. Ct. (ea. dist.) Mich. 1986, U.S. Ct. Appeals (6th and 8th cirs.) 1986, U.S. Ct. Appeals (Fed. cir.) 1990, U.S. Ct. Internat. Trade 1990, U.S. Dist. Ct. (we. dist.) Mich. 1992. Assoc. Sullivan & Cromwell, N.Y.C., 1967-74, ptnr., 1974—. Mem. ABA, N.Y. State Bar Assn., Assn. of the Bar of the City of N.Y. Antitrust, General civil litigation, Mergers and acquisitions. Office: Sullivan & Cromwell 125 Broad St Fl 28 New York NY 10004-2489

NORGLE, CHARLES RONALD, SR., federal judge; b. Mar. 3, 1937; BBA, Northwestern U., Evanston, Ill., 1964; JD, John Marshall Law Sch., Chgo., 1969. Asst. state's atty. DuPage County, Ill., 1969-71, dep. pub. defender, 1971-73, assoc. judge, 1973-77, 78-81, cir. judge, 1977-78, 81-84; judge U.S. Dist. Ct. (no. dist.) Ill., Chgo., 1984—. Mem. exec. com. No. Dist. Ill.; mem. 7th Cir. Jud. Coun., 7th Cir. Jud. Conf. planning com., subcom. grant requests Fed. Defender Orgn., Fed. Defender Svcs. Com.; adj. faculty Northwestern U. Sch. Law, John Marshall Law Sch., Chgo.; pres. Atticus Finch Inn Ct. Mem. ABA, Fed. Bar Assn., Fed. Circuit Bar Assn., Ill. Bar Assn., DuPage County (Ill.) Bar Assn., Nat. Attys. Assn., DuPage Assn. Women Attys., Chgo. Legal Club, Northwestern Club. Office: US Dist Ct 219 S Dearborn St Ste 2346 Chicago IL 60604-1802

NORMAN, ALBERT GEORGE, JR., lawyer; b. Birmingham, Ala., May 29, 1929; s. Albert G. and Ila Mae (Carroll) N.; m. Catherine Marshall DeShazo, Sept. 3, 1955; children: Catherine Marshall, Albert George III. BA, Auburn U., 1953; LLB, Emory U., 1958; MA, U. N.C., 1960. Bar: Ga. 1957. Assoc. Moise, Post & Gardner, Atlanta, 1958-60, ptnr., 1960-62, Hansell & Post, Atlanta, 1962-86, Long, Aldridge & Norman, Atlanta, 1986-2000. Dir. Atlanta Gas Light Co., 1976-2000. Served with USAF, 1946-49. Mem. ABA, Ga. Bar Assn., Atlanta Bar Assn., Lawyers Club Atlanta (pres. 1973-74), Am. Law Inst., Am. Judicature Soc. (dir. 1975-78), Old War Horse Lawyers Club, (pres. 1991-92), Cherokee Town and Country Club. Episcopalian. General civil litigation, Communications, Utilities, public. E-mail: almarnorman@mingspring.com.

NORRIS, ALAN EUGENE, federal judge; b. Columbus, Ohio, Aug. 15, 1935; s. J. Russell and Dorothy A. (Shrader) N.; m. Nancy Jean Myers, Apr. 15, 1962 (dec. Jan. 1986); children: Tom Edward Jackson, Tracy Elaine; m. Carol Lynn Spohn, Nov. 10, 1990. BA, Otterbein Coll., 1957, HLD (hon.), 1991; cert., U. Paris, 1956; LLB, NYU, 1960; LLM, U. Va., 1986; HLD, Capital U. Law Sch., 2001. Bar: Ohio 1960, U.S. Dist. Ct. (so. dist) Ohio 1962, U.S. Dist. Ct. (no. dist) Ohio 1964. Law clk. to judge Ohio Supreme Ct., Columbus, 1960-61; assoc. Vorys, Sater, Seymour & Pease, Columbus, 1961-62; ptnr. Metz, Bailey, Norris & Spicer, Westerville, Ohio, 1962-80; judge Ohio Ct. Appeals (10th dist.), Columbus, 1981-86, U.S. Ct. Appeals (6th cir.), Columbus, 1986—. Contbr. articles to profl. jours. Mem. Ohio Ho. of Reps., Columbus, 1967-80. Named Outstanding Young Man, Westerville Jaycees, 1971; recipient Legislator of Yr. award Ohio Acad. Trial Lawyers, Columbus, 1972. Mem. Ohio Bar Assn., Columbus Bar Assn. Lodges: Masons (master 1966-67). Republican. Methodist. Office: US Ct Appeals 328 US Courthouse 85 Marconi Blvd Columbus OH 43215-2823

NORRIS, GLENN L. lawyer; b. Clarinda, Iowa, Sept. 25, 1946; s. Harold E. and Darlene Louise (Crane) N.; m. Dale Bailey, Jan. 28, 1967 (div. June 1990); m. Tiffinny C. Sparks, Nov. 14, 1998; children: Christopher Steven, Catherine Beth, Glenn Leonard Jr., Janet Darlene. BA, Simpson Coll., 1968; JD with honors, U. Iowa, 1971. Bar: Iowa 1971, So. Dist. Iowa 1971, U.S. Dist. Ct., no. dist., Iowa, 8th circuit, 1972, U.S. Supreme Ct., 1976. Law clerk U.S. Dist. Judge Hanson, Ft. Dodge, Iowa, 1971-73; assoc. Hawkins, Hedberg & Ward, Des Moines, Iowa, 1973-78; ptnr. Hawkins & Norris, P.C., Des Moines, Iowa, 1978—. Editor: Iowa Academy of Trial Lawyers Handbook, 3d edit., 1999. Mem. tech. com. Iowa Supreme Ct. Commn. for Planning for 21st Century, 1996-98, Iowa Supreme Ct. Budget Adv. Com., 1997—; dir. men's chorus Sacred Heart Knights of Columbus. Recipient St. George award for Disting. Svc. to Cath. Scouting, Boy Scouts Am., Eagle Scout. Fellow Iowa Acad. Trial Lawyers; master C. Edwin Moore Am. Inn of Ct. (pres. 1998-2000); mem. Am. Bd. Trial Advs. (cert. civil trial advocate 2000—), Iowa State Bar Assn. (mem. fed. practice com. 1999—), Iowa Assn. Trial Lawyers (bd. govs. 1987-98). Roman Catholic. General civil litigation. Home: 6205 Oakwood Hills Dr Johnston IA 50131-1962 Office: Hawkins & Norris PC 2501 Grand Ave Ste C Des Moines IA 50312-5311 E-mail: gnorrislaw@hotmail.com.

NORRIS, JOHN E. lawyer; b. Childersburg, Ala., Nov. 18, 1965; s. James Lloyd and Joyce Elizabeth (Smith) Norris; m. Victoria Lee Ann Valkenburg, June 25, 1988; children: William Powell, Elizabeth Chason. BA in Polit. Sci. magna cum laude, Birmingham So. Coll., 1988; JD, U. Ala., 1992. Bar: Ala. 1991, U.S. Dist. Ct. (no. dist.) Ala. 1992, U.S. Dist. Ct. (ctrl. dist.) Ala. 1995, U.S. Dist. Ct. (so. dist.) Ala. 1996, U.S. Supreme Ct. 1995, U.S. Ct. Appeals (11th cir.) 2000. Law clk. Hon. William M. Acker, Jr., U.S. Dist. Ct. (no. dist.) Ala., Birmingham, 1991—92; assoc. Berkowitz, Lefkovits, Isom & Kushner, Birmingham, 1992—94, Burr & Forman LLP, Birmingham, 1994—99, ptnr., 2000—. Mem.: ABA (sects. of litigation and labor and employment), ATLA, Ala. Bar Assn. General civil litigation, Labor (including EEOC, Fair Labor Standards Act, labor-management relations, NLRB, OSHA). Office: Burr & Forman LLP 420 N 20th St Birmingham AL 35203 Office Fax: 2054585100. E-mail: jnorris@burr.com.

NORRIS, KENNETH MICHAEL, lawyer; b. Ludlow, Mass., Jan. 22, 1952; s. Kenneth Richard and Santa (LiAntonio) N. BS in Nuclear Engring., USCG Acad., 1973; MSChemE, Purdue U., 1977; MBA, U. Md., 1979; JD, George Washington U., 1983. Bar: D.C. 1984, Tex. 1988, Calif. 1992, Wash. 1998; registered profl. engr., Tex. Marine engr. USCG, Seattle, 1973-75, chem. engr. Washington, 1977-82; del. Internat. Maritime Orgn., London, 1978-82, UN Com. on Trade and Devel., Geneva, 1979-82; resigned USCG, 1984; patent atty. Sandler & Greenblum, P.C., Arlington, Va., 1984-85; sr. cons. Booz, Allen & Hamilton, Inc., Washington, 1985-86; corp. counsel Resource Engring., Inc., Houston, 1986-88; environ. atty. Butler & Binion, Houston, 1988-90; ptnr., dir. environ. law dept. Norton & Blair, Houston, 1990-91; environ. atty. Morgan, Lewis & Bockius, L.A., 1991-93; sr. environ. counsel Chem. Waste Mgmt., Houston, 1993-96; sr. counsel Fluor Hanford, Inc., Richland, Wash., 1997—. Rep. Am. Nat. Standards Inst. Com. N-14 and Com. N-522; adj. prof. environ. law U. Houston Law Ctr., 1989-97; faculty Columbia Basin Coll., 1999—; mil. aide to Pres. Carter, Pres. Reagan, 1978-82. Contbr. articles to profl. publs. Treas. Westchester Found., Arlington, 1982-86; atty. Arlington Coun. on Fin., 1984; pres. Wroxton Owners Assn.; v.p. Benton Franklin Dispute Resolution Ctr., 1999-2000, bd. dirs. 1999-2002; bd. dirs. Willowbrook Cmty. Assn., 2002—; bd. dirs. Neurol. Ctr., 1998—, pres., 1999—. With USCG, 1969-84, capt. USCGR, 1984-96. Mem. ABA, AAAS, D.C. Bar, Tex. Bar, Calif. Bar, Wash. Bar Assn., Am. Chem. Soc., Am. Nuc. Soc., Neurol. Ctr. (bd. dirs. 1999—, pres. 2000—), Houston Striker Rugby Club, West Potomac Rugby Club (Washington) (pres.), Masons. Republican. Avocation: rugby. Admiralty, Environmental. Home: 227 Sitka Ct Richland WA 99352 E-mail: Kenneth-M-Ken-norris@rl.gov.

NORRIS, PASCALE DANIELLE, lawyer; b. Vienna, Jan. 16, 1969; d. Robert Norman and Françoise Anne-Marie Norris; life ptnr. Arnaud Vanhelle; children: Lucas Vanhelle, Rosalie Vanhelle. LLB in English Law, King's Coll., London, 1989; M in French Law, Sorbonne, Paris, 1991. Bar: N.Y. 1997, Paris 2000. Assoc. Salans Hertzfeld and Heilbronn, Paris, 1999—. Cons. Human Rights Watch, N.Y.C., 1996—97, Coalition for an Internat. Criminal Ct., N.Y.C., 1997—99. Commercial, contracts (including sales of goods; commercial financing), General civil litigation. Office: Salans 9 rue Boissy d Anglas 75008 Paris France

NORRIS, ROBERT WHEELER, military officer; b. Birmingham, Ala., May 22, 1932; s. Hubert Lee and Georgia Irene (Parker) N.; m. Martha Katherine Cummins, Feb. 19, 1955; children— Lisha Katherine Norris Utt, Nathan Robert BA in Bus. Adminstrn., U. Ala., 1954, LL.B., 1955; LL.M., George Washington U., 1979; postgrad., Air Command & Staff Coll., 1968, Nat. War Coll., 1975. Commd. 2d lt. USAF, advanced through grades to maj. gen., dep. judge advocate gen., 1983-85, judge advocate gen., 1985-88; gen. counsel Ala. Bar Assn., Montgomery, 1988-95; ptnr. London & Yancey, Birmingham, Ala., 1995—2002; ret. Decorated D.S.M., Legion of Merit, Meritorious Svc. medal. Mem. ABA. Methodist. Military, Personal injury (including property damage), Ethics. Office: London & Yancey 2001 Park Pl Ste 400 Birmingham AL 35203-2787

NORSTRAND, HANS PETER, lawyer, real estate public official, municipal official; b. Cambridge, Mass., Aug. 1, 1940; s. Hans Donald and Marion (Hardy) N.; m. Janet Hoover, Dec. 30, 1967 (div.); children: Rachel Bell, Hans Christopher; m. Katherine Tallman, Feb. 5, 1994. AB, Dartmouth Coll., 1963; JD, Boston Coll., 1966. Bar: Mass., 1966; U.S. Supreme Ct., 1994. Asst. atty. gen., Mass., 1966-69; assoc. Sullivan & Worcester, Boston, 1969-74; v.p., gen. csl Kuras & Co., Inc., Boston, 1974-76; pvt. practice Boston, 1977-80; v.p., gen. counsel Boston Co. Real Estate Counsel, Inc., 1980-81; prin. Aldrich, Eastman & Waltch, Boston, 1981-91; mng. dir. Sun Capital Adv.,Inc., Boston, 1991-93; prin. State St. Global Advs., 1994—99; v.p. ASB Capital Mgmt., Inc., 1999; pvt. practice Brookline, Mass., 2000; dir. real estate Commonwealth of Mass. Divsn. Capital Asset Mgmt., Boston, 2000; dir. real estate and dep. commr, divsn. capital asset mgmt. Commonwealth of Mass., Boston, 2001—. Property, real (including real estate development, water). Office: 1 Ashburton Pl 15th Fl Boston MA 02108 E-mail: ksthpn@aol.com., HPeter.Norstrand@state.ma.us.

NORSWORTHY, ELIZABETH KRASSOVSKY, lawyer; b. N.Y.C., Feb. 26, 1943; d. Leonid Alexander and Wilma (Hudgens) Krassovsky; m. John Randolph Norsworthy, June 24, 1961 (div. 1962), m. Nov. 26, 1977 (div. 1984); 1 child, Alexander. AB magna cum laude, CUNY, 1965; MA, U. N.C., 1966; JD, Stanford U., 1977. Bar: D.C. 1978, Mass. 1992, Vt. 1998, U.S. Ct. Appeals (D.C. cir.) 1979. Atty. applications, disclosure rev. and investment adviser regulation, divsn. investment mgmt. SEC, Washington, 1978-79, 80-82, atty. operating brs. and disclosure policy divsn. corp. fin., 1979-80, chief, spl. counsel office of regulatory policy divsn. investment mgmt., 1983-86; assoc. Kirkpatrick & Lockhart, Washington, 1986-90; ptnr. Sullivan & Worcester, Boston, 1990-92; pvt. practice Norfolk, Mass., 1992, Concord, Vt., 1996—. Pub. arbitrator, chairperson NASD; mediator, facilitator Cmty. Justice Ctr., St. Johnsbury. Mem. North Country Chorus, Wells River; chair investment com. North Congl. Ch., St. Johnsbury; mem. adv. bd. Natural Resources, Concord. Mem.: Vt. Coverts, Vt. Grass Farmers, Am. Farmland Trust, Jacob Sheep Breed Assn., Am. Livestock Breed Conservancy, Vt. Bar Assn. (ADR com., family law com.), College Club (St. Johnsbury), Athenaeum (St. Johnsbury), Catamount Arts Club (St. Johnsbury), Phi Alpha Theta, Phi Beta Kappa. Democrat. Mem. United Church of Christ. Avocations: farming, swimming, singing, environmental protection. Juvenile, Alternative dispute resolution. Office: Winterbrook Farm 1342 Woodward Rd Concord VT 05824-9620 Fax: 802-695-2516. E-mail: ekn@kingcon.com.

NORTELL, BRUCE, lawyer; b. Nov. 19, 1946; s. Joseph and Dorothy Nortell; children: Adam, Daniel, Anthony. AB, Boston U., 1968; JD, U. Chgo., 1971. Bar: Ill. 1971, U.S. Dist. Ct. (no. dist.) Ill. 1971, U.S. Supreme Ct. 1979. Sole practice, Chgo., 1971—74; asst. dir. legal affairs AMA, Chgo., 1974—81, counsel, sec. jud. coun., 1976—81; dir. tax and fin. planning Loyola U., Chgo., 1981—88, North Ctrl. Coll., Naperville, Ill., 1988—. Contbr. articles to profl. jours.; , author two books novels. Mem.: ABA, Chgo. Bar Assn., Ill. Bar Assn. (Lincoln award 1975), Phi Beta Kappa (bd.). Home: 1124 Dickens Ln Naperville IL 60563-4301 Office: 30 N Brainard St Naperville IL 60540-4607

NORTH, WILLIAM T. lawyer; b. EMporia, Kans., Feb. 13, 1950; s. Stanley J. and Mildred I. N.; m. Ann K. Winters, Aug. 12, 1972; children: Thomas A., Jennifer A. BA, Emporia State U., 1972; JD, Washburn U., 1976. Bar: Kans., U.S. Surpeme Ct., U.S. Dist. Ct. Kans. Ptnr. Masoner & North, Cottonwood Falls, Kans., 1976-91; atty. pvt. practice, Cottonwood Falls, Kans., 1991—. City atty. City of Cottonwood Falls, 1976—, sch. atty. United Sch. Dist. No 248, Chase County, Kans., 1976—. Mem. Kans. Bar Assn., Chase/Lyon County Bar Assn. Republican. Episcopalian. Avocation: golf. Criminal, Estate planning, General practice. Office: 308 Broadway Cottonwood Falls KS 66845

NORTHERN, RICHARD, lawyer; b. Louisville, Dec. 17, 1948; s. James William and Mary Helen (Barry) N.; m. Mary Lou Grundy, Aug. 28, 1971; children: James Barry, Nancy Hope, Mary Grace. BA in English, U. Louisville, 1970, JD, 1976; MPA, Harvard U., 1977. Bar: Ky. 1976, U.S. Dist. Ct. (we. and ea. dists.) Ky. 1977. Staff writer Courier-Jour., Louisville, 1970-72; dir. planning devel. Jefferson County Govt., Louisville, 1972-76; legis. dir. Office of U.S. Rep. Romano Mazzoli, Washington, 1977-78; spl. asst. U.S. Sec. of Interior, Washington, 1979-80; ptnr. Wyatt, Tarrant & Combs, Louisville, 1980—. Dir. Nugent Sand Co., 1998—. Chmn. bd. dirs. Cath. Edn. Found., Inc., Louisville, 1998—; dir. Caister Health Svcs., 1981—. White House fellow, 1979, U.S.-Japan Leadership fellow Japan Soc., Inc., 1988. Democrat. Roman Catholic. Administrative and regulatory, Corporate, general, Private international. Office: Wyatt Tarrant & Combs 2800 Citizens Plz Louisville KY 40202-2898

NORTHROP, EDWARD SKOTTOWE, federal judge; b. Chevy Chase, Md., June 12, 1911; s. Claudian Bellinger and Eleanor Smythe (Grimke) N.; m. Barbara Middleton Burdette, Apr. 22, 1939; children: Edward M., St. Julien (Mrs. Kevin Butler), Peter. LLB, George Washington U., 1937. Bar: Md. 1937, D.C. 1937. Village mgr., Chevy Chase, Md., 1934-41; pvt. practice, Rockville, Md., 1937-61; mem. Md. Senate, 1954-61, chmn. fin. com., joint com. taxation fiscal affairs, majority leader, 1959-61; judge U.S. Dist. Ct. Md., Balt., 1961-70; chief judge U.S. Dist. Ct. of Md., Balt., 1970-81, sr. judge, 1981—. Mem. Met. Chief Judges Conf., 1970-81; mem. Jud. Conf. Com. on Adminstrn. of Probation System, 1973-79, Adv. Corrections Council U.S., 1977, Jud. Panel on Multidist. Litigation, 1979; judge U.S. Fgn. Intelligence Surveillance Ct. of Rev., 1985—1992. Trustee Woodberry Forest Sch.; founder Washington Met. Area Coun. Govts. & Mass Transp. Agy. Served to comdr. USNR, 1941-45. Decorated Army commendation medal, Navy commendation medal; recipient Profl. Achievement award George Washington U., 1975, Disting. Citizen award State of Md., 1981, Spl. Merit citation Am. Judicature Soc., 1982. Mem. ABA, Md. Bar Assn. (Disting. Svc. award 1982), D.C. Bar Assn., Montgomery County Bar Assn., Barristers, Washington Ctr. Met. Studies. Clubs: Chevy Chase (Md.). Lodges: Rotary. Democrat. Episcopalian. Office: US Dist Ct 101 W Lombard St Ste 8A Baltimore MD 21201-2903*

NORTON, ELIZABETH WYCHGEL, lawyer; b. Cleve., Mar. 25, 1933; d. James Nicolas and Ruth Elizabeth (Cannell) Wychgel; m. Henry Wacks Norton Jr., July 16, 1954 (div. 1971); children: James, Henry, Peter, Fred; m. James Cory Ferguson, Dec. 14, 1985 (div. Apr. 1988). BA in Math., Wellesley Coll., 1954; JD cum laude, U. Minn., 1974. Bar: Minn. 1974. Summer intern Minn. Atty. Gen.'s Office, St. Paul, 1972; with U.S. Dept. Treasury, St. Paul, 1973; assoc. Gray, Plant, Mooty, Mooty & Bennett, P.A., Mpls., 1974-79, prin., 1980-94, of counsel, 1995-96. Mem. Minn. Lawyers Bd. Profl. Responsibility, 1984-89; mem. U. Minn. Law Sch. Bd. Visitors, 1987-92. Trustee YWCA, Mpls., 1979-84, 89-91, co-chmn. deferred giving com., 1980-81, chmn. by-laws com., bd. dirs., 1976-77, lectr.; treas. Minn. Women's Campaign Fund, 1985, guarantor, 1982-83, budget and fin. com. bd. dirs., 1984-87; trustee Ripley Meml. Found., 1980-84; treas. Jones-Harrison Home, 1967, bd. dirs., 1962-69, 2d v.p., chmn. fin., 1968-69; mem. Sen. David Durenberger's Women's Network, 1983-88. Durant scholar. Fellow Am. Bar Found.; mem. ABA (mediation task force family law sect. 1983-84), Minn. Bar Assn. (human rights com. family law sect., task force uniform marital property act 1984-85), Minn. Bar Found. (dir. 1991-94), Hennepin County Bar Assn. (pres. 1987-88, chmn. task force on pub. edn. 1984, chmn., mem. exec. com. family law sect. 1979-94), Minn. Inst. Legal Edn., Minn. Women's Lawyers (exec. com.), Hemlock Soc. of S.W. Fla. (co-chmn. 1999-2001), U. Minn. Law Sch. Alumni Assn. (dir. 1975-81, exec. com. 1981-83), Wellesley Club (Naples, pres. 2002—), Phi Beta Kappa. Home: 26 Water Oaks Way Naples FL 34105-7157

NORTON, GALE ANN, federal official; b. Wichita, Mar. 11, 1954; d. Dale Bentsen and Anna Jacqueline (Lansdowne) N.; m. John Goethe Hughes, Mar. 26, 1990. BA, U. Denver, 1975, JD, 1978. Bar: Colo. 1978, U.S. Supreme Ct. 1981. Jud. clk. Colo. Ct. of Appeals, Denver, 1978-79; sr. atty. Mountain States Legal Found., Denver, 1979-83; nat. fellow Hoover Instn. Stanford (Calif.) U., 1983-84; asst. to dep. sec. USDA, Washington, 1984-85; assoc. solicitor U.S. Dept. of Interior, Washington, 1985-87; pvt. practice law Denver, 1987-90; atty. gen. State of Colo., Denver, 1991-99; atty. Brownstein, Hyatt & Farber, P.C., sr. counsel, 1999-2000; sec. U.S. Dept. Interior, Washington, 2001—. Lectr. U. Denver Law Sch., 1989; transp. law program dir. U. Denver, 1978-79. Contbr. chpts. to books, articles to profl. jours. Past chair Nat. Assn. Attys. Gen. Environ. Com.; co-chair Nat. Policy Forum Environ. Coun.; candidate for 1996 election to US Senate; chair environ. commn. Rep. Nat. Lawyers Assn. Named Young Career Woman Bus. and Profl. Wome, 1981, Young Lawyer of Yr., 1991, Mary Lathrop Trailblazer award Colo. Women's Bar Assn., 1999. Mem. Federalist Soc., Colo. Women's Forum, Order of St. Ives. Republican. Methodist. Avocation: skiing. Office: Dept of the Interior Office of the Sec 1849 C St NW Washington DC 20240

NORTON, SALLY PAULINE, lawyer; b. Elkhart, Ind., Jan. 28, 1964; d. Ronald and Peggy Hale; m. Peter Norton, Aug. 28, 1993; children: Alexander, Aileen. BA, Ind. U., 1986, JD, 1989. Bar: Ind. 1991, U.S. Dist. Ct. (no. and so. dists.) Ind. 1991. Law clk. Kalamaros & Assocs., South Bend, Ind., 1990-91, assoc., 1991—2002, Doran-Blackmond LLP, South Bend, 2000—02, prnt., 2002—. Mem. Ind. Bar Assn., St. Joseph County Bar Assn., Def. Trial Counsel Ind., Def. Rsch. Inst., Robert A. Grant Inn of Ct. Avocation: martial arts. Insurance, Personal injury (including property damage), Workers' compensation. Home: 10628 N Pheasant Cove Dr Granger IN 46530-7576 Office: Doran Blackmond LLP 211 W Washington South Bend IN 46601

NORTON, WILLIAM ALAN, lawyer; b. Garretsville, Ohio, Apr. 26, 1951; s. Hugh Delbert and Tommie (Leet) N.; m. Denise Ann, May 2, 1991; children: Rachel, Sarah Megan, William Tucker. AA, U. Fla., 1972, BS, 1973, JD, 1976. Bar: Fla. 1977, U.S. Dist. Ct. (so. and mid. dist.) Fla. 1995. Assoc. Law Office of David Paul Horan, Key West, Fla., 1978-79; asst. pub. defender 16th Jud. Cir., Monroe County, Fla., 1979-81, 1st Jud. Cir., Ft. Walton Beach, Fla., 1981-85; assoc. Jones & Foster, P.A., West Palm Beach, Fla., 1985-88, Montgomery Searcy & Denney, West Palm Beach, 1988-89, Searcy Denney Scarola Barnhart & Shipley, P.A., 1989-93, atty./shareholder, 1989—, shareholder. Lectr. in civil trial and securities litigation. Mem. Fla. Bar Assn. (cert. civil trial litigation), Pub. Investors Arbitration Bar Assn., Palm Beach County Bar Assn., Acad. Fla. Trial Lawyers. Federal civil litigation, General civil litigation, State civil litigation. Home: 12710 Drake Ln Palm Beach Gardens FL 33410 Office: Searcy Denney Scarola et al 2139 Palm Beach Lakes Blvd West Palm Beach FL 33409-6601 E-mail: wan@searcylaw.com.

NORWITZ, TREVOR S. lawyer; b. Cape Town, South Africa, Oct. 21, 1964; came to the U.S., 1989; s. Rubin Gabriel and Marionne Joyce Norwitz; m. Shannon Lieberman, Jan. 19, 1992; children: Raphael Shai, Herschel Sam. B in Bus. Sci., U. Cape Town, 1986; BA in Juris, Oxford (Eng.) U., 1989, MA, 1993; LLM, Columbia U., 1990. Bar: N.Y. 1991. Assoc. Cravath, Swaine & Moore, N.Y.C., 1990-94, Wachtell, Lipton, Rosen & Katz, N.Y.C., 1994-98, ptnr., 1999—. Contbr. articles to profl. jours. Rhodes scholar, 1987. Mem. ABA (bus. sect. com., com. corp. laws). Corporate, general, Mergers and acquisitions, Securities. Office: Wachtell Lipton Rosen & Katz 51 W 52nd St Fl 29 New York NY 10019-6150

NORWOOD, DEBORAH ANNE, law librarian; b. Honolulu, Nov. 12, 1950; d. Alfred Freeman and Helen G. (Papsch) N.; 1 child, Nicholas. BA, U. Wash., 1972; JD, Willamette U., 1974; M in Law Librarianship, U. Wash., 1979. Bar: Wash., U.S. Dist. Ct. (we. dist.) 1975, U.S. Ct. Appeals (9th cir.) 1980. Ptnr. Evans and Norwood, Seattle, 1975-79; law librarian U.S. Courts Library, Seattle, 1980-89; state law librarian Wash. State Law Libr., Olympia, 1989—2002, reporter of decisions, 1994-2001; asst. dir. pub. svcs. Jacob Burns Law Libr. George Washington U., Washington, 2002—. Mem. Freedom to Read Found. Mem. Am. Assn. Law Librs. (chmn. state, ct. and county spl. interest section 1995-96, chair legal info. svcs. to pub. spl. interest sect. 2001-02). Office: Jacob Burns Law Libr George Washington U 716-20th St NW Washington DC 20052 E-mail: dnorwood@law.gwu.edu.

NOSEK, FRANCIS JOHN, lawyer, diplomat; b. Evanston, Ill., Apr. 13, 1934; s. Francis J. and Loretto (Brannan) N.; m. Janet Child, Dec. 30, 1964; children: Francis J. III, Peter C. BA in Polit. Sci., U. Idaho, 1956, JD, 1960. Bar: Calif. 1961, U.S. Dist. Ct. (no. dist.) Calif. 1961, U.S. Ct. Appeals (9th cir.) 1961, Alaska 1962, U.S. Dist. Ct. Alaska 1962, D.C. 1978. Pvt. practice, Anchorage, 1960-67, 75—; assoc. Bell, Sanders & Tallman, Anchorage, 1961-62; sr. ptnr. Nosek, Bradberry, Wolf and Schlossberg, Anchorage, 1967-75; hon. consul Czech Republic. Adj. prof. U. Alaska, Mat-Su C.C., Anchorage, 1976-82; lectr. Anchorage C.C., 1979-83, SBA, 1975-97; editor State of Alaska Real Estate Commn., Anchorage, 1983; presenter in field; bd. of dirs. on real estate and bus. topics. Author: Alaska Mortgage Law, How to Buy and Sell a Business; contbr. articles to law jours. Chmn. Anchorage Parks and Recreation, 1968-83, IIHF World Jr.

Championships, Anchorage, 1988; named hon. Consul for Czech Republic. Mem. Am. Coll. Real Estate Lawyers, Alaska Bar Assn. (chmn. real estate law 1978, mem. internat. law exec. com. 1991-95), Calif. Bar Assn. (real estate law coms.), D.C. Bar Assn. (internat. law com.), Anchorage Bar Assn. Avocations: mountain climbing, ice hockey, antique cars. Private international, Property, real (including real estate development, water). Office: 310 K St Ste 601 Anchorage AK 99501-2041

NOTT, GREGORY ANTONY, lawyer; b. Durban, KZN, South Africa, June 2, 1960; s. Cecil Alexander and Mavourneen Nott; m. Ann Mary Nott, Mar. 24, 1990; children: Joshua, Ben, Thomas. BA, Univ. Witwatersand, JHB, 1980; LLB, Univ. Natal, Durban, 1983; diploma in corp. govt., Univ. Rand, JHB, 1998. Ptnr. Beu, Dewar & Hall, Johannesburg, 1987—99; sr. counsel LeBonef, Lamb, Green & Macrae, Johannesburg, 2000—. Contbr. chapters to books. Com. mem. Am. C. of C. Mem.: Nat. Assn. Democratic Lawyers (v.p.). Avocations: reading, running, fishing, theater , internat. affiars. Home: 42 Cawdor Ave Murlingham Johannesburg South Africa Office: Leboeuf Lamb Greene Macrae Standard Bank Bldg W wing 2nd flr 11 Alice Ln Johannesburg South Africa

NOTTINGHAM, EDWARD WILLIS, JR., federal judge; b. Denver, Jan. 9, 1948; s. Edward Willis and Willie Newton (Gullett) N.; m. Cheryl Ann Card, June 6, 1970 (div. Feb. 1981); children: Amelia Charlene, Edward Willis III; m. Janis Ellen Chapman, Aug. 18, 1984 (div. Dec. 1998); 1 child, Spencer Chapman. AB, Cornell U., 1969; JD, U. Colo., 1972. Bar: Colo. 1972, U.S. Dist. Ct. Colo. 1972, U.S. Ct. Appeals (10th cir.) 1973. Law clk. to presiding judge U.S. Dist. Ct. Colo., Denver, 1972-73; assoc. Sherman & Howard, Denver, 1973-76, 78-80, ptnr., 1980-87, Beckner & Nottingham, Grand Junction, Colo., 1987-89; asst. U.S. atty. U.S. Dept. Justice, Denver, 1976-78; U.S. dist. judge Dist. of Colo., Denver, 1989—. Mem. Jud. Conf. of the U.S. Com. on Automation and Tech., 1994-2000, chmn., 1997-2000. Bd. dirs. Beaver Creek Met. Dist., Avon, Colo., 1980-88, Justice Info. Ctr., Denver, 1985-87, 21st Jud. Dist. Victim Compensation Fund, Grand Junction, Colo., 1987-89. Mem. ABA, Colo. Bar Assn. (chmn. criminal law sect. 1983-85, chmn. ethics com. 1988-89), Order of Coif, Denver Athletic Club, Delta Sigma Rho, Tau Kappa Alpha. Episcopalian. Office: US Dist Ct 1929 Stout St Denver CO 80294-1929 E-mail: Edward_W._Nottingham@cod.uscourts.gov.

NOVAK, JOSEPH ANTHONY, law librarian; b. Detroit; s. Thomas Paul and Mary Cecilia N. AA, Macomb C.C., Warren, Mich., 1984; BA, Oakland U., 1986; JD, Mich. State U., 1991; M Libr. and Info. Sci., Wayne State U., 1998. Intern Wayne County Pub. Defender's Office, Detroit, 1986; intern Office of Jud. Assistance 3d Jud. Ct. Mich., Detroit, 1993, law clk. to Hon. Diane M. Hathaway, intern, 1996; law libr. St. Louis Correctional Facility, 2000—01, Mid-Mich. Correctional Facility, 2001—. Vol., Vol. Income Tax Assistance Program, Detroit, 1995-2001. Recipient Outstanding Vol. Volunteer Income Tax Assistance Program, 1995, 96, 98, 99, 2000, The Spirit of Am. Is In the Heart of Its Volunteers IRS, 1995, 96, 97, 99. Mem. Am. Assn. Law Librs., Am. Corrections Assn., Spl. Librs. Assn., Acctg. Aid Soc., Coun. of State Agy. Librs., Mich. Corrections Assn. Democrat. Roman Catholic. Avocations: coin and stamp collecting, biking, walking. Home and Office: PO Box 12 Saint Louis MI 48880-0012

NOVAK, THOMAS J. lawyer; b. Chgo., July 17, 1940; s. Edward W. and Margaret R. (Rocket) N.; children: Tricia, Amie, Brandi. BBA, Marquette U., 1964; JD, Loyola U., Chgo., 1967. Bar: Ariz. 1968, U.S. Dist. Ct. Ariz. 1968, U.S. Supreme Ct. 1972. Chief adminstrv. dep. Maricopa County, Phoenix, 1968-72; ct. commr. Maricopa County Superior Ct., Phoenix, 1973-77; ptnr. Sullivan & Novak, Phoenix, 1977-79; judge pro tempore Superior Ct. Ariz., 1978—; pvt. practice Phoenix, 1979—. Instr. Glendale (Ariz.) C.C., 1972-79; lectr. Ariz. State Bar, Phoenix, 1973—. Recipient Outstanding Svc. award Boy Scouts Am., 1978, Top Lawyers, Phoenix Mag., 1998. Mem. Ariz. State Bar Assn. (past chmn. family law com. 1972-73), Ariz. Dist. Atty. Assn. (charter pres. 1972-73). Avocation: bowling. Family and matrimonial. Office: 301 E Bethany Home Rd # 200 Phoenix AZ 85012-1263

NOVIKOFF, HAROLD STEPHEN, lawyer; b. N.Y.C., Apr. 5, 1951; s. Eugene Benjamin and Vivian (Hirsch) N.; m. Amy Pearl, Aug. 20, 1972; children: Sara Heather, Elyse Fana. AB, Cornell U., 1972; JD, Columbia U., 1975. Bar: N.Y. 1976, U.S. Dist. Ct. (so. dist.) N.Y. 1976. Ptnr. Wachtell, Lipton, Rosen & Katz, N.Y.C., 1975—. Mem. ABA, N.Y. State Bar Assn., Assn. Bar City N.Y. (bankruptcy and reorgn. com. 1995-99, chair 1999-2002), Nat. Bankruptcy Conf. Bankruptcy, Finance. Office: Wachtell Lipton Rosen Katz 51 W 52nd St Fl 29 New York NY 10019-6150 Business E-Mail: hsnovikoff@wlrk.com.

NOVOTNY, F. DOUGLAS, lawyer; b. Mineola, N.Y., Mar. 10, 1952; s. Frank Joseph and Eleanor Evans (Rose) N.; m. Norma R. Federici, Sept. 7, 1991; children: Nicholas, Christina, Alexander. BA cum laude, SUNY, Albany, 1974; postgrad., NYU, Hofstra U., C.W. Post U.; JD cum laude, Albany Law Sch., 1979. Bar: N.Y. 1980, U.S. Dist. Ct. (no. dist.) N.Y. 1980. Confidential law asst. Appellate Divsn. 3d Dept., Albany, 1979-80; ptnr. DeGraff, Foy, Conway, Holt-Harris & Mealey, Albany, 1980-91; pvt. practice Saratoga, N.Y., 1991-93; mng. atty. Law Offices of F. Douglas Novotny, 1993—; staff counsel Am. Internat. Group, Inc., 1993—. Mem. Albany County Arbitration Panel, 1984-88. Editor Albany Law Rev., 1978-79; contbr. articles to profl. jours. Mem. ATLA, Justinian Soc., Assn. Trial Lawyers Am., Capital Dist. Trial Lawyers Assn. Presbyterian. Federal civil litigation, State civil litigation. Home: 27 Mallard Lndg S Waterford NY 12188-1037

NOVOTNY, PATRICIA SUSAN, lawyer, educator; b. Omaha, Nov. 22, 1953; d. John Albert and Lauretta Lee (Waters) N. BA, Reed Coll., 1976; JD, U. Wash., 1983. Bar: Wash. 1983, U.S. Supreme Ct. 1995. Staff atty. Wash. Appellate Defender Assn., Seattle, 1989-91, 92-95, asst. dir., 1994-95; spl. counsel Wash. Defender Assn., Seattle, 1991-92; pvt. practice, Seattle, 1986-89, 95—. Lectr. U. Wash. Sch. Law, U. Wash. Women Studies, Seattle, 1996—; mem. legal com. N.W. Women's Law Ctr., Seattle, 1990—, chmn., 1995-97. Contbr. articles to profl. jours. Recipient Individual Artist award Seattle Arts Commn., 1990. Mem.: Wash. Appellate Lawyers Assn., Wash. Assn. Criminal Def. Lawyers. Avocations: creative writing, birdwatching, gardening, hiking, jazz. Appellate, Criminal, Family and matrimonial. Office: 3418 NE 65th St Ste A Seattle WA 98115-7341

NOWACKI, JAMES NELSON, lawyer; b. Columbus, Ohio, Sept. 12, 1947; s. Louis James and Betty Jane (Nelson) N.; m. Catherine Ann Holden, Aug. 1, 1970; children: Carrie, Anastasia, Emma. AB, Princeton U., 1969; JD, Yale U., 1973. Bar: Ill. 1973, N.Y. 1982, U.S. dist. Ct. (no. dist.) Ill. 1973, U.S. Ct. Appeals (7th cir.) 1978, U.S. Ct. Appeals (6th cir.) 1987, U.S. Supreme Ct. 1992. Assoc. Isham, Lincoln & Beale, Chgo., 1976-79; ptnr. Kirkland & Ellis, Chgo., 1980—. Mem. Winnetka Sch. Bd. Dist. 36, Ill. 1983-91, bd. pres., 1989-91; mem. New Trier Sch. Bd., 1997-99, pres., 1997-98. Harlan Fiske Stone prize Yale U., 1972. Mem. ABA (forum com. on constrn. industry, litigation sect.), Mid-Am. Club, Skokie Country Club. Federal civil litigation, State civil litigation, Construction. Home: 708 Prospect Ave Winnetka IL 60093-2320 Office: Kirkland & Ellis 200 E Randolph St Fl 60 Chicago IL 60601-6636

NOWAK, JOHN E. law educator; b. Chgo., Jan. 2, 1947; s. George Edward and Evelyn (Bucci) N.; m. Judith Johnson, June 1, 1968; children: John Edwin, Jeffrey Edward. AB, Marquette U., 1968; JD, U. Ill., 1971. Law clk. Supreme Ct. of Ill., Chgo., 1971-72; asst. prof. U. Ill., Urbana, 1972-75, assoc. prof., 1975-87, law prof., 1978—, grad. coll. faculty, 1982—, Baum prof. Law, 1993—. Chmn. Constl. Law Sch. Sect.; faculty rep. Big Ten Intercollegiate Conf., Schaumburg, 1981—91; vis. prof. law U. Mich., Ann Arbor, 1985; Lee disting. vis. prof. Coll. William and Mary, 1993; Williams vis. prof. law U. Richmond, 2003. Co-author: Constitutional Law, 6th edit. 2000, Treatise on Constitutional Law, 1986, 3d edit., 1999, Story's Commentaries on the Constitution, 1987. Scholar-in-Residence, U. of Ariz., Tucson, 1985, 87. Mem. Assn. of Am. Law Schs. (chmn. constl. law sect., accreditation com. 1980-88), Nat. Collegiate Athletic Assn. (mem. infractions com. 1987—), Am. Law Inst., Am. Bar Assn., Ill. Bar Assn., Order of the Coif (Triennial Book award com.). Roman Catholic. Home: 1701 Mayfair Rd Champaign IL 61821-5522 Office: U Ill Coll Law 504 E Pennsylvania Ave Champaign IL 61820-6909

NOWLIN, JAMES ROBERTSON, federal judge; b. San Antonio, Nov. 21, 1937; s. William Forney and Jeannette (Robertson) N. BA, Trinity U., 1959, MA, 1962; JD, U. Tex., Austin, 1963. Bar: Tex. 1963, Colo. 1993, U.S. Dist. Ct. D.C. 1966, U.S. Ct. Claims 1969, U.S. Supreme Ct. 1969, U.S. Dist. Ct. (we. dist.) Tex. 1971. Assoc. Kelso, Locke, & King, San Antonio, 1963-65; assoc. Kelso, Locke & Lepick, San Antonio, 1966-69; legal counsel U.S. Senate, Washington, 1965-66; propr. Law Offices James R. Nowlin, San Antonio, 1969-81; mem. Tex. Ho. of Reps., Austin, 1967-71, 73-81; judge U.S. Dist. Ct. for Western Dist. Tex., Austin, 1981-99, chief judge, 2000—03, sr. judge, 2003—. Instr. Am. govt. and history San Antonio Coll., 1964-65, 71-73. Capt. U.S. Army, 1959-60, USAR, 1960-68. Fellow State Bar Found (life); mem. San Antonio Bar Assn., Colo. Bar Assn. Republican. Presbyterian. Avocations: pilot, skiing, hiking, jogging. Office: US Courthouse 200 W 8th St Austin TX 78701-2325 Fax: 512-916-5680.

NUCCIARONE, A. PATRICK, lawyer; b. Denville, N.J., Aug. 29, 1947; s. H. Joseph and Alice Marie (McGuirk) N. BA, U. So. Calif., 1969; JD, George Washington U., 1973. Bar: N.J. 1973, N.Y. 1981, Vt. 1984, U.S. Dist. Ct. N.J. 1973, U.S. Dist. Ct. (no. dist.) Ohio 1986, U.S. Ct. Appeals (3d cir.) 1976, U.S. Supreme Ct. 1995. Com. staff asst. U.S. House of Reps., Washington, 1971-72; staff asst. Exec. Office of Pres. of U.S., Washington, 1972-73; asst. U.S. Atty. Office of U.S. Atty., Newark, 1974-83, chief environ. sect., 1978-83; spl. asst. Atty. Gen. Office of Atty. Gen., Montpelier, Vt., 1984; ptnr. Hannoch Weisman, Roseland, N.J., 1984-91, Dechert, Price & Rhoads, Princeton, N.J., 1991-95. Co-chmn. N.J. Hazardous Task Force, Trenton, 1978-83; supr. Rutgers U. Environ. Law Clinic, Newark, 1978-83; mem. Environ. Expn. Adv. Bd., Trenton, 1985-90; chmn. ann. seminar on impacts of environ. law bus. trans. Practicing Law Inst., 1986-92, mem. adv. com. on environ. law, 1986—; mem. faculty NYU Summer Inst. on Environ. Law, 1991-94. Contbr. articles to profl. jours. Recipient Outstanding Service award U.S. Dept. Justice, Washington, 1980, Spl. Achievement awards U.S. Dept. Justice, 1978, 79, Presdl. Citation for Excellent Performance Exec. Office of Pres., Washington, 1973. Mem. ABA (vice chmn. sect. on natural resources, energy and environ. law 1987-93), N.J. State Bar Assn. (bd. dirs. environ. law sect. 1985-89). Criminal, Environmental. Office: 1540 Hwy 138 Ste 107 Wall NJ 07719-3766

NUDING, DORIS LEONA, law librarian, legal assistant, researcher; b. Chgo., Dec. 26, 1949; d. Donald Harold and Leona Elvira (Fremgen) Thompson; m. William E. Nuding Jr., July 13, 1949; children: Tracy, Kelly. Cert. legal asst., Roosevelt U., 1987. Lic. real estate assoc. Clk./typist Continental Ill. Nat. Bank, Chgo., 1968-70; clk./typist Personal Trust Banking Attys. W. Clement & Jesse Stone Found., 1972-74; sec., asst. to dir. pub., dir. achievment motivation Nat. Com. for Prevention of Child Abuse, Chgo., 1974-83; sales coord. Arnstein & Lehr, Chgo., 1981-91; legal asst., sec. Querry & Harrow, Chgo., 1991—; real estate assoc. Barid & Warner, 2003. Mem. Am. Assn. Law Librs., Chgo. Assn. Law Librs., Solo Libr. Soc., Am. Legion Aux. (pres. 1995-98, sec. 1999-2003). Avocations: reading, computers, grandchildren. Office: 175 W Jackson Blvd Ste 1600 Chicago IL 60604-2827 E-mail: dnuding@querrey.com., dnuding1@juno.com.

NUERNBERG, WILLIAM R(ICHARD), lawyer; b. Pitts., July 7, 1946; s. William W. and Frances (Hubler) N. BA cum laude, Denison U., 1968; JD cum laude, U. Mich., 1971. Bar: Pa. 1971, U.S. Dist.Ct. (we. dist.) Pa. 1971, Fla. 1995. Mem. Eckert Seamans Cherin & Mellott LLC, 1981-98; ptnr. Duane Morris LLP, Miami, 1999—. Bd. govs. Big Bros. Big Sisters Greater Miami. Pitt fellow U. Pitts. Sch. Bus., 1987-88. Mem. ABA, Pa. Bar Assn., Fla. Bar Assn., Miami City Club. Corporate, general, Mergers and acquisitions, Securities. Office: Duane Morris LLP 200 S Biscayne Blvd Ste 3400 Miami FL 33131-2318

NUGEE, EDWARD GEORGE, Queen's counsel; b. Godalming, Surrey, U.K., Aug. 9, 1928; s. George Travers Nugee and Violet Mary Richards; m. Rachel Elizabeth Makower, Dec. 1, 1955; children: John Francis, Christopher George, Andrew James, Richard Edward. BA with 1st class honors jurisprudence, Oxford U., 1952, MA, 1956. Barrister-at-law, 1955. Pvt. practice, London, 1955—; Queen's counsel, 1977—; dep. high ct. judge Supreme Ct. Eng. and Wales, London, 1982-97. Mem., vice chmn. and chmn. bd. studies Coun. Legal Edn. Eng., 1967-90; mem. Lord Chancellor's Law Reform Com., Eng., 1973—; mem., chmn. Common Professional Edn. Bd., Eng., 1976-90. Author: Nathan on Charities Act 1960, 1962; editor: Halsbury's Laws of England, Landlord and Tenant, 3d edit., 1958, Real Property, 3d edit., 1960, 4th edit., 1982, reissue, 1998, others. Ch. commr. Ch. of Eng., 1989—2001; trustee Lambeth Palace Libr., 1999—2001; chmn. Govt. Com. on Mgmt. of Blocks of Flats, England and Wales, 1984—85; mem. legal adv. commn. Gen. Synod of the Ch. of Eng., 2001—; mem. coun. Radley Coll., 1975—95. Decorated Territorial Decoration, Her Majesty the Queen, 1964; Eldon Law scholar Oxford U., 1953. Mem. Bar of Eng. and Wales (gen. coun. 1962-66), The Inst. (pres. 1986-87), Inner Temple (treas. 1996). Pension, profit-sharing, and employee benefits, Probate (including wills, trusts), Finance, Landlord-tenant, Property, real (including real estate development, water). Home: 10 Heath Hurst Rd London NW3 2RX England Office: Wilberforce Chambers 8 New Square, Lincoln's Inn London WC2A 3QP England E-mail: enugee@wilberforce.co.uk.

NUGENT, LORI S. lawyer; b. Peoria, Ill., Apr. 24, 1962; d. Walter Leonard and Margery (Frost) Meyer; m. Shane Vincent Nugent, June 14, 1986; children: Justine Nicole, Cole Tyler. BA in Polit. Sci. cum laude, Knox Coll., 1984; JD, Northwestern U., Chgo., 1987. Bar: Ill. 1987, U.S. Dist. Ct. (no. dist.) Ill. 1988, U.S. Ct. Appeals (7th cir.) 1995. Assoc. Peterson & Ross, Chgo., 1987-94, Blatt, Hammesfahr & Eaton, Chgo., 1994, ptnr., chmn. nat. punitive damages practice, 1994-2000; ptnr. Cozen O'Connor, Chgo., 2000—. Co-author: Punitive Damages: A Guide to the Insurability of Punitive Damages in the United States and Its Territories, 1988, Punitive Damages: A State-by-State Guide to Law and Practice, 1991, 2d edit., 2002, 3d edit., 2003, Japanese edit., 1995; contbr. articles to law jours. Alternative dispute resolution, Insurance. Office: Cozen O'Connor Ste 1500 222 S Riverside Plz Chicago IL 60606-6000 E-mail: lnugent@cozen.com.

NULL, WILLIAM SETH, lawyer; b. N.Y.C., Apr. 15, 1954; s. Douglas P. Null and Barbara M. (Black) Schacker; m. Lauren E. Thaler, May 10, 1981; children: Danielle, Evan. BA, Hampshire Coll., 1977; JD, Yeshiva U., 1980. Bar: N.Y. 1981, U.S. Dist. Ct. (ea. and so. dists.) N.Y. 1981, U.S. Supreme Ct. 1987. With Null & Null, P.C., Garden City, N.Y., 1980-83, Kraver & Martin, N.Y.C., 1983-85, Cuddy & Feder LLP (now Cuddy & Feder & Worby LLP), White Plains, NY, 1985—99, mng. ptnr., 1999—. Dir. The Housing Partnership, Elmsford, NY, 1995—2001, White Plains Bridge of Friendship Found., 1994—, Juvenile Diabetes Rsch. Found. Internat., 1998—, Gilda's Club Westchester, 2001—, The Briarcliff Manor Edn. Found., 2001—, White Plains Hosp. Ctr., 2002—. Land use and zoning (including planning), General civil litigation, Property, real (including real estate development, water). Office: Cuddy & Feder & Worby LLP 90 Maple Ave White Plains NY 10601-5105 E-mail: wnull@cfwlaw.com.

NUNCIO, PAULO, lawyer; b. Lisbon, Jan. 23, 1968; s. Luis and Teresa Nuncio; m. Marta Roque Nuncio, Oct. 9, 1993; children: Antonio, Bernardo, Marin. Degree in law, U. Cat. Portuguese, 1991. Assoc. Morias Leitao J. Galvao Teles, Funehal, Portugal, 1997—2001, sr. assoc. Lisbon, 2001—. Mem.: Internat. Bar Assn., Portuguese Tax Assn., Portuguese Bar Assn. Avocations: tennis, golf, soccer, rugby . Corporate taxation, Taxation, general, Estate taxation. Office: Morais Leitao J Galvao TEles Rua Castilho N 75 1 1250-068 Lisbon Portugal Fax: 352 21 3817490. E-mail: plnuncio@mlgt.pt.

NUNES, FRANK M. lawyer; b. Fresno, Calif., Oct. 25, 1968; s. Marvin Frank and Phyllis Mae Nunes; m. Sharon L. Nunes, July 20, 1996. BS, Calif. State U., Fresno, 1991; JD, San Joaquin Coll. Law, Fresno, 1994. Bar: Calif. 1995, U.S. Dist. Ct. (ea. dist.) Calif. 1995. Dep. dist. atty. Tulare County Dist. Atty., Visalia, Calif., 1995-97; assoc. Marderosian, Oren & Paboojian, Fresno, 1997-99; Fresno county counsel, 1999—2002; assoc. David J. Wells & Assocs., Fresno, 2002—. Mem. Fresno County Young Lawyers, Delta Theta Phi, Alpha Gamma Rho (pres. 1990), Alpha Zeta. Roman Catholic. State civil litigation, Personal injury (including property damage), Property, real (including real estate development, water). Office: David J Wells & Assocs 7576 N Ingram Ste 104 Fresno CA 93711 Office Fax: 559-434-1750. E-mail: frank_nunes@farmersinsurance.com.

NUNES, MORRIS A. lawyer; b. Oceanside, N.Y., Apr. 9, 1949; s. Myron A. and Betty Ann (Ecoff) Nunes; m. Jane S. Chargar, Aug. 30, 1970 (dec. Aug. 2002); 2 children. BA, BS, U. Pa., 1970; JD, Georgetown U., 1975. Bar: Va. 1975, D.C. 1976. Auditor Arthur Young & Co. CPAs, Boston, 1970; controller Sanitary Group, Inc., West Haven, Conn., 1970-72; securities analyst Donatelli, Rudolph & Schoen, Washington, 1972-74; group controller Potomac Electric Power Co., Washington, 1974-77; pvt. practice Falls Church, Va., 1977—. Adj. prof. Cath. U. Law Sch., 1991—, Georgetown U. Law Sch., 1999—, Georgetown MBA program, 2001—; arbitrator Am. Arbitration Assn., Washington, 1980—87; bus. appraiser, pres. Net Worth, Inc., 1988—; hearing officer Va. Supreme Ct., 1996—2000; bus. adv. bd. James Monroe Bank, 1998—2001. Author: Operational Cash Flow, 1982, Balance Sheet Mgmt., 1987, The Right Price for Your Business, 1988; co-author: Property Logbook, 1985, Basic Legal Forms for Business, 1989; contbr. Apptd. mem. Va. State Bd. Profl. and Occupl. Regulations, 1995—, chmn., 1997—; mem. Fairfax County Edn. Adv. Bd., 1983—87; del. Rep. State Conv., 1993, 1994. Mem.: Internat. Churchill Soc., Nat. Fedn. Ind. Bus., Nat. Assn. Corp. Dirs., Am. Soc. Appraisers, Washington Ind. Writers, D.C. Bar Assn., Va. State Bar Assn., Wharton Club of D.C., Sigma Chi, Alpha Lit. and Philosophy Soc. Avocations: racquetball, chess, wargames, music appreciation, squash. Commercial, contracts (including sales of goods; commercial financing), Corporate, general, Property, real (including real estate development, water). Office: 7247 Lee Hwy Falls Church VA 22046-3710 E-mail: man.apc@verizon.net.

NÚÑEZ MÜLLER, MARCO A. lawyer; b. Hamburg, Germany, Dec. 18, 1960; s. Diego A. Núñez Villarejo and Gefion R. Müller de Núñez; m. Chantal U. Núñez Müller, Nov. 13, 2000; 1 child, Rafael. LLM, Columbia U., 1992; Dr. iur., Hamburg U., 1993. Bar: Hamburg 1991. Rsch. asst. Hamburg U., 1987—90; clk. Hamburg Supreme Ct., 1988—91; assoc. Bruckhaus, Hamburg, 1993—94, Schön Nolte, Brussels, 1994—98, ptnr., 1998—99, Gaedertz, Hamburg, 1999—2001, Latham & Watkins, Hamburg, 2001—, Brussels, 2001—. Author: Nationality of Ships, 1993. Antitrust, Mergers and acquisitions. Office: Latham & Watkins Wartburgstr 50 20354 Hamburg Germany

NUNNALLY, KNOX DILLON, lawyer; b. Haynesville, La., Jan. 26, 1943; s. Miles Dillon and Linnie Mat (Knox) Nunnally; m. Kay Clyde Webb; 1 child, Kevin Knox. BBA, U. Tex., 1965, LLB, 1968. Bar: Tex. 1968, U.S. Dist. Ct. (ea. dist.) : Tex. 1970, U.S. Dist. Ct. (so. dist.) : Tex. 1969, U.S. Dist. Ct. (we. dist.) : Tex. 1976, U.S. Ct. Appeals (5th cir.): 1978, Diplomate Tex. Bd. Legal Specialization:. Ptnr. Vinson & Elkins LLP, Houston, 1976—. Mem.: ABA, Houston Bar Assn., Tex. Bar Assn., Am. Coll. Trial Lawyers. Federal civil litigation, State civil litigation, Personal injury (including property damage). Home: 3421 Meadow Lake Ln Houston TX 77027-4106 Office: Vinson & Elkins LLP 1001 Fannin St Ste 2300 Houston TX 77002-6760

NUSS, LAWTON R. judge; b. Salina, Kans., Dec. 30, 1952; m. Barbara Nuss; 5 children. BA in English and History, U. Kans., 1975, JD, 1982. With Clark Mize & Linville law firm, 1982; justice Kans. Supreme Ct., Topeka, 2002—. Mediator U.S. Dist. Ct. (Kans.). Combat engring. officer USMC. Mem.: Kans. Assn. Def. Counsel (pres.), Kans. Bar Assn. (chmn. bd. editors jour.). Office: Kans Jud Ctr 301 W 10th Topeka KS 66612-1507

NUSSBAUM, BERNARD J. lawyer; b. Berlin, Mar. 11, 1931; came to U.S., 1936; s. William and Lotte (Frankfurther) N.; m. Jean Beverly Enzer, Sept. 4, 1956; children— Charles, Peter, Andrew AB, Knox Coll., 1948-52; JD, U. Chgo., 1955. Assoc. Proskauer Rose Goetz & Mendelsohn, N.Y.C., 1955-56; assoc. Sonnenschein Nath & Rosenthal, Chgo., 1959-65, sr. ptnr., 1965—. Master bencher Am. Inns of Ct., 1986—; appointed to com. on civility 7th cir. U.S. Ct. Appeals, 1989-92. Editor U. Chgo. Law Rev., 1954-55; mem. nat. adv. bd. BNA Civil Trial Man., 1985— ; contbr. articles to profl. jours. Mem. vis. com. U. Chgo. Law Sch., 1977-83. Served to capt. U.S. Army, 1956-59 Fellow Am. Bar Found., Ill. Bar Found. (charter); mem. ABA, Chgo. Bar Assn. (chmn. com. on fed. civil procedure 1968-69, mem. com. on judiciary 1970-76), Ill. Bar Assn. (council Antitrust sect. 1971-73, assembly del. 1972-80), U. Chgo. Law Sch. Nat. Alumni Assn. (pres. 1981-83). Avocations: skiing; cycling. Federal civil litigation, State civil litigation. Office: Sonnenschein Nath & Rosenthal 8000 Sears Tower 233 S Wacker Dr Ste 8000 Chicago IL 60606-6491

NUTTER, ROBERT HEINRICH, lawyer; b. Little Rock, Dec. 23, 1939; s. Robert Alspaugh and Vera (Henry) N.; m. Linda Frances Crunk, June 18, 1960; children: Amy Lynne, Nathan Brook. BS in Pharmacy, U. Fla., 1963; JD, Stetson U., 1970. Bar: Fla. 1970, U.S. Dist. Ct. (mid. dist.) Fla. 1974, U.S. Dist. Ct. Appeals (11th cir.) 1981, U.S. Ct. Appeals (5th cir.), U.S. Supreme Ct. 1978. Pharmacist Walgreen Drug Co., Tampa, Fla., 1964-67; asst. county solicitor Hillsborough County, Tampa, Fla., 1970-73; asst. state's atty. for Hillsborough County, State of Fla., 1973-75; chief asst. spl. prosecutor statewide grand jury, 1974-75; ptnr. Ferlita, Nutter & Rosello, P.A., Tampa, 1975—. Mem. Fla. Bar, Hillsborough County Bar Assn. (grievance com. 1978-81), Assn. Trial Lawyers Am., Acad. Fla. Trial Lawyers, Hillsborough Pharm. Assn. (pres. 1975), Masons. Republican. Avocations: hunting, fishing, reading, family. General civil litigation, Criminal, Personal injury (including property damage). Office: Ferlita Nutter & Rosello PA 610 W Azeele St Tampa FL 33606-2206 Fax: (813) 254-6214.

NUZUM, ROBERT WESTON, lawyer; b. Evanston, Ill., Dec. 11, 1952; s. John Weston and Janet Marie (Talbot) N.; m. Julia Ann Abadie, Sept. 16, 1983. BS in Fin., La. State U., 1974, JD, 1977; LLM in Taxation, N.Y.U., 1978. Bar: La. 1977, D.C. 1979. Assoc. Office Chief Counsel, Washington, 1978-81, Jones, Walker, Waechter, Poitevent, Carrere & Denegre, New Orleans, 1981-85; ptnr. Jones, Walker, Waechter, Poitevent, Carrere & Denegre, New Orleans, 1985-88, Deutsch, Kerrigan & Stiles, New Orleans, 1988-89, Phelps Dunbar, L.L.P. and predecessor firm, New Orleans, 1989—2003. Prof. law, state and local taxation Tulane U. Sch. Law, New Orleans, 1998—. Editor La. Law Rev., 1977; contbr. articles to profl. jours.

Wallace scholar N.Y.U., 1978. Mem.: Tulane Tax Inst. (planning com. 1993—, tax specialization adv. commn.), New Orleans Bar Assn. (chmn. tax sect. 2001—), La. Bar Assn. (program chmn. tax sect. 1992—93, sec.-treas. 1993—94, vice chmn. 1994—95, chmn. 1995—96), Order of Coif. Republican. Roman Catholic. Avocations: golf, reading, fishing. Corporate taxation, Taxation, general, State and local taxation. Office: Law Offices Robert W Nuzum & Assocs LLC 474 Metainie Rd Ste 201 Metairie LA 70005-4313 Office Fax: 504-833-1037. Business E-Mail: law@robertnuzum.com. E-mail: nuzumr@bellsouth.net.

NWELE, KENNETH F. lawyer, bank executive; b. Abakaliki, Nigeria, Nov. 23, 1962; s. Augistine B. and Josephine Nwokocha Nwele; m. Blessing R.S. Nwele, May 30, 1998; 1 child, Kenneth Chukwudi Akanya. BSc in Acctg., S.E. Mo. State U., 1985; MBA in Fin., St. John's U., 1989; JD, Seton Hall U., 1999. CPA NY; bar: NY 2000, NJ 2000. Sr. auditor Citibank/Citigroup, N.Y.C., 1989—93; asst. treas. Natwest Bank, Jersey City, 1993—94; v.p. J.P. Morgan Chase Bank, N.Y.C., 1994—. Mem.: AICPA, ATLA, ABA, NY County Lawyers' Assn. Avocations: reading, travel, soccer. Personal injury (including property damage), Property, real (including real estate development, water), Immigration, naturalization, and customs. Home: PO Box 24105 2472 JFK Blvd #5B Jersey City NJ 07304

NYCE, JOHN DANIEL, lawyer; b. York, Pa., Sept. 7, 1947; s. Harry Lincoln and Dorothy (Wagner) Nyce; m. Deborah Dvorak; children: Joshua David, Laura Kimberly. BA, SUNY, Buffalo, 1970; JD, U. Miami, 1973. Bar: Fla. 1973, U.S. District Ct. (so. dist.) Fla. 1973, U.S. Dist. Ct. (middle dist.), Fla. 1973, U.S. Ct. Appeals (5th and 11th cirs.) 1986, U.S. Supreme Ct. 1984. Assoc. Ralph P. Douglas, Pompano Beach, Fla., 1974, Coleman, Leonard & Morrison, Ft. Lauderdale, Fla., 1975-78; ptnr. Nyce and Smith, Ft. Lauderdale, 1979; sole practice Ft. Lauderdale, 1980—. Adj. prof. bus. law, inernat. bus. law and orgn. Lynn U., Boca Raton, Fla., 2001—. Author books in field; author: Proof of God's Existence in the Seven C's and Christian Handbook of Lists, 2002. Mem. Social Register Ft. Lauderdale; mem. Broward County Right to Life, Operation Rescue, South Fla., Beach Street Aid to the Homeless of Ft. Lauderdale, Legis. Adv. Coun. on Adoptions, Nat. Right to Life Com., Inc.; founder, past pres., bd. dirs. Broward County Christian Lawyers Assn.; mem. Christian Legal Soc.; mem. exec. com. Broward County Rep. Party; Broward Citizens bd. U. Miami; mem. Conservative Caucus of Broward County; bd. dirs. Shepherd Care Ministries, Inc.; co-founder Christian Adoption Svcs. of Shepherd Care Ministries, Inc.; cert. trainer Evangelism Explosion III Internat., Inc.; legal counsel and evangelism trainer Coral Ridge Presbybn. Ch., Christ the Rock Cmty. Ch., First Bapt. Ch., West Hollywood, Fla., Calvary Chapel of Ft. Lauderdale Ch.; bd. dirs. Alliance for Responsible Growth, Inc. Mem.: Nat. Acad. Elder Law Attys., Attys. Title Ins. Fund, S.D. Rifle and Hunting Assn., U. Miami Alumni Assn., SUNY Buffalo Alumni Assn., Holiday Park Tennis Ctr., U.S. Tennis Assn., U. Miami Hurricane Club, Sports Fitness Clin., Palm Aire Golf and Country Club. Republican. Presbyterian. Estate planning, Property, real (including real estate development, water), Family and matrimonial. Office: PO Box 11071 Fort Lauderdale FL 33339-1071 E-mail: miamijd73@aol.com.

NYCUM, SUSAN HUBBELL, lawyer; BA, Ohio Wesleyan U., 1956; JD, Duquesne U., 1960; postgrad., Stanford U. Bar: Pa. 1962, U.S. Supreme Ct. 1967, Calif. 1974. Sole practice law, Pitts., 1962-65; designer, adminstr. legal rsch. sys. U. Pitts., Aspen Sys. Corp., Pitts., 1965-68; mgr. ops. Computer Ctr., Carnegie Mellon U., Pitts., 1968-69; dir. computer facility Computer Ctr., Stanford U., Calif., 1969-72, Stanford Law and Computer fellow, 1972-73; cons. in computers and law, 1973-74; sr. assoc. MacLeod, Fuller, Muir & Godwin, Los Altos, Los Angeles and London, 1974-75; ptnr. Chickering & Gregory, San Francisco, 1975-80; ptnr.-in-charge high tech. group Gaston Snow & Ely Bartlett, Boston, NYC, Phoenix, San Francisco, Calif., 1980-86; mng. ptnr. Palo Alto office Kadison, Pfaelzer, Woodard, Quinn & Rossi, Los Angeles, Washington, Newport Beach, Palo Alto, Calif., 1986-87; sr. ptnr., chmn. U.S. intellectual property/info. tech. practice group Baker & McKenzie, Palo Alto, 1987—, mem. U.S. leadership team, 1987-97, mem. Asia Pacific regional coun., 1995—. Founder Tech. Disputes Resolution Svcs., Inc., 2002—; trustee EDUCOM, 1978-81; mem. adv. com. for high tech. Ariz. State U. Law Sch., Santa Clara U. Law Sch., Stanford Law Sch., U. So. Calif. Law Ctr., law sch. Harvard U., U. Calif.; U.S. State Dept. del. OECD Conf. on Nat. Vulnerabilities, Spain, 1981; invited speaker Telecom, Geneva, 1983; lectr. N.Y. Law Jour., 1975—, Law & Bus., 1975—, Practicing Law Inst., 1975—; chmn. Office of Tech. Assessment Task Force on Nat. Info. Sys., 1979-80. Author:(with Bigelow) Your Computer and the Law, 1975, (with Bosworth) Legal Protection for Software, 1985, (with Collins and Gilbert) Women Leading, 1987; contbr. monographs, articles to profl. publs. Fellow Am. Bar Found.; mem. Town of Portola Valley Open Space Acquisition Com., Calif., 1977; mem. Jr. League of Palo Alto, chmn. evening div., 1975-76 NSF and Dept. Justice grantee for studies on computer abuse, 1972— Fellow Am. Bar Found., Assn. Computer Machinery (mem. at large of coun. 1976-80, nat. lectr. 1977—, chmn. standing com. on legal issues 1975—, mem. blue ribbon com. on rationalization of internat. propr. rights protection on info. processing devel. in the '90s 1990—), Coll. Law Practice Mgmt. (trustee 2002—); mem. ABA (chmn. sect. on sci. and tech. 1979-80), Computer Law Assn. (v.p. 1983-85, pres. 1986—, bd. dirs. 1975—), Calif. State Bar Assn. (founder first chmn. econs. of law sect., vice chmn. law and computers com.), Internat. Bar Assn. (U.S. mem. computer com. of corps. sect.), Nat. Conf. Lawyers and Scientists (rep. ABA), Strategic Forum on Intellectual Property Issues in Software of NAS, Internat. Coun. for Computer Comm. (gov. 1998). Commercial, contracts (including sales of goods; commercial financing), Computer, Trademark and copyright. Home: 35 Granada Ct Portola Valley CA 94028-7736 Office: Baker & McKenzie PO Box 60309 Palo Alto CA 94306-0309

NYE, W. MARCUS W. lawyer; b. N.Y.C., Aug. 3, 1945; s. Walter R. and Nora (McLaren) N.; m. Eva Johnson; children: Robbie, Stephanie, Philip, Jennifer. BA, Harvard U., 1967; JD, U. Idaho, 1974. Bar: Idaho 1974, U.S. Dist. Ct. Idaho 1974, U.S. Ct. Appeals (9th cir.) 1980; lic. pilot. Ptnr. Racine, Olson, Nye, Budge & Bailey, Pocatello, Idaho, 1974—. Vis. prof. law U. Idaho, Moscow, 1984; adj. prof. Coll. Engring. Idaho State U., 1993-96; pres. Idaho State U. Found., U. Idaho Coll. Law Found. Commr., Idaho State Centennial Found., 1985-90. Recipient Alumni Svc. award U. Idaho, 1988. Fellow ABA (bd. govs. 1997-2000), Am. Bar Found. (stat. chmn. 1992-95); mem. Am. Bd. Trial Advs. (nat. bd. dirs.), Am. Coll. Trial Lawyers, Idaho State Bar Assn. (pres. 1987-88), Idaho Def. Counsel Assn. (pres. 1982), 6th Dist. Bar Assn. (pres. 1982). Avocation: flying. General civil litigation, Product liability. Home: 173 S 15th Ave Pocatello ID 83201-4056 Office: Racine Olson Nye Budge & Bailey PO Box 1391 Pocatello ID 83204-1391

NYS, JOHN NIKKI, lawyer; b. Duluth, Minn., May 3, 1948; s. Leslie Leo and Kathleen Cecilia (Beaudin) N.; m. Sandra Ann Stephenson, Aug. 20, 1977; 1 child, John Stephenson. BA, Dartmouth Coll., 1970; JD, Stanford U., 1973. Bar: Minn. 1973, U.S. Dist. Ct. Minn. 1973, U.S. Ct. Appeals (8th cir.) 1984, U.S. Dist. Ct. (we. dist.) Wis. 1985, Wis. 1986. Ptnr. Johnson, Killen & Seiler, Duluth, 1973—. Pres., treas., bd. dirs. Duluth Regional Care Ctr., 1979-85; v.p., bd. dirs. Western Community Coun., 1980-86; cubmaster Lake Superior coun. Boy Scouts Am., 1987-90; mem. state cen. com. Dem. Farmer Labor Party, 1976-78; pres., bd. dirs. Morgan Park Smithville Community Club, 1978-85. Mem. ABA, Duluth Young Lawyers (pres. 1974-75), Minn. State Bar Assn. (chmn. lawyers referral com. 1986-88, bd. govs. 1990-98, pres. 1996-97), 11th Dist. Bar Assn. (pres. 1989-90). Lutheran. Banking, Bankruptcy, Corporate, general. Office: Johnson Killen & Seiler 811 Wells Fargo Ctr Duluth MN 55808 E-mail: jnys@duluthlaw.com.

OAKES, JAMES L. federal judge; b. Springfield, Ill., Feb. 21, 1924; m. Evelena S. Kenworthy, Dec. 29, 1973 (dec. Oct. 1997); m. Mara A. Williams, Jan. 1, 1999; m. Rosalyn Landon, Oct. 2, 1945; 3 children. AB, Harvard Coll., 1945; LLB, Harvard U. Law Sch., 1947; LLD, New Eng. Coll., 1976, Suffolk U., 1980, Vt. Law Sch., 1995. Bar: Calif. 1949, Vt. 1950. Pvt. practice, Brattleboro, Vt.; spl. counsel Vt. Pub. Svc. Commn., 1959—60; counsel Vt. Statutory Revision Commn., 1957—60; mem. Vt. Senate, 1961—65; atty. gen. Vt., 1967—69; U.S. dist. judge, 1970—71; judge U.S. Ct. Appeals 2d Cir., Brattleboro, 1971—, chief judge, 1989—92. Adj. faculty Duke U. Law Sch., 1985—96, Iowa U. Coll. Law, 1993—97. Office: US Ct Appeals PO Box 696 Brattleboro VT 05302-0696

OAKLEY, JOEL NEESE, lawyer; b. Greensboro, N.C., Jan. 30, 1960; s. Julius H. Oakley and Yvonne P. Berkerly; m. Nancy Calvin, Nov. 25, 1989; 1 child, Erica Danielle. BA, Appalachain State, 1982; JD summa cum laude, N.C. Ctrl. Sch. Law, 1986. Bar: N.C. 1986, U.S. Dist. Ct. (mid. dist.) N.C. 1986. Atty. N.C. Bar, Greensboro, 1986—. Mem. Greensboro Criminal Def. Lawyers Assn. (bd. dirs. 1993-2002, pres. 1994-95, 2002-03), Guilford Inns Ct., Triad Rugby Dogs. Democrat. Avocation: rugby. Criminal. Office: 322 S Eugene St Greensboro NC 27401-2322

OAKLEY, MARY ANN BRYANT, lawyer; b. Buckhannon, W.Va., June 22, 1940; d. Hubert Herndon and Mary F. (Deeds) Bryant; m. Godfrey P. Oakley, Jr., Sept. 2, 1961; children: Martha, Susan, Robert. AB, Duke U., 1962; MA, Emory U., 1970, JD, 1974. Tchr. Winston-Salem/Forsyth County Schs., N.C., 1961-65; assoc. Margie Pitts Hames, Atlanta, 1974-80; ptnr. Stagg Hoy & Oakley, Atlanta, 1980-83, Oakley & Bonner, Atlanta, 1984-90; pvt. practice, 1990-96; ptnr. Holland & Knight LLP, Atlanta, 1996—. Adj. prof. trial practice Ga. State U., 1986-95; adj. prof. pretrial Emory U. Law Sch., 1991, 95; bd. dirs. Nat. Employment Lawyers Assn., 1989-94; founding coord. NELA, Ga.; mem. Ga. Supreme Ct. Commn. on Racial and Ethnic Bias, 1994-95; mem. Ga. Bd. Bar Examineres, 1990-94, chmn., 1994. Author: Elizabeth Cady Stanton, 1972; mem. editl. rev. bd.: The Ga. Labor Letter, 1997—2001, notes and comments editor: Emory Law Jour., 1973—74; contbr. articles to law jours. Bd. dirs. Atlanta Met. YWCA, 1975-79, 1st v.p., 1978-79; mem. Leadership Atlanta, 1979; bd. dirs. Ga. chpt. ACLU, 1981-83, Holland & Knight Charitable Found., 2002—, Ga. Legal Svcs. Program, 1991-98; trustee Unitarian Universalist Congregation Atlanta, 1977-80, pres., 1979-80, mem. Unitarian Universalist Commn. Appraisal, 1980-85; bd. dirs. Unitarian Universalist Service Com., 1984-90, v.p., 1986-88, pres., 1988-90. Nat. Merit scholar, 1958. Fellow: Ga. Bar Found., Am. Bar Found.; mem.: ABA, Gate City Bar Assn., Ga. State Bar Disciplinary Bd. (investigative panel 1985—88, chmn. 1987—88), Ga. Assn. Women Lawyers (Kathleen Kessler award 1998), Lawyers Club Atlanta, Atlanta Bar Assn., State Bar Ga. (chmn. individual rights sect. 1979—81, Disting. Svc. award 1998, H. Sol Clark Pro Bono award 1996), Am. Judicature Soc., Order of Coif, Phi Beta Kappa, Bleckley Inn of Ct. (pres. 1996—99). Labor (including EEOC, Fair Labor Standards Act, labor-management relations, NLRB, OSHA), Alternative dispute resolution, Appellate. Home: 2224 Kodiak Dr NE Atlanta GA 30345-4152 Office: 1201 W Peachtree St 1 Atlantic Ctr Ste 2000 Atlanta GA 30309-3400

OAKLEY, ROBERT LOUIS, law librarian, educator; b. N.Y.C., Nov. 6, 1945; s. Bert Tuttle Oakley and Allese (Duffin) Vestigo; m. Madeleine Cohen, Aug. 13, 1971 (div. 2002); children: Esther Shulamit, Daniel Isaac-Meir. BA, Cornell U., 1968; MLS, Syracuse U., 1972; JD, Cornell U., 1976. Bar: N.Y. 1977, U.S. Dist. Ct. (no. dist.) N.Y. 1977. Assoc. dir. law libr. Cornell U., Ithaca, N.Y., 1976-79; dir. law libr., assoc. prof. Boston U. Law, 1979-82, Georgetown U., Washington, 1982-87, dir. law libr., prof., 1987—. Contbr. articles to profl. jours. Mem. Libr. of Congress, mem. Network Adv. Com., 1986-92, 95—; adv. nat. commn. on Preservation and Access, 1988-94; bd. dirs. Montgomery County (Md.) Pub. Librs., 1988-92. Mem. ABA, ALA, Am. Assn. Law Librs. (Washington Affairs rep. 1989—, mem. exec. bd. 1991-94, v.p. 1999-2000, pres. 2000-01), Assn. Am. Law Schs. Avocations: photography, music, personal computers, amateur radio. Office: Georgetown U Law Ctr 111 G St NW Washington DC 20001-1417

OAKS, DALLIN HARRIS, lawyer, church official; b. Provo, Utah, Aug. 12, 1932; s. Lloyd E. and Stella (Harris) Oaks; m. June Dixon, June 24, 1952 (dec. July 1998); children: Sharmon, Cheri Lyn, Lloyd D., Dallin D., TruAnn, Jenny June; m. Kristen McMain, Aug. 25, 2000. BA with high honors, Brigham Young U., 1954, LLD (hon.) , 1980; JD cum laude, U. Chgo., 1957; LLD (hon.) , Pepperdine U., 1982, So. Utah U., 1991. Bar: Ill. 1957, Utah 1971. Law clk. to Chief Justice Earl Warren U.S. Supreme Ct., 1957—58; with firm Kirkland, Ellis, Hodson, Chaffetz & Masters, Chgo., 1958—61; mem. faculty U. Chgo. Law Sch., 1961—71, assoc. dean and acting dean, 1962, prof., 1964—71, mem. vis. com., 1971—74; pres. Brigham Young U., Provo, Utah, 1971—80; also prof. law J. Reuben Clark Law Sch., 1974—80; justice Utah Supreme Ct., 1981—84; mem. Coun. of Twelve Apostles Ch. Jesus Christ of Latter Day Sts., 1984—. Legal counsel Bill of Rights com. Ill. Constl. Conv., 1970. Author (with G.G. Bogert): Cases on Trusts, 1967, 1978; author: (with W. Lehman) A Criminal Justice System and The Indigent, 1968; author: The Criminal Justice Act in the Federal District Courts, 1969; author: (with M. Hill) Carthage Conspiracy, 1975; author: Trust Doctrines in Church Controversies, 1984, Pure in Heart, 1988, The Lord's Way, 1991, His Holy Name, 1998, With Full Purpose of Heart, 2002; editor: The Wall Between Church and State, 1963; contbr. Mem. adv. com. Nat. Inst. Law Enforcement and Criminal Justice, 1974—76; mem. Wilson coun. Woodrow Wilson Internat. Ctr. for Scholars, 1973—80; trustee Intermountain Health Care Inc., 1975—80; regional rep. Ch. of Jesus Christ of Latter-day Saints, 1974—80, past 1st counselor Chgo. South Stake; bd. dirs. Notre Dame Ctr. for Constl. Studies, 1977—80, Rockford Inst., 1980—2000, Pub. Broadcasting Svc., 1977—85, chmn., 1980—85; bd. dirs. Polynesian Cultural Ctr., 1987—96, chmn., 1988—96. Fellow: Am. Bar Found. (exec. dir. 1970—71); mem.: Am. Assn. Pres. Ind. Colls. and Univs. (pres. 1975—78, dir. 1971—78), Order of Coif. Mem. Ch. Of Jesus Christ Of Latter-Day Saints. Office: Quorum of Twelve 47 E South Temple Salt Lake City UT 84150-9701

OATES, CARL EVERETTE, lawyer, director; b. Harlingen, Tex., Apr. 8, 1931; s. Joseph William and Grace (Watson) O.; m. Eileen Noble Hudnall; children: Carl William, Gregory Carl Hudnall, Patricia O. Chase, Matthew Noble Hudnall. BS, U.S. Naval Acad., 1955; LLB, So. Meth. U., 1962. Bar: Tex. 1962, D.C. 1977, Nebr. 1985. Assoc. Akin, Gump, Strauss, Hauer & Feld, Dallas, 1962-64, ptnr., 1965-91. Asst. atty. gen. State of Texas, 1992-94, spl. coun., Tex. Dept. Banking, 1994-95, prin. Carl E. Oates, P.C. Chmn. bd. trustees S.W. Mus. Sci. and Tech., Dallas; v.p. S.W. Sci. Mus. Found., Dallas; bd. dirs. Kiwanis Wesley Dental Ctr., Inc., Dallas; pres. Wesley Dental Found., Dallas. Lt. USN, 1955-59. Mem. ABA, D.C. Bar Assn., Tex. Bar Assn., Dallas Bar Assn., Barristers, Northwood Club, Delta Theta Phi. Administrative and regulatory, Corporate, general, Property, real (including real estate development, water). E-mail: coates00@aol.com.

O'BARR, BOBBY GENE, SR., lawyer; b. Houston, May 5, 1932; s. Walter Morris and Maggie (Whitt) O'B.; children: Morris Clayton, William Clinton, Candace Jean, Bobby G.; m. Jennifer Ryals, Dec. 5, 1984; 1 child, Richard. BA, U. Miss., 1959, JD, 1958. Bar: Miss. 1958, U.S. Dist. Ct. (no. dist.) Miss. 1958, U.S. Dist. Ct. (so. dist.) Miss. 1966, U.S. Ct. Appeals (5th cir.) 1970, U.S. Supreme Ct. 1971. Pvt. practice, Houston, 1958-59; assoc. W.M. O'Barr, Jr., Okolona, Miss., 1959-60; adminstrv. judge Miss. Workmen's Compensation Commn., 1960-65; assoc. Cumbest, Cumbest, O'Barr and Shaddock, Pascagoula, Miss., 1965-68, Hurlbert & O'Barr, O'Barr, Hurlbert and O'Barr, Biloxi, Miss., 1968-80; pvt. practice, owner Bobby G. O'Barr, P.A., Biloxi, 1980—. Mem., pres. Biloxi Port Commn., 1975-90; mem. mgmt. coun. Gulf Mex. Fishery, 1979-82. With USAF, 1951-54. Mem. VFW, State Bar Found., Southeastern Admiralty Law Inst., Miss. Trial Lawyers Assn., Am. Legion, Masons, Shriners. Admiralty, Personal injury (including property damage), Workers' compensation. Office: PO Box 541 Biloxi MS 39533-0541

OBER, RICHARD FRANCIS, JR., lawyer, banker; b. Balt., Dec. 12, 1943; s. Richard Francis and Caroline Fisher Ober; m. Carol Laycock Munger, Aug. 25, 1973; children: Julia Keyser, Margaret Delancey. AB cum laude, Princeton U., 1965; LLB, Yale U., 1968. Bar: Md. 1968, Pa. 1970, N.J. 1977. Law clk. to chief judge Md. Ct. Appeals, Annapolis, 1968; assoc. Ballard, Spahr, Andrews & Ingersoll, Phila., 1969-75; gen. counsel Summit Bancorp, Princeton, NJ, 1975—2001. Sec. Summit Bancorp, Princeton, 1978-2001, sr. v.p., 1982-88, exec. v.p., 1988-2001; bd. dirs. sec. Summit Credit Life Ins. Co., Summit Credit Corp.; sec. Summit Bank, Summit Leasing Co., Summit Venture Capital, Inc. Fire commr. South Brunswick (N.J.) Fire Dist. 3, 1981-85; Republican county committeeman, 1975—; v.p. Republican Assn. Princeton, 1995-96; trustee Princeton Day Sch., 1986-92, treas., 1988-92, vice-chmn., 1990-92; trustee Yale Law Sch. Assn. N.J.; first vice-chmn., dir N.J. Spl. Olympics. Mem. ABA, Bank Corp. Counsel Com. (chmn. 1979-80), N.J. Bar Assn. (gen. coun. 1982-85, 93-94, exec. com. banking law sect. 1979-94, sec. sect. 1980-81, vice-chmn. 1981-82, chmn. 1984-85), N.J. Corp. Counsel Assn. (exec. com. 1980-91, 2d v.p. 1982-85, pres. 1985-86, chmn. banking and fin. instns. com. 1984-85), Am. Bankers Assn. (exec. com. bank counsel unit 1990-95, vice-chmn. 1993-94, chmn. 1994-95), N.J. Bankers Assn. (chmn. bank lawyers coun. 1993-94, chmn. legal and tax com. 1994-95), N.J. Bus. and Industry Assn. (legis. affairs com.), Pa. Bankers Assn. (legal affairs com.), Phila. Bar Assn., Assn. Corp. Counsel Am., Princeton Bar Assn., Fin. Svcs. Roundtable, Lawyers Coun., Bedens Brook Club (Princeton). Episcopalian. Banking, Corporate, general, Securities.

OBERDORFER, LOUIS F. federal judge; b. Birmingham, Ala., Feb. 21, 1919; s. A. Leo and Stella Maud (Falk) O.; m. Elizabeth Weil, July 31, 1941; children: John Louis, Kathryn Lee, Thomas Lee, William L. AB, Dartmouth, 1939; LL.B., Yale, 1946. Bar: Ala. bar 1946, D.C. bar 1949. Law clk. to Justice Hugo L. Black, 1946-47; pvt. practice, 1947-51; mem. firm Wilmer, Cutler, & Pickering (and predecessors), 1951-61, 65-77; asst. atty. gen. tax div. Dept. of Justice, 1961-65; judge, now sr. judge U.S. Dist. Ct. (D.C. dist.), 1977—. Vis. lectr. Yale Law Sch., 1966-71; adv. com. Fed. Rules Civil Procedure, 1962-84; co-chmn. lawyers com. Civil Rights Under Law, 1967-69; adj. prof. law Georgetown U., Washington, 1993-97. Editor-in-chief Yale Law Jour., 1941. Served to capt. AUS, 1941-46. Mem. ABA, D.C. Bar Assn. (bd. govs. 1972-77, pres. 1977), Ala. Bar Assns., Am. Law Inst., Yale Law Sch. Assn. (pres. 1971-73) Office: US Dist Ct 333 Constitution Ave NW Washington DC 20001

OBERHELMAN, HARRY ALVIN, III, lawyer; b. Oak Park, Ill., Mar. 30, 1947; s. harry Alvin Jr. and Betty Jane (Porter) O.; m. Leslie Ann Vickers, May 11, 1991; children: Nicholas, Linsdsey, Andrew. BS, Stanford U., 1969; JD, Golden Gate U., 1976. Bar: Calif. 1977, U.S. Ct. Appeals (9th cir.) 1977, U.S. Supreme Ct. 1996. House counsel Eldorado Ins. Co., Palo Alto, Calif., 1977-78; pvt. practice Palo Alto, 1978-80; dep. county counsel Madera (Calif.) County, 1980-83; asst. county counsel Santa Cruz (Calif.) County, 1983—. Trustee, pres. bd. dirs. County Law Libr., Santa Cruz, 1985-95. Office: County of Santa Cruz 701 Ocean St Santa Cruz CA 95060-4003

OBERLE, ANDREAS, lawyer; b. Jan. 26, 1955; LLM, U. Zurich, Switzerland, 1983. CLU Switzerland, 1985; bar: Zurich 1985. Mgr. tax and legal Deloitte & Touche, Zurich, 1987—94; mng. ptnr. Bellerive Treuhaud, Zurich, 1995—2000; ptnr. Oberle, Law Firm, Zurich, 2001—. Mem.: Zurich Bar Assn., Swiss Bar Assn. Corporate, general, Immigration, naturalization, and customs, Taxation, general. Office: Oberle Law Firm Klausstrasse 4 8034 Zürich Switzerland

OBERLY, KATHRYN ANNE, lawyer; b. Chgo., May 22, 1950; d. James Richard and Lucille Mary (Kraus) Oberly; 1 child, Michael W. Goelzer; m. Haynes B. Johnson, June 29, 2002. Student, Vassar Coll., 1967-69; BA, U. Wis., 1971, JD, 1973. Bar: Wis. 1973, D.C. 1981, N.Y. 1995. Law clk. U.S. Ct. Appeals, Omaha, 1973-74; trial atty. U.S. Dept. Justice, Washington, 1974-77, spl. asst., 1977-81, spl. litigation counsel, 1981-82, asst. to Solicitor Gen., 1982-86; ptnr. Mayer, Brown & Platt, Washington, 1986-91; assoc. gen. counsel Ernst & Young LLP, Washington, 1991-94, vice-chair, gen. counsel N.Y.C., 1994—. Exec. com. CPR Ctr. for Dispute Resolution. Named one of 50 Most Influential Women Lawyers in Am., Nat. Law Jour., 1998. Mem. ABA, Am. Law Inst. (coun. mem.), Am. Acad. Appellate Lawyers, Wis. Bar Assn., D.C. Bar Assn. Democrat. Office: Ernst & Young LLP 5 Times Sq New York NY 10036 E-mail: kathryn.oberly@ey.com.

OBERMAN, MICHAEL STEWART, lawyer; b. Bklyn., May 21, 1947; s. Hyman Martin and Gertrude O.; m. Sharon Land, Oct. 8, 1975; 1 child, Abigail Land. AB, Columbia U., 1969; JD, Harvard U., 1972. Bar: N.Y. 1973, U.S. Dist. Ct. (so. and ea. dists.) N.Y. 1973, U.S. Ct. Appeals (2d cir.) 1973, U.S. Supreme Ct. 1976, Calif. 1981, U.S. Dist. Ct. (no. dist.) Calif. 1981, U.S. Ct. Appeals (9th cir.) 1981, U.S. Dist. Ct. (so. and cen. dists.) Calif. 1982, U.S. Ct. Appeals (5th cir.) 1989, D.C. 1992, U.S. Ct. Appeals (7th cir.) 1993. Law clk. to Hon. Milton Pollack, U.S. Dist. Ct. (so. dist.) N.Y., 1972-73; assoc. Kramer Levin Naftalis & Frankel LLP, N.Y.C., 1973-79, ptnr., 1980—. Contbr. articles to profl. jours. Recipient Nathan Burkan prize ASCAP, 1973. Mem. N.Y. State Bar Assn. (mem. ho. of dels. 1989-91, exec. com. comml. and fed. litigation sect.). General civil litigation, Intellectual property. Office: Kramer Levin Naftalis & Frankel LLP 919 3rd Ave New York NY 10022-3902

OBERMAN, STEVEN, lawyer; b. St. Louis, Sept. 21, 1955; s. Albert and Marian (Kleg) O.; m. Evelyn Ann Simpson, Aug. 28, 1977; children: Rachael Diane, Benjamin Scott. BA in Psychology, Auburn U., 1977; JD, U. Tenn., 1980. Bar: Tenn. 1980, Tenn. Supreme Ct. 1980, Tenn. Criminal Ct. Appeals 1980, U.S. Dist. Ct. (ea. dist.) Tenn. 1980, U.S. Ct. Appeals (4th cir.) 1981, U.S. Ct. Appeals (6th cir.) 1983, U.S. Supreme Ct. 1985. Law clk. Daniel, Duncan & Claiborne, Knoxville, Tenn., 1978-80; assoc. Daniel, Claiborne & Lewallen, Knoxville, Tenn., 1980-82, Daniel, Claiborne, Oberman & Buuck, Knoxville, 1983-85, Daniel & Oberman, Knoxville, 1986—. Pres. Project First Offender, Knoxville, 1983—86; bd. dirs. Fed. Defender Svcs. Ea. Tenn., Inc., 1994—97, pres., 1998—2000; guest instr. U. Tenn., 1988—90, guest instr. legal clinic, trial advocacy program, 1984—; guest lectr. U. Tenn. Law Sch., 1982—88, adj. prof., 1993—, coach nat. trial team, 1991—96; guest instr. U. Tenn. Grad. Sch. Criminal Justice Program, 1983, 84; guest spkr. Ct. Clk.'s Meeting, Cambridge, England, 1984; spl. judge criminal divsn. Knox County Gen. Session Ct.; spkr. in field. Author: D.U.I.: The Crime and Consequences in Tennessee, 1991, supplemented annually; co-author: D.W.I. Means Defend With Ingenuity, 1987, Drunk Driving Defense, 5th edit., 2003; contbr. legal articles on drunk driving to profl. jours. Bd. dirs. Knoxville Legal Aid Soc., Inc., 1986-88 (pres. 1990), Arnstein Jewish Community Ctr., 1987-91, pres. 1990; bd. dirs. Knoxville Racquet Club, 1991-93, pres. 1992-93. Named Col. Aide de Camp, Tenn. Gov.'s Staff, 1983; recipient Forrest W. Lacey award for outstanding faculty contbn. to moot ct. program, U. Tenn. Coll. Law, 1993—94, Moot Ct. Bd. Spl. Svc. award, 1995—96. Mem.: ATLA, Knoxville Bar Assn., Tenn. Assn. Criminal Def. Lawyers (bd. dirs. 1983—89), Nat. Coll. DUI Def. (founding, bd. regents 1999—), Nat. Assn. Criminal Def. Lawyers (chair/co-chair DUI advocacy com. 1995—, editl. bd. The Champion). Jewish. Criminal, Personal injury (including property damage). Office: Daniel & Oberman 550 W Main St Ste 950 Knoxville TN 37902-2536

OBERT, PAUL RICHARD, lawyer, manufacturing company executive; b. Pitts. s. Edgar F. and Elizabeth T. Obert. BS, Georgetown U., 1950; JD, U. Pitts., 1953. Bar: Pa. 1954, D.C. 1956, Ohio 1972, Ill. 1974, U.S. Supreme Ct. 1970. Sole practice, Pitts., 1954-60; asst. counsel H.K. Porter Co., Inc., Pitts., 1960—62, sec., gen. counsel, 1962-71, Addressograph-Multigraph Corp., Cleve., 1972-74; v.p. law Marshall Field & Co., Chgo., 1974-82, sec., 1976-82; v.p., gen. counsel, sec. CF Industries, Inc., Long Grove, Ill., 1982—, also officer, dir. various subs. Served to lt. col. USAF. Mem. ABA (corp. gen. counsel com.), Pa. Bar Assn., Allegheny County Bar Assn., Ill. Bar Assn., Chgo. Bar Assn., Am. Soc. Corp. Secs., Am. Retail Fedn. (bd. dirs. 1977-80), Georgetown U. Alumni Assn. (bd. govs.), Pitts. Athletic Assn., Univ. Club (Chgo.), Delta Theta Phi. Administrative and regulatory, Commercial, contracts (including sales of goods; commercial financing), Corporate, general. Office: CF Industries Inc 1 Salem Lake Dr Long Grove IL 60047-8401

OBNINSKY, VICTOR PETER, lawyer; b. San Rafael, Calif., Oct. 12, 1944; s. Peter Victor and Anne Bartholdi (Donston) Obninsky; m. Clara Alice Bechtel, June 8, 1969 (div. Nov. 1, 2002); 1 child, Mari. BA, Columbia U., 1966; JD, U. Calif., Hastings, 1969. Bar: Calif. 1970. Sole practice, Novato, Calif., 1970-2001, Tiburon, Calif., 2001—02, Sonoma, Calif., 2003—. Arbitrator Marin County Superior Ct., San Rafael, 1979—; superior ct. judge pro tem, 1979—; lectr. real estate and partnership law. Author: The Russians in Early California, 1966. Bd. dirs. Calif. Young Reps., 1968-69, Richardson Bay San. Dist., 1974-75, Marin County Legal Aid Soc., 1976-78; baseball coach Little League, Babe Ruth League, 1970-84; mem. nat. panel consumer arbitrators Better Bus. Bur., 1974-88; leader Boy Scouts Am., 1970-84; permanent sec. Phillips Acad. Class of 1962, 1987—; mem. Phillips Acad. Alumni Coun., 1991-95; bd. cmty. advisors Buck Ctr. for Rsch. on Aging, 1990-2001. Mem ABA, State Bar Calif., Marin County Bar Assn. (bd. dirs. 1985-91, treas. 1987-88, pres.-elect 1989, pres. 1990), Sonoma Bar Assoc. Phi Delta Phi, Phi Gamma Delta. Republican. Russian Orthodox. Corporate, general, General practice, Probate (including wills, trusts). Home and Office: 21453 Shainsky Sonoma CA 95476-8412 Fax: 707-935-7310.

O'BRIEN, CHARLES H. lawyer, retired state supreme court chief justice; b. Orange, N.J., July 30, 1920; s. Herbert Rodgers and Agnes Sidman (Montanya) O'B.; m. Anna Belle Clement, Nov. 9, 1966; children: Merry Diane, Steven Shawn (dec.), Heather Lynn. LLB, Cumberland U., 1947. Rep. Tenn. Legislature, Memphis, 1963-65, senator, 1965-67; assoc. judge Tenn. Ct. Criminal Appeals, Crossville, 1970-87; assoc. justice Tenn. Supreme Ct., 1987-94, chief justice, 1994-95; ret., 1995; pvt. practice, 1995—. Bd. dirs. Lake Tansi Village Property Owners Assn., 1984-89, chmn., 1989. With U.S. Army, 1938-45, ETO, 1950, UN Command, Tokyo. Decorated Bronze Star, Purple Heart with oak leaf cluster. Fellow Tenn. Bar Found.; mem. Tenn. Bar Assn., Cumberland County Bar Assn., Am. Legion, Lake Tansi Village Chowder and Marching Soc. (pres.). Democrat. Avocation: outdoor activities. Estate planning, Finance, Probate (including wills, trusts).

O'BRIEN, DANIEL WILLIAM, lumber company executive; b. St. Paul, Jan. 6, 1926; s. Daniel W. and Kathryn (Zenk) O'B.; m. Sarah Ward Stoltze, June 20, 1952; children: Bridget Ann, Daniel William, Kevin Charles, Timothy John. Student, U. Dubuque, 1943, Ill. State U., 1944; BSL, U. Minn., 1948, JD, 1949. Bar: Minn. 1949. Practice in, St. Paul, 1950—; partner Randall, Smith & Blomquist, 1955-65; of counsel Doherty, Rumble & Butler, 1965-99; pres., chmn. bd. dirs. F.H. Stoltze Land & Lumber Co., 1964—; pres. Maple Island, Inc., 1968—. Served to ensign USNR, 1943-46. Mem. Minn., Ramsey County bar assns., World Pres's. Orgn., Chief Execs. Orgn. Office: 2497 7th Ave E Ste 105 North Saint Paul MN 55109-2902 Home (Winter): 3951 S Placita de la Moneda Green Valley AZ 85614-5063 Home: 4734 Bouleau Rd White Bear Lake MN 55110-3355 E-mail: dwobrien@maple-island.com.

O'BRIEN, DANIEL J. lawyer; b. Los Alamos, N.Mex., Nov. 18, 1951; BS, U. N.Mex., 1975, MBA, 1980, JD, 1983. Bar: N.Mex. 1983, Tex. 1993, U.S. Dist. Ct. N.Mex. 1984, U.S. Ct. Appeals (10th cir.) 1987. Atty. DAniel J. O'Brien & Assocs., Albuquerque. Mem.: ABA, Albuquerque Bar Assn., N.Mex. Trial Lawyers Assn., N.Mex. Def. Lawyers Assn. (pres. 1999—2000), State Bar N.Mex. (bd. commrs. 1994—2000, v.p. 2002). Insurance. Office: Daniel J O'Brien and Assocs 6301 Indian Sch NE Ste 800 Albuquerque NM 87110*

O'BRIEN, DANIEL ROBERT, lawyer; b. Peoria, Ill., May 7, 1951; s. William Patrick and Irene Cornelia O'Brien; m. Eileen Mary Kahn, Aug. 17, 1974; children: Colleen, Patrick, Bridget. BS, No. Ill. U., 1973; JD, Wash. U., St. Louis, 1976. Bar: U.S. Dist. Ct. (so. dist.) Ill. 1977. Ptnr. Smith Moos Schmitt & O'Brien, Peoria, 1976-82, Moos, Schmitt & O'Brien, Peoria, 1982—. Lectr. Peoria County Bar Assn., Ill. Continuing Legal Edn., Springfield. Dem. precinct committeeman Dem. Party, 1986. Named to Greater Peoria Sports Hall of Fame, 2000. Fellow Ill. Bar Found. (charter mem., Leading Ill. Atty. award), Beta Gamma Sigma. Avocation: coaching children's basketball. Personal injury (including property damage), Workers' compensation. Office: Moos Schmitt & O'Brien 331 Fulton St Ste 740 Peoria IL 61602-1499

O'BRIEN, DARLENE ANNE, lawyer; b. Cleve., July 14, 1955; d. Joseph and Suzanne (Belica) Mason; m. Thomas C. O'Brien, Feb. 2, 1984; children: John Michael, Lauren Katherine. BA summa cum laude, U. Toledo, 1977; JD, U. Notre Dame, 1980. Bar: Ind. 1980, Mich. 1981. Law clk. to presiding justice U.S. Bankruptcy Ct. (no. dist.), Ind., 1980-81; assoc. Smith and Brooker P.C., Saginaw, Mich., 1981-84, O'Brien and O'Brien, Ann Arbor, Mich., 1984—. Commentator, panelist Inst. Continuing Legal Edn. Contbng. author Mich. Causes of Action Formbook, Inst. Continuing Legal Edn., 1996, 1998, 2000. Mem. ABA, Nat. Inst. Trial Advocacy, Advocates Assn., Mich. Bar Assn., Women's Law Assn. Mich., Washtenaw County Bar Assn, Washtenaw Trial Lawyers Assn. State civil litigation, Criminal, Personal injury (including property damage). Office: O'Brien & O'Brien 300 N 5th Ave Ste 150 Ann Arbor MI 48104-1499 Fax: 734-996-5555.

O'BRIEN, DAVID A. lawyer; b. Sioux City, Iowa, Aug. 30, 1958; s. John T. and Doris K. (Reisch) O'B. BA, George Washington U., 1981; JD with distinction, U. Iowa, 1984. Bar: Iowa 1985, U.S. Dist. Ct. (no. dist.) Iowa 1985, Nebr. 1990, U.S. Dist. Ct. Nebr. 1990. Legis. asst. Nat. Transp. Safety Bd., Washington, 1978-81; assoc. O'Brien, Galvin & Kuehl, Sioux City, 1985-88; ptnr. O'Brien, Galvin Moeller & Neary, Sioux City, 1989-94; chair Wage Appeals Bd. & Bd. of Svc. Contract Appeals U.S. Dept. Labor, Washington, 1994-96, acting dir. Office Adminstrv. Appeals, 1995-96, chair adminstrv. review bd., 1996-98; atty. White & Johnson, P.C., Cedar Rapids, Iowa, 1998-2000; ptnr. Willey, O'Brien, Mullin, Laverty & Hanrahan, PLC, Cedar Rapids, 2000—. Dem. candidate for Congress, 6th dist. of Iowa, Sioux City, 1988; chmn. Woodbury County Dem. Party, Sioux City, 1992-94, chair Iowa campaign Clinton for Pres., Des Moines, 1992; bd. dirs. Mid-Step Svcs. Inc., Sioux City, 1986-91, Mo. River Hist. Devel., Sioux City, 1989-94. Mem.: Iowa Trial Lawyers Assn. (bd. govs. 1991—94, bd. govs. 2002—), Nat. Assn. Trial Lawyers. Roman Catholic. Avocations: sports, politics. Labor (including EEOC, Fair Labor Standards Act, labor-management relations, NLRB, OSHA), Personal injury (including property damage), Workers' compensation. Office: Willey O'Brien Mullin Laverty Hanrahan 3519 Center Pointe Rd NE Cedar Rapids IA 52402 Home Fax: 319-378-1413.

O'BRIEN, DENNIS SEAN, lawyer; b. June 19, 1953; s. Edward Patrick and Virginia (Davlin) O'B.; m. Laurie Lynne Barnes, Aug. 6, 1977; children: Sean, Patrick, Kathleen Erin, Elizabeth Honora, Conor James. AA, Springfield Coll., Ill., 1973; BA, Rosary Coll., 1975; JD, Loyola U., Chgo., 1978. Bar: Ill. 1978, U.S. Dist. Ct. (no. dist.) Ill. 1978; U.S. Dist. Ct. (cen. dist.) Ill. 1980. Asst. states atty. felony div. Lake County States Atty.'s Office, Waukegan, Ill., 1978-80; ptnr. Livingstone, Mueller, O'Brien & Davlin, Springfield, 1980—, v.p., sec., 1999—. Presenter seminar Ill. State Bar Asn,. Nat. Bus. Inst., Lohrman Edn. Svcs. Bd. dirs. Springfield Mcpl. Opera, 1971-75, 88-92, 94-97, 99-2003, pres., 1990-92; bd. dirs. Springfield Theatre Ctr., 1986-88. Named to Outstanding Young Men. Am., U.S. Jaycees, 1976. Mem.: ABA, Ill. Bar Assn. (workers compensation sect. coun. 1988—90), Sangamon County Bar Assn. (bd. dirs. 1995—97). Roman Catholic. Municipal (including bonds), Workers' compensation. Home: 2013 S Glenwood Ave Springfield IL 62704-4517 Office: Livingstone Mueller O'Brien and Davlin 620 E Edwards St Springfield IL 62703-1639 E-mail: dsob@livingstonelaw.com.

O'BRIEN, DONALD EUGENE, federal judge; b. Marcus, Iowa, Sept. 30, 1923; s. Michael John and Myrtle A. (Toomey) O'B.; m. Ruth Mahon, Apr. 15, 1950; children: Teresa, Brien, John, Shuivaun. LL.B., Creighton U., 1948. Bar: Iowa bar 1948, U.S. Supreme Ct. bar 1963. Asst. city atty., Sioux City, Iowa, 1949—54; county atty. Woodbury County, Iowa, 1955—59; mcpl. judge Sioux City, Iowa, 1959-60; U.S. atty. No. Iowa, 1961-67; pvt. practice law Sioux City, 1948—61; U.S. Dist. judge, 1978—; chief judge U.S. Dist. Ct. (no. dist.) Iowa, Sioux City, 1985-92, sr. judge, 1992—; pvt. practice law Sioux City, 1967—78. Rep. 8th cir. dist. ct. judges to Jud. Conf. U.S., 1990-97. Served with USAAF, 1942-45. Decorated D.F.C., air medals. Mem. Woodbury County Bar Assn., Iowa State Bar Assn. Roman Catholic. Office: US Dist Ct PO Box 267 Sioux City IA 51102-0267 E-mail: Don_OBrian@iand.uscourts.gov.

O'BRIEN, EDWARD IGNATIUS, private investor, corporation director; b. N.Y.C., Sept. 15, 1928; s. Edward I. and Marguerite (Malone) O'B.; m. Margaret M. Feeney, June 29, 1957; children: Edward Ignatius III, Margaret Mary, Thomas Gerard, John Joseph. AB, Fordham U., 1950; LLB, St. John's U., 1954; grad., Advanced Mgmt. Program, Cornell U., 1965. Bar: N.Y. 1954. With firm Hale, Kay & Brennan, N.Y.C., 1954-55; with Bache & Co., Inc., N.Y.C., 1955-74, gen. counsel, 1960, gen. ptnr., 1964, sec., 1968, v.p., 1965-68, sr. v.p., mem. exec. com., 1969, exec. v.p., 1969, chmn. exec. com., 1971-74; pres. Securities Industry Assn., 1974-93; retired, 1993. Bd. dirs. 8 corps.; lectr. Am. Law Inst., Practising Law Inst., Am. Mgmt. Assn.; exch. ofcl. Am. Stock Exch., 1972; mem. adv. bd., mem. exec. com. Securities Regulation Inst., U. Calif., 1975—. Mem. Cardinal's com. Laity Cath. Archdiocese N.Y., mem. Cardinal's com. for edn.; chmn. Fordham U. Coun., 1971-73; bd. dirs. 3 non-profit orgns.; chmn. corp. devel. com. Fordham U.; trustee, chmn. bd. trustees Fordham Prep. Sch., 1975-77, Capt. USAR. Mem. N.Y. State Bar Assn,. Am. Arbitration Assn., Am. Soc. Internat. Law, Guild Cath. Lawyers, Securites Industry Assn. (chmn. publicly owned firms com. 1972), Nat. Assn. Securities Dealers (dist. com. 1973-74), Shenorock Shore Club (Rye, N.Y.), Town Club (Scarsdale, N.Y.), Met. Club (Washington). Home and Office: 12 Woods Ln Scarsdale NY 10583-6408

O'BRIEN, JOAN SUSAN, lawyer, educator; b. New York, Apr. 14, 1946; d. Edward Vincent O'Brien and Joan Therese (Kramer) Quinn; m. Michael P. Wilpan, May 27, 1979; children: Edward B. Wilpan, Anabel T. Wilpan. BA, NYU, 1967; JD, Georgetown U., 1970. Bar: N.Y. 1971, Mass. 1971, U.S. Dist. Ct. (so. and ea. dist.) N.Y. 1972, U.S. Ct. Appeals (2d cir.) 1971. Law clk. to Hon. Frank J. Murray U.S. Dist. Ct. Mass., Boston, 1970-71; asst. U.S. atty. Office of U.S. Atty. U.S. Dist. Ct. (ea. dist.) N.Y., Bklyn., 1972-76; pvt. practice N.Y.C., 1976-79; trial atty. Mendes & Mount, N.Y.C., 1979-84; asst. prof. St. Johns U., Jamaica, N.Y., 1984-90; adminstrv. law judge N.Y. State Workers Compensation Bd., Hempstead, N.Y., 1990-93; appellate atty. Scheine, Fusco, Brandenstein & Rada, Woodbury, N.Y., 1993-97; trial atty. Grey & Grey, L.L.P., Farmingdale, N.Y., 1997—. Editor: Georgetown Law Jour., 1968-70. Pres. Nassau County Dem. Com. Women's Caucus, Westbury, N.Y., 1988-90; leader Girl Scouts Nassau County, 1990-93. Unitarian-Universalist. Personal injury (including property damage), Product liability, Workers' compensation. Office: Grey & Grey LLP 360 Main St Farmingdale NY 11735-3592

O'BRIEN, JOHN GRAHAM, lawyer; b. N.Y.C., May 12, 1948; s. John Edward and Marian Helen (FitzGerald) O'B.; m. Phyllis Mary Eyth, Apr. 10, 1976; children: John Graham Jr., Jennifer A. BS cum laude, Mt. St. Mary's Coll., Emmitsburg, Md., 1970; JD, Am. U., 1973. Bar: N.J. 1974, D.C. 1974, N.Y. 1982, U.S. Supreme Ct. 1982. Law clk. to Hon. F.C. Kentz and J.H. Coleman, Superior Ct. of N.J., Elizabeth, N.J., 1973-74; assoc. Carpenter, Bennett & Morrissey, Newark, 1975-81; sr. counsel GAF Corp., Wayne, N.J., 1981-90; assoc. gen. counsel Keene Corp., N.Y.C., 1990-93, ISS Internat. Svc. Sys., N.Y.C., 1994-95; cons. GE, Fairfield, Conn., 1993-94; mng. ptnr. Atkins O'Brien Ekblom LLP, N.Y.C., 1995-2000; of counsel McGivney, Kluger & Gannon, N.Y.C., 2000—01; gen. counsel Brickforce Staffing Inc., Edison, NJ, 2001—03; of counsel Karasik & Einbinder, LLP, 2003. Author: (monograph) Responding to Products Liability Claims, 1986, also supplements; contbg. author: Toxic Torts Practice Guide, 1992. Recipient Disting. Young Alumni award Mt. St. Mary's Coll., 1976. Mem. N.J. Bar Assn., D.C. Bar, Echo Lke Country Club (assoc.), Coll. Mens Club. Roman Catholic. General civil litigation, Insurance, Personal injury (including property damage). Office: 2 Ethel Rd Ste 204B Edison NJ 08817-2839 E-mail: obriennj2@aol.com.

O'BRIEN, STEPHEN MAZYCK, III, lawyer; b. Louisville, Jan. 24, 1947; s. Stephen Mazyck Jr. O'Brien and Jane Hartman OBrien; m. Michele Marie Legris, May 20, 1972 (div. May 1993); children: Anne Chambers, William Teige; m. Sarah Catherine Sturgill, Dec. 3, 1994; children: John Patrick Jennings, Conor Francis. BA, U. Va., 1969; JD, U. Ky., 1974. Bar: Ky. 74, Fla. 76, U.S. Dist. Ct. (ea. and we. dists.) Ky., U.S. Ct. Appeals (6th cir.). Assoc. McDonald, Alford & Roszell, Lexington, Ky., 1974—76; ptnr. Landrum & Shouse, Lexington, 1976—93; pvt. practice Lexington, 1993—2000; ptnr. Savage, Garmer, Elliott & O'Brien PLLC, Lexington, 2000—. 1st lt. U.S. Army, 1969—71, Vietnam. Product liability, Personal injury (including property damage). Home: 225 Henry Clay Blvd Lexington KY 40502 Office: Savage Garmer Elliott & O'Brien PLLC 141 N Broadway Lexington KY 40507 Fax: 859-223-3397. E-mail: sobrien@sgelaw.com.

O'BRIEN, TERRENCE LEO, federal judge; b. Lincoln, Nebr., Aug. 8, 1943; s. Leo James and Luella Mildred (Benting) O'B.; m. Dorothy Marguerite Driskill, Mar. 30, 1966; children: Sean Brendan, Heather Kathleen. BS in Acctg., U. Wyo., 1965, JD with honors, 1972. Bar: Wyo. 1972, U.S. Dist. Ct. Wyo. 1972, U.S. Ct. Appeals (7th and 10th cirs.) 1972, U.S. Ct. Appeals (8th, 9th and D.C. cirs.) 1973, U.S. Ct. Appeals (2d and 4th cirs.) 1974, U.S. Supreme Ct. 1975. Staff atty. Land and Natural Resources-U.S. Dept. Justice, Washington, 1972-74; ptnr. Omohundro & O'Brien, Buffalo, Wyo., 1974-80; judge 6th Jud. Dist. Wyo., Gillette, 1980—2001, U.S. Ct. Appeals (10th Cir.), 2002—. Justice of Peace Johnson County, Buffalo, 1975-80. Mem. Wyo. Community Coll. Commn., 1978-80. Capt. U.S. Army, 1966-69. Mem.: Rotary. Republican. Office: US Courthouse 2120 Capitol Ave Ste 2212 Cheyenne WY 82001*

O'BRIEN, WALTER JOSEPH, II, lawyer; b. Apr. 22, 1939; s. Walter Joseph O'Brien and Lorayne (Stouffer) Steele; children: Kelly A., Patrick W., Kathleen; m. Sharon Ann Curling, July 8, 1978; 1 child, John Joseph. BBA, U. Notre Dame; JD, Northwestern U. Bar: Ill., U.S. Dist. Ct. (no. dist.) Ill., U.S. Supreme Ct. Assoc. Nicholson, Nisen, Elliott & Meier, Chgo., 1966-70; pres. Capstan Co., Chgo., 1970-73, Walter J. O'Brien II, Ltd., Oak Brook, Ill., 1973-78, O'Brien & Assocs., P.C., Oakbrook Terrace, Ill., 1978—. Chmn., bd. dirs. Atty. Title Guaranty Fund, Inc., Champaign, Ill., 1979—; arbitrator chairperson 18th Judicial Ct., DuPage County, Ill. Contbr. articles to legal jours. Commr. Oak Brook Plan Commn., 1980-85; mem. Oak Brook Zoning Bd. Appeals, 1985-87, Bd. Edn. Elem. Dist. # 53, Oak Brook, 1991-95; commr. Ill. and Mich. Canal, Nat. Heritage Corridor Commn.; v.p. Oak Brook Civic Assn., 1972; trustee St. Isaac Jogues Ch., Hinsdale, Ill., 1975-76. Capt. Q.M.C., U.S. Army, 1964-66. Fellow Ill. Bar Found.; mem. Ill. State Bar Assn. (mem. assembly), DuPage Bar Assn. (bd. dirs. 1987-88, elected Man of Yr. 1988), Am. Inn of Ct. (master DuPage chpt.), Butterfield Country Club (bd. dirs. 1982-88). Roman Catholic. Corporate, general, Probate (including wills, trusts), Property, real (including real estate development, water). Office: O'Brien & Assocs PC Ste 501 1900 Spring Rd Oak Brook IL 60523

O'BRIEN, WILLIAM J., III, lawyer; BS, Holy Cross Coll., 1965; LLB, Yale U., 1969. Bar: N.Y. 1970, Mich. 1985. With Hughes Hubbard and Reed, N.Y.C. and Paris, 1969-75; asst. gen. counsel Chrysler Corp., Highland Park, 1983, assoc. gen. counsel, 1984, dep. gen. counsel, 1986, v.p., gen. counsel, sec., 1987; sr. v.p., gen. counsel DaimlerChrysler AG, 1998—2002, exec. v.p., gen. counsel, 2002—. Office: DaimlerChrysler Corp CIMS 485-14-96 1000 Chrysler Dr Auburn Hills MI 48326-2766

O'BRIEN, WILLIAM JEROME, II, lawyer; b. Darby, Pa., Oct. 22, 1954; s. Richard James O'Brien and Margaret (McGill) Hahn. BA in Econ. and Polit. Sci., Merrimack Coll., 1976; JD, Del. Law Sch., 1981. Bar: Pa. 1982, U.S. Dist. Ct. (ea. dist.) Pa. 1983, U.S. Supreme Ct. 1986. Law clk. Commonwealth Ct. of Pa., Harrisburg, 1982-83; assoc. Philips, Curtin and DiGiacomo, Phila., 1983-86, O'Brien & Assocs. PC, Phila., 1986—. Bd. dirs. New Manayunk Corp., Phila. counselor, 1987-98. Bd. dirs. North Light Inc., 1986-94, sec., 1988-90, pres., 1990-92; bd. dirs. Manayunk Cmty. Ctr. for Arts, 1988-90, chmn. Chaminouix Mansion, 1989—, chmn., 1991—; spl. asst. to U.S. Senator H. John Heinz, 1976-78; Rep. candidate for Phila. City Coun., 1991, for Phila. City Contr., 1997; mem. Rep. State Com. Pa., 1998-2000; mem. Phila. Rep. Exec. Com. Mem. Phila. Bar Assn., Pa. Bar Assn., Del. Law Sch. Alumni Assn. (sec. 1985-87), Bus. Assn. Manayunk (bd. dirs. 1987-89), Racquet Club (mem. com. 1985-87). Roman Catholic. Avocations: squash, court tennis, scuba, golf. Corporate, general, General practice, Property, real (including real estate development, water). Office: O'Brien & Assocs PC 4322 Main St Philadelphia PA 19127-1421

O'CALLAGHAN, R.J. PATRICK, lawyer; b. Mpls., Aug. 8, 1924; s. Robert Desmond and Claire Marie (Moe) O'C.; married Albina Julie Sepich, June 4, 1949; children: Michael, Edward, Catherine, Diana, Robert, Daniel. BA, Drake U., 1949; JD, U. Denver, 1951. Bar: Colo. 1951, U.S. Dist. Ct. Colo. 1956, U.S. Tax Ct. 1971, U.S. Ct. Appeals (10th cir.) 1978. Pvt. practice law, Denver, 1952-53, Rangely, Colo., 1953-63; real estate broker Grand Junction, Colo., 1963-65; ptnr. Bellinger, Faricy, Tursi & O'Callaghan, Pueblo, Colo., 1965-73; pvt. practice law Pueblo, 1973-76; ptnr. Lattimer, O'Callaghan & Ware P.C., Pueblo, 1978-81; of counsel Quiet & Dice, Denver, 1981-83; pvt. practice law Pueblo, 1983—. Atty. Town of Rangely, 1953-63; bd. atty. Pueblo Bd. Realtors, 1971-82; instr. real estate U. Colo., 1968-79; sr. cert. valuer Internat. Real Estate Inst. Pres. Homes for Sr. Citizens Inc., Pueblo, 1978-80; pres. Mt. Carmel Credit Union, 1972-74; adv. bd. dirs. Pueblo Salvation Army, 1987-91. With USNR, 1943-46. Mem. ABA, Colo. Bar Assn., Pueblo County Bar Assn., Nat. Network Estate Planning Attys., Elks (exalted ruler Rangley Lodge No. 1907). Republican. Roman Catholic. Avocation: photography. Estate planning, Probate (including wills, trusts), Property, real (including real estate development, water). Address: 125 E 7th Ste 100 Pueblo CO 81003-3407 E-mail: patoc@qwest.net.

O'CALLAGHAN, WILLIAM LAWRENCE, JR., lawyer; b. Atlanta, Aug. 6, 1941; s. William Lawrence and Martha Kathryn (Fitzpatrick) O'C.; m. Bonnie Faye Whitmire, Dec. 18, 1964; children: Diana Lee, John Patrick, Michael Lawrence. BBA, U. Ga., 1963, JD cum laude, 1965; LLM in Taxation, Georgetown U., 1968. Bar: Ga. 1965, U.S. Supreme Ct. 1971. Assoc. Sutherland, Asbill & Brennan, Atlanta, 1965; ptnr. Gambrell, Russell et al, Atlanta, 1968-74; chmn. O'Callaghan, Saunders & Stumm, Atlanta, 1974-90; ptnr. Branch, Pike, Ganz & O'Callaghan, Atlanta, 1990—93, O'Callaghan & Stumm LLP, 1993—2002, Alston & Bird, LLP, Atlanta, 2002—. Bd. dirs. Atlanta Jr. Golf Assn., pres., 1987-88; bd. dirs. Phoenix Soc. of Atlanta, 1985-87. Served as capt. U.S. Army, 1965-68. Mem. ABA (chmn. 1985-89, mem. com. on fed. tax real property sect., mem. real property sect., mem. tax sect.), Atlanta Estate Planning Coun., Atlanta Bar Assn., Sandy Springs (Ga.) C. of C. (bd. dirs. 1982-83), State Bar Georgia. Presbyterian (elder). Clubs: Atlanta Athletic (dir. 1987-96, pres. 1992-94), Georgian. Lodges: Rotary (v.p. Sandy Springs chpt. 1986), Optimists (pres. Sandy Springs chpt. 1978). Avocations: golf, travel. Mergers and acquisitions, Property, real (including real estate development, water), Taxation, general. Office: Alston & Bird LLP 1201 W Peachtree St Atlanta GA 30309-3424

OCKEY, RONALD J. lawyer; b. Green River, Wyo., June 12, 1934; s. Theron G. and Ruby O. (Sackett) O.; m. Arline M. Hawkins, Nov. 27, 1957; children: Carolyn S. Ockey Baggett, Deborah K. Ockey Christiansen, David, Kathleen M. Ockey Hellewell, Valerie Ockey Sachs, Robert. BA, U. Utah, 1959, postgrad., 1959-60; JD with honors, George Washington U., 1966. Bar: Colo. 1967, Utah 1968, U.S. Dist. Ct. Colo. 1967, U.S. Dist. Ct. Utah 1968, U.S. Ct. Appeals (10th cir.) 1969, U.S. Ct. Claims 1987. Missionary to France for Mormon Ch., 1954-57; law clk. to judge U.S. Dist. Ct. Colo., 1966-67; assoc. ptnr., shareholder, v.p., treas., dir. Jones, Waldo, Holbrook & McDonough, Salt Lake City, 1967-91; pres. IntelliTrans Internat. Corp., 1992-94; mem. Utah Ho. of Reps., 1988-90, Utah State Senate, 1991-94; of counsel Mackey Price & Williams, Salt Lake City, 1995-98; asst. atty. gen. Utah, 1998—. Trustee SmartUtah, Inc., 1995-2002; trustee Utah Tech. Fin. Corp., 1995-98; lectr. in securities, pub. fin. and bankruptcy law. Mem. editl. bd. Utah Bar Jour., 1973-75; mem. staff and bd. editors George Washington Law Rev., 1964-66; contbr. articles to profl. jours. State govtl. affairs chair Utah Jaycees, 1969; del. state Rep. Convs., 1972-74, 76-78, 80-82, 84-86, 94-96, del. Salt Lake County Rep. Conv., 1978-80, 88-92; sec. Wright for Gov. campaign, 1980; legis. dist. chmn. Utah Rep. Party, 1983-87; trustee Food for Poland, 1981-85, pres., trustee Unity to Assist Humanity Alliance, 1992-95; bd. dirs. Utah Opera Co., 1991-94; trustee Utah Info. Tech. Assn., 1991-2000. Lt. U.S. Army, 1960-66, to capt. JAG, USAR, 1966-81. Mem. ABA, Utah State Bar Assn. (various coms.), Nat. Assn. Bond Lawyers (chmn. con. on state legislation 1982-85), George Washington U. Law Alumni Assn. (bd. dirs. 1981-85), Order of Coif, Phi Delta Phi. Commercial, contracts (including sales of goods; commercial financing), Computer, Corporate, general. Home: 4502 Crest Oak Cir Salt Lake City UT 84124-3825 E-mail: rao@netutah.net.

O'CONNELL, DANIEL JAMES, lawyer; b. Evergreen Park, Ill., Aug. 14, 1954; s. Edmund J. and Kathryn J. (Hanna) O'C.; m. Nancy L. Eichler, March 21, 1992; children: Kelly Jacklyn, Kirby Kathryn. BS, Millikin U., 1976; JD, ITT, 1980; postgrad., DePaul U., 1981, U. Mich., 1997—2001, U. Ill., 1999—. Bar: Ill. 1980, U.S. Dist. Ct. (no. dist.) Ill. 1980, U.S. Dist. Ct. (ctrl. dist.) Ill. 2000, U.S. Dist. Ct. Ariz. 1989. Ins. regulatory counsel Kemper Group, Long Grove, Ill., 1980-81, environ. claims counsel, 1981-82; sr. home office claim counsel Zurich Ins. Cos., Schaumburg, Ill., 1982-83; assoc. Clausen, Miller, Gorman et al, Chgo., 1983-86; ptnr. environ. toxic tort litigation O'Connell & Moroney, P.C., Chgo., 1986-90; ptnr. toxic tort litigation Burditt, Bowles & Radzius, Chgo., 1990-91; ptnr. Daniel J. O'Connell & Assocs., P.C., Elgin, 1991—2002, O'Connell & O'Sullivan, P.C., Elgin, 2002—. James S. Kemper Found. scholar, 1972-76.

Mem. ABA, APHA, AAAS, Ill. Bar Assn., Kane County Bar Assn., Def. Rsch. Inst., N.Y. Acad. Scis. Environmental, Insurance, Product liability. Home: 177 Macintosh Ct Glen Ellyn IL 60137-6478 E-mail: doconn3@uic.edu.

O'CONNELL, KEVIN, lawyer; b. Boston, Sept. 4, 1933; s. Michael Frederick and Kathryn Agnes (Kelley) O'C.; m. Mary Adams, July 14, 1990; children: Tiffany W., Elizabeth H., Dana A., Liesel E. AB, Harvard, 1955, JD, 1960. Bar: Calif. 1961. Assoc. firm O'Melveny & Myers, L.A., 1960-63; asst. U.S. atty. criminal div. Cen. Dist. Calif., L.A., 1963-65; staff counsel Gov. Calif. Commn. to Investigate Watts Riot, L.A., 1965-66; ptnr. Tuttle & Taylor, L.A., 1966-70, Coleman & O'Connell, L.A., 1971-75; pvt. practice law L.A., 1975-78; of counsel firm Simon & Sheridan, L.A., 1978-89; ptnr. Manatt, Phelps & Phillips, L.A., 1989—; adj. prof. law U. So. Calif. Law Sch., 2002—. Bd. editors: Harvard Law Rev, 1958-60. Mem. Los Angeles County (Calif.) Democratic Central Com., 1973-74; bd. dirs. Calif. Supreme Ct. Hist. Soc. Lt. USMCR, 1955-57. Mem. Am. Law Inst. Home: 426 N Mccadden Pl Los Angeles CA 90004-1026 Office: Manatt Phelps & Phillips Trident Ctr E Tower 11355 W Olympic Blvd Los Angeles CA 90064-1614 E-mail: koconnell@manatt.com.

O'CONNELL, MARGARET SULLIVAN, lawyer; b. N.Y.C., Feb. 16, 1942; d. Thomas J. and Nora (Ryan) Sullivan; m. Anthony F. O'Connell, May 11, 1968 (dec. Mar. 1975); children: Noreen Anne, Joan Margaret, Alison Marie. Nursing diploma, St. Clare's Hosp. Sch. Nursing, N.Y.C., 1962; BA, Jersey City State Coll., 1973; JD, St. John's U., 1983. Bar: N.Y. 1984, U.S. Dist. Ct. (so. and ea. dists.) 1996; RN, N.Y. Staff nurse St. Clare's Hosp., N.Y.C., 1962-64, head nurse, 1964-67; clin. instr. medicine and surgery St. Clare's Sch. Nursing, N.Y.C., 1967-70; nursing supr. Menorah Home and Hosp., Bklyn., 1974-75; assoc. Costello, Shea & Gaffney, N.Y.C., 1987-95, ptnr., 1995—. Mem. ABA, N.Y. State Bar Assn., Assn. Bar City N.Y. (com. on med. malpractice 1996-2000), Am. Assn. Nurse Attys., Brehon Law Soc., Soc. Med. Jurisprudence (trustee). General civil litigation, Insurance, Personal injury (including property damage). Office: Costello Shea & Gaffney 44 Wall St New York NY 10005-2401

O'CONNELL, MAURICE DANIEL, lawyer; b. Ticonderoga, N.Y., Nov. 9, 1929; s. Maurice Daniel and Leila (Geraghty) O'C.; m. Joan MacLure Landers, Aug. 2, 1952; children: Mark M., David L., Ann M., Leila K., Ellen A. Grad., Phillips Exeter Acad., 1946; AB, Williams Coll., 1950; LLB, Cornell U., 1956. Bar: Ohio 1956. Since practiced in, Toledo; assoc. Williams, Eversman & Black, 1956-60; ptnr. Robison, Curphey & O'Connell, 1961-95, of counsel, 1996—; spl. hearing officer in conscientious objector cases U.S. Dept. Justice, 1966-68. Mem. complaint rev. bd. Bd. Commrs. on Grievance and Discipline of Supreme Ct. Ohio, 1987. Mem. Ottawa Hills Bd. Edn., 1963-66, pres., 1967-69; former trustee Toledo Soc. for Handicapped; past trustee Woodlawn Cemetery; past trustee Toledo Hearing and Speech Center, Easter Seal Soc.; mem. alumni council Phillips Exeter Acad. Served to 1st lt. USMCR, 1950-53. Fellow Ohio State Bar Found.; mem. NW Ohio Alumni Assn. of Williams Coll. (past pres.), Ohio Bar Assn., Toledo Bar Assn. (chmn. grievance com. 1971-74), Kappa Alpha, Phi Delta Phi. Clubs: Toledo. Corporate, general, Labor (including EEOC, Fair Labor Standards Act, labor-management relations, NLRB, OSHA). Home: 3922 W Bancroft St Toledo OH 43606-2533 Office: 9th Flr Four SeaGate Toledo OH 43604

O'CONNOR, BRUCE EDWARD, lawyer; b. Cin., Ohio, Dec. 12, 1942; s. John J. and Dorothy R. O'Connor; m. Janet Louise Wright, July 30, 1966; 1 child, Matt. BEE, U. Cin., 1965; JD, Georgetown U., 1969. Bar: Wash. 1969, U.S. Dist. Ct. (we. dist.) Wash. 1969, U.S. Dist. Ct. (ea. dist.) Wash. 1969, U.S. Dist. Ct. (no. dist.) Calif. 1969, Can. Patent Office 1969, Can. Trade-Marks Office 1969, U.S. Appeals Ct. (fed. cir.) 1970, U.S. Appeals Ct. (8th cir.) 1970, U.S. Appeals Ct. (D.C. cir.) 1970, U.S. Patent and Trademark Office 1966, Supreme Ct. Wash. 1969, U.S. Supreme Ct. 2002. Computer programmer, operator Addressograph Multigraph Corp., Cleve., 1963—64; patent agt. GE, Washington, 1965—69; sr. ptnr. Christensen O'Connor Johnson Kindness, Seattle, 1969—. Relay engr., draftsman Cin. Gas and Electric Co., 1961—63, constrn. supr. power plant, 1964—65. Trustee Seattle Opera Assn., 1985—2002; bd. legal counsel Seattle Symphony, 1998—. Mem.: ABA (patent, trademark and copyright and litigation sects.), Comml. Arbitration Assn. Taiwan (panel arbitrators), King County Bar Assn., Wash. State Patent Law Assn., Wash. State Bar Assn., U.S. Trademark Assn., Internat. Trademark Assn., Internat. Fedn. Indsl. Property Attys., World Intellectual Property Orgn. Arbitration and Mediation Ctr. (domain name panel), Am. Arbitration Assn. (comml. arbitration panel, domain name panel), Am. Intellectual Property Law Assn., Ranier Club of Seattle, Eta Kappa Nu. Achievements include patents in field; trademarks protected. Avocations: boating, fishing, piano, photography, gardening. Intellectual property, Alternative dispute resolution. Office: Christensen O'Connor Johnson Kindness 1429 Fifth Ave Ste 2800 Seattle WA 98101

O'CONNOR, CHARLES P. lawyer; b. Boston, Sept. 29, 1940; m. Mary Linda Hogan; children: Jennifer, Amy, Austin, Catherine. Bachelors degree, Holy Cross Coll., Worcester, Mass., 1963; LLB, Boston Coll., 1966. Bar: Mass. 1966, D.C. 1968, U.S. Supreme Ct. 1974. Atty., gen. counsel's office NLRB, Washington, 1966-67; assoc. Morgan, Lewis & Bockius, LLP, Washington, 1968-71; ptnr. Morgan, Lewis & Bockius, Washington, 1971—, chmn. labor and employment law sect., 1996-99, mng. ptnr. Washington office, 1995-97. Gen. counsel Major League Baseball Player Rels. Com., N.Y.C., 1989-94. Contbr. numerous articles on labor and employment law to law jours. Spl. counsel elections com. U.S. Ho. of Reps., Washington, 1968-69. Fellow Coll. Labor and Employment Lawyers; mem. ABA, D.C. Bar Assn., Met. Club Washington, Belle Haven Country Club, N.Y. Athletic Club, Cape Cod Nat. Golf Club. Entertainment, Labor (including EEOC, Fair Labor Standards Act, labor-management relations, NLRB, OSHA). Home: 424 S Lee St Alexandria VA 22314 Office: Morgan Lewis & Bockius LLP 1111 Pennsylvania Ave NW Washington DC 20004

O'CONNOR, EDWARD GEARING, lawyer; b. Pitts., May 5, 1940; s. Timothy R. and Irene B. (Gearing) O'C.; m. Janet M. Showalter, June 17, 1972; children: Mark G., Susan M. BA, Duquesne U., 1962, JD, 1965. Bar: Pa. 1965, U.S. Dist. Ct. (we. dist.) Pa. 1965, U.S. Ct. Appeals (3d cir.) 1968, U.S. Supreme Ct. 1976. Assoc. Eckert, Seamans, Cherin & Mellott, Pitts., 1965-72, ptnr., 1973-99, sr. counsel, 2000—. Mem. adv. com. on appellate ct. rules Supreme Ct. Pa., 1986—92, mem. procedure rules com., 1998—; bd. dirs., mem. audit com. Federated Investors, Inc. Editor Duquesne U. Law Rev., 1964-65. Chmn. Hampton (Pa.) Twp. Planning Commn., 1986-87; mem. Hampton (Pa.) Twp. Zoning Hearing Bd., 1997—; bd. dirs. Duquesne U. Recipient Disting. Alumni award Duquesne U. Law Rev., 1985, Disting. Law Alumni award Duquesne U. Sch. Law, 1991, Disting. Svc. award Hampton Twp., 1991, McAnurlty Svc. award Duquesne U., 1992; named Century Club Disting. Alumni, Duquesne U., 1985. Fellow: Pa. Bar Found., Am. Bar Found.; mem.: Ally City Bar Found. (chair fellows com. 2000—01), Acad. Trial Lawyers Allegheny County (bd. govs. 1986—89, 1998—), Pa. Bar Assn. (ho. of dels. 1985—90), Pitts. Athletic Assn., Duquesne U. Alumni Assn. (pres. 1980—82, 1988—90, bd. govs. 1982—90, bd. dirs. 1988—89), Duquesne Club. Republican. Roman Catholic. Antitrust, Federal civil litigation, State civil litigation. Home: 4288 Green Glade Ct Allison Park PA 15101-1202 Office: Eckert Seamans Cherin & Mellott 600 Grant St Ste 44th Pittsburgh PA 15219-2702 E-mail: ego@escm.com.

O'CONNOR, EDWARD VINCENT, JR., lawyer; b. Yokosuka, Japan, Nov. 9, 1952; s. Edward Vincent and Margaret (Robertson) O'C.; m. Kathy J. Hunt, May 23, 1992. BA, Duke U., 1975; JD, N.Y. Law Sch., 1981. Bar: Va. 1982, D.C. 1983. Assoc. Lewis, Kinsey, Dack & Good, Washington, 1982-87; ptnr. Lewis, Dack, Paradiso & Good, Washington, 1988-89, Lewis, Dack, Paradiso, O'Connor & Good, Washington, 1989-94, The Lewis Law Firm, 1994, Byrd, Mische, Bevis, Bowen, Joseph & O'Connor, Fairfax, Va., 1995—2003; pvt. practice, 2003—. Arbitrator D.C. Superior Ct.; neutral case evaluator and concilliator Fairfax County Cir. Ct.; lectr. Va. Trial Lawyers Assn., Arlington County Bar Assn. Bd. dirs., treas. Potomac Legal Aid Soc., 2001—. Named One of Best 50 Divorce Lawyers Washingtonian mag., 1995, 2000. Mem. Va. State Bar (lectr., spl. com. on access to legal svcs. 1994—, 5th dist. discipline com. 2001—), D.C. Bar, Fairfax County Bar Assn. (lectr., vice chair family law sect. 1995-96, continuing edn. com. 1988-95, chair 1995, mem. pub. svc. com. 1995, chair 1996-98, mem. cir. ct. com. 1994-96, 99-2001, judicial selection com., pro bono com., James Keith award for pub. svc. 1999), Legal Svcs. No. Va. (bd. dirs., chmn. pro bono com., sec.-treas. 1998-2002, pres. 2002-2003, treas. 2003, pro bono award for outstanding svc. 1997). Entertainment, Family and matrimonial, Probate (including wills, trusts).

O'CONNOR, GAYLE MCCORMICK, law librarian; b. Rome, N.Y., July 8, 1956; d. John Joseph and Barbara Jane (Molyneaux) McC. Head libr. Bolling, Walter & Gawthrop, Sacramento, 1987-88, Weintraub, Genshlea & Sproul, Sacramento, 1988-93, Brobeck, Phleger & Harrison, San Diego, 1993-96; legal cons., author, 1996—; owner Automated legal Solutions, Ft. Lauderdale, Fla., 1996—98; legal industry mktg. specialist CourtLink, Seattle, 1998—99; dir. mktg. ABC Legal Svcs., 1999—2000; legal cons., 2000—. Instr. law Lincoln U., Sacramento. Assoc. editor, rsch. advisor Alert Publs., Chgo.; contbr. articles to profl. jours. Mem. ABA (tech. show bd.), No. Calif. Assn. Law Libs., So. Calif. Assn. Law Librs., Am. Assn. Law Librs., Spl. Librs. Assn. (chair legal divsn. 1997-98). Avocations: bodybuilding, skiing. E-mail: goconnor@cybersleuther.com.

O'CONNOR, JOSEPH A., JR., lawyer; b. N.Y.C., Aug. 12, 1937; s. Joseph A. and Louise G. (Lucht) O'C.; children: Joseph A. III, Edward W. BA, Yale U., 1959; LLB, Columbia U., 1962. Bar: N.Y. 1963, U.S. Supreme Ct. 1968, Pa. 1973, Fla. 1978. Assoc. Davis, Polk & Wardwell, N.Y.C., 1963-72; ptnr. Morgan, Lewis & Bockius, Phila., 1972—2002, spl. coun., 2002—; exec. dir. E. Rhodes & Leona B. Carpenter Fedn., 2002—. Mem. ABA, N.Y. State Bar Assn., Pa. Bar Assn., Fla. Bar Assn., Phila. Bar Assn., Assn. of Bar of City of N.Y. Clubs: Racquet (Phila.). Roman Catholic. Office: Morgan Lewis & Bockius LLP 1701 Market St Philadelphia PA 19103-2903

O'CONNOR, JOSEPH DANIEL, lawyer; b. Chgo., Sept. 13, 1953; s. Joseph D. and Donna M. (Birmingham) O.; m. Cinda Zehner, Aug. 14, 1976; children: Timothy, Ann. BS in Math., Purdue U., 1975; JD cum laude, Ind. U., 1978. Bar: Ind. 1978, U.S. Dist. Ct. (so. dist.) Ind. 1978, U.S. Dist. Ct. (no. dist.) Ind. 1987, U.S. Ct. Appeals (7th cir.) 1989. Assoc. Bunger & Robertson, Bloomington, Ind., 1978-82, ptnr., 1983—. Bd. dirs. Western Golf Assn., Boys' Clubs of Bloomington; co-chair profl. div. United Way of Monroe County, 1992; sec. Bloomington Hosp. Adv. Coun. Fellow Am. Bar Found., Ind. Bar Found.; mem. ABA (bd. govs. 1998-2001, exec. com. of bd. 2000-01, chair bd. govs. ops. and comms. com. 2000-01, ho. of dels. 1986-90, 91—, chair standing com. on meetings and travel 1997-98), Ind. State Bar Assn. (chmn. young lawyers divsn. 1986-87, treas. 1987-88, sec. 1989-90, bd. mgrs. 1990-92, v.p. 1992-93, pres.-elect 1993-94, pres. 1994-95), Bloomington Country Club (bd. govs.). Avocations: golf, reading, travel. General practice, Insurance, Personal injury (including property damage). Office: Bunger & Robertson PO Box 910 Bloomington IN 47402-0910

O'CONNOR, KARL WILLIAM (GOODYEAR JOHNSON), lawyer; b. Washington, Aug. 1, 1931; s. Hector and Lucile (Johnson) O'C.; m. Sylvia Gasbarri, Mar. 23, 1951 (dec.); m. Judith Ann Byers, July 22, 1972 (div. 1983); m. Eleanor Celler, Aug. 3, 1984 (div. 1986); m. Alma Hepner, Jan. 1, 1987 (div. 1996); children: Blair, Frances, Brian, Brendan; m. Allie O'Connor, Jul. 15, 2000. BA, U. Va., 1952, JD, 1958. Bar: Va. 1958, D.C. 1959, Am. Samoa 1976, Calif. 1977, Oreg. 1993. Law clk. U.S. Dist. Ct. Va., Abingdon, 1958-59; practice law Washington, 1959-61; trial atty. U.S. Dept. Justice, Washington, 1961-65; dep. dir. Men's Job Corps OEO, Washington, 1965-67; mem. civil rights div. Dept. of Justice, chief criminal sect., prin. dep. asst. atty. gen., 1967-75, spl. counsel for intelligence coordination, 1975; v.p., counsel Assn. of Motion Picture and Television Producers, Hollywood, Calif., 1975-76; assoc. justice Am. Samoa, 1976; chief justice, 1977-78; sr. trial atty. GSA Task Force, Dept. Justice, 1978-81; insp. gen. CSA, 1981-82; spl. counsel Merit Systems Protection Bd., Washington, 1983-86; U.S. atty. for Guam and the No. Marianas, 1986-89; ret.; pvt. practice, 1989—; Am. counsel O'Reilly Vernier Ltd., Hong Kong, 1992-93; ptnr. O'Connor & Vernier, Medford, Oreg., 1993-94; pvt. practice Medford, 1994—. Served with USMC, 1952-55. Mem. Oreg. Bar Assn., D.C. Bar Assn., Va. Bar Assn., Calif. Bar Assn., Am. Samoa Bar Assn., Soc. Colonial Wars, Phi Alpha Delta, Sigma Nu. Federal civil litigation, Criminal, Labor (including EEOC, Fair Labor Standards Act, labor-management relations, NLRB, OSHA). Home: Box 126 6743 Griffin Ln Jacksonville OR 97530 Office: Brehon House 915 W 10th St Medford OR 97501-3018

O'CONNOR, KATHLEEN MARY, lawyer; b. Camden, Jan. 14, 1949; d. John A. and Marie V. (Flynn) O'C. BA, U. Fla., 1971, JD, 1981. Bar: Fla. 1981, U.S. Ct. Appeals (11th cir.) 1982, U.S. Supreme Ct. 1987. Atty. Walton, Lantaff, Schroeder & Carson, Miami, Fla., 1981-84, Thornton, Davis & Murray PA, Miami, 1984-98, Thornton, Davis & Fein, P.A., Miami, 2002—. Exec. editor U. Fla. Law Rev., 1981; contbr. articles to profl. jours. Legal advocate Miami Project to Cure Paralysis, 1992-97. Mem. ABA, Dade County Bar Assn. (vice-chair appellate cts. com. 1981), Def. Rsch. Inst., Fla. Def. Lawyers Assn., Fla. Assn. for Women Lawyers (bd. dirs. Miami-Dade County chpt.), Fla. Bar (mem. appellate rules com. 2002—). Appellate, Aviation, Insurance. Office: Thornton Davis & Fein PA 80 SW 8th St Ste 2900 Miami FL 33130 E-mail: oconnor@tdflaw.com.

O'CONNOR, KEVIN JAMES, lawyer; b. Hartford, Conn., May 3, 1967; s. Dennis Edmund and Mary Theresa (Leahy) O'Connor. BA, U. Notre Dame, Ind., 1989; JD, U. Conn., Hartford, 1992. Conn. 1992, N.Y. 1993, U.S. Dist. Ct. Conn. (so. and ea. dists.) N.Y. 1994, U.S. Ct. Appeals (2d cir.) 1994. Law clerk Hon. William H. Timbers, U.S. Ct. Appeals (2d cir.), N.Y.C., 1992-93; assoc. Cahill, Gordon & Reindel, N.Y.C., 1993-95; sr. counsel Divsn. Enforcement U.S. Securities & Exchg. Commn., Washington, 1995-97; assoc. LeBoeuf, Lamb, Greene & MacRae, Hartford, Conn., 1997—2002; US atty. U.S. Dept. of Justice, Conn., 2003—. Adj. prof. George Washington U. Law Sch., Washington, 1996-97, U. Conn. Law Sch., 1998—. Bd. dirs. Old State House, John Rogers African Am. Cultural Ctr., 1999— Mem. Am. Assn. Bar City of N.Y., Conn. Bar Assn. Republican. Roman Catholic. Office: Connecticut Financial Center PO Box 1824 New Haven CT 06508*

O'CONNOR, MAUREEN, judge; b. Washington, Aug. 7, 1951; d. Patrick and Mary E. O'Connor; children: Alex, Ed. BA, Seton Hill Coll., 1973; postgrad., SUNY, 1975-76; JD, Cleve. State U., 1980. Pvt. practice, 1981-85; referee Probate Ct., 1985-93; judge Common Pleas, 1993-95; prosecutor Summit County, 1995-99; lt. gov., dir. Dept. Pub. Safety State of Ohio, 1999—2003; Supreme Ct. Ohio Supreme Ct. Justice, Ohio, 2003. Dir. Summit County Child Support Enforcement Agy.; spkr. in field. Parishioner St. Vincent's Ch.; vol. Comty. Drug Bd., Am. Cancer Soc., bd. dirs.; bd. dirs. Victim Assistance, St. Edward Home, Fairlawn, Furnace St. Mission. Recipient MADD Law Enforcement award, 1997, Cleve. State Disting. Alumnae award for Civic Achievement, 1997. Mem. MADD, Nat. Dist. Attys. Assn., Nat. Child Support Enforcement Assn., Nat. Coll. Dist. Attys. Assn., Ohio Prosecuting Attys. Assn. (exec. com.), Ohio Family Support Assn., Atty. Gen.'s Prosecutor Liaison Com., Summit County Police Chiefs Assn., Summit Forum, Summit County Child Mortality. Republican. Office: Ohio Supreme Ct 30 E Broad St Fl 3 Columbus OH 43215*

O'CONNOR, OTIS LESLIE, lawyer, director; b. Charleston, W.Va., July 6, 1935; s. Robert Emmett and Julia Elizabeth (Aultz) O'C.; m. Elizabeth Frances Morris, Aug. 7, 1965; children: Otis Leslie, James M. AB, Princeton U., 1957; JD, Harvard U., 1963; MBA, W.Va. Coll. Grad. Studies, 1979; MA, Trinity Theol. Sem., 2003. Bar: W.Va. 1963, U.S. Dist. (so. dist.) W.Va. 1963. Assoc. Steptoe & Johnson, Charleston, 1963-69, ptnr., 1969—. Pres. Daymark, Inc., 1981—82. Served with USN, 1957—60, served to comdr. JAGC USNR, 1960—81. Mem. ABA, W.Va. Bar Assn., Kanawha County Bar Assn., Res. Officers Assn., Rotary Internat. Club (Charleston). Presbyterian. Banking, Probate (including wills, trusts), Property, real (including real estate development, water). Home: 890 Chester Rd Charleston WV 25302-2817

O'CONNOR, ROBERT EDWARD, JR., lawyer; b. Omaha, June 1, 1950; s. Robert Edward Sr. and Agnes (Flynn) O'C.; m. Jean Patricia Mergens; children: Maureen, Kathleen. undergrad. degree, JD, Creighton U., 1974. Bar: Nebr. 1974, U.S. Dist. Ct. Nebr., U.S. Ct. Appeals (8th cir.). Sole practice, Omaha, 1974—. Mem. Nebr. State Bar Assn. (del. 1982-84, pres. 2001-02), Nebr. Assn. Trial Attys. (del.), Assn. Trial Lawyers Am. (del.). Democrat. Roman Catholic. Avocation: sailing. State civil litigation, Appellate, Aviation. Office: 2433 S 130th Cir Omaha NE 68144-2528

O'CONNOR QUINN, DEIRDRE, lawyer; b. N.Y.C., Feb. 19, 1966; d. Raymond and Roisin O'Connor; m. Patrick T. Quinn, Sept. 8, 1990; children: Malachy, Oona, Maeve, Rory. BS in Commerce, U. Va., 1987; JD, Boston Coll., 1990; LLM in Taxation, NYU, 1994. CPA Va.; bar: N.Y. 1991. Assoc. White & Case, N.Y.C., 1990-95; v.p., corp. counsel tax sect. Prudential Fin., Newark, N.J., 1995—. Mem. AICPA, Assn. of Bar of City of N.Y., N.Y. State Bar Assn. Corporate taxation, Taxation, general. Office: Prudential 213 Washington St Newark NJ 07102-2917 E-mail: deirdre.o'connor_quinn@prudential.com.

O'DEA, DENNIS MICHAEL, lawyer; b. Lowell, Mass., Nov. 1, 1946; s. James Lawrence and Carol France (Gibbons) O'D.; m. Mary Gail Frawley; children: Emily C., Dennis C., Daniel P., Mollie G., Sally K. Igor Ibradzic. BA in Govt., U. Notre Dame, 1968; JD magna cum laude, U. Mich., 1972. Bar: Mass. 1972, D.C. 1980, Ill. 1981, N.Y. 1994. Assoc. Goodwin, Procter & Hoar, Boston, 1972-74, Fine & Ambrogne, Boston, 1974-77; assoc. prof. Syracuse U. Coll. Law, 1977-78; vis. assoc. prof. Nat. Law Ctr., George Washington U., 1978-80; ptnr. Keck Mahin & Cate, N.Y.C., 1980-96; pvt. practice, 1996-97; ptnr. Wolf, Block, Schorr and Solis-Cohen LLP, N.Y.C., 1997—. Co-dir. The Gilmore Inst., 1995—. Mem. Order of the Coif, Chgo. Lit. Club (pres. 1993). Presbyterian. Bankruptcy, State civil litigation, Commercial, contracts (including sales of goods; commercial financing). Home: 5 Opal Ct New City NY 10956-7021 Office: Wolf Block Schorr & Solis-Cohen 250 Park Ave Ste 1000 New York NY 10177-0001

O'DELL, EDWARD THOMAS, JR., retired lawyer; b. Lowell, Mass., Nov. 26, 1935; s. Edward Thomas and Helen Louise (Shaw) O'Dell; m. Kerstin Lilly Sjoholm, Mar. 18, 1962; children: Edward Thomas III, Brian Patrick, Christine Marie. BA, Brown U., 1957; JD, U. Chgo., 1960. Bar: N.Y. 1961, Mass. 1968, U.S. Dist. Ct. Mass. 1968, U.S. Ct. Appeals (1st cir.) 1968. Ptnr. Goodwin, Procter, LLP, Boston, 1966—2000; ret., 2000. Dir, trustee ING/Aetna Mut. Funds, Hartford, Conn., 2002—. Trustee Gov. Dummer Acad., Byfield, Mass., 1982—87. Mem.: ABA, Internat. Bar Assn. (chmn. investment cos. and mutual funds com. 1994—98), Mass. Bar Assn. Home: 96 Wildwood Rd Andover MA 01810-5126 Office: Goodwin Procter LLP Exchange Pl Boston MA 02109-2803

ODELL, HERBERT, lawyer; b. Phila., Oct. 20, 1937; s. Samuel and Selma (Kramer) O.; m. Valerie Odell; children: Wesley, Jonathan, James, Sarah, Samuel. BS in Econs., U. Pa., 1959; LLB magna cum laude, U. Miami, 1962; LLM, Harvard U., 1963. Bar: Fla. 1963, Pa. 1968, D.C. 2002. Trial atty. tax div. U.S. Dept. Justice, Washington, 1963-65; assoc. Walton, Lantaff, Schroeder, Carson & Wahl, Miami, Fla., 1965-67; from assoc. to ptnr. Morgan, Lewis & Bockius, Phila., 1967-89; ptnr. Zapruder & Odell, Phila., 1989-98, Odell & Ptnrs., Phila., 1998-99, Miller & Chevalier (PA) LLC, Phila., 2000—. Adj. prof. U. Miami, Villanova U.; lectr. various tax insts. Contbr. articles to profl. jours. Ford fellow, 1962-63. Mem.: ABA, D.C. Bar Assn., Phila. Bar Assn., Pa. Bar Assn., Fla. Bar Assn., Harvard Club, Beta Alpha Psi, Omicron Delta Kappa, Phi Kappa Phi. Avocations: sailing, running, tennis, scuba diving, fishing. Corporate taxation, Taxation, general, Personal income taxation. Office: Miller & Chevalier 401 E City Ave Ste 815 Bala Cynwyd PA 19004-1121 E-mail: hodell@milchev.com.

O'DELL, JOAN ELIZABETH, lawyer, mediator, business executive, educator; b. East Dubuque, Ill., May 3, 1932; d. Peter Emerson and Olive (Bonnet) O'D.; children: Dominique R., Nicole L. BA cum laude, U. Miami, 1956, JD, 1958. Bar: Fla. 1958, DC 1974, Ill. 1978, Va. 1987, U.S. Supreme Ct. 1972; lic. real estate broker Ill., Va., W.Va. Trial atty. SEC, Washington, 1959-60; asst. state atty. Office State Atty., Miami, Fla., 1960-64; asst. county atty. Dade County Atty.'s Office, Miami, 1964-70; county atty. Palm Beach County Atty.'s Office, West Palm Beach, Fla., 1970-71; regional gen. counsel Region IV EPA, Atlanta, 1971-73, assoc. gen. counsel Washington, 1973-77; sr. counsel Nalco Chem. Co., Oakbrook, Ill., 1977-78; v.p., gen. counsel Angel Mining, Washington and Tenn., 1979-96; pres. S.W. Land Investments, Miami, 1979-88; v.p. Events U.S.A., Washington, 1990—. Mem. Exec. Women's Coun., Tucson, 1982—85; co-chmn. sch. improvement coun. Harpers Ferry Jr. H.S., 2000—; bd. dirs. Tucson Women's Found., 1982—84, U. Ariz. Bus. and Profl. Women's Club, Tucson, 1981—85, LWV, Tucson, 1981—85, pres., 1984—85; bd. dirs. LWV Ariz., 1984—85, chmn. nat. security study; bd. dirs. LWV, Palm Beach County, Fla., 1990—92. Mem. Fla. Bar Assn., D.C. Bar Assn., Va. State Bar Assn., Ill. Bar Assn. Avocations: camping, hiking, skiing. Commercial, contracts (including sales of goods; commercial financing), Estate planning, General practice. E-mail: jeod@aol.com.

ODELL, STUART, lawyer; b. Phila., Jan. 1, 1940; s. P. Samuel and Selma Odell; m. Andrea L. Villegas; children: Stuart Irwin Jr., Benjamin Eaton, Manuela, Sebastian Patricio. BS in Econs., U. Pa., 1961; LLB cum laude, U. Miami, 1964; LLM in Tax, NYU, 1965. Bar: Fla. 1965, Pa. 1966, N.Y. 1982. Assoc. Morgan, Lewis & bockius, N.Y.C., 1966-70, ptnr., 1970-88, Dewey Ballantine, N.Y.C., 1988—. Lectr. law NYU, 1965-66, adj. prof. law, 1966-80; adj. lectr. Temple U. Law Sch., 1972. Assoc. editor U. Miami Law Rev., 1963-64. Recipient Harry J. Ruddick award NYU. Mem. ABA, N.Y. State Bar Assn., Fla. Bar Assn., Assn. of Bar of City of N.Y. Corporate taxation, Private international, Taxation, general. Office: Dewey Ballantine 1301 Avenue Of The Americas New York NY 10019-6022 also: Dewey Ballantine 1 Undershaft London EC3A 8LP England E-mail: sodell@DBLLP.com.

O'DESS, MARY ABIGAIL, lawyer; b. Detroit, May 21, 1954; d. Laurence G. and Naomi V. (Michau) O'Dess.; m. William J. Hein, Nov. 19, 1983. (dec.). BS, No. Mich. U., 1975; JD, U. Mich., 1977. Bar: Wis. 1978, U.S. Dist. Ct. (ea. dist.) Wis. 1978. Assoc. Jacobson & Hupy, S.C., Milw., 1978-91; ptnr. Maculak, Robertson, & O'Dess S.C., Milw., 1991—. Mem. Jr. League Milw., 1983-85; sec. Wis. Coalition for Adv., Madison, 1982-83; bd. dirs. Milw. Women's Ctr., 1981-83, pres., 1983. Mem. Wis. Bar Assn., Phi Kappa Phi, Omicron Delta Nu, Phi Alpha Theta. Avocations: volunteer activities, reading. Office: Macuulak Mutchinson Robertson O'Dess Reilly SC 1733 N Farwell Ave Milwaukee WI 53202-1805

ODGERS, RICHARD WILLIAM, lawyer; b. Detroit, Dec. 31, 1936; s. Richard Stanley and Elsie Maude (Trevarthen) O.; m. Gail C. Bassett, Aug. 29, 1959; children: Thomas R., Andrew B. AB, U. Mich., 1959, JD, 1961. Bar: Calif. 1962. Assoc. Pillsbury Winthrop, San Francisco, 1961-69, ptnr., 1969-87, 98-2000; exec. v.p., gen. counsel Pacific Telesis Group, San Francisco, 1987-98; ptnr. Pillsbury Winthrop, San Francisco, 2001—. Chmn., bd. dirs. Legal Aid Soc. Employment Law Ctr.; dir. Legal Cmty. Against Violence; dir., sec./treas. Van Loben Sels Charitable Found.; dir. Immigrant Legal Resource Ctr.; mem. Calif. Legal Svcs. Trust Fund Commn. Served with USNR. Fellow Am. Bar Found., Am. Judicature Soc., Am. Coll. Trial Lawyers; mem. ABA (spl. com. on gun violence), Am. Law Inst., Coll. Law Practice Mgmt. Administrative and regulatory, Antitrust, Utilities, public. Office: Pillsbury Winthrop 50 Fremont St San Francisco CA 94105-2228 E-mail: rwodgers@pillsburywinthrop.com.

ODONER, ELLEN J. lawyer; b. N.Y.C., Jan. 23, 1952; BA magna cum laude, Yale U., 1973; JD, Harvard U., 1977. Bar: N.Y. 1978. Mem. Weil, Gotshal & Manges, N.Y.C. Mem. Assn. of Bar of City of N.Y. (com. on mergers, acquisitions and corp. control contests). Office: Weil Gotshal & Manges LLP 767 Fifth Ave New York NY 10153-0119

O'DONNELL, ANTHONY JOSEPH, JR., lawyer, educator; b. Miami, Fla., Apr. 13, 1945; s. Anthony Joseph O'Donnell and Margaret S. (Sloan) Blue; m. Gloria Germain Dworet, Aug. 5, 1967 (div. Dec.c 1977); children: Anthony Joseph, William Tyler; m. Sonia Escobio, Apr. 21, 1978; children: Lara Escobio, Robert Anthony. BA in History, Emory U., 1967; MA in History, Princeton U., 1970, PhD in History, 1974; JD, U. Fla., 1977. Bar: Fla. 1977, U.S. Dist. Ct. (so. dist.) Fla. 1985, U.S. Ct. Appeals (11th cir.) 1985, U.S. Supreme Ct. 1988. Pol. Peace Corps, Malaysia, 1968-69; asst. prof. history U. Mo., St. Louis, 1972-75; assoc.c Mershon, Sawyer et al, Miami, 1977-80; assoc., then ptnr. Greenberg, Traurig, Askew et al, Miami, 1981-88; ptnr. Akerman, Senterfitt Eidson, Miami, 1988-90; of counsel Baker & McKenzie, Miami, 1991—2000. Adj. prof. law U. Miami Law Sch., 1983-95. Pro bono legal counsel St. Thomas Episcopal Ch., Miami, 1985-98, Charlee, abused children charity, Miami, 1988-98; trustee Palmer-Trinity Sch., Miami, 1990-99 Mem. Fla. Bar (CLE com. 1988-90, CLE lectr. 1986, 89, 90, lectr. bus. law seminar 1989, environ. seminar 1990), Dade County Bar Assn., Lambda Alpha. Avocations: sailing, musical theater, classical piano. Home: 1129 Palermo Ave Coral Gables FL 33134-6324

O'DONNELL, BARBARA BOURDONNAY, lawyer; b. New Orleans, La., Feb. 25, 1961; d. Charles Leon and Doris Maroney Bourdonnay; m. Phillip Arthur O'Donnell, Aug. 13, 1997; children: Darby Guay, Robin Drew. BA in Polit. Sci., U. New Orleans, 1982; JD, Tulane U., 1986. Bar: La. 1988, U.S. Dist. Ct. (ea. dist.) La. 1988, U.S. Dist. Ct. (mid. and we. dist.) La. 1990. Atty. W.M. Hingle & Assocs., Slidell, La., 1988-95, Hailey, McNamara, Hall, Larmann & Papale, LLP, Metairie, La., 1995—. Mem. Am. Soc. Law, Medicine and Ethics, Def. Rsch. Inst., La. Assn. Def. Counsel. Insurance, Toxic tort, Environmental. Office: Hailey McNamara Hall et al Ste 1400 One Galleria Blvd Metairie LA 70001

O'DONNELL, CATHERINE ROSE, lawyer; b. South Charleston, W.Va., Feb. 15, 1964; d. Philip John and Madeline Marie Ripepi; m. Neil Taney O'Donnell, May 6, 1989; children: Neil Philip, Renata Marie. BA in Bus. and Econs., U. Pitts., 1984, JD, MBA, U. Pitts., 1987. Bar: D.C. 1988, Pa. 1988, U.S. Dist. Ct. (ea. dist.) Pa. 1988, U.S. Dist. Ct. (ctrl. dist.) Pa. 1990. Assoc. Drinker Biddle & Reath, Phila., 1988—90; assoc. to shareholder Elliott Reihner Siedzikowski & Egan, Scranton, Pa., 1990—2000; dist. justice Wilkes-Barre, Pa., 2000—02; assoc. O'Donnell Law Offices, Wilkes-Barre, Pa., 2002—. Mem. parish coun. St. Therese Ch., Wilkes-Barre, 1990—93, mem. fin. coun., 2000—, cantor, 2001—; bd. dirs. Wyoming Valley Montessori Sch., Kingston, Pa., 1997—2000; pres. Wyoming Valley Montessori Sch. PTA, Kingston, Pa.; bd. dirs. Osterhout Libr., Wilkes-Barre, 1999—2000, Cath. Youth Ctr., Wilkes-Barre, 1996—99, Wyoming Valley Habitat for Humanity, Kingston, 1991—93, Luzerne County LWV, Kingston, 1999—2000, Wyo. Sem. Lower Sch. Parents Assn., 2003—. Mem.: ATLA, ABA, Lackawanna County Bar Assn., Wilkes-Barre Law and Libr. Assn., Pa. Trial Lawyers Assn., Pa. Bar Assn. Personal injury (including property damage), Probate (including wills, trusts). Office: O'Donnell Law Offices 22 E Union St Wilkes Barre PA 18701 Office Fax: 570-821-5799 .

O'DONNELL, DENISE ELLEN, lawyer; BS in Polit. Sci., Canisius Coll., 1968; MSW, SUNY, Buffalo, 1973, JD summa cum laude, 1982. Bar: NY 1983, U.S. Dist. Ct. (we., no., ea. and so. dists.) NY, U.S. Ct. Appeals (2d cir.), U.S. Supreme Ct. Law clk. Hon. M. Dolores Denman NY Appellate Divsn. 4th Dept., Buffalo, 1982-85; asst. U.S. atty. Western Dist. N.Y., Buffalo, 1985-90, appellate chief, 1990-93, 1st asst. U.S. atty., 1993—97, U.S. atty., 1997-2001; ptnr. Gen. Litigation Practice Group, Hodgson, Russ, LLP, Buffalo, 2001—. Part-time instr. trial technique program SUNY, 1990—; lectr. ethics, evidence and trial practice Office Legal Edn.U.S. Dept. Justice, 1988—2000; lectr. NITA seminar Western NY Trial Acad., 1994, 98; mem. Atty. Gen.'s Adv. Com., 1999—2001, vice-chair, 2000—01. Mem. Vol. Lawyers Program, 1997—2001; bd. dirs. NCCJ, 2000—; sec. Nat. Women's Hall of Fame, 2001—, bd. dirs., 2001—. Mem.: ABA, Nat. Assn. Former U.S. Attys. (bd. dirs.), Western NY Trial Lawyers Assn., Women's Bar Assn. State NY (founding mem. Western NY chpt. 1985), Bar Assn. Erie County (dep. treas. 1992—93, treas. 1993—94), West Side Rowing Club. Office: Hodgson Russ LLP One M&T Plz Ste 2000 Buffalo NY 14203-2931 E-mail: dodonnel@hodgsonruss.com.

O'DONNELL, EDWARD FRANCIS, JR., lawyer; b. Waterbury, Conn., May 13, 1950; s. Edward Francis and Dorothy Patricia (Breheny) O'D.; m. Jayne Ann DeSantis, Dec. 29, 1972; children: Ryan Anderson, Brooke Stires. BA, St. Anselm Coll., Manchester, N.H., 1972; JD, U. Conn., 1977. Bar: S.C. 1978, Conn. 1977, U.S. Dist. Ct. S.C. 1978, U.S. Dist. Ct. Conn. 1980, U.S. Ct. Appeals (1st and 2d cirs.) 1980. Assoc. Ogeltree, Deakins, Nash, Smoak & Stewart, Greenville, S.C., 1977-79; ptnr. Siegel, O'Connor, Zagari, O'Donnell & Beck, P.C., Hartford, Conn., 1979—. Contbr. articles to profl. jours. Mem. ABA, Conn. Bar Assn., S.C. Bar Assn., Hartford Bar Assn., Hartford Club, Phi Alpha Theta. Roman Catholic. Labor (including EEOC, Fair Labor Standards Act, labor-management relations, NLRB, OSHA). Office: Siegel O'Connor Zangari O'Donnell & Beck PC 150 Trumbull St Fl 5 Hartford CT 06103-2400

O'DONNELL, JOHN LOGAN, lawyer; b. Chgo., Mar. 6, 1914; s. William Joseph and Elizabeth (McLogan) O'D.; m. Mary Ellen Sipe, Sept. 2, 1939 (dec. Dec. 29, 1979); 1 son, John Logan; m. Michele G. Fischer, May 9, 1981. BA, Williams Coll., 1934; JD, Northwestern U., 1937. Bar: Ill. 1937, N.Y. 1943, D.C. 1977. Asso. firm Defrees, Buckingham, Jones and Hoffman, Chgo., 1937-38; staff atty. Office Gen. Counsel, SEC, 1938-41; instr. Cath. U. Law Sch., 1938-41; assoc. Cravath, Swaine & Moore, N.Y.C., 1941-52; ptnr. Olwine, Connelly, Chase, O'Donnell & Weyher, N.Y.C., 1952-91, of counsel, 1991, Twomey, Hoppe & Gallanty, N.Y.C., 1991—. Bd. dirs. Near East Found., 1968-84. Fellow Am. Coll. Trial Lawyers; mem. Assn. Bar City N.Y., Am., Fed., bar assns., Beta Theta Pi, Phi Delta Phi. Clubs: Union, Univ., Williams, (N.Y.C.). Roman Catholic. Avocations: piano, sports. Federal civil litigation, State civil litigation, Securities. Home: 181 E 73rd St New York NY 10021-3549 Office: Twomey Hoppe and Gallanty 757 3rd Ave New York NY 10017-2013

O'DONNELL, LAWRENCE, III, lawyer; b. Houston, Dec. 14, 1957; s. Lawrence Jr. and Annell (Haggart) O'D.; m. Dare Boswell, May 22, 1981; children: Linley, Lawrence IV. BS in Archtl. Engring., U. Tex., 1980; JD cum laude, U. Houston, 1983. Bar: Tex. 1983. Assoc. Wood, Campbell, Moody & Gibbs, Houston, 1983-84; ptnr. Campbell & Riggs, Houston, 1984-91; dep. gen. counsel Baker Hughes Inc., Houston, 1991-94; v.p., gen. counsel Baker Hughes Oilfield Ops., Houston, 1993-95; corp. sec. Baker Hughes Inc., Houston, 1991-96, v.p., gen. counsel, 1995-2000; sr. v.p., gen. counsel, sec. Waste Mgmt., Inc., Houston, 2000-01, exec. v.p., gen. counsel, corp. sec., 2001—; exec. v.p. Western Operations, 2001—03, Operations Support & CAO, 2003—. Bd. dirs., mem. exec. com. Spring Br. Edn. Found.; bd. dirs. Am. Arbitration Assn., U. Tex. Med. Br. Trustee Houston Police Activities League. Fellow Tex. Bar Found., Houston Bar Found.; mem. ABA, ASCE, Tex. State Bar (corp. law com. of bus. law sect.), Houston Bar Assn., Am. Corp. Counsel Assn., Am. Soc. Corp. Sec., Tex. Bus. Law Found., Houston Bar Assn., Tex. Gen. Counsel Forum (pres. Houston chpt. 2000-01), Order of Barons, Phi Delta Phi. Avocations: golf, sailing, skiing. Commercial, contracts (including sales of goods; commercial financing), Corporate, general, Mergers and acquisitions. Office: Waste Mgmt Inc 1001 Fannin St Ste 4000 Houston TX 77002-6711

O'DONNELL, TERRENCE, lawyer; b. N.Y.C., Mar. 3, 1944; s. Emmett and Lorraine (Muller) O'Donnell; m. Margaret Lynne Kidder; children: Stephanie T., Erin K., Victoria L. BS, U.S. Air Force Acad., 1966; JD, Georgetown Law Sch., 1971. Bar: D.C. 1971, U.S. Ct. Appeals (D.C. cir.) 1978, U.S. Ct. Appeals (4th cir.) 1987, U.S. Dist. Ct. Md. 1986, U.S. Ct. Mil. Appeals 1990, U.S. Ct. Fed. Claims, U.S. Supreme Ct., others. Commd. 2d lt. USAF, 1966, advanced through grades to capt., various positions, 1966-72, resigned, 1972; spl. asst. Pres. of U.S., The White House, Washington, 1972-77; appointments sec. Pres. Ford, Washington, 1974-77; assoc. Williams & Connolly, Washington, 1977-82, ptnr., 1982-89; gen. counsel Dept. Def., Washington, 1989-92; ptnr. Williams and Connolly, Washington, 1992—; exec. v.p., gen. counsel Textron Inc., 2000—. Presdl. appointee to bd. visitors U.S. Air Force Acad., Colorado Springs, 1982-87, chmn., 1985-86; U.S. corr. and rep. UN Program to Prevent Crime, Washington and N.Y.C., 1977-81; bd. dirs. IGI Inc., MLC Holdings. Trustee Gerald R. Ford Found., Grand Rapids, Mich., 1987—; mem. Adminstrv. Conf. U.S., 1991-92; mem. adv. com. U.S. Ct. Fed. Claims; mem. code com. U.S. Ct. of Mil. Appeals for the Armed Forces, 1993-95; bd. dirs. Falcon Found., 1988—. Decorated Bronze star; recipient Disting. Pub. Svc. medal Dept. of Def., 1992, Disting. Svc. award U.S. Atty. Gen., 1992. Mem. ABA, D.C. Bar Assn., Bar of U.S. Supreme Ct., and others. Administrative and regulatory, General civil litigation. Home: 5133 Yuma St NW Washington DC 20016-4336 Office: Williams and Connolly 725 12th St NW Washington DC 20005-5901 E-mail: todonnell@textron.com., todonnell@wc.com.

O'DONNELL, THOMAS ALEXANDER, lawyer; b. Phila., June 3, 1947; s. Robert James and Sara Esther (Hall) O'D.; m. Cathlene Janine Moreno, May 26, 1973; 1 child, James. BA, Swarthmore (Pa.) Coll., 1969; PhD, Rutgers U., 1979; JD, U. Cin., 1983. Bar: D.C. 1983, U.S. Tax Ct. 1983, U.S. Ct. Appeals (fed. cir.) 1983, U.S. Ct. Appeals (4th cir.) 1985, U.S. Supreme Ct. 1989. Asst. prof. Transylvania U., Lexington, Ky., 1974-79; assoc. Baker & McKenzie, Washington, 1983-92, ptnr., 1992-98, Paris, 1998-2001, Zurich, 2001—; coord. European-Am. Tax Inst., Paris, 1998-2001. Author: Passive Foreign Investment Companies, 1991; co-author: Business Operations in the USSR, 1991; contbr. articles to profl. jours. Woodrow Wilson Found. fellow, 1972. Mem. ABA, Order of Coif, Phi Beta Kappa. Email: Thomas.A.O'Donnell@Bakernet.com. Estate taxation, Corporate taxation, Taxation, general. Office: Baker & McKenzie Zollikerstr 225 PO Box 8034 Zürich Switzerland

O'DONOHOE, JUDITH MACK, lawyer; b. Phila., Apr. 25, 1951; d. Charles Lawrence and Jane Cridland Mack; m. Christopher Franklin O'Donohoe, Sept. 2, 1974; children: Jennifer Grace, Emily Joy. BA, Carleton Coll., 1973; JD, N.Y.U., 1976. Bar: Iowa 1976, U.S. Supreme Ct. Assoc. McCoutney and Erb, Charles City, Iowa, 1976—79; ptnr. Erb, O'Donohoe and Frye, Charles City, 1979—88, Eggert, Erb, O'Donohoe and Frye, Charles City, Elwood, O'Donohoe, Stochl, Braun and Churbuk, Charles City, 1997—. Juvenile referee Floyd and Mitchell Counties, Iowa, 1983—87. Bd. dirs. legal svs. corp., Des Moines, 1982—85; coach Odyssey of Mind, New Hampton, Iowa, 1988—2003. Recipient Gov.'s Vol. award, State of Iowa, 1992, New Hampton Edn. Assn. award, Friend of Edn., New Hampton, Iowa, 1996. Mem.: Iowa State Bar Assn., Am. Trial Lawyers Assn., Iowa Assn. Trial Lawyers, Iowa Supreme Cts. Com. Achievements include setting the paramters of public employee and employer rights under the law in Charles City Education Association versus the public employment relations board; altered the interpretation of FIFRA and preamption in Ackerman versus American Tyinumid, Estate of Leonard versus Henkels, Iowa Supreme Court decision. Avocations: working with children, reading, volleyball, volunteer work. Appellate, Education and schools, Personal injury (including property damage). Home: 271 South Locust Ave New Hampton IA 50659 Office: Elwood ODonohoe Stohl Braun & Churbuk 116 N Main St Charles City IA 50616 Office Fax: 641-228-8057. E-mail: elwood@fiai.net.

ODZA, RANDALL M. lawyer; b. Schnectady, May 6, 1942; s. Mitchell and Grace (Mannes) O.; m. Rita Ginness, June 19, 1966; children: Kenneth, Keith. BS in Indsl. and Labor Rels., Cornell U., 1964, LLB, 1967. Bar: N.Y. 1967, U.S. Ct. Appeals (2d cir.) 1970, U.S. Dist. Ct. (so. and ea. dists.) N.Y. 1969, U.S. Dist. Ct. (we. dist.) N.Y. 1970. Assoc. Proskauer, Rose, Goetz & Mandelsohn, N.Y.C., 1967-69, Jaeckle, Fleischmann & Mugel, Buffalo, 1969-72, ptnr., 1972—. Trustee, legal counsel, past treas. Temple Beth Am; bd. dirs. Buffalo Philharm. Orch. Soc. Fellow Coll. Labor & Employment Lawyers; recipient Honow award Western N.Y. Retail Mchts. Assn., 1980. Fellow Coll. Labor and Employment Lawyers; mem. ABA, Indsl. Rels. Rsch. Assn. Western N.Y., Erie County Bar Assn., N.Y. State Bar Assn., Buffalo Philharm. Soc. (bd. dirs.). Labor (including EEOC, Fair Labor Standards Act, labor-management relations, NLRB, OSHA). Office: Jaeckle Fleischmann & Mugel 12 Fountain Plz Rm 700 Buffalo NY 14202-2292

OECHLER, HENRY JOHN, JR., lawyer; b. Charlotte, N.C., Apr. 9, 1946; s. Henry J. and Convere Jones (McAden) O. AB, Princeton U., 1968; JD, Duke U., 1971. Bar: N.Y. 1972, U.S. Ct. Appeals (2d cir.) 1974, U.S. Ct. Appeals (D.C. cir.) 1975, U.S. Ct. Appeals (8th cir.) 1986, U.S. Ct. Appeals (9th cir.) 1995. Assoc. Chadbourne & Parke, N.Y.C., 1971-80, ptnr., 1980—. Avocation: studying airline schedules. General civil litigation, Labor (including EEOC, Fair Labor Standards Act, labor-management relations, NLRB, OSHA), Transportation. Office: Chadbourne & Parke 30 Rockefeller Plz Fl 31 New York NY 10112-0129

OEHLER, RICHARD DALE, lawyer; b. Iowa City, Dec. 9, 1925; s. Harold Lawrence Oehler and Bernito Babb; m. Rosemary Heineman, July 11, 1952, (div.); m. Maria Luisa Holguin-Zea, June 11, 1962; children: Harold D., Richard L. BA in Med. Scis., U. Calif., Berkeley, 1951; JD, Loyola U., L.A., 1961. Bar: Calif. 1962, Fla. 1968. Sales rep. Abbott Labs., Pasadena, Calif., 1951-63; with claims dept. Allstate Ins., Tampa, 1963-70; pvt. practice Tampa, 1970—. Instr. Dale Carnegie Courses West Fla. Inst., Tampa, Scott Hitchcock & Assocs., Tampa, 1969—. Pres. U. South Fla. Parents Assn., Tampa, 1986-87. Mem. Fla. Bar Assn., Hillsborough County Bar Assn., Acad. of Fla. Trial Lawyers, Assn. of Trial Lawyers of Am., Masons (32d degree), Shriners, Phi Beta Kappa. Republican. Presbyterian. Avocations: jogging, road races, target shooting, fishing. Personal injury (including property damage), Probate (including wills, trusts). Office: 200 N Pierce St Tampa FL 33602-5020 E-mail: doehler@mindspring.com.

OETTING, ROGER H. lawyer; b. Ft. Wayne, Ind., Dec. 17, 1931; s. Martin W. and Valetta E. (Holman) O.; m. Marcia J. Highlands, Aug. 10, 1957; children: Richard H., Susan E., Catherine R. BBA, U. Mich., 1953, MBA, JD, U. Mich., 1956; LLM in Taxation, Georgetown U., 1958. Ptnr. Touche Ross & Co., Detroit, 1960-80, Warner Norcross & Judd LLP, Grand Rapids, Mich., 1980—. Adj. prof. taxation Grand Valley State U., 1984-99. Past pres., dir. treas. Chamber Music Soc. Grand Rapids, 1980-89; past dir., treas. Opera Grand Rapids, 1980-87; dir. Porter Hills Presbyn. Village, 1989—, treas., 1990—; dir., chair fin. Aquinas Emeritus Coll. Fellow Am. Coll. Tax Lawyers; mem. State Bar Mich. (coun. fed. tax sect. 1991—), Grand Rapids Bar Assn. (chair fin. com. 1983—), Econ. Club (past treas., bd. dirs. 1982-91), Sugar Bush Assn. (dir., sec., treas. 1985—), Kent Country Club (fin. com.), Leland Country Club, Leland Yacht Club, Univ. Club (bd. dirs., treas.), Rotary (bd. dirs. 1989-93), Delta Kappa Epsilon. Corporate taxation, Taxation, general, Personal income taxation. Office: Warner Norcross & Judd LLP 900 Fifth Third Ctr 111 Lyon St NW Grand Rapids MI 49503-2487

OETTINGER, JULIAN ALAN, lawyer, pharmacy company executive; BS, U. Ill., 1961; JD, Northwestern U., 1964. Bar: Ill. 1964. Atty. SEC, 1964-67, Walgreen Co., Deerfield, Ill., 1967-72, sr. atty., 1972-78, dir. law, 1978-89, v.p., gen. counsel, corp. sec., 1989-2000, sr. v.p., 2000—. Corporate, general, Property, real (including real estate development, water), Securities. Office: Walgreen Co 200 Wilmot Rd Deerfield IL 60015-4616*

OFFER, STUART JAY, lawyer; b. Seattle, June 2, 1943; m. Judith Spitzer, Aug. 29, 1970; children: Rebecca, Kathryn. BA, U. Wash., 1964; LLB, Columbia U., 1967. Bar: D.C. 1968, U.S. Tax Ct. 1968, Calif. 1972. Atty., advisor U.S. Tax Ct., Washington, 1967-68; assoc. Morrison & Foerster, LLP, San Francisco, 1972-76, ptnr., 1976—. Trustee Am. Tax Policy Inst. Served as capt. U.S. Army, 1968-72. Mem. ABA (chmn. taxation sect., corp. tax com. 1991-92, coun. dir. 1995-98, vice chair adminstrn. 1998-2000), Internat. Fiscal Assn., Am. Coll. Tax Counsel. Private international, Corporate taxation. Office: Morrison & Foerster LLP 425 Market St San Francisco CA 94105-2482 E-mail: soffer@mofo.com.

OFFNER, ERIC DELMONTE, lawyer; b. Vienna, June 23, 1928; came to U.S., 1941, naturalized, 1949; s. Sigmund J. and Kathe (Delmonte) O.; m. Julie Cousins, 1955 (dec. 1959); m. Barbara Ann Shotton, July 2, 1961; 1 son, Gary Douglas; m. Carol Sue Marcus, Jan. 12, 1980 (dec. 1983) BBA, CCNY, 1949; JD in Internat. Affairs, Cornell U., 1952. Bar: N.Y. 1952. Assoc. Langner, Parry, Card & Langner, N.Y.C., 1952-57; ptnr. Haseltine, Lake, Waters & Offner, N.Y.C., 1957-77; sr. ptnr. Offner & Kuhn, 1978-83; pvt. practice N.Y.C., 1983—. Instr. George Washington U. Law Sch., Cornell U. Law Sch.; spl. prof. law Hofstra Law Sch., 1974-92. Author: International Trademark Protection, 1964, Japanese edit., 1977, International Trademark Service, Vols. I-III 1970, Vol. IV, 1972, Vol. V., 1973, Vol. VI, 1976, Vol. VII, 1981, Vols. I-VII, 2d edit., 1981, Legal Training Course on Trademarks, 1982; editor in chief: Cornell Law Forum, 1950-51; mem. editorial bd.: Trademark Reporter, 1961-64, 69-72; book reviewer Jour. Humanism and Ethical Religion; contbr. articles to profl. jours.; prodr. jazz concerts N.Y.C., 1996—, jazz video and jazz CDs. V.p. Riverdale Mental Health Clinic, N.Y.C., 1966-67; pres. Riverdale Mental Health Assn., 1967-69,pres. Ethical Culture Soc., Riverdale-Yonkers, 1964-67,pres. Ethical Cultural Retirement Ctr., 1975-94; trustee Am. Ethical Union, 1967-73, Internat. Alliance of Holistic Lawyers; bd. dirs. Fit Kids; pres. The Sidney Bechet Soc., Ltd., 1997—. Mem. N.Y. Patent Law Assn. (assoc. editor Bull. 1961-66, gov. 1973-76), ABA, City N.Y. Bar Assn. (sec. 1962-64), U.S. Trademark Assn., World Peace Through Law (charter), Trademark Soc. Washington (charter), Inst. Trade Mark Agts. (London), Sidney Bechet Soc. Ltd. (pres. 1997—), Australian Patent Inst., Internat. Assn. Protection Indsl. Property, Nat. Coun. Patent Law Assn., Internat. Patent, Trademark Assn., Phi Alpha Delta. Intellectual property, Trademark and copyright. Home: 20 Joy Dr New Hyde Park NY 11040-1109 E-mail: eoffner@optonline.net.

OFFUTT, DENVER CLYDE, JR., lawyer; b. Marlinton, W.Va., Feb. 21, 1949; s. Denver Clyde and Mary Margaret (Beard) O.; m. Cheryl Ann Eifert; children: Kimberly Dawn, Jody Monroe, Kelsey Devon, Andrew Bryant. BA, W.Va. U., 1971, MPA, 1972, JD, 1978. Bar: W.Va. 1978, U.S. Dist. Ct. (so. dist.) W. Va. 1978, U.S. Ct. Appeals (4th cir.) 1988, U.S. Supreme Ct. 1983, Ky. 1989, U.S. Ct. Appeals (6th cir.) 1997, U.S. Dist. Ct. (ea. dist.) Ky. 1997. Gen. counsel State of W.Va. div. vocat. rehab., Charleston, 1978-79, dep. dir., 1979-81; assoc., ptnr. Jenkins, Fenstermaker, Krieger, Kayes & Farrell, Huntington, W.Va., 1981-93; mng. ptnr. Offutt, Fisher & Nord, Huntington, 1993—. Bd. dirs., Goodwill Industries, Huntington, 1981-92, pres., 1987. Mem. ABA, W.Va. State Bar (bd. govs. 1992-95, v.p. 1995-96, pres.-elect 1996-97, pres. 1997-98), W.Va. Bar Assn., Cabell County Bar (pres. 1987-88), Def. Trial Counsel W.Va. (bd. govs. 1990-92), Ky. Bar Assn. Democrat. Episcopalian. General civil litigation, Insurance, Personal injury (including property damage). Office: Offutt Fisher & Nord PO Box 2868 Huntington WV 25728-2868

OFNER, WILLIAM BERNARD, investor; b. L.A., Aug. 24, 1929; s. Harry D. and Gertrude (Skoss) Offner; m. Florence Ila Maxwell, Apr. 13, 1953 (div. 1956). AA, L.A. City Coll., 1949; BA, Calif. State U., L.A., 1953; LLB, Loyola U., L.A., 1965; postgrad., Sorbonne, 1951; cert. de Langue Francaise, 1987; postgrad., U. So. Calif., 1966, Glendale Community Coll., 1986-92. Bar: Calif. 1966, U.S. Dist. Ct. Calif. 1966, U.S. Supreme Ct. 1972. Assoc. Thomas Moore and Assocs., L.A., 1967-69; pvt. practice L.A., 1969-70, 74—; assoc. Peter Lam, L.A., 1981-94, mng. atty., 1993—. Assoc. C.M. Coronel, 1986-87, Jack D. Janofsky, 1987-89, Mario P. Gonzalez, 1990-92, Genaro Legorreta, Jr., 1997-98; lectr. Van Norman U., 1975; property mgr., 1982—; investor 1984—. Electronics instr. USNR, 1949—54. Mem. Inst. Gen. Semantics, Toastmasters, Safari Athletic Club. Democrat. Avocations: photography, linguistics, tutoring, travel, watercolor. Office: PO Box 163 Chino Hills CA 91709

OGBOGU, CECILIA IFY, lawyer; b. Enugu, Nigeria, Sept. 19, 1964; d. Samuel and Cecilia Ogbogu; children: Jason, Osita. BL with honors, Nigerian Law Sch., Lagos, Nigeria, 1986; LLB with honors, Imo State U., Aba, Nigeria, 1985. Bar: Calif. 1996, U.S. Dist. Ct. (ctrl. dist.) Calif. 1996, Nigerian Bar 1986. Staff counsel Cooperative and Commerce, Bank of Nigeria Plc, Enugu, Nigeria, 1988-93; vol. atty. Legal Aid Found. of L.A., 1996, Bet Tzedek Legal Svcs., L.A., 1996; pvt. practice L.A., 1996—. Fellow The Alliance for Children's Rights, L.A., 1998—. Recipient Wiley Manuel award State Bar of Calif., 1997, Merit award Nat. Ctr. for Missing and Exploited Children, 1997. Mem. ABA (Child Advocacy Nat. Cert. Recognition young lawyers divsn. 2000), ATLA, L.A. County Bar Assn. (barristers' com. 1996—). Democrat. Roman Catholic. Avocations: writing, reading, stamp collecting. General civil litigation, Family and matrimonial, Personal injury (including property damage). Office: 315 W 9th St Ste 603 Los Angeles CA 90015-4207 E-mail: ceeogbogu@lawyer.com.

OGBURN, THOMAS LYNN, III, lawyer; b. Winston-Salem, N.C., Sept. 15, 1969; s. Thomas Lynn Jr. and Anita O. BA in Polit. Sci. and Econs., U. N.C., 1992; MBA, JD, Wake Forest U., 1996. Bar: N.C. 1996, S.C. 1996. Atty. Poyner & Spruill, L.L.P., Charlotte, NC, 1996—. Swim instr. Ctrl. YMCA, Charlotte, 1996—; CPR instr. ARC, Charlotte, 1996—. Mem. N.C. Bar, S.C. Bar, N.C. Bar Assn. General civil litigation, Commercial, consumer (including collections, credit). Office: Poyner & Spruill LLP 301 S College St Ste 2300 Charlotte NC 28202

OGDEN, ANNE D. lawyer; b. New Orleans, Sept. 28, 1974; d. Henry Duplessis IV and Diana Hayden Ogden. BGS, La. State U., 1996; JD, Nova Southeastern U., 2000. Bar: Fla. 00, U.S. Dist. Ct. (no. and so. dists) Fla. 01. Law clk., then assoc. Atlas Pearlman, P.A., Ft. Lauderdale, Fla., 1999—2001; assoc. Bazinsky & Guerra, P.A., Plantation, Fla., 2001—. Adj. prof. English Fla. Internat. U., Miami, 2002. Mem.: Broward County

Bar Assn. (bd. dirs. young lawyers divsn. 2002). Personal injury (including property damage), Product liability, Insurance. Office: Bazinsky & Korman PA 7901 SW 6th Ct Ste 450 Plantation FL 33324

OGG, ELTON JERALD, JR., educator, academic administrator; b. Springfield, Mo., Aug. 25, 1955; s. Elton Jerald Sr. and Janett Northam O.; m. Mary Jane Nichols, Dec. 28, 1973; children: Jennifer Lauren, Jana Elizabeth. JD, U. Tenn., 1978; MJ, La. State U., 1987; PhD, So. Ill. U., 1994. Bar: Tenn. 1979, La. 1984. Pvt. practice law, Baton Rouge, 1983-87; asst. prof. comm. U. Tenn., Martin, 1987-97, chmn. dept. comm., 1997-2000; dean Coll. Humanities and Fine Arts, 2000—; prof. Tenn. Govs. Sch. Humanities, Martin, 1991-2000, dir., 2000—. Contbr. articles to profl. jours. Pres. Parent-Tchr. Orgn., Martin, 1989—90; coach Martin Girls Softball Assn., 1993—2001; dir. Lifeline Blood Svcs., Weakley County, Tenn., 1993—. Res. judge adv. USAFR, 1983—. Avocations: golf, softball, tennis, reading. Office: U Tenn 225 Humanities Martin TN 38238-0001

OGG, WILSON REID, lawyer, judge, poet, lyricist, curator, publisher, educator, philosopher, social scientist, parapsychologist; b. Alhambra, Calif., Feb. 26, 1928; s. James Brooks and Mary (Wilson) Ogg. Student, Pasadena Jr. Coll., 1946; AB, U. Calif., Berkeley, 1949; JD, U. Calif., 1952; Cultural D in Philosophy of Law, World U. Roundtable, 1983. Bar: Calif. 1955. Assoc. trust dept. Wells Fargo Bank, San Francisco, 1954-55; pvt. practice Berkeley, 1955—. Adminstv. law judge, 1974—93; real estate broker, cons., 1974—; curator-in-residence, Pinebrook, 1964—; owner Pinebrook Press, Berkeley, 1988—; rsch. atty., legal editor dept. of continuing edn. bar U. Calif., 1958—63; instr. 25th Sta. Hosp., Taegu, Republic of Korea, 1954, Taegu English Lang. Inst., 1954; trustee World U., 1976—80; dir. admissions internat. Soc. Phil. Enquiry, 1981—84; dep. dir. gen. Internat. Biographical Ctr., England, 1986—; dep. gov. Am. Biographical Inst. Rsch. Assn., 1986—. Author: (book) The Unified Theory; contbr. articles to profl. jours., poems to mags. With AUS, 1952—54. Named to Internat. Poetry Hall of Fame, Nat. Libr. Poetry, 1997; recipient Internat. Peace prize, Auth. of United Cultural Conv., U.S., 2002. Mem.: ACLU, ASCAP, ABA, AAAS, VFW, London Diplomatic Acad., Inst. Noetic Scis., Triple Nine Soc., Intertel, Calif. Soc. Psychical Study (pres., chmn. bd. 1963—65), Am. Arbitration Assn. (nat. panel arbitrators), San Francisco Bar Assn., State Bar Calif., Internat. Soc. Individual Liberty, Internat. Soc. Unified, Internat. Platform Assn., Faculty Club of the U. Calif. at Berkeley (emeritus), Men's Inner Cir. Achievement, Amnesty Internat., Marines Meml. Club, Elks, Shriners, Masons, Am. Legion. Unitarian Universalist. Constitutional, General practice, Probate (including wills, trusts). Home: Pinebrook 8 Bret Harte Way Berkeley CA 94708-1607 Office: 1104 Keith Ave Berkeley CA 94708-1607 Fax: 510-540-6052. E-mail: wilsonogg@alum.calberkeley.org.

OGILVIE, GAIL, arbitrator, mediator, lawyer; b. Boston, July 10, 1944; d. Leon Russell and Dorothy Burt Ogilvie. AB in Math., Mount Holyoke Coll., 1966; MEd, Tufts U., 1970; JD, U. Maine, 1977. Bar: Maine 1977, U.S. Dist. Ct. Maine 1977, U.S. Supreme Ct. 1996. Asst. atty. gen. Maine Dept. Atty. Gen., Augusta, 1977-89; worker's compensation commr. Worker's Compensation Commn., Augusta, 1989-94; sr. trial atty. Piampiano & Gavin, Portland, Maine, 1994-96; chair med. malpractice screening panel Maine Superior Ct., Augusta, 1994—; adminstrv. hearing officer Maine Dept. Labor, 2002—. Mem. Maine State Bar Assn., Alternative Dispute Resolution Profls. Avocations: traveling, skiing, sailing, hiking. Home and Office: 25 Gardiner St Richmond ME 04357-1345

OGLE, ROBBIN SUE, criminal justice educator; b. North Kansas City, Mo., Aug. 28, 1960; d. Robert Lee and Carol Sue (Gray) O. BS, Ctrl. Mo. State U., 1982; MS, U. Mo., 1990; PhD, Pa. State U., 1995. State probation and parole officer Mo. Dept. Corrections, Kansas City, 1982-92; collector J.C. Penney Co., Mission, Kans., 1990-92; instr. U. Mo., Kansas City, 1990-92; grad. lectr. Pa. State U., University Park, 1992-95; prof. criminal justice dept. U. Nebr., Omaha, 1995—. Contbr. articles to profl. jours. Athletic scholar Ctrl. Mo. State U., Warrensburg, 1978-82. Mem. AAUW, ACLU, NOW, Am. Soc. Criminology, Acad. Criminal Justice Scis., Am. Correctional Assn., Phi Kappa Phi. Avocations: reading, watching basketball, walking dog. Office: U Nebr Dept Criminal Justice 1100 Neihardt Lincoln NE 68588-0630 Home: 2410 N 99th St Omaha NE 68134-5642 E-mail: RSOgle@webtv.net.

O'GRADY, DENNIS JOSEPH, lawyer; b. Hoboken, N.J., Nov. 16, 1943; s. Joseph A. and Eileen (Broderick) O'Grady; m. Mary Anne Amoruso, Sept. 9, 1966 (div. Apr. 1984); 1 child, Kara Anne. AB, Seton Hall Coll., 1965; MA, U. So. Calif., 1969; JD, Rutgers U., 1973. Bar: N.J. 1973, U.S. Ct. Appeals (3d cir.) 1975, U.S. Dist. Ct. N.J., U.S. Supreme Ct. 2000. Ptnr. Riker, Danzig, Scherer, Hyland & Perretti, Newark, Trenton and Morristown, N.J., 1974—. Adj. asst. prof. of bus. law St. Peter's Coll., Jersey City, 1973—; adj. prof. law Rutgers U. Law Sch., 1997—. Fellow: Am. Coll. Bankruptcy Lawyers (bus./bankruptcy sect.); mem.: ABA, Am. Bd. Cert. (faculty subcom.), Am. Bankruptcy Inst. (health career subcom., bd. profl. cert.), Fed. Bar Assn., N.J. State Bar Assn. (debtor/creditor sect.). Democrat. Roman Catholic. Banking, Bankruptcy, General civil litigation. Office: Riker Danzig Scherer Hyland & Perretti 1 Speedwell Ave Ste 2 Morristown NJ 07960-6823 E-mail: dogrady@riker.com.

O'GRADY, JOHN JOSEPH, III, lawyer; b. N.Y.C., Mar. 21, 1933; s. John Joseph and Terese (O'Rourke) O'G.; m. Mary E. McHugh, June 28, 1958; children— Glennon, Ellen, Carol, Paul AB, Holy Cross Coll., 1954; JD, Harvard U., 1957. Bar: N.Y. 1958. Assoc. Cadwalader, Wickersham & Taft, N.Y.C., 1958-66, ptnr., 1966-96, counsel, 1997—. Estate planning, Probate (including wills, trusts), Estate taxation. Office: Cadwalader Wickersham & Taft 100 Maiden Ln New York NY 10038-4818

O'HARA, PATRICIA A. dean, law educator; BA summa cum laude, Santa Clara U., 1971; JD summa cum laude, Notre Dame, 1974. Bar: Calif. 1974. Assoc. Brobeck, Phleger & Harrison, 1974—79, 1980—81; assoc. prof. law Notre Dame Law Sch., 1981, prof., 1990, v.p. student affairs, 1990—99, dean, law educator, 2001—. Contbr. chapters to books, articles to law jours. Office: U Notre Dame 203 Law Sch PO Box R Notre Dame IN 46556 Office Fax: 574-631-8400. E-mail: Patricia.A.O'Hara.3@nd.edu.

O'HARA, ROBERT SYDNEY, JR., lawyer; b. Englewood, N.J., Apr. 26, 1939; s. Robert Sydney and Katharine (Drayton) O'Hara; m. Elizabeth Crocker, June 17, 1961 (div.); children: Jennifer, Isabelle; m. Bonnie Durkin, July 19, 1975. AB, Princeton U., 1960; JD, U. Pa., 1963. Bar: N.Y. 1964. Ptnr. Milbank, Tweed, Hadley & McCloy, N.Y.C., 1965—. Served to capt. AUS, 1963—65. Banking, Corporate, general. Office: Milbank Tweed Hadley & McCloy 1 Chase Manhattan Plz Fl 47 New York NY 10005-1413

O'HARA, WILLIAM DESMOND, JR., lawyer; b. Corning, N.Y., July 18, 1938; s. William D. Sr. and Mary Margaret (Fleming-Burke) O'H.; m. LaVerne Mary Smith, Nov. 22, 1980. BA, U. Notre Dame, 1960; JD, Chgo.-Kent Coll. Law, 1968. Bar: Ill. 1968, U.S. Supreme Ct. 1971, Colo. 1971, Minn. 1976, U.S. Dist. Ct. Ill., U.S. Dist. Ct. Minn., U.S. Ct. Appeals (7th and 8th cirs.). Atty. McKenna Storer Rowe White and Haskell, Chgo., Law Office Dale Schlafer, Chgo., Ruff & Grotefeld, Chgo., Sachs Latz & Kirschbaum, Mpls., O'Hara Fossum Hill & Lothspeich, Brainerd, Minn., William D. O'Hara Jr. Ltd., Brainerd. Mem. Minn. Trial Lawyers Assn., Minn. State Bar Assn., Trial Lawyers Club Chgo., Elks Club, Sertoma. General practice, Personal injury (including property damage), Property, real (including real estate development, water). Home: 20446 Legionville Point Tr Brainerd MN 56401 Office: 417 Laurel St PO Box 624 Brainerd MN 56401-0624 E-mail: oharalaw@brainerd.net.

O'HERN, DANIEL JOSEPH, retired state supreme court justice; b. Red Bank, N.J., May 23, 1930; s. J. Henry and Eugenia A. (Sansone) O'H.; m. Barbara Ronan, Aug. 8, 1959; children: Daniel J., Eileen, James, John, Molly. AB, Fordham Coll., 1951; LLB, Harvard U., 1957. Bar: N.J. 1958. Clk. U.S. Supreme Ct., Washington, 1957-58; assoc. Abramoff, Apy & O'Hern, Red Bank, N.J., 1966-78; commr. N.J. Dept. Environ. Protection, 1978-79; counsel to Gov. N.J. Trenton; assoc. justice N.J. Supreme Ct., Trenton, 1981—2000; counsel Gibbons, Del Deo, Dolan, Griffinger & Vecchione, Newark, 2000—. Former mem. adv. com. profl. ethics N.J. Supreme Ct.; commr. Nat. Conf. Commrs. Uniform State Laws, 2001-. Past trustee Legal Aid Soc. Monmouth County, (N.J.); mayor Borough of Red Bank, 1969-78, councilman, 1962-69. Served as lt. (j.g.) USNR, 1951-54. Fellow Am. Bar Found.; mem. ABA, N.J. Bar Assn., Monmouth County Bar Assn., Harvard Law Sch. Assn. N.J. (past pres.) Office: NJ Supreme Ct 151 Bodman Pl Red Bank NJ 07701-1070 also: NJ Supreme Ct PO Box 970 Trenton NJ 08625-0970 Office: Gibbons Del Deo Dolan et al One Riverfront Plaza Newark NJ 07102*

OHLGREN, JOEL R. lawyer; b. Mpls., July 21, 1942; BA, UCLA, 1965, JD, 1968. Bar: Calif. 1969. Ptnr. Sheppard, Mullin, Richter & Hampton LLP, L.A. Fellow Am. Coll. Bankruptcy; mem. ABA, State Bar Calif., Los Angeles County Bar Assn. (past chmn. comml. law and bankruptcy sect.), Order of Coif, Financial Lawyers Inst., Am. Bankruptcy Inst., Turnaround Management Assn., Internat. Insolvency Inst. Bankruptcy, Commercial, consumer (including collections, credit). Office: Sheppard Mullin Richter & Hampton LLP 333 S Hope St Fl 48 Los Angeles CA 90071-1406

OHMAN, JOHN MICHAEL, lawyer; b. Dec. 22, 1948; s. John W. and D. Jeanne (Forster) O.; m. Desiree Ohman; children: Brittany Michelle, Andrea Michaela. BS in Bus. Adminstrn., Creighton U., 1971, JD, 1972. Bar: Nebr. 1972, Idaho 1973, U.S. Dist. Ct. Idaho 1973, U.S. Dist. Ct. Nebr. 1973, U.S. Ct. Appeals (9th cir.) 1978., U.S. Supreme Ct. 1978. Atty. Cox & Ohman, Idaho Falls, Idaho, 1978—. Lectr. various locations; chmn. Idaho Transp. Dept. Author: Federal Judges: The Complexity of Recruitment, Appointment, Tenure and Removal; contbr. articles to profl. jours. Exec. bd. Assn. Humanities in Idaho, legal advisor; active United Way, YMCA; past pres. Am. Cancer Soc.; judge advocate Intermountain dist. Civitan Internat., also past pres. Idaho Falls chpt.; legal adv. Mayor's Com. for Handicapped, Mayor's Com. for Swimming Pool, Community Concert Assn., Idaho Falls Symphony Soc., Eastern Idaho Spl. Services Agy.; dir. Group Homes, Inc.; campaign coordinator Gov. Idaho; mem. State Dem. Cen. Com.; precinct committeeman. Served to capt. U.S. Army. Recipient Outstanding Pres. award Civitian Internat., Century Club mem. YMCA, Idaho Safe Pilot award; named del. to Hong Kong, to People's Republic of China and Japan by Idaho Bus. Leaders. Mem. ABA (litig. sect., family law sect., tort and ins. practice sect., divsn. law and procedures com.), Am. Soc. Law and Medicine, Am. Judicature Soc., Idaho State Bar Assn. (adv. coun. continuing legal edn.), Nebr. State Bar. Assn., Seventh Jud. Dist. Bar Assn., Am. Trial Lawyers Assn., Idaho Trial Lawyers Assn., Idaho Assn. Def. Counsel, Def. Rsch. Inst., Idaho Law Found., Unauthorized Practice Law Com., Western Assn. State Hwy. and Transp. Officials, Assn. Humanities Idaho (past mem. exec. bd.), Am. Assn. State Hwy. and Transp. Officials, Smithsonian Inst. (assoc.), Internat. Platform Assn., Assn. Interstate Commerce Practitioners, 7th Jud. Dist. Bar Assn., Am. Mus. Natural History, Airplane Owners and Pilots Assn., Nat. Arbor's Day Found., Idaho Falls C. of C. (chmn. legis. com.), Phi Alpha Delta, Omicron Delta Epsilon, Phi Kappa Psi. Lodges: Elks (legal advisor). Democrat. Roman Catholic. Avocations: aquatic sports, numismatics, reading, aviation, racquetball. General practice, Personal injury (including property damage). Office: Cox and Ohman PO Box 51600 Idaho Falls ID 83405-1600 Fax: 208 520-8618. E-mail: johman3419@aol.com., cobjmo@ida.net.

OHRT, HANS-CHRISTIAN, lawyer; b. Ribe, Denmark, Jan. 10, 1966; s. Svend Ohrt and Ingrid Ohrt Johansen; m. Malene Holm Ohrt, Aug. 5, 1995; children: Alexander Holm, William Holm. JD, U. Aarhus, Denmark, 1991. Bar: Danish High Ct. 1995. Legal asst. Bech-Bruun Dragsted, Copenhagen, 1991—94, lawyer, 1994—96, Cameron McKenna, London, 1996—97; gen. counsel Bang and Olufsen, Struer, Denmark, 1997—99; lawyer, ptnr. Dahl, Koch and Boll, Kolding, Denmark, 1999—. Mem.: DSV V.L. Gruppe 50. Mergers and acquisitions, Commercial, contracts (including sales of goods; commercial financing), Antitrust. Home: Trapholtparken 20 DK-6000 Kolding Denmark Office: Dahl Koch and Boll Jernbanegade 29 DK-6000 Kolding Denmark

O'KEEFE, EDWARD FRANKLIN, lawyer; b. S.I., N.Y., June 9, 1937; s. Francis Franklin and Bertha (Hall) O'K.; m. Toni Lynne McGohan; children: Kira Kathleen, Douglas Franklin, Andrew Franklin, Alison Elizabeth, Theadore William, Nigel Francis. AB, U. N.C., 1959; JD, U. Denver, 1961. Bar: Colo. 1962. Law clk. Colo. Supreme Ct., Denver, 1962-63; assoc. gen. counsel Hamilton Mgmt. Corp., Denver, 1966-69, sec., 1968-76, v.p. legal, gen. counsel, 1969-76; ptnr. Moye, Giles O'Keefe, Vermeire & Gorrell, Denver, 1976—. Assoc. gen. counsel, sec. ITT Variable Annuity Ins. Co., Denver, 1969, v.p. legal, gen. counsel, 1969-70; sec. Hamilton Funds Inc., Denver, 1968-76 Served with USNR, 1963-66. Mem. Nat. Assn. Security Dealers (dist. conduct com., chmn. 1976), Colo. Assn. Corporate Counsel (pres. 1974-75) also: 2680 Mariners Way SE Southport NC 28461 Office: Moye Giles O'Keefe Vermeire 1225 17th St Fl 29 Denver CO 80202-5534 Home: 2680 Mariners Way SE Southport NC 28461-8512 E-mail: ed.okeefe@moyelaw.com.

O'KEEFE, RAYMOND PETER, lawyer, educator; b. N.Y.C., Jan. 16, 1928; s. William Bernard and Catherine Irene (Smith) O'Keefe; m. Stephanie Ann Fitzpatrick, June 19, 1954; children: Raymond, William, Ann, Kevin, Mary, James, John. AB cum laude, St. Michael's Coll., 1950; JD, Fordham U., 1953. Bar: N.Y. 1954, Fla. 1976, U.S. Dist. Ct. (so. dist.) : N.Y. 1955, U.S. Ct. Claims : 1960, U.S. Ct. Appeals (2d cir.) : 1963, U.S. Supreme Ct. : 1971. Assoc. Thayer & Gilbert, N.Y.C., 1953—55; prof. law Fordham U. Sch. Law, N.Y.C., 1955—63; sr. assoc. Carter, Ledyard & Milburn, N.Y.C., 1963—68; ptnr. Ide & Haigney, N.Y.C., 1968—74; sr. ptnr. McCarthy, Fingar, Donovan, Drazen & Smith, White Plains, NY, 1974—. Adj. prof. Pace U. Sch. Law, White Plains, 1979—, Fordham U. Sch. Law, 1983—; lectr. N.Y. Med. Coll., Valhalla, NY, 1979—; prof. St. Thomas of Villanova Miami Sch. Law, 1984—; vis. prof. Thomas M. Cooley Sch. Law, Lansing, 1991, Fordham U. Sch. Law, 1992; justice State of N.Y. Justice Ct., 1978—81. Trustee Am. Irish Hist. Soc.; chmn. bd. Westchester Halfway House, 1974—78; bd. dirs. Westchester Youth Shelter, 1980. With USN, 1945—48. Recipient Alumni award, St. Michael's Coll., 1961, Humanitarian award, Fordham Law Sch., 1999. Mem.: ABA (commn. on youth, drugs and alcoholism 1984), Assn. of Bar of City of N.Y., N.Y. State Trial Lawyers Assn., Assn. Trial Lawyers Am., Fla. Bar Assn., N.Y. State Bar Assn. (chmn. spl. com. on lawyer alcoholism and drug abuse 1979—), Surf Club, Harbor View Club, Larchmont Shore Club. General practice. Home: 802 Kure Village Way Kure Beach NC 28449-4900 Office: St Thomas Law Sch 16400 NE 32nd Ave Miami FL 33160

O'KELLEY, WILLIAM CLARK, federal judge; b. Atlanta, Jan. 2, 1930; s. Ezra Clark and Theo (Johnson) O'K.; m. Ernestine Allen, Mar. 28, 1953; children: Virginia Leigh O'Kelley Wood, William Clark Jr. AB, Emory U., 1951, LLB, 1953. Bar: Ga. 1952. Pvt. practice, Atlanta, 1957-59; asst. U.S. atty. No. Dist. Ga., 1959-61; partner O'Kelley, Hopkins & Van Gerpen, Atlanta, 1961-70; U.S. dist. judge No. Dist. Ga., Atlanta, 1970—, chief judge, 1988-94. Mem. com. on adminstrn. of criminal law Jud. Conf. U.S., 1979-82, exec. com., 1983-84, subcom. on jury trials in complex criminal cases, 1981-82, dist. judge rep. 11th cir., 1981-84, mem. adv. com. of fed. rules of criminal procedure, 1984-87; bd. dirs. Fed. Jud. Ctr., 1987-91, adv. com. history program, 1989-91, com. on orientation of newly appointed dist. judges, 1985-88; mem. Com. Jud. Resources, 1989-94; mem. Jud. Coun. 11th Cir., 1990-96, exec. com., 1990-96; mem. Fgn. Intelligence Surveillance Ct., 1980-87; mem. Alien Terrorist Removal Ct., 1996—; corp. sec., dir. Gwinnett Bank & Trust Co., Norcross, Ga., 1967-70. Mem. exec. com., gen. counsel Ga. Republican Com., 1968-70; mem. fin. com. Northwest Ga. Girl Scout Coun., 1958-70; trustee Emory U., 1991-97. Served as 1st lt. USAF, 1953-57; capt. USAFR. Mem. Fed. Bar Assn., Ga. State Bar, Atlanta Bar Assn., Dist. Judges Assn. 5th Cir. (sec.-treas. 1976-77, v.p. 1977-78, pres. 1978-80), Lawyers Club Atlanta, Kiwanis (past pres.), Atlanta Athletic Club, Sigma Chi (named Significant Sig 1983), Phi Delta Phi, Omicron Delta Kappa. Baptist. Home: 550 Ridgecrest Dr Norcross GA 30071-2158 Office: US Dist Ct 1942 US Courthouse 75 Spring St SW Atlanta GA 30303-3309

O'KIEF, W. GERALD, lawyer; b. Portland, Oreg., Feb. 19, 1937; s. William G. and Alice M. (Zilmer) O'K.; m. Sharon M. Moran, June 26, 1966; children: Gregory, Mary, John, Paul. AB, LLB, Creighton U., 1960; LLM, Harvard U., 1961. Pvt. practice, Valentine, Nebr., 1961—. Bd. dirs. First Nat. Bank, Valentine, Nebr. Mem. Nebr. Bar Assn. Banking, Estate planning, General practice. Office: Box 766 111 E 3rd St Valentine NE 69201-1809

OKINAGA, CARRIE KIYONO, lawyer; b. Honolulu, Sept. 9, 1967; d. Lawrence Shoji and Carolyn (Hisako) O.; m. Scott Wai Hin Seu, Nov. 14, 1998. BA, Pomona Coll., 1989; JD, Stanford U., 1992. Bar: Calif., Hawaii, 1993; U.S. Dist. Ct. Hawaii, 1993. Ptnr. McCorriston, Miller Mukai MacKinnon LLP, Honolulu, 1992—. Asst. editor: (newsletter) The Affiliate, 1998. Mem. P.A.R.E.N.T.S., 1994-98. Pacific Century fellow, Honolulu, 1998-99. Mem. ABA (dist. rep. young lawyers divsn. 1996-98, vice-chair minorities in the profession com. 1997-99, liaison to sect. labor and employment law 1999-2000, co-editor Minority Trial Lawyer 2003-), Hawaii State Bar Assn. (bd. dirs. young lawyers divsn. 1995-99). General civil litigation, Environmental, Labor (including EEOC, Fair Labor Standards Act, labor-management relations, NLRB, OSHA). Office: McCorriston Miller Mukai MacKinnon LLP Five Waterfront Plz 4th Fl 500 Ala Moana Blvd Honolulu HI 96813-4989 E-mail: okinaga@m4law.com.

OKINAGA, LAWRENCE SHOJI, lawyer; b. Honolulu, July 7, 1941; s. Shohei and Hatsu (Kakimoto) O.; m. Carolyn Hisako Uesugi, Nov. 26, 1966; children: Carrie, Caryn, Laurie. BA, U. Hawaii, 1963; JD, Georgetown U., 1972. Bar: Hawaii 1972, U.S. Dist. Ct. Hawaii 1972, U.S. Ct. Appeals (9th cir.) 1976. Adminstrv. asst. to Congressman Spark Matsunaga, Honolulu, 1964, 65-69; law clk. to chief judge U.S. Dist. Ct. Hawaii, Honolulu, 1972-73; assoc. Carlsmith Ball, Honolulu, 1973-76, ptnr., 1976—. Mem. Gov.'s Citizens Adv. Com. Coastal Zone Mgmt., 1974-79; sec. Hawaii Bicentennial Corp., 1975-77, chmn., 1985-87, vice chmn., 1983-85; mem. Jud. Selection Commn., State of Hawaii, 1979-87, vice chmn., 1986; mem. consumer adv. coun. Fed. Res. Bd., 1984-86; chmn. State of Hawaii Jud. Conduct Commn., 1991-94; apptd. mem. Fed. Savs. and Loan Adv. Coun., Washington, 1988-89; mem. nat. adv. coun. U.S. SBA, 1994-2000; mem. adv. coun. Fed. Res. Bank of San Francisco, 1995-2002. Bd. dirs. Moiliili Cmty. Ctr., Honolulu, 1965-68, 73-86, trustee 1993—; bd. visitors Georgetown U. Law Ctr., 1993—; trustee Kuakini Med. Ctr., 1984-88, 89-96. Capt. USAFR, 1964-72, 74-76. Mem. ABA (ho. of dels. 1991-94, standing com. on jud. selection tenure and compensation 1993-96, standing com. on jud. independence 1999-2002), Hawaii Bar Assn. (sec., bd. dirs. 1981), Am. Judicature Soc. (bd. dirs. 1986, treas. 1995-97, pres. 1997-99), Georgetown U. Law Alumni Assn. (bd. dirs. 1986-91), Omicron Delta Kappa. Banking, Corporate, general, Property, real (including real estate development, water). Office: Carlsmith Ball PO Box 656 Honolulu HI 96809-0656

OLD, WILLIAM ABNER, lawyer; b. Norfolk, Va., Aug. 14, 1953; s. William Abner and Melba Phelps Old; m. Elizabeth K. Old, Jan. 7, 1984; children: William A. III, Meriwether E. BS, U. Va., 1975, MS, 1977; JD, William and Mary Coll., 1980. CPA. Pres., chmn. Hofhimer Nusbaum, Norfolk, Va., 1980—2002. Mem.: ABA, Am. Soc. Corp. (sec.). Republican. Methodist. Avocations: surfing, mountain biking, swimming. Securities, Mergers and acquisitions, Taxation, general. Office: Hofheimer Nusbaum 1700 Dominion Tower Norfolk VA 23510 Fax: 757-629-0660. E-mail: wold@hnlaw.com.

OLDAKER, BRADLEY RUSSELL, lawyer; b. Washington, Sept. 5, 1962; s. William B. and Lois L. (Westfall) O.; m. Marianne E. Kaufman. BA magna cum laude, W.Va. Wesleyan Coll., 1984; JD, W.Va. U., 1987. Bar: W.Va. 1987, Ky 2002, Sup. Ct. US 2002, U.S. Dist. Ct. (no. and so. dists.) W.Va. 1987, U.S. Ct. Appeals (4th cir.) 1989. Assoc. Wilson & Bailey, Weston, W.Va., 1987-88, ptnr., 1988—. Contbr. W.Va. Law Rev., 1986. Mem. ATLA, W.Va. Trial Lawyers Assn. Democrat. Methodist. Toxic tort, Personal injury (including property damage). Office: Wilson & Bailey 122 Court Ave Weston WV 26452-1966

OLDENBURG, RONALD TROY, lawyer; b. Eldora, Iowa, June 2, 1935; s. Lorenz Frank and Bess Louise (Lewis) O.; m. Vickie Yu; children: John, Keith, Mark. BA, U. N.C., 1957; postgrad., Brunnsvik Folkhogskola, Sorvik, Sweden, 1957-58; JD, U. Miss., 1961. Bar: Miss. 1961, Hawaii 1975. Mgr. Continental Travel Svc., Chapel Hill, N.C., 1956-57, Meridian Travel Svc., Raleigh, N.C., 1961, Linmark Internat. Devel., Seoul, 1972-74; fgn. atty. Li Chun Law Office, Taipei, Taiwan, 1965-67; pvt. practice, Taipei, 1967-72, Honolulu, 1975—. Adj. prof. immigration law U. Hawaii Sch. Law, 1985—97. Compiler: International Directory of Birth, Death, Marriage and Divorce Records, 1985; contbr. articles on immigration law to legal jours. Capt. JAGC, USAF, 1962-65. Mem. Am. Immigration Lawyers Assn. Immigration, naturalization, and customs. Office: 700 Bishop St Ste 2100 Honolulu HI 96813-3215 Also: 94-229 Waipahu Depot Rd Ste 204 Waipahu HI 96797 E-mail: rtoibm@attglobal.net.

OLDERSHAW, LOUIS FREDERICK, lawyer; b. New Britain, Conn., Aug. 30, 1917; s. Louis A. and Annie Louise (Bold) O.; m. Virginia Wakelin, Nov. 30, 1940; children: Peter W., Robert L., David L. AB, Dartmouth Coll., 1939; LL.B., Yale U., 1942. Bar: Mass. 1946, Fed. 1947. Mem. legal staff Army Ordnance Dist., Springfield, Mass., 1942-43; with firm Lyon, Green, Whitmore, Doran & Brooks, Holyoke, Mass., 1947-49; partner firm Davenport, Millane & Oldershaw, Holyoke, 1949-64; treas. Nat. Blank Book Co., Inc., Holyoke, 1964-65, pres., 1965-78, chmn. bd., 1978-83; group v.p., dir. Dennison Mfg. Co., Framingham, Mass., 1967-82; counsel Bulkley, Richardson & Gelinas, Springfield, Mass., 1983—2002, ret., 2002. Mem. editorial bd.: Yale Law Jour, 1941-42. Trustee Mt. Holyoke Coll., 1966-76, Greater Holyoke YMCA; bd. dirs. emeritus Holyoke C.C. Found., Sta. WGBY-TV. Lt. USNR, 1943-47. Mem.: Rotary, Mill Reef Club (Antigua), Colony Club (Springfield, Mass.), Longmeadow (Mass.) Country Club. Republican. Mem. United Congl. Ch. Home: 30 Bayon Dr South Hadley MA 01075 Office: Baybank Tower 1500 Main St Ste 2700 Springfield MA 01115-0001 E-mail: loldershaw@bulkley.com.

OLDFIELD, E. LAWRENCE, lawyer; b. Lake Forest, Ill., Dec. 21, 1944; s. W. Ernest and Evelyn Charlotte (Gyllenberg) O.; m. Kaaren Elaine Sabey, Aug. 24, 1974; 1 stepchild, Kimberly Jo; 1 child, Lauren Elizabeth. Student, L.I. U., 1961-62, Wheaton Coll., 1962-64, Near East Sch. Archeology, Jordan, 1964; BA in Polit. Sci., No. Ill. U., 1969; JD, DePaul U., 1973. Bar: Ill. 1973, U.S. Dist. Ct. (no. dist.) Ill. 1973, U.S. Ct. Appeals (7th cir.) 1974, U.S. Supreme Ct. 1979, U.S. Ct. Appeals (3d cir.) 1985, U.S. Ct. Appeals (10th cir.) 1986, U.S. Ct. Appeals (8th cir.) 1990. Fed. agt. Dept. HUD, 1969-70; assoc. Ruff & Grotefeld Ltd., Chgo., 1973-77; gen. counsel livestock dept. Hartford Fire Ins. Co., Chgo., 1977-87; prin. E. Lawrence Oldfield & Assocs., Oak Brook, 1987-2000, Oldfield & Fox, P.C., Oak Brook, 2000—. Mediator, arbitrator U.S. Arbitration and Mediation, 1994-

97, Resolute Systems, Inc., 1997-2001; ind. arbitrator, 2002—. Dir. Edgewater Cmty. Coun., 1973-74; precinct capt. 50th Ward Dems., 1974-77; trustee North Shore Bapt. Ch., 1974-77, chmn. constn. com., 1976-77; dir. Chgo. Bapt. Assn., 1974-77, treas., 1976-77; dir. Ctrl. Bapt. Children's Home, 1978-81, chmn. pers. com., 1980-81; deacon, 1981-83, chmn. bd. deacons, 1983, First Presbyn. Ch. Glen Ellyn, 1983-84; dir. Chgo. Bible Soc., 1980-84; v.p., 1983-84; trustee Village of Glen Ellyn, 1981-85; committeeman Milton Twp., DuPage County Reps., Wheaton, Ill., 1985-88; publicity chmn. Milton Twp. Reps., Wheaton, 1986-88; mem. Dist. 41 Sch. Bd., 1991-95; elder Christ Ch. of Oak Brook, 1993-2000; bd. govs. Execs. Breakfast Club of Oak Brook 1993—, 1st v.p., 1997-99, pres., 1999-2001. Served in U.S. Army, 1964-67. Mem. ABA, Ill. State Bar Assn., Chgo. Bar Assn., DuPage County Bar Assn., West Suburban Bar Assn., Ill. Trial Lawyers' Assn., Assn. Trial Lawyers Am., Fed. Trial Bar, U.S. Golf Assn., Safari Club Internat., Wheaton Comty. Radio Amateurs, Am. Legion, VFW, Kiwanis, Moose, Masons, Shriners (mem. sec. 1998-2001), Jesters, Elks. Avocations: fishing, hunting, golf, amateur radio, chess. General civil litigation, Corporate, general, General practice. Home: 1050 Crescent Blvd Glen Ellyn IL 60137-4276 Office: Oldfield & Fox PC 2021 Midwest Rd Ste 201 Oak Brook IL 60523-1367 also: 30 N Lasalle St Ste 1524 Chicago IL 60602-2502 also: 1622 W Colonial Pkwy Palatine IL 60067-4795 E-mail: eloesq@oldfieldfox.com.

OLDHAM, DARIUS DUDLEY, lawyer; b. Beaumont, Tex., July 6, 1941; s. Darius Saran and Mary Francis (Carraway) O.; m. Judy J. White, Jan. 23, 1965; children: Steven, Michael BA, U. Tex., Austin, 1964; JD, U. Tex., 1966. Bar: Tex. 1966, U.S. Dist. Ct. (so., no., ea. and we. dists.) Tex. 1966, U.S. Supreme Ct. 1974, U.S. Ct. Appeals (3rd, 5th and 11th cirs.) 1968; cert. arbitrator and mediator. Assoc. Fulbright & Jaworski, Houston, 1966-74, ptnr., 1974—, mem. policy com., 1980—97, 2001—, mem. exec. com., former chmn. litigation mgmt. com., 1997—. Mem. faculty grad. litigation program U. Houston; lectr. on corp. def. ins. and product liability. Former mem. bd. editors Aviation Litigation Reporter, Personal Injury Def. Reporter; country corr. Internat. Ins. Law Rev.; contbr. articles to profl. jours. Mem. Nat. Jud. Coll. Adv. Coun.; mem. liberal arts adv. coun. U. Tex.; bd. dirs. FICC Found.; past bd. dirs. Houston Pops Orch. Fellow Am. Coll. Trial Lawyers (complex litigation and judicial relations com.), Tex. Bar Found. (life), Am. Bar Found. (life), Houston Bar Found. (life), Am. Bd. Trial Advs. (pres. Houston chpt. 1999); mem. ABA (mem. ho. of dels. 1996-98, chair tort and ins. practice sect. 1994-95, mem. coun. tort and ins. practice sect. 1988-98, chmn. presdl. emissary 1993-95, chmn. Standing Com. on Independence of the Judiciary 2001—, chmn. Commn. on Jud. Campaign Fin. 2000-01), Tex. Bar Assn. (chmn. liaison fed. jud. com. 1989-90, pattern jury charges Vol. IV com. 1988-92), Tex. Young Lawyers Assn. (bd. dirs., chmn.), Fed. Ins. and Corp. Counsel (pres. 1989-90, chmn. bd. 1990-91, exec. com. 1988-91), Tex. Assn. Def. Counsel, Maritime Law Assn. U.S., Am. Counsel Assn. (bd. dirs. 1982-83, 89-94), Def. Rsch. Inst. (chmn. aerospace com. 1984-87, Presdl. Achievement award 1987, bd. dirs. 1989-92, exec. com. 1991-92), Lawyers for Civil Justice (bd. dirs. 1988-98, chmn. 1998, exec. com. 1990-98, pres. 1997), River Oaks Country Club, Houston Ctr. Club, Sigma Chi, Phi Delta Phi. General civil litigation, Corporate, general, Toxic tort. Office: Fulbright & Jaworski 1301 Mckinney St 51st Fl Houston TX 77010-3031 E-mail: doldham@fulbright.com.

OLDWEILER, THOMAS PATRICK, lawyer; b. Lawrence, Kans., May 13, 1961; s. Harry Eldon and Jeanne Teresa (Boyle) O.; m. Laura Elise Busby, Dec. 31, 1988; children: T. Patrick Jr., Alexander B., Madeline A. AB, Duke U., 1983; JD, Vanderbilt U., 1986. Bar: Ala. 1986, Mo. 1987, Miss. 1987, U.S. Dist. Ct. (so. dist.) Miss. 1987. Assoc. Miller, Hamilton, Snider & Odom, Mobile, Ala., 1986-92, ptnr., 1993-94, Zieman, Speegle, Oldweiler & Jackson, L.L.C., Mobile, 1994—98; mem. Armbrecht Jackson, LLP, Mobile, 1999—. Faculty mem. Ala. Bar Inst., Tuscaloosa, 1988—. Mem. ABA, Mobile Bar Assn., Athelstan Club. Banking, Corporate, general, Mergers and acquisitions. Office: Armbrecht Jackson LLP 63 S Royal St Ste 1300 Mobile AL 36602

O'LEARY, DANIEL VINCENT, JR., lawyer; b. Bklyn., May 26, 1942; s. Daniel Vincent and Mary (Maxwell) O'L.; m. Marilyn Irene Gavigan, June 1, 1968; children: Daniel, Katherine, Molly, James. AB cum laude, Georgetown U., 1963; LLB, Yale U., 1966. Bar: Ill. 1967. Assoc. Wilson & Mc Ilvaine, Chgo., 1967—75, ptnr., 1975—87, Peterson & Ross, Chgo., 1987—94, Schwartz & Freeman, Chgo., 1994—95; of counsel Mandell, Menkes & Surdyk, LLC, Chgo., 1995—. Pres., bd. dirs. Jim's Cayman Co., Ltd.; pres. TV and Radio Purchasing Group Inc.; asst. sec. L.M.C. Ins. Co. Bermuda, 1990—; pres. Wagering Ins. N.Am. Purchasing Group Inc., 1997—. Lt. comdr. USNR, ret. Roman Catholic. Avocations: fishing, scuba diving. Office: Mandel Menkes & Surdyk LLC Ste 300 333 W Wacker Dr Chicago IL 60606 E-mail: doleary@mms-law.net.

O'LEARY, PRENTICE L. lawyer; b. L.A., May 6, 1942; BA, UCLA, 1965, JD, 1968. Bar: Calif. 1969. Ptnr. Sheppard, Mullin, Richter & Hampton, L.A., 1974—. Bd. dirs. Legal Aide Found. L.A., 1987—93, 2000—. Mem. ABA (bus. bankruptcy com.), State Bar Calif., Los Angles County Bar Assn. (chmn. bankruptcy com., chmn. comml. law and bankrupt sect. 1985-86), Am. Coll. Bankruptcy Profls., Order of Coif. Bankruptcy, Commercial, consumer (including collections, credit), Commercial, contracts (including sales of goods; commercial financing). Office: Sheppard Mullin Richter & Hampton 333 S Hope St Fl 48 Los Angeles CA 90071-1406

O'LEARY, SEAN EDWARD, lawyer; b. Newton, Mass., Dec. 9, 1940; s. Stephen Blake and Marion Elizabeth (Barrett) O'L.; m. Joanne Pariseau, Aug. 22, 1964; children: Kathleen, Sean B., Brian E., Timothy P. BA, U. Mass., 1965; JD, Western New Eng. Law Sch., 1975. Bar: Mass. 1977, U.S. Dist. Ct. (fed. dist.) Mass. 1977. Pvt. practice, Easthampton, Mass., 1977—. Treas. Hampshire Bar Advs., Inc., Northampton, 1994—. Town counsel Town of Easthampton, 1980-84. General civil litigation.

O'LEARY, THOMAS MICHAEL, lawyer; b. N.Y.C., Aug. 16, 1948; s. James and Julia Ann (Connolly) O'L.; m. Luise Ann Williams, Jan. 13, 1978; 1 child, Richard Meridith. BA, CUNY, 1974; JD, Seattle U., 1977. Bar: Wash. 1977, U.S. Ct. Mil. Appeals 1978, U.S. Ct. Appeals (9th cir.), U.S. Supreme Ct. 1983. Dep. pros. atty. Pierce County, Tacoma, 1978; commd. 1st lt. U.S. Army, 1978, advanced through grades to capt., 1978; chief trial counsel Office of Staff Judge Adv., Ft. Polk, La., 1978-79, trial def. counsel, trial def. svc., 1979-81; chief legal advisor Office Insp. Gen., Heidelberg, Fed. Republic of Germany, 1981-82; sr. def. counsel Trial Def. Svc., Giessen, Fed. Republic of Germany, 1982-84; asst. chief adminstrv. law U.S. Army Armor Ctr., Ft. Knox, Ky., 1984-85, chief adminstrv. law, 1985, chief legal asst., 1985-86; ret. U.S. Army, 1996; sr. trial atty. Immigration and naturalization Svc., Phoenix, 1987; sector counsel, spl. asst. U.S. atty., U.S. Border Patrol, Tucson, 1987-90; enforcement counsel U.S. Immigration and Naturalization Svc., Tucson, 1990-95, asst. dist. counsel Phoenix litigation, 1995-97. Apptd. U.S. Immigration Judge, U.S. Immigration Ct., Imperial, Calif., 1997-2000, apptd. sr. U.S. Immigration Judge, Tucson, 2000—; adj. prof. Embry-Riddle Aero. U., Tucson, 2002-Decorated Purple Heart, Cross of Gallantry (Vietnam). Mem. Judge Advs Assn., Wash. State Bar Assn., Order Ky. Cols. (commd. col. 1985). Immigration, naturalization, and customs, Military, Labor (including EEOC, Fair Labor Standards Act, labor-management relations, NLRB, OSHA). Home: 9080 E 25th St Tucson AZ 85710-8675 Office: US Immigration Ct 1705 E Hanna Rd Ste 366 Eloy AZ 85231-9612

OLENDER, JACK HARVEY, lawyer; b. McKeesport, Pa., Sept. 8, 1935; m. Lovell Olender. BA, U. Pitts., 1957, JD, 1960; LLM, George Washington U., 1961. Bar: D.C. 1961, U.S. Supreme Ct. 1965, Md. 1966, Pa. 1985; diplomate Am. Bd. Trial Advocates,Inner Cir. Advocates. Pvt. practice, Washington, 1961-79; prin. Jack H. Olender & Assocs., P.C., Washington, 1979—. Contbr. articles to profl. jours. Active World Peace through Law, Washington. Named to Hall of Fame Nat. Assn. Black Women Attys., 1987, D.C. Hall of Fame, 2000, Washington Bar Assn. Hall of Fame, 2000; recipient Presdl. award Nat. Bar Assn., 1996, 2000, 02, Advocate for Justice award Nat. Bar Assn., 2000, Internat. B'nai B'rith Pursuit of Justice award, 2001. Fellow Am. Coll. Trial Lawyers, Internat. Acad. Trial Lawyers and Inner Cir. Advs.; mem. ATLA, Nat. Bar Assn. (adv. for justice 2000), Am. Bd. Profl. Liability Attys. (bd. dirs.), Trial Lawyers Pub. Justice (bd. dirs.), Internat. Assn. Jewish Lawyers and Jurists (bd. dirs.), Bar Assn. of D.C. (pres. 1999-2000). Personal injury (including property damage), Product liability, Professional liability. Office: Jack H Olender & Assocs PC 888 17th St NW Fl 4 Washington DC 20006-3939

OLES, STUART GREGORY, lawyer; b. Seattle, Dec. 15, 1924; s. Floyd and Helen Louise (La Violette) O.; m. Ilse Hanewald, Feb. 12, 1954; children: Douglas, Karl, Stephen. BS magna cum laude, U. Wash., 1947, JD, 1948. Bar: Wash., 1949, U.S. Supreme Ct. 1960. Dep. pros. atty. King County, Wash., 1949, chief civil dept., 1949-50; gen. practice law Seattle, 1950-95; sr. ptnr. firm Oles, Morrison & Rinker and predecessor, 1955-90, of counsel, 1991-95. Author: A View From the Rock, 1994, On Behalf of My Clients -- A Lawyer's Life, 1998. Chmn. Seattle Cmty. Concert Assn., 1955; pres. Friends Seattle Pub. Libr., 1956; mem. Wash. pub. Disclosure Commn., 1973-075; trustee Ch. Divinity Sch. of Pacific, Berkeley, Calif., 1974-75; mem. bd. curators Wash. State Hist. Soc., 1983; former mem. Seattle Symphony Bd.; pres. King County Ct. House Rep. Club, 1950, U. Wash. Young Rep. Club, 1947; Wash. conv. floor leader Taft, 1952, Goldwater, 1964; Wash. chmn. Citizens for Goldwater, 1964; chmn. King County Rep. convs., 1966, 68, 76, 84, 88, 90, 92, 96, Wash. State Rep. Conv., 1980. Served with USMCR, 1943-45. Mem. ABA (past regional vice-chmn. pub. contract law sect.), Wash. Bar Assn., Order of Coif, Scabbard and Blade, Am. Legion, Kapoho Bay Club (pres.), Am. Highland Cattle Assn. (v.p. and dir.), Phi Beta Kappa, Phi Alpha Delta. Construction, General practice, Government contracts and claims. Home: 22715 SE 43rd Ct Issaquah WA 98029-5200 also: RR 2 Pahoa HI 96778-9802

OLIAN, ROBERT MARTIN, lawyer; b. Cleve., June 14, 1953; s. Robert Meade and Doris Isa (Hessing) O.; m. Terri Ellen Ruther, Aug. 10, 1980; children: Andrew Zachary, Alix Michelle, Joshua Brett. AB, Harvard U., 1973, JD, M in Pub. Policy, 1977. Bar: Ill. 1977, U.S. Dist. Ct. (no. dist.) Ill. 1977, U.S. Ct. Appeals (7th cir.) 1983, U.S. Dist. Ct. (no dist. trial bar) Ill. 1992, U.S. Dist. Ct. (we. dist.) Mich. 1994. Assoc. Sidley & Austin, Chgo., 1977-84; ptnr. Sidley Austin Brown & Wood, Chgo., 1985—. Editor: Illinois Environmental Law Handbook, 1988, 97. Panel atty. Chgo. Vol. Legal Svcs., Chgo., 1983—; mem. regional strategic planning/mktg. com. Alexian Bros. Ill., Inc., Elk Grove, 1985-88; trustee North Shore Congregation Israel, 1990—, sec., 1995-96, v.p., 1996-2003; bd. dirs. Chgo. Friends of IDF, 2003-. Mem. ABA, Chgo. Bar Assn., Std. Club, Harvard Club (Chgo.). Jewish. Environmental. Home: 85 Oakmont Rd Highland Park IL 60035-4111 Office: Sidley Austin Brown & Wood Bank One Plaza 10 S Dearborn St #5200 Chicago IL 60603-2003 E-mail: rolian@sidley.com.

OLIPHANT, CHARLES FREDERICK, III, lawyer; b. Chattanooga, Sept. 25, 1949; s. Charles Frederick and Jayne (Shutting) O.; m. Nancy Ann Stewart, May 15, 1976; children: James Andrew, Alexander Stewart. BA in Econs., U. N.C., 1971; JD, U. Mich., 1975. Bar: D.C. 1975. Assoc. Miller & Chevalier, Chartered, Washington, 1975-81, mem. firm, 1982—. Bd. adv. Jour. of Pension Planning and Compliance. Fellow Am. Coll. Employee Benefits Counsel; mem. ABA, Bar Assn. D.C. Episcopalian. Avocations: music, reading. Pension, profit-sharing, and employee benefits, Taxation, general. Office: Miller & Chevalier Chartered 655 15th St NW Ste 900 Washington DC 20005-5799

OLIVAS, DANIEL ANTHONY, lawyer; b. L.A., Apr. 8, 1959; s. Michael A. and Elizabeth M. (Velasco) O.; m. Susan L. Formaker, Oct. 19, 1986; 1 child, Benjamin Formaker-Olivas. BA in English Lit., Stanford U., 1981; JD with honors, UCLA, 1984. Bar: Calif. 1987, U.S. Dist. Ct. (cen. dist.) Calif. 1988, U.S. Ct. Appeals (9th cir.) 1988, U.S. Supreme Ct. 1995. Law clk., atty. Hunt & Cochran-Bond, L.A., 1984-88; atty. Heller, Ehrman, White & McAuliffe, L.A., 1988-90; dep. atty. gen. dept. of justice antitrust div. State of Calif., L.A., 1990-91, dep. atty. gen. dept. of justice land law sect., 1991—. State apptd. bd. dirs. Western Ctr. Law and Poverty, L.A., 1988-94; mem. Hispanic employees adv. com. Calif. Dept. Justice, 1990—; mem. exec. com. eviron. law sect. State Bar Calif., 2002--. Contbr. articles to L.A. Daily Jour., and others; writer fiction and poetry. Recipient Atty. Gen.'s award for outstanding achievement in litigation, 1994; named one of Outstanding Young Men of Am., 1984. Mem. Mex.-Am. Bar Assn., Mex.-Am. Bar Found. (bd. dirs. 1993-94), L.A. County Bar Assn. (Jud. Appointments Com 1993-97), Stanford Chicano/Latino Alumni Assn. (pres.-elect 1992-93, pres. 1993-94). Democrat. Jewish. Administrative and regulatory, General civil litigation, Environmental. Office: State of Calif 300 S Spring St Ste 5212 Los Angeles CA 90013-1230 E-mail: olivasdan@aol.com.

OLIVEIRA-RAMOS, LUIZ GUSTAVO, lawyer; b. São José dos Campos, São Paulo, Brazil, Feb. 15, 1971; s. João Francisco Ramos and Maria Célia Oliveira-Ramos. JD, U. São Paulo, 1993. Brazilian Jurisdiction: 1993. Ptnr. Rayes, Fagundes & Oliveira Ramos Advogados Assocs., São Paulo, 1999—; pvt. practice Advocacia Luiz Gustavo de Oliveira Ramos, São José dos Campos, 1996—99. Mem.: São Paulo Assn. Lawyers (assoc.). Commercial, consumer (including collections, credit), General civil litigation. Office: Rayes Fagundes & Oliveira Ramos Líbero Badaró 425/11o andar São Paulo 01009-000 Brazil Office Fax: (55 11) 3293-2000. E-mail: luiz.ramos@rayesfagundes.com.br.

OLIVER, DALE HUGH, lawyer; b. Lansing, Mich., June 26, 1947; s. Alvin Earl and Jean Elizabeth (Stanton) Oliver; m. Sarah Elyse Sanders, Mar. 18, 2001; children: Nathan Corey, John Franklin. BA, Mich. State U., 1969; JD cum laude, Harvard U., 1972. Bar: DC 1973, Calif. 1991, US Dist. Ct. (DC dist.) 1973, US Ct. Appeals (DC cir.) 1976, US Supreme Ct. 1980, US Ct. Appeals (fed. cir.) 1983, US Ct. Claims 1983. Assoc., ptnr. Jones, Day, Reavis & Pogue, Washington, 1975—79; ptnr. Crowell & Moring, Washington, 1979—84, Gibson, Dunn & Crutcher, Washington, 1984—87, Jones, Day, Reavis & Pogue, Washington, 1987—92, Quinn Emanuel Urquhart & Oliver, L.A., 1992—. Editor: (jour.) Pub. Contracts Law, 1980—86; contbr. articles to profl. jours. Spl. counsel 1980 Presdl. Inaugural Com., Washington, 1980; bd. dirs. L.A. coun. Boy Scouts Am., 1991—. Capt. USAF, 1973—75. Mem.: ABA (con. chmn. pub. contract sect. 1979—), Nat. Security Indsl. Assn., Nat. Contract Mgmt. Assn., Harvard Law Sch. Assn., Mich. State U. Alumni Club of Washington (pres., dir. 1984—88). Federal civil litigation, Government contracts and claims, Private international. Office: Quinn Emanuel Urquhart & Oliver & Hedges 865 S Figueroa St Fl 10 Los Angeles CA 90017-2543 E-mail: dho@quinnemanuel.com.

OLIVER, JOHN PERCY, II, lawyer, consultant; b. Alexander City, Ala., Dec. 3, 1942; s. Samuel William and Sarah Pugh (Coker) D.; m. Melissa Vann, June 11, 1966. AB, Birmingham (Ala.) So. Coll., 1964; JD, U. Ala., 1967. Bar: Ala. 1967, U.S. Dist. Ct. (mid. dist.) Ala. 1969, U.S. Supreme Ct. 1971, U.S. Ct. Appeals (5th cir.) 1975, U.S. Ct. Appeals (11th cir.) 1981, U.S. Dist. Ct. (mid. dist.) Ga. 1989. Assoc. Samuel W. Oliver, Atty., Dadeville, Ala., 1967; prin. John P. Oliver II, Atty., Dadeville, 1967-71; ptnr. Oliver & Sims, Attys., Dadeville, 1972-83, Oliver, Sims & Jones, Attys., Dadeville, 1984-85, Oliver & Sims, Attys., Dadeville, 1985—2002, Oliver-Treadwell Attys., Dadeville, 2002—. Dir. Bank of Dadeville. Mem. State Dem. Exec. Com., Tallapoosa County, Ala., 1986-94; judge Tallapoosa County Dist. Ct., Dadeville, 1973-76; mcpl. judge, Dadeville, 19765; spl. probate judge Tallapoosa County Probate Ct., Dadeville, 1987-88. Mem. Ala. State Bar Assn. (bd. bar commrs. 1992-98), Ala. Trial Lawyers Assn. (exec. com. 1975-77), Tallapoosa County Bar Assn. (pres. 1990). Baptist. Avocations: sailing, skiing. General civil litigation, Property, real (including real estate development, water), Workers' compensation. Office: Oliver-Treadwell 129 W Columbus St Dadeville AL 36853-1308

OLIVER, JOSEPH MCDONALD, JR., lawyer; b. Savannah, Ga., July 26, 1946; s. Joseph McDonald and Louise (Myers) O.; m. Patricia Clark, Sept. 8, 1965 (div. Mar. 1983); children: Joseph McDonald III, Catherine McCay; m. Meredith Bennett, May 11, 1985. BA, U. Va., 1967; JD, U. Ga., 1970. Bar: Ga. 1970, D.C. 1971. Law clk. U.S. Ct. Claims, 1970-71; assoc. Jones, Day, Reavis & Pogue, Washington, 1971-77, ptnr., 1978-79, Crowell & Moring LLP, Washington, 1979—2000, sr. counsel, 2000—. Mem. ABA, Fed. Energy Bar Assn. Episcopalian. FERC practice, Utilities, public. Home: PO Box 446 Washington VA 22747 Office: Crowell & Moring LLP 1001 Pennsylvania Ave NW Fl 10 Washington DC 20004-2595

OLIVER, MILTON MCKINNON, lawyer, German translator, patent database searcher; b. Columbia, S.C., 1951; s. Caldwell Hardy and Eleanor (McKinnon) Oliver; m. Joan Nichols, July 12, 1981; children: John, James, Lindsay. BA, Harvard U., 1972; JD, Golden Gate U., 1975. Bar: Calif. 1975, Mass. 1975, Patent and Trademark Office 1976, Fla. 1978, D.C. 1983, N.Y. 1984, U.S. Supreme Ct. 1979, U.S. Ct. Appeals (fed. cir.) 1982. Assoc. Wolf, Greenfield & Sacks, P.C., Boston, 1977—83; assoc., then ptnr. Frishauf, Holtz, Goodman & Woodward, P.C., N.Y.C., 1983—94; of counsel Dike, Bronstein, Roberts & Cushman, Boston, 1994—97; ptnr. Ware, Fressola, Van Der Sluys & Adolphson, LLP, Monroe, Conn., 1997—. Mem.: AIPLA, IEEE, Computer Law Assn., Calif. State Bar, Boston Patent Law Assn., Conn. and N.Y. I.P. Assns., Aircraft Owners and Pilots Assn. Episcopalian. Computer, Patent, Trademark and copyright. Home: 72 Green St Canton MA 02021-1020 Office: Ware Fressola Van Der Sluys & Adolphson LLP 755 Main St Monroe CT 06468-2830

OLIVER, PHILIP DUDLEY, law educator; b. Albertville, Ala., Aug. 13, 1947; s. Bruce and Bobby (Clay) O.; m. Ranko Shiraki, May 29, 1974. BA, U. Ala., 1969; JD, Yale U., 1976. Fgn. service officer, 2d sec. embassy, vice consul U.S. Dept. of State, Washington and Mex. City, 1970-73; assoc. Sutherland, Asbill & Brennan, Atlanta, 1976-80; prof. law U. Ark. Sch. of Law, Little Rock, 1980—. Republican. Methodist. Home: 716 Providence Dr Bryant AR 72022-7016 Office: U Ark at Little Rock William H Bowen Sch Law 1201 McMath Ave Little Rock AR 72202-5142

OLIVER, SOLOMON, JR., judge; b. Bessemer, Ala., July 20, 1947; s. Solomon Sr. and Willie Lee (Davis) O.; married; 2 children. BA, Coll. of Wooster, 1969; JD, NYU, 1972; MA, Case Western Res. U., 1974. Bar: Ohio 1973, U.S. Dist. Ct. (no. dist.) Ohio 1977, U.S. Ct. Appeals (6th cir.) 1977, U.S. Supreme Ct. 1980. Asst. prof. dept. polit. sci. Coll. of Wooster, Ohio, 1972-75; sr. law clk. to Hon. William H. Hastie U.S. Ct. Appeals (3d cir.), Phila., 1975-76; asst. U.S. atty. U.S. Atty.'s Office, Cleve., 1976-82, chief civil divsn., 1978-82; spl. asst. U.S. atty., chief appellate divsn. Dept. Justice, Cleve., 1982, spl. asst. U.S. atty., 1982-85; prof. law Cleve. State U., 1982-94, assoc. dean faculty and adminstrn., 1991-94. Lectr. in law, trial practice Case Western Res. U., Cleve., 1979-82; vis. scholar Stanford U. Coll. Law, 1987; vis. prof. Comenius U., Bratislava, Czechoslovakia, 1991, Charles U., Prague, Czechoslovakia, 1991. Chair O.K. Hoover Scholarship com. Bapt. Ch., 1987-89; trustee Coll. of Wooster, Ohio, 1991-97, 2000—. Mem. ABA, Nat. Bar Assn. Office: 801 W Superior Ave Cleveland OH 44113-1838 Fax: 216-357-7176.

OLIVERI, PAUL FRANCIS, lawyer; b. Far Rockaway, N.Y., Feb. 27, 1954; s. Alphonse J. and Rita (Gregorace) O.; m. Debra Lynn Malkin, Aug. 7, 1977; children: Jason, Evan, Rebecca. BA, NYU, 1976; JD, St. John's U., Queens, N.Y., 1978. Bar: N.Y. 1979, U.S. Dist. Ct. (ea. and so. dists.) N.Y. 1980. Assoc. Fuchsberg & Fuchsberg, N.Y.C., 1979-83; ptnr. Oliveri & Schwartz, N.Y.C., 1983—. Mem. N.Y. State Bar Assn., Am. Trial Lawyers Assn., N.Y. State Trial Lawyers Assn. (dir. emeritus). Avocations: music, numismatics. State civil litigation, Insurance, Personal injury (including property damage). Office: Oliveri & Schwartz 30 Vesey St New York NY 10007-2914

OLIVIER, WILLIAM K. lawyer; b. NJ, Aug. 8, 1945; s. William E. Olivier and Mary E. Perez. BA, Ripon Coll.; MS in Jud. Adminstrn., JD, U. Denver, 1974. Bar: Colo. 74, DC, Calif. 82, U.S. Supreme Ct., U.S. Ct. Appeals (9th, 10th, DC and Fed. cirs.), U.S. Dist. Ct. Colo., U.S. Dist. Ct. DC, U.S. Ct. Fed. Claims. Law clk. Colo. Ct. Appeals, Denver, 1974—75; atty. Adminstrv. Office U.S. Cts., Washington, 1975—78, Merit Sys. Protection Edn., Washington, 1978—79, U.S. Dept. Justice, Washington, 1987—; supervising atty. Office of Spl. Counsel, San Francisco, 1979—82; pvt. practice Denver, 1982—83, Newport Beach, Calif., 1982—87. Editor-in-chief: Denver Jour. Internat. Law, U. Denver, 1972—73. Capt. U.S. Army, 1968—71. Decorated Bronze Star with oak leaf cluster, Air medal. Avocations: skiing, golf, tennis, canoeing, coaching soccer.

OLK, FREDERICK JAMES, county official, paralegal; b. Clintonville, Wis., Apr. 30, 1952; s. James Howard and Bernice Helen (Durben) O. Student, Inst. Comp. Polit.& Econ. Sys., 1973; BS in Liberal Arts, U. Wis. River Falls, 1976; cert., Wis. Sch. Real Estate, Milw., 1980. Notary pub., Ill. Libr. asst. U. Wis., Stevens Point and Oshkosh, 1977-80; contract libr. U.S. Dept. Justice, Oxford, Wis., 1980; editl. libr. The Chgo. Cath. newspaper Archdiocese of Chgo., 1980-89; tax. examiner Cook County, Chgo., 1990—. Congl. intern U.S. Ho. of Rep., Washington, 1973; sales rep. Waupaca (Wis.) Pub. Co., 1978-79; freelance paralegal, Chgo., 1988—; security guard, account mgr. Glenbrook Security Svcs., Glenview, Ill., 1988—; asst. reference libr. Cicero (Ill.) Pub. Libr., 1989; genealogy rschr. Lineage Search Assocs., Mechanicsville, Va., 1980-99; v.p. New World Credit Union, Chgo., 1981-86. Columnist Looking back Chgo. Cath., 1985-89. Tutor Mercy Home for Boys, Chgo., 1987—88; coord. Friends of Vatican Libr., Chgo., 1995—; mem. exec. bd. customer adv. coun. U.S. Postal Svc., Cicero, 1997—; Cicero rep. for Ill. 43d dist. Anti-Crime Adv. Bd., 1999—2001; precinct capt. Wis. and Ill. Rep. coms., 1973—; Rep. judge of election Cook County, 1980—; mem. Rome tour St. John Cantius Parish Resurrection Choir, 2001, sang at St. Peter's Basilica, 2001. Named adm. Nebr. Navy, State of Nebr., 1982, col. State of Ala., 1988, Internat. Citizen of Yr., Hutt River Province, Australia, 1995; recipient Legion of Merit Rep. Nat. Com., 1997, Order of the Arrow, Boy Scouts Am., 1971. Mem. Am. Soc. Notaries (life, chmn. govt. rels. 1984-85), Nat. Assn. Investigative Specialists, Am. Legion (life), Amtrak Hist. Soc. (asst. archivist 1996—), Chgo. Geneal. Soc. (life, bd. dirs. 1988-90), 20th Century R.R. Club (sec. 1994-98, Century Club 1996, dir. 1998-2000), KC (del. archdiocesan pastoral coun. 1996—). Avocations: rail travel, genealogy, reading, history, stamp collecting. Home: 5550 W 22nd Pl Apt 306 Cicero IL 60804-2769 Office: Cook County Clk 118 N Clark St Ste 434 Chicago IL 60602-1382

OLLEY, MICHAEL JOSEPH, lawyer; b. Phila., Feb. 7, 1963; s. Francis Robert Olley and Patricia Regina Dougherty; m. Kristine Erin Kelly, Apr. 25, 1998. BS magna cum laude, St. Joseph's U., 1985; JD, Villanova U., 1989. Bar: Pa. 1989, N.J. 1989, U.S. Dist. Ct. (ea. dist.) Pa. 1989, U.S. Dist. Ct. N.J. 1990, U.S. Ct. Appeals (3d cir.) 1992. Rsch. assoc. Chase Econometrics, Bala Cynwyd, Pa., 1985-86; assoc. Marks, Kent & O'Neill, Phila., 1989-92, White and Williams, Phila., 1992-97; trial atty. Coffey & Kaye, Bala Cynwyd, Pa., 1997—. Fellow Acad. of Advocacy; mem. Pa. Bar Assn., St. Joseph's U. Law Alumni Assn. (mem. exec. bd. 1995—), Million Dollar Advocates Forum. Roman Catholic. Avocations: travel, theater, golf.

General civil litigation, Personal injury (including property damage), Product liability. Home: 525 Rock Glen Dr Wynnewood PA 19096-2620 Office: Coffey & Kaye 2 Bala Plz Ste 718 Bala Cynwyd PA 19004-1501

OLLINGER, W. JAMES, lawyer, director; b. Kittanning, Pa., Apr. 5, 1943; s. William James and Margaret Elizabeth (Reid) Ollinger; m. Susan Louise Gerspacher, Oct. 20, 1979; children: Mary Rebecca, David James. BA, Capital U., Columbus, Ohio, 1966; JD, Case Western Res. U., 1968. Bar: Ohio 1968, US Dist Ct (no dist) Ohio 1971. Ptnr. Baker & Hostetler, Cleve., 1968—. Mem Bentleyville Village Coun, Ohio, 1990—93; mayor Bentleyville, 1997—99. Mem.: Order of Coif, Phi Delta Phi. Corporate, general, Pension, profit-sharing, and employee benefits, Taxation, general. Office: Baker & Hostetler 3200 Nat City Ctr 1900 E 9th St Ste 3200 Cleveland OH 44114-3475 E-mail: jollinger@bakerlaw.com.

OLMSTEAD, CECIL JAY, lawyer; b. Jacksonville, Fla., Oct. 15, 1920; s. Cecil Jay Sr. and Bessie (Irby) O.; m. Frances Hughes; children: Cecil Jay III, Frank Hughes, Jane Olmstead Murphy, Amy Olmstead Vanecek. BA, U. Ga., 1950, LLB, 1951; Sterling Grad. fellow, Yale Law Sch., 1951-52; LLD (hon.), U. Hull, Eng., 1978. Bar: Ga. 1950, U.S. Supreme Ct 1964, D.C. 1978. Asst. to legal adviser Dept. State, counsel Mut. Security Agy., counsel Hoover Commn. on Orgn. Exec. Br. of Govt., 1952-55; prof. N.Y. U. Sch. Law, 1953-61; dir. Inter-Am. Law Inst., 1958-61, adj. prof. law, 1961-69; atty. Texaco, Inc., N.Y.C., 1961-62, asst. to chmn. bd., 1962-70, v.p., asst. to chmn. bd., 1970, v.p., asst. to pres., 1970-71, v.p., asst. to chief exec. officer, 1971-73, exec. dept., v.p., 1973-80; mem. firm Steptoe & Johnson, Washington, 1980—. Wang Disting. vis. prof. St. Johns U., 1987-90; mem. adv. panel on internat. law to sec. state; adv. com. law of sea State Dept.; also adv. com. transnat. enterprise; U.S. del. UN Com. on Law of Sea, 1972-73; U.S. del. UN Conf. on Law of Sea, 1974-76; Eisenhower lectr. Nat. War Coll., 1973; mem. U.S. del. UN Conf. on Code of Conduct for Transnat. Corps., ann. 1984-90; mem. World Bank's panel of conciliators of the Internat. Ctr. for Settlement of Investment Disputes, 1988-95; vis. fellow All Souls Coll., Oxford U., 1988; vis. scholar Yale Law Sch., 1990-91. With USAF, 1943-46, 8th and 20th Air Forces. ETO, PTO. Recipient Gold medal City of Brussels (Belgium, 1973, Gold medal City of Paris (France), 1984; named Commdr. Brit. Empire (hon.), 1990. Mem. Internat. Law Assn. (pres. Am. br. 1966-73, pres. 1972-75, vice chmn. exec. coun. 1975-86, chmn. exec. coun. 1986-88, patron 1989—), Am. Law Inst. (assoc. reporter Restatement of the Fgn. Rels. Law of the U.S., 1st edit. 1964, advisor 3d edit.), Coun. on Fgn. Rels., Washington Inst. Fgn. Affairs, Nat. Fgn. Trade Coun. (dir.), Am. Coun. on Germany (hon. dir.), Coun. on Ocean Law (dir.), Knickerbocker Club, Yale Club, Fairfield County Hunt Club (Westport), Cosmos Club (Washington), Order of Coif, Phi Beta Kappa. Home: 4 Sprucewood Ln Westport CT 06880-4021 Office: 1330 Connecticut Ave NW Washington DC 20036-1704

OLOFSSON, DANIEL JOEL, lawyer; b. Chgo., Sept. 29, 1954; s. Joel Gustav and Patricia Marie (Casey) O.; children: Nicole Lynn, Gustave Daniel, Jonathon Leonard; m. Catherine Elaine Baehler, July 24, 1999; AA, Thornton C.C., 1974; BA, U. Ill., 1976; JD with honors, Chgo.-Kent Coll. Law, Ill. Inst. Tech., 1979. Bar: Ill. 1979, U.S. Dist. Ct. (no. dist.) Ill. 1979, U.S. Ct. Appeals (7th cir.) 1979, U.S. Tax Ct. 1980. Assoc. Jerry L. Lambert, Flossmoor, Ill., 1979-80, John P. Block, Chgo., 1980-82; sole practice, Dolton, Ill., 1982-94; gen. mgr. ops Signature Mortgage, Inc., 1994—. Elected trustee Village of Dolton, 1985. James scholar U. Ill., Champaign, 1976. Mem. Chgo. Bar Assn., South Suburban Bar Assn., Ill. State Bar Assn., ABA, Phi Theta Kappa. Democrat. Roman Catholic. Lodges: Rotary, Elks. General civil litigation, Criminal, Family and matrimonial. Home: 18521 S Marshfield Homewood IL 60430 E-mail: dolofsson@signatureservicesinc.com.

OLSCHWANG, ALAN PAUL, lawyer; b. Chgo., Jan. 30, 1942; s. Morton James and Ida (Ginsberg) O.; m. Barbara Claire Miller, Aug. 22, 1965; children: Elliot, Deborah, Jeffrey. BS, U. Ill., 1963, JD, 1966. Bar: Ill. 1966, N.Y. 1984, Calif. 1992. Law clk. Ill. Supreme Ct., Bloomington, 1966-67; assoc. Sidley & Austin and predecessor firms, Chgo., 1967-73; with Montgomery Ward & Co. Inc., Chgo., 1973-81, assoc. gen. counsel, asst. sec., 1979-81; ptnr. Seki, Jarvis & Lynch, Chgo., 1981-84, dir., mem. exec. com.; dir. Mitsubishi Electric & Electronics USA, Inc. and predecessors, N.Y.C., 1983-91, Cypress, Calif., 1991—. Mem. ABA, Am. Corp. Counsel Assn., Calif. Bar Assn., Ill. Bar Assn., Chgo. Bar Assn., N.Y. State Bar Assn., Bar Assn. of City of N.Y., Am. Arbitration Assn. (panel arbitrators). Commercial, contracts (including sales of goods; commercial financing), Corporate, general, Mergers and acquisitions. Office: Mitsubishi Elec & Electronics USA Inc PO Box 6007 5665 Plaza Dr Cypress CA 90630-0007

OLSEN, ALFRED JON, lawyer; b. Phoenix, Oct. 5, 1940; s. William Hans and Vera (Bearden) O.; m. Susan K. Smith, Apr. 15, 1979. BA in History, U. Ariz., 1962; MS in Acctg., Ariz. State U., 1964; JD, Northwestern U., 1966. Bar: Ariz. 1966, Ill. 1966, U.S. Tax Ct. 1970, U.S. Supreme Ct. 1970; C.P.A., Ariz., Ill. cert. tax specialist. Acct. Arthur Young & Co., C.P.A.s, Chgo., 1966-68; dir. firm Ehmann, Olsen & Lane (P.C.), Phoenix, 1969-76; dir. Streich, Lang, Weeks & Cardon (P.C.), Phoenix, 1977-78; v.p. Olsen-Smith, Ltd., Phoenix, 1978—. Chmn. tax adv. commn. Bd. Legal Specialization, 1990-92. Bd. editors: Jour. Agrl. Law and Taxation, 1978-82, Practical Real Estate Lawyer, 1983-95. Mem. Phoenix adv. bd. Salvation Army., 1973-81. Fellow: Am. Coll. Tax Counsel, Am. Coll. Trust and Estate Counsel (state chair); mem.: ABA (chmn. com. on agr., sect. taxation 1976—78, chmn. CLE com. sect. taxation 1982—84), AICPA, Internat. Acad. Estate and Trust Law (exec. coun. 1994—99), Nat. Cattlemen's Assn. (tax com. 1979—88), Am. Law Inst. (life; chmn. tax planning for agr. 1971—82), Ctrl. Ariz. Estate Planning Coun. (pres. 1972—73), State Bar Ariz., Ariz. Soc. CPAs, Phi Beta Kappa, Phi Kappa Phi, Beta Gamma Sigma, Sigma Nu Internat. (pres. 1986—88). Estate planning, Probate (including wills, trusts), Corporate taxation. Office: 3300 Virginia Fin Pla 301 E Virginia Ave Phoenix AZ 85004-1218

OLSEN, HANS PETER, lawyer; b. Detroit, May 21, 1940; s. Hans Peter and Paula M. (Olsen) O.; m. Elizabeth Ann Gayton, Sept. 14, 1968; children: Hans Peter, Heidi Susanne, Stephanie Elizabeth BA, Mich. State U., 1961; JD, Georgetown U., 1965; LLM, NYU, 1966. Bar: Mich. 1967, Pa. 1969, R.I. 1974. Law clk. Monaghan, McCrone, Campbell & Crawmer, Detroit, 1964, U.S. Ct. of Claims, Fed. Appellate Ct., Washington, 1966—68; assoc. Pepper, Hamilton & Scheetz, Phila., 1968—72; ptnr. Hinckley, Allen, & Snyder, Providence, 1974—. Adv. planning com. U. R.I. Fed. Taxation Inst.; continuing legal edn. adv. bd., tax symposium adv. bd. Bryant Coll.; mem. Gov.'s State Task Force, R.I. Pub. Expenditure Coun.; cons. Bur. Nat. Affairs; liaison Bar Assn. and North Atlantic region IRS; tax adminstrs. adv. com. R.I.; lectr. tax insts. and other profl. groups N.Y., L.A., Phila., Boston, R.I.; advisor R.I. Econ. Policy com. Contbr. numerous articles on taxation to legal jours. Fellow Am. Bar Found.; mem. ABA (sect. taxation, exempt orgns. com., subcom. healthcare, corp.-shareholders rels. com., partnerships com.), R.I. Bar Assn. (sect. taxation, sec.-treas. 1977-80, liaison with CPAs, specialization com., mem. various coms.), Providence C. of C., R.I. C. of C. (chmn. com. on bus. taxes and public spending, mem., past chmn. legis. action council), Mich. State Bar, Pa. State Bar. Corporate, general, Health, Taxation, general. Home: 274 Olney St Providence RI 02906-2305 Office: 1500 Fleet Ctr Providence RI 02903 also: 28 State St Boston MA 02109-1775 also: 14 South St Concord NH 03301-3744 E-mail: holsen@haslaw.com., hpeterolsen@cox.net.

OLSEN, HAROLD FREMONT, lawyer; b. Davenport, Wash., Oct. 17, 1920; s. Oscar E. and Dorothy (Sprowls) O.; m. Jeanne L. Rounds, Aug. 30, 1942; children: Eric O., Ronald R., Margaret Ruth. BA, Wash. State U., 1942; LL.B., Harvard U., 1948. Bar: Wash. 1948, U.S. Ct. Claims 1970, U.S. Supreme Ct. 1982; C.P.A., Wash. Instr. Oxford Bus. Sch., Cambridge, Mass., 1946-47; examiner Wash. State Dept. Pub. Utilities, 1948; with firm Perkins Coie (and predecessors), Seattle, 1949—, ptnr., 1954-88, of counsel, 1989—. Trustee Exec. Svcs. Corp. Wash., 1990-96. Bd. dirs. Northwest Hosp. Found., Northwest Hosp., 1980-90; trustee Wash. State U. Found., chmn. 1986-88; mem. adv. coun. Wash. State U. Sch. Bus. and Econs., 1978-90; trustee, mem. exec. com., pres. Mus. of Flight, 1991-92, chmn., 1993; trustee Horizon House, 1994-97. Maj. USAAF, 1942-45, NATOUSA, Mid. East, ETO. Decorated Silver Star. Mem. ABA, Wash. Bar Assn., Seattle Bar Assn., Aircraft Industry Assn. (chmn. legal com. 1957), Phi Beta Kappa, Phi Kappa Phi, Tau Kappa Epsilon, Rainier Club, Queenstown (New Zealand) Golf Club, Seattle Golf Club (pres. 1986-87), Sr. N.W. Golf Assn. Congregationalist. Commercial, contracts (including sales of goods; commercial financing), Government contracts and claims, Private international. Home: 8875 Overlake Dr W Medina WA 98039-5347 Office: 1201 3rd Ave Ste 4500 Seattle WA 98101-3029 E-mail: olseh@perkinscoie.com., olseh@seanet.com.

OLSEN, M. KENT, lawyer, educator; b. Denver, Mar. 10, 1948; s. Marvin and F. Winona (Wilker) O.; m. Shauna L. Casement; children: Kristofor Anders, Alexander Lee, Nikolaus Alrik, Amanda Elizabeth. BS, Colo. State U., 1970; JD, U. Denver, 1975. Bar: Colo., U.S. Dist. Ct. Colo. 1982, U.S. Tax Ct. Law clk. Denver Probate Ct., 1973-75; assoc. ptnr. Johnson & McLachlan, Lamar, Colo., 1975-80; assoc. Buchanan, Thomas and Johnson, Lakewood, Colo., 1981-82, William E. Myrick, P.C., Denver, 1982-83; referee Denver Probate Ct., Denver, 1983-89; ptnr. Haines & Olsen, P.C., Denver, 1989-95; pvt. practice Denver, 1995—2001; ptnr. Olsen & Traeger, LLP, 2001—. Adv. bd. Denver Paralegal Inst., 1993—, Elder Law Inst., 1994—. Mem. Gov.'s Commn. on Life and the Law, Denver, 1991-2000; bd. dirs. Adult Care Mgmt., Inc., Denver, 1985-95; bd. dirs. Arc of Denver, Inc., 1990—, pres., 1995-97; bd. dirs. Colo. Guardianship Alliance, Denver, 1990-91; bd. dirs. Colo. Fund for People with Disabilities, 1994—, pres., 1994-2000. Recipient Outstanding Vol. Svc. award Adult Care Mgmt., 1990, Outstanding Svc. award The Arc of Denver, 1991, Vol. Svc. award Colo. Gerontol. Soc., 1997, Pres.'s award Arc of Denver, 1998. Mem. ABA, Colo. Bar Assn. (past chair probate sect.), Am. Assn. Home for Aging, Nat. Acad. Elder Law Attys., Colo. Assn. Homes and Svcs. to the Aging, Denver Bar Assn., Denver Estate Planning Coun. Avocations: running, skiing, racquetball, art, hiking. Estate planning, Probate (including wills, trusts), Estate taxation. Home: 3030 S Roslyn St Denver CO 80231-4153 Office: 650 S Cherry St Ste 850 Denver CO 80246-1805 E-mail: mkolsen@olsentraeger.com.

OLSEN, MARY ANN, lawyer; b. Hoboken, N.J., Aug. 5, 1948; d. Charles Joseph and Margaret Nora (Power) O.; 1 child, Matthew Ellisen. AAS, Purdue U., 1973; BS, St. Peter's Coll., Jersey City, 1973; JD, Rutgers U., 1989. Bar: N.J. 1990, N.Y. 1991. Pvt. practice, Bayonne, N.J., 1991—. Cons. atty. Hudson County Protective Svc., West New York, N.J., 1993-96. Chmn. money mgmt. com. Bayonne Office on Aging, 1996-97; trustee Jersey City Cmty. Charter Sch.; bd. dirs. St. Joseph's Home for the Blind, Guardianship Assn. N.J., Inc. Mem. N.J. Bar Assn., Hudson County Bar Assn., Hudson Inn of Ct. Bankruptcy, Family and matrimonial, Probate (including wills, trusts). Office: 8 E 35th St Bayonne NJ 07002-3925

OLSEN, ROBERT ERIC, lawyer, educator, writer; b. Easton, Pa., July 10, 1944; s. Robert Thorvald and Frances (Wallburg) O.; m. Barbara Edith Mackay, July 25, 1992; 1 child, Alexander. AB, Harvard Coll., 1966; MA, U. Pa., 1967; JD, U. Denver, 1975. Bar: Md., Colo. Corp. planner Indsl. Valley Bank, Phila., 1968-73; sr. v.p. First Am. Indsl. Bank and First Am. Leasing Co., Denver, 1973-75; assoc. Calkins, Kramer, Grimshaw & Harring, Denver, 1975-79, Brenman, Epstein, Zerobnick, Raskin & Friedlob, Denver, 1979-80; ptnr. Olsen & Guardi, Denver, 1980-90; fgn. svc. officer U.S. Dept. of State, Washington, 1992-94; of counsel Goldstein & Baron, College Park, Md., 1995-97; atty. Olsen Law Firm, McLean, Va., 1997—99, 2001—; counsel to Greenberg Traurig, McLean, Va., 1999—2001; instr. U. Phoenix and U. Phoenix Online, 2001—. Democrat. Avocations: opera, photography, political policy development. Mergers and acquisitions, Securities, Transportation. Home: 922 Ridge Dr Mc Lean VA 22101-1632 E-mail: olsenr@cox.net.

OLSON, DENNIS ALAN, law educator; b. Frankfurt, Hesse, Germany, May 27, 1959; came to U.S., 1960; s. Rodger Dale and Nancy Elizabeth (French) O.; m. Julie Ann Arthur, Apr. 28, 1983; children: Emily Nicole, Peter Arthur, Caitlin Marie, Spencer Christian, Benjamin Thomas, Natalie Elizabeth, Valerie Ann. BA, Brigham Young U., 1978, JD, 1984. Bar: Idaho 1984, U.S. Dist. Ct. Idaho 1984, Oreg. 1985, U.S. Dist. Ct. Oreg. 1985. Law clk. to judge Idaho State Trial Ct., Boise, 1984-85; assoc. Kell, Alterman & Runstein, Portland, Oreg., 1985-86; vis. asst. prof. Ill. Inst. Tech., Chgo., 1986-88, U. Okla., Norman, 1988-89, vis. assoc. prof., 1989-90; assoc. dean, assoc. prof. Tex. Wesleyan U., 1990-93, assoc. prof., 1993-96; dean, prof. Appalachian Sch. of Law, 1996-98, prof., 1998-99; provost, v.p. acad. affairs, prof. Univ. Gt. Falls, Mont., 2000—02, prof., 2002—. Disting. vis. prof., spl. asst. to pres. So. Va. Coll., 1999-2000. Rep. committeeman Utah, 1976-78. Mem. ABA. Mem. Lds Ch. Avocation: football official. E-mail: dolson01@ugf.edu.

OLSON, DENNIS OLIVER, lawyer; b. Seminole, Tex., Oct. 19, 1947; s. Edwin and Beulah Matilda (Strang) O.; m. Leonee Lynn Claud, Jan. 30, 1971; children: James Edwin, Stacy Rae. BA in English, U. Tex., 1969; JD, Tex. Tech U., 1974. Bar: Tex. 1974, U.S. Ct. Mil. Appeals 1974, U.S. Dist. Ct. (no. dist.) Tex. 1978, U.S. Dist. Ct. (we. dist.) Tex. 1978, U.S. Ct. Appeals (5th cir.) 1984, U.S. Supreme Ct. 1985, U.S. Dist. Ct. (ea. dist.) Tex. 2002. Commd. USMC, 1969, advanced through grades to capt., 1973, infantry officer various locations including Vietnam, 1969-74, judge advocate, 1974-78, resigned, 1978; assoc. Carr, Evans, Fouts & Hunt, and predecessor, Lubbock, Tex., 1978-81, ptnr., 1981-85; pvt. practice Dallas, 1985-88; shareholder, co-chmn. bankruptcy sect. Godwin & Carlton, P.C., Dallas, 1989-94; ptnr. Olson Nicoud & Gueck, LLP & predecessor, Dallas, 1994—. Bd. dirs. Presbyn. Ctr. Doctor's Clinic, Lubbock, 1983-85, United Campus Ministry, Tex. Tech U., Lubbock, 1984-85, Discovery Sch.of Canyon Creek, Richardson, 1999-2002; elder Canyon Creek Presbyn. Ch., Richardson, Tex.; v.p. bd. dirs. Quantico, Va. chpt. ARC, 1975-77; v.p., bd. dirs. Quantico chpt. ARC, 1975-77, treas., bd. dirs. Lubbock chpt., 1981-83; vol. Lubbock United Way, 1978-80. Decorated Bronze Star; named Outstanding Young Man of Am., 1983. Fellow Tex. Bar Found. (sustaining life); mem. Dallas Bar Assn., Lubbock County Bar Assn. (bd. dirs. 1983-85), Tex. Young Lawyers Assn. (bd. dirs. 1981-83), Judge Advocates Assn. (bd. dirs. 1976-78), Lubbock C. of C. (grad. Leadership Lubbock program 1981), U. Tex. NROTC Alumni Found., (bd. dirs. 2001-), Phi Delta Phi. Bankruptcy, General civil litigation, General practice. Home: 313 Forest Grove Dr Richardson TX 75080-1937 E-mail: denniso@dallas-law.com.

OLSON, JOHN KARL, lawyer; b. Springfield, Mass., Aug. 14, 1949; s. Harold Gunnar and Louise Theodora (Shukis) Olson; m. Ann Catherine Sullivan, June 16, 1973; children: Elizabeth Ann, Katherine Louise. AB, Harvard Coll., 1971; JD, Boston Coll., 1975. Bar: Fla. 1975, U.S. Dist. Ct. (mid. and so. dists.) Fla. 1976, U.S. Ct. Appeals (5th cir.) 1979, U.S. Supreme Ct. 1979, U.S. Ct. Appeals (11th cir.) 1981. From assoc. to ptnr. Carlton, Fields, Ward et al., Tampa, Fla., 1975-86; exec. v.p., gen. counsel, dir. Jet Fla., Inc., Miami, 1986-88; ptnr. Stearns Weaver Miller Weissler Alhadeff & Sitterson P.A., Tampa, 1988—. Author: (book) Creditors and Debtors Rights in Florida, 1979, 1989, Collier Bankruptcy Practice Guide, 1986. Trustee Tampa Mus. Art, 1992—98; mem. parent bd. U. Del., 1998—2002, co-pres., 2000—02. Fellow, U. Tampa, 1986—. Mem.: ABA (vice chmn. bankruptcy com. 1984—86), Fla. Bar (chmn. bus. law sect. 1988—89), Am. Bankruptcy Inst., Harvard Club (pres. 1982—84). Bankruptcy, General civil litigation, Commercial, contracts (including sales of goods; commercial financing). Home: 2632 W Prospect Rd Tampa FL 33629-5358 Office: Sun Trust Fin Ctr 401 E Jackson St Tampa FL 33602-5233

OLSON, KEVIN LORY, lawyer; b. Berkeley, Calif., Dec. 2, 1956; s. Lorimer Reuben and Norma Carolyn Olson; m. Linda Sue Gladish, June 16, 1978; children: Lisa Marie, Kimberly Ann, Karen Amanda. BS in Math., Ariz. State U., 1977; JD, Yale U., 1980. Bar: Ariz. 1980. Assoc. Lewis and Roca, Phoenix, 1980-85, ptnr., 1985-97, Steptoe & Johnson LLP, Phoenix, 1997—. Bd. dirs. East Valley Partnership, Mesa, Ariz., 1990—, pres.-elect, 2000-01, pres., 2001-02. Mem. ABA, State Bar of Ariz., Maricopa County Bar Assn., Tempe C. of C. (pres. 1995-96), Greater Phoenix C. of C. (v.p. transp. 2000-03). Commercial, contracts (including sales of goods; commercial financing), Corporate, general, Securities. Office: 201 E Washington St Ste 1600 Phoenix AZ 85004 E-mail: kolson@steptoe.com.

OLSON, ROBERT GRANT, lawyer; b. Ft. Dodge, Iowa, Mar. 29, 1952; s. Grant L. and R. June (Pohlmann) O.; m. Cynthia Lynn Murray, Sept. 7, 1978; children: Brendon, Elisabeth, Jeffrey, Daniel. BS, Iowa State U., 1973; JD, U. Iowa, 1976. Bar: Mo., 1976, Ill. 1977. Ptnr. Thompson & Mitchell, St. Louis, 1976-92, Riezman & Blitz, P.C., St. Louis, 1992-2000, Stone, Leyton & Gershman, P.C., St. Louis, 2000—. Editor Jour. Corp. Law, 1975-76. Vol. Gephardt for Pres. Campaign, 1988, Carnahan for Lt. Gov. Campaign, 1988, Carnahan for Gov. Campaign, 1992., Habitat for Humanity; arbitrator Better Bus. Bur. Taxpayer assistance program. Mem. ABA, Mo. Bar Assn., Ill. Bar Assn., Met. St. Louis Bar Assn., Downtown St. Louis Lions Club (pres. 1990-91). Commercial, contracts (including sales of goods; commercial financing), Finance, Property, real (including real estate development, water). Home: 424 E Jackson Rd Saint Louis MO 63119-4128 Office: Stone Leyton & Gershman 7733 Forsyth Blvd Ste 500 Saint Louis MO 63105-1817

OLSON, ROBERT WYRICK, lawyer; b. Madison, Wis., Dec. 19, 1945; s. John Arthur and Mary Katherine (Wyrick) O.; m. Carol Jean Duane, June 12, 1971; children: John Hagan, Mary Catherine Duane. BA, Williams Coll., 1967; JD, U. Va., 1970. Assoc. Cravath, Swaine & Moore, N.Y.C., 1970-79; asst. gen. counsel Penn Cen. Corp., Cin., 1979-80, assoc. gen. counsel, 1980-82, v.p., dep. gen. counsel, 1982-87; sr. v.p., gen. counsel, sec. Am. Premier Underwriters, Inc. (formerly Penn Cen. Corp.), Cin., 1987-95; sr. v.p., gen. counsel and sec. Chiquita Brands Internat., Inc., Cin., 1995—. Mem. ABA. Corporate, general, Mergers and acquisitions, Securities. Office: Chiquita Brands Internat 250 E 5th St Ste 29 Cincinnati OH 45202-4119 E-mail: bolson@chiquita.com.

OLSON, STEPHEN M(ICHAEL), lawyer; b. Jamestown, N.Y., May 4, 1948; s. Charles R. and Marilyn (Dietzel) O.; m. Linda C. Hanson, Aug. 24, 1968; children: Kevin, Darren. AB cum laude, Princeton U., 1970; JD, U. Chgo., 1973. Bar: Pa. 1973, U.S. Dist. Ct. (we. dist.) Pa. 1973, U.S. Ct. Appeals (3d cir.) 1975, U.S. Ct. Appeals (1st and D.C. cirs.) 1986, U.S. Ct. Appeals (7th cir. and 8th cir. 1988), U.S. Supreme Ct. 1986. Assoc. Kirkpatrick & Lockhart, Pitts., 1973-81, ptnr., 1981—. Bd. dirs. Sweetwater Art Ctr. Mem.: ABA (rlwy./airline labor law com.), Allegheny County Bar Assn., Pa. Bar Assn., Princeton Alumni Assn. West Pa., Duquesne Club. Avocations: photography, bicycling. Labor (including EEOC, Fair Labor Standards Act, labor-management relations, NLRB, OSHA). Office: Kirkpatrick & Lockhart Henry W Oliver Bldg 535 Swithfield St Pittsburgh PA 15222-2312

OLSON, THEODORE BEVRY, federal agency administrator, lawyer; b. Chgo., Sept. 11, 1940; 2 children. BA, U. Pacific, 1962; LL.B., U. Calif.-Berkeley, 1965. Bar: Calif. 1965, D.C. 1982. Assoc., ptnr. Gibson, Dunn & Crutcher, Los Angeles, 1972-81, 84—; asst. atty. gen. Dept. Justice, Washington, 1981—84; ptnr. Gibson, Dunn & Crutcher, Washington, 1984—2001; U.S. solicitor gen. Dept. Justice, Washington, 2001—. Mem. Calif. Commn. on Uniform State Laws, 1972-74; del. Republican Nat. Conv., 1976, 80. Fellow Am. Acad. of Appellate Lawyers, Am. Coll. Trial Lawyers; mem. ABA, L.A. County Bar Assn. Republican. Office: Office Solicitor Gen 950 Pennsylvania Ave NW Rm 5143 Washington DC 20530-0001

OLSON, WALTER GILBERT, lawyer; b. Stanton, Nebr., Feb. 2, 1924; s. O.E. Olson and Mabel A. Asplin; m. Gloria Helen Bennett, June 26, 1949; children: Clifford Warner, Karen Rae Olson. BS, U. Calif., Berkeley, 1947, JD, 1949. Bar: Calif. 1950, U.S. Dist. Ct. (no. dist.) Calif. 1950, U.S. Tax Ct. 1950, U.S. Ct. Appeals (9th cir.) 1950. Assoc. Orrick, Herrington and Sutcliffe (formerly Orrick, Dahlquist, Herrington and Sutcliffe), San Francisco, 1949-54, ptnr., 1954-88, of counsel, 1989—. Bd. dirs. Alltel Corp., Little Rock, 1988-94; mem. Commn. to Revise Calif. Corp. Securities Law, 1967-69, Securities Regulatory Reform Panel, 1978-80; mem. corp. security adv. com. Calif. Commr. of Corps, 1975-88. Editor-in-chief Calif. Law Review, 1948-49. Bd. dirs. Internat. Ho., Berkeley, 1981-86. With U.S. Army, 1943-46, ETO. Fellow Am. Bar Found.; mem. ABA (trust divsn. nat. conf. of lawyers and reps. of Am. Bankers Assn.), Calif. Bar Assn. (chmn. corps com. 1975-76, exec. com. bus. law sect. 1977-78), San Francisco Bar Assn., U. Calif. Alumni Assn., Boalt Hall Alumni Assn. (bd. dirs. 1982-90, sec. 1985, v.p. 1987, pres. 1988), Order of Coif, Menlo Country Club (Woodside, Calif.), Pacific-Union Club. Commercial, contracts (including sales of goods; commercial financing), Corporate, general, Securities. Office: Orrick Herrington & Sutcliffe 400 Sansome St San Francisco CA 94111-3143

OLSON, WILLIAM JEFFREY, lawyer; b. Paterson, N.J., Oct. 23, 1949; s. Walter Justus and Viola Patricia (Trautvetter) O.; m. Janet Elaine Bollen, May 22, 1976; children: Robert J., Joanne C. AB, Brown U., 1971; JD, U. Richmond, 1976. Bar: Va. 1976, D.C. 1976, U.S. Ct. Claims 1976, U.S. Ct. Appeals (4th, 6th, 10th, and D.C. cirs.) 1976, U.S. Supreme Ct. 1982. Assoc. Jackson & Campbell, Washington, 1976-79; ptnr. Gilman, Olson & Pangia, Washington, 1980-92; prin. William J. Olson PC, McLean, Va. and Washington, 1992—. Sec., treas. bd. dirs. Victims Assistance Legal Orgn., McLean, Va., 1979—; presdl. transition team leader Legal Svcs. Corp., Washington, 1980; chmn. and bd. dirs. nat. Legal Svcs. Corp., 1981-82; mem. Pres.'s Export Coun. Subcom. on Export Adminstrn., Washington, 1982-84; spl. counsel bd. govs. U.S. Postal Svc., Washington, 1984-86. Author: Tuition Tax Credits and Alternatives, 1978; co-author: Debating National Health Policy, 1977, Executive Orders and National Emergencies, 1999, An Evaluation of Postal Service Worksharing, 2003. Trustee Davis Meml. Goodwill Industries, Washington, 1980-86, 88-93; chmn. Fairfax County Rep. Com., Fairfax, Va., 1980-82; mem. Rep. State Ctrl. Com., Richmond, Va., 1982-86. Mem. Va. Bar Assn., Assn. Trial Lawyers Am., Va. Trial Lawyers Assn. Republican. Baptist. Avocation: gardening. Administrative and regulatory, Constitutional, Non-profit and tax-exempt organizations. Office: 8180 Greensboro Dr Ste 1070 Mc Lean VA 22102-3860 E-mail: wjo@mindspring.com.

O'MALLEY, CARLON MARTIN, judge; b. Phila., Sept. 7, 1929; s. Carlon Martin and Lucy (Bol) O'M.; m. Mary Catherine Lyons, Aug. 17, 1957; children: Carlon Martin III, Kathleen B. O'Malley Aikman, Harry Tighe, John Todd, Cara M. O'Malley Colombo. BA, Pa. State U., 1951; LLB, Temple U., 1954. Bar: Pa. 1955, Fla. 1973, U.S. Supreme Ct. 1973. Practiced law, 1957-61; asst. U.S. atty. for Middle Dist. Pa., Dept. Justice, 1961-69, U.S. atty., 1979-82; ptnr. O'Malley & Teets, 1970-72, O'Malley, Jordan & Mullaney (and predecessor firms), 1976-79; pvt. practice Pa. and Fla., 1972-79, 82-87; judge Ct. Common Pleas of Lackawanna County (45th Judicial Dist.), 1987-97, sr. judge, 1998—. Dir. pub. safety City of Scranton, 1983-86; lectr. Lackawanna Coll., 1982-86. Editorial bd.: Temple

Law Rev, 1952-53. Pres. Lackawanna County (Pa.) unit Am. Cancer Soc., 1966-67; bd. dirs. Pa. Cancer Soc., 1967-68, Lackawanna county chpt. ARC, 1967-69; mem. solicitation team, govtl. divsn. Lackawanna United Fund, 1963-68; chmn. profl. divsn. Greater Scranton (Pa.) YMCA Membership Drives; trustee Everhart Mus., Scranton, 1987—. Pilot USAF, 1955-57, Pa. N.G., 1957-59. Mem. Am. Judges Assn., Nat. Assn. Former U.S. Attys., Pa. Bar Assn., Lackawanna County Bar Assn. (bd. dirs., fin. sec.), Fla. Bar Assn., Country Club of Scranton, Elks (pres. Pa. chpt. 1978-79, judiciary com. 1985-89, justice Grand Forum 1991, 1995-97, chief justice 1992-93, nat. pres. 1997-98), K.C., Phi Kappa (pres.), Delta Theta Phi (pres.). Democrat. Office: Judges Chambers Lackawanna County Courthouse Scranton PA 18503

O'MALLEY, DENISE MARGARET, judge; b. Chgo., Mar. 15, 1940; d. Edward O'Malley and Muriel McGuirl; m. Thomas Murphy, Sept. 16, 1961 (div. Apr. 1971); children: Brian Murphy, Brigid Murphy, Patrick Murphy. BA, Mundelein Coll., 1961; MA, U. Chgo., 1971; JD, John Marshall Law Sch., 1981. Bar: Ill. 1981, U.S. Dist. Ct. (no. dist.) Ill. 1982. Sch. social worker Matteson Dist. 162, Ill., 1971—78; with State Atty's Appellate Office, 1981—85; atty. Chgo. Transit Authority, 1985—86, Fasano & Farina, Chgo., 1986—87, O'Connor Schiff and Meyer, Chgo., 1987—89; sr. trial counsel, torts divsn. City of Chgo., 1989—92; trial judge, domestic rels. Chgo., 1992—94; trial judge, law divsn., 1994—2002; appellate ct. judge Ill. Appellate Ct., Chgo., 2002—. Adj. prof. law John Marshall Law Sch., Chgo., 1998—. Office: 1103 N Damen Ave Chicago IL 60602

O'MALLEY, KEVIN FRANCIS, lawyer, writer, educator; b. St. Louis, May 12, 1947; s. Peter Francis and Dorothy Margaret (Cradick) O'M.; m. Dena Hengen, Apr.2, 1971; children: Kevin Brendan, Ryan Michael. AB, St. Louis U., 1970, JD, 1973. Bar: Mo. 1973, U.S. Ct. Appeals D.C. 1974, U.S. Ct. Appeals (8th cir.) 1979, Ill. 1993. Trial lawyer U.S. Dept. Justice, Washington, 1973-74, Los Angeles, 1974-77, Phoenix, 1977-78, asst. U.S. atty. St. Louis, 1978-83. Adj. prof. law St. Louis U., 1979—; lectr. Ctrl. and Ea. European Law Initiative, Russian Fedn., 1996, Poland, 1999. Author: (with Devitt, Blackmar, O'Malley) Federal Jury Practice and Instruction, 1990, 92, (with O'Malley, Grenig & Lee), 1999, 2000, 01; contbr. articles to law books and jours. Community amb. Expt. in Internat. Living, Prague, Czechoslovakia, 1968; bd. dirs. St. Louis-Galway (Ireland) Sister Cities. Capt. U.S. Army, 1973. Recipient Atty. Gen.'s Disting. Service award U.S. Dept. Justice, 1977, John J. Dwyer Meml. Scholarship award, 1967-70. Fellow Am. Coll. Trial Lawyers; mem. ABA (chmn. govt. litigation counsel com. 1982-86, chmn. jud. com. 1986-87, chmn. com. on ind. and small firms, chmn. trial practice com. 1991-94, health care litigation 1994-98), Am. Law Inst., Met. Bar Assn. St. Louis (chmn. criminal law sect.), Nat. Inst. Trial Advocacy, Mo. Athletic Club. Roman Catholic. Office: 10 S Brentwood Blvd Ste 102 Saint Louis MO 63105-1694 E-mail: komalley@omalleylaw.com.

O'MALLEY, SUSAN MARIE, lawyer; b. Evergreen Park, Ill., Apr. 11, 1968; d. Arthur Stephen and Mary Catherine O'Malley. BS cum laude, U. N.C., Charlotte, 1990; JD, U. N.C., 1994. Bar: N.C. 1994, D.C. 1996, U.S. Dist. Ct. (ea. dist.) N.C. 1998, U.S. Ct. Appeals (4th cir.) 2003. Atty. Keel Law Offices, Tarboro, NC, 1995-98; ptnr. Keel, Kessler & O'Malley, LLP, Tarboro, 1998-2000, Keel O'Malley LLP, Tarboro, 2001—. Contbr. articles to publs. Mem.: ATLA (social security sect. chair-elect 2000—01, chair 2001—03), N.C. Acad. Trial Lawyers (disability adv. sect. edn. chair 1998—99, vice-chair 2000, chair 2002—03), Jaycees (v.p. 1998—99). Pension, profit-sharing, and employee benefits, Personal injury (including property damage), Workers' compensation. Office: PO Box 1158 Tarboro NC 27886-1158

OMAN, RICHARD HEER, lawyer; b. Columbus, Ohio, Jan. 4, 1926; s. B. R. Oman and Marguerite H. (Oman) Andrews; m. Jane Ellen Wert, Oct. 5, 1963; children: Sarah M., David W. BA, Ohio State U., 1948, JD, 1951. Bar: Ohio 1951. Atty. Ohio Nat. Bank, Columbus, 1951-55; ptnr. Isaac, Postlewaite, O'Brien & Oman, Columbus, 1955-71; dir. Columbus Found., 1955-77, counsel, 1955—; ptnr. Porter, Wright, Morris and Arthur (and predecessor firm), Columbus, 1972-89; of counsel Vorys, Sater, Seymour and Pease, Columbus, 1990, ptnr., 1991-96, of counsel, 1997—. Mem. Columbus Airport Commn., 1960-64; trustee Reinberger Found., Cleve., 1980—, Columbus Acad., 1981-87, Grant Hosp., 1978-86, Harding Hosp., 1978-86; sr. warden Trinity Epsic. Ch., 1985-88. Fellow Ohio State Bar Found.; mem. ABA, Am. Coll. Trust and Estate Counsel, Ohio State Bar Assn. (past mem. bd. govs. probate and trust law sect.), Columbus Bar Assn., Columbus Club, Rocky Fork Hunt and Country Club, Nantucket (Mass.) Yacht Club, Kit Kat Club. Republican. Episcopalian. Estate planning, Non-profit and tax-exempt organizations, Estate taxation. Office: Vorys Sater Seymour & Pease PO Box 1008 52 E Gay St Columbus OH 43215-3161 Fax: 614.714.4731. E-mail: rhoman@ussp.com.

O'MARA, JAMES WRIGHT, lawyer; b. McComb, Miss., Jan. 7, 1940; s. Junior and Mary Jane (Wright) O'M.; m. Jeanette Walter, June 28, 1963; children: James W. Jr., Angela J. BA, U. Miss., 1962, JD with distinction, 1967. Bar: Miss. 1967. Ptnr. Butler, Snow, O'Mara, Stevens & Cannada, Jackson, Miss., 1967-97, chmn., 1990-97; sr. ptnr. Phelps & Dunbar, Jackson, Miss., 1997—. Vis. prof. Jackson Sch. Law, 1970-72. Editor-in-chief Miss. Law Jour., 1966-67. Pres. Jackson Prep. Sch., 1984-85, Woodland Hills Bapt. Acad., Jackson, 1973-84. Capt. U.S. Army, 1962-64. Fellow Miss. Bar Found.; mem. ABA, Miss. Bar Assn., Am. Bankruptcy Inst., Miss. Bankruptcy Conf. (pres. 1980-81). Baptist. Bankruptcy, General civil litigation, Commercial, contracts (including sales of goods; commercial financing). Home: 42 Eastbrooke St # I Jackson MS 39216-4714 Office: Phelps & Dunbar PO Box 23066 Jackson MS 39225-3066 E-mail: omaraj@phelps.com.

O'MEILIA, DAVID E. lawyer; b. July 1951; Grad. Okla. State U.; grad. in law, Tulsa Coll. Atty. Tulsa County Dist. Atty.'s Office, 1980—84; asst. U.S. atty. U.S. Atty.'s Office, Tulsa, Okla., 1986—96; atty. Nichols, Wolfe, Stamper, Nally, Fallis & Robertson, 1996—99; ptnr. Lyons, Clark, Daniel-son & O'Meilia, Tulsa, Okla., 1999—2002; U.S. atty. No. Dist. Okla., 2002—. Office: 333 W Fourth St Ste 3460 Tulsa OK 74103*

OMINSKY, ANDREW MICHAEL, lawyer; b. Phila., Jan. 8, 1965; s. Albert and Elaine Ominsky; m. Emma G. Ominsky, June 5, 1994; children: Jared, Emily, Elizabeth. BA, Duke U., 1987; JD, U. Denver, 1990. Bar: Colo. 1990, U.S. Dist. Ct. Colo. 1991, Pa. 1996, U.S. Dist. Ct. (ea. dist.) Pa. 1996, Pa. (U.S. Dist Ct. (middle dist.)) 1997, (U.S. Ct. of Appeals (4th cir.)) 2000, (U.S. Ct. of Appeals (3rd cir.)) 2002. Jud. clk. Colo. Dist. Ct., Englewood, 1989-91; lawyer Burg & Eldredge, PC, Denver, 1991-96, Ominsky & Ominsky PC, Phila., 1996—. Apptd. to appellate ct. procedural rules com. Pa. Supreme Ct., 1999—. Bd. dirs. Linda Creed Breast Cancer Found., Phila., 1997—, J/CHAI, Phila., 1996—; founder Elaine Ominsky Circle of Friends, Wistar Inst., Gladwyne, Pa., 1997—. Mem. Colo. Bar Assn., Pa. Bar Assn., Pa. Trial Lawyers Assn., Phila. Bar Assn. General civil litigation, Commercial, contracts (including sales of goods; commercial financing). Office: Two Penn Ctr 1500 JFK Blvd Ste 1210 Philadelphia PA 19102 E-mail: ominskylaw@yahoo.com.

OMINSKY, HARRIS, lawyer; b. Phila., Sept. 14, 1932; s. Joseph and Lillian (Herman) O.; m. Rosalyn Rita Rutenberg; children— Michelle, David BS in Econs., U. Pa., 1953, LLB cum laude, 1956. Bar: Pa. 1956. Ptnr. Ominsky & Ominsky, Phila., 1958-64; ptnr. Blank, Rome, Comisky & McCauley, Phila., 1964—, Balnk Rome LLP, 1964—; mem. mgmt. com. Blank, Rome, Comisky & McCauley, Phila., 1981-84, 88-92, co-chmn. real estate dept., 1988-93. Lectr. Law Sch., Temple U., Phila., 1969-71, lectr. Real Estate Inst., 1996—. Author: Real Estate Practice: New Perspectives, 1996, Real Estate Practice: Breaking New Ground, 2001, If I'm Still Around, I Can't Be Dead, 2002; weekly columnist Ominsky's Terrain, Phila. Legal Intelligencer, 1999—; contbr. numerous articles to profl. jours. Pres. bd. Phila. Singing City Choir, 1984-88; chmn. zoning com. Merion Civic Assn., Pa., 1984-91. Fellow Am. Bar Found.; mem. ABA (Harrison Tweed spl. merit award 1988), Pa. Bar Assn. (ho. of dels. 1984—), Pa. Bar Inst. (bd. dirs. 1981—, exec. com. 1986-93, v.p. 1988-89, pres. 1989-90, lectr., planner 1969—), Phila. Bar Assn. (chmn. real estate taxes subcom. 1984-85, real property sect. 1991-92, Leon J. Obermayer Edn. award 1989, Good Deed award real property sect. 1999), Am. Coll. Real Estate Lawyers (bd. govs. 1993-95), Order of Coif. Landlord-tenant, Property, real (including real estate development, water), State and local taxation. Home: 526 Baird Rd Merion Station PA 19066-1302 Office: Blank Rome LLP One Logan Sq Philadelphia PA 19103-6998

O'NEAL, LEE C. lawyer; b. Greensboro, N.C., July 9, 1971; d. Richard Lee and Betty Lou Calhoun; m. Cam O'Neal, Mar. 8, 1997; 1 child, Cameron. BA, U. N.C., Greensboro, 1995, JD, 1997. Bar: N.C. 1998. Solo practitioner, Greensboro, 1998—. Mem.: N.C. Acad. Trial Lawyers, N.C. Bar Assn., Guilford Inn of Ct. Avocations: reading, travel, cooking, volunteering. Criminal. Office: 330 S Greene St Ste 304 Greensboro NC 27401 Office Fax: 336-273-7304.

O'NEAL, MICHAEL RALPH, state legislator, lawyer; b. Kansas City, Mo., Jan. 16, 1951; s. Ralph D. and Margaret E. (McEuen) O'N.; children from a previous marriage: children: Haley Anne, Austin Michael; m. Cindy Wulfkuhle, Apr. 9, 1999. BA in English, U. Kans., 1973, JD, 1976. Bar: Kans. 1976, U.S. Dist. Ct. Kans. 1976, U.S. Ct. Appeals (10th cir.) 1979. Intern Legis. Counsel State of Kans., Topeka, 1975-76; assoc. Hodge, Reynolds, Smith, Peirce & Forker, Hutchinson, Kans., 1976-77; ptnr. Reynolds, Peirce, Forker, Suter, O'Neal & Myers, Hutchinson, 1980-88; shareholder Gilliland & Hayes, P.A., Hutchinson, 1988—, mng. ptnr., 1999—2000; mem. Kans. Ho. of Reps., 1984, chmn. jud. com., 1989-90, 93-94, 97—; pres. Gilliland & Hayes, P.C., 1999-2000; minority whip Kans. Ho. of Reps., 1991-92, majority whip, 1995-96, chmn. edn. com., 1995-96, mem. fiscal oversight com., 1997—, chair redistricting com., 2001—02, mem. bus., commerce, labor com., mem. tax, commerce, transp. and jud. budget com., 2003—, chmn. reappointment com., 2001—02. Instr. Hutchinson C.C., 1977-88. Vice chmn. Rep. Ctrl. Com., Reno County, Kans., 1982-86; bd. dirs. Reno County Mental Health Assn., Hutchinson, 1984-89, YMCA, 1984-86, Crime Stoppers (ex-officio), Hutchinson; chmn. adv. bd. dirs. Wesley Towers Retirement Cmty., 1984-96; mem. Kans. Travel and Tourism Commn., 1990-94; mem. bd. govs. U. Kans. Law Sch., 1991-94; mem. Kans. Sentencing Commn., 1997-2000. Recipient Leadership award Kans. C. of C. and Industry, 1985; named one of Outstanding Young Men Am., 1986. Mem. ABA, Nat. Conf. State Legislatures (criminal justice com.), Kans. Assn. Def. Counsel, Def. Rsch. Inst., Kans. Bar Assn. (prospective legis. com., Outstanding Svc. award), Hutchinson C. of C. (ex-officio bd. dirs., Leadership award 1984), Am. Coun. Young Polit. Leaders (del. to Atlantic conf. biennial assembly), Kans. Jud. Coun., Commn. on Uniform State Laws. Avocations: basketball, tennis, golf. Home: 8 Windemere Ct Hutchinson KS 67502-2020 Office: Gilliland & Hayes PA 2d Flr Box 2977 20 W 2nd Ave Hutchinson KS 67504-2977 E-mail: mroneal@southwind.net.

O'NEAL, MICHAEL SCOTT, SR., lawyer; b. Jacksonville, Fla., Dec. 22, 1948; s. Jack Edwin and Lucille (Colvin) O'N.; m. Barbara Louise Hardie, Jan. 30, 1971 (div. Sept. 1974); 1 child, Jennifer Erin; m. Helen Margaret Joost, Mar. 18, 1985; children: Mary Helen, Angela Marie, Michael Scott O'Neal Jr. AA, Fla. Jr. Coll., 1975; BA in Econs. summa cum laude, U. No. Fla., 1977; JD cum laude, U. Fla., 1979. Bar: Fla. 1980, U.S. Dist. Ct. (mid. dist.) Fla. 1980, U.S. Dist. Ct. (no. dist.) Fla. 1981, U.S. Ct. Appeals (5th and 11th cirs.) 1981, U.S. Supreme Ct. 1986. Assoc. Howell, Liles, Braddock & Milton, Jacksonville, Fla., 1980-83; ptnr. Commander, Legler, Werber, Dawes, Sadler & Howell, Jacksonville, 1983-91, Foley & Lardner, Jacksonville, 1991-93, Howell O'Neal & Johnson, Jacksonville, 1993-96, Howell & O'Neal, Jacksonville, 1996—. Pro bono atty. Legal Aid Soc., Jacksonville, 1980—; practicing atty. Lawyers Reference, Jacksonville, 1980—. Pres. Julington Landing Homeowners Assn., Jacksonville, 1980-83. Served to staff sgt. USAF, 1968-74. Mem. ATLA, ABA, Jacksonville Bar Assn., Fed. Bar Assn., Am. Bd. Trial Advocates, Fla. Def. Lawyers Assn., Northeast Fla. Med. Malpractice Claims Coun. (pres. 1996), Jacksonville Assn. Def. Counsel (pres. 1999), Internat. Assn. Def. Counsel, Def. Rsch. Inst., Univ. Club, San Jose Country Club (Jacksonville). Republican. Methodist. Avocations: golf, music. Federal civil litigation, State civil litigation, Personal injury (including property damage). Home: 1299 Norwich Rd Jacksonville FL 32207-7525 Office: Howell O'Neal 200 N Laura St Ste 1100 Jacksonville FL 32202-3500 E-mail: msoneal@hotmail.com.

O'NEIL, JOHN JOSEPH, lawyer; b. Detroit, July 20, 1943; s. John J. and Dora J. (Collins) O'N.; children: Meghan, Kathryn. BA, Trinity Coll., 1965; LLB, U. Va., 1968. Bar: N.Y. 1969, U.S. Ct. Appeals (2d cir.) 1969, Fla. 1979, D.C. 1982. Assoc. Jackson & Nash, N.Y.C., 1968-71, Paul, Weiss, Rifkind, Wharton & Garrison, N.Y.C., 1971-77, ptnr., 1977—. Fellow Am. Coll. Trusts and Estates Counsel; mem. ABA (com. on spl. problems of aged), N.Y. State Bar Assn. (com. on taxation, trusts and estates sect.), Assn. Bar City N.Y. (com. on trusts and estates), Pi Gamma Mu. Family and matrimonial, Probate (including wills, trusts). Office: Paul Weiss Rifkind Wharton & Garrison Ste 3221 1285 Avenue Of The Americas Fl 21 New York NY 10019-6064

O'NEIL, ROBERT MARCHANT, university administrator, law educator; b. Boston, Oct. 16, 1934; s. Walter George and Isabel Sophia (Marchant) O'N.; m. Karen Elizabeth Elson, June 18, 1967; children— Elizabeth, Peter, David, Benjamin AB, Harvard U., 1956, AM, 1957, LLB, 1961; LLD, Beloit Coll., 1985, Ind. U., 1987. Bar: Mass. 1962. Law clk. to Justice William J. Brennan Jr. U.S. Supreme Ct., 1962-63; acting assoc. prof. law U. Calif.-Berkeley, 1963-66, prof., 1966-67, 69-72; exec. asst. to pres., prof. law SUNY-Buffalo, 1967-69; provost, prof. law U. Cin., 1972-73, exec. v.p., prof. law, 1973-75; v.p., prof. law Ind. U., Bloomington, 1975-80; pres. U. Wis. System, 1980-85; prof. law U. Wis.-Madison, 1980-85, U. Va., Charlottesville, 1985—, pres., 1985-90; gen. counsel AAUP, 1970-72, 91-92. Author: Civil Liberties: Case Studies and the Law, 1965, Free Speech: Responsible Communication Under Law, 2d edit., 1972, The Price of Dependency: Civil Liberties in the Welfare State, 1970, No Heroes, No Villians, 1972, The Courts, Government and Higher Education, 1972, Discriminating Against Discrimination, 1976, Handbook of the Law of Public Employment, 1978, 2d rev. edit., 1993, Classrooms in the Crossfire, 1981, Free Speech in the College Community, 1997, The First Amendment and Civil Liability, 2001; co-author: A Guide to Debate, 1964, The Judiciary and Vietnam, 1972, Civil Liberties Today, 1974. Trustee Tchrs. Ins. and Annuity Assn.; bd. dirs. Commonwealth Fund, Nat. Coalition Against Censorship, Am. Law Inst. Home: 1839 Westview Rd Charlottesville VA 22903-1632 Office: Thomas Jefferson Ctr Protection Free Expression 400 Peter Jefferson Pl Charlottesville VA 22911-8691

O'NEIL, THOMAS FRANCIS, III, lawyer, business executive; b. Fairfield, Conn., Apr. 8, 1957; s. Thomas F. Jr. and Carmen A. (Therrien) O'N.; m. Nancy D., Aug. 14, 1982; children: Caley Elizabeth, Patrick McGee. AB magna cum laude, Dartmouth Coll., 1975-79; JD, Georgetown U., 1979-82. Bar: Md. 1982, U.S. Dist. Ct. Md. 1983, U.S. Ct. Appeals (4th cir.) 1983, D.C. 1992. Legis. asst. Congressman Stewart B. McKinney, Washington, 1980-82; law clk. Hon. Alexander Harvey II U.S. Dist. Ct. Md.; assoc. Venable, Baetjer & Howard, Balt., 1984-86; asst. U.S. atty. U.S. Dept. Justice, Balt., 1986-89; assoc. Hogan & Hartson, Balt., 1990-91, ptnr., 1992-95; chief litigation counsel MCI Comms. Corp., Washington, 1995-98; chief legal counsel, sr. v.p. MCI Worldcom, Inc., 1998—; sr. v.p., gen. counsel MCI Group, 2001—02; sr. ptnr. Piper Rudnick LLP, 2002—. Bd. govs. Fed. Bar Assn., Balt., 1992; Walters Art Museum, ex officio trustee, 1995-96, trustee, 1999-2002; chair William T. Walters Assocs., Georgetown U. Law Ctr. mem., bd. visitors, 1999—; mem. adv. bd. Marbury Inst., 2000-02; trustee The Contemporary Mus., 2001-02. Recipient Chief Postal Insps. Spl. award U.S. Postal Svc., Washington, 1988, Letter of Commendation award Bur. of Investigation, Washington, 1989, Spl. Achievement award U.S. Dept. Justice, 1989. Mem. Serjeants Inn Law Club. Republican. Roman Catholic. Federal civil litigation, Criminal, Health. Office: Piper Rudnick 1200 19th St Washington DC 20036

O'NEIL, WILLIAM JOSEPH, judge; b. Casa Grande, Ariz., May 17, 1951; s. James Thomas and Mary Elizabeth (Smarden) O'N.; m. Tammy Gail Holmes; children: Christopher James, Michael Caleb, Sarah Caitlin, Kevin Joseph. BBA, U. Ariz., 1974; JD, Stetson U., 1977. Bar: Ariz. 1978, U.S. Dist. Ct. Ariz. 1978. Assoc. firm J. Lavell Harper Law Office, Casa Grande, 1977-79; ptnr. Harper & O'Neil, Casa Grande, 1979-80, Cole & O'Neil, Casa Grande, 1980-90; judge Superior Ct. Ariz., 1990—, presiding judge juvenile ct., 1991—, presiding judge, 2001—. Lectr. Cen. Ariz. Coll., Casa Grande, 1980-84; family law commr. Superior Ct. Ariz. Pinal County, Florence, 1987-90; mem. adv. bd. dirs. United Bank Ariz., Casa Grande, Mera Bank, Casa Grande; chmn. Ariz. Commn. on Juvenile Cts., 1991-2001; mem. Juvenile Justice Task Force Govs., Ariz. Com. Superior Ct., Ariz. Capital Litigation Com; mem. Ariz. Jud. Coun., 2001—. Chmn., bd. dirs. West Pinal Family Health Ctr., Casa Grande; mem. Cen. Ariz. Found. Bd., 1986—; chmn. deacons Trinity So. Bapt. Ch., Casa Grande, 1985-86. Mem. Nat. Coun. Juvenile and Family Ct. Judges, Nat. Lawyer's Assn., Assn. Trial Lawyers Am., Pinal County Bar Assn. (pres. 1989-90), Ariz. Bar Assn. (disciplinary com. 1985-90), Rotary (bd. dirs. 1987-90, pres. 1989-90). Office: Superior Ct Ariz PO Box 847 Florence AZ 85232-0847

O'NEILL, ALBERT CLARENCE, JR., lawyer; b. Gainesville, Fla., Nov. 25, 1939; s. Albert Clarence and Sue Virginia (Henry) O'N.; m. Vanda Marie Nigels, Apr. 26, 1969; 1 child, Heather Marie. BA with high honors, U. Fla., 1962; LL.B. magna cum laude, Harvard U., 1965. Bar: Fla. bar 1965. Law clk. to judge U.S. Dist. Ct. (mid. dist.) Fla., 1965-66; assoc. Fowler, White, Collins, Gillen, Humkey & Trenam, Tampa, Fla., 1966-69; ptnr. Trenam, Simmons, Kemker, Scharf & Barkin, Tampa, 1970-77; mem. firm Trenam, Kemker, Scharf, Barkin, Frye, O'Neill & Mullis (P.A.), Tampa, 1977—, also bd. dirs. Vis. lectr. law Stetson Law Sch., 1970-73; mem. adv. coun. IRS, 2001—. Exec. editor Harvard Law Rev., 1964-65; contbr. articles to profl. jours. Bd. dirs. Fla. Gulf Coast Symphony, Inc., 1975-86, U. Fla. Found., Inc., 1976-84, 97-2001, 2003- , Fla. Orch., 1988—, Gator Boosters, Inc., 2002—; mem. adv. coun. IRS, 2001- . Mem. ABA (chmn. tax sect. 1992-93), Am. Law Inst., Am. Coll. Tax Counsel, Fla. Bar (chmn. tax sect. 1975-76), Am. Bar Retirement Assn. (pres. 2000-01, bd. dirs.), Phi Beta Kappa. Corporate, general, Estate planning, Taxation, general. Office: Trenam Kemker Scharf Barkin Frye O'Neill & Mullis 101 E Kennedy Blvd Ste 2700 Tampa FL 33602-5150 E-mail: aconeill@trenam.com.

O'NEILL, BRIAN DENNIS, lawyer; b. Phila., Feb. 21, 1946; s. Harry William and Margaret Elizabeth (Miller) O'N.; m. Bonnie Anne Ryan, Aug. 17, 1968; children: Aimee Kathleen, Catherine Margaret. BA, Fla. State U., 1968, JD, 1971. Bar: Fla. 1971, D.C. 1975, U.S. Ct. Appeals (D.C. cir.) 1978, U.S. Ct. Appeals (5th and 11th cirs.) 1981, U.S. Ct. Appeals (10th cir.) 1985. Trial atty. Fed. Power Commn., Washington, 1972-75; assoc. Farmer, Shibley, McGuinn & Flood, Washington, 1975-80; ptnr. LeBoeuf, Lamb, Greene & MacRae, Washington, 1980—. Lectr. in field. Editorial bd. Energy Law Jour., Washington, 1983-84; contbr. articles to profl. jours. Bd. dirs. Immaculata Coll., Rockville, Md., 1989-91; bd. trustees Acad. of Holy Cross, Kensington, Md., 1994—; bd. visitors Fla. State U. Coll. of Law, 1994—. 2d lt. USAF, 1971-72. Mem.: ABA (vice-chmn. coun., pub. utilities, comm. and transp. law sect.), Energy Bar Assn. (chmn. coms. 1983—84), Fla. Bar, Congl. Country Club (Bethesda, Md. bd. govs. 2002—), Phi Alpha Delta. Democrat. Roman Catholic. Administrative and regulatory, FERC practice, Utilities, public. Office: LeBoeuf Lamb Green & MacRae 1875 Connecticut Ave NW Washington DC 20009-5728

O'NEILL, HARRIET, state supreme court justice; Undergrad. degree with honors, Converse Coll.; JD, JD, U. S.C., 1982. Practice law, Houston; with Porter & Clements, Morris & Campbell; pvt. practice, 1982-92; judge 152d Dist. Ct., Houston, 1992; justice 14th Ct. Appeals, Houston, 1995, Tex. Supreme Ct., 1998—. Lectr. continuing edn. courses; adv. bd. CLE Inst., 1996; panelist Tex. Ctr. Advanced Jud. Studies., Austin, 1993. Contbr. articles to profl. publs. Mem. U. S.C. academic honors soc.; law sch. rep. ABA. Office: Supreme Ct PO Box 12248 Austin TX 78711-2248

O'NEILL, JOSEPH DEAN, lawyer; b. Bayonne, N.J. s. Austin Joseph and Ann (Lynch) O'N. AB, Allegheny Coll.; JD, N.Y. Law Sch. Bar: N.J. 1968; cert. civil and criminal trial atty. Nat. Bd. Trial Advocacy. Pvt. practice, Vineland, N.J. Pres. Cumberland County Legal Aid Soc., Vineland, 1974-87. Contbr. articles to profl. publs. Assoc. counsel N.J. Jaycees. Recipient Outstanding Contbn. and Leadership award Nat. Assn. Criminal Def. Lawyers, 1978-79. Mem. Assn. Trial Lawyers Am. (pres. N.J. chpt. 1988-89, N.J. Legal PAC chmn. 1991-95), Cert. Trial Attys. (bd. dirs. 1988-90), Am. Bd. Trial Advocates (diplomate). General civil litigation, Criminal. Office: PO Box 847 30 W Chestnut Ave Vineland NJ 08360-5401

O'NEILL, PHILIP DANIEL, JR., lawyer, educator; b. Boston, Sept. 19, 1951; s. Philip Daniel Sr. and Alice Maureen (Driscoll) O'N.; m. Lisa G. Arrowood, June 25, 1983; children: Alexander Edwin, Sean Matthew, Madeleine Clarice. BA, Hamilton Coll., 1973; JD cum laude, Boston Coll., 1977. Bar: Mass. 1977, N.Y. 1985, R.I. 1988. Assoc. Hale and Dorr, Boston, 1977-83, ptnr., 1983-87, Edwards & Angell, Boston, 1987—. Adj. rsch. fellow John F. Kennedy Sch. Govt., Ctr. for Sci. and Internat. Affairs Harvard U., 1983—86; adj. prof. law Boston U., 1992, 2001—, Boston Coll., 1988—; cons. Arms Control and Disarmament Agy. U.S. Dept. Def., 1983—84; guest lectr., commentator Boston Coll. Law Sch., Kennedy Sch. Govt., 1985, Boston U. Law Sch., 1990—91, Harvard Law Sch., 1994—95, 1998; current or past internat. and domestic comml. arbitrator Am. Arbiration Assn., Hong Kong Ctr. for Internat. Arbitration, N.Am. Free Trade Agreement, Internat. C. of C., London Ct. Internat. Arbitration, Stockholm and Milan Arb. Ctrs., Euro-Arab C. of C, World Intellectual Property Orgn.; panelist in internat. and domestic legal programs. Contbr. chpts. to books and articles to profl. jours. Fellow Chartered Inst. Arbitrators (Eng.); mem. ABA (vice chmn. nat. security and arms control com.), Internat. Law Assn. (chmn. Am. br. arbitration com. 1985-89, rep. internat. arbitration com. 1989—), Boston Bar Assn. (chmn. internat. law sect. 1994-96, past chmn. internat. litigation and arbitration com.), Am. Soc. Internat. Law. Alternative dispute resolution, Corporate, general, Private international. Home: 11 Blackburnian Rd Lincoln MA 01773-4317 Office: Edwards & Angell 101 Federal St Fl 23 Boston MA 02110-1800

O'NEILL, THOMAS NEWMAN, JR., federal judge; b. Hanover, Pa., July 6, 1928; s. Thomas Newman and Emma (Cornpropst) O'N.; m. Jeanne M. Corr., Feb. 4, 1961; children: Caroline Jeanne, Thomas Newman, III, Ellen Gitt. AB magna cum laude, Catholic U. Am., 1950; LL.B. magna cum laude, U. Pa., 1953; postgrad. (Fulbright grantee), London Sch. Econs., 1955-56. Bar: Pa. 1954, U.S. Supreme Ct. 1959. Law clk. to Judge Herbert F. Goodrich U.S. Ct. Appeals (3d cir.), 1953-54; to Justice Harold H. Burton U.S. Supreme Ct., 1954-55; assoc. Montgomery, McCracken, Walker & Rhoads, Phila., 1956-63, ptnr., 1963-83; judge U.S. Dist. Ct. (ea. dist.) Pa., 1983—; counsel 1st and 2d Pa. Legis. Reapportionment Commns., 1971, 81. Lectr. U. Pa. Law Sch., 1973 Articles editor: U. Pa. Law Rev, 1952-53. Former trustee Lawyers Com. for Civil Rights Under Law; former mem.

Gov.'s Trial Ct. Nominating Commn. for Phila. County; former mem. bd. overseers U. Pa. Mus. Fellow Am. Coll. Trial Lawyers; mem. Am. Law Inst. (life), Phila. Bar Assn. (chancellor 1976), Pa. Bar Assn. (gov. 1978-81), U. Pa. Law Alumni Soc. (pres. 1976-77), Pa. Conf. County Bar Officers (pres. 1981-82), Am. Inn of Ct. (founding chmn. U. Pa.), Order of Coif (pres. U. Pa. chpt. 1971-73), Merion Cricket Club, Edgemere Club, Broadacres Trouting Assn., Phi Beta Kappa, Phi Eta Sigma. Office: US Dist Ct 4007 US Courthouse 601 Market St Philadelphia PA 19106-1713

O'NEILL, THOMAS TYRONE, lawyer; b. Wichita, Kans., June 9, 1956; s. John Joseph and Dorothy Marie O'Neill; 1 child, Allison Rutherford Jones. BS in Geology, U. Kans., 1983, JD, 1986. Bar: Kans. 1986, U.S. Dist. Ct. Kans. 1986, U.S. Ct. Appeals (10th cir.) 1990. Assoc. Carson & Fields, Kansas City, Kans., 1987-91, ptnr., 1991-96, Carson & O'Neill, Kansas City, 1997—. Republican. Avocations: snow skiing, travel. General civil litigation, General practice, Personal injury (including property damage). Office: Carson & O'Neill 753 State Ave #460 Kansas City KS 66101

ONG, COLIN YEE CHENG, barrister; b. Bandar Seri Begawan, Brunei, Sept. 7, 1967; s. Pang Ting Ong and Theresa Liew. LLB with honors, U. Sheffield, Eng., 1990; LLM, U. London, 1992, PhD in Law, 1996. Cert.: (barrister-at-law). Pvt. practice, London, 1991-97; rschr. U. London, 1993-97; advocate and solicitor Brunei Supreme Ct., 1997—. Cons. various corps., 1990—94; barrister Essex Ct. Chambers, England, 1992; prin. legal cons. ASEAN Ctr. for Energy, Jakarta, Indonesia, 2002. Author: Cross-Border Litigation, 1996; contbr. articles to profl. jours. Mem. Chartered Inst. Arbitrators (assoc.), Bar Assn., Internat. Bar Assn., London Court Internat. Arbitration. Home: PO Box 354 BSB BS 8670 BSB BS 8670 Bandar Seri Begawan Brunei Office: Stes 2-2to 2-5 Gadong Properties Ctr Km 3-6 Jalan Gadong Bandar Seri Begawan BA 1511 Negara Brunei Fax: (6732) 420911.

ONG, GEORGE E. lawyer; b. Oakland, Calif., Jan. 6, 1936; s. Chester T.H. Ong and Lee Foon Young; m. Jennie Yep, Aug. 29, 1965; children: Gail, Lori, Ryan. BA, Stanford U., 1958; JD, Golden Gate U., 1969. Bar: Calif. Sr. trial dep. Alameda County Dist. Atty.'s Office, Oakland, 1971-79; pvt. practice, Oakland, 1979—. Adv. dir. Golden Coin Savs. Bank, Oakland, 1985-88. Scoutmaster Boy Scouts Am., Piedmont, Calif., 1990—, bd. dirs. Piedmont coun. 1993—; lectr. youth leadership tng. Chinese Am. Citizens Alliance, Oakland, 1994—. Recipient svc. award Lions Club, Oaklandt, 1989; Disting. Scouter award Piedmont coun. Boy Scouts Am., 1991, award of merit for scoutmasters Nat. coun., 1996. Mem. Asian Am. Bar Assn., Oakland County Bar Assn. (appreciation award 1981), Oakland Chinatown C. of C. (pres. 1988, svc. award 1990). Avocations: scouting, skiing, boating, youth. Commercial, contracts (including sales of goods; commercial financing), Corporate, general, Property, real (including real estate development, water). Office: 701 Franklin St Oakland CA 94607-3931

ONGKIKO, MARIO ELBO, lawyer, educator; b. Manila, Philippines, Oct. 29, 1931; s. Felipe Calma Ongkiko and Rosario Tobias Elbo; m. Sonia Palma Gil Ongkiko; children: Jose, Rosario, Zenaida, Ricardo, Teresa Gregoria, Bella, Virginia, Milagros. BSc in Bus. Adminstrn., U. of the East, Manila, Philippines, 1951; BSc in Law, U. of the Philippines, 1956. Bar: Philippines 57. Assoc. atty. Sycip Salazar, Manila, 1957—69; ptnr. Angel Cruz Law Office, 1970—74, Luna Puruganan Sison Cruz Ongkiko, Manila, 1975—80, Ongkiko Kalaw Manhit & Acorda, Makati, Philippines, 1981—. Dep. gen. coun. fact finding bd. Agrava Commn., 1983—84; legal cons. Met. Waterworks and Sewerage Sys., 1989—90; spl. coun. presdl. commn. on good govt. Office of Solicitor Gen., 1991—99; lectr. U. Philippines, Diliman, Philippines, 1983—; spkr. in field. Host (radio program) Kasangga Mo sa Batas, Radio Veritas 846 khz AM, 2001—. Pres. Caritas Found. Inc., Laguna, Philippines, Christ the King Parish Coun., 1978—85; mem. adoracion Nocturna Christ the King Parish, 1986. Mem.: ATLA, Philippine Bar Assn., Internat. Law Assn., Integrated Bar of Philippines, Law Alumni Assn. of U. Philippines, Valley Golf & Country Club, Inc. (bd. dir. 1998—99, pres. 1999—2001), Philippine Jaycees (gen. legal counsel 1966—67, senator 1989—). Roman Catholic. Avocation: golf. Criminal. Office: Ongkiko Kalaw Manhit & Acorda 101 Aguirre St 4th Fl Legaspi Village Makati Philippines

ONKEN, GEORGE MARCELLUS, retired lawyer; b. Bklyn., Aug. 15, 1913; s. William Henry and Lillian Charlotte (Dawe) O.; m. Mildred Ann Tausch, Dec. 13, 1958; children: Jane Elizabeth, Nancy Catherine. AB, Princeton U., 1936; LLB, Columbia U., 1948; LLM, NYU, 1952. Bar: N.Y. 1949. Asst. to pres. Welsbach Engrng. and Mgmt. Corp., Phila., 1939-43; mem. legal staff L.I. R.R., 1949-78, gen. counsel, 1963-78, v.p., 1966-78, sec., 1968-78. Bd. dirs. Orphan Asylum Soc., Bklyn., 1958—, YMCA Greater N.Y., 1963-80, Pop Warner Little League, 1976-78; bd. mgrs. Pa. R.R. br. YMCA, N.Y.C., 1957-80, chmn., 1967-80; trustee Bklyn. YWCA, 1976-92. Lt. (j.g.) USNR, 1943-46. Recipient Man of Year award YMCA, 1977; Outstanding Svc. award Bklyn. Chpt. ARC Greater N.Y., 1994, Lifetime Commitment award Brookwood Child Care, 1998. Republican. Episcopalian (vestry 1958-64, 76-85). Clubs: Union League (N.Y.C.), Univ. (N.Y.C.), Church (N.Y.C.); Rembrandt (Bklyn.), Heights Casino (Bklyn.), Ihpetonga (Bklyn.). Home: 215 Adams St Brooklyn NY 11201-2856

OPALA, MARIAN P(ETER), state supreme court justice; b. Lódz, Poland, Jan. 20, 1921; JD, Oklahoma City U., 1953, BSB in Econs., 1957, LLD (hon.), 1981; LLM, NYU, 1968; HHD, Okla. Christian U. Sci. & Arts, 1981. Bar: Okla. 1953, U.S. Supreme Ct. 1970. Asst. county atty., Oklahoma County, 1953—56; practiced law Oklahoma City, 1956—60, 1965—67; referee Okla. Supreme Ct., Oklahoma City, 1960—65; prof. law Oklahoma City U. Sch. Law, 1965—69; asst. to presiding justice Supreme Ct. Okla., 1967—68; administrv. dir. Cts. Okla., 1968—77; presiding judge Okla. State Indsl. Ct., 1977—78; judge Workers Compensation Ct., 1978; justice Okla. Supreme Ct., 1978—, chief justice, 1991—92. Adj. prof. law Okla. City U., 1962—, U. Okla. Coll. Law, 1969—; prof. law U. Tulsa Law Sch., 1982—; mem. permanent faculty Am. Acad. Jud. Edn., 1970—; mem. NYU Inst. Jud. Adminstrn.; mem. faculty Nat. Jud. Coll., U. Nev., 1975—; chmn. Nat. Conf. State Ct. Adminstrs., 1976-77; mem. Nat. Conf. Commrs. on Uniform State Laws, 1982—. Co-author: Oklahoma Court Rules for Perfecting a Civil Appeal, 1969 Mem. Adminstrn. Conf. U.S., 1993-95. Recipient Herbert Harley award Am. Judicature Soc., 1977, Disting. Alumni award Oklahoma City U., 1979, Americanism medal Nat. Soc. DAR, 1984, ABA/Am. Law Inst. Harrison Tweed Spl. Merit award, 1987, Humanitarian award NCCJ, 1991, Jour. Record award, 1995, Constn. award Rogers State U., 1996, Jud. Excellence award Okla. Bar Assn., 1997, Leo H. Whinery Disting. Svc. award, 1999, Lifetime Achievement award Oklahoma City Univ. Sch. Law, 2000, First Amendment award FOI Okla., Inc., 2002; inductee Okla. Hall of Fame, 2000. Mem. AbA (edn. com. appellate judges conf. 1984-93), Okla. Bar Assn. (Earl Sneed Continuing Legal Edn. award 1988, Jud. Excellence award 1997), Okla. County Bar Assn., Am. Soc. Legal History, Oklahoma City Title Lawyers Assn., Am. Judicature Soc. (bd. dirs. 1988-92), Am. Law Inst. (elected), Order of Coif, Phi Delta Phi (Oklahoma City Alumni award). Office: Okla Supreme Ct State Capitol Rm 238 Oklahoma City OK 73105

OPAT, MATTHEW JOHN, lawyer; b. Riceville, Iowa, Nov. 5, 1952; s. Wesley John and Dolores Genevieve (Ludwig) O.; m. Therese Ann Dusheck, Aug. 13, 1977; children: Michael, Kristin, Steven. BA in History, U. Iowa, 1974; JD, Hamline U., 1977. Bar: Iowa 1977, Minn. 1977. Prin. Opat Law Office, Chatfield, Minn., 1977—. Atty. Fillmore County, 1997-2003. Mem. Fillmore County Bar Assn. (pres. 1984-85), Minn. State Bar Assn. (bd. dirs. 1985-87), Tenth Dist. Bar Assn. (chmn. ethics com. 1989-96, pres. 2001-02). General practice, Probate (including wills, trusts), Property, real (including real estate development, water). Office: 22 2nd St SE Chatfield MN 55923-1203

OPDAHL, CLARK DONALD, lawyer; b. St. Paul, June 22, 1956; s. Donald Arthur and Elizabeth Claire O.; m. Cynthia Ann Slipka, Sept. 2, 1977; children: Kyle, Shannon, Kelsey. BA, U. Minn., 1978; JD magna cum laude, William Mitchell Coll. of Law, St. Paul, 1986. Bar: Minn. 1987, U.S. Dist. Ct. Minn. Account exec., v.p. D.A. Opdahl & Assocs., Inc., Roseville, Minn., 1978-86; law clk. David G. Johnson, P.A., North St. Paul, 1984-86; atty. Henson & Efron, P.A., Mpls., 1986—. Baseball coach Blaine/Spring Lake Park Athletic Assn., Blaine, 1987-92, softball coach Spring Lake Park Athletic Assn., 1996-97. Mem. Minn. State Bar Assn., Hennepin County Bar Assn. (co-chmn. cmty. rels. 1989-93, 97-2000, co-chmn. publs. com. 1994-97). Avocations: golf, fishing. Commercial, contracts (including sales of goods; commercial financing), Corporate, general, Mergers and acquisitions. Office: Henson & Efron PA 220 S 6th St Ste 1800 Minneapolis MN 55402 E-mail: copdahl@hensonfron.com.

OPPENHEIMER, FRANZ MARTIN, lawyer; b. Mainz, Germany, Sept. 7, 1919; s. Arnold and Johanna (Mayer) O.; m. Margaret Spencer Foote, June 17, 1944; children: Martin Foote, Roxana Foote, Edward Arnold. BS, U. Chgo., 1942; student, U. Grenoble, France, 1938-39; LL.B. cum laude (note editor Law Jour. 1945), Yale U., 1945. Bar: N.Y. 1946, D.C. 1955. Rsch. asst. com. human devel. U. Chgo., 1942-43; law clk. to Judge Swan, U.S. Circuit Ct. of Appeals, N.Y., 1945-46; assoc. atty. Chadbourne, Wallace, Parke & Whiteside, N.Y.C., 1946-47; atty. IBRD, Washington, 1947-57; individual practice law, 1958-59; ptnr. firm Leva, Hawes, Symington, Martin & Oppenheimer, 1959-83, Fort & Schlefer, Washington, 1984-94; pvt. practice Washington, 1995—2001; sr. of counsel Swidler Berlin Shereff Friedman (formerly Swidler & Berlin), Washington, 1996—2001; individual consulting and law practice, 2001—. Contbr. articles to profl. and other jours, chpts. to books. Bd. dirs. Internat. Student House; founding mem. Company of Christian Jews. Decorated officer's cross Order of Merit (Fed. Republic Germany), chevalier Nat. Order of Merit (France). Mem. ABA, Am. Soc. Internat. Law (hon. v.p., treas. 1964-76), Coun. Fgn. Rels., Yale Club, Century Assn. (N.Y.), City Tavern, Met. Club (Washington). Anglican. Banking, Finance. Home: 3248 O St NW Washington DC 20007-2847 E-mail: franzmfmo@aol.com.

OPPENHEIMER, MARTIN J. lawyer; b. Apr. 11, 1933; s. Julius and Sylvia (Haas) O.; m. Suzanne Rosenhirsch, July 3, 1958; children: Marcy, Evan, Joshua, Alexandra. BS with honors, U. Pa., 1953; LLB, Yale U., 1956. Assoc. Hays, Sklar & Hertzberg, Mendes & Mount; ptnr. Proskauer Rose Goetz & Mendelsohn, N.Y.C., 1958—. Contbr. articles to profl. jours. Chmn. City Ctr. of Music and Drama, Lincoln Ctr., N.Y., 1984—; vice chmn. N.Y.C. Opera, 1985—; bd. dir. 92nd St. YWCA, N.Y., 1985—, Lincoln Ctr. for Performing Arts, 1987—; bd. advs. Mailman Sch. of Pub. Health, Columbia U., 1991; chmn. Lincoln Ctr. Constituent Devel. Corp., 2001-02. Fulbright scholar Goethe U., Frankfurt, Fed. Republic Germany, 1956-57. Entertainment, Labor (including EEOC, Fair Labor Standards Act, labor-management relations, NLRB, OSHA), Pension, profit-sharing, and employee benefits. Home: 400 Claflin Ave Mamaroneck NY 10543-3906 Office: Proskauer Rose et al 1585 Broadway Fl 21-76 New York NY 10036-8299

OPPENHEIMER, RANDOLPH CARL, lawyer; b. N.Y.C., Feb. 5, 1954; s. Bennett and Sandra (Haber) O.; m. Cynthia Ellen Shatkin, June 19, 1976; children: Benjamin David, Adam Jeremy, Jacob Aaron, Jordan Michael, Daniel Corey. BA, U. Vt., 1976; JD, Case Western Res. U., 1979. Bar: N.Y. 1980, U.S. Dist. Ct. (we. dist.) N.Y. 1980, U.S. Dist. Ct. (no. dist.) N.y. 1995, U.S. Bankruptcy Ct. 1980, U.S. Ct. Appeals (2d cir.) 1981. Assoc. Kavinoky & Cook, Buffalo, 1979-84, ptnr., 1984—. Instr. legal research, writing and adv., Case Western Res. U., 1978-79. Assoc. editor Case Western Reserve Law Rev., 1977-79. Mem. ABA, N.Y. Bar Assn., Erie County Bar Assn. Commercial, contracts (including sales of goods; commercial financing), Corporate, general, Labor (including EEOC, Fair Labor Standards Act, labor-management relations, NLRB, OSHA). Home: 195 Greenaway Rd Buffalo NY 14226-4165 Office: Kavinoky & Cook 120 Delaware Ave Rm 600 Buffalo NY 14202-2793 E-mail: roppenheimer@kavinokycook.com.

OPPERWALL, STEPHEN GABRIEL, lawyer; b. Racine, Wis., Aug. 14, 1953; s. Raymond and Helen Bertha Opperwall; m. Kathleen O'Neill, Oct. 27, 1990; children: Christopher Stephen, Scott O'Neill. BA, Calvin Coll., 1975; JD, U. Santa Clara, 1981. Bar: Calif. 1981, U.S. Dist. Ct. (no., ea., ctrl. and so. dists.) Calif. 1981, U.S. Tax Ct. 1994, U.S. Ct. Appeals (9th cir.) 1984; cert. specialist in creditor's rights. Tchg. asst. U. Santa Clara (Calif.) Sch. Law, 1979; judge's law clk. U.S. Ct. Appeals, 9th Cir., San Francisco, 1980; assoc. Pitto & Ubhaus, San Jose, Calif., 1980-82, Germino, Layne & Brodie, Palo Alto, Calif., 1982-87, Tarkington, O'Connor & O'Neill, San Jose, 1988-90, Smith & Smith, San Jose, 1990-92; pvt. practice Law Offices of Stephen G. Opperwall, Pleasanton, Calif., 1992—. Judge pro tem Santa Clara County Cts., 1986—, Alameda County (Calif.) Cts., 1992—; mem. adv. bd. Fremont (Calif.) Bank, 1996. Editor Santa Clara Law Review, 1980. Mem. bd. dirs. Fremont Symphony, 1994. Mem. Coml. Law League Am., Pleasanton C. of C. Avocations: golf, tennis, computers. Bankruptcy, General civil litigation, Commercial, consumer (including collections, credit). Office: 4900 Hopyard Rd Ste 100 Pleasanton CA 94588-3149 E-mail: lawofcsgo@aol.com.

ORCE, KENNETH W. lawyer; b. Yonkers, N.Y., Apr. 3, 1943; s. Edmund John and Helen (Mulcahy) O.; m. Helene Mary Sparti, Aug. 20, 1966; children: Kenneth W., Kimberley J., Brian C. B.S. with honors, Manhattan Coll., 1965; LL.B. cum laude, Harvard U., 1968. Bar: N.Y. 1969. Assoc. Cahill Gordon & Reindel, LLP, N.Y.C., 1968-76, ptnr. 1976—; bd. dirs. Burlington Resources, Inc. Mem. ABA, Assn. Bar City N.Y., Down Town Assn. (N.Y.C.), Scarsdale (N.Y.) Golf Club, Met. Opera Club, Hudson (N.Y.) Nat. Golf Club. Editor: Harvard Law Rev. 1966-68. Corporate, general, Securities. Home: 22 Hearthstone Cir Scarsdale NY 10583 Office: Cahill Gordon & Reindel LLP 80 Pine St Fl 17 New York NY 10005-1702 Business E-Mail: korce@cahill.com.

ORDEN, STEWART L. lawyer; b. N.Y.C., Jan. 13, 1953; s. Charles Quigley and Esther (Ash) O.; m. Bonnie Lynn Raymond, Nov. 12, 1988; children: Molly, Justin, Tyler. BA, Clark U., 1975; JD, Bklyn. Law Sch., 1979. Bar: N.Y. 1979. Sr. trial atty. Kings Dist. Atty., Bklyn., 1979-87; ptnr. Orden & Cohen, N.Y.C., 1987-91; pvt. practice, N.Y.C., 1991—. Expert on trial techniques, complex personal injury, med. malpractice, comml. and white collar cases; won largest pub. settlement against NYC in discrimination case; profiled on 60 Minutes. Mem. N.Y. Coun. Def. Lawyers, Assn. Bar City N.Y., N.Y. Criminal Bar Assn., N.Y. State Def. Lawyers Assn., Nat. Assn. Def. Lawyers. Democrat. Avocations: skiing, windsurfing, swimming, rollerblading, biking. Civil rights, General civil litigation, Criminal. Office: Rm 1300 299 Broadway New York NY 10007-1932

ORDIN, ANDREA SHERIDAN, lawyer; m. Robert Ordin; 1 child, M. Victoria; stepchildren: Allison, Richard. AB, UCLA, 1962, LLB, 1965. Bar: Calif. 1966. Dep. atty. gen. Calif., 1965-72; So. Calif. legal counsel Fair Employment Practices Commn., 1972-73; asst. dist. atty. L.A. County, 1975-77; U.S. atty. Central Dist. Calif., 1977-81; adj. prof. UCLA Law Sch., 1982; chief asst. atty. gen. Calif. L.A., 1983-90; ptnr. Morgan, Lewis & Bockius, L.A., 1993—. Mem. L.A. County Bar Assn. (past pres., past exec. dir.). Office: Morgan Lewis & Bockius 300 S Grand Ave Ste 22 Los Angeles CA 90071-3109 E-mail: aordin@morganlewis.com.

ORDOVER, ABRAHAM PHILIP, lawyer, mediator; b. Far Rockaway, N.Y., Jan. 18, 1937; s. Joseph and Bertha (Fromberg) O.; m. Carol M. Ordover, Mar. 23, 1961 (dec. 1999); children: Andrew Charles, Thomas Edward; m. Eleanor Musick, Feb. 24, 2001. BA magna cum laude, Syracuse U., 1958; JD, Yale U., 1961. Bar: N.Y. 1961, U.S. Dist. Ct. (so. and ea. dists.) N.Y., U.S. Ct. Appeals (2d cir.), U.S. Supreme Ct. Assoc. Cahill, Gordon & Reindel, N.Y.C., 1961-71; prof. law Hofstra U., Hempstead, N.Y., 1971-81; L.Q.C. Lamar prof. law Emory U., Atlanta, 1981-91; CEO Resolution Resources Corp., Atlanta, 1991—; mediator and arbitrator. Vis. prof. Cornell U., Ithaca, N.Y., 1977; vis. lectr. Tel Aviv U., 1989, Am. Law Inst.; team leader nat. program Nat. Inst. Trial Advocacy, Boulder, Colo., 1980, 82, 84, 86, 89, tchr. program Cambridge, Mass., 1979-84, 88, adv. program Gainesville, Fla., 1978-79, northeast regional dir., 1977-81; team leader SE regional program, 1983; team leader Atlanta Bar Trial Tech. Program, 1981-91; lectr. in field; sr. v.p. Resolute Sys. Inc., bd. dirs. Author: Argument to the Jury, 1982, Problems and Cases in Trial Advocacy, 1983, Advanced Materials in Trial Advocacy, 1988, Alternatives to Litigation, 1993, Cases and Materials in Evidence, 1993, Art of Negotiation, 1994; prodr. ednl. films; contbr. articles to profl. jours. Bd. dirs. Atlanta Legal Aid Soc., 1984-91, 7 Stages Theatre, 1991-96. Recipient Gumpert award Am. Coll. Trial Lawyers, 1984, 85, Jacobsen award Roscoe Pound Am. Trial Lawyer Found., 1986. Fellow Am. Coll. Civil Trial Mediators; mem. ABA, N.Y. State Bar Assn., Assn. Am. Law Schs. (chair litigation sect.), Atlanta Lawyers Club, Am. Law Inst., Am. Acad. of Civil Trial Mediators. Avocation: photography. Office: Resolution Resources Corp 303 Peachtree St Atlanta GA 30308-3201 E-mail: ordover@rrcatlanta.com.

O'REILLY, ANN CATHERINE, lawyer; b. Rochester, Minn., Dec. 18, 1970; BA with distinction, U. Wis., 1992; JD cum laude, U. Minn., 1996. Bar: Minn. 1996, U.S. Dist. Ct. Minn. 1998, U.S. Dist. Ct. (no. dist.) Ill. 1998. Law clk. to Hon. John Sommerville Minn. 4th Jud. Dist., Mpls., 1996-97; shareholder LeVander, Gillen & Miller, PA, South St. Paul, Minn., 1997—. Contbr. chpt. to book. Bd. dirs., pres. Dakota County Legal Assistance, 1997-01; bd. dirs. Animal Ark. Mayo Clinic scholar, 1989. Mem. ABA, Minn. State Bar Assn., Hennepin County Bar Assn., Dakota County Bar Assn., Minn. Women Lawyers (jud. endorsement com.). Democrat. Avocation: antique refinishing and collecting. General civil litigation, Criminal, Municipal (including bonds). Office: LeVander Gillen & Miller PA 633 Concord St S Ste 400 South Saint Paul MN 55075-2423 E-mail: aoreilly@levander.com.

O'REILLY, JAMES THOMAS, lawyer, educator, author; b. N.Y.C., Nov. 15, 1947; s. Matthew Richard and Regina (Casey) O'R.; children: Jean, Ann. BA cum laude, Boston Coll., 1969; JD, U. Va., 1974. Bar: Va. 1974, Ohio 1974, U.S. Supreme Ct. 1979, U.S. Ct. Appeals (6th cir.) 1980. Atty. Procter & Gamble Co., Cin., 1974-76, counsel, 1976-79, sr. counsel for food, drug and product safety, 1979-85, corp. counsel, 1985-93, assoc. gen. counsel, 1993-98; adj. prof. in adminstrv. law U. Cin., 1980-97, vis. prof. law, 1998—. Cons. Adminstrv. Conf. U.S., 1981-82, 89-90, Congl. Office of Compliance, 1995-96; arbitrator State Employee Rels. Bd.; mem. Ohio Bishops Adv. Coun., Mayor's Infrastructure Commn., Cin. Environ. Adv. Coun. Author: Federal Information Disclosure, 1977, Food and Drug Administration Regulatory Manual, 1979, Unions' Rights to Company Information, 1980, Federal Regulation of the Chemical Industry, 1980, Administrative Rulemaking, 1983, Ohio Public Employee Collective Bargaining, 1984, Protecting Workplace Secrets, 1985, Emergency Response to Chemical Accidents, 1986, Product Defects and Hazards, 1987, Protecting Trade Secrets Under SARA, 1988, Toxic Torts Strategy Deskbook, 1989, Complying With Canada's New Labeling Law, 1989, Solid Waste Management, 1991, Ohio Products Liability Handbook, 1991, Toxic Torts Guide, 1991, ABA Product Liability Resource Manual, 1993, RCRA and Superfund Practice Guide, 1993, Clean Air Permits Manula, 1994, United States Environmental Liabilities, 1994, Elder Safety, 1995, Environmental and Workplace Safety for University and Hospital Managers, 1996, Indoor Environmental Health, 1997, Product Warnings, Defects & Hazards, 1999, Accident Prevention Manual, 2000, Food Crisis Management Manual, 2002, Police Racial Profiling, 2002; mem. editl. bd. Food and Drug Cosmetic Law Jour.; contbr. articles to profl. jours. Mem. Hamilton County Dem. Ctrl. Com. Served with U.S. Army, 1970-72. Mem. ABA (chmn. AD law sect.), FBA, Food and Drug Law Inst. (chair program com.), Leadership Cin. Democrat. Roman Catholic. Administrative and regulatory, Environmental. Office: 24 Jewett Dr Cincinnati OH 45215-2648

O'REILLY, TERENCE JOHN, lawyer; b. Farnborough, Eng., Apr. 12, 1945; came to U.S., 1960, naturalized, 1965; s. Arthur Francis and Doris Eileen (Burden) O'R.; m. Katharine Van Dyke Wallace, Sept. 26, 1970; children: Tobin Cooper, Matthew Wallace. BA, Loyola U., 1966; JD, U. Calif., Berkeley, 1969. Bar: Calif. 1970. Assoc. Voegelin, Barton, L.A., 1969-70, Walkup, Downing & Sterns, San Francisco, 1970-75; mem. Walkup, Shelby, Bastian, Melodia, Kelly & O'Reilly, San Francisco, 1975-87; prin. O'Reilly, Collins & Danko, San Mateo, Calif., 1987—. Lectr. Kennedy Law Sch., Moraga, Calif., 1975-76, Inner Cir. of Advocates, 1998—; bd. govs. Consumer Attys. of Calif., 1995— bd. govs., diplomate Am. Bd. Profl. Liability Lawyers, 1989—. V.p. No. Calif. Rugby Football, San Francisco, 1975-80, bd. dirs., 1975—; trustee U.S. Rugby Football Found., 1987—; trustee The Philip Brooks Sch., 1986-89, Coun. of Bancroft Libr., U. Calif. Mem. Boalt Hall Alumni (bd. dirs. 1982-85), Assn. San Francisco Trial Lawyers (bd. dirs. 1985—), Assn. San Mateo Trial Lawyers (dir. 1992—, pres. 2003), Bohemian Club, Burlingame Country Club, Menlo Circus Club, Pacific Union Club. Roman Catholic. Personal injury (including property damage), Product liability. Office: attn Debra Foster 1900 O'Farrell St Ste 360 San Mateo CA 94403 E-mail: toreilly@oreillylaw.com.

O'REILLY, TIMOTHY PATRICK, lawyer; b. San Lorenzo, Calif., Sept. 12, 1945; s. Thomas Marvin and Florence Ann (Ohlman) O'R.; m. Susan Ann Marshall, July 18, 1969; children: T. Patrick Jr., Sean M., Colleen K. BS, Ohio State U., 1967; JD, NYU, 1971. Bar: Pa. 1971, U.S. Dist. Ct. (ea. dist.) Pa. 1971, U.S. Dist. Ct. (mid. dist.) Pa. 1972, U.S. Ct. Appeals (3d cir.) 1977, U.S. Supreme Ct. 1988. Ptnr. Morgan, Lewis & Bockius, Phila., 1978—. Editor: Developing Labor Law, 1989; contbr. articles to profl. jours. Bd. dirs. Notre Dame Acad. and Devon Preparatory Sch.; bd. govs. Aronimink Golf Club, J. Wood Platt Caddie Scholarship Trust. Elected to Coll. of Labor and Employment Lawyers. Mem. ABA (chmn. com. on devel. of the law under the Nat. Labor Rels. Act., editor-in-chief The Developing Labor Law jour., elected mem. coun. labor and employment sect.), Pa. Bar Assn., Phila. Bar Assn., Ohio State U. Alumni Assn., Aronimink Golf Club (bd. govs.). Avocation: golf. Labor (including EEOC, Fair Labor Standards Act, labor-management relations, NLRB, OSHA), Pension, profit-sharing, and employee benefits. Home: 1127 Cymry Dr Berwyn PA 19312-2056 Office: Morgan Lewis & Bockius 1701 Market St Philadelphia PA 19103-2903 E-mail: toreilly@morganlewis.com.

ORLEBEKE, WILLIAM RONALD, retired lawyer, writer; b. El Paso, Tex., Jan. 5, 1934; s. William Ronald and Frances Claire (Cook) O.; m. Barbara Raye Pike, 1955 (div. 1981); children: Michelle, Julene, David; m. Susan K. Nash, 2000. BA, Willamette U., 1956; MA, Kans. U., 1957; JD, Willamette U., 1966. Bar: Calif. 1966, U.S. Dist. Ct. (no. dist.) Calif. 1967, U.S. Ct. Appeals (9th cir.) 1967, U.S. Ct. Appeals (7th cir.) 1989, U.S. Dist. Ct. (no. dist.) Ill. 1989, U.S. Dist. Ct. (cen. dist.) Calif. 1989. Mem. staff Travelers Ins. Co., Sacramento, 1957-61; branch claim mgr. N.Y. Life Ins. Co., 1961-62, Transamerica Ins. Co., San Francisco, 1962-63; assoc. Eliassen & Postel, San Francisco, 1966-69; ptnr. Coll, Levy & Orlebeke, Concord, Calif., 1969-77, Orlebeke & Hutchings, Concord, Calif., 1977-89; prin. Law Offices W. Ronald Orlebeke, 1989-98; hearing officer Contra Costa County, Calif., 1981-98; arbitrator Contra Costa County Superior Ct., 1977-98, U.S. Dist. Ct. No. Calif., 1978-98, Mt. Diablo Mcpl. Ct., 1987-89; ret., 1998. Judge pro tem Mt. Diablo Mcpl. Ct., 1973-75; criminology prof. Pioneer-Pacific Coll., 2002-03. Author: Orlebeke Family in Europe and America, 1570-1990, 1988, Don't Tell Me I Can't, 2003. Alumni bd. dirs. Willamette U., 1978-81, trustee, 1980-81 scholar chmn. Concord Elks,

1977-79; del. Joint U.S./China Internat. Trade Law Conf., Beijing, 1987. With USMCR, 1952-59. Sr. scholar Willamette U., 1955-56; Woodrow Wilson fellow Kans. U., 1956-57, U.S. Bur. Nat. Affairs fellow, 1966, others. Mem. SAR, Sons of Confederate Vets. (Merit award 1989), Sons of Union Vets. Civil War, First Marine Divsn. Assn., Order Ea. Star (worthy patron 1980), Masons (sec. Salem, Oreg. chpt. 2002—), Shriners, Elks, Rotary (charter pres. Clayton Valley/Concord Sunrise club 1987-88, chmn. dist. 5160 Calif. membership devel. 1989-90, dist. govs. liaison dist. 5160 1990-92, dist. Rotarian of Yr. 1989-90, Paul Harris fellow 1988, 1992 dist. conf. chmn. benefactor 1990, Merit award 1990). Republican. Administrative and regulatory, State civil litigation, General practice.

ORLOFF, NEIL, lawyer, artist; b. Chgo., May 9, 1943; s. Benjamin R. and Annette (Grabow) O.; m. Jan Krigbaum, Oct. 9, 1971 (div. 1979); m. Gudrun Mirin, Oct. 2, 1992. BS, MIT, 1964; MBA, Harvard U., 1966; JD, Columbia U., 1969. Bar: D.C. 1969, N.Y. 1975, Calif. 1989, Utah 1993. Ops. officer World Bank, Washington, 1969-71; dir. regional liaison staff EPA, Washington, 1971-73; legal counsel Pres.'s Council on Environ. Quality, Washington, 1973-75; prof. dept. environ. engring. Cornell U., Ithaca, N.Y., 1975-88; sch. law UCLA, 1992; dir. Ctr. for Environ. Rsch., 1984-87, Am. Ecology Corp., 1986-88; of counsel Morgan, Lewis & Bockius, N.Y.C., 1986-87; ptnr. Irell & Manella, L.A., 1986-92, Parsons, Behle & Latimer, Salt Lake City, 1992—2001. Vice chmn. bd. dirs. S.W. Research and Info. Ctr., Albuquerque, 1975-84; vice chmn. air quality commn. ABA, Chgo., 1983-92, co-chmn. intensive course in environ. law ABA, 1994-96, co-chmn. roundtable sr. environ. lawyers ABA, 1996-97, membership officer sect. on natural resources, energy and environ. law, 1997-98; coun. mem. sect. on environ., energy and natural resources, 1998-2001; adviser Internat. Joint Com. Can., 1979-81; governing bd. N.Y. Sea Grant Inst., 1984-87; vice chmn. City of Ithaca Environ. Commn., 1976-77; adviser N.Y. Dept. Environ. Conservation, 1984-87; artist-in-residence MacDowell Colony, 2000, Yaddo, 2001; vis. prof. art Cornell U., 2001. Author: The Environmental Impact Statement Process, 1978, The National Environmental Policy Act, 1980, Air Pollution-Cases and Materials, 1980, Community Right-to-Know Handbook, 1988, Under the Fifth Street Overpass, 2000; mem. editl. bd. Natural Resources and Environ., 1984-87. Environmental. E-mail: norloff@alum.mit.edu.

ORLOVSKY, DONALD ALBERT, lawyer; b. East Orange, N.J., May 15, 1951; s. Manuel Martin and Eleanor Marie Orlovsky. AB, Cornell U., 1973; JD, Rutgers U., 1976. Bar: Fla. 1976, U.S. Ct. Appeals (5th cir.) 1976, N.J. 1977, U.S. Dist. Ct. (so. dist.) Fla. 1977, U.S. Dist. Ct. N.J. 1977, U.S. Supreme Ct. 1980, U.S. Ct. Appeals (11th cir.) 1981. Assoc. Smathers & Thompson, Miami, 1976-77; ptnr. McCune, Hiaasen, Crum, Ferris & Gardner, P.A., Ft. Lauderdale, Fla., 1978-86, Kamen & Orlovsky PA, West Palm Beach, 1988—. Pres. bd. dirs. Comprehensive Alcoholism Treatment Program, Inc.; treas., bd. dirs. Fla. Lawyers Assistance, Inc., supervising monitor and counselor, 1991—. Author: Nova U. Law Review, 1977, U. Miami Law Review, 1978. Recipient All-Am. recognition in springboard diving, 1966-69; inducted Hall of Fame Newark Acad., Livingston, N.J., 1997. Mem. ABA, Fla. Bar (civil procedure rules com. 1981), Acad. Fla. Trial Lawyers, Assn. Trial Lawyers Am. Episcopalian. Federal civil litigation, State civil litigation. Office: 1601 Belvedere Rd Ste 402 West Palm Beach FL 33406-1541 E-mail: dao4law@aol.com.

ORMAN, LEONARD ARNOLD, lawyer; b. Balt., June 15, 1930; s. Samuel and Bertie (Adler) O.; m. Barbara Gold, June 9, 1978; children: Richard Harold, Robert Barton. AB summa cum laude, U. Md., 1952, JD, 1955. Bar: Md. 1955, U.S. Ct. Appeals (4th cir.) 1956, U.S. Dist. Ct. Md. 1955, Ct. Appeals Md. 1955, U.S. Supreme Ct. 1977, U.S. Ct. Claims 1990, D.C. Ct. Appeals 1987; cert. civil trial advocate by Nat. Bd. Trial Advocacy. Law clk. Hon. Frederick W. Brune, Chief Judge Md. Ct. of Appeals, 1955-56; mem. dept. legis. reference Md. Legislature, 1957-58; mem. Gov.'s Commn. to Revise Criminal Code, 1958-59; pvt. practice law Balt., 1956—. Lectr. trial tactics. Mem. editl. bd. Md. Law Rev., 1953-55; contbr. articles to profl. jours. Pres. Young Dems. 2d Dist., Balt., 1960-63. With AUS, 1948-49; lt. col. USAF Res. ret. Rosco Pound Found. fellow, trustee. Mem. Md. State Bar Assn. (com. mem.), Balt. City Bar Assn. (com. mem.), Nat. Coll. Trial Advocacy (trustee), Assn. Trial Lawyers Am. (com. mem., nat. committeeman 1976-80, bd. govs. 1985—, exec. com. 1988-90, chmn. orgn. rev. com., home office and budget com., orgn. and home office com., election com., key man com., past mem. steering com., past mem. publ. com., past mem. edn. adv. group 1989-90, chmn. Stalwarts Hall of Fame com., past vice-chair ABA-ATLA liaison com., M Club, co-chair conv. site planning com., co-chairpolit. insight com., long-range planning com., auth-hwy. adv. com., toy safety conf., med. malpractice adv. com., product liability adv. com., co-chair home office capital improvements adv. com., co-chmn. conv. planning com. Washington, Wiedmann/Wysocki award 1989-90, 96, 2002), Md. Trial Lawyers Assn. (bd. govs., pres. 1984-85, Lifetime Achievement award, 2002), Order of Coif, Masons. Professional liability, Personal injury (including property damage), Aviation. Home: 2 Celadon Rd Owings Mills MD 21117-3010 Office: 26 South St Baltimore MD 21202-3215 Fax: 410-962-0402. E-mail: lorman@triallaw.com.

ORMASA, JOHN, retired utility executive, lawyer; b. Richmond, Calif., May 30, 1925; s. Juan Hormaza and Maria Inocencia Olondo; m. Dorothy Helen Trumble, Feb. 17, 1952; children: Newton Lee, John Trumble, Nancy Jean Davies. BA, U. Calif.-Berkeley, 1948; JD, Harvard U., 1951. Bar: Calif. 1952, U.S. Supreme Ct. 1959. Assoc. Clifford C. Anglim, 1951-52; assoc. Richmond, Carlson, Collins, Gordon & Bold, 1952-56, ptnr., 1956-59; with So. Calif. Gas Co., L.A., 1959-66, gen. atty., 1963-65, v.p., gen. counsel, 1965-66; v.p., sys. gen. counsel Pacific Lighting Service Co., Los Angeles, 1966-72; v.p., gen. counsel Pacific Lighting Corp., Los Angeles, 1973-75, v.p., sec., gen. counsel, 1975. Acting city atty., El Cerrito, Calif., 1952. Served with U.S. Navy, 1943-46. Mem. ABA, Calif. State Bar Assn., Richmond (Calif.) Bar Assn. (pres. 1959), Kiwanis (v.p. 1959). Republican. Roman Catholic.

ORNDORFF, LORETTA FRANCES, law librarian; b. Balt., Oct. 8, 1949; d. Joseph Franklin and Elsie May Orndorff; m. Carl Steffens Yaller, May 26, 1974 (div. Feb. 1995); children: Josie Orndorff Yaller, Max Ross Yaller. BA in Russian Lang., U. Md., 1971, MLS, 1975; JD, U. Balt., 1980. Libr. Gordon Feinblatt, Balt., 1976—80; libr. dir. Piper Marbury, Balt., 1980—84; ref. libr. Villanova (Pa.) Law Sch., 1984—86; libr. Prickett Jones, Wilmington, Del., 1986—91; libr. dir. Dilworth Paxson, Phila., 1991—97; head libr. Cozen O'Connor, Phila., 1997—. Mem.: Greater Phila. Law Libr. Assn. (bd. mem. at-large 1987), Law Libr. Assn. Md. (pres. 1984, v.p. 1983), Am. Assn. Law Librs. Avocation: singing. Office: Cozen O'Connor 1900 Market St Philadelphia PA 19103 Office Fax: 215-864-8037. Business E-Mail: lorndorff@cozen.com.

O'ROURKE, C. LARRY, lawyer; b. Colusa, Calif., Dec. 10, 1937; s. James Harold and Elizabeth Janice (Jenkins) O'R.; m. Joy Marie Phillips, May 22, 1965; children: Ryan, Paula, Alina. BSEE, Stanford U., 1959, MBA, 1961; JD, George Washington U., 1972. Bar: Va. 1971, D.C. 1974, Calif. 2002, U.S. Ct. Appeals (fed. cir.) 1973, U.S. Patent and Trademark Office 1971, U.S. Supreme Ct. Patent atty. Westinghouse Elec., Washington, 1969-70, Pitts., 1970-73; assoc. Finnegan, Henderson, Farabow, Garrett & Dunner, Washington, 1974-79, ptnr., 1979—, mng. ptnr. Palo Alto, Calif. Dir. Zest Inc., Md., 1988, chmn. bd. dirs., 1990-95; mem. George Washington Law Sch. I.P. adv. coun., mem. bd. dirs. Stanford Bus. Sch. Alumni and mem. devel. coun. Stanford GSB. Mem. ABA, Am. Intellectual Property Law Assn., Inter-Pacific Bar Assn. Democrat. Presbyterian. Federal civil litigation, Patent. Office: Finnegan Henderson Farabow Garrett & Dunner 700 Hansen Way Palo Alto CA 94304-1016

O'ROURKE, JAMES LOUIS, lawyer; b. Bridgeport, Conn., July 5, 1958; s. James G. and Margaret Elizabeth (Fesco) O'R.; m. Margaret C. DiCicco, Sept. 18, 1994. BS, U. Bridgeport, 1984, JD, 1987. Bar: Conn. 1988, U.S. Dist. Ct. Conn. 1989, Mashantucket Pequot Tribal Bar 1995, Supreme Ct. of U.S., 1998. Pvt. practice, Stratford, Conn., 1987—. With USN, 1976-79. Mem. ABA, ATLA, Conn. Trial Lawyers Assn., Conn. Bar Assn., Greater Bridgeport Bar Assn. Roman Catholic. Avocations: boating, gardening, fishing, cycling, swimming. General practice, Personal injury (including property damage), Workers' compensation. Office: The Barnum Profl Bldg 1825 Barnum Ave Ste 201 Stratford CT 06614-5333

OROZCO, RODRIGO, lawyer; b. Mexico City, Mar. 15, 1971; s. Alfonso Orozco and Patricia Waters; m. Martha Fernanda Gonzalez Solache, Aug. 9, 1997; 1 child, Nicolas Orozco Gonzalez. Degree in law, Escuela Libre de Derecho, Mexico City, 1995; M in Law, Columbia U., 1997. Bar: N.Y. 1999. Legal intern Notary Pub. No. 6, Mexico City, 1992—94; assoc. White & Case, S.C., Mexico City, 1994—97, 1999—, White & Case, L.L.P., N.Y.C., 1997—98, London, 1998—99. Office: White & Case SC Av Palmas 405-5 Lomas de Chapultepec 11000 Mexico City Mexico Office Fax: (5255) 5540-9698.

ORR, ROBERT F. judge; b. Norfolk, Va., Oct. 11, 1946; married; 4 children. AB, U. N.C., 1971, JD, 1975. Bar: N.C. 1975. Pvt. practice, Asheville, NC, 1975—86; assoc. judge N.C. Ct. Appeals, 1986—94; assoc. justice N.C. Supreme Ct., Raleigh, 1994—. Mem. N.C. Beverage Control Commn., 1985—86; adj. prof. appellate advocacy N.C. Ctrl. U. Sch. Law, 1989—, adj. prof. N.C. State constl. law, 1998. Mem. Asheville-Revitalization Commn., 1977—81, Asheville-Buncombe Hist. Resources Commn., 1980—81; bd. trustees Hist. Preservation Found. NC, 1982—85; mem. Nat. Park Sys. Adv. Bd., 1990—95, chmn., 1992—93; bd. visitors U. NC-Chapel Hill, 1993—; mem. NCBAs Appellate Rules Study com., 1999—, Gov.'s Crime Commn. With U.S. Army, 1968—71. Mem.: N.C. Bar Assn., 28th Jud. Dist., N.C. State Bar. Republican. Office: PO Box 1841 Raleigh NC 27602-1841 also: 302 Justice Bldg 2 E Morgan St Raleigh NC 27601-1428*

ORSATTI, ERNEST BENJAMIN, lawyer; b. Pitts., Nov. 14, 1949; s. Ernest Ubaldo and Dorothy Minerva (Pfeiffer) O.; m. Ingrid Zalman, May 3, 1975; 1 child, Benjamin E. BA, Marquette U., 1971; JD, Duquesne U., 1974; postgrad., Army Command and Gen. Staff Coll., 1984. Bar: Pa. 1974, U.S. Dist. Ct. (we. dist.) Pa. 1974, U.S. Ct. Appeals (3d cir.) 1977, U.S. Supreme Ct. 1978, U.S. Ct. Appeals (6th cir.) 1992. Assoc. Jubelirer, Pass & Intrieri, Pitts., 1974-81, ptnr., 1981—. Contbg. editor: The Developing Labor Law, 4th edit., 1992—2002; chpt. editor The Developing Labor Law, 4th edit., 2002. Bd. dirs. Am. Italian Cultural Inst., Pitts. Served to capt. U.S. Army, 1975, lt. col., USAR, ret. Mem. ABA, ACLU (legal com. 1996—), Am. Arbitration Assn., Pa. Bar Assn., Allegheny County Bar Assn. (profl. ethics com. 2000—), Am. Legion. Democrat. Roman Catholic. Labor (including EEOC, Fair Labor Standards Act, labor-management relations, NLRB, OSHA), Military. Home: 9343 N Florence Rd Pittsburgh PA 15237-4815 Office: Jubelirer Pass & Intrieri 219 Fort Pitt Blvd Pittsburgh PA 15222-1576 E-mail: ebo@jpilaw.com., eborsatti@aol.com.

ORSINI, ROSEMARY, lawyer; b. Lodi, N.J., Aug. 21, 1955; d. Camillo Michael Orsini and Mary Margaret (Edell) Orsini. BA, U. Colo., Boulder, 1976; JD, U. Denver, Colo., 1992. Bar: Colo. 1993, Nebr. 1994, U.S. Dist. Ct.: Colo. 1994, U.S. Ct of Appeals: 10th Circuit 1998. Law clk. for justice Nebr. Supreme Ct., Lincoln, Nebr., 1993—94; shareholder Burg Simpson Eldredge Hersh & Jardine, P.C., Englewood, Colo., 1994—. Recipient Order of St. Ives, U. of Denver Coll. of Law, 1993. Fellow: Inns of Ct.; mem.: Colo. Bar Assn., Nat. Employee Lawyers Assn., Arapahoe Bar Assn., Denver Bar Assn., Phi Alpha Delta. Avocations: triathalon, mountain biking. Labor (including EEOC, Fair Labor Standards Act, labor-management relations, NLRB, OSHA), Insurance, General civil litigation. Office: Burg Simpson Eldredge Hersh & Jardine P 40 Inverness Dr E Englewood CO CO Office Fax: 303-708-0527. E-mail: rorsini@burgsimpson.com.

ORTH, PAUL WILLIAM, retired lawyer; b. Balt., May 7, 1930; s. Paul W. and Naomi (Howard Bevard) O.; m. Isle Haertle, June 15, 1956; children: Ingrid, Ilse Christine. AB, Dartmouth Coll., 1951; JD, Harvard U., 1954. Bar: Mass. 1954, Conn. 1957, U.S. Dist. Ct. Conn. 1958, U.S. Ct. Appeals (2d cir.) 1960, U.S. Ct. Appeals (1st cir.) 1983, U.S. Supreme Ct. 1960. Assoc. Hoppin, Carey & Powell, Hartford, Conn., 1957-62, ptnr., 1962-86, Shipman & Goodwin, Hartford, 1987-2000, MacDermid, Reynolds & Glissman P.C., Hartford, 2000—. Instr. Sch. Law U. Conn., 1959-81. Editor: Every Employee's Guide to the Law, 1993, 96. Chmn. Farmington Conservation Commn., 1982-83; mem. town com. Town of Farmington, 1973-81; dir. Conn. Opera Assn., 2000-02. With AUS, 1954-56. Fellow Am. Bar Found., Conn. Bar Found.; mem. ABA, Hartford County Bar Assn. (pres. 1983-84), Conn. Bar Assn. (chmn. coms.). Democrat. Alternative dispute resolution, General civil litigation, Labor (including EEOC, Fair Labor Standards Act, labor-management relations, NLRB, OSHA). Office: MacDermid Reynolds & Glissman PC 86 Farmington Ave Hartford CT 06105 E-mail: porth@mrglaw.com.

ORTIQUE, REVIUS OLIVER, JR., city official, retired state supreme court justice; b. New Orleans, June 14, 1924; s. Revius Oliver and Lillie Edith (Long) O.; m. Miriam Marie Victorianne, Dec. 29, 1947; 1 child: Rhesa Marie (Mrs. Alden J. McDonald). AB, Dillard U., 1947; MA, Ind. U., 1949; JD, So. U., 1956; LLD (hon.) , Campbell Coll., 1960; LHD (hon.) , Ithaca Coll., 1971; LLD (hon.) , Ind. U., 1983, Morris Brown Coll., 1992, Loyola U. South, 1993, Dillard U., 1996. Bar: La. 1956, U.S. Dist. Ct 1956, Eastern Dist. La 1956, U.S. Fifth Circuit Ct. of Appeals 1956, U.S. Supreme Ct 1964. Practiced in, New Orleans, 1956-78; judge Civil Dist. Ct. for Orleans Parish, 1978-92; assoc. justice La. Supreme Ct., 1993-94; chmn. New Orleans Aviation Bd., 1994—2002. Lectr. labor law Dillard U., 1950-52, U. West Indies, 1986; formerly assoc. gen. counsel Cmty. Improvement Agy.; former gen. counsel 8th Dist. A.M.E. Ch.; former mem. Fed. Hosp. Coun., 1966, Pres.'s Commn. on Campus Unrest, 1970, Bd. Legal Svcs. Corp., 1975-83; chief judge civil cts. Orleans Parish, 1986-87; spkr. in field; U.S. alt. rep. to 54th Gen. Assembly UN, 1999-2000. Contbr. articles to profl. jours. Former pres. Met. Area Com.; former mem. Bd. City Trusts, New Orleans, New Orleans Legal Assistance Corp. Bd., Ad Hoc Com. for Devel. of Ctrl. Bus. Dist. City of New Orleans; bd. dirs. Cmty. Rels. Coun., Am. Lung Assn.; trustee Antioch Coll. Law, New Orleans chpt. Operation PUSH, 1981-84; pres. Louis A. Martinet Soc., 1959; active World's Fair, New Orleans, 1984, Civil Rights Movement, 1960-79; bd. dirs., mem. exec. com. Nat. Sr. Citizens Law Ctr., L.A., 1970-76, Criminal Justice Coordinating Com., UN Assn. New Orleans, 1980—; former mem. exec. bd. Nat. Bar Found.; mem. exec. com. Econ. Devel. Coun. Greater New Orleans; past chmn. Health Edn. Authority of La.; trustee, mem. exec. com. Dillard U.; former mem. bd. mgmt. Flint Goodridge Hosp.; former mem. adv. bd. League Women Voters Greater New Orleans; former mem. men's adv. bd. YWCA; trustee AME Ch., former connectional trustee; former chancellor New Orleans Fedn. Chs.; bd. dirs. Nat. Legal Aid and Defender Assn.; trustee Civil Justice Found.; served on over 50 bds., commns. 1st lt. AUS, 1943-47, PTO. Recipient Arthur von Briesen medal Disting. Svcs. Disadvantaged Ams. NLADA, 1971, Weiss award NCCJ, 1975, Brotherhood award NCCJ, 1976, Nat. Black Achievement award, 1979, Poor People's Banner award, 1979, William H. Hastie award, 1983, Outstanding Citizen award Kiwanis of Pontchartrain, 1986, Civil Justice award, 1989, Daniel E. Byrd award NAACP, 1991, A.P. Tureaud Meml. medal La. State NAACP, 1993; Revius O. Ortique Jr. Law Libr. named in his honor, Lafayette, La., 1988; named Outstanding Young Man Nat. Urban League, 1958, Outstanding Person in La. Inst. Human Understanding, 1976, Citizen of Yr. Shreveport, 1993. Mem. ABA (del., Legal Svcs. program, Nat. adv. coun., 1964-71, jud. divsn., Thurgood Marshal award 2000), Nat. Bar Assn. (pres. 1965-66, exec. bd., Raymond Pace Alexander award, jud. coun. 1987, William Hastie award 1982, Gertrude E. Rush award 1991, Thurgood Marshall award 2000), La. State Bar Assn. (former mem. ho. of dels., Lifetime Achievement award 1986, WTC award for Exceptional Internat. Distinction, 2001), Nat. Legal Aid and Defender Assn. (past pres., mem. exec. bd.), La. District Judges Assn., Am. Judicature Soc. (bd. dirs. 1975-79), Civil Justice Found. (trustee 1989-93), Louis A. Martinet Legal Soc., World Peace Through Law (charter mem.), Blue Key Honor Soc., Phi Delta Kappa, Alpha Kappa Delta. Home: 10 Park Island Dr New Orleans LA 70122-1229

ORTIZ, ALBERT, protective services official; Joined San Antonio Police Dept., 1972, dep. chief police, 1994—99, chief of staff, 1999—2002, chief police, 2002—. Office: San Antonio Police Dept PO Box 839966 San Antonio TX 78283-3966*

ORTIZ, JAY RICHARD GENTRY, lawyer; b. Washington, Mar. 21, 1945; s. Charles and Catherine Gentry (Candlin) Ortiz; m. Lois Wright Hatcher Greer, June 12, 1982. BA, Yale U., 1967; postgrad., Stanford U., 1967—68; JD, U. N.Mex., 1972. Bar: N.Mex. 1973, Mo. 1978, Tenn. 1982, Ga. 1991, U.S. Dist. Ct. N.Mex. 1973, U.S. Ct. Appeals (10th cir.) 1973, U.S. Supreme Ct. 1977, U.S. Dist. t. (we. dist.) Mo. 1978, U.S. Dist. t. (no. dist.) Ga. 1991, U.S. Ct. Appeals (8th cir.) 1978, U.S. Ct. Appeals (11th cir.) 1991. Assoc. Rodey, Dickason, Sloan, Akin & Robb, Albuquerque, 1972—75; ptnr. Knight, Sullivan, Villella, Skarsgard & Michael, Albuquerque, 1975—77; litigation atty. Monsanto Co., St. Louis, 1977—81; environ. atty. Eastman Kodak Co., Kingsport, Tenn., 1981—84; sr. atty. AT&T, Atlanta, 1984—91; gen. counsel AMS Group, Inc., 1991—96, 1998—, ConsultaAmerica Internat., 1994—97, Vision Net, Inc., 1994—, Cross Constrn. Internat., Inc., 1996—97, Ophthalmic Solutions LLC, 1996—97, Univest Ltd., 1996—97; pres. VMS, Inc., 1994—. Precinct vice chmn. Dem. Party, Albuquerque, 1971—77. Lt. (j.g.) USN, 1969—70. Mem.: ABA, English Speaking Union, Tenn. Bar Assn., Mo. Bar Assn., N.Mex. Bar Assn., Ga. Bar Assn., Yale Club of Ga., Order of the Coif, Delta Theta Phi (tribune 1972—77). Episcopalian. Federal civil litigation, Corporate, general, Environmental. Home: 1000 Buckingham Cir NW Atlanta GA 30327-2704

ORTIZ MAYAGOITIA, GUILLERMO IBERION, judge; b. Feb. 10, 1941; Grad., U. Veracruzana. Magistrate Fed. Electoral Ct., 1993—94; min. Supreme Ct. Mexico, 1995—. Office: Suprema Corte de Justicia de la Nacion Pino Suarez 2 Col Centro 06065 Mexico City Mexico*

ORWIG, MATTHEW DANE, lawyer; b. Ardmore, Okla., Jan. 2, 1959; s. Richard R. and Mary E. (Pyle) O.; m. Melissa L. Vaughan, July 11, 1981; children: Joshua Matthew, Rachel Elizabeth, Jacob Andrew. BS, Tex. Tech. U., 1981, JD, 1984. Bar: Tex. 1985, U.S. Dist. Ct. (no. dist.) Tex. 1985, U.S. Ct. Appeals (5th cir.) 1985. Legal intern for n. dist. Tex. U.S. Dept. Justice, Dallas, 1983; briefing atty. for judge U.S. Dist. Ct., Lubbock, Tex., 1984-86; ptnr. Jones, Flygare, Galey, Moody and Brown, Lubbock, 1986-89; asst. U.S. atty. U.S. Dept. Justice, Dallas, 1989—2001, U.S. atty. ea. dist., 2001—. Adj. prof. So. Meth. U. Law Sch, 1990—, Tex. Wesleyan U. Sch. Law, 1990—; legal advisor Exec. Office of U.S. Atty., Office of Legal Counsel, 1997—. Mem. ABA, State Bar Tex., Lubbock County Bar Assn., Lubbock County Young Lawyers Assn. (bd. dirs. 1987-89), Tex. Trial Lawyers Assn. Methodist. General civil litigation, Insurance, Personal injury (including property damage). Office: 350 Magnolia Ave Ste 150 Beaumont TX 77701-2237*

ORWOLL, GREGG S. K. lawyer; b. Austin, Minn., Mar. 23, 1926; s. Gilbert M. and Kleonora (Kleven) O.; m. Laverne M. Flentie, Sept. 15, 1951; children: Kimball G., Kent A., Vikki A., Tristen A., Erik G. BS, Northwestern U., 1950; JD, U. Minn., 1953. Bar: Minn. 1953, U.S. Supreme Ct. 1973. Assoc. Dorsey & Whitney, Mpls., 1953-59, ptnr., 1959-60; assoc. counsel Mayo Clinic, Rochester, Minn., 1960-63, gen. counsel, 1963-87, sr. legal counsel, 1987-91, sr. counsel, 1991-92. Gen. counsel, dir. Rochester Airport Co., 1962-84, v.p., 1981-84; gen. counsel Mayo Med. Svcs., Ltd., 1972-90; bd. dirs., sec. and gen. counsel Mayo Found. for Med. Edn. and Rsch., 1984-90; gen. counsel Mid-Am. Orthop. Assn., 1984—, Minn. Orthop. Soc., 1985-95; counsel Norwegian Am. Orthopaedic Soc., 1999—, Intl. Soc. of Amyloidosis 2002—; asst. sec./sec. Mayo Found., Rochester, 1972-91; sec. Mayo Emeritus Staff, 1998-99, vice chair, 1999-2000, chair, 2000-2001; bd. dirs. Charter House, 1986-90; dir., officer Travelure Motel Corp., 1968-86; dir., v.p. Echo Too Ent., Inc.; dir., v.p. Oberhamer Inc., 1989-99; bd. dirs. Am. Decal and Mfg. Co., 1989-93, sec., 1992-93; adj. prof. William Mitchell Coll. Law, 1978-84. Contbr. articles and chpts. to legal and medico-legal publs.; mem. bd. editors HealthSpan, 1984-93; mem. editl. bd. Minn. Law Rev., 1952-53. Trustee Minn. Coun. on Founds., 1977-82, Mayo Found., 1982-86; trustee William Mitchell Coll. Law, 1982-88, 89-98, mem. exec. com. 1990-98; bd. visitors U. Minn. Law Sch., 1974-76, 85-91; mem. U. Minn. Regent Candidate Adv. Coun., 1988-99, Minn. State Compensation Coun., 1991-97. With USAF, 1944-45. Recipient Outstanding Svc. medal U.S. Govt., 1991. Mem. ABA, AMA (affiliate), Am. Corp. Counsel Assn., Minn. Soc. Hosp. Attys. (bd. dirs. 1981-86), Minn. State Bar Assn. (chmn. legal/med. com. 1977-81), Olmsted County Bar Assn. (v.p., pres. 1977-79), Rochester C. of C., U. Minn. Law Alumni Assn. (bd. dirs. 1973-76, 85-91), Rochester U. Club (pres. 1977), The Doctors Mayo Soc., Mid Am. Orthop. Assn. (hon.), Mayo Alumni Assn. (hon.), Phi Delta Phi, Phi Delta Theta. Republican. Corporate, general, Personal injury (including property damage). Home: 2233 5th Ave NE Rochester MN 55906-4017 Office: Mayo Clinic 200 1st St SW Rochester MN 55905-0002

OSAKWE, CHRISTOPHER, lawyer, educator; b. Lagos, Nigeria, May 8, 1942; came to U.S. 1970, naturalized 1979; s. Simon and Hannah (Morgan) O.; m. Maria Elena Amador, Aug. 19, 1982; 1 child, Rebecca E. LLB, Moscow State U., 1967, PhD, 1970; JSD, U. Ill., 1974. Bar: Moscow, 1967, Kazakhstan, 1997. Prof. sch. law Tulane U., New Orleans, 1972-81, 86-88; ptnr. firm Riddle and Brown, New Orleans, 1989—; Eason-Weinmann prof. comparative law, dir. Eason-Weinmann Ctr. for Comparative Law Tulane U., New Orleans, 1981-86. Vis. prof. U. Pa., 1978, U. Mich., 1981, Washington and Lee U., 1986; vis. fellow St. Anthony's Coll., Oxford U., Eng., 1980, Christ Ch. Coll., Oxford U., 1988-89, Lomonosov Moscow State U., 1999-2002; cons. U.S. Dept. Commerce, 1980-85. Author: The Participation of the Soviet Union in Universal International Organizations, 1972, The Foundations of Soviet Law, 1981, Joint Ventures with the Soviet Union: Law and Practice, 1990, Soviet Business Law, 2 vols., 1991, (with others) Comparative Legal Traditions in a Nutshell, 1982, Comparative Legal Traditions--Text, Materials and Cases, 1985, 2d edit., 1994, The Russian Civil Code Annotated: Translation and Commentary, 2000, Comparative Law in Diagrams: General and Special Parts, 2000, 2d edit., 2002; editor Am. Jour. Comparative Law, 1978-85. Carnegie doctoral fellow Hague Acad. Internat. Law, 1969; Russian rsch. fellow Harvard U., 1972; USSR sr. rsch. exch. fellow, 1982, rsch. fellow Kennan Inst. for Advanced Russian Studies, 1988. Mem. ABA, Am. Law Inst., Am. Soc. Internat. Law, Supreme Ct. Hist. Soc., Soc. de Legislation Comparée, Order of Coif. Republican. Roman Catholic. Home: 339 Audubon Blvd New Orleans LA 70125-4124 Office: 201 S Charles Ave Ste 3100 New Orleans LA 70170 E-mail: osakwec@aol.com.

OSBORN, DONALD ROBERT, lawyer; b. N.Y.C., Oct. 9, 1929; s. Robert W. and Ruth C. (Compton) O.; m. Marcia Lontz, June 4, 1955; children: David, Judith, Robert; m. Marie A. Johnson, Sept. 11, 1986. BA, Cornell U., 1951; LLB, Columbia U., 1957. Bar: N.Y. 1957, U.S. Tax Ct. 1958, U.S. Ct. Claims 1961, U.S. Ct. Appeals (2d cir.) 1974, U.S. Ct. Appeals (8th cir.) 1974, U.S. Dist. Ct. (so. and ea. dists.) N.Y. 1975, U.S. Supreme Ct. 1975.

Assoc. Sullivan & Cromwell, N.Y.C., 1957-64, ptnr., 1964-96, sr. counsel, 1997—. Trustee Hamilton Coll., 1978-88, Mus. of Broadcasting, 1975-80; trustee, treas. Kirkland Coll., 1969-78; mem. coun. White Burkett Miller Ctr. Pub. Affairs, 1976-82; bd. dirs., pres. Stevens Kingsley Found., 1967—; sec., treas. Dunlevy Milbank Found., 1974—; bd. dirs. Spanel Found., 1978-88, CBS, Inc., 1975-80. Served with USN, 1951-54. Mem. ABA, N.Y. State Bar Assn., Assn. of Bar of City of N.Y., Am. Bar Found., Scarsdale Golf Club, India House, Regency Whist Club, Country Club of the Rockies. Presbyterian. Private international, Probate (including wills, trusts), Corporate taxation. Home: 1049 Park Ave New York NY 10028-1061 Office: Sullivan & Cromwell 125 Broad St Fl 32 New York NY 10004-2498

OSBORN, JOE ALLEN, lawyer; b. Friona, Tex., Mar. 1, 1932; s. Sloan H. and Ilene (McFarland) O.; m. Carolyn Culbert, July 5, 1955; children: William, Claire. BA, U. Tex., 1954, LLB, 1958. Bar: Tex. 1958. Asst. atty. gen. State of Tex., Austin, 1958-62; assoc. Wilson, Kendall, Koch & Randall, Austin, 1962-65, ptnr., 1966—. Served to 1st lt., U.S. Army, 1955-57. Presbyterian. Probate (including wills, trusts), Property, real (including real estate development, water), Estate planning. Home: 3612 Windsor Rd Austin TX 78703-1538 Office: Kendall and Osborn 515 Congress Ave Austin TX 78701-3504 Fax: 512-474-2461. E-mail: joeosborn@kendallosborn.com.

OSBORN, JOHN EDWARD, lawyer, pharmaceutical and biotechnology industry executive, former government official, writer; b. Davenport, Iowa, Sept. 4, 1957; s. Edward Richard and Patricia Anne (O'Donovan) O.; m. Deborah Lynn Powell, Aug. 11, 1984; children: Delaney Powell, Keeley Rush. Student, Coll. William and Mary, 1975-76; BA, U. Iowa, 1979; cert., Georgetown U., 1980; JD, U. Va., 1983; cert., Wadham Coll., Oxford U., 1987; M Internat. Pub. Policy, Johns Hopkins U., 1992; cert., Wharton Sch., U. Pa., 1994-95; postgrad., Princeton U., 1997-99. Bar: Mass. 1985, U.S. Supreme Ct. 2001. Staff U.S. Rep. Jim Leach, 1978, Congl. Budget Office, 1979—80, U.S. Senator John Heinz, 1981; law clk. to Hon. Albert V. Bryan U.S. Ct. Appeals (4th cir.), Alexandria, Va., 1983-84; assoc. Sidley & Austin, Chgo., 1982, Hale and Dorr, Boston, 1983—88, Dechert Price & Rhoads, Phila., 1988-89; spl. asst. to legal adviser U.S. Dept. State, Washington, 1989-92; sr. counsel DuPont Merck Pharm. Co., Wilmington, Del., 1992-94, assoc. gen. counsel, 1994-96, v.p., assoc. gen. counsel, asst. sec., 1996—97; v.p. legal affairs Cephalon, Inc., West Chester, Pa., 1997—98, sr. v.p., gen. counsel, sec., 1998—. Vis. lectr. U. Mich. Bus. Sch., 1997—2002; vis. scholar East European studies Woodrow Wilson Internat. Ctr. for Scholars, Washington, 1991; vis. fellow politics Princeton U., 2002—. Contbr. articles to profl. jours. and newspapers; articles editor Va. Jour. Internat. Law, 1982—83. Bd. advisors U. Pa. Inst. Law and Econs., Phila., 1999—; mem. Friends of Child Devel. Ctr., Georgetown U. Med. Ctr., Washington, 1999—, Johns Hopkins U. Alumni Coun., Balt., 1997—2003, U. Va. Law Sch. Bus. Adv. Coun., Charlottesville, 1996—, U. Iowa Liberal Arts Dean's Adv. Bd., Iowa City, 1999—; trustee Tower Hill Sch., Wilmington, Del., 1997—, Del. Art Mus., 1999—, asst. sec., 2001—; mem. Del. Rep. State Com., 1995—99; del. Rep. Nat. Conv., San Diego, 1996; rsch. aide, speechwriter George Bush for Pres. Com., 1979—80, 1987—88; bd. dirs. Del. Ctr. for the Contemporary Arts, 1995—, v.p., 1997—99; bd. dirs. Am. Civil Liberties Found. Del., 1995—98, adv. bd., 1998—; bd. dirs. World Affairs Coun. of Wilmington, 2001—. Recipient study grant, Andrew W. Mellon Found., 1999; Eisenhower fellow, Ireland and No. Ireland, 1998. Mem. Am. Law Inst., Atlantic Coun. of the U.S., Coun. Fgn. Rels., Greenville Country Club, Princeton Club N.Y., Fieldstone Golf Club, Met. Club Washington, Mortar Bd., Phi Beta Kappa, Phi Delta Phi, Omicron Delta Kappa, Omicron Delta Epsilon. Republican. Roman Catholic. Commercial, contracts (including sales of goods; commercial financing), Corporate, general, Private international. Home: 5 Doe's Lane Way Ridge Wilmington DE 19807-1548 also: 75 Baxter Rd PO Box 198 Siasconset MA 02564 Office: 145 Brandywine Pkwy West Chester PA 19380-4245 E-mail: josborn@cephalon.com., jeosborn@princeton.edu.

OSBORN, JOHN SIMCOE, JR., lawyer; b. Louisville, Jan. 14, 1926; s. John S. and Ruby (Pinnell) O.; m. Mary Jo Fishback, Sept. 6, 1947; children— Robert, John, Donna LLB, U. Louisville, 1949. Bar: Ky. 1949, U.S. Dist. Ut. (ea. and we. dists.) Ky. 1952. Exec. v.p., gen. counsel Louisville Title Ins. Co., 1954-72; ptnr. Tarrant Combs & Bullitt (name changed to Wyatt Tarrant & Combs 1980), Louisville, 1972—. Chmn. bd. Beargrass Corp. Capt. JAGC, U.S. Army, 1952-54. Fellow Am. Bar Found.; mem. Ky. Bar Assn., Louisville Bar Assn., ABA, Am. Land Title Assn., Am. Coll. Real Estate Lawyers, Rotary. Democrat. Lutheran. General practice, Insurance, Property, real (including real estate development, water). Office: Wyatt Tarrant & Combs 2800 Citizens Plz Louisville KY 40202

OSBORN, MALCOLM EVERETT, lawyer; b. Bangor, Maine, Apr. 29, 1928; s. Lester Everett and Helen (Clark) O.; m. Claire Anne Franks, Aug. 30, 1953; children: Beverly, Lester, Malcolm, Ernest. BA, U. Maine, 1952; postgrad., Harvard U., 1952-54; JD, Boston U., 1956, LLM, 1961. Bar: Maine 1956, Mass. 1956, U.S. Dist. Ct. Mass. 1961, U.S. Tax Ct. 1961, U.S. Claims Ct. 1961, N.C. 1965, U.S. Supreme Ct. 1979, U.S. Ct. Appeals (4th cir.) 1980, Va. 1991. Tax counsel State Mut. Life Assurance Co., Worcester, Mass., 1956-64; v.p., gen. tax counsel Integon Corp. and other group cos., Winston-Salem, N.C., 1964-81; ptnr. House, Blanco & Osborn, P.A., Winston-Salem, N.C., 1981-88; v.p., gen. counsel, dir. Settlers Life Ins. Co., Bristol, Va., 1984-89; prin. Malcolm E. Osborn, P.A., Winston-Salem, 1988—. Lectr. The Booke Seminars, Life Ins. Co., 1985-87; adj. prof. Wake Forest U. Sch. Law, Winston-Salem, 1974-82; Disting. guest lectr. Ga. State U., 1965; guest lectr. NYU Ann. Inst. Fed. Taxation, 1966, 68, 75, 80. Com. editor The Tax Lawyer, ABA, 1974-76; author numerous articles in field. Trustee N.C. Coun. Econ. Edn., 1968-76; bd. dirs. Christian Fellowship Home, 1972-80; co-founder Bereaved Parents Group Winston-Salem, 1978—. Mem. ABA (chmn. com. ins. cos. of taxation sect. 1980-82, chmn. subcom. on continuing legal edn. and publs. 1982-88), Am. Bus. Law Assn. (mem. com. fed. taxation 1968—, chmn. 1972-75), Assn. Life Ins. Counsel (com. on co. tax, tax sect. 1965—), N.C. Bar Assn. (com. taxation 1973—), Fed. Bar Assn. (taxation com. 1973—), Maine State Bar Assn., Va. State Bar Assn., Internat. Bar Assn. (com. on taxes of bus. law sect. 1973—), AAUP, Southeastern Acad. Legal Studies in Bus., Masons (Lincoln, Maine). Insurance, Corporate taxation, Personal income taxation. Office: PO Box 5192 Winston Salem NC 27113-5192

OSBORNE, DUNCAN ELLIOTT, lawyer; b. Orange, N.J., May 24, 1944; s. Walter Dodd Osborne and Anne (Boaz) Treanor; m. Elizabeth May Bachman, Dec. 29, 1965; children: Ellen Osborne Ray, Mark Elliott, Michael Cleveland. BA, Stanford U., 1966; MA, U. Tex., 1968, JD with honors, 1971. Bar: Tex. (cert. estate planning and probate law) 1971, U.S. Supreme Ct. 1975, U.S. Tax Ct. 1975, U.S. Fed. Ct. Claims 1997. Atty. Graves Dougherty, Austin, Tex., 1971-93, Osborne, Lowe, Helman & Smith L.L.P., Austin, 1993-2000, Osborne & Helman L.L.P., Austin, 2001—. Bd. dirs. Boatmen's Nat. Bank Austin, 1995-97, Hill Country Bank, Austin, 1998. Author, editor: Asset Protection: Domestic and International Law and Tactics; contbr. articles to profl. jours.; mem. Tex. Law Rev. Trustee Susan Vaughan Found., Houston, Still Water Found., Austin; chair bd. trustees St. Stephens Episcopal Sch., Austin, 1985-91, St. Andrews Episcopal Sch., Austin, 1978. Fellow Am. Coll. Trust and Estate Counsel, Coll. of State Bar of Tex.; mem. ABA, Internat. Tax Planning Assn., Offshore Inst., Internat. Acad. Estate and Trust Law (exec. com.), Asset Protection Planning Commn. (chair 1996-98)), Order of Coif. Avocation: scuba diving. Estate planning, Non-profit and tax-exempt organizations, Estate taxation. Office: Osborne & Helman LLP 301 Congress Ave Ste 1910 Austin TX 78701-2959 E-mail: deosborne@osbornehelman.com.

OSBORNE, FRANK R. lawyer, educator, lecturer; b. Cleve., Dec. 7, 1946; s. Thomas L. and Doris E. O.; m. Charlotte A. Caston, July 8, 1972; children: James, Thomas, Patricia, Janet, Karen, Kathleen, Linda, Jennifer. AB in Polit. Sci., John Carroll U., 1969; JD, Cleve. State U., 1973. Bar: Ohio 1973, U.S. Dist. Ct. (no. dist.) 1975, U.S. Supreme Ct. 1979, U.S. Ct. Appeals (6th cir.) 1979, U.S. Tax Ct. 1980, U.S. Ct. Appeals (7th cir.) 1982. Law clk. to Hon. John V. Corrigan Ohio Ct. Appeals (8th appellate dist.), Cleve., 1973-76; atty. Roudebush, Brown & Ulrich, LPA, Cleve., 1976-86, Arter & Hadden, LLP, Cleve., 1986—. Adj. faculty mem. Ohio civil procedure Cleve. Marshall Coll. Law, Cleve. State U., 1994—; alternative dispute resolution neutral U.S. Dist. Ct. (no. dist.), Cleve., 1990—; lectr. civil procedure Rossen Bar Rev., 2001—. Co-author: Civil Discovery Practice in Ohio, 1995. Mem. Ohio State Bar Assn., Cleve. Bar Assn. Appellate, General civil litigation, Commercial, contracts (including sales of goods; commercial financing). Home: 1278 Croyden Rd Lyndhurst OH 44124-1413 Office: Arter & Hadden LLP 1100 Huntington Bldg Cleveland OH 44115 Fax: 216-696-2645. E-mail: frank.osborne@arterhadden.com.

OSBORNE, JOHN EDWARDS, lawyer; b. Tucson, Feb. 10, 1953; s. Earle Dean and Helen Edwards Osborne; m. Diana Kuhel, Apr. 10, 1976; children: Monica, Valerie. AB with honors, Stanford U., 1975; JD, U. Tex., 1981. Bar: Ariz. Supreme Ct. 1981, U.S. Dist. Ct. Ariz. 1981, U.S. Ct. Appeals (9th cir.) 1990, U.S. Supreme Ct. 1994, White Mountain Apache Tribal Ct. Assoc. Chandler, Tullar, Udall & Redhair, Tucson, 1981-85; mng. atty. Tucson br. personal injury dept. Jacoby & Meyers Law Offices, Tucson, 1985-89; mng. ptnr. Goldberg & Osborne, Tucson, 1989—. Referee adminstr. Am. Youth Soccer Orgn., Tucson, 1997—. Fellow Ariz. Bar Found.; mem. ATLA, ABA, Am. Bd. Trial Advs. (assoc. mem., Tucson chpt.), Ariz. Trial Lawyers Assn. (sustaining mem., bd. govs.), State Bar Ariz. (cert. specialist in personal injury and wrongful death, pub. rels. com. 1985-89, trial practice sect. 1988—), Pima County Bar Assn. (pro bono com. 1982-95, v.p. young lawyers divsn. 1987-88). Avocations: private pilot, scuba diving, skiing, hunting, soccer referee. Insurance, Personal injury (including property damage), Product liability. Office: Goldberg & Osborne 33 N Stone Ave Ste 1850 Tucson AZ 85701-1426

O'SCANNLAIN, DIARMUID FIONNTAIN, federal judge; b. N.Y.C., Mar. 28, 1937; s. Sean Leo and Moira (Hegarty); m. Maura Nolan, Sept. 7, 1963; children: Sean, Jane, Brendan, Kevin, Megan, Christopher, Anne, Kate. BA, St. John's U., 1957; JD, Harvard U., 1963; LLM, U. Va., 1992; LLD (hon.) , U. Notre Dame, 2002. Bar: Oreg. 1965, N.Y. 1964. Tax atty. Standard Oil Co. (N.J.), N.Y.C., 1963—65; oassoc. Davies, Biggs, Strayer, Sotel & Boley, Portland, Oreg., 1965—69; dep. atty. gen. State of Oreg., 1969—71, pub. utility commr., 1971—73; dir. Oreg. Dept. Environ. Quality, 1973—74; sr. ptnr. Ragen, Roberts, O'Scannlain, Robertson & Neill, Portland, 1978—86; judge U.S. Ct. Appeals (9th cir.), San Francisco, 1986—, mem. exec. com., 1988—89, 1993—94; mem. Jud. Coun. 9th Cir., 1991—93. Mem. U.S. Jud. Conf. Com. on Automation and Tech. , 1990—; cons. Office of Pres.-elect and mem. Dept. Energy Transition Team (Reagan Transition), Washington, 1980—81; chmn. com. adminstrv. law Oreg. State Bar, 1980—81. Mem. coun. of legal advisors Rep. Nat. Com., 1981—83, mem., 1983—86; chmn. Oreg. Rep. Party, 1983—86; del. Rep. Nat. convs., 1976, 1980, chmn. Oreg. del., 1984; nominee U.S. Ho. of Reps., 1st Congl. Dist., 1974; team leader energy task force Pres.'s Pvt. Sector Survey on Cost Control, 1982—83; trustee Jesuit H.S.; bd. visitors U. Oreg. Law Sch., 1988—; mem. citizens adv. bd. Providence Hosp., 1986—92. Maj. USAR, 1955—78. Mem.: ABA (sec. Appellate Judges Conf. 1989—90, exec. com. 1990—, chmn. 1994—95, chmn. jud. divsn. 2001—02), Fed. Judges Assn., Fed. Bar Assn., Multnomah Club. Roman Catholic. Office: US Ct Appeals 313 Pioneer Courthouse 555 SW Yamhill St Portland OR 97204-1396 E-mail: JudgeO'Scannlain@ca9.uscourts.gov.

OSER, JUDI, lawyer, artist; b. Phila., Sept. 18, 1933; d. James Isadore and Mildred (Greenspan) O.; m. Richard Hunter Hollinger, Nov. 4, 1965 (div. Nov. 1975). BA in English with honors, U. Pa., 1956; JD, New Coll. Calif., 1980; student, Sarah Lawrence Coll., Pa. Acad. Fine Arts. Bar: Calif. 1980, U.S. Dist. Ct. (no. dist.) Calif. 1980, U.S. Ct. Appeals (9th crct.) 1982. Law clk. immigration law unit North Beach-Chinatown br. San Francisco Neighborhood Legal Assistance Found., 1979; immigration atty. Law Offices of Fred C. Hite, San Francisco, 1979-81, Wong, Main and Wu, Palo Alto, Calif., 1981; assoc. Law Offices of C. H. Blagburn, San Francisco, 1981-82; staff atty. Am. Ind. Hist. Soc., San Francisco, 1982; sole practice Piedmont, Calif., 1982—. One-woman shows include Lotus Gallery, Berkeley, Calif., Mus. Coastal Arts League, Spanishtown Galleries, Half Moon Bay, Calif., Clark's Corner, San Francisco, Heart's Content, Lyndell, Pa.; exhibited in numerous group shows and pvt. collections; contbr. articles to profl. jours. Mem. Calif. Lawyers for the Arts (atty.'s ref. panel), Eastbay Watercolor Soc. (2d place award 1992), San Francisco Women Artists (bus. sec., bd. dirs., Merit award 1988, 94), Oakland Art Assn. (corp. counsel, bd. dirs., 1st place award 1991, Merit award 1988, 90, 1st prize 30th ann. exhbn. 1987), Phila. Watercolor Club (signature membership), Pa. Acad. Fine Arts (fellowship mem. alumni assn.), Calif. Bar Assn. Office: PO Box 21342 Piedmont CA 94620-1342

OSGOOD, RUSSELL KING, academic administrator; b. Fairborn, Ohio, Oct. 25, 1947; s. Richard M. and Mary Russell Osgood; m. Paula Haley, June 6, 1970; children: Mary, Josiah, Micah, Iain. BA, Yale U., 1969, JD, 1974. Bar: Mass. 1974, U.S. Dist. Ct. Mass. (admitted to) 1976. Assoc. Hill & Barlow, Boston, 1974—78; assoc. prof. Boston U., 1978—80; prof. Cornell U., Ithaca, NY, 1980—88, dean law sch., 1988—98; pres. Grinnell (Iowa) Coll., 1998—. Lt. USNR, 1969—71. Mem.: Selden Soc., Stair Soc., Mass. Hist. Soc. Office: Grinnell Coll 1121 Park St Grinnell IA 50112-1640 E-mail: osgood@grinnell.edu.

O'SHAUGHNESSY, CHRISTOPHER T. lawyer; b. Princeton, N.J., Jan. 19, 1971; s. Thomas G. and Geraldine M. O'Shaughnessy; m. Renée M. Pilliod, Aug. 13, 1994; 1 child, Michael J. BA, Ohio State U., 1993; JD, Capital U., Columbus, Ohio, 1997. Bar: Ohio 1998, U.S. Dist. Ct. (no. and so. dists.) Ohio 1999. Law clk. State of Ohio's Atty. Gen., Columbus, 1995, Ray, Alton, Todaro and Kirstein, LPA, Columbus, 1995—97, Lane, Alton & Horst, LLC, Columbus, 1997—98, atty. at law, 1998—, mem. profl. recruiting com. Atty., cons. Action Children Counsel Franklin County, Columbus, 1999—. Co-editor: (book) The ePolicy Handbook, 2001. Vol. Rep. John Kasich's Re-election, Columbus, 1990, Sen. Michael Dewine's Campaign, Columbus, 1992. Mem.: Franklin Am. Inn of Ct., Ohio Acad. of Trial Lawyers, Def. Rsch. Inst. Republican. Roman Catholic. Avocations: basketball, golf, music. State civil litigation, Construction, Professional liability. Office: Lane Alton and Horst LLC 175 S Third St Columbus OH 43215 Office Fax: 614-228-6885. Business E-Mail: cto@lah4law.com.

O'SHAUGHNESSY, JAMES PATRICK, lawyer; b. Rochester, N.Y., Mar. 3, 1947; s. John Andrew and Margaret May (Yaxley) O'S.; m. Terry Lee Wood. BS cum laude, Rensselaer Poly. Inst., 1972; JD, Georgetown U., 1977. Bar: Va. 1977, Ohio 1979, Wis. 1987. Assoc. Squire, Sanders & Dempsey, Cleve., 1978-81; ptnr. Hughes & Cassidy, Sumas, Wash., 1981-84; patent counsel Kimberly-Clark Corp., Neenah, Wis., 1984-85; ptnr. Foley & Lardner, Milw., 1986-96; v.p., chief intellectual property counsel Rockwell Automation, Inc., Milw., 1996—, corp. officer. Founder Innovatech Co., 1996—; mem. tech. adv. coun. Ideation Internat., Inc., 1999—; mem. adv. bd. Licensing Econs. Rev.; mem. bd. visitors Georgetown U. Sch. Nursing, 1996-2000; mem., bd. dir. Intellectual Property Owners; frequent lectr., chmn. seminars to legal and bus. groups. Contbg. author: Technology Licensing: Corporate Strategies for Maximizing Value, 1996, Profiting From Intellectual Capital: Extracting Value From Innovation, 1998; contbr. articles to profl. jours. Bd. dirs. Skylight Opera Theatre, 1991-92, Milw. Florentine Opera Co., 1999—. With USN, 1964-68. Mem. CPR Inst. for Dispute Resolution (mediation/arbitration panel), Lic. Execs. Soc., Am. Intellectual Property Law Assn., Assn. Chief Patent Coun.; Disabled Am. Vets., Tau Beta Pi, Alpha Sigma Mu. Computer, Patent, Trademark and copyright. Home: 3207 W Donges Bay Rd Mequon WI 53092-5119 Office: Rockwell Automation Inc 777 E Wisconsin Ave Ste 1400 Milwaukee WI 53202-5302

O'SHEA, PATRICK JOSEPH, lawyer, electrical engineer; b. Chgo., Apr. 10, 1950; s. John Raymond and Alta M. (Bauert) O'S.; m. Patricia Ann Dalaker, Aug. 11, 1980; children: Erin, Tarah, Brian, Maghan. BSEE, U. Ill., 1972; JD, John Marshall Law Sch., 1979. Bar: Ill. 1979, U.S. Dist. Ct. (no. dist.) Ill. 1979, U.S. Patent Office 1982. Elec. engr. elec. div. City of Chgo. Police Dept., 1976-79; elec. engr. Commonwealth Edison, Chgo., 1972-76; atty. Patricik Mazza & Assocs., Chgo., 1979-80, Richard E. Alexander & Assocs., Chgo., 1980-81; sole pratice Chgo. and Lombard, Ill., 1981—; spl. asst. states atty. Du. Page County, Ill., 1988. Spl. appellate prosecutor, 1989. Elected Rep. committeeman, York Twp., Ill., 1982, chmn. rep. committeeman's orgn., 1996; mem. exec. com. York Twp. Rep. Committeeman's Orgn., vice-chmn., 1992, chmn., 1996; mem. exec. com. DuPage County Bd., 1989—, chmn. landfill com., 1989, 94, vice chmn. legis. com., 1994; commr. Forest Preserve, 1992; gen. counsel Ill. Rep. Party; gen. counsel Ill. Rep. Party. Mem. Ill. Bar Assn., DuPage Bar Assn., Chgo. Bar Assn., Lombard C. of C., Lombard Rotary. Roman Catholic. Avocations: politics, golf, chess. Federal civil litigation, Criminal, Personal injury (including property damage). Home: 1051 S Fairview Ave Lombard IL 60148-4035 Office: 156 S Main St Lombard IL 60148-2628

OSHIMA, MICHAEL W. lawyer; b. Big Rapids, Mich., Apr. 4, 1957; s. Walter W. and Mitsue Oshima. AB, Brown U., 1979; MA, Harvard U., 1984; JD, NYU, 1987. Bar: N.Y. 1988, D.C. 1989. Sr. rsch. asst. Harvard U. John F. Kennedy Sch. Govt., Cambridge, Mass., 1981-84; assoc. Davis Polk & Wardwell, N.Y.C., 1987-90, Arnold & Porter, N.Y.C., 1990-96, ptnr., 1997—. Contbr. articles, reports to profl. publs. Mem. Am. Sociol. Assn., Law and Soc. Assn., N.Y. State Bar Assn., Assn. Bar City N.Y. Banking, Private international, Securities. Office: Arnold & Porter 399 Park Ave Fl 35 New York NY 10022-4690 E-mail: michael_oshima@aporter.com.

OSIS, DAIGA GUNTRA, lawyer; b. Riga, Latvia, July 24, 1943; d. Voldemars and Sandra (Seja) Amatnieks; m. Aivars Osis, Dec. 2, 1967; 1 child, Andre. BA cum laude, CUNY, Bklyn., 1971; JD, U. (Bridgeport) Conn., 1980. Bar: Conn. 1980, U.S. Dist. Ct. Conn. 1981, U.S. Ct. Appeals (2d cir.) 1982, U.S. Supreme Ct. 1984. Assoc. DePiano & Palmesi, Bridgeport, 1980-85; ptnr. Gans, Leo & Osis, Bridgeport, 1985-88, Gans, Osis, Reynolds & Riccio, Bridgeport, 1989-90, Gans, Osis & Reynolds, Bridgeport, 1990-94; pvt. practice law Bridgeport, 1994—. Asst. prof. law U. Bridgeport, 1982-83. Research editor U. Bridgeport Law Review, 1979-80. Mem. Bd. Edn., Trumbull, Conn., 1982-84; bd. dirs. Conn. Inst. of Vocal Arts, Southport, Conn., 1984-87. Mem.: Conn. Bar Assn. Democrat. Lutheran. State civil litigation, Family and matrimonial, Personal injury (including property damage). Home: 175 Middlebrooks Ave Trumbull CT 06611-3016 Office: 325 Reef Rd Ste 212 Fairfield CT 06824 E-mail: osisatty@aol.com.

OSMAN, EDITH GABRIELLA, lawyer; b. N.Y.C., Mar. 18, 1949; d. Arthur Abraham and Judith (Goldman) Udem; children: Jacqueline, Daniel. BA in Spanish, SUNY, Stony Brook, 1970; JD cum laude, U. Miami, 1983. Bar: Fla. 1983, U.S. Dist. Ct. (so. dist.) Fla. 1984, U.S. Dist. Ct. (mid. dist.) Fla. 1988, U.S. Ct. Appeals (11th cir.) 1985, U.S. Supreme Ct. 1987, U.S. Ct. Mil. Appeals 1990; cert. family law mediator Fla. Supreme Ct. Assoc. Kimbrell & Hamann, PA, Miami, 1984-90, Dunn & Lodish, PA, Miami, 1990-93; pvt. practice Miami, 1993-98; shareholder Carlton Fields, Miami, 1998—. Spkr. in field. Adv. com. for Implementation of the Victor Posner Judgement to Aid the Homeless, 1986-89. Recipient Breaking the Glass Ceiling award Ziff Mus., 2000, In the Company of Women award Dade County, 2000, Judge Mattie Belle Davis award, 2000, FAWL's Rosemary Barkett Achievement award, 1997, Outstanding Past Vol. Bar Pres.'s award, 1996; selected for photographic exhibit Florida Women of Achievement, 2000, Top Lawyers So. Fla. Legal Guide, 2001-03; named 100 Women to Watch MIA Metro Mag., 2000. Fellow Am. Bar Found.; mem. ABA (family law, Ho. of Dels. 1998—, standing com. on independence of judiciary 2000—), Fla. Bar Assn. (budget com. 1989-92, 97-98, voluntary bar liaison com. 1989-90, spl. com. on formation of All-Bar Conf. 1988-89, chair mid-yr. conv. 1989, long range planning com. 1988-90, bd. govs. 1991-98, spl. commn. on delivery of legal svcs. to the indigent 1990-92, bus. law cert. com. 1995-96, practice law mgmt. com. 1995-96, chair program evaluation com., 1993-94, exec. com. 1992-93, 96—, rules and bylaws com., 1993-94, vice-chair disciplinary rev. com. 1994-95, investment com. 1994-95, vice-chair rules com. 1994-95, All-Bar Conf. chair 1997, chair grievance mediation com. 1997-99, pres.-elect 1998-99, pres. 1999-2000, exec. coun. family law sect. 2001-, vice-chair legis. 2001-2002), Dade County Bar Assn. (fed. ct. rules com. 1985-86, chmn. program com. 1988-91, 96-97, exec. com. 1987-88), Fla. Assn. Women's Lawyers Assn. (Dade County chpt. bd. dirs. 1984-85, treas. 1985-86, v.p. 1986-87, pres. 1987-88), Fla. Assn. Women Lawyers (v.p. 1988-89, pres. 1989-90), Fla. Bar Found. (dir. 1998—), Nat. Conf. Women's Bar Assn. (dir. nat. conf. 1990-91), Fla. Acad. Trial Lawyers, Dade County Trial Lawyers Assn., Nat. Conf. Bar Pres., So. Conf. Bar Pres., Leading Attys. (bd. dirs. 2000—). General civil litigation, Commercial, contracts (including sales of goods; commercial financing), Family and matrimonial. Office: Carlton Fields PA 100 SE 2nd St Ste 4000 Miami FL 33131-2148 E-mail: eosma@carltonfields.com.

OSSTYN, RANDOLPH BEIER, lawyer; b. Royal Oak, Mich., Apr. 24, 1943; s. Alouis and Doris Helen (Finnie) O.; children: Alicia Anne, Neal Randolph; m. Carrie Ann Wood, May 3, 1997. BA, MA, U. Mich.; JD magna cum laude, U. Detroit. Bar: U.S. Supreme Ct. 1980; bd. cert. creditors rights specialist. Tchr., dept. head Detroit Bd. Edn., 1969-76; founding ptnr. Osstyn, Bays, Ferns & Spray, Marquette, Mich., 1979—. Lectr. collection law in Mich., 2002. Treas. Prince of Peach Luth. Ch., Marquette, 1978-81; founding mem. Save the Janzen Com., Marquette, 1983-85; mem ch. council Messiah Luth. Ch., Marquette, 1984-85; bd. dirs. Marquette Mountain Racing Team, 1982-90, pres., 1986-89. Mem. ABA, Wis. Bar Assn., Mich. Bar Assn., Comml. Law League Am. Democrat. Avocations: skiing, running, bridge. Commercial, consumer (including collections, credit). Home: 43 White Oak Dr Marquette MI 49855-9450 Office: Osstyn Bays Ferns & Quinnell 419 W Washington St Ste 500 Marquette MI 49855-4322

O'STEEN, VAN, lawyer; b. Sweetwater, Tenn., Jan. 10, 1946; s. Bernard Van and Laura Emelyne (Robinson) O.; m. Deborah Ann Elias, May 18, 1974; children— Jonathan Van, Laura Ann. B.A., Calif. Western U., 1968; J.D. cum laude, Ariz. State U., 1972. Bar: Ariz. 1972, U.S. Dist. Ct. Ariz. 1972, U.S. Ct. Appeals (9th cir.) 1973, U.S. Supreme Ct. 1975. Staff atty. Maricopa Legal Aid Soc., Phoenix, 1972-74; atty. Bates & O'Steen, Legal Clinic, Phoenix, 1974-77; atty. O'Steen Legal Clinic, Phoenix, 1977-80; mng. ptnr. Van O'Steen and Ptnrs., Phoenix and Tucson, 1980—; pres. Van O'Steen Mktg. Group, Inc., Phoenix, 1985—. Author numerous self-help legal books. Founding dir. Ariz. Ctr. for Law in the Pub. Interest, 1974-80. Served with USNR, 1963-69. Mem. ABA (chmn. spl. com. delivery legal services 1982-85), Am. Legal Clinic Assn. (pres. 1979), Assn. Trial Lawyers Am. Democrat. Administrative and regulatory, Personal injury (including property damage). Address: 3605 N 7th Ave Phoenix AZ 85013-3638

OSTEEN, WILLIAM L. federal judge; b. 1930; BA, Guilford Coll., 1953; LLB, U. N.C., 1956. With Law Office of W.H. McElwee, Jr., North Wilkesboro, N.C., 1956-58; pvt. practive Greensboro, N.C., 1958-59; with Booth & Osteen, Greensboro, 1959-69; U.S. atty. U.S. Attys. Office, Greensboro, 1969-74; ptnr. Osteen, Adams & Osteen, Greensboro, 1974-91;

fed. judge U.S. Dist. Ct. (mid. dist.) N.C., Greensboro, 1991—. With USAR, 1958-51. Fellow Am. Coll. Trial Lawyers; mem. ABA, N.C. State Bar, N.C. Bar Assn. (mem. and chair subcom. N.C. sentencing commn.), U. N.C. Law Alumni Assn. Office: US Dist Ct PO Box 3485 Greensboro NC 27402-3485*

OSTENDORF, LANCE STEPHEN, lawyer, investor, financial consultant and planner; b. New Orleans, Aug. 16, 1958; 1 child, Christine Marie Ostendorf. BBA summa cum laude, Loyola U., 1976, JD, 1980. Bar: La. 1980, U.S. Dist. Ct. (ea. dist.) La. 1981, U.S. Dist. Ct. La., U.S. Supreme Ct. 1980, U.S. Dist. Ct. (we. and mid. dists.) La. 1983. Owner RCO Internat. Inc., GO Entertainment, Balt./Washington DC, L.A./Orange County, San Diego/Riverside; founder Ostendorf, Tate, Barnett & Wells PLC, Orange County, Calif., Riverside, Houston, Baltimore, Tucson. Treas., CFO La. State U. Med. Ctr. Found., New Orleans, 1992—; lectr. Lorman Ednl. Seminars; bd. dirs. La. State U. Med. Ctr. Found., New Orleans, tech. transfer com.; speaker and tchr. Lorman Ednl. Svcs., Inc. Author: Insurance Law; contbr. articles to profl. jours. Mem. ABA, Fed. Bar Assn., Internat. Bar Assn., La. Bar Assn., Metairie Bar Assn., Maritime Law Assn., Comite Maritime Internat., Assn. for Transp. Law, Trucking Industry Def. Assn., Logistics and Policy, Assn. Average Adjusters of U.S., Jefferson Bar Assn., New Orleans Bar Assn., La. Restaurant Assn., Am. Trial Lawyers Assn., La. Bar Assn., Jefferson Bar Assn., Fifth Cir. Bar Assn., Def. Rsch. Inst., La. Trial Lawyers Assn., Law Def. Lawyers Assn., Houston Mariners Club, Southeastern Adm. Law Inst., St. Thomas Moore Club, La. Notary Soc., Blue Key Honor Soc. Federal civil litigation, Personal injury (including property damage), Transportation. Office: The Poydras Ctr Ste 1460 650 Poydras St New Orleans LA 70130 Fax: 504-527-5111. E-mail: lance.ostendorf@otbw-law.com.

OSTERBERG, EDWARD CHARLES, JR., lawyer; b. Honolulu, Jan. 1, 1942; s. Edward Charles and Emily Julia (Preston) O.; m. Susan Rhea Snider, Aug. 26, 1967; 1 child, Edward Charles III. BA, Northwestern U., 1963, JD cum laude, 1966; LLM in Taxation, So. Meth. U., 1972. Bar: Tex. 1966, Ill. 1966. Assoc. Vinson & Elkins, Houston, 1967-73, ptnr., 1974—. Reporter Internat. Fiscal Assn., Sydney, Australia, 1978, Barcelona, Spain, 1991. Contbr. articles to profl. publs. Mem. ABA (chmn. taxation com.), Houston Bar Assn. (chmn. taxation sect. 1987), Petroleum Club, Metro. Racquet Club. Methodist. Corporate taxation, Estate taxation, Taxation, general. Home: 11222 Wilding Ln Houston TX 77024-5308 Office: Vinson & Elkins LLP 1001 Fannin St Ste 3300 Houston TX 77002-6760 E-mail: eosterberg@velaw.com.

OSTERGAARD, JONI HAMMERSLA, lawyer; b. Seattle, May 26, 1950; d. William Dudley and Carol Mae (Gillett) Hammersla; m. Gregory Lance Ostergaard, May 22, 1976 (div. 1985); 1 child, Bennett Gillett; m. William Howard Patton, Jan. 1, 1988; 1 child, Morgan Hollis; stepchildren: Colin W., Benjamin C. BS, U. Wash., 1972; MS, Purdue U., 1974; JD, U. Wash., 1980. Bar: Wash. 1980, U.S. Dist. Ct. (we. dist.) Wash. 1980, U.S. Ct. Appeals (9th cir.) 1981, U. S. Ct. Claims 1983. Clin. psychol. intern Yale Med. Sch., 1976-77; law clk. U.S. Ct. Appeals (9th cir.), Seattle, 1980-81; assoc. Roberts & Shefelman, Seattle, 1982-86, ptnr., 1987, Foster Pepper & Shefelman, Seattle, 1988-92; sole practitioner Seattle, 1996—. Contbr. articles to profl. jours.; notes and comments editor Wash. Law Rev., 1979-80. Recipient Sophia and Wilbur Albright scholarship U. Wash. Law Sch., 1979-80, law sch. alumni scholarship U. Wash. Law Sch., 1978-79; fellow NIMH. Avocations: gardening, reading. Appellate, Municipal (including bonds), Utilities, public. Fax: 206-725-8121. E-mail: jostergaard@att.net.

OSTERHOUT, RICHARD CADWALLADER, lawyer; b. Abington, Pa., Nov. 16, 1945; s. Robert Edward and Charlotte Leedom (Cadwallader) O.; m. Diane Renee Higgins, Sept. 15, 1982; children: Steven M., Schuyler C., Cody R. BA in History magna cum laude, Pa. State U., 1967; JD, Temple U., 1974. Bar: Pa. 1974, U.S. Dist. Ct. (ea. dist.) Pa. 1974, U.S. Ct. Appeals (3d cir.) 1984. Assoc. Wood & Floge, Bensalem, Pa., 1974-77; pvt. practice Trevose, Pa., 1978-85, Feasterville, Pa., 1985—. Solicitor Zoning Hearing Bd., Hulmeville, Pa., 1983—. Contbr. articles to publs. of various hist. socs. Mem. Langhorne Borough Planning Commn. (Pa.), 1974; candidate Rep. Nat. Conv., 1984. With U.S. Army, 1968-70. Mem. Pa. Bar Assn., Bucks County Bar Assn., Feasterville Business Assn. (treas. 1985, 86, v.p. 1987), Nat. Assn. Outlaw and Lawman History, Inc., Phi Beta Kappa. State civil litigation, Family and matrimonial, General practice. Home: 309 Hemlock Ave Bensalem PA 19020-7331 Office: 1744 Bridgetown Pike Feasterville Trevose PA 19053-2362

OSTERTAG, ROBERT LOUIS, lawyer; b. N.Y.C., June 21, 1931; s. Frederick C. and Lillian (Bishop) O.; m. Ann Mary Flynn, Aug. 28, 1954; children— Thomas J., Daniel V., Debra A. BA, Fordham U., 1953; LL.B., St. John's U., Bklyn., 1956; LL.M., Georgetown U., 1960. Bar: N.Y. 1957, U.S. Dist. Ct. (so. dist.) N.Y. 1969, U.S. Tax Ct. 1965, U.S. Ct. Mil. Appeals 1959, U.S. Supreme Ct. 1960. Atty. office chief counsel IRS, Washington, 1958-60; ptnr. Guernsey, Butts & Walsh, Poughkeepsie, N.Y., 1963-90, Guernsey, Butts, Ostertag & O'Leary, Poughkeepsie, N.Y., 1991-95, Ostertag, O'Leary & Barrett, Poughkeepsie, 1995—; adj. prof. paralegal studies Marist Coll., Poughkeepsie, 1975-91; adj. prof. Fordham U. Sch. of Law, N.Y.C., 1993—. Counsel Agr. Com., N.Y. State Assembly, 1967-68; mem. Gov.'s Jud. Screening Com., 1987-93; counsel to cons. and draftsman of proposed county charters and adminstrv. codes for Sullivan, Fulton, Orange and Onondaga Counties, N.Y., City of Poughkeepsie, N.Y.; mem. 9th Jud. Dist. Grievance Com., 1975-79, 9th Jud. Dist. Med. Malpractice Panel, 1975-91, mem. 9th Jud. Dist. Arbitration Panel, 1980—; mem. Chief Judges Com. on Pro Bono Legal Svc., 1992-93. Trustee Joseph F. Barnard Meml. Law Libr., Poughkeepsie, 1979—; dir. Hudson Valley Philharm. Soc., 1973—76; v.p., dir. High Tor Opera Co., 1967—70; dir. United Fund of Dutchess County, 1973—78; dir. Dutchess County chpt. Am. Heart Assn., 1975—81, 1984—89; trustee Sports Mus. Dutchess County, 1989—93, chmn., 1989—90; dir. Hudson Valley Stadium Corp., 1995—, chair, 1998—; mem. Dutchess County (N.Y.) Charter Commn., 1966—67, Dutchess County Bd. Health, 1964—70, pres., 1966—70; chmn. Dutchess County Charter Revision Task Force, 1979—88; dep. supr. Town of Poughkeepsie, 1976; bd. dirs. Com. for Modern Cts., 1975—99; dir. Std. Gage Co., 1972—88; mem. adv. coun. Pace U. Sch. Law, 1975—84; paralegal adv. coun. Marist Coll., 1975—. Served to capt. JAGC USAF, 1956—58. Recipient Recognition award Cen. Poughkeepsie Exch. Club, 1967, Marist Coll. Pres.'s award, 1991. Mem.: ABA (chmn. conf. of state bar gen. practice leaders of gen. practice sect. 1980—87, mem. coun. 1982—86, ho. of dels. 1985—98, Gavel awards com. 1989—, standing com. on solo and small firm practitioners 1992—95, standing com. on profl. discipline), Dutchess County Bar Assn. (sec. 1969—79, pres. 1984—85), N.Y. State Bar Assn. (ho. of dels. 1973—79, chmn. unlawful practice of law com. 1977—81, chmn. sect. on gen. practice of law 1980—82, ho. of dels. 1980—, chmn. com. on law office econs. and mgmt. 1982, exec. com. 1983—85, com. profl. ethics 1986—90, exec. com. 1986—93, pres. 1991—92, com. profl. ethics 1996—99, chmn. comm. on future of profession 1998, spl. com. on law governing firm structure and operation 1999—, com. profl. ethics 2000—), N.Y. Bar Found., Am. Bar Found., Hudson Valley Estate Planning Coun. (pres. 1965—66, dir. 1969—74), Delta Theta Phi. State civil litigation, Estate planning, Personal income taxation. Home: 5 Pat Dr Poughkeepsie NY 12603-5626 Office: 17 Collegeview Ave Poughkeepsie NY 12603-2406 E-mail: rlodmo@vh.net.

OSTROV, JEROME, lawyer; b. Boston, Dec. 2, 1942; s. Harold S. and Etta (Resnick) O.; m. Roberta S. Baruch, Sept. 3, 1978; children: Rebecca Ann, Max Abraham, Julia Grace. BSBA cum laude, Boston U., 1964; JD, Union U., 1967; LLM in Taxation, NYU, 1968; MPA, Harvard U., 1980. Bar: N.Y. 1968, D.C. 1971, Md. 1991. Mem. Friedlander, Misler, Sloan, Kletzkin & Ochsman PLLC, 1985—; ptnr. N.Y.C., 1968-69; law clk. to presiding judge U.S. Tax Ct., Washington, 1969-71; pvt. practice Washington, 1971-73; dep. assoc. gen. counsel U.S. EPA, Washington, 1973-79; fellow John F. Kennedy Sch. Govt., Harvard U., 1979-80; staff counsel U.S. Ho. of Reps., Washington, 1982-83; pvt. practice Washington, 1983—. Bd. dirs. Am. Assocs. Ben Gurion U. of Negev, N.Y.C. Author: (law treatise) Tax Planning with Real Estate, 2001; contbr. articles. Bd. dirs. Jewish Social Svcs. Agy. Mem. ABA. Democrat. Jewish. Avocations: family, jogging, hiking, skiing, classical music, ballet. Estate planning, Probate (including wills, trusts), Taxation, general. Office: Friedlander Misler Sloan Kletzkin Ochman PLLC 1101 17th St NW Ste 700 Washington DC 20036-4711 E-mail: jostrov@dclawfirm.com.

OSTROVSKY, LAWRENCE ZELIG, lawyer; b. Cleve., June 1, 1956; s. Peter and Yetta Ostrovsky. BA, St. John's Coll., Annapolis, Md., 1978; JD, Lewis and Clark Coll., 1982. Bar: Ohio 1982, Alaska 1983. Assoc. Berger & Kirschenbaum, Cleve., 1982, Birch, Horton, Bittner, Pestinger & Anderson, Anchorage, 1983—87; spl. asst. to the commr. of natural resources Alaska Dept. Natural Resources, Anchorage, 1987—91; assoc. dir. for energy and public lands Alaska Gov. Office, Washington, 1991—94; asst. atty. gen. oil, gas, and mining sect., Alaska Dept. Law, Anchorage, 1994—. Mem. Commonwealth North, Anchorage, 1986, Alaska Bar Assn.(bd. of governors, 1998—, pres. elect, 2003-) Banking, Bankruptcy, Criminal. Office: Alaska Dept Law 1031 W 4th Ave Ste 200 Anchorage AK 99501-1994*

OSTROW, MICHAEL JAY, lawyer; b. Baldwin, N.Y., Apr. 25, 1934; s. Oscar I. and Ethel M. (Morganstern) O.; m. Judith L. Loewenthal, Aug. 25, 1957; children: Thomas L., Kenneth A., Nancy M. BA, Alfred U., 1955; JD, Cornell U., 1958. Bar: N.Y. 1958, U.S. Supreme Ct. 1964, U.S. Dist. Ct. (so. and ea. dists.) N.Y. 1970; diplomate Am. Coll. Family Trial Lawyers. Ptnr. Taylor & Ostrow, Mineola, N.Y., 1961-69, Taylor Atkins & Ostrow, Garden City, N.Y., 1969-96, Ostrow and Taub, Garden City, 1996-2000. Bd. dirs., lectr Advanced Practice Inst. Hofstra Law Sch., Hempstead; lectr. Practicing Law Inst., N.Y.C. Mem. ABA, Acad. Matrimonial Lawyers (pres. N.Y. chpt. 1980-81, sec. nat. acad. 1988-90, nat. v.p. 1990-94, pres.-elect 1995-96, pres. 1996-97), Internat. Acad. Matrimonial Lawyers (bd. govs. 1990-92), Am. Coll. Family Trial Lawyers (diplomate), N.Y. State Bar Assn. (chmn. family law sect. 1976-78, mem. exec. com.), Nassau County Bar Assn. (pres. 1984-85, chmn. judiciary com. 1992-93), Order of Coif, Zeta Beta Tau, Phi Delta Phi. Family and matrimonial. Home: 8 Randolph Dr Dix Hills NY 11746-8308 Office: Schlissel Ostrow Karabatos Poepplein Cender & Fisher PLLC 200 Garden City Plz Suite 301 Garden City NY 11530 E-mail: MJODIX@aol.com.

OSUKA, AKIRA, law educator; b. Yokohama, Japan, Jan. 21, 1934; s. Minoru and Teiko (Ogura) O.; m. Reiko Fujikawa, May 10, 1961; children: Jun, So. BA in Law, Waseda U., Tokyo, 1958, MA in Law, 1960, LLD, 1984. With Waseda U., 1964—, assoc. prof. Sch. Law, 1969-74, prof. Sch. Law, 1974—; vis. scholar Harvard Yencheng Inst., 1985-86; examiner National Legal Examiniation, 1988-94; dir. Inst. Comparative Law, Waseda U., 1994-98; prof. emeritus Northwest U., China, 1997—. Author, editor: Constitutional Theory of the Social State, 1994, State Legal Intervention and Freedom: Comparative Studies on Asian-Oceanic Legal Systems, 2001, Right to a Decent Life, 1977, Lectures on Modern Law, Constitutional Law, 1984; author: Theory of Fundamental Rights to a Decent Life, 1984, Social State and Constitutional Law, 1992; co-editor: The Annual Typical Statute Book, 1981—; Commentary on Japanese Constitutional Adjudications, vols. 1-3, 1993-94, Dictionary of Constitutional Law, 2001. Mem. Japan Assn. for Studies of Constnl. Law (pres. 1997-99), Japan Pub. Law Assn. (dir.), Internat. Assn. of Constnl. Law (dir.). Avocations: golf, ice skating, traveling. Home: 6-10-10 Jindaijikita-machi Chyofu-shi Tokyo 182-0011 Japan Office: Waseda U Sch Law 1-6-1 Nishiwaseda Shinjuku-ku Tokyo 169-8050 Japan

O'SULLIVAN, JUDITH ROBERTA, lawyer, author, artist; b. Pitts., Jan. 6, 1942; d. Robert Howard and Mary Olive (O'Donnell) Gallick; m. James Paul O'Sullivan, Feb. 1, 1964; children: Kathryn, James. BA, Carlow Coll., 1963; MA, U. Md., 1969, PhD, 1976; JD, Georgetown U., 1996. Editor Am. Film Inst., Washington, 1974—77; assoc. program coord. Smithsonian Resident Assocs., Washington, 1977—78; dir. instl. devel. Nat. Archives, Washington, 1978—79; exec. dir. Md. State Humanities Coun., Balt., 1979—81, 1982—84, Ctr. for the Book, Libr. of Congress, Washington, 1981—82; dep. asst. dir. Nat. Mus. Am. Art, Washington, 1984—87, acting asst. dir., 1987—89; pres., CEO The Mus. at Stony Brook, NY, 1989—92; exec. dir. Nat. Assn. Women Judges, Washington, 1993; clk. Office Legal Adviser U.S. Dept. State, Washington, 1994—96; trial atty. Atty. Gen.'s honors program U.S. Dept. Justice, 1996—; spl. asst. U.S. atty. U.S. Dist. (ea. dist.) Va., 1998—; asst. U.S. atty. U.S. Dist. Ariz., Tucson, 1999—2000. Summer assoc. Piper & Marbury, Balt., 1995; chair Smithsonian Women's Coun., Washington, 1988-89. Author: The Art of the Comic Strip, 1971 (Gen. Excellence award Printing Industry Am.); Workers and Allies, 1975; (with Alan Fern) The Complete Prints of Leonard Baskin, 1984, The Great American Comic Strip, 1991; editor Am. Film Inst. Catalogue: Feature Films, 1961-70, 1974-77; mem. editl. bd. Am. Film Inst. Catalog, 1979-1990. Trustee Child Life Ctr., U. Md., College Pk., 1971-74; chair Smithsonian Women's Coun., 1988-89. Univ. fellow U. Md., 1967-70, Mus. fellow, 1970-71, Smithsonian fellow Nat. Collection Fine Arts, Washington, 1972-73. Mem.: Mystery Writers of Am., D.C. Bar Assn., Md. Bar Assn. Avocations: landscape painting, mystery writing. Home: # 606 7111 Woodmont Ave Chevy Chase MD 20815 Office: US Dept Justice Domestic Security Sect Criminal Divsn Washington DC 20530 E-mail: Judith.O'Sullivan@usdoj.gov.

O'SULLIVAN, LYNDA TROUTMAN, lawyer; b. Oil City, Pa., Aug. 30, 1952; d. Perry John and Vivian Dorothy (Schreffler) Troutman; m. P. Kevin O'Sullivan, Dec. 15, 1979; children: John Perry, Michael Patrick. BA, Am. U., 1974; JD, Georgetown U., 1978, postgrad., 1982-83. Bar: D.C. 1978. Ptnr. Perkins Coie, Washington, 1985-92, Fried, Frank, Harris, Shriver & Jacobson, Washington, 1993-97, Miller & Chevalier, Washington, 1997—. Mem. adv. bd. Fed. Contracts Report, 1991-97, Govt. Contract Costs, Pricing & Acctg. Report, 1997-99; mem. faculty govt. contracts program George Washington U., 1993-99; lectr. in field. Contbr. articles to profl. jours. Fellow Am. Bar Found.; mem. ABA (chair truth in negotiations com. 1991-94, chair acctg., cost and pricing com. 1996-2000, coun. sect. pub. contract law 1993-95). Federal civil litigation, Government contracts and claims. Office: Miller & Chevalier 655 15th St NW Ste 900 Washington DC 20005-5799 E-mail: losullivan@milchev.com.

O'SULLIVAN, THOMAS J. lawyer; b. New Haven, Apr. 7, 1940; s. Thomas J. and Marjorie (Hession) O'S.; m. Anita Brady, Aug. 10, 1968; children: Kathleen, Margaret, Mary Tess, Anne Elizabeth. BA in History, Yale U., 1961; LLB, Harvard U., 1966. Bar: Conn. 1966, U.S. Dist. Ct. Conn. 1967, N.Y. 1967, U.S. Dist. Ct. (so. and ea. dists.) N.Y. 1967, U.S. Ct. Appeals (2d cir.) 1971, U.S. Supreme Ct. 1971, U.S. Dist. Ct. (no. dist.) N.Y. 1976. Assoc. White & Case, N.Y.C., 1966-74, ptnr., 1974—. 1st lt. U.S. Army, 1961-63. Mem. ABA, N.Y. State Bar Assn., Assn. of Bar of City of N.Y., Internat. Bar Assn. Clubs: Milbrook (Greenwich, Conn.); Yale (N.Y.C.). Federal civil litigation, State civil litigation, Private international. Home: 56 Hillside Rd Greenwich CT 06830-4835 Office: White & Case Bldg Ll 1155 Avenue of The Americas New York NY 10036-2787

OTERO, BRIAN V. lawyer; b. N.Y.C., Oct. 26, 1963; s. Philip V. and Maureen A. Otero; m. M. Natasha Ferens, July 25, 1987; children: Conor K., Ian W., India A., Madison R. BA, U. Va., 1985; JD, U. Chgo., 1990. Bar: Va. 1990, N.Y. 2002, U.S. Dist. Ct. (ea. and we. dists.) Va. 1990, U.S. Ct. Appeals (4th cir.) 1990, U.S. Dist. Ct. (so. dist.) N.Y. 2002. Assoc. Hunton & Williams, Richmond, Va., 1990—98, ptnr., 1998—2001, N.Y.C., 2001—. Dir. John Marshall Found., Richmond, 1993—98. Mem.: ABA, Ctrl. Va. Legal Aid Soc. (vol. housing lawyer 1991—99), Federalist Soc. (pres. Richmond chpt. 1991—93), Va. Bar Assn. (exec. coun. young lawyers divsn. 1994—99, judiciary com. 1998—2001), U. Va. Club of N.Y. Republican. Roman Catholic. Avocations: music, soccer, hiking, computers. Product liability, Libel, Commercial, contracts (including sales of goods; commercial financing). Office: Hunton & Williams 200 Park Ave 143d Fl New York NY 10166 E-mail: botero@hunton.com.

OTIS, ROY JAMES, lawyer; BA, Stanford (Calif.) U., 1968; JD, Golden Gate U., 1980. Bar: Calif. 1980, U.S. Dist. Ct. (no. dist.) Calif. 1980; cert. specialist in workman's compensation. Ptnr. Gearheart & Otis, Pleasant Hill, 1996—. Mem. Calif. Applications Atty. Assn. (pres. no. Calif. chpt., 1994-96, bd. govs. 1997—), Assn. of Trial Lawyers of Am. (workplace injury litigation group sect. 1996—). Democrat. Workers' compensation. Office: Gearheart & Otis 367 Civic Dr Ste 17 Pleasant Hill CA 94523-1935

O'TOOLE, AUSTIN MARTIN, lawyer; b. New Bedford, Mass., Oct. 5, 1935; s. John Brian, Jr. and Helen Veronica O'T.; m. Valerie Sherlock O'Toole; children: Erin Ann, Austin Martin Jr. BBA, Coll. Holy Cross, 1957; JD, Georgetown U., 1963. Bar: N.Y. 1965, D.C. 1963, Tex. 1975. Law clk. to judge U.S. Ct. Appeals, Washington, 1962-63; assoc. White & Case, N.Y.C., 1963-74; sr. v.p., sr. counsel, sec. Coastal Corp., Houston, 1974—2001. Bd. editors Georgetown Law Jour., 1962-63. Bd. dirs. Nat. Coun. on Alcoholism and Drug Dependency, Inc., 2001—; charter mem., certificated mediator Inst. for Responsible Dispute Resolution, Houston, 2000—; bd. dirs. Houston Marathon Com., 1973—2002. Officer USMC, 1957—60. Mem. ABA, Am. Soc. Corp. Secs. (bd. dirs. 1982-85), State Bar of Tex., Houston Bar Assn. (past chmn. corp. counsel sect. 1979-80), Am. Arbitration Assn. (comml. com.). Corporate, general, Finance, Mergers and acquisitions. Home: 2200 Willowick (10-H) Houston TX 77027 Office: 509 Nineteenth St Galveston TX 77550 E-mail: austinotoole@msn.com.

OTOROWSKI, CHRISTOPHER LEE, lawyer; b. Teaneck, N.J., Nov. 20, 1953; s. Wladyslaw Jerzy and Betty Lee (Robbins) O.; m. Shawn Elizabeth McGovern, Aug. 4, 1978; children: Kirsten, Hilary. BSBA cum laude, U. Denver, 1974, MBA, JD, U. Denver, 1977. Bar: Wash. 1977, Colo. 1977, U.S. Dist Ct. (we. dist.) D.C. 1977, U.S. Dist. Ct. (we. dist.) Wash. 1978. Asst. atty. gen. Wash. State Atty. Gen., Spokane, 1978-79; atty. Bassett, Gemson & Morrison, Seattle, 1979-81; pvt. practice Seattle, 1981-88; atty. Sullivan, Golden & Otorowski, Seattle, 1988-91, Morrow & Otorowski, Bainbridge Island, 1996—; pvt. practice Morrow and Otorowski, Bainbridge Island, Wash., 1991-96. Contbr. articles to profl. jours. Bd. dirs. Bainbridge Edn. Support Team, Bainbridge Island, 1991-97. Mem. Fed. Bar Assn. We. Dist. Wash. (sec. 1979-82, trustee 1990-93), Wash. State Trial Lawyers Assn. (bd. govs. 1991-93), Assn. Trial Lawyers Am., Seattle Tennis Club, Seattle Yacht Club. Avocations: photography, sailing. General civil litigation, Personal injury (including property damage). Office: 298 Winslow Way W Bainbridge Island WA 98110 E-mail: clo@medilaw.com.

OTT, ANDREW EDUARD, lawyer; b. Vancouver, B.C., Can., Sept. 23, 1962; s. Eduard Karl and Elfriede Marie (Petryc) O. BA in English, Seattle U., 1986, JD, 1989; D (hon.), U. Graz, Austria, 1986. Bar: Wash. 1990, U.S. Dist. Ct. (we. dist.) Wash. 1992. Contract atty. Keller Rohrback, Seattle, Lieff Cabraser Heimann & Bernstein, San Francisco, Jamin, Ebell, Schmitt & Mason, Kodiak, Alaska, 1989—. Cons. OMNI Tech. Engring., Bothell, Wash., 1986-2000. Actor musicals and theater, 1992, 93, 95, 96, 98, 99, 2000; musician Cmty. Orch. and Jazz, 1990-2000. Trustee Kodiak Arts Coun. Mem. ABA, ATLA, Nat. Assn. Self-Employed. Avocations: snow skiing, soccer, bike riding, running, acting. General civil litigation, Environmental, General practice. Office: Jamin Ebell Schmitt & Mason 323 Carolyn Ave Kodiak AK 99615-6348 E-mail: Andrew@JESMKOD.com.

OTTEN, ARTHUR EDWARD, JR., lawyer, corporate executive; b. Buffalo, Oct. 11, 1930; s. Arthur Edward Sr. and Margaret (Ambrusko) O.; m. Mary Therese Torri, Oct. 1, 1960; children: Margaret, Michael, Maureen Staley, Suzanne Hoodecheck, Jennifer Shankle. BA, Hamilton Coll., 1952; JD, Yale U., 1955. Bar: N.Y. 1955, Colo. 1959. Assoc. Hodges, Silverstein, Hodges & Harrington, Denver, 1959-64; ptnr. Hodges, Kerwin, Otten & Weeks (predecessor firms), Denver, 1964-73, Davis, Graham & Stubbs, Denver, 1973-86; gen. counsel Colo. Nat. Bankshares, Inc., 1973-93; mem. Otten, Johnson, Robinson, Neff & Ragonetti, P.C., Denver, 1986—. Rec. sec. Colo. Nat. Bankshares, Inc., Denver, 1983-93; gen. counsel Regis U., Denver, 1994-99; mediator Denver Dist. Ct., 1997-99; com. bd. Centura Health, Denver, St. Anthony Hosps., Denver. Bd. dirs. Cath. Charities Archdiocese of Denver, 1998—. Lt. USN, 1955-59. Mem. ABA, Colo. Bar Assn., Denver Bar Assn., Am. Arbitration Assn. (panel arbitrators, large complex case panel, mediator panel), Nat. Assn. Securities Dealers (bd. arbitrators), Law club, Univ. Club, Denver Mile High Rotary (pres. 1992-93), Phi Delta Phi. Republican. Roman Catholic. Avocations: hiking, biking, church activities. Banking, Corporate, general, Education and schools. Home: 3774 S Niagara Way Denver CO 80237-1248 Office: Otten Johnson Robinson Neff & Ragonetti PC 950 17th St Ste 1600 Denver CO 80202-2828 E-mail: aeotten@ojrnr.com.

OTTINGER, RICHARD LAWRENCE, dean emeritus; b. N.Y.C., Jan. 27, 1929; s. Lawrence and Louise (Lowenstein) O.; children from previous marriage: Ronald, Randall, Lawrence, Jenny Louise; m. June Godfrey. BA, Cornell U., 1950; LLB, Harvard U., 1953. Assoc. Cleary, Gottlieb, Friendly & Hamilton, N.Y.C., 1955-56; ptnr. William J. Kridel, Law Firm, N.Y.C., 1956-60; second staff mem., dir. programs Peace Corps, L.Am., 1961-64; mem. 89th-91st Congresses, 1965-71, 94th-98th Congresses, 1975-85; prof. Pace U. Sch. Law, White Plains, N.Y., 1985—, dean, 1994—99, dean emeritus, 1999—. Bd. dirs. Environ. and Energy Study Inst., Washington. Author: Environmental Costs of Electricity, 1990. Contract mgr. Internat. Coop. Adminstrn., 1960-61; organizer Grassroots to Action, 1971-73. Office: Pace U Sch Law 78 N Broadway White Plains NY 10603-3710 E-mail: rottinger@law.pace.edu.

OTTO, BYRON LEONARD, lawyer, state administrator; b. Battle Creek, Mich., Oct. 4, 1940; s. Henry John and Mildred Alice (Wagner) O. BBA, St. Edward's U., 1964, MBA, 1979; JD, U. Tex., 1968. Bar: U.S. Dist. Ct. (we. dist.) 1976. Staff atty. State Welfare Dept., Austin, Tex., 1968-75; sole practice Austin, Tex., 1975-77; assoc. James R. Sloan, Austin, Tex., 1978-79; adminstr. State Comptroller, Austin, Tex., 1980—; ret., 2000. Author articles and monographs. St. Edward's U. scholar, Austin, 1978. Mem. ABA, Tex. Bar. Democrat. Roman Catholic. Home: 4604 S Lamar Blvd, Apt C-109 Austin TX 78745-1356

OUDERKIRK, MASON JAMES, lawyer; b. Des Moines, Feb. 1, 1953; s. Mason George and Florence Astor (Lowe) O.; m. Kari Aune Hormel, May 28, 1983; 1 child, Mason Christopher. BA, Drake U., 1975, JD, 1978. Bar: Iowa 1978, U.S. Dist. Ct. (so. dist.) Iowa 1978, U.S. Ct. Appeals (8th cir.); lic. real estate broker. Assoc. M.G. Ouderkirk Law Office, Indianola, Iowa, 1978-79; ptnr. Ouderkirk Law Firm, Indianola, 1979-96; sr. mem. Ouderkirk, Ouderkirk & Dougherty, P.L.C., Indianola, 1996-98; proprietor Ouderkirk Law Firm, Indianola, Iowa, 1998—; pres. Avanti Realty Co. (formerly Landmark Real Estate, Ltd.), Indianola, 1978—2002, Avanti Builders Co., Indianola, 1991—2002. Mem. Vol. Lawyers Project of Iowa, 1987-93. Mem. Indianola Police Retirement Bd., 1983-88; instr. Eric Heintz Black Belt Acad., 1988-93, Indianola Parks and Recreation Dept., 1988-93; mem. Nominating Commn., Warren County Assoc. Dist. Ct., 1999—; mem. Jud. Nominating Commn. for 5A Jud. Dist. of Iowa, 2002--. Mem. ABA, Iowa Bar Assn. (pub. rels. com. 1989-94, family law com. 1989-90), Warren County Bar Assn. (sec., treas. 1985-89, v.p. 1989-90, pres. 1990-92), 5th

Jud. Dist. Bar Assn. (sec., treas. 1995), Assn. Trial Lawyers Am., Iowa Trial Lawyers Assn. Episcopalian. Avocations: fishing, hunting, gardening. Family and matrimonial, Personal injury (including property damage), Probate (including wills, trusts). Office: Ouderkirk Law Firm 108 S Howard St PO Box 156 Indianola IA 50125-0156 Home: PO Box 156 Indianola IA 50125-0156 Fax: 515-961-0304. E-mail: ouderkirklaw@aol.com.

OVERGAARD, FINN, lawyer; b. Copenhagen, Nov. 6, 1958; Law Degree, U. Copenhagen, 1982. Bar: High Cts. Denmark 1987, Supreme Ct. Denmark 1993. Counsel legal dept. Copenhagen Handelsbank, 1982—85; lawyer Lett & Co., Attys. at Law, Copenhagen, 1985—, ptnr., 2002—. Asst. prof. corp. law faculty law U. Copenhagen, 1986—. Co-author: International Liability of Corporate Directors, 1993. Mem.: Danish Banking and Fin. Soc., Danish Corp. Law Soc., Danish Bar and Law Soc. Commercial, contracts (including sales of goods; commercial financing), Corporate, general, Mergers and acquisitions. Office: Lett & Co 4 Radhuspladsen 1550V Copenhagen Denmark E-mail: fov@lettco.dk.

OVERGAARD, MITCHELL JERSILD, lawyer; b. Chgo., Jan. 9, 1931; s. Kristen Mikkelsen and Rose Eunice (Jersild) O.; m. Joan Marquardt, Aug. 2, 1958; children: Wade, Kristin Bond, Neil. BA, U. Chgo., 1950, JD, 1953. Bar: Ill. 1957, U.S. Supreme Ct. 1975. Assoc. Dale, Haffner & Grow, Chgo., 1957-63; ptnr. Overgaard & Davis, Chgo., 1963-2000, of counsel, 2001—. Dir. Cmty. Bank of Homewood-Flossmoor, Homewood, Ill., 1973—83. Trustee Village of Homewood, 1965-69, 85-95; commr. Homewood-Flossmoor Park Dist., 1969-77; past pres., bd. dirs. Family Svcs. and Mental Health Ctr. of South Cook County, Homewood Youth Coun.; bd. dirs. Ill. Philharm. Orch., 1992-95, South Star Svcs., 1998—. With U.S. Army, 1953-56. Mem.: Rotary. Mem. Reformed Ch. in America (elder) Home: 19137 Loomis Ave Homewood IL 60430-4431 Office: Overgaard & Davis 134 N La Salle St Chicago IL 60602-1086

OVERHOLT, HUGH ROBERT, lawyer, retired army officer; b. Beebe, Ark., Oct. 29, 1933; s. Harold R. and Cuma E. (Hall) O.; m. Laura Annell Arnold, May 5, 1961; children: Sharon, Scott. Student, Coll. of Ozarks, 1951-53; BA, U. Ark., 1955, LL.B., 1957. Bar: Ark. 1957. Commd. 1st lt. U.S. Army, 1957, advanced through grades to maj. gen., 1981; chief Criminal Law Div., JAG Sch., Charlottesville, Va., 1971-73; chief personnel, plans and tng. Office of JAG, U.S. Army, Washington, 1973-75; staff judge adv. XVIII Airborne Corps, Ft. Bragg, N.C., 1976-78; spl. asst. for legal and selected policy matters Office of Dep. Asst., 1978-79; asst. judge adv. gen. for mil. law office of JAG, Washington, 1979-81, asst. judge adv. gen., 1981-85, judge adv. gen, 1985-89; atty. Ward & Smith, New Bern, N.C., 1989—. Notes and comment editor Ark. Law Rev, 1956-57. Decorated Army Meritorious Service medal with oak leaf cluster, Army Commendation medal with 2 oak leaf clusters., Legion of Merit, Def. Meritorious Service medal, D.S.M. Mem. ABA, N.C. Bar Assn., Ark. Bar Assn., Assn. U.S. Army, Delta Theta Phi, Omicron Delta Kappa, Sigma Pi. Presbyterian. Office: Ward and Smith 1001 College Ct New Bern NC 28562-4972

OVERTON, GEORGE WASHINGTON, lawyer; b. Hinsdale, Ill., Jan. 25, 1918; s. George Washington and Florence Mary (Darlington) O.; m. Jane Vincent Harper, Sept. 1, 1941; children— Samuel Harper, Peter Darlington, Ann Vincent AB, Harvard U., 1940; JD, U. Chgo., 1946. Bar: Ill. 1947, U.S. Dist. Ct. (no. dist.) Ill. 1947, U.S. Supreme Ct. 1951. Assoc. Pope & Ballard, Chgo., 1946-48; ptnr. Overton & Babcock, Chgo., 1948-51, Taylor, Miller, Busch & Magner, Chgo., 1951-60; pvt. practice Chgo., 1960; sr. prin. Overton, Schwartz & Fritts and predecessor cos., Chgo., 1961-81; of counsel Wildman Harrold Allen & Dixon, Chgo., 1981—. Bd. dirs. Ill. Inst. Continuing Legal Edn., 1974-81, chmn. 1980-81; mem. com. on profl. responsibility of Ill. Supreme Ct., 1986-97, chmn., 1990-93. Contbr. articles to profl. jours. Ill. reporter Cornell U. Nat. Legal Ethics Project, 1981—; bd. dirs. Open Lands Project, 1961—, pres., 1978—81; bd. dirs. Canal Corridor Assn., 1981—, chmn., 1981—84. 1st lt. U.S. Army, 1942—45. Mem. ABA (mem. com. on counsel responsibility 1985—, com. on nonprofit corps., adv. coun. ethics 2000), Ill. Bar Assn., Chgo. Bar Assn. (bd. mgrs. 1981-83), Assn. of Bar of City of N.Y., Am. Law Inst., Univ. Club. Office: Wildman Harrold Allen & Dixon 225 W Wacker Dr Chicago IL 60606-1224 E-mail: overton@wildmanharold.com.

OWEN, ALLAN JACOBS, lawyer; b. Ft. Hood, Tex., Aug. 20, 1952; s. William J. and Pauline (Jacobs) O.; m. Linda Kay Whitney, Oct. 15, 1988. BS with high honors, U. Calif.-Davis, 1974; JD with distinction, U. of Pacific, 1979. Bar: Calif. 1979, U.S. Dist. Ct. (ea. dist.) Calif. 1979, U.S. Ct. Appeals (9th cir.) 1981. Assoc. Friedman, Collard Poswall & Thompson, Sacramento, 1979-84; ptnr. Friedman, Collard & Poswall, Sacramento, 1984-94, Owen & Owen, 1994-96; mng. ptnr. Ordas, Timmons, Owen & Owen, Sacramento, 1996-99, Timmons, Owen & Owen, Sacramento, 2000—. Mem. ABA, Consumer Attys. of Calif., Sacramento Consumer Attys., Sacramento County Bar Assn. Democrat. Jewish. Avocations: golf, reading. Personal injury (including property damage), Product liability. Office: Timmons Owen & Owen 906 G St Ste 610 Sacramento CA 95814-1812 E-mail: ajowen@saclaw.net.

OWEN, H. MARTYN, lawyer; b. Decatur, Ill., Oct. 23, 1929; s. Honore Martyn and Virginia (Hunt) O.; m. Candace Catlin Benjamin, June 21, 1952; children: Leslie W., Peter H., Douglas P. AB, Princeton U., 1951; LLB, Harvard U., 1954. Bar: Conn. 1954, U.S. Ct. Appeals (2d cir.) 1961, U.S. Dist. Ct. Conn. 1962, U.S. Supreme Ct. 1963, U.S. Dist. Ct. Vt. 1965. Assoc. Shipman & Goodwin, Hartford, Conn., 1958-61, ptnr., 1961-94, of counsel, 1995-96. Mem. Simsbury (Conn.) Zoning Bd. Appeals, 1961-67, Simsbury Zoning Commn., 1967-79; sec. Capitol Region Planning Agy., 1965-66; bd. dirs. Symphony Soc. Greater Hartford, 1967-73; trustee Renbrook Sch., West Hartford, Conn., 1963-72, treas. 1964-68, pres., 1968-72, hon. life trustee, 1972—; trustee Simsbury Free Libr., 1970-84; pres. Hartford Grammar Sch., 1987-98, trustee; corporator Hartford Hosp., 1984-96; vestry St. Alban's Ch., Simsbury, 1988-94; warden, vestry St. Paul's Ch., Brunswick, Maine, 1999-2001. Lt. USNR, 1954-57. Mem. ABA, Conn. Bar Assn., Hartford County Bar Assn., Am. Law Inst., Princeton (N.Y.C.) Club, Ivy Club (Princeton, N.J.). Democrat. Episcopalian. Antitrust, Corporate, general, Municipal (including bonds). Home: 80 Matthew Dr Brunswick ME 04011-3275

OWEN, LANGDON TALBOT, JR., lawyer; b. Pitts., Oct. 6, 1951; s. Langdon Talbot Owen and Kathryn Agnes (Kropp) Pymm; m. Ann Nebeker, June 16, 1981; children: Brooke, Lisa, Clark, Kate. AB, U. Calif.-Berkeley, 1973; JD, U. Utah, 1977. Bar: Utah 1977, U.S. Dist. Ct. Utah 1977, U.S. Ct. Appeals (10th cir.) 1978, U.S. Tax Ct. 1978. Pvt. practice, Salt Lake City, 1977; assoc. Reynolds and Arnold, Salt Lake City, 1978-80, Watkiss & Saperstein, Salt Lake City, 1980-92; ptnr. Parsons, Kinghorn, Peters, Salt Lake City, 1992—. Comment editor, Contbr. Utah Law Rev., 1976-77. Mem.: ABA, Ctr. for Interant. Legal Studies, Am. Arbitration Assn., Salt Lake County Bar Assn., Utah Bar Assn., Am. Health Lawyers Assn. Democrat. Estate planning, Health, Probate (including wills, trusts). Office: Parsons Kinghorn Peters 111 E Froadway Fl 11 Salt Lake City UT 84111 E-mail: lto@pklawyers.com.

OWEN, PRISCILLA RICHMAN, state supreme court justice; BA, Baylor U., JD, 1977. Bar: Tex. 1978, U.S. Ct. Appeals (4th, 5th, 8th and 11th cirs.). Former ptnr. Andrews & Kurth, L.L.P., Houston; justice Supreme Ct. Tex., Austin, 1995—. Liaison to Tex. Legal Svcs. for Poor Spl. Supreme Ct. Tex., Supreme Ct. Adv. Com. on Ct.-Annexed Mediations. Named Young Lawyer of Yr., Baylor U., Outstanding Young Alumna. Office: Supreme Ct Tex PO Box 12248 Austin TX 78711-2248

OWEN, RICHARD, federal judge; b. N.Y.C., Dec. 11, 1922; s. Carl Maynard and Shirley (Barnes) O.; m. Lynn Rasmussen, June 6, 1960; children: Carl R., David R., Richard. AB, Dartmouth Coll., 1947; LLB, Harvard U., 1950; MusD (hon.), Manhattan Sch. Music, 1989. Bar: N.Y. 1950. Practiced in, N.Y.C., 1950-74; assoc. Willkie Owen Farr Gallagher & Walton, 1950-53, Willkie Farr Gallagher Walton & Fitzgibbon, 1958-60; pvt. practice, 1960-65; ptnr. Owen & Aarons, 1965-66, Owen & Turchin, 1966-74; asst. U.S. atty. So. Dist. N.Y., 1953-55; trial atty. antitrust div. U.S. Dept. Justice, 1955-58; U.S. dist. judge So. Dist. N.Y., 1974-89, sr. judge, 1989—. Asst. prof. N.Y. Law Sch., 1951-53; adj. prof. law Fordham U. Sch. Law, 1996—. Composer, librettist operas Dismissed with Prejudice, 1956, A Moment of War, 1958, A Fisherman Called Peter, 1965, Mary Dyer, 1976, The Death of the Virgin, 1980, Abigail Adams, 1987, Tom Sawyer, 1989, Sadie Thompson, 1997. Trustee Manhattan Sch. Music, N.Y.C.; founder, bd. dirs. Maine Opera Assn., 1975-85; pres., bd. dirs. N.Y. Lyric Opera Co. 1st lt. USAAC, 1942-45. Decorated D.F.C. with oak leaf cluster, Air medal with 3 oak leaf clusters. Mem. ASCAP, Century Assn., Chelsea Yacht Club. Republican. Mem. Soc. Of Friends. Office: US Dist Ct US Courthouse Foley Sq New York NY 10007-1501

OWEN, ROBERT DEWIT, lawyer; b. St. Louis, Nov. 15, 1948; s. Kenneth Campbell Owen and Mary Elenor (Fish) Luebbers; m. Rebecca Roberts Baxter, June 4, 1977; children: Abigail Mary, James Roy, Charlotte Grace. BA, Northwestern U., 1970; JD cum laude, U. Pa., 1973. Assoc. Sullivan & Cromwell, N.Y.C., 1973-81; ptnr. Towne, Dolgin, Furlaud, Sawyier & Owen, N.Y.C., 1981-83, Owen & Fennell, N.Y.C., 1983-87, Owen & Davis, N.Y.C., 1987—2002, Fulbright & Jaworski, LLP, N.Y.C., 2002—. Instr. Nat. Inst. Trial Advocacy, Boulder, Colo., 1988—; faculty mem. ABA Nat. Inst. 1992, 93. Bd. dirs. St. Christopher's-Jennie Clarkson Child Care Svcs., Dobbs Ferry, N.Y., 1991-97. Mem. Assn. Bar City N.Y., Fed. Bar Coun., Nat. Assn. Securities Dealers (bd. arbitrators 1985—), Nat. Futures Assn. (bd. arbitrators 1999—), Colonial Springs Club (pres. 1986-94), India House. Episcopalian. Avocations: boating, running. General civil litigation, Commercial, contracts (including sales of goods; commercial financing), Oil, gas, and mineral. Office: Fulbright & Jaworski LLP 666 5th Ave New York NY 10103-3198

OWEN, ROBERTS BISHOP, lawyer, arbitrator; b. Boston, Feb. 11, 1926; s. Roberts Bishop and Monica Benedict (Burrell) O.; m. Kathleen Comstock von Schrader, Aug. 27, 1966; children— David Roberts, Lucy Leffingwell, William Atreus. Student, Dartmouth Coll., 1943-44; AB cum laude, Harvard U., 1948, LL.B. cum laude, 1951; Dip.C.L.S., Cambridge U., Eng., 1952. Bar: D.C. 1952, U.S. Ct. Appeals (D.C. cir.) 1953, U.S. Supreme Ct. 1958. Assoc. Covington & Burling, Washington, 1952-60, ptnr., 1960-79, 81—; the legal advisor U.S. Dept. State, Washington, 1979-81. Sr. advisor Sec. of State former Yugoslavia, 1995; arbitrator Fedn. Bosnia and Herzegovina, 1995; mem. Permanent Ct. Arbitration, The Hague, The Netherlands, 1980—86, 1993—98; mem. arbitration panel Internat. Ctr. for Settlement of Investment Disputes, 1995—; chair bd. dirs. Internat. Human Rights Law Group, 1996—99; mem. Claims Resolution Tribunal for Dormant Accounts in Switzerland, 1998—2000; sr. U.S. negotiator U.S.-Can. Pacific Salmon Treaty dispute, 1998; vice chair, sr. claims judge Claims Resolution Tribunal , 2001—02. Served to ensign USN, 1943-46. Fulbright scholar, 1951-52; recipient Disting Honor award Dept. of State, 1981, Sec. of State Disting. Svc. award, 1996, Sec. of Defense's medal for outstanding pub. svc., 1996. Fellow Am. Coll. Trial Lawyers; mem. ABA, Council Fgn. Relations, Am. Soc. Internat. Law (exec. council 1981-85). Clubs: Royal Ocean Racing (London); Metropolitan (Washington). Antitrust, Federal civil litigation, Private international. Office: Covington & Burling PO Box 7566 1201 Pennsylvania Ave NW Washington DC 20004

OWENS, BETTY RUTH, lawyer; b. Texas City, Tex., Dec. 21, 1951; d. Marvin Lee Jr. and Ellen Frances (Nunnally) O.; m. Robert Foster Geary, Oct. 1, 1994. BS, La. State U., 1973, MA, 1975; JD with high honors, U. Tex., 1988. Bar: Tex., U.S. Dist. Ct. (so. dist.) Tex. 1989, U.S. Ct. Appeals (5th cir.) 1989, U.S. Dist. Ct. (we. dist.) Tex. 1999. Ptnr. Vinson & Elkins LLP, Houston, 1988—, dir. atty. devel., 2002—. Author: (with others) ABA Antitrust Law Developments, 4th edit., ABA Annual Review of Antitrust Law Developments, 1992-95; editor ABA Antitrust Summary Judgment Newsletter, 1996-98. Mem. adv. com. Seniors Place, 1994—98, mem. pers. com., 1999—2001; trustee St. Luke's United Meth. Ch., Houston, 1998—2000, chair com. on women's ministry, 2002—; dir. St. Luke's United Meth. Ch. Found., 2002—. Recipient U. Tex. Sch. Law Faculty Service Award, 2001. Mem. ABA (vice chair civil practice and procedure com., antitrust sect. 1993-98, v. chair books and treatises com. 2000-2001), Am. Law Inst., Tex. Bar Found., Houston Bar Found. Avocations: reading, cooking, travel. Antitrust, Appellate, General civil litigation. Office: Vinson & Elkins LLP 1001 Fannin St Ste 2300 Houston TX 77002-6760 E-mail: bowens@velaw.com.

OWENS, DENNIS JAMES CAMPBELL, lawyer; b. Kansas City, Mo., Dec. 4, 1944; s. James Charles and Josephine Augusta (Wright) O.; m. Cathy Diane Campbell, Dec. 28, 1968; children: James Campbell, Mollie Kathleeen, Mary Theda, Sean Padraic Washington. BA, Rockhurst Coll., 1967; JD, U. Notre Dame, 1975. Bar: Mo. 1975, U.S. Dist. Ct. (we. dist.) Mo. 1975, U.S. Tax Ct. 1976, U.S. Ct. Claims 1976, U.S. Ct. Appeals (8th and D.C. cirs.) 1976, U.S. Supreme Ct. 1978, U.S. Ct. Internat. Trade 1983, U.S. Air Force Ct. Mil. Rev. 1983, U.S. Ct. Mil. Appeals 1983, U.S. Ct. Appeals (D.C. cir.) 1983, U.S. Ct. Appeals (6th and 11th cirs.) 1985, U.S. Ct. Appeals (9th cir.) 1986, U.S. Ct. Appeals (5th cir.) 1987, U.S. Ct. Appeals (3d cir.) 1988, U.S. Ct. Appeals (7th cir.) 1989, U.S. Ct. Appeals (4th cir.) 1991, U.S. Ct. Appeals (2d cir.) 1992, U.S. Dist. Ct. (ea. dist.) Mo. 1997, U.S. Dist. Ct. Kans. 1998, U.S. Ct. Appeals (1st cir.) 2002. Law clk. to chief justice Supreme Ct. of Mo., Jefferson City, 1975-76; sole practice Kansas City, 1976—. Editor-in-chief Notre Dame Jour. of Legis., 1974-75; author: Missouri Appellate Courts Research Manual, 1976; editor: Missouri Appellate Practice & Extraordinary Remedies, 4th edit., 1989; contbr. articles to law revs. Bd. govs. Citizens Assn. Kansas City, 1976, Mo. Bar, 1997-99; trustee (mid-Am. chpt.) Nat. Multiple Sclerosis Soc., Kansas City, 1977; bd. dirs. NCCJ, Kansas City, 1978; vice chmn. Human Rels. Commn. Kansas City, 1979-82; bd. dirs. Rockhurst Coll. Alumni Assn., 1977-79, 1984-87; ambassador Mo. Colls. Fund, Kansas City, 1982-83, chmn. bd. dirs. Coop. Social Svcs., Kansas City, 1983-87; asst. scoutmaster Boy Scouts Am., Kansas City, 1983-2002; pres. Friends of Kansas City Pub. Library, 1984-88, gen. chmn. Alliance for Better Libraries, Kansas City, 1986-88; hon. consul Repub. of Austria for Mo. and Kans., 1987-93, for Kans. and Ea. Mo., 1993—; bd. visitors Ave Maria Law Sch., Ann Arbor, Mich, 1996—; presdl. elector, Mo., 2000. 1st lt. USMC, 1968-71, Vietnam. Recipient Meritorious Achievement award Mo. Libr. Assn., 1985, Disting. Svc. award Greater Kansas City Jaycees, 1980, Jefferson award for Outstanding Cmty. Svc., Am. Inst. for Pub. Service, 1988, Steve Harvey Human Rights Hero award Justice Campaign Am., 2001, Outstanding Citizenship award SAR Del. Crossing chpt., 2002; named Outstanding Young Missourian, Mo. Jaycees, 1980, Tchr. of Yr., U. Mo.-Kansas City Dental Sch., 1980. Fellow: Am. Acad. Appellate Lawyers; mem.: ABA (8th cir. editor Cir. Ct. Newsletter 1983—87, editor-in-chief Appellate Practice Jour. 1988—, Mo. chmn. appellate practice com., Outstanding Editor award 2000—01), Assn. Bar of U.S. Ct. Appeals for 8th Cir. (bd. dirs. 2002—), Am. Soc. Writers on Legal Subjects (SCRIBES), Nat. Lawyers Assn. (chmn. appellate practice sect. 1997—), Assn. Bar of U.S. Ct. Appeals for 10th Cir. (pres. 2002—), Lawyers Assn. Kansas City (Judge James A. Moore award 2002), Kansas City Met. Bar Assn. (chmn. appellate com. 1984—85), Kansas City (Mo.) Bar Assn., Notre Dame Law Assn. (chmn. Mo. chpt.), Mo. Bar Assn., Federalist Soc. Law and Policy Studies, Native Sons Kansas City, U.S. Supreme Ct. Hist. Soc., Notre Dame Club (pres.), K.C. Republican. Roman Catholic. Appellate, Constitutional. Home: 1115 Valentine Rd Kansas City MO 64111-3821 Office: 1100 Main St Ste 1900 Kansas City MO 64105-5176

OWENS, ROBERT PATRICK, lawyer; b. Spokane, Wash., Feb. 17, 1954; s. Walter Patrick and Cecile (Phillippay) O.; children: Ryan Barry, Meghan Jane. BA, Wash. State U., 1976; JD, Gonzaga U., 1981; LLM in Admiralty Law, Tulane U., 1983. Bar: Wash. 1982, Alaska 1984, U.S. Dist. Ct. (ea. dist.) Wash. 1982, U.S. Dist. Ct. Alaska 1984, U.S. Ct. Appeals (5th cir.) 1983. Assoc. Groh, Eggers & Price, Anchorage, 1983-88; mng. atty. Taylor & Hintze, Anchorage, 1988-90; Anchorage office mgr. Copeland, Landye, Bennett and Wolf, Anchorage, 1990-99; prin. Law Offices of Robert P. Owens, PC, Anchorage, 2000—. V.p. bd. dirs. Hope Cmty. Resources, Inc., 1999-2001, pres., 2001-2003. Coord. supplies Insight Seminars, Anchorage, 1985-86. Mem. ABA (dist. 27 rep. young lawyers div. 1988-90), Alaska Bar Assn., Wash. State Bar Assn., Anchorage Bar Assn. (pres. 1991-92, v.p. 1990-91, pres. young lawyers sect. 1986-88), Alaska Fly Fishers, Phi Alpha Delta. Roman Catholic. Avocations: fishing, photography, skiing, softball. Admiralty, Commercial, contracts (including sales of goods; commercial financing), Environmental. Office: Law Offices Robert P Owens PC 310 K St Ste 200 Anchorage AK 99501 E-mail: rpowens@alaska.com.

OWENS, RODNEY JOE, lawyer; b. Dallas, Mar. 7, 1950; s. Hubert L. and Billie Jo (Foust) O.; m. Sherry Lyn Bailey, June 10, 1972; 1 child, Jonathan Rockwell. BBA, So. Meth. U., 1972, JD, 1975. Bar: Tex. 1975, U.S. Dist. Ct. (no. dist.) Tex. 1975, U.S. Tax Ct. 1975, U.S. Ct. Appeals (5th cir.) 1975. Assoc. Durant & Mankoff, Dallas, 1975-78, ptnr., 1978-83, Meadows, Owens, Collier, Reed, Cousins & Blau, Dallas, 1983—. Contbr. articles to profl. jours. Baptist. Estate planning, Estate taxation, Taxation, general. Home: 6919 N Jan Mar Dr Dallas TX 75230-3111 Office: Meadows Owens Collier Reed 901 Main St Ste 3700 Dallas TX 75202-3725 E-mail: rowens@meadowsowens.com.

OWENS, SUSAN, state supreme court justice; b. Kinston, N.C., Aug. 19, 1949; BA, Duke U., 1971; JD, U. N.C., Chapel Hill, 1975. Bar: Oreg. 1975, Wash. 1976. Judge Dist. Ct., Western Clallam County, 1981—2001; justice Wash. State Supreme Ct., 2001—. Mem.: Dist. and Mcpl. Ct. Judges' Assn. (bd. dirs., sec.-treas., v.p., pres.-elect). Office: PO Box 40929 Olympia WA 98504-0929

OWENS, WILBUR DAWSON, JR., federal judge; b. Albany, Ga., Feb. 1, 1930; s. Wilbur Dawson and Estelle (McKenzie) O.; m. Mary Elizabeth Glenn, June 21, 1958; children: Lindsey, Wilbur Dawson III, Estelle, John. Student, Emory U., 1947-48; JD, U. Ga., 1952. Bar: Ga. 1952. Mem. firm Smith, Gardner & Owens, Albany, 1954-55; v.p., trust officer Bank of Albany, 1955-59; sec.-treas. Southeastern Mortgage Co., Albany, 1959-65; asst. U.S. atty. Middle Dist. Ga., Macon, 1962-65; assoc., then ptnr. Bloch, Hall, Hawkins & Owens, Macon, 1965-72; judge U.S. Dist. Ct. for Mid. Dist. Ga., Macon, 1972—, now sr. U.S. dist. judge. Served to 1st lt., JAG USAF, 1952-54. Mem. State Bar Ga., Macon Bar Assn., Am. Judicature Soc., Phi Delta Theta, Phi Delta Phi. Clubs: Rotarian, Idle Hour Golf and Country. Republican. Presbyterian. Office: US Dist Ct PO Box 65 Macon GA 31202-0065

OWLES, PETER GARY, lawyer; b. Christchurch, New Zealand, Feb. 6, 1963; m. Michele Hollis; children: Samuel, Katie. LLB, Auckland U., 1984. Bar: barrister and solicitor High Ct. of New Zealand; solicitor Eng. and Wales. Lawyer Clifford Chance, London, 1991-94, Buddle Findlay, Auckland, New Zealand, 1987-91, ptnr., 1995—. Mem. Inter Pacific Bar Assn. (chair banking, finance and securities com.). Corporate, general, Finance, Mergers and acquisitions. Office: Buddle Findlay 188 Quay St Auckland New Zealand E-mail: peter.owles@buddlefindlay.com.

OWNBY, JERE FRANKLIN, III, lawyer; b. Chicago Heights, Ill., Oct. 1, 1956; s. Jere Franklin Jr. and Emogene (Stephens) O.; m. Melissa Cooley, Mar. 17, 1990. BA, U. Tenn., 1986, JD, 1991. Bar: Tenn. 1991. Assoc. Law Offices of Peter G. Angelos, Knoxville, Tenn., 1991-2000, The Neal Law Firm, Knoxville, Tenn., 2000—02; pvt. practice, 2002—. Mem. Order of Barristers, William B. Spong Invitational Moot Ct. Team. Mem. ABA, Assn. Trial Lawyers Am., Am. Inn of Ct., Tenn. Bar Assn., Knoxville Bar Assn., Tenn. Trial Lawyers Assn., Omicron Delta Epsilon, Pi Sigma Alpha. Democrat. Avocations: gardening, raising dogs, the Life Training program. Personal injury (including property damage), Product liability, Workers' compensation. Home: 3902 Glenfield Dr Knoxville TN 37919-6635 Office: PO Box 51930 Knoxville TN 37950-1930

OXMAN, DAVID CRAIG, lawyer; b. Summit, N.J., Mar. 10, 1941; s. Jacob H. and Kathryn (Grear) O.; m. Phyllis Statter; children— Elena, Lee AB, Princeton U., 1962; LL.B., Yale U., 1969. Bar: N.Y. 1970, N.J. 1974, U.S. Dist. Ct. (so. and ea. dists.) N.Y. 1974, U.S. Ct. Appeals (2d cir.) 1974, U.S. Tax Ct. 1977, U.S. Supreme Ct. 1974. Assoc. Davis Polk & Wardwell, N.Y.C., 1970-76, ptnr., 1977-95, sr. counsel, 1995—. Served with USN, 1962-66 Fellow Am. Coll. Trust and Estate Counsel; mem. ABA, N.Y. State Bar Assn., Assn. of Bar of City of N.Y. Probate (including wills, trusts). Office: Davis Polk & Wardwell 450 Lexington Ave New York NY 10017-3982

OZ, YILMAZ, lawyer; b. Ankara, Turkey, Apr. 10, 1930; s. Hilmi and Zuhtiye (Muslim) O.; m. Nihal Ipek, Nov. 29, 1951; children: F. Simin, Y. Sinan, Selmin. LLB, U. Ankara, 1951; LLM, Yale U., 1952. Bar: Turkey 1956. Atty.-at-law, Ankara, 1956—. Panelist Ctr. European Legal Studies, U. Cambridge, Eng., 1994. Editor: English-Turkish Dictionary of Legal Terms, 2002; co-editor: (chpt.) Comparative Report on Force Majeure in Western Europe (Turkey), 1982; translator: Quotations from Ataturk, 1981; reviser (law directory) Martindale-Hubbell Law Directory, 1986—; contbr. articles to profl. jours. Recipient Ataturk's Centennial award State Min., Ankara, 1982. Mem. Ankara Bar Assn., World Jurist Assn., Yale Law Sch. Alumni Assn., Turkish-Am. Assn. (pres. 1965-74), Rotary (Ankara club pres. 1966-67, internat. svc. consultative com. 1967). Avocations: historical research, tennis, skiing. Commercial, contracts (including sales of goods; commercial financing), Oil, gas, and mineral, Private international.

PACE, NICHOLAS JOSEPH, lawyer; b. Cleve., Ohio, Oct. 10, 1970; s. Nicholas Joseph Pace and Mary Catherine Cihon; m. Liane Rose Liguori, Aug. 30, 2002. BS in Acctg./Fin., Miami U., Ohio, 1993; MBA, JD, U. Richmond, 1996. Bar: Va. 1996, Calif. 2001. Cons. Ernst & Young LLP, Richmond, Va., 1996—98; assoc. LeClair Ryan PC, Richmond, 1998—2000; sr. assoc. Morrison & Foerster LLP, Palo Alto, Calif., 2000—03, CarMax Inc, 2003—. Mem.: ABA, Calif. Bar Assn., Va. Bar Assn. Corporate, general, Mergers and acquisitions, Corporate taxation. Office: CarMax Inc 4900 Cox Rd Glen Allen VA 23060

PACE, ROSA WHITE, lawyer; b. Borger, Tex., Nov. 5, 1932; d. John Herron and Anna Mae (Caldwell) White; m. M. Carroll Pace, Jan. 3, 1968; children: Ann Catherine, Virginia Gale, Mary Jane. BA, William Jewell Coll., 1953; JD, U. Tex., 1956. Bar: Tex. 1956. Ptnr. White & White Attys., Borger, 1956-62, White, White & White Attys., Borger, 1962-65; pvt. practice Borger, 1966—. Co-author: Borger, a History, Hutchinson County History, 1983. Chmn. Hutchinson County Hist. Commn., 1985-94. Recipient Professionalism award Coll. of State Bar of Tex., 1996. Mem. ABA, State Bar Assn. Tex., Borger Bar Assn., DAR (local regent 1975-76), Beta Sigma Phi (women of yr. 1978). General practice, Probate (including wills, trusts), Personal income taxation. Office: 431 Deahl St Borger TX 79007-4113

PACE, STANLEY DAN, lawyer; b. Dayton, Ohio, Dec. 10, 1947; s. Stanley Carter and Elaine (Cutchall) P.; m. Judy Roehm, Sept. 8, 1973; children: Stanley Carter, Barbara Roehm. BA, Denison U., Granville, Ohio, 1970; JD, U. Toledo (Ohio), 1975. Bar: U.S. Dist. Ct. (so. dist.) Ohio 1975, U.S. Dist. Ct. (no. dist.) Ohio 1977, U.S. Ct. Appeals (6th cir.) 1975. Atty. ARMCO Steel Corp., Middletown, Ohio, 1975-77; assoc. Spieth, Bell, McCurdy & Newell, Cleve., 1977-82, dir., 1982—, co-mng. dir., 1987—. Bd. mem. Indsl. Rels. Rsch. Assn., Cleve., 1985. Bd. pres. Judson Retirement Community, Cleve., 1985; bd. mem. Arthritis Found. N.E. Ohio, Cleve., 1984, Western Res. Hist. Soc., 1998. Mem. ABA, Ohio Bar Assn., Greater Cleve. Bar Assn., The Country Club, Pepper Pike Club, Tavern Club, Rolling Rock Club. Labor (including EEOC, Fair Labor Standards Act, labor-management relations, NLRB, OSHA). Office: Spieth Bell McCurdy & Newell 2000 Huntington Bldg Cleveland OH 44115

PACE, THOMAS M. lawyer; b. Mesa, Ariz., Feb. 5, 1952; s. Lemuel Max and Ann (Green) P.; m. Vi Garrett Pace, Jan. 24, 1981; children: Melanie, Brittany. BA, Stanford U., 1973; JD, U. Ariz., 1976. Bar: Ariz.; cert. real estate specialist. Assoc. Martin, Feldhacker & Freidl, Phoenix, 1976-77, Trew & Woodford, Phoenix, 1977-78; ptnr. Hecker, Phillips & Hooker, Tucson, 1978-88; sr. ptnr. O'Connor Cavanagh, Tucson, 1988-95; pvt. practice Law Office of Thomas M. Pace, Tucson, 1995—. Mem. Mayor's Housing Task Force, Tucson, 1993; bd. dirs. Tucson Urban League, 1986-96; chmn. So. Ariz. Homebuilders Polit. Action Com., 1995, 96. Mem. So. Ariz. Homebuilders (tech. com), Stanford Club So. Ariz. Democrat. Corporate, general, Property, real (including real estate development, water), Securities. Office: 2525 E Broadway Blvd Ste 102 Tucson AZ 85716-5398 E-mail: tpace2@mindspring.com.

PACHECO, HUMBERTO, JR., lawyer; b. San José, Costa Rica, Jan. 10, 1940; s. Humberto and Julia (Alpizar) P.; m. Cynthia Ortiz, Mar. 7, 1975; children: Humberto III, Miguel. JD, U. Costa Rica, 1964; MCL, U. Miami, Fla., 1971; postgrad., Harvard U., 1972, 76. Costa Rican Bar: 1965. With Pacheco Coto, San José, 1959-64, sr. ptnr., 1964—. Legal adviser to pres. Costa Rica, sec. state fgn. affairs, 1970-78; scholar in residence Law Sch., U. San Diego, 1984; dir. Internat. Fin. Adv. Corp. Contbr. articles to profl. jours. Mem. Internat. Bar Assn., Inter-Am. Bar Assn., Costa Rican Bar Assn., Assn. of Bar of City of N.Y., Internat. Fiscal Assn., Am. C. of C. Costa Rica, Union Club, Costa Rica Country Club. Office: PO Box 6610 1000 San José Costa Rica

PACK, STUART HARRIS, lawyer; b. N.Y.C., Nov. 2, 1950; s. Irving and Ruth (Blum) P.; m. Robin Carol Levine, Nov. 28, 1976; children: Jennifer, Allison. BA, U. Rochester, 1972; JD, Georgetown U., 1975. Bar: Colo. 1975, U.S. Dist. Ct. Colo. 1975, U.S. Ct. Appeals (10th cir.) 1977. Ptnr. Sherman & Howard, Denver, 1975-91, Cox, Buchanan & Pack, P.C., Denver, 1991; pvt. practice Denver, 1992-96; ptnr., litigation dept. Gorsuch Kirgis LLC, Denver, 1997—. Mem. ATLA, Def. Rsch. Inst., Phi Beta Kappa. General civil litigation, Insurance, Personal injury (including property damage). Office: Gorsuch Kirgis LLC 1515 Arapahoe St Ste 1000 Denver CO 80202-2120 E-mail: spackl@gorsuch.com.

PACKARD, STEPHEN MICHAEL, lawyer; b. Hartford, Conn., Nov. 26, 1953; s. Charles David and Anne (Moriarty) P.; m. Eileen Mary Joyce, May 23, 1981; children: Stephen Michael Jr., Sheila Marie, James Charles, Brian Joseph. BS, Fairfield U., 1975; JD magna cum laude, N.Y. Law Sch., 1981. Bar: N.Y. 1981, U.S. Dist. Ct. (ea. and so. dists.) N.Y. 1981, U.S. Dist. Ct. Conn. 1983, Conn. 1984. Assoc. Mudge, Rose, Guthrie, Alexander & Ferdon, N.Y.C., 1981-83, Wiggin & Dana, New Haven, 1983-87; atty. Aetna Life & Casualty, Hartford, 1987-96; ptnr. Accenture, N.Y.C., 1996—. Adj. prof. law U. Bridgeport Law Sch., Conn., 1987. Bd. dirs. New Haven Literacy vols., 1985-87. Mem. Conn. Bar Assn., N.Y.C. Bar Assn., Fed. Bar Coun., Conn. Def. Lawyers Assn. Roman Catholic. General civil litigation, Insurance. Office: Accenture One Financial Plz Hartford CT 06103

PACKENHAM, RICHARD DANIEL, lawyer; b. Newton, Pa., June 23, 1953; s. John Richard and Mary Margaret (Maroney) P.; m. Susan Patricia Smillie, Aug. 20, 1983. BA, Harvard U., 1975; JD, Boston Coll., 1978; LLM in Taxation, Boston U., 1985. Bar: Mass. 1978, Conn. 1979, U.S. Dist. Ct. Mass. 1979, U.S. Dist. Ct. Conn. 1979, U.S. Ct. Appeals (1st cir.) 1981, U.S. Supreme Ct. 1985. Staff atty. Conn. Superior Ct., 1978-79; ptnr. McGrath & Kane, Boston, 1979-94, Packenham, Schmidt & Federico, Boston, 1994—. Mem. ABA, Mass. Bar Assn., Conn. Bar Assn., Boston Bar Assn., Mass CLE (faculty). Clubs: Harvard (Boston). Democrat. Roman Catholic. State civil litigation, Family and matrimonial. Home: 1062 North St Walpole MA 02081-2307 Office: Packenham Schmidt & Federico 10 St James Ave Boston MA 02116

PACKERT, G(AYLA) BETH, retired lawyer; b. Corpus Christi, Tex., Sept. 25, 1953; d. Gilbert Norris and Virginia Elizabeth (Pearce) P.; m. James Michael Hall, Jan. 1, 1974 (div. 1985); m. Richard Christopher Burke, July 18, 1987; children: Christopher Geoffrey Makepeace Burke Packert, Jeremy Eliot Marvell Packert Burke. BA, La. Tech. U., 1973; MA, U. Ark., 1976; postgrad., U. Ill., 1975-81, JD, 1985. Bar: Ill. 1985, U.S. Dist. Ct. (no. dist.) Ill. 1985, U.S. Ct. Appeals (7th cir.) 1987, Va. 1988, U.S. Dist. Ct. (we. dist.) Va. 1989. Assoc. Jenner & Block, Chgo., 1985-88; law clk. U.S. Dist. Ct. Va. (we. dist.), Danville, 1988-89; asst. commonwealth atty. Commonwealth of Va., Lynchburg, Va., 1989-95; pvt. practice Lynchburg, 1995—2002; ret., 2002. Notes and comments editor U. Ill. Law Rev., 1984-85. Mem. Phi Beta Kappa. General civil litigation, Criminal, Family and matrimonial. Home: 3900 Faculty Dr Lynchburg VA 24501-3110

PADDISON, DAVID ROBERT, lawyer; b. Savannah, Ga., May 15, 1949; s. Richard Milton and Josephine Butler (Bowles) P.; m. Frances M. Phares (div. Mar. 1995); children: Hunt, Brian, Margery; m. Jane Ingrid Caddell, Mar. 30, 1996; 1 child, Ethan David. BSBA, La. State U., 1971; JD, Tulane U., 1976. Bar: La. 1976; U.S. Dist. Ct. (ea. dist.) 1976; U.S. Ct. Appeals (5th cir.) 1976; bd. cert. specialist in family law La. State Bar Assn., 1995; U.S. Tax. Ct. 2001. Asst. dist. atty. Dist. Atty.'s Office, Covington, La., 1983-86, New Orleans, La., 1978-83; pvt. practice Covington, La., 1986—. Advisor Contemporary Arts Ctr., New Orleans, 1978-79; clin. advisor Tulane U. Sch. Law, New Orleans, 1980-81; spl. cons. Dist. Atty.'s Office, New Orleans, 1981. Legal advisor Christ Episcopal Church (sch. planning com., lector, usher). Mem. Covington Bar Assn., La. Trial Lawyers Assn., ATLA. Republican. Episcopalian. Avocations: golf, sailing, snow skiing. Criminal, Family and matrimonial, Personal injury (including property damage). Office: PO Box 1830 Covington LA 70434-1830

PADGETT, GREGORY LEE, lawyer; b. Greenfield, Ind., May 9, 1959; s. William Joseph and Anna Katherine (Hyre) Padgett; m. Ruth Anne Dorworth, June 5, 1982; children: Joshua David, William Joel, Emily Xiao Lei. BA summa cum laude, DePauw U., 1981; JD, Northwestern U., 1984. Bar: Ill., U.S. Dist. Ct. (no. dist.) Ill. 1984, U.S. Ct. Appeals (7th cir.) 1986, Ind. 1988, U.S. Dist. Ct. (no. & so. dists.) Ind. 1988. Assoc. Kirkland & Ellis, Chgo., 1984-88, Baker & Daniels, Indpls., 1988-92; ptnr. Johnson, Lawhead, Buth & Pope, P.C., Indpls., 1992-2000; of counsel Barnes & Thornburg, Indpls., 2000—. Adj. prof. Butler U., 1989-90. Mem. Marion County Prosecutor's Rev. Task Force, Indpls., 1991; pres., bd. dirs. Theatre on the Square, Indpls., 1994-95; mem. coun. Hope Evang. Covenant Ch., 1992-96; bd. dirs. Meridian St. Found., 1994-96. Mem. Ind. State Bar Assn., Indpls. Bar Assn. (exec. com. alternative dispute resolution sect.), Christian Legal Soc., Phi Beta Kappa. Avocations: theatre arts, vocal music, hiking, writing. Estate planning, Probate (including wills, trusts), Securities. Office: Barnes & Thornburg 11 S Meridian St Indianapolis IN 46204 E-mail: greg.padgett@btlaw.com.

PADGETT, NANCY WEEKS, law librarian, consultant, lawyer; b. Newberry, S.C., June 3, 1932; d. Price John and Caroline (Weeks) P.; m. David Lazar, Aug. 6, 1953 (div. Feb. 1994). BS, Northwestern U., 1953; MLS, U. Md., 1972; JD, Georgetown U., 1977. Bar: D.C. 1977. Asst. law libr. U.S. Ct. Appeals for D.C., Washington, 1972—74, supervisory law libr., 1974—84, circuit libr., 1984—. Mem. ALA, D.C. Bar Assn., Am. Assn. Law Librs. Home: 5301 Duvall Dr Bethesda MD 20816-1873 Office: US Ct Appeals for DC Cir Judges' Libr 5518 US Court House Washington DC 20001-5618

PADILLA, JAMES EARL, lawyer; b. Miami, Fla., Dec. 28, 1953; s. Earl George and Patricia (Bauer) P. BA, Northwestern U., 1975; JD, Duke U., 1978. Bar: Ill. 1978, U.S. Ct. Appeals (5th and 7th cir.) 1978, U.S. Supreme Ct. 1981, Colo. 1982, U.S. Ct. Appeals (10th cir.) 1982, D.C. 1985, N.Y. 1989. Assoc. Mayer, Brown & Platt, Chgo. and Denver, 1978-84, ptnr. Denver, 1985-87, N.Y.C., 1988-96; private investor, 1996—. Contbg. author: Mineral Financing, 1982, Illinois Continuing Legal Education, 1993. Mem. ABA, Ill. Bar Assn., D.C. Bar Assn., Colo. Bar Assn., N.Y. State Bar Assn. Avocation: golf. Banking, Bankruptcy, Commercial, contracts (including sales of goods; commercial financing).

PADOVAN, LIRA RENARDINI, lawyer; b. São Paulo, Brazil, Aug. 23, 1975; d. Sergio and Maria Cecilia (Prenardini) Padovan. LLB, U. of Sao Paulo, Sch. of Law, 1997; LLM, Columbia U., Sch. of Law, 2002. Bar: Sao Paulo 1998, NY 2002. Mem. Araujo e Policastro, Sao Paulo; fgn. assoc. Curtis Mallet Prevost, Colt., NYC; assoc. Araujo e Policastro, legal trainee. Olin fellow, Ctr. for Law and Economics, Columbia Law Sch., 2001—02. Administrative and regulatory, Antitrust, Banking, Corporate, general, Intellectual property, Mergers and acquisitions, Oil, gas, and mineral, Trademark and copyright. Office: Araujo e Policastro Advogados AV Brig Faria Lima 2094 11th Fl 01452-9 São Paulo Brazil Office Fax: 5511 3078 6120. Business E-Mail: lpadovan@araujopolicastro.com.br.

PAGANO, EUGENE SALVATORE ROONEY, lawyer; b. N.Y.C., Apr. 29, 1951; s. Vito Venero and Virginia Marie (Rooney) P. BA summa cum laude, Spring Hill Coll., Mobile, Ala., 1973; JD, U. Va., 1976; LLM, Harvard U., 1983. Bar: N.Y. 1977, D.C. 1977, U.S. Dist. Ct. (so. dist.) N.Y. 1978, U.S. Dist. Ct. (ea. dist.) N.Y. 1979, U.S. Ct. Appeals (D.C. cir.) 1981, U.S. Ct. Appeals (2d cir.) 1985, U.S. Supreme Ct. 1987. Law clk. to Hon. Stanley S. Harris D.C. Ct. Appeals, Washington, 1976-77; self-employed. Contbr. articles to profl. jours. Mem. Nassau County Bar Assn. (vice chair appellate practice com. 2000—, Pres.'s award 1991). Roman Catholic. Avocation: history. Appellate, General civil litigation. E-mail: jurisconsultus@earthlink.net.

PAGE, ALAN C. state supreme court justice; b. Canton, Ohio, Aug. 7, 1945; s. Howard F. and Georgianna (Umbles) P.; m. Diane Sims, June 5, 1973; children: Nina, Georgianna, Justin, Khamsin. BA, U. Notre Dame, 1967; JD, U. Minn., 1978; LLD, U. Notre Dame, 1993; LLD (hon.), St. John's U., 1994, Westfield State Coll., 1994, Luther Coll., 1995, U. New Haven, 1999. Bar: Minn. 1979, U.S. Dist. Ct. Minn. 1979, U.S. Supreme Ct. 1988. Profl. athlete Minn. Vikings, Mpls., 1967-78, Chgo. Bears, 1978-81; assoc. Lindquist & Vennum, Mpls., 1979-85; former atty. Minn. Atty. Gen.'s Office, St. Paul, 1985-92; assoc. justice Minn. Supreme Ct., St. Paul, 1993—. Cons. NFL Players Assn., Washington, 1979-84. Commentator Nat. Pub. Radio, 1982-83. Founder Page Edn. Found., 1988. Named NFL's Most Valuable Player, 1971, one of 10 Outstanding Young Men Am., U.S. Jaycees, 1981; named to NFL Hall of Fame, 1988, Coll. Football Hall of Fame, 1993. Mem. ABA, Minn. Bar Assn., Hennepin County Bar Assn., Minn. Minority Lawyers Assn., Minn. Assn. Black Lawyers. Avocations: running, biking. Office: 423 Minnesota Judicial Ctr 25 Rev Dr Martin Luther King Jr Blvd Saint Paul MN 55155-1500

PAGE, ERIC MICHAEL, lawyer; b. Wash., Feb. 9, 1953; s. Mack and Sylvia Page; m. Mary Foye, Aug. 19, 1978; children: Kiersten Elizabeth, Alexander Kenneth. AB, Cornell U., 1975; JD, U. Richmond, 1978. Bar: Va. 1978, U.S. Dist. Ct. (ea. dist.) Va. 1979, U.S. Ct. Appeals (4th cir.) 1979, U.S. Supreme Ct. 1984. Asst. atty. gen. Va. Atty. General's Office, Richmond, Va., 1979—83; assoc. Wallerstein, Goode & Dobbins, Richmond, Va., 1983—85; ptnr. Thorsen Page & Marchant, Richmond, 1985—95, LeClair Ryan, Glen Allen, Va., 1996—. Chair Va. State Bar Adminstrv. Law Sect., Richmond, 1997—98. Musician: (violinist, concertmaster) Richmond Philharmonic, 1982—97. Parish pastoral coun. St. Bridget's Ch., Richmond, Va., 2002—; commr. Richmond Neighborhood Soccer Assn., Richmond, Va., 1990—95. Scholar Cornell Nat. scholar, Cornell U., 1971—75. Mem.: St. Thomas More Soc., Westwood Racquet Club. Roman Catholic. Avocations: tennis, golf, violin. Administrative and regulatory, Communications, Utilities, public. Home: 4318 Fauquier Ave Richmond VA 23227 Office: LeClair Ryan 4201 Dominion Blvd Ste 200 Glen Allen VA 23060 Office Fax: 804-783-7682. E-mail: epage@leclairryan.com.

PAGE, JACK RANDALL, lawyer; b. Waco, Tex., Aug. 1, 1956; s. Jack Bennett and Mary Elizabeth (Cobbs) P.; m. Shirley Jean Hull, Aug. 5, 1978; children: Anna Christine, Sara Elaine. BBA magna cum laude, Baylor U., 1977, JD, 1980. Bar: Tex. 1980, U.S. Tax Ct. 1985, U.S. Dist. Ct. (we. dist.) Tex. 1987, U.S. Ct. Appeals (5th cir.) 1989; cert. in tax law Tex. Bd. Legal Specialization; CPA, Tex. Acct. Allie B. Gates Jr., CPA, Waco, 1975-78; assoc. Pakis, Giotes, Page & Burleson, P.C., Waco, 1980-86, ptnr., 1986—. Chmn. exploring sales team Heart O' Tex. coun. Boy Scouts Am., 1983, dist. chmn., 1984—85, v.p., 1986—88, coun. commr., 1989—91, coun. pres., 1991—94, asst. coun. commr., 1994—95, v.p., 1995—96, mem. adv. coun. Longhorn Coun., 2000—02, dist. chmn., 2002—; mem. adv. coun. dept. acctg. Baylor U., 1993—2002; co-chmn. Food for Families, 1995—. Recipient Dist. Award of Merit Heart O' Tex. coun. Boy Scouts Am., 1985, Silver Beaver award 1993, Commrs. Key, 1994. Life Fellow Tex. Bar Found.; mem. AICPA, Tex. Bar Assn., Coll. of State Bar of Tex., Waco-McLennan County Bar Assn., Tex. Soc. CPAs, Waco Estate Planning Coun. (pres. 1983), Rotary (Paul Harris fellow), Order of Demolay (chevalier 1975). Roman Catholic. Avocations: fly fishing, outdoor activities. Corporate, general, Estate planning, Taxation, general. Office: Pakis Giotes Page & Burleson PC 801 Washington Ave Ste 800 Waco TX 76701-1266

PAGE, TIMOTHY A.C. lawyer; b. England, Nov. 16, 1963; LLB with honors, U. Bristol, 1985. Qualified solicitor: England 1989. Assoc. Freshfields, London, 1987—89; exec. Marriott Moore, 1989—90; assoc., sr. assoc. Freshfields, 1990—96; sr. assoc. Laboruf, Lamb, Greene & McRae, 1996—99; ptnr. Clifford Chance, 1999—. Mem.: Life Assurance Legal Soc., Law Soc. England & Wales, City of London CLub. Mergers and acquisitions, Corporate, general, Insurance. Office: CLifford Chance LLP 200 Aldersgate St London EC1A 4PR England Fax: +44 (0) 20 7600 5555. E-mail: tim.page@cliffordchance.com.

PAGEL, SCOTT B. dean, law librarian, law educator; BA, Mich. State U.; MA in Libr. Sci., U. Mich.; JD, U. Calif., Berkeley. Pub. svcs. libr. Golden Gate U.; assoc. law libr. Columbia Law Sch.; dir. law libr., assoc. prof. U. Okla.; assoc. dean info. svcs., dir. law libr., prof. law Jacob Burns Law Libr. George Washington U., Washington, 1993—. Contbr. articles to profl. jours. Mem.: Am. Assn. Law Librs. Office: George Washington Univ 2000 H St NW Washington DC 20052*

PAGNI, ALBERT FRANK, lawyer; b. Reno, Nev., Jan. 28, 1935; s. Bruno and Daisy Rose (Recami) Pagni; m. Nancy Lynne Thomas, Aug. 12, 1961; children: Elisa, Michelle, Melissa, Michael. AB, U. Nev., 1961; JD, U. Calif., 1964. Bar: Nev. 1964. Assoc. Vargas, Dillon, Bartlett & Dixon, Reno, 1965—70; ptnr. Vargas & Bartlett and Jones Vargas, Reno, 1970—. Adv. bd. Nev. Cir. Ct. Mem. Nev. Dist. Appeal Bd.; mem. hospice coun. St. Mary's Hosp.; mem. adminstrv. coun. U. Nev., 1974—81; treas. U. Nev. Legis. Commn., 1973—74, pres., 1975; bd. dirs. Better Bus. Bur. With U.S. Army, 1955—57. Recipient Outstanding Alumni award, U. Nev., 1978. Master: Am. Inns Ct.; fellow: Am. Bd. Trial Advocates (nat. bd.), Nev. Law Found. (trustee, vice chair), Am. Coll. Barristers, Am. Coll. Trial Lawyers (state chair); mem.: ATLA, ABA, State Bar Nev. (bd. govs. 1976—87, v.p. 1984—85, pres.-elect 1985—86, pres. 1986—87, mediator, arbitrator 1990—), Am. Judicature Assn., Assn. Def. Counsel Calif. and Nev. (no. state chmn. 1983—85), Def. Rsch. Inst., Nev. Trial Lawyers Assn., Washoe County Bar Assn., Am. Softball Found. (bd. dirs.), Wolf Club, Elks, Order of the Coif. State civil litigation, Insurance, Personal injury (including property damage). Office: 12th Fl 100 W Liberty St Fl 12 Reno NV 89501-1962

PAGTER, CARL RICHARD, lawyer; b. Balt., Feb. 13, 1934; s. Charles Ralph and Mina (Amelung) P.; m. Judith Elaine Cox, May 6, 1978; 1 child by previous marriage: Corbin Christopher. AA, Diablo Valley Coll., 1953; BA, San Jose State U., 1955; LLB, U. Calif., Berkeley, 1964. Bar:Calif. 1965, D.C. 1977, U.S. Supreme Ct. 1976. Law clk. Kaiser Industries Corp., Oakland, Calif., 1963-64, counsel, 1964-70, assoc. counsel Washington, 1970-73, counsel Oakland, Calif., 1973-75, dir. govt. affairs Washington, 1975-76; v.p., sec., gen. counsel Kaiser Cement Corp., Oakland, Calif., 1976-88, cons., gen. counsel San Ramon, 1988-98, cons., 1998—. Author: (with A. Dundes) Urban Folklore from the Paperwork Empire, 1975, More Urban Folklore from the Paperwork Empire, 1987, Never Try to Teach a Pig to Sing, 1991, Sometimes the Dragon Wins, 1996, Why Don't Sheep Shrink When It Rains, 2000. With USNR, 1957-61, to comdr., 1978. Mem. Calif. Bar, Am. Folklore Soc., Calif. Folklore Soc., Calif. Bluegrass Assn. (founder), Mariners Square Athletic Club. Republican. Antitrust, Corporate, general, Product liability. Home and Office: 17 Julianne Ct Walnut Creek CA 94595-2610

PAINTER, MARK PHILIP, judge; b. Cin., Apr. 6, 1947; s. John Philip and Marjorie (West) P.; m. Sue Ann Painter. BA, U. Cin., 1970, JD, 1973. Bar: Ohio 1973, U.S. Dist. Ct. (so. dist.) Ohio 1973, U.S. Supreme Ct. 1980. Assoc. Smith & Schnacke (now part of Thompson Hine), 1973-78; pvt. practice Cin., 1978-82; judge Hamilton County Mcpl. Ct., Cin., 1982-95, Ohio 1st Dist. Ct. Appeals, Cin., 1995—. Adj. prof. law U. Cin., 1990—; lectr. in field. Author: The Legal Writer: 30 Rules for the Art of Legal Writing, 2002; co-author: Ohio DUI Law, 1988, 12th edit., 2003; mem. editl. bd.: Criminal Law Jour. Ohio, 1989—92; contbr. articles to profl. jours. Mem. bd. commrs. on grievances and discipline Ohio Supreme Ct., 1993—95; mem. Rep. Ctrl. Com., Cin., 1972—82; bd. dirs. Citizens Sch. Com., Cin., 1974—76; trustee Freestore Foodbank, Cin., 1984—90, Friends of William Howard Taft Birthplace, 2002—, Mary Jo Brueggeman Meml. Found., Cin., 1981—92. Recipient Superior Jud. Svc. award Ohio Supreme Ct., 1982, 84, 85. Mem. ABA, Ohio State Bar Assn., Cin. Bar Assn. (trustee 1988-90), Am. Judges Assn., Am. Judicature Soc., Am. Soc. Writers on Legal Subjects, Potter Stewart Inn of Ct. (master of bench emeritus), Bankers Club. Home: 2449 Fairview Ave Cincinnati OH 45219-1170 Office: Ct of Appeals William Howard Taft Law Ctr 230 E 9th St Cincinnati OH 45202-2174 E-mail: JuqPainter@aol.com.

PAINTON, RUSSELL ELLIOTT, lawyer, mechanical engineer; b. Port Arthur, Tex., Dec. 5, 1940; s. Clifford Elliott and Edith Virginia (McCutcheon) P.; m. Elizabeth Ann Mullins, July 2, 1965 (div. Dec. 1977); 1 child, Todd Elliott; m. Mary Lynn Weber, May 9, 1981. BS in Mech. Engring., U. Tex.-Austin, 1963, JD, 1972. Bar: Tex. 1972; registered profl. engr., Tex. Engr. Gulf States Utilities, Beaumont, Tex., 1963-66, Tracor, Inc., Austin, Tex., 1966-70, corp. counsel, 1973-83, v.p., gen. counsel, 1983-98, corp. sec., 1991-98; atty. Brown, Maroney, Rose, Baker & Barber, Austin, 1972-73, Childs, Fortenbach, Beck & Guyton, Houston, 1973; corp. sec. Westmark Systems, Inc., Austin, 1990-91; sole practitioner, 1998—. Gen. counsel Paramount Theatre for Performing Arts, 1977-83, 2d vice chmn., 1978-80, 1st vice chmn., 1980-82, chmn. bd., 1982-84, retiring chmn., 1984-85; mem. Centex chpt. ARC; mem. adv. bd. Austin Sci. Acad., 1985-88, 93-95; mem. adv. coun. Austin Transp., 1985-88; bd. dirs. Tex. Industries for the Blind and Handicapped, 1988-95, vice chmn., 1990-91; bd. dirs. Aransas County Ind. Sch. Dist. Found., 2002—, Key Allegro Homeowners Assn., 2002—. Named Boss of Yr. Austin Legal Secs. Assn., 1981. Mem.: Rockport Yacht Club (rear commodore 2001—02, vice commodore 2003), Am. Electronics Assn. (chmn. Austin coun. 1985—86), Better Bus. Bur. (arbitrator 1983—), Nat. Chamber Litigation Ctr., Tex. Bar Assn. (treas. corp. counsel sect. 1982—83), ABA, Houston Yacht Club, Order Blue Gavel, Austin Yacht Club (race commdr. 1968—69, treas. 1970—71, sec. 1972, 1975, vice commodore 1980, commodore 1981, fleet comdr. 1986), Delta Theta Phi. Republican. Episcopalian. Corporate, general, Alternative dispute resolution, Mergers and acquisitions. E-mail: sailor44@swbell.net.

PAIRO, PRESTON ABERCROMBIE, JR., lawyer; b. June 5, 1927; s. Preston Abercrombie and Blossom Winona (Pritchett) P.; m. Carol May Rupprecht, Aug. 12, 1950; 1 child, Preston Abercrombie III. AA, U. Balt., 1948; JD, 1951. Bar: Md. 1951. Legal investigator Office of City Solicitor, Balt., 1947-50; mem. Md. Ho. Dels., 1950-54; asst. states atty. State of Md., Balt., 1954-58; atty. Liquor Bd. City of Balt., 1958-60; savs. and loan atty., 1960—90. Mem. Md. Criminal Def. Bar (bd. dirs., past pres.), Assn. Trial Lawyers Am., Md. Bar Assn., Howard County Bar Assn. Democrat. Episcopalian. Club: Ellicott City Optimists (pres. 1968). Lodges: Ben Franklin, Masons, Shriners, Jesters. Home: 9032 Overhill Dr Ellicott City MD 21042-5221 Office: Pairo & Pairo 9050 Frederick Dr # A Ellicott City MD 21042-4014 E-mail: pairojr@aol.com., pairo@pairo.com.

PAJAK, DAVID JOSEPH, lawyer, consultant; b. Buffalo, N.Y., June 19, 1956; s. William H. and Theresa A. (Granato) P.; m. Peggy J. Fisher, Aug. 1, 1981; children: Andrew J., Karl W. BA, State Coll. Buffalo, 1978; JD, U. Buffalo, 1982. Bar: N.Y. 1983, U.S. Dist. Ct. (we. dist.) N.Y., 1991. Social svcs. counsel Genesee County Dept. Social Svcs., Batavia, N.Y., 1984-93; pvt. practice Corfu, N.Y., 1983—, Buffalo, N.Y., 1993—; town justice Town of Pembroke, N.Y., 1994—; with Genesee County Attys. Office, 2001—. Mem. legis. com. N.Y. Fed. on Child Abuse and Neglect, Albany, 1986—99, bd. dirs., 1987—89; cons. N.Y. Pub. Welfare Assn., Inc., Albany, 1987—92; pres. Social Svcs. Attys. Assn. N.Y. State, 1990—91; instr. Bill Adam's Martial Arts & Fitness Ctr., Buffalo, 1999—2002, Klassic Karate Studies, 1990—98, Filipino Karate Acad., 1989—90. Contbr. articles to profl. jours. Mem.: Western Genesee County Bus. Assn., Corfu Area Bus. Assn., Genesee County Magistrate's Assn., Genesee County Bar Assn., Erie County Bar Assn., N.Y. State Magistrate's Assn., N.Y. State Bar Assn. Republican. Avocations: Karate, martial arts. Personal injury (including property damage), Product liability, Professional liability. Home: 17 E Main St Corfu NY 14036-9665 Office: 170 Franklin St Ste 701 Buffalo NY 14202-2412 E-mail: dave@djpajak.com.

PAKDEEJIT, WYNN, lawyer; b. Bangkok, Oct. 30, 1969; s. Anavic Pakdeejit and Praneet Bumrerjit. LLB, Thammasat U., Bangkok, 1993; LLM, So. Meth. U., 1995. Lawyer Baker & McKenzie, Bangkok, 1995—96, assoc., 1996—2001, ptnr., 2002—. Mem. com. to propose revision of the bankruptcy act Ministry Justice, 2000—01. Mem.: Thai Bar Assn., Law Soc. Thailand. Office: Baker & McKenzie 990 Rama IV Rd Abdulrahim Bangkok Thailand

PALANS, LLOYD ALEX, lawyer; b. St. Louis, Aug. 6, 1946; s. Hyman Robert and Mae (Sherman) P.; m. Deborah Regn, Aug. 5, 1972; children: Emily Rebecca, Samantha Jane. BS, Tulane U., 1968; JD, U. Mo., 1972. Bar: Mo. 1972, U.S. Dist. Ct. (ea. and we. dists.) Mo. 1972, U.S. Ct. Appeals

(8th cir.) 1972, U.S. Ct. Appeals (5th cir.) 1974, U.S. Supreme Ct. 1975, U.S. Ct. Appeals (9th cir.) 1992. Ptnr. Kramer, Chused, Kramer, Shostak & Kohn, St. Louis, 1972-77, Blumenfeld, Marx & Tureen, P.C., St. Louis, 1978-81, Gallop, Johnson & Neuman, St. Louis, 1981-90, Bryan Cave, LLP, St. Louis, 1990—. Adj. prof. Washington U. Sch. Law, St. Louis, 1989—. Bd. dirs. St. Louis Chpt. ARC, 1987—, St. Louis Chpt. Leukemia Soc., 1988—, Combined Health Appeal Greater St. Louis, 1988—, Combined Health Appeal of Am., 1990. Fellow Am. Coll. Bankruptcy; mem. ABA, Mo. Bar, St. Louis Met. Bar Assn. Bankruptcy, Federal civil litigation, Commercial, contracts (including sales of goods; commercial financing). Office: Bryan Cave LLP 1 Metro Sq 211 N Broadway Saint Louis MO 63102-2733

PALERMO, ANTHONY ROBERT, lawyer; b. Rochester, N.Y., Sept. 30, 1929; s. Anthony C. and Mary (Palvino) P.; m. Mary Ann Coyne, Jan. 2, 1960; children: Mark Henry, Christopher Coyne, Peter Stuart, Elisabeth Megan McCarthy, Julie Coyne Lawther, Gregg Anthony. BA, U. Mich., 1951; JD, Georgetown U., 1956. Bar: DC 1956, NY 1957, U.S. Supreme Ct. 1961. Trial atty. U.S. Dept. Justice, Washington, 1956-58, asst. U.S. atty. N.Y.C., 1958-60, asst. U.S. atty. in charge Rochester, N.Y., 1960-61; ptnr. Brennan, Centner, Palermo & Blauvelt, Rochester, 1962-81, Harter, Secrest & Emery, Rochester, 1981-94, Hodgson, Russ, Andrews, Woods & Goodyear, LLP, Rochester, 1994-97, of counsel, 1998, Woods Oviatt Gilman LLP, Rochester, 1999—. Note editor Georgetown Law Jour., 1956. Bd. dirs. McQuaid Jesuit H.S., Rochester, 1978-84, St. Ann's Home for Aged, Rochester, 1974-2001; bd. dirs., sec. St. Ann's Found., Rochester, 1989-2001; trustee, charter chmn. Clients' Security Fund N.Y. (now Lawyer's Fund for Client Protection), 1981-90; chmn. Govs. Jud. Screening Com. 4th Jud. Dept., mem. statewide com., 1987-89; chair magistrate selection com. U.S. Dist. Ct. (we. dist.) N.Y., 1995, 98; mem. N.Y. Chief Judge's Commn. on Jud. Salaries, 1997—; mem. N.Y. Office Ct. Adminstrn. Commn. on Fiduciary Appointments, 2000—. Fellow Am. Bar Found., N.Y. State Bar Found. (bd. dirs. 1978-91), Am. Coll. Trial Lawyers; mem. ABA (ho. dels. 1980-98, state del. 1982-85, bd. govs. 1985-88, 1989-93, sec. 1990-93), N.Y. State Bar Assn. (pres. 1979-80, ho. dels. 1973-75, 77—), Monroe County Bar Assn. (pres. 1973), Oak Hill Country Club. Roman Catholic. Avocation: golf. Personal injury (including property damage), Estate planning, General practice. Home: 38 Huntington Meadow Rochester NY 14625-1813

PALERMO, NORMAN ANTHONY, lawyer; b. Whittier, Calif., Mar. 14, 1937; s. Anthony and Alice Lucille (Ingram) P.; m. Wynne Harrison Kieffer, Apr. 12, 1989; children by previous marriage: David I., Pamela B. BS in Geology, Tulane U., 1958; LLB, Georgetown U., 1966. Bar: Colo. 1966, U.S Dist. Ct. Colo. 1966, U.S. Ct. Appeals (10th cir.) 1966, U.S. Supreme Ct. 1971. Assoc., ptnr. Quigley Wilder & Palermo, Colorado Springs, Colo., 1966-75; v.p. Quigley & Palermo, P.C., Colorado Springs, 1975-85; pres. Norman A. Palermo, P.C., Colorado Springs, 1985—. Chmn. El Paso County Rep. Cen. Com., Colorado Springs, 1985-87; bd. dirs. Goodwill Industries, Colorado Springs, 1973—; mem. State Commn. on Jud. Performance, 1993-97; bd. dirs. Colorado Springs Symphony, 1981-87; bd. dirs. Centura Health Penrose-St. Francis Health Svcs. Cmty. Bd., 2000—, chmn., 2001—; co-chmn. SPRINGS 2000; mem. Colo. Commn. on Taxation, 2000-2002. Comdr. USNR, 1958-66. Mem. ABA, Colo. Bar Assn. (bd. govs. 1999-2001), El Paso County Bar Assn., Colorado Springs C. of C. (bd. dirs. 1980-83, 93-97, chmn. bd. dirs. 1993-95, chmn. Chamber Found. 1996-97). Republican. Avocations: golf, travel. Corporate, general, Estate planning, Property, real (including real estate development, water). Home: 1835 Cantwell Grv Colorado Springs CO 80906-6911 Office: 102 E Pikes Peak Ave 5th Fl Colorado Springs CO 80903-1823 also: PO Box 1718 Colorado Springs CO 80901-1718 E-mail: norm@palermolaw.com.

PALEY, GERALD LARRY, lawyer; b. Albany, N.Y., Sept. 11, 1939; s. Arthur and Mary (Peckner) P.; m. Joyce R., June 25, 1961 (div. June 1985); children: Jonathan, Eric, Suzanne; m. Sheryl Gae, Aug. 14, 1985. BA, Union Coll., 1961; JD with distinction, Cornell U., 1964. Bar: N.Y. 1964. Assoc. Nixon, Hargrave, Devans & Doyle, Rochester, N.Y., 1964-69; assoc. solicitor Dept. Labor, Washington, 1969-71; ptnr. Nixon, Hargrave, Devans & Doyle, Rochester, 1971-87, Phillips, Lytle, Hitchcock, Blaine & Huber, Rochester, 1987—. Author: Handbook of Federal Labor Relations Laws, 1981, Understand Employee Regulations, 1984. Mem. ABA. Republican. Jewish. Labor (including EEOC, Fair Labor Standards Act, labor-management relations, NLRB, OSHA). Office: Phillips Lytle Hitchcock et al 1400 First Federal Plz Rochester NY 14614-1981

PALIOTTA, ARMAND, lawyer; b. N.Y.C., Mar. 17, 1967; s. Armand R. and Margaret R. Paliotta; m. Amanda M. Dry, Aug. 29, 1992; 1 child, Joshua Armand. BBA, U. Okla., 1989, JD, 1992. Bar: Okla. 1992. Ptnr. Hartzog Conger Cason & Neville, Oklahoma City, Okla., 1992—. Corporate, general, Mergers and acquisitions, Corporate taxation. Office: Hartzog Conger Cason & Neville 1600 Bank of Oklahoma Plz Oklahoma City OK 73102 E-mail: apaliotta@hartzoglaw.com.

PALLARES, IGNACIO, lawyer; b. Barcelona, Mar. 7, 1973; s. Rafael Pallares and Maria Teresa Capdevila. Lic. Derecho, U. Barcelona, 1997; LLM, Duke U., 2000. Bar: Barcelona 1997. Assoc. Cuatrecasas, Barcelona, 1997—99, Madrid, 1997—99; internat. assoc. Wilmer, Cutler & Flickering, Washington, 2000—01; assoc. Cuatrecasas, Barcelona, 2001—. Legal advisor Barcelona Stock Exch., 2002—. With Spanish Army, 1996—97. Avocations: reading, travel, music, sports. Mergers and acquisitions, Commercial, contracts (including sales of goods; commercial financing), Corporate, general. Office: Cuatrecasas Paseo De Gracia 1111 4th Fl 08008 Barcelona Spain Fax: +34 932905535. E-mail: ignacio.pallares@cuatrecasas.com.

PALLMEYER, REBECCA RUTH, judge; b. Tokyo, Sept. 13, 1954; arrived in U.S., 1957; d. Paul Henry and Ruth ((Schrieber)) Pallmeyer; m. Dan P. McAdams, Aug. 20, 1977; 2 children. BA, Valparaiso U., Ind., 1976; JD, U. Ill., Chgo., 1979. Bar: Ill. 1980, U.S. Ct. Appeals (7th cir.) 1980, U.S. Ct. Appeals (11th and 5th cir.) 1982. Judge clk. Minn. Supreme Ct., St. Paul, 1979-80; assoc. Hopkins and Sutter, Chgo., 1980-85; judge, administrv. law Ill. Human Rights Commn., Chgo., 1985-91; magistrate judge U.S. Dist. Ct. (No. Dist.), Chgo., 1991-98, dist. judge, 1998—. Mem. jud. resources com. Jud. Conf. U.S., 1994—2000. Nat. adv. coun. Christ Coll., Valparaiso U., 2001—; bd. dirs. Augustana Ctr., 1990—91. Recipient Profl. Achievement award, Chgo.-Kent Coll. of Law, 2002, President's Award for Disting. Svc., N.W. Suburban Bar Assn., 2003. Mem.: FBA (bd. mgrs. Chgo. chpt. 1995—99), Chgo. Bar Assn. (chair devel. law com. 1992—93, David C. Hilliard award 1990—91), Fed. Magistrate Judges Assn. (bd. dirs. 1994—97), Nat. Assn. Women Judges, Womens Bar Assn. Ill. (bd. mgrs. 1995—98), Valparaiso U. Alumni Assn. (bd. dirs. 1992—94). Lutheran. Avocations: choral music, sewing, running. Office: US Dist Ct 219 S Dearborn St Ste 2178 Chicago IL 60604-1877

PALLOT, JOSEPH WEDELES, lawyer; b. Coral Gables, Fla., Dec. 23, 1959; s. Richard Allen Pallot and Rosalind Brown (Wedeles) Spak; m. Linda Fried, Oct. 12, 1956; children: Richard Allen, Maxwell Ross. BS, Jacksonville U., 1981; JD cum laude, U. Miami, Coral Gables, Fla., 1986. Bar: Fla. 1986. Comml. lending officer S.E. Bank, N.A., Miami, 1981-83; ptnr. Steel Hector & Davis, Miami, 1986-2000, Devine Goodman Pallot & Wells, P.A., Miami, 2000—. Trustee MOSAIC: Jewish Mus. Fla., Miami Beach, 1993—; dir. Fla. Grand Opera, 1996—, The Beacon Coun., 1997—, exec. com., 2001—, sec., 2002—. Avocations: golf, tennis. Commercial, contracts (including sales of goods; commercial financing), Corporate, general, Property, real (including real estate development, water). E-mail: jpallot@devinegoodman.com.

PALM, GREGORY K. lawyer, investment company executive; b. Binghamton, N.Y., Sept. 25, 1948; SB, MIT, 1970; MBA, JD, Harvard U., 1974. Bar: N.Y. 1977, DC 1978. Assoc. Sullivan & Cromwell, 1976—82, ptnr., 1982—92; exec. v.p., gen. counsel Goldman, Sachs & Co., N.Y.C., 1992—. Mem. Harvard Law Rev. Mem.: Am. Law Inst., DC Bar. Office: Goldman Sachs and Co Legal Dept 1 New York Plz 37th Fl New York NY 10004 Office Fax: 212-902-3876.*

PALMA, NICHOLAS JAMES, lawyer; b. Newark, Oct. 28, 1953; s. James Thomas and VeniceMaria (DiBenedetto) Palma; m. Mary Jo Cugliari, Sept. 1, 1973; children: Nicholas J., Valerie Michele, James Michael. BS cum laude, William Paterson U., 1975; JD, Seton Hall U., 1979. Bar: N.J. 1979, U.S. Dist. Ct. N.J. 1979, U.S. Ct. Appeals (3d cir.) 1985, N.Y. 1986, U.S. Dist. Ct. (ea. and so. dists.) N.Y. 2002, cert.: Hudson County, N.J. (firearms expert). Investigator N.J. Pub. Defender's Office, Essex Region, Newark, 1974—75, Hudson County Prosecutor's Office, Jersey City, 1975—79, asst. prosecutor, 1979—81; ptnr. A.J. Fusco, Jr., P.A., Passaic, NJ, 1981—90; sole practitioner Clifton, NJ, 1990—. Recipient commendation, Dade County Sheriff, Fla., 1976. Mem.: N.J. State Bar Assn., Passaic County Bar Assn. Roman Catholic. State civil litigation, Criminal, Personal injury (including property damage). Home: 221 Cedar St Cedar Grove NJ 07009-1615 Office: 1425 Broad St Clifton NJ 07013-4201

PALMER, ANN THERESE DARIN, lawyer; b. Detroit, Apr. 25, 1951; d. Americo and Theresa (Del Favero) Darin; m. Robert Towne Palmer, Nov. 9, 1974; children: Justin Darin, Christian Darin. BA, U. Notre Dame, 1973, MBA, 1975; JD, Loyola U., Chgo., 1978. Bar: Ill. 1978, U.S. Supreme Ct. 1981. Intern Wall Street Jour., Detroit, 1974; freelancer Time Inc. Fin. Publs., Chgo., 1975-77; extern, Midwest regional solicitor U.S. Dept. Labor, 1976-78; tax atty. Esmark Inc., 1978; counsel Chgo. United, 1978-81; ind. contractor Legal Tax Rsch., 1981-89; fin. and legal news contbr. The Chgo. Tribune, 1991—, Bus. Week Chgo. Bur., 1991—, Automotive News, 1993-97, Crain's Chgo. Bus., 1994-2000. Mem.: Woman's Athletic Club Chgo. Labor (including EEOC, Fair Labor Standards Act, labor-management relations, NLRB, OSHA), Corporate taxation, Taxation, general. Home: 873 Forest Hill Rd Lake Forest IL 60045-3905

PALMER, BRIAN EUGENE, lawyer; b. Mpls., May 16, 1948; s. Eugene Philip and Virginia Breeze (Rolfshus) P.; m. Julia Washburn Morrison, Dec. 29, 1972; 1 child, Julia Hunter. AB, Brown U., 1970; JD, William Mitchell Coll. of Law, 1974. Bar: Minn. 1974, U.S. Dist. Ct. Minn. 1975, U.S. Dist. Ct. (ea. dist.) Wis. 2001, U.S. Ct. Appeals (8th cir.) 1980, U.S. Ct. Fed. Claims 1984, U.S. Supreme Ct. 1980. Asst. pub. defender Hennepin County Pub. Defender, Mpls., 1974-78; assoc. Dorsey & Whitney LLP, Mpls., 1978-82, ptnr., 1983—. Banking, General civil litigation, Criminal. Home: 1190 Lyman Ave Wayzata MN 55391-9671 Office: Dorsey & Whitney LLP 50 South Sixth St Ste 1500 Minneapolis MN 55402-1498 E-mail: palmer.brian@dorseylaw.com.

PALMER, DAVID GILBERT, lawyer; b. Lakewood, N.J., Jan. 10, 1945; s. Robert Dayton and Lois (Gilbert) P.; m. Susan Edmundson Walsh, Aug. 17, 1968; children: Jonathan, Megan. AB, Johns Hopkins U., 1967; JD, U. Colo., 1970. Bar: Colo. 1970, U.S. Dist. Ct. Colo. 1970, U.S. Ct. Appeals (9th and 10th cirs.) 1970, U.S. Supreme Ct. 1970. Ptnr., chmn. litigation dept. Holland & Hart, Denver, 1970-87, Gibson, Dunn & Crutcher, Denver, 1987-97; mng. ptnr. Zevnik, Horton, Palmer, Denver, 1997-2001; mng. shareholder Greenberg Traurig LLP, Denver, 2001—. Chmn. N.W. region Am. Heart Assn., Dallas, 1986—, bd. dirs., 1986—, sec., 1990—, nat. chmn., 1992-93; pres., bd. dirs. Colo. Heart Assn., Denver, 1974; bd. dirs. C.H. Kempe Nat. Ctr. for Prevention of Child Abuse, Denver, 1984-90, pres., 1989-90; bd. dirs. Goodwill Industries, Denver, 1981-84. Mem. ABA, Colo. Bar Assn., Denver Law Club, Univ. Club, Mile High Club. Federal civil litigation, Criminal. Home: 3120 Ramshorn Dr Castle Rock CO 80108-9073 Office: Greenberg Traurig 1200 17th St Ste 2400 Denver CO 80202 E-mail: palmerdg@gtlaw.com.

PALMER, DENNIS DALE, lawyer; b. Alliance, Nebr., Apr. 30, 1945; s. Vernon D. Palmer and Marie E. (Nelson) Fellers; m. Rebecca Ann Turner, Mar. 23, 1979; children: Lisa Marie, Jonathan Paul. BA, U. Mo., 1967, JD, 1970. Bar: Mo. 1970, U.S. Dist. Ct. (we. dist.) Mo. 1970, U.S. Ct. Appeals (8th and 10th cirs.) 1973, U.S. Supreme Ct. 1980. Staff atty. Legal Aid Soc. Western Mo., Kansas City, 1970-73; assoc. Shughart, Thomson & Kilroy, P.C., Kansas City, 1973-76, ptnr., bd. dirs., 1976—. Contbr. articles on franchise and employment law to legal jours. Bd. dirs., chmn. legal assts. adv. bd. Avila Coll., Kansas City, 1984-87. 2d lt. U.S. Army, 1970. Mem. ABA (litigation com. 1980, forum com. on franchising 1987), Mo. Bar Assn. (antitrust com. 1975—, civil practice com. 1975—), Kansas City Bar Assn. (chmn. franchise law com. 1987—), Univ. Club. Avocations: jogging, golf, tennis, outdoor activities, reading. Federal civil litigation, General civil litigation, Franchising. Home: 13100 Canterbury Rd Leawood KS 66209-1700 Office: Shughart Thomson & Kilroy 12 Wyandotte Plz 120 W 12th St Fl 17 Kansas City MO 64105-1902

PALMER, DOUGLAS S., JR., lawyer; b. Peoria, Ill., Mar. 15, 1945; AB cum laude, Yale U., 1966; JD cum laude, Harvard U., 1969. Bar: Wash. 1969. Mem. Foster Pepper & Shefelman PLLC, Seattle, 1975—2002, Hillis Clark Martin & Peterson, P.S., Seattle, 2002—. Corporate, general, Private international, Property, real (including real estate development, water). Office: Hillis Clark Martin & Peterson PS 500 Galland Bldg 1221 Second Ave Seattle WA 98101-2925

PALMER, JANICE MAUDE, lawyer; b. Greeley, Colo., Sept. 7, 1951; d. William L. and Cleo E. (White) P.; children: Emilie Halladay, Eileen Halladay, Michael W. Halladay III. BS, Ariz. State U., 1979, JD, 1982. Bar: Ariz. 1983, U.S. Dist. Ct. Ariz. 1983, U.S. Ct. Appeals (9th cir.) 1985. Assoc. Law Office of Guy Buckley, Mesa, Ariz., 1983-86, Slater & Santiquida, Mesa, 1986-89; pvt. practice Phoenix, 1989-92, Mesa, 1992—. Democrat. Bankruptcy, State civil litigation, Family and matrimonial. Office: 2111 E Baseline Rd Ste F-8 Tempe AZ 85283-1519

PALMER, JOHN BERNARD, III, lawyer; b. Ft. Wayne, Ind., May 18, 1952; s. John Bernard and Dorothy Alma (Lauer) P. BA, Mich. State U., 1974; JD, U. Mich., 1977. Bar: Ill. 1977, U.S. Dist. Ct. (no. dist.) Ill. 1977, U.S. Tax Ct. 1979. Assoc. Mayer Brown & Platt, Chgo., 1977-80, Hopkins & Sutter, Chgo., 1980-83, ptnr., 1983-2001, Foley & Lardner, Chgo., 2001—. Adj. prof. Ill. Inst. Tech.- Kent Coll. of Law, Chgo., 1984—. Mem. ABA. Corporate taxation, State and local taxation. Office: Foley & Lardner 321 N Clark St Chicago IL 60610

PALMER, JUDITH GRACE, university administrator; b. Washington, Ind., Apr. 2, 1948; d. William Thomas and Laura Margaret (Routt) P. BA, Ind. U., 1970; JD cum laude, Ind. U., Indpls., 1973. Bar: Ind. 1974, U.S. Dist. Ct. (so. dist.) Ind. 1974. State budget analyst State of Ind., Indpls., 1969-76, exec. asst. to gov., 1976-81, state budget dir., 1981-85; spl. asst. to pres. Ind. U., 1985-86, v.p. for planning, 1986-91, v.p. for planning and fin. mgmt., 1991-94, v.p., CFO, 1994—. Bd. dirs. Ind. Fiscal Policy Inst., Kelley Exec. Ptnrs.; bd. dirs., treas. Advanced Rsch. and Tech. Inst. Bd. dirs., sec.-treas. Columbian Found., 1990-94, 2000—; bd. dirs. Columbia Club, 1989-98, pres. 1995; bd. dirs. Commn. for Downtown, 1984, mem. exec. bd., 1989-92, chmn. cmty. rels. com., 1989-93; mem. State Budget Commn., 1981-85. Named one of Outstanding Young Women in Am., 1978; recipient Sagamore of the Wabash award, 1977, 85, Citation of Merit, Ind. Bar Assn. of Young Lawyers, 1978, Appreciation award, 1980. Mem. ABA, Ind. Bar Assn., Indpls. Bar Assn. Roman Catholic. Office: Ind Univ Bryan Hall Rm 204 Bloomington IN 47405 E-mail: jgpalmer@indiana.edu.

PALMER, RICHARD CRIST, lawyer; b. New London, Conn., June 8, 1964; s. Richard Crist and Alice Frances (Linzen) P. AA, Mitchell Coll., New London, 1985; BA, Ea. Conn. State U., 1987; JD, Western New Eng. Law, Springfield, Mass., 1990. Bar: Conn. 1991, U.S. Dist. Ct. 1991. Law clk. Faulkner & Boyce P.C., New London, 1988-92; indexing editor Conn. Trial Lawyers Assn., Hartford, 1992; atty. Law Offices Theodore Ladwig, Mystic, Conn., 1993-95; indexing cons. publ. divsn. Mass. Continuing Legal Edn., Inc., Boston, 1995; sole practice Stonington, Conn., 1993—. Campaign field coord. Friends of Chris Dodd, Hartford, 1992, Clinton-Gore, 1992; registrar of voters Town of Stonington, 1997-2000, Justice of the Peace, 1995—, econ. devel. commr., 1993-98, constable, 1993-94; mem. Dem. Town Com., 1991-2000, vice chmn., 1994-95. Mem. Knights of Columbus (advocate 1992-93), Phi Alpha Delta. Democrat. Roman Catholic. General practice, Probate (including wills, trusts). Office: PO Box 126 Mystic CT 06355-0126 E-mail: crisp@snet.net.

PALMER, RICHARD DOUGLAS, lawyer; b. Ann Arbor, Mich., Jan. 18, 1950; s. Donnally Woodruff and Louise (Greiner) P.; m. Jemery Mae Van Sickle, Jan. 20, 1973; children: Justin Donnally, Vanessa Louise. BA, Alma (Mich.) Coll., 1972; JD, U. Ill., 1976. Bar: Mich. 1976. Pvt. practice, Greenville, Mich., 1976—. Twp. atty. Eureka, Cato, Winfield, Crystal, Belvidere, Sidney twps.; atty. coach Greenville H.S. Mock Trial Team. Dir. Greenville Danish Festival; baseball coach Pony League, Greenville; debate instr. Greenville Pub. Sch. Saturday Scholars; lay leader First United Meth. Ch.; pres. Greenville H.S. Band Boosters; mem. dramatic prodns. Cmty. Players. Mem. Mich. Bar Assn., Montcalm-Ionia Bar Assn. (pres.). Avocations: antiques and old cars, water skiing, song writing, tennis. General practice, Municipal (including bonds). Office: 111 S Lafayette St Greenville MI 48838-1933

PALMER, RICHARD N. state supreme court justice; b. Hartford, Conn., May 27, 1950; BA, Trinity Coll., 1972; JD with high honors, U. Conn., 1977. Bar: Conn. 1977, U.S. Dist. Ct. Conn. 1978, D.C. 1980, U.S. Ct. Appeals (2nd cir.) 1981. Law clk. to Hon. Jon O. Newman U.S. Ct. Appeals (2nd cir.), 1977-78; assoc. Shipman & Goodwin, 1978-80; asst. U.S. atty. Office U.S. Atty. Conn., 1980-83, 87-90, U.S. atty. dist. Conn., 1991, chief state's atty. Conn., 1991-93; ptnr. Chatigny and Palmer, 1984-86; assoc. justice Conn. Supreme Ct., Hartford, 1993—. Mem. Phi Beta Kappa. Office: Connecticut Supreme Ct 231 Capitol Ave Hartford CT 06106-1548

PALMER, RICHARD WARE, lawyer; b. Boston, Oct. 20, 1919; s. George Ware and Ruth French (Judkins) P.; m. Nancy Fernald Shaw, July 8, 1950; children: Richard Ware Jr., John Wentworth, Anne Fernald. AB, Harvard U., 1942, JD, 1948. Bar: N.Y. 1950, Pa. 1959. Sec., dir. N.Am. Mfg. Co., Natick, Mass., 1946-48; assoc. Burlingham, Veeder, Clark & Hupper, Burlingham, Hupper & Kennedy, N.Y.C., 1949-57; ptnr. Rawle & Henderson, Phila., 1958-79; co-founder, ptnr. Palmer, Biezup & Henderson, Phila., 1979-95, of counsel, 1998—. Sec., bd. dirs. Underwater Technics, Inc., Camden, N.J., 1967-85; adv. on admiralty law to U.S. del. Inter-Govtl. Maritime Consultative Orgn., London, 1967, U.S. del. 30th-34th internat. confs.; mem. U.S. Shipping Coordinating Com., Washington legal sub com., 1967—; titular mem. Comité Maritime Internat.; v.p., sec., bd. dirs. Phila. Belt Line R.R.; bd. dirs. Mather (Bermuda) Ltd. Editor: Maritime Law Reporter. Mem., permanent adv. bd. Tulane Admiralty Law Inst., Tulane U. Law Sch., New Orleans, 1975—; trustee Seamen's Ch. Inst., Phila., 1967—2001, pres., 1972—84; mem. exec. com. Harvard Law Sch. Assn., Phila., 1986—; bd. dirs. Havrford (Pa.) Civic Assn., 1972—85, pres., 1976—79; consul for Denmark State of Pa., 1980—91, consul emeritus, 1992—; bd. dirs. Woodlands Cemetary Co. of Phila., Woodlands Trust for Historic Preservation. Lt. comdr. USNR, 1942—46. Fellow World Acad. Art and Sci. (treas. 1988-2002); mem. ABA (former chmn. stdg. com. on admiralty and maritime law 1978-79), N.Y.C. Bar Assn., Phila. Bar Assn., Am. Judicature Soc., Maritime Law Assn. (chmn. limitation liability com. 1977-83, 2d v.p. 1984-86, 1st v.p. 1986-88, pres. 1988-90, immediate past pres. 1990-92), Assn. Average Adjusters USA and Gt. Britain, Port of Phila. Maritime Soc., Harvard Law Sch. Assn. of Phila. (exec. com. 1986—), Consul Assn. of Phila., The Colonial Soc. Pa., Danish Order of Dannebrog, Colonial Soc. Pa., Merion Cricket Club, Phila. Club, Rittenhouse Club, Geneal. Soc. Pa. (bd. dirs. 1997—), Harvard Club of N.Y.C. and Phila. (exec. com. 1983-86, 94-97). Republican. Episcopalian. Admiralty, Marine Insurance, International Law. Home: 432 Montgomery Ave Haverford PA 19041-1527 Office: Palmer Biezup & Henderson Pub Ledger Bldg 620 Chestnut St Philadelphia PA 19106-3409

PALMER, ROBERT ALAN, lawyer, educator; b. Somerville, N.J., June 29, 1948; BA, U. Pitts., 1970; JD, George Washington U., 1976. Bar: Va. 1977. Dir. labor relations Nat. Assn. Mfrs., Washington, 1976-79; assoc. gen. counsel Nat. Restaurant Assn., Washington, 1979-85, gen. counsel, 1985-87; assoc. prof. Pa. State U., State College, 1987-88, Calif. State Poly. U., 1988-92, prof., 1992—. Mem. ABA, Va. State Bar Assn. Home: 557 Fairview Ave Arcadia CA 91007-6736 Office: 3801 W Temple Ave Pomona CA 91768-2557

PALMER, ROBERT LESLIE, lawyer; b. Porterville, Calif., Apr. 10, 1957; s. Harrison Rowe and Margaret Elizabeth (Witty) P.; m. Huisuk Kim, Feb. 1, 1986; 1 child, Aaron Rowe. BA, Tulane U., 1979; JD, Georgetown U., 1982. Bar: D.C. 1982, U.S. Ct. Mil. Appeals 1985, Tex. 1987, Ala. 1987, U.S. Dist. Ct. (no. dist.) Ala. 1987, U.S. Ct. Appeals (11th cir.) 1987. Assoc. Lewis Martin Burnett & Dunkle, P.C., Birmingham, Ala., 1987-89, Lewis and Martin, Birmingham, Ala., 1989-90, Martin, Drummond and Woosley, Birmingham, 1990-91, bd. dirs., 1991-92, Martin, Drummond, Woosley and Palmer, Birmingham, 1992-95; atty. Environ. Litig. Group, P.C., Birmingham, Ala., 1995—. Ala. del. 6th Joint Conf. between Korea and S.E. U.S., Kyongju, Republic of Korea, 1991, 7th Joint Conf., Atlanta, 1992. Capt. JAGC, U.S. Army, 1983-87, USAR, 1987-91. Recipient commendation Republic of Korea Ministry of Justice, 1984. Mem. ATLA, Christian Legal Soc., Phi Beta Kappa, Omicron Delta Kappa. Independent. Baptist. Environmental, Personal injury (including property damage), Toxic tort. Home: 1408 E Whitehaway Helena AL 35080-4102 Office: Environ Litig Group PC 3529 7th Ave S Birmingham AL 35222-3210

PALMER, ROBERT TOWNE, lawyer, banker; b. Chgo., May 25, 1947; s. Adrian Bernhardt and Gladys (Towne) P.; m. Ann Therese Darin, Nov. 9, 1974; children: Justin Darin, Christian Darin. BA, Colgate U., 1969; JD, U. Notre Dame, 1974. Bar: Ill. 1974, D.C. 1978, U.S. Supreme Ct. 1978. Law clk. to Hon. Walter V. Schaefer Ill. Supreme Ct., 1974-75; assoc. McDermott, Will & Emery, Chgo., 1975-81, ptnr., 1982-86, Chadwell & Kayser, Ltd., Chgo., 1987-88, Connelly, Mustes, Palmer & Schroeder, Chgo., 1988-89; of counsel Garfield & Merel Ltd., Chgo., 1990-2000. Adj. faculty Chgo. Kent Law Sch., 1975—77, Loyola U., 1976—78; adv. com. Fed. Home Loan Mortgage Corp., 1988—89; bd. dirs. Ctrl. Fed. Savs. & Loan Assn. of Chgo., chmn., 2000—; dir. Chgo. Assn. Fin. Insts., 2001—03, sec., 2002—03; mem. Chgo. Ctr. Adv. Bd. Voyageur Outward Bound Sch., 1988—91; chmn. Lake Forest Cemetery Commn., 2001—; mem. Chgo. Crime Commn., 2001—, dir., 2002—. Contbr. articles to legal jours. and textbooks. Mem. ABA, Ill. State Bar Assn. (Lincoln award 1983), Chgo. Bar Assn., Chgo. Club, Dairymen's Country Club, Lambda Alpha. Federal civil litigation, State civil litigation, Insurance. Office: Central Fed Savs 1601 W Belmont Ave Chicago IL 60657-3044

PALMER, RUSSELL SCOTT, lawyer; b. Longmont, Colo., July 24, 1951; children: Lauren Elizabeth, Dane Andrew. BA, U. Colo., 1973; JD, U. Oreg., 1976. Bar: Oreg. 1976, U.S. Dist. Ct. Oreg. 1976, U.S. Ct. Appeals (9th cir.) 1982. Assoc. Johnson, Harrang & Swanson, Eugene, Oreg., 1976—82, ptnr., 1983—92; shareholder Muhlheim Palmer & Wade, P.C., Eugene, 1992—2001, Watkinson Laird Rubenstein Baldwin & Burgess, P.C., Eugene, 2002—; mcpl. judge Cresswell, Oreg., 1984—2003. Articles editor: Oreg. Law Rev., 1975—76, contbg. author: Oregon Civil Pleading and Practice, 1980. Mem.: Lane County Bar Assn. (bd. dirs. 1985—88, law day chmn. 1984—86), Rotary, Phi Beta Kappa. Democrat. Bankruptcy, State civil litigation, Commercial, contracts (including sales of goods; commercial financing). Home: 85954 Cherokee Dr Eugene OR 97402-9019 Office: Watkinson Laird Rubenstein Baldwin & Burgess PC 100 E Broadway Ste 200 Eugene OR 97401-3114

PALMER, VENRICE ROMITO, lawyer, educator; b. Springfield, Mass., Jan. 11, 1952; s. Venrice Wellesley and Mildred Adlay (Foster) P. Higher diploma, U. Besançon, France, 1973; AB maxima cum laude, King's Coll., Wilkes-Barre, Pa., 1974; JD, Harvard U., 1977. Bar: N.Y. 1978, U.S. Dist. Ct. (so. and ea. dists.) N.Y. 1979, Ill. 1986, Calif. 1997. Spl. asst. atty. gen. Office N.Y. Atty. Gen., N.Y.C., 1977-79; staff atty. SEC, N.Y.C., 1979-82, br. chief, 1982-83, spl. trial counsel, 1983-85, acting asst. regional adminstr., 1984-85; sr. counsel Sears, Roebuck and Co., Hoffman Estates, Ill., 1985-97, Bank of Am., San Francisco, 1997-99; counsel McCutchen, Doyle, Brown & Enersen, LLP, San Francisco, 1999—2002, Bingham McCutchen LLP, San Francisco, 2002—. Guest lectr. St. John's U. Bus. Sch., N.Y.C., 1984; lectr. Practicing Law Inst., N.Y.C., 1995—, Glasser LegalWorks, Little Falls, N.J., 1997—, Am. Soc. Corp. Secs., 1997-99, Nat. Bus. Inst., Eau Claire, Wis., 2000—. Contbr. articles to various law publs. Recipient cert. of appreciation N.Y. State Bar Assn., 1978, Benaglia award King's Coll., 1974. Mem. ABA, Calif. State Bar Assn. (mem. fin. instns. com. 2000—), Delta Epsilon Sigma, Alpha Mu Gamma. Avocations: opera, ballet, reading. Corporate, general, Finance, Securities. Home: 1200 Gough St Apt 7A San Francisco CA 94109-6616 Office: Bingham McCutchen LLP Three Embarcadero Ctr San Francisco CA 94111 E-mail: venricepalmer@bingham.com.

PALMER, VERNON VALENTINE, law educator; b. New Orleans, Sept. 9, 1940; s. George Joseph and Juliette Marie (Wehrmann) P. BA, Tulane U., 1962, LL.B., 1965; LL.M., Yale U., 1966; PhD, Pembroke Coll., Oxford U., 1985. Bar: La. 1965, U.S. Supreme Ct. 1981. Asst. prof. law Ind. Sch. Law, Indpls., 1966-70; lectr. law U. Botswana, Lesotho & Swaziland, Roma, Lesotho, 1967-69; prof. Tulane Law Sch., New Orleans, 1970—, Clarence Morrow research prof. law, 1980—, Thomas Pickles prof. law, 1989—; external examiner Nat. U. Lesotho, Roma, 1978-81. Dir. Tulane Paris Inst. European Legal Studies, European Legal Studies; reporter for revision of civil code La. Law Inst. 1979; vis. prof. Faculty Law, U. Strasbourg, 1988, The Sorbonne, U. Paris, 1986, 92, Universite des Antilles, Martinique, 1998, Universidad Ramon Llull, Barcelona, 1998, U. Trento, 1999—, U. Laussanne, 2000, U. Geneva, 2000. Author: The Roman-Dutch and Lesotho Law of Delict, 1970, The Legal System of Lesotho, 1971, The Paths to Privity, 1992, The Civil Law of Lease in Louisiana, 1997, Louisiana: Microcosm of a Mixed Jurisdiction, 1999, Mixed Jurisdictions Worldwide: The Third Legal Family, 2001; (with Bussani) Pure Economic Loss Europe, 2003; contbr. numerous articles to profl. jours. Pres. French Quarter Residents Assn., 1973-75, Alliance for Good Govt., 1974-75; del. Nat. Democratic Conv., N.Y.C., 1976; chmn. World Congress on Mixed Jurisdictions, 2002, pres., pres. WOrld Soc. of Mixed Jursdiction Jurists, Titulary Mem. Internat. Acad. of Compatative Law, 2003. Decorated chevalier L'ordre des Palmes Académiques. Mem. La. Law Inst., World Soc. Mixed Jurisdiction Jurists (pres.), Titulaire Internat. Acad. Comparative Law (The Hague). Democrat. Roman Catholic. Home: 3311 Coliseum St New Orleans LA 70115-2401 Office: 6329 Freret St New Orleans LA 70118-6231 E-mail: vpalmer@law.tulane.edu .

PALMER, WALTER WHELAN, lawyer; b. Huntsville, Ala., Feb. 6, 1966; m. Angela Cristina Pinheiro-Palmer. BA, U. Miami, 1988, MA, 1990; JD, George Washington U., 1995. Bar: Fla. 1995, U.S. Dist. Ct. (so. and mid. dists.) Fla., U.S. Ct. Appeals (11th cir.). Atty. Amlong & Amlong, Ft. Lauderdale, Fla., 1995—97, Gunster Yoakley & Stewart, West Palm Beach, 1997—2000, Daniel Advogados, Rio de Janeiro, 2000—. Mem.: ABA, Brazilian Intellectual Property Assn. Intellectual property. Office: Daniel Advogados Av Republica Chile 230 6th Fl 20031-170 Rio de Janeiro Brazil Fax: 55-21 2524-3344. E-mail: walter.palmer@daniel-advogados.com.

PALMER, WILLIAM D. judge; b. Adrian, Mich., 1952; BS in Mgmt. cum laude, Rensselaer Poly. Inst., 1973; JD cum laude, Boston Coll., 1976. Bar: Fla. 1976; cert. civil mediator, family mediator, arbitrator, Fla. Assoc. Carlton, Fields, Ward, Emmanuel, Smith & Cutler, Orlando, Fla., 1976-82, ptnr., 1982-97, Palmer & Palmer, PA, Orlando, 1997-2000; dist. judge 5th dist. Fla. Ct. Appeal, Daytona Beach, 2000—. Lectr. in field. Editor-in-chief Boston Coll. Environ. Affairs Law Rev., 1975-76. Past bd. dirs. Fla. Hosp. Found., Life for Kids Adoption Agy.; past chmn. bd. dirs. Ctrl. Fla. Helpline; bd. dirs. Boys and Girls Club of Ctrl. Fla. Mem.: Orange County Bar Assn. (chmn. various coms.), Fla. Bar (chair jud. nominating procedures com. 1992—94, chair Fla. Bar jour. com. 1993—95, vice chair family section amicus com. 1993—95, mem. jud. adminstrn. selection and tenure com. 1995—98, mem. litigation, appellate law and family law sects.). Office: 5th Dist Ct Appeal 300 S Beach St Daytona Beach FL 32114-5097 E-mail: palmerw@flcourts.org.

PALMETER, N. DAVID, lawyer; b. Elmira, N.Y., Jan. 29, 1938; s. Neal Henry and Elizabeth Jane (McHale) P.; m. Mary Lee Morken, 1964 (div. 1979); m. Mary Faith Tanney, Jan. 15, 1983; children: Stephen Michael, John David, Elizabeth Jane, James Martin. AB, Syracuse U., 1960; JD, U. Chgo., 1963. Bar: N.Y. 1963, D.C. 1969. Trial atty. U.S. Dept. Justice, Washington, 1966-68; assoc. Daniels & Houlihan, Washington, 1969-73, ptnr., 1973-75, Daniels, Houlihan & Palmeter, Washington, 1975-84, Mudge, Rose, Guthrie, Alexander & Ferdon, Washington, 1984-95, Graham & James, Washington, 1995-98, Powell, Goldstein, Frazer and Murphy, 1998—2002, Sidley Austin Brown and Wood, 2002—. Co-author: Dispute Settlement in the World Trade Organization, 1999; contbr. articles to profl. publs. Mem. ABA, Internat. Bar Assn. (chmn. internat. trade and customs law com. 1989-93, liaison to World Trade Orgn. 1993—), N.Y. State Bar Assn., D.C. Bar Assn., Washington Fgn. Law Soc. (pres. 1992-93), Am. Soc. Internat. Law, Can. Coun. on Internat. Law, Brit. Inst. Internat. and Comparative Law. Private international, Public international. Home: 2804 29th St NW Washington DC 20008-4112 E-mail: dpalmeter@sidley.com.

PALMIGIANO, ALESSANDRO, lawyer; b. Palermo, Italy, May 4, 1967; s. Gaetano Palmigiano and Sonia Sarno; m. Elvira Lo Giudice, Sept. 4, 1999; 1 child, Ennio. Grad. cum laude in law, U. Palermo, Italy, 1993. Bar: Italy 1996. Ptnr. Palmigiano Law Firm, Palermo, Italy, 1995—; head of legal rsch. dept. Ronelli Found. Cons. in field. Author: (book) Legal Aspects of Electromagnetic Fields, Unfair Teams and Consumer Protection. Mem.: ATLA, Washington Fgn. Law Soc., European Assn. Law and Econs., Union Internat. Advocates, Palermo Law Soc., Rotary. Roman Catholic. Avocations: reading, soccer. Commercial, consumer (including collections, credit), Family and matrimonial, Communications. Office: Palmigiano Law Firm Via Wagner 9 90139 Palermo Italy Fax: +39 091 6110983. E-mail: palmigianolawfirm@tin.it.

PALMORE, JOHN STANLEY, JR., retired lawyer; b. Ancon, C.Z., Aug. 6, 1917; s. John Stanley and Antoinette Louise (Gonzalez) P.; m. Eleanor Anderson, July 31, 1938 (dec. 1980); 1 child, John Worsham (dec.); m. Carol Pate, Jan. 1, 1982. Student, Western Ky. State Coll., 1934-36; LL.B. cum laude, U. Louisville, 1939. Bar: Ky. 1938. Practice law, Henderson, 1939-42, 47-59; judge Ct. Appeals Ky. (name changed to Supreme Ct. Ky. 1975), 1959-82, chief justice, 1966, 73, 77-82; practice law Frankfort, Ky., 1983-84; ptnr. Palmore & Sheffer, Henderson, 1984-86; sr. counsel Jackson & Kelly, Lexington, Ky., 1986-92; ret., 1992. City pros. atty., Henderson, 1949-53, city atty., 1953-55; commonwealth's atty. 5th Circuit Ct. Dist. Ky., 1955-59 Served to lt. USNR, 1942-46, 51-52. Mem. VFW, Ky. Bar Assn., Am. Legion, Ky. Hist. Soc., Frankfort Country Club, Lexington Club, Frankfort Rotary Club (pres. 1993-94), Masons, Shriners, Elks, Phi Alpha Delta. Episcopalian (past vestryman, sr. warden). Home: 2310 Peaks Mill Rd Frankfort KY 40601-9437

PALOTIE, TAUNO VEIKKO, lawyer; b. Helsinki, Dec. 29, 1947; s. Veikko and Irina (Grunberg) P.; m. Monica Roschier-Holmberg, May 30, 1969 (d9v. Oct. 1995); children: Juha, Ira; m. Barbara Roos, Aug. 31, 1996. LLM, U. Helsinki, 1972, Vrie U., Brussels, 1978. Assoc. Veikko Palotie & Co., Helsinki, 1972-74; head legal dept. Ctrl. C. of C., Finland, 1974-77; fin. advisor Kansallis-Osake-Pankki, 1978-79; atty. Oy Partek Ab, Helsinki, 1979-81; ptnr. Veikko Palotie & Co., Helsinki, 1981—. Bd. dirs. Indsl. Property Rights Assn.; sec. fair trading com. Ctrl. C. of C., 1974-77, arbitration com., 1975-77. Avocation: skiing. Office: Veikko Palotie & Co Aleksanterinkatu 44 A FIN-00100 Helsinki Finland

PAMPANIN, ALAN MARK, lawyer; b. San Francisco, Calif., Apr. 18, 1949; s. Vincent Mark and Francesca Lilian Pampanin; m. Kimberly Darden, Dec. 3, 1988; children: Emma Elizabeth, Mark Christopher. B in Lit., U. Calif. Berkeley, 1971; JD, Hastings Coll., 1976. Bar: Mass. 1980, Calif. 1977, U.S. Dist. Ct. Mass., U.S. Ct. Appeals (1st cir.). Prin. Pampanin Law Offices, Cambridge, Mass., 1986—. Contbr. Exec. bd. Refugee Immigration Ministry, Malden, Mass., 2002—. Office: 2343 Mass Ave Cambridge MA 02140

PANCHOT, DUDLEY BRADFORD, lawyer; b. Yakima, Wash., Feb. 25, 1930; s. Kenneth Bradford and Marion Roberts (Dudley) P.; m. Anne Louise Swanson, Oct. 28, 1950; children— Yvonne Marie, Jeanne Louise, Marianne Margarite, John Robert. Student U. Puget Sound, 1947-48; B.A. in Econs., U. Wash., 1951, J.D., 1955. Bar: Wash. 1956, U.S. Dist. Ct. (we. dist.) Wash. 1956, U.S. Ct. Appeals (9th cir.) 1957. Assoc. R. Wayne Cyphers, Seattle, 1956, 57, Reaugh, Hart & Allison, Seattle, 1957-62; assoc. Wolfstone & Piehler, Seattle, 1962-63, ptnr., 1964; ptnr. Wolfstone & Panchot, Seattle, 1965-67, Wolfstone, Panchot & Kleist, Seattle, 1968, Wolfstone, Panchot, Kleist & Bloch, Seattle, 1969-70, Wolfstone, Panchot & Bloch, Seattle, 1970-77; ptnr. Wolfstone, Panchot, Bloch & Kelley, Seattle, 1977-81; sr. ptnr., 1981-84; sr. ptnr. Wolfstone, Panchot & Bloch, 1985— ; lectr. Bellevue Community Coll., state bar assn. seminars; town coun. Medina (Wash.), 1970-72. Bd. visitors U. Wash. Sch. Law, 1982—95; trustee Seattle Central YMCA, 1978—95. Mem. ABA, Seattle Bar Assn., King County Bar Assn., Am. Coll. Trust and Estate Counsel, Wash. State Bar Assn. (past chmn. tax sect.), Seattle Estate Planning Council, Phi Kappa Delta. Congregationalist. Club: Harbor (Seattle). Estate planning, Probate (including wills, trusts), Property, real (including real estate development, water). Home: 110 E Smith Cove Way Shelton WA 98584-9472 Office: Norton Bldg Ste 1500 Seattle WA 98104

PANCIERA, RICHARD CONNER, lawyer; b. Westerly, R.I., Mar. 11, 1947; s. Louis and Grace (Conner) P. BA, U. Tex., 1969; JD, U. Ariz., 1973. Bar: Ariz. 1974, U.S. Dist. Ct. Ariz. 1974, R.I. 1975, U.S. Dist. Ct. R.I., 1975, U.S. Ct. Appeals (1st cir.) 1978, U.S. Supreme Ct. 1984, U.S. Ct. Mil. Appeals 1988, U.S. Tax Ct. 1991, U.S. Claims Ct. 1991, U.S. Ct. Customs 1991, U.S. Ct. Appeals (fed. cir.) 1991, U.S. Dist. Ct. Conn. 1999. Pvt. practice, Westerly, 1975—. Legal counsel Hope Valley-Wyoming Fire Dist., R.I., 1979—. Lt. col. JAGC, USAR, 1969-2000. Mem. ATLA, R.I. Bar Assn., Ariz. Bar Assn., Washington County Bar Assn. Bankruptcy, Probate (including wills, trusts), Property, real (including real estate development, water). Office: PO Box 504 Westerly RI 02891-0504

PANDOLFE, JOHN THOMAS, JR., lawyer; b. Neptune, N.J., Dec. 15, 1941; s. John T. and Jeannette R. (Pullen) P.; m. Linda Lee Fritzsche, July 12, 1969; children: Leslie, Matthew. AB, U. Miami, 1965; MS, Monmouth Coll., 1973; JD, U. Miami, 1975. Bar: Fla. 1976, N.J. 1976, U.S. Dist. Ct. N.J. 1976. Ptnr. Pandolfe, Shaw & Rubino, Spring Lake, N.J. Mem. ABA, Fla. Bar Assn., N.J. Bar Assn., Monmouth Bar Assn., Spring Lake Golf Club. General practice. Office: Pandolfe Shaw and Rubino 215 Morris Ave Spring Lake NJ 07762-1360

PANEK, EDWARD STANLEY, JR., lawyer; b. Phila., Jan. 10, 1945; s. Edward S. and Clara S. P.; m. Marlene Lazzaro, Sept. 26, 1981; 1 child, Marilyn O. Primiano. BA, St. Joseph's U., Phila., 1966; JD, Villanova U., 1969. Bar: Pa. 1971, U.S. Cir. Ct. (8th cir.) 1976, U.S. Cir. Ct. (3d cir.) 1982. Counsel Phila. Civil Svc. Commn., 1969; trial atty. antitrust divsn. U.S. Dept. Justice, Phila., 1971—. Mem. Logan Sq. Neighborhood Assn., Phila., 1990—. With U.S. Army, 1969-71. Mem. Union League Phila. Roman Catholic. Avocations: sports, investing, wines, real estate, dining. Home: 2137 Race St Philadelphia PA 19103-1009 Office: US Dept Justice Antitrust Divsn 650 Curtis Ctr 7th & Walnut Philadelphia PA 19106 E-mail: edward.panek@usdoj.gov.

PANICCIA, PATRICIA LYNN, journalist, writer, lawyer, educator; b. Glendale, Calif., Sept. 19, 1952; d. Valentino and Mary (Napoleon) P.; m. Jeffrey McDowell Mailes, Oct. 5, 1985; children: Alana Christine, Malia Noel. BA in Comm., U. Hawaii, 1977; JD, Pepperdine U., 1981. Bar: Hawaii 1981, Calif. 1982, U.S. Dist. Ct. Hawaii 1981. Extern law clk. hon. Samuel P. King U.S. Dist. Ct., Honolulu, 1980; reporter, anchor woman Sta. KEYT-TV, Santa Barbara, Calif., 1983-84; reporter Sta. KCOP-TV, L.A., 1984-88; reporter CNN, L.A., 1989-93. Adj. prof. comm. law Pepperdine Sch. Law, 1987, gender & the law, 1994—, adj. prof.; profl. surfer, 1977-81. Author: Worksmarts for Women: The Essential Sex Discrimination Survival Guide, 2000. Recipient Clarion award Women in Comm., Inc., 1988. Mem. ABA (chair of law and media com. young lawyers divsn. 1987-88, nat. conf. com. lawyers and reps. of media 1987-91), Calif. State Bar (mem. com. on fair trial and free press 1983-84, pub. affairs com. 1985-87), Hawaii Bar Assn., Phi Delta Phi (historian 1980-81). Office: PO Box 881 La Canada CA 91012-0881

PANICH, DANUTA BEMBENISTA, lawyer; b. East Chicago, Ind., Apr. 9, 1954; d. Fred and Ann Stephanie (Grabowski) B.; m. Nikola Panich, July 30, 1977; children: Jennifer Anne, Michael Alexei. AB, Ind. U., 1975, JD, 1978. Bar: Ill. 1978, U.S. Dist. Ct. (no. dist.) Ill. 1978, U.S. Dist. Ct. (ctrl. dist.) Ill. 1987, U.S. Ct. Appeals 1987, U.S. Dist. Ct. (no. dist.) Ind. 2001. Assoc. Mayer Brown & Platt, Chgo., 1978-86, ptnr., 1986—2001, Mayer Brown Rowe & Maw, Chgo., 2002—. Bd. dirs. Munster (Ind.) Med. Rsch. Found., 1990—. Mem. ABA, Ill. Bar Assn. Republican. Roman Catholic. General civil litigation, Labor (including EEOC, Fair Labor Standards Act, labor-management relations, NLRB, OSHA). Office: Mayer Brown Rowe & Maw 190 S La Salle St Ste 3100 Chicago IL 60603-3441 E-mail: dpanich@mayerbrownrowe.com.

PANIOTO, RONALD ANGELO, judge; b. Dec. 18, 1935; s. Judith K. Panioto; 1 child, Ronald A. Jr. BBA, U. Cin., 1963; JD, No. Ky. U., 1967. Bar: Ohio 1967. Constable Ct. Common Pleas, Cin., 1958-63, 1963-67; adminstrv. asst. U.S. Congressman Donald Clancy, Cin. and Washington, 1967-68; asst. pros. atty. Hamilton County Prosecutor's Office, Cin., 1968-75; judge Hamilton County Mcpl. Ct., Cin., 1975-82, Hamilton County Ct. Common Pleas, Cin., 1982-83, adminstrv. judge, 1983—, judge domestic rels. divsn., 1982—. Mem. Ohio State Bar Assn., Order Sons of Italy, Lawyers' Club Cin., Queen City Club, United Italian Soc. Greater Cin. (pres.), DaVinci U. Club, So. OHio Dog and Game Protective Assn., Cin. Athletic Club, Met. Club, Order Sons of Italy (pres.). Republican. Roman Catholic. Avocation: golf. Office: Hamilton County Ct Domestic Rels 800 Broadway Rm 225 Cincinnati OH 45202

PANKEN, PETER MICHAEL, lawyer; b. NYC, Dec. 30, 1936; s. Harold Ira and Sylvia Rita (Haimes) P.; m. Beverly Muriel Goldner, June 19, 1960; children: Aaron, Melinda. BA cum laude, Haverford Coll., 1957; LLB magna cum laude, Harvard U., 1962. Bar: N.Y. 1962, U.S. Dist. Ct. N.Y. 1962, U.S. Ct. Appeals (2d cir.) 1969, 3d cir. 1988, (10th cir.) 1989, U.S. Supreme Ct. 1989. Assoc. Paul Weiss Rifkind Wharton Garrison, N.Y.C., 1962-66, Poletti Freiden Prashker Feldman & Gartner, N.Y.C., 1966-67, Parker Chapin Flattau & Klimpl, N.Y.C., 1967-72, ptnr., 1973-99, chair employment and labor law dept., 1986-99; mem. Epstein Becker & Green PC, N.Y.C., 1999—. Editor: Harvard Law Rev., 1961-62; author: A State-by-State Survey of the Law of Religion in the Workplace, 2001; contbg.: Employment Law Desk Book for Human Resources Professionals; contbr. articles to profl. jours. Pres., bd. dirs. Fedn. of Handicapped, N.Y.C., 1984-92; bd. dirs. Fedcap Rehab. Svcs., 1993—; pres. metro N.Y. chpt. Soc. for Human Resource Mgmt., 1990-92, gen. counsel, 1993-2003. Mem. ABA (labor and employment sect., com. on NLRB law), NY State Bar Assn. (labor and employment law sect., continuing legal edn. com.), Am. Law Inst.-ABA (chmn. employment and labor law programs, editor-in-chief Resource Materials on Labor and Employment Law 1982—), Am. Law Inst. (com. on restatement of agy. and restatement of employment law), Soc. for Human Resource Mgmt. (com. on employment practices 1990-99). General civil litigation, Labor (including EEOC, Fair Labor Standards Act, labor-management relations, NLRB, OSHA), Pension, profit-sharing, and employee benefits. Office: Epstein Becker & Green PC 250 Park Ave Ste 1200 New York NY 10177-1211 E-mail: ppanken@ebglaw.com.

PANKOPF, ARTHUR, JR., lawyer; b. Malden, Mass., Feb. 1, 1931; BS in Marine Transp., Mass. Maritime Acad., 1951; BS in Fgn. Svc. and Internat. Transp., Georgetown U., 1957, JD, 1965. Bar: Md. 1965, D.C. 1966, U.S. Supreme Ct. 1977. Ea. area mgr. Trans Ocean Van Service of Consol. Freightway, 1958-61; with U.S. Maritime Adminstrn., 1961-65; assoc. firm Preston, Thorgrimson, Ellis & Holman, Washington, 1976-77; minority chief counsel Com. on Mcht. Marine & Fisheries U.S. Ho. of Reps., Washington, 1965-69; minority chief counsel, staff dir. Com. on Commerce, U.S. Senate, 1969-76; mng. dir. Fed. Maritime Commn., 1977-81; pvt. practice Washington, 1981-84; dir. legis. affairs Corp. Pub. Broadcasting, 1984-86, v.p., gen. counsel, sec., 1986-88; pvt. practice Washington, 1988-90, 96—; dir. fed. affairs Matson Navigation Co. Inc., Washington, 1990-95. Mem. Maritime Adminstrv. Bar Assn. (pres. 1995-96), Propeller Club Port of Washington (bd. govs. 1992—). Administrative and regulatory, Legislative, Transportation. Address: 7819 Hampden Ln Bethesda MD 20814-1108 E-mail: a.pankopf@worldnet.att.net.

PANNER, OWEN M. federal judge; b. 1924; Student, U. Okla., 1941-43, LL.B., 1949. Atty. Panner, Johnson, Marceau, Karnopp, Kennedy & Nash, 1950-80; judge, now sr. judge U.S. Dist. Ct. Oreg., Portland, 1980—, sr. judge, 1992—. Recipient Am. Bd. Trial Advocates Trial Lawyer of Yr., 1973. Mem. Am. Coll. Trial Lawyers, Am. Bd. Trial Advs., Order of Coif. Office: US Dist Ct 1000 SW 3rd Ave Ste 1207 Portland OR 97204-2942

PANNILL, WILLIAM PRESLEY, lawyer; b. Houston, Mar. 5, 1940; s. Fitzhugh H. and Mary Ellen (Goodrum) P.; m. Deborah Detering, May 9, 1966 (div. Nov. 1986); children: Shelley, Katherine, Elizabeth. BA, Rice U., 1962; MS, Columbia U., 1963; JD, U. Tex., 1970. Bar: Tex. 1970, U.S. Ct. Appeals (5th cir.) 1973, U.S. Ct. Appeals (D.C. cir.) 1974, U.S. Dist. Ct. (so. dist.) Tex. 1975, U.S. Supreme Ct. 1975, U.S. Ct. Appeals (10th cir.) 1980, U.S. Dist. Ct. (no. dist.) Tex. 1991. Assoc. Vinson, Elkins, Searls & Connally, 1970-71, Vinson, Elkins, Searls, Connally & Smith, 1972-75; staff asst. to sec. Treasury Treasury Dept., Washington, 1971-72; pvt. practice, Houston, 1975-76, 85-88, 2000—; ptnr. Pannill and Hooper, Houston, 1977-80, Pannill and Reynolds, Houston, 1982-85, Pannill, Moser, Mize & Hermann, Houston, 1988-90, Pannill & Moser, L.L.P., Houston, 1990-93, Pannill, Moser & Barnes, L.L.P., Houston, 1993-2000; atty. pvt. practice, 2000—. Assoc. editor Litigation Jour. sect. litigation, ABA, 1979-81, exec. editor, 1981-82, editor-in-chief, 1982-84, dir. publs., 1984-86, mem. coun., 1986-89; lectr. Southwestern Legal Found., 1980; chmn., Legal Found. Am., 1981-82, bd. dirs., 1983-97. Contbr. articles to profl. jours. Bd. dirs. Houston Grand Opera, 1989-92, mem. adv. bd., 1995-97; mem. adv. bd. Houston Symphony Soc., 1990-98. With USMCR, 1963-64. Mem. ABA, Tex. Bar Assn., Houston Bar Assn., Rice U. Alumni Assn. (bd. dirs. 1989-92). Episcopalian. Alternative dispute resolution, Appellate, General civil litigation. Office: 3262 Westheimer PMB 570 Houston TX 77098 Personal E-mail: william.pannill@william.pannillcom.

PANSEGRAU, PHAEDRA RENÉE, lawyer; b. Rantoul, Ill., Jan. 19, 1967; d. Robert A. and Shonna Noles Leidecker; children: Lauren, Reed. BBA, Baylor U., 1989, JD, 1991. Bar: Tex. 1991, U.S. Dist. Ct. (so. dist.) Tex. Assoc. Wesley, Wilson & Herzog, Houston, 1991-95; corp. counsel Compass Group USA, Inc., Charlotte, N.C., 1996-99, sr. ops. counsel Columbia, SC, 2000—01, sr. corp. counsel, 2002—. Commercial, contracts (including sales of goods; commercial financing), Corporate, general. Office: Compass Group USA Inc 104 Hurlingham Dr Columbia SC 29223 E-mail: phaedra_pansegrau@exch.compass-usa.com.

PANTEL, GLENN STEVEN, lawyer; b. Plainfield, N.J., Sept. 25, 1953; s. Donald and Sarah Libby (Pearlman) P.; m. Lisa Pamela Krop, June 28, 1981; 1 child, Adam Scott. AB, Johns Hopkins U., 1975; JD, U. Pa., 1978. Bar: N.J. 1978, U.S. Dist. Ct. N.J. 1978, Pa. 1978, Fla. 1980, U.S. Ct. Appeals (3d cir.) 1982. Law clk. to presiding judge U.S. Dist. Ct. (so. dist.), Miami, Fla., 1978-79; from assoc. to ptnr. Shanley & Fisher P.C., Morristown, N.J., 1979-99, also bd. dirs.; ptnr. Drinker Biddle and Reath LLP, Florham Park, NJ, 1999—. Trustee Integrity, Inc., Drug and Alcohol Abuse Program, Newark; trustee, mem. scholarship com. 200 Club of Somerset County. Mem. ABA, Fla. Bar Assn., N.J. Bar Assn., Morris County Bar Assn., Phi Beta Kappa. Avocations: skiing, sailing. Environmental, Property, real (including real estate development, water). Home: 3 Cross Way Mendham NJ 07945-3120 Office: Drinker Biddle & Reath LLP 500 Campus Dr Florham Park NJ 07932-1047

PANZER, MITCHELL EMANUEL, lawyer; b. Phila., Aug. 2, 1917; s. Max and Cecelia P.; m. Edith Budin, Apr. 13, 1943; children: Marcy C. Pokotilow, Leslie S. Katz. AB with distinction and 1st honors, Temple U., 1937; JD magna cum laude, U. Pa., 1940; LLD honoris causa, Gratz Coll., 1972. Bar: Pa. 1942, U.S. Dist. Ct. (ea. dist.) Pa. 1948, U.S. Ct. Appeals (3d cir.) 1949, U.S. Supreme Ct. 1961. Gowen Meml. fellow U. Pa. Law Sch., 1940-41; law clk. Phila. Ct. Common Pleas, No. 7, 1941-42; assoc. Wolf, Block, Schorr and Solis-Cohen, Phila., 1946-54, ptnr., 1954-88, of counsel, 1988—; spl. adv. counsel Fed. Home Loan Mortgage Corp., Fed. Nat. Mortgage Assn., 1972-82; dir. emeritus, former counsel St. Edmond's Fed. Savs. Bank; former dir. State Chartered Group, Pa. Bldg. and Loan Assn. Treas., Jewish Fedn. Greater Phila., 1981-82, v.p., 1982-86, trustee, 1963—, mem. exec. com., 1981-86, hon. life trustee, 1992—; trustee emeritus Pa. Land Title Inst., 1992—; bd. regents Gratz Coll., 1958—, pres., 1962-68. Served to capt. USAF, 1942-46. Decorated Bronze Star medal; recipient Man of Year award Gratz Coll. Alumni Assn., 1964. Mem. Am. Coll. Real Estate Lawyers, ABA (chmn. spl. com. on residential real estate transactions 1972-73), Pa. Bar Assn. (mem. spl. com. on land titles), Phila. Bar Assn. (chmn. com. censors 1966, chmn. bd. govs. 1971, parliamentarian 1965-67, 71, chmn. charter and by-laws com. 1972), Jewish Publ. Soc. (trustee 1966-81, 85-88, v.p. 1972-75, sec. 1975-78), Order of Coif (pres. 1961-63, exec. com.). Jewish. Clubs: 21 Jewel Square (Phila.); Masons. Patentee in field. Landlord-tenant, Property, real (including real estate development, water). Home: 505 Oak Ter Merion Station PA 19066-1340 Office: Wolf Block Schorr & Solis-Cohen 22nd Fl Arch St Philadelphia PA 19103-2097 Personal E-mail: mepanzer@erols.com. Business E-Mail: mpanzer@wolfblock.com.

PAPADEMETRIOU, OURANIA, lawyer; b. Newburyport, Mass., Sept. 9, 1952; d. Spyridon C. Papademetriou and Maxine Zerveas; m. Jon J. Belisonzi, Oct. 2, 1981; children: Eleni P. Belisonzi, Lisa P. Belisonzi. BA in English, Salve Regina Coll., 1974; JD, Temple U., 1981. Bar: Pa. Asst. dist. atty., Phila., 1984—97; counsel Women Against Abuse Legal Ctr., Phila., 1997—2002, dir., 2002—. Office: Women Against Abuse Legal Ctr 100 S Broad St 5th Fl Philadelphia PA 19110

PAPANTONOPOULU, KATIA, lawyer; b. Kyparissia, Greece, Nov. 27, 1941; d. Gregory Ioannidis and Vassiliki Ioannidoy; m. Anthony Papantonopoulos, Jan. 29, 1967; children: Vassiliki, Dimitra. Law Degree, Athens (Greece) U., 1965. In-house counsel Olympic Airways S.A., Athens, 1973—99; counsel M. & P. Bernitsas Law Offices, Athens, 2000—. Rep. Olympic Airways S.A. Legal Com. of IATA and Tax Sub-Com. of IATA, Montreal, Canada, 1983—89. Mem.: Athens Bar Assn. Greek Orthodox. Avocations: travel, gardening. Aviation, Commercial, contracts (including sales of goods; commercial financing). Office: M & P Bernitsas Law Offices 5 Lykavittou St 10672 Athens Greece

PAPAZISSIS, MICHAEL GEORGE, lawyer, consultant; b. 1935; s. George and Zoe (Katsaridou) Papazissis; m. Athena Vogassari, Oct. 25, 1959; children: Byron, Joan, Georgia, Natalie. LLB, U. Thessaloniki, Greece, 1961, postgrad. diploma law, 1967; LLM, U. Montreal, 1968. Bar: Thessaloniki 1965, Supreme Ct. Athens 1969, Athens 1980. Pvt. practice, Athens, 1981-82, B.I.A.O. of Paris, Athens, 1982-85. Mem. Youth for Understanding Student Exch. Program, nat. chmn. Hellenic com., 1970—2002. Recipient medal Youth for Understanding, Student Exch. Program, Ann Arbor, Mich., 1974; Ford Found. scholar, U. Montreal, 1968—69. Greek Orthodox. Home: 41 Spefsippou St 10676 Athens Greece Office: 5 Xanthou St 10673 Athens Greece

PAPE, STUART M. lawyer; b. Paterson, N.J., Dec. 24, 1948; BA, U. Va., 1970, JD, 1973. Bar: Va. 1973, U.S. Ct. Appeals (6th cir.) 1975, U.S. Supreme Ct. 1976, D.C. 1980. Law clk. to Hon. Leonard Braman Superior Ct. D.C., 1973-74; exec. asst. to commr. FDA, 1979; mng. ptnr. Patton Boggs LLP and predecessors, Washington. Mem. ABA (com. food and drug law, sect. adminstrv. law 1973-2002), Va. State Bar, D.C. Bar. Administrative and regulatory, Banking. Address: 2950 Chain Bridge Rd NW Washington DC 20016-3408 E-mail: spape@pattonboggs.com.

PAPERNIK, JOEL IRA, lawyer; b. N.Y.C., May 4, 1944; s. Herman and Ida (Titefsky) Papernik; m. Barbara Ann Barker, July 28, 1972; children: Deborah, Ilana. BA, Yale U., 1965; JD cum laude, Columbia U., 1968. Bar: NY 1969. Assoc. Shea & Gould, N.Y.C., 1968-76, ptnr., 1976-91; ptnr., chmn. corp. and securities dept., mem. mgmt. com. Squadron, Ellenoff, Plesent & Sheinfeld, N.Y.C., 1991-2000; ptnr., chair mergers and acquisitions practice group, mem. bus. fin. dept. and opinion com. Mintz, Levin, Cohn, Ferris, Glovsky and Popeo PC, N.Y.C., 2000—. Lectr various panels. With 11th Spl. Forces USAR, 1967—73. Mem.: ABA (sect. corp. law), Negotiated Acquisitions Com., NY Tri-Bar Opinion Com., Assn. Bar City NY (mem. securities regulation com. 1992—95, chmn., lectr., mem. corp. law com.), NY State Bar Assn. (lectr. various panels, mem. securities law com.), NY Biotech. Assn. (lectr. various panels), Yale Club. Corporate, general, Entertainment, Securities. Office: Mintz Levin Cohn Ferris Glovsky and Popeo PC 666 3rd Ave New York NY 10017-4011 E-mail: jpapernik@mintz.com.

PAPPAS, DAVID CHRISTOPHER, lawyer; b. Kenosha, Wis., Mar. 18, 1936; s. theros and Marion Lucille (Piperas) P.; m. Laurie Jean LaCaskey, Nov. 26, 1956 (div. 1969); children: Christopher David, Andrea Lynn; m. Nancy Marie Pratt, June 11, 1983. BS, U. Wis., 1959, JD, 1961. Bar: Wis. 1961, U.S. Dist. Ct. (ea. and we. dists.) Wis. 1965, U.S. Supreme Ct. 1971; lic. master mariner. Asst. corp. counsel Racine County (Wis.), 1961; atty., advisor U.S. Dept. Labor, Washington, 1961-62; staff atty. U.S. Commn. Civil rights, Washington, 1962-63; asst. city atty. City of Madison (Wis.), 1963-65; atty. pvt. practice, Madison, 1965—. Chmn. Madison Mayor's Citizen Adv. Com., 1964-65; pres. Wis. Cup Assn., Madison, 1965; c0-chmn. 2d Congl. Dist. Humphrey for Pres., Madison, 1972. Recipient commendation for Supreme Ct. work Madison County Coun., 1965, commendation resolution City of Madison, 1965. Mem. Wis. Bar Assn., Dane County Bar Assn., Wis. Acad. Trial Lawyers, Am. Assn. Trial Lawyers, Lawyer-Pilot Bar Assn. (master mariner), Gt. Lakes Hist. Soc., Madison Club, South Shore Yacht Club (Milw.). General civil litigation, Family and matrimonial, General practice. Home and Office: 1787 Strawberry Rd Deerfield WI 53531-9779

PAPPAS, EDWARD HARVEY, lawyer; b. Midland, Mich., Nov. 24, 1947; s. Charles and Sydell (Sheinberg) P.; m. Laurie Weston, Aug. 6, 1972; children: Gregory Alan, Steven Michael. BBA, U. Mich., 1969, JD, 1973. Bar: Mich. 1973, U.S. Dist. Ct. (ea. dist.) Mich. 1973, U.S. Dist. Ct. (we. dist.) Mich. 1980, U.S. Ct. Appeals (6th cir.) 1983, U.S. Supreme Ct. 1983. Ptnr. firm Dickinson & Wright, P.L.L.C., Detroit and Bloomfield Hi, Mich., 1973—. Mediator Oakland County Cir. Ct., Pontiac, Mich., 1983—; hearing panelist Mich. Atty. Discipline Bd., Detroit, 1983—, chmn., 1987—; mem. bus. tort subcom. Mich. Supreme Ct. Com. Standard Jury Instructions, 1992-94; bd. commrs. State Bar Mich., 1999—. Trustee Oakland Community Coll., Mich., 1982-90, Oakland-Livingston Legal Aid, 1982-90, v.p., 1982-85, pres., 1985-87; trustee, adv. bd. Mich. Regional Anti-Defamation League of B'nai B'rith, Detroit, 1983-90; planning commr. Village of Franklin, Mich., 1987-91, chmn. 1989-91, councilman, 1991-92, chmn. charter com., 1993-94; chmn. State Bar Mich. Long Range Planning com.; pres.-elect Oakland County Bar Assn., 1996-97, pres., 1997-98, chmn. Jud. Selection Task Force, 1997; bd. dirs. Franklin Found., 1989-92; trustee The Oakland Medication Ctr., 1992-96. Master Oakland County Bar Assn. Inn of Ct.; fellow Mich. State Bar Found., Oakland Bar-Adams Pratt Found., ABA Found.; mem. ABA, Fed. Bar Assn., State Bar Mich. (co-chmn. nat. moot ct. competition com. 1974, 76, com. on legal aid, chmn. standing com. on atty. grievances 1989-92, comml. litigation com., civil procedure com. 1992-94, bd. commrs. 1999—), Oakland County Bar Assn. (vice-chmn. continuing legal edn. com., chmn. continuing legal edn. com. 1985-86, mediation com. 1989-90, chmn. mediation com. 1990-91, bd. dirs. 1990-98, chmn. select com. Oakland County cir. ct. settlement week 1991, chmn. strategic planning com. 1992-93, editor Laches monthly mag. 1986-88, co-chair task force to improve justice systems in Oakland County 1993—, pres.-elect, bd. dirs. 1996-97, pres. 1997-98), Am. Judicature Soc., Mich. Def. Trial Lawyers, Def. Rsch. and Trial Lawyers Assn. (com. practice and procedure), B'nai B'rith Barristers. Federal civil litigation, State civil litigation. Home: 32223 Scenic Ln Franklin MI 48025-1702 Office: Dickinson Wright Moon Van Dusen & Freeman 525 N Woodward Ave Bloomfield Hills MI 48304-2971

PAPPAS, GEORGE FRANK, lawyer; b. Washington, Oct. 5, 1950; s. Frank George and lora Marie (Stauber) P.; m. Susan Elizabeth Bradshaw, Apr. 25, 1980; children: Christine Bradshaw, Alexandra Stauber. BA, U. Md., 1972, JD, 1975. Bar: Md. 1976, D.c. 1991, u.S. Dist. Ct. Md. 1976, U.S. Dist. Ct. (d.C. cir.) 1986, U.S. Dist. Ct. (we. dist.) Tex. 1993, U.S. Ct. Appeals (4th cir.) 1976, U.S. Ct. Appeals (d.c. cir.) 1984, U.S. Ct. Appeals 9fed. cir.) 1991, U.S. Ct. Appeals (2d cir.) 1993, U.S. Ct. Appeals (6th and 7th cirs.) 1994, U.S. Supreme Ct. 1984, U.S. Ct. of Fed. Claims, 1995. Assoc. H. russell Smouse, Balt., 1976-81, Melnicove, Kaufman, Wiener & Smouse, Balt., 1981-83, prin., 1983-88; ptnr. Venable, Baetjer and Howard, Balt., 1986—. Lectr. Wash. Coll. Law, Am. U., Washington, 1980-84; mem. moot ct. bd., 1974-75; Master of the Bench , Inn XIII, Am. Inns of Ct., 1989; mem. U.S. Dist. Ct. of Delaware Judges' Intellectual property Adv. Com., 1998—; mem. Dist. Judge Edn. Adv. Com. for the Fed. Jud. Ctr., 2001—, chmn. Gov. Commn. on Devel. of Tech. Bus., 2003-. Founding editor-in-chief Internat. Trade law Jour., 1974-75. Mem. bd. vis. U. Md. Sch. of Law, 2000—. 1st lt. USAF, 1972-76. Mem. ABA, Am. Law Inst. 2002-, Internat. Assn. Def. Counsel, Md. Bar Assn. (chmn. internat. coml. law sect., 1980-81), Am. Intellectual Property Law Assn., U.S. Trademark Assn., Omicron Delta kappa, Phi Kappa Phi, Phi Beta Kappa, L'Hirondelle Club, Baltimore Country Club. Republican. Greek Orthodox. Federal civil litigation, State civil litigation, Intellectual property. Home: 9 Roland Ct Baltimore MD 21204-3550 Office: Venable Baetjer & Howard 2 Hopkins Plz Ste 2100 Baltimore MD 21201-2982 also: 1201 New York Ave NW Ste 1000 Washington DC 20005-6197

PAPROCKI, THOMAS JOHN, lawyer, priest; b. Chgo., Aug. 5, 1952; s. John Henry and Veronica Mary (Bonat) P. BA, Loyola U., Chgo., 1974; student Spanish lang. study, Middlebury Coll., 1976, student Italian lang. study, 1987; MDiv, St. Mary of the Lake Sem., 1978; student Spanish lang. study, Instituto Cuannahuac, 1978; Licentiate in Sacred Theology, St. Mary of the Lake Sem., 1979; JD, DePaul U., 1981; JCD, Gregorian U., Rome, 1991; student Polish lang. study, Cath. U. Lublin, Poland, 1989, Jagiellonian U., Cracow, Poland, 2000. Bar: Ill. 1981, U.S. Dist. Ct. (no. dist.) Ill. 1981, U.S. Supreme Ct. 1994. Assoc. pastor St. Michael Ch., Chgo., 1978-83; pres. Chgo. Legal Clinic, 1981-87, 91—; exec. dir. South Chgo. Legal Clinic, 1981-85, bd. dirs., 1987—; adminstr. St. Joseph Ch., Chgo., 1983-86; vice-chancellor Archdiocese of Chgo., 1985-92, chancellor, 1992-2000; adj. faculty Loyola U. of Law, 1999—; pastor St. Constance Parish, 2001—03; Titular Bishop of Vulturara, Auxiliary Bishop of Chgo., Episc. Vicar, Vicariate IV Archdiocese of Chgo., 2003—. Senator Presbyteral senate Archdiocese of Chgo., 1985-87, mem. Presbyteral coun., 1992-2000, mem. Cardinal's cabinet, 1992-2000, sec. coll. consultors, 1992-2000; chmn. incardination com., 1991-2000, chmn. policy devel. com., 1998-2000, chmn. Fgn. Priests Initiative, 1998-2000; asst. to the Gen. Sec., Vatican Synod of Bishops, Spl. Assembly for Am., Rome, 1997, cardinal's del. to profl. rev. bd., 1991-2003, chmn. profl. conduct adminstrv. com., 1991-2002; bd. dirs. Cath. Conf. Ill., 1985-87. Mem. editl. adv. bd. Chgo. Cath. Newspaper, 1984-85; contbr. articles to profl. jours. Bd. dirs. United Neighborhood Orgn., Chgo., 1982-85, S.E. Community Youth Svc. Bd., Chgo., 1985, Ctr. for Neighborhood Tech., Chgo., 1986-87, Chgo. Area Found. for Legal Svcs., 1994-2002; active Chgo. Cmty. Trust Com. on Children, Youth and Families, 1991-2002, Ill. Family Violence Coordinating Coun., 1994—. Recipient Humanitarian award Polish Am. Congress, 1997, Alumni award for Outstanding Pub. Svc., DePaul Coll. of Law, 2001; named Man of Yr., Nat. Advs., 1999. Fellow Leadership Greater Chgo.; mem. Ill. Bar Assn., Chgo. Bar Assn. (bd. mgrs. 1999-2001, Maurice Weigle award 1985), Advs. Soc. (award of merit 1996), Cath. Lawyers Guild, Canon Law Soc. Am., Polish Am. Leadership Initiative (bd. dirs. 2001—), Polish Am. Assn. (bd. dirs. 1998—), The Chgo. Jr. Assn. Commerce and Industry (Ten Outstanding Young Citizens award 1986), Union League Club of Chgo., Pi Sigma Alpha, DePaul U. Alumni Assn. Avocations: hockey, running, reading. Immigration, naturalization, and customs, Non-profit and tax-exempt organizations. Home and Office: St Constance Parish 5843 W Strong St Chicago IL 60630-2098

PAQUIN, JEFFREY DEAN, lawyer; b. Milw., Dec. 7, 1960; s. James DeWayne and Helen Ann (Walter) P. BA, U. Wis., 1983; JD, U. Ky., 1986. Bar: Ga. 1986, U.S. Dist. Ct. (no. dist.) Ga. 1986, U.S. Ct. Appeals (11th cir.) 1986, U.S. Dist. Ct. (mid. dist.) Ga. 1987, D.C. 1989, U.S. Ct. Appeals (D.C. cir.) 1989, U.S. Supreme Ct. 1990. Assoc. Powell, Goldstein, Frazer & Murphy, Atlanta, 1986—94; chief litigation counsel United Parcel Svc., Atlanta, 1994—98; nat. practice leader ADR and litig. mgmt. Price Waterhouse, Atlanta, 1998; global practice leader Legal Mgmt. Svcs. Ernst & Young, LLP, Atlanta, 1998—2000; practice leader ADR and conflict mgmt. svcs. Kritzer & Levick, Atlanta, 2000—01; ptnr. Paquin Victor LLP, Atlanta, 2001—. V.p. Prodn. Values, Inc., Atlanta, 1987-88. Exec. editor U. Ky. Law Rev., 1985-86. Bd. dirs. Children's Motility Disorder Found., 1995-2000, Ctr. Corp. Counsel Innovation, 2000-02. Mem. ABA, FBA, The Ombudsman Assn., Am. Corp. Counsel Assn. (bd. dirs. Ga. 1997-98), D.C. Bar Assn., Ga. Bar Assn., Atlanta Bar Assn. (v.p., dir. alternative dispute resolution sect.), Mortar Board, Phi Delta Phi, Sigma Epsilon Sigma, Psi Chi. Roman Catholic. Federal civil litigation, General civil litigation, State civil litigation. Home: 3620 Woodshire Chase Marietta GA 30066-8719 Office: Paquin Victor LLP 4403 Northside Parkway Ste 1101 Atlanta GA 30327 E-mail: jeff.paquin@adrcms.com.

PAQUIN, THOMAS CHRISTOPHER, lawyer; b. Quincy, Mass., Feb. 12, 1947; s. Henry Frederick and Rita Marie (St. Louis) P.; m. Jean Jacqueline O'Neill, Aug. 5, 1972; children: Martha, Edward. BS in Acctg., Bentley Coll., 1969; JD, U. Notre Dame, 1974. Bar: Mass. 1974, U.S. Dist. Ct. Mass. 1976. Tax atty. Coopers and Lybrand, Boston, 1974-76; assoc. Cargill, Masterman & Cahill, Boston, 1976, Wilson, Curran & Malkasian, Wellesley, Mass., 1976-77; ptnr. Bianchi and Paquin, Hyannis, Mass., 1977-98; shareholder, dir. Quirk and Chamberlain, P.C., Yarmouthport, Mass., 1998—2001; of counsel Quirk, Chamberlain & Marsh, P.C., Yarmouthport, 2002—. Bd. dirs., chmn. nominating com. Elder Svcs. Cape Cod and Islands, Inc., Dennis, Mass., 1986-91; bd. dirs., corporator Vis. Nurse Assn. Cape Cod Found., Inc., Dennis, 1988-97; pres. Life Svcs. Inc., 1991-95; bd. dirs. Woodside Cemetery Corp., 1998—, pres., 1999—. Mem. Bass River Golf Commn., Yarmouth, Mass., 1980-83, chmn., 1982-83; chmn. Yarmouth Golf Course Bldg. Com., 1985-89; mem. hearing com. bd. Bar Overseers of the Supreme Jud. Ct., 1989-95; bd. dirs. Project Coach, Inc., 1990-97; conciliator Barnstable Superior Ct., 1992—; trustee, asst. treas. Cape Symphony Orch., 1999—. Fellow Mass. Bar Found.; mem. ABA, Mass. Bar Assn. (del. 1986-87, mem. com. on bicentennial U.S. Constn. 1986-88, fee arbitration bd. 1985-86, chmn. spkrs. and writers subcom. 1986-88), Barnstable County Bar Assn. (chmn. seminar com. 1979-83, mem. exec. com. 1981-84, v.p. 1984-86, pres. 1986-87), Estate Planning Coun. Cape Cod (exec. com. 1985-98, sec. 1991-93, pres.-elect 1993-95, pres. 1995-97), Mass. Conveyancers Assn., Mid-Cape Men's Club (v.p. 1992, pres. 1993), Cummaquid Golf Club. Estate planning, Probate (including wills, trusts), Property, real (including real estate development, water), Estate taxation. Office: Thomas C Paquin Atty at Law 99 Willow St PO Box 38 Yarmouth Port MA 02675-0038

PARA, GERARD ALBERT, lawyer, real estate broker, consultant; b. Oak Park, Ill., June 27, 1953; s. Bruno Joseph and Bernice Agnes Para; m. Gayle Louise Keegan, Sept. 15, 1979; children: Eric, Teresa. BA with honor, De Paul U., 1973, JD, 1976. Bar: Ill. 1977, U.S. Dist. Ct. (no. dist.) Ill. 1977, U.S. Ct. Appeals (7th cir.) 1977, Fed. Trial Bar. 1984; lic. real estate broker, Ill., 1981. Jud. law clk. Ill Appellate Ct. (1st dist.), Chgo., 1977-78; divsnl. counsel Household Internat. Franchisor Divsns., Prospect Heights, Ill., 1978-85; v.p. Bannockburn (Ill.) Pk. Concepts, Inc., 1986-93; dir. real estate ops., asst. gen. counsel Ben Franklin Stores, Carol Stream, Ill., 1994-96; v.p., gen. counsel DiMucci Devel. Corp., Palatine, Ill., 1996-97; gen. counsel Urban Investment Trust Inc., Chgo., 1998-99; prin. Franchise ESQ.sm, Lincolnshire, Ill., 1999—; arbitrator 19th Jud. Cir., Lake County, Ill., 1999—, 18th Jud. Cir., DuPage County, Ill., 2000—, Cir. Ct. of Cook County, Ill., 2000—; candidate 19th Jud. Cir. Judge, Dem. Party, Lake and McHenry Counties, Ill., 2002. Real estate broker, Long Grove, Ill., 1987—; franchise cons. Elliotts' Off Broadway Deli, Oak Brook, Ill., 1993—. Editor: Medical Malpractice, 1975, Trial Technique, 1975. Asst. coach Little League Buffalo Grove (Ill.) Recreation Assn., 1988-2000; asst. scoutmaster Boy Scouts Am., Long Grove, 1995—. Mem. ABA, Internat. Coun. Shopping Ctrs., Internat. Corp. Real Estate Execs. (bd. dirs. Chgo. chpt.), Chgo. Bar Assn., Internat. Franchise Assn., Coun. Franchise Suppliers. Roman Catholic. Avocations: lap swimming, boating, scuba diving, weightlifting. Corporate, general, Franchising, Property, real (including real estate development, water). Office: Franchise ESQ sm 125 Shelter Rd #450 Lincolnshire IL 60069 E-mail: franchiseesq@aol.com.

PARDAU, STUART LLOYD, market research company executive, lawyer, educator; b. L.A., June 30, 1962; arrived in Japan, 1994; s. Leon S. and Yvette Pardau. BA, U. Calif., Santa Barbara, 1984; MPhil, Cambridge (Eng.) U., 1985; JD, Stanford U., 1992. Bar: D.C. 1992, Ariz. 1994, Calif., 2001. Atty. Weil, Gotshal & Manges, 1992-93, Morrison & Hecker, 1993-94; fgn. legal advisor Matsuo & Kosugi, Tokyo, 1994-97; mng. dir., regional counsel Fed. Express, Tokyo, 1997—; sr. dir. bus. and legal affairs JD Power and Assocs., Calif. Adj. prof. law and bus. Temple U. Del. Dem. Nat. Conv., Atlanta, 1988. Fellow Kyoto U., 1991. Mem. Am. C. of C. (chmn. corp. counsel subcom. 1998—), Tokyo Am. Club. Office: JD Power and Assocs 2625 Townsgate Rd Westlake Village CA 91361

PARDIECK, ROGER LEE, lawyer; b. Seymour, Ind., Mar. 1, 1937; s. Martin W. and Lorna (Wente) P.; m. Mary Ann Pardieck; children: Amy, Andrew, Melissa, Duncan. AB, Ind. U., 1959, LLB, 1963; student, Internat. Grad. Sch., Stockholm, 1960. Bar: Ind. 1963, U.S. Dist. Ct. (so. dist.) Ind. 1964, U.S. Ct. Appeals (7th cir.) 1965; diplomate Am. Bd. Trial Advocates. Tchg. asst. Ind. U., Bloomington, 1963-64; spl. prosecutor Jackson County, Ind., 1964-65; ptnr. Montgomery, Elsner and Pardieck, 1965-84; prin. Pardieck & Gill, PC, Seymour, Ind., 1985—. Faculty Nat. Inst. Trial Advocacy, Ind.; lectr. in field. Contbr. articles to profl. jours. Bd. dirs. Seymour Girls Club, 1968-72, Seymour C. of C., 1971-75; bd. dirs. Luth. Comty. Home, 1964-82, pres., 1970; trustee Immanuel Luth. Ch., 1977-80, bd. Immanuel Luth. Sch., 1980-83; adv. bd. Ind. U., Purdue U.-Indpls., 1981-83. Fellow Am. Coll. Trial Lawyers, Ind. Trial Lawyers Assn. (bd. dirs. 1969—, pres. 1975), Ind. Coll. Trial Lawyers, Roscoe Pound Found., Ind. Bar Assn.; mem. FBA, ATLA (bd. govs. 1985-88), Ind. State Bar Assn. (bd. govs. 1980-82), Inst. for Injury Reduction (bd. dirs. 1992-95), Nat. Bd. Trial Advocacy, Safety Attys. Fedn. (bd. dirs. 1993-95), Internat. Soc. Primerus Law Firms (bd. dirs. 1995—), Am. Bd. Trial Advocates, Trial Lawyers Pub. Justice (IN coord. 1991-), Am. Judicature Soc., Inner Cir. Advocates. Federal civil litigation, State civil litigation, Personal injury (including property damage). Office: 100 N Chestnut St PO Box 608 Seymour IN 47274-0608 E-mail: rlp@pardieckgill.com.

PARENT, LOUISE MARIE, lawyer; b. San Francisco, Aug. 28, 1950; d. Jules D. and Mary Louise (Bartholomew) P.; m. John P. Casaly, Jan. 5, 1980. AB, Smith Coll., 1972; JD, Georgetown U., 1975. Bar: N.Y. 1976, U.S. Dist. Ct. (so. dist.) N.Y. 1976. Assoc. Donovan Leisure, N.Y.C., 1975-77; various positions, then gen. counsel Am. Express Info. Svcs. Corp., N.Y.C., 1977-92; dep. gen. counsel Am. Express Co., N.Y.C., 1992-93, exec. v.p., gen. counsel, 1993—. Bd. dirs. A Better Chance Inc., Cooke Ctr. for Learning and Devel., YWCA N.Y., Nat. Ctr. State Cts.; mem. adv. bd. Studio in a Sch. Mem. ABA (com. depts. corp. law; mem. steering com. commerce and industry), N.Y.C. Bar Assn., N.Y. State Bar Assn., Coun. on Fgn. Rels. Corporate, general, Mergers and acquisitions, Securities. Home: 1170 5th Ave New York NY 10029-6527 Office: Am Express Co Am Express Tower World Fin Ctr New York NY 10285-0001*

PARIENTE, BARBARA J. state supreme court justice; b. Dec. 24, 1948; m. Frederick A. Hazouri. Grad. with high honors, Boston U., 1970; JD with highest honors, George Washington U., 1973. Bar: Fla. 1973; cert. civil trial lawyer Fla. Bar; cert. Nat. Bd. Trial Advocacy. Law clk. to hon. Norman C. Roettger, Jr. U.S. Dist. Ct. (so. dist.) Fla., 1973-75; ptnr. Cone Wagner Nugent, 1975-83, Pariente & Silber, P.A., 1983; pvt. practice; judge U.S. Ct. of Appeals (4th dist.), 1993-97; justice Fla. Supreme Ct., Tallahassee, 1997—. Participant Twenty-First Century Justice Conf.; mem. Judicial Cir. Grievance Com., 1989-92, chair, 1990-92; mem. nominating com. U.S. Ct. Appeals (15th cir.), 1980-84. Contbr. articles to profl. jours. Bd. dirs. Fla. Bar Found.; mentor Take Stock in Children; active Palm Beach County Youth Ct. program, 1997, Cities in Schs. mentoring program, 1993, Temple Judea, Palm Beach County Sephardi Fedn., Jewish Cmty. Ctr., Ballet Fla., Palm Beach County Commn. on Status of Women. Recipient award for disting. svc. to the arts Palm Beach County Bar Assn., 1987, Civil Litigation Pro Bono award Legal Aid Soc., 1993. Mem. ABA, Nat. Assn. Women Judges, Am. Inns. of Ct. (founding mem. Palm Beach County chpt.), Acad. Fla. Trial Lawyers (bd. dirs., chair Spkr.'s Bur. program 1984-87, outreach com. 1991-92, co-chair Workhorse Seminar 1991-92), Assn. Trial Lawyers Am. (vice chair profl. rsch. and devel. dept. 1980-82, chair comml. litigation sect. 1984-85, women's trial lawyer caucus 1986-87; mem. ethics com. 1989-90, conv. planning com. 1992-93), Fla. Assn. Women Lawyers. Office: State Supreme Ct of Florida 500 S Duval St Tallahassee FL 32399-1925

PARISH, J. MICHAEL, lawyer, writer; b. Decatur, Ill., Nov. 9, 1943; s. John Mitchell and Gladys Margaret (Daulton) P.; m. Susan Lee Sgarlat, July 24, 1976 (div.); m. Ellen R. Harnett, Dec. 3, 1991; children: Margaret Ruth, William Walter. AB cum laude, Princeton U., 1965; LLB, Yale U., 1968. Assoc. LeBoeuf Lamb et al, N.Y.C., 1968-73, ptnr., 1974-89, Winthrop Stimson Putnam & Roberts, N.Y.C., 1989-95, Thelen, Reid & Priest, N.Y.C., 1995—2002, Wolf, Block, Schorr & Solis-Cohen, N.Y.C., 2002—. Bd. dirs. Forum Funds, Portland, Maine, Core Trust. Contbr. stories and poetry to mags. Dir. PBS Am. Poetry Project, 1985-90; coord. Yale Law Sch. Clinton Election com.; class sec. Princeton Class of 1965. Univ. scholar Princeton U., 1965, Nat. scholar Yale U., 1968. Mem. Princeton Club N.Y. Avocation: creative writing. Corporate, general, Utilities, public, Securities. Home: 100 Riverside Dr New York NY 10024-4822 Office: Wolf Block 250 Park Ave New York NY 10177

PARISH, WILLIAM HENRY, lawyer; b. Oakland, Calif., July 28, 1954; s. Harry and Elaine Katherine (Triplett) P.; m. Kathryn Annette, Aug. 14, 1976; children: Michael Erik, Jennifer Christine, Melissa Ann. AA, Hartnell Coll., 1974; BA, Calif. State U., 1977; JD, U. Pacific, 1980. Bar: Calif. 1980, U.S. Dist. Ct. (ea. dist.) Calif. 1980, U.S. Ct. Appeals (9th cir.) 1980, U.S. Supreme Ct. 1990. Assoc. Cavalero, Bray, Geiger & Rudquist, Stockton, Calif., 1980-82, ptnr., 1982-87, Bray, Geiger, Rudquist, Nuss & Parish, Stockton, Calif., 1987; prin. Law Offices of William H. Parish, Stockton, Calif., 1987—96, Parish & Nelson, A Profl. Corp., Stockton, Calif., 1997—2002, Parish & Small, A Profl. Corp., Stockton, Calif., 2003—. Mem. ABA (litigation sect. 1980—), Order of Coif, Am. Heart Assn., San Joaquin County, mem. bd. dirs. (2001-), pres. (2002-). Federal civil litigation, State civil litigation. Office: Parish & Small Profl Corp 1919 Grand Canal Blvd Ste A-5 Stockton CA 95207

PARISIER, CARLOS, lawyer, economist; b. Buenos Aires, Oct. 21, 1930; m. Alicia Parisier, Nov. 25, 1965; children: Martin, Jacqueline. BA, Colegio Nacional de Buenos Aires, 1948; LLB cum laude, U. Buenos Aires, 1954. Bar: Argentina, 1954, Uruguay, 1955, Spain, 1985. Owner, sr. ptnr. Estudio Parisier, Buenos Aires, 1954—; pres. Hermitage Hotel S.A., Mar del Plata, Argentina, 1958-75; founder Fundacion Pro Justitia, Buenos Aires, 1980. Film producer, 1963—. Author: La nueva ley argentina en materia de convenciones de trabajo, 1955; contbr. articles on corp. and bankruptcy law to legal publs. Recipient motion picture award, Acapulco, Mexico, 1963. Mem. ABA, Buenos Aires Bar Assn., Uruguay Bar Assn., Madrid Bar Assn., Argentine Inst. Comml. Law, Comml. Bank Lawyers Argentina. General practice, Private international, Commercial, consumer (including collections, credit), Corporate, general. Office: Estudio Parisier Callao 220 4th Fl Buenos Aires Argentina E-mail: carlos@parisier.com.

PARK, BEVERLY GOODMAN, lawyer; b. Boston, Nov. 10, 1937; d. Morris and Mary (Keller) Goodman; divorced; children: Glynis Forcht, Seth, Elyse. BS, Simmons Coll., 1959; MS, Ea. Conn. State U., 1968; JD, Western N.E. Coll. Law, 1998. Bar: Mass. 1998. Asst. dir. comty. svc. Hartford (Conn.) Courant, 1976-79; mayor Borough of Colchester, Conn., 1979-83; lifestyle editor Chronicle, Willimantic, Conn., 1980-82, suburban editor, 1982-84; officer mktg. & comm. U. Conn. Health Ctr., Farmington, 1984-97; assoc. Etheredge and Steuer, Northampton, Mass., 1998—. Selected team mem. radiation exposure info. study Belorussia, 1993; mem. adv. bd. Hosp. News; mem. women's affairs com. U. Conn. Health Ctr. Women's Networking Task Force; mem. Univ. Adminstrv. Staff Coun.; mem. minority awards com. U. Conn. Health Ctr., mem. John N. Dempsey hosp. disaster plan com. Designer: (libr. studies curriculum) Classroom Instruction on the Use of Books and Libraries, 1972; pub.: (ednl. booklets) Have You Made Plans for the Future?, 1977-78; editor of edn. holiday and bridal supplements The Chronicle, 1980-84; editor: U. Conn. Health Ctr. Anniversary Mag., 1986, U. Conn. Health Ctr. Med. Catalog, 1986, (ann. pub.) Salute, 1988, U. Conn. Health Ctr. 30th Anniversary Supplement, 1991. Bd. dirs. Ea. Conn. Found. for Pub. Giving, Norwich, 1990-96; women's club officer Dem. Town Com., Colchester, Conn., 1963-90; active Hadassah, Northampton/Amherst, 1996—, Women's League for Conservative Judaism. Recipient Lifestyle Page award New England Press Assn., 1980, Media Excellence in Covering Human Svcs. award Conn. chpt. NASW, 1982, Ragan Report Arnold's Admirables award for excellence in graphics and typography, 1985, Gold award Healthcare Mktg. Report, 1987, award for video ACS, 1990. Mem. NOW (membership com. Southea. chpt., mem. legis. task force, Meritorious Svc. award Southea. Conn. chpt. 1985), Am. Soc. for Hosp. Mktg. and Pub. Rels., Am. Mktg. Assn., Assn. Am. Med. Colls. (mem. group on pub. affairs), Conn. Hosp. Assn. (participant hosp. pub. rels. conf.), State of Conn. Pub. Info. Coun. (mem. steering com.), Mass. Bar Assn., Hampshire County and Franklin County Bar Assns., New England Hosp. Pub. Rels. and Mktg. Assn. (bd. dirs. 1987, 88). Avocations: swimming, hiking, spending time with grandchildren. General civil litigation, Commercial, consumer (including collections, credit), Constitutional. Home and Office: 116 N Main St Florence MA 01062-1220 E-mail: parklegal@aol.com.

PARK, ELENA, lawyer; b. Toronto, Ont., Can. arrived in U.S., 1995; BA with honors, U. Toronto, 1994; JD, Temple U., 1998. Bar: Pa. 1998, U.S. Dist. Ct. (ea. dist.) Pa. 1999. Jud. law clk. Phila. Ct. Common Pleas, 1998—99; atty. Cozen O'Connor, P.C., 1999—. Vol. atty. for indigent, Phila., 1998—. Recipient Gomez award Pub. Svc., Phila. Bar Assn., 1996. Mem.: Asian Am. Bar Assn. Delaware Valley. Immigration, naturalization, and customs, Insurance. Office: Cozen O'Connor 1900 Market St Philadelphia PA 19103 Home: 133 Golphi Hills Rd Wayne PA 19087

PARK, JERROLD ELLIOTT, lawyer; b. Mitchell, S.D., Jan. 18, 1921; s. Ronald Ray and Crystal Blanche (Elliott) P.; m. Merna Dyce, Aug. 24, 1946; children— Sherri Wood, Debra Park Schmidt, Ron, Crys Harpole, Jill Karber. Student Augustana Coll., Sioux Falls, S.D., 1939, U. Colo., 1946-47; B.A., U. Denver, 1948; LL.B., U. Wis., 1951. Bar: Ill. 1951, Colo. 1954, Idaho 1962. Assoc., Sidley, Austin, Burgess & Smith, Chgo., 1951-54; with legal dept. Shell Oil Co., 1954-61; ptnr. McFadden & Park, St. Maries, Idaho, 1962-77, Park & Rogers, St. Maries, 1977—, ret. 2000 ; sec., bd. dirs. Benewah County Devel. Corp., St. Maries, 1963— , E.C. Hay & Sons, Inc., Tekoa, Wash., 1965— . Exec. editor Wis. Law Rev., 1950-51. Mem. council, mayor pro tem City of Arvada, Colo., 1957-61; chmn. Met. Sewage Dist., Denver, 1960-61. Served to lt. U.S. Army, 1940-45, PTO. Mem. Idaho State Bar, 1st Dist. Bar Assn. (pres. 1972-73), Order of Coif, Elks, Phi Beta Kappa. Democrat. Presbyterian. Estate planning, General practice, Probate (including wills, trusts). Home: 322 S 9th St Saint Maries ID 83861-1706

PARK, WILLIAM WYNNEWOOD, law educator; b. Phila., July 2, 1947; s. Oliver William and Christine (Lindes) Park. BA, Yale U., 1969; JD, Columbia U., 1972; MA, Cambridge U., 1975. Bar: Mass. 1972, DC 1980. Law practice, Paris, 1972-79; prof. law Boston U., 1979—. V.p. London Ct. Internat. Arbitration; dir. Boston U. Ctr. Banking Law Studies, 1990-93; vis. prof. U. Dijon, France, 1983-84, Inst. U. Hautes Etudes Internat., Geneva, 1983, U. Hong Kong, 1990; fellow Selwyn Coll., Cambridge, Eng., 1975-77; arbitrator Claims Resolution Tribunal for Dormant Accts., Switzerland. 1998-2002. Author: International Chamber of Commerce Arbitration, 3d edit., 2000, International Forum Selection, 1995, International Commercial Arbitration, 1997, Annotated Guide to the 1998 ICC Arbitration Rules, 1998, Arbitration in Banking and Finance, 1998; contbr. articles to profl. jours. Trustee Mass. Bible Soc.; sr. warden King's Chapel, Boston. Fellow Chartered Inst. Arbitrators (U.K.), Coll. Comml. Arbitrators; mem. ABA (chmn. internat. dispute resolution com.). Home: 36 King St Cohasset MA 02025-1304 Office: Boston U Law Sch 765 Commonwealth Ave Boston MA 02215-1401

PARKER, BARRINGTON D., JR., federal judge, lawyer; b. Washington, Aug. 21, 1944; BA, Yale U., 1965, JD, 1969. Bar: N.Y. 1971. Law clk. to Hon. Aubrey E. Robinson, U.S. Dist. Ct. for D.C., Washington, 1969-70; assoc. Sullivan & Cromwell, N.Y.C., 1970-77; ptnr. Parker Auspitz Neesemann & Delehanty, P.C., N.Y.C., 1977-87, Morrison & Foerster, N.Y.C., 1987-94; judge U.S. Dist. Ct. for so. dist. N.Y., White Plains, 1994—2001, U.S. Ct. Appeals (2nd Ct.), NY, 2001—. Bd. dirs., v.p. NAACP Legal Def. and Educational Fund, Inc., 1980—; com. on grievances, com. on civil discovery U.S. Dist. Ct. (so. dist.) N.Y., 1983—; com. on pre-trial phase civil cases U.S. Ct. Appeals (2d cir.) 1983—. Trustee Governance Inst., Greenwich Acad., South Africa Legal Svcs. and Legal Edn. Project, Inc.; successor trustte an mem. Yale Corp. Mem. ABA, Fed. Bar Coun., Assn. Bar City N.Y. (com. on the judiciary 1978-82, exec. com. 1982-86, nominating com. 1987), Coun. on Fgn. Rels. Office: US Courthouse 300 Quarropas St Rm 633 White Plains NY 10601-4150 also: Thurogood Marshall US Courthouse 40 Foley Square New York NY 10007*

PARKER, BRET I. lawyer; b. N.Y.C., 1968; m. Katharine; children: Matthew, Benjamin. BA, U. Pa., 1990; JD, Fordham U., 1993. Bar: N.Y. 1994, U.S. Dist. Ct. (so. dist.) N.Y., U.S. Dist. Ct. (ea. dist.) N.Y. Law clk. to Hon. K. Michael Moore U.S. Dist. Ct. (so. dist.) Fla., Miami, 1993-94; assoc. Townley & Updike, N.Y.C., 1994-95, Dorsey & Whitney, N.Y.C., 1995-97; asst. gen. counsel Colgate-Palmolive Co., N.Y.C., 1997—. Mem. Internat. Trademark Assn. (bd. dirs. 2002), N.Y.C. Bar Assn. (chair com. trademarks and unfair competition 2000-03). Intellectual property, Private international, Trademark and copyright. Office: Colgate-Palmolive Co 300 Park Ave New York NY 10022-7499

PARKER, DALLAS ROBERT, lawyer; b. Houston, Oct. 16, 1947; s. Richard Henry and Rosemary (McMillan) P.; m. Ingrid Elayne Thompson, July 1, 1972; children: Dallas Robert Jr., Nicholas Mattsson. BA, Vanderbilt U., 1969; JD, U. Tex., 1972. Bar: Tex. 1972. Assoc. Fulbright & Jaworski, Houston, 1972—79, ptnr., 1979—82, Brown Parker & Leahy, Houston, 1982—99, Thompson & Knight LLP, Houston, 1999—. Editor U. Tex. Law Rev., 1971. Dir. Odyssey House, Tex.; adv. dir., chair adv. bd. Houston Tech. Ctr. Named to Chancellors U. Tex. Fellow Houston Bar Found., Tex. Bar Found.; mem. ABA, Tex. Bar Assn., Houston Bar Assn. Corporate, general, Securities. Office: Thompson & Knight 3300 Three Allen Ctr Houston TX 77002

PARKER, ELLIS JACKSON, III, lawyer, broadcaster; b. Haleyville, Ala., Oct. 2, 1931; s. Ellis J. and Elizabeth (Funderburg) P.; m. Nancy Elizabeth Bealer; children: Francis Hill, Ellis Stuart. Student, U.S. Mil. Acad., West Point, N.Y., 1953-57; AB, U. Ala., 1958, LLB, 1960, JD, 1961; diploma, Droit Compare, Luxembourg, 1959; cert., Acad. Internat. Law, Hague, The Netherlands, 1960. Bar: Ala. 1960, U.S. Tax Ct. 1960, U.S. Supreme Ct. 1966, D.C. Ct. Appeals 1972, U.S. Ct. Appeals D.C. 1972, Md. Ct. Appeals 1973, U.S. Ct. Claims 1977. Legis. atty. IRS, Washington, 1961-62; chief of staff to U.S. Congressman Grant Ala., 1963-64; pvt. practice, 1964-84; spl. advisor to Pres. Richard Nixon White House, Washington, 1968-69; v.p., counsel Birmingham Broadcasting Co., 1964-83; ptnr. Taylor, Smith & Parker Law Office, Upper Marlboro, Md., 1970-86; prin., owner Ellis J. Parker, Law Office, Washington, 1986—. V.p., sec. Constrn. Components Corp., Upper Marlboro, Md., 1968-72; pres. Washington-Ala. News Reports, Washington, 1980-01; pres. Sta. WNPT-AM-FM, Tuscaloosa, Ala.; v.p. Sta. WLPH, Birmingham, Parker Real Estate, Birmingham, N.B. Devel. Co., Washington; chmn. bd. Blackbelt Broadcasting Co., Selma, Ala.; founding mem. Women's Nat. Bank, Washington; CEO Birmingham Broadcasting Co.; ptnr. Linden Radio Joint Venture, Faunsdale, Ala., 1969-89; bd. dirs. 17th St L.L.C., Bealer-Parker, LLC, Washington. Mem. Presdl. Inaugural Com., inaugural protocol officer V.p. Agnew, 1968; mem. steering com. Rep. Party, Balt., 1972; chmn. bd. trustees Prince George's Hist. and Cultural Trust, Upper Marlboro, 1974; chmn. bd. advisors Prince George's Equestrian Ctr., Upper Marlboro, 1980; founder, pres. bd. dirs. Hospice of Prince George's County, Upper Marlboro, 1982; mem. Upper Marlboro Devel. Com. Mem. IEEE, ABA, FCC Bar Assn., Fed. Bar Assn., Inter-Am. Bar Assn., Ala. Bar Assn., Md. Bar Assn., Nat. Assn. Broadcasters, Ala. Broadcasters Assn., Balt. Coun. Fgn. Affairs, Assn. Grads. U.S. Mil. Acad., Chevy Chase Club, Md. Club, St. Andrews Soc., Met. Club, Ala. Alumni Assn., Scabbard and Blade (chmn. nat. alumni coun.), Pi Kappa Alpha, Sigma Delta Kappa. Home and Office: 9220 Cranford Dr Potomac MD 20854-2229 Home: Chateau Rambouillet 2165 Ibis Island Palm Beach FL 33480 E-mail: eparker124@aol.com.

PARKER, EUGENE LEROY, III, lawyer; b. Arlington, Mass., Oct. 17, 1949; s. Eugene LeRoy Jr. and Jane Gates (Washburn) P.; m. Jo Ann Williams, June 24, 1978; children: Willis Washburn, Jones Griffith, Alden Jackson, Eliza Ann. Student, Hampden-Sydney (Va.), 1969; AB, Rutgers U., 1972; JD, Memphis State U., 1976. Bar: Tenn. 1977. Sole practice, Etowah, Tenn., 1977—. Judge City of Etowah, 1986-95. Regional dir. Am. Youth Soccer Orgn., 1985-95. Mem. Tenn. Trial Lawyers Assn., McMinn County Bar Assn. Republican. Presbyterian. Avocations: walking, coaching, scout activities, reading, yard work. General practice, Personal injury (including property damage), Workers' compensation. Home and Office: PO Box 804 Etowah TN 37331-0804

PARKER, HAROLD ALLEN, lawyer, real estate executive; b. Denver, Sept. 14, 1924; s. Hyman and Sophia P.; m. Gertrud Parker; children: David, Rodney, Diana, Jesse, Jonathan. JD, Golden Gate U., 1971. Bar: Calif. 1972. Pvt. practice, San Francisco; gen. ptnr. Harold Parker Properties, San Francisco. Legal cons. San Francisco Craft and Folk Art Mus.; past mem. Bay Area Lawyers for the Arts; spkr. in field; prime developer Union St. Comml. Corridor, San Francisco, 1963—. Pub.: Wolfgang Paalen, His Art and His Writings, 1980, Richard Bowman, Forty Years of Abstract Painting, 1986. Chmn. Fine Arts Commn., Tiburon, Calif., 1976-78. Mem. Family Club (San Francisco). Avocations: music, art, tennis. Office: 1844 Union St San Francisco CA 94123-4308

PARKER, JAMES AUBREY, federal judge; b. Houston, Jan. 8, 1937; s. Lewis Almeron and Emily Helen (Stuessy) P.; m. Florence Fisher, Aug. 26, 1960; children: Roger Alan, Pamela Elizabeth. BA, Rice U., 1959; LLB, U. Tex., 1962. Bar: Tex. 1962, N.Mex. 1963. With Modrall, Sperling, Roehl, Harris & Sisk, Albuquerque, 1962-87; judge U.S. Dist. Ct. N.Mex., Albuquerque, 1987—2000, chief judge, 2000—. Mem. Standing Commn. on Rules of Practice and Procedures of U.S. Cts., 1993-99, N.Mex. Commn. on Professionalism, 1986—; bd. visitors U. N.Mex. Law Sch., 1996—; bd. dirs. Fed. Jud. Ctr. Articles editor Tex. Law Rev., 1961-62. Mem. Fed. Judges Assn., Am. Judicature Soc., Am. Bd. Trial Advocates, N.Mex. Bar Assn. (Outstanding Judge award 1994), Albuquerque Bar Assn. (Outstanding Judge award 1993, 2000), Order of Coif, Chancellors, Phi Delta Phi. Avocations: ranching, fly fishing, running, skiing. Office: US Dist Ct 333 Lomas Blvd NW Ste 770 Albuquerque NM 87102-2277 Fax: 505 348-2225. E-mail: jparker@mncourt.fed.us.

PARKER, JOHN HILL, lawyer; b. High Point, N.C., Feb. 1, 1944; s. George Edward and Tullia Virginia (Hill) P.; children from previous marriage: Alice Lindsey, Elizabeth Shelby (dec.); m. Lynette Becton Smith, July 7, 1977. BA, U. N.C., 1966; JD, U. Tenn., 1969. Bar: N.C. 1969, U.S. Dist. Ct. (ea dist.) N.C. 1970, U.S. Supreme Ct. 1975. Assoc. Sanford, Cannon, Adams & McCullough, Raleigh, N.C., 1969-73; pvt. practice Raleigh, 1974-76; judge N.C. Dist. Ct., Raleigh, 1976-82; ptnr. Cheshire & Parker, Raleigh, 1982—. Instr. judges seminars Inst. Govt. Chapel Hill, N.C., 1977-82. Parlementarian Wake County Young Dems., 1971-73; mem. Raleigh Arts Commn., 1981-84, chmn. 1983. Fellow Am. Acad. Matrimonial Lawyers (ethics com. 1995-97, pres. N.C. chpt. 1999-2000); mem. ABA, N.C. Bar Assn. (editor family law sect. 1984-85, chmn. 1985-86, 96-97, continuing legal edn. for family law 1979—, chmn. 1985-87, 96-98, chmn. ethics com. 1989-90, chmn. gen. curriculum com. 1989-2003), N.C. Acad. Trial Lawyers, Wake County Bar Assn. Episcopalian. Avocations: travel, backpacking, fishing, reading, music. State civil litigation, Family and matrimonial. Home: 1620 Park Dr Raleigh NC 27605-1609 Office: Cheshire & Parker PO Box 1029 133 Fayetteville St Mall Raleigh NC 27601-1356 E-mail: John.Parker@Cheshirepark.com.

PARKER, JOHN VICTOR, federal judge; b. Baton Rouge, La., Oct. 14, 1928; m. Mary Elizabeth Fridge, Sept. 3, 1949; children: John Michael, Robert Fridge, Linda Anne. BA, La. State U., 1949, JD, 1952. Bar: La. 1952. Atty. Parker & Parker, Baton Rouge, 1954-66; asst. parish atty. City of Baton Rouge, Parish of East Baton Rouge, 1956-66; atty. Sanders, Downing, Kean & Cazedessus, Baton Rouge, 1966-79; chief judge U.S. Dist. Ct., Middle Dist. La., Baton Rouge, 1979—. Vis. lectr. law La. State U. Law Sch. Served with Judge Adv. Gen.'s Corps U.S. Army, 1952-54. Mem. ABA, Am. Judicature Soc., Am. Arbitration Assn., La. State Bar Assn. (past mem. bd. govs.), Baton Rouge Bar Assn. (past pres.), Order of Coif, Phi Delta Phi. Clubs: Baton Rouge Country. Lodges: Masons (32 deg.); Kiwanis (past pres.). Democrat. Office: Russell B Long Fed Bldg & Courthouse 777 Florida St Ste 355 Baton Rouge LA 70801-1717

PARKER, R. JOSEPH, lawyer; b. St. Louis, June 29, 1944; s. George Joseph and Ann Rosalie Parker; m. Theresa Gaynor, Aug. 26, 1967; children: Christa Michele, Kevin Blake. AB, Georgetown U., 1966; JD, Boston Coll., 1969. Bar: Ohio 1969. Law clk. to judge U.S. Ct. Appeals (6th Cir.), Akron, Ohio, 1969-70; assoc. Taft, Stettinius & Hollister, Cin., 1970-78, ptnr. Arbitrator Am. Arbitration Assn., Cin., 1980—; faculty Nat. Inst. for Trial Advocacy, 1990—; faculty advanced trial advocacy program IRS, 1993. Editor Law Rev. Ann. Survey Mass. Law, 1967-69; contbg. author: Fed. Civil Procedure Before Trial-6th Circuit. Bd. dirs. West End Health Ctr., Inc., Cin., 1972-76, Legal Aid Soc. Cin., 1982-85; chmn. bd. dirs. Vol. Lawyers for Poor Found., Cin., 1986-88; master Am. Inn of Court, 1984—. Fellow Am. Coll. Trial Lawyers; mem. Ohio State Bar Assn., Cin. Bar Assn., Cin. Country Club, Order of Coif. Democrat. Roman Catholic. General civil litigation, Construction, Environmental. Office: 425 Walnut St Ste 1800 Cincinnati OH 45202-3923

PARKER, RICHARD WILSON, lawyer, rail transportation executive; b. Cleve., June 14, 1943; s. Edgar Gael and Pauline (Wilson) P.; m. Helen Margaret Shober, Jan. 3, 1998; children from previous marriage: Brian Jeffrey, Lauren Michelle, Lisa Christine. BA in Econs. cum laude, U. Redlands, 1965; JD cum laude, Northwestern U., 1968. Bar: Ohio 1968, Va. 1974. Assoc. Arter & Hadden, Cleve., 1968-71; asst. gen. atty. Norfolk & Western Ry. Co., Cleve. and Roanoke, Va., 1971-74, asst. gen. solicitor Roanoke, 1974-78, gen. atty., 1978-84, Norfolk So. Corp., 1985-88, sr. gen. atty., 1988-93, asst. v.p. real estate, 1993-99, v.p. properties, 1999-2000, v.p. real estate, 2000—. Mem. ABA, Va. State Bar, Norfolk-Portsmouth Bar Assn. Presbyterian. Commercial, contracts (including sales of goods; commercial financing), Environmental, Property, real (including real estate development, water). Office: 3 Commercial Pl Norfolk VA 23510-2108

PARKER, SARAH ELIZABETH, state supreme court justice; b. Charlotte, N.C., Aug. 23, 1942; d. Augustus and Zola Elizabeth (Smith) P. AB, U. N.C., 1964, JD, 1969; LHD (hon.), Queens Coll., 1998. Bar: N.C. 1969, U.S. Dist. Ct. (mid., ea. and we. dists.) N.C. Vol. U.S. Peace Corps, Ankara, Turkey, 1964-66; pvt. practice Charlotte, 1969-84; judge N.C. Ct. Appeals, Raleigh, 1985—92; assoc. justice N. C. Supreme Ct., Raleigh, 1993—. Bd. visitors U. N.C., Chapel Hill, 1993—97; pres. Mecklenburg County Dem. Women, Charlotte, 1973; N.C. ct. commr., 1999—; bd. dirs. YWCA, Charlotte, 1982—85. Recipient Disting. Woman of N.C. award, 1997, Woman of Achievement award Nat. Fedn. Women's Clubs, 1997. Mem. ABA, Inst. Jud. Adminstrn., N.C. Bar Assn. (v.p. 1987-88), Mecklenburg County Bar (sec.-treas. 1982-84), Wake County Bar Assn., N.C. Internat. Women's Forum, Women Attys. Assn. (Gwyneth David Pub. Svc. award 1986). Episcopalian. Office: NC Supreme Ct PO Box 2448 Raleigh NC 27602-2448*

PARKER, WILMER, III, lawyer, educator; b. Ozark, Ala., Oct. 3, 1951; s. Wilmer and Anne Laura (Ragsdale) P.; m. Rebecca Joy Skillern, Aug. 25, 1984; children: R. Virginia, J. William; m. Beverly Laura Barnard, Dec. 23, 1972 (div. Dec. 1977). BS in Commerce, U. Ala., 1972, MBA, JD, U. Ala., 1975; LLM, Emory U., 1976. Bar: Ala. 1975, Ga. 1976, Fla. 1976, U.S. Dist. Ct. (no. dist.) Ga. 1976, U.S. Tax Ct. 1976, U.S. Ct. Appeals (11th cir.) 1986, U.S. Dist. Ct. (mid. dist.) Ga. 1997. Assoc. Nall, Miller & Cadenhead, Atlanta, 1975-78; trial atty. tax divsn. U.S. Dept. Justice, Washington, 1978-83; asst. U.S. atty. Organized Crime Drug Enforcement Task Force, Atlanta, 1983-97; ptnr. Kilpatrick Stockton LLP, Atlanta, 1997—2002, Gillen Cromwell Parkker & Withers, Atlanta, 2002—. Lectr. trial advocacy Emory U. Law Sch., Atlanta, 1984—. Named Outstanding Trial Atty. Tax Divsn., U.S. Dept. Justice, Washington, 1979; recipient Spl. Commendation award U.S. Dept. Justice, 1985, 87, Superior Performance as Asst. U.S. Atty. Dirs. award, 1986, 94. Mem. ABA, Internat. Bar Assn., Atlanta Bar Assn., Lawyers Club Atlanta. Presbyterian. Office: Gillen Cromwell Parker & Withers Ste 1050 3490 Piedmont Rd NW Atlanta GA 30305

PARKERSON, HARDY MARTELL, lawyer; b. Longview, Tex., Aug. 22, 1942; s. James Dee and Winifred Lenore (Robertson) P.; m. Janice Carol Johnson, Aug. 3, 1968; children: James Blaine, Stanley Andrew, Paul Hardy. BA, McNeese State U., Lake Charles, La.; JD, Tulane U., 1966. Bar: La. 1966, U.S. Supreme Ct. 1971. Assoc. Rogers, McHale & St. Romain, Lake Charles, 1967-69; pvt. practice Lake Charles, 1969—. Chmn. 7th Congl. Dist. Crime and Justice Task Force, La. Priorities for the Future, 1980; asst. prof. criminal justice La. State U., 1986, instr., Delta Sch. Bus. and Tech., 1988, pres., So. Christian U., 1991—. Bd. dirs. 1st Assembly of God Ch., Lake Charles, 1980—; bd. dirs., sec.-treas. Phi Kappa Phi Housing Corp. of Lake Charles, 1985—; bd. regents So. Christian U., Lake Charles, 1993—; mem. La. Dem. State Ctrl. Com., 1992-96, Calcasieu Parish Dem. Com., 1988—, past sec.-treas., exec. com.; former mem. Gulf Assistance Program, Lake Charles; 7th Congl. Dist. La. mem. Imports and Exports Trust Authority, Baton Rouge, 1984-88. Mem. Fed. Bar Assn., Pi Kappa Phi. Democrat. Mem. Assembly of God Ch. Avocations: political activism, hosting television talk show. Federal civil litigation, State civil litigation, Toxic tort. Home: 127 Greenway St Lake Charles LA 70605-6821 Office: # B 3309 Common St Lake Charles LA 70601-8603

PARKHURST, TODD SHELDON, lawyer; b. Evanston, Ill., Mar. 8, 1941; s. Don A. and Ruth Ellen (Sheldon) P.; m. Karen Judy Hucklebery, Sept. 2, 1968 (dec. Sept. 1969); m. Beverly Ann Susler, Aug. 15, 1976. BS in Gen. Engring., U. Ill., 1963; JD, U. Pa., 1966. Bar: Ill. 1968, U.S. Dist. Ct. (no. dist.) Ill. 1968, U.S. Dist. Ct. (ea. dist.) Wis. 1989, U.S. Ct. Appeals (7th cir.) 1977, U.S. Ct. Appeals Fed. Cir. 1978, U.S. Ct. Mil. Appeals, 1968, U.S. Patent and Trademark Office, 1973, U.S. Supreme Ct. 1973. Assoc. Wolfe, Hubbard, Voit & Osann, 1968-72; assoc. and ptnr. Trexler, Wolters, Bushnell & Fosse, Chgo., 1972-84; ptnr. Jenner & Block, Chgo., 1984-87; ptnr., mgr. intellectual property practice Schiff Hardin & Waite, Chgo., 1987-96; ptnr. Gardner, Carton & Douglas, 1996-98, Hill & Simpson, Chgo., 1998-2000; ptnr., mgr. intellectual property practice Holland & Knight, Chgo., 2000—. Adj. prof. John Marshall Law Sch., Chgo., 1980-84, Ill. Inst. Tech.-Chgo. Kent Law Sch., 1989—. Contbr. articles to profl. jours. Mem. Lifeline Pilots, Inc., pres. 1994-96; hearing officer Ill. Pollution Control Bd., 1972-96. Mem. Am. Intellectual Property Law Assn., Licensing Execs. Soc., Chgo. Bar Assn., Patent Law Assn. Chgo., Chgo. Lit. Club (pres. 1989-90), Adventurers Club Chgo. (sec. 1988). Methodist. Avocations: flying, scuba diving, photography, theatrical acting. Federal civil litigation, Patent, Trademark and copyright. Home: 260 E Chestnut St Apt 4301 Chicago IL 60611-2474 Office: Holland & Knight 55 W Monroe St Ste 800 Chicago IL 60603-5004 E-mail: tparkhur@hklaw.com.

PARKS, ALBERT LAURISTON, lawyer; b. Providence, July 18, 1935; s. Albert Lauriston and Dorothy Isabel (Arnold) P.; m. Martha Ann Anderson, Jan. 12, 1961; children: Amy Woodward, George Webster, Reed Anderson. BA, Kent State U., 1958; JD, U. Chgo., 1961. Bar: R.I. 1962, U.S. Dist. Ct. R.I. 1963, U.S. Ct. Appeals (1st cir.) 1966, U.S. Supreme Ct. 1980. Assoc. Hanson, Curran, Parks & Whitman, Providence, 1961-65, ptnr., 1966-2000. Town solicitor, North Kingstown, R.I., 1978-80, 97—. Fellow Am. Coll. Trial Lawyers; mem. ABA, Maritime Law Assn., R.I. Bar Assn., Saunderstown Yacht Club, Wickford Yacht Club. Republican. Episcopalian. Municipal (including bonds), General civil litigation, Land use and zoning (including planning). Office: 10 Coronado St Jamestown RI 02835 Home: 14 Church Ln North Kingstown RI 02852-5004 E-mail: alp@hcpw.com.

PARKS, JAMES WILLIAM, II, public facilities executive, lawyer; b. Wabash, Ind., July 30, 1956; s. James William and Joyce Arlene (Lillibridge) P.; m. Neil Ann Armstrong, Aug. 21, 1982; children: Elizabeth Joyce, Helen Frances, James William III. BS, Ball State U., 1978; JD, U. Miami, 1981. Bar: La. 1981, U.S. Dist. Ct. (ea. dist.) La. 1981, U.S. Ct. Appeals (5th and 11th cirs.) 1981. Fla. 1982, U.S. Dist. Ct. (mid. dist. La.) 1982.. Atty. Jones, Walker, Waechter, Poitevent, Carrere et al., New Orleans, 1981-83, Foley & Judell, New Orleans, 1983-88, McCollister & McCleary, pc, Baton Rouge, 1988-95; pres., CEO La. Pub. Facilities Authority, Baton Rouge, 1995—. Mem. AICPA, Nat. Assn. Bond Lawyers, La. State Bar Assn., Fla. Bar Assn., Assn. for Gifted and Talented Students, Baton Rouge (treas. 1994-96, pres.-elect 1996-97, pres. 1997-98), Soc. La. CPA (govt. acctg. and auditing com. 1994-95), Nat. Assn. Higher Edn. Facilities Authorities (bd. dirs. 1996-2001, v.p. 1997-99, pres. 1999-2001), Coun. of Devel. Fin. Agys. (bd. dirs. 2002—), La. Assistive Tech. Access Network (bd. dirs. 2002—). Avocations: travel, computers. Home: 5966 Tennyson Dr Baton Rouge LA 70817-2933 Office: La Pub Facilities Authority 2237 S Acadian Thruway Ste 650 Baton Rouge LA 70808-2380 E-mail: jameswparks2@hotmail.com., parks@lpfa.com.

PARKS, JANE DELOACH, retired law librarian, legal assistant; b. Atlanta, June 7, 1927; d. John Keller and Martha Lorena (Lee) deLoach; m. James Bennett Parks, Dec. 28, 1951 (dec. Sept. 1983); children: Carrie Anne Parks-Kirby, Susan Jane, Lora Beth Parks-Maury. BA magna cum laude, Vanderbilt U., 1949; postgrad., Emory U., 1950-51; tchr. cert., U. Chattanooga, 1954; postgrad., U. Tenn., Chattanooga, 1971-73. Med. rsch./writing dept. surgery Emory U., Atlanta, 1949-51; sec. to med. dir. Tenn. Tuberculosis Hosp., Chattanooga, 1951-53; tchr. Signal Mountain (Tenn.) Elem. Sch., 1954-55; tchr., dean jr. sch. Cleve. (Tenn.) Day Sch., 1963-70; law firm libr., legal asst. Stophel, Caldwell & Heggie, Chattanooga, 1972-85, Caldwell, Heggie & Helton, Chattanooga, 1985-93, Heiskell, Donelson, Bearman, Adams, Williams & Caldwell, Chattanooga, 1993-94, Baker, Donelson, Bearman & Caldwell, Chattanooga, 1994-99; ret., 1999. Tchr. various seminars on legal rsch. and writing, organizing one-person librs. and ch. librs., Chattanooga Legal Secs. Assn., Chattanooga-Hamilton County Bicentennial Libr. Editor (mag.) The Gadfly, 1947-49; editorial asst.: Studio Collotype, 1988 and to profl. jours., 1949—. Tchr. Chattanooga Area Literacy Movement, 1984-86; exec. coun. Friends of Chattanooga-Hamilton County Bicentennial Libr., 1989-94; del. Gov.'s Conf.-White House Conf. on Librs. and Info. Svcs., Nashville, 1990; libr. vol. Tenn. Aquarium. Environ. Learning Lab. 1993—; allocations com. United Way, 1994—, Signal Mountain Cmty. Guild, 1999—; dir. Lit. Dept.,

2000—02, pub. chmn., 2002-. Mem. Tenn. Paralegal Assn., Chattanooga Area Libr. Assn. (2d v.p. 1989-90, sec. 1992-93), Non-Atty. Profl. Assn. (chmn. 1989-93), Phi Beta Kappa, Mortar Bd. Republican. Methodist. Avocations: ceramics, reading, storytelling, needlework, genealogy.

PARKS, PATRICIA JEAN, lawyer; b. Portland, Oreg., Apr. 2, 1945; d. Robert and Marion (Crosby) P.; m. David F. Jurca, Oct. 17, 1971 (div. 1976). BA in History, Stanford U., 1963-67; JD, U. Penn., Phila., 1967-70. Bar: N.Y. 1971, Wash. 1974. Assoc. Milbank, Tweed, Hadley & McCoy, N.Y.C., 1970-73, Shidler, McBroom, Gates & Lucas, Seattle, 1974-81, ptnr., 1981-90, Preston, Thorgrimson, Shidler, Gates & Ellis, Seattle, 1990-93; pvt. practice Seattle, 1993-99; spl. counsel Karr Tuttle Campbell, 1999—. Active Vashon Allied Arts, Mountaineers. Mem.: ABA, Pension Roundtable, Western Pension Conf., Employee Stock Ownership Plan Assn., Seattle-King County Bar Assn., Washington Women in Tax, Wash. State Bar Assn. (past pres. tax sect., past chair gift and estate tax com.), Vashon Athletic Club, Wash. Athletic Club. Avocations: kayaking, hiking, contra dancing, bird watching, Karate. Pension, profit-sharing, and employee benefits, Taxation, general. Office: 1201 3rd Ave Ste 2900 Seattle WA 98101-3284

PARKS, ROBERT L. lawyer; b. Nassau, New Providence, Bahamas, May 29, 1938; s. Ralph Lionel and Merle Florine Parks; m. Lvn Sears (div.); children: Carey Parks Guerra, Rob, Greg, Josh D'Alemberte, Gabrielle D'Alemberte. BA, U. Fla., 1960; JD, Georgetown U., 1963. Ptnr. Haggard Parks Haggard & Bologna PA, Coral Gables, Fla. Mem. adv. bd. Nat. Jud. Coll., Reno; bd. dirs. Trial Lawyers for Pub. Justice, Kristi House, Miami. Chmn. Miami River Commn., 1998—; mem. Gov.'s Commn. on Property Rights, 1993—94; chmn. Miami River Coordinating Com., 1984—89, Environ. Regulation Commn., 1979—87; mem. Environ. Land Mgmt. Study Com., 1982—84. Fellow: ABA, Roscoe Pound Found., Fla. Bar Found., Am. Bd. Trial Advocates, Internat. Soc. Barristers, Internat. Acad. Trial Lawyers (pres. 2000—01, pres.-elect 1999—2000, v.p. 1998—99, dean 1996—97, sec. internat. rels. 1995—96), Am. Coll. Trial Lawyers; mem.: Fla. Supreme Ct. Commn. on Professionalism, Am. Law Inst. Methodist. Avocation: scuba diving. Home: 2901 S Bayshore Dr Apt 2-C Miami FL 33133 Office: Haggard Parks Haggard & Bologna PA 330 Alhambra Cir Coral Gables FL 33134

PARLIN, CHARLES C., JR., retired lawyer; b. Trenton, Feb. 12, 1928; s. Charles C. and Miriam (Boyd) P.; m. Joan Bona, June 28, 1948; children: C. Christopher, Robert B., Timothy B. BA, U. Chgo., 1946; LL.B., U. Pa., 1949. Bar: N.Y. 1951. Assoc. firm. Shearman & Sterling, N.Y.C., 1950-59, ptnr., 1959-90, of counsel, 1990-92, ret., 1992. Home: 5220-303 W Harbor Village Dr Vero Beach FL 32967

PARMLEY, ROBERT JAMES, lawyer, consultant; b. Madison, Wis., Oct. 23, 1950; s. Loren Francis and Dorothy Louise (Turner) P.; m. Debra Paliszewski, Dec. 23, 1982; children: Michelle Hope, Matthew Turner. BA, U. Va., 1972; JD, U. S.C., 1975. Bar: S.C. 1975, Tex. 1976, U.S. Dist. Ct. (so. dist.) Tex. 1976, U.S. Dist. Ct. (we. and no. dists.) Tex. 1980, U.S. Ct. Appeals (5th cir.) 1978, U.S. Tax Ct. 1976, U.S. Supreme Ct. 1980. Staff atty., Vista vol. Tex. Rural Legal Aid, Inc., Alice, 1975-76, mng. atty. Kingsville, 1976-79, sr. staff atty. Kerrville, 1979-81; sole practice Kerrville, 1981—. Mem. State Bar Tex., State Bar S.C., Kerr County Bar Assn. Episcopalian. Commercial, contracts (including sales of goods; commercial financing), General practice, Property, real (including real estate development, water). Office: Ste 615 222 Sidney Baker St S Kerrville TX 78028-5900 E-mail: law@ktc.com.

PARNESE, JOHN S. lawyer; b. Bklyn., Oct. 7, 1968; s. Irene M. and Salvatore Parnese; m. Elvira S. Carlino, July 31, 1993; 1 child, Salvatore Parnese. BS, St. John's U., Jamaica, N.Y., 1989; JD, Bklyn. Law Sch., 1993. Bar: N.Y. 1994, N.J. 1995, U.S. Dist. Ct. (ea. dist.) N.Y. 1996. Lawyer/ptnr. The Law Office of Scano & Parnese, Staten Island, NY, 1997—2000; sr. lawyer/owner The Law Office of John S. Parnese, Staten Island, 2000—. Adj. prof. St. John's U., 1999—2001; bd. dirs. Silver Line, Inc./GTS, Inc., Carlstadt, NJ, 2001—. Cub scout leader Boy Scouts Am., Staten Island, 2001—; mentor/student advisor St. John's U., Staten Island; bd. dirs., com. chmn. St. John's U. Alumni Assn., Staten Island. Recipient award in torts, Am. Jurisprudence Pub., 1990, award in conflicts of laws, 1993, Ad Altari Dei, Boy Scouts Am., Order of the Arrow. Mem.: ABA, ATLA, Xaverian Bar Assn., Richmond County Bar Assn., N.Y. Civil and Criminal Bench & Bar Assn., N.J. State Bar Assn., N.Y. State Bar Assn. Republican. Roman Catholic. Achievements include obtaining highest non-medical malpractice jury verdict in Staten Island. Avocations: reading, travel, billiards, music. General civil litigation, Personal injury (including property damage), Family and matrimonial. Office: 1110 South Ave Staten Island NY 10314 Office Fax: 347-273-1302. E-mail: jsparnese@aol.com.

PAROLA, LORENZO, lawyer; b. Cuneo, Italy, Apr. 10, 1969; m. Carla Zagarella, Sept. 30, 2000; 1 child, Martina. JD, Cath. U. Milan, 1995; post grad M for Legal Cons., U. Turin, Italy, 1998; postgrad., BPP Law Sch., London, 2001. Bar: Italy 1998, solicitor: Eng. and Wales 2002. Trainee Paolo Emilio Ferreri Law Firm, Turin, 1997—98; assoc. Brosio Casati Allen & Overy, Milan, 1998—2001, Allen & Overy, London, 2001—02, sr. assoc. Milan, 2002—. Lectr. Learning Resources Assocs., 2002—, Istituto di Ricerca Internat., 2001—, Somedia-LaRepubblica, 2001—; former profl. basketball player. Contbr. Mem.: Law Soc. Eng. and Wales. Roman Catholic. Oil, gas, and mineral, Mergers and acquisitions, FERC practice. Office: Allen & Overy Via Manzoni 43 20121 Milan Italy E-mail: lorenzo.parola@allenovery.com.

PARRES, CYNTHIA DILLARD, lawyer; b. Columbia, Mo., July 3, 1964; d. Robert Howard and Martha Ann Dillard. Student, Vanderbilt U., 1982-83; BS, S.E. Mo. State U., 1986; JD, U. Mo., Columbia, 1990. Bar: Mo. 1990, Kans. 1991. Assoc. Blackwell Sanders et al, Kansas City, Mo., 1990-92; ptnr. Bryan Cave LLP, Kansas City, Mo., 1992—. Adminstrv. asst. Mayor's Fast Forward Com., Kansas City, 1996—; mem. Downtown Coun.; vol. Jr. League Kansas City, Mo., 1991—. Mem.: Kansas City Bankruptcy Bar Assn., Kansas Women Attys. Assn., Ctrl. Exchange (chair membership com. 1992—), Kansas City Met. Bar Assn. (bankruptcy com. 1990—, bankruptcy com. chair 1999), Assn. Women Lawyers (bd. dirs. 1999—), Am. Bankruptcy Inst., Workout Profls. Assn. (pres. of bd.), Kansas City Club (athletic com.), Rotary. Roman Catholic. Banking, Bankruptcy, Commercial, contracts (including sales of goods; commercial financing). Office: Bryan Cave LLP 3500 One KC Pl 1200 Main St Kansas City MO 64105-2122 E-mail: cdparres@bryancave.com.

PARRETT, SHERMAN O. lawyer; b. Cin., Jan. 8, 1943; s. Earl and Ruby (Angel) P.; m. Rosalind K. Brooks, Sept. 21, 1985; children: Laura, Samantha. BSEE, U. Cin., 1965; JD with honors, George Washington U., 1969. Bar: Calif. 1970, D.C. 1975, Ariz. 1992. Assoc. Flehr, Hohbach et al., San Francisco, 1970-73; ptnr. Cushman, Darby & Cushman, Washington, 1973-86, Irell & Manella, L.A., 1986-91, Streich Lang, Phoenix, 1991-94, Snell & Wilmer, Phoenix, 1994-98. Address: 111 Honeysuckle Ln Owings MD 20736 E-mail: parretts@aol.com.

PARRETTE, LESLIE JACKSON, lawyer; b. Mt Pleasant, Mo., Aug. 25, 1961; s. Leslie Jackson and Janet Parrette. AB, Harvard Coll., 1983; JD, Harvard Law Sch., 1986. Assoc. Hale & Dorr, Boston, 1986-89, Watson Ess Marshall & Enggas, Kansas City, Mo., 1989-91, Bryan Cave, Kansas City, Mo., 1991-92; ptnr. Blackwell Sanders Peper Martin, Kansas City, Mo., 1992-2000; gen. coun., sr. v.p., corp. sec. Aquila Inc., Kansas City, Mo., 2000—. Mem. Sister City Commn. of Kansas City, Mo., 1999—; bd. dirs. Am. Jazz Mus., 2002—03. Commercial, contracts (including sales of goods; commercial financing), Corporate, general, Private international. Office: Aquila Inc 20 W 9th St Kansas City MO 64105-1711 E-mail: les.parrette@aquila.com.

PARRIGIN, ELIZABETH ELLINGTON, lawyer; b. Colon, Panama, May 23, 1932; d. Jesse Cox and Elizabeth (Roark) Ellington; m. Perry G. Parrigin, Oct. 8, 1975. BA, Agnes Scott Coll., 1954; JD, U. Va., 1959. Bar: Tex. 1959, Mo. 1980. Atty., San Antonio, 1960-69; law libr. U. Mo., Columbia, 1969-77, rsch. assoc., 1977-82; atty. pvt. practice, Columbia, 1982—. Elder, clk. of session First Presbyn. Ch., Columbia; mem. permanent jud. commn. Presbyn. Ch. U.S., 1977-83, mem. advisory com. on constitution, 1983-90. Mem. ABA, Mo. Bar Assn. (chmn. sub-com. revision of Mo. trust law 1988-92), Columbia Kiwanis Club (pres. 1997-98). Democrat. Presbyterian. Avocations: music, gardening, reading. Family and matrimonial, Non-profit and tax-exempt organizations, Probate (including wills, trusts). Home: 400 Conley Ave Columbia MO 65201-4219 Office: 224 N 8th St Columbia MO 65201-4844

PARRISH, DAVID WALKER, JR., legal publishing company executive; b. Bristol, Tenn., Feb. 8, 1923; BA, Emory and Henry Coll., 1948, LLD, 1978; BS, U.S. Mcht. Marine Acad., 1950; LLB, U. Va., 1951. Pres. The Michie Co., Charlottesville, Va., 1969-89, vice chmn., 1989-96; pub. cons., 1996—. Home: 114 Falcon Dr Charlottesville VA 22901-2013 Office: 300 Preston Ave Ste 103 Charlottesville VA 22902-5044

PARRISH, JOHN EDWARD, circuit judge; b. Lebanon, Mo., June 10, 1940; s. Folie and Thelma (Osborn) P.; m. Claudia Barbee, Sept. 1, 1962; 1 child, Mark Everett. BBA, U. Mo., 1962, JD, 1965. Acct. Arthur Andersen & Co., St. Louis, 1965-66; ptnr. Phillips & Parrish, Camdenton, Mo., 1968-73; prosecuting atty. Camden County, Camdenton, 1969-73; circuit judge State of Mo., Camdenton, 1973-1990, judge Mo. Ct. Appeals (southern dist.), 1990-; mem. State Adv. Group on Juvenile Justice, Jefferson City, Mo., 1981—;Bd. dirs. Lake Regional Health System., Osage Beach, Mo., 1977—, pres. 1983-85, 1991-93, 1999-2001. Capt. U.S. Army, 1966-68. Mem. Mo. Bar Assn., Mo. Coun. Juvenile Ct. Judges (pres. 1978-79), Mo. Jud. Conf. (exec. council 1980-87), Nat. Council Juvenile and Family Ct. Judges, Nat. Juvenile Ct. Found Inc. (trustee 1987-90), Rotary (pres. 1977-78). Mem. Christian Ch. (Disciples of Christ). Office: MO Ct Appeals 300 Hammons Pky Springfield MO 65806

PARROTT, NANCY SHARON, lawyer; b. Atoka, Okla., Jan. 11, 1944; d. Albert L. and Willie Jo (Parkhill) Furr. BA, Okla. U., 1967; MA, No. Tex. U., 1974; JD, Okla. City U., 1982. Bar: Okla. 1984, U.S. Supreme Ct. 1984. Ptnr. Chapman & Chapman, Oklahoma City, 1984-85; chief legal asst. marshal Okla. Supreme Ct., Oklahoma City, 1985—. Mem. Leadership Oklahoma, Leadership Oklahoma City; bd. dirs. Youth Leadership Exch. treasurer, exec. bd. mem., recruitment chmn., mentor. Mem. ABA, Okla. Bar Assn. (awards com., civil procedure com.), Okla. County Bar Assn. (bd. dirs., del., mem. cmty. svc. com., Law Day co-chair), Am. Judicature Soc. Office: Okla Supreme Ct State Capital Bldg 245 Oklahoma City OK 73105

PARSKY, GERALD LAWRENCE, lawyer; b. West Hartford, Conn., Oct. 18, 1942; s. Isadore and Nettie (Sanders) P.; m. Susan Haas, June 26, 1966; children: Laura, David; m. Robin Cleary, Jan. 27, 1980. AB, Princeton U., 1964; JD, U. Va., 1968. Bar: N.Y. 1969, D.C. 1974, Calif. 1983. Assoc. Mudge Rose Guthrie & Alexander, N.Y.C., 1968-71; spl. asst. to under sec. U.S. Treasury Dept., Washington, 1971-73, exec. asst. to dep. sec. Fed. Energy Office, 1973-74, asst. sec. internat. affairs, 1974-77; sr. ptnr. Gibson, Dunn & Crutcher, Los Angeles, 1977-90; of counsel Gibson, Dunn & Cruther, L.A., 1990-92; chmn. Aurora Capital Ptnrs., L.A., 1990—. Bd. dirs. James A. Baker III Inst. Pub. Policy. Bd. govs. Performing Arts Coun., L.A. Music Ctr.; trustee George Bush Presdl. Libr. Found., 1993—, Ronald Reagan Presdl. Found., 1995—; bd. dirs. Music Ctr. Found., 1998—. Recipient Alexander Hamilton award U.S. Treasury, 1976, Woodrow Wilson award, 2000. Mem. ABA, Coun. Fgn. Rels., N.Y. Princeton Club, Calif. Club, Racquet Club N.Y., Rolling Rock Club, Rancho Santa Fe Golf Club. Corporate, general, Private international. Office: Aurora Capital Group 10877 Wilshire Blvd Ste 2100 Los Angeles CA 90024-4376

PARSON, JASON A. lawyer; b. Madisonville, Ky., Jan. 30, 1963; s. Dewey Allen and Peggy Sue Parson; m. Valerie Ann Schmidt, Mar. 28, 1992; 1 child, Samuel Ayres. BA, Ind. Ctrl. U., Indpls., 1985; JD, Washington U., St. Louis, 1988. Bar: Ill. 1989, U.S. Dist. Ct. (no. dist.) Ill. 1991. Fed. clk. to Hon. John F. Nangle U.S. Dist. Ct. (ea. dist.) Mo., St. Louis, 1988-90; assoc. Lord, Bissell & Brook, Chgo., 1990-98, ptnr., 1998-2000; founding ptnr. Anderson, Bennett & Ptnrs., Chgo., 2000—. Editor-in-chief Washington U. Law Quar., 1987-88; contbr. articles to profl. jours. Hagelskamp scholar, 1984. Mem. Ill. State Bar Assn., Def. Rsch. Inst., Ill. Assn. Healthcare Attys., Ill. Assn. Def. Trial Counsel. Avocation: vocal music. Federal civil litigation, State civil litigation, Health. Office: Anderson Bennett & Ptnrs 55 E Monroe St Ste 3650 Chicago IL 60603 E-mail: Jason.Parson@ABandPartners.com.

PARSONS, CHARLES ALLAN, JR., lawyer; b. Mpls., July 16, 1943; s. Charles Allan and Grace Adelaide (Covert) P.; m. JoAnne Ruth Russell, Oct. 16, 1965; children: Charles, Daniel, Nancy. BS, U. Minn., 1965, JD cum laude, 1972. Bar: Minn. 1972, U.S. Dist. Ct. Minn. 1972, U.S. Supreme Ct. 1995. Ptnr. Moss & Barnett, P.A., 1972—. Bd. dirs. Legal Advice Clinics Ltd., Mpls., 1975-93, Legal Aid Soc. Mpls., 1999—, first v.p., 2000-2002, pres., 2002—; bd. dirs. Mid-Minn. Legal Assistance, 2001—; chair steering com. S.E. Asian Legal Assistance Project, Mpls., 1988-93. Named Vol. Atty. of Yr., Legal Advice Clinics, Ltd., Mpls., 1990. Mem. ABA, Am. Coll. Real Estate Lawyers, Minn. State Bar Assn. (co-chair legis. com. real property sec. 1986—, coun. mem. 1986—, chair real property sect. 1993-94), Hennepin County Bar Assn. (chair real property sect. 1988-89, Van Valkenburg award for pub. svc. 2002). Roman Catholic. Avocations: reading, walking, biking, hiking. Finance, Property, real (including real estate development, water). Office: Moss & Barnett PA 4800 Wells Fargo Ctr 90 S 7th Minneapolis MN 55402-4129 E-mail: parsonsc@moss-barnett.com.

PARSONS, INGA L. law educator; b. Jackson Hole, Wyo., Oct. 24, 1962; m. Sept. 6, 1992; children: Ara, Ethan. AB in Govt., Harvard U., 1985; JD, Columbia U., 1986. Bar: N.Y. 1990. Legis. intern U.S. Senate, Washington, 1983; summer assoc. Spence, Moriarity & Schuster, Jackson Hole, 1986-89; legis. intern Office Atty. Gen., N.Y.C., 1987-89; fed. jud. law clerk USDC CDCA, L.A., 1989-90; asst. fed. defender Legal Aid Soc., N.Y.C., 1990-95; acting asst. prof. clin. law NYU, N.Y.C., 1995—. Guest commentator Ct. TV, N.Y.C., 1993—, Fox News, 1998—; instr. trial advocacy Harvard U., 1998—, Fordham U., 1994-96, Cardozo U., 1993—; lectr. law, Columbia U. Sch. Law, fall 1999. Co-author: Practice Commentaries, Federal Rules of Criminal Procedure; contbg. editor: Criminal Defense Weekly. Recipient Jane Marks Murphy prize Columbia U., 1989, Cmty. Recognition NYU Law Student Body, 1996; G.G. Michelson fellow Helena Rubenstein Found., 1992-93. Mem. ABA, Nat. Assn. Criminal Def. Lawyers, N.Y. Women's Bar Assn., Adv. Bd. of Justice Without Borders. Office: NYU Sch Law 161 Ave of the Americas New York NY 10013 E-mail: parsonsi@juris.law.nyu.edu.

PARTLETT, DAVID F. dean, law educator; b. 1947; LLB, Sydney U., 1970; LLM, Mich. U., 1972, 74; SJD, U. Va., 1980. Bar: New South Wales 1971, Australian Cap. Terr. 1978. Vis. asst. prof. U. Ala., 1972-73; legis. officer Australia Atty. Gen.'s Office, 1974—75; dir, rsch. Australian Law Reform Commn. , 1975—78; lectr. Australian Nat. U., 1978-80, sr. lectr., 1980-87, assoc. dean, 1982—85; vis. prof. Vanderbilt U., Nashville, 1987-88, prof. law, 1988-2000, acting dean, 1996-97; v.p., dean, prof. Sch. Law Washington & Lee U., Lexington, Va., 2000—. Sparkman Dist. vis. prof. Ala. U., 1986-87. Office: Washington & Lee U Sydney Lewis Hall Lexington VA 24450

PARTNOY, RONALD ALLEN, lawyer; b. Norwalk, Conn., Dec. 23, 1933; s. Maurice and Ethel Marguerite (Roselle) P.; m. Diane Catherine Keenan, Sept. 18, 1965. BA, Yale U., 1956; LL.B., Harvard U., 1961; LL.M., Boston U., 1965. Bar: Mass. 1962, Conn. 1966. Atty. Liberty Mut. Ins. Co., Boston, 1961-65; assoc. counsel Remington Arms Co., Bridgeport, Conn., 1965-70, gen. counsel, 1970-88, sec., 1983-93; sr. counsel E.I. du Pont de Nemours & Co., Wilmington, Del., 1985-95. Served with USN, 1956-58; to capt. USNR (ret.) Mem.: ABA, Naval Res. Assn. (3d dist. pres., nat. exec. com. 1981—85, 1997—99, 2001—, nat. v.p. 1997—99, 2001—), U.S. Navy League (pres. Bridgeport coun. 1975—77, nat. dir., Conn. pres. 1977—80, v.p. Empire region 1980—85), Am. Judicature Soc., Sporting Arms and Ammunition Mfrs. Inst. (chmn. legis. and legal affairs com. 1971—86), Assn. of Yale Alumni (del. 1997—2000), Yale Club of N.Y.C., Harvard Club of Phila., Harvard Club of Boston, Chancery Club. Antitrust, Commercial, contracts (including sales of goods; commercial financing), Corporate, general. Home: 616 Bayard Rd Kennett Square PA 19348-2504

PARTRIDGE, BRUCE JAMES, lawyer, educator, writer; b. Syracuse, N.Y., June 4, 1926; arrived in Can., 1969; s. Bert James and Lida Marion (Rice) P.; m. Mary Janice Smith, June 13, 1948 (dec. 1986); children: Heather Leigh, Eric James, Brian Lloyd, Bonnie Joyce; m. May S. Archer, May 28, 1988; stepchildren: Sheila Archer, Laurel Archer. AB cum laude, Oberlin Coll., Ohio, 1946; LLB, Blackstone Coll., Chgo., 1950, JD, 1952; LLB, U. B.C., 1974. Bar: B.C. 1976, N.W.T. 1980. Rsch. physicist Am. Gas Assn., Cleve., 1946-48; bus. mgr. Cazenovia (N.Y.) Coll., 1948—51; bus. mgr., purchasing agt., asst. treas. Rochester Inst. Tech., NY, 1953—58; bus. adminstr. Baldwin-Wallace Coll., Berea, Ohio, 1951-53; v.p. bus. and mgmt. U. Del., Newark, 1958-63; v.p. adminstrn. Johns Hopkins U., Balt., 1963-69; pres. U. Victoria, B.C., Can., 1969-72; assoc. Clark, Wilson & Co., Vancouver, B.C., Can., 1975-78; successively solicitor, mng. solicitor, gen. solicitor, v.p. law and gen. counsel, sec. Cominco Ltd., Vancouver, 1978-88; exec. dir. Baker & McKenzie, Hong Kong, 1988-90; v.p. Pacific Creations, Inc., 1990-92; faculty Camosun Coll., 1992-99. Author: Management in Canada: The Competitive Challenges, 2000; co-author: College and University Business Administration, 1968; chmn. editl. com. Purchasing for Higher Education, 1962; contbr. numerous articles to profl. jours. Chmn. commn. on adminstrv. affairs Am. Coun. on Edn., Washington, 1966-69; mem. Pres.'s Com. on Employment of Handicapped, Washington, 1967-69; mem. adv. coun. Ctr. for Resource Studies, Queen's U., 1983-88; bd. dirs. L'Arche in the Americas, 1984-88; mem. adv. coun. Westwater Rsch. Ctr., 1982-88 U. B.C. Mem. Law Soc. B.C., 1975-91, Law Soc. of N.W. Ters., Assn. Can. Gen. Counsel, Fedn. Ins. and Corp. Counsel, 1985-88, Def. Rsch. Inst. (product liability com.), Am. Corp. Counsel Assn., 1985-89 Vancouver Club, Aberdeen Marina Club, Hong Kong Football Club, 1988-91. Unitarian Universalist. E-mail: brucepart@telus.ca.

PARTRIDGE, MARK VAN BUREN, lawyer, educator, writer; b. Rochester, Minn., Oct. 16, 1954; s. John V.B. and Constance (Brainerd) P.; m. Mary Roberta Moffitt, Apr. 30, 1983; children: Caitlin, Lindsay, Christopher. BA, U. Nebr., 1978; JD, Harvard U., 1981. Bar: Ill. 1981, U.S. Dist. Ct. (no. dist.) Ill. 1981, U.S. Dist. Ct. (ea. dist.) Mich. 1983, U.S. Ct. Appeals (fed. cir.) 1983, U.S. Ct. Appeals (4th cir.) 1986, U.S. Ct. Appeals (7th cir.), 1992, U.S. Ct. Appeals (5th cir.) 1993, U.S. Ct. Appeals (3rd cir.) 1998. Assoc. Pattishall, McAuliffe, Newbury, Hilliard & Geraldson, Chgo., 1981-88, ptnr., 1988—. Adj. prof. John Marshall Law Sch., Chgo., 1987—; arbitrator Cook County Mandatory Arbitration Program, 1989-2003; v.p. Harvard Legal Aid Bur., 1980-81; mediator no. dist. Ill. Voluntary Mediation Program, 1997—; panelist World Intellectual Property Orgn., Domain Name Dispute Resolution Svc., 1999—. Contbr. articles to profl. jours.; mem. editl. bd. The Trademark Reporter, 1994-97; adv. bd. IP Litigator, 1995—. Vol. Chgo. Vol. Legal Svcs., 1983—; mem. Chgo. coun. Boy Scouts Am., troop treas., 2002—. Mem. ABA (com. chmn. 1989-91, 94-99), Internat. Trademark Assn. (com. vice chmn. 1996), World Intellectual Property Orgn. (experts panel internet domain name process 1998-99), Am. Intellectual Property Law Assn. (com. chmn. 1989-91, 96-98, bd. dirs. 1998-2001), Intellectual Property Law Assn. Chgo. (com. chmn. 1993-96), Brand Names Ednl. Found. (moot ct. regional chmn. 1994-96, nat. vice-chmn. 1997-98, nat. chmn. 1998-99), Legal Club (v.p. 1998, pres. 1999), Lawyers Club Chgo. (pres. 2000, bd. dirs. 2000-01), Union League Club. Avocations: writing, music, genealogy, travel, internet. Alternative dispute resolution, Trademark and copyright, Intellectual property. Office: Pattishall McAuliffe Newbury Hilliard & Geraldso 311 S Wacker Dr Ste 5000 Chicago IL 60606-6631 E-mail: mpartridge@pattishall.com.

PARTRIDGE, WILLIAM FRANKLIN, JR., lawyer; b. Newberry, S.C., July 16, 1945; s. William F. and Clara (Eskridge) P.; m. Ilene S. Stewart, Aug. 16, 1969; children: Allison, William F. BA in History, The Citadel, 1967; JD, U. S.C., 1970. Bar: S.C. 1970, U.S. Ct. Claims 1971, U.S. Ct. Mil. Appeals 1971, U.S. Tax Ct. 1971, U.S. Supreme Ct. 1973, U.S. Dist. Ct. S.C. 1980. Instr. internat. law Chapman Coll., 1973-74; pub. issue com. S.C. Bar, 1982-83. Lt. Col. USAFR. Mem. Newberry Bar Assn. (pres. 1982-83), Palmetto Club, County of Newberry Club, Cotillion Club, Assn. Citadel Mens Club, Masons, Phi Delta Phi. Democrat. Methodist. Oil, gas, and mineral, Family and matrimonial. Home: 2029 Harrington St Newberry SC 29108-3055 Office: 1201 Boyce St Newberry SC 29108-2705

PARTSCH, KARL JOSEF H. legal educator; b. Freiburg, Germany, June 24, 1914; s. Josef and Ilse E. (Roesler) P.; m. Juliane Bernhardt; 1 child, Susanna. D, U. Freiburg, 1937; assessor, Cologne Ct. Appeals, 1948. Legal adviser bank and machine factory, Berlin, Cologne and Ulm, Germany, 1938-41; constl. analyst Deutscher Städtetag, Cologne, 1948-50; asst. legal adviser Auswärtiges Amt, Bonn, Fed. Republic Germany, 1950-54; consul Fed. Republic Germany Naples, Italy, 1955-57; prof. law U. Kiel, Fed. Republic Germany, 1957-60, U. Mainz, Fed. Republic Germany, 1960-66, U. Bonn, 1966-79, prof. emeritus, from 1979. Lectr. law U. Bonn, 1953-57, rector, 1968-69; mem., reporter com. on elimination racial discrimination UN, 1970—; mem. com. on human rights UNESCO, Paris, 1981—. Author: Europ Menschenrechte, 1966, Zoologische Station Neapel, 1980; co-author: Victims of Armed Conflicts, 1982; contbr. articles to profl. jours. Bd. dirs. German Civil Liberties Union, Cologne, 1949-54. Recipient Gt. Cross Merit, Pres. Fed. Republic Germany, 1984, Peace medal Sec. Gen. UN, 1984. Mem. Deutsche Staatsrechtslehrer, Gesellschaft Für Völkerrecht, Am. Soc. Internat. Law, German Assn. UN. Avocation: Italian history and culture. Home: Ingelheim am Rhein, Germany. Died Dec. 30, 1996.

PARZEN, STANLEY JULIUS, lawyer; b. N.Y.C., Feb. 6, 1952; BA, Earlham Coll., 1973; LLB cum laude, Harvard U., 1976. Bar: Ill. 1978, U.S. Dist. Ct. (no. dist.) Ill. 1978, U.S. Dist. Ct. (no. dist.) Calif. 1989, U.S. Dist. Ct. (we. dist.) Mich. 1995, U.S. Ct. Appeals (7th cir.) 1981, U.S. Ct. Appeals (8th cir.) 1983, U.S. Ct. Appeals (5th cir.) 1992, U.S. Ct. appeals (D.C. cir.) 1992, U.S. Ct. Appeals (2d cir.) 1990, U.S. Ct. Appeals (9th cir.) 1996. Law clk. to judge U.S. Ct. Appeals 4th cir., 1976-77; ptnr. Mayer, Brown & Platt, Chgo. Mem. Phi Beta Kappa. Office: Mayer Brown Rowe & Maw 190 S La Salle St Ste 3100 Chicago IL 60603-3441 E-mail: sparzen@mayerbrownrowe.com.

PASAHOW, LYNN H(AROLD), lawyer; b. Ft. Eutiss, Va., Mar. 13, 1947; s. Samuel and Cecelia (Newman) P.; m. Leslie Aileen Cobb, June 11, 1969; 1 child, Michael Alexander. AB, Stanford U., 1969; JD, U. Calif., Berkeley, 1972. Bar: Calif. 1972, U.S. Ct. Appeals (9th cir.) 1972, U.S. Dist. Ct. (no. dist.) Calif. 1973, U.S. Dist. Ct. (cen. dist.) Calif. 1974, U.S. Supreme Ct. 1976, U.S. Dist. Ct. (ea. dist.) Calif. 1977, U.S. Ct. Appeals (fed. cir.) 1990.

Law clk. judge U.S. Dist. Ct. (no. dist.) Calif., San Francisco, 1972-73; with McCutchen, Doyle, Brown & Enersen, Palo Alto, Calif., 1973—2001; ptnr. Fenwick & West LLP, 2001—. Bd. dirs. Bay Area Biosci. Ctr., 2002—, Boalt Hall Alumni Assn., 2003—; mem. adv. bd. Berkeley Ctr. for Law and Tech., 1998—. Author: Pretrial and Settlement Conferences in Federal Court, 1983; co-author: Civil Discovery and Mandatory Disclosure: A Guide to Effective Practice, 1994; contbr. articles to profl. jours. Mem. ABA, Calif. Bar Assn., Boalt Hall Alumni Assn. (bd. dirs. 2003—). Democrat. Federal civil litigation, Patent, Trademark and copyright. Office: Fenwick & West LLP Silicon Valley Ctr 801 California St Mountain View CA 94041 E-mail: lpasahow@fenwick.com.

PASCAL, ROGER, lawyer; b. Chgo., Mar. 16, 1941; s. Samuel A. and Harriet E. (Hartman) P.; m. Martha Hecht, June 16, 1963; children: Deborah, Diane, David AB with distinction, U. Mich, 1962; JD cum laude, Harvard U., 1965. Bar: Ill. 1965, U.S. Dist. Ct. (no. dist.) Ill. 1965, U.S. Ct. Appeals (7th cir.) 1969, U.S. Supreme Ct. 1976, Wis. 1985, U.S. Ct. Appeals (2d, 6th, 9th and 10th cirs.) 186. Assoc. Schiff Hardin & Waite, Chgo., 1965-71, ptnr., 1972—. Adj. prof. law Northwestern U. Law Sch., 1994—. Bd. dirs., mem. exec. com. Chgo. Law Enforcement Study Group, 1975-80, pres., 1978-80; pres. Harvard Law Soc. Ill., 1976-78; bd. dirs. ACLU of Ill., 1984—, gen. counsel, 1986—. Mem. ABA (antitrust, intellectual property, and litigation sects.), Pub. Interest Law Initiative (bd. dirs. 1989—, v.p. 1995-97, pres. 1997-98), Fund for Justice (v.p., bd. dirs. 1986-97), Chgo. Coun. Lawyers (bd. dirs. 1970-74, 80-84), Chgo. Legal Assistance Found. (bd. dirs. 1985-88), Univ. Club, Met. Club, Phi Beta Kappa. Antitrust, Federal civil litigation, Securities. Office: Schiff Hardin & Waite 6600 Sears Tower Chicago IL 60606

PASCARELLA, HENRY WILLIAM, lawyer; b. New Haven, Conn., Aug. 15, 1933; s. John Manlio and Mary (Iannotti) P.; m. Tessa Peruzzi, Jan. 28, 1967; children: Averardo, Leonora, Cassandra. BS in Econs., U. Pa., 1955; LLB, Yale U., 1958. Bar: Conn. 1958, U.S. Supreme Ct. 1963. Ptnr. Badger, Fisher, Cohen & Barnett and predecessors, Greenwich, Conn., 1959-73; sr. counsel to Taylor Cooper & Alcorn, Greenwich, Conn., 1978—. Pres., dir. The Timber Trails Corp. Sherman, Conn.; dir. Nine West Group, Inc., 1995-99. Author column, theater critic Greenwich Times, 1964-67. Dir. Planned Parenthood League of Conn., Greenwich coun. Boy Scouts Am., 1990-96. Served to lt. (j.g.) USCG, 1959. Me.m ABA, Greenwich Bar Assn. (pres. 1967), Conn. Bar Assn., Yale Club (N.Y.C.), Belle Haven Club (Greenwich). Environmental, Probate (including wills, trusts), Property, real (including real estate development, water). Home: 675 Steamboat Rd Greenwich CT 06830-7140 E-mail: henry@pascarellalaw.com.

PASCHALIDIS, NICKOLAS M. lawyer, writer; b. Thessaloniki, Greece, Mar. 17, 1936; s. Menelaus and Aphrodite (Kargiotakis) P.; m. Helen Hatsiasemidis, Feb. 25, 1967 (div. June 1975); 1 child, Menelaus; m. Marianna Asimakopoulos, Apr. 14, 1985. Law Degree, U. Thessaloniki, 1959. Lawyer Bar Assn., Thessaloniki, 1963-67, Ct. of Appeal, Thessaloniki, 1967-80, Supreme Ct., Athens, Greece, 1980-2000. Legal collaborator High Commr. UN for Refugees, 1971-80. Author: Nomopsychosis, 1980, Labyrinth, 1981, Trap for Sophists, 1985, Macedonian Roulette, 1993 (award Thessaloniki Municipality 1993), Code: Agent Macedonian, 1995 (award Thessaloniki's Bar Assn. 1996), The British Commander Nicholas Hammond, 1995 (award Met. Lions 1995), Konstantin Armenopoulus, The Byzantine Guardian of law and Justice of Thessaloniki, 1996, The British Conflict and the Greek Resistance, Anatomy of a Riddle, 1997 (award Thessaloniki Municipality Ctr. of History 1997). Recipient awards Greek-Am. C. of C., 1995, Assn. Pubs. No. Greece, 1995, Assn. Greek Writers, 1995. Mem. Soc. for Macedonian Studies, Soc. Writers Thessaloniki, Greek-Am. C. of C., Assn. Jurists No. Greece. Office: 13 Frangon St 54626 Thessaloniki Greece Fax: 543297.

PASCHETTO, JOHN J. lawyer; b. Long Branch, N.J., Sept. 18, 1959; s. Edward and Elizabeth McCue Paschetto; m. Katherine Anne Dobrosky, Feb. 20, 1982. BA, Rutgers U., 1981; MA, U. Del., 1988; JD, Harvard U., 1998. Bar: Del. 1998, U.S. Dist. Ct. Del. 1999. Assoc. Young Conaway Stargatt & Taylor, LLP, Wilmington, Del., 1998—. Contbr. chapters to books. Mem.: ABA, Del. State Bar Assn., Harvard Law Sch. Assn. Del. (treas. 1998—). Commercial, contracts (including sales of goods; commercial financing), Corporate, general. Office: Young Conaway Stargatt & Taylor LLP 1000 West St Wilmington DE 19801 Office Fax: 302-576-3324. E-mail: jpaschetto@ycst.com.

PASCO, HANSELL MERRILL, retired lawyer; b. Thomasville, Ga., Oct. 7, 1915; s. John and Katherine (Merrill) P.; m. Williamine Carrington Lancaster, June 28, 1941; children: Hansell Merrill, Dabney, Robert, Elizabeth, Carrington. BA, Va. Mil. Inst., 1937; LL.B., U. Va., 1940. Bar: Va. bar 1939. Ptnr. Hunton & Williams, Richmond, Va., 1948-81, sr. counsel, 1981—, mng. partner, 1968-76. Chmn. State Counsel Higher Edn. for Va., 1978-80; trustee Protestant Episcopal Sem., Alexandria, Va., 1980-85. Served with U.S. Army, 1940-45. Office: Hunton & Williams Riverfront Plz E Tower PO Box 1535 Richmond VA 23218-1535

PASCOTTO, ALVARO, lawyer; b. Rome, Mar. 8, 1949; came to U.S., 1984; s. Antonio and Anna Ludovica (Habig) P.; m. Linda Haldan, July 20, 1985. JD, U. Rome, 1973. Bar: Italy 1976, Calif. 1987, U.S. Dist. Ct. (cen. dist.) Calif. 1987, U.S. Ct. Appeals (9th cir.) 1987. Ptnr. Studio Legale Pascotto, Rome, 1976-86, Pascotto, Gallavotti & Gardner, L.A. and Rome, 1986-90, Pascotto & Gallavotti, L.A., 1990—; of counsel Irell & Manella LLP, L.A., 1994—2003, Morrison & Forrester, LLP, L.A., 2003. Ofcl. counsel Consulate Gen. Italy, L.A., 1987—. Mem. ABA, Calif. Bar Assn., Italian-Am. Bar Assn., Am. Mgmt. Assn., Consiglio dell'Ordine Degli Avvocati e Procuratori di Roma. Clubs: Circolo del Golf (Rome); Malibu (Calif.) Racquet Club, Regency Club (L.A.), L.A. Country Club. Aviation, Entertainment, Private international. Home: 6116 Merritt Dr Malibu CA 90265-3847 Office: Ste 2200 1925 Century Park E Los Angeles CA 90067-2701 Fax: 310-203-4036. E-mail: apascotto@mofo.com.

PASEK, JEFFREY IVAN, lawyer; b. Pitts., Apr. 4, 1951; m. Kathryn Ann Hirsh, Aug. 17, 1975; children: Joshua, Benjamin, Michael. BA, U. Pitts., 1973; JD, U. Pa., 1976. Bar: Pa. 1976, U.S. Dist. Ct. (ea. dist.) Pa. 1976, U.S. Ct. Appeals (3d cir.) 1976, U.S. Dist. Ct. (we. dist.) Pa. 1977, U.S. Supreme Ct. 1980, U.S. Dist. Ct. (mid. dist.) Pa. 1984, N.Y. 1988, N.J. 1988, U.S. Dist. Ct. N.J. 1988, U.S. Dist. Ct. (so. and ea. dists.) N.Y. 1989, U.S. Dist. Ct. Vt. 1990, U.S. Dist. Ct. (we. dist.) N.Y. 1996, U.S. Dist. Ct. (no. dist.) N.Y. 2000, U.S. Ct. Appeals (2d cir.) 1989, U.S. Dist. Ct. Vt. 1990, U.S. Dist. Ct. (no. dist.) Ill. 2000. Assoc. Cohen, Shapiro, Polisher, Shiekman & Cohen, Phila., 1976-84, ptnr., 1985-95; sr. mem. Cozen O'Connor, Phila., 1995—. Lectr. Pa. Bar Inst., Harrisburg, 1980-83, 86, 95—, course planner, 1986, 2000-03; instr. Inst. for Paralegal Tng., Phila., 1981-82. Mem. nat. governing coun. Am. Jewish Congress, N.Y.C., 1985, 88-96, pres. Pa. region, 1992-95; co-chmn. Commn. on Law and Social Action, Phila., 1985-92; bd. dirs. Jewish Employment and Vocat. Svc. Phila., 1982—, asst. treas., 1986-87, v.p., 1987-95, pres., 1995-98; bd. dirs. Fairmount Geriatric Ctr., 1986-88, sec., 1985-87, v.p., 1987-88; bd. dirs. Pa. Legal Svcs. Ctr., 1987-88, treas., 1988. Mem. ABA (equal employment opportunity law com., labor law sect.), Pa. Bar Assn., Phila. Bar Assn. (co-chmn. labor and employment law com. 1997), Indsl. Rels. Rsch. Assn., Pa. Chamber of Bus. and Industry (exec. com. 1991-96, bd. dirs. 1988—, chmn. indsl. rels. com. 1984-87, chmn. edn. com. 1988-91). Civil rights, General civil litigation, Labor (including EEOC, Fair Labor Standards Act, labor-management relations, NLRB, OSHA). Office: Cozen O'Connor 1900 Market St Philadelphia PA 19103-3527

PASICH, KIRK ALAN, lawyer; b. La Jolla, Calif., May 26, 1955; s. Chris Nick and Iva Mae (Tormey) P.; m. Pamela Mary Woods, July 30, 1983; children: Christopher Thomas, Kelly Elizabeth, Connor Woods. BA in Polit. Sci., UCLA, 1977; JD, Loyola Law Sch., L.A., 1980. Bar: Calif. 1980, U.S. Dist. Ct. (no., so., ea. and cen. dists.) Calif. 1981, U.S. Ct. Appeals (9th cir.) 1982, U.S. Ct. Appeals (1st cir.) 1992. Assoc. Paul, Hastings, Janofsky & Walker, L.A., 1980-88, ptnr., 1988-89, Troop Steuber Pasich Reddick & Tobey, LLP, L.A., 1989-2000, Howrey Simon Arnold & White LLP, L.A., 2001—. Author: Casualty and Liability Insurance, 1990, 2000, 03; co-author: Officers and Directors: Liabilities and Protections, 1996, 2000, 03, The Year 2000 and Beyond: Liability and Insurance for Computer Code Problems, 2000; contbg. editor: West's California Litigation Forms: Civil Procedure Before Trial, 2000; entertainment law columnist, ins. law columnist L.A. and San Francisco Daily Jour., 1989—; contbr. articles to profl. jours. Active bd. dirs. Nat. Acad. Jazz, L.A., 1988-89, chmn. bd. dirs. Woody Herman Found., L.A., 1989-92, Constnl. Rights Found., 2000; active L.A. City Atty's. Task Force for Econ. Recovery, 1992-93. Named to Calif's. Legal Dream Team as 1 of state's top 25 litigators, Calif. Law Bus., 1992, as one of the nation's top 45 lawyers under age 45, The Am. Lawyer, 1995. Mem. ABA (mem. Task Force on Complex Insurance Coverage Litigation). General civil litigation, Entertainment, Insurance. Home: 10419 Lindbrook Dr Los Angeles CA 90024-3323 Office: Ste 2100 1925 Century Park E Los Angeles CA 90067 E-mail: pasichk@howrey.com.

PASSER-MUSLIN, JULIETTE MAYABELLE, lawyer; b. USSR; MusB, Manhattan Sch. Music, 1981, MA in Music Edn., 1984; postgrad., NYU, 1985-86, Columbia U., 1988-89; JD cum laude, Yeshiva U., 1990. Bar: N.Y. 1990. Solist, music dir. mus. theater cos. in U.S. and Europe, 1977-87; dir. admissions and pub. rels. St. Sergius Sch., N.Y.C., 1981-83; tchg. asst. edn. dept. NYU, N.Y.C., 1985-86; assoc. Debevoise & Plimpton, N.Y.C., 1990-94, Patterson, Belknap, Webb & Tyler, LLP, N.Y.C., 1994-96; pres., gen. counsel Internat. Project Devel. Group, LLC, N.Y.C., 1996—. Adj. lectr. Hunter Coll. CUNY, and Hunter Coll. H.S., 1981-82; tchg. asst., substitute lectr. Manhattan Sch. Music, N.Y.C., 1981-83; judge numerous music competitions, including Bklyn. Acad. Music, 1985, 86. Contbr. numerous articles to law and other publs.; performer, dir. musicals, including Camelot, Sound of Music, Fantasticks, Grease, West Side Story, Show Boat, Little Night Music, Carousel, King and I, and Jesus Christ Superstar; spl. guest 3d Internat. Festival Contemporary Music, Leningrad, USSR, 1988. Bd. dirs. Coun. for Trade and Econ. Cooperation, U.S.-Uzbekistan Coun., St. Petersburg Found. Scholar Jewish Found. for Edn. Women, 1977-78, Manhattan Sch. Music. Mem. Internat. Law Soc., N.Y. State Bar Assn., Bar Assn. City N.Y., Women in Internat. Trade, Coun. on Fgn. Rels. Corporate, general, Finance, Private international. Office: Internat Project Devel Group 730 5th Ave 9 flr New York NY 10019 Fax: 212-541-2486.

PASSONNEAU, POLLY NICOLE, lawyer; b. St. Louis, Nov. 4, 1956; d. Joseph Russell and Janet Vivian P. AB cum laude, Washington U., St. Louis, 1978; Diplome, U. Strasbourg, 1978; MA in Comparative Lit., U. N.C., 1987, JD, 1984. Bar: N.Y. 1986, Mass. 1985, U.S. Dist. Ct. (ea. dist.) N.Y. 1987, U.S. Dist. Ct. (so. dist.) N.Y. 1987, U.S. Ct. Appeals (2d cir.) 1987. Contbr. short stories to The Sun, 1989, Spit, 1990, 91, The S.C. Rev., 1995; contbr. articles to profl. jours. Recipient Am. Jurisprudence award Lawyers' Cooperative Pub. Co., 1982. Mem. Nat. Orgn. Criminal Def. Lawyers, N.Y. Criminal Bar Assn., N.Y. County Lawyers. Appellate, Criminal, Family and matrimonial. Office: 20 Vesey St Rm 400 New York NY 10007-2913

PASTORIZA, JULIO, lawyer; b. Havana, Cuba, Sept. 22, 1948; came to U.S., 1960; s. Julio S. and Emilia (Bardanca) P.; m. Gloria M. Alvarez-Pedroso, Jan. 5, 1974; 1 child, Gloria Cristina. AA, Miami Dade C.C., 1967; BA, U. Fla., 1969; JD, U. Miami, 1973. Bar: Fla. 1973, U.S. Tax Ct. 1974, U.S. Supreme Ct. 1977. Assoc. Miguel A. Suarez P.A., Miami, Fla., 1973-77; ptnr. Sulli, Pastoriza & Hill, Miami, 1977-82; shareholder Julio Pastoriza, P.A., Coral Gables, Fla., 1982-85; ptnr. LaCapra & Wiser, Miami, 1985-87; pvt. practice Coral Gables, 1987—. Agent Attys. Title Ins. Fund, Miami, 1979—; instr. Biscayne Coll., Miami, 1972-76. Spkr. pre-marital conf. St. Theresa Cath. Ch., Coral Gables, 1981-88, mem. adv. bd., 1987-89; mem. adv. bd. Our Lady of Lourdes Acad., Miami, 1991-95; counselor St. Robert Bellarmine Cath. Ch., 2000-01. Avocations: fishing, photography. Bankruptcy, Family and matrimonial, Property, real (including real estate development, water). Home: 2601 San Domingo St Coral Gables FL 33134-5534 Office: 7101 SW 99 Ave Ste 109B Miami FL 33173-4661

PATE, JAMES LAVERT, lawyer; b. Shreveport, La., Feb. 16, 1952; s. Barney Fain and Mary Elizabeth (Stancil) P.; m. Andrea Carol Cofer, Nov. 7, 1975; children: Allison, Erin, Caitlin. BS, La. State U., 1975; JD, Loyola U., New Orleans, 1979. Bar: La. 1979, U.S. Dist. Ct. (ea., mid. and we. dists.) La. 1979. Assoc. Bailey & Leininger, New Orleans, 1979-80; ptnr. Onebane, Donohoe, Lafayette, La., 1982-87, Laborde & Neuner, Lafayette, 1987—. Bd. mem. Acadiana Safety Assn., Lafayette, 1987—. Mem. ABA, Am. Arbitration Assn., La. Bar Assn., La. Assn. Def. Counsel, Def. Rsch. Inst. Republican. Episcopalian. General civil litigation. Office: Laborde and Neuner 1 Petroleum Ctr 1001 W Pinhook Rd Lafayette LA 70503-2407

PATE, MICHAEL LYNN, lawyer; b. Ft. Worth, Tex., July 9, 1951; s. J.B. and Mary Anna (Hable) P.; m. Barbara Ann Linch, May 28, 1977. AA, Schreiner Coll., 1971; BS, Tex. Wesleyan Coll., 1973; JD, U. Tex., 1975. Bar: Tex. 1976, D.C. 1983, U.S. Tax Ct. 1986, U.S. Supreme Ct. 1987. Adminstrv. asst. to Senator Sherman, counsel natural resources com. Tex. Senate, 1976-77; adminstrv. asst. to Lt. Gov. Bill Hobby, Austin, Tex., 1977-79; legis. asst. Senator Bentsen, Washington, 1979-81, legis. dir., 1981-86; ptnr., head Washington office Bracewell & Patterson, Washington, 1986—. Trustee Schreiner U. Mem. ABA, Tex. Bar Assn., D.C. Bar Assn. Democrat. Methodist. Avocations: basketball, tennis, golf. Legislative. Office: Bracewell & Patterson 2000 K St NW Ste 500 Washington DC 20006-1872 E-mail: mpate@bracepatt.com.

PATERSON, BASIL ALEXANDER, lawyer; b. N.Y.C., Apr. 27, 1926; s. Leonard J. and Evangeline (Rondon) P.; m. Portia Hairston, 1953; children: Daniel, David. BS, St. John's Coll., 1948; JD, St. John's U., 1951. Bar: N.Y. 1952. Ptnr. Paterson, Michael, Jones and Cherot, N.Y.C., 1956-77, Meyer, Suozzi, English & Klein, P.C., Mineola, N.Y., 1983—; mem. N.Y. State Senate, 1965-70; dep. mayor for labor rels. City of N.Y., 1978; sec. of state State of N.Y., 1979-82. Pres. Inst. Mediation and Conflict Resolution, 1971-77; chmn. 2d Jud. Screening Com., 1985-95; assoc. chmn. N.Y. State Sentencing Guidelines Com.; commr. Port Authority N.Y. and N.J., 1989-95; mem. commn. to promote confidence in judicial elections, 2003-. Bd. dirs. St. Benedict's Day Nursery, 1999—; vice chmn. Dem. Nat. Com., 1972-78, mem., 1972-78. Recipient Eagleton Inst. Politics award, Disting. Svc. award Guardians Assn. N.Y. Police Dept., City Club N.Y. award, Black Expo award, Excellence medal St. John's U., Kibbe award CUNY. Roman Catholic. Labor (including EEOC, Fair Labor Standards Act, labor-management relations, NLRB, OSHA). Office: Meyer Suozzi English & Klein PC 1505 Kellum Pl Ste 3 Mineola NY 11501-4824

PATERSON, ROBERT, lawyer, director; b. Ballarat, Australia, Sept. 7, 1944; s. William Arbuckle and Joan Patricia Paterson; m. Barbara Frances Lugg, Nov. 8, 1980; children: Jacqueline, Lucille, Amanda. B of Commerce, U. Melbourne, 1967, LLB with honors, 1968; MBA, Deakin U., Geelong, Australia, 1992. Bar: Victoria 1970, NSW 1985, Australian Capital Territory 1985, Western Australia 1988. From solicitor to ptnr. Blake & Riggall, Melbourne, 1970—88; ptnr. Blake Dawson Waldron, Melbourne, 1988—93; group gen. counsel Australia & New Zealand Banking Group Ltd., Melbourne, 1993—98; ptnr. Norton Smith & Co., Melbourne, 1998—. Bd. dirs. Rolex Australia Pty. Ltd., Melbourne. Trustee Honda Found., Melbourne, 1991—. Mem.: Melbourne Cricket Club, Royal Melbourne Golf Club, Melbourne Club. Banking, Commercial, contracts (including sales of goods; commercial financing), Corporate, general. Home: 5/58 Clarendon St East Melbourne Vi 3002 Australia Office: Norton Gledhill 459 Collins St Level 23 Melbourne 3000 Australia Office Fax: 613 96291475. Business E-Mail: robert.paterson@norgled.com.au.

PATHE, ILMO, lawyer, tax specialist; b. Wuppertal, Germany, Aug. 2, 1968; parents Helmut and Renate Pathe. First state exam, U. Wuerzburg, Germany, 1994, JD, 1999; second state exam, Oberlandesgericht Duesseldorf, Germany, 1997; tax advisor, Steuerberatungskammer Duesseldorf, 2001. Bar: Wuppertal 1997, Düsseldorf 2001, Steuerberaterkammer Duesseldorf 2001, Düsseldorf 2002. Lawyer Dr. Breidenbach & Ptnr., CPA, Wuppertal, 1997—2001; lawyer, tax advisor White & Case, Feddersen, Duesseldorf, 2001—. Author: Der deutsche Familienname im Sach-und Verweisungsrecht, 1999. Lt. Germany Inf., 1987—89. Mem.: Steuerberaterverein Duesseldorf, Deutscher Anwalt Verein, Internat. Fiscal Assn. Avocations: history, music, sports. Taxation, general, Corporate, general, Mergers and acquisitions. Home: Meertal 64 41464 Neuss Germany Office: White & Case Feddersen Jaegerhofstraße 29 40479 Düsseldorf Germany

PATMAN, PHILIP FRANKLIN, lawyer; b. Atlanta, Nov. 1, 1937; s. Elmer Franklin and Helen Lee (Miller) P.; m. Katherine Sellers, July 1, 1967; children: Philip Franklin, Katherine Lee. BA, U. Tex., 1959, LLB, 1964; MA, Princeton U., 1962. Bar: Tex. 1964, U.S. Supreme Ct. 1970, U.S. Dist. Ct. (so. dist.) Tex. 1971, U.S. Dist. Ct. (we. dist.) Tex. 1975. Atty. office of legal adviser Dept. State, Washington, 1964-67; dep. dir. office internat. affairs HUD, Washington, 1967-69; pvt. practice Austin, Tex., 1969—. Contbr. articles to legal jours. Ofcl. rep. of Gov. Tex. to Interstate Oil Compact Commn., 1973-83, 87-91. Woodrow Wilson fellow, 1959. Fellow Tex. Bar Found. (life); mem. ABA, State Bar Tex., Tex. Ind. Prodrs. and Royalty Owners Assn., Tex. Oil and Gas Assn., Tex. Law Rev. Assn., Austin Club, Headliners Club, Westwood Country Club, Rotary, Phi Beta Kappa, Phi Delta Phi. Administrative and regulatory, Oil, gas, and mineral, Environmental. Office: Patman & Osborn 515 Congress Ave Ste 1704 Austin TX 78701-3503

PATRICK, DANE HERMAN, lawyer; b. San Antonio, Oct. 18, 1960; s. Kae Thomas and Joyce Lynn (von Scheele) P.; m. Kelly Marie Carlson, May 17, 1986. BA in Econs. with honors, U. Tex., 1983; JD, So. Meth. U., 1987. Cert.: Tex. Bd. of Legal Specialization (personal injury trial law). Assoc. Law Office of Earl Luna, Dallas, 1987-88, Veitch & Davis, San Antonio, 1988-91; pvt. practice, San Antonio, 1991—. Mem. ATLA, San Antonio Trial Lawyers Assn. (bd. dirs.), San Antonio United Shareholder Assn. (chmn. 1988-92). Democrat. Methodist. Avocations: weight lifting, hunting, martial arts. General civil litigation, Insurance, Personal injury (including property damage). Office: 111 Soledad St Ste 705 San Antonio TX 78205-2298

PATRICK, DEVAL LAURDINE, lawyer; b. Chgo., July 31, 1956; s. Laurdine Kenneth and Emily Mae (Wintersmith) P.; m. Diane Louise Bemus, May 5, 1984; children: Sarah Baker, Katherine Wintersmith. AB cum laude, Harvard Coll., 1978, JD, 1982, Dist. Columbia Law Sch., 1994, Morris Brown Coll., 1996, Curry Coll., 1997, Clark U., 1999, New Eng. Sch. of Law, 1999, Suffolk U., 2000, Northeastern U., 2002. Bar: Calif. 1983, D.C. 1985, Mass. 1987, U.S. Dist. Ct. Mass. 1987, U.S. Dist. Ct. (cen. dist.) Calif. 1983, U.S. Ct. Appeals (1st and 5th cirs.) 1984, U.S. Ct. Appeals (9th and 11th cirs.) 1984, U.S. Supreme Ct. 1988. Law clk. to Hon. Stephen Reinhardt U.S. Ct. Appeals (9th cir.), L.A., 1982-83; asst. counsel NAACP Legal Def. Fund, N.Y.C., 1983-86; ptnr. Hill & Barlow, Boston, 1986-94; asst. atty. gen. civil rights divsn. U.S. Dept. Justice, Washington, 1994-97; ptnr. Day, Berry & Howard, Boston, 1997-99; v.p., gen. counsel Texaco Inc., White Plains, N.Y., 1999-2001; exec. v.p., gen. counsel The Coca-Cola Co., Atlanta, Ga., 2001—. Herman Phleger disting. vis. prof. Stanford Law Sch., 1997; lectr. Boston Coll. Sch. Law, 1997, Harvard Law Sch., 1998; mem. various corp. bd. dirs.; bd. overseers Harvard U., 1998—2003; dir. UAL Corp., 1997-2001, Reebok Internat. Ltd., 2001-, Coca-Cola Enterprises Inc., 2001-. Dir., mem. exec. com., chmn. New Eng. steering com. NAACP Legal Def. and Edn. Fund., Inc., 1991-94, vice chmn. Mass. Jud. Nominating Coun., 1991-93; trustee, mem. exec. com. Milton Acad., 1985-97; overseer WGBH, 1993-94; trustee Nathan Cummings Found., 1998-2000, Ford Found., 2000--. Recipient George Leisure award Harvard Law Sch., 1981; Rockefeller Traveling fellow, 1978. Mem. ABA (numerous bds. and coms.), Mass. Bar Assn., Mass. Black Lawyers Assn., Boston Bar Assn. (coun. mem. 1993), Harvard Alumni Assn. (dir. 1993-96). Avocations: squash, cooking, gardening. Civil rights, Federal civil litigation, Criminal. Office: The Coca-Cola Co One Coca-Cola Plz Atlanta GA 30301

PATRICK, H. HUNTER, judge; b. Gasville, Ark., Aug. 19, 1939; s. H. Hunter Sr. and Nelle Frances (Robinson) P.; m. Charlotte Anne Wilson, July 9, 1966; children: Michael Hunter, Colleen Annette. BA, U. Wyo., 1961, JD, 1966. Bar: Wyo. 1966, U.S. Dist. Ct. Wyo. 1966, Colo. 1967, U.S. Supreme Ct. 1975. Mcpl. judge City of Powell (Wyo.), 1967-68; sole practice law Powell, 1966-88; atty. City of Powell, 1969-88; justice of the peace County of Park, Wyo., 1971-88; bus. law instr. Northwest Community Coll., Powell, 1968-98; dist. judge State of Wyo. 5th Jud. Dist., 1988—. Mem. Wyo. Dist. Judges Conf., sec.-treas., 1993-94, vice chair, 1994-95, chair, 1995-96. Editor: Bench Book for Judges of Courts of Limited Jurisdiction in the State of Wyoming, 1980-90. Dir. cts. Wyo. Girls State, Powell, 1982-85, 89-99; elder, deacon, moderator of deacons Powell Presbyn. Ch., 1997; mem. Wyo. Commn. Jud. Conduct & Ethics, 1997-2003; judge, chair mgmt. com. Park County Drug Ct., 2002—. Recipient Wyo. Crime Victims Compensation Commn. Judicial award, 1995. Fellow Am. Bar Found. (life), Wyo. Jud. Adv. Coun.; mem. ABA (Wyo. state del. to ho. of dels. 1994-2001, Wyo. del. judicial adminstrn. divsn., exec. com. nat. conf. trial ct. judges representing Wyo., Colo., Kans., Nebr., N.Mex. 1996-2000, bd. govs. 2001—, Pub. Svc. award for ct.-sponsored Law Day programs 1990, 92), Wyo. Bar Assn. (Cmty. Svc. award 1999, Ann. Pub. Svc. award 1999), Colo. Bar Assn., Park County Bar Assn. (sec. 1969-70, pres. 1970-71), Wyo. Assn. Cts. Ltd. Jurisdiction (pres. 1973-80), Wyo. Dist. Judges Conf. (chair 1996), Am. Judicature Soc. (bd. dirs. 2002—). Avocations: photography, travel, fishing, reading, writing. Home: PO Box 941 Powell WY 82435-0941 Office: PO Box 1868 Cody WY 82414-1868 E-mail: hpatrick@parkco.wtp.net.

PATRICK, PHILIP HOWARD, lawyer; b. Bridgend, Wales, Aug. 12, 1946; s. Frederick Harry and Phyllis Mair (Vaulters) P.; m. Rosalind Elizabeth Davies, Aug. 5, 1969. MusB, U. Wales, 1969; MFA, Princeton U., 1971, PhD, 1973; JD, Washington (D.C.) Coll. Law, 1980. Bar: D.C. 1980, Md. 1981. Asst. prof. Am. U., Washington, 1973-77; cons., Washington, 1978-81; pvt. practice, Silver Springs, Md., 1980-89; pres. Computing Community Services Corp., Silver Springs, 1980-89; gen. counsel The Orcutt Group Ltd., Rockville, Md., 1989-92; dir. contracts FileTek, Inc., Rockville, Md., 1992—. Founder, sec. Nat. Welsh-Am. Found., Washington, 1981-84, mem. adv. coun., 1984—. Computer, Corporate, general. Home: 2523 Oakenshield Dr Potomac MD 20854-2926 Office: FileTek Inc 9400 Key West Ave Rockville MD 20850-3322 E-mail: php@filetek.com.

PATRICK, VICTOR PHILLIP, lawyer; b. Lake Forest, Ill., Jan. 7, 1958; s. Rodger Ralph Patrick and Phyllis Elaine Bachler; m. Elizabeth Fletcher, Aug. 9, 1985; children: Kathryn Elaine, Stephen James, Diane Elizabeth, Marie Christine, Thomas Grant, John Wallace, Daniel Victor. AB in Politics magna cum laude, Princeton U., 1982; JD cum laude, Harvard U., 1985. Bar: D.C. 1986, N.Y. 1986, U.S. Ct. Appeals (10th cir.) 1986. Law clk. U.S. Ct. Appeals 10th Cir., Denver, 1985-86; assoc. Cleary, Gottlieb, Steen & Hamilton, Washington, 1986-88, 92-94, Brussels, 1988—91; from asst. gen.

counsel to v.p., sec. and dep. gen. counsel Honeywell Internat. Inc. (formerly AlliedSignal Inc.), Morristown, NJ, 1994—97, 1999—2002, Torrance, Calif., 1997—99; sr. v.p., gen. counsel, sec. Walter Industries, Inc., Tampa, Fla., 2002—. Mem. ABA. Mem. Lds Ch. Corporate, general, Finance, Mergers and acquisitions. Home: 410 S Armenia Ave Apt 939C Tampa FL 33609 E-mail: vpatrick@walterind.com.

PATT, HERBERT JACOB, lawyer; b. Chgo., Feb. 12, 1935; s. Abraham and Esther Blanch (Kuchinsky) P.; m. Yvonne Phyllis Shavell, Oct. 9, 1958 (dec. Mar. 1986); children: Aldon Wayne, Bradley Earl, Colette Emile; m. Lynn Cheryl Feingold, December 26, 1993. BA, Northwestern U., 1956, JD, 1958; Diploma, Indsl. Coll., Johannesburg, South Africa. Bar: Ill. 1959, U.S. Dist. Ct. (no. dist.) Ill. 1959, U.S. Supreme Ct. 1977, Calif. 1986, U.S. Dist. Ct. (ctrl. and so. dists.) Calif. 1987, U.S. Ct. Appeals (9th cir.) 1987, U.S. Ct. Appeals (4th cir.) 2002. Assoc. Andres & Andres, Santa Ana, Calif. Pres. Jewish Nat. Fund Orange Co., Santa Ana, 1994-95, chmn., 1996-98, nat. bd. dirs., N.Y., 1994-98; pres. Temple Judea, Laguna Hills, Calif., 1992-93. General civil litigation, Personal injury (including property damage), Probate (including wills, trusts). Office: Andres & Andres 2041 N Main St Santa Ana CA 92706 E-mail: pattlaw@aol.com.

PATTE, GEORGE DAVID, JR., lawyer; b. Batavia, N.Y., Dec. 16, 1945; s. George David and Patricia Elmira (O'Cain) P.; m. Mary Christine Crass, Dec. 28, 1969; children: Chesua Conkling, George David V. BA in Internat. Relations, Ithaca Coll., 1967; JD, U. Louisville, 1974. Bar: N.Y. 1976, U.S. Dist. Ct. (no. dist.) N.Y. 1976. Tchr. spl. studies Dryden (N.Y.) High Sch., 1970-72; sole practice Ithaca, N.Y., 1976-80, 88—; ptnr. Greenburg & Patte, Ithaca, 1981-88. Lectr. bus. law Ithaca Coll., 1985-86. Author: (with Greenburg) A Legal View of Your Rights if Injured on the Job, 1986. Pres. Tompkins County Soc. for Prevention Cruelty to Animals, Ithaca, 1980, bd. dirs. 1977-81; mem. Instl. Animal Care and Use Com., Cornell U., Ithaca, 1986-88; bd. dirs. United Way of Tompkins County, 1987-94; trustee Ithaca Coll., 1991-96. Mem. N.Y. State Bar Assn., Tompkins County Bar Assn., N.Y. Trial Lawyers Assn. (pres. so. tier affiliate 1987-89, bd. dirs. 1987-95), Ithaca Coll. Alumni Assn. (bd. dirs. 1990—, chmn. nominations com. 1985, pres. 1990-93, chair Fall Creek watershed com. 2003—, Disting. Alumni award 1997). Roman Catholic. Avocation: stream fishing for trout. State civil litigation, Construction. Home: 1167 Taughannock Blvd Ithaca NY 14850-9573 Office: 121 E Buffalo St Ithaca NY 14850-4222 E-mail: george.patte@verizon.net.

PATTEN, EDWARD ELLIS, JR., judge; s. Edward Ellis Patten, Sr. and Jane Elizabeth Patten; m. Jacqueline Randolph, Aug. 17, 1974; children: Erin Elise Lane, Elizabeth Green, Katherine Randolph. AA, Pearl River Jr. Coll., Poplarville, Miss., 1972; JD, U. of Miss., 1977, BS in Pharmacy, 1975. Bar: Miss. 1978, U.S. Dist. Ct. (no. and so. dist.) Miss. 1978, U.S. Supreme Ct. 1998. Assoc. Armstrong & Hoffman, Hazlehurst, Miss., 1978—81, ptnr., 1981—98; chancellor State of Miss., 15th Chancery Ct. Dist., Brookhaven and Hazlehurst, Miss., 1998—. Mem. Miss. Supreme Ct. Adv. Com. on Rules, Jackson, 2002—. Spkr. New Judges' Orientation Conf., 2002, Judges' Conf. Rule 81, 2003, Chancery Ct. Clks. Seminar, 2003; mem. Hazlehurst C. of C., Miss.; rep. of chancery judges Conf. on Legis. Study Commn. on Miss. Jud. Sys., Jackson, Miss., 2001. Fellow: Miss. Bar Found.; mem.: ABA (family law and jud. sects.), Miss. Bar Assn. (chmn. bylaws com. 22d Cir. Ct. Dist. 1996—97). Baptist. Avocations: golf, gardening. Office: 15th Chancery Court District PO Drawer 707 Hazlehurst MS 39083 Office Fax: 601-894-4081. E-mail: epatten@15thchancerydistrictms.org.

PATTEN, VALERIE LYNN, lawyer; b. L.A., Apr. 8, 1950; d. Russell Carl and Donna D. Patten; 1 child, Elizabeth Nicole Wood. AB, Stanford U., 1972; MFA, San Jose State U., 1981; JD, Georgetown U., 1992. Bar: Calif. 1992. Legal intern Washington Area Lawyers for the Arts, 1990—90; law clk. Garfinkle & Assocs., Washington, 1990—92; staff atty. Legal Advocates for Children and Youth, San Jose, Calif., 1992—93; assoc. atty. Law Offices of Robert L. Hoover, San Jose, 1994—96; pvt. practice Law Offices of Valerie L. Patten, Palo Alto, Calif., 1996—. Freelance writer Bay Area (Calif.) Art Publ., 1980—84; writer arts & entertainment Palo Alto (Calif.) Weekly, 1982—84; instr. art dept. U. Mont., Missoula, 1984—84; referral atty., lectr. Calif. Lawyers for the Arts, San Francisco, 1993—2003; lectr. continuing edn. art dept. legal issues for artists San Jose State U., 1993—93; asst. prof. art dept. San Francisco State U., 1994—95; atty. mem. Graphic Artists Guild, San Francisco, 1997—; presenter, continuing edn. seminar on custody and visitation in calif. Nat. Bus. Inst., Eau Claire, Wis., 2003. One-woman shows include DeSaisset Mus. , Pro Arts Gallery, Oakland , Henry Art Gallery, Seattle , exhibited in group shows at Am. Acad. and Inst Arts and Letters, N.Y. (selected for Hassam and Speicher fund Purchase Exhbn., 1983). Pro tem judge Superior Ct. Santa Clara County, San Jose, 1999—2003, property divsn. mediator, 1998—2001; pro bono panel mem. Santa Clara County Bar Assn. Law Found., San Jose, 1993—2003; vol. tchr. Prisoners' Info. Svcs., Palo Alto, 1977—84; vol. atty. Pro Bono Project, San Jose, 2002—03; bd. mem., sec. Young Audiences San Jose, 1998—2001; bd. mem. DanceVisions, Palo Alto, 1993—2003. Recipient Am. Jurisprudence award, Lawyers Coop. Pub., 1991; Charles Warren Kendrick Meml. scholar, Stanford U., 1968—72. Mem.: San Mateo County Bar Assn. (family law sect. 2003—), Calif. State Bar Assn., ABA (family law sect. 1992—), Santa Clara County Bar Assn. (family law sect. com. 1995—), State Bar Calif. Episcopalian. Avocations: painting, art history, hiking. Family and matrimonial, Trademark and copyright, Art Law. Office: Law Offices Valerie L Patten Ste 7 744 San Antonio Rd Palo Alto CA 94303 Office Fax: 650-855-9580. E-mail: valpatten@prodigy.net.

PATTERSON, CHRISTOPHER NIDA, lawyer; b. Washington Courthouse, Ohio, Apr. 17, 1960; s. Donis Dean and JoAnne (Nida) O.; m. Vicky Patterson; children: Travis, Kirsten. BA, Clemson U., 1982; JD, Nova U., 1985. Bar: Fla. 1985, U.S. Dist. Ct. (mid. dist.) Fla. 1985, U.S. Ct. Mil. Rev. 1986, U.S. Ct. Mil. Appeals 1987, U.S. Dist. Ct. (ea. dist.) Va. 1987, U.S. Supreme Ct. 1990, U.S. Ct. Appeals (11th cir.) 1992, U.S. Dist. Ct. (no. dist.) Fla. 1992, U.S. Dist. Ct. (so. dist.) Tex. 1995; cert. criminal trial lawyer Fla. Bar. and Nat. Bd. Trial Advocacy. Pros. Fla. State Attys. Office, Orlando, Fla., 1985; spl. asst. U.S. Atty. U.S. Dist. Ct. (ea. dist.) Va., 1987-90; ptnr. Patterson & Hauversburk, Panama City, Fla., 1992—. Adj. prof. law Gulf Coast Coll.; mem. Fla. Supreme Ct. Mediators Qualifications Bd.; family law mediator Fla. Supreme Ct., dependency law mediator, county ct. mediator, mem. mediators qualifications bd.; mediator County Ct.; on-air legal analyst Nex Media-WYOO-FM. Author: Queen's Pawn, 1996, Treasure Trove, 1997; contbr. Nat. DAR Mag., Fla. Defender mag. Chancellor St. Thomas Episcopal Ch. Capt. JAGC, U.S. Army, 1986-92, Desert Storm. Recipient U.S. Army Chief of Staff award for legal excellence, 1989, Guardian ad litem commendation, Fla. Supreme Ct., 1999. Mem. ABA, ATLA, FBA, SAR, NACDL (life), Am. Coll. Barristers, Fla. Assn. Criminal Def. Lawyers, Acad. Fla. Trial Lawyers, Assn. Fed. Def. Attys., Fla. Acad. Profl. Mediators, Fla. Bar Spkrs. Bur. (criminal law sect., mil. law standing com., del. 11th cir. jud. conf. 1999, Pro Bono Svc. award, nominee Jefferson award for pub. svc. 1999), Bay County Bar Assn., The Ret. Officers' Assn., Christian Legal Soc., Am. Legion, Fellowship of Christian Athletes, Nat. Triathlon Fedn., Soc. Colonial Wars, Mil. Order Fgn. Wars. Episcopalian. Avocations: athletics, triathlons. Office: PO Box 9474 415 Beckrich Rd Ste 290 Panama City Beach FL 32417

PATTERSON, DONALD ROSS, lawyer, educator; b. Sept. 9, 1939; s. Sam Ashley and Marguerite (Robinson) P.; m. Peggy Ann Schulte, May 1, 1965; children: D. Ross, Jerome Ashley, Gretchen Anne. BS, Tex. Tech U., 1961; JD, U. Tex., 1964; LLM, So. Meth. U., 1972. Bar: Tex. 1964, U.S. Ct. Claims 1970, U.S. Ct. Customs and Patent Appeals 1970, U.S. Ct. Mil. Appeals 1970, U.S. Supreme Ct. 1970, U.S. Dist. Ct. (ea. dist.) Tex. 1982, U.S. Ct. Appeals (5th cir.) 1991, U.S. Ct. Appeals (D.C. cir.) 1994; bd. cert. in immigration and naturalization law, Tex. Commd. lt. (j.g.) USN, 1964, advanced through grades to lt. comdr., 1969; asst. officer in charge Naval Petroleum Res., Bakersfield, Calif., 1970-72; staff judge adv. Kenitra, Morocco, 1972-76; officer in charge Naval Legal Svcs. Office, Whidbey Island, Wash., 1976-79; head mil. Justice divsn., Subic Bay, The Philippines, 1979-81; ret. USN, 1982; pvt. practice Tyler, Tex., 1982—. Former instr. U. Md., Chapman Coll., U. LaVerne, Tyler Jr. Coll., Jarvis Christian Coll., U. Tex., Tyler. Mem. East Tex. Estate Planning Coun. Mem. Coll. of State Bar of Tex., Tex. Bar Assn., Smith County Bar Assn., Am. Immigration Lawyers Assn., Masons, Rotary (past pres.), Shriners, Toastmasters (past pres.), Phi Delta Phi. Republican. Baptist. Bankruptcy, Commercial, consumer (including collections, credit), Immigration, naturalization, and customs. Home: 703 Wellington St Tyler TX 75703-4666 Office: 777 S Broadway Ave Ste 106 Tyler TX 75701-1648 E-mail: oneworld2gether@cs.com.

PATTERSON, JOHN DE LA ROCHE, JR., lawyer; b. Schenectady, N.Y., July 8, 1941; s. John de la Roche Sr. and Jane C. (Clay) P.; m. Michele F. Demarest, Nov. 28, 1987; children: Daniel C., Sara R., Amy C. BA, Johns Hopkins U., 1963; LLB, Harvard U., 1966. Bar: Mass. 1968. Vol. Peace Corps, Chad, 1966-67; assoc. Foley, Hoag & Eliot, Boston, 1967-73, ptnr., 1974—, exec. com., 1989-97. Chmn. Kodaly Ctr. Am. Inc., Newton, Mass., 1977-87. Mem. ABA, Boston Bar Assn. Democrat. Avocations: sailing, tennis, travel, reading. Corporate, general, Intellectual property, Mergers and acquisitions. Office: Foley Hoag LLP 155 Seaport Blvd Boston MA 02210- E-mail: jpatters@FoleyHoag.com.

PATTERSON, JOHN B. lawyer, educator; b. Ft. Lauderdale, Fla., Apr. 29, 1968; s. George Anthony and Miriam (Bledsoe) Patterson; m. Amy Aline Hoodecheck, Aug. 29, 1998; 1 child, Kayla Aline. BBA, U. Notre Dame, 1990; JD, Nova Southeastern U., Ft. Lauderdale, 1994. Bar: Fla. 1994, U.S. Dist. Ct. (so. dist.) Fla. 2000, U.S. Dist. Ct. (mid. dist.) Fla. 2002. Asst. state atty. State's Atty. Office, 17th Jud. Cir., Ft. Lauderdale, 1994—2000; assoc. Wicker, Smith, O'Hara, et. al., Ft. Lauderdale, 2000—01, Montgomery & Larson, LLP, West Palm Beach, Fla., 2001—. Instr. Broward County Criminal Justice Inst., Ft. Lauderdale, 2000—. Roman Catholic. Avocations: golf, fishing. Personal injury (including property damage), Product liability, Professional liability. Office: Montgomery and Larson LLP 1016 Clearwater Pl West Palm Beach FL 33402 Office Fax: 561-832-0887. Business E-Mail: jbp@rmmjr.com.

PATTERSON, ROBERT EDWARD, lawyer; b. Los Angeles, Sept. 14, 1942; s. Ellis Elwood and Helen (Hjelte) P.; m. Christina Balboni, Oct. 2, 1971; 1 child, Victor Ellis. BA, UCLA, 1964; JD, Stanford U., 1972, grad. bus. exec. program, 1986; vis. scholar, Amos Tuck School Dartmouth Coll., 1998. Bar: Calif. 1972. Ptnr. Squire Sanders & Dempsey LLP, Palo Alto, Calif., 1972—. Bd. dirs. Procyte Corp., Peninsula Equity Ptnrs., Foster Ctr. for Pvt. Equity, Amos Tuck Sch., Dartmouth Coll., Sumida Corp., HK Pharmaceuticals, Inc, Synzyme Techs., LLC, Calif. State Parks Found., Acuity Ventures; mem. adv. bd. Borealis Ventures. Served to lt. comdr. USN, 1964-69. Mem. Rotary, Palo Alto Club, Menlo Circus Club, Bohemian Club, Band of Angels. Democrat. Corporate, general, Private international, High technology. Office: Squire Sanders & Dempsey 600 Hansen Way Ste 100 Palo Alto CA 94304-1043 E-mail: rpatterson@ssd.com.

PATTERSON, ROBERT HOBSON, JR., lawyer; b. Richmond, Va., Jan. 30, 1927; s. Robert Hobson and Margaret S. (Sargent) P.; m. Luise Franklin Wyatt, June 15, 1952 (dec.); children— India, Robert Hobson, Margaret. B.A., Va. Mil. Inst., 1949; LL.B., U. Va., 1952. Bar: Va. 1952, U.S. Ct. Appeals (4th cir.) 1953, U.S. Supreme Ct. 1955. Assoc. McGuireWoods LLP, Richmond, 1952-56, ptnr., 1956— , sr. ptnr., chmn. exec. com., 1978-89, chmn., 1984-89. Pres. bd. visitors Va. Mil. Inst., 1975; pres. Va. Home for Boys, 1975. Served with USNR, 1945-46. Fellow Am. Coll. Trial Lawyers, Am. Bar Found., Va. Mil. Inst. Alumni Assn. (pres. 1963-65), Commonwealth Club, Country Club of Va. Republican. Episcopalian. Antitrust, Federal civil litigation, State civil litigation. Office: McGuire-Woods LLP 1 James Ctr 901 E Cary St Richmond VA 23219-4057

PATTERSON, ROBERT PORTER, JR., federal judge; b. N.Y.C., July 11, 1923; s. Robert Porter and Margaret (Winchester) P.; m. Bevin C. Daly, Sept. 15, 1956; children: Anne, Robert, Margaret, Paul, Katherine. AB, Harvard U., 1947; LLB, Columbia U., 1950. Bar: N.Y. 1951, D.C. 1966. Law clk. Donovan, Leisure, Newton & Lumbard, N.Y.C., 1950-51; asst. counsel N.Y. State Crime Commn. Waterfront Investigation, 1952-53; asst. U.S. atty. Chief of Narcotics Prosecutions and Investigations, 1953-56; asst. counsel Senate Banking and Currency Com., 1954; assoc. Patterson, Belknap, Webb & Tyler, N.Y.C., 1956-60, ptnr., 1960-88; judge U.S. Dist. Ct. (so. dist.) N.Y., 1988—. Counsel to minority select com. pursuant to house resolution no. 1, Washington, 1967; mem. Senator's Jud. Screening Panel, 1974-88, Gov.'s Jud. Screening Panel, 1975-82, Gov.'s Sentencing Com., 1978-79. Contbr. articles to profl. jours. Chmn. Wm. T. Grant Found., 1974-94, Prisoners' Legal Services N.Y., 1976-88; dir. Legal Aid Soc., 1961-88, pres., 1967-71; chmn. Nat. Citizens for Eisenhower, 1959-60, Scranton for Pres., N.Y. State, 1964; bd. mgrs. Havens Relief Fund Soc., 1994—, Millbrook Sch., 1966-78, Vera Inst. Justice, 1981-99, New Sch. for Social Rsch., 1986-94, George C. Marshall Found., 1987-93; mem. exec. com. Lawyers Com. for Civil Rights Under Law, 1968-88; mem. Goldman Panel for Attica Disturbance, 1972, Temporary Commn. on State Ct. System, 1971-73, Rockefeller U. Council, 1986-88, exec. com. N.Y. Vietnam Vets. Meml. Commn., 1982-85, Mayor's Police Adv. Com., 1985-87. Served to capt. USAAF, 1942-46. Decorated D.F.C. with cluster, Air medal with clusters. Mem. ABA (ho. of dels. 1976-80), N.Y. State Bar Assn. (pres. 1978-79), Assn. Bar City N.Y. (v.p. 1974-75), N.Y. County Lawyers Assn., Am. Law Inst., Am. Judicature Soc. (bd. dirs. 1979). Republican. Episcopalian. Home: Fair Oaks Farm 1657 Route 9D Cold Spring NY 10516-3543 Office: US Dist Ct So Dist NY US Court House 500 Pearl St New York NY 10007-1316

PATTERSON, WILLIAM ROBERT, retired lawyer; b. Wathena, Kans., Feb. 25, 1924; s. George Richard and Jessie (Broadbent) P.; m. Lee Rhyne, Aug. 16, 1947; children: Martha, Robert, Elizabeth. Student, U. Rochester, 1943-44; AB, Lenoir-Rhyne Coll., 1947; LL.B. with distinction, Duke U., 1950. Bar: Ga. 1951, D.C. 1962. Asso. firm Sutherland, Asbill & Brennan, Atlanta, 1950-58, partner, 1958—; trustee Ga. Tax Conf., 1980-83, pres., 1980-82. Lectr. in field. Mem. bd. visitors Duke U. Law Sch., 1973-87, chmn., 1977-87, life mem., 1987—; trustee Pace Acad., Atlanta, 1958-89, trustee emeritus, 1989—; mem. devel. bd. Lenoir-Rhyne Coll., 1976-79, trustee, 1980-89; elder Trinity Presbyterian Ch., Atlanta. With USN, 1942-46. Fellow Am. Coll. Mortgage Attys. (bd. regents 1993-99, pres. 1997-98); mem. ABA, Ga. State Bar, Atlanta Bar Assn., D.C. Bar Assn., Am. Coll. Real Estate Lawyers (bd. govs. 1987-90), Am. Law Inst., So. Fed. Tax Inst. (trustee 1957-90, adv. trustee 1990—, pres. 1974-75, chmn. 1975-76), Atlanta Tax Forum (trustee 1977-83, pres. 1981-82), Order of Coif, Cherokee Town and Country Club, Commerce Club, Peachtree Club. Home: 2939 Rivermeade Dr NW Atlanta GA 30327-2039 Office: Sutherland Asbill & Brennan First Union Pla 23d Fl 999 Peachtree St NE Ste 2300 Atlanta GA 30309-3996

PATTON, BRUCE M. law educator, management consultant; b. Terre Haute, Ind., Oct. 14, 1956; s. William Eugene and Carol Ann P.; m. Diana McLain Smith, Oct. 21, 1994. AB, Harvard U., 1977, JD, 1984. Bar: Mass. Co-founder, assoc. dir. Harvard Negotiation Project, Cambridge, Mass., 1979-84, dep. dir., 1984—; co-founder, assoc. dir. Program on Negotiation at Harvard Law Sch., Cambridge, Mass., 1983—2002; co-founder, ptnr. Vantage Partners, LLC, Cambridge, 1997—. Co-founder, prin. Conflict Mgmt. Inc., Cambridge, 1984—; co-founder, dir. Conflict Mgmt. Group, Cambridge, 1984-2000; Thaddeus R. Beal lectr. Harvard Law Sch., Cambridge, 1985-99. Co-author: The Mainstream of Alegbra and Trigonometry, 2d edit., 1980, Getting To Yes, 2d edit., 1991, Difficult Conversations, 1999; contbr. articles to profl. jours. Fellow: Coll. of Trial Mediators (hon.). Avocations: squash, hiking, tennis. Office: Harvard Negotiation Project Pound Hall 524 Harvard Law Sch Cambridge MA 02138 also: Vantage Ptnrs Brighton Landing W Ste 350 10 Guest St Boston MA 02135 E-mail: bpatton@post.harvard.edu.

PATTON, CHARLES HENRY, lawyer, educator; b. Asheville, N.C., Jan. 13, 1953; s. Charles Robert and Sarah (Gulledge) P. BA, Memphis State U., 1975, JD, 1979. Bar: Tenn. Assoc. Holt, Bachelor, Spicer & Ryan, Memphis, 1979-80; fin. exec. Felsenthal Planning Service Co., Memphis, 1980-81; sole practice Memphis, 1981—; prof. Memphis State U., 1982—. Planned giving dir. Christ United Meth. Ch., Memphis, 1986; mem. Planned Giving Coun. Memphis. Mem. S.E. Regional Bus. Law Professors Assn., Memphis Bar Assn., Estate Planning Coun. Memphis. Republican. Avocations: classic automobile restoration, model trains. Estate planning, Probate (including wills, trusts), Estate taxation. Office: 5100 Poplar Ave Ste 2701 Memphis TN 38137-4000

PATTON, PETER MARK, lawyer; b. Chgo., Dec. 23, 1955; s. James T. and Dorothy R. Patton; m. Anne E. Castimore, Oct. 12, 1985; 1 child, William James. AB, Harvard Coll., 1977; JD, U. Calif., Berkeley, 1985. Bar: Pa. 1987, U.S. Dist. Ct. (ea. dist.) Pa. 1987, U.S. Ct. Appeals (4th cir.) 1986, U.S. Ct. Appeals (3rd cir.) 1988. Law clk. U.S. Ct. Appeals (4th cir.), Richmond, Va., 1985-87; assoc. Galfand, Berger, Phila., 1987-93, ptnr., 1993—. Committeeman Dem. Orgn., Delaware County, 1998. Reciient Profl. Responsibility award Am. Jurisprudence, 1985. Mem. Pa. Trial Lawyers Assn., Phila. Trial Lawyers Assn., Million Dollar Advocates Forum. Avocation: running. Personal injury (including property damage), Product liability. Office: Galfand Berger 1818 Market St Ste 2300 Philadelphia PA 19103-3648

PATTY, CLAIBOURNE WATKINS, JR., lawyer; b. Cleve., Feb. 19, 1934; s. Claibourne Watkins and Eleanor (Todd) P.; m. Barbara Benton, May 4, 1968; children— Claibourne Watkins III, William Jordan. BA, U. of South, 1955; JD, U. Ark., 1961. Bar: Ark. 1961. Law clk. U.S. dist. judge, Ft. Smith, 1961-63; pvt. practice Little Rock, 1963-68; asst. ins. commr. State of Ark., 1968-69; trust officer Union Nat. Bank of Little Rock, 1969-77; asst. dean U. Ark. Sch. Law, Little Rock; also exec. dir. Ark. Inst. for Continuing Legal Edn., 1977-86; law clk. 2d Div. Chancery Ct., Pulaski County, 1986-89; of counsel Gruber Law Firm, North Little Rock, 1989-2001; prin. Patty Law Firm, North Little Rock, 2001—. Lectr. law Ark. Sch. Law, 1965; bd. dirs., chmn. Pulaski County Legal Aid Bur., 1966-69; mem. com. on civil practice Ark. Supreme Ct., 1998—. Bd. dirs., pres. Family Svc. Agy. of Ctrl. Ark., 1976-81, 86-93, 99—; bd. dirs., pres. Good Shepherd Ecumenical Retirement Ctr., 1975-2002; bd. dirs. Am. Diabetes Assn., Ark. Affil., 1996—, Ark. Gerontol. Soc. 1996—; mem. Ark. adv. com. U.S. Commn. on Civil Rights, 1985-89. With AUS, 1955-57. Mem.: Phi Alpha Delta, Beta Theta Pi. Estate taxation, Probate (including wills, trusts), Commercial, consumer (including collections, credit). Office: Patty Law Firm 315 N Broadway St North Little Rock AR 72114-5379 E-mail: clairgpm@swbell.net.

PATZ, EDWARD FRANK, retired lawyer; b. Balt., Aug. 25, 1932; s. Maurice A. and Violet (Furman) P.; m. Betty Seldner Levi, Nov. 18, 1956; children— Evelyn Anne, Edward Frank, Thomas L. BS, U. Md., 1954, LLB, 1959. Bar: Md. 1959, U.S. Dist. Ct. Md. 1959, U.S. Ct. Appeals (4th cir.) 1959, U.S. Supreme Ct. 1980. Ptnr. Weinberg and Green and predecessor firms, Balt., 1959-97; ret., 1997. Bd. dirs. Jewish Family and Children's Service, 1965-71; regional bd. dirs. NCCJ; pres. Suburban Club Balt. County, 1977-79; bd. trustees, exec. com. Flagler Ecumenical Social Svcs. Ctr., Inc., 1999-2002. Mem.: Hammock Dunes Club. Banking, Bankruptcy, Corporate, general. Home: 39 Island Estates Pkwy Palm Coast FL 32137-2203 E-mail: efpatz@pcfl.net.

PAUCIULO, JOHN WILLIAM, lawyer; b. N.Y.C., Nov. 6, 1965; m. Johanna Choate; children: Michael, Nina. BA, Villanova U., 1987; JD, Temple U., 1990. Staff atty. U.S. Securities and Exch. Commn., N.Y.C., 1990-92; assoc. Lamb, Windle & McErlane, West Chester, Pa., 1992-96; assoc. counsel Pep Boys, Phila., 1996-98; assoc., then ptnr. White & Williams, Phila., 1998—. Judge of elections Chester County, Pa., 1995-2001. Mem. Pa. Bar Assn. Corporate, general, Property, real (including real estate development, water), Securities. Home: 22 Hickory Ln Malvern PA 19355-3005 Office: White & Williams 1800 One Liberty Pl Philadelphia PA 19103 E-mail: pauciuloj@whitewms.com.

PAUL, DAVID AARON, lawyer; b. West Orange, N.J., Dec. 18, 1969; s. Mike S. and Stephanie E. (Kelsh) P.; m. Melissa Lynne Haralson. BS, Stetson U., 1991, JD with honors, 1994. Bar: Fla. 1994, U.S. Dist. Ct. (mid. dist.) Fla. 1994. Atty. Fisher, Rushmer et al, Orlando, Fla., 1994-97, Justin C. Johnson, St. Petersburg, Fla., 1997-98, Maher, Gibson & Guiley, Orlando, 1998-99, Dalton & Paul, P.A., Orlando, 1999—. Bd. dirs. Orange County Children's Safety Village, Orlando, 1996-97, Ctrl Fla. YMCA, Orlando, 1996-97, YMCA Camping Svcs., Orlando, 1996-97. Named Best Advocate in the Nat. ABA/Am. Coll. Trial Lawyers, 1993, Nat. Champion, Nat. Trial Competition, 1993. Mem. ATLA, Acad. Fla. Trial Lawyers, Million Dollar Advs. Forum, Order of Barristers. General civil litigation, Personal injury (including property damage). Office: 720 Rugby St Ste 100 Orlando FL 32804 E-mail: dpaul@daltonpaul.com.

PAUL, EVE W. retired lawyer; b. N.Y.C., June 16, 1930; d. Leo I. and Tamara (Sogolow) Weinschenker; m. Robert D. Paul, Apr. 9, 1952; children: Jeremy Ralph, Sarah Elizabeth. BA, Cornell U., 1950; JD, Columbia U., 1952. Bar: N.Y. 1952, Conn. 1960, U.S. Ct. Appeals (2nd cir.) 1975, U.S. Supreme Ct. 1977. Assoc. Botein, Hays, Sklar & Herzberg, N.Y.C., 1952-54; pvt. practice Stamford, Conn., 1960-70; staff atty. Legal Aid Soc., N.Y.C., 1970-71; assoc. Greenbaum, Wolff & Ernst, N.Y.C., 1972-78; v.p. legal affairs Planned Parenthood Fedn. Am., N.Y.C., 1979—91, v.p., gen. counsel, 1991—2003; ret., 2003. Bd. dirs. Ctr. Advancement of Women, Inc. Contbr. articles to profl. jours. Trustee Cornell U., Ithaca, N.Y., 1979-84; mem. Stamford Planning Bd., Conn., 1967-70; bd. dirs. Stamford LWV, 1960-62. Harlan Fiske Stone scholar Columbia Law Sch., 1952. Mem. ABA, Conn. Bar Assn., Assn. of Bar of City of N.Y., Stamford/Norwalk Regional Bar Assn., Internat. Trademark Assn. (chair dictionary listings com. 1988-90), Phi Beta Kappa, Phi Kappa Phi. Health, Intellectual property, Non-profit and tax-exempt organizations. E-mail: evewpaul@aol.com.

PAUL, HERBERT MORTON, lawyer, accountant, taxation educator; b. N.Y.C. s. Julius and Gussie Paul; m. Judith Paul; children: Leslie Beth, Andrea Lynn. BBA, Baruch Coll.; MBA, LLM, NYU; JD, Harvard U. Ptnr. Touche Ross & Co., N.Y.C., assoc. dir.-tax, dir. fin counseling; mng. ptnr. Herbert Paul, P.C., N.Y.C., 1983—. Prof. taxation, trustee NYU. Author: Ordinary and Necessary Expenses; editor: Taxation of Banks; adv. tax editor The Practical Acct.; mem. adv. bd. Financial and Estate Planning, Tax Shelter Insider, Financial Planning Strategist, Tax Shelter Litigation Report; bd. dirs. Partnership Strategist, The Business Strategist; cons. Profl. Practice Mgmt. Mag.; mem. panel The Hot Line; advisor The Partnership Letter, The Wealth Formula; cons. The Insider's Report for Physicians; mem. tax bd. Business Profit Digest; cons. editor physician's Tax Advisor; bd. fin. cons. Tax Strategies for Physicians; tax and bus. advisor Prentice Hall; contbg. editor. Jour. of Accountancy; mem. editl. bd. Family Bus. Advisor. Trustee NYU, mem. bd. overseers Grad. Sch. Bus.; mem. com. on trusts and estates Rockefeller U.; trustee Alvin Alley Am. Dance Theatre, Assoc. Y's of N.Y.; mem. accts. divsn. Fedn. Philanthropies; mem. adv. bd. Family Bus.

Advisor. Mem. NYU Alumni Assn. (pres., bd. dirs.). Mem. ABA, Inst. Fed. Taxation (adv. com. chmn.), Internat. Inst. on Tax and Bus. Planning (adv. bd.), Assn. Bar City N.Y., NYU Tax Soc. (pres.), Bur. Nat. Affairs-Tax Mgmt. (adv. com. on exec. compensation), Am. Inst. CPAs (com. on corp. taxation), Tax Study Group, N.Y. County Lawyers Assn., N.Y. State Soc. CPAs Dir. (chmn. tax div. com. on fed. taxation, gen. tax com., furtherance com., com. on rels. with IRS, bd. dirs.), Nat. Assn. Accts., Assn. of Bar of City of N.Y., Accts. Club of Am., Pension Club, Nat. Assn. Estate Planners (bd. dirs.), N.Y. Estate Planning Coun. (bd. dirs.), N.Y. C. of C. (tax com.), Grad. Sch. Bus. of NYU Alumni Assn. (pres.), NYU Alumni Assn. (pres.). Clubs: Wall St., City Athletic (N.Y.C.), Inwood Country. Estate planning, Corporate taxation, Personal income taxation. Office: Herbert Paul PC 450 7th Ave Ste 3000 New York NY 10123

PAUL, JAMES WILLIAM, lawyer; b. Davenport, Iowa, May 3, 1945; s. Walter Henry and Margaret Helene (Hillers) P.; m. Sandra Kay Schmid, June 15, 1968; children: James William, Joseph Hillers. BA, Valparaiso U., 1967; JD, U. Chgo., 1970. Bar: N.Y. 1971, U.S. Ct. Appeals (2d cir.) 1971, U.S. Dist. Ct. (so. and ea. dists.) N.Y. 1972, U.S. Supreme Ct. 1977, U.S. Ct. Appeals (6th cir.) 1981, Ind. 1982, U.S. Dist. Ct. (no. dist.) Ind. 1982, U.S. Claims Ct. 1989, U.S. Dist. Ct. (ea. dist.) Mich. 1989, U.S. Ct. Appeals (fed. cir.) 1991. Assoc. Rogers & Wells, N.Y.C., 1970-78, ptnr., 1978—. Dir., officer Musica Sacra, Inc., 1972-81 Bd. dirs. Turtle Bay Music Sch., Am. Luth. Publicity Bur., Wartburg Found. Recipient Disting. Alumnus award Valparaiso U., 1994. Mem. ABA (antitrust sect. ins. com.), Assn. Bar City N.Y. (com. on legal and jud. ethics, com. on civil ct.), Fed. Bar Council. Democrat. Insurance, Private international, Professional liability. Home: 360 E 72nd St Apt A-710 New York NY 10021-4755 also: 5 Curtis Dr Sherman CT 06784-1220 Office: Clifford Chance US LLP 200 Park Ave Ste 5200 New York NY 10166-0005

PAUL, RICHARD WRIGHT, lawyer; b. Washington, May 23, 1953; s. Robert Henry Jr. and Betty (Carey) P.; m. Paula Ann Coolsaet, July 25, 1981; children: Richard Haven, Timothy Carey, Brian Davis. AB magna cum laude, Dartmouth Coll., 1975; JD, Boston Coll., 1978. Bar: Mich. 1978, U.S. Dist. Ct. (ea. dist.) Mich. 1978, U.S. Ct. Appeals (6th cir.) 1982, U.S. Supreme Ct. 1989, U.S. Dist. Ct. (we. dist.) Mich. 1991. Assoc. Dickinson, Wright, Moon, Van Dusen & Freeman, Detroit, 1978-85, ptnr., 1985—. Mediator Wayne County Cir. Ct., Oakland County Dist. Ct. Co-author, Barbarians At The Gate: Daubert Two Years Later, 1995; contbr. articles to profl. publs. Trustee Bloomfield Village Assn., Birmingham, Mich., 2001—; sec., bd. dirs. Little League, Birmingham, 2000—,. Mem. ABA, State Bar of Mich. (treas. litig. sect. 1998-99, sec. litig. sect. 1999-2000, chmn. elect litig. sect. 2000-01, chairperson litigation sect. 2001-02), Def. Rsch. Inst., Detroit Bar Assn., Mich. Def. Trial Counsel, Dartmouth Lawyers Assn., Oakland County Bar Assn., Assn. Def. Trial Counsel, Alumni Coun. Dartmouth Coll., Dartmouth Detroit Club (pres. 1980—). Avocations: tennis, cycling. General civil litigation, Product liability, Professional liability. E-mail: rpaul@dickinson-wright.com.

PAUL, ROBERT CAREY, lawyer; b. Washington, May 7, 1950; s. Robert Henry and Betty Jane (Carey) P. AB, Dartmouth Coll., 1972; JD, Georgetown U., 1978. Assoc. Milbank, Tweed, Hadley & McCloy, N.Y.C., 1978-85; ptnr. Dechert Price & Rhoads, N.Y.C., 1986-89, Kelley Drye & Warren, Brussels, 1989-93; counsel Rockefeller & Co., Inc., N.Y.C., 1995—2003. Finance, Private international, Property, real (including real estate development, water). Home: 310 E 46th St Apt 19E New York NY 10017-3029 E-mail: rpaul@aviaamerica.com.

PAUL, THOMAS FRANK, lawyer; b. Aberdeen, Wash., Sept. 23, 1925; s. Thomas and Loretta (Ounstead) P.; m. Dolores Marion Zaugg, Apr. 1, 1950; chilren: Pamela, Peggy, Thomas Frank. BS in Psychology, Wash. State U., 1951; JD, U. Wash., 1957. Bar: Wash. 1958, U.S. Dist. Ct. (no. and so. dists.) Wash. 1958, U.S. Ct. Appeals (9th cir.) 1958, U.S. Supreme Ct. 1970. Ptnr., shareholder, pres. LeGros, Buchanan & Paul, Seattle, 1958—. Lectr. on admiralty and maritime law; bd. advisors U. San Francisco Law Jour., 1996—2002; mem. mediation and arbitration panel U.S. Dist. Ct. Seattle. Mem.: ATLA, ABA (chmn. com. on admiralty and maritime litig. 1982—86), Asia Pacific Lawyers Assn., Am. Arbitration Assn., Transp. Lawyers Assn., Wash. Def. Trial Lawyers, Def. Rsch. Inst., Wash. State Trial Lawyers Assn., Maritime Law Assn. U.S.A. (com. on nav. and C.G. matters 1981—82, com. on U.S. Mcht. Marine program 1981—82, com. on practice and proc. 1982—86, com. on limitation of liability 1982—86, com. on maritime legislation 1982—, nominating com. 1998—99), Wash. State Bar Assn. Republican. Admiralty, General civil litigation, Product liability. Home: 1323 Willard Ave W Seattle WA 98119-3460 Office: LeGros Buchanan & Paul 701 5th Ave Ste 2500 Seattle WA 98104-7051 E-mail: tpaul@legros.com.

PAUL, VIVIAN, lawyer; b. N.Y.C., July 3, 1925; d. A. Spencer and Simonson Feld; m. M.B. Paul, Sept. 10, 1966; children: Leslie Vivian, Melissa Beth. BA, U. Miami, 1944; LLB, U. So. Calif., 1949. Bar: Calif. 1949, U.S. Dist. Ct. (so. dist.) Calif. 1950. Pvt. practice, Cathedral City, Calif., 1949—. Editor-in-chief U. So. Calif. Law Rev., 1944. Los Angeles County Bar Assn. Democrat. Insurance, Personal injury (including property damage). Home and Office: 69864 Via Del Norte Cathedral City CA 92234-1726 E-mail: ranchovillage@aol.com.

PAUL, WILLIAM GEORGE, lawyer; b. Pauls Valley, Okla., Nov. 25, 1930; s. Homer and Helen (Lafferty) P.; m. Barbara Elaine Brite, Sept. 27, 1963; children: George Lynn, Alison Elise, Laura Elaine, William Stephen. BA, U. Okla., 1952, LL.B., 1956. Bar: Okla. bar 1956. Pvt. practice law, Norman, 1956; ptnr. Oklahoma City, 1957-84; with Crowe & Dunlevy, 1962-84, 96—; sr. v.p., gen. counsel Phillips Petroleum Co., Bartlesville, Okla., 1984-95; ptnr. Crowe & Dunlevy, Oklahoma City, 1996—. Assoc. prof. law Oklahoma City U., 1964-68; adv. bd. Martindale Hubbell, 1990—. Author: (with Earl Sneed) Vernon's Oklahoma Practice, 1965. Bd. dirs. Nat. Ctr. for State Cts., 1993-99, Am. Bar Endowment, 1986—; trustee Nat. Constitution Ctr., 2000—. 1st lt. USMCR, 1952-54. Named Outstanding Young Man Oklahoma City, 1965, Outstanding Young Oklahoman, 1966 Fellow Am. Bar Found. (chmn. 1991), Am. Coll. Trial Lawyers; mem. ABA (bd. govs. 1995—, pres. 1999), Okla. Bar Assn. (pres. 1976), Oklahoma County Bar Assn. (past pres.), Nat. Conf. Bar Pres. (pres. 1986), U. Okla. Alumni Assn. (pres. 1973), Order of Coif, Phi Beta Kappa, Phi Delta Phi, Delta Sigma Rho. Democrat. Presbyterian. Federal civil litigation, State civil litigation, Corporate, general. Home: 13017 Burnt Oak Rd Oklahoma City OK 73120-8919 Office: Crowe & Dunlevy Mid-Am Tower 20 N Broadway Ave Ste 1800 Oklahoma City OK 73102-8273

PAUL, WILLIAM MCCANN, lawyer; b. Cambridge, Mass., Feb. 9, 1951; s. Kenneth William and Mary Jean (Lamson) P.; m. Janet Anne Forest, Feb. 25, 1984; children: Emily L'Engle, Andrew Angwin, Elizabeth Seton. Student, U. Freiburg, Fed. Republic of Germany, 1971-72; BA, Johns Hopkins U., 1973; JD, U. Mich., 1977. Bar: D.C. 1978, U.S. Dist. Ct. D.C. 1978, U.S. Ct. Claims 1984, U.S. Ct. Appeals (4th cir.) 1980, U.S. Ct. Appeals (fed. cir.) 1983, U.S. Tax Ct. 1990. Law clk. to judge U.S. Ct. Appeals (5th cir.), Austin, Tex., 1977-78; assoc. Covington & Burling, Washington, 1978-87, ptnr., 1987-88, 89—; dep. tax legis. counsel U.S. Treasury Dept., 1988-89. Mem. ABA (asst. sec. tax sect. 1995-97, sec. 1997-99, coun. mem. 1999-2002), D.C. Bar Assn., Am. Law Inst., Am. Coll. Tax Counsel, Order of Coif. Presbyterian. Corporate taxation, Personal income taxation. Home: 5604 Chevy Chase Pkwy NW Washington DC 20015-2520 Office: Covington & Burling PO Box 7566 1201 Pennsylvania Ave NW Washington DC 20004-2401 E-mail: wpaul@cov.com.

PAULUS, NORMA JEAN PETERSEN, lawyer; b. Belgrade, Nebr., Mar. 13, 1933; d. Paul Emil and Ella Marie (Hellbusch) Petersen; m. William G. Paulus, Aug. 16, 1958; children: Elizabeth, William Frederick. LL.B., Willamette Law Sch., 1962; LL.D. (hon.), Linfield Coll., 1985; LittD (hon.), Whitman Coll., 1990; LHD (hon.), Lewis & Clark Coll., 1996. Bar: Oreg. 1962. Sec. to Harney County Dist. Atty., 1950-53; legal sec., 1953-55; sec. to chief justice Oreg. Supreme Ct., 1955-61; of counsel Paulus and Callaghan, Salem; mem. Oreg. Ho. of Reps., 1971-77; sec. of state State of Oreg., Salem, 1977-85; supt. pub. instrn., 1990-99; of counsel Paulus, Rhoten & Lien, 1985-86. Mem. Oreg. exec. bd. U.S. West, 1985-97; adj. prof. Willamette U. Grad. Sch., 1985; mem. N.W. Power Planning Com., 1986-89. Mem. adv. com. Def. Adv. Com. for Women in the Svc., 1986, Nat. Trust for Hist. Preservation, 1988-90; trustee Willamette U., 1978—; bd. dirs. Oreg. Grade Instn. Sci. and Tech., 1985-2001, Edn. Commn. States, 1991-99, Coun. Chief State Sch. Officers, 1995-98, Nat. Assessment Governing Bd., 1996-99, Oreg. Garden Found., 1997—, Oreg. Coast Aquarium, 1999—; bd. dirs., adv. bd. World Affairs Coun. Oreg., 1997—; overseer Whitman Coll., 1985—; bd. cons. Marion-Polk Boundary Commn., 1970-71; mem. Presdl. Commn. to Monitor Philippines Election, 1986; dir. Oreg. Hist. Soc., 2001—. Recipient Disting. Svc. award City of Salem, 1971, LWV, 1995, Path Breaker award Oreg. Women's Polit. Caucus, 1976; named One of 10 Women of Future, Ladies Home Jour., 1979, Woman of Yr. Oreg. Inst. Managerial and Profl. Women, 1982, Oreg. Women Lawyers, 1982, Woman Who Made a Difference award Nat. Women's Forum, 1985; Eagleton Inst. Politics fellow Rutgers U. Mem. Oreg. State Bar, Nat. Order Women Legislators, Women Execs. in State Govt., Women's Polit. Caucus Bus. and Profl. Women's Club (Golden Torch award 1971), Delta Kappa Gamma.

PAVALON, EUGENE IRVING, lawyer; b. Chgo., Jan. 5, 1933; m. Lois M. Frenzel, Jan. 15, 1961; children: Betsy, Bruce, Lynn. BSL, Northwestern U., 1954, JD, 1956. Bar: Ill. 1956. Sr. ptnr. Pavalon, Gifford, Laatsch & Marino, Chgo., 1970—. Adj. prof. Northwestern U. Sch. Law; mem. com. on discovery rules Ill. Supreme Ct., 1981—; lectr., mem. faculty various law schs.; bd. dirs. ATLA Mut. Ins. Co.; 01740982. Author: Human Rights and Health Care Law, 1980, Your Medical Rights, 1990; contbr. articles to profl. jours., chpts. in books. Former mem. state bd. dirs. Ind. Voters Ill. bd. overseers Inst. Civil Justice, Rand Corp., 1993-99; mem. vis. com. Northwestern U. Law Sch., 1990-96. Capt. USAF, 1956-59. Fellow Am. Coll. Trial Lawyers, Internat. Soc. Barristers, Internat. Acad. Trial Lawyers, Roscoe Pound Found. (life, pres. 1988-90); mem. ABA, Chgo. Bar Assn. (bd. mgrs. 1978-79), Ill. Bar Assn., Ill. Trial Lawyers Assn. (pres. 1980-81), Trial Lawyers for Pub. Justice (founding mem., v.p. 1991-92, pres.-elect 1992-93, pres. 1993-94), Assn. Trial Lawyers Am. (parliamentarian 1983-84, sec. 1984-85, v.p. 1985-86, pres.-elect 1986-87, pres. 1987-88), Am. Bd. Profl. Liability Attys. (diplomate), Am. Bd. Trial Advocates, Inner Circle of Advocates, Chgo. Athletic Assn., Std. Club. Personal injury (including property damage), Product liability, Professional liability. Home: 1540 N Lake Shore Dr Chicago IL 60610-6684 Office: Pavalon Gifford et al 2 N La Salle St Chicago IL 60602-3702 E-mail: pavalon@pglmlaw.com.

PAVEC, ARNAUD, lawyer; b. Saint Germain en Laye, France , Sept. 14, 1973; s. Joel and Mitou Pavec; m. Laure Pavec, Apr. 6, 2002. Master, Ecole Supérieur de Commerce de Paris, Paris, 1991—94, Univ. Paris X, 1997. Bar: France 1999. Assoc. Stibbe Simont Monahan Duhot, Paris, 1999—2000, SCP Philippe Clément, Paris, 2000—. Corporate, general, Mergers and acquisitions. Office: SCP Philippe Clément 50 Ave Victor Hugo Paris 75116 France Office Fax: 00 33 1 45 02 39 01.

PAVETTI, FRANCIS JAMES, lawyer; b. New Haven, Dec. 14, 1931; s. Frank and Ellen (Dawson) P.; m. Sally Thomas, July 5, 1958; 1 child, Leah Thomas. BS, U. Conn., 1953; JD cum laude, Boston coll., 1959. Bar: Conn. 1959, U.S. Dist. Ct. Conn. 1960, U.S. Ct. Appeals (2d cir.) 1966, U.S. Supreme Ct. 1966. Law clk. to judge U.S. Ct. Appeals (2d cir.), Conn., 1959-60; sole practitioner New London, Conn. Commr. from Conn. Nat. Conf. Commrs. on Uniform State Laws; chair drafting com. Revised Uniform Arbitration Act. Mem. Conn. Dem. State Ctrl. Commn., 1968-72; trustee, corp. sec., gen. counsel Eugene O'Neill Theater Found., 1964—; trustee, treas. Cmty. Found. of S.E. Conn., 1982-97. Mem. ABA, Conn. Bar Assn. (chmn. planning and zoning law sect. 1983-86), Fed. Bar Council (v.p., sec. 1974-80). Clubs: Players (N.Y.C.). Democrat. Roman Catholic. Alternative dispute resolution, Commercial, contracts (including sales of goods; commercial financing), Property, real (including real estate development, water). Office: Law Offices Francis J Pavetti 18 The Strand Waterford CT 06385

PAVEY, JUDITH ANN, lawyer; b. Indpls., Aug. 4, 1951; d. Ricahrd and Phyllis May Pavey; m. Kali Kuamoo Watson, July 1, 1989; 1 child, Jesse Nainoa Watson. BA, Purdue U., 1973; JD, Ind. U., Indpls., 1977. Bar: Ind. 77, U.S. Dist. Ct. Hawaii 77, Hawaii 77, U.S. Ct. Appeals (9th and 11th cirs.). Assoc., then ptnr. Schutter Pavey Cayeteau, Honolulu, 1977—84; pvt. practice Honolulu, 1984—86, 1999—; ptnr. Pavey & Wilson, Honolulu, 1987—94, Pavey Wilson & Gachstein, Honolulu, 1991—94, Pavey & Gachstein, Honolulu, 1998—99. Bd. dirs. ACLU, 1987—90, Hawaii Ctr. for Ind. Living, 1988—89. Mem.: ATLA, Consumer Lawyers Hawaii, Am. Inns of Ct. (barrister), Am. Bd. Trial Advocates, Honolulu Rotary Club. Personal injury (including property damage). Office: 1188 Bishop St Ste 907 Honolulu HI 96813-3303

PAVIA, GEORGE M. lawyer; b. Genoa, Italy, Feb. 14, 1928; s. Enrico L. and Nelly (Welisch) P.; m. Ellen Salomon, June 15, 1952; children— Andrew, Alison; m. 2d, Antonia Pearse, Dec. 2, 1976; children— Julian, Philippa. B.A., Columbia U., 1948, LL.B., 1951; postgrad. U. Genoa, 1954-55. Bar: N.Y. 1951, U.S. Supreme Ct. 1956, U.S. Dist. Ct. (so. and ea. dists.) N.Y. 1956. Assoc., Fink & Pavia, N.Y.C., 1955-65; sr. ptnr. Pavia & Harcourt, N.Y.C., 1965— . Served to capt. JAGC, U.S. Army, 1951-54. Mem. ABA, Internat. Law Soc., Consular Law Soc. Corporate, general, Private international. Home: 18 E 73rd St New York NY 10021-4130 Office: 600 Madison Ave New York NY 10022-1615

PAWLIK, JAMES DAVID, lawyer, historian; b. Cleve., May 26, 1958; s. Eugene Joseph and Eleanor Therese Marie (Gorzelanczyk) P. BA cum laude, Ohio State U., 1980, MA, 1991; JD cum laude, Harvard U., 1983. Bar: Calif. 1984, Ohio 1990, U.S. Dist. Ct. (no. dist.) Calif. 1984, U.S. Dist. Ct. (ctrl. and ea. dists.) Calif. 1986, U.S. Dist. Ct. (no. and so. dists.) Ohio 2001, U.S. Ct. Appeals (9th cir.) 1985, U.S. Ct. Appeals (6th cir.) 1994, U.S. Supreme Ct. 2002. Intern Dept. Def., Washington, 1980; assoc. Chandler, Wood, Harrington & Maffly, San Francisco, 1983-87, ptnr., 1988-89; teaching assoc. Ohio State U., 1990-91; pvt. practice Law Offices of James D. Pawlik, Cleve., 1991-93; ind. contractor Gallagher, Sharp, Fulton & Norman, Cleve., Ohio, 1992-93; jud. law clk. to Hon. Robert J. Krupansky U.S. Ct. Appeals (6th cir.), Cleve., 1993—. Instr. dept. history Cuyahoga C.C., Parma, Ohio, 1993—; instr. dept. polit. sci. Lourdes Coll., Sylvania, Ohio, 1993; co-founder, co-owner The Vicar Sauce Co. Ltd., 2000—. Mem. staff Harvard Internat. Law Jour., 1981-83. Campaign mgr. for city coun. candidate, Westerville, Ohio, 1977; bd. trustees Midpark H.S. Alumni Assn., 1999—, vice chair, 2000—. William Green Meml. scholar 1979, Kosciuszko scholar 1989-91; Ohio State U. fellow, 1989-90; named Midpark H.S. Acad. Hall of Fame, 1997. Mem. AAUP, State Bar Ohio, Fed. Bar Assn., Mensa, Ohio State U. Alumni Assn., Harvard Alumni Assn., Ohio State U. Undergrad. Student Govt. Alumni Assn., Phi Beta Kappa, Phi Kappa Phi, Phi Alpha Theta. E-mail: jdpesq546@msn.com.

PAYMENT, KENNETH ARNOLD, lawyer; b. Aug. 6, 1941; s. Arnold F. and Eleanor J. (Kinsey) Payment; m. Jane A. Conrad, Aug. 16, 1996; children: Simone, Elise, Ryan. BS, Union Coll., 1963; LLB, Cornell U., 1966. Bar: NY 66, U.S. Dist. Ct. (we. dist.) NY 67, U.S. Ct. Appeals (2d cir.) 68, U.S. Supreme Ct. 89. Assoc. Wiser, Shaw, Freeman, Van Graafeiland, Harter & Secrest, Rochester, 1966—75; ptnr. Harter, Secrest & Emery, Rochester, 1975—. Instr. Rochester Inst. Tech., 1969, U. Rochester, 1970, Cornell U. Law Sch., Ithaca, NY, 1971—72. Mem.: ABA, Best Lawyers in Am. (bus. litigation 1989—, antitrust 2003), Rochester C. of C., Monroe County Bar Assn. (trustee), NY State Bar Assn. (chmn. constrn. and suretyship divsn. 1978), Cornell Club. Antitrust, Federal civil litigation, State civil litigation. Home: 268 Harmon Rd Churchville NY 14428-9518 Office: Harter Secrest & Emery 1600 Bausch & Lomb Place Rochester NY 14604-2006

PAYNE, LUCY ANN SALSBURY, law librarian, educator, lawyer; b. Utica, N.Y., July 5, 1952; d. James Henry and Dorothy Eileen (Seavy) Salsbury; m. Albert E. Payne, June 2, 1973 (div. 1983); 1 child, Joni Eileen. MusB, Andrews U., 1974; MA, Loma Linda (Calif.) U., 1979; JD, U. Notre Dame, Ind., 1988; MLS, U. Mich., 1990. Bar: Ind. 1988, Mich. 1988, U.S. Dist. Ct. (no. and so. dists.) Ind. 1988, U.S. Ct. Appeals (7th cir.) 1992. Rsch. specialist Kresge Libr. Law Sch. U. Notre Dame, 1988—90, asst. libr., 1990—91, assoc. libr., 1991—96, libr., 1996—2002. Vis. prof. Notre Dame London Law Programme, 2001. Contbr. articles to profl. jours. Recipient Rev. Paul J. Foik award, 2001, Commitment award Notre Dame Black Student Law Assn., 2002. Adventist. Home and Office: 4420 Barrett NW Albuquerque NM 87114

PAYNE, MARGARET ANNE, lawyer; b. Aug. 10, 1947; d. John Hilliard and Margaret Mary (Naughton) P. Student, Trinity Coll., Washington, 1965-66; BA magna cum laude, U. Cin., 1969; JD, Harvard U., 1972; LLM in Taxation, NYU, 1976. Bar: N.Y. 1975, U.S. Dist. Ct. (so. dist.) N.Y. 1975, Calif. 1979, U.S. Dist. Ct. (so. dist.) Calif. 1979. Assoc. Mudge, Rose, Guthrie, and Alexander, N.Y.C., 1972-75, Davis, Polk and Wardwell, N.Y.C., 1976-78, Seltzer, Caplan, Wilkins and McMahon, San Diego, 1978-79, Higgs, Fletcher and Mack, San Diego, 1980-82, ptnr., 1983-90, of counsel, 1991—. Adj. prof. grad. tax program U. San Diego Sch. Law, 1979-89, Calif. Western Sch. Law, San Diego, 1980-82; judge pro tem Mcpl. Ct., San Diego Jud. Dist., 1983, 92. Bd. dirs. Artist Chamber Ensemble, Inc., 1983-86, Libr. Assn. La Jolla, Calif., 1983-86, San Diego County Crimestoppers, Inc., 1993-95, San Diego Crime Commn., 1994-95, St. Augustine's H.S., 1994-95, San Diego Hist. Soc., 1993-95. Mem. ABA, Calif. State Bar Assn., San Diego County Bar Assn., Mortar Bd., Guidon Soc., Charter 100, Phi Beta Kappa. Estate planning, Probate (including wills, trusts), Estate taxation. Office: Higgs Fletcher & Mack 401 W A St Ste 2600 San Diego CA 92101-7913

PAYNE, ROY STEVEN, judge; b. New Orleans, Aug. 30, 1952; s. Fred J. and Dorothy Julia (Peck) P.; m. Laureen Fuller, Sept. 8, 1973; children: Julie Elizabeth, Kelly Kathryn, Alex Steven, Michael Lawrence. BA with distinction, U. Va., 1974; JD, La. State U., 1977; LLM, Harvard U., 1980. Bar: La. 1977, U.S. Dist. Ct. (we. dist.) La. 1980, U.S. Ct. Appeals (5th cir.) 1980, U.S. Supreme Ct. 1983. Law clk. to judge U.S. Dist. Ct., Shreveport, La., 1977-79; assoc. Blanchard, Walker, O'Quin & Roberts, Shreveport, 1980-83, ptnr., 1984-87; U.S. Magistrate judge We. Dist. La., Shreveport, 1987—. Instr. New Eng. Sch. Law, Boston, 1979-80. Contbr. articles to profl. jours. Chmn. Northwest La. Legal Svcs. Assn., Shreveport, 1984-85. Mem. 5th Cir. Bar Assn., 5th Cir. Jud. Coun. (magistrate judges com. 1992—), La. State Bar Assn. (editorial bd. Forum jour., 1983-87, legal aid com.), Fed. Magistrate Judges Assn., Shreveport Bar Assn., La. Assn. Def. Counsel (bd. dirs. 1987), Harry V. Booth Am. Inn of Ct. (pres. elect 1994-95, pres. 1996-98), Order of Coif, Rotary, Phi Kappa Phi, Phi Delta Phi. Republican. Methodist. Home: 12494 Harts Island Rd Shreveport LA 71115-8505 Office: US Courthouse 300 Fannin St Ste 4300 Shreveport LA 71101-3122 E-mail: Payne@lawd.uscourts.gov.

PAYNE, TIMOTHY RICHARD, prosecutor; b. Columbus, Ohio, Oct. 1, 1959; s. Carl Richard Payne and Helen Louise Holland; m. Patricia Cecilia Corrales, Dec. 2, 1995; children: Christina, Paulina, Erica. BA in Philosophy, Ohio State U., 1982; JD, Cath. U. Am., Washington, 1985. Bar: Md. 1985, D.C. 1987, Ohio 2000, U.S. Ct. Appeals (6th cir.) 2001, U.S. Dist. Ct. (no. and so. dists.) Ohio 2001. Staff atty. Jones, Day, Reeves & Pogue, Washington, 1986—88; trial atty. Civil Rights divsn. U.S. Dept. Justice, Washington, 1988—98; asst. pub. defender Death Penalty divsn., Fed. Habeas Corpus sect. Ohio Pub. Defender, Columbus, 1998—. Recipient Spl. Achievement award, U.S. Dept. Justice, 1991, 1994, 1996, 1997, Outstanding Performance award, 1989, Cmty./Vol. Svc. award, 1991, 1993, 1998. Mem.: ATLA. Office: Office of Ohio Public Defender 8 E Long St 11th Fl Columbus OH 43215

PAYTON, JOHN, lawyer; b. Dec. 27, 1946; BA, Pomona Coll., 1973; JD, Harvard U., 1977. Law clk. to Hon. Cecil F. Poole U.S. Dist. Ct., Northern Dist. Calif.; corp. counsel D.C., 1991—94; ptnr. Wilmer, Cutler & Pickering. Mem.: D.C. Bar (pres. 2001—02). Commercial, contracts (including sales of goods; commercial financing), Civil rights, Libel. Office: Wilmer Cutler & Pickering 2445 M St NW Washington DC 20037

PEACE, JOHN ROBERT, lawyer; b. Greenville, S.C., July 25, 1967; s. Winfred Marshall and Martha Elizabeth Peace; m. Mary Laura Branyon, Aug. 22, 1998; 1 child, John Marshall. BS in Fin. and Econs., U. S.C., 1988, MBA, 1992. Bar: S.C. 1998, N.C. 2000, U.S. Dist. Ct. S.C. 2000, U.S. Ct. Appeals (4th cir.) 2000. Lawyer Office of Suzanne Coe, Greenville, 1998—99, Joel Bieber Firm, Easley, SC, 1999—2002; pvt. practice Greenville, 2002—. Office: Ste B 408 N Church St Greenville SC 29601

PEACOCK, JAMES DANIEL, lawyer; b. Moorestown, N.J., Dec. 19, 1930; s. L. Lawrence and Esther H. Peacock; m. Joan Peacock, June 14, 1953; children: Elizabeth Holcomb, Martha McLaughlin, Margaret Mae Daly, Mary Anne Freidman. AB, Duke U., 1952; LLB, U. Md., 1957. Bar: M. 1957, U.S. Ct. Appeals (4th cir.) 1959, U.S. Dist. Ct. Md. 1957, U.S. Supreme Ct. 1976. Of counsel Semmes Bowen & Semmes, Balt., 1957-97. Trustee Sheppard and Enoch Pratt Hosp., Towson, Md., 1964-97, chmn., 1993-97, assoc. trustee, 1998—. Fellow Am. Coll. Trial Lawyers (state chmn. 1985-86, adj. state chmn. 1992-93), Am. Bar Found., Md. Bar Found. Home: 105 Bonnie Hill Rd Baltimore MD 21204-4209

PEACOCK, JUDITH ANN See ERWIN, JUDITH ANN

PEAR, CHARLES E., JR., lawyer; b. Macon, Ga., June 18, 1950; s. Charles Edward and Barbara Jane P.; m. Linda Sue King; children: Jennifer Sue, Charles Edward III, Stephanie Sue. BA, U. Hawaii, 1972 with honors; JD, U. Calif., Berkeley, 1975. Bar: Hawaii 1976, Fla. 1977, Colo. 1994, U.S. Ct. of Appeals (9th cir.) 1976. Assoc. Rush, Moore, Craven, Sutton, Morry & Beh, Honolulu, 1976-77, of counsel, 1987-90; assoc., ptnr. Carlsmith & Dwyer, Honolulu, 1977-82; ptnr. Burke, Sakai, McPheeters, Bordner & Gilardy, Honolulu, 1983-87; vis. prof. law and computers U. British Columbia, 1990-93; of counsel Holland & Hart, Denver, 1993-96; counsel, ptnr. McCorriston, Miller, Mukai, MacKinnon, Honolulu, 1996—. Mem. Hawaii Real Estate Commn. com. on condominium and resort real estate legis., 1978-79; spl. counsel to consumer protection com. Hawaii State Ho. of Reps., 1981-82; chair real property and fin. svcs. sect. Hawaii State Bar Assn., ABA. Editor-in-Chief Hawaii Conveyance Manual II, 1987; editor Hawaii Commercial Real Estate Manual, 1988; bd. editors Hawaii Inst. of Continuing Legal Edn.; co-author: Nat. Assn. of Real Estate Licensing Law Officials and Nat. Timesharing Coun. Model Timesharing Act, 1981-82; contbg. author: Winning With Computers, 1992, Hawaii Real Estate Manual, 1997; lectr. in field, 1981—. Mem. ABA . Computer, Finance, Property, real (including real estate development, water).

PEARCE, HARRY JONATHAN, lawyer; b. Bismarck, N.D., Aug. 20, 1942; s. William R. and Jean Katherine (Murray) P.; m. Katherine B. Bruk, June 19, 1967; children: Shannon Pearce Baker, Susan J., Harry M. BS, USAF Acad., Colorado Springs, Colo., 1964; JD, Northwestern U., 1967; Degree in Engring. (hon.), Rose-Hulman Inst. Tech., 1997; LLD (hon.), Northwestern U., 1998. Bar: N.D. 1967, Mich. 1986. Mcpl. judge City of Bismarck, 1970-76, U.S. magistrate, 1970-76, police commr., 1976-80; sr. ptnr. Pearce & Durick, Bismarck, 1970-85; assoc. gen. counsel GM, Detroit, 1985-87, v.p., gen. counsel, 1987-92, exec. v.p., gen. counsel, 1992-94, exec. v.p., 1994-95, vice chmn., 1996—2001; chmn. Hughes Electronics, El Segundo, Calif., 2001—. Bd. dirs. GM Corp., Hughes Electronics Corp., GM Acceptance Corp., Delphi Automotive Sys. Corp., Alliance of Automobile Mfrs. of Marriott Internat. Inc., Econ. Strategy Inst., Theodore Roosevelt Medora Found., MDU Resources Group, Inc., Nat. Def. U. Found., Detroit Investment Fund. Mem. law bd. Sch. Law, Northwestern U.; mem. bd. visitors U.S. Air Force Acad.; chmn. Product Liability Adv. Coun. Found.; founding mem. minority counsel demonstration program Commn. on Opportunities for Minorities in the Profession, ABA; chmn. The Sabre Soc., USAF Acad.; trustee Howard U., U.S. Coun. for Internat. Bus., New Detroit, Inc.; mem. The Mentor's Group Forum for U.S.-European Union Legal-Econ. Affairs, The Conf. Bd., Network of Employers for Traffic Safety's Leadership Coun., Pres.'s Coun. on Sustainable Devel., World Bus. Coun. for Sustainable Devel., World Economic Forum Coun. Innovative Leaders in Globalization. Capt. USAF, 1964-70. Named Michiganian of Yr., The Detroit News, 1997; Hardy scholar Northwestern U., Chgo., 1964-67, recipient Alumni Merit award, 1991. Fellow Am. Coll. Trial Lawyers, Internat. Soc. Barristers; mem. Am. Law Inst. Avocations: amateur radio, woodworking, sailing. Corporate, general. Office: Hughes Electronics 200 N Sepulveda Blvd El Segundo CA 90245*

PEARCE, JOHN Y. lawyer; b. New Orleans, Mar. 26, 1948; s. John Young II and Marina (Harris) P.; m. Marjorie Pamela Doyle, May 22, 1971 (div.); children: Andrea Elizabeth, Roger Wellington. BA, La. State U., 1973, JD, 1976. Bar: La. 1977, U.S. Dist. Ct. (ea., mid. and we. dists.) La., U.S. Ct. Claims, U.S. Ct. Appeals (5th and 11th cirs.). Assoc. Doyle, Smith & Doyle, New Orleans, 1977-79, ptnr., 1979-80, mng. ptnr., 1980-84; ptnr. Montgomery, Barnett, Brown, Read, Hammond & Mintz, New Orleans, 1984—. Pres. New Orleans Legal Assistance Corp., 1999—2002, S.E. La. Legal Svcs. Corp., 2002—. Sgt. U.S. Army, 1969—71. Mem.: ABA (ho. of dels. 1998—2003), New Orleans Bar Assn. (pres. 1997—98, exec. com.), La. Bar Assn. (chmn. mineral law coun. 1994—95). Republican. Episcopalian. General civil litigation, Oil, gas, and mineral, Environmental. Office: Montgomery Barnett Brown Read Hammond & Mintz 1100 Poydras St New Orleans LA 70163-1101

PEARCE, NORMAN STANLEY, law librarian; b. Hampton, Va., May 12, 1958; s. Stanley Leroy and Erma Louise (Carpenter) Pearce; m. Beth Ann Hill, July 17, 1981. BA in History, Christopher Newport Coll., 1988; MLS, MS in History, So. Conn. State U., 1994. Libr. asst. Yale U., New Haven, 1988—93, Yale Law Sch., New Haven, 1993—94; libr. Mich. Dept. of Corrections, Ionia, 1995—. Instr. USCG Aux., Grand Rapids, 1997—. With USCG, 1979—86. Mem.: ALA, Am. Assn. Law Librs., Am. Correctional Assn. Office: Bellamy Creek Correctional Facility 1727 W Bluewater Hwy Ionia MI 48846 E-mail: nsbapearce@juno.com.

PEARCE, RICHARD LEE, lawyer; b. Racine, Wis., Apr. 11, 1959; s. John Wallace and Betty Jane P.; m. Cynthia Diane Davis, June 11, 1983; 1 child, Melissa Lauren. BS in Chemistry, U. S.C., 1981, JD, 1984. Bar: S.C. 1984, U.S. Dist. Ct. S.C. 1985, U.S. Ct. Appeals (4th cir.) 1985. Law clk. to resident cir. judge Edward B. Cottingham, 1984-85; assoc. Fox, Zier, Burkhalter & Verenes, Aiken, S.C., 1985-86; ptnr. Toole & Toole, Aiken, 1986-96; asst. pub. svcs. dir., legis. liaison S.C. Bar, 1996-98; city solicitor, staff atty. City of Aiken, 1998—. Instr. Am. Banking Inst., Nat. Advocacy Ctr., Nat. Dist. Attys. Assn.; guest lectr., adj. instr. U. S.C., Aiken; legal advisor Bd. of Zoning Appeals, Hist. Preservation Commn., Neighborhoods Com., City Dept. Heads, Leadership Aiken County Class of 2003, Soc. Prevention of Cruelty to Aminals, 2000-01; U.S. Dept. Justice Operation Cease Fire. Emcee Sch. Bd. Acad. Tournament, Aiken, 1986; bd. dirs. Tri-Devel. Ctr., Aiken, 1985-86; spl. events com. Downtown Aiken Devel. Corp.; fundraiser com. Am. Cancer Soc., 1985-2000, Am. Heart Assn., 2000-01; legal advisor Children's Place, Inc.; judge mock trial high sch. competition, 1991-96; trustee Aiken, Barnwell, Bamberg, and Edgefield Libr. Sys.; organizer, coord. Aiken Youth Ct. Mem. S.C. Bar Assn. (ho. of dels. 1989-95, pro bono program 1989-97, resolution of fee disputes bd., lawyers' fund for client protection, task force on justice for all, ethics adv. com., unauthorized practice law com., co-editor Legis. Update, editor Ethics Adv. Opinion Summaries, coord. annual jud. evaluation, sec. govtl. law sect.), Aiken County Bar Assn. (pres. 1990-92), Aiken C. of C. (legal liaison 1986), Internat. Mcpl. Lawyers Assn., Nat. Dist. Attys. Assn., S.C. Solicitors Assn., Rotary Internat. (bd. dirs. 1994-96, pres.-elect 1994-95, pres. 1995-96, group study exch. coord., Aiken-Llandrindod, Wales, U.K., Exch. Program, Paul Harris fellow, Sustaining Paul Harris fellow), Omicron Delta Kappa, Hitchcock Woods Axe Club. Presbyterian (vice-chair bd. deacons 1999-2000, chair 2000-02). Avocations: antique phonographs/records, camping, outdoor activities, historical research, cycling. Appellate, Constitutional, Government contracts and claims. Office: City of Aiken PO Box 1177 Aiken SC 29802-1177 E-mail: rpearce@aiken.net.

PEARLMAN, PETER STEVEN, lawyer; b. Orange, N.J., June 11, 1946; s. Jack Kitchener and Tiela Josephine (Fine) P.; m. Joan Perlmutter, June 19, 1969; children: Heather, Christopher, Megan. BA, U. Ill., 1967; JD, Seton Hall U., 1970. Bar: N.J. 1970, U.S. Dist. Ct. N.J. 1970, U.S. Tax Ct. 1973, U.S. Supreme Ct. 1974, U.S. Ct. Appeals (2d cir.) 1981, U.S. Ct. Appeals (3d cir.) 1983, U.S. Ct. Appeals (7th cir.) 1985, U.S. Ct. Appeals (D.C. cir.) 1998, U.S. Ct. Appeals (4th cir.) 1999, U.S. Ct. Claims 2000; cert. civil trial atty., 1982. Assoc. Cohn & Lifland, Esquires, Saddle Brook, N.J., 1970-72; ptnr. Cohn, Lifland, Pearlman, Herrmann & Knopf, Saddle Brook, 1972—. Lectr. Nat. Inst. Trial Advocacy, Hempstead, N.Y., 1988—; active trial advocacy program Widener Law Sch.; adj. faculty mem. trial advocacy program Hofstra Law Sch.; master C. Willard Heckel Inn of Ct.; guest lectr. appellate advocacy Roger Williams Law Sch., 1995—; mem. panel arbitrators Am. Arbitration Assn.; lectr. for Inst. Continuing Legal Edn. for State of N.J. Mem. ABA, ATLA, N.J. Bar Assn. Federal civil litigation, State civil litigation, Corporate, general. Home: 9 Harvey Dr Short Hills NJ 07078-1122 Office: Cohn Lifland Pearlman Herrmann & Knopf 1 Park 80 Plz W Ste 4 Saddle Brook NJ 07663-5808 E-mail: psp@njlawfirm.com.

PEARLMAN, SAMUEL SEGEL, lawyer, educator; b. Pitts., May 28, 1942; s. Merle Maurice and Bernice Florence (Segel) P.; m. Cathy Schwartz, Aug. 16, 1964; children: Linda P. Kraner, Caren E. AB, U. Pa., 1963, LLB magna cum laude, 1966. Bar: Pa. 1966, Ohio 1967, U.S. Ct. Appeals (3d cir.) 1967. Law clk. U.S. Dist. Ct. for Ea. Dist. Pa., Phila., 1966-67; assoc. Burke, Haber & Berick, Cleve., 1967-72, prin., 1973-86, Berick, Pearlman & Mills, Cleve., 1986-99; ptnr. Squire, Sanders & Dempsey L.L.P., Cleve., 2000—. Lectr. law Case Western Res. U. Sch. Law, 1978-82; mem. registration com. Ohio Div. Securities, 1979-89; adv. dir. Midland Title Security, Inc.; trustee Realty ReFund Trust, N.Y. Stock Exch., 1990-98. Author: Cases, Forms and Materials for Modern Real Estate Transactions, 1978, 82. Mem. ABA, Ohio Bar Assn., Greater Cleve. Bar Assn. (chmn. securities law sect. 1985-86), Order of Coif. Republican. Jewish. Corporate, general, Finance, Property, real (including real estate development, water). Office: Squire Sanders & Dempsey 4900 Key Tower 127 Public Sq Ste 4900 Cleveland OH 44114-1304 E-mail: spearlman@ssd.com.

PEARLMUTTER, FREDI L. lawyer, educator; b. Paterson, N.J., Nov. 15, 1946; d. Paul and Rose H. Pearlmutter; m. Paul D. Cohen, Oct. 18, 1987. AB cum laude, Brown U., 1968; JD, Harvard U., 1971. Bar: N.J. 1987, N.Y. 1972, U.S. Dist. Ct. N.J. 1987, U.S. Dist. Ct. (so. dist.) N.Y. 1973, U.S. Dist. Ct. (ea. dist.) N.Y. 1973). Assoc. Fried, Frank, Harris, Shriver & Jacobson, N.Y.C., 1971-74; atty. U.S. Mktg. and Refining divsn. Mobil Oil Corp., N.Y.C., 1974-80; asst. gen. counsel Amerada Hess Corp., N.Y.C., 1980-86; adj. prof. Seton Hall U. Sch. Law, Newark, 1994—99; of counsel Cooper, Rose & English, Summit, N.J., 1987—. Former advisor to environ. com. N.J. State Assembly. Contbr. articles to profl. jours. Mem. Warren Twp. (N.J.) Environ. Commn.; mem. ad. hoc com. on land use Warren Twp. 1998-2002. Mem. ABA, N.J. State Bar Assn. (chair environ. law sect. 1997-98, founder and co-chair environ. ins. com.), Assn. Bar City N.Y. (com. on energy law, com. on adminstrv. law); trustee, Harvard Law Sch. Assn. of NJ. Administrative and regulatory, Environmental, Insurance. Office: Cooper Rose & English LLP 480 Morris Ave Summit NJ 07901-1523

PEARLSTEIN, PAUL DAVIS, lawyer; b. Berlin, N.H., Jan. 3, 1938; s. Victor and Sophia (Davis) Pearlstein; m. Patricia Hurston, June 1964 (div.); children: Laura Sue, David Seth; m. Marilyn Mills, Jan. 11, 1981; children: Adam Lowell, Susanna Lee. AB, U. Pa., 1959; LLB, U. Va., 1962. Bar: Va. 1962, D.C. 1963, Md. 1990, U.S. Supreme Ct. 1970, cert.: Comml. Law League, Am. Arbitration Assn. (arbitrator), Nat. Assn. Securities Dealers, Am. Bd. of Cert. (bus. bankruptcy specialist). Atty. HUD, Washington, 1964-66; adminstr. contrn. and purchasing activities Cafritz Co. and affiliated cos., Washington, 1966-68; pvt. practice Washington, 1968-96; ptnr. Pearlstein & Jacques, Washington, 1989—, Pearlstein & Assocs., Washington, 1997—. Chair adv. rules com. U.S. Bankruptcy Ct. D.C., Washington; bankruptcy trustee Washington and Va., 1973—90; spkr. in the field. Editor, contbg. author: Real Estate Practice in DC, Md. and Va., 1995, contbg. author, editor: articles and books revs. to legal jours. Mandolinist, guitarist Takoma Mandoleers, 1971—, Orgn. Anacostia Rowing and Scullings, Coun. Ct. Excellence; bd. dirs., sec. Met. Washington, DC Trial Lawyers Found., 1991—96; bd. dirs. DC shpt. Am. Diabetes Assn., 1987—89; pres. brotherhood Washington Hebrew Congregation, 1974—75, bd. mgrs., 1979—85; mem. inter group rels. com. Jewish Cmty. Coun., 1973—90. Capt. U.S. Army, 1962—64. Fellow: Am. Bar Found.; mem.: ABA (real property and probate sects.), D.C. Land Title Assn. (v.p. 1989—90), Washington Estate Planning Coun., Washington Assn. Realtors, Jud. Conf. D.C. cir., Bar Assn. D.C. (chmn. real property law com. 1976—78, pres. rsch. found., Chmn. of the Yr. 1977, Spl. Projects award 1987). Democrat. Avocations: kayaking, hiking, mandolin, guitar, rowing. Bankruptcy, Estate planning, Property, real (including real estate development, water). Office: Ste 505 1730 Rhode Island Ave NW Washington DC 20036-3101 Fax: 202-223-8737. E-mail: merraul@aol.com.

PEARSALL, JOHN WESLEY, lawyer; b. Richmond, Va., Aug. 21, 1914; BS, Randolph-Macon Coll., 1935; LLB, U. Richmond, 1941. Bar: Va. 1940. Assoc. McGuire, Riely & Eggleston, Richmond, 1941-50; ptnr. McGuire, Eggleston, Bocock & Woods, Richmond, 1950-53; gen. counsel Va.-Carolina Chem. Corp., Richmond, 1953-56; sole practice Richmond, 1956-60; ptnr. McCaul, Grigsby & Pearsall, Richmond, 1960-86, Pearsall & Pearsall, 1986—; gen. counsel, dir. Estes Express Lines, 1972—. Chpt. chmn. ARC, Chesterfield County, Va., 1944-49, campaign chmn., 1949, campaign chmn. Richmond, Henrico, and Chesterfield, Va., 1950, nat. vice chmn. fund dr., 1956, nat. gov., 1953-55; mem. budget com. Richmond Area Community Chest, 1946-47, mem. exec. com., 1947-55, trustee, 1946-50, campaign chmn., 1951, pres., 1955, United Giver's Fund, 1970; v.p. Children's Aid Soc., Richmond, 1950-55, trustee, 1948-55; active Boy Scouts Am., 1953-56; mem. exec. com. Randolph-Macon Coll., 1958-76, chmn. long range plan com., 1960-76, trustee, 1955-76, mem. alumni bd., 1994-99; mem. Chesterfield County Welfare Bd., 1951-55; trustee Sheltering Arms Hosp., Richmond, 1949-80; dir. Jr. Achievement, 1975-81; vestryman St. Stephens Ch., 1967-70, ch. bearer, 1986-87; mem. exec. com. Hist. Richmond Found. (1965-70), Falls of James adv. bd., 1979—, Chesterfield Hist. Soc., 1985-95. Served to lt. j.g. USNR, 1944-46. Mem. ABA, Va. Bar Assn., Richmond Bar Assn., Chesterfield County Bar Assn. (pres. 1963-64), Am. Judicature Soc., Va. State Bar Council (chmn. judicial ethics com. 1970-71), Am. Archaeol. Soc. (local chpt., pres. 1976), Phi Beta Kappa (pres. Richmond area chpt. 1976-77), Jr. C. of C. (Disting. Svc. award 1948, state pres. 1948-49), Omicron Delta Kappa, Lambda Chi Alpha. Condemnation (eminent domain), Corporate, general, General practice. Home: 7701 Riverside Dr Richmond VA 23225-1036 Office: Ellen Glasgow House 1 W Main St Richmond VA 23220-5623

PEARSON, APRIL VIRGINIA, lawyer; b. Martinsville, Ind., Aug. 11, 1960; d. Clare Grill and Sheila Rosemary (Finch) Rayner; m. Randall Keith Pearson, Dec. 10, 1988; children: Randall Kyle, Austin Finch, Autumn Virginia. BA, Calif. State U., Long Beach, 1982; JD, Pepperdine U., 1987; cert. indsl. fire brigade, HAZWOPER Tex. A&M U. Bar: Calif. 1987, Idaho 1993, D.C. 1989. Assoc. counsel Union Oil Co. Calif., L.A., 1988-2001; owner Avrilex, Chino Hills, Calif., 2001—. V.p. Pa's Bier, Long Beach, Calif., 1988—98, Ammonia Safety Tng. Inst., sec., 1995—98, gen. counsel, 1997—; mem. pub. works commn. City of Chino Hills, 1999—. Mem.: Chem. Industry Coun. Calif. (chair regulatory affairs com. 1995), Am. Corp. Counsel Assn., Women Lawyers Long Beach (v.p. 1990—93). Avocations: running, Tae Kwon Do. Antitrust, Corporate, general, Environmental. Office: Avrilex 13462 Montserrat Ct Chino Hills CA 91709-1327 E-mail: april@avrilex.com.

PEARSON, CHARLES THOMAS, JR., lawyer, director; b. Fayetteville, Ark., Oct. 14, 1929; s. Charles Thomas and Doris (Pinkerton) P.; m. Wyma Lee Hampton, Sept. 9, 1988; children: Linda Sue, John Paddock. BS, U. Ark., 1953, JD, 1954; postgrad., U.S. Naval Postgrad. Sch., 1959; A.M., Boston U., 1963. Bar: Ark. bar 1954. Practice in, Fayetteville, 1963—. Dir. officer N.W. Comms., Inc., Dixieland Devel., Inc., Jonlin Investments, Inc., World Wide Travel Svc., Inc., Okliania Farms, Inc., N.W. Arl. Land & Devel., Inc., Garden Plaza Inns, Inc. Word Data, Inc., M.P.C. Farms, Inc., Fayetteville Enterprises, Inc., NWA Devel.Co., Delta Comm., Inc.; past. dir., organizer N.W. Nat. Bank. Adviser Explorer Scouts, 1968— ; past pres. Washington County Draft Bd.; past pres. bd. Salvation Army. Served to comdr. Judge Adv. Gen. Corps USNR, 1955-63. Mem. ABA, Ark. Bar Assn., Washington County Bar Assn., Judge Advs. Assn., N.W. Ark. Ret. Officers Assn. (past pres.), Methodist Men (past pres), U. Ark. Alumni Assn. (past dir.), Sigma Chi (past pres. N.W. Ark. alumni, past chmn. house corp.), Alpha Kappa Psi, Phi Eta Sigma, Delta Theta Phi. Clubs: Mason (32 deg., K.T., Shriner), Moose, Elk, Lion, Metropolitan. Republican. Methodist. General practice, Personal injury (including property damage), Property, real (including real estate development, water). Office: 9 N College Ave Fayetteville AR 72701-5301 E-mail: tpesq1101@aol.com.

PEARSON, DAVID BROOKSBANK, lawyer, educator; b. Springfield, Mo., Mar. 6, 1935; s. Otis Brackingham and Mary Helen (Brooksbank) P.; m. Betty Jean Sloan, Feb. 5, 1955; children— Marlon Kim, Julie Michele Logan. Student Los Angeles City Coll., 1958-59, U.C.L.A., 1982-84, USC, 1980; LL.B., LaSalle Sch. Law, 1967. Bar: Calif. 1967, U.S. Dist. Ct. Calif. 1967, U.S. Supreme Ct. 1971, U.S. Ct. Appeals (9th cir.) Calif. 1973; cert. in criminal law Calif. Bd. Legal Specialization. Dep. sheriff Los Angeles County Sheriff, 1960-62; Dist. Atty.'s investigator Los Angeles County Dist. Atty., 1962-67; dep. dist. atty., 1967-69, 1969-93; sole practice, Los Angeles, 1969; prof. criminal law Glendale Sch. Law, 1972-75, USC Law Center, 1981, Beverly Sch. Law, 1976, USC Sch. Pub. Adminstrn., 1984; adj. prof. Pepperdine Law Sch., Malibu, Calif., 1977-84; asst. prof. clin. law USC Sch. Psychiatry and Law, 1976- 78; instr. Cerritos Coll. Norwalk, Calif., 1972-75; lectr. Nat. Coll. Dist. Attys., Houston, 1975-84; Calif. Inst. for Trial Advocacy Skills, Los Angeles, 1979-80; Calif. Continuing Edn. of the Bar, 1979-84, Rossi-Field Center for Clinical Hypnotherapy, 1983; faculty mem. Los Angeles Coll. Trial Advocacy, 1979-84; tech. adv. Columbia Pictures TV, 1978; legal advisor Atty. Coun. Altanta, 1993-. Editor, author booklet Law Enforcement Legal Bulletin, 1980. Inventor parlor game 1979. Adv. bd. mem. El Camino Coll., Torrance, Calif., 1976-84; active mem. Nat. Conf. Christians and Jews criminal justice com., Los Angeles, 1983-84, Crime, Violence and Vandalism on Campus Com., Los Angeles, 1976-84. Served as pfc. USMCR, 1953-57. Named Heavy Weight Boxing Champion Sr. Olympics, 1977-79; Recipient Western States Police Pistol Combat Champion Team award Nat. Rifle Assn., 1965; Outstanding Contribution to Youth award Constl. Rights Found., 1975-77; Disting. Faculty award Nat. Coll. Dist. Attys., 1982. Mem. Calif. Dist. Attys. Assn., Assn. Dep. Dist. Attys., ABA, South Bay Policetraining Assn., Southeast Policetraining Assn., Northeast Police Training Assn. Home: 3139 S Las Marias Ave Hacienda Heights CA 91745-6219

PEARSON, HENRY CLYDE, judge; b. Ocoonita Lee County, Va., Mar. 12, 1925; s. Henry James and Nancy Elizabeth (Seals) P.; m. Jean Calton, July 26, 1956; children: Elizabeth, Frances, Timothy Clyde. Student, Union Coll., 1947-49; LLB, U. Richmond, 1952. Bar: Va. 1952, U.S. Ct. Appeals (4th cir.) 1957, U.S. Supreme Ct. 1958. Sole practice, Jonesville, Va., 1952-56; asst. U.S. atty. Western Dist. Va., Roanoke, 1956-61; ptnr. Hopkins, Pearson & Engleby, Roanoke, 1956-61; judge U.S. Bankruptcy Ct. Western Dist. Va., Roanoke, 1970-98; ret., 1998. Participant Va. Continuing Edn. Seminars; mem. adv. com. fed. rules bankruptcy procedure; mem. Va. Ho. of Reps., 1954-56, Va. Senate, 1968-70; Republican nominee Gov. of Va., 1961. Editl. bd. Am. Survey Bankruptcy Law, 1979. Served with USN, 1943-46, PTO. Mem. Va. State Bar, ABA, Va. Trial Lawyers Assn., Assn. Trial Lawyers Am., Am. Judicature Soc., Am. Judges Assn., Fed. Bar Assn., Delta Theta Phi, Tribune Jefferson Senate, Am. Legion, VFW, Masons, Shriners. Methodist. Office: 1910 Mcvitty Rd Salem VA 24153-7406

PEARSON, JOHN EDWARD, lawyer; b. Jamaica, N.Y., Aug. 20, 1946; s. Stanley Charles and Rose Margaret (Manning) P.; m. Laura Marie Johannes, Dec. 28, 1968; children: Laura Rose, Jack. BA, Manhattan Coll., 1968; JD, St. John's U., 1972. Bar: N.Y. 1973, Fla. 1981, U.S. Dist. Ct. (so. dist.) N.Y. 1977, U.S. Dist. Ct. (so. dist.) Fla. 1982, U.S. Ct. Appeals (11th cir.) 1982, U.S. Ct. Appeals (5th cir.) 1982. Assoc. Sage, Gray, Todd & Sims, N.Y.C., 1972-78, ptnr., 1979, Miami, Fla., 1980-87, Hughes, Hubbard & Reed, Miami, 1987-91, 94-98, counsel, 1998—2002; ptnr. Hughes, Hubbard & Reed , N.Y.C., 1992-93. Author jour. article (Best Article award 1971). With USMCR, 1968-69. Mem. ABA, Fla. Bar Assn., N.Y. State Bar Assn., Assn. Bar City N.Y., Dade County Bar Assn., N.Y. County Lawyers Assn., Greater Miami C. of C. (trustee). Republican. Roman Catholic. Avocations: sailing, running. Corporate, general, Government contracts and claims, Property, real (including real estate development, water). Home: 180 Harbor Dr Key Biscayne FL 33149-2409 E-mail: jep8436@aol.com.

PEARSON, JOHN YEARDLEY, JR., lawyer; b. Norfolk, Va., July 23, 1942; BA, Washington & Lee U., 1964; JD, U. Va., 1971. Bar: Va. 1971. Atty. Willcox & Savage P.C., Norfolk, Va. Bd. editors: Va. Law Rev., 1969-71. Fellow Am. Coll. Trial Lawyers; mem. ABA (litigation sect.), Internat. Assn. Def. Counsel, Va. Assn. Def. Attys., Order of Coif. General civil litigation, Commercial, contracts (including sales of goods; commercial financing), Professional liability. Office: Willcox & Savage PC 1800 Bank of America Ctr Norfolk VA 23510-2197

PEARSON, PAUL DAVID, lawyer, mediator; b. Boston, Jan. 22, 1940; s. Bernard J. and Ruth (Bayla) Horblit; m. Carol A. Munschauer; children: David Todd, Lisa Kari, Grant M. BA, Bucknell U., 1961; LLB, U. Pa., 1964. Bar: Mass. 1966, N.Y. 1987. Staff atty., tech. assoc. lab. cmty. psychiatry dept. psychiatry Med. Sch. Harvard U., Boston, 1966-68; assoc. Snyder Tepper & Berlin, Boston, 1968-71; ptnr., 1971-77; ptnr., chmn. family law dept. Hill & Barlow, 1977-87; ptnr. chmn. family law dept. Hodgson, Russ, Andrews, Woods and Goodyear, Buffalo, 1987-96; of counsel Sullivan Oliverio & Gioia, 1996—. Lectr. Mass. Con. Legal Edn., New Eng. Law Inst., dept. psychiatry SUNY Sch. of Medicine, Buffalo, 1989—; instr. law and mental health Boston Psychoanalytic Soc. and Inst., 1975-87; lectr. in law, mental health, alternative dispute resolution. Contbr. articles to profl. jours. and interdisciplinary publs. Founding mem. Alliance for Dispute Resolution, 1996, Buffalo Collaborative Law Coun.; bd. dirs. Jewish Cmty. Ctr. Greater Buffalo, 1991-96, Am. Jewish Com. Buffalo, 1991—, pres., 1995-97, nat. bd. govs., 1997—; bd. dirs. Arts Coun. Buffalo and Erie County, 1992-99; legal coord. Parent Edn. And Custody Effectiveness program N.Y. 8th jud. dist.; pres., trustee, legal counsel Wayland (Mass.) Townhouse; trustee Family Counseling Svc. (region West); mem., chmn., clk. Wayland Zoning Bd. Appeals, 1970-80; v.p., counsel Arts Wayland Found., 1982-87; vis. fellow Woodrow Wilson Found., 1985-87, Mass. Gov.'s Spl. Commn. on Divorce, 1985-87. Capt. Mil. Police Corps USAR. Fellow Am. Acad. Matrimonial Lawyers (pres., bd. mgrs. Mass); mem. Mass. Bar Assn. (chmn. family law sect.), Assn. Conflict Resolution (advanced practitioner), N.Y. State Coun. on Divorce Mediation, Assn. Family and Conciliation Cts., Boston Bar Assn. (family law com., legis. chmn.), N.Y. Bar Assn. (family law com., ADR com.), Erie County Bar Assn. (chmn. alternative dispute resolution com. 1992-96, family law com., judiciary com.). Alternative dispute resolution, Family and matrimonial. Home: 605 Lebrun Rd Amherst NY 14226-4232 Office: 600 Main Place Tower Buffalo NY 14202-3706 Fax: 716-854-5299. E-mail: ppearson@soglawny.com.

PECCARELLI, ANTHONY MARANDO, lawyer; b. Newark, Apr. 12, 1928; s. Adolph and Mary (Marano) P.; m. Mary Dearborn Hutchison, Dec. 23, 1953; children: Andrew Louis, David Anthony, Laura Elizabeth. BS, Beloit Coll., 1953; JD, John Marshall Law Sch., 1959; M in Jud. Studies, U. Nev., 1990. Bar: Ill. 1961, U.S. Dist. Ct. (no. dist.) Ill., U.S. Supreme Ct. Supr. real estate and claims Gulf Oil Corp., Chgo., 1956-61; asst. state's atty. DuPage County, Wheaton, Ill., 1961-65; first asst. state's atty. DuPage County State's Atty., Wheaton, Ill., 1965-69; mem.-del. Ill. Constnl. Conv., Springfield, 1969-70; exec. dir. Ill. State's Atty. Assn., Elgin, 1970-71; ptnr. Barclay, Damisch & Sinson, Chgo., 1971-79; assoc. cir. judge 18th Jud. Cir. Ct., Wheaton, 1979-82, cir. judge, 1982-93, chief judge, 1989-93, presiding judge domestic rels. divsn., 1982-83, presiding judge law divsn., 1987-89, chief judge, 1989-93; justice 2nd dist. Ill. Appellate Ct., Wheaton, 1993-94; state's atty. DuPage County, Wheaton, Ill., 1995-96; assoc., of counsel Ottosen Trevarthen Britz Kelly & Cooper, Ltd., Wheaton, Ill., 1996—. Exec. Conflict Resolution Ltd.; chair Ill. Jud. Conf. Ill. Supreme Ct., Springfield, 1987-89. Contbr. articles to profl. jours. Bd. dirs., treas. DuPage Coun. for Child Devel.; bd. dirs. Ctrl. DuPage Pastoral Counseling Ctr.; chair Wheaton Com. for Jud. Reform, 1962; trustee Midwestern U., 1993—, vice chmn., bd. trustees 1997-99. Cpl. USMC, 1946-48. Mem. DuPage County Bar Assn. (pres. 1972-73), DuPage County Legal Assistance Fedn. (pres. 1973-74), DuPage County Lawyer Referral Svc. (pres. 1972). Alternative dispute resolution, Appellate, State civil litigation.

PECK, AUSTIN H., JR., lawyer; b. Pomona, Calif., Dec. 25, 1913; s. Austin H. and Helen (Templeton) P.; m. Jean Albertson, Nov. 9, 1939 (dec. Aug. 1997); children: Julie (dec.), Francesca, Lisa; m. Janice Galloway, Apr. 3, 1998 (dec. May 2001). AB with distinction, Stanford, 1935, JD, 1938. Bar: Calif. 1938. Practiced in, L.A., from 1938; mem. Latham & Watkins, 1946-76, of counsel, 1976-92. Mem. nat. coun. House Ear Inst. Mem. ABA, Calif. Bar Assn., L.A. Bar Assn., Calif. Club, L.A. Country Club, Birnam Wood Club (Montecito, Calif.), Valley Club (Montecito), Zeta Psi, Phi Delta Phi. Home: 2108 Forge Rd Santa Barbara CA 93108-2262 Office: 633 W 5th St Los Angeles CA 90071-2005

PECK, KENNETH E. lawyer; b. Carson City, Nev., June 20, 1950; s. Donald Leon and Thelma Louise (Robinson) P.; m. Katherine Louise Weeks, Oct. 20, 1973; children: Jason Z., Jennifer D., Joy H., Jessica K. BA in Polit. Sci. cum laude, U. Colo., 1971; MA in Pub. Adminstrn., U. Va., 1975; JD, Georgetown U., 1979. Bar: Colo. 1979, U.S. Dist. Ct. Colo. 1979, U.S. Ct. Appeals (10th cir.) 1980, U.S. Supreme Ct. 1983. Rsch. analyst Va. Hwy. Rsch. Coun., Charlottesville, 1972-73; budget and mgmt. analyst Prince Georges County Schs., Upper Marlboro, Md., 1974-76; chief legis. asst. U.S. Rep. Paul Trible, Washington, 1977-79; atty. Holland & Hart, Denver, 1979-83, Hopper & Kanouff, Denver, 1983-85, Phelps, Singer & Dunn, Denver, 1985-90, Law Firm of Kenneth E. Peck, Denver, 1990-98, Bushell & Peck, L.L.C., Denver, 1999—. Mem. nat., regional and state adv. councils SBA, 1981-86; mem. bd. appeals U.S. Dept. Edn., Washington, 1982-84; profl. lobbyist Colo. Legis., Denver, 1983-84; nat. commr. of econ. policy 1986 White House Conf. on Small Bus. Asst. campaign mgr. Jim Tate for Congress, Fairfax, Va., 1976; bd. dirs. Jefferson County Srs.' Resource Ctr., Wheatridge, Colo., 1982-88; pres. Arvada Rep. Club, Colo., 1982; mem. bd. mgrs. Northwest YMCA, Arvada, 1982-88. William McIntyre fellow U. Va., 1971-72; law fellow Georgetown U. Law Ctr., 1976-77. Mem. ABA (litigation sect., various coms.), Colo. Bar Assn. (various coms.), Colo. Assn. Comml. Industry (chmn. small bus. legis. com. 1983-85), Denver Bar Assn. (various coms.). Republican. Mem. Ch. of Christ. Avocations: golf, hiking, coaching youth sports. General civil litigation, Personal injury (including property damage), Property, real (including real estate development, water). Home: 10935 W 68th Ave Arvada CO 80004-2744

PECK, LEONARD WARREN, JR., lawyer; b. El Paso, Tex., June 3, 1948; s. Leonard Warren and Perry Elizabeth (Lewis) Peck; m. Johanna Lee Blaschke, July 23, 1976; 1 child, Margaret Elizabeth. AB, Harvard U., 1970; JD, U. Tex., 1973. Bar: Tex. 1973, US Dist. Ct. (so. dist.) Tex. 1980, US Dist. Ct. (ea. dist.) Tex. 1980, US Dist. Ct. (we. dist.) Tex. 1980, US Dist. Ct. (no. dist.) Tex. 1984, US Ct. Appeals (11th cir.) 1981, US Supreme Ct. 1980. Analyst Tex. Gov.'s Office, Austin, 1974—75; cons. Atty. Gen. Tex. Office, Austin, 1976—80, asst. atty. gen., 1981; dir. R & D Tex. Dept. Corrections, Huntsville, Tex., 1981—82, legal counsel, 1982—2002. Trustee Tri-County MHMR Svcs., 1985—. Home: 489 Elkins Lk Huntsville TX 77340-7312

PECKERMAN, BRUCE MARTIN, lawyer; b. Milw., Sept. 28, 1949; s. Joseph and Doris (Kassel) P.; m. Jeanette Chrustowski. BA, U. Wis., 1971; JD, Washington U., St. Louis, 1973. Bar: Wis. 1974, U.S. Dist. Ct. (we. dist.) Wis. 1974, U.S. Ct. Appeals (7th cir.) 1977. Sole practice, Milw., 1985—2002; ptnr. Peckerman & Klein, Milw., 2002—. Recipient young leadership award Milw. Jewish Fedn. Mem. ABA, Wis. Bar Assn. (past chmn. family law sect.), Milw. Bar Assn. (bench/bar com. 1987-88), Am. Acad. Matrimonial Lawyers (past pres.). Family and matrimonial. Office: 920 E Mason St Milwaukee WI 53202-4015 E-mail: bmp@peckermanlaw.com.

PECORARO, STEVEN JOHN, lawyer; b. N.Y.C., Apr. 27, 1961; m. Frances P. Ferraro, Feb. 18, 1996. BA in Polit. Sci., Queens Coll. of CUNY, Flushing, 1982; JD, St. John's U., Jamaica, N.Y., 1985. Bar: N.Y. 1986, U.S. Dist. Ct. (so. and ea. dists.) N.Y. 1993. Asst. dist. atty. Dist. Atty.'s Office, Queens County, N.Y., 1985-87; sr. staff atty. Law Offices of Stewart H. Friedman, Lake Success, N.Y., 1987-91; sr. trial atty. Alio & Caiati, N.Y.C., 1991-95; ptnr. Pecoraro & Schiesel, N.Y.C., 1995—. Mem. N.Y. State Bar Assn., N.Y. State Trial Lawyers Assn., Million Dolla Advs. Forum. Personal injury (including property damage). Office: Pecoraro & Schiesel Ste 1800 One Whitehall St New York NY 10004

PEDDICORD, ROLAND DALE, lawyer; b. Van Meter, Iowa, Mar. 29, 1936; s. Clifford Elwood and Juanitas Irene (Brittain) P.; m. Teri Linn O'Dell; children: Erin Sue, Robert Sean. BSBA with honors, Drake U., 1961, JD with honors, 1962. Bar: Iowa 1962; cert. civil trial specialist Nat. Bd. Trial Advs. Asst. atty. gen. State of Iowa, 1962-63; assoc. Steward, Crouch & Hopkins, Des Moines, 1962-65; ptnr. Peddicord, Wharton, Spencer & Hook, Des Moines, 1965—. Lectr. in law Drake U., 1962-68; lectr. law Coll. Osteo. Medicine, Des Moines, 1965-72 Editor and chief Drake Law Rev., 1961-62 Past mem. nat. bd. dirs., nat. coun. YMCA of U.S.A., past vice chmn. nat. bd.; bd. dirs., past chmn. Greater Des Moines YMCA, 1968-89. With USMC, 1954-57. Mem. ABA, ATLA, Iowa Bar Assn., Polk County Bar Assn., Iowa Trial Lawyers Assn., Iowa Acad. Trial Lawyers, Am. Bd. Trial Advs. (mem. nat. bd., past pres. Iowa chpt.). Republican. Methodist. Federal civil litigation, Insurance, Personal injury (including property damage). Office: 405 6th Ave Ste 700 Des Moines IA 50309-2415 also: Peddicord Wharton Spencer & Hook PO Box 9130 Des Moines IA 50306-9130 E-mail: Dale.Peddicord@Peddicord-Law.com.

PEDEN, JAMES ALTON, JR., lawyer; b. Gainesville, Fla., Apr. 24, 1944; s. James Alton and Frances Merle (Wilson) P. BA summa cum laude, U. Miss., 1966, JD, 1970; postgrad., U. Bristol, England, 1966-67. Bar: Miss. 1970, U.S. Dist. Ct. (no. and so. dists.) Miss., U.S. Ct. Appeals (5th cir.) 1970, U.S. Supreme Ct. 1973. Staff asst. to Sen. John C. Stennis U.S. Senate, Washington, 1964-65; assoc. Stennett, Wilkinson & Ward (now Stennett, Wilkinson & Peden), Jackson, Miss., 1970-73, ptnr., 1973—. Staff asst. to lt. gov. State of Miss., Jackson, 1972-75; services officer Miss. Senate, Jackson, 1972-75; staff judge adv. Miss. Air N.G., Jackson, 1974-99; mem. Miss. Gov.'s Jud. Nominating Com., 1980-83. Mem. Leadership Jackson, 1991-92. Col. Miss. Air N.G., 1968-99. Named Fulbright scholar, 1966-67; Inst. Politics in Miss. fellow, 1971-72. Fellow Miss. Bar Found.; mem. ABA (fellow young lawyers divsn.), Miss. Bar Assn. (pres. young lawyers sect. 1978-79, 2d v.p. 1979-80, pres. fellows young lawyers 1989-90), Hinds County Bar Assn., Supreme Ct. Hist. Soc., Miss. Law Inst. (chmn. 1979). Baptist. Avocations: american and military history, baseball, basketball. Administrative and regulatory, Land use and zoning (including planning), Property, real (including real estate development, water). Office: PO Box 13308 Jackson MS 39236-3308

PEDERSEN, WILLIAM FRANCIS, lawyer; b. N.Y.C., Apr. 4, 1943; s. William F. and Priscilla S. (Auchincloss) P.; m. Ellen L. Frost, Feb. 2, 1974; children: Mark Francis, Claire Ellen. BA, Harvard U., 1965, LLB, 1968. Bar: Mass. 1969, D.C. 1978. Assoc. Ropes & Gray, Boston, 1969-72; staff atty. EPA, Washington, 1972-75, dep. gen. counsel, then assoc. gen. counsel, 1976-85; staff counsel Senate Com. on Govt. Ops., Washington, 1975-76; lectr. Harvard Law Sch., 1985-86; of counsel Perkins Coie, Washington, 1987—89, ptnr., 1989-94, Shaw, Pittman, Potts & Trowbridge, Washington, 1994-2001; pvt. practice Washington, 2001—. Vis. prof. Law Sch., U. Mich., 1997-98. Contbr. articles to profl. jours. Mem. ABA (standing com. on environ. law 1987-89). Republican. Episcopalian. Office: William F Pedersen PLLC Ste 800 1752 N St NW Washington DC 20036 E-mail: bill.pedersen@billpedersen.com.

PEDREIRA, JORGE, lawyer, bank executive; b. N.Y.C., Sept. 14, 1958; s. Jose and Juana Pedreira; m. Jane Prentzel, Jan. 1, 1997 (div. June 4, 2002); 1 child, Christine Marie. BS, John Jay Coll., 1989; JD, St. John's U., Jamaica, N.Y., 1993. Bar: N.J. 1993, U.S. Dist. Ct. N.J. 1993, N.Y. 1994. Police officer N.Y. Police Dept., N.Y.C., 1983—89, detective, 1989—93; assoc. Willkie, Farr & Galagher, N.Y.C., 1993—97; head investment banking legal group SG Cowen, N.Y.C., 1997—. Mem.: ABA, N.Y. County Lawyers, Securities Industry Assn. (mem. legal and compliance divsn.). Securities, Mergers and acquisitions, Finance. Office: SG Cowen Securities Corp 1221 Ave of the Americas New York NY 10020 Office Fax: 212-278-7995. Business E-Mail: jorge.pedreira@us.socgen.com.

PEGRAM, JOHN BRAXTON, lawyer; b. Yeadon, Pa., June 29, 1938; s. William Bement and Marjorie (Rainey) P.; m. Patricia Jane Narbeth; Aug. 21, 1965; children: Catherine, Stephen. AB in Physics, Columbia U., 1960; LLB, NYU, 1965. Bar: N.Y. 1965, U.S. Dist. Ct. (ea. and so. dists.) N.Y. 1967, U.S. Supreme Ct. 1971. Engr. Fairchild Camera and Instrument Corp., Clifton, N.J., 1960-66; assoc. Davis Hoxie Faithfull and Hapgood, LLP, N.Y.C., 1966-71; ptnr. Davis Hoxie Faithfull and Hapgood, N.Y.C., 1972-95; prin. Fish & Richardson P.C., N.Y.C., 1995—2002, sr. counsel, 2003—. Mem. intellectual property litig. adv. com. U.S. Dist. Ct. for the Dist. Del., 1994-96; mem. neutral evaluation and mediation panels U.S. Dist. Ct. for the Eastern Dist. of N.Y., 1994-97; mem. mediation panel U.S. Dist. Ct. for the So. Dist. N.Y., 1994-97. Editor The Trademark Reporter jour., 1984-86, mem. editorial adv. bd., 1986—; contbr. articles to profl. jours. Fellow Am. Bar Found. (life); mem. IEEE, ABA (chmn. antitrust law sect. com. on patents, trademarks and know how 1986-89, mem. legal econs. sect., bus. law sect., chmn. intellectual property law divsn. IV 1995-96), Am. Phys. Soc. (life), Fed. Bar Coun., Fed. Cir. Bar Assn., N.Y. State Bar Assn., Assn. of Bar of City of N.Y., Am. Intellectual Property Law Assn. (chmn. fed. practice and procedure com. 1974-76, chmn. unauthorized practice com. 1977-79, chmn. trade secrets com. 1992-94, mem. Japan practice com. 1992—, mem. editl. bd. Quar. Jour., 1994-95, chmn. fed. litig. com. 1995-97, chmn. internat. com. 1998-2000, bd. dirs. 2000—), N.Y. Intellectual Property Law Assn. (sec. 1981-84, dir. 1984-86, pres. 1989-90), U .S. Bar/Japan Patent Office Liaison Coun. (del. 1990—), Am. Judicature Soc., Internat. Intellectual Property Soc., Internat. Patent and Trademark Assn. (U.S. group AIPPI), Internat. Trademark Assn. (bd. dirs. 1985-87, fin. com. 1987-95, pub. com. 1997-98). Intellectual property, Patent, Trademark and copyright. Office: Fish & Richardson PC 45 Rockefeller Plz Fl 28 New York NY 10111-2889

PEIRCE, FREDERICK FAIRBANKS, lawyer; b. Torrington, Conn., Jan. 28, 1953; s. Everett L. and Frederica (Fairbanks) P.; m. Sandra Marie MacMillan, Dec. 16, 1989. BS with high honors, Colo. State U., 1975; JD, U. Colo., 1979. Bar: Colo. 1979, U.S. Dist. Ct. Colo. 1979. Assoc. Bratton & Zimmerman, Gunnison, Colo., 1979-80; staff atty. Holland & Hart, Aspen, Colo., 1980-82; assoc. Austin, McGrath & Jordan, Aspen, 1982-84, Austin & Jordan, Aspen, 1984-87; ptnr. Austin, Jordan, Young & Peirce, Aspen, 1987-89, Austin & Peirce, Aspen, 1989-92, Austin, Peirce & Smith, P.C., Aspen, 1992—. Bd. dirs. Aspen Nordic Coun. Inc., 1985-88, Aspen Velo Club Inc., 1986-88, Aspen Cycling Club, Inc., 1988-93, Kids First, 1997—, pres., 2000—; bd. dirs. Aspen Ctr. for Environ. Studies, 1991-97, v.p., 1992-94, pres., 1994-97; bd. dirs. Pitkin County Pks. Assn., Inc., 1990-98, v.p., 1991-92, pres., 1992-95; mem. Aspen Valley Land Trust, 1990-98, v.p., 1991-92, pres., 1992-95; mem. bd. edn. Aspen Sch. Dist., 1997—; mem. open space and trails adv. bd. City of Aspen, 2002—, pres., 2002—; mem. Kids First adv. bd. City of Aspen, 1997—, pres., 1998—. NSF grantee, 1975. Mem. Colo. Bar Assn. (bd. govs. 1989-93, exec. coun. 1993-95, v.p. 1995-96, ethics com., 1995-97), Pitkin County Bar Assn. (v.p. 1985-86, pres. 1986-88, bd. govs. rep. 1989-93), Phi Kappa Phi. Avocations: skiing, hiking, fly fishing, cycling, flying. Corporate, general, Landlord-tenant, Property, real (including real estate development, water). Office: Austin Peirce & Smith PC Ste 205 600 E Hopkins Ave Aspen CO 81611-2933 E-mail: fpeirce@aps-pc.com., feircto@rof.net.

PELLECCHIA, JOHN MICHAEL, lawyer; b. Orange, N.J., Dec. 6, 1958; BA, Lafayette Coll., 1980; JD cum laude, Tulane U., 1983. Bar: N.J. 1983, U.S. Dist. Ct. N.J. 1983, U.S. Supreme Ct. 1994. Assoc. Pitney, Hardin, Kipp & Szuch, Morristown, N.J., 1983-86; asst. counsel to gov. Thomas H. Kean State of N.J., Trenton, 1986-88; ptnr. Riker, Danzig, Scherer, Hyland & Perretti, LLP, Morristown and Trenton, 1988—. Mem. mgmt. com. Riker, Danzig, Scherer, Hyland & Perretti LLP, Morristown and Trenton, 1995-98; jud. extern to fed. dist. ct. judge, U.S. Dist. Ct., New Orleans, 1982-83; sr. fellow Tulane Law Sch., 1982-83; bd. dirs. Proformance Ins. Co.; mem. N.J. Supreme Ct. Com. on Tax Ct., 1993-96, 2000—; mem. bus. and fin. svcs. task force of Gov. Whitman's Econ. Master Plan Commn., 1994. Trustee, v.p. Leukemia Soc. Am. North Jersey chpt., 1991—; trustee N.J. Shakespeare Festival, 1996—, Schiff Natural Lands Trust, 2002—. Vol. of Yr., Leukemia Soc. Am. North Jersey chpt., 1994. Administrative and regulatory, General civil litigation, Legislative. Office: Riker Danzig Scherer Hyland & Perretti LLP Hdqrs Plaza One Speedwell Ave Morristown NJ 07962-1981

PELLER, STEFAN, lawyer; b. Switzerland, Apr. 11, 1967; M in Legal Studies with merits, U. St. Gall, Switzerland, 1992; postgrad., London U., 1996. Asst. for Civil Procedure U. St. Gall, 1990—91; intern Law Firm Schellenberg Wittmer, Zurich, Switzerland, 1993—94, atty., 1997—2000; secondment Herbert Smith, Solicitors, London, 1996—97; ptnr. Law Firm Nick & Ineichen, Zug, Switzerland, 2000—. Gen. sec. Internat. Union Marine Ins., 1997—2002. Mem.: India House. Corporate, general. Office: Nick & Ineichen Gotthardstr 3 6304 Zug Switzerland

PELLETT, JON MICHAEL, lawyer; b. Orlando, Fla., Nov. 16, 1961; s. Milton Francis and Jean Ellen (Avery) P.; m. Karen Walker, July 21, 1984 (div. Sept. 1990). BS in Biology, U. Ctrl. Fla., Orlando, 1984, BS in Stats., 1985; JD, Fla. State U., 1993. Bar: Fla. 1995, U.S. Dist. Ct. (mid. dist.) Fla. 1996. Legal trainee Dept. Bus. and Profl. Regulation, Tallahassee, 1993-95; staff atty. Agy. for Health Care Adminstrn., Tallahassee, 1995-96; assoc. Freeman, Hunter & Malloy, Tampa, Fla., 1996-2000, Barr, Murman, Tonelli et al, Tampa, 2000—. Vol. guardian ad litem Guardian ad Litem Program, Tallahassee, 1991-95. Bd. dirs. Friends of Arboretum, Orlando, 1998—. Mem. ABA, ATLA, Hillsborough County Bar Assn. Avocations: racquetball, beach volleyball. Administrative and regulatory, Appellate, Health. Office: Barr Murman Tonelli Et Al 201 E Kennedy Blvd Ste 1750 Tampa FL 33602-5829

PELOSO, JOHN FRANCIS XAVIER, lawyer; b. N.Y., Oct. 7, 1934; s. Rocco C. and Victoria P.; m. Elizabeth Byrne Peloso, Oct. 7, 1961; children: Alycia, John, Matthew. BA, Fordham U., 1956, LLB, 1960. Bar: N.Y. 1960, U.S. Dist. Ct. (so. dist.) N.Y. 1962, U.S. Ct. Appeals (2nd cir.) 1967, U.S. Supreme Ct. 1968. Law clk. to judge U.S. Dist. Ct. (so. dist.) N.Y., 1960-61; asst. U.S. Atty. U.S. Atty.'s Office, N.Y., 1961-65; assoc. Carter Ledyard & Milburn, N.Y., 1965-70; chief trial counsel NYRO-SEC, N.Y., 1970-75; ptnr. to chmn. Sage Gray Todd & Sims, N.Y., 1975-87; ptnr. to mng. ptnr. Morgan, Lewis & Bockius, LLP, N.Y.C., 1987-95, 95-99, sr. counsel, 2000—. Adj. prof. law Fordham Law Sch., 2000—; speaker in field. Contbr. articles to profl. jours. Capt. inf. USAR, 1956-64. Mem. ABA (sect. corp., banking and bus. law, com. fed. regulation securities 1975—, com. bus. and corp. litigation, chair subcom. securities litigation 1993-99, litigation co-chmn. com. securities 1983-87, com. on liaison with jud. 1987-88, coun. 1989-91, co-chmn. com. trial evidence 1994-95, co-chmn. task force on the ind. lawyer 1995-99), Assn. of Bar of City of N.Y. (arbitration com. 1970-73, fed. legis. com. 1975-78, fed. cts. com. 1982-86), Nat. Assn. Securities Dealers (nat. panel arbitrators 1975—, nat. arbitration com. 1982-85), CPR Inst. for Dispute Resolution (Disting. Neutral). Office: Morgan Lewis & Bockius LLP 101 Park Ave Fl 44 New York NY 10178-0060

PELTIN, SHERWIN CARL, lawyer; b. Milw., Aug. 2, 1929; s. Alvin Leonard and Rebecca (Weisfeldt) P.; m. Julie Marion Stern, Mar. 15, 1953; children: Laurie Peltin Merar, Steven, William. BBA, U. Wis., 1950, LLB, 1952; LLM in Taxation, NYU, 1955; SJD, George Washington U., 1962. CPA Wis.; bar: Wis. 1952, U.S. Tax Ct. 1958, U.S. Fed. Claims Ct. 1960. Atty.-advisor U.S. Tax Ct., Washington, 1955-58; atty. Offices of Louis L. Meldman, Milw., 1958-62; ptnr. Laikin, Swietlik & Peltin, Milw., 1962-68, Peregrine, Marcuvitz & Peltin, SC, Milw., 1968-87, Weiss, Berzowski, Brady, LLP, Milw., 1987—. Elected trustee Village Bd. Trustees, Bayside, 1967-73. Capt. U.S. Army, 1952-54, Korea. Mem. ABA, State Bar Wis., Milw. Bar Assn., Estate Counselors' Forum, Profl. Inst. Tax Study. Estate planning, Probate (including wills, trusts), Taxation, general. Office: Weiss Berzowski Brady LLP 700 N Water St Milwaukee WI 53202-4206

PELTON, RUSSELL MEREDITH, JR., lawyer; b. Chgo., May 14, 1938; BA, DePauw U., 1960; JD, U. Chgo., 1963. Bar: Ill. 1963, U.S. Supreme Ct. 1979. Assoc. Peterson, Ross, Schloerb & Seidel, Chgo., 1966-72, ptnr., 1972-90, Oppenheimer, Wolff & Donnelly, Chgo., 1990-2000, Chgo. mng. ptnr., 1992-95, 98-2000; ptnr. Ross & Hardies, Chgo., 2000—. Co-founder, gen. counsel Chgo. Opportunities Industrialization Ctr., 1969—83; gen. counsel Delta Dental Plan Ill., 1979—96, Am. Assn. Neurol. Surgeons, 1983—. Pres. Wilmette Jaycees, 1970; chmn. Wilmette Sch. Bd. Caucus, 1970-71; Wilmette Dist. 39 Bd. Edn., 1972-80; bd. dirs. Wilmette United Way, 1980-86, campaign chmn., 1983-85, pres., 1985-86; Wilmette Zoning Bd. Appeals, 1989-2000, chmn., 1990-2000. Served to capt. USAF, 1963-66. Mem.: ABA, Soc. Trial Lawyers, Chgo. Bar Assn., Ill. Bar Assn., Ill. State Dental Soc. (hon.). Labor (including EEOC, Fair Labor Standards Act, labor-management relations, NLRB, OSHA), General civil litigation, Health. Office: Ross & Hardies 150 N Michigan Ave Ste 2500 Chicago IL 60601-7567 E-mail: russell.pelton@rosshardies.com.

PELZ, ROBERT LEON, lawyer; b. N.Y.C., Nov. 18, 1918; s. Leon S. and Fanny M. (Berk) P.; m. Mary Jane Gips, Feb. 11, 1949; children: Kathryn Louise, Robert Leon Jr. AB, Columbia U., 1939, JD, 1942. Bar: N.Y. 1942. Since practiced in, N.Y.C.; ptnr. Hess Segall Guterman Pelz Steiner & Barovick, 1953-86, Loeb and Loeb, N.Y.C., 1986-2000. Life trustee, former v.p. Fedn. Jewish Philanthropies; bd. dirs., former chmn. bd. dirs. Fedn. Jewish Philanthropies Svc. Corp.; past trustee Coll. Pharm. Scis. Columbia U.; former chmn. bd. trustees Am. Jewish Com. Capt. AUS, WWII. Corporate, general. Office: Loeb and Loeb 345 Park Ave Fl 18 New York NY 10154-1895

PEMBERTON, BRADLEY POWELL, lawyer; b. Ft. Scott, Kans., June 15, 1952; s. Howard Duane and Juanita Lucille (Powell) P.; m. Kathleen Frances Querrey, May 22, 1976 (div. Feb. 1984); m. Lori Scott, June 18, 1994. BSBA, U. Mo., Columbia, 1974; JD, U. Mo., Kansas City, 1977. Bar: Mo. 1977, U.S. Dist. Ct. (we. dist.) Mo. 1981, U.S. Tax Ct. 1981; CPA, Mo. Tax acct. Alexander Grant & Co., Kansas City, Mo., 1977-79; shareholder Polsinelli, Shalton & Welte, Kansas City, 1979—; also bd. dirs. Kansas City. Active Vol. Atty. Project, Kansas City, 1984—; bd. dirs. Synergy House Inc., Kansas City, 1985-88, Youth Vol. Corps of Am., 1991—, March of Dimes, 1995—. Mem. ABA, Internat. Entrepreneurs Coun. (bd. dirs.), Mo. Bar Assn., Kansas City Bar Assn., AICPAs, Mo. Soc. CPAs, Kansas City C. of C. Avocations: tennis, golf, water skiing, snow skiing, private aviation. Corporate, general, Mergers and acquisitions, Taxation, general. Home: 5806 W 131st St Shawnee Mission KS 66209-3639 Office: Polsinelli Shalton & Welte 700 W 47th St Ste 1000 Kansas City MO 64112-1805 E-mail: bpemberton@pswlaw.com.

PEMBERTON, WILLIAM BERTRAM, II, lawyer; b. Nashville, Nov. 11, 1949; s. William Bertram and Martha Carolyn (Hutsell) P.; m. Sue Zan Williams, June 9, 1973 (div. Sept. 1987); children: Jennifer Leigh, William Bertram III, Charles Williams; m. Martha Louise Lewis, Nov. 5, 1988. BS, U. Tenn., 1971, JD, 1974; MBA, Millsaps Coll., 1990. Bar: Tenn. 1974, Miss. 1977, U.S. Dist. ct. (so. dist.) Miss. 1987. Land mgr. R.E. Williams Oil & Gas Co., Jackson, Miss., 1975-83; assoc. Smith, Clement, Rudolph & Pemberton, Nashville, 1984; ind. landman, Jackson, 1985-91; ptnr. Pemberton & Williams, Jackson, 1992; sole practice Jackson, 1992—. 2d lt. U.S. Army, 1974-75. Mem. ABA, ATLA, Miss. Trial Lawyers Assn., Miss. Bar, Beta Gamma Sigma. Republican. Episcopalian. Avocations: golf, bridge, skiing. Family and matrimonial, Probate (including wills, trusts), Property, real (including real estate development, water). Home: 5103 Meadow Oaks Park Dr Jackson MS 39211-4818 Office: Atty at Law 682 Towne Ctr Blvd Ridgeland MS 39157 Fax: 601-952-0904. E-mail: pembertn@bellsouth.net.

PENA, RICHARD, lawyer; b. San Antonio, Feb. 13, 1948; s. Merced and Rebecca (Trejo) P.; m. Carolyn Sarah Malley, May 25, 1979; 1 stepchild, Jason Charles Schubert. BA, U. Tex., 1970, JD, 1976. Bar: Tex. 1976, Colo. 1986. Pvt. practice, Austin, Tex., 1976—. Instr. bus. law St. Edwards U., Austin, 1983, Austin C.C., 1981-82; broker Tex. Real Estate Commn., 1980—; sports editor Austin Light, 1982. Bd. dirs. Ctr. for Battered Women, Austin, 1979-82, Austin Assn. Retarded Citizens, 1980-82; chmn. Austin Travis County Mental Health/Mental Retardation Pub. Responsibility Com., 1979-84; chmn. pvt. facilities monitoring com. Austin Assn. Retarded Citizens, 1981; bd. dirs. Boys Club of Austin, 1987-88; chair Homeless Task Force Austin, 1999—. Named to Outstanding Young Men. of Am., 1982. Fellow Tex. Bar Found. (sustaining life; trustee 1994, sec., treas. 1994, vice-chmn. 1995, chmn. 1996); mem. ABA (ho. dels., nominating com. 1998—, immigration bono com. 2000—, vice chair credentials com. 2001, state del. 2002), Am. Bar Found. (bd. dirs. 2000), Nat. Conf. Bar Pres. (exec. com. 2001—), State Bar Tex. (bd. dirs. Dist. 9 1991—, exec. com. 1992—, chmn. minority representation com. 1991-92, chair James Watson Inn 1997-98, pres. 1998-99, chmn. profl. devel. com. 1991-92, policy manual com. 1993, fed. jud. appts. com. 1984-86, opportunities for minorities in the profession com. 1990-91, mem. advt. rev. com., pres.-elect 1997, pres. 1998-99), Travis County Bar Assn. (trustee lawyer referral svc. 1984-85, bd. dirs. 1986-88, sec. 1988, pres. 1990-91, chmn. jud. screening com. 1987, chmn. 1988-89, ins. com. 1988, 89, chmn. law day banquet com. 1988-89, lawyer referrel svc. com. 1983-84, trustee 1984-86, membership com. 1989), Capitol Area Mex. Am. Lawyers (pres. 1985, Outstanding Hispanic Lawyer Austin 1989), Legal Aid Soc. Ctrl. Tex. (bd. dirs. 1984), Austin Young Lawyers Assn., Tex. Trial Lawyers Assn., Austin C. of C. (Leadership Austin 1985-86). Democrat. Personal injury (including property damage), Workers' compensation. Home: 107 Top O The Lake Dr Austin TX 78734-5234 Office: 2028 E Ben White #220 Austin TX 78741

PENCE, STEPHEN BEVILLE, prosecutor; MBA, Ea. Ky. U.; JD, U. Ky. Assoc. Taustine and Post, 1987—88, Borowitz and Goldsmith, 1988—90; served in U.S. Attys. Office we. dist. Ky., 1990—95; ptnr. Sheffer and Hoffman, 1995—96; former U.S. Atty. We. Dist. Ky. Office Fax: 502-582-5067.*

PENDELL, TERRY ASHLEY, lawyer, mediator; b. Great Bend, Kans., July 26, 1937; d. John J. and Ida Berniece (Littrell) Ashley; m. George M. Pendell Jr., June 25, 1960 (div. July 1977); children: George III, Wade A.; m. Cal K. Moser, Feb. 18, 1994. BA, U. Okla., 1960, MEd, 1965; JD, Oklahoma City Univ., 1967. Bar: Okla. 1967, U.S. Dist. Ct. (we. dist.) Okla. 1967, U.S. Dist. Ct. (no. dist.) Okla. 1972, U.S. Supreme Ct. 1980. Pvt. practice, Oklahoma City, 1966—; ptnr. Pendell & Pendell Lawyers, Oklahoma City, 1967-73; assoc. Pritchett & Pendell, Oklahoma City, 1973-75; judge Oklahoma City Mcpl. Ct., Oklahoma City, 1975-90, Okla. Worker's Compensation Ct., State of Okla., Oklahoma City, 1990-96; ptnr. Pritchett, Snyder & Pendell, Oklahoma City, 1996—2001; chief admin. law judge Okla., 2003—. Adj. law prof. Okla. City U., 1998. Dir. Cmty. Coun. Okla., Oklahoma City, 1980—; chmn. to TB Task Force to the Homeless, Oklahoma City, 1997—. Recipient Spotlight award Okla. Bar Assn. Women in Law sect., 1999, Okla. Exec. Woman of the Yr. award High Noon, 2001. Mem. Okla. City U. Law Alumni Assn. (bd. dirs. 1997-99, Outstanding Law Sch. Alumni award 1994), Nat. Assn. Women Judges (bd. dirs. 1982-84), Ruth Bader Ginsberg Inn of Ct. (officer 1995—), Iota Tau Tau, Zeta Phi Eta (Outstanding Svc. award 1975-87), Gamma Phi Beta. Alternative dispute resolution, Labor (including EEOC, Fair Labor Standards Act, labor-management relations, NLRB, OSHA), Probate (including wills, trusts). Office: 524 S 2d St Mcalester OK 74501 E-mail: oktap@yahoo.com.

PENNAMPED, BRUCE MICHAEL, lawyer; b. Kearney, Nebr., July 16, 1948; s. Matthew Paul and Betty Fern (Harper) P.; mm. Victoria A. Crull, May 13, 1972 (div. Dec. 1980); 1 child, Katheryn A.; m. Melissa J. Barth, July 22, 1985. BS in Mgmt., Ind. U., 1970, JD, 1972. Bar: Ind. 1972, U.S. Dist. Ct. (no. and so. dists.) Ind. 1972, U.S. Ct. Appeals (7th cir.) 1978; cert. family law specialist. Assoc. Rocap Rocap Reese & Young, Indpls., 1972-76; pvt. practice Indpls., 1976-78, 88-91; ptnr. Forbes & Pennamped, Indpls., 1978-88, Lowe Gray Steele & Hoffman, Indpls., 1991-96, Lowe Gray Steele & Darko, Indpls., 1996—2002, Pennamped & Assocs., Indpls., 2002—. Chair and panelist Ind. Continuing Legal Edn. Forum; mem. Ind. Child Custody and Support Adv. Commn. Contbr. articles to profl. jours. Majority atty. Ind. Ho. of Reps., Indpls. Cpl. USMCR, 1967-69. Fellow Am. Acad. Matrimonial Lawyers, Ind. Family Law Specialist Bd. (co-chair). Family and matrimonial. Home: 9662 Decatur Dr Indianapolis IN 46256-9654 Office: Pennamped & Associates 3925 River crossing Parkway Ste 280 Indianapolis IN 46240 Fax: 317-843-0718. E-mail: bruce@pennamped-associates.com.

PENNELL, WILLIAM BROOKE, lawyer; b. Mineral Ridge, Ohio, Oct. 28, 1935; s. George Albert and Katherine Nancy (McMeen) P. AB, Harvard U., 1957; LLB cum laude, U. Pa., 1961; m. Peggy Polsky, June 17, 1958; children: Katherine, Thomas Brooke. Bar: N.Y. 1963, U.S. Dist. Ct. (so. dist.) N.Y. 1964, U.S. Dist. Ct. (ea. dist.) N.Y. 1964, U.S. Ct. Appeals (2d cir.) 1966, U.S. Ct. Claims 1966, U.S. Tax Ct. 1967, U.S. Supreme Ct. 1967. Clk. U.S. Dist. Ct., (so. dist.) N.Y., N.Y.C., 1961-62; assoc. Shearman & Sterling, N.Y.C., 1962-71, ptnr., 1971-91. Recent case editor U. Pa. Law Rev., 1960-61. Bd. govs. Bklyn. Heights Assn., 1964-74, pres., 1969-71; chmn. bd. Willoughby House Settlement, 1972-95. Served with U.S. Army, 1957. Fellow Salzburg Seminar Am. Studies, 1965. Mem. Rembrandt Club. Federal civil litigation, State civil litigation, Private international. Office: PO Box 249 Canaan NY 12029-0249

PENNINGTON, ALYCE LORAINE, lawyer; b. Scotia, Calif., Dec. 19, 1953; d. Ronald Duane and Bernice June (Coleman) Stutz; m. Richard Allen Trapp, July 4, 1985. BS, U. Ariz., 1978, JD, 1982. Bar: Ariz. 1982, U.S. Dist. Ct. Ariz. 1982, U.S. Ct. Appeals (9th cir.) 1989. Clk., personnel asst. City of Tucson, Ariz., 1971-79; pvt. practice Tucson, 1982-84; atty. Pima County Pub. Fiduciary, Tucson, 1984-86; ptnr. Richards & Pennington and predecessor firm, Tucson, 1986-97, Deconini McDonald Yetwin & Lacy, Tucson, 1997—. Contbr. articles to profl. jours. Mem. Ariz. Women Lawyers Assn., Ariz. State Bar Assn. (mem. exec. coun., family law sect., 2001-, cert. family law specialist). Democrat. Family and matrimonial, Personal injury (including property damage), Probate (including wills, trusts).

PENNOYER, ROBERT M. lawyer; b. N.Y.C., Apr. 9, 1925; BA, Harvard U., 1946; LL.B., Columbia U., 1950. Bar: N.Y. 1951, U.S. Supreme Ct. 1971. Asst. U.S. atty. criminal div. So. Dist., N.Y., 1953-55; asst. to gen. counsel Office of Sec. of Def., Dept. Def., Washington, 1955-57, spl. asst. to asst. sec. of def. for internat. security affairs, 1957-58; ptnr. Patterson, Belknap, Webb & Tyler, N.Y.C., 1962-95, of counsel, 1995—. Trustee Carnegie Instn., Washington, 1968-79, John Merck Fund, 1982—, Mrs. Giles Whiting Found., 1970—, Met. Mus. Art, 1966—, Pierpont Morgan Libr., 1969—, Columbia U., 1982-88, Boyce Thompson Inst. for Plant Rsch., Cornell U., 1974-97, Inst. Democracy Studies, 1999-2002. Lt. (j.g.) USNR, 1944-46. Mem. ABA, N.Y. State Bar Assn., Assn. Bar City N.Y., Century Assn. Office: Patterson Belknap Webb & Tyler Rm 2200 1133 Ave of the Americas New York NY 10036-6731 E-mail: rmpennoyer@pbwt.com.

PENSKAR, MARK HOWARD, lawyer; b. Detroit, Mar. 4, 1953; s. Sol Leonard and Frances (Rosenthal) P.; m. Carol Ann Stewart, Aug. 7, 1977; children: David, Rebecca. BA, U. Mich., 1974, M in Pub. Policy, 1975, JD cum laude, 1977. Bar: Calif. 1977, U.S. Dist. Ct. (no. dist.) Calif. 1977, (ea. and cen. dists.) Calif. 1983, (so. dist.) 1988, U.S. Ct. Appeals (9th cir.) 1987, U.S. Tax Ct. 1993. Assoc. Pillsbury, Madison and Sutro, San Francisco, 1977-84, ptnr., 1985-96; sr. bus. litigation atty. Pacific Gas and Electric Co., San Francisco, 1996—, sect. head comml. and contracts sect., 2001—. Mediator Superior Ct. early settlement program, San Francisco; mediator and early neutral evaluator U.S. Dist. Ct. Alternative Dispute Resolution Program; former bd. dirs. Legal Aid Soc. of San Francisco Employment Law Ctr. Mem. ABA, San Francisco Bar Assn., Commonwealth Club, Phi Gamma Delta (past pres. Bay Area grad. chpt.). Avocations: camping, golf, wine collecting, fishing. Administrative and regulatory, General civil litigation, Environmental. Home: 29 E Altarinda Dr Orinda CA 94563-2415 Office: Pacific Gas & Electric Co Law Dept B30A PO Box 7442 San Francisco CA 94120-7442 E-mail: MHP5@pge.com.

PENZER, MARK, lawyer, editor, corporate trainer, former publisher; b. Bklyn., Nov. 22, 1932; s. Ed and Fay (Weinberg) P.; m. Eileen Malen, Aug. 12, 1962; children: Matthew, Nicole; m. Nydia A. Rey, Nov. 25, 1984. BBA, CCNY; JD, Fordham U. Bar: N.Y. 1968, D.C. 1973, Fla. 1982, U.S. Dist. Ct. (ea. dist.) N.Y. 1976, U.S. Dist. Ct. (so. dist.) Fla. 1991; cert. instr. DMA, 1986. Free-lance writer, 1950-83; editorial asst. Hearst mags., N.Y.C., 1955, asst. editor, 1956, assoc. editor, 1957-66; columnist N.Y. Jour.-Am., 1960-62; editor in chief Rudder mag., 1967-69, editorial dir., 1970-74; editor in chief True, 1970-73, editor at large, 1973-75; pub., editor in chief Jour. Energy Medicine, 1978-81; Medicare hearing officer Miami, Fla., 1981-82; pres. Success Internat., Inc., Coral Gables, Fla., 1984-85; adj. prof. bus. and tech. writing Fla. Internat. U., small bus. mgmt., U. Miami, 1986-89; pres. Heroica, Inc., Miami Lakes, Fla., 1989-90; pvt. practice Law Offices of Mark Penzer, Hialeah and Miami Lakes, Fla., 1991—. Tchr. creative writing Dade County Off Campus Edn. Author: The Motorboatman's Bible, 1965, The Powerboatman's Bible, 1977; asst. editor: The Path of Least Resistance, 1989, Do It!, 1991. Served with AUS, 1953-55. Mem. Hialeah-Miami Lakes Bar Assn. (pres. 1990-92). Administrative and regulatory, Corporate, general, Health. E-mail: mpenz@aol.com.

PEPE, LOUIS ROBERT, lawyer, educator; b. Derby, Conn., Mar. 7, 1943; s. Louis F. and Mildred R. (Vollaro) P.; m. Carole Anita Roman, June 8, 1969; children: Marissa Lee, Christopher Justin, Alexander Drew. B in Mgmt. Engring., Rensselaer Poly. Inst., 1964, MS, 1967; JD with distinction, Cornell U., 1970. Bar: Conn. 1970, U.S. Dist. Ct. Conn. 1970, U.S. Ct. Appeals (2d cir.) 1971, U.S. Supreme Ct. 1975, U.S. Ct. Claims 1978. Assoc. Alcorn, Bakewell & Smith, Hartford, Conn., 1970-75, ptnr., 1975-82; sr. ptnr. Pepe & Hazard, Hartford, 1983—. Adj. assoc. prof. Hartford Grad. Ctr., 1972-87; adj. prof. U. Conn. Law Sch., 2000—. Mem. New Hartford Housing Authority, 1971-72, New Hartford Planning Zoning Commn., 1973-84, chmn., 1980-84, New Hartford Inland Wetlands Commn., 1975-78; mem. dean's adv. coun. Cornell Law Sch., 1990—; dir. Capitol Area Found. Equal Justice, 1993—, pres., 1999-2001. 1st lt. U.S. Army, 1964-66. Decorated Army Commendation medal. Fellow Am. Bar Found., Am. Coll. Constl. Lawyers, Am. Coll. Trial Lawyers (assoc.); mem. Am. Bd. Trial Advocates (assoc.), Conn. Bar Assn. (chmn. constrn. law sect. 1989-92, chmn. standing com. on professionalism 2000—, v.p. 2003—), Conn. Trial Lawyers Assn., Hartford County Bar Assn., Phi Kappa Phi. Federal civil litigation, State civil litigation, Construction. Home: 3 Metacom Dr Simsbury CT 06070-1851 Office: Pepe & Hazard Goodwin Sq Hartford CT 06103-4300 E-mail: lpepe@pepehazard.com.

PEPE, STEVEN DOUGLAS, federal magistrate judge; b. Indpls., Jan. 29, 1943; s. Wilfrid Julius and Roselda (Gehring) P.; m. Janet L. Pepe. BA cum laude, U. Notre Dame, 1965; JD magna cum laude, U. Mich., 1968; postgrad., London Sch. Econs. and Polit. Sci., 1970-72; LLM, Harvard U., 1974. Bar: Ind. 1968, U.S. Dist. Ct. Ind. 1968, D.C. 1969, U.S. Dist. Ct. D.C. 1969, Mass. 1973, Mich. 1974, U.S. Dist. Ct. (ea. dist.) Mich., 1983. Law clk. Hon. Harold Leventhal U.S. Cir. Ct. Appeals, Washington, 1968-69; staff atty. Neighborhood Legal Svcs. Program, 1969-70; cons. Office of Svcs. to Aging, Lansing, Mich., 1976-77, Administrn. Aging, Dept. Health and Human Svcs., 1976-78; U.S. magistrate judge Eastern Dist., Ann Arbor, Mich., 1983—. Mem. Biregional Older Am. Advocacy Assistance Resource and Support Ctr., 1979-81; cons., bd. dirs. Ctr. Social Gerontology (1988-93); clin. prof. law, dir. Mich. Clin. Law Program, U. Mich. Law Sch., 1974-83; adj. prof. law Detroit Mercy Sch. Law, 1985; lectr. U. Mich. Law Sch., 1985-97. Editor Mich. Law Rev.; contbr. articles to profl. jours. Recipient Reginald Heber Smith Cmty. Lawyer fellowship, 1969-70; Mich.-Ford Internat. Studies fellow, 1970-72, Harvard Law Sch. Clin. Teaching fellow, 1972-73. Mem. State Bar Mich., State Bar Ind., Fed. Bar Assn., Washtenaw County Bar Assn., Am. Inn Court XI, U. Detroit Mercy, Pi Sigma Alpha, Order of Coif. Office: US District Court PO Box 7150 Ann Arbor MI 48107-7150 E-mail: Steven_Pepe@mied.uscourts.gov.

PEPER, CHRISTIAN BAIRD, lawyer; b. St. Louis, Dec. 5, 1910; s. Clarence F. and Christine (Baird) P.; m. Ethel C. Kingsland, June 5, 1935 (dec. Sept. 1995); children: Catherine K. Peper Larson, Anne Peper Perkins, Christian B.; m. Barbara C. Pleiter, Jan. 25, 1996. AB cum laude, Harvard U., 1932; LLB, Washington U., 1935; LLM, Yale U., 1937. Bar: Mo. 1934. Pvt. practiced, St. Louis; of counsel Blackwell Sanders Peper Martin LLP. Lectr. various subjects Washington U. Law Sch., St. Louis, 1943-61; ptnr. A.G. Edwards & Sons, 1945-67; pres. St. Charles Gas Corp., 1953-72; bd. dirs. El Dorado Paper Bag Mfg. Co., Inc. Editor: An Historian's Conscience: The Correspondence of Arnold J. Toynbee and Columba Cary-Elwes, 1986. Mem. vis. com. Harvard Div. Sch., 1964-70; counsel St. Louis Art Mus. Sterling fellow Yale U., 1936. Mem. ABA, Mo. Bar Assn., St. Louis Bar Assn., Noonday Club, Univ. Club, Harvard Club, East India Club (London), Order of Coif, Phi Delta Phi. Roman Catholic. Home: 1454 S Mason Rd Saint Louis MO 63131-1211 Office: Blackwell Sanders Peper Martin LLP 720 Olive St Saint Louis MO 63101-2338 E-mail: cpeper@blackwellsanders.com.

PEPPET, SCOTT R. law educator; b. Mpls., Dec. 11, 1969; s. Russell F. and Rosemary M. Peppet; m. Kellie Zell; children: Jessica, Lauren, Anna. BA, Cornell U., 1991; JD, Harvard U., 1996. Bar: Mass. Law clk. to Justice Charles Fried Mass. Superior Jud. Ct., Boston, 1997—98; lectr. law Harvard U. Law Sch., Cambridge, Mass., 1997—98, 1998—2000; assoc. prof U. Colo. Sch. Law, Boulder, 2000—. Author: Beyond Winning, 2000 (CPR Book award, 00), Processes of Dispute Resolution: The Role of Lawyers, 2001. Office: U Colo Sch Law Campus Box 401 Boulder CO 80309

PEPPLES, CANDACE BRANNEN, lawyer; b. Fitzgerald, Ga., Dec. 15, 1974; d. Donald Neal and Blanche Davis Brannen; m. Lloyd Chandler Peeples III, June 29, 2002. BA, U. Ga., 1997; JD, Samford U., 2000. Bar: Ala., U.S. Dist. Ct. (mid. dist.) Ala. Assoc. Crittenden Martin, Birmingham, Ala., 2000—. Mem.: Birmingham Bar Assn., Rotary Club. Family and matrimonial. Office: Crittenden Martin Ste 210 813 Shades Creek Pkwy Birmingham AL 35209

PEPYNE, EDWARD WALTER, lawyer, psychologist, former educator; b. Springfield, Mass., Dec. 27, 1925; s. Walter Henry and Frances A. (Carroll) P.; m. Carol Jean Dutcher, Aug. 2, 1958; children— Deborah, Edward, Jr., Susan, Byron, Shari, Randy, David, Allison, Jennifer BA, Am. Internat. Coll., 1948; MS, U. Mass., 1951, Ed.D., 1968; postgrad., NYU, 1952-55; prof. diploma, U. Conn., 1964; JD, Western New Eng. Coll., 1978. Bar: Mass. 1978, U.S. Supreme Ct. 1981. Prin., tchr. Gilbertville Grammar Sch., Hardwick, Mass., 1948-49; sch. counselor West Springfield High Sch., Mass., 1949-53; instr. NYU, 1953-54; supt. schs. New Shoreham, R.I., 1954-56; asst. prof. edn. Mich. State U., 1956-58; sch. psychologist, guidance dir. Pub. Sch. System, East Long, Mass., 1958-62; lectr. Westfield State Coll., 1961-65; dir. pupil services Chicopee Pub. Sch., 1965-68; assoc. prof. counselor edn. U. Hartford, West Hartford, Mass., 1968-71, prof., 1971-85, dir. Inst. Coll. Counselors Minority and Low Income Students, 1971-72, dir. Div. Human Services, 1972-77; cons. Aetna Life & Casualty Co., Hartford, 1962-75; hearing officer Conn. State Bd. Edn., 1980-99; exec. dir. Sinapi Assocs., 1959-78; pvt. practice, Ashfield, Mass., 1978—. Co-author: Better Driving, 1958; assoc. editor: Highway Safety and Driver Education, 1954; chmn. editorial com.: Man and the Motor Car, 5th edit., 1954; contbr. numerous articles to profl. jours. Chief Welfare Svcs. Civil Def., Levittown, N.Y., 1953-54; chmn. Ashfield Planning Bd., Mass., 1979-83; moderator Town of Ashfield, 1980-81, town counsel, Charlemont, Mass., 1983-84; mem. jud. nominating coun. Western Regional Com., 1993-99; mem. Mohawk Regional Sch. Com., 1999-2000. Mem. ABA, APA, Mass. Bar Assn., Mass. Acad. Trial Attys., Am. Pers. and Guidance Assn., New Eng. Pers. and Guidance Assn. (bd. dirs.), New Eng. Ednl. Rsch. Orgn. (pres. 1971), Am. Assn. Sch. Adminstrs., Am. Ednl. Rsch. Assn., Mt. Tom Amateur Radio Assn., Franklin County Amateur Radio Club, Elks, Kiwanis (pres. 1988-89, lt. gov. div. 12, 1991-92), Masons (master 1994-96), Shriners, Phi Delta Kappa. Administrative and regulatory, State civil litigation, Education and schools. Home: PO Box 31 134 Ashfield Mountain Rd Ashfield MA 01330-9505 Office: PO Box 345 134 Ashfield Mountain Rd Ashfield MA 01330-9505 Home: 3808 Airport Rd Coventry VT 05855 E-mail: pepyne@pshift.com.

PERALTA, FEDERICO, lawyer; b. San Jose, Costa Rica, Sept. 5, 1974; s. Federico Peralta Sr. and Magda Calzada; m. Maria Paula Robles, June 23, 2000; 1 child, Felipe. BA in Law, U. Costa Rica, 1997, JD in Law, 1998; spl. courses internat. law, Georgetown Univ., 1999; LLM, U. Chgo., 2002. Bar: Costa Rica 1998; notary pub. Costa Rica, 1999. Legal asst. Facio & Cañas, San Jose, Costa Rica, 1994—98, assoc., 1999—. Pro-bono legal svcs. Clin. Program U. Costa Rica, 1995—96; asst. internat. trade law U. Costa Rica, 1999. Scholar, U. Costa Rica, 1993—98. Avocations: reading, sports. Corporate, general, Mergers and acquisitions, Property, real (including real estate development, water). Office: Facio & Cañas Barrio Tournon San Jose 5173-1000 Costa Rica Home: Villas San Antonio condo no 5 Escazú Costa Rica Fax: 011 506 2339091. E-mail: fperalta@fayca.com.

PERDOMO, MICHELLE, lawyer; b. Miami, Fla., Nov. 25, 1967; d. Jose and Migdalia Perdomo; m. Mauricio Buendia, Dec. 21, 2001. BA, U. So. Calif., 1991; JD, George Washington U., 1995. Bar: Fla. 96, U.S. Dist. Ct. (so. dist.) Fla. 97, U.S. Dist. Ct. (mid. dist.) Fla. 00, U.S. Ct. Appeals (11th cir.) 00. Assoc. Douglas S. Luv, P.A., Miami, 1996—99; pvt. practice Michelle Perdomo and Assocs., PA, Miami, 1999—. Mem. Dade Ptnrs. Dade County Pub. Schs., Miami, 2000. Mem.: Am. Immigration Lawyers Assn., ABA. Immigration, naturalization, and customs, consular law. Office: Michelle Perdomo and Assocs PA 100 N Biscayne Blvd Ste 3000 Miami FL 33132

PEREIRA DOS SANTOS, SANDRO WILSON, tax specialist; LLB, postgrad. in tax law, Cath. U. Paraná, 1997, postgrad. Prof. postgrad. course tax law Cath. U. Parana; mem. Pereira dos Santos Advogados, Curitiba, Brazil. Mem.: Norwegian-Brazilian C. of C., Brazilian-French C. of C., Brazilian-Am. C. of C., Brazilian Assn. Fin. Law, Brazilian Bar Assn., Tax Law Coun., Internat. C. of C., Environ. Law Group, Internat. Fiscal Assn., Internat. Bar Assn. Office: Periera dos Antos Advogados Rua Santa Rita Cássia 130 80 540 200 Curitiba Brazil

PERELL, EDWARD ANDREW, lawyer; b. Stamford, Conn., Mar. 30, 1940; s. Sydney C. and Dorothy (Barger) P.; m. Nan Lifflander, Oct. 10, 1959; children: Stephanie Perell, Timothy R. BA, Yale Coll., 1962, LLB, 1965. Bar: N.Y. 1966. Assoc. Debevoise & Plimpton, N.Y.C., 1965-72, ptnr., 1973-88, 93—, N.Y.C. and London, 1989-93. Contbr. numerous articles on securities laws, mergers and acquisitions to profl. publs. Chmn. bd. dirs. Fedn. Protestant Welfare Agys., N.Y.C., 1983-87; pres., bd. dirs. Graham-Windham Family Svcs., N.Y.C., 1970-77. Mem. ABA, Assn. of Bar of City of N.Y. Corporate, general, Private international, Securities. Home: 333 E 57th St New York NY 10022 also: 90 Dorland Rd Old Chatham NY 12136 Office: Debevoise & Plimpton 919 3rd Ave New York NY 10022

PERERA, LAWRENCE THACHER, lawyer; b. Boston, June 23, 1935; s. Guido R. and Faith (Phillips) P.; m. Elizabeth A. Wentworth, July 5, 1961; children: Alice V. Perera Lucey, Caroline F. Perera Barry, Lucy E., Lawrence Thacher, Jr., Perera Adams. BA, Harvard U., 1957, LL.B., 1961. Bar: Mass. 1961, U.S. Supreme Ct. 1973. Clk. Judge R. Ammi Cutter, Mass. Supreme Jud. Ct., Boston, 1961-62; assoc. Palmer & Dodge, Boston, 1962-69, ptnr., 1969-74; judge Middlesex County Probate Ct., East Cambridge, Mass., 1974-79; ptnr. Hemenway & Barnes, Boston, 1979—. Mem. nat. coun. Hon. Nat. Jud. Coll., Reno, prof./pres. Mass. Continuing Legal Edn., Inc., 1988-90. Chmn. Boston Fin. Commn., 1969-71; overseer Boston Lyric Opera; chmn. bd. overseers Boston Opera Assn.; chmn. Back Bay Archtl. Commn., 1966-72; trustee emeritus Sta. WGBH Ednl. Found., Boston Athenaeum, Wang Ctr. Performing Arts. Fellow Am. Acad. Matrimonial Lawyers, Am. Coll. Trust and Estate Counsel; mem. ABA, Am. Bar Found., Am. Law Inst., Mass. Bar Assn., Mass. Bar Found., Boston Bar Assn., Boston Bar Found. Family and matrimonial, General practice, Probate (including wills, trusts). Home: 18 Marlborough St Boston MA 02116-2101 Office: 60 State St Boston MA 02109-1800

PEREYRA-SUAREZ, CHARLES ALBERT, lawyer; b. Paysandu, Uruguay, Sept. 7, 1947; came to U.S., 1954, naturalized, 1962; s. Hector and Esther (Enriquez-Sarano) P.-S.; m. Susan H. Cross, Dec. 30, 1983. BA in History magna cum laude, Pacific Union Coll., 1970; postgrad., UCLA, 1970-71; JD, U. Calif., Berkeley, 1975. Bar: Calif. 1975, D.C. 1980. Staff atty. Western Ctr. Law and Poverty, Inc., Los Angeles, L.A., 1976; trial atty. civil rights div. U.S. Dept. Justice, Washington, 1976-79, asst. U.S. atty., criminal div. Los Angeles, L.A., 1979-82; sr. litigation assoc. Gibson, Dunn & Crutcher, Los Angeles, L.A., 1982-84; sole practice Los Angeles, L.A., 1984-86; ptnr. McKenna & Cuneo, Los Angeles, L.A., 1986-95, Davis Wright Tremaine, L.A., 1995-98; pvt. practice L.A., 1998—. Democrat. Avocations: tennis, jogging, travel. Federal civil litigation, State civil litigation, Criminal.

PEREZ, JOSE RAFAEL, JR., lawyer; b. Victoria de las Tunas, Oriente, Cuba, May 14, 1955; s. Jose Rafael Perez and Yolanda Ramona Sosa; m. Joan Anne Terp, Dec. 9, 1984; children: Alexander Rafael, Gabriella Susanna. BA in History, St. Mary's U., San Antonio, 1977, MA in History, 1980; JD, Tex. So. U., 1985. Cert.: Tex. Bd. Legal Specialization (immigration and nationality law) 1993, bar: Tex. Shareholder Quan, Burdette & Perez, PC, Houston, 1986—. Spkr. in field; consular liaison with U.S. consulate Tex. Am. Immigration Lawyers Assn., Ciudad Juarez, Mexico, 1997—99. Pres. Immigration Counseling Ctr., Houston, 1996—. Mem.: Am. Immigration Assn. (spkr.). Avocations: reading, exercise. Home: 6111 Riverview Way Houston TX Office: Quan Burdette and Perez PC 5177 Richmond Ave Ste 800 Houston TX 77056 E-mail: jperez@quanlaw.com.

PEREZ, PAUL IGNATIUS, lawyer; b. Cuba; Bachelor, Jacksonville U.; Master, U. Fla.; grad. in Law, George Washington U. Asst. U.S. atty., Jacksonville, Fla., 1988—92; fed. criminal def. atty. Booth, Arnold & Perez, Jacksonville, Fla., 1994—2002; U.S. atty. Mid. Dist. Fla., 2002—. Office: Mid Dist Fla 400 N Tampa St Ste 3200 Tampa FL 33602*

PEREZ, RODRIGO ELIZUNDIA, lawyer; b. Mexico City, DF, Mexico, July 18, 1973; s. Guillermo Zuñiga and Maria Carmen (Elizundia) Perez. JCL, Panamericana U, Mexico City, Mexico, 1993—98; fgn. student, summer, Baker & McKenzie, Chgo, Ill, 1997; LLM corp. law, NYU, NY, NY, 2000—01. Law clk. BMW, Mexico City, 1995, Baker & McKenzie, Mexico City, 1995—98; fgn. atty. Gleiss Lutz Hootz Hirsch, Stuttgart, Germany, 2001—02; assoc. atty. Barrera, Sigueiros & Torres Landa, Mexico City, 1999—. Scholar Ad-Honorem, Panamericana U, 1993—98, NYU Grad. Merit, NYU, 2000—01, Fulbright, Mexico, 2000—01. Catholic. Avocations: bicycling, swimming, guitar, culture. Home: Moctezuma 11 Colonia Coyoacán 04000 Mexico City Mexico Office: Barrera, Sigueiro & Torres Landa Montes Urales 470,Lomas of Chapultepec 11000 Mexico City Mexico

PEREZ ELIZUNDIA, RODRIGO, lawyer; b. Mexico City, July 18, 1973; s. Guillermo Perez Zuniga and Maria del Carmen Elizundia. Degree in law, U. Panamericana, Mexico City, 1998; LLM in Corp. Law, NYU, 2001. Law clk. BMW, Mexico City, 1995, Baker and McKenzie, Mexico City, 1995—98; fgn. atty. Gleiss, Lutz, Hootz & Hirsch, Stuttgart, Germany, 2001—02; assoc. Barrera, Siqueiros y Torres Landa, Mexico City, 1999—. Commercial, contracts (including sales of goods; commercial financing), Corporate, general, Mergers and acquisitions. Office: Barrera Siqueiros y Torres Landa Colonia Lomas de Chapultepec Montes Urales 470 11000 Mexico City Mexico Home: Moctezuma No 11 Colonia Coyoacan (entre Arco y Aviora) CH 04000 Mexico DF Mexico

PERIERA, SANTHAPAT, lawyer; b. Bangkok, May 22, 1965; s. Rojvit Periera and Thaveeval Tovidaya; m. Ratree Putthmuan Periera, Jan. 9, 1998. LB, Thammasat U., 1985; diploma, U. Fla., 1987; ML, U. Miami, 1988; LLM, Boston U., 1989; cert., Harvard U., 2000. Intern Banking Internat. Investing Group Skadden, Arps, Slate, Meagher & Flom, N.Y.C., 1989—90; atty. and head Banking and Fin. Group Tilleke & Gibbins Internat. Ltd., Bangkok, 1990—98, group dir. Comml. Dept., 1998—. Mem.: Law Soc. Thailand, Thai Bar Assn., The Chartered Inst. Arbitrators. Banking, Mergers and acquisitions, Commercial, contracts (including sales of goods; commercial financing). Office: Tilleke & Gibbins International Ltd 64/1 Soi Tonson Ploenchit Pathumwan Bangkok 10330 Thailand Fax: 66-2 263-7710-3. E-mail: santhapat@tillekeandgibbins.com.

PERKINS, JAMES WOOD, lawyer; b. New Bedford, Mass., Oct. 14, 1924; s. Ralph Chamberlain and Louise Bartlett (Allen) P.; m. Margaret Neale Heard, Feb. 3, 1951; children: Charles H., James A., George H. AB, Havard U., 1945, JD, 1948; MTS, Harvard Div. Sch., 1996. Bar: Mass. 1948, U.S. Dist. Ct. Mass. 1948. Engr. Sylvania Electric Products, Inc., Salem, Mass., 1944-45; assoc. Palmer & Dodge LLP, Boston, 1948-54, ptnr., 1955-91, mng. ptnr., 1986-89, of counsel, 1992—. Mem. ABA (chmn. sect. local govt. law 1970-71, sect. del. 1974-78), Nat. Assn. Bond Lawyers (pres. 1985-86). Municipal (including bonds).

PERKINS, JOHN ALLEN, lawyer; b. New Bedford, Mass., Sept. 13, 1919; s. Ralph Chamberlain and Louise Bartlett (Allen) P.; m. Lydia Bullard Cobb, Sept. 9, 1944; children: John A., Susan W., Robert C., William B. AB, Harvard U., 1940, LL.B., 1943. Bar: Mass. Of counsel Palmer & Dodge LLP, Boston; clk. Social Law Library, 1961-83; grad. researcher Univ. Coll., Oxford U., 1978. Bd. dirs. Greater Boston Legal Services, Inc., 1972-91. Author: The Prudent Peace— Law as Foreign Policy, 1981; contbr. articles to profl. jours. Mem. Dedham (Mass.) Sch. Com., 1959-65, chmn., 1963-65, town counsel, Dedham, 1971-72. Mem. Am. Law Inst., Am. Coll. Trust and Estate Counsel, Mass. Bar Assn. (dir. 1973-75), Internat. Acad. Estate and Trust Law (exec. coun. 1990-94), Boston Bar Assn. (council 1972-75, v.p. 1981-82, pres. 1982-84). Banking, Estate planning, Probate (including wills, trusts). Home: 100 Newbury Court Ste 610 Concord MA 01742-5835 Office: Palmer & Dodge LLP 111 Huntington Ave at Prudential Ctr Boston MA 02199-7613

PERKINS, ROGER ALLAN, lawyer; b. Port Chester, N.Y., Mar. 4, 1943; s. Francis Newton and Winifred Marcella (Smith) P.; m. Katherine Louise Howard, Nov. 10, 1984; children: Marshall, Morgan, Matthew, Justin,

Ashley. BA, Pa. State U., 1965; postgrad., U. Ill., 1965-66; JD with honors, George Washington U., 1969. Bar: Md. 1969, Mass. 1975. Trial atty. Nationwide Ins. Co., Annapolis, Md., 1969-72; assoc. Arnold, Beauchemin & Huber, PA, Balt., 1973; from assoc. to ptnr. Goodman & Bloom, PA, Annapolis, 1973-76; ptnr. Luff and Perkins, Annapolis, 1976-78; pvt. practice Annapolis, 1978—. Temp. adminstrv. hearing officer Anne Arundel County, 1984—; asst. city atty., Annapolis, 1980-82; atty. Bd. Appeals of City of Annapolis, 1986-2003; mem. Appellate Jud. Nominating Commn., 1995—. Editl. adv. bd. Daily Record, 1996-97. Mem. Gov.'s Task Force on Family Law, 1991-94; adv. coun. on family legal need of low income persons MLSC, 1991; coach youth sports. Fellow Am. Acad. Matrimonial Lawyers, Am. Bar Found., Md. Bar Found. (bd. dirs. 1992-95); mem. ABA (ho. dels. 1991-93, 94-96, standing com. on solo and small firm practitioners 1993-97, chair 1996-97), Md. State Bar Assn. (pres. 1992-93, treas. 1988-91, bd. govs. 1985-87, chair membership com. 2002-03, chair spl. com. on lawyer profl. responsibility 1994-95, family and juvenile law sect. coun. 1983-89, chair 1987-88), Anne Arundel County Bar Assn. (pres. 1984-85). State civil litigation, Family and matrimonial. Home: 503 Bay Hills Dr Arnold MD 21012-2001 Office: The Courtyards 133 Defense Hwy Ste 202 Annapolis MD 21401-8907 E-mail: roger@perkinslaw.com.

PERKINS, ROSWELL BURCHARD, lawyer; b. Boston, May 21, 1926; AB cum laude, Harvard U., 1945, LLB cum laude, 1949; LLD, Bates Coll., 1988. Bar: Mass. 1949, N.Y. 1949. Assoc. Debevoise, Plimpton & McLean, N.Y.C., 1949-53; ptnr. Debevoise & Plimpton and predecessor firm, N.Y.C., 1957-96; of counsel, head rep. office Debevoise & Plimpton LLC, Moscow, 1997-01. Asst. sec. U.S. Dept. Health, Edn. and Welfare, 1954-56; counsel to Gov. Nelson A. Rockefeller State of N.Y., 1959; asst. counsel spl. subcom. Senate Commerce Com. to investigate organized crime in interstate commerce, 1950; chmn. N.Y.C. Mayor's Task Force on Transp. Reorgn., 1966; mem. Pres.'s Adv. Panel on Pers. Interchange, 1968, chmn. adv. com. Medicare Adminstrn. Contracting, Subcontracting HEW, 1973-74; dir. Fiduciary Trust Co., N.Y., 1963-2000; trustee Bowery Savs. Bank, 1975-82; mem. legal com. to bd. dirs. N.Y. Stock Exch., 1995-2000. Editor Harvard Law Rev., 1948-49. Mem. N.Y. Lawyers Com. Civil Rights, 1970-73; mem. nat. exec. com., 1973-1980, co-chmn. 1973-75; mem. adv. coun. Woodrow Wilson Sch. Pub. and Internat. Affairs, Princeton U., 1967-69; bd. dirs. The Commonwealth Fund, 1974-97, Sch. Am. Ballet, 1974-85, chmn. bd. 1976-80; dir., sec. N.Y. Urban Coalition, 1967-74; trustee Pomfret Sch., 1961-76; The Brearley Sch., 1969-75; dir. Salzburg Seminar Am. Studies, 1970-80; mem. overseers vis. com. Kennedy Sch. Govt., Harvard U., 1971-77, Harvard and Radcliffe Colls., 1958-64, 1971-77, Davis Ctr. for Russian and Eurasian Studies, 2000—. Recipient Spl. Merit citation Am. Judicature Soc., 1989, Harvard Law Sch. Assn. award, 1994, 50 Yr. award Fellows of ABA, 2002. Mem. ABA (commn. on law and economy, 1975-79, mem. ho. of dels. 1980-93), N.Y. State Bar Assn., Assn. of the Bar of the City of N.Y. (chmn. spl. com. on fed. conflict of interest laws 1958-60). Harvard Alumni Assn. (pres. 1970-71), Am. Law Inst. (mem. coun. 1969, pres. 1980-93, chmn. coun. 1993—), Am. Arbitration Assn. (bd. dirs. 1966-71), Russian Inst. Dirs. (mem. expert coun. 2002-), Ind. Dirs. Assn. (mem. adv. com. Russia 2002-). Corporate, general, Private international, Mergers and acquisitions. Home: 1120 5th Ave New York NY 10128-0144 Office: Debevoise & Plimpton 919 3rd Ave 46th Fl New York NY 10022-3902 E-mail: rbperkins@debevoise.com.

PERKO, KENNETH ALBERT, JR., lawyer, art dealer; b. Iron Mountain, Mich., Feb. 9, 1943; s. Kenneth Albert and Alice Ellen (Hamad) P.; m. Susan Jane Roodenburg, Oct. 5, 1968; children: Kathryn Ann, Kenneth Albert. AB in Math. with honors magna cum laude, Princeton U., 1964; JD, Harvard U., 1967. Bar: Ohio, N.Y.; cert. real estate broker, N.Y. Assoc. Milbank, Tweed, Hadley & McCloy, N.Y.C., 1967-79; asst. sec. The Rockefeller Group, N.Y.C., 1979—96, 1998—2002; counsel Radio City Music Hall, N.Y.C., 1985-96, Tishman Speyer Properties, 1996-97; pres. Petrarch LLC, 2002—. Lectr. Cambridge U., 1979, U. Paris, 1979; reviewer Math. Revs., 1980—. Contbr. articles to profl. jours. Trustee Princeton Libr., N.Y.C., 1968—, Rockette Alumnae Found., 1992—. Grantee NSF, Blacksburgh, Va., 1982. Democrat. Roman Catholic. General civil litigation, Corporate, general, Insurance. Home: 325 Old Army Rd Scarsdale NY 10583-2643

PERL, SANFORD ERIC, lawyer; b. Poughkeepsie, N.Y., Nov. 12, 1965; s. Stephen C. and Elyse A. Perl; m. Jody Frances Sacks, Oct. 10, 1993; children: Hannah, David, Lauren. BS in Accountancy, U. Ill., 1987; JD, U. Mich., 1990. Bar: Ill. 1990. Assoc. Kirkland & Ellis, Chgo., 1990—96, ptnr., 1996—. Recipient Elijah Watt Sells award, AICPA, 1990. Mergers and acquisitions. Office: Kirkland & Ellis 200 E Randolph Dr Chicago IL 60601

PERLE, EUGENE GABRIEL, lawyer; b. N.Y.C., Dec. 21, 1922; s. Philip and Simme (Meschenberg) P.; m. Ellen Carlotta Kraus, Nov. 26, 1953 (dec. 1964); 1 child, Elizabeth Anne Perle; m. Ruth Friedberg Lerner, May 23, 1972 (div. 1977); m. Patricia Fitzpatrick Sinnott, Jan. 24, 1981. BA, Queens Coll., 1943; JD, Yale U., 1949. Bar: N.Y. 1950, Conn. 1995. Assoc. Cravath, Swaine & Moore, N.Y.C., 1949-53; asst. counsel N.Y. State Moreland Commn. Investigation Harness Racing, N.Y.C., 1953-54; assoc. Gordon, Brady, Caffrey & Keller, N.Y.C., 1954-56; assoc. gen. atty. Time Inc., N.Y.C., 1956-66, pub. counsel, 1966-73, v.p. law, 1973-80, corp. v.p. law, 1980-85; counsel Proskauer & Rose, N.Y.C., 1985-92, Chapman & Fennell, 1992-94; mem. Ohlandt, Greeley, Ruggiero & Perle, Stamford, Conn., 1995-97, sr. counsel, 1998—. Co-author: Publishing Law, 1988-2002; mem. editl. bd. Yale Law Jour., 1948-49; mem. adv. bd. Bur. Nat. Affairs Patent, Trademark and Copyright Jour., 1972-86; contbr. to Bull. Copyright Soc. U.S.A. Trustee Baron deHirsch Fund, 1959-87, hon. trustee, 1988—; commr. Nat. Commn. New Technol. Uses Copyrighted Works, 1975-78; bd. dirs. N.Y. Sch. for Circus Arts, Inc., 1979-87, Am. Arbitration Assn., 1979-84; justice of peace City of Norwalk, Conn., 1960-63. Lt. USNR, 1943-46. Mem. ABA (chmn. copyright divsn. 1970-71, 86-87, chmn. com. copyright and new tech. 1971-73, chmn. com. econs. profession 1976, coun. patent, trademark and copyright sect. 1979-83, governing bd. forum com. comms. law 1979-85, chmn. related fields and future devels. divsn. forum com. entertainment and sports industries 1979), Copyright Soc. U.S.A. (trustee 1962-64, 69-70, 71-74, pres. 1976-78, hon. trustee 1978—), U.S. Trademark Assn. (bd. dirs. 1969-72, 74-77, v.p. 1972-73), Assn. of Bar of City of N.Y., Sunningdale Country Club, Century Assn., Banyan Golf Club of Palm Beach. Democrat. Office: Ohlandt Greeley Ruggiero & Perle One Landmark Sq Stamford CT 06901 E-mail: egperle@ix.netcom.com.

PERLIS, SHARON A. lawyer; b. New Orleans; d. Rogers I. and Dorothy Perlis. BA in French, Principia Coll., 1967; JD, Tulane U., 1970. Officer, dir. Perlis, Inc., New Orleans, 1973—2003; pres. SILREP Internat. Co., Metairie, 1984—; officer, dir. Internat. Adv. Svcs., Inc., New Orleans, 1985-89; prin. Perlis & Assocs., Metairie, 1985-01; pres. Sharon A. Perlis P.C., 2001—. Legal counsel La. Ins. Rating Commn., 1980-84; adminstrv. law judge State of La., 1980-84, mem. Econ. Devel. Adv. Coun., 1982-84; exec. com. small bus. coun. Bd. of Trade, 1987-89, chmn. small bus. coun., 1988, exec. com. East Jefferson coun., 1989-96; dir. World Trade Ctr., 1985-2003, vice chmn. internat. bus. com.; dir. New Orleans br. Fed. Res. Bank of Atlanta, 1982-88, chmn., 1984, 86, 88; dir. Metairie Bank & Trust, 1997-2003; bd. of commr. Port of New Orleans, 1992-96, vice chmn., 1995, chmn. bd., 1996; del. U.S. Def. Dept.'s Joint Civilian Orientation Conf., 1997; bd. dirs. Metairie Bank & Trust. Mem. human rels comm. City of New Orleans, 1992-93, Commn. To Reorganize Govt., Leadership La., 2001; mem. exec. bd. La. Coun. Econ. Edn., 1986-89, Pvt. Enterprise Edn. Found., 1986-89; state del. White House Conf. on Small Bus., La. rep. internat. trade issues, 1986; dir. Metro YMCA, 1990-97; exec. com. agy. rels. United Way, 1987-90; mem. exec. com. Jr. Achievement Project Bus., 1987; vice chmn. La. Dist. Export Coun.; bd. dir. Bur. Govermental Rsch.; mem. bd. La. Internat. Trade Commn. Recipient Achiever's award Woman Bus. owners Assn., 1994, Jefferson Econ. Devel. Commn. award, 1994, Advocacy of Yr. award Small Bus. Adminstrn., 1988, 89, Iberville award New Orleans Pub. Group, 1996, Women of the Yr. award New Orleans Pub. Group, 2000, Patty Strong award Jefferson-25, 2000; named Young Leadership Coun. Role Model, 2001. Mem. ABA, Banker's Assn., Am. Arbitration Assn. (arbitrator/mediator), Jefferson Bar Assn., Orleans Bar Assn., Federal Bar Assn., Adv. Coun. Federalist Soc., La. Estate Planning Coun., La. Bar Assn., Gov.'s Commn. on Internat. Trade Devel., New Orleans Regional C. of C. (bd. dirs. 1990—), New Orleans Regional Leadership Inst., New Orleans Area Polit. Action Coun. (pres.). Avocations: reading, sailing, tennis. Office: Perlis & Assocs 6069 Magazine St New Orleans LA 70118-6006

PERLMAN, B. ARTHUR, lawyer; b. Denver, July 22, 1959; s. L.H. and Marie (Stearns) P.; m. Joanne Marie Jakicic, Feb. 14, 1987. BA, U. Denver, 1981; JD, Southwestern U., 1985. Bar: Colo. 1985, U.S. Bankruptcy Ct. 1987, U.S. Dist. Ct. Colo. 1987. Assoc. Duran & Duran, Denver, 1986-88, Hyatt Legal Svcs., Lakewood, Colo., 1988-90, Dodd, Scott, & Stockton, Lakewood, 1990-91, Kurtz & Peckham, Denver, 1991-92; 13th jud. dist. atty. Ft. Morgan, Colo., 1993; sole practitioner Littleton, Colo., 1993—. Atty. coach Abe Lincoln mock trial, Denver, 1988, 89, 90. Mem. Assn. Trial Lawyers Am., Colo. Trial Lawyers Assn., Colo. Criminal Def. Bar, Phi Alpha Theta, Phi Sigma Iota. Democrat. Jewish. Avocations: model clipper ship building, coin collecting, american history. Bankruptcy, Criminal, Juvenile. Office: PO Box 620086 Littleton CO 80162-0086

PERLMAN, BURTON, judge; b. Dec. 17, 1924; s. Phillip and Minnie Perlman; m. Alice Weihl, May 20, 1956; children: Elizabeth, Sarah, Nancy, Daniel. BE, Yale U., 1945, ME, 1947; LLB, U. Mich., 1952. Bar: Ohio 1959, N.Y. 1953, Conn. 1952, U.S. Dist. Ct. (so. and ea. dists.) N.Y. 1954, U.S. Dist. Ct. (so. dist.) Ohio 1959, U.S. Ct. Appeals (2d cir.) 1953, U.S. Ct. Appeals (6th cir.) 1959. Assoc. Armand Lackenbach, N.Y.C., NY, 1952—58; pvt. practice Cin., 1958—61; assoc. Paxton and Seasongood, Cin., 1961—67; ptnr. Schmidt, Effton, Josselson and Weber, Cin., 1968—71; U.S. magistrate U.S. Dist. Ct. (so. dist.) Ohio, 1971—76, U.S. bankruptcy judge, 1976—. Chief bankruptcy judge so. dist. Ohio, 1986—93; adj. prof. U. Cin. Law Sch., 1976—. Served with U.S. Army, 1944—46. Mem.: ABA, Cin. Bar Assn., Am. Judicature Soc., Fed. Bar Assn. Office: US Bankruptcy Ct Atrium 2 8th Fl 221 E 4th St Cincinnati OH 45202-4124

PERLMAN, MATTHEW SAUL, lawyer; b. Washington, Aug. 30, 1936; s. Jacob and Helen (Aronson) P.; m. Julia Gertrude Hawks, June 22, 1966; children— Penelope Leah, Deborah Jane, Sarah Louise, Jacob Henry AB, Brown U., 1957; LLB, Harvard U., 1960. Bar: D.C. 1960, Md. 1960, U.S. Supreme Ct. 1965. Atty. Air Force Gen. Counsel's Office, Washington, 1960-65; mem. Armed Services Bd. of Contract Appeals, Washington, 1965-67; gen. counsel Pres.' Commn. on Postal Orgn., Washington, 1967; asst. gen. counsel Dept. Transp., Washington, 1967-69; ptnr. Arent, Fox, Kintner, Plotkin & Kahn, Washington, 1969—2001, arbitrator, 2002—. Mem. Pres. Reagan's Transition Team for GSA, Washington, 1980-81; mem. adv. bd. Fed. Contracts Report, Washington, 1970-97; overseas corr. Internat. Constn. Law Rev., London, 1983—. Contbr. articles to profl. jours. Pres. Civic Assn. River Falls, Potomac, Md., 1975-77; mem. Montgomery County Md. Citizens Adv. Commn. for Rock Run AWT Plant, 1979-85. Served to capt. USAF, 1960-63 Mem. ABA (pub. contracts sect.), Fed. Bar Assn., Cosmos Club. Republican. Jewish. Construction, Government contracts and claims. Home: 10517 Stable Ln Potomac MD 20854-3867 Office: Arent Fox Kintner Plotkin & Kahn 1050 Connecticut Ave NW Ste 500 Washington DC 20036-5303 E-mail: perlmanm@arentfox.com., mpjp@erols.com.

PERLMUTH, WILLIAM ALAN, lawyer; b. N.Y.C., Nov. 21, 1929; s. Charles and Roe (Schneider) P.; m. Loretta Kaufman, Mar. 14, 1951; children: Carolyn, Diane. AB, Wilkes Coll., 1951; LLB, Columbia U., 1953. Bar: N.Y. 1954. Assoc. Cravath, Swaine & Moore, N.Y.C., 1955-61; ptnr. Stroock & Stroock & Lavan, N.Y.C., 1962—. Editor Columbia U. Law Rev., 1952-53. Trustee Aeroflex Found., N.Y.C., 1965—, City Ctr. 55th St. Theater Found., 1995—, Harkness Found. for Dance, N.Y.C., 1976—, Sch. Am. Ballet, 1997—, Wilkes U., Wilkes-Barre, Pa., 1980—, Weininger Found., 1985—, NYU Hosps. Ctr., 1994—, Hosp. for Joint Diseases Orthopaedic Inst., N.Y.C., 1980—, chmn. bd. trustees, 1994—. Mem. N.Y. State Bar Assn., Assn. of Bar of City of N.Y. Jewish. Corporate, general, Mergers and acquisitions, Securities. Home: 880 5th Ave New York NY 10021-4951 Office: Stroock & Stroock & Lavan 180 Maiden Ln Fl 34 New York NY 10038-4982

PERLOFF, JEAN MARCOSSON, lawyer; b. Lakewood, Ohio, June 25, 1942; d. John Solomon and Marcella Catherine (Borngen) Marcosson; m. Lawrence Storch, Stpe. 8, 1991. BA magna cum laude, Lake Erie Coll., 1965; MA in Italian, UCLA, 1967; JD magna cum laude, Ventura Coll. Law, 1976. Bar: Calif. 1976, U.S. Dist. Ct. (cen. dist.) Calif. 1978. Assoc. in Italian U. Calif.-Santa Barbara, 1967-70; law clk., paralegal Ventura County Pub. Defender's Office, Ventura, Calif., 1975; sole practice Ventura, 1976-79; co-prin. Clabaugh & Perloff, A Profl. Corp., Ventura, 1979-82; sr. jud. atty. to presiding justice 6th divsn. 2d Dist. Ct. Appeals, L.A., 1982-97; comml. property mgr. Santa Barbara, Calif., 1997—. Instr. Ventura Coll. Law, 1976-79. Pres., bd. dirs. Santa Barbara Zool. Gardens, 1987-88; bd. dirs. Montecito Found., 1999—; trustee Lake Erie Coll., 1993—; mem. 19th Agrl. Dist. Bd., 2001—. Named Woman of Yr., 18th Senatorial dist. and 35th Assembly dist. Calif. Legislature, 1993; recipient Disting. Alumnae award Lake Erie Coll., 1996; sesquicentennial fellow Lake Erie Coll., 2001. Mem. Calif. Bar Assn. (appellate ct. com. 1993-95), Fiesta City Club, Kappa Alpha Sigma. Democrat. Avocations: tennis, jogging, biking, reading, music. Home: 1384 Plaza Pacifica Santa Barbara CA 93108-2877

PERLSTEIN, WILLIAM JAMES, lawyer; b. N.Y.C., Feb. 7, 1950; s. Justin Sol and Jane (Goldberg) P.; m. Teresa Catherine Lotito, Dec. 20, 1970; children: David, Jonathan. Student, London Sch. Econs., 1969-70; BA summa cum laude, Union Coll., 1971; JD, Yale U., 1974. Bar: Conn. 1974, D.C. 1976, U.S. Dist. Ct. D.C. 1977, U.S. Ct. Appeals (D.C. cir.) 1978, U.S. Supreme Ct. 1993, N.Y. 2000. Law clk. to judge Marvin Frankel U.S. Dist. Ct., N.Y.C., 1974-75; assoc. Wilmer, Cutler & Pickering, Washington, 1975-82, ptnr., 1982—, mem. mgmt. com., 1995—, chmn., 1998—. Mng. editor Yale Law Jour., 1973-74; contbg. author The Workout Game, 1987. Dir. Neighborhood Legal Svcs. program. Mem.: Am. Bar Found., Am. Coll. Bankruptcy (gen. counsel), Am. Law Inst., Am. Bankruptcy Inst. (chmn. legis. com. 1986—89, bd. dirs. 1989—93, 1997—), ABA (bus. bankruptcy com 1983—, v.chmn. executory contracts subcom. of bus. bankruptcy com. 1988—90, bankruptcy cts. subcom. 1990—97, chmn. legislation subcom. 1997—), Phi Beta Kappa. Jewish. Bankruptcy, Legislative. E-mail: wperlstein@wilmer.com.

PERMUT, SCOTT RICHARD, lawyer; b. N.Y.C., Apr. 23, 1954; arrived in Israel, 1980; BA magna cum laude, Queens Coll., N.Y.C., 1977; JD, St. Johns Law Sch., 1980. Ptnr. Goldsobel & Permut, Haifa, Israel, 1980—. With Israeli Def. Forces, 1986. Intellectual property, Probate (including wills, trusts), Property, real (including real estate development, water). Office: 5 Hantke St Haifa Israel Fax: 972.4.8253663. E-mail: srp@permlaw.com.

PERON, SABRINA, lawyer; b. Milan, Dec. 16, 1964; d. Giancarlo Peron and Rosaria Previtera Degree in law, Milan U., 1991. Bar: Milan 1995. Asst. Studio Valli-Donvito, Milan, 1991-94; assoc. Studio Prof. AVV. Granelli, Milan, 1995-97, Franzosi Dal Negro Avvocati Associati, Milan, 1997-99; ptnr. Studio Legale Avvocati Associati, Milan, 2000—. Asst. lectr. Pavia U., 1994-96, Milan U., 1997-2002; lectr. Istituto Formazione Giornalismo, 1998-99; spkr. in field. Contbr. articles to profl. jours. Avocations: philosophy, journalism. Communications, Entertainment, Libel. Office: Studio Legale Avvocati Assn Via U Foscolo 4 20121 Milan Italy Fax: 0039/02/866935. E-mail: stleaa@tiscalinet.it.

PEROTTI, ROSE NORMA, lawyer; b. St. Louis, Aug. 10, 1930; d. Joseph and Dorothy Mary (Roleski) Perotti. BA, Fontbonne Coll., St. Louis, 1952; JD, St. Louis U., 1957. Bar: Mo. 1958. Trademark atty. Sutherland, Polster & Taylor, St. Louis, 1958-63, Sutherland Law Office, 1964-70, Monsanto Co., St. Louis, 1971-85, sr. trademark atty., 1985-91, assoc. trademark counsel, 1991-94, trademark counsel, 1994-96, Polster, Lieder, Woodruff & Lucchesi, 1996—. Honored with dedication of faculty office in her honor, St. Louis U. Sch. Law, 1980. Mem. ABA, Mo. Bar, Bar Assn. Met. St. Louis, Am. Judicature Soc., Friends St. Louis Art Mus., Mo. Bot. Garden. Trademark and copyright. Office: Polster Lieder Woodruff & Lucchesi 763 S New Ballas Rd Ste 160 Saint Louis MO 63141-8750 E-mail: rperotti@patpro.com.

PEROUTKA, HYNEK, lawyer; b. Most, Czech Republic, Nov. 29, 1973; Baccalaureat, Lycee Carnot, Dijon, France, 1993; ML, Charles U. of Prague, 1998. Bar: Czech Republic 2001. Legal clk. Klimova & Klima, Prague, 1994—98; jr. atty. at law Andrej Peterka, Prague, 1998—2000, Peterka & Leuchterova v.o.s., 2000—01; ptnr. Peterka, Leuchterova & Ptnrs. v.o.s., 2001—. Translator, interpreter, Prague, 1996—98. Mem.: Czech Light Aircraft Assn. Bankruptcy, Commercial, contracts (including sales of goods; commercial financing), Intellectual property. Office: Peterka Leuchterova & Partners vos Na Prikope 15 Prague 110 00 Czech Republic

PERRETT, ROSS GRAHAM, lawyer; b. Ipswich, Australia, Nov. 2, 1957; s. Graham F. and Glenice A.; m. Jennifer Anne Dunning, Dec. 20, 1980; children: Sarah, Elise, Jonathon. B of Law, Queensland U., Brisbane, Australia, 1981, B of Commerce, 1979. Clk. Clayton Utz, Brisbane, Australia, 1979-80, solicitor, 1981-84, ptnr., 1984-98, mng. ptnr., 1998—. Mem. Queensland Law Soc., Valley Cricket Club (life), Royal Queensland Golf Club, Brisbane Club. Administrative and regulatory, General civil litigation, Alternative dispute resolution. Office: Clayton Utz 215 ADelaide St Brisbane QLD 4000 Australia Fax: 61 7 30031366. E-mail: rperrett@claytonutz.com.

PERRY, BRYAN LLOYD, lawyer; b. Baltimore, Md., Jan. 31, 1972; JD, U. Md., Baltimore, 1993—96. Atty. Law Offices of Bryan L. Perry, Owings Mills, Md., 2000—. Mem.: ABA (mem. forum on entertainment and sports law), Md. Bar Assn. (mem. com. on entertainment and sports law), Wash. Area Lawyers for the Arts, Black Entertainment and Sports Lawyers Assn., Nat. Assn. Rec. Industry Profls., Nat. Acad. Rec. Arts Sci. Office: Law Offices Bryan L Perry 8367 Township Drive Owings Mills MD 21117 Office Fax: 410-998-9760. E-mail: bryanperry@entertainmentlawcenter.net.

PERRY, GEORGE R. lawyer; b. Wyandotte, Mich., Sept. 8, 1927; s. John H. and Claire R. Perry; m. Mary Lou Owens, Sept. 11, 1948; children: David J., Douglas J., Denise Perry Doinavin. JD, U. Detroit, 1952. Bar: Mich. 1954, U.S. Dist. Ct. (ea. dist.) Mich. 1954, U.S. Ct. Appeals (6th cir.) 1954, U.S. Supreme Ct. 1965. Justice of the Peace Nankin Twp., Mich., 1955—64; planning commn. chmn. City and Village of Inkster, Mich., 1956—62. Cpl. U.S. Army, 1945—47, U.S. and Japan. Mem.: KC. Democrat. Roman Catholic. Avocations: bridge, golf, bowling. Home: 8401 S Kolb Rd Unit 415 Tucson AZ 85706-9624

PERRY, GEORGE WILLIAMSON, lawyer; b. Cleve., Dec. 4, 1926; s. George William and Melda Patricia (Arther-Holt) P. BA in Econs., Yale U., 1949; JD, U. Va., 1953. Bar: Ohio 1953, D.C. 1958, U.S. Supreme Ct. 1958, U.S. Ct. Appeals (D.C. cir.) 1959. Atty. U.S. Dept. Justice, Washington, 1954-56; assoc. Roberts and McInnis, Washington, 1957-59; atty. assoc. counsel Com. on Interstate Fgn. Commerce, U.S. Ho. Reps., Washington, 1960-65; atty., advisor ICC, Washington, 1965-68; assoc. dir. devel. Yale U., New Haven, 1968-70; trust officer The No. Trust Co., Chgo., 1970-71; dir. tax rsch. Pan Am. World Airways, N.Y.C., 1973-75; hearing officer Indsl. Commn. Ohio, Cleve., 1978-81; sole practice Cleve., 1981—. With U.S. Army, 1945-46. Mem. Soc. Cin. in State of Conn., Ancient and Hon. Artillery Co. (mem. Boston-hereditary), Concord Coalition, Phi Delta Phi, Chi Delta Theta. Episcopalian. Administrative and regulatory, General practice.

PERRY, JON ROBERT, lawyer; b. Kane, Pa., May 14, 1965; s. James Felix and Judith Rose (Zelina) P.; m. Joni Lee Detrick, Aug. 10, 1991; children: Alex Joseph, Trevor James. BA summa cum laude, Pa. State U., 1987; JD magna cum laude, Duquesne U., 1991. Bar: Pa. 1991, U.S. Dist. Ct. (we. dist.) Pa. 1991, U.S. Ct. Apppeals (3d, 6th, 7th and fed. cirs.). Assoc. Reed Smith Shaw & McClay, Pitts., 1990-94; ptnr. Betts & Perry, Pitts., 1994-97, Meyers Rosen Louik & Perry, Pitts., 1998—. Bd. dirs. Flying Pig Theatre, Pitts., J's Place, Inc., Kane, RBCI, Inc., Cranberry, Pa., CDS, Inc., Pitts. Exec. editor Duquesne Law Rev., 1991. Vol. mentor/spkr. elem. and high schs., Pitts., 1992—; founder Pennies From Heaven Children's Charity. Mem. ATLA, Pa. Trial Lawyers Assn., Pa. Bar Assn., Allegheny County Bar Assn., Allegheny County Acad. Trial Lawyers, Phi Beta Kappa. General civil litigation, Personal injury (including property damage), Product liability. Office: Meyers Rosen Louik and Perry 437 Grant St Pittsburgh PA 15219-6002

PERRY, LEE ROWAN, retired lawyer; b. Chgo., Sept. 23, 1933; s. Watson Bishop and Helen (Rowan) P.; m. Barbara Ashcraft Mitchell, July 2, 1955; children: Christopher, Constance, Geoffrey. BA, U. Ariz., 1955, LLB, 1961. Bar: Ariz. 1961. Since practiced in, Phoenix; clk. Udall & Udall, Tucson, 1960-61; mem. firm Carson, Messinger, Elliott, Laughlin & Ragan, 1961-99. Mem. law rev. staff, U. Ariz., 1959-61. Mem. bd. edn. Paradise Valley Elem. and H.S. Dists., Phoenix, 1964-68, pres., 1968; mem. bd. edn. Osborn Elem. Sch. Dist., Phoenix, 2002; bd. dirs. Osborn Sch. Dist. Found., 2003—; treas. troop Boy Scouts Am., 1970-72; mem. Ariz. adv. bd. Girl Scouts U.S.A., 1972-74, mem. nominating bd., 1978-79; bd. dirs. Florence Crittenton Services Ariz., 1967-72, pres., 1970-72; bd. dirs. U. Ariz. Alumni, Phoenix, 1968-72, pres., 1969-70; bd. dirs. Family Service Phoenix, 1974-75; bd. dirs. Travelers Aid Assn. Am., 1985-89; bd. dirs. Vol. Bur. Maricopa County, 1975-81, 83-86, pres., 1984-85; bd. dirs. Ariz. div. Am. Cancer Soc., 1978-80, Florence Crittenton div. Child Welfare League Am., 1976-81; bd. dirs. Crisis Nursery for Prevention of Child Abuse, 1978-81, pres., 1978-80; Ariz. dir. Devereux Found., 1996-2000, vice chmn. 1996-98. 1st lt. USAF, 1955-58. Mem. State Bar Ariz. (conv. chmn. 1972), Rotary (dir. 1971-77, 95-96, pres. 1975-76, West Leadership award 1989), Ariz. Club (bd. dirs. 1994-2002, pres.-elect 1997-98, pres. 1998-99), Phoenix Country Club, Phi Delta Phi, Phi Delta Theta (pres. 1954). Republican. Episcopalian. Corporate, general, Finance, Property, real (including real estate development, water). Home: 106 N Country Club Dr Phoenix AZ 85014-5443 E-mail: imlerp@att.net.

PERRY, RALPH BARTON, III, lawyer; b. NYC, Mar. 17, 1936; s. Ralph Barton Jr. and Harriet Armington (Seelye) P.; m. Mary Elizabeth Colburn, Sept. 2, 1961; children: Katherine Suzanne, Daniel Berenson. AB, Harvard U., 1958; LL.B., Stanford U., 1963. Bar: Calif. 1964. Assoc. and mem. Keatinge & Sterling, Los Angeles, 1963-68; mem. firm Graven Perry Block Brody & Qualls, Los Angeles, 1968—. Bd. dirs. Planning and Conservation League, 1968—, Coalition for Clean Air, 1961—, pres. 1972-80, 85-88. Served with U.S. Army, 1956-58. Mem. ABA (ho. of dels. 1975-95), State Bar Calif., LA County Bar Assn., Lawyers Club LA County (gov. 1968-82),

Nat. and Internat. Wildlife Fedns., Sierra Club, LA Athletic Club Home: 296 Redwood Dr Pasadena CA 91105-1339 Office: Graven Perry 523 W 6th St Ste 723 Los Angeles CA 90014-1223 E-mail: rbp3@earthlink.net.

PERRY, RONALD, lawyer; b. Pitts., Feb. 20, 1952; s. Joseph E. and Margaret (Majhan) P.; m. Deborah Lauer, July 19, 1975; children: Meredith Lyn, Erin Michelle. BA in Polit. Sci., Ind. U., Pa., 1974; JD, Western New Eng. U., 1978; LLM in Taxation, Temple U., 1982. Bar: Pa. 1978, U.S. Dist. Ct. (mid. dist.) Pa. 1979, U.S. Tax Ct. 1980, U.S. Supreme Ct. 1984. Pvt. practice, York, Pa., 1978-82; ptnr. Carn, Vaughn & Perry, York, 1982-85, Countess, Gilbert, Andrews, York, 1985—. Asst. dist. atty., York County, 1982-85. Pres. Self-Help Counseling, York, 1978-84; bd. dirs. West York (Pa.) Sch. Dist., 1983-85, York County Jr. Achievement, 1998—, dir. White Rose Invitational track and Field Meet, 1998-2001; solicitor West York Zoning Bd., 1987-88; chmn. Manchester Twp. Planning Commn., 1992-98; pres. York County Literacy Coun., 1992-98; bd. dirs. Jr. Achievement York County. Mem. ABA, Pa. Bar Assn., York County Estate Planning Coun. (bd. dirs. 1986-91), Rotary Club. Avocation: music. Commercial, contracts (including sales of goods; commercial financing), Property, real (including real estate development, water), Taxation, general. Office: Countess Gilbert Andrews 29 N Duke St York PA 17401-1204

PERRY, ROTRAUD MEZGER, lawyer; b. Berlin, Aug. 29, 1927; came to U.S., 1927; d. Fritz and Luise (Scheuerle) M.; m. John Wilson Perry, Sept. 9, 1950; children: Erik David, Julia Louise, Kathleen Anne, Duncan Gerrit, Ellen Eva. AB, Bryn Mawr Coll., 1948; JD, U. Mich., 1952. Bar: D.C. 1954, Md. 1974, U.S. Supreme Ct. 1962. Various positions Library of Congress, Washington, 1947-50; atty. USN, Washington, 1955-56; sole practice Washington, 1957-78; ptnr. Perry & Perry, Washington, 1978-97; retired. Mem. Bar Assn. D.C., D.C. Bar Assn., Women's Bar Assn. D.C. (pres. 1975-76). Democrat. General practice, Public international, Probate (including wills, trusts). Home: 3511 Idaho Ave NW Washington DC 20016-3151

PERRY, SIR WILLIAM JOHN, solicitor; b. Bexley, Kent, England, Nov. 19, 1952; s. William H. and Margaret Bennett (Annear) P.; m. Jane Ann Sherlock, July 15, 1978; children: Alexandra, Caroline, Michael. BA, Oxford U., England, 1973, MA, 1977, PhD, 1993. Articled clk. Norton, Rose, Botterell, Roche, London, 1974-77, asst. solicitor, 1977-85; ptnr., head litigation Pickering, Kenyon, London, 1986-95, sr. ptnr., 1990-95; ptnr. Charles Russell, London, 1995—, head litigation, 2002—. Chmn. bd. dirs. Spencer Hill Mgmt. Ltd., London, 1978-81. Contbr. articles to profl. jours. Bd. dirs. London Handel Soc. Ltd., 1990-95. Named Hon. Solicitor Royal Soc. Musicians of Great Britain, 1990-95. Fellow: Royal Soc. Arts; mem.: Chartered Inst. Arbitrators, Chartered Mgmt. Inst., Law Soc., City of London Solicitors Co, Carlton Club. Anglican. Avocations: ballet, opera, oenology, political history, walking. Office: Charles Russell 8-10 New Fetter Lane EC4A London 1RS England E-mail: billjperry@aol.com., billp@cr-law.co.uk.

PERSCHBACHER, REX ROBERT, dean, law educator; b. Chgo., Aug. 31, 1946; s. Robert Ray and Nancy Ellen (Beach) P.; children: Julie Ann, Nancy Beatrice. AB in Philosophy, Stanford U., 1968; JD, U. Calif., Berkeley, 1972. Bar: Calif. 1972, U.S. Dist. Ct. (no. dist.) Calif. 1973, U.S. Dist. Ct. (so. dist.) Calif. 1979, U.S. Ct. Appeals (9th cir.) 1980, U.S. Dist. ct. (ea. dist.) Calif. 1985. Law clk. to judge U.S. Dist. Ct. (no. dist.) Calif., San Francisco, 1973-74; asst. prof. law U. Tex., Austin, 1974-75; assoc. Heller, Ehrman, White & McAuliffe, San Francisco, 1975-78; asst. prof. law U. San Diego, 1978-79, assoc. prof. law, 1980-81; mem. faculty Inst. on Internat. and Comparative Law, London, 1984—; acting prof. law U. Calif., Davis, 1981-85, prof., 1988—, assoc. dean, 1993-98, dean Law Sch., 1998—. Dir. clin. edn. Univ. Calif., Davis, 1981-93, acad. senate, law sch. rep., 1989-91; vis. prof. law Univ. Santa Clara (Calif.), summer 1986. Co-author: California Civil Procedure and Practice, 1996, California Legal Ethics, 2nd edit., 1997, Problems in Legal Ethics, 4th edit., 1997, Cases and Materials on Civil Procedure, 3d edit., 1998; contbr. articles to legal jours. Bd. dirs. Legal Svcs. of No. Calif., 1990-96. Mem. ABA, Calif. Bar Assn., Am. Assn. Law Schs., Inn of Ct. Democrat. Avocation: travel. Office: UC Davis Sch Law Dean Office 400 Mrak Hall Dr Davis CA 95616*

PERSHAN, RICHARD HENRY, lawyer; b. N.Y.C., Jan. 4, 1930; s. Benjamin and Sadie (Aronowsky) P.; m. Kathryn Schaefler, June 11, 1952; children: Lee S., Richard H. Jr., Pamela P. Hochman, Julia B. BA, Yale U., 1951, LLB, 1956. Bar: N.Y. 1956, U.S. Supreme Ct.1969. Assoc. Davis, Polk & Wardwell, N.Y.C., 1956-60; ptnr. Finch & Schaefler, N.Y.C., 1960-85, LeBoeuf, Lamb, Greene & MacRae, N.Y.C., 1986-94, of counsel, 1995—. Counsel Mcpl. Art Soc., N.Y.C., 1965-70, Fine Arts Fedn., N.Y.C., 1975-80. Served to 1st lt. USAF. Fellow Am. Coll. Trust and Estate Counsel (author, editor, articles and studies 1960—); mem. Assn. of Bar of City of N.Y., Yale Club (N.Y.C.), N.Y. Croquet Club. Democrat. Avocations: indoor rowing, croquet, weightlifting. Estate planning, Probate (including wills, trusts), Estate taxation. Home: 1435 Lexington Ave New York NY 10128-1625 Office: LeBoeuf Lamb Greene & MacRae 125 W 55th St New York NY 10019-5389 E-mail: rpershan@yahoo.com., rpershan@llgm.com.

PERSONS, W. RAY, lawyer, educator; b. Talbottan, Ga., July 22, 1953; s. William and Frances (Crowell) P.; m. Wendy-Joy Mottley, Sept. 24, 1977; children: Conrad Ashley, April Maureen. BS cum laude, Armstrong State Coll., 1975; JD, Ohio State U., 1978. Bar: Ga. 1979, U.S. Dist. Ct. (so. dist.) Ga. 1980, U.S. Dist. Ct. (no. dist.) Ga. 1986, U.S. Ct. Appeals (11th cir.) 1986. Assoc. Troutman, Sanders, Lockerman & Ashmore, Atlanta, 1978-79; atty. Nat. Labor Rels. Bd., Atlanta, 1980-82; legis. counsel U.S Ho. Reps., Washington, 1983-86; atty. Mack & Bernstein, Atlanta, 1986-87; ptnr. Arrington & Hollowell, Atlanta, 1987-95, Swift, Currie, McGhee & Hiers, Atlanta, 1995-99, Hunton and Williams, Atlanta, 1999—2001, King & Spalding, Atlanta, 2001—. Adj. prof. litigation Ga. State U., Atlanta, 1989—; spl. asst. atty. gen. State of Ga., Atlanta, 1988—. Master Am. Inns of Ct. (Lamar chpt.); fellow Am. Coll. Trial Lawyers; mem. ABA, Internat. Soc. Barristers, Am. Bd. Trial Advocates, State Bar Ga., Atlanta Bar Assn., Lawyers Club of Atlanta. Roman Catholic. General civil litigation, Insurance. Office: King & Spalding LLP 191 Peachtree St NE Atlanta GA 30303-1763

PERWIN, JEAN SHAPIRO, lawyer; b. Boston, June 26, 1949; d. Leon Nathan and Rose Selma (Kurhan) S.; m. Joel Stephen Perwin, Aug. 23, 1970; children: Amanda Julia, Samuel Harris. BA, Sarah Lawrence Coll., 1971; JD, Boston Coll., 1975. Bar: Mass. 1975, D.C. 1976, Fla. 1981. Counsel commerce, consumer and monetary affairs subcom. U.S. Ho. Reps., Washington, 1975-78; counsel oversight of govt. mgmt. subcom. U.S. Senate, Washington, 1978-80; counsel Spl. Asst. to Pres. for Consumer Affairs, Washington, 1980-81; assoc. Seiler and Seiler, PA, Miami, Fla., 1982-85, Stuzin and Camner, Miami, 1985-87; pvt. practice Miami, 1987—. Author: (book) Electronic Copyright, 1996; co-author: (book) The Artist's Friendly Legal Guide, 1988. Mem. majority coun. Emily's List, Washington, 1986—. Mem. Internat. Trademark Assn., Fla. Bar (computer law com. 1994—, chair entertainment, arts and sports sect. 1991). Computer, Corporate, general, Intellectual property. Office: 25 SE 2nd Ave Ste 1144 Miami FL 33131-1607

PESHKIN, SAMUEL DAVID, lawyer; b. Des Moines, Oct. 6, 1925; s. Louis and Mary (Grund) P.; m. Shirley R. Isenberg, Aug. 17, 1947; children: Lawrence Allen, Linda Ann. BA, State U. Iowa, 1948, JD, 1951. Bar: Iowa 1951. Ptnr. Bridges & Peshkin, Des Moines, 1953-66, Peshkin & Robinson, Des Moines, 1966-82. Mem. Iowa Bd. Law Examiners, 1970—. Bd. dirs. State U. Iowa Found., 1957—, Old Gold Devel. Fund, 1956—, Sch. Religion U. Iowa, 1966—. Fellow Am. Bar Found., Internat. Soc. Barristers; mem. ABA (chmn. standing com. membership 1959— , ho. of dels. 1968— , bd. govs. 1973—), Iowa Bar Assn. (bd. govs. 1958—, pres. jr. bar sect. 1958-59, award of merit 1974), Inter-Am. Bar Assn., Internat. Bar Assn., Am. Judicature Soc., State U. Iowa Alumni Assn. (dir., pres. 1957) Corporate, general, Private international, Corporate taxation.

PESIKOFF, BETTE SCHEIN, lawyer; b. N.Y.C., Oct. 9, 1942; d. Stephen and Ethel (Barrett) Schein; m. Richard B. Pesikoff, June 7, 1964; children: David, Josh, Daniel. BS, NYU, 1963, MA, 1964; JD, U. Houston, 1974. Bar: Tex. 1974, U.S. Dist. Ct. (so. dist.) Tex. 1975, U.S. Patent and Trademark Office 1995. Tchr. N.Y.C. Bd. Edn., 1964-68; pvt. practice Houston, 1977—. Chmn. social action com. Cong. Emam El, Houston, 1985-87, bd. dirs., sec., 1986-88; mem. community rels. com. Jewish Fedn. Houston, 1986-88; mem. Tex. Supreme Ct. Child Support Guidelines Commn., 1986-87. Fellow Tex. Bar Found.; mem. ABA, Houston Bar Assn. (sec. family law sect. 1986-87), Gulf Coast Family Law Specialists. Democrat. Family and matrimonial, General practice, Intellectual property. Office: 1715 North Blvd Houston TX 77098-5413

PESSANHA, TOMAS VASCONCELOS, lawyer; b. Lisbon, Portugal, Apr. 22, 1972; s. Joao Vasconcelos Pessanha and Maria Cabral Moraes; m. Margarida Pinto Leite, July 4, 1998; children: Margarida, Tomás. Degree, U. Lisbon Law Sch., Portugal, 1995; postgrad., U. Coimbra, Portugal, 1997-98. Trainee Jose Maria Calheiros & Assocs., Lisbon, Portugal, 1995-97, assoc., 1997-2000, PMBGR, Lisbon, Portugal, 2000—01, PLMJ, Porto, Portugal, 2001—03. Author: Legal Implications of the Millenium Bug, 1999. Mem. Ctr. internat. Legal Studies (hon.). Commercial, contracts (including sales of goods; commercial financing), Mergers and acquisitions, Corporate, general. Home: Rua Prof Mota Pinto 197 Porto Portugal Office: Av Boavista 2121 4-407 4100-134 Porto Portugal E-mail: tvp@plmj.pt.

PETER, ANNE-MARIE, lawyer; b. Manheim, Baden-Wüttemberg, Germany, Apr. 20, 1963; d. Klaus Karl Friedrich and Eveline Jeanne André Peter. Diploma, U. Munich, 1987. Bar: Regional Cts. Germany, Regional Ct. Frankfurt/Main, Ct. Appeals Frankfurt/Main. Lawyer Schwarz, Schniewind, Kelwing, Munich, 1987—91, Feddersen, Laule, et al., Frankfurt/Main, Germany, 1992—95, ptnr., 1995—2000, Schulte Lawyers, Frankfurt/Main, 2000—. Mergers and acquisitions, Corporate, general, Commercial, contracts (including sales of goods; commercial financing). Office: Schulte Lawyers Hochstraße 49 60313 Frankfurt Germany Office Fax: (069) 900 26-999. Business E-Mail: schulte@schulte-lawyers.de.

PETER, BERNARD GEORGE, lawyer; b. Balt., July 28, 1949; S. Bernard George and Ella (Galvin) P.; m. Ellen Cherobina Carosselli; children: Kyle, Jared. AB, Coll. Holy Cross; JD, U. Md. Bar: Md. 1969, Ill. 1974. Lawyer, asst. sec. C.F. Industries, Inc., Long Grove, Ill., 1974-78; assoc. gen. counsel Joslyn Corp., Chgo., 1978-80; asst. gen. counsel Marshall Field & Co., Chgo., 1980-84; atty./cons. William M. Mercer Inc., Chgo., 1984-89; atty./sr. cons. Alexander & Alexander Cons. Group, Chgo., 1989-94; atty., sr. cons. Watson Wyatt and Co., Chgo., 1994—. Bd. dirs. John T. Galvin, Inc., Balt., treas., 2000. Contbr. articles to profl. jours. Usher St. Mary's Ch., Lake Forest, 1983—; recruiter high sch. athletes. Mem. Ill. State Bar Assn. (com. mem. sect. coun. corp. law), Chgo. Bar Assn. (vice-chmn. corp. law depts. 1988-90), John Purdue Club. Avocations: Purdue U. sports, swimming, tennis. Corporate, general, Labor (including EEOC, Fair Labor Standards Act, labor-management relations, NLRB, OSHA), Pension, profit-sharing, and employee benefits. Home: 622 Timber Ln Lake Forest IL 60045 Office: Watson Wyatt Co 191 N Wacker Dr Ste 2100 Chicago IL 60606-1615

PETER, PHILLIPS SMITH, lawyer; b. Washington, Jan. 24, 1932; s. Edward Compston and Anita Phillips (Smith) P.; m. Jania Jayne Hutchins, Apr. 8, 1961; children: Phillips Smith Peter Jr., Jania Jayne Hutchins Stone. BA, U. Va., 1954, JD, 1959. Bar: Calif. 1959. Assoc. McCutchen, Doyle, Brown, Enerson, San Francisco, 1959-63; with GE (and subs.), various locations, 1963-94, v.p. corp. bus. devel., 1973-76, v.p., 1976-79, v.p. corp. govtl. rels., 1980-94; counsel, head govt. rels. dept. Reed Smith Shaw & McClay, Washington, 1994—. Chmn. bd. govs. Bryce Harlow Found., 1990-92, bd. dirs. Mem. editl. bd. Va. Law Rev., 1957-59. Trustee Howard U., 1981-89; bd. dirs., exec. com. Nat. Bank of Washington, 1981-86; v.p. Fed. City Coun., Washington, 1979-85; bd. dirs. Carlton, 1987-90, 95-98, pres., 1995-96; bd. dirs. Tudor Place Found., 1999—, v.p., 2001-02, pres., 2002--. With transp. corps U.S. Army, 1954-56. Mem. Calif. Bar Assn., Order of Coif, Wee Burn Club, Ea. Yacht Club, Farmington Country Club, Landmark Club, Congl. Country Club, Georgetown Club, Chevy Chase Club, Carlton Club (bd. dirs. 1990-98), Coral Beach and Tennis Club, Johns Island Club, The Windsor Club, Omicron Delta Kappa. Episcopalian. Home: 10805 Tara Rd Potomac MD 20854-1341 also: Johns Island 1000 Beach Rd & 690 Ocean Vero Beach FL 32963-3429 E-mail: ppeter@reedsmith.com.

PETERKA, ONDREJ, lawyer; b. Prague, Czech Republic, Aug. 2, 1969; s. Josef Peterka and Jana Peterkova; m. Charlotte Thuesen, 1996; children: Christopher, Caroline. Maitrise pvt. law, U of Reims, Reims, France, 1991; DEA internat. pvt. law, Sorbonne U of Paris, Paris, France, 1992; ML, Charles U of Prague, Prague, Czech Republic, 1994; CAPA, School for Attys., Paris, France, 1994. Bar: Paris Bar, France 1995, Czech Bar, Czech Republic 1996. Assoc. Coudert Brothers, Paris, 1992—94, Sokolow, Dunaud, Mercadier & Carreras, Paris, 1994—96, Gide, Loyrette, Nouel, Prague, Czech Republic, 1996—97; ind. atty. GLN, Prague, Czech Republic, 1998—2000; ptnr. Peterka & Leuchterova, Prague, Czech Republic, 2000—01; mng. ptnr. Peterka, Leuchterova & ptnrs., Prague, Czech Republic, 2001—. Avocations: family, history, politics. Mergers and acquisitions, Commercial, contracts (including sales of goods; commercial financing), General civil litigation. Office: Peterka, Leuchterova & ptnrs vos Na Prikope 15 Prague 11000 Czech Republic

PETERS, ELLEN ASH, judge, trial referee, retired state supreme court justice; b. Berlin, Mar. 21, 1930; came to U.S., 1939, naturalized, 1947; d. Ernest Edward and Hildegard (Simon) Ash; m. Phillip I. Blumberg; children: David Bryan Peters, James Douglas Peters, Julie Peters Dreisch. BA with honors, Swarthmore Coll., 1951, LLD (hon.), 1983; LLB cum laude, Yale U., 1954, MA (hon.), 1964, LLD (hon.), 1985, U. Hartford, 1983; LLD (hon.) , Georgetown U., 1984; LLD (hon.), Yale U., 1985, Conn. Coll., 1985, N.Y. Law Sch., 1985; HLD (hon.), St. Joseph Coll., 1986; LLD (hon.), Colgate U., 1986, Trinity Coll., 1987, Bates Coll., 1987, Wesleyan U., 1987, DePaul U., 1988; HLD (hon.), Albertus Magnus Coll., 1990; LLD (hon.), U. Conn., 1992; LLD, U. Rochester, 1994, Detroit Mercy Coll. Law, 2001. Bar: Conn. 1957. Law clk. to judge U.S. Circuit Ct., 1954-55; assoc. in law U. Calif., Berkeley, 1955-56; prof. law Yale U., New Haven, 1956-78, adj. prof. law, 1978-84; assoc. justice Conn. Supreme Ct., Hartford, 1978-84, chief justice, 1984-96; judge trial referee Superior Ct., Hartford, 2000—. Author: Commercial Transactions: Cases, Texts, and Problems, 1971, Negotiable Instruments Primer, 1974; contbr. articles to profl. jours. Bd. dirs. Nat. Ctr. State Cts., 1992—96, chmn., 1994; bd. mgrs. Swarthmore Coll., 1970—81; trustee Yale-New Haven Hosp., 1981—86, Yale Corp., 1986—92; mem. conf. Chief Justices, 1984—, pres., 1994; hon. chmn. U.S. Constl. Bicentennial Com., 1986—91; mem. Conn. Permanent Commn. on Status of Women, 1973—74, Conn. Bd. Pardons, 1978—80, Conn. Law Revision Commn., 1978—84; bd. dirs. Hartford Found., 1997—. Recipient Ella Grasso award, 1982, Jud. award Conn. Trial Lawyers Assn., 1982, citation of merit Yale Law Sch., 1983, Pioneer Woman award Hartford Coll. for Women, 1988, Disting. Svc. award U. Conn. Law Sch. Alumni Assn., 1993, Raymond E. Baldwin Pub. Svc. award Quinnipiac Coll. Law Sch., 1995, Disting. Svc. award Conn. Law Tribune, 1996, Nat. Ctr. State Cts., 1996; named Laura A. Johnson Woman of Yr. Hartford Coll., 1996. Mem. ABA, Conn. Bar Assn. (Jud. award 1992, Spl. award 1996), Am. Law Inst. (coun.), Am. Acad. Arts and Scis., Am. Philos. Soc. Office: Superior Ct 95 Washington St Hartford CT 06106-4431 Fax: 860-548-2887.

PETERS, FREDERICK WHITTEN, lawyer; b. Omaha, Aug. 20, 1946; s. Jordan Holt and Elizabeth (O'Bryant) P.; children: Mary Irvin, Elizabeth Holt, Margaret Etheridge. BA magna cum laude, Harvard U., 1968; MS with distinction, London Sch. Econs., 1973; JD magna cum laude, Harvard U., 1976. Bar: D.C. 1978, U.S. Dist. Ct. D.C. 1978, U.S. Dist. Ct. Md., 1994, U.S. Ct. Appeals (3d and D.C. cirs.) 1979, U.S. Ct. Claims 1981, U.S. Ct. Appeals (11th cir.) 1986, U.S. Ct. Mil. Appeals 1993. Law clk. to Hon. J. Skelly Wright U.S. Ct. Appeals (D.C. cir.), Washington, 1976-77; law clk. to justice William J. Brennan U.S. Supreme Ct., Washington, 1977-78; assoc. Williams & Connolly, Washington, 1978-84, ptnr., 1984-95, 2001—; prin. dep. gen. counsel Dept. of Defense, 1995-97, undersec., acting sec. USAF, 1997-99, sec. USAF, 1999-2001; ptnr. Williams & Connolly LLP, Washington, 2001—. Legal ethics com. DC Bar, 1988-94, chmn. rules rev. com., 1991-96; rules com. US Ct. Mil. Appeals, 1993-95. Pres. Harvard Law Rev., 1975-76. Bd. dirs. Cleveland Park Hist. Soc., Washington, 1986-91, 2001-02, Washington Area Lawyers for the Arts, 1987-93, Air Force Enlisted Found., 2001—, Air Force Aid Soc., 2002—; adv. com. on streamlining procurement laws DOD, 1991-93, vice chmn. adv. com. on future of US aerospace industry, 2001-2002. Lt. USNR, 1969-72. Fellow Am. Bar Found.; mem. ABA. Democrat. Episcopalian. Avocations: sailing, computer science, golf. Federal civil litigation, Computer, Criminal. Home: 735 S Union St Alexandria VA 22314-3889 Office: Williams & Connolly 725 12th St NW Washington DC 20005 E-mail: secaf19@aol.com., wpeters@wc.com.

PETERS, JOHN DOUGLAS, lawyer, artist; b. Dover, N.H., Jan. 23, 1948; s. John Philip Peters, Helen Irene Hurst; m. Christine K. Consales, June 23, 1973. BA, U. N.H., 1971; JD, U. Toledo, 1975. Exec. dir. PSRO 4th Ohio Area PSR Coun., Toledo, 1974—75; shareholder Charfoos & Christensen, P.C., Detroit, 1975—. Legal dir. Mich. Med. Schs. Coun. of Deans, Ann Arbor, 1978—80; lectr. law U. Toledo, 1978—88; assoc. prof. Sch. Medicine Wayne State U., Detroit, 1978—; cons. Georgetown U. Inst. for Health Policy, Washington, 1989, Office of Tech. Assessment, Washington, 1992—96, Robert Wood Johnson Found., Washington, 1994—98. Author: (book) Anesthesiology and the Law, 1983, Obstetrics/Gynecology and the Law, 1984, The Law of Medical Practice in Pennsylvania and New Jersey, 1984, Social Security Disability Claims, 2002, The Law of Medical Practice in Michigan, 1981; editor: Legal and Ethical Aspects of Treating Terminally Ill Patients, 1982; contbr. articles to profl. jours. Bd. dirs. Am. Lung Assn., Detroit, 1978—83, Vis. Nurse Assn., Detroit, 1987—96, Preservation Wayne, 1992—. Avocations: Persian textiles, folk art, collecting and studying antiquities. Drug and Medical Device Litigation, Complex Litigation, Personal injury (including property damage). Office: Charfoos and Christensen PC 5510 Woodward Ave Detroit MI 48202

PETERS, LEE IRA, JR., public defender; b. Jamestown, N.Y., Dec. 17, 1946; s. Lee Ira and Carrie Irene (Roberson) P.; m. Mabel Luisa Thompson, June 21, 1969; children: Tammy M., Lee III, Ryan J. BA in Criminology, Fla. State U., 1971; JD, U. Fla., 1984. Bar: Fla. 1984, U.S. Dist Ct. (mid. dist.) Fla. 1989. Sr. intern Pub. Defender State of Fla., Gainesville, Fla., 1983; spl. asst. U.S. Atty No. Dist. Fla., Tallahassee, 1987-89; asst. states atty. 3d cir. State's Atty. Office, Live Oak, Fla., 1984-89; asst. pub. defender, felony divsn. chief 3rd cir. Pub. Defender's Office, Live Oak, 1989—. Spl. agt. crim. investigation Bur. ATF- U.S. Treas., Anniston, Ala., Boise, Idaho, 1971-77, resident agt.-in-charge Portland, Oreg., 1977-81; assoc. counsel (pro bono) Nat. Assn. Treas. Agts., 1993—. With USN, 1965-67, Vietnam, U.S. Army Res., 1981-95. Recipient Disting Svc. award Fla. Coun. Crime & Delinquency, Chpt. XV, 1989; Meritorious Svc. Sec. Army U.S., 1997. Mem. ACLU, Fla. Assn. Criminal Def. Lawyers, Fla. Bar Assn. (3d cir. grievance com. 1993-96), Acad. Fla. Trial Lawyers, 3d Cir. Bar Assn., Am. Legion (fin. officer post 107, Live Oak), McAlpin Comty. Club (pres. 1990-96), Rotary Club, Elks, Phi Alpha Delta. Avocation: cattle and arabian horse raising. Office: Third Cir Pub Defender 106 Ohio Ave S Live Oak FL 32064-3212 E-mail: pd3liveoak@hotmail.com.

PETERS, R. JONATHAN, lawyer, manufacturing company executive; b. Janesville, Wis., Jan. 6, 1927; m. Ingrid H. Varvayn, 1953; 1 dau., Christina. BS in Chemistry, U. Ill., 1951; JD, Northwestern U., 1954. Bar: Ill. 1954. Chief patent counsel Englehard Industries, 1972-82, Kimberly-Clark Corp., Neenah, Wis., 1982-85; gen. counsel Lanxide Corp., Newark, Del., 1985-87; pvt. practice Chgo., 1985—. Served with CIC, U.S. Army, 1955-57. Patentee in field. Mem. ABA, Am. Intellectual Property Law Assn., Lic. Execs. Soc., Assn. Corp. Patent Counsel, North Shore Golf (Menasha, Wis.), Masons, Scottish Rite, Shriners. Patent, Trademark and copyright.

PETERS, ROBERT TIMOTHY, judge; b. Memphis, Dec. 28, 1946; s. Rhulin Earl and Bertie Nichols (Moore) P.; m. Ruth Audrey Allen, Dec. 11, 1973; children: Lindsay Elizabeth, Christopher Andrew. AA, St. Petersburg Jr. Coll., 1969; BA, U. Fla., 1971, JD, 1973. Bar: Fla. 1973, U.S. Dist. Ct. (mid. dist.) Fla. 1977, U.S. Ct. Appeals (5th cir.) 1981; cert. real estate lawyer. Ptnr. Goza, Hall & Peters P.A., Clearwater, Fla., 1973-84; sole practice Clearwater, 1984-95; apptd. cir. judge, 1995—. Gov. Fla.'s appointee Condominium Study Commsn., Clearwater, 1990-91. Columnist Clearwater Sun newspaper, 1985—. 1st Lt. U.S. Army, 1966-68, Vietnam. Decorated Silver Star, Purple Heart, Bronze Star with oak leaf cluster. Avocations: reading, exercise. Office: Criminal Justice Ctr 14250 49th St N Clearwater FL 33762 Address: PO Box 6316 Clearwater FL 33758-6316

PETERSEN, BENTON LAURITZ, paralegal; b. Salt Lake City, Jan. 1, 1942; s. Lauritz George and Arleane (Curtis) P.; m. Sharon Donnette Higgins, Sept. 20, 1974 (div. Aug. 9, 1989); children: Grant Lauritz, Tashya Eileen, Nicholas Robert, Katrina Arleane. AA, Weber State Coll., 1966, BA, BA, Weber State Coll., 1968; M of Liberal Studies, U. Okla., 1980; diploma, Nat. Radio Inst. Paralegal Sch., 1991; JD, Monticello U., 1999. Registered paralegal. Announcer/news dir. KWHO Radio, Salt Lake City, 1968-70, KDXU Radio, St. George, Utah, 1970-73, KSOP Radio, Salt Lake City, 1973-76; case worker/counselor Salvation Army, Midland, Tex., 1976-84; announcer/news dir. KBRS Radio, Springdale, Ark., 1984-86; case worker/counselor Office of Human Concern, Rogers, Ark., 1986-88; announcer KAZM Radio, Sedona, Ariz., 1988-91; paralegal Benton L. Petersen, Manti, Utah, 1991—. Cons. Sanpete County Srs., Manti, 1992—. Award judge Manti City Beautification, 1992-96; treas. Manti Destiny Com., 1993-98; tourism com. Sanpete County Econ. Devel., Ephraim, Utah, 1993-96. Served with U.S. Army N.G., 1959-66. Mem. Nat. Assn. Attys. in Fact (past pres.). Mem. Lds Ch. Avocation: reading. Home: 470 E 120 N Manti UT 84642-1164 E-mail: bpfreedom@hotmail.com.

PETERSEN, CATHERINE HOLLAND, lawyer; b. Norman, Okla., Apr. 24, 1951; d. John Hays and Helen Ann (Turner) Holland; m. James Frederick Petersen, June 26, 1973 (div.); children: T. Kyle, Lindsay Diane. BA, Hastings Coll., 1973; JD, Okla. U., 1976. Bar: Okla. 1976, U.s. Dist. Ct. (we. dist.) Okla. 1978. Legal intern, police legal advisor City of Norman, 1974-76; sole practice Norman, 1976-81; ptnr. Williams Petersen & Denny, Norman, 1981-82; pres. Petersen Assocs., Inc., Norman, 1982—. Adj. prof. Oklahoma City U. Coll. Law, 1982, U. Okla. Law Ctr., 1987; instr. continuing legal edn. U. Okla. Law Ctr., Norman, 1977, 79, 81, 83, 84, 86, 89-95; instr. Okla. Bar Assn., ABA, Am. Acad. Matrimonial Lawyers. Bd. dirs. United way, Norman, 1978-84, pres., 1981; bd. dirs. Women's Resource Ctr., Norman, 1975-77, 82-84; mem. Jr. League, Norman, 1980-83, Norman Hosp. Ayx., 1982-84; trustee 1st Presbyn. Ch., 1986-87. Named to Outstanding Okla. Women of 1980s, Women's Polit. Caucus, 1980, Outstanding Young Women of Am., 1981, 83. Fellow Am. Acad. Matrimonial Lawyers (pres. Okla. chpt. 1990-91, bd. govs. 1991-95); mem.

ABA (family law sect.), Cleveland County Bar Assn., Okla. Bar Assn. (chmn. family law sect. 1987-88), Phi Delta Phi. Republican. Family and matrimonial. Home: 4716 Sundance Ct Norman OK 73072-3900 Office: PO Box 1243 314 E Comanche St Norman OK 73069-6009

PETERSEN, DAVID L. lawyer; AA, Concordia Jr. Coll., Milw., 1963; BA, Concordia Sr. Coll., Ft. Wayne, Ind., 1965; JD, Valparaiso U., Ind., 1968. Bar: Wis. 1968, U.S. Dist. Ct. (ea. dist.) Wis. 1969, U.S. Ct. Appeals (7th cir.) 1972, U.S. Supreme Ct. 1988, Fla. 1989. Ptnr. Quarles & Brady, Milw. and Naples, Fla., 1968—. Author: Wisconsin Condominium Law, 1988, 98; editor Valparaiso U. Law Rev., 1967-68; contbr. articles to profl. jours. Mem. Greater Milw. Com. Cmty. Devel., 1983; bd. dirs. Goals for Greater Milw. 2000, 1982, Broward Com. of 100; mem. nat. adv. bd. Nat. Ctr. for Missing and Exploited Children, Washington, Adam Walsh Children's Fund, Palm Beach, Fla.; dir. Boys and Girls Club Collier County. Lt. col., instr. pilot USAF/Wis. Air N.G., 1970-90. Mem. ABA, Wis. Bar Assn., Milw. Bar Assn., Fla Bar Assn., Broward County Bar Assn., Palm Beach County Bar Assn., Collier County Bar Assn., Wis. Mortgage Bankers Assn., Am. Coll. Real Estate Lawyers, Milw. Yacht Club, Palm Beach Yacht Club. Banking, Finance, Property, real (including real estate development, water). Office: Quarles & Brady LLP 4501 Tamiami Trail N Naples FL 34103-3060 also: Quarles & Brady LLP 411 E Wisconsin Ave Ste 2550 Milwaukee WI 53202-4409 E-mail: dlp@quarles.com.

PETERSEN, DONALD SONDERGAARD, lawyer; b. Pontiac, Ill., May 14, 1929; s. Clarence Marius and Esther (Sondergaard) P.; m. Alice Thorup, June 5, 1954; children: Stephen, Susan Petersen Schuh, Sally Petersen Riordan. Student, Grand View Coll., 1946-48; BA, Augustana Coll., Rock Island, Ill., 1951; JD, Northwestern U., 1956. Bar: Ill. 1957. Assoc. Norman & Billick and predecessors, Chgo., 1956-64, ptnr., 1965-78; counsel Sidley & Austin, Chgo., 1978-80, ptnr., 1980-93, ret., 1993. Pres. Chgo. Exhibitors Corp., Chgo., 1972-85. Bd. dirs. Mount Olive Cemetery Co. Inc., Chgo., 1972-90; bd. dirs. Augustana Hosp., 1983-87, Danish Old People's Home, 1976—; bd. dirs. Luth. Gen. Hosp., Park Ridge, Ill., 1968—, chmn., 1979-81, 89-91; bd. dirs. Luth. Gen. Health System and predecessors, Park Ridge, 1980-95, chmn., 1980-81, 83-85; bd. dirs., chmn. Parkside Health Mgmt. Corp., Parkside Home Health Svcs., 1985-88. With U.S. Army, 1951-53. Mem. Chgo. Bar Assn., Ill. State Bar Assn. Clubs: Union League (Chgo.). Home: 241 N Aldine Ave Park Ridge IL 60068-3009 Office: 55 W Monroe St Ste 2000 Chicago IL 60603-5008

PETERSEN, JAMES L. lawyer; b. Bloomington, Ill., Feb. 3, 1947; s. Eugene and Cathryn Theresa (Hemmele) P.; m. Helen Louise Moser, Nov. 20, 1971; children: Christine Louise, Margaret Theresa. BA, Ill. State U., 1970; MA, U. Ill., Springfield, 1973; JD magna cum laude, Ind. U., 1976. Bar; Ind. 1976, Fla. 1980, U.S. Dist. Cts. (no. and so. Ind.), U.S. Ct. Appeals (7th cir.), U.S. Supreme Ct. Admissions officer U. Ill., Springfield, 1970-71, asst. to v.p., 1971-72, registrar, 1972-73; assoc. Ice Miller, Indpls., 1976-83, ptnr., 1983—. Pres. United Cerebral Palsy of Ctrl. Ind., 1981-83, pres. Found., 1988-90. Mem. ABA, Fla. Bar Assn., Ind. Bar Assn., Internat. Assn. Def. Counsel, Ill. State U. Alumni Assn. (pres. 1990-92), Ind. U. Law Alumni Assn. (bd. dirs. 1992—, pres. 1998-99), Order of Coif. General civil litigation, Franchising, Product liability. Home: 11827 Sea Star Dr Indianapolis IN 46256-9400 Office: Ice Miller PO Box 82001 One American Sq Indianapolis IN 46282

PETERSEN, MICHAEL JOHN, lawyer; BA, U. No. Colo., 1976, MSBA, 1979; MA, U. Ala., 1994; JD, Jones Sch. Law, Montgomery, Ala., 1998. Bar: Ala. 1999, U.S. Dist. Ct. (ea. dist.) Ala. 1999, U.S. Ct. Appeals (11th cir.) 1999. Commd. 2d lt. USAF, 1979, advanced through grade to maj., ICBM ops., 1979—84, computer ops. Offutt AFB, Nebr., 1984—88, airborne ops. plans, 1988—92; doctrine analyst USAF Air U., Maxwell AFB, Ala., 1992—95, asst. editor Air Power Jour., 1995—96, sr. editor, 1996—98, editor, 1998—99; pvt. practice law Montgomery, 1999—. Editor: (book) Cumulative Index - Air Power Journal, 1998. Mem.: ABA, Ala. Criminal Def. Lawyers Assn., Fed. Bar Assn. Criminal, Family and matrimonial, Juvenile. Office: 631 S Perry St Montgomery AL 36104 Personal E-mail: attymike@directvinternet.com.

PETERSEN, WILLIAM OTTO, lawyer; b. Chgo., Nov. 28, 1926; s. William Ferdinand and Alma Schmidt P.; m. Jane Browne, Nov. 25, 1978. AB cum laude, Harvard U., 1949, LLB, 1952. Bar: Ill., 1952. Atty. No. Trust. Co., Chgo., 1952-55; ptnr. Vedder, Price, Kaufman & Kamholz, Chgo., 1955-2001, of counsel, 2001—. Mem. exec. bd. Ct. Theatre, 1992-97; mem. vis. to U. Chgo. Libr., 1992—; bd. dirs. Chgo. Youth Ctrs., 1958—, pres., 1971, 72; bd. dirs., v.p. Luther I. Replogle Found., Chgo. and Washington, 1986—. With USN, 1944-46. Mem. ABA, Ill. State Bar Assn., Chgo. Bar Assn. (chmn. corp. law com. 1976), Racquet Club of Chgo. (pres. 1981, 82), Univ. Club, Lake Geneva (Wis.) Country Club, Lake Geneva Yacht Club, Caxton Club. Lutheran. Home: 1120 N Lake Shore Dr Chicago IL 60611-1036

PETERSON, CHARLES GORDON, retired lawyer; b. Lansing, Mich., May 21, 1926; s. Russell V. and Edna E. (Jones) P.; m. Clara Elizabeth Parmelee, Mar. 8, 1947; children— Wendy, Pamela, Christopher BS, Columbia U. Sch. Gen. Studies, 1954; LL.B., Columbia U. Sch. Law, 1956. Bar: N.Y., 1957. Legal assoc. Beekman & Bogue, N.Y.C., 1956-67; mem. Gaston & Snow, N.Y.C., 1967-91; of counsel Reid & Priest, N.Y.C., 1991-93; ret., 1993. Trustee The Riverside Ch., N.Y.C., 1968-80, 82-89, mem. bd. deacons, 1960-68; pres. Lincoln Guild Housing Corp., N.Y.C., 1961-62, 84-87, v.p., 1987-89, 94-96, bd. dirs., 1961-62, 84-89, 94-96. Mem. Phi Beta Kappa. Republican. Mem. United Ch. of Christ. Avocations: piano, reading, travel. Home: 303 W 66th St Apt 20ee New York NY 10023-6330

PETERSON, DAVID ROBERT, lawyer, former Canadian government official; b. Toronto, Dec. 28, 1943; s. Clarence and Laura Marie (Scott) P.; m. Shelley Peterson, Jan. 16, 1974; children: Benjamin David, Chloe Matthews, Adam Drake Scott BA, U. Western Ont., 1964; LLB, U. Toronto, 1967; LLD (hon.), U. Ottawa, Am. U. of Caribbean, U. Tel Aviv, U. Toronto. Bar: Ont. 1969, Queens counsel 1981. Chmn., pres. C.M. Peterson Co. Ltd., 1969-75, Cambridge Acceptance Corp., 1969-75; M.P. Ontario Parliament, Can., 1975—; leader Ont. Liberal Party, 1982; premier Province of Ont., 1985-90; chmn. Cassels Brock & Blackwell LLP, Toronto, 1991—. Bd. dirs. Rogers Comms., Ltd., Nat. Life Assurance Co., Industrielle-Alliance Life Assurance Co., BNP Paribas (Can.), SMK Speedy Inc., Franc-Nev. Mining Corp. Ltd., Rogers AT&T Wireless, others; founding chmn. Chpts. Inc., Cassels-Pouiliot Noriega; mem. strategic adv. bd. Xerox Can. Inc. Leader of the official opposition party, Liberal Party, Ont., 1982-85; dir. Legal Svcs., Yorkville; mem. Kidney Found. Can., Ont., Cystic Fibrosis Found. Fellow McLaughlin Coll., 1985; appointed Knight of Order of Legion of Honor, Govt. France, 1994; recipient Ordre de la Pléiade, Internat. Assembly French-Speaking Parliamentarians, 1995. Mem. Law Soc. U.C., Young Pres. Orgn., London C. of C., London Hunt Country Club, London Racquets Club, Can. Club, Toronto Raptors Basketball Club Inc. (foundg chmn.). Mem. United Ch. Christ. Avocations: theatre, riding, jogging, skiing, tennis. Office: Cassels Brock Blackwell LLP 40 King St W Ste 2100 Toronto ON Canada M5H 3C2

PETERSON, EDWARD ADRIAN, lawyer; b. St. Louis, May 19, 1941; s. Adrian J. and Virginia (Hamlin) P.; m. Catherine Frances Younghouse, Dec. 17, 1960; children: Kristin, Kendra. BSBA, Washington U., St. Louis, 1963; LLB, So. Methodist U., 1966. Bar: Tex. 1966, U.S. Dist. Ct. (no. and so. dists.) Tex. Instr. bus. law and acctg. Midwestern U., Wichita Falls, Tex., 1966-67; assoc. Schenk & Wesbrooks, Wichita Falls, 1966-67, Newman & Pickering, Dallas, 1967-72; ptnr. Moore & Peterson, Dallas, 1972-89, Winstead Sechrest & Minick P.C., Dallas, 1989—. Speaker in field. Contbr. articles to legal jours. Bd. dirs. Leukemia Soc., 1970-71, North Tex. Commn., 1992-96, South Dallas/Fair Park Trust Fund, 1992, Tex. Ch. Extension Fund, Tex. Dist., Tex. Dist. Luth. Ch. Mo. Synod. Fellow Tex. Bar Found. (life), Coll. State Bar Tex.; mem. ABA, Am. Coll. Real Estate Lawyers (title ins. com.), State Bar Tex., Tex. Coll. Real Estate Attys., Dallas Bar Assn., Phi Alpha Delta, Sigma Alpha Epsilon. Lutheran. Banking, Corporate, general, Property, real (including real estate development, water). Home: Ste 617 2808 McKinney Ave Dallas TX 75204-2562 also: 131 Hilton Head Island Dr Mabank TX 75147-9325 Office: Winstead Sechrest & Minick PC 5400 Renaissance Tower 1201 Elm St Dallas TX 75270-2199 E-mail: epeterson@winstead.com.

PETERSON, EDWIN J. retired judge, mediator, law educator; b. Gilmanton, Wis., Mar. 30, 1930; s. Edwin A. and Leora Grace (Kitelinger) P.; m. Anna Chadwick, Feb. 7, 1971; children: Patricia, Andrew, Sherry. BS, U. Oreg., 1951, LL.B., 1957. Bar: Oreg. 1957. Assoc. firm Tooze, Kerr, Peterson, Marshall & Shenker, Portland, 1957-61, mem. firm, 1961-79; assoc. justice Supreme Ct. Oreg., Salem, 1979-83, 91-93, chief justice, 1983-91; ret., 1993; disting. jurist-in-residence, adj. instr. Willamette Coll. of Law, Salem, Oreg., 1994—. Chmn. Supreme Ct. Task Force on Racial Issues, 1992-94; standing com. on fed. rules of practice and procedure, 1987-93; bd. dirs. Conf. Chief Justices, 1985-87, 88-91. Chmn. Portland Citizens Sch. Com., 1968-70; vice-chmn. Young Republican Fedn. Orgn., 1951; bd. visitors U. Oreg. Law Sch., 1978-83, 87-93, chmn. bd. visitors, 1981-83; pres., bd. dirs. Understanding Racism Found., 1999-2002. 1st lt. USAF, 1952-54. Mem. Oreg. State Bar (bd. examiners 1963-66, gov. 1973-76, vice chmn. profl. liability fund 1977-78), Multnomah County Bar Assn. (pres. 1972-73), Phi Alpha Delta, Lambda Chi Alpha. Episcopalian. Home: 3365 Sunridge Dr S Salem OR 97302-5950 Office: Willamette Univ Coll Law 245 Winter St SE Salem OR 97301-3916 E-mail: epeterso@willamette.edu.

PETERSON, ERIC H. lawyer, energy executive; m. Tonya Peterson; 2 children. BA, JD, So. Meth. U. Ptnr. Worsham Forsythe & Wooldridge; sr. v.p., gen. counsel DTE Energy, Mich.; exec. v.p., gen. counsel TXU, Dallas, 2002—. Presbyterian. Office: TXU Energy Plz 1601 Bryan St Dallas TX 75201*

PETERSON, FRANKLIN DELANO, lawyer; b. Braham, Minn., Nov. 11, 1932; s. John Erick and Myrtle M. (Anderson) P.; m. Beverly Ann Crabb, Aug. 2, 1958; children: Heidi, Durward, Heather. Student, Augsburg Coll., 1950-51; BA, St. Cloud State Coll., 1955; LLB, William Mitchell Coll. Law, 1961. Bar: Minn. 1961. Field claims adjuster Farmers Mut. Ins. Co., St. Paul, 1955-57; asst. dist. claims mgr. Minn. Farmers Ins. Group, Mpls., 1957-62; sole practice Kenyon, Minn., 1963—. Atty. City of Kenyon, 1964-82; v.p. Kenyon Devel. Corp., bd. dirs.; sec. Tri-Valley Constrn. Co., Kenyon, bd. dirs. Chmn. Goldwater for Pres. campaign, Village of Kenyon Reps., 1964, Goodhue County LeVander for Gov., 1966, Goodhue County Reps, 1969-70; sec. Goodhue Selective Service Bd., 1968—; pres. Mineral Springs Chem. Dependency Ctr., 1974-85; mem. Kenyon Pub. Sch. Bd. Edn., 1976-82, treas. 1980-82, Kenyon Booster Club (charter), v.p. 1983; mgr. mgr. Kenyon Legion Baseball, 1979—; bd. dirs. Kenyon Roseview Apts., 1967—, pres. 1985—. Served with USAF, 1950-52. Mem. ABA, Minn. Bar Assn. (jud. dist. del., pres. 1st dist. 1979-80), Goodhue County Bar Assn., Minn. Assn. Plaintiffs Attys., Nat. Assn. Claimants Counsel, Sons of Norway (pres. Kenyon lodge 1969), Kenyon Comml. Club, Kenyon Country Club (pres. Osman Shrine Clowns 1993), Masons, Shriners, Lions (pres. Kenyon chpt.), royal Order Jesters, Ct. of St. Paul and Shriner Clowns. Lutheran. Estate planning, General practice, Probate (including wills, trusts). Home: RR Box B Kenyon MN 55946 Office: 634 2nd St Kenyon MN 55946-1334

PETERSON, H. DALE, lawyer; b. Amherst, Wis., Jan. 4, 1951; s. Harold C. and Eva I. (Hansen) P.; m. Julie A. Goplin, Jan. 1, 1995; children: Matt, David, Alex, Ellen. BS with honors, U. Wis., Stevens Point, 1973; JD cum laude, U. Wis., 1978. Bar: U.S. Dist. Ct. (we. dist.) Wis., U.S. Ct. Appeals (7th cir.) Wis. Rsch. analyst U.S. Dept. Justice, Washington, 1973-75; ptnr. Stroud, Willink & Howard, LLC, Madison, Wis., 1978—. Dir. Wis. Farm Bur. Svc. Bd., Inc., Madison, 1994—. Co-author: Contract Law in Wisconsin, 1995. Mem. Dane County Bar Assn. (dir./treas. 1987-91). General civil litigation, Commercial, contracts (including sales of goods; commercial financing), Corporate, general. Office: Stroud Willink & Howard LLC PO Box 2236 Madison WI 53701-2236

PETERSON, HOWARD COOPER, lawyer, accountant; b. Decatur, Ill., Dec. 12, 1939; s. Howard and Lorraine (Cooper) P. BEE, Ill., 1963; MEE, San Diego Sate Coll., 1967; MBA, Columbia U., 1969; JD, Calif. Western Sch. Law, 1983; LLM in Taxation, NYU, 1985. Bar: Calif.; CFP; CPA, Tex.; registered profl. engr., Calif.; cert. neuro-linguistic profl. Elec. engr. Convair divsn. Gen. Dynamics Corp., San Diego, 1963-67, sr. electronics engr., 1967-68; v.p., dirl Equity Programs Corp., San Diego, 1973-83; gen. ptrn. Costumes Characters & Classics Co., San Diego, 1979-86; pres., dir. Coastal Properties Trust, San Diego, 1979-89, Juno Securities, Inc., 1983-96, Juno Real Estate Inc., 1974—, Juno Fin. Svcs., Inc., 1999—, Scripps Mortgage Corp., 1987-90, Juno Transport Inc., 1988-89. CFO, dir. Imperial Screens of San Diego, 1977-96, Heritage Transp. Mgmt. Inc., 1989-91, A.S.A.P. Ins. Svcs. Inc., 1983-85. Mem.: ABA, Am. Assn. Atty.-CPAs, Assn. Enrolled Agts., Internat. Assn. Fin. Planning, Interam. Bar Assn. Estate planning, Property, real (including real estate development, water), Taxation, general.

PETERSON, JAN ERIC, lawyer; b. Seattle, Apr. 28, 1944; s. Theodore Dare and Dorothy Elizabeth (Spofford) P.; children: Nels Andrew, Anne Elizabeth; m. Marguerite Victoria Caggiano, Mar. 31, 1984. AB in History, Stanford U., 1966; JD, U. Wash., 1969. Bar: Wash. 1969, U.S. Dist. Ct. (we. and ea. dists.) Wash. 1970, U.S. Ct. Appeals (9th cir.) 1970. Gen. counsel ACLU, Seattle, 1969-71; assoc. Daniel F. Sullivan, Seattle, 1972-73; sr. ptnr. Peterson, Young, Putra, Fletcher, Zeder, Massong & Knopp, Seattle, 1973—. Mem. Wash. State Salary Commn., 2002—. Drafter (state statute) Tap Water Regulation Act, 1983. Fellow Am. Coll. Trial Lawyers; mem. ABA (editor assoc. 1976-78), Damages Attys. Round Table (founding, pres. 1997-98), ATLA (del. 1985-86), Wash. State Trial Lawyers Assn. (bd. 1973-85, pres. 1982-83, Trial Lawyer of Yr. 1999), Wash. State Bar Assn. (jud. selection 1985-87, bd. govs. 1992-95, pres. 2000-01), Am. Bd. Trial Adv. (diplomate, pres. Wash. chpt. 1990), ACLU, Bd. Legal Found. Wash. Democrat. Avocations: piano, baseball, basketball, golf. Personal injury (including property damage), Product liability, Professional liability. Office: Peterson Young Putra Fletcher Zeder Massong & Knopp 1501 4th Ave Ste 2800 Seattle WA 98101-1609 E-mail: janeric@pypfirm.com.

PETERSON, LINDA S. lawyer; b. Grand Forks, N.D., Mar. 15, 1952; BA summa cum laude, U. N.D., 1973; JD, Yale U., 1977. Bar: N.D. 1977, D.C. 1978, U.S. Dist. Ct. D.C. 1979, U.S. Ct. Appeals (D.C. cir.) 1979, U.S. Ct. Appeals (3d cir.) 1982, Calif. 1986, U.S. Ct. Appeals (fed. cir.) 1986. Law clk. Ct. of Appeals for D.C., Washington, 1977-78; ptnr. Sidley & Austin, L.A., 1978—. Dep. counsel Webster Commn., 1992; mem. bd. trustees Southwestern U. Sch. Law, 1995. Recipient Dean Phillips Memorial Award, Vietnam Veterans of America. Mem. State Bar Calif. (rules of ct. com. 1988-91), L.A. County Bar Assn. (conf. dels. 1987-90), Women Lawyers Assn. L.A. (bd. dirs. 1989-95), Phi Beta Kappa. General civil litigation. Office: Sidley & Austin 555 W 5th St Ste 4000 Los Angeles CA 90013-3000

PETERSON, MARK BRADLEY, lawyer; b. Mpls., Aug. 16, 1957; s. C. Donald and Gretchen Elaine (Palen) P.; m. Teresa Mahoney, Apr. 21, 1990; children: Stephen James, John Donald, David Michael. BA magna cum laude, St. Olaf Coll., 1979; JD, U. Minn., 1982. Bar: Minn. 1982, U.S. Dist. Ct. Minn. 1983, U.S. Ct. Appeals (8th cir.) 1991, U.S. Supreme Ct. 1992. Law clk. Hennepin County Dist. Ct., Mpls., 1982-83; assoc. Popham, Haik, Schnobrich & Kaufman, Ltd., Mpls., 1983—95; shareholder Plunkett, Schwartz, Peterson, P.A., 1995-2000, Moss & Barnett, P.A., Mpls., 2000—; adjunct prof. William Mitchell Coll. Law, 1994-95. Deacon Christ Presbyn. Ch., Edina, Minn., 1988-91, elder, 1993-97; bd. dirs. Cystic Fibrosis Found., Mpls., 1991-96; mem. Minn. Internat. Ctr., Mpls.; mem. Hennepin County Vol. Lawyers Network, 1994-98; bd. dirs. Southdale YMCA, 1999—. Mem. ABA, Minn. Bar Assn., Hennepin County Bar Assn., Golden Key, Phi Beta Kappa. Avocations: skiing, sailing, golf. Commercial, contracts (including sales of goods; commercial financing), Corporate, general, Securities. Office: Moss & Barnett PA 4800 Wells Fargo Ctr Minneapolis MN 55402-4129 Fax: (612) 339-6686. E-mail: Petersonm@moss-barnett.com.

PETERSON, OSLER LEOPOLD, lawyer; b. Mpls., Oct. 19, 1946; s. Osler Luther and Delores (Kealy) P.; m. Sandra Ann Freeto, Jan. 2, 1971 (div. Dec. 1983); m. Deborah Jean Bero, July 30, 1989. BA, Brown U., 1969; JD cum laude, Suffolk U., 1976. Bar: Mass. 1976, U.S. Dist. Ct. Mass. 1976. Pvt. practice, Newton, Mass., 1976-84; ptnr. Freeto, Peterson & Scoll, Newton, 1984—. Bd. mem. Riverside Cmty. Care (formerly Neww Ctr., Inc.), 1976-96, clk., 1978-84, pres., 1984-89; bd. mem. Lasell Coll. (formerly Lasell Jr. Coll.), 1983-97, 98—, clk., 1984-91; bd. mem. Lasell Village, Inc., 1990-2000, 2001-, chmn., 1992-2000; bd. mem. Medfield Zoning Bd. Appeals, 1993-2000;, Beth Israel Deaconess Hosp.-Needham Campus, 2001—; selectman Town of Medfield, 2000—, chair, 2002—. Mem. ABA, ATLA, Mass. Bar Assn., Mass. Conveyancers Assn. General civil litigation, Personal injury (including property damage), Property, real (including real estate development, water). Home: 10 Copperwood Rd Medfield MA 02052-1034 Office: Freeto Peterson & Scoll 580 Washington St Newton MA 02458-1416 also: 66 North St PO Box 358 Medfield MA 02052-0358 E-mail: osler.peterson@verizon.net.

PETERSON, PAUL AMES, lawyer, educator; b. Los Angeles, Feb. 17, 1928; s. Ames and Norma (Brown) P.; m. Cynthia Peterson, June 21, 1953 (div.); children: Daniel C., Andrew G., Matthew A., James F.; m. Barbara J. Henderson, Sept. 12, 1976. BS in Econs., U. Calif., Berkeley, 1953, JD, 1956. Bar: Calif. 1956, U.S. Ct. Appeals (9th cir.) 1956, U.S. Supreme Ct. 1964. Assoc. Peterson & Price, San Diego, 1958—. Assoc. prof. Calif. Western Coll. Law, San Diego, 1960—63, U. San Diego Law Sch. , 1958—60, U. Calif., San Diego, 1984—87, chmn. bd. overseers, 1994—, chmn., 2000—02; bd. trustees U. Calif. Found., San Diego, 1988—2002; bd. dirs. Children's Advocacy Inst., San Diego Regional Airport Authority, 2002—. Contbr. articles to profl jours. Bd. dirs. San Diego Conv. Ctr. Corp., 1985—90; mem. San Diego County Regional Airport Authority, 2002—; bd. dirs. San Diego Stadium Authority, 1964—72, San Diego County Water Authority, 1984—90, San Diego Regional Govt. Efficiency Commn., 2001—02. Fellow Am. Judicature Soc.; mem. State Bar of Calif., Phi Beta Kappa, Order of Coif. Democrat. Avocation: hiking. Administrative and regulatory, Environmental, Property, real (including real estate development, water). Home: 7020 Neptune Pl La Jolla CA 92037-5328 Office: Peterson & Price 7979 Ivanhoe Ave Ste 520 La Jolla CA 92037-4513 E-mail: ppeterson@price-entities.com.

PETERSON, RANDALL THEODORE, law educator and librarian; b. Sioux City, Iowa, Aug. 27, 1944; s. Theodore Melvin and Ileann Grace (Wendrich) P.; m. Judith Ashcroft, Aug. 24, 1967; children— Kristin, Randall, Heidi, Travis, Robert, Quinn. Student Dixie Coll., 1962-63; BS, Brigham Young U., 1968, MLS, 1974; JD, U. Utah, 1972. Asst. law librarian Brigham Young U., Provo, Utah, 1972-74, assoc. law librarian, 1974-77; asst. prof. law , dir. libr. svcs. John Marshall Law Sch., Chgo., 1977-86, assoc. prof., , 1986—, dir. libr. svcs., 1986-90. Mem. ABA. Mormon. Office: John Marshall Law Sch 315 S Plymouth Ct Chicago IL 60604-3968 E-mail: 7rtp@jmls.edu.

PETERSON, RICHARD WILLIAM, retired judge, lawyer; b. Council Bluffs, Iowa, Sept. 29, 1925; s. Henry K. and Laura May (Robinson) P.; m. Patricia Mae Fox, Aug. 14, 1949; children: Katherine Ilene Peterson Sherbondy, Jon Eric, Timothy Richard. BA, U. Iowa, 1949, JD with distinction, 1951; postgrad., U. Nebr.-Omaha, 1972-80, 86. Bar: Iowa 1951, U.S. Dist. Ct. (so. dist.) Iowa 1951, U.S. Supreme Ct. 1991, U.S. Ct. Appeals (8th cir.) 1997. Pvt. practice law, Council Bluffs, 1951—; U.S. commr. U.S. Dist. Ct. (so. dist.) Iowa, 1958-70. U.S. magistrate judge U.S. Dist. Ct. (so. dist.) Iowa, 1970-99; nat. faculty Fed. Jud. Ctr., Washington, 1972-82; emeritus trustee Children's Square, U.S.A.; verifying ofcl. Internat. Prisoner Transfer Treaties, Mexico City, 1977, La Paz, Bolivia, 1980-81, Lima, Peru, 1981. Author: The Court Moves West: A Study of the United States Supreme Court Decision of Appeals from the United States Circuit and District Court of Iowa, 1846-1882, 1988, West of the Nishnabotna: The Experiences of Forty Years of a Part-Time Judicial Officer as United States Commissioner, Magistrate and Magistrate Judge, 1958-1998, 1998; co-author: (with George Mills) No One is Above the Law: The Story of Southern Iowa's Federal Court, 1994; contbr. articles to legal publs. Bd. dirs. Pottawattamie County (Iowa) chpt. ARC, state fund chmn., 1957-58; state chmn. Radio Free Europe, 1960-61; dist. chmn. Trailblazer dist. Boy Scouts Am., 1952-55; mem. exec. coun. Mid-Am. Coun., 1976—. With inf. U.S. Army, 1943-46. Decorated Purple Heart, Bronze Star; named Outstanding Young Man Council Bluffs C. of C., 1959 Fellow Am. Bar Found. (life); mem. ABA, Am. Judicature Soc., Iowa Bar Assn. (chmn. com. fed. practice 1978-80, probate and trust coun. and sect. 1997—), Pottawattamie County Bar Assn. (pres. 1979-80), Fed. Bar Assn., Inter-Am. Bar Assn., Supreme Ct. Hist. Soc., Fed. Magistrate Judges Assn. (pres. 1978-79), Iowa Conf. Bar Assn. (pres. 1985-87), Hist. Soc. of U.S. Cts. Eighth Jud. Cir. (pres. 1989-99, ct. historian U.S. Dist. Ct. S.D. and Iowa 2000-), Kiwanis (pres. Council Bluffs chpt. 1957), Masons, Phi Delta Phi, Delta Sigma Rho, Omicron Delta Kappa. Republican. Lutheran. Home: 1007 Arbor Ridge Cir Council Bluffs IA 51503-5000 Office: PO Box 248 25 Main Pl Ste 200 Council Bluffs IA 51503-0790

PETERSON, RONALD ROGER, lawyer; b. Chgo., July 27, 1948; married; children: Elizabeth G., Ronald W. AB, Ripon, 1970; JD, U. Chgo., 1973. Bar: Ill. 1974, U.S. Dist. Ct. (no. dist.) Ill. 1974, U.S. Ct. Appeals (7th cir.) 1974, U.S. Dist. Ct. (ea. dist.) Wis. 1975, U.S. Dist. Ct. (no. dist.) Ind. 1978, U.S. Dist. Ct. (cen. dist.) Ill. 1980, U.S. Dist. Ct. (we. dist.) Mich. 1999, U.S. Ct. Appeals (8th cir.) 1984, U.S. Ct. Appeals (6th cir.) 1990, U.S. Ct. Appeals (9th cir.) 1996, U.S. Ct. Appeals (3rd cir.) 2001. Ptnr. Jenner & Block, Chgo., 1974—; commd. 2d lt. U.S. Army, 1968, advanced through grades to 1st lt., 1973, ret., 1978, with mil. intelligence, 1968-78. Mem. ABA, Chgo. Bar Assn., Internat. Soc. Insolvency Practitioners, Comml. Law League, Am. Bankruptcy Inst., Am. Coll. Bankruptcy Lawyers, U.S. Supreme Ct. Hist. Soc. Avocation: skiing. Bankruptcy, Commercial, contracts (including sales of goods; commercial financing), State and local taxation. Office: Jenner & Block 1 E Ibm Plz Fl 4000 Chicago IL 60611-7603 E-mail: rpeterson@jenner.com.

PETERSON, STEVEN A. lawyer; b. Princeton, Minn., Sept. 9, 1953; s. Albin Arthur and Patricia Ann (Samuelson) P.; m. Michelle Behring, Jan. 11, 1980; children: Michael Charles, Stephanie Rose. BA, U. Minn., 1975; JD, Hamline U., 1978. Bar: Minn. 1978, U.S. Dist. Ct. Minn. 1979. Pvt. practice, Milaca, Minn., 1978-92, Chanhassen, Minn., 1984—. Mem. Minn. Bar Assn. Republican. Lutheran. General practice, Probate (including wills, trusts), Property, real (including real estate development, water). Home: 736 Ashley Dr Chaska MN 55318-1536 Office: 80 W 78th St Chanhassen MN 55317-8716

PETERSON, WILLIAM ALLEN, lawyer; b. Marshall, Mo., Oct. 1, 1934; s. R.O. and Marjorie E. (Mallot) P.; m. Mary Kay Moore, July 26, 1958; children: Laura, Clayton, Mary M., Sarah. BS, Drury Coll., Springfield, Mo., 1958; JD, Washington U., 1963. Bar: Mo. 1963, U.S. Dist. Ct. (ea. dist.) Mo. 1964, U.S. Dist. Ct. (we. dist.) Mo. 1965, U.S. Supreme Ct. 1967. Assoc. Riddle, O'Herin & Newberry, Malden, Mo., 1963-65; asst. atty. gen. State of Mo., Jefferson City, 1965-70; legislator Mo. Ho. Reps., Jefferson City, 1970-74; pvt. practice Marshall, 1974—. Atty. City of Marshall, 1976-78, City of Slater, Mo., 1988-89; judge mcpl. divsn. State Cir. Ct., Marshall, 1979-80, 2000—, Slater, 1990-94; pros. atty. County of Saline, Marshall, 1979-80, 84-88. With USN, 1954-56. Mem. ABA, Mo. Bar Assn., Assn. Trial Lawyers Am., Am. Legion, VFW. Methodist. Criminal, Family and matrimonial, Personal injury (including property damage). Home: 503 E Eastwood St Marshall MO 65340-1535 Office: 54 W Arrow St PO Box 9 Marshall MO 65340-0009

PETH, HOWARD ALLEN, lawyer, educator; b. Calif., Apr. 20, 1955; s. Howard Allen and Diane Marie (Munyan) P.; m. Gloria Gene Stockton, Aug. 9, 1992; children: Andrew Howard, Rachel Gloria. BA, U. Calif., San Diego, 1980; MD, U. Santiago, 1984; JD, U. Mo., 1991. Bar: Calif. 1993, U.S. Ct. Appeals (9th cir.) 1993, U.S. Ct. Claims, U.S. Ct. Appeals (fed. cir.) 1993, U.S. Dist. Ct. (so. dist.) Calif. 1993, U.S. Supreme Ct. 1997; diplomate Am. Bd. Internal Medicine, Am. Bd. Emergency Medicine; lic. physician, Calif., Mo., Wis. Asst. prof. U. Mo. Sch. Medicine, Columbia, 1997—. Fellow Am. Coll. Legal Medicine; mem. AMA, ABA (health law sect.), ACP, Am. Coll. Emergency Physicians. Republican. Episcopalian. Office: U Mo Hosp and Clinic One Hospital Dr Columbia MO 65212 Business E-Mail: pethh@health.missouri.edu. E-mail: hpethmdjd@aol.com.

PETILLON, LEE RITCHEY, lawyer; b. Gary, Ind., May 6, 1929; s. Charles Ernest and Blanche Lurene (Mackay) P.; m. Mary Anne Keeton, Feb. 20, 1960; children: Andrew G., Joseph R. BBA, U. Minn., 1952; LLB, U. Calif., Berkeley, 1959. Bar: Calif. 1960, U.S. Dist. Ct. (so. dist.) Calif. 1960. V.p. Creative Investment Capital, Inc., L.A., 1969-70; corp. counsel Harvest Industries, L.A., 1970-71; v.p., gen. counsel, dir. Tech. Svcs. Corp., Santa Monica, Calif., 1971-78; ptnr. Petillon & Davidoff, L.A., 1978-92, Gipson Hoffman & Pancione, 1992-93; pvt. practice Torrance, Calif., 1993-94; ptnr. Petillon & Hansen, Torrance, Calif., 1994—. Co-author: R&D Partnerships, 2d edit., 1985, Representing Start-Up Companies, 1992, 9th edit., 2002; contbr. chapters to books. Chmn. Neighborhood Justice Ctr. Com., 1983-85, Middle Income Co., 1983085; active Calif. Senate Commn. on Corp. Governance, State Bar Calif. Task Force on Alternative Dispute Resolution, 1984-85; chmn. South Bay Sci. Found., Inc.; vice-chmn. Calif. Capital Access Forum, Inc.; dir., legal counsel ACE-Net.org, Inc. Recipient Cert. of Appreciation L.A. City Demonstration Agy., 1975, United Indian Devel. Assn., 1981, City of L.A. for Outstanding Vol. Svcs., 1984, Outstanding Vol. award Torrance C. of C., 2000, Small Bus. Adv. of Yr. award Torrance C. of C., 2001; named Small Bus. Adv. of Yr. Calif. C. of C., 2001. Mem.: ABA (venture capitol and equity com.), Los Angeles County Bar Assn. (trustee 1984—85, alt. dispute resolution sect. 1992—94, bus. and corp. law sect. 2000—, chmn. law tech. sect., Griffin Bell Vol. Svc. award 1993), Los Angeles County Bar Found. (bd. dirs.), Calif. State Bar Assn. (pres., Pro Bono Svcs. award 1983). Avocations: backpacking, reading, music, painting. Corporate, general, Securities. Home: 1636 Via Machado Palos Verdes Estates CA 90274-1930 Office: Petillon & Hansen 21515 Hawthorne Blvd Ste 1260 Torrance CA 90503-6503 E-mail: lpetillon@corplawp-h.com.

PETITTI, MICHAEL JOSEPH, JR., lawyer; b. Canton, Ohio, July 25, 1955; s. Michael Joseph and Shirley Darlene Petitti; m. Anita Jean Charley, Aug. 27, 1977; 1 child, Michael Joseph III. BA in Edn., Ari. State U., 1982, JD cum laude, 1987. Bar: Ariz. 1987, U.S. Dist. Ct. Ariz. 1987, U.S. Ct. Appeals (9th cir.) 1987. Social worker Tempe (Ariz.) Ctr. for the Handicapped, 1982-84; atty. Evans, Kitchel & Jenckes, P.C., Phoenix, 1987-88, Beus, Gilbert & Morrill, P.C., Phoenix, 1988-90, Gomez & Petitti, P.C., Phoenix, 1990—. Spkr. in field. Pedrick scholar, 1984, 85, 86. Mem. ABA, State Bar Ariz. (mem. exec. coun. state bar employment and labor law sect. 1997—, sec. 2002-2003), Maricopa County Bar Assn., Nat. Employment Lawyers Assn., Ariz. Employment Lawyers Assn. Democrat. Federal civil litigation, State civil litigation, Labor (including EEOC, Fair Labor Standards Act, labor-management relations, NLRB, OSHA). Office: Gomez & Petitti PC 2525 E Camelback Rd Ste 860 Phoenix AZ 85016-4279 E-mail: mjp@gomezlaw.net.

PETKOV, PETKO ANGELOV, lawyer; b. Rousse, Bulgaria, Mar. 4, 1971; s. Angel Petkov Georgiev and Lipiana Petkova Georgieva; m. Rositsa Rossenova Nedelsheva, Aug. 21, 1999. ML, Sofia (Bulgaria) U., 1998. Bar: Sofia 2000. Expert Privatization Agy., Sofia, 1998; sr. assoc. Djingov, Gouginski, Kyutchugov & Velichkov Law Firm, Sofia, 1998—. Avocations: football, bridge. Property, real (including real estate development, water). Home: Drujba 2 bi 221 entr 4 Sofia Bulgaria Office: DGKV Law Firm 8A Tzar Osvoboditel Blvd 1000 Sofia Bulgaria

PETRASICH, JOHN MORIS, lawyer; b. Long Beach, Calif., Oct. 13, 1945; s. Louis A. and Margaret A. (Moris) P.; children from previous marriage: Jason, Jacquelyn; m. Mary T. Nevin, Aug. 22, 1997. BA, U. So. Calif., 1967, JD, 1970. Bar: Calif. 1971, U.S. Dist. Ct. (cen. dist.) 1971, U.S. Ct. Appeals (9th cir.) 1973, U.S. Dist. Ct. (no. dist.) Calif. 1974, U.S. Ct. Appeals (ea. dist.) Calif. 1976. Assoc. Fulop, Rolson, Burns & McKittrick, Beverly Hills and Newport Beach, Calif., 1971-74, ptnr., 1975-82; ptnr., head litigation McKittrick, Jackson, DeMarco & Peckenpaugh, Newport Beach, 1983-93; shareholder, head litigation Jackson, DeMarco & Peckenpaugh, Newport Beach, 1993—; also bd. dirs. McKittrick, Jackson, DeMarco & Peckenpaugh, Newport Beach. Mem. editorial staff U. So. Calif. Law Rev., 1969-70. Mem. ABA, Beverly Hills Bar Assn., L.A. Bar Assn., Assn. Trial Lawyers Am., Orange County Bar Assn., Lawyers Club L.A., Order of Coif. General civil litigation, Insurance, Property, real (including real estate development, water). Office: Jackson DeMarco Peckenpaugh PO Box 19704 Irvine CA 92623-9704 E-mail: jpetrasich@jdplaw.com.

PETRIE, BRUCE INGLIS, lawyer; b. Washington, Nov. 8, 1926; s. Robert Inglis and Marion (Douglas) P.; m. Beverly Ann Stevens, Nov. 3, 1950 (dec. Oct. 1993); children: Laurie Ann Roche, Bruce Inglis, Karen Elizabeth Medsger. BBA, U. Cin., 1948, JD, 1950. Bar: Ohio 1950, U.S. Dist. Ct. (so. dist.) Ohio 1951, U.S. Ct. Appeals (6th cir.) 1960, U.S. Supreme Ct. Assoc. Kunkel & Kunkel, Cin., 1950-51, Graydon, Head & Ritchey, 1951-57, ptnr., 1957—. Exec. prodr. (sch. video) Classical Quest, 2000; author: How To Get the Most Out of Your Lawyer, 2002; contbr. articles to legal jours. Mem. bd. Charter Com. Greater Cin., 1952—; pres. Charter Rsch. Inst., 2000-2003; mem. bd. edn. Indian Hill Exempted Village Sch. Dist., 1965-67, pres., 1967; mem. adv. bd. William A. Mitchell Ctr., 1969-86; mem. Green Areas adv. com. Village of Indian Hill, Ohio, 1969-80, chmn., 1976-80; mem. Ohio Ethics Com., 1974-75; co-founder Sta. WGUC-FM; mem. WGUC-FM Cmty. Bd., 1974—, chmn., 1974-76; bd. dirs. Murray Seasongood Good Govt. Fund, 1975—, pres., 1989—; bd. dirs. Nat. Civic League, Cin. Vol. Lawyers for Poor Found., Linton Music Series, Amernet Chamber Music Soc.; founder Parents as Tchrs. Metro Housing Authority Commn., 1991—; elder, trustee, deacon Knox Presbyn. Ch.; a prin. advocate merit selection judges, Ohio; trustee, mem. bd., Seven Hills Neighborhood Houses, Inst. for Learning in Retirement; mem. bd. Hamilton County Good Govt. League; organizer Late Great Lakes Book Distbn. project, global vol. tchr. China, 2003. Recipient Pres.'s award U. Cin., 1976, Disting. Alumnus award, 1995. Fellow Am. Bar Found.; mem. ABA, Ohio Bar Assn., Cin. Bar Assn. (pres. 1981, Trustee's award 2000), Am. Judicature Soc. (Herbert Lincoln Harley award 1973, dir.), Nat. Civic League (Disting. Citizen award 1985, coun. 1984—), Am. Law Inst., Ohio State Bar Assn. Found. (Outstanding Rsch. in Law and Govt. award 1986, Charles P. Taft Civic Gumption award 1988, Ohio Bar medal 1988), Cincinnatus Assn., Order of Coif, Lit. Club, Univ. Club, Cin. Club. Avocations: tennis, squash, woodworking, writing, horticulture, music. Corporate, general, Estate planning, Property, real (including real estate development, water). Home: 2787 Walsh Rd Cincinnati OH 45208-3428 Office: Graydon Head & Ritchey 1900 Fifth 3d Ctr 511 Walnut St Ste 1900 Cincinnati OH 45202-3157

PETRIE, GREGORY STEVEN, lawyer; b. Seattle, Feb. 25, 1951; s. George C. and Pauline P.; m. Margaret Fuhrman, Oct. 6, 1979; children: Kathryn Jean, Thomas George. AB in Polit. Sci and Econs., UCLA, 1973; JD, Boston U., 1976. Bar: Wash. 1976, U.S. Dist. Ct. (we. dist.) Wash. 1976. Adminstr. Action/Peace Corps, Washington, 1973, Fed. Power Commn., Washington, 1974; assoc. Oles Morrison et al, Seattle, 1976-80; ptnr. Schwabe Williamson Ferguson & Burdell, Seattle, 1981-94; mng. shareholder Krutch Lindell Bingham Jones & Petrie, Seattle, 1994—. Mem. Seattle-King County Bar Assn., Profl. Liability Architects and Engrs., Wash. Athletic Club. Avocations: woodworking, skiing. Construction, Estate planning, State civil litigation. Office: Krutch Lindell Bingham Jones & Petrie 1420 Fifth Ave Ste 3150 Seattle WA 98101 E-mail: gsp@nwlink.com.

PETRIE, RICHARD ALLEN, retired lawyer, tax consultant; b. Milw., Oct. 11, 1930; s. Elmer Jacob and Ella Emma (Hass) P.; m. Helen Ann Brunner, July 31, 1965; children: Paula Erin Schmidt, Brenda Marie Williams. BS in Bus. Adminstrn. magna cum laude, Marquette U., U. Wis., Milw., 1953; LLM cum laude, U. Wis., 1956. Assoc. Paul P. Lipton, Milw., 1956-71; ptnr. Lipton & Petrie, Milw., 1971-74; shareholder Lipton & Petrie, Ltd., Milw., 1974-80, Meldman, Case & Weine, Ltd., Milw., 1980-85, Mulcahy & Wherry, S.C., Milw., 1986-91, Richard A. Petrie, S.C., Milw., 1991—2002. Tax cons. Reinhart, Boerner, Van Deuren, Norris & Rieselbach, S.C., Milw., 1991—. Co-author: Federal Taxation Practice and Procedure, 4th edit., 1992; bd. editors Wis. Law Rev., 1954-56; contbr. articles to profl. jours. Mem. ABA, State Bar Wis., Order of the Coif. Avocations: reading, golfing, gardening, bowling. Corporate taxation, Taxation, general, Personal income taxation.

PETRIN, HELEN FITE, lawyer, consultant, mediator; b. Bklyn., June 22, 1940; d. Clyde David and Connie Marie Keaton; m. Michael Richard Petrin, June 29, 1963; children: Jennifer Lee, Michael James, Daniel John. BS, Rider Coll. (now Rider U.), 1962, MA, 1980; postgrad., Glassboro (N.J.) Coll. (now Rowan U.), 1981; JD, Widener U., 1987. Bar: Pa. 1989, N.J. 1990, U.S. Dist. N.J. 1990. Tchr. bus. edn. Pennsville (N.J.) Meml. High Sch., 1962-66; asst. prof. Salem Community Coll., Carney's Point, N.J., 1977-81; asst. prof. Brandywine Coll. Widener U., Wilmington, Del., 1981-87, asst. prof., adminstr., dir. paralegal program, 1987-88; dir. continuing legal edn. Widener U. Sch. Law, Brandywine, 1987-88; pvt. practice computer cons. Del., Pa., N.J., Del., Pa., N.J., 1988—; pvt. practice law Salem, N.J., 1989—; prosecutor Pilesgrove Township, N.J., 1990-91; dep. surrogate Salem County, N.J., 1991-2000. Word processing cons. New Castle County (Del.) Pers. Dept., 1983; mem. dist. I ethics com. N.J. Supreme Ct., 1993-96; instr. N.J. Inst. for CLE, 1995—; adv. com. on minority concerns Superior Ct. N.J. Vicinage 15, 1995—; judge mock trial N.J. State Bar, 1994—; mem. women's advocacy panel Salem C.C., 1998—. Pres. bd. Salem County YMCA, 1983; dir. mediator Salem County YMCA Mediation Svcs., 1995—2001; vol. atty. Phila. Vols. for Indigent Program, 1990—95, Camden Legal Svcs., Inc. for Salem County, 1990—2001; mem. Hope III com. (Home Ownership and Opportunity for People Everywhere), Salem, NJ, 1992—2001; vol. atty. Salem County N.J. Office Aging Sr. Law Day, 1991—2001; vol. dir. Guardianship Monitoring Program, 1993—2001; sec.-treas. Stand Up for Salem, Inc., 1997—2002; bd. dirs. Salem County YMCA, 1980—98, United Way Salem County, 1991—97, treas., 1994—95; bd. dirs. United Ways of Pa. & N.J., 1994—97, Stand Up for Salem, Inc., 1991—2002, Salem Main St. Program, 2000—03; bd. dirs., chair pers. com. Salem County Hist. Soc., 2002—. Mem.: ABA (chmn. young lawyers econs. com. 1990—93, vice chmn. mktg. legal svcs. com. gen. practice sect. 1993—98), Salem County Bar Assn. (treas. 1991—92, sec. 1992—93, v.p., pres.-elect 1993—94, pres. 1994—95, dir. of Salem County, N.J. YMCA Family Ct. Mediation program 1995—2001), Phila. Bar Assn. (probate adv. panel 1992—94), Pa. Bar Assn., N.J. State Bar Assn. (exec. com. young lawyers divsn. 1990—93, pro bono com. 1998—2000, fin. and ops. com. 2002—, resolutions com. 2002—, meeting arrangements and program com. 2002—), Salem County Hist. Soc. (bd. dirs. 2002—, chmn. pers. com. 2002—), Delta Pi Epsilon (sec. bd. dirs. 1980—82). Avocations: swimming, music, walking, reading. Civil rights, General practice, Probate (including wills, trusts). Home: 99 Marlton Rd Woodstown NJ 08098-2722 Office: 51 Market St Salem NJ 08079-1909

PETRO, JAMES MICHAEL, state attorney general; b. Cleve., Oct. 25, 1948; s. William John and Lila Helen (Janca) P.; m. Nancy Ellen Bero, Dec. 16, 1972; children: John Bero, Corbin Marie. BA, Denison U., 1970; JD, Case Western Res., 1973. Bar: Ohio 1973, U.S. Dist. Ct. (no. dist.) Ohio 1974, U.S. Ct. Appeals (6th cir.), U.S. Supreme Ct. Spl. asst. U.S. senator W.B. Saxbe, Cleve., 1972-73; asst. pros. atty. Franklin County, Ohio, 1973-74; asst. dir. law City of Cleve., 1974; ptnr. Petro & Troia, Cleve., 1974-84; dir. govt. affairs Standard Oil Co., Cleve., 1984-86; ptnr. Petro, Rademaker, Matty & McClelland, Cleve., 1986-93, Buckingham, Doolittle & Burroughs, Cleve., 1993-95; auditor State of Ohio, 1995—, atty. gen., 2003—. Mem. city coun. Rocky River, Ohio, 1977-79, dir. law, 1980; mem. Ohio Ho. of Reps., Columbus, 1981-84, 86-90; commr. Cuyahoga County, Ohio, 1991-95. Mem. ABA, Ohio State Bar Assn., Cleve. Bar Assn. Republican. Methodist. Home: 1933 Lake Shore Dr Columbus OH 43204-4963 Office: 30 E Broad St Columbus OH 43266 E-mail: petro@agstate.oh.us.

PETRONY, JOHN FRANCIS, lawyer; b. Youngstown, Ohio, May 26, 1968; s. Francis Leon and Dorothy Jane (Dubos) P.; m. Mari Michele Wren, July 29, 1995. BA in Polit. Sci. summa cum laude, Youngstown State U., 1990; JD, Ohio State U., 1993. Bar: Ohio 1993, U.S. Dist. Ct. (no. dist.) Ohio 1994. Assoc. atty. Harrington, Huxley, Smith, Mitchell & Reed, Youngstown, 1993—97; assoc. Nadler, Nadler & Burdman, Youngstown, 1997—. Faculty mem. National Bus. Inst., 2001—02. Downtown Youngstown Revitalization Com., 1998-. Mem.: ABA (bus. law sect, real property sect., com. partnerships and unincorporated bus. orgs., negotiated acquisitions com.), Ohio St. Bar Assn. (corp. law com., limited liability company subcommittee). Republican. Roman Catholic. Avocations: golf, tennis, music. Mergers and acquisitions, Corporate, general, Property, real (including real estate development, water). Home: 7395 Cobblers Run Youngstown OH 44514-5313 Office: Nadler Nadler & Burdman 20 Fed Plz W Youngstown OH 44503

PETRUSH, JOHN JOSEPH, lawyer; b. Rochester, Pa., Oct. 15, 1942; s. Joseph Anthony and Helen Rosemarie (Klucarich) P.; children: John Joseph, Joshua Laurence. AB cum laude, Princeton U., 1964; LLB, Stanford U., 1967. Bar: Calif. 1967, Pa. 1970. Assoc. Bernard Petrie, San Francisco, 1967-68; law clk. to judge Common Pleas Ct. Beaver County, Pa., 1969; assoc. Buchanan, Ingersoll, Rodewald, Kyle & Buerger, Pitts., 1970-75; pvt. practice Beaver, Pa., 1976—. Mem. Beaver Town Coun., 1973-88; bd. dirs. Beaver County unit Am. Cancer Soc., 1976-90, United Way of Beaver County, 1986-92; trustee Beaver Area Sch. Dist. Edn. Found. With USMCR, 1961-63. Mem. ABA, ATLA, Pa. Bar Assn., Pa. Trial Lawyers Assn. (bd. govs. western chpt. 1984-90), Allegheny County Bar Assn., Beaver County Bar Assn. (treas. 1987-2002). Republican. State civil litigation, Personal injury (including property damage), Corporate, general. Home: 331 Wilson Ave Beaver PA 15009-2323 Office: 348 College Ave Beaver PA 15009-2209 E-mail: john.j.petrush@verizon.net.

PETTIBONE, PETER JOHN, lawyer; b. Schenectady, N.Y., Dec. 11, 1939; s. George Howard and Caryl Grey (Ketchum) P.; m. Jean Kellogg, Apr. 23, 1966; children: Stephen, Victoria. AB summa cum laude, Princeton U., 1961; JD, Harvard U., 1964; LLM, NYU, 1971. Bar: Pa. 1965, D.C. 1965, N.Y. 1968, U.S. Supreme Ct. 1974, Russia (fgn. legal cons.) 1995. Lectr. Heidelberg (Fed. Republic Germany) U., 1965-67; assoc. Cravath, Swaine & Moore, N.Y.C., 1967-74, Lord Day & Lord, Barrett Smith, N.Y.C., 1974-76, ptnr. N.Y.C. and Washington, 1976-94, Patterson, Belknap, Webb & Tyler LLP, N.Y.C. and Moscow, 1994-99, Hogan & Hartson LLP, N.Y.C. and Moscow, 2000—. Pres. 1158 Fifth Ave. Corp., N.Y.C., 1991-94; pres. North Ferry Co., Shelter Island, N.Y., 1987-90; bd. dirs., vice-chmn. N.Y. State Facilities Devel. Corp., N.Y.C., 1983-89. Editor USSR Legal Materials, 1990-92. Trustee, treas. Hosp. Chaplaincy Inc., N.Y.C., 1980-86, Civitas, N.Y.C., 1984-92; mem. Coun. Fgn. Rels., 1993—; trustee Union Chapel, Shelter Island, N.Y., 1990—, CEC Internat. Ptnrs., 1996-2002; bd. dirs., vice chmn. Geonomics Inst., Middlebury, Vt., 1991-98; mem. vestry Ch. of Heavenly Rest, N.Y.C., 1987-93; mem. Nat. Adv. Coun. Harriman Inst. Columbia U., 1996—; mem. Russia com. Episcopal Diocese of N.Y. Capt. U.S. Army, 1965-67, Heidelberg, Germany. Mem. ABA, Assn. Bar City N.Y. (chmn. com. on CIS affairs 1991-94), U.S.-USSR Trade and Econ. Coun. Inc. (U.S. co-chmn. legal com. 1980-92), U.S.-Russia Bus. Coun. (bd. dirs.), Soc. of Cin., Anglers Club N.Y.C., N.Y. Yacht Club, Shelter Island Yacht Club, Moscow Country Club, Amateur Ski Club N.Y. (pres. 1980-82), Canterbury Choral Soc. (pres. 1983-84), Phi Beta Kappa. Episcopalian. Corporate, general, Private international, Securities. Home: 1158 5th Ave New York NY 10029-6917 also: 10 Wesley Ave Shelter Island Heights NY 11965 Office: Hogan & Hartson LLP 875 3rd Ave New York NY 10022

PETTIETTE, ALISON YVONNE, lawyer; b. Brockton, Mass., Aug. 16, 1952. Student Sorbonne, Paris, 1971-72; BA, Sophie Newcomb Coll., 1972; MA, Rice U., 1974; JD, Bates Coll., 1978. Bar: Tex. 1979, U.S. Dist. Ct. (so. dist.) Tex. 1980, U.S. Ct. Appeals (5th cir.) 1981. Ptnr. Harvill & Hardy, Houston, 1979-83; pvt. practice, Houston, 1983-84; assoc. O'Quinn & Hagans, Houston, 1984-86, Jones & Granger, Houston, 1986-88; pvt. practice, Houston, 1988—. Editor Houston Law Rev. U. Houston, 1976-78. Exercise instr. YWCA, Houston, 1976-81, U. St. Thomas, Houston. NDEA fellow Rice U., Houston, 1972-74; Woodrow Wilson scholar, Tulane U., New Orleans, 1972. Mem. ABA, Assn. Trial Lawyers Am., Tex. Trial Lawyers Assn., Houston Trial Lawyers Assn., Phi Delta Phi, Phi Beta Kappa. Federal civil litigation, Personal injury (including property damage), Product liability. Home: PO Box 980847 Houston TX 77098-0847 E-mail: aypettiett@sbcglobal.net., aypettiett@hotmail.com.

PETTUS, E. LAMAR, lawyer; b. 1945; m. Donna C.; children: Evan Lamar, Carrie Anne, Samuel Chase. BSME, U. Ark., 1968, JD with honors, 1973. Bar: U.S. Dist. Ct. 1974 Ark., U.S. Ct. Appeals (8th cir.) 1974, Ark. Supreme Ct. 1974, U.S. Supreme Ct. 1979. Canton works plant engr. trainee Internat. Harvester, 1971; assoc. Pearson & Woodruff Law Firm, 1973; pvt. practice Pettus Law Firm, Fayetteville, Ark., 1974—. City atty. Farmington, 1981; mem. com. bar examiners Ark. Supreme Ct., 1986, chmn., 1988-89. Bus. mgr. Ark. Law Rev.; participant: televised "Ask Your Lawyer Program", 1981-83. Fin. chair Ctrl. United Meth. Ch., 1994-96, chair adminstrv. bd., 1997-2000; mem. Fayette Sch. Bd., 1991-97; active Assn. Voluntary Lawyers for Elderly, 1990—, Washington County Rep. Party. Comdr. USN, 1968-71, Vietnam, res. 1971-86. Recipient Navy Achievement medal, Navy Commendation medal. Mem. Ark. Bar Assn (pres. 1993-94, various positions and coms.), Ark. Trial Lawyers Assn., Washington County Bar Assn. (pres. 1989-90, v.p. 1989-90, sec.-treas. 1978-79), Fayetteville C. of C. (legis. com. 1994—), Rotary Internat. (various coms.). Commercial, consumer (including collections, credit), Corporate, general, Property, real (including real estate development, water). Office: PO Box 1665 151 W Dickson St Fayetteville AR 72702 E-mail: lpettus@pettuslaw.com.

PETTYJOHN, SHIRLEY ELLIS, lawyer, real estate executive; b. Liberty, Ky., Aug. 16, 1935; d. Wesley Barker and Ada Lou (Bryant) Ellis; m. Flem D. Pettyjohn, Sept. 24, 1955; children: Deena Renee, Ellisa Denise. BS in Commerce, U. Louisville, 1974, JD, 1977. Bar: Ky. 1978, Ind. 1988; lic. real estate broker, Ky., Ind.; cert. mediator. Pres. Universal Devel. Corp., Ky. and Fla., 1984—, Pettyjohn Inc., Ky. and Ind., 1967—, Ind. Mediation Svcs., Inc., 1990—, Ky. Mediation Svcs., Inc., 1991—; v.p. Continental Investments Corp., 1986—; sr. ptnr. Pettyjohn & Assocs., Attys., 1987—. Editor Law-Hers Jour. Vice chmn. Louisville and Jefferson County Planning Commn., 1971-75; mem. Gov.'s Conf. on Edn., 1977, jud. nominee, 1981, Met. Louisville Women's Polit. Caucus, Bluegrass State Skills Corp., 1992-96, Ky. Opera Assn. Guild; elected mem. Ky. State Dem. Exec. Com., 1988-92; del. Nat. Dem. Conv. and Dem. Nat. Platform Com., 1988; bd. dirs. Ky. Dem. Hdqs., Inc., 1988-92, Pegasus Rising, Inc.; chmn. Okolona Libr. Task Force; mem. Clinton-Gore Nat. Steering Com., 1995; hon. mem. Gore 2000 Presdl. Campaign Com. Recipient Mayor's Cert. Recognition, 1974, Mayor's Fleur de lis award, 1969-73, Excellence in Writing award Arts Club Louisville, 1986, 87, 93, 99; inducted into Casey County Alumni Hall of Fame, 1997. Mem. ABA, NAFE, Nat. Assn. Adminstrv. Law Judges, Ky. Bar Assn., Louisville Bar Assn., Women Lawyers Assn. of Jefferson County, Am. Judicature Soc., Clark County Bar Assn., Ind. Bar Assn., Ind. Assn. Mediators, Am. Inst. Planners, Women's C. of C. of Ky. (past bd. dirs., chmn. legis. com.), Am. Legion (aux.), Fraternal Order Police Assn. (award 1982), Louisville Legal Secs. (past pres., editor Law-Hers Jour.), Coun. of Women Pres. (past pres., Woman of Achievement award 1974), Louisville Visual Arts Assn. (past bd. dirs.), Louisville Ballet Guild (chair audience devel. 1989-91), Fern Creek Woman's Club, Ky. Fedn. Women's Clubs, Gen. Fedn. Women's Clubs, Dem. Leadership Coun., Casey County Alumni Assn. (pres. 1998-2000), Poplar Level Area Bus. Assn., Jefferson County Dem. Women's Club (past v.p.), Nat. Fedn. Dem. Women's Clubs, Spirit of 46th Club, Mose Green Club, North End Club, 12th Ward Club, S. End Club, 3rd Ward Club, Highland Pk. Club, Grass Roots Club, Harry S. Truman Club, Beargrass Club, Arts Club of Louisville (past pres.), Sigma Delta Kappa (life), Chi Thi Theta, Century 2000 Democrat Club. Administrative and regulatory, General practice, Probate (including wills, trusts). Home: 6924 Norlynn Dr Louisville KY 40228-1471 Office: 4500 Poplar Level Rd Louisville KY 40213-2124

PETZOLD, JOHN PAUL, judge; b. 1938; BA, U. Maine, 1961; LLB, Washington & Lee U., 1962. Bar: Ohio 1962, Va. 1962. Pvt. practice law, Ohio, 1962-91; asst. atty. gen. State of Ohio, 1964-71; law dir. City of Miamisburg, Ohio, 1979-91; judge Montgomery County Common Pleas Ct., Dayton, Ohio, 1991—. Bd. tax appeals City of Kettering, Ohio, 1971-91. Mem. ABA, Ohio State Bar Assn. (bd. govs., former chairperson young lawyers sect., chairperson pub. rels. com., vice chairperson lawyers assistance com., eminent domain com., banking, comml., and bankruptcy law com., pres. 1998-99), Dayton Bar Assn. (pres. 1989-90), Common Pleas Judge Assn. (mem. bd. commrs. on grievances and discipline 1995-97). Avocations: golf, swimming, writing, teaching, reading, genealogy. Office: Montgomery County Common Pleas Ct 41 N Perry St Dayton OH 45402-1431

PFAFF, ROBERT JAMES, lawyer; b. Pitts., Jan. 12, 1943; s. William Michael and Elizabeth (Ludwig) P.; m. Carol Pillich, June 18, 1977. BS in Edn., Slippery Rock U., 1965; JD, Duquesne U., 1973. Bar: Pa. 1973, U.S. Dist. Ct. (we. dist.) Pa. 1973, U.S. Supreme Ct. 1980. Tchr. secondary schs., Norwin and Jeanette, Pa., 1965-66; suit group supr. Liberty Mut. Ins. Co.,

Pitts., 1966-70; assoc. Egler, McGregor & Reinstadtler, Pitts., 1973-76; ptnr. Leopold, Eberhardt & Pfaff, Altoona, Pa., 1976-80; sr. ptnr. Meyer, Darragh, Buckler, Bebenek & Eck, Pitts., 1980-84, Pfaff, McIntyre, Dugas, Hartye & Schmitt, Hollidaysburg, Pa., 1984—2001, Thomson, Rhodes & Cowie, Pitts., 2001—. Mem. Def. Rsch. Inst., Pa. Bar Assn., Allegheny County Bar Assn., Pa. Assn. Mut. Ins. Cos. (claims com.), Pa. Def. Inst. Republican. Roman Catholic. Avocations: golf, music, licensed pilot. General civil litigation, State civil litigation, Insurance. Home: 405 Kingsberry Cir Pittsburgh PA 15234-1065 Office: Thomson Rhodes & Cowie 1010 Two Chatham Ctr Pittsburgh PA 15219-3499 E-mail: rjmpfaff@aol.com.

PFALTZ, HUGO MENZEL, JR., lawyer; b. Newark, Sept. 23, 1931; s. Hugo M. and Mary E. (Horr) Pfaltz; m. Marilyn M. Muir, Sept. 29, 1956; children: Elizabeth W., William M., Robert L. BA, Hamilton Coll., 1953; JD, Harvard U., 1960; LLM, NYU, 1965. Bar: N.J. 1960, U.S. Dist. Ct. N.J. 1960, U.S. Supreme Ct. 1977. Assoc. McCarter & English, Newark, 1960—61, Bourne & Noll, Summit, NJ, 1961—74; sole practice Summit, 1974—82; ptnr. Pfaltz & Woller, 1983—. Mem. Battleship N.J. Commn., 1985—, N.J. Law Revision Commn., 1986—. Assoc. editor N.J. Law Jour., 1966—2002, editor, 1984—86. Chmn. Summit Rep. City Com., 1966; mem. N.J. Constl. Conv., 1966, N.J. Assembly, 1968—72. Served to lt. USNR, 1953—62. Mem.: ABA, Summit Bar Assn., Union County Bar Assn., N.J. Bar Assn., Summit Tennis Club, Beacon Hill Club (Summit), Baltusrol Club (Springfield, N.J.), Univ. Club (Washington), Univ Club (N.Y.C.). Banking, Probate (including wills, trusts), Estate taxation. Home: 118 Prospect St Summit NJ 07901-2472 Office: 382 Springfield Ave Summit NJ 07901-2707

PFEIFER, PAUL E. state supreme court justice; b. Bucyrus, Ohio, Oct. 15, 1942; m. Julia Pfeifer; 3 children. BA, Ohio State U., 1963, JD, 1966. Asst. atty. gen. State of Ohio, 1967-70; mem. Ohio Ho. of Reps., 1971-72; asst. prosecuting atty. Crawford County, 1973-76; mem. Ohio Senate, 1976-92, minority floor leader, 1983-84, asst. pres. pro-tempore, 1985-86; ptnr. Cory, Brown & Pfeifer, 1973-92; justice Ohio Supreme Ct., 1992—. Chmn. jud. com. Ohio Senate, 10 yrs. Mem. Grace United Meth. Ch., Bucyrus. Mem. Bucyrus Rotary Club. Office: Supreme Court of Ohio 30 E Broad St Fl 3 Columbus OH 43215

PFEIFFER, MARGARET KOLODNY, lawyer; b. Elkin, N.C., Oct. 7, 1944; d. Isadore Harold and Mary Elizabeth (Brody) K.; m. Carl Frederick Pfeiffer II, Sept. 2, 1968. BA, Duke U., 1967; JD, Rutgers U., 1974. Bar: N.J. 1974, N.Y. 1976, D.C. 1981, U.S. Supreme Ct. 1979. Law clk. to Hon. F.L. Van Dusen U.S. Ct. Appeals 3d cir., Phila., 1974-75; assoc. Sullivan & Cromwell, N.Y.C. and Washington, 1975-82, ptnr., 1982—. Contbr. articles to profl. jours. Trustee Am. Found. for Blind, Nat. Law Ctr. on Homelessness and Poverty; mem. bd. visitors Trinity Coll. of Duke U. Mem. ABA, Internat. Bar Assn., D.C. Bar Assn., N.Y. State Bar Assn., Assn. of Bar of City of N.Y., Am. Soc. of Intl. Law. Avocations: gardening, reading, music. Antitrust, Federal civil litigation, Intellectual property. Office: Sullivan & Cromwell 1701 Pennsylvania Ave NW Washington DC 20006-5866

PFEIFFER, PHILIP J. lawyer; b. Houston, Aug. 16, 1947; BS, Sam Houston State U., 1969; JD, So. Meth. U., 1972. Bar: Tex. 1972. Mem. Fulbright & Jaworski L.L.P., San Antonio. Mem. ABA, State Bar Tex., San Antonio Bar Assn., Order of Coif, Phi Alpha Delta. Labor (including EEOC, Fair Labor Standards Act, labor-management relations, NLRB, OSHA), Alternative dispute resolution. Office: Fulbright & Jaworski 300 Convent St Ste 2200 San Antonio TX 78205-3792 E-mail: ppfeiffer@fulbright.com.

PFEIFFER, STEVEN BERNARD, lawyer; b. Orange, N.J., Jan. 19, 1947; s. Bernard Victor and Elizabeth Sophia (Bissell) P.; m. Kristin Reagan, June 27, 1970; children: Victoria Elizabeth, Rachel Catherine, Emily Dorothea, Stephanie Kristin Bissell, Andrew Steven Bernard. BA in Govt., Wesleyan U., 1969; BA in Jurisprudence, Oxford U., 1971, MA, 1983; MA in African Studies, U. London, 1973; JD, Yale U., 1976. Bar: N.J. 1976, D.C. 1978. Assoc. Fulbright & Jaworski, Houston, London, 1976—83, ptnr. London, Washington, 1983—, ptnr.-in-charge London, 1983—86, 1989—, head internat. dept. Washington office, 1989—, ptnr.-in-charge Washington office, 1998—. Bd. dirs., chmn. internat. com. Riggs Nat. Corp., Washington; bd. dirs., non-exec. chmn. Riggs Bank Europe Ltd., London; bd. dirs. The Africa Am. Inst., N.Y.C., Barloworld Ltd., Johannesburg. Contbr. articles to profl. jours. Alumni-elected trustee Wesleyan U., Middletown, Conn., 1976-79, charter trustee, 1980-92, vice chmn. bd. trustees, 1986-87, chmn. bd. trustees, 1987-92, chmn. emeritus, 1992—; trustee St. Andrews Sch., Middletown, Del., 1995—. With USN, 1969, 72-74; asst. cinceur plans officer, Office of CNO, Washington, 1972-73; spl. asst. to Sec. of Navy, Washington, 1973-74. Rhodes scholar, 1969-72; Thomas Watson Travel fellow, The Watson Found., 1969. Mem. ABA, N.J. State Bar Assn., Am. Soc. Internat. Law, Internat. Bar Assn. (past chmn. sect. energy and natural resources law 1992-94), Naval Res. Assn., Internat. Inst. Strategic Studies (London), Coun. Fgn. Rels. Avocations: tennis, history, fishing, books. Home: 301 N View Ter Alexandria VA 22301-2609 Office: Fulbright & Jaworski LLP 801 Pennsylvania Ave NW Washington DC 20004-2623

PFENNIGSTORF, WERNER, lawyer; b. Hamburg, Germany, Sept. 28, 1934; s. Walter and Ilse (Schroeter) P.; m. Heika Helene Droenner, Apr. 6, 1963. Habilitation, U. Hamburg, Germany, 1974; JD, 1960; MCL, U. Mich. 1961. Bar: Germany 1962. Wissenschaftl asst. U. Hamburg, 1963-66; staff atty. Ins. Laws Rev. Commn., State Wis., Madison, 1967-70; rsch. fellow U. Hamburg, 1970-72; project dir. Am. Bar Found., Chgo., 1973-86; pvt. practice, 1986— . Author: Legal Expense Insurance, 1975, German Insurance Laws, 3rd edit., 1995, A Comparative Study of Liability Law and Compensation Schemes in Ten Countries and the U.S., 1991, Public Law of Insurance, 1996; co-editor: Legal Service Plans, 1977; editor: Personal Injury Compensation, 1993, Pollution Insurance, 1993. Mem. Deutscher Verein für Versicherungswissenschaft, ABA (assoc.), Internat. Assn. Ins. Law. Lutheran. Insurance, Private international, Personal injury (including property damage). Office: Roethkampstr 3 21709 Duedenbuettel Germany

PHAIR, JOSEPH BASCHON, lawyer; b. N.Y.C., Apr. 29, 1947; s. James Francis and Mary Elizabeth (Baschon) P.; m. Bonnie Jean Hobbs, Sept. 04, 1971; children: Kelly I., Joseph B., Sean P. BA, U. San Francisco, 1970, JD, 1973. Bar: Calif., U.S. Dist. Ct. (no. dist.) Calif., U.S. Ct. Appeals (9th cir.). Assoc. Berry, Davis & McInerney, Oakland, Calif., 1974-76, Bronson, Bronson & McKinnon, San Francisco, 1976-79; staff atty. Varian Assocs., Inc., Palo Alto, Calif., 1979-83, corp. counsel, 1983-86, sr. corp. counsel, 1986-87, assoc. gen. counsel, 1987-90, v.p., gen. counsel, 1990-91, v.p., gen. counsel, sec., 1991-99; v.p. adminstrn., gen. counsel, sec. Varian Med. Sys., Inc., Palo Alto, 1999—. Mem. devel. bd. St. Vincent de Paul Devel. Coun., San Francisco, 1992—. Mem. Bay Area Gen. Counsel, Silicon Valley Assn. Gen. Counsel, The Olympic Culb. Roman Catholic. Corporate, general, Mergers and acquisitions, Securities. Office: Varian Med Sys Inc M S V 250 3100 Hansen Way Palo Alto CA 94304-1030

PHARAOH, PAUL GRENVILLE, lawyer; b. Chesterfield, Eng., Apr. 16, 1947; s. Morton Grenville and Kathleen Jean Pharaoh; m. Lynn Margaret Francis, Oct. 27, 1969; children: Claire, Richard. LLB, Manchester (Eng.) U., 1968. Ptnr. Bettinsons, Birmingham, England, 1973—90, Shakespeares, Birmingham, 1990—96, Martineau Johnson, Birmingham, 1996—. Coun. mem. Law Soc. Eng. and Wales, London, 1990—2002; gov. Lakes Coll. West Cumbria, 1998—. Author: How to Manage a Merger, 1998; contbr. chapters to books. Mem.: Chartered Inst. Pub. Fin. and Accountancy (investigations com. 2002—). Avocations: theater , walking, tennis. Education and schools. Office: Martineau Johnson St Philips House St Philips Pl Birmingham B3 2PP England

PHELAN, CHARLES SCOTT, retired lawyer; b. Saranac Lake, N.Y., Mar. 21, 1926; m. Ruth Rene Kuntzleman, Sept. 4, 1948; children: Susan P. Moser, Donna K. Merrick, Barbara K. Glumac. BSEE, Pa. State U., 1949; LLB, George Washington U., 1954. Bar: N.Y. 1955, U.S. Patent Office, 1956, U.S. Ct. Appeals (fed. cir.) 1982. Elec. engr. GE, Schenectady, N.Y., 1949-52, patent asst., 1950-54; sr. atty. AT&T Bell Labs., Whippany, N.J. and other cities, 1954-86; pvt. practice Millington, N.J., 1987-95; ret., 1995. Active Passaic Twp. (N.J.) Bd. Edn., 1962-64. 2d lt. U.S. Army, 1944-47. Mem. ABA, Am. Intellectual Property Law Assn., N.J. Patent Law Assn. (pres. 1964-65), Tau Beta Pi, Eta Kappa Nu. Avocations: fishing, hiking, sketching. Patent, Personal income taxation.

PHELAN, JOHN M. lawyer; b. Phila., Jan. 12, 1939; s. James J. and Gertrude (Murphy) P.; m. Joanne D'Arcy, Sept. 10, 1966; children: D'Arcy, John Jr., Sean. BS in Econs., U. Pa., 1960; LLB, Temple U., 1963. Bar: Pa. 1964, U.S. Dist. Ct. (ea. dist.) Pa. 1964, U.S. Ct. Appeals (3d cir.) 1972. Law clerk to chief justice Supreme Ct. of Pa., Phila., 1964-65; asst. dist. atty., Phila., 1966-69; assoc. Morgan, Lewis & Bockius, Phila., 1965-66, 1969-81; ptnr. Phelan, Pettit & Biedrzycki, Phila., 1981—. Mem. Pa. Bar Assn., Phila. Bar Assn. Republican. Roman Catholic. Clubs: Phila. Country (Gladwyne, Pa.) (tennis chmn. 1981-83); Union League (Phila.). Federal civil litigation, State civil litigation, Product liability. Office: Phelan Pettit & Biedrzycki 121 S Broad St Ste 1600 Philadelphia PA 19107-4533

PHELAN, ROBIN ERIC, lawyer; b. Steubenville, Ohio, Dec. 28, 1945; s. Edward John and Dorothy (Borkowski) P.; m. JoAnn Keach, June 27, 1970 (dec. May 1994); children: Travis McCoy, Tiffany Marie, Trevor Monroe; m. Melinda Jo Rickets, May 27, 1995; 1 child, Taezja Monet. BSBA, Ohio State U., 1967, JD, 1970. Bar: Tex. 1971, U.S. Ct. Appeals (5th cir.) 1981, U.S. Ct. Appeals (11th cir.) 1981, U.S. Ct. Appeals (6th cir.) 1986, U.S. Ct. Appeals (10th cir.) 1988, U.S. Supreme Ct. Ptnr. Haynes and Boone, Dallas, 1970—. Co-author: Bankruptcy Practice and Strategy, 1987, Cowans Bankruptcy Law and Practice, 1987, Annual Survey of Bankruptcy Law, 1988, Bankruptcy Litigation Manual; contbr. articles to profl. jours. Mem. ABA (chmn. insolvency and secured transactions com. internat. law sect.), Internat. Bar Assn., Internat. Insolvency Inst. (bd. dirs.), Am. Bankruptcy Inst. (dir., past pres.), Am. Coll. Bankruptcy, State Bar Tex. (chmn. bankruptcy law com. sect. bus. law 1989-91), Dallas Bar Assn. Roman Catholic. Avocation: athletics. Bankruptcy. Home: 4214 Woodfin St Dallas TX 75220-6416 E-mail: phelanr@haynesboone.com.

PHELPS, ANTHONY DAVID, lawyer; b. Oklahoma City, June 5, 1963; s. David Lemoine and Carol Joy Phelps; m. Monica Marie Marcinek, Jan. 18, 2000; 1 child, Kaitlyn Marie. BA, U. Okla., 1991, JD, 1994. Bar: Okla. 1994, U.S. Dist. Ct. (we., no., ea. dists.) Okla. 1994. Assoc. Lawter & Pitts, P.C., Oklahoma City, 1994—95, Hiltgen & Brewer, P.C., Oklahoma City, 2000—01, Merritt & Assocs., P.C., Oklahoma City, 2002—; ptnr. Moore & Phelps, LLC, Chickasha, Okla., 1995—2000. Mem.: ATLA, ABA, Oklahoma County Bar Assn., Okla. Trial Lawyers Assn. Democrat. Lutheran. Personal injury (including property damage), Product liability, Toxic tort. Office: Merritt and Assocs PC 917 N Robinson Oklahoma City OK 73102 Office Fax: 405-232-8360. Business E-Mail: anthony.phelps@merrittfirm.com.

PHELPS, ROBERT FREDERICK, JR., lawyer; b. Evanston, Ill., Aug. 20, 1956; s. Robert F. and Hanna (Kulej) P.; m. Joan Ann Brisky, Oct. 6, 1984; children: Jennifer Katherine, William Robert. BA, Trinity Coll., Hartford, Conn., 1978; JD cum laude, U. Mich., 1981; LLM, NYU, 1987. Bar: Conn. 1981, U.S. Tax Ct. 1987. Atty. Cummings & Lockwood, Stamford, Conn., 1981-87; atty. Day, Berry & Howard, Stamford, 1987-91; mng. dir. J.P. Morgan, N.Y.C., 1991—. Cons. Conn. Safe Deposit Assn., 1983-87; mem. Fairfield County Estate Planning Coun., 1987-98; mem. Conn. Tax and Estate Planning Coun., 1990-92, Denver Estate Planning Coun., Rocky Mountain Estate Planning Coun., 2000—. Contbr. articles to profl. jours. Bd. dirs. Greenwich Coun. on Youth and Drugs, Inc., 1985-89, Ctrl. City Opera Ho. Assn., Denver, 2002—; elder Noroton Presbyn. Ch., Darien, Conn., 1990-93; mem. Rep. Town Meeting, Darien, 1992-95; res. elder Highland Park Presbyn. Ch., 1998—; mem. adv. bd. So. Meth. U. Cox Sch. Bus., 2000-02. Mem. ABA (real property and probate sect., tax sect., lectr. tax sect. fall meeting 2000), Conn. Bar Assn. (estates sect., tax and real property sects.), Middlesex Club, Denver Press Club, Phi Beta Kappa. Republican. Avocation: tennis. Estate planning, Probate (including wills, trusts), Estate taxation. Home: 5495 Preserve Dr Greenwood Village CO 80121 Office: JP Morgan 370 17th St Ste 3200 Denver CO 80202 E-mail: robert.phelps@jpmorgan.com.

PHELPS, ROBERT J. lawyer; b. Davenport, Iowa, Apr. 20, 1946; s. Lowell Dean and Helen Berniece (Hall) P.; m. Cheryl Ann O'Brien, Sept. 3, 1966 (div. Nov. 1983); children: Kristin Marie, Randall L.; m. Lauren Gail McNaughton, June 16, 1984 (div. Dec. 2000). BA in History, U. Iowa, 1971; MA in Internat. Relations, U. Ark., 1972; JD, U. Tulsa, 1974. Bar: Okla. 1975, U.S. Dist. Ct. (no. dist.) Okla. 1975, Iowa 1987, U.S. Dist. Ct. (so. dist.) Iowa 1987. Assoc. Drummond and Raymond, Pawhuska, Okla., 1975; from assoc. to ptnr. Byers and Phelps, Cleve., 1975-83; sole practice Cleve., 1983-87, Davenport, Iowa, 1987—. Mem. Pawnee County Rep. Cen. Com., Cleve., 1986; bd. dirs. Cleve. Area Health Care Found., 1977-87; mem. Davenport City Rep. Party Cen. Com., 1987-89. Served as sgt. USAF, 1968-72. Mem. Iowa Bar Assn., Scott County Bar Assn., Davenport C. of C., Cleve. C. of C. (chmn. indsl. devel. com. 1986-87). Avocations: reading, swimming, tennis. Commercial, consumer (including collections, credit), Criminal, General practice. Office: 1622 E Lombard St Davenport IA 52803-2448 E-mail: rjp5555@aol.com.

PHILIP, MARIANNE, lawyer; b. Copenhagen, July 14, 1957; d. Allan and Birthe Philip; m. Per Haakon Schmidt, Apr. 11, 1981; children: Mikael, Jesper, Frederik. JD, U. Copenhagen, 1980; LLM, Duke U., 1983. Bar: Denmark 1983. Assoc. Reumert & Ptnrs. (now Kromann Reumert), Copenhagen, 1980—82, assoc., 1984—89, ptnr., 1989—; fgn. assoc. Shearman & Sterling , N.Y.C., 1983—84. Chmn. bd. dirs. Irwin Indsl. Tool Co. A/S, Aamund A/S, Bisca Holding A/S, Sehested Consulting A/S; bd. dirs. Bacardi-Martini Danmark A/S, Cubic Transp. Sys. (Nordic) A/S, Klinger Danmark A/S, ProActive A/S, Brenntag Nordic A/S, Ferdinand Andersens Legat and Ingrid Zachariaes Found., Duke U. Law Sch., NC. Author: Selskabsret, 2000; contbr. articles to profl. jours. Avocations: travel, skiing, cooking. Corporate, general, Mergers and acquisitions, Securities. Home: Tranegårdsvej 5 2900 Hellerup Denmark Office: Kromann Reumert Sundkrogsgade 5 2100 Copenhagen Denmark

PHILIPSBORN, JOHN TIMOTHY, lawyer, writer; b. Paris, Oct. 19, 1949; s. John David and Helen (Worth) P. AB, Bowdoin Coll., 1971; MEd, Antioch Coll., 1975; JD, U. Calif., Davis, 1978. Bar: Calif. 1978, U.S. Dist. Ct. (no., ctrl. and ea. dists.) Calif. 1978, U.S. Ct. Appeals (9th cir.) 1985, U.S. Supreme Ct. 1985; cert-specialist in criminal law State of Calif. VISTA vol. Office of Gov. State of Mont., Helena, 1972-73; cons. U.S. Govt., Denver, 1974; lectr. Antioch New Eng. Grad. Sch., Keene, N.H., 1973-75, U. N.H., Durham, 1973-75; ptnr. Philipsborn & Cohn, San Jose, Calif., 1978-80; atty., supr. Defenders Inc., San Diego, 1980-83; assoc. Garry, Dreyfus & McTernan, San Francisco, 1983-87; pvt. practice, San Francisco, 1987—. Cons. Nicaraguan ct. evaluation projects, 1987-88, UN Internat. Tribunal, 1995—; coord. Internat. Conf. Adversarial Sys., Lisbon, Portugal, 1990; mem. adj. faculty New Coll. Law, San Francisco, 1991—; legal asst. project refugee camps S.E. Asia, 1992, legal edn. projects, Cambodia, 1995, Pakistan, 2001; cons. on continuing edn. of bar, 1995—. Bd. editors Champion, Forum; contbr. articles to profl. jours., chpts. to book. Founder trial program San Francisco Schs., 1986; bd. dirs. Calif. Indian Legal Svcs., 1990-96. Fulbright scholar, Portugal, 1989, Pakistan, 2001—. Mem. Nat. Assn. Criminal Def. Lawyers (assoc., co-chmn. death penalty impact litigation group 1989, co-chmn. govtl. misconduct com. 1990-92, vice chmn. task force on emerging democracies 1990-91), Calif. State Bar (evaluation panel criminal law specialists 1986—, com. on continuing edn. of bar 1991-94, criminal law subcom. state bd. legal specialists 1995-96), Calif. Attys. for Criminal Justice (bd. govs. 1989-94, 2003—, assoc. editor jour. 1987—, chmn. Amicus Curiae com. 1992—, co-chmn. govtl. misconduct com. 1989-92), WorldCoun. Criminal, Public international. Office: 507 Polk St Ste 250 Civic Ctr Bldg San Francisco CA 94102-3375

PHILLIPOFF, MARK JAMES, lawyer; b. Kansas City, Mo., Dec. 28, 1951; s. James George Phillipoff and Dorothy L. (Bartley) Probst; m. Sigrid M. Henn, July 6, 1974; children: Lyndsey Ann, James Alexander. AB, U. Notre Dame, 1974; JD, Ind. U., 1980. Bar: Ind. 1980, U.S. Dist. Ct. (so. dist.) Ind. 1980, U.S. Dist. Ct. (no. dist.) Ind. 1983, U.S. Ct. Appeals (7th cir.) 1983, Mich. 1983, U.S. Supreme Ct. 1983, U.S. Dist. Ct. (we. dist.) Mich. 1985. Dep. prosecuting atty. Greene County, Bloomfield, Ind., 1980-81; assoc. Mellen, Mellen & Wood, Bedford, Ind., 1981-83; ptnr. Jones, Obenchain LLC, South Bend, Ind., 1983—. Bd. dirs. Hospice St. Joseph County, Inc., South Bend, 1986-92. Mem. ABA, ATLA, Ind. State Bar Assn., Mich. State Bar Assn., Notre Dame Club of St. Joseph County. Democrat. Roman Catholic. Avocations: boating, skiing, photography. General civil litigation, Family and matrimonial, Health. Home: 17927 Augusta Ct Granger IN 46530-8417 Office: Jones Obenchain LLC PO Box 4577 South Bend IN 46634-4577

PHILLIPS, ANTHONY FRANCIS, lawyer; b. Hartford, Conn., May 18, 1937; s. Frank and Lena Phillips; m. Rosemary Karran McGowan, Jan. 28, 1967; children: Karran, Antonia, Justin. BA, U. Conn., 1959; JD, Cornell U., 1962. Bar: N.Y. 1964, U.S. Dist. Ct. (so. dist., ea. dist.) N.Y. 1965, (ctrl. dist.) Calif. 1980, U.S. Tax Ct. 1981, U.S. Ct. Appeals (2nd cir.) 1967, (3d cir.) 1985, (4th cir.) 1983, (5th cir.) 1972, (7th cir.) 1987, (9th cir.) 1983, (10th cir.) 1983, U.S. Supreme Ct. 1971. Assoc. Willkie, Farr & Gallagher, N.Y.C., 1963-69, ptnr., 1969—. Mem. adv. com. Cornell U. Law Sch., 1994—. Fellow Am. Bar Found.; mem. ABA, N.Y. State Bar Assn., N.Y. County Bar Assn. (bd. dirs. 1989-95), Assn. of Bar of City of N.Y. Federal civil litigation, State civil litigation. Home: 3 Elm Rock Rd Bronxville NY 10708-4202 Office: Willkie Farr & Gallagher 787 7th Ave Lbby 2 New York NY 10019-6018 E-mail: aphillips@willkie.com.

PHILLIPS, BARNET, IV, lawyer; b. New York, N.Y., July 5, 1948; s. Barnet III and Isabelle (Auriema) P.; m. Sharon Walsted Packey, Jan. 2, 1981; children: Victoria Ilonka, Caroline Walsted. BA, Yale U., 1970; JD, Fordham U., 1973; LLM, NYU, 1977. Bar: N.Y. 1974. Assoc. Hughes Hubbard & Reed, N.Y.C., 1973-76, Skadden, Arps, Slate, Meagher & Flom, N.Y.C., 1977-81, ptnr., 1981—. Adj. assoc. prof. Fordham U., N.Y.C., 1987-88; articles editor The Tax Lawyer, 1989-91. Co-author: Structuring Corporate Acquisitions--Tax Aspects. Bd. dirs Student/Sponsor Partnership, N.Y.C., 1990-95; bd. cons. Portsmouth (R.I.) Abbey Sch., 1991-96, chmn.,1997-2002. Republican. Avocations: skiing, opera, triathlons. Corporate taxation, Taxation, general, Personal income taxation. Home: 6 Hycliff Rd Greenwich CT 06831-3223 Office: Skadden Arps Slate Meagher & Flom Four Times Square 42nd Flr New York NY 10036-6522 E-mail: bphillip@skadden.com.

PHILLIPS, BARRY, lawyer; b. Valdosta, Ga., Feb. 16, 1929; s. W. Otis and Gypsy (Mercer) P.; m. Grace Greer, Aug. 3, 1957; children: Mary Grace, Barry Jr., Greer, Quinton. AB, U. Ga., 1949, LLB, 1954. Bar: Ga. 1951, D.C. 1977. Assoc. Kilpatrick Stockton, Atlanta, 1954-60, ptnr., 1960-97, of counsel, 1997—. Bd. dirs., mem. exec. com., credit com. Bank South Corp., 1978-96. Mem. bd. regents Univ. Sys. Ga., 1988-94, vice chmn., 1991-93, chmn., 1993-94; trustee U. Ga. Found., Atlanta, 1983-87, treas., 1985-87; mem. bd. visitors U. Ga. Law Sch., 1983-87, chmn., 1985; dir. Ctrl. Atlanta Progress, 1985-86; dir. USA-ROC Econ. Coun., 1985-91; bd. dirs. Ga. Coun. Internat. Visitors, Atlanta, 1986-93, sec., 1986-87, pres., 1987-88; bd. dirs. Atlanta Conv. and Visitors Bur., 1986-91, sec., 1986-87, v.p., 1987-88; bd. dirs. Ga. Region NCCJ, 1980-98, co-chair, 1982-83; chmn. Met. Atlanta Olympic Games Authority, 1990-91; bd. dirs. Ga. Sports Hall of Fame, 1990—, vice chmn., 1993-95, chmn., 1995-96; attache Can. Olympic Team for 1996 Olympics, 1995-96. 1st lt. U.S. Army, 1951-53, Korea. Decorated Air medal; recipient Brotherhood-Sisterhood award Ga. Regional NCCJ, 1993. Fellow Am. Coll. Investment Counsel (bd. dirs. 1986-88), Ga. Bar Found., Soc. Internat. Bus. Fellows; mem. Ga. Bar Assn. (chmn. corp. and banking law sect. 1977-78), Atlanta Bar Assn., D.C. Bar Assn., Lawyers Club Atlanta, U. Ga. Law Sch. Alumni Assn. (trustee 1979-84, pres. 1982-83), Can. Am. Soc. (bd. dirs. 1981-90, pres. 1981-83), Brit. Am. Bus. Group (bd. dirs. 1985-95), Sphinx, Gridiron, Phi Beta Kappa, Phi Kappa Phi, Omicron Delta Kappa. Democrat. Methodist. Avocations: reading, travel. Home: 4850 Tanglewood Ct NW Atlanta GA 30327-4558 Office: Kilpatrick Stockton 1100 Peachtree St NE Ste 2800 Atlanta GA 30309-4530 E-mail: bphillips@kilstock.com., bphilatl@aol.com.

PHILLIPS, CARTER GLASGOW, lawyer; b. Canton, Ohio, Sept. 11, 1952; s. Max Dean and Virginia Scott (Carter) P.; m. Sue Jane Henry, June 5, 1976; children: Jessica, Ryan. BA, Ohio State U., 1973; MA, Northwestern U., 1975, JD, 1977. Bar: Ill. 1977, D.C. 1979, U.S. Dist. Ct. (no. dist.) Ill., U.S. Dist. Ct. (D.C. dist.), U.S. Ct. Appeals (1st, 2d, 3d, 4th, 5th, 6th, 7th, 8th, 9th, 10th, 11th, D.C. and Fed. cirs.). Law clk. U.S. Ct. Appeals (7th cir.), Chgo., 1977—78; law clk. to chief Justice Warren E. Burger U.S. Supreme Ct., Washington, 1978—79; asst. prof. law U. Ill., Champaign, 1979—81; asst. solicitor gen. U.S. Dept. Justice, Washington, 1981—84; ptnr. Sidley & Austin, Washington, 1984—; mng. ptnr. Sidley Austin Brown & Wood LLP, Washington, 1995—. Contbr. articles to profl. jours. Chief counsel Spina Bifida Assn. Am., Rockville, Md., 1987—; mem. bd. advisors state and local legal ctrs., Washington, 1985-91. Mem.: Am. Coll. Trial Lawyers, Acad. Appellate Lawyers, Am. Law Inst. Republican. Episcopalian. Administrative and regulatory, Federal civil litigation, Appellate. Office: Sidley Austin Brown & Wood LLP 1501 K St NW Fl 10 Washington DC 20005-3705 E-mail: cphillips@sidley.com.

PHILLIPS, DOROTHY KAY, lawyer; b. Nov. 2, 1945; d. Benjamin L. and Sadye (Levinsky) Phillips; children: Bethann P., David M. Schaffzin. BS in English Lit. magna cum laude, U. Pa., 1964; MA in Family Life & Marriage Counseling, NYU, 1975; JD, Villanova U., 1978. Bar: Pa. 1978, N.J. 1978, U.S. Dist. Ct. (ea. dist.) Pa. 1978, U.S. Dist. Ct. N.J., 1978, U.S. Ct. Appeals (3d cir.), 1984, U.S. Supreme Ct. 1984. Tchr. Haddon (N.J.) Twp. H.S., Haddon Heights H.S., 1964-70; lectr., counselor Marriage Coun. of Phila., U. Pa., Hahnemann Med. Schs., Phila., 1970-75; atty. Adler, Barish, Daniels, Levin & Creskoff, Phila., 1978-79, Astor, Weiss & Newman, Phila., 1979-80; ptnr. Romisher & Phillips. P.C., Phila., 1981-86; prin. Dorothy K. Phillips & Assocs., LLC, 1986—. Faculty Sch., of Law Temple U.; guest spkr. on domestic rels. issues on radio and TV shows; featured in newspaper and mag. articles; bd. mem. Anti-Defamation League of B'nai B'rith, Nat. Mus. Jewish History; mem. friend's circle, Athenaeum, Phila., shareholder. Contbr. articles to profl. jours. Mem. ABA, ATLA (membership com. 1990-91, co-chair 1989-90), Pa. Trial Lawyers Assn. (chair membership com. family sect. 1989-90, presenter ann. update civil litigators-family law, author procedures practice of family law Phila. County Family Law Litigation Sect. County practiced database 1991) Pa. Bar Assn. (continuing legal edn. com. 1990-92, faculty, lectr. Pa. Bar Inst. Continuing Legal Edn. 1990, panel mem. summer meeting 1991), N.J. Bar

Assn., Phila. Bar Assn. (chmn. early settlement program 1983-84, mem. custody rules drafting com. for Supreme Ct. Pa., spl. events spkr. on pensions, counsel fees, written fee agreements 1989-91, co-chair and moderator of panel mandatory continuing legal edn. 1994), Nat. Bus. Inst. (lectr. 1997—), Phila. Trial Lawyers Assn., Montgomery County Bar Assn., Lawyers Club. Appellate, State civil litigation, Family and matrimonial. Office Fax: 215-568-1711. E-mail: DKPhil@aol.com.

PHILLIPS, DWIGHT WILBURN, lawyer; b. Detroit, Dec. 19, 1951; s. Wilburn Raymond and Inez Marie (Sims) P. BA, U. San Francisco, 1973; JD, U. Mich., 1976. Bar: Mich. 1976. Assoc. Ronald Crenshaw and Assocs., Detroit, 1976-81; ptnr. Patterson, Phifer & Phillips, Detroit, 1981—. Chmn. bd. Eastside Br. YMCA, 1987-90. Mem. ABA, Mich. Bar Assn. (workers compensation sect., panel chmn., atty. discipline bd.), Wolverine Bar Assn. (treas. 1979-81), Assn. Trial Lawyers Am., Alpha Phi Alpha. Avocation: model trains. Personal injury (including property damage), Workers' compensation. Home: 1233 Audubon Rd Grosse Pointe MI 48230-1151 Office: Phifer, Phillips & White PC 1274 Library St Ste 500 Detroit MI 48226-2283 E-mail: dphillips@ppwlegal.com.

PHILLIPS, ELVIN WILLIS, lawyer; b. Tampa, Fla., Feb. 27, 1949; s. Claude Everett and Elizabeth (Willis) P.; m. Sharon Gayle Alexander, June 20, 1970; children: Natasha Hope, Tanya Joy, Trey Alexander. BA, U. Fla., 1971; MA, Western Carolina U., 1974, EdS, 1975; JD, Stetson U., 1980. Bar: Fla. 1980, U.S. Dist. Ct. (mid. dist.) Fla. 1981, U.S. Dist. Ct. (so. dist.) Fla. 1982, U.S. Ct. Appeals (11th cir.) 1988. Tchr. Monroe County Schs., Key West, Fla., 1970-73; asst. prin. Habersham County Schs., Clarksville, Ga., 1973-77; assoc. Dixon, Lawson & Brown, Tampa, Fla., 1980-81, Yado, Keel, Nelson et al, Tampa, Fla., 1981; ptnr. Lawson, McWhirter, Grandoff & Reeves, Tampa, Fla., 1981-88, Williams, Parker, Harrison, Dietz & Getzen, Sarasota, Fla., 1988—. Leadership Devel. Program fellow Southern Regional Coun., Atlanta, 1975. Mem. ABA (forum com. constrn. industry 1989-96), Assn. Legal Adminstrs., Fla. Bar (chmn. 1991-92, vice chmn. 1990-91, mem. benefits com.), Sarasota County Bar Assn., Phi Kappa Phi, Phi Alpha Delta, Phi Delta Kappa. Democrat. Baptist. Alternative dispute resolution, Construction, Government contracts and claims. Home: 3310 Del Prado Ct Tampa FL 33614-2721 Office: Williams Parker Harrison Dietz & Getzen 200 S Orange Ave Sarasota FL 34236-6802 E-mail: ephillips@williamsparker.com.

PHILLIPS, GARY STEPHEN, lawyer; b. Far Rockaway, N.Y., June 26, 1957; s. Lawrence and Ilene (Kaufman) P.; m. Debbie J. Kanner, Mar. 27, 1983; children: Joshua Charles, Allison Ilyse. BA with high honors, U. Fla., 1978, JD with honors, 1981. Bar: Fla. 1982, U.S. Dist. Ct. (so. dist.) Fla. 1982, U.S. Ct. Appeals (11th cir.) 1982, U.S. Supreme Ct. 1986. With Sparber, Shevin, Shapo & Heilbronner, Miami, Fla., 1981-87; pvt. practice law Miami, 1987-90; with Buchanan Ingersoll P.C., Miami, 1990-95, Phillips, Eisinger & Brown, P.A., Hollywood, Fla., 1996—. Contbr. editor U. Fla. Law Rev., 1980-81. Named one of Leading Fla. Attys.-Comml. Litig., Best of the Bar, South Fla. Bus. Jour., 2003, South Fla. Legal Guide Top Lawyers, 2003. Mem.: ABA, North Dade Bar Assn. (treas. 1992), Dade County Bar Assn., Fla. Bar Assn. (litig., real property, probate and trust law sects.), Am. Judicature Soc., Omicron Delta Epsilon, B'nai B'rith, Omicron Delta Kappa, Phi Beta Kappa. Democrat. Jewish. Federal civil litigation, State civil litigation, Personal injury (including property damage). Office: 4000 Hollywood Blvd Ste 265 Hollywood FL 33021-6782

PHILLIPS, JAMES EDGAR, lawyer; b. N.Y.C., Aug. 30, 1947; s. Jack Louis Phillips and Jacqueline (Kasper) Ehrman; children: Zachary J., Mark H. BA, Boston U., 1971; JD, Case Western Reserve U., 1975. Bar: Ohio 1975, U.S. Supreme Ct. 1977, U.S. Dist. Ct. (so. dist.) 1978, U.S. Ct. Appeals (6th cir.) 1981, U.S. Dist. Ct. (no. dist.) 1982. Asst. prosecutor Franklin County Prosecutor Office, Columbus, Ohio, 1975-77, sr. asst. prosecutor, 1977-79; assoc. Vorys, Sater, Seymour & Pease, Columbus, 1979-84, ptnr., 1984—; spl. prosecutor State of Ohio, 1993—. Gen. counsel Nat. Fraternal Order of Police, Washington, 1987—, Conrail Police #1, U.S. Postal Police #2; mem. Bd. Profl. Law Enforcement Certification; pres. Ohio Ctr. for Law-Related Edn., 1985-95; mem. Wong Sun Soc., 1997—. Author: Civil Recovery in Ohio, 1986, Collective Bargaining in the Pub. Sector, 1988; editor Bar Briefs; contbr. articles Jours., 1987-89. Fellow Ohio Bar Found., Columbus Bar Found., Ohio Bar Assn. (chmn. com. law-related edn. 1982-86), Columbus Bar Assn., Am. Judicature Soc., Sixth Cir. Jud. Conf. (life); bd. dirs. Ohio Assn. Criminal Defense Lawyers. General civil litigation, Criminal, General practice. Office: Vorys Sater Seymour & Pease PO Box 1008 52 E Gay St Columbus OH 43215-3161 E-mail: phillips@vssp.com.

PHILLIPS, JAMES HAROLD, lawyer; b. Dec. 18, 1934; s. Frank Carroll and Mabel Lorraine (James) Phillips; m. Jean Kier Woodruff, Oct. 2, 1959; children: Susan, John(dec.) , Sara, Jamie. BSEE, Rose-Hulman Inst. Tech., 1960; JD, George Washington U., 1967. Bar: Ariz. 68, U.S. Dist. Ct. Ariz. 68, U.S. Patent Office 68, U.S. Supreme Ct. 72, U.S. Ct. Customs & Patent Appeals 74, Tex. 80, U.S. Ct. Appeals (fed. cir.) 82. Patent atty. GE, 1967—68; ptnr. Drummond, Cahill & Phillips, Phoenix, 1968—73; asst. patent counsel NCR Corp., Dayton, Ohio, 1973—76; sr. profl. atty. Sun Co. Inc., Dallas, 1976—84; ptnr. Cates & Phillips, Phoenix, 1984—88; asst. patent counsel Bull HN Info. Sys., Phoenix, 1988—95; patent cons. Bull NH Info. Sys., Phoenix, 2000—; counsel Squire, Sanders and Dempsey, Phoenix, 1995—2000. Contbr. articles to profl. jours. Charter mem. Phoenix Symphony Coun.; pres. AMICA-Tex. chpt. With USN, 1952—55. Mem.: Tex. Bar Assn., Ariz. Bar Assn. (chmn. patent, trademark and copyright sect. 1985—86). Patent, Trademark and copyright. Home: 410 E Braeburn Dr Phoenix AZ 85022-3624 Office: Bull HN Info Sys Inc 13430 N Black Canyon Hwy Phoenix AZ 85029-1361

PHILLIPS, JOHN BOMAR, lawyer; b. Murfreesboro, Tenn., Jan. 28, 1947; s. John Bomar Sr. and Betty Blanche (Primm) P.; m. Ellen Elizabeth Ellis, Aug. 9, 1969; children: John Bomar III, Anna Carroll, Ellis Elizabeth. BS, David Lipscomb Coll., 1969; JD, U. Tenn., 1974. Bar: Tenn. 1974, U.S. Dist. Ct. (ea. dist.) Tenn. 1975, U.S. Ct. Appeals (6th cir.) 1980. Assoc. Stophel, Caldwell & Heggie, Chattanooga, 1974-79; ptnr. Caldwell, Heggie & Helton, Chattanooga, 1979-91, Miller & Martin, Chattanooga, 1991—, mng. ptnr., 1997—2002; deputy gen. counsel labor and employment Coca-Cola Enterprises Inc., 2002—. Author: Tennessee Employment Law, 1989, 3d edit., 2000, Employment Law Desk Book for Tennessee Employers, 1989; editor: Tennessee Employment Law Letter, 1986—; host Danger Zones Video Tng. Series for Suprs., 1998—; mem. nat. moot ct. team U. Tenn. Law Rev. Pres. Chattanooga State coll. Found., 1992-94, Boys Club of Chattanooga, 1983-84; sec. Tenn. Aquarium, 1989—; chmn. Chattanooga Conv. and Visitors Bur., 1996-97; bd. dirs. Vol. Comty. Sch., Chattanooga, 1980-85, Coun. for Alcohol and Drug Abuse, Chattanooga, 1981-83, Creative Discovery Mus., 1994-99, Girls Prep. Sch., 1997-2002, Allied Arts of Gtr. Chattahooga, 1997-2002; mem. Hamilton County Juvenile Ct. Commn., 1995-99. Fellow Tenn. Bar Found., Chattanooga Bar Found.; mem. ABA (labor law sect.), Tenn. Bar Assn. (chair labor law sect. 1992-93, Justice Joseph W. Henry award 1986-87), Chattanooga Bar Assn. (bd. govs. 1978-79), Chattanooga C. of C. (bd. dirs. 1998-2001), Order of Coif, Fairyland Country Club (Lookout Mountain, Tenn.), Walden Club (bd. govs. 1992-95), Mountain City Club, Kiwanis (pres. Chattanooga 1986-87). Episcopal. Avocations: reading, writing. Labor (including EEOC, Fair Labor Standards Act, labor-management relations, NLRB, OSHA), Libel. Home: 1107 E Brow Rd Lookout Mountain TN 37350-1015 Office: Miller & Martin 832 Georgia Ave Ste 1000 Chattanooga TN 37402-2289 E-mail: jphillips@millermartin.com.

PHILLIPS, JOHN C. lawyer; b. S.I., N.Y., June 6, 1948; s. John D. G. and Eleanor (Stier) P.; m. Karen Francis McKenna, June 5, 1971; children: James, Thomas, Robert. AB in Govt., Cornell U., 1970; MA in Polit. Sci., Rutgers U., 1972, JD, 1975. Bar: N.J. 1975, U.S. Dist. Ct. N.J. 1975, N.Y. 1982, U.S. Supreme Ct. 1985, U.S. Ct. Appeals (3d cir.) 1985, Fla. 1988. Assoc. Carpenter, Bennett & Morrisey, Newark, 1975-79, Buttermore, Mullen & Jeremiah, Westfield, N.J., 1979-80; mng. ptnr. Buttermore, Mullen, Jeremiah & Phillips, Westfield, 1981-85, 87-2001; with DeVos, Phillips & Co. PC, 1986-87; of counsel Price, Meese, Shulman & D'Arminio, 2001—. Trustee, dir. Animal Care Fund Inc., East Smithfield, Pa., 1983-98. Author: (with others) New Jersey Transactins, Zoning and Planning, 1993. Dir., coach Police Athletic League, Berkeley Heights, N.J., 1967-99; mem. Kappa Alpha Literary Soc., 1967—, trustee Kappa Alpha Assn., 1974-90, v.p. Kappa Alpha Assn. Found., 1978-87, vice-chmn., 1983, chmn., 1984; dir. Youth Soccer Club, Berkeley Heights, 1983-94; mem. Berkeley Heights Twp. Com., 1985-87, dep. mayor, 1986, 87; Twp. atty., Berkeley Heights, 1989, 91, 94-2002; planning bd. atty. Twp. Warren, 1987-2001; mem. N.J. Hotel and Multiple Dwelling Safety Bd., 1988—, vice chmn., 1998—; mem. Rep. Mcpl. Com., 1985-2000, vice chmn., 1990-92, 98-2000, mem. dist. XII ethics com., 1993-97, dist. XII fee arbitration com., 1998-2002. Recipient award for Assistance and Dedication to youth, Police Athletic League, Berkeley Heights, 1975, Dedicated Svc. award Berkeley Heights Twp. Com., 1983. Mem.: ABA, Inst. of Mcpl. Attys., Fedn. of Planning Ofcls., Urban Land Inst., Union County Bar Assn., N.J. State Bar Assn., Canoe Brook Country Club, Jaycees (sec. New Providence-Berkeley Heights chpt. 1982, Jaycee of Yr. 1982). Republican. Methodist. State civil litigation, Land use and zoning (including planning), Personal injury (including property damage). Home: 56 Emerson Ln Berkeley Heights NJ 07922-2414 Office: Price Meese Shulman & D'Arminio 50 Tice Blvd Woodcliff Lake NJ 07677 E-mail: jphillips@pricemeese.com.

PHILLIPS, JOSEPH BRANTLEY, JR., lawyer; b. Greenville, S.C., Dec. 5, 1931; BS in Bus. Adminstrn., U. S.C., 1954, JD, 1955. Bar: S.C. 1955. Assoc. Leatherwood, Walker, Todd & Mann, Greenville, 1958-63, ptnr., 1963—. Chmn. bd. deacons Presbyterian Ch., 1970-71, pres. Men of Ch., 1968-69, chmn. Christian Service Ctr., 1972-73; bd. dirs. Greenville Urban Ministry, 1978. Mem. ABA, S.C. Bar Assn., Greenville Bar Assn., Greenville Young Lawyers Club (pres. 1961-62), Lawyers Pilots Bar Assn., Kiwanis (pres. 1973). Clubs: Greenville Country (pres. 1977). Antitrust, Aviation, Corporate, general. Home: 207 Butler Springs Rd Greenville SC 29615-2261 Office: PO Box 87 Greenville SC 29602-0087 E-mail: jbphillipsjr@aol.com.

PHILLIPS, KAREN BORLAUG, economist, railroad industry executive; b. Long Beach, Calif., Oct. 1, 1956; d. Paul Vincent and Wilma (Tish) Borlaug. Student, Cath. U. P.R., 1973-74; BA, BS, U. N.D., 1977; postgrad., George Washington U., 1978-80. Rsch. asst. rsch. and spl. programs adminstrn. U.S. Dept. Transp., Washington, 1977—78, economist, office of sec., 1978—82; profl. staff mem. (majority) Com. Commerce Sci., Transp. U.S. Senate, Washington, 1982—85, tax economist (majority) com. on fin., 1985—87, chief economist (majority) senate com. on fin., 1987—88; commr. Interstate Commerce Commn., Washington, 1988—94; v.p. legis. Assn. Am. Railroads, Washington, 1994—95, sr. v.p. policy, legis. and comm., 1995—98; pres. Policy & Advocacy Assocs., Alexandria, Va., 1998—2000; v.p. U.S. govt. affairs Can. Nat. Rlwy. Co., Washington, 2000—. Contbr. articles to profl. jours. Recipient award for Meritorious Achievement, Sec. Transp., 1980, Spl. Achievement awards, 1978, 80, Outstanding Performance awards, 1978, 80, 81. Mem. Am. Econ. Assn., Women's Transp. Seminar (Woman of Yr. award 1994), Transp. Rsch. Forum, Assn. Transp. Law, Logistics and Policy, Tax Coalition, Can.-Am. Bus. Coun. (bd. dirs.), Blue Key, Phi Beta Kappa, Omicron Delta Epsilon. Republican. Lutheran. Office: Can Nat Rlwy Co Ste 500 601 Pennsylvania Ave NW Washington DC 20004 E-mail: karen.phillips@cn.ca.

PHILLIPS, LARRY EDWARD, lawyer; b. Pitts., July 5, 1942; s. Jack F. and Jean H. (Houghtelin) P.; m. Karla Ann Hennings, June 5, 1976; 1 son, Andrew H.; 1 stepson, John W. Dean IV. BA, Hamilton Coll., 1964; JD, U. Mich., 1967. Bar: Pa. 1967, U.S. Dist. Ct. (we. dist.) Pa. 1967, U.S. Tax Ct. 1969. Assoc. Buchanan, Ingersoll, Rodewald, Kyle & Buerger, P.C., Pitts., 1967-73, mem., 1973—. Mem. ABA (sect. taxation, com. on corp. tax and sect. real property, probate and trust law), Am. Coll. Tax Counsel, Pa. Bar Assn., Tax Mgmt. Inc. (adv. bd.), Pitts. Tax Club, Allegheny County Bar Assn., Duquesne Club. Republican. Presbyterian. Corporate taxation, Estate taxation, Personal income taxation. Office: Buchanan Ingersoll PC One Oxford Ctr 301 Grant St Fl 20 Pittsburgh PA 15219-1410 E-mail: phillipsle@bipc.com.

PHILLIPS, LEO HAROLD, JR., lawyer; b. Jan. 10, 1945; s. Leo Harold and Martha C. (Oberg) P.; m. Patricia Margaret Halcomb, Sept. 3, 1983. BA summa cum laude, Hillsdale Coll., 1967; MA, U. Mich., 1968, JD cum laude, 1973; LLM magna cum laude, Free U. of Brussels, 1974. Bar: Mich. 1974, N.Y. 1975, U.S. Supreme Ct. 1977, D.C. 1979. Fgn. lectr. Pusan Nat. U., Korea, 1969-70; assoc. Alexander & Green, N.Y.C., 1974-77; counsel Overseas Pvt. Investment Corp., Washington, 1977-80, sr. counsel, 1980-82, asst. gen. counsel, 1982-85, Manor Care, Inc., Gaithersburg, Md., 1985-91, asst. sec., 1988-99, assoc. gen. counsel, 1991-99, v.p., 1996-99. Vol. Peace Corps, Pusan, 1968-71; mem. program for sr. mgrs. in govt. Harvard U., Cambridge, Mass., 1982. Contbr. articles to legal jours. Chmn. legal affairs com. Essex Condominium Assn., Washington, 1979-81; mem. fin. com., cmty. leadership bd. Miami City Ballet, 2001—; deacon Chevy Chase Presbyn. Ch., Washington, 1984-87, moderator, 1985-87, supt. ch. sch., elder, trustee, 1987-90, pres., 1988-90, mem. nominating com., 1995-96; treas. Delray Beach Rotary Club, 2003-. Recipient Alumni Achievement award Hillsdale Coll., 1980; Meritorious Honor award Overseas Pvt. Investment Corp., 1981, Superior Achievement award, 1984. Mem. ABA (internat. fin. transactions com., vice-chmn. com. internat. ins. Law), Am. Soc. Internat. Law (Jessup Internat. Law moot ct. judge semi-final rounds 1978-83, chair corp. counsel com. 1993-97), Internat. Law Assn. (Am. br.; com. sec. 1982), D.C. Bar, N.Y. State Bar Assn., Royal Asiatic Soc. (Korea br.), State Bar Mich., Washington Fgn. Law Soc. (sec.-treas. 1980-81, bd. dirs., program coord. 1981-82, v.p. 1982-83, pres.-elect 1983-84, pres. 1984-85, chmn. nominating com. 1986, 88), Washington Internat. Trade Assn. (bd. dirs. 1984-87), Bar City N.Y., Hillsdale Coll. Alumni Assn. (co-chmn. Washington area 1977-90), Univ. Club (N.Y.C.). Commercial, contracts (including sales of goods; commercial financing), Corporate, general, Private international.

PHILLIPS, RICHARD MYRON, lawyer, educator; b. N.Y.C., Sept. 8, 1931; s. Morris and Henrietta (Schatz) P.; m. Elda Marie, June 11, 1955; children— Laurie, David, Stephen. B.A., Columbia U., 1951; LL.B., Yale U., 1956. Bar: D.C. 1957. Atty. Office Gen. Counsel Bur. Aero., 1956-57; with SEC, Washington, 1960-68, spl. counsel Office Gen. Counsel, 1964-66, asst. gen. counsel, 1966-68; mem. Surrey, Karasik, Greene & Hill, Washington, 1968-71, Kirkpatrick & Lockhart, and predecessor firms, Washington, 1971—; Trustee SEC Historical Soc.; mem. legal adv. com. Nat. Assn. Securities Dealers, Inc. Served with U.S. Navy. Mem. ABA, Fed. Bar Assn. Contbr. articles to profl. jours. Federal civil litigation, Corporate, general, Securities. Office: Kirkpatrick & Lockhart Four Embarcadero Ctr San Francisco CA 94111

PHILLIPS, ROBERT JAMES, JR., lawyer, corporate executive; b. Houston, 1955; s. Robert James and Mary Josephine Phillips; m. Nancy Norris, Apr. 24; 1 child. BBA, So. Meth. U., 1976, JD, 1980. Bar: Tex. 1980. Vp., gen. counsel Aegis Shipping Ltd., London, 1980-81; assoc. Bishop, Larrimore, Lamsens & Brown, 1981-82; pres. Phillips Devel. Corp., Ft. Worth, 19825; pvt. practice Ft. Worth, 1982-87, 895; assoc. Haynes and Boone, Ft. Worth, 1988-89; sr. v.p. Am. Real Estate Group, 1989-93, Am. Savs. Bank, N.A., New West Fed. Savs. and Loan Assn., 1989-93, Am. Savs. Bank, Ft. Worth, 1991-92; chmn., CEO creative risk control Environ. Risk Mgmt. Inc., Ft. Worth, 1992-94; pres., CEO Pangburn Candy Co., 1996-99; exec. v.p. Ancor Holdings, 1999—2002; chmn., CEO Am. Staff Resources Corp., 1999—. Bd. dirs. Tex. Heritage, Inc.; chmn., CEO Am. Staff Resources Corp., 1999—. Bd. dirs., exec. com. Ft. Worth Ballet Assn., 1984-85, Van Cliburn Found.; v.p. planning, bd. dirs., exec. com. Ft. Worth Symphony Orch., 1984-85; bd. dirs. Mus. Modern Art, 1986; bd. dirs., exec. com., chmn. investment com. Tex. Boys Choir, 1983-85. Mem. ABA, Tex. Bar Assn., Ft. Worth Bd. Realtors, Crescent Club, Phi Delta Phi, Kappa Sigma, Beta Gamma Sigma. Clubs: River Crest Country, Ft. Worth. Avocations: hunting, fishing, photography. Estate planning, General practice, Property, real (including real estate development, water). Home and Office: PO Box 470099 Fort Worth TX 76147-0099

PHILLIPS, ROBERT JOHN, lawyer; b. Bournemouth, Hampshire, Eng., May 15, 1947; s. Geoffrey Charles and Betty Eileen P.; m. Eleanor Jean Jack, Dec. 12, 1974; children: Nicola, Hannah, James. Bar: solicitor Eng. and Wales, Hong Kong; barrister and solicitor Victoria, Australia. Ptnr. CMS Cameron McKenna, London, 1977—, McKenna & Co., London, 1979—83, 1988—, Hong Kong, 1983—88. Mem.: Major Projects Assn. Utilities, public. Office: CMS Cameron McKenna Mitre House 160 Aldersgate EC1A 4DD London England Fax: 02073672000. E-mail: robert.phillips@cmlk.com.

PHILLIPS, RONALD FRANK, university administrator; b. Houston, Nov. 25, 1934; s. Franklin Jackson and Maudie Ethel (Merrill) P.; m. Jamie Jo Bottoms, Apr. 5, 1957 (dec. Sept. 1996); children: Barbara Celeste Phillips Oliveira, Joel Jackson, Phil Edward. BS, Abilene Christian U., 1955; JD, U. Tex., 1965. Bar: Tex. 1965, Calif. 1972. Bldg. contractor Phillips Homes, Abilene, Tex., 1955-56; br. mgr. Phillips Weatherstripping Co., Midland and Austin, Tex., 1957-65; corp. staff atty. McWood Corp., Abilene, 1965-67; sole practice law Abilene, 1967-70; mem. adj. faculty Abilene Christian U., 1967-70; prof. law Pepperdine U., Malibu, Calif., 1970—, dean Sch. Law, 1970-97, dean emeritus, 1997—, vice chancellor, 1995—. Deacon North A and Tenn. Ch. of Christ, Midland, 1959-62; deacon Highland Ch. of Christ, Abilene, 1965-70; elder Malibu Ch. of Christ, 1978-95; mgr., coach Little League Baseball, Abilene, Huntington Beach and Malibu, 1968-78, 90-95; coach Youth Soccer, Huntington Beach, Westlake Village and Malibu, 1972-80, 85-86, 91. Recipient Alumni citation Abilene Christian U., 1974 Fellow Am. Bar Found. (life); mem. ABA, State Bar Tex., State Bar Calif., Christian Legal Soc., L.A. Bar Assn., Assn. Am. Law Schs. (chmn. sect. on adminstrn. law schs. 1982, com. on cts. 1985-87), Am. Law Inst., Nat. Conf. Commrs. on Uniform State Laws. Republican. Office: Pepperdine U 24255 Pacific Coast Hwy Malibu CA 90263-0002 E-mail: ronald.phillips@pepperdine.edu.

PHILLIPS, T. STEPHEN, lawyer; b. Tennyson, Ind., Oct. 1, 1941; AB, DePauw U., 1963; LLB, Duke U., 1966. Bar: Ohio 1966, Ind. 1967. Assoc. Frost & Jacobs, Cin., 1966-72; ptnr. Frost & Jacobs (now Frost Brown Todd LLC), Cin., 1972—. Adj. prof. North Ky. U. Chase Coll. Law, Highland Hights, 1983—. Contbg. editor: Ohio Probate Practice (Addams and Hosford), Page on Wills. Trustee Spring Grove Cemetery, Cin.; chmn. Bethesda Found. Methodist. Estate planning, Probate (including wills, trusts), Estate taxation. Office: Frost Brown Todd LLC 2500 PNC Ctr 201 E 5th St Ste 2500 Cincinnati OH 45202-4182

PHILLIPS, THOMAS ROYAL, judge; b. Dallas, Oct. 23, 1949; s. George S. and Marguerite (Andrews) P.; m. Lyn Bracewell, June 26, 1982; 1 son, Daniel Austin Phillips; 1 stepson, Thomas R. Kirkham. BA, Baylor U., 1971; JD, Harvard U., 1974; LLD (hon.), Tex. Tech. U., 1997; DHL (hon.), St. Edwards U., 1998. Bar: Tex. 1974; cert. in civil trial law Tex. Bd. Legal Specialization. Briefing atty. Supreme Ct. Tex., Austin, 1974-75; assoc. Baker & Botts, Houston, 1975-81; judge 280th Dist. Ct., Houston, 1981-88; chief justice Supreme Ct. Tex., Austin, 1988—. Mem. com. on fed.-state rels. Jud. Conf. U.S., 1990-96; chair Tex. Jud. Dists. Bd., 1988—; mem. Tex. Jud. Coun., 1988—, chair, 1998&; mem. State Judges Mass Tort Litig. Com., 1991-96; bd. dirs. Elmo B. Hunter Citizens Ctr. for Jud. Selection, 1992-94, Ctr. Am. Internat. Law.; mem. Nat. Conf. Chief Justices, 1988—, pres., 1997-98; adv. dir. Rev. of Litig., U. Tex. Law Sch., 1990—; chair Nat. Mass Tort Conf. Planning Com., 1993-94. Bd. advisors Ctr. for Pub. Policy Dispute Resolution, U. Tex. Law Sch., 1993—; mem. planning com. South Tex. Coll. of Law Ctr. for Creative Legal Solutions, 1993—; adv. dir. Austin Habitat for Humanity, 1993-96. Recipient Outstanding Young Lawyer award Houston Young Lawyers Assn., 1986, Outstanding Tex. Leader award John Ben Shepperd Pub. Leadership Forum, 1989, award of excellence in govt. Tex. C. of C., 1992, Disting. Svc. award Nat. Ctr. for State Cts., 1999, Rosewood Gavel award St. Mary's U. Sch. Law, 2002; named Appellate Judge of Yr., Tex. Assn. Civil Trial and Appellate Specialists, 1992-93, Disting. Alumnus, Baylor U., 1998. Mem. ABA (task force lawyers polit. contbns. 1997-98, com. on 21st Century judiciary, 2002-03), Am. Law Inst. (advisor Fed. Jud. Code Project 1996-2001), Nat. Ctr. for State Ctrs. (chair, bd. dirs. 1997-98), State Bar Tex. (chmn. pattern jury charges IV com. 1985-87, vice chmn. adminstrn. justice com. 1986-87), Am. Judicature Soc. (bd. dirs. 1989-95, 99—, exec. bd. 1995-96), Tex. Philol. Soc., Houston Philol. Soc., Houston Bar Assn., Travis County Bar Assn., Bastrop County Bar Assn., Order of Coif. Republican. Episcopalian. Office: Tex Supreme Ct PO Box 12248 Austin TX 78711-2248 E-mail: cj@tomphillips.com.

PHILLIPSON, DONALD E. lawyer; b. Denver, July 22, 1942; BS, Stanford U., 1964, JD, 1968; MS, U. Calif., Berkeley, 1965. Former mem. Davis, Graham & Stubbs, Denver; now cons., writer. Mem. Nat. Soccer Hall of Fame (adminstr.). Federal civil litigation, Patent. Office: 14325 Braun Rd Golden CO 80401-1431

PHIPPS, DAVID LEE, lawyer; b. Fairfield, Iowa, Jan. 11, 1945; s. Sherman Richard and Dorthy Helen Phipps; children: Rachelle, Martin, Robin, Kelly. BA, Drake U., 1967, JD with honors, 1969. Bar: Iowa 1969, U.S. Dist. Ct. (so. dist.) Iowa, 1969, U.S. Dist. Ct. (no. dist.) Iowa 1974, U.S. Ct. Appeals (8th cir.) 1975. Assoc. Whitfield & Eddy, Des Moines, 1969-74, ptnr., 1974—. Contbr. articles to profl. jours. Mem. ABA, Internat. Assn. Def. Counsel, Am. Coll. Trial Lawyers, Am. Bd. Trial Advocates, Iowa State Bar Assn., Iowa Def. Counsel Assn. (past pres.), Def. Rsch. Inst. (bd. dirs. 1999-2002), Iowa Acad. Trial Lawyers, Polk County Bar Assn. Mem. Cmty. Of Christ Ch. Avocations: reading, woodworking, collecting. Federal civil litigation, General civil litigation, Insurance. Office: Whitfield & Eddy PLC 317 6th Ave Ste 1200 Des Moines IA 50309-4195

PIANKO, THEODORE A. lawyer; b. Dennville, N.J., Sept. 5, 1955; s. Theodore and Pasqualina (Liguori) Pianko; m. Beatriz Maria Olivera (div. Dec. 1985); m. Kathryn Anne Lindley, Feb. 18, 1990; children: Matthew James, Samuel Wahoo, Zoe Wahoo. BA, SUNY, 1975; JD, U. Mich., 1978. Bar: Mich. 1978, Ill. 1979, Calif. 1980. Atty. Ford Motor Co., Dearborn, Mich., 1978-80; assoc. Lillick McHose & Charles, L.A., 1980-83; ptnr. Sidley & Austin, L.A., 1983-94, Christie, Parker & Hale, Newport Beach, Calif., 1994—. Intellectual property. E-mail: ted@pianko.com.

PIAZOLO, KATHRIN BARBARA, lawyer; b. Rosenheim, Germany, Feb. 5, 1967; d. Klaus Hugo Piazolo and Eleonore Edith Groffebert. Grad., Ruhr U., 1993; PhD, U. Hamburg, 1998. Bar: Germany 1997. Atty., Villingen, Germany, 1997—. Author: Social Dialog, 1998. Trainer Youth for Understanding, Germany. Mergers and acquisitions, Corporate, general. Office: Schrade & Ptnr Karlsruher Strasse 21 D-78048 Villingen Germany E-mail: kathrin.piazolo@schrade-partner.de.

PICADIO, ANTHONY PETER, lawyer; b. Latrobe, Pa.,.Dec. 7, 1941; s. Peter J. and Elsie M. (Caldarelli) P.; m. Lynette Norton. BA, U. Pitts., 1965, JD, 1970. Bar: Pa. 1970, U.S. Dist. Ct. (we. dist.) Pa. 1970, U.S. Ct. Appeals (3d cir.) 1971, U.S. Supreme Ct. 1998. Asst. atty. gen. Dept. Environ Protection Commonwealth Pa., 1970-72; ptnr. Reding, Blackstone, Rea & Sell, Pitts., 1972-75, Tucker, Arensberg, P.C., Pitts., 1975-85; founder, sr. ptnr. Picadio, Sneath, Miller & Norton, Pitts., 1985—. Mem.: Order of Coif. General civil litigation, Construction, Environmental. Office: Picadio Sneath Miller & Norton PC US Steel Tower 600 Grant St Ste 4710 Pittsburgh PA 15219-2703 E-mail: picadio@psmn.com.

PICCO, STEVEN JOSEPH, lawyer; b. N.Y.C., Sept. 9, 1948; s. Carl and Constance (Speers) P.; m. Ada T. Ryan, July 15, 1972; children: Christopher, Timothy, Kaitlin. BS, Rider Coll., Lawrenceville, N.J., 1970; JD, Seton Hall U., 1975. Bar: N.J. 1975, U.S. Dist. Ct. N.J. 1975, U.S. Ct. Appeals (3d cir.) 1975. Data processing programmer-sys. engring. N.J. Dept. Labor and Industry, Trenton, 1970-75; project specialist N.J. Dept. Environ. Protection, Trenton, 1975-76, dir. regulatory and govtl. affairs, 1976-78, acting dep. commr., 1979-80, asst. commr., 1979-81, N.J. Dept. Energy, Newark, 1978-79; ptnr. Greenstone & Sokol, Trenton, 1981-87, Picco Mack Herbert Kennedy Jaffe & Yoskin, Trenton, 1988-97, Reed Smith LLP, Princeton, N.J., 1997—. Bd. dirs. Northeast-Midwest Inst., Robert Wood Johnson Univ. Hosp. at Hamilton; treas. N.J. Orgn. for a Better State; mem. N.J. Seed., Am. Heart Assn., Heritage bd. Mem. Am. Credit Assn. (pres. 2001—). Avocations: golf, reading, community volunteer work. Administrative and regulatory, Environmental. Office: Reed Smith LLP Princeton Forrestal Village 136 Main St Ste 250 Princeton NJ 08540 E-mail: spicco@reedsmith.com.

PICCOLO, GERARD ANTHONY, lawyer; b. Omaha, Oct. 11, 1955; s. Salvatore and Maria Rose Piccolo. BSBA, Creighton U., 1977, JD, 1979. Bar: Nebr. 1979, U.S. Dist. Ct. Nebr. 1979, U.S. Supreme Ct. 1983. Pvt. practice, Omaha, 1984-88; dep. pub. defender Hall County Pub. Defender's Office, Grand Island, Nebr., 1988-90, pub. defender, 1990—. Judge advocate USAF, 1980-84. Republican. Roman Catholic. Avocations: chess, basketball, running. Home: 2020 N Sycamore St Grand Island NE 68801-2343 Office: Hall County Pub Defender 117 E 1st St Ste 2 Grand Island NE 68801-6022 E-mail: gerardp@hcgi.org.

PICHEDVANICHOK, ARKRAPOL, lawyer; b. Bangkok, Jan. 23, 1967; LLB, Chulalongkorn U., Bangkok, 1989; LLM, Boston U., Eng., 1991, Georgetown U., 1992. Bar: Law Soc. Thailand. Assoc. Denton Hall, Bangkok, 1993, Arthur Anderson, Bangkok, 1993—94; sr. assoc. MPS & Assocs., Bangkok, 1995—98; seconment Allen & Overy, Hong Kong, 1998, sr. assoc. Bangkok, 1998—2001, ptnr., 2001—. Mem.: Law Soc. Thailand. Corporate, general, Mergers and acquisitions, Securities. Office: Allen & Overy Thailand Co Ltd 130 22nd Fl Sindhorn Bldg 3 Wireless Rd Bangkok 10330 Thailand

PICKER, MARC, lawyer; b. Glen Cove, N.Y., Feb. 15, 1954; s. Sidney and Pearl (Sussman) P.m. Nancy Ann Stilwell, 1979 (div. 1985); m. Larri Ann Lightner, Mar. 26, 1988; children: Angela Lightner, Sarah Lightner, Seth. BA in Journalism, U. Nev., 1978; JD, U. Calif., 1988. Bar: Nev. 1988, U.S. Dist. Ct. Nev. 1988, U.S. Ct. Appeals (9th cir.) 1992. Assoc. Michael L. Melner & Assocs., Reno, 1988-89; atty. pvt. practice, Reno, 1989-91, 93—; pres. Plater & Picker, Reno, 1991-93. Pres. Truckee Meadows Youth Soccer, Reno, 1989-92; 1st v.p. Nev. State Youth Soccer Assn., 1992-98; chmn. Parks and Recreation Bd., Ely, Nev., 1983-85; pres. Temple Sinai, Reno, 1991-98. Mem. ABA, Am. Trial Lawyers Assn., No. Nev. Criminal Defense Lawyers, Nev. Bar Assn. Nev. Trial Lawyers Assn. Avocations: soccer, tennis. Bankruptcy, Criminal, Personal injury (including property damage). Office: 691 Sierra Rose Dr PO Box 3344 Reno NV 89505-3344

PICKERING, JOHN HAROLD, lawyer; b. Harrisburg, Ill., Feb. 27, 1916; s. John Leslie and Virginia Lee (Morris) P.; m. Elsa Victoria Mueller, Aug. 23, 1941 (dec. Nov., 1988); children: Leslie Ann, Victoria Lee; m. Helen Paton Wright, Feb. 3, 1990. AB, U. Mich., 1938, JD, 1940, LLD, 1996, D.C. Sch. Law, 1995. Bar: N.Y. 1941, D.C. 1947. Practiced in N.Y.C., 1941; practiced in Washington, 1946—; assoc. Cravath, de Gersdorff, Swaine & Wood, 1941; law clk. to Justice Murphy, Supreme Ct. U.S., 1941-43; assoc. Wilmer & Broun, 1946-48, ptnr., 1949-62, Wilmer, Cutler & Pickering, 1962-79, Wilmer & Pickering, 1979-81, Wilmer, Cutler & Pickering, 1981-88, sr. counsel, 1989—. Vis. lectr. U. Va. Law Sch., 1958; mem. com. visitors U. Mich. Law Sch., 1962-68, chmn. devel. com., 1973-81; mem. com. on adminstrn. of justice U.S. Ct. Appeals (D.C. cir.), 1966-72, chmn. adv. com. on procedures, 1976-82, chmn. mediation project, 1988—; bd. govs. D.C. Bar, 1975-78, pres., 1979-80; dir. Nat. Ctr. for State Cts., 1987-93. Lt. comdr. USNR, 1943-46. Recipient Outstanding Achievement award U. Mich., 1978, Disting. Svc. award Nat. Ctr. for State Cts., 1985, 50 Yr. award from Fellows Am. Bar Found., 1993, Paul. C. Reardon award Nat. Ctr. for State Cts., 1994, Pro Bono award NAACP Legal Def. Fund, 1990, Am. Bar Assn. medal, 1999, Justice William J. Brennan Jr. award, D.C. Bar, 1998, Justice Potter Stewart award, Coun. for Court Excellence, 1999, numerous other awards. Mem. ABA (state del. 1984-93, chmn. commn. on legal problems of elderly 1985-93, sr. advisor 1993-95, chmn. 1995-96, commr. emeritus 1996—, chmn. sr. lawyers divsn. 1996-97), D.C. Bar Assn. (Lawyer of the Yr. 1996), Am. Law Inst., Barristers Washington, Lawyers Club, Met. Club, Chevy Chase Club, Wianno Club, Order of Coif, Phi Beta Kappa, Phi Kappa Phi. Democrat. Mem. United Ch. Christ. Home: 8100 Connecticut Ave Chevy Chase MD 20815 Office: Wilmer Cutler & Pickering 2445 M St NW Ste 8 Washington DC 20037-1435 E-mail: jpickering@wilmer.com.

PICKETT, OWEN B. lawyer, congressman; b. Richmond, Va., Aug. 31, 1930; BS, Va. Poly. Inst., 1952; LLB, U. Richmond, 1955. CPA Va.; bar: Va. 1955, D.C. 1962. Lawyer practice, Virginia Beach, Va., 1955—72; mem. Va. Ho. of Dels., Richmond, 1972—86, U.S. Congress from 2d Va. dist., Washington, 1987—2001; of counsel Troutman, Sanders, Mays & Valentine, Virginia Beach, Va., 2001—. Mem. resources com. Armed Svcs. Com.; chmn. Va. Dem. State Ctrl. Com., 1980—82. Mem.: D.C. Bar Assn., Va. Bar Assn. Office: Troutman Sanders Mays & Valentine 4425 Corporation Ln Virginia Beach VA 23462*

PICKLE, JERRY RICHARD, lawyer; b. Paris, Tex., Feb. 2, 1947; s. Joseph Rambert and Martha Marie (Biggers) P.; m. Helen Leigh Russell, May 3, 1975; children: Jonathan Russell, Stephen Richard (dec.), Sarah Elizabeth. BA in History, U. Houston, 1969, JD, 1971. Bar: Tex. 1972, U.S. Dist. Ct. (no. dist.) Tex. 1974. Mem. Luna, Ballard & Pickle, Garland, Tex., 1972-74; assoc. Hightower & Alexander, Dallas, 1974-76, Cuba & Johnson, Temple, Tex., 1976-77; sr. corp. counsel Scott & White Clinic, Temple, 1977—. Asst. prof. Tex. A&M U. Coll. of Medicine, Temple, 1986—. Contbr. articles to profl. jours. V.p. The Caring House, Temple, 1989, Tex. divsn. Am. Cancer Soc., Temple, 1976-77; adv. bd. R.R. & Pioneer Mus., Temple, 1982-84; hist. preservation bd. City of Temple, 1979-90; chmn. Bell County Hist. Commn., 1980-82; bd. dirs. Bell County Mus., 1992-96, Temple Coord. Child Care Coun., 1991-93, Sr. Citizens Activites Ctr., Temple, 1993-94, pres., 1994-95; bd. dirs. Temple Cultural Activities Ctr., 1992-98, 2001—, pres., 1994-95; chair Heart o'Tex. Coun., Chisholm Trail Dist., Boy Scouts Am., 1987-88. Mem.: ABA, Temple C. of C. (bd. dirs. 1983—85, 1988—90), Coun. Med. Group Practice Attys. (chair 2001—02), Am. Health Lawyers Assn. (chair tchg. hosp. and acad. med. ctrs. 1997—99), Bell-Lampasas-Mills Counties Young Lawyers Assn. (pres. 1980—81), Bell-Lampasas-Mills Counties Bar Assn. (bd. dirs. 1985—90, pres. 1988—89), State Bar Coll., Tex. Bar Found., Tex. Young Lawyers Assn., State Bar Tex. (health law sect. councilman 1980—84, chmn. 1983—84, health law sect. councilman 1985—87), Jaycees (chpt. dir. 1977—78), Rotary (chpt. dir. 1981—85, 1986—87). Democrat. Episcopalian. Avocations: reading, golf, music. Corporate, general, Health, Insurance. Office: Scott & White Clinic 2401 S 31st St Temple TX 76508-0001 Fax: 254-724-4501. E-mail: jpickle@swmail.sw.org.

PICKLE, L. SCOTT, lawyer; b. Kosciusko, Miss., Jan. 21, 1965; m. Shelia G. Pickle, Mar. 13, 1993; children: Griffin, Taylor. BBA, U. Miss., 1987, JD, 1990. Bar: Miss. 1990. Judge Kosciusko Mcpl. Ct., 1995—; pvt. practice, Kosciusko, 1990—. Federal civil litigation, General practice, Property, real (including real estate development, water). Office: PO Box 701 Kosciusko MS 39090-0701 E-mail: picklelaw@kopower.com.

PIDGEON, STEVEN D. lawyer; b. Norwood, Mass., Mar. 28, 1957; s. Norman L. and Dorothy H. Pidgeon; m. Kathryn A. Pierson, Sept. 12, 1981; children: Tyler Steven, Gregory Michael, Austin Robert. BA, U. Miami, 1978, JD, 1981. Ptnr. Streich, Lang, P.A., Phoenix, 1981-94, Snell & Wilmer, LLP, Phoenix, 1994—. Bd. dirs. Enterprise Network, Phoenix, 1986—; mem. Ariz. Securities Coun., Phoenix, 1995—. Author articles. Mem. ABA, State Bar Ariz., Maricopa County Bar Assn. Avocation: golf. Corporate, general, Securities. Office: Snell & Wilmer LLP 400 E Van Buren St Phoenix AZ 85004-2223 E-mail: spidgeon@swlaw.com.

PIDOT, WHITNEY DEAN, lawyer; b. N.Y.C., Mar. 2, 1944; s. George B. and Virginia (Ulrich) P.; m. Jeanne Stoddard, April 23, 1973; children: Whitney Dean Jr., Philip Martin, Seth Thayer. AB magna cum laude, Harvard U., 1966; JD, MBA, Columbia U., 1970. Bar: N.Y. 1971. Ptnr. Shearman & Sterling, N.Y.C., 1970, global mng. ptnr., 1998—2002; ptnr. Executive Group, 1998—2003; Asia Managing ptnr., 2001—03. Adv. bd. Barclays Bank N.Y., 1989-92, Molecular Tool, Inc. (biotech.) Balt., 1991-96, Equine Genetic Rsch. Ptnrs., Balt., 1991-95; trustee, vice chair Winthrop Univ. Hosp., Mineola, N.Y.; bd. dirs. Oneida Ltd., NORIC Corp., North Ctrl. Oil Corp., Houston, Goslet Corp., Cold Spring Harbor Labs., N.Y. Mayor, Village of Matinecock, Locust Valley, N.Y., 1977-92; vice chmn. North Shore Mayors Com., Long Island, N.Y., 1980-92; bd. dirs. Nassau County (N.Y.) Village Officials Assn., 1978-80; commr. Locust Valley Fire Dist., 1979-93. Mem. Piping Rock Club (pres. 1988-94), Links Club N.Y.C. (v.p., sec.), New York Bar Assoc., Phi Delta Phi. Republican. Banking, Corporate, general, Finance. Home: 42 Ryefield Rd Locust Valley NY 11560-1922 Office: 599 Lexington Ave Ste C-2 New York NY 10022-6030

PIEPER, DAROLD D. lawyer; b. Vallejo, Calif., Dec. 30, 1944; s. Walter A. H. and Vera Mae (Ellis) P.; m. Barbara Gillis, Dec. 20, 1969; 1 child, Christopher Radcliffe. AB, UCLA, 1967; JD, USC, 1970. Bar: Calif. 1971. Ops. rsch. analyst Naval Weapons Ctr., China Lake, Calif., 1966-69; assoc. Richards, Watson & Gershon, L.A., 1970-76, ptnr., 1976—; gen. counsel Foothill Transit, 2000—; spl. counsel L.A. Unified Sch. Dist., 2000—; gen. counsel Greater L.A. County Vector Control Dist., 2001—. Spl. counsel L.A. County Transp. Commn., 1984-93, L.A. County Met. Transp. Authority, 1993-94; commr. L.A. County Delinquency and Crime Commn., 1983-94, pres., 1987-94; chmn. L.A. County Delinquency Prevention Planning Coun., 1987-90. Contbr. articles to profl. jours. Peace officer Pasadena (Calif.) Police Res. Unit, 1972-87, dep. comdr., 1979-81, comdr., 1982-84; chmn. pub. safety commn. City of La Canada Flintridge, Calif., 1977-82, commr. 1977-88; bd. dirs. La Canada Flintridge Coordinating Council, 1975-82, pres. 1977-78; exec. dir. Cityhood Action Com., 1975-76; chmn. Youth Opportunities United, Inc., 1990-96, vice-chmn. 1988-89, bd. dirs. 1988-96; mem. L.A. County Justice Systems Adv. Group, 1987-92; trustee Lanterman Hist. Mus. Found., 1989-94, Calif. City Mgmt. Found., 1992—. Recipient commendation for Community Service, L.A. County Bd. Suprs., 1978, Commendation for Svc. to Youth, 1996. Mem. La Canada Flintridge C. of C. and Cmty. Assn. (pres. 1981, bd. dirs. 1976-83), Peace Officers Assn., L.A. County, UCLA Alumni Assn. (life), L.A. County Bar Assn., Calif. Bar Assn., ABA, U. So. Calif. Law Alumni Assn. Construction, Government contracts and claims, Transportation. Office: Richards Watson & Gershon 40th Fl 355 S Grand Ave Los Angeles CA 90071-3101

PIERCE, DELANA S. lawyer; b. Burkesville, Ky., Aug. 26, 1972; d. Willie Raymond Pierce and Loretta Keathley. BA, Morehead State U., 1994; JD, No. Ky. U., 1998. Bar: Ky. 1998, U.S. Dist. Ct. (ea. dist.) Ky. 1998. Law clk. Robert E. Sanders & Assocs., 1996—98; assoc. lawyer Sanders, Tismo & Assocs., Covington, Ky., 1998—. Mem.: ATLA, ABA, No. Ky. Bar Assn., Ky. Acad. Trial Lawyers, Am. Inn Cts. Democrat. Roman Catholic. Personal injury (including property damage), Product liability. Office: Sanders Tismo and Assocs PC 1017 Russel St Covington KY 41011 Office Fax: 859-655-4642. Business E-Mail: dpierce@sanderstismolaw.com.

PIERCE, DONALD FAY, lawyer; b. Bexley, Miss., Aug. 28, 1930; s. Percy O. and Lavada S. (Stringfellow) P.; m. Norma Faye Scribner, June 5, 1954; children: Kathryn Pierce Peake, D. F. Jr., John S., Jeff G. BS, U. Ala., 1956, JD, 1958. Bar: Ala. 1958, U.S. Ct. Appeals (5th cir.) 1958, U.S. Dist. Ct. (no., mid. and so. dists.) Ala. 1958, U.S. Ct. Appeals (11th cir.) 1982. Law clk. to presiding judge U.S. Dist. Ct. (so. dist.) Ala., 1958-59; ptnr. Hand, Arendall, Bedsole, Greaves & Johnston, Mobile, Ala., 1964-91, Pierce, Carr, Alford, Ledyard & Latta, P.C., Mobile, 1991—; pvt. practice, Mobile. Trustee, UMS Prep. Sch., 1980-87; mem. Products Liability Adv. Coun., 1990—; bd. overseers The Vanderbilt Cancer Ctr., 1994—. 1st lt. U.S. Army, 1951-53. Mem. Ala. Def. Lawyers Assn. (past pres.), Fedn. Ins. and Corp. Counsel, Am. Acad. Hosp. Attys., Internat. Assn. Def. Counsel, Def. Counsel Trial Acad. (bd. dirs. 1983-84), Def. Research Inst. (pres. 1987, chmn. 1988). Baptist. Contbr. articles to profl. jours. Federal civil litigation, Environmental, Health. Home: 4452 Winnie Way Mobile AL 36608-2221 Office: Pierce Ledyard PC PO Box 161389 3801 Airport Blvd Mobile AL 36616 Office Fax: 251-338-1305.

PIERCE, JOHN GERALD (JERRY PIERCE), lawyer; b. Winter Haven, Fla., Jan. 12, 1937; s. Francis E. and Margaret (Butler) P.; m. Kathleen E., Dec. 1, 1989; children: Kathleen M. Cooke, Nancy A., John Gerald Jr., Michael J. B in Chem. Engring., U. Fla., 1959, JD with honors, 1965. Bar: Fla. 1966, U.S. Dist. Ct. (mid. dist.) Fla. 1966, U.S. Ct. Appeals (11th cir.). Assoc. Anderson & Rush, Dean & Lowndes, Orlando, Fla., 1966-68, Arnold, Matheny & Eagen, Orlando, 1968-70; ptnr. Pierce, Lewis & Dolan, Orlando, 1970-74; sole practice Orlando, 1974—2002; ptnr. Pierce & Klein, PLC, Orlando, 2003—. Served to 1st lt. U.S. Army, 1959-62. Mem. ABA, Fla. Bar Assn., Orange County Bar Assn. Republican. Roman Catholic. Avocations: golf, boating, skiing. Corporate, general, Property, real (including real estate development, water), Securities, General civil litigation, Commercial, contracts (including sales of goods; commercial financing). Home: 605 Fox Valley Dr Longwood FL 32779-2417 Office: 800 N Ferncreek Ave Orlando FL 32803-4127 E-mail: jerry@johnpierce.com.

PIERCE, LAWRENCE WARREN, retired federal judge; b. Phila., Dec. 31, 1924; s. Harold Ernest and Leora (Bellinger) Pierce; m. Wilma Taylor, 1948 (dec. May 1978); m. Cynthia Straker, July 8, 1979; children: Warren Wood, Michael Lawrence, Mark Taylor. BS, St. Joseph's U., Phila., 1948, DHL, 1967; JD, Fordham U., 1951, LLD, 1982, Fairfield U., 1972, Hamilton Coll., 1987, St. John's U., 1990. Bar: N.Y. 1951, U.S. Supreme Ct. 1968. Civil law practice, N.Y.C., 1951—61; asst. dist. atty. Kings County, N.Y., 1954—61; dep. police commr. N.Y.C., 1961—63; dir. N.Y. State Divsn. for Youth, Albany, 1963—66; chmn. N.Y. State Narcotic Addiction Control Commn., 1966—70; vis. prof. criminal justice SUNY, Albany, 1970—71; dist. judge U.S. Dist. Ct. , So. Dist. N.Y., 1971—81; judge U.S. Fgn. Intelligence Surveillance Ct., Washington, 1979—81; cir. judge U.S. Ct. Appeals 2d Cir., 1981—95; ret., 1995. Dir. Cambodian ct. tng. project Internat. Human Rights Law Group, 1995. Past bd. dirs. CARE, Havens Fund Soc., Lincoln Hall for Boys, S-R and S.A.R., N.Y. chpts., Cath. Interracial Coun., Practising Law Inst. Mem.: ABA (com. on corr. svc. and facilities 1970—71, alt. observer U.S. Mission to UN 1988—90, site evaluation com., sec. legal edn. 1996—98), Spl. Com. Army Confinement Facilties (office of sec. of army 1970), Urban League, Nat. Bar Assn., Am. Law Inst., Coun. Fgn. Rels. Home: PO Box 2234 Sag Harbor NY 11963-0111

PIERCE, MORTON ALLEN, lawyer; b. Liberec, Czechoslovakia, June 25, 1948; m. Nancy Washor, Dec. 14, 1975; children: Matthew J., Nicholas L. BA, Yale Coll., 1970; JD, U. Pa., 1974; postgrad., Oxford U., 1974-75. Bar: N.Y. 1975. Assoc. Reid & Priest, N.Y.C., 1975-83, ptnr., 1983-86, Dewey Ballantine, N.Y.C., 1986—, vice-chmn., 2002—. Mem. mgmt. com. 1988—, chmn. corp. dept., 1999—, chmn., mergers and acquisitions group, 1990—, mem. exec. com., 2001—. Contbr. articles to profl. jours. Mem. ABA (chmn. subcom. on internat. securities matters 1985-91, adv. com. to fed. regulation of securities com. 1991-2000, task force on rev. of the fed. securities law 1991-2000), Assn. of the Bar of the City of N.Y. (securities law com. 1988-91, chmn. subcom. on securities and exch. commn. enforcement matters 1990-91); Internat. Bar Assn. (com. on securities transactions). Mergers and acquisitions, Securities, Corporate, general. Home: 188 E 76th St New York NY 10021-2826 Office: Dewey Ballantine LLP 1301 Ave Of The Americas New York NY 10019-6022

PIERCE, RICKLIN RAY, lawyer; b. Waukegan, Ill., Sept. 16, 1953; s. Forest Ellsworth and Mildred Colleen (Cole) P. BBA in Acctg., Washburn U., 1975; BA in Econs., 1978, JD, 1978. Bar: Kans. 1978, U.S. Dist. Ct. Kans. 1978, U.S. Ct. Appeals (10th cir.) 1981, U.S. Supreme Ct. 1986. Assoc. Law Firm of C. C. Whittaker, Jr., Eureka, Kans., 1978-79; trust officer Smith County State Bank & Trust Co., Smith Center, Kans., 1979-80; staff atty. Northwest Kans. Legal Aid Soc., Goodland, 1980-81; assoc. Jochems, Sargent & Blaes, Wichita, Kans., 1981-82, Garden City, Kans., 1982-83; pvt. practice, Garden City, 1983-88; atty. County of Finney, 1988-93; pvt. practice, Garden City, 1993—. Pres., chmn. bd. dirs. Volunteers, Inc. of Finney County. Mem. Western Kans. Coun. Estate Planning & Giving. Mem. ABA, Assn. Trial Lawyers Am., Kans. Bar Assn., Southwest Kans. Bar Assn., Kans. Trial Lawyer Assn., Finney County Bar Assn. (treas.). Republican. Methodist. State civil litigation, Corporate, general, Criminal. Home: 2015 Campus Dr Garden City KS 67846-3706 Office: 206 W Pine St Garden City KS 67846-5347

PIERLUISI, PEDRO R. lawyer; b. San Juan, P.R., Apr. 26, 1959; s. Jorge A. and Doris (Urrutia) Pierluisi; children: Anthony, Michael, Jacqueline, Rafael. BA , Tulane U., 1981; JD, George Washington U., 1984. Bar: D.C. 1984, U.S. Dist. Ct. D.C. 1985, U.S. Ct. Appeals (D.C. cir.) 1985, P.R. 1990, U.S. Dist. Ct. P.R. 1990, U.S. Supreme Ct. 1990, U.S. Ct. Appeals (1st cir.) 1993. Assoc. Verner, Liipfert, Bernhard, McPherson & Hand, Washington, 1984—85, Cole, Corette & Abrutyn, Washington, 1985—90; ptnr. Pierluisi Pierluisi & Mayol-Bianchi, San Juan, 1990—93; atty. gen. Govt. of P.R., 1993—96; ptnr. O'Neill & Borges, San Juan, 1997—. Mem.: ABA (ho. of dels. 1995—96, standing com. on substance abuse 1995—98, coordinating com. on gun violence 1998—2001, state membership chair 2000—), Am. Arbitration Assn. (arbitrator), Nat. Assn. Securities Dealers (arbitrator), George Washington U. Internat. Law Soc. (pres. 1982—83), Nat. Assn. Attys. Gen. (chair ea. region 1996), Puerto Rico Homebuilders Assn. (bd. dirs. 1999—), N.Y. Stock Exch. (arbitrator), Phi Alpha Delta (hon.; Munoz chpt.). Avocation: jogging. Administrative and regulatory, General civil litigation, Corporate, general. Office: O'Neill & Borges 250 Ave Munoz Rivera Am Internat Plz San Juan PR 00918-1808

PIERNO, ANTHONY ROBERT, lawyer; s. Anthony M. and Mary Jane (Saporita) P.; m. Beverly Jean Kohn; children: Kathryn Ann, Robert Lawrence, Linda Jean Derengowski, Diane Marie Leonard. BA with highest honors, Whittier Coll., 1954; JD, Stanford U., 1959; LLD (hon.), Whittier Coll., 2000. Bar: Calif. 1960, D.C. 1979, Tex. 1994. Assoc. Adams, Duque & Hazeltine, L.A.; ptnr. Poindexter & Barger, L.A.; chief dep. commr. State of Calif., 1967-69, commr. of corps., 1969-71; ptnr. Wyman, Bautzer, Rothman & Kuchel, Beverly Hills, Calif.; sr. ptnr. Memel, Jacobs, Pierno & Gersh, L.A., 1976-86; ptnr. Pillsbury, Madison & Sutro, L.A., 1986-89; sr. v.p., gen. counsel MAXXAM, Inc., L.A. and Houston, 1989-97. Author: Corporate Disaggregation, 1982; editor Stanford U. Law Rev. Trustee Whittier Coll., 1977-2000, chmn. bd. trustees, 1994-2000, chmn. presdl. selection com., 1989-90; chmn. Marymount Coll., Palos Verdes, Calif., 1989-92, trustee, 1976-93; past mem. Los Angeles County Children's Svcs. Commn. With U.S. Army, 1954-56. Recipient Emcalian award Marymount Palos Verdes Coll., 1983. Mem. ABA, Los Angeles County Bar Assn., State Bar Calif. (chmn. com. on corps. 1971-75, advisor to com. on corps. 1975-76, mem. exec. com. bus. law sect. 1976-80, chmn. spl. com. on franchise law), Calif. Club (L.A.). Republican. Roman Catholic. Administrative and regulatory, Alternative dispute resolution, Corporate, general. Office: 73255 El Paseo Ste 11 Palm Desert CA 92260-4125

PIERSOL, LAWRENCE L. federal judge; b. Spirit Mound Township, S.D., Oct. 21, 1940; s. Ralph Nelson and Mildred Alice (Millette) P.; m. Catherine Anne Vogt, June 30, 1962; children: Leah C., William M., Elizabeth J. BA, U. S.D., 1962, JD summa cum laude, 1965. Bar: S.D. 1965, U.S. Ct. Mil. Appeals, 1965, U.S. Dist. Ct. S.D. 1968, U.S. Supreme Ct. 1972, U.S. Dist. Ct. Wyo. 1980, U.S. Dist. Ct. Nebr. 1986, U.S. Dist. Ct. Mont. 1988. Ptnr. Davenport, Evans, Hurwitz & Smith, Sioux Falls, S.D., 1968-93; judge U.S. Dist. Ct., Sioux Falls, 1993—; chief judge Dist. of S.D., 1999—. Mem. budget com. chair, economy sub com., Jud. Conf. U.S.; chmn. tribal ct. com., security com. 8th Cir. Jud. Coun.; editor-in-chief Law Review. Majority leader S.D. Ho. of Reps., Pierre, 1973-74, minority whip, 1971-72; del. Dem. Nat. Conv., 1972, 76, 80; S.D. mem. del. select commn. Dem. Nat. Com., 1971-75. Mem. ABA, State Bar S.D., Fed. Judges Assn. (bd. dirs., pres.). Roman Catholic. Avocations: reading, running, painting, sailing. Office: US Dist Ct 400 S Phillips Ave Sioux Falls SD 57104-6824

PIERSON, GREY, lawyer; b. Abilene, Tex., Dec. 31, 1950; s. Don and Annette (Grubbs) P. Student in history Baylor U., 1971, JD, 1974; student in internat. law Coll. William and Mary, Exeter, Eng., summer 1973. Bar: Tex. 1974, U.S. Dist. Ct. (no. dist.) Tex. 1974, U.S. Ct. Appeals (5th cir.) 1983, U.S. Supreme Ct. 1984. Assoc. Law Office of Tom Sneed, Odessa, Tex., 1974-76, Duke, Duke, & Jelinek, Arlington, Tex., 1976-78; ptnr. Duke & Pierson, Arlington, 1978-79, Pierson & Galyen, Arlington, 1983-88, Pierson, Baker & Ray, 1988-95, Pierson & Behr, 1995—; sole practice, Arlington, 1979-83; gen. counsel Mercer Internat. Transp., Ft. Worth, 1979-84; sr. legal adviser Dominica Caribbean Freeport Authority, Roseau, W.I., 1979; ptnr. Sta. KVMX-FM, Eastland, Tex., 1981-86. Contbr. articles to City Digest mag., 1979-80. Pres. Eastland Youth Council, 1967, Arlington Community Theatre, 1979; mem. Tarrant 2000 Commn. on Civil Justice, 1988; chmn. Tarrant County Rep. Jud. Recruitment Com., 1988; del. Rep. Nat. Conv., New Orleans, 1988. Recipient Disting. Svc. award Nat. Assn. Disabled Ams., Washington, 1982. Corporate, general, Private international, Property, real (including real estate development, water). Home: 301 W Abram St Arlington TX 76010

PIERSON, STUART F. lawyer; b. Washington, D.C., June 25, 1943; s. W. Theodore and Barbara F. Pierson; m. Jennifer M. Pierson, June 20, 1987; children: Stuart, Jr., Sean, Jody Skye, Emily J.; m. Carole S. (div. 1985). BA cum laude, Hobart Coll., 1965; diploma, L.S. ID, 1968. Bar: D.C. 1969, N.Y. 1984, U.S. Supreme Ct. 1974. Atty. U.S. Dept. Justice Civil Rights Divsn., Washington, 1968—71, AUSA WD Washington, Washington, 1971—73, Spec. AUSA WD, Washington, 1974, Verner Liipfert, Washington, 1975—88, Davis Wright, Washington, 1988—96, Levine Pierson, Washington, 1996—98, Troutman Sanders, Washington, 1998—. Media law, Libel, Criminal. Office: Troutman Sanders LLP 401 9th St NW Washington DC 20004

PIERSON, WILLIAM GEORGE, lawyer; b. Pontiac, Mich., Oct. 13, 1951; s. Robert D. and Elizabeth C. (Brode) P.; m. Mary K. Grossa, Sept. 25, 1986; children: Megan Ewing, Robert John. BBA, Cen. Mich. U., 1973; JD, Detroit Coll. Law, 1980. Bar: Mich. 1980, U.S. Dist. Ct. (ea. dist.) Mich. 1982, U.S. Supreme Ct. 1985. Sr. assoc. Kohl, Secrest, Wardle, Lynch, Clark & Hampton, Farmington Hills, Mich., 1980-89, Schwartz & Jalkanen, Southfield, Mich., 1989-90; sole practice Howell, Mich., 1991-99; counsel Oakland County Corp., Pontiac, Mich., 1999—. Mem. ABA, Mich. Bar Assn. (negligence sect., elected to rep. assembly 1999—), Oakland County Bar Assn (dist. ct. com. 1983-84, cir. ct. com. 1984-85, negligence com. 1987—, chair negligence com. 2002, med.-legal com. 1989-96, pub. adv. com. on jud. candidates 2002—), Livingston County Bar Assn. Avocations: golf, skiing, boating, camping. State civil litigation, Insurance, Personal injury (including property damage). Home: 2153 Ridge Rd White Lake MI 48383-1742 Office: Oakland County Dept Corp Counsel 1200 N Telegraph Rd Dept 419 Pontiac MI 48341-0419 E-mail: piersonw@co.oakland.mi.us., megrob1@msn.com.

PIETROWSKI, R. SCOTT, lawyer; b. Dearborn, Mich., Feb. 8, 1970; s. Richard Louis and Rhonda Diane Pietrowski; m. Amy Kathryn Piercey, Jan. 8, 1990; children: Alexandria Nicole, Blake Ashton James. AA, Barstow Coll., 1993, AS, 1994; BA, U. Miss., Oxford, 1995, JD, 1998. Bar: U.S. Dist. Ct. (no. dist.) Miss. 1999, U.S. Dist. Ct. (we. dist.) Tenn., Tenn., Miss. 1999. Rsch. asst. to Hon. James D. Todd U.S. Dist. Ct., Jackson, Tenn., 1998; atty. Spragins, Barnett, Cobb & Butler, Jackson, 1998—. Mem. hearing com. Tenn. Bd. Profl. Responsibility, Jackson, 2001—. Cpl. USMC, 1989—92. Mem.: Jackson-Madison County Bar Assn. (bd. dirs. 1998—99). Appellate, General practice, Personal injury (including property damage). Office: Spragins Barnett Cobb & Butler 312 E Lafayette St Jackson TN 38301

PIETZSCH, MICHAEL EDWARD, lawyer; b. Burlington, Iowa, Aug. 1, 1949; s. Walter E. and Leanna (Moore) P.; m. Ellen G. Hart; children: Christine E., Catherine M. AB, Stanford U., 1971; JD, U. Chgo., 1974. Bar: Ill. 1974, Ariz. 1976. Assoc. Schwartz & Freeman, Chgo., 1974-75; ptnr. McCabe & Pietzsch, Phoenix, 1975-90, Pietzsch & Williams, Phoenix, 1990-95, Polese, Pietzsch, Williams & Nolan, Phoenix, 1995—. Contbr. articles to profl. jours.; speaker at profl. confs. Del. White House Conf. Small Bus., Washington, 1986, White House Savs. Summit, 1998; chmn. bd. trustees Ariz. Sci. Ctr., 1994-98; pres. The Group, Inc., 1995-98. Fellow Am. Coll. Tax Counsel, Am. Coun. on Tax Policy, Am. Coll. Employee Benefits Counsel; mem. ABA (chmn. personal svc. orgns. com. tax sect. 1986-90), Stanford Phoenix Club (pres. 1982-84). Corporate, general, Health, Pension, profit-sharing, and employee benefits. Office: 3101 East Marshall Avenue Phoenix AZ 85016

PIGA, STEPHEN MULRY, retired lawyer; b. Bklyn., Apr. 9, 1929; s. Stephen Paul and Ella (Mulry) P.; married, Feb. 23, 1952 (div.); children: Maureen, Stephen, Susan, Elizabeth; m. Emilie Halliday, Aug. 1, 1975; 1 dau., Margaret. AB, Princeton U., 1950; LL.B., Columbia u., 1955. Bar: N.J. 1955, N.Y. 1956. Assoc. White & Case, N.Y.C., 1955-63, ptnr., 1964-92; ret., 1992. Lectr. Practicing Law Inst. N.Y. and various insts., bar assns. Served to capt. USMCR, 1951-53. Mem. ABA, N.Y. State Bar Assn. (exec. com. tax sect. 1981-89, chmn. employee benefits com.), Assn. of Bar of City N.Y., N.J. Bar Assn., Am. Contract Bridge League (life master), Profl. Bowlers' Assn. Am. Republican. Avocations: fishing, golf, bowling. Pension, profit-sharing, and employee benefits.

PIKE, LARRY SAMUEL, lawyer; b. Savannah, Ga., Feb. 23, 1939; s. Abram and Ida (Feinberg) P.; m. Bonnie Jo Haykin, June 21, 1959; children: Douglas, Stacey, Scott. BA, Emory U., 1960, LLB, 1963; postgrad., Leeds (Eng.) U., 1960-61. Assoc. L. Jack Swertfeger Jr. Atty., Decatur, Ga., 1963-65; ptnr. Swertfeger, Scott, Pike & Simmons, Decatur, 1966-75, Simmons, Pike & Warren, Decatur, 1975-76, Lefkoff, Pike & Sims, Atlanta, 1976-85, Branch, Pike & Ganz, Atlanta, 1985-95, Holland & Knight LLP, Atlanta, 1995—. Pres. Ansley Park Civic Assn., Atlanta, 1977-79, Northshore Homeowners Assn., Tybee Island, Ga., 1992-95, The Temple, Atlanta, 1979-81, trustee, 1977—, Am. Cancer Soc., DeKalb County, Ga. unit, 1970-71, crusade chmn., 1969-70; trustee Ansley Park Beautification Found., Inc., Atlanta, 1984—, treas., 2000—; trustee The Temple Endowment Fund, Atlanta, 1979-87, Atlanta Jewish Cmty. Ctr., 1973-76; bd. overseers Hebrew Union Coll., Cin., 1987-93; alumni coun. Emory U., Atlanta, 1966-72; bd. trustees Union of Am. Hebrew Congregations, 1991-99; mem. Rabbinical Placement Commn., 1994-2000. Editor-in-chief law jour. and newspaper; contbr. articles to profl. jours. Fulbright fellow, 1960-61; named Outstanding Young Man of Yr. North DeKalb Jaycees, 1968. Mem. ABA, State Bar Ga. (exec. coun. Young Lawyers sect. 1968-72), Atlanta Bar Assn., Decatur-DeKalb Bar Assn. (sec. 1965-66), Atlanta Legal Aid Soc. (pres. 1974-75, past bd. dirs.), Atlanta Tax Forum, Lawyers Club Atlanta, B'nai B'rith (pres. Atlanta lodge 1970-71, Ga. pres. 1974-75, dist. 5 bd. govs. 1973-76, chair Youth Orgn. Bd. 1971-73), Phi Beta Kappa, Omicron Delta Kappa. Corporate, general, Probate (including wills, trusts), Taxation, general. Office: Holland & Knight LLP 2000 One Atlantic Ctr Atlanta GA 30309 E-mail: lpike@hklaw.com.

PIKL, JAMES ALAN, lawyer; b. Athens, Tenn., Sept. 20, 1956; s. Ignatz James Pikl and Jeannette Louise Jiacoletti; m. Joanie Lisa Kriegel, Jan. 26, 1991; children: Lisa, Ryan, Laura. BS, Ea. Wash. U., 1981; JD, Gonzaga U., 1985. Bar: Tex. 1986, U.S. Dist. Ct. Tex. 1987, U.S. Supreme Ct. 1991. Atty. Boyd, Veigel & Hawce, Dallas, 1986—87, Johnson, Bromberg & Leeds, Dallas, 1987—90, Vial, Hamilton, Roch & Knox, Dallas, 1990—94, True & Sewell, Dallas, 1994—99; pvt. practice McKinney, Tex., 1999—. Author: (law review) Tex. Tech. Law Rev., 1993; contbr. articles to profl. jours. With USN, 1974—75, PTO. Avocations: scuba diving, golf, fishing, writing. Commercial, consumer (including collections, credit), Product liability, Criminal. Office: PO Box 2939 Mc Kinney TX 75070 Fax: 214-544-7001. E-mail: jimpikl@flash.net.

PILCHER, JAMES BROWNIE, lawyer; b. Shreveport, La., May 19, 1929; s. James Reece and Martha Mae (Brown) P.; m. Lorene Pilcher; children: Lydia, Martha, Bradley. BA, La. State U., 1952; JD summa cum laude, John Marshall Law Sch., 1955; postgrad., Emory U., 1957. Bar: Ga. 1955. Legal aide to Spkr. of Ho. of Reps., Ga., 1961-64; assoc. city atty. City of Atlanta, 1964-69; pvt. practice law Atlanta, 1969—. Exec. committeeman Dem. Exec. Com. of Fulton County, Ga., 1974-86; bd. dirs. Whitehead Boys Club, 1961-89; trustee Ga. Inst. Continuing Legal Edn., 1988-89; pres. Altana Jaycees, 1961-62. Fellow Lawyers Found. Ga., 1996—. Mem. ABA, State Bar Ga. (chmn. 1988-89, gen. practice and trial sect., chmn. criminal law sect. 1986-87), Atlanta Bar Assn., Ga. Assn. Criminal Def. Lawyers (pres. 1980-82), Ga. Trial Lawyers Assn. (life), Ga. Claimants Attys. Assn. (pres. 1983-84), NACDL (bd. dirs. 1980-85), Ga. Inst. Trial Advocacy (bd. dirs. 1986-89), South Fulton Bar Assn. (pres. 1987-88), Am. Bankruptcy Inst., Nat. Assn. Consumer Bankruptcy Attys., Trial Lawyers for Pub. Justice, Atlanta Consumer Bankruptcy Attys. Group (pres. 2001—), Kiwanis (Peachtree, Atlanta pres. 1983-84, gov. Ga. dist. 1992-93), Sierra Club of Am. (life). Presbyterian. Criminal, Personal injury (including property damage). Home: 1195 W Wesley Rd NW Atlanta GA 30327-1407 Office: One Northside 75 Atlanta GA 30318-7715 E-mail: pilcherj@bellsouth.net.

PILLANS, CHARLES PALMER, III, lawyer; b. Orlando, Fla., Feb. 22, 1940; s. Charles Palmer Jr. and Helen (Scarborough) P.; m. Judith Hart, July 6, 1963; children: Charles Palmer IV, Helen Hart. BA, U. Fla., 1962, JD, 1966. Bar: Fla. 1967, U.S. Dist. Ct. (mid. dist.) Fla. 1967, U.S. Ct. Appeals (2d cir.) 1968, U.S. Supreme Ct. 1971, U.S. Ct. Appeals (3d cir.) 1976, U.S. Ct. Appeals (5th and 11th cirs.) 1981. Assoc. Bedell, Bedell, Dittmar, Smith & Zehmer, Jacksonville, Fla., 1966-70; asst. state atty. 4th jud. cir. Jacksonville, 1970-72; asst. gen. counsel City of Jacksonville, 1972; ptnr. Bedell, Dittmar, DeVault Pillans & Coxe, P.A., Jacksonville, 1972—. Mem. Fla. Bd. Bar Examiners, Tallahassee, 1979-84, chmn., 1983-84, Jud. Nominating Commn., 1988-92, chmn., 1990-91, 1st Dist. Ct. Appeal, Tallahassee, 1988-92, chmn., 1990-91, Supreme Ct. com. on standard jury instructions in civil cases, 1998—. Master Chester Bedell Inn of Ct.; fellow Am. Coll. Trial Lawyers, ABA; mem. Am. Bar Found., Fla. Bar Assn. (chmn. profl. ethics com. 1998—, chmn. 1998-99). Methodist. Federal civil litigation, State civil litigation, Criminal. Home: 10 Buckthorne Dr Amelia Island FL 32034-6518 Office: Bedell Dittmar DeVault Pillans & Coxe PA Bedell Bldg 101 E Adams St Jacksonville FL 32202-3303 E-mail: cpillans@bedellfirm.com.

PINCHAK, ANN SIMCHA, lawyer; b. Waco, Tex., Sept. 6, 1957; d. Louis E. and Alice (Wright) P.; m. Richard Tomlinson, July 1, 1983; children: Will Tomlinson, David Tomlinson. BA, Rice U., Houston, 1979; student, U. Houston Coll. Law, 1982. Bar: Tex. 1982, U.S. Dist. Ct. (so. dist.) 1991, U.S. Ct. Appeals (5th cir.) 1988. Atty. East Tex. Legal Svcs., Tyler, 1982-84, Nelkin & Nelkin, Houston, 1984-85, Immigration Law, Houston, 1985-96, Pinchak and Assocs., Houston, 1996—. Lectr. Houston and Tex. chpt. Am. Immigration Law Assn., 1991—; pro bono asylum YMCA Internat. Svc. Houston, 1985-96; Coliason-Houston sect. Tex. Am. Immigration Law Assn., Houston, 1993-94. Contbr. articles to profl. jours. V.p. Hadassah, Houston, 1989-90; frequent spkr. bus. immigration, bus. immigration issues. Mem. Am. Immigration Law Assn., Nat. Access to Healthcare Coalition, State Bar Tex. Immigration, naturalization, and customs. Office: 1 E Greenway Plz Ste 325 Houston TX 77046-0198

PINCKNEY, CHARLES COTESWORTH, lawyer; b. Richmond, Va., Oct. 23, 1939; s. Thomas and Charlotte (Kent) P.; m. Helen Raney, Aug. 13, 1966; children: Sarah Whitley, Thomas. BA, Yale U., 1961; LLB, U. Va., 1967. Bar: Va. 1967. Assoc. Mays, Valentine, Davenport & Moore, Richmond, 1967-72; ptnr. Mays & Valentine, LLP, Richmond, 1972-2000, Troutman Sanders LLP , Richmond, 2001—. Bd. dirs. Sweet Briar Coll., 1996-2000; pres. Sheltering Arms Hosp., Richmond, 1986-87, bd. dirs., 1970-99; trustee William H.-John G.-Emma Scott Found., 1974—, sec., 1994-99, v.p., 1999—; campaign chmn. United Way Svcs., 1998. Ensign lt. j.g. USNR, 1961-64. Mem. ABA, Va. Bar Assn., Phila. Quarry Club (pres. 1985-91), Country Club of Va., Commonwealth Club (bd. govs. 1986-92, pres. 1991-92), Richmond German (pres. 1996-98), Soc. of Cin. Republican. Episcopalian. Banking, Bankruptcy, Commercial, contracts (including sales of goods; commercial financing). Home: 2 Roslyn Rd Richmond VA 23226-1610 Office: Troutman Sanders LLP 1111 E Main St PO Box 1122 Richmond VA 23218-1122 E-mail: cotes.pinckney@troutmansanders.com.

PINCUS, SHELDON H. lawyer; b. Bklyn., May 4, 1952; s. Nat and Frances P.; m. Sherry A. Beltramini, July 11, 1982; children: Matthew A., Lauren N. BS with distinction, Pa. State U., 1973; JD, Rutgers Sch. Law, 1977. Bar: N.J. 1977, DC 1981, U.S. Ct. Appeals (3d cir.). Assoc. Goldberg & Simon, P.A., Clifton, N.J., 1978-81; sr. ptnr. Bucceri, Pincus, Clifton, N.J., 1981—. Dir. Mental Health Assn. Essex County, Montclair, N.J., 1993-98, Friends of Montclair Coop., 1996-97. Named 1 of Top 10 Leading Employment Attys. in N.J., Survey by Digital Press Internat., Fort Lee, N.J. Mem.: Nat. Employment Lawyers Assn. (chmn. N.J.' chpt. amicus com.), N.J. Bar Assn. (labor and employment sect.). Avocations: skiing, backpacking, home renovation. Education and schools, General practice, Labor (including EEOC, Fair Labor Standards Act, labor-management relations, NLRB, OSHA). Office: Bucceri & Pincus 1200 Rte 46 Clifton NJ 07013-2440 E-mail: bucceri_pincus@msn.com.

PINCZOWER, KENNETH EPHRAIM, lawyer; b. N.Y.C., Aug. 24, 1964; s. Joachim and Dinah Pinczower; m. Julie Rieder; children: Devorah, David C., Chana. BA, Queens Coll., 1985; postgrad., Rabbinical Sem. Am., N.Y.C., 1983-86; JD, Benjamin N. Cardozo Sch. Law, 1989. Bar: N.Y. 1990, N.J. 1990, U.S. Dist. Ct. (so. and ea. dists.) N.Y. 1990, U.S. Dist. Ct. N.J. 1990, DC 1991, Fla. 1993. Auditor Seidman & Seidman/B.D.O., N.Y.C., 1986-87; summer assoc. U.S. Attys. Office, So. Dist. N.Y., N.Y.C., 1988; Alexander jud. fellow U.S. Dist. Judge, So. Dist. N.Y., N.Y.C., 1987-88; asst. corp. counsel N.Y.C. Law Dept., 1989-95; atty. Barron, McDonald, Carroll & Cohen, N.Y.C., 1995—. Editor: Cardozo Arts & Entertainment Law Jour., 1988—89. Com. mem. Nat. Conf. Synagogue Youth, 1991—; vol. instr. Jewish Edn. Program, N.Y.C., 1983—86; instr. Aish Ha Torah, 1994—98; Shulchan Aruch Sar Eleph Machon Yerushalayim, 2000—; chmn. Torah Chesed Fund Yeshiva U., 1993—. Avocations: talmudic law, tennis, basketball. Civil rights, General civil litigation, Personal injury (including property damage). Home: 3950 Blackstone Ave Bronx NY 10471-3703 Office: Barron McDonald et al 1 Whitehall St New York NY 10004-2109 E-mail: pinczok@nationwide.com.

PINDERSKI, JEROME WILBERT, JR., lawyer; b. Chgo., Jan. 12, 1957; s. Jerome W. P.; m. Karen Marie Peterson, Oct. 1, 1983; children: Shaun, Heather, Victoria. BA magna cum laude, Marquette U., 1978; JD, Loyola U., Chgo., 1981. Bar: Ill. 1981, U.S. Dist. Ct. (no. dist.) Ill. 1981, U.S. Ct. Appeals (7th cir.) 1983, U.S. Supreme Ct., 1988, U.S. Ct. Appeals (fed. cir.) 1989, U.S. Ct. Internat. Trade, 1989, D.C. 1990. Mng. ptnr. Pinderski & Pinderski Ltd., Palatine, Ill., 1981—; panel atty. Legal Assistance Found., Chgo., 1982—; bd. dirs. First Bank and Trust Co. Ill., Palatine, Performance Home Med. Equipment, Ft. Worth, Tex.; commr. Algonquin Econ. Devel. Commn., 1994—. Bd. dirs. United Way of Palatine, Inverness, Rolling Meadows, 1985—, sec., 1986-88, 1st v.p., 1988-90, pres., 1990-92; mem. N.W. 2001 Planning Conf., 1994—; strategic planning com. United Way Crusade of Mercy, Chgo., 1991-93, bd. dirs., 1995-99; active Palatine Twp. Human Needs Com., 1989—, Palatine-Inverness Healthier Communities Project, 1995—; chmn. candidate slating com. Palatine Twp. Rep. Orgn., 1990-92; del. U.S. Japan bilateral session on law and econs., Tokyo, 1988, Moscow conf. on law and econ. coop., 1990; trustee Palatine Libr. Dist. Found., 1993-95; arbitrator, Cook County Cir. Ct. Arbitration Program, 1990-95. Mem. ABA, ATLA, Ill. State Bar Assn., D.C. Bar Assn., Internat. Bar Assn. (London), Ill. Jaycees (gen. coun. 1989), Palatine Jaycees (sec. 1984-85, legal counsel 1983—, John H. Ambruster Keyman award 1984-85, Dick Bayer Mr. Reliability award 1985-86), Chgo. Coun. Fgn. Rels., Greater Palatine C. of C. and Industry (dir. 1982-89, v.p. 1985-86, 1st vice chmn. 1987, chmn. 1988), Terrace Hill Golf Club (Algonquin, Ill.), Rotary, Phi Beta Kappa, Alpha Sigma Nu. Republican. Roman Catholic. Corporate, general, General practice, Property, real (including real estate development, water). Home: 622 Greens View Dr Algonquin IL 60102-4408 Office: Pinderski & Pinderski Ltd 115 W Colfax St Palatine IL 60067-5086 E-mail: pinderlaw@aol.com.

PINEAU, JOHN KENNETH, lawyer; b. Detroit, July 2, 1960; s. Kenneth John and Rosemary Louise P.; m. Cynthia Pineau, Aug. 3, 1991. Student, U. Mich., 1981; BA with honors, Oberlin Coll., 1982; JD, U. Colo., 1994. Bar: Colo. 1994, U.S. Dist. Ct. Colo. 1994. Adminstrv. hearings advocate Wayne Legal Svcs., Detroit, 1984-91; pvt. practice Boulder, 1994—. Ct. appointed counsel for Boulder County, Alt. Def. Counsel. Recipient Am. Jurisprudence award Lawyer Coop. Pub., Boulder, 1993, 94. Mem. Colo. Bar Assn., Colo. Trial Lawyers Assn., Boulder Crime Def. Bar. General civil litigation, Criminal. Office: # 300 1244 Grant St Denver CO 80203-2306 E-mail: johnpineau@yahoo.com.

PINGREE, BRUCE DOUGLAS, lawyer; b. Salt Lake City, June 6, 1947; s. Howard W. and Lois (Ivie) P.; m. Lorraine Bertelli, Oct. 11, 1981; children: Christian James, Matthew David, Alexandra Elizabeth, Meredith Gillian, Lauren Ashley, Geoffrey Nicholas. BA in Philosophy, U. Utah, 1970, JD, 1973. Bar: Ariz. 1973, Tex. 1990. Ptnr. Snell & Wilmer, Phoenix, 1973-89; shareholder Johnson & Gibbs, Dallas, 1989-93; ptnr. Gardere & Wynne, Dallas, 1993-95, Baker Botts, L.L.P., Dallas, 1995—. Lectr. in field of taxation. Contbr. articles to profl. jours. Served to capt. USAR. Fellow Am. Coll. Employee Benefit Counsel, Inc. (charter); mem. ABA (tax sect., past chair employee benefits com., past vice chair, past chmn. various sub-coms., 1993-94, chair joint com. on employee benefits 1994-95), Tex. State Bar Assn. (chair, tax sect. benefits and compensation com. 2000), Dallas Bar Assn. (chair employee benefits sect. 2001-2002), S.W. Benefits Conf., Nat. Assn. Stock Plan Profls., Order of Coif. Episcopalian. Pension, profit-sharing, and employee benefits, Corporate taxation, Personal income taxation. Home: 4065 Bryn Mawr Dr Dallas TX 75225-7032 Office: Baker & Botts LLP 2001 Ross Ave Ste 600 Dallas TX 75201-2900

PINHEIRO, GUILHERME MARTINS, lawyer; b. São Paulo, Brazil, May 5, 1973; s. José Martins Pinheiro and Theresa Brandão Teixeira; m. Maria Rita Raggio, May 12, 2001 (div. May 2002); 1 child, Maria Cristina Magalhaes Pinto Pinheiro. Degree in law, PUC-Cath. U., Rio de Janeiro, 2003. Bar: Rio de Janeiro 1999. Trainee contracts Boavista Bank, Rio de Janeiro, 1995—96; trainee labor and civil litigation Jose Thomaz Nabvco Law Firm, Rio de Janeiro, 1996—97; trainee civil contracts Pinheiro Neto Advogados, Rio de Janeiro, 1997—99, lawyer real estate, 1999—. Lawyer oil and gas Esso Brasileira de Petrólec, Rio de Janeiro, 2000—01; legal advisor Exxon, Rio de Janeiro, 2000—01. Avocations: sports, soccer. Property, real (including real estate development, water), Sports, Landlord-tenant. Home: Rua Arauiária 90 ap 201 Jardin Botânico Brazil Office: Pinheiro Neto Advogados Av Nilo Peçanha 11 20020-100 Rio de Janeiro Brazil

PINHEIRO-GUIMARÃES, PLINIO, lawyer; b. Rio de Janeiro, Mar. 5, 1967; s. Francisco and Anna Maria Pinheiro-Guimarães; m. Cristiana Pinheiro-Guimarães, July 27, 2000; 1 child, Maria Vitoria. LLB, Candido Mendes Law Sch., Rio de Janeiro, 1990; LLM, cert. in recognition with honors in internat. law, Columbia U., 1994. Bar: Rio de Janeiro 1990, São Paulo 1996, N.Y. 1995, Appelate Divsn. Supreme Ct. N.Y. Law clk. Pinheiro-Guimarães Advogados, Rio de Janeiro, 1986—88, assoc., 1989—91, ptnr., 1995—; legal asst. Banco Interatlantico, Rio de Janeiro, 1988—89; fgn. assoc. Shearman & Sterling, N.Y.C., 1991—94. Contbr. articles to profl. jours. Recipient Cert. Appreciation, Brazilian Am. C. of C. Inc., 1992. Mem.: Am. C. of C. (mem. legis. com. 1995—). Roman Catholic. Avocation: golf. Banking, Corporate, general, Finance. Office: Pinheiro-Guimarães Advogados Av Rio Branco 181 27th Fl 20040-007 Rio de Janeiro Brazil

PINKERTON, ALBERT DUANE, II, lawyer; b. Portland, Oreg., Aug. 28, 1942; s. Albert Duane and Barbara Jean Pinkerton; 1 child, Albert Duane III. BA, Willamette U., 1964, JD, 1966. Bar: Oreg. 1966, U.S. Dist. Ct. Oreg. 1966, U.S. Ct. Appeals (9th cir.) 1966, Alaska 1985, Calif. 1986, U.S. Dist. Ct. Calif. 1987. Gen. practice, Springfield, Oreg., 1966-69, Burns, Oreg., 1969-86, Concord, Calif., 1986-88; assoc. Sellar Hazard McNeely & Manning, Walnut Creek, Calif., 1988—2002. Mem. Oreg. State Bar (com. Uniform Jury Instrns. sec. 1972-73, 82-83, chmn. 1973-74, 83-84; com. Procedure and Practice sec. 1985-86, chmn. 1986-87), Am. Judicature Soc., Masons (master 1980-81), Grand Lodge of Oreg. (dist. dep. 1983-86). State civil litigation, General practice, Insurance. Home: PO Box 2045 Walnut Creek CA 94595-0045 E-mail: duane02@sbcglobal.net.

PINNEY, SIDNEY DILLINGHAM, JR., lawyer; b. Hartford, Conn., Nov. 17, 1924; s. Sydney Dillingham and Louisa (Griswold) Wells P.; m. Judith Munch, Sept. 30, 1990; children from previous marriage: William Griswold, David Rees. Student, Amherst Coll., 1941-43, Brown U., 1943; also, M.I.T., 1943-44; BA cum laude, Amherst Coll., 1947; LLB, Harvard U., 1950. Bar: Conn. 1950. Pvt. practice, Hartford, 1950; assoc. Shepherd, Murtha and Merritt, Hartford, 1950-53; ptnr. Murtha, Cullina, Richter & Pinney (1967) (name changed to Murtha Cullina LLP 2000), 1953-92; of counsel Shepherd, Murtha and Merritt (name changed to Murtha Cullina LLP 2000), 1993—. Lectr. on estate planning. Contbr. to: Estate Planning mag. Bd. dirs. Greater Hartford Area TB and Respiratory Diseases Health Soc., 1956-69, pres., 1966-67; mem. Wethersfield (Conn.) Town Coun., 1958-62; trustee Hartford Conservatory Music, 1967-71, 75-81; trustee, pres. Historic Wethersfield Found., 1961-81; bd. dirs. Hartford Hosp., 1971-80, adv. bd., 1980—; mem. adv. com. Jefferson House, 1978-82; mem. Mortensen Libr. Bd. of Visitors U. Hartford, 1984—; corporator Hartford Pub. Libr., 1969—, Renbrook Sch., West Hartford, Conn., 1970-75. 1st lt. USAF, 1943-46. Fellow Am. Coll. Trust and Estate Counsel; mem. ABA, Nat. Acad. Elder Law Attys., Conn. Bar Assn. (com. elder law sect.), Hartford County Bar Assn. Republican. Congregationalist. Office: City Place 185 Asylum St Hartford CT 06103-3408

PINNOCK, DAVID BRUCE, lawyer; b. Johannesburg, Aug. 10, 1973; s. Bruce Graham and Elaine Isabelle Pinnock; m. Colleen Gillian Ann Yates, Feb. 5, 2000. BA, U. Witwatersrand, Johannesburg, 1994, LLB, 1996. Bar: High Ct. South Africa 1999. Candidate atty. Cliffe Dekker & Todd, Gauteng, South Africa, 1997—98, profl. asst., 1999; assoc. Cliffe Dekker Fuller Moore, Gauteng, South Africa, 2000; dir. Cliffe Dekker Inc., Gauteng, South Africa, 2001—. Mem.: Johannesburg Attys. Assn., Law Soc. No. Provinces. Avocations: hockey, golf, literature. Mergers and acquisitions, Commercial, contracts (including sales of goods; commercial financing), Corporate, general. Office: Cliffe Dekker Inc 1 Protea Pl Sandton 2010 South Africa

PINOVER, EUGENE ALFRED, lawyer; b. N.Y.C., Jan. 8, 1948; s. Maurice Alfred and Harriet (Ortner) P.; m. Diana Elzey, Feb. 14, 1974; children: Julia, Benjamin, Hannah. BA cum laude, Dartmouth Coll., 1969; JD cum laude, NYU, 1973. Bar: N.Y. 1974, U.S. Dist. Ct. (so. and ea. dists.) N.Y. 1974. Ptnr. Willkie Farr & Gallagher, N.Y.C. Property, real (including real estate development, water). Office: Willkie Farr & Gallagher 787 7th Ave Lbby 2 New York NY 10019-6099 E-mail: epinover@willkie.com.

PINSKY, ROY DAVID, lawyer; b. Syracuse, N.Y., Feb. 1, 1948; s. Norman M. and Rose C. Pinsky; m. Stephanie V. Pinsky, June 9, 1968; children: Alissa Jill, Todd Justin. BS, Syracuse U., 1969, JD, 1971. Bar: N.Y. 1972, Fla. 1981. Ptnr. Pinsky, Canter and Pinsky, Syracuse, 1972, Pinsky and Pliskin, Syracuse, 1972-88, Pinsky & Skandalis, 1988—. Spl. cons. Syracuse Bd. Edn., 1972-74. Contbr. articles to profl. jours. Bd. dirs. Young Israel-Shaarei Torah of Syracuse; past trustee Jewish Home of Ctrl. N.Y. Served with U.S. Army, 1969-75. Mem. N.Y. State Bar Assn., Fla. Bar Assn., Onondaga County Bar Assn., Transp. Lawyers Assn. (past trustee), Def. Rsch. Inst., Can. Transport Lawyers Assn. General civil litigation, Health, Transportation. Home: 4623 Glencliffe Rd Manlius NY 13104-2378 Office: PO Box 250 5790 Widewaters Pkwy Syracuse NY 13214-0250 E-mail: pinskyskan@aol.com.

PINSON, JERRY D. lawyer; b. Harrison, Ark., Sept. 7, 1942; s. Robert L. and Cleta (Keeter) P.; m. Jane Ellis, Sept. 11, 1964; 1 child, Christopher Clifton. BA, U. Ark., 1964, JD, 1967. Bar: Ark. 1967, U.S. Ct. Appeals (8th cir.) 1967, U.S. Supreme Ct. 1967, U.S. Dist. Ct. (ea. and we. dists.) Ark. 1968. Dep. atty. gen. State of Ark., Little Rock, 1967-70; ptnr. Pinson & Reeves, Harrison, 1973-88; sole practice Harrison, 1970-73, 88—. Mem. Ark. Supreme Ct. com. on the unauthorized practice of law in Ark., 1979-91, chmn. 1990-91; spl. justice Ark. Supreme Ct., 1991, 94; active state bd. law examiners, 1997—. Pres. United Way Boone County, Harrison, 1974. Mem. Ark. Bar Assn., Boone County Bar Assn., Harrison C. of C. (sec. bd. dirs. 1977), Rotary (bd. dirs. 1975, v.p. 1976, pres. 1977). General practice, Personal injury (including property damage), Estate planning. Office: Atty at Law PO Box 1111 Harrison AR 72602-1111

PIPKIN, JAMES HAROLD, JR., lawyer; b. Houston, Jan. 3, 1939; s. James Harold and Zenda Marie (Lewis) P. BA, Princeton U., 1960; JD, Harvard U., 1963; Diploma in Law, Oxford (Eng.) U., 1965. Bar: D.C. 1964, U.S. Supreme Ct. 1969, D.C. Ct. Appeals, 1972. Law ck. to assoc. justice U.S. Supreme Ct., Washington, 1963-64; assoc. Steptoe and Johnson, Washington, 1965-70, ptnr., 1971-93; counselor to The Sec. of the Interior U.S. Dept. of the Interior, 1993-98; U.S. spl. negotiator for Pacific Salmon, Dept. of State, 1994-2001; rank of amb. Dept. of State, 1995-96; dir. office policy analysis U.S. Dept. Interior, 1998-2001; fgn. affairs officer U.S. State Dept., 2001—02. Counsel Friends of Music, Smithsonian Inst., Washington, 1984-88; mem. Nat. Arbitration Panel, 1983-94. Author or co-author: The English Country House: A Grand Tour, 1985, The Country House Garden: A Grand Tour, 1987, Places of Tranquility, 1990; contbr. photographs and articles to mags. including House & Garden, Smithsonian mag., The Mag. Antiques, Archtl. Digest. Grand officier Confrérie des Chevaliers du Tastevin, 1989—. Mem. ABA, D.C. Bar Assn., Met. Club. Administrative and regulatory, Alternative dispute resolution, Environmental. Home: 6109 Davenport Ter Bethesda MD 20817-5827

PIPKIN, MARVIN GRADY, lawyer; b. San Angelo, Tex., Nov. 15, 1949; s. Raymond Grady and Lillie Marie (Smith) P.; m. Dru Cheatham, July 24, 1971; children: Lacey Elizabeth, Matthew Todd. BBA, U. Tex., 1971, JD, 1974. Bar: Tex. 1974, U.S. Dist. Ct. (we. dist.) Tex. 1979, U.S. Ct. Appeals (5th cir.) 1983. Assoc. Green & Kaufman, San Antonio, 1974-79, ptnr., 1979-82, Kendrick & Pipkin, San Antonio, 1982-93, Drought & Pipkin L.L.P., San Antonio, 1993-98, Pipkin, Oliver & Bradley, LLP, San Antonio, 1998—. Mem. coms. on ethics and admissions Tex. Supreme Ct., admissions com.; adv. dir. Trinity Nat. Bank, San Antonio, 1983; bd. dirs. Allied Am. Bank, San Antonio, First Interstate Bank, San Antonio. Bd. dirs. Monte Vista Hist. Assn., San Antonio, 1975-78. Fellow Tex. Bar Found., San Antonio Bar Found.; mem. ABA, Tex. Assn. Def. Counsel, Tex. Bar Assn., Tex. Assn. Bank Counsel, San Antonio Bar Assn. Republican. Methodist. Avocations: sports, outdoor activities. General civil litigation, Corporate, general, Property, real (including real estate development, water). Home: 2 Dorchester Pl San Antonio TX 78209-2203 Office: Pipkin Oliver & Bradley LLP 1020 NE 600 P 410 #810 San Antonio TX 78209 Fax: 210-820-0077. E-mail: mpipkin@pobllp.com.

PIRAINO, ANDREW NORMAN, lawyer; b. Syracuse, N.Y., Dec. 12, 1954; s. Martin J. and Mary C. Piraino; m. Anne Marie Francoeur, June 6, 1987; 1 child, Maria. BA, St. Bonaventure U., 1977; JD, Albany Law Sch., 1981. Bar: N.Y. 1983, U.S. Dist. Ct. (no. dist.) N.Y., 1984. Asst. counsel N.Y. State Senate, Albany and Syracuse, 1982-84, N.Y. State Assembly, Syracuse, 1984-93; judge Town of Salina Justice Ct., Liverpool, N.Y., 1994—; pvt. practice Syracuse, 1983—. Chmn. legis. com. Cen. N.Y. Workers' Compensation Bar, Syracuse, 1996—. Mem. Town of Salina Rep. Com., 1984-93. Mem. N.Y. State Bar Assn., N.Y. State Magistrates Assn., Onondaga County Magistrates Assn. (rec. sec. 1997-98, v.p. 1998-99, pres. 2000), Onondaga County Bar Assn. Roman Catholic. Avocation: sports card collector. Personal injury (including property damage), Workers' compensation. Home: 211 Victoria Park Dr Liverpool NY 13088-5437 Office: 117 South State St Syracuse NY 13202

PIRCHER, LEO JOSEPH, lawyer, director; b. Berkeley, Calif., Jan. 4, 1933; s. Leo Charles and Christine (Moore) P.; m. Phyllis McConnell, Aug. 4, 1956 (div. Apr. 1981); children: Christopher, David, Eric; m. Nina Silverman, June 14, 1987. BS, U. Calif., Berkeley, 1954, JD, 1957. Bar: Calif. 1958, (N.Y.) 1985, cert.: Calif. Bd. Legal Specialization (cert. specialist taxation law). Assoc. Lawler, Felix & Hall, L.A., 1957-62, ptnr., 1962-65, sr. ptnr., 1965-83, Pircher, Nichols & Meeks, L.A., 1983—. Adj. prof. Loyola U. Law Sch., L.A., 1959—61; corp. sec. Am. Metal Bearing Co., Gardena, Calif., 1975—; dir. Varco Internat., Inc., Orange, Calif.; spkr. various law schs. and bar assns. edn. programs. Author (with others): (novels) Definition and Utility of Leases, 1968. Chmn. pub. fin. and taxation sect. Calif. Town Hall, L.A., 1970—71. Mem.: ABA, Nat. Assn. Real Estate Investment Trusts Inc. (cert. specialist taxation law), L.A. County Bar Assn. (exec. com. comml. law sect.), N.Y. State Bar, Calif. State Bar, Regency (L.A.). Republican. Corporate, general, Property, real (including real estate development, water), Corporate taxation. Office: Pircher Nichols & Meeks Ste 1700 1925 Century Park E Los Angeles CA 90067-6022 E-mail: lpircher@pircher.com.

PIROK, EDWARD WARREN, lawyer, consultant; b. Chgo., June 2, 1947; s. Edward Warren and Elinor Jean Pirok; m. Christine Merk, Jan. 23, 1972; children: Edward, Christopher, Jennifer, Elizabeth. BS, Ill. Inst. Tech., 1970; JD, Loyola U., 1973. Bar: N.Y. 1988, Ill. 1973, U.S. Supreme Ct., U.S. Ct. Appeals (2d and 7th cirs.) U.S. Dist. Ct. (so. and ea. dists.) N.Y., U.S. Dist. Ct. (no. dist.) Ill. Trial atty. Burlington No., Inc., Chgo., 1975-77; asst. gen. counsel Regional Transp. Authority, Chgo., 1977-82; gen. counsel Metra, The N.E. Ill. R.R. Corp., Chgo., 1982-87; trial atty. Metro-North Commuter R.R., N.Y.C., 1987-89; of counsel Peltz & Walker, N.Y.C., 1990-93; ptnr. Frank & Assocs., Ltd., Chgo., 1999. 1st lt. Ill. Army N.G. Mem. ATLA, Ill. Trial Lawyers Assn. Roman Catholic. Avocations: golf, tennis. Environmental, Personal injury (including property damage), Corporate, general. Office: Frank & Assocs Ltd 734 N Wells St Chicago IL 60610 Home: 299 Mallard Point Lake Barrington IL 60010-1783

PIRTLE, H(AROLD) EDWARD, lawyer; b. Detroit, Apr. 6, 1948; s. Edward Bensen Pirtle and Lorraine Virginia (La Pointe) Schwartz; m. Maxine Mary Stencel, June 10, 1971 (div. May 1981); children: Kimberly, Jeffrey, Michelle; m. Betsy Yvonne Mark, Sept. 1, 1984. AS, Macomb County Cmty. Coll., Warren, Mich., 1977; B in applied sci., Siena Heights Coll., 1983; JD, U. Toldeo, 1990. Bar: Mich. 1990, U.S. Dist. Ct. (ea. dist.) Mich. 1990, U.S. Ct. Appeals (6th cir.) 1997. Assoc. Beaman & Beaman, Jackson, Mich., 1990-91; pvt. practice, H. Edward Pirtle, Atty. at Law, Detroit, 1991-96; assoc. Calligaro & Meyering, PC, Taylor, Mich., 1996-97; mng. mem. H. Edward Pirtle, PLC, Detroit, 1997—. With U.S. Navy, 1967-72. Mem. ABA, Macomb County Bar Assn., Met. Detroit Bar Assn., Am. Mensa (gen. rep. 1984-85, legal counsel Mensa Edn. and Rsch. Found., trustee, found. sec.). Avocations: computers, financial markets. Bankruptcy, Family and matrimonial, Criminal. Office: 1402 Ford Bldg 615 Griswold Detroit MI 48226-3989 E-mail: epirtle@aol.com., detroitlaw1@aol.com.

PISANO, VINCENT JAMES, lawyer; b. Englewood, N.J., Sept. 12, 1953; s. Vincent Paul and Georgette (Cernek) P.; m. Lissa Roth, May 4, 1996; children: Catherine Callahan Steele, Elisabeth Lynden Steele. BA, Vassar Coll., 1975; JD, St. Johns U., 1978. Bar: N.Y. 1979. With Skadden, Arps, Slate, Meagher and Flom, N.Y.C., 1978—2003; ptnr. Skadden, Arps, Slate and Meagher, N.Y.C., 1986—2003, Kirkland & Ellis, N.Y.C., 2003—. Bd. dirs. Make a Wish Found. Met. N.Y., 1988-90. Mem. N.Y. Bar Assn., N.Y.C. Bar Assn., Vassar Coll. Alumni Assn. Corporate, general, Mergers and acquisitions, Securities. Office: Kirkland & Ellis 153 W 53d St New York NY 10022 E-mail: vpisano@kirkland.com.

PITMAN, ROBERT L. judge; JD, U. Tex., 1988. Atty. advisor Executive Office for US Atty., Office of Legal Council, Washington, DC, 1996; cheif Austin Div., Western Dist., Tex.; asst US atty.; US atty. Western Dist., Tex., 2001—02; U.S. magistrate judge Tex., 2003—. Recipient commendations from Exec. Office for US Atty, Fed. Bureau of Investigation, US Dept. of State, US Drug Enforcement Adminstrn., US Secret Service. Office: US Magistrate Judge 200 W 8th St Austin TX 78701 Fax: 210-384-7105.*

PITTMAN, EDWIN LLOYD, state supreme court chief justice; b. Hattiesburg, Miss., Jan. 2, 1935; s. Lloyd H. and Pauline P.; m. Virginia Lund, 1996; children: Melanie, Win, Jennifer. BS, U. So. Miss.; JD, U. Miss., 1960. Bar: Miss. Practiced law until, 1964; mem. Miss. Senate, 1964-72; treas. State of Miss., Jackson, 1976-80, sec. of state, 1980-84, atty. gen., 1984-88; justice Supreme Ct. Miss., Jackson, 1990—; chief justice Miss. Supreme Ct. , Jackson, Miss., 2000—. Trustee William Carey Coll. 2nd lt., Inf. U.S. Army. Mem. U. Miss. Alumni Assn., U. So. Miss. Alumni Assn., Miss. Jaycees (past state dir.), ABA, South Central Miss. Bar Assn. Clubs: Lions, Masons. Democrat. Baptist. Office: Miss Supreme Ct Gartin Justice Bldg PO Box 249 Jackson MS 39205-0117

PITTMAN, STEUART LANSING, lawyer; b. Albany, N.Y., June 6, 1919; s. Ernest Wetmore and Estelle Young (Romeyn) P.; children by previous marriage— Andrew Pinchot, Nancy Steuart, Rosamond Pinchot, Tamara Pickering; m. Barbara Milburn White, Mar. 29, 1958; children— Patricia Milburn, Steuart Lansing, Anne Romeyn. Grad., St. Paul's Sch., Concord, N.H., 1937; BA, Yale U., 1941, LLB, 1948. Bar: N.Y. 1948, D.C. 1954. With Pan Am. Airways Africa Ltd., Cairo, 1941-42, China Nat. Aviation Co., Calcutta, India, 1942; with firm Cravath, Swaine & Moore, N.Y.C., 1948-50; with govt. agys. ECA, Mut. Security Agy. and FOA, 1950-54; founder Shaw Pittman (and predecessors), Washington, 1954-61, 64—; asst. sec. of def., 1961-64. Cons. 2d Hoover Commn., 1954-55, Dept. State, 1955, Devel. Loan Fund, 1958-59; sr. fellow Inst. Def. Analysis. Bd. dirs. Hudson Inst., Chesapeake Environ. Protection Assn.; mem. Atlantic Coun. 1st lt. USMCR, WWII, CBI. Decorated Silver Star. Mem. Met. Club (Washington). Office: Shaw Pittman 2300 N St NW Washington DC 20037-1172

PITTMAN, VIRGIL, federal judge; b. Enterprise, Ala., Mar. 28, 1916; s. Walter Oscar and Annie Lee (Logan) P.; m. Floy Lasseter, 1944 (dec.) 2000; children— Karen Pittman Gordy, Walter Lee. BS, U. Ala., 1939, LL.B., 1940. Bar: Ala. bar 1940. Spl. agt. FBI, 1940-44; practice law Gadsden, Ala., 1946-51; judge Ala. Circuit Ct., Circuit 16, 1951-66; U.S. dist. judge Middle and So. Dist. Ala., 1966-71; chief judge U.S. Dist. Ct. for Ala. So. Dist., 1971-81, sr. judge, 1981—; periodically sat as judge U.S. Ct. Appeals 11th Cir., 1981—96. Lectr. bus. law, econs. and polit. sci. U. Ala. Center, Gadsden, 1948-66 Author: Circuit Court Proceedings in Acquisition of a Tract of Right of Way, 1959, A Judge Looks at Right of Way Condemnation Proceedings, 1960, Technical Pitfalls in Right of Way Proceedings, 1961. Mem. Ala. Bd. Edn., 1951; bd. trustees, life trustee Samford U, 1975-. Lt. (j.g.) USN, 1944-46, USS Wharton, Pacific Supply Corp. Mem. Ala. State Bar, Etowah County Bar Assn. (pres. 1949), Baptist Oaks (bd. dirs. lower income housing), Omicron Delta Kappa. Democrat. Baptist. Office: US Dist Ct 113 St Joseph St Mobile AL 36602

PITTS, GARY BENJAMIN, lawyer; b. Miss., Aug. 23, 1952; s. Dextar Derward Pitts and Eva Margaret Bush; m. Nicole Palmer; children: Andrew Ross, Caitlan Taylor, Austin Palmer. Student, U. Miss., Oxford, 1970-71, Coll. Charleston (S.C.), 1971-73; BA, McGill U., Montreal, Que., Can., 1973-74; JD, Tulane U., New Orleans, 1979. Bar: Tex. 1979, U.S. Ct. Appeals (5th cir.) 1980, U.S. Supreme Ct. 1983. Assoc. Julian & Seele, Houston, 1979-84, Ogletree, Pitts & Collard, Houston, 1984-85; ptnr. Pitts & Collard LLP, Houston and Dallas, 1985-96; owner Pitts & Assocs., Houston, 1996—. V.p., gen. counsel EnviroSec, 2002—. Organizer, legal counsel for Neighborhood Watch Coalition. Capt. USNG, 1975-87. Admiralty, Personal injury (including property damage), Workers' compensation. Office: Pitts & Assocs 8866 Gulf Fwy Ste 117 Houston TX 77017-6528

PITZNER, RICHARD WILLIAM, lawyer; b. Fond du Lac, Wis., Sept. 19, 1946; s. Robert J. and Almira (Wurtz) P.; m. Georgene J. Thuerwachter, July 6, 1968 (div. 1991); children: Christie, Kyle; m. Ricki L. Mundstock, Jan. 4, 1998. BBA, U. Wis., 1968, MBA, 1969, JD, 1972. Bar: Wis. 1972, U.S. Dist. Ct. (we. dist.) Wis. 1972, U.S. Tax Ct. Ptnr. Murphy & Desmond, Madison, Wis., 1972—. Tchr. U. Wis., Madison, 1975-78. Mem. ABA, AICPA, Nat. Assn. Accts., Wis. Inst. CPAs, State Bar Wis., Wis. Inst. CPAs, Kensington Golf and Country Club, Nakoma Golf Club, Order of Coif, Beta Gamma Sigma. Avocations: golf, swimming. Probate (including wills, trusts), Corporate taxation, Estate taxation. Home: 3123 Harlan Circle Madison WI 53711 Office: Murphy & Desmond 2 E Mifflin St Madison WI 53703-2889

PIZZULLI, FRANCIS COSMO JOSEPH, lawyer, bioethicist; b. Bklyn., May 16, 1950; s. Dominick Lawrence and Rose Nancy (Ieracitano) P. BA in Math with high honors, U. Calif., Santa Barbara, 1971; JD, U. So. Calif., 1974. Bar: Calif. 1975. NEH fellow Inst. Soc., Ethics and Life Scis./Hastings Ctr., Hastings-on-Hudson, N.Y., 1974-75; law clk. U.S. Ct. Appeals (9th cir.), 1975-76; pvt. practice Santa Monica, Calif., 1981—. Cons. Nat. Commn. for Protection Human Subjects of Biomed. and Behavioral Rsch., Washington, 1976-77; spkr., lectr., panelist in bioethics field. Editor So. Calif. Law Rev., 1973-74; contbr. articles to profl. jours. Mem. Italian-Am. Lawyers Assn., Order of Coif, KC. Roman Catholic. General civil litigation, Constitutional, Entertainment. Office: 718 Wilshire Blvd Santa Monica CA 90401-1708

PLACHTA, THOMAS J. lawyer; b. Bay City, Mich., May 4, 1948; s. Joseph W. and Maureen B. Plachta; m. Laura A. Parker; children: Thomas Parker, Dominic David. BA in Comm., Mich. State U., 1970; JD, Wayne State U., 1973. Bar: Mich. 1974, U.S. Dist. Ct. (ea. dist.) Mich. 1974, U.S. Dist. Ct. (we. dist.) Mich. 1976, U.S. Ct. Appeals (6th cir.) 1976. Assoc. dir. Misdemeanor Defender Office, Detroit, 1974—75; atty. Campbell & Plachta, Detroit, 1975—76; pvt. practice Grand Rapids, Mich., 1976—78; chief asst. pros. Isabella County Prosecutor, Mt. Pleasant, Mich., 1979—86; pvt. practice Mt. Pleasant, 1986—. Mem.: ABA, Criminal Def. Attys. Mich., Nat. Assn. Criminal Def. Attys. Democrat. Methodist. Criminal, Family and matrimonial, General civil litigation. Home: 301 West Dr Mount Pleasant MI 48858 Office: Plachta Law Office 405 S Main St Mount Pleasant MI 48858

PLAEGER, FREDERICK JOSEPH, II, lawyer; b. New Orleans, Sept. 10, 1953; s. Edgar Leonard and Bernice Virginia (Schiwetz) P.; m. Kathleen Helen Dickson, Nov. 19, 1977; children: Douglas A., Catherine E. BS, La. State U., 1976, JD, 1977. Bar: La. 1978, Tex. 1999, U.S. Dist. Ct. (ea. dist.) La. 1978, U.S. Ct. Appeals (5th cir.) 1981, U.S. Supreme Ct. 1989. Law clk. U.S. Dist. Ct. (ea. dist.) La., New Orleans, 1977-79; assoc. Milling, Benson, Woodward, Hillyer, Pierson & Miller, New Orleans, 1979-85, ptnr., 1985-89; v.p., gen. counsel, corp. sec. La. Land and Exploration Co., New Orleans, 1989-97; v.p., gen. counsel Burlington Resources Inc., Houston, 1997—. Selected mem. Met. Area Com. Leadership Forum, 1986; bd. dirs. Soc. Environ. Edn., La. Nature and Sci. Ctr., 1992—94; trustee Houston Ballet, 2001—; mem. adv. bd. Inst. for Energy Law, 2001—, mem. exec. com., 2002—; bd. dirs. New Orleans Speech and Hearing Ctr., 1985—91, pres., 1988—90; bd. dirs. Children's Oncology Svcs. La. (Ronald McDonald Ho. of New Orleans), 1987—90. Recipient Service to Mankind award Sertoma, 1989. Mem. ABA, La. Bar Assn., Am. Corp. Counsel Assn. (bd. dirs. New Orleans chpt. 1995-98), Am. Petroleum Inst. (mem. gen. commn. law), Univ. Club, Lakeside Country Club. Republican. Avocations: computers, hunting, fishing. Corporate, general, Oil, gas, and mineral, General practice. Home: 5105 Longmont Dr Houston TX 77056-2417 Office: Burlington Resources Inc 5051 Westheimer Rd Ste 1400 Houston TX 77056-5686

PLAGER, S. JAY, judge; b. Long Branch, N.J., May 16, 1931; s. A. L. and Clara L. Plager; children: Anna Katherine, David Alan, Daniel Tyler. AB, U. N.C., 1952; JD, U. Fla., 1958; LLM, Columbia U., 1961. Bar: Fla. 1958, Ill. 1964. Asst. prof. law U. Fla., 1958—62, assoc. prof., 1962—64; assoc. prof. law U. Ill., Champaign-Urbana, 1964—65, prof., 1965—77; dir. Office Environ. and Planning Studies, 1972—74, 1975—77; dean, prof. law Ind. U. Sch. Law, Bloomington, 1977—84, prof. law, 1984—90; counselor to undersec. U.S. Dept. Health and Human Svcs., 1986—87; assoc. dir. Office of Mgmt. and Budget Office of Mgmt. and Budget, 1987—88; adminstr. info. and regulatory affairs Exec. Office of the Pres., 1988—89; cir. judge U.S. Ct. Appeals (fed. cir.), 1989—. Vis. rsch. prof. law U. Wis., 1967—68; vis. scholar Stanford U., 1984—85. Author (with others): Water Law and Administration, 1968; author: Social Justice Through Law-New Approaches in the Law of Property, 1970; author: (with others) Florida Water Law, 1980. Chmn. Gainesville (Fla.) Planning Commn., 1962—63; mem. Urbana Plan Commn., 1966—70; mem. nat. air pollution manpower devel. adv. com., 1971—75; cons. Ill. Inst. for Environ. Quality, U.S. EPA; chmn. Ill. Task Force on Noise, 1972—76; vice chmn. Nat. Commn. on Jud. Discipline and Removal, 1991—93. With USN, 1952—55. Office: US Ct Appeals for Fed Cir The National Courts Bldg 717 Madison Pl NW Washington DC 20439-0002

PLAINE, LLOYD LEVA, lawyer; b. Washington, Nov. 3, 1947; d. Marx Leva and Shirley P. Leva, MD; m. James W. Hill. BA, U. Pa., 1969; postgrad., Harvard U.; JD, Georgetown U., 1975. Bar: DC 1975. Legis. asst. to US Rep. Sidney Yates, 1971-72; with Sutherland, Asbill & Brennan, Washington, 1975-82, ptnr., 1982—. Fellow Am. Bar Found., Am. Coll. Trust and Estate Counsel (past regent), Am. Coll. Tax Counsel; mem. ABA (past chmn. real property, probate and trust law sect.). Estate planning, Probate (including wills, trusts), Estate taxation. Office: Sutherland Asbill & Brennan Ste 6 1275 Pennsylvania Ave NW Washington DC 20004-2415

PLANKENSTEINER, MARCO, lawyer, researcher; b. Bolzano, Italy, Mar. 29, 1974; s. Mario Angelo P. and Mitzi Baldessari; life ptnr. Virginie Rue. D, Cath. U., Milan, 1998; LLM, PhD, U. Paris II, 1999. Bar: Ct. Milan 1998, Ct. Paris 2002. Atty. Kramer, Lebin, Naftalis & Frankel LLP, Paris, 2002. Rschr. U. Paris II, 1999—. Avocation: international history. Banking, Public international, Taxation, general. Home: 22 Rue Rouget De Lisue 94100 Saint Naur Des Fosses France Office: Kramer Levin Naftalis & Frankel LLP 47 Ave Hoche 75008 Paris France Fax: 00390277197260. E-mail: m_planke@hotmail.com., mp@santalex.com.

PLANT, ALBIN MACDONOUGH, lawyer; b. Balt., Md., July 30, 1937; s. Albin Joseph and Ruth E. (French) P.; m. Anne Warwick Brown, June 17, 1961; children: Katherine, Albin MacDonough Jr., Elizabeth Ashby. BA, Princeton U., 1959; LLB, U. Va., 1963; MLA, Johns Hopkins U., 1978. Bar: Md. 1963, U.S. Dist. Ct. Md. 1963, U.S. Ct. Appeals 1970. Assoc. Semmes, Bowen & Semmes, Balt., 1963-71, ptnr., 1971-91, Stewart, Plant & Blumenthal, Balt., 1991—. Adj. prof. law U. Balt., 1979, U. Md., 1979-83, 84-85. Bd. dir. Ctr. Stage, Am. Horticulture Soc., Md. Club, T. Rowe Price Savings Bank, Balt. Choral Arts Soc. Mem. Am. Coll. Trust and Estate Counsel, life fellow, Am. Bar Foud., Lawyers Roundtable, Md. Club, Wednesday Law Club. Democrat. Probate (including wills, trusts), Estate taxation. Office: 7 St Paul St Baltimore MD 21202-1626 E-mail: amplant@spblaw.com.

PLANT, DAVID WILLIAM, lawyer; b. Ottawa, Ill., Apr. 22, 1931; s. Arthur Percival and Margery Elmina (Flick) P.; children: Susan W. BME, Cornell U., 1953, LLB, 1957. Bar: N.Y. 1957, U.S. Dist. Ct. (ea. and so. dists.) N.Y., U.S. Supreme Ct., 1968, U.S. Patent Office 1982; cert. CEDR mediator. Assoc. Fish & Neave, N.Y.C., 1957-70, ptnr., 1970-98, mng. ptnr., 1981-84. Domestic and internat. arbitrator, mediator, panel mem., arbitration cons. com. World Intellectual Property Orgn., 1994—; mem. panels of neutrals CPR, 1990—, AAA, 1982—, Internat. C. of C., 1992—, London Ct. Internat. Arbitration, 1992—, ea. dist. N.Y., so. dist. N.Y., dist. N.H.; adj. prof. Franklin Pierce Law Ctr., 1998—; sr. fellow U. Melbourne Law Sch., 2002; lectr. in field. Contbr. articles to profl. jours. Past mem. bd. dirs. Cornell Rsch. Found. Fellow Chartered Inst. Arbitrators, Coll. Comml. Arbitrators, Am. Coll. Civil Trial Mediators; mem. ABA, Assn. of Bar of City of N.Y. (com. on patents 1980-83, chmn. 1983-86, com. on arbitration and alternative dispute resolution 1987-90, 91-94, 97-99, chmn. 1994-97), Am. Arbitration Assn. (various coms. and panels of neutrals), N.Y. Intellectual Property Law Assn. (chmn. arbitration com. 1989-91, bd. dirs. 1994-96), Am. Intellectual Property Law Assn. (chmn. alternative dispute resolution com. 1993-95), Ctr. Pub. Resources (panels of neutrals, co-chmn. tech. com. 1995—), Cornell Law Assn. (exec. com., pres. 1994-96), Lic. Execs. Soc. (co-chmn. alternative dispute resolution com. 1995-97).13291786 Patent, Trademark and copyright. Home: 1451 Little Sunapee Rd New London NH 03257-4211 E-mail: DPlantADR@aol.com.

PLATKIN, RICHARD M. lawyer; b. 1963; m. Laurie Conway. BS, Rensselaer Poly. Inst., 1985; JD, Union U., Albany, 1993. Bar: N.Y. 1994. Computer engr.; law clk. to Hon. Roger J. Miner U.S. Ct. Appeals (2d cir.); asst. counsel Office Gov. State of N.Y., Albany, 1995—97, sr. asst. counsel, 1997—98, dep. counsel to gov., 1998—2003, counsel to gov., 2003—. Exec. editor: Union U. Law Rev. Office: State Capitol Albany NY 12224-0341*

PLATT, LESLIE A. lawyer; b. Bronx, N.Y., Aug. 7, 1944; s. Harold and Ann (Bienstock) P.; m. Marcia Ellin Berman, Aug., 1969; 1 son, Bill Lawrence. BA, George Washington U., 1966; JD, NYU, 1969. Bar: N.Y. 1970, U.S. Dist. Ct. D.C. 1972. Atty. advisor Office Gen. Counsel HUD, Washington, 1971-72, legis. atty., 1972-75, asst. gen. counsel for legis. svcs., 1975-78, assoc. gen. counsel for legis., 1978-80; dep. gen. counsel-legal counsel HEW (HHS 1980) Office Gen. Counsel, Washington, 1980-81, legal counsel and staff dir. White House Agent Orange group, 1980-81; pvt. practice Washington, 1982-91; exec. asst. to dir. NIH, 1991-92; exec. v.p., COO, gen. counsel The Inst. for Genomic Rsch., Gaithersburg, Md., 1992-95; sr. v.p. strategic devel., gen. counsel Am. Type Culture Collection, Manassas, Va., 1996-98; prin., litig. adv. svcs., assurance and adv. bus. practice Ernst & Young LLP, McLean, Va., 1999—. Pres, dir. Found. for Genetic Medicine, Inc., 1997—. Patentee in field. Chmn. cmty. adv. bd. Fairfax Hosp. Assn. Cameron Glen Facility; chair steering com. Reston/Herndon Bus.-H.S. Partnership; mem. Loudoun County Sci. and Tech. Cabinet, 2002—; bd. dirs. No. Va. Tech. Coun., 2002—. Recipient Disting. Svc. award HUD, 1978. Mem. ABA, Fed. Bar Assn., Am. Jud. Soc., Fed. Sr. Exec. Svc. (charter), Internat. Bar Assn. Administrative and regulatory, Health, Legislative. Home: 11901 Triple Crown Rd Reston VA 20191-3015

PLATT, NINA, law librarian; d. Harlan and Ethel (Byron) Thorlacius; m. Vernon Platt, Dec. 21, 1984. BS, U. ND, Grand Forks, 1980; Masters of Libr. and Info. Sci., Dominican U., River Forest, Ill., 1997. Libr. dir. Carnegie Libr., Devils Lake, ND, 1982—85; tech. svcs. mgr. Dorsey & Whitney, Mpls., 1986—95; systems libr. Minn. Office of Atty. Gen., St. Paul, 1995—97; dir. of libr. services Faegre & Benson LLP, Mpls., 1998—. Cons. Nina Platt & Associates, Prior Lake, Minn., 1993—98. Contbr. textbook, articles to profl. jours. and web sites. Mem.: Spl. Libraries Assn., Minn. Assn. of Law Libraries, Am. Assn. of Law Libraries (exec. bd. mem. 2002—), Minn. Libr. Assn. (assoc.), Hekla Club (pres. 1996—97). Achievements include development of Minnesota Appellate Court Opinions Archive (1997); Led development of use of customization within law firm research intranets. Avocations: motorcycling, gardening. Office: Faegre & Benson LLP 90 South Street Minneapolis MN 55402 Office Fax: 612-766-1600. E-mail: nplatt@faegre.com.

PLATT, STEVEN IRVING, lawyer, judge; b. Woodstock, Va., Jan. 1, 1947; s. Nathan and Adele P. (Lober) Platt; children: Jason Benjamin, Sarah Edan. BA, U. Va., 1969; JD, Am. U., 1973; cert. of completion, Nat. Jud. Coll., 1980, Nat. Coll. of Probate Judges, 1983. Bar: Md. 1973, U.S. Dist. Ct. Md., 1976. Ptnr. Stern, Platt & Risner, Oxon Hill, Md., 1976-79; judge Orphans Ct., Prince Georges County, Md., 1978-85; ptnr. Platt & Risner, Clinton, Md., 1980-86; chief judge Orphans Ct., Prince Georges County, Md., 1985-86; assoc. judge Dist. Ct. Md., Upper Marlboro, Md., 1986-88, adminstrv. judge Prince Georges County, 1988-90; assoc. judge Cir. Ct., Prince Georges County, Md., 1990—. Instr. Paralegal Inst. U. Md.; chmn. Jud. Adminstrn. Com., Md. Jud. Conf., 1989-90. Bd. dirs. United Way, Prince Georges, 1980; bd. mgrs. YMCA, Prince Georges, 1980; chmn. Labor Law Revision Task Force, Prince Georges, 1981—; chmn. bd. trustees Henson Valley Montessori Sch., Temple Hills, Md., 1985-86. With Md. NG, 1970-76; v.p. Md. Bus. and Tech. Case Mgmt. Task Force; chmn. Cong. of Cir. Ct. Judges Bus. & Tech. Case Mgmt. Implementation Com. Mem. ABA, Md. Bar Assn., Prince Georges Bar Assn. (bd. dirs. 1978-85, treas. 1985-86, sec. 1986-87), Am. Trial Lawyers Assn., Nat. Coll. Probate Judges (state rep. 1985-86), Md. State Bar Assn. (bd. govs., sect. coun. jud. adminstrn.), Prince Georges County Bar Assn. (pres. 1988—), Delta Theta Phi. Jewish. Home: 8607 Grey Fox Trl Upper Marlboro MD 20772-9618 Office: Cir Ct Judges Chambers 2D Fl Courthouse Upper Marlboro MD 20772

PLATT, THOMAS COLLIER, JR., federal judge; b. N.Y.C., N.Y., May 29, 1925; s. Thomas Collier and Louise Platt; m. Ann Byrd Symington, June 25, 1948; children: Ann Byrd, Charles Collier, Thomas Collier, III, Elizabeth Louise. BA, Yale U., 1947, LL.B., 1950. Bar: N.Y. 1950. Assoc. Root, Ballantine, Harlan, Bushby & Palmer, N.Y.C., 1950-53; asst. U.S. atty. Bklyn., 1953-56; assoc. Bleakley, Platt, Schmidt, Hart & Fritz, N.Y.C., 1956-60, ptnr., 1960-74; judge U.S. Dist. Ct. (ea. dist.) N.Y., 1974—, chief judge, 1988-95. Former dir. Phoenix Mut. Life Ins. Co., RAC Corp., McIntyre Aviation, Inc.; atty. Village of Laurel Hollow, N.Y., 1958-74; acting police justice Village of Lloyd Harbor, N.Y., 1958-63 Alt. del. Republican Nat. Conv., 1964, 68, 72; del. N.Y. State Rep. Conv., 1966; trustee Brooks Sch., North Andover, Mass., 1968-82, pres., 1970-74. Served with USN, 1943-46 Mem. Fed. Judges Assn. (sec., bd. dirs. 1982-91). Clubs: Phelps Assn. (New Haven) (bd. govs. 1960-98); Cold Spring Harbor Beach (N.Y.) (bd. mgrs. 1964-70); Yale of N.Y.C. Episcopalian. Office: US Dist Ct 1044 Federal Plaza Central Islip NY 11722-4442*

PLATT, WARREN E. lawyer; b. McNary, Ariz., Aug. 5, 1943; BA, Mich. State U., 1965; JD, U. Ariz., 1969. Bar: Ariz. 1969, Calif. 1991, Texas 1993. Atty. Snell & Wilmer, Phoenix. Mng. editor: Ariz. Law Rev., 1968-69. Fellow Am. Coll. Trial Lawyers; mem. Blue Key, Order of Coif, Phi Alpha Delta General civil litigation, Product liability, Accountant. Office: Snell & Wilmer One Arizona Ctr Phoenix AZ 85004-0001

PLATT, WILLIAM HENRY, judge; b. Allentown, Pa., Jan. 25, 1940; s. Henry and Genevieve (McElroy) P.; m. Maureen Hart, Nov. 29, 1969; children: Meredith H., William H., James H. AB, Dickinson Coll., 1961; JD, U. Pa., 1964. Bar: Pa. 1967, U.S. Supreme Ct. 1971. Ptnr. Yarus and Platt, Allentown, 1967-77; asst. pub. defender Lehigh County (Pa.), 1972-75, chief pub. defender, 1975-76, dist. atty., 1976-91; ptnr. Eckert, Seamans, Cherin & Mellott, 1991-95; city solicitor City of Allentown, 1994-95; judge Ct. Common Pleas of Lehigh County, Allentown, 1996—, pres. judge, 2002—. Mem. criminal procedural rules com. Supreme Ct. Pa., 1982-92, chmn., 1986-92; mem. Gov.'s Trial Ct. Nominating Commn. Lehigh County, 1984-87; mem. Pa. Commn. on Crime and Delinquency Victim Services Adv. Com., 1983-91. Served with M.P., U.S. Army, 1964-66. Mem.: ABA, Pa. Conf. of State Trial Judges (edn. com. 1997—2002), Pa. Assn. Dist. Attys. (exec. com. 1980—86, pres. 1983—84, chmn. 1986—87, tng. inst. mem. 1986—91), Nat. Assn. Dist. Attys. (state dir. 1982—84), Lehigh County Bar Assn., Pa. Bar Assn., Pa. Bar Inst. (hon.) (life; bd. dirs. 1989—2000, exec. com. 1994—2000, pres. 1997—98). Office: Lehigh County Courthouse 455 W Hamilton St Allentown PA 18101-1614

PLATTNER, RICHARD SERBER, lawyer; b. N.Y.C., Aug. 10, 1952; s. Milton and Sallee Sarah (Serber) P.; m. Susan M. Madden, June 4, 1976 (div. June 1979); m. Susan K. Morris, Mar. 30, 1983; children: Samuel Morris, Katherine Elise. BA cum laude, Mich. State U., 1973; JD, Ariz. State U., 1977. Bar: Ariz. 1977, U.S. Dist. Ct. Ariz. 1977, U.S. Ct. Appeals (9th cir.) 1987; cert. specialist personal injury and wrongful death. Assoc. Wolfe & Harris, Pa., 1977-79, Monbleau, Vermeire & Turley, Phoenix, 1979-81, Phillips & Lyon, Phoenix, 1981; sole practice Phoenix, 1982-91; ptnr. Plattner Verderame, P.C., 1991—. Posse comdr. Maricopa County Sheriff Exec. Posse, 1986-87; judge pro tem Maricopa County Superior Ct., 1986—, Ariz. Ct. Appeals, 1993—. Editor: Trial Judges of Maricopa County, 1985; co-editor Jury Verdict Research newsletter, 1982-83. Mem. ATLA (sustaining mem.), Am. Bd. Trial Advs. (assoc. 1997—), Ariz. Trial Lawyers Assn. (sustaining mem., editor Ariz. Appellate Highlights, 1985—, bd. dirs., 1987—, pres. 1991), Ariz. Bar Assn. (mem. civil practice and procedure com. 1988-99, civil jury instrn. com. 1991), Maricopa County Bar Assn., Phoenix Trial Lawyers Assn. (bd. dirs. 1983-95, pres. 1986-87), Ariz. Bus. and Profl. Assn. (pres. 1984-86). Insurance, Personal injury (including property damage), Product liability. Office: PO Box 36570 Phoenix AZ 85067-6570 E-mail: rplattner@plattner-verderame.com.

PLAX, KAREN ANN, lawyer; b. St. Louis, June 29, 1946; d. George J. and Evelyn G. Zell; m. Stephen E. Plax, Dec. 19, 1968; 1 child, Jonathan. BA magna cum laude, U. Mo., St. Louis, 1969; JD with distinction, U. Mo., Kansas City, 1976. Bar: Mo. 1976, U.S. Supreme Ct. 1980. Atty. Thayer, Gum & Wickert, Grandview, Mo., 1976-84, Plax & Cochet, Kansas City, Mo., 1984-87; pvt. practice Kansas City, 1987—. Past chair divsn. 3, region IV Mo. Supreme Ct. Com. to review ethical conduct of attys., 1997-98. Author: Missouri Bar Practical Skills, 1998; asst. editor: Racial Integration in the Inner Suburb, 1970; contbr. articles to profl. jours. Recipient Pub. Svc. award U. Mo. Kansas City Law Found., 1998, Woman of Yr. award Assn. Women Lawyers of Greater Kansas City, 1999. Fellow: Am. Acad. Matrimonial Lawyers (pres. Mo. chpt. 1999—2001); mem.: ABA (family law sect. 1976—), Mo. Bar Family Law (legis. chair 1997—98, v.p. 1999—2000, Spl. Commendation for Legis. Role in Family Law 1998), Kansas City Met. Bar Assn. Family and matrimonial. Office: Ste 300 1310 Carondelet Dr Kansas City MO 64114-4803 E-mail: kaplax@swbell.net.

PLAZA, EVA M. lawyer; b. Torreon, Coahuila, Mex., Feb. 13, 1958; d. Sergio and Eva (Torres) P. BA cum laude, Harvard U., 1980; JD, U. Calif., Berkeley, 1984. Trial atty. U.S. Dept. Justice, Washington, 1984-86; assoc. Arent, Fox, Kintner, Plotkin, Washington, 1986-88, Seyfarth, Shaw, Fairweather & Geraldson, Washington, 1988-93; dep. asst. atty. gen. U.S. Dept. Jutice, 1993-97; asst. sec. U.S. Dept. Housing and Urban Devel., 1997—. Mem. ABA, Tex. Bar Assn., Pa. Bar Assn., D.C. Bar Assn., Hispanic Bar Assn. (pres. D.C. chpt.). Democrat. Roman Catholic.

PLEASANT, JAMES SCOTT, lawyer; b. Anniston, Ala., July 14, 1943; s. James C. and Barbara (Scott) P.; m. Susan M. Pleasant, May 17, 1966; children: Deborah Kaye, Carol Ann, Julie Ruth. BS, Oreg. State U., 1965; JD summa cum laude, Williamette U., 1972. Bar: Tex. 1972, U.S. Dist. Ct. (no. dist.) Tex. 1973, U.S. Ct. Appeals (5th cir.) 1975, U.S. Supreme Ct. 1977. Ptnr. Gardere Wynne Sewell, LLP, Dallas, 1972—. Mem. Smithsonian Assn., Washington, 1985—, Dallas Mus. of Art, 1987—. Capt. U.S. Army, 1966-69, Vietnam. Mem. ABA (partnership law sect. 1969—), Tex. Bar Assn. (partnership law sect. 1989—), Vietnam Pilots Assn., Dustoff Assn. Corporate, general, Property, real (including real estate development, water), Securities. Office: Gardere Wynne Sewell LLP 1601 Elm St Ste 3000 Dallas TX 75201-4761 E-mail: pleja@gardere.com.

PLEICONES, COSTA M. state supreme court justice; b. Greenville, SC, Feb. 29, 1944; BA in English, Wofford Coll., 1965; JD, U. SC, 1968. Pub. defender Richland County, SC; pvt. practice law; resident cir. ct. judge 5th Judicial Cir., 1991—2000; assoc. justice SC Supreme Ct., 2000. With JAG U.S. Army, 1968—73, with USAR, 1973—99. Office: 1231 Gervais St Columbia SC 29201-3206 also: PO Box 11330 Columbia SC 29211

PLEICONES, LAURA, lawyer; b. Fort Rucker, Ala., Sept. 21, 1972; d. Costa Michael and Donna (Singletary) Pleicones. AB in English, U. Ga., 1994; cert. in pub., U. Denver Pub. Inst., 1995; MA in English, U. S.C., 1999, JD cum laude, 2000. Bar: SC 2000, NC 2001. Editl. asst., indexer Bruccoli Clark Layman, Columbia, SC, 1994—97; rsch. asst. U. S.C. Sch. Law, Columbia, 1998—99; summer assoc. Poyner & Spruill, LLP, Charlotte, NC, 1999; atty. Kennedy Covington Lobdell & Hickman, LLP, Charlotte, NC, 2000—. Mem.: ABA (real property, probate and trust law sect., taxation sect.), Charlotte Estate Planning Coun., Mecklenburg County Bar Assn. (estate planning and probate sect.), SC Bar Assn. (probate, estate planning and trust sect.), NC Bar Assn. (estate planning and fiduciary law sect., elder law sect.). Probate (including wills, trusts), Estate planning, Estate taxation. Office: Kennedy Covington Lobdell & Hickman LLP 214 N Tryon St Fl 47 Charlotte NC 28202 Office Fax: 704-331-7598.

PLENDER, RICHARD OWEN, barrister; b. Epsom, England, Oct. 9, 1945; s. George and Louise Mary Plender; m. Patricia Clare Ward, Dec. 16, 1978; children: Sophie Clare, Amy Louise. BA, Cambridge U., 1968; LLM, U. Ill., 1971; PhD, U. Sheffield, 1971; LLD, Cambridge U., 1980. Bar: England 1972. Lectr. Sheffield U., England, 1968—70, Exeter U., 1971—74; dir. Ctr. European Law King's Coll., London, 1974—80; rep. Ct. Justice European Cmtys., Luxembourg, 1980—83; barrister London, 1983—. Author: European Courts Procedure, 1990. Office: Essex St 20 Chambers Iain Milligan QC 20 Essex St London WC2R 3AL England Fax: 0044 2075831341. E-mail: rplender@20essexst.com.

PLESS, LAURANCE DAVIDSON, lawyer; b. Jacksonville, Fla., Dec. 22, 1952; s. James William Pless III and Anne (Dodson) Martin; m. Dana Halberg, June 20, 1980; children: Anna Amesbury, William Davidson, Deane Ahlgren. AB cum laude with distinction, Duke U., 1975; JD, U. N.C., Chapel Hill, 1980. Bar: Georgia 1980, U.S. Supreme Ct. 2001. Assoc. Neely & Player, P.C., Atlanta, 1980-86, ptnr., 1986-92, Welch Spell Attys., Atlanta, 1992—. Contbr. articles to profl. jours.; mem. staff N.C. Law Rev. Vol. Saturday Vol. Lawyer's Found., Atlanta, 1980-92; mem. bd. visitors U. N.C., Chapel Hill, 2001—; bd. dirs. Christian Coun. Met. Atlanta, 1999-2002; trustee Asheville Sch., 2002—. Mem. ABA, Lawyer's Club of Atlanta, Atlanta Bar Assn. (bd. dirs. bus. and fin. law sect. 1999—), Capital City Club, Lake Rabun Assn. Democrat. Episcopalian. Avocations: hiking, tennis, coaching kid's sports, canoeing. Corporate, general, General practice, Mergers and acquisitions. Home: 25 Palisades Rd NE Atlanta GA 30309-1530 E-mail: ldp@welchspell.com.

PLETZ, THOMAS GREGORY, lawyer; b. Toledo, Oct. 3, 1943; s. Francis G. and Virginia (Connell) P.; m. Carol Elizabeth Connolly, June 27, 1969; children: Anne M., John F. BA, U. Notre Dame, 1965; JD, U. Toledo, 1971. Bar: Ohio 1971, U.S. Ct. Appeals (6th cir.) 1978, U.S. Supreme Ct. 1985. Ct. bailiff Lucas County Common Pleas Ct., Toledo, 1967-71; jud. clk. U.S. Dist. Ct. (no. dist.) Ohio, Toledo, 1971-72; assoc. Shumaker, Loop & Kendrick, Toledo, 1972-76, litigation ptnr., 1976—. Acting judge Sylvania (Ohio) Mcpl. Ct., 1990—; mem. Ohio Bar Bd. Examiners, 1993-2003, chmn., 1996-99. Active Toledo Parish Coun., 1987-2003; chmn., trustee Kiroff Trial Adv. Com., Toledo, 1982-91; mem. Nat. Conf. Bar Examiners Com., 1996-2001. With USNR, 1965-92; ret. CDR. Recipient Toledo Jr. Bar award, 1995. Mem. ABA, Ohio State Bar Assn., Toledo Bar Assn. (trustee 1981-93), Diocesan Attys. Bar Assn., 6th Cir. Jud. Conf. (life). Roman Catholic. General civil litigation, Education and schools, Libel. Office: Shumaker Loop & Kendrick 1000 Jackson St Toledo OH 43624-1573 E-mail: tpletz@slk-law.com.

PLOSCOWE, STEPHEN ALLEN, lawyer; b. N.Y.C., Jan. 30, 1941; s. Samuel Stuart and Molly Florence (Slutsky) P.; m. Wendie Sue Malkin, Sept. 5, 1964; children— Jon, Lauren. B.S., Cornell U., 1962, LL.B., 1965. Bar: N.J. 1965, U.S. Dist. Ct. N.J. 1965, U.S. Ct. Appeals (3d cir.) 1979. Assoc. Cole, Berman & Belsky (and predecessor firm) Paterson, N.J. also Rochelle Park, N.J. 1965-69, ptnr., 1970-78; ptnr. Grotta, Glassman & Hoffman, Newark also Roseland, N.Y., 1979— ; borough atty. North Caldwell, N.J., 1973-79. Mem. Passaic County Bar Assn., Bergen County Bar Assn., N.J. State Bar Assn., Indsl. Relations Research Assn., ABA. Republican. Jewish. Club: Green Brook Country. Labor (including EEOC, Fair Labor Standards Act, labor-management relations, NLRB, OSHA). Home: 76 Brookside Ter Caldwell NJ 07006-4413 Office: Grotta Glassman & Hoffman PA 75 Livingston Ave Ste 13 Roseland NJ 07068-3701 E-mail: ploscowe@gghlaw.com.

PLOTKIN, LOREN H. lawyer; b. Bklyn., Feb. 8, 1943; s. Arthur and Betty Ann (Strugatz); m. Carol Baxter, Aug. 25, 1990; children: Lily, Kate. BA, Harpur Coll., SUNY, Binghamton, 1963; JD, St. John's U., N.Y.C., 1966. Bar: N.Y. 1966, U.S. Dist. Ct. (so. and ea. dists.) N.Y. 1972, U.S. Tax Ct. 1976. Law asst. appellate divsn., first dept. N.Y. State Supreme Ct.; ptnr. Lans Feinberg & Cohen, N.Y.C., 1969-81; mem. Levine & Thall, P.C., N.Y.C., 1981-84, Levine Thall and Plotkin, N.Y.C., 1984-96, Levine Thall, Plotkin & Menin, L.L.P., N.Y.C., 1996-99, Levine, Plotkin & Menin, L.L.P., N.Y.C., 2000—. Lectr. on entertainment law. Notes and comments editor St. John's U. Law Rev., 1965-66. Entertainment, General practice, Property, real (including real estate development, water). Home: 34 Lawrence Ln Palisades NY 10964-1604 Office: Levine Plotkin & Menin LLP 1740 Broadway Fl 22 New York NY 10019-4315

PLOTNICK, PAUL WILLIAM, lawyer; b. Chgo., Mar. 16, 1947; s. Sam and Mary P.; m. Eleanor Levy, Jan. 18, 1970; 1 child, Sarah Jennie. BA, So. Ill. U., 1969; JD, DePaul U., 1974. Bar: Ill. 1974., U.S. Dist. Ct. (no. dist.) Ill. 1974, U.S. Ct. Appeals (7th cir.) 1974, U.S. Tax Ct. 1975, U.S. Supreme Ct. 1977. Tchr. Chgo. Pub. Schs., 1969-74; pvt. practice Chgo., 1974-75; pres. Paul W. Plotnick, Ltd., Skokie, Ill., 1979—; asst. pub. defender Cook County Pub. Defender's Office, Chgo., 1975-79. Felony asst. Cook County Pub. Defender's Office, Evanston, Ill., 1976-79. Contbr. articles, poem to profl. publs. Pres. Budlong Woods Civic Group, Chgo., 1982—83; candidate for judge Circuit Ct. Cook County, 1998—2000, 2002—. Staff sgt. U.S. Army, 1969. Named Man of the Yr. Midwest Fedn. Men's Clubs, 1995; recipient Disting. Svc. award Chgo. Vol. Legal Svcs., 1995. Mem. ABA, ATLA, Ill. State Bar Assn., Chgo. Bar Assn., N.W. Suburban Bar Assn., N. Suburban Bar Assn., Kiwanis (pres. Skokie Valley chpt. 1989-90, Disting. Sec. award 1987, Disting. Pres. award 1991, Lay Person of the Yr. I.I. Dist. divsn. 7), Beth Hillel Men's Club (pres. 1991-93), Decalogue Soc., Phi Kappa Phi (DePaul U. chpt. Disting. Alumnus). State civil litigation, Criminal, Property, real (including real estate development, water). Office: Paul W Plotnick Ltd 9933 Lawler Ave Ste 312 Skokie IL 60077-3706

PLOWMAN, JACK WESLEY, lawyer; b. Blairsville, Pa., Sept. 12, 1929; s. Ralph Waldo, Sr., and Ethel Beatrice (Nicely) P.; m. Barbara Ellen Brown, Apr. 5, 1952; children: Linda Ellen, Judith Lynn AB, U. Pitts., 1951, LL.B. with honors, 1956. Bar: Pa. 1956, U.S. Dist. Ct. (we. dist.) Pa. 1956, U.S. Ct. Appeals 1960, U.S. Supreme Ct. 1978. Assoc. Campbell, Houck & Thomas, Pitts., 1956-57; ptnr. Rose, Houston, Cooper & Schmidt, Pitts., 1957-63, Plowman & Spiegel, Pitts., 1963-2000; of counsel Bentz Law Firm, P.C., Pitts., 2000—. Adj. prof. emeritus Duquesne U. Sch. Law, 1963—80, 1983—2002. Editor-in-chief Pitts. Legal Jour., 1971-81, U. Pitts. Law Rev., 1955-56 Bd. dirs. United Meth. Pub. House, 1984-96, Ward Home for Children, United Meth. Ch. Union, 1977-83, Wesley Inst., 1977-81, Neighborhood Legal Svcs. Assn., 1969-74; chancellor emeritus Western Pa. Ann. Conf., United Meth. Ch. Fellow Am. Bar Found. (life mem.), Am. Coll. Trial Lawyers, Allegheny County Bar Found. (trustee, sec.); mem. ABA, Pa. Bar Assn., Allegheny County Bar Assn. (pres. 1982), Pa. Bar Inst. (bd. dirs. 1988-92), Am. Law Inst., Supreme Ct. Pa. Hist. Soc. (trustee, pres.). Republican. Federal civil litigation, State civil litigation. Home: 1025 Lakemont Dr Pittsburgh PA 15243-1817 Office: The Washington Ctr Bldg 680 Washington Rd Pittsburgh PA 15228

PLUCIENNIK, THOMAS CASIMIR, lawyer, former assistant county prosecutor; b. Irvington, N.J., Apr. 8, 1947; s. Casimir Stanley and Helen Victoria (Sienicki) P.; m. Maria Anne Soriano, June 16, 1974. BS in Acctg., Seton Hall U., 1969, JD, 1983; MA in Criminal Justice, CUNY, 1976. Bar: N.J. 1983, U.S. Ct. Mil. Appeals 1986, U.S. Dist. Ct. N.J. 1983, D.C. 1994, U.S. Supreme Ct. 1995, N.Y. 1996, U.S. Ct. Appeals (3rd cir.), U.S. Dist. Ct. (so., ea., fed. dists.) N.Y. 1998; cert. criminal trial atty., mil. trial atty.; lic. pvt. investigator. Mng. ptnr. Joe Bell's Tavern & Restaurant, Newark, 1979; police officer City of Newark, 1972-79; criminal investigator Essex County Prosecutor, Newark, 1980-84, asst. prosecutor, 1984-88; sr. asst. prosecutor Warren County, N.J., 1988-89; atty. Voorhees & Acciavatti Esq., Morristown, N.J., 1989-94; defense atty. Picillo Caruso, 1994-96; assoc. Netchert, Dineen & Hillman, 1996-97; litigator Francis J. Dooley, 1998-99; pvt. practice, 1999—. Cert. instr. N.J. State Police Tng. Commn., Trenton, 1984; asst. dir. instruction Officers Candidate Sch. N.J. Mil. Acad., Sea Girt. Committeeman South Orange Republican Club, N.J., 1978-83; treas., founder Tuxedo Park Neighborhood Assn., South Orange, 1977; fin. sec. J. T. Kosciusko Assn., Irvington, N.J., 1979. Served to 1st lt. U.S. Army, 1969-71, maj. (ret.) JAGC, 1985-90. Recipient Class C. Commendations, Newark Police Dept., 1973, 74, 75, Command Citations, 1973, 74, 75, 77, 78. Master: Worrall F. Mountain Inn of Ct.; mem.: ABA, ATLA, D.C. Bar Assn., N.Y. State Bar Assn., Morris County Bar Assn., N.J. Def. Assn., N.J. State Bar Assn., Trial Attys. N.J. (trustee), Polish Univ. Club, South Orange Lions Club (charter), Picatinny Officers Club, Mil. Officers Club (pres. Sea Girt, N.J. 1979—81), Masons (master), Ret. Officers Assn., Am. Legion. Republican. Roman Catholic. General civil litigation, Criminal, Insurance. Home: 11 Laurel Ln Morris Plains NJ 07950-3216

PLUMMER, RISQUE WILSON, retired lawyer; b. Mobile, Ala., Oct. 13, 1910; s. Frederick Harvey and Caroline (Wilson) P.; m. Constance M. Burch, Feb. 21, 1939; children: Risque Wilson Jr., Richard Randolph. JD, U. Va., 1933. Bar: Va. 1932, Md. 1938. Atty. in charge of litigation Balt. Regional Office HOLC, 1933-38; pvt. practice law, 1938—; counsel U.S. Maritime Commn., 1942; partner firm Griffin & Plummer, 1951-73; counsel O'Connor, Preston, Glenn & Smith, Balt., 1979—. Prof. law Am. Inst. Banking, 1948—52; chmn. spkrs. com. ARC Blood Bank for Md. Contbr. articles to profl. jours. Exec. sec. Md. Commn. on Anti-Subversive Activities, 1949-50; co-founder, pres. Roland Park Baseball Leagues, Inc., 1956-57; co-founder, pres. Wyndhurst Improvement Assn., Inc., 1957-59; mem. Selective Service Adv. Bd., 1940-42. Served to lt. USNR, 1943-46, ATO, PTO, Philippines Area Ops.; gunnery officer, WWII. Fellow Internat. Acad. Law and Sci.; mem. ABA (council sect. of family law 1966-70), Md. Bar Assn. (council sect. of family and juvenile law 1968-70), Md. Assn. Trial Lawyers (gov. 1966-67), Bar Assn. Baltimore City (com. on grievances 1966-69, chmn. com. on profl. ethics 1969-70, exec. com. 1969-70), Am. Judicature Soc., Md. Health Claims Arbitration Commn. (chair arbitration panels), Am. Contract Bridge League (Silver life master, cert. dir., author The Small Club), Soc. Colonial Wars, Sons of the Revolution, Delta Tau Delta (pres. U. Va. chpt.), Phi Delta Phi, Hon. Law Soc. Episcopalian. Personal injury (including property damage), Probate (including wills, trusts), General civil litigation. Home: Highfield House Unit 512 4000 N Charles St Baltimore MD 21218-1760

PLYMALE, RONALD ELTON, lawyer; b. Huntington, W.Va. s. Arthur L. and R. Ellene Plymale; m. Nancy L. Papp, June 21, 1989. BA, Ohio State U., 1963, JD, 1968. Bar: Ohio 1968, U.S. Dist. Ct. (so. dist.) Ohio 1969, U.S. Ct. Appeals (6th cir.) 1973, U.S. Supreme Ct. 1976; cert. civil trial lawyer; cert. trial adv. Lawyer Barkan & Neff, Columbus, Ohio, 1968-70; city atty. City of Grove City, Ohio, 1971-79; lawyer Plymale & Assocs., Columbus, Ohio, 1980—. Fellow Roscoe Pound Found.; mem. Assn. of Trial Lawyers of Am., Nat. Bd. of Trial Advocacy, Million Dollar Advocates Forum. General civil litigation, Personal injury (including property damage), Professional liability. Office: Plymale Partnership 495 S High St Columbus OH 43215-4510

PODBOY, ALVIN MICHAEL, JR., law library director, lawyer; b. Cleve., Feb. 10, 1947; s. Alvin Michael and Josephine Esther (Nagode) P.; m. Mary Ann Gloria Esposito, Aug. 21, 1971; children: Allison Marie, Melissa Ann. AB cum laude, Ohio U., 1969; JD, Case Western Res. U., 1972, MLS, 1977. Bar: Ohio 1972, U.S. Dist. Ct. (no. dist.) Ohio 1973, U.S. Supreme Ct. 1992. Assoc. Joseph T. Svete Co. LPA, Chardon, Ohio, 1972-76; dir. pub. svcs. Case Western Res. Sch. Law Libr., Cleve., 1974-77, assoc. law libr., 1977-78; libr. Baker & Hostetler, LLP, Cleve., 1978-88, dir. librs., 1988—. Instr. Notre Dame Coll. of Ohio, Cleve., 1991-2002, Ursuline Coll., Cleve., 2003—, Am. Inst. Paralegal Studies, Cleve., 1991-96. Bd. overseers Case Western Res. U., 1981-87, mem. vis. com. sch. libr. sci., 1980-86, mem. Westlaw adv. bd., 1987-92, bd. govs. law sch. alumni assn., 1992-95, West's Legal Directory Ohio Adv. Panel, 1990-91; mem. adv. com. West's Info. Innovators Inst., 1995-97; chmn. Case Western Res. Libr. Sch. Alumni Fund, 1979-80; Rep. precinct committeeman Cuyahoga County, Cleve., 1981-95, mem. exec. com., 1984-87. 1st lt. USAF, 1972. Mem.: Am. Assn. Law Librs. (chmn. pvt. law librs. spl. interest sect. 1994—95, mem. exec. bd. 2001—, cert.), ABA, Arnold Air Soc., Case Western Res. U. Libr. Sch. Alumni Assn. (pres. 1981), Ohio Regional Assn. Law Librs. (pres. 1985), Cleve. Bar Assn., Ohio State Bar Assn. (chmn. librs. com. 1989—91), Phi Alpha Theta, Pi Gamma Mu. Roman Catholic. Avocation: alpine skiing. Home: 417 East Parkway Blvd Aurora OH 44202 Office: Baker & Hostetler LLP 3200 National City Ctr Cleveland OH 44114-3485 E-mail: apodboy@bakerlaw.com.

PODGOR, ELLEN SUE, law educator; b. Bklyn., Jan. 30, 1952; d. Benjamin and Yetta (Shilensky) Podgor. BS magna cum laude, Syracuse U., 1973; JD, Ind. U., Indpls., 1976; MBA, U. Chgo., 1987; LLM, Temple U., 1989. Bar: Ind. 1976, N.Y. 1984, Pa. 1987. Dep. prosecutor Lake County Prosecutor's Office, Crown Point, Ind., 1976-78; ptnr. Nicholls & Podgor, Crown Point, 1978-87; instr. Temple U. Sch. Law, 1987-89; assoc. prof. law St. Thomas U., Miami, Fla., 1989-91, Ga. State U., Atlanta, 1991—. Vis. scholar Yale Law Sch., 1998; vis. prof. U. Ga., 2000; John S. Stone vis. endowed chair U. Ala., 2000. Author: (with Israel) White Collar Crime in a Nutshell, (with Israel and Borman) White Collar Crime: Law and Practice, (with Wise) International Criminal Law: Cases and Materials; assoc. editor Ind. Law Rev., 1975-76; contbr. articles to legal jours; mem. adv. bd. BNA Criminal Practice Manual. Del. Ind. Dem. Conv., 1982. Mem. ABA, NACDL (bd. dirs.), Am. Law Inst., Ind. Bar Assn. Democrat. Jewish. Office: Ga State U Coll Law PO Box 4037 Atlanta GA 30302-4037

PODHURST, AARON SAMUEL, lawyer; b. N.Y.C., Apr. 29, 1936; s. Louis and rae (Pomerantz) P.; m. Dorothy Ellen Podhurst, Sept. 7, 1958; children: Karen Beth Dern, Laura Koffsky, Julie Weinberg. BBA, U. Mich., 1957; JD, Columbia U., 1960. Bar: Fla., 1961, N.Y., 1961. Assoc. Nichols, Gaither, Miami, Fla., 1962-67; founding ptnr. Podhurst, Orseck, Josefsberg, Eaton, Meadow, Olin & Perwin, P.A., Miami, 1967—. Vice pres. Miami Coalition for Safe Cmty., 1994—; mem. Orange Bowl Com., Miami, 1996—. Recipient Nat. Medallion award NCCJ, 1994; Harlan Fiske Stone scholar, 1960. Mem. ABA (aviation com.), Internat. Acad. Trial Lawyers (pres. 1990), Acad. Fla. Trial Lawyers (pres. 1978, aviation com.), Am. Coll. Trial Lawyers, Assn. Trial Lawyers Am. (bd. govs., aviation com.), Internat. Soc. Barristers, Inner Cir. of Advocates. Aviation, Commercial, consumer (including collections, credit), Personal injury (including property damage). Office: Podhurst Orseck PA 25 W Flagler St Ste 800 Miami FL 33130-1712

PODOLSKY, ARNOLD MARK, lawyer, physician; b. Detroit, Oct. 11, 1951; BA, Oakland U., 1972; MD, Wayne State U., 1977; JD, Detroit Coll. Law, 1986. Diplomate Am. Bd. Anesthesiology; Bar: Mich. 1986. Med. cons. Lopatin & Miller PC, Detroit, 1984-86, atty., 1986-91; ptnr. Ravid & Podolsky PC, Southfield, Mich., 1991-93; CEO Podolsky & Assocs. PC,

Birmingham, Mich., 1993—. Faculty scholar Detroit Coll. Law, 1983-86. Fellow Am. Coll. Legal Medicine; mem. Am. Soc. Anesthesiologists, Mich. Soc. Anesthesiologists, Mich. Trial Lawyers Assn. (mem. exec. bd. 1991-95)., Mich. State Med. Soc., Assn. Trial Lawyers Am., State Bar Assn. Mich. Office: Podolsky and Assocs PC 999 Haynes St Ste 395 Birmingham MI 48009-6775 E-mail: medical-legal@consultant.com.

POE, LUKE HARVEY, JR., lawyer; b. Richmond, Va., Jan. 29, 1916; s. Luke Harvey and Alice Morris (Reddy) Poe; m. Josephine Jaster, Mar. 20, 1998. BS in Math, U. Va., 1938, JD, 1941; postgrad. (Rhodes scholar), Oxford (Eng.) U., 1939; D.Phil., Christ Ch., 1957. Bar: Va. bar 1940, D.C. bar and D.C. Ct. Appeals bar 1967, U.S. Supreme Ct. bar 1969, Md. bar 1974. Asso. firm Cravath, Swaine & Moore, N.Y.C., 1941-42; tutor St. John's Coll., Annapolis, Md., 1946-50, asst. dean, 1947-49, tenure tutor, 1953-60, dir. physics and chemistry lab., 1959-60; asst. chmn. Nat. Citizens Com. for Kennedy and Johnson and chmn. Citizens Com., Pres.'s Inaugural Com., 1960-61; asst. to chmn. bd. Aerojet-Gen. Corp., El Monte, Calif., 1961-63; div. pres. Internat. Tech. Assistance and Devel. Co., Washington, 1963-66; ptnr. Howard, Poe & Bastian, Washington, 1966-83; pvt. practice law, 1983—. Bd. dirs. First Am. Bank of Md.; cons. Dept. Transp., Dept. State, NEH; lectr. War Coll. of USAF, Gen. Studies program U. Va.; seminar leader Aspen Inst. Humanistic Studies; guest panelist Panel on Sci. and Tech. of Com. on Sci. and Astronautics, U.S. Ho. of Reps., 1970; pres. bd. dirs. Watergate East, Inc., 1976-79, 90-92; organizer U. Va. Unified Liberal Arts Program, 1988—. Author: The Combat History of the Battleship U.S.S. Mississippi, 1947, The Transition From Natural Law to Natural Rights, 1957; (with others) lab. manuals Einstein's Theory of Relativity, 1957, Electro-Magnetic Theory, 1959; editor: (with others) Va. Mag., 1936-38, U. Va. Law Rev., 1940-41. Dean's adv. coun. Lehigh U., 1962-65, mem. Seminar on Sci., Tech. and Pub. Policy, Brookings Instn., 1964-66; coun. on trends and perspectives U.S. C. of C., 1966-69; chmn. bd. Bristol Property Mgmt. and Svcs., Inc., 1967-88; chmn. Annapolis Bd. Zoning Appeals, 1966-75; mem. Annapolis Mayor's Task Force, 1967-74, Md. Gov.'s Commn. on Capital City, 1970-76. Lt. comdr. USNR, 1942-46. Decorated Jhalavada Order of Durbargadh, Dhrangadhara. Mem. Am. Law Inst., AAUP, Raven Soc. (pres.), Soc. of Cincinnati, Sr. Common Room and High Table (Christ Church), Met. Club (Washington), Travellers Club (London), Brook Club (N.Y.C.), New Providence Club (Annapolis), Vincent's Club (Oxford), Phi Beta Kappa, Phi Delta Phi. Episcopalian. Constitutional, Corporate, general, Private international. Home: 139 Market St Annapolis MD 21401-2628 also: 2500 Virginia Ave NW Washington DC 20037-1901 Office: 2600 Virginia Ave NW Washington DC 20037-1905

POFF, RICHARD HARDING, retired state supreme court justice; b. Radford, Va., Oct. 19, 1923; s. Beecher David and Irene Louise (Nunley) P.; m. Jo Ann R. Topper, June 24, 1945 (dec. Jan. 1978); children: Rebecca, Thomas, Richard Harding; m. Jean Murphy, Oct. 26, 1980. Student, Roanoke Coll., 1941-43; LL.B., U. Va., 1948, LL.D., 1969. Bar: Va. 1947. Partner law firm Dalton, Poff, Turk & Stone, Radford, 1949-70; mem. 83d-92d congresses, 6th Dist. Va.; justice Supreme Ct. Va., 1972-89, sr. justice, 1989—2002. Vice chmn. Nat. Commn. on Reform Fed. Crime Laws; chmn. Republican Task Force on Crime; sec. Rep. Conf., House Rep. Leadership. Named Va.'s Outstanding Young Man of Year Jr. C. of C., 1954; recipient Nat. Collegiate Athletic Assn. award, 1966, Roanoke Coll. medal, 1967, Distinguished Virginian award Va. Dist. Exchange Clubs, 1970, Presdl. certificate of appreciation for legislative contbn., 1971, legislative citation Assn. Fed. Investigators, 1969, Thomas Jefferson Pub. Sesquicentennial award U. Va., 1969, Japanese Am. Citizens League award, 1972, Carrio Professionalism award Va. State Bar Assn. Criminal Law Sect., 1998; named to Hall of Fame, Am. Legion Boys State, 1985; fellow Va. Law Found., 1997. Mem. Bar Assn., VFW, Am. Legion, Pi Kappa Phi, Sigma Nu Phi. Clubs: Mason, Moose, Lion. Office: Va Supreme Ct 100 N 9th St Richmond VA 23219-2335

POGREBIN, BERTRAND B. lawyer; b. Bklyn., Apr. 10, 1934; s. Abraham and Esther Pogrebin; m. Letty Cottin; children: Abigail, Robin, David. AB, Rutgers U., 1955; LLB, Harvard U., 1958. Bar: N.Y. 1959, U.S. Dist. Ct. (ea. and so. dists.) N.Y. 1963, U.S. Ct. Appeals (2d cir.) 1965, U.S. Ct. Appeals (4th cir.) 1965, U.S. Ct. Appeals (6th cir.) 1970, U.S. Ct. Appeals (9th cir.) 1987, U.S. Supreme Ct. 1991. Pres. Rains & Pogrebin, P.C., N.Y.C., 1959—. Adj. prof. law NYU, 1975-90, Hofstra Law Sch., 1980-82, 86-91, 97-98; vis. lectr. Yale Law Sch., 1983. Co-author: Labor Relations: The Basic Process, Law and Practice, 1988, 2d edit., 1999; mem. editl. bd. N.Y. Law Jour. Mem. Am. Jewish Congress; v.p., bd. dirs. Appleseed Found. Mem. ABA, N.Y.C. Bar Assn., Nassau County Bar Assn., Suffolk County Bar Assn., Indsl. Rels. Rsch. Assn. Education and schools, Labor (including EEOC, Fair Labor Standards Act, labor-management relations, NLRB, OSHA), Pension, profit-sharing, and employee benefits. Home: 33 W 67th St New York NY 10023-6224 Office: 210 Old Country Rd Mineola NY 11501-4218 also: 375 Park Ave New York NY 10152-0002 E-mail: BPogrebin@Rainslaw.com.

POGUE, L(LOYD) WELCH, lawyer; b. Grant, Iowa, Oct. 21, 1899; s. Leander Welch and Myrtle Viola (Casey) P.; m. Mary Ellen Edgerton(dec. 2001), Sept. 8, 1926; children: Richard Welch, William Lloyd, John Marshall. AB, U. Nebr., 1924; JD, U. Mich., 1926; SJD, Harvard U., 1927. Bar: Mass., N.Y., D.C., Ohio, U.S. Supreme Ct. Assoc. Ropes, Gray, Boyden and Perkins, 1927-33; ptnr. affiliated firm Searle, James and Crawford, N.Y.C., 1933-38; asst. gen. counsel CAB, 1938-39, gen. counsel, through 1941, chmn. bd., 1942-46; mem., mng. ptnr. Pogue & Neal, Washington, 1946-67; Washington mng. ptnr. Jones, Day, Reavis & Pogue, Washington, 1967-79, ret., 1981. Lindbergh Meml. lectr. Nat. Air and Space Mus., Smithsonian Inst., 1991; presenter essay 50th Ann. Internat. Civil Aviation Orgn., Montreal, 1994; Wright Bros. Meml. lectr., 1999; spkr. and lectr. in field. Author: International Civil Air Transport—Transition Following WW II, 1979, Pogue/Pollock/Polk Genealogy as Mirrored in History, 1990 (1st pl. in Anna Ford Family history book contest 1991, Nat. Geneal. Soc. award for excellence genealogy and family history 1992, William H. and Benjamin Harrison Book award Coun. Ohio Genealogists 1992, Outstanding Achievement award County and Regional History category Ohio Assn. Hist. Socs. and Mus. 1992, 1st pl. award Iowa Washington County Geneal. Soc. 1994, cert. commendation Am. Assn. State and Local History 1994, 1st place award Lake Havasu Geneal. Soc. 1996), Airline Deregulation, Before and After: What Next? (Lindbergh Meml. lectr. 1991), The International Civil Aviation Conference, 1944, and Its Sequel, The Anglo-American Bermuda Air Transport Agreement, 1946, 1994; The Wright Brothers Memorial Lecture (Annually given) NASA Langley Research Center, 1999; contbr. articles to profl. publs. Mem. U.S. dels.: Chgo. Internat. Civil Aviation Conf., 1944; vice chmn. Bermuda United Kingdom-U.S. Conf., 1946; vice chmn. Provisional Internat. Civil Aviation Orgn. Assembly, 1946; active Internat. Civil Aviation Orgn. Assembly, 1947. With AUS, 1918. Recipient Elder Statesman of Aviation award Nat. Aeronautic Assn., Golden Eagle award Soc. Sr. Aerospace Execs., 1st annual recipient of L. Welch Pogue award for Aviation Achievement, McGraw-Hill Orgn.'s Aviation Week Group, 1994, Laurel Legend award and named to Laureate Hall of Fame, 2002; fellow Am. Helicopter Soc., Benjamin Franklin fellow Royal Soc. Arts. Fellow Royal Aero. Soc.; mem. AIAA (hon., Certificate of 60 yrs. continuous membership), Soc. of Sr. Aerospace Execs. (hon.), Helicopter Assn. Internat. (hon. mem.), Am. Air Mus. in Britain (founding mem.), Can. Aeronautics and Space Inst., Nat. Aeronautic Assn. (pres. 1947), Nat. Air and Space Soc. (founder), Nat. Geneal. Soc., Soc. Sr. Aerospace Execs., New Eng. Hist. Geneal. Soc. (life, former trustee), Ohio Geneal. Soc. (life), Md. Geneal. Soc. (life), Md. Hist. Soc. (life), Provincial Families of Md., First Families of Ohio, Met. Club, Univ. Club, Wings Club (hon., N.Y.C.), Bohemian Club (San Francisco), Cosmos Club, Masons, Order of the First World War (charter), Nat. Aviation Club, Aero Club of Washington (hon. mem., Donald D. Engen trophy for aviation excellence 2001), Am. Legion (cert. of 80 years continuous membership, Life Membership, 2002). Aviation, Corporate, general, Finance. Home: Chevy Chase, Md. Died May 10, 2003.

POHL, AMY KIRBY, lawyer; b. Pitts., Apr. 30, 1973; d. John Joseph and Mary Jean Kirby; m. Joseph Paul Pohl, III, Sept. 19, 1998. BA, John Carroll U., Cleve., 1995; JD, U. Pitts., 1998. Bar: Pa. 1998. Assoc. Jones Day Reavis & Pogue, Pitts., 1998—. Mem.: Allegheny County Bar Assn. Roman Catholic.

POINDEXTER, WILLIAM MERSEREAU, lawyer; b. Los Angeles, June 16, 1925; s. Robert Wade and Irene M. Poindexter; m. Jani Jennifer Wohlgemuth, Feb. 14, 2000; children: James Wade, David Graham, Honour Hêlenê, Timothy John, Cory Todd, E.W. Greg. BA, Yale U., 1946; postgrad., U. Chgo., 1946-47; LL.B., U. Calif., Berkeley, 1949. Bar: Calif. 1952. Practiced in, San Francisco, 1952-54, Los Angeles, 1954—; mem. firm Poindexter & Doutre, Inc., 1964—. Pres. Consol. Brazing & Mfg. Co., Riverside, Calif., 1949-52. Pres. South Pasadena-San Marino (Calif.) YMCA, 1963; Mem. San Marino Sch. Bd., 1965-69, pres., 1967; pres. Conf. of Ins. Counsel, 1975. Served with USMCR, 1943. Fellow Am. Coll. Trust and Probate Counsel; mem. ABA, L.A. County Bar Assn., State Bar Calif., Yale Club (pres. So. Calif. chpt. 1961), Calif. Lincoln Clubs (L.A. downtown chpt. chmn. 1997-2002). Republican. Presbyterian. Office: 1 Wilshire Bldg Ste 2420 Los Angeles CA 90017

POINTER, SAM CLYDE, JR., retired federal judge, lawyer; b. Birmingham, Ala., Nov. 15, 1934; s. Sam Clyde and Elizabeth Inzer (Brown) P.; m. Paula Purse, Oct. 18, 1958; children: Minge, Sam Clyde III. AB, Vanderbilt U., 1955; JD, U. Ala., 1957; LL.M., NYU, 1958. Bar: Ala. 1957. Ptnr. Brown, Pointer & Pointer, 1958-70; judge U.S. Dist. Ct. (no. dist.) Ala., Birmingham, 1970-2000, chief judge, 1982-99; judge Temp. Emergency Ct. Appeals, 1980-87; mem. Jud. Panel Multi-dist. Litigation, 1980-87; ptnr. Lightfoot, Franklin & White, 2000—. Mem. Jud. Conf. U.S., 1987-90; mem. Jud. Coun. 11th Cir., 1987-90, mem. standing com. on rules, 1988-90, chmn. adv. com. on civil rules, 1990-93. Bd. editors: Manual for Complex Litigation, 1979-91. Mem. ABA, Ala. Bar Asn., Birmingham Bar Assn., Am. Law Inst., Am. Judicature Soc., Farrah Order of Jurisprudence, Phi Beta Kappa. Episcopalian. Office: Lightfoot Franklin & White The Clark Bldg 400 N 20th St Birmingham AL 35203 E-mail: spointer@lfwlaw.com.

POIRIER, ROLAND ALBERT, lawyer; b. Villemomble, France , Jan. 25, 1963; m. Delphine Claudie Bocquet, Aug. 16, 1996. DESS Fiscalité, Pantheon Sorbonne U., Paris, 1985. Bar: Paris Bar Assn. 1993. Assoc. Linklaters, Paris, 1987—91, Arthur Andersen, Paris, 1991—93, landwell, Paris, 1994—99; ptnr. Rambaud Martel, Paris, 2000—. Mem.: IFA. Corporate taxation, Personal income taxation, Taxation, general. Office: Rambaud Martel 25 Blvdf de l'Amiral Bruix Paris 75782 France Office Fax: 01 40 67 28 80. E-mail: r.poirier@rambaud-martel.com.

POITEVENT, EDWARD BUTTS, II, lawyer; b. New Orleans, Oct. 19, 1949; s. Eads and Elizabeth (Schramm) P.; m. Julia Dunbar Baños, Dec. 29, 1972; children: Sarah Dunbar,Elizabeth Grehan, Edward Scott, Mary McCutchen. BA, Tulane U., 1971, JD, 1974. Assoc. Jones, Walker, Waechter, Poitevent, Carrere & Denegre, New Orleans, 1974-79, ptnr., 1979-91, Phelps Dunbar, New Orleans, 1991—2001; of counsel King & Spalding, Houston, 2002—. Mem. ad hoc com. Pipeline div. La. Office of Conservation; mem. adv. coun. La. Mineral Law Inst. Mem. editorial bd. Oil and Gas Law and Taxation Rev.; contbr. articles to profl. jours.; presenter in field. Pres. La. chpt. Leukemia Soc. Am., Inc., New Orleans, 1991; trustee Ea. Mineral Law Found., 1988-93; co-chmn. oil and gas sect. Rocky Mountain Mineral Law Found. 36th Ann. Inst., Santa Fe; trustee-at-large Rocky Mountain Mineral Law Found., 1995-97. Mem. ABA (sect. on natural resources, energy and environ. law natural gas and oil coms., litigation sect. energy litigation com., chair program com., editor energy litigation com. newsletter, chair energy litigation com. natural gas mktg. and trans. com., mem. coun. 1994-98, mem. nominating com. 1995-96, CLE officer 1995-96, mem. exec. com. 1996-97), La. State Bar Assn., Fed. Energy Bar Assn., Am. Assn. Petroleum Landmen (chair ad hoc com. on model form gas Balancing Agreement). Republican. Roman Catholic. Oil, gas, and mineral. Office: King & Spalding LLP 1100 Louisiana St Ste 4000 Houston TX 77002

POKEMPNER, JOSEPH KRES, lawyer; b. Monessen, Pa., June 11, 1936; s. Leonard and Ethel Lee (Kres) P.; m. Judith Montague Stephens, Aug. 23, 1970; children: Elizabeth, Jennifer, Amy. AB, Johns Hopkins U., 1957; LLB, U. Md., 1962. Bar: Md. 1962. Law clk. to judge Supreme Bench Balt., 1960-62; field atty. 5th region NLRB, 1962-64; pvt. practice labor law Balt., 1964—; ptnr. Wolf, Pokempner & Hillman, Balt., 1972-86, Whiteford, Taylor & Preston, Balt., 1986—. Contbr. articles to legal jours. Capt. AUS, 1969-74. Mem. ABA, Fed. Bar Assn. (pres. Balt. chpt. 1979-80), Md. Bar Assn., Balt. Bar Assn. (pres. 1984-85), Serjeant's Inn Law Club. Jewish. Labor (including EEOC, Fair Labor Standards Act, labor-management relations, NLRB, OSHA). Home: 1500 Willow Ave Baltimore MD 21204-3611 E-mail: jpokempner@wtplaw.com.

POKOTILOW, MANNY DAVID, lawyer, educator; b. Patterson, N.J., June 26, 1938; s. Samuel Morris and Ruth (Fuchs) P.; children: Mali, Charyse, Mona, Andrew. BEE, Newark Coll. Engring., 1960; LLB, Am. U., 1964. Bar: Pa. 1964, U.S. Supreme Ct. 1969. Examiner Patent Office, Washington, 1960-64; ptnr. Caesar, Rivise, Bernstein, Cohen & Pokotilow Ltd., Phila., 1965—. Lectr. Pa. Bar Inst., various trade assns., expert witness on protection of computer software, patents, trademarks, trade secrets and copyrights; faculty Temple U. Sch. Law, 1985-94. Vol. Support Ctr. for Child Advs., Phila., 1979—; bd. dirs., organizer Phila. Bar Assn. 10k Race, Phila., 1980-, Packard Press Road Run Grand Prix, 1986; bd. dirs. Hist. Soc. U.S. Dist. Ct. (ea. dist.) Pa., 1989-, v.p. 1998-2002, pres. 2002-. Recipient Chair award for vol. excellence Am. Diabetes Assn., 1991; honored by Support Ctr. for Child Advocates, 1992 and Am. Diabetes Assn., 1997; named to Million Dollar Club, Am. Diabetes Assn., 2002; named Best Lawyer in Greater Phil. area Phil. Mag., 1999. Mem. ABA (chmn. proprietary rights in software com., coun. sci. and tech. sect. 1989—), IEEE, Assn. Trial Lawyers Am., Phila. Bar Assn. (bd. govs. 1982-84, chmn. sports and recreation com. 1977—, hon. trustee campaign for qualified judges 1993), Phila. Patent Law Assn. (bd. govs. 1982-84, chmn. fed. practice and procedure com. 1983-88), Phila. Trial Lawyers (chmn. fed. cts. com. 1986-90), Lawyers Club Phila. (bd. govs. 1984-94, chmn. publicity 1994-98), Pa. Trial Lawyers, Tau Epsilon Rho (vice chancellor Phila. grad. chpt. 1986-88, chancellor 1988-90). Federal civil litigation, Patent, Trademark and copyright. Office: Caesar Rivise Bernstein Cohen & Pokotilow Ltd 1635 Market St Fl 12 Philadelphia PA 19103-2212

POL, RONALD FRANCISCUS, lawyer; b. Jutphaas, The Netherlands, May 16, 1965; arrived in New Zealand, 1967; s. Bernardus Johannes and Francina Johanna Pol; m. Alison Reay MacKay, Aug. 14, 1992; 1 child, Oliver James. B of Econs., LLB with honors, Auckland U., 1988. Bar: New Zealand 1989, England & Wales 1994. Law clk. Connell Lamb Gerard & Co., Whangarei, New Zealand, 1987—88; solicitor Russell McVeagh, Auckland, 1989—92; sr. solicitor Slaughter and May, London, 1992—95, Russell McVeagh, Auckland, 1995—97; group litig. counsel Telecom NZ Ltd., Wellington, 1997—2001, corp. counsel, cons., 2001—03. Contbr. articles to profl. jours. Recipient Law Rev. award, Auckland U., 1989. Mem.: ABA, Law Coun. Australia (sect. mem. 2002—), Australian Corp. Lawyers Assn., Am. Corp. Counsel Assn., New Zealand Law Soc. (bd. dir. 2002—, coun. mem. 2002—, Writers award 1999), Corp. Lawyers Assn. New Zealand (pres. 2002—, Pres. award 2001). Avocations: travel, photography. General civil litigation, Alternative dispute resolution, Antitrust. Office: Telecom NZ Ltd 68 Jervois Quay Wellington 6015 New Zealand Fax: +64-4 4735926. E-mail: rfp@xtra.co.nz.

POLAKOV, ANTHONY SCOTT, lawyer; b. Encino, Calif., Sept. 24, 1956; s. Howard David and Lois Hoyce Polakov; m. Wendy C. Hertz-Polakov, Apr. 26, 1997; children: Jackson, Emily. BA, UCLA, 1978; JD, Southwestern Sch. Law, 1981. Bar: Calif. 85, U.S. Dist. Ct. (cen. dist.) Calif. 85. Ptnr. Stoll, Nussbaum & Polakov, L.A., 1982—. Judge pro tem Workers Compensation Appeals Bd., Santa Monica, Van Nuys and L.A., Calif., 1990—95. Mem.: Consumer Attys. L.A. (fund raiser 1996), Calif. Applicant Attys. Assn. Democrat. Avocations: golf, sports, baseball, wine. Personal injury (including property damage), Workers' compensation. Office: Stoll Nussbaum & Polakov 11601 Wilshire Blvd # 200 Los Angeles CA 90025

POLANSKY, LARRY PAUL, court administrator, consultant; b. Blkyn., July 24, 1932; s. Harry and Ida (Gershgom) P.; m. Eunice Kathryn Neun; children: Steven, Harriet, Bruce. BS in Acctg., Temple U., 1958, JD, 1973. Bar: Pa. 1973, U.S. Dist. Ct. (ea. dist.) Pa. 1973, U.S. Ct. Appeals (3d cir.) 1973, D.C. 1978, U.S. Supreme Ct. 1980. Acct., systems analyst City of Phila., 1956-63; data processing mgr. Jefferson Med. Coll. and Hosp., Phila., 1963-65; systems engr. IBM Corp., Phila., 1965-67; dep. ct. adminstr. Common Pleas Cts. of Phila., 1967-76; dep. state ct. adminstr. Pa. Supreme Ct., Phila., 1976-78; exec.officer D.C. Cts., Washington, 1979-90. Presdl. appt. to bd. dirs. State Justice Inst., 1985-89; bd. dirs. Search Group, Inc. Author: A Primer for the Technologically Challenged Judge, 1995; contbr. articles to profl. jours. Served as cpl. U.S. Army, 1951-53, Korea. Fellow Inst. for Ct. Mgmt., Denver, 1984; recipient Reardon award Nat. Ctr. for State Cts., 1982, Disting. Svc. award Nat. Ctr. for State Cts., 1986, Justice Tom C. Clark award Nat. Conf. of Metro. Cts., 1991, award of merit Nat. Assn. Ct. Mgmt., 1996. Mem. ABA (jud. adminstrn. divsn., chmn. tech. com. 1991-93, 95, exec. com. lawyers conf. 1985-98, chmn. 1991-92, JAD coun. 1994-97), Conf. State Ct. Adminstrn. (bd. dirs. 1980-86, pres. 1984-85). Republican. Jewish. Avocations: tennis, skiing, computers, golf. Home and Office: PO Box 752 Lake Harmony PA 18624-0752 E-mail: polanskyl@aol.com.

POLETTINI, ALESSANDRO, lawyer; b. Modena, Italy, May 29, 1956; s. Umberto Polettini and Mariarosa Corna Pellegrini; m. Michela Paglianti, Sept. 17, 1988; 1 child, Luca. Law Degree, U. Padua, Italy. Bar: Italy 1984, Padua 1984. Assoc. Studio Legale Miele & Croze, Padua, 1982—86; ptnr. Studio Legale Camilotti-Ceccon-Polettini, Padua, 1986—2001, Studio LCA, Padua, 2001—. Contbr. articles to profl. jours. Avocations: skiing, sailing, reading, travel. Mergers and acquisitions, Commercial, contracts (including sales of goods; commercial financing), Property, real (including real estate development, water). Office: Studio Associato LCA Galleria Borromeo 3 Padua Italy

POLI, FRÉDÉRIC CHARLES, lawyer; Maîtrise de droit des affaires, Paris I Panthéon Sorbonne, 1985. Avocat: Barreau des Hauts-de-Seine, France, cert.: N.Y. State Bar (fgn. legal cons.). Conseil juridique and avocat Caubet Chouchana Meyer, Paris, 1986—95; avocat HSD Ernst & Young, Paris La Défense, France, 1995—98; french legal desk Ernst & Young LLP, N.Y.C., 1998—2000, Donahue & Ptnrs. LLP, N.Y.C., 2000—02; avocat, ptnr. HSD Ernst & Young, Paris-La Défense, 2002—. Mergers and acquisitions, Corporate, general, Commercial, consumer (including collections, credit). Office: HSD Ernst & Young Tour Ernst & Young 92037 Paris France Office Fax: 33 1 58 47 52 28. E-mail: frederic_poli@ernst-young.fr.

POLIAKOFF, GARY A. lawyer, educator; b. Greenville, S.C, Nov. 25, 1944; s. Herman and Dorothy (Ravitz) P.; m. Sherri D. Dublin, June 24, 1967; children: Ryan, Keith. BS, U. S.C., 1966; JD, U. Miami, 1969. Bar: Fla. 1969, D.C. 1971, Colo. 1999. Founding prin., pres. Becker & Poliakoff, P.A., Hollywood, Miami, Naples, Sarasota, West Palm Beach, Largo, Jacksonville, Orlando, Ft. Walton Beach, Fla., Prague and Beijing, 1973—. Adj. prof. condominium law and practice Nova Southeastern U.; panelist Nat. Confs. Community Assns.; testified before coms. of the U.S. Senate on Condominiums; lectr. ann. condominium seminars Fla. Bar; participant Fla. Law Revision Council; cons. to State Legis. and the White House in drafting Condominium and Coop. Abuse Relief Act, 1980; mem. condominium study commn. State of Fla., 1990; chmn. State of Fla. Advisory Coun. on Condominiums, 1992, 93.; atty. Town of Southwest Ranches. Author: The Law of Condominium Operations, 1988; co-author: Florida Condominium Law and Practice, 1982, The Florida Bar Continuing Legal Education, 1982; contbr. articles to legal jours. Mem. pres.'s adv. group U. S.C., U.S.C. Ednl. Found., 1999—. Recipient Judge Learned Hand award Am. Jewish Com. for devel. of co-ownership housing law, 1999. Mem. Fla. Bar, Coll. Cmty. Assn. Lawyers (bd. govs.), Scribes. Property, real (including real estate development, water).

POLICY, VINCENT MARK, lawyer; b. Warren, Ohio, Mar. 29, 1948; s. Vincent James and Anna Marie (Berardi) P.; m. Katherine Anne Veazey; children: Nicholas, Katherine Nicole. BA, U. Md., 1970; JD, Georgetown U., 1973. Bar: N.Y. 1974, D.C. 1975, U.S. Supreme Ct. 1977. Assoc. Cahill Gordon & Reindel, Washington and N.Y.C., 1973-78, Hogan & Hartson, Washington, 1978-85; prin. Pohoryles & Greenstein PC, Washington, 1985-89, Greenstein, Delorme & Luchs, P.C., Washington, 1989—. Author: Speedy Trial, A Constitutional Right in Search of Definition, 1973. Mem. D.C. Bar Assn. (chmn. rental housing com. 1985-88), D.C. Assn. Realtors (speaker 1984—), Apt. and Office Bldg. Assn. (lectr. 1985—), Greater Washington Bd. Trade (subcom. on initiatives, econ. growth com.), D.C. Builders Assn. (legis. affairs com.), Phi Beta Kappa, Omicron Delta Kappa. Lodges: KC. Democrat. Roman Catholic. Avocation: sailing. Banking, State civil litigation, Property, real (including real estate development, water). Office: Greenstein DeLorme & Luchs 1620 L St NW Ste 900 Washington DC 20036-5613

POLIN, ALAN JAY, lawyer; b. N.Y.C., Sept. 5, 1953; s. Mortin and Eleanor (Clarke) P.; m. Sharon Lynn Hirschfeld, Oct. 10, 1976; children: Jay Michael, Meryl Beth. Student, Cornell U., 1971-74; BA cum laude, Seton Hall U., 1978; JD, Nova U., 1981. Bar: Fla. 1981, N.Y. 1990; lic. athlete agt. Fla., life, health and variable annuities agt. Fla. Assoc. Berryhill, Avery, Williams & Jordan, Esq., Ft. Lauderdale, Fla., 1981-82, Greenspoon & Marder, P.A., Miami, Fla., 1982-83; pvt. practice Ft. Lauderdale, 1983-86; ptnr. Mousaw, Vigdor, Reeves & Hess, Ft. Lauderdale, 1986-90; pvt. practice Coral Springs, Fla., 1990—. Adj. faculty mem. Nova U.; mem. grievance com. Fla. Bar, 1989-92, vice chair, 1990-91, chair, 1991-92. Chmn. Broward County Crct. Ct. Handbook, 1988; contbr. chpt. to Bridge the Gap Attorney's Handbook, 1987. Mem. Anti-Defamation League Fla. Regional Bd., 1994—; chmn. Fla. Intergovtl. Fin. Commn., 2002—; mem. exec. com. Broward County Dem., 1989—96; vice mayor City of Coral Springs, 1994—96, commr., 1991—; vice chmn. Fla. Intergovtl. Fin. Commn., 2001; vice mayor City of Coral Springs, 2002—; dir. Temple Beth Am, Margate, Fla., 1991—93; bd. dirs. Fla. Regional Bd. of Anti-Defamation League, 1994—, Children's Cardiac Rsch. Found., Inc., 1996—, The Irving Fryer Found., Inc., 1995—96, Am. Heart Assn., 1997—, Jr. Achievement So. Fla., 2001—. Recipient Am. Jurisprudence award Nova U. Law Ctr., 1981, Disting. Pub. Svc. award, Anti-Defamation League, 2000. Mem. Fla. Bar Assn. (bd. govs. young lawyers divsn. 1987-89), Broward County Bar Assn. (exec. com. young lawyers sect. 1986-87), North Broward Assn. Realtors, Inc. (affiliate, std. contract forms com. 1989-95, atty./realtor rels. com. 1989-91), Kiwanis (Key Club advisor 1990-91). Commercial, contracts (including sales of goods; commercial financing), Estate planning, Property, real (including real estate development, water). Office: 3300 University Dr Ste 601 Coral Springs FL 33065-4132 E-mail: alanpolin@polinlaw.com.

POLITI, STEPHEN MICHAEL, lawyer, educator; b. Mass., Mar. 30, 1948; s. Selvi J. and Anne (Gargiulo) P.; m. Joan Spignesi, June 29, 1985. AB in Econs. cum laude, U. Mass., 1970; JD, Boston U., 1973, LLM in Taxation, 1974. Bar: Mass. 1973, U.S. Tax Ct. 1977, U.S. Dist. Ct. Mass. 1977. Counsel Joint Legis. Com. on Taxation, Boston, 1973-74; staff atty. Mass. Dept. Revenue, Boston, 1974-79, chief counsel, 1979-83; pvt. practice Boston, 1983-86; ptnr. Hennessy, Killgoar & Politi, Boston, 1986—2001; of counsel Engel & Schultz, P.C., Boston, 2001—. Prof. Bentley Coll. Grad. Sch. of Taxation, Waltham, Mass., 1977—. Contbr. articles to profl. jours. Former chmn. Lexington Mass. Bd. of Selectman; former pres. Lexington Hist. Soc.; chmn. Lexington Hist. Dists. Commn., 1990-2000. Mem. Mass. Bar Assn., Boston Bar Assn. General practice, State and local taxation. Office: Engel & Schultz PC 125 High St Boston MA 02110

POLITZ, NYLE ANTHONY, lawyer; b. Lake Charles, La., May 7, 1953; s. Henry Anthony and Jane Marie (Simoneaux) P.; children: Brandon, Jared, Caroline. Student, La. State U., Shreveport, 1971-72, U. Guadalajara, 1972, La. State U., 1972-74, JD, 1977. Bar: La. 1978, U.S. Dist. Ct. (ea., mid. and we. dists.) La. 1978, U.S. Ct. Appeals (5th cir.) 1979. Assoc. Booth, Lockard, Jack, Pleasant & LeSage, Shreveport, La., 1978-79; ptnr. Booth, Lockard, Politz, LeSage & D'Anna, L.L.C., Shreveport, 1979-96; assoc. Pendley Law Firm, Plaquemine, La., 1996-98; ptnr. Jones, Odom, Davis & Politz, LLP, Shreveport, 1998—. Lectr. La. State U., Shreveport. Resolutions com. La. Dem. Party, 1980; bd. dirs. Liberty Bank & Trust, Greenwood, La., 1980-86. Mem.: ATLA, ABA, Shreveport Bar Assn. (exec. com. 1983—85, 1993—94, bd. dirs. pro bono project, chmn. 1993—94), La. Trial Lawyers Assn. (bd. govs. 1983—94), La. State Bar Assn. (ho. of dels. 1986—98, 2002—), KC. Democrat. Roman Catholic. Avocations: whitetail deer and wild turkey hunting, golf. Personal injury (including property damage), Family and matrimonial, Insurance. Office: Jones Odom et al PO Box 1320 Shreveport LA 71164-1320 E-mail: nyle.politz@jodplaw.com.

POLKING, PAUL J. lawyer; BS, U. Notre Dame, 1959, JD, 1966. Bar: Iowa 1966, N.C. 1978. Atty. office of comp. of currency Dept. of Treasury, 1966-70; asst. v.p. Bank of Am., Charlotte, NC, 1970—88, gen. coun., 1988; chmn. The Fin. Svc. Roundtable Lawyers Coun., 2000. Office: Bank of Am Corp Ctr NC1-007-56-11 Charlotte NC 28255*

POLL, LOTHAR CHRISTOPH, lawyer; b. Berlin, Dec. 25, 1937; s. Bernhard and Elsbeth (Carbyn) P.; m. Eva Keller; 1 child, Nana. Student, U. Tübingen, U. Koeln, U. Bonn, U. Berlin. Cert. jubior judge. Editor Der Tagesspiegel, Berlin, 1984-94; gen. mgr. Tagesspiegel Group, Berlin, 1984-94; lawyer, prin. Lothar C. Poll Lawyers, Berlin, 1994—; gen. mgr. MittePresse Verlagsgesellschaft mbH, Berlin, Art Found. Poll Gemeinnützige Gesellschaft mbH, Berlin. Author: Hommage a Max Beckmann, 1984. Mem. Habimah-Freundeskreis Verein zur Foerderung Jüdischer Kulturtage in Berlin e.V. (pres. 1987—). Office: Lothar C Poll Lawyers Lützowplatz 7 Tiergarten Berlin D-10785 Germany E-mail: kanzlei@poll-berlin.de.

POLLACK, ALAN JAY, lawyer; b. Staten Island, N.Y., Apr. 4, 1969; BA, U. Mich., 1991; JD, Bklyn. Law Sch., 1994. Bar: N.J. 1994, U.S. Dist. Ct. N.J. 1994, N.Y. 1999, U.S. Ct. Appeals (2d cir.). Assoc. Levitt & Needlemar, N.Y.C., 1996—97, Lebanhoff & Coren, N.Y.C., 1997—99; ptnr. Baron & Pollack, P.C., N.Y.C., 1999—. Mem.: ABA, Am. Immigration Lawyers Assn. Immigration, naturalization, and customs. Office: Baron & Pollack PC Ste 3507 233 Broadway New York NY 10279

POLLACK, MICHAEL, lawyer; b. N.Y.C., July 14, 1946; s. Irving and Bertha (Horowitz) P.; m. Barbara Linda Shore, Aug. 23, 1970; children: Matthew, Ilana. BEng, Cooper Union, 1967; MS, U. Pa., 1970; JD, Temple U., 1974. Bar: Pa. 1974, U.S. Dist. Ct. (ea. dist.) Pa. 1974, N.Y. 2000. Rsch. scientist Pa. Rsch. Assocs., Phila., 1968-69; engr. GE Co., Valley Forge, Pa., 1969-70, Burroughs Corp., Great Valley, Pa., 1970-71; assoc. Blank, Rome, Comisky & McCauley, Phila., 1974-82, ptnr., mgr. dept. real estate, 1982—. Lectr., course planner Pa. Bar Inst., Phila. Mem. ABA, Pa. Bar Assn., Phila. Bar Assn., Internat. Assn. Attys. and Execs. in Corp. Real Estate (bd. dirs.), Eta Kappa Nu, Tau Beta Pi. Republican. Avocations: music, tennis. Property, real (including real estate development, water). Office: Blank Rome LLP 1 Logan Sq Fl 3 Philadelphia PA 19103-6998 E-mail: pollack@blankrome.com.

POLLACK, MILTON, federal judge; b. N.Y.C., Sept. 29, 1906; s. Julius and Betty (Schwartz) P.; m. Lillian Klein, Dec. 18, 1932 (dec. July 1967); children: Stephanie Pollack Miller, Daniel A.; m. Moselle Baum Erlich, Oct. 24, 1971. AB, Columbia U., 1927, JD, 1929. Bar: N.Y. 1930. Assoc. Gilman & Unger, N.Y.C., 1929-38; ptnr. Unger & Pollack, N.Y.C., 1938-44; propr. Milton Pollack, N.Y.C., 1945-67; dist. judge U.S. Dist. Ct. (so. dist.) N.Y., 1967—, sr. status, 1983. Mem. com. on ct. adminstrn. Jud. Conf., 1968-87, mem. Jud. Panel on Multi-dist. Litigation, 1983-95. Mem. Prospect Park So. Assn., Bklyn., pres., 1948-50, counsel, 1950-60, bd. dirs., 1945-60; mem. local SSS, 1952-60; chmn. lawyers div. Fedn. Jewish Philanthropies, 1957-61, vice chmn., 1954-57; chmn. lawyers div. Am. Jewish Com., 1964-66, bd. dirs., from 1967; hon. dir. Beth Isreal Hosp.; trustee Temple Emanu-El, from 1977, v.p., from 1978. Decorated chevalier Legion of Honor (France); recipient Learned Hand award Am. Jewish Com., 1967, Proskauer medal lawyers divsn. Fedn. Jewish Philanthropies, 1968, Disting. Svc. medal N.Y. County Lawyers Assn., 1991, Fordham-Stein Prize award, 1994, Devitt award Disting. Svc. to Justice, 1995. Mem. ABA, N.Y. State Bar Assn., Assn. of Bar of City of N.Y., Columbia Law Sch. Alumni Assn. (pres. 1970-72), Harmonie Club (past bd. trustees). Office: US Dist Ct US Courthouse Foley Sq New York NY 10007-1501

POLLAK, LOUIS HEILPRIN, judge, educator; b. N.Y.C., Dec. 7, 1922; s. Walter and Marion (Heilprin) P.; m. Katherine Weiss, July 25, 1952; children: Nancy, Elizabeth, Susan, Sarah, Deborah. AB, Harvard U., 1943; LLB, Yale U., 1948; LLD (hon.) , Wilkes U., 2002. Bar: N.Y. bar 1949, Conn. bar 1956, Pa. bar 1976. Law clk. to Justice Rutledge U.S. Supreme Ct., 1948-49; with Paul, Weiss, Rifkind, Wharton & Garrison, N.Y.C., 1949-51; spl. asst. to Amb. Philip C. Jessup State Dept., 1951-53; asst. counsel Amalgmated Clothing Workers Am., 1954-55; mem. faculty Yale Law Sch., 1955-74, dean, 1965-70; Greenfield prof. U. Pa., 1974-78, dean Law Sch., 1975-78, lectr., 1980—; judge U.S. Dist Ct. (ea. dist.) Pa., Phila., 1978—, now sr. judge. Vis. lectr. Howard U. Sch. Law, 1953; vis. prof. U. Mich. Law Sch., 1961, Columbia Law Sch., 1962 Author: The Constitution and the Supreme Court: A Documentary History, 1966. Mem. New Haven Bd. Edn., 1962-68; chmn. Conn. adv. com. U.S. Civil Rights Commn., 1962-63; mem. bd. NAACP Legal Def. Fund, 1960-78, v.p., 1971-78. Served with AUS, 1943-46. Recipient ABA Spirit of Excellence award, 2003. Mem.: ABA (chmn. sect. individual rights 1970—71, Spirit of Excellence award 2003), Am. Law Inst. (coun. 1978—), Am. Acad. Polit. and Social Sci. (bd. dirs. 2001—), Am. Philos. Soc., Am. Acad. Arts and Scis., Assn. Bar City N.Y., Phila. Bar Assn., Fed. Bar Assn. Office: US Dist Ct 16613 US Courthouse 601 Market St Philadelphia PA 19106-1713

POLLAK, MARK, lawyer; b. Paris, July 16, 1947; came to U.S., 1955; s. Joseph and Zofia (Berkowitz) P.; m. Joanne Elizabeth Harris, Dec. 26, 1976; children: Joshua David, Jonathan Stephen, Benjamin Eric, Rebecca Lynn. BA, Bklyn. Coll., 1968; MA in City Planning, JD, U. Pa., 1972. Bar: Md. 1972. Assoc. Piper & Marbury, Balt., 1972-81, ptnr., 1981-99, Wilmer, Cutler & Pickering, Washington, 1999—. Bd. dirs. Jack Kent Cook Found. Author: Sports Leagues and Teams--An Encyclopedia 1871 to 1996, 1997. Bd. dirs. Balt. Children's Mus., Downtown Partnership of Balt., Inc. Mem. ABA, Md. Bar Assn., Am. Coll. Real Estate Lawyers, Am. Planning Assn., Nat. Assn. Bond Lawyers. Land use and zoning (including planning), Municipal (including bonds), Property, real (including real estate development, water). Office: Wilmer, Cutler & Pickering 100 Light St Baltimore MD 21202-1036

POLLAN, STEPHEN MICHAEL, lawyer, personal finance expert, speaker, author; b. N.Y.C., May 19, 1929; m. Corinne Stoller; children: Michael, Lori, Tracy, Dana. LLB, Bklyn. Law Sch., 1951; BBS, L.I. U., 1985. Bar: N.Y. 1951. Asst. prof. Marymount Coll., 1960-70; pres. Royal Bus. Funds AMEX, 1970-76; sr. real estate cons. Nat. Westminster Bank, 1976-78; asst. prof. fin. C.W. Post Coll., L.I. U. Sch. Bus., 1994-96; prin. Stephen M. Pollan, P.C., N.Y.C., 1980—. Mem. President's Commn. on Small Bus. Co-author: Die Broke, Live Rich, The Total Negotiator, 1994, Lifescripts, 1996, also other personal bus. books; contbr. numerous articles to nat. bus. publs. Pres. Gay Head Cmty. Coun., 1975; vice chmn. UN Com. for UN Day, 1971-72. Mem. Nat. Assn. Small Bus. Investment Cos. (regional pres. 1975, bd. govs.). Commercial, contracts (including sales of goods; commercial financing), Estate planning, Property, real (including real estate development, water). Home: 1095 Park Ave New York NY 10128-1154 also: Warshaw Burstein Cohen Schlesinger & Kuh 555 5th Ave New York NY 10017-2416 Office: 555 5th Ave Fl 11 New York NY 10017-2416

POLLARD, DENNIS BERNARD, lawyer, educator; b. Phila., May 12, 1968; BS in Psychology, Pa. State U., 1990; JD, Ohio State U., 1993; postgrad., U. Mich., 1996. Bar: Ohio 1993, U.S. Dist. Ct. (no. dist.) Ohio 1994, U.S. Ct. Appeals (6th cir.) 1994. freelance cons., 1993-. Staff atty. The Legal Aid Soc. Cleve., 1993-95; atty. student affairs, student life Pa. State U., 1995-96; acad. adminstrv. intern U. Mich. Law Sch., Ann Arbor, 1996-97; asst. dean student affairs U. Tenn. Coll. Law, Knoxville, 1997-98; program dir. tenants' rights unit Tenants' Action Group of Phila., 1998-99, dir. devel., 1999—2001. Mem. ABA, Ohio State Bar Assn., Assn. Fundraising Profls., Phi Delta Phi. Avocation: biking. Home: PO Box 41884 Philadelphia PA 19101-1884

POLLARD, OVERTON PRICE, state agency executive, lawyer; b. Ashland, Va., Mar. 26, 1933; s. James Madison and Annie Elizabeth (Hutchinson) P.; m. Anne Aloysia Meyer, Oct. 1, 1960; children: Mary O., Price, John, Anne, Charles, Andrew, David AB in Econs., Washington and Lee U., 1954, JD, 1957. Bar: Va. Claims supr. Travelers Ins. Co., Richmond, Va., 1964-67; asst. atty. gen. State of Va., Richmond, 1967, 70-72; spl. asst. Va. Supreme Ct., Richmond, 1968-70; exec. dir. Pub. Defender Commn., Richmond, 1972—; ptnr. Pollard & Boice and predecessor firms, Richmond, 1972-87. Bd. govs. Va. Criminal Law Sect., Richmond, 1970-72, 91-93; chmn. prepaid legal svcs. com. Va. State Bar, Richmond, 1982-85, chair sr. lawyers sect., 1999; pres. Met. Legal Aid, Richmond, 1978 Del. to State Dem. Cong., Richmond, 1985; mem. Va. Commn. on Family Violence Prevention, 1995; bd. dirs. Henrico Cmty. Housing Corp., 1999. With USN, 1957-59. Recipient Svc. award, Criminal Law Bd. of Govs. for Pub. Defender Study, 1971, Outstanding Svc. award, Pub. Defender Commn., 1998. Mem. ABA, Va. Bar Assn. (chmn. criminal law sect. 1991-93), Richmond Bar Assn., Nat. Legal Aid and Defender Assn. (Reginald Heber Smith award 1991), Va. Bar Assn. (Pro Bono Publico award 1995). Democrat. Baptist. Avocation: fishing. Home: 7726 Sweetbriar Rd Richmond VA 23229-6622 Office: Pub Defender Commn 701 E Franklin St Ste 1416 Richmond VA 23219-2510 E-mail: opollard@pdcmail.state.va.us.

PÖLLATH, REINHARD, lawyer; b. Marktredowtiz, Germany, Jan. 15, 1948; s. Georg and Else (Weiss) Pollath; m. Raimunda Fischer, Dec. 31, 1974; 1 child, Jakob;1 child, Johanna. JD, U., 1973; LLM, Harvard Law Sch., 1974. Bar: Munich, Germany 1977. Ptnr. Radler Raupach, Munich, 1980—93; mng. dir. Deubche Interhotel, Berlin, 1993—97; ptnr. Pollath & Ptnrs., Munich, Frankfurt, Berlin, 1997—. Chmn. Up Micro Loans Found., 1999—; CEO Tchibo Holding AG, Hamburg, 2002—03; chmn. of bd. Deubche Woolworth, Frankfurt, 2001—; OHO Vemand, Hamburg, 2001—; bd. mem. Beiepdoof AG, Hamburg, 2002—. Author: (book) German M&A Manual, 1982—2003, German Foundation Manual, 2001. Pvt. U.S. Army, 1969—70, Germany. Avocations: skiing, travel. Office: Pöllath & Partners Kardinal-Faulhaber Str 10 80333 Munich Germany Office Fax: 0049 89 2424 0997. E-mail: reinhard.poellath@pplaw.com.

POLLEN, RAYMOND JAMES, lawyer; b. Manitowoc, Wis., June 10, 1956; s. Frank R. and Clara R. (Aulik) P.; m. Kay A. Wifler, Dec. 31, 1983; 1 child, Joseph. BS, U. Wis., 1978; JD, Marquette U., 1983. Bar: Wis. 1983, U.S. Dist. Ct. Wis. 1983, U.S. Ct. Claims, U.S. Ct. Appeals (7th cir.) 1985, U.S. Supreme Ct. 1986, U.S. Dist. Ct. Ill. 1994. Shareholder Crivello Carlson & Mentkowski, Milw., 1983—. Village atty. Shorewood, Wis., 1995—. Assessor Alverno Coll., Milw., 1981—; bd. dirs. Marian Ctr., 1989-95, 97-2001. Mem. ABA, Wis. Bar Assn., Internat. Mcpl. Lawyers Assn. Civil rights, Federal civil litigation, State civil litigation. Office: Crivello Carlson Mentkowski 710 N Plankinton Ave Milwaukee WI 53203-2404 Fax: 414-271-4438. E-mail: ray@milwlaw.com.

POLLET, SUSAN L. lawyer; b. Manhasset, N.Y., Dec. 17, 1954; d. Myron J. and Barbara Audrey (Kananack) Feldman; m. Richard Pollet, June 30, 1985; children: Katharine Ann, Eve Whitney. BS in Consumer Econ. and Pub. Policy, Cornell U., 1976; JD, Emory U., 1979. Bar: Ga. 1979, N.Y. 1980. Legal asst. ICC Industries, Inc., N.Y.C., 1979; lawyer Dwyer, Peltz & Walker, N.Y.C., 1980-82, Acito & Klein P.C., N.Y.C., 1982-84; supervising atty. litigation Long Island Lighting Co., Hicksville, N.Y., 1984-86; part-time county atty. Westchester County Family Ct., N.Y., Putnam County Dept. of Social Svcs., 1994-97; sr. ct. atty. Westchester County Family Ct., N.Y., 1997—. Adj. prof. Mercy Coll., N.Y., 1991-97; pvt. practice, 1988-97; law guardian for children, 1988-97. Contbr. articles to profl. jours. Legal facilitator P.E.A.C.E. Program; former mem. 9th Jud. Dist. Task Force; nominating com. Temple Bethel, 1999—2001; bd. dirs. Chappaqua Children's Workshop, 1991—92, Pleasantville Children's Ctr., 1988—89; amb. Cornell Alumni Admissions, 1991—. Mem.: Women's Bar Assn. of the State of N.Y. (co-chair legis. com. 1999—2001, v.p. 2001—02, co-chair legal rights children com. 2002—03, state dir. 1997—2003), Westchester County Bar Assn. (family ct. com. 1991—92), Westchester Women's Bar Assn. (v.p. 1993—95, pres. 1995—97, co-chair archives and historian com. 2001—, co-chair subcom. women and politics 2002—), Westchester Children's Assn. (bd. dirs. 2000—, Gagliardi award com. 2002). Avocations: reading, art, hiking, writing. Home: 67 Ludlow Dr Chappaqua NY 10514-1222 E-mail: susanpollet@aol.com.

POLLI, ROBERT PAUL, lawyer; b. Miami, Fla., Nov. 22, 1947; BA, U. South Fla., 1969, MA, 1971, 78; JD, Stetson U., 1983. Bar: Fla. 1983. Tchr. Project Headstart, various locations, 1968-69; exceptional child educator Hillsborough County Schs., Tampa, Fla., 1974-76, guidance counselor, 1976-80; profl. photographer Tampa, 1972—; assoc. Bennie Lazzara, Jr., P.A., Tampa, 1983-87; ptnr. Lazzara, Caskey, Polli and Paul, Tampa, 1987-91, Law Firm Robert P. Polli, P.A., Tampa, 1991—. Contbr. articles to profl. jours. Mem. ABA, Fla. Bar Assn. (chmn. grievance com.), Fla. Assn. Criminal Def. Lawyers, Hillsborough County Assn. Criminal Def. Lawyers (pres.). Democrat. Roman Catholic. Criminal. Office: PO Box 1427 Kilauea HI 96754

POLLIHAN, THOMAS HENRY, lawyer; b. St. Louis, Nov. 15, 1949; s. C.H. and Patricia Ann (O'Brien) P.; m. Donna M. Bickhaus, Aug. 25, 1973; 1 child, Emily Christine. BA in Sociology, Quincy U., 1972; JD, U. Notre Dame, 1975; Exec. Masters in Internat. Bus., St. Louis U., 1992. Bar: Mo. 1975, Ill. 1976. Jud. law clk. to judge Mo. Ct. of Appeals, St. Louis, 1975-76; from assoc. to ptnr. Greenfield, Davidson, Mandelstamm & Voorhees, St. Louis, 1976-82; asst. gen. counsel Kellwood Co., St. Louis, 1982-89, gen. counsel, sec., 1989-93, v.p., sec., gen. counsel, 1993—2002, sr. v.p., 2002—. Trustee Quincy (Ill.) U., 1987-93, 97—, pres. alumni bd., 1986-87; pres. S.W. Neighborhood Improvement Assn., St. Louis, 1984, Quincy (Ill.) U. Found., 1993-94, 97—; dir., sec. New Piasa Chautauqua, Ill., 1996-97. Named Quincy U. Alumnus of Yr., 1997. Mem. Bar Assn. Met. St. Louis. Roman Catholic. Avocations: soccer, cycling. Commercial, contracts (including sales of goods; commercial financing), Corporate, general, Property, real (including real estate development, water). Home: 415 Spring Ave Saint Louis MO 63119-2634 Office: Kellwood Co 600 Kellwood Pkwy Ste 300 Chesterfield MO 63017-5897 E-mail: tom_pollihan@kellwood.com.

POLLOCK, BRADLEY NEIL, lawyer; b. St. Charles, Ill., Sept. 23, 1970; s. Neil Edward and Karen Irene Pollock; m. Tara Lynne Kozlowski, Aug. 23, 1997; 1 child, Kent Bradley. BA with distinction, U. Ill., 1992; JD, Loyola U., Chgo., 1995. Bar: Ill. 1995, U.S. Dist. Ct. (no. dist.) Ill. 1995. Assoc. Williams & Montgomery, Ltd., Chgo., 1995, Robert N. Wadington & Assocs., Chgo., 1995-2000, Walsh, Knippen, Knight & Diamond, Wheaton, Ill., 2000—. Recipient Am. Jurisprudence award in Appellate Practice Lawyers Coop. Pub., 1993. Mem. ATLA, Ill. Bar Assn., DuPage County Bar Assn., Ill. Trial Lawyers Assn. Avocations: fly fishing, backpacking, other outdoor activities. Personal injury (including property damage), Product liability, Professional liability. Home: IN281 Prairie Ave Glen Ellyn IL 60137 Office: Walsh Knippen Knight & Diamond 601 W Liberty Dr Wheaton IL 60187

POLLOCK, BRUCE GERALD, lawyer; b. Providence, Feb. 18, 1947; s. Reuben and Stella (Reitman) P.; m. Sheri Barbara Tepper, Dec. 21, 1969; children: Dawn, Meah. BA, U. R.I., 1968; JD, Suffolk U., 1974. Bar: R.I. 1974, U.S. Supreme Ct. 1978, U.S. Dist. Ct. R.I. 1980. Law clk. R.I. Superior Ct., Providence, 1974, adminstrv. asst. to chief justice, 1975; asst. pub. defender R.I. Dept. Pub. Defender, Providence, 1975-80; pvt. practice Warwick and West Warwick, R.I., 1980—. Adj. instr. So. N.E. Law Sch., New Bedford, Mass., 1990. Dist. chmn. Narragansett Coun. Shawomet Dist. Boy Scouts Am., 1996-98. Fellow R.I. Bar Found. (bd. dirs. 1990-2000; v.p. 2000—); mem. ABA, Nat. Conf. Bar Pres., New Eng. Bar Assn. (del. 1991-93), R.I. Bar Assn. (pres. 1992-93, ho. of dels. 1986—, award of merit 1995). Democrat. Avocations: golf, skiing, stained glass craftsman, bicycling, tai chi. Criminal, General practice, Landlord-tenant. Office: 45 Providence St West Warwick RI 02893-3714 E-mail: brucepollock@juno.com., bgpollock@yahoo.com.

POLLOCK, DAVID SAMUEL, lawyer; b. Altoona, Pa., Dec. 11, 1949; s. Arthur Edgar and Judith Jaffe Pollock; m. Rita Lee, June 27, 1971; children: Adam, Joshua. BA, Pa. State U., 1970; JD, Duquesne U., 1974. Bar: Pa. 1974, U.S. Dist. Ct. (we. dist.) Pa. 1974. Law clk. Ct. Common Pleas, Pitts., 1974-76; assoc. Jubelirer, Pass & Intrieri PC, Pitts., 1976-82; prin. Pollock & Adams, Pitts., 1982-92; ptnr. Wittlin Goldston Caputo & Pollock PC, Pitts., 1992-94, Reed Smith Shaw & McClay LLC, Pitts., 1994-98; prin. David S. Pollock & Assocs., Pitts., 1998—2000; ptnr. Pollock Begg Komar Glasser LLC, Pitts., 2000—. Lectr. in field. Contbr. articles to law revs., jours. and presentations Bd. dirs. Jewish Comty. Ctr., 1988-97, sec., 1993-95, treas., 1992-93, asst. treas. 1991-92, exec. com. 1990-98, chair Emma Kaufmann Camp, 1991-94, other offices; past bd. dirs., founding dir., atty. Oakland Bus. and Civic Assn.; intergenerational choir, past mem. brotherhood, bd. trustees Temple Sinai. With USAR, 1970-76. Recipient Ida and Samuel Latterman Vol. Mitzvah award Jewish Comty. Ctr., 1989. Fellow Internat. Acad. Matrimonial Lawyers, Am. Acad. Matrimonial Lawyers (co-chmn. membership com., bd. examiners Pa. chpt. 1993-95, 97-98, 2000-03, mem. program com. Pa. chpt. 1993-96); mem. ABA (family law sect.), Am. Inns of Matrimonial Cts. (Master 1995-96, 97—), Pa. Bar Assn. (past chair and various offices family law sect., coun. mem. 1987—, co-chair program com. 1984-87, 88-89, 91-95, editor-in-chief Pa. Family Lawyer 1996—, task force on family ct. reform 1997—, Outstanding Contbn. award 1988-89, Spl. Achievement award 1993, 94, 95, 96, 97, 98), Pa. Futures Commn. (family law task group 1996-97), Westmoreland County Bar Assn. (family law sect.), Allegheny County Bar Assn. (vice chair, sec., treas., coun. mem. family law sect. 1984-87, 88-91, 92-95, 96—, co-chair rules com. 1996-97, co-chair ct. rels. com. 1994-95, opinions com. 1993—, co-chair procedures and rulees com. 1985-88), Washington County Bar Assn. (family law sect.), Duquesne U. Law Alumni Assn. (bd. govs. 1993-96). Avocations: snow and water skiing, swimming, jogging, bicycling, canoeing. Family and matrimonial. Office: 501 Frick Bldg 437 Grant St Pittsburgh PA 15219-6002 Fax: (412) 471-9001. E-mail: dpollock@pbkg.net.

POLLOCK, EARL EDWARD, lawyer; b. Decatur, Nebr., Feb. 24, 1928; s. Herman and Della (Rosenthal) P.; m. Betty Sokol, Sept. 8, 1951; children: Stephen, Della, Naomi. BA, U. Minn., 1948; JD, Northwestern U., 1953; LLD (hon.), Morningside Coll., 1995. Bar: D.C. 1955, Va. 1955, Ill. 1959, U.S. Supreme Ct. 1960. Law clk., chief justices Vinson and Warren, U.S. Supreme Ct. Washington, 1953-55; atty. antitrust div. Dept. Justice, Washington, 1955-56, asst. to solicitor gen., 1956-59; ptnr. Sonnenschein Nath & Rosenthal, Chgo., 1959—. Trustee Loyola U., Chgo., 1983-92; life trustee Northwestern Meml. Hosp.; dir. Fla. West Coast Symphony, (exec. com.). Mem. Chgo. Bar Assn. (chmn. antitrust law com. 1967-68), ABA (chmn. antitrust law sect. 1979-80), Alumni Assn. Northwestern U. Sch. Law (pres. 1974-75, svc. award 1976). Antitrust, Federal civil litigation. Office: Sonnenschein Nath 233 S Wacker Dr Ste 8000 Chicago IL 60606-6491

POLLOCK, JOHN PHLEGER, lawyer; b. Sacramento, Apr. 28, 1920; s. George Gordon and Irma (Phleger) P.; m. Juanita Irene Gossman, Oct. 26, 1945; children: Linda Pollock Harrison, Madeline Pollock Chiotti, John, Gordon. AB, Stanford U., 1942; JD, Harvard U., 1948. Bar: Calif. 1949, U.S. Supreme Ct. 1954. Ptnr. Musick, Peeler & Garrett, L.A., 1953-60, Pollock, Williams & Berwanger, L.A., 1960-80, Rodi, Pollock, Pettker, Galbraith & Cahill, L.A., 1980-89, of counsel, 1989—. Contbr. articles to profl. publs. Active Boy Scouts Am.; trustee Pitzer Coll., Claremont, Calif., 1968-76, Pacific Legal Found., 1981-91, Fletcher Jones Found., 1969—, Good Hope Med. Found., 1980—. Fellow Am. Coll. Trial Lawyers; mem. ABA, Los Angeles County Bar Assn. (trustee 1964-66). Home: 30602 Paseo Del Valle Laguna Niguel CA 92677-2317 Office: 444 S Flower St Ste 1700 Los Angeles CA 90071-2918 E-mail: Phleger1@msn.com.

POLLOCK, R. JEFFREY, lawyer; b. San Francisco, Jan. 5, 1946; BA, DePauw U., 1968; MT, Harvard U., 1971; JD, Northeastern U., 1976. Bar: Ohio 1976. Asst. sec. dept. community devel. Commonwealth of Mass., 1972-73; atty. McDonald, Hopkins, Cleve. Mem. ABA, Ohio State Bar Assn., Cleve. Bar Assn. Federal civil litigation, General civil litigation, State civil litigation. Office: McDonald Hopkins 2100 Bank One Ctr 600 Superior Ave E Ste 2100 Cleveland OH 44114-2653

POLLOCK, STEWART GLASSON, lawyer, former state supreme court justice; b. East Orange, N.J., Dec. 21, 1932; BA, Hamilton Coll., 1954, LLD (hon.), 1995; LLB, NYU, 1957; LLM, U. Va., 1988. Bar: N.J. 1958. Asst. U.S. atty., Newark, 1958-60; ptnr. Schenck, Price, Smith & King, Morristown, N.J., 1960-74, 76-78; commr. N.J. Dept. Pub. Utilities; counsel to gov. State of N.J., Trenton, 1978-79; assoc. justice N.J. Supreme Ct., Morristown, 1979-99; of counsel Riker Danzig Hyland & Perretti, Morristown, 1999—. Mem. N.J. Commn. on Investigation, 1976-78; chmn. coordinating coun. on life-sustaining med. treatment decision making Nat. Ctr. for State Cts., 1994-96; bd. dirs. NYU Law Ctr. Found., Inst. Jud. Adminstrn., N.J. Conservation Found., 1999-2003; chmn. commn. on the rules of profl. conduct N.J. Supreme Ct., 2000—. Assoc. editor N.J. Law Jour.; contbr. articles to legal jours. Trustee Coll. Medicine and Dentistry, N.J., 1976. Fellow Am. Coll. Comml. Arbitrators; mem. ABA (chmn. appellate judges conf. 1991-92), N.J. Bar Assn. (trustee 1973-78), Am.

Judicature Soc. (dir. 1984-88), Morris County Bar Assn. (pres. 1973). Alternative dispute resolution, Appellate, General civil litigation. Office: Riker Danzig Scherer Hyland & Perretti LLP Hdqs Plz 1 Speedwell Ave Morristown NJ 07962-1981

POLOZOLA, FRANK JOSEPH, federal judge; b. Baton Rouge, Jan. 15, 1942; s. Steve A. Sr. and Caroline C. (Lucito) P.; m. Linda Kay White, June 9, 1962; children: Gregory Dean, Sheri Elizabeth, Gordon Damian. Student bus. adminstrn., La. State U., 1959-62, JD, 1965. Bar: La. 1965. Law clk. to U.S. Dist. Ct. Judge E. Gordon West, 1965-66; assoc. Seale, Smith & Phelps, Baton Rouge, 1966-68, ptnr., 1968-73; part-time magistrate U.S. Dist. Ct. (mid. dist.) La., Baton Rouge, 1972-73, magistrate, 1973-80, judge, 1980—, chief judge, 1998—. Adj. prof. Law Ctr., La. State U., 1977-95. Bd. dirs. Cath. High Sch. Mem. La. Bar Assn., Baton Rouge Bar Assn., Fed. Judges Assn., 5th Cir. Dist. Judges Assn., La. State U. L Club, KC, Wex Malone Inns of Ct., Omicron Delta Kappa. Roman Catholic. Office: US Dist Ct Russell B Long Fed Bldg & US Courthouse 777 Florida St Ste 313 Baton Rouge LA 70801-1717

POLSKY, HOWARD DAVID, lawyer; b. Phila., Sept. 10, 1951; s. Herman and Meriam Polsky. BA, Lehigh U., 1973; JD, Ind. U., 1976. Bar: Pa. 1976, N.J. 1977, D.C. 1978, U.S. Ct. Appeals (D.C. cir.) 1976. Atty. FCC, Washington, 1976-79; assoc. Kirkland & Ellis, Washington, 1979-83; ptnr. Wiley, Rein & Fielding, Washington, 1983-92; v.p. fed. policy and regulation COMSAT Corp., Bethesda, Md., 1992-2000; v.p., gen. counsel Lockheed Martin Global Telecomms., Bethesda, 2000—02. Adj. prof. law Del. Law Sch. Widner U., 1981-84. Mem. ABA, Fed. Comm. Bar Assn. Administrative and regulatory, Communications, Utilities, public.

POLSTRA, LARRY JOHN, lawyer; b. Lafayette, Ind., June 28, 1945; s. John Edward and Elizabeth (Vandergraff) P.; m. Joan Marie Blair Rozier, Sept. 2, 1972 (dec.); 1 stepchild, Shawn M. Rozier; m. Barbara Dominy, Mar. 18, 1988; stepchildren: Tobi Shawn Hoff, Teri Lane Kelly. BS in Bus. Mgmt., Bob Jones U., 1968; JD, Atlanta Law Sch., 1976, LLM, 1977. Bar: Ga. 1976, U.S. Dist. Ct. (no. dist.) Ga. 1976, U.S. Ct. Appeals (11th cir.) 1990, U.S. Supreme Ct. 1994. Mktg. dir. N.Am. Security, Atlanta, 1972-73; acctg. supr. Allstate Ins. Co., Atlanta, 1973-76; sole practice Atlanta, 1976-77; ptnr. Law Smith (formerly Smith & Polstra), Atlanta, 1977-94, of counsel, 1995, England & McKnight, 1996-97, Hays & Maysilles, P.C. (now known as Gary Martin Hays and Assoc., P.C., 1997—. Arbitrator Fulton County Superior Ct., Atlanta, 1986. Served to 1st lt. USMC, 1968-71, Vietnam. Mem. ATLA, Atlanta Bar Assn., Ga. Assn. Trial Lawyers, Ga. Assn. Criminal Def. Lawyers, Marine Corps Assn. Ga. Lawyers. Avocation: golf. Home: 2597 Regency Dr E Tucker GA 30084-2326 Office: PO Box 451068 1979 Lakeside Pkwy Ste 220 Tucker GA 30084-5813 E-mail: lpolstra@aol.com.

POLYZOGOPOULOS, CONSTANTIN, lawyer, law educator; b. Athens, Greece, Mar. 25, 1950; s. Panayotis and Paraskevi (Morfopoulou) P.; m. Katherine Papadopoulou, July 19, 1979; 1 child, Eva. LLB, U. Athens, 1973; PhD, U. Tübingen, Germany, 1975. Bar: Athens, 1974, Ct. Appeal, 1979, Supreme Ct., 1982. Asst. U. Athens, 1976-82, lectr., 1982-89, asst. prof. law, 1989—; practice Athens. Author: Cross-Examination of the Parties and Oral Affidavits in their Relationship to Each Other, 1976, Execution on Copyright, 1987, Juridical Studies, 1996. Mem. Automobile Club of Greece (pres. disciplinary ct. appeal 1990-96, Medal 1993, 95, v.p. 2000—), Greek Assn. Procedural Law, Internat. Assn. Procedural Law, Assn. Tchg. and Rsch. in Intellectual Property, Internat. Assn. Artistic Literature (treas. Greek section 1982—), Wissenschaftliche Vereinigung für Internationales Verfahrensrecht, U. Tubingen Alumni Assn., German Acad. Exch. Svc. Alumni Assn., German Sch. Athens Alumni Assn., Salzburg Seminar Alumni Assn., Yacht Racing Club Athens. Avocations: sailing, boating. Office: Law Office Skoufa 60A GR-10680 Athens Greece E-mail: kpolizog@law.uoa.gr.

POMERANTZ, JERALD MICHAEL, lawyer; b. Springfield, Mass., July 9, 1954; s. Lawrence Louis Pomerantz and Dolores (Barez) Chaudoir. BA in Econs. cum laude, Brandeis U., 1976; JD, Vanderbilt U., 1979; student, Am. Inst. Banking, 1983-99. Attys., McAllen, Tex., 1979-80, Weslaco, Tex., 1980-85; gen. counsel, sec. Tex. Valley Bancshares, Inc., Weslaco, 1985-87; atty. for Hidalgo County Rural Fire Prevention Dist., Tex., 1982-88; atty. SBA, Harlingen, Tex., 1987; pvt. practice Weslaco, Tex., 1987-89; adv. dir. South Tex. Fed. Credit Union, 1995-98. Atty. Elsa (Tex.) Housing Authority, 1993—, Weslaco (Tex.) Housing Authority, 1995—, Econ. Devel. Corp. Weslaco, 2001—02. Mem. Weslaco Charter Review Com., 1981-82,; drafted S.B. 139 (amending Tex. bus. and commerce code sect. 9.402(g)) regular session Tex. Legislature), 1989, S.B. 140, 1989, enacted as H.B. 2005 (amending Tex. Credit Code sect. 1.06) regular session Tex. Legislature, 1993; commr. Weslaco Planning and Zoning Com., 2002—. Recipient continuing edn. award Banking Law Inst., 1992. Mem.: Rio Grande Valley Bankruptcy Bar Assn. (v.p. 2000—01), Hidalgo County Bar Assn. (law libr. com. 1999—), Coll. State Bar Tex. (bd.dirs. 1990—95), Conf. on Consumer Fin. Law, State Bar Tex., Tex. Assn. Bank Counsel (bd. dirs. 1990—95, 1997—2000, v.p. 2001—02, pres.-elect 2002—03, pres. 2003—). Banking, Commercial, consumer (including collections, credit), Property, real (including real estate development, water). Home and Office: PO Box 10 Weslaco TX 78599-0010 E-mail: jmp@justice.com.

POMEROY, CHRISTOPHER DONALD, lawyer; b. Waterbury, Conn., Nov. 11, 1970; BS in Biology cum laude, Fairfield (Conn.) U., 1992; JD with high honors, George Washington U., 1996. Bar: Va. 1996, U.S. Dist. Ct. (ea. and we. dists.) Va. 1997, U.S. Ct. Appeals (4th cir.) 1997. Assoc. atty. Williams, Mullen, Christian & Dobbins, Richmond, Va., 1996-98, McGuire Woods, LLP, Richmond, 1998—2002; founding ptnr. Aqualaw, PLC, 2002—. Chair, bd. govs. environ. law sect. Va. State Bar, 2000-2001. Environmental. Office: Aqualaw PLC 801 E Main St Ste 1002 Richmond VA 23219

POMEROY, GREGG JOSEPH, lawyer; b. Flushing, N.Y., June 22, 1948; s. George Bart and Dianne (Marshall) P.; m. Deborah Christina Pomeroy, Feb. 16, 1985 (div.); children: Christopher William, Glenn David; m. Suzanne R. Pomeroy, July 25, 1992; children: Adam Barton, Sarah Nicole. BA, U. Fla., 1971; JD, Samford U., 1974. Bar: Fla. 1974, U.S. Dist. Ct. Fla. 1974, U.S. Ct. Appeals (5th and 11th cirs.) 1974. Asst. pub. defender 17th Jud. Cir., Ft. Lauderdale, Fla., 1974-75; ptnr. Pomeroy, Pomeroy & Pomeroy, Ft. Lauderdale, 1976-86, Pomeroy & Pomeroy, P.A., Ft. Lauderdale, 1987-96; pvt. practice Fort Lauderdale, 1996—. Served to specialist class 4 USNG, 1970-76. Mem. ABA, Def. Research Inst., NRA, Coral Ridge Power Squadron, Harleys Owners Group. Clubs: Boat U.S., NRA. Roman Catholic. Avocations: boating, motorcycling. Insurance, Personal injury (including property damage), Product liability. Office: 900 E Broward Blvd Fort Lauderdale FL 33301

PONCELET, ALINE, lawyer; b. Paris, Apr. 5, 1961; Degree in Bus. Law, U. Paris II, 1982; grad. degree bus. law, U. Paris I., 1983; HEC, Ecole Hautes Etudes Commerciales, France, 1985. Bar: Paris, Brussels. Assoc. Cabinet Moquet Borde and Assocs., Paris, 1985—93, ptnr., 1993—. Contbr. articles to profl. jours. Mem.: HEC Alumni Legal and Jud. Group, Woman Internat. Group, HEC Alumni Banking and Securities Group (pres.), Internat. Union Lawyers, IBA Securities Law Com. Capital Market, Securities, Mergers and acquisitions. Office: Moquet Borde 3o ave Messine 75008 Paris France Fax: 33145 639149. E-mail: aponcelet@moquet-borde.com.

PONCET, DOMINIQUE MATTEO, lawyer, educator; b. Geneva, Aug. 31, 1929; s. Jean Francis and Giuseppina Poncet; m. Eliane Uldry, July 12, 1967; children: Isabelle, Philippe. Licentiate of Laws, U. Geneva, 1951, Doctor of Laws, 1967. With Lord Nathan Oppenheimer's Chambers, London, 1954; lawyer Geneva, 1953—; sr. ptnr. Poncet Turrettini Amaudruz Neyroud & Assocs., Geneva, 1953—; prof. criminal procedure U. Geneva, 1967-97. Dir. various cos.;mem. expert commn. to draft New Swiss Criminal Code; alternate mem. Geneva State Ct. Cassation; pres. Fiat Auto Suisse. Author: L'information contradictoire dans le système de la procédure pénale genevoise, 1967, Droit à l'assistance de l'avocat, 1970, L'extradition et le droit d'asile, 1976, La protection de l'accusé par la Convention Européenne des droits de l'homme, 1977, Le nouveau code de procédure pénale annoté, 1978, Extradition: The European Model, 1986, Le statut du dirigeant d'entreprise en Suisse, 1989, La surveillance des banques étrangères, 1993, Systeme accusatoire: Etats Unis, 1994; La responsabilité pénale des personnes morales, 2000. Decorated comdr. Order of Merit (Italy). Mem. Swiss Fedn. Lawyers, Geneva Law Soc., Swiss Soc. Jurists, Swiss Soc. Criminal Law, Rotary Club. Mem. Conservative Party. Avocations: golf, skiing, conjuring. Home: 21 route de Pressy 1253 Vandoeuvres Switzerland Office: Poncet Turrettini Amaudruz Neyroud Assoc 8-10 rue de Hesse 1204 Geneva Switzerland Fax: 41-22 312 14 31. E-mail: info@ptan.ch.

PONEMAN, DANIEL BRUCE, lawyer; b. Toledo, Mar. 12, 1956; s. Meyer and Delores Suzanne (Shapiro) P.; m. Susan Anne Danoff, Aug. 12, 1984; children: Claire Gillian, Michael Bruder, William Meyer. AB in Govt. and Econs. magna cum laude, Harvard Coll., 1978; MLitt in Politics, Lincoln Coll., Oxford, Eng., 1981; JD cum laude, Harvard U., 1984. Bar: D.C. 1985, N.Y., 1985. Vis. fellow Internat. Inst. Strategic Studies, London, 1980-81; rsch. fellow ctr. sci. and internat. affairs Kennedy sch. govt. Harvard U., 1981-84; assoc. Covington & Burling, 1985-89; White House fellow U.S. Dept. of Energy, 1989-90; dir. def. policy and arms control NSC, Washington, 1990-93, spl. asst. to the Pres., sr. dir. nonproliferation and export controls, 1993-96; counsel Hogan & Hartson L.L.P., 1996-97, ptnr., 1999—2002; prin. The Scowcroft Group, 2001—. Author: Nuclear Power in the Developing World, 1982, Argentina: Democracy on Trial, 1987; contbr. articles to profl. jours. and newspapers including N.Y. Times, Washington Post, Wall Street Jour., L.A. Times, Boston Globe. Mem. Commn. to Asses the Orgn. of Govt. to Combat the Proliferation of Weapons of Mass Distruction, 1997-99; mem. Pres.' Export Coun. Subcom. on Export Adminstrn. Grantee Corp. Pub. Broadcasting; Lord Crewe scholar. Mem. D.C. Bar, N.Y. Bar, Coun. Fgn. Rels., Phi Beta Kappa. Home: 1541 Forest Ln Mc Lean VA 22101 Office: The Scowcroft Group 900 17th St NW Ste 500 Washington DC 20006 E-mail: poneman@scowcroft.com.

PONG, YUEN SUN LOUIS, lawyer; b. Hong Kong, May 5, 1957; s. Che Yue and Leung King (Tam) P.; m. Lai Kuen Grace Brigid Chan, Aug. 5, 1982; children: Sze Ngok Kandor, Sze Lok Portia. BSc, U. Hong Kong, 1979. Qualified lawyer. Asst. solicitor Johnson Stokes & Master, Hong Kong, 1984-88; ptnr. Liau Ho & Chan, Hong Kong, 1988—. Pres. Hong Kong Chinese Family for Christ, 1997—; mem. synod Diocese of Hong Kong and Macao, 1994-98; mem. gen. synod Hong Kong Sheng Kung Hui, 1999—; supr. S.K.H. Tang Shiu Kin Secondary Sch., 2002—. Mem. Law Soc. Hong Kong. Avocations: couples and family ministry, singing. Home: Flat A 5th fl Avon Ct 2 Fessenden Rd Kowloon Tong Hong Kong Office: 6th Fl United Chinese Bank 31-37 Des Voeux Rd Ctrl Hong Kong China

PONITZ, JOHN ALLAN, lawyer; b. Battle Creek, Mich., Sept. 7, 1949; m. Nancy J. Roberts, Aug. 14, 1971; children: Amy, Matthew, Julie. BA, Albion Coll., 1971; JD, Wayne State U., 1974. Bar: Mich. 1974, U.S. Dist. Ct. (ea. dist.) Mich. 1975, (we. dist.) Mich. 1986, U.S. Ct. Appeals (6th cir.) Mich. 1981, U.S. Supreme Ct. 1992. Assoc. McMachan & Kaichen, Birmingham, Mich., 1973-75; atty. Grand Trunk Western R.R., Detroit, 1975-80, sr. trial atty., 1980-89, gen. counsel, 1990-95; ptnr. Hopkins & Sutter, Detroit, 1995-2000, Maxwell, Ponitz & Sclawy, Troy, Mich., 2000—01; of counsel Fabrizio & Brook, P.C., Troy, 2002—; gen. counsel A&M Hospitality, Southfield, Mich., 2002—. V.p. Beverly Hills (Mich.) Jaycees, 1981. Served to capt. USAR, 1974-82. Mem. Mich. Bar Assn., Nat. Assn. R.R. Trial Counsel, Oakland County Bar Assn. Lutheran. Avocation: golf. Federal civil litigation, Corporate, general, Personal injury (including property damage). Office: A&M Hospitality 24725 Greenfield Rd Southfield MI 48075 E-mail: japonitz@pbmaxwell.com.

PONOROFF, LAWRENCE, law educator, legal consultant; b. Chgo., Sept. 10, 1953; s. Charles Melvin and Jean Eileen (Kramer) P.; m. Monica J. Moses, July 25, 1981; children: Christopher J., Devon E., Laura J., Scott C. AB, Loyola U., Chgo., 1975; JD, Stanford U., 1978. Bar: Colo. 1978, Ohio 1988, U.S. Dist. Ct. Colo., U.S. Dist. Ct. (no. dist.) Ohio, U.S. Ct. Appeals (10th cir.). Assoc. Holme Roberts & Owen, Denver, 1978-84, ptnr., 1984-86; asst. prof. law U. Toledo, 1986-88, assoc. prof. coll. of law, 1988-90, prof. law, assoc. dean academic affairs, 1990-92, prof., 1990-95, Tulane U. Sch. Law, New Orleans, 1995-00, Mitchell Franklin prof., 2000—, vice dean, 1998-2001, dean, 2001—. Vis. prof. Wayne State U. Law Sch., 1993, U. Mich. Law Sch., 1997, lectr. fed. juc. ctr.; cons. long range planning subcom. of com. on adminstrn. of bankruptcy system Jud. Conf. of the U.S.; dir. Am. Bd. Certification, 2000—; bd. advr. editors Am. Bankruptcy Inst. Law Rev., 2000—; bd. dirs. Am. Bs. Certification. Co-author: (with S.E. Snyder) Commerical Bankruptcy Litigation, 1989, (with J. Dolan) Basic Concepts in Commercial Law, 1998, (with Epstein and Markell) Making and Doing Deals: Contracts in Context, 2001. Mem. ABA, Am. Bar Ist., Am. Law Inst., La. State Bar Assn. (bd. govs.). Home: 6025 Pitt St New Orleans LA 70118-6010 Office: Tulane Law Sch Coll Law 6329 Freret St New Orleans LA 70118-6231 E-mail: lponoroff@law.tulane.edu.

PONS, ELIZABETH S. lawyer, health facility administrator; b. Cali, Colombia, Feb. 25, 1961; arrived in U.S., 1965; d. Jaime Julio Sanchez and Stella; m. Francisco Pons, Sept. 28, 1991; children: Eric Jonathan, Jacqueline. BA magna cum laude, Dartmouth Coll., 1982; postgrad. in clin. psychology, Yale U., 1982—83; JD, Harvard U., 1988. Bar: Fla., U.S. Dist. Ct. (so. and mid. dist.) Fla. Assoc. Tew Jorden Schulte Beasley, Miami, 1988—91, Coffrey Aragon Burlington, et al, Miami, 1991—93; pvt. practice Miami, 1997—2001; sr. counsel Am. Bankers, Miami, 1997—2001; CEO, gen. counsel Kidney Treatment Ctr. South Fla., Miami, 2001—. Bd. dirs. Coconut Grove Theatre, Miami, 2000—01. Named to Pres.'s Adv. Coun., 2002; recipient Small Bus. award, Congressman Tom Delay, 2002; Remsden Hon. scholar. Mem.: Mensa Internat., St. Louis Outreach Ministry, Dartmouth Lawyers Club, Harvard Club. Republican. Roman Catholic. Avocations: travel, reading, dancing, fishing. Health, Corporate, general. Home: 16153 SW 73d Pl Miami FL 33158 Office: Kidney Treatment Ctr S Fla 13500 N Kendall Dr Ste 131 Miami FL 33186

PONTAROLO, MICHAEL JOSEPH, lawyer; b. Walla Walla, Wash., Sept. 1, 1947; s. Albert and Alice Mary (Fazzari) P.; m. Elizabeth Louise Onley, July 18, 1970; children: Christie, Amy, Nick, Angela. BA, Gonzaga U., 1969, JD, 1973. Bar: Wash. 1973, US Dist. Ct. (ea. dist.) Wash. 1974. Assoc. Mullin & Etter, Spokane, Wash., 1973-74, William Iunker, Spokane, 1974-75, Delay, Curran & Boling, Spokane, 1975-77; prin. Delay, Curran, Thompson & Pontarolo, P.S., Spokane, 1977-97, Delay, Curran, Thompson, Pontarolo & Walker, Spokane, 1997—. Mem. Spokane County Med. Legal Com., 1987-88, 91; chmn. liaison com. Superior Ct., 1987-88, 94-97, chair, 1994-95, mem. arbitration bd., 1987-2002; mem. Bench Bar Com., 1987-88; bd. gov., nom. com., superior ct. judge adv. com. to Gov. Locke, Wa.; adj. prof. Gonzaga U. Sch. Law, 1987—, bd. advisors, 2000—. Bd. dir. Community Ctr. Found., Spokane, 1986-89; active Spokane C.C. Legal Secretary Adv. Com.; mem. adv. bd. Spokane C.C., 1992—. Recipient Cert. of Recognition, Superior Ct. Clk., Spokane, 1986; named one of Best Lawyers in Am., 2003--. Mem.: ABA, ATLA, Wash. State Bar Assoc., Bd. of Gov. (elected 2003—06), Spokane County Bar Assn. (trustee 1984—86, sec.-treas. 1987—88, v.p. 1988—89, pres. 1989—90, membership com. chair 1992—93), Wash. State Trial Lawyers Assn. (v.p. east 1979—80, CLE program chmn. 1984, chair 1995—96, mem. awards com. 1995—99, Cert. of Appreciation 1982, 1990, 1992, Leadership award 1984), Wash. State Bar Assn. (spl. dist. counsel 1984—, interprofl. com. 1987—90, character and fitness com. 1991—94, com. chair 1993—94, mem. jud. recommendation com. 1994—98, co-chair jud. recommendation com. 1996—, chair jud. recommendation com. 1997—98, consumer protection com. 2000—01, rules of profl. conduct com. 2000—03, spl. disciplinary counsel 2001), Alpha Sigma Nu. Insurance, Personal injury (including property damage), Workers' compensation. Office: Delay Curran Thompson Pontarolo & Walker PS 601 W Main Ave Ste 1212 Spokane WA 99201-0684 E-mail: mikep@dctpw.com.

POOLE, GORDON LEICESTER, lawyer; b. Mpls., Dec. 25, 1926; s. Arthur Bensell and Mildred Loyal (Wood) P.; m. Lois Claire Teasdale, Oct. 30, 1954; children— David Wilson, Edward Gray, Elisabeth Claire AB, Harvard U., 1949, LL.B., 1952. Assoc. Treadwell & Laughlin, San Francisco, 1953-54, Lillick, McHose & Charles, San Francisco, 1955-63, ptnr., 1963-97, mem. exec. com., 1977-81, chmn. mgmt. com., 1981-84, chmn., 1984-86; of counsel Lillick & Charles LLP, 1997-2001, Nixon Peabody LLP, 2001—. Contbr. articles to profl. jours. Pres. Young Republicans, San Mateo County, Calif., 1958-59; vestryman Trinity Episcopal Parish, Menlo Park, Calif., 1968, 70, 76-78, sr. warden, 1970. Served as sgt. U.S. Army, 1944-47, Korea Mem. Calif. Bar Assn., San Francisco Bar Assn., Maritime Law Assn. (com. on marine financing), Maritime Adminstrv. Bar Assn., ABA, Mng. Ptnrs. Assn. Clubs: Bohemian, World Trade (San Francisco); Ladera Oaks (Menlo Park). Avocations: stamp collecting, marine paintings, prints and memorabilia. Home: 2280 Stockbridge Ave Woodside CA 94062-1130 Office: Nixon Peabody LLP 2 Embarcadero Ctr Ste 2700 San Francisco CA 94111-3996

POOLE, HEATHER L. lawyer; b. Thousand Oaks, Calif., Feb. 6, 1974; d. Randolph Earle and Valerie Jeanne Poole. BA in Philosophy, BA in History, Calif. Poly. Inst., Pomona, 1997; JD, NY Law Sch., 2000. Bar: Calif. 01, U.S. Dist. Ct. (cen. dist.) Calif. 01. Law clk. Lambda Legal Def. and Edn. Fund., Inc., L.A., 1998; law clk. to Justice Lorraine Miller NY Supreme Ct., N.Y.C., 1998; rsch. asst. NY Law Sch., N.Y.C., 1999, discrimination claims investigator Civil and Human Rights Clinic, 1999; law clk. Sabel & Sabel, P.C., Montgomery, Ala., 1999; litigation clk. Planned Parenthood Fedn. Am., Inc., N.Y.C., 1999—2000, U.S. EEOC, N.Y.C., 2000; assoc. Bernard P. Wolfsdorf, PLC, Pacific Palisades, Calif., 2000—01; mng. atty. Heather L. Poole, PC, PLC, Pasadena, Calif., 2001—. Cons. Stop Violence Grant Office Calif. Poly. Inst., Pomona, 2002. Mem. adv. bd. L.A. Commn. on Assaults Against Women, Pasadena, 2002; vol. atty. Barrister's Domestic Violence Project, Pasadena, 2001—02; legal cons. Domestic Violence Prevention Coalition, Pasadena, 2001—02; mem. workplace domestic violence prevention tng. com. Pasadena-Altadena Domestic Violence Prevention Coailtion, 2001—02; courtroom advocate Domestic Violence Law Sch. Consortium NY, 1999. Mem.: ABA, Women Lawyers Assn. L.A., Pasadena Bar Assn., L.A. County Bar Assn. (family law sect., immigration law sect.), Am. Immigration Lawyers Assn., Nat. Network Behalf of Battered Immigrant Women. Democrat. Immigration, naturalization, and customs, domestic violence, Civil rights. Office: 221 E Walnut Pasadena CA 91101 Fax: 626-599-8260. E-mail: heather@humanrightsattorney.com.

POOLEY, CHRISTOPHER J. lawyer; b. Ann Arbor, Apr. 5, 1963; s. Beverley John and Patricia Joan Pooley. BBA, We. Mich. U., 1989; JD, U. Toledo, 1997. Immigration advisor U. Mich., Ann Arbor, 1991—95; paralegal Shindler Lap & Kendrick, Toledo, 1995—97, atty., 1997—2000, Berry, Appleman & Leiden, San Francisco, 2000—01; solo practitioner Toledo, 2002—. Mem.: Toledo Bar Assn. Criminal, Immigration, naturalization, and customs, Juvenile. Office: 520 Madison Ste 851 Toledo OH 43604

POPE, ANDREW JACKSON, JR., (JACK POPE), retired judge; b. Abilene, Tex., Apr. 18, 1913; s. Andrew Jackson and Ruth Adelia (Taylor) P.; m. Allene Esther Nichols, June 11, 1938; children: Andrew Jackson III, Walter Allen. BA, Abilene Christian U., 1934, LLD (hon.), 1980; LLB, U. Tex., 1937; LLD (hon.), Pepperdine U., 1981, St. Mary's U., San Antonio, 1982, Okla. Christian U., 1983. Bar: Tex. 1937. Practice law Corpus Christi, Corpus Christi, 1937-46; judge 94th Dist. Ct., Corpus Christi, 1946-50; justice Ct. Civil Appeals, San Antonio, 1950-65, Supreme Ct. of Tex., Austin, 1965-82, chief justice, 1982-85. Author: John Berry & His Children, 1988; chmn. bd. editors Appellate Procedure in Tex., 1974; author numerous articles in law revs. and profl. jours. Pres. Met. YMCA, San Antonio, 1956-57; chmn. Tex. State Law Libr. Bd., 1973-80; trustee Abilene Christian U., 1954—. Seaman USNR, 1944-46. Recipient Silver Beaver award Alamo council Boy Scouts Am., 1961, Distinguished Eagle award, 1983; Rosewood Gavel award, 1962, St. Thomas More award, St. Mary's U., San Antonio, 1982; Outstanding Alumnus award Abilene Christian U., 1965; Greenhill Jud. award Mcpl. Judges Assn., 1980; Houston Bar Found. citation, 1985; San Antonio Bar Found. award, 1985; Disting. Jurist award Jefferson County Bar, 1985; Outstanding Alumnus award U. Tex. Law Alumni Assn., 1988; George Washington Honor medal Freedom Found., 1988; Disting. Lawyer award Travis County, 1992. Fellow Tex. Bar Found. (Law Rev. award 1979, 80, 81); mem. ABA, State Bar Tex. (pres. jud. sect. 1962, Outstanding Alumnus U. Tex. Sch. of Law 1994, Outstanding Fifty Years Lawyer award 1994), Tex. Bar Found., Order of Coif, Nueces County Bar Assn. (pres. 1946), Travis County Bar Assn., Bexar County Bar Assn., Tex. Philos. Soc., Austin Knife and Fork (pres. 1980), Am. Judicature Soc., Tex. State Hist. Assn., Tex. Supreme Ct. Hist. Soc. (v.p.), Sons of Republic of Tex., Statesmanship award State Bar Tex., 1998, Christian Chronicle Coun. (chmn.), Masons, K.P. (grand chancellor 1946), Alpha Chi, Phi Delta Phi, Pi Sigma Alpha. Mem. Ch. of Christ. Home: 2803 Stratford Dr Austin TX 78746-4626

POPE, CHARLES WILSON, JR., prosecutor; b. Knoxville, Tenn., Apr. 18, 1970; s. Charles Wilson and Jean Cook Pope; m. Shauna Adams Pope, May 30, 1998; children: Bryce Daniel Adams, Bradleigh Elizabeth Adams, Charles W. III, Allyson Jane. Bachelor Degree summa cum laude, U. Tenn., 1993; JD, Regent U., 1996. Bar: Tenn. 1998, U.S. Dist. Ct. Tenn. 1998. Assoc. atty. Kennedy Law Firm, Clarksville, Tenn., 1998—99; ast. dist. atty. gen. Office of Dist. Atty., Athens, Tenn., 1999—. Tchr. Police Acad. Cleveland (Tenn.) State C.C., 2001. Active Christ Cmty. Ch., Athens, 2001—02. Recipient Trial Advocacy award, Va. Trial Lawyers Assn., 1996. Mem.: Alliance Def. Fund (affiliate), Tenn. Bar Assn., Nat. Dist. Attys. Assn., Optimist Club. Republican. Evangelical. Avocations: reading, hunting, fishing, fitness. Home: 153 CR 142 Riceville TN 37370 Office: Office Dist Atty Gen 130 NE Washington Ave Athens TN 37303

POPE, MARK ANDREW, lawyer, university administrator; b. Munster, Ind., May 22, 1952; s. Thomas A. and Eleanor E. (Miklos) P.; m. Julia Risk Pope, June 15, 1974; children: Brent Andrew, Bradley James. BA, Purdue U., 1974; JD cum laude, Ind. U., 1977. Bar: Ind. 1977, U.S. Dist. Ct. (so. dist.) Ind. 1977, U.S. Ct. Appeals (7th cir.) 1984. Assoc. Johnson & Weaver, Indpls., 1977-79, Rocap, Rocap, Reese & Young, Indpls., 1980-82, Dutton & Overman, Indpls., 1982-88, ptnr., 1988-89; asst. gen. counsel Lincoln Nat. Corp., Fort Wayne, Ind., 1989-91, sr. counsel, 1991-95, v.p. govt. rels., 1995-2001; dir. athletics Ind. U.-Purdue U., Ft. Wayne, 2001—. Bd. dirs. Ft. Wayne Bicentennial Coun.; pres., bd. dirs. ARCH, Inc., 1994-97. Bd. editors, devel. editor Ind. U. Law Rev., 1976-77 Mem. pres.'s coun. Purdue U., 1977—; applied econs. cons. Jr. Achievement, 1989—95; bd. dirs. Jr. Achievement of No. Ind., 1992—94; grad. Leadership Ft. Wayne, 1992;

adv. coun. Ind. U. Bus. Sch., Purdue U., Ft. Wayne, 2000—02; trustee Allen County War Meml. Coliseum, 2002—; mem. parish coun. St. Elizabeth Ann Seton Ch., 1993—96, pres., 1993—95; bd. edn. mem. Bishop Luers H.S., 2000—03, pres., 2002—03. Named Disting. Hoosier, Gov. of Ind., 1974. Fellow Ind. Bar Found., Indpls. Bar Found. (disting.); mem. ABA (dist. rep. young lawyers divsn. 1981-83, dir. 1983-84, liaison coord. 1985-86, 87-88, exec. coun. 1981-88, cabinet 1982-88, gen. practice sect. coun. mem. 1986—, membership chmn. 1987-89, chmn. career and family com. 1990-92, dir. 1991-93), Indpls. Bar Assn. (v.p. 1983, chmn. young lawyers divsn. 1981), 500 Festival Assocs. (vice-chmn. of 500 festival parade 1985-89), Orchard Ridge Country Club (bd. dirs. 1995-2001, sec. 1996-97, pres. 1999-2001). Avocations: tennis, golf, running. Education and schools, General civil litigation, Commercial, contracts (including sales of goods; commercial financing). Office: Ind U-Purdue U at Fort Wayne Gates Sports Ctr 2101 E Coliseum Blvd Fort Wayne IN 46805-1499 E-mail: popem@ipfw.edu.

POPE, MICHAEL ARTHUR, lawyer; b. Chgo., June 27, 1944; s. Arthur Wellington and Phyllis Anne (O'Connor) P.; m. Christine Collins, Nov. 19, 1966; children: Jennifer, Amy, Katherine. BS, Loyola U., Chgo., 1966; JD cum laude, Northwestern U., 1969. Bar: Ill. 1969, N.Y. 1985, U.S. Dist. Ct. (no. dist.) Ill. 1969, U.S. Ct. Appeals (7th cir.) 1970, U.S. Supreme Ct. 1980. Tchg. asst. U. Ill. Coll. Law, Champaign, 1969-70; assoc. Isham, Lincoln & Beale, Chgo., 1970-76; ptnr. Phelan, Pope & John, Ltd., Chgo., prin., 1976—95; capital ptnr. McDermott, Will & Emery, Chgo., 1995—. Adj. prof. law Chgo.-Kent Law Sch. Ill. Inst. Tech., 1982-85; chmn. bd. trustees Nat. Jud. Coll., 2002-03. Mem. ABA, Ill. Bar Assn., Chgo. Bar Assn., Am. Bd. Profl. Liability Attys. (pres. 1985-87), 7th Cir. Bar Assn. (1st v.p.), Internat. Assn. Def. Counsel (pres. 1993-94), Internat. Soc. Barristers, Am. Coll. Trial Lawyers, Internat. Acad. Trial Lawyers, Am. Law Inst., Econ. Club Chgo., The Chgo. Club, Skokie Country Club (Glencoe Ill.), East Bank Club (Chgo.). General civil litigation, Environmental, Insurance. Office: McDermott Will & Emery 227 W Monroe St Ste 3100 Chicago IL 60606-5096 E-mail: mpope@mwe.com.

POPE, PATRICK HARRIS, lawyer, business executive; b. Dunn, NC, Aug. 27, 1944; s. Claude Efton and Rochelle Olive (Jackson) P.; m. Mary Norfleet Tilghman, Aug. 21, 1965; children: Patrick Tilghman, Wiley Jackson, Caroline Denning. BS in Bus. Adminstrn., U. N.C., 1966, JD with honors, 1969. Bar: N.C. 1969, U.S. Dist. Ct. (ea. dist.) N.C. 1969. Ptnr. Doffermyre & Pope, Dunn, 1969-72; sr. ptnr. Pope & Tart and predecessor firms, Dunn, 1972—. Bd. dirs. Master Developers, Inc. Rsch. editor N.C. Law Rev., 1969; contbr. articles to profl. jours. Bd. dirs. Gen. William C. Lee Meml. Commn., Inc., Dunn, 1983—; trustee Betsy Johnson Regional Hosp., Inc., Dunn, 1977-82, 96-2001, vice-chmn., 1983-84, 99-2001, chmn., 1984. Mem. N.C. Bar Assn., N.C. State Bar, Hartnett County Bar Assn. (pres. 1974-75), 11th Jud. Dist. Bar Assn. (pres. 1974-75, v.p. 1973-74), N.C. Acad. Trial Lawyers, Order of Coif, Masons. Republican. Presbyterian. State civil litigation, General practice, Personal injury (including property damage). Home: 208 W Pearsall St Dunn NC 28334-5236 Office: Pope & Tart 403 W Broad St Dunn NC 28334-4807

POPE, ROBERT DANIEL, lawyer; b. Screven, Ga., Nov. 29, 1948; s. Robert Verlyn and Mae (McKey) P.; children: Robert Daniel Jr., Veronica Teres, Jonathan Chase, Byron Christopher, Jessica Victoria. BS in Criminal Justice magna cum laude, Valdosta (Ga.) State Coll., 1975; JD, John Marshall Law Sch., Savannah, Ga., 1980. Bar: Ga. 1981, U.S. Dist. Ct. (no., mid. and so. dist.) Ga. 1983, U.S. Ct. Appeals Ga. 1982. Pvt. practice, Cartersville, 1981—. Mem. Valdosta Indigent Def. Atty. Panel, 1981-83, Bartow County Indigent Def. Panel, Cartersville, 1987-91, So. Dist. of Ga. Indigent Def. Panel, Brunswick, 1982-84; mem. Cobb County Cir. Defender's Panel for Indigent Criminal Def., Marietta, Ga., 1986— Recognized as one of most successful criminal def. lawyers Cobb County Cir. Defenders Office, 1994. Mem. Ga. Assn. Criminal Def. Lawyers, Ga. Bar Assn. (criminal law sect.), Am. Criminal Justice Orgn. (Valdosta chpt. pres. 1974-75). Criminal, Personal injury (including property damage), Product liability. Home: 74 Spruce Ln SE Cartersville GA 30121-7643 Office: PO Box 1043 Acworth GA 30101

POPE, WILLIAM L. lawyer, judge; b. Brownsville, Tex., Nov. 5, 1960; s. William E. and Maria Antonieta P.; m. Sandra Solis, May 16, 1992; children: Ana Lauren, William E.H. AA, Tex. Southmost Coll., 1980; postgrad., U. Tex., 1980-81, Tex. Christian U., 1982, Tex. Coll. Osteo. Medicine, 1982-83; JD, Baylor U., 1986; MD (hon.), Cosmopolitan U. & Rsch. Inst., Vina del Mar, Chile, 1998. Bar: Tex. 1986, U.S. Dist. Ct. (so. dist.) Tex. 1988, U.S. Supreme Ct. 1990. Assoc. Adams & Graham, Harlingen, Tex., 1986-91, ptnr., 1991—; mcpl. ct. judge City of La Feria, Tex., 1987—. Bd. trustees Episcopal Day Sch., Brownsville, Tex., 1999—2000. Mem.: Cameron County Bar Assn., Am. Coll. Legal Medicine, Tex. State Bar Assn. (mem. judiciary rels. com. 1999—). Ch. Of Christ. General civil litigation, Health, Professional liability. Office: Adams & Graham L L P PO Drawer 1429 Harlingen TX 78551-1429 E-mail: Pope@adamsgraham.com.

POPKIN, ALICE BRANDEIS, lawyer; b. N.Y.C. d. Jacob H. and Susan Brandeis Gilbert; m. Jordan J. Popkin; children: Susan Cahn, Anne, Louisa. AB magna cum laude, Radcliffe Coll., 1949; JD, Yale U., 1953. Bar: N.Y. 1953, U.S. Dist. Ct. (so. dist.) N.Y. 1956, U.S. Ct. Appeals (2nd cir.) 1959, U.S. Supreme Ct. 1962, D.C. 1972, Mass. 1987. Assoc. Cahill Gordon & Reindel, 1953—61; dir. internat. programs Peace Corps, 1961—63; project co-dir. Georgetown Inst. Criminal Law and Procedure, 1967—72; spl. counsel Senate Sub-Com. to Investigate Juvenile Delinquency, 1972—74; atty., prof. Antioch Sch. Law, 1974—77; assoc. adminstr. EPA, 1977—79; pvt. practice cons. on internat. environ. issues, 1979—81; practicing atty., 1981—87; of counsel Toabe and Riley, Chatham, Mass., 1987—. Fellow Brandeis U.; bd. trustees Radcliffe Coll.; mem. Chatham Harbor Mgmt. Com.; trustee Eldredge Pub. Libr., 1994—. Mem. ABA, Mass. Bar Assn., Barnstable County Bar Assn., Estate Planning Coun. Cape Cod, Planned Giving Coun. Cape Cod. Office: Toabe & Riley Box 707 154 Crowell Rd Chatham MA 02633-2800

POPOFSKY, MELVIN LAURENCE, lawyer; b. Oskaloosa, Iowa, Feb. 16, 1936; s. Samuel and Fannye Charlotte (Rosenthal) P.; m. Linda Jane Seltzer, Nov. 25, 1962; children: Mark Samuel, Kaye Sylvia. BA in History summa cum laude, U. Iowa, 1958; BA in Jurisprudence (first class honors), Oxford U., Eng., 1960; LLB cum laude, Harvard U., 1962. Bar: Calif. 1962. Assoc. Heller, Ehrman, White & McAuliffe, San Francisco, 1962-69, ptnr., 1969—, mem. exec. com., 1980-93, co-chair, 1988-93. Contbr. articles to law jours. Bd. dirs. Mt. Zion Hosp., San Francisco, 1982-88, U.S. Dist. Ct. (no. dist.) Calif. Hist. Soc., 1988—, Jewish Home for Aged, San Francisco, 1989-96, Golden Gate U., 1997-2000, Jewish Cmty. Fedn., 1997-2001. Recipient Anti-Defamation League's Disting. Jurisprudence award, 2000; named State Bar of Calif. Antitrust Lawyer of the Yr., 2000; Rhodes scholar, 1958. Fellow Am. Bar Found., Am. Coll. Trial Lawyers; mem. ABA, Calif. Bar Assn., San Francisco Bar Assn., Bur. Nat. Affairs (adv. bd. antitrust sect.), Calif. Acad. Appellate Lawyers. Democrat. Jewish. Antitrust, Federal civil litigation, General civil litigation. Home: 1940 Broadway Apt 10 San Francisco CA 94109-2216 Office: Heller Ehrman 333 Bush St Ste 3000 San Francisco CA 94104-2834

POPPLER, DORIS SWORDS, lawyer; b. Billings, Mont., Nov. 10, 1924; d. Lloyd William and Edna (Mowre) Swords; m. Louis E. Poppler, June 11, 1949; children: Louis William, Kristine, Mark J., Blaine, Claire, Arminda. Student, U. Minn., 1942-44; JD, Mont. State U., 1948. Bar: Mont. 1948, U.S. Dist. Ct. Mont. 1948, U.S. Ct. Appeals (9th cir.) 1990. Pvt. practice law, Billings, 1948-49; sec., treas. Wonderpark Corp., Billings, 1959-62; atty. Yellowstone County Attys. Office, Billings, 1972-75; ptnr. Poppler and Barz, Billings, 1972-79, Davidson, Veeder, Baugh, Broeder and Poppler, Billings, 1979-84, Davidson and Poppler, P.C., Billings, 1984-90; U.S. atty. Dist. of Mont., Billings, 1990-93; field rep. Nat. Indian Gaming Commn., Washington, 1993-2000. Pres. Jr. League, 1964-65; bd. dirs., pres. Yellowstone County Metre Bd., 1982; trustee Rocky Mt. Coll., 1984-90, mem. nat. adv. bd., 1993—; mem. Mont. Human Rights Commn., 1988-90; bd. dirs. Miss Mont. Pageant, 1995—; elected to Billings City Coun., Billings, Mont., 2002; elected dep. mayor coun. woman Ward4, 2002—. Recipient Mont. Salute to Women award, Mont. Woman of Achievent award, 1975, Disting. Svc. award Rocky Mt. Coll., 1990, 1st ann. U. Montana Law Sch. Disting. Female Alumna award, 1996. Mem. AAUW, Mont. Bar Assn., Nat. Assn. Former U.S. Attys., Nat. Rep. Lawyers Assn., Internat. Women's Forum, Yellowstone County Bar Assn. (pres. 1990), Alpha Chi Omega. Republican.

PORFILIO, JOHN CARBONE, federal judge; b. Denver, Oct. 14, 1934; s. Edward Alphonso Porfilio and Caroline (Carbone) Moore; m. Joan West, Aug. 1, 1959 (div. 1983); children: Edward Miles, Joseph Arthur, Jeanne Kathrine; m. Theresa Louise Berger, Dec. 28, 1983; 1 stepchild, Katrina Ann Smith. Student, Stanford U., 1952—54; BA, U. Denver, 1956, LLB, 1959, LLD (hon.) , 2000. Bar: Colo. 1959, U.S. Supreme Ct. 1965. Asst. atty. gen. State of Colo., Denver, 1962—68, dep. atty. gen., 1968—72, atty. gen., 1972—74; U.S. bankruptcy judge Dist. of Colo., Denver, 1975—82; judge U.S. Dist. Ct. Colo., Denver, 1982—85, U.S. Ct. Appeals (10th cir.), Denver, 1985—99, sr. judge, 1999—. Instr. Colo. Law Enforcement Acad., Denver, 1965—70, State Patrol Acad., Denver, 1968—70; guest lectr. U. Denver Coll. Law, 1978. Committeeman Arapahoe County Rep. Com., Aurora, Colo., 1968; mgr. Dunbar for Atty. Gen., Denver, 1970. Mem.: ABA. Roman Catholic. Office: US Ct Appeals Byron White US Courthouse 1823 Stout St Denver CO 80257-1823

PORITZ, DEBORAH T. state supreme court chief justice, former attorney general; b. 1936; BA Brooklyn Coll., City U. of NY, JD U. Penn. Atty. gen. State of N.J., 1994—96; chief justice Supreme Ct. N.J., Trenton, 1996—. Office: Supreme Ct NJ Hughes Justice Complex PO Box 23 Trenton NJ 08625-0023*

PORTEOUS, G. THOMAS, JR., judge; b. 1946; BA, La. State U., 1968, JD, 1971. Spl. counsel, atty. gen., 1971-73; asst. dist. atty. Dist. Atty. Office Parrish of Jefferson, 1973-75; ptnr. Edward, Porteous & Amato, Grenta, La., 1973-74, Edwards, Porteous & Lee, Grenta, 1974-76, Porteous, Lee & Mustakas, 1976-80, Porteous & Mustakas, Metairie, La., 1980-84; city atty. City of Harahan, La., 1982-84; dist. ct. judge divsn. A State of La., 1984-94; dist. judge U.S. Dist. Ct. (ea. dist.), La., 1994—. Mem. ABA, Fed. Bar Assn., La. State Bar Assn., 4th and 5th Cir. Judges Assn., Jefferson Bar Assn., Am. Judges Assn., La. Dist. Atty. Assn. Office: US Dist Ct E Dist 500 Camp St Rm C-206 New Orleans LA 70130-3313

PORTER, CHARLES RALEIGH, JR., retired lawyer; b. Waco, Tex., Sept. 22, 1922; s. Charles Raleigh and Virginia Louise (Bowen) P.; m. Alice Mungall, Sept. 16, 1946; children: Charles Raleigh III, Melissa Ann, Alice Marguerite, Daniel Bowen. BBA, U. Tex., 1943, JD, 1949. Bar: Tex. 1948, U.S. Dist. Ct. (so. dist.) Tex. 1949, U.S. Ct. Appeals (5th cir.) 1955, U.S. Dist. Ct. (we. dist.) Tex. 1972, U.S. Dist. Ct. (no. dist.) Tex. 1977. Asst. Nueces County Attys. Office, Corpus Christi, Tex., 1949-50, Dist. Attys. Office, Corpus Christi, 1950-53; ptnr. Anderson & Porter, Corpus Christi, 1953-63, Sorrell, Anderson & Porter, 1964-68, Porter, Rogers, Dahlman & Gordon, 1969-92; ret., 1992. Mem. adv. bd. dirs. Frost Nat. Bank, San Antonio. Past mem. exec. bd. Perkins Sch. Theology, So. Meth. U.; past chairperson adminstrv. bd. First United Meth. Ch.; mem. chancellor's com. U. Tex.; past mem. adv. bd. U. Tex. Marine Sci. Inst.; active Dean's Roundtable, U. Tex. Sch. Law, 2001; Past mem. bd. dirs. Meth. Home, Waco. Mem.: Spanish Oaks Golf Club, Spanish Oaks Golf Club (Austin, Tex.), Rockport Country Club, Scottish Rite, Masons. Banking, State civil litigation, Oil, gas, and mineral. Home: 33 Blue Heron Dr Rockport TX 78382-3771 E-mail: crockport@aol.com.

PORTER, CHEAIRS MAYES, lawyer; b. Birmingham, Ala., May 20, 1970; BA in English, Birmingham So. Coll., 1992; JD, U. Ala., Tuscaloosa, 1996; LLM in Health Law, DePaul U., 2001. Bar: Ala. 1996, U.S. Dist. Ct. (mid. dist.) Ala. 1996. Asst. dist. atty. Montgomery (Ala.) County Dist. Atty., 1997—2000; atty. Kaufman & Rothfeder, P.C., Montgomery, 2001—. Mem. health care task force Envision 20/20, Montgomery, 2002. Mem.: Montgomery County Bar Assn., Ala. Bar Assn., Am. Health Lawyers Assn. Avocations: running, golf, hunting, writing. Health, Administrative and regulatory, Criminal. Office: Kaufman and Rothfeder PC 2740 Zelda Rd Montgomery AL 36106 Office Fax: 334-244-1969. Business E-Mail: cporter@krlegal.com.

PORTER, JAMES KENNETH, retired judge; b. Newport, Tenn., Apr. 6, 1934; s. John Calhoun and Bessie Betis (Crouch) P.; m. Evelyn Janet Rhodes, Sept. 17, 1955; children: Jane Caroline, James Kenneth Jr. BS, U. Tenn., 1955, JD, 1957. Bar: Tenn. 1957, U.S. Dist. Ct. (ea. dist.) Tenn. 1958, U.S. Ct. Appeals (6th cir.) 1971. Ptnr. Porter, Porter & Dunn, Porter & Porter, Newport, 1957-74; state rep. Tenn. Gen. Assembly, Nashville, 1961-65, minority fl. leader, 1963-65; county atty. Cocke County, Tenn., 1961-63, commr. County Election Commn., 1966-72, chmn., 1968-70; mem. Tenn. Senate, Nashville, 1972-74; state cir. judge 4th Jud. Cir., Newport, 1974-93; ret., 1993; state presiding judge 4th Jud. Cir., Newport, 1984-86, 88-90, 1992-93; judgeship nominee U.S. Dist. Ct. (ea. dist.), Tenn., 1986; Tenn. Ct. Appeals nominee, 1990. Del. S.E. Law Rev. Conf., Durham, N.C., 1957, Nat. Conf. State Legislator Leaders, Boston, 1963; discussion leader Nat. Jud. Coll., Reno, 1981, faculty adviser, 1982; mem. Gov.'s Correction Overcrowding Commn., Nashville, 1985-86. Contbr. articles to U. Tenn. Law Rev., 1956-57, editor in chief, 1957. Active Farm Bur., 1962-82; mem. adv. coun., trustee Walters State Community Coll., Morristown, Tenn., 1975-86. Mem. ABA (Tenn. jud. del. 1984), Tenn. Jud. Conf. (v.p. 1980-81), Tenn. Trial Judges Assn. (bd. dirs. 1976-86, pres. 1982-85), Tenn. Bar Assn. (spl. trial counsel 1973-76), Cocke County Bar Assn., Smoky Mountain Country Club (bd. dirs. 1964-67, v.p. 1966-67), Order of Coif, Sigma Alpha Epsilon (Highest Effort Law award 1986), Phi Delta Phi. Republican. Baptist. Avocations: golf, gardening, guitar. Home: 306 North St Newport TN 37821-2413 Office: 106 S Mims Ave Newport TN 37821-3125 E-mail: porterk@planetc.com.

PORTER, JAMES MORRIS, retired judge; b. Cleve., Sept. 14, 1931; s. Emmett Thomas and Mary (Connell) P.; m. Helen Marie Adams, May 31, 1952; children: James E., Thomas W., William M., Daniel J. AB, John Carroll U., 1953; JD, U. Mich., 1957. Bar: Ohio 1957. Assoc. firm M.B. & H.H. Johnson, Cleve., 1957-62, McAfee, Hanning, Newcomer, Hazlett & Wheeler, Cleve., 1962-67; ptnr. firm Squire, Sanders & Dempsey, Cleve., 1967-92; judge Ohio Ct. Appeals, 8th Dist., Cleve., 1993-2000, Cuyahoga County Common Pleas Ct., Cleve., 2001. 1st lt. U.S. Army, 1953-55. Fellow Am. Coll. Trial Lawyers; mem. The Country Club (Cleve.). Republican. Roman Catholic.

PORTER, MICHAEL PELL, lawyer; b. Indpls., Mar. 31, 1940; s. Harold Troxel and Mildred Maxine (Pell) P.; m. Alliene Laura Jenkins, Sept. 23, 1967 (div.); 1 child, Genevieve Natalie Porter Eason; m. Janet Kay Smith Hayes, Feb. 13, 1983 (div.). Student, DePauw U., 1957-58; BA, Tulane U., 1961, LLB, 1963. Bar: La. 1963, U.S. Ct. Mil. Appeals 1964, N.Y. 1969, Hawaii 1971. Clk. U.S. Ct. Appeals (5th cir.), New Orleans, 1963; assoc. Sullivan & Cromwell, N.Y.C., 1968-71, Cades Schutte Fleming & Wright, Honolulu, 1971-74, ptnr., 1975-94; mem. faculty Addis Ababa (Ethiopia) U. Sch. Law, 1995-99; sr. regulatory advisor Egyptian Capital Market Authority, Cairo, 1999—2002; advisor capital market Palestinian Nat. Authority, 2002—03. Legal advisor St. Matthews Anglican Ch. Addis Ababa, 1995-99; cons. Rep. of Yemen, 1997; mem. deans coun. Law Sch. Tulane U., 1981-88; dep. vice chancellor Episcopal Diocese Hawaii, 1980-88, chancellor, 1988-94; chancellor Episcopal Ch., Micronesia, 1988-95. Author: Hawaii Corporation Law & Practice, 1989; Hawaii reporter State Limited Partnership Laws, 1992-94. Bd. dirs. Jr. Achievement Hawaii, Inc., 1974-84, Inst. Human Svcs., Inc., 1980-88; donor Michael P. Porter Dean's Scholastic Award, U. Hawaii Law Sch., 1977—. With JAGC, U.S. Army, 1963-66, Vietnam. Fulbright scholar, 1997-99; Tulane U. fellow, 1981; lectorship named in his honor, Addis Abba, 1994-97; established Michael P. Porter Prizes on Ethnic Harmony and Religious Tolerance in a Dem. Soc. at Addis Ababa, 1995. Mem. ABA, Hawaii State Bar Assn. Republican. Corporate, general, Securities. E-mail: porterconsultant@yahoo.com.

PORTER, ROBERT CARL, JR., lawyer; b. Cin., Sept. 21, 1927; s. Robert Carl and Lavinia (Otte) P.; m. Joanne Patterson, July 5, 1952; children: Robert Carl III, David M., John E. BA with distinction, U. Mich., 1949; JD, Harvard U., 1952. Bar: Ohio 1952, U.S. Dist. Ct. (so. dist.) Ohio 1954, U.S. Ct. Appeals (6th cir.) 1954, U.S. Ct. Mil. Appeals 1956, U.S. Tax Ct. 1980, U.S. Supreme Ct. 1956. Ptnr. Porter & Porter, Cin., 1953-54; sole practice Cin., 1954-63; sr. ptnr. Porter & McKinney, Cin., 1963-88, Porter & Porter, Cin., 1989—. Dir. and officer numerous cos. Served with JAGC, USAF, 1952-53. Mem. ABA, Ohio State Bar Assn., Cin. Bar Assn., Cin. Country Club, Univ. Club, U. Mich. Club, Harvard Law Sch. Assn., Masons, Scottish Rite, Shriners, Phi Beta Kappa. Presbyterian. Corporate, general, Probate (including wills, trusts), Taxation, general. Home: 2365 Bedford Ave Cincinnati OH 45208-2656 Office: Porter & Porter 2100 4th and Vine Tower Cincinnati OH 45202

PORTER, VERNA LOUISE, lawyer; b. May 31, 1941; BA, Calif. State U., 1963; JD, Southwestern U., 1977. Bar: Calif. 1977, U.S. Dist. Ct. (ctrl. dist.) Calif. 1978, U.S. Ct. Appeals (9th cir.) 1978. Ptnr. Eisler & Porter, L.A., 1978-79, mng. ptnr., 1979-86; pvt. practice, 1986—. Judge pro-tempore L.A. Mcpl. Ct., 1983—, L.A. Superior Ct., 1989—, Beverly HIlls Mcpl. Ct., 1992—; mem. subcom. landlord tenant law, State Calif., panelist conv.; mem. real property law sect. Calif. State Bar, 1983; mem. client rels. panel, vol. L.A. County Bar Dispute Resolution; ct. appointed arbitrator civil cases, fee arbitrator L.A. Superior Ct.; mem. Better Bus. Bur. Abitrator Automobile Lemon Laws, 2000—. Editl. asst., contbr. Apt. Bus. Outlook, Real Property News, Apt. Age. Mem. adv. coun. Freddie Mac Vendor, 1995—; mem. World Affairs Coun. Mem. ABA, L.A. County Bar Assn. (client-rels. vol. dispute resolution fee arbitration 1981—; arbitrator lemon law claims), L.A. Trial Lawyers Assn., Wilshire Bar Assn. Women Lawyers' Assn., Landlord Trial Lawyers Assn. (founding, pres.), Da Camera Soc. Republican. Commercial, consumer (including collections, credit), Landlord-tenant, Property, real (including real estate development, water). Office: 2500 Wilshire Blvd Ste 1226 Los Angeles CA 90057-4365

PORTMAN, GLENN ARTHUR, lawyer; b. Cleve., Dec. 26, 1949; s. Alvin B. and Lenore (Marsh) P.; m. Katherine Seaborn, Aug. 3, 1974 (div. 1984); m. Susan Newell, Jan. 3, 1987. BA in History, Case Western Res. U., 1968; JD, So. Meth. U., 1975. Bar: Tex. 1975, U.S. Dist. Ct. (no. dist.) Tex. 1975, U.S. Dist. Ct. (so. dist.) Tex. 1983, U.S. Dist. Ct. (we. and ea. dists.) Tex. 1988. Assoc. Johnson, Bromberg & Leeds, Dallas, 1975-80, ptnr., 1980-92, Arter, Hadden, Johnson & Bromberg, Dallas, 1992-95, Arter & Hadden LLP, Dallas, 1996—. Chmn. bd. dirs. Physicians Regional Hosp., 1994-96; mem. exec. bd. So. Meth. U. Sch. Law, 1994—; lectr. bankruptcy topics South Tex. Coll. Law, State Bar Tex.; mem. vis. com. Coll. Arts and Scis., Case Western Res. U., 1999—. Asst. editor-in-chief Southwestern Law Jour., 1974-75; contbr. articles to profl. jours. Firm rep. United Way Met. Dallas, 1982-92; treas. Lake Highlands Square Homeowners Assn., 1990-93. Mem. ABA, Am. Bankruptcy Inst., State Bar Tex. Assn., Dallas Bar Assn., So. Meth. U. Law Alumni Assn. (council bd. dirs., v.p. 1980-86, chmn. admissions com., chmn. class agt. program 1986-89, chmn. fund raising 1989-91), 500 Club Inc., Assemblage Club. Republican. Methodist. Bankruptcy, Commercial, contracts (including sales of goods; commercial financing), Property, real (including real estate development, water). Home: 9503 Winding Ridge Dr Dallas TX 75238-1451 Office: Arter & Hadden LLP 1717 Main St Ste 4100 Dallas TX 75201-7389 E-mail: g.portman@att.net., gportman@anterhadden.com.

PORTNOY, SARA S. lawyer; b. N.Y.C., Jan. 11, 1926; d. Marcus and Gussie (Raphael) Spiro; m. Alexander Portnoy, Dec. 13, 1959 (dec. 1976); children: William, Lawrence. BA, Radcliffe Coll., 1946; LLB, Columbia U., 1949. Bar: N.Y. 1949, U.S. Dist. Ct. (so. dist.) N.Y. 1952, U.S. Dist. Ct. (eas. dist.) N.Y. 1975, U.S. Ct. Appeals (2d cir.) 1975, U.S. Supreme Ct. 1975. Assoc. Seligsberg, Friedman & Berliner, N.Y.C., 1949-51; atty. AT&T, N.Y.C., 1951-61; vol. atty. Legal Aid Soc. of Westchester, N.Y., 1966-74; assoc. Proskauer Rose Goetz & Mendelsohn, N.Y.C., 1974-78, ptnr., 1978-94; ret., 1994. Mem. Commn. on Human Rights, White Plains, N.Y., 1973-78; mem. bd. visitors Columbia Law Sch., 1996—; bd. dirs. Legal Aid Soc. of Westchester County, N.Y., 1975-83, Columbia Law Sch. Assn., 1990-94, Mosholu Montifiore Cmty. Ctr., 1998—; mem. Pres.'s Coun. Yaddo; dir. Muscular Dystrophy Assn., 2000—. Mem. Assn. Bar City of N.Y. (chair com. legal support staff 1994, mem. Com. on Homeless, Sr. Lawyer's Com. and Pub. Svc. Network), South Fork Country Club (dir. 1997—), The Children's Storefront (dir. 1998—). Civil rights, Labor (including EEOC, Fair Labor Standards Act, labor-management relations, NLRB, OSHA), Pension, profit-sharing, and employee benefits.

POSCOVER, MAURY B. lawyer; b. St. Louis, Jan. 13, 1944; s. Edward and Ann (Chapnick) P.; m. Lorraine Wexler, Aug. 14, 1966; children: Michael, Daniel, Joanna. BA, Lehigh U., 1966; JD, Washington U., 1969. Bar: Mo. 1969. Assoc. Husch & Eppenberger LLC, St. Louis, 1969-75, ptnr., mem., 1975—. Lectr. Washington U., St. Louis, 1972—79. Editor-in-chief: The Business Lawyer, 1995-96; contbr. articles to profl. jours. Bd. dirs. Childhaven, St. Louis, 1978-92, pres. 1986; pres. Jewish Community Rels. Coun., 1990-92. Mem.: Am.-Israel C. of C. (pres. 2000—02, chair 2002—), Wash. U. Alumni Law Assn. (pres. 1980—81), Am. Judicature Soc. (dir. 1981—87), Mo. Bar Assn. (bd. govs. 1979—81), Bar Assn. Met. St. Louis (pres. 1983—84), ABA (chair bus. law sect. 1997—98, bd. govs. 1999—2002, mem. exec. com. bd. govs. 2001—02, chair ops. and comms. com. 2001—02, chmn. comml. fin. svcs. com. bus. law sect. coun., editor-in-chief jour.). Jewish. Banking, Commercial, contracts (including sales of goods; commercial financing), Corporate, general. Office: Husch & Eppenberger LLC 190 Carondelet Plz Ste 600 Saint Louis MO 63105-3441 E-mail: maury.poscover@husch.com.

POSEN, RICHARD L. lawyer; b. N.Y.C., May 26, 1950; AB, Johns Hopkins U., 1972; JD, NYU, 1975. Bar: N.Y. 1976. Mem. Willkie, Farr & Gallagher, N.Y.C. Artilces editor Annual Survey Am. Law, 1974-75. Mem. ABA, Assn. of Bar of City of N.Y. Office: Willkie Farr & Gallagher 787 7th Ave New York NY 10019-6018

POSEN, SUSAN ORZACK, lawyer; b. N.Y.C., Nov. 5, 1945; BA, Sarah Lawrence Coll., 1967; JD, Bklyn. Law Sch., 1978. Bar: N.Y. 1979. Assoc. Stroock & Stroock & Lavan, N.Y.C., 1978-83, 84-86; ptnr. Stroock, Stroock & Lavan, LLP, N.Y.C., 1987-2000; asst. gen. counsel Cablevision Systems Corp., Woodbury, N.Y., 1983-84; co-founder, ptnr. DIVA Capital LLC, N.Y.C., 2000—01; CEO Outspoke LLC, 2001—. Corporate, general, Mergers and acquisitions, Securities. Office: Outspoke LLC 13-17 Laight St New York NY 10013

POSGAY, MATTHEW NICHOLS, lawyer; b. Ft. Lauderdale, Fla., Sept. 23, 1970; s. Raymond Joseph and Mary Lynn P. BA in Polit. Sci., U. Fla., 1991, JD, 1994. Bar: Fla. 1995, U.S. Dist. Ct. (mid. dist.) Fla. Shareholder

Kubicki Draper, Jacksonville, Fla., 1995—. Bd. dirs. Family Farm of N.E. Fla. Mem. Fla. Bar Spkrs. Bur., 1997—. Mem. Fla. Bar Assn., Jacksonville Bar Assn., Fla. Defense Lawyers Assn., Defense Rsch. Inst., U. Fla. Coll. Law Alumni Assn., Phi Alpha Delta, Phi Kappa Phi, Sigma Phi Epsilon, Fla. Blue Key. Avocations: scuba diving, rowing. General civil litigation, Insurance, Product liability. Office: 1650 Prudential Dr Ste 110 Jacksonville FL 32207 E-mail: mp@kubickidraper.com.

POSHTAKOVA, DORA HRISTOVA, lawyer; b. Sofia, Bulgaria, Jan. 2, 1973; d. Hristo Dimitrov Poshtakov and Nadia Tsvetanova Poshtakova. LLM, St. Kliment Ohridski U. , 1996; BA in Econs. (hon.) , St. Kliment Ohridski U., 1996. Bar: Sofia. Lawyer IKRP Rokas and Partners, Sofia, 1997—2001; staff atty. Judicial Devel. Project USAID , Sofia, 2001; office mgr. and sr. lawyer Hayhurst, Berlad, Robinson, Sofia, 2001—. Atty. Sofia (Bulgaria) Arbitration Ct. Banking, Bankruptcy, Commercial, contracts (including sales of goods; commercial financing). Home: 145 G Rakovski Street 1000 Sofia Bulgaria Office: Hayhurst Berlad Robinson 24 Vassil Levski Blvd 1st Floor 1000 Sofia Bulgaria

POSNER, DAVID S. lawyer; b. Pitts., Dec. 27, 1945; s. Mortimer B. and Lillian P.; m. Marilyn Hope Ackerman, Aug. 14, 1966; children: Morton J., Jennifer L. BS, Carnegie Mellon U., 1969; JD, U. Pitts., 1972. Bar: Pa. 1972, U.S. Supreme Ct. 1981. Ct. adminstr. Washington County, Pa., 1972-76, asst. dist. attys., 1976-79; ptnr. Goldfarb & Posner, Washington, Pa., 1979-97, Goldfarb, Posner, Beck, DeHaven & Drewitz, Washington, 1997—. Pres. Pa. Council of Trial Ct. Adminstrs., 1972-76; solicitor Clk. of Cts., Washington, 1983—. Mem. sect. 85 YMCA, Washington, 1980-85; chmn. East Washington Zoning Hearing Bd., 1992—; bd. dirs. Washington County Redevel. Authority, 2002—, chmn., 2003—; bd. dirs. United Way, Washington, 1979-85; pres. Beth Israel Congregation, 1992-94. With USAR, 1966-72. Mem. ABA, Pa. Bar Assn. (ho. of dels. 1995-97), Washington County Bar Assn. (treas. 1982-83, pres. 1995), B'nai B'rith (past pres.). Banking, Probate (including wills, trusts), Property, real (including real estate development, water). Home: 149 S Wade Ave Washington PA 15301-4926 Office: Goldfarb Posner Beck DeHaven & Drewitz 26 S Main St Ste 200 Washington PA 15301-6812 E-mail: dsp.gpbdd@verizon.net.

POSNER, LOUIS JOSEPH, lawyer, accountant; b. N.Y.C., May 29, 1956; s. Alex Pozner and Hilda G. (Gottlieb) Weinberg; m. Betty F. Osin, June 21, 1986; 1 child, Daniel. BS in Acctg., Drexel U., 1979; MS in Taxation, Pace U., 1985; JD, N.Y. Law Sch., 1989. Bar: N.Y. 1990, N.J. 1990, U.S. Dist. Ct. (so. and ea. dists.) N.Y., 1990, D.C. 1991, U.S. Ct. Appeals (2d cir.) 1993, U.S. Supreme Ct. 1994. Auditor Arthur Andersen & Co., CPAs, Phila., 1979-81; tax sr. Kenneth Leventhal & Co., CPAs, N.Y.C., 1981-82; tax mgr. Mann Judd Landau, CPAs, N.Y.C., 1983-86; tax dir. Integrated Resources, Inc., N.Y.C., 1986-89; pvt. practice, N.Y.C., 1989—. Spkr. in field. Producer, dir. TV show Your Legal Rights. Founder, exec. dir. Voter March, 2000—. Mem.: AICPA, ABA, Nat. Lawyers Guild, N.Y. State Bar Assn. (trusts and estates sect.), Assn. Atty CPA's, N.Y. County Lawyers Assn. (trusts and estates sect.), N.Y. State Soc. CPA's (tax. com. 1985—90, mem. faculty N.Y.C. chpt. Found. for Acctg. Edn. 1989—90), Assn. Bar. City of N.Y., Mensa (coord. spl. interest group N.Y.C. chpt. 1978—99). Bankruptcy, Estate planning, Taxation, general. Home: 160 E 48th St Apt 12T New York NY 10017-1225 Office: 39th Fl 245 Park Ave New York NY 10167 E-mail: lawline@nyc.rr.com.

POSNER, RICHARD ALLEN, federal judge; b. N.Y.C., Jan. 11, 1939; s. Max and Blanche Posner; m. Charlene Ruth Horn, Aug. 13, 1962; children: Kenneth A., Eric A. AB, Yale U., 1959, LLD (hon.) , 1996; LLB, Harvard U., 1962; LLD (hon.) , Syracuse U., 1986; LLD (hon.) , Georgetown U., 1992, U. Pa., 1997; LLD (hon.) , Northwestern, 2001, Aristotle Univ. Thessaloniki, 2002; PhD (hon.) , U. Ghent, 1995, Univ. Athens, 2002. Bar: N.Y. 1963, U.S. Supreme Ct. 1966. Law clk. to Hon. William J. Brennan Jr. U.S. Supreme Ct., Washington, 1962—63; asst. to commr. FTC, Washington, 1963—65; asst. to solicitor gen. U.S. Dept. Justice, Washington, 1965—67; gen. counsel Pres.'s Task Force on Comm. Policy, Washington, 1967—68; assoc. prof. Stanford U. Law Sch., Calif., 1968—69; prof. U. Chgo. Law Sch., 1969—78, Lee and Brena Freeman prof., 1978—81, sr. lectr., 1981—; circuit judge U.S. Ct. Appeals (7th cir.), Chgo., 1981—, chief judge, 1993—2000. Rsch. assoc. Nat. Bur. Econ. Rsch., cambridge, Mass., 1971—81; pres. Lexecon Inc., Chgo., 1977—81. Author: Antitrust Law: An Economic Perspective, 1976, Economic Analysis of Law, 5th edit., 1998, The Economics of Justice, 1981, The Essential Holmes, 1992; author: (with William M. Landes) The Economic Structure of Tort Law, 1987; author: The Problems of Jurisprudence, 1990, Cardozo: A Study in Reputation, 1990, Sex and Reason, 1990, Sex and Reason, 1992; author: (with Tomas J. Philipson) Private Choices and Public Health: The AIDS Epidemic in an Economic Perspective, 1993; author: Overcoming Law, 1995, Aging and Old Age, 1995, The Federal Courts: Challenge and Reform, 1996, Law and Legal Theory in England and America, 1996, Law and Literature, revised and enlarged edit., 1998, The Problematics of Moral and Legal Theory, 1999, An Affair of State: The Investigation, Impeachment, and Trial of President Clinton, 1999, Frontiers of Legal Theory, 2001, Breaking the Deadlock: The 2000 Election, The Constitution, and the Courts, 2001, Antitrust Law, 2d edit., 2001, Public Intellectuals, 2001; pres. Harvard Law Rev., 1961—62, editor Jour. Legal Studies, 1972—81, Am. Law and Econs. Rev., 1999—. Fellow: Am. Acad. Arts and Scis., Brit. Acad., Am. Law Inst.; mem.: Am. Law and Econ. Assn. (pres. 1995—96), Am. Econ. Assn., Century Assn. Office: US Ct Appeals 7th Cir 219 S Dearborn St Chicago IL 60604-1702

POST, BERNARD GERALD, lawyer; b. N.Y.C., Oct. 9, 1942; s. Hyman and Rachel Post. BA, NYU, 1964; JD, Bklyn. Law Sch., 1967. Bar: N.Y. 1968, U.S. Dist. Ct. (so. and ea. dists.) N.Y., U.S. Ct. Appeals (2d cir.). Atty. Feigen Post Holm & Drath, 1988—95, Post & Frank, 1995—99; ptnr. Bernard G. Post, N.Y.C., 1999—. Fellow: Am. Acad. Matrimonial Lawyers (bd. mgrs.); mem.: N.Y. State Bar Assn., Assn. of Bar City of N.Y. (matrimonial law com.), Novac Golf Club. Avocations: golf, sailing, music, art. Family and matrimonial. Office: 950 3rd Ave New York NY 10022

POST, PETER DAVID, lawyer; b. Reading, Pa., Jan. 2, 1947; s. Carl B. and Frances (Gaughan) P.; children: Michael, Elizabeth. BS, Pa. State U., 1968; JD, Harvard U., 1971. Bar: Pa. 1971, La. 1974. Assoc. Reed, Smith, Shaw & McClay, Pitts., 1975-81, ptnr., 1982—, dept. head, 1992—2000. Commr. Upper St. Clair (Pa.) Twp., 1989-93. Lt. USN, 1971-75. Avocations: golf, skiing. Labor (including EEOC, Fair Labor Standards Act, labor-management relations, NLRB, OSHA). Office: Reed Smith Shaw & McClay 435 6th Ave Pittsburgh PA 15219-1886

POST, RUTH-ELLEN, lawyer, educator; b. Audubon, N.J., Mar. 6, 1946; d. Theodore J. and Margaret E. Post; m. D.R. Karklin (div. 1981); 1 child, Kenneth D. Karklin; m. Dale H. Corliss, May 23, 1984; 1 child, Rebecca Post Corliss. BA, Montclair State U., 1967; JD, Rutgers U., Camden, N.J., 1975. Bar: N.J. 1976, Mass. 1979, N.H. 1987. Gen. practice law William V. Eisenberg, Esq., Haddonfield, N.J., 1975-76; sole practitioner Medford, N.J., 1976-78, Pittsfield, Mass., 1983-84, Pelham, N.H., 1987-88; prof., chmn. dept. Rivier Coll., Nashua, NH, 1988—2001; prof. legal skills Franklin Pierce Law Ctr., Concord, NH, 2001—02; arbitrator Nat. Assn. Securities Dealers, 2001—. Mem. certifying bd. Nat. Assn. Legal Assts., Tulsa, 1994-98; bd. dirs. Am. Assn. for Paralegal Edn., Overland Park, Kans., 1996-98. Author: (textbook) Paralegal Internships: Finding, Managing, and Transitioning Your Career, 1999; co-author: (manual) Preventing Unauthorized Practice of Law: For the Paralegal in New Hampshire, 1998. Mem. Pelham Planning Bd., 1986-88. Named Atty. of Yr., Paralegal Assn. N.H., 1996. Mem. N.H. Bar Assn. (chair paralegal task force 1994, mem. com. on unauthorized practice of law 1996—).

POSTAL, DAVID RALPH, lawyer; b. Grand Rapids, Mich., Jan. 12, 1945; s. Ralph Bernard and Eleanor Postal; children: Bryan Charles, Stephanie Lynn. BA, Mich. State U., 1967; JD cum laude, U. Mich., 1974. Bar: Ariz. 1975, U.S. Dist. Ct. Ariz. 1975, U.S. Ct. Appeals (9th cir.) 1981. Assoc. Powers, Boutell, Fannin & Kurn, Phoenix, 1974-75; staff atty. Ariz. Supreme Ct., Phoenix, 1975-76; sole practice Phoenix, 1976-78, 83—; ptnr. Holland & Postal, Phoenix, 1978-83. Lectr. in real estate, 1976. Pres. New Hope for the Blind, Phoenix, 1976-82; chmn. bd. dirs. Trinity United meth. Adminstrn., Phoenix, 1980; trustee New Beginnings Transitional Home, 1995—; bd. dirs. Westside Foodbank, 1998—. Served to 1st lt., U.S. Army, 1969-72. Mem. Maricopa County Bar Assn., Kiwanis (pres. Phoenix 1984-85). Republican. General civil litigation, Commercial, contracts (including sales of goods; commercial financing), Property, real (including real estate development, water). Office: 3601 N 7th Ave Phoenix AZ 85013-3638

POSTER, MICHAEL SOLLOD, lawyer; b. N.Y.C., Nov. 7, 1971; s. Paul Michael and Sandra Sollod P.; m. Kendra Lynn Schwartz, Nov. 29, 1997. BA magna cum laude, U. Mass., 1993; JD, NYU, 1997. Bar: N.Y. 1998. Assoc. Katten Muchin Zavis Rosenman, N.Y.C., 1997—. Avocations: Judo, film, music. Corporate, general, Entertainment, Mergers and acquisitions. Office: Katten Muchin Zavis Rosenman 575 Madison Ave New York NY 10022 Fax: 212 940-8776.

POSTON, ANITA OWINGS, lawyer; b. Sylacauga, Ala., Sept. 24, 1949; d. John T. and Margaret Owings; m. Charles E. Poston, June 9, 1973; children: Charles E. Jr., John W., Margaret Elizabeth. BA, U. Md., 1971; JD, Coll. William & Mary, 1974. Bar: Va. 1974. Atty. Vandeventer Black LLP, Norfolk, Va., 1974—. Substitute judge Norfolk (Va.) Gen. Dist. Cts., 1982-90; mem. Bar Examiners Bd. Mem. State Bd. for Community Colls., Richmond, 1985-90, chmn. 1988-89; mem. Norfolk Sch. Bd., 1990-2002; bd. dirs. WHRO Pub. Broadcasting, chair, 2002-03; bd. dirs. Learning Bridge Acad., Govs. Sch. for the Arts Found. Mem. ABA (law fellows), Va. Bar Assn. (exec. com., pres. 2000), Norfolk-Portsmouth Bar Assn. (pres. 1998-99), Va. Law Fellows, Am. Inn of Ct. Corporate, general, Estate planning, Health. Office: Vandeventer Black LLP 500 World Trade Ctr Norfolk VA 23510-1679 Fax: 757-446-8670. E-mail: aposton@vanblk.com.

POSTON, REBEKAH JANE, lawyer; b. Wabash, Ind., Apr. 20, 1948; d. Bob E. and April (Ogle) P. BS, U. Miami, 1970, JD, 1974. Bar: Fla. 1974, Ohio 1977, U.S. Dist. Ct. (so. and mid. dists.) Fla., U.S. Ct. Appeals (11th cir.). Asst. U.S. atty. U.S. Atty.'s Office, Miami, Fla., 1974-76; spl. atty. organized crime and racketeering sect. Strike Force, Cleve., 1976-78; ptnr. Fine, Jacobson, Schwartz, Nash & Block, Miami, 1978-94, Steel Hector & Davis, Miami, 1994—. Adj. prof. U. Miami Law Sch., Coral Gables, 1986; mem. U.S. sentencing guidelines com. So. Dist. of Fla., Miami, 1987-88. Named one of Best Lawyers in Am. Mem. Fla. Bar Assn., Nat. Assn. Criminal Def. Attys., Nat. Directory Criminal Lawyers, Am. Immigration Lawyers Assn., Dade County Bar Assn. Democrat. Lutheran. Avocations: power boat racing, swimming. Criminal, Immigration, naturalization, and customs, Private international. Home: 1541 Brickell Ave Apt 3706 Miami FL 33129-1229 Office: 200 SE 2nd St Miami FL 33131 E-mail: rposton@steelhector.com.

POTENZA, JOSEPH MICHAEL, lawyer; b. Stamford, Conn., June 27, 1947; s. Michael Joseph Sr. and Rose Elizabeth (Coppola) P.; m. Karen Louise Yankee, Jan. 28, 1978; children: Wendy Lynn, Chiara Micol. BSEE cum laude, Rochester Inst. Tech., 1970; JD, Georgetown U., 1975. Bar: Va. 1975, D.C. 1976, U.S. Dist. Ct. D.C., U.S. Ct. Appeals (fed. cir.), U.S. Ct. Appeals (6th cir.), U.S. Supreme Ct. Patent examiner U.S. Patent and Trademark Office, Arlington, Va., 1970-74, law clk. bd. appeals, 1974-75, law clk. to presiding judge 6th cir. U.S. Ct. Appeals, 1975-76; assoc. Banner, Birch, McKie & Beckett, Washington, 1976-80, ptnr., 1980—. Adj. prof. Georgetown U. Law Ctr., Washington, 1985—; faculty Nat. Inst. Trial Advocacy--Patent Inst., 1996—. Editor (monographs) Sorting Out Ownership Rights in Intellectual Property, 1980, Recent Developments in Licensing, 1981. Bd. dirs. Found. for a Creative Am., 1991—. Recipient Patent and Trademark Office Superior Performance award Dept. Commerce, 1973-75. Fellow Am. Bar Found.; mem. ABA (young lawyers divsn. exec. coun. 1979—, chmn. legis. action com. 1980—, chmn. patent trademark and copyright com. 1977—, house of dels. 1984-86, sci. and tech. sect., coun. mem. 1985—, membership chmn. 1985—, budget co-chmn. 1987—, budget officer 1988—, vice chmn. 1991—, chmn.-elect 1992-93, chmn. 1993, chmn. standing com. on pub. oversight, 1996—, fed. practice and procedure com. intellectual property law sect. 1995-96, spring CLE program 1997-98, chmn. summer CLE 1999, 2001, chair fed. practice and procedure com. div. chmn., div. VI IP law sec. 1995-97, sec. sec. 2001—), IEEE, AAAS (nat. conf. lawyers and scientists), Am. Intellectual Property Law Assn. (chmn. unfair competition com. 1980-81), D.C. Bar Assn. (sec. patent, trademark, copyright sect.), Va. Bar Assn., Wash. Patent Lawyers Club (pres. 1988-89), Am. Inns of Ct. (founding mem. and exec. com. Giles S. Rich 1991—, v.p. 1997, pres. 1998-99), Phi Sigma Kappa, Alpha Sigma (pres. 1979-80), Tau Beta Pi. Intellectual property, Federal civil litigation, Trademark and copyright. Home: 1238 Gilman Ct Herndon VA 20170-2418 Office: Banner & Witcoff 1001 G St NW Ste 1100 Washington DC 20001-4545

POTH-WYPASEK, ANGELA KAY, prosecutor; b. Ashland, Ohio, Apr. 17, 1975; d. Timothy and Juanita Poth-Wypasek. B of Criminal Justice, Tiffin U., 1997; JD, U. Akron, 2000. Bar: Ohio. Atty. Summit County Jevenile Ct., Akron, Ohio, 2000—02; asst. prosecutor Summit County Prosecutor's Office, Ohio, 2002—. Mem.: ABA, Ohio State Bar Assn., Akron Bar Assn. Avocations: physical fitness, gardening, dancing, pets. Office: Summit County Prosecutors Office 650 Dan St Akron OH 44310

POTTER, FRED LEON, lawyer, insurance company executive, consultant; b. Kansas City, Kans., Dec. 15, 1948; s. Donald Warren and Olive Lucile (Ater) P.; m. Mertie Lorraine Scribner, June 13, 1970; children: Mark, Amy, Joy. BA, Harvard U., 1970, MBA, 1972; JD, U. Mich., 1975. Bar: N.H. 1975, U.S. Dist. Ct. N.H. 1975. Atty. Sulloway, Hollis & Soden, Concord, NH, 1975-80, 96—; pres., gen. counsel Christian Mut. Life Ins. Co., Concord, NH, 1980-96; exec. dir. NH Health Plan, NH, 2002, NH Vaccine Assoc., NH, 2002. Ptnr., mgmt. cons. Potter-Brock Assn., Tucson, 1969-82; trustee Gordon-Conwell Theol. Seminar, South Hamilton, Mass., 1983—; bd. dirs. N.H. Savs. Bank Corp., Concord, 1987-90; exec. dir. N.H. Health Plan N.H. Vaccine Assn., 2002--. Clk. Concord Union Sch. Dist., 1978-84; deacon 1st Bapt. Ch., Concord, 1978-85; elder Grace Bible Fellowship, 1993—; coach Concord Little League, 1985-87, 90-93. Mem. ABA, N.H. Bar Assn. (treas. 1980-84, v.p. 1984-85, pres. 1986-87, Pres. Disting. Service award 1983), Merrimack County Bar Assn. (sec. 1976-80), Christian Legal Soc., Computer Law Assn., Order of Coif. Evangelical. Commercial, contracts (including sales of goods; commercial financing), Corporate, general, Mergers and acquisitions. Home: 4 Pond Place Ln Concord NH 03301-3033 Office: 9 Capitol St Concord NH 03301-6310 E-mail: FPotter@sulloway.com.

POTTER, JOHN WILLIAM, federal judge; b. Toledo, Ohio, Oct. 25, 1918; s. Charles and Mary Elizabeth (Baker) P.; m. Phyllis May Bihn, Apr. 14, 1944; children: John William, Carolyn Diane, Kathryn Susan. PhB cum laude, U. Toledo, 1940; JD, U. Mich., 1946. Bar: Ohio 1947. Assoc. Zachman, Boxell, Schroeder & Torbet, Toledo, 1946-51; ptnr. Boxell, Bebout, Torbet & Potter, Toledo, 1951-69; mayor City of Toledo, 1961-67; asst. atty. gen. State of Ohio, 1968-69; judge 6th Dist. Ct. Appeals, 1969-82, U.S. Dist. Ct., Toledo, 1982—, sr. judge, 1992—. Presenter in field. Sr. editor U. Mich. Law Rev., 1946. Pres. Ohio Mcpl. League, 1965; past assoc. pub. mem. Toledo Labor Mgmt. Commn.; past pres., bd. dirs. Commn. on Rels. with Toledo (Spain); past bd. dirs. Cummings Sch. Toledo Opera Assn., Conlon Ctr.; past trustee Epworth United Meth. Ch.; hon. chmn. Toledo Festival Arts, 1980. Capt. F.A., U.S. Army, 1942-46. Decorated Bronze Star; recipient Leadership award Toledo Bldg. Congress, 1965, Merit award Toledo Bd. Realtors, 1967, Resolution of Recognition award Ohio Ho. of Reps., 1982, Outstanding Alumnus award U. Toledo, 1966, conf. rm. named in his honor, U.S. Courthouse, Toledo, 1998; named to Field Arty. Officer Candidate Sch. Hall of Fame, 1999. Fellow Am. Bar Found., Am. Judicature Soc., 6th Jud. Cir. Dist. Judges Assn., Fed. Judges Assn.; mem. ABA, Ohio Bar Assn. (Found. Outstanding Rsch. award 1995), Toledo Bar Assn. (exec. com. 1962-64, award 1992), Lucas County Bar Assn., U. Toledo Alumni Assn. (past pres.), Toledo Zool. Soc. (past bd. dirs.), Old Newsboys Club, Toledo Club, Kiwanis (past pres.), Phi Kappa Phi. Home: 2418 Middlesex Dr Toledo OH 43606-3114 Office: US Dist Ct 307 US Courthouse 1716 Spielbusch Ave Toledo OH 43624-1363

POTTER, ROBERT DANIEL, federal judge; b. Wilmington, N.C., Apr. 4, 1923; s. Elisha Lindsey and Emma Louise (McLean) P.; m. Mary Catherine Neilson, Feb. 13, 1954; children: Robert Daniel, Mary Louise, Catherine Ann. AB in Chemistry, Duke U., 1947, LLB, 1950; LLD (hon.), Sacred Heart Coll., Belmont, N.C., 1982. Bar: N.C. 1951. Pvt. practice law, Charlotte, N.C., 1951-81; dist. judge U.S. Dist. Ct. (we. dist.) N.C., 1981-2000; chief judge, 1984-91; now sr. judge U.S. Dist. Ct. (we. dist.) N.C. Commr. Mecklenburg County, Charlotte, 1966-68. Served as 2d lt. U.S. Army, 1944-47, ETO Mem. N.C. Bar Assn. Clubs: Charlotte City. Republican. Roman Catholic.

POTTER, TANYA JEAN, lawyer; b. Washington, Oct. 30, 1956; d. John Francis and Tanya Agnes (Kristof) P.; m. Howard Bruce Adler; 1 child, Alexandra Potter Adler. BA, Georgetown U., 1978, JD, 1981. Bar: D.C. 1982, U.S. Ct. Appeals (D.C. cir.), U.S. Ct. Appeals (fed. cir.), U.S. Dist. Ct. (D.C. dist.), U.S. Ct. Internat. Trade. Assoc. Ragan and Mason, Washington, 1981-88; atty.-adviser Office of Chief Counsel for Import Adminstrn., U.S. Dept. Commerce, Washington, 1989-92. Mediator D.C. Superior Ct., 1982-84. Author: Practicing Before the Federal Maritime Commission, 1986, supplement, 1988, Preferentiality Under the Proposed Commerce Department Regulations, 1990, Oil Refining in U.S. Foreign-Trade Zones, 1990. Rep. Avenel Homeowners Adv. Coun., 1994-97; dir. Avenel Bd. Dirs., 1997, 98, 99-2001. Recipient Cmty. Svc. Recognition award ARC, Washington, 1986. Mem. ABA, Bar Assn. of D.C. (exec. coun. ad law sect. 1985-89). Avocations: sports, travel, visiting museums and art galleries. Administrative and regulatory, Private international.

POTTS, DENNIS WALKER, lawyer; b. Santa Monica, Calif., Dec. 17, 1945; s. James Longworth and Donna (Neely) P.; m. Chung Wan; children: Brandon Earl Woodward, Trevor Shipley. BA, U. Calif., Santa Barbara, 1967; JD, U. Calif., San Francisco, 1970. Bar: Hawaii 1971, Calif. 1971, U.S. Dist. Ct. Hawaii 1971, U.S. Ct. Appeals (9th cir.) 1973, U.S. Supreme Ct. 1978, U.S. Dist. Ct. (cen. dist.) Calif. 1983. Assoc. Chuck Mau, Honolulu, 1971-74; sole practice Honolulu, 1974—. Mem. litigation com. ACLU Hawaii, 1977-82; former mem. Hawaii Acad. Plaintiff's Attys. Disting. Svc. Cert. ACLU Hawaii. Fellow Internat. Napoleonic Soc.; mem. ATLA (sustaining), Consumer Lawyers Hawaii (treas., bd. govs.), Honolulu Club. Federal civil litigation, State civil litigation, Personal injury (including property damage). Office: 2755 Pacific Tower 1001 Bishop St Honolulu HI 96813-3429

POTTS, RAMSAY DOUGLAS, lawyer, aviator; b. Memphis, Oct. 24, 1916; s. Ramsay Douglas and Ann Clifton (VanDyke) P.; m. Veronica Hamilton Raynor, Dec. 22, 1945 (dec. May 1993); children: Ramsay Douglas, David Hamilton, Lesley Ann, Lindsay Veronica. BS, U. N.C., 1941; LL.B., Harvard U., 1948. Bar: Tenn. 1948, D.C. 1954, U.S. Supreme Ct. 1957. Commd. 2d lt. USAAF, 1941, advanced through grades to maj. gen. Res., 1961; various combat and operational assignments (8th Air Force and Air Force Res.), 1942-60; chmn. Air Force Res. Policy Com., 1967-68; practice law, Washington, 1955—; spl. asst. to chmn. Nat. Security Resources Bd., 1951; pres. Ind. Mil. Air Transport Assn., 1952-55; ptnr. Shaw, Pittman, Potts & Trowbridge, 1956-86, sr. counsel, 1986—. Publisher: Air Power History, 1989-93; contbr. articles to profl. jours. Mem. State Council Higher Edn. for Va., 1968-71; Trustee Air Force Hist. Found., pres., 1971-75; pres. Washington Area Tennis Patrons Found., 1984-87; trustee emeritus. Physicians for Peace, 199789—. Decorated D.S.C., other combat decorations Mem. ABA, D.C. Bar Assn., Met. Club (Washington), Army Navy Country Club (Arlington, Va.), Internat. Lawn Tennis Club (U.S., Gt. Brit., India), Phi Beta Kappa. Home: 2818 27th St N Arlington VA 22207-4921 Office: Shaw Pittman Potts & Trowbridge 2300 N St NW Washington DC 20037-1128

POTTS, STEPHEN DEADERICK, lawyer; b. Memphis, Nov. 20, 1930; s. Ramsay Douglas and Anne (Van Dyke) P.; m. Irene Potter, Mar. 14, 1953; children: Lori Potts-Dupre, Stephen Deaderick Jr., Stacy Potts Krogh. AB, Vanderbilt U., 1952, LLB, 1954. Bar: Tenn. 1954, D.C. 1961. Assoc. Farris, Evans & Evans, Nashville, 1957-61; ptnr. Shaw, Pittman, Potts & Trowbridge, Washington, 1961-90; dir. U.S. Office Gov. Ethics, Washington, 1990-2000; chmn. fellows program, sr. ethics counselor Ethics Resource Ctr., Washington, 2001—. Past mem. Pres.'s Coun. on Integrity and Efficiency, Pres.'s Commn. on the Fed. Appt. Process. Past pres. Washington Tennis Patrons Found., 1970—72; chmn. USTA Olympic com. 1st lt. U.S. Army, 1954—57. Mem. ABA, U.S. Supreme Ct. Bar Assn., D.C. Bar Assn., Chevy Chase Club (bd. govs. 1982-86), Met. Club (bd. govs. 2000), Alibi Club, U.S. Tennis Assn. (bd. dirs., won 5 nat., 1 internat. father/son championships, twice ranked 1st in U.S.). Methodist. Office: Ethics Resource Ctr Ste 400 1747 Pennsylvania Ave Washington DC 20006

POTUZNIK, CHARLES LADDY, lawyer; b. Chgo., Feb. 11, 1947; s. Charles William and Laverne Frances (Zdenek) P.; m. Mary Margaret Quady, Jan. 2, 1988; children: Kylie Brommell, Kathryn Mary. BA with high honors, U. Ill., 1969; JD cum laude, Harvard U., 1973. Bar: Minn. 1973. Assoc. Dorsey & Whitney LLP, Mpls., 1973-78, ptnr., 1979—. Co-head Broker-Dealer and Investment Markets Regulation Practice Group. Mem. Minn. State Bar Assn. (chmn. state securities law subcom. 1987-2000), Hennepin County Bar Assn., Minn. Securities Adv. Com., Phi Beta Kappa. Mem. Evang. Free Ch. Avocations: hunting, fishing, camping, canoeing, foreign travel. Finance, Securities. Office: Dorsey & Whitney LLP 50 South Sixth St Minneapolis MN 55402-1498 E-mail: potuznik.charles@dorseylaw.com.

POUL, FRANKLIN, lawyer; b. Phila., Nov. 6, 1924; s. Boris and Anna P.; m. Shirley Weissman, June 26, 1949; children— Leslie Poul Melman, Alan M., Laurie Price.. Student, U. Pa., 1942-43, Haverford Coll., 1943-44; LL.B. cum laude, U. Pa., 1946. Bar: Pa. 1949, U.S. Supreme Ct. 1955. Asso. firm Gray, Anderson, Schaffer & Rome, Phila., 1948-56, Wolf, Block, Schorr and Solis-Cohen, Phila., 1956-60, partner, 1960-93. Bd. dirs. ACLU, Phila., 1955-80, pres., 1975-76. Served with AUS, 1943-46. Mem. ABA, Am. Law Inst., Order of Coif. Antitrust, Federal civil litigation, Securities. Office: Wolf Block Shorr & Solis-Cohen 1650 Arch St Philadelphia PA 19103-2097

POUND, JOHN BENNETT, lawyer; b. Champaign, Ill., Nov. 17, 1946; s. William R. and Louise Catherine (Kelly) P.; m. Mary Ann Hanson, June 19, 1971; children: Meghan Elizabeth, Matthew Fitzgerald. BA, U. N.Mex., 1968; JD, Boston Coll., 1971. Bar: N. Mex. 1971, U.S. Dist. Ct. N. Mex. 1971, U.S. Ct. Appeals (10th cir.) 1972, U.S. Supreme Ct., 1993. Law clk. to Hon. Oliver Seth, U.S. Ct. Appeals, 10th Cir., Santa Fe, 1971-72. Asst. counsel Supreme Ct. Disciplinary Bd., 1977-83, dist. rev. officer, 1984—; mem. Supreme Ct. Com. on Jud. Performance Evaluation, 1983-85; bd. dirs. Archdiocese Santa Fe Cath. Social Svcs., 1995—. Contbr. articles to profl. jours. Pres. bd. dirs. N.Mex. Ind. Coll. Fund, Santa Fe; chmn. N.Mex. Dem. Leadership Coun., 1991—; bd. dirs. Santa Fe Boys Club, 1989-92; rules com. N.Mex. Dem. Party, 1982—; v.p. Los Alamos Nat. Lab. Comm. Coun., 1985-90; fin. chmn. N.Mex. Clinton for Pres. campaign, 1992; co-chmn. Clinton-Gore Re-election Campaign, N.Mex., 1996, 2000 Fellow Am. Bar Found., Am. Coll. Trial Lawyers, N.Mex. Bar Found.; mem. ABA, Am. Bd. Trial Advocates, N.Mex. Bar Assn. (health law sect. 1987—), Santa Fe County Bar Assn. Democrat. Roman Catholic. Avocations: history, foreign language, literature, swimming, baseball. General civil litigation, Corporate, general, Health. Office: Herrera Long Pound Komer PA PO Box 5098 2200 Brothers Rd Santa Fe NM 87505-6903 E-mail: HLPLaw@aol.com.

POVICH, DAVID, lawyer; b. Washington, June 8, 1935; s. Shirley Lewis and Ethyl (Friedman) Povich; m. Constance Enid Tobriner, June 14, 1959; children: Douglas, Johanna, Judtih, Andrew. BA, Yale U., 1958; LLB, Columbia U., 1962. Bar: D.C. 1962, U.S. Ct. Appeals (4th cir.) 1980, U.S. Tax Ct. 1981, U.S. Ct. Appeals (5th and 11th cirs.) 1984, U.S. Dist. Ct. Md., U.S. Ct. Appeals (3d cir.) 1997. Law clk. to assoc. judge D.C. Ct. Appeals, Washington, 1962-63; ptnr. Williams & Connolly, Washington, 1963—, exec. com., 1986-87. Bd. dirs., officer Lisner Home for Aged. Mem.: ABA, Barristers (exec. com. 1992—93), Bar Assn. D.C., D.C. Bar Assn. Federal civil litigation, Criminal, Personal injury (including property damage). Office: Williams & Connolly 725 12th St NW Washington DC 20005-5901 E-mail: dpovich@wc.com.

POWDERLY, WILLIAM H., III, lawyer; b. Pitts., Feb. 23, 1930; BS, Georgetown U., 1953; LLB, U. Pitts., 1956. Bar: Pa. 1956. Of counsel Tucker Arensberg PC, Pitts. Office: Tucker Arensberg PC 1500 One PPG Pl Pittsburgh PA 15222 E-mail: wpowderly@tuckerlaw.com.

POWELL, EDMUND WILLIAM, lawyer; b. St. Paul, Dec. 23, 1922; s. George L. and Mary (Sexton) P.; m. Ellen M. Williams, May 7, 1949; children— Susan Marie, Sarah Ann, Daniel. Student, St. Thomas Coll., St. Paul, 1941-43, U. Minn., 1943, 46; LL.B., Marquette U., 1948. Bar: Wis. bar 1948. Pvt. practice, Milw., 1948-97; pres. firm Borgelt, Powell, Peterson & Frauen and predecessors, 1948-90. Served with USNR, 1943-45; to capt. USMCR, 1945-46, 52-53. Fellow Am. Coll. Trial Lawyers; mem. State Bar Wis. (sec. 1964-65, bd. govs. 1961-63, 65-67, sec., dir. ins. sect. 1962-69), Marquette Law Alumni Assn. (pres., dir. 1957-60), Town Club (Milw.), Country Club of Hilton Head. Home: 3113 E Hampshire Ave Milwaukee WI 53211-3117

POWELL, JAMES HENRY, lawyer; b. N.Y.C., May 1, 1928; s. Milton Jerome and Doris (Unterberg) P.; m. Connie Lu Egger, Oct. 5, 1958; children: David E., Andrew J., Jeffrey K. AB, Harvard U., 1949; LLB, Yale U., 1952. Bar: N.Y. 1952. Assoc. McLaughlin and Stern, N.Y.C., 1955-69; atty. ABC, N.Y.C., 1969-72; assoc. Fried Frank Harris Shriver & Jacobson, N.Y.C., 1972-76, Patterson Belknap Webb & Tyler, N.Y.C., 1976-80, ptnr., 1980-95; pvt. practice N.Y.C., 1996—. Mem. exec. com. Lexington Dem. Club, 1961-63. With U.S. Army, 1953-55. Mem. Assn. of Bar of City of N.Y., City Athletic Club N.Y.C. (mem. bd. govs. 1973-81), Phi Beta Kappa. Landlord-tenant, Property, real (including real estate development, water). Office: 477 Madison Ave New York NY 10022-5802

POWELL, KATHLEEN LYNCH, lawyer, real estate executive; b. N.Y.C., Dec. 30, 1949; d. Daniel Francis and Mary Margaret (Flynn) L.; m. P. Douglas Powell. BA in Math. cum laude, Coll. of Mt. St. Vincent, 1970; postgrad., U. Pa., 1976-77; JD cum laude, U. Md., 1977; LL.M. in Taxation, NYU, 1991. Bar: Pa. 1977, N.J. 1978, N.Y. 1984, D.C. 1985, Conn. 1995, U.S. Ct. Appeals (3d cir.) 1980, U.S. Supreme Ct. 1981. Research analyst, claims rep. Social Security Adminstrn., Balt., 1973-76; assoc. Drinker, Biddle & Reath, Phila., 1977-84, ptnr., 1984-86; v.p., gen. counsel M. Alfieri Co., Inc., Edison, N.J., 1987-89; v.p., counsel Berwind Property Group, Phila., 1992—. Instr. Inst. for Paralegal Tng., Phila. 1984—. Vol. atty. Support Ctr. for Child Advocates, Phila., 1979-86, Queen Village Neighbors Assn., Phila., 1984-86; pres. Soc. Hill Towers Buyers Assn., Phila., 1979-80; bd. dirs. Soc. Hill Civic Assn., 1980. Mem. ABA, Pa. Bar Assn., Phila. Bar Assn. (chair zoning and land use com. 1985-86), Conn. Bar Assn.

POWELL, KENNETH EDWARD, investment banker; b. Danville, Va., Oct. 5, 1952; s. Terry Edward and C. Anne (Wooten) P.; m. Cicely Grandin Moorman, Jan. 3, 1976; children: Tanner, Priscilla. Student, Hampden-Sydney Coll., 1971-73; BA in Polit. Sci., U. Colo., 1975; JD, U. Richmond, 1978; LLM in Taxation, Coll. of William and Mary, 1982. Bar: Va. 1978, U.S. Dist. Ct. (ea. dist.) Va. 1979, U.S. Tax Ct. 1980. Ptnr. Maloney, Yeatts & Barr, Richmond, Va., 1978-87; ptnr., owner Hazel & Thomas, P.C., Richmond, 1987-94, mem. bus./tax team, internat. bus. team; v.p. Legg Mason, Richmond, Va., 1994—. Vice chmn. Sci. Mus. Va., Richmond, 1984-91; chmn. Va. Police Found., Inc., 1987; bd. dirs. State Edn. Assistance Authority, 1991—; mem. adv. bd. Va. Opera, 1991—; candidate U.S. Congress, Va., 1986. Recipient Disting. Svc. award Fraternal Order of Police, 1986; named Outstanding Young Man of the Yr., Jaycees, 1981, Outstanding Young Alumni, U. Colo., 1982. Mem. ABA, Va. Bar Assn. (chmn. profl. responsibility com. 1989-92, chmn. com. on legal edn. and admission to the Bar 1991—), Richmond Bar Assn., Richmond C. of C. (bd. dirs. 1988), Va. Econ. Developers Assn. (gen. counsel), Va. Econ. Bridge Initiative. Episcopal. Office: Legg Mason Wood Walker Inc 2234 Monument Ave Richmond VA 23220

POWELL, ROGER NORMAN, lawyer; b. Balt., Sept. 26, 1942; s. Philip C. and Roslyn (Goldberger) P.; m. Michele Rae Cohen, Aug. 10, 1965 (div. 1978); children: Alan, Tamara; m. Iris Sondra Quirmbach, Oct. 15, 1978. BA, U. Md., 1965; JD, U. Balt., 1970. Bar: Md. 1971. Pvt. practice, Pikesville, Md., 1971—; atty. Md. State Fireman's Assn., Annapolis, 1974—. Editor: Fire Laws of Maryland, 1982-02, 10th edit. Bd. dirs. Md. affiliate Am. Diabetes Assn., 1988-90, Sugar Ball com., 1999-02; founder, dir. Reister's Towne Festival. Named Vol. of Yr. Pikesville Vol. Fire Co., 1974. Mem. Md. Bar Assn., Md. State Fireman's Assn., Balt. County Bar Assn. Democrat. Jewish. General civil litigation, General practice. Office: 107 Old Court Rd Baltimore MD 21208-4011

POWELL-SMITH, MARC EDGAR RAOUL, lawyer; b. Levallois-Perret, France, June 13, 1970; s. David Edward and Teresa (Bonvecchiato) P.-S.; m. Sabine Louvet, Apr. 8, 2000. Diploma in Anglo-Am. Bus. Law, Maitrise in Bus. Law, U. Paris, 1992; DESS in Internat. Comml. Law, U. Paris X, 1993; LLM in Corp. Law, Widener U., Wilmington, Del., 1994; DESS in Litigation Law, U. Rouen, France, 1996. Bar: France 1996. Assoc. Lette Lette & Ptnrs., Paris, 1997-99, Jobard Chemla & Assocs., Paris, 1999-2001; pvt. practice Paris, 2001—. With French Air Force, 1994-95. Mem. Franco-Brit. Lawyer's Soc., Franco-Brit. C. of C. and Industry, Chambre de Commerce Italienne pour la France, Chambre de commerce Franco-Arabe. Avocations: travel, tennis, open water diving, fencing, languages. General civil litigation, Commercial, contracts (including sales of goods; commercial financing), Labor (including EEOC, Fair Labor Standards Act, labor-management relations, NLRB, OSHA). Home: 57 bis ave Motte-Picquet Paris 75015 France Office: 148 avenue de Wagram Paris 75017 France Fax: 1-56-79-01-55.

POWER, JOHN BRUCE, lawyer; b. Glendale, Calif., Nov. 11, 1936; m. Sandra Garfield, Apr. 27, 1998; children by previous marriage: Grant, Mark, Boyd. AB magna cum laude, Occidental Coll., 1958; JD, NYU, 1961; postdoctoral, Columbia U., 1972. Bar: Calif. 1962. Assoc. O'Melveny & Myers, L.A., 1961-70, ptnr., 1970-97, resident ptnr. Paris, 1973-75; Sheffelman disting. lectr. Sch. Law, U. Wash., Seattle, 1997. Mem. Social Svcs. Commn. City of L.A., 1993, pres., 1993; pres. circle, exec. com. Occidental Coll., 1979-82, 91-94, chair, 1993-94. Contbr. articles to jours. Bd. dirs. Met. L.A. YMCA, 1988—, treas., 1998-2001; mem. bd. mgrs. Stuart Ketchum Downtown YMCA, 1985-92, pres., 1989-90; mem. Los Angeles County Rep. Ctrl. Com., 1962-63; trustee Occidental Coll., 1992—, vice-chmn., 1998-2001, chmn., 2001—. Root Tilden scholar. Fellow Am. Coll. Comml. Fin. Lawyers (bd. regents 1999-2003); mem. ABA (comml. fin. svcs. com., com. 3d party legal opinions, UCC com., bus. law sect.), Am. Bar Found. (life), Calif. Bar Assn. (chmn. partnerships and unincorporated assns. com. 1982-83, chmn. uniform commn. code com. 1984-85, chmn. opinions com. 2000—, exec. com. 1987-91, chmn. bus. law sect. 1990-91, chmn. coun. sect. chairs 1992-93, liaison to state bar commn. on future of legal profession and state bar 1993-95), L.A. County Bar Assn. (exec. com. comml. law and bankruptcy sect. 1970-73, 86-89), Internat. Bar Assn., Fin. Lawyers Conf. (bd. govs. 1982—, pres. 1984-85), Exec. Svc. Corps (sec. 1985-2000, vice-chmn. 2000—, dir. 1994—), Occidental Coll. Alumni Assn. (pres. 1967-68), Phi Beta Kappa (councilor So. Calif. 1982—, pres. 1990-92). Corporate, general, Commercial, contracts (including sales of goods; commercial financing), Mergers and acquisitions. Office: O Melveny & Myers 400 S Hope St Los Angeles CA 90071-2899

POWER, JOSEPH EDWARD, lawyer; b. Peoria, Ill., Dec. 2, 1938; s. Joseph Edward and Margaret Elizabeth (Birkett) P.; m. Camille June Repass, Aug. 1, 1964; children— Joseph Edward, David William, James Repass Student, Knox Coll., Galesburg, Ill., 1956-58; BA, U. Iowa, 1960, JD, 1964. Bar: Iowa 1964. Law clk. to judge U.S. Dist. Ct., 1964-65; mem. Bradshaw, Fowler, Proctor & Fairgrave, P.C., Des Moines, 1965—. Bd. dirs. Moingona coun. Girl Scouts U.S.A., 1968-77, pres., 1971-74; bd. dirs. Des Moines United Way, 1976-82, v.p., 1979-81; trustee Am. Inst. Bus., 1987-2002, chmn., 1992-2002; bd. dirs. Iowa Law Sch. Found., 1992—, Plymouth Ch. Found., 1991-99; bd. dirs. Des Moines Found, 1996—, sec.-treas., 2001-; bd. dirs. Iowa Natural Heritage Found., 1995—, vice chmn., 2001-; mem. Des Moines Civil War Roundtable. Fellow Am. Coll. Trust and Estate Counsel (state chair 1994-2000), Am. Coll. Real Estate Lawyers; mem. ABA, Iowa Bar Assn. (chmn. probate, property and trust law com. 1983-87), Polk County Bar Assn., Des Moines Estate Planners Forum (pres. 1982-83) Republican. Mem. United Ch. of Christ. Clubs: Des Moines, Rotary. Home: 1928 Elm Cr West Des Moines IA 50265 Office: Bradshaw Fowler Proctor & Fairgrave 801 Grand Ave Ste 3700 Des Moines IA 50309-2727 E-mail: www.power.edward@bradshawlaw.com.

POWERS, EDWARD HERBERT, lawyer; b. Jersey City, N.J., June 21, 1942; s. Samuel and Ruth (Handman) P.; m. Phyllis Elinor Alpern, May 29, 1966; children: Alexander, Jill, Annette. BA, U. Mich., 1964, JD, 1967. Bar: Mich. 1968, U.S. Dist. Ct. (ea. dist.) Mich. 1968, U.S. Ct. Appeals (6th cir.) 1989, U.S. Supreme Ct. 1990. Owner, mem. Pelavin, Powers & Behm PC., Flint, Mich., 1968-2001; sole practitioner, Flint, 2001—; instr. Mott Adult Edn., Flint, 1970-74 Chmn. region XI U. Mich. Law Sch. Fund, 1980-81; v.p. Flint Jewish Fedn., 1978-82; chmn. Flint United Jewish Appeal, 1978; v.p. Congregation Beth Israel, 1979-82. Mem. Assn. Trial Lawyers Am., Mich. Trial Lawyers Assn., State Bar Mich., ABA (forum on constrn. industry), Genesee County Bar Assn., Am. Mensa Soc., Univ. Club (Flint). Commercial, contracts (including sales of goods; commercial financing), General practice, Property, real (including real estate development, water). Home: 1071 Briarcliffe Dr Flint MI 48532-2102 Office: 300 Phoenix Bldg 801 S Saginaw St Flint MI 48502

POWERS, ELIZABETH WHITMEL, lawyer; b. Charleston, S.C., Dec. 16, 1949; d. Francis Persse and Jane Coleman Cotten (Wham) P.; m. John Campbell Henry, June 11, 1994 (dec. Jan. 1997); m. Henry C. B. Lindh, June 16, 2000. AB, Mt. Holyoke Coll., 1971; JD, U. S.C., 1978. Bar: S.C. 1978, N.Y. 1979. Law clk. to justice S.C. Cir. Ct., Columbia; assoc. Reid & Priest, N.Y.C., 1978-86, ptnr., 1986-97; of counsel LeBoeuf, Lamb, Greene & MacRae, N.Y.C., 1997—. Exec. editor S.C. Law Rev., Columbia, 1977-78. Vol. N.Y. Jr. League, N.Y.C., 1983—; bd. dirs. The Seamen's Ch. Inst., 1996—; sec. The Seamen's Ch. Inst. , 1999—; trustee Ch. Club, 1991—94, 1997—2001, v.p., 1992—94. Mem.: Nat. Soc. Colonial Dames in State of N.Y. (pres. 1992—95), Nat. Soc. Colonial Dames of Am. (parliamentarian 1994—2000, regent Gunston Hall 2001—02), S.C. Bar Assn., ABA. Corporate, general, Utilities, public, Securities.

POWERS, WILLIAM CHARLES, JR., dean, law educator; b. 1946; AB, U. Calif., Berkeley, 1967; JD, Harvard U., 1973. Bar: Wash. 1974, Tex. 1980. Law clk. to Hon. E. A. Wright U.S. Ct. Appeals (9th cir.), Seattle, 1973-74; asst. prof. Wash. U. , Seattle, 1974-77; assoc. prof. Wash. U., Seattle, 1977-78; prof. law U. Tex., Austin, 1978—, assoc. dean acad. affairs, 1984—87, 1994—95, univ. disting. prof. and Hines H. Baker and Thelma Kelly Baker chair in law, 1997—, John Jeffers Rsch. Chair in law, 2000—, dean Sch. Law, 2000—. Office: U Tex Sch Law 727 E Dean Keeton St Austin TX 78705-3224*

POZNER, LOUIS-JACK, lawyer; b. N.Y.C., Dec. 12, 1946; s. Harry Bear and Regina (Lindsey) P.; m. Rona Judkowitz, June 9, 1968; children: Samantha Brooke, Jo-Ellen, Zachary Blair. BA with honors in History, U. Rochester, 1968; JD, Bklyn. Law Sch., 1971. Bar: N.Y. 1972, U.S. Dist Ct. (no. dist.) N.Y. 1972, U.S. Dist. Ct. (so. and ea. dists.) N.Y. 1991, U.S. Supreme Ct. 1983. Law clk. N.Y. State Supreme Ct. Appellate Divsn. 3rd Dept., Albany, 1971-72; law clk. to Judge James Gibson N.Y. State Ct. Appeals, Albany, 1972; assoc. DeGraff Foy Conway Holt-Harris & Meeley, Albany, N.Y., 1973-74; pvt. practice Albany, N.Y., 1974—; pres. Louis-Jack Pozner, P.C., Albany, N.Y., 1993—. Judge Albany Law Sch. Moot Ct. Competition, 1979, 80, 84, 86, 89-2003; advisor in 1982 State Mock Trial Tournament. Pres. Electronic Body Art Inc., 1979-80, bd. dirs., 1976-79; trustee Temple Israel Albany, 1976-82, 98-2003, v.p., 1980-82, exec. v.p., 1995-96, pres., 1996-98; bd. dirs. Friends of Albany Pub. Libr., 1982-84, Greater Albany Jewish Fedn., 1979-85, Horizon House, 1982-83, Bet Shraga Hebrew Acad. the Capital Dist., 1978-88, v.p., 1980-85, pres., 1985-88; co-chmn. cmty. rels. com. Greater Albany Jewish Fedn., 1980-82; trustee Daus. of Sarah Found., 1983-2002, v.p., 1988-90, pres., 1990-93; bd. trustees Greater Jewish Fedn. Northeastern N.Y., 1999—, bd. govs. endowment fund, 1999—. Recipient of Greater Albany Jewish Fedn. Samuel E. Aronowitz Young Leadership award, 1981. Mem. ABA (mem. character and fitness coms. 3d dist. 1990-99, mem. com. on profl. stds. 1999-2002), Albany County Bankruptcy Bar Assn., Albany County Bar Assn., N.Y. State Bar Assn. General civil litigation, Family and matrimonial, General practice. Home: 258 Lenox Ave Albany NY 12208-1408 Office: 11 N Pearl St Ste 1405 Albany NY 12207-2771

PRABHAKARAN, PRATHISH, lawyer; b. Mumbai, Bombay, India, May 2, 1975; LLM, Univ. Conn. Law Sch., Hartford, Conn., 1999. Ptnr. Cons. Juris, Mumbai, India, 1999—. Office: Cons Juris 1st Flr 2 of Maruti Ln Mumbai 400001 India

PRADELL, STEVEN, lawyer; b. Fairbanks, Alaska, June 29, 1960; s. David Edward and Lila (Charney) P. BA cum laude, Brandeis U., 1982; JD, U. Oreg., 1986. Bar: Alaska 1986, U.S. Dist. Ct. Alaska 1986, U.S. Ct. Appeals (9th cir.) 1990. Assoc. Kelly & Assocs., Anchorage, 1986-88, Birch, Horton, Bittner & Cherot, Anchorage, 1988-93; owner Pradell and Assocs., Anchorage, 1993—. Author: Winning The War Against Life Threatening Diseases, 1994, Alaska Family Law Handbook, 1998. Avocations: magic, music. Criminal, Family and matrimonial, Personal injury (including property damage). Home: PO Box 102062 Anchorage AK 99510-2062 Office: Pradell & Assocs 1009 W 7th Ave Anchorage AK 99501-3323 E-mail: pradell@alaska.net.

PRAGER, SUSAN WESTERBERG, law educator, provost; b. Sacramento, Dec. 14, 1942; d. Percy Foster Westerberg and Aileen M. (McKinley) P.; m. James Martin Prager, Dec. 14, 1973; children: McKinley Ann, Case Mahone. AB, Stanford U., 1964, MA, 1967; JD, UCLA, 1971. Bar: N.C. 1971, Calif. 1972. Atty. Powe, Porter & Alphin, Durham, N.C., 1971-72; acting prof. law UCLA, 1972-77, prof. Sch. Law, 1977—, Arjay and Frances Fearing Miller prof. of law, 1992-99, assoc. dean Sch. Law, 1979-82, dean, 1982-98; provost Dartmouth Coll., Hanover, N.H., 1999—. Bd. dirs. Pacific Mut. Life Holding Co., Newport Beach, Calif. Editor-in-chief, UCLA Law Rev., 1970-71. Trustee Stanford U., 1976-80, 87-97. Mem. ABA (council of sect. on legal edn. and admissions to the bar 1983-85), Assn. Am. Law Schs. (pres. 1986), Order of Coif. Address: Dartmouth College Office of the Provost 6004 Parkhurst Hall Rm 204 Hanover NH 03755-3529

PRANGE, ROY LEONARD, JR., lawyer; b. Chgo., Sept. 12, 1945; s. Roy Leonard and Marjorie Rose (Kauppi) P.; m. Carol Lynn Poels, June 5, 1971; children: David, Ellen, Susan. BA, U. Iowa, 1967; MA, Ohio State U., 1968; JD, U. Wis.-Madison, 1975. Bar: Wis. 1975, U.S. Dist. Ct. (we. and ea. dists.) Wis. 1975, U.S. Ct. Appeals (7th cir.) 1978, U.S. Supreme Ct. 1978. Assoc. Ross & Stevens, Svc. Corp., Madison, Wis., 1975-79, ptnr., 1979-90, Quarles & Brady, Madison, 1990—. Lectr. bankruptcy, debtor-creditor rights, U. Wis., Madison, 1982-. Contbr. Wis. Lawyer's Desk Reference Manual, 1987, Comml. Litigation in Wis. Practice Handbook, 1995, West's Bankruptcy Exemption Manual, 1997—. 1st lt. U.S. Army, 1969-72. Fellow Am. Coll. Bankruptcy; mem. ABA, Wis. State Bar (dir. bankruptcy, insolvency, creditors rights sect. 1985-91, chair 1990-92, mem. continuing legal edn. com. 1990-95), Am. Bankruptcy Inst., Dickens Fellowship (v.p. 1980-84). Avocations: swimming, bicycling, scuba diving. Bankruptcy, General civil litigation, Commercial, consumer (including collections, credit). Office: Quarles & Brady PO Box 2113 1 S Pinckney St Madison WI 53703-2892

PRATER, WENDY LEA, lawyer; b. Houston, Aug. 23, 1964; d. Walter LeRoy and Dolores Marie (Bartula) P.; m. Peter Robert Dear, Nov. 4, 1995. BA, Baylor U., 1986, JD, 1989. Bar: Tex. 1990, U.S. Dist. Ct. (so. dist.) Tex. 1991, U.S. Ct. Appeals (5th cir.) 1992, U.S. Supreme Ct. 1993. Assoc. Jim S. Adler, P.C., Houston, 1990-92; pvt. practice Houston, 1992—. Mem. Magic Cir. Rep. Women's Club, Houston, 1996—; bd. dirs. N.W. YMCA, Houston, 1995—; life mem. Houston Livestock Show & Rodeo, Houston, 1993—. Mem. State Bar Tex., Houston Bar Assn., Coll. of State of Tex. Avocations: sailing, water skiing, jetskiing, travel, sports. General civil litigation, Family and matrimonial, General practice. Office: 1919 North Loop W Ste 490 Houston TX 77008-1366

PRATHER, DAVID C. lawyer; b. Bronx, N.Y., Jan. 16, 1965; s. Rufus James Prather and Jeanette Peggy Long; m. Glynette D. Jefferson, Feb. 23, 1983; children: Christopher, Taylor, Ashley. BA in Polit. Sci. and Econs., CUNY, 1987; JD, Rutgers U., 1990. Bar: Fla. 1991, U.S. Dist. Ct. (no., so. and ctrl. dists.) Fla. 2002. Asst. pub. defender Palm Beach County Pub. Defenders Office, West Palm Beach, Fla., 1990—92; asst. state atty. Palm Beach County State Atty., West Palm Beach, Fla., 1992—95; assoc. Lytal, Reiter, Clark, Fountain & Williams LLP, West Palm Beach, Fla., 1995—. Palm Beach County rep. Fla. Bar Bd. Govs., 1996—2000. Bd. dirs. Palm Beach County Edn. Found., 1999—, Urban League Palm Beach County, 1996—99. Named one of Best Lawyers in South Fla., Miami Metro Publ., 2000. Mem.: Palm Beach County Trial Lawyers Assn. (bd. dirs. 1996—), Kiwanis. Democrat. Baptist. Avocations: bicycling, basketball, skiing. Criminal, Personal injury (including property damage), Product liability. Office: Lytal Reiter Clark Fountain & Williams 515 N Flagler Dr West Palm Beach FL 33401 Office Fax: 561-832-2932. E-mail: dprather@palmbeachlaw.com.

PRATHER, JOHN GIDEON, lawyer; b. Somerset, Ky., Dec. 12, 1919; s. James Frederick and Josephine Linnwood (Collier) P.; m. Marie Jeanette Moore, Oct. 1945; children: John G., Jerome Moore. B.A., U. Ky., 1940, J.D., 1947. Bar: Ky. 1947, U.S. Dist. Ct. (ea. dist.) Ky. 1950. Pros. atty. Somerset, Ky., 1950-63; commonwealth atty. 28th Jud. Dist., 1963-64; sole practice, Somerset; sr. ptnr. Law Offices of John G. Prather, Somerset; dir. First & Farmers Bank, Somerset. Served to lt. USN, 1942-46; Mem. Pulaski County Bar Assn., Ky. Bar Assn. (ethics com., com. on fees), ABA (probate sect.), Def. Research Inst. Democrat. Mem. Christian Ch. (Disciples of Christ). Clubs: Kiwanis (Somerset), Shriners, Odd Fellows, Masons. General practice, Probate (including wills, trusts), Estate taxation. Office: PO Box 616 Somerset KY 42502-0616

PRATHER, JOHN GIDEON, JR., lawyer; b. Lexington, Ky., Sept. 10, 1946; s. John Gideon Sr. and Marie Jeanette (Moore) P.; m. Hilma Elizabeth Skonberg, Aug. 4, 1973; children: John Hunt, Anna Russell. BS in Acctg., U. Ky., 1968, JD, 1970. Bar: Ky. 1971, U.S. Dist. Ct. (ea. dist.) Ky. 1978, U.S. Dist. Ct. (we. dist.) Ky. 1984, U.S. Ct. Appeals (6th cir.) 1988, U.S. Supreme Ct. 1988. Ptnr., prin. Law Offices John G. Prather, Somerset, Ky., 1972—; dir. Ky. Higher Edn. Assistance Authority, Somerset, 2002—. Bd. dirs. Lawyers Mutual Ins. Co. Ky., 1989—, treas., 1995-2002, chmn. bd., 2002—. Bd. dirs. United Way, 1978—; mem. state cen. com. Ky. Young. Dems., Frankfort, 1972. Served to 1st lt. USAF, 1971-72, JAG, 1972. Fellow U. Ky., 1998—. Mem. ABA (house dels.), ATLA, Am. Bd. Trial Advs., Am. Coll. Trial Lawyers, Am. Bd. Trial Attys., Ky. Bar Assn. (ho. of dels. 1984-85, bd. govs. 1985-91, v.p. 1991-92, pres.-elect 1992-93, pres. 1993-94, lectr.), Coun. Sch. Bd. Attys. (state pres., bd. dirs. 1986—, lectr.), Ky. Def. Coun. (bd. dirs. 1987-91), Pulaski County Indsl. Found. (bd. dirs. 1982-95), Phi Delta Phi. Mem. Christian Ch. Avocations: boating, flying. General practice, Personal injury (including property damage), Probate (including wills, trusts). Home: 510 N Main St Somerset KY 42501-1434 Office: PO Box 616 Somerset KY 42502-0616 E-mail: pratherlaw@msn.com.

PRATHER, KENNETH EARL, lawyer; b. Detroit, May 9, 1933; s. Earl and Agnes (Mesanko) P.; m. Shirley Armstrong, Dec. 26, 1955; children: Eric, Kimberly, Jon, Laura, Lisa; m. Jeanette M. Elder, June 30, 1973; 1 child, Kenneth. PhB, U. Detroit, 1955, JD 1960. Bar: Mich. 1960. Assoc. Kenney, Radom, Rockwell & Kenney, Detroit, 1960-66; ptnr. Kenney, Kenney, Chapman & Prather, Detroit, 1966-76; pvt. practice, Detroit, 1976-82; ptnr. Prather, Hilborn & Harrington, P.C., Detroit, 1982, Prather & Assocs., P.C., Detroit, 1982—; adj. prof. law U. Detroit. Fellow Am. Acad. Matrimonial Lawyers (bd. govs. 1988-89), Internat. Acad. Matrimonial Lawyers (bd. mgrs. 1989); mem. Am. Coll. Family Law Trial Lawyers, State Bar Mich. (chairperson family law sect. 1983-84), Detroit Athletic. Contbr. articles to legal jours. Family and matrimonial, Personal injury (including property damage). Home: 5 Stratford Pl Grosse Pointe MI 48230-1907 Office: Prather & Garwood PC 19846 Mack Ave Grosse Pointe Woods MI 48236

PRATHER, LENORE LOVING, former state supreme court chief justice; b. West Point, Miss., Sept. 17, 1931; d. Byron Herald and Hattie Hearn (Morris) Loving; m. Robert Brooks Prather, May 30, 1957; children: Pamela, Valerie Jo, Malinda Wayne. BS, Miss. Univ. Women, 1953; JD, U. Miss., 1955. Bar: Miss. 1955. Practice with B. H. Loving, West Point, 1955-60; sole practice, 1960-62, 65-71; assoc. practice, 1962-65; mcpl. judge City of West Point, 1965-71; chancery ct. judge 14th dist. State of Miss., Columbus, 1971-82, supreme ct. justice Jackson, 1982-92, presiding justice, 1993-97, chief justice, 1998-2001; interim pres. Miss. U. for Women, Columbus, Miss., 2001—02. V.p. Conf. Local Bar Assn., 1956-58; sec. Clay County Bar Assn., 1956-71 1st woman in Miss. to become chancery judge, 1971, and supreme ct. justice, 1982, and chief justice, 1998-2000. Mem. ABA, Miss. State Bar Assn., DAR, Rotary, Pilot Club, Jr. Aux. Columbus Club. Episcopalian. Fax: 662-328-7119.

PRATHER, ROBERT CHARLES, SR., lawyer; b. Kansas City, Mo., Feb. 16, 1945; s. Charles William and Shirley Anne P.; m. Lana Jo Ball, Jan. 25, 1969; children: Robert Charles Jr., Lisa Michelle. BSc in Comm., U. Tex., 1967, JD, 1970; postgrad., U. Tasmania, Australia, 1968. Bar: Tex. 1971, U.S. Dist. Ct. (no. dist.) Tex. 1978, U.S. Ct. Appeals (5th and 11th cirs.) 1981, U.S. Supreme Ct. 1978. Staff atty., com. clk. Senator W.T. Moore State Affairs Com. Tex. State Senate, Austin, 1971; asst. dist. atty. Dallas, 1971-74; asst. atty. U.S. No. Dist. Tex., Dalls, 1974-80; econ. crime enforcement specialist U.S. Dept. Justice, Dallas, 1980-81; assoc. trial atty. Turner, Rodgers, Sailers, Jordan & Calloway, Dallas, 1981-83; ptnr., trial atty. Jordan, Dunlap, Prather & Harris LLP, Dallas, 1983—. Author: (with others) A Document Numbering System, 1981, Texas ADR Practice Guide West, 1995. Gen. counsel, bd. dirs. Childrens Cancer Fund Dallas, Inc., 1982-91; soccer coach YMCA, North Dallas C. of C., 1979-84. Recipient Spl. Achievement award U.S. Dept. Justice, Washington, 1976; Rotary Found. fellow, 1968. Mem. ABA, Dallas Bar Assn., Assn. Atty.-Mediators (pres. North Tex. chpt. 2003), Am. Arbitration Assn. (panel 1992—), Argyle Club (pres. Dallas), Park City Club (bd. dirs.), Rotary (parliamentarian, bd. dirs.), Phi Alpha Delta. Baptist. Alternative dispute resolution, Property, real (including real estate development, water), Commercial, contracts (including sales of goods; commercial financing). Office: Jordan Dunlap Prather & Harris LLP 8111 Preston Rd Ste 400 Dallas TX 75225-6373 E-mail: prather@jdplegal.com.

PRATT, DARRELL, judge; b. Radnor, W.Va., Jan. 5, 1954; s. Fred and Vangie P. Pratt; m. Barbara L. Lycan, Dec. 15, 1973; children: Evan Elizabeth, Austin Harrison. BA in Social Studies, Marshall U., 1975; JD, W.Va. U., 1981. Bar: W.Va. 1981. Tchr. Wayne County Schs., Buffalo, W.Va., 1975—78; ptnr. Lycan & Pratt L.C., Wayne, W.Va., 1981—92; pros. atty. Wayne County Prosecutor, Wayne, 1984—96; judge Wayne County Cir. Ct., Wayne, 1997—. Mem. 5th dist. character com. W.Va. State Bar, Wayne, 1985—97; mem. juvenile justice com. Gov.'s Com. for Juvenile Justice, Charleston, W.Va., 1998—. Chmn. bd. dirs. Wayne County Cmty. Svc. Orgn., Wayne, 1983—, Stepping Stones Boys Home, Buffalo, 1984—90, Green Acres Ctr. for Mental Disabilities, Huntington, W.Va., 1982—. Avocations: antique cars, horses, golf. Home: Rt 2 Box 14 Prichard WV 25555 Office: Wayne County Cir Ct PO Box 68 Wayne WV 25570 Fax: 304-272-3246. E-mail: darrellpratt@courtswv.org.

PRATT, GEORGE CHENEY, law educator, retired federal judge; b. Corning, N.Y., May 22, 1928; s. George Wollage and Muriel (Cheney) Pratt; m. Carol June Hoffman, Aug. 16, 1952; children: George W., Lise M., Marcia Pratt Burke, William T. BA, Yale U., 1950, JD, 1953. Bar: N.Y. 1953, U.S. Supreme Ct. 1964, U.S. Ct. Appeals 1974. Law clk. to Charles W. Froessel (Judge of N.Y. Ct. Appeals), 1953—55; assoc. then ptnr. Sprague & Stern, Mineola, NY, 1956—60; ptnr. Andromidas, Pratt & Pitcher, Mineola, 1960—65, Pratt, Caemmerer & Cleary, Mineola, 1965—75; partner Farrell, Fritz, Pratt, Caemmerer & Cleary, 1975—76; judge U.S. Dist. Ct. (Ea. Dist. of N.Y.), 1976—82, U.S. Cir. Ct. Appeals for 2d cir. (Uniondale), NY, 1982—93; sr. circ. judge U.S. Cir. of Appeals for 2d Cir., NY, 1993—95; counsel Parnon & Pratt L.L.P., N.Y.C., 1995—2000, Farrell Fritz PC, 2001—. Prof. Touro Law Sch., Huntington, NY, 1993—. Fellow: Coll. Comml. Arbitrators; mem.: ATLA, ABA, Soc. Am. Law Tchrs., Nassau County Bar Assn., N.Y. State Bar Assn. United Ch. Of Christ. Office: Farrell Fritz PC EAB Plaza West Tower 14th Fl Uniondale NY 11556-0120 E-mail: gpratt@farrellfritz.com.

PRATT, ROBERT WINDSOR, lawyer; b. Findlay, Ohio, Mar. 6, 1950; s. John Windsor and Isabelle (Vance) P.; m. Catherine Camak Baker, Sept. 3, 1977; children: Andrew Windsor, David Camak, James Robert. AB, Wittenberg U., Springfield, Ohio, 1972; JD, Yale U., 1975. Bar: Ill. 1975, U.S. Dist. Ct. (no. dist.) Ill. 1976, U.S. Dist. Ct. (we. dist.) Mich. 1995, U.S. Ct. Appeals (fed. cir.) 1984, U.S. Ct. Appeals (7th cir.) 1996. Assoc. Keck, Mahin & Cate, Chgo., 1975—81, ptnr., 1981—97; pvt. practice Wilmette, Ill., 1998—99; sr. asst. atty. gen. Office Ill. Atty. Gen., 1999—2001, chief antitrust bur., 2001—. Bd. dirs. Chgo. region ARC, 1985-96, vice chmn., 1988-92, chmn., 1992-96, bd. dirs. Mid-Am. chpt., 1992-96. Mem. ABA, Chgo. Bar Assn., Yale Club (Chgo.). Antitrust, Commercial, contracts (including sales of goods; commercial financing), Finance. Personal E-mail: rowpr50@msn.com. Business E-Mail: rpratt@atg.state.il.us.

PRATT, SCOTT OWEN, lawyer; b. Glendale, Calif., Oct. 18, 1955; s. Donald Hugh and Marlene Fay (Johnson) P.; m. Teresa Jean Browning, Sept. 6, 1996; 1 child, Avery J. BS, U. Wis., Eau Claire, 1978; JD, Willamette U., 1981. Bar: Oreg., Wash., U.S. Dist. Ct. (we. dist.) Wash., U.S. Dist. Ct. Oreg.; U.S. Ct. Appeals (9th cir.) Oreg. Assoc. Webb & Martinez, Salem, 1981-82; pvt. practice Portland, Oreg., 1983—. Pres. Laurelhurst Neighborhood Assn., Portland, 1994-96; chair Oreg. League of Conservation Voters, Portland, 1987-93; candidate for bd. of Portland Met. Area Regional Govt., 1998. Corporate, general, Estate planning, Property, real (including real estate development, water). Office: 806 SW Broadway Ste 1200 Portland OR 97205-3314 E-mail: scopratt@netscape.net.

PRATTE, GEOFFREY LYNN, lawyer, arbitrator; b. Bonne Terre, Mo., Sept. 14, 1940; s. Charles John and Ruth Jane (Thornton) P.; m. Gretchen Ann Westendorf, Mar. 15, 1969; children: Stephen Charles, Geoffrey Marc, Nicole Elizabeth, Gregory Lynn, Robert Wendell. BA in Philosophy, Kilroe Coll., 1963; MA in French, St. Louis U., 1967; JD, Wash. U., 1974. Bar: Mo. 1974, U.S. Dist. Ct. (ea. dist.) Mo. Tchr. Divine Heart Sem., Donaldson, Ind., 1963-65; analyst CIA, McLean, Va., 1967-71; assoc. Roberts & Roberts, Farmington, Mo., 1974-87; pvt. practice Farmington, Mo., 1987—; asst. pros. atty. St. Francois County, Farmington, Mo., 1987-93; city pros. atty. Bonne Terre, Mo., 1988—. Labor arbitrator Fed. Mediation and Conciliation Svc., Washington, 1988—. Bd. dirs. Terre du Lac Property Owners Assn., 1976-87. Mem. Order of the Coif, KC. Roman Catholic. Avocations: jogging, gardening. Office: 205 E Liberty St Farmington MO 63640-3129

PRAVEL, BERNARR ROE, lawyer; b. Feb. 10, 1924; BSChemE, Rice U., 1947; JD, George Washington U., 1951. Bar: D.C. 1951, Tex. 1951, U.S. Supreme Ct. 1951. Ptnr. Pravel, Hewitt firm, 1956—99; sr. counsel Akin, Gump, Houston, 1999—2002. Patent editor George Washington U. Law Rev., 1950. Precinct chmn. Houston Rep. Com., 1972-74. Served to lt. (j.g.) USNR. Fellow Am. Bar Found., Tex. Bar Found.; mem. ABA (chair intellectual property sect. 1991-92), Tex. Bar Assn. (chmn. patent, trademark sect. 1968-69, bd. dirs. 1976-79, Outstanding Contbn. 1982), Nat. Coun. Patent Law (chmn. 1970-71), Am. Intellectual Property Law Assn. (pres. 1983-84), Houston Intellectual Property Law Assn. (pres. 1983-84, Outstanding Svc. award 1986), Order of Coif, Kiwanis, Tau Beta Pi. Intellectual property, Patent, Trademark and copyright. Home: 10806 Oak Hollow St Houston TX 77024-3017 E-mail: bpravel@sbcglobal.net.

PREBLE, LAURENCE GEORGE, lawyer; b. Denver, Apr. 24, 1939; s. George Enos and Ruth (Jewett) Preble; m. Deborah Joan Horton, Aug. 24, 1963; children: Robin Lee, Randall Laurence. B in Petroleum Refining Engring., Colo. Sch. Mines, 1961; JD cum laude, Loyola U., Los Angeles, 1968. Bar: Calif. 1969, D.C. 1983, N.Y. 1987, U.S. Dist. Ct. (cen. dist.) Calif. 1969. Assoc. firm O'Melveny & Myers, Los Angeles, 1968-76, ptnr. L.A., 1976—2000; dir. devel. KUD Internat. LLC, 2001—. Adj. prof. law Southwestern U., 1970-75, Loyola U. of L.A. Sch. Law, 1984-92, 99-2000, Fordham U. Sch. Law, 1992-98, Calif. Continuing Edn. of the Bar; lectr., author Practicing Law Inst. Trustee Harvey Mudd Coll., 1991-94, Citizens Bidget Commn. N.Y.C., 1994-98, Ho. Ear Inst., 1998—, vice-chmn., 2001—. Recipient Disting. Achievement medal, Colo. Sch. Mines, 1998. Mem. Los Angeles County Bar Assn. (chmn. real property sect. 1979-80, Outstanding Leadership award 1999), Assn. Bar City of N.Y. (real property sect. exec. com. 1993-96), N.Y. State Bar Assn. (exec. com. real property sect. 1996—), Calif. Bar Assn. (mem. exec. com. real property sect.), ABA, Am. Coll. Real Estate Lawyers (bd. govs. 1986—), Anglo-Am. Real Property Inst., La Canada-Flintridge C. of C. (pres. 1974-75), Loyola Law Sch. Alumni Assn. (pres. 1978). Banking, Commercial, contracts (including sales of goods; commercial financing), Property, real (including real estate development, water). Office: KUD Internat LLC 100 Wilshire Blvd Ste 1800 Santa Monica CA 90401

PREDOIU, CATALIN MARIAN, lawyer, law educator; b. Buzău, Romania, Aug. 27, 1968; s. Gheorghe Predoiu; m. Alina Andreea Zamfirescu, Aug. 26, 2000; 1 child, Toma Andrei. BA in Law, U. Bucharest, Romania, 1991. Bar: Bucharest 1991. Prof. U. Bucharest, 1994—; sr. ptnr. Racotti, Predoiu & Ptnrs., Bucharest, 1996—. Bd. dirs. Dorna Apemin S.A., Bucharest, Dorna Lactate S.A., Bucharest. Co-author: Company Law, 2001. Lt. Romanian Mil., 1986—87. Recipient I.L. Georgescu award, Romanian Dem. Union Legal Counselors, 2001. Mem.: Insol Europe, Romanian Bar Assn. (counselor), Internat. Bar Assn. Avocations: internat. politics, philosophy, sports. Commercial, contracts (including sales of goods; commercial financing), Banking, Alternative dispute resolution. Office: Univ Bucharest Law Sch Mihail Kogalniceanu 36-46 70609 Bucharest Romania Home: 12 Aurel Vlaicu St Apt 4 2nd dist Bucharest Romania

PREISENBERGER, SIMON ANDREAS, lawyer; b. Erlangen, Germany, Oct. 24, 1968; s. Ernst and Johanna Preisenberger; m. Carmen Stocker-Preisenberger, Sept. 8, 1995; 1 child, Paul. Grad., U. Tuebingen, 1995, State Baden-Wuerttemberg, 1997; Dr. Iur., U. Tuebingen, 1999. Bar: Freiburg 1997, Munich 1999, Ct. Appeals Munich 2002. Apprentice Deutsche Bank, Ludwigsburg, Germany, 1989—90; assoc. Kaspar & Ptnr., Freiburg, 1997—99, Haarmann Hemmelrath & Ptnr., Munich, 1999—2001, ptnr., 2001—. Avocation: clarinet. Mergers and acquisitions, Corporate, general, Commercial, contracts (including sales of goods; commercial financing). Office: Haarmann Hemmelrath & Ptnr Maximillianstrasse 35 80539 Munich Germany Fax: 49-89 21636133. E-mail: simon.preisenberger@haarmannhemmelrath.com.

PREM, F. HERBERT, JR., lawyer; b. N.Y.C., Jan. 14, 1932; s. F. Herbert Prem Sr. and Sybil Gertrude (Nichols) Prem; m. Patricia Ryan, Nov. 18, 1978; children from previous marriage: Julia Nichols, F. Herbert III(dec.). AB, Yale U., New Haven, 1953; JD, Harvard U., Mass., 1959. Bar: N.Y., 1960. Assoc. Whitman and Ransom, N.Y.C., 1959-66; ptnr. Whitman and Ransom, N.Y.C., 1967-93; co-chmn. exec. com. Whitman and Ransom, N.Y.C., 1988-92, chmn., 1993, Whitman, Breed ,Abbott , and Morgan LLP, N.Y.C., 1993-99; of counsel Whitman ,Breed, Abbott, and Morgan LLP, N.Y.C., 2000; vol. atty. The Legal Aid Soc., N.Y.C., 2000—03. Bd. dir., Fuji Photo Film U.S.A., Inc., Fuji Film Med. Sys. U.S.A., Inc., Seiko Instruments Am., Inc. Bd. dir., Bagaduce Music Lending Libr., Inc., 1988—95, pres., 1989—93; bd. dir., The Health Care Chaplaincy, Inc., Inter Faith Neighbors, Inc.; bd. dir. Legal Aid Soc., N.Y.C., 1969—73; bd. dir., Cmty. Action for Legal Svc., Inc., 1967—70, treas. Lt. j.g. USNR, 1953—56. Mem. ABA, Assn. of Bar of N.Y.C., (sec. 1967-69), N.Y. State Bar Assn., Am. Law Inst. (life), Union Club, Yale Club. Episcopalian. Corporate, general, Private international, Education and schools.

PRENDERGAST, TERRY NEILL, lawyer; b. Sioux Falls, S.D., May 25, 1953; s. Harry Neill and Dorothy Gretchen (Angerhofer) P.; m. Susan Jane Larson, Aug. 2, 1980; children, Christopher Neill, Steven Robert. B.A. cum laude, Augustana Coll., 1975; M.B.A., U. S.D., 1978, J.D. magna cum laude, 1978. Bar: S.D. 1978, U.S. Dist. Ct. S.D. 1978, U.S. Tax Ct. 1981, U.S. Ct. Appeals (8th cir.) 1981. Law clk. U.S. Dist. Ct., Sioux Falls, 1978-79; ptnr. Boyce, Murphy, McDowell & Greenfield, Sioux Falls, 1979—2002; founding ptnr. Murphy, Goldammer & Prendergast, L.L.P., Sioux Falls, 2003--; chmn. continuing legal edn. com. State Bar S.D., Pierre, 1984-87, Bar Commr., 1987-90; city atty. Lennox, S.D., 1980-82. Mem. ABA (coms. on corp., banking and bus. law, sci. and tech.), Assn. Trial Lawyers Am., S.D. Trial Lawyers Assn., Comml. Law League Am., Am. Judicature Soc., Assn. Coll. and Univ. Attys. Republican. Methodist. Lodges: Kiwanis (bd. dirs. 1981-83, v.p. 1986-87, pres. 1987-88), Elks. Banking, Federal civil litigation, Property, real (including real estate development, water). Home: 2904 S 1st Ave Sioux Falls SD 57105-4915 Office: Murphy Goldammer & Prendergast LLP 402 Wells Fargo Bldg PO Box 1728 Sioux Falls SD 57101-1728

PRENTKE, RICHARD OTTESEN, lawyer; b. Cleve., Sept. 8, 1945; s. Herbert E. and Melva B. (Horbury) P.; m. Susan Ottesen, June 9, 1974; children: Catherine, Elizabeth. BSE, Princeton U., 1967; JD, Harvard U., 1974. Assoc. Perkins Coie, Seattle, 1974-80, ptnr., 1981—, CFO, 1989-94. Author: School Construction Law Deskbook, 1989, rev. 2d edit. 1998; contbr. articles to profl. jours. Pres., trustee Seattle County Day Sch., 1990-95; trustee Pocock Rowing Found., 1996—. With USN, 1967-70. Fellow Leadership Tomorrow, Seattle, 1985-86. Mem. ABA, Wash. State Bar Assn. (mem. jud. screening com. 1985-91, chmn. 1987-91), Seattle-King County Bar Assn. (chmn. jud. task force 1990-93), Am. Arbitration Assn. (arbitrator 1988—), Princeton U. Rowing Assn. (pres. 1993—, trustee 1976—), Rainier Club, Princeton Club Wash. (trustee 1986—, pres. 1990-92), Seattle Tennis Club. Avocations: art, carpentry, travel, rowing, sports. Computer, Construction. Office: Perkins Coie 1201 3rd Ave Fl 40 Seattle WA 98101-3029

PRESANT, SANFORD CALVIN, lawyer, educator, writer, tax specialist; b. Buffalo, N.Y., Nov. 15, 1952; s. Allen and Reeta Presant; children: Jarrett, Danny, Lauren; m. Nancy Loeb. BA, Cornell U., 1973; JD cum laude, SUNY, Buffalo, 1976; LLM in Taxation, Georgetown U., NYU, 1981. Bar: N.Y. 1977, D.C. 1977, U.S. Tax Ct. 1977, U.S. Ct. Claims 1978, Calif. 1992, U.S. Supreme Ct. 1982. Staff atty. SEC Options Task Force, Washington, 1976-78; assoc. Barrett Smith Schapiro, N.Y.C., 1978-80, Trubin Sillcocks, N.Y.C., 1980-81; ptnr. Carro, Spanbock, Fass, Geller, Kaster, N.Y.C., 1981-86, Finley, Kumble, Wagner, Heine, Underberg, Manley, Myerson & Casey, N.Y.C., 1987, Kaye, Scholer, Fierman, Hays & Handler, N.Y.C., 1987-95, Battle Fowler LLP, L.A., 1995-2000, Ernst & Young, L.A., 2000—; nat. dir. real estate tax strategies, opportunity funds Ernst & Young LLP, L.A., 2000—. Adj. assoc. prof. real estate NYU, 1984—; frequest lectr. in tax law; regular TV appearances on Nightly Business Report, Pub. Broadcasting System, 1986-88; co-chmn. NYU Conf. Fed. Taxation of Real Estate Transactions, 1987, PLI Advanced Tax Planning for Real Estate, 1987, PLI Ann. Real Estate Tax Forum, 1999—; conf. chmn. various confs. in field. Author: (with others) Tax Aspects of Real Investments, 2002, Understanding Partnership Tax Allocations, 1987, Realty Joint Ventures, 1980-86, Tax Sheltered Investments Handbook-Special Update on Tax Reform Act of 1984, Real Estate Syndication Handbook, 1986, Real Estate Syndication Tax Handbook, 1987, The Tax Reform Act of 1986, 1987, The Final Partnership Nonrecourse Debt Allocation Regulations, 1987, Taxation of Real Estate Investments, 1987, Understanding Partnership Tax Allocations, 1987, Tax Aspects of Environmental (Superfund) Settlements, 1994, The Proposed Publicly Traded Partnership Regulations, 1995, others. Kripke Securities Law fellow NYU, 1976. Mem. ABA (nat. chmn. audit subcom. of tax sect. partnership com. 1984-86, partnership tax allocation subcom. chmn. 1986-90, nat. chmn. partnership com. 1992-94, chmn. task force publicly traded partnerships 1995—, others), N.Y. State Bar Assn. (tax sect. partnership com. 1980—), Assn. of Bar of City of N.Y. Republican. Jewish. Securities, Corporate taxation, Personal income taxation. Office: Ernst & Young LLP Ste 1800 2049 Century Park E Los Angeles CA 90067-3119 Fax: 310-284-7970. E-mail: sanford.presant@ey.com.

PRESCOTT, DANA E. lawyer; b. Aug. 1958; BA, Western New Eng. Coll.; JD, Vt. Law Sch. Bar: Maine 1983. Atty. Prescott Lemoine Jamieson & Nelson, PA, Saco, Maine. Mem.: Maine State Bar Assn. (pres.-elect). Office: Prescott Lemoine Jamieson and Nelson PO Box 1190 Saco ME 04072-1190*

PRESKA, LORETTA A. federal judge; b. 1949; BA, Coll. of St. Rose, 1970; JD, Fordham U., 1973; LLM, NYU, 1978; LHD (hon.), Coll. of St. Rose, 1995. Assoc. Cahill, Gordon & Reindel, N.Y.C., 1973-82; ptnr. Hertzog, Calamari & Gleason, N.Y.C., 1982-92; fed. judge U.S. Dist. Ct. (so. dist.) N.Y., N.Y.C., 1992—. Mem. N.Y. State Bar Assn., N.Y. County Lawyers Assn., Fed. Bar Coun., Fordham Law Alumni Assn. (v.p.). Office: US Courthouse 500 Pearl St Rm 1320 New York NY 10007-1316

PRESSLEY, FRED G., JR., lawyer; b. N.Y.C., June 19, 1953; s. Fred G. Sr. and Frances (Sanders) P.; m. Cynthia Denise Hill, Sept. 5, 1981. BA cum laude, Union Coll., 1975; JD, Northwestern U., 1978. Bar: Ohio 1978, U.S. Dist. Ct. (so. dist.) Ohio 1979, U.S. Dist. Ct. (no. dist.) Ohio 1985, U.S. Dist. Ct. (ea. dist.) Wis. 1980, U.S. Ct. Appeals (6th cir.). Assoc. Porter, Wright, Morris & Arthur, Columbus, Ohio, 1978-85, ptnr., 1985—. Bd. dirs. Columbus Area Leadership Program, 1981-84, Franklin County Bd. Mental Retardation and Devel. Disabilities, Columbus, 1989-97, Union Coll., Schenectady, N.Y., 1992—. Recipient Civic Achievement award Ohio Ho. of Reps., 1988. Mem. ABA. Avocations: jogging, golf, basketball, military history. Civil rights, Labor (including EEOC, Fair Labor Standards Act, labor-management relations, NLRB, OSHA). Office: Porter Wright Morris & Arthur 41 S High St Ste 2800 Columbus OH 43215-6194

PRESTI, GERALYN MARIE, lawyer; b. Cleve., July 15, 1955; d. Joseph Carl Presti and Josephine Joanne Ambrogio; m. John Reid Sedor, Aug. 16, 1980; 2 children. BMus, Ohio U., 1979; M of Social Sci. Adminstrn. magna cum laude, JD, Case Western Res. U., 1988. Bar: Ohio 1989. Music therapist Bellefaire, Cleve., 1978-79, The Cleve. Music Sch. Settlement, Cleve., 1979-84; gen. counsel, sr. v.p. Forest City Enterprises, Inc., Cleve., 1989—. Admissions counsellor Case Western Res. U., Cleve., 1993-96, rsch. asst., law prof., 1994-96, adv. bd. LLM degree fgn. students, 1998—. Trustee Homeowners Assn., Bentleyville, Ohio, 1992-94; treas. bd. trustees Cleve. Music Sch. Settlement, 1999—; trustee, Bus. Vol. Unlimited, 2003; co-chmn. ann. fund U. Sch., Shaker Heights, Ohio, 1998—; dir. Ohio U. Sch. of Music, Athens, 1985-86; project mem. Reorgn. of the Cuyahoga County Dept. Human Svcs., Cleve., 1985. Recipient Greater Cleve. Woman of Profl. Excellence award YWCA, 1996. Mem. Greater Cleve. Gen. Counsel Assn. (trustee), Vis. Com. Case Western Res. U. law sch., Order of the Coif. Avocations: pianist, travelling, art, reading, films. Property, real (including real estate development, water), Corporate, general. Office: Forest City Enterprise Inc 50 Public Sq Cleveland OH 44113-2267

PRESTON, BRUCE MARSHALL, lawyer, educator; b. Trinidad, Colo., Feb. 24, 1949; s. Marshall Caldwell and Juanita (Killgore) P.; m. Mariannina Erra, Aug. 10, 1974; children: Charles Marshall, Robert Arthur. BS summa cum laude, Ariz. State U., 1971; MA, U. Ariz., 1972, JD, 1975. Bar: Ariz. 1975, Colo. 2002, U.S. Ct. Appeals (9th cir.) 1976, U.S. Ct. Claims 1983, U.S. Tax Ct. 1983, U.S. Supreme Ct. 1983, Colo. 2002; cert. fin. planner. Atty. Maricopa County Office of Pub. Defender, Phoenix, 1975-84; ptnr. Simonsen & Preston, Phoenix, 1985-86, Simonsen, Preston, Sargeant & Arbetman, Phoenix, 1986; atty. office of atty. gen. State of Ariz., 1987-90; assoc. Broening, Oberg and Woods, Phoenix, 1989-96, ptnr., 1997—. Judge pro tem Mcpl. Ct., Phoenix, 1984-86; licensee in sales Ariz. Dept. Real Estate, Phoenix, 1981-87; adj. faculty Phoenix Coll. for Fin. Planning, Denver, 1984-87, Maricopa County Community Coll. Dist., Phoenix, 1985-87, Ariz. State U. Coll. of Bus., Tempe, 1986-87, Ottawa U., Phoenix, 1986. Chmn. com., treas., pres. bd. dirs. Kachina Country Day Sch., 1982-90; bd. dirs. Family Svc. Agy., Phoenix, 1988—, treas., 1990-91; bd. dirs. Clearwater Hills Homeowners Assn., Paradise Valley, Ariz., 1989—, v.p., 1990, treas., 1991; bd. dirs. Phoenix Boys Choir, 1989-90. Mem. Ariz. Assn. Def. Counsel, Ariz. Bar Assn. (cert. specialist criminal law 1982-84), Colo. Bar Assn., Maricopa County Bar Assn., Ariz. State U. Coll. Liberal Arts Alumni Assn. (bd. dirs. 1978-80, 87-88), Phi Kappa Phi. Avocations: computers, skiing, boating, running. General civil litigation, Insurance, Personal injury (including property damage). Home: 7247 N Black Rock Trl Paradise Valley AZ 85253-2802 Office: Broening Oberg & Woods 1122 E Jefferson St Phoenix AZ 85034-2224 E-mail: bmp@bowwc.com.

PRESTON, CAROLINE MARY, lawyer; b. London, Apr. 12, 1955; d. Robert Edmund and Barbara ALice Orr; m. John Peter Preston, June 6, 1981; children: Eliza, Arthur. BA (hon.) in History, Polit. Sci., Dublin, Ireland, 1977; Solicitor, Law Soc. of Ireland, 1980. Qualified solicitor. Solicitor A&L Goodbody, Dublin, Ireland, 1980-86, ptnr., 1986—, head of litigation, 1997—. Personal solicitor Atty. Gen. of Ireland, 1994—97. Dir. St. Patrick's Hosp., Dublin, 1993—, Cancer Soc. Ireland, 1990-95. Mem. IWF Ireland. Avocations: fox hunting, fishing, travel. General civil litigation, Product liability, Professional liability. Home: Swainstown Kilmessan 25256 Ireland Office: A&L Goodbody 1 North Wall Dublin 1 Ireland E-mail: cpreston@algoodbody.ie.

PRESTON, CHARLES GEORGE, lawyer; b. Nov. 11, 1940; s. Charles William and Gudveig Nicoline (Hoem) P.; m. Hilde Delphine van Stappen, Mar. 12, 1970; children: Charles William, Stephanie Delphine, Christina Nicoline. BA, U. Wash., 1963, MPA, 1968; JD, Columbia U., 1971. Bar: Wash. 1971, D.C. 1981, U.S. Dist. Ct. D.C. 1981, U.S. Dist. Ct. (we. dist.) Wash. 1971, U.S. Ct. Appeals (9th cir.) 1972, U.S. Ct. Appeals (4th cir.) 1979, U.s. Ct. Appeals (5th and D.C. cirs.) 1978, U.S. Ct. Appeals (2d cir.) 1980, U.S. Ct. Appeals (11th cir.) 1981, U.S. Supreme Ct. 1977, U.S. Ct. Claims 1982, U.S. Ct. Appeals (1st cir.) 1984, U.S. Ct. Appeals (3d, 6th and 7th cirs.) 1987, Va. 1987, U.S. Dist. Ct. (ea. dist.) Va. 1989, U.S. Dist. Ct. (we. dist.) Wash. 1971, U.S. Dist. Ct. (no. dist.) Calif. 1981, U.S. Bankruptcy Ct. Va. 1990. Assoc. Jones, Grey, Bayley & Olson, Seattle, 1971-72; atty., asst. counsel for litigation Officer of Solicitor U.S. Dept. Labor, Seattle, 1972-76, Washington, 1976-81; atty. Air Line Pilots Assn., Washington, 1981-82; mng. ptnr. MacNabb, Preston & Waxman, Washington, 1981-86, Preston & Preston, Great Falls, Va., 1986-95, Charles G. Preston, P.C., 1995—. Pres. Preston Group, Inc. 1989-98; lectr. seminars. Mem. Wash. State Bar, D.C. Bar Assn., Va. Bar Assn., Tng. Law Inst. (pres. 1985-95), Gt. Falls Bus. and Profl. Assn. (pres. 1990), The Serbian Crown, Va. (pres. 1989-99). State civil litigation, Corporate, general, Property, real (including real estate development, water). Office: Charles G Preston PC 774C Walker Rd Great Falls VA 22066-2639 E-mail: preston.law@verizon.net.

PRESTON, CHARLES MICHAEL, lawyer; b. Balt., Oct. 11, 1945; s. Carlton Edward and Jeannette Thorn (Baker) P.; m. Carol Ann Armacost, June 21, 1969 (div. Dec. 1978). BA, Western Md. Coll., 1967; JD, U. Balt., 1970. Bar: Md. 1970, U.S. Dist. Ct. Md. 1972, U.S. Supreme Ct. 1974, U.S. Dist. Ct. (trial bar) 1984. Law clk. to Hon. E.O. Weant, Jr., Westminster, Md., 1970-71; assoc. Hoffman & Hoffman, Westminster, 1972-75; ptnr. Hoffman, Hoffman & Preston, Westminster, 1976-77, Hoffman, Stoner & Preston, Westminster, 1978-79; ptnr., v.p. Stoner, Preston & Boswell Chartered, Westminster, 1980—. Rev. bd., panel mem. Atty. Grievance Commn., Annapolis, Md., 1978-95; mem. Md. Ct. Appeals Commn. on alternate dispute resolution, 1998-2000, adv. bd., Md. Mediation and Conflict Resolution Office (co-chair, Circuit Courts Com.), 2001-, Md. Ct. of Appeals Task Force on Professionalism, 2002-. Contbr. articles to profl. jours. Mem. Carroll County Gen. Hosp., Westminster, 1983—; trustee Raymond I. Richardson Found., Middleburg, Md., 1979-93; bd. dirs. Carroll County Agrl. Ctr., Westminster, 1975—; dir. N.W. dist. ARC, Balt., 1987-95; trustee Balt. Opera Co., 1998-2001. With U.S. Army, 1970-71. Fellow Md. Bar Found. (dir. 1998-), Am. Bar Found.; mem. ABA (del. ho.

of dels., 1997-2000), Md. State Bar Assn. (treas. 1991-96, bd. govs. 1985-86, 91-2000, pres.-elect 1997, pres. 98), Carroll County Bar Assn. (pres. 1985), Pro Bono Resource Ctr. Md. (bd. dirs. 1997-2000), Elks. Presbyterian. Avocations: snow skiing, ice skating, woodworking, music, travel. Appellate, Criminal, Land use and zoning (including planning). Office: Stoner Preston & Boswell PO Box 389 188 E Main St Westminster MD 21157-5017

PRESTON, DAVID RAYMOND, lawyer; b. Harlingen, Tex., Feb. 12, 1961; s. Raymond C., Jr. and Janet (Bowman) P. BS, U. Fla., 1983, MS, 1985, PhD, 1989; JD, George Mason Sch. Law, 1996. Bar: Calif., U.S. Patent and Tradmark Office. Postdoctoral rsch. U.S. Army, Frederick, Md., 1989-90; patent examiner U.S. Patent and Trademark Office, Washington, 1990-94; tech. devel. specialist Nat. Cancer Inst., NIH, Bethesda, Md., 1994-96; intern for Judge Rader U.S. Ct. Appeals (fed. cir.), Washington, 1995; patent attorney Campbell & Flores, San Diego, 1996-97; asst. patent counsel Aurora Bioscis. Corp., San Diego, 1997-98; pres. David R. Preston & Assocs., San Diego, 1999—. Judge internat. sci. fair U.S. Patents and Trademark Office, 1991. NIH fellow, 1987, Pres.'s fellow Am. Soc. Microbiology, 1988. Mem. AAAS, ABA, Am. Intellectual Property Law Assn., Fed. Cir. Bar Assn., San Diego Intellectual Property Law Assn. Republican. Avocations: tennis, golf, skiing, surfing, windsurfing. Intellectual property, Patent. Office: David R Preston & Assocs 12625 High Bluff Dr Ste 205 San Diego CA 92130- E-mail: preston@drpna.com.

PRESTON, JAMES YOUNG, lawyer; b. Atlanta, Sept. 21, 1937; s. James William and Mary Lou (Young) P.; m. Elizabeth Buxton Gregory, June 13, 1959; children: Elizabeth P. Carr, Mary Lane P. Lennon, James Brenton Preston. BA in English, U. N.C., 1958, JD with high honors, 1961. Bar: N.C. 1961. Assoc. to ptnr. Parker, Poe, Adams & Bernstein L.L.P. and predecessors, Charlotte, N.C., 1961—. Pres. Charlotte Area Fund, 1968, Cmty. Sch. of Arts, 1976-78; pres. Arts and Sci. Coun. Charlotte/Mecklenburg, Inc., 1986-87, chair The Nat. Conf. for Cmty. and Justice, Charlotte, 1996-99, Wildacres Leadership Initiative, 1994—; vice chair N.C. Dance Theatre, 1995-97. Mem. ABA (ho. dels. 1988-92, 95-97), N.C. State Bar (pres. 1987-88), Am. Law Inst., Nat. Conf. Bar Presidents (exec. coun. 1989-92), Phi Beta Kappa, Phi Eta Sigma. Democrat. Episcopalian. Avocations: travel, tennis, profl. and civic activities. Corporate, general, Estate planning, Taxation, general. Office: Parker Poe Adams Bernstein LLP 3000 Three Wachovia Ctr 401 S Tryon St Charlotte NC 28202 E-mail: jimpreston@parkerpoe.com.

PRESTON, ROBERT BRUCE, retired lawyer; b. Cleve., Feb. 24, 1926; s. Robert Bruce and Erma May (Hunter) P.; m. Agnes Ellen Stanley, Jan. 29, 1949; children— Robert B., Patricia Ellen Preston Kiefer, Judith Helen Preston Yanover. AB, Western Res. U., 1950, JD, 1952. Bar: U.S. Dist. Ct. (no. dist.) Ohio 1953, U.S. Ct. Appeals (6th cir.) 1959, U.S. Supreme Ct. 1964. Assoc. Arter & Hadden, Cleve., 1952-63, ptnr., 1964-93; ret., 1994. Dir. Service Stampings Inc., Willoughby, Ohio. Vice pres. Citizens League Cleve., 1965; chmn. Charter Rev. Com., Cleveland Heights, Ohio, 1972; mem. Zoning Bd. Appeals, Cleveland Heights, 1974-76; trustee Women's Philanthropic Union, 1977—. Mem. Ohio Bar Assn., Greater Cleve. Bar Assn. Republican. Presbyterian. Avocations: tennis, fishing, travel. Home: 117 Manor Brook Dr Chagrin Falls OH 44022-4163 Office: Arter & Hadden 1100 Huntington Bldg Cleveland OH 44115

PRESTON, STEPHEN W. lawyer; BA summa cum laude, Yale U., 1979; diploma., Trinity Coll., U. Dublin, 1980; JD magna cum laude, Harvard U., 1983. Bar: D.C. Law clk. to Hon. Phyllis A. Kravitch U.S. Ct. Appeals (11th cir.), 1983-84; vis. fellow Ctr. for Law in Pub. Interest, Washington, 1984-85; ptnr. Wilmer, Cutler & Pickering, Washington, 1986-93; prin. dep. gen. counsel, acting gen. counsel Dept. of Def., 1993-95; dep. asst. atty. gen. Dept. of Justice, 1995-98; gen. counsel Dept. of Navy, 1998-2000; ptnr. Wilmer, Cutler & Pickering, Washington, 2001—. Recipient Disting. Pub. Svc. medal Dept. of Def., 1995, 2000, Dept. of Navy, 2000. Office: Wilmer Cutler & Pickering 2445 M St NW Washington DC 20037-1420 E-mail: stephen.preston@wilmer.com.

PRESTRIDGE, PAMELA ADAIR, lawyer; b. Delhi, La., Dec. 25, 1945; d. Gerald Wallace Prestridge and Louis Baugh and Peggy Adair (Arender) Martin. BA, La. Poly. U., 1967; M in Edn., La. State u., 1968, JD, 1973. Bar: U.S. Dist. Ct. (mid. dist.) La. 1975, U.S. Dist. Ct. (so. dist.) Tex. 1982, U.S. Ct. Appeals (5th cir.) 1982, U.S. Supreme Ct. 1990. Law clk. to presiding justice La. State Dist. Ct., Baton Rouge, 1973-75; ptnr. Breazeale, Sachse & Wilson, Baton Rouge, 1975-82, Hirsch & Westheimer P.C., Houston, 1982-92; pvt. practive, Houston, 1992—. Counselor Big Bros./Big Sisters, Baton Rouge, 1968-70; legal cons., bd. dirs. Lupus Found. Am., Houston, 1984-93; bd. dirs. Quota Club, Baton Rouge, 1979-82, Speech and Hearing Found., Baton Rouge, 1981-82, The Actors Workshop, Houston, 1988-93, Tex. Satsang Soc., 2000—; active Tex. Accts. and Attys. for the Arts. Recipient Pres.'s award Lupus Found. Am., 1991, cert. of appreciation Assn. Atty. Mediators, 1992, Outstanding Profl. Woman of Houston award Fedn. Profl. Women, 1984. Mem. ABA, La. Bar Assn., Tex. Bar Assn., Houston Bar Assn., Houston Bar Found., Assn. Atty. Mediators (bd. dirs. 1994-96, Citation for Outstanding Mems. 1993), Profl. Atty.-Mediators Coop. (v.p. 1994, bd. dirs. 1994-96, pres. 1995), Phi Alpha Delta. Eckankar. Avocations: acting, ultralite flying. Alternative dispute resolution, Bankruptcy, General civil litigation. Home: 1701 Hermann Dr Unit 407 Houston TX 77004-7345 Office: 3200 Southwest Freeway Ste 3300 PO Box 130987 Houston TX 77219-0987

PRETTYMAN, ELIJAH BARRETT, JR., lawyer; b. Washington, June 1, 1925; s. Elijah Barrett and Lucy Courtney (Hill) P.; children by previous marriage: Elijah Barrett III, Jill Savage Lukoschek. BA, Yale U., 1949; LLB, U. Va., 1953. Bar: Wash., D.C. 1954, U.S. Supreme Ct. 1957. Pvt. practice, Washington, 1955—; law clk. to Hon. Justices Jackson, Frankfurter and Harlan U.S. Supreme Ct., 1953-55; assoc. Hogan & Hartson, Washington, 1955—63, ptnr., 1964—2001, of counsel, 2002—; inspector gen. Dist. of Colo., Washington, 1998—99. Spl. asst. to Atty. Gen. U.S., 1963, White House, 1963-64; also Pres. rep. to Interagy. Com. on Transport Mergers; spl. cons. subcom. to investigate problems connected with refugees and escapees, U.S. Senate Judiciary Com., Vietnam, 1967-68; outside cons. to subcom. on oversight and investigations, Ho. of Reps. com. on internal and fgn. commerce, 1978; spl. cons. for ABSCAM investigation to Com. on Standards of Ofcl. Conduct, U.S. Ho. of Reps., 1980-81; trustee emeritus, past exec com. Am. U., Washington; past trustee, mem. exec. com. Washington Journalism Ctr.; past adv. com., Media Law Reporter. Author: Death and the Supreme Court, 1961 (Edgar Allan Poe award); Editor: (with William E. Jackson) The Supreme Court in the American System of Government (Justice Robert H. Jackson), 1955; contbr. articles to profl. jours. Past corp. mem. Salvation Army; past mem. adv. com. Procedures of Jud. Coun., D.C.; past mem. adv. bd. Inst. Comm. Law Studies, Cath. U.; bd. govs., St. Albans Sch., 1957-63, 65-72, chmn., 1965-67; past mem. nat. adv. com., Nat. Inst. for Citizen Edn. in Law; bd. dirs., past pres. PEN/Faulkner Found.; v.p., chmn. publ. com., exec. com. Supreme Ct. Hist. Soc.; past internat. adv. group Toshiba Corp.; past commr. Supreme Ct. Jud. Fellows Comm. With AUS., 1943-45. Chmn. recipient Pub. Achievement award Common Cause, 1999, Justice Potter Stewart award Coun. for Ct. Excellence, 2000, disting. pub. svc. award D.C. 1999. Fellow: ABA; mem.: D.C. Cir. Hist. Soc. (pres. 2000—), Am. Acad. Appellate Lawyers (past pres.), Am. Judicature Soc. (past vice chair exec. com.), Met. Washington Bd. Trade, DC Bar Assn. (bd. govs., Lawyer of Yr. award 1998), DC Bar (1st pres. 1972—73, bd. govs. 1973—74, jud. evaluation com.), DC Bar Found. (pres. 1983—84), Jud. Conf. DC Cir., Am. Coll. Trial Lawyers, Chevy Chase Club, Met. Club, Alfalfa Club, Barristers Club, Lawyers Club (past pres.). Methodist Antitrust, Federal civil litigation, General practice. Home: 2737 Devonshire Pl NW # 424 Washington DC 20008-5148 Office: Columbia Sq 555 13th St NW Washington DC 20004-1109

PREWOZNIK, JEROME FRANK, lawyer; b. Detroit, July 15, 1934; s. Frank Joseph and Loretta Ann (Parzych) Prewoznik; m. Marilyn Ruth Johnson, 1970; 1 child, Frank Joseph II. AB cum laude, U. Detroit, 1955; JD with distinction, U. Mich., 1958. Bar: Calif. 1959. Pvt. practice, Calif., 1960-91. Served in U.S. Army, 1958—60, ret. U.S. Army. Mem.: State Bar Calif. Republican. Home: Pelican Lodge on Fisher Cove PO Box 120017 Big Bear Lake CA 92315-8913

PRIBANIC, VICTOR HUNTER, lawyer; b. McKeesport, Pa., Apr. 7, 1954; s. John Edward and Marlene Cecilia (Hunter) P. BA, Bowling Green State U., 1976; JD, Duquesne U., 1979. Bar: Pa. 1979, U.S. Dist. Ct. (we. dist.) Pa. 1979, U.S. Ct. Appeals (3d cir.) 1979, U.S. Supreme Ct. 1989, U.S. Ct. Claims 1990. Asst. dist. atty. Office of Dist. Atty., Pitts., 1980-82; law clk. to presiding justice Pa. Ct. Common Pleas, Pitts., 1982-85; pvt. practice Pitts. and McKeesport, 1982—; pres. Pribanic & Pribanic, P.C., 1987—. Mem.: ATLA, Million Dollar Adv. Forum, Roscoe Pound Found., Acad. Trial Lawyers Allegheny County, Pa. Trial Lawyers Assn., Nat. Assn. Criminal Def. Lawyers. Democrat. Roman Catholic. State civil litigation, Criminal, Personal injury (including property damage). Home: 100 Victoria Dr Mc Keesport PA 15131-1224 Office: 1735 Lincoln Way White Oak PA 15131-1715 Address: 513 Court Pl Pittsburgh PA 15219-2002

PRICE, CHARLES STEVEN, lawyer; b. Inglewood, Calif., June 10, 1955; s. Frank Dean Price and Ann (Rounds) Bolling; m. Sandra Helen Laney, Feb. 26, 1983; children: Katherine Laney, Courtney Ann, Diana Emily. BA, U. Calif., Santa Barbara, 1976; JD, U. Chgo., 1979. Bar: Ariz. 1980, U.S. Dist. Ariz. 1980, U.S. Ct. Appeals (9th cir.) 1982. Assoc. Brown & Bain P.A., Phoenix, Ariz., 1979-85, ptnr., 1985-96, Allen & Price P.L.C., Phoenix, Ariz., 1996-2000, Allen, Price & Padden, Phoenix, 2000—. Antitrust, Intellectual property, Securities. Office: Allen Price & Padden PLC 3131 E Camelback Rd Ste 110 Phoenix AZ 85016-4597 E-mail: price@aplaw.com.

PRICE, CHARLES T. lawyer; b. Lansing, Mich., Feb. 11, 1944; BA, Ohio Wesleyan U., 1966; JD, Harvard U., 1969. Bar: Ohio 1969, U.S. Dist. Ct. (no. dist.) Ohio 1974, U.S. Ct. Appeals (6th cir) 1981, U.S. Supreme Ct. 1982, Ill. 1989. Former ptnr. Baker & Hostetler, Cleve.; pres., pub. Chgo. Sun-Times, 1987-88; exec. v.p. Sun-Times Co., 1989-92; ptnr. Foley & Lardner, Chgo., 2000—. Office: Foley & Lardner 330 N Wabash Ave Chicago IL 60611-3603

PRICE, DANIEL MARTIN, lawyer; b. St. Louis, Aug. 23, 1955; s. Albert and Edith S. (Werner) P.; m. Kim Ellen Heebner, July 15, 1984; children: Emma Rachel, Joseph Armin, Joshua Simon. BA, Haverford Coll., 1977; diploma in law, Cambridge U., 1979; JD, Harvard U., 1981. Bar: D.C. 1981, Pa. 1987. Assoc. Drinker, Biddle & Reath, Phila., 1981-82, 86-89; dep. gen. counsel Office of U.S. Trade Rep., Washington, 1989-92; ptnr. Powell, Goldstein, Frazer & Murphy, Washington, 1992—2002, Sidley Austin Brown & Wood, Washington, 2002—. Atty., adviser Dept. State, Washington, 1982-84; dep. agt. U.S. Iran-U.S. Claims Tribunal, Hague, The Netherlands, 1984-86; lectr. Haverford Coll., 1982; mem. adv. bd. Can.-U.S. Law Inst. Articles editor Harvard Law Rev., 1980-81; contbr. articles to profl. jours. including Am. Jour. Internat. Law, Internat. Lawyer, Internat. Fin. Law Rev., Harvard Internat. Law Jour., others. Mem. arbitration panel Internat. Ctr. for Settlement of Investment Disputes; mem. state dept. adv. com. Internat. Econ. Policy; mem. adv. bd. Georgetown U. Law Ctr. Inst. Internat. Econ. Rels.; mem. Bush-Cheney Transition Team, 1999—2000. Am. Keasbey scholar Cambridge U., 1977-78. Mem. ABA, Internat. Bus. Forum (legal adv. bd. 1987-89), Am. Arbitration Assn. (panel arbitrators), Internat. C. of C. (arbitrator), Orgn. for Internat. Investment (counsel), Coun. on Fgn. Rels., Phi Beta Kappa., Intl. Ctr. for Settlement of Investment Disputes (mem. panel of arbirators), Dept. of State Adv. Com. on Intl. Economic Policy, Georgetown U. Law Center Inst. of Intl. Economic Law (mem. adv. bd.). Private international, Public international. Office: 1001 Pennsylvania Ave NW Washington DC 20004-2505

PRICE, GRIFFITH BALEY, JR., lawyer; b. Lawrence, Kans., Aug. 15, 1942; s. Griffith Baley and Cora Lee (Beers) P.; m. Maria Helena Martin, June 29, 1968 (div.); children: Andrew Griffith, Alexandra Helena; m. Nancy Culver Rhodes, Aug. 17, 1997; 1 child, Carolyn Rhodes. AB (cum laude), Harvard U., 1964; LLB, NYU, 1967. Bar: N.Y. 1967, D.C. 1991, U.S. Ct. Appeals (6th cir.) 1975, U.S. Ct. Appeals (2nd cir.) 1978, U.S. Ct. Appeals (3d, 5th and 11th cirs.) 1981, U.S. Ct. Appeals (1st cir.) 2002, U.S. Ct. Appeals (fed. cir.) 1984, U.S. Supreme Ct. 2001. Assoc. Dewey, Ballantine, Bushby, Palmer & Wood, N.Y.C., 1967-75; ptnr. Milgrim Thomajan & Lee, N.Y.C., 1976-86; of counsel, ptnr. Finnegan, Henderson, Farabow, Garrett & Dunner, LLP, Washington, 1987—. Adj. prof., lectr. George Washington U. Law Ctr., Washington, 1989—93; mem., chair pub. adv. com. U.S. Patent and Trademark Office, 1999—; lectr., spkr. in field. Author: (with others, treatise) Milgrim on Trade Secrets, 1986; contbr. articles to publs. Root-Tilden scholar NYU Law Sch., 1964-67. Mem.: ABA (intellectual property sec., com. chmn.), Fed. Cir. Bar Assn., Licensing Execs. Soc., Am. Intellectual Property Law Assn. (bd. dirs., com. chmn.), Internat. Trademark Assn. (bd. dirs., com. chmn.), Cosmos Club, Nat. Press Club, Harvard Club (Washington), N.Y. Athletic Club. Presbyn. Federal civil litigation, Intellectual property, Trademark and copyright. Office: Finnegan Henderson Farabow Garrett & Dunner LLP 1300 I St NW Ste 700 Washington DC 20005-3314 E-mail: gbprice@finnegan.com.

PRICE, JAMES TUCKER, lawyer; b. Springfield, Mo., June 22, 1955; s. Billy L. and Jeanne Adele Price; m. Francine Beth Warkow, June 8, 1980; children: Rachel Leah, Ashley Elizabeth. BJ, U. Mo., 1977; JD, Harvard U., 1980. Bar: Mo. 1980. Assoc. firm Spencer Fane Britt & Browne, Kansas City, 1980-86; ptnr. Spencer Fane Britt & Browne LLP, Kansas City, 1987—, chair environ. practice group, 1994—, mem. exec. com., 1997—. Mem. Brownfields Commn., Kansas City, 1999—; mem. steering com. Kansas City Bi-State Brownfields Initiative, 1997—. Contbr. to monographs, other legal publs. Mem. ABA (coun. sect. environ, energy and resources 1992-95, vice chmn. solid and hazardous waste com. 1985-90, chmn. 1990-92, chmn. brownfields task force 1995-97, vice chmn. environ. transactions and brownfield com. 1998-2000), Mo. Bar Assn., Kansas City Met. Bar Assn. (chmn. environ. law com. 1985-86), Greater Kansas City C. of C. (co-chair Brownfields Working Group, 1996-98, chmn. energy and environ. com. 1987-89). Federal civil litigation, State civil litigation, Environmental. Office: Spencer Fane Britt & Browne LLP 1000 Walnut St Ste 1400 Kansas City MO 64106-2140 E-mail: jprice@spencerfane.com.

PRICE, JOHN ALEY, lawyer; b. Maryville, Mo., Oct. 7, 1947; s. Donald Leroy and Julia Catherine (Aley) P.; m. Deborah Diadra Gunter, Aug. 12, 1995; children: Theodore John, Joseph Andrew. BS, N.W. Mo. State U., 1969; JD, U. Kans., 1972. Bar: Kans. 1972, U.S. Dist. Ct. Kans. 1972, U.S. Ct. Appeals (10th cir.) 1972, Tex. 1984, U.S. Ct. Appeals (5th cir.) 1984, U.S. Supreme Ct. 1987; cert. civil trial law Tex. Bd. Legal Specialization. Law clk. U.S. Dist. Ct. Kans., Wichita, 1972-74; from assoc. to ptnr. Weeks, Thomas and Lysaught, Kansas City, Kans., 1974-82; ptnr. Winstead, Sechrest & Minick, Dallas, 1982-96, litigation sect. coord., 1990-92, intellectual property sect. litigation coord., 1993-95; gen. counsel Travelhost Inc., Dallas, 1996—, Club Co., Inc., 1999-2001. Pres. Umansys, Inc., Dallas, 2000—; spl. prosecutor Leavenworth County Office Dist. Atty., 1970-71, Sedgwick County Offce Dist. Atty., Wichita, Kans., 1971-72. Author: Our Boundless Self (A Call to Awake), 1992, A Gathering of Light: Eternal Wisdom for a Time of Transformation, 1993; co-author: Soular Reunion: Journey to the Beloved, 1998; editor (mag.) Academic Analyst, 1968-69; assoc. editor U. Kans. Law Rev., 1971-72, Dallas Bus. Jour.; contbr. articles to profl. jours. Co-dir. Douglas County Legal Aid Soc., Lawrence, Kans., 1971-72; co-pres. Northwood Hills PTA, Dallas, 1984, Westwood Jr. H.S. PTA, 1989-90; founder New Frontiers Found., 1993; co-founder Wings of Spirit Found., 1994, dir., v.p. 1994—. Mem. ABA, Kans. Bar Assn. (mem. task force for penal reform; Pres.'s Outstanding Svc. award 1981), Tex. Bar Assn., Pro Bono Coll., State Bar Tex., World Bus. Acad., Inst. Noetic Scis., UN Assn. (human rights com. Dallas chpt. 1991-93, bd. dirs. 1991-93), Campaign for the Earth (chpt. coord. Global Report 1991-92, coord. govt. and polit. area 1991-92), Blue Key, Order of Coif, Phi Delta Phi, Sigma Tau Gamma (v.p. 1968-69). Mem. Unity Ch. Antitrust, Federal civil litigation, Trademark and copyright. Office: Travelhost Inc 10701 N Stemmons Fwy Dallas TX 75220-2419 E-mail: japrice@travelhost.com.

PRICE, JOHN RICHARD, lawyer, law educator; b. Indpls., Nov. 28, 1934; s. Carl Lee and Agnes I. P.; m. Suzanne A. Leslie, June 22, 1963; children: John D., Steven V. BA with high honors, U. Fla., 1958; LL.B. with honors, NYU, 1961. Bar: Calif. 1962, Wash. 1977, U.S. Ct. Appeals (9th cir.), U.S. Dist. Ct. (we. dist.) Wash. Assoc. McCutchen, Doyle, Brown & Enersen, San Francisco, 1961-69; prof. law U. Wash., Seattle, 1969-97, dean, 1982-88; of counsel Perkins Coie, Seattle, 1976—. Author: Contemporary Estate Planning, 1983, Price on Contemporary Estate Planning, 1992, 2d edit., 2000, Conflicts, Confidentiality and Other Ethical Issues, 2000. Served with U.S. Army, 1953-55 Root-Tilden fellow NYU Sch. Law, 1958-61 Fellow Am. Coll. Trust and Estate Counsel (former regent); mem. ABA, Am. Law Inst., Order of Coif, Phi Beta Kappa. Congregationalist. Home: 3794 NE 97th St Seattle WA 98115-2564 Office: 1201 3rd Ave Ste 4800 Seattle WA 98101-3029 E-mail: jprice@perkinscole.com.

PRICE, JOSEPH HUBBARD, lawyer; b. Montgomery, Ala., Jan. 31, 1939; s. Aaron Joseph and Minnie Jule (Reynolds) P.; m. Cynthia Winant Ramsey, Sept. 14, 1963 (div. 1980); children: Victoria Reynolds, Ramsey Winant; m. Courtney McFadden, Apr. 25, 1980. AB, U. Ala., 1961; LLB, Harvard U., 1964; postgrad., London Sch. Econs., 1964-65. Bar: Ala. 1964, D.C. 1968. Law clk. to justice Hugo L. Black U.S. Supreme Ct., Washington, 1967-68; assoc. Leva, Hawes, Symington, Martin & Oppenheimer, Washington, 1968-71; v.p. Overseas Pvt. Investment Corp., Washington, 1971-73; ptnr. Leva, Hawes, et. al., Washington, 1973-83, Gibson, Dunn & Crutcher, Washington, 1983—. Mem. CARE Com. Washington; mem. adv. com. Hugo Black Meml. Libr., Ashland, Ala. Capt. U.S. Army, 1966-67, Vietnam. Decorated Bronze Star; Frank Knox Meml. fellow London Sch. Econs., 1964-65. Mem. ABA, Am. Soc. Internat. Law, Supreme Ct. Hist. Soc., Phi Beta Kappa, Met. Club. Administrative and regulatory, Corporate, general, Private international. Home: 3104 Cathedral Ave NW Washington DC 20008-3419 Office: Gibson Dunn & Crutcher 1050 Connecticut Ave NW Ste 900 Washington DC 20036-5306

PRICE, PAUL L. lawyer; b. Chgo., Apr. 21, 1945; s. Walter S. and Lillian (Czerepkowski) L.; m. Dianne L. Olech, June 3, 1967; children: Kristen, Kathryn. BBA, Loyola U., Chgo., 1967; JD with honors, Ill. Inst. Tech., 1971. Bar: Ill. 1971, U.S. Dist. Ct. (no. dist.) Ill., U.S. Ct. Appeals (7th cir.). Tax acct. Arthur Anderson & Co., Chgo., 1970—71; assoc. Doyle & Tarpey, Chgo., 1971—75, Gordon & Assocs., Chgo., 1975—76; from assoc. to ptnr. Pretzel & Stouffer, Chartered, Chgo., 1976—96; ptnr. Price, Tunney, Reiter, Chgo., 1996—. With USMC, 1969—70. Fellow: Am. Coll. Trial Lawyers; mem.: ABA, Ill. Inst. Tech.-Chgo. Kent Coll. Law Alumni Assn. (pres. 1989—90), Assn. Def. Trial Attys., Lawyers for Civil Justice (bd. dirs. 1999—2001), Def. Rsch. Inst. (bd. dirs. 1999—2001), Fedn. Def. and Corp. Counsel (pres. 1999—2000), Ill. Assn. Def. Trial Counsel (pres. 1990—91), Soc. Trial Lawyers, Ill. Bar Assn. Roman Catholic. General civil litigation, Product liability, Professional liability. Office: Price Tunney Reiter 123 N Wacker Dr Ste 2220 Chicago IL 60606-

PRICE, PAUL MARNELL, lawyer; b. Binghamton, N.Y., July 23, 1959; s. Paul B. and Rita E. (Marnell) P.; m. Teresa Lynn Doll, Sept. 26, 1987; children: Kayla Marie, Tyler Marnell. BS in Chemistry-Bus. cum laude, Scranton (Pa.) U., 1981; JD magna cum laude, Syracuse U., 1984. Bar: N.Y. 1985, Pa. 1995, U.S. Supreme Ct. 2001. Assoc. Levene, Gouldin & Thompson, Binghamton, 1984-87; mem. Hickey, Sheehan & Gates, P.C., Binghamton, 1987-95; prin. Law Office of Paul M. Price, Binghamton, N.Y., 1995—. Bd. dirs. United Way of Broome County, Inc., Broome County Bar Assn., Mothers and Babies Perinatal Network South Ctrl. N.Y. Inc. Mem. ABA, ATLA, N.Y. State Bar Assn., Broome County Bar Assn. Democrat. Roman Catholic. Avocations: masters swimming, skiing. Estate planning, Personal injury (including property damage), Property, real (including real estate development, water). Office: Proctor Bldg 25 Main St Binghamton NY 13905-3121 E-mail: pmpesqlaw@aol.com.

PRICE, RICHARD EDWARD, lawyer; b. Stanford, Calif., Apr. 30, 1969; s. Richard Maxwell and Mary Frances Price; m. Brook Renee Gauntz, Sept. 14, 2002. BA, U. Mass., 1991; JD, George Washington U., 1994; LLM, Cambridge U., England, 1995. Bar: N.Y. 1995, Mass. 1995, D.C. 1996, U.S. Ct. Appeals (D.C. cir.) 1997. Atty. Koteen & Naftalin, L.L.P., Washington, 1996—99, Vinson & Elkins L.L.P., 1999—. Mem.: Federalist Soc., Fed. Comm. Bar Assn., U. Club of Wash., DC, Golden Key, Pi Sigma Alpha. Administrative and regulatory, Communications. Office: Vinson & Elkins LLP 1455 Pennsylvania Avenue NW Washington DC 20004

PRICE, ROBERT ALLAN, lawyer; b. Phila., Dec. 25, 1946; s. Harold James and Marie (Werner) P.; m. Margaret Price (div. 1972); 1 child, Karen Elaine Price Vretto; m. Donna Elaine Walding, Nov. 22, 1975; children: Robert Allan Jr., Jamie Leigh. BS, Troy State U., Dothan, Ala., 1989; JD, Jones Sch. Law, Montgomery, Ala., 1994. Bar: Ala. Enlisted man U.S. Army, 1967, advanced through grades to chief warrant officer 4, pilot; ret., 1987; director, Primary Flight Training Lear Siegler Svcs., Ft. Rucker, Ala., 1987—; pvt. practice, Enterprise, Ala., 1994—. Decorated DFC. Mem. ABA, Ala. Bar Assn. Avocations: golf, fishing. Bankruptcy, Family and matrimonial, Personal injury (including property damage). Office: PO Box 310968 Enterprise AL 36331-0968 E-mail: Robert@snowhill.com.

PRICE, ROBERT DEMILLE, lawyer; b. N.Y.C., Oct. 11, 1915; s. Willard DeMille Price and Eugenia Reeve; m. Newell Potter, Aug. 15, 1940 (div. May 1946); 1 child, Jonathan; m. Ruth Bentley, July 5, 1946; children: Katharine, Susannah, Rebecca. AB in Econs. with honors, Cornell U., 1936; JD, Harvard U., 1940; MBA, Clark U., 1973. Bar: Mass. 1940, U.S. Dist. Ct. Mass. 1941, U.S. Ct. Appeals (1st cir.) 1976, U.S. Tax Ct. 1977, U.S. Supreme Ct. 1978. Assoc. Ropes & Gray, Boston, 1940-43, 1946-50; ptnr. Vaughan, Esty, Crotty & Mason, Worcester, Mass., 1950-53, Sibley, Blair & Mountain, Worcester, 1953-70, Corbin, Sarapas, Madaus & Arakelian, Worcester, 1970-73, Price & Madaus, Worcester, 1973-87; pres. Robert D. Price, PC, Holden, Mass., 1987—. Dir. Appian Way Pizza, Ltd., Worcester, 1951-61, Food Specialties, Inc., Worcester, 1951-61, James Monroe Wire and Cable Co., S. Lancaster, Mass., 1973—; mem. Fin. Com., Holden, 1989-95, conservation com., 1999—. Moderator (TV series) Am. Bar Assn. Jr. Bar Assn., 1947-50. Bd. dirs., treas. Friends Gale Free Libs., Inc., Holden, 1988—; mem. adv. bd. Met. Dist. Commn., 1990—96; pres. Humanist Chaplaincy at Harvard, 1995—; bd. dirs., sec. Humanist Assn. Mass., 1979—, Am. Humanist Assn., 1991—94; trustee AHA Humanist Found., 1999—. Lt. USNR, 1943—50. Mem. Mass. Bar Assn., Worcester County Bar Assn., Worcester Club (dir. 1953-56), Boston Athenaeum (propr. 1949—). Avocations: museum and art shows, photography, alpine climbing, sailing. Corporate, general, Estate planning, Estate taxation. Office: 11 Malden St Holden MA 01520-1827

PRICE, ROBERT GRANT, lawyer; b. Elizabethtown, Ill., Mar. 30, 1936; s. Robert Lee and Virginia Rose (Gullett) P.; m. Ann Carol Hall, Aug. 8, 1964; children— Robert Grant, Ann Sloan. B.S., So. Ill., U., 1959; J.D., U. S.C., 1969. Bar: S.C. 1969, U.S. Ct. Appeals (4th cir.) 1969, U.S. Supreme Ct. 1975. Ptnr. Kennedy & Price, Columbia, S.C., 1969— ; dir. Coastal Coca Cola Bottling Co., Marion, S.C., 1975— ; dir., pres. Music Festival Assn., Columbia, 1980-83. Precinct committeeman S.C. Republican party, Columbia, 1980-84. Served to capt. USAF, 1959-66. Presbyterian. Lodge: Richland Sertoma (bd. dirs. 1978-82) (Columbia). Banking, Corporate, general, Property, real (including real estate development, water). Home: 11 Lake Point Rd Columbia SC 29206-4511 Office: Kennedy & Price 1321 Lady St Columbia SC 29201-3330

PRICE, STEPHEN CONWELL, lawyer; b. Hornell, NY, July 17, 1949; s. Ralph and Berta Lee (Davis) Conwell; m. Dianna R. Johnson; children from previous marriage: Margaret Davis, Mary Darden, John Tyler, Diana Allison, Thomas Garrett. BA in History, Va. Mil. Inst., 1971; JD, U. Va., 1974; LLM, U. Cambridge, Eng., 1977. Bar: Va. 1974, U.S. Dist. Ct. (ea. dist.) Va. 1974, U.S. Ct. Appeals (4th cir.) 1976, U.S. Supreme Ct. 1977. Assoc. McCandlish, Lillard, Church & Best, Fairfax, Va., 1974-76; pvt. practice Leesburg, Va., 1977-82; ptnr. Price & Zimmerman, Leesburg, Va., 1982—98; prin. McCandlish & Lillard PC, Leesburg, Va., 1998—. Substitute judge Gen. Dist. Ct., 20th Dist. Va., 1982-91; escheator for Loudoun County, Va., 1983-94. Chmn. Loudoun County Dem. Com., 1981; sec., bd. dirs. Oatlands of the Nat. Trust, Leesburg, 1981—; pres., bd. dirs. Am. Friends Cambridge U., 1983-2000; dedication chmn. George C. Marshall Meml., Leesburg, 1980; chmn. colonial bd. George Washington U., 1996-98; pres. George C. Marshall Internat. Ctr. at Dodona Manor, 2000—. Capt. U.S. Army, 1973. Mem. Va. Bar Assn., Selden Soc., Sons of Confederate Vets., United Oxford and Cambridge U. Club (London), Hawks Club (Cambridge), Colonnade Club (Charlottesville), Kappa Alpha. Democrat. Episcopalian. General civil litigation, Condemnation (eminent domain), Commercial, contracts (including sales of goods; commercial financing). Home: PO Box 374 Leesburg VA 20178 Office: McCandlish & Lillard PC 305 Harrison St SE Leesburg VA 20175-3729 E-mail: sprice@mccandlaw.com.

PRICE, WILLIAM RAY, JR., state supreme court judge; b. Fairfield, Iowa, Jan. 30, 1952; s. William Ray and Evelyn Jean (Darnell) P.; m. Susan Marie Trainor, Jan. 4, 1975; children: Emily Margret, William Joseph Dodds. BA with distinction, U. Iowa, 1974; postgrad., Yale U., 1974-75; JD cum laude, Washington and Lee U., 1978. Bar: Mo. 1978, U.S. Dist. Ct. (we. dist.) Mo. 1978, U.S. Ct. Claims 1978, U.S. Ct. Appeals (8th cir.) 1985. Assoc. Lathrop & Norquist, Kansas City, Mo., 1978-84, ptnr., 1984-92, chmn. bus. litigation sect., 1987-88, 90-92, exec. com., 1989-92; judge Supreme Ct. Mo., Jefferson City, 1992—, chief justice, 1999—2001. G.L.V. Zumwalt monitoring com. U.S. Dist. Ct. (we. dist.) Mo., Kansas City. Pres. Kansas City Bd. Police Commrs.; mem. Together Ctr. & Family Devel. Ctr., Kansas City; chmn. merit selection com. U.S. marshal Western Dist. of Mo., Kansas City; bd. dirs. Truman Med. Ctr., Kansas City. Rockefeller fellow, 1974-75; Burks scholar Washington & Lee U., 1976. Mem. Christian Ch. Office: Supreme Ct Mo PO Box 150 207 W High St Jefferson City MO 65102-0150

PRICHARD, VINCENT MARVIN, lawyer; b. Kirksville, Mo., July 16, 1946; s. George William and Mary Elizabeth (Love) P. BS, U. Colo., 1969; JD, U. Denver, 1974. Bar: Colo. 1975, U.S. Dist. Ct. Colo. 1975. Atty. Bur. Hearings and Appeals Social Security Adminstrn., Denver, 1975-79; asst. regional counsel Dept. Energy, Lakewood, Colo., 1979-82; atty. Fed. Legal Info. Through Electronics, Denver, 1982-93; info. tech. profl. U. Colo. Health Scis. Ctr., Denver, 1994-99; info. tech. mgr. Colo. Water Conservation Bd., Denver, 2000—. With U.S. Army, 1969-71. Mem. Colo. Bar Assn., 1st Jud. Dist. Bar Assn. Home: 30191 Peggy Ln Evergreen CO 80439-7227 Office: Colo Water Conservation Bd 1313 Sherman St Ste 721 Denver CO 80203

PRIEST, GEORGE L. law educator; b. 1947; BA, Yale U., 1969; JD, U. Chgo., 1973. Assoc. prof. U. Puget Sound, Tacoma, 1973-75; law and econ. fellow U. Chgo., 1975-77; prof. U. Buffalo, 1977-80, UCLA, 1980-81, Yale U., New Haven, 1981—. Dir. program in civil liability; John M. Olin prof. law and econs., 1986—. Mem. Pres.' Com. on Privatization, 1987-88. Office: PO Box 208215 New Haven CT 06520-8215

PRIEST, PETER H. lawyer; b. Norwood, Mass., Sept. 12, 1955; s. William G. and Mary E. (Horne) P.; children: William, Sarah. BSEE, U. Maine, Orono, 1977; JD, U. Maine, Portland, 1980. Bar: N.Y. 1981, N.C., 1996, U.S. Dist. Ct. (so., ea. dists.) N.Y. 1981, U.S. Patent Office 1981, U.S. Ct. Appeals (Fed. cir.) 1987. Assoc. Davis, Hoxie, Faithfull, Hapgood, N.Y.C., 1980-88, ptnr., 1989-95; atty. Law Offices of Peter H. Priest, PLLC, Chapel Hill, NC, 1995—. Mem. ABA, Am. Intellectual Property Law Assn., Fed. Cir. Bar Assn., Internat. Intellectual Property Soc., Union Internat. Avocats. Patent. Office: 5015 Southpark Dr Ste 230 Durham NC 27713-7736 Home: 200 Telluride Trail Chapel Hill NC 27514-1854

PRIKRYLOVA, PAVLA, atty. at law; b. Prague, Czech Republic, May 10, 1974; d. Ivo Prikryl and Jarmila Prikrylova. DEUE, DMI, U of Toulouse, Toulouse, France, 1995; ML, Charles U of Prague, Prague, Czech Republic, 1998. Bar: Czech Republic 2001. Legal clk. Brobeck, Hale & Dorr Internat., Prague, Czech Republic, 1993—94, Ondrej Peterka, Prague, Czech Republic, 1996—98, jr. atty., 1998—2000, Peterka & Leuchterova v.o.s., Prague, Czech Republic, 2000—01; ptnr. Peterka, Leuchterova & Ptnrs. v.o.s., Prague, Czech Republic, 2001—. Avocations: skiing, bicycling, hiking, ballroom dancing, reading. Office: Peterka, Leuchterova & Ptnrs vos Na Prikope 15 11000 Prague Czech Republic

PRIM, JOSEPH ANTHONY, lawyer; b. Phila., June 29, 1944; s. Joseph A. and Leila A. P.; children: Joseph A. III, Jennifer L.; m. Jeanne C. Mullen, May 29, 1992; children: Marian S., Thomas J. BA, U. Pa., 1967; JD, Boston U., 1970. Bar: Pa. 1970, U.S. Dist. Ct. (ea. dist.) Pa. 1970, U.S. Ct. Appeals (3d cir.) 1974, U.S. Supreme Ct. 1991. Assoc. O'Halloran, Stack & Smith, Phila., 1970-73, Stephen A. Sheller & Assocs., Phila., 1980-87; pvt. practice Phila., 1974-80; ptnr. Duca & Prim, Phila., 1987—. Mem. Pa. Bar Assn., Phila. Bar Assn. (chmn. worker's compensation com. 1993-94, treas. 1994—), Union League Phila. Workers' compensation. Office: 1500 Walnut St Ste 900 Philadelphia PA 19102-3505

PRIMPS, WILLIAM GUTHRIE, lawyer; b. Ossining, NY, Sept. 8, 1949; s. Richard Byrd and Mary Elizabeth (Guthrie) P.; m. Sophia Elizabeth Beutel, Aug. 25, 1973; children: Emily Ann, Elizabeth Armstrong, William Andrew. BA, Yale U., 1971; JD, Harvard U., 1974. Bar: N.Y., 1975. Assoc. LeBoeuf, Lamb, Leiby & MacRae, N.Y.C., 1974-82; ptnr. LeBoeuf, Lamb, Greene & MacRae, N.Y.C., 1983—. Counsel to Bd. Zoning Appeals, Bronxville, 1988-89, chmn., 1989-91. Class coun. Yale U., New Haven, 1986-91; trustee Village of Bronxville, 1991-98, dep. mayor, 1995-98; deacon Reformed Ch. Bronxville, 1989-94, elder, 1998-2002; bd. dirs. Bronxville Sch. Fdn. 1998—, Ivy Football Assn., 2003—. Mem. ABA, N.Y. State Bar Assn., Assn. Yale Alumni (class rep. 1986-91), Yale Club, Bronxville Field Club. Republican. Antitrust, Federal civil litigation, Insurance. Home: 71 Summit Ave Bronxville NY 10708-1815 Office: LeBoeuf Lamb Greene & MacRae 125 W 55th St New York NY 10019-5369

PRINCE, DAVID CANNON, lawyer; b. Hawkinsville, Ga., July 4, 1950; s. Carl Willis and Carobel (Cannon) P.; m. Mary MacIntyre, June 30, 1973. BA in Econs., Clemson U., 1972; JD, St. John's U., Jamaica, N.Y., 1980. Bar: N.Y. 1981, Ga. 1982, U.S. Dist. Ct. (no. dist.) Ga. 1982. Atty. enforcement SEC, Atlanta, 1981-86; regional counsel Shearson Lehman Bros. Inc., Atlanta, 1986-92; gen. counsel Robinson-Humphrey Co., Inc., Atlanta, 1992—2001; chief legal officer SunTrust Capital Markets, Inc., 2001—. Capt. USAF, 1972-78. Mem. ABA (co-chairperson young lawyers div. 1986-88). Democrat. Avocations: sailing, running. Administrative and regulatory, Federal civil litigation, Securities. Home: 1824 Lenox Rd NE Atlanta GA 30306-3031 Office: 3333 Peachtree Rd NE Atlanta GA 30326-1070

PRINCE, KENNETH STEPHEN, lawyer; b. Newton, Mass., Jan. 28, 1950; s. Samuel and Edna L. Prince; m. Patricia Denning, Jan. 15, 1977 (dec. Nov. 1985); 1 child, Kenneth Stephen Jr.; m. Jane M. McCabe, Sept. 5, 1987; 1 child, Allison Pamela. BA, U. Pa., 1972; JD, Boston Coll., 1975. Bar: N.Y. 1976, Mass. 1975, U.S. Dist. Ct. (so. and ea. dists.) N.Y. 1978. Assoc. Shearman & Sterling, N.Y.C., 1975-83, ptnr., 1984—, antitrust group practice leader, 1992—2003. Mem. N.Y. Law Inst. (exec. com. 1984-96), Order of Coif. Antitrust, Mergers and acquisitions. Home: 15 Dellwood Rd Darien CT 06820-2915 E-mail: kprince@shearman.com.

PRINCE, WILLIAM TALIAFERRO, retired federal judge; b. Norfolk, Va., Oct. 3, 1929; s. James Edward and Helen Marie (Taliaferro) P.; m. Anne Carroll Hannegan, Apr. 12, 1958; children: Sarah Carroll Prince Pishko, Emily Taliaferro, William Taliaferro, John Hannegan, Anne Martineau Thompson, Robert Harrison. Student, Coll. William and Mary, Norfolk, 1947-48, 49-50; AB, Williamsburg, 1955, BCL, 1957, MLT, 1959. Bar: Va. 1957. Lectr. acctg. Coll. William and Mary, 1955-57; lectr. law Marshall-Wythe Sch. Law, 1957-59; assoc. Williams, Kelly & Greer, Norfolk, 1959-63, ptnr., 1963-90; U.S. magistrate judge Eastern Dist. of Va., Norfolk, 1990-2000; ret., 2000; recalled Ct. Appeals 4th Cir., 2000—03, Ct. Appeals 10th Cir., 2002, Ct. Appeals 3d Cir., 2002, Ct. Appeals 6th Cir., 2003. Pres. Am. Inn of Ct. XXVII, 1987-89. Bd. editors: The Virginia Lawyer, A Basic Practice Handbook, 1966. Bd. dirs. Madonna Home, Inc., 1978-93, Soc. Alumni of Coll. William and Mary, 1985-88. Fellow Am. Coll. Trial Lawyers, Am. Bar Found., Va. Law found. (bd. dirs. 1976-90); mem. ABA (ho. of dels. 1984-90), Am. Judicature Soc. (bd. dirs. 1984-88), Va. State Bar (coun. 1973-77, exec. com. 1975-80, pres. 1978-79). Roman Catholic. Home: 1227 Graydon Ave Norfolk VA 23507-1006 Office: Walter E Hoffman US Courthouse 600 Granby St Ste 341 Norfolk VA 23510-1915 E-mail: WTPrince1@aol.com.

PRIOR, GARY L. lawyer; b. Niagara Falls, New York, June 26, 1943; s. Harold D. and Adeline Thelma (Lee) Prior; m. Nancy (O'Shaughnessy), Aug. 23, 1975; children: Joseph Lee, Julia Elizabeth. BS, Tulane U., 1965; JD, U. Chgo., 1968. Bar: Ill., 1968, U.S. Dist. Ct. (no. dist.), Ill. 1968, U.S. Ct. Appeals (7th cir.) 1973, U.S. Ct. Appeals (3d cir.) 1974, U.S. Trial Bar 1983, U.S. Supreme Ct. 1989, U.S. Dist. Ct. (we. dist.) Wis. 1992, U.S. Dist. Ct. (ea. dist.) Wis. 1993, U.S. Dist. Ct. Minn. 1994, U.S. Ct. Appeals (Fed. Cir.) 2002. Assoc. Rooks, Pitts, and Poust, Chgo., 1968-71, McDermott, Will, and Emery, Chgo., 1971-74, ptnr., 1974—2002, dir. trial dept. tng., 1980-85, mem. securities approval com., 1986—94, mem. nominating com., chmn., 1988-89, partnership com., 1989-92, mem mgmt. com., 1991-93; of counsel Tabet, DiVito, and Rothstein, LLC, 2002—. Mem.: ISBA, Ill. State Bar Assn., Ill. Appellate Lawyers Assn., Sports Law. Avocations: farming, scuba diving, charities trustee: Prin. Family Charitable Found. and Funny Friends Found.. Federal civil litigation, State civil litigation, Securities. Home: 2512 N Burling St Chicago IL 60614-2510 Office: Tabet DiVito & Rothstein 180 N La Salle Ste 1510 Chicago IL 60601

PRISSEL, BARBARA ANN, paralegal, law educator; b. Plum City, Wis., July 7, 1946; d. John Henry and Mary Ann Louise (Dankers) Seipel; m. Stephen Joseph Prissel, Dec. 16, 1967; children: Angela, Benjamin. Graduate with honors, Mpls. Bus. Coll., 1966; student, Moraine Park Tech. Coll., Wis., 1983—. Cert. interactive TV, adult edn. instr. Legal sec. Mott, Grose, Von Holtum & Hefferan, Mpls., 1966-67, Whelan, Morey & Morey Attys. at Law, Durand, Wis., 1967-70, Murry Law Office, River Falls, Wis., 1968-70, Potter, Wefel & Nettesheim, Wisconsin Rapids, Wis., 1970-71; sec. to adminstr. Moraine Park Tech. Coll., Fond du Lac, Wis., 1971-72; paralegal Kilgore Law Office, Ripon, Wis., 1985—. Chmn. legal adv. com. Moraine Park Tech. Coll., Fond du Lac, Wis., 1996-98, mem. adminstrv. assts. adv. com., 1984-86; mem. legal adv. commn. Moraine Park Tech. Coll., 1984—. Contbr. poems to newspapers. Ch. rep. Ch. Women United, Ripon, Wis., 1984-87; pianist Christian Women's Orgn., Ripon, 1985-95; pianist, organist Our Lady of Lake Ch., Green Lake, Wis., 1987—. Mem.: NAFE, Legal Profls. Assn. (East Ctrl. Wis. pres. 1994—95, sec. 1995—96, chmn. Day-In-Ct. 1999, NALS Fedn. liaison 2000—02, sec. 2001—02, v.p. 2003—, chmn. edn. lisison com., state legal ed. task force 2003—, Legal award of Excellence 1995—96), Wis. Assn. Legal Secs. (state legal ednl. liaison com. 1997—), Nat. Assn. Legal Secs. Roman Catholic. Avocations: teaching and playing piano, creative writing, cooking, swimming, exercising. Home: 129 Wolverton Ave Ripon WI 54971-1144 E-mail: prissel@powercom.net.

PRITCHARD, LLEWELYN G. lawyer; b. N.Y.C., Aug. 13, 1937; s. Llewelyn and Anne Mary (Streib) P.; m. Joan Ashby, June 20, 1959; children: David Ashby, Jennifer Pritchard Vick, Andrew Harrison, William Llewellyn. AB with honors, Drew U., 1958; LLB, Duke U., 1961. Ptnr. Helsell & Fetterman, Seattle. Trustee, corp. counsel Allied Arts Found.; pres. Allied Arts Seattle, 1974-76; trustee Meth. Ednl. Found., 1970-85, pres., 1991-92; life trustee Poncho Patrons of Pacific N.W. Civil, Cultural and Charitable Orgns., pres., 1972-73; bd. dirs. Planned Parenthood of Seattle/King County, 1972-78; trustee Seattle Symphony Orch., 1979-83, chmn. bd., 1980-82, hon. trustee; trustee U. Puget Sound., 1972-99, mem. exec. com., chmn. bd. visitors to Law Sch., 1984-88; trustee, exec. com. Mus. of Glass, 2000—; chancellor Pacific N.W. Ann. conf. United Meth. Ch., 1969—. Fellow Am. Bar Found. (life, state chmn. 1988-98); mem. ABA (bd. govs. 1986-89, chmn. program com. 1988-89, exec. com. 1988-89, Ho. of Dels. 1979—, nat. dir. young lawyers divsn. 1971, chmn. sect. of individual rights and responsibilities 1975-76, exec. coun. family law sect. 2002—, chair standing com. on legal aid and indigent defendants 1973-75, chair legal needs study 1995-98, chair adv. com. to pro bono immigration project 1991-2001, dir. Ctr. for Human Rights 2001—), Wash. State Bar Assn. (bd. govs. King County 1972-75), King County Bar Assn. (chair young lawyers sect. 1970). Avocations: reading, art collector. Family and matrimonial, General practice. Home: 5229 140th Ave NE Bellevue WA 98005-1024 Office: Helsell & Fetterman 1001 Fourth Ave Ste 4200 Seattle WA 98154 E-mail: lpritchard@helsell.com.

PRITCHETT, MICHAEL EUGENE COOK, lawyer; b. Louisiana, Mo., Mar. 14, 1960; s. Lloyd Thornton and Wanda Maxine P.; m. Lila Sue Cook, July 30, 1983; children: Andrew Jacob, Courtney Elizabeth. BA in Econs. & Polit. Sci., U. Mo., 1982, MA in Econs., 1983, JD, 1986. Bar: U.S. Dist. Ct. (we. dist.) Mo., 1986, U.S. Ct. Appeals (8th cir.), 1989, U.S. Supreme Ct., 2000. Law clk. Supreme Ct. Mo., Jefferson City, 1986-88; assoc. Inglish, Monaco, Riner & Lockenvitz, Jefferson City, 1988-89; asst. atty. gen. Mo. Atty. Gen.'s Office, Jefferson City, 1989—, chmn. CLE com., 2000—, dep. chief counsel Labor divsn., 2001—02, trial team leader Litigation divsn., 1983—2001, 2002—. Mem. Mo. Law Rev., 1984-86. Gregory fellow U. Mo., 1982-83. Mem. Mo. Bar Assn., Order of the Coif. Office: Atty Gen's Office PO Box 899 Jefferson City MO 65102-0899 E-mail: mike.pritchett@mail.ago.state.mo.us.

PRITCHETT, REBECCA WRIGHT, lawyer; b. Mobile, Ala., Jan. 7, 1967; d. William Marvin and Peggy Wilson Wright; m. Matthew D. Pritchett, Apr. 20, 1996. BS in Journalism, U. So. Miss., 1990; JD, U. Oreg., 1993. Bar: Calif. 1993, Ala. 1995. Atty. Sasser and Littleton PC, Montgomery, Ala., 1994—97; shareholder Sirote and Permutt PC, Birmingham, Ala., 1997—. 2d v.p., bd. dirs. Ala. Wildlife Fedn., 2001—; trustee Ala. Forever Wild Land Trust, Montgomery, 1999—; commr. Ala. Commn. Environ. Initiatives, Montgomery, 2000-02. Recipient Pres.'s award Ala. Wildlife Fedn., 2000. Mem.: Jr. League Birmingham, Exec. Womens Roundtable. Avocations: sporting clays, hunting, fishing, cooking, wine tasting. Environmental, Government contracts and claims, Property, real (including real estate development, water). Office: Sirote and Permutt PC PO Box 55727 Birmingham AL 35255-5727 Home: PO Box 55727 Birmingham AL 35255-5727

PRITCHETT, RUSSELL WILLIAM, lawyer, educator; b. Missoula, Mont., Feb. 16, 1951; s. Floyd Wiley and Mary Almeda (Brewer) P.; m. Meg Jesse Jacobson, June 23, 1974; 1 child, Arundel B. BA in History, U. Wash., 1974; JD, Northwestern Sch. of Law, 1977; LLM Maritime & Internat., U. London, 1979. Bar: Wash. 1978, Alaska 1979, U.S. Dist. Ct. Alaska 1979, U.S. Ct. Appeals (9th cir.) 1980, U.S. Dist. Ct. (we. dist.) Wash. 1984. In-house counsel Steamship Mut. Underwriting Assn., Ltd., London, 1978; assoc. Graham & James, Anchorage, 1978-81, Braun, Moriya, Hoashi & Kubota, Tokyo, 1981-83; pvt. practice Bellingham, Wash., 1983-95; ptnr. Pritchett & Jacobson, Bellingham, Wash., 1995—. Adj. prof. internat. trade Western Wash. U., Bellingham, 1986-98. Contbr. articles to profl. jours. Pres. Bellingham Maritime Found., 1985. Mem. Maritime Law Assn. U.S. (com. on fisheries 1985—, proctor), Am. Immigration Lawyers Assn. Avocations: cross country skiing, hiking. Admiralty, Immigration, naturalization, and customs, Private international. Home and Office: 870 Democrat St Bellingham WA 98229-8829 E-mail: PandJ@nas.com.

PRITIKIN, JAMES B. lawyer; b. Chgo., Feb. 18, 1939; s. Stan and Anne (Schwartz) P.; m. Barbara Cheryl Demovsky, Apr. 20, 1968 (dec. 1988); children: Gregory, David, Randi; m. Mary Szatkowski, July 7, 1990; 1 child, Peyton. BS, U. Ill., 1961; JD, DePaul U., 1965. Bar: Ill. 1965, U.S. Dist. Ct. (no. dist.) Ill. 1965, U.S. Supreme Ct. 1985; cert. matrimonial arbitrator. Pvt. practice, Chgo., 1965-68, 1984—; ptnr. Sudak, Grubman, Pritikin, Rosenthal & Feldman, Chgo., 1969-80, Pritikin & Sohn, Chgo., 1980-84, Nadler, Pritikin & Mirabelli, Chgo., 1997—. Hearing officer State of Ill. Atty. Registration and Disciplinary Commn. Fellow Internat. Acad. Matrimonial Lawyers, Am. Acad. Matrimonial Lawyers (past pres.); mem. ABA, Am. Acad. Matrimonial Lawyers (past pres. Ill. chpt.), Ill. Bar Assn., Chgo. Bar Assn. (cir. ct. Cook County liaison com.). Family and matrimonial. Office: 1 Prudential Plz 130 E Randolph Dr Chicago IL 60601-6207

PRIVETT, CARYL PENNEY, judge; b. Birmingham, Ala., Jan. 7, 1948; d. William Kinnaird Privett and Katherine Speake (Binford) Ennis. BA, Vanderbilt U., 1970; JD, NYU, 1973. Bar: Ala. 1973, U.S. Dist. Ct. (so. dist.) Ala. 1973, U.S. Dist. Ct. (no. dist.) Ala. 1974, U.S. Ct. Appeals (5th cir.) 1974, U.S. Ct. Appeals (11th cir.) 1981. Assoc. Crawford & Blacksher, Mobile, Ala., 1973—74, Adams, Baker & Clemon, Birmingham, Ala., 1974—76; asst. US atty. no. dist. Ala. US Atty.'s Office, US Dept. Justice, Birmingham, Ala., 1976—94, first asst. US atty., 1992—93, US atty., 1995—97, chief asst., 1997—98; pvt. practice Birmingham, Ala., 1998—2003; city prosecutor City of Mountain Brook, 1998—2003; cir. judge 10th Jud. Cir. of Ala., 2003—. Adj. prof. Cumberland Sch. Law Samford U., 1998—. Active Downtown Dem. Club, Birmingham, Ala.; bd. dir. Planned Parenthood Ala., Birmingham, Ala., Legal Aid Soc., Birmingham, Ala., 1986—88, pres., 1988; sec., founder Lawyers for Choice Ala., 1989—92; chair domestic violence com. City of Birmingham, Ala., 1989—91; sustaining mem. Jr. League Birmingham, Ala.; mem. Photography Guild; active Birmingham Mus. Art, Ala. Named, Outstanding Young Women Am., 1977, 1978; recipient Cert. in Color Photography, U. Ala. Birmingham, 1989, Commr.'s Spl. citation, Food and Drug Adminstrn. Mem.: ABA, Ala. Law Inst., Adminstrv. Dir., Ala. Acad. Atty. Mediators (pres. 2002), Birmingham Bar Found. (pres. 2001), Birmingham Bar Assn. (exec. com. 1996-98), Ala. Bar Assn. (chmn. women in the profession com. 1997-99), Fed. Bar Assn. (pres. Birmingham chpt. 1979), Ala. Solution, Leadership Birmingham, Women's Network, Women's Fund, Altamont Alumni Assn., Summit Club. Presbyterian. Avocation: photography. Home: 30 Norman Dr Birmingham AL 35213-4310 Office: 660 Jefferson County Courthouse 716 Richard Arrington Blvd Birmingham AL 35203 E-mail: carylprivett@mindspring.com.

PRO, PHILIP MARTIN, judge; b. Richmond, Calif., Dec. 12, 1946; s. Leo Martin and Mildred Louise (Beck) P.; m. Dori Sue Hallas, Nov. 13, 1982; 1 child, Brenda Kay. BA, San Francisco State U., 1968; JD, Golden Gate U., 1972. Bar: Calif. 1972, Nev. 1973, U.S. Ct. Appeals (9th cir.) 1973, U.S. Dist. Ct. Nev. 1973, U.S. Supreme Ct. 1976. Pub. defender, Las Vegas, 1973-75; asst. U.S. atty. Dist. Nev., Las Vegas, 1975-78; dep. atty. gen. State of Nev., Carson City, 1979-80; U.S. magistrate U.S. Dist. Ct. Nev., Las Vegas, 1980-87, U.S. dist. judge, 1987—2002, chief U.S. dist. judge, 2002—. Instr. Atty. Gen.'s Advocacy Inst., Nat. Inst. Trial Advocacy, 1992; chmn. com. adminstrn. of magistrate judge system Jud. Conf. U.S., 1993—. Bd. dirs. NCCJ, Las Vegas, 1982—, mem. program com. and issues in justice com. Mem. ABA, Fed. Judges Assn. (bd. dirs. 1992—, v.p. 1997-2001), Nev. State Bar Assn., Calif. State Bar Assn., Nev. Judges Assn. (instr.), Assn. Trial Lawyers Am., Nev. Am. Inn Ct. (pres. 1989-91), Ninth Cir. Jury (instructions com.), Nat. Conf. U.S. Magistrates (sec.). Republican. Episcopalian. Office: US Dist Ct 7015 Fed Bldg 300 Las Vegas Blvd S Ste 4650 Las Vegas NV 89101-5883 E-mail: Philip_Pro@nvd.uscourts.gov.

PROBUS, MICHAEL MAURICE, JR., lawyer; b. Louisville, Jan. 26, 1963; s. Michael Maurice and Jerilyn Ann (Burks) P.; m. Luz Marie Probus, May 22, 1985; children: Michael Julian, Lauren Michael. BA, U. Dallas, 1985; JD, U. Tex., 1988. Bar: Tex. 1988, U.S. Dist. Ct. (we. dist.) Tex. 1990, U.S. Ct. Appeals (5th cir.) 1993. Jud. law clk. to chief judge U.S. Dist. Ct. Tex., Houston, 1988-90; assoc. Law Offices of Michael A. Wash, Austin, Tex., 1990-97; pvt. practice, Austin, 1997—. Pro bono atty. Vol. Legal Svcs., Austin, 1994—. Mem.: Travis County Bar Assn. Democrat. Roman Catholic. Personal injury (including property damage), Product liability, Professional liability. Office: Law Office M Probus 111 Congress Ave Ste 2230 Austin TX 78701 E-mail: mprobusjr@msn.com.

PROCHNOW, DOUGLAS LEE, lawyer; b. Omaha, Jan. 9, 1952; s. Albert Delmer and Betty Jean (Wood) P. BA with high distinction, U. Nebr., 1974; JD, Northwestern U., 1977. Bar: Ill. 1977, U.S. Dist. Ct. (no. dist.) Ill. 1977, U.S. Ct. Appeals (7th cir.) 1989, U.S. Supreme Ct. 2000. Assoc. Wildman, Harrold, Allen & Dixon, Chgo., 1977-84, ptnr., 1985—. Spl. asst. corp. counsel City of Chgo., 1986—87. Bd. dirs. Chgo. chpt. Prevent Child Abuse Am. Mem. ABA, ATLA (assoc.), Ill. Bar Assn., Chgo. Bar Assn., Soc. Trial Lawyers, Def. Rsch. Inst., Am. Health Lawyers Assn., Phi Beta Kappa, Phi Eta Sigma. State civil litigation, Insurance, Product liability. Home: 1230 N State Pky Apt 6D Chicago IL 60610-2261 Office: Wildman Harrold Allen & Dixon 225 W Wacker Dr Ste 2700 Chicago IL 60606-1224 E-mail: prochnow@wildmanharrold.com.

PROCHNOW, HERBERT VICTOR, JR., retired lawyer; b. Evanston, Ill., May 26, 1931; s. Herbert V. and Laura (Stinson) P.; m. Lucia Boyden, Aug. 6, 1966; children: Thomas Herbert, Laura. AB, Harvard U., 1953, JD, 1956; A.M., U. Chgo., 1958. Bar: Ill. 1957, U.S. Dist. Ct. (no. dist.) Ill. 1961. With 1st Nat. Bank Chgo., 1958-91, atty., 1961-70, sr. atty., 1971-73, counsel, 1973-91, adminstrv. asst. to chmn. bd., 1978-81; pvt. practice, 1991—; ret., 2003. Author: (with Herbert V. Prochnow) A Treasury of Humorous Quotations, 1969, The Changing World of Banking, 1974, The Public Speaker's Treasure Chest, 1986, The Toastmaster's Treasure Chest, 1988; also articles in legal publs. Mem.: Am. Soc. Internat. Law, Chgo. Bar Assn. (chmn. com. internat. law 1970—71), Ill. Bar Assn., ABA, Chgo. Club, Lawyers Club (Chgo.), Harvard Club (N.Y.C.), Univ. Club (Chgo.),

Econ. Club, Onwentsia, Phi Beta Kappa. Banking, Private international. Home: 949 Woodbine Pl Lake Forest IL 60045-2275 Office: 155 N Michigan Ave Chicago IL 60601-7511

PROCHNOW, THOMAS HERBERT, lawyer; b. Chgo., May 29, 1967; s. Herbert Victor Jr. and Lucia (Boyden) P. AB, Harvard U., 1989; postgrad., U. London, 1989; student, U. Paris, Sorbonne, 1990; JD, Yale U., 1993. Bar: N.Y. 1994, U.S. Dist. Ct. (so. and ea. dists.) N.Y. 1994, U.S. Ct. Appeals (fed. cir.) 1998. Assoc. Debevoise & Plimpton, N.Y.C., 1993-99; assoc. counsel intellectual property NHL Enterprises, L.P., N.Y.C., 1999—2001, sr. counsel legal and bus. affairs, 2001—. Contbr. chpt. to book, articles to profl. jours. Vol. atty., asylum program Lawyers Com. for Human Rights, N.Y.C., 1994-99. Recipient award of Excellence, Vol. Lawyers for the Arts, 1996. Mem.: ABA (intellectual property sect.), Internat. Trademark Assn. (internet com.), Assn. of Bar of City of N.Y. Computer, Intellectual property. Office: NHL Enterprises LP 47th Fl 1251 Ave of Americas New York NY 10020-1192

PROCOPIO, JOSEPH GUYDON, lawyer; b. Paterson, N.J., May 1, 1940; s. Joseph A. and V. Genevieve (Kievitt) P.; m. Joanne Julia Roccato, June 30, 1962 (div. Aug. 1980); children: Jennifer Tehani Tyler, Joseph Christian; m. Frances Mary Hansen Schmieder, Apr. 16, 1988 (div. Oct. 1998); stepchildren: Timothy James Schmieder, Julie Ann Schmieder. BS, U.S. Naval Acad., 1962; MS in Ops. Rsch., Naval Postgrad. Sch., 1971; JD, Cath. U. Am., 1979; LLM, George Washington U., 1987. Bar: Va. Commd. ensign USN, 1962, served to comdr., 1978, ret., 1983; gen. counsel, sec. Presearch, Inc., Fairfax, Va., 1983-85; dir. bus. devel., then v.p. corp. communications ERC Internat., Fairfax, Va., 1985-90; pres., CEO Advanced Engring. Group, Inc., Fairfax, 1990-92; chmn., CEO JP Fin. Group Ltd., Fairfax, 1992—; exec. USPS. Prin. The Poretz Group, 1996-98, Viking Profl. Seminars; bd. dirs. Solomon Group; prin. The Millenium Group, Ltd. (formerly Ashley-Boden-Keenan, Inc.); v.p. Valuation Techs., LLC, 1999-2001; corp. comm. cons., 1999-2001; substitute tchr. Douglas County; cons. VR Bus. Brokers, Engelwood, Colo., 2002. Chmn. Pub. Works & Utilities Commn., Castle Rock, Colo., mem. budget sub-com.; pres. Navy League U.S., Denver Coun.; election judge Douglas Co. Decorated Bronze Star, Meritorious Svc. medal, 3 Joint Svc. Commendation medal, Nat. Def. medal (Cambodia), Navy Achievement medal, Combat Action ribbon. Mem. Internat. Inst. Strategic Studies, Va. Bar Assn., The Atlantic Coun., George Washington U. Law Alumni Assn., U.S. Naval Acad. Alumni Assn., U.S. Naval Acad. Class of 1962 Assn. (bd. dirs. 1978-80, 87—, spl. asst. to pres. 1984-87), U.S. Naval Acad. Alumni Colo. (bd. dirs.), Nat. Eagle Scout Assn. Avocations: reading, history, legal, theology, military, naval, economic, golf, cooking. Corporate, general, Finance, Private international. Home: 237 Cherry St Castle Rock CO 80104-3206 E-mail: JoePro@aol.com.

PROCTOR, DAVID RAY, lawyer; b. Nashville, Apr. 18, 1956; s. Raymond Douglas and Margaret Florence (Coffey) P.; m. Robbin Lynn Fuqua, May 12, 1984 (div.); children: Rachael Lynne, Benjamin David; m. Shana T. Murdoch, Mar. 30, 2002; stepchildren: Sarah-Rachael, Rebecca Caroline. AA in Polit. Sci., Cumberland Jr. Coll., 1976; BA in Polit. Sci., Vanderbilt U., 1978; JD, Cumberland Sch. Law, 1981; LLM in Taxation, U. Fla., 1983. Bar: Ala. 1981, Tenn. 1983, U.S. Tax Ct. 1983. Law clk. to presiding justice Ala. Supreme Ct., Montgomery, 1981-82; assoc. Thrailkill & Goodman, Nashville, 1983-84; v.p. taxes Alfa Mut. Ins. Co., Montgomery, 1984—. Contbg. editor Cumberland Law Rev., 1980-81; contbr. articles to profl. jours. Tchr. Rsch. Bd., Birmingham, Ala., 1980; active Montgomery Area United Way, 1985—; mem. adv. bd. Montgomery Therapeutic Recreation Ctr., 2000—, pres., 2001; treas. Taylor Rd. Bapt. Ch., 1994—95, asst. treas., 1996, treas., 1997—98. Mem. ABA, Nat. Assn. Ind. Insurers (exec. tax com. 2000—), Nat. Assn. Mut. Ins. Cos. (tax com. 1988—, chmn. 1997-99, exec. tax com. 2000—), Ala. Bar Assn., Tenn. Bar Assn., Sunrise Exch. Club Montgomery (treas. 1989-91), Phi Alpha Delta, Pi Sigma Alpha. Baptist. Avocations: running, music, sports, charities. Corporate taxation, Personal income taxation, State and local taxation. Home: 9224 Sturbridge Pl Montgomery AL 36116 Office: Alfa Mut Ins Co 2108 E South Blvd Montgomery AL 36116-2015

PROCTOR, JOHN FRANKLIN, lawyer; b. Scottsboro, Ala., May 6, 1931; s. James Moody and Lucy (May) P.; children: James Moody, Laura. BS, U. Ala., 1953, LL.B., 1957. Bar: Ala. bar 1957. Asst. atty. gen., 1957-59; pvt. practice, 1959-90; judge Jackson County Ct., 1959-63; pvt. practice, 1963-66, 68-90; judge 9th Jud. Circuit, 1966-68; fed. adminstrv. law judge, 1990—. Served with U.S. Army, 1953-55. Mem. Ala. Bar Assn. (commr. 1979-90), Sigma Chi, Phi Alpha Delta. Methodist. Home: 3110 Olde Towne Ln Chattanooga TN 37415-5903 Office: Office Hearings and Appeals 300 Uplain Bldg Chattanooga TN 37411

PROFAIZER, JOSEPH RUDOLPH, lawyer; b. Cedar Rapids, Iowa, Oct. 5, 1967; s. Rudolph Henry and Lore Sophie (Schaefer) P. BA, U. Tex., 1990, JD, 1993; LLM, London Sch. Econs., 1999. Bar: Tex. 1993, U.S. Dist. Ct. (so. dist.) Tex. 1994. Law clk. to Hon. George P. Kazen U.S. Dist. Ct. So. Dist. Tex., Laredo, Tex., 1993-94; counsel Wilmer Cutler and Pickering, 1998; solicitor Supreme Ct. of Eng. and Wales. Contbr. articles to profl. jours. Named Dean's Disting. Grad., U. Tex., 1990. Mem. ABA. Roman Catholic. Alternative dispute resolution, General civil litigation, Private international. Office: Wilmer Cutler & Pickering 2445 M St NW Washington DC 20037 Home: 5115 Knapp Pl Alexandria VA 22304

PROFUSEK, ROBERT ALAN, lawyer; b. Cleve., Jan. 14, 1950; s. George John and Geraldine (Hobl) P.; m. Linda Gail Schmidt, May 7, 1972; children: Robert Charles, Kathryn Anne. BA, Cornell U., 1972; JD, NYU, 1975. Bar: Ohio 1975, Tex. 1981, NY 1994. Assoc. Jones Day, Cleve., 1975-81, Dallas, 1981-82, ptnr., 1982—, NY, 1993. bd. dir., CTS Corporcitum and Valero, LP; Contbr. articles to profl. jour. Mem. ABA, NY Bar Assn., Assn. Bar City of NY, Tex. Bar Assn., Greenwich Country Club. Republican. Episcopalian. Corporate, general, Securities. Home: 541 North St Greenwich CT 06830-3424 Office: Jones Day 15th Fl 222 E 41st St New York NY 10017

PROM, STEPHEN GEORGE, lawyer; b. Jacksonville, Fla., July 8, 1954; s. George W. and Bonnie M. (Porter) P.; divorced; children: Ashley Brooke, Aaron Jacob, Adam Glenn; m. Charlotte Rutter. AA in Polit. Sci. with high honors, Fla. Jr. Coll., 1974; BA in Polit. Sci. with high honors, U. Fla., 1977, JD with honors, 1979. Bar: Fla. 1980, U.S. Dist. Ct. (mid. dist.) Fla. 1980, U.S. Dist. Ct. (no. dist.) Fla. 1981, U.S. Tax Ct. 1982, U.S. Ct. Appeals (11th cir.) 1985, U.S. Supreme Ct. 1985. Assoc. Rogers, Towers, Bailey, Jones & Gay, Jacksonville, 1979-83, Foley & Lardner, Jacksonville, 1983-86; ptnr. Christian & Prom, Jacksonville, 1986-87, Prom, Korn & Zehmer, P.A., Jacksonville, 1987-95, Brant, Moore, MacDonald & Wells, P.A., 1995-2001, Akerman, Senterfitt & Eidson, P.A., 2001—. Sr. mgmt. editor U. Fla. Law Rev., 1978-79. Mem. Leadership Jacksonville, 1984, Jacksonville Cmty. Coun. Inc., 1985-86; bd. dirs. Mental Health Resource Ctr., Jacksonville, 1984-87, Mental Health Resource Foun., Jacksonville, 1985-87, Mental Health Found., Inc., 1987-89, mem. cmty. bd., 1989-91; bd. dirs. Youth Crisis Ctr., Jacksonville, 1984-86, Young Profls. Bd. Multiple Sclerosis Soc., 1988-89; bd. dirs. The Team, Inc., 1992-94; vol. Jacksonville, Inc., 1993-96, Jacksonville Found., Inc., 1993-96, Positively Jacksonville!, Inc., 1993-95, We Care of Jacksonville, Inc., 2002—. Mem. ABA (tax, health law sects.), Fla. Bar Assn. (tax, health law bd., bd. govs. young lawyers sect. 1983-87), Jacksonville Bar Assn. (chmn. health law sect.), Am. Acad. Healthcare Attys., Am. Hosp. Assn., Nat. Health Lawyers Assn., Fla. Acad. Healthcare Attys. (bd. dirs. 1994-97), Jacksonville Sailing Found., Inc. (bd. dirs. 1997—), N.E. Fla. Sailboat Rating Assn., Inc. (bd. dirs. 1997-98, chair 1998), Epping Forest Yacht Club (bd. govs.,commodore, vice commodore, rear commodore and sail fleet capt.), Ponte Vedra Club, North Fla. Cruising Club, Phi Beta Kappa, Phi Theta Kappa, Phi Kappa Phi. Republican. Baptist. Avocations: sailing, surfing, weightlifting, tennis, jogging. Commercial, contracts (including sales of goods; commercial financing), Health. Office: Akerman Senterfitt 50 N Laura St Ste 2500 Jacksonville FL 32202 E-mail: sprom@akerman.com.

PROMISLO, DANIEL, lawyer; b. Bryn Mawr, Pa., Nov. 15, 1932; s. Charles and Pearl (Backman) P.; m. Estelle Carasso, June 10, 1961; children: Mark, Jacqueline, Steven. BSBA, Drexel U., 1955; JD magna cum laude, U. Pa., 1966. Bar: Pa. 1966. Pres., owner Hist. Souvenir Co., Phila., 1957—; assoc. Wolf, Block, Schorr & Solis-Cohen, Phila., 1966-70, ptnr., 1977-94, exec. com., 1987-89, of counsel, 1994—, mng. dir., 1997-2001; founder, pres. dir. Inst. for Paralegal Tng., Phila., 1970-75, cons., 1975-77. Editor: Corporate Law, 1970, Real Estate Law, 1971, Estates and Trusts, 1971, Civil Litigation, 1972, Employee Benefit Plans, 1973, Criminal Law, 1974; contbr. articles to profl. jours. Bd. dirs. Phila. Drama Guild, 1977-95, chmn., 1982-86; bd. dirs. Phila. Israel Econ. Devel. Program, 1983-88, Inst. for Arts in Edn., 1990-93, WHYY, Inc., 1994—, vice-chmn., 1995-96, chmn., 1996-97; bd. dirs. U.S. Physicians, Inc., 1995-98; trustee Resource Asset Investment Trust (now RAIT Investment Trust), 1997—; bd. advisors Drexel U. Coll. Arts & Scis., 2001-. Mem. Order of Coif, Drexel U. 100, Blue Key, Phi Kappa Phi. Democrat. Jewish. Avocations: movies, basketball, tennis, golf. Corporate, general, Mergers and acquisitions, Securities. Office: Wolf Block Schorr & Solis-Cohen 1650 Arch St Fl 22 Philadelphia PA 19103-2097 E-mail: dpromislo@comcast.net.

PROPST, ANDREW J. lawyer; b. Burlington, Vt., Oct. 24, 1967; s. Michael Truman Propst and Judith Frances Libby; m. Elizabeth C. Emory, Apr. 26, 1997; children: Lillian Carley, Clara Emory. BA, U. Mo., 1990; JD cum laude, Gonzaga U., Spokane, Wash., 1994; LLM in Taxation, U. of Wash., 1998. Bar: Wash. 1994. Atty. Buzzard & Assocs., Centralia, Wash., 1995—97; sr. tax cons. Deloitte & Touche, Seattle, 1998—2000; atty. Karr Tuttle Campbell, Seattle, 2000—. Corporate, general, Finance, Mergers and acquisitions. Office: Karr Tuttle Campbell 1201 Third Ave Ste 2900 Seattle WA 98101 Office Fax: 206-682-7100. E-mail: apropst@karrtuttle.com.

PROSSER, DAVID THOMAS, JR., state supreme court justice, retired state legislator; b. Chgo., Dec. 24, 1942; s. David Thomas, Sr. and Elizabeth Averell (Patterson) Prosser. BA, DePauw U., 1965; JD, U. Wis., 1968. Bar: Wis. 1968. Lectr. Ind. U., Indpls., 1968-69; advisor U.S. Dept. Justice, Washington, 1969-72; adminstrv. asst. to U.S. Rep. Harold V. Froehlich, Washington, 1973-74; pvt. practice Washington, 1975, Appleton, Wis., 1976; dist. atty. Outagamie County, Appleton, 1977-78; state rep. State of Wis., Madison, 1979-96; commr. Tax Appeals Commn., 1997-98; justice Supreme Ct. Wis., 1998—, Jud. Coun., 2002—. Commr. Nat. Conf. Commrs. Uniform State Laws, 1982—96; mem. Wis. Sesquicentennial Commn., Madison, 1993—99; minority leader Wis. Assembly, 1989—94, spkr., 1995—96. Mem.: Outagamie Bar Assn., Milw. Bar Assn., Dane Bar Assn., Wis. Bar Assn. Presbyterian. Avocation: art collector of American prints. Home: 3156 Ridgeview Ave Madison WI 53704 Office: Supreme Ct Wis PO Box 1688 Madison WI 53701-1688 E-mail: david.prosser@courts.state.wi.us.

PROST, SHARON, federal judge; b. Newburyport, Mass., May 24, 1951; m. Kenneth F. Greene, June 24, 1984; 1 child, Matthew Prost-Greene. BS, Cornell U., 1973; MBA, George Washington U., 1975, LLM in Taxation, 1984; JD, Am. U., 1979. Bar: D.C. Labor rels. specialist Office of Personnel Mgmt., 1973-76; with Gen. Acctg. Office, 1976-79; trial atty. Fed. Labor Rels. Authority, 1980-83; atty. chief counsel's office Dept. of Treasury, 1983-84; assoc. solicitor Nat. Labor Rels. Bd., 1984-89; chief minority labor counsel Senate Com. on Labor and Human Resources, 1989-93; minority chief counsel Senate Com. on the Judiciary, 1993—2001; judge U.S. Court of Appeal , Federal Cir., 2001—. Office: US Court Appeals Fed Cir 717 Madison Pl NW Washington DC 20439*

PROUTY, CHARLES S. federal agency administrator; b. Jersey City; BS, U.S. Naval Acad., 1967; MA in Econs., George Mason U., 1982, JD, 1991. Bar: Va. Joined as spl. agt. FBI, 1973, supr. hostage rescue team, 1986—87, supr. violent crimes and major offenders sect. criminal investigative divsn., 1987—89, unit chief spl. ops. and rsch. unit tng. divsn. FBI Acad. Quantico, Va., 1989—92, inspector's aide inspection divsn., 1992—93, spl. asst. to the dep. asst. dir. tng. divsn., 1993—94, asst. spl. agt. in charge, 1994—97, sect. chief bur. applicant recruit and selection sect. Washington, 1997—98, spl. agt. in charge Little Rock divsn., 1998—2000, spl. agt. in charge Boston divsn., 2000—02, exec. asst. dir. law enforcement svcs. divsn. Washington, 2002—. With USN, 1967—73, ret. capt. USNR. Office: FBI J Edgar Hoover Bldg 935 Pennsylvania Ave NW Washington DC 20535*

PROVINE, JOHN CALHOUN, retired lawyer; b. Asheville, N.C., May 15, 1938; s. Robert Calhoun and Harriet Josephine (Thoms) P.; m. Martha Ann Monson, Aug. 26, 1966 (div. Jan. 1975); m. Nancy Frances Lunsford, Apr. 17, 1976 (div. Mar. 1996); children: Robert, Frances, Harriet. AB, Harvard U., 1960; JD, U. Mich., 1966; MBA, NYU, 1972, LLM in Taxation, 1975. Bar: N.Y., Tenn., U.S. Dist. Ct. (so. and ea. dists.) N.Y., U.S. Ct. Appeals (2nd and 6th cirs.), U.S. Dist. Ct. (mid. dist.) Tenn., U.S. Supreme Ct. From assoc. to ptnr. White & Case, N.Y.C., 1966—74, ptnr., 1974—82, 1992—94, Jakarta and Ankara, 1982—91; counsel Dearborn & Ewing, Nashville, 1981—82; ret., 1994. Lt. USN, 1960-63. Mem. ABA, N.Y. Bar Assn., Tenn. Bar Assn., Assn. of Bar of City of N.Y. Avocations: bluegrass music, rural activities. Commercial, contracts (including sales of goods; commercial financing), Corporate, general, Private international. Home and Office: 6630 Manley Ln Brentwood TN 37027-3401 E-mail: jprovine@compuserve.com.

PROVINZINO, JOHN C. lawyer; b. Long Prairie, Minn., Apr. 30, 1947; s. John T. and Jean M. Provinzino; m. Jannine M. Provinzino, Dec. 29, 1970; children: Alan, Laura, Anne. BA, St. John's U., 1969; JD, U. Minn., 1972. Bar: Minn. 1972, U.S. Dist. Ct. Minn. 1972. Ptnr. Murphy, Neils & Provinzino, St. Cloud, Minn., 1972-76, Reichert, Wenner, Koch & Provinzino, St. Cloud, 1976—. Mem. St. Cloud Newman Ctr., 1992-94, Epilepsy Found., 1975-80. Capt. Army N.G., 1969-77. Mem. Minn. Bar Assn., Stearns-Benton County Bar Assn., St. Cloud C. of C., Kiwanis. Avocations: racquetball, golf. State civil litigation, Criminal, Pension, profit-sharing, and employee benefits. Office: Reichert Wenner Koch & Provinzino 501 W Saint Germain St Saint Cloud MN 56301-3633 Fax: 320-252-2678.

PROVORNY, FREDERICK ALAN, lawyer, educator; b. Bklyn., Sept. 7, 1946; s. Daniel and Anna (Wurm) P.; m. Nancy Ileene Wilkins, Nov. 21, 1971; children: Michelle C., Cheryl A., Lisa T., Robert D. BS summa cum laude, NYU, 1966; JD magna cum laude, Columbia U., 1969. Bar: N.Y. 1970, U.S. Supreme Ct. 1973, D.C. 1975, Mo. 1977, Md. 1987, Calif. 1989; CPA, Md., Mo. Law clk. to Judge Harold R. Medina U.S. Ct. Appeals (2d cir.), N.Y.C., 1969-70; asst. prof. law Syracuse (N.Y.) U., 1970-72; assoc. Debevoise, Plimpton, Lyons & Gates, N.Y.C., 1972-75, Cole & Groner P.C., Washington, 1975-76; with Monsanto Co., St. Louis, 1976-86, asst. co. counsel, 1978-86; pvt. practice Washington, 1986-89; ptnr. Provorny & Jacoby, Washington, 1989-91; counsel Shaw, Pittman, Potts & Trowbridge, Washington, 1991-93; ptnr. Tydings & Rosenberg, Balt., 1993-94; pvt. practice Balt., 1994—98; Harold R. Tyler prof. of law and tech., dir. Sci. and Tech. Law Ctr., Albany (N.Y.) Law Sch., 1998—; pres. Empire State Venture Group, Inc., 2001—. Lect. Bklyn Law Sch., 1973-74; adj. prof. U. Balt. Sch. of Law, 1996-98; pres. Sci. and Tech. Assocs., Inc., 1986-91. Contbr. articles to profl. jours. Trustee Christian Woman's Benevolent Assn. Youth Home, 1979-83, Jewish Family Svcs. of N.E. N.Y., 1999—. Mem. ABA, Am. Law Inst., Am. Arbitration Assn. (panel comml. abitrators), Am. Intellectual Property Lawyers Assn., Licensing Execs. Soc. (U.S., Can.), Assn. Rsch. Tech. Mgrs., Philo-Mt. Sinai Lodge 968, Masons, Beta Gamma Sigma. Jewish. Corporate, general, Finance, Intellectual property. Home: 11803 Kemp Mill Rd Silver Spring MD 20902-1511 Office: Albany Law School 80 New Scotland Ave Albany NY 12208-3494

PRUDEN, JAMES NORFLEET, III, lawyer; b. Edenton, N.C., Sept. 1, 1948; s. James Norfleet Jr. and Helen (Goodwin) P.; m. Cynthia Haines Gridley, Aug. 7, 1971; children: Matthew Gridley, Haines Goodwin. AB, U. N.C., 1970; JD, U. Va., 1973. Assoc. Kennedy Covington Lobdell & Hickman, Charlotte, N.C., 1973-78, ptnr., 1979—. Author manuscripts for continuing legal edn. programs, 1979—. Mem. county selection com. John Motley Morehead Found., Chapel Hill, N.C., 1990-92, chmn. 1993-95; vestryman Christ Episcopal Ch., 1990-92, 2000-02, sr. warden, 2002. Recipient John Motley Morehead award, 1966-70. Mem. ABA, N.C. Bar Assn. (chmn. bus. law sect. 1991-92, pres. 2002-03). Democrat. Corporate, general, Securities, Mergers and acquisitions. Home: 1139 Queens Rd Charlotte NC 28207-1849 Office: Kennedy Covington Hearst Tower 214 N Tryon St 47th Fl Charlotte NC 28202

PRUELLAGE, JOHN KENNETH, lawyer; b. St. Louis, Feb. 4, 1941; s. John H. P. and Bertha Kunkel; m. Patricia Marré, Dec. 30, 1966 (div. Apr. 1993); children: Jill Shannon Pruellage Hunt, John Kenneth, Jr., William Marré; m. Vicky L. Fehl, Aug. 29, 1993. BS, St. Louis U., 1962; JD, U. Mo., 1965; LLM, George Washington U., 1968. Tax staff Coopers & Lybrand, St. Louis, 1965-66; ptnr., chmn. Lewis, Rice & Fingersh, LLC, St. Louis, 1970—. Bd. dirs. Unity Health Sys., St. Louis. Bd. dir. St. Anthony's Med. Ctr., St. Louis, 1996—; trustee St. Louis U., 1998—. Capt. USAF, 1966-70. Mem. ABA, Mo. Bar Assn., St. Louis Bar Assn., Noonday Club (pres., bd. dirs. 1996—), Old Warson Country Club (pres. 2001-02, bd. dirs. 1997—). Office: Lewis Rice Fingersh LLC 500 N Broadway Ste 2000 Saint Louis MO 63102-2147

PRUESSNER, DAVID MORGAN, lawyer; b. Corpus Christi, Tex., May 13, 1955; s. Harold Trebus and Alma (Morgan) P.; m. Becky McKinney, May 21, 1977; children: Jennifer, Daniel, Heather. BA cum laude, Baylor U., 1977, JD cum laude, 1980. Bar: Tex. 1980, U.S. Dist. Ct. (no. dist.) Tex. 1980, U.S. Ct. Appeals (5th cir.) 1986, U.S. Supreme Ct. 1989. Atty. Coke & Coke, Dallas, 1980-83, Shank, Irwin & Conant, Dallas, 1983-90, Pettit & Martin, Dallas, 1990-92, Fletcher & Springer, Dallas, 1992-99; pvt. practice Law Office of David Pruessner, Dallas, 1999—. Instr. legal assts. program So. Meth. U., Dallas, 1989-91. Mem. editl. bd. Baylor Law Rev., 1980. Avocations: world religions, history, chess. Appellate, General civil litigation, Insurance. Office: Law Offices of David M Pruessner Ste 600 10100 N Central Expy Dallas TX 75231-4156 Fax: 214-692-6474. E-mail: david@prulaw.com.

PRUETT, CATHERINE EILEEN, lawyer; b. Louisville, Mar. 5, 1950; d. Herbert Milton and Charlesetta Lindsey Pruett; m. David S. Jump, Aug. 31, 1986; 1 child, Lindsey Jump. AB, Ind. U., 1972; JD, Ohio State U., 1981. Bar: Ohio. Dir. intake and night pros. program Columbus (Ohio) City Atty., 1991—92, intake counselor, hearing officer, 1980—82, asst. city prosecutor, 1982—85, asst. city atty., 1985—91; coord. dispute resolution program Supreme Ct. Ohio, Columbus, 1992—. Adj. faculty mem. Capital U. Law and Grad. Ctr., Columbus, 1996—. Contbr. articles to profl. jours.; sr. staff mem.: Ohio State U. Law Jour. Fellow: Ohio Bar Found.; mem.: Assn. Family and Conciliation Cts. (bd. dirs., chmn. profl. devel. and tech. assistance com., Pres.' award 2002), Ohio Mediation Assn., Assn. Conflict Resolution, Columbus Br Found., Columbus Bar Assn., Ohio State Bar Assn. (chmn. dispute resolution com. 2001—). Office: Supreme Ct of Ohio 30 E Broad St Columbus OH 43215-3431

PRUETZ, ADRIAN M. lawyer; Student, U. Wis., 1966—69; BA, Loyola U., Chgo., 1972, postgrad., 1972—73; JD magna cum laude, Marquette U., 1982. With Quinn Emanual et al, L.A. Spkr., lectr. Price Waterhouse Intellectual Property Forum, Licensing Execs. Soc., Am. Soc. Indsl. Security. Named one of Most Influential Trial Lawyers in Calif., L.A. Daily Jour., 2002, State's Top 25 Copyright, Trademark and Patent Legal Minds, head STRONG, 2003, Calif.'s Most Successful Lawyers, Calif. Law Bus. Mem.: ABA (past chair com. U.S. lit. affecting internat. patent problems, past chair com. impact 1991 amendments), Women Lawyer's Assn. L.A., Los Angeles County Bar, State Bar Calif., Fed. Bar Assn. (spkr., lectr.). Intellectual property, Antitrust, Commercial, contracts (including sales of goods; commercial financing). Office: 865 S Figueroa St 10th Fl Los Angeles CA 90017 Office Fax: 213-624-0634. Business E-Mail: emp@quinnemanuel.com.*

PRUGH, GEORGE SHIPLEY, lawyer; b. Norfolk, Va., June 1, 1920; s. George Shipley and Florence (Hamilton) P.; m. Katherine Buchanan, Sept. 27, 1942; children: Stephanie Dean, Virginia Patton. AB, U. Calif., Berkeley, 1941; JD, U. Calif., San Francisco, 1948; postgrad., Army War Coll., 1961-62; MA, George Washington U., 1963. Bar: Calif. 1949, U.S. Supreme Ct. 1954. Legal advisor U.S. Mil. Assistance Command, Vietnam, 1964-66; legal adviser U.S. European Command, Stuttgart, Ger., 1966-69; Judge Adv., U.S. Army Europe, Heidelberg, Ger., 1969-71; Judge Adv. Gen. Washington, 1971-75; ret., 1975. Prof. law Hastings Coll. Law, U. Calif., San Francisco, 1975-82 Author: (with others) Law at War, 1975; (play) Solferino; contbr. articles to profl. jours. Mem. Sec. Def. Task Force on Racial Discrimination in Adminstrn. Mil. Justice, 1973; mem. U.S. del. Diplomatic Conf. on Law of War, Geneva, 1974, 75. 2d lt. U.S. Army; maj. gen. JAGC, 1971. Decorated D.S.M. with oak leaf cluster, Legion of Merit with oak leaf cluster. Mem. ABA, Am. Judicature Soc., Internat. Soc. Mil. Law and Law of War (hon. pres.), Civil Affairs Assn. (hon. dir.), Selden Soc., Calif. Bar, Order of Coif, Bohemian Club, Army and Navy Club (Washington), Phi Delta Phi. Episcopalian.

PRUITT, REBECCA LEE, lawyer; b. Decatur, Ill., Oct. 30, 1952; d. Harold and Barbara Lee Pruitt. BS, U. Ill., 1974, MSW, 1981; JD, Loyola U., Chgo., 1992; M in Pastoral Studies, Loyola U., New Orleans, 2001. Bar: Ill. 1992, U.S. Dist. Ct. (no. dist.) Ill. 1992, Mo. 2002, U.S. Dist. Ct. (w. dist.) Mo. 2002. Social worker Luth. Gen. Hosp., Park Ridge, Ill., 1987—95; ethics cons. Park Ridge Ctr., Chgo., 1995—96; ethicist St. John's Health Sys., Springfield, Mo., 1996—99; v.p. mission and ethics Mercy Health Sys. Okla., Oklahoma City, 1999—2001; founding mem. Zerrer & Pruitt, LLC, Springfield, 2002—. Mem. adv. bd. The Mirror Diocesan Newspaper, Springfield, 2002—; Nat. Acad. Elder Law Attys.; bd. mem. Springfield Mid Am. Singers, 2002. Mem.: ABA, Nat. Acad. of Elder Law Attys., Mo. Bar, Ill. State Bar Assn., Alpha Sigma Nu. Estate planning, Probate (including wills, trusts). Office: Zerrer & Pruitt LLC 1147 E Walnut Springfield MO 65806

PRUNA, LAURA MARIA, lawyer; b. La Habana, Cuba, Apr. 23, 1954; came to U.S., 1961; d. Max and Martha Luz P. BBA, U. Miami, 1976; JD, Fla. State U., 1988. Bar: Fla. 1989, U.S. Ct. Appeals (11th cir.), U.S. Ct. Mil. Appeals, Ill. 1989. Law clk. Dept. Profl. Regulation, State of Fla., Tallahassee, 1987-88; atty. Carl Di Bernardo, P.A., South Miami, Fla., 1989-90, Pruna & Milian, Miami, Fla., 1991-93, Pruna Law Offices, Miami, 1993—. Atty., Fundacion Centro Americana, Miami, 1997-98. Mem. Colombian Am. Bar (bd. dirs. 1997-98), Cath. Lawyers Guild (pres. 1989-92). Republican. Avocations: fishing, reading. Family and matrimonial, Immigration, naturalization, and customs, Private international. Office: Pruna Law Offices 2525 SW 3d Ave Ste 205 Miami FL 33129-2057 E-mail: pruna@lawyer.com., prunaesq@aol.com.

PRUSAK, MAXIMILIAN MICHAEL, lawyer; b. Granite City, Ill., Mar. 22, 1943; s. Max Emil and Catherine Theresa (Jakich) P.; m. Carolyn Irene Pinkel, July 2, 1966; children: Scott Michael, Stephanie K. BS in Math., U.

Ill., 1965, JD, 1968. Bar: Ill. 1968, U.S. Dist. Ct. (so. dist.) Ill. 1973. Staff atty. Atty.'s Title Guaranty Fund, Champaign, Ill., 1968-69; ptnr. Goldsworthy, Fifield & Prusak, Peoria, Ill., 1973-80, Nicol, Newell, Prusak & Winne, Peoria, 1980-83, Prusak & Winne, Peoria, Ill., 1983-88, Prusak, Winne & Wombacher, Peoria, 1988-93, Prusak & Winne, Ltd., Peoria, 1993—. Contbr. articles to profl. publs. Bd. dirs. Human Svc. Ctr., Peoria, 1970's, Friendship House, Peoria, 1980, Southside Mission, Peoria, 1988-89; pres. adminstrv. bd. 1st United Meth. Ch., Peoria, 1990—. Capt. USAF, 1969-73. Mem. Ill. State Bar Assn. (chmn. law office cons. sect. coun. 1997-98), PeoriaCounty Bar Assn. (bd. dirs. 1982, 94, 98, 99, v.p. 1999, pres. 2000), Union League Club Chgo., Ill. Valley Yacht Club. Avocations: computers, sailing, reading. General civil litigation, Insurance, Personal injury (including property damage). Home: 5821 N Mar Vista Dr Peoria IL 61614-3850 Office: Prusak & Winne Ltd 704 Jefferson Bldg 331 Fulton St Peoria IL 61602-1499 E-mail: mprusak@mtco.com.

PRUZANSKY, JOSHUA MURDOCK, lawyer; b. N.Y.C., Mar. 16, 1940; s. Louis and Rose (Murdock) P.; m. Susan R. Bernstein, Aug. 31, 1980; 1 child, Dina Gabrielle. BA, Columbia Coll., 1960, JD, 1965. Bar: N.Y., 1965, U.S. Dist. Ct. (ea. and so. dists.) N.Y., 1968, U.S. Supreme Ct., 1980. Ptnr. Scheinberg, DePetris & Pruzansky, Riverhead, N.Y., 1965-85, Greshin, Ziegler & Pruzansky, Smithtown, N.Y., 1985-2000, Pruzansky & Besunder, LLP, Islandia, N.Y., 2001—. Mem. exec. coun. N.Y. State Conf. Bar Leaders, 1984—, chmn., 1988-89; mem. grievance com. Appellate Divsn. 10th Judicial Dist., 1992-96; mem. adv. bd. Ticor Title Guarantee Co., 1992-2001; mem. L.I. adv. bd. HSBC Bank, 1995—; dir. N.Y. State Com. for Modern Cts., 1998—; mem. adv. task force N.Y. Dept. State Corps., 1998—. Mem. bd. visitors Columbia Law Sch., 1998—; chair bd. visitors Touro Law Sch., 1998—; dir., sec. L.I. Mus., 1998—. Fellow ABA Found., N.Y. State Bar Found. (bd. dirs. 1994-2003); mem. ABA (ho. of dels. 1997-2003, probate and real property sect., standing com. on solo and small firm practitioners 1998-2000, N.Y. state del. Caucus of State Bar Assns.), N.Y. State Bar Assn. (ho. dels. 1982—, pres. 1997-98, exec. com. 1992-99, spl. com. women and law 1986-91, task force on small firms 1991-92, spl. com. on MDP 1999-2000, chair spl. com. on fiduciary appts. 2002—, nominating com. 1999-2003, chair 2000-01, trusts and estates sect., gen. practice, elder law sects.), Suffolk County Bar Assn. (bd. dirs. 1979-89, pres. 1985-86), N.Y. County Lawyers Assn., Nassau County Bar Assn. Corporate, general, Probate (including wills, trusts), Property, real (including real estate development, water). Office: Pruzanksy & Besunder LLP One Suffolk Sq Ste 315 Farmingville NY 11749 E-mail: pruzansk@villagenet.com.

PRYOR, MARK LUNSFORD, senator; b. Fayetteville, Ark. m. Jill Pryor; children: Adams, Porter. BA in History, U. Ark., 1985, JD, 1988. Pvt. practice Wright, Lindsey & Jennings, Little Rock, 1988—97; mem. Ark. Ho. of Reps., 1990—98, chmn. Freshman Caucus, mem. judiciary com., com. on aging and legis. affairs; atty. gen. State of Ark., 1999—2002; U.S. senator from Ark., 2003—. Democrat. Office: US Senate 825 Hart Senate Off Bldg Washington DC 20510*

PRYOR, SHEPHERD GREEN, III, lawyer; b. Fitzgerald, Ga., June 27, 1919; s. Shepherd Green Jr. and Jeffie (Persons) P.; m. Lenora Louise Standifer, May 17, 1941 (dec.); m. Ellen Wilder, July 13, 1984; children from previous marriage: Sandra Pryor Clarkson, Shepherd Green IV, Robert Stephen, Patty Pryor Smith (dec.), Alan Persons, Susan Lenora. BSAE, Ga. Inst. Tech., 1947; JD, Woodrow Wilson Coll. Law, Atlanta, 1974. Bar: Ga. 1974, U.S. Dist. Ct. (no. dist.) Ga. 1974, U.S. Ct. Appeals (5th cir.) 1974, U.S. Ct. Appeals (11th cir.) 1982, U.S. Supreme Ct. 1977; registered profl. engr., Ga. Comml. pilot engr. Hartford Accident and Indemnity Co., 1947-56; nuclear engr. Lockheed Ga. Co., 1956-64, research and tech. rep., 1964-76; real estate salesman Cole Realty Co. and Valient Properties, 1955-74; sole practice law Atlanta, 1974—. Chmn. bd. adv. Rerimeter Adult Learning Svcs. Past pres. Loring Heights Civic Assn.; former trustee Masonic Children's Home of Ga.; bd. advisors Reinhardt Coll.; former chmn. Bd. Equalization Fulton County, Ga.; chmm. bd. advisors Perimeter Adult Learning Svcs. Capt. U.S. Army, 1942-45, USAFR, 1942-55. Mem. Ga. Bar Assn., Ga. Trial Lawyers Assn., Mensa, Intertel, Soc. Automotive Engrs., Assn. Old Crows, The Old Guard of the Gate City Guard (past commandant), Masons, Shriners, Sigma Delta Kappa, Pi Kappa Phi, Kappa Kappa Psi. Republican. Methodist. Corporate, general, General practice, Property, real (including real estate development, water). Address: 135 W Spalding Dr NE Atlanta GA 30328-1912

PRYOR, WILLIAM HOLCOMBE, JR., state attorney general; b. Mobile, Ala., Apr. 26, 1962; s. William Holcombe Sr. and Laura Louise (Bowles) Pryor; m. Kristan Camille Wilson, Aug. 15, 1987; children: Caroline Elizabeth, Victoria Camille. BA in Legal Studies with honors, U. of La. (now N.E. La. U.), Monroe, 1984; JD with honors, Tulane U., 1987. Law clk. U.S. Ct. Appeals (5th cir.), Judge John Minor Wisdom, New Orleans, 1987—88; assoc. Cabaniss, Johnston, Gardner, Dumas & O'Neil, Birmingham, Ala., 1988—91, Walston, Stabler, Wells, Anderson & Bains, Birmingham, 1991—95; dep. atty. gen. State of Ala., Montgomery, 1995—97, atty. gen., 1997—. Adj. prof. Samford U. Cumberland Sch. Law, Birmingham, 1989—94. Bd. student editors: Tulane Law Rev., 1985—86, editor-in-chief: , 1986—87, bd. adv. editors: , 1995—. La. nat. com. Young Rep. Nat. Fedn., 1984—86; mem. Ala. Rep. Exec. Com., 1994—95. Mem.: Order of Coif, Omicron Delta Kappa, Phi Kappa Phi. Republican. Roman Catholic. Office: Office Atty Gen 11 S Union St Montgomery AL 36130-2103 E-mail: billpryor@ago.state.al.us.

PUCCINELLI, ANDREW JAMES, lawyer; b. Elko, Nev., July 21, 1953; BA cum laude, U. of the Pacific, 1975, JD, 1978. Bar: Nev. 1978. Ptnr. Puccinelli & Puccinelli, Elko, Nev., 1978—2002; dist. judge 4th Judicial Dist. Ct., 2002—. Bus. law adj. prof. No. Nev. C.C., 1982-93; legal advisor Nev. Home Health Svcs., 1980-88. Bd. dirs. Nev. Legal Svcs., 1986-93. Mem. ATLA, Nev. Trial Lawyers Assn., Nev. State Bar Assn. (bd. govs. 1993-2000, v.p. 1996-97, pres.-elect 1997-98, pres. 1998-99, No. Nev. disciplinary bd. 1988-93, CLE com. 1981-85), Elko County Bar Assn. (pres. 1985-86), Phi Delta Phi. Office: Puccinelli & Puccinelli 700 Idaho St Elko NV 89801-3824

PUCCIO, THOMAS P. lawyer; b. N.Y.C., 1944; BA, Fordham U., 1966, JD, 1969. Bar: N.Y. 1969, U.S. Ct. Appeals (2d cir.) 1970, D.C. 1982, U.S. Supreme Ct. 1982, U.S. Ct. Appeals (4th and 9th cirs.) 1993. Lawyer Office U.S. Atty. Ea. Dist. N.Y., 1969—76, chief criminal divsn., 1973—75; exec. asst. U.S. atty., 1975—76; chief U.S. Dept. Justice Strike Force, 1976—82; pvt. practice N.Y.C., 1982—. Mem.: Assn. Bar City N.Y., D.C. Bar, Fed. Bar Coun. General civil litigation, Criminal. Office: Ste 301 230 Park Ave New York NY 10169*

PUCHTA, RANDOLPH E. lawyer; b. Hermann, Mo., May 31, 1928; s. Everett Adam and Marie Katherine (Sexauer) P.; m. Eunice Marie Rohlfing, Apr. 7, 1951 (wid. Apr. 1995); children: Kristine Marie Puchta-Brown, Timothy John Puchta, Matthew Paul Puchta; m. Lois Lydia Verena Hoerstkamp, July 28, 1996. BA, U. Mo., 1950, JD, 1955. Pvt. practice, Hermann, Mo., 1955-78; prosecuting atty. Gasconade County, Hermann, 1957-67, assoc. cir. judge, 1978-98, sr. assoc. cir. judge, 1998—. Chmn. Gasconade County Rep. Cen. Com., Mo., 1950-51; dir. Hermann Indsl. Devel. Corp., Hermann, 1956—, Gasconade County Hist. Soc., Hermann, 1980s—, Emmaus Homes, Inc., 2000—; mem. numerous other orgns. Served USAF, 1951—53, Korean War, ret. as lt. col. USAF, 1978. Named to Outstanding Young Men of Mo., Jaycees, 1961; recipient Disting. Svc. award Jaycees, Hermann, 1961. Mem. Mo. Bar Assn., 20th Cir. Bar Assn., Gasconade County Bar Assn., U. Mo. Alumni Assn. Republican. Mem. United Ch. of Christ. Avocations: reading, mil. history, gardening, woodworking, antique collecting. Home: PO Box 231 Hermann MO 65041-0231 Office: Sr Assoc Cir Judge Hermann MO 65041 E-mail: ranlo@ktis.net.

PUCKETT, PAUL WALTER, lawyer; b. Honolulu, July 31, 1946; s. Paul James and Jean Haruko (Tsuda) P.; m. Peggy Hope, Nov. 29, 1969; children: Christopher, Paul Casey, Curtis James. BA, Colo. U., 1971, JD, 1974. Bar: Colo., U.S. Dist. Ct. Colo., U.S. Ct. Appeals (10th cir.). Right-of-way coord. Colo.-Ute Elec. Co., Montrose, 1975-76; pvt. practice Gunnison & Crested Butte, Colo., 1976-86, Denver, 1986-92; asst. prosecutor Glendale, Colo., 1988-92; asst. city atty. City and County of Denver, 1992—. Bd. dirs. Rocky Mountain Ski Assn., Denver, 1978-82; pres., bd. dirs. Concerned Lawyers, Inc., Wheat Ridge, Colo., 1987-92; bd. dirs., v.p. Mile High Coun. on Alcohol and Drug Abuse, Denver, 1990-92. Home: 2701 S Utica St Denver CO 80236-2102 Office: City Attys Office 201 W Colfax Ave Dept 1207 Denver CO 80202

PUGH, FRANCIS LEO, lawyer; b. Detroit, Dec. 8, 1934; s. Charles Herbert and Elizabeth Sonetta (Brown) P.; m. Mary Louise Hake, Oct. 4, 1958; children: Jane Marie, Thomas Scott, Francis Leo II, Patrick Kevin. BS, Auburn U., 1957; MS, St. Louis U., 1959; JD, Ventura Coll Law, 1979. Bar: Calif., U.S. Dist. Ct. (cen. dist.) Calif. 1980, U.S. Ct. Appeals (9th cir.) 1981, U.S. Tax Ct. Atty. sole practitioner, Somis, 1980-83, Masci & Pugh, Inc., Thousand Oaks, Calif., 1983-85, sole practitioner, Camarillo, Calif., 1985—2003. Adj. faculty So. Calif. Inst. Law, Ventura, 1982—85; mem. oversight com. Lawyer Referral Svc., Ventura, 1994—2003; mem. Estate Planning Coun., 1983—2002; past pres. and dir.; chmn. Multidisciplinary Estate Planning reg. workshops, 1998—99; notary pub. State of Calif., Ventura County, 1992—2004. Mem. editl. bd.: Citations monthly mag. of Ventura Bar Assn. Dir., v.p., pres. Dos Caminos Plz. Assoc., Camarillo, 1994—98; dir., pres. Ponderosa Heights HOA, 1989—97, 2001—02; lay min. Work Furlough Corrections, Camarillo, 1987—2000. Capt. USAF, 1959—62. Mem. AIAA (sr.), Fed. Bar Assn., Calif. Bar Assn., Calif. Bar Tax Sect., Lawyer Pilots Bar Assn, Aircraft Owners & Pilots Bar Assn. Republican. Roman Catholic. Avocations: commercial pilot, certified flight instructor. Estate planning, Taxation, general. Office: 2460 Ponderosa Dr N #A110 Camarillo CA 93010-2375

PUGH, RANDALL SCOTT, lawyer; b. Jamestown, N.Y., Mar. 31, 1950; s. H. Theodore and Jeanne M. (Crossley) P.; m. Christie S., Sept. 3, 1978; 1 child, Theodore Clifford. BA, Hobart Coll., 1972; JD, U. Richmond, 1976. Bar: Va. 1976, U.S. Dist. Ct. Va. 1982, U.S. Bankruptcy Ct. 1982. Law clk. to justice Supreme Ct., Richmond, Va., 1976-77; asst. county atty. Prince William County, Manassas, Va., 1977; assoc., ptnr. Whitticar, Sokol, Ledbetter & Haley, Fredericksburg, Va., 1978-87; prin. R. Scott Pugh, Fredericksburg, 1987—. Pres. Lawyer Assistance and Support Svc., Fredericksburg, 1987—; dep. county atty. Spotsylvania County, Va., 1988-90; instr. criminal law Rappahannock Criminal Justice Acad., 1978-90. Editor: Cir. Writer, 1991—98. Bd. dirs. Rappahannock Boy Scouts Am., Fredericksburg, 1982-86, Big Bros. & Sisters, 1978-81; chmn. Spotsylvania County Dem. Com., 1987-91; mem., chair Spotsylvania County Sch. Bd., 1993-96; mem. Spotsylvania County Bd. of Zoning Appeals, 1997—, now chair; TV host and panelist Rappahannock Rev., 1997—2002. Mem. ABA, Va. Trial Lawyers Assn., Fredericksburg Area Bar Assn. (pres.), Fredericksburg C. of C. (legal counsel), Fredericksburg Area Jaycees (bd. dirs. 1978-82), Hobart Coll. Alumni, U. Richmond Alumni Assn. Democrat. Methodist. Avocation: computers. Appellate, General civil litigation, Commercial, consumer (including collections, credit). Office: PO Box 999 9108 Courthouse Rd Spotsylvania VA 22553-1902

PUGH, RICHARD CRAWFORD, lawyer; b. Phila., Apr. 28, 1929; s. William and Myrtle P.; m. Nanette Bannen, Feb. 27, 1954; children: Richard Crawford, Andrew Lembert, Catherine Elizabeth. AB summa cum laude, Dartmouth Coll., 1951; BA in Jurisprudence, Oxford (Eng.) U., 1953; LLB, Columbia U., 1958. Bar: N.Y. 1958. Assoc. firm Cleary, Gottlieb, Steen & Hamilton, N.Y.C., 1958—61, ptnr., 1969—89; disting. prof. law U. San Diego, 1989—, univ. prof., 1998—99. Mem. faculty Law Sch. Columbia U., 1961-89, prof., 1964-69, adj. prof., 1969-89; lectr. Columbia-Amsterdam-Leyden (Netherlands) summer program Am. law, 1963, 79; dep. asst. atty. gen. tax div. U.S. Dept. Justice, 1966-68; Cons. fiscal and fin. br. UN Secretariat, 1962, 64. Editor: Columbia Law Rev., 1957—58; co-editor (with W. Friedmann): Legal Aspects of Foreign Investment, 1959; co-editor: (with others) International Law, 2001, Taxation of International Transactions, 2001, Taxation of Business Enterprises, 2002, International Income Taxation: Code and Regulations, 2003. Served with USNR, 1954-56. Rhodes scholar, 1951-53. Mem. ABA, Am. Law Inst., Am. Coll. Tax Counsel, Am. Soc. Internat. Law, Internat. Fiscal Assn. (pres. U.S. br. 1978-79). Private international, Public international, Corporate taxation. Home: 7335 Encelia Dr La Jolla CA 92037-5729 Office: U San Diego Sch Law Alcala Park San Diego CA 92110-2429 E-mail: rpugh@sandiego.edu.

PUGH, TODD SELBY, lawyer; b. Pitts., Nov. 13, 1967; s. David and Mary Alice Pugh; m. Kimberly Rene Mabry, Aug. 3, 1996. BS, Fla. Atlantic U., Boca Raton, 1993; JD with honors, DePaul U., Chgo., 1997. Bar: U.S. Dist. Ct. (no. dist.) Ill. 2002, U.S. Supreme Ct. 2002, State of Ill. 1997, U.S. Ct. of Appeals (7th cir.) 1998. Summer assoc. Jenner & Block, Chgo., 1996; assoc. Martin, Breen & Merrick, Chgo., 1997—2000, Thomas M. Breen & Assocs., Chgo., 2000—. Recipient CALI Award for Excellence in the Study of Evidence, DePaul Coll. of Law, 1996, CALI Award for Excellence in the Study of Advanced Criminal Procedure, 1996, CALI Award for Excellence in the Study of Pretrial Criminal Procedure, 1997. Mem.: Ill. State Bar Assn., Chgo. Bar Assn., Nat. Assn. Criminal Def. Attys., Am. Acad. of Forensic Sciences, Order of the Coif. Criminal, Appellate. Office: Thomas M Breen & Assocs 53 West Jackson Blvd Ste 1460 Chicago IL 60604 Office Fax: 312-362-9907. E-mail: darrow@interaccess.com.

PUGH, WILLIAM WHITMELL HILL, III, lawyer; b. Baton Rouge, La., June 25, 1954; s. George Willard and Jean (Hemphill) P.; m. Beth Smith, Mar. 12, 1983; children: Brendan Kelly, Bryan Clayton, Katharine Elaine. BA, U. Va., 1976; JD, La. State U., 1979. Bar: La. 1979, U.S. Supreme Ct. 1986, U.S. Ct. Appeals (5th and 11th cirs.) 1983. Law clk. to presiding justice U.S. Ct. Appeals (5th cir.), New Orleans, 1979-80. Editor-in-chief La. Law Rev., 1978-79. Mem. Maritime Law Assn., La. Assn. Def. Counsel, La. State Bar Assn., Coun. of La. State Law Inst. (young lawyers rep. 1988-91, mem. 1992—). Admiralty, General civil litigation, Commercial, contracts (including sales of goods; commercial financing). Office: Liskow & Lewis One Shell Sq 50th Fl New Orleans LA 70139-5001

PUGSLEY, FRANK BURRUSS, lawyer; b. Kansas City, Mo., Apr. 3, 1920; s. Charles Silvey and Emma (Burruss) P.; m. Aline East, May 7, 1943; children— John, Susan Pugsley Patterson, Nancy Pugsley Young BS in Mech. Engring, U. Tex., Austin, 1942; JD, DePaul U., Chgo., 1950. Bar: Ill. 1950, Tex. 1953, U.S. Supreme Ct. 1960. Engr. Gen. Electric Co., Schenectady, 1946-50, patent atty., 1950-52; assoc. Baker & Botts, Houston, 1952-60, ptnr., 1960-84, sr. ptnr., 1974-84. Lectr. Southwestern Legal Found., Practising Law Inst., Bur. Nat. Affairs Conf. Contbr. articles to legal jours. Trustee West Univ. Methodist Ch., Houston, 1959-65; bd. dirs. St. Stephens Episcopal Day Sch., 1960-62; adminstrv. bd. St. Luke's United Meth. Ch., 1981-83. Served to lt. USNR, 1942-46. Fellow Tex. Bar Found.; mem. ABA (chmn. intellectual property law sec. 1980-81), Am. Intellectual Property Law Assn. (pres. 1966-67), Tex. Bar Assn. (chmn. intellectual property law sect. 1960-61), Houston Bar Assn., Petroleum Club, Frisch Auf! Valley Country Club, Friars. Federal civil litigation, Patent, Trademark and copyright. Home: 3602 Nottingham St Houston TX 77005-2221

PUGSLEY, ROBERT ADRIAN, law educator; b. Mineola, N.Y., Dec. 27, 1946; s. Irvin Harold and Mary Catherine (Brusselars) P. BA, SUNY-Stony Brook, 1968; JD, NYU, 1975, LLM in Criminal Justice, 1977. Instr. sociology New Sch. Social Rsch., N.Y.C., 1969-71; coord. Peace Edn. programs The Christophers, N.Y.C., 1971-78; assoc. prof. law Southwestern U., L.A., 1978-81, prof., 1981—, Paul E. Treusch prof. law, 2000-01. Adj. asst. prof. criminology and criminal justice Southampton Coll.-Long Island U., 1975-76; acting dep. dir. Criminal Law Edn. and Rsch. Ctr., NYU, 1983-86; bd. advisors Ctr. Legal Edn. CCNY-CUNY, 1978, Sta. KPFK-FM, 1985-86; founder, coord. The Wednesday Evening Soc., L.A., 1979-86; vis. prof. Jacob D. Fuchsberg Law Ctr. Touro Coll., L.I., N.Y., summers, 1988, 89; lectr. in criminal law and procedure Legal Edn. Conf. Ctr., L.A., 1982-96; prof., dir. Comparative Criminal Law and Procedure Program U. B.C., Vancouver, summers, 1994, 98, 99, 2000, 01, 02, 03; chair pub. interest law com. Southwestern U., 1990-2001; lectr. legal profl. responsibility West Bar Rev. Faculty, Calif., 1996-98; legal analyst/commentator for print and electronic media, 1992—. Creative advisor Christopher Closeup (nationally syndicated pub. svc. TV program), 1975-83; host Earth Alert, Cable TV, 1983-87; prodr., moderator (pub. affairs discussion program) Inside L.A., Sta. KPFK-FM, 1979-86, Open Jour. program, Sta. KPFK-FM, 1991-94; contbr. articles to legal jours. Founding mem. Southwestern U. Pub. Interest Law com., 1992—; mem. L.A. County Bar Assn. Adv. Com. on Alcohol & Drug Abuse, 1991-95, co-chair, 1993-95; mem. exec. com. non-govtl. orgns. UN Office Pub. Info., 1977; mem. issues task force L.A. Conservancy, 1980-81, seminar for law tchrs. NEH UCLA, 1979; co-convenor So. Calif. Coalition Against Death Penalty, 1981-83, convener, 1983-84; mem. death penalty com. Lawyer's Support Group, Amnesty Internat., U.S.A.; founding mem. Ch.-State Coun., L.A., 1984-88; bd. dirs. Equal Rights Sentencing Found., 1983-85, Earth Alert, Inc., 1984-87; mem. adv. bd. First Amendment Info. Resources Ctr., Grad. Sch. Libr. and Info. Scis., UCLA, 1990—; mem. coun. Friends UCLA Libr., 1993—, pres., 1996-2002; mem. adv. bd. Children Requiring a Caring Kommunity, 1998—. Robert Marshall fellow Criminal Law Edn. and Rsch. Ctr., NYU Sch. Law, 1976-78. Mem. Am. Legal Studies Assn., Am. Soc. Polit. and Legal Philosophy, Assn. Am. Law Schs., Inst. Soc. Ethics and Life Scis., Soc. Am. Law Tchrs., Internat. Platform Assn., Internat. Soc. Reform of Criminal Law, The Scribes. Roman Catholic. Office: Southwestern U Sch Law 675 S Westmoreland Ave Los Angeles CA 90005-3905 E-mail: rpugsley@swlaw.edu.

PULEO, FRANK CHARLES, lawyer; b. Montclair, N.J., Nov. 25, 1945; s. Frank and Kathren (Despenzerie) P.; m. Alice Kathren Leek, June 1, 1968; children— Frank C., Richard James. B.S.E., Princeton U., 1967; J.D., N.Y.U., 1970. Bar: N.Y., 1971. Ptnr., Milbank, Tweed, Hadley & McCloy, N.Y.C., 1970— . Mem. ABA (mem. com. on fed. regulation securities), N.Y. State Bar Assn. Banking, Commercial, contracts (including sales of goods; commercial financing), Corporate, general. Office: Milbank Tweed Hadley & McCloy 1 Chase Manhattan Plz Fl 49 New York NY 10005-1413

PULLEY, LEWIS CARL, lawyer; b. Oklahoma City, Aug. 19, 1954; s. Harriet Ruth (Meyers) P.; foster sons: Tuan Le, Chien Hoang. Student, Oxford U., England, 1974; BA with high honors, U. Okla., 1976; JD, Am. U., 1979. Bar: Pa. 1981, D.C. 1987, U.S. Ct. Mil. Appeals 1982, U.S. Ct. Appeals (D.C. cir.) 1985, U.S. Supreme Ct. 1985. Commd. 1st lt. USAF, 1982, advanced through grades to capt., 1982, judge advocate, 1982-88; atty. Def. Logistics Agy., Alexandria, Va., 1988-90; atty. EEO staff mass media bur. FCC, 1990-97, supr. atty. EEO staff mass media bur., 1997—2002, acting chief EEO staff mass media bur., 2001—02, asst. chief policy divsn. media bur., 2002—. Contbr. over 500 articles to 11 newspapers and mags. (recipient Investigative Reporting award, Okla. City Gridiron Found., 1975, Media award for Econ. Understanding, Dartmouth Bus. Sch., 1980). Vol. Nat. Pub. Radio, Washington, 1989-90, Connections, 1990-98, White House, 1993-94; mem. Ams. for Med. Progress Ednl. Found. Ewing Found. fellow, 1975. Democrat. Jewish. Avocations: travel, collecting polit. paraphernalia. Office: FCC Media Bur Policy Divsn 445 12th St SW Washington DC 20554

PULOS, WILLIAM WHITAKER, lawyer; b. Hornell, N.Y., Aug. 29, 1955; s. William Leroy and Juanita (Whitaker) P. BA in Econs. magna cum laude, Alfred U., 1977; JD, Union U., 1980. Bar: N.Y. 1982, U.S. Supreme Ct. 1987. Pvt. practice, Alfred, NY, 1982—92, Hornell, NY, 1992—. Adj. prof. law Alfred U., 1981-90; prof. bus. adminstrn. SUNY-Alfred, 1982-84; tutor Empire State Coll., 1982-85; atty. Town of Alfred, 1982-2000, Village of Almond (N.Y.), 1983-98, Town of West Almond (N.Y.), 1987-97, Town of Almond, 1990-98, Town of West Union (N.Y.), 1992-98, Town of Birdsall (N.Y.), 1993-97; mem. Allegany County and Steuben County Assigned Counsel Program for Indigent Defendants, 1982-85; spl. prosecutor Allegany County, 1984-88; asst. counsel N.Y. State Assembly, 1980; hearing officer NY State Small Claims Assessment Rev., 1983-87, NY State Bd. Equalization and Assessment, 1988-91; tax atty. NY State Dept. Tax and Fin., 1984-91; pres. Alfred Dombec, Ltd., 1985-99, Maple City Way, Inc., 1990-97. Active Alfred Sta. Vol. Fireman's Assn., Inc., 1985-98, 2d chief, 1988-92, pres. 1994-96, life mem. Recipient Outstanding Young Man Am. award U.S. Jaycees, 1982, 86, Internat. Humanitarian award Lions Club Internat., 1991. Mem. ABA, ATLA, N.Y. State Bar Assn. (lawyer referral program 1983-90, 98—, Steuben County Bar Assn., Phi Kappa Phi, Pi GAmma Mu, Delta Mu Delta, Alpha Iota Delta. Personal injury (including property damage), Workers' compensation, Property, real (including real estate development, water). Office: PO Box 337 70 Main St Hornell NY 14843-0337

PUMPHREY, GERALD ROBERT, lawyer; b. Flushing, N.Y., May 31, 1947; s. Fred Paul and Anne (Afferman) P.; m. Joann DeLillo, Oct. 6, 1968; children: Gerald, Christopher, Elena. BBA, St. John's U., 1969, MBA, 1974; JD, Nova U., 1978. Bar: Fla. 1978. Assoc. Walden & Walden, Dania, Fla., 1978; v.p. legal svcs. Golden Bear, Inc., North Palm Beach, Fla., Jack Nicklaus & Assocs., Air Bear, Inc., also bd. dirs.; v.p., sec. Triple P., Inc., 1978-83; pvt. practice, 1983—. Bd. advdisor Benjamin Sch. Found. Athletics Assn., 1980-83; coord. Benjamin Sch. Found., Inc.; mem. golf com. St. Clare's Sch.; pres. Home and Sch. Assn., 1983-84; bd. dirs. Deaf Svc. Ctr. Palm Beach County Inc., 1988-89. Mem. Palm Beach County Bar Assn., North Palm Beach County Bar Assn. (pres. 1991-92), Palm Beach Gardens C. of C., Kiwanis (charter mem., bd. dirs. Palm Beach Gardens 1983-87), No. Palm Beaches C. of C. (counsel 1987—), Rotary North Palm Beach (bd. dirs. 1998—, pres. 2001-2002), Phi Alpha Delta. General civil litigation, General practice, Property, real (including real estate development, water). Office: Ste 300 11000 Prosperity Farms Rd Palm Beach Gardens FL 33410-3462 Fax: 561-626-4824. E-mail: pumphreypa@aol.com.

PUNDT, RICHARD ARTHUR, lawyer; b. Iowa City, Iowa, Apr. 18, 1944; s. Arthur Herman and Johanna Celeste (Pasterik) P.; B.A., State U. Iowa, 1966; J.D., Drake U., 1969; m. Joyce Kay Schoenfelder, Dec. 1, 1968; children— Vincent Arthur, Jennifer Johanna, Heather Ann. Temporary claims dep. Iowa Employment Security Commn., 1968-69; admitted to Iowa bar, 1969; staff atty. Polk County Legal Aid, Office Econ. Opportunity, 1969; spl. agt. FBI, 1969-71; prin. Richard A. Pundt Law Office; dir. Cedar Rapids Profl. Football Corp., 1972-73, pres., 1972-73. Exec. dir. Iowans for Rockefeller, 1968; exec. dir. Polk County Republican Com. 1968-69; mem. Linn County Rep. Central Com., 1972-78; chmn. Linn County Rep. party, 1977-78; asst. prosecuting atty. Linn County, 1972-76. Mem. Am., Iowa, Linn County bar assns., Metro Athletic Assn. (dir. 1976—). Roman Catholic. Club: Sertoma. Home: 3851 Hickory Ridge Ln SE Cedar Rapids IA 52403-3765 Office: 330 1st St SE Cedar Rapids IA 52401-1702

PURDOM, THOMAS JAMES, lawyer; b. Seymour, Tex., Apr. 7, 1937; s. Thomas Exer and Juanita Florida (Kuykendall) P.; m. Betty Marie Shoemaker, May 31, 1969; 1 son, James Robert. Student, U. Syracuse, 1956-57, U. Md., 1958-59; BA, Tex. Tech. Coll., 1962; JD, Georgetown U., 1966. Bar: Tex. 1966, U.S. Supreme Ct. 1978, U.S. Ct. Appeals (5th cir.) 1983. Ptnr. Griffith & Purdom, Lubbock, Tex., 1966-67; asst. dist. atty. 72d Jud. Dist., Lubbock, 1967-68; county atty. Lubbock County, Tex., 1968-72; pres. Purdom & Atchley, Lubbock, Tex., 1972—. Mem. com. for Vol. 5 pattern jury charges, 1988-97. Author: West's Texas Forms Vols. 16, 17, 18, 1984-96, Family Law, Texas Practice and Procedure, 1981. Served with USAF, 1956-60. RecipientSam Emison award Tex. Acad. Family Law Specialists, 2000. Fellow Tex. Bar Found.; mem ABA, Lubbock County Bar Assn. (bd. dirs. 1970, Disting. Sr. Lawyer award 2000), State Bar Assn. Tex. (sec. family law sect. 1974-75, chmn. family law sect. 1975-76, mem. examining commn. for family law specialization), Am. Acad. Matrimonial Lawyers (cert. family law, Tex. bd. legal specialization), Delta Theta Phi. Democrat. Baptist. Family and matrimonial, Insurance, Personal injury (including property damage). Home: 3619 55th St Lubbock TX 79413-4713 Office: Purdom & Atchley 6307 Indiana Ave Lubbock TX 79413-5713 E-mail: paplaw6307@aol.com.

PURDY, WILLIAM RICHARD, lawyer; b. Statesville, N.C., May 3, 1946; s. Frank Kerr and Catherine Ritchie Purdy; m. Susan Clark Smith, Aug. 18, 1968; children: Kathryn Blythe Purdy Barton, Susanna Grey. BA, U. N.C., 1972, JD, 1975. Assoc. Smith, Currie & Hancock, Atlanta, 1975—77; v.p. Southeastern Svcs., Inc., Jackson, Miss., 1977—80; ptnr., prin. Ott & Purdy, P.A., Jackson, 1980—. Gen. counsel Miss. Rd. Bldrs. Assn., Jackson, 1993—, Assoc. Gen. Contrs. of Miss., Jackson, 1995—, Miss. Assn. Bldrs. and Contrs., Jackson, 1990—, Miss. Asphalt Pavers Assn., Jackson, 1998—; lectr. in field. Author (editor): Contractor's Desk Book on Mississippi Construction Law, 1996. 1st lt. USMC, 1968—72. Decorated Bronze Star; named Master of the Bench, Charles Clark Inn, Am. Inns of Ct., 1994—; recipient Commendation for Disting. Profl. Achievement, Joint Resolution of Miss. Senate and Ho. of Reps., 2000. Fellow: Miss. Bar Found., Internat. Soc. Barristers, Am. Coll. Constrn. Lawyers; mem.: ABA (mem. pub. contract law sect., state chair 1980—83, mem. forum com. on constrn. law 1980—). Avocations: jogging, rock and roll, college sports. Alternative dispute resolution, Construction, Government contracts and claims. Office: Ott & Purdy PA PO Drawer 1079 Jackson MS 39215-1079

PURNELL, MAURICE EUGENE, JR., lawyer; b. Dallas, Feb. 17, 1940; s. Maurice Eugene Sr. and Marjorie (Maillot) P.; m. Diane Blake, Aug. 19, 1966; children: Maurice Eugene III, Blake Maillot. BA, Washington and Lee U., 1961; MBA, U. Pa., 1963; LLB, So. Meth. U., 1966. Bar: Tex. 1966. Ptnr. Locke, Purnell, Boren, Laney & Neely, Dallas, 1966-87; shareholder Locke Purnell Rain Harrell PC, Dallas, 1987-99; ptnr. Locke Liddell & Sapp LLP, Dallas, 1999—2002, of counsel, 2002—. Bd. dirs. Leggett & Platt, Inc. Bd. dirs. Dallas Summer Musicals. Mem. ABA, Tex. Bar Assn., Tex. Bar Found., Dallas Bar Assn. Am. Judicature Soc., Dallas C. of C, Brook Hollow Golf Club. Home: 4409 S Versailles Ave Dallas TX 75205-3044 Office: Locke Liddell & Sapp LLP 2200 Ross Ave Ste 2200 Dallas TX 75201-6776

PURNELL, OLIVER JAMES, III, judge; b. Richmond, Va., Jan. 18, 1949; s. Oliver James Jr. and Margaret Helen (Hodges) P.; m. Cheryl Naomi Williams, June 30, 1973; children: Oliver James IV, Amy Susan. AA, U. Hartford, 1969; AB, Middlebury Coll., 1972; MSLS, Case Western Res. U., 1976; JD, Western New England Sch. Law, 1982. Bar: Conn. 1982, U.S. Dist. Ct. Conn. 1982. Dir., pharmacy libr. U. Conn. Sch. Pharmacy, Storrs, Conn., 1977-81; assoc. Lavitt, Hutchinson & Kaplan, Vernon, Conn., 1981-84, DuBeau & Ryan, Vernon, Conn., 1984-87, Howard, Kohn Sprague & Fitzgerald, Hartford, Conn., 1987-89; pvt. practice Vernon, 1989-92; reference libr. U. Conn. Sch. Law, Hartford, 1992-98; regional info. mgr. Lexis-Nexis, Vernon, 1998—99; judge Ellington Dist. Probate Ct., Vernon, 1999. Contbr. articles to profl. jours. Scoutmaster Boy Scouts Am., Rockville, Conn., 1990—; trustee Rockville (Conn.) Pub. Libr.; corporator Ea. Conn. Health Network; mem. U. Hartford Alumni Coun. Mem. Am. Assn. Law Libraries, So. New England Law Libr. Assn. (pres. 1998-99), Conn. Bar Assn. (coun. of bar pres. 1995-96), Tolland County Bar Assn. (pres. 1995-96), Nat. Coll. Probate Judges (chrm. Conn. probate tech. com., Masonic Lodge, A.F. & A.M. (master Fayette Lodge 1970). Avocations: skiing, camping, hiking, church organist. Office: 6 Forestview Dr Vernon Rockville CT 06066-4807 Mailing: PO Box 891 Vernon Rockville CT 06066-0891 E-mail: jpurnell3@att.net.

PURTELL, LAWRENCE ROBERT, lawyer; b. Quincy, Mass., May 2, 1947; s. Lawrence Joseph and Louise Maria (Loria) P.; m. Cheryl Lynn Tymon, Aug. 3, 1968; children: Lisa Ann, Susan Elizabeth. AB, Villanova U., 1969; JD, Columbia U., 1972. Bar: N.Y. 1973, N.J. 1978, Conn. 1988. Assoc. White & Case, N.Y.C., 1972-73; judge advocate USMC, Washington, 1973-76; assoc. White & Case, N.Y.C., 1977-79; corp. counsel Great Atlantic & Pacific Tea Co., Montvale, N.J., 1979-81; asst. gen. counsel United Techs. Corp., Hartford, Conn., 1981-84, assoc. gen. counsel, 1984-92, sec., gen. counsel, 1989-92; v.p., gen. counsel and sec. Carrier Corp., 1992-93; sr. v.p., gen. counsel and corp. sec. Mc Dermott Internat., New Orleans, La., 1993-96; sr. v.p., gen. counsel Koch Industries, Wichita, Kans., 1996-97; exec. v.p., gen. counsel Alcoa, Pitts., 1997—. Capt. USMC, 1973-76. Roman Catholic. Avocation: running. Finance, Mergers and acquisitions, Securities. Home: 637 Shoreline Dr Naples FL 34119 Office: Alcoa 390 Park Ave New York NY 10022*

PURTLE, JOHN INGRAM, lawyer, former state supreme court justice; b. Enola, Ark., Sept. 7, 1923; s. John Wesley and Edna Gertrude (Ingram) P.; m. Marian Ruth White, Dec. 31, 1951 (dec. 1995); children: Jeffrey, Lisa K.; m. Phyllis Kelly Purtle. Student, U. Central Ark., 1946-47; LLB, U. Ark., Fayetteville, 1950. Bar: Ark. 1950, U.S. Dist. Ct. (ea. dist.) Ark. 1950. Pvt. practice, Conway, Ark., 1950-53, Little Rock, 1953-78; mem. Ark. State Legislature, 1951-52, 69-70; assoc. justice Ark. Supreme Ct., 1979-90; pvt. practice Little Rock, 1990—. Tchr., deacon Baptist Ch. Served with U.S. Army, 1940-45. Mem. ABA, Ark. Bar Assn., Am. Judicature Soc., Ark. Jud. Council. Democrat. Criminal, General practice, Personal injury (including property damage).

PURVIS, JOHN ANDERSON, lawyer, educator; b. Aug. 31, 1942; s. Virgil J. and Emma Lou (Anderson) P.; m. Charlotte Johnson, Apr. 3, 1976; 1 child, Whitney; children by previous marriage: Jennifer, Matt. BA cum laude, Harvard U., 1965; JD, U. Colo., 1968. Bar: Colo. 1968, U.S. Dist. Ct. Colo. 1968, U.S. Ct. Appeals (10th cir.) 1978. Dep. dist. atty., Boulder, Colo., 1968-69; asst. dir., dir. legal aid U. Colo. Sch. Law, 1969; assoc. Williams, Taussig & Trine, Boulder, 1969; head Boulder office Colo. Pub. Defender Sys., 1970-72; assoc., ptnr. Hutchinson, Black, Hill, Buchanan & Cook, Boulder, 1972-85; ptnr. Purvis, Gray, Schuetze and Gordon, 1985-98, Purvis, Gray & Gordon, LLP, 1999—2001, Purvis Gray LLP, 2001—. Acting Colo. State Pub. Defender, 1978; adj. prof. law U. Colo., 1981, 84-88, 94, others; lectr. in field; chmn. Colo. Pub. Defender Commn., 1979-89; mem. nominating commn. Colo. Supreme Ct., 1984-90; mem. com. on conduct U.S. Dist. Ct., 1991-97, chmn., 1996-97; chmn. Boulder County Criminal Justice Com., 1975-81. Recipient Ames award Harvard U., 1964, Outstanding Young Lawyer award Colo. Bar Assn., 1978, Dist. Achievement award U. Colo. Law Sch. Alumni Assn., 1997. Mem.: ATLA, Am. Bar Found., Colo. Bar Found., Trial Lawyers for Pub. Justice, Colo. Trial Lawyers Assn., Boulder County Bar Assn., Colo. Bar Assn. (chair litigation sect. 1994—95), Am. Coll. Trial Lawyers (state chmn. 1998—2000), Am. Bd. Trial Advs., Internat. Acad. Trial Lawyers, Internat. Soc. Barristers, Faculty of Fed. Advs. (bd. dirs. 1999—2001), Supreme Ct. Hist. Soc. (state chmn. 1998—2002). Democrat. Federal civil litigation, State civil litigation, Personal injury (including property damage). Address: 1050 Walnut St Ste 501 Boulder CO 80302-5144

PURVIS, RANDALL W. B. lawyer; b. Summit, N.J., Mar. 2, 1957; s. Merton B. and Marjory L. (Baker) P.; m. Robin Head Intemann Purvis; children: Zachary, Timothy, Andrew. BS, Ohio State U., 1979; JD, Georgetown U., 1982. Bar: Colo. 1983, U.S. Dist. Ct. Colo. 1983, U.S. Ct. Appeals (10th cir.) 1983. Pvt. practice, Colorado Springs, Colo., 1983—. Bd. dirs. Nova Resources Corp., Dallas, 1985-88; adj. prof. Colo. Coll. Mem. steering com. Nat. League of Cities, Washington; trustee Meml. Hosp. Colorado Springs, 1991—99; councilman Colorado Springs City Coun., 1987—99, re-elected, 1991, 1995, 2003; elder 1st Presbyn. Ch., Colorado Springs, 1987—91. Mem. Colo. Bar Assn., El Paso County Bar Assn. (com. chmn. 1986), Colorado Springs C. of C. (com. chmn. 1986), Colorado Springs Bridge Club, Phi Beta Kappa. Republican. Avocations: bridge, woodworking. General civil litigation, Probate (including wills, trusts), Property, real (including real estate development, water). Office: 128 S Tejon Ste 402 Colorado Springs CO 80903-1520

PUSATERI, JAMES ANTHONY, judge; b. Kansas City, Mo., May 20, 1938; s. James A. and Madeline (LaSalle) P.; m. Jacqueline D. Ashburne, Sept. 1, 1962; children: James A., Mark C., Danielle L. BA, U. Kans., 1960, LLB, 1963. Bar: Kans. 1963, U.S. Dist. Ct. Kans. 1963, U.S. Ct. Appeals (10th cir.) 1964. Assoc. Payne, Jones, Chartered, Olathe, Kans., 1963-65, James Cashin, Prairie Village, Kans., 1965-69; asst. U.S. atty. Dept. Justice, Kansas City, Kans., 1969-76; judge U.S. Bankruptcy Ct. Dist. Kans., Topeka, 1976—. Active Prairie Village City Coun., 1967-69. Mem. Kans. Bar Assn., Topeka Bar Assn., Nat. Conf. Bankruptcy Judges, Am. Bankruptcy Inst., Sam A. Crow Am. Inn of Ct.

PUSATERI, LAWRENCE XAVIER, lawyer; b. Oak Park, Ill., May 25, 1931; s. Lawrence E. and Josephine (Romano) P.; m. Eve M. Graf, July 9, 1956; children: Joanne J., Eva M., Lawrence F., Paul L., Mary Ann. JD summa cum laude, DePaul U., 1953. Bar: Ill. 1953. Asst. state's atty. Cook County, 1957-59; ptnr. Newton, Wilhelm, Pusateri & Naborowski, Chgo., 1959-77; justice Ill. Appellate Ct., Chgo., 1977-78; ptnr. Peterson, Ross, Schloerb & Seidel, Chgo., 1978-95; of counsel Peterson & Ross, Chgo., 1996—2000. Pres. Conf. Consumer Fin. Law, 1984-92, chmn. gov. com., 1993-99; mem. Ill. Supreme Ct. Com. on Pattern Jury Instrns., 1981-96; mem. adv. bd. Ctr. for Analysis of Alt. and Dispute Resolution, 1999—; mem. U.S. Senate Jud. Nominations Commn. State Ill., 1993, 95; exec. dir. State of Ill. Jud. Inquiry Bd., 1995-96; panel chmn. Cook County mandatory arbitration, 1990—, judicate Am. Arbitration; mem. Merit Selection Panel for U.S. Magistrate; lectr. law DePaul U., Chgo., 1962, Columbia U., N.Y.C., 1965, Marquette U., Milw., 1962-82, Northwestern U. Law Sch., Def. Counsel Inst., 1969-70; apptd. by U.S. Senator Paul Simon to Merit Screening Com. Fed. Judges, U.S. Atty. and U.S. Marshal, 1993, others; mem. task force indigent appellate def. Cook County Jud. Adv. Coun., 1992-95; mem. Ill. Gen. Assembly, 1964-68. Contbr. articles to profl. jours. Chmn. Ill. Crime Investigating Commn., 1967-68, chmn. Ill. Parole and Pardon Bd., 1969-70; bd. dirs. Ill. Law Enforcement Commn., 1970-72; chmn. Com. on Correctional Facilities and Services; exec. v.p. and gen. counsel Ill. Fin. Svcs. Assn., 1980-95; chmn. law forum Am. Fin. Svcs. Assn., 1975-76; mem. spl. commn. on adminstrn. of justice in Cook County, Ill. (Greylord Com.) 1984-90, bd. dirs. Chgo. Crime Commn., 1986-91; mem. Ill. Supreme Ct. Spl. Commn. on the Adminstrn. of Justice, Ill. Supreme Ct. Appointment, 1991; adv. bd. mem. Ctr. for Analysis of Alternative Dispute Resolution Systems, 1998-; Served to capt. JAGC, AUS, 1955-58. Named One of Ten Outstanding Young Men in Chgo., Chgo. Jr. Assn. Commerce and Industry, 1960, 65; recipient Outstanding Legislator award Ill. Gen. Assembly, 1966. Mem. ABA (com. consumer fin. svcs. 1975-99, ho. dels. 1981-90, judicial adminstrn. divsn. 1980-95, mem. exec. com. lawyer's conf. 1994-95, mem. bench and bar rels. com. 1994-96, mem. adv. com. to Ill. State Del., Jud. Adminstrn. Divsn. in Recognition of Leadership in Improvement of Adminstrn. of Justice award 1993), Ill. State Bar Assn. (pres. 1975-76, com. on fed. jud. and related appointments; Abraham Lincoln Legal Writing award 1959, mem. adv. com., state del., 1994-99, bd. dirs., co-chmn. joint com. jud. compensation 2002-), Chgo. Bar Assn. (bd. mgrs. 1965-66), Fred B. Snite Found. (sec., counsel 1976-90), Gertrude and Walter Swanson Found. (sole trustee 1995—), Mid-Am. Club Chgo. Republican. Roman Catholic. Finance.

PUSEY, WILLIAM ANDERSON, lawyer; b. Richmond, Va., Mar. 17, 1936; s. Paul H. and Vernelle (Barnes) P.; m. Patricia Powell, Sept. 3, 1960; children: Patricia Brent, William A. Jr., Margaret Glen. AB, Princeton U., 1958; JD, U. Va., 1962. Bar: Va. 1964. Assoc. McCutchen, Brown, et al, San Francisco, 1962-63; dep. dist. atty. Alameda County, Oakland, Calif., 1963-64; assoc., ptnr., sr. counsel Hunton & Williams, Washington, Fairfax and Richmond, Va., 1964—. Trustee Ea. Mineral Law Found., Morgantown, W.Va., 1985—, pres., 1987-88. Chmn. bd. dirs. Presbyn. Sch. Christian Edn., Richmond, 1984-85. Mem. Am. Hort. Soc. (bd. dirs. and sec. 1995-2002)—, Order of Coif (gen. counsel), Phi Beta Kappa, Omicron Delta Kappa. Corporate, general, Mergers and acquisitions, Securities. Home: 3910 N Glebe Rd Arlington VA 22207-4340 Office: Hunton & Williams 1900 K St NW Washington DC 20006-1110

PUSHINSKY, JON, lawyer; b. N.Y.C., May 30, 1954; s. Paul and Harriet (Rosenberg) P.; m. M. Jean Clickner, July 31, 1982; children: Matthew Clickner-Pushinsky, Jeremy Clickner-Pushinsky. BA, MA, U. Pa., 1976; JD, U. Pitts., 1979. Bar: Pa. 1979, U.S. Dist. Ct. (we. dist.) Pa. 1979, U.S. Ct. Appeals (3rd cir.) 1980, U.S. Supreme Ct. 1988. Staff counsel W.Va. Legal Svcs. Plan, Wheeling, 1979—80; pvt. practice Pitts., 1980—. Dem. candidate Superior Ct. Pa., 1993, 95; solicitor Cmty. Human Svcs. Corp., Pitts., 1992—; consulting lawyer ARC-Allegheny, Pitts., 1981—. Recipient Civil Libertarian award ACLU of Pa., 1994, Cmty. Citation of Merit Allegheny County Mental Health/Mental Retardation Bd., 1992, Cert. Appreciation Pitts. Commn. on Human Rels., 1992. Mem. Pa. Trial Lawyers Assn., Allegheny County Bar Assn. (appellate practice com., civil rights com.), Acad. Trial Lawyers Allegheny County. Democrat. Avocations: reading, hiking, movies. Civil rights, Constitutional, General practice. Office: 429 4th Ave Pittsburgh PA 15219-1500

PUSTILNIK, DAVID DANIEL, lawyer; b. N.Y.C., Mar. 10, 1931; s. Philip and Belle (Gerberholtz) P.; m. Helen Jean Todd, Aug. 15, 1959; children: Palma Elyse, Leslie Royce, Bradley Todd. BS, NYU, 1952, JD, 1958, LLM, 1959; postgrad., Air War Coll., 1976. Bar: N.Y. 1959, U.S. Supreme Ct. 1962, Conn. 1964. Legis. tax atty. legis. and regulations div. Office Chief Counsel, IRS, Washington, 1959-63; atty. Travelers Ins. Co., Hartford, Conn., 1963-68, assoc. counsel, 1968-73, counsel, 1973-75, assoc. gen. counsel, 1975-87, dep. gen. counsel, 1987-93. Mem. adv. coun. Hartford Inst. on Ins. Taxation, 1978-93, vice chmn., 1991-92, chmn., 1992-93. Grad. editor NYU Tax Law Rev., 1958-59. Trustee Hartford Coll. for Women, 1985-91; life sponsor Am. Tax Policy Inst.; dir. Congregation Beth Yam, 1996-99. Served to col. USAFR. Kenneson fellow NYU, 1958-59. Fellow Am. Coll. Tax Counsel; mem. ABA (chmn. ins. cos. com. 1976-78), Am. Coun. Life Ins. (chmn. cos. tax com. 1982-84), Am. Ins. Assn. (chmn. tax com. 1979-81), Assn. Life Ins. Counsel (chmn. tax sect. 1991-93), Twentieth Century Club, Sea Pines Country Club (co-chair social com. 1997-99). Pension, profit-sharing, and employee benefits, Corporate taxation.

PUTKA, ANDREW CHARLES, lawyer; b. Cleve., Nov. 14, 1926; s. Andrew George and Lillian M. (Koryta) P. Student, John Carroll U., 1944, U.S. Naval Acad., 1945-46; AB, Adelbert Coll., Western Res. U., 1949, JD, 1952. Bar: Ohio 1952. Practice law, Cleve.; instr. govt. Notre Dame Coll.; v.p. Koryta Bros. Coal Co., Cleve., 1952-56; supt. divsn. bldg. and loan assns. Ohio Dept. Commerce, 1959-63; pres., chmn. bd., CEO Am. Nat. Bank, Parma, Ohio, 1963-69; dir. fin. City of Cleve., 1971-74; dir. port control, 1974-78; dir. Cleve. Hopkins Internat. Airport, 1974-78. Mem. Ohio Ho. of Reps., 1953-56, Ohio Senate, 1957-58; dep. auditor, acting sec. Cuyahoga County Bd. Revision, 1970-71; mem. exec. com. Cuyahoga County Democratic Com., 1973-81, Assn. Ind. Colls. and Univs. Ohio, 1983-89; bd. govs. Sch. Law, Western Res. U., 1953-56; mem. exec. com. World Service Student Fund, 1950-52; U.S. rep. Internat. Pax Romana Congress, Amsterdam, 1950, Toronto, 1952; mem. lay advisory bd. Notre Dame Coll., 1968-90, trustee, 1990-93, hon. trustee, 1993—; mem. adv. bd. St. Andrew's Abbey, 1976-88 ; trustee Case-Western Res. U., Newman Found. No. Ohio, 1980-93, hon. trustee, 1993—; 1st v.p. First Cath. Slovak Union of U.S., 1977-80; pres. USO Council of Cuyahoga County, 1980-83. Voted an outstanding legislator Ohio Press Corrs., 1953; named to All-Star Legislative team Ohio Newspaper Corrs., 1955; named one of Fabulous Clevelanders Cleve. Plain Dealer, John Henry Newman honor Soc. Mem. Cuyahoga County, Cleve. Bar Assn., Nat. Assn. State Savs. and Loan Suprs. (past. nat. pres.), U.S. Savs. and Loan League (mem. legis com, 1960-63), Am. Legion, Ohio Mcpl. League (bd. trustees 1973), Parma C. of C. (bd. dirs., treas. 1965-67), Newman Fedn. (past nat. pres.), NCCJ, Catholic Lawyers Guild (treas.), Am. Ohio Bankers Assn., Am. Inst. Banking, Adelbert Alumni Assn. (exec. com.), Cathedral Latin Alumni Assn. (trustee 1952—), Internat. Order of Alhambra (internat. parliamentarian 1971—, past grand comdr., supreme advocate 1973), Amvets, KC, Pi Kappa Alpha, Delta Theta Phi (past. pres. Cleve. alumni senate, master inspector 1975). Office: 28 Pond Dr Cleveland OH 44116-1062

PUTMAN, MICHAEL (MICHAEL JAMES PUTMAN), lawyer; b. San Antonio, May 12, 1948; s. Harold David and Elizabeth Finley (Henderson) P.; m. Kris J. Bird. BBA, S.W. Tex. State U., 1969; JD, St. Mary's U., 1972. Bar: Tex. 1972, U.S. Dist. Ct. (we. dist.) Tex. 1980, U.S. Ct. Appeals (5th and 11th cirs.) 1981, U.S. Supreme Ct., 2003; cert. personal injury trial law specialist Tex. Bd. Legal Specialization. Ptnr. Putman & Putman (Inc. 1981), San Antonio, 1972-81, officer, dir., 1981—. Mem. ATLA, State Bar Tex., Nat. Employment Lawyers Assn., Tex. Trial Lawyers Assn. (assoc. dir. 1995, dir. 1996-99, dir. emeritus 1999), Tex. Employment Lawyers Assn. (founding mem. 1998—), San Antonio Trial Lawyers Assn. (dir., officer 1975—, Am. Bd. Trial Advocates. Labor (including EEOC, Fair Labor Standards Act, labor-management relations, NLRB, OSHA), Personal injury (including property damage), Product liability. Office: 310 S Saint Marys St Fl 27 San Antonio TX 78205-3113

PUTNEY, PAUL WILLIAM, lawyer; b. Phila., Feb. 6, 1940; s. R. Emerson and Dorothea (Schulz) P.; m. Joan E. High, June 9, 1961; children: Joanna E., Andrew E. AB, Princeton U., 1962; JD, Harvard U., 1965. Bar: Pa. 1965, U.S. Dist. Ct. (ea. dist.) Pa. 1966, U.S. Supreme Ct. 1977, N.Y. 1988. Assoc. Dechert Price & Rhoads, Phila., 1965-73, ptnr., 1973—74, Dechert Price & Rhoads LLP, 1977—, mng. ptnr. N.Y.C., 1987—94, chmn. trust and estates dept., 1994—2001; dep. chief broadcast bur. FCC, Washington, 1974-77. Chmn. Phila. Presbytery Homes, Inc., 1987-93. Mem.: ABA. Estate planning, Probate (including wills, trusts). Office: Dechert LLP 4000 Bell Atlantic Tower 1717 Arch St Philadelphia PA 19103-2793

PUTNEY, WAINSCOTT WALKER, lawyer; b. Pitts., Nov. 10, 1957; s. Charles Walker and Karen (Albright) P.; m. Sharon Lynn Smith, Apr. 11, 1982. BS in Physics, Va. Mil. Inst., 1978; JD, U. Tulsa, 1981; LLM, George Washington U., 1991. Bar: Fla. 1981, D.C. 1990, Va. 1993, Okla. 2001, U.S. Dist. Ct. (mid. dist.) Fla. 1981, U.S. Ct. Appeals (11th cir.) 1984, U.S. Dist. Ct. (so. dist.) Fla. 1985, U.S. Ct. Appeals (D.C. cir.) 1987, U.S. Dist. Ct. (ea. and we. dists.) Va. 1995, U.S. Ct. Appeals (4th cir.) 1993, U.S. Dist. Ct. (no. dist.) Okla. 1999, U.S. Ct. Appeals (10th cir.) 1999, U.S. Ct. Fed. Claims, 1989, U.S. Ct. Appeals (fed. cir.) 1990, U.S. Supreme Ct. 1985. Assoc. Sanders, McEwan, Mims & Martinez, Orlando, Fla., 1981-85; pvt. practice Orlando, 1985-89; trial atty. U.S. Dept. Justice, Washington, 1989-99; asst. U.S. atty. U.S. Atty.'s Office, Tulsa, 1999—. Bankruptcy trustee, Orlando, 1985-89; lectr. comml. law Mary Washington Coll., Fredericksburg, Va., 1997-99. Contbr. articles to profl. jours. Precinct committeeman Orange County Rep. Exec. Com., 1987-88. Recipient cert. of appreciation Legal Aid Soc., 1988. Mem. Fla. Bar Assn. (bd. govs. young lawyers divsn. 1991-93), IEEE. Bankruptcy, Criminal, Taxation, general.

PUTTER, DAVID SETH, lawyer; b. N.Y.C., Mar. 11, 1944; s. Norton Seth and Ruth Crystal P. Student, U. Granada, Spain, 1964; BA in Biology, Beloit Coll., Spain, 1965; JD, Syracuse U., 1968. Bar: Vt. 1970, N.Y. 1971, U.S. Dist. Ct. Vt. 1970, U.S. Ct. Appeals (2d cir.) 1975, U.S. Ct. Claims 1998. Atty. Putter & Carrington, Arlington, Vt., 1970-73; Bennington County pub. defender State of Vt., Bennington, 1973-76, law clk. to Superior Ct. judges Burlington, 1976-78, asst. atty. gen. Montpelier, 1979-81; with Putter & Unger, Montpelier, 1981-88; assoc. Saxer, Anderson, Wolinsky & Sunshine, Montpelier, 1988-2000; ptnr. Putter and Edson, LLP, Montpelier, 2001—02; pvt. practice Law Offices of David Putter, 2002—. Contbr. articles to profl. jours. Acting Superior Ct. judge, 1997-2001; chair legal panel ACLU Vt., 1988—; sponsored advisor on assembly, free press, free speech USIA, Lusaka, Zambia, Kampala, Uganda, 1996. Recipient Jonathan Chase award, ACLU Vt., 1991, 1997. Avocations: hiking, camping, theater, travel, music (folk and rock). Appellate, General civil litigation, Constitutional, Civil rights. Home: 6 Towne St Montpelier VT 05602-4231 Office: 15 E State St Montpelier VT 05602-3010

PUTZEL, CONSTANCE KELLNER, lawyer; b. Balt., Sept. 5, 1922; d. William Stummer and Corinne (Strauss) Kellner; m. William L. Putzel, Aug. 28, 1945; 1 son, Arthur William. AB, Goucher Coll., 1942; LLB, U. Md., 1945, JD, 1969. Bar: Md. 1945. Social worker Balt. Dept. Pub. Welfare, 1945-46; atty. New Amsterdam Casualty Co., Balt., 1947; staff atty. Legal Aid Bur., Balt., 1947-49; mem. Putzel & Putzel, P.A., Balt., 1950-89; pvt. practice Balt., 1989—; instr. U. Balt. Sch. Law, 1975-77, Goucher Coll., 1976-77. Chair character com. Ct. Appeals for 3d Cir., 1976-97. Author: A Practice Guide to Divorce, 1999, Representing the Older Client in Divorce, 1992. Commr. Md. Com. on Status of Women, 1972-76, Com. to Implement ERA, 1973-76; Pres. U. Md. Law Alumni Assn., 1978; bd. dirs. Legal Aid Bur., 1951-52, 71-73. Fellow Am. Acad. Matrimonial Lawyers (chair elder issues com. 1996); mem. ABA (co-chair elder issues com., mem. coun. sr. lawyers divsn. 1996-2000, editl. bd. 1996-99), Md. Bar Assn. (bd. govs. 1972-73, chmn. family law sect. 1978-79, chair sr. lawyers divsn. 2001-03). Family and matrimonial. Home: 7121 Park Heights Ave Unit 401 Baltimore MD 21215-1610 Office: 401 Washington Ave Ste 803 Towson MD 21204 E-mail: lawtowson@aol.com.

PUTZELL, EDWIN JOSEPH, JR., lawyer, mayor; b. Birmingham, Ala., Sept. 29, 1913; s. Edwin Joseph and Celeste (Joseph) Putzell; m. Dorothy Corcoran Waters, Aug. 5, 1967; children from previous marriage: Cynthia Putzell Reidy, Edwin Joseph, III. AB, Tulane U., 1935; LLB, Harvard U., 1938. Bar: N.Y. 1939, U.S. Supreme Ct. 1945, Mo. 1947. Atty. Donovan, Leisure, Newton & Lumbard, N.Y.C. and Washington, 1937-42; asst. dir., exec. officer Office of Strategic Svcs., 1942-45; asst. treas. Monsanto Co., St. Louis, 1945-46, asst. sec., atty., 1946-51, sec., 1951-77, dir. law dept., 1953-68, v.p., gen. counsel, 1963-77; ptnr. Coburn, Croft, Shepherd, Herzog & Putzell, St. Louis, 1977-79; of counsel Coburn, Croft & Putzell, St. Louis, 1979-96; mayor City of Naples, Fla., 1986-90; of counsel Thompson & Coburn, St. Louis, 1996—. Dir. St. Louis Symphony Soc., 1955—69; pres. The Conservancy, Inc., 1981—85, chmn. bd. dirs., 1984—85; pres. Social Planning Coun., St. Louis, 1954—57; vice chmn. Westminster Coll., 1976—79; chmn. Sta. KETC-TV, St. Louis, 1977—79; trustee St. Luke's Hosp., St. Louis, 1973—79; pres. Hospice of Naples (Fla.) Cmty. Found., Collier County., 2002—; bd. dirs. The Moorings, Inc., Fla., Collier/Naplescape, Inc., Fla., Greater Naples Civic Assn., Naples Bot.

Garden; vice chmn. St. Louis County Bd. Police Commrs., 1964—72; Big Cypress Basin bd. S. Fla. Water Mgmt. Dist., 1985—86; chmn. Naples Airport Authority, 1979—83, 1993—97. Mem.: ABA, Assn. Gen. Counsel, Am. Soc. Corp. Secs. (pres. 1968—69), St. Louis Bar Assn., Mo. Bar Assn., Naples Area C. of C., Naples Yacht Club, Bogey Club, Forum Club (v.p. 1998—2000, pres. 2002—), Port Royal Golf Club, Hole in the Wall Golf Club, Delta Sigma Phi, Phi Beta Kappa. Episcopalian. Home: 1285 Gulf Shore Blvd N Naples FL 34102-4911 E-mail: dcpnaples@aol.com.

PYFER, JOHN FREDERICK, JR., lawyer; b. Lancaster, Pa., July 25, 1946; s. John Frederick and Myrtle Ann (Greiner) P.; m. Carol Trice, Nov. 25, 1970; children: John Frederick III, Carol Lee. Grad. cum laude, Peddie Sch., 1965; BA in Polit. Sci. and Econs., Haverford Coll., 1969; JD, Vanderbilt U., 1972. Bar: Pa. 1972, U.S. Dist. Ct. (ea. dist.) Pa. 1973, U.S. Tax Ct. 1975, U.S. Supreme Ct. 1975, U.S. Dist. Ct. (mid. dist.) Pa. 1984, U.S. Ct. Appeals (3d cir.) 1986. Law clk. to presiding justice Ct. Common Pleas, Lancaster, Pa., 1972-74; assoc. Xakellis, Perezous & Mongiovi, Lancaster, 1972-76; founding ptnr. Allison & Pyfer, Lancaster, 1976-85; pres. Pyfer & Assocs., Lancaster, 1986-88, Pyfer & Reese, Lancaster, 1988—. Prof. para-legal tng. Pa. State Ext. Svc., 1989-93; fed. ct. mediator, 1992-2001. Contbr. articles to law revs., law treatises. Pres. Lancaster-Lebanon Coun., Boy Scouts Am., 1989—93, coun. commr., 1987—89, mem. nat. com., 1996—, exec. bd. N.E. region, 1998—, area pres., 2000—03; bd. dirs. World of Scouting Mus.; achieved Eagle Scout , 1962; named Disting. Eagle Scout , 2001. Recipient Silver Beaver and Silver Antelope, Boy Scouts Am. Fellow Am. Bd. Criminal Lawyers, Lancaster Heritage Ctr. (vice-chair 2003—); mem. ABA (First prize Howard C. Schwab Nat. Essay Contest in Writing 1972), ATLA, SAR, Nat. Assn. Criminal Def. Lawyers, Pa. Trial Lawyers Assn., Pa. Criminal Def. Lawyers Assn., Am. Arbitration Assn., Pa. Bar Assn., Lancaster Bar Assn., Inns Ct. (founder, pres. W. Hensel Brown 1993-94), Christian Lawyers Soc., Train Collector Assn. (divsn. pres. 1984), Am. Orchid Soc. (affiliate pres. 1998), Lions Club (pres. 1980-82, 2000-01) (Willow Street, Pa.), Masons (Lancaster). Republican. United Ch. of Christ (elder, pres. 1989, 95). Criminal, Family and matrimonial, General practice. Home: 1100 Little Brook Rd Lancaster PA 17603-6116 Office: Pyfer & Reese 128 N Lime St Lancaster PA 17602-2951 E-mail: pyfer@comcast.net., law@pyferreese.com.

PYLE, HOWARD, lawyer, consultant; b. Richmond, Va., Feb. 1, 1940; s. Wilfrid and Anne Woolston (Roller) P.; children: Elizabeth Roller Ross, Howard. AB, Princeton U., 1962; JD, U. Va., 1967. Bar: Va. 1967, D.C. 1969. Career trainee CIA, Washington, 1967-69; adminstrv. asst. to Congressman Odin Langen, U.S. Ho. of Reps., Washington, 1969-70, to Congressman Hastings Keith, 1971; asst. to sec. Dept. Interior, Washington, 1971-73; Washington rep. Std. Oil Co. Ind., 1973-77; mgr. fed. pub. affairs R.J. Reynolds Industries, Inc., Winston-Salem, N.C., 1977-80; dir. fed. rels. Houston Industries, Washington, 1980-99; pres. HPYLE Cons., Alexandria, Va., 1999—. Bd. govs., pres. Episcopal Sr. Ministries, 1986-96; bd. dirs., pres. Friendship Terrace, 1986-96; chair D.C. area ann. giving Princeton U. Capt. USNR, 1962-89, ret. Mem.: SAR, NRA, Va. Bar, DC Bar, Res. Officers Assn., Naval Res. Assn., Princeton Club of Washington (mem. coun. 1998—, chmn. comms. com., chair DC ann. giving), Va. Country Club, Delta Theta Phi. Republican. Episcopalian. Home: 125 N Lee St Alexandria VA 22314-3260 also: PO Box 19645 Alexandria VA 22320-0645 Office: HPYLE Cons Po Box 19645 Alexandria VA 22320-0645 E-mail: hpyle@alumni.Virginia.EDU.

PYLE, KURT H. lawyer; b. Oakland, Calif., Mar. 11, 1941; s. Thomas H. and Jean W. P.; m. Beth R., Apr. 30, 1977; children: Christopher, Brendan, Hilary. BS, U. Calif., Berkeley, 1962; JD, Hastings Coll. Law, 1965. Bar: Calif. 1966, U.S. Dist. Ct. (ctrl. dist.) Calif. 1966, D.C. 1972, U.S. Ct. Appeals (9th cir.) 1978, U.S. Dist. Ct. (no. and so. dists.) Calif. 1982, U.S. Dist. Ct. (ea. dist.) Calif. 1983, U.S. Claims Ct. 1984, U.S. Tax Ct. 1984. Capt., judge advocate USAF, Wright-Patterson AFB, Ohio, 1962-65; from atty. to mng. ptnr. Schramm & Raddue, Santa Barbara, Calif., 1965-96; ptnr. Reicker, Pfau Pyle McRoy & Herman LLP, Santa Barbara, 1996—. Bd. dirs. Santa Barbara Counseling Ctr., 1996-2000. Mem. ATLA, Santa Barbara County Bar Assn., Assn. Bus. Trial Lawyers, Consumers Attys. Calif., Santa Barbara Inn of Ct. General civil litigation, Labor (including EEOC, Fair Labor Standards Act, labor-management relations, NLRB, OSHA), Personal injury (including property damage). Home: 520 Grove Ln Santa Barbara CA 93105-2428 Office: Reicker Pfau Pyle McRoy & Herman LLP PO Box 1470 Santa Barbara CA 93102-1470 E-mail: kpyle@rppmh.com.

PYLE, WALTER K. lawyer; b. Chgo. s. Garland K. and Agnes G. (O'Connor) P.; m. Frances S. Kaminer; children: Michael K., James B., Isaac David. JD, Loyola U., Chgo., 1964; postgrad, NYU, 1964-65. Bar: Ill. 1965, Calif. 1981, U.S. Supreme Ct. 1972, U.S. Ct. Appeals (1st cir.) 1979, U.S. Ct. Appeals (7th cir.) 1992, U.S. Ct. Appeals (8th cir.) 1977, U.S. Ct. Appeals (9th cir.) 1980, U.S. Dist. Ct. (no. dist.) Ill. 1965, U.S. Dist. Ct. (no. dist.) Calif. 1981, U.S. Dist. Ct. (ea. dist.) Calif. 1982, U.S. Dist. Ct. (cen. dist.) Calif. 1989, U.S. Dist. Ct. (so. dist.) Calif. 1991; cert. specialist appellate law and criminal law, State Bar Calif., Bd. Legal Specialization; bd. cert. civil trial advocate Nat. Bd. Trial Advocacy. Asst. state's atty. Criminal Div. Cook County (Ill.) State's Atty.'s Office, Chgo., 1967-69; asst. atty. gen. Ill. Atty. Gen.'s Office, Chgo., 1969-78; pvt. practice law Chgo., 1978-80, San Francisco, 1981-88, Berkeley, Calif., 1988—. Arbitrator Alameda County (Calif.) Superior Ct., 1993—; judge pro tempore Alameda County (Calif.) Superior Ct., 1989-. Mem. ABA, Calif. Bar Assn., Ill. Bar Assn., Alameda County Bar Assn. (dir. 1992-93), DuPage County Bar Assn., Bar Assn. San Francisco, Chgo. Bar Assn., Calif. Appellate Def. Counsel (sec. 2002--), Calif. Assn. Toxicologists. Avocations: running, cooking. General civil litigation, Appellate, Criminal. Office: 2039 Shattuck Ave Ste 202 Berkeley CA 94704-1150 E-mail: walt@wfkplaw.com.

PYTELL, ROBERT HENRY, retired lawyer, former judge; b. Detroit, Sept. 27, 1926; s. Henry Carl and Helen (Zielinski) P.; m. Laurie Mazur, June 2, 1956; children: Mary Beth, Mark Henry, Robert Michael. JD, U. Detroit, 1951. Bar: Mich. 1952. Of counsel Pytell & Varchetti, P.C., Detroit, 1952-2001; asst. U.S. atty. Ea. Dist. Mich., 1962-65; judge Mcpl. Ct., Grosse Pointe Farms, Mich., 1967-85. With USNR, 1945-46. Mem. Am. Coll. Trust and Estate Coun., State Bar Mich. (mem. probate coun. probate sect. 1998-2000), Crescent Sail Yacht Club (Grosse Pointe), Delta Theta Phi. Roman Catholic. Commercial, consumer (including collections, credit), Corporate, general, Probate (including wills, trusts). Office: 20100 Mack Ave Grosse Pointe Woods MI 48236

QIAN, JIN, law librarian; b. Shanghai; came to the U.S., 1987; s. Bingchun and Shiyi Qian. BA, Shanghai Tchrs. U., ;, 1981; MA, Fordham U., 1988; MLS, St. John's U., 1990. Libr. trainee N.Y. Pub. Libr., N.Y.C., 1988; reference asst. N.Y. Hist. Soc., N.Y.C., 1989-90; asst. libr. Wilson, Elser et al., N.Y.C., 1990-92, head libr., 1992—. Presdl. scholar Fordham U., 1987. Mem. Law Libr. Assn. Greater N.Y., Am. Assn. Law Librs., Spl. Librs. Assn., ALA. Home: PO Box 811 New York NY 10163-0811 Office: Wilson Elser & Moskowitz 150 E 42nd St New York NY 10017-5612 E-mail: QianJ@wemed.com.

QUACKENBUSH, JUSTIN LOWE, federal judge; b. Spokane, Wash., Oct. 3, 1929; s. Carl Clifford and Marian Huldah (Lowe) Q.; m. Marie McAtee; children: Karl Justin, Kathleen Marie, Robert Craig. Student, U. Ill., 1947-49; BA, U. Idaho, 1951; LLB, Gonzaga U., Spokane, 1957. Bar: Wash. 1957. Dep. pros. atty., Spokane County, 1957-59; ptnr. Quackenbush, Dean, Bailey & Henderson, Spokane, 1959-80; dist. judge U.S. Dist. Ct. (ea. dist.) Wash., Spokane, 1980—, now sr. judge. Part-time instr. Gonzaga U. Law Sch., 1960-67 Chmn. Spokane County Planning Commn., 1969-73. Served with USN, 1951-54. Mem. Wash. Bar Assn., Spokane County Bar Assn. (trustee 1976-78), Internat. Footprint Assn. (nat. pres. 1967), Shriners. Episcopalian. Office: US Dist Ct PO Box 1432 Spokane WA 99210-1432

QUADE, VICKI, editor, writer, playwright, producer; b. Chgo., Aug. 15, 1953; d. Victor and Virginia (Uryasz) Q.; m. Charles J. White III, Feb. 15, 1986 (div. Aug. 1996); children: Michael, David, Catherine. BS in Journalism, No. Ill. U., 1974. Staff reporter news divsn. The News-Tribune, LaSalle, Ill., 1975-77; staff writer news divsn. The News-Sun, Waukegan, Ill., 1977-81; staff writer ABA Jour., Chgo., 1981-85; mng. editor ABA Press, Chgo., 1985-90, editor, 1990-2000, sr. editor, 1994-2000. Author: (poetry) Rain and Other Poems, 1976, Laughing Eyes, 1979, Two Under the Covers, 1981, (biography) I Remember Bob Collins, 2000; playwright Late Nite Catechism, 1993, (with Maripat Donovan) Room for Advancement, 1994, Mr. Nanny, 1997, (musical) Lost in Wonderland, 1998, (musical) Here Come the Famous Brothers, 2001; prodr. Late Nite Catechism, Mr. Nanny, Here Come the Famous Brothers, Christopher Carter Messes With Your Mind; contbr. to numerous anthologies and publs.; contbd. to: 20th Century Chicago: 100 Years, 100 Voices (contbd. the year 1953), owner/operator Crossroads Theater, Naperville, Ill. Recipient numerous awards from Soc. Nat. Assn. Publs., AP, UPI. Mem. Am. Soc. Bus. Press Editors (award), Chgo. Newspaper Guild (award), Am. Soc. Assn. Execs. (Gold Circle award 1989, 90). Avocations: travel, photography.

QUADRI, FAZLE RAB, lawyer, government official; b. Dacca, Pakistan, Aug. 5, 1948; came to U.S., 1967; s. Gholam Moula and Jehan (Ara) Q.; children: Ryan F., Tania M. AA, Western Wyo. Coll., 1969; BA, Calif. State U., 1972; JD, Western State U., 1978; postgrad. cert. in criminal advocacy, U. Calif., San Francisco, 1988. Bar: Calif. 1981. Sr. adminstrv. analyst San Bernardino County, Calif., 1978-82, acting legis. adv., 1982, sr. legis. analyst, 1982-90, county legis. analyst, 1990-93, acting pub. defender, 1984; dist. counsel Mojave Desert Air Quality Mgmt. Dist., Victorville, Calif., 1993—; dist. cousnel Antelope Valley Air Pollution Control Dist., 1997—. Local gov. rep. State Hazardous Waste Mgmt. Council, Sacramento, Calif., 1982-84; chmn.'s rep. County Projects Selection Coms., San Bernardino, 1983-91; county rep. South Coast Air Quality Mgmt. Dist., El Monte, Calif., 1983-87. Advisor Mcpl. Adv. Couns., San Bernardino, 1984-87; mem. Law Libr. Bd. Trustees, 1984-85, 93-95. Mem. ABA, Calif. Bar Assn. (mem. exec. com. pub. law section 2000—, vice chair 2002-.), Calif. State U. Alumni Assn. (bd. dirs. 1985-86), Masons, Shriners. Republican. Islamic. Avocations: personal computers, reading, music, Karate, water sports. Home: 535 E Mariposa Dr Redlands CA 92373-7351 Office: Mojave Desert AQMD 14306 Park Ave Victorville CA 92392-2310 E-mail: quadri@mdaqmd.ca.gov.

QUALE, ANDREW CHRISTOPHER, JR., lawyer; b. Boston, July 7, 1942; s. Andrew Christopher and Luella (Meland) Q.; m. Sally Sterling Ellis, Oct. 15, 1977; children: Andrew, Addison. BA magna cum laude, Harvard U., 1963, LLB cum laude, 1966; postgrad., Cambridge (Eng.) U., 1966-67. Bar: Mass. 1967, N.Y. 1971. Fellow Internat. Legal Ctr., Bogota, Colombia, 1967-68; cons. Republic of Colombia, Bogota, 1968-69; assoc. Cleary, Gottlieb, Steen and Hamilton, N.Y.C., 1969-75; ptnr. Coudert Brothers, N.Y.C., 1975-82, Sidley Austin Brown & Wood, N.Y.C., 1982—. Adj. prof. Sch. of Law U. Va., Charlottesville, 1976—88; cons. privatizations World Bank, UN, Harvard Inst. Internat. Devel., 1982—; bd. dirs. Botelle Stoeckel Assocs., Norfolk. Contbr. to profl. publs. Pres. Bronxville (N.Y.) Sch. Bd., 1991-93; founder, bd. dirs. Bronxville Sch. Found., 1991-95, 96-2002; bd. dirs. Coun. The Ams. Knox fellow, 1966—67. Mem.: ABA, The Little Forum (co-chair Bronxville), Colombian-Am. Assn. (v.p., bd. dirs.), NY State Bar Assn., Assn. Bar City NY (chmn. Inter-Am. affairs com. 1982—85), Norfolk (Conn.) Country Club, Bronxville Field Club. Banking, Private international, Mergers and acquisitions. Office: Sidley Austin Brown & Wood 787 7th Ave New York NY 10019

QUALE, JOHN CARTER, lawyer; b. Boston, Aug. 16, 1946; s. Andrew C. and Luella (Meland) Q.; m. Diane Zipursky, Jan. 19, 1992; children: Virginia Ann, Jane Harris, John Andrew; stepchildren: Rachel Goldman, Alisa Goldman. AB cum laude, Harvard U., 1968, JD cum laude, 1971. Bar: Mass. 1971, D.C. 1972. Assoc. Kirkland & Ellis, Washington, 1971-78, ptnr., 1978-83, Wiley, Rein & Fielding, Washington, 1983-96, Skadden, Arps, Slate, Meagher & Flom L.L.P., Washington, 1996—. Spkr. mass media trade groups. Contbr. articles to profl. jours. Trustee Fed. Comm. Bar Assn. Found., 1992-93. Mem. ABA, Fed. Comm. Bar Assn. (treas. 1982-83, 98-99, mem. exec. com. 1993-98), Barristers, Met. Club. Administrative and regulatory, Communications, Corporate, general. Office: Skadden Arps Slate Meagher & Flom LLP 1440 New York Ave NW Ste 600 Washington DC 20005-6000 E-mail: jquale@skadden.com.

QUANDT, JOSEPH EDWARD, lawyer, educator; b. Port Huron, Mich., May 21, 1963; s. Herbert Raymond and Mary Katherine (West) Q.; m. Christine Ann Reilly, Aug. 21, 1993. BA, Oakland U., 1990; JD, Thomas M. Cooley Law Sch., Lansing, Mich., 1993. Bar: Mich. 1994, U.S. Dist. Ct. (ea. and we. dists.) Mich. 1994. Exec. dir. Lord & Taylor, Sterling Heights, Mich., 1985-90; compliance and enforcement specialist Mich. Dept. Environ. Quality, Lansing, 1990-93, adv. bd., 1997—; assoc. Stowe, Draling & Boyd, Traverse City, Mich., 1993-94, Smith & Johnson, Traverse City, 1994-98; ptnr. Menmuir, Zimmerman, Kuhn, Taylor and Quandt, Traverse City, 1998—. Lectr., commentator Inst. CLE, Ann Arbor, Mich., 1994—; adj. prof. Thomas M. Cooley Law Sch., 1997—; co-chair environ. law sect. State Bar Mich. Contbr. articles to profl. jours. Bd. dirs. Involved Citizens Enterprises, Traverse City, 1995—. Mem. Nat. Honor Soc. for Polit. Scientists, Ancient Order Hibernians, Pi Sigma Alpha. Republican. Roman Catholic. Avocations: ice hockey, golf, fly fishing. Environmental, Natural resources, Property, real (including real estate development, water). Office: Zimmerman Kuhn Darling Boyd Taylor and Quandt PLC 412 S Union St Traverse City MI 49684-2404

QUAY, THOMAS EMERY, lawyer; b. Cleve., Apr. 3, 1934; s. Harold Emery and Esther Ann (Thomas) Q.; divorced; children: Martha Wyndham, Glynis Cobb, Eliza Emery; m. Winnifred B. Cutler, May 13, 1989. AB in Humanities magna cum laude (Univ. scholar), Princeton U., 1956; LLB (Univ. scholar), U. Pa., 1963. Bar: Pa. 1964. Assoc. Pepper, Hamilton & Scheetz, Phila., 1963-65; with William H. Rorer, Inc., Ft. Washington, Pa., 1965—, sec., counsel, 1974-79, v.p., gen. counsel, sec., 1979-88; v.p. legal planning and adminstrn. Rorer Group, 1988-90; counsel Reed Smith Shaw and McClay, Phila., 1991-93; v.p., gen. counsel Athena Inst., Chester Springs, Pa., 1993—. Bd. dirs. Main Line YMCA, Ardmore, Pa., 1971-73, chmn. bd., 1972-73; editor 10th Reunion Book Princeton Class of 1956, 1966, 25th Reunion Book, 1981—, class sec., 1966-71, class v.p., 1971-81, pres., 1981-86. Lt. (j.g.) USNR, 1957-60. Recipient Commendation award, Main Line YMCA, 1984. Mem. ABA, Pa. Bar Assn., Phila. Bar Assn., Pharm. Mfrs. Assn. (chmn. law sect. 1983), Pa. Biotech. Assn. (chmn. legis. com., mem. exec. com. 1991-93), Phila. Drug Exch. (chmn. legis. com. 1975-78), Cannon Club of Princeton U., Sharswood Law Club of U. Pa., Princeton Club of Phila. Democrat. Presbyterian. Antitrust, Corporate, general, Intellectual property. Office: 601 Swedesford Rd Ste 201 Malvern PA 19355-1573

QUIAT, MARSHALL, lawyer; b. Denver, Mar. 10, 1922; s. Ira Louis and Esther Quiat; m. Ruth Laura Saunders, Nov. 26, 1950 (dec. Nov. 1995); 1 child, Matthew Philip; m. Jane Cooley, May 1, 1996. BA, U. Colo., 1947, JD, 1948. Bar: Colo. 1949, U.S. Dist. Ct. Colo. 1949, U.S. Ct. Appeals (10th cir.) 1968. Pvt. practice, Denver, 1949—. Judge Gilpin County (Colo.) Ct., 1956, 1st Jud. Dist. Ct., Golden, Colo., 1959; mem. com. on jud. reform Colo. Legis. Commn., 1958. Mem. Colo. Ho. of Reps., Denver, 1949-51; bd. dirs. Luth. Med. Ctr., Denver, 1961-87. 1st lt. F.A., U.S. Army, 1941-46, MTO, ETO. Mem. Am. Radio Relay League (nat. bd. dirs. 1986-99, honorary v.p. 1999—), Pi Gamma Mu, Delta Sigma Rho, Phi Alpha Delta. Avocations: amateur radio, skiing, mathematics, history. State civil litigation, Communications, Family and matrimonial. Home: 714 Pontiac St Denver CO 80220-5540 Office: PO Box 200878 Denver CO 80220-0878 E-mail: quiat@msn.com.

QUICK, ALBERT THOMAS, lawyer, educator; b. Battle Creek, Mich., June 28, 1939; s. Robert and Vera Quick; m. Brenda Jones; children: Lori, Traci, Becki, Breton, Regan, Leigh. BA, U. Ariz., 1962; MA, Cen. Mich. U., 1964; JD, Wayne State U., 1967; LLM, Tulane U., 1974. Bar: Mich. 1968. Asst. prosecutor Calhoun County, Marshall, Mich., 1968-69; assoc. Hatch & Hatch, Marshall, 1969-70; asst. prof. U. Maine, Augusta, 1970-73; prof. law U. Louisville, 1974-87, spl. asst. to univ. provost, 1983-87; dean, prof. law Ohio No. U., Ada, 1987-95; prof. law, dean U. Toledo, Ohio, 1995-99, dean and prof. emeritus, 1999—; of counsel Smith Haughey Rice & Roegge, Traverse City, Mich., 2002—. Co-author: Update Federal Rules of Criminal Procedure; contbr. articles to profl. jours. Trustee Traverse Dist. Libr.; 3rd sec. bd. Human Rights Commn., mem. Recipient Medallion of Justice Nat. Bar Assn., 1995. Mem. ABA, ACLU, Mich. State Bar Assn., Willis Soc., Ohio State Bar Assn., Phi Kappa Phi, Coif. Episcopalian. Avocations: golf, art, reading. Federal civil litigation. Office: 202 E State St Traverse City MI 49685-0848 E-mail: atquick@aol.com.

QUIGLEY, LEONARD VINCENT, lawyer; b. Kansas City, Mo., June 21, 1933; s. Joseph Vincent and Rosemary (Cannon) Q.; m. Lynn Mathis Pfohl, May 23, 1964; children: Leonard Matthew, Cannon Louise, Daniel Pfohl, Megan Mathis. AB, Coll. Holy Cross, 1953; LL.B. magna cum laude, Harvard U., 1959; LL.M. in Internat. Law, NYU, 1962. Bar: N.Y. 1960. Assoc. Cravath, Swaine & Moore, N.Y.C., 1959-67; ptnr. Paul, Weiss, Rifkind, Wharton & Garrison, N.Y.C., 1968—; gen. counsel Archaeol. Inst. Am., Boston. Served to lt. USN, 1953-56. Mem. ABA, Can. Bar Assn., N.Y. State Bar, Coun. Fgn. Rels., Assn. Bar City N.Y., Harvard Club (N.Y.C.), West Side Tennis Club (Forest Hills, N.Y.). Corporate, general, Oil, gas, and mineral, Private international. E-mail: lquigley@paulweiss.com.

QUILLEN, CECIL DYER, JR., lawyer, consultant; b. Kingsport, Tenn., Jan. 21, 1937; s. Cecil D. and Mary Louise (Carter) Q.; m. Vicey Ann Childress, Apr. 1, 1961; children: Cecil D. III, Ann C. BS, Va. Poly. Inst., 1958; LLB, U. Va., 1962. Bar: Va. 1962, N.Y. 1963, Tenn. 1974. Atty. patent dept. Eastman Kodak Co., Rochester, NY, 1962—65; atty. patent sect. Tenn. Eastman Co. (divsn. Eastman Kodak), Kingsport, 1965—69, mgr. patent sect., 1969—72, mgr. licensing, 1972—74, sec. and asst. chief counsel, 1974—76, v.p., chief counsel, 1983—85; dir. patent litigation Eastman Kodak, 1976—82, dir. antitrust litigation, 1978—82, v.p., assoc. gen. counsel, 1986, sr. v.p., gen. counsel, dir., 1986—92; sr. advisor Putnam, Hayes, Bartlett and PHB Hagler Bailly, Washington, 1992, Cornerstone Rsch., Washington, 2000—. Mem. ABA, Va. State Bar, Am. Intellectual Property Law Assn., Va. Poly. Inst. Com. of 100, Assn. Gen. Counsel. Antitrust, General civil litigation, Intellectual property. E-mail: cquillen@cornerstone.com.

QUILLEN, CECIL DYER, III, lawyer; b. Rochester, N.Y., Aug. 15, 1963; s. Cecil Dyer, Jr. and Vicey Ann (Childress) Q.; m. Mary Stuart Humes, Oct. 20, 1990; children: Caroline, James C.D., George. AB magna cum laude, Harvard U., 1985; JD, U. Va., 1988. Bar: N.Y. 1989, D.C. 1991, U.S. Ct. Appeals (4th cir.) 1989. Law clk., Sr. Cir. Judge U.S. Ct. Appeals (4th cir.), Richmond, Va., 1988-89; assoc. Sullivan & Cromwell, N.Y.C., 1989-95, Linklaters, N.Y.C., 1995-96, ptnr., 1996—, ptnr. London office, 2000—. Spkr. various profl. confs. Notes editor Va. Law Rev., 1987-88. Mem. ABA, N.Y. State Bar Assn., Assn. Bar City of N.Y., Raven Soc., Order of Coif, Phi Beta Kappa. Banking, Private international, Securities. Office: Linklaters One Silk St London EC2Y 8HQ England

QUIN, WILLIAM MONROE, II, lawyer; b. McComb, Miss., Sept. 9, 1971; s. William Monroe and Donna Hornsby Quin; m. Christy Anne Risher, Nov. 13, 1999. BBA, U. Miss., 1994; JD, La. State U., 1997. Bar: La. 1997, Miss. 1998, U.S. Dist. Ct. (no., so. dists.) Miss. 1998, U.S. Dist. Ct. (ea. dist.) La. 1998, U.S. Ct. Appeals (5th cir.) 1998. Law clk. to Hon. Michael P. Mills Miss. Supreme Ct., Jackson, 1997—98; assoc. atty. Lemle & Kellcher, LLP, New Orleans, 1998—2001, Allred Law Firm, Jackson, 2001—. Mem.: ATLA, Miss. Trial Lawyers Assn. Methodist. Avocations: golf, running. Personal injury (including property damage), Insurance, Professional liability. Office: Allred Law Firm 1911 Dunbarton Dr Jackson MS 39216 Office Fax: 601-713-3259. Business E-Mail: bquin@llredlaw.com.

QUINA, MARION ALBERT, JR., lawyer; b. Mobile, Ala., Apr. 18, 1949; s. Marion Albert Sr. and Tallulah (Dunlap) Q.; children: Marion Albert III, Elliott Richardson; m. Jamie Mayhall Curtis, May 2, 1998. BS, U. Ala., 1971; JD, Samford U., 1974. Bar: Ala. 1974, U.S. Dist. Ct. (so. dist.) Ala. 1975, U.S. Ct. Appeals (5th cir.) 1977, U.S. Ct. Appeals (11th cir.) 1981. Assoc. Lyons, Pipes & Cook, Mobile, 1974-77, ptnr., 1978-87; shareholder Lyons, Pipes & Cook, P.C., Mobile, 1988—. Past mem., bd. dirs. Mobile Touchdown Club, Presch. for the Sensory Impaired; mem. United Way, 1989—; chmn. adv. bd. Cumberland Sch. of Law, Birmingham; sec., treas., vice chmn., chmn. Southeastern Admiralty Law Inst., Athens, Ga., 1996—. 1st lt. U.S. Army. Mem. ABA, Ala. Bar Assn., Mobile Bar Assn. (chmn. admiralty and maritime law com.), Maritime Law Assn. U.S. (assoc.), Ala. Wildlife Fedn. (past dir.), Mobile Area C. of C. (past vice chmn., gen. counsel), Kiwanis (past dir.), Mobile County Wildlife Assn., Mobile Propeller Club, Mobile Area C. of C. Diplomat Club, among others. Avocations: hunting, fishing. Admiralty, Property, real (including real estate development, water), Commercial, contracts (including sales of goods; commercial financing). Office: Lyons Pipes & Cook PC 2 N Royal St Mobile AL 36602-3896

QUINBY, WILLIAM ALBERT, lawyer, mediator, arbitrator; b. Oakland, Calif., May 28, 1941; s. George W. and Marge (Diaz) Q.; m. Marion Bach, Nov. 27, 1964; 1 child, Michelle Kathleen. BA, Harvard U., 1963; JD, U. Calif., San Francisco, 1967. Bar: Calif. 1967. V.p., dir., shareholder Crosby, Heafey, Roach & May, Oakland, Calif., 1967-96; mediator, arbitrator Am. Arbitration Assn. and AAA Ctr. for Mediation, San Francisco, 1996—. Bd. dirs. Haws Drinking Faucet Co., Berkeley, Calif.; mem. faculty Hastings Coll. Advocacy, San Francisco, 1980, instr. Boalt Hall Sch. Law, 1997; co-moderator Counsel Connect's Calif. ADR Discussion Group; lectr. currents devels. in banking arbitration and mediation; mem. fellowship rev. com. HEW; mem. panel disting. neutrals Ctr. for Pub. Resources, Inc.; mem. mediation panel Nat. Assn. Securities Dealers; trustee Nat. Pre-Suit Mediation Program; adj. prof. Hastings Coll. of the Law, U. Calif., 1998, 99. Author: Six Reasons--Besides Time and Money--to Mediate Rather Than Litigate, Why Health Care Parties Should Mediate Rather Than Litigate, Starting an ADR Practice Group in a Law Firm, Mediation Process Can Amicably Solve Business Disputes and Not a Gold Rush (But Silver, Maybe), ADR Practice in a Large Law Firm Produces No Overnight Bonanzas, Making The Most of Mediation (Effective Mediation Advocacy). Bd. dirs. Big Bros. East Bay, Oakland, 1983-87, Easter Seals Soc. East Bay, 1973; past bd. dirs. Oakland East Bay Symphony, Oakland Pub. Libr. Found.; chmn. bd. dirs. Bay Area Tumor Inst. Scholar Harvard U., 1962-63. Fellow Coll. Comml. Arbitrators; mem. ABA (sect. on dispute resolution, chair programs, mediation coms.), Calif. Bar Assn., Alameda County Bar Assn., San Francisco Bar Assn., Contra Costa County Bar Assn., Calif. Bus. Trial Lawyers Assn., Am. Arbitration Assn. (large, complex case panel, comml. mediation and arbitration panels), Oakland C. of C. (past bd. dirs., exec. com.), Alameda County Barristers Club (bd. dirs., pres. 1972), Harvard Club, San Francisco Calimari Club. Republican. Avocations: running, skiing, tennis, travel, gardening. General civil litigation, Alternative dispute resolution. Office: Wulff Quinby & Sochynsky Dispute Resolution 1901 Harrison St Ste 1420 Oakland CA 94612-3582 E-mail: wquinby@aol.com.

QUINCE, PEGGY A. state supreme court justice; b. Norfolk, Va., Jan. 3, 1948; m. Fred L. Buckine; children: Peggy LaVerne, Laura LaVerne. BS in Zoology, Howard U., 1970; JD, Cath. U. of Am., 1975. Hearing officer Rental Accomodations Office, Washington; pvt. practice Norfolk, 1977-78, Bradenton, Fla., 1978-80; asst. atty. gen. criminal divsn. Atty. Gen.'s Office, 1980; apptd. 2d Dist. Ct. of Appeals, 1994-98; state supreme ct. justice Fla. Supreme Ct., 1998—. Lectr. in field. Asst. Sunday sch. tchr., mem. #3 usher bd. New Hope Missionary Bapt. Ch.; active Jack and Jill of Am., Inc., Urban League, NAACP, Tampa Orgn. for Black Affairs. Recipient award Cath.'s Neighborhood Legal Svcs. Clinic. Mem. Nat. Bar Assn., Fla. Bar, Va. State Bar, George Edgecomb Bar Assn., Hillsborough County Bar Assn., Fla. Assn. Women Lawyers, Hillsborough Assn. Women Lawyers, Tampa Bay Inn of Ct., Alpha Kappa Alpha. Office: 500 S Duval St Tallahassee FL 32399-6556 E-mail: supremecourt@mail.flcourts.org.*

QUINLAN, GUY CHRISTIAN, lawyer; b. Cambridge, Mass., Oct. 28, 1939; s. Guy Thomas and Yvonne (Carver) Q.; m. Mary-Ella Holst, Apr. 18, 1987. AB, Harvard Coll., 1960; JD, Harvard U., 1963. Bar: N.Y. 1964, U.S. Dist. Ct. (so. and ea. dists.) N.Y. 1965, U.S. Ct. Appeals (2d cir.) 1967, U.S. Supreme Ct. 1969, U.S. Ct. Appeals (8th cir.) 1973, (10th cir.) 1977, (4th cir.) 1993, (11th cir.) 1995, U.S. Tax Ct. 1977. Assoc. Clifford Chance, N.Y.C., 1963-70, ptnr., 1970—90, of counsel, 1991—. Past pres. Unitarian Universalist Svc. Com., Yorkville Common Pantry; Unitarian Universalist Dist. of Met. N.Y.; mem. adv. council on ministerial studies Harvard U. Div. Sch.; chair nuclear disarmament task force All Souls Unitarian Ch. Mem.: Lawyers Com. on Nuclear Policy, Amnesty Internat. Legal Network, Am. Assn. Internat. Commn. Jurists, Fed. Bar Coun., N.Y. State Bar Assn., ABA, Arm Control Assn., Harvard Club. Democrat. Antitrust, Environmental, Insurance. Office: Clifford Chance US LLP 200 Park Ave Fl 8E New York NY 10166-0899

QUINN, ANDREW PETER, JR., lawyer, insurance executive retired; b. Providence, Oct. 22, 1923; s. Andrew Peter and Margaret (Canning) Q.; m. Sara G. Bullard, May 30, 1952; 1 child, Emily H. AB, Brown U., 1945; LLB, Yale U., 1950. Bar: R.I. 1949, Mass. 1960, U.S. Tax Ct. 1960, U.S. Supreme Ct. 1986. Pvt. practice, Providence, 1950-59; ptnr. Letts & Quinn, 1950-59; with Mass. Mut. Life Ins. Co., Springfield, 1959—88, exec. v.p., gen. counsel, 1971-88; of counsel Day, Berry & Howard, Hartford, Conn. and Boston, 1988-99; retired, 1999. Pres., trustee MML Series Investment Fund, 1971-88; bd. dirs. Sargasso Mut. Ins. Co., Ltd., 1986-95, pres., 1986-89, chmn. bd. dirs., 1989-93. Trustee, MacDuffie Sch., 1974-87, chmn. bd., 1978-85; trustee Baystate Med., Springfield, 1977-80. Lt. (j.g.) USNR, 1944-46. Mem. ABA (co-chmn. nat. conf. lawyers and life ins. cos. 1973), Assn. Life Ins. Counsel (pres. 1983-84), Am. Coun. Life Ins. (chmn. legal sect. 1971, Anderson Disting. Svc. award 1998), Life Ins. Assn. Mass. (chmn. exec. com. 1975-77), Brown U. Alumni Assn. (bd. dirs. 1969-72), N.Y. Yacht Club, Longmeadow Country Club, Dunes Club, Hillsboro Club, Colony Club (Springfield, Mass.), Conn. Valley Brown U. (past pres.). Corporate, general, Insurance. Home: 306 Ellington Rd Longmeadow MA 01106-1559

QUINN, FRANCIS XAVIER, arbitrator, mediator, author, lecturer; b. Dunmore, Pa., June 9, 1932; s. Frank T. and Alice B. (Maher) Q.; m. Marlene Stoker Quinn; children: Kimberly, Catherine, Cameron, Lindsay, Megan, Savannah, Jackson Blair. BA, Fordham U., 1956, MA, 1958; STB, Woodstock Coll., 1964; MS in Indsl. Rels., Loyola U., Chgo., 1966; PhD in Indsl. Rels., Calif. Western U., 1966. Assoc. dir. Inst. Indsl. Rels. St. Joseph's Coll., Phila., 1966-68; Manpower fellow Temple U., Phila., 1969-74, asst. to dean Sch. Bus. Adminstrn., 1972-78. Arbitrator Fed. Mediation and Conciliation Svc., Nat. Mediation Bd., Am. Arbitration Assn., Nat. Assn. Railroad Referees, Dem. Nat. Steering Com.; ; apptd. to Rail Emergency Bd., 1975, to Fgn. Service Grievance Bd., 1976, 78, 80. Author: The Ethical Aftermath of Automation, 1963, Ethics and Advertising, 1965, Population Ethics, 1968, The Evolving Role of Women in the World of Work, 1969, Developing Community Responsibility, 1970; editor: The Ethical Aftermath Series; contbr. articles to profl. jours. Chmn. Hall of Fame com. Internat. Police Assn., 1990-92, Tulsa City-County Mayor's Task Force to Combat Homelessness, 1991-92; mem. exec. bd. Tulsa Met. Ministries, 1990-92, Labor-Religion Coun. Okla., 1990-98; pastoral coun. Holy Family Roman Cath. Ch., 2000-03, formation adv. bd., 2002-04. Named Tchr. of Yr. Freedom Found., 1959; recipient Human Rels. award City of Phila.; inducted into Hall of Fame, Internat. Police Assn., 2000. Mem. Nat. Acad. Arbitrators (v.p. 1999-2001), Indsl. Rels. Rsch. Assn., Assn. for Social Econs., Soc. for Dispute Resolution, Am. Arbitration Assn. (arbitrator), Nat. Assn. Railroad Refs. (pres. 2000-04, arbitrator), Internat. Soc. Labor Law and Social Security. Democrat. Home: 4213 Blackhaw Ave Fort Worth TX 76109-1618 E-mail: FXQ@prodigy.com.

QUINN, JOHN PETER, lawyer, software designer; b. Bay City, Mich., Aug. 20, 1944; s. William Joseph and Helen Marie (Darland) Q.; m. Dana Elizabeth Hillman, June 1969 (div. 1974); 1 child, Adrianne; m. Sharon Margaret Goode, June 27, 1981; children: William, Catherine, Mary Margaret, John, Daniel. BS in Chemistry, Xavier U. La., New Orleans, 1968; JD cum laude, U. Mich., 1972. Bar: Mich. 1974, U.S. Dist. Ct. (ea. dist.) Mich. 1977, U.S. Ct. Appeal (6th cir.) 1977, U.S. Supreme Ct. 1985. Police officer Detroit Police Dept., 1973-74; counsel Detroit Bd. Police Commrs., 1974-76; chair bd. dirs. Quinn & Budaj, P.C., Detroit, 1977-85; asst. corp. counsel Detroit Law Dept., 1976-77, prin./supervising chief asst. corp. counsel, 1985—. Def. mediator Mediation Tribunal Assn., Detroit, 1995—; spkr. profl. seminars and confs. Contbr. articles to profl. jours. Chair bd. dirs. S.W. Alliance of Neighborhoods, Detroit, 1995-2000; founding mem. bd. dirs. S.W. Cmty. and Neighborhood Devel. Orgn., Detroit, 1990. With U.S. Army, 1968-70, Munich. Recipient Spirit of Detroit award Detroit City Coun., 1979. Mem. Detroit Bar Assn. (pub. adv. com., mediator, chair dist. ct. sect.), Assn. Def. Trial Counsel. Roman Catholic. Avocations: cottage living, camping, woodworking, classical languages. Office: City of Detroit Law Dept 1650 First Nat Bldg Detroit MI 48226

QUINN, LINDA CATHERINE, lawyer; b. Rockville Centre, N.Y., 1948; BA, Mt. Holyoke Coll., 1969; JD, Georgetown U., 1972. Bar: N.Y. 1973. Law clk. Hon. J. Joseph Smith U.S. Ct. Appeals (2d cir.), 1972-73; assoc. Sullivan & Cromwell, 1973-80; atty. fellow SEC, 1980-82, assoc. dir. divsn. corp. fin., 1982-84, exec. asst. to chmn., 1984-86, dir. corp. fin. divsn., 1986-96; ptnr. Shearman & Sterling, N.Y.C., 1996—. Named one of 50 Top Women Lawyers Nat. Law Jour., 1998. Mem.: ABA. Corporate, general, Securities. Office: Shearman & Sterling 599 Lexington Ave Fl 16 New York NY 10022-6069 E-mail: lquinn@shearman.com.

QUINN, R. JOSEPH, district judge; m. Carole Quinn. BA, St. John's U.; JD, Hamline U. Minn. State rep., 1983-90; formerly judge Minn. Supreme Ct., 1991-99; now. judge Dist. Ct., 1999; chief judge 10th judicial dist., Minn. Office: Anoka County Court 325 E Main St Anoka MN 55303-2483

QUINN, WILLIAM FRANCIS, lawyer, director; b. Rochester, N.Y., July 13, 1919; s. Charles Alvin and Elizabeth (Dorrity) Q.; m. Nancy Ellen Witbeck, July 11, 1942; children: William Francis, Stephen Desford, Timothy Charles, Christopher Thomas, Ann Cecily, Mary Kaiulani, Gregory Anthony. BS summa cum laude, St. Louis U., 1940; LL.B. cum laude, Harvard U., 1947. Bar: Hawaii 1948. Ptnr. Robertson, Castle & Anthony, Honolulu, 1947-57; gov. Ter. of Hawaii, Honolulu, 1957-59, State of Hawaii, Honolulu, 1959-62; ptnr. Quinn & Moore, Honolulu, 1962-64; exec. v.p. Dole Co., Honolulu., 1964-65, pres., 1965-72; ptnr. Jenks, Kidwell, Goodsill & Anderson, Honolulu, 1972-73, Goodsill Anderson & Quinn, 1973-82, Goodsill Anderson Quinn & Stifel, 1982-91; ret., 1991. Mem. sr. adv. bd. 9th Cir. Jud. Coun. Served with USNR, 1942-46. Decorated knight of Holy Sepulchre Order. Mem. Pacific Club (Honolulu). Republican. Roman Catholic. Home: 4340 Pahoa Ave Apt 13C Honolulu HI 96816-5023

QUINN, YVONNE SUSAN, lawyer; b. Spring Valley, Ill., May 13, 1951; d. Robert Leslie and Shirley Eilene (Morse) Quinn. BA, U. Ill., 1973; JD, U. Mich., 1976, MA in Econs., 1977. Bar: N.Y. 1978, U.S. Dist. Ct. (ea. and so. dists.) N.Y. 1978, U.S. Ct. Appeals (3d, 5th, 9th, 10th and D.C. cirs.) 1982, U.S. Ct. Appeals (2d cir.) 1992, U.S. Ct. Appeals (4th cir.) 1994, U.S. Supreme Ct. 1982. Assoc. Cravath, Swaine & Moore, N.Y.C., 1977-80, Sullivan & Cromwell, N.Y.C., 1980-84, ptnr., 1984—. Mem. ABA, Assn. of Bar of City of N.Y., India House Club. Antitrust, Federal civil litigation, State civil litigation. Office: Sullivan & Cromwell 125 Broad St New York NY 10004-2489

QUINT, ARNOLD HARRIS, lawyer; b. Boston, Jan. 3, 1942; s. Milton and Esther (Kirshen) Q.; m. Susan Arenson, July 23, 1967; children: Edward, Michael. AB, Haverford (Pa.) Coll., 1963; LLB, Yale U., 1966. Bar: D.C. 1967. Supervisory atty. Power Commn., Washington, 1967-70; assoc. Hunton & Williams, Washington, 1970-74, ptnr., 1974—. Mem. ABA, Energy Bar Assn. (com. chmn. 1979-83, bd. dirs. 1989-92). Administrative and regulatory, FERC practice. Office: Hunton & Williams 1900 K St NW Washington DC 20006-1110 E-mail: aquint@hunton.com.

QUINTIERE, GARY GANDOLFO, lawyer; b. Passaic, N.J., Nov. 26, 1944; s. Benjamin and Sadie (Riotto) Q.; m. Judy Rosenthal, Aug. 16, 1966; children: Karen, Geoffrey. AB in Govt., Lafayette Coll., 1966; JD, George Washington U., 1969. Bar: Va. 1969, D.C. 1970. Law clk. to Judge Philip Nichols, Jr. U.S. Ct. Appeals (Fed. cir.), Washington, 1969-70; from assoc. to ptnr. Miller & Chevalier, Washington, 1970-85; ptnr. Morgan, Lewis & Bockius, Washington, 1985—. Mem. ABA, D.C. Bar Assn., Va. Bar Assn., Am. Coll. Employee Benefits Counsel. Avocations: tennis, skiing, golf. Pension, profit-sharing, and employee benefits. Home: 14 Mercy Ct Potomac MD 20854-4540 Office: Morgan Lewis & Bockius 1111 Pennsylvania Ave NW Washington DC 20004

QUIRANTES, ALBERT M. lawyer; b. Cuba, Jan. 25, 1963; came to U.S., 1966; s. Alberto adn Haydee (Mendez) Q. B in Bus., U. Miami, Fla., 1984; JD, U. Fla., 1987. Bar: Fla. 1988, U.S. Dist. Ct. (so. dist.) Fla. 1990, U.S. Dist. Ct. (mid. dist.) Fla. 1990, U.S. Ct. Appeals (11th cir.) 1990, U.S. Supreme Ct. 1991, U.S. Dist. Ct. Ariz. 1991. Pub. defender Ct. 8th cir., Gainsville, Fla., 1988-89; pvt. practice Miami, Fla., 1989—; sr. ptnr. Ticket Law Ctr., P.A., Miami, Fla., 1990—. Mem. Fla. Traffic Ct. Rules Com., Tallahassee, 1991—. Mem. Fla. Assn. Criminal Def. Attys., Dade Bar (cts. com. 1992—, criminal cts. com. 1992—), Latin C. of C., Jaycees. Administrative and regulatory, Criminal, Health. Home and Office: 1800 NW 7th St Miami FL 33125-3504 E-mail: lawyer@ticketlawyer.com.

QUIROGA-LEON, ANIBAL, lawyer, consultant, arbitrator, law educator; b. Cuzco, Peru, May 14, 1957; s. Anibal Quiroga and Vilma Leon; children: Alonso, Sol Maria. LLB, Pontificia Univ. Cath. del Peru, Lima, 1983; postgrad., U. Complutense, Madrid, 1983—85. Exec. sec. Nat. Coun. Human Rights, Lima, 1986—87; legal adviser of chamber Min. Justice, Lima, 1987—88; counselor Dist. Counsel of LIma Magistrature, Lima, 1989—90; alt. superior mem. Ct. Appeal Justice, Lima, 1990—97; mem. Conciliation and Arbitraje Ctr. of the C. of C. , Lima, 1998. Assoc. Luis Echecopar Garcia Law Office, Lima, 1989—96; external cons. World Bank, Washington, 1993; prin. ptnr. Anibal Quiroga Leon, Law Office, Lima, 1996; sr. prof. Pontificia Univ. Cath. del Peru, Lima, 1997; amb. in spl. mission Spl. Sr. Commn., Lima, 1999. Compilator, co-author: About the Constitutional Jurisdiction, 1990. Mem.: Peruvian Assn. Constnl. Law, World Soc. Mixed Jurisdictions Jurist, Internat. Procedural Assn., Iberoamerican Inst. Procedure Law, Lima Bar Assn. Civil rights, Human Rights, Constitutional. Office: Calle Roma 254 Lima 27 Peru

QUIST, GORDON JAY, federal judge; b. Grand Rapids, Mich., Nov. 12, 1937; s. George J. and Ida F. (Hoekstra) Q.; m. Jane Capito, Mar. 10, 1962; children: Scot D., George J., Susan E., Martha J., Peter K. BA, Mich. State U., 1959; JD with honors, George Washington U., 1962. Bar: D.C. 1962, Ill. 1964, U.S. Dist. Ct. (no. dist.) Ill. 1964, U.S. Supreme Ct. 1965, Mich. 1967, U.S. Dist. Ct. (we. dist.) Mich. 1967, U.S. Ct. Appeals (6th cir.) 1967. Assoc. Hollabaugh & Jacobs, Washington, 1962-64, Sonnenschein, Levinson, Carlin, Nath & Rosenthal, Chgo., 1964-66, Miller, Johnson, Snell & Cummiskey, Grand Rapids, 1967-72, ptnr., 1972-92, mng. ptnr., 1986-92; judge U.S. Dist. Ct. (we. dist.) Mich., Grand Rapids, 1992—. Mem. Code of Conduct Com. for U.S. Cts., 2001—. Bd. dirs. Wedgewood Acres-Ch. Youth Home, 1968-74, Mary Free Bed Hosp., 1979-88, Christian Ref. Publs., 1968-78, 82-88, Opera Grand Rapids, 1986-92, Mary Free Bed Brace Shop, 1988-92, Better Bus. Bur., 1972-80, Calvin Theol. Sem., 1992-93; bd. dirs. Indian Trails Camp, 1970-78, 82-88, pres., 1978, 88; code of conduct com., U.S. Cts., 2000—. Recipient Disting. Alumnus award George Washington U. Law Sch.. 1998 Mem. Am. Indicature Soc., Mich. State Bar Found., Univ. Club Grand Rapids, Order of Coif, Am. Inns Ct. Avocations: reading, travel. Office: 482 Ford Fed Courthouse 110 Michigan St NW Grand Rapids MI 49503-2313 E-mail: Gordon_J_Quist@miwd.uscourts.gov.

RAAB, IRA JERRY, lawyer, judge; b. N.Y.C., June 20, 1935; s. Benjamin and Fannie (Kirschner) R.; m. Regina Schneider, June 4, 1957 (div. 1978); children: Michael, Shelley; m. Katie Rachel McKeever, June 30, 1979 (div. 1991); children: Julie, Jennifer, Joseph; m. Gloria Silverman, Nov. 7, 1996; children: Jill, Todd, John. BBA, CCNY, 1955; JD, Bklyn. Law Sch., 1957; MPA, NYU, 1959, postgrad.; MS in Pub. Adminstrn., L.I. U., 1961; MBA, Adelphi U., 1990. Bar: N.Y. 1958, U.S. Dist. Ct. (so. and ea. dists.) N.Y. 1960, U.S. Supreme Ct. 1967, U.S. Tax Ct. 1976, U.S. Ct. Appeals (2d cir.) 1977. Pvt. practice, Woodmere, N.Y., 1958-96; agt. Westchester County Soc. Prevention of Cruelty to Children, White Plains, N.Y., 1958; counsel Dept. Correction City of N.Y., 1959, trial commr. Dept. Correction, 1976, asst. corp. counsel Tort divsn. N.Y.C. Law Dept., 1963-70; staff counsel SBA, N.Y.C., 1961-63; counsel Investigation Com. on Willowbrook State Sch., Boro Hall, S.I., N.Y., 1970; gen. counsel Richmond County Soc. Prevention of Cruelty to Children, Boro Hall, 1970-81; pro bono counsel N.Y.C. Patrolmen's Benevolent Assn., 1974-81; rep. to UN Internat. Criminal Ct., 1977-78; arbitrator Small Claims Ct. Day Cts., N.Y.C., 1970-96; arbitrator L.I. Better Bus. Bur., 1976-93, Nassau County Dist. Ct., 1978-93, arbitrator Small Claims Ct., 1978-96; spl. master N.Y. County Supreme Ct., 1977-96; judge N.Y.C. Parking Violations Bur., 1991-93. Small claims arbitrator N.Y.C. Civil Ct., 1970-96; arbitrator U.S. Dist. Ct. (ea. dist.) N.Y., 1986-96; lectr. comty. and ednl. orgns.; instr. paralegal course Lawrence Sch. Dist., N.Y., 1982-84; law prof. Briarcliff Coll., Bethpage, N.Y., 1997. Chmn. Businessmen's Luncheon Club, Wall St. Synagogue, 1968-79; exec. sec. Cmty. Mediation Ctr., Suffolk County, 1978-80, exec. v.p., 1980-81; vice chmn. Woodmere Inc., Com., 1980-81; mem. adv. bd. Nassau Expressway Com., 1979-80; bd. dirs. Woodmere Mchts. Assn., 1979-80, v.p., 1979-83, chmn., 1984-93; sec. Congregation Aish Kodesh, Woodmere, 1992-2002; candidate for dist. ct. judge Nassau County, 1987, 88, 89, 91, 93, 94, 2000; candidate for supreme ct. justice Nassau and Suffolk Counties, 1995, 98; elected judge Nassau County Dist. Ct., 1997-99; candidate for county ct., Nassau County, 1997; elected presiding judge dist. ct., 1999-2000; elected justice Nassau County Supreme Ct., 2000-. Recipient Consumer Protection award FTC, 1974, 76, 79, Recognition award Pres. Ronald Reagan, 1986, Man of Yr. award L.I. Coun. of Chambers, 1987, N.Y. State Ct. Reporters Assn., 1999. Mem. ABA (chmn. cts. and comty. com. 1988-93, exec. com. jud. adminstrn. divsn. lawyers conf. 1989-95), Am. Judges Assn. (rep. to UN 2000—, bd. govs. 1973-78, 82-88, 89-96, 97—, nat. treas. 1978-82, chmn. civil ct. ops. com. 1975-76, chmn. ednl. film com. 1974-77, editl. bd. Ct. Rev. mag. 1975-79, 82-86, chmn. spkrs. bur. com. 1976-77, chmn. legis. com. 1983-95, chmn. resolutions com. 1995-98, 2000-2002, chmn. jud. concerns com. 1997-99, historian 1988—, William H. Burnett award 1983), Am. Judges Found. (pres. 1977-79, chmn. bd. trustees 1979-83, treas. 1974-75, 76-77, trustee 1983-97, 2000—), Assn. Arbitrators of Civil Ct. City of N.Y. (past pres.), N.Y. State Bar Assn. (sec. dist., city, town and village cts. com.), Nassau County Bar Assn. (criminal cts. com., matrimonial and family ct. com., ct. com., ethics com., Supreme Ct. com.), Profl. Group Legal Svc. Assn. (past pres.), Internat. Assn. Jewish Lawyers and Jurists (com. to draft Internat. Bill of Rights to Privacy 1982, coun. 1981-95, bd. govs. 1984-95), adv. bd. comty. dispute ctr. 1979-81), K.P. (past chancellor comdr.). Democrat. State civil litigation, General practice, Personal injury (including property damage). Home: 375 Westwood Rd Woodmere NY 11598-1624 Office: Supreme Court 100 Supreme Ct Dr Mineola NY 11501 Fax: 516-571-2555. E-mail: iraab@courts.state.ny.us.

RAAB, SHELDON, lawyer, Bklyn. Nov. 30, 1937; s. Morris and Eva (Shereshevsky) R.; m. Judith Deutsch, Dec. 15, 1963; children: Michael Kenneth, Elisabeth Louise, Andrew John. AB, Columbia U., 1958; LLB cum laude, Harvard U., 1961. Bar: N.Y. 1961, U.S. Ct. Appeals (2d cir.) 1963, U.S. Dist. Ct. (so. and ea. dists.) 1967. Dep. asst. atty. gen. State of N.Y., 1961-63, asst. atty gen., 1963-64; assoc. Fried, Frank, Harris, Shriver & Jacobson and predecessor firm, N.Y.C., 1964-69, ptnr., 1970-81, inc. ptnr., 1981—. Mem. exec. com. lawyers' div. United Jewish Appeal, 1982—. Mem. ABA, Am. Law Inst., N.Y. State Bar Assn. (trial lawyers sect. 1968—), Assn. of Bar of City of N.Y. (adminstrv. law com. 1968-71, spl. com. electric power and environment 1971-73, chmn. energy com. 1974-79, fed. cts. com. 1981-84, state superior cts. juris. com. 1985-88). Democrat. Appellate, General civil litigation, Securities. Office: Fried Frank Harris Shriver & Jacobson 1 New York Plz Fl 22 New York NY 10004-1980

RAAS, DANIEL ALAN, lawyer; b. Portland, Oreg., July 6, 1947; s. Alan Charles and Mitzi (Cooper) R.; m. Deborah Ann Becker, Aug. 5, 1973; children: Amanda Beth, Adam Louis. BA, Reed Coll., 1969; JD, NYU, 1972. Bar: Wash. 1973, Calif. 1973, U.S. Dist. Ct. (we. dist.) Wash. 1973, U.S. Ct. Appeals (9th cir.) 1975, U.S. Supreme Ct. 1977, U.S. Tax Ct. 1983, U.S. Ct. Claims 1984. Atty. Seattle Legal Svcs, VISTA, 1972-73; reservation atty. Quinault Indian Nation, Taholah, Wash., 1973-76, Lummi Indian Nation, Bellingham, Wash., 1976-97, spl. counsel, 1997—; mem. Raas, Johnsen & Stuen, P.S., Bellingham, 1982—. Cons. Falmouth Inst., Fairfax, Va., 1992-2000, Nat. Am. Ind. Ct. Judges Assn., McLean, Va., 1976-80. Rules chmn. Whatcom County Dem. Conv., Bellingham, 1988, 92, 94, 96; bd. dirs. Congregation Beth Israel, Bellingham, 1985-2000, pres., 1990-92; mem. adv. com. legal asst. program Bellingham Vocat. Tech. Inst., 1985-91; trustee Whatcom County Law Libr., 1978-2002; pres. Vol. Lawyer Program, 1990-93, bd. dirs., 1988-94; pres. Cliffside Cmty. Assn., 1978-80, bd. dirs., 1977-89; bd. dirs. Friends Maritime Heritage Ctr., 1983-86, Samish Camp Fire Coun., 1988-94, pres. 1991-94, v.p., 1989-91, regional v.p. Union Am. Hebrew Congregations, 1986-93, nat. trustee, 1995—, exec. com., 1995-99, sec. Pacific N.W. region, 1993-95, pres., 1995-99. John Ben Snow scholar, NYU, 1969-70, Root-Tilden scholar, NYU, 1970-72. Mem. Wash. State Bar Assn. (trustee Ind. law sect. 1989-95, Pro Bono award 1991), Whatcom County Bar Assn. (v.p. 1981, pres. 1982, Pro Bono award 1991), Grays Harbor Bar Assn. (v.p. 1976). General civil litigation, Commercial, consumer (including collections, credit), Native American. Home: 1929 Lake Crest Dr Bellingham WA 98226-4510 Office: Raas Johnsen & Stuen PS 1503 E St Bellingham WA 98225-3007

RABB, BRUCE, lawyer; b. Cambridge, Mass., Oct. 4, 1941; s. Maxwell M. and Ruth (Criedenberg) R.; m. Harriet Rachel Schaffer, Jan. 4, 1970; children: Alexander Charles, Katherine Anne. AB, Harvard U., 1962; Cert. d'Etudes Politiques, Institut d'Etudes Politiques, Paris, 1963; LLB, Columbia U., 1966. Bar: N.Y. 1966. Law clk. to judge U.S. Ct. Appeals (5th cir.), 1966-67; assoc. Stroock & Stroock & Lavan, N.Y.C., 1967-68, 71-75, ptnr., 1976-91, Kramer Levin Naftalis & Frankel LLP, N.Y.C., 1991—. Staff asst. to Pres. U.S., 1969-70; vice-chmn. Lawyers Com. Human Rights, 1977-95, nat. coun., 1996—; supr. bd. dirs. Agora-Gazeta, sp.zo.o., 1993-98, Agora-Druk, sp.zo.o., 1995-98; pub. mem. Adminstrv. Conf. U.S., 1982-86, 89-92, spl. counsel, 1986-88. Sec. Lehrman Inst., 1978-88; bd. dirs. Citizens Union of N.Y., 1981-87, 88-94, 95-2001, 02--, treas., 2002--; bd. dirs. Am. Friends of Alliance Israelite Universelle, 1987-2001, Human Rights Watch, 1987—, Welfare Law Ctr., 1997—, Sabre Found., 2003—; mem. Human Rights Watch/Ams., 1982—, Human Rights Watch/Helsinki, 1985-97, Fund for Free Expression, 1987-97, Human Rights Watch/Middle East and No. Africa, 1989—, vice chmn., 1990—; mem. internat. adv. com. Internat. Parliamentary Group for Human Rights in the Soviet Union, 1984-88, Prin. of the Coun. for Excellence in Govt., 1990—; adv. coun. Doctors of the World USA, 1996—, FilmAid Internat., 2000-2003, dir., sec., 2003—. Mem. ABA (adv. panel Internat. Human Rights Trial Observer project), Am. Law Inst., Assn. of Bar of City of N.Y. (fed. legis., internat. law chair 1992-95, internat. human rights, civil rights, legal edn. and admission to bar, internat. trade coms., coun. fgn. affairs), Coun. Fgn. Rels., Harvard Club N.Y.C., Met. Club of Washington. Corporate, general, Finance, Private international. Office: Kramer Levin et al 919 3rd Ave New York NY 10022-3902

RABB, HARRIET SCHAFFER, university administrator, government official, lawyer, educator; b. Houston, Sept. 12, 1941; d. Samuel S. and Helen G. Schaffer; m. Bruce Rabb, Jan. 4, 1970; children: Alexander, Katherine. BA in Govt., Barnard Coll., 1963; JD, Columbia U., 1966. Bar: N.Y. 1966, U.S. Supreme Ct. 1969, D.C. 1970. Instr. seminar on constl. litigation Rutgers Law Sch., 1966-67; staff atty. Center for Constl. Rights, 1966-69; spl. counsel to commr. consumer affairs N.Y.C. Dept. Consumer Affairs, 1969-70; sr. staff atty. Stern Community Law Firm, Washington, 1970-71; asst. dean urban affairs Law Sch., Columbia U., N.Y.C., 1971-84, prof. law, dir. clin. edn., 1984-99, George M. Jaffen prof. law and social responsibility, 1991-99, vice dean, 1992-93; gen. counsel Dept. Health and Human Svcs., Washington, 1993—2001; v.p., gen. counsel Rockefeller U., 2001—. Mem. faculty employment and tng. policy Harvard Summer Inst., Cambridge, Mass., 1975-79 Author: (with Agid, Cooper and Rubin) Fair Employment Litigation Manual, 1975, (with Cooper and Rubin) Fair Employment Litigation, 1975. Bd. dirs. Ford Found., 1977-89, N.Y. Civil Liberties Union, 1972-83, Lawyers Com. for Civil Rights Under Law, 1978-86, Legal Def. Fund NAACP, 1978-93, Mex. Am. Legal Def. and Edn. Fund, 1986-90, Legal Aid Soc., 1990-93; mem. exec. com. Human Rights Watch, 1991-93; trustee Trinity Episcopal Sch. Corp., 1991-93. Office: Rockefeller U 1230 York Ave New York NY 10021

RABB, LLOYD LEATH, lawyer; b. Corona, Calif., June 11, 1953; s. Lloyd Leath Rabb, Jr. and Mildred Marie Rabb; children: Matthew, Michael. BS in Bus. Adminstrn., U. Ariz., 1982, JD, 1985. Bar: Ariz. 1985, Tex. 1993, Colo., N.Mex. 1996. Locomotive engr. So. Pacific R.R., Tucson, 1973—86; atty. Dickerson Butler & Rabb, Tucson, 1987—98, The Crow Law Firm, Tucson, 1998—2001, The Rabb Penny Firm, Tucson, 2001—. Designated legal counsel United Transp. Union, Tucson, 1992—. Mem.: Acad. Rail Labor Attys. (pres. 1992). Personal injury (including property damage), Product liability, Labor (including EEOC, Fair Labor Standards Act, labor-management relations, NLRB, OSHA). Office: The Rabb Penny Law Firm 3320 N Campbell Ave #150 Tucson AZ 85719

RABBITT, DANIEL THOMAS, JR., lawyer; b. St. Louis, Sept. 19, 1940; s. Daniel Thomas and Charlotte Ann (Carpenter) R.; m. Susan Lee Scherger, July 26, 1969. BA in Commerce, St. Louis U., 1962, JD cum laude, 1964.

Bar: Mo. 1964, U.S. Supreme Ct. 1970. Assoc. Moser, Marsalek, Carpenter, Cleary, Jaeckel, Keaney & Brown and predecessor, St. Louis, 1964-68; ptnr. Moser, Marsalek, Carpenter, Cleary, Jaeckel, Keaney & Brown, St. Louis, 1969-81, Brown, James & Rabbitt, P.C., St. Louis, 1981-91, Rabbitt, Pitzer & Snodgrass, P.C., St. Louis, 1991—. Recipient Lon Hocker Meml. Trial Atty. award Mo. Bar Found., 1975. Fellow: Am. Coll. Trial Lawyers; mem.: ABA (chmn. young lawyers sect. 1973—74, product liability adv. counsel), Bar Assn. Met. St. Louis, Internat. Assn. Def. Counsel (product liability com.), Mo. Bar Assn., Mo. Athletic Club (gov. 1978—81, v.p. 1980—81). Personal injury (including property damage), Product liability, Toxic tort. Office: 100 S 4th St Ste 400 Saint Louis MO 63102 E-mail: rabbitt@rabbitt.law.com.

RABECS, ROBERT NICHOLAS, lawyer; b. Scranton, Pa., Mar. 19, 1964; s. Nicholas and Anne Marie (Stull) R.; m. Kimberly Ann Rabecs. BA summa cum laude, U. Scranton, 1986; JD cum laude, Georgetown U., 1990. Bar: Pa. 1990, D.C. 1992. Assoc. Reed Smith Shaw & McClay, Washington, 1990-94, Hogan & Hartson, Washington, 1994—. Adj. prof. law George Washington U. Law Sch., Washington, 2002—. Columnist Managed Healthcare News, Belle Meade, N.J., 1994-98. Fulbright scholar, 1986-87; NEH undergrad. fellow, 1985. Mem. ABA, Am. Health Lawyers Assn., Pa. Bar Assn. (health law com.), D.C. Bar Assn. (health law sect.), Alpha Sigma Nu. Roman Catholic. Health. Home: 6809 Rannoch Rd Bethesda MD 20817- Office: Hogan & Hartson 555 13th St NW Washington DC 20004-1161 E-mail: rnrabecs@hhlaw.com.

RABEKOFF, ELISE JANE, lawyer; b. N.Y.C., June 26, 1959; d. Sidney and Natalie (Kaufman) R.; m. Christopher Gladstone, June 7, 1986; children: Katherine, Nicholas. AB, Princeton U., 1980; JD, Yale U., 1986. Bar: Pa. 1986, D.C. 1988, U.S. Dist. Ct. (fed. dist.) D.C. 1988. Legis. asst. Sen. D.P. Moynihan, Washington, 1980-83; law clk. judge Charle Robert Richey U.S. Dist. Ct. D.C., Washington, 1986—88; assoc. Shea & Gardner, Washington, 1988-93; v.p., gen. counsel Quadrangle Devel. Corp., Washington, 1993—. Bd. dirs. Chelsea Sch., Silver Spring, Md., 1990-95. Fellow: Am. Bar Found. Corporate, general, Labor (including EEOC, Fair Labor Standards Act, labor-management relations, NLRB, OSHA), Property, real (including real estate development, water). Office: Quadrangle Devel Corp 1001 G St NW Washington DC 20001-4545 E-mail: eliserabekoff@quad1.com.

RABIN, JACK, lawyer; b. Aug. 19, 1930; s. Leo and Bertha Rabin; m. Roberta Edith Libson, Oct. 25, 1953; children: Keith Warren, Michael Jay, Adam Douglas. Student, Bklyn. Coll., 1948-50; LLB, Bklyn. Law Sch., 1953. Bar: N.Y. 1953, U.S. Tax Ct. 1960, U.S. Ct. Claims 1964, U.S. Supreme Ct. 1964, U.S. Ct. Appeals (2d cir.) 1968. Ptnr. Hoffberg, Rabin & Engler and predecessor firms, N.Y.C., 1968-82, Javits, Hinckley, Rabin & Engler, N.Y.C., 1982-84, Phillips, Nizer, Benjamin, Krim & Ballon, N.Y.C., 1984-94, counsel, 1994—. Arbitrator gen. comml. and constrn. panel Am. Arbitration Assn., 1968—; instr. Real Estate Inst., NYU, 1976-78; ct. apptd. mediator U.S. Dist. Ct. (so. dist.), N.Y., 1994—, N.Y. Supreme Ct., N.Y. County, 1999. Assoc. editor Bklyn. Law Rev., 1952, editor-in-chief, 1953, also author law rev. note. 1st lt. JAGC, U.S. Army, 1954-57, col. res., ret., 1983. Mem. N.Y. State Bar Assn., Res. Officers Assn. U.S. (pres. Rockland County chpt. 1967-68), B'nai B'rith (pres. New City, N.Y. 1965-66). Jewish. State civil litigation, Corporate, general, Property, real (including real estate development, water). Home: Box 233 Goshen CT 06756-0233 Office: 10 W 66th St Ste 8G New York NY 10023 E-mail: sutleg@earthlink.net.

RABINOVITZ, DANIEL M. lawyer; b. Boston, Sept. 5, 1964; s. Mayer and Carol Singer Rabinovitz; m. Holly A. Rabinovitz, May 29, 1994; children: Louis I., Peter H. Grad., Union Coll., 1986; JD, Boston U., 1990. Bar: Mass., Ill. Asst. states atty. Cook County States Atty. Office, Chgo., 1990—97; assoc. Abrams, Roberts, Krickhein & Levy, Boston, 1997—99, Dwyer & Collora, LLP, Boston, 2000—. Civil rights, Criminal. Office: Dwyer & Collora LLP 600 Atlantic Ave Boston MA 02210

RABINOWITZ, SAMUEL NATHAN, lawyer; b. Hazleton, Pa., Sept. 16, 1932; s. Morris M. and Bodia (Janowitz) R.; m. Barbara Cohen, Mar. 27, 1955; children— Fredric E., Mark I., Joshua A. BA, Pa. State U., 1955; JD, Temple U., 1959. Bar: D.C. 1959, Pa. 1960. Agt. IRS, Phila., 1956—60; sole practice Phila., 1960—61; ptnr. Blank Rome, LLP, Phila., 1961—. Mem. trust com. Continental Bank, Phila., 1983-91; faculty Temple U. Sch. Law Contbr. articles to profl. jours. Active Phila. Friends Boys Town Jerusalem; bd. dirs. Jerusalem Soc. Boys Town, Phila., Friends of Ben Gurion U. the Negev, Jewish Nat. Fund Coun., Phila., Fellow Am. Coll. Trust and Estate Counsel; mem. ABA, Pa. Bar Assn., Phila. Bar Assn. (chmn. probate and trust sect. 1985-86), Green Valley Country Club, Elkview Country Club, Belaire Country Club (Delray Beach, Fla.), Pyramid Club, Golden Slipper, Maccabi/USA Sports for Israel (exec. com., counsel). Estate planning, Probate (including wills, trusts), Estate taxation. Home: 1161 Norsam Rd Gladwyne PA 19035-1419 Office: Blank Rome LLP One Logan Sq 8th Fl Philadelphia PA 19103-6998

RABY, KENNETH ALAN, lawyer, retired army officer; b. Dec. 29, 1935; s. Carl George and Helen Josette (Milne) R.; m. Shirley Rae Nelson, June 2, 1957; children: Randolph Carlton, Shelly Ann. BA, U. S.D., 1957, JD, 1960; grad. with honors, Command and Gen. Staff Coll., 1975, U.S. Army War Coll., 1981. Bar: S.D. 1960, Ga. 1988, Supreme Ct. Ga., Supreme Ct. S.D., Ga. Ct. Appeals, U.S. Supreme Ct. Commd. 2d lt. U.S. Army, 1957, advanced through grades to col. JAGC, 1979, ret., 1987; dep. staff judge adv. Am. Divsn., Chu Lai, Vietnam, 1968-69; chief legal team U.S. Army Inf. Sch., Ft. Benning, Ga., 1969-71; team chief, acting divsn. chief adminstrv. law divsn. Office JAG, Dept. Army, 1971-74; staff judge adv. Hdqs. 24th Inf. Divsn., Ft. Stewart, Ga., 1974-79; staff judge adv. U.S. Army Armor Ctr., Ft. Knox, Ky., 1979; chief criminal law divsn. Office of JAG, Washington, 1981-84; sr. judge Army Ct. Mil. Rev., Falls Church, Va., 1984-87; staff atty. Ga. Ct. Appeals, 1987—; chief mil. def. counsel U.S. vs. Calley (My Lai Massacre) U.S. Army, 1969—71. Former chmn., mem. Joint Service Com. on Mil. Justice, 1981-84; mem. Mil. Justice Act of 1983 Adv. Commn., 1984-87; army liaison to criminal law sect. ABA, 1981-84. Eagle Scout Boy Scouts Am., 1952—53. Decorated Legion of Merit, Bronze Star with oak leaf cluster, Meritorious Svc. medal with 2 oak leaf clusters, Joint Svc. Commendation medal, Air medal, Army Commendation medal with oak leaf cluster, Army Achievement medal. Mem.: FBA (chmn. law enforcement liaison com. 1986—87), Ga. Bar Assn., Assn. U.S. Army, Scottish Rite (32d degree, KCCH), Shriners, Masons, Order Ea. Star (grand chpt. Ga. 1999—2000, worthy grand patron, gen. grand chpt. parliamentarian 2003—), Theta Xi, Delta Theta Phi. Home: 575 Spender Trce Atlanta GA 30350-5017 Office: Staff Atty Ga Ct Appeals Jud Bldg Rm 336 Capitol Sq Atlanta GA 30334-9003 E-mail: alan.raby@juno.com.

RACHANOW, GERALD MARVIN, lawyer, pharmacist; b. Balt., Aug. 7, 1942; s. Louis and Lillyan (Binstock) R.; m. Sally Davis, July 26, 1964; children: Mindy, Shelly, Gary. BS in Pharmacy, U. Md., 1965; JD, U. Balt., 1972. Bar: Md. 1973, U.S. Dist. Ct. Md. 1977, U.S. Supreme Ct. 1977. Consumer safety officer FDA, Rockville, Md., 1973-96, dep. dir. divsn. OTC drug evaluation, 1978-96, regulatory counsel divsn. OTC drug products, 1996—; ptnr. Rachanow & Wolfson, Owings Mills, Eldersburg, Md., 1975—. Contbr. fed. drug law exam. Nat. Assn. Bds. Pharmacy, 1985. Contbr. articles to profl. jours. Fellow Am. Soc. Pharmacy Law; mem. ABA, Soc. FDA Pharmacists, Heuisler Honor Soc. Avocations: chess, stamp and coin collecting, sports. Administrative and regulatory, Probate (including wills, trusts), Personal income taxation. Home: 6700 Sweet Clover Ct Eldersburg MD 21784-6385 Office: US FDA 5600 Fishers Ln Rockville MD 20857-0001 E-mail: rachanow@cder.fda.gov.

RACHIE, CYRUS, retired lawyer; b. Willmar, Minn., Sept. 5, 1908; s. Elias and Amanda (Lien) R.; m. Helen Evelyn Duncanson, Nov. 25, 1936; children: John Burton Rachie, Janice Carolyn MacKinnon, Elisabeth Dorthea Becker. Student, U. Minn., 1927-28; JD, George Washington U., 1932, William Mitchell Coll. Law, 1934. Bar: Minn. 1934, U.S. Supreme Ct. Atty. Minn. Hwy. Dept., 1934-43; spl. asst. atty. gen. Minn., 1946-50; counsel Luth. Brotherhood (fraternal life ins. co.), 1950-61; pvt. practice law Mpls., 1961-62; v.p., counsel Gamble-Skogmo, Inc., Mpls., 1962-64; v.p., gen. counsel Aid Assn. Lutherans, Appleton, Wis., 1964-70, sr. v.p., gen. counsel, 1970-73; with Rachie & Rachie, 1973-83; pvt. practice Minn., 1983—2001; part-time spl. master Minn. 4th Jud. Dist., 1977; ret., 2001. One of eleven com. mems. planning 1957 Luth. World Fedn. in Mpls. Councillor Nat. Luth. Coun., 1959-66, sec., 1962-64, mem. exec. com., 1965-66; United Luth. Ch. in Am. del. to 4th Assembly Luth. World Fedn., Helsinki, 1963; past pres. Luth. Welfare Soc. Minn.; past chmn. Mpls. Mayor's Coun. on Human Rels.; chmn. finance United Fund drive, 1967-68; past mem. bd. dirs. Mpls. YMCA; trustee emeritus William Mitchell Coll. Law Augsburg Coll. With USNR, 1943-46. Recipient Disting. Alumnus award William Mitchell Coll. Law, 1987. Mem. ABA, Minn. Bar Assn., Am. Legion, Minn. Fraternal Congress (past pres.), Rotary. Lutheran. Probate (including wills, trusts). Home: 7500 York Ave S Apt 101 Minneapolis MN 55435-4736

RACHLIN, ALAN SANDERS, lawyer; b. N.Y.C., Mar. 14, 1942; s. Irving Louis and Blanche (Klein) R.; m. Gail S. Kaufman, June 11, 1972 (dec. Apr. 1987); m. Charlotte D. Moslander, Aug. 15, 1992. BA, CCNY, 1965; MPA, CUNY, 1971; JD, N.Y. Law Sch., 1975. Bar: N.Y. 1976, U.S. Dist. Ct. (so. and ea. dists.) 1976, U.S. Supreme Ct. 1983. Atty. N.Y. State Dept. Ins., N.Y.C., 1976-79, sr. atty., 1979-81, assoc. atty., 1981-87, supervising atty., 1987-96, prin. atty., 1996—. With U.S. Army, 1966-67. Mem. ABA, Assn. Bar City N.Y., N.Y. State Bar Assn., N.Y. County Lawyers Assn., Med. Jurisprudence. Democrat. Jewish. Avocations: science fiction, mysteries. Office: NY State Ins Dept 25 Beaver St New York NY 10004-2310 E-mail: arachlin@ins.state.ny.us.

RACHLIN, LAUREN DAVID, lawyer; b. Buffalo, Feb. 6, 1929; s. Harry A. and Thelma (Goldberg) R.; m. Jean K. Rachlin, June 27, 1954; children: Laura Gail, Ellen Joan, James N. BS, U. Buffalo, 1948; JD, Harvard U., 1951. Bar: N.Y. 1952, U.S. Dist. Ct. (no. and we. dists.) N.Y. 1952, U.S. Supreme Ct. 1958, U.S. Ct. Appeals (2nd cir.) 1967, U.S. Tax Ct. 1952, U.S. Ct. Internat. Trade 1978. Ptnr. Rachlin & Rachlin, Buffalo, 1952-81; sr. ptnr. Kavinoky & Cook, Buffalo, 1981—. U.S. appointee to Bi-nat. Dispute Settlement Panel created under U.S.-Can. Free Trade Agreement, 1989-93; U.S. appointee N. Am. Free Trade Agreement Bi-Nat. Dispute Settlement Panel, 1994-96; arbitrator Internat. C. of C., Am. Arbitration Assn.; founder and dir. Can./U.S. Border Alliance regionalizing the bi-national trade corridor linking Toronto, Hamilton, Buffalo, Syracuse and Rochester, 1996—; founder, past pres., dir. World Trade Ctr.-Buffalo Niagara, 1986—; lectr. in field. U.S. del. to UN Human Rights Commn., 1970; cons. to temporary commn. N.Y. State Constl. Conv.; mem. Erie County Charter Rev. Commn.; mem.-at-large U.S. Nat. Commn. for UNESCO, 1972-76, chmn. human rights task force; mem. industry functional adv. com. Customs for Trade Policy Matters of U.S. Dept. Commerce, Office U.S. Trade Rep., 1987—. Mem. ABA (fgn. investment in U.S. real estate com., internat. bus. law com., subcom. on trade import), N.Y. State Bar Assn. (founding chmn. internat. sect. 1987-89, chmn. internat. divsn. 1989-94, chair legal edn. and admission to bar com. 1999-2002), World Arbitration Inst. (adv. bd., bd. dirs.), Am. Assn. Exporters & Importers (trade policy com.), Interpacific Bar Assn., Interam. Bar Assn., Customs and Internat. Trade Bar Assn., Erie County Bar Assn. Corporate, general, Estate planning, Private international. Office: Kavinoky & Cook 120 Delaware Ave Rm 600 Buffalo NY 14202-2793

RACHOFSKY, DAVID J. lawyer; b. Oceanside, N.Y., Nov. 17, 1936; s. Lester M. and Marjorie A.; m. Faith Allen; children: Robert, Patricia, Edward. BSEE, MIT, 1958; JD, Temple U., 1968. Bar: Pa., U.S. Dist. Ct. (ea. dist.) Pa., U.S. Tax. Ct., U.S. Ct. Fed. Claims, Pa. Supreme Ct. 1968. Ptnr. Dechert LLP, Phila., 1968—. Lectr. law Temple U. Law Sch., 1976-95. Contbr. articles to profl. jours. With USAF, 1969-72. Mem. ABA, Phila. Bar Assn., Internat. Fiscal Assn. (chmn. mid-Atlantic region 1985-87, mem. coun. 1986—, mem. exec. com. 1992—, v.p., sec. 1992-96, exec. v.p. 1996-98, pres. 1998-2000). Corporate taxation, International taxation. Office: Dechert LLP 4000 Bell Atlantic Tower 1717 Arch St Lbby 3 Philadelphia PA 19103-2713

RADDING, ANDREW, lawyer; b. N.Y.C., Nov. 30, 1944; m. Bonnie A. Levinson, Oct. 7, 1972; children: Judith Lynne, Joshua David. BBA, CCNY-Baruch Sch., 1965; JD, Boston U., 1968. Bar: N.Y. 1968, Md. 1977, D.C. 1977, U.S. Supreme Ct. Grad. fellow Northwestern U. Sch. Law, 1968-69; asst. counsel U.S. Ho. of Reps. Select Com. on Crime, 1969-72; asst. U.S. atty. for Dist. Md., 1972-77; ptnr. Francomano, Radding & Mannes, Balt., 1977-80, Burke, Gerber, Wilen, Francomano & Radding, Balt., 1980-85, Blades & Rosenfeld P.A., Balt., 1985-97, Adelberg, Rudow, Dorf and Hendler LLC, Balt., 1997—. Mem. adj. faculty clin. practice skills, criminal law, fed. criminal practice U. Balt. Sch. Law, 1980—; mem. trial experience com. U.S. Dist. ct., 1986-88; apptd. by gov. State Adminstrv. Bd. of Election Laws, 1995-96; instr. professionalism course Md. State Bar Assn., 1999—. Bd. dirs. Copper Hill Condominium, 1979-82, pres., 1981-82; vice chair Lawyers for Erlich for Gov. Com., 2002; mem. subcom. Md. Republican Conv., 1981; sen. C.M. Mathias Jud. Selection com., 1986, chmn. U.S. Dist. Ct. Bicentennial Program, 1989-90; mem. Mayor's Domestic Violence Coord. com., 2001—. Mem.: Nat. Arbitration Forum (arbitrator), U.S. Arbitration and Mediation (inquiry panel and peer rev. panel atty. grievance com. 1991—, arbitrator and mediator), Md. Inst. Continuing Profl. Edn. for Lawyers (bd. govs. 1987—92), U.S. Atty. Alumni Assn. Md. (pres. 1978—), Fed. Bar Assn. (Balt. chpt. pres. 1986—87), Balt. City Bar Assn. (jud. selection com. 1990—92, 1994—, chmn. 1996—97, exec. coun. 1998—99, co-chmn. membership com. 1999—2000, exec. coun. 2000—, 2000—, fee arbitration chmn. 2001—02, co-chair 2002—03), Md. Bar Assn., ABA. Jewish. Federal civil litigation, State civil litigation, Criminal. Office: Adelberg Rudow et al LLC 2 Hopkins Plz Baltimore MD 21201-2930 E-mail: aradding@adelbergrudow.com.

RADER, RALPH TERRANCE, lawyer; b. Clarksburg, W.Va., Dec. 5, 1947; s. Ralph Coolidge and Jeanne (Cover) R.; m. Rebecca Jo Vorderman, Mar. 22, 1969; children: Melissa Michelle, Allison Suzanne. BSME, Va. Poly. Inst., 1970; JD, Am. U., 1974. Bar: Va. 1975, U.S. Ct. Customs and Patent Appeals, 1977, U.S. Dist. Ct. (ea. dist.) Mich. 1978, Mich. 1979, U.S. Ct. Appeals (6th cir.) 1979, U.S. Dist. Ct. (we. dist.) Mich. 1981, U.S. Ct. Appeals (fed. cir.) 1983. Supervisory patent examiner U.S. Patent Office, Washington, 1970-77; patent atty., ptnr. Cullen, Sloman, Cantor, Grauer, Scott & Rutherford, Detroit, 1977-88; ptnr. Dykema, Gossett, Detroit, 1989-96, Rader, Fishman & Grauer, Bloomfield Hills, Mich., 1996—. Contbr. articles to profl. jours. Mem. adminstrv. bd. 1st United Meth. Ch., Birmingham, Mich., 1980—. With U.S. Army, 1970-76. Mem. ABA, Am. Patent Law Assn., Mich. Patent Law Assn., Mich. Bar (governing coun. patent, trademark and copyright law sect. 1981-84), Engring. Soc. Detroit, Masons, Tau Beta Pi, Pi Tau Sigma, Phi Kappa Phi. Methodist. Federal civil litigation, Patent, Trademark and copyright. Home: 4713 Riverchase Dr Troy MI 48098-4186 Office: Rader Fishman & Grauer 39533 Woodward Ave Ste 140 Bloomfield Hills MI 48304-5098 E-mail: rtr@raderfishman.com.

RADER, STEVEN PALMER, lawyer; b. Charlotte, N.C., Dec. 30, 1952; s. Alvin Marion Jr. and Shirley Ninabelle (Palmer) Rader; m. Victoria Rolinsky, 2001. AB, Duke U., 1975; postgrad., Stetson U., 1975-76; JD, Wake Forest U., 1978. Bar: N.C. 1978, U.S. Dist. Ct. (ea. dist.) N.C. 1979. Assoc. Wilkinson and Vosburgh, Washington, N.C., 1978-81; pvt. practice Washington, 1981-88; spl. asst. to sec. N.C. Dept. Human Resources, Raleigh, 1988-89, asst. dir. office legal affairs, 1989-91, gen. counsel, 1991-93; ptnr. Wilkinson & Rader, P.A., Washington, 1993—. Commr. Nat. Conf. Commrs. on Uniform State Laws, 1985-93; gen. counsel N.C. Rep. Party, 1992-97; commr. N.C. Rules Rev. Commn., 1997-99. Mem., sec. City of Washington Human Rels. Coun., 1981-83; chmn. Beaufort County Rep. party, Washington, 1983-87, 1st Congl. Dist. Rep. party, N.C., 1985-92; v.p. East Main St. Area Neighborhood Assn., 1983-85, 1st v.p., Ocean Villas Homeowners Assn., 1999—; del. Rep. Nat. Conv., 1984, 88, 92; Presdl. elector from N.C., U.S. Electoral Coll., 2000. Mem. N.C. State Bar, 2d Jud. Dist. Bar, Beaufort County Hist. Soc. (v.p. 1981-85, pres. 1985-86). Lutheran. Avocations: boating, classic automobiles, travel. Home: PO Box 1901 Washington NC 27889-1901 Office: Wilkinson & Rader PA PO Box 732 Washington NC 27889-0732

RADIN, STEVEN S. lawyer; b. Newark, N.J. s. Morris and Sara Radin; m. Karen Burman; children: Jonathan, Elizabeth Radin Jacobs. AB, Seton Hall U., 1957; LLB, JD, Columbia Law Sch., 1960. Atty. Sills Cummis Radin Tischman Gross & Epstein, Newark. 2d lt. U.S. Army. Banking, Bankruptcy, Insurance. Office: Sills Cummis Radin Tischman Gross & Epstein One Riverfront Plaza Newark NJ 07102

RADLO, EDWARD JOHN, lawyer, mathematician; b. Pawtucket, R.I., Mar. 7, 1946; s. Edward Zygmund and Sue Mary (Borek) R.; m. Patricia Jackson, Feb. 22, 1989; children: Heather Sue, Graeme Michael, Connor Andrew. BS, MIT, 1967; JD, Harvard U., 1972. Bar: Calif. 1972, U.S. Dist. Ct. (no. dist.) Calif. 1972, R.I. 1973, U.S. Patent Office 1973, Can. Patent Office 1974. Staff dir. Atty. Gen.'s Adv. Commn. on Juvenile Code Revision, Boston, 1970-72; law clk. R.I. Supreme Ct., 1972-73; patent atty. Honeywell Info. Systems, Waltham, Mass., 1973-74, Varian Assocs., Palo Alto, Calif., 1974-78, Ford Aerospace Corp., Palo Alto, Calif., 1978-83, patent counsel, 1983-90; ptnr. Fenwick & West LLP, Mountain View, Calif., 1991—; lectr. law U. Calif., San Jose State U., U. Santa Clara, 1975-78; organizer So. Peninsula Emergency Comms. Sys., 1979— . Mem., Lawyers' Alliance for Nuclear Arms Control, 1982-83, Environ. Def. Fund., 1979— , Los Altos Hills (Calif.) Emergency Comms. Com. With USPHS, 1967-69. Mem. Silicon Valley Intellectual Property Law Assn., San Francisco Intellectual Property Law Assn., ABA, Calif. Bar (intellectual property sect.), No. Calif. Contest Club (pres. 1984-85), Assn. Radio Amateurs of So. New England Inc. (sec. 1962-63), Sigma Xi. Intellectual property, Private international, Patent. Home: 28040 Elena Rd Los Altos Hills CA 94022-2454 Office: Fenwick & West LLP 801 California St Mountain View CA 94041-

RADNOR, ALAN T. lawyer; b. Cleve., Mar. 10, 1946; s. Robert Clark and Rose (Chester) R.; m. Carol Sue Hirsch, June 22, 1969; children: Melanie, Joshua, Joanna. BA, Kenyon Coll., 1967; MS in Anatomy, Ohio State U., 1969, JD, 1972. Bar: Ohio 1972. Ptnr. Vorys, Sater, Seymour & Pease, Columbus, Ohio, 1972—. Adj. prof. law Ohio State U., Columbus, 1979-99. Author: Cross-Examining Doctors: A Practical Guide, 1999; contbr. articles to profl. jours. Bd. dirs., trustee Congregation Tifereth Israel, Columbus, 1975—, pres., 1985-87; trustee Columbus Mus. Art, 1995-98. Named Boss or Yr., Columbus Assn. Legal Secs., 1983. Fellow Am. Coll. Trial Lawyers; mem. ABA, Ohio State Bar Assn., Columbus Bar Assn., Def. Rsch. Inst., Internat. Assn. Def. Counsel. Avocations: reading, sculpture. Personal injury (including property damage), Product liability. Home: 400 S Columbia Ave Columbus OH 43209-1629 Office: Vorys Sater Seymour & Pease 52 E Gay St PO Box 1008 Columbus OH 43216-1008

RADOGNO, JOSEPH ANTHONY, lawyer; b. Chgo., Dec. 7, 1958; s. Nunzio Concetto and Bernice M. Radogno; m. Randi Ellen Weinberg, Sept. 28, 1991; 1 child, Celestina Nicole. BA, U. Ill., 1980; JD, Ill. Inst. Tech., 1984. Bar: Ill. 1984. Counsel Allstate Ins. Co., Northbrook, Ill., 1989—. Insurance.

RADON, JENIK RICHARD, lawyer; b. Berlin, Jan. 14, 1946; came to U.S., 1951, naturalized, 1956; s. Louis and Irmgard (Hinz) R.; m. Heidi B. Duerbeck, June 10, 1971 (dec. Sept. 1999); 1 child, Kaara H.D. BA, Columbia Coll., 1967; MCP, U. Calif., Berkeley, 1971; JD, Stanford U., 1971. Bar: Calif. 1972, N.Y. 1975, U.S. Ct. Appeals (2d cir.) 1975, U.S. Dist. Ct. (so. dist.) N.Y. 1975. Atty. Radon & Ishizumi, N.Y.C. and Tokyo, 1981—; counsel Walter, Conston, Alexander & Green, N.Y.C., 1991—2000, ptnr., 2000. Lectr. Polish Acad. Scis., 1980, Tokyo Arbitration Assn., 1983, Japan External Trade Orgn., 1983, 86, Japan Mgmt. Assn., 1983, 90, Japan Inst. Internat. Bus. Law, 1983-84, Va. Ctr. World Trade, 1985, UN Indsl. Devel. Orgn., Warsaw, 1987, Wichita World Trade Coun., 1987, Inst. Nat. Economy of Poland, 1987, Hungarian Econ. Roundtable, 1987, Tallinn, 1988, USSR Com. on Sci. and Tech., 1988, USSR Fgn. Trade Ministry, 1988, Tallinn Tech. Inst., 1988, Tartu State U., 1988, U. Ottawa, 1988-89, Palm Beach World Trade Coun., 1988, Fla. Atlantic U., 1988, Bus. Assn. Latin Am. Studies, 1989—, Assn. France-Poland, 1989, Russian and East European Studies Inst. Stanford U., 1989, Ukrainian Profl. Assn. N.Y. and N.J., 1989, Columbia U. Harriman Inst., 1989, Inst. East-West Security Studies, 1989, Friedrich-Schiller U. Jena, East Germany, 1990, East European Inst. Free U. Berlin, numerous others; bd. dirs. Gland Pharma Ltd., India, 1996—, HTM Sport, Estonia, 1993—; pub. Baltic Rev., 1993—, City Paper (Baltic), 1993—; mem. exec. com. Vetter Group, Germany; adj. mem. faculty/lectr. Stanford Sch. of Law, 2000-02, Stanford Bus. Sch., 2000-01, Columbia Sch. Internat. Pub. Affairs, 2002—, Indira Gandhi Inst. for Devel. Rsch., Bombay, 2003—. Editor-in-chief Stanford Jour. Internat. Studies, 1970-71; contbr. The International Acquisitions Handbook, 1987, Negotiating and Financing Joint Ventures Abroad, 1989, How to Form and Manage Successful Strategic Alliances, 1990, Risks Management in International Business, 1991, Comrade Goes Private, 1992, Investing in Reform, 1991, Fordham Internat. Law Jour., 1996, various jours. in U.S., Germany, Canada. Active Am. Coun. on Germany, N.Y.C., 1978—; vice-chmn. U.S.-Polish Econ. Coun., 1989-93; mem. exec. com. Afghanistan Relief Com., N.Y.C., 1980-95; bd. dirs. Columbia Coll. Alumni Assn., 1988-92, nat. coun., 1996-98, Freedom Medicine, 1987-94, chmn., 1989-94; trustee Direct Relief Internat., Santa Barbara, Calif., 1987-89; founder and dir. Eesti and Eurasian Fellowship of Columbia U., 1990—; profl. advisor Harriman Inst., 1993—; advisor Estonian Ministries of Economy, Reform and Justice, 1991-95; advisor to Parliament Republic of Georgia, 1996-98, to Pres. of Georgia, 1999—; advisor Min. of Fin. of Georgia, 1998-2000, Georgian Internat. Oil Corp., 1998—; chmn. Estonian-Am. C. of C., 1990-93, Deutsche Stiftung fuer internationale rechtliche Zusammenarbeit, Estonia Commn., Beirat, 1992-94. Recipient Order of Honor award Republic of Georgia, 2000. Mem. ABA, Asia-Pacific Lawyers Assn., German-Am. Law Assn. Roman Catholic. Banking, Corporate, general, Private international. Office: Radon & Ishizumi 269 W 71st St New York NY 10023-3701

RADTKE, DEREK PAUL, lawyer; b. Edmonds, Wash., May 5, 1970; AA in Audio Engring., Shoreline C.C., Seattle, 1990; BA in English Composition, U. Wash., 1993; JD, Gonzaga U., 1997. Bar: Wash. 97, U.S. Ct. Appeals (9th cir.) 98, U.S. Dist. Ct. (we. dist.) Wash. 99, U.S. Supreme Ct. 02. Assoc. Buckley & Assocs., Seattle, 1998—. Mem.: Wash. State Trial Lawyers. Personal injury (including property damage), Insurance, General civil litigation. Office: Buckley & Assocs 675 S Lane St Ste 300 Seattle WA 98104 Fax: 206-622-0688.

RADVANYI, ILDIKO, lawyer; b. Budapest, Hungary, Oct. 26, 1961; m. István Z. Skrinyár; 1 child, Bianca Lilla. JD, Eötvös Lóránd U., Budapest, 1985, Internat. Comml. Law Expert, 1994; DMS, Brunel U., Eng., 1997; MBA, Buckinghamshire Univ. Coll., Eng., 1999. Bar: Hungary 1988.

Assoc. practice Law Firm No. 5, Budapest, 1985-88, ptnr., 1988-92; mng. ptnr. Radványi & Ptnrs., Budapest, 1992—. Co-author: Hungary: Rules and Regulations for Doing Business, 1997, Doing Business in Hungary, 2002; author: legal column in periodical Print Info. Mem. Can. C. of C. in Hungary (bd. dirs. 1992-93), Am. C. of C., Brill and Carat Bus. Club. Avocations: skiing, scuba diving, travel. Office: Radványi & Ptnrs Magyar jakobinusok tere 2 3 1122 Budapest Hungary

RAE, MATTHEW SANDERSON, JR., lawyer; b. Pitts., Sept. 12, 1922; s. Matthew Sanderson and Olive (Waite) R.; m. Janet Hettman, May 2, 1953; children: Mary-Anna, Margaret Rae Mallory, Janet S. Rae Dupree. AB, Duke, 1946, LLB, 1947; postgrad., Stanford U., 1951. Bar: Md. 1948, Calif. 1951. Asst. to dean Duke Sch. Law, Durham, N.C., 1947-48; assoc. Karl F. Steinmann, Balt., 1948-49, Guthrie, Darling & Shattuck, L.A., 1953-54; nat. field rep. Phi Alpha Delta Law Frat., L.A., 1949-51; research atty. Calif. Supreme Ct., San Francisco, 1951-52; ptnr. Darling, Hall & Rae (and predecessor firms), L.A., 1955—. Mem. Calif. Commn. Uniform State Laws, 1985—, chmn., 1993-94; chmn. drafting com. for revision Uniform Prin. and Income Act of Nat. Conf., 1991-97, Probate and Mental Health Task Force, Jud. Coun. Calif., 1996-2000. Vice pres. L.A. County Rep. Assembly, 1959-64; mem. L.A. County Rep. Ctrl. Com., 1960-64, 77-90, 2000—, exec. com., 1977-90; vice chmn. 17th Congl. Dist., 1960-62, 28th Congl. Dist., 1962-64; chmn. 46th Assy. Dist., 1962-64, 27th Senatorial Dist., 1977-85, 29th Senatorial Dist., 1985-90, sec. 53d Assembly Dist., 2000-; mem. Calif. Rep. State Ctrl. Com., 1966—, exec. com., 1966-67; pres. Calif. Rep. League, 1966-67; trustee Rep. Assocs., 1979-94, pres., 1983-85, chmn. bd. dirs., 1985-87. 2d lt. USAAF, WWII. Fellow Am. Coll. Trust and Estate Counsel; academician Internat. Acad. Estate and Trust Law (exec. coun. 1974-78); mem. ABA, L.A. County Bar Assn. (chmn. probate and trust law com. 1964-66, chmn. legis. com. 1980-86, chmn. program com. 1981-82, chmn. membership retention com. 1982-83, trustee 1983-85, dir. Bar Found., 1987-93, Arthur K. Marshall award probate and trust law sect. 1984, Shattuck-Price Meml. award 1990), South Bay Bar Assn., State Bar of Calif. (chmn. state bar jour. com. 1970-71, probate com. 1974-75; exec. com. estate planning trust and probate law sect. 1977-83, chmn. legis. com. 1977-89; co-chmn. 1991-92; probate law cons. group Calif. Bd. Legal Specialization 1977-88; chmn. conf. dels. resolutions com. 1987, exec. com. conf. dels. 1987-90), Lawyers Club L.A. (bd. govs. 1981-87, 1st v.p. 1982-83), Am. Legion (comdr. Allied post 1969-70), Legion Lex (bd. dirs. 1964-99, pres. 1969-71), Air Force Assn., Aircraft Owners and Pilots Assn., Town Hall (gov. 1970-78, pres. 1975), World Affairs Coun., Internat. Platform Assn., Breakfast Club (law, pres. 1989-90), Commonwealth Club, Chancery Club (pres. 1996-97), Rotary, Phi Beta Kappa (councilor Alpha Assn. 1983—, pres. 1996), Omicron Delta Kappa, Phi Alpha Delta (supreme justice 1972-74, elected to Disting. Svc. chpt. 1978), Sigma Nu. Presbyterian. Estate planning, Probate (including wills, trusts), Estate taxation. Home: 600 John St Manhattan Beach CA 90266-5837 Office: Darling Hall & Rae LLP 520 S Grand Ave Fl 7 Los Angeles CA 90071-2645

RAEDER, MYRNA SHARON, lawyer, educator; b. N.Y.C., Feb. 4, 1947; d. Samuel and Estelle (Auslander) R.; m. Terry Oliver Kelly, July 13, 1975; children: Thomas Oliver, Michael Lawrence. BA, Hunter Coll., 1968; JD, NYU, 1971; LLM, Georgetown U., 1975. Bar: N.Y. 1972, D.C. 1972, Calif. 1972. Spl. asst. U.S. atty. U.S. Atty's Office, Washington, 1972-73; asst. prof. U. San Fransisco Sch. Law, 1973-75; assoc. O'Melveny & Myers, L.A., 1975-79; assoc. prof. Southwestern U. Sch. Law., L.A., 1979-82, prof., 1983—, Irwin R. Buchalter prof. law, 1990, Paul E. Treusch prof. law, 2002; mem. faculty Nat. Judicial Coll., 1993—. Prettyman fellow Georgetown Law Ctr., Washington, 1971-73. Author: Federal Pretrial Practice, 3d edit., 2000; co-author: Evidence, State and Federal Rules in a Nutshell, 3d edit., 1997, Evidence, Cases, Materials and Problems, 2d edit., 1998. Recipient Margaret Brent Women Lawyers of Achievement award, 2002. Fellow Am. Bar Found.; mem. ABA (trial evidence com. litigation sect. 1980—, criminal justice sect. 1994-97, vice-chair planning 1997-98, chair elect 1997-98, chair 1998-99, mem. mag. bd., 2000—, adv. to nat. conf. commrs. uniform state laws drafting com. uniform rules of evidence 1996-1999, Commn. Women in the Profession), Am. Law Inst., Assn. Am. Law Schs. (chair women in legal edn. sect. 1982, com. on sects. 1984-87, chair elect evidence sect. 1996, chair 1997), Nat. Assn. Women Lawyers (bd. dirs. 1991-98, pres.-elect 1993, pres. 1994-96), Women Lawyers Assn. L.A. (bd. dirs., coord. mothers support group 1987-96), Order of Coif, Phi Beta Kappa. Office: Southwestern U Sch Law 675 S Westmoreland Ave Los Angeles CA 90005-3905 E-mail: mraeder@swlaw.edu.

RAFEEDIE, EDWARD, senior federal judge; b. Orange, N.J., Jan. 6, 1929; s. Fred and Nabeeha (Hishmeh) R.; m. Ruth Alice Horton, Oct. 8, 1961; children: Fredrick Alexander, Jennifer Ann. BS in Law, U. So. Calif., 1957, JD, 1959; LLD (hon.), Pepperdine U., 1978. Bar: Calif. 1960. Pvt. practice, Santa Monica, Calif., 1960-69; mcpl. ct. judge Santa Monica Jud. Dist., 1969-71; judge Superior Ct. State of Calif., L.A., 1971-82; dist. judge U.S. Dist. Court (cen. dist.) Calif., L.A., 1982-96, sr. judge, 1996—. With U.S. Army, 1950-52, Korea. Office: US Dist Ct 312 N Spring St Ste 244P Los Angeles CA 90012-4704

RAFFALOW, JANET TERRY, law librarian; b. Burbank, Calif., Oct. 11, 1947; d. Melvin and Honey (Sobel) Whitney; m. Richard Elliott Raffalow, June 9, 1984; 1 child, Melissa Rose. BA, UCLA, 1968, MLS, 1969, cert. in pub. adminstrn., 1980. Cert. community coll. tchr., Calif. Young adult libr. L.A. Pub. Libr., 1969-70; libr. Calif. Atty. Gen.'s Libr., L.A., 1970-78; supervising libr. Calif. Atty. Gen.'s Library, Los Angeles, 1978—. Vol. Pub. TV-KCET, Los Angeles, 1973—; vice chmn. Los Angeles Jr. C. of C., 1979-81; vol. citizens commn. Los Angeles Olympic Organizing Com., 1982-84; mem. City of Hope. Recipient Atty. Gen.'s award for excellence, 1991. Mem. L.A. Law Librs. Assn. (long-range planning com.), Am. Assn. Law Librs. (cert.), So. Calif. Assn. Law Librs., UCLA Libr. Sch. Alumni Assn., Sunshines of Cedars Sinai (v.p. 1971-73). Democrat. Jewish. Avocations: tennis, photography, travel. Office: Calif Atty Gen's Libr 300 S Spring St 7th Flr Los Angeles CA 90013 E-mail: janet.raffalow@doj.ca.gov.

RAFFERTY, JAMES GERARD, lawyer; b. Boston, July 9, 1951; s. James John and Helen Christine (Kennedy) R.; m. Rhonda Beth Friedman, May 17, 1981; children: Jessica Faith, Evan Louis Quinn. BA, Brown U., 1974; MA, Princeton U., 1980; JD, Georgetown U., 1984. Bar: Md. 1985, D.C. 1985, U.S. Tax Ct. 1988, U.S. Ct. Appeals (4th cir.) 1989, U.S. Ct. Appeals (3d cir.) 1992. Assoc. Piper & Marbury, Washington, 1984-91, Pepper, Hamilton & Scheetz, Washington, 1991-92; founding ptnr. Harkins Cunningham, Washington, 1992—. Contbr. articles to legal jours. Brown U. Club of Boston scholar, 1969-70. Mem. ABA (chmn. com. on affiliated and related corps. tax sect. 1994-95). Roman Catholic. Avocation: golf. Corporate, general, Mergers and acquisitions, Corporate taxation. Office: Harkins Cunningham 801 Pennsylvania Ave NW Ste 600 Washington DC 20004-2664 E-mail: jrafferty@harkinscunningham.com.

RAFFIN, MARIE-HÉLÈNE J. lawyer; b. Paris, Jan. 23, 1963; d. Jacques and Françoise Raffin. 1st cert., Cambridge U., Paris, 1980; diploma in Econs., Spanish C. of C., Paris, 1981, Brit. C. of C., 1983; BA with honors, U. Paris II, 1984, LLM, 1985, degree in Tax Law, 1986; degree in Advanced Business, Ecole Supérieure des Scis. Econs. Commerciales, Paris, 1984; degree in Acctg., D.E.S.C.F., 1985. Bar: France. Asst. to mem. Nat. Assembly, Paris, 1986-87; from assoc. to ptnr. Arthur Andersen, Paris, 1987—2002; ptnr. Willkie Farr & Gallagher, Paris, 2002—. Prof. in Tax U. Paris, 1995—; cons. Assn. Française des Entreprises Privées, 1996—, Nat. Fedn. French Entrepreneurs, 1997—. Author: La révolution fiscale à refaire, 1986, La Fiscalité des fusions et des apports partiels d'actifs, 1994; contbr. articles to profl. jours. Mem. Paris Bar Assn. Avocations: classical music, theater, philosophy. Mergers and acquisitions, Corporate taxation, Taxation, general. Office: Willkie Farr & Gallagher 21-23 rue de la Ville l'Evêque 75008 Paris France Office Fax: 33140069606. E-mail: mhraffin@willkie.com.

RAGALEVSKY, STANLEY VICTOR, lawyer; b. Everett, Mass., Aug. 31, 1948; s. Stanley G. Ragalevsky. AB, Boston Coll., 1970; JD, Harvard U., 1973. Bar: Mass. 1973, U.S. Dist. Ct. Mass. 1974, U.S. Ct. Appeals (1st cir.) 1979, U.S. Supreme Ct. 1981. Assoc. firm Warner & Stackpole, Boston, 1973-80, ptnr., 1981-99, Kirkpatrick & Lockhart, LLP, Boston, 1999—. Author: Asset Protection Strategies, 2002, Massachusetts Bank Lending Powers Handbook, 1999; contbr. articles to profl. jours. Banking, Property, real (including real estate development, water). Home: 15 Fuller Farms Rd Topsfield MA 01983-1300 Office: Kirkpatrick & Lockhart LLP 75 State St Ste 6 Boston MA 02109-1807

RAGAN, CHARLES OLIVER, JR., lawyer; b. Knoxville, Tenn., Dec. 23, 1935; s. Charles Oliver and Jeanette (Butler) R.; m. Pauline Iona Kimsey, Apr. 19, 1958. BSBA, U. Tenn., 1958, JD, 1963. Bar: Tenn. 1964, U.S. Dist. Ct. (ea. dist.) Tenn. 1965; cert. consumer bankruptcy specialist. Staff atty. State of Tenn., Chattanooga, 1964-69; atty. Bean & Phillips, Chattanooga, 1969-73; sr. ptnr. Ragan & Schulman, Chattanooga, 1973-75, Ragan & Littleton, Chattanooga, 1975-80, Ragan & Wulforst, Chattanooga, 1980-84; pvt. practice Chattanooga, 1984—. Tenn. commnr. Nat. Conf. Commrs. on Uniform State Laws, 1976-80. Campaign treas. for Dem. candidates. Democrat. Methodist. Bankruptcy, Commercial, consumer (including collections, credit). Home: 185 Woodcliff Cir Signal Mountain TN 37377-3142 Office: 707 Georgia Ave Ste 300 Chattanooga TN 37402-2047

RAGAN, CHARLES RANSOM, lawyer; b. N.Y.C., Aug. 13, 1947; s. Charles Alexander Jr. and Josephine Forbes (Parker) R.; m. Barbara Thiel McMahon, Aug. 30, 1969; children: Alexandra Watson, Madeline McCue. AB, Princeton U., 1969; JD, Fordham U., 1974. Bar: N.Y. 1975, U.S. Ct. Appeals (3d cir.) 1975, Calif. 1976, U.S. Ct. Appeals (9th cir.) 1976, U.S. Dist. Ct. (no. dist.) Calif. 1976, U.S. Supreme Ct. 1981, U.S. Dist. Ct. (so. dist.) N.Y. 1982, U.S. Ct. Appeals (2d cir.) 1984. Law clk. to Hon. R.J. Aldisert U.S. Ct. Appeals (3rd cir.), 1974-76; assoc. Pillsbury, Madison & Sutro, San Francisco, 1976-81, ptnr., 1982-97, Palo Alto, 1997-2000, Pillsbury Winthrop, Palo Alto, San Francisco , 2001—. Mem. exec. com. 9th Cir. Judicial Conf., 1987-91. Avocations: biking, swimming, spectator sports. Federal civil litigation, Private international. Office: Pillsbury Winthrop LLP 50 Fremont St San Francisco CA 94105

RAGATZ, THOMAS GEORGE, lawyer; b. Madison, Wis., Feb. 18, 1934; s. Wilmer Leroy and Rosanna (Kindschi) Ragatz; m. Karen Christensen, Dec. 19, 1965; children: Thomas Rolf, William Leslie, Erik Douglas. BBA, U. Wis., 1957, LLB, 1961. CPA Wis.; bar: Wis. 1961, U.S. Dist. Ct. (ea. and we. dists.) Wis. 1961, U.S. Tax Ct. 1963, U.S. Ct. Appeals (7th cir.) 1965, U.S. Supreme Ct. 1968. Staff acct. Peat, Marwick, Mitchell & Co., Mpls., 1958; instr. Sch. Bus., U. Wis., Madison, 1958-60; formerly lectr. in acctg. and law Law Sch. U. Wis.; law clk. Wis. Supreme Ct., 1961-62; assoc. Boardman Suhr Curry & Field, Madison, 1962-64, ptnr., 1965-78, Foley & Lardner, Madison, 1978—, mng. ptnr., 1984-93, chmn. budget com., 1994-98. Dir. Sub-Zero Freezer Co., Inc., Mortenson, Matzell & Meldrem, Inc., Norman Bassett Found., Wis. Sports Found., United Way Found.; pres. Courtier Found.; dir., pres. Wis. Sports Devel. Corp.; lectr. seminars on tax subjects. Author: The Ragatz History, 1989; contbr. articles to profl. jours. Formerly dir. United Way, Meth. Hosp. Found; mem. U. Wis. Found.; chmn. site selection com. U. Wis. Hosp. Com.; past pres. 1st Congl. Ch. Found.; bd. dirs. Found. for Madison Pub. Schs.; pres. Bus. and Edn. Partnership, 1983—89, bd. dirs.; past pres. First Congl. Ch. Found.; chmn. site selection com. U. Wis. Hosp.; bd. regents U. Wis., panel provision of legal svcs.; bd. dirs. Met. YMCA, Madison, 1983—90, YMCA Found., Norman Bassett Found., Courtier Found.; pres. Bus. & Edn. Partnership, 1983—89. Fellow: Am. Bar Found.; mem.: ABA, Dane County Bar Assn. (pres. 1978—79, chmn. jud. qualification com., sec.), Wis. Inst. CPA, State Bar Wis. (sec. 1969—70, bd. govs. 1971—75, chmn. fin. com. 1975—80, chmn. tax sect., chmn. spl. com. on econs., chmn. svcs. for lawyers com.), Wis. Bar Found., Seventh Cir. Bar Assn., Am. Judicature Soc., Order of Constantine, Bascom Hill Soc., Order of Coif, Madison Club (pres. 1980—81), Madison Club House Corp. (pres. 1999—, bd. dirs.), Sigma Chi, Beta Gamma Sigma. Republican. General civil litigation, Corporate, general, Corporate taxation. Home: 3334 Lake Mendota Dr Madison WI 53705-1469 Office: Foley & Lardner PO Box 1497 Madison WI 53701-1497 also: Foley & Lardner 1st Wisconsin Ctr 777 E Wisconsin Ave Ste 3800 Milwaukee WI 53202-5302

RAGGI, REENA, circuit judge; b. Jersey City, May 11, 1951; BA, Wellesley Coll., 1973; JD, Harvard U., 1976. Bar: N.Y. 1977. U.S. atty. Dept. Justice, Bklyn., 1986; ptnr. Windels, Marx, Davies & Ives, N.Y.C., 1987; judge U.S. Dist. Ct. (Ea. dist.) N.Y., 2002, U.S. Ct. Appeals (2nd Cir.), N.Y.C., 2002—. Office: US Courthouse 40 Foley Square New York NY 10007

RAGLAND, ROBERT ALLEN, lawyer; b. Bartlesville, Okla., Apr. 18, 1954; s. Thomas Martin and Joan Ethel (Murphy) R. BA, U. Md., 1976; JD, George Mason Sch. of Law, 1980. Dir. regulatory reform and govt. orgn. Nat. Assn. Mfrs., Washington, 1979-82, asst. v.p. taxation, 1983-86; mgr. congl. rels. The Clorox Co., Oakland, Calif., 1982-83; dir. tax rsch. U.S. C. of C., Washington, 1988-93. Chief tax counsel, mng. dir. Nat. Chamber Found., Washington, 1989-93; v.p. Wachovia Bank, 1995—, officer, 1995—. Author: Transportation Reform, 1980, Employee Stock Ownership Plans, 1989, Taxation of Foreign Source Income, Distributional Impact of Excise Taxes, 1990; editor Taxation of Intercorporate Profits, 1990, Jour. Regulation and Social Costs, 1992—, Jour. Regulation, 1992-93. Active Boy Scouts Am., Washington, 1967—, bd. dirs. nat. capital area coun.; dep. dir. duPont for Pres., 1987-88; v.p. Nat. Chamber Found. U.S. C. of C., 1989-93, dir., Liz Lerman Dance Exchange, 1993-2001, dir. Our House, Inc., 1988-2000. Republican. Roman Catholic. Home: 3510 Inverness Dr Chevy Chase MD 20815

RAIGN, MICHAEL STEPHEN, lawyer; b. Glendale, Ariz., Mar. 11, 1960; s. Phillip Harry and Stephanie Elizabeth (Medoff) R.; m. Sherie Leslie Gee, July 2, 1995; 1 child, Kelsie Gee. BBA in Acctg., U. Tex., 1982, BA in Govt., 1983; JD, St. Mary's U., San Antonio, 1986. Bar: Tex. 1987; cert. in criminal law Tex. Bd. Legal Specialization, 1997. Prosecutor Bexar County Dist. Atty.'s Office, San Antonio, 1987-95; pvt. practice, San Antonio, 1995—. Player San Antonio Soccer Assn.; mental health master, 2002—. Mem.: San Antonio Criminal Def. Lawyers Assn. (dir. 1999—, treas. 2001—02, sec. 2002—03, v.p. 2003—), Tex. Dist. and County Attys. Assn., Tex. Criminal Def. Lawyers Assn. Republican. Roman Catholic. Avocations: music, soccer, backpacking, photography, antiques. Criminal. Office: 313 S Main Ave San Antonio TX 78204-1016

RAIKES, CHARLES FITZGERALD, retired lawyer; b. Mpls., Oct. 6, 1930; s. Arthur FitzGerald and Margaret (Hawthorne) R.; m. Antonia Raikes, Dec. 20, 1969; children: Jennifer Catherine, Victoria Samantha. BA, Washington U., 1952; MA, Harvard U., 1955, LL.B., 1958. Bar: N.Y. State 1959. Assoc. White & Case, N.Y.C., 1958-69; assoc. gen. counsel Dun & Bradstreet, Inc., N.Y.C., 1969-72, v.p., gen. counsel, 1972-73, The Dun & Bradstreet Corp., N.Y.C., 1973-76, sr. v.p., gen. counsel, 1976-94, of counsel, 1994-95; ret., 1995. Cons. Bd. Govs. Fed. Reserve System, 1958-95. Served with U.S. Army, 1952-54. Woodrow Wilson fellow, 1952 Mem. Assn. Bar City of N.Y., Harvard Club, Phi Beta Kappa. Corporate, general. Home: 26 Crooked Trl Norwalk CT 06853-1106

RAILTON, WILLIAM SCOTT, retired lawyer; b. Newark, July 30, 1935; s. William Scott and Carolyn Elizabeth (Guiberson) R.; m. Karen Elizabeth Walsh, Mar. 31, 1979; 1 son, William August; children by previous marriage: William Scott, Anne Greenwood. BSEE, U. Wash., 1962; JD with honors, George Washington U., 1965. Bar: D.C. 1966, Md. 1966, Va. 1993, U.S. Patent Office 1966. Assoc., then ptnr. Kemon, Palmer & Estabrook, Washington, 1966-70; sr. trial atty. Dept. Labor, Washington, 1970-71, asst. counsel for trial litigation, 1971-72; chief counsel U.S. Occupational Safety and Health Rev. Commn., Washington, 1972-77, acting gen. counsel, 1975-77; ptnr. Reed Smith LLP, Pitts., 1977—2002, ret., 2002; appointed commr., chmn. U.S. Occupl. Safety and Health Rev. Commn., 2002—. Lectr. George Washington U. Law Sch., 1977-79, seminar chmn. Occupational Safety and Health Act, Govt. Inst., 1979-96; lectr. Practicing Law Inst., 1976-79; apptd. commr., chmn. U.S. Occupl. Safety and Health Rev. Commn., 2002. Author: (legal handbooks) The Examination System and the Backlog, 1965, The OSHA General Duty Clause, 1977, The OSHA Health Standards, 1977; OSHA Compliance Handbook, 1992; contbg. author: Occupational Safety and Health Law, 1988, 93. Regional chmn. Montgomery County (Md.) Republican party, 1968-70; pres. Montgomery Sq. Citizens Assn., 1970-71; bd. dirs., pres. Foxvale Farms Homeowners Assn., 1979-82; pres. Orchards on the Potomac Homeowners Assn., 1990-92; dir. Great Falls Hist. Soc., 1991-94; scoutmaster Troop 55 Boy Scouts Am., 1993-98. With USMC, 1953-58. Recipient Meritorious Achievement medal Dept. Labor, 1972, Outstanding Service award OSHA Rev. Commn., 1977, elected fell. Coll. Labor and Employment Lawyers, 1998. Fellow Coll. Labor and Employment Lawyers; mem. ABA (mgmt. co-chmn. occupational safety and health law com. 1995-98), Md. Bar Assn., Va. Bar Assn., Bar Assn. D.C. (vice chmn. young lawyers sect. 1971), Order of Coif, Sigma Phi Epsilon, Phi Delta Phi. Federal civil litigation, Labor (including EEOC, Fair Labor Standards Act, labor-management relations, NLRB, OSHA), Patent. Home: 10102 Walker Lake Dr Great Falls VA 22066-3502 Office: US Occupational Safety and Health Rev Commn 1120 20th Street NW Washington DC 20036

RAIMI, BURTON LOUIS, lawyer; b. Detroit, May 5, 1938; s. Irving and Rae (Abel) R.; m. Judith Morse, Mar. 31, 1963 (div. Mar. 1985); children: Diane L., and Matthew D. BA, Brandeis U., 1960; JD with honors, U. Mich., 1963; LLM, George Washington U., 1964. Bar: Mich. 1963, DC 1964, Fla. 1991, U.S. Ct. Appeals (4th, 7th, 8th, 9th, 10th, 11th and DC cirs.), U.S. Ct. Fed. Claims, U.S. Supreme Ct. Atty. appelate ct. sect. NLRB, Washington, 1964-69; assoc. Morgan, Lewis & Bockius, Washington, 1969-71; dep. gen. counsel FDIC, Washington, 1971-78; ptnr. Rosenman and Colin, Washington, 1978-86, Dechert Price & Rhoads, Washington, 1986-93; shareholder McCaffrey & Raimi, P.A., Naples and Sarasota, Fla., 1994—2002, Law Offices of Burton L. Raimi PA, Sarasota, Fla., 2003—. Speaker various insts. Mem. ABA (past chmn. bank receiverships subcom. of banking com.), D.C. Bar Assn. (past chmn. banking law com., com. on interest on lawyers trust accounts), Fla. Bar (bus. law com.). Avocations: sailing, travel, golf, fishing. Banking, Corporate, general, Securities. Home: 4452 Staghorn Ln Sarasota FL 34238-5626 Office: 1800 2d St Ste 753 Sarasota FL 34236-5900 Fax: 941-957-0449. E-mail: burt@moneylaw.com.

RAIMO, BERNARD (BERNIE RAIMO), lawyer; b. Kansas City, Mo., May 29, 1944; m. Sharon Marie Brady, Aug. 23, 1974; children: Sarah Elizabeth, Peter Bernard. BA, U. Notre Dame, 1965; MA, U. Md., 1967; JD with honors, George Washington U., 1972. Bar: D.C. Staff asst. to Sen. Stuart Symington, Mo., 1968-72; asst. corp. counsel D.C., Washington, 1972-76; legis. analyst Am. Petroleum Inst., 1976-78; counsel Permanent Select Com. Intelligence U.S. Ho. Reps., Washington, 1978-91, chief counsel Ho. Com. Standards of Official Conduct, 1991-95; minority counsel Ho. Com. Standards of Official Conduct, 1995-97; counsel to Dem. leader U.S. Ho. of Reps., 1997—. Office: Office of the Dem Leader H-204 The Capitol Washington DC 20515-0001 E-mail: bernard.raimo@mail.house.gov.

RAINER, G. BRADLEY, lawyer; b. Phila., June 5, 1947; s. Francis J. and Ruth J. Rainer; m. Joan Klamkin, Mar. 27, 1949; children: Daniel, Julia. BA, Wesleyan U., Middletown, Conn., 1969; JD, Temple U., 1972. Bar: Pa. 1972, U.S. Dist. Ct. (ea. dist.) Pa. 1972. Assoc. Duryea, Larzelere & Hepburn, Ardmore, Pa., 1972-74, ptnr., 1975-76; sole practitioner Haverford, Pa., 1976-79; ptnr. Hecker Rainer and Brown, Phila., 1980-88; shareholder Rubin Quinn Moss & Patterson PC, Phila., 1988-93; shareholder, chair bus. dept., mem. exec. com. Eckell, Sparks, Levy, Auerbach, Monte, Rainer & Sloane, PC, Media, Pa., 1993—. Pres. Phila. Bar Edn. Ctr., 1998—; adj. prof. Temple U. Sch. Law, Phila., 1995—; spkr. at seminars on estate planning, bus. law and lawyer ethics. Pres. Voyage House, Phila., 1992-94; bd. dirs. Crisis Intervention Network, Phila., 1983-89, Phila. Estate Planning Coun., 1998—; pres. A Better Chance in Lower Merion, Ardmore, 1977-79. Mem. Assn. Profl. Responsibility Lawyers. Corporate, general, Estate planning, Ethics. Office: Eckell Sparks et al 344 W Front St Media PA 19063-2632 E-mail: brainer@eckellsparks.com.

RAINEY, JOHN DAVID, federal judge; b. Freeport, Tex., Feb. 10, 1945; s. Frank Anson and Jewel Lorene (Hortman) R.; m. Judy Davis, Aug. 17, 1968; children, John David Jr., Jacob Matthew, Craig Thomas. BBA, So. Meth. U., 1967, JD, 1972. Bar: Tex. 1972, U.S. Dist. Ct. (no. dist.) Tex. 1974, U.S. Tax Ct. 1974, U.S. Ct. Appeals (5th cir.) 1981, U.S. Supreme Ct. 1981, U.S. Dist. Ct. (so. dist.) Tex. 1986. Assoc. Taylor, Mizell, Price, Corrigan & Smith, Dallas, 1973-79; ptnr. Gilbert, Gilbert & Rainey, Angleton, Tex., 1979-82, Rainey & LeBoeuf, Angleton, 1982-86; judge 149th Dist. Ct., Brazoria County, Tex., 1987-90, U.S. Dist. Ct. (so. dist.) Tex., 1990—. Bd. dirs. Angleton Bank of Commerce. Mem. City of Angleton Planning and Zoning Commn., 1981-84; mem. Angleton Charter Rev. Commn., 1984, chmn. 1982. Served with U.S. Army, 1969-70. Mem. State Bar Tex., Brazoria County Bar Assn. (pres. 1983-84). Lodges: Lions (pres. Angleton 1986-87). Methodist. Avocations: hunting, fishing, woodworking. Office: US Dist Ct 312 S Main St Rm 406 Victoria TX 77901

RAINEY, WILLIAM JOEL, lawyer; b. Flint, Mich., Oct. 11, 1946; s. Ralph Jefferson and Elsie Matilda (Erickson) R.; m. Cynthia Hetsko, June 15, 1968; children: Joel Michael, Allison Elizabeth. AB, Harvard U., 1968; JD, U. Mich., 1971. Bar: N.Y. 1973, Wash. 1977, Ariz. 1987, Mass. 1992, Kans. 1997, U.S. Dist. Ct. (so. and ea. dists.) N.Y. 1973, U.S. Ct. Appeals (2nd cir.) N.Y. 1973, U.S. Dist. Ct. (we. dist.) Wash. 1977, U.S. Supreme Ct. 1976, U.S. Ct. Appeals (9th cir.) Wash. 1978, U.S. Dist. Ct. Ariz. 1987, U.S. Dist. Ct. Mass. 1992. Assoc. atty. Curtis, Mallet-Prevost, Colt & Mosle, N.Y.C., 1971-76; atty., asst. corp. sec. Weyerhaeuser Co., Tacoma, 1976-85; v.p., corp. sec., gen. counsel Southwest Forest Industries Inc., Phoenix, 1985-87; sr. v.p., corp. sec., gen. counsel Valley Nat. Corp. and Valley Nat. Bank, Phoenix, 1987-91; v.p., gen. counsel Cabot Corp., Boston, 1991-93; exec. v.p., gen. coun., corp. sec. Fourth Fin. Corp., Wichita, Kans., 1994-96; sr. v.p., gen. counsel, corp. sec. Payless ShoeSource, Inc., Topeka, 1996—2003, Longs Drug Stores Corp., Walnut Creek, Calif., 2003—. Editor U. Mich. Jour. Law Reform, 1970-71 Bd. dirs. Big Bros./Big Sisters, 1994-96. Maj. USAR, 1970-91. Mem. ABA (chmn. task force 1984-91, com. of corp. gen. counsel, exec. com. 2002—), Wash. State Bar Assn., State Bar of Ariz., Assn. Bank Holding Cos. (steering com. 1989-91, chmn. lawyers com. 1990-91), Am. Corp. Counsel Assn., Harvard Club of Phoenix (bd. dirs. 1989-91). Avocations: backpacking, running, fishing, bicycling. Mergers and acquisitions, Pension, profit-sharing, and employee benefits, Securities. Home: 901 Deer Run Dr Lawrence KS 66049-4731 Office: Longs Drug Stores Corp 141 N Civic Dr Walnut Creek CA 94596

RAINONE, MICHAEL CARMINE, lawyer; b. Phila., Mar. 4, 1918; m. Ledena Tonioni, Apr. 10, 1944; children: Sebastian, Francine. LLB, U. Pa., 1941. Bar: Pa. 1944, U.S. Dist. Ct. Pa. 1944, U.S. Supreme Ct. 1956. Del. 3d cir. Jud. Conf., 1984-95. Bd. dirs. C.C., Phila. 1970-85; past pres.

Nationalities Svc. Ctr., hon. bd. dirs.; commr. Fellowship Commn., 1973-82; internat. pres. Orphans of Italy, Inc., 2975-83; bd. dirs., mem. govt. rels. com. Mental Health Assn. Southeastern Pa., 1979-91; pres. Columbus Civic Assn. Pa., Inc., 1984-91; chmn. Lawyers' Biog. Com. Hist. Soc., U.S. Dist. Ct.; trustee Balch Inst. for Ethnic Studies, 1989-92; regional v.p. Nat. Italian-Am. Found.; pres. Seaview Harbor Civic Assn., 1990-95, pres. emeritus, 1996—; apptd. judge Final Law Sch. Trial Advocacy Program for the Northeast, 1996; counsel, v.p. Piccola Opera Com., Phila., 1997—; pres. Grad. Club, bd. dirs., 2000; task force chmn. Mazzei Nat. Constn. Ctr., 2001. Recipient Disting. Svc. award Nationalities Svc. Ctr., 1975, Man of Yr. award Columbus Civic Assn., 1969, Legion of Honor, Chapel of Four Chaplains, 1979, Bronze Medallion award, 1982, commendation Pa. Senate, 1982, Villanova Law Sch. Appreciation award 1993, Syracuse U. Achievement award 1994, Hon. Lifetime award KC, 1997, Resolution of Praise, pres. City Coun. of Phila., 1999, Svc. to Legal Profession and Cmty. award City Coun. of Phila., 2003. Mem. ABA (chmn. U.S. Surpeme Ct. admissions com. 2001), ATLA (Supervising Judge Advocacy award Phila. region 2000, supr. judge law sch. trial advocacy competition, 2000, Phila. chpt. emeritus chmn. of Justice Michael A. Musmanno award 2000), Internat. Acad. Law and Sci., Justinian Soc. (bd. govs. 1980-83, sr. lawyer award 2000), Pa. Bar Assn., Pa. Trial Lawyers Assn. (bd. govs. 1982-84), N.Y. Trial Lawyers Assn. (assoc.), Phila. Bar Assn. (bd. dirs. 1980-83, asst. sec. 1983, 84, chmn. emeritus Beccaria award, 1993—), Lawyers Club Phila. (pres. 1982-84, chmn. Centennial Celebration 2001, Achievement and Svc. award 2003), Phila. Trial Lawyers Assn. (pres. 1982-83, Disting. Svc. award 2000), Nat. Italian-Am. Bar Assn. (bd. govs. 1986-2003, historian 1987-90, pres. 1991-93, bd. chmn. 1993-95, chmn. Supreme Ct. admissions com. 2000), Am. Arbitration Assn. (arbitrator 1950—), Sons of Italy (Man of Yr. award 1995). General civil litigation, Commercial, contracts (including sales of goods; commercial financing), Estate planning. Home: 2401 Pennsylvania Ave Philadelphia PA 19130-3010 Office: 1530 Chestnut St Fl 4 Philadelphia PA 19102-2739

RAINS, M. NEAL, lawyer; b. Burlington, Iowa, July 26, 1943; s. Merritt and Lucille (Lepper) R.; m. Jean Baldwin, July 26, 1980 (div. 1995); children: Robert Baldwin, Kathleen Kellogg. BA in Polit. Sci. with honors, U. Iowa, 1965; JD, Northwestern U., 1968. Bar: Ohio 1968. Assoc. Arter & Hadden, Cleve., 1968-76, ptnr., 1976—2001, mem. exec. com., 1981-90, mem. mgmt. com., 1987-90, mng. ptnr., 1990-92; ptnr. Frantz Ward LLP, Cleve., 2001—. Lectr. on profl. topics, including alternative dispute resolution, distbn. law, litigation practice and procedure, and antitrust. Contbr. articles to profl. jours. Former trustee Legal Aid Soc. Cleve.; trustee Cleve. Play House, mem. adv. coun., 1988—; trustee Citizens League Greater Cleve., Cleve. Art Assn. With U.S. Army, 1968-70 Fellow: Am. Bar Found.; mem.: ABA, William K. Thomas Am. Inn Ct. (pres. 1999—2000), Cleve. Bar Found. (trustee 1999—), Ohio Assn. Civil Trial Attys., Internat. Assn. Def. Counsel, Def. Rsch. Inst., Bar Assn. Greater Cleve. (chmn. young lawyers sect. 1975—76, chmn. CLE com.), Ohio Bar Assn., Rowfant Club, City Club, Cleve. Skating Club, Print Club (trustee 2001—), Union Club, Phi Delta Phi, Omicron Delta Kappa, Phi Beta Kappa. Antitrust, General civil litigation. Home: 18400 Shelburne Rd Shaker Heights OH 44118 Office: Frantz Ward LLP 55 Public Sq Cleveland OH 44113 E-mail: nrains@frantzward.com.

RAINVILLE, CHRISTINA, lawyer; b. N.Y.C., Feb. 7, 1962; d. Dewey and Nancy Rainville; m. Peter S. Greenberg, May 1994. BS, Northwestern U., 1984, JD, 1988. Atty. Schnader Harrison Segal & Lewis, Phila., 1988—. Mem. ABA (pro bono publico award 1999), Nat. Assn. Criminal Def. Lawyers. Presbyterian. Civil rights, Federal civil litigation, Criminal. Office: Schnader Harrison et al 1600 Market St Ste 3600 Philadelphia PA 19103-7287 E-mail: trainville@schnader.com.

RAISIG, PAUL JONES, JR., lawyer; b. Jamestown, N.Y., June 21, 1932; s. Paul Jones and Marian Elizabeth (Christian) R.; m. Carolyn Virginia Sides, June 12, 1955; children: Dawn Virginia, Paul Christian, Anne Sibley. B.G.E., U. Nebr., 1961; MBA, U. Ala., 1965; JD, Campbell U., 1989. Bar: N.C., 1989, D.C. 1991, U.S. Supreme Ct. 1992. Commd. 2d lt. U.S. Army, 1953, advanced through grades to col., 1973, ret., 1977, served in Vietnam, 1963, btn. comdr., Vietnam, 1968; dep. dir. U.S. Army Reorganization, 1973; v.p. Armed Forces Relief and Benefit Assn., Washington, 1977-79; sr. cons. Dept. Def., Washington, 1979-80; exec. dir. Am. Fedn. Info. Processing Socs., Arlington, Va., 1980-84; v.p., dir. Designs, Ltd., Alexandria, Va., 1985-86; ptnr. Barrington, Herndon & Raisig, P.A., Fayetteville, N.C., 1989-92. Adj. prof. bus. law and bus. mgmt. Campbell U., 1992-2003; cons. in field. Decorated Legion of Merit (4), Bronze Star medal (2), Air medal (5), Purple Heart (2), Meritorious Service medal, Army Commendation medal with V Device (3), Combat INf. badge. Mem. U.S. Council for World Communications, Beta Gamma Sigma. Alternative dispute resolution, Education and schools. Home and Office: Buffalo Lake 325 Mallard Rd Sanford NC 27332-1142 E-mail: pjr4u2@aol.com.

RAISLER, KENNETH MARK, lawyer; b. New Rochelle, N.Y., May 15, 1951; s. Herbert A. and Norma (Glaubach) R.; m. Sara Ann Kelsey, June 11, 1978; children: Caroline Elisabeth, Katharine Kelsey, David Mark. BSBA, Yale Coll., 1973; JD, NYU, 1976. Bar: N.Y. 1977, D.C. 1977, U.S. Dist. Ct. (so. dist.) N.Y. 1977, U.S. Dist. Ct. D.C. 1977, U.S. Ct. Appeals (2d cir.) 1977, U.S. Ct. Appeals (D.C. cir.) 1977, U.S. Ct. Appeals (7th cir.) 1982, U.S. Ct. Appeals (10th cir.) 1983, U.S. Supreme Ct. 1985. Law clk. U.S. Dist. Ct. (so. dist.) N.Y., N.Y.C., 1976-77; asst. U.S. atty., Washington, 1977-82; dep. gen. counsel Commodity Futures Trading Commn., Washington, 1982-83, gen. counsel, 1983-87; ptnr. Rogers & Wells, N.Y.C., 1987-92, Sullivan & Cromwell, N.Y.C., 1992—. Mem. Assn. of Bar of City of N.Y. (chair futures regulation com. 1988-91). Office: Sullivan & Cromwell 125 Broad St 33d Fl New York NY 10004-2489 E-mail: raislerk@sullcrom.com.

RAK, LORRAINE KAREN, lawyer; b. Trenton, N.J., Jan. 8, 1959; d. Charles Walter and Lottie Mary (Debiec) R. BA in Polit. Sci., Seton Hall U., South Orange, N.J., 1981; JD, Cornell U., 1984. Bar: N.J. 1986, N.Y. 1986, U.S. Dist. Ct. N.J. 1986, U.S. Dist. Ct. (so. and ea. dists.) N.Y. 1988, U.S. Dist. Ct. (no. dist.) N.Y. 1991, U.S. Ct. Appeals (4th cir.) 1989, U.S. Ct. Appeals (2d cir.) 1990, U.S. Ct. Appeals (3d cir.) 1991. Assoc. Shearman & Sterling, N.Y.C., 1984-91, Robinson, St. John & Wayne, N.Y.C., 1992-93; dep. atty. gen. State of N.J., Newark, 1993—. Active Lawyers' Com. for Human Rights, N.Y.C. Mem. ABA, ACLU, LWV, Cornell Law Assn., Amnesty Internat., Polish Arts Club Trenton. Democrat. Roman Catholic. Federal civil litigation, State civil litigation, Commercial, consumer (including collections, credit). Office: 124 Halsey St Fl 5 Newark NJ 07102-3017 E-mail: raklor@law.dol.lps.state.nj.us.

RAKER, IRMA STEINBERG, judge; b. Bklyn. m. Samuel K. Raker, Apr. 3, 1960; children: Mark, Stefanie, Leslie. BA, Syracuse U., 1959; cert. of attendance (hon.), Hague (The Netherlands) Acad. Internat. Law, 1959; JD, Am. U., 1972. Bar: Md. 1973, D.C. 1974, U.S. Dist. Ct. Md. 1977, U.S. Ct. Appeals (4th cir.) 1977. Asst. state's atty. State's Atty.'s Office of Montgomery County, Md., 1973-79; ptnr. Sachs, Greenebaum & Tayler, Washington, 1979-80; judge Dist. Ct. Md., Rockville, 1980-82, Cir. Ct. for Montgomery County, Md., 1982-94, Ct. of Appeals of Md., 1994—. Adj. prof. Washington Coll. Law, Am. U., 1980—; faculty seminar leader child abuse course Nat. Coll. Dist. Attys. at U. Mass., 1977; mem. faculty Md. Jud. Inst., Nat. Criminal Def. Inst., 1980, 81, 82; instr. litigation program Georgetown Law Ctr.-Nat. Inst. Trial Advocacy; mem. legis. com. Md. Jud. Conf., mem. exec. com., 1985-89, mem. commn. to study bail bond and surety industry in Md.; mem. spl. com. to revise article 27 on crimes and punishment State of Md., 1991—; mem. inquiry com. atty. Grievance Commn. Md., 1978-81; chairperson jud. compensation com. Md. Jud. Conf., 1997—. Past editor Am. U. Law Rev. Treas., v.p. West Bradley Citizens Assn., 1964-68; mem. adv. com. to county exec. on child abuse Montgomery County, 1976-77, mem. adv. com. to county exec. on battered spouses, 1977-78, mem. adv. com. on environ. protection, 1980; mem. citizens adv. bd. Montgomery County Crisis Ctr., 1980. Recipient Robert C. Heeney award Md. State Bar Assn., 1993, Dorothy Beatty Meml. award Women's Law Ctr., 1994, Rita Davidson award Women's Bar Md., 1995, Margaret Brent Trailblazers award ABA Commn. on Women in the Profession/Women's Bar Assn. Md., 1995, Elizabeth Dole Woman of Achievement award ARC, 1998, Leadership in Law award The Daily Record, 2001, Nat. Assn. Social Workers' Pub. Citizen of Yr. award, 2001, others; named of Md.'s Top 100 Women Warfield's Bus. Record, 1997, 99, 2001. Fellow Md. Bar Found.; mem. ABA (chairperson criminal justice stds. com. 1995-96, mem. coun. criminal law sect. 1997—, del. nat. conf. state trial judges, active various coms.), Md. State Bar Assn. (chairperson coun. criminal law and practice sect., mem. bd. govs. 1981, 82, 85, 86, 90, mem. coun. litigation sect., active coms., chairperson com. to draft pattern jury instrns. in civil and criminal cases 1980—), Nat. Assn. Women Judges, Internat. Acad. Trial Judges, Am. Law Inst., Montgomery County Bar Assn. (chairperson criminal law sect. 1978-79, mem. exec. com. 1979-80, active other coms., Outstanding Jurist award 2000), Montgomery County Bar Leaders, Women's Bar Assn. Md., Women's Bar Assn. D.C., Hadassah Women's Orgn. (life), Pioneer Women Na'amat (hon. life, Celebration of Women award 1985), Pi Sigma Alpha. Avocations: photography, tennis, needlework. Office: Ct of Appeals of Md 50 Maryland Ave Rockville MD 20850-2320

RALEY, JOHN W., JR., lawyer; b. May 23, 1932; s. John Wesley and Helen Thames; children: John Wesley III, Robert Thames. AB, Okla. Baptist U., 1954; JD, U. Okla., 1959. Bar: Okla. 1959, U.S. Supreme Ct. 1973, U.S. Ct. Appeals (10th cir.), 1962, U.S. Dist. (we. dist.) 1961, U.S. Dist. Ct. (no. dist.) 1988, U.S. Dist. Ct. (ea. dist.) 1989 Okla. Asst. U.S. atty. We. Dist. Okla. U.S. Dept. Justice, 1961-69; ptnr. Northcutt, Raley, Clark and Gardner, Ponca City, Okla., 1969-90; U.S. atty. Ea. Dist. Okla. U.S. Dept. Justice, 1990-97; of counsel Northcutt, Clark, Gardner & Hron, Ponca City, 1997—; mcpl. ct. judge Ponca City, 2001—. Mem. State Ethics Commn., 2003—. Mayor of Ponca City, Okla., 1980-83; commr. Okla. Ehtics Commn., 2003—. Capt. USNR, 1950-84, ret. Recipient George Washington Honor medal Freedoms Found. at Valley Forge, 1971, Spl. Initiative award U.S. Dept. Justice, 1994, Outstanding Alumni Achievement award Okla. Bapt. U., 1981, Outstanding Citizen award Ponca City, 1984. Fellow Am. Coll. Trial Lawyers; mem. ABA, Am. Bd. Trial Advs., Okla. Bar Assn. (mem. bd. govs.), Kay County Bar Assn. (pres. 1980), Am. Legion, Mason, Reserve Officers Assn., Naval Reserve Assn., VFW. Republican. Southern Baptist. Personal injury (including property damage), General practice, Criminal. Office: 400 E Central Ave Ste 401 Ponca City OK 74601-5428 Address: PO Box 1412 Ponca City OK 74602-1412

RALEY, JOHN WESLEY, III, lawyer; b. Oklahoma City, Oct. 19, 1959; s. John Wesley Raley Jr. and Mary Lane Mallett; m. Kelly Elaine Williams, Sept. 22, 1984; children: Katherine Elise, William Thomas, James Wesley. BA summa cum laude, U. Okla., 1981, JD, 1984; LLM, U. Aberdeen, Scotland, 1988. Bar: Tex. 1985, U.S. Dist. Ct. (so. dist.) Tex. 1985, U.S. Ct. Appeals (5th cir.) 1985; bd. cert. personal injury trial law Tex. Bd. Legal Specialization. With Fulbright & Jaworski, LLP, Houston, 1985-96, ptnr., 1996-2000; shareholder, mng. ptnr. Cooper & Scully, P.C., Houston, 2001—. Lectr. civil litigation U. Houston CLE, 1995—; on-air spokesman Houston Pub. TV, 1996—. Vol. Habitat for Humanity, Houston, 1998. Fellow Tex. Bar Found. (life); mem. ABA, State Bar Tex., Houston Bar Assn. (interdisciplinary ednl. alliance, spkrs. bur.), U. Okla. Varsity O Club, Phi Beta Kappa. Avocations: basketball, golf, tennis, local amateur drama performances. General civil litigation, Intellectual property, Personal injury (including property damage). Home: 5 Falling Leaf Ln Houston TX 77024-4513 Office: 2700 Chase Tower 600 Travis St Houston TX 77002-3009

RALLI, CONSTANTINE PANDIA, lawyer; b. Bronxville, N.Y., Apr. 6, 1948; s. Pandia C. and Mary (Motter) R.; m. Alison Rhoads, Aug. 11, 1973; children: Pandia C., Christopher A. BA, Middlebury Coll., 1970; JD, Fordham U., 1973; LLM in Taxation, NYU, 1986. Bar: N.Y. 1974, U.S. Ct. Appeals (2nd cir.) 1974, U.S. Dist. Ct. (so. and ea. dists.) N.Y. 1975, U.S. Tax Ct. 1977, Fla. 1985, Conn. 1985, U.S. Dist. Ct. Conn. 1987. Assoc. Davis Polk & Wardwell, N.Y.C., 1973-81; ptnr. Hall, McNicol, Hamilton & Clark, N.Y.C., 1981-88, LeBoeuf, Lamb, Greene & MacRae, N.Y.C., 1988—. Sec., bd. dirs. Fairfield-Maxwell Ltd., Campo Tankers SA, N.Y.C., 1987-95. Bd. dirs. Samaritan Counseling Ctr., Rye, N.Y., 1987-90, Rye Free Reading Room, 1990-93, Rye Presbyn. Ch., 1986-89. Mem. Union Club, Am. Yacht Club, Ekwanok Country Club (Manchester, Vt.). Republican. Presbyterian. Estate planning, Probate (including wills, trusts), Estate taxation. Home: 11 Rockridge Rd Rye NY 10580-4130 Office: LeBoeuf Lamb Greene & MacRae 125 W 55th St New York NY 10019-5369 also: 411 Pequot Ave Southport CT 06490-1386

RALLO, DOUGLAS, lawyer; b. Orange, N.J., Nov. 22, 1953; s. Vito and Mary (Spiduro) Rallo. BA, Montclair (N.J.) State U., 1975; cert., Inst. Internat. and Comparative Law, 1977; JD, John Marshall Law Sch., 1978. Bar: Ill 1979, US Dist Ct (no dist) Ill 1979, US Ct Appeals (7th cir) 1979, US Dist Ct (ea dist) Wis 1995, Wis 1998, US Dist Ct (we dist) Wis 2001. Corp. lawyer Bendix Corp., N.Y.C., 1979-81; assoc. David T. Rallo & Assocs., Ltd., Chgo., 1981-83, Horwitz & Assocs., Ltd., Chgo., 1983-84, Semmelman & Bertucci Ltd., Lake Forest, Ill., 1984-98; pvt. practice Law Offices of Douglas Rallo, P.C., Libertyville, Ill., 1998—. Research asst A Functional Analysis of the Criminal Code Reform Act of 1978 for US Congress; panel atty Ill State Appellate Defender's Office, 1980; profiled in Newsweek mag, 1989, Chicago Tribune, 1989; tchr adult legal educ programs Libertyville High Sch, Ill., 1988—90, Mundelein High Sch, Ill., 1989; Notable cases include: Sherrod vs. Berry, 629F. Supp. 159 (1985) and 589F Supp. 433 (1984). Contbr. articles to profl jours. Vpres Lake County chpt NW Ill MADD, 1989—91; comnr Libertyville Youth Comn, 1990—94; bd dirs Civic Ctr Found, Libertyville. Mem.: Vernon Hills, Mundelien and Libertyville C. of C., Lake County Bar Assn., State Bar Wis., Ill. Trial Lawyers Assn., Ill. State Bar Assn. (lectr hedonic damages, civil practice procedure, sem expert witnesses 1989), Pi Sigma Alpha. Avocations: water sports, swimming, softball. Personal injury (including property damage), Product liability, Workers' compensation. Office: Law Offices Douglas Rallo P C 611 S Milwaukee Ave Libertyville IL 60048-3256

RAMBO, SYLVIA H. federal judge; b. Royersford, Pa., Apr. 17, 1936; d. Granville A. and Hilda E. (Leonhardt) R.; m. George F. Douglas, Jr., Aug. 1, 1970. BA, Dickinson Coll., 1958; JD, Dickinson Sch Law, 1962; LLD (hon.), Wilson Coll., 1980, Dickinson Sch. Law, 1993, Dickinson Coll., 1994, Shippensburg U., 1996, Widener U., 1999. Bar: Pa. 1962. Atty. trust dept. Bank of Del., Wilmington, 1962-63; pvt. practice Carlisle, 1963-76; from public defender to chief public defender Cumberland County, Pa., 1974-76; judge Ct. Common Pleas, Cumberland County, 1976-78, U.S. Dist. Ct. (mid. dist.) Pa., Harrisburg, 1979-92, chief judge, 1992-99; federal judge U.S. Dist. Ct., Harrisburg, 2000—. Asst. prof., adj. prof. Dickinson Sch. Law, 1974—76; mem. Jud. Conf. Com. on Adminstrn. of Magistrate Judges Sys., 1996—2002, Pa. Bar Assn. Task Force on Legal Svcs. to the Needy, 2000—03. Bd. govs. Dickinson Sch. Law., Pa. State U., 2000—. Mem. Phi Alpha Delta. Democrat. Presbyterian. Office: US Dist Ct Federal Bldg PO Box 868 Harrisburg PA 17108-0868

RAMEY, CECIL EDWARD, JR., lawyer; b. Shreveport, La., Nov. 9, 1923; s. Cecil Edward and Blanche (Gwin) R.; m. Betty Loper, June 15, 1945; children— Martha L., L. Christine, Stephen E. BS summa cum laude, Centenary Coll., 1943; LLB, Yale U., 1949; postgrad., Tulane U., 1950-51. Bar: Wis. 1949, La. 1951. Assoc. Miller, Mack & Fairchild, Milw., 1949-50; mem. faculty Tulane U., 1950-54; assoc. Hargrove, Guyton, Van Hook and Hargrove, Shreveport, 1954-56, ptnr., 1956-63, Hargrove, Guyton, Van Hook and Ramey, Shreveport, 1963-73, Hargrove, Guyton, Ramey and Barlow, Shreveport, 1973-89, of counsel, 1989-94, Barlow and Hardtner, L.C., Shreveport, 1994-2001, Lemle Kelleher Barlow and Hardtner, Shreveport, 2001—03, Lemle & Kelleher LLP, Shreveport, 2003—. Adj. prof. Centenary Coll., 1992—98. Former chmn. Citizens Capital Improvements com. City of Shreveport; former mem. governing bd. Shreveport YMCA; former chmn. bd. trustees Broadmoor Meth. Ch., Shreveport, chmn. bd. stewards; former bd. dirs., former chmn. Shreveport-Bossier Found.; trustee Centenary Coll. With AC, U.S. Army, 1943-46. Named Shreveport's Outstanding Young Man of Yr., 1956, Mr. Shreveport, 1968; recipient Clyde E. Fant Meml. award community service United Way, 1979 Fellow Am. Coll. Trust and Estate Counsel; mem. ABA, La. Bar Assn., Shreveport Bar Assn., La. Law Inst., Shreveport C. of C. (pres. 1974), Centenary Coll. Alumni Assn. (past pres.), Shreveport Club, Order of Coif, Phi Delta Phi, Kappa Sigma. Clubs: Shreveport. Home: 139 Oscar Ln Shreveport LA 71105-3566 Office: Lemle & Kelleher LLP 401 Edwards St 10th Fl Shreveport LA 71101-3289 E-mail: cramey@lemle.com.

RAMEY, DENNY L. bar association executive director; b. Portsmouth, Ohio, Feb. 22, 1947; s. Howard Leroy and Norma Wylodine (Richards) R.; m. Jeannine Gayle Dunmyer, Sept. 24, 1971 (div. Nov. 1991); children: Elizabeth Michelle, Brian Michael. BBA, Ohio U., 1970; MBA, Capital U., 1976. Cert. assn. exec. Adminstrv. mgr. Transit Warehouse div. Elston Richards Storage Co., Columbus, Ohio, 1970-73; mgr. continuing profl. edn. Ohio Soc. CPA's, Columbus, 1973-79; exec. dir. Engrs. Found. of Ohio, Columbus, 1979-80; asst. exec. Ohio State Bar Assn., Columbus, 1980-86, exec. dir., sec., treas., 1986—. Treas., exec. com., bd. dirs. Ohio Bar Liability Ins. Co., Columbus, 1986—; treas. Ohio State Bar Found., 1986—; treas. Ohio Legal Ctr. Ins., Columbus, 1988-91; sec. Ohio Printing Co., Ltd., 1991; v.p. Osbanet, Inc., 1993—; chmn. Lawriter LLC, 2000—; bd. dirs. OSBA.com, LLC. Mem.: Ohio Soc. Assn. Execs., Am. Soc. Assn. Execs., Nat. Assn. Bar Execs., Brookside Golf & Country Club, Scioto Country Club. Methodist. Avocations: tennis, golf, sports, music, wine appreciation. Office: Ohio State Bar Assn 1700 Lake Shore Dr PO Box 16562 Columbus OH 43216-6562 E-mail: dramey@ohiobar.org.

RAMIL, MARIO R. judge; b. Quezon City, The Philippines, June 21, 1946; came to U.S., 1956; s. Quintin A. and Fausta M. (Reyes) R.; m. Judy E. Wong, Nov. 6, 1971; children: Jonathan, Bradley. BA in Polit. Sci., Calif. State U., Hayward, 1972; JD, U. Calif., San Francisco, 1975. Bar: Calif. 1976, Hawaii 1976, U.S. Dist. Ct. Hawaii, U.S. Dist. Ct. (no. dist.) Calif., U.S. Ct. Appeals (9th cir.) Law clk. San Francisco Neighborhood Legal Aid Found., 1973-75; legal counsel Sandigan-Newcomers Svcs., Inc., San Francisco, 1975-76; dep. atty. gen. Dept. Labor and Indsl. Rels., 1976-79; dep. atty. gen. cen. adminstrn. U. Hawaii, 1979-80; staff atty. house majority atty.'s office Hawaii Ho. of Reps., 1980; pvt. practice, 1980-82; dep. atty. gen. adminstrv. div. State of Hawaii, 1982-84, ins. commr., 1984-86; dir. Hawaii State Dept. Labor and Indsl. Rels., Honolulu, 1986-91; of counsel Lyons, Brandt, Cook and Hiramatsu, 1991-93; assoc. justice Hawaii Supreme Ct., Honolulu, 1993—. Bd. dirs. Hawaii Youth-At-Risk, 1989; co-chair state conv. Dem. Party State of Hawaii, 1984; mem. Adv. Coun. on Housing and Constrn., State of Hawaii, 1981; pres., bd. dirs. Hawaii Non-Profit Housing Corp.; exec. sec., chmn. adminstrv. budget com. Oahu Filipino Community Coun.; bd. dirs, legal advisor Oahu Filipino Jaycees, 1978-81. Office: Ali'iolani Hale Hawaii Supreme Ct 417 S Kinga St Honolulu HI 96813-2902

RAMO, ROBERTA COOPER, lawyer; b. Denver, Aug. 8, 1942; d. David D. and Martha L. (Rosenblum) Cooper; m. Barry W. Ramo, June 17, 1964. BA magna cum laude, U. Colo., 1964; JD, U. Chgo., 1967; LLD, U. Mo., 1995, U. Denver, 1995; LHD (hon.) , U. Colo., 1995; JD (hon.) , Golden Gate U., 1996; LLD (hon.) , U. S.C., 2001. Bar: N.Mex. 1967, Tex. 1971. With NC. Fund, Durham, 1967-68; nat. tchg. fellow Shaw U., Raleigh, N.C., 1968-70; mem. Sawtelle, Goode, Davidson & Troilo, San Antonio, 1970-72, Rodey, Dickason, Sloan, Akin & Robb, Albuquerque, 1972-74; sole practice law Albuquerque, 1974-77; dir., shareholder Poole, Kelly & Ramo, Albuquerque, 1977-93; shareholder Modrall, Sperling, Roehl, Harris & Sisk, Albuquerque, 1993—. Lectr. in field., bd. dirs. Merrill Lynch Asset Mgmt., Ednl. Credit Mgmt. Corp. Co-author: New Mexico Estate Administration System, 1980; editor: How to Create a System for the Law Office, 1975; contbg. editor: Tex. Probate Sys., 1974; contbr. articles to profl. jours., chpts. to books. Mem. steering com. World Conf. Domestic Violence, 1996—99; mem. Am. Law Inst. Coun., 1997—, exec. com., 2000—; mem. Martindale-Hubbell Legal Adv. Bd., 1996—2000; bd. dirs., past pres. N.Mex. Symphony Orch., 1977—86; bd. dirs. Albuquerque Cmty. Found., N.Mex. First, 1987—90, Santa Fe Opera, Santa Fe, 2001—; bd. regents U. N.Mex., 1989—94, pres., 1991—93; founding bd. mem. Think N.Mex., 1998—; mem. Civitas Initiative, 1997—; chmn. bd. Cooper's Inc., 1999—. Recipient Disting. Pub. Svc. award Gov. of N.Mex., 1993. Fellow: Am. Bar Found.; mem.: ABA (pres. 1995, bd. govs. 1994—97, chmn. London 2000 com., Asia Law Initiatives Coun. 1999—, others), Am. Arbitration Assn. (bd. dirs. 1997—, bd. trustees Global Ctr. Dispute Resolution Rsch. 1999—), Law Inst. Coun., Am. Judicature Soc. (bd. dirs. 1988—91), Am. Bar Retirement Assn. (bd. dirs. 1990—94), N.Mex. Bar Assn. (Outstanding Contbn. award 1981, 1984), Albuquerque Bar Assn. (bd. dirs., pres. 1980—81), Greater Albuquerque C. of C. (bd. dirs., exec. com. 1987—91). Pension, profit-sharing, and employee benefits, Probate (including wills, trusts), Property, real (including real estate development, water). Address: Modrall Sperling Roehl Harris & Sisk PO Box 2168 Albuquerque NM 87103-2168

RAMOS, CARLOS E. law educator; b. Caguas, P.R., Oct. 20, 1952; s. Francisco E. and Olga (Gonzalez) R.; m. Lesbia Hernandez, July 30, 1988; children: Carlos Francisco, Isabel Maria, Macarena Eugenia. BA, U. P.R., 1974, JD, 1978; diploma, U. Stockholm, 1975; LLM, U. Calif., Berkeley, 1987. Bar: P.R. 1978, U.S. Dist. Ct. P.R. 1978, U.S. Ct. Appeals (1st cir.) 1979. Staff atty. P.R. Legal Svcs., San Juan, P.R., 1978-79; asst. prof. law InterAm. U. P.R., San Juan, 1979-86, assoc. prof., 1986-93, dean, 1993-2000, prof. law, 1993—; exec. dir. Santurce Law Firm, San Jose, 1983-86. Co-author: Derecho Constitucional de Puerto Rico y los Estados Unidos, 1990, Teoria y Practica de la Litigacion en Puerto Rico. Mem. ABA, ATLA, Am. Judicature Soc., P.R. Bar Assn. Office: InterAm U PR Sch Law PO Box 70351 San Juan PR 00936-8351 E-mail: ceramos@inter.edu.

RAMSAUR, ALLAN FIELDS, lawyer, lobbyist; b. Rocky Mount, NC, Dec. 30, 1951; s. Carl Hamilton and Celestine (Fields) R.; m. Jimmie Lynn Brewer, Sept. 2, 1972; children: Katherine Celeste, Benjamin Allan. BA in Polit. Sci., Lambuth U., 1974; JD, U. Tenn., 1977. Bar: Tenn. 1977. Staff atty. Tenn. Dept. Mental Health, Nashville, 1977-80; dir. Tenn. Assn. Legal Services, Nashville, 1980-86; campaign dir. Steve Cobb, Nashville, 1986; exec. dir. Nashville Bar Assn., 1986-98, Tenn. Bar Assn., 1999—. Pres. Woodland-in-Waverly Neighborhood Assn., Nashville, 1985; bd. dirs. SAGA, Nashville, 1984-86, Bethlehem Center, Nashville, 1990-96 (sec. 1992, v.p. 1994-95). Recipient Leadership Nashville award, 1988. Mem. ABA (liaison to standing com. on legal aid and indigent defendants 1984-86, spl. com. on prepaid legal svcs. 1988-89, standing com. on lawyer referral and info. svc. 1990-92), Nat. Assn. Bar Execs. (chair edn. com.), Tenn. Bar Assn. (pres. young lawyers divsn. 1985-86), Nat. Legal Aid and Defender Assn. (chmn. legis com. 1984-86), Tenn. Soc. Assn. Execs. (pres. 2000). Democrat. Methodist. Home: 1417 Beddington Park Nashville TN 37215-5815 E-mail: aramsaur@tnbar.org.

RAMSAY, LOUIS LAFAYETTE, JR., lawyer, banker; b. Fordyce, Ark., Oct. 11, 1918; s. Louis Lafayette and Carmile (Jones) R.; m. Joy Bond, Oct. 3, 1945; children: Joy Blankenship, Richard Louis. JD, U. Ark., 1947; LLD (hon.), U. Ark., Fayetteville, 1988, U. Ark., Pine Bluff, 1992. Bar: Ark. 1947, U.S. Dist. Ct. Ark. 1947, U.S. Ct. Appeals (8th cir.) 1948, U.S. Supreme Ct. 1952. Of counsel Ramsay, Bridgforth, Harrelson & Starling and predecessor firm Ramsay, Cox, Lile, Bridgforth, Gilbert, Harrelson & Starling, Pine Bluff, Ark., 1948—; pres. Simmons First Nat. Bank, Pine Bluff, Ark., 1970-78, CEO, chmn. bd. dirs., 1978-83. Chmn. exec. com., bd. dirs. Blue Cross-Blue Shield of Ark., Usable Life Ins. Co.; chmn. exec. com. Simmons First Nat. Corp. With USAF, 1942-45, maj. Res., 1945-49. Recipient Disting. Alumnus award U. Ark., 1982, Outstanding Lawyer award Ark. Bar Assn./Ark. Bar Found., 1966, 87; named to Ark. Bus. Hall of Fame, 2003. Mem. ABA (mem. spl. com. on presdl. inability and vice presdl. vacancy 1966), Ark. Bar Assn. (pres. 1963-64), Ark. Bar Found. (pres. 1960-61, Joint Bar Assn.,-Bar Found. Outstanding Lawyer award 1966, Lawyer Citizen award 1987), Ark. Bankers Assn. (pres. 1980-81), Pine Bluff C. of C. (pres. 1968), Rotary (pres. Pine Bluff 1954-55). Methodist. Corporate, general, Probate (including wills, trusts). Office: Ramsay Bridgforth Harrelson & Starling 11th Fl Simmons 1st Nat Bldg 501 S Main St Pine Bluff AR 71601-4327 E-mail: firm@ramsaylaw.com.

RAMSEY, EDWARD LAWRENCE, judge; b. Dothan, Ala., Dec. 9, 1941; s. Joseph Robert and Hilda (Hawkins) R.; m. Pamela Thuss, 1971 (div. 1976); 1 child, Matthew Edward. Student, Emory U., 1960-62; BA, U. Ala., Tuscaloosa, 1965, JD, 1966. Bar: Ala. 1966, Calif. 1970, U.S. Ct. Appeals (5th and 11th cirs.) 1972. Dep. dist. atty. Office of Dist. Atty., San Diego, 1970-72; pvt. practice Birmingham, Ala., 1972-94; judge civil divsn. Cir. Ct. Jefferson County, Birmingham, 1995—. Capt. USMC, 1967-70. Republican. Episcopalian.

RANA, HARMINDERPAL SINGH, lawyer; b. Bombay, July 4, 1968; came to U.S., 1970; s. Baljit Singh and Devinder (Kaur) R.; m. Aasjot Kaur Sidhu, Mar. 8, 1998. BS in Fgn. Svc., cert. in Asian studies, Georgetown U., 1990; JD, honors cert. in internat. law, Rutgers U., Camden, N.J., 1994; cert. info. sys. analysis, Columbia U., 2002. Bar: N.J. 1994, U.S. Dist. Ct. N.J. 1994, N.Y. 1995, U.S. Dist. Ct. (so. and ea. dists.) N.Y. 1995. Pvt. practice, Warren, N.J., 1994—. Assoc. staff analyst N.Y.C. Dept. Mental Health, Bklyn., 1995-97, region coord., Bklyn. and S.I., 1997; pool atty. family law litigation N.J. Office Pub. Defender, Middlesex and Somerset counties, 1995. Mem. traffic safety com. Warren Twp. (N.J.) Coun., 1997-2000. NYU Trustees scholar, 1986, N.Y. State Regents scholar, 1986. Mem. ABA, Assn. Bar City N.Y. (health law com. 1997-2000). Sikh. Avocations: literature, philosophy, world affairs, athletic cross training, public service. Commercial, contracts (including sales of goods; commercial financing), General practice, Immigration, naturalization, and customs. Office: 3 Krausche Rd Warren NJ 07059 E-mail: rajranaesq@aol.com.

RANALOW, JOHN VIVIAN APLIN, solicitor; b. Barnes, Surrey, Eng., Apr. 17, 1930; Arrived in Portugal, 1969; s. Arthur Vivian and Alfreda Althea (Aplin) R. Degree in law, U. London. Jr. ptnr. Beddington Hughes & Hobart, London, 1956-58; pvt. practice Ranalow, Charles & Co., Hornchurch, England, 1958-69, cons., 1969-72; pvt. practice J.V.A. Ranalow Solicitor, Madeira, Portugal, 1972-92; assoc. SMS Advogadas, Madeira, Portugal, 1992—. Oral examiner in English Cambridge U., Funchal, Portugal, 1982-94. Author: (textbook) Law of Conveyancing, 1984. Sec. Assn. Friends of Conservatory of Music Found., 1994—; lay asst., trustee Holy Trinity Church, Funchal, 1981—; supt. Brit. Cemetary, Madeira, 1983—. Mem. Law Soc., Offshore Inst. Anglican. Avocations: music, reading. Fax: 351-291-776-998.

RANCHOD, KAUSHIK, lawyer; BS, U. So. Calif., L.A., 1995; JD, U. Calif., Hastings, 1998. Bar: Calif. 1998, U.S. Dist. Ct. (no. dist.) Calif. 1999, U.S. Dist. Ct. (ea. dist.) Calif. 1999. Pvt. practice, San Francisco. Mem.: U. So. Calif. Pub. Adminstrn., Am. Immigration Lawyers Assn., Phi Beta Kappa. Immigration, naturalization, and customs. Address: Ste 102 211 Gought St San Francisco CA 94102-6805

RAND, ANTHONY EDEN, lawyer; b. Garner, N.C., Sept. 1, 1939; s. Walter and Geneva R., Jr.; m. Karen Skarda; children: Ripley E., Craven M. AB, U. N.C., 1961, LLB, 1964; LLB (hon.), U. N.C., Fayetteville, N.C., 2000. Ptnr. Mitchiner, Andrews, Rand, Raleigh, N.C., 1965-68, Rose, Thorp, Rand & Ray, Fayetteville, N.C., 1968-81, Rose, Rand, Winfrey & Gregory, Fayetteville, 1982-89, Rand, Finch & Gregory, Fayetteville, 1989-93; mem. from 24th dist. N.C. Senate, Fayetteville, 1995—2001, chmn. rules and operations, 1995—, majority leader, 2001—, mem. from 19th dist., 2003—. Sec., legal counsel Sonorex, Inc., 1989-96; cons., Prime Med. Svcs., 1996-2000, Sonorex, Inc., 2001—. Mem. N.C. State Dem. Exec. Com., 1975-77; chmn. exec. com. Cumberland County Dem. party (N.C.), 1977-81; bd. visitors U. N.C.-Chapel Hill, Meth. Coll.; bd. dirs., mem. exec. com. Pub. Sch. Forum; bd. dirs. Fayetteville Area Sentencing, 1985; mem. adv. bd. Mus. Cape Fear, 1989—; mem. nat. adv. panel Child Care Action Com., 1989—; pres. Med-Tech Investments, 1989—. Mem. ABA, ATLA (state commiteeman 1968-72), N.C. Bar Assn., Am. Judicature Assn., Govtl. and Legis. Affairs C. of C., Alpha Tau Omega, Delta Theta Phi. Episcopalian. Office: 2014 Litho Pl Fayetteville NC 28304 E-mail: Tonyr@ncleg.net.

RAND, HARRY ISRAEL, lawyer; b. N.Y.C., July 27, 1912; s. Samuel and Rose (Hirth) R.; m. Anna Tulman, Oct. 22, 1938; children: Steven, Deborah, Naomi. BS, CCNY, 1932; JD, NYU, 1936. Bar: N.Y. 1936, U.S. Supreme Ct. 1943, D.C. 1947, U.S. Dist. Cts. (so. and ea. dists.) N.Y. 1959, 60, U.S. Ct. Appeals (2d cir.) 1966. Atty. U.S. Pub. Works Adminstrn., 1938-39, U.S. Dept. Interior, 1939-43, U.S. Dept. Justice, 1943-48; pvt. practice Washington, 1948-58; mem. Weisman, Celler, Allan, Spett & Sheinberg, N.Y.C., 1959-67, Botein, Hays & Sklar, N.Y.C., 1967-89; counsel Herrick, Feinstein, N.Y.C., 1990—. Mem. Assn. of Bar of City of N.Y., Am. Law Inst. Federal civil litigation, State civil litigation, Private international. Home: 66 Hillandale Rd Westport CT 06880-5319 also: 320 W 86th St New York NY 10024-3139 Office: Herrick Feinstein LLP Two Park Ave New York NY 10016 E-mail: hrand@herrick.com.

RAND, WILLIAM, lawyer, former state justice; b. N.Y.C., Oct. 11, 1926; s. William and Barbara (Burr) R.; married; children: Alicia, Carley Coudert, William Coudert, Paula Burr. AB, Harvard U., 1948; LLB, Columbia U., 1951. Bar: N.Y. 1951, U.S. Dist. Ct. N.Y. 1951, U.S. Supreme Ct., 1958, U.S. Ct. Appeals (2d cir.) 1961, U.S. Ct. Appeals (4th cir.) 1985. Asst. dist. atty. New York County, 1954-59; asst. counsel to gov. of State of N.Y., 1959-60; assoc. Coudert Bros., N.Y.C., 1961-62, ptnr., 1963-98; justice N.Y. State Supreme Ct., 1962. Justice Village of Cove Neck, Oyster Bay, N.Y., 1974-98. Mem. exec. com. New York County Reps., 1968-72. Served with USN, 1944-46, PTO. Mem.: Racquet and Tennis Club (N.Y.C.), Piping Rock Club (Locust Valley, N.Y.). General civil litigation, Private international. Home: 73 Cove Neck Rd Oyster Bay NY 11771-1821 Office: Coudert Bros Fl 43 1114 Avenue of the Americas New York NY 10036-7710 E-mail: paulrand@aol.com., randw@coudert.com.

RANDALL, KENNETH C. dean, law educator; JD, Hofstra U., 1981; Master's, Yale U., 1982, Columbia U., 1985, Doctorate, 1988. Practice law Simpson Thacher & Bartlett, N.Y.C., 1982-84; with faculty U. Ala. Sch. Law, Tuscaloosa, 1985—, vice dean, 1989-93, dean, 1993—. Author book on international law; contbr. articles to law jours. and revs. W. Bayard Cutting Jr. fellow of internat. law Columbia U. Sch. Law, 1984-85. Office: U Ala Law Sch PO Box 870382 Tuscaloosa AL 35487-0001

RANDALL, RONALD RAY, lawyer; b. Los Angeles, Aug. 4, 1939; m. Joanne Menu, Aug. 7, 1959 (div. July 1971); children: Marjorie, Ronald Jr., John; m. Jane Warriner, June 17, 2000. BSEE, U. Nev., 1961; JD, U. Calif., Berkeley, 1967. Bar: Calif. 1968, U.S. Dist. Ct. (so. dist.) Calif. 1968, U.S. Ct. Appeals (9th cir.) 1978, Tex. 1990. Assoc. Fowler, Knobbe & Martins, Orange, Calif., 1967-69; gen. counsel Gen. Automation, Inc., Anaheim, Calif., 1969-75; ptnr. Randall & Engle, Tustin, Calif., 1975-79; gen. counsel Smith Internat., Inc., Houston, 1979-90; v.p., gen. counsel, sec. Camco Internat., Inc., Houston, 1990—98; cons., 1998—.

RANDAZZO, ANTHONY J. lawyer; b. Paterson, N.J., Apr. 17, 1967; s. Dominick George and Joyce Kathleen Randazzo. BA, Temple U., 1989; JD, Hofstra U., 1992. Bar: N.J. 1995, U.S. Dist. Ct. N.J. 1995, U.S. Supreme Ct. 1999. Pvt. practice, Clifton, NJ, 1995—. Author poetry. Named Outstanding Young Man of Am., 1989. Mem.: ATLA, Assn. Criminal Def., Phi Alpha Delta. Avocations: art, theater , music. Criminal, Family and matrimonial, Personal injury (including property damage). Office: 1135 Clifton Ave Clifton NJ 07013

RANDELS, ED L. lawyer; b. Albuquerque, Nov. 17, 1953; s. James L. and Betty J. (Ridgeway) R.; m. Kathryn J. Eddleman, July 11, 1975; children: Nancy L, Joshua L. BA, Mid-Am. Nazarene Coll., Olathe, Kans., 1975; JD, U. Kans., 1982. Bar: Kans. 1982, U.S. Dist. Ct. Kans. 1982, U.S. Ct. Appeals (10th cir.) 1994. Asst. county atty. Montgomery County, Indpendence, Kans., 1982-85, Miami County, Paola, Kans., 1985-86; asst. city atty. City of Wichita, Kans., 1986-92; asst. county counselor Sedgwick County, Wichita, Kans., 1992—. Law day dir. Miami County Bar Assn., Paola, Kans., 1985-86. Contbr. articles to profl. jours. Mem. ABA, Kans. Bar Assn., Wichita Bar Assn. (chair law in edn. com. 1999-2000, mem. mcpl. practice com.), Christian Legal Soc. (pres. Wichita chpt. 1998-99, 2000-01). Republican. Nazarene. Office: Sedgwick County Counselor 525 N Main St Ste 359 Wichita KS 67203-3731 E-mail: erandels@sedgwick.gov.

RANDOLPH, A(RTHUR) RAYMOND, federal judge; b. Riverside, N.J., Nov. 1, 1943; m. Eileen J. O'Connor, May 18, 1984; children: John Trevor, Cynthia Lee. BS, Drexel U., 1966; JD summa cum laude, U. Pa., 1969. Bar: Calif. 1970, D.C. 1973, U.S. Supreme Ct. 1973. Law clk. to Hon. Henry J. Friendly U.S. Ct. Appeals (2d cir.), N.Y.C., 1969—70; asst. to solicitor gen. U.S. Dept. Justice, Washington, 1970—73, dep. solicitor gen., 1975—77; ptnr. Sharp, Randolph & Green, Washington, 1977—83, Randolph & Truitt, Washington, 1983—87, Pepper, Hamilton & Scheetz, Washington, 1987—90; judge U.S. Ct. Appeals (D.C. cir.), Washington, 1990—. Spl. asst. atty. gen. State of Mont., 1983—90, State of N.Mex., 1985—90, State of Utah, 1986—90; adv. panel Fed. Cts. Study Com., 1989—90; spl. counsel Com. on Stds. Ofcl. Conduct, U.S. Ho. of Reps., 1979—80; adj. prof. Georgetown U. Law Ctr., 1974—78; exec. sec. Atty. Gen.'s Com. on Reform of Fed. Jud. Sys., 1975—77; com. on fed. rules evidence U.S. Justice Dept., 1972; chmn. Com. on Govtl. Structures, McLean, Va., 1973—74; adj. prof. law sch. George Mason U., 1992, disting. prof., 1998—; com. codes conduct Jud. Conf. U.S., 1992—95, chmn., 1995—98. Recipient Spl. Achievement award, U.S. Dept. Justice, 1971. Mem.: D.C. Bar Assn., Calif. Bar Assn., Am. Law Inst., Order of Coif. Office: US Court of Appeals 333 Constitution Ave NW Washington DC 20001-2866

RANDOLPH, CHRISTOPHER CRAVEN, lawyer; b. Washington, May 26, 1956; s. William Barksdale and Elizabeth Page (Craven) R.; m. Linda Bubernak Dressler, June 6, 1982; children: Alexander Dressler, Brian Donovan. BA summa cum laude, U. Va., 1978; JD cum laude, Harvard U., 1982. Bar: D.C. 1983, N.Y. 1983. Assoc. Debevoise & Plimpton, N.Y.C., 1982-86, Washington, 1987-92; atty. advisor Agy. for Internat. Devel., Washington, 1992-95; investor, entrepreneur Vienna, Va., 1995—2002; assoc. gen. counsel Peace Corps, 2002—. Editor Harvard Law Rev., 1980-82; contbr. articles to profl. jours. Mem. ABA, D.C. Bar Assn., Phi Beta Kappa. Republican. Episcopalian. Avocations: travel, reading, sports. Corporate, general, Government contracts and claims, Securities. Home: 2784 Marshall Lake Dr Oakton VA 22124-1148

RANDOLPH, ELIZABETH T. elementary school educator; b. Milw., Nov. 19, 1946; d. George Graham and Thelma Henrietta Thompson; m. Richard Alfred Randolph, June 3, 1948; children: Brett Alexander, Rebecca Renee. BA in Spanish, Chico State Coll., 1968; MA in Edn., Stanford U., 1979. Tchr. Oronville Sch. Dist., Calif., 1969—70, Sunnyvale Sch. Dist., 1971—. Presenter in field. Mem.: Sunnyvale Edn. Assn. Democrat. Episcopalian. Avocations: skiing, singing, travel, bicycling, hiking. Home: 10927 Northridge Sq Cupertino CA 95014

RANDOLPH, ROBERT DEWITT, lawyer; b. Sligo, Pa., Mar. 6, 1929; s. DeWitt Lyman and Hazel Irene (McCall) R.; m. Betty Ann McElhattan, May 8, 1953 (dec. Aug. 1979); children: Douglas, Andrew; m. Susan Denise Hopkins, Oct. 15, 1988 BA, Westminster Coll., 1951; LLB, Harvard U., 1957. Bar: Ohio 1958, Pa. 1960, U.S. Supreme Ct. 1981. Assoc. Buckingham, Doolittle & Burroughs, Akron, Ohio, 1957-59, Rose, Houston, Cooper & Schmidt, Pitts., 1959-60, 61-65; fgn. svc. officer U.S. Dept. State, Washintgon, 1960-61; ptnr. Houston, Cooper, Spear & German, Pitts., 1965-70, Randolph & O'Connor, Pitts., 1970-74, Buchanan Ingersoll P.C., Pitts., 1974-93. Pres. Assn. Retarded Citizens Allegheny, Pitts., 1990-92; mem. Allegheny County Mental Health/Mental Retardation Bd., 2002—. With U.S. Army, 1951-54. U.S. Army, 1951—54. Mem. Duquesne Club, St. Clair Country Club. Democrat. Presbyterian. Avocations: golf, skiing. Home: 750 Washington Rd Pittsburgh PA 15228-2051

RANDT, CLARK THORP, JR., lawyer; b. Cleve., Nov. 24, 1945; s. Clark Thorp and Mary-Louise (Mitchell) R.; m. Sarah Talcott, Nov. 3, 1979; children: Clark Thorp III, Paull Mitchell, Clare Talcott. BA, Yale U., 1968; JD, U. Mich., 1975; People's Republic China law diploma, U. East Asia, 1988. Bar; N.Y. 1976. Assoc. Milbank, Tweed, Hadley & McCloy, N.Y.C., Hong Kong and Tokyo, 1975-82; lst sec., comml. attache Am. Embassy, Beijing, 1982-84; ptnr. Heller, Ehrman, White & McAuliffe, San Francisco and Hong Kong, 1985-87; resident ptnr. Gibson, Dunn and Crutcher, Hong Kong, 1987—. Cons. People's Republic China Ministry Fgn. Econ. Rels. and Trade joint legal seminars U.S. Dept. Commerce, 1983-85; legal advisor Nat. Coun. U.S.-China Trade, 1974. Contbr. articles to profl. jours. and books. Mem. nat. steering com. George Bush for Pres., l988; vice chmn. Reps. Abroad Com., Hong Kong, 1988—. With USAF, l968-72. Recipient Disting. Svc. medal U.S. Dept. Commerce, 1984. Mem. ABA, Am. Soc. Internat. Law, Am. C. of C. in Hong Kong (v.p., gov.), Yale Club, Univ. Club, Am. Club in Hong Hong, Ladies Recreation Club. Commercial, contracts (including sales of goods; commercial financing), Corporate, general. Home: 4B Eredine 38 Mt Kellett Rd The Peak Hong Kong Hong Kong Office: Caxton House 17/F 1 Duddell St Hong Kong Hong Kong

RANKIN, CLYDE EVAN, III, lawyer; b. Phila., July 3, 1950; s. Clyde Evan, Jr. and Mary E. (Peluso) R.; m. Camille Cozzone, Aug. 24, 1997; A.B., Princeton U., 1972; J.D., Columbia U., 1975; postgrad. Hague Acad. Internat. Law, 1975. Bar: N.Y., N.J., D.C., U.S. Supreme Ct. Law clk. to judge U.S. Dist. Ct. So. Dist. N.Y., 1975-77; assoc. Debevoise, Plimpton, Lyons & Gates, N.Y.C., 1977-79; assoc. Coudert Bros., N.Y.C., 1979-83, ptnr., 1984—. Trustee The Rensselaerville (N.Y.) Inst., 1989—, Coun. on Fgn. Rels., 1996—. Stone scholar, 1974. Mem. ABA, Assn. of Bar of City of N.Y., N.Y. State Bar Assn., D.C. Bar Assn., N.J. Bar Assn. Roman Catholic. Club: Amateur Comedy (N.Y.C.). Contbr. article to legal jour. E-mail: rankinc@coudert.com. Corporate, general, Private international. Office: Coudert Bros 1114 Ave of Americas New York NY 10036-7703

RANKIN, GENE RAYMOND, lawyer; b. Madison, Wis., Sept. 29, 1940; s. Eugene Carleton and Mildred Florence (Blomster) R.; m. Katherine E. Hundt, Aug. 25, 1979; 1 child, Abigail Hundt. BS, U. Wis., 1966, MS in Planning, 1973, JD, 1980. Bar: Wis. 1980, U.S. Dist. Ct. (we. dist.) Wis. 1980, U.S. Ct. Appeals (7th cir.) 1992. Systems analyst U. Wis. Primate Research Ctr., Madison, 1967-72; planner Dane County Regional Planning Commn., Madison, 1973-79; pres. Mendota Rsch., 1978—; with Risser and Risser, Madison, 1980-89; dir. land regulation and records dept. Dane County, Madison, 1984-89; pvt. practice Madison, Wis., 1989—; dir. bd. examiners Wis. Supreme Ct., Madison, 1994—. Planning cons., Madison, 1973-77; guest lectr. land use, ethics and admiralty law Law Sch. U. Wis., 1982, 86, 93, 94, 95, 96, guest lectr. land econs. Planning Sch., 1973-81; guest lectr. various legal subjects U. Wis. Ext., 1988—. Author: Historic Preservation Law in Wisconsin, 1982; The First Bite at the Apple: State Supreme Court Takings Jurisprudence Antedating First English, 1990; (with others) Boundary Law in Wisconsin, 1991; contbr. articles to profl. jours. Bd. dirs. Madison Trust for Hist. Preservation, 1984-87, Madison Zoning Bd. of Appeals, 1986-94, Dane County Humane Soc., 1988-90, Dane County Housing Devel. Corp., 1975-79; spl. counsel City of Fitchburg, 1983-84, Nat. Trust for Hist. Preservation, 1989-90, City of Shullsburg, 1990-98; gen. counsel Cat Fanciers' Assn. Midwestern Region, 1990-95, Hist. Madison, Inc., 1981—, Wis. Lead Region Hist. Trust, Inc., 1992—; mem. legis. coun. Spl. Com. on Condo. Issues, Madison, 1984-85; commr. and vice-chmn. Dane County Housing Authority, 1979-84; chmn. Wis. Chamber Orch. Bd., 1979-81; state chmn. McCarthy 1976 campaign, Madison, 1974-76. With USCGR, 1958-60. Fellow Nat. Endowment for the Arts and Humanities, 1972; Olympic finalist for Internat. 470 yachting competition, 1976. Mem. Am. Planning Assn., Urban Land Inst., Urban and Regional Info. Sys. Assn., Wis. Bar Assn. (bd. dirs., treas., founder environ. law sect.), Dane County Bar Assn., Coun. Bar Admission Adminstrs., U. Wis. Hoofers Sailing Club (vice commodore 1972), Meml. Union Club, U.S. Yacht Racing Union, Downtown Madison Rotary, Ixion. Avocations: sailing, racquet sports, music, skating, motorcycling. Environmental, Land use and zoning (including planning), Property, real (including real estate development, water). Home: 2818 Ridge Rd Madison WI 53705-5224 Office: 715 Tenney Bldg 110 E Main St Madison WI 53703-3395

RANNIGER, LESLIE JEAN, lawyer; b. Dallas, Mar. 5, 1957; BA, U. Colo., Boulder, 1979; MBA, U. Denver, 1982, JD, 1985. Bar: Colo. 1985, U.S. Dist. Ct. Colo., 1985. Atty. Cosgiff Dunn & Abplanalp, Vail, Colo., 1985-87, Frascona & Joiner, Boulder, 1987-89; in-house counsel Ameralq Inc., Boulder, 1989-90; pvt. practice Boulder, 1990—. V.p., bd. dirs. Boulder County YWCA, 1985-87; dir. Cherryvale Fire Protection Dist., 1982-83. General civil litigation, Commercial, contracts (including sales of goods; commercial financing), Property, real (including real estate development, water). Office: PO Box 15 Boulder CO 80306-0015

RANSBOTTOM, JENNIFER DICKENS, lawyer; b. Pontiac, Mich., Oct. 7, 1966; d. David Noel and Suzanne Lynch Dickens; m. Barry Don Ransbottom, July 4, 1997. BS, Marshall U., 1988; JD, W.Va. U., 1994. Bar: Ga. 1994, W.Va. 1994, U. S. Dist. Ct. (so. dist.) W.Va. 1994. Sole practitioner Ransbottom Law Office, Huntington, W.Va. Mem. ABA, Ga. Bar Assn., W.Va. Bar Assn. (family law com. 1997—), Cabell County Bar Assn. Democrat. Roman Catholic. Family and matrimonial, Juvenile. Office: Ransbottom Law Office PO Box 1388 Huntington WV 25715 E-mail: JenRansbottom@aol.com.

RANSOM-MARTIN, EVA KATHRYN, law librarian, researcher; b. San Francisco, Jan. 31, 1957; m. Steven Ransom-Jones; children: Christopher Ian, Philip. Fgn. student acknowledgement, U. Moscow, 1979; BA cum laude, U. Tex., 1980; cert., Notre Dame Summer London Law Programme, 1995; JD, Wesleyan U., 1998; postgrad., Tex. Woman's U. Rschr., author Martin Law, Inc., Tex., 1996—. Author: Fleeting Vowels in Russian Verbs of Motion (Russian lang. edit.), 1979; guest author The Super Antioxidants, 1998. Bd. dirs. Health Counseling, Inc., Tex., 1997—2001. Mem.: Am. Assn. Law Librs., Phi Delta Phi. Avocations: Slavic-based languages, quantum physics, law. Home: 7901 Rampston Pl Fort Worth TX 76137 Fax: 817-427-5267. E-mail: evarmjd@aol.com.

RAPADAS, LEONARDO M. lawyer; b. 1960; BS, Pacific Univ.; JD, Williamette Univ. Coll of Law. Pros. Guam Atty. Gen. office, 1989—97, chief pros., 1997—99; US Atty. Dept. of Justice, Guam and Mariana Islands, 2003. Office: Sirena Plz Ste 500 108 Hernan Cortez Hagatna 96950-0377 Japan*

RAPER, WILLIAM CRANFORD, lawyer; b. Asheville, N.C., Aug. 17, 1946; s. James Sidney and Kathryn (Cranford) R.; m. Patricia Dotson, Sept. 28, 1974; children: Kimber-leigh, Heather, James. AB, U. N.C., 1968; JD, Vanderbilt U., 1972. Bar: N.C. 1972, U.S. Ct. Appeals (4th cir.) 1972, U.S. Supreme Ct. 1977, U.S. Ct. Appeals (fed. cir.) 1985. Law clk. to Senator Sam Ervin Jr., Washington, 1970; law clk. to presiding justice U.S. Ct. Appeals (4th cir.), Richmond, Va., 1972-73; ptnr. Womble, Carlyle, Sandridge & Rice, Winston-Salem, N.C., 1974—. Fellow Am. College Trial Lawyers; mem. ABA, N.C. Bar Assn., N.C. Assn. of Def. Attys. (charter). Federal civil litigation, State civil litigation, Personal injury (including property damage). Office: Womble Carlyle Sandridge & Rice One Wachovia Ctr 301 S Coll St Ste 3300 Charlotte NC 28202-6025 E-mail: braper@wcsr.com.

RAPINET, CRISPIN WILLIAM, lawyer; b. London, Feb. 18, 1964; s. Michael William and Christina Mary R.; m. Ruth Margaret Ingledow, May 3, 1998; children: Francesca Hero, Juliette Eloise, Zachary Paris William. BA with honors, Corpus Christi Coll., Cambridge, Eng., 1987; Law Soc. Finals, Coll. Law, London, 1988. Bar: solicitor Eng., Wales, 1990, Hong Kong, 1998. Articled clk., solicitor Lovell White Durrant, London, 1990-98; ptnr., 1998, 1998-2000, Lovells, Hong Kong, 2000—. Mem. Soc. Practitioners of Insolvency/R3, Insolvency Interest Group. Bankruptcy, General civil litigation, Private international. Office: Lovells 23rd Fl Cheung Kong Ctr 2 Queens Rd Ctrl Hong Kong China Fax: (852) 2219-0222. E-mail: crispin.rapinet@lovells.com.

RAPOPORT, DAVID E. lawyer; b. Chgo., May 27, 1956; s. Morris H. and Ruth (Teckteil) R.; m. Andrea Gail Albun; children: Alyson Faith, Steven Andrew. BS in Fin., No. Ill. U., 1978; JD with high honors, Ill. Inst. Tech., 1981; cert. trial work, Lawyers Postgrad. Inst., Chgo., 1984; cert. civil trial specialist, Nat. Bd. Trial Adv., 1991. Bar: Ill. 1981, Wis. 1995, U.S. Dist. Ct. (no. dist.) Ill. 1981, U.S. Dist. Ct. (trial bar) Ill. 1993, U.S. Dist. Ct. (so. and ctrl. dists.) Ill., U.S. Ct. Appeals (7th cir.) 1981, U.S. Ct. Appeals (4th cir.) 1996. Assoc. Katz, Friedman, Schur & Eagle, Chgo., 1981-90, of counsel, 1990—; ptnr. Baizer & Rapoport, Chgo., of counsel Highland Park, Ill., 1990-95; founder, pres. Rapoport Law Offices, P.C. (formerly Rapoport & Kupets P.C.), 1995—. Instr. legal writing Ill. Inst. Tech.-Kent Coll. Law, Chgo., 1981, guest lectr., 1985-92; instr. Ill. Inst. CLE, 1995—; arbitrator Million Dollar Advs. Forum, 1995—; state coord. Nat. Bd. Trial ADvocacy; lead trial counsel, mem. plaintiff's steering com. In Air Disaster at Charlotte Douglas Airport, 1994; mem. lead counsel com. In Air Disaster at Morrisville, N.C., 1994; lead trial counsel, In The Air Disaster at Sioux Gateway Airport, 1989. Fellow Roscoe Pound Found.; mem. ABA, ATLA (sustaining mem.), Ill. Bar Assn., Ill. Trial Lawyers Assn., Chgo. Bar Assn., Ill. Inst. for CLE, Trial Lawyers for Pub. Justice, Trial Lawyers for Pub. Justice, Trial Lawyers for Civil Justice, Lake County Bar Assn. Aviation, Personal injury (including property damage), Product liability. Office: Rapoport Law Offices PC 20 N Clark St Ste 3500 Chicago IL 60602-2801

RAPOPORT, NANCY B. dean, law educator; b. Bryan, Tex., June 29, 1960; m. Jeffrey D. Van Niel, Oct. 13, 1996. BA in legal studies, honors psychology summa cum laude, Rice U., 1982; JD, Stanford Law Sch., 1985. Bar: Calif. 1987, U.S. Dist. Cts. (no., ea., ctrl., and so. dists.) Calif. 1987, Ohio 1993, Nebr. 1999, U.S. Ct. Appeals (ninth cir.) 1987. Jud. clerk Hon. Joseph T. Sneed, United States Ct. Appeals for Ninth Cir. , San Francisco, 1985—86; assoc. bus.dept. of bankruptcy and workouts group Morrison & Foerster, San Francisco, 1986—91; asst. prof. Ohio State U. Coll. Law, Columbus, Ohio, 1991—95, tenured assoc. prof., 1995—98, assoc. dean student affairs, 1996—98, prof., 1998; dean, prof. law U. Nebr. Coll. Law , Lincoln, 1998—2000, U. Houston Law Ctr., 2000—. Invited spkr., panelist, and presenter in field; mem. Robert Wood Johnson Found. Partnership Initiative, Policy and Enforcement Workgroup , 1998—2000; mem. , chancellor spl. budget adv. com., 1999; chair UNL search com. Dean Coll. Arch., 1999—2000, Dean Coll. Arts & Scis., 2000. Note editor (rev.) Stanford Law; author: (with co-author Jeffrey D. Van Niel) "Retail Choice" Is Coming: Have you Hugged Your Utility Lawyer Today? , 2001; contbr. articles to profl. jours. and revs. ; (mem. editl. bd.) Calif. Bankruptcy Jour., 1995—, State Bar Tex., Bar Jour. Editl. Bd. Com., 2001—04. Bd. trustees Law Sch. Admissions Coun., 2001—; bd. dirs. Friends of Girl Scouting Adv. Bd., 2001—, Pro Bono Rsch. Group, 2000—, St. Elizabeth Found., 1999—2000, ADL Southwest Regional Bd., 2001—, Houston Area Women's Ctr. Named Legal Pioneer for Women in Law (first woman to serve as dean of Nebr. Law Sch.), Nebr. State Bar Assn., 2000, Outstanding Prof. of Yr., Ohio State U. Coll. Law., 1997; named to Louis Nemzer meml. lectr., 1998; fellow 1998 Fellowship, Am. Bankruptcy Law Jour. Fellow: Am. Bar Found.; mem.: ABA (task force on law student debt 2001—), A.A. White Inn of Ct. (exec. com. 2000—), Assn. Am. Law Sch.'s Profl. Develop. Com., Ohio State Bar Assn. (legal edn. com. 1997—98), Am. Bankruptcy Inst. (law sch. com. 1994—), Bar Assn. San Francisco, Nebr. Continuing Legal Edn. (long-range planning com. 1998—2000), Nat. Assn. Coll. and U. Attys., Nebr. State Bar Assn. (bankruptcy sect. 1998—2000, exec.com., bankruptcy sect. 1999—2000, access to profession com. 1999—2001), Houston Bar Found. (selection com. Best Article award 2000—), Houston Bar Assn., Am. Law Inst. Avocations: tae kwon do, ballroom dancing, Latin dancing, black and white photography, music. Office: U Houston Law Ctr 100 Law Ctr Houston TX 77204-6060 Business E-Mail: nrapoport@uh.edu.

RAPP, GERALD DUANE, lawyer, manufacturing company executive; b. Berwyn, Nebr., July 19, 1933; s. Kenneth P. and Mildred (Price) R.; children: Gerald Duane Jr., Gregory T., Amy Frances Wanzek. BS, U. Mo., 1955; JD, U. Mich., 1958. Bar: Ohio bar 1959. Practice in, Dayton, 1960—; ptnr. Smith & Schnacke, 1963-70; asst. gen. counsel Mead Corp., Dayton, 1970, v.p. human resources and legal affairs, 1973, v.p., corp. sec., 1975, v.p., gen. counsel, corp. sec., 1976, v.p., gen. counsel, 1979, sr. v.p., gen. counsel, 1981-91, counsel to bd. dirs., 1991-92; of counsel Bieser, Greer & Landis, 1992—. Pres. R-J Holding Co., Weber Canyon Ranch, Inc. Sr. editor U. Mich. Law Rev., 1957-58. Past chmn. Oakwood Youth Commn.; past v.p., bd. dirs. Big Bros. Greater Dayton; mem. pres.'s visitors com. U. Mich. Law Sch.; past trustee Urbana Coll.; past pres., trustee Ohio Ctr. Leadership Studies, Robert K. Greenleaf Ctr., Indpls.; past pres. bd. trustees Dayton and Montgomery County Pub. Libr.; past. mem. bd. visitors Law Schs. of Dayton. 1st lt. U.S. Army, 1958-60. Mem. ABA, Ohio Bar Assn., Dayton Bar Assn., Moraine Country Club, Dayton Racquet Club, Dayton Lawyers Club, Met. Club Washington, Phi Kappa Psi, Phi Delta Phi, Beta Gamma Sigma. Presbyterian. Office: 108 Green St Dayton OH 45402-2835 Fax: 937-224-0403.

RAPP, JAMES ANTHONY, lawyer, author; b. Williamson, W.Va., Feb. 25, 1949; s. Roy Thomas and Lucille (Middendorf) R.; m. Martha Brune, Dec. 28, 1972; children: Rebecca, Elizabeth Marie, Amy Christine. BS in Comm., U. Ill., Urbana, 1971; JD, Washington U., 1974. Bar: Ill. 1974, Mo. 1975, D.C. 2001, U.S. Dist. Ct. (so. dist.) Ill. 1975, U.S. Ct. Appeals (7th cir.) 1976, U.S. Ct. Appeals (8th cir.) 1976, U.S. Tax Ct. 1976, U.S. Supreme Ct. 1979, U.S. Dist. Ct. (cen. dist.) Ill. 1980. Prin. Hutmacher & Rapp PC and predecessors, Quincy, Ill., 1974—. Asst. corp. counsel City of Quincy, 1976-85; cons. Ill. Corps. Legal System, 1984. Author: Education Law, 1984, Victims Rights: Law and Litigation, 1988; co-author: Illinois Public Community College Act: Tenure Policies and Procedures, 1980, School Crime and Violence: Victims Rights, 1986, Illinois Domestic Relations Legal System, 1983; contbr. chpts. to books, articles to profl. jours. Bd. dirs. United Way Adams County, Inc., Quincy, 1975-81, pres., 1981-82; bd. dirs. Quincy Symphony Orch. Assn., 1976-79, pres., 1979-82. Mem. ABA, Ill. State Bar Assn., Mo. Bar Assn., Adams County Bar Assn., Chgo. Bar Assn. Corporate, general, General practice. Home: 1223 Scotia Trl Quincy IL 62301-6287 Office: Hutmacher & Rapp PC 428 N 6th St Quincy IL 62301-2502

RAPP, STEPHEN JOHN, international prosecutor; b. Waterloo, Iowa, Jan. 26, 1949; s. Spurgeon John and Beverly (Leckington) R.; m. Donna J.E. Maier, 1981; children: Alexander, Stephanie. AB cum laude, Harvard U., 1971; JD with honors, Drake U., 1973. Bar: Iowa 1974, U.S. Dist. Ct. (no. and so. dists.) Iowa 1978, U.S. Ct. Appeals (8th cir.) 1979, U.S. Supreme Ct. 1979. Rsch. asst. Office of U.S. Senator Birch Bayh, Ind., 1970; community program asst. HUD, Chgo., 1971; mem. Iowa Ho. Reps., 1972-74, 79-83, Coun. to Majority Caucus, Iowa Ho. Reps., 1975; staff dir., counsel subcom. on juvenile delinquency U.S. Senate, Washington, 1977-78; ptnr. Rapp & Gilliam, Waterloo, 1979-83; pvt. practice Waterloo, 1983-93; U.S. atty. U.S. Dist. Ct. (no. dist.) Iowa, 1993—2001; sr. prosecuting atty. United Nations Internat. Crime Tribunal for Rwanda, 2001—. Del., mem. com. Dem. Nat. Conv., 1976, 80, 84, 88, 92; mem. Dem. Nat. Adv. Com. on Econ., 1982-84, chmn. Black Hawk Dem. Com., 1986-91; mem. Iowa Dem. Com., 1990-93, chair 2d C.D. Dem. Com., 1991-93. Mem. ABA, Iowa Bar Assn., Order of Coif. Methodist. Home: 219 Highland Blvd Waterloo IA 50703-4229 Office: K-708 UN-ICTR PO Box 6016 Arusha Tanzania E-mail: rapp@un.org.

RAPPAPORT, CHARLES OWEN, lawyer; b. N.Y.C., May 15, 1950; s. Edward and Edith (Novick) R.; m. Valerie B. Ackerman, Oct. 11, 1987; children: Emily Randle, Sarah Elisabeth. BA, Columbia U., 1970; JD, NYU, 1975. Bar: N.Y. 1976. Assoc. Simpson, Thacher & Bartlett, N.Y.C., 1975-82, ptnr., 1982—. Corporate taxation. Home: 26 N Moore St Apt 4W New York NY 10013-2436 Office: Simpson Thacher & Bartlett 425 Lexington Ave 14th Fl New York NY 10017-3954 E-mail: corappaport@stblaw.com.

RAPPAPORT, STUART RAMON, lawyer; b. Detroit, Apr. 13, 1935; s. Reuben and Zella (Golechen) R.; m. Anne M. Plotnick; children: Douglas, Erica Rappaport Witt. BA in History, U. Mich., 1956; JD, Harvard U., 1959. Bar: Calif. 1962. Trial lawyer, chief trials, bur. chief, chief. asst. pub. defender L.A. County Pub. Defender's Office, L.A., 1962-87; pub. defender Santa Clara County, San Jose, Calif., 1987-95; pvt. practice, 1995—. Mem. standing adv. com. on criminal law Jud. Coun. Calif., San Francisco, 1993—; mem. discipline evaluation com. State Bar of Calif. Contbr. articles to profl. jours. Recipient Lifetime Achievement award Calif. Attys. for Criminal Justice. Mem. Calif. Pub. Defenders Asn. (pres. 1982-83, Lifetime Achievement award), L.A. County Pub. Defenders Assn. (pres.). Democrat. Jewish. Address: 1415 Arch St Berkeley CA 94708 E-mail: sturap@mcn.

RARDON, LARRY L. lawyer; b. Arcadia, Fla., Oct. 4, 1946; s. Wayne V. and Nellie Rardon; m. Hilda M. Rardon, Dec. 12, 1986; children: Shawn, Adria. BA, U. South Fla., 1968; JD, Stetson U., 1971. Bar: Fla. 1971. Specialist in trial work Rardon, Rodriguez & Assocs. PA, Tampa, Fla. Personal injury (including property damage), Workers' compensation. Office: 3918 N Highland Ave Tampa FL 33603

RARICK, PHILIP JOSEPH, judge; b. Collinsville, Ill., Nov. 10, 1940; s. Philip J. and Mary (Buckman) R.; m. Janet N. Arnovitz, Feb. 1, 1963; 1 child, Philip J. IV. BA, So. Ill. U., 1962; JD, St. Louis U., 1966. Bar: Ill. 1966, U.S. Dist. Ct. Ill. 1966. Twp. atty. Collinsville & Jarvis, Collinsville, Ill., 1966-75; asst. state's atty. Madison County, Edwardsville, Ill., 1966-75; city atty. City of Collinsville, 1967-75; cir. judge Third Jud. Cir., Edwardsville, 1975-88; presiding judge Criminal Div. in Madison County, Ill., 1982—85; chief cir. judge Third Jud. Cir., Edwardsville, 1985-87; mem. exec. com. Ill. Jud. Conf., Springfield, 1985—; presiding judge Criminal Div. in Madison County, Ill., 1987—88; elected judge Appellate Ct., Fifth Dist., Ill., 1988; mem., chmn. complex litigation com. Ill. Jud. Conf., Springfield, 1988—96; judge indsl. commn. divsn. Ill. Appellate Ct., 1988—; served Industrial Comm. Div. of the Appellate Ct., 1992; mem. Ill. Cts. Commn. State of Ill., Springfield, 1992—99; mem. Courts Comm., Ill., 1992—99; elected judge, retained Appellate Ct., Fifth Dist., Ill., 1998; alt. mem. Courts Comm., Ill., 1999—; mem., chmn. complex litig. com. Springfield, Ill., 1999—2001. Chmn. (manual) Illinois Manual for Complex Litigation. Mem. Ill. State Bar Assn., Ill. Judges Assn. (dir. 1977—), Madison County Bar Assn., Tri-City Bar Assn. Office: Supreme Ct Bldg Springfield IL 62701 also: State of Ill Bldg 160 N LaSalle St Chicago IL 60601*

RASCH, STEPHEN CHRISTOPHER, lawyer; b. Cambridge, Mass., Jan. 20, 1962; s. Philip John and Lynne (Whiteman) R.; m. Ellen Rasch; children: Lauren Byrne, Hilary Daniel, Stephen Charles. BA, U. Notre Dame, 1983; JD, U. Tex., 1986. Bar: Tex. 1986, U.S. Dist. Ct. (no., so. & ea. dists.) Tex., U.S. Ct. Appeals (5th cir.). Law clk. Hon. Joseph T. Sneed U.S. Ct. Appeals (9th cir.), San Francisco, 1986-87; assoc. Thompson & Knight, Dallas, 1987-92, ptnr., 1993—. Mem. Tex. Bar Assn., Dallas Bar Assn., Order of Coif, Phi Beta Kappa. Republican. Roman Catholic. General civil litigation. Office: Thompson & Knight 1700 Pacific Ave Ste 3300 Dallas TX 75201-4693 E-mail: raschs@tklaw.com.

RASHIDMANESH, HAMID REZA, solicitor; b. Tehran, Iran, Feb. 3, 1972; s. T. and S. Rashidmanesh; married. BSc in Govt. Law, London Sch. Econs., 1992, MSc in Internat. Rels., 1993; diploma in law, The Coll. Law, 1994, diploma in legal practice, 1995; postgrad., London Sch. Econs., 2002—. Bar: England & Wales. Trainee solicitor Nabarro Nathanson, London, 1996—98, solicitor, 1998—99, McDermott, Will & Emery, 1999—2001, Morrison & Foerster, 2001—. Contbr. articles to profl. jours. Pro bono legal counsel Friends of Benjamin Franklin Ho., London, 2001—. Mem.: Law Soc. England and Wales. Corporate, general, Communications, Commercial, contracts (including sales of goods; commercial financing). Office: Morrison & Foerster 21 Garlick Hill London EC4V 2AU England Fax: +44 20 7815 1159. E-mail: hrashidmanesh@mofo.com.

RASHKIND, ALAN BRODY, lawyer; b. N.Y.C., June 6, 1947; s. Julian and Eleanor (Brody) R.; m. Suzette DeBell, July 9, 1972; children: Graham Brody, Douglas Cormack. BA, Randolph-Macon Coll., 1969; JD, U. Va., 1972. Bar: Va. 1972, U.S. Dist. Ct. (ea. dist.) Va. 1972, U.S. Ct. Appeals (4th cir.) 1980, U.S. Supreme Ct. 1992. Assoc. Furniss, Davis and Sachs, Norfolk, Va., 1972-75; ptnr., shareholder Furniss, Davis Rashkind and Saunders P.C. and predecessors, Norfolk, 1976—. Mem. faculty Va. State Bar Law Sch., 2000—, State Bar Professionalism Course, 1996-99; adj. prof. law William and Mary Law Sch., 2003—. Co-author: Virginia Insurance Case Finder, 1st edit., 1994, 2d edit., 2002; contbr. articles to profl. jours. Trustee Randolph-Macon Coll., Ashland, Va., 1991-2003, pres. Soc. of Alumni, 1987-89; trustee, mem. exec. com. Chesapeake Bay Acad., Virginia Beach, Va., 1989—, vice chmn., 1996-2002, chmn., 2002—. Fellow Va. Law Found., Am. Coll. Trial Lawyers; mem. ABA, Va. State Bar Assn., Va. Bar Assn., Fed. Bar Assn., Norfolk-Portsmouth Bar Assn., Virginia Beach Bar Assn., Va. Assn. Def. Attys., Def. Rsch. Inst., Fedn. Def. and Corp. Counsel, Boyd-Graves Conf., (chmn. 1995-97), I'Anson-Hoffman Inn of Court (master of the bench 1987-94). General civil litigation, Insurance, Personal injury (including property damage). Office: Furniss Davis et al 6160 Kempsville Cir Norfolk VA 23502-3933

RASHKIND, PAUL MICHAEL, lawyer; b. Jamaica, N.Y., May 21, 1950; s. Harvey and Norma (Dorfman) Rashkind; m. Robin Shane Rashkind, Dec. 20, 1975; children: Adam Charles, Noah Hamilton, Jennifer Elizabeth. AA, Miami-Dade Jr. Coll., 1970; BBA, U. Miami, Coral Gables, Fla., 1972, JD, 1975. Bar: Fla. 1975, D.C. 1981, N.Y. 1981, U.S. Dist. Ct. (so. dist.) Fla. 1975, U.S. Ct. Appeals (5th cir.) 1976, U.S. Supreme Ct. 1978, U.S. Dist. Ct. (mid. dist.) Fla. 1979, U.S. Ct. Appeals (2d and 11th cirs.) 1981, U.S. Ct. Appeals (4th and 6th cirs.) 1986, U.S. Dist. Ct. (no. dist.) Fla. 1987, U.S. Dist. Ct. (no. dist.) Calif. 1989; diplomate Nat. Bd. Trial Advocacy-Criminal Law (bd. examiners), bd. cert. Criminal Trial Law, Fla. Bar. Asst. state atty. Dade County State Attys. Office, Miami, Fla., 1975-78, chief asst. state atty. in charge of appeals, 1977-78; atty. Sams, Gerstein & Ward, P.A., Miami, 1978-83; ptnr. Bailey, Gerstein, Rashkind & Dresnick, Miami, 1983-92, supr. asst. Fed. Defender Chief of Appeals, 1992—. Spl. master Ct. Appointment, Miami, 1982-83; arbitrator Dade County Jail Inmates Grievance Program, Miami, 1981-92; mem. Fla. Bar Unauthorized Practice of Law Com. C, 11th Jud. Cir., Miami, 1980-84, Fed. Ct. Practice Com., 1992—; mem. So. Dist. Fla. Fed. Ct. Rules Com., 1996—. Contbr. articles on ethics and criminal law to profl. jours. Pres., bd. dirs. Lindgren Homeowners Assn., Miami, 1981-86. Fellow: Am. Bd. Criminal Lawyers (bd. govs. 1980—86); mem.: ATLA, ABA (ethics com. criminal justice sect. 1979—92, vice chmn. 1985—87, chmn. 1987—89, ethics advisor to chair 1992—97, criminal justice sect. coun. 1998—, vice chair criminal justice sect. 2001—), Soc. Bar and Gavel, Nat. Assn. Criminal Def. Lawyers, Acad. Fla. Trial Lawyers (chmn. criminal law sect. 1985—86, diplomate 1986—), Fla. Assn. Criminal Def. Lawyers (Miami pres. 2002—, v.p. 2001—02, bd. dirs. 1992—2000), Dade County Bar Assn., D.C. Bar Assn., N.Y. Bar Assn., Fla. Bar Assn. (commn. on lawyer professionalism 1988—89, criminal law cert. com. 1989—94, standing com. on professionalism 1989—94), Hon. Order Ky. ols., Iron Arrow, Delta Theta Phi, Phi Rho Pi, Pi Sigma Alpha, Tau Kappa Alpha, Delta Sigma Rho, Omicron Delta Kappa. Democrat. Jewish. Appellate, Constitutional, Criminal. Office: Fed Pub Defender's Office SD FL 150 W Flagler St Ste 1500 Miami FL 33130-1555 E-mail: paul@rashkind.com.

RASK, KELLY SCOTT, lawyer; b. Mpls., Dec. 18, 1950; s. Otis Henry and Patricia Ann Rask. BA, Macalester Coll., 1972; JD, U. Minn., 1982. Bar: Minn. 1984, U.S. Dist. Ct. Minn. 1984. Assoc. counsel various law offices, Minn., 1984—87; pvt. practice St. Paul, 1988—. Mem. transition team Pres.-Elect Reagan, 1980-81. Author: The American Experiment Plan, 1990. Bankruptcy, Family and matrimonial, Landlord-tenant. Office: PO Box 683 Owatonna MN 55060-0683

RASMUS, JOHN CHARLES, trade association executive, lawyer; b. Rochester, N.Y., Dec. 27, 1941; s. Harold Charles and Myrtle Leota (Dybevik) R.; m. Elaine Green Reeves, Mar. 19, 1982; children: Kristin, Stuart, Karin. AB, Cornell U., 1963; JD, U. Va., 1966. Bar: Va. 1970, U.S. Supreme Ct. 1974. Spl. agt. Def. Dept., Washington, 1966-70; v.p., adminstrv. officer, legis. rsch. counsel U.S. League Savs. Instns., Washington, 1970-83; asst. to exec. v.p. Nat. Assn. Fed. Credit Unions, 1983-84; sr. fed. adminstrv. counsel, mgr. regulatory & trust affairs Am. Bankers Assn., 1985—. Bd. trustees The Appraisal Found. Mem. ABA, FBA (disting. svc. award 1980, 82, past chmn. long range planning com., past chmn. coun. fin. instns. and economy), Univ. Club, Exchequer Club, Masons. Home: 303 Kentucky Ave Alexandria VA 22305-1739 Office: Am Bankers Assn 1120 Connecticut Ave NW Washington DC 20036 E-mail: jrasmus@aba.com.

RASMUSSEN, ANN C. paralegal; b. Orlando, Fla., July 9, 1952; s. Edward DAvid Champagne and Mary Ruth Hoffpauier-Champagne; m. Paul Edward Pearson, Mar. 31, 1972 (div. Feb. 14, 1980); children: Paul Eric Pearson, Brandon Emile Pearson; m. Robert H. Rasmussen. Student, Southwestern La. U., La. State Paralegal Sch. Litigation paralegal Taylor, Porter, Brooks & Phillips, Baton Rouge, Kean, Miller, Hasthorne, D'Armond, McCowan & Jarman, Baton Rouge; pres., dir. ops. Legal Solutions, Baton Rouge; pres. Legal Profls., LLC, Baton Rouge. Mem. bd. advisors La. State U. Paralegal Sch., 1998—99; mentor for paralegal interns, 1998—99; instr. PIE and PCA seminars. Mem.: La. State Paralegal Assn. (dist. IV dir.), Baton Rouge Paralegal Assn. (pres. 1998—99, chmn. cmty. involvement com. 1999—2002), Baton Rouge Bar Assn. (mem. Ball Maul com. 2001—02, mem. Holiday Star com. 2001—02, ac hoc mem. pro bono com.). Address: PO Box 80011 Baton Rouge LA 70898

RASMUSSEN, DOUGLAS JOHN, lawyer; b. Mt. Clemens, Mich., Jan. 18, 1941; s. Kenneth Edward and Laura Jean (Fletcher) R.; m. Andrea Marie Smart, Aug. 22, 1964; children: Mark Douglas, Michael Andrew. BBA, U. Mich., 1962, MBA, JD, 1965. Bar: Mich. 1965, U.S. Dist. Ct. (ea. dist.) Mich. 1965, U.S. Tax Ct. 1973, U.S. Ct. Appeals (6th cir.) 1973. Assoc. Clark Hill plc, Detroit, 1965—73; mem. Detroit, 1973—; CEO, 1994-2000. Trustee Community Found. for S.E. Mich., Holley Found., bd. dirs. S.E. chpt. ARC, Detroit, 1987—, chmn., 1994-96; bd. dirs. YMCA of Metro Detroit, chmn., 1992-93; unit chmn. United Way, Detroit, 1987-92; bd. dirs. Detroit Symphony Orch., 1999—, Friends of Detroit Pub. Libr., 2000—, pres., 2001-03. Recipient Outstanding Vol. award Mich. Chpt. Nat. Assn. Fund Raising Execs., 1988, Fundraiser of Yr. award Nat. ARC, 1997, Outstanding Vol. award Mich. ARC, 2002. Fellow Am. Coll. Trust and Estate Counsel (regent 1987-93); mem. ABA, State Bar Mich., Internat. Acad. Estate and Trust Law, Fin. and Estate Planning Coun. Met. Detroit (pres. 1986-87), Detroit Athletic Club (bd. dirs. 1992, pres. 1997), Econ. Club Detroit (bd. dirs. 1999—), Rotary (Paul Harris fellow, Stanley S. Kresge award). Republican. Presbyterian. Avocations: music, photography, nordic skiing, golf. Estate planning, Probate (including wills, trusts), Taxation, general. Home: 466 Lakeland St Grosse Pointe MI 48230-1655 Office: Clark Hill PLC 500 Woodward Ave Ste 3500 Detroit MI 48226-3435 E-mail: drasmussen@clarkhill.com.

RASMUSSEN, RICHARD ROBERT, lawyer; b. Chgo., July 5, 1946; s. Robert Kersten Rasmussen and Marisa Bruna Batistoni; children: Kathryn, William. BS, U. Oreg., 1970, JD, 1973. Bar: Oreg. 1973. Atty. U.S. Bancorp, Portland, Oreg., 1973-83, 95-00, v.p. law divsn., 1983-87, mgr. law divsn, 1983-95, sr. v.p., 1987-95, mgr. corp. sec. divsn., 1990—95; exec. v.p., gen. counsel, sec. West Coast Bancorp, Lake Oswego, Oreg., 2000—. Mem. editl. bd. Oreg. Bus. Law Digest, 1979-81, Oreg. Debtor/Creditor newsletter, 1980-84; contbr. articles to profl. jours. Chmn. mgmt. com. YMCA of Columbia-Willamette, Portland, 1978-79; bd. dirs. Camp Fire, 1988-89, v.p., 1990-91; bd. dirs. Portland Repertory Theatre, 1994-96. Mem.: ABA, Am. Bankers Assn. (bank counsel com. 1996—99), Multnomah County Bar Assn., Oreg. State Bar Assn. (chmn. corp. counsel com. 1979—81, debtor/creditor sect. 1982—83, sec. com. on sects. 1982—83, award of merit, debtor/creditor sect. 2003), Beta Gamma Sigma. Avocations: mountaineering, white-water rafting, tennis, basketball. Banking, Corporate, general, Finance. Office: West Coast Bancorp 5335 Meadows Rd Ste 201 Lake Oswego OR 97035

RASMUSSEN, ROBERT CARL, lawyer; b. Oelwein, Iowa, Aug. 22, 1949; s. Leo Lyle and Gloria Servoin (Ballinger) R.; m. Marlene Francis Schneider, June 30, 1990. BSBA, The Am. U., 1971; JD, U. Iowa, 1974. Bar: Iowa 1974, Fla. 1975. Dir. ednl. mktg. svcs. div. Nat. Student Mktg. Corp., Washington, 1968-70; dir. youth activity div. and spl. projects Distributive Edn. Clubs of Am., Falls Church, Va., 1970-72; assoc. Holland & Knight, Tampa, Fla., 1974-78, ptnr., 1979-83; founding ptnr. Glenn, Rasmussen, Fogarty & Hooker, P.A., Tampa, 1983—. Ex-officio mem. Pres.'s Task Force on Edn. and Tng. for Minority Bus. Enterprises, Washington, 1971-72. Chmn. Leadership Tampa Alumni, 1992; founding chmn. Tampa Heights Neighborhood Revitalization Alliance, 1991-93; mem. Regional Telephone Svc. Steering Com., Tampa, 1991. Recipient Golden Eagle award Am. Acad. of Achievement, 1968. Mem. Fla. Bar, Iowa Bar Assn., Hillsborough County Bar Assn., Greater Tampa C. of C., Tampa Club, Harbour Island Athletic Club,Palma Ceia Golf and Country Club. Republican. Methodist. Corporate, general, Mergers and acquisitions, Securities. Office: Glenn Rasmussen Fogarty & Hooker PA 100 S Ashley Dr Ste 1300 Tampa FL 33602-5309

RASMUSSEN, THOMAS VAL, JR., lawyer, small business owner; b. Salt Lake City, Aug. 11, 1954; s. Thomas Val and Georgia (Smedley) R.; m. Donita Gubler, Aug. 15, 1978; children: James, Katherine, Kristin. BA magna cum laude, U. Utah, 1978, JD, 1981. Bar: Utah 1981, U.S. Dist. Ct. Utah 1981, U.S. Supreme Ct. 1985, U.S. Ct. Appeals (10th cir.) 1999. Atty. Salt Lake Legal Defender Assn., Salt Lake City, 1981-83, Utah Power and Light Co., Salt Lake City, 1983-89; of counsel Hatch, Morton & Skeen, Salt Lake City, 1989-90; ptnr. Morton, Skeen & Rasmussen, Salt Lake City, 1991-94, Skeen & Rasmussen, Salt Lake City, 1994-97; pvt. practice, Salt Lake City, 1997—. Co-owner, developer Handi Self-Storage, Kaysville, Utah, 1984-93; instr. bus. law Brigham Young U., Salt Lake City, 1988-90. Adminstrv. editor Jour. Contemporary Law, 1980-81, Jour. Energy Law and Policy, 1980-81. Missionary Ch. of Jesus Christ of Latter-Day Sts., Brazil, 1973-75. Mem. Utah, Salt Lake County Bar Assn., Intermountain Miniature Horse Club (pres. 1989, 2d v.p. 1990), Phi Eta Sigma, Phi Kappa Phi, Beta Gamma Sigma. Avocations: tennis, scuba diving, showing horses, travel, collecting art. General civil litigation, Criminal, Juvenile. Home: 3094 Whitewater Dr Salt Lake City UT 84121-1561 Office: 4659 Highland Dr Salt Lake City UT 84117-5137

RASMUSSON, THOMAS ELMO, lawyer; b. Lansing, Mich., Dec. 5, 1941; s. William and Mary Jane Rasmusson; m. Alice Wolo, Oct. 1, 1989; children: David, Jane. BA, Mich. State U., 1963; JD, U. Mich., 1966; MA, Fletcher Sch., 1988. Bar: Mich. 1967, U.S. Ct. Appeals (6th cir.) 1982, U.S. Supreme Ct. 1982. Law clk. to presiding justice Mich. Supreme Ct., Lansing, 1966-68; asst. prosecutor Ingham Prosecutor's Office, Lansing, 1968-72, criminal divsn. chief, 1972-75; spl. prosecutor Ingham County, Lansing, 1975-76; pvt. practice Lansing, 1975—. Trustee Lansing Cmty. Coll., 1998-; Fulbright prof. U.S. Info. Svc., Washington, 1986-88; cons. U.S. AID, Monrovia, Liberia, 1989-90; contractor U.S. Dept. of State, Monrovia, 1987-90; adj. prof. Cooley Law Sch., Lansing, 1991-97; rsch. assoc. program on negotiation Harvard U., Cambridge, 1987-88; mem. Ct. Rule Com., Lansing, 1979-81; dir. Capital Area Sch. Employees Credit Union, 1996-, Educated Solutions, LLC, 2000-. Editor: Jurisprudence and System Science, 1986, Interactive Systems, 1988, (series) Liberian Law Reports, 1988-90; contbr. articles to profl. jours. Chair fin. Ingham Rep. Party, Lansing, 1994-98, mem. exec. com., 1994—; mem. 8th Congl. Com., Lansing, 1997—; trustee Lansing C.C., 1998—; dir. Case Credit Union, Lansing, 1996; dir. MyWebConnect ISP, Lansing, 1998—. Recipient Outstanding Svc. award U.S. Edn. Found., 1987; grantee U.S. Edn. Found., 1987. Mem. AAAS, State Bar Mich. Republican. Methodist. Avocations: physics, history of science. Federal civil litigation, State civil litigation, Criminal. Home: 1818 Redbud Lansing MI 48917 Office: Rasmusson and Assoc 2201 E Grand River Lansing MI 48912

RASSAS, MARK A. lawyer; b. Clarksville, Tenn., Feb. 11, 1951; BS with honors, U. Tenn., 1973, JD, 1975. Bar: Tenn. 1976. Assoc. prof. bus. law Austin Peay State U., 1976, 77; atty. Rassas & Rassas, Clarksville, Tenn. Contbr. articles to profl. jours. Col. U.S. Army Res., 1991. Fellow Tenn. Bar Found.; mem. ATLA (vice chmn. mil. law sect. 1989-91), Montgomery County Bar Assn. (pres. 1983), Tenn Bar Assn., Am. Bd. Trial Advocates (pres. Tenn. chpt. 2002), Tenn. Trial Lawyers Assn. (cert. civil trial specialist), Phi Alpha Delta. Office: Glenn Bldg Ste 101 120 S 2d St Clarksville TN 37040 E-mail: rassaslaw@aol.com.

RATCHFORD, DAVID MAURICE, lawyer; b. Charlotte, N.C., Dec. 29, 1944; s. Clyde Banks and Rubye (Valentine) R.; m. Sylvia McNair, Sept. 2, 1966; 1 child, Melissa. BS in Bus. Adminstrn., U. S.C., 1966, JD, 1969. Bar: S.C. 1969, U.S. Dist. Ct. S.C. 1969, U.S. Ct. Appeals (4th cir.) 1976. Sole practice, Columbia, S.C., 1969-72; ptnr. Ratchford & Eleazer, Columbia, 1973-77, Ratchford & Cooper, Columbia, 1977-87, Ratchford & ASsocs., Columbia, 1987—97, Ratchford & Hamilton, LLP, 1998—. Commr., Irmo (S.C.) Fire Dept., 1974-79; tchr., former deacon Cornerstone Presbyn. Ch., Columbia, 1973—, elder, 1986—; bd. dirs. St. Andrew Christian Acad. Mem. S.C. Bar Assn., Richland County Bar Assn., S.C. Trial Lawyers Assn., Christian Legal Soc., Sertoma (charter pres. 1974), Phi Alpha Delta. Aviation, Federal civil litigation, General civil litigation. Home: PO Box 1607 Irmo SC 29063-160 Office: Ratchford & Hamilton LLP 1531 Laurel St Columbia SC 29201-2697

RATH, FRANCIS STEVEN, lawyer; b. N.Y.C., Oct. 10, 1955; s. Steven and Elizabeth (Chorin) R.; m. Denise Stephania Thompson, Aug. 2, 1980. BA cum laude, Wesleyan U., Middletown, Conn., 1977; JD cum laude, Georgetown U., 1980; postgrad., Harvard U., 1999-2000. Bar: D.C. 1980, U.S. Dist. Ct. D.C. 1981, U.S. Ct. Appeals (D.C. cir.), 1981, U.S. Supreme Ct. 1987, Va. 1988; nationally registered EMT-I. Atty., advisor Comptr. of the Currency, Washington, 1980-84; assoc. Verner, Liipfert, Bernhard, McPherson & Hand, Washington, 1984-85; founding mem. Wolf, Arnold & Monroig (merged with Burnham, Connolly, Oesterly & Henry), Washington, 1986-88; pvt. practice Great Falls, Va., 1989—. Internat. cons. Fried, Frank, Harris, Shriver and Jacobson, 1991-95; counsel Seward & Kissel, Washington, 1995-98; of counsel, Squire Sanders & Dempsey, Washington, 1998—. Editor: Law and Policy in Internat. Bus., 1979-80; contbg. author Business Ventures in Eastern Europe and Russia; contbr. articles to profl. jours. Trustee Dunn Loring (Va.) Vol. Fire Dept., 1986. Mem. ABA, D.C. Bar Assn., Va. Bar Assn., Bar of U.S. Supreme Ct., U.S. Combined Tng. Assn. (legal com. 1989-91, 96-99, safety com. 1990-91, 96-99, bd. govs. 1995-98). Corporate, general, Private international, Public international. Home and Office: 1051 Kelso Rd Great Falls VA 22066-2032 E-mail: frath@fsrpc.com.

RATH, THOMAS DAVID, lawyer, former state attorney general; b. East Orange, N.J., June 1, 1945; s. Harvey and Helen R.; m. Christine Casey, Dec. 18, 1971; children— Erin, Timothy. AB, Dartmouth Coll., 1967; JD, Georgetown U., 1971. Bar: N.J. 1971, N.H. 1972, U.S. Supreme Ct. 1978. Law clk. Judge Clarkson Fisher, U.S. Dist. Ct. N.J., 1971-72; atty. criminal div. Office of Atty. Gen., State of N.H., 1972-73, asst. atty. gen., 1973-76, dep. atty. gen., 1976-78, atty. gen., 1978-80; ptnr. Orr & Reno, P.A., Concord, N.H., 1980-87, Rath & Young, P.A., Concord, 1987-91; founding ptnr. Rath, Young, Pignatelli & Oyer, P.A., Concord, 1991—. Polit. analyst WHDH-TV, Boston, WGBH Pub. TV, Boston, WENH, N.H. Pub. TV, WBUR-Boston Radio; chief strategist Alexander for Pres.; vice chmn. of bd. Primary Bank, 1995-97; pres. Play Ball, N.H., 1994—; commentator, polit. analyst WMUR-TV and Yankee Network; bd. dirs. Assoc. Grocers New England, Chubb Am. Fund. Host State of the State, Yankee Cable Network; co-host Close-Up, WMUR-TV. Chmn. campaign Warren B. Rudman for U.S. Senate, 1980, 86; bd. overseers Aquinas House, Dartmouth Coll., com. on trustees Rockefeller Ctr. Bd. Visitors; bd. oversers Dartmouth Med. Sch.; nat. dir. Baker Exploratory Com., 1986-87; sec. bd. trustees Concord Hosp.; treas. N.H. Rep. party, 1981-93; trustee DWC, 1981-87, chmn., 1982-86; mem. Baker Exploratory Com., 1986-87; trustee Concord Hosp., 1980-86; sr. nat. cons. Dole for Pres.; del. Rep. Nat. Conv., 1984, 88, 92, rules com., 1988, 92, N.H. committeeman, 1996—; Rep. nat. committeeman State of N.H., 1996; bd. dirs. New Eng. Coun., 1997. Mem. Nat. Assn. Attys. Gen. (vice-chmn. Eastern region, vice chmn. standing com. on energy), N.H. Bar Assn. (Spl. Pres. award 1992). Clubs: Dartmouth Coll. (v.p. Merrimack County). Roman Catholic. Administrative and regulatory, General civil litigation, Legislative. Office: Rath Young and Pignatelli One Capital Plaza PO Box 1500 Concord NH 03302-1500 E-mail: tdr@rathlaw.com.

RATHJEN, JON LAURENCE, lawyer, mediator; b. Elizabeth, N.J., June 28, 1951; s. Theodore A. Rathjen and Marie Betty Ahrendtsen; 1 child, Daniel Laurence. AB, Brown U., 1973; JD, U. Calif., Berkeley, 1977. Bar: Calif. 1978, U.S. Dist. Ct. (no. dist.) Calif. 1980. Atty. Paul & Baker, Oakland, Calif., 1979-81, Warwick, Gardner & Rathjen, Oakland, 1981-88, Pearce & Rathjen, Walnut Creek, Calif., 1988—. Cons. Bay Area Lawyers for the Arts, San Francisco, 1981-85; bd. dirs. Dancer's Repertory Theater, Oakland, 1978-81. Mem. Contra Costa County Bar Assn. (family law sect., mediation sub-sect.). Bankruptcy, General civil litigation, Family and matrimonial. Office: 1333 N California Blvd Ste 525 Walnut Creek CA 94596-4576

RATHKOPF, DAREN ANTHONY, lawyer; b. Lynbrook, N.Y., May 12, 1933; s. Arden Herman and Florence Marie (Gortikov) R.; m. Mira Torgersen, Mar. 30, 1963; children: Ann, Erika. BA, Columbia U., 1955, LLB, 1958. Bar: N.Y. 1958, U.S. Dist. Ct. (ea., so. dists.) N.Y. 1962. Assoc. Mendes & Mount, N.Y.C., 1961-62, Rathkopf & Rathkopf, N.Y.C., 1962-66, ptnr. Glen Cove, N.Y., 1966-81, Payne, Wood & Littlejohn, Glen Cove and Melville, N.Y., 1982-98, of counsel Melville, Bridgehampton, Locust Valley, NY, 1999-2001, Farrell Fritz, P.C., Uniondale, Melville, Bridghampton, Locust Valley, NY, 2001—02; ptnr. Chase, Rathkopf & Chase, LLP, Glen Cove, NY, 2002—. Author: (with others) The Law of Zoning and Planning, 4th edit., 1977. Mem.: Nassau County Bar Assn., NY State Bar Assn. Land use and zoning (including planning). Home: 149 Turkey Ln Cold Spring Harbor NY 11724-1712 Office: Chase Rathkopf & Chase LLP 48 Forest Ave Glen Cove NY 11542 E-mail: chaserathkopf@aol.com.

RATHMAN, WILLIAM ERNEST, retired lawyer, minister; b. Middletown, Ohio, Jan. 10, 1927; s. Ernest Daniel and Marguerite (Sebald) R.; m. Constance Schedler, Nov. 28, 1958; children: Marchie, William E. Jr. Grad., Phillips Exeter Acad., 1944; BA, Kenyon Coll., 1948; postgrad., Harvard U., 1950, Ohio State U. Coll. of Law, 1951, United Theol. Seminary, Dayton, Ohio, 1975. Bar: Ohio 1952; ordained to ministry Episc. Ch., 1975. Pvt. practice law, Middletown, Ohio, 1952-78; sr. ptnr. Rathman, Elliott & Boyd, Middletown, 1979-84, Rathman, Combs, Schaefer, Valen & Kaup, Middletown, 1985-88, Rathman, Combs, Schaefer & Kaup, Middletown, 1989-95, ret., 1995—. Spl. counsel to County of Butler, 1956-64, City of Middletown, 1965-66, Ohio Atty. Gen., 1967-69; acting judge Middletown Mcpl. Ct., 1969-74. Pres. Middletown Community Found., 1972-76, Middletown Chamber Found., 1977-80, Butler County Park Commn., 1986-90; trustee-at-large Ohio Found. of Ind. Colls., Columbus, 1972-90; trustee, mem. exec. com. Middletown United Way, 1963-90; trustee Middleton Req. Hosp. Found., 1986-90; adv. bd. Middletown campus Miami U., 1984-90. With USN, 1944-46, capt. USAF, 1959, comdr. Am. Legion, 1965. Named Exec. Yr., Middletown chpt. Nat. Secs. Assn., 1969; recipient Outstanding Community Svc. award Middletown post Am. Legion, 1975, Outstanding Svc. award Parstoral Counselling Svc., 1983, Vol. of Yr. award Middletown Area United Way, 1986. Fellow Am. Coll. Trust and Estate Counsel; mem. ABA (estate tax com. 1966-69), Ohio Bar Assn. (coun. del. 1980-93), Butler County Bar Assn. (pres. 1980), Middletown Bar Assn. (pres. 1967), Fed. Bar Assn. (pres. Cin. chpt. 1975), Ohio State Bar Found. (trustee 1992-96, Ohio Supreme Ct. bd. commrs. on grievances and discipline 1996-99), Browns Run Country Club, Masons (Jefferson lodge, master 1959-60), Scottish Rite Valley of Cin. (treas. 1986, chmn. bd. 1990, 33d degree mason 1988—). Episcopalian. Home: 501 Thornhill Ln Middletown OH 45042-3750 also: 1924 S Beach Club Hilton Head Island SC 29928-3750 E-mail: crathman@aol.com.

RATHWELL, PETER JOHN, lawyer; b. Windsor, Ont., Can., Aug. 20, 1943; came to U.S., 1947; s. Harold Wilfred and Jean Isabel (Lucas) R.; m. Ann Wickstrom Williams, Sept. 10, 1977; 1 child, James Michael BA, U. Ariz., 1965, JD, 1968. Bar: Ariz. 1968. Assoc. Boettcher, Crowder & Schoolitz, Scottsdale, Ariz., 1972-73; ptnr. Snell & Wilmer, Phoenix, 1973—. Seminar lectr. Nat. Bus. Inst., Inc., 1987—90, Ariz. Ann. Bankruptcy Symposium, 1995, 97, Am. Agrl. Lawyers Assn., 1997, 99, Lormans Bus. Seminars, 2000—, Sterling Edn. Sems., 2001—. Mem. exec. com. Jr. Achievement Ariz., Phoenix, 1980-92, 2000—, bd. advisors, 1980—; chmn. scholarship fund St. Mary H.S., 1982-91; mem., chmn. Phoenix Parks Bd., 1982-87; trustee Orme Sch., 1991—, chair devel. com., 1994—; treas., trustee Smith Scholarship Trust U. Ariz. Law Sch., 1985—; bd. advisors, S.W. Bankruptcy Conf. 1995—. Capt. JAGC, USAF, 1969-72. Fellow State Bar Ariz. Found. (founding mem.), Maricopa County Bar Found. (founding mem.); mem. Am. Bankruptcy Inst., Ariz. Bar Assn. (bar counsel 1982-87, 97, chmn. discipline hearing com. 1987-93, mem. bankruptcy sect.), Maricopa County Bar Assn. (seminar lectr. 1987), Comml. Law League Am., Phoenix Zoo Wildest Club in Town (founding mem. 1972). Republican. Avocations: fishing, raising cattle. Bankruptcy, Federal civil litigation, Commercial, contracts (including sales of goods; commercial financing). Home: 4523 E Mountain View Rd Phoenix AZ 85028-5213 Office: Snell & Wilmer 1 Arizona Ctr Phoenix AZ 85004

RATNER, DAVID LOUIS, retired law educator; b. London, Sept. 2, 1931; AB magna cum laude, Harvard U., 1952, LLB magna cum laude, 1955. Bar: N.Y. 1955. Assoc. Sullivan & Cromwell, N.Y.C., 1955-64; assoc. prof. Cornell Law Sch., Ithaca, N.Y., 1964-68, prof., 1968-82; prof. law U. San Francisco Law Sch., 1982-99, dean, 1982-89, prof. emeritus, 1999—. Exec. asst. to chmn. SEC, Washington, 1966-68; chief counsel Securities Industry Study, Senate Banking Com., Washington, 1971-73; vis. prof. Stanford (Calif.) U., 1974, Ariz. State U., Tempe, 1974, U. San Francisco, 1980, Georgetown U., Washington, 1989-90, U. Calif., Hastings, San Francisco, 1992; mem. Larkspur (Calif.) Planning Commn., 1992—. Author: Securities Regulation: Cases and Materials, 6th edit., 2002, Securities Regulation in a Nutshell, 7 edit., 2002, Institutional Investors: Teaching Materials, 1978. Fulbright scholar Monash U., Australia, 1981. Mem. Cosmos Club (Washington), Harvard Club of San Francisco (pres. 1999-2000), Phi Beta Kappa. Home and Office: 84 Polhemus Way Larkspur CA 94939-1928 E-mail: dlratner@aol.com.

RATTRAY, JAMES BAILEY, lawyer; b. Watertown, N.Y., July 26, 1950; s. Clifford M. and Dora M. (Bailey) R.; m. Paula Cataldi, Nov. 30, 1998. AB cum laude, Syracuse U., 1972; JD, Coll. William and Mary, 1975, MLT, 1982. Bar: Va. 1975, D.C. 1976. Assoc. firm Ernest C. Consolvo, Norfolk, Va., 1975; dep. city atty. City of Hampton, Va., 1976—92; exec. dir. Hampton Redevel. and Housing Authority, 1992—2001; asst. office dir. Ga. Dept. Cmty. Affairs, Atlanta, 2002—. Instr. St. Leo Coll., Tidewater Center, Langley AFB, Va., 1982-99, Golden Gate U., Resident Ctr., Langley AFB, 1978-82, Hampton U., Va., 1985-90. Contbr. articles to profl. jours. Mem. ABA, D.C. Bar Assn., Va. Bar Assn., Local Govt. Attys. of Va., Nat. Assn. Housing and Redevel. Ofcls., Pub. Housing Authority Dirs. Assn. Episcopalian. Home: 1015 Lake Windward Overlook Alpharetta GA 30005-9010 Office: Dept Cmty Affairs 60 Executive Park S Atlanta GA 30329-2231 E-mail: jbrattray@aol.com.

RAU, LEE ARTHUR, lawyer; b. Mpls., July 22, 1940; s. Arthur W. and Selma A. (Lund) R.; m. Janice R. Childress, June 27, 1964; children: Brendan D., Patrick C., Brian T. BSB, U. Minn., 1962; JD, UCLA, 1965. Bar: Calif. 1966, D.C. 1972, Va. 1986, U.S. Dist. Ct. D.C. 1973, U.S. Dist. Ct. (ea. dist.) Va. 1988, U.S. Ct. Mil. Appeals 1966, U.S. Ct. Appeals (D.C. cir.) 1972, U.S. Ct. Appeals (3d cir.) 1975, U.S. Ct. Appeals (6th cir.) 1980, U.S. Ct. Appeals (4th cir.) 1988, U.S. Supreme Ct. 1971. Trial atty. evaluation sect. antitrust div. U.S. Dept. Justice, Washington, 1965-66, appellate sect., 1970-72; assoc. Reed Smith Shaw & McClay, Washington, 1972-74, ptnr., 1975—2002; commr. Fairfax County Redevel. and Housing Authority, 2002—. Former mem. constl. and adminstrv. law adv. com. Nat. Chamber Litigation Ctr. Inc.; sec., bd. dirs. Old Dominion Land Co., Inc. Contbr. articles to profl. jours. Sec. bd. dris. Reston Found., 1982-93; bd. dirs. Reston Interfaith Inc., 1973-89, pres, 1984-88; bd. dirs. Greater Reston Arts Ctr., 1988-96, pres., 1989-91, sec., 1991-95; mem. Washington Dulles Task Force, 1982-91; mem. exec. com. and ops. com. Fairfax-Falls Ch. United Way, mem. regional coun., 1988-92. Capt. JAGC, U.S. Army, 1966-70. Named Restonian of Yr., 1990; decorated Commendation with oak leaf cluster; recipient Best of Reston award. Mem. ABA (antitrust, adminstrv. law, corp. banking and bus., sci. and tech. sects.), D.C. Bar Assn. (past chmn. energy study group), Calif. Bar Assn., U.S. C. of C. (antitrust policy com.). Democrat. Lutheran. Administrative and regulatory, Antitrust, Corporate, general. Home: 11654 Mediterranean Ct Reston VA 20190-3401

RAUCH, GEORGE WASHINGTON, lawyer, director; b. Marion, Ind., July 18, 1919; s. George W. and Emma Asenath (Nolen) R.; m. Audrey M. Cranfield, Feb. 28, 1943 (div.); children: George Washington III, Nancy Lynn, Jane Nolen; m. Dorothy D. Farlow, June 26, 1970. BS, Ind. U., 1941; LL.B., U. Va., 1947. Bar: Ind. 1948, Ill. 1957, Mass. and Fla. 1972. Practice law Batton, Harker and Rauch (and predecessor firms), Marion, Ind., 1948-57; v.p., gen. counsel The Greyhound Corp., Chgo., 1957-61; mem. firm Hubachek & Kelly Ltd. and predecessor firms, Chgo., 1961-82; pres. Hubachek & Kelly Ltd., 1972-80; of counsel firm Chapman and Cutler, Chgo., 1982-95; gen. counsel Household Finance Corp., 1967-78, dir., 1967-92, mem. fin. com., 1969-92, exec. com., 1972-92; dir. Edwards Engrng. Corp., Constrn. Materials Co., Indsl. Air & Hydraulics Co., 1976-90, Burch Co., 1972-97, pres., 1975-97; dir. 1242 Lake Shore Dr. Corp., 1971-83, pres., 1973-74. Mem. Nat. Conf. Commrs. on Uniform Laws, 1955-57. Served as aviator USNR, 1941-45; lt. comdr. Mem. Raven Soc., Sankaty Head Golf Club (Nantucket, Mass.), Casino Club (Nantucket), Beach Club (Palm Beach, Fla.), Masons, Shriners, Phi Delta Phi, Delta Tau Delta. Home: 455 Australian Ave Palm Beach FL 33480-4532 also: PO Box 149 83 Baxter Rd Siasconset MA 02564

RAUCH, MICHAEL H. lawyer; BA, Princeton U., 1960; LLM, Harvard U., 1963. Bar: N.Y., U.S. Supreme Ct., U.S. Ct. Appeal (2d, 4th, 5th, 7th, 9th, and 10th cirs.). With Fried Frank Harris Shrivers & Jacobson, N.Y.C., 1968, ptnr., 1972—. Office: 1 New York Plz New York NY 10004

RAUDONIS, VALERIE CHRISTINE, lawyer; b. Nashua, N.H., July 30, 1953; d. Alphonse J. and Sophie C. (Raucykevich) R.; children: Ryan, Laura. BA, Boston Coll., 1975; JD, New England Sch. Law, Boston, 1978. Bar: N.H. 1978, U.S. Dist. Ct. N.H. 1978, U.S. Tax Ct. 1979, U.S. Ct. Appeals (1st cir.) 1979. Pvt. practice, Nashua, N.H., 1978—. Mem. part-time faculty Rivier Coll. Paralegal Studies, Nashua, 1984-86, 91-92, mem. adv. bd., 1993-2001, chairperson, 1999. Bd. dirs. Nashua Children's Assn., 1980-88, v.p., 1982-84, pres., 1984-85, assoc., 1988—; bd. dirs. YWCA, 1979-84, mem. YM-YW coun., 1981-84, 2d v.p., 1983-84; trustee Mt. St. Mary Sem., 1981-86, Tacy House, Inc., 1981-86; bd. dirs. Nashua Youth Coun., 1982-83, Adult Learning Ctr., 1995-2001; mem. N.H. Action Com. for Foster Children, 1983-86; mem. adv. com. to bd. dirs. Souhegan Theatre Coun., 1990-95; mem. St. Casimir's Ladies Guild, 1981-86. Recipient N.H. Young Career Woman, Nat. Fed. Bus. and profl. Women, Catherine M. McAuley award. Fellow N.H. Bar Found.; mem. ABA (custody com. family law sect. 1983-84), N.H. Bar Assn. (chmn. com. on juvenile problems and family law 1980-81, 82-83, com. on needs of children 1984-85), Nashua Bar Assn. (pres. 2001), Nat. Fedn. Bus. and Profl. Women (chmn. young career woman com. 1982-83, 2d v.p. Nashua 1983-85, pres. 1985-86, N.H. Young Career Woman award 1982). Avocations: downhill skiing, children. General civil litigation, Family and matrimonial, Probate (including wills, trusts). Office: 7 Auburn St Nashua NH 03064-2615 E-mail: raudonislaw@aol.com.

RAUH, CARL STEPHEN, lawyer; b. Washington, Dec. 14, 1940; s. Joseph L. and Olie (Westheimer) R. AB, Columbia U., 1962; LL.B., U. Pa., 1965; LL.M., Georgetown U., 1968. Bar: D.C. 1966, U.S. Supreme Ct. 1969. Asst. U.S. atty. for D.C., 1966-69; atty. Dep. Atty Gen.'s Office Dept. Justice, Washington, 1969-71; 1st asst. atty. gen. U.S. V.I., 1971-73; prin. asst. U.S. atty. for D.C., 1974-79; U.S. atty. for D.C., 1979; ptnr. Dunnells, Duvall, Bennett & Porter, Washington, 1980-90, Skadden, Arps, Slate, Meagher & Flom, Washington, 1990—. Mem. D.C. Jud. Nomination Commn., 1985-90. Recipient Dir.'s award Dept. Justice, 1976; Atty. Gen.'s Disting. Service award, 1980 Fellow Am. Coll. Trial Lawyers; mem. ABA, D.C. Bar Assn., Nat. Assn. Former U.S. Attys., Asst. U.S. Attys. Assn. (Harold J. Sullivan award 1980). Office: 1440 New York Ave NW Washington DC 20005-2111

RAUL, ALAN CHARLES, lawyer; b. Bronx, N.Y., Sept. 9, 1954; s. Eugene and Eduarda (Müller-Mañas) R.; m. Mary Tinsley, Jan. 30, 1988; children: Caroline Tinsley, William Eduardo Tinsley, Alexander Tinsley. AB magna cum laude, Harvard U., 1975, MPA, 1977; JD, Yale U., 1980. Bar: N.Y. 1982, D.C. 1982, U.S. Ct. Appeals (D.C. cir.) 1982, U.S. Supreme Ct. 1988. Law clk. to judge U.S. Ct. Appeals (D.C. cir.), Washington, 1980-81; assoc. Debevoise & Plimpton, N.Y.C., 1981-86; White House assoc. counsel Pres. Reagan, Washington, 1986-88; gen. counsel Office Mgmt. and Budget, Washington, 1988-89, USDA, Washington, 1989-93; prin. Beveridge & Diamond P.C., Washington, 1993-97; ptnr. Sidley Austin Brown & Wood, Washington, 1997—. Cons. Reagan-Bush campaign, N.Y.C., 1984; mem. implementation task force Internet Corp. for Assigned Names and Numbers, 2000—. Author: (book) Privacy and the Digital State, 2001. Co-chairperson, co-founder Lawyers Have Heart; chmn. bd. USDA Grad. Sch., 1991-93; bd. dirs. Nation's Capital affiliate Am. Heart Assn., 1993-97, Greater Washington region, 2002—; treas., dir. Citizens Assn. Georgetown, 1993-97; mem. Nat. Policy Forum's Environ. Policy Coun.; mem. adv. coun. Atlantic Legal Found., 2001—. Recipient Disting. Achievement award Am. Heart Assn., 1991, Vol. of Yr. award, 1993, Lifetime Achievement award, 1999. Mem. ABA (coun. sect. internat. law and practice 1992-98, chmn. com. on nat. security and internat. law 1990-92, standing com. on election law 1995-99, sect. internat. law and practice govt. affairs officer 1996-98), Assn. of Bar of City of N.Y. (chmn. subcom. on Cen. Am. issues 1985, mem. com. on inter-Am. affairs 1983), Federalist Soc. (mem. nat. practitioners adv. coun., chair environ. and property rights practice group 1996-99), Coun. on Fgn. Rels. Administrative and regulatory, Environmental, Private international. Office: Sidley Austin Brown & Wood 1501 K St NW Washington DC 20005 E-mail: araul@sidley.com.

RAVED, YORAM, lawyer; b. Jerusalem, June 22, 1956; s. Dan and Miryam R.; m. Ayala Levanon Raved, Aug. 24, 1982; children: Tomer, Itai, Roy, Yuval. LLB, Tel Aviv U., Israel, 1982. Israel Bar: 1983; lic. notary Israeli Min. Justice. Mng. ptnr. Raved, Magriso, Beokel & Co., Tel Aviv, Israel, 1990—. Dir. Memet, 1991-96, Hasin Esh, Israel, 2000. Mem. Barelq Governors Yeladim, Israel, 1999—, Um Yafe Um Ehad, 1994—. With Intelligence, 1974-77. Commercial, contracts (including sales of goods; commercial financing), Property, real (including real estate development, water), Hi-tech and venture. Office: Raved Magriso Benkel & Co 37 Shaul Hamelech Blvd 64928 Tel Aviv Israel also: Raved Magriso Benkel & Co PO Box 21411 61213 Tel Aviv Israel E-mail: Raved@rmblaw.co.il.

RAWKINS, JASON W.D. lawyer; b. Norwich, England, Apr. 4, 1965; s. David J. and A. Tessa Rawkins; m. Alison J. Eyet, July 31, 1999; 1 child, George. Grad., Oxford U., 1988, degree in law, 1990; IP diploma, Bristol U., 1993. Assoc. solicitor Taylor Wessing, London, 1992—97, ptnr., 1997—. Editor: International Protection of Intellectual Property, 2000. Mem.: Internat. Trademark Assn. (sub-com. 2002—). Avocations: tennis, travel, sailing. Intellectual property, Trademark and copyright, Computer. Office: Taylor Wessing 50 Victoria Embankment London EC4Y 0DX England

RAWLES, EDWARD HUGH, lawyer; b. Chgo., May 7, 1945; s. Fred Wilson and Nancy (Hughes) R.; m. Margaret Mary O'Donoghue, Oct. 20, 1979; children: Lee Kathryn, Jacklyn Ann. BA, U. Ill., 1967; JD summa cum laude, Ill. Inst. Tech., 1970. Bar: Ill., 1970, Colo. 1984, U.S. Dist. Ct. (cen. dist.) Ill. 1970, U.S. Ct. Appeals (7th cir.) 1983, U.S. Supreme Ct. 1973. Assoc. Reno, O'Byrne & Kepley, Champaign, Ill., 1970-73, ptnr., 1973-84; pres. Rawles, O'Byrne, Stanko & Kepley P.C., Champaign, 1984-98, pres., 1990-97; mem. student legal svc. adv. bd. U. Ill., Urbana, 1982—; hearing officer Ill. Fair Employment Practice Commn., Springfield, 1972-74; mem. rules com. U.S. Dist. Ct. for Ctrl. Dist. Ill., 1994—. Diplomate Nat. Bd. Trial Advocacy. Fellow Ill. State Bar Found., 1984. Mem. Ill. Bar Assn., Bar Assn. 7th Fed. Cir., Rules Com. U.S. Dist. Court (ctrl. dist. Ill.), Assn. Trial Lawyers Am., Ill. Trial Lawyers Assn., Colo. Trial Lawyers Assn., Kent Soc. Honor Men, Phi Delta Theta. Roman Catholic. Federal civil litigation, State civil litigation, Personal injury (including property damage). Home: 6 Alice Dr White Heath IL 61884-9747 Office: Rawles O'Byrne Stanko & Kepley PC 501 W Church St Champaign IL 61820-3412

RAWLEY, JAMES ALBERT, lawyer; b. N.Y.C., May 3, 1952; s. James Albert and Ann (Keyser) R.; m. Gay Finlayson, Sept. 9, 1978 (div. 2001); children: Asae Elizabeth, Marit Terry, James Neil. BA, U. Calif., Berkeley, 1973; JD, U. Nebr., 1977. Bar: N.Mex. 1979, U.S. Dist. Ct. N.Mex. 1979, U.S. Ct. Appeals (10th cir.) 1979, U.S. Supreme Ct. 1993, Trust Territory Dist. No. Marianas 1978. Pub. defender U.S. Trust Territory/Truk Dist.; pvt. practice Albuquerque, 1979—. Mem. N.Mex. Trial Lawyers (worker's compensation com. 1996-97). Democrat. Avocation: painting. Personal injury (including property damage), Workers' compensation. Office: 919 Gold Ave SW Albuquerque NM 87102-3082

RAWLINS, DONALD R. lawyer; b. Dyersburg, Tenn., Apr. 28, 1965; s. Dal M. and Rebecca S. Rawlins. BBA, U. Memphis, 1987; JD, Am. U., 1990. Bar: Tenn., 1990. V.p., asst. gen. counsel, asst. sec. AutoZone, Inc., Memphis, 1990—. Recipient Best Brief award ATLA, 1990. Corporate, general, Securities. Office: AutoZone Inc 123 S Front St Memphis TN 38103-3618

RAWLINSON, JOHNNIE BLAKENEY, federal judge; b. Concord, NH, Dec. 16, 1952; BS in Psychology summa cum laude, NC A&T State U., 1974; JD, U. of Pacific, 1979. Private practice, Las Vegas, 1979—80; staff atty. Nevada Legal Services, 1980; from dep. dist. atty. to asst. dist. atty. Clark County Dist. Atty.'s Office, 1980—98; judge U.S. Dist. Ct. Nev., 1998—2000, U.S. Ct. Appeals (9th cir.), 2000—. Office: 333 Las Vegas Blvd S Rm 7072 Las Vegas NV 89101

RAWLS, CHARLES RICHARDSON, lawyer, government official; b. Wilmington, N.C. m. Deanne Elizbeth Maynard. BA in Bus. Mgmt., N.C. State U., 1979; JD, Campbell U., 1982. Bar: N.C. 1982. Counsel to subcom. on forests, family farms, and energy Ho. of Reps., Washington, 1983—85, assoc. gen. counsel com. on agr., 1985—88, legis. dir. Congressman Martin Lancaster, 1988—90, adminstrv. asst., 1991—93; asst. to dep. sec. agr. Richard Rominger USDA, Washington, 1993—98, gen. counsel, 1998—2001; gen. counsel, v.p. for legal, tax, and acctg. Nat. Coun. of Farmer Cooperatives, 2002—03; gen. counsel FCA, McLean, Va., 2003—. Office: Farm Credit Admin 1501 Farm Credit Dr Mc Lean VA 22102-5090*

RAWLS, FRANK MACKLIN, lawyer; b. Suffolk, Va., Aug. 24, 1952; s. John Lewis and Mary Helen (Macklin) R.; m. Sally Hallum Blanchard, June 26, 1976; children: Matthew Christopher, John Stephen, Michael Andrew. BA in History cum laude, Hampden Sydney Coll., 1974; JD, U. Va., 1977. Bar: Va. 1977, U.S. Dist. Ct. (ea. dist.) Va. 1977, U.S. Ct. Appeals (4th cir.) 1977. Assoc. Rawls, Habel & Rawls, Suffolk, 1977-78, ptnr., 1978-91, Ferguson & Rawls, Suffolk, 1991-96, Ferguson, Rawls, MacDonald,

Overton & Grissom PC, Suffolk, 1996-98, Ferguson, Rawls, MacDonald & Overton PC, Suffolk, 1999—2002, Ferguson, Rawls & Raines, P.C., 2002—. Sec., bd. dirs. Suffolk Title Ltd., 1986-95; bd. dirs Old Dominion Investors Trust, Inc. 1994—, Secure Title, Inc., 1996—. Deacon Westminster Reformed Presbyn. Ch., Suffolk, 1979-83, elder, clk. of session, 1984-91, 94-99; chmn. bd. dirs. Suffolk Crime Line, 1982-90, Suffolk Cheer Fund, 1982—, Covenant Christian Schs., Suffolk, 1982-84; bd. dirs. Norfolk Christian Schs., 1990—, v.p., 1998-99, pres., 1999—; pres. Parent Tchr. Fellowship, 1995-97, vice-chmn. steering com. for capital campaign, 1996-98, v.p., 1997-98; adv. bd. dirs. Salvation Army, Suffolk, 1977-95, chmn., 1989-90; chmn. Suffolk Com. on Affordable Housing, 1989-90; bd. dirs. Suffolk YMCA, 1988-90, Suffolk Youth Athletic Assn., 1999-2000. Mem. ATLA, Suffolk Bar Assn. (past pres.), Va. State Bar, Va. Bar Assn., Christian Legal Soc., Va. Trial Lawyers Assn., Suffolk Bar Assn. Corporate, general, General practice, Personal injury (including property damage). E-mail: frawls@frrlaw.com.

RAWLS, JOHN D. lawyer; b. Jacksonville, Fla., Sept. 16, 1943; s. Hugh Miller Sr. and Katherine (Dickenson) R. BA, Williams Coll., 1965; JD, Fla. State U., Tallahassee, 1974. Bar: Fla. 1975, La. 1986, U.S. Dist. Ct. (mid. dist.) Fla. 1975, U.S. Dist. Ct. (ea. dist.) La. 1986, U.S. Dist. Ct. (no. dist.) Fla. 1989, U.S. Dist. Ct. (we. dist.) La. 1996, U.S. Ct. Appeals (5th cir.) 1986. Assoc. Foerster & Hodge, Jacksonville Beach, Fla., 1975-78; ptnr. Thames, Rawls & Skinner, Jacksonville, 1978-80; pvt. practice, Jacksonville, 1980-85; pres. At Your Svc. Supply Co., New Orleans, 1985-86; assoc. Oestreicher, Whalen & Hackett, New Orleans, 1986-87; pvt. practice, New Orleans, 1987—. Charter mem. Fla. Commn. on Ethics, Tallahassee, 1974-75. Mem. Fla. State U. Law Rev., 1973-74. Bd. dirs. Celebration '86, New Orleans, 1985-86; vol. NO/AIDS Task Force, New Orleans, 1986—; bd. dirs. La. Lesbian and Gay Polit. Action Caucus, New Orleans, 1987-89, Nat. Lesbian and Gay Law Assn., Washington, 1992-94, Supreme Ct. of La. Hist. Soc., New Orleans, 1992-96; founder, sec., bd. dirs. La. Electorate of Gays and Lesbians, New Orleans, 1993-96; chair La. Gov.'s Commn. on HIV and AIDS, Baton Rouge, 1994-95; unofcl. advisor on Gay and AIDS issues Gov. of La., Baton Rouge, 1992-96. Capt. U.S. Army, 1968-72, Vietnam. Nat. Merit scholar, 1961; Forum for Equality ACCLAIM award Outstanding Polit. Activist, 1999, Champion for Equality award La. Lesbian and Gay Polit. Action Caucus, 2000. Fellow: La. Bar Found.; mem.: La. Landmarks Soc., Inc. (trustee 2001—02), New Orleans Bar Assn. Democrat. Episcopalian. Avocation: reading. Civil rights, Personal injury (including property damage).

RAWSON, RICHARD J. corporate lawyer; b. Florham Park, N.J. BS, Notre Dame U.; JD, Rutgers U. Formerly with Sullivan & Cromwell, N.Y.C. and Washington; with Law Divsn. AT&T, 1984-92; sr. v.p., gen. counsel Lucent Technologies, Murray Hill, N.J., 1992—. Mem. ABA, Am. Corp. Counsel Assn. Office: Lucent Technologies 600 Mountain Ave New Providence NJ 07974-2008*

RAY, BETTY JEAN G. retired lawyer; b. New Orleans, June 7, 1943; d. William E. George and Iris U. (Berthold) Grizzell; m. Gerald L. Ray, June 9, 1962; children: Gerald L. Ray, Jr., Brian P. BS Psychology, La. State U., 1976, JD, 1980. Bar: La., 1980; U.S. Dist. Ct. (ea., mid. and we. dists.) La. 1981; U.S. Ct. Appeal (5th cir.) 1981. Jud. law clk. 19th Jud. Dist. Ct., Baton Rouge, 1980-81; atty. Jean G. Ray, Baton Rouge, 1981-83; counsel Gulf Stream, Inc., Baton Rouge, 1982-83; staff atty. La. Dept. Justice, Baton Rouge, 1983-84, asst. atty. gen., 1984-87; staff atty. FDIC, Shreveport, La., 1987-88, mng. atty., 1988-94; spl. dep. receiver Receivership Office, La. Dept. Ins., Baton Rouge, 1994-95; spl. counsel Brook, Pizza & van Loon, L.L.P., Baton Rouge, 1995-2000. Mem. La. Bar Assn., Order of Coif, Phi Beta Kappa, Phi Delta Phi (scholar 1980). Episcopalian. Home: 12154 County Rd 99 Lillian AL 36549-5120 E-mail: jeangray@gulftel.com.

RAY, BRUCE DAVID, lawyer, writer; b. Denver, Dec. 19, 1955; s. John Denver Ray and Jane (Guiney) Mitchell; m. Faith Theofanus, Aug. 20, 1978 (div. 2001); children: Ellena, Constance, Christian, Zoe. BA magna cum laude, U. Colo., 1978; JD, Union U., Albany, N.Y., 1981. Bar: Colo. 1981. Spl. environ. counsel URS-Berger, San Bernardino, Calif., 1982-84; asst. regional counsel EPA, Denver, 1984-90; spl. asst. U.S. atty. U.S. Dept. Justice, Denver, 1987-90; assoc. gen. counsel Johns-Manville Corp., Denver, 1990—. Asst. editor Natural Resources and Environment, 1989—; contbr. articles to legal jours. First v.p. St. Catherine Greek Orthodox Ch. of S.E. Denver, 1994-95. Recipient bronze medal EPA, 1986, 91, gold medal, 1989, Environ. Excellence award, 1987, Best Article award, 1988, Roasch prize Albany Law Sch., 1981. Mem. ABA (sect. on environment, energy and resources law), Colo. Bar Assn. (environ. law coun. 1987—, chmn. 1995-96), Aurora Bar assn., Environ. Law Inst., Air and Waste Mgmt. Assn., Phi Beta Kappa. Avocations: german language and literature, modern greek, writing. Environmental. Office: Johns-Mannville 717 17th St Denver CO 80202-3330 E-mail: rayb@jm.com.

RAY, FRANK ALLEN, lawyer; b. Lafayette, Ind., Jan. 30, 1949; s. Dale Allen and Merry Ann (Fleming) R.; m. Carol Ann Olmutz, Oct. 1, 1982; children: Erica Fleming, Robert Allen. BA, Ohio State U., 1970, JD, 1973. Bar: Ohio 1973, U.S. Dist. Ct. (so. dist.) Ohio 1975, U.S. Supreme Ct. 1976, U.S. Tax Ct. 1977, U.S. Ct. Appeals (6th cir.) 1977, U.S. Dist. Ct. (no. dist.) Ohio 1980, U.S. Dist. Ct. (ea. dist.) Mich. 1983, U.S. Ct. Appeals (1st cir.) 1986; cert. civil trial adv. Nat. Bd. Trial Advocacy. Asst. pros. atty. Franklin County, Ohio, 1973-75, chief civil counsel, 1976-78; dir. econ. crime project Nat. Dist. Attys. Assn., Washington, 1975-76; assoc. Brownfield, Kosydar, Bowen, Bally & Sturtz, Columbus, Ohio, 1978, Michael F. Colley Co., L.P.A., Columbus, 1979-83; pres. Frank A. Ray Co., L.P.A., Columbus, 1983-93, 2000—, Ray & Todaro Co., LPA, Columbus, 1993-94, Ray, Todaro & Alton Co., L.P.A., Columbus, 1994-96, Ray, Todaro, Alton & Kirstein Co., L.P.A., Columbus, 1996, Ray, Alton & Kirstein Co., L.P.A., Columbus, 1996—98; sr. ptnr. Ray & Alton, L.L.P., Columbus, 1998—2000; adj. prof. Moritz Coll. of Law, Ohio State U., Ohio, 2003—. Mem. seminar faculty Nat. Coll. Dist. Attys., Houston, 1975-77; mem. nat. conf. faculty Fed. Jud. Ctr., Washington, 1976-77; bd. editors Man. for Complex Litigation, Fed. Jud. Ctr., 1999—; bd. mem. bar examiners Ohio Supreme Ct., 1992-95, Rules Adv. Com., 1995-99; adj. prof. law Mortiz Coll. Law, Ohio State U., 2003—. Editor: Economic Crime Digest, 1975-76; co-author: Personal Injury Litigation Practice in Ohio, 1988, 91. Mem. fin. com. Franklin County Rep. Orgn., Columbus, 1979-84; trustee Ohio State U. Coll. Humanities Alumni Soc., 1991-93, Nat. Coun. Ohio State U. Coll. Law Alumni Assn., 1998—; mem. Legal Aid Soc. of Columbus Capital Campaign Fund Cabinet, 1998. Capt. inf. U.S. Army, 1976. Named to Ten Outstanding Young Citizens of Columbus, Columbus Jaycees, 1976; recipient Nat. award of Distinctive Svc., Nat. Dist. Attys. Assn., 1977. Fellow: Ohio Acad. Trial Lawyers (pres. 1989—90, Pres.'s award 1986), Ohio State Bar Found., Roscoe Pound Found., Am. Coll. Trial Lawyers, Internat. Soc. Barristers, Columbus Bar Found.; mem.: ATLA (state del. 1990—92), ABA, Franklin County Trial Lawyers Assn. (pres. 1987—88, Pres.'s award 1990), Ohio State Bar Assn. (com. negligence law 1990—97), Million Dollar Advs. Forum, Columbus Bar Assn. (pres. 2001—02, Profl. award 1987), Am. Bd. Trial Advs. (pres.-elect, Ohio Chpt. 2003—), Inns. of Ct. (pres. Judge Robert M. Duncan chpt. 1993—94). Presbyterian. General civil litigation, Personal injury (including property damage), Product liability. Home: 2030 Tremont Rd Columbus OH 43221-4330 Office: 175 S 3rd St Ste 350 Columbus OH 43215-5188 E-mail: far@raylaw.com.

RAY, GILBERT T. lawyer; b. Mansfield, Ohio, Sept. 18, 1944; s. Robert Lee Ray and Renatha (Goldie) Washington; m. Valerie J. Reynolds, June 14, 1969; children: Tanika, Tarlin. BA, Ashland Coll., 1966; MBA, U. Toledo, 1968; JD, Howard U., 1972. Assoc. O'Melveny & Myers, L.A., 1972-79, ptnr., 1980-2000, ret. ptnr., 2000—. Bd. dirs. HMS Host Co., Sierra Monolithics, Inc., Watson, Wyatt & Co., Advance Auto Parts, Automobile Club of So. Calif., Haynes Found., Anchor Pathway Fund, Seasons Series Fund, SunAmerica Series Trust. Mem. The Calif. Club, L.A. Country Club. Democrat. Office: 400 S Hope St Ste 1900 Los Angeles CA 90071-2899

RAY, HUGH MASSEY, JR., lawyer; b. Vicksburg, Miss., Feb. 1, 1943; s. Hugh Massey and Lollie Landon (Powell) R.; m. Carol Robertson, Sept. 7, 2002; children: Hugh, Hallie. BA, Vanderbilt U., 1965, JD, 1967. Bar: Tex. 1967, U.S. Dist. Ct. (so. dist.) Tex. 1967, U.S. Dist.Ct. (we. dist.) La. 1979, U.S. Dist. Ct. (we. dist.) Tex. 1979, U.S. Dist Ct. (no. dist.) Tex. 1980, U.S. Ct. Appeals 1st, 5th, 9th, 11th cirs.) 1982, U.S. Dist. Ct. (no. dist.) Calif. 1989, N.Y. 1992; cert. Tex. Bd. Legal Specialization. Asst. U.S. atty. So. Dist. Tex., 1967-68; assoc. Andrews & Kurth, Houston, 1968-77, ptnr., 1977—. Lectr. Ctrl. and Ea. European Law Initiative, Vilnius, Lithuania, 1996. Co-author: Bankruptcy Investing, 1992, Creditor's Rights in Texas, vol. 1 & 2, 1998; contbr. articles to profl. jours. Mem. ABA (chmn. real property practice com. 1975-77, chmn. continuing legal edn. com. young lawyers divsn. 1976-78, vice-chmn. 1979, chmn. oil and gas subcom. bus. bankruptcy com. 1985-89, chmn. executory contracts subcom. 1989-93, chmn. bus. bankruptcy com. 1993-96, chmn. com. on trust indentures and indenture trustees 1995-97, mem. standing com. on jud. selection, tenure and compensation 1996-97, coun. mem. bus. law sect. 1997-2001, chmn. ad hoc com. on bankruptcy ct. structure 1996-2001, chair energy bus. com. 2001—), Houston Bar Assn., Tex. Bar Assn. (chmn. bankruptcy com. 1985-88), Am. Law Inst., Houston Country Club, Tex. Club, Houston Club. Episcopalian. Bankruptcy, Federal civil litigation, State civil litigation. Home: 3036 Locke Ln Houston TX 77019- Office: Andrews & Kurth 600 Travis St Ste 4200 Houston TX 77002-2910

RAY, JEANNE CULLINAN, lawyer, insurance company executive; b. N.Y.C., May 5, 1943; d. Thomas Patrick and Agnes Joan (Buckley) C.; m. John Joseph Ray, Jan. 20, 1968 (dec. Mar. 1993); children: Christopher Lawrence, Douglas James. Student, Univ. Coll., Dublin, Ireland, 1963; AB, Coll. Mt. St. Vincent, Riverdale, N.Y., 1964; LLB, Fordham U., 1967. Bar: N.Y. 1967. Atty. Mut. Life Ins. Co. N.Y. (MONY), N.Y.C., 1967-68, asst. counsel, 1969-72, assoc. counsel, 1972-73, counsel, 1974-75, asst. gen. counsel, 1976-80, assoc. gen. counsel, 1981-83, v.p. pension counsel, 1984-85, v.p. area counsel group and pension ops., 1985-87, v.p. sector counsel group and pension ops., 1988, v.p., chief counsel exec. and corp. affairs, 1988-89; v.p. law, sec. MONY Securities Corp., N.Y.C., 1980-85, MONY Advisers, Inc., N.Y.C., 1980-88; sec. MONYCO, Inc., N.Y.C., 1980-85; v.p., counsel MONY Series Fund, Inc., Balt., 1984-87; v.p., assoc. gen. counsel Tchrs. Ins. and Annuity Assoc. Coll. Ret. Equities Fund (TIAA-CREF), N.Y.C., 1989-91, v.p., chief counsel ins., 1991-99. Contbr. articles to legal jours. Cubmaster, den mother Greater N.Y. coun. Boy Scouts Am., N.Y.C., 1978-84, mem. bd. rev. and scouting com., 1985-99. Mem. ABA (chmn. employee benefits com. tort and ins. practice sect. 1981-82, vice-chmn. 1983-96), Assn. Life Ins. Counsel (chmn. policy holders tax com. tax sect. 1982-91, vice chmn. tax sect. 1991-93, chmn. 1993-99), Assn. Bar City N.J. (chmn. employee benefits com. 1992-95), Investment Co. Inst. (mem. pension com. 1993-99), Am. Coun. Life Ins. (chmn. fiduciary task force of pension com. 1990-99), Am. Coun. Life Ins. Democrat. Roman Catholic. Corporate, general, Pension, profit-sharing, and employee benefits, Securities. Address: 304 E 20th St Apt 3E New York NY 10003-1814

RAY, MARY LOUISE RYAN, lawyer; b. Houston, Dec. 8, 1954; d. Cornelius O'Brien and Mary Anne (Kelley) R.; m. Marshall Ransome Ray, Jan. 30, 1982; children: Siobhan Elisabeth Kelley, Johanna Frances Morris, Jonathan Jordan Willson. BA with honors, U. Tex., 1976; JD, St. Mary's Univ., San Antonio, Tex., 1980. Bar: Tex. 1980, U.S. Dist. Ct. (so. dist.) Tex. 1981, U.S. Ct. Appeals (5th cir.) 1993, U.S. Supreme Ct. 1994. Assoc. Kelley & Ryan, Houston, 1980-82, R.W. Armstrong, Brownsville, Tex., 1982-83; ptnr. Armstrong & Ray, Brownsville, Tex., 1983-87; shareholder Ransome and Ray, P.C., Brownsville, Tex., 1987—. Bd. dirs. Brownsville Soc. for Crippled Children, 1984-95, pres., 1992-93; bd. dirs. Valley Zool. Soc., 1990-2003, v.p., 2003; bd. dirs. United Way of Southern Cameron County, 1989-95, pres., 1994; bd. dirs. Crippled Children's Found., Brownsville, 1989—; bd. dirs. Episcopal Day Sch. Found., 1995-2002, pres., 1995-2002. Fellow Tex. Bar Found.; mem. Tex. Bar Assn., Cameron County Bar Assn. (bd. dirs. 1990-99, pres. 1998), Tex. Assn. Bank Counsel, Brownsville C. of C. (bd. dirs. 1998-99). Episcopalian. General civil litigation, Corporate, general, Probate (including wills, trusts), Estate planning, Property, real (including real estate development, water), Probate (including wills, trusts). Office: Ransome & Ray PC 550 E Levee St Brownsville TX 78520-5343

RAY, RONALD DUDLEY, lawyer; b. Hazard, Ky., Oct. 30, 1942; BA in Psychology and English, Centre Coll., 1964; JD magna cum laude, U. Louisville, 1971. Assoc. Greenebaum, Doll & McDonald, 1971-75, ptnr., 1975-84, 85-86, Ray & Morris, Louisville, 1986-89; mng. ptnr. Ronald Ray Attys., Louisville, 1990—; dep. asst. sec. def. Pentagon, Washington, 1984-85. Adj. prof. law U. Louisville Sch. Law, 1972-80; commr. Presdl. Commn. on Assigment of Women in Mil., 1992. Author: Military Necessity & Homosexuality, 1993; sr. legal editor: Personnel Policy Manual, Bank Supervisory Policies, The Bank Employee Handbook, 1985-86; mil. historian. State fin. chmn. Nat. Fin. Com. for George Bush for Pres.; chmn. Vietnam Vets. Leadership Program in Ky., 1982-85, Ky. Vietnam Vets. Meml. Fund, 1985-91; trustee Marine Corps Command and Staff Found., 1985-92; mem. exec. com. State Cen. Com., Ky. Rep. Party, 1986-90; mem. Am. Battle Monuments Commn., 1990-94; chmn. Vets. for Bush in Ky., 2000; mem. Nat. Com. Vets. for Bush, 2000; spokesman Coalition of Am. Vets., 1998—, chmn., 1999—. With USMC, 1964-69; col. USMCR (ret.). Decorated Silver Star medal with gold star, Bronze Star medal, Purple Heart, Vietnamese Cross of Gallantry, Vietnamese Honor Medal; recipient Nat. Eagle award Nat. Guard Assn., 1985. Mem. Naval Inst. (life), Marine Corps Res. Officers' Assn. General civil litigation, Legislative, Military. Home: Halls Hill Farm 3317 Halls Hill Rd Crestwood KY 40014-9523 E-mail: euniceray@aol.com.

RAY, STEPHEN ALAN, academic administrator, lawyer; b. Oklahoma City, Aug. 26, 1956; s. Thompson Eugene and Dorothea Hodges. BA summa cum laude, St. Thomas Sem., 1978; PhD, Harvard U., 1986; JD, U. Calif., Hastings, 1990. Bar: Calif. 1990, Mass. 1994. Assoc. Richards, Watson & Gershon, L.A., 1990—93; lectr. theology Boston Coll., Chestnut Hill, Mass., 1993—95; staff counsel Houghton Miffin Co., Boston, 1995—96; assoc. dean acad. affairs Harvard Law Sch., Cambridge, 2001—, dir. acad. affairs, 1996—98, asst. dean acad. affairs, 1998—2001. Vis. lectr. religion Harvard Divinity Sch., spring 1995; adv. bd. Harvard Native Am. Program, 1999—. Author: The Modern Soul, 1987. Vol. AIDS action com., Boston, 1994-96; atty. vol. AIDS Project L.A., 1991-93; Native Am. Adv. Com. on Repatriation, Peabody Mus., 1999-2002. Mem. ABA, Cherokee Nation Okla. Office: Harvard Law Sch Griswold Hall 207 Cambridge MA 02138 E-mail: aray@law.harvard.edu.

RAYIS, JAMES Y. lawyer; b. Detroit, Nov. 15, 1957; s. Afram Dinkha and Juliet Patros Rayis; 1 child, Ashur S. BA in Econs., Mich. State U., 1979; JD, U. Ga., 1982. Bar: Ga. 1982, Mich. 1982, Colo. 1994. Assoc. Powell, Goldstein, Frazer & Murphy, Atlanta, 1989—94; v.p., gen. counsel Omnivest Internat., Inc., Denver, 1994—99; of counsel Meadows, Ichter & Bowers (now Balch & Bingham LLP), Atlanta, 2000—. Chmn. Ga. Bar Internat. Law Soc., Atlanta, 2002—; exec. mem. Internat. Assn. Jeunes Avocats, Brussels, 1996—; chmn. Ga. Bar YLD Internat. Com., Atlanta, 1988—90. Contbr. articles to profl. jours. Mem. bd. dirs. Atlanta MSU Alumni Club, Atlanta, 2002—; spl. legal advisor Assyrian Universal Alliance, Chgo., 1988—95; internat. counsel Assyrian Am. League, 2002—. Mem.: ABA, SILP, ABA Middle East Law Com., So. Ctr. Internat. Studies, First Tuesday Atlanta (bd. dirs. 2001—). Avocations: running, soccer, coaching. Private international, Intellectual property, Corporate, general. Office: Balch & Bingham LLP 14 Piedmont Ctr #1100 Atlanta GA 30305 Fax: 404-261-3656. E-mail: jyr@miblaw.com.

RAYLESBERG, ALAN IRA, lawyer; b. N.Y.C., Dec. 6, 1950; s. Daniel David and Sally Doris (Mantell) R.; m. Caren Thea Coven, Nov. 20, 1983; children: Lisa Maris, Jason Todd. BA, NYU, 1972; JD cum laude, Boston U., 1975. Bar: N.Y. 1976, U.S. Dist. Ct. (so. dist.) N.Y. 1976, U.S. Dist. Ct. (ea. dist.) N.Y. 1978, U.S. Tax Ct. 1981, U.S. Ct. Appeals (2d and 5th cirs.) 1982, U.S. Ct. Appeals (1st cir.) 1986, U.S. Ct. Appeals (9th cir.) 1996. Assoc. Orans, Elsen & Polstein, N.Y.C., 1975-77, Guggenheimer & Untermyer, N.Y.C., 1977-83, ptnr., 1983-85; ptnr. Rosenman & Colin, N.Y.C., 1985—2002, co-chmn. litigation dept., 1998-99, chmn. litigation dept., 1999—2002; ptnr., sect. head litigation group Vinson & Elkins, N.Y.C., 2002—. Adj. instr. N.Y. Law Sch., 1980-83; instr. Nat. Inst. of Trial Advocacy; mem. adv. group comml. divsn., mem. mediation panel N.Y. State Supreme Ct.; mem. arbitration panel U.S. Dist. Ct. (ea. dist.) N.Y.; judge Nat. Moot Ct. Competition, 1980—. Bd. dirs. Fund for Modern Cts., 1994—. Mem. ABA, Fed. Bar Coun., Assn. Bar City N.Y., N.Y. County Lawyers Assn. (bd. dirs. 1995-98, 99-2002, fed. ct. com. 1988—, appellate ct. com. 1990—, co-chmn. appellate ct. com. 1992-93, chair appellate ct. com. 1993-96), N.Y. County Lawyers Assn. Found. (bd. dirs. 1998—), N.Y. State Bar Assn. (ho. delegates 1996-2000), Securities Industry Assn. (legal and compliance divsn) N.Y. Coun. Def. Lawyers, Town Club of New Castle (mem. exec. com. 1987-91). Democrat. Jewish. Federal civil litigation, State civil litigation, Securities. Office: Vinson & Elkins 666 Fifth Ave New York NY 10103 E-mail: araylesberg@velaw.com., alan.raylesberg@verizon.net.

RAYMOND, DARIN JAMES, lawyer; b. Sioux Falls, S.D., Sept. 9, 1966; m. Beth Ann Farley; children: Walker James, Katelyn Ann. BA, Drake U., 1988, JD, 1991. Bar: Iowa. Pvt. practice, Iowa, 1991—94; counsel Plymouth County, Lemars, Iowa, 1994—. Mem. Fight Crime Invest in Kids, Washington, 1999—; chair Domestic Violence Coalition, Lemars, 1994—; mem. Death Rev. Team Iowa Domestic Violence, Des Moines, 2001—. Mem.: ATLA, Plymouth County Bar Assn. (pres. 1992—94), Plymouth County Peace Officers Assn., Iowa County Attys. Assn., Iowa State Bar Assn., Nat. Dist. Atty. Assn. Office: Plymouth County Attys Office 215 4th Ave SE Le Mars IA 51031

RAYMOND, DAVID WALKER, lawyer; b. Chelsea, Mass., Aug. 23, 1945; s. John Walker and Jane (Beck) R.; m. Sandra Sue Broadwater, Aug. 12, 1967 (div.); m. Margaret Byrd Payne, May 25, 1974; children: Pamela Payne, Russell Wyatt. BA, Gettysburg Coll., 1967; JD, Temple U., 1970. Bar: Pa. 1970, D.C. 1971, Ill. 1975, U.S. Dist. Ct. (no. dist.) Ill. 1981, U.S. Supreme Ct. 1974. Govtl. affairs atty. Sears, Roebuck and Co., Washington, 1970-74, atty. Sears Hdqrs. law dept. Chgo., 1974-80, asst. gen. counsel advt., trademarks and customs, 1981-84, asst. gen. counsel adminstrn., 1984-86, mgr. planning and analysis corp. planning dept., 1986-89, sr. corp. counsel pub. policy corp. law dept., 1989-90; assoc. gen. counsel litigation and adminstrn. law dept. Sears Mdse. Group, 1990-92, dep. gen. counsel, 1992-93, v.p., gen. counsel, 1993-95; v.p. law Sears Roebuck and Co., 1996; of counsel Winston & Strawn, Washington, 1996-2001; v.p., gen. counsel C-NAV Systems, Inc., Gettysburg, Pa., 2001—. Mem. staff Temple Law Quar., 1968-69, editor, 1969-70. Trustee No. Ill. U., 1996-98; mem. bd. visitors Christopher Newport U., 1999—; mem. bd. fellows Gettysburg Coll., 1999-2003; bd. dirs. ATO House Corp., 1997—. Mem.: ABA, Phi Alpha Delta. Presbyterian. Administrative and regulatory, Corporate, general, Legislative.

RAYNOR, STEVEN LEIGH, lawyer; b. Charlottesville, Va., May 20, 1960; s. Robert Cook Raynor and Eleanor Laing; m. Chloe Payne Raynor, Jan. 8, 1983; children: Austin L., Jean L., Natalie J. BA in Philosophy, Randolph-Macon Coll., 1982; JD, U. Va., 1985. Bar: W.Va. 1985, Va. 1987. Mng. atty. Martin & Raynor, Charlottesville, Va., 1994—. Chmn. bd. dirs. Masters Trucking Co., Charlotteville, 2002. Author: Separation and Divorce Handbook, 2002. Mem.: ABA, Charlotteville Bar Assn. (chair 1999—2001), Va. State Bar Assn. Family and matrimonial. Home: 2121 Whippoorwill Rd Charlottesville VA 22901 Office: Martin & Raynor 415 4th St NE Charlottesville VA 22902 Fax: 434-817-3110. E-mail: raynor@mrlaw.com.

RAYO, MARK JAMES, lawyer; b. Bklyn., Aug. 1, 1957; s. Ignazio and Aurora (Trivisani) R.; m. Diana Digangi, Aug. 4, 1979 (dec. Oct. 1989); children: Jason, Danielle; m. Ivette Rayo, July 8, 1995; 1 child, Jennifer. BS, NYU, 1978. Bar: N.Y. 1983. Ptnr. Rayo & Rayo, Bklyn., 1983-96; pvt. practice Bklyn., 1996—. Mem. ATLA, N.Y. State Trial Lawyers Assn., Bklyn. Bar Assn., Columbian Lawyers Assn. Avocations: skiing, fishing, hunting, golf, tennis. Personal injury (including property damage). Office: 26 Court St Brooklyn NY 11242-0103

RAYSON, EDWIN HOPE, lawyer; b. Earlville, Ill., Jan. 13, 1923; s. Edwin H. and Lillian (Astley) R.; m. Evelyn Sherry Kirkland, Oct. 1, 1983; children: Jane Rayson Young, Edwin Hope III, G. Scott. AB, U. Tenn., 1944, LL.B., 1948. Bar: Tenn. 1948. Pvt. practice, Knoxville, 1948—; ptnr. Kramer, Rayson, Leake, Rodgers & Morgan, 1949—. Lectr. labor law U. Tenn. Coll. Law, 1951-71 Served to lt. (j.g.) USNR, 1944-46. Mem. Order of Coif, Sigma Chi, Omicron Delta Kappa. Home: 501 River Rd Loudon TN 37774-5583 Office: 25th Fl 1st Tennessee Plaza Knoxville TN 37901

RAZZANO, FRANK CHARLES, lawyer; b. Bklyn., Feb. 25, 1948; s. Pasquale Anthony and Agnes Mary (Borgia) R.; m. Stephanie Anne Lucas, Jan. 10, 1970; children: Joseph, Francis, Catherine. BA, St. Louis U., 1969; JD, Georgetown U., 1972. Bar: N.Y. 1973, U.S. Dist. Ct. (so. dist.) N.Y. 1973, U.S. Dist. Ct. (es. dist.) N.Y. 1973, N.J. 1976, D.C. 1981, Va. 1984, U.S. Dist. Ct. N.J. 1976, U.S. Dist. Ct. Md. 1977, U.S. Dist. Ct. (no. dist.) Calif. 1981, U.S. Dist. Ct. D.C. 1982, U.S. Dist. Ct. (ea. dist.) Va. 1989, U.S. Dist. Ct. (we. dist.) Va. 1990, U.S. Ct. Appeals (2d cir.) 1973, U.S. Ct. Appeals (3d cir.) 1975, U.S. Ct. Appeals (D.C. and 5th cirs.) 1983, U.S. Ct. Appeals (4th cir.) 1984, U.S. Ct. Appeals (6th cir.) 1990, U.S. Ct. Appeals (8th and 9th cirs.) 2000, U.S. Supreme Ct. 1976. Assoc. Shea & Gould, N.Y.C., 1972-75; asst. U.S. atty. Dist. of N.J., Newark, 1975-78; asst. chief trial atty. SEC, Washington, 1978-82; ptnr. Shea & Gould, Washington, 1982-94, mng. ptnr., 1991-92; ptnr. Camhy Karlinsky Stein Razzano & Rubin, Washington, 1994-96, Dickstein, Shapiro, Morin & Oshinsky, Washington, 1996—. Lectr. in field; adv. bd. Securities Litigation Reform Act Reporter, Securities Regulation Law Jour.; adj. prof. law U. Md. Sch. Law. Civil law editor Rico Law Reporter; mem. adv. bd. Corp. Confidentiality and Disclosure Letter; hon. adv. com. Jour. Internat. Law and Practice, Detroit Coll. Law; contbr. articles to legal jours. Scoutmaster Vienna coun. Boy Scouts Am., 1984. Recipient spl. achievement award Justice Dept., 1977, spl. commendation, 1978, Outstanding Achievement award Detroit Coll. of Law, 1993. Mem. ABA (chmn. criminal law com., sect. bus. law 1996—), Va. Bar, D.C. Bar (chmn. litigation sect. 1987-89, vice-chmn. coun. sects. 1988-89), Assn. Securities & Exch. Commn. Alumni (pres. 1993-95), Phi Beta Kappa, Eta Sigma Phi. Roman Catholic. Criminal, State civil litigation, Securities. Home: 1713 Paisley Blue Ct Vienna VA 22182-2326

RAZZANO, PASQUALE ANGELO, lawyer; b. Bklyn., Apr. 3, 1943; s. Pasquale Anthony and Agnes Mary (Borgia) R.; m. Maryann Walker, Jan. 29, 1966; children: Elizabeth, Pasquale, Susan, ChristyAnn. BSCE, Poly. Inst. Bklyn., 1964; student law, NYU, 1964-66; JD, Georgetown U., 1969. Bar: Va. 1969, N.Y. 1970, U.S. Ct. Appeals (2d, 3d, 7th, 9th and fed. cirs.), U.S. Supreme Ct., U.S. Dist. Ct. (so., ea. and western dists.) N.Y., U.S. Dist.

Ct. (we. dist.) Tex., U.S. Dist. Ct. Hawaii, U.S. Dist. Ct. Conn. Examiner U.S. Patent Office, 1966-69; assoc. Curtis, Morris & Safford, P.C., 1969-71, ptnr., 1971-91, Fitzpatrick, Cella, Harper & Scinto, 1991—. Guest lectr. U.S. Trademark Assn., Am. Intellectual Property Law Assn., Practicing Law Inst., NYU Law Ctr., ABA, N.Y. Intellectual Property Law Assn. Mem. bd. editors Licensing Jour., 1986—; mem. bd. editors Trademark Reporter, 1987—, book rev. editor, 1989-91, pub. articles editor, 1991-94, domestic articles editor, 1992-93, 95, editor-in-chief 1996-98. Rep. committeeman Rockland County. Recipient Robert Ridgeway award, 1964. Mem.: FBA (chmn. patent law com. 1999—2002, bd. govs. 2002—), ABA (guest lectr.), Columban Laws Assn., Bar Assn. City N.Y., Italian Am. Bar Assn., Va. Bar Assn., N.Y. Coun. Bar Leaders (exec. coun. 1993—94), N.Y. Bar Assn., Am. Intellectual Property Law Assn., Internat. Trademark Assn. (bd. dirs. 1996—99), Licensing Exec. Soc. (chmn. N.Y. chpt. 1996—99), N.Y. Intellectual Property Law Assn. (bd. dirs. 1985—93, sec. 1988—91, pres. 1994—95), Shorehaven Golf Club, Minute Man Yacht Club, N.Y. Athletic Club. Republican. Roman Catholic. Federal civil litigation, Patent, Trademark and copyright. Address: 21 Covlee Dr Westport CT 06880-6407 also: 14 Deerwood Trl Lake Placid NY 12946-1834

RE, EDWARD DOMENIC, law educator, retired federal judge; b. Santa Marina, Italy, Oct. 14, 1920; s. Anthony and Marina (Maetta) R.; m. Margaret A. Corcoran, June 3, 1950; children: Mary Ann, Anthony John, Marina, Edward, Victor, Margaret, Matthew, Joseph, Mary Elizabeth, Mary Joan, Mary Ellen, Nancy Madeleine. BS cum laude, St. John's U., 1941, LLB summa cum laude, 1943, LLD (hon.), 1968; JSD, NYU, 1950; DPed (hon.), Aquila, Italy, 1960; LL.D. (hon.), St. Mary's Coll., Notre Dame, Ind., 1968, Maryville Coll., St. Louis, 1969, N.Y. Law Sch., 1976, Bklyn. Coll., CUNY, 1978, Nova U., 1980, Roger Williams Coll., 1982, Dickinson Sch. Law, Carlisle, Pa., 1983, Seton Hall U., 1984, Stetson U., 1990, William Mitchell Coll. Law, 1992, St. Francis Coll., Bklyn., 1993; L.H.D. (hon.), DePaul U., 1980, Coll. S.I., CUNY, 1981, Pace U., 1985, Am. U. of Rome, 1995; D.C.S. (hon.), U. Verona, Italy, 1987; JD (hon.), U. Bologna, Italy, 1988, U. Urbino, 1994. Bar: N.Y. 1943. Appointed faculty St. John's U., N.Y., 1947, prof. law, 1951-69, adj. prof. law, 1969-80, Disting. prof., 1980—2002; vis. prof. Georgetown U. Sch. Law, 1962-67; adj. prof. law N.Y. Law Sch., 1972-82, Martin disting. vis. prof., 1982-90; spl. hearing officer U.S. Dept. Justice, 1956-61; chmn. Fgn. Claims Settlement Commn. of U.S., 1961-68; asst. sec. ednl. and cultural affairs U.S. Dept. State, 1968-69; judge U.S. Customs Ct. (now U.S. Ct. Internat. Trade), N.Y.C., 1969-91, chief judge, 1977-91, chief judge emeritus, 1991—. Mem. Jud. Conf. U.S., 1986-91, adv. com. on appellate rules, 1976-88, com. on internat. jud. rels., 1994-97; chmn. adv. com. on experimentation in the law Fed. Jud. Ctr., 1978-81; mem. bd. higher edn. City of N.Y., 1958-69, emeritus, 1969—; Jackson lectr. Nat. Coll. State Trial Judges, U. Nev., 1970. Author: Foreign Confiscations in Anglo-American Law, 1951, Selected Essays on Equity, 1955, (chpt., freedom in internat. soc.) Concept of Freedom, 1955, Cases and Materials on Equitable Remedies, 1975, Cases and Materials on Remedies, 1982; co-author (with Joseph R. Re), 2000, Law Students' Manual on Legal Writing and Oral Argument, 1991, Brief Writing and Oral Argument, 1999; co-author: (with Lester D. Orfield) Cases and Materials on International Law, 1965; co-author: (with Zechariah Chafee Jr.) Cases and Materials on Equity, 1967; contbr. articles to legal jours. Served with USAAF, 1943-47; col. JAGD, ret. Decorated Grand Cross Order of Merit Italy; recipient Am. Bill of Rights citation; Morgenstern Found. Interfaith award; USAF commendation medal; Distinguished service award Bklyn. Jr. C. of C., 1956 Mem. ABA (ho. of dels. 1976-78, chmn. sect. internat. and comparative law 1965-67), Am. Fgn. Law Assn. (pres. 1971-73), Am. Law Inst., Fed. Bar Coun. (pres. 1973-74), Am. Soc. Comparative Law (pres. 1969-91), Am. Justinian Soc. Jurists (pres. 1974-76), Internat. Assn. Jurists: Italy-USA (pres. 1991—), Internat. Assn. Judges (prin. rep. to UN 1993-2000), Scribes Am. Soc. Writers on Legal Subjects (pres. 1978). Home: 305 B 147th St Neponsit NY 11694 Office: 305 B 147th St Neponsit NY 11694

READ, NICHOLAS CARY, lawyer; b. Florence, Italy, Nov. 9, 1951; came to U.S., 1952; s. Forrest Godfrey III and Virginia (Cary) R.; m. Anne Parker Renfro, May 16, 1976; children: Sarah, Joanna. BFA, U. N.C., 1974; MA in History, U. Va., 1979, JD, 1982. Bar: Mass. 1982, U.S. Dist. Ct. Mass. 1982. Assoc. Craig & Macauley, Boston, 1982-85; counsel N.E. Merchants Leasing Co., Boston, 1985-87; sr. counsel Boston Safe Deposit and Trust Co., Boston, 1987—. Banking, Commercial, consumer (including collections, credit), Commercial, contracts (including sales of goods; commercial financing). Office: Boston Safe Deposit & Trust Co 1 Boston Pl Boston MA 02108-4407

READ, SUSAN, judge; Bachelor's degree, Ohio Wesleyan U., 1969; JD, U. Chgo., 1972. In-house counsel GE Co., 1977—88; dep. counsel to Gov. Pataki, 1995—97; judge Ct. of Claims, 1998—; ptnr. Bond, Schoeneck & King, Albany, NY; asst. counsel SUNY; assoc. judge N.Y. State Ct. Appeals, Albany, NY, 2003—. Office: NY State Ct Appeals 20 Eagle St Albany NY 12207-1095

READ, THOMAS BUCHANAN, lawyer; b. Des Moines, Apr. 7, 1949; s. Thomas Buchanan and Betty (Sherrill) R.; m. Elizabeth Rhoads, June 3, 1972; children: Peter Thomas, Katherine Elizabeth. B.A., Cornell Coll., 1971; J.D., Drake U., 1975. Bar: Iowa 1975, U.S. Dist. Ct. (no. dist.) Iowa 1975, U.S. Dist. Ct. (so. dist.) Iowa 1983, U.S. Tax Ct. 1976, U.S. Ct. Appeals (8th cir.) 1984. Assoc., ptnr. Keyes & Crawford, Cedar Rapids, Iowa, 1975-79; ptnr. Crawford, Sullivan & Read, Cedar Rapids, 1979-83, Crawford, Sullivan, Read & Roemerman, Cedar Rapids, 1983— . Bd. dirs. Jane Boyd Community House, Cedar Rapids, 1981-87 , treas., 1983, pres., 1985; mem. Linn County Ethics and Griveance Com., 1988—. Fellow Iowa Acad. Trial Lawyers; mem. Iowa State Bar Assn., Iowa Assn. Workers' Compensation Lawyers, Def. Rsch. Inst., Linn County Bar Assn., Iowa Def. Counsel Assn. State civil litigation, Personal injury (including property damage), Workers' compensation. Home: 3951 Hickory Ridge Ln SE Cedar Rapids IA 52403-3766 Office: Crawford Sullivan Read & Roemerman Alliant Tower 200 1st St SE Ste 1910 Cedar Rapids IA 52401

READE, CLAIRE ELIZABETH, lawyer; b. Waltham, Mass., June 2, 1952; d. Kemp Brownell and Suzanne Helen (Dorntge) R.; m. Earl Phillip Steinberg, Nov. 22, 1980; children: Evan Samuel, Emma Miriam. BA, Conn. Wesleyan U., 1973; JD, Harvard U., 1979; MA in Law and Diplomacy, Tufts U., 1979. Bar: Mass. 1980, D.C. 1983. Sheldon fellow Harvard U., Cambridge, Mass. and, Republic of China, 1979-80; assoc. Ropes & Gray, Boston, 1980-82, Arnold & Porter, Washington, 1982-86, ptnr., 1987—. Exec. editor: International Trade Policy: The Lawyer's Perspective, 1985; contbr. articles to profl. jours. Mem. ABA (co-chair internat. trade com.), D.C. Bar Assn., Am. Soc. Internat. Law, Washington Coun. Lawyers, Women in Internat. Trade. Private international, Public international, Legislative. Office: Arnold & Porter 555 12th St NW Washington DC 20004-1206 E-mail: readecl@aporter.com.

REAGAN, GARY DON, state legislator, lawyer; b. Amarillo, Tex., Aug. 23, 1941; s. Hester and Lois Irene (Marcum) R.; m. Nedra Ann Nash, Sept. 12, 1964; children: Marc Kristi, Kari, Brent. BA, Stanford U., 1963, JD, 1965. Bar: N.Mex. 1965, U.S. Dist. Ct. N.Mex. 1965, U.S. Supreme Ct. 1986. Assoc. Smith & Ransom, Albuquerque, 1965-67; ptnr. Smith, Ransom, Deaton & Reagan, Albuquerque, 1967-68, Williams, Johnson, Houston, Reagan & Porter, Hobbs, N.Mex., 1968-77, Williams, Johnson, Reagan, Porter & Love, Hobbs, N.Mex., 1977-82; pvt. practice pvt. practice, Hobbs, N.Mex., 1982—; city atty. City of Hobbs, 1978-80, 97—, City of Eunice, N.Mex., 1980—; mem. N.Mex. State Senate, 1993-96. Instr. N.Mex. Jr. Coll. and Coll. of S.W., Hobbs, 1978-84; N.Mex. commr. Nat. Conf. Commrs. Uniform State Laws, 1993-96; adv. mem. N.Mex. Constl. Revision Commn., 1993-95. Mayor City of Hobbs, 1972-73, 76-77, city commr., 1970-78; pres., dir. Jr. Achievement of Hobbs, 1974-85; pres., trustee Landsun Homes, Inc., Carlsbad, N.Mex., 1972-84; trustee Lydia Patterson Inst., El Paso, Tex., 1972-84, N.Mex. Conf. United Meth. Ch., 1988—, Coll. S.W. Hobbs, 1989-2001; chmn. County Dem. Com., 1983-85. Mem. ABA, State Bar N.Mex. (coms. 1989-96, v.p. 1992-93, pres. 1994-95), Lea County Bar Assn. (pres. 1976-77), Hobbs C. of C. (pres. 1989-90), Rotary (pres. Hobbs 1985-86), Hobbs Tennis Club (pres. 1974-75). Home: 200 E Eagle Dr Hobbs NM 88240-5323 Office: 1819 N Turner Ste G Hobbs NM 88240-3834 E-mail: lglregan@nm.net.

REAGAN, HARRY EDWIN, III, lawyer; b. Wichita, Kans., Sept. 9, 1940; s. Harry E. II and Mary Elizabeth (O'Steen) R.; m. Marvene R. Rogers, June 17, 1965; children: Kathleen, Leigh, Mairen. BS, U. Pa., 1962, JD, 1965. Bar: Pa. 1965, U.S. Dist. Ct. (ea. dist.) Pa. 1965, U.S. Ct. Appeals (3d cir.) 1965. From assoc. to ptnr. Morgan, Lewis & Bockius, Phila., 1965-98. Chmn. Northampton Twp. Planning Commn., Bucks County, Pa., 1974-79; mem. Warwick Twp. Planning Commn., 1980-95, chmn., 1994; supr. Warwick Twp., 1996-98; mem. San Miguel County (Colo.) Open Space Commn., 1998—, chmn., 2001—, San Miguel County Planning Commn.; mem. Town of Telluride Open Space Commn., 1999-2002, San Miguel County Planning Commn., 2002—. Mem. ABA (labor sect.), Pa. Bar Assn. (labor sect.), Phila. Bar Assn. (labor sect.), Indsl. Rels. Assn. (pres. Phila. chpt. 1990-91). Republican. Presbyterian. Avocations: coaching rugby, skiing, raising horses, bicycling. Labor (including EEOC, Fair Labor Standards Act, labor-management relations, NLRB, OSHA), Pension, profit-sharing, and employee benefits. Home and Office: 12350 McKenzie Springs Rd Placerville CO 81430

REAM, JACK FRANTZ, lawyer; b. York, Pa., Nov. 15, 1946; s. Jack Francis and Doris Gertrude (Frantz) Ream; m. Diane M. Shostak; children: Michael Brady, Bryan Andrew, Jack F. III. BA, Gettysburg Coll., 1968; LLD, Dickinson Sch., 1971; postgrad. in Comml. Law. Bar: Pa. 1971, U.S. dist. Ct. (mid. dist.) Pa. 1972, U.S. Dist. Ct. (ea. dist.) Pa. 1974, U.S. Ct. Appeals (3d cir.) 1979. Ptnr. Morris, Vedder & Ream, York, Pa., 1983—87, Kain, Brown & Roberts, York, 1987—. Instr. bankruptcy law Pa. State U., 1983—. Mem.: ABA, Comml. Law League, Am. Trial Lawyers Assn., Pa. Bar Assn. Republican. Bankruptcy, Commercial, consumer (including collections, credit), Commercial, contracts (including sales of goods; commercial financing). Office: Kain Brown & Roberts 119 E Market St York PA 17401-1221

REAMS, BERNARD DINSMORE, JR., lawyer, educator; b. Lynchburg, Va., Aug. 17, 1943; s. Bernard Dinsmore and Martha Eloise (Hickman) Reams; m. Rosemarie Bridget Boyle, Oct. 26, 1968 (dec. Oct. 1996); children: Andrew Dennet, Adriane Bevin; m. Lee Anne Oberhofer, Apr. 19, 2003. BA, Lynchburg Coll., 1965; MS, Drexel U., 1966; JD, U. Kans., 1972; PhD, St. Louis U., 1983. Bar: Kans. 1973, Mo. 1986, N.Y. 1996, Tex. 2002. Instr., asst. librarian Rutgers U., 1966-69; asst. prof. law, librarian U. Kans., Lawrence, 1969-74; mem. faculty law sch. Washington U., St. Louis, 1974-95, prof. law, 1976-95, prof. tech. mgmt., 1990-95, librarian, 1974-76, acting dean univ. libraries, 1987-88; prof. law, assoc. dean, dir. Law Libr. St. John's U. Sch. Law, Jamaica, N.Y., 1995-97, assoc. dean acad. affairs, 1997-98; prof., dir. law libr. and info. tech. St. Mary's U., San Antonio, 2000—03, prof. law, 2000. Vis. fellow Max-Planck Inst., Hamburg, 1995, 97-98, 2001; vis. prof. law Seton Hall U., 1998-2000. Author: Law For The Businessman, 1974, Reader in Law Librarianship, 1976, Federal Price and Wage Control Programs 1917-1979: Legis. Histories and Laws, 1980, Education of the Handicapped: Laws, Legislative Histories, and Administrative Documents, 1983, Internal Revenue Acts of the United States: The Revenue Act of 1954 with Legislative Histories and Congressional Documents, 1983, Congress and the Courts: A Legislative History 1978-1984, 1984, University-Industry Research Partnerships: The Major Issues in Research and Development Agreements, 1986, Deficit Control and the Gramm-Rudman-Hollings Act, 1986, The Semiconductor Chip and the Law: A Legislative History of the Semiconductor Chip Protection Act of 1984, 1986, American International Law Cases, 2d series, 1986, Technology Transfer Law: The Export Administration Acts of the U.S., 1987, Insider Trading and the Law: A Legislative History of the Insider Trading Sanctions Act, 1989, Insider Trading and Securities Fraud, 1989, The Health Care Quality Improvement Act of 1989: A Legislative History of P.L. No. 99-660, 1990, The National Organ Transplant Act of 1984: A Legislative History of P.L. No. 98-507, 1990, A Legislative History of Individuals with Disabilities Education Act, 1994, Federal Legislative Histories: An Annotated Bibliography and Index to Officially Published Sources, 1994, Electronic Contracting Law, 1996, Health Care Reform, 1994, The American Experience: Clinton and Congress, 1997, The Omnibus Anti-Crime Act, 1997, The Law of E-SIGN: A Legislative History of the Electronic Signature in Global and National Commerce Act, 2001; co-author: Segregation and the Fourteenth Amendment in the States, 1975, Historic Preservation Law: An Annotated Bibliography, 1976, Congress and the Courts: A Legislative History 1787-1977, 1978, Federal Consumer Protection Laws, Rules and Regulations, 1979, A Guide and Analytical Index to the Internal Revenue Acts of the U.S., 1909-1950, 1979, The Numerical Lists and Schedule of Volumes of the U.S. Congressional Serial Set: 73d Congress through the 96th Congress, 1984, Human Experimentation: Federal Laws, Legislative Histories, Regulations and Related Documents, 1985, American Legal Literature: A Guide to Selected Legal Resources, 1985, U.S.A. Patriot Act: A Legislative History, 2002. Bd. trustees Quincy Found. for Med. Rsch. Charitable Trust, San Francisco. Fellow Am. Bar Foun.; recipient Thornton award for excellence Lynchburg Coll., 1986, Joseph L. Andrews Bibliog. award, 1995; named to Hon. Order Ky. Cols., 1992. Mem. ABA, Am. Law Inst., ALA, Am. Soc. Law and Medicine, Nat. Health Lawyers Assn., Am. Assn. Higher Edn., Spl. Librs. Assn., Internat. Assn. Law Libr. Coll. and Univ. Attys., Order of Coif, Phi Beta Kappa, Sigma Xi, Beta Phi Mu, Phi Delta Phi, Phi Delta Epsilon, Kappa Delta Pi, Pi Lambda Theta. Office: St Marys U Sch Law One Camino Santa Maria San Antonio TX 78228 E-mail: breams@stmarytx.edu.

REARDON, ROBERT IGNATIUS, JR., lawyer; b. N.Y.C., Nov. 28, 1945; s. Robert I. and Mildred (Lomax) R.; m. Lise Hofffman; children: Colleen Brooke, Kelly Elizabeth. BS in Econs., Boston Coll., 1967; JD, Fordham U., 1970. Bar: Conn. 1970, U.S. Dist. Ct. Conn. 1974, U.S. Ct. Mil. Appeals 1971, U.S. Ct. Appeals (2d cir.) 1974, U.S. Supreme Ct. 1974, U.S. Ct. Claims 1986. Ptnr. Shapiro & Reardon, P.C., New London, Conn., 1973-83; pres. Reardon Law Firm P.C., New London, 1983—. State trial referee Conn. Superior Ct., 1985—. Chmn. Bd. Fin. Town of Waterford, Conn., 1974-79; mem. Bd. Edn. Town of East Lyme, Conn., 1981-84; trustee Eugene O'Neill Meml. Theater, Inc., 1978-84; active Conn. Commn. Pub. Trust, 1998-2000. Served as capt. USMC, 1970-73. Mem. ABA (award of achievement young lawyers sect. 1975), ATLA (bd. dirs. 1998—), Conn. Trial Lawyers Assn. (pres. 1997-98), Conn. Bar Assn. (bd. govs. 1979-81, ho. of dels. 1975-79), New London County Bar Assn. (mem. exec. com. 1975-79). General civil litigation, Personal injury (including property damage), Product liability. Home: 95 Quarry Dock Rd Niantic CT 06357-1908 Office: 160 Hempstead St New London CT 06320-5638

REASONER, BARRETT HODGES, lawyer; b. Houston, Apr. 16, 1964; s. Harry Max and Macey (Hodges) R.; m. Susan Hardig; children: Matthew Joseph, Caroline Macey, William Harry, Olivia Lucille, Eloise Susan. BA cum laude, Duke U., 1986; Grad. Dipl., London Sch. Econs., 1987; JD with honors, U. Tex., 1990. Bar: Tex. 1990, U.S. Dist. Ct. (ea., so., we., and no. dists.) Tex. 1993, U.S. Ct. Appeals (5th cir.) 1993, U.S. Supreme Ct. 1997. Asst. dist. atty. Harris County Dist. Atty.'s Office, Houston, 1990-92; ptnr. Gibbs & Bruns, L.L.P., Houston, 1992—. Fellow Tex. Bar Found., Houston Bar Found.; mem. Am. Law Inst., Am. Judicature Soc. (bd. dirs. 1994-99, exec. com. 1997-99), Am. Law Inst., State Bar Tex. (jud. rels. com. 1999-2001), Houston Bar Assn. (bd. dirs. 2000—, outstanding com. chmn. 2003), Houston Young Lawyers Assn. (pub. schs. and pub. edn. com. 1994-99, chmn. pub. schs. and pub. edn. com. 1997-99, outstanding com. chair 1999), Houston Vol. Lawyers Program (bd. dirs.), Order of Barristers. Episcopalian. General civil litigation. Office: Gibbs & Bruns LLP 1100 Louisiana St Ste 5300 Houston TX 77002-5215 E-mail: breasoner@gibbs-bruns.com.

REASONER, HARRY MAX, lawyer; b. San Marcos, Tex., July 15, 1939; s. Harry Edward and Joyce Majorie (Barrett) Reasoner; m. Elizabeth Macey Hodges, Apr. 15, 1963; children: Barrett Hodges, Elizabeth Macey Reasoner Stokes. BA in Philosophy summa cum laude, Rice U., 1960; JD with highest honors, U. Tex., 1962; postgrad., U. London, 1962—63. Bar: Tex., DC, NY. Law clk. U.S. Ct. Appeals (2d cir.), 1963—64; assoc. Vinson & Elkins, Houston, 1964—69, ptnr., 1970—, mng. ptnr., 1992—2001. Vis. prof. U. Tex. Sch. Law, 1971, Rice U., 1976, U. Houston Sch. Law, 1977; chair adv. group U.S. Dist. Ct. (so. dist.) Tex.; mem. adv. com. Supreme Ct. Tex. Author (with Charles Alan Wright): Procedure: The Handmaid of Justice, 1965. Trustee U. Tex. Law Sch. Found., Ctr. Am. and Internat. Law, Baylor Coll. Medicine; chair Tex. Higher Edn. Coordinating Bd., 1991; chair. Houston Annenberg Challenge, Houston, 1997—; mem. Supreme Ct. of U.S. Bd. Hist. Soc., 2000—; bd. dirs. Houston Music Hall Found. Bd., 1996—, Tex. So. Univ. Found., 2001—; mem. Tex. Supreme Ct. Hist. Soc. Bd., 1997—. Named Disting. Alumnus, U. Tex., 1997, U. Tex. Sch. Law, 1998, Rice U., 2003; fellow, Rotary Found., 1962—63. Fellow: Tex. Bar Found., ABA Found., Internat. Soc. Barristers, Am. Coll. Trial Lawyers, Internat. Acad. Trial Lawyers; mem.: ABA (chmn. antitrust sect. 1989—90), Am. Bd. Trial Advocates, Philos. Soc. Tex., Houston Philos. Soc., Am. Law Inst., Assn. Bar City of NY, Houston Bar Assn., Century Assn. N.Y.C., Chancellors, Cosmos Club (DC), Phi Delta Phi, Phi Beta Kappa. Antitrust, Federal civil litigation, State civil litigation. Office: Vinson & Elkins 2800 First City Tower 1001 Fannin St Houston TX 77002-6760

REASONER, STEPHEN M. federal judge; b. 1944; BA in Econs., U. Ark., 1966, JD, 1969. Mem. firm Barret, Wheatley, Smith & Deacon, Jonesboro, Ark., 1969-88; from judge to chief judge U.S. Dist. Ct. (ea. dist.) Ark., Little Rock, 1991-98, dist. judge. Bd. dirs. U. Ark. Law Rev.; mem. judicial coun. 8th cir., 1990-93. Trustee Craighead-Jonesboro Pub. Libr., 1972—, chmn. 1984-88; bd. dirs. Jonesboro C. of C., 1981-84, Ark. IOLTA, 1987—, Abilities Unltd., 1974-81; mem. St. Marks Episcopal Ch. Vestry, 1976-79, sr. warden, 1979. With USAR, 1969-73. Mem. ABA, Am. Counsel Assn., Am. Judicature Soc., Ark. Bar Assn. (exec. com., ho. of dels. 1984-87), Craighead County Bar Assn. (pres. 1983-84). Avocation: flying. Office: Courthouse 600 W Capitol Ave Ste 560 Little Rock AR 72201-3327

REASONER, WILLIS IRL, III, lawyer; b. Hamilton, Ohio, Dec. 24, 1951; s. W. Irl Jr. and Nancy Jane (Mitchell) R.; m. Lana Jean Mayes, Apr. 19, 1975 (div. Sept. 1985); 1 child, Erick; m. Joan Marie Mogil, Dec. 30, 1985; children: Scott, Sally. BA in History, Ind. U., 1974; JD cum laude, U. S.C., 1978. Bar: Ohio 1978, U.S. Dist. Ct. (so. dist.) Ohio 1978, U.S. Dist. Ct. (no. dist.) Ohio 1979, U.S. Ct. Appeals (6th cir.) 1988, U.S. Ct. Appeals (1st cir.) 1991, U.S. Ct. Appeals (7th cir.) 1999. Assoc. Porter, Wright, Morris & Arthur, Columbus, Ohio, 1978-83; ptnr. Baker & Hostetler, Columbus, 1983-94, Habash, Reasoner & Frazier, 1994—. Mem. ABA, Ohio Bar Assn., Columbus Bar Assn. Civil rights, Federal civil litigation, Labor (including EEOC, Fair Labor Standards Act, labor-management relations, NLRB, OSHA). Home: 4005 Redford Ct New Albany OH 43054-9500 Office: Habash, Reasoner & Frazier 471 E Broad St Ste 800 Columbus OH 43215-3854

REATH, GEORGE, JR., lawyer, mediator, arbitrator; b. Phila., Mar. 14, 1939; s. George and Isabel Duer (West) R.; children from a previous marriage: Eric (dec. 1995), Amanda; m. Ann B. Rowland, 1990. BA, Williams Coll., 1961; LLB, Harvard U., 1964. Bar: Pa. 1965, U.S. Dist. Ct. (ea. dist.) Pa. 1966, U.S. Ct. Appeals (3d cir.) 1996. Assoc. Dechert Price & Rhoads, Phila., 1964-70, Brussels, 1971-74; atty. Pennwalt Corp., Phila., 1974-78, mgr. legal dept., asst. sec., 1978-87, sr. v.p.-law, sec., 1987-89; sr. v.p., gen. counsel, sec. Elf Atochem N.Am., Inc. (formerly Pennwalt Corp.), Phila., 1990-92; sr. v.p., gen counsel, sec. Legal Triage Svcs., Inc., Phila., 1993-98; sr. v.p., gen. counsel, sec. Triage Mediation Svcs., Inc., Phila., 1999—. Bd. dirs. Internat. Bus. Forum, Inc., 1978-91; arbitrator Am. Arbitration Assn. Trustee Children's Hosp., Phila., 1974-2003, sec., 1980-81, vice chmn., 1984-97; bd. mgrs. Phila. City Inst. Libr., 1974—, treas., 1981-88, pres., 1989-99; bd. dirs. Phila. Festival Theatre for New Plays, 1983-94, Ctrl. Phila. Devel. Corp., 1987-93; bd. dirs. Bach Festival Phila., 1990-98, v.p., 1992-93; bd. dirs. Citizens Crime Commn. Delaware Valley, 1st vice chmn., 1992-94, chmn., 1994-96; exec. com., 1996—; bd. coun. mem. Episcopal Cmty. Svcs. 1999—, treas., 2000—. Mem.: ABA, Assn. for Conflict Resolution, Am. Corp. Counsel Assn., Phila. Bar Assn., Pa. Bar Assn., Am. Arbitration Assn., Penn Club, Winter Harbor Yacht Club, Penllyn Club, Phi Beta Kappa. Alternative dispute resolution, Commercial, contracts (including sales of goods; commercial financing). Personal E-mail: greath@mindspring.com. Business E-Mail: gr@triagemediation.com.

REAVLEY, THOMAS MORROW, federal judge; b. Quitman, Tex., June 21, 1921; s. Thomas Mark and Mattie (Morrow) Reavley; m. Florence Montgomery Wilson, July 24, 1943; children: Thomas Wilson, Marian, Paul Stewart, Margaret. BA, U. Tex., 1942; JD, Harvard U., 1948; LLD, Austin Coll., 1974, Southwestern U., 1977, Tex. Wesleyan, 1982; LLM, U. Va., 1983; LLD, Pepperdine U., 1993. Bar: Tex. 1948. Asst. dist. atty., Dallas, 1948—49; mem. Bell & Reavley, Nacogdoches, Tex., 1949—51; county atty. Nacogdoches, Tex., 1951; with Collins, Garrison, Renfro & Zeleskey, 1951—52; mem. Fisher, Tonahill & Reavley, Jasper, Tex., 1952—55; sec. state Tex., 1955—57; mem. Powell, Rauhut, McGinnis & Reavley, Austin, Tex., 1957—64; dist. judge Austin, Tex., 1964—68; justice Tex. Supreme Ct., Tex., 1968—77; counsel Scott & Douglass, 1977—79; judge U.S. Ct. Appeals (5th cir.), Austin, Tex., 1979—90, sr. judge, 1990—. Lectr. Baylor U. Law Sch., 1976—94; adj. prof. U. Tex. Law Sch., 1958—59, 1978—79, 1988—95. Chancellor S.W. Tex. conf. United Meth. Ch., 1972—93. Lt. USNR, 1943—45. Mem.: Masons (33 degree). Office: US Ct Appeals Homer Thornberry Judicial Bldg 903 San Jacinto Blvd Ste 434 Austin TX 78701-2450 E-mail: tmr@ca5.uscourts.gov.

REBACK, JOYCE ELLEN, lawyer; b. Phila., July 11, 1948; d. William and Sue (Goldstein) R.; m. Itzhak Brook, Aug. 2, 1981; children: Jonathan Zev, Sara Jennie. BA magna cum laude, Brown U., 1970; JD with honors, George Washington U., 1976. Bar: D.C. 1976, U.S. Dist. Ct. D.C. 1976, U.S. Ct. Appeals (D.C. cir.) 1976, U.S. Ct. Appeals (3d cir.) 1983, U.S. Ct. Appeals (Fed. cir.) 1985. Assoc. Fulbright & Jaworski, Washington, 1976-84, ptnr., 1984-87; legal cons. IMF, Washington, 1987—. Contbr. articles to profl. jours. Mem. ABA, D.C. Bar Assn., Phi Beta Kappa. Jewish. Office: Internat Monetary Fund 700 19th St NW Washington DC 20431-0001

REBANE, JOHN T. lawyer; b. Bamberg, Germany, Oct. 29, 1946; s. Henn and Anna (Inna) R.; m. Linda Kay (Morgan), Sept. 22, 1972; children: Alexis Morgan, Morgan James. BA, U. Minn., 1970, JD, 1973. Bar: Minn. 1973. Atty. Land O'Lakes, Inc., Arden Hills, Minn., 1973-80, assoc. gen. counsel, 1983, v.p., gen. counsel, 1984—. Sec. Land O' Lakes Farmland Feed, LLC; sec., bd. dirs. Land O' Lakes Internat. Devel. Corp.; bd. dir. Cheese & Protein Internat., LLC. Mem. ABA; Minn. Bar Assn.; Hennepin County Bar Assn.; Nat.Coun.Farm Coop. (gen.coun.com.chmn.). Commercial, contracts (including sales of goods; commercial financing), Corporate, general, Mergers and acquisitions. Office: Land O'Lakes Inc PO Box 64101 Saint Paul MN 55164-0101 E-mail: jreba@landolakes.com.

REBAZA, ALBERTO, lawyer; b. Lima, Peru, Sept. 14, 1965; s. Alberto and Gloria Rebaza; m. Patricia Mendoza, Nov. 15, 1991; 1 child, Micaela. BA summa cum laude, U. Catolica, Lima, 1991, degree in Law summa cum laude, 1992; LLM, U. Va., 1995. Prin. rschr. Liberty and Democracy Inst., Lima, 1990-93; ptnr. Yori & Bustamente, Lima, 1994-95, Rodrigo, Elias & Medrano Abogados, Lima, 1996—. Prof. econ. law analysis U. Catolica, Lima, 1994-95, prof. corp. law, 1996—; supervising com. Wiese Investment Fund, Lima, 2000—; cons. in fgn. trade regulations Govt. Honduras. Contbr. articles to profl. jours. Advisor Inst. de Arte Contemporáneo, Lima, 1999-2000. Fulbright fellow, Washington, 1995. Mem. ABA, Internat. Bar Assn., Soc. Sol and Armonla, Club Nacional. Avocations: running, triathlons, music, painting, reading. Antitrust, Corporate, general, Mergers and acquisitions. Office: Rodrigo Elias & Medrano Av San Felipe 758 Lima 11 Peru Office Fax: (511) 619-1919. E-mail: arebaza@estudiorodrigo.com.

REBER, JOSEPH E. lawyer; b. Butte, Mont., Aug. 9, 1940; s. Joseph B. and Marie Terry (Tauriainen) R. BA in Hist., U. Mont., 1962, JD, 1965; LLM in Tax, NYU, 1982. Bar: Mont. 1965, U.S. Supreme Ct. 1970, N.Y. 1980, Calif. 1989. Law clk. Mont. Supreme Ct., Helena, 1965; ptnr. Heron & Reber, Helena, 1965-70; pvt. practice Helena, 1970-80; assoc. various law firms, N.Y.C., 1980-84; v.p. Pension & Actuarial Co., Colorado Springs, Colo., 1984-89; gen. counsel Great Am. Life Ins., L.A., 1989-90; pvt. practice Marina Del Rey, Calif., 1990—. Presenter in field. Author: Trust and Tax Estate Planning, 1993; editor law rev. U. Mont., 1964-65; contbr. articles to Fin. Planning Mag., 1987-89. State chmn. Robert F. Kennedy for Pres., Mont., 1968, Senator Frank Church for Pres., 1976; del. platform com. Dem. Nat. Conv., 1976-80; active endowment steering com. L.A. Philharmonic, 1992—; dir. SOM Found., 1995—. Capt. USMSC, 1966-72. Mem. ABA (minorities vice-chmn., internat. law com. 1995—), Nat. Acad. Elder Law Attys., Calif. Bar Assn. (trust com. 1992—), Mont. State Hist. Soc. (v.p. 1979-80), Marina-Culver City Bar Assn. (pres. 1994-95), L.A. County Bar Assn. (ho. of dels.), Beverly Hills Bar Assn., N.Y. Bar Assn. Avocations: art, history, skiing, music, scuba. Estate planning, Probate (including wills, trusts), Estate taxation.

REBOLLO-LOPEZ, FRANCISCO, judge; Justice Supreme Ct. of Puerto Rico, San Juan, 1992—. Office: Supreme Court PO Box 2392 San Juan PR 00902-2392

RECTOR, JOHN MICHAEL, association executive, lawyer; b. Seattle, Aug. 15, 1943; s. Michael Robert and Bernice Jane (Allison) R.; m. Mary Kaaren Sueta Jolly, Feb. 8, 1977 (div. 1994); m. Carmen De Ortiz Nouri, 1994; children: Christian Phillip, Ciera Rose, Zachary Ryan. BA, U. Calif., Berkeley, 1966; JD, U. Calif., Hastings, 1969; PharmD (hon.), Ark. State Bd. Pharmacy, 1991. Bar: Calif. 1970, U.S. Supreme Ct. 1974. Trial atty. civil rights div. Dept. Justice, 1969-71; dep. chief counsel judiciary com. U.S. Senate, 1971-73, counsel to Sen. Birch Bayh, 1971-77, chief counsel, staff dir., 1973-77; confirmed by U.S. Senate as assoc. adminstr. to Law Enforcement Assistance Adminstn. and adminstr. of Office Juvenile Justice Dept. Justice, 1977-79; spl. counsel to U.S. Atty. Gen., 1979-80; dir. govt. affairs Nat. Assn. Retail Druggists, Washington, 1980-85; sr. v.p. govt. affairs, gen. counsel Nat. Cmty. Pharmacists Assn., 1986—. Chmn. adv. bd. Nat. Juvenile Law Center, 1973-77; mem. Hew panel Drug Use and Criminal Behavior, 1974-77; mem. cons. panel Nat. Commn. Protection Human Subjects of Biomed. and Behavioral Research, 1975-76; mem. bd. Nat. Inst. Corrections, 1977-79; chmn. U.S. Interdepartmental Council Juvenile Justice, 1977-79; mem. bd. com. civil rights and liberties Am. Democratic Action, 1976-80, Pres.'s Com. Mental Health-Justice Group, 1978; com. youth citizenship ABA, 1978-84; mem. Pharm. Industry Adv. Com.; exec. dir., treas. polit. action com. Nat. Pharmacists Assn., 1981—; exec. dir. Retail Druggist Legal Legis. Def. Fund, 1985—, founder, chmn. Washington Pharmacy Industry Forum; mem. numerous fed. narcotic and crime panels and coms.; owner Second Genesis, an antique and furniture restoration co. Mem. editorial bd. Managed Care Law; contbr. articles to profl. jours. Exec. com. small bus. and fin. couns. Dem. Nat. Com., 1988-92; dir. Dem. Leadership Coun.'s Network, 1989-92, bd. advisers, 1992-94, Clinton-Gore Washington Bus. adv. com.; bd. dirs. Small Bus. Legis. Coun., 1987—, sec., 1999, treas., 2000, chmn. elect 2001, chmn., 2002; bd. dirs. Nat. Bus. Coalition for Fair Competition, 1984—. Perry E. Towne scholar, 1966-67; mem. U.S. Atty. Gen.'s Honors Program, 1968-71; recipient Children's Express Juvenile Justice award, 1981. Mem. Calif. Bar Assn., Nat. Health Lawyers Assn., Am. Soc. Assn. Execs. (govt. affrs sect.), Washington Coun. Lawyers, Assn. of Former Senior Senate Aides, Vinifera Wine Growers Assn. Va. (life), Health R Us, Am. League of Lobbyists, Theta Chi. Democrat. Avocations: collecting antique furniture, books and documents. Office: Nat Cmty Pharmacists Assn 205 Daingerfield Rd Alexandria VA 22314-2885

RECTOR, SUSAN DARNELL, lawyer; b. Wilmington, Del., Feb. 14, 1959; d. W. Thomas and Barbara Joan (Shafer) Darnell; m. Neil Kenyon Rector, Aug. 7, 1982. BA in Economics, Wake Forest U., Winston-Salem, N.C., 1981; JD, U. N.C., Chapel Hill, 1984. Bar: Ohio 1984. Lawyer Ohio Legislative Svc. Commn., Columbus, Ohio, 1984-87; assoc. Schottenstein, Zox & Dunn, Columbus, Ohio, 1987-93, ptnr., 1993—. Bd. trustees Firstlink, Inc., 1990-95, v.p., 1993, pres., 1994; apt. to Ohio Small Bus. and Entrepreneurship Coun., 1991-95. Contbr. articles to profl. jours. Mem. allocation com. United Way, Columbus, 1990-96, campaign cabinet, 1991, co-chair planning, evaluation and allocation com., 1993-94, bd. trustees, 1996—, chair health vision coun., 1996-99; trustee Columbus Zool. Park Assn., 2001—, chmn. devel. com., 2001, chmn. zoo fund, 2000; bd. dirs., sec., treas. Cmty. Rsch. Ptnrs., 2000-02. Named Harry S. Truman scholar, Truman Scholarship Found., 1979, 1 of 10 Outstanding Young Citizens, Columbus Jaycees, 1993, 1 of 40 under 40, Business (Columbus); grad. Columbus Area Leadership program. Mem. ABA, Ohio Bar Assn., Columbus Bar Assn. (Cmty. Svc. award 1997), Columbus Bar Found. (trustee 1995—, pres. 2003), Women Lawyers of Franklin County, Jr. League of Columbus (bd. trustees, sec. 1989-90, 95-98, pres. 1997-98), Columbus Met. Club, Columbus Women's Network (Cmty. Leader award), Mortar Bd., Phi Beta Kappa, Omicron Delta Kappa. Corporate, general, Trademark and copyright, Computer. Home: 67 E Deshler Ave Columbus OH 43206-2655 Office: Schottenstein Zox & Dunn 41 S High St Ste 2600 Columbus OH 43215-6109

REDA, ROBERT L. lawyer; b. Suffern, N.Y., May 31, 1969; s. Louis and Kathleen Reda; married, June 19, 1998. BA, Allegheny Coll., 1991; JD, NYU, 1994. Bar: N.Y., Conn., U.S. Dist. Ct. (so. and ea. dists.) N.Y. Assoc. Moloney & Ankar, N.Y.C., 1992—96; mng. ptnr. Wieder, MAstrioanni & Rede, 1996; atty. pvt. practice, 1996—. Property, real (including real estate development, water), General practice. Office: 1 Exec Blvd Ste 201 Suffern NY 10901 Fax: 845-357-3333. E-mail: redalaw@aol.com.

REDD, CHARLES APPLETON, lawyer; b. Quincy, Ill., Aug. 13, 1954; s. Charles Lambert and Julia (Harrell) R.; m. Susan Backer, June 2, 1978; children: Elizabeth Appleton, Christopher O'Leary, Thomas Charles, Daniel Louis. BA, St. Louis U., 1976, JD, 1979. Bar: Wis. 1979, U.S. Dist. Ct. (ea. and we. dists.) Wis. 1979, Mo. 1980, Ill. 1991. Trust adminstr. First Wis. Trust Co., Milw., 1979-80; asst. counsel Centerre Trust Co. of St. Louis (now Bank of Am., N.A.), 1980-83; assoc. Armstrong, Teasdale, Schlafly & Davis, St. Louis, 1983-85; ptnr. Armstrong, Teasdale LLP and predecesssor firm, St. Louis, 1986-94; chmn. trust and estates dept., 1993-94. Adj. prof. law in fed. estate tax and estate planning Northwestern U. Mem. Estate Planning Coun. of St. Louis; bd. dirs. Make-A-Wish Found. of Metro. St. Louis; mem. planned giving and endowment coun. Archdiocese of St. Louis. Recipient Mo. Bar Pres.'s award, 1991. Fellow Am. Coll. of Trust and Estate Counsel (mem. fiduciary litig. comn., estate and gift tax com.); mem. ABA (real property, probate and trust law sect.), Wis. Bar Assn., Mo. Bar Assn. (probate and trust com.), Ill. State Bar Assn., Bar Assn. Met. St. Louis (past chmn. probate and trust sect.). Estate planning, Probate (including wills, trusts), Estate taxation. Home: 7245 Maryland Ave University City MO 63130-4419 Office: Sonnenschein Nath & Rosenthal 1 Metropolitan Sq Ste 3000 Saint Louis MO 63102-2741 E-mail: credd@sonnenschein.com.

REDDEN, JAMES ANTHONY, federal judge; b. Springfield, Mass., Mar. 13, 1929; s. James A. and Alma (Cheek) R.; m. Joan Ida Johnson, July 13, 1950; children: James A., William F. Student, Boston U., 1951; LL.B., Boston Coll., 1954. Bar: Mass., 1954, Oreg., 1955. Pvt. practice, Mass., 1954-55; title examiner Title & Trust Ins. Co., Oreg., 1955; claims adjuster Allstate Ins. Co., 1956; mem. firm Collins, Redden, Ferris & Velure, Medford, Oreg., 1957-73; treas. State of Oreg., 1973-77; atty. gen., 1977-80; U.S. dist. judge, now sr. judge U.S. Dist. Ct. Oreg., Portland, 1980—. Chmn. Oreg. Pub. Employee Relations Bd.; mem. Oreg. Ho. of Reps., 1963-69, minority leader, 1967-69. With AUS, 1946-48. Mem. ABA, Mass. Bar Assn., Oreg. State Bar. Office: US Dist Ct 1527 US Courthouse 1000 SW 3d Ave Portland OR 97204-2902*

REDDEN, JOE WINSTON, JR., lawyer; b. Houston, Jan. 24, 1951; s. Joe Winston and Katherine Louise (Fickessen) R; children: Rebecca Kay, Forrest Winston II. BA, Tex. Christian U., 1972; JD, U. Tex., 1975. Bar: U.S. Dist. Ct. (so., ea. and we. dists.) Tex., U.S. Ct. Appeals (5th cir.), U.S. Supreme Ct. 1993. Assoc. Fulbright & Jaworski, Houston, 1975-83, ptnr., 1983-91, Beck, Redden & Secrest, Houston, 1993—. Fellow ACTL, Tex. Bar Found.; mem. ABA, Am. Bd. Trial Advocates, Internat. Assn. Def. Counsel, Tex. Bar Assn., Order of Coif, Chancellors, Phi Beta Kappa, Phi Delta Phi. Federal civil litigation, State civil litigation, Personal injury (including property damage). Home: 2405B Brun Rd Houston TX 77019-6701 Office: Beck Redden & Secrest 1221 Mckinney St Ste 4500 Houston TX 77010-2010

REDDIEN, CHARLES HENRY, II, lawyer, corporate executive, consultant; b. San Diego, Aug. 27, 1944; s. Charles Henry and Betty Jane (McCormick) R.; m. Paula Gayle, June 16, 1974; 1 child, Tyler Charles. BSEE, U. Colo., Boulder, 1966; MSEE, U. So. Calif., 1968; JD, Loyola U., L.A., 1972. Bar: Calif. 1972, Colo. 1981, U.S. Dist. Ct. 1981. Mgr. Hughes Aircraft Co., 1966-81; pvt. practice, 1972—. Pres., broker R&D Realty Ltd., 1978-91; mem. spl. staff, co-dir. tax advantage group OTC Net Inc., 1981-82; pres., chmn. Heritage Group Inc., investment banking holding co., 1982-84, Plans and Assistance Inc., mgmt. cons., 1982-83, Orchard Group Ltd., investment banking holding co., 1982-84, J.W. Gant & Assocs., Inc., investment bankers, 1983-84; mng. ptnr., CEO J.W. Gant & Assocs., Ltd., 1984-85; chmn. bd. Kalamath Group Ltd., 1985-87, Heritage group Ltd. Investment Bankers, 1985-87; dir. Virtusonics Corp., 1985-92; v.p., dir. Heritage Fin. Planners Inc., 1982-83; pres., chmn. PDN Inc., 1987-89; pub., exec. v.p., dir. World News Digest Inc., 1987-90, LeisureNet Entertainment, Inc., 1989-90; chief exec. officer, Somerset Group Ltd., 1988-93, Inland Pacific Corp., 1989-91, World Info. Network, Inc., 1990-92, pres., CEO, chmn., Europa Cruises Corp., 1992-94; CEO, chmn. Casino World Inc., 1993-97, Miss. Gaming Corp., 1993-97; pres., chmn., CEO Chart Group Ltd., 1997—, SkyData Corp., 2000—; pres., Miss. Corrections, L.L.C., 2000—. Contbr. articles to profl. jours. Pres. Diamondhead Business and Profl. Assn.; commr. Diamondhead Fire Dist.; dir. Internat. Trade Club South Miss. Recipient tchg. internship award, 1964. Mem. AIAA, IEEE (chmn. U. Colo. chpt. 1965), Calif. Bar Assn., Nat. Assn. Securities Dealers, Phi Alpha Delta, Tau Beta Pi, Eta Kappa Nu. Corporate, general. Office: PO Box 6133 Diamondhead MS 39525-6002 E-mail: chartgroup@aol.com.

REDDING, BOBBIE NEWMAN, lawyer; b. Guilford County, N.C., Mar. 30, 1935; d. John J. Newman and Flora Pearl (Kirkman) Brower; m. Marshall S. Redding, June 2, 1957 (div. 1982); children: Joan Lucile, Rebecca Marie Redding Greene. Student, U. N.C., Greensboro, 1952-54; BA in Edn., U. N.C., 1956, MSLS, 1957; JD, Campbell U., 1985. Bar: N.C. 1986. Staff atty. Lumbee River Legal Svcs., Fayetteville, N.C., 1986-88, Cumberland County Dept. Social Svcs., Fayetteville, 1988—. Mem. ABA, N.C. Bar Assn., N.C. Assn. Social Svcs. Attys., N.C. State Bar Assn., Cumberland County Bar, Twelth Judicial Bar. Home: Box F 1100 Clarendon St Fayetteville NC 28305-4800 Office: Cumberland County DSS 1225 Ramsey St Fayetteville NC 28302

REDDING, ROBERT ELLSWORTH, lawyer; b. South Bend, Ind., Mar. 23, 1919; s. Harry Ellsworth and Lorraine (Livengood) R.; m. Blanche Breisch, Apr. 14, 1941 (div.); children: Rosemary, Robert Ellsworth, Douglas; m. A. Virginia Boender, July 22, 1972. AB, Ohio State U., 1940; LLB, JD, Georgetown U., 1946. Bar: D.C. 1946, Md. 1949, U.S. Supreme Ct. 1950. Legal asst. to mem. CAB, Washington, 1949-51; mem. Bradshaw Shearin Redding & Thomas, Silver Spring, Md., 1951-59; v.p., gen. counsel Transp. Assn. Am., Washington, 1960-69; dir. Office Facilitation Dept. Transp., 1970-76; sole practice Washington, Md., 1976—. Sec. Cert. Claims Profl. Accreditation Council, Washington, 1981-85; chief judge Appeal Tax Ct., Rockville, Md., 1953-55; dir. fed. affairs Shippers Nat. Freight Claim Council, Washington, 1979-89; cons. UN Devel. Program, N.Y.C., 1980-81, Montgomery County, Md. Office of Inspector Gen., 1999—. Author: Community Planning for Air Transportation, 1960; Washington editor Handling and Shipping mag., 1976-81. Pres. Allied Civic Group (50 assns.), Silver Spring, 1956-58; chmn. rsch. com. Md. Rep. Com., 1965-70; chmn. fin. adv. com. to county coun., Rockville, 1965-70; exec. dir. Montgomery County Taxpayers League, 94-97. 2d lt. U.S. Army, 1943-46. Mem. Assn. of Former Intelligence Officers (v.p. corp. devel.), Univ. Club (bd. govs., Washington), Masons, Scottish Rite, Phi Beta Kappa, Phi Alpha Delta (supreme justice 1966-68, exec. v.p. Pub. Svc. Ctr. 1984-91). Estate planning, Legislative, Transportation. Home: 9105 Falls Chapel Way Potomac MD 20854-2452 Fax: 301-340-6468.

REDFEARN, PAUL L., III, lawyer; b. Camp Cook, Calif., Oct. 1, 1951; s. Paul Leslie Jr. and Alice Ruby Redfearn; children: Ashley, Lauren; m. Denise Jean Davis, July 24, 1993. BS, S.W. Mo. State U., 1973; JD, Oklahoma City U., 1976. Bar: Mo. 1977, U.S. Dist. Ct. (we. and ea. dists.) Mo., U.S. Dist. Ct. Kans., U.S. Dist. Ct. N.D., U.S. Dist. Ct. Mont., U.S. Ct. Appeal (8th ant 11th cirs.); bd. cert. civil trial advocate. Assoc. Sheridan, Sanders & Simpson, P.C., 1977-79, William H. Pickett, P.C., 1979-84; ptnr. The Redfearn Law Firm, P.C., Kansas City, Mo., 1984—. Bd. dirs. Lawyers Encouraging Acad. Performance; lectr. and presenter in field. Contbr. chpts. to books. Bd. govs. S.W. Mo. State U., 1998-2003. Mem. ABA, ATLA, Mo. Bar Assn., Mo. Assn. Trial Attys. (bd. govs. 1986-94, exec. com. 1990—, pres. 1992), Am. Bd. Trial Advocates (charter, pres. chpt. 1996-97), Trial Lawyers for Pub. Justice, Kansas City Met. Bar Assn., East Jackson County Bar Assn. Democrat. Avocation: tennis. State civil litigation, Personal injury (including property damage), Product liability. Office: The Redfearn Law Firm PC 1125 Grand Blvd Ste 814 Kansas City MO 64106-2518 E-mail: predfearn@aol.com.

REDLICH, MARC, lawyer; b. N.Y.C., Nov. 25, 1946; s. Louis and Mollie R.; m. Janis Redlich, Jan. 16, 1982; children: Alison, Suzanne, Rachel. BA, Queens Coll., 1967; JD, Harvard U., 1971. Bar: Mass. 1971, U.S. Dist. Ct. 1971, U.S. Ct. Appeals (1st cir.) 1974, U.S. Ct. Appeals (5th cir.) 1984. Assoc. Rubin & Rudman, Boston, 1971-75; mem., sr. dir. Widett, Slater & Goldman, Boston, 1975-84; prin. Law Offices of Marc Redlich, Boston, 1984—. Seminar chmn. Mass. Continuing Legal Edn., Inc., 1996. Mem. Mass. Bar Assn. (governing coun. civil litigation sect., participant/panelist chpt. 93A in the bus. context seminar 1996), participant/panelist, Cambridge Bar Assn., Nat. Assn. Coll. and Univ. Attys., Harvard Sq. Bus. Assn. (bd. dirs. 1989-92, 93-94), Friends of Switzerland Inc. (bd. dirs. 1984—, assoc. pres. 1991-93, pres. 1993—), German Am. Bus. Club of Boston (exec. com. 1997-2001), Harvard Club Boston (co-chair music com. 1997-98, chair 1998—), Am. Council on Germany (Boston Chpt. Coord., 2001—) , Phi Beta Kappa. General civil litigation, Corporate, general, General practice. Office: Three Center Plz Boston MA 02108

REDLICH, NORMAN, lawyer, educator; b. N.Y.C., Nov. 12, 1925; s. Milton and Pauline (Durst) R.; m. Evelyn Jane Grobow, June 3, 1951; children: Margaret Bonny-Claire, Carrie Ann, Edward Grobow. AB, Williams Coll., 1947, LLD (hon.), 1976; LLB, Yale U., 1950; LLM, NYU, 1955; LLD (hon.), John Marshall Law Sch., 1990. Bar: N.Y. 1951. Practiced in, N.Y.C., 1951-59; assoc. prof. law NYU, 1960-62, prof. law, 1962-74, assoc. dean Sch. Law, 1974-75, dean Sch. Law, 1975-88, dean emeritus, 1992—, Judge Edward Weinfeld prof. law, 1982—; counsel Wachtell, Lipton, Rosen & Katz, N.Y.C., 1988—. Editor-in-chief Tax Law Rev., 1960-66; mem. adv. com. Inst. Fed. Taxation, 1963-68; exec. asst. corp. counsel, N.Y.C., 1966-68, 1st asst. corp. counsel, 1970-72, corp. counsel, 1972-74; asst. counsel Pres. Commn. on Assassination Pres. Kennedy, 1963-64; mem. com. on admissions and grievances U.S. 2d Circuit Ct. Appeals, 1978—, chmn., 1978-87. Author: Professional Responsibility: A Problem Approach, 1976, Constitutional Law, Cases and Materials, 1983, rev. edit., 1996, 2001, Understanding Constitutional Law, 1995, rev. edit., 1999; contbr. articles in field. Chmn. commn. on law and social action Am. Jewish Congress, 1978—, chmn. governing coun., 1996; mem. Borough Pres.'s Planning Bd. Number 2, 1959-70, counsel N.Y. Com. to Abolish Capital Punishment, 1958-77; mem. N.Y.C. Bd. Edn., 1969; mem. bd. overseers Jewish Theol. Sem., 1973—; trustee Law Ctr. Found. of NYU, 1975—, Freedom House, 1976-86, Vt. Law Sch., 1977-99, Practicing Law Inst., 1980-99; trustee Lawyers Com. for Civil Rights Under Law, 1976—, co-chmn., 1979-81; bd. dirs. Legal Aid Soc., 1983-88, NAACP Legal Def. Fund, 1985—, Greenwich House, 1987—. Decorated Combat Infantryman's Badge. Mem. ABA (coun. legal edn. and admissions to bar 1981—, vice chmn. 1987-88, chmn. 1989-90, equal opportunities in legal profession 1986-92, ho. of dels. 1991—), Assn. of Bar of City of N.Y. (exec. com. 1975-79, professionalism com. 1988-92), com. on capital punishment 1998—). Office: 51 W 52nd St Fl 30 New York NY 10019-6119

REDMAN, CLARENCE OWEN, lawyer; b. Joliet, Ill., Nov. 23, 1942; s. Harold F. and Edith L. (Read) R.; m. Barbara Ann Pawlan, Jan. 26, 1964 (div.); children: Scott, Steven; m. 2d, Carla J. Rozycki, Sept. 24, 1983. BS, U. Ill., 1964, JD, 1966, MA, 1967. Bar: Ill. 1966, U.S. Dist. Ct. (ea. dist.) Ill. 1970, U.S. Ct. Appeals (7th cir.) 1973, U.S. Ct. Appeals (4th cir.) 1982, U.S. Supreme Ct. 1975. Assoc. Keck, Mahin & Cate, Chgo., 1969-73, ptnr., corp. ptnr., 1973—, CEO, 1986-97; of counsel Lord, Bissell & Brook, Chgo., 1997—. Spl. asst. atty. gen. Ill., 1975-8; bd. dirs. AMCOL Internat. Corp. Mem. bd. visitors U. Ill. Coll. of Law, 1991-95. Capt. U.S. Army, 1967-69. Decorated Bronze Star. Mem. Ill. State Bar Assn. (chmn. young lawyers sect. 1977-78, del. assembly 1978-81, 84-87), Seventh Cir. Bar Assn. Federal civil litigation, Corporate, general, Labor (including EEOC, Fair Labor Standards Act, labor-management relations, NLRB, OSHA). Office: Lord Bissell & Brook 115 S Lasalle St Ste 3200 Chicago IL 60603-3902

REDMAN, ERIC, lawyer; b. Palo Alto, Calif., June 3, 1948; s. M. Chandler and Marjorie Jane (Sachs) R.; children: Ian Michael, Graham James, Jing; m. Heather Bell, 1996. AB, Harvard U., 1970, JD, 1975; BA, Oxford U., 1972, MA, 1980. Bar: Wash. 1975, U.S. Dist. Ct. (we. dist.) Wash. 1975, D.C. 1979, U.S. Ct. Appeals (9th cir.) 1981, U.S. Supreme Ct. 1983. Asst. U.S. senator W.G. Magnuson, Washington and Seattle, 1968-71, 74-75; assoc. Preston, Thorgrimson et al, Seattle, 1975-78, ptnr., 1979-82, Heller, Ehrman, White & McAuliffe, Seattle, 1983—. Author: Dance of Legislation, 1973; also book revs., articles. Administrative and regulatory, Environmental, Utilities, public. Office: Heller Ehrman White & McAuliffe 701 5th Ave Ste 6100 Seattle WA 98104-7098

REDMANN, JOHN WILLIAM, lawyer, consultant; b. New Orleans, Sept. 10, 1963; s. William Vincent and Ana Maria (Macouzet) R. BA in Psychology, BA in French, Loyola U. of the South, 1986, JD, 1989. Bar: La. 1990, U.S. Dist. Ct. (ea. dist.) La. 1990; cert. notary pub., La. Litigation law clk. Orleans Sewerage and Water Bd., New Orleans, 1989-90; law clk. to Hon. Judge Connolly Orleans Civil Dist. Ct., New Orleans, 1990-92; atty. Exnicios & Nungesser, New Orleans, 1992-94; prin. Law Offices of John W. Redmann, New Orleans, 1994—; v.p., gen. counsel Meridian Group, LLC, New Orleans, 1999—, 5 Lights, LLC, 2000—. V.p. L'Ecole Maternelle, 1998, also bd. dirs.; charter mem. alumni com. Loyola Law Sch. Moot Ct., 1991-96, also chmn. 1980's decade ann. fund campaign. Chmn. 1995 Loyola Law Ann. Fund Campaign, New Orleans; charter mem./officer Lawyers Against Crime, Inc., New Orleans, 1995—. Mem. ATLA (traumatic brain injury litigation group 1997-2000), Nat. Inst. Trial Advocacy (diplomate), La. Trial Lawyers Assn. (mem. leadership and membership coms. 1994-96, treas. Bench and Bar sect. 2001—), Assn. of New Orleans Trial Lawyers, Supreme Ct. of La. Hist. Soc. (charter), So. Trial Lawyers Assn. (bd. dirs. 1998-2000—), La. Hispanic C. of C. (bd. dirs. 1998—, sec. 1999, gen. counsel 1999—, 1st v.p. 1999—), Young Leadership Counsel, Bards Bohemia (mem. exec. bd. 1998-99, 2001—), Celtic Club of New Orleans (pres. 1997-98). Roman Catholic. Avocations: travel, foreign languages. Admiralty, General civil litigation, Personal injury (including property damage). Home: 1327 Short St New Orleans LA 70118-4043 Office: 9701 Lake Forest Blvd Ste 103 New Orleans LA 70127-5403 E-mail: advice@redmannlaw.com.

REDMOND, CHRISTOPHER JOHN, lawyer; b. Oakland, Calif., May 8, 1947; s. Owen Joseph and Josephine Alice (Hanswirth) R.; m. Rosalyn Lee Finney, June 8, 1970; children: Kirk, Renee, Megan. BA, U. Kans., 1968, JD, 1970. Bar: Kans. 1970, U.S. Dist. Ct. Kans. 1970, U.S. Ct. appeals (10th cir.) 1973, U.S. Supreme Ct. 1974. Mem. Husch & Eppenberger LLC, Kansas City, Mo., 1996—. Mem. U.S. delegation to UN Commn. on Internat. Trade Law. Assoc. editor Am. Bankruptcy Inst. Jour. Mem. ABA (chmn., subcom. internat. law, bus. bankruptcy com., 1995—), Wichita Bar Assn. (bd. govs.). Bankruptcy, Federal civil litigation, Private international. Office: Husch & Eppenberger LLC 1200 Main St Ste 1700 Kansas City MO 64105-2100 E-mail: christopher.redmond@husch.com.

REDMOND, DAVID DUDLEY, lawyer; b. Hartford, Conn., May 12, 1944; s. Robert LaVere and Dorothy Iva (Mylchreest) R.; m. Eugenia Blount Scott, Aug. 24, 1968; children: R. Scott, Sarah D. BA, Washington and Lee U., 1966, LLB, 1969. Bar: Va. 1970, U.S. Dist. Ct. (ea. dist.) Va. 1972, U.S. Ct. Appeals (4th cir.) 1972. Ptnr. Christisn & Barton LLP, Richmond, Va., 1972—. Edtl. bd. Washington and Lee U. Law Rev., 1968-69. Served to capt. U.S. Army, 1970-71. Decorated Bronze Star. Mem.: Richmond Bar Assn. (exec. com. 1980), Va. Bar Assn., Va. State Bar, Washington and Lee Law Alumni Assn. (pres. 1995—96, bd. dirs. 1990—2002), Washington and Lee U. Alumni Assn. (pres. Richmond chpt. 1980—82, bd. dirs. 1997—99, 2003—), Omicron Delta Kappa. Corporate, general, Land use and zoning (including planning), Property, real (including real estate development, water). Office: Mutual Bldg Ste 1200 Richmond VA 23219 E-mail: dredmond@cblaw.com.

REDMOND, RICHARD ANTHONY, lawyer; b. Chgo., Oct. 4, 1947; s. Richard Aloysius and Mary Jane (Berger) R.; m. Merrilee Clark, May 5, 1984; children: Richard William, Michael Clark. BA, U. Notre Dame, 1969; JD, Cornell U., 1972. Bar: Ill. 1972, U.S. Dist. Ct. (no. dist.) Ill. 1972, U.S. Ct. Appeals (7th cir.) 1975, U.S. Supreme Ct. 1976. Assoc. Freeman & Tingler, Chgo., 1972-75; from assoc. to ptnr. Kennedy, Golan & Morris, Chgo., 1975-81; ptnr. Walsh, Case, Coale & Brown, Chgo., 1981-89, McBride, Baker and Coles, Chgo., 1989—2002, Holland and Knight, 2002—. Mem. com. of profl. responsibility Ill. Supreme Ct., 1983-97, chmn., 1993-97. Trustee Chgo. Acad. Sci., 1986-95, chmn. bd. trustees, 1990-94. Mem. ABA, Chgo. Bar Assn. (chmn. eminent domain subcom. 1982—), Law Club Chgo., Mich. Shores Club. Roman Catholic. Federal civil litigation, State civil litigation, Condemnation (eminent domain). Office: Holland & Knight 131 S Dearborn St Chicago IL 60603

REDMOND, ROBERT, lawyer, educator; b. Astoria, N.Y., June 18, 1934; s. George and Virginia (Greene) R.; m. Georgine Marie Richardson, May 21, 1966; children: Kelly Anne, Kimberly Marie, Christopher Robert. BA, Queens Coll., 1955; MPA, CUNY, 1962; JD, Georgetown U., 1970. Bar: D.C. 1971, Va. 1974, U.S. Supreme Ct. 1974. Commd. 2d lt. USAF, 1955, advanced through grades to lt. col., 1972, ret., 1978; served as spl. investigations officer Korea, Vietnam, W. Germany; adj. prof., acad. dir. mil. dist. Washington Resident Ctr. Park U., Parkville, Mo., 1977—; pvt. practice Falls Church, Va., 1980—. Precinct capt. Fairfax County Rep. Party, Va., 1981-87; pres. PTO, Falls Church, 1984-86; bd. dirs. Chaconas Home Owners Assn., 1984—, Social Ctr. Psychiat. Rehab., 1987-93. Mem. ATLA, Va. Trial Lawyers Assn., Fairfax Bar Assn., Assn. Former Air Force Office Spl. Investigations Agts. (chpt. pres. 1984-86, nat. membership com. 1986—), Comml. Law League, Delta Theta Phi, K.C. (4th deg.). Roman Catholic. Commercial, consumer (including collections, credit), General practice, Personal injury (including property damage). Home: 7802 Antiopi St Annandale VA 22003-1405 Office: Ste 700 2010 Corporate Ridge Mc Lean VA 22102-7838 Address: PO Box 2103 Falls Church VA 22042-0103 E-mail: collectlaw@aol.com.

REDPATH, JOHN S(LONEKER), JR., lawyer, publishing company executive; BA, Princeton U., 1966; JD, U. Mich., 1973; LLM, NYU, 1978. Bar: U.S. Dist. Ct. (so. dist.) N.Y. 1975. Assoc. Dewey, Ballantine, Bushby, Palmer & Wood, N.Y.C., 1974-78; assoc. counsel film programming Home Box Office, Inc., N.Y.C., 1978-79, chief counsel programming, 1979-80, asst. gen. counsel, 1980-81, v.p., gen. counsel, 1981-83, sr. v.p., gen. counsel, 1983-94, exec. v.p., gen. counsel, 1994—2002; sr. v.p., gen. counsel Time Inc., N.Y.C., 2003—. Lt. USNR, 1966-69. Mem. ABA, N.Y. State Bar Assn., Assn. Bar City N.Y. Communications. Office: Time Inc 1271 Ave of the Americas New York NY 10020

REED, ANTHONY W. lawyer; b. Austin, Tex., June 29, 1969; s. Walter C. and Nora E. Reed. BA in Polit. Sci., S.W. Tex. State U., San Marcos, 1996; JD, Thurgood Marshall Sch. of Law, Houston, 1999. Bar: Tex. 2001. Contract mgr. Sprint Comm. Co., L.P., Houston, 1997—2002; assoc. v.p. NEC BNS, Inc., Irving, Tex., 2002—. Mem.: ATLA (assoc.), ABA (assoc.), Houston ProDuffers Golf Club USA, Inc. (assoc.; pres. 2002—02), Kappa Alpha Psi. D-Conservative. Avocations: golf, outdoor activities, reading, travel. Corporate, general. Office: NEC Business Network Solutions Inc 6555 N State Hwy 161 8th Flr Irving TX 75039-2402

REED, D. GARY, lawyer; b. Covington, Ky., June 4, 1949; m. Mary Elizabeth Goetz, May 20, 1972; children: Mark, Stacey. BA, Xavier U., 1971; JD, Catholic U. Am., 1974. Bar: Ohio 1974, Ky. 1975, U.S. Ct. Appeals (6th cir.) 1975, U.S. Dist. Ct. (so. dist.) Ohio 1974, U.S. Dist. Ct. (ea. dist.) Ky. 1977, U.S. Dist. Ct. (we. dist.) Ky. 1980. Law clk. to judge U.S. Dist. Ct. (so. dist.) Ohio, Cin., 1974-75; assoc. Dinsmore & Shohl, Cin., 1976-82, ptnr., 1982-90; dir. legal svcs. Choice Care Health Plans, Inc., Cin., 1991-96; asst. gen. coun., 1996-97; ins. counsel Humana, Inc., Louisville, 1998—. Asst. sec. Choice Care Found., 1996-97. Contbg. author: Woodside, Drug Product Liability, vol. 3, 1987. Asst. sec. The Choice Care Found., 1996-97. Mem. ABA, Ky. Bar Assn., Ohio Bar Assn., Nat. Health Lawyers Assn., No. Ky. C. of C. (Leadership award 1988), Greater Cin. Coun. for Epilepsy (bd. dirs. 1990-97), Leadership No. Ky. Alumni Assn. Corporate, general, Health, Insurance. Office: Humana Inc Insurance Cons-Law Dept 500 W Main St Ste 300 Louisville KY 40202-4268 E-mail: dgaryreed@aol.com., greed@humana.com.

REED, EDWARD CORNELIUS, JR., federal judge; b. Mason, Nev., July 8, 1924; s. Edward Cornelius Sr. and Evelyn (Walker) R.; m. Sally Torrance, June 14, 1952; children: Edward T., William W., John A., Mary E. BA, U. Nev., 1949; JD, Harvard U., 1952. Bar: Nev. 1952, U.S. Dist Ct. Nev. 1957, U.S. Supreme Ct. 1974. Atty. Arthur Andersen & Co., 1952-53; spl. dep. atty. gen. State of Nev., 1967-79; judge U.S. Dist. Ct. Nev., Reno, 1979—, chief judge, now sr. judge. Former vol. atty. Girl Scouts Am., Sierra Nevada Council, U. Nev., Nev. Agrl. Found., Nev. State Sch. Adminstrs. Assn., Nev. Congress of Parents and Teachers; mem. Washoe County Sch. Bd., 1956-72, pres. 1959, 63, 69; chmn. Gov.'s Sch. Survey Com., 1958-61; mem. Washoe County Bd. Tax Equalization, 1957-58, Washoe County Annexation Commn., 1968-72, Washoe County Personnel Com., 1973-77, chmn. 1973; mem. citizens adv. com. Washoe County Sch. Bond Issue, 1977-78, Sun Valley, Nev., Swimming Pool Com., 1978, Washoe County Blue Ribbon Task Force Com. on Growth, Nev. PTA (life); chmn. profl. div. United Way, 1978; bd. dirs. Reno Siver Sox, 1962-65. Served as staff sgt. U.S. Army, 1943-46, ETO, PTO. Mem. ABA (jud. adminstrn. sect.), Nev. State Bar Assn. (adminstrv. com. dist. 5, 1967-79, lien law com. 1965-78, chmn. 1965-72, probate law com. 1963-66, tax law com. 1962-65), Am. Judicature Soc. Democrat. Baptist. Named in his honor Edward C. Reed H.S., Sparks, Nev., 1972. Office: US Dist Ct 400 S Virginia St Ste 606 Reno NV 89501-2182

REED, HELEN SKUGGEDAL, law librarian, musician; b. Halifax, N.S., Can., June 19, 1948; came to U.S., 1971; d. Johan Martin Skuggedal and Anna Gurine (Ringdal) Burns; m. Robert Douglas Reed, Aug. 14, 1971 (div. 1996); 1 child, Eric Douglas Reed. BA with honors, Dalhousie U., Halifax, 1969; MM, U. Mich., 1971. Libr. Hochstein Sch. Music, Rochester, 1972-75; organist Neu Chapel U. Evansville, 1976-83; acting archivist U. So. Ind., Evansville, 1978-80; organist Washington Ave. Presbyn., Evansville, 1984-90; prin. harpsichordist Evansville Philharm., 1984—; law libr. William H. Miller Law Libr., Evansville, 1985—. Archival cons. Evansville Mus. of Arts and Scis., 1984-85; exec. bd. mem. Four Rivers area Libr. Svcs. Authority, Evansville, 1988-91; bd. dirs., mem. adv. coun. Ind. Coop. Libr. Svcs. Authority, 1995—. Recitalist Royal Can. Coll. of Organists Conv., 1973; artist-fellow Bach Aria Festival and Inst., 1992. Founding mem. Evansville Chamber Orch., 1981—; organist Eastminster Presbyn. Ch., Evansville, 1991—. Grantee Nova Scotia Talent Trust, 1969-70. Mem. Am. Assn. Law Librs., Am. Guild Organists (Evansville chpt. exec. 1982-91, 94—), Evansville Area Librs. Consortium, Friends of UE Music (sec., treas. 1988-91), Ohio Regional Assn. Law Librs., Midwestern Hist. Keyboard Soc., Evansville Philharmonic Youth Orch. (mem. adv. coun.). Home: 1435 Brookside Dr Evansville IN 47714-2043 Office: William H Miller Law Libr 825 Sycamore St Ste 207 Evansville IN 47708-1849 E-mail: hsr@evansville.net.

REED, JOHN SQUIRES, II, lawyer; b. Lexington, Ky., Mar. 20, 1949; s. John Squires and Mary Alexander (O'Hara) R.; m. Nancy Claire Battles, Dec. 29, 1973; children: Alexandra Simmons, John Squires III. AB in Polit. Sci., U. Ky., 1971; JD, U. Va., 1974. Bar: Ky. 1974, U.S. Dist. Ct. (we. dist.) Ky. 1975, U.S. Ct. Appeals (6th cir.) 1975, U.S. Dist. Ct. (ea. dist.) Ky. 1979, U.S. Supreme Ct. 1980, U.S. Ct. Appeals (fed. cir.) 1985. Assoc. Greenbaum Doll & McDonald, Louisville, 1974-79, ptnr., 1979-87, Hirn, Doheny, Reed & Harper, Louisville, 1987-96, Reed Weitkamp Schell & Vice PLLC, Louisville, 1996—. Mem. Leadership Louisville, 1982, treas., mem. exec. com. Leadership Louisville Alumni Assn., 1984, pres., 1985; bd. dirs. Econs. Am. in Ky., 1985-2002, Nat. Assn. Cmty. Leadership, 1986-91, treas., 1987-88, v.p., 1988-89, pres., 1989-90, Leadership Louisville Found., Inc., 1986-92, Greater Louisville Econ. Devel. Partnership, 1987-97; chair Leadership USA, Inc., 1997—, Louisville Collegiate Sch., 1996—. 1st lt. U.S. Army, 1974. Mem. ABA (antitrust, intellectual property, litig. sects.), Ky. Bar Assn., Louisville Bar Assn. (bd. dirs. 1985-86, treas. 1988, sec. 1989, v.p. 1990, pres. 1992), Louisville Boat Club, Valhalla Golf Club, Phi Beta Kappa. Democrat. Presbyterian. Antitrust, General civil litigation, Patent. Office: Reed Weitkamp Schell & Vice PLLC 2400 Citizens Plz Louisville KY 40202 E-mail: jreed@rwsvlaw.com.

REED, JOHN WESLEY, lawyer, educator; b. Independence, Mo., Dec. 11, 1918; s. Novus H. and Lilian (Houchens) R.; m. Imogene Fay Vonada, Oct. 5, 1946 (div. 1958); m. Dorothy Elaine Floyd, Mar. 5, 1961; children: Alison A., John M. (dec.), Mary V., Randolph F., Suzanne M. AB, William Jewell Coll., 1939, LLD, 1995; LLB, Cornell U., 1942; LLM, Columbia U., 1949, JSD, 1957. Bar: Mo. 1942, Mich. 1953. Assoc. Stinson, Mag, Thomson, McEvers & Fizzell, Kansas City, Mo., 1942-46; assoc. prof. law U. Okla., 1946-49; assoc. prof. U. Mich., 1949-53, prof., 1953-64, 68-85, Thomas M. Cooley prof., 1985-87, Thomas M. Cooley prof. emeritus, 1987—; dean, prof. U. Colo., 1964-68, Wayne State U., Detroit, 1987-92, prof. emeritus, 1992—. Vis. prof. NYU, 1949, U. Chgo., 1960, Yale U., 1963-64, Harvard U., 1982, U. San Diego, 1993; dir. Inst. Continuing Legal Edn., 1968-73; reporter Mich. Rules of Evidence Com., 1975-78, 83-84; mem. faculty Salzburg Sem., 1962, chmn., 1964. Author: (with W.W. Blume) Pleading and Joinder, 1952; (with others) Introduction to Law and Equity, 1953, Advocacy Course Handbook series, 1963-81; editor in chief Cornell Law Quar., 1941-42; contbr. articles to profl. jours. Pres. bd. mgrs. of mins. and missionaries benefit bd. Am. Bapt. Chs. U.S.A., 1967-74, 82-85, 88-94; mem. com. visitors JAG Sch., 1971-76; trustee Kalamazoo Coll., 1954-64, 68-70. Recipient Harrison Tweed award Assn. Continuing Legal Edn. Adminstrs., 1983, Samuel E. Gates award Am. Coll. Trial Lawyers, 1985, Roberts P. Hudson award State Bar Mich., 1989. Fellow Internat. Soc. Barristers (editor jour. 1980—); mem. ABA (mem. coun. litigation sect.), Assn. Am. Law Schs. (mem. exec. com. 1965-67), Am. Acad. Jud. Edn. (v.p. 1978-80), Colo. Bar Assn. (mem. bd. govs. 1964-68), Mich. Supreme Ct. Hist. Soc. (bd. dirs. 1991—), Sci. Club Mich., Order of Coif. Office: U Mich Sch Law Ann Arbor MI 48109-1215 E-mail: reedj@umich.edu.

REED, JOHN WILSON, lawyer; b. Manchester, Eng., May 31, 1945; came to U.S., 1954; s. Firmin P. and Isabel (Woollam) R.; m. Leslee King, Dec. 27, 1969; children— Ashley King, Cameron King. B.A., Yale U., 1966; J.D., Harvard U., 1969. Bar: La. 1970, U.S. Dist. Ct. (ea. dist.) La. 1970, U.S. Ct. Apls. (5th cir.) 1970, U.S. Ct. Appeals (11th cir.) 1970, N.Y., 1980, U.S. Dist. Ct. (so. dist.) Ala., 1982. Vista vol. New Orleans Legal Assistance Corp., 1969-70, staff atty., 1970-72; sole practice, New Orleans, 1972-78; ptnr. Glass & Reed, New Orleans, 1978— ; gen. counsel ACLU of La., New Orleans, 1974-78; mem. faculty New Orleans Bar Rev., 1979— , Nat. Inst. Trial Advocacy, Boulder, Colo., 1984, 89, 97. Mem. Nat. Assn. Criminal Def. Lawyers, Am. Trial Lawyers Assn., La. Trial Lawyers Assn., La. Assn. Criminal Def. Lawyers (v.p. 1985—). Democrat. Criminal. Office: Glass & Reed 530 Natchez St New Orleans LA 70130-2700

REED, KEITH ALLEN, lawyer; b. Anamosa, Iowa, Mar. 5, 1939; s. John Ivan and Florence Lorine (Larson) R.; m. Beth Illana Kesterson, June 22, 1963; children: Melissa Beth, Matthew Keith. BBA, U. Iowa, 1960, JD, 1963. Bar: Ill. 1963, Iowa 1963. Ptnr. Seyfarth Shaw, Chgo., 1963—. Co-author: Labor Arbitration in Healthcare, 1981; co-editor: Chicagoland Employment Law Manual, 1994, Employment and Discrimination, 1996, Federal Employment Law and Regulations, 1989-99, 2001-; co-contbr. articles to Am. Hosp. Assn. publs., 1986-89. Trustee Meth. Hosp. Chgo., 1985—; mem. ad hoc labor adv. com. Am. Hosp. Assn., Chgo., 1980—; bd. dirs. Lyric Opera Chgo. Ctr. for Am. Artists, pres., 1983-86. Mem. ABA (dir. health law forum 1979-82), Chgo. Bar Assn. (chair labor and employment law com. 1996-), Union League Club Chgo. (bd. dirs. 1985-88), Sunset Ridge Country Club (Northbrook, Ill.). Republican. Methodist. Avocations: music, community theater, tennis, golf. Health, Labor (including EEOC, Fair Labor Standards Act, labor-management relations, NLRB, OSHA). Office: Seyfarth Shaw 55 E Monroe St Ste 4200 Chicago IL 60603-5863

REED, LELAND, lawyer; b. Hector, Ark., Sept. 17, 1921; s. Albert McCain and Hattie Mae (Hogins) R.; 1 child, Starla Jacobs. BS, U. So. Calif., 1948; JD, Van Norman U., 1969. Bar: Calif. 1976, D.C. 1994, U.S. Ct. Appeals (9th cir.) 1976, U.S. Supreme Ct. 1980. Pub. acct. Haskings Sells-Arthur Young, L.A. and N.Y.C., 1948-55; plant contr. Dunlop Rubber Co., Buffalo, N.Y., 1955-60; acct. cons. Kirk Mayer Engring. Co., L.A., 1960-62, Daniel, Mann, Johnson, L.A., 1963-65; contract specialist USN, Long Beach, Calif., 1966-73; contracting officer USAF, L.A., 1973-80, Europe and Middle East, 1980-83; pvt. practice L.A. and Washington, 1983—. Mem. State Bar Calif., D.C. Bar Assn., L.A. County Bar Assn. Avocations: fishing, travel. General civil litigation, Criminal, Immigration, naturalization, and customs. Home: 4223 Verdugo Rd Los Angeles CA 90065 Office: 1186 W Sunset Blvd Los Angeles CA 90012

REED, LOWELL A., JR., federal judge; b. Westchester, Pa., 1930; s. Lowell A. Sr. and Catherine Elizabeth R.; m. Diane Benson; four children. BBA, U. Wis., 1952; JD, Temple U., 1958. Bar: Pa. 1959, U.S. Dist. Ct. (ea. dist.) Pa. 1961, U.S. Ct. Appeals (3d cir.) 1962, U.S. Supreme Ct. 1970. Corp. trial counsel PMA Group, Phila., 1958-63; assoc. Rawle & Henderson, Phila., 1963-65, gen. ptnr., 1966-88; judge U.S. Dist Ct., Phila., 1988-99; sr. judge U.S. Dist. Ct., Phila., 1999—. Lectr. law Temple U., 1965-81, faculty Acad. Advocacy, 1988—, Pa. Bar Inst., 1972—. Contbr. articles to profl. jours. Elder Abington (Pa.) Presbyn. Ch.; past. mem. Pa. Senate Select Com. Med. Malpractice; past pres., bd. dirs. Rydal Meadowbrook Civic Assn.; bd. dirs. Abington Sch. Bd., 1971, World Affairs Coun. Phila., 1983-88; trustee Abington Health Care Corp., 1983-88, 90-93. Lt. Comdr. USNR, 1952-57. Recipient Alumni Achievement award Temple U. 1988, Cert. of Honor, 2001. Mem. ABA, Phila. Bar Assn. (chmn. medico legal com. 1975, constl. bicentennial com. 1986-87, commn. on jud. selection and retention 1983-87), Temple Am. Inn of Ct. (pres. 1990-93, master of bench 1990—), Am. Judicature Soc., Temple U. Law Alumni Assn. (exec. com. 1987-90, 99—), Hist. Soc. U.S. Supreme Ct., Hist. Soc. U.S. Dist. Ct. Ea. Dist. Pa. Republican. Office: US Dist Ct US Courthouse Independence Mall W Philadelphia PA 19106

REED, MICHAEL HAYWOOD, lawyer; b. Phila., Jan. 17, 1949; s. Soloman Taylor and Vivian (Haywood) Reed; m. Yalta Gilmore, Aug. 12, 1978; children: Alexandra Haywood, Michael Haywood Jr. BA in Polit. Sci., Temple U., 1969; JD, Yale U., 1972. Bar: Pa. 1972, U.S. Dist. Ct. (ea. dist.) Pa. 1972, U.S. Dist. Ct. (ea. dist.) Mich. 1982, U.S. Supreme Ct. 1982, U.S. Ct. Appeals (3d cir.) 1985. Assoc. Pepper, Hamilton & Scheetz, Phila., 1972-80, ptnr., 1980—. Co-adj. prof. law Rutgers U., Camden, N.J., 1983, 85; adj. prof. sch. law Temple U., Phila., 1989; mem. Pa. Judicial Inquiry and Rev. Bd., 1990-93; mem. steering com. Ea. Dist. Pa. Bankruptcy Conf., 1992—. Contbr. articles to profl. jours. Advisor Post 913 Law Explorers, Phila., 1974-84; trustee Acad. Natural Scis., Phila., 1988—, Episcopal Hosp., Phila., 1986—; mem. bd. advisors Pub. Interest Law Ctr., Phila., 1992—; mem. exec. bd. Com. of Seventy, Phila., 1985—. Recipient cert. of honor Alumnus of Yr. Coll. of Arts and Scis. Temple U., 1995, Award of Excellence, Thurgood Marshall Scholarship Fund, Inc., 2003. Fellow Am. Coll. Bankruptcy; mem. ABA (chmn. subcom. labor and employment law, bus bankruptcy com. sect. bus. law 1991-97, chmn. subcom. on labor and employment law 1997-2002), Nat. Bar Assn., Pa. Bar Assn. (mem. ho. of dels. 1985—, chmn. minority bar com. 1988-90, mem. bd. govs. 1993-96, co-chairperson 1994, v.p. 2002-03, pres.-elect 2003-, ann. meeting, Spl. Achievement award 1989, Cert. of Honor award 1995), Barristers Assn. Phila. (1st v.p. 1974-76), Alpha Phi Alpha, Yale Club (Phila.). Democrat. Baptist. Avocations: racquetball, film, theatre, biking, piano. Bankruptcy, Corporate, general, Health. Home: 225 N 23rd St Philadelphia PA 19103-1005 Office: Pepper Hamilton & Scheetz 3000 Two Logan Sq 18th and Arch Streets Philadelphia PA 19103-2799 Office Fax: 215-981-4750.*

REED, ROBERT PHILLIP, lawyer; b. Springfield, Ill., June 14, 1952; s. Robert Edward and Rita Ann (Kane) R.; m. Janice Leigh Kloppenburg, Oct. 8, 1976; children: Kevin Michael, Matthew Carl, Jennifer Leigh, Rebecca Ann. AB, St. Louis U., 1974; JD, U. Ill., 1977. Bar: Ill. 1977, U.S. Dist. Ct. (ctrl. dist.) Ill. 1979, U.S.Ct. Appeals (7th cir.) 1983, U.S. Dist. Ct. (so. dist.) Ill. 1992, Colo. 1993. Intern Ill. Legislature, Springfield, 1977-78; assoc. Traynor & Hendricks, Springfield, 1979-80; ptnr. Traynor, Hendricks & Reed, Springfield, 1981-88; pvt. practice Springfield, 1988—. Pub. defender Sangamon County, Ill., Springfield, 1979-81; hearing examiner Ill. State Bd. Elections, Springfield, 1981-88; spl. asst. atty. gen. State of Ill., Springfield, 1983—; instr. Lincoln Land Community Coll., Springfield, 1988. Trustee Springfield Pk. Dist., 1985-89. Mem.: Am. Immigration Lawyers Assn., Attys Title Guaranty Fund, Inc., Colo. Bar Assn., Ill. State Bar Assn., Nat. Assn. Securities Dealers, Inc. (arbitrator 1996—), Phi Beta Kappa. Roman Catholic. Family and matrimonial, Probate (including wills, trusts), Property, real (including real estate development, water). Office: 1129 S 7th St Springfield IL 62703-2418

REED, RONALD ERNST, lawyer; b. Frankfort, Ky., Mar. 24, 1958; s. Thomas B. and Gerhild M. Reed; m. Lisa J. Hayden, Mar. 7, 1994; 1 child, Spencer Thomas. BA, U. Fla., 1980, JD, 1983. Bar: Fla. 1983, U.S. Dist. Ct. (mid. dist.) Fla. 1987. Asst. states atty. State Atty.'s Office, Jacksonville, Fla., 1983-86; ptnr. Fallin & Reed, Jacksonville, 1986-87, Bullock, Childs, Pendley & Reed, P.A., Jacksonville, 1987—. Democrat. Methodist. Avocations: golfing, reading, sports. Insurance, Personal injury (including property damage), Product liability. Office: Bullock Childs Pendley & Reed PA 1551 Atlantic Blvd 2d Fl Jacksonville FL 32207 E-mail: rreed@bcprlaw.com.

REED, SAMUEL LEE, lawyer; b. Selma, Ind., July 29, 1934; s. Merritt C. and Ivy Jane (Williams) R.; m. Joan C. Guinn, Aug. 27, 1955; children: Scott, Craig, Steven, Jennifer. BS in Bus., Ind. U., 1956; JD, 1959. Bar: Ind. 1959, U.S. Dist Ct. (so. dist.) Ind. 1959. Ptnr. DeFur, Voran, Hanley, Radcliff & Reed, Muncie, Ind., 1959-2003, mng. ptnr., 1981-89; dep. pros. atty. Delaware County, Ind., 1961-63; magistrate U.S. Dist. Ct. (so. dist.) Ind., 1978-85; mem. Ind. Gen. Assembly, 1973-77; former chmn. bd. dirs. Westminster Village Muncie, Inc. Mem. Muncie Community Sch. Bd., 1969-73, pres., 1973; pres. Ind. Pub. Broadcasting Soc., 1979-82; bd. dirs. Muncie Children's Mus., 1980-84; elder First United Presbyterian Ch., Muncie; mem. Community Adv. Council Med. Edn., Muncie; chmn. Delaware County Coalition for Legis. Interests, 1984-85; chmn. Delaware County Rep. Fin. Com., 1984-86; mem. nominating com. Ind. Pub. Service Commn., 1984-86. Recipient Big Ten medal Ind. U., 1956, Disting. Service award Muncie Jaycees, 1968. Mem. ABA, Ind. Bar Assn., Muncie Bar Assn. (pres. 1966), Muncie-Delaware C. of C. (vice chmn. bd. dirs. 1986-89), Exch. Club (pres. club 1969). Republican. General practice, Probate (including wills, trusts), Property, real (including real estate development, water). Office: 201 E Jackson St Suite 400 Muncie IN 47305

REED, SUSAN D. prosecutor; m. Robert D. Reed; 1 child. B in Econs., U. Tex., JD, 1974. Bar: Tex., U.S. Dist. Ct. (we. dist.) Tex., Fed. Ct., U.S. Supreme Ct., bd. cert. criminal law: Tex. Bd. Legal Specialization. Judge 144th Dist. Ct.; pvt. practice Souls and Reed; chief pros. 144th and 187th Dist. Cts.; adminstrv. judge Dist. Cts. Bexar County, 1996—97; asst. dist. atty. Bexar County, San Antonio, 1974—82, criminal dist. atty., 1998—. Mem. Criminal Justice Policy Coun., Govs. Juvenile Justice Adv. Bd., Bush-Cheney Transition Team for Dept. Justice, Nat. Adv. Coun. on Violence Against Women. Mem. Regional Anti-Terrorism Task Force; co-chair Anti-Crime Commn., 2002. Recipient Judge of Yr. award, Tex. Gang Investigators Assn. Mem.: Nat. Dist. Attys. Assn., Tex. Dist. and County Attys. Assn. Office: Bexar County Criminal Dist Atty 5th Fl 300 Dolorosa San Antonio TX 78205-3630*

REED, W. FRANKLIN, lawyer; b. Louisville, Dec. 30, 1946; s. William Ferguson and Stella Elizabeth (Richardson) R.; m. Sharon Ann Coss, June 16, 1973; children: Jonathan Franklin, William Brian, Carrie Ann. BA, Williams Coll., 1968; JD, Columbia U., 1971. Bar: N.Y. 1972, U.S. Dist. Ct. (so. dist.) N.Y. 1975, U.S. Ct. Appeals (2d cir.) 1975, Pa. 1982, U.S. Dist. Ct. (we. dist.) 1983. Assoc. Milbank, Tweed, Hadley & McCloy, N.Y.C., 1971-82, Reed Smith Shaw & McClay, Pitts., 1982-83; ptnr. Reed, Smith, Shaw & McClay, Pitts., 1984—. With Instnl. Devel. Com., The Pitts. Cultural Trust. Mem. ABA, Pa. Bar Assn., Allegheny Bar Assn., Carnegie 100, Williams Coll. Alumni Soc. W. Pa. (sec. 1983—), Rivers Club (Pitts.), St. Clair Country Club (Upper St. Clair, Pa.), Duquesne Club (Pitts.), Phi Beta Kappa. Democrat. Presbyterian. Avocations: fishing, golf. Corporate, general, Utilities, public, Property, real (including real estate development, water). Home: 525 Miranda Dr Pittsburgh PA 15241-2039 Office: Reed Smith LLP 435 6th Ave Pittsburgh PA 15219-1886 E-mail: wreed@reedsmith.com.

REEDE, MICHAEL BARRINGTON, lawyer; b. Sydney, Australia, June 14, 1965; s. Kevin B. Reede and Margaret C. Spurret; m. Katherine Margaret McCosker, 1991; children: Daniel, Phoebe. LLB, B. Comm., U. NSW, Australia, 1988, MA, 1993. Solicitor Minter Ellison, Sydney, Australia, 1990—93, Gilbert & Tobin, Sydney, Australia, 1993—96, ptnr., 1996—2000, Paul, Weiss, Rifkind, Wharton & Garrison, Hong Kong, 2000—. Office: Paul Weiss Rifkind Wharton & Garrison 12th Fl Hong Kong Club Bldg 3A Chater Rd Central Hong Kong China

REEDER, F. ROBERT, lawyer; b. Brigham City, Utah, Jan. 23, 1943; s. Frank O. and Helen H. (Heninger) R.; m. Joannie Anderson, May 4, 1974; children: David, Kristina, Adam. JD, U. Utah, 1967. Bar: Utah 1967, U.S. Ct. Appeals (1oth cir.) 1967, U.S. Ct. Appeals (D.C. and 5th cirs.) 1979, U.S. Ct. Mil. Appeals 1968, U.S. Supreme Ct. 1972. Shareholder Parsons, Behle & Latimer, Salt Lake City, 1968—. Bd. dirs. Holy Cross Found., 1981-90, chmn., 1987-90; bd. dirs. Holy Cross Hosp., 1990-93, treas., 1986-87, vice chmn., 1987-93; bd. dirs. Holy Cross Health Svcs. Utah, 1993-94, treas., 1993-94; bd. dirs. Sale Lake Regional Med. Ctr., 1995—, vice chmn., 1995-2000, chmn., 2000—; trustee Univ. Hosp. Found.; hon. col. Salt Lake City Police, Salt Lake County Sheriff. Served with USAR, 1967-73. Mem. ABA, Utah State Bar, Salt Lake County Bar (ethics adv. com. 1989-94), Cottonwood Country Club (bd. dirs. 1978-82, 83-86, pres. 1981-82), Rotary. General civil litigation, Commercial, contracts (including sales of goods; commercial financing), Utilities, public. Office: Parsons Behle & Latimer PO Box 45898 Salt Lake City UT 84145-0898

REEDER, JAMES ARTHUR, lawyer; b. Baton Rouge, June 29, 1933; s. James Brown and Grace (Britt) R.; m. Mary Leone Guthrie, Dec. 30, 1958; children: Mary Virginia, James Jr., Elizabeth Colby. BA, Washington and Lee U., Lexington, Va., 1955; LLB, U. Tex., 1960; JD, La. State U., 1961. Ptnr. Booth, Lockard, Jack et al, Shreveport, La., 1961-72; pres. and mgng. ptnr. Shreveport Broadcasting Co., 1972-86; CEO, mng. gen. ptnr. Radio USA Limited, Houston, 1986-89; pres. SW subsidiaries Sun Group, Inc., Houston, 1990-92; atty. Patton & Boggs, LLP, Washington, 1991-94; ptnr. Patton, Boggs LLP, Washington, 1994—. Dir. ABC Radio Sta. Affiliates adv. bd., N.Y.C., 1978-84. Dir. Boys Country, Houston, 1986-90; pres. Holiday in Dixie, Shreveport, 1968; chmn. Ambassadors Club, Shreveport, 1979. 1st Lt. U.S. Army, 1955-57. Named La. Outstanding Young Man, La. Jaycees, 1969. Mem. ABA (bd. dirs. young lawyers sect. 1967-68, Gavel awards com. 1980), La. Bar Assn. (pres. young lawyers sect. 1966, La. Outstanding Young Lawyer award 1968), D.C. Bar Assn., Tex. Bar Assn., Nat. Assn. Broadcasters, Houston Country Club, Allegro Club (Houston). Roman Catholic. Legislative.

REEG, KURTIS BRADFORD, lawyer; b. St. Louis, Sept. 1, 1954; s. Jay Flory and Mary Louise (Braun) R.; m. Cynthia Diane Wable, June 25, 1994. BA cum laude, DePauw U., 1976; JD, St. Louis U., 1979. Bar: U.S. Dist. Ct. (ea. dist.) Mo. 1979, U.S. Dist. Ct. Ariz. 1994, U.S. Dist. Ct. (ctrl. dist.) Ill. 1997, U.S. Dist. Ct. (we. dist.) Mo. 2000, U.S. Dist. Ct. Colo. 2003, U.S. Ct. Appeals (8th cir.) 1984, U.S. Ct. Appeals (7th cir.) 1986, U.S. Ct.

Appeals (2nd cir.) 1994, U.S. Supreme Ct. 1994. Law clk. to presiding justice Ill. Appellate Ct. (5th dist.), Granite City, 1979-80; assoc. Coburn, Croft & Putzell, St. Louis, Mo. and Belleville, Ill., 1980-86, ptnr., 1986-91; ptnr., chmn. tort and ins. group, co-chmn. litigation dept. Gallop, Johnson & Neuman, L.C., St. Louis, 1991-98, mem. mgmt. com., 1991-98, mng. ptnr. Belleville, Ill., 1997-98; ptnr. Sonnenschein Nath & Rosenthal, St. Louis, 1998-2000; ptnr., chmn. product liability group Kohn, Shands, Elbert, Gianoulakis & Giljum, LLP, St. Louis, 2001—02; ptnr. Leritz, Plunkert & Bruning, P.C., St. Louis, 2002—. Instr. legal rsch. and writing St. Louis U., 1979-80. Mem. Police, Fire Commns., City of Town and Country, Mo., 1987-89; Rep. committeeman 24th ward, St. Louis, 1980. Mem.: ABA, Mo. Orgn. Def. Lawyers, Def. Rsch. Inst., Fedn. Def. and Corp. Counsel (chmn. toxic tort and environ. law sect. 2001—), Mo. Orgn. Def. Counsel, Internat. Assn. Def. Counsel, Bar Assn. Met. St. Louis, Mo. Bar Assn., Ill. State Bar Assn., Pi Sigma Alpha, Phi Alpha Delta. Republican. Avocations: hunting, fishing, golf, astronomy. Insurance, Product liability, Toxic tort. also: 12720 Willowyck Dr Saint Louis MO 63146-3726 Office: Leritz Plunkert & Bruning PC 1 City Centre Ste 2001 Saint Louis MO 63101 E-mail: kreeg@leritzlaw.com.

REES, THOMAS DYNEVOR, lawyer; b. S.I., N.Y., Sept. 25, 1949; s. Thomas and Caroline (Bridgman) Rees; m. Josephine Stephanie Madej, Apr. 8, 1978; 1 child, Thomas D. III. AB in Polit. Sci., Stanford U., 1971; JD, U. Pa., 1975. Bar: N.Y. 1976, Pa. 1977, U.S. Supreme Ct. 1982. Assoc. Lovejoy, Wasson, Lundgren & Ashton, N.Y.C., 1975-77, Morgan, Lewis & Bockius, Phila., 1977-81; dep. gen. counsel Office of Gov. of Pa., Harrisburg, 1981-85; counsel High, Swartz, Roberts & Seidel, Norristown, Pa., 1985-86, ptnr., 1987—. CLE course planner, author, faculty mem. Pa. Bar Inst., 1990—; employment panel arbitrator Am. Arbitration Assn., Phila., 1991—. Solicitor Upper Merion Twp., King of Prussia, Pa., 1987—88, 1990—95, Abington Twp., Pa., 1986—87; pres. Gladwyne Civic Assn., Pa., 1995—97. Mem.: ABA, Montgomery County Bar Assn. (co-chair employment law com. 1996—2000), Pa. Bar Assn. (chair mcpl. law sect. 1993—95), King of Prussia C. of C. (solicitor 1996—, v.p., gen. counsel 1999—). Republican. Episcopalian. Education and schools, Labor (including EEOC, Fair Labor Standards Act, labor-management relations, NLRB, OSHA), Land use and zoning (including planning). Office: High Swartz Roberts & Seidel LLP 40 E Airy St Norristown PA 19401-4803 E-mail: trees@highswartz.com.

REESE, CHARLES WOODROW, JR., lawyer, real estate developer; b. San Antonio, June 21, 1944; s. Charles Woodrow and Mary Ruth (Gott) R.; m. Jill Fritschi, Aug. 10, 1979; children— Clarissa, Alexandra. B.A. cum laude, Washington and Lee U., 1966; J.D., U. Calif., Berkeley, 1969. Bar: Calif. 1970, U.S. Sup. Ct. 1976. Assoc. McCutchen, Doyle, Brown & Enersen, San Francisco, 1969-75; staff atty. Kaiser Industries Corp., Oakland, Calif., 1975-78; asst. gen. csl. Kaiser Cement Corp., Oakland, 1978-86 ; gen. ptnr. Reese Interests, Houston, 1978— ; mng. trustee Clotilde deMartini Trusts, San Francisco, 1977—; prin Lempres & Wulfsberg PC, Okland, 1986-98; exec. v.p. Wulfsberg Reese & Sykes PC, 1998-2002; pres. and CFO Wulsberg Reese Colvig & Firstman PC, 2002-. Hon. trustee Orinda Found., 1976— ; bd. dirs. Planned Parenthood Alameda/San Francisco, 1981—83 , Brown and Caldwell, Walnut Creek, 1987-, PLA Holdings, Inc., Port Costa, 1991-. Robert E. Lee research scholar, 1965-66. Mem. State Bar Calif., ABA, Bar Assn. San Francisco, Alameda County Bar Assn. (coms.), Omicron Delta Upsilon, Pac. Union Club (San Francisco). Republican. Episcopalian. Clubs: Orinda (Calif.) Country. Corporate, general, Pension, profit-sharing, and employee benefits, Property, real (including real estate development, water). Home: 89 La Salle Piedmont CA 94611 Office: 300 Lakeside Dr 24th Fl Oakland CA 94612-3534 E-mail: creese@wulfslaw.com.

REESE, JOHN ROBERT, lawyer; b. Salt Lake City, Nov. 3, 1939; s. Robert McCann and Glade (Stauffer) R.; m. Francesca Marroquin Gardner, Sept. 5, 1964 (div.); children— Jennifer Marie, Justine Francesca; m. Robin Ann Gunsul, June 18, 1988. AB cum laude, Harvard U., 1962; LLB, Stanford U., 1965. Bar: Calif. 1966, U.S. Dist. Ct. (no. dist.) Calif. 1966, U.S. Ct. Appeals (9th cir.) 1966, U.S. Dist. Ct. (cen. dist.) Calif. 1974, U.S. Supreme Ct. 1976, U.S. Dist. Ct. (ea. dist.) Calif. 1977, U.S. Ct. Appeals (6th cir.) 1982, U.S. Ct. Appeals (8th cir.) 1985, U.S. Ct. Appeals (10th cir.) 1992, U.S. Ct. Appeals (Fed. cir.) 1994. Assoc. McCutchen, Doyle, Brown & Enersen, San Francisco, 1965—74, ptnr., 1974—2002, Bingham McCutchen, San Francisco, 2002—. Adj. asst. prof. law Hastings Coll. of Law, 1991; lectr. U. Calif., Berkeley, 1987, 92. Mem. editl. and adv. bds.: Antitrust Bull., Jour. Reprints for Antitrust Law and Econs., 1981—99. Bd. dirs. Friends of San Francisco Pub. Libr., 1981-87; bd. vis. Stanford U. Law Sch., 1983-86. Capt. U.S. Army, 1966-68 Decorated Bronze Star. Mem. ABA, Am. Acad. Appellate Lawyers, State Bar Calif., San Francisco Bar Assn., U.S. Supreme Ct. Hist. Soc., Ninth Jud. Cir. Hist. Soc., Calif. Acad. Appellate Lawyers, Order of the Coif. Avocations: aviculture, gardening. General civil litigation. Home: 9 Morning Sun Dr Petaluma CA 94952-4780 Office: Bingham McCutchen 3 Embarcadero Ctr San Francisco CA 94111-4003

REESE, KEVIN WAYNE, lawyer; b. Newport News, Va., May 6, 1970; s. William and Shirley Holly Reese; m. Ann Elizabeth McNamara. BA in Pub. Rels. Journalism, Bob Jones U., 1992; JD, U. SC, 1996. Assoc. Law Offices Douglas A. Cherob, Greenville, SC, 1996—97, McNay Law Firm, P.A., Greenville, 1997—99; corp. counsel Michelin N.Am., Inc., Greenville, 2000—. Corporate, general, Finance, Property, real (including real estate development, water). Home: 411 Falling Rock Way Greenville SC 29615 Office: Michelin NAm Inc One Parkway S Greenville SC 29615 Fax: 864-458-6110. E-mail: kevin.reese@us.michelin.com.

REEVES, GENE, judge; b. Meridian, Miss., Feb. 27, 1930; s. Clarence Eugene and May (Philyaw) R.; m. Brenda Wages, Sept. 26, 1980. JD, John Marshall U., 1964; cert. judge spl. ct. jurisdiction; postgrad., U. Nev., 1995. Bar: Ga. 1964, U.S. Ct. Appeals (11th cir.) 1965, U.S. Supreme Ct. 1969. Ptnr. Craig & Reeves, Lawrenceville, Ga., 1964-71; sole practice Lawrenceville, 1971-85; prin. Reeves Law Firm, 1985-94; judge City Ct., Lawrenceville, 1969-70, Magistrate Ct. of Gwinnett County, Ga., 1994—. Sgt. USAF, 1951-54. Mem. ABA, ATLA, GTLA, Am. Jud. Soc., Gwinnett County Bar Assn. (pres. 1970-72), Criminal Def. Lawyers Assn., Atlanta Bar Assn. Baptist. Home: 221 Pineview Dr Lawrenceville GA 30045-6035 Office: 75 Langley Dr Lawrenceville GA 30045-6935 E-mail: GREEV@mindspring.com.

REEVES, SIMON, lawyer; b. Middleton, Eng., Dec. 1, 1967; arrived in Switzerland, 2001; LLB in English and French Law, King's Coll., London, 1988; Maitrise en Droit Prive, U. Paris I, 1990. Bar: Law Soc. Eng. and Wales 1994. Trainee solicitor Trowers & Hamlins, London, 1992—94; solicitor Lordship Estates, Prague, Czech Republic, 1995—98, Clifford Chance, Prague, 1998—2001; sr. counsel Philip Morris Internat. Mgmt. SA, Lausanne, Switzerland, 2001—. Mem.: Law Soc. Eng. and Wales. Computer, Property, real (including real estate development, water), Commercial, contracts (including sales of goods; commercial financing). Office: Philip Morris Internat Mgmt SA Avenue de Cour 107 1003 Lausanne Switzerland

REGAN, MICHAEL PATRICK, lawyer; b. Bklyn., Feb. 22, 1941; s. Cornelius Francis and Marguerite (Cann) R.; m. Susan Ann Light, July 13, 1974; children: Michael Patrick, Brian Christopher, Mark Dennis. BA in English, U. Notre Dame, 1963; LLB, Albany Law Sch., Union U., 1967, JD, 1968. Bar: N.Y. 1967, Va. 1975. Assoc. Medwin & McMahon, Albany, N.Y., 1967-69; asst. dist. atty. Albany County, N.Y., 1969; corp. atty. Mohasco Corp., Amsterdam, N.Y., 1969-74; asst. gen. csl. Dan River Inc., Danville, Va., 1975, assoc. gen. counsel, 1981-84, assoc. gen. counsel, asst. sec., 1984, acting gen. counsel, asst. sec., 1988, gen. counsel, asst. sec., 1989, assoc. gen. counsel, asst. sec. Dan River Holding Co., 1984-88, acting gen. counsel, asst. sec., 1988, gen. counsel, asst. sec., 1989; assoc. gen. counsel, asst. sec. Dan River Svc. Corp. of Va., 1984-88; gen. counsel, Wunda Weve Carpets, Inc., Greenville, S.C., 1990-93; mem. Danville Symphony Orch., 1991-; pvt. practice, Danville, Va., 1990—. Clarinetist, saxophonist Tightsqueeze Philharm. Band, 1981-; leader: The DanceNotes, 1986-; sec. DanPac Polit. Action Com., 1976-89; prin. Danville Symphony Orch., 1991-; mem. Starmont Swing Band, 1999-. Mem. ATLA, ABA, N.Y. State Bar Assn., Va. Bar Assn., Danville Bar Assn., Va. Trial Lawyers Assn., Rotary. Corporate, general, Pension, profit-sharing, and employee benefits, Trademark and copyright. Home: 236 Cambridge Cir Danville VA 24541-5233 Office: 703 Patton St Danville VA 24541-1905

REGAN, PAUL MICHAEL, lawyer; b. Detroit, May 8, 1953; s. Timothy J. and Adele (Anthony) R. BA, Duke U., 1975; JD, Cath. U., 1979. Bar: N.Y. 1983. Clearance officer, counsel Ticor Title Guarantee Co., Syracuse, N.Y., 1980-84; assoc. Van Epps & Shulman, Syracuse, 1984-87, Shulman Law Firm, Syracuse, 1987-91; ptnr. Shulman Curtin Grundner & Regan, P.C., Syracuse, 1992—. Speaker Nat. Bus. Inst., 1991, N.Y. State Bar Seminars, 1990-94, 99. Vestry Christ Ch., Malius, N.Y., 1991-96; bd. dirs. Cazenovia (N.Y.) Childrens House, 1990-94; counsel Save Our Cmty., Inc., Cazenovia, 1989-93. Mem. N.Y. State Bar Assn., Onondaga County Bar Assn. (chmn. real estate contract com. 1990-96, com. on title standards 1990-96, spkr. 1998). Environmental, Property, real (including real estate development, water). Office: Shulman Curtin Grundner & Regan PC 250 S Clinton St Ste 502 Syracuse NY 13202-1262 E-mail: pregan@scgrslaw.com.

REGENBOGEN, ADAM, judge; b. Steyer, Austria, June 12, 1947; s. William and Pauline (Feuerstein) R.; m. Paula Ruth Rothenberg, June 27, 1970 (div. Oct. 1992); children: Stacy, Candice; m. Helen Busuttil Drwal, Apr. 20, 1996; 1 stepchild, Jason A. Drwal. BA, Temple U., 1969; MSW, U. Pa., 1972; JD, Temple U., 1980. Bar: N.Y. 1983. Social worker VA, Coatesville, Pa., 1974—78, supr. Northport, NY, 1978—80, quality assurance dir., 1980—87; dir. quality assurance N.Y. State Office Mental Health, Willard, 1987—91; workers compensation law judge Binghamton, Oneonta, Norwich, Ithaca, Manhattan, 1998—; pvt. practice NY, 1983—98; conciliator, acting judge Workers Compensation Bd., NY, 1992—98, judge, 1998—; judge assigned to World Trade Ctr. 9/11 cases, 2002. Organizer/incorporator Ithaca (N.Y.) Reform Temple, 1992; organizer Parents Without Partners, Ithaca, 1992. Recipient Pro Bono Svc. award Suffolk County Bar Assn., 1986. Home: 14 Grant St Port Dickinson Binghamton NY 13901 Office: Workers Compensation Bd 44 Hawley St Binghamton NY 13901-4434 E-mail: adam.regenbogen@wcb.state.ny.us.

REGENSTREIF, HERBERT, lawyer; b. N.Y.C., May 13, 1935; s. Max and Jeannette (Hacker) R.; m. Patricia Friedman, Dec. 20, 1967 (div. July 1968); m. Charlotte Lois Levy, Dec. 11, 1980 (div. Sept. 2002); 1 child, Cara Rachael. BA, Hobart Coll., 1957; JD, N.Y. Law Sch., 1960; MS, Pratt Inst., 1985. Bar: N.Y. 1961, Ky. 1985, U.S. Dist. Ct. (ea. and so. dists.) N.Y. 1962, U.S. Dist. Ct. (ea. dist.) Ky. 1998, U.S. Tax Ct. 1967, U.S. Ct. Appeals (2d cir.) 1962, U.S. Supreme Ct. 1967. Ptnr. Fried & Regenstreif, P.C., Mineola, N.Y., 1963—; reservist atty. Fed. Emergency Mgmt. Agy., 1998-99. Cons. in field; arbitrator Dist. Ct., Nassau County, N.Y., 1989—, N.Y.C. Civil Ct., 1984-86; sec.-treas. Sta. WAHY-FM, Inc., 1998-2000. Contbr. articles to profl. jours. County committeeman Dem. Com., Queens County, N.Y., 1978-79. Mem. Bar Assn. Nassau County, Ky. Bar Assn., Phi Delta Phi, Beta Phi Mu, Hobart Club of N.Y. (gov. 1968-69). General practice, Religion, Property, real (including real estate development, water).

REGNIER, JAMES, state supreme court justice; b. Aurora, Ill., July 22, 1944; m. Linda Regnier; 3 children. BS, Marquette U., 1966; JD, U. Ill., 1973. Judicial Fellow ACTL, Internat. Soc. Barristers; completed atty. mediator tng., Atty.-Mediator Tng. Inst., Dallas, 1993. Lawyer pvt. practice, Rochelle, Ill., 1973-78; co-founder, ptnr. Regnier, Lewis and Boland, Great Falls, Mont., 1979-91; lawyer pvt. practice, Missoula, Mont., 1991-97; justice Mont. Supreme Ct., Helena, 1997—. Appt. Mont. Supreme Ct. Commn. on Civil Jury Instrn.; appt. lawyer-rep. to 9th Cir. Judicial Confs., 1987, 88, 89, chair Mont. lawyer delegation, 1989; lectr. U. Mont. Sch. Law, numerous continuing legal edn. seminars. Contbr. Mont. Pattern Jury Instrns. for Civil Cases, 1985. Co-founder Mont. chpt. Am. Bd. Trial Advocates, 1989—, pres. Officer USN, Vietnam. Office: Montana Supreme Ct Justice Bldg 215 N Sanders St Helena MT 59601-4522 also: PO Box 203001 Helena MT 59620-3001

REHBOCK, RICHARD ALEXANDER, lawyer; b. New Haven, Sept. 12, 1946; s. Morton J. and Evelyn (Norris) R.; m. Nanette DiFalco, June 5, 1997; 1 stepchild: Gregory. BA, Fairleigh Dickinson U., 1968; JD, St. John's U., 1973. Bar: N.Y. 1974, U.S. Dist. Ct. (ea. and so. dists.) N.Y. 1974, U.S. Ct. Appeals (2d cir.) 1977, U.S. Ct. Appeals (3d cir.) 1996, U.S. Supreme Ct. 1978, U.S. Dist. Ct. (we. dist.) N.Y. 1983, Fla. 1987. Atty. criminal divsn. Legal Aid Soc., N.Y.C., 1973-77; staff atty. U.S. Dist. Ct. N.Y. Legal Aid Soc., Bklyn., 1977-79; ptnr. Rehbock, Fishman & Kudisch, Kew Gardens, N.Y., 1979-83; pvt. practice law N.Y.C., 1983—. Staff sgt. U.S. Army, 1969-70, Vietnam. Fellow Am. Bd. Criminal Lawyers; mem. Criminal Ct. Bar Assn. (bd. dirs. Queens County chpt.), Am. Trial Lawyers Assn., Nat. Assn. Criminal Def. Attys. (vice chmn legis. com.), Nat. Assn. Trial Attys., Fed. Bar Coun., N.Y. State Bar Assn., Queens Bar Assn., N.Y. County Lawyers Assn., N.Y. State Assn. Criminal Def. Attys. (chair fed. legis com.), Fla. Bar Assn. Federal civil litigation, Commercial, contracts (including sales of goods; commercial financing), Criminal. Home and Office: 1 Maple Run Dr Jericho NY 11753-2827 E-mail: rrehbock@msn.com.

REICH, ALLAN J. lawyer; b. Chgo., July 9, 1948; s. H. Robert and Sonya (Minsky) R.; m. Lynne Susan Roth, May 23, 1971; children: Allison, Marissa, Scott. BA, Cornell U., 1970; JD cum laude, U. Mich., 1973. Bar: Ill. 1973, U.S. Dist. Ct. (no. dist.) Ill. 1973. Ptnr. McDermott, Will & Emery, Chgo., 1973-93; vice chmn. D'Ancona & Pflaum LLC, Chgo., 1993—. Trustee Oakmark Family of Mutual Funds, 1994—. V.p., mem. exec. com. Coun. for Jewish Elderly, 1989—97; mem. men's coun. Mus. Contemporary Art, Chgo., 1988—89; mem. Chgo. exec. bd. Am. Jewish Com., 1989—, nat. bd. govs.; mem. met. Chgo. bd. Am. Heart Assn.; bd. dirs. Young Men's Jewish Coun., Chgo., 1974—84, Coun. for Jewish Elderly, 1986—97. Fellow: Am. Bar Found.; mem.: ABA, Chgo. Bar Assn., Econ. Club Chgo., Northmoor Country Club (Highland Park, Ill.), Standard Club (Chgo.). Corporate, general, Finance, Securities. Home: 936 Skokie Ridge Dr Glencoe IL 60022-1434 Office: D'Ancona & Pflaum LLC 111 E Wacker Dr Chicago IL 60601-3713 E-mail: areich@dancona.com.

REICH, LARRY SAM, lawyer; b. Bklyn., Sept. 24, 1946; s. Sidney and Regina (Brown) R.; children: Ilysa Jill, Shari Beth; m. Marcia S. Koltun, Mar. 17, 2002. BA, Hofstra U., 1969; JD, Bklyn. Law Sch., 1973. Bar: N.Y. 1974, U.S. Dist. Ct. (so. and ea. dists.) N.Y. 1974, U.S. Ct. Appeals (2d cir.) 1974, U.S. Ct. Appeals (3d cir.) 2002, U.S. Supreme Ct. 1980. Assoc. S. Edward Orenstein PC, N.Y.C., 1973-78; ptnr. Herzfeld & Rubin PC, N.Y.C., 1978-98, Blank Rome LLP, N.Y.C., 1999—. Arbitrator U.S. Dist. Ct. for Ea. Dist. N.Y., Bklyn., 1986—; mem. guest faculty Hofstra U. Sch. Law, 1994—. Mem. ABA, N.Y. State Bar Assn. (chmn. com. on supreme cts. 1986-89, chmn. com. on jud. adminstrn. 1989-92, com. jud. adminstrn. 1989-94), N.Y. County Bar Assn., Nassau County Bar Assn., Assn. Trial Lawyers Am., N.Y. State Trial Lawyers Assn. Avocations: running, rowing, biking, reading. Federal civil litigation, State civil litigation. Office: Blank Rome LLP The Chrysler Bldg New York NY 10174

REICH, PETER LESTER, legal educator, legal and historical consultant; b. L.A., Mar. 20, 1955; s. Jack Edward and Lillian (Lerner) R.; m. Alisa Schulweis, Sept. 8, 1985; children: Gabriel, Eli. BA in History, UCLA, 1976, PhD in History, 1991; JD, U. Calif., Berkeley, 1985. Bar: Calif. 1985, U.S. Dist. Ct. (ctrl. dist.) Calif. 1986. Rsch. atty. Calif. Ct. Appeal, Ventura, 1985-86; assoc. Parker, Milliken et al, L.A., 1986-88; asst. prof. law Whittier Law Sch., L.A., 1988-91, assoc. prof. law, 1991-93, prof. law Costa Mesa, Calif., 1993—. Vis. prof. of history U. Calif., Irvine, 1999—2003. Author: Mexico's Hidden Revolution, 1995; mem. editl. bd. Western Legal History, 1995—; contbr. articles to profl. jours. Recipient Hubert Herring Meml. award Pacific Coast Coun. on Latin Am. Studies, 1991, Ray A. Billington award Western History Assn., 1995; Fulbright-Hays fellow, 1979-80; Rocky Mountain Mineral Law Found. rsch. grantee, 1993, 95, 99; Huntington Libr. fellow Andrew Mellon Found., 1997. Mem. Am. Soc. for Legal History, Assn. Am. Law Scs. (sec.-treas. immigration sect., treas. legal history sect.), Calif. Supreme Ct. Hist. Soc. Democrat. Jewish. Avocations: sea kayaking, hiking, ice skating. Office: Whittier Law Sch 3333 Harbor Blvd Costa Mesa CA 92626-1501

REICH, WILLIAM ZEEV, lawyer; b. Tel Aviv, Oct. 5, 1947; came to U.S., 1958; s. Louis and Helen (Skura) R.; children: Eric, Justin, Zabrina, Aviva. BA, Queens Coll., CUNY, 1969; JD, SUNY, Buffalo, 1974. Bar: N.Y. 1974, U.S. Supreme Ct. 1980. Assoc. Serotte, Reich & Harasym, Buffalo, 1974-76; ptnr. Serotte, Reich, & Seipp, Buffalo, 1976—. Mem. ABA, N.Y. State Bar Assn., Erie County Bar Assn., Am. Immigration Lawyers Assn. (treas. Upstate chpt. 1982—, overseas practice com. 1984—, nat. liaison com. 1997). Immigration, naturalization, and customs. Home: 467 N Forest Rd Buffalo NY 14221-5036 Office: Serotte Reich & Seipp 300 Delaware Ave Ste 4 Buffalo NY 14202-1807

REICHBACH, GUSTIN LEWIS, state supreme court justice; b. Bklyn., Oct. 9, 1946; s. Herman and Lee (Klein) R.; m. Ellen Meyers, Oct. 24, 1984; 1 child, Hope Isadora. BA in Polit. Sci. with high honors(hon.) , SUNY, Buffalo, 1967; JD, Columbia U., 1970. Bar: N.Y. 1972, U.S. Dist. Ct. (ea. and so. dists.) N.Y. 1972, Calif. 1975, U.S. Dist. Ct. (ea. and no. dists.) Calif. 1975, U.S. Supreme Ct. 1984. Pvt. practice, NY, 1972-90, 1975-90; judge Civil Ct. City of N.Y., Bklyn., 1991-98; justice Supreme Ct. N.Y., Bklyn., 1998—. Counsel to commr. Calif. Agrl. Labor Rels. Bd., Sacramento, 1975-76. Co-author: The Bust Book, 1970, (Grove Press, NY); Litigating Electronic Surveillance Claims in Criminal Cases, 1977. (Lakes Law Books, S.F.) Recipient David Michael award N.Y. State Bar Assn., 1992. Mem. Phi Beta Kappa. Office: Supreme Ct State NY 120 Schermerhorn St Brooklyn NY 11201-5108

REICHE, FRANK PERLEY, lawyer, former federal commissioner; b. Hartford, Conn., May 8, 1929; s. Karl Augustus and LaFetra (Perley) R.; m. Janet Taylor, Sept. 26, 1953; children: Cynthia Reiche Schumacker, Dean S. AB, Williams Coll., 1951; LLB, Columbia U., 1959; MA, George Washington U., 1959; LLM in Taxation, NYU, 1966. Bar: N.J. 1960, D.C. 1981. Assoc. Stryker, Tams & Dill, Newark, 1959-61, Smith, Stratton, Wise & Heher, Princeton, NJ, 1962-64, ptnr., 1964-79; commr. Fed. Election Commn., Washington, 1979-85, chmn., 1982; ptnr. Katzenbach, Gildea & Rudner, Lawrenceville, NJ, 1986-93; pvt. practice law Princeton, 1993-97; of counsel Schragger, Lavine & Nagy, West Trenton, NJ, 1997-2000, Archer & Greiner, Princeton, 2001—. Trustee Westminster Choir Coll., Princeton, 1974-86, Ctr. Theol. Inquiry, Princeton, 1991-97, Wells Coll., Aurora, N.Y., 1994—; mem. planned giving com. Williams Coll., Williamstown, Mass., 1973-87, nat. chmn. planned giving, 1983-87; dir., Ctr. Responsive Politics, Washington, 2002—. Lt. USN, 1952-56. Mem. ABA, D.C. Bar Assn., N.J. Bar Assn., Am. Coll. Trust and Estate Counsel (N.J. state chair 1995-2000, bd. regents 2001—). Clubs: Washington Golf and Country, Capitol Hill. Republican. Presbyterian. Estate planning, Probate (including wills, trusts), Estate taxation.

REICHEL, AARON ISRAEL, lawyer, rabbi, editor; b. N.Y.C., Jan. 30, 1950; s. Oscar Asher and Josephine Hannah (Goldstein) R. BA, Yeshiva U., 1971, MA, 1974; JD, Fordham U., 1976. Bar: N.J. 1977, N.Y. 1978; ordained rabbi, 1975. Atty. editor Securities Regulation Prentice-Hall, Englewood Cliffs, N.J., 1977-78, editor, founder govt. disclosure service Paramus, N.J., 1978-82, atty. editor fed. taxation, 1982-89; tech. editor Warren, Gorham & Lamont, Practical Acct., N.Y.C., 1989-90; assoc. Firm A. Edward Major, N.Y.C., 1990-91, Firm Allen L. Rothenberg, N.Y.C., 1991-93; pvt. practice N.Y.C., 1993—. Author: The Maverick Rabbi, 1984, 2d edit. 1986, Back to the Past for Inspiration for the Future—West Side Institutional Synagogue Jubilee 1937-87, 1987; co-author (manual) Style and Usage, 1984; contbr. The 1986 Jewish Directory and Almanac, 1986, The 1987-88 Jewish Almanac, 1988; contbg. editor Complete Guide to the Tax Reform Act of 1986, Prentice-Hall's Explanation of the Tax Reform Act of 1986, 1986, Prentice Hall's Complete Guide to the Tax Law of 1987, 1988, Prentice Hall's Explanation of the Technical & Miscellaneous Revenue Act of 1988, 1988, Guide to Equal Employment Practices, 1997; contbr. articles to profl. jours. Bd. dirs. Union Orthodox Jewish Congregations Am., N.Y.C., 1973-74, Harry and Jane Fischel Found., N.Y.C., 1977—, West Side Instl. Synagogue, 1987-98, Amalgamated Dwellings, Inc., 1992-96; nat. pres. YAVNEH, N.Y.C., 1973-74; mem. youth commn. Am. Jewish Congress, N.Y.C., 1973-76. Mem. ABA, N.Y. State Bar Assn. (various coms.), N.Y. County Lawyers Assn. (various coms.), Am. Soc. Access Profls. (founder, 1st chmn. N.Y. chpt.), Nat. Jewish Commn. on Law and Pub. Affairs (family law com.), Yeshiva U. Alumni Assn. (exec. com. 1971-87, editor-in-chief Bull. 1974-78). Avocations: writing, baseball, tennis, compiling proverbs. Civil rights, General practice, Personal injury (including property damage). Home: 83-28 Abingdon Rd Kew Gardens NY 11415-1714

REICHERT, DAVID, lawyer; b. Cin., Nov. 23, 1929; s. Victor E. and Louise F. Reichert; m. Marilyn Frankel, May 31, 1959; children— James G., Steven F., William M. BA, Bowling Green State U., 1951; JD, U. Cin., 1954. Bar: Ohio 1954, U.S. Supreme Ct. 1963. Ptnr. firm Porter, Wright, Morris & Arthur, formerly sr. ptnr. Reichert, Strauss & Reed and predecessors, Cin. Dir. numerous corps. Monthly columnist: Scrap Age mag, 1966-74; bd. editors: U. Cin. Law Rev, 1953-54. Pres. brotherhood Rockdale Temple, Cin., 1960-61, temple treas., 1973-75, v.p., 1975-79, pres., 1979-81; mem. Amberley Village Planning Commn. & Zoning Bd. Appeals, 1972-79, Ohio Solid Waste Adv. Group, 1974; treas. Contemporary Arts Ctr., Cin., 1973-75, pres., 1976-77, trustee, 1982-88; trustee Cin. Art Mus., 1978-93, v.p., 1992-93, chmn. vis. com. for contemporary art, 1990-92; trustee Jewish Publ. Soc., 1980-86, Cin. Sculpture Coun., 1984-87; mem. acquisitions com. Miami U. Art Mus., 1982-85. Mem. Cin. Print and Drawing Cir. (pres. 1974-76), The Literary Club (sec. 1988-91, v.p. 1991-92, pres. 1992-93), Losantiville Country Club (bd. govs. 1985-92, sec. 1986-90, pres. 1990-92), ISRI 20th Century Club (hon. 1998), Omicron Delta Kappa, Sigma Tau Delta, Phi Delta Phi, Zeta Beta Tau. Office: Porter Wright Morris & Arthur 250 E 5th St Ste 2200 Cincinnati OH 45202-5177

REICHGOTT JUNGE, EMBER D. small business owner, former state senator, lawyer, writer, broadcast analyst, radio personality; b. Detroit, Aug. 22, 1953; d. Norbert Arnold and Diane (Pincich) Reichgott; m. Michael Junge. BA summa cum laude, St. Olaf Coll., Minn., 1974; JD, Duke U., 1977; MBA, U. St. Thomas, 1991. Bar: Minn. 1977, D.C. 1978. Assoc. Larkin, Hoffman, Daly & Lindgren, Bloomington, Minn., 1977-84; counsel Control Data Corp., Bloomington, Minn., 1984-86; ptnr. The Gen. Counsel, Ltd., 1987—; mem. Minn. State Senate, 1983-2000, chmn. legis. com. on econ. status of women, 1984-86, vice chmn. senate edn. com., 1987-88, senate majority whip, 1990-94, chmn. property tax divsn. senate tax com., 1991-92, chmn. senate judiciary com., 1993-94, senate asst. majority leader, 1995-2000, chmn. spl. subcom. on ethical conduct; pres. Video on Wings, video to web co., Mpls., 2000—. Dem. endorsed candidate Minn. Atty.

Gen., 1998; instr. polit. sci. St. Olaf Coll., Northfield, Minn., 1993; bd. dirs. Citizens Ind. Bank, St. Louis Park, Minn. Host cable TV monthly series Legis. Report, 1985-92. State co-chair Clinton/Gore Presdl. Campaign, Minn. Dem. Farmer-Labor Party, 1992, 1996; del. Nat. Dem. Conv., 1984, 1992, 1996; trustee, bd. dirs. N.W. YMCA, New Hope, Minn., 1983—88, United Way Mpls., 1989—, Greater Mpls. ARC, 1988—, chair, 2001—03. Recipient Woman of Yr. award North Hennepin Bus. and Profl. Women, 1983, award for contbn. to human svcs. Minn. Social Svcs. Assn., 1983, Clean Air award Minn. Lung Assn., 1988, Disting. Svc. award Mpls. Jaycees, 1984, Minn. Dept. Human Rights award, 1989, Myra Bradwell award Minn. Women Lawyers, 1993, Disting. Alumnae award Lake Conf. Schs., 1993, Disting. Alumnae award St. Olaf Coll., 1998, awards for leadership Am. Lung Assn., 1999, Am. Heart Assn., 1997, Everyday Hero award Up with People, 1995, Unsung Hero award United Way of Mpls., 1999, 1st recipient of award named in her honor for prevention of sexual assault, 2000; charter inductee Robbinsdale H.S. Hall of Fame, 2000; author of Minn. charter sch. law, winner of "2000 Innovations in Am. Govt." award Harvard U. and Ford Found., others; named One of ten Outstanding Young Minnesotans, Minn. Jaycees, 1984, Policy Advocate of Yr., NAWBO, 1988, Woman of Achievement, Twin West C. of C., 1989, Marvelous Minn. Woman, 1993; youngest woman ever elected to Minn. Senate, 1983. Mem. Minn. Bar Assn. (bd. govs. 1992-96, Pro Bono Publico Atty. award 1990), Hennepin County Bar Assn., Corp. Counsel Assn. (v.p. 1989-96); pres. Minn. Women's Political Caucus, 2002-. Home: 7701 48th Ave N Minneapolis MN 55428-4515 Fax: 763-536-1447. E-mail: emberrj@msn.com.

REICIN, RONALD IAN, lawyer; b. Chgo., Dec. 11, 1942; s. Frank Edward and Abranita (Rome) R.; m. Alyta Friedland, May 23, 1965; children: Eric, Kael. BBA, U. Mich., 1964, MBA, JD cum laude, U. Mich., 1967. Bar: Ill. 1967, U.S. Tax Ct. 1967; CPA, Ill. Mem. staff Price Waterhouse & Co., Chgo., 1966; ptnr. Jenner & Block, Chgo., 1967—. Bd. dirs. Nat. Kidney Found., Ill., 1978—, v.p., 1992-95, pres., 1995-98; bd. dirs. Ruth Page Found., 1985—, v.p., 1990—; bd. dirs. Scoliosis Assn. Chgo., 1981-90, Kohl Children's Mus., 1991-95, River North Chgo. Dance Co., 1999—. Mem.: Ill. State Bar Assn., Chgo. Mortgage Attys. Assn., Chgo. Bar Assn., ABA, Lawyers Club (Chgo.), Exec. Club, Beta Alpha Psi, Beta Gamma Sigma, Phi Kappa Phi. Corporate, general, General practice, Property, real (including real estate development, water). Office: Jenner & Block LLC 1 E IBM Plz Fl 38 Chicago IL 60611-3586 E-mail: rreicin@jenner.com.

REID, CHARLES ADAMS, III, lawyer; b. Plainfield, N.J., Apr. 21, 1947; s. Charles Adams Jr. and Gertrude C. (Egan) R.; m. Teresa Keenan, May 11, 1974. BA, Colgate U., 1969; JD, Columbia U., 1974. Bar: N.Y. 1974, N.J. 1976, U.S. Ct. Appeals (3d cir.) 1983, U.S. Ct. Appeals (fed. cir.) 1989, U.S. Ct. Appeals (2d cir.) 1991, U.S. Ct. Appeals (9th cir.) 2002, Calif. 2002. Law clk. to hon. John R. Bartels U.S. Dist. Ct. (ea. dist.) N.Y., Bklyn., 1974-75; assoc. Coudert Bros., N.Y.C., 1975-77, Shanley & Fisher, Newark, 1977-82, ptnr. Newark and Morristown, N.J., 1983-99, Drinker Biddle & Reath LLP, Florham Park, N.J. and San Francisco, 1999—. Mem. planning bd. Peapack-Gladstone, N.J., 1984-88, chmn., 1987-88; bd. dirs. Morris Ctr. YMCA, Cedar Knolls, N.J., 1986-93. Served with U.S. Army, 1970-72, Vietnam. Mem. ABA (litigation sect.), N.J. Bar Assn., Morris County Bar Assn., Essex County Bar Assn., Calif. State Bar, Park Avenue Club (Florham Park). General civil litigation, Insurance, Pension, profit-sharing, and employee benefits. Home: 1150 Greenwich St Apt 3 San Francisco CA 94107 Office: Drinker Biddle & Reath LLP 500 Campus Dr Florham Park NJ 07932-1047 also: Drinker Biddle & Reath LLP 225 Bush St, 15th Fl San Francisco CA 94104

REID, EDWARD SNOVER, III, lawyer; b. Detroit, Mar. 24, 1930; s. Edward S. Jr. and Margaret (Overington) Reid; m. Carroll Grylls, Dec. 30, 1953; children: Carroll Reid Highet, Richard Gerveys, Jane Reid McTigue, Margaret Reid Boyer. BA, Yale U., 1951; LL.B. magna cum laude (Sheldon fellow), Harvard U., 1956. Bar: Mich. 1957, N.Y. 1958, D.C. 1982, Gaikokuho jimu-bengoshi, Tokyo 1991-96. Assoc. Davis, Polk & Wardwell, N.Y.C., 1957-64, partner, 1964-95, sr. counsel, 1996—; dir. Gen. Mills, Inc., 1974-89. Mem. N.Y.C. Bd. Higher Edn., 1971—73; trustee Bklyn. Inst. Arts and Scis., 1966—93, chmn., 1974—79; trustee Bklyn. Mus. Art, 1973—93, 1994—; bd. dirs. Bklyn. Bot. Garden Corp., 1977—92, 1996—, Bargemusic Ltd., 1990—93. Active duty USMCR, 1951—53. Mem. ABA, N.Y. State Bar Assn., Assn. of Bar of City of N.Y., Am. Law Inst., Internat. Bar Assn., Heights Casino Club, Rembrandt Club, Century Assn. Club, Yale Club, Quoque Beach Club, Shinnecock Yacht Club, Quoque Field Club. Corporate, general, Mergers and acquisitions, Securities. Home: PO Box 39 Quogue NY 11959-0039 Office: Davis Polk & Wardwell 450 Lexington Ave New York NY 10017-3982 E-mail: ereid@dpw.com.

REID, INEZ SMITH, lawyer, educator; b. New Orleans, Apr. 7, 1937; d. Sidney Randall Dickerson and Beatrice Virginia (Bundy) Smith. BA, Tufts U., 1959; LLB, Yale U., 1962; MA, UCLA, 1963; PhD, Columbia U., 1968. Bar: Calif. 1963, N.Y. 1972, D.C. 1980. Assoc. prof. Barnard Coll. Columbia U., N.Y.C., 1972-76; gen. counsel youth divsn. State of N.Y., 1976-77; dep. gen. counsel HEW, Washington, 1977-79; inspector gen. EPA, Washington, 1979-81; chief legis. and opinions, dep. corp. counsel Office of Corp. Counsel, Washington, 1981-83; corp. counsel D.C., 1983-85; counsel Laxalt, Washington, Perito & Dubuc, Washington, 1986-90, ptnr., 1990-91; counsel Graham & James, 1991-93, Lewis, White & Clay, P.C., 1994-95; assoc. judge D.C. Ct. Appeals, 1995—. William J. Maier, Jr. vis. prof. law W.Va. U. Coll. Law, Morgantown, 1985-86. Contbr. articles to profl. jours. and publs. Trustee emeritus Lancaster Sem., Pa., 2002—; bd. dirs. Homeland Ministries bd. United Ch. of Christ, N.Y.C., 1978—83, vice chmn., 1981—83; chmn. bd. govs. Antioch Law Sch., Washington, 1979—81; chmn. bd. trustees Antioch U., Yellow Springs, Ohio, 1981—82; trustee Tufts U., Medford, Mass., 1988—98, trustee emeritus, 1999—; trustee Lancaster (Pa.) Sem., 1988—2001; bd. govs. D.C. Sch. Law, 1990—96, chmn., 1991—95. Recipient Emily Gregory award Barnard Coll., 1976, Arthur Morgan award Antioch U., 1982, Service award United Ch. of Christ, 1983, Disting. Service (Profl. Life) award Tufts U. Alumni Assn., 1988. General civil litigation, Constitutional, Corporate, general. Office: DC Ct Appeals 500 Indiana Ave NW Fl 6 Washington DC 20001-2138

REID, LORINE MAY, lawyer; b. Toledo, Ohio, Apr. 29, 1932; d. Edwin McKechnie and Eleanora Mary (DeMars) R. B.A. in Speech, Wayne State U., 1958; M. Social Work, U. Mich., 1965; J.D., U. Toledo, 1969. Bar: Ohio 1973. Exec. dir. Mental Health Bd., 1970-72; planning dir. Pilot Cities Project, Dayton, Ohio, 1972-75; sole practice, Dayton, 1974-88; asst. prosecutor Montgomery County, Ohio, 1988-99; ret., 1999; legal dir. Childrens Service Bd., 1977-81; tchr. U. Dayton, 1977-80. Citizens adv. bd. Dayton Mental Health Ctr., 1978-85. Recipient Mental Health Service award Gov. of Ohio, 1984. Mem. Dayton Women Voters League, ABA, Ohio State Bar Assn., Dayton Bar Assn., Nat. Assn. Women Lawyers. Democrat. Club: Altrusa Internat. (pres. 1985—). Avocation: community theatre.

REID, RUST ENDICOTT, lawyer; b. NYC, Dec. 31, 1931; Atty. firm Thompson & Knight, Dallas. Trustee Child Care Group, Dallas, 1968-72, 1996-2002, Hockaday Sch., Dallas, 1972-82, chmn., 1976-78; trustee Tex. coun. Girl Scouts U.S.A., 1982-83, Vis. Nurse Assn., Dallas, 1984-93, chmn., 1991-93; trustee Grace Presbyn. Village Fedn., 1996—. Lt. (j.g.) USNR, 1954-57. Fellow Am. Coll. Probate Counsel; mem. Tex. Bar Found., Dallas Estate Planning Coun. (pres. 1988-89). Estate planning, Probate (including wills, trusts), Personal income taxation. Office: Thompson & Knight 1700 Pacific 1700 Pacific 3300 Dallas TX 75201 Home: 6715 Golf Dr Dallas TX 75205-1213

REIDENBERG, JOEL R. law educator; AB in Govt., Dartmouth, 1983; JD, Columbia U., 1986; DEA, U. Paris-Sorbonne, 1987, Doctorat en droit, 2003. Bar: N.Y. 1986, D.C. 1988. Friedmann fellow PROMETHEE, Paris, 1986-87; assoc. Debevoise & Plimpton, Washington, 1987-90; prof. law Fordham U. Sch. Law, N.Y.C., 1990—, dir. grad. program, 1998—2001. Cons. FTC, Washington, 1997-99; expert advisor European Commn., Luxembourg, 1993-96, Brussels, 1997-98. Co-author: Data Privacy Law, 1996, Online Services and Data Protection and Privacy: Regulatory Responses, 1998; contbr. articles to profl. jours. Mem. Assn. Am. Law Schs. (chair sect. law and computers 1997, chair sect. defamation and privacy 1998). Fax: 212-636-6899.

REIFLER, STEWART, lawyer; b. Poughkeepsie, N.Y., May 5, 1954; s. Aaron and Sally Reifler; m. Sheryl Louise Perry, Sept. 19, 1982; 1 child, Jonathan Perry. Student, McGill U., 1972—75; BA, Bard Coll., 1979; JD magna cum laude, NY Law Sch., 1992. Bar: N.Y. 1992, Conn. 1992, U.S. Tax Ct. 1992. Assoc. Law Offices of Joseph E. Bachelder, N.Y.C., 1992—95, Weil, Gotshal & Manges, 1995—98; dir. PricewaterhouseCoopers, 1998—2001; ptnr. Vedder, Price, Kaufman & Kammholz, 2001—. Steering com. mem., exec. compensation AICPA. Contbr. articles to profl. jours. Trustee Westport Pub. Libr., Conn. Recipient Outstanding Editl. Contbn., NY Law Sch. Law Rev., 1991, Law Rev., NY Law Sch., Am. Jurisprudence award, 1991. Mem.: ABA, N.Y. State Bar Assn., Conn. State Bar Assn., Assn. of Bar of City of N.Y., WorldatWork, Nat. Assn. Stock Plan Profls., Minuteman Yacht Club, The Sky Club. Pension, profit-sharing, and employee benefits, Taxation, general, Mergers and acquisitions, executive compensation. Home: 8 Brightfield Ln Westport CT 06880 Office: Vedder Price Kaufman & Kammholz 805 Third Ave New York NY 10022 E-mail: sreifler@vedderprice.com.

REILLY, CHARLES JAMES, lawyer, educator, accountant; b. Pawtucket, R.I., Oct. 10, 1950; s. Thomas Joseph and Florence Marie (McKenna) R.; m. Barbara Bouffard, Aug. 7, 1971; children: Kristen, Elizabeth. BSBA, Providence Coll., 1972; JD, Suffolk U., 1979. Bar: R.I. 1979, U.S. Dist. Ct. R.I. 1979, U.S. Ct. Appeals (1st cir.) 1979, U.S. Supreme Ct. 1984, U.S. Ct. Claims, 1985; CPA, R.I. Agt. IRS, Providence, 1972-75; appellate conferee U.S. Dept. Treasury, Boston, 1976-81; ptnr. Arcaro & Reilly, Providence, 1981-91, Reilly Law Assocs., Providence, 1991—. Assoc. prof. Grad. MST program Bryant Coll., Smithfield, R.I., 1983—. Mem. AICPA, R.I. Soc. CPAs, ABA, R.I. Bar Assn. (chair tax sect. 1996-2000). Clubs: R.I. Country. Democrat. Roman Catholic. Avocation: golf. Corporate taxation, Personal income taxation, State and local taxation. Office: Reilly Law Assocs 1040 Turks Head Bldg Providence RI 02903 E-mail: reillylaw1@aol.com.

REILLY, CONOR DESMOND, lawyer; b. Kansas City, Mo., Feb. 12, 1952; s. Desmond M. and Patricia (Carton) R.; m. Margaret M. Cannella, June 8, 1975; children: Katherine C., Michael C. BS, MIT, 1972; JD cum laude, Harvard U., 1975. Bar: N.Y. 1976, U.S. Dist. Ct. (ea. and so. dists.) N.Y. 1976, U.S. Ct. Appeals (2d. cir.) 1977, U.S. Dist. Ct. (D.C. cir.) 1979, U.S. Dist. Ct. (no. dist.) Calif. 1981, U.S. Dist. Ct. (cen. dist.) Calif. 1982. Law clk. to judge U.S. Dist. Ct. (ea. dist.), Bklyn., 1975-76; assoc. Cravath, Swaine & Moore, N.Y.C., 1976-77, Coudert Bros., N.Y.C., 1977-83, LeBoeuf, Lamb, Leiby & MacRae, N.Y.C., 1983-84, ptnr., 1985-88, Gibson, Dunn & Crutcher, N.Y.C., 1988—. Vice-chmn Memorex-Telex N.V., 1988-90; chmn. bd. dirs. Acorn Products Inc., 1996-99. Editor Harvard U. Law Rev., 1973-74. Hearing officer N.Y.C. Bd. Edn., 1977-79; elected mem. Millburn Twp. Bd. Edn., 1987-92. Mem. ABA, Am. Arbitration Assn. (arbitrator). Democrat. Avocation: tennis. Bankruptcy, Corporate, general, Insurance. Home: 62 Joanna Way Short Hills NJ 07078-3241 Office: Gibson Dunn & Crutcher 200 Park Ave Fl 47 New York NY 10166-0193

REILLY, DANIEL M. lawyer, educator, arbitrator; b. Groton, Conn., Mar. 21, 1953; s. Daniel R. and Rosalind T. Reilly; m. Mary J. Kelly, June 13, 1981; children: Michael, Kathleen, Daniel. BA, Mich. State U., 1975; JD, U. Denver, 1981. Bar: Colo. 1981, U.D. Dist. Ct. Colo. 1981, U.S. Ct. Appeals (10th cir.) 1983, U.S. Supreme Ct., N.Mex., Ariz., Wash., Oregon, Utah, Minn., Iowa, Wyoming, Mont., S.D., N.D., Calif., U.S. Dist. Ct. (no. dist.) Iowa, U.S. Dist. Ct. (no. dist.) Fla. Atty. McDermott, Hansen and Reilly, Denver, 1981—95, McKenna and Cuneo, LLP, Denver, 1995—2000, Hoffman Reilly Pozner and Williamson LLP, Denver, 2000—. Arbitrator in field; guest lectr. in field; mem. faculty, lectr. trial expert witness, demonstrative evidence, tactics and advocacy skills Nat. Inst. Trial Advocacy; lectr. U. Colo. Sch. Law; lectr. conf. Colo. Jud. Conf., 2000, 01, 02. Recipient Moot Ct. Barrister's Cup Disting. Achievement in Oral Advocacy. Mem.: ABA (tort and ins. practice sect.), William E. Doyle Am. Inns of Ct. (founding mem., past pres.), Colo. Trial Lawyers Assn. (lectr. seminars), Am. Bd. Trial Advocates, Am. Coll. Trial Lawyers, Denver Bar Assn. (cert., lectr.), Colo. Bar. Assn. (lectr. ann. litig. symposium 2001, 2002, cert.). Avocations: running, basketball, surfing. Insurance, Personal injury (including property damage), Commercial, contracts (including sales of goods; commercial financing). Office: Hoffman Reilly Pozner & Williamson LLP 511 16th St Ste 700 Denver CO 80202 Fax: 303-893-6110. E-mail: dreilly@hrpwlaw.com.

REILLY, EDWARD ARTHUR, lawyer; b. N.Y.C., Dec. 17, 1943; s. Edward Arthur and Anna Marguerite (Sautter) R.; children: M. Teresa, Edward A. AB, Princeton U., 1965; JD, Duke U., 1968. Bar: N.Y. 1969, N.C. 1971, Fla. 1979, Conn. 1983. Asst. dean law sch. Duke U., 1970-72; assoc. Shearman & Sterling, N.Y.C., 1972-80, ptnr., 1980-87, Harlow, Reilly, Derr & Stark, Research Triangle Park, N.C., 1988-90; counsel Morris & McVeigh, N.Y.C., 1991-93, ptnr., 1993—. Pres. Am. Friends of Paris Opera and Ballet, Inc.; sec. The Camille and Henry Dreyfus Found., Inc.; sec. The Owen Cheatham Found. Decorated Chevalier de l'Ordre des Arts et des Lettres, French Govt.-Ministry of Culture and Comm., 1992. Fellow Am. Coll. Trust & Estate Counsel; mem. N.Y. State Bar Assn., Fla. Bar Assn., Conn. Bar Assn. Episcopalian. Non-profit and tax-exempt organizations, Probate (including wills, trusts), Estate taxation. Office: Morris & McVeigh 767 3rd Ave New York NY 10017-2023 Home: 5 Old Field Pl Norwalk CT 06853-1116

REILLY, FRANCIS X. lawyer, consultant; b. Westborough, Mass., Sept. 18, 1916; s. Francis Xavier and Blanche Marie (Marshall) R.; m. Beverly E. Blackwell, Oct. 7, 1941 (dec. July 1982); children: Martha J. Reilly Hinchman, John F. AB, Dartmouth Coll., 1938; JD, Harvard U., 1941. Bar: Mass. 1941, Ill. 1954. Atty., treas. Wilson & Co., Inc., Chgo., 1963-67; v.p. LTV Corp., Dallas, 1967-70; v.p., treas. B. F. Goodrich Co., Akron, Ohio, 1970-73, Katy Industries, Inc., Elgin, 1973-76; gen. counsel, v.p. Rollins Burdick Hunter, Chgo., 1976-84; pvt. practice law and cons. Barrington, Ill., 1984-99. Lt. comdr. USNR, 1943-46. Mem. ABA, U. Club of Chgo. General practice. Address: The King Home 1555 Oak Ave Apt 202 Evanston IL 60201-4233

REILLY, JOHN B. lawyer; b. Bangor, Maine, Sept. 12, 1947; s. Louis J. and Evelyn I. (Lindsay) R.; children: Carolyn, Bridget. BA, U. R.I., 1970; JD cum laude, Suffolk U., 1976. Bar: R.I. 1976, Mass. 1985, U.S. Dist. Ct. R.I. 1976, U.S. Dist. Ct. Mass. 1985, U.S. Dist. Ct. Conn. 1995, U.S. Claims Ct. 1980, U.S. Ct. Appeals (1st and 2d cirs.) 1984, U.S. Ct. Appeals (3d cir.) 1985, U.S. Supreme Ct. 1983; cert. fraud examiner. Sole practice, Providence, 1976-81, Warwick, RI, 1981-83; sr. ptnr. John Reilly & Assocs. and predecessor firms, Warwick, RI, 1984—89, 2002—, Reilly & Nikolyszyn, LLP, Warwick, RI, 2000—01. Mem. Gov.'s Automobile Ins. Task Force, 1992-93. Mem. ABA, R.I. Bar Assn., Def. Rsch. Inst., R.I. Assn. Auth Theft and Arson Investigators (sec. 1995-96, pres. 1997—), Trucking Ind. Def. Assn., Pi Sigma Alpha, Phi Kappa Psi. General civil litigation, Environmental, Insurance. Home: 80 Paterson Ave Warwick RI 02886-9110 Office: John Reilly & Assocs 300 Centerville Rd Warwick RI 02886-0200 E-mail: jrasoc@gis.net.

REILLY, PATRICK JOHN, lawyer; s. William Henry and Lorraine Marie (De Vito) Reilly; m. Brigid Mary Higgins, Nov. 4, 1995; 1 child, William Henry. BA, U. So. Calif., L.A., 1988; JD, Loyola, L.A., 1996. Bar: Nev. 1996, U.S. Dist. Ct., Nev. 1996, U.S. Ct. of Appeals (ninth cir.) 1998, U.S. Supreme Ct. 2000. Law clk. to dist. ct. judge US Dist. Ct., L.A., 1996—97; shareholder Hale Ln. Peek Dennison and Howard, Las Vegas, 1997—. Federal civil litigation, State civil litigation. Office: Hale Lane Peek Dennison and Howard 2300 West Sahara Ave 8th Fl Las Vegas NV 89102 Office Fax: 702-365-6940. E-mail: preilly@halelane.com.

REILLY, THOMAS F. state attorney general; b. Springfield, Mass. m. Ruth Reilly; 3 children. BA, Am. Internat. Coll., 1964; JD, Boston Coll., 1970. Atty. Civil Rights divsn. Atty. Gen.'s Office; dist. atty. Middlesex County Dist. Atty. Office, 1991—99; atty. gen. State of Mass., Springfield, 1999—. Founder The Cmty. Based Justice Program. Democrat. Office: One Ashburton Pl Boston MA 02108-1698 also: 436 Dwight St Springfield MA 01103 also: One Exchange Place Worcester MA 01608*

REILLY, WILLIAM THOMAS, lawyer; b. Passaic, N.J., Feb. 25, 1949; s. Thomas Edwin and Edna May (Dorritie) R.; m. Sheila Mary Brogan, Aug. 1, 1981; children: Kathleen Anne, Brendan Thomas, Timothy John. BS, Boston Coll., 1971; JD, Harvard U., 1974. Bar: N.J. 1974, U.S. Dist. Ct. N.J. 1974, U.S. Supreme Ct. 1979, U.S. Ct. Appeals (3rd cir.) 1984, U.S. Ct. Claims, 1996, U.S. Ct. Appeals (fed. cir.) 1997. Assoc. McCarter & English LLP, Newark, 1974-81, ptnr., 1982—. Trustee United Hosps. Med. Ctr., Newark, 1983-89, One-to-One/N.J., Inc., 1990-97, chmn., 1993-97. Mem. ABA, N.J. State Bar Assn., Harvard Law Sch. Assn., Eastward Ho Country Club. Avocation: golf. General civil litigation, Federal civil litigation, Professional liability. Home: 302 Kensington Dr Ridgewood NJ 07450-1822 Office: McCarter & English LLP Four Gateway Ctr 100 Mulberry St Newark NJ 07102-4004

REIN, BERT WALTER, lawyer; b. Bklyn., Feb. 7, 1941; s. Moe and Florence (Fishman) R.; m. Jennifer Christine Bulson, July 11, 1966 (dec. Mar. 1989); children: Joanna, Benjamin, Samantha; m. Barbara Jean Kahn, Oct. 18, 1992. BA, Amherst Coll., 1961; LLB, Harvard U., 1964. Bar: D.C. 1965, U.S. Dist. Ct. D.C. 1965, U.S. Ct. Appeals (D.C. cir.) 1968, U.S. Ct. Appeals (2d cir.) 1973, U.S. Ct. Appeals (8th cir.) 1974, U.S. Ct. Appeals (4th cir.) 1976, U.S. Ct. Appeals (11th cir.) 1982, U.S. Supreme Ct. 1982. Law ck. to Justice John M. Harlan U.S. Supreme Ct., Washington, 1966-67; assoc. Kirkland & Ellis, Washington, 1967-69, ptnr., 1973-83; spl. asst. U.S. Dept. State, Washington, 1969-70, dep. asst. sec., 1970-73; ptnr. Wiley, Rein & Fielding, Washington, 1983—. Bd. dirs., chmn. govt. and regulatory affairs com. U.S. C. of C., 1986-90; bd. dirs. Nat. Chamber Litigation Ctr.; advisor Reagan Dept. Justice Transition, Washington, 1980; mem. adv. com. U.S. Sentencing Commn., 1988-89; edn. gen. counsel Comty. Learning and Info. Network, 1992—. Contbr. articles to profl. publs. Mem. Capitol Area adv. bd. Salvation Army. Capt. USAR, 1964-68. Mem. ABA, Am. Law Inst., Internat. Trade Commn. Trial Lawyers Assn. (pres. 1990-91), Internat. Aviation Club. Republican. Jewish. Antitrust, Federal civil litigation, Private international. Home: 6423 Shadow Rd Chevy Chase MD 20815-6613 Office: Wiley Rein & Fielding 1776 K St NW Washington DC 20006-2304 E-mail: brein@wrf.com.

REINER, LEONA HUDAK, consultant, attorney; b. Cleve., Apr. 07; d. Stephen and Anna (Ilko) Hudak; 1 child, Eric. BA, Case Western Res. U.; MA in Libr. Sci., MA in Spanish, U. Wis.; JD, LLM, Cleve. State U., 1971; LLM, Yale U., 1987, D in Jusrisprudential Law, 1991. Bar: Pa. 1973. Pres. Reiner Assocs., New Haven, 1971—, Ctr. for Jud. Accountability, New Haven, 1994—. Author: (book) Early American Women Printers & Publishers, 1978, Lehrnfreiheit: Freedom to Learn, 1991; contbr. articles to profl. jours. Sterling fellow Yale Law Sch., 1981-83, 87-91; Regent's Scholar U. Wis. Mem. Internat. Soc. Needlecrafts (pres.), Phi Beta Kappa, Beta Phi Mu. Avocation: collecting embroidered and needlepoint artwork. Federal civil litigation, Family and matrimonial. Home and Office: 65 Judwin Ave New Haven CT 06515-2312

REINGLASS, MICHELLE ANNETTE, lawyer; b. L.A., Dec. 9, 1954; d. Darwin and Shirley (Steiner) R. Student, U. Calif., Irvine, 1972-75; BSL, Western State U., 1977; JD, Western State U., Coll. Law, 1978. Bar: Calif. 1979, U.S. Dist. Ct. (ctrl. dist.) Calif. 1979, U.S. Ct. Appeals (9th cir.) 1981, U.S. Dist. Ct. (so. dist.) Calif. 1990. Pvt. practice employee litig., Laguna Hills, Calif., 1979—. Instr. Calif. Continuing Edn. of Bar, 1990—, Western State Coll., 1991, Rutter Group, 1994—; chmn. magistrate selection com. U.S. Dist. Ct. (ctrl. dist.) Calif., L.A., 1991, 93, 94, 95, mem. com., 1997; lectr. in field. Contbr. articles to profl. jours. Pres., bd. dirs. Child or Parental Emergency Svcs., Santa Ana, Calif., 1982-92; bd. dirs. Pub. Law Ctr., Santa Ana, Coalition for Justice, Working Wardrobes; mem. exec. com. and cast CHOC Follies. Recipient Jurisprudence award Anti-Defamation League, 1997; named to Hall of Fame, Western State U., 1993; named one of Best Lawyers, Bestlawyers.com, 2001, 02, 03, one of Top 100 Most Influential Lawyers in Calif., L.A. Daily Jour., 2001, one of Top 30 Female Litigators in Calif., L.A. Daily Jour., 2002. Mem. State Bar Calif., Orange County Bar Assn. (del. to state conv. 1980-94, bd. dirs. 1983-94, chmn. bus. litigation sect. 1989, sec. 1990, treas. 1991, pres.-elect 1992, pres. 1993), Orange County Trial Lawyers Assn. (bd. dirs. 1987-89, Bus. Trial Lawyer of Yr. award 1995), Orange County Women Lawyers (Lawyer of Yr. award 1996), Vols. in Parole (chmn. adv. com. 1990-91), Peter Elliot Inns Ct. (master), Am. Bd. of Trial Advocates. Avocations: distance running, skiing. Federal civil litigation, State civil litigation, Labor (including EEOC, Fair Labor Standards Act, labor-management relations, NLRB, OSHA). Office: 23161 Mill Creek Dr Ste 170 Laguna Hills CA 92653-1650 E-mail: michelle@reinglasslaw.com.

REINHARD, PHILIP G. federal judge; b. LaSalle, Ill., Jan. 12, 1941; s. Godfrey and Ruth R.; married Virginia Reinhard; children: Bruce, Brian, David, Philip. BA, U. Ill., Champaign, 1962, JD, 1964. Asst. state atty. Winnebago County, 1964-67; atty. Hyer, Gill & Brown, 1967-68; state atty. Winnebago County, 1968-76; judge 17th Jud. Cir., 1976-80, Appellate Ct., 1980-92, U.S. Dist. Ct. (no. dist.) Ill., 1992—. Mem. Am. Acad. Jud. Edn., Winnebago County Bar Assn. Office: US Courthouse 211 S Court St Rockford IL 61101-1219

REINHARD, STEVEN IRA, lawyer; b. Schenectady, N.Y., June 9, 1961; s. Arnold and Lenore (Bluthe) R.; m. Susan Marie Parham, June 15, 1986; children: Laura Suzanne, Samuel Jacob. BSBA, U. N.C., Chapel Hill, 1982, JD, 1985. Bar: N.C. 1985, U.S. Dist. Ct. (ea. dist.) N.C. 1985, U.S. Dist. Ct. (mid. dist.) N.C. 1989. Assoc. Graham & James, Raleigh, N.C., 1985-93, Johnson, Mercer, Hearn & Vinegar, PLLC, Raleigh, N.C., 1994-97, Ragsdale Liggett, PLLC, Raleigh, N.C., 1997-2000; assoc. gen. counsel Spectrasite Comm., Inc., Cary, N.C., 2000—. Mem. N.C. Bar Assn. (chair real property sect. 1998-99), Wake County Real Property Lawyers Assn. (pres. 1994-95). Communications, Corporate, general, Property, real (including real estate development, water). Office: Spectrasite Comm Inc Ste 4000 100 Regency Forest Dr Cary NC 27511 E-mail: steve.reinhard@spectrasite.com.

REINHARDT, BENJAMIN MAX, lawyer, arbitrator, mediator; b. N.Y.C., Dec. 29, 1917; s. Meyer and Miriam (Fischer) R.; children: Dennis, Dixie, Sara, Shawn; m. Rosa Reinhardt. BA, Harvard U., 1940; JD magna cum laude, Southwestern U., L.A., 1956. Bar: Calif. 1956, U.S. Supreme

Ct. 1960. Pvt. practice, Van Nuys, Calif., 1957-87, Palm Desert, Calif., 1987—. Chief legal counsel Northridge (Calif.) Hosp. Found., 1965-75; atty. Calif. Psychol. Assn., San Francisco, 1965-70; tchr. law Los Angeles County Bd. Edn., L.A., 1965-73; instr. law U. So. Calif., L.A., 1963-69, Coll. of Desert, Palm Desert, Calif., 1992-94; arbitrator Superior Ct. Calif., Palm Springs, 1994—; atty. Sr. T.V., Indian Wells, Calif., 1992—. Mem. Palm Desert Police Adv. Com., 1993-98; mem. adv. bd. Ret. Sr. Vol. Program, Palm Desert, 1994-96; instr. law Elderhostel, Indian Wells, Calif., 1993-98. Capt. U.S. Army, 1941-46. Mem. State Bar Calif., Desert Bar Assn. Republican. Avocations: golf, reading. Estate planning, Family and matrimonial, Probate (including wills, trusts). Office: Palm Desert Greens 38-101 Story Creek Dr Palm Desert CA 92260-8617 Fax: 760-346-0936. E-mail: reino81@earthlink.net.

REINHARDT, GEORGE ROBERT, lawyer; b. Tifton, Ga., Mar. 1, 1954; BBA magna cum laude, U. Ga., 1975; JD, U. Va., 1978. Bar: Ga. 1979. Atty. Reinhardt, Whitley, Wilmot, Summerlin & Pittman, PC, Tifton, Ga. Mem.: Tifton Bar Assn., State Bar Ga. (program com. 1998—, chair fin. com. 1999—2000, fin. com. 1996—, exec. com. 1998—, bd. govs. 1992—, state disciplinary bd. review panel 1993—98, chmn. 1996—98, treas. 2000—01, pres.-elect 2003—), Sphinx Soc. Corporate, general, Estate planning. Office: Reinhardt Whitley Wilmot et al PO Drawer 1287 1001 N Central St Tifton GA 31794*

REINHARDT, STEPHEN ROY, federal judge; b. N.Y.C., Mar. 27, 1931; s. Gottfried and Silvia (Hanlon) Reinhardt; children: Mark, Justin, Dana. BA cum laude, Pomona Coll., 1951; LLB, Yale, 1954. Bar: Calif. 1958. Law clk. to Hon. Luther W. Youngdahl U.S. Dist. Ct. , Washington, 1956—57; atty. O'Melveny & Myers, L.A., 1957—59; ptnr. Fogel Julber Reinhardt Rothschild & Feldman LC, L.A., 1959—80; judge U.S. Ct. Appeals (9th cir.), L.A., 1980—. Adj. prof. Loyola Law Sch., L.A., 1988—90. Pres. L.A. Recreation and Parks Commn., 1974—75; active Coliseum Commn., 1974—75, L.A. Police Commn., 1974—78, pres., 1978—80; sec., exec. organizing com. L.A. Olympics, 1980—84; exec. com. Dem. Nat. Com., 1969—72; nat. Dem. committeeman State of Calif., 1976—80; bd. dirs. Amateur Athletic Found. L.A, 1984—92. 1st lt. USAF, 1954—56. Mem.: ABA (labor law coun. 1975—77).

REINHART, PETER SARGENT, corporate executive, lawyer; b. Mineola, N.Y., May 17, 1950; s. Charles Woodham and Martha Way (Sargent) R.; m. Susan Stockwell, Aug. 29, 1970 (div. Jan. 1976); 1 child, Amy Lynn; m. Gale McElroy, Oct. 16, 1976 (div. May 1985); 1 child, James Gharrett; m. Carol O. Gaffney, Jan. 4, 1992 (div. Jan. 2001). BA, Franklin and Marshall Coll., 1971; JD, Rutgers U., 1975. Bar: N.J. 1975. Atty. Pillsbury and Russell, Atlantic Highlands, N.J., 1975-78; corp. counsel K. Hovnanian Enterprises, Inc., Red Bank, N.J., 1978-81, sr. v.p., gen. counsel, 1981—; also bd. dirs. Pres. Inst. Multi-Family Housing, Plainsboro, N.J., 1989-90. Trustee, mem. editorial bd. Housing N.J. mag., 1991—. Trustee Community Assns. Inst., Arlington, Va., pres. N.J. chpt., 1988; trustee Assn. for Children of N.J., Newark, 1988-93, Keep Middlesex Moving, New Brunswick, 1990-93, Bayshore Cmty. Hosp., Holmdel, N.J., 1992-01, v.p., 1995, chmn., 1997, Meridian Hosp. Corp., 2002—; chmn. Jersey Shore Partnership, 2003—; pres. Greater Red Bank Jaycees, 1978-79, Atlantic Highlands Rep. Club, 1978; v.p. Monmouth coun. Boy Scouts Am., Oakhurst, N.J., 1987-94, pres., 1994-95; v.p. Garden State Games, Edison, N.J., 1991-94; mem. Coun. Affordable Housing, Trenton, N.J., 1993—. Named to Community Assns. Inst. Hall of Fame, 1988; named Jaycee of Yr. Greater Red Bank Jaycees, 1977. Mem. N.J. State Bar Assn., N.J. Shore Builders Assn. (pres. 1989-90, Builder of Yr. 1987, Hall of Fame 1991), Nat. Assn. Indsl. and Office Parks (bd. dirs. 1990-92), N.J. Builders Assn. (v.p. 1992-94, pres. 1995-96, Builder of Yr. award 1995, Shore Athletic Club (Oakhurst), Ea. Monmouth C. of C. (trustee 1992-98, Vol. of Yr. 1995). Avocations: road racing, marathon running, golf. Office: Hovnanian Enterprises Inc PO Box 500 10 Hwy 35 Red Bank NJ 07701-5902

REINHART, RICHARD PAUL, lawyer; b. Cleve., Sept. 1, 1954; s. Richard A. and Carole F. (Kaspar) R.; m. Debra Rae Hitchcock, June 20, 1976; children: Geoffrey, Richelle Marie. BA with honors, Rollins Coll., 1976; JD with distinction, Emory U., 1979. Bar: Ga. 1979, Fla. 1980. Ptnr. Morris, Manning & Martin, Atlanta, 1979-89; officer McMillen Reinhart and Voght, P.A., Orlando, Fla., 1989—, also bd. dirs. Mem. ABA, ATLA, Fla. Bar Assn., Ga. Bar Assn., Orange County Bar Assn., Acad. Fla. Trial Lawyers, Order of Coif, Omicron Delta Kappa. Federal civil litigation, State civil litigation. Office: McMillen Reinhart and Voght PA PA 111 N Orange Ave Ste 1450 Orlando FL 32801-4641 E-mail: reinhart@floridamalpractice.com.

REINHART, ROBERT ROUNTREE, JR., lawyer; b. Chgo., Oct. 21, 1947; s. Robert Rountree and Ruth (Duncan) R.; m. Elizabeth Aileen Plews, July 26, 1969; children: Andrea Jean, Jessica Elizabeth, Rebecca Jill. BA, Northwestern U., 1968; JD, U. Mich., 1971. Bar: Ill. 1971, Mich. 1972, Minn. 1973, U.S. Supreme Ct. 1976. Law clk. to judge U.S. Dist. Ct. (we. dist.) Mich., Grand Rapids, 1971-73; assoc. Oppenheimer Wolff & Donnelly, Mpls., 1973-77, ptnr., 1978-96, chair labor and employment bus. group, 1985-92; ptnr. Dorsey & Whitney, Mpls., 1996—, chair labor and employment practice group, 2000—. Co-chmn. Upper Midwest Employment Law Inst., Mpls., 1984—; gen. counsel Minn. Empoyment Law Coun., 1990—. Mem. ABA (labor and employment, civil litigation sects.), Minn. Bar Assn. General civil litigation, Labor (including EEOC, Fair Labor Standards Act, labor-management relations, NLRB, OSHA). Office: Dorsey & Whitney Ste 1500 50 S 6th St Minneapolis MN 55402-1498 E-mail: reinhart.robert@dorseylaw.com.

REINHOLD, RICHARD LAWRENCE, lawyer; b. Buffalo, Feb. 24, 1951; s. Richard J. and Ann J. R.; m. Beth Stacey Grossman, May 11, 1991; children: Elizabeth Jane, Eleanor Terese, Rebecca Hope. AB, Cornell U., 1973; JD, SUNY, Buffalo, 1976. Bar: N.Y. 1977, Fla. 1977. With office of tax legis. counsel U.S. Dept. Treasury, Washington, 1982-84; ptnr., head tax dept. Willkie Farr & Gallagher, N.Y.C., 1985—. Contbr. articles to profl. jours. Bd. dirs. The Adirondack Coun.; mem. dean's adv. coun. sch. of law SUNY, Buffalo. Fellow Am. Coll. of Tax Counsel; mem. N.Y. State Bar Assn. (chair tax sect. 1996-97), Internat. Fiscal Assn., Tax Forum, Tax Club, Am. Alpine Club. Office: Willkie Farr & Gallagher 787 7th Ave New York NY 10019-6099

REINIGER, DOUGLAS HAIGH, lawyer; b. Mt. Kisco, N.Y., Nov. 8, 1948; s. Haigh McDiarmid and Virginia (Munson) R.; m. Margaret Vrablic, Aug. 31, 1968 (div. Jan. 1983); 1 child, Brian Christopher; m. Anne Fanning, Aug. 5, 1984. BA, Iona Coll., 1970; MSW, Fordham U., 1974, JD, 1980. Bar: N.Y. 1981, Wyo. 1996, U.S. Dist. Ct. (so. dist.) N.Y. 1982, U.S. Dist. Ct. (ea. dist.) N.Y., 1991, U.S. Cir. Ct. Appeals (2d cir.) 1997, U.S. Supreme Ct 1986. Psychiat. aide St. Vincent's Psychiat. Hosp., Harrison, N.Y., 1968-69; child care worker Cardinal McCloskey Home for Children, White Plains, N.Y., 1969-71, social worker, 1971-75, dir. legal affairs, 1975-81; sole practice N.Y.C., 1981-83; ptnr. Rosin & Reiniger, N.Y.C., 1983—; assoc. prof. Sch. Social Work Columbia U., N.Y.C., 1991-99, coord. law minor program, Sch. Social Work, 1994-99. Lectr. appellate divsn. N.Y. Supreme Ct., N.Y.C., 1985, 99, Fedn. Protestant Welfare, N.Y.C., 1987-91, Ct. Apptd. Spl. Advs., N.Y.C., 1987-94, Practicing Law Inst., N.Y.C., 1988, 99, 2000, 01. Mem. ABA (family law sect., com. on adoption, com. on custody 1992-2001), N.Y. State Bar Assn. (lectr. 1988, 99, family law sect., com. on family ct., com. on adoption), Assn. Bar City N.Y. (lectr. 1995, 99, com. on family law and family ct. 1985-88, com. on juvenile justice 1989-91, com. on children and the law 1993-97), Am. Acad. Adoption Attys. (lectr. 1995-96, 2000-01, chmn. adoption agy. com. 1998-2001, trustee 2000—, pres.-elect 2002-03, pres. 2003-), N.Y. State Foster and Adoptive Parents Assn. (bd. dirs. 1992—, lectr. 1992-2001), New York County Lawyers Assn. (lectr. 1994-2001). Roman Catholic. Family and matrimonial, Juvenile. Office: Rosin & Reiniger 630 3rd Ave New York NY 10017-6705 E-mail: dreiniger@aol.com.

REINISCH, AUGUST ALEXANDER, lawyer, educator; b. Vienna, Jan. 29, 1965; s. August and Herta (Lenninger) R.; m. Elisabeth Feitzinger, July 3, 1993; children: Johanna, August. LLM, NYU, 1989; JD, U. Vienna, 1991; diploma, Acad. Internat. Law, The Hague, The Netherlands, 1994. Bar: N.Y. 1990, Conn. 1990. Law clk. fed. cts., Vienna, 1990-91; univ. asst. Inst. Internat. Law, Vienna, 1991-92, lectr., 1993-98; prof. pub. internat. and European law U. Vienna Sch. Law, 1998—. Cons. Legal Advisor's Office/Fgn. Ministry, Vienna, 1992-93; vis. scholar Sch. Advanced Internat. Studies Johns Hopkins U., Washington, 1995-96, adj. prof., 1996; lectr. Austrian Diplomatic Acad., Vienna, 1993—; professorial lectr. Sch. Advanced Internat. Studies, Johns Hopkins U., Bologna, 1999—; vis. prof. Bocconi U., Milan, 2002-03; mem. panel arbitrators ICSID, Washington; univ. prof. pub. internat. law and European law U. Vienna Sch. of Law. Author: US-Exportkontrollrecht in Österreich, 1991 (Vienna Juridical Soc. award 1992), State Responsibility for Debts, 1995, International Organizations Before National Courts, 2000; co-author: Staatensukzession und Schuldenübernahme, 1995; contbr. articles to profl. jours. including Austrian Jour. Pub. and Internat. Law, German Yearbook Internat. Law, Nordic Jour. Internat. Law, Am. Jour. Internat. Law, and European Jour. Internat. Law. Recipient scholarship Fulbright Commn., 1988. Mem. ABA, Am. Soc. Internat. Law, Internat. Law Assn. Avocations: tennis, skiing, opera, medieval music. Office: Inst Internat Law Universitatsstr 2 A-1090 Vienna Austria E-mail: August.Reinisch@univie.ac.at.

REINKE, STEFAN MICHAEL, lawyer; b. Concord, Calif., May 7, 1958; s. Albert Richard and Patricia Eleanor (Stefan) R.; m. Lisa Elaine Williams, June 7, 1997. AA, Bakersfield Coll., 1978; AB, U. So. Calif., 1981; JD, U. Calif., Davis, 1984. Bar: Hawaii 1984, U.S. Dist. Ct. Hawaii 1984, U.S. Ct. Appeals (9th and Fed. cirs.) 1985. Assoc. Carlsmith, Wichman, Case, Mukai & Ichiki, Honolulu, 1984-86; dir. Lyons, Brandt, Cook & Hiramatsu, Honolulu, 1986—. Lectr. Windward C.C., 1995-98; lawyer rep. 9th Cir. Jud. Conf., 1995; lawyer rep. Jud. Conf. for the U.S. Dist. Ct. Hawaii, 1996-98, 2002--. Bd. dirs. Hawaii Ctrs. for Ind. Living, Honolulu, 1985-91, Prevent Child Abuse Hawaii, 1995—, v.p., 1999-2000, pres., 2000-2001; ofcl. U.S. Cycling Fedn. Mem. ABA, FBA (pres. Hawaii chpt. 1994-96, 98-99), Hawaii Bar Assn. (mem. jud. adminstrn. com.), Am. Arbitration Assn. (arbitrator and mediator), Def. Rsch. Inst., Hawaii State Cycling Assn. (bd. dirs. 1998-2001), Phi Beta Kappa, Phi Alpha Delta. General civil litigation, Insurance, Labor (including EEOC, Fair Labor Standards Act, labor-management relations, NLRB, OSHA). Office: Lyons Brandt Cook & Hiramatsu 841 Bishop St Ste 1800 Honolulu HI 96813-3992 E-mail: sreinke@iwon.com.

REINKE, WILLIAM JOHN, lawyer; b. South Bend, Ind., Aug. 7, 1930; s. William August and Eva Marie (Hein) R.; m. Sue Carol Colvin, 1951 (div. 1988); children: Sally Sue Taelman, William A., Andrew J.; m. Elizabeth Beck Lockwood, 1991. AB cum laude, Wabash Coll., 1952; JD, U. Chgo., 1955. Bar: Ind. 1955. Assoc. Barnes & Thornburg and predecessors, South Bend, Ind., 1957-61, ptnr., 1961-96, of counsel, 1996—; former chmn. compensation com.; former mem. mgmt. com. Trustee Stanley Clark Sch., 1969-80, pres., 1977-80; mem. adv. bd. Salvation Army, 1973—, pres., 1990-92; bd. dirs. NABE Mich. chpt., 1990-94, pres. 1993-94, Isaac Walton League, 1970-81, United Way, 1979-81; pres. South Bend Round Table, 1963-65; trustee First Meth. Ch., 1976-70. Served with U.S. Army, 1955-57. Recipient Outstanding Local Pres. award Ind. Jaycees, 1960-61, Boss of Yr. award, 1979, South Bend Outstanding Young Man award, 1961. Mem. ABA, Ind. State Bar Assn., St. Joseph County Bar Assn., Ind. Bar Found. (patron fellow), Am. Judicature Soc., Ind. Soc. Chgo., Summit Club (past gov., founders com.), Rotary (bd. dirs. 1970-73, 94-97). General civil litigation, Commercial, contracts (including sales of goods; commercial financing), Construction. Home: 51795 Waterton Square Cir Granger IN 46530-8317 Office: Barnes & Thornburg 1st Source Bank Ctr 100 N Michigan St Ste 600 South Bend IN 46601-1632

REINSTEIN, JOEL, lawyer; b. N.Y.C., July 23, 1946; s. Louis and Ruth Shukovsky; children: Lesli, Louis, Mindy. BSE, U. Pa., 1968; JD cum laude, U. Fla., 1971; LLM in Taxation, NYU, 1974. Bar: Fla. 1971, U.S. Tax Ct. 1973, U.S. Dist. Ct. (so. dist.) Fla. 1976. Atty., office of chief counsel IRS, 1971-74; ptnr. Capp, Reinstein, Kopelowitz and Atlas, P.A., Ft. Lauderdale, Fla., 1975-85; dir., ptnr. Greenberg, Traurig, Hoffman, Lipoff, Rosen & Quentel, P.A., Ft. Lauderdale, 1985-92; gen. counsel Internat. Magnetic Imaging, Inc., Boca Raton, Fla., 1992-94; prin. Law Offices of Joel Reinstein, Boca Raton, 1993—. Lectr. Advanced Pension Planning, Am. Soc. C.L.U.s; lectr. in field. Mem. editl. bd. U. Fla. Law Rev. 1970-71; contbr. articles to profl. jours. Mem. Fla. Bar Assn. (tax sect.), ABA (tax sect.), Order of Coif, Phi Kappa Phi, Phi Delta Pi. Corporate, general, Estate planning, Corporate taxation. Office: 925 S Federal Hwy Ste 325 Boca Raton FL 33432

REINTHALER, RICHARD WALTER, lawyer; b. N.Y.C., Feb. 27, 1949; s. Walter F. and Maureen C. (Tully) R.; m. Mary E. Maloney, Aug. 8, 1970; children: Brian, Scott, Amy. BA in Govt. magna cum laude, U. Notre Dame, 1970, JD summa cum laude, 1973. Bar: N.Y. 1974, U.S. Dist. Ct. (so. and ea. dists.) N.Y. 1974, U.S. Ct. Appeals (2d cir.) 1974, U.S. Ct. Appeals (9th cir.) 1976, U.S. Ct. Appeals (5th cir.) 1978, U.S. Ct. Appeals (11th cir.) 1981, U.S. Supreme Ct. 1977. Assoc. White & Case, N.Y.C., 1973—81, ptnr., 1981—95, Dewey Ballantine LLP, N.Y.C., 1995—, co-chmn. litigation dept., 2002—. Mem. adv. group U.S. Dist. Ct. (ea. dist.) N.Y., 1992—, chairperson subgroup on ethics, 1993—. Contbr. articles to profl. jours. Served to 1st lt. U.S. Army, 1974. Fellow Am. Bar Found.; mem. ABA (2d cir. chmn. discovery com. 1982-87, program coord. 1986, ann. meeting litigation sect., vice chmn. com. on fed. procedure 1988-89, co-chmn. com. on profl. responsibility 1989-92, vice chmn. securities litigation com. 1993-94, vice chair Hong Kong meeting 1995, co-chair energy litigation com. 1996-97, co-chair antitrust litigation com. 1997-2000, mem. Ethics 2000 task force 1999-2000), N.Y. State Bar Assn., Assn. of Bar of City of N.Y. (mem. com. to enhance diversity in the profession 1990-95, mem. Orison S. Marden Meml. Lectrs. com. 1994-2000, chair 1997-2000, spl. com. on mergers, acquisitions and corp. control contests 1995-2002), Scarsdale Golf Club (Hartsdale, N.Y., bd. govs. 1994—, pres. 2002-2003), Capital Hill Club (Washington). Republican. Roman Catholic. Avocations: golf, tennis. Antitrust, Federal civil litigation, Securities. Office: Dewey Ballantine LLP 1301 Avenue Of The Americas New York NY 10019-6022

REIS, HAROLD F. lawyer; b. July 22, 1916; s. Bernard and Rose (Frank) Reis; m. Ruthanne Abram, June 11, 1951; children: Alan B., Kate Reis Grogan, Deborah Reis Kennedy. BS, CCNY, 1937; LLB, Columbia U., 1940. Bar: NY 1941, DC 1953. With U.S. Dept. Justice, Washington, 1942—67; 1st asst. Office of Legal Counsel, 1960—63, exec. asst. to Atty. Gen., 1963—67; pvt. practice Washington, 1967—83; ptnr. Newman Holtzinger, P.C., Washington, 1983—94; sr. advisor Morgan, Lewis & Bockuis, Washington, 1994—96. Recipient Rockefeller Pub. Svc. award in law, legislation and adminstrn., 1964. Mem.: ABA, DC Bar Assn., Cosmos Club (Washington). Personal E-mail: reis8508@aol.com.

REISMAN, JASON ERIC, lawyer; b. Atlanta, Feb. 15, 1969; s. Stuart Ronald and Donna Faye Reisman; m. Suzanne Gail Barrett, Dec. 31, 1994. BS in Econs. summa cum laude, U. Pa., 1991; JD cum laude, Georgetown U., 1994. Bar: Pa. 1994, N.J. 1994, U.S. Dist. Ct. (ea. dist.) Pa. 1994, U.S. Dist. Ct. (mid. dist.) Pa. 2002, U.S. Dist. Ct. N.J. 1994, U.S. Ct. Appeals (8th cir.) 1998, U.S. Ct. Appeals (3d cir.) 1999. Lawyer Obermayer Rebmann Maxwell & Hippel LLP, Phila., 1994—. Vol. lawyer Homeless Advocacy Project, Phila., 1994—; vol. basketball coach Ridley Jr. ABA, Ridley Park, Pa., 1995-99; vol. co-leader Explorers Program, Phila., 1997-98. Mem. ABA, Pa. Bar Assn., Phila. Bar Assn. Democrat. Jewish. Avocations: sports, family, coaching kids. Labor (including EEOC, Fair Labor Standards Act, labor-management relations, NLRB, OSHA). Office: Obermayer Rebmann Maxwell & Hippel LLP One Penn Ctr 19th Fl 1617 Jfk Blvd Ste 1950 Philadelphia PA 19103-1895

REISS, JEROME, lawyer; b. Bklyn., Dec. 7, 1924; s. William and Eva (Marenstein) Reiss; m. Naomi Betty Plutzik, June 15, 1947; children: Robert Scott, Harlan Morgan, Andrea Ellen, Samantha Glynis. BA, Bklyn. Coll., 1948; JD, Harvard U., 1951. Bar: N.Y. 1951, U.S. Dist. Ct. (so. dist.) N.Y. 1954, U.S. Ct. Claims 1960, U.S. Dist. Ct. (ea. dist.) N.Y. 1964, DC 1967, U.S. Dist. Ct. (we. dist.) N.Y. 1979, U.S. Supreme Ct. 1989. Staff atty. civil br. Legal Aid Soc., N.Y.C., 1951—54; staff atty. City of N.Y., 1954-58; assoc. Max E. Greenberg, 1958-67; sr. ptnr. Max E. Greenberg, Trayman, Cantor, Reiss & Blasky, 1967-80, Max E. Greenberg, Cantor & Reiss, N.Y.C., 1980-88, Thelen, Marrin, Johnson & Bridges, N.Y.C., 1989-97, Thelen, Reid & Priest, 1997-2000. Lectr. constrn. law Practicing Law Inst., Gen. Svcs. Adminstrn., Engring. News Record, Medger Evers C.C., Am. Arbitrators Assn., Internat. Contr. Assn., Prof. Edn. Sys.; arbitrator Small Claims Ct., 1960—88; advisor Fed. Pub., Inc.; chmn. bd. AMT-Pacific, Israel, 2000—02. Contbr. articles to profl. jours., chapters to books. Trustee Brownsville Boys Club and Alumni Assn.; gen. counsel Artist Fellowship, Inc. With USAAF, 1943—46. Fellow: Am. Coll. Constrn. Lawyers (founding mem.); mem.: IBA, ABA, N.Y. Bar Assn., Jacob K. Javits Conv. Ctr. Oper. Corp. (bd. dirs.), Mcpl. Assist. Corp. City of N.Y. (bd. dirs.), Am. Arbitrators Assn. Federal civil litigation, Construction, Government contracts and claims.

REISS, JOHN BARLOW, lawyer; b. London, Aug. 29, 1939; arrived in U.S., 1963; s. James Martin and Margaret Joan (Ping) R.; m. Mary Jean Maudsley, Aug. 6, 1967 (div. 1978); m. Kathleen Strouse, Aug. 2, 1979; 1 child, Juliette Blanche. BA with honors, Exeter U., Devon, Eng., 1961; AM, Washington U., St. Louis, 1966, PhD, 1971; JD, Temple U., 1977. Bar: Pa. 1977, N.J. 1977, U.S. Dist. Ct. N.J. 1977, D.C. 1980, U.S. Supreme Ct. 1981, U.S. Dist. Ct. D.C. 1982. Economist Commonwealth Econ. Com., London, 1962-63; asst. prof. Allegheny Coll., Meadville, Pa., 1967-71; assoc. prof. Stockton State Coll., Pomona, N.J., 1971-75; asst. health commr. State of N.J., Trenton, 1975-79; dir. office of health regulation U.S. Dept. HHS, Washington, 1979-81; assoc. Baker & Hostetler, Washington, 1981-82, Dechert Price & Rhoads, Phila., 1982-86, ptnr., 1986-93, asst. chair health law group, 1984-91, chmn. health law group, 1991-93; ptnr. Saul Ewing LLP, Phila., 1993—, chmn. health law dept., 1995—2002. Mem. editl. bd. Topics in Hosp. Law, 1985-86, Hosp. Legal Forms Manual, 1985-2002, Jour. Health Care Tech., 1984-86; contbr. Hosp. Contracts Manual, 1983-2002; contbr. articles to profl. jours., chpts. to books. Bd. dirs. Gateway Sch. Little Children, Phila., 1986-99; bd. dirs. ECRI, Plymouth Meeting, Pa., 1994—, chmn. bd., 2001—; mem. bd. vestry All Saints Ch., Wynnewood, Pa., 1993, 96-2001. Pub. Health Svc. fellow, 1979-81, English Speaking Union fellow, 1963-66, Econ. Devel. Adminstr. fellow Washington U., 1966-67. Mem. Nat. Health Lawyers Assn., Phila. Bar Assn., Brit. Am. C. of C. of Greater Phila. (bd. dirs. 1991), Union League of Phila., Univ. Barge Club, Brit. Officers Club of Phila. (first v.p. 2003—). Avocations: gardening, house restoring, reading, sculling. Administrative and regulatory, Corporate, general, Health. Home: 415 Wister Rd Wynnewood PA 19096-1808 Office: Saul Ewing LLP 3800 Centre Sq W Philadelphia PA 19102 E-mail: jreiss@saul.com.

REISS, STEVEN ALAN, lawyer, law educator; b. N.Y.C., Dec. 18, 1951; s. Louis and Ruth (Harrow) R.; m. Mary A. Mattingly; children: Alexandra Mattingly Reiss, Tyler Brennan Reiss. BA, Vassar Coll., 1973; JD, Stanford (Calif.) U., 1976. Bar: N.Y., D.C., Calif. Law clk. to John Minor Wisdom U.S. Ct. Appeals for 5th Cir., New Orleans, 1976-77; law clk. to justice William J. Brennan U.S Supreme Ct., Washington, 1977-78; assoc. Miller, Cassidy, Larroca & Lewin, Washington, 1978-80; vis. prof. Georgetown U. Law Ctr., Washington, 1981; asst. prof. Law Sch., NYU, 1981-83, assoc. prof., 1984-87, prof., 1987-91; ptnr. Weil, Gotshal & Manges, N.Y.C., 1990—. Editor-in-chief White Collar Crime Reporter, 1987-91, contbg. editor, 1991—. Trustee Vassar Coll. Poughkeepsie, N.Y., 1978-82; bd. dirs. NYU Cmty. Fund, 1984-87, Concert Artists Guild, 1991-94, Lyrics Chamber Music Soc., 2000-; gen. counsel Brennan Ctr. for Justice, 1996—; bd. trustees Vols. of Legal Svcs. Mem. N.Y. State Bar Assn., D.C. Bar Assn., Calif. Bar Assn., Assn. of Bar of City of N.Y. (fed. legis. com. 1981-87), 2d Jud. Conf. (reporter 1984—). Federal civil litigation, Criminal, Private international. Home: 25 E 86th St New York NY 10028-0553 Office: Weil Gotshal & Manges 767 5th Ave Fl Concl New York NY 10153-0119 E-mail: steven.riess@weil.com.

REITER, GLENN MITCHELL, lawyer; b. N.Y.C., Feb. 1, 1951; s. Bernard Leon and Helene (Edson) R.; m. Marilyn Beckhorn, Sept. 5, 1976; children: Benjamin, Diana, Julie. BA, Yale U., 1973, JD, 1976. Bar: N.J. 1976, Pa. 1977, D.C. 1978, N.Y. 1979. Law clk. to judge U.S. Ct. Appeals, Phila., 1976-77; assoc. Schnader, Harrison, Segal & Lewis, Phila., 1977-78, Simpson Thacher & Bartlett, N.Y.C., 1978-84, ptnr., 1984—, resident ptnr. London, 1986-90. Mem. Phi Beta Kappa. Banking, Corporate, general, Securities.

REITER, JOSEPH HENRY, lawyer, retired judge; b. Phila., Mar. 21, 1929; s. Nicholas and Barbara (Hellmann) Reiter; m. Beverlee A. Bearman, Nov. 8, 1993. AB, Temple U., 1950, LLB, 1953. Bar: D.C. 1953, Pa. 1954. Atty. advisor U.S. Army, 1955—61; asst. U.S. atty. Ea. Dist. Pa., 1961—63, asst. U.S. atty. in charge of civil div., 1963—69; chief organized crime and racketeering strike force Western N.Y. State U.S. Dept. Justice, 1969—70, sr. trial atty. tax divsn., 1970—72, regional dir. office of drug abuse law enforcement, 1972—73; dep. atty. gen., dir. Drug Law Enforcement Office of Pa., 1973—77; ptnr. Stassen, Kostos and Mason, Phila., 1978—85, Kostos Reiter & Lamer, 1985—89; judge Armed Svcs. Bd. of Contract Appeals, Falls Church, Va., 1989—95; of counsel Kostos & Lamer, Phila., 1995—. Mem. adv. com. Joint State Commn. on Procurement; lectr. in field. Contbr. articles to profl. jours. With U.S. Army, 1953—55. Recipient Meritorious Svc. award, U.S. Atty. Gen. Clark, 1967, Spl. Commendation, Asst. U.S. Atty. Gen. Tax Divsn., 1969, Outstanding Performance award, U.S. Atty. Gen. Richardson, 1973. Mem.: ABA, Phila. Bar Assn., D.C. Bar Assn., Fed. Bar Assn., Pan Am. Assn. Phila., Vesper Club, Am. Legion. Office: Kostos & Lamer 1608 Walnut St Ste 1300 Philadelphia PA 19103-5407

REIVE, KEVIN CHRISTOPHER, lawyer; b. Wayne, Mich., Sept. 3, 1975; s. Christopher Lawrence and Susan Frances Reive; m. Amanda Marisa Reive, Jan. 10, 1999. BA, Wash. State U., 1996; MBA, JD, U. Miami, Fla., 2000. Bar: Fla. 2000, U.S. Dist. Ct. (mid. dist.) Fla. 2001, U.S. Ct. Appeals (9th and 11th cirs.) 2001, U.S. Dist. Ct. (so. and no. dists.) 2002. Assoc. White & Case LLP, Miami, 2000—. Property, real (including real estate development, water), Commercial, contracts (including sales of goods; commercial financing). Office: White & Case LLP 200 S Biscayne Blvd Ste 4900 Miami FL 33131

REIVER, JOANNA, lawyer; b. Oct. 20, 1946; d. Julius and Iona (Peterson) R.; m. Robert E. Schlusser, July 16, 1982; children: Amelia, Daniel. Student, U. Del., 1964-65; AB, W. Va. U., 1968; JD, Catholic U. Am., 1976. Bar: Del. 1976, N.Mex. 1994. Reporter Del. State News, Dover, 1968-69, San Diego Evening Tribune, 1969-71; asst. editor Epilepsy Found. Am., Washington, 1972-73; asst. to dean Cath. U. Am. Law Sch., Washington, 1973-76; assoc. Murdoch & Walsh, P.A., Wilmington, Del., 1976-81, dir., 1980-82; ptnr. Schlusser & Reiver, Wilmington, Del., 1982-87, Schlusser, Reiver, Hughes and Sisk, Wilmington, Del., 1987-94; dir. Schlusser & Reiver, P.A., Wilmington, Del., 1995—2002; ptnr. Gollatz,

Griffin & Ewing PC, Wilmington, 2002—. Adj. prof. Delaware Law Sch. Widener U., 1987—. Pres. Estate Law Specialist Bd., Inc., 1998-2000; v.p. Del. Care Plan, Inc., 1999-2000. Fellow Am. Coll. Trust and Estate Counsel; mem. Del. Bar Assn. (sec. estates and trusts sect. 1982-84, vice chmn. 1984-85, chmn. 1985-86), Estate Planning Council Del. (bd. dirs. 1983-85, chmn. membership com. 1983-84, 1987-88, pres. 1991-92), Nat. Assn. Estate Planners and Couns. (bd. dirs. 1993, treas. 1998-99, v.p. 2000, pres. 2001). Estate planning, Probate (including wills, trusts), Estate taxation. Office: Gollatz Griffin & Ewing PC 1700 W 14th St Wilmington DE 19806-4012 E-mail: jreiver@ggelaw.com.

REMAR, ROBERT BOYLE, lawyer; b. Boston, Nov. 19, 1948; s. Samuel Roy and Elizabeth Mary (Boyle) R.; m. Victoria A. Greenhood, Nov. 11, 1979; children: Daniel A.G., William B.G. BA, U. Mass., 1970; JD, Boston Coll., 1974. Bar: Ga. 1974, Mass. 1975, U.S. Ct. Appeals (5th cir.) 1978, U.S. Ct. Appeals (11th cir.) 1981, U.S. Ct. Appeals (2d cir.) 1995, U.S. Supreme Ct. 1981. Staff atty. Ga. Legal Svcs. Program, Savannah, 1974-76, Western Mass. Legal Svcs., Greenfield, 1976-77; sr. staff atty. Ga. Legal Svcs. Program, Atlanta, 1977-82; ptnr. Remar & Graettinger, Atlanta, 1983-95, Kirwan, Parks, Chesin & Remar PC, Atlanta, 1993-96, Rogers & Hardin, Atlanta, 1996—. Bd. dirs., exec. com. ACLU, N.Y.C., pres. Ga. chpt., 1985-87, gen. counsel, 1980-83; hearing officer Ga. Pub. Svc. Commn., Atlanta, 1985-98; adj. prof. Ga. State U., Atlanta, 1984-98, spl. asst. atty. gen., 1990-2003; bd. experts Lawyers Alert, Boston, 1985-94. Mem. Ga. Energy Regulatory Reform Commn., Gov. of Ga., 1980-82, Ga. Consumer Adv. Bd., 1981-82; pres. Ga. Consumer Ctr. Inc., 1988-91; bd. dirs., exec. com. Ga. Resource Ctr.; v.p. Ga Ctr. Law Pub. Inst., 1991-94. Fellow Am. Coll. Trial Lawyers; mem. ABA (chmn. individual rights access to civil justice com. 1988-99), Ga. Bar Assn. (chmn. individual rights sect. 1981-83, co-chmn. consumer rights and remedies com. 1979-83, chmn. death penalty re. com. 1993—, mem. legis. adv. com. 1994-97, mem. indigent def. com. 2000—), Atlanta Bar Assn., Lawyers Club Atlanta, Lamar Inn of Ct. (master of the bench). Democrat. Avocations: golf, gardening. Administrative and regulatory, Federal civil litigation, Labor (including EEOC, Fair Labor Standards Act, labor-management relations, NLRB, OSHA). Home: 1714 Meadowdale Ave NE Atlanta GA 30306-3114 Office: Rogers & Hardin Internat Tower Peachtree Ctr 229 Peachtree St NE Ste 2700 Atlanta GA 30303-1638 E-mail: RBR@RH-LAW.COM.

REMBOLT, JAMES EARL, lawyer; b. Nov. 13, 1943; s. Earl Lester and Dorothy Elouise (Mehring) Rembolt; m. Marilyn Sue Schmadeke, July 16, 1972; children: Tami Anne, Michelle Sue. BBA, U. Nebr., 1965; MA in Bus. Orgn. and Mgmt., 1967, JD with distinction, 1972. Bar: Nebr. 1972, U.S. Dist. Ct. Nebr. 1972, U.S. Tax Ct. 1978, U.S. Ct. Claims 1978. Pres. Nebr. Moot Ct. Bd., 1972; pilot Nebr. Air Nat. Guard, Lincoln, 1969-74; lecr. legal writing U. Nebr. Coll. Law, 1973-74; ptnr. Rembolt, Ludtke & Berger, LLP, Lincoln, 1976—. Chmn. bd. trustees YWCA, Lincoln, 1982—83; mem., past pres. Lincoln/Lancaster Sr. Ctrs. Found., Inc., bd. dirs., 1988—90; mem., past chair bd. dirs. Madonna Found., Inc., 1989—91; trustee, past bd. dirs. U.Nebr. Found., U. Nebr.-Lincoln Com. of Visitors; past bd. dirs., pres. Nebr. Continuing Legal Edn., Inc.; bd. elders Eastridge Presbyn. Ch., Lincoln, 1979—82. Fellow: ABA, Nebr. State Bar Found., Am. Coll. Probate Counsel; mem.: U. Nebr. Lincoln Coll. Bus. Adminstrn. Alumni Assn. (past pres.), Lincoln Estate Planning Coun. (past pres.), Lincoln Probate Discussion Group (charter mem., exec. coun. ho. of dels.), Am. Jud. Soc., Nebr. State Bar Assn. (pres. 2002—03, exec. coun., ho. of dels.), Lincoln Bar Assn. Estate planning, Mergers and acquisitions, Probate (including wills, trusts). Office: Rembolt Ludtke & Berger LLP 1201 Lincoln Mall Ste 102 Lincoln NE 68508-2839 E-mail: jrembolt@remlud.com.

RENAU, DONALD IRWIN, lawyer; b. Louisville, Ky., Apr. 28, 1936; m. Scholl, Dec. 21, 1961. BA, Principia Coll., 1958; JD, U. Louisville, 1967. Bar: Ky. 1968, U.S. Ct. Appeals (6th cir.) 1968. Pvt. practice, Louisville, 1968—. Columnist Am. Agt. & Broker, 1997—. Bd. dirs. Salvation Army Adv. Bd., Louisville, 1990—; past pres. Lions club, 1966—. Avocation: horses. Corporate, general, Probate (including wills, trusts). Office: PO Box 7669 Louisville KY 40257-0669

RENCH, STEPHEN CHARLES, lawyer; b. Coffeyville, Kans., Oct. 11, 1930; s. Stephen and Gladys Mae (Carpenter) R.; m. Loraine Pennock, Oct. 11, 1966. BA in Econs., U. Kans., 1952; JD, Georgetown U., 1959. Bar: Colo. 1959, U.S. Dist. Ct. Colo. 1959, U.S. Ct. Appeals (10th cir.) 1961, U.S. Supreme Ct. 1979. Law clk to judge U.S. Ct. Appeals (10th cir.), Denver, 1959; law clk. to chief judge U.S. Dist. Ct. Colo., Denver, 1960-61; assoc. Tippit and Haskell, Denver, 1961-63; clk. Probate Ct., Denver, 1964-65; dep. state pub. defender Denver, 1966-74; tng. dir. Colo. State Pub. Defender System, Denver, 1974-77, tng. dir. as ind. contractor tng. seminars, 1980-82; pvt. practice Denver, 1977—. Mem. permanent lecturing faculty for summer sessions and seminars Nat. Coll. Criminal Def., Houston, 1974— , course dir., 1977; instr. trial tactics and strategy, evidence courses U. Denver Law Sch., 1979-91; lectr. in field throughout U.S. Author: Fingertip Law for Colorado Public Defenders, 1975, Strategy for Colorado Public Defenders, 1979, The Rench Book, Trial Tactics and Strategy, 1990, Courtbook, 1982, monthly columnist Trade Secrets of a Trial Lawyer, Washington Memo, 1977-78; contbr. articles to profl. jours. 1st lt. USAF, 1952-56. Mem. ABA, Colo. Trial Lawyers Assn., Colo. Criminal Def. Bar, Nat. Assn. Criminal Def. Lawyers, Nat. Legal Aid and Defenders Assn., Nat. Practice Inst., Assn. Trial Lawyers Am., Denver Bar Assn., Colo. Bar Assn. Appellate, General civil litigation, Criminal. Office: 580 S Franklin St Denver CO 80209-4502

RENDALL, DONALD JAMES, JR., lawyer; b. Phila., Jan. 31, 1956; s. Donald James and Mary (Hough) R.; m. Sandra Smallwood, July 28, 1979; children: Samuel, Katherine, Ann. AB summa cum laude, Dartmouth Coll., 1978; JD, Duke U., 1981. Bar: Ill. 1982, U.S. Dist. Ct. (no. dist.) Ill. 1983, U.S. Dist. Ct. Vt. 1984, Vt. 1985, U.S. Ct. Appeals (2d cir.) 1986. Law clk. to Hon. James S. Holden U.S. Dist. Ct. for Vt., Rutland, 1981-82; assoc. Jenner & Block, Chgo., 1982-84; asst. U.S. atty. U.S. Atty.'s Office for Dist. Vt., Rutland, 1984-87; assoc. Sheehey Furlong Rendall & Behm PC, Burlington, Vt., 1987, ptnr., 1988—; v.p. & gen. counsel Green Monster Power Corp., 2002—. Mem. ABA, Vt. Bar Assn.(pres. 2002-03), Chittenden County Bar Assn., Order of Coif, Phi Beta Kappa. General civil litigation, Environmental, Insurance. Home: 51 Old Farm Rd South Burlington VT 05403-6804 Office: Green Mountain Power Corp 163 Acorn Ln Burlington VT 05446-6611 E-mail: rendall@greenmountainpower.biz.

RENFREW, CHARLES BYRON, lawyer; b. Detroit, Oct. 31, 1928; s. Charles Warren and Louise (McGuire) R.; m. Susan Wheelock, June 28, 1952 (div. June 1984); children: Taylor Allison Ingham, Charles Robin, Todd Wheelock, James Bartlett; m. Barbara Jones Orser, Oct. 6, 1984; 5 stepchildren. AB, Princeton U., 1952; JD, U. Mich., 1956. Bar: Calif. 1956. Assoc. Pillsbury, Madison & Sutro, San Francisco, 1956-65, ptnr., 1965-72, 81-82; U.S. dist. judge No. Dist. Calif., San Francisco, 1972-80; dep. atty. gen. U.S. Washington, 1980-81; instr. U. Calif. Boalt Hall Sch. Law, 1977-80; v.p. law Chevron Corp. (formerly Standard Oil Co. Calif.), San Francisco, 1983-93, also bd. dirs.; ptnr. LeBoeuf, Lamb, Greene & McRae, San Francisco, 1994-97; pvt. practice San Francisco, 1998—. Mem. exec. com. 9th Cir. Jud. Conf., 1976-78, congl. liaison com. 9th Cir. Jud. Council, 1976-79, spl. com. to propose standards for admission to practice in fed. cts. U.S. Jud. Conf., 1976-79; chmn. spl. com. to study problems of discovery Fed. Jud. Ctr., 1978-79; mem. council on role of cts. U.S. Dept. Justice, 1978-83; mem. jud. panel Ctr. for Pub. Resources, 1981—; head U.S. del. to 6th UN Congress on Prevention of Crime and Treatment of Offenders, 1980; co-chmn. San Francisco Lawyers Com. for Urban Affairs, 1971-72, mem., 1983—; bd. dirs. Internat. Hospitality Ctr., 1961-74, pres., 1967-70; mem. adv. bd. Internat. Comparative Law Ctr., Southwestern Legal Found., 1983-93; trustee World Affairs Council No. Calif., 1984-87, 94—, Nat. Jud. Coll., 1985-91, Grace Cathedral, 1986-89. Contbr. articles to profl. jours. Bd. fellow Claremont U., 1986-94; bd. dirs. San Francisco Symphony Found., 1964-80, pres., 1971-72; bd. dirs. Coun. Civic Unity, 1962-73, pres., 1971-72; bd. dirs. Opportunity Through Ownership, 1969-72, Marin County Day Sch., 1972-74, No. Calif. Svc. League, 1975-76, Am. Petroleum Inst., 1984—, Nat. Crime Prevention Coun., 1982—; alumni trustee Princeton U., 1976-80; mem. vis. com. u. chgo. Law Sch., 1977-79, u.Mich. Law Sch., 1977-81; bd. visitors J. Reuben Clark Law Sch., Brigham Young U., 1981-83, Stanford Law Sch., 1983-86; trustee Town Sch. for Boys, 1972-80,pres. 1975-80; gov. San Fransciso Symphony Assn., 1974—; mem. nat. adv. bd. Ctr. for Nat. Policy, 1982—; bd. dirs. Nat. Coun. Crime and Deliquency, 1981-82,NAACP Legal Def. and Edn. Fund, 1982—; parish chancellor St. Luke's Episcopal Ch., 1968-71, sr. warden, 1974-76; mem. exec. coun. San Francisco Deanery, 1969-70; mem. diocesan coun. Episcopal Diocese of Calif., 1970; chmn. Diocesan Conv., 1977, 78, 79. Served with USN, 1946-48, 1st lt. U.S. Army, 1952-53. Fellow Am. Bar Found.; mem. ABA (coun. mem. sect. antitrust law 19778-82, vice c hmn. sect. antitrust law 1982-83), San Francisco Bar Assn. (past bd. dirs.), Assn. Gen. Counsel, State Bar Calif., Am. Judicature Soc., Am. Coll. Trial Lawyers (pres. 1995-96), Am. Law Inst., Coun. Fgn. Rels., Order of Coif, Phi Beta Kappa, Phi Delta Phi. Federal civil litigation, Corporate, general. Office: 710 Sansome St San Francisco CA 94111-1704

RENFRO, WILLIAM LEONARD, futurist, lawyer, inventor, entrepreneur; b. West Palm Beach, Fla., Sept. 9, 1945; s. Ernest Leonard and Oine Warren (McAdams) R. BS in Physics, Rensselaer Poly. Inst., 1967, MS in Nuclear Engring., 1972; postgrad., Yale U., 1967-68; JD, U. Conn., 1972. Bar: Conn. 1973, U.S. Ct. Fed. Claims, Fed. Ct. Appeals (D.C. cir.). Physicist Compustion Engring., Windsor Locks, Conn., 1968-69; pvt. practice law, Hartford, Conn., 1973-74; sr. rsch. assoc. The Futures Group, Glastonbury, Conn., 1973-76; analyst futures rsch. Congl. Rsch. Svc., U.S. Congress, Washington, 1976-80; pres. Policy Analysis Co., Inc., Washington, 1980—. Vis. fellow Ark. Inst.; guest lectr. Georgetown U., Brookings Inst., Nat. War Coll.; adj. prof. George Washington U., Indsl. Coll. Armed Forces Nat. Def. U.; mem. nat. foresight network U.S. Congress. Author: (with others) The Futures Research Handbook, 1997, Anticipatory Democracy, 1978, The Public Affairs Handbook, 1983, The Legislative Role of Corporations, 1982, Applying Methods and Techniques of Futures Research, 1983, Future Research and the Straegic Planning Process, 1985, Non-Extrapolative Forecasting in Business, 1988, Futures Research Methodology: The UN Millennium Project, 1999; author: Issue Management in Stratetic Planning, 1993, Vision-2020, 1999; editor Futures Rsch. Quar. World Futures Soc.; issues mgmt. editor the Futurist, 1982—, Tech. Analysis and Strategic Mgmt. Mem. long range planning com. United Way; trustee World Tech. Found., Am. Friends of Romania, 2002—; lic. pastoral vis. lay eucharistic min. Wash. Diocese. Mem.: ABA, Hartford County Bar Assn., Conn. Bar Assn., Internat. Pub. Rels. Assn., Assn. Former Intelligence Officers, World Futures Soc., Issues Mgmt. Assn. (bd. dirs. 1981—98, v.p. 1986—88, pres. 1988—96), Pub. Rels. Soc. Am., St. Andrews Soc., Clan Hamilton Soc., English Speaking Union (trustee Washington br.). Episcopalian. Achievements include U.S. and foreign patents.

RENFROW, JAY ROYCE, lawyer; b. Canon City, Colo., Feb. 19, 1943; s. J.F. and Fern W. Renfrow; m. Evelyn Lee Renfrow, July 25, 1964; children: Seadon T., Stephanie J. BS in Bus., U. Colo., 1964, JD, 1969. Bar: Colo. 1969, U.S. Dist. Ct. Colo. 1969, U.S. Ct. Appeals (10th cir.) 1970, U.S. Supreme Ct. 1970. Pres. J. Royce Renfrow, P.C., Colorado Springs, Colo., 1969-96, Speedway Gas and Oil Co., Colorado Springs, 1969—, Wine Corp. of N.Am., Colorado Springs, 1982-88; v.p., gen. counsel MedLogic Global Corp., Colorado Springs, 1991-92; sec., gen. counsel InnterCircle Group, Inc., Colorado Springs, 1996-97; mgr. J. Royce Renfrow PLLC, Mt. Crested Butte, Colo., 1997-98, Renfrow & Frazier PLLC, Mt. Crested Butte, 1998-2000; pvt. practice J. Royce Renfrow PLLC, Mt. Crested Butte, 2000—. Patentee in field. Bd. dirs. ARC, Colorado Springs, 1970-94, Colo. Opera Festival, Colorado Springs, 1990-96, Crested Butte Reel Fest, 2002—. Avocations: skiing, backpacking, astronomy, food and wine, hunting. Corporate, general, Estate planning, Property, real (including real estate development, water). Office: J Royce Renfrow PLLC PO Box 608 Crested Butte CO 81224 E-mail: jrr@renfrowlaw.com.

RENKENS, MADELINE A. lawyer; BA, U. Rochester, N.Y., 1973; MLS, Queens Coll., 1974; JD cum laude, Fordham U., 1979. Bar: N.Y. 1980, Conn. 1981, Wash. 1984, Alaska 1986, U.S. Dist. Ct. Alaska, U.S. Dist. Ct. (so. dist.) N.Y., U.S. Dist. Ct. (we. dist.) Wash., U.S. Ct. Appeals (9th cir.), U.S. Supreme Ct. Tchr., library media specialist Southampton (N.Y.) Pub. Schs., 1974-76; law clk. U.S. Dept. Justice, 1978-79, trial atty. anti-trust div., 1979-82; assoc. Willkie Farr & Gallagher, N.Y.C., 1982-84, Barokas & Martin, Seattle, 1984-87; pvt. practice, Snohomish, Wash., 1988—. Active Snohomish County Hist. Soc., Families with Children from China. Mem. Wash. Women Lawyers, Everett Rowing Assn., Snohomist County Bar Assn. Home and Office: 329 Ave C Snohomish WA 98290-2732

RENKES, GREGG, state attorney general; m. Maureen Renkes; 2 children. BA, Vassar Coll.; MS, Yale U.; JD, U. Colo. Bar: Alaska 1987. Law clk., magistrate State Alaska Ct. Sys.; chief of staff, chief counsel to U.S. Senator Frank Murkowski; majority staff dir. U.S. Senate Com. on Energy and Natural Resources, 1995—98; pres. The Renkes Group, Ltd.; atty. gen. State of Alaska, Juneau, 2003—. Spkr. in field. Contbr. articles to profl. jours. Mem. Campaign to Re-elect Senator Frank Murkowski, 1992, 1998, Murkowski 2002 Alaska Gubernatorial Campaign; active Rep. Nat. Conv. Platform Com., 1996. Republican. Office: Diamond Courthouse PO Box 110300 Juneau AK 99811-0300*

RENNER, ROBERT GEORGE, federal judge; b. Nevis, Minn., Apr. 2, 1923; s. Henry J. and Beatrice M. (Fuller) R.; m. Catherine L. Clark, Nov. 12, 1949; children: Robert, Anne, Richard, David. BA, St. John's U., Collegeville, Minn., 1947; JD, Georgetown U., 1949. Bar: Minn. 1949. Pvt. practice, Walker, 1949-69; U.S. atty. Dist. of Minn., 1969-77, U.S. magistrate, 1977-80, U.S. dist. judge, 1980-92, assumed sr. status, 1992—. Mem. Minn. Ho. of Reps., 1957-69. Served with AUS, 1943-46. Mem. FBA. Roman Catholic. Office: US Dist Ct 748 US Courthouse 316 Robert St N Saint Paul MN 55101-1495

RENO, OTTIE WAYNE, former judge; b. Pike County, Ohio, Apr. 7, 1929; s. Eli Enos and Arbannah Belle (Jones) Reno; m. Janet Gay McCann, May 22, 1947; children: Jennifer Lynn, Lorna Victoria, Ottie Wayne II. A in Bus. Adminstrn., Franklin U., 1949; LLB, Franklin Law Sch., 1953; JD, Capital U., 1966; grad. Coll. Juvenile Justice, U. Nev., 1973. Bar: Ohio 1953. Practiced in Pike County; recorder Pike County, 1957-73, common pleas judge probate and juvenile divsn., 1973-79. Author: Story of Horseshoes, 1963, Pitching Championship Horseshoes, 1971; 2d rev. edit., 1975; author: The American Directory of Horseshoe Pitching, 1983, Ohio vs. Smith, Murder, 1990, Reno and Apsaalooka Survive Custer, 1996. Del. Dem. Nat. Conv., 1972, 1996; mem. Camp Creek precinct Dem. Ctrl. Com., 1956—72, 1983—90, 1999—; sec. Pike County Dem. Exec. Com., 1971—72, 1988—90; mem. Ohio Dem. Ctrl. Com., 1969—70; Dem. candidate 6th Ohio dist. U.S. Ho. of Reps., 1966; Dem. candidate 88th Ohio dist. Ohio Ho. of Reps., 1992; pres. Scioto Valley Local Sch. Dist., 1962—66. Named to Nat. Horseshoe Pitchers Hall of Fame, 1978; recipient Disting. Svc. award, Ohio Youth Commn., 1974, 6 Outstanding Jud. Svc. awards, Ohio Supreme Ct., 17 times Ala. horseshoe pitching champion. Mem.: Pike County Bar Assn., Nat. Coun.Juvenile Ct. Judges, Ohio Bar Assn., Am. Legion. Mem. Ch. Of Christ In Christian Union. Home: 148 Reno Rd Lucasville OH 45648-9580

RENO, ROGER, lawyer; b. Rockford, Ill., May 16, 1924; s. Guy B. and Hazel (Kinnear) R.; m. Janice Marie Odelius, May 17, 1952; children: Susan Marie, Sheri Jan Reno-Rudolph, Michael Guy. Student, Kenyon Coll., 1943-44, Yale U., 1944, U. Wis., 1946; AB, Carleton Coll., 1947; LL.B., Yale U., 1950. Bar: Ill. 1950. Practiced in Rockford, 1950; assoc. firm Reno, Zahm, Folgate, Lindberg & Powell, 1950-56, partner, 1956-84, of counsel, 1984—. Chmn. Amcore Fin. Inc., 1982-95; atty. Rockford Bd. Edn., 1955-64. Past pres., bd. dirs. Childrens Home Rockford; trustee Swedish-Am. Hosp. Assn., 1967-77, Keith Country Day Sch. Served to 1st lt. USAAF, 1943-46. Mem. ABA, Ill. Bar Assn., Winnebago County Bar Assn. (pres. 1979-80) Clubs: Forest Hills Country (Rockford). Republican. Methodist. Home: 2515 Chickadee Trl Rockford IL 61107 Office: Reno Zahm Folgate Lindberg & Powell Amcore Fin Plaza Rockford IL 61104 Fax: 815-961-7723.

RENO, RUSSELL RONALD, JR., lawyer; b. Gary, Ind., Nov. 28, 1933; s. Russell Ronald Sr. and Katherine Narcissus (White) R.; m. Mary Ellen Klock, Jan. 30, 1956; children: Mary Hall, Russell III, William, Elizabeth. AB, Haverford Coll., 1954; JD, U. Pa., 1957. Bar: Md. 1957, D.C. 1983. Assoc. Venable, Baetjer & Howard, Balt., 1958-66, ptnr., 1966—; asst. atty. gen. State of Md., Balt., 1962-64. Author: Maryland Real Estate Law-Practice, 1983. Bd. dirs. Balt. Choral Arts Soc., 1966—; trustee Goucher Coll., Balt., 1978-98, trustee emeritus, 1998—; chancellor Episcopal Diocese of Md., Balt., 1985—; bd. mgrs. Haverford Coll., 1990-2002. Fellow Am. Bar Found., Md. Bar Found.; mem. ABA, Md. State Bar Assn., Am. Coll. Real Estate Lawyers, Hamilton St. Club, Wednesday Law Club. Education and schools, Finance, Property, real (including real estate development, water). Home: 706 W Joppa Rd Baltimore MD 21204-3810 Office: Venable Baetjer & Howard 2 Hopkins Plz Ste 2100 Baltimore MD 21201-2982 E-mail: rrreno@venable.com.

RENOUX, VINCENT ANDRE, lawyer; b. Paris, Apr. 23, 1963; s. Andre and Nicole (Chenu) Renoux; m. Valerie Aelion, Aug. 7, 1995; children: Marion, Paul, Juliette; m. Valerie Le Meur, July 10, 1988 (div. July 1, 1993); 1 child, Emmanuelle. LLM, Univ. Paris XII, 1985, DESS Fiscalite, 1986; diploma politics, IEP Paris, 1988. Assoc. Coopers & Lybrand, Paris, 1989—92, mgr., 1992—96, dir., 1996—99; ptnr. PWC, Paris, 1999—2000, Landwell, Paris, 2000—01, Stehlin and Assoc., Paris, 2001—. Prof. IEP Paris, 1999—2001. Mem.: IFA, Paris. Taxation, general, Corporate taxation, Estate taxation. Office: Stehlin and Assoc 48 Ave Victor Hugo 75116 Paris France

RENWICK, EDWARD S. lawyer; b. L.A., May 10, 1934; AB, Stanford U., 1956, LLB, 1958. Bar: Calif. 1959, U.S. Dist. Ct. (cen. dist.) Calif. 1959, U.S. Ct. Appeals (9th cir.) 1963, U.S. Dist. Ct. (so. dist.) Calif. 1973, U.S. Dist. Ct. (no. dist.) Calif. 1977, U.S. Dist. Ct. (ea. dist.) Calif. 1981, U.S. Supreme Ct. 1985. Ptnr. Hanna and Morton LLP, L.A. Mem., bd. vis. Stanford Law Sch., 1967-69; mem. environ. and natural resources adv. bd. Stanford Law Sch. bd. dirs. Calif. Supreme Ct. Hist. Soc. Fellow Am. Coll. Trial Lawyers, Am. Bar Found.; mem. ABA (mem. sect. on litigation, antitrust law, bus. law, chmn. sect. of nat. resources, energy and environ. law 1987-88, mem. at large coord. group energy law 1989-92, sect. rep. coord. group energy law 1995-97, Calif. del. legal com., interstate oil compact com.), Calif. Arboretum Assn. (trustee 1986-92), L.A. County Bar Assn. (chmn. natural resources law sect. 1974-75), The State Bar of Calif., Chancery Club (pres. 1992-93), Phi Delta Phi. Environmental, General civil litigation, Natural resources. Office: Hanna and Morton LLP 444 S Flower St Ste 1500 Los Angeles CA 90071-2922 E-mail: erenwick@hanmor.com.

RENZ, WILLIAM TOMLINSON, lawyer; b. Washington, Feb. 26, 1947; s. William C. and Anna T. (Tomlinson) R.; m. Suellen Gilson, Feb. 3, 1968; children: William T. Jr., Michelle, Michael. BA, Pa. State U., 1969; JD, Dickinson Sch. Law, 1972. Bar: Pa. 1972, U.S. Supreme Ct. 1979, U.S. Ct. Appeals (3d cir.) 1982. From assoc. to ptnr. Power, Bowen & Valimont, Doylestown, Pa., 1972—99; ptnr. Fox, Rothschild, O'Brien & Frankel, LLP, 1999. Served to capt. U.S. Army, 1969-77. Mem. ABA, Pa. Bar Assn. (treas. young lawyers div.), Bucks County Bar Assn. (bd. dirs. 1984-86), Deep Run Sports Assn. (v.p.), Am. Legion (parliamentarian Dept. Pa., judge adv. 1994-99). Republican. Avocations: racquetball, baseball, chess. Federal civil litigation, State civil litigation. Office: 102 N Main St Doylestown PA 18901-3711

REPHAN, JACK, lawyer; b. Little Rock, Mar. 16, 1932; s. Henry and Mildred (Frank) R.; m. Arlene Clark, June 23, 1957; children: Amy Carol, James Clark. BS in Commerce, 1954; LLB, U. Va., 1959. Bar: Va. 1959, D.C. 1961. Assoc. Kanter & Kanter, Norfolk, Va., 1959-60; law clk. to Judge Sam E. Whitaker, U.S. Ct. Claims, Washington, 1960-62; assoc. Pierson, Ball & Dowd, Washington, 1962-64; ptnr. Danzansky, Dickey, Tydings, Quint & Gordon, Washington, 1964-77; mem. Braude, Margulies, Sacks & Rephan, Washington, 1977-87; ptnr. Porter, Wright, Morris & Arthur, Washington, 1987-88, Sadur, Pelland & Rubinstein, Washington, 1988-93; counsel Hofheimer Nusbaum P.C., Norfolk, Va., 1993-00; principal Rephan Lassiter, PLC, Norfolk, 2001—. Mem. nat. panel arbitrators Am. Arbitration Assn., NASD Bd. Arbitrators; lectr. joint com. continuing legal edn. State Bar Va. Contbr. articles to legal jours. Pres. Patrick Henry PTA, Alexandria, Va., 1968-69, Linkhorn Bay Condominium Assn., 2000—; treas. John Adams Mid. Sch. PTA, Alexandria, 1970-71; pres. Seminary Ridge Citizens Assn., 1976-77; Dem. candidate for Alexandria City Com., 1969. 1st lt. AUS, 1955-57. Mem. ABA (chmn. subcom. on procurement of jud. remedies pub. contract sect. 1973-74), Va. Bar Assn. (govt. sect. constrn. law 1979-81, 99—, vice chmn. 1980-81, chmn. 1981-82), D.C. Bar Assn., Assoc. Gen. Contractors, Hampton Roads Utility and Heavy Contractors Assn. (gen. counsel), Cavalier Golf and Yacht Club, Kiwanis (pres. Landmark Club 1969). Jewish. Home: 1276 Laskin Rd Ste 402 Virginia Beach VA 23451-5272 Office: 500 E Main St Ste 1200 Norfolk VA 38510-2204 E-mail: jrephan@rephanlassiter.com.

REPPER, GEORGE ROBERT, lawyer; b. Topeka, Dec. 22, 1954; s. George Vincent Jr. and Maria Magdalena (Bullert) R.; m. Helen Linda Zeichner, Aug. 23, 1981; children: Brian Lawrence, Kevin Michael, Michelle Suzanne. BS, SUNY, Albany, 1977; JD, Albany Law Sch., 1981. Bar: N.Y. 1982, D.C. 1982, U.S. Patent and Trademark Office 1984, U.S. Ct. Appeals (fed. cir.) 1989. V.p. Rothwell, Figg, Ernst & Manbeck, Washington, also bd. dirs. Contbr. articles to profl. jours. including Patent World. Mem. ABA (patents, trademarks and copyrights sect.), D.C. Bar Assn. (patents, trademarks and copyrights sect.), Am. Intellectual Property Law Assn., Internat. Intellectual Property Assn., Internat. Fedn. Indsl. Property Attys., Intellectual Property Owners, Internat. Trademark Assn. Republican. Mergers and acquisitions, Patent, Trademark and copyright. Office: Rothwell Figg Ernst & Manbeck 1425 K St NW Ste 800 Washington DC 20005

REPPERT, NANCY LUE, former county official, legal consultant; b. Kansas City, Mo., June 17, 1933; d. James Everett and Iris R. (Moomey) Moore; m. James E. Cassidy, 1952 (div.); children: James E., II, Tracy C. Student, Ctrl. Mo. State U., 1951-52, U. Mo., Kansas City, 1971-75; cert. legal asst., Rockhurst Coll., Kansas City, 1980, cert. risk mgr., 1979. With Kansas City chpt. ARC, 1952-54, N. Ctrl. Region Boy Scouts Am., 1963-66, Clay County Health Dept., Liberty, Mo., 1966-71, city of Liberty, 1971-80; risk mgr. City of Dallas, 1982-83; dir. Dept. Risk Mgmr., Pinellas County, Fla., 1984-94; ind. legal cons. Cedar Rapids, Iowa, 1994—. Mem. faculty William Jewell Coll., Liberty, 1975-80; vis. prof., U. Kans., 1981; adj. prof. dept. polit. sci. masters program, U. South Fla., 1990; seminar leader, cons. in field. Author: Kids are People, Too, 1975, Pearls of Potentiality, 1980; also contbr. articles to publs. Lay min., United Meth. Ch., 1965—; dir. youth devel., Hillside United Meth. Ch., Liberty; co-chmn. youth dir. Collegiate United Meth. Ch. scouting coord. Palm Lake

Christian Ch., Exec. Fellow U. South Fla., mem. Coun. Ministries; advancement chmn. Mid-Iowa Coun. Boy Scouts Am., membership chmn. White Rock Dist. Coun., health and safety chmn. West Ctrl. Fla. Coun., 1985—; scouting coord., chmn. youth dept., bd. dirs., pastor's cabinet, diaconate Palm Lake Christian Ch., 1987—; skipper Sea Explorer ship, 1986—; bd. dirs. Neighborly Sr. Svcs., Inc.; vol. sailing master, instr., Boys & Girls Clubs and Hawkeye Coun. Boy Scouts Am., Cedar Rapids. Recipient Order of Merit, Boy Scouts Am., 1979, Living Sculpture award, 1978, 79; Svc. award Rotary Internat., 1979; Internat. awrd of Merit/Leadership Excellence, IBA, 1992; Exec. fellow, U. South Fla., 1988. Mem. NAFE, Am. Mgmt. Assns., Internat. Platform Assn., Risk Mgrs. Soc., Pub. Risk & Ins. Mgmt. Asns., Am. Soc. Profl. & Exec. Women, Am. Film Inst., U.s. Naval Inst., Nat. Inst. Mcpl. Law Officers. Home: 257 38th Street Dr SE Apt 8 Cedar Rapids IA 52403-1116 E-mail: windsongsailor@netzero.com.

RESCINIO, ALBERT JOHN, lawyer; b. Red Bank, N.J., June 15, 1964; s. Umberto Nicholas and Margaret Elizabeth Rescinio; m. Tara Rescinio, Jan. 15, 2000. BS, Villanova U., 1986, JD, 1989. Bar: N.J. 1989, Pa. 1989, U.S. Dist. Ct. N.J. 1990. Tax atty. Arthur Andersen & Co., Phila., 1989—90; atty. Gulkin & Beinhaker, Livingston, NJ, 1990—91, Domenichetti & Hook, Woodbridge, NJ, 1992; pvt. practice Oakhurst, NJ, 1992—. Mem. adv. bd. Cmty. Bank N.J., Freehold, 1999—. Mem. Colombus Day Parade com., Long Branch, NJ, 1992—; chmn. Man of Y. dinner Amerigo Vespucci, Long Branch, NJ; head parade marshal Columbus Day Parade, Long Branch, NJ, 1999—. Mem.: ABA, Monmouth City Bar, Pa. Bar, N.J. Bar, Fraternal Order Police. Commercial, consumer (including collections, credit), Personal injury (including property damage), Banking. Office: 1806 Hwy 35 Oakhurst NJ 07755 Office Fax: 732-531-8080. Business E-Mail: arescinio@monmouth.com.

RESKE, STEVEN DAVID, lawyer, writer; b. Mpls., May 31, 1962; s. Albert Edgar Reske and Florence Mae Altland. BA with distinction, St. Olaf Coll., Northfield, Minn., 1985; JD cum laude, Boston U., 1988. Bar: Ill. 1988, Minn. 1989, D.C. 1998, U.S. Dist. Ct. Minn. 1991, U.S. Ct. Appeals (5th cir.) 1989, (7th and 8th cir.) 1992, (D.C. circuit) 1998, U.S. Supreme Ct. 1993. Intern U.S. Senator Durenberger, Washington, 1981-82, Citizens for Ednl. Freedom, Washington, D.C., 1981-82, Abbott-Northwestern Hosp., Mpls., 1984, U.S. Dist. Ct. Judge Magnuson, St. Paul, 1986; summer assoc. Faegre & Benson, Mpls., 1987; assoc. Sidley & Austin, Chgo., 1988; law clk. to Hon. Judge Politz U.S. Ct. Appeals 5th cir., Shreveport, La., 1988-89; pvt. practice, 1989—; writer, 1989—. Contbr. CD Rev., 1993-95, JAZZIZ, 1996—, Skyway News, 1997—, City Pages, 2000—; contbr. articles to profl. jours.; mem. Am. Jour. Law and Medicine, 1986-87, editor, 1987-88; legal editor-at-large Law and Politics, 1998—; columnist Twin Cities Revue, 1998—. Recipient Minn. Super Lawyer award, 1998, Am. Jurisprudence award, 1988; Edward F. Hennessey scholar, 1988, G. Joseph Tauro scholar, 1986. Mem. ABA (antitrust divsn.), Minn. State Bar Assn., Hennepin County Bar Assn., Am. Econ. Assn., Am. Philos. Assn. Antitrust, Federal civil litigation, Constitutional. Office: 3422 Douglas Dr N Crystal MN 55422-2414 E-mail: stevenresk@aol.com.

RESNICK, ALICE ROBIE, judge; b. Erie, Pa., Aug. 21, 1939; d. Adam Joseph and Alice Suzanne (Spizarny) Robie; m. Melvin L. Resnick, Mar. 20, 1970 PhB, Siena Heights Coll., 1961; JD, U. Detroit, 1964. Bar: Ohio 1964, Mich. 1965, U.S. Supreme Ct. 1970. Asst. county prosecutor Lucas County Prosecutor's Office, Toledo, 1964-75, trial atty., 1965-75; judge Toledo Mcpl. Ct., 1976-83, 6th Dist. Ct. Appeals, State of Ohio, Toledo, 1983-88; instr. U. Toledo, 1968-69; justice Ohio Supreme Ct., 1989—. Co-chairperson Ohio State Gender Fairness Task Force. Trustee Siena Heights Coll., Adrian, Mich., 1982— ; organizer Crime Stopper Inc., Toledo, 1981— ; mem. Mayor's Drug Coun.; bd. dirs. Guest House Inc. Mem. ABA, Toledo Bar Assn., Lucas County Bar Assn., Nat. Assn. Women Judges, Am. Judicature Soc., Toledo Women's Bar Assn., Ohio State Women's Bar Assn. (organizer), Toledo Mus. Art, Internat. Inst. Toledo. Roman Catholic. Home: 2407 Edgehill Rd Toledo OH 43615-2321 Office: Supreme Ct Office 30 E Broad St Fl 3 Columbus OH 43215

RESNICK, DONALD IRA, lawyer; b. Chgo., July 19, 1950; s. Roland S. and Marilyn B. (Weiss) R.; m. Jill Allison White, July 3, 1977; children: Daniel, Allison. BS with high honors, U. Ill., 1972; JD, Harvard U., 1975. Bar: Ill. 1975, U.S. Dist. Ct. (no. dist.) Ill. 1975. Assoc. Arvey, Hodes, Costello & Burman, Chgo., 1975-80, ptnr., 1981-83; sr. ptnr. Nagelberg & Resnick, Chgo., 1983-89, Levenstein & Resnick, Chgo., 1989-91; chmn. real estate dept. Jenner & Block, Chgo., 1992—. Mem. mgmt. com. Jenner & Block, Chgo. Mem. ABA, Birchwood (Highland Park, Ill.) Club. Property, real (including real estate development, water). Office: Jenner & Block 1 E Ibm Plz Fl 4000 Chicago IL 60611-7603 E-mail: dresnick@jenner.com.

RESNICK, JEFFREY LANCE, federal magistrate judge; b. Bklyn., Mar. 5, 1943; s. Bernard and Selma (Monheit) R.; m. Margery O'Connor, May 27, 1990. BA, U. Conn., 1964; LLB, U. Conn., West Hartford, 1967. Bar: Conn. 1967, N.Y. 1968, U.S. V.I. 1968, D.C. 1979, U.S. Ct. Appeals (3d cir.) 1979. Assoc. Office of J.D. Marsh, Christiansted, St. Croix, V.I., 1967-69; asst. atty. gen. Dept. Law, Christiansted, 1969-73; ptnr. James & Resnick, Christiansted, 1973-89; magistrate judge U.S. Dist. Ct. V.I., Christiansted, 1989—. Active V.I. Bridge Team, 1971—. Jewish. Avocation: writing poetry and palindromes. Office: US District Court 3013 East Golden Rock Christiansted VI 00820-4256

RESNICK, MELVIN L. judge; b. N.Y.C., June 27, 1927; s. Jack and Ida Resnick; m. Alice Robie Resnick, Mar. 20, 1970; children: Kenneth, Gary, Cynthia. Grad., U. Toledo, 1949; JD, Ohio State U., 1952. Bar: U.S. Supreme Ct. 70. Assoc. Streicher, Gorman & Barone, Toledo, 1952—76; asst. prosecutor Lucas County, Toledo, 1961—76; judge Lucas County Common Please Ct., Toledo, 1976—89, presiding adminstrv. judge, 1989; judge 6th Dist. Ct. Appeals, Toledo, 1990—, presiding judge, 1996—97. With USN, 1945—46. Named Number 1 Appellate Judge for 6th Dist., Toledo Jr. Bar Assn., 1993—; recipient Supreme Ct. award for outstanding or excellent svc., 1976—88, Outstanding Judge award, Ohio Acad. Trial Lawyers, 1982, Order of the Heel award, Toledo Jr. Bra Assn., 1981. Mem.: ABA, Ohio Jud. Conf. (former chmn. civil law sect.), Ct. Appeals Assn. (former chmn. jud. adminstrv. and proc. com.), Ohio Ct. Appeals Assn., Am. Judicature Soc., Lucas County Bar Assn., Toledo Bar Assn., Ohio State Bar Assn., Toledo Mus. Art, Old Newsboys Toledo, Tau Epsilon Rho, Delta Theta Phi, Alpha Epsilon Pi. Office: 6th Dist Ct Appeals 800 Jackson St Toledo OH 43624 Fax: 419-213-4844.

RESNICK, PHILLIP STANLEY, lawyer; b. Mpls., July 19, 1944; s. Sidney L. and Rae J. (Barres) Resnick; children: Allison, David. BA, U. Minn., 1967; JD, William Mitchell Coll., 1971. Bar: Minn. 1971, U.S. Dist. Ct. Minn. 1972, U.S. Ct. Appeals (8th cir.) 1972, U.S. Supreme Ct. 1977. Pres. Phillip S. Resnick & Assocs., Mpls. Mem.: ABA, Hennepin County Bar Assn., Minn. Assn. Criminal Def. Lawyers (bd. dirs., pres. 1995—), Minn. Trial Lawyers Assn., Minn. Bar Assn., Nat. Assn. Criminal Def. Lawyers. Criminal. Address: Phillip S Resnick & Assocs 527 Marquette Ave Ste 1925 Minneapolis MN 55402-1334

RESNICK, STEPHANIE, lawyer; b. NYC, Nov. 12, 1959; d. Diane Gross. AB, Kenyon Coll., 1981; JD, Villanova U., 1984. Bar: Pa. 1984, N.J. 1984, U.S. Dist Ct. (ea. dist.) Pa. 1984, U.S. Dist Ct. N.J. 1984, N.Y. 1990, U.S. Ct. Appeals (3d cir.) 1993, U.S. Dist. Ct. (so. dist.) N.Y. 1996, U.S. Dist. Ct. (ea. dist.) N.Y. 2001, U.S. Supreme Ct. 1998. Assoc. Cozen and O'Connor, Phila., 1984-87, Fox, Rothschild, O'Brien & Frankel, Phila., 1987-92, ptnr., 1992—. Mem. Vols. for Indigent Program, Phila., 1987-92. Mem.: ABA, Womens Way (vice-chair 2002, chair 2003), N.Y. Bar Assn., N.J. Bar Assn., Phila. Bar Assn. (investigative divsn. Commn. on Jud. Selection and Retention 1988—94, profl. guidance com. 1992—96, profl. responsibility com. 1992—2000, women's rights com., women in the profession com. 1993—, Comm. on Jud. Selection and Retention 1995—2001, vice-chair 1996, chair 1997, fed. cts. com. 2000—, vice-chair 2001—02, chair 2002—03), Pa. Bar Assn. (disciplinary bd. and study com. 1989—91, prof. liability com. 1991—92, commr. on Women in the Profession 1997—99). Federal civil litigation, General civil litigation, Insurance. Home: 233 S 6th St Apt 2306 Philadelphia PA 19106-3756 Office: Fox Rothschild O'Brien & Frankel 2000 Market St Ste 10 Philadelphia PA 19103-3231

RESNICOW, NORMAN JAKOB, lawyer; b. N.Y.C., July 23, 1947; s. Herbert and Melly (Engelberg) R.; m. Barbara Jane Roses, June 14, 1970; children: Daniel Ilan, Joel Ethan. BA summa cum laude, Yale U., 1969, JD, 1972. Bar: N.Y. 1973, U.S. Dist. Ct. (so. and ea. dists.) N.Y. 1973. Assoc. Baker & McKenzie, N.Y.C., 1972-79, ptnr., 1979-98, Piper, Marbury Rudnick & Wolff, N.Y.C., 1998-2000, Fox Horan & Camerini, N.Y.C., 2000—. Term mem. Council Fgn. Relations, N.Y.C., 1976-81; exec. com., vice chair, v.p., treas., bd. dirs. Hebrew Immigrant Aid Soc., N.Y.C., 1981—; mem. nat. young leadership cabinet United Jewish Appeal, N.Y.C., 1978-83. Recipient Young Leadership award United Jewish Appeal-Fedn. Jewish Philanthrophies, 1978. Mem. ABA (corp. bus. and banking law, internat. law sects.), Assn. of Bar of City of N.Y. (internat. trade com. 1987-89, com. nuclear law and tech. 1992-98), N.Y. State Bar Assn. (internat. law com. 1985-87, internat. employement law com. 1997—), Phi Beta Kappa. Democrat. Avocation: internat. polit. relations. Commercial, contracts (including sales of goods; commercial financing), Private international, Mergers and acquisitions. Home: 4701 Iselin Ave Bronx NY 10471-3323 Office: Fox Horan & Camerini LLP 825 Third Ave New York NY 10022 E-mail: njresnicow@foxlex.com.

RESOR, STANLEY ROGERS, lawyer; b. N.Y.C., Dec. 5, 1917; s. Stanley Burnet and Helen (Lansdowne) R.; m. Jane Lawler Pillsbury, Apr. 4, 1942 (dec.); children: Stanley R., Charles P., John L., Edmund L., William B., Thomas S., James P.; m. Louise Mead Walker, May 1, 1999. BA, Yale U., 1939, LLB, 1946. Bar: N.Y. 1947. Assoc., then ptnr. firm Debevoise & Plimpton, N.Y.C., 1946-65, 71-73, 79-87, of counsel, 1988-90; undersec. Dept. Army, 1965, sec., 1965-71, ambassador negotiations for Mut. and Balanced Force Reductions in Central Europe, 1973-78; undersec. for policy Dept. Def., 1978-79; ret. Fellow Yale Corp., 1979-86. Served to maj. AUS, 1942-45. Decorated Silver Star, Bronze Star, Purple Heart; recipient George C. Marshall award Assn. U.S. Army, 1974, Sylvanus Thayer award Assn. Graduates of U.S. Mil. Acad., 1984. Mem. ABA, Assn. of Bar of City of N.Y. (chmn. com. internat. arms control and security affairs 1983-86), Atlantic Coun., Arms Control Assn. (chmn. bd. 1994-2000), UN Assn. U.S.A., Coun. Fgn. Rels., Lawyers Alliance for World Security (bd. dirs.), Internat. Inst. Strategic Studies. Republican. Episcopalian. Home: 809 Weed St New Canaan CT 06840-4023 Office: 1824 Phelps Pl NW #1804 Washington DC 20008 Home Fax: 202-966-3965; Office Fax: 202-462-7081. E-mail: srresor@aol.com.

RESTA, MANUELA, lawyer; b. Trieste, Italy, Jan. 10, 1973; d. Nicola and Teresa (Gargaro) Resta. ML, Catholic U, Milan, Italy, 1991—96; JCL jud. processing , U of Milan, Italy, 1991, ML indsl. law, 1995. Bar: Milan Bar Assoc., course: judge and lawyer, Milan, comml. arbitration, Milan, teacher: Cereda. Lawyer Assoc. study, Milan, 1997, Assoc. study fellow, Milan, 1998—99, Assoc. study Franzosi, Milan, 2000—01, assoc. study DE Luca, Milan, 2001—02; juridical and economic matters secondary school, Brindisi, Milan, Italy, 2002. Recipient studies merit, 1991. Mem.: Lunedi Letterario, Merco Letterario, Foundation of Scala Theatre of Milan. Avocations: gymnastics, fencing. Home: Via Manzoni 81 76021 Trancavilla FNA BR Italy Office: Studio Legale FDE Luca Piazza Borromeo 12 20123 Milan Italy

RESTIVO, JAMES JOHN, JR., lawyer; b. Pitts. s. James J. and Dorothy (Ardolino) R.; m. Gail Sharon Hackenburg, July 11, 1970; 4 children BA in History, U. Pa., 1968; JD, Georgetown U., 1971. Bar: Pa. 1971, U.S. Dist. Ct. (we. and ea. dists.) Pa. 1971, U.S. Ct. Appeals (3d cir.) 1971, U.S. Supreme Ct. 1979. Ptnr. Reed Smith, Pitts., 1979—; head litigation dept. Reed, Smith, Shaw & McClay, Pitts., 1986-97. Mem. editl. staff Georgetown Law Rev., 1970-71. Bd. dirs. Greater Pitts. C. of C., Rebuilding Together-Greater Pitts., Pitts. Regional Alliance. Fellow Am. Coll. Trial Lawyers; mem. Acad. Trial Lawyers Allegheny County, Allegheny County Bar Assn., Pa. Economy League (Western divsn.), Def. Rsch. Inst. Banking, General civil litigation, Insurance. Home: 209 Deer Meadow Dr Pittsburgh PA 15241-2253 Office: Reed Smith 435 6th Ave Ste 2 Pittsburgh PA 15219-1886 E-mail: jrestivo@reedsmith.com.

RETANA, VANESSA, lawyer; b. San José, Costa Rica, Apr. 17, 1970; d. Manuel Enrique Retana Jimenez and Elizabeth Barrantes Bosques; m. Juan Eduardo Medina Alvarado, Dec. 21, 2002. Law Degree, U. Costa Rica, San José, 1992, Agrarian Law Specialist (hon.) , 1995; Magister Scientae, U. Nantes, France, 1998. Rschr. and asst. to the exec. dir. Estudios para el Futuro Consultores; stagiere Hunsperger & Weston, Ltd. and The Hannon Law Firm, Denver, 1999—99; lawyer Guardia, Cubero & Facio, 2001—01, Facio Abogados, San José, 2001—. Prof. U. for Internat. Cooperation, San José, 1999—99, U. Costa Rica, San José, 1999—2001; cons. Fundación Arias para la Paz y el Progreso Humano, San José, 2001—02. Contbr. , chapters to books, articles to profl. jours. Mem.: Colegio de Abogados de Costa Rica. Administrative and regulatory, Environmental, Corporate, general. Home: Barrio La Granja San Pedro San José Costa Rica Office: Apdo 67-1260 Plaza ColonialRoble Escazú San José Costa Rica Office Fax: 201-8707. Personal E-mail: vretana@hotmail.com. E-mail: vretana@faciolaw.com.

RETSON, NICHOLAS PHILIP, lawyer, military officer; b. Appleton, Wis., Oct. 20, 1947; s. Philip Nicholas and Catherine Retson; m. Birgit Maria Abromaitis, Dec. 30, 1977; children: Philip N., Kathryn L., Nicholas Peter. BA in Chemistry, Ripon Coll., 1969; JD, Marquette U., 1972; LLM in Govt. Procurement, George Washington U., 1983. Bar: Wis. 1972, U.S. Dist. Ct. (ea. and we. dists.) Wis. 1972; cert. ct. mediator Va. Commd. 2nd lt. U.S. Army, 1969, advanced through grades to col., 1990-01; ops. officer Trial Def. Svc., Falls Church, Va., 1976-78; prof. contract law Judge Adv. Gen.'s Sch., Charlottesville, Va., 1979-82; trial team chief Office Chief Trial Atty., Falls Church, 1983-86; chief contract law divsn. Hdqrs. U.S. Army Europe, Heidelberg, Germany, 1986-90; chief counsel U.S. Army Test and Evaluation Command, Aberdeen Proving Ground, Md., 1990-93; chief contract law divsn. Office Judge Adv. Gen., Washington, 1993-95; army chief trial atty. U.S. Army Litigation Ctr., Arlington, Va., 1995-00; pres. ADRbizLLC, 2001—; chief stds. of conduct and profl. responsibility U.S. Army Litigation Ctr., 2000-01, dep. gen. counsel, def. contract mgmt. agy., 2002—. Fellow Wis. Bar Found.; mem. ABA (vice chair alternative disputes resolution subcom. sect. on pub. contract law 1995—), State Bar Wis. (dir. non resident lawyers divsn. 1980—), Ripon Coll. Alumni Assn. (dir. 1995-2001), Fed. Bar Assn., Assn. for Conflict Resolution (treas. com. sec., 2001-.). Greek Orthodox. Avocations: travel, stocks, scouting. Office: Def Contract Mgmt Agy Office Gen Counsel 6350 Walker Ln Ste 300 Alexandria VA 22310-3241

REUBEN, DON HAROLD, lawyer; b. Chgo., Sept. 13, 1928; s. Michael B. and Sally (Colucci) R.; m. Evelyn Long, Aug. 27, 1948 (div.); children: Hope Reuben Boland, Michael Barrett, Timothy Don, Jeffrey Long, Howard Ellis; m. Jeannette Hurley Haywood, Dec. 13, 1971; stepchildren: Harris Hurley Haywood, Edward Gregory Haywood. BS, Northwestern U., 1949, JD, 1952. Bar: Ill. 1952, Calif. 1996. With firm Kirkland & Ellis, Chgo., 1952-78, sr. ptnr., until 1978, Reuben & Proctor, Chgo., 1978-86, Isham, Lincoln & Beale, Chgo., 1986-88; sr. counsel Winston & Strawn, 1988-94; of counsel Altheimer & Gray, Chgo., 1994—. Spl. asst. atty. gen. State of Ill., 1963-64, 69, 84; gen. coun. Tribune Co., 1965-88, Chgo. Bears Football Club, 1965-88, Cath. Archdiocese of Chgo., 1975-88; coun. spl. session Ill. Ho. of Reps., 1964, for Ill. treas. for congl., state legis. and jud. reapportionment, 1963; spl. fed. ct. master, 1968-70; dir. Lake Shore Nat. Bank, 1973-93; dir. Heitman Fin., 1993-98; mem. citizens adv. bd. to sheriff County of Cook, 1962-66, mem. jury instrn. com., 1963-68; rules com. Ill. Supreme Ct., 1963-73; past mem. pub. rels. com. Nat. Conf. State Trial Judges; mem. com. study caseflow mgmt. in law div. Cook County Cir. Ct., 1979-88; mem. adv. implementation com. U.S. Dist. Ct. for No. Dist. Ill., 1981-82; mem. Chgo. Better Schs. Com., 1968-69, Chgo. Crime Commn., 1970-80; mem. supervisory panel Fed. Defender Program, 1971-78; gen. counsel Palm Springs Air Mus., 1996—; dir. News-Gazette, Champaign, Ill., 1997-99; lectr. on libel, slander, privacy and freedom of press. Bd. dirs. Lincoln Park Zool. Soc., 1972-84 ; trustee Northwestern U., 1977—; mem. vis. com. U. Chgo. Law Sch., 1976-79; bd. dirs. Blood Bank of the Desert, 1999—, vice-chmn. 2001—; sec., gen. counsel Palm Springs Air Mus., 2000—. Recipient Northwestern U. Law Sch. Alumni Achievement medal, 2002. Fellow Internat. Acad. Trial Lawyers; mem. Ill. Bar Assn., Chgo. Bar Assn. (chmn. subcom. on propriety and regulation of contingent fees com. devel. law 1966-69, subcom. on media liaison 1980-82, mem. com. on profl. info. 1980-82), ABA (standing com. on fed. judiciary 1973-79, standing com. on jud. selection, tenure and compensation 1982-85), Am. Law Inst., Fellow: Am. Bar Found., Am. Coll. Trial Lawyers (Rule 23 com. 1975-82, judiciary com. 1987-91), Am. Arbitration Assn. (nat. panel arbitrators), Calif. Bar Assn., Desert Bar Assn., Tavern Club, Mid-Am. Club, Lawyers Club Chgo., Casino Club, Desert Riders of Palm Springs, Com. of 25 Palm Springs, The Chgo. Club, Mission Hills Country Club, Phi Eta Sigma, Beta Alpha Psi, Beta Gamma Sigma, Order of Coif. Office: 20 Jill Ter Rancho Mirage CA 92270-2635

REUBEN, LAWRENCE MARK, lawyer; b. Akron, Ohio, Apr. 5, 1948; s. Albert G. and Sara I. (Rifkin) R. Student, London Sch. Econs., 1969; BS, Ind. U., 1970; JD, Ind. U., Indpls., 1973. Bar: Ind. 1973, U.S. Dist. Ct. (so. dist.) Ind. 1973, U.S. Dist. Ct. (no. dist.) Ind. 1975, U.S. Ct. Appeals (7th cir.) 1975, U.S. Supreme Ct. 1976, U.S. Ct. Appeals (9th cir.) 1978, U.S. Ct. Appeals (D.C. cir.) 1994, U.S. Ct. Appeals (fed. cir.) 1999. Ptnr. Atlas, Hyatt & Reuben, Indpls., 1976-87, Atlas & Reuben, Indpls., 1987-90; chief counsel Ind. Dept. Ins., 1990-91; gen. counsel Ind. Dept. Transp., 1991-93; chief deputy Ind. Atty. Gen., Indpls., 1993-94; gen. counsel State Lottery Commn. Ind., Indpls., 1994-97; pvt. practice Indpls., 1997—. V.p. Ind. Civil Liberties Union, 1975-84; sec., bd. dirs. Indpls. Humane Soc., 1974-85; fellow Indpls. C. of C.-Lacey Leadership Program, 1982; sec., v.p., bd. dirs. Julian Ctr., Inc., 1983-89; mem. ch.-state commn. Nat. Jewish Community Relations Adv. Council, N.Y.C., 1982-89; bd. dirs. Indpls. Consumer Credit Counseling Bur., 1983-89; pres. Bur. Jewish Edn., 1984-86; parliamentarian Ind. State Dem. Party, 1985-86; mem. Indpls. Police Community Relations Rev. Com., 1983. Recipient Robert Risk award Ind. Civil Liberties Union, 1981, David M. Cook Meml. award Indpls. Jewish Community Rels. Coun., 1982; L.L. Goodman Leadership award, Jewish Fed. Indpls., 1989. Mem. Fed. Bar Assn., Ind. State Bar Assn., Indpls. Bar Assn. Federal civil litigation, Civil rights, Labor (including EEOC, Fair Labor Standards Act, labor-management relations, NLRB, OSHA). Office: Jefferson Plaza 1 Virginia Ave Ste 600 Indianapolis IN 46204-3671 E-mail: Lmreubenlaw@yahoo.com.

REUM, JAMES MICHAEL, lawyer; b. Oak Park, Ill., Nov. 1, 1946; s. Walter John and Lucy (Bellegay) R. BA cum laude, Harvard U., 1968, JD cum laude, 1972. Bar: N.Y. 1973, D.C. 1974, U.S. Dist. Ct. (so. dist.) N.Y. 1974, Ill. 1979, U.S. Dist. Ct. (no. dist.) Ill. 1982. Assoc. Davis Polk & Wardwell, N.Y.C., 1973-78; assoc. Minority Counsel Com. on Judiciary U.S. Ho. of Reps., Washington, 1974; ptnr. Hopkins & Sutter, Chgo., 1979-93, Winston & Strawn, Chgo., 1994—. Midwest advance rep. Nat. Reagan Bush Com., 1980; nominee commr. Securities and Exchange Comm., Pres. Bush, 1992; mem. G.W. Bush fin. com, 2000. Served to SP4 USAR, 1969-75. Recipient Harvard U. Honorary Nat. Scholarship, 1964-72. Mem. Monte Carlo Country Club (Monaco), Univ. Club (NYC), Racquet Club Chgo. Republican. Finance, Mergers and acquisitions, Securities. Home: 12 E Scott St Chicago IL 60610-2320 Office: Winston & Strawn 35 W Wacker Dr Ste 4200 Chicago IL 60601-1695 E-mail: jreum@winston.com.

REUTER, MICHAEL F.M. law educator; b. Simmern, Germany, Sept. 15, 1954; s. Heinrich and Gertrud R. Degree in law & econs., U. Bonn, Germany; PhD, U. Muenster, Germany; LLM, U. B.C. With Deutsche Bank, Dusseldorf, Germany, 1973-75, U. Muenster, Germany; prof. U. Cologne, Germany, 1991-98; lectr. U. Essen, Germany, 1996-2000. Chmn. Hattinger Studienkreis Wirtschaftsfragen, Germany. Mem. ABA, IFA, IBA. Office: Reuter & Ptnr Lotharstr 94 D-47057 Duisburg Germany Fax: 0049-203-370065. E-mail: reuterpart@aol.com.

REUTIMAN, ROBERT WILLIAM, JR., lawyer; b. Mpls., June 4, 1944; s. Robert William and Elsbeth Bertha (Doering) R.; m. Virginia Lee Traxler, June 25, 1983; children: Robert James, Joseph Lee. BA magna cum laude, U. Minn., 1966, JD, 1969. Bar: Minn. 1969, U.S. Ct. Mil. Appeals 1969, U.S. Dist. Ct. Minn. 1973, U.S. Ct. Appeals (8th cir.) 1976, U.S. Tax. Ct. 1979. Mem. Armstrong, Phleger, Reutiman & Vinokour, Ltd., Wayzata, Minn., 1973-76; ptnr. Phleger & Reutiman, Wayzata, 1976-81; pvt. practice Wayzata, 1981—. Chmn. Spring Pk. Planning Commn., 1978. Capt. U.S. Army, 1969-73. Decorated Army Commendation medal. Mem. ABA, Minn. Bar Assn., Hennepin County Bar Assn., Am. Arbitration Assn. (panel of arbitrators), Phi Beta Kappa. Lutheran. Avocations: fishing, rose growing. General civil litigation, Commercial, consumer (including collections, credit), Probate (including wills, trusts). Home: 11610 3rd Ave N Plymouth MN 55441-5919 Office: 305 Rice St E Wayzata MN 55391-1615

REVELEY, WALTER TAYLOR, III, dean; b. Churchville, Va., Jan. 6, 1943; s. Walter Taylor and Marie (Eason) R.; m. Helen Bond, Dec. 18, 1971; children: Walter Taylor, George Everett Bond, Nelson Martin Eason, Helen Lanier. AB, Princeton U., 1965; JD, U. Va., 1968. Bar: Va. 1970, D.C. 1976. Asst. prof. law U. Ala., 1968-69; law clk. to Justice Brennan U.S. Supreme Ct., Washington, 1969-70; fellow Woodrow Wilson Internat. Ctr. for Scholars, 1972-73; internat. affairs fellow Coun. on Fgn. Rels., N.Y.C., 1972-73; assoc. Hunton & Williams, Richmond, Va., 1970-76, ptnr., 1976-98, mng. ptnr., 1982-91, cons., 1998—; dean William and Mary Law Sch., 1998—. Lectr. Coll. William and Mary Law Sch., 1978-80; cons. in field. Author: War Powers of the President and Congress: Who Holds the Arrows and Olive Branch, 1981; mem. editl. bd. Va. Law Rev., 1966-68; contbr. articles to profl. jours. Trustee Princeton U., 1986-90, 91-2001, Presbyn. Ch. (U.S.A.) Found., 1991-97, Va. Hist. Soc., 1991-96, 2003—, Union Theol. Sem., 1992-2000, Andrew W. Mellon Found., 1994—, JSTOR, 1995—, Va. Mus. Fine Arts, 1995—, pres. 1996-99, St. Christopher's Sch., 1996-01, Carnegie Endowment for Internat. Peace, 1999—; bd. dirs. Fan Dist. Assn., Richmond, Inc., 1976-80, pres., 1979-80; bd. dirs. Richmond Symphony, 1980-92, pres., 1988-90, pres. symphony coun., 1994-99; bd. dirs. Presbyn. Outlook Found., 1985-2003, pres., 1992-95; bd. dirs. Va. Mus. Found., 1990-99; elder Grace Covenant Presbyn. Ch.; bd. dirs. New Covenant Trust Co., 1997-99, Va. Found. Humanities, 2001-. Mem. ABA, Va. Bar Assn., D.C. Bar Assn., Am. Bar Found., Va. Bar Found., Princeton Assn. Va. (bd. dirs. 1981—, pres. 1983-85), Va. State Bar (edn. Lawyers sect. bd. govs. 1992—, chmn. 1992-95), Raven Soc., Phi Beta Kappa, Omicron Delta Kappa. Home: 2314 Monument Ave Richmond VA 23220-2604 Office: William and Mary Law Sch PO Box 8795 Williamsburg VA 23187-8795 E-mail: Taylor@wm.edu.

REVERCOMB, HORACE AUSTIN, III, judge; b. Richmond, Va., Sept. 22, 1948; s. Horace Austin Jr. and Mary Virginia (Kelley) R.; m. Annie S. Anthony, July 10, 1976; children: Brian Austin, Suzanne Melanie. BA, Pembroke State U., 1971; JD, George Mason U., 1977. Bar: Va. 1978. Pvt. practice law, King George, Va., 1978-82; ptnr. Revercomb & Revercomb, King George, 1982-90; judge Gen. Dist. Cts. of 15th Jud. Dist. Va., 1990-99, Cir. Cts. 15th Jud. Cir. Va., 1999—. Mem. Va. Bar Assn. Methodist. Avocation: music. Home: PO Box 216 King George VA 22485-0216 E-mail: HRevercomb@aol.com.

REVESZ, RICHARD LUIS, law educator; b. Buenos Aires, May 9, 1958; BSE in Civil Engring. summa cum laude, Princeton U., 1979; MS, Mass. Inst. Tech., 1980; JD, Yale U., 1983. Bar: N.Y. 1986, D.C. 1986, U.S. Supreme Ct. 1989, U.S. Ct. Appeals (D.C. cir.) 1986, U.S. Dist. Ct. (so. dist.) N.Y. 1986. Jud. clerk for Chief Judge Wilfred Feinberg U.S. Ct. Appeals (2d cir.) N.Y., 1983-84; jud. clerk for Justice Thurgood Marshall U.S. Supreme Ct., 1984-85; asst. prof. NYU Law Sch., 1985-88, assoc. prof., 1988-90, prof., 1990—. Cons. superfund settlements Adminstrv. Conf. U.S., 1991-92, cons. nonacquiescence by agys., 1986-89; term mem. Coun. Fgn. Rels., 1989—; pro-bono rep. Natural Resources Def. Coun., 1987; cons. dept. tech. coop. for devel. UN, 1980-81. Contbr. articles to profl. jours. Cons. Carnegie Commn. Sci., Tech. and Govt., 1989-90. Recipient Exploratory Rsch. grant EPA, 1991—. Mem. ABA (vice chmn. com. jud. review sect. adminstrv. law 1988—), Am. Law Inst. (mem.'s consultative group 1993—), N.Y. State Bar Assn. (chmn. com. adminstrv. law 1988-91, sec. com. second century 1986-88, mem. com. environ. law 1986-88), Phi Beta Kappa, Sigma Xi, Tau Beta Pi (prize winner). Office: NYU Sch Law Vanderbilt Hall 40 Washington Sq S Ste 406 New York NY 10012-1099

REW, LAWRENCE BOYD, lawyer; b. Eugene, Oreg., June 22, 1936; BA, Whitman Coll., 1958; JD, Willamette U., 1961. Bar: Oreg. 1961. Ptnr. Corey, Byler, Rew, Lorenzen & Hojem, LLP, Pendleton, Oreg., 1965—. Fellow Am. Bar Found.; mem. ABA, Oreg. State Bar Assn. (pres. 2000, Pub. Svc. award 1991, bd. bar examiners 1975-79, bd. govs. 1996-2000). Estate planning, Probate (including wills, trusts), General practice. Office: Corey Byler Rew Lorenzen & Hojem LLP PO Box 218 222 SE Dorion Ave Pendleton OR 97801-2553

REY, JOSE M. lawyer; b. Madrid, Oct. 21, 1967; s. Jose Rey and M. Oliva Garcia. Degree in law, Complutense U. Madrid, 1991, M of Tax Law, 1992. Bar: Madrid. Atty. Gomez-Acebo & Pombo, Madrid, 1991—95. Tchr. Inst. Emoresa, Madrid, 1999—2002, INESE, 1997—98, ALITER, 2002—03. Intellectual property, Trademark and copyright. Office: Larrauri & Lopez Ante Hermosilla 30 28001 Madrid Spain Fax: 34 91 577 0763. E-mail: jmrey@larraurilopezante.com.

REY, PATRICIA FATIMA, lawyer; b. Principality of Monaco, Aug. 21, 1966; d. Henry and Susan (Zanganeh) R. Maitrise de droit, U. Droit, Nice, France, 1989; LLM, Georgetown U., Washington, 1990. Bar: Principality of Monaco. Paralegal O'Connor & Hannan, Washington, 1990; Soc. Civil Profl. Piasezzi, Cardix, Carlotti, Nice, 1991; paralegal Gide, Loyrette & Nouel, Brussels, 1992; rschr. Price Waterhouse, Brussels, 1992; paralegal EEC Commn., Brussels, 1992; pvt. practice Principality of Monaco, 1996—. Mem. Dem. Nat. Union. Avocations: golf, painting. Office: Avocat 19 Bvd des Moulins MC 98000 Monaco Monaco E-mail: etudeprey@atlantis.mc., avocat@patriciarey.com.

REYES ROBBINS, ANN MARIE, magistrate, judge; b. Los Angeles, Calif., Mar. 9, 1966; d. Raymond Alexander and Flora (Sanchez) Reyes; m. Jeffrey Warren Schroeder, Sept. 20, 1986 (div. July 22, 1997); 1 child, Andrew Nicholas Reyes-Schroeder; m. Bruce Anthony Robbins, Nov. 7, 1997. BA, Am. Lit., U. of So. Calif., Los Angeles, California, 1991—94; JD, U. Mich., Ann Arbor, 1998. Bar: Ind. 1999, cert.: ICO (Family Law Specialist) 2002, registered: Ind. Jud. Ctr. (Probation Officer) 1998, Domestic Relations Mediator: Ind. 1998, So Dist. Ct.: Ind. 1999, bar: Ind. (No. Dist. Ct.) 1999. Edn. track liaison Allen Superior Ct. Family Rels. Divsn., Fort Wayne, Ind., 1998, asst. chief juvenile probation officer, 1999—99; assoc. Avery & Van Gilder, Fort Wayne, Ind., 1999—2000; assoc. jr. ptnr. Blume Connelly Jordan & Stucky, LLP, Fort Wayne, Ind., 2000—01, ptnr., 2002—02; magistrate Allen Superior Ct. Family Rels. Divsn., Fort Wayne, Ind., 2003—. Mem. 3rd Dist. Pro Bono Commn., Fort Wayne, 2002. V.p. League of United Latin Am. Citizens, Fort Wayne, Ind., 1999—2000; bd. dirs. United Hispanic Americans, Fort Wayne, 1999—2001, Vol. Lawyers Program, Fort Wayne, 2002; pres. Allen County Minority Health Coalition, Fort Wayne, 2001; vice chair Allen County Dem. Party, Fort Wayne, Ind., 2002, latino/hispanic liaison, 2001. Fellow Kellog/Bergstom Child Welfare Law Summer Fellow, U. Mich. Law Sch., 1997, Mexican Am. Legal Def. and Edn. Fund, Pub. Interest Law Initiative (PILI), 1997; scholar Juan Luis Tienda Scholarship, U. of Mich. Law Sch., 1996. Mem.: ABA (15th Ann. Family Law Trial Advocacy Inst. 2001), Am. Inns of Court, Nat. Ct. Appointed Spl. Advocates, Nat. Assn. of Counsel for Children, Ind. State Bar Assn., Allen County Bar Assn. (women lawyers sect.), Hispanic Nat. Bar Assn., Benjamin Harrison Chpt. Office: Allen Superior Ct 715 S Calhoun St Rm 208 Fort Wayne IN 46802 Office Fax: 260-449-3161. E-mail: ann.reyes.robbins@co.allen.in.us.

REYNARDUS, JORGE EDGARDO, lawyer; b. N.Y.C., Dec. 15, 1964; s. Jorge and Clara Reynardus; m. Tania Tejera Reynardus, July 25, 1992; children: Johannes, Kristine, Hannah. BA in History, Fla. Internat. U., 1992, MA in Am. History, MA in Internat. Studies, Fla. Internat. U., 1995; JD, U. Pa., 1998. Bar: Fla. 1998, U.S. Dist. Ct. (so. dist.) Fla. 1999, U.S. Dist. Ct. (mid. dist.) Fla. 2001, U.S. Ct. Appeals (11th cir.) 2002. Traffic mgr. GS&B Advt., 1989—90; assoc. Holland & Knight LLP, Miami, Fla., 1998—. Dir. Internat. Businessman's Assn., Miami, 2002—. Vol. atty. ad litem Lawyers for Children Am., 1999—; bd. mem. Miami Dade County (Fla.) Affirmative Action Adv. Bd., 1999—2002, Miami Dade County Supt. Rev. Panel, 2002—. Sgt. U.S. Army, 1985—89. Louis L. Redding fellow, Del. Bar, 1996. Mem.: ABA, Dade County Bar Assn., Cuban Am. Bar Assn. Presbyterian. Avocations: substitute teaching leader, Bible study fellowship. Product liability, Labor (including EEOC, Fair Labor Standards Act, labor-management relations, NLRB, OSHA). Office: Holland & Knight LLP Ste 3000 701 Brickell Ave Miami FL 33131

REYNOLDS, BRADLEY KENNETH, lawyer; b. St. Petersburg, Fla., May 23, 1966; s. Jay J. and Maxine V.E. Reynolds; m. Rhona Eileen Forbes, July 16, 1988; children: Connor Forbes, Senaidra Siobhain. BA with honours, Stirling U., Scotland, 1988; JD with high honors, Fla. State U., 1991. Bar: Ga. 1992, U.S. Dist. Ct. (no. dist.) Ga. 1997, U.S. Ct. Appeals (11th cir.) 2000, U.S. Ct. Internat. Trade 2001. Law clk., U.S. Magistrate Judge John E. Dougherty U.S. Dist. Ct. (no. dist.) Ga., Atlanta, 1991—93; staff atty. U.S. Ct. Appeals, 11th cir., Atlanta, 1993—95; atty. Lockheed Martin Corp., Marietta, Ga., 1995—2001; corp. atty. Ga. Gulf Corp., Atlanta, 2001—. Mem.: ABA, Order of Coif. Avocation: Tae Kwon Do (black belt). Antitrust, Private international, Commercial, contracts (including sales of goods; commercial financing). Office: Georgia Gulf Corp Ste 495 400 Perimeter Center Terrace Atlanta GA 30346

REYNOLDS, MICHAEL TIMOTHY, lawyer; b. N.Y.C., June 29, 1968; s. Timothy John and Patricia Mary Reynolds. AB in History magna cum laude, Dartmouth Coll., 1990; MPhil in Medieval History, Cambridge (Eng.) U., 1991; JD, Yale U., 1995. Bar: N.Y. 1996, U.S. Dist. Ct. (so. and ea. dists.) N.Y. 1996. Law clk. to Hon. Diarmuid F. O'Scannlain, U.S. Ct. Appeals for 9th Cir., Portland, Oreg., 1995—96; ptnr. Cravath, Swaine & Moore, N.Y.C., 2003—. Exec. editor Yale Law Jour., 1994-95. Mem. bd. proprietors The Dartmouth, Inc., Hanover, NH, 2001—. Keasbey Found. scholar Cambridge U., 1990-92. Mem.: Assn. Bar City NY, Phi Beta Kappa. Antitrust, General civil litigation, Non-profit and tax-exempt organizations. Office: Cravath Swaine & Moore 825 8th Ave Fl 38 New York NY 10019-7475

REYNOLDS, ROBERT HUGH, lawyer; b. St. Louis, Jan. 3, 1937; s. Leslie A. and Rebecca (McWaters) R.; m. Carol Jemison, Apr. 8, 1961; children: Stephen H., Cynthia C., Laura M. BA, Yale U., 1958; JD, Harvard U., 1964. Assoc. Barnes & Thornburg, Indpls., 1964-70, ptnr., 1970—, chmn. bus. dept., 1983-91; chmn. internat. practice group, 1992—; vice-chmn. TerraLex, 1996—2003, chmn., 2003—. Co-chmn., editor Comml. Real Estate Financing for Ind. Attys., 1968; vice-chmn., co-editor Advising Ind. Businesses, 1974; chmn., editor Counseling Ind. Businesses, 1981, The Purchase and Sale of a Business, 1987. Bd. dirs. Crossroads Am. Coun. Boy Scouts Am., v.p., 1971-75, pres., 1987-89; v.p. Area 4 Ctrl. Region Boy Scouts Am., 1989-92, pres., 1992-93, pres. Ctrl. Region, 1993-96, Nat. Exec. Bd., 1993— (Silver Buffalo award); bd. dirs. Family Svc. Assn. Indpls., 1974-81, pres., 1978-80; bd. dirs. Family Svc. Am., 1979-88, Greater Indpls. Fgn. Trade Zone, 1987-2000, Indpls. Conv. and Visitors Assn., 1989-2000, Indpls. Econ. Devel. Corp., 1983-99, Greater Indpls. Progress Com., 1986-2000, exec. com., vice chmn. (Charles L. Whistler award); hon. trustee Children's Mus. Indpls., trustee, 1988-96, chmn., 1992-94; bd. dirs. Indpls. Downtown Inc., chmn., 1996-99; bd. gov. Legacy Fund, 1992—, v.chmn., 2000-; bd. dirs. Noyes Meml. Found., Japan-Am. Soc. Ind., pres., 1994—, Ctrl. Ind. Cmty. Found., 2003—. Named Hon. Consul Gen. of Japan, 1999—. Fellow Ind. Bar Found., Indpls. Bar Found.; mem. ABA, Ind. Bar Assn. (chmn. corp., banking and bus. law sect. 1981-82, chmn. internat. sect. 1994-96), Internat. Bar Assn., Indpls. Bar Assn., Greater Indpls. C. of C. (bd. dirs., sec. 2000—), Econ. Club Indpls. (bd. dirs.). Clubs: Univ., Skyline (Indpls.). Lodges: Kiwanis. Republican. Corporate, general, Private international, Mergers and acquisitions. Office: Barnes & Thornburg 11 S Meridian St Indianapolis IN 46204-3535 E-mail: rreynolds@btlaw.com.

REZANKA, THOMAS W. lawyer; b. Plainfield, N.J., Mar. 3, 1954; s. William L. and Helen G. Rezanka; m. Karen T. Rezanka, May 21, 1977. BA, Montclair State U., Upper Montclair, N.J., 1976; JD, Stetson U., 1980. Bar: Fla. 1980, U.S. Ct. Appeals (5th and llth cirs.) 1980. Pvt. practice, Palm Harbor, Fla., 1980—. Presenter Joint Conf. on Law and Aging, Washington, 1995. Monthly legal columnist Tropical Breeze, 1995-2001, Countryside Cougar, East Lake Eagle, Palm Harbor Panther, Dunedin Highlander, 1995—. Mem. adv. com. Countryside H.S., Clearwater, Fla., 1998-99; bd. dirs. Tampa Bay Area Planned Giving Coun., Tampa, 2001. Mem. ABA, Nat. Acad. Elder Law Attys., Fla. Bar Assn. (former mem. legis. drafting com. real property, probate and trust law sect., exec. coun. elder law sect. 1995-99, faculty counseling your Fla. client seminar for out-of-state attys. 1999, faculty elder law bd. cert. rev. course 1998, editor The Advocate newsletter 1996-97), Clearwater Bar Assn. (estate planning columnist 1996-97, 2000-01, probate, guardianship and trust practice com.), Pinellas County Estate Planning Coun. (bd. dirs. 1995-99). Office: 2672 West Lake Rd Palm Harbor FL 34684

REZNECK, DANIEL ALBERT, lawyer; b. Troy, N.Y., Apr. 26, 1935; s. Samuel and Elizabeth (Fishburne) R.; m. Beverly Ann Macht, Mar. 7, 1971; children: Jonathan Noah, Abigail Rebecca. BA, Harvard U., 1956, JD, 1959. Bar: N.Y. 1959, D.C. 1961. Rsch. asst. Harvard U. Law Sch., Cambridge, Mass., 1959-60; law clk. to Justice William J. Brennan U.S. Supreme Ct., Washington, 1960-61; asst. U.S. atty. Dept. Justice, Washington, 1961-64; assoc. Arnold & Porter, Washington, 1964-68, ptnr., 1969-95; gen. counsel D.C. Fin. Responsibility and Mgmt. Assistance Authority, Washington, 1995—2001, D.C. Office of the Corp. Counsel, 2001—. Adj. prof. law Georgetown U., Washington, 1963—; mem. D.C. Commn. on Jud. Disabilities and Tenure, 1979-86, D.C. Bd. Profl. Responsibility, 1994-2000; trustee D.C. Pub. Defender Svc., 1981-87. Contbr. articles to profl. jours. Named Young Lawyer of Yr. for D.C., 1971 Fellow Am. Coll. Trial Lawyers, Am. Bar Found.; mem. ABA, D.C. Bar (pres. 1975-76, pres. Bar Found. 1994-97), Bar Assn. D.C., Asst. U.S. Attys. Assn. Jewish. Avocations: american history, reading, writing. General civil litigation, Criminal. Home: 2852 Albemarle St NW Washington DC 20008-1036 Office: CD Corp Counsel 441 4th St NW 6th Fl S Washington DC 20001 E-mail: daniel.rezneck@dc.gov.

RHEE, ALBERT, lawyer, author; b. Pa., June 25, 1958; s.S.K. Rhee and B.C. Chun; m. I.Y. Choi, June, 1992. AB, Wabash (Ind.) Coll., 1980; JD, U. So. Calif., 1985; postgrad., Oxford U.; M Jurisprudence, U. Calif., Berkeley, 1990, postgrad., 1990—94. Bar: N.Y. 1986. Fellow Bryn Mawr (Pa.) Coll., 1985-87; instr. U. Calif. Boalt Hall Sch. Law, 1987-95, Columbia U., 1999—. Editor: Patent Law in Korea, 1994, Intellectual Property in Korea, 1995. Recipient Franklin award, 1985, fellowship Bryn Mawr Coll., 1985-87, U. Calif. Berkeley grad. fellowship, 1988-90, Boalt Hall fellowship, 1990-92. Avocations: tennis, music, fine arts. E-mail: albersjr@aol.com.

RHEINSTEIN, PETER HOWARD, healthcare company executive, consultant, physician, lawyer; b. Cleve., Sept. 7, 1943; s. Franz Joseph Rheinstein and Hede Henrietta (Neheimer) Rheinstein Lerner; m. Miriam Ruth Weissman, Feb. 22, 1969; 1 child, Jason Edward BA with high honors, Mich. State U., 1963, MS, 1964; MD, Johns Hopkins U., 1967; JD, U. Md., 1973. Bar: Md. 1973, D.C. 1980, U.S. Supreme Ct. 2000; diplomate Am. Bd. Family Practice; cert. added qualifications in geriatric medicine. Intern USPHS Hosp., San Francisco, 1967-68, resident in internal medicine Balt., 1968-70; instr. internal medicine U. Md., Balt., 1970-73; med. dir. extended care facilities CHC Corp., Balt., 1972-74; dir. drug advt. and labeling divsn. FDA, Rockville, Md., 1974-82, acting dep. dir. Office Drugs, 1982-83, acting dir. Office Drugs, 1983-84, dir. Office Drug Standards, 1984-90, dir. medicine staff Office Health Affairs, 1990-99; sr. v.p. for med. and clin. affairs Cell Works, Inc., Balt., 1999—. Chmn. Com. on Advanced Sci. Edn., 1978-86, Rsch. in Human Subjects Com., 1990-92; adj. prof. forensic medicine George Washington U., 1974-76; WHO cons. on drug regulation Nat. Inst. for Control Pharm. and Biol. Products, China, 1981-90; advisor on essential drugs WHO, 1985-90; FDA del. to U.S. Pharmacopeial Conv., 1985-90, coord. com. for assessment and transfer of tech. NIH, 1990-99, mem. health care fin. adminstrn. tech. adv. com., 1990-98, Nat. Adv. Coun. on Healthcare Policy, Rsch. and Evaluation, 1990-99, Healthy People 2000/2010 Steering Com., 1990-99, CDC and Prevention Task Force on Cmty. Preventive Svcs., 1996-99, Nat. Task Force on CME Industry/Provider Collaboration, 1992—, ann. meeting chmn., 2003; cons. in legal medicine and regulatory affairs, 1999—. Co-author: (with others) Human Organ Transplantation, 1987; spl. editorial advisor Good Housekeeping Guide to Medicine and Drugs, 1977-80; mem. editorial bd. Legal Aspects Med. Practice, 1981-89, Drug Info. Jour., 1982-86, 91-95; pub. Discovery Medicine, 2001–; contbr. articles to profl. jours. V.p. Intercultural Friends Found., 1998—. Recipient Commendable Svc. award, FDA, 1981, Group award of merit, 1983, 1988, Group Commendable Svc. award, 1989, 1992, 1993, 1995, 1995, 1999, Commr.'s Spl. citation, 1993; grantee NIH Nat. Cancer Inst. SBIR grant, 2001. Fellow Am. Coll. Legal Medicine (bd. govs. 1983-93, treas., chmn. fin. com. 1985-88, 90-91, chmn. publs. com. 1988-93, jud. coun. 1993-95; Pres.'s awards 1985, 86, 89-91, 93, Gold medal 2003), Am. Acad. Family Physicians; mem. Am. Acad. Pharm. Phys. (bd. trustees 1999—, v.p. AMA rels. 1999—, pres. Washington-Balt. chpt. 1999—), AMA (life; ho. of dels. 2002--), ABA, Drug Info. Assn. (bd. dirs. 1982-90, pres. 1984-85, 88-89, v.p. 1986-87, chmn. ann. meeting 1991, 94, steering com. Ams. 1991—, Outstanding Svc. award 1990), Fed. Bar Assn. (chmn. food and drug com. 1976-79, Disting Svc. award 1977), Med. and Chirurgical Faculty Md., Balt. City Med. Soc., Johns Hopkins Med. and Surg. Assn., APHA, Md. Bar Assn., Math. Assn. Am., Soc. Indsl. and Applied Math., Mensa (life), U. Md. Alumni Assn. (life), Fed. Exec. Inst. Alumni Assn. (life), Johns Hopkins U. Alumni Assn. (life), Mich. State U. Alumni Assn. (life), Mich. State U. Honors Coll. Alumni Assn. (bd. dirs. 1998-2001, pres. 2000-2001, Food and Drug Adminstrn. Alumni Assn.), Chartwell Golf and Country Club, Annapolis Yacht Club, Johns Hopkins Club, Delta Theta Phi (life). Avocations: boating, electronics, physical fitness, real estate investments. Home: 621 Holly Ridge Rd Severna Park MD 21146-3520 Office: Cell Works Inc 6200 Seaforth St Baltimore MD 21224-6506 E-mail: phr@jhu.edu., peter@cell-works.com.

RHIND, JAMES THOMAS, lawyer; b. Chgo., July 21, 1922; s. John Gray and Eleanor (Bradley) R.; m. Laura Haney Campbell, Apr. 19, 1958; children: Constance Rhind Robey, James Campbell, David Scott. Student, Hamilton Coll., 1940-42; AB cum laude, Ohio State U., 1944; LL.B. cum laude, Harvard U., 1950. Bar: Ill. bar 1950. Japanese translator U.S. War Dept., Tokyo, Japan, 1946-47; congl. liaison Fgn. Operations Adminstrn., Washington, 1954; atty. Bell, Boyd & Lloyd, Chgo., 1950-53, 55—, ptnr., 1958-92, of counsel, 1993—. Bd. dirs. Kewaunee Scientific Corp., Statesville, N.C. Commr. Gen. Assembly United Presbyn. Ch., 1963; life trustee Ravinia Festival Assn., Hamilton Coll., Clinton, N.Y., U. Chgo.; Northwestern Univ. Assocs.; chmn. Cook County Young Republican Orgn., 1957; Ill. Young Rep. nat. committeeman, 1957-58; v.p., mem. bd. govs. United Rep. Fund Ill., 1965-84; pres. Ill. Childrens Home and Aid Soc., 1971-73, life trustee; bd. dirs. E.J. Dalton Youth Center, 1966- 69; governing mem. Chgo. Symphony Orch., Chgo.; mem. Ill. Arts Council, 1971-75; mem. exec. com. div. Met. Mission and Ch. Extension Bd., Chgo. Presbytery, 1966-68; trustee Presbyn. Home, W. Clement and Jessie V. Stone Found., U. Chgo. Hosps. Served with M.I. AUS, 1943-46. Mem. ABA, Ill. Bar Assn., Chgo. Bar Assn. (bd. mgrs. 1967-69), Fed. Bar Assns., Chgo. Council on Fgn. Relations, Japan Am. Soc. Chgo., Lawyers Club Chgo., Phi Beta Kappa, Sigma Phi. Clubs: Chicago, Glen View (Ill.), Commercial (Chgo.), Mid-Day Club (Chgo.), Economic (Chgo.). Corporate, general, Securities. Home: 830 Normandy Ln Glenview IL 60025-3210 Office: Bell Boyd & Lloyd 3 First National Pla 70 W Madison St Ste 3200 Chicago IL 60602-4244 E-mail: jrhind@bellboyd.com.

RHINE, JOHN E. lawyer; b. Eldorado, Ill., Nov. 12, 1952; s. R.L. and Iris Faye (Harlow) R.; children: Oliver Sampson, Tison Hausser, Julia Eva. BA, So. Ill. U., 1974; JD magna cum laude, U. Ill., 1977. Bar: Ill. 1977, U.S. Dist. Ct. (so. dist.) Ill. 1979, U.S. Ct. Appeals (7th cir.) 1985. Law clk. to justice Ill. Supreme Ct., Springfield, 1977-78; pvt. practice law Mt. Carmel, Ill., 1978-79; ptnr. Rhine, Ernest & Vargo, Mt. Carmel, 1979—. Bd. dirs. Koester Cos., Nat. Land & Mineral Co., Inc., Starlight TV Corp., chmn., 1989-94; vis. prof. law Moscow State Inst. Internat. Rels., 1993, 95. Adv. coun. mineral lands mgmt. U. Evansville (Ind.), 1984-88; active Mt. Carmel Planning Commn., 1986-88; del. Moscow Conf. on Law and Econs., 1990; bd. dirs. Voices Ill. Children, 1990—, chmn. bd. dirs., 1993-96. Mem. Ill. Bar Assn. (mineral law subcom. 1984, law office econs. sect. coun. 1986-93, chmn. 1991-92, mineral law sect. coun. 1993—). Presbyterian. Oil, gas, and mineral. Office: Rhine Ernest & Vargo 631 N Market St Mount Carmel IL 62863-1458

RHOADES, JOHN SKYLSTEAD, SR., federal judge; b. 1925; m. Carmel Rhoades; children: Mark, John, Matthew, Peter, Christopher. AB, Stanford U., 1948; JD, U. Calif., San Francisco, 1951. Prosecuting atty. City of San Diego, 1955-56, dep. city atty., 1956-57; pvt. practice San Diego, 1957-60; ptnr. Rhoades, Hollywood & Neil, San Diego, 1960-85; judge U.S. Dist. Ct. (so. dist.) Calif., San Diego, 1985—. With USN, 1943-46. Office: US Dist Ct 940 Front St San Diego CA 92101-8994

RHOADS, NANCY GLENN, lawyer; b. Washington, Oct. 15, 1957; d. Donald L. and Gerry R. R.; m. Robert A. Koons, June 23, 1984. BA, Gettysburg Coll., 1980; JD, Temple U., 1983. Bar: Pa., U.S. Dist. Ct. (ea. dist.) Pa. 1983. Rsch. asst. Prof. Mikochick, Phila., 1982-83; law clk. Phila. Ct. of Common Pleas, 1983-85; assoc. Post and Schell P.C., Phila., 1985-90, Sheller, Ludwig and Badey, Phila., 1990—. Co-author: Aging and the Aged: Problems, Opportunities, Challenges, 1980. Vol. Spl. Olympics. Mem. ATLA, Pa. Bar Assn., Phi Beta Kappa, Phi Alpha Theta, Pi Delta Epsilon, Eta Sigma Phi. Avocations: classical piano, horticulture, swimming. Personal injury (including property damage). Home: 401 Audubon Ave Wayne PA 19087-4006 Office: Sheller Ludwig and Badey 1528 Walnut St Philadelphia PA 19102-3604

RHOADS, PAUL KELLY, lawyer; b. La Grange, Ill., Sept. 4, 1940; s. Herbert Graves and Mary Margaret (Gurrie) R.; m. Katheryn Virginia Reissaus, Sept. 14, 1963; children: Elizabeth S. R. Saline, Katheryn B.R. Meek, Julia C. Rhoads Brenneman. BA, Washington & Lee U., 1962; JD, Loyola U., Chgo., 1967. Bar: Ill. 1967, U.S. Dist. Ct. (no. dist.) Ill. 1967, U.S. Tax Ct. 1980. Trust officer 1st Nat. Bank Chgo., 1963-69; with Schiff Hardin & Waite, Chgo., 1969-98, ptnr., 1973-98; sole practitioner Western Springs, Ill., 1999—. Author: Starting a Private Foundation, 1993, Managing a Private Foundation, 1997; contbr. articles to profl. jours. and chpts. to books. Trustee Ill. Inst. Tech., 1985-95, Western Springs (Ill.) Hist. Soc., 1983-92, Philanthropy Roundtable, Washington, 1992-2000; bd. dirs. Cyrus Tang Scholarship Found., 1984-91, McKay Enterprises, Chgo., 1981-2002; bd. overseers Ill. Inst. Tech. Chgo.-Kent Coll. Law, 1985-95; pres., bd. dirs. Grover Hermann Found., Chgo., 1984—; sec., bd. dirs. Western Springs Svc. Club, 1976-86; sec. Vandivort Properties, Inc., Cape Girardeau, Mo., 1990-2002; mem. adv. com. estate, tax and fin. planning Loyola U., 1986-92; adv. com. Thomas A. Roe Inst. for Econ. Policy Studies, Heritage Found., 1989—. Fellow Am. Coll. Trust and Estate Coun.; mem. Ill. State Bar Assn., Chgo. Bar Assn., Union League Club Chgo., Portage Lake Yacht Club (Onekama, Mich.) (commodore 1988, bd. dirs. 1985-89), Healthlands Golf Club (Onekama). Republican. Avocations: sailing, golf, tennis. Estate planning, Probate (including wills, trusts), Estate taxation. Office: 1000 Hillgrove Ave Western Springs IL 60558-1420 E-mail: paulkrhoads@ameritech.net.

RHODE, DEBORAH LYNN, law educator; b. Jan. 29, 1952; BA, Yale U., 1974, JD, 1977. Bar: D.C. 1977, Calif. 1981. Law clk. to judge U.S. Ct. Appeals (2d cir.), N.Y.C., 1977-78; law clk. to Hon. Justice Thurgood Marshall U.S. Supreme Ct., D.C., 1978-79; asst. prof. law Stanford (Calif.) U., 1979-82, assoc. prof., 1982-85, prof., 1985—; dir. Inst. for Rsch. on Women and Gender, 1986-90, Keck Ctr. of Legal Ethics and The Legal Profession, 1994—; sr. counsel jud. com. Ho. of Reps., Washington, 1998. Trustee Yale U., 1983-89; pres. Assn. Am. Law Schs., 1998; Ernest W. McFarland prof. Stanford Law Sch., 1997—; sr. counsel com. on the jud. U.S. Ho. of Reps., 1998; dir. Stanford Ctr. on Ethics. Author: Justice and Gender, 1989, (with Geoffrey Hazard) the Legal Profession: Responsibility and Regulation, 3d edit., 1993, (with Annette Lawson) The Politics of Pregnancy: Adolescent Sexuality and Public Policy, 1993, (with David Luban) Legal Ethics, 2001, (with Barbara Allen Babcock, Ann E. Freedman, Susan Deller Ross, Wendy Webster Williams, Rhonda Copelon, and Nadine H. Taub) Sex Discrimination and the Law, 1997, Speaking of Sex, 1997, Professional Responsibility: Ethics by the Pervasive Method, 1998, In the Interests of Justice, 2000 (with Geoffrey Hazard, Jr.) Professional Responsibility and Regulation, 2002; editor: Theoretical Perspectives on Sexual Difference, 1990, Ethics in Practice, 2000, The Difference Difference Makes: Women and Leadership, 2002 ; contbr. articles to profl. jours. Mem.: ABA (chmn. commn. on women 2000—02). Office: Stanford U Law Sch Crown Quadrangle Stanford CA 94305

RHODES, ALICE GRAHAM, lawyer; b. Phila., June 15, 1941; d. Peter Graham III and Fannie Isadora (Bennett) Graham; m. Charles Milton Rhodes, Oct. 14, 1971 (div. Apr. 21, 1997); children: Helen, Carla, Shauna. BS, East Stroudsburg U. Pa., 1962; MS, U. Pa., 1966, LLB, 1969, JD, 1970. Bar: N.Y. 1970, U.S. Dist. Ct. (so. and ea. dists.) N.Y. 1971, U.S. Ct. Appeals (2d cir.) 1971, Ky. 1983, U.S. Dist. Ct. (ea. dist.) Ky. 1985. Staff atty. Harlem Assertion Rights, Mobilization for Youth Office Econ. Opportunity, N.Y.C., 1969-70, coord. Cmty. Action Legal Svcs., 1970-72; assoc. dir. in charge of civil representation HUD Model Cities Cmty. Law Offices, N.Y.C., 1972-73; resource assoc. Commn. on Edn. & Employment of Women, N.C. Dept. Adminstrn., Raleigh, 1975-76; mgr. policies and procedures Div. for Youth, N.C. Dept. Human Resources, Raleigh, 1976; in-house counsel, petroleum transactional atty. Ashland, Inc. (formerly Ashland Oil, Inc.), 1980-82; corp. atty. core group Ashland, Inc., 1985-87, 88-91; mem. Ashland City Commn. Human Rights, 1993-99; mem. bd. regents Ea. Ky. U., 1994-2001; exec. bd., chmn. internal affairs com., academic affairs, 1997-98; asst. county atty. family ct. Jefferson County, 1999—2000. Mem. Property Valuation Appeals Commn., 1994; cons. pub. mem. selection and performance stds. review bd. Fgn. Svc., U.S. Dept. State, 1995, Fgn. Agrl. Svc. USDA, 1997; prison program planner, cons. N.Y. City Dept. Corrections, 1971; lectr. N.Y.C. Corrections Acad., Riker's, 1971; lectr. juvenile justice N.C. Law Enforcement Acad., Salemburg, 1976. Mem. usher bd. New Hope Bapt. Ch., Ashland, 1980-94; bd. dirs. YWCA Ashland, 1983-84, Ashland Heritage Pk. Commn., 1983-85; bd. dirs., budget com. United Way, Greenup County, Ky., Ashland, 1988-92; driver Meals on Wheels, 1983-91; vol. Am. Heart Assn., 1982-91; bd. dirs. Our Lady of Bellefonte Hosp. Found. Franciscan Sisters of the Poor, Ky. Health System, 1996-99, Carter G. Woodson Found. Study Afro-Am. Life and History, 1997; mem. adv. com. task force post secondary edn. Gov. of Ky.; bd. dirs. exec. com. Boyd County Dem. Women, 1996-2000; mem. presdl. search com. Ea. Ky. U., 1997-98, Ky. Gov.'s Conf. on Postsecondady Edn., 1999. Recipient Cmty. Svc. award Queens Community Corp., N.Y.C., 1972, Ashland C.C., 1986, Cmty. Svc. award NAACP, Ky.; NSF fellow, 1964, 65, ; faculty friends of Penn scholar U. Pa., 1966-69, Reginald Heber Smith postgrad. fellow cmty. law, 1969-71; named to Hon. Order of Ky. Cols., 1989. Fellow Ky. Bar Found.; mem. AAUW (bd. dirs. Phila. chpt. 1963-65), Nat. Bar Assn., N.Y. Bar, Ky. Bar Assn. (mem. edn. law, corp. house counsel, workers compensation law sects.), Pilot Club (exec. bd. Ashland 1983), Links, Inc., Penn Club (charter mem. N.Y. chpt.), Assn. Gov. Bds. Colls. and Univs., Jefferson Club, Bellefonte Country Club. Democrat. Avocations: interior decorating, sports, dancing, gourmet cooking, gardening. Home: PO Box 12488 Philadelphia PA 19151 Address: 658 N 65th St Philadelphia PA 19151

RHODES, GEORGE FREDERICK, JR., lawyer; b. Houston, Nov. 2, 1952; s. George F. and Marion Kathleen Rhodes; m. Bebe Lyn Burns, Nov. 30, 1980; 1 child, Elizabeth Kathleen. BS, U. Tex., 1974; JD, U. Houston, 1991. Bar: Tex. 1991, U.S. Dist. Ct. (all dists.) Tex. 1992. Reporter KTBC-TV, Austin, 1974-76; reporter KHOU-TV, Houston, 1977-79, KTVI-TV, St. Louis, 1979-82; dir. pub. rels. Inn on the Park Four Season Hotel, Houston, 1982-84; editor in chief Houston City Mag., 1984-86; dir. pub. affairs Tex. Children's Hosp., Houston, 1986-88; assoc. Hirsch & Westheimer, P.C., Houston, 1991-94, Haynes and Boone, LLP, Houston, 1994-99, Gibson-Gruenert, 1999—2002; ptnr. Golden & Rhodes, LLP, 2002—. Co-author: Annual Survey of Texas Privacy and Related Claims Against the Media, 1996-98; author: Will Contests and Other Probate Litigation, 1998-2003. Pres. The Park People, Houston, 1987-88; bd. dirs. U. Houston Law Alumni Assn., 1994-96. Avocations: reading, traveling. General civil litigation, Commercial, consumer (including collections, credit), Probate (including wills, trusts). Office: Frost Bank Bldg 6750 West Loop South Ste 920 Bellaire TX 77401-4103 E-mail: fred@golden-rhodes.com.

RHODES, JOHN JACOB, retired lawyer, former congressman; b. Council Grove, Kans., Sept. 18, 1916; s. John Jacob and Gladys Anne (Thomas) R.; m. Mary Elizabeth Harvey, May 24, 1942; children: John Jacob 3d, Thomas H., Elizabeth C. Rhodes Reich, James Scott. BS, Kans. State U., 1938; LLB, Harvard U., 1942. Bar: Kans. 1942, Ariz. 1945, D.C. 1965. Mem. 83d-97th congresses from 1st Dist. Ariz., chmn. Republican policy com. 89th-93d congresses, house minority leader, 1973-81; of counsel Hunton & Williams, Washington, 1985-97; mem. bd. overseers Hoover Instn., 1984-92. Chmn. platform com. Nat. Rep. Conv., 1972, permanent chmn., 1976, 80 Mem. Ariz. Bd. Pub. Welfare, 1951-52. Served with AUS, World War II; Col., ret. Mem. Mesa C. of C. (pres. 1950), SAR, Am. Legion, Ariz. Club, Mesa Golf and Country Club, Capitol Hill Club, Met. Club, Burning Tree Club (Bethesda, Md.), Pinetop Country Club, Masons (33 deg., Grand Cross), KP, Elks, Moose, Rotary, Beta Theta Pi (internat. pres. 1984-87). Republican. Methodist.

RHODES, THOMAS WILLARD, lawyer; b. Lynchburg, Va., Mar. 9, 1946; s. Howard W. and Ruth R.; m. Ann Bloodworth, May 31, 1975; children: Mildred, Andrew. AB, Davidson (N.C.) Coll., 1968; JD, U. Va., 1971. Bar: Ga. 1971. Assoc. Smith, Gambrell & Russell and predecessor firms, Atlanta, 1971-76, ptnr., 1976—. Dir., pres. Atlanta Vol. Lawyers Found., 1984-89, Fed. Defender Program, Atlanta, 1989-94, 2002—. Contbr. articles to profl. jours.; editor: Nonprofit News. Capt. USAR, 1968—72. Recipient Heiner award, Atlanta Vol. Lawyers Found., 1989. Fellow Am. Law Inst.; mem. Ga. Bar Assn. (past chmn. antitrust law sect.), ABA. Antitrust, Non-profit and tax-exempt organizations, General civil litigation. Office: Smith Gambrell & Russell Promenade II 1230 Peachtree St NE Ste 3100 Atlanta GA 30309-3592

RHYNE, SIDNEY WHITE, lawyer; b. Charlotte, N.C., Apr. 2, 1931; s. Sidney White and Ruth (Dry) R.; m. Rosemarie Kennedy, July 11, 1959; children: Patricia Ruth, Kendall Sidney, Randall Sylvanus. AB, Roanoke Coll., 1952; LLB, U. Pa., 1955; LLM, Georgetown U., 1961. Bar: Pa. 1955, D.C. 1957, U.S. Supreme Ct. 1959, Md. 1987. Assoc. Rhyne, Mullin, Connor and Rhyne, Washington, 1957-60; mem. Mullin, Rhyne, Emmons and Topel, Washington, 1961-97; individual practice law Washington, 1997—. Lectr. law ctr. Georgetown U., Washington, 1964-70. Pres. Legal Aid Soc. of D.C., 1976-78, trustee, 1968-80, pres. coun., 1991—; trustee Luth. Theol. Sem. at Phila., 1988-93, pres. coun., 1993—. With U.S. Army, 1955-57. Prettyman fellow Georgetown U., 1960-61. Fellow Am. Bar Found. (life); mem. ABA (mem. house delegates 1972-73, 75, 76-78, 98-2001), Bar Assn. D.C. (bd. dirs. 1969-73, 92-94, 98-2002, trustee Found., v.p. 1990-91, presdl. award 2000-2001), Fed. Comm. Bar Assn. (mem. exec. com. 1988-96, treas. 1991-92, Disting. Svc. award 1992, pres. 1994-95). Republican. Lutheran. Communications, Probate (including wills, trusts), Appellate. Office: 3250 Arcadia Pl NW Washington DC 20015-2330 E-mail: swrhyne@abanet.org.

RHYNEDANCE, HAROLD DEXTER, JR., lawyer, consultant; b. New Haven, Conn., Feb. 13, 1922; s. Harold Dexter and Gladys (Evans) R.; m. Barbara Ann Hall (dec.); 1 child, Harold Dexter III; m. Ruth Cosline Hakanson. BA, Cornell U., 1943, JD, 1949; grad., U.S. Army Command and Gen. Staff Coll., 1961, U.S. Army War Coll., 1970. Bar: N.Y. 1949, D.C. 1956, U.S. Tax Ct. 1950, U.S. Ct. Mil. Appeals 1954, U.S. Supreme Ct. 1954, U.S. Ct. Appeals (D.C. cir.) 1956, (2d cir.) 1963, (3rd cir.) 1965, (4th cir.) 1973, (5th cir.) 1968, (7th cir.) 1973, (9th cir.) 1964, U.S. Temporary Emergency Ct. Appeals 1975, U.S. Dist. Ct. D.C. 1956, U.S. Dist. Ct. (so. and ea. dist.) N.Y. 1963. Pvt. practice, Buffalo, Eggertsville, N.Y., 1949-50; examiner/gen. atty. ICC, Washington, 1950-51; atty.-advisor Subversive Activities Control Bd., Washington, 1951-52; trial atty., spl. asst. to atty. gen., asst. U.S. atty. U.S. Dept. Justice, Washington, 1953-62; sr. trial atty., asst. gen. counsel, gen. counsel FTC, Washington, 1962-73; counsel Howrey & Simon, Washington, 1973-76; mng. atty., asst. gen. counsel, corp. counsel Washington Gas Light Co., 1977-87; counsel Conner & Wetterhahn, 1987-90; cons. Fairview, N.C., 1990—. Exec. sec. adv. coun. on rules of practice and procedures FTC; mem. Jud. Conf. (D.C. Cir.), 1967—; chmn. legal and regulatory subcom. Solar Energy Com., Am. Gas Assn., Washington, 1978-84; lectr. George Washington U. Law Ctr., 1974; faculty moderator Def. Strategy Seminar Nat. War Coll., 1973; participant spl. programs Indsl. Coll. of Armed Forces, 1962, 69, Armed Forces Staff Coll., 1964. V.p. bd. dirs. Peninsula Symphony Assn., Palos Verdes Peninsula, Calif., 1989-94; bd. dirs. Help-The-Homeless-Help-Themselves, Inc., Palos Verdes Peninsula, 1991-93. 1st lt. U.S. Army, 1943-46, PTO; col. AUS, 1982—. Mem.: The Selden Soc. (London), Cornell Lawyers Club D.C. (pres. 1959—61), Washington Met. Area Corp. Counsel Assn. (bd. dirs. 1981—84), Bar Assn. of D.C., D.C. Bar Assn., Fed. Bar Assn., ABA, Cornell Alumni Assn., Leadership Asheville Forum, Officers Assn. (life), U.S. Army War Coll. Alumni Assn. (life), Mil. Officers Assn. of Am., Res., Mil. Order Carabao, Downtown Club Asheville (past pres.), Scottish Soc., Montreat (N.C.), Biltmore Forest Country Club (Asheville, N.C.), Am. Legion (life), Phi Delta Phi, Sigma Chi. Republican. Episcopalian. Administrative and regulatory, Antitrust, Federal civil litigation. Home and Office: Eagles View 286 Sugar Hollow Rd Fairview NC 28730-9559

RICCIO, FRANK JOSEPH, lawyer, educator; b. Somerville, Mass. BS, Boston Coll., 1973; JD, Suffolk U., 1985; D of Dental Medicine, Boston Coll., 1986. Bar: Mass. 1985, U.S. Dist. Ct. Mass. 1986, U.S. Ct. Appeals (1st cir.) 1986. Dentist, Lowell, Mass., 1977-83, Metheun, Mass., 1983-84; assoc. Sugarman & Sugarman, Boston, 1985-87; pvt. practice Braintree, Mass., 1987. Clin. instr. oral medicine Harvard U., Boston, 1995—. Dental extern USPHS, 1976. Mem. Am. Assn. Trial Attys., Nat. Bd. Trial Attys. (cert. civil trial specialist), Mass. Bar Assn., Mass. Acad. Trial Attys., Million Dollar Advocates Forum. Personal injury (including property damage). Office: Law Offices of Frank J Riccio PC 25 Braintree Hill Park Ste 208 Braintree MA 02184-8702 E-mail: fjriccio@socialaw.com.

RICCOMAGNO, MARIO, lawyer; b. Genoa, Italy, July 13, 1948; s. Domenico and Licia (Benzi) R.; m. Franca Galanti, Oct. 13, 1979; children: Francesco-Domenico, Edoardo. JD, U. Milan, 1972; postgrad., State U. Milan, 1972-76; Diploma, City of London Poly., 1972; student, Columbia U., 1980. Bar: Italy 1974, Supreme Ct. 1989. Lawyer Studio Legale Riccomagno, Genoa. Co-author: Code of International Conventions, 1977; contbr. numerous articles to profl. jours. Mem. Italian Bar Assn., Internat. Bar Assn., Internat. Law Assn., Am. Fgn. Law Assn., Associazione Italiana di Diritto Marittimo, London Maritime Arbitration Assn., Mediterranean and Middle East Inst. Arbitration, Mediterranean Maritime Arbitration Assn. (sec.-gen.), European Maritime Law Orgn. (dir.), Columbia Law Sch. Alumni Assn. Avocations: jogging, mountain climbing, travel, reading. Office: Studio Legale Riccomagno 4 Via Assarotti Genoa 16122 Italy

RICE, CANICE TIMOTHY, JR., lawyer; b. St. Louis, Apr. 4, 1950; s. Canice Timothy and Jane Elizabeth (Tobin) R. AB, Holy Cross Coll., 1972; JD, U. Mo., 1976. Bar: Mo. 1976, Ill. 1977, U.S. Dist. Ct. (cen. and so. dists.) Ill. 1977, U.S. Ct. Appeals (2d and 8th cirs.) 1977, U.S. Dist. Ct. (ea. dist.) Mo., U.S. Dist. Ct. (we. dist.) Mo. 2003, U.S. Ct. Appeals (2d cir.) 1991. Pvt. practice law, St. Louis, 1976—. Mem. Bar Assn. Met. St. Louis (chair fed. litigation and practice com. 1996-97, co-chair 1997-2002), Ill. Bar Assn., Mo. Assn. Trial Attys., Lawyers Assn. Federal civil litigation, State civil litigation, Personal injury (including property damage). Home: 6624 Kingsbury Blvd Saint Louis MO 63130-4605 Office: 319 N 4th St Ste 602 Saint Louis MO 63102

RICE, DONALD SANDS, lawyer, entrepreneur; b. Bronxville, N.Y., Mar. 25, 1940; s. Anton Henry and Lydia Phipps (Sands) R.; m. Edgenie Higgins, Aug. 27, 1966; children: Alice Higgins, Edgenie Rice Thomas. AB magna cum laude, Harvard U., 1961, LLB/JD cum laude, 1964; LLM in Taxation, NYU, 1965. Bar: N.Y. 1964, U.S. Ct. Claims 1965, U.S. Supreme Ct. 1981. Law clk. to judge U.S. Ct. Claims, 1965-67; assoc. Barrett, Smith, Schapiro & Simon, N.Y.C., 1967-71; ptnr. Barrett, Smith, Schapiro, Simon & Armstrong, N.Y.C., 1971-86; vice chmn. bd. The Bowery Savs. Bank, N.Y.C., 1986-88; ptnr. Chadbourne & Parke, N.Y.C., 1988-96; mng. dir. and prin. Ravitch Rice & Co. LLC, N.Y.C., 1996—; ptnr. Rice & Ravitch LLP, N.Y.C., 1996—. Bd. dirs. B-Line, LLC, N.Y. Port Terminal Devel. Co., LLC; lectr. Nat. Assn. Real Estate Investment Trusts, Bank Adminstrs. Inst., Bank Tax Inst., 1971-86; chmn., bd. dirs. Corp. of Yaddo, 1986—; co-chmn. Russian-Am. Banking Law Working Group, 1991-; v.p., treas., bd. dirs. Soviet Bus. and Comml. Law Edn. Found., 1991-96; vol. lectr. Fin. Svcs. Vol. Corps Mongolian Bank Tng. Program, 1993, Georgetown Internat. Law Inst., NYU Sch. Continuing Edn., Russian Trade Fair-U.S. Dept. Commerce, 1994; mem. nat. com. Am. fgn. policy study group dels. to China, Taiwan, 1996, 2000, 01, Roundtable on U.S.-China Policy and Cross-Strait Rels., 1996—; mem. real estate adv. bd. to N.Y. State Comptr., 1987-93; bd. advisors Am.-Russian Investment Forum, 1999—. Trustee Nat. Com. Am. Fgn. Policy, 1994—, sr. v.p., 1996—; trustee Marimed Found., 1984—97, Chapin Sch., 1980—91, v.p., 1989—91; trustee The Hackley Sch., 1974—81, St. Philip's Episcopal Ch., Mattapoisett, Mass., 1987—; pres. Quadequina Co./Mattapoisett Casino, 2001—; bd. dirs. African Med. Rsch. Found. , 1978—2002. Mem. ABA, Coun. Fgn. Rels., N.Y. State Bar Assn., Assn. of the Bar of the City of N.Y., Century Assn., Harvard Club N.Y., N.Y. Yacht Club. General practice, Mergers and acquisitions, Corporate taxation. Home: 1120 Fifth Ave New York NY 10128-0144 Office: Ravitch Rice & Co LLC 610 5th Ave Rm 420 New York NY 10020-2403 E-mail: ravricellc@aol.com.

RICE, GEORGE LAWRENCE, III, (LARRY RICE), lawyer; b. Jackson, Tenn., Sept. 24, 1951; s. George Lawrence Jr. and Judith W. (Pierce) R.; m. Joy Gaia, Sept. 14, 1974; children: George Lawrence IV (Nick), Amy Colleen. Student british studies, Oxford U., 1972-73; BA with honors, Rhodes Coll., 1974; JD, U. Memphis, 1976, Nat. Coll. Advocacy, ATLA, 1978. Bar: Tenn. 1977, U.S. Supreme Ct. 1980; cert. family law trial advocate Nat. Bd. Trial Advocacy, family law specialist, Tenn. Assoc. Rice, Admundsen & Capenton LLPC, 1976—, ptnr., 1981—. Cert. family law trial advocate NBTA and Family Law Specialist by Tenn. Author: Divorce Practice in Tenn., 1987, 2d edit., 1987, Family Law, 1988, Winning for Your Client, 1988, Divorce Practice A to Z, 1989, Divorce Lawyer's Handbook, 1989, (video) Divorce: What You Need to Know When it Happens to You, 1990, Rice's Divorce Practice Manual, 1990, Child Custody in Tennessee, 1992, Divorce Trial, Tribulations, Tactics and Triumphs, 1993, The Complete Guide to Divorce Practice, 1993, 2d edit., 1998, Divorce Practice Made Easier, 1993, Divorce Practice, 1994, Visual Persuasion, AIDS 1996 Clients, Prenuptial Agreements, 1996, The Ethical Effective Lawyer, 1996, Wiley Family Law Update, Discovery Supplement, 1997, Tennessee Evidence Workshop Handbook, 1997, Hot Topics in Family Law, 1997, Child Custody and Visitation in Tennessee, 1998, Larry Rice on Divorce: How to Run an Efficient and Effective Divorce Practice and Improve Client Satisfaction, 1998, Client Communications, 1998, Post Nuptial Agreement A Proposal for Consideration, 1998, Larry Rice of Divorce, 1998; mem. bd. editors Matrimonial Strategist, 1995-2002, Hunt, Hide Shoot--a Guide to Paintball, 1996; contbr. articles to profl. jours. Founding chmn. Student Legal Assistance Program, 1975; active Supreme Ct. Child Support Guidelines Commn., 1989, Family Law Revision Commn., 1990—91, 1998—2001; mem. Timberwolves Paintball Team, 1988—2000; exec. com. Rhodes Coll. Red and Black Soc., 1999—2002, chmn., 2001—01; treas. Rocky Mountain Elk Found., Memphis, 2001. Named one of Best Lawyers in Am., 1993, 94; recipient Excellence in Edn. award PESI, 1997; Outstanding intern supr. Rhodes Coll., Mentor award, 1997-98, award Amicus Curi Family Laws Sect. Wilson-Wilson, 1997-98. Mem. ABA (conv. lectr. 1993, 94, 98, 99, 01), ATLA, Tenn. Bar Assn. (chmn., co-founder family law sect. 1987-88), Memphis Bar Assn. (founding chmn. family law sect.), Tenn. Trial Lawyers Assn. Family and matrimonial. Office: Rice Amundsen & Capenton 275 Jefferson Memphis TN 38103-2251 E-mail: lrice@ricelaw.com.

RICE, JAMES BRIGGS, JR., lawyer; b. Kansas City, Mo., Dec. 31, 1940; s. James Briggs and Oma J. (Smoyer) R.; m. Carolyn Ryan, Aug. 11, 1962 (div.); children: James Briggs III, Cynthia L.; m. Beverly Sue, Oct. 24, 1980. AB, U. Mo., 1962, JD, 1965. Bar: Mo. 1965, U.S. Dist. Ct. (we. dist.) Mo. 1968. Assoc., Rogers, Field & Gentry, Kansas City, 1967-72; ptnr. Wesner, Wesner & Rice, Sedalia, Mo., 1972-75, Rice & Romines, Sedalia, 1975-80; pvt. practice, Sedalia, 1980—; atty. Sedalia Area Devel. Corp., 1976-79. Chmn., Police Pers. Bd., Sedalia, 1976. Served as capt. U.S. Army, 1965-67; Vietnam. Mem. ABA, Mo. Bar Assn., Pettis County Bar Assn. (pres. 1975), , Am. Judicature Soc., Mo. Assn. Trial Atty.'s, VFW, Vietnam Vets. of Pettis County. Republican. Methodist. Lodges: Kiwanis (pres. 1975), Noon-day Optimist, Masons, Shriners. General practice, Personal injury (including property damage), Workers' compensation. Office: 701 S Ohio Ave Sedalia MO 65301-4415 Home: 1940 Ashwood Cir Sedalia MO 65301-9296

RICE, JIM, state supreme court justice; b. Ramore Air Force Base, Ont., Canada, Nov. 15, 1957; (parents Am. citizens); BA in Polit. Sci., Mont. State U., 1979; JD U. Mont., 1982. Pub. defender Lewis and Clark County; ptnr. Jackson & Rice, Helena, Mont., 1985—2001; assoc. justice Mont. Supreme Ct., 2001—. Mem. Mont. Ho. Reps., 1989—95, ho. majority whip, 1993. Office: Justice Bldg Rm 323 PO Box 203003 Helena MT 59620-3003

RICE, JULIAN CASAVANT, lawyer; b. Miami, Fla., Dec. 31, 1923; s. Sylvan J. and Maybelle (Casavant) R.; m. Dorothy Mae Haynes, Feb. 14, 1958; children— Scott B., Craig M. (dec.), Julianne C., Linda D., Janette M. Student, U. San Francisco, 1941-43; JD cum laude, Gonzaga U., 1950. Bar: Wash. 1950, Alaska 1959, U.S. Tax Ct. 1988. Pvt. practice law, Spokane, 1950-56, Fairbanks, Alaska, 1959—; prin. Law Office Julian C. Rice (and predecessor firms), Fairbanks, 1959, Salcha, Alaska, 1999. Founder, gen. counsel Mt. McKinley Mut. Savs. Bank, Fairbanks, 1965-99, chmn. bd., 1979-80; v.p., bd. dirs., gen. counsel Skimmers, Inc., Anchorage, 1966-67; gen. counsel Alaska Carriers Assn., Anchorage, 1960-71, Alaska Transp. Conf., 1960-67. Mayor City of Fairbanks, 1970-72. Served to maj. USNG and USAR, 1943-58. Decorated Bronze Star, Combat Infantryman's Badge. Fellow Am. Bar Found. (life); mem. ABA, Wash. State Bar Assn. (50-Yr. mem. award 2000), Alaska Bar Assn., Transp. Lawyers Assn., Alternative Dispute Resolution Com., Am. Arbitration Assn. (mem. transp. comml., transp. panel), Spokane Exch. Club (pres. 1956). Alternative dispute resolution, Commercial, contracts (including sales of goods; commercial financing), Probate (including wills, trusts). Home and Office: 10104 Salcha Dr Salcha AK 99714-9624 Fax: 907-490-0018. E-mail: salcha@worldnet.att.net.

RICE, NANCY E. judge; b. Denver, June 2, 1950; 1 child. BA cum laude, Tufts U., 1972; JD, U. Utah, 1975. Law clerk U.S. Dist. Ct. of Colo., 1975-76, dep. state pub. defender, appellate divn., 1976-77; asst. U.S. atty. Dist. of Colo., 1977-87; dep. chief civil divn. U.S. Attorney's Office, 1985-88; judge Denver Dist. Ct., 1988-98; apptd. judge Colo. Supreme Ct., 1998—. Contbr. articles to profl. jours. Mem. Denver Bar Assn., Colo. Bar Assn. (bd. govs. 1990-92, exec. coun., 1991-92), Women's Bar Assn., Rhone-Brackett Inn of Ct. (master 1993-97), Women Judges Assn. (co-chair nat. conf. 1990). Office: Colo Supreme Ct Colo State Jud Bldg 2 E 14th Ave Fl 4 Denver CO 80203-2115

RICE, PAUL JACKSON, lawyer, educator; b. East St. Louis, Ill., July 15, 1938; s. Ray Jackson and Mary Margaret (Campbell) Rice; m. Carole Jeanne Valentine, June 6, 1959; children: Rebecca Jeanne Ross, Melissa Ann Hansen, Paul Jackson Jr. BA, U. Mo., 1960, JD, 1962; LLM, Northwestern U., 1970; student, Command and Gen. Staff Coll., 1974-75, Army War Coll., 1982-83. Bar: Mo. 1962, Ill. 1969, U.S. Dist. Ct. (no. dist.) Ill. 1970, U.S. Supreme Ct. 1972, U.S. Ct. Appeals (DC cir.) 1991, DC 1993, U.S. Dist. Ct. DC 2000. Commd. 1st lt. U.S. Army, 1962, advanced through grades to col., 1980; asst. judge advocate 4th Armored Div., Goeppingen, Germany, 1966-69; dep. staff judge advocate 1st Cavalry Div., Vietnam, 1970-71; inst., prof. Judge Adv. Gen. Sch., Charlottesville, Va., 1971-74, commdt., dean, 1985-88; br. chief Gen. Law Br., Pentagon, 1975-78; chief adminstrv. law div. Office Judge Adv. Gen., Pentagon, Washington, 1978-79; staff judge adv. 1st Inf. Div., Ft. Riley, Kans., 1979-82, V Corps U.S. Army, Frankfurt, Germany, 1983-85, USACAC, Ft. Leavenworth, Kans., 1989-90; faculty Indsl. Coll. Armed Forces, 1988-89; chief counsel Nat. Hwy. Traffic Safety Adminstrn., Washington, 1990-93; ptnr. Arent Fox Kintner Plotkin & Kahn, Washington, 1993—. Contbr. articles to profl. jours. Recipient Granted Legal Svc. award, State of Hessen, Germany, 1985, cert. of merit, U. Mo. Alumni Assn., 1987. Mem.: Ctr. Law and Nat. Security, Mo. Bar Assn., Lion Tamers, Phi Delta Phi. Methodist. Avocations: writing, reading, golf. Administrative and regulatory, Product liability, Transportation. Home: 7835 Vervain Ct Springfield VA 22152-3107 Office: Arent Fox Kintner Plotkin & Kahn 150 Connecticut Ave NW Washington DC 20036-5339 E-mail: ricepj@arentfox.com.

RICE, SHAWN G. lawyer; b. Milw., Aug. 11, 1968; s. Jeremiah K. and Catherine (Fountain) R.; m. Liesl M. Testwuide, July 6, 1996. BA, Creighton U., 1990; JD, Marquette U., 1993. Bar: Wis. 1993, U.S. Dist. Ct. (ea. dist.) Wis. 1993, U.S. Dist. Ct. (we. dist.) Wis. 1995. Jud. intern Wis. Ct. Appeals, Waukesha, 1992, U.S. Bankruptcy Ct. (ea. dist.) Wis., Milw., 1992-93; assoc. Kohner, Mann & Kailas, Milw., 1993-97; gen. coun. Schreier Malting Co., Sheboygan, Wis., 1997-98; assoc. Godfrey & Kahn, S.C., Milw., 1998—2002; pres. Inst. for Viral Pathogenesis, Inc., 1999—; shareholder Davis & Kuelthav, Shegoygan, 2002—. Pres., gen. counsel. Wis. Zeta Alumni Corp., Sigma Phi Epsilon, Marquette U., 1994-98. Law Class of 1948 and Stellman scholar, Marquette U., 1992-93; recipient Alumni of Yr. award Sigma Phi Epsilon Frat., Milw., 1996. Republican. Roman Catholic. Avocations: golf, politics. E-amil. Commercial, contracts (including sales of goods; commercial financing), Corporate, general, Mergers and acquisitions. Home: 3017 N 6th St Sheboygan WI 53081 Office: Davis & Keulthav 605 N 8th St #610 Sheboygan WI 53081 E-mail: srice@dkatttornegs.com.

RICE, WALTER HERBERT, federal judge; b. Pitts., May 27, 1937; s. Harry D. and Elizabeth L. (Braemer) R.; m. Bonnie Rice; children: Michael, Hilary, Harry, Courtney Elizabeth. BA, Northwestern U., 1958; JD, MBA, Columbia U., 1962; LLD (hon.), U. Dayton, 1991; DHL (hon.), Wright State U., 2000. Bar: Ohio 1963. Asst. county prosecutor, Montgomery County, Ohio, 1964-66; assoc. Gallon & Miller, Dayton, Ohio, 1966-69; 1st asst. Montgomery County Prosecutor's Office, 1969; judge Dayton Mcpl. Ct., 1970-71, Montgomery County Ct. Common Pleas, 1971-80, U.S. Dist. Ct. (so. dist.) Ohio, 1980-95, chief judge, 1996—. Adj. prof. U. Dayton Law Sch., 1976— , bd. visitors, 1976— ; chmn. Montgomery County Supervisory Council on Crime and Deliquency, 1972-74; vice chmn. bd. dirs. Pretrial Release, Inc., 1975-79 Author papers in field. Pres. Dayton Area Coun. on Alcoholism and Drug Abuse, 1971-73; chmn. bd. trustees Stillwater Health Ctr., Dayton, 1976-79, Family Svc. Assn. Dayton, 1978-80; chmn. RTA in 2000 Com., 2003 Com. Designed To Bring Nat. Park to Dayton To Honor Wright Bros. and Birth of Aviation; chmn. Martin Luther King Jr. Meml. Com., Dayton Aviation Heritage Commn.; trustee Montgomery County Vol. Lawyers Project, Miami Valley Cultural Alliance, Barbara Jordan Com. Racial Justice; co-chmn., Dayton Dialogue on Race Rels.; former bd. mem. Sinclair C.C., U.S. Air & Trade Show. Recipient Excellent Jud. Service award Ohio Supreme Ct., 1976, 77, Outstanding Jud. Service award, 1973, 74, 76, Man of Yr. award Disting. Service Awards Council, Dayton, 1977, Outstanding Jurist in Ohio award Ohio Acad. Trial Lawyers, 1986, Pub. Ofcl. of Yr. award Ohio region of Nat. Assn. Social Workers, 1992, Humanitarian award NCCJ, 1993, City Mgr.'s Cmty. Svc. award City of Dayton, 1994, Paul Laurence Dunbar Humanitarian award, 1996, Pres.' award NAACP, 1996, greater Dayton Peace Bridge (civil rights) Hall of Fame, Mark of Excellence award Nat. Forum Black Pub. Adminstrs., 2001, Conservation Svc. award U.S. Dept. of the Interior, 2002. Mem. Dayton Bar Assn., Fed. Judges Assn., Carl D. Kessler Inn of Ct. (founder, former chmn.).

RICE, WINSTON EDWARD, lawyer; b. Shreveport, La., Feb. 22, 1946; s. Winston Churchill and Margaret (Coughlin) R.; m. Barbara Reily Gay, Apr. 16, 1977; 1 child, Andrew Hynes; children by previous marriage: Winston Hobson, Christian MacTaggart. Student, Centenary Coll. La., 1967; JD, La. State U., 1971. Bar: La. 1971, Colo. 1990, Tex. 1992. Cons. geologist, Gulfport, Miss., 1968-70; ptnr. Phelps, Dunbar, New Orleans, 1971-88; sr. ptnr. Rice, Fowler, New Orleans, Houston, Miami, Fla., London and Bogota, 1988-2000; gen. mgr. Winston Edw. Rice LLC, Covington, La., 2000—. Instr. law La. State U., Baton Rouge, 1970-71. Assoc. editor La. Law Rev., 1970-71. Mem.: Trucking Industry Def. Assn., Ctr. Transp. Law and Policy, Soc. Ins. Trainers and Educators, Assn. Average Adjusters (U.K.), Assn. Average Adjusters U.S., Maritime Law Assn. U.S. (chmn. subcom. on offshore exploration and devel. 1985—88, vice chmn. com. internat. law of the sea 1988—91, chmn. 1991—95, membership sec. 1998—2002), Com. Maritime Internat. (titulary mem.), Fedn. Ins. and Corp. Counsel, La. Assn. Def. Counsel, New Orleans Assn. Def. Counsel, Can. Transp. Lawyers Assn., New Orleans Bar Assn., Tex. State Bar, Colo. State Bar Assn., La. Bar Assn., Stratford Club, Boston Club, Mariners Club (treas. 1974—75, 1978—79, sec. 1975—76, v.p. 1976—77, pres. 1977—78), Kappa Alpha, Phi Kappa Phi, Phi Delta Phi, Order of Coif. Republican. Episcopalian. Admiralty, Insurance, Private international. Office: 328 N Columbia St Covington LA 70433-2918

RICH, ROBERT STEPHEN, lawyer; b. NYC, Apr. 30, 1938; s. Maurice H. and Natalie (Priess) R.; m. Myra N. Lakoff, May 31, 1964; children: David, Rebecca, Sarah. AB, Cornell U., 1959; JD, Yale U., 1963. Bar: N.Y. 1964, Colo. 1973, U.S. Tax Ct. 1966, U.S. Supreme Ct. 1967, U.S. Ct. Claims 1968, U.S. Dist. Ct. (so. dist.) N.Y. 1965, U.S. Dist. Ct. (ea. dist.) N.Y. 1965, U.S. Dist. Ct. Colo. 1980, U.S. Ct. Appeals (10th cir.) 1978; conseil juridique, Paris, 1968. Assoc. Shearman & Sterling, N.Y.C., Paris, London, 1963-72; ptnr. Davis, Graham & Stubbs, Denver, 1973—. Adj. faculty U. Denver Law Sch., 1977—; mem. adv. bd. U. Denver Ann. Tax Inst., 1985—, global bus. and culture divsn., U. Denver, 1992—, Denver World Affairs Coun., 1993—; mem. Colo. Internat. Trade Coun., 1985—; mem. Rocky Mt. Dist. Export Coun., US Dept. Commerce, 1993—; tax adv. com. US Senator Hank Brown; bd. dirs. Clos du Val Wine Co. Ltd., Danskin Cattle Co., Ouray Ranch, Areti Wines, Ltd., Taltarni Vineyards, Christy Sports, others. Contbr. articles to profl. jours. Actor, musician N.Y. Shakespeare Festival, 1960; sponsor Am. Tax Policy Inst., 1991—; adv. bd. Denver World Affairs Coun., 1993—, Middle Park Land Trust, Granby, Colo., 2003—; pres. So. Boulder Park Ecol. Assn., 1999—; sec. Bhutan Found., Citizens for Arts to Zoo; bd. dirs. Alliance Francaise, 1977—, Copper Valley Assn., Denver Internat. Film Festival, 1978—79, Anschutz Family Found.; trustee, sec. Denver Art Mus., 1982—; pres., bd. dirs. Ouray Ranch, Granby, Colo., 2001—. Capt. U.S. Army, 1959—60. Fellow Am. Coll. Tax. Coun. (bd. regents 10th cir. 1992—), Soc. Fellows Aspen Inst.; mem. ABA, Internat. Bar Assn., Colo. Bar Assn., NY State Bar Assn., Assn. Bar City of NY, Asia-Pacific Lawyers Assn., Union Internat. des Avocats, Internat. Fiscal Assn. (pres. Rocky Mt. br. 1992—, US regional v.p. 1988—), Japan-Am. Soc. Colo. (bd. dirs. 1989—, pres. 1991-93), Confrerie des Chevaliers du Tastevin, Rocky Mt. Wine and Food Soc., Meadowood Club, Denver Club, City Club Denver, Mile High Club, Cactus Club Denver, Yale Club, Denver Tennis Club. Private international, Corporate taxation, Taxation, general. Office: Cherry Creek Sta PO Box 61429 Denver CO 80206-8429 also: Antelope Co 555 17th St Ste 2400 Denver CO 80202-3941 E-mail: robertrich@aya.yale.edu.

RICHARDS, ALAN EDWARD, lawyer; b. Chgo., Mar. 7, 1949; s. Robert E. and Ann R. (Ekhart) R.; m. Meridee G. Johnson, June 13, 1970; children: Kate Elizabeth, Zachary Stephen. B.A., Carthage Coll., Kenosha, Wis., 1970; J.D., Marquette U., 1976. Bar: Wis. 1976, Ill. 1977, U.S. Dist. Ct. (no. dist.) Ill. 1977. Ptnr. Richards & Ralph, Chartered, Libertyville, Ill., 1977-87, Richards, Ralph & Schwab Chartered, Vernon Hills, Ill., 1987- . Editor Marquette U. Law Rev., 1975-76. Mem. ABA, Ill. Bar Assn., Lake County Bar Assn. State civil litigation, Commercial, contracts (including sales of goods; commercial financing). Office: Richards Ralph & Schwab Chartered 175 E Hawthorne Pkwy Vernon Hills IL 60061-1463 E-mail: arichards@rrs-chartered.com.

RICHARDS, ANNE C. mediator; b. Morristown, N.J., Nov. 18, 1943; d. Oscar Henry and Elsie (Fishbein) Cohen; m. Fred L. Richards, July 5, 1969. BA, Brandeis U., Waltham, Mass., 1965; MST, U. Chgo., 1966; EdD, U. Fla., Gainesville, 1971. Reg. Neutral: Ga. Office of Dispute Resolution 1997. Tchr. Grover Cleveland Jr. H.S., Caldwell, NJ, 1966—68; asst. prof. Northeast La. U., Monroe, 1970; asst./assoc. prof. U. No. Colo., Greeley, 1971—75; asst./assoc./full prof. State U. West Ga., Carrollton, 1975—2001; mediator Carroll County Magistrate Ct., Carrollton, Ga., 1997—, Carroll County Juvenile Ct., Carrollton, Ga., 2002—; prof. emerita State U. West Ga, 2001—. Trustee Field Psych Trust, Carrollton, Ga., 1999—. Co-author (with A.W. Combs and F. Richards): Perceptual Psychology: A Humanistic Approach to the Study of Persons, 1976; co-editor (with T. Schumrum): Invitations to Dialogue: The Legacy of Sidney M. Jourard, 1999; Author or Co-author of 5 books and over 25 articles on implications of Humanistic Psychology for understanding persons and improving education; contbr. chapters to books. Co-recipient Dora Byron Citizenship award, Carroll County League of Women Voters, 2002; named to, State U. of W. Ga. ODK Circle, 1992; Paul Harris fellow, Rotary Club of Carrollton, 1999. Mem.: AAUP (pres., State U. of W. Ga. chpt. 1985—86, exec. bd. mem. 1992—96, co-editor, AAUP Summary, Ga. Conf. 1992—96, pres., State U. of W. Ga. chpt. 1995—96, exec. bd. mem. 2000—, co-editor, AAUP Summary, Ga. Conf. 2000—), Am. Psychology Law Soc. (mem.). Democrat. Avocations: swimming, walking, reading. Home: 301 Dixie St Carrollton GA 30117 Office: Field Psych Trust 301 Dixie St Carrollton GA 30117 E-mail: arichard@westga.edu.

RICHARDS, BONNIE E. lawyer, accountant; b. Salisbury, Md., July 25, 1969; d. Gerald W. and Sue Ann Richards. BS in Acctg. and Fin. cum laude, Drexel U., 1992; student, U. Oxford, 1997; JD, Temple U., 1999; postgrad., NYU. Bar: Pa. 1999, NJ 1999. Tax cons. PriceWaterhouseCoopers, LLP, 1993—94; sr. tax. cons. Ernst & Young, N.Y.C., 1995—96; intern bankruptcy unit U.S. Atty.'s Office, 1998; intern frauds bur. NY County Dist. Atty.'s Office, 1998; assoc. Reed Smith LLP, Phila., 1999—2000; ptnr. Horvitz Richards LLP, Phila., 2001—. Recipient Joseph W. Price III Meml. award; Robert S. Kravitz Meml. scholar. Mem.: Am. Assn. Atty.-CPAs, Phila. Estate Planning Coun., NJ Bar Assn. (probate and trust sect.), Pa. Bar Assn. (bus. law and taxation sects.), Phila. Bar Assn. (probate, trust and taxation sects.). Avocations: piano, reading. Taxation, general, Estate taxation. Office: Horvitz Richards LLP 1800 JFK Blvd #1601 Philadelphia PA 19103

RICHARDS, DAVID ALAN, lawyer; b. Dayton, Ohio, Sept. 21, 1945; s. Charles Vernon and Betty Ann (Macher) R.; m. Marianne Catherine Del Monaco, June 26, 1971; children: Christopher, Courtney. BA summa cum laude, Yale U., 1967, JD, 1972; MA, Cambridge (Eng.) U., 1969. Bar: N.Y. 1973. Assoc. Paul, Weiss, Rifkind, Wharton & Garrison, N.Y.C., 1972-77, Coudert Bros., N.Y.C., 1977-80, ptnr., 1981-82; ptnr., head real estate group Sidley & Austin, N.Y.C., 1983-2000; ptnr. McCarter & English, N.Y.C., 2001—, mng. ptnr. N.Y. office, 2002—. Gov. Anglo-Am. Real Property Inst. U.S./U.K., 1983-88, chair, 1993; mem. Chgo. Title N.Y. Realty Adv. Bd., 1992—. Co-editor: Kipling and His First Publisher, 2001; co-author: The Commercial Office Lease Handbook, 2003, Comml. Office Leave Handbook, 2003; contbr. articles to profl. jours. Trustee Scarsdale Pub. Libr., 1984-89, pres., 1988-89; co-chair N.Y. Lawyers for Clinton/Gore, 1996. Fellow Am. Bar Found.; mem. ABA (real property, probate and trust sect., coun. 1982-88, chair 1991-92), Am. Coll. Real Estate Lawyers (gov. 1987-93), Assn. of Bar of City of N.Y. (real property com. 1978-80, 84-87), Kipling Soc. (N.Am. rep.), Shenorock Shore Club (Rye, N.Y.), The Grolier Club (N.Y.C., coun. 2003—), Yale Club (N.Y.C.); trustee, Yale Libr. Assoc. 2003-. Democrat. Property, real (including real estate development, water). Home: 18 Forest Ln Scarsdale NY 10583-6464 Office: McCarter & English 300 Park Ave Fl 18 New York NY 10022 E-mail: darichards21@aol.com., drichards@mccarter.com.

RICHARDS, GERALD THOMAS, lawyer, consultant, educator, writer; b. Monrovia, Calif., Mar. 17, 1933; s. Louis Jacquelyn Richards and Inez Vivian (Richardson) Hall; children: Patricia M. Richards Grauf, Laura J., Dag Hammarskjold; m. Mary Lou Richards, Dec. 27, 1986. BS magna cum laude, Lafayette Coll., 1957; MS, Purdue U., 1963; JD, Golden Gate U., 1976. Bar: Calif. 1976, U.S. Dist. Ct. (no. dist.) Calif. 1977, U.S. Patent Office 1981, U.S. Ct. Appeals (9th cir.) 1984, U.S. Supreme Ct. 1984. From computational physicist to asst. lab. counsel Lawrence Livermore Nat. Lab., Calif., 1967—84, asst. lab. counsel, 1984—93; sole practice Livermore, Calif., 1976-78, Oceanside, Calif., 1994-97; emeritus atty. pro bono participant Calif. State Bar, 1998—; staff atty. Contra Costa Sr. Legal Svcs., Concord, 1998—. Constrn. law instr. Contrs. State License Schs., Van Nuys, Calif., 1998; mem. exec. com., policy advisor Fed. Lab. Consortium for Tech. Transfer, 1980-88; panelist, del. White House Conf. on Productivity, Washington, 1983; del. Nat. Conf. on Tech. and Aging, Wingspread, Wis., 1981. Commr. Housing Authority, City of Livermore, 1977, vice chairperson, 1978, chairperson, 1979; mem. Bd of Administrn. Appeals, City of Antioch, CA, 2003-; pres. Housing Choices, Inc., Livermore, 1980-84; bd. dirs. Valley Vol. Ctr., Pleasanton, Calif., 1983, pres., 1984-86; mem. staff Calif. Boys' State Am. Legion, 1996—. Served to maj. U.S. Army, 1959-67. Recipient Engrng. award GE, 1956. Mem. ABA, Calif. State Bar (conv. alt. del. 1990-92, del. 2000, mem. com. on sr. lawyers 2002—), Alameda County Bar Assn., Contra Costa County Bar Assn., Ea. Alameda County Bar Assn. (sec. 1978, bd. dirs. 1991-92, chair lawyers referral com. 1992-93), Santa Barbara County Bar Assn., San Diego County Bar Assn., Bar Assn. No. San Diego County, San Francisco Bar Assn., Phi Beta Kappa, Tau Beta Pi, Sigma Pi Sigma. Commercial, contracts (including sales of goods; commercial financing), General practice, Probate (including wills, trusts). Home: 2505 Whitetail Dr Antioch CA 94531-7744 E-mail: hesiod@calbears.com.

RICHARDS, JOHN THOMAS, JR., lawyer; b. Pitts., Aug. 11, 1930; s. John Thomas and Hannah B. (Williams) R.; m. Rosemary Brennen, June 27, 1953; children— John Thomas III, Veronica A. Richards Arnstein, Charles B., Lynn Ellen. B.S. in Bus. Adminstrn., Ohio State U., 1953; J.D., Duquesne U., 1959. Bar: Pa. 1960, U.S. Dist. Ct. (we. dist.) Pa. 1960, U.S. Supreme Ct. 1965. Assoc. firm McMonigle-Vesely, Pitts., 1959-65; sole practice, Pitts., 1965-68; ptnr. firm Richards & Kelly, Pitts., 1968— ; pres. Stone Lodge Inc., Pitts., 1982-97. Served to 1st lt. U.S. Army, 1953-55. Mem. Allegheny County Bar Assn. (officer, mem. real estate council 1980—). Republican. Baptist. Club: Wildwood Country (Pitts.) (bd. dirs., sec., counsel 1971-80). Condemnation (eminent domain), Probate (including wills, trusts), Property, real (including real estate development, water). Home: 4193 Rothschild Ct Allison Park PA 15101-2868 Office: Richards & Kelly 429 4th Ave Ste 900 Pittsburgh PA 15219-1546

RICHARDS, MARTA ALISON, lawyer; b. Mar. 15, 1952; d. Howard Jay and Mary Dean (Nix) Richards; m. Richard Peter Massony, June 16, 1979 (div. Apr. 1988); 1 child, Richard Peter Massony Jr. Student, Vassar Coll., 1969-70; AB cum laude, Princeton U., 1973; JD, George Washington U., 1976. Bar: La. 1976, U.S. Dist. Ct. (ea. dist.) La. 1976, U.S. Ct. Appeals (5th cir.) 1981, U.S. Supreme Ct. 1988, U.S. Dist. Ct. (mid. dist.) La. 1991. Assoc. Phelps, Dunbar, Marks, Claverie & Sims, New Orleans, 1976-77; assoc. counsel Hibernia Nat. Bank, New Orleans, 1978; assoc. Singer, Hutner, Levine, Seeman & Stuart, New Orleans, 1978-80, Jones, Walker, Waechter, Poltevent, Carrere & Denegre, New Orleans, 1980-84; ptnr. Mmahat, Duffy & Richards, 1984, Montgomery, Barnett, Brown, Read, Hammond & Mintz, 1984-86, Montgomery, Richards & Ballin, 1986-89, Gelpi, Sullivan, Carroll and Laborde, 1989; gen. counsel Maison Blanche Inc., Baton Rouge, 1990-92, La. State Bond Commn., 1992-97; pvt. practice, cons., 1998—. Lectr. paralegal inst. U. New Orleans, 1984-89, adj. prof., 1989. Contbr. articles to legal jours. Treas. alumni coun. Princeton U., 1979-81. Mem. ABA, La. State Bar Assn., New Orleans Bar Assn., Baton Rouge Bar Assn., Nat. Assn. Bond Lawyers, Princeton Alumni Assn. New Orleans (pres. 1982-86), Princeton Alumni Assn. Baton Rouge (pres. 2002—). Episcopalian. Commercial, contracts (including sales of goods; commercial financing), Corporate, general, Municipal (including bonds). Home and Office: 4075 S Ramsey Dr Baton Rouge LA 70808-1653

RICHARDS, NORMAN BLANCHARD, lawyer; b. Melrose, Mass., May 27, 1924; s. Henry Edward and Annie Jane (Blanchard) R.; m. Diane Maionchi, July 9, 1977; children— Terri, Jeffrey. BS, Bowdoin Coll., 1945; JD, Stanford U., 1951. Bar: Calif. bar 1951. Mem. firm McCutchen Doyle Brown & Enersen, San Francisco, 1951—, partner, 1960—. Mem. faculty Tulane Admiralty Law Inst., Hastings Coll. Advocacy. Bd. visitors Stanford Law Sch. With USN, 1943-46. Fellow Am. Coll. Trial Lawyers; mem. ABA, Calif. State Bar, San Francisco Bar ASsn., Maritime Law Assn. U.S. Admiralty, Federal civil litigation, State civil litigation. Home: 85 Platt Ave Sausalito CA 94965-1897 Office: Bingham McCutchen 3 Embarcadero Ctr San Francisco CA 94111-4003

RICHARDS, STEVEN GEORGE, lawyer; b. Milw., Aug. 19, 1960; s. Joseph and Bessie A. Richards; m. LaNor L. Burgermeister, Feb. 17, 2000; children: Jessica, Michelle, Leilani, Gabrielle, Christian. AAS, Gateway Tech. Coll., Kenosha, WIs., 1985; BS in Applied Sci. and Tech., Thomas Edison State Coll., 1991; JD, John Marshall Law Sch., 1999. Bar: Wis. 2001, U.S. Dist. Ct. (ea. dist.) Wis. 2002, U.S. Dist. Ct. (we. dist.) Wis. 2003, Wis. 2003. Clk. William A. Pangman, Waukesha, Wis., 1994—98; intern Wis. State Ct. Appeals, Dist. I, Milw., 1995; clk. Robin Shellow, Milw., 1995—97; pvt. practice Van Dyne, Wis., 2001—03; of counsel Anderegg & Mutschler, Fond Du Lac, Wis. Assigned counsel Wis. State Pub. Defender. Mem. Wis. Coalition Against the Death Penalty. Mem.: ABA, Wis. Acad. Trial Lawyers, Calif. Def. Attys. for Criminal Justice, Wis. Assn. Criminal Def. Lawyers, Nat. Assn. Criminal Def. Lawyers. Serbian Orthodox. Avocations: fishing, golf. Criminal, Appellate. Home and Office: PO Box 8 127 Main St Casco WI 54205 Office Fax: 920-837-2924. E-mail: sgr@wisconsinattorney.org.

RICHARDS, SUZANNE V. lawyer; b. Columbia, S.C., Sept. 7, 1927; d. Raymond E. and Elise C. (Gray) R. AB, George Washington U., 1948, JD with distinction, 1957, LLM, 1959. Bar: D.C. 1958. Sole practice, Washington, 1974—. Lectr. in family and probate law; mem. D.C. Jud. Conf., 1975—2003. Bd. dirs. Coun. for Ct. Excellence. Recipient John Bell Larner award George Washington U., 1958; named Woman Lawyer of Yr., Women's Bar Assn. D.C., 1977. Mem. ABA (ho. of dels. 1988-90), Bar Assn. D.C. (pres. 1989-90, named Lawyer of Yr. 2002), Women's Bar Assn. (pres. 1977-78), Trial Lawyers Assn. of D.C. (bd. govs. 1978-82, 85-2001, treas. 1982-85), D.C. Bar, Fed. Bar Assn. Family and matrimonial, General practice, Probate (including wills, trusts). Home: 530 N St SW Washington DC 20024-4546 Office: PO Box 65466 Washington DC 20035-5466

RICHARDSON, ARTHUR WILHELM, lawyer; b. Glendale, Calif., Apr. 3, 1963; s. Douglas Fielding and Leni (Tempelaar-Lietz) R.; m. Noriko Satake, Nov. 14, 1998. Student, London Sch. Econs., 1983; AB, Occidental Coll., 1985; JD, Harvard U., 1988. Bar: Calif. 1989, Ohio 2002. Assoc. Morgan, Lewis and Bockius, L.A., 1988—90; staff lawyer U.S. SEC, L.A., 1990—92, br. chief, 1992—96, sr. counsel, 1996—2001; of counsel Arter and Hadden, Columbus, Ohio, 2002—03. Mem. ABA, Calif. Bar Assn., L.A. County Bar Assn., Harvard/Radcliffe Club So. Calif., Town Hall Calif., L.A. World Affairs Coun., Sierra Club, Phi Beta Kappa. Presbyterian. Home: 2328 Mallard Ln #6 Beavercreek OH 45431

RICHARDSON, BETTY H. lawyer, former prosecutor; b. Oct. 3, 1953; BA, U. Idaho, 1976; JD, Hastings Coll. Law, 1982. Staff aid U.S. Senator Frank Church, 1976-77; tchg. asst. Hastings Coll. Law, 1980-82, 1980-82; legal rsch. asst. criminal divsn. San Francisco Superior Ct., 1982-84; jud. law clk. Chamber of Idaho Supreme Ct. Justice Robert C. Huntley Jr., 1984-86; atty. U.S. Dept. Justice, Boise, Idaho, 1993-2001, Richardson & O'Leary, Eagle, Idaho, 2001—. Instr. Boise State U., 1987, 89; mem. U.S. Atty. Gen.'s Adv. Com. subcoms. on environ., civil rights and native Am. issues, others, 1993-2001; mem. hon. adv. bd. for Crime Victims Amendment in Idaho, 1994; mem. Dist. of Idaho Judges and Lawyer Reps. com., gender fairness com., Civil Justice Reform Act com. and criminal adv. com., 1993-2001; Dem. nominee Dist 1 Idaho, U.S. Ho. of Reps., 2003. Mem. Idaho Indsl. Commn., 1991-93, chmn., 1993; mem. adv. bd. Family and Workplace Consortium, 1995-2001; mem. Assistance League of Boise, 2001—; bd. dirs. Tony Patino Fellowship. Recipient Harold E. Hughes Exceptional Svc. award Nat. Rural Inst. on Alcohol and Drug Abuse, 1999; Tony Patino fellow Hastings Coll. Law, 1982. Mem. Idaho Bar Assn. (governing coun. govt. and pub. sectors lawyers sect. 1999-2001, Pro Bono Svc. award 1988), Idaho Women Lawyers, Idaho Dem. Women's Caucus, City Club Boise. Office: Richardson & O'Leary 99 E State St Eagle ID 83616 also: 5796 N Dalspring Boise ID 83713

RICHARDSON, DANIEL RALPH, lawyer; b. Pasadena, Calif., Jan. 18, 1945; s. Ralph Claude and Rosemary Clare (Lowery) R.; m. Virginia Ann Lorton, Sept. 4, 1965; children: Brian Daniel, Neil Ryan. BS, Colo. State U., 1969; MBA, St. Mary's Coll. of Calif., 1977; JD, JFK U., 1992. Bar: Calif., U.S. Patent and Trademark Office. Systems engr. Electronic Data Systems, San Francisco, 1972-73; programmer/analyst Wells Fargo Bank, San Francisco, 1973-74; systems analyst Crown-Zellerbach Corp., San Francisco, 1974; programming mgr. Calif. Dental Svc., San Francisco, 1974-75, Fairchild Camera and Inst., Mountain View, Calif., 1975-77; sr. systems analyst Bechtel Corp., San Francisco, 1977; pres. Richardson Software Cons., Inc., San Francisco, 1977-99; pvt. practice San Francisco, 1993—. Instr. data processing Diablo Valley Coll., Concord, Calif., 1979-80. Author: (book) System Development Life Cycle, 1976, (computer software) The Richardson Automated Agent, 1985. Asst. scoutmaster Boy Scouts Am., Clayton, Calif., 1983-91; soccer coach Am. Youth Soccer League, Clayton, 1978-83. 1st lt. USAF, 1966-72. Mem. State Bar Calif., Am. Immigration Lawyers Assn., Am. Intellectual Property Assn. Avocations: travel, reading, writing. General civil litigation, Patent, Immigration, naturalization, and customs. Office: 870 Market St San Francisco CA 94102-3010

RICHARDSON, DAVID ALEXANDER, lawyer; b. Hong Kong, Sept. 15, 1954; LLB, U. Hong Kong, 1977, Postgrad. Cert. of Laws, 1978; LLB, U. B.C., 1982. Bar: Hong Kong, B.C. Solicitor Fraser & Beatty, Vancouver, B.C., Can., 1984-85; trainee solicitor, solicitor Wilkinson & Grist, Hong Kong, 1985-88; solicitor Victor Chu & Co., Hong Kong, 1988-91, ptnr., 1991-2001, Bird & Bird, Hong Kong, 2001—. Corporate, general, Securities. Office: Ste 602-4 6th Fl Asia Pacif Finance Twr Citibank Plaza 3 Garden Rd Hong Kong Hong Kong

RICHARDSON, JOHN CARROLL, lawyer, tax legislative consultant; b. Mobile, Ala., May 3, 1932; s. Robert Felder and Louise (Simmons) R.; m. Cicely Tomlinson, July 27, 1961; children: Nancy Louise, Robert Felder III, Leslie. BA, Tulane U., 1954; LLB cum laude, Harvard U., 1960. Bar: Colo. 1960, N.Y. 1965, D.C. 1972. Assoc. Holland & Hart, Denver, 1960-64; legal v.p. Hoover Worldwide Corp., N.Y.C., 1964-69; v.p., gen. counsel Continental Investment Corp., Boston, 1969; dep. tax legis. counsel U.S. Dept. Treasury, Washington, 1970-71, tax legis. counsel, 1972-73; ptnr. Brown, Wood, Ivey, Mitchell & Petty, N.Y.C., 1973-79, LeBoeuf, Lamb, Leiby & MacRae, N.Y.C., 1979-88, Morgan, Lewis & Bockius, N.Y.C., 1988-93; ret., 1993. Tax legis. cons., Orford, N.H., 1993—; adj. prof. Law Sch. Fordham U., 1990-94. Served to lt. comdr. USN, 1954-57 Mem. ABA (chmn. com. adminstrv. practice tax sect. 1984-86), N.Y. State Bar Assn. (exec. com. tax sect. 1975-84), D.C. Bar Assn., Am. Coll. Tax Counsel, N.Y. Athletic Club, Royal Automobile Club.

RICHARDSON, PATRICK WILLIAM, lawyer; b. Huntsville, Ala., Oct. 5, 1925; s. Schuyler Harris and Suzane Agnes (Smith) R.; m. Martha Alice Holliman, Dec. 23, 1949; m. Mary McAlpine Moore, Oct. 9, 1970; children: Schuyler Harris, III, James Holiman. BS, U. Ala., 1946, JD, 1948, LLD (hon.), 1976. Bar: Ala. 1948, U.S. Ct. Appeals (5th cir.) 1955, U.S. Supreme Ct. 1957, U.S. Ct. Appeals (11th cir.) 1981. Ptnr. Bell Richardson LLP, Huntsville, 1948—; dep. atty. gen. State of Ala., 1996—. Spl. cir. solicitor 23d Cir. Ala., 1951. Bd. dirs. U. Ala. Huntsville Found., 1962—, pres., 1962-74. Fellow Am. Coll. Trial Lawyers; mem. Ala. State Bar (pres. 1969-70), Huntsville-Madison County Bar Assn. (pres. 1966-67), Ala. Law Inst. (council), Am. Coll. Mortgage Attys. (regent 1975-77), Rotary. Republican. Methodist. General civil litigation, Probate (including wills, trusts), Property, real (including real estate development, water). Office: 116 Jefferson St S Huntsville AL 35801-4818 E-mail: pwr@bellrich.com.

RICHARDSON, WILLIAM WINFREE, III, lawyer; b. Williamsburg, Va., Aug. 12, 1939; s. William Winfree Jr. and Ellen Blanche (Johnson) R.; m. Constance Diane Niver (div. July 1985); children: Christine Marie, Kenneth Erik. BA, Coll. William and Mary, 1963, Bachelor of Civil Law, 1966, JD, 1967. Bar: Va. 1968. Pvt. practice, Providence Forge, Va., 1968—; commr. accounts New Kent Cir. Ct., Providence Forge, 1968—2000, atty. correctional field unit, 1968—; asst. commr. accounts Charles City Cir. Ct., Providence Forge, 1970—2000. Bd. dirs. C.H. Evelyn Piling Co. Inc., Providence Forge. Advisor Selective Svc. System, New Kent County, Va., 1972. Internat. Order Kings Daus. and Sons scholar, 1957. Mem. Williamsburg Bar Assn., Colonial Bar Assn., Sigma Pi. Avocations: hist. restoration, collecting antiques. General practice, Probate (including wills, trusts), Property, real (including real estate development, water). Home: Chelsea Plantation West Point VA 23181 Office: PO Box 127 Providence Forge VA 23140-0127

RICHESON, HUGH ANTHONY, JR., lawyer; b. Aberdeen, Md., Apr. 22, 1947; s. Hugh Anthony Sr. and Mary Evelyn (Burford) R.; m. Melissa Anne Baum, Apr. 4, 1970; children: Hugh Anthony III, Heidi E., Holly K., Hagin G., Herald Joshua. BBA, U. Richmond, 1969; JD, U. Fla., 1973; student, St. Catherine's Coll., Oxford U., Eng., summer 1973. Bar: Fla. 1974, U.S. Dist. Ct. (mid. dist.) Fla. 1975, U.S. Supreme Ct. 1992. Assoc. Bryant, Dickens, Rumph, Franson & Miller, Jacksonville, Fla., 1974—76, ptnr., 1977; sole practice Orange Park, Fla., 1977—82; ptnr. Smith, Hallowes & Richeson, Orange Park, 1982—83; sole practice Palm Harbor, Fla., 1984—98; of counsel Carey Leisure & Battle, Clearwater, Fla., 1998—. Author: Legally Yours, 2002. Pres. Full Gospel Bus. Men's Fellowship Internat., Orange Park, 1983-84, Palm Harbor, 1985-92, field rep., 1987—. Mem. ATLA, Fla. Coun. Bar Assn. Pres. (life), Christian Legal Soc., Gideons Internat., Phi Delta Phi, Sigma Phi Epsilon. Republican. Methodist. State civil litigation, Personal injury (including property damage).

RICHIE, BOYD LYNN, lawyer; b. Breckenridge, Tex., July 11, 1945; s. Bradie Eugene adn Billie June (Robinson) R.; m. Betty Zoe Furr, May 28, 1966; children: Christophber Robin, Tracy Lynn. BA in Polit. Sci. and History, Midwestern State U., 1967; JD, Tex. Tech. U., 1970. Bar: Tex. 1970, U.S. Dist. Ct. (no. dist.) Tex. 1975. Trial atty. Fed. Power Commn., Washington, 1970-71; assoc. John Bradshaw, Graham, Tex., 1971-72; sole practice Graham, 1972-77; dist. atty. 90th Jud. Dist., Graham, 1977-80; asst. dist. atty. Wichita County, Wichita Falls, Tex., 1980-81; ptnr. Neal, Neal, Richie & Hill, Graham, 1981—; atty. Young County, Tex., 1996—. Co-op, Inc, Bluegrove, Tex., 1979-83, Ft. Belknap Electric Coop., Inc., Olney, Tex., 1984—. Mem. State Bar Tex., Young County Bar Assn. (pres. 1972-73). Democrat. Episcopalian. Criminal, Family and matrimonial. Home: 1307

Roanoake Dr Graham TX 76450-4037 Office: Young County Courthouse Rm 102 PO Box 390 Graham TX 76450-0390 E-mail: ycatty@wf.net., brichie@wf.net.

RICHINS, KENT ALAN, lawyer; b. Evanston, Wyo., Oct. 13, 1959; s. Robert H. and Betty L. (Evert) R.; m. Rosie Ramos, May 27, 1978; children: Mike, Jason, Jennifer. BS in Psychology, Polit. Sci., Utah State U., 1982; JD, Washburn U., 1985. Bar: Kansas 1985, U.S. Dist. Ct. Kans. 1985, Wyo. 1986, U.S. Dist. Ct. Wyo. 1986, U.S. Tax Ct. 1987. Sole practice, Worland, Wyo., 1985—. V.p. Cloud Peak Investment, Inc., Worland, 1983—, also bd. dirs. City atty. City of Worland, 1989—. Mem. Lds Ch. Avocations: oil painting, golf. Criminal, General practice, Property, real (including real estate development, water). Office: 721 Big Horn Ave PO Box 1858 Worland WY 82401-1858

RICHMAN, JOEL ESER, lawyer, mediator, arbitrator; b. Brockton, Mass., Feb. 17, 1947; s. Nathan and Ruth Miriam (Bick) R.; m. Elaine R. Thompson, Aug. 21, 1987; children: Shawn Jonah, Jesse Ray, Eva Rose. BA in Psychology, Grinnell Coll., 1969; JD, Boston U., 1975. Bar: Mass. 1975, U.S. Dist. Ct. Mass. 1977, U.S. Supreme Ct. 1980, U.S. Ct. Appeals (1st cir.) 1982, Hawaii 1985, U.S. Dist. Ct. Hawaii 1987. Law clk. Richman & Perenyi, Brockton, Mass., 1973-75, atty., 1975-77; pvt. practice pvt. practice, Provincetown, Mass., 1977-82, Paia, Hawaii, 1985—. Arbitrator Am. Arbitration Assn., Paia, 1992—, mediator, 1994—. Pres. Jewish Congregation Maui (Hawaii), 1989-97, bd. dirs., 1984-89; bd. dirs. Pacific Primate Ctr., 1991, pres., 1994. Mem. Haiku Cmty. Assn. (dir. 1998, pres. 2000, v.p. 2001-), Kalama Band Boosters (pres. 2001). Avocations: wind-surfing, youth soccer, t'ai chi. Commercial, contracts (including sales of goods; commercial financing), Construction, Property, real (including real estate development, water). Office: PO Box 791539 Paia HI 96779-0046 E-mail: jer@haikulaw.com.

RICHMAN, MARTIN FRANKLIN, lawyer; b. Newark, Feb. 23, 1930; s. Samuel L. and Betty E. (Goldstein) R.; stepson Doris (Bloom) R.; m. Florence E. Reif, May 6, 1962; children— Judith, Andrew. BA magna cum laude, St. Lawrence U., 1950; LL.B. magna cum laude, Harvard U., 1953. Bar: N.Y. 1953. Law clk. to Judge Calvert Magruder and Chief Justice Earl Warren, 1955-57; assoc., mem. firm Lord Day & Lord, Barrett Smith (and predecessors), N.Y.C., 1957-66, 69-94; of counsel Kirkpatrick & Lockhart, LLP, N.Y.C., 1994—; dep. asst. atty. gen. Office Legal Counsel, Dept. Justice, Washington, 1966-69. Public mem. Adminstrv. Conf. U.S., 1970-76; bd. dirs. Community Action for Legal Services, 1977-80 Trustee St. Lawrence U., 1979-95, trustee emeritus, 1995—, vice chmn. bd., 1988-95; bd. dirs. Friends of Law Libr. of Congress, 1992-99. Recipient Alumni citation St. Lawrence U., 1972 Fellow Am. Bar Found., N.Y. Bar Found.; mem. ABA (chmn. sect. adminstrv. law 1983-84), N.Y. State Bar Assn. (ho. of dels. 1981-84), Assn. of Bar of City of N.Y. (sec. and mem. exec. com. 1976-79, chmn. com. fed. legislation 1972-75, com. lawyer's pro bono obligations 1977-81), Am. Law Inst. Office: Kirkpatrick & Lockhart LLP 599 Lexington Ave New York NY 10022-6030 E-mail: mrichman@kl.com.

RICHMAN, STEPHEN I. lawyer; b. Washington, Pa., Mar. 26, 1933; m. Audrey May Gefsky. BS, Northwestern U., 1954; JD, U. Pa., 1957. Bar: Pa. 1958, U.S. Dist. Ct. (we. dist.) Pa. With McCune Greenlee & Richman, 1960-63, Greenlee Richman Derrico & Posa, 1963-84, ptnr. Richman, Smith Law Firm, P.A., Washington, 1985—; bd. dirs. Three Rivers Bank; lectr. U. South Fla. Sch. Medicine, Mine Safe Internat. Chamber of Mines of Western Australia, W.Va. U. Med. Ctr. Grand Rounds, Am. Coll. Chest Physicians, Pa. Thoracic Soc., Am. Thoracic Soc., The Energy Bur., Coll. of Am. Pathologists, Allegheny County Health Dept., APHA, Internat. Assn. Ind. Accident Bds. and Commns., Indsl. Health Found., Nat. Coun. Self-Insurers Assn., Am. Iron and Steel Inst., Can. Thoracic Soc., I.L.O./N.I.O.S.H., Univs. Associated for Rsch. and Edn. in Pathology, Am. Ceramics Soc., Nat. Sand Assn.; mem. adv. com. U.S. Dist. Ct. Western Dist. Pa., 1994—; lectr. in field. Author: Meaning of Impairment and Disability, Chest, 1980, Legal Aspects for the Pathologist, in Pathology of Occupational and Environmental Lung Disease, 1988, A Review of the Medical and Legal Definitions of Related Impairment and Disability, Report to the Department of Labor and the Congress, 1986, Medicolegal Aspects of Asbestos for Pathologists, Arch. Pathology and Laboratory Medicine, 1983, Legal Aspects of Occupational and Environmental Disease, Human Pathology, 1993, Impairment and Disability in Pneunoconiosis, State of the Art Reviews in Occupational Medicine-The Mining Industry, 1993, other publs. and articles; author House Bills 2103 and 885 co-author Act 44 and 57 amending Pa. Workmen's Compensation Act. Mem. legal com. Indsl. Health Found., Pitts.; bd. dirs. Pitts. Opera Soc., 1994—, Pitts. Jewish Fedn., 1994-97; dir. Jewish Family and Children's Svc., Pitts., 1995—. Mem. ABA (former vice chair workers compensation and employers liability law com., toxic and hazardous substance and environ. law com., lectr.), ATLA, Pa. Bar Assn. (former mem. coun. of worker's compensation sect., lectr., contbg. author bar assn. quarterly 1992, 93), Pa. Chamber Bus. and Industry (workers' compensation com., chmn. subcom. on legis. drafting, lectr.). General civil litigation, Personal injury (including property damage), Workers' compensation. Home: 820 E Beau St Washington PA 15301-2906 Office: Washington Trust Bldg Ste 200 Washington PA 15301

RICHMOND, ALICE ELENOR, lawyer; b. N.Y.C. d. Louis A. and Estelle (Muraskin) R.; m. David L. Rosenbloom, July 26, 1981; 1 child, Elizabeth Lara. BA magna cum laude, Cornell U., 1968; JD, Harvard U., 1972, grad. Owners and Pres.'s Mgmt. Program, 2001; DLH (hon.) , North Adams State U., 1987. Bar: Mass. 1973, U.S. Dist. Ct. Mass. 1975, U.S. Ct. Appeals (1st cir.) 1982, U.S. Supreme Ct. 1985. Law clk. to justices Superior Ct., Boston, 1972-73; asst. dist. atty. Office of Dist. Atty., Boston, 1973-76; spl. asst. atty. gen. Office of Atty. Gen., Boston, 1975-77; asst. prof. New Eng. Sch. of Law, Boston, 1976-78; assoc. Lappin, Rosen, Boston, 1978-81; ptnr. Hemenway & Barnes, Boston, 1982-92, Deutsch, Williams, Boston, 1993-95, Richmond, Pauly & Ault, Boston, 1996—2002; prin. Richmond & Assocs., Boston, 2002—. Asst. team leader, faculty Trial Advocacy Course, 1978—82; examiner Mass. Bd. Bar Examiners, Boston, 1983—; trustee Mass. Continuing Legal Edn., Inc., Boston, 1985—96, Boston, 1998—; treas. Nat. Conf. Bar Examiners, 1995—, chmn. elect., 2002—03; v.p., bd. dirs. Am. Bar Ins., Inc., 1996—. Author (2 chpts.) Rape Crisis Intervention Handbook, 1976; contbr. articles to profl. jours. Mem. Pres. Adv. Com on the Arts, 1995—99; bd. overseers Handel & Haydn Soc., 1985—94, bd. govs., 1994—2002, v.p., 1996—2002; mem. Boston 2000 Millennium Commn., 1997—98; sec., dir. Boston 2000, Inc., 1998—2001; mem., pres. Coun. of Cornell Women, Cornell U. Coun.; trustee Red Auerbach Youth Found., Fund for Justice and Edn.; mem. adv. bd. Ctrl. and Ea. European Law Initiative; mem. Angell Meml. Hosp. Coun. of Fellows, 2001—. Named one of Outstanding Young Leaders Boston Jaycees, 1982; Sloan Found. Urban fellow, N.Y.C., 1969 Fellow: Am. Coll. Trial Lawyers; mem.: NOW, Legal Def. and Edn. Fund (trustee 1995—2002, sec. 1998—2002), ABA (ho. of dels. 1980—, vice chmn. com. on rules and calendar 1986—88, bd. govs. 2002—), Internat. Jud. Acad., Latin Am. Legal Initiatives Coun., Mass. Bar Found. (pres. 1988—91), Mass. Bar Assn. (pres. 1986—87), Am. Law Inst., Boston Club, Harvard Club. General civil litigation, Insurance, Personal injury (including property damage). Office: Richmond & Assocs 39 Brimmer St Boston MA 02108 E-mail: arichmond@rpalaw.com.

RICHMOND, DAVID WALKER, lawyer; b. Silver Hill, W.Va., Apr. 20, 1914; s. David Walker and Louise (Finlaw) R.; m. Gladys Evelyn Mallard, Dec. 19, 1936; children: David Walker, Nancy L. LL.B., George Washington U., 1937. Bar: D.C. 1936, Ill. 1946, Md. 1950. Partner firm Miller & Chevalier, Washington. Lectr. fed. taxation. Contbr. to profl. jours. Served from ensign to lt. comdr. USNR, 1942-46. Decorated Bronze Star; recipient Disting. Alumni Achievement award George Washington U., 1976 Fellow Am. Bar Found., Am. Coll. Tax Counsel; mem. ABA (chmn. taxation sect. 1955-57, ho. of dels. 1958-60), Am. Law Inst., Lawyers' Club of Washington, Union League (Chgo.), Masons. Republican. Methodist. Legislative, Corporate taxation. Home: 7979 S Tamiami Trl Apt 359 Sarasota FL 34231-6819 Office: 655 15th St NW Washington DC 20005-5701

RICHMOND, DIANA, lawyer; b. Milw., July 5, 1946; d. Lee and Laurel Jean (Bohlmann) Schultz; 1 child, Kavana. BA, U. Chgo., 1967; JD with highest honors, Golden Gate U., 1973. Bar: Calif. 1973, U.S. Dist. Ct. (no. dist.) Calif. 1973. Assoc. Stern, Stotter & O'Brien, San Francisco, 1973—77; sole practice San Francisco, 1977—80, 1983—2001; ptnr. Sideman & Bancroft, LLP, San Francisco, 2001—. Chmn. exec. com. family law sect. Calif. State Bar, 1984-85. Editor: California Marital Termination Settlements, 1988; editl. cons. Calif. Family Law Practice, 1984—; cons. editor: California Family Law Practice and Procedure II, 1995—. Recipient Outstanding Alumna award, Golden Gate U. Sch. Law, 1985, Golden Gate U., 1990. Fellow Am. Acad. Matrimonial Lawyers (pres. No. Calif. chpt. 1988-89, C. Rich Chamberlain award No. Calif. chpt. 2000), Bar Assn. San Francisco (bd. dirs. 1983-84, cert. of merit 1977), Barrister Club San Francisco. Democrat. Alternative dispute resolution, Appellate, Family and matrimonial. Office: Sideman & Bancroft LLP 8th Fl One Embarcadero Ctr San Francisco CA 94111 E-mail: drichmond@sideman.com.

RICHMOND, HAROLD NICHOLAS, lawyer; b. Elizabeth, N.J., Apr. 5, 1935; s. Benjamin I. and Eleanor (Turbowitz) R.; m. Elaine Zemel, June 16, 1957 (div. Nov. 1972); children: Bonnie J. Ross, Michele Weinfeld; m. Marilyn A. Wenrich, Aug. 26, 1973; children: Eric L., Kacy L. BA, Tulane U., 1957; LLB, NYU, 1961, LLM in Taxation, 1965. Estate tax examiner IRS, Newark, 1963-65; tax mgr. Puder & Puder/Touche Ross & Co., CPAs, Newark, 1965-73; ptnr. Sodowick Richmond & Crecca, Newark, 1973-84; prin. Harold N. Richmond, West Orange, N.J., 1984-86; ptnr. Wallerstein Hauptman & Richmond, West Orange, 1986-91, Hauptman & Richmond, West Orange, 1992—. With U.S. Army, 1959-60. Mem. ABA (tax sect. closely held bus. com., real property and probate sect.), N.J. Bar Assn. (tax, real property and probate sects.), Essex County Bar Assn. (chmn. tax com. 1989, real property and probate sect.). Avocations: running, tennis. Estate planning, Corporate taxation, Taxation, general. Office: Hauptman & Richmond 100 Executive Dr Ste 330 West Orange NJ 07052-3309

RICHMOND, JAMES GLIDDEN, lawyer; b. Sacramento, Feb. 20, 1944; s. James Gibbs and Martha Ellen (Glidden) R.; m. Lois Marie Bennett, Oct. 22, 1988; 1 child, Mark R. BS in Mgmt., Ind. U., 1966, postgrad., 1966-69, JD, 1969. Bar: Ind. 1969, Ill. 1991, U.S. Dist. Ct. (no. dist.) Ind. 1971, U.S. Dist. Ct. (so. dist.) Ind., 1969, U.S. Ct. Appeals (7th cir.) 1975, U.S. Tax Ct. 1980. Spl. agent FBI, 1970-74; spl. agent Criminal Investigation Divsn. IRS, 1974-76; asst. U.S. atty. no. dist. U.S. Atty. Office, Ind., 1976-80; assoc. Galvin, Stalmack & Kirschner, Hammond, Ind., 1980-81; pvt. practice Highland, Ind., 1981-83; ptnr. Goodman, Ball & Van Bokkelen, Highland, Ind., 1983-85; U.S. atty. no. dist. State of Ind., Hammond, 1985-91; spl. counsel to dep. atty. gen. of the U.S. U.S. Dept. Justice, Washington, 1990-91; mng. ptnr. Ungaretti and Harris, Chgo., 1991-92, ptnr., 1995—2002; exec. v.p., gen. counsel Nat. Health Labs., 1992-95; shareholder Greenberg Traurig, Chgo., 2002—. Practitioner in residence Ind. U. Sch. Law, Bloomington, 1989. Minority counsel senate republicans October Surprise Hearings, 1992. Fellow Am. Coll. Trial Lawyers. Republican. Avocation: fly fishing. Office: Greenberg Traurig 77 W Wacker Dr Ste 2500 Chicago IL 60601

RICHMOND, LYLE L. judge; LLB, Yale U., 1955. Dep. dist. atty., San Diego, 1959—64; pvt. practice, 1964—70; atty. gen., 1975—78; adminstr., legal mgr. Samoa Packing Co., Pago Pago, 1989—91; assoc. justice High Ct., Pago Pago, 1991—; legal counselor to American Samoa govs. Peter T. Coleman and A. P. Lutali, 1978—89; head legal divsn. atty.'s gen. office, 1973—75; dist. atty. Truk/Ponape dists., 1970—73. Capt. USNR. Office: Courthouse PO Box 309 Pago Pago AS 96799

RICHTER, DONALD PAUL, lawyer; b. New Britain, Conn., Feb. 15, 1924; s. Paul John and Helen (Racoske) R.; m. Jane Frances Gumpright, Aug. 10, 1946; children: Christopher Dean, Cynthia Louise. AB, Bates Coll., 1947; LL.B., Yale U., 1950. Bar: N.Y. 1951, Conn. 1953. Assoc. Winthrop, Stimson, Putnam & Roberts, N.Y.C., 1950-52; ptnr. Murtha, Cullina, Richter and Pinney, Hartford, Conn., 1954-94; counsel Murtha Cullina LLP, Hartford, Conn., 1994—. Trustee Bates Coll., 1962-94, Manchester (Conn.) Meml. Hosp., 1963-94, Hartford Sem., 1973-85; trustee Suffield Acad., 1974—, pres., 1982-89; bd. dirs. Met. YMCA Greater Hartford, 1970-94, pres., 1976-81, trustee, 1994—; mem. nat. coun. YMCA, 1978-82; bd. dirs. Church Homes, 1967-81; trustee, v.p., Silver Bay Assn., 1971-96. With USNR, 1943-46. Fellow Am. Coll. Trust and Estate Counsel; mem. ABA, Conn. Bar Assn., Univ. Club, Hartford Club, 20th Century Club, Rotary (Paul Harris fellow 1996), Phi Beta Kappa, Delta Sigma Rho. Congregationalist. Corporate, general, Estate planning. Home: 140 Boulder Rd Manchester CT 06040-4508 Office: Murtha Cullina LLP City Place I 185 Asylum St Hartford CT 06103-3469

RICHTER, TOBIN MARAIS, lawyer; b. Washington, Dec. 31, 1944; s. Vivian Craig and Leora Chapelle (Aultman) R.; m. Elizabeth Mills Dunlop, July 11, 1970; children: Ian, Lauren. B in City Planning, U. Va., 1967, JD, 1973. Bar: Ill. 1973, U.S. Dist. Ct. (no. dist.) Ill. 1973, U.S. Ct. Fed. Claims, 1976, U.S. Ct. Appeals (7th cir.) 1977, U.S. Supreme Ct. 1979, U.S. Dist. Ct. (ea. dist.) Wis. 1987. Assoc. Ross & Hardies, Chgo., 1973-80, ptnr., 1981-84, Spindell, Kemp & Kimball, Chgo., 1984-89; pvt. practice Chgo., 1989—. Adj. instr. U. Wis., Osh Kosh, 1976; ct. apptd. arbitrator Cir. Ct. Cook County, 1991—; chancellor Seabury-Western Theol. Sem., 1998-2001. Co-author: Federal Land Use Regulation, 1977; contbr. articles to profl. jours. Legal counsel 44th Ward Community Zoning Bd., Chgo., 1980; v.p., Aux. Bd. Chgo. Architecture Found., 1983; pres., bd. dirs. Landmarks Preservation Council Ill., Chgo., 1986; v.p., bd. dirs. Counseling Ctr. of Lakeview, 1997—. 1st lt. U.S. Army, 1968-70, Vietnam. Mem. ABA, Chgo. Bar Assn., Soc. Am. Mil. Engrs. (v.p. 1980, 84, 86), Econ. Club (Chgo.). Avocations: tennis, pottery, genealogy. Federal civil litigation, State civil litigation, Property, real (including real estate development, water). Office: 53 W Jackson Blvd Ste 560 Chicago IL 60604-3667 E-mail: tmrichter@corecomm.net.

RICKERT, BRIAN PATRICK, lawyer; b. Mankato, Minn., Dec. 10, 1972; s. Marvin LeRoy and Marie Annette Rickert. BBA in Fin., U. Iowa, 1995; JD with honors, Drake U., 1998. Bar: Mo. 1998, U.S. Dist. Ct. (we. dist.) Mo. 1998, Kans. 1999, Iowa 1999, U.S. Dist Ct. Kans. 1999, U.S. Dist. Ct. (no. and so. dists.) Iowa 2000, U.S. Ct. Appeals (8th cir.) 2002. Assoc. Dysart, Taylor, Lay, Cotter & McMonigle, Kansas City, Mo., 1998—2000, Brown, Winick, Graves, Gross, Baskerville & Schoenebaum, Des Moines, 2000—. Mem. staff Drake Law Rev., 1996-98. Mem. ABA, Kansas City Met. Bar Assn. Lutheran. Avocations: golf, volleyball, outdoor activities. General civil litigation, Federal civil litigation, Construction. Office: Brown Winick et al 666 Grand Ave Ste 2000 Des Moines IA 50309

RICKS, CECIL EARL, JR., lawyer; b. Bell, Calif., Oct. 4, 1939; s. Cecil Earl and Harriett C. R.; m. Sharon Ann Klusmeyer, Sept. 7, 1957; children— Gregory Paul, Kathleen Ann. B.A., UCLA, 1960, J.D., 1963. Bar: Calif. 1964, U.S. Supreme Ct. 1972. Assoc. Hill, Farrer & Burrill, Los Angeles, 1964-68; ptnr. Kurilich, Slack, Ballard, Batchelor, Maher & Ricks, Fullerton, Calif., 1968-72; ptnr. Maher, Moore, Rheinheimer & Ricks, Anaheim, Calif., 1972-75; ptnr. Ricks & Ricks, Anaheim, 1975-82; mem. Cecil E. Ricks, Jr., P.C., Anaheim, 1982—87, Ricks & Anderson PLC, 1987- ; judge pro tem Orange County, Calif., 1980—87 . Former pres. Anaheim YMCA, Fullerton Civic Light Opera Assn.; former mem. bd. dirs. No. Orange County YMCA, Muckenthaler Ctr., Los Angeles Jr. C. of C. Mem. ABA, State Bar Calif. (past hearing officer and dir.), Orange County Trial Lawyers Assn. (dir. 1983-85), Assn. Trial Lawyers Am., Calif. Trial Lawyers Assn., Barristers, Phi Delta Phi (magister). Republican. Administrative and regulatory, State civil litigation, Personal injury (including property damage).

RICKS, LYNDON LEE, lawyer; b. Rexburg, Idaho, Dec. 19, 1955; s. LaVere Arnold and Lucille (Johnson) R.; m. Elizabeth Ann Gardner, Aug. 20, 1980; children: Daniel, Heather, Adam, Whitney, Amanda. AAS, Ricks Coll., 1978; BA, Brigham Young U., 1979; JD, J. Reuben Clark Sch. Law, Provo, Utah, 1981. Bar: Utah 1982, U.S. Dist. Ct. Utah 1982, U.S. Ct. Appeals (10th cir.) 1986. Intern U.S. Senator James McClure, Washington, 1980; assoc. Kesler & Rust, Salt Lake City, 1981—82; shareholder Allen, Nelson, Hardy & Evans, Salt Lake City, 1983—92; mem. Kruse, Landa, Maycock & Ricks, Salt Lake City, 1992—. Spkr. in field. Author, editor: Brigham Young U. Jour. Legal Studies, 1981-82. Mem. Centerville (Utah) Planning and Zoning Commn., 1991—, 1996, chmn., 1994-96; active Utah State Rep. Ctrl. Com., 1991-93; cubmaster Boy Scouts Am., Centerville, 1992-93; coach Jr. Jazz Basketball, Little League Baseball and Utah Youth Soccer, Centerville, 1989—. Mem.: J. Reuben Clark Law Soc., Nat. Assn. Stock Plan Profls., Utah State Bar Assn. (chmn. securities law sect.). Mem. Lds Ch. Corporate, general, Mergers and acquisitions, Securities. Office: Kruse Landa Maycock & Ricks PO Box 45561 Salt Lake City UT 84145-0561 E-mail: lricks@klmlaw.com.

RIDDICK, WINSTON WADE, SR., lawyer; b. Crowley, La., Feb. 11, 1941; s. Hebert Hobson and Elizabeth (Wade) R.; m. Patricia Ann Turner, Dec. 25, 1961;1 child, Winston Wade. BA, U. Southwestern La., 1962; MA, U. N.C., 1963; PhD, Columbia U., 1965; JD, La. State U., 1973. Bar: La. 1974, U.S. Dist. Ct. (so., mid. and we. dists.) La., U.S. Ct. Appeals (5th cir.), U.S. Supreme Court. Asst. prof. gov., dir. Inst. Gov. Research, La. State U., Baton Rouge, 1966-67; dir. La. Higher Edn. Facilities Commn., Baton Rouge, 1967-72; exec. asst. state supt. La. Dept. Edn., Baton Rouge, 1972-73; law ptnr. Riddick & Riddick, Baton Rouge, 1973—; asst. commnr., gen. counsel La. Dept. Agr., Baton Rouge, 1981-82. Cons. Riddick & Assoc., Baton Rouge, 1973—; part-time law faculty mem. So. Univ. Law Ctr., Baton Rouge, 1974-95; assoc. prof., 1995-99, prof. law, 1999—, exec. asst. atty. gen. State of La., 1987-91. Spl. asst. to Gov. John J. McKeithen on Nat. Ctr. for Edn. in Politics Fellowship, 1966-67; state campaign mgr. Gillis W. Long for Gov., Baton Rouge, 1971; mem. East Baton Rouge Parish Dem. Exec. Com., 1981-84. Mem. La. Trial Lawyers Assn. (bd. govs. 1978-80), real estate investor and property mgr., 1975—. Presbyterian. Constitutional, Health, Insurance. Office: Riddick & Assocs Inc 1563 Oakley Dr Baton Rouge LA 70806-8622 E-mail: wriddick@sus.edu.

RIDDLE, CHARLES ADDISON, III, district attorney, former state legislator; b. Marksville, La., June 8, 1955; s. Charles Addison Jr. and Alma Rita (Gremillion) R.; m. Margaret Susan Noone, Mar. 24, 1978; children: Charles Addison IV, John H., Michael J. BA, La. State U., 1976, JD, 1980. Bar: La. 1980, U.S. Dist. Ct. (mid. and we. dists.) La. 1983, U.S. Ct. Appeals (5th cir.) 1988, U.S. Supreme Ct. 1991, U.S. Ct. Vets. Appeals 1994. Assoc. Riddle & Bennett, Marksville, 1980; pvt. practice Marksville, 1981—; mem. La. Ho. of Reps., Baton Rouge, 1992—2003; reelected La. House of Reps., Baton Rouge, 1995—99, 1999—2003; dist. atty. Avoyelles Parish 12th Jud. Dist., 2003—. Elected La. State Dem. Cen. com., Avoyelles Parish, 1983-87, Parish Exec. Demo. Com. 1987-91. Mem. Avoyelles Bar Assn. (pres. 1987-88), Bunkie Rotary (bd. dirs.), Marksville Lions, Marksville C. of C. (pres. 1988-92). Office: PO Box 608 208 E Mark St Marksville LA 71351-2416 E-mail: criddle777@aol.com.

RIDDLE, MICHAEL LEE, lawyer; b. Oct. 7, 1946; s. Joy Lee and Francis Irene (Brandes) R.; m. Suzan Ellen Shaw, May 25, 1969 (div.); m. Carol Jackson, Aug. 13, 1977; 1 child, Robert Andrew. BA, Tex. Tech U., 1969, JD with honors, 1972. Bar: Tex. 1972, U.S. Dist. Ct. (no. dist.) Tex. 1972, U.S. Ct. Appeals (5th cir.) Tex. 1972. Assoc. Geary Brice Barron & Stahl, Dallas, 1972-75; ptnr. Baker Glast Riddle Tuttle & Elliott, Dallas, 1975-80; ptnr., mng. ptnr. Middleburg, Riddle & Gianna, 1980—; chmn., CEO MRG Document Techs., 2000—. Bd. dirs. Dallas Opera. Bd. dirs. U.S.A. Film Festival, pres., 1984-86, North Tex. Pub. Broadcasting, 1992-97; chmn., bd. dirs. Provident Bancorp Tex., 1987-90. Mem. ABA, Tex. Bar Assn., Dallas Bar Assn., Coll. of State Bar of Tex., Lakewood Country Club, Crescent Club. Democrat. Lutheran. Banking, Property, real (including real estate development, water). Office: 717 N Harwood Ste 2400 Dallas TX 75201 E-mail: mriddle@midrid.com.

RIDENOUR, CHARLES EDWARD, lawyer; b. Lebanon, Tenn., Nov. 5, 1950; s. Billy R. and Jaunita J. (Jacobs) R.; m. Kathy Chlorine Bilderback, Sept. 2, 1972; children: Tracey Kristine, Mary Kathryn. BS in Mgmt., Tenn. Wesleyan Coll., 1972; JD, Nashville Sch. Law, 1978. Bar: Tenn. 1980. Pvt. practice law, Sweetwater, Tenn., 1980—. Legal counsel Sweetwater Utility Bd., Sweetwater Housing Authority, Vestal's Employee's Credit Union; faculty mem. Cleve. State C.C., 1988-89, Tenn. Wesleyan Coll., 1995. Active Boy Scouts Am., asst. scoutmaster, Sweetwater, 1971—, bd. mem. Great Smokey Mountain Coun., 1984—, exec. bd. mem. Great Smokey Mountain Coun., 1987-90, advancement chmn. Unaka dist., 1984—, chmn. Unaka Dist.-Great Smokey Mountain Coun., 1986-89 (coun. camping chmn., 2003); active First Bapt. Ch., Sweetwater, chmn. pers. com., 1984-85, 99-2002, chmn. 2002, mem. by-laws com., 1986-90, mem. fin. com., 1991-93, trustee, 1995—; pres. Knox County Chpt., Tenn. State Employees Assn., 1979-80; sec. Monroe County Election Commn., 1980-84; mem. Sweetwater Valley Citizens for the Arts, 1982—, chmn., 1984-86; mem. Monroe County United Way, 1982-95, 99—, chmn., 1984-95; mem. chmn. Better Schs. adv. bd. Sweetwater City Schs., 1985-86. Mem. Monroe County Bar Assn. (pres. 1984, 2000), Kiwanis (pres. Sweetwater Club 1982-83, Disting. lt. gov. divsn. four 1985-86, 87-88, dist. chmn. by-laws and resolution com. 1987-94, 96-97, dist. chmn. Bi-Centennial Celebration of the Bill of Rights 1990-91, Disting. past gov. 1994-95, life mem. Ky./Tenn. dist. 22., others.), Odd Fellows Lodge, Sweetwater Masonic Lodge. Commercial, contracts (including sales of goods; commercial financing), General practice, Probate (including wills, trusts). Home: 510 Broad St Sweetwater TN 37874-1611 Office: PO Box 444 107 W North St Sweetwater TN 37874-2627

RIDER, BRIAN CLAYTON, lawyer; b. San Antonio, Oct. 8, 1948; s. Ralph W. and Emmie(Rider); m. Patsy Anne (Ruppert), Dec. 27, 1970; children: Christopher, David, James, Andrew. BA, Rice U., 1969; JD, U. Tex., 1972. Bar: Tex., 1972. Assoc. then ptnr. Dow, Cogburn, and Friedman, Houston, 1972-83; ptnr. Brown, McCarroll, Oaks, and Hartline, Austin, Tex., 1983-96. Adj. prof. U. Tex., 1997—; lectr. in field. Contbr. articles to profl. jour. Mem. Am. Coll. Real Estate Lawyers; Travis County Bar Assn. (bd. dirs. 1986-88, chmn. Travis County real estate sect. 1986-88); State Bar of Tex. (coun. real estate and probate sect. 1992-96),; Tex. Coll. Real Estate Lawyers (chair 1999-2002, sec. treas. 2003—). Environmental, Finance, Property, real (including real estate development, water). Home: 2906 Hatley Dr Austin TX 78746-4613 Office: 1300 S Mopac Austin TX 78746 E-mail: brider@lumbermensinv.com.

RIDGE, THOMAS JOSEPH, federal agency administrator, former governor, former congressman; b. Munhall, Pa., Aug. 26, 1945; m. Michele Moore, 1979, children, Lesley & Tommy. BA, Harvard U., 1967; JD, Dickinson Sch. Law, Carlisle, Pa., 1972. Bar: Pa. 1972. Pvt. practice, Erie, Pa., 1972-82; asst. dist. atty., 1979-82; mem. 98th-103rd Congresses from Pa. 21st dist., Washington, 1983-1995; mem. Banking, Fin., Urban Affairs com., subcoms. Econ. Growth and Credit Formation, Housing and Community Devel., Veteran's Affairs com.; gov. State of Pa., 1995—2001; dir. Dept. Homeland Security, Washington, 2001—02, sec., 2003—. Mem. banking, fin., urban affairs com., subcoms. econ. growth and credit formation, housing and cmty. devel., vets. affairs com.; subcom. Hosps. and Healthcare, Oversight and Investigation, Post Office and Civil Svc., com., subcom. Census and Population, Civil Svc. With U.S. Army, 1968-70, Vietnam. Republican. Office: Office Homeland Security 3801 Nebraska Ave NW Washington DC 20016*

RIEGER, MITCHELL SHERIDAN, lawyer; b. Chgo., Sept. 5, 1922; s. Louis and Evelyn (Sampson) R.; m. Rena White Abelmann, May 17, 1949 (div. 1957); 1 child, Karen Gross Cooper; m. Nancy Horner, May 30, 1961 (div. 1972); stepchildren: Jill Levi, Linda Hanan, Susan Perlstein, James Geoffrey Felsenthal; m. Pearl Handelsman, June 10, 1973; stepchildren: Steven Newman, Mary Ann Malarkey, Nancy Halbeck. AB, Northwestern U., 1944; JD, Harvard U., 1949. Bar: Ill. 1950, U.S. Dist. Ct. (no. dist.) Ill. 1950, U.S. Supreme Ct. 1953, U.S. Ct. Mil. Appeals 1953, U.S. Ct. Appeals (7th cir.) 1954. Legal asst. Rieger & Rieger, Chgo., 1949-50, assoc., 1950-54; asst. U.S. atty. No. Dist Ill., Chgo., 1954-60, 1st asst., 1958-60; assoc. gen. counsel SEC, Washington, 1960-61; ptnr. Schiff Hardin & Waite, Chgo., 1961—, sr. counsel, 1998—. Instr. John Marshall Law Sch. Chgo., 1952-54. Contbr. articles to profl. jours. Active Chgo. Crime Commn., bd. dirs., 1998—; pres. Park View Home for Aged, 1969-71; Rep. precinct committeeman, Highland Park, Ill., 1964-68; bd. dirs. Spertus Mus. Judaica, 1987-91, vis. com., 1991—. Served to lt. (j.g.) USNR, 1943-46, PTO. Fellow Am. Coll. Trial Lawyers; mem. ABA, FBA (pres. Chgo. chpt. 1959-60, nat. v.p. 1960-61), Chgo. Bar Assn., Ill. Bar Assn., Am. Judicature Soc., 7th Circuit Bar Assn., Standard Club, Lawyers Club Chgo., Vail Racquet Club, Phi Beta Kappa. Jewish. Avocations: photography, skiing, sailing. Professional liability. Office: Schiff Hardin & Waite 6600 Sears Tower Chicago IL 60606 E-mail: mrieger@schiffhardin.com., msheridanr@aol.com.

RIEKE, DAVIN ERIC, lawyer, military officer; b. West Palm Beach, Fla. m. Amanda K. Rieke. BS in Internat. Bus., Fla. Atlantic U., 1996; MBA, JD, Stetson U., 1999. Bar: Fla. 2000, U.S. Ct. Appeals for Armed Forces 2002. Intern mid. dist. U.S. Dist. Ct., Tampa, Fla., 1998; clk. mid. dist. Fla. U.S. Atty., Tampa, 1999; legal assistance counsel Navy Legal Svc. Office NW USN, Silverdale, Wash., 2000—01, tax officer Bremerton, Wash., 2001—02, def. counsel, 2002—. Lt. USN, 2000—. Mem.: ABA. Office: Navy Legal Svc Office NW 365 S Barclay Bremerton WA 98314 E-mail: riekede@jag.navy.mil.

RIEKE, FORREST NEILL, lawyer; b. Portland, Oreg., May 26, 1942; s. Forrest Eugene and Mary Neill (Whitelaw) R.; m. Madonna Bernardi, Apr. 2, 1966; children: Mary Jane, Forrest Ermelindo. AB in Polit. Sci., Stanford U., 1968; JD, Willamette U., 1971. Bar: Oreg. 1971, U.S. Dist. Ct. Oreg. 1974, U.S. Ct. Appeals (9th cir.) 1975, U.S. Supreme Ct. 1977. Sr. dep. dist. atty. Multnomah County, Portland, 1971-76; ptnr. Rieke & Savage P.C., Portland, 1977—. Instr. Oreg. State Police Acad., Ft. Rilea, 1979-2001 Contbr. editor Williamette U. Law Rev., 1971. Pres., bd. dirs. Council Great City Schs., Washington, 1985-93; trustee Emanuel Hosp. Found., 1987-93; bd. dirs. Portland Pub. Schs., 1978-93. Mem. ABA, Oreg. Bar Assn. (indigent accused def. com., chmn. law related edn. com. 1985, bd. dirs. criminal law sect. 1979-84, mem. pub. info. com. 1987-90, ho. dels. 1995-98), Nat. Criminal Def. Lawyers Assn., Multnomah County Bar Assn., Oreg. Criminal Def. Lawyers Assn., Multnomah Athletic, Rotary. Presbyterian. Avocations: skiing, reading, coaching youth sports. General civil litigation, Criminal, Personal injury (including property damage). Home: 820 SW 2nd Ave Apt 6 Portland OR 97204-3086 Office: Rieke & Savage PC 140 SW Yamhill St Portland OR 97204-3007 E-mail: joe@rieke_savage.com.

RIES, WILLIAM CAMPBELL, lawyer; b. Pitts., Apr. 8, 1948; s. F. William and Dorothy (Campbell) R.; m. Mallory Burns, Oct. 26, 1968; children: William Sheehan, Sean David. AB, Cath. U. Am., 1970; JD, Duquesne U., 1974; cert. Grad. Sch. Indsl. Adminstrn., Carnegie Mellon U., 1980. Bar: Pa. 1974, U.S. Dist. Ct. (we. dist.) Pa. 1974, U.S. Supreme Ct. 1979. Atty., then mng. counsel trust and investment svc. Mellon Bank, N.A., Pitts., 1974-90; ptnr. Dickie, McCamey and Chilcote, Pitts., 1990-98; mem. Sweeney, Metz, Fox, McGrann & Schermer, LLC, 1998-2001; shareholder Tucker Arensberg, 2001—. Mem. adv. com. decedents' estates and trust law Pa. Joint State Govt. Commn., 1981—; adj. prof. Duquesne U., 1984—. Author: The Regulation of Investment Management and Fiduciary Services West, 1997. Pres. McCandless Twp. Civic Assn., Pitts., 1981—, McCandless Town Coun., chair pub. safety com., vice chair fin com.; sec. McCandless Indsl. Devel. Auth.; liaison McCandless zoning hearing bd. Fellow Am. Bar Found.; mem. ABA (chmn. fiduciary svcs. subcom.), Pa. Bar Assn., Allegheny County Bar Assn., Pitts. Estate Planning Coun., Am. Bankers Assn. (co-chmn. nat. conf. lawyers and corp. fiduciaries, chmn. trust counsel com.), Pa. Bankers Assn. (trust com., trust legis. com.), Rivers Club, Treesdale Golf and Country Club. Republican. Avocations: golf, sailing, cross-country skiing, fitness. Banking, Pension, profit-sharing, and employee benefits, Securities. Home: 9602 Fawn Ln Allison Park PA 15101-1737 E-mail: wries@tuckerlaw.com.

RIESELBACH, ALLEN NEWMAN, lawyer; b. Milw., June 2, 1931; s. Allen Saxe and Renee (Newman) R.; m. Patricia Fried, May 27, 1956; children: Anne, William. AB, Harvard U., 1953, LLB, 1956. Bar: Wis. 1956, Fla. 1971, Colo. 1986. Shareholder Reinhart, Boerner, Van Deuren, S.C., Milw., 1959-99, sr. counsel, 1999—. Gov. Am. Coll. Real Estate Lawyers, 1989-92. Editor: Wisconsin Condominium Law, 1980. Mem. exec. bd. Milw. County Boy Scouts, 1975-92, 99—; bd. dirs. Milw. Repertory Theater, 1984-90; pres. Milw. Symphony Orch., 1995-98, mem. exec. com., 1992—. Recipient Lifetime Achievement award, Milw. Bar Assn., 2002. Avocations: sailing, biking. Construction, Land use and zoning (including planning), Property, real (including real estate development, water). Office: Reinhart Boerner Van Deuren SC 1000 N Water St Ste 2100 Milwaukee WI 53202-3197 E-mail: arieselb@reinhartlaw.com.

RIFKIND, ROBERT S(INGER), lawyer; b. N.Y.C., Aug. 31, 1936; s. Simon H. and Adele (Singer) R.; m. Arleen Brenner, Dec. 24, 1961; children: Amy, Nina. BA, Yale U., 1958; JD, Harvard U., 1961; LHD (hon.), Jewish Theol. Sem. Am., 1998. Bar: N.Y. 1961, U.S. Supreme Ct. 1965. Asst. to solicitor gen. Dept. Justice, 1965-68; assoc. firm Cravath, Swaine & Moore, N.Y.C., 1962-65, 68-70, ptnr., 1971—2001, sr. counsel, 2002—. Trustee Dalton Sch., N.Y.C., 1975-83, hon. trustee, 1983—, pres., 1977-79; trustee Brandeis U., 1998—, The Loomis Inst., 1987-95, Citizens Budget Commn.; bd. dirs. Charles H. Revson Found., 1991—, chmn., 1997—; bd. dirs. Jewish Theol. Sem. Am., 1983—, Jerusalem Found., 1998–, Leo Baeck Inst., 1999—, Benjamin N. Cardozo Sch. Law, 1984-89; pres. Am. Jewish Com., 1994-98; chmn., adminstr. coun., Jacob Blaustein Inst. Advancement of Human Rights, 1999-. Fellow Am. Coll. Trial Lawyers, Am. Bar Found.; mem. ABA, Coun. Fgn. Rels., Am. Law Inst., Assn. of Bar of City of N.Y., Phi Beta Kappa. Democrat. Antitrust, Federal civil litigation, State civil litigation. Office: Cravath Swaine & Moore Worldwide Pla 825 8th Ave Fl 38 New York NY 10019-7475

RIGGIO, MICHAEL V. lawyer; b. Tacoma, Oct. 27, 1944; s. Vincent F. and Genevieve Riggio; m. Janet M. Lind, June 16, 1967; children: Mark, Amy, Sarah, Aaron. BA, U. Wash., 1967, LLM, 1985; JD, Seattle U., 1976. Bar: Wash. 1976, U.S. Supreme Ct. 1980, U.S. Dist. Ct. (we. dist.) Wash. 1986, U.S. Ct. Appeals (9th cir.) 1986, Oreg. 2002. Dep. pros. atty. Pierce County, Tacoma, 1987—89; atty. Graham & Dunn, Seattle, 1989—95, Luce, Lombino & Riggio, Tacoma, 1995—. Comdr. USN, 1967—87, atty. JAGC USN, 1976—87. Roman Catholic. Personal injury (including property damage), Admiralty, Aviation. Office: Luce Lombino and Riggio 4505 Pacific Hwy E # A Tacoma WA 98424 Office Fax: 253-922-2802. E-mail: michael.riggio@llrwa.com.

RIGGIO, NICHOLAS JOSPEH, SR., lawyer; b. St. Louis, Oct. 1, 1930; s. Joseph and Anna (Trapani) R.; m. Etta G. Riggio, Nov. 6, 1954; children: Nicholas Jr., Michael John, Joy Ann. BS, St. Louis U., 1953; LLB, Washington U., 1959, JD, 1968. Pvt. practice, St. Louis, 1959—. Co-founder Hill 2000 Orgn., St. Louis, 2000. Inducted into St. Louis Soccer Hall of Fame, 1985. General civil litigation, Commercial, consumer (including collections, credit), Condemnation (eminent domain). Office: 5149 Daggett Ave Saint Louis MO 63110-3039

RIGGS, ARTHUR JORDY, retired lawyer; b. Nyack, N.Y., Apr. 3, 1916; s. Oscar H. and Adele (Jordy) R.; m. Virginia Holloway, Oct. 15, 1942 (dec.); children: Arthur James (dec.), Emily Adele Riggs Freeman, Keith Holloway, George Bennett; m. Priscilla McCormack, Jan. 16, 1993. AB, Princeton U., 1937; LLB, Harvard U., 1940. Bar: Mass. 1940, Tex. 1943; cert. specialist in labor law. Assoc. Warner, Stackpole, Stetson & Bradlee, Boston, 1940-41; staff mem. Solicitors Office U.S. Dept. Labor, Washington, Dallas, 1941-42; mem. Johnson, Bromberg, Leeds & Riggs, Dallas, 1949-81; of counsel Geary & Spencer, Dallas, 1981-91. Mem. ABA, State Bar Tex., Phi Beta Kappa. Avocations: maya archeology, history, photography. Home and Office: 2110 Antibes Dr Carrollton TX 75006-4326

RIGGS, DAN BRITT, lawyer; b. Oklahoma City, Dec. 26, 1949; s. Carroll A. and Mayme B. (Britt) R.; m. Kathryn Ann Elliott, Aug. 17, 1975. BA with honors, U. Wyo., 1972, LLB with honors, 1975. Bar: Wyo. 1975, U.S. Dist. Ct. Wyo. 1975, U.S. Ct. Appeals (10th cir.) 1975. From assoc. to ptnr. Lonabaugh & Vanderhoof, Sheridan, Wyo., 1975-81; ptnr. Lonabaugh & Riggs, Sheridan, 1981—. Adv. com. 10th cir. U.S. Ct. Appeals, 2002—. Articles editor Land & Water Law Rev., 1974-75. Mem. Sheridan Planning Commn., 1977-84. Mem. ABA, Wyo. State Bar Assn., Am. Trial Lawyers Assn., Wyo. Trial Lawyers Assn., Sheridan County Bar Assn. (pres. 1985-86). Republican. Avocations: tennis, horseback riding. General civil litigation, Corporate, general, Insurance. Home: 155 Scott Dr Sheridan WY 82801-3257

RIGGS, R. WILLIAM, judge; Grad., Portland State U., 1961; JD, U. Oreg., 1968. Atty. Willner Bennett & Leonard, 1968—78; judge circuit ct. 4th Jud. Dist., 1978—88; judge Oreg. Ct. of Appeals, 1988—98, Oreg. Supreme Ct., 1998—. Active mem. Cmty. Law Project; founder Integra Corp. Capt. USNR. Office: Supreme Ct Bldg 1163 State St Salem OR 97310-0260 E-mail: r.william.riggs@ojd.state.or.us.

RIGOR, BRADLEY GLENN, lawyer; b. Cheyenne Wells, Colo., Aug. 9, 1955; s. Glenn E. and Lelia (Teed) R.; m. Twyla G. Helweg, Sept. 4, 1983; children: Camille, Brent, Tiffany, Lauren. BS in Mktg., Ft. Hays State U., 1977; JD, Washburn U., 1980. Bar: Kans. 1980, U.S. Dist. Kans., 1980, U.S. Tax Ct. 1981, U.S. Ct. Appeals (10th cir.) 1982, U.S. Supreme Ct. 1986, Colo. 1990, Tex. 1991, U.S. Dist. Ct. Colo. 1991, Mo. 1993, Fla. 1998; cert. trust and fin. advisor Inst. Cert. Bankers; cert. fin. planner. Ptnr. Zuspann & Rigor, Goodland, Kans., 1980-82; city atty. Goodland, 1981-82; asst. county atty. Wallace County, Sharon Springs, Kans., 1982-84, county atty., 1984; city atty. Sharon Springs, 1983-84; judge Mcpl. Ct., Goodland, 1988-93; ptnr. Fairbanks, Rigor & Irvin, P.A., Goodland, 1982-93; v.p., mgr. personal trusts Merc. Bank, St. Joseph, Mo., 1993-96; sr. v.p., mgr., personal trust adminstr. SunTrust Bank, Naples, Fla., 1996-98; ptnr. Bond Schoeneck & King P.A., Naples, Fla., 1998—. Mem. Estate Planning Coun., Naples. Mem. Kans. Bar Assn., Tex. Bar Assn., Mo. Bar Assn., Colo. Bar Assn., Fla. Bar Assn., Collier County Bar Assn. (trust and estates sect.). Republican. Baptist. Estate planning. Office: Ste 250 4001 Tamiami Trl N Naples FL 34103-3555 E-mail: rigorb@bsk.com.

RIGOS, GEORGE, retired judge; b. Athens, Greece; s. Constantine and Helen (Rorri) R.; m. (div.); 1 child, Constantine. Law degree, Athens, 1961. Lawyer, Athens, 1964-66; judge of 1st instance Athens, Xanthi, Nafplia, 1966-78; pres. of 1st instance Edessa, 1978-81; appellate judge Corfu, Patras, Athens, 1981-93; pres. ct. appeals Piraeus, 1993-97; judge supreme ct. Athens, 1997—2002; ret. Author: Liberty and Language, 1995; editor: (periodical) Greek Justice-Organ of the Greek Judges Union; contbr. articles to profl. jours. Mem. Union of Greek Judges, Assn. of Greek Constitutionalists, Soc. Judicial Studies. Avocations: reading, travel, movies, theater, concerts. Home: 37 Gouda St 11476 Athens Greece

RIGSBY, LINDA FLORY, lawyer; b. Topeka, Kans., Dec. 16, 1946; d. Alden E. and Lolita M. Flory; m. Michael L. Rigsby, Aug. 14, 1963; children: Michael L. Jr., Elisabeth A. MusB, Va. Commonwealth U., 1969; JD, U. Richmond, 1981. Bar: Va. 1981, D.C. 1988. Assoc. McGuire, Woods, Battle & Boothe, Richmond, Va., 1981-85; dep. gen. counsel and corp. sec. Crestar Fin. Corp., Richmond, 1985-99, gen. counsel, 1999-2000; mng. atty. Sun Trust Banks Inc., 2000—. Recipient Disting. Svc. award U. Richmond, 1987; named Vol. of Yr. U. Richmond, 1986, Woman of Achievement, Met. Richmond Women's Bar, 1995. Mem. Va. Bar Assn. (exec. com. 1993-96), Richmond Bar Assn. (bd. dirs. 1992-95), Va. Bankers Assn. (chair legal affairs 1992-95), U. Richmond Estate Planning Coun. (chmn. 1990-92). Roman Catholic. Avocations: music, gardening. Home: 163 W Square Pl Richmond VA 23233-6157 Office: SunTrust Bank 919 E Main St Richmond VA 23219-4625

RIKON, MICHAEL, lawyer; b. Bklyn., Feb. 2, 1945; s. Charles and Ruth (Shapiro) R.; m. Leslie Sharon Rein, Feb. 11, 1968; children: Carrie Rachel, Joshua Howard. BS, N.Y. Inst. Tech., 1966; JD, Bklyn. Law Sch., 1969; LLM, NYU, 1974. Bar: N.Y. 1970, U.S. Dist. Ct. (so. and ea. dists.) N.Y. 1971, U.S. Ct. Appeals (2d cir.) 1972, U.S. Supreme Ct. 1973, U.S. Ct. Appeals (5th and 11th cirs.) 1981. Asst. corp. counsel City of N.Y., 1969-73; law clk. N.Y. State Ct. Claims, 1973-80; ptnr. Rudick and rikon, P.C., N.Y.C., 1980-88; pvt. practice N.Y.C., 1988-94; ptnr. Goldstein, Goldstein and Rikon, P.C., N.Y.C., 1994—. Contbr. articles to profl. jours. Pres. Village Greens Residents Assn., 1978-79; chmn. bd. Arden Heights Jewish Ctr., Staten Island, N.Y., 1976-77; pres. North Shore Repub. Club., 1977; mem. cmty. bd. Staten Island Borough Pres., 1977. Fellow Am. Bar Found.; mem. ABA (chair com. Condemnation) ATLA, TLPJ Found., N.Y. State Bar Assn. (spl. com. of condemnation law), Suffolk County Bar Assn., N.Y. County lawyers Assn. (chair Condemnation com.), Assn. Bar of City of N.Y. (condemnation com.), Mt. Vernon Bar Assn. Republican. Jewish. Avocations: collecting stamps, photography, collecting miniature soldiers. State civil litigation, Condemnation (eminent domain), Property, real (including real estate development, water). Home: 133 Avondale Rd Ridgewood NJ 07450-1301 Office: 80 Pine St New York NY 10005-1702

RILEY, JAMES KEVIN, lawyer; b. Nyack, N.Y., July 21, 1945; s. Charles A. and Mary Lenihan R.; m. Joan Leavy Riley, Oct. 4, 1969; children: Carolyn, Tara, Sean. AB, Fordham Coll., 1967; JD, Rutgers U., 1970. Bar: N.Y. 1971, N.J. 1983, U.S. Supreme Ct. 1984; cert. fin. planner., estate planner. Asst. dist. atty. Rockland County, New City, NY, 1973-74; ptnr. Amend & Amend, N.Y.C., 1974-78, O'Connell & Riley, Pearl River, NY, 1978—. Pub., pres. 1099 Express Software, 1099 Express Ltd., Pearl River, 1987-97; adj. prof. estate planning Pace Univ., White Plains, N.Y.; atty. Town of Orangetown. Bd. dirs. United Way of Rockland County, N.Y., 1974-80, Rockland Family Shelter for Victims of Domestic Violence, 1981-85, Literacy Vols. Rockland County, 1989—; chmn. bd. dirs. New Hope Manor, Barryville, N.Y., 1985-88. Mem. ABA, Am. Soc. Hosp. Attys., Nat. Coun. Sch. Dist. Attys., N.Y. State Bar Assn. (ho. of dels. 1988-92, 2002—), Rockland County Bar Assn. (bd. dirs. 1986—, pres. 1997-98), Internat. Platform Assn., Rotary Club of Pearl River (pres. 1999—). Democrat. Roman Catholic. Education and schools, Estate planning, Municipal (including bonds). Home: 145 Franklin Ave Pearl River NY 10965-2510 Office: O'Connell & Riley 144 E Central Ave Pearl River NY 10965 also: 103 Chestnut Ridge Rd Montvale NJ 07645

RILEY, JOHN FREDERICK, lawyer; b. Salisbury, N.C., Oct. 18, 1938; s. John Horace and Beatrice (Williams) R.; m. Jan Colby, June 20, 1965; children: John Michael, Jennifer Lynn, Julia Grace. BA, Wake Forest U., 1960; JD, U. N.C., 1967. Bar: N.C. 1967. Law clk. to presiding justice N.C. Supreme Ct., Raleigh, 1967-68; assoc. Leroy, Wells, Shaw & Hornthal, Elizabeth City, N.C., 1968-70; ptnr. Leroy, Wells, Shaw, Hornthal & Riley, Elizabeth City, N.C., 1970-85, Hornthal, Riley, Ellis & Maland, Elizabeth City, N.C., 1985-2001, of counsel, 2001—. Chmn. adv. bd. Salvation Army, Elizabeth City, 1976-77; trustee Elizabeth City State U., 1981-86. Hankins scholar Wake Forest U., Winston-Salem, N.C., 1956. Mem. ABA, N.C. Bar Assn. (bd. dirs. real property sect. 1979-83), N.C. Land Title Assn., Elizabeth City Bar Assn. (pres. 1973-74), 1st Jud. Dist. Bar Assn. (pres. 1985-86), Rotary, Pine Lakes Country. Democrat. Methodist. Avocations: golf, tennis, boating. Corporate, general, Probate (including wills, trusts), Property, real (including real estate development, water). Home: 101 Inlet Dr Elizabeth City NC 27909-3225 Office: Hornthal Riley Ellis & Maland 301 E Main St # 220 Elizabeth City NC 27909-4425 E-mail: friley@hrem.com.

RILEY, MICHAEL HYLAN, lawyer; b. Ardmore, Okla., Oct. 26, 1951; s. Paul Emerson and Anne (Hylan) R. AB cum laude, Harvard U., 1973; JD, Northea. U., 1978. Bar: Mass. 1978, U.S. Dist. Ct. Mass. 1980, U.S. Ct. Appeals (1st cir.) 1980. Assoc. White, Inker, Aronson, Boston, 1979-83, Chaplin & Milstein, Boston, 1984-86, Goldstein & Manello, Boston, 1986-91; ptnr. Goldstein & Manello, P.C., Boston, 1992-95; of counsel King & Navins, P.C., Wellesley, Mass., 1995—. Lectr. Met. Coll. Boston U., 1986-92. Author: Estate Administration, 1985, 2nd edit., 1993. Mem. ABA, Boston Bar Assn. Democrat. Avocations: books, music, food, wine, backpacking. Estate planning, Probate (including wills, trusts), Estate taxation. Home: 83 Grove Hill Ave Newton MA 02460-2336 Office: King & Navins PC 20 William St Wellesley MA 02481-4103 E-mail: rileymh@sprynet.com.

RILEY, RICHARD WILSON, lawyer, federal official; b. Greenville, S.C., Jan. 2, 1933; s. Edward Patterson and Martha Elizabeth (Dixon) Riley; m. Ann Osteen Yarborough, Aug. 23, 1957; children: Richard Wilson, Anne Y., Hubert D., Theodore D. BA, Furman U., 1954; JD, U. S.C., 1959. Bar: S.C. 1960. Ptnr. Riley & Riley, Greenville, 1959—78, Nelson, Mullins, Riley & Scarborough, Greenville and Columbia, 1987—93, Greenville, 2001—; gov. State of S.C., 1979—87; sec. U.S. Dept. Edn., Washington, 1993—2001; disting. univ. prof. U. S.C., Columbia, 2001—. Spl. asst. to subcom. U.S. Senate Jud. Com., 1960; mem. S.C. Ho. of Reps., 1963—66, S.C. Senate senate form Greenville-Laurens Dist., 1966—76. Lt. (j.g.) USNR, 1954—56. Recipient Dist. Svc. award, Coun. Chief State Sch. Officers, 1994, James Bryant Conant award, Edn. Commn. of the States, 1995, T.H. Bell award for outstanding edn. advocacy, Com. for Edn. Funding, 1996, Dist. Svc. award, Am. Coun. on Edn., 1998. Mem.: Greenville Bar Assn., S.C. Bar Assn., Furman U. Alumni Assn. (pres. 1968—69), Rotary, Phi Beta Kappa. Banking, Corporate, general, Education and schools. Office: Nelson Mullins Riley & Scarborough Poinsett Plaza Ste 900 104 S Main St Greenville SC 29601 E-mail: rwr@nmrs.com.

RILEY, SCOTT C. lawyer; b. Bklyn., Oct. 5, 1959; s. William A. and Kathleen (Howe) R.; m. Kathleen D. O'Connor, Oct. 6, 1984; children: Matthew, Brendan. BA, Seton Hall U., South Orange, N.J., 1981; JD, Seton Hall U., Newark, 1984. Bar: N.J. 1985, U.S. Dist. Ct. N.J. 1985. Assoc. Dwyer, Connell & Lisbona, Montclair, N.J., 1985-87; assoc. gen. counsel, v.p. Consolidated Ins. Group, Wilmington, Del., 1987-91; counsel Cigna Ins. Group, Phila., 1991-94; assoc. gen. counsel KWELM Cos., N.Y.C., 1994-98, head U.S. legal ops., 1998—; head U.S. ops. KMSIS Ltd., 1998—. Mem. ABA (com. on environ. ins. coverage), Fedn. of Ins. and Corp. Counsel, Excess and Surplus Lines Claims Assn., N.J. State Bar Assn., Profl. Liability Underwriting Soc. Environmental, Insurance, Toxic tort. Office: KWELM Companies 599 Lexington Ave New York NY 10022-6030

RILEY, WILLIAM JAY, federal judge; b. Lincoln, Nebr., Mar. 11, 1947; s. Don Paul and Marian Frances (Munn) R.; m. Norma Jean Mason, Dec. 27, 1965; children: Brian, Kevin, Erin. BA, U. Nebr., 1969, JD with distinction, 1972. Bar: Nebr. 1972, U.S. Dist. Ct. Nebr. 1972, U.S. Ct. Appeals (8th cir.) 1974; cert. civil trial specialist Nat. Bd. Trial Advocacy. Law clk. U.S. Ct. Appeals (8th cir.), Omaha, 1972-73; assoc. Fitzgerald, Schorr Law Firm, P.C., LLO, Omaha, 1973-79; shareholder Fitzgerald, Schorr Law Firm, Omaha, 1979—2001; US Circuit Judge 8th Circuit Ct. Appeals , 2001—. Adj. prof. trial practice Creighton U. Coll. Law, Omaha, 1991—; chmn. fed. practice com. Fed. Ct., 1992-94. Scoutmaster Boy Scouts Am., Omaha, 1979—89, scout membership chair Mid. Am. coun., 1995—98, trustee, 2001—. Recipient Silver Beaver award Boy Scouts Am., 1991. Fellow Am. Coll. Trial Lawyers (chair state com. 1997-99), Nebr. State Bar Found.; mem. Am. Bd. Trial Advs. (Nebr. chpt. pres. 2000), Nebr. State Bar Assn. (chmn. ethics com. 1996-98, ho. of dels. 1998—), Omaha Bar Assn. (treas. 1997-98, pres. 2000-01), Robert M. Spire Inns of Ct. (master 1994—, counselor 1997-98), Order of Coif, Phi Beta Kappa. Republican. Methodist. Avocations: reading, hiking, cycling. Office: Roman L Hruska US Courthouse 111 S 18th Plaza Ste 4179 Omaha NE 68102-1322

RILL, JAMES FRANKLIN, lawyer; b. Evanston, Ill., Mar. 4, 1933; s. John Columbus and Frances Eleanor (Hill) R.; m. Mary Elizabeth Laws, June 14, 1957; children: James Franklin, Roderick M. AB cum laude, Dartmouth Coll., 1954; LLB, Harvard, 1959. Bar: D.C. bar 1959. Legis. asst. Congressman James P. S. Devereux, Washington, 1952; pvt. practice Washington, 1959-89; assoc. Steadman, Collier & Shannon, 1959-63; ptnr. Collier, Shannon & Rill, 1963-69, Collier, Shannon, Rill & Scott, 1969-89; asst. atty. gen., antitrust div. U.S. Dept. Justice, Washington, 1989-92; ptnr. Collier, Shannon, Rill & Scott, Washington, 1992-2000; co-chair internat. competition policy adv. com. U.S. Dept. Justice, 1997-2000; ptnr. Howrey Simon Arnold & White, Washington, 2000—. Pub. mem. Adminstrv. Conf. of U.S., 1992-94; coun. prin. Coun. for Excellence in Govt.; mem., advisor panel Office of Tech. Assessment of Multinat. Firms and U.S. Tech. Base. Contbr. articles to profl. jours. Trustee emeritus Bullis Sch., Potomac, Md. Served to 1st lt. arty. AUS, 1954-56. Fellow: Am. Bar Found.; mem.: ABA (antitrust law sect., past chmn.), DC Bar Assn., Loudoun Valley Club, Met. Club, Phi Delta Theta. Home: 7305 Masters Dr Potomac MD 20854-3850 Office: Howrey Simon Arnold & White, LLP Rm 621 1299 Pennsylvania Ave NW Washington DC 20004-2402

RIME, FINN, lawyer; b. Kråkstad, Norway, Jan. 2, 1926; s. Thorleif and Berit Rime; m. Randi Brun, Dec. 29, 1951; children: Karen Margrethe, Dagfinn. LLB, U. Oslo, 1952. Lawyer before Supreme Ct. of Norway. Assisting judge, Alesund, Norway, 1955-57; lawyer Oslo, 1957-64; prin. firm, 1964—. Lectr. seminars for Norwegian trade and industry leaders. Mem. ABA, Norwegian Bar Assn. (chmn. bankruptcy com. 1975-86),European Insolvency Practitioners Assn. (Eng.), Am. Club (Oslo). Mem. Conservative Party. Christian. Avocations: classical music, antiques, literature, art. Office: Øvre Slottsgt 12 B 0157 Oslo Norway

RINAMAN, JAMES CURTIS, JR., lawyer; b. Miami, Fla., Feb. 8, 1935; s. James Curtis and Ruth Marie (Rader) R.; m. Gloria Margaret Kaspar; children: James, Mark, Christine, Karen BA, U. Fla., 1955, JD, 1960. Bar: Fla. 1960, U.S. Dist. Ct. (so. dist.) Fla. 1960, U.S. Ct. Appeals (5th cir.) 1960, U.S. Supreme Ct. 1963, U.S. Dist. Ct. (mid. dist.) Fla. 1967, U.S.

Dist. Ct. (no. dist.) Fla. 1981, U.S. Ct. Appeals (11th cir.) 1981, U.S. Ct. Claims 1991, U.S. Ct. Mil. Appeals 1994; cert. civil trial lawyer Fla. Bar. With Marks, Gray, Conroy & Gibbs, P.A., Jacksonville, Fla., 1960—. Gen. counsel Fla. Bd. Architecture, 1965-79, City of Jacksonville, 1970-71, Jacksonville C. of C., 1973-76, 90; adj. prof. Coll. Architecture, U. Fla., 1975-90; dir. gen. The Southern Acad. Letters, Arts and Scis., 1997—. Pres. Jacksonville Cmty. Coun. Inc., 1985. Leadership Jacksonville, Inc., 1987; mem. Jacksonville Transp. Authority, 1971-80, Jacksonville Base Realignment and Closure Commn., 1993-95. Jacksonville Cecil Field Devel. Commn., 1994-96; chmn. N.E. Fla. chpt. ARC, 1996. With U.S. Army, 1955-57, Fla. NG, 1957-92. ret. brig. gen., 1992. Named to U. Fla. Hall of Fame. Fellow Am. Coll. Trial Lawyers, Am. Bar Found., Fla. Bar Found. (bd. dirs. 1982-87, 88, Disting. Svc. award 1983, 86, Medal of Honor 1988); mem. ABA (ho. of dels. 1982-86), Jacksonville Bar Assn. (pres. 1972-73, Lawyer of Yr. 1994), The Fla. Bar (pres. 1982-83), Def. Rsch. Inst. (so. regional v.p. 1980-83, bd. dirs. 1976-78, 83-87), Am. Judicature Soc. (Herbert Harley award 1987), Fla. Coun. Bar Pres. (Outstanding Past Pres. award 1989), Lawyers for Civil Justice (pres. 1989-91, chmn. bd. dirs. 1991-94), Vol. Lawyers Resource Ctr. of Fla., (pres. 1984-89, chmn. bd. dirs. 1989-93), So. Conf. of Bar, Nat. Conf. of Bar, Assn. Def. Trial Attys. (internat. pres. 1976-77), Internat. Assn. Def. Counsel, Jacksonville Assn. Def. Counsel, Fla. Defense Lawyers Assn. (pres. 1973), Fla. C. of C., Jacksonville C. of C. (chmn. 1994), Meninak Civic Club (pres. 1986), Jacksonville Commodores League, The Army War Coll. Alumni Assn. (life), Fla. Blue Key, San. Jose Country Club, River Club, Phi Gamma Delta (bd. trustees ednl. found. 1995—), Phi Alpha Delta. Republican. Methodist. Administrative and regulatory, General civil litigation, Corporate, general. Office: Marks Gray Conroy & Gibbs 1200 Riverplace Blvd Ste 800 Jacksonville FL 32207-1805 also: PO Box 447 Jacksonville FL 32201-0447 E-mail: jrinaman@marksgray.com

RINER, JAMES WILLIAM, lawyer; b. Jefferson City, Mo., Dec. 25, 1936; s. John Woodrow and Virginia Loraine (Jackson) R.; m. Carolyn Ruth Hicke, May, 14 1976; children: Alicia Gayle, Angela Gayle, Amity Gayle. BA, U. Mo., 1957, LLB, 1960. Bar: Mo. 1960, U.S. Dist. Ct. (we. dist.) Mo. 1982, U.S. Ct. Appeals (8th cir.) 1989. Asst. atty. gen. Atty. Gen's. Office Mo., Jefferson City, 1960; commd. 1st lt. U.S. Air Force, 1960, advanced through grades to lt. col., 1974, retired, 1981; ptnr. Inglish & Monaco, P.C., Jefferson City, 1985-91, Hendricks, Riner & Smith, P.C., Jefferson City, 1991-96, Riner & Turnbull, P.C., 1996-98, Riner, Turnbull & Walker, P.C., Jefferson City, 1998-99, Riner & Walker PC, Jefferson City, 1999—2003; pvt. practice Jefferson City, Mo., 2003—. City pros. Jefferson City, 1983-91; city atty. California, Mo., 1985-87. Contbr. author: Mo. Ins. Practice Manual, 1995, 4th edit., 2000. Decorated Bronze Star, Meritorious Svc. Medal. Mem. Am. Trial Lawyers Assn., Mo. Bar Assn. Democrat. General civil litigation, Personal injury (including property damage), Labor (including EEOC, Fair Labor Standards Act, labor-management relations, NLRB, OSHA). Home: 1205 Moreau Dr Jefferson City MO 65101-3522 Office: Law Offices of James W Riner PC PO Box 104623 Jefferson City MO 65110 E-mail: rinerlaw@earthlink.net.

RING, LUCILE WILEY, lawyer; b. Kearney, Nebr., Jan. 2, 1920; d. Myrtie Mercer and Alice (Cowell) W.; m. John Robert Ring, Mar. 28, 1948; children: John Raymond, James Wiley, Thomas Eric. AB, U. Nebr., Kearney, 1944; JD, Washington U., 1946. Bar: Mo. 1946, U.S. Dist. Ct. (ea. dist.) Mo. 1947, U.S. Ct. Appeals (8th cir.) 1972. Atty.-adviser, chief legal group adjudications br. Army Fin. Ctr., St. Louis, 1946-52; exec. dir. lawyer referral svcs. St. Louis Bar, 1960-70; pvt. practice St. Louis, 1960-2000; staff law clk. U.S. Ct. Appeals (8th cir.), St. Louis, 1970-72; exec. dir. St. Louis Com. on Cts., 1972-85. Legal advisor Mo. State Anat. Bd., 1965-95; adj. prof. adminstrv. law Webster Coll., Webster Groves, Mo., 1977-78; mem. Mo. Profl. Liability Rev. Bd., State of Mo., 1977-79. Author, editor: Guide to Community Services - Who Do I Talk To, 1974, 75, 76-79, St. Louis Court Directories, 1972, 73, 74, 75, Felony Procedures in St. Louis Courts, 1975; author: Breaking Barriers: The St. Louis Legacy of Women in Law 1869-1969, 1996; author (series): Women Lawyers in St. Louis History, 1996, Women Breaking Barriers, 1998; contbr. articles to profl. jours. Mem. Mo. Mental Health Authority, 1964-65; bd. dirs., v.p. Drug and Substance Abuse Coun., met. St. Louis, 1976-83; mem. adv. coun. St. Louis Agy. on Tng. and Employment, 1976-83; mem. Mayor's Jud. Reform Subcom., St. Louis, 1974-76. Washington U. Sch. Law scholar, 1944-46; 1st Mo. woman nominated for St. Louis Ct. Appeals, Mo. Appellate Commn., 1972; 1st woman nominated judgeship Mo. Non-Partisan Ct. Plan, 1972; recipient letter of commendation Office of Chief of Fin., U.S. Army, 1952, Outstanding Alumni award U. Nebr., Kearney, 1994. Mem. Bar Assn. Met. St. Louis (v.p. 1975-76), Legal Svcs. Ea. Mo., Inc. (v.p. 1978-79, dir.), Legal Aid Soc. St. Louis City and County (bd. dirs. 1977-78), HUD Women and Housing Commn. (commr. 1975), Women's Bar Assn. (treas. St. Louis chpt. 1949-50), Mo. Assn. Women Lawyers (treas. 1959-60, pres. 1960-61), Washington U. Dental Faculty Wives (pres. 1972-74), Mortar Board, Pi Kappa Delta, Sigma Tau Delta. Methodist. General practice. Home and Office: 2041 Reservoir Loop Rd Selah WA 98942-9616

RING, RENEE ETHELINE, lawyer; b. Frankfurt, Germany, May 29, 1950; arrived in U.S., 1950; d. Vincent Martin and Etheline Bergetta (Schoolmeesters) R.; m. Paul J. Zofnass, June 24, 1982; Jessica Renee, Rebecca Anne. BA, Catholic U. Am., 1972; JD, U. Va., 1976. Bar: N.Y. 1977. Assoc. Whitman & Ransom, N.Y.C., 1976-83, Carro, Spanbock, Fass, Geller, Kaster & Cuiffo, N.Y.C., 1983-86, ptnr., 1986, Finley Kumble Wagner et. al., N.Y.C., 1987; of counsel Kaye, Scholer, Fierman, Hays & Handler, N.Y.C., 1988; ptnr. Kaye, Scholer, Fierman, Hays & Handler, LLP, N.Y.C., 1989-97, Hunton & Williams, N.Y.C., 1997—2002. Trustee The Spence Sch., 2001—02; advisor WestWind Found., 2001—, 2001—; mem. exec. com. Lawyers for Clinton, Washington, 1991—92; team capt. Clinton Transition Team, Washington, 1992—93; mem. Nat. Lawyers Coun. Dem. Nat. Com., 1993—98; trustee The Clinton Legal Expense Trust, 1998—2002; mem. Alumni Coun. U. Va. Sch. of Law, 1997—, 2d v.p., 2000—01, 1st v.p., 2001—03, 2003—. Mem. ABA, N.Y. Women's Bar Assn. Democrat. Roman Catholic. Banking, Corporate, general, Securities.

RING, RONALD HERMAN, lawyer; b. Flint, Mich., Nov. 30, 1938; s. Herman and Lydia (Miller) R.; m. Joan Kay Whitener, Aug. 5, 1966. AB, U. Mich., 1961, LLB, 1964. Bar: Mich. 1964, U.S. Dist. Ct. (ea. dist.) Mich. 1966. Assoc. Beagle, Benton & Hicks, Flint, 1964-69; ptnr. Beagle & Ring, Flint, 1970-80, Beagle, Ring & Beagle, Flint, 1980-85, Ring, Beagle & Busch, Flint, 1985-93, Ronald H. Ring, P.C., Flint, 1993-95; pvt. practice Flint, 1991—. Mem. meml. com. Crossroads Village, Flint, 1981; pres. Family Service Agy., Genesee County, Mich., 1986. Mem. ABA, Assn. Trial Lawyers Am., Mich. Bar Assn. (delivery of legal service com. 1986, med. malpractice panel 1986), Genesee County Bar Assn. (pres. 1980-81, bd. dirs. 1979-82, cir. ct. mediation panel 1986). Clubs: Ostego Ski (Gaylord, Mich.). Avocations: skiing, sailing. State civil litigation, General practice, Personal injury (including property damage). Office: 7993 Bussa Ln Rapid City MI 49676-9203 E-mail: ronhring@cs.com.

RINGEL, DEAN, lawyer; b. N.Y.C., Dec. 12, 1947; m. Ronnie Sussman, Aug. 24, 1969; children: Marion, Alicia. BA, Columbia Coll., 1967; JD, Yale U., 1971. Bar: N.Y. 1972, U.S. Ct. Appeals (6th cir.) 1972, U.S. Ct. Appeals (2d and D.C. cirs.) 1974, U.S. Supreme Ct. 1976, U.S. Ct. Appeals (10th cir.) 1982, U.S. Ct. Appeals (11th cir.) 1997, U.S. Ct. Appeals (9th cir.) 2000. Law clk. to Judge Anthony J. Celebrezze U.S. Ct. Appeals (6th cir.), 1971-72; assoc. Cahill Gordon & Reindel, N.Y.C., 1972-79; ptnr. Cahill, Gordon & Reindel, N.Y.C., 1979—. Mem.: ABA (vice chmn. com. on freedom of speech and press 1978—79), Pub. Edn. Assn. (trustee, sec. 1997—2000, trustee CEI-PEA 2000—), Assn. Bar City NY (commn. comm., fed. litigation, antitrust and trade regulation), NY State Bar (chmn. antitrust litigation com., sect. comml. and fed. litigation 1994—96, co-chmn. fed. judiciary com. 1997—2001, co-chair newsgathering com. Media Law Resource Ctr. 2001—, media law com.). lectr., practicing Law Antitrust Institute (2002-)., Communications, Libel. Office: Cahill Gordon & Reindel 80 Pine St 17th Fl New York NY 10005-1790

RINGER, DARRELL WAYNE (DAN RINGER), lawyer; b. Elizabeth, N.J., Apr. 14, 1948; s. Darrell Wayne and Elva (Brown) R.; m. Rebecca Ruth Bonner, Feb. 23, 1979; children: Daniel Benjamin, Darren Wayne. BS in Physics, W.Va. U., 1971; MBA, U. N.D., 1975; JD, W.Va. U., 1978. Bar: W.Va. 1978, U.S. Dist. Ct. (no. and so. dists.) W.Va. 1978. Assoc. Jones, Williams, West & Jones, Clarksburg, W.Va., 1978-80, Moreland & Ringer, Morgantown, W.Va., 1980-83, Reeder, Shuman, Ringer & Wiley, Morgantown, 1983-91, Ringer Law Offices, Morgantown, 1991—2001, Ringer & Sal, PLLC, Morgantown, 2002—. 1st asst. prosecutor Monongalia County, W.Va., 1985-87; host W.Va. Pub. TV, PBS Pub. Affairs Programming, 1991—. Bd. dirs. Monongalia County (W.Va.) Mental Health Assn., Morgantown, 1981-83; mem. W.Va. U. Animal Care and Use Com., 1985—. Capt. USAF, 1971-75. Named W.Va. Bar Found. Lawyer Citizen of Yr., 1996. Fellow W.Va. Bar Found.; mem. ABA (named Sole Practitioner of Yr., 2000), ATLA, W.Va. State Bar (pres. 1999-2000), Monongalia County Bar Assn. (sec. 1980-92, pres. 2001), W.Va. Trial Lawyers Assn. (bd. govs. 1982-91, Pres.'s award 2001). Democrat. Avocation: amateur radio. Personal injury (including property damage), Family and matrimonial. Home: 18 W Front St Morgantown WV 26501-4507 Office: 823 Fairmont Rd Morgantown WV 26501-3812

RINGER, JAMES MILTON, lawyer; b. Orlando, Fla., July 9, 1943; s. Robert T. and Jessie M. (Rowe) R.; m. Jaquelyn Hope, Apr. 10, 1965; children— Carolyn Hope, James Matthew AB, Ohio U., 1965; JD, Cornell U., 1968. Bar: N.Y. 1968, U.S. Dist. Ct. (no. dist.) N.Y. 1968, U.S. Dist. Ct. (so. and ea. dists.) N.Y. 1972, U.S. Ct. Appeals (2d cir.) 1972, U.S. Ct. Claims 1976, U.S. Dist. Ct. (we. dist.) N.Y. 1978, U.S. Ct. Appeals (4th cir.) 1981, U.S. Ct. Appeals (9th cir.) 1983. Assoc. Clifford Chance U.S., LLP, N.Y.C., 1968-78, ptnr., 1978—. Instr. bus. law U. Alaska, 1970-71 Editor Cornell Law Rev., 1967-68 Served to lt. JAGC, USNR, 1969-72 Republican. Episcopalian. Federal civil litigation, Alternative dispute resolution, Securities. Office: Clifford Chance US LLP 200 Park Ave Fl 8E New York NY 10166-0899

RINGKAMP, STEPHEN H. lawyer, educator; b. St. Louis, Nov. 14, 1949; s. Aloysius G. and Melba Ann (Finke) Ringkamp; m. Patricia Sue Fuse, July 5, 1971; children: Christa, Angela, Laura, Stephen M., Kara. BSEE, St. Louis U., 1971, JD cum laude, 1974. Bar: Mo. 1974, U.S. Dist. Ct. (ea. dist.) Mo. 1974, U.S. Ct. Appeals (8th cir.) 1974, U.S. Supreme Ct. 1990. Law clk. 22d Jud. Cir. Mo., St. Louis, 1974-75; mng. prin. The Hullverson Law Firm, St. Louis, 1976—. Chmn., mem. com. on civil instrns. Mo. Supreme Ct., 1981— ; adj. prof. law St. Louis U., 1983— ; mem. faculty Mo. Jud. Coll., 1993-2002; lectr. legal seminars. Contbr. articles to legal jours. Recipient Trial Lawyer award Mo. Bar Found. 1983, Smithson award for Excellence, 1996. Mem. ABA, ATLA, Mo. Bar Assn. (vice chmn. civil practice com. 1983-84), Mo. Assn. Trial Attys. (pres. 1991), Bar Assn. Met. St. Louis, Lawyers Assn. St. Louis. General civil litigation, Personal injury (including property damage), Product liability. Office: The Hullverson Law Firm 1010 Market St Ste 1550 Saint Louis MO 63101-2091 E-mail: sringkamp@hullverson.com.

RINGLE, BRETT ADELBERT, lawyer, petroleum company executive; b. Berkeley, Calif., Mar. 17, 1951; s. Forrest A. and Elizabeth V. (Darnall) R.; m. Sue Kinslow, May 26, 1973. BA, U. Tex., 1973, JD, 1976. Bar: Tex. 1976, U.S. Dist. Ct. (no. dist.) Tex. 1976, U.S. Supreme Ct. 1980, U.S. Ct. Appeals (5th cir.) 1984. Ptnr. Shank, Irwin & Conant, Dallas, 1976-86, Jones, Day, Reavis & Pogue, Dallas, 1986-96; v.p. Hunt Petroleum Corp., Dallas, 1996—. Adj. prof. law So. Meth. U., Dallas, 1983. Author: (with J.W. Moore and H.I. Bendix) Moore's Federal Practice, 2d edit., Vol. 12, 1980, Vol. 13, 1981, (with J.W. Moore) Vol. 1A, 1982, Vol. 1A Part 2, 1989. Mem. Dallas Bar Assn. Federal civil litigation, State civil litigation, General practice. Home: 3514 Gillon Ave Dallas TX 75205-3220 Office: Hunt Petroleum Corp 5000 Thanksgiving Tower 1601 Elm St Dallas TX 75201 E-mail: bar@huntpetroleum.com.

RINSKY, JOEL CHARLES, lawyer; b. Bklyn., Jan. 29, 1938; s. Irving C. and Elsie (Millman) R.; m. Judith L. Lynn, Jan. 26, 1963; children: Heidi M., Heather S., Jason W. BS, Rutgers U., 1961, LLB, 1962, JD, 1968. Bar: N.J. 1963, U.S. Dist. Ct. N.J. 1963, U.S. Supreme Ct. 1967, U.S. Ct. Appeals (3d cir.) 1986. Pvt. practice, Livingston, N.J., 1964-97; sr. ptnr. Rinsky & Marley L.L.C., Livingston, 1997-98; of counsel Gonzalez and Weichert P.C., Livingston, 1999—. Committeeman Millburn-Short Hills (N.J.) Dem. Com., 1982-97, vice chmn., 1983-87; trustee Student Loan Fund, Millburn, 1983-91. Fellow Am. Acad. Matrimonial Lawyers; mem. N.J. Bar Assn., Essex County Bar Assn. (exec. com. sect. family law). Jewish. Avocations: tennis, chess, golf, piano. Family and matrimonial, Personal injury (including property damage), Property, real (including real estate development, water). Home: 87 Sullivan Dr West Orange NJ 07052-2262 Office: 127 E Mount Pleasant Ave Livingston NJ 07039-3005 E-mail: Rinsky3@aol.com.

RINTAMAKI, JOHN M. automotive executive; BBA, U. Mich., 1964, JD, 1967. Bar: Mich. 1968, Pa. 1973. Sr. atty. internat. Ford Motor Co., 1978-84, assoc. counsel corp. and financings, 1984-86, asst. sec., assoc. counsel, 1986-92, sec., asst. gen. counsel, 1993-98, v.p., gen. counsel, sec., 1999-00, chief staff, 2000—. Office: Ford Motor Co One American Rd Dearborn MI 48126-1899

RINTELMAN, DONALD BRIAN, lawyer; b. Madison, Wis., May 25, 1955; s. Donald Carl Rintelman and Eugenie Elizabeth Kroll; m. Ann Marie Gall, Aug. 2, 1980; children: Katherine Ann, Brian James. BA, U. Wis., 1976; JD, U. Mich., 1980. Bar: Wis. 1980, U.S. Dist. Ct. (ea. dist.) Wis. 1980, U.S. Dist. Ct. (we. dist.) Wis. 1984. Assoc. Whyte & Hirschboeck, S.C., Milw., 1980-86, shareholder, 1986—; mng. dir. Whyte Hirschboeck Dudek, S.C., Milw., 1994—. Chmn. comml. practice group Am. Law Firm Assn. Internat., L.A., 1998-2001. Bd. dirs. Ozaukee County United Way Allocations, Mequon, Wis., 1986-88; treas. Cedarburg (Wis.) Cmty. Scholarship Fund, 1991-93; coun. pres. Advent Luth. Ch., Cedarburg, 1996-97; bd. dirs. Greater Cedarburg Cmty. Found., Inc., 2002—. Fellow Am. Coll. Investment Counsel; mem. ABA, Wis. Bar Assn., Milw. Bar Assn. Republican. Avocations: travel, golf, enjoying children's soccer, swimming. Commercial, contracts (including sales of goods; commercial financing), Corporate, general, Mergers and acquisitions. Home: N108W7365 Balfour St Cedarburg WI 53012-3248 Office: Whyte Hirschboeck Dudek SC 111 E Wisconsin Ave Ste 2100 Milwaukee WI 53202-4861

RINTOUL, DAVID SKINNER, lawyer; b. Westport, Conn., July 11, 1961; s. Stephen Rich and Eve Clark (Green) R.; m. Judy Mae Duncan, Aug. 7, 1988; children: Emily Grace, Maxwell Duncan. BA, Johns Hopkins U., 1983; JD with high honors, U. Conn., Hartford, 1986. Bar: Ill. 1986, Conn. 1989, U.S. Dist. Ct. (no. dist.) Ill. 1987, U.S. Dist. Ct. Conn. 1989, U.S. Ct. Appeals (2d cir.) 1997. Atty. Schwartz & Freeman, Chgo., 1986-89, Levin & D'Agostino, Hartford, Conn., 1989-91; ptnr. Rintoul & Rintoul, Glastonbury, Conn., 1991-2001, Brown, Paindiris & Scott, Glastonbury, 2001—. Mem. Nat. Employment Lawyers Assn., Conn. Employment Lawyers Assn. (bd. dirs. 1996-2001). Democrat. Episcopalian. Avocations: bicyle racing, skiing. Labor (including EEOC, Fair Labor Standards Act, labor-management relations, NLRB, OSHA), Federal civil litigation, General civil litigation. Home: Lake Rd Marlborough CT 06447 Office: Brown Paindiris & Scott 2252 Main St Glastonbury CT 06033 E-mail: drintoul@bpslawyers.com.

RIOS-FARJAT, MARGARITA, lawyer, consultant; d. Rodolfo Rios-Vazquez and Ana Mary Farjat de Rios; m. Gabriel Cavazos-Villanueva, Sept. 10, 1998. Law Degree, Autonomous U. of Nuevo Leon, Mexico, 1996; Diploma in Amparo & Constl. Law, Inst. Supreme Ct. Justice, Mexico, 1998. Bar: Fed. Govt. of Mex. 1996. Law clk. Third Fed. Ct. of the Fourth Circuit, Monterrey, Mexico, 1996—99; assoc. Treviño Zambrano & Assocs., Baker & McKenzie, 1999—. Guest lectr., rschr. Inst. Tecnologico y de Estudios Superiores de Monterrey Sch. Law, 1996—97; arbitrator Centro de Arbitraje de Mex., 2002—. Co-author (book) Doing Bus. in Mex., U.S.A., co-editor A guide to Internat. Arbitration in Mex., co-author Perspectivas del Derecho en Mex.; author: (book of poetry) Si las horas llegaran para quedarse. Recipient first pl., state poetry contest, Grupo Cultural del Estado de Nuevo Leon, 1998; grantee, Govt. of Nuevo Leon, 1997—98. Mem.: Barra Mexicana de Abogados (assoc.). Avocations: travel, photography, writing, swimming, movies, music. General civil litigation, Commercial, consumer (including collections, credit), Private international. Office: Baker & McKenzie Torre I piso 10 A L Rodriguez 1884 pte Santa María Nuevo Leon Monterrey 64650 Mexico Office Fax: (5281)8399-1399. E-mail: margarita.rios-farjat@bakernet.com.

RIPPLE, KENNETH FRANCIS, federal judge; b. Pitts., May 19, 1943; s. Raymond John and Rita (Holden) Ripple; m. Mary Andrea DeWeese, July 27, 1968; children: Gregory, Raymond, Christopher. AB, Fordham U., 1965; JD, U. Va., 1968; LLM, George Washington U., 1972, LLD (hon.) , 1992. Bar: Va. 1968, N.Y. 1969, U.S. Supreme Ct. 1972, U.S. Supreme Ct. 1972, D.C. 1976, Ind. 1984, U.S. Ct. Appeals (7th cir.), U.S. Ct. Mil. Appeals, U.S. Dist. Ct. (no. dist.) N.Y. Atty. IBM Corp., Armonk, NY, 1968; legal officer U.S. Supreme Ct., Washington, 1972—73, spl. asst. to chief justice Warren E. Burger, 1973—77; prof. law U. Notre Dame, 1977—; judge U.S. Ct. Appeals (7th cir.), South Bend, 1985—. Reporter Appellate Rules Com., Washington, 1978—85; commn. on mil. justice U.S. Dept. Def., Washington, 1984—85; cons. Supreme Ct. Ala., 1983, Calif. Bd. Bar Examiners, 1981, Anglo-Am. Jud. Exch., 1977; adv. com. Bill of Rights to Bicentennial Constn. Commn., 1989; adv. com. on appellate rules Jud. Conf. U.S., 1985—90, chmn., 1990—93; chmn. adv. com. on appellate judge edn. Fed. Jud. Ctr., 1996—2003. Author: Constitutional Litigation, 1984. With JAGC USN, 1968—72. Mem.: ABA, Am. Law Inst., Phi Beta Kappa. Office: US Ct of Appeals 208 US Courthouse 204 S Main St South Bend IN 46601-2122 also: Fed Bldg 219 S Dearborn St Ste 2660 Chicago IL 60604-1803

RIPPLINGER, GEORGE RAYMOND, JR., lawyer; b. East St. Louis, Ill., Apr. 19, 1945; s. George Raymond and Virginia Lee (Toupnot) R. AB, U. Ill., 1967, JD, 1970. Bar: Ill. 1970, U.S. Dist. Ct. (so. dist.) Ill. 1970, U.S. Ct. Appeals (7th cir.) 1970, U.S. Dist. Ct. (cen. dist.) Ill. 1972, U.S. Tax Ct. 1971, U.S. Claims Ct. 1973, U.S. Ct. Mil. Appeals 1985, U.S. Supreme Ct. 1973, U.S. Ct. Internat. Trade 1973, U.S. Dist. Ct. (ea. dist.) Mo. 1977, U.S. Ct. Appeals (8th cir.) 1977. Assoc. Meyer & Meyer, Belleville and Greenville, Ill., 1970-72; assoc. Meyer & Kaucher, Belleville and Highland, Ill., 1972-73; sole practice Belleville, 1974; ptnr. Ripplinger & Walsh, Clayton, Mo., 1974-76, Ripplinger, Dixon & Johnston, Belleville, Ill., St. Louis, Scott AFB, and Bellvue, Neb., 1976-94; prin. George Ripplinger & Assoc., Belleville, Ill., 1994—. Bd. visitors Coll. of Law U. Ill., 1979-86, pres., 1983-84; chmn. Southwestern Ill. chpt. ACLU, 1971-74, 76-80; mem. exec. com. Sierra Club, 1981-85. Col. USAR, 1970-2001. Fellow Am. Bar Found., Ill. Bar Found. (bd. dirs. 1988—, treas. 1998—); mem. ABA (ho. of dels. 1989-93, 95-99, chmn. workers compensation com. 1985-88, divsn. dir. 1988-89, 95-99, mem. coun. 1989-93, 99-2003, sec. 1999-2000, vice-chmn. 2000-2001, chmn. 2001-02, gen. practice/solo and small firm sect.), ATLA, Lawyers Trust Fund Ill. (bd. dirs. 1988-94), Ill. Bar Assn. (bd. govs. 1981-83, 87-93, sec. 1991-92), St. Clair County Bar Assn., Bar Assn. Met. St. Louis, Mo. Bar Assn., Ill. Trial Lawyers Assn. (bd. advs. 1993—), Land of Lincoln Legal Assistance Found. (bd. dirs. 1982-88, vice-chmn. 1987-88), Res. Officers Assn. Democrat. Personal injury (including property damage), Product liability, Professional liability. Office: George Ripplinger & Assoc 2215 W Main St Belleville IL 62226-6668 E-mail: george@ripplingerlaw.com.

RISBJOERN, PHILIP, lawyer; b. Frederiksberg, Denmark, July 11, 1965; s. Erik and Marie Michèle Risbjoern; m. Alice Verghese, Sept. 1, 2002; 1 child, Jasmine Aurélia. Master in Law, U. Copenhagen, 1991; LLM, U. Cambridge, Eng., 1995. Bar: Danish High Ct. 1994. Jr. assoc. B. Helmer Nielsen Law Firm, Copenhagen, 1991—94; sr. assoc. Nabarro Nathanson Law Firm, London, 1995—96, Bech-Bruun & Trolle Law Firm, Copenhagen, 1996—2001; ptnr. Bech-Bruun Dragsted Law Firm, Copenhagen, 2002—. A Practitioner's Guide to Takeovers and Mergers in the European Union, 2001. Mem.: Danish Corp. Law Assn., Danish Bar Assn., Internat. Bar Assn. Office: Bech-Bruun Dragsted Law Firm Langelinie Allé 35 Copenhagen Denmark

RISCH, JAMES E. lawyer, lieutenant governor, former state legislator; b. Milw., May 3, 1943; s. Elroy A. and Helen B. (Levi) R.; m. Vicki L. Choborda, June 8, 1968; children— James E., Jason S., Jordan D. BS in Forestry, U. Idaho, 1965, JD, 1968. Dep. pros. atty. Ada County, Idaho, 1968-69, chief dep. pros. atty., 1969-70, pros. atty., 1971-75; mem. Idaho Senate, Dist. 18, Boise, 1974—88, 1995—2002; majority leader Idaho Senate, 1977—82, 1997—2002, pres. pro tem, 1983-88; ind. counsel to Gov. of Idaho, 1996; ptnr. Risch Goss & Insinger, Boise, Idaho, 1975—; lt. gov. State of Idaho, 2003—. Prof. law Boise State U., 1972-75. Bd. dirs. Nat. Dist. Attys. Assn., 1973,, Idaho Co., 1992-94; chmn. bd. dris. Am. Trailer Mfg. Co., 1995—; pres. Idaho Prosecuting Attys., 1970-74; chmn. George Bush Presdl. Campaign, Idaho, 1988; gen. counsel Idaho Rep. Party, 1991-2002. Mem. ABA, Idaho Bar Assn., Boise Bar Assn., Ducks Unlimited, Nat. Rifle Assn., Nat. Cattlemans Assn., Idaho Cattlemans Assn., Am. Angus Assn., Idaho Angus Assn., Am. Legis. Exch. Coun., Boise Valley Angus Assn., Phi Delta Theta, Xi Sigma Pi Republican. Roman Catholic. Avocations: hunting, fishing, skiing. Federal civil litigation, State civil litigation, Corporate, general. Home: 5400 S Cole Rd Boise ID 83709-6401 Office: Risch Goss & Insinger 407 W Jefferson St Boise ID 83702-6012

RISSETTO, HARRY A. lawyer; b. Dec. 1, 1943; AB, Fairfield U., 1965; JD, Georgetown U., 1968. Bar: N.Y. 1969, D.C. 1970. Law clk. to Hon. John J. Sirica U.S. Dist. Ct. D.C., 1968-69; law clk. to Chief Justice Warren E. Burger U.S. Supreme Ct., 1969-70; ptnr. Morgan, Lewis & Bockius, Washington. Adj. prof. law Georgetown U. Law Ctr., 1986-89. Mem. ABA (co-chmn. railway labor act com. sect. of labor and employment law 1987-89). Labor (including EEOC, Fair Labor Standards Act, labor-management relations, NLRB, OSHA). Office: Morgan Lewis & Bockius 1111 Pennsylvania Ave NW Washington DC 20004

RISSMAN, BURTON RICHARD, lawyer; b. Chgo., Nov. 13, 1927; s. Louis and Eva (Lyons) R.; m. Francine Greenberg, June 15, 1952; children: Lawrence E., Thomas W., Michael P. BS, U. Ill., 1947, JD, 1951; LLM, NYU, 1952. Bar: Ill. 1951, U.S. Dist. Ct. (no. dist.) Ill. 1954, U.S. Ct. Appeals (7th cir.) 1978, U.S. Supreme Ct. 1982. Assoc. Schiff, Hardin & Waite, Chgo., 1953-59, ptnr., 1959—, mem. mgmt. com., 1984-92, chmn. mgmt. com., 1986-90. Mem. faculty Practicing Law Inst. Bd. editor U. Ill. Law Forum, 1949-51; contbr. articles to profl. jours. 1st lt. JAGC USAF, 1952—53. Food Law fellow, 1951. Mem. ABA, Ill. Bar Assn., Chgo. Bar Assn., Chgo. Coun. Lawyers, Carlton Club. Office: Schiff Hardin & Waite 6600 Sears Tower Chicago IL 60606-6473

RISTAU, KENNETH EUGENE, JR., lawyer; b. Knoxville, Tenn., Feb. 14, 1939; s. Kenneth E. and Frances (Besch) R.; m. Mary Emily George, Nov. 27, 1967 (div. Apr. 1985); children: Heidi, Mary Robin, Kenny, Michael, Robert; m. Emily Pettis, Mar. 31, 1990; 1 child, James Patrick. BA, Colgate U., 1961; JD, NYU, 1964. Bar: U.S. Ct. Appeals (9th cir.) 1968, U.S. Ct. Appeals (D.C. cir.) 1974, U.S. Supreme Ct. 1974, U.S. Dist. Ct., Southern Dist. of Calif., 1993. Assoc. Gibson, Dunn & Crutcher, L.A., 1964-69, ptnr. Irvine, Calif., 1969-2000, adv. ptnr., 2000—. Fellow Coll. Labor and Employment Lawyers (charter); mem. Orange County Indsl. Rels. Rsch. Assn. (pres. 1992-93), Big Canyon Country Club, Rancho Las Palmas Country Club, Orange County Hunt Club, Santa Fe Hunt Club. Administrative and regulatory, Labor (including EEOC, Fair Labor Standards Act, labor-management relations, NLRB, OSHA). Office: Gibson Dunn & Crutcher LLP Jamboree Ctr 4 Park Plz Irvine CA 92614-8557

RISTAU, MARK MOODY, lawyer, petroleum consultant; b. Warren, Pa., Mar. 21, 1944; s. Harold J. and Eleanor K. (Moody) Ristau. BA, Pa. Mil. Coll., 1966, Widner Coll., 1966; JD, Case Western Res. U., 1969. Bar: Pa. 1970, D.C. 1972, U.S. Supreme Ct. 1973, N.Y. 1982. Pvt. practice, Warren, Pa., 1970—85, Warren and Vancouver, Canada, 1976—85, Jamestown, NY, 1982—85; sr. ptnr. Ristau & McKeirnan, Warren, 1986—2002; sr. dir. Pa. Allied Oil Prodrs., 1972—78; atty. Pa. Field Prodrs., 1981—85; ptnr. SAR Devel., 1984—91, Slagle Almendinger & Ristau, 1983—89. Counsel United Refining Co., Pennbank, Enhanced Oil Recovery, Consol. Svcs., 1982—84; chmn. bd. Comml. Svc. Corp., U.S. interim trustee, 1979—88, bankruptcy trustee, 1988—98; CEO Silicon Electro-physics Corp., Inc., 1988—91, Phoenix Materials Corp., Inc., 1988—91; dirs. Warren Industries, Inc., 1991—94; bd. dirs. Petrex, Inc., A & A Metal Fabricating; U.S. counsel Brazilian Promotions, Inc. of Brazilian Govt., 1981—85; v.p. Daytona Apts., Inc., Daytona Beach, Fla.; case reporter Legal Intelligencer, 1972—79. Contbr. Sec. Daytona Devel. League; mem. Warren County Bd. Pub. Assistance, 1970—71, chmn., 1971—72; mem. Broward County (Fla.) Devel. League, 1981—83, Fla. Profl. Recruitment Assn., 1980—83. Recipient Tate Meml. award, 1981, Sambas award, 1981. Mem.: ATLA, Warren County Bar Assn. (past pres.), Am. Arbitration Assn., Conewango (Warren), Ipanema (Brazil), Eagles (life). Banking, Bankruptcy, Commercial, contracts (including sales of goods; commercial financing). Home and Office: PO Box 885 Warren PA 16365-0885

RISTUBEN, KAREN R. lawyer; b. Malden, Mass., Sept. 28, 1956; d. James Francis and Jane Dale Ristuben; m. Eric N. Stafford, Apr. 16, 1988 (div. Apr. 12, 1994); 1 child, James Hunter. BFA, Tufts U., 1982; JD, Suffolk U., 1987. Bar: Mass., U.S. Dist. Ct. Mass. 1987. Paralegal Parker Coulter Daley & White, Boston, 1982-83, Meehan, Boyle, Black & Fitzgerald and predecessor firm, Boston, 1983-87, assoc., 1987-94, dir., 1994—. Chair, bd. dirs. Ctr. for Health Care Negotiation, Boston. Author: Containing and Using Medical Records in Massachusetts, 1993; contbr. articles to profl. jours. Bd. govs. Sch. of the Mus. of Fine Arts, 1996-97. Mem. ABA (vice chair medicine and law com. 1995—), Mass. Bar Assn. (budge and fin. com. 1998, chair health law sect. coun. 1996-98), Mass. Acad. of Trial Attys. (bd. govs. 1995—), Womens Bar Assn. Avocations: sea kayaking, biking, running, art, music. Alternative dispute resolution, Health, Personal injury (including property damage). Office: Meehan Boyle Black & Fitzgerald 2 Center Plz Ste 600 Boston MA 02108-1922

RITCHIE, ALBERT, lawyer; b. Charlottesville, Va., Sept. 29, 1939; s. John and Sarah Dunlop (Wallace) R.; m. Jennie Wayland, Apr. 29, 1967; children: John, Mary. BA, Yale U., 1961; LLB, U. Va., 1964. Bar: Ill. 1964, Tenn. 2000. Assoc. Sidley & Austin, Chgo., 1964-71, ptnr., 1972-99, ret., 1999. Bd. dirs. Erie Neighborhood House, Chgo., 1978-88; bd. dirs. United Charities of Chgo., 1979-90; trustee U. Va. Law Sch. Found., 1997-99. Capt. U.S. Army, 1965-67. Mem. ABA, Am. Coll. Real Estate Lawyers, Chgo. Legal Aid Soc., Legal Club Chgo. (pres. 1986-87), U. Va. Law Sch. Alumni Assn. (v.p. 1989-93, pres. 1993-95), Cherokee Country Club, Hillsboro Club, Indian Hill Club. Episcopalian. Landlord-tenant, Property, real (including real estate development, water). Home: 436 Boxwood Sq Knoxville TN 37919-6627 E-mail: ritchiea@bellsouth.net.

RITCHIE, ALEXANDER BUCHAN, lawyer; b. Detroit, Apr. 19, 1923; s. Alexander Stevenson and Margaret (May) R.; m. Sheila Spellacy, June 1998; 1 child, Barbara Ritchie Drolshagen. BA, Wayne State U., 1947, JD, 1949. Bar: Mich. 1949. Pvt. practice, Detroit, 1949-52, 84—; asst. gen. counsel, asst. v.p. Maccabees Mutual Life Ins. Co., Detroit, 1952-65, v.p., sec., gen. counsel Southfield, Mich., 1977-84; sec., house counsel Wayne Nat. Life Ins. Co., Detroit, 1966-67; ptnr. Fenton, Nederlander, Dodge & Ritchie, Detroit, 1967-77. Spl. asst. atty. gen. State Mich., 1974-77. Bd. mem. Detroit Bd. Edn., 1971-77, Detroit Ctrl. Bd. Edn., 1971-73; bd. Police Commrs., Detroit, 1974-77; bd. dirs. Doctor's Hosp., Detroit, 1974-89. With U.S. Army, 1943-46. Recipient Key to the City of Detroit, Mayor Coleman Young, 1977. Mem. Mich. State Bar Assn. Avocations: reading, golf, theatre, gourmet. Home: 29255 Laurel Woods Dr Apt 201 Southfield MI 48034-4647

RITT, ROGER MERRILL, lawyer; b. N.Y.C., Mar. 26, 1950; m. Mimi Santini, Aug. 25, 1974; children: Evan Samuel, David Martin. BA, U. Pa., 1972; JD, Boston U., 1975, LLM, 1976. Bar: Mass. 1977, Pa. 1975, U.S. Tax Ct. Sr. ptnr. Hale and Dorr, Boston, 1984—. Adj. prof. grad. tax program Boston U., 1979-92; panelist Am. Law Inst., Mass. Continuing Legal Edn., World Trade Inst., NYU Inst. on Fed. Taxation; mem. exec. com. Fed. Tax Inst. New Eng. Treas. Found. for Tax Edn. Mem. ABA (tax sect.), Boston Bar Assn. Corporate taxation, Taxation, general, Personal income taxation. Office: Hale and Dorr 60 State St Boston MA 02109-1816

RITTER, ANN L. lawyer; b. N.Y.C., May 20, 1933; d. Joseph and Grace (Goodman) R. BA, Hunter Coll., 1954; JD, N.Y. Law Sch., 1970; postgrad. Law Sch., NYU, 1971-72. Bar: N.Y. 1971, U.S. Ct. Appeals (2d cir.) 1975, U.S. Supreme Ct. 1975. Writer, 1954-70; editor, 1955-66; tchr., 1966-70; atty. Am. Soc. Composers, Authors and Pubs., N.Y.C., 1971-72, Greater N.Y. Ins. Co., N.Y.C., 1973-74; sr. ptnr. Brenhouse & Ritter, N.Y.C., 1974-78; sole practice N.Y.C., 1978—. Editor N.Y. Immigration News, 1975-76. Mem. ABA, Am. Immigration Lawyers Assn. (treas. 1983-84, sec. 1984-85, vice-chair 1985-86, chair 1986-87, chair program com. 1989-90, chair spkrs. bur. 1989-90, chair media liaison 1989-90), N.Y. State Bar Assn., N.Y. County Lawyers Assn., Assn. Trial Lawyers Am., N.Y. State Trial Lawyers Assn., N.Y.C. Bar Assn., Watergate East Assn. (v.p., asst. treas. 1990—). Democrat. Jewish. Family and matrimonial, Immigration, naturalization, and customs, Personal injury (including property damage). Home: 47 E 87th St New York NY 10128-1005 Office: 420 Madison Ave Rm 1200 New York NY 10017-1171

RITTER, DANIEL BENJAMIN, lawyer; b. Wilmington, Del., Apr. 6, 1937; s. David Moore and Bernice Elizabeth (Carlson) R.; m. Shirley F. Sether, Jan. 29, 1971 (dec. Jan. 1998); 1 child, Roxane Elise. AB with honors, U. Chgo., 1957; LLB, U. Wash., 1963. Bar: Wash. 1963, U.S. Dist. Ct. (we. dist.) Wash. 1963, U.S. Tax Ct. 1965, U.S. Ct. Appeals (9th cir.) 1963. Assoc. Davis, Wright Tremaine LLP (formerly Davis, Wright and Jones), 1963-69, ptnr., 1969—. Lectr. Bar Rev. Assocs. Wash., Seattle, 1964-86; chmn. internat. dept. Davis, Wright and Jones, Seattle, 1984-85, chmn. banking dept., 1986-89. Casenote editor U. Wash. Law Rev., 1962-63; editor-in-chief, contbg. author Washington Revised Article 9 Deskbook, 2003; contbg. author: Washington Commercial Law Desk Book, 1982, rev. edit., 1987, Washington Community Property Desk Book, 1977. Trustee Cathedral Assoc., Seattle, 1980-86; legal counsel Wash. State Reps., Bellevue, 1983-92; bd. dirs. U. Chgo. Club Puget Sound, Seattle, 1982-95, pres., 1984-86; bd. dirs. Am. Lung Assn. Wash., Seattle, 1983-92; mem. vis. com. U. Wash. Law Sch., 1984-88; trustee U. Wash. Law Sch. Found., 1989-92; chmn. alumni rels. coun. U. Chgo., 1986-88; mem. statute law com. State of Wash., 1978-87; bd. dirs. Seattle Camerata, 1991-93; bd. dirs. Early Music Guild, Seattle, 1993-96. Mem. ABA (bus. law sect.), Wash. State Bar Assn. (chmn. bus. law sect. 1988-89, uniform comml. code com. 1980—, chmn. 1980-86, chmn. internat. law com. 1979-81, judicial recommendations com. 1991-93), Seattle-King County Bar Assn. (chmn. internat. and comparative law sect. 1980-82), Rainier Club, Order of Coif. Republican. Lutheran. Avocations: reading, theater, early music. Banking, Commercial, contracts (including sales of goods; commercial financing). Home: 907 Warren Ave N Apt 202 Seattle WA 98109-5635 Office: Davis Wright Tremaine 2600 Century Sq 1501 4th Ave Seattle WA 98101-1688

RITTER, ROBERT THORNTON, lawyer; b. N.Y.C., Nov. 4, 1956; s. Robert J. and Barbara W. (Foust) R.; m. Rebecca L. Grubbs, July 25, 1981; children: Sarah, Luke, Robert R. BA, Duke U., 1979; JD, Washington U., 1984. Bar: Mo., 1984, U.S. Dist. Ct. (ea. dist.) Mo., 1985. Assoc. William Brown, Atty. at Law, Bridgeton, Mo., 1984-85, Kopsky & Vouga, Chesterfield, Mo., 1986; pvt. practice Clayton, Mo., 1987-89; ptnr. Ritter & Gusdorf, Clayton, 1990-96; mem. Ritter & Gusdorf L.C., Clayton, 1997—2002; ptnr., mem. Belz & Jones, P.C., Clayton, 2002—03; pvt. practice St. Charles, Mo., 2003—. Treas. Campaign Election of State Rep. Steve Moore, 1988; coach Little League Baseball; head coach Christian H.S. Baseball. Mem.: St. Louis Assn. Christian Attys. (treas.), Bar Assn. Met. St. Louis, Mo. Bar Assn. Republican. Avocations: tennis, baseball. Family and matrimonial, Personal injury (including property damage), Property, real (including real estate development, water). Office: 820 S Main St Ste 300 Saint Charles MO 63301

RITVO, ELIZABETH ANN, lawyer; b. Washington, July 14, 1951; d. Martin and Zelma Ritvo; m. Robert G. Kunzendorf, June 5, 1971; children: Jennifer, Rebecca. AB, Yale Coll., 1973; JD, U. Va., 1976. Bar: Va. 1976, D.C. 1978, U.S. Dist. Ct. D.C. 1978, Mass. 1980, U.S. Ct. Appeals (D.C. cir.) 1978, U.S. Dist. Ct. Mass. 1980, U.S. Ct. Appeals (1st cir.) 1980, U.S. Supreme Ct. 1987. Staff atty. U.S. Dept. Transp., Washington, 1976—77; assoc. Kirlin Campbell & Keating, Washington, 1977—79, Brown Rudnick Freed & Gesmer, Boston, 1980—84; ptnr. Brown Rudnick Berlack Israels, Boston, 1985—. Trustee Women's Bar Found., 1994—99, pres., 1998—99. Appellate, General civil litigation. Office: Brown Rudnick Berlack Israels One Financial Ctr Boston MA 02111 E-mail: eritvo@brbilaw.com.

RITZ, STEPHEN MARK, lawyer; b. Midland, Mich., Aug. 23, 1962; s. Alvin H. and Patricia M. (Padway) R. BA, Northwestern U., 1985; JD, Ind. U., 1989. Bar: Ill. 1990, U.S. Dist. Ct. (no. dist.) Ill. 1990, Ind. 1996. Atty. Chapman & Cutler, Chgo., 1990-93; CEO Newport Pension Mgmt. LLC, Carmel, Ind., 1993—97, atty., 1997—. Pension, profit-sharing, and employee benefits, Taxation, general, Personal income taxation. Office: Newport Pension Mgmt PO Box 502448 Indianapolis IN 46250

RIVA, DAVID MICHAEL, lawyer; b. Herrin, Ill., Sept. 19, 1948; s. Charles David and Maryann (Peek) R.; m. Paula Jean Calvert, July 31, 1971; children: Allison, Jennifer, Katie, Sarah. BA, Knox Coll., 1970; JD, Washington U., 1974. Bar: Ill. 1974, U.S. Dist. Ct. (so. dist.) Ill. 1974. Pvt. practice, West Frankfort, Ill., 1974—. Officer West Frankfort Bd. Edn., 1983-93; bd. dirs. West Frankfort Recreation Assn. Mem. Masons. Avocation: coaching girls fast pitch softball. General practice, Probate (including wills, trusts), Property, real (including real estate development, water). Home: 1270 Ramsey Heights Rd West Frankfort IL 62896-4971 Office: 226 E Main St West Frankfort IL 62896-2406 E-mail: mriva@midwest.com.

RIVELLESE, VINCENT WOODROW, lawyer; b. Smithtown, N.Y., Apr. 27, 1969; s. Vincent Joseph and Lynne Joan R.; m. Nadine Mary-Cecille Rapacioli, Oct. 25, 1997. AB, Harvard U., 1991; JD, Am. U., 1994. Bar: N.Y. 1995, U.S. Dist. Ct. (so. dist.) N.Y. 1998. Asst. dist. atty. Manhattan Dist. Attys. Office, N.Y.C., 1994—2002; prin. law clerk Hon. William C. Donnino, N.Y. State Supreme Ct., 2002—. Mem. N.Y. County Lawyers Assn. Avocations: jazz, saxophone, science fiction, puzzles. Office: Queens County Supreme Ct 125-01 Queens Blvd Kew Gardens NY 11415

RIVERA, JOSE DE JESUS, lawyer; b. Zacatecas, Mex., 1950; m. Nina Rivera; 5 children. BA, No. Ariz. U.; JD, Ariz. State U. Atty. civil rights divsn. Dept. of Justice, 1976—77; asst. U.S. atty. Dist. Ariz., 1977—81; with Langerman, Begam, Lewis and Marks, 1981—84; ptnr. Rivera, Scales and Kizer, 1984—98; atty. City of El Mirage, U.S. Atty., Dist. of Ariz., 1998—2001; with Haralson, Miller, Pitt & McAnally PLC, Phoenix, 2001—. Vice-chair adv. com. civil rights Atty. Gen. Ariz. dist., 1998-2001, adv. com. native Am. issues, domestic terrorism subcom., 1998-2001, chair subcom. no Mem. com. Los Abogados; bd. dirs. Inst. for Cmty. Initiatives, 1996-98; coach Little League. With N.G. Mem. Ariz. State Bar. (bd. govs. 1995-98, bd. officer, sec. treas. 1996, 2d v.p. 1997-98, exec. dir. search com. 1996-97, chair appointments com. 1997-98), Hispanic Bar Assn., Los Abogados Bar Assn. (bd. dirs. 1981-83). Democrat. Avocation: reading. General civil litigation, Private international, Personal injury (including property damage). Office: Haralson Miller Pitt & McAnally PLC 3003 N Central Ave Ste 1400 Phoenix AZ 85012 E-mail: jrivera@hmpmlaw.com.*

RIVERA, OSCAR R. lawyer, corporate executive; b. Havana, Cuba, Dec. 8, 1956; s. Alcibiades R. and Marian (Fernandez) R.; children: Peter, Taylor. BBA, U. Miami, 1978; JD, Georgetown U., 1981. Bar: Fla. 1981, U.S. Dist. Ct. (so. dist.) Fla. 1982, U.S. Tax Ct. 1982. Assoc. Corrigan. Zelman & Bander P.A., Miami, Fla., 1981-83; ptnr. Siegfried, Rivera, Lerner De La Torre & Sobel P.A., Miami, 1984—. Adj. prof. law U. Miami, 1987—. Asst. mgr. campaign to elect Michael O'Donovan, Miami, 1976; mem. youth adv. bd., Miami, 1975-78, youth planning council Dade County, Miami, 1975-78. Mem. ABA, Cuban Am. Bar Assn., Internat. Coun. Shopping Ctrs. (pres. Fla. polit. action com., v.p. Fla. govtl. affairs com., state dir. Fla.), Little Havana Kiwanis, Orange Key, Omicron Delta Kappa, Phi Kappa Phi. Avocations: photography, skiing. Corporate, general, Landlord-tenant, Property, real (including real estate development, water).

RIVERA, RAMON E. lawyer, law educator; b. Columbia, S.C., Jan. 4, 1964; s. Angel Luis Rivera-Estrada and Jacqulin C. Murray; m. Elise Renee Farr-Rivera, Feb. 11, 1982; children: Laura B., Jessica Renee. BS in Philosophy, U. Calif., Davis, 1991; JD, Syracuse U., 1994. Bar: N.Y., U.S. Dist. Ct. (no. dist.) N.Y., U.S. Supreme Ct. Staff atty. Frank Hiscock Legal Aid Soc., Syracuse, NY, 1995—96; pvt. practice Rivera Law Firm, Syracuse, 1996—99; mng. ptnr. Micale & Rivera, LLP, Syracuse, 1999—2001; gen. ptnr. Mackenzie Hughes LLP, Syracuse, 2001—. Adj. prof. Syracuse U., 1999—, Syracuse U. Coll. Law, 2001—. V.p. Onondaga County Spanish Action League, Syracuse, 2001—; mem. torchbearer com. U.S. Olympic Com., Syracuse, 2002; dir. Leadership Greater Syracuse, Syracuse, 2001—. Named grad., Leadership Greater Syracuse, 2001; recipient 40 Under 40 Bus. Leadership award, Syracuse C. of C., 2001. Mem.: Onondaga County Bar Assn. (dir. 2001—). Immigration, naturalization, and customs, Private international. Office: Mackenzie Hughes LLP Ste 600 101 S Salina St Syracuse NY 13202-4304

RIVERA, WALTER, lawyer; b. N.Y.C., Jan. 18, 1955; s. Marcelino and Ana Maria (Reyes) R. BA, Columbia U., 1976; JD, U. Pa., 1979. Bar: N.Y. 1980. Law clk. to cen. legal research staff N.Y. State Ct. Appeals, Albany, 1979-81; asst. atty. gen. State of N.Y., N.Y.C., 1981-85; sole practice N.Y.C., 1985-88; shareholder Rivera & Muniz, P.C., N.Y.C., 1988-93, Law Offices of Walter Rivera P.C., 1994-97; ptnr. Rivera, Hunter, Colon & Dobshinsky, LLP, N.Y.C., 1998—. Chmn. Third World Lawyers Caucus, N.Y. State Atty. Gen.'s Office, N.Y.C., 1984; arbitrator City Ct. N.Y.C., 1985. Bd. dirs. Andrew Glover Youth Program. Mem. ABA, Puerto Rican Bar Assn., Nat. Hispanic Bar Assn., N.Y. State Bar Assn., Assn. Bar City N.Y. (past chmn. com. on small law firm mgmt.), Sch. of Visual Arts (bd. dirs.). Avocations: golf, travel. Personal injury (including property damage), General civil litigation, State civil litigation. Home: 19 Orchard Ln Elmsford NY 10523 Office: Rivera Hunter Colon & Dohshinsky LLP 61 Broadway Rm 1030 New York NY 10006-2701 E-mail: wrivera@rhcdlaw.com.

RIVERA PEREZ, EFRAIN E. state supreme court justice; b. Mayaguez, P.R., July 15, 1951; s. Efrain Padilla Rivera and Irene Perez Camacho; m. Border Mariluz; 1 child, Mariela Mariluz. B in Adminstrn. of Cos. , U. Enclosure Mayaguez, 1971; JD, Pontifica Cath. U. Ponce Sch. Right, Ponce, P.R. , 1975. Dist. judge Judicial Region Mayaguez, 1983—84, superior judge, 1984—85; pvt. practice law Maguayez, 1985—92; chmn. U. Enclosure Mayaguez U. P.R., 1986—92; adviser judicial subjects, dir. office judicial appts.; dir. office of commn. Judicial Reformation; temp. sec. justice, 1993—95; judge Ct. Cir. Appeals, 1995—2000; assoc. justice Supreme Ct. of P.R., 2000—. Office: PO Box 902 2392 San Juan PR 00902-2392*

RIVERS, KENNETH JAY, retired judicial administrator, consultant; b. N.Y.C., Feb. 13, 1938; s. Alexander Maximillian and Albertina Ray (Gay) R.; m. Leah B. Files, Sept. 21, 1957 (div.); children: Londa Denise, Nancy Laura, Terrie Ruth, Kenneth J. Jr. AAS in Criminal Justice, BS in Criminal Justice, St. Francis Coll., Bklyn., 1978; MPA, L.I. Univ., 1981. Correction officer N.Y.C. Dept. Correction, 1965-69; ct. officer N.Y. State Unified Ct. System, N.Y.C., 1969-71, asst. ct. clk., 1971-73, sr. ct. clk., 1973-85, assoc. ct. clk., 1985-88, prin. ct. clk., 1988-90, dep. chief clk., 1991-93; ret., 1993. Tng. instr. N.Y. State Unified Ct. System, N.Y.C., 1985—, pers. assessor, 1985—; lectr. John Jay Coll. NYU, N.Y.C., 1987. Author: Juvenile Crime Survey, 1982, New York State Jury Selection, 1984. Bd. dirs. Parkway Consumers Med. Coun., Bklyn., 1983—, Cen. Bklyn. Tenant's Rights, 1988—. Recipient Leadership award Tribune Soc., N.Y. State Cts., 1987, Svc. award, 1988, Cert. of Merit award Fedn. Afro-Am. Civil Svc. Orgns., 1987. Mem. ASPA, Internat. Pers. Mgmt. Assn., Acad. Polit. Sci., Conf. Minority Pub. Adminstrs., Masons. Democrat. Methodist. Avocation: jazz musician. E-mail: kchiefclerk@aol.com.

RIVERS, RICHARD ROBINSON, lawyer; b. Dallas, June 9, 1942; s. Stewart Robinson and Madge (Fiske) R.; children : Laura Ellen, Jonathan Stewart. BA, Tulane U., 1964; JD, Cath. U. of Am., 1974; MA, Johns Hopkins U., 2003. Bar: D.C. 1974. Writer Bauerlein, Inc., New Orleans, 1965-68; staff asst. Office of House Majority Whip, Washington, 1968-70, Office of House Majority Leader, Washington, 1971-73; internat. trade counsel Com. on Fin. U.S. Senate, Washington, 1973-77; gen. counsel Office Spl. Trade Rep., Washington, 1977-79; ptnr. Akin, Gump, Strauss, Hauer & Feld, Washington, 1979-96. Instr. Dalian (Peoples Republic of China) Inst. Tech., 1986. Trustee Am. Indian Coll. Fund. Mem. ABA, D.C. Bar Assn., Coun. Fgn. Rels., Met. Club of City of Washington. Democrat. Episcopalian. Private international, Public international, Legislative. Home: 4809 V St NW Washington DC 20007

RIVET, DIANA WITTMER, lawyer, developer; b. Auburn, N.Y., Apr. 28, 1931; d. George Wittmer and Anne (Jenkins) Wittmer Hauswirth; m. Paul Henry Rivet, Oct. 24, 1952; children: Gail, Robin, Leslie, Heather, Clayton, Eric. BA, Keuka Coll., 1951; JD, Bklyn. Law Sch., 1956. Bar: N.Y. 1956, U.S. Dist. Ct. (ea. and so. dists.) N.Y. 1975; cert. organic NOFA, 2001. Sole practice, Orangeburg, NY, 1957—2000; farmer Danny's Backyard Organic Farm, Orangeburg, 2000—. County atty. Rockland County (N.Y.), 1974-77; asst. to legis. chmn. Rockland County, 1978-79; counsel, adminstr. Indsl. Devel. Agy., Rockland County, 1980-91, Rockland Econ. Devel. Corp., 1981-90; counsel, exec. dir. Pvt. IndustryCoun. Rockland county, 1980-90; pres., CEO Environ. Mgmt. Ltd., Orangeburg, 1980-98; mem. air mgmt. adv. com. N.Y. State Dept. Environ. Conservation 1984-92, Orangetown Planning Bd., 1993-2000, master plan com., 2000—. Pres. Rockland County coun. Girl Scouts U.S., 1981-84; chmn. Rockland County United Way, 1996-97, mem. campaign com., 1983-84, 88-89, 93, sec., 1997-99, bd. dirs., 1988-94, 95—; mem. Leadership Rockland, 1991-94. Recipient Cmty. Svc. award Keuka Coll., 1965, Disting. Svc. award Town of Orangetown, 1970, Disting. Svc. award Rockland County, 1989, Econ. Devel. award Rockland Econ. Devel. Corp., 1990; named Businessperson of Yr. Jour. News, Rockland County, 1982. Mem. ABA, N.Y. State Bar Assn. (mcpl. law sect. exec. com. 1976-83, environ. law sect. exec. com. 1974-86), Rockland County Bar Assn. (chair environ. law com. 1994-96), Rockland Bus. Assn. (bd. dirs. 1981-97, small bus. adv. com. 1998, gov. affairs com. 1998—), Rockland Computer Users' Group (bd. dirs. 1998-99). Democrat. Mem. Religious Soc. of Friends. Environmental, Municipal (including bonds), Property, real (including real estate development, water). Home: 1 Lester Dr Orangeburg NY 10962-2316 E-mail: danny@ucs.net.

RIVETTE, FRANCIS ROBERT, lawyer; b. Syracuse, N.Y., May 1, 1952; s. Francis Patrick and Barbara Parker (Smith) R.; m. Judith A. La Manna, 1993. BA, Allegheny Coll., 1974; JD, Syracuse U., 1977. Bar: N.Y. 1978, D.C. 1980, U.S. Dist. Ct. (no. dist.) N.Y. 1978, U.S. Supreme Ct. 1993. Ptnr. Rivette & Rivette P.C., Syracuse, 1978—; corp. counsel Nicom Techs., Inc., 1995—, Group 52, Inc., 2002—. Corp. counsel Fangand Enterprises Ltd., 1978—; co-founder Apex Racing. Mem. ATLA, N.Y. State Trial Lawyers Assn., Syracuse Corvette Club (pres. 1985-86), Sportscar Vintage Racing Assn., Nat. Corvette Restorers Soc. (nat. judge, 1985, 88, 95, 97), Historic Sportscar Racing Ltd., Phi Delta Phi, Phi Gamma Mu. Republican. Corporate, general, General practice, Personal injury (including property damage). Home: 200 Old Liverpool Rd Liverpool NY 13088-6354 Office: Rivette & Rivette PC 224 Harrison St Ste 306 Syracuse NY 13202-3067 E-mail: frr-rr@accucom.net.

RIVKIN, STEVEN ROBERT, lawyer; b. Boston, Jan. 11, 1937; s. Bernard Morris and Ruth (Lasker) R.; m. Mary Stimpson Seckinger, Aug. 17, 1975; children: Caroline Seckinger Carlson, Robert Edward Seckinger, Sarah Edith Rivkin, Jesse Stimpson Rivkin. AB, Harvard U., 1958, LLB, 1962. Bar: Mass. 1963, D.C. 1967, Md. 1992, U.S. Supreme Ct. 1968. Analyst Weapons Systems Evaluation Group, Washington, 1958-59; tech. asst. for legal affairs White House Staff and Exec. Office of Pres., Washington, 1961-65; assoc. Foley Hoag & Eliot, Boston, 1965-67; counsel Fisher Sharlitt & Gelband, Washington, 1967—68; counsel, ptnr. Nicholson & Carter, Washington, 1971-75; ptnr. Rivkin & Lewis, Washington, 1982-83; pvt. practice, Washington, 1968-70, 75-81, 83—. Vis. fellow Progressive Policy Inst. of Dem. Leadership Coun., Washington, 1992; counsel Sloan Commn. on Cable Comms., N.Y.C., 1970-71; mem. adv. bd. N.Am. Cmty. Svc., Santa Fe, 2001—. Author, editor 5 books; contbr. articles to profl. jours., mags. and newspapers. With USAR, 1962-67. Recipient Travel and Study award Ford Found., 1970. Democrat. Jewish. FERC practice, Environmental, Securities. Home and Office: 8013 Maple Ridge Rd Bethesda MD 20814-1307 Office Fax: 301-907-9851. E-mail: srrivkin@msn.com.

RIZOR, STEFAN, lawyer; b. Hannover, Germany, July 7, 1961; s. Kurt Carl and Gisela Anna Rizor; m. Ursula Finken, Dec. 12, 1991; children: David, Anton. LLM, McGill U., Montréal, 1989; Abitur, Kaiser-Wilhelm-Gymnasium, Hannover, 1979; First State Exam (Law Sch.), Ludwig Maximilian U., Würzburg, 1985; LLM, Oberlandesgericht Celle, 1989. Bar: dist. ct. of Cologne 1990. Assoc. Graf von Westphalen & Ptnr., Cologne, Germany, 1990—93; ptnr. Graf von Westphalen Fritze & Modest, Cologne, Germany, 1994—2001, Osborne Clarke, Cologne, Germany, 2001. Chmn. German-Canadian Bus. Club, Northrhine-Westfalia, Germany, 2002; bd. mem. Canadian-German Lawyers Assn., Germany, 1992. Property, real (including real estate development, water), Corporate, general, Mergers and acquisitions. Office: Osborne Clarke Innere Kanalstrasse 15 Northrhine-Westfalia Cologne 50823 Germany Office Fax: +49 221 5108 4027. E-mail: stefan.rizor@osborneclarke.com.

RIZOWY, CARLOS GUILLERMO, lawyer, educator, political analyst; b. Sarandi Grande, Uruguay, Mar. 5, 1949; came to U.S., 1973, naturalized, 1981; s. Gerszon and Eva (Visnia) R.; m. Charlotte Gordon, Mar. 14, 1976; children: Brian Isaac, Yael Deborah, Michal Evie. BA, Hebrew U., Jerusalem, 1971; MA, U. Chgo., 1975, PhD, 1981; JD, Chgo. Kent Coll. Law, Ill. Inst. Tech., 1983. Bar: Ill. 1983, U.S. Dist. Ct. (no. dist.) Ill. 1983, U.S. Ct. Appeals (7th cir.) 1983. Asst. prof. polit. sci. Roosevelt U., Chgo., 1982-89, chmn. dept. polit. sci., 1983-86, dir. internat. studies program, 1986-89; mng. ptnr. Ray, Rizowy & Fleischer, Chgo., 1983-90; ptnr. corp. law dept. Gottlieb and Schwartz, 1990-92; ptnr. Levenfeld, Eisenberg, Janger, Glassberg, Samotny & Halper, 1993-94; of counsel Sonnenschein, Nath & Rosenthal, 1994—. Hon. consul of Uruguay, Chgo., 1994—; adj. assoc. prof. Spertus Coll. Judaica, Chgo., 1984—; weekly polit. analyst on Middle East, internat. law and fgn. policy, resource specialist Sta. WBEZ Pub. Radio and BBC Latin Am.; mem. panel of arbitrators of Mediation and Arbitration Ctr., Internat. Arbitration Ct. for Mercosur Bolsa de Comercio, Uruguay, 1999—. Author: Avoiding Premises Liability Suits by Improving Security, 1991, Middle East Security: Five Areas to Watch, 1997. V.p., resource specialist to exec. com. Orgn. Children of Holocaust Survivors, Chgo., 1982; pres. Assn. Children Holocaust Survivors, 1986-91; pres. bd. dirs. Soviet Jewry Legal Advocacy Ctr., 1986-88; rsch. com. Nat. Strategy Forum, bd. dirs. UN Assn. U.S., 1985-89; mem. cmty. rels. com. Jewish Fedn. Met. Chgo., 1983-84; mem. adv. bd., chmn. internat. affairs commn. Am. Jewish Congress, Chgo., 1983-85, chmn. subcom. for Israel, 1986-88; mem. Nat. Spkrs. Bur. United Jewish Appeal, Nat. Spkrs. Bur. Devel. Corp. for Israel; mem. adv. bd. Chgo. Action for Soviet Jewry, 1983-85; bd. dirs. Am. Friends of Hebrew U., Chgo., 1984-86, Florence Heller Jewish Cmty. Ctr., 1986-88, Soviet Jewry Legal Advocacy Ctr., 1986-88; mem. human rights com. Anti-Defamation League, 1986, bd. dirs., 1989—; bd. dirs. Bd. Jewish Edn., 1989-91, Hispanic Coalition for Jobs, 1991-94; chmn. univ. educators divsn. Jewish United Fund, 1988-90; mem. consular corp. adv. bd. Internat. Vis. Ctr. Chgo., 1995—, com. fgn. affairs Chgo. Coun. Fgn. Rels., 1994—. Scholar Hebrew U., 1967-72, U. Chgo., 1972-78, Hillman Found., 1978, Peter Volid Found., 1980; recipient Globalist award Heritage Internat. Trade Assn., 1997. Mem. ATLA, ABA (chmn. bus. com. 1993-95), Assn. Ibero-Am. Consuls of Chgo., Ill. State Bar Assn., Chgo. Bar Assn. (internat. trade com.), Latin Am. Bar Assn., Nat. Hispanic Bar Assn., Am. Immigration Lawyers Assn., Am. Polit. Sci. Assn., Am. Judicature Soc., Exec. Club Chgo., Internat. Platform Assn., Wexner Heritage Found., Am. Forum, Latin Am. C. of C. (bd. dirs. 1991—, gen. counsel 1992—), Anshe Emet Congregation, Masons. Private international, Public international, Mergers and acquisitions. Office: Sonnenschein Nath & Rosenthal 8000 Sears Tower Chicago IL 60606

RIZZO, RONALD STEPHEN, lawyer; b. Kenosha, Wis., July 15, 1941; s. Frank Emmanuel and Rosalie (Lo Cicero); children: Ronald Stephen Jr., Michael Robert. BA, St. Norbert Coll., 1963; JD, Georgetown U., 1965, LLM in Taxation, 1966. Bar: Wis. 1965, Calif. 1967, Ill. 1999. Assoc. Kindel & Anderson, L.A., 1966-71, ptnr., 1971-86, Jones, Day, Reavis & Pogue, L.A., 1986-93, Chgo., 1993—. Bd. dirs. Guy LoCicero & Son Inc., Kenosha, Wis. Contbg. editor ERISA Litigation Reporter, 1994-99; mem. internat. adv. editl. bd. Jour. Pensions Mgmt. and Mktg. Schulte zur Hausen fellow Inst. Internat. and Fgn. Trade Law, Georgetown U., 1966. Fellow Am. Coll. Tax Counsel, Am. Coll. Employee Benefits Counsel (charter); mem. ABA (chmn. com. on employee benefits sect. on taxation 1988-89, vice chair com. on govt. submissions 1995-99), Los Angeles County Bar Assn. (chmn. com. on employee benefits sect. on taxation 1977-79, exec. com. 1977-78, 90-92), State Bar Calif. (co-chmn. com. on employee benefits sect. on taxation 1980), West Pension Conf. (steering com. L.A. chpt. 1980-83). Avocations: reading, golf, travel. Pension, profit-sharing, and employee benefits, Corporate taxation. Home: 1040 N Lake Shore Dr #19C Chicago IL 60611-6164 Office: Jones Day 77 W Wacker Ste 3500 Chicago IL 60601-1692 E-mail: rsrizzo@jonesday.com.

ROACH, JON GILBERT, lawyer; b. Knoxville, Tenn., June 17, 1944; s. Walter Davis and Lena Rose (Chapman) R.; m. Mintha Marie Evans, Oct. 22, 1977; children: Jon G., II, Evan Graham. BS, U. Tenn., 1967, JD, 1969. Bar: Tenn. 1970, D.C. 1981, U.S. Ct. Appeals (6th cir.). Assoc. Stone & Bozeman, Knoxville, 1970—71; pvt. practice Knoxville, 1971—75; delinquent tax atty. Sevier County, 1971—76; city atty., dir. of law City of Knoxville, 1976-83; ptnr. Peck, Shaffer & Williams, Knoxville, 1983-90, Watson, Hollow & Reeves, PLC, Knoxville, 1990—2002, Watson & Hollow, P.L.C., Knoxville, 2002—. City atty. City of Plainview, 1999—, City of Maynardville, 2000—; faculty Knoxville Bus. Coll., 1973-74; mem. Tenn. Commn. on Continuing Legal Edn. and Specialization of Tenn. Supreme Ct., 1995-2000. Mem. bd., Bapt. Health Sys. Found. Mem. ABA, Tenn. Bar Assn. (mem. ho. of dels.), Knoxville Bar Assn., D.C. Bar Assn., Internat. Mcpl. Lawyers Assn., Kiwanis (East Knoxville). Democrat. Baptist. General civil litigation, Municipal (including bonds), Probate (including wills, trusts). Office: Watson & Hollow PLC PO Box 131 1500 Riverview Tower Knoxville TN 37901-0131 Home: 722 Cheowa Cir Knoxville TN 37919-6676

ROACH, WESLEY LINVILLE, lawyer, insurance executive; b. Norlina, N.C., Oct. 8, 1931; s. Joseph Franklin and Florence G. (Sink) R.; m. Mary Jon Gerald, Aug. 13, 1955; children: Gerald, Mary Virginia. BS, Wake Forest U., 1953, JD, 1955. Bar: N.C. 1955. With Pilot Life Ins. Co., Greensboro, N.C., 1958-86, also bd. dirs.; sr. v.p., gen. counsel Jefferson-Pilot Life Ins. Co., Greensboro, 1986-88; sec. Great Ea. Lif. Ins. Co., 1975-85; of counsel Smith, Anderson, Blount, Dorsett, Mitchell & Jernigan, Attys. at Law, Raleigh, N.C., 1988—. Former chmn. bd. dirs. N.C. Life and Accident and Health Ins. Guaranty Assn., Va. Life, Accident and Health Guaranty Assn., S.C. Life, Accident and Health Guaranty Assn.; sec. JP Investment Mgmt. Co., Jefferson-Pilot Equity Sales, Inc., Spl. Services Agy., Inc., 1974-84; mem. exec. com., bd. dirs. N.C. Ins. Edn. Found., 1978—; trustee In-Home Care, Inc., 1999—, chmn., 2001. Mem. fin. com. Greensboro United Fund, 1964-65; mem. fin. com. Greensboro 1st Bapt. Ch., 1963-66, 83-86, chmn., 1983-85, chmn. bd. deacons, 1974-76, 80-81; nat. chmn. alumni coun. coll. fund Wake Forest U., 1971-76, pres. nat. alumni coun., 1975-76, trustee univ., 1978-82, emeritus trustee, 1999—; trustee So. Bapt. Theol. Sem., Louisville, 1973-84; trustee Bapt. Retirement Homes N.C., Inc., 1992-2000, chmn., 1993-94, emeritus trustee, 2001-; trustee In Home Care, Inc., 1997—, chmn., 2001. With USNR, 1955-58. Mem. ABA, N.C. Bar Assn., Raleigh Bar Assn., Assn. Life Ins. Counsel (bd. govs. 1984-88), Greensboro C. of C. (chmn. nat. legis. com. 1973—), Nat. Orgn. Life Guaranty Assn. (bd. dirs. 1982-87). Democrat. Home: PO Box 1690 601 Selma Rd Wendell NC 27591-8648 Office: 2500 First Union Capitol Ctr PO Box 2611 Raleigh NC 27602-2611

ROADES, JOHN LESLIE, lawyer; b. El Campo, Tex., Mar. 29, 1951; s. Ora E. and Carolyn Elizabeth (Roten) R.; m. Therese Carol Pavlas, Mar. 20, 1982; children: Leslie Carol, Elizabeth Ann. AA, Wharton Coll., 1971; BBA, U. Tex., 1973, JD, 1975. Bar: Tex. 1976. Assoc. Manske and Hajovsky, El Campo, Tex., 1976-77; county atty. Wharton County, 1981-83; dist. atty. 23rd Jud. Dist., Wharton and Matagorda counties, 1983-84; pvt. practice law Wharton, 1977—. Chmn. Wharton County Dem. Party, 1978-79, 91-95, state exec. com., 1981-82; state pres. Young Dems., 1981-82; U.S. del. Am. Coun. Young Polit. Leaders, 1981. Mem. Tex. Bar Assn. (coun. mem. gen., solo and small firm sect., 1995—, sec./treas. 2000-01, chair 2002-03, local bar svcs. com. 1990-95), Wharton County Bar Assn. (pres. 1989-90), Lions (v.p. 1992-94, pres. 1994-95). Methodist. Family and matrimonial, General practice, Personal injury (including property damage). Office: 1201 N Alabama Rd PO Box 1219 Wharton TX 77488-1219 E-mail: roades@intertex.net.

ROAN, FORREST CALVIN, JR., lawyer; b. Waco, Tex., Dec. 18, 1944; s. Forrest Calvin and Lucille Elizabeth (McKinney) R.; m. Vickie Joan Howard, Feb. 15, 1969 (div. Dec. 1983); children: Amy Katherine, Jennifer Louise; m. Leslie D. Hampton Roan, Jan. 2, 1999. BBA, U. Tex., Austin, 1973, JD, 1976. Bar: Tex. 1976, U.S. Dist. Ct. (we. dist.) Tex. 1977, U.S. Dist. Ct. (so. dist.) Tex. 1998, U.S. Ct. Appeals (5th cir.) 1977, U.S. Supreme Ct. 1979, U.S. Ct. Appeals (11th cir.) 1981, U.S. Ct. Appeals (fed. cir.) 1998, U.S. Ct. Internat. Trade, 1998. Prin. Roan & Assocs., Austin, 1969-71; counsel, com. dir. Tex. Ho. of Reps., 1972-75; assoc. Heath, Davis & McCalla, Austin, 1975-78; prin. Roan & Gullahorn, P.C., Austin, 1978-85, Roan & Autrey (formerly Roan & Simpson), P.C., 1986-99; sr. ptnr. Cantey, Hanger, Roan & Autrey, 1999—. Bd. dirs. Lawyers Credit Union, chmn., 1982-83; bd. dirs. pub. law sect. State Bar Tex., 1980-84; mem. chancellor's coun. U. Tex. With Tex. Army N.G., 1966-74. Fellow Tex. Bar Found.; mem. ABA, Tex. Assn. Def. Counsel, Tex. Assn. Bank Counsel, Def. Rsch. Inst., Travis County Bar Assn., Tex.-Mexico Bar Assn., Knights of the Symphony (Lord Chancellor 2003—), Tex. Lyceum Assn. (v.p., bd. dirs. 1980-87), Austin C. of C., Austin Club, Headliners Club, Masons, Shriners (Parsons Masonic master 1976-77). Methodist. Administrative and regulatory, Mergers and acquisitions, Insurance. Office: Cantey Hanger Roan & Autrey 200 Wells Fargo Bank Tower 400 W 15th St Austin TX 78701-1600 E-mail: froan@canteyhanger.com.

ROARK, CANDICE RENAU, lawyer; b. Lawton, Okla., Dec. 21, 1970; d. Thomas T. Renau and Michele D. Binkowski; children: Andrew, Elizabeth, Rory. BSc in Psychology & Sociology, U. State N.Y., Albany, 1993; MBA, Cardinal Stritch U., 1997; JD, Hamline U., 2000. A.G.E. mechanic USAF, Germany, 1988—92, 1988—92; orgnl. cons. Minn., 1996—99; atty. Pub. Defenders Office, Minn., 1999—2000; arbitrator BBB; mediator internat. law, contract lawyer, bd. dirs., min. DEA. Arbitrator; nat. spkr. in field. Author: Adolescent God, 1999. Fin. dir. Cmty. Caring for Life, Minn., 1998—99; coord. for jr./sr. h.s. Cmty. Youth, Minn., 1989—98; native am. publicity dir. Native Am. Coun., Incircik, Turkey, 1991—92; mem. parish coun. Minn., 1998—99. Named 2,000 Notable Am. Women; recipient Women's Military Meml. award, USAF, Nat. Defense Svc. medal, Humanitarian Svc. medal, MJF award Pub Svc. Mem.: Mensa. Roman Catholic. Avocations: rollerblading, skiing, writing, fencing.

ROARK, JIMMY LEE, lawyer; b. Hazard, Ky., Dec. 5, 1948; s. John and Emma Lou (Fowler) R.; m. Deborah Louise McIntyre, July 6, 1983. BBA, Morehead State U., 1973; JD, U. Ky., 1977. Bar: Ky. 1977, U.S. Dist. Ct. (ea. and we. dists.) Ky. 1979, U.S. Ct. Appeals (6th cir.) 1979. Ptnr. Cook & Roark, Whitesburg, Ky., 1977-80; asst. county atty. Letcher County, 1978-80; ptnr. Barrett, Haynes, May, Carter & Roark P.S.C., Hazard, 1980—. Served with U.S. Army, 1970-72. Mem. ABA, Assn. Trial Lawyers Am., Ky. Bar Assn., Ky. Acad. Trial Attys., Perry County Bar Assn. Federal civil litigation, State civil litigation, Insurance. Office: Barret Haynes May et al 113 Lovern St Hazard KY 41701-1725

ROBB, GARY CHARLES, lawyer; b. Kansas City, Mo., May 17, 1955; m. Anita Candace Porte, Apr. 30, 1983. B.A. with distinction in Polit. Sci. and Communications, U. Mo.-Kansas City, 1977, M.A. in Econs., 1978; J.D. cum laude, U. Mich., 1981. Bars: Ill. 1981, U.S. Dist. Ct. (no. dist.) Ill. 1981, Mo. 1982, U.S. Dist. Ct. (we. dist.) Mo. 1982, U.S. Ct. Appeals (8th cir.) 1982. Assoc. Mayer, Brown & Platt, Chgo., 1981-82, Shughart, Thomson & Kilroy, Kansas City, Mo., 1982-84; ptnr. Robb & Robb, Kansas City, Mo., 1984— ; adj. prof. law U. Mo., Kansas City; lectr., program chmn. Nat. Conf. on Products Liability Law, Chgo., 1983, lectr., 1984. Contbg. author: Tort Law, Missouri Bar Handbook, 1982; Products Liability, 1984. Exec. articles editor U. Mich. Jour. Law Reform, 1980-81; contbg. editor Products Liability, 1983; mem. bd. editors Products Liability Newsletter, 1982— ; mem. bd. experts Lawyers Alert Newsmag. Contbr. articles to profl. jours. Mem. ABA (chmn. future programs and projects subcom., trial evidence com., sect. litigation, mem. products liability and consumer law com., tort and ins. practice sect.), Kansas City Bar Assn., Mo. Bar Assn. (fed. practice com.), Lawyers Assn. Kansas City, Assn. Trial Lawyers Am. (tort and aviation sects.), Mo. Assn. Trial Attys. (bd. govs.,pres.-elect), Univ. Mo.-Kansas City Alumni Assn. (chmn. career planning com.), Phi Kappa Phi, Omicron Delta Epsilon, Pi Sigma Alpha (pres.), Pi Kappa Delta. Republican. Club: Kansas City. Aviation, Product liability, Medical Negligence. Office: 1200 Main St Ste 3900 Kansas City MO 64105-2100

ROBBINS, IRA PAUL, law educator; b. Bklyn., Jan. 2, 1949; AB, U. Pa., 1970; JD, Harvard U., 1973. Bar: N.Y. 1974, U.S. Ct. Appeals (2d cir.) 1975, D.C. 1984. Law clk. to presiding justice U.S. Ct. Appeals (2d cir.), N.Y.C., 1973-75; assoc. prof. law, dir. Kans. Defender Project U. Kans., Lawrence, 1975-79; prof. law and justice Am. U., Washington, 1979—. Vis. prof. law Georgetown U. Law Ctr., Washington, 1982, 90; cons. Nat. Inst. Corrections, Washington, 1983—, Fed. Jud. Ctr., Washington, 1983—, also acting dir. Continuing Edn. and Tng. Div. Fed. Jud. Ctr., 1986; bd. dirs. D.C. Prisoners Legal Svcs. Inc.; cons. editor The Am. Univ. Press, Jour. Criminal Law & Criminology, Judicature, Fed. Probation, Justice Quar., Justice System Jour., State-Fed. Jud. Observer; cons. criminal rules com. Conf. of the U.S., 2001—. Author: Comparative Postconviction Remedies, 1980; Judicial Sabbaticals, 1987, The Legal Dimensions of Private Incarceration, 1988, Toward a More Just and Effective System of Review in State Death Penalty Cases, 1990, Habeas Corpus Checklists, 2003; editor, contbr. Prisoners' Rights Sourcebook, 1980, The Law and Processes of Post-Conviction Remedies, 1982, Prisoners and the Law, 2003; contbr. articles to profl. jours. Ethel and Raymond F. Rice scholar, 1978, Pauline Ruyle Moore scholar, 1980, 90, Barnard T. Welsh scholar, 1982—; Supreme Ct. fellow, 1985-86; named one of Outstanding Young Men Am., U.S. Jaycees, 1982. Recipient of Chief Judge John R. Brown Award for Jud. Scholarship and Edn., 1998. Mem. ABA (reporter study on pvt. prisons 1986-88, cons. 1986-90, study on death penalty habeas corpus 1988-90), Am. Law Inst., Assn. Am. Law Schs. (exec. coun. criminal justice sect. 1983-89), Internat. Assn. Penal Law, Am. Judicature Soc. (nat. coun. crime and delinquency 1997—), Phi Beta Kappa. Office: Am U Washington Coll Law 4801 Massachusetts Ave NW Washington DC 20016-8001

ROBBINS, JACK WINTON, lawyer; b. Flemington, Mo., Nov. 1, 1919; s. Winnie and Opal (Pitts) R.; m. Hilda Haynes, Feb. 2, 1946; children: Randel Bliss Brodrique, Mark Haynes Robbins. BS, U. North Tex., 1941; JD, Columbia U., 1943. Bar: N.Y. 1944, Pa. 1956, U.S. Supreme Ct. 1953. Law clk. N.Y. Ct. of Appeals, Albany, 1943-44; assoc. atty. Cravath, Swaine & Moore, N.Y.C., 1944-53; prosecutor Nuremberg (Germany) War Crimes Trials, 1946-48; counsel Pitcairn Trust Co., Jenkintown, Pa., 1953—. Bd. dirs. Upper Dublin Twp. Sch. Bd., Ft. Washington, Pa., 1960-73, Ursinus Coll., Collegeville, Pa., 1984—. Mem. ABA, Pa. Bar Assn., Phila. Bar Assn. Republican. Methodist. Corporate, general, Estate planning, General practice. Home: 3500 West Chester Pike Newtown Square PA 19073-Office: Pitcairn Trust Co 165 Township Line Rd Jenkintown PA 19046-3531

ROBBINS, NORMAN NELSON, lawyer; b. Detroit, Sept. 27, 1919; s. Charles and Eva (Gold) R.; m. Pamela Anne Eldred, April 22, 1946; children: Susan, Aimee. LLB, JD, Wayne State U., 1943. Bar: Mich. 1943. Pvt. practice, Birmingham, Mich., 1943—. Chmn. Mich. Bd. for Marriage Counselors, 1971-75; lectr. Inst. Continuing Legal Edn. Editor Mich. Family Law Jour., 1974—; mem. editorial bd. Am. Jour. Family Law; co-editor: Michigan Family Law, 2 vols., 1988; contbr. 600 articles to legal publs. Chmn. Wayne County unit Am. Cancer Soc., Detroit, 1971-76, Mich. Dept. Vets. Trust Fund, 1977-8. Capt. USMCR, 1943-46, PTO. Recipient Gov.'s award State of Mich., Cert. of Appreciation, Gov. of Mich., Cert. of Recognition, Detroit Common Coun. award Mich. Assn. Marriage Counselors, Lifetime Achievement award Mich. Family Law Sect. Mem. ABA (mem. family law coun. 1993-95, sr. editor ABA Family Adv. 1991—), Mich. Bar Assn. (chmn. family law sect. 1974-75), Oakland County Bar Assn., Am. Acad. Matrimonial Lawyers (pres. Mich. chpt. 1982), Am. Legion (judge adv. Mich. dept. 1968-69, comdr. Detroit chpt. 1970-71). Family and matrimonial. Office: 5543 Tadworth Pl West Bloomfield MI 48322-4016

ROBBINS, STEPHEN J. M. lawyer; b. Seattle, Apr. 13, 1942; s. Robert Mads and Aneita Elberta (West) R.; m. Nina Winifred Tanner, Aug. 11, 1967; children: Sarah E.T., Alicia S.T. AB, UCLA, 1964; JD, Yale U., 1971. Bar: D.C. 1973, U.S. Dist. Ct. D.C. 1973, U.S. Ct. Appeals (D.C. cir.) 1973, U.S. Ct. Appeals (3d cir.) 1973, U.S. Dist. Ct. (ea. and no. dists.) Calif. 1982, U.S. Dist. Ct. (cen. dist.) Calif. 1983, Supreme Ct. of Republic of Palau, 1994. Pres. U.S. Nat. Student Assn., Washington, 1964-65; dir. scheduling McGovern for Pres., Washington, 1971-72; assoc. Steptoe & Johnson, Washington, 1972-75; chief counsel spl. inquiry on food prices, com. on nutrition and human needs U.S. Senate, Washington, 1975; v.p., gen. counsel Straight Arrow Pubs., San Francisco, 1975-77; dep. dist. atty. City and County of San Francisco, 1977-78; regional counsel U.S. SBA, San Francisco, 1978-80; spl. counsel Warner-Amex Cable Communications, Sacramento, 1981-82; ptnr. McDonough, Holland and Allen, Sacramento, 1982-84; v.p. Straight Arrow Pubs., N.Y.C., 1984-86; gen. legal counsel Govt. State of Koror, Rep. of Palau, Western Caroline Islands, 1994-95; pvt. practice law, 1986—. Adj. prof. govt. Calif. State U., Sacramento, 1999—. Staff sgt. U.S. Army, 1966-68. Mem. ABA (sect. urban, state and local govt. sect. real property, probate and trust law, sect. natural resources energy, environ. law, forum com. on affordable housing and cmty. devel.), D.C. Bar, State Bar of Calif., Urban Land Inst., Am. Hist. Assn., Supreme Ct. Hist. Soc., Acad. Polit. Sci., Chamber Music Soc. of Sacramento, Oreg. Shakespeare Festival, Shaw Island Hist. Soc. Democrat. Unitarian Universalist. Avocations: theatre, art, hiking. Environmental, Land use and zoning (including planning), Property, real (including real estate development, water). Office: 2150 3rd Ave Sacramento CA 95818-3102

ROBEL, LAUREN, law educator; b. Dec. 1953; BA, Auburn U., 1978; JD, Ind. U., 1983. Law clk. to Hon. Jesse Eschbach, U.S. Ct. Appeals (7th cir.), 1983—85; acting dean, Val Nolan prof. law Ind. U. Sch. Law, Bloomington. Vis. faculty U. Panthenon-Assas, Paris; reporter rules com. U.S. Dist. Ct. (so. dist.) Ind.; mem. rules com. Ind. Supreme Ct. Contbr. articles to profl. jours.; author: Les États des Noirs: Federalisme et question raciale aux États-unis, 2000. Mem.: Ind. State Bar Women (Law Recognition award), Ind. Bar Found. (Pro Bono Publico award), Order of Coif. Office: Ind Univ Sch Law 211 S Indiana Ave Bloomington IN 47405*

ROBENALT, JOHN ALTON, lawyer; b. Ottawa, Ohio, May 2, 1922; s. Alton Ray and Kathryn (Straman) R.; m. Margaret Morgan Durbin, Aug. 25, 1951 (dec. July 1990); children: John F., William A., James D., Robert M., Mary K., Margaret E., Thomas D.; m. Nancy Leech Kidder, Sept. 21, 1991. BA, Miami U., 1943; LL.B., JD, Ohio State U., 1948. Bar: Ohio 1948. Asst. atty. gen., Ohio, 1949-51; practice in, 1951-59; acting municipal judge Lima Municipal Ct., 1955-59; partner Robenalt, Daley, Balyeat & Balyeat, 1959-82; ptnr. Robenalt, Kendall & Robenalt, 1983-85, Robenalt, Kendall, Rodabaugh & Staley, 1985-92, Robenalt & Robenalt, 1993—. Chmn. Lima March of Dimes, 1957-58; Bd. dirs. Lima Civic Center, pres., 1971-72; bd. dirs. Lima Rotating Fund; trustee Allen County Regional Transit Authority, Lima, pres., 1975— . Served with AUS, 1943-45. Mem. ABA, Ohio Bar Assn., Allen County Bar Assn. (pres. 1969-70), Am. Legion, Lima Automobile Club (bd. dirs., pres. 1975-82), Shawnee Country Club (pres. 1968-70), Ohio Automobile Club (trustee 1982-2002, chmn. 1995-97), Elks (bd. trustees 1991-97), Rotary, Delta Tau Delta, Phi Delta Phi. General practice, Probate (including wills, trusts), Property, real (including real estate development, water). Home: 1755 Shawnee Rd Apt 700 Lima OH 45805-3857

ROBERSON, BRUCE HEERDT, lawyer; b. Wilmington, Del., Mar. 7, 1941; s. A. L. and Virginia Amelia (Heerdt) R.; m. Mary E. Abrams; children: Cheryl Anne, David B., Douglas M. BS cum laude, Washington and Lee U., 1963; JD, U. Va., 1966. Bar: Va. 1966, Del. 1966, Fla. 1969. Assoc. Morris, Nichols, Arsht & Tunnell, Wilmington, 1966-67; assoc. Holland & Knight, Tampa, Fla., 1969-74; ptnr. Holland & Knight LLP, Tampa, Fla., 1975—. Contbg. editor Pratt's Banking and Lending Institution Forms, 1992—. Capt. U.S. Army, 1967-69 Decorated Bronze Star. Fellow Am. Bar Found. (life), Fla. Bar Found.(life); mem. ABA (bus. law sect. com. on consumer fin. svcs. 1976—, banking law com. 1980—, savs. instns. com. 1989-96), Am. Judicature Soc., Fla. Bar Assn. (corp. banking and bus. law sect. exec. coun. 1978-86, chmn. banking law com. 1982-84), Del. Bar Assn., Va. Bar Assn., Hillsborough County Bar Assn., Univ. Club, Tampa Yacht and Country Club, Lambda Chi Alpha. Republican. Methodist. Banking, Commercial, consumer (including collections, credit), Corporate, general. Office: Holland & Knight LLP PO Box 1288 Tampa FL 33601-1288 E-mail: broberso@hklaw.com.

ROBERSON, G. GALE, JR., lawyer, arbitrator; b. Chgo., Mar. 22, 1933; s. G. Gale and Charlotte D. R.; m. Ann Griesedieck, Jan. 3, 1957; children: Michael G., Christine R. Hurd. BA, Dartmouth Coll., 1955; LLB, Harvard U., 1960. Bar: Ill. 1960, U.S. Dist. Ct. (no. dist.) Ill. 1961. Assoc. Leibman, Williams, etc., Chgo., 1960-65; asst. counsel Fed. Res. Bank, Atlanta, 1965-66; ptnr., assoc. Quinn, Jacobs & Barry, Chgo., 1966-81; of counsel, ptnr. McBride Baker & Coles, Chgo., 1981—2002; of counsel Holland & Knight, LLC, Chgo., 2002—. Arbitrator, mediator NASD, N.Y.C., 1998—; lectr. in field. Contbr. articles to profl. jours. Bd. dirs. Jobs For Youth/Chgo., Inc., 1979—, pres., 1980-95; mem., chmn. Zoning Bd. Appeals, Wilmette, Ill., 1979-91. Lt. j.g. USN, 1955-57. Mem. ABA, Ill. State Bar Assn., Chgo. Bar Assn., Mich. Shores club. General civil litigation, Corporate, general, Securities. Home: 1351 Ashland Ave Wilmette IL 60091-1607 Office: Holland & Knight LLC 131 S Dearborn St Fl 31 Chicago IL 60603

ROBERSON, KELLY MCINTOSH, lawyer; b. Mobile, Ala., May 29, 1970; m. Richard James Roberson, Jr.. AB, U. Ga., 1993; JD, U. Miss., Oxford, 1996. Bar: Fla. 1997, U.S. Dist. Ct. (no. dist.) Fla. 1998. Assoc. Daniel & Komarek, Panama City, Fla., 1996—2001; asst. pub. defender Office of Herman Laramore Pub. Defender, 14th Jud. Cir., Panama City, 2001—. Unlicensed practice law com. Fla. Bar 14th Jud. Cir., 1999—2001; mem. young lawyer's divsn. 14th Jud. Cir., Panama City, 2000—. Mem. Jr. Svc. League, Panama City, 1998—. Mem.: Bay County Bar Assn. (pres., v.p., sec., treas. 1998—2001), Nat. Assn. Criminal Def. Attys., St. Andrew Bay Am. Inn of Ct. (barrister 1997—), Fla. Assn. Criminal Def. Attys. Republican. Episcopalian. Office: Office of Herman Laramore Pub Defender 115 E 4th St PO Box 580 Panama City FL 32402 Office Fax: 850-784-6160 . E-mail: kroberso@pd14.state.fl.us.

ROBERSON, LINDA, lawyer; b. Omaha, July 15, 1947; d. Harlan Oliver and Elizabeth Aileen (Good) R.; m. Gary M. Young, Aug. 20, 1970; children: Elizabeth, Katherine, Christopher. BA, Oberlin Coll., 1969; MS, U. Wis., 1970, JD, 1974. Bar: Wis. 1974, U.S. Dist. Ct. (we. dist.) Wis. 1974. Legis. atty. Wis. Legis. Reference Bur., Madison, 1974-76, sr. legis. atty., 1976-78; assoc. Rikkers, Koritzinsky & Rikkers, Madison, 1978-79; ptnr. Koritzinsky, Neider, Langer & Roberson, Madison, 1979-85, Stolper, Koritzinsky, Brewster & Neider, Madison, 1985-93, Balisle & Roberson, Madison, 1993—. Adj. faculty U. Wis. Law Sch., Madison, 1978—. Co-author: Real Women, Real Lives, 1981, Wisconsin's Marital Property Reform Act, 1984, Understanding Wisconsin's Marital Property Law, 1985, A Guide to Property Classification Under Wisconsin's Marital Property Act, 1986, Workbook for Wisconsin Estate Planners, 2d edit., 1993, 5th edit., 2003, Look Before You Leap, 1996, Family Estate Planning in Wis., 1992, rev. edit. 2003, The Marital Property Classification Handbook, 1999. Fellow Am. Acad. Matrimonial Lawyers (pres. Wis. chpt. 2001), Am. Bar Found.

(del. family law coun. of cmty. property states 1996—, chair-elect 2002—); mem. ABA, Wis. Bar Assn., Dane County Bar Assn., Legal Assn. Women, Nat. Assn. Elder Law Attys., Internat. Soc. Family Law, Family Law Coun. Cmty Property States (del. 1996, chair elect 2003). Estate planning, Family and matrimonial, Probate (including wills, trusts). Office: Balisle and Roberson PO Box 870 Madison WI 53701-0870 E-mail: lr@b-rlaw.com.

ROBERT, MAPIE, lawyer; b. Paris, Aug. 5, 1974; d. Jean Pierre and Nicole (Etcheto) Robert. ML private law, Paris U, Paris, France, 1996, ML pub. law, 1997; DEA bus. law, Paris, France, 1998. Bar: Paris. Assoc. Jeantet & Assoc., Paris, Ashurst, Norris, Crisp, Paris, White & Case, Paris. Home: 12 Rue de Veaduu 92100 Bon Cogue France Office: White & Case Bd de le Nade Ceine 75001 Paris France

ROBERT CARTERET, JEAN-YVES, lawyer; b. Paris, Feb. 20, 1948; s. Yves and Monique Robert Carteret; m. Valérie Constant, Oct. 1, 1977; children: Gwendoline, Tiffany, Soazic. Lic. in law, U. Paris, 1972; diploma, Sch. Oriental Langs., Paris, 1972; hon. degree, Inst. Higher Studies Nat. Def., Paris, 1983. Bar: Paris 1973. Pvt. practice, Paris, 1973—. Def. counsellor adviser to prefect of Paris, 1993-94; judge Cons. Prud'hommes, 1992-2002. Served with French Navy, 1974. Mem. Internat. Union Lawyers, Internat. Bar Assn., Amnesty Internat., Racing Club France, Yacht Club France, Wig and Pen Club (London). Roman Catholic. Avocations: golf, hunting, skiing, yachting. Home: 7 bd de la Reine 78000 Versailles France Office: 9 Av Frédéric Le Play 75007 Paris France E-mail: bobcart@carteret.org., law@carteret.org.

ROBERTS, BRIAN MICHAEL, lawyer; b. Cin., May 28, 1957; s. Shearl Joseph and Mary Ruth (Christian) R.; m. Carol Denise Zimmerman, July 28, 1979; children: Nicholas Brian, Mary Katelin, Kevin Matthew. BS in Bus., Miami U., Oxford, Ohio, 1979; JD, U. Dayton, 1982. Bar: Ohio 1982, U.S. Dist. Ct. (so. dist.) Ohio 1983, U.S. Ct. Appeals (6th cir.) 1984, U.S. Supreme Ct. 1988. Ptnr. Jablinski, Folino, Roberts & Martin Co. LPA, Dayton, 1982—. Organizer, scheduler legal presentations to engaged couples Family Life Office, Archdiocese of Cin., Dayton, 1982-92. Mem. Ohio State Bar Assn., Ohio Acad. Trial Lawyers, Dayton Bar Assn., Miami Valley Trial Lawyers Assn., Assn. Trial Lawyers Am. Republican. Roman Catholic. State civil litigation, Estate planning, Probate (including wills, trusts). Home: 3830 Gardenview Pl Dayton OH 45429-4517 Office: Jablinski Folino Roberts & Martin Co LPA PO Box 1266 Dayton OH 45402-9766 E-mail: brianr@jfrmlaw.com.

ROBERTS, BURK AUSTIN, lawyer; b. Albuquerque, Apr. 8, 1968; s. Thomas Franklin Jr. and Judy Jane Roberts; m. Cindy Rene Breaux, June 6, 1998. BA, U. Tex., 1989; JD, Baylor U., 1991. Bar: Tex. 1992. Ptnr. Roberts & Roberts LLP, Killeen, Tex., 1992—; city atty. City of Harker Heights, Tex., 1994—. Co-chair region 5 devel. Tex. Ctr. Legal Ethics & Professionalism, Austin, 1998-99. Mem. adv. bd. Killeen Salvation Army, 1993—, chair, 1996. Named Outstanding Young Man of Am., 1998. Fellow Tex. Bar Found., mem. Coll. State Bar Tex. State civil litigation, Family and matrimonial. Office: Roberts & Roberts LLP 324 E Avenue C Killeen TX 76541-5233

ROBERTS, BURTON BENNETT, lawyer, retired judge; b. N.Y.C., July 25, 1922; s. Alfred S. and Cecelia (Schanfein) R.; m. Gerhild Ukryn. BA, NYU, 1943, LL.M., 1953; LL.B., Cornell U., 1949. Bar: N.Y. 1949. Asst. dist. atty., New York County, 1949-66; chief asst. dist. atty. Bronx County, Bronx, N.Y., 1966-68, acting dist. atty., 1968-69, dist. atty., 1969-72; justice Supreme Ct. State N.Y., 1973-98, adminstrv. judge criminal br. Bronx County 12th Jud. Dist., 1984-98, adminstrv. judge civil br. Bronx County 12th Dist., 1988-98; ret., 1998; counsel Fischbein, Badillo, Wagner & Harding, 1999—. Pres. Bronx div. Hebrew Home for Aged, 1967-72. With U.S. Army, 1943-45. Decorated Purple Heart, Bronze Star with oak leaf cluster. Mem. Assn. Bar City N.Y., Am. Bar Assn., N.Y. Bar Assn., Bronx County Bar Assn., N.Y. State Dist. Attys. Assn. (pres. 1971-72) Jewish (exec. bd. temple). Home: 215 E 68th St Apt 19A New York NY 10021-5727 Office: Fischbein Badillo et al 909 3rd Ave New York NY 10022-4731 E-mail: broberts@fbwhlaw.com.

ROBERTS, CARL GEOFFREY, lawyer; b. Boston, June 17, 1948; s. Simon Matthew and Ruth (Gorfinkle) Roberts; m. Sharon Ash, Mar. 24, 1979 (div. June 19, 2002); 1 child, Dennis; m. Susan Busch, Dec. 28, 2002. BA, Harvard U., 1970; JD, U. Pa., 1974. Bar: Pa. 1974, U.S. Dist. Ct. (ea. dist.) Pa. 1974, U.S. Ct. Appeals (3d cir.) 1978, U.S. Supreme Ct. 1980, U.S. Ct. Claims 1980, U.S. Dist. Ct. (mid. dist.) Pa. 1986. Law clk. U.S. Dist. Ct. (ea. dist.) Pa., Phila., 1974-76; assoc. Dilworth, Paxson, Kalish & Kauffman, Phila., 1978-82, ptnr., 1982-92, Ballard, Spahr, Andrews & Ingersoll, Phila., 1992—. Bd. dirs. Phila. Chamber Ensemble, sec., 1977-92, pres., 1992-95; mem. Hillel com. U. Pa., 1999—, chair 2001—; bd. dirs. Hillel of Greater Phila., 2000—. Mem.: ABA (law practice mgmt. sect. sec. 2002—). Federal civil litigation, General civil litigation, Construction. Office: Ballard Spahr Andrews & Ingersoll 1735 Market St Fl 51 Philadelphia PA 19103-7599

ROBERTS, CHARLES BREN, lawyer; b. Washington DC, Oct. 28, 1949; s. Ray Oliver and Ruth B. (Barlow) R.; children: Elisha Ruthanne, Jacquelyn Celene. BS, Wright State U., 1974; JD, U. Dayton, 1978; postgrad., Ohio State U., 1980, Harvard Law Sch., 1984. Bar: Ohio 1978, D.C. 1983, Va. 1986, U.S. Supreme Ct. 1987, U.S. Dist. Ct. (ea. dist.) Va., 1988, U.S. Ct. Appeals (4th cir.) 1990. Legal intern U.S. Atty's Office, Dayton, Ohio, 1977-78; law clk. Ohio Supreme Ct., Columbus, Ohio, 1978-80; congl. intern U.S. Gen. Acctg. Office, Washington, summer 1977, atty. advisor, 1980-86; sr. ptnr. Charles B. Roberts and Assocs. P.C., Woodbridge, Va., 1986—. Mem. bus. adv. coun. Nat. Rep. Congl. Com. With USN, 1971—77. Recipient Disting. Svc. award Washington Songwriter's Assn., 1986, Acad. scholarship U. Dayton Law Sch., 1977, 78, Registry of America's Outstanding Profls. Award. Mem. ABA, Va. Trial Lawyers Assn., Fairfax County Bar Assn., Prince William County Bar Assn., Woodbridge C. of C., Republican Nat. Congressional Com. Bus. Adv. Coun. Avocations: racquetball, running. General civil litigation, Family and matrimonial, Personal injury (including property damage). Office: Charles B Roberts & Assocs PC 1308 Devils Reach Rd Ste 303 Woodbridge VA 22192 E-mail: info@charlesrobertslaw.com.

ROBERTS, CHRISTOPHER CHALMERS, lawyer; b. Washington, Oct. 12, 1950; s. Chalmers McGeagh and Lois (Hall) R.; m. Mary Hammond Higgins, Apr. 23, 1983; children: Kevin, Morgan, Rachel, Sarah. BA, Amherst Coll., 1972; JD, Georgetown U., 1975, MLT, 1981. Bar: Md. 1975, D.C. 1976, U.S. Dist. Ct. Md. 1978, U.S. Ct. Appeals (4th cir.) 1979, U.S. Dist. Ct. D.C. 1980, U.S. Ct. Appeals (D.C. cir.) 1980. Law clk. to presiding justice Ct. Appeals of Md., Annapolis, 1974-76; assoc. Shulman, Rogers, Gandal, Pordy & Ecker, P.A., Rockville, Md., 1978-83, ptnr., 1984—98. Counsel Montgomery County Students Automotive Trades Found., Md., 1984-99. Editor: Jour. Georgetown Law, 1973—75; contbr. articles to legal jours. Mem. Amherst Alumni Assn. Washington (past officer, pres.). Corporate, general, Mergers and acquisitions, Securities. Office: Shulman Rogers Gandal Pordy & Ecker 11921 Rockville Pike Ste 300 Rockville MD 20852-2743 E-mail: croberts@srgpe.com.

ROBERTS, DELMAR LEE, editor; b. Raleigh, N.C., Apr. 9, 1933; s. James Delmer and Nellie Brockelbank (Tyson) R. BS in Textile Mgmt., NC State U., 1956; postgrad., Inst. Polit. Studies, U. Paris, 1963; MA in Journalism, U. SC, 1974. Product devel. engr. U.S. Rubber Co. (Uniroyal), Winnsboro, SC, 1959—63; process improvement engr. Allied Chem. Co., Irmo, S.C., 1965-67; assoc. editor S.C. History Illustrated Mag., Columbia, 1970; editor-in-chief, editl. v.p. Sandlapper-The Mag. of S.C., Columbia, 1968-74; mng. editor, art dir. Legal Econs. mag. of the ABA, Chgo., 1975-89, Law Practice Mgmt. mag. of the ABA, Chgo., 1990-2000, editor emeritus, 2000—. Editor: The Best of Legal Economics, 1979; freelance editor and/or designer of over 35 books. Active World Affairs Coun. Columbia, 1997—; 1st v.p. English-Speaking Union, 1996-97, pres. 1997—. With U.S. Army, 1956-58. Hon. fellow Coll. of Law Practice Mgmt., Golden, Colo., 1995—. Mem. Soc. Profl. Journalists, Capital City Club (Columbia), Phi Kappa Tau, Kappa Tau Alpha. Avocations: european travel, turkish carpet/kilim collecting, antique collecting.

ROBERTS, DERRICK STACY, federal official; b. Tallahassee, Aug. 5, 1970; s. Kelly Carl and Beverly (Peoples) Roberts; m. Kenya Antrel Jones, Aug. 18, 1996; 1 child, Kaiya Danielle. BS in Polit. Sci., Fla. State U., 1992; JD, U. Miami, 1996. Bar: Fla. 1996, U.S. Dist. Ct. (so. dist.) Fla. 1998. Asst. state atty. State Atty.'s Office, West Palm Beach, Fla., 1996—2001; asst. atty. gen. Atty. Gen.'s Office, Ft. Lauderdale, Fla., 2001—. Office: Office Atty Gen 110 Tower 110 SE 6th St Fort Lauderdale FL 33301 Office Fax: 954-713-3077.

ROBERTS, E. F. lawyer, educator; b. 1930; m. Alice A. Dunn, July 4, 1955; children: Martha, Ernest III, Michael, Marianne. BA, Northeastern U., Boston, 1952; LL.B., Boston Coll., 1954. Bar: Mass. 1954. Asst. prof. law Villanova U., Pa., 1957-59, assoc. prof. law, 1959-60, prof. law, 1960-64, Cornell U., Ithaca, N.Y., 1964-96, Edwin H. Woodruff prof. law, emeritus prof., 1996. Vis. prof. Nottingham U., Eng., 1962-63, Harvard U., 1983; mem. edn. panel Environ. Law Reporter, 1971-80; cons. in field. Author: Public Regulation of Title Insurance, 1960, Land Use Planning, 2d edit., 1975, Law and the Preservation of Agricultural Land, 1982, (with Strong et al) McCormick on Evidence, 5th edit., 1999. Mem. Am. Law Inst. (life). Office: Cornell U Sch Law Ithaca NY 14853 E-mail: e-f-roberts@postoffice.law.cornell.edu.

ROBERTS, JACK EARL, lawyer, ski resort operator, wood products company executive, real estate developer; b. L.A., Nov. 5, 1928; s. James Earle and Illa Ann (Morgan) R.; m. Marilyn Humphreys, Sept. 13, 1954; children: Ronda, Cyndi, Scott, Robynne, Craig. BS in Acctg. and Bus. Adminstrn., Brigham Young U., 1952; JD, George Washington U., 1955, LLM in Taxation (Teaching fellow), 1956. Bar: Calif. 1957; CPA, Ariz. Pvt. practice, L.A.; atty. Office Chief Counsel, IRS, L.A., 1956-60; mem. firm Roberts, Carmack, Johnson, Poulson & Harmer, L.A., 1961-78; pres. Park West Ski Resort, Park City, Utah, 1975-88; pres., dir. Accudyne Corp., Los Angeles, 1972-89, Richmark Corp., Los Angeles, 1972-77; chmn., dir. Comml. Wood Products Co., Los Angeles, 1968—; pres., dir. Snyderville Devel. Co., Inc., Utah, 1978-94, Community Water Co., Salt Lake City, 1987-2000, Roberts Mgmt. Corp., Salt Lake City, 1988—, Ste. Vacations, Inc., Salt Lake City, 1989—. Contbr. articles on legal subjects to tech. jours. Pres. Westwood Rep. Club, 1968; mem. cen. coms. Calif. State, L.A. County Rep. Party, 1974-77; mem. Utah State Cen. and Exec. Coms., 1981-96, Summit County Rep. cen. and exec. coms., 1978-84; chmn. Summit County, 1981-83; chmn. Utah State Rep. Com., 1988-89, state sec., 1986-88. Mem. Calif. Bar Assn., D.C. Bar Assn. Office: 2726 E Wasatch Dr Salt Lake City UT 84108-1929

ROBERTS, JEAN REED, lawyer; b. Washington, Dec. 19, 1939; d. Paul Allen and Esther (Kishter) Reed; m. Thomas Gene Roberts, Nov. 26, 1958; children: Amy, Rebecca, Nathanial. AB in Journalism, U. N.C., 1966; JD, Ariz. State U., 1973. Bar: Ariz. 1974. Pvt. practice Jean Reed Roberts P.C., Scottsdale, Ariz., 1975—; with Fin. Health Advisors, Scottsdale Healthcare. Judge pro tem Superior Ct., Maricopa County, Ariz., 1979-92; judge pro tem Ariz. Ct. Appeals, 1995-99; chmn., adv. endowment bd. City of Scottsdale, Ariz., 1994-98; past pres. Charter 100 of Phoenix. Recipient Dorothy Wiley award YWCA Maricopa County, 1999. Mem. AAUW, Ariz. Bar Assn., Ariz. Women's Town Hall, Scottsdale Bar Assn. Democrat. Jewish. Estate planning, Probate (including wills, trusts), Elder. Office: 8669 E San Alberto Dr Ste 101 Scottsdale AZ 85258-4309 E-mail: jean.roberts@azbar.org.

ROBERTS, JOHN DERHAM, lawyer; b. Orlando, Fla., Nov. 1, 1942; s. Junius P. and Mary E. Roberts; m. Malinda K. Swineford, June 11, 1965; 1 child, Kimberlyn Amanda. Cert., Richmond (Va.) Bus. Coll., 1960; BS, Hampden-Sydney (Va.) Coll., 1964; LLB, Washington & Lee U., 1968. Bar: Va. 1968, Fla. 1969, U.S. Supreme Ct. 1969, U.S. Ct. Customs and Patent Appeals 1970, U.S. Tax Ct. 1970, U.S. Ct. Appeals (5th cir.) 1970, U.S. Ct. Appeals (9th cir.) 1974, U.S. Supreme Ct. 1969. Law clk. U.S. Dist. Ct., Jacksonville, Fla., 1968-69; assoc. Phillips, Kendrick, Gearhart & Aylor, Arlington, Va., 1969-70; asst. U.S. Atty. mid. dist. Fla. U.S. Dept. Justice, Jacksonville, 1970-74, Dist. of Alaska, Anchorage, 1974-77, U.S. magistrate judge, 1977—. Bd. dirs. Teen Challenge Alaska, Anchorage, 1984-93; chmn. Eagle Scout Rev. Bd., 1993—; bd. dirs. Alaska Youth for Christ, 1993-96; govs.'s Prayer Breakfast Com., 1994—, vice-chair, 1998—. Recipient Citizenship award DAR, Anchorage, 1984, plaque, U.S. Navy, Citizen Day, Adak, Alaska, 1980. Mem. ABA, Nat. Conf. Spl. Ct. Judges (exec. bd. 1985-92), 9th Cir. Conf. Magistrates (exec. bd. 1982-85, chmn. 1984-85), Alaska Bar Assn., Anchorage Bar Assn., Chi Phi, Psi Chi, Phi Alpha Delta. Republican. Office: US Magistrate Judge 222 W 7th Ave Unit 46 Anchorage AK 99513-7504

ROBERTS, MARK SCOTT, lawyer; b. Fullerton, Calif. s. Emil Seidel and Theda (Wymer) R. BA in Theater, Pepperdine U., 1975; JD, Western State U., 1978; cert. civil trial advocacy program, U. Calif., San Francisco, 1985; cert. program of instrn. for lawyers, Harvard U., 1990. Bar: Calif. 1980, U.S. Dist. Ct. (cen. dist.) Calif. 1980, U.S. Supreme Ct. 1989, U.S. Ct. Mil. Appeals 1989, U.S. Tax Ct. 1990. Prin. Mark Roberts & Assocs., Fullerton, Calif., 1980—. Instr. bus. law Biola U., La Mirada, Calif., 1980-84; judge pro tem Orange County Superior Ct., Santa Ana, 1989—; adj. prof. wills and trusts Trinity Law Sch., Santa Ana, 2000—. Co-author: Legacy-Plan, Protect and Preserve Your Estate, 1996, Generations Planning Your Legacy, 1999. Mem. Calif. State Bar Assn., Orange County Bar Assn. (charter), Nat. Network Estate Planning Attys., Soc. Cert. Sr. Advisors. Estate planning, Probate (including wills, trusts). Office: 1440 N Harbor Blvd Ste 900 Fullerton CA 92835-4122

ROBERTS, MARY ELLEN, judge; b. Bellingham, Wash., Oct. 12, 1958; d. James Gerald and Lois Jean Roberts; m. James Lawrence Brewer, Apr. 1, 1990; children: Emma Elizabeth Brewer Hite, Alexander Roberts Brewer. BS in Math., U. Puget Sound, 1981; JD, U. Wash., 1984. Bar: Wash. 1985, U.S. Dist. Ct. (we. dist.) Wash. 1986, U.S. Dist. Ct. (ea. dist.) Wash. 2002, U.S. Ct. Appeals (9th cir.) 1987, U.S. Supreme Ct. 1990. Law clk. to Hon. Gerard M. Shellan King County Superior Ct., Seattle, 1984—85; staff atty. Pub. Defender, Seattle, 1985—86; dep. pros. atty. King County Pros. Office, Seattle, 1986—92; assoc. Frank and Rosen, Seattle, 1992—95; ptnr. Frank Freed Roberts Subit & Thomas LLP, Seattle, 1996—2003; judge King County Superior Ct., Seattle, 2003—. Coop. atty. ACLU, Seattle, 1992—2003; mediator, arbitrator U.S. Dist. Ct. (we. dist.) Wash., Seattle, 2002—03; arbitrator King County Superior Ct., Seattle, 1990—2003. Spkr., mem. N.W. Women's Law Ctr., Seattle, 1986—; mem. civil rights pro bono screening panel U.S. Dist. Ct., Seattle, 1997—2001; chmn. Pacific Coast Labor and Employment Law Conf., Seattle, 2000—01. Mem.: King County Bar Assn. (chmn. labor and employment sect. 2001—02), Nat. Employment Lawyers Assn. (convention chmn. 2001), Wash. State Trial Lawyers Assn. (chmn. employment sect. 1998—2000), Wash. Employment Lawyers Assn. (bd. dirs. 1993—2003, chmn. 1999—2000). Avocations: reading, hiking. Office: King County Superior Ct 516 Third Ave Seattle WA 98104-2381

ROBERTS, PAMELA J. lawyer; BA in Econs., U. Calif., Berkeley, 1977; JD, Southwestern U., 1980. Cert.: Supreme Ct. S.C. (mediator) 1997, bar: S.C., Ga., Calif., U.S. Dist. Ct. S.C., U.S. Dist. Ct. (no. and mid. dists.) Ga., U.S. Dist. Ct. (no. dist.) Calif., U.S. Ct. Appeals (4th, 9th and 11th cirs.), U.S. Supreme Ct. Ptnr. Nelson, Mullins, Riley & Scarborough LLP, Colubmia, SC. Instr. Harvard Law Sch., 1999; mediation instr. U.S. Dept. Justice Advocacy Ctr.; presenter in field. Chairwoman bd. trustees EdVenture Children's Mus.; mem. adv. bd. Trinity Housing Corp.; bd. dirs. YWCA of the Midlands. Fellow: S.C. Bar Found., Am. Bar Found.; mem.: ABA (bd. govs. 2002—, former mem. Commn. on Women in the Profession, former mem. Commn. on Opportunities for Minorities in the Profession, chairwoman young lawyers divsn., mem. nominating com., mem. spl. com. on governance), U.S. Fourth Cir. Jud. Conf., Richland County Bar Assn., S.C. Women Lawyers Assn. (bd. dirs., pres. 1999—2001), S.C. Bar (bd. govs., ho. dels.), Nat. Bar Assn., Am. Judicature Soc., Phi Alpha Delta. Office: 3rd Fl 1330 Lady St PO Box 11070 Columbia SC 29211*

ROBERTS, PATRICIA SUSAN, lawyer; b. Hammond, Ind., Sept. 1, 1953; d. Wayne Thomas and Lois (Schurgers) R.; m. James Stanley Kowalik, July 27, 1985. BA, Ind. U., 1975, JD, 1978. Bar: U.S. Dist. Ct. (so. dist.) Ind. 1978, U.S. Supreme Ct. 1987. Rep. State Farm Ins. Co., Indpls., 1978-79; atty. United Farm Bur. Mut. Ins. Co., Indpls., 1979-85; sr. corp. counsel Farm Family Ins. Cos., Indpls., 1985—. Mem. ABA (corp. counsel com. 1988). Corporate, general, Insurance, Pension, profit-sharing, and employee benefits. Home: 2018 E 106th St Carmel IN 46032-4008 Office: United Farm Family Ins Co 225 S East St Indianapolis IN 46202-4058 E-mail: pat.roberts@infarmbureau.com.

ROBERTS, PATRICK KENT, lawyer; b. Waynesville, Mo., Feb. 9, 1948; s. J. Kent and Winona (Clark) R.; m. Jeanne Billings, April 17, 1976; children: Christopher, Kimberly, Courtney. Student, U. Ill., Urbana, 1970; AB, U. Mo., 1970, JD, 1973. Bar: Mo. 1974, U.S. Dist. Ct. (we. dist.) Mo. 1974, U.S. Ct. Appeals (8th cir.) 1979. Lawyer U.S. Senator Stuart Symington, Columbia, Mo., 1973-76; ptnr. Daniel, Clampett, Powell & Cunningham, Springfield, Mo., 1976—2001; of counsel Cunningham, Harpool & Cordonnier, Springfield, 2002—. Adj. prof. Webster U., 2000—. Mem. ctrl. com. Greene County Dems., Springfield, 1982-84, 88-90. Mem. ABA, Mo. Orgn. Def. Lawyers, Mo. Bar Assn., Springfield Met. Bar Assn. Lodges: Rotary. Democrat. Methodist. General civil litigation, Insurance, Personal injury (including property damage). Office: Cunningham Harpool & Cordonnier PO Box 10306 3171 E Sunshine St Springfield MO 65804-2056

ROBERTS, RICHARD C., III, lawyer; b. Jackson, Miss., Mar. 18, 1951; BA, U. Miss., 1973, JD with distinction, 1976. Bar: Miss. 1976, U.S. Dist. Ct. (no. and so. dists.) Miss. 1976, U.S. Ct. Appeals (5th cir.) 1976, U.S. Ct. Appeals (11th cir.) 1981, U.S. Supreme Ct. 1989. Pvt. practice, Jackson, Miss. Mem.: ABA (sect. on family law, gen. practice, solo and small firm practice), Nat. Lawyer's Assn., Bar Assn. 5th Fed. Cir., Miss. Bar (chmn. solo and small firm practitioner's task force 1993—94, exec. com. family law sect. 1994—95, bd. bar commrs. 1996—99, nominating com. 1998—99, bench-bar liaison standing com. 2001—, sect. litigation and gen. practice, labor and employment, chmn. 1996), Hinds County Bar Assn. (bd. dirs. 1990—96, sec.-treas. 1992—93, pres. 1994—95, chmn. long range planning com. 1995—97), Fed. Bar Assn. (pres. Miss. chpt. 1987—88, nat. coun. 1988, jud. liaison for U.S. Dist. Cts.-So. Dist. Miss. 1989), Am. Inss of Ct., Phi Kappa Phi. Family and matrimonial, Labor (including EEOC, Fair Labor Standards Act, labor-management relations, NLRB, OSHA). Office: Richard C Roberts III PO Box 55882 814 N President St Jackson MS 39296-5882*

ROBERTS, SIDNEY I. lawyer; b. Bklyn., Nov. 29, 1913; s. David I. and Ray (Bleicher) Robinovitz; m. Arlene Lee Aron, June 4, 1961; 1 son, Russell Lewis. BBA, CCNY, 1935; LL.B. magna cum laude, Harvard U., 1938. Bar: N.Y. 1938; C.P.A., N.Y. With Michael Schimmel & Co. (C.P.A.s), N.Y.C., 1938-39, S.D. Leidesdorf & Co. (C.P.A.s), N.Y.C., 1939-49; with firm Roosevelt, Freidin & Littauer, N.Y.C., 1950-56, Anderson & Roberts, N.Y.C., 1956-57, Roberts & Holland, N.Y.C., 1957-94. Adj. prof. law Columbia U., 1971-78; mem. adv. council Internat. Bur. Fiscal Documentation. Author (with William C. Warren): U.S. Income Taxation of Foreign Corporations and Nonresident Aliens, 1966; author: (with others) Annotated Tax Forms: Practice and Procedure, 1970; editor: Legislative History of United States Tax Conventions, 18 vols., 1986—2001; contbr. articles to profl. jours. Mem. Internat. Bar Assn., ABA (sect. on taxation, council dir. 1970-73, chmn. com. on cooperation with state and local bar assns. 1968-70, chmn. com. on taxation of fgn. income 1963-64), N.Y. State Bar Assn. (tax sect. exec. com. 1967-87, chmn. com. on tax sect. planning 1968-70, chmn. com. on tax policy 1970-72), Assn. of Bar of City of N.Y., N.Y. State Soc. CPA's, Internat. Fiscal Assn. (mem. exec. com. 1972-77, pres. U.S.A. br. 1972-73). Jewish. Corporate taxation, Personal income taxation. Office: 145 Central Park W New York NY 10023-2004 E-mail: arsir@erols.com.

ROBERTS, THOMAS ALBA, lawyer; b. Ft. Wayne, Ind., Sept. 7, 1946; s. Jack and Elizabeth (Wallace) R.; m. Mary Alice Buckley, Aug. 11, 1973; children: Kaitrin M., John A., Kara B. BA, Georgetown U., 1969, JD, 1972. Bar: N.Y. 1973, U.S. Dist. Ct. (so. dist.) N.Y. 1973, U.S. Ct. Appeals (2d cir.) 1973, Tex. 1976, U.S. Supreme Ct. 1977, U.S. Dist. Ct. (so. dist.) Tex. 1978, U.S. Ct. Appeals (5th and 11th cirs.) 1982. Assoc. Winthrop, Stimson, Putnam & Roberts, N.Y.C., 1972-76; ptnr. Moore & Peterson, Dallas, 1976-89, mng. ptnr., 1980-88; ptnr. Johnson & Gibbs, Dallas, 1989-92; sr. ptnr. Weil, Gotshal & Manges, Dallas, N.Y.C., 1992—. Chmn. Internat. Corp. Practice Group, 1997—, chmn. corp. dept., 2001—, mem. mgmt. com., 1997—2001; adj. prof. law So. Meth. U., Dallas, 1977—78; lectr. in field. Lectr. in field. Mem. fin. com. St. Rita Ch., Dallas, 1983—88; mem. Ch. of the Resurrection; bd. dirs. Make-A-Wish Found. Met. N.Y., 1998—, Make-A-Wish of Am., 2002—. Mem. ABA, Tex. Bar Assn., Dallas Bar Assn., Assn. of Bar of City of N.Y. Roman Catholic. Avocations: skiing, golf, literature. Corporate, general, Mergers and acquisitions, Securities. Home: 133 Grandview Ave Rye NY 10580-2030 E-mail: thomas.roberts@weil.com.

ROBERTS, VIRGIL PATRICK, lawyer, business executive; b. Ventura, Calif., Jan. 4, 1947; s. Julius and Emma D. (Haley) R.; m. Brenda Cecilia Banks, Nov. 10, 1979; children: Gisele Simone, Hayley Tasha. AA, Ventura Coll., 1966; BA, UCLA, 1968; JD, Harvard U., 1972. Bar: Calif. 1972. Assoc. Pacht, Ross, Warne Bernhardt & Sears, L.A., 1972-76; ptnr. Manning, Reynolds & Roberts, L.A., 1976-79, Manning & Roberts, 1980-81; mng. ptnr. Bobbitt & Roberts, 1995—; exec. v.p., gen. counsel Solar Records, L.A., 1981—; pres. Dick Griffey Prodns., L.A., 1982—, Solar Records, 1988—; judge pro tem L.A., Beverly Hills Mcpl. Cts., 1975—. Bd. dirs. Broadway Fed. Bank. Past bd. dirs. L.A. Black Leadership Coalition, L.A. Mus. African Am. Art, Beverly Hills Bar Assn., L.A. Legal Aid Found.; bd. dirs. Coro Found., 1984-90, L.A. Ednl. Alliance for Restructuring Now, Cmty. Build; bd. dirs. Calif. Cmty. Found., 1991—, chmn. bd., 1999—; past pres. Beverly Hills Bar Scholarship Found.; commr. Calif. Commn. for Tchr. Credentialing, 1980-83; chmn. L.A. Ednl. Partnership, 1989—, v.p. 1983-89; vice-chmn. Nat. Pub. Edn. Fund Network; chmn. bd. dirs. L.A. Annenberg Met. Project; trustee Com. Econ. Devel., 1991—, Occidental Coll., Marlborough Sch.; mem. bd. councillors UCLA. Recipient NAACP Legal Def. Fund Equal Justice award, 1988, Rose award U. So. Calif., 1998. Mem. Recording Industry Assn. Am., Black Entertainment and Sports Lawyers (treas., bd. dirs. 1982—). Lead atty. for NAACP in Crawford vs. Bd. Edn. desegregation case, L.A., 1979-80. Entertainment. Address: 4820 Vista De Oro Ave Los Angeles CA 90043-1611 Office: Bobbitt & Roberts 1620 26th St Ste 150 Santa Monica CA 90404-4067

ROBERTS, WILLIAM B. lawyer, business executive; b. Detroit, Aug. 23, 1939; s. Edwin Stuart and Marjorie Jean (Wardle) R.; m. Cathleen Anne Thompson, Sept. 1, 1962; children: Bradford William, Brent William, Katrina Marjorie. BA, Mich. State U., 1961; JD with distinction, U. Mich., 1963; China law diploma, U. East Asia, Macau, 1989. Bar: Mo. 1964, Fla. 1983, U.S. Dist. Ct. (ea. dist.) Mo. 1964, U.S. Dist. Ct. (mid. dist.) Fla. 1993. Mem. firm Thompson & Mitchell, St. Louis, 1963-67; atty. Monsanto Co., 1967-70; sr. exec. v.p. adminstrn., sec., gen. counsel Chromalloy Am. Corp. (successor Segua Corp. N.Y.), St. Louis, 1970-78, exec. v.p.-adminstrn., gen. counsel, sec. Clayton, Mo., 1978-82; pvt. practice law, 1983-87; mng. ptnr. Roberts and Nordahl, St. Louis and Naples, Fla., 1988-89, Law Offices of William B. Roberts, St. Louis and Naples, 1989-90, Darrow & Roberts, P.A., Naples, 1992-93; pres., mng. dir. Law Offices of William B. Roberts, Naples, 1994—, Kansas City, Mo., 1999—. Pres., mng. dir. The Fairborne Group, Ltd., St. Louis and Naples, 1988-91, William B. Roberts & Assocs. Co., Merger and Acquisitions Specialists, 1982—; mem. exam. com. of policyowners Northwestern Mut. Life Ins. Co., Milw., 1978; del. to U.S.-China Joint Session on Trade Investment and Econ. Law, Beijing, 1987; sports rep. Steve Carlton, St. Louis Cardinals, Phila. Phillies baseball clubs, 1987-89; pres., CEO Tropical Tracks, Inc., Naples, 1994—. Mem. ABA, Fed. Bar Assn. (Mid. Dist. Fla.), Mo. Bar Assn., St. Louis Bar Assn. (chmn. antitrust sect. 1973), Fla. Bar Assn., Collier County Bar Assn., Delta Theta Phi. Methodist. Corporate, general, Private international, Public international. Home: 133 Crestview Terr Lake Placid FL 33852 Also: 321 NE Landings Dr Lees Summit MO 64064-1586

ROBERTS, WILLIAM EVERETT, lawyer; b. Pierre, S.D., May 12, 1926; s. Everett David and Bonnie (Martin) R.; m. Cynthia Cline, July 18, 1953; children: Catherine C. Roberts-Martin, Laura M., Nancy F., David H. BS, U. Minn., 1947; LLB, Yale U., 1950. Bar: Ind. 1950, U.S. Supreme Ct. 1964. Employee, ptnr. Duck and Neighbours, Indpls., 1950-58; ptnr. Cadick, Burns, Duck & Neighbours, Indpls., 1958-60, Roberts, Ryder, Rogers & Scism, Indpls., 1960-85, Barnes & Thornburg, Indpls., 1986-93, of counsel, 1994—. Pres., bd. dirs. Park-Tudor Sch., Indpls., 1982-83; elder Second Presbyn. Ch., Indpls., 1962—; trustee Indpls. Mus. Art, 1978—; pres. New Hope of Ind., Indpls., 1986-87. Fellow Am. Bar Found.; mem. ABA, Ind. Bar Assn., Indpls. Bar Assn., Rotary, Meridian Hills Country Club (pres. 1983-84). Republican. Home: 10466 Spring Highland Dr Indianapolis IN 46290-1101 Office: Barnes & Thornburg 11 S Meridian St Ste 1313 Indianapolis IN 46204-3535

ROBERTS, WILLIAM H. lawyer; b. Buffalo, June 14, 1945; s. Esther C. Roberts and William H. Roberts, Jr.. JD, U. Pa., Phila., 1970; AB, Harvard Coll., Cambridge, MA, 1967. Bar: Pa. 1970, U.S. Ct. Appeals (3d cir.) 1972, U.S. Supreme Ct. 1974, U.S. Ct. Appeals (11th cir.) 1982, U.S. Claims Ct. 1986, U.S. Ct. Appeals (4th cir.) 1987, U.S. Ct. Appeals (9th cir.) 2000. Ptnr. Blank Rome Comisky & McCauley LLP, Phila., 1977—. Co-author: (book) Com. Free Speech, 1985. Trustee The Curtis Inst. of Music, Phila., 1997—2002; trustee and Pres. Chamber Orch. of Phila., Phila., 1988—2002; Trustee Harvard Rev. of Philosophy, Cambridge, Mass., 1993—2002. Named Disting. Honoree, Nat. Assn. of Fundraising Execs., 2002. Mem.: Phila. Bot. Club, Harvard Club NYC. Avocations: violin, botany, salmon fishing. Antitrust, Appellate, Professional liability.

ROBERTSON, EDWIN DAVID, lawyer; b. Roanoke, Va., July 5, 1946; s. Edwin Traylor and Norma Burns (Bowles) R.; m. Anne Littelle Ferratt, Sept. 7, 1968, 1 child, Thomas Therit. BA with honors, U. Va., 1968, LLB, 1971. Bar: N.Y. 1972, U.S. Ct. Appeals (2d cir.) 1972, U.S. Dist. Ct. (ea. and so. dists.) N.Y. 1973, U.S. Supreme Ct. 1975, U.S. Dist. Ct. (ea. dist.) Mich. 1986. Assoc. Cadwalader, Wickersham & Taft, N.Y.C., 1972-80, ptnr., 1980—. Bd. dirs. Early Music Found. N.Y.C., 1983-99, chmn., 1993-99; bd. dirs. Oratorio Soc. of N.Y.C., 1988—, sec., 1991—. 1st lt. USAF, 1971-72. Echols scholar. Mem. ABA, Fed. Bar Coun., N.Y. County Lawyers Assn. (chmn. bankruptcy com. 1983-87, chmn. fin. com., bd. dirs. 1985-88, 95-99, 2000—, investment com. 1992—, exec. com. 1996—, treas. 2001-2002, v.p. 2002-), N.Y. State Bar Assn. (ho. of dels. 2001—, nominatng com. 2002-), Assn. Bar City N.Y., Soc. Colonial Wars, Down Town Assn., Jefferson Soc., Echols Scholar, judge, Ct. of Review, Protestant Episcopal Ch., Order of Coif, Phi Beta Kappa, Phi Kappa Psi. Republican. Episcopalian. Federal civil litigation, Libel, Securities. Home: 315 E 72nd St New York NY 10021-4625 Office: Cadwalader Wickersham & Taft 100 Maiden Ln New York NY 10038-4818 E-mail: darob@cwt.com.

ROBERTSON, HUGH DUFF, lawyer; b. Grosse Pointe, Mich., Mar. 14, 1957; s. Hugh Robertson and Louise (Grey) Bollinger; m. Mercedes Dano, May 3, 1997. BBA in Fin., U. Wis., Whitewater, 1978; JD, Whittier Coll., 1982. Bar: Calif. 1983, U.S. Tax Ct. 1984, U.S. Supreme Court, 1999. Pres., CEO, A. Morgan Maree Jr. & Assocs., Inc., L.A., 1979—. Mem. ABA (forum com. on entertainment 1982—), State Calif., L.A. County Bar Assn., Beverly Hills Bar Assn., Acad. TV Arts and Scis., Am. Film Inst., Phi Alpha Delta. Republican. Episcopalian. Avocations: sports, swimming. Entertainment, Finance, Property, real (including real estate development, water). Office: A Morgan Maree Jr & Assocs 1125 Gayley Ave Los Angeles CA 90024-3403

ROBERTSON, J. MARTIN, lawyer; b. Danville, Ill., Apr. 30, 1952; s. Calloway Middleton and Barbara (Holland) R. AB in Polit. Sci., Miami U., Oxford, Ohio, 1974; JD, U. Cin., 1978; postgrad., Ohio State U., 1978-79. Bar: Ohio 1978, U.S. Dist. Ct. (so. dist.) Ohio 1980, U.S. Dist. Ct. (no. dist.) Calif. 1984, Calif. 1989, U.S. Dist. Ct. (so. dist.) Calif. 1989, U.S. Dist. Ct. (ea. and ctrl. dists.) Calif. 1992, U.S. Ct. Appeals (9th cir.) 1992, U.S. Dist. Ct. (no. dist.) Tex. 1998, U.S. Ct. Appeals (5th cir.) 1998, Tex. 1999, Alaska 2001, U.S. Dist. Ct. Alaska 2002. Atty. Southeastern Ohio Legal Services, Chillicothe and Steubenville, 1979-80; staff atty., asst. dist. counsel Dept. of the Army, C.E. Office of Counsel, Huntington, W.Va. and Jacksonville, Fla., 1980-83; asst. atty. gen. State of Ohio, Columbus, 1983-84; trial atty., sr. trial atty. Dept. of Navy Office of Gen. Counsel, Washington and San Francisco, 1984-92; mem., ptnr. Ware & Freidenrich, Palo Alto, Calif., 1992-93; ptnr. Gray, Cary, Ware & Freidenrich, Palo Alto, 1994-97, San Francisco, 1997—. Mem. ABA (natural resources law sect.), Bar Assn. San Francisco (environment and water law sect.). Federal civil litigation, Environmental, Land use and zoning (including planning). Office: Gray Cary Ware & Friedenrich Ste 800 153 Townsend St San Francisco CA 94107-0630 E-mail: mrobertson@graycary.com.

ROBERTSON, JERRY D. lawyer; b. Port Clinton, Ohio, Dec. 16, 1948; s. Edgar N. and Delores E. (Brough) R.; m. Kathryn A. Behlmer, Aug. 1, 1970; children: Matthew, Adam. BS, Bowling Green State U., 1971; JD, U. Toledo, 1974. Bar: Ohio 1974, U.S. Ct. Mil. Appeals 1974, U.S. Dist. Ct. (no. dist.) Ohio 1977, U.S. Supreme Ct. 1980. Pvt. practice, Oak Harbor, Ohio, 1977—. Instr. real estate law Terra tech. Coll., Fremont, Ohio, 1978-82; asst. pros. atty. Ottawa County, Ohio, 1980-84; law dir. Village of Oak Harbor, Ohio, 1982-98; bd. dirs. Luther Home of Mercy, Williston, Ohio; cert. estate planning, trust & probate law specialist, Ohio State Bar Assoc. Capt. U.S. Army, 1974-77. Decorated Meritorious Svc. medal. Mem. ABA, Nat. Network of Estate Planning Attys., Nat. Acad. Elder Law Attys., Ohio Bar Assn., Toledo Estate Planning Coun., Am. Legion. Lutheran. Estate planning, Probate (including wills, trusts), Estate taxation. Office: PO Box 26 132 W Water St Oak Harbor OH 43449-1332 Home: 307 S Robinson Dr Oak Harbor OH 43449-1527

ROBERTSON, LEWIS HAROLD, lawyer; b. Oct. 2, 1946; s. Edgar Harold and Margaret Ruth (Yeates) R.; m. Justine Decker, Aug. 17, 1985. BS, U.S. Mil. Acad., 1968; MSSM, U. So. Calif., 1975; JD, Seton Hall U., 1976. Bar: (N.J.) 1976, Fla. 1980, U.S. Dist. Ct. N.J. 1976, U.S. Ct. Appeals (3rd cir.) 1980, U. S. Ct. Appeals (11th cir.) 1983, U.S. Dist. Ct. (so. dist.) Fla. 1984, U.S. Supreme Ct. 1980. Law sec. Hon. Marhsall Selikoff Superior Ct. N.J., Freehold, 1976—77; mem. firm Levy & Robertson, Asbury Park, NJ, 1977—90; of counsel Evans Osborne & Kreizman, Little Silver, NJ, 1990—97; pvt. practice Lewis H. Robertson, P.C., Little Silver, NJ, 1997—. Capt. USAF, 1968—73. Mem.: ACLU, Monmouth Bar Assn. Civil rights, Federal civil litigation, State civil litigation. Office: Lewis H Robertson PC 116 Oceanport Ave Little Silver NJ 07739

ROBERTSON, WILLIAM WITHERS, lawyer; b. Morristown, N.J., Nov. 3, 1941; s. Thomas Withers and Jessie (Swain) R.; m. Elizabeth Jeanne Robertson; children: Barbara Ellen Richmond, William Withers, Jr., Jessie Swain Wilt. BA, Rutgers U., 1964, LL.B., 1967. Bar: N.J. 1968. Law sec. to judge Superior Ct. N.J., 1967-68; asst. U.S. atty., 1972-76; 1st asst. U.S. atty., 1978-80; U.S. atty. Dist. N.J., 1980-81; chief Newark Organized Crime Strike Force, 1976-78; ptnr. Hannoch Weisman, Roseland, NJ, 1981-99, Robertson, Freilich, Bruno & Cohen, LLC, Newark, 1999—. Mng. editor: Rutgers Law Rev., 1966—67. Trustee Rutgers U., 1984-88. Served to capt. JAGC USAR, 1968-72. Mem. Nat. Assn. Former U.S. Attys. (bd. dirs. 1990-93, pres. 2002-2003), Rutgers U. Law Sch. Alumni Assn. (pres. 1990-91), Rutgers U. Alumni Fedn. (pres. 1981-83). Federal civil litigation, State civil litigation, Criminal. Office: Robertson Freilich Et Al 4th Fl 1 Riverfront Plz Newark NJ 07102-5401 E-mail: wrobertson@rtbclaw.com.

ROBILIO, KAY SPALDING, judge; b. Sept. 25, 1941; m. Victor L. Robilio, Jr.; children: Cecilia Ann, Catherine Robilio Womack. BA cum laude, Memphis State U., 1973, JD, 1980. Law clk. divsn. III and IV Cir. Ct., Memphis, 1979—81; assoc. Bowling and Scruggs Law Firm, Memphis, 1981; prosecutor City of Memphis, 1982—83; judge divsn. I Memphis City Ct., 1983—90; judge divsn. V Cir. Ct. 30th Jud. Dist., Memphis, 1990—. Host (TV show) A Question of Law. Former bd. dirs. Neighborhood Watch, Parenting Ctr.; ex officio, founding bd. dirs. Tenn. Assn. Children and Adults Learning Disabilities; pres. Eastwood Manor Neighborhood Assn., 1982—83. Named Outstanding Grad., U. Memphis Dept. Arts and Scis., 1998; named one of the Oustanding Women Mid-South, Tenn-Ark-Miss Girl Scouts, 1985; named to Memphis Heroes, Jr. Achievment, 1997; recipient White Rose award, March of Dimes, 1993. Mem.: ABA, Memphis Assn. Women Attys., Memphis Bar Assn., Tenn. Jud. Conf., Tenn. Lawyers Assn. Women (chair organizing com. 2002, pres. 2002), Tenn. Trial Lawyers Assn., Tenn. Bar Assn., Am. Judges Assn., Rotary (bd. dirs. 2001—). Office: Cir Ct Divsn V 140 Adams Rm 212 Memphis TN 38103 Office Fax: 901-545-5659. Business E-Mail: robili-k@shelby.tn.us.

ROBIN, THEODORE TYDINGS, JR., lawyer, engineer, consultant; b. New Orleans, Aug. 29, 1939; s. Theodore Tydings and Hazel (Corbin) R.; m. Helen Jones, June 8, 1963; children: Corbin, Curry, Ted, Phil. BME, Ga. Inst. Tech., 1961, MS in N.E., 1963, PhD, 1967; LLB, Blackstone Sch. Law, 1979. Bar: Calif. 1980, U.S. Patent and Trademark Office 1982; registered profl. engr., Ala., Calif. Rsch. engr. Oak Ridge (Tenn.) Nat. Lab., 1967; asst. prof. radiology and physics Emory U., Atlanta, 1968-69; project engr. Atomic Internat. divsn. N.Am. Rockwell, Canoga park, Calif., 1970-72; engr. mgmt. engring. divsn. So. Co. Svcs., Birmingham, Ala., 1972-83, mgr. nuclear support and quality assurance, 1989-90, mgr. quality assurance and resources, 1991-92; mgr. Hatch Design Configuration, 1993-94; program mgr. pooled inventory mgmt. program So. Electric Internat., Birmingham, 1984-88, bd. dirs. polit. action com., 1985-87; dir. nuclear stds., radiation safety officer, sr. patent counsel, prin. nuclear engring., cons. Theragenics Corp., Atlanta, 1996—. Mem. ABA, ASME (mem. nuclear quality assurance subcom. on stds. coordinating and radioactive waste 1991-99), Am. Assn. Physicists Medicine (legal info./risk mgmt. subcom. 2000—, mem. TG No6 Dose Equivalence in Br. Therapy 2001—), Am. Nuclear Soc. (chmn. Birmingham sect. 1987-88, nuclear power plant stds. com. 1989-94), Ga. Tech. Alumni Assn. (trustee 1997-00), Rotary (pres. Shades Valley club 1987-88, chmn. dist. 6860 internat. youth exch. com. 1989-90, dist. gov. 6860 1994-95, tech. task force zone 30 coord 2000-01), Sigma Xi. Achievements include research on power plant performance and reliability and effect of coal quality, space radiation effects on human cells, radiation safety, med. physics, boiling heat transfer, nuclear reactor safety, multi-utility contracting, reliability economics, benchmarking and total quality management; patent law. Nuclear power, Environmental, Patent. Home and Office: 4524 Pine Mountain Rd Birmingham AL 35213-1828 E-mail: robinty@mindspring.com.

ROBINER, DONALD MAXWELL, lawyer, former federal official; b. Detroit, Feb. 4, 1935; s. Max and Lucia (Chassman) Robiner; m. Phyllis F Goodman; children: Brian Roberts, Marc Roberts, Steven Ralph, Lawrence Alan. BA, U. Mich., 1957; postgrad., Wayne State U., 1957-58; JD, Case Western Res. U., 1961. Bar: Ohio 1961, US Supreme Ct 1964, US Ct Appeals (6th cir) 1965. Assoc. Metzenbaum, Gaines, Schwartz, Krupansky, Finley & Stern, Cleve., 1961-67; ptnr. Metzenbaum, Gaines, Krupansky, Finley & Stern, Cleve., 1967-72; v.p. Metzenbaum, Gaines, Finley & Stern Co., L.P.A., Cleve., 1972-77, Gaines, Stern, Schwarzwald & Robiner Co., Cleve., 1977-81; exec. v.p., sec. Schwarzwald, Robiner & Rock Co. LPA, Cleve., 1981-90; prin. Buckingham, Doolittle & Burroughs Co, LPA, Cleve., 1991-94; U.S. Trustee Ohio and Mich. region 9 U.S. Dept. of Justice, 1994—2001; of counsel Belkin, Billick & Harrold Co., LPA, Cleve., 2002—. V.p., sec. Richard L. Bowen & Assocs. Inc., Cleve., 1969—94; acting judge Shaker Heights Mcpl. Ct., 1973; mem. bd. bar examiners State of Ohio, Columbus, 1974—79; life mem. 6th Cir. Jud. Conf.; mediator alternate dispute resolution panel U.S. Dist. Ct. (no. dist.) Ohio, 1993—94. Sec. Friends of Beachwood Libr. Inc, Ohio, 1981—88; trustee Friends of Beachwood Libr. Inc., Ohio, 1981—96. Recipient Cert Appreciation, Ohio Supreme Ct, 1974—79, Appreciation Award, Am Soc Appraisers, 1975. Mem.: Ohio State Bar Assn., Cleve. Bar Assn., Ohio Coun. Sch. Bd. Attys. (mem. exec. com. 1990—94), Am. Arbitration Assn. (Serv Award 1975), Am. Bankruptcy Inst., Jud. Conf. 8th Appellate Dist. Ohio (life; charter mem.), KP. Home: 3094 Richmond Rd Beachwood OH 44122-3247 Office: Commerce Park Four 23240 Chagrin Blvd Ste 450 Cleveland OH 44122 Fax: 216-831-1326. E-mail: DonRobiner@msn.com.

ROBINETTE, CHRISTOPHER JOHN, lawyer; b. Raleigh, N.C., June 22, 1971; s. Kim V. and Billie Kaye Robinette; m. Amanda Irene Lenz, Oct. 13, 1996. BA, Coll. William and Mary, 1993; JD, U. Va., 1996. Bar: Va. 1996, U.S. Dist. Ct. (we. dist.) Va. 1997, U.S. Ct. Appeals (4th cir.) 1997, U.S. Dist. Ct. (ea. dist.) Va. 1998. Assoc. Tremblay & Smith LLP, Charlottesville, Va., 1996—. Contbr. to profl. jours. Adv. bd. mem. Salvation Army, Charlottesville, Va., 1997—; mem. Recreational Facilities Authority, Albemarle County, Va., 1998—. Mem. Va. State Bar (young lawyers divsn., litigation sect.), Va. Trial Lawyers' Assn., Charlottesville-Albemarle Bar Assn. Avocations: reading, jogging, weight lifting, traveling. General civil litigation, Commercial, contracts (including sales of goods; commercial financing), Communications. Office: Tremblay & Smith LLP 105-109 E High St Charlottesville VA 22902 E-mail: chris.robinette@tremblaysmith.com.

ROBINOWITZ, CHARLES, lawyer; b. White Plains, N.Y., Sept. 29, 1942; s. Seymour and Shirley (Horowitz) R.; m. Selene Bea Greenberg, June 17, 1973; children: Scott, Mark. BA, Cornell U., 1964; LLB, U. Va., 1968. Bar: Oreg. 1969, N.Y. 1969, U.S. Dist. Ct. (all dists.) Oreg. 1969, U.S. Ct. Appeals (9th cir.) 1973, U.S. Supreme Ct. 1974. Law clk. U.S. Dist. Ct., N.Y.C., 1968-69; assoc. Dusenbery, Martin et al, Portland, Oreg., 1969-71; pvt. practice Portland, 1971—. Bd. dirs. Jewish Fedn. Portland, 1991-97; pres. Cornell Club Oreg., 1991-95, Temple Beth Israel, Portland, 1988-94; bd. dirs. Friends of Chamber Music, Portland, 1975-79. Mem. ABA, ATLA, Oreg. Trial Lawyers Assn., Oreg. State Bar Assn., Multnomah County Bar Assn. Avocations: running, classical music. Admiralty, Personal injury (including property damage), Workers' compensation. Office: 1211 SW 5th Ave Ste 1150 Portland OR 97204-3729 E-mail: cr@teleport.com.

ROBINS, MARTIN B. lawyer; b. Chgo., Oct. 20, 1956; s. Sam I. and June (Tikulski) R.; m. Elizabeth Bangs Eaton, May 28, 1993. BS summa cum laude, U. Pa., 1977; JD cum laude, Harvard U., 1980. Bar: Ill. 1980, U.S. Dist. Ct. (no. dist.) Ill. 1980. Assoc. Sonnenschein Carlin Nath & Rosenthal, Chgo., 1980-83, Gottlieb & Schwartz, Chgo., 1983-85; v.p., gen. counsel, sec. IDC Svcs., Inc., Chgo., 1985-89; sr. v.p., gen. counsel Meridian Leasing Corp., Deerfield, Ill., 1990-99; ptnr. Law Office Martin B. Robins, Buffalo Grove, Ill., 1999—. Cons. in field. Author: Equipment Leasing-Matthew Berler Monograph, 2000, Cyberfinance: Financing the E-Business, 2001; contbr. articles to profl. jours. Mem. ABA, Chgo. Bar Assn. Avocations: participatory athletics, reading, gardening, cooking. Commercial, contracts (including sales of goods; commercial financing), Corporate, general, Finance. Office: 1110 Lake Cook Rd #355 Buffalo Grove IL 60089

ROBINS, RONALD ALBERT, JR., lawyer; b. Columbus, Ohio, Nov. 19, 1963; s. Ronald Albert and Barbara (Feibel) R.; m. Mary Wales Leslie, Nov. 29, 1967.; 1 child: Leslie Pearl. BA, Duke U., 1985; JD, Harvard U., 1989. Jud. clk. Hon. Milton Pollack, N.Y.C., 1989-90; assoc. Davis Polk & Wardwell, N.Y.C., 1990-93, Vorys Sater Seymour and Pease LLP, Columbus, 1993-96, ptnr., 1997—. Chmn. alumni bd. Columbus Acad., 1997-99; chmn. adv. bd. for Columbus, Duke U., 1998—; trustee Columbus Symphony Orch., 2002—. Mem. Columbus Bar Assn. Corporate, general, Mergers and acquisitions, Securities. Office: Vorys Sater Seymour and Pease LLP 52 E Gay St Columbus OH 43215-3161 E-mail: rarobins@vssp.com.

ROBINSON, ADELBERT CARL, lawyer, judge; b. Shawnee, Okla., Dec. 13, 1926; s. William H. and Mayme (Forston) R.; m. Paula Kay Settles, Apr. 16, 1988; children from previous marriage: William, James, Schuyler, Donald, David, Nancy, Lauri. Student, Okla. Bapt. U., 1944-47; JD, Okla. U., 1950. Bar: Okla. 1950. Pvt. practice, Muskogee, Okla., 1956-97; with legal dept. Phillips Petroleum Co., 1950-51; adjuster U.S. Fidelity & Guaranty Co., 1951-54, atty., adjuster-in-charge, 1954-56; ptnr. Fite & Robinson, 1956-62, Fite, Robinson & Summers, 1963-70, Robinson & Summers, 1970-72, Robinson, Summers & Locke, 1972-76, Robinson, Locke & Gage, 1976-80, Robinson, Locke, Gage & Fite, 1980-83, Robinson, Locke, Gage, Fite & Williams, Muskogee, 1983-95, Robinson, Gage, Fite & Williams, Muskogee, 1995-97. Police judge City of Muskogee, 1963—64, mcpl. judge, 1964—70; prin. justice 84Temp. Divsn. 36 Okla. Ct. Appeals, 1981—84, spl. dist. judge, 1997—; pres., dir. Wall St. Bldg. Corp., 1969—78, Three Forks Devel. Corp., 1968—77, Rolo Leasing Inc., 1971—97, Suroya II Inc.1, 1977—99; mng. ptnr. RLG Ritz, 1980—97; ptnr. First City Real Estate Partnership, 1985—94; del. to U.S./China Jt. Session on Trade, Investment and Econ. Law, Beijing, 1987. Chmn. Muskogee County (Okla.) Law Day, 1963, Muskogee Area Redevel. Authority, 1963, Muskogee County chpt. Am. Cancer Soc., 1956; pres., bd. dirs. United Way of Muskogee Inc., 1980-88, v.p., 1982, pres., 1983; bd. dirs. Muskogee Cmty. Concert Assn., Muskogee Tourist Info. Bur., 1964-68; bd. dirs., gen. counsel United Cerebral Palsy Eastern Okla., 1964-68; trustee Connors Devel. Found., Connors Coll., 1981-99, chmn., 1987-89; active Muskogee Housing Authority, 1992-95. With inf. AUS, 1945-46. Mem. ABA, Okla. Bar Assn. (chmn. uniform laws com. 1970-72, chmn. profl. coop. com. 1965-69, past regional chmn. grievance com.), Muskogee County Bar Assn. (pres. 1971, mem. exec. coun. 1971-74), Okla. Assn. Def. Counsel (dir. 1970-74), Okla. Assn. Mcpl. Judges (dir. 1968-70), Muskogee c. of C., Delta Theta Phi, Rotary (pres. 1971-72). Methodist. Banking, Estate planning, Property, real (including real estate development, water). Home: 3702 Club Estates Dr Muskogee OK 74403 Office: Muskogee County Courthouse PO Box 1350 Muskogee OK 74402-1350

ROBINSON, BARBARA PAUL, lawyer; b. Oct. 19, 1941; d. Leo and Pauline G. Paul; m. Charles Raskob Robinson, June 11, 1965; children: Charles Paul, Torrance Webster. AB magna cum laude, Bryn Mawr Coll., 1962; LLB, Yale U., 1965, Order of the Coif. Bar: N.Y. 1966, U.S. Dist. Ct. (so. and ea. dists.) N.Y. 1975, U.S. Tax Ct. 1972, U.S. Ct. Appeals (2d cir.) 1974. Assoc. Debevoise & Plimpton (formerly Debevoise, Plimpton, Lyons & Gates), N.Y.C., 1966-75, ptnr., 1976—; commr. Mayor's Commn. on Women's Issues, 2003—. Mem. adv. bd. Practicing Law Inst.; bd. dirs. Am. Arbitration Assn., 1987—, Sch. Choice Scholarships Found. Mem. bd. editors: Chase Jour., 1997—2001; contbr. articles. Mem. adv. coun., bd. vis. CUNY Law Sch., Queens, 1984—90; active Coun. on Fgn. Rels.; trustee Trinity Sch., 1982—86, pres., 1986—88; bd. dirs. Found. for Child Devel., 1989—2000, 2001—, chmn., 1991—2000; bd. dirs. Catalyst, 1993—, Fund for Modern Courts, 1990—2003, Wave Hill, 1994—, Garden Conservancy, 1996—2002, Lawyers Com. for Civil Rights Under Law, 1997—, William Nelson Cromwell Found., 1993—, Irish Legal Rsch. Found. Inc., 1996—, Citizens Union Found. Inc., 1996—; trustee Bryn Mawr Coll., 2000—. Recipient Laura Parsons Pratt award, 1996. Fellow Am. Coll. Trust and Estate Counsel, Am. Bar Found., N.Y. Bar Found.; mem. ABA (commn. on women in profession 1999-2002), N.Y. State Bar Assn. (vice chmn. com. on trust adminstrn., trusts and estates law sect. 1977-81, ho. of dels. 1984-87, 90-92, com. ann. award 1993-94), Assn. of Bar of City of N.Y. (chmn. com. on trusts, estates and surrogates cts. 1981-84, judiciary com. 1981-84, coun. on jud. adminstrn. 1982-84, chair nominating com. 1984-85, 99—, exec. com. 1986-91, chair 1989-90, v.p. 1990-91, pres. 1994-96, chair com. on honors 1993-94, com. on long-range planning 1991-94, co-chair coun. on childen 1997-99), Assn. of Bar of City of N.Y. Fund Inc. (bd. dirs., pres.), Women's Forum, Yale Coun., Yale Law Sch. Assn. N.Y. (devel. bd., exec. com. 1981-85, pres. 1988-93), Yale Club, Washington Club. Estate planning, Probate (including wills, trusts), Estate taxation. Office: Debevoise & Plimpton 919 Third Ave New York NY 10022 E-mail: bprobinson@debevoise.com.

ROBINSON, DAVID HOWARD, lawyer; b. Hampton, Va., Nov. 24, 1948; s. Bernard Harris and Phyllis (Canter) R.; m. Nina Jane Briscoe, Aug. 20, 1979. BA, Calif. State U., Northridge, 1970; JD, Cabrillo Pacific U., 1975. Bar: Calif. 1977, U.S. Dist. Ct. (so. dist.) Calif. 1977, U.S. Ct. Claims, 1979, U.S. Supreme Ct. 1980. Adminstr. Cabrillo Pacific U. Coll. Law, 1977; assoc. Gerald D. Egan, San Bernardino, Calif., 1977-78, Duke & Gerstel, San Diego, 1978-80, Rand, Day & Ziman, San Diego, 1980-81; pvt. practice, San Diego, 1981-88; ptnr. Robinson and Rubin, San Diego, 1988-95; dep. atty. gen. State of Calif., San Diego, 1995—. Mem. Foothills Bar Assn. (bd. dirs., past treas.). Office: 110 West A St San Diego CA 92101-3711

ROBINSON, DAVID SPENCER, lawyer, consultant; b. Jacksonville, Fla., Mar. 16, 1965; BS, Georgetown U., 1987; postgrad., Sophia U., Tokyo, 1986; JD, George Washington U., 1990. Bar: N.C. 1990. Atty. Graham & James, Raleigh, NC, 1990—96; atty., of counsel Moore & van Allen, Raleigh; pres. Am. Labor, Inc., Research Triangle Park, NC, 1998; pvt. practice Raleigh, 1998—. Adj., bd. dirs. N.C. Japan Ctr., Raleigh, 1994—, dep. dir., 2000—02; advisor, mem. com. Wake Tech. Bus. & Industry, 2002. Pro bono advisor, bd. dirs. various non-profit orgns., NC; candidate N.C. Legislature, Raleigh, 1994; founding dir. N.C. China Ctr., 2002. Paul Harris fellow, Rotary. Mem.: N.C. Bar Assn. (chair internat. legis. 1994—, mem. exec. com. 1996—, chair law sect. 2001—02). Avocations: triathlons, competitive athletics. Private international, Commercial, contracts (including sales of goods; commercial financing), Immigration, naturalization, and customs. Office: PO Box 99766 Raleigh NC 27624-9766

ROBINSON, DAVIS ROWLAND, lawyer; b. N.Y.C., July 11, 1940; s. Thomas Porter and Cynthia (Davis) R.; m. Suzanne Walker, June 11, 1966; children: Christopher Champlin II, Gracyn Walker. BA magna cum laude, Yale U., 1961; LLB cum laude, Harvard U., 1967. Bar: N.Y. 1968, D.C. 1971, U.S. Supreme Ct. 1972. Fgn. svc. officer U.S. Dept. State, Washington, 1961-69; assoc. Sullivan & Cromwell, N.Y.C., 1969-71; assoc., then ptnr. Leva, Hawes, Symington, Martin and Oppenheimer, Washington, 1971-81; the legal adviser U.S. Dept. State, Washington, 1981-85; ptnr. Pillsbury, Madison & Sutro, Washington, 1985-88, Le Boeuf, Lamb, Greene & MacRae LLP, Washington, 1988—2002, ret., 2002—. Dir. Mid. East Policy Coun., Washington, 1999—. Pres. Harvard Legal Aid Bur., 1966-67. Mem. Assn. of Bar of City of N.Y., Am. Law Inst. (adviser fgn. rels. law of U.S.), Am. Soc. Internat. Law, Internat. Centre for Settlement of Investment Disputes (U.S. panel, 2002-), Coun. on Fgn. Rels., Phi Beta Kappa. Corporate, general, Private international, Public international. Office: Le Boeuf Lamb Greene & MacRae LLP 1875 Connecticut Ave NW Washington DC 20009-5728 Business E-Mail: drrobins@llgm.com.

ROBINSON, E. GLENN, lawyer; b. Charleston, W.Va., Jan. 1, 1924; s. Elmer George and Eva Elena (Rexrode) Robinson; m. Emma Lou Legg, Dec. 23, 1947; children: Richard G., Martha L., William E., Ann K. BSc, Ohio State U., 1948; JD, W.Va. U., 1950. Bar: W.Va. 1950, U.S. Ct. Appeals (4th cir.) 1953, U.S. Ct. Appeals (3d cir.) 1980, U.S. Supreme Ct. 1982. Ptnr. Shannon & Robinson, Charleston, 1950—52, Love, Wise, Robinson & Woodroe, Charleston, 1952—83, Robinson & McElwee, Charleston, 1983—91, of counsel, 1991—. Served with AUS, 1942—45. Fellow: Am. Bar Found.; mem.: Am. Bd. Trial Advocates, Am. Coll. Trial Lawyers, Kanawha County Bar Assn. (pres. 1968—69), W.Va. Bar Assn. (pres. 1982—83), W.Va. State Bar (pres. 1972—73), Rotary. Republican. General civil litigation. Home: 507 Superior Ave Charleston WV 25303-2024 Office: 600 United Ctr Charleston WV 25301-2135

ROBINSON, EDWARD NORWOOD, lawyer; b. Roseboro, N.C., June 18, 1925; s. Edward Croswell and Lolita (Underwood) R.; m.Pauline L. Gray, Mar. 20, 1952; children: Edward Norwood Jr., James Gray, Michael Lindsay, Mark Alvin. BS in Engring., U.S. Mil. Acad., 1945; JD, Duke U., 1952. Atty. Robinson & Lawing, L.L.P., Winston-Salem, N.C. N.C. civilian aide to Sec. of Army, 1994-2001; apptd. to 5th Dist. Acad. Selection Bd.; mem. ethics com. Bowman Gray Sch. Medicine; bd. visitors Duke U. Sch. Law, Wake Forest U. Sch. Law, Duke Divinity Sch.; lectr. in field. Co-editor Duke Law Jour. Past pres. Winston-Salem Rotary Club; past campaign chmn. United Way; past pres. C. of C.; past pres. local chpt. ARC; past dir. Winston-Salem Housing Found.; mem. Centenary United Meth. Ch., Winston-Salem, tchr. Chapel class, chmn. bd. stewards; past chmn. Winston-Salem Dist. United Meth. Ch., Ch. Ext.; past dir., campaign chmn. Triad United Meth. Home. 1st Lt. U.S. Army, 1942-49. Recipient Charles L. Rhyne award Duke U. Law Alumni, 1997. Fellow Am. Coll. Trial Lawyers; mem. ABA (antitrust and litigation sects.), U.S. 4th Cir. Jud. Conf. (life), N.C. Bar Assn. (past dir.), Forsyth County Bar Assn. (past pres.), Pvt. Adjudication Ctr. Duke U. (past chmn. bd.), U.S. Mil. Acad. Assn. Grads. (bd. trustees emeritus), Order of the Coif, Joseph Branch Inns of Ct., Am. Inns of Ct. Avocations: golf, travel. Office: Robinson and Lawing LLP 370 Knollwood St Ste 600 Winston Salem NC 27103-1830 E-mail: nrobinson@robinson-lawing.com.

ROBINSON, IRWIN JAY, lawyer; b. Bay City, Mich., Oct. 8, 1928; s. Robert R. and Anne (Kaplan) R.; m. Janet Binder, July 7, 1957; children: Elizabeth Binder Schubiner, Jonathan Meyer, Eve Kimberly Wiener. AB, U. Mich., 1950; JD, Columbia U., 1953. Bar: N.Y. 1956. Assoc. Breed Abbott & Morgan, N.Y.C., 1955-58; asst. to ptnrs. Dreyfus & Co., N.Y.C., 1958-59; assoc. Greenbaum Wolff & Ernst, N.Y.C., 1959-65, ptnr., 1966-76; sr. ptnr. Rosenman & Colin, N.Y.C., 1976-90; of counsel Pryor, Cashman, Sherman & Flynn, 1990-92; sr. ptnr. Phillips, Nizer, Benjamin, Krim & Ballon, N.Y.C., 1992-99; pvt. practice N.Y.C., 1999—. Treas. Saarsteel, Inc., Whitestone, N.Y., 1970—. Bd. dirs. Henry St. Settlement, N.Y.C., 1960-85, Jewish Cmty. Ctr. Assn. N.Am., N.Y.C., 1967-94, mem. adv. bd., 1998—; bd. dirs. Heart Rsch. Found., 1989-94, pres., 1991-93. Mem. ABA, N.Y. State Bar Assn., Assn. Bar City of N.Y., Internat. Bar Assn., Thai-Am. C. of C. (founder, bd. dirs. 1992-95, pres. 1992-95), Vietnam-Am. C. of C. (founder, bd. dirs. 1992-95, pres. 1992-95), Philippine-Am. C. of C. (bd. dirs. 1960-98), Sunningdale Country Club, The Desert Mountain Club. Jewish. Private international, Corporate, general, Securities. Home: 4622 Grosvenor Ave Bronx NY 10471-3305 Office: care Kramer Levin Naftalis & Frankel 919 3d Ave 40th Fl New York NY 10022-3902 E-mail: ijrjbr@aol.com.

ROBINSON, JOHN WILLIAM, IV, lawyer; b. Atlanta, Apr. 29, 1950; s. J. William III and Elizabeth (Smith) R.; m. Ellen Showalter, Dec. 28, 1976; children: William, Anna. BA with honors, Washington & Lee U., 1972; JD, U. Ga., 1975. Bar: Fla., Ga., U.S. Dist. Ct. (no., so. and mid. dists.) Fla., U.S. Ct. Mil. Appeals, U.S. Ct. Appeals (5th and 11th cirs.), U.S. Supreme Ct.; cert. labor & employment law, civil trial and bus. litigation lawyer, Fla., Nat. Bd. Trial Advocacy. Trial atty. Nat. Labor Rels. Bd., New Orleans, 1975-76; trial def. counsel 8th infantry U.S. Army, Mainz, Germany, 1977-78, trial counsel 8th infantry, 1979; law clerk, commr. Ct. Mil. Review, Washington, 1980; atty. Fowler, White, Boggs & Banker, PA, Tampa, Fla., 1980—, head labor and employment law dept., 1993—, dir., 1998—, sec./treas, ops. com., 2001—. Mem. faculty U. Md., 1977-79; arbitrator U.S. Dist. Ct. (mid. dist.) Fla. Editor-in-chief: Employment & Labor Relations Law, 1991-95; editor: Developing Labor Law, 1982—, Model Jury Instructions for Employment Litigation, 1994—; editor: Employment Litigation Handbook, 1998. Chmn. Tampa Bay Internat. Trade Coun., 1990-91, Rough Riders Dist. Boy Scouts Am., 1990; legal counsel Drug Free Workplace Task Force, 1999-00, Greater Tampa C. of C., 1996, gen. counsel, bd. dirs., 1999—. Capt. U.S. Army, 1976-80. Named one of Best Lawyers in Am. for labor and employment law. Mem.: ABA (chmn. employment and labor rels. com. 1993—96, divsn. dir. 1996—2000, litig. sect., mem. coun., chmn. com. on multijurisdictional practice 2000—), Am. Inn of Ct. (pres., dir. and master barrister, trustee Am. Inns of Ct. Found.), Washington & Lee U. Bd. (pres. nat. alumni bd. 1990—91, trustee 1995—), Fla. Bar Assn. (chmn. labor and employment law sect. 1992—93), Rotary (pres. Tampa Bay chpt.). Avocations: tennis, history. General civil litigation, Labor (including EEOC, Fair Labor Standards Act, labor-management relations, NLRB, OSHA), Pension, profit-sharing, and employee benefits. Office: Fowler White Boggs Banker PA 501 E Kennedy Blvd Tampa FL 33602-5237

ROBINSON, KENNETH PATRICK, lawyer, electronics company executive; b. Hackensack, N.J., Dec. 12, 1933; s. William Casper and Margaret Agnes (McGuire) r.; m. Catherine Esther Lund, Aug. 26, 1961; children: James, Susan. BS in Elec. Engring., Rutgers U., 1955; JD, NYU, 1962. Bar: N.Y. 1962, U.S. Ct. Appeals (fed. cir.) 1990. With Hazeltine Corp., Greenlawn, N.Y., 1955-88, patent counsel, 1966-69, gen. counsel, 1969-88, sec., 1971-88; v.p. Hazeltine Rsch. Inc., Chgo., 1966-88; of counsel Brumbaugh, Graves, Donohue & Raymond, N.Y.C., 1989-92; prin. Kenneth P. Robinson, Huntington, N.Y., 1992—. Dir. Hazeltine Ltd., London, 1973-80; dir. Imlac Corp., Needham, Mass., 1978-83. Served to 1st lt. USAF, 1955-57. Mem. ABA, IEEE, Am. Intellectual Law Assn., Licensing Execs. Soc. Roman Catholic. Patent, Trademark and copyright, Technology. Home: 137 Darrow Ln Greenlawn NY 11740-2923 Office: 474 New York Ave Huntington NY 11743-3542

ROBINSON, LOGAN GILMORE, lawyer; b. Cin., Ohio, Dec. 26, 1949; s. Landon Graves and Alis (Rule) R.; m. Edrie Baker Sowell, Sept. 22, 1983; children: Leyland G., Landon G. BA, Cornell U., 1972; JD, Harvard U., 1976; Cert. Competence in German, Goethe Inst., Freiburg, Germany, 1978. Bar: Ohio 1977, N.Y. 1979, U.S. Ct. Internat. Trade 1983. Rsch. faculty Leningrad State U., Russia, 1976-77; research officer U. Leiden, The Netherlands, 1977-78; assoc. Wender, Murase & White, NYC, 1978-81, Coudert Bros., NYC, 1981-83; sr. counsel TRW Inc., Cleve., 1983-87; asst. gen. counsel Chrysler Corp., Detroit, 1987—95; sec., v.p., gen. counsel ITT Automotive, Auburn Hills, Mich., 1996—97; counsel Dickinson Wright PLLC, 1998; v.p., gen. counsel Delphi Corp., 1999—. Author: An American in Leningrad, 1982, paperback, 1984, Evil Star, 1986, paperback, 1987. Mem. Am. Fgn. Law Assn. (past sec.), Am. Soc. Internat. Law, German-Am. Law Assn., Phi Beta Kappa. Commercial, contracts (including sales of goods; commercial financing), Corporate, general, Private international. Office: Delphi Corp World Headquarters 5725 Delphi Dr Troy MI 48098-2815*

ROBINSON, MALCOLM S. lawyer; b. Chgo. JD, U. Kans., 1975. Bar: Ill., Tex. With law dept. SCOR Reinsurance Co., Dallas, 1979—84, v.p., gen. counsel, corp. sec.; co-founder, ptnr. Robinson & Hoskins, LLP, Dallas, 1984—. Immediate past chmn. Dallas Conv. and Visitors Bur., 1998—2000; past chmn. Greater Dallas Crime Commn.; past chmn. bd. trustees State Bar Tex. Ins. Trust; mem. Dallas Together Forum, past co-chair So. Sector Initiative; past mem. bd. North Tex. Commn. Mem.: Dallas Black C. of C. (chmn. 1990—92, bd. dirs., gen. counsel), Nat. Bar Assn. (pres. 2002—03), Salesmanship Club Dallas. Office: Robinson & Hoskins LLP Bank of Am Oak Cliff Tower 400 Zang Blvd Ste 600 Dallas TX 75208*

ROBINSON, MARIETTA S. lawyer; BA, U. Mich., 1973; JD, UCLA, 1978. Bar: Calif. 1978, Mich. 1979, U.S. Dist. Ct. (ea. dist.) Mich. 1979, U.S. Ct. Appeals (6th cir.) 1983, U.S. Supreme Ct. 1989. Data processing mktg. rep. IBM Corp., Flint, Mich., 1973-75; assoc. The Bank of Bermuda Legal Dept., Hamilton, 1978-79; from assoc. to ptnr. Dickinson, Wright, Moon, VanDusen & Freeman, Detroit, 1979-94; ptnr. Sommers, Schwartz, Silver & Schwartz, P.C., Southfield, Mich., 1985-89; owner Law Offices of Marietta S. Robinson, Detroit, 1989—. Dem. nominee for Mich. Supreme Ct., 2000; adj. prof. U. Detroit Sch. of Law, 1982-83, Wayne State U., Detroit, 1983-84; lectr. in field. Contbr. articles to profl. jours. Trustee Dalkon Shield Claimants Trust, 1989-97; appointee Gov. James Blanchard, State of Mich. Bldg. Authority, 1985-89, State Bar Mich./Mich. State Med. Soc. Coalition, 1993—; appointee Transition Team of Wayne County Exec. Robert Ficano, 2002—. Named one of ten Mich. Lawyers of Yr., Lawyers Weekly, 2000. Fellow ABA, Internat. Soc. Barristers (bd. govs.), Am. Bar Found., Mich. State Bar Found.; mem. State Bar Mich., State Bar Calif., ATLA, Mich. Trial Lawyers Assn., Women Lawyers Mich., Detroit Bar Assn., Oakland Bar Assn., U.S. Ct. Appeals (6th cir.) Jud. Conf. (life). Office: 185 Oakland Ave Ste 260 Birmingham MI 48009 E-mail: mrobin6510@aol.com.

ROBINSON, MARY LOU, federal judge; b. Dodge City, Kans., Aug. 25, 1926; d. Gerald J. and Frances Strueber; m. A.J. Robinson, Aug. 28, 1949; 3 children. BA, U. Tex., 1948, LL.B., 1950. Bar: Tex. 1949. Ptnr. Robinson & Robinson, Amarillo, 1950-55; judge County Ct. at Law, Potter County, Tex., 1955-59, (108th Dist. Ct.), Amarillo, 1961-73; assoc. justice Ct. of Civil Appeals for 7th Supreme Jud. Dist. of Tex., Amarillo, 1973-77, chief justice, 1977-79; U.S. dist. judge No. Dist. Tex., Amarillo, 1979—. Named Woman of Year Tex. Fedn. Bus. and Profl. Women, 1973. Mem. Nat. Assn. Women Lawyers, ABA, Tex. Bar Assn. (Outstanding 50-Yr. Lawyer award 2002), Amarillo Bar Assn., Delta Kappa Gamma. Presbyterian. Office: US Dist Ct Rm 226 205 E 5th Ave # F13248 Amarillo TX 79101-1559

ROBINSON, NEIL CIBLEY, JR., lawyer; b. Columbia, S.C., Oct. 25, 1942; s. Neil C. and Ernestine (Carns) R.; m. Judith Ann Hunter, Sept. 4, 1971 (div. Nov. 1979); 1 child, Hunter Leigh; m. Vicki Elizabeth Kornahrens, Mar. 2, 1985; children: Neil C. III, Taylor Elizabeth. BS in Indsl. Mgmt., Clemson U., 1966; JD, U. S.C., 1973. Bar: S.C. 1974, U.S. Ct. Appeals (4th cir.) 1974, U.S. Dist. Ct. S.C. 1976. Asst. to dean U. S.C. Law Sch., Columbia, 1973-74; law clk. to Hon. Charles E. Jr. Simons Jr. U.S. Dist. Ct. S.C., Aiken, 1974-76; assoc. Grimball & Cabaniss, Charleston, S.C., 1976-78; ptnr. Grimball, Cabaniss, Vaughan & Robinson, Charleston, 1978-84; ptnr., pres. Robinson, Wall & Hastie, P.A., Charleston, 1984-91; ptnr., exec. com. Nexsen, Pruet, Jacobs, Pollard & Robinson, Charleston, 1991—. Permanent mem. 4th Cir. Jud. Conf., 1982—; pres. Coastal Properties Inst., Charleston, 1981—. Bd. dirs. Southeastern Wildlife Exposition, Charleston, 1987—, pres. 1994-99, Charleston Maritime Festival, 1993-99, pres. 1994-98, Parklands Found. of Charleston County; pres. S.C. Tourism Coun., Columbia, 1991-99; co-founder, chmn. Charleston Planning Project Pub. Edn., 1996—; bd. dirs. Charleston Edn. Found., Clemson U. Humanities Found., Charleston Edn. Network, chmn. bd. dirs., 2000—; edn. adv. bd. Coll. of Charleston; pres. Clemson Advancement Found., 2003, bd. dirs. Clemson U. Found. 2003-, mem. Gov. Sanford's Quality of Life Task Force, 2003. Cpl. USMCR, 1960-66. Recipient Order of Palmetto, Gov. David Beasley, S.C., 1996. Mem. ABA, Urban Land Inst. (recreational devel. coun.), S.C. Bar Assn., Fed. Bar Assn., S.C. Def. Trial Lawyers Assn., Hibernian Soc. (mgmt. com. 1984—, sec. 1998-2000, chmn. 2000-2002, v.p. 2002-), Kiawah Club, Haig Point Club, Country Club of Charleston, Carolina Yacht Club, Phi Delta Phi. Presbyterian. Avocation: golf. Environmental, Land use and zoning (including planning), Property, real (including real estate development, water). Home: PO Box 121 Charleston SC 29402-0121 Office: Nexsen Pruet Jacobs Pollard & Robinson 205 King St Charleston SC 29401 E-mail: nrobinson@npjp.com.

ROBINSON, RANDAL D. lawyer; b. Newark, Ohio, Apr. 2, 1949; s. Paul Alden and Bonnie J. C. R.; m. C. Brittney Copeland, Oct. 1, 1993; children: Brandon M., Frances M. BA, Denison U., 1971; JD, Capital U., 1975. Bar: Ohio 1975, U.S. Dist. Ct. (so. dist.) Ohio 1983, U.S. Ct. Appeals (6th cir.). Assoc. Harris, Lias & Strip, Columbus, Ohio, 1975-79; ptnr. Burman & Robinson, Columbus, 1979—. Instr. bus. law Columbus (Ohio) Tech. Inst., 1983-84; instr., lectr. Franklin County Trial Lawyers Assn., 1998. Mem. ABA, Am. Arbitration Assn., Nat. Panel Arbitrators, Ohio State Bar Assn., Columbus Bar Assn. (lectr. family law legal assts. program 1980-82), Comml. Law League Am., Austin Healey Club N. Am., Inc. (bd. dirs., gen. counsel 1976—). Commercial, consumer (including collections, credit), Commercial, contracts (including sales of goods; commercial financing). Office: Burman & Robinson 601 S High St Fl 2 Columbus OH 43215-5680

ROBINSON, RUSSELL MARABLE, II, lawyer; b. Charlotte, N.C., Mar. 13, 1932; s. John Moseley and Camilla Croom (Rodman) R.; m. Sally Gossett Dalton, Sept. 4, 1953; children: Camilla, Russell III, Sally. Student, Princeton U., 1950-52; LLB, Duke U., 1956. Bar: N.C. 1956, U.S. Dist. Ct. (ea., mid. and we. dists.) N.C. 1956, U.S. Ct. Appeals (4th cir.) 1960. From assoc. to ptnr. Lassiter, Moore & Van Allen, Charlotte, 1956-60; ptnr. Robinson, Bradshaw & Hinson P.A., Charlotte, 1960—. Author: Robinson on North Carolina Corporation Law, 7th edit., 2002. Gen. Counsel Morehead Found., Chapel Hill, N.C., 1965—; chmn. The Duke Endowment, 2002-. Fellow Am. Bar Found.; mem. ABA, Am. Law Inst., N.C. Bar Assn., Order of Coif, Phi Beta Kappa. Episcopalian. Corporate, general, Securities. Home: 3829 Bonwood Dr Charlotte NC 28211-1752 Office: Robinson Bradshaw & Hinson 1900 E Independence Blvd Charlotte NC 28205-6117

ROBINSON, VIANEI LOPEZ, lawyer; b. Houston, Mar. 6, 1969; d. David Tiburcio and Romelia Gloria (Guerra) Lopez. AB in Psychology cum laude, Princeton U., 1988; JD, U. Tex., 1991. Bar: Tex. 1991; mediator's cert. Assoc. Bracewell & Patterson LLP, Houston, 1991-94, Wagstaff Law Firm, Abilene, Tex., 1994-97; owner Robinson Law Firm, Abilene, 1997—. Contbr. articles to profl. jours., chpts. to School Law in Texas, A Practical Guide, 1996, Texas Employment Law, 1998; weekly wine columnist, Abilene Reporter News. Bd. dirs., sec. Historic Paramount Theatre, 2003, bd. dirs. Ctr. for Contemporary Arts, pres., 2000, sec., 2001, 2003; mem. adv. bd., Day Nursery of Abilene. Presdl. scholar, Nat. Merit scholar, Nat. Hispanic scholar, 1985, Vinson & Elkins scholar U. Tex. Sch. Law, Austin, 1988-91. Fellow Tex. Bar Found.; mem. ABA, State Bar Tex. (minority dir. 2000-05, various coms.), Coll. of the State Bar of Tex. (bd. dirs. 2000-01), Tex. Young Lawyers Assn. (bd. dirs. 1994-97), Abilene Bar Assn., Abilene Young Lawyers Assn., Big Country Soc. for Human Resource Mgmt. (pres. 1999). Avocations: theater and dance, fine art, food and wine. Education and schools, Health, Labor (including EEOC, Fair Labor Standards Act, labor-management relations, NLRB, OSHA). Home: 2410 Wyndham Ct Abilene TX 79606-4370 Office: Robinson Law Firm First Nat Bank Tower 400 Pine St Ste 1070 Abilene TX 79601-5173 Fax: 915-677-6044. E-mail: vlr@robinsonlawfirm.com.

ROBINSON, W. LEE, lawyer; b. Rome, Ga., Sept. 24, 1943; m. Irene Scales, 1966; children: Christine, Jacquelyn. BS, Ga. Inst. Tech.; MBA, JD, Mercer U., 1985. With Robinson Hardware Store, Macon, Ga., 1954-86; mem. Ga. Senate, Atlanta, 1975-83; mayor City of Macon, Macon, 1988-92; pvt. practice Macon, 1985—. Judge mcpl. ct. (part time), Macon. 2d lt. U.S. Army; col. USAR. Decorated Bronze Star with two oak leaf clusters, Legion of Merit with oak leaf cluster. Named to U.S. Army Officer Candidate Sch. Hall of Fame. Mem. Ga. Assn. Criminal Def. Lawyers, Macon C. of C. (former bd. dirs.), Macon Bar Assn. Address: 3824 Overlook Ave Macon GA 31204-1325 Office: 201 2nd St Ste 580 Macon GA 31201-8282 also: PO Box 4852 Macon GA 31208-4852 E-mail: wlrmcnlaw@aol.com.

ROBINSON, WARREN A. (RIP ROBINSON), lawyer; b. Denver, Mar. 23, 1957; s. William A. and Mary Jane Robinson; m. Janice M. Koerwer, Aug. 18, 1979; children: John William, Robert Joseph, Matthew Laurence, Sarah Elizabeth. BA, Seton Hall U., 1979; JD, U. Denver, 1982. Bar: Colo. 1982, U.S. Dist. Ct. Colo. 1982, U.S. Ct. Appeals (10th cir.) 1984. Assoc. Greengard, Blackman & Senter, Denver, 1982-83; assoc., ptnr. Silver & Hayes, P.C., Denver, 1983-89; ptnr. Silver, Robinson & Barrick, P.C., Denver, 1989-91; shareholder Robinson & Schuyler, P.C., Denver, 1991-2000; pvt. practice Littleton, Colo., 2000—. Mem. Colo. Bar Assn., Arapahoe County Bar Assn. Democrat. Christian. Avocations: sports, stained glass, coaching children. General civil litigation, Family and matrimonial, Personal injury (including property damage). Office: 7931 S Broadway # 308 Littleton CO 80122 E-mail: warjd@aol.com.

ROBINSON, WILKES COLEMAN, retired federal judge; b. Anniston, Ala., Sept. 30, 1925; s. Walter Wade and Catherine Elizabeth (Coleman) R.; m. Julia Von Poellnitz Rowan, June 24, 1955; children: Randolph C., Peyton H., Thomas Wilkes Coleman. BA, U. Ala., 1948; JD, U. Va., 1951. Bar: Ala. 1951, Va. 1962, Mo. 1966, Kans. 1983. Assoc. Bibb & Hemphill, Anniston, Ala., 1951-54; city recorder City of Anniston, 1953-55; judge Juvenile and Domestic Relations Ct. of Calhoun County, Ala., 1954-56; atty. legal dept. GM&O R.R., Mobile, Ala., 1956-58; commerce counsel, asst. gen. atty. Seaboard Air Line R.R., Richmond, Va., 1958-66; chief commerce counsel Monsanto Co., St. Louis, 1966-70; gen. counsel, v.p. Marion Labs., Inc., Kansas City, Mo., 1970-79; pres. Gulf and Gt. Plains Legal Found., Kansas City, Mo., 1980-85, also bd. dirs.; atty. Howard, Needles, Tammen & Bergendoff, Kansas City, 1985-86, also bd. dirs.; v.p. S.R. Fin. Group, Inc., Overland Park, Kans., 1986-87; judge U.S. Ct. Fed. Claims, Washington, 1987-97, sr. judge, 1997—. Bd. govs. Kansas City Philharmonic Orch., 1975-77. Served with USNR, 1943-44. Mem. Indian Bayou Golf Club, Scottish Rite, Phi Beta Kappa (past treas. Kansas City, Mo. chpt.), Phi Eta Sigma, Phi Alpha Theta, Kappa Alpha. Episcopalian. Home: 12 Weekewachee Cir Destin FL 32541-4426

ROBINSON, WILLIAM ADAMS, lawyer; b. Flushing, N.Y., Sept. 7, 1936; s. William E. and Marjorie Robinson. BA in Internat. Econs., Stanford U., 1958, postgrad. Law Sch., 1960—62; JD, Golden Gate U., 1964. Bar: (Calif.) 1965, (U.S. Supreme Ct.) 1984. Assoc. Barfield, Barfield & Dryden, San Francisco, 1970—71; ptnr. Goldeen, Goldeen & Robinson, Lafayette, Calif., 1966—70; assoc. Miller, Van Dorn & Bowen, San Francisco, 1970—71; sr. trial counsel Calif. State Automobile Assn., San Francisco, 1971—96; mediator, arbitrator, pvt. adminstrv. law judge Law Offices William A. Robinson, San Francisco, 1996—. Dep. sheriff Santa Clara County, Calif., 1962; claims authorizer Social Security Adminstrn., San Francisco, 1963—64; lectr. C.E.B. Golden Gate U. Law Sch., 1978—; referee State Bar Ct. state and fed. jud. arbitrator; prof. Monterey Coll. Law. Author: Practicing California Judicial Arbitration, CEB, 1983—89. Pres. Easter Seal Soc., Marin County, Calif., 1978—79; foreman Monterey County Civil Grand Jury, 2003. Capt. politico-mil. affairs USNR, 1955—88. Mem.: Bar Assn. San Francisco (chmn. arbitration com.), Am. Arbitration Assn. (arbitrator), U.S. Naval Order, Tiburon Yacht Club (commodore 1983), Naval Air Sta. Aero Club. Office: 3033 Strawberry Hill Rd Pebble Beach CA 93953-2922

ROBINSON, ZELIG, lawyer; b. Balt., July 7, 1934; s. Morton Matthew and Mary (Ackerman) R.; m. Karen Ann Bergstrom (div. Oct. 1987); children: John, Christopher, Kristin; m. Linda Portner Strangmann, Dec. 23, 1987. BA, Johns Hopkins U., 1954; LLB, Harvard U., 1957. Bar: Md. 1958. Legis. analyst Md. House of Dels., Annapolis, 1958; tech. asst. IRS, Washington, 1958-60; pvt. practice Balt., 1960-62; assoc. gen. counsel commerce com. U.S. Ho. of Reps., Washington, 1962-64; assoc. Weinberg & Green, Balt., 1964-66; special legal cons. commerce com. U.S. Ho. of Reps., Washington, 1966-68; pvt. practice Balt., 1966-72; mem. Gordon, Feinblatt, Rothman, Hoffberger & Hollander, LLC, 1972—. Bd. dirs. Durapak Mfg. Co., Balt., Vac Pac, Inc., Balt., Universal Die Casting Co., Inc., Saline, Mich.; chmn. Balt. City Minimum Wage Commn., 1974-82, Md. Pub. Broadcasting, 1991-95; mem. Gov.'s Commn. to revise Md. Code, Annapolis, 1968-89. Contbr. articles to profl. jours. Bd. dirs., v.p./sec. Gov.'s Mansion Found., Annapolis, Md.; v.p. bd. dirs. Md. Cmtys. and Citizens Fund, Chestertown, Md.; sec. bd. dirs. William Donald Schaefer Civic Fund; bd. dirs. Md. Arts Pl., Balt., Balt. Coalition of Homeowners, 1989—, v.p., Everyman Theatre, 2002-; mem. Found. for Md. Pub. Broadcasting; trustee Hist. Soc.; bd. dirs., pres. Celebration 2000, Inc., 1998—; founder, bd. dirs. Baltimore Efficiency and Econ. Found., 1999—. With U.S. Army, 1958. Mem. ABA, Md. State Bar Assn. (laws com., internat. law com.). Democrat. Corporate, general, Private international, Mergers and acquisitions. Office: Gordon Feinblatt Rothman Hoffberger & Hollander LLC 233 E Redwood St Baltimore MD 21202-3332 E-mail: zrobinson@gfrlaw.com.

ROBINSON-DORN, MICHAEL JAY, lawyer, director; b. N.Y.C., Apr. 14, 1966; s. Elke Angelica Davenport and Paul Myron Robinson; m. Trilby Constance Elizabeth Dorn, Oct. 19, 2002; children: Grace Karen Robinson children: Hannah Elizabeth Robinson, Max Aaron Robinson. BA, U. (Can.) Victoria, 1988; J.D. cum laude, Cornell U., Ithaca, NY, 1991. Bar: Calif. 1992, DC 1993, Wash. 2000, U.S. Supreme Ct. 1999. Law clk. Hon. Morton A. Brody, U.S. Dist. Judge, Bangor, Maine, 1991—92; assoc. Jones Day Reavis & Pogue, Washington, 1992—95; trial atty. U.S. Dept. Justice, ENRD-Environment & Natural Resources Divsn., Washington, 1995—99; ptnr. Riddell Wiliams, PS, Seattle, 1999—2002; dir., environ. protection sect. Seattle (Wash.) City Attorney's Office, 2002—. Mem. 9th Circuit Pro Bono Panel, Seattle; mem. editl. bd. Wash. State Bar, Environment and Land Use Sect., Seattle, 2001. Mem.: ABA (vice chair, marine resources committee 1994—96). Achievements include Named a Rising Star in Law and Politics Magazine (2002). Environmental, Natural resources, Federal civil litigation. Office: Seattle City Atty's Office 600 Fourth Ave 10th Fl Seattle WA 98104 Office Fax: 206-684-8284. E-mail: michaelj.robinson-dorne@seattle.gov.

ROBINSON-DORN, TRILBY C. E. lawyer; b. Spokane, Wash., Aug. 20, 1970; d. Charles Stuart Dorn and Karen Dorn-Steele; m. Michael J. Robinson-Dorn; 1 child, Grace Karen. BA with honors, Swarthmore Coll., 1992; JD cum laude, Tulane U., 1997. Bar: Wash. 1997, U.S. Dist. Ct. (We. Dist.) Wash. 1997. Ea. Wash. field dir. Wash. Dem. Party Coordinated Campaign, Spokane, 1992, Wash. Environ. Coun., Spokane, 1992-94; law clk. Fed. Pub. Defender of Western Wash., Seattle, 1995, Wash. Environ. Coun., Seattle, 1995, Riddell Williams, Seattle, 1996, atty., 1997—2002,

Tousley Brain Stephens, 2002—. Mem. Washington Women Lawyers Bd., 2001—. Mem. adv. bd. Tulane Environ. Law Jour., 1998-99, editor-in-chief, 1997. Ea. Wash. field organizer Clinton Campaign, Spokane, 1992; coop. atty. ACLU, Seattle, 1998-99, mem., 1998-99; vol. N.W. Immigrants' Rights Project, Seattle, 1998-99. Mem. Wash. Bar Assn., King County Bar Assn., King County Wash. Women Lawyers (bd. dirs. 1998-2000), ACLU, (bd. dir. 2003-). Democrat. Avocations: reading, travel, hiking, dogs, cooking. General civil litigation, Environmental. Office: Tousley Brain Stephens 700 5th St Ste 5600 Seattle WA 98104

ROBISON, WILLIAM ROBERT, lawyer; b. Memphis, May 5, 1947; s. Andrew Cliffe and Elfrieda (Barnes) R. AB, Boston U., 1970; JD, Northeastern U., 1974. Bar: Mass. 1974, D.C. 1975, U.S. Dist. Ct. Mass. 1975, U.S. Ct. Appeals (1st cir.) 1975, U.S. Dist. Ct. Conn. 1977, U.S. Supreme Ct. 1977, Calif. 1978, U.S. Dist. Ct. (cen. dist.) Calif. 1979, U.S. Ct. Appeals (9th cir.) 1979. Assoc. Meyers, Goldstein, et al, Boston, 1975-76, Cooley, Shrair, et al, Springfield, Mass., 1976-78, Hertzberg, et al, Los Angeles, 1978-79, Marcus & Lewi, Santa Monica, Calif., 1980-81; pvt. practice, Santa Monica, 1981—. Lectr. Northeastern U., Boston, 1975-76; judge pro-tem., Mcpl. Ct., Los Angeles, 1984—, Los Angeles Superior Ct., 1987—. Co-author: Commercial Transactions, 1976. Bd. dirs. Boston Legal Asst. Project, 1972-75, Action for Boston Community Devel., Inc., 1971-75. Mem. ABA, Los Angeles County Bar Assn., Santa Monica Bar Assn. (Cert. of Appreciation 1987). Democrat. Unitarian Universalist. State civil litigation, Construction, Property, real (including real estate development, water). Home and Office: 2546 Amherst Ave Los Angeles CA 90064-2712

ROBLES-ROMAN, CAROL A. municipal official; b. Bronx, N.Y., 1962; m. Nelson Roman; 1 child, Adriana Roman. BA, Fordham U.; JD, NYU. Bar: N.Y. 1990. Sr. v.p., gen. counsel P.R. Indsl. Devel. Co.; asst. atty. gen. civil rights bur. N.Y. State Dept. of Law; chief staff, counsel to dep. chief adminstrv. judge Hon. Barry Cozier N.Y. State Unified Ct. Sys., spl. insp. gen. bias matters, dir. pub. affairs, spl. counsel to chief adminstrv. judge Hon. Jonathan Lippman; dep. mayor legal affairs, counsel to Mayor Mike Bloomberg City of New York. Counsel to com. promote pub. trust and confidence Unified Ct. Sys. Bd. dirs. N.Y. State Jud. Com. Women and Cts. Named one of N.Y.'s 50 Outstanding Latinas, El Diario/La Prensa. Mem.: NYU Black, Latino, and Asian Pacific Alumni Assn. (pres. 1999—2000). Office: City Hall New York NY 10007*

ROBOL, RICHARD THOMAS, lawyer; b. Norfolk, Va., Feb. 8, 1952; s. Harry James and Lucy Henley (Johnson) R. BA, U. Va., 1974; JD, Harvard U., 1978. Bar: Va. 1979, Ohio 1996, U.S. Dist. Ct. (ea. dist.) Va. 1979, U.S. Ct. Appeals (4th cir.) 1979, U.S. Dist. Ct. (we. dist.) Va. 1981, U.S. Supreme Ct. 1982, D.C. 1991, U.S. Ct. Appeals (4th, 6th and 9th cirs.) 1995. Law clk. to presiding justice U.S. Dist. Ct. (ea. dist.) Va., 1978-79; ptnr. Seawell, Dalton, Hughes & Timms, Norfolk, 1979-87, Hunton and Williams, Norfolk, 1987-92; exec. v.p., gen. counsel Columbus Am. Discovery Group, Inc., 1992—. Adj. prof. U. Dayton Law Sch.; asst. prof. mil. sci. Capital U.; pro bono counsel Nat. Commn. for Prevention Child Abuse, Norfolk, 1983, Tidewater Profl. Assn. on Child Abuse, 1983, Parents United Va., 1981-82, Sexual Abuse Help Line, 1983-86; mem. Boyd-Graves Conf. on Civil Procedure in Va., 1981-87. Contbr. articles to law revs.; contbg. editor: International Law for General Practitioners, 1981. Bd. dirs. Va. Opera Assn. Guild, Norfolk, 1983-87, Tidewater br. NCCJ, 1991-92; deacon Ctrl. Bapt. Ch., Norfolk, 1980-83. Capt. USAR, 1992—. Fulbright scholar, 1974. Mem. Va. State Bar Assn. (bd. dirs. internat. law sect. 1984-87, chmn. 1982-83), Va. Young Lawyers Assn. (cir. rep. 1984-88), Va. Assn. Def. Attys., Maritime Law Assn., Norfolk-Portsmouth Bar assn. (chmn. speakers bur. 1987-88), Assn. Def. Trial Attys. (chmn. Va. 1987), Def. Rsch. Inst., 1982-88. Avocations: camping, rowing, scuba diving. General civil litigation, Intellectual property, Personal injury (including property damage). Home: 60 Kenyon Brook Dr Worthington OH 43085-3629 Office: Columbus Am Discovery Group 433 W 6th Ave Columbus OH 43201-3136 E-mail: robol@ee.net.

ROBRENO, EDUARDO C. federal judge; b. 1945; BA, Westfield State Coll., 1967; MA, U. Mass., 1969; JD, Rutgers U., 1978. With antitrust divsn. U.S. Dept Justice, Phila., 1978-81; ptnr. Meltzer & Schiffrin, Phila., 1981-86, Fox, Rothschild, O'Brien & Frankel, Phila., 1987-92; judge U.S. Dist. Ct. for Ea. Dist. Pa., Phila., 1992—. Mem. Jud. Conf. Com. on Bankruptcy Rules. Fellow Am. Law Inst. Office: US Courthouse Rm 3810 Philadelphia PA 19106

ROBSON, DOUGLAS SPEARS, lawyer; b. Balt., Jan. 25, 1967; s. Martin C. Robson and Susan Robson Eck; m. Anne Marie Schreiber, July 27, 1991; children: Meghan, Brendan, Kevin. BA, Ind. U., 1989; JD, DePaul U., 1992. Bar: Ill., 1992, U.S. Dist. Ct. (no. dist.) Ill. 1993. Assoc. Wolfe & Polovin, Chgo., 1992-95, Hickey, Driscoll, Kurfirst, Patterson & Melia, Chgo., 1995-98, ptnr., 1999—2001, Handler, Thayer & Duggam, Chgo., 2002—. Mem. Chgo. Bar Assn. (mem. corp. and bus. law com., probate and trust law com.), Ill. State Bar Assn. Corporate, general, Estate planning, Property, real (including real estate development, water). Home: 2609 Oriole Trl Long Beach IN 46360-1651 Office: Ste 680 333 W Wacker Dr Chicago IL 60606-1225

ROBY, DANIEL ARTHUR, lawyer; b. Anderson, Ind., Aug. 16, 1941; s. Virgil A. and Frances E. R. A.B. with honors, Ind. U., 1963, J.D., 1966. Bar: Ind. 1966, U.S. Dist. Ct. (no. dist.) Ind. 1967, U.S. Dist. Ct. (so. dist.) Ind. 1966, U.S. Ct. Appeals (7th cir.) 1968. Practice law, Ft. Wayne, Ind.; faculty lectr. Ind. U.; mem. Ind. Jud. Nominating Com., 1997-99; mem. Allen County Jud. Nominating Commn., 1983—. Past pres. Allen County (Ind.) Heart Assn., Northeastern Ind. Heart Assn.; chmn. bd. Ind. affiliate Am. Heart Assn.; past pres. bd. mgrs. Faith Bapt. Ch. Mem. Ind. State Bar Assn., Allen County Bar Assn. (bd. dirs. 1983), Assn. Trial Lawyers Am., Ind. Trial Lawyers Assn. (bd. dirs. 1980—, pres. 1993, named Lawyer of Yr. 1986, Lifetime Achievement award 2004), Am. Arbitration Assn. (bd. arbitrators). Contbr. articles to legal jours. Product liability, Professional liability. Office: Standard Fed Pla 200 E Main St Ste 520 Fort Wayne IN 46802-1998

ROCH, MICHAEL PETER, lawyer; b. Munich, Mar. 20, 1970; s. Heinz Peter and Ingeborg Roch. BS, MA in Acctg., U. Denver, 1991, JD, 1996. Bar: Colo. 1996. Auditor KPMG, Atlanta, 1991—92; mgmt. cons. ITEO, Ljubljana, Slovenia, 1993; atty. Dufford & Brown, Denver, 1996—2000, Holland & Hart, Denver, 2000—01, Norton Rose, Frankfurt, Germany, 2001—. Strategic adv. GEA Coll., Ljubjana, 1993; adj. prof. U. Denver Coll. Law, 1998—2000, U. Denver Sch. Accountancy, 1994—96; adj. prof. dept. econs. Colo. Sch. Mines, 1997. Co-author: Expert Regulations, The Law of Transnational Business Transactions, 1997; co-editor: Doing Bus. in the U.S., 1989—98; contbr. articles to profl. jours. Treas. Rocky Mountain Human Rights Law Group, Denver, 1990—. Mem.: ABA, German and Am. Lawyers Assn., Denver Bar Assn. (pub. edn. com. 1996—), Colo. Bar Assn. (interprof. com. 1996—). Avocations: tennis, skiing, travel, running, writing. Securities, Mergers and acquisitions, Private international. Office: Norton Rose Stephanstrasse 15 60313 Frankfurt Germany

ROCHE, DONAL AIDAN, lawyer; b. Dublin, Oct. 3, 1954; s. Donal Michael and Eileen Roche; m. Mary Roche, 1978; children: Eileen, Celeste, Alice, Donal. M of Legal Sci., Trinity Coll., 1975. Ptnr. Matheson Ormoby Prentice, Dublin, 1984—95, mng. ptnr., 1995—. Office: Matheson Ormsby Prentice 30 Herbert St Dublin 2 Ireland

ROCHE, JOHN JEFFERSON, lawyer; b. N.Y.C., Apr. 12, 1934; s. William and Florence E. (Garvey) R.; m. Judith J. Stackpole, Sept. 4, 1980; 1 child from previous marriage, Forrest B. AB, Brown U., 1957; LL.B., Boston U., 1964. Bar: Mass. 1964, U.S. Tax Ct. 1976. Asst. atty. gen. Dept. Atty. Gen., Boston, 1964-67; ptnr. Hale and Dorr, Boston, 1967-90; pvt. practice Cambridge, Mass., 1991-2001; ptnr. Taylor, Ganson & Perrin LLP, Boston, 2001—. Trustee The Hotchkiss Sch., 1986-91, Archaeol. Inst. Am., 1998—; bd. dirs. Indian Soc., Bostonian Soc. Served with U.S. Army, 1959-62. Fellow Am. Coll. Trusts and Estates, Internat. Acad. Estate and Trust Law; mem. ABA, Mass. Bar Assn., Boston Bar Assn., Masons, Wig and Penn Club (London), Winchester Country Club. Republican. Congregationalist. Estate planning, Probate (including wills, trusts), Estate taxation. Office: Taylor Ganson & Perrin 160 Federal St Boston MA 02110-1700

ROCHELLE, ROBERT THOMAS, lawyer, former state legislator; b. Nashville, Nov. 25, 1945; s. James Marcell and Katherine (Purnell) R.; m. Janice Johnson, Aug. 18, 1973; 1 son, Aaron Marcellus. BS, Cumberland Coll. Bar: Tenn. Sole practice law, Lebanon, Tenn.; county atty. Wilson County, Tenn., 1974—87; mem. Tenn. Senate, 1982—2002, Rochelle, McCulloch, Aulds P.L.L.C., 2003—. Democratic del. Nat. Conv. from Wilson County, 1974; coord. 4th Congl. Dist. for Carter for Pres., 1976, 80; state vice chmn. Mondale for Pres., 1984; bd. dirs. YMCA, 1971-76; chmn. Children's Hosp. Fund Drive, 1977-78; legacies chmn. Cancer Crusade, 1977-83; bd. dirs. Wilson County Promotions, Inc. Served with U.S. Army, 1969-71. Decorated Army Commendation medal with oak leaf cluster, Bronze Star, Vietnam Svc. medal; recipient Svc. to Youth award YMCA, 1974; named Outstanding Young Man of Yr., Lebanon Jr. C. of C., 1978. Mem. ABA, Wilson County Bar Assn., Tenn. Bar Assn., U. Tenn. Alumni Assn. (pres. 1974), Lebanon/Wilson County C. of C., West Wilson C. of C. Methodist. Office: 109 Castle heights Ave N Lebanon TN 37087*

ROCHELLE, VICTOR CLEANTHUS, lawyer; b. Nov. 4, 1918; s. Floyd Emerson and Goldie Opal (Dunbar) Rochelle; m. Marjorie Armitage, Dec. 20, 1946 (div. 1956); children: Vickie Adrianne, Margo Renee; m. Patricia Ann Leary, Mar. 20, 1964; children: Elizabeth Ann, Linda Raquel. BA, U. Tex., 1940; LLB, Columbia U., 1947. Bar: Tex. 48, U.S. Dist. Ct. Ill. 53. Assoc. Tom Hartley, Atty., Pharr, Tex., 1947—49, Kelly, Looney, McLean & Littleton, Edinburg, Tex., 1949—52; personal injury supr. County Mut. Ins. Co., Chgo., 1952—57, claims mgr., 1957—61, Bloomington, Ill., 1961—69; cons., dir. litigation Country Mut., Country Casualty, Mid-Am., 1969—84; ins. law cons., 1984—. Lectr. in field.; arbitrator Mut. Casualty, 1965—70. Lt. comdr. USN, 1941—45. Mem.: ABA, Am. Judicature Soc., Def. Rsch. Inst., Property Loss Bur., Internat. Assn. Ins. Counsel, McLean County Bar Assn., Ill. Bar Assn., Tex. Bar Assn. Reform. Address: 27 Lateer Dr Normal IL 61761-3925

ROCKEFELLER, EDWIN SHAFFER, lawyer; b. Sept. 10, 1927; s. Edwin and Nancy Rhea (McCullough) R.; m. Marilie Gould Wallace, Dec. 22, 1952; children: Ben Wallace, Edwin Palmer. AB, Yale U., 1948, LLB, 1951; M in Internat. Pub. Policy, Johns Hopkins U., 1989. Bar: Conn. 1951, D.C. 1956, U.S. Supreme Ct. 1957. Atty. FTC, 1956—61, asst. to gen. counsel, 1958—59, exec. asst. to chmn., 1960—61; pvt. practice Washington, 1961; chmn. adv. bd. bna.antitrust rept., 1961—. Mem. USIA Inspection Team, Pakistan, 1971; adj. prof. Georgetown U. Law Ctr., Washington, 1987. Author: Antitrust Questions & Answers, 1974, Desk Book of FTC Practice & Procedure, 3d edit., 1979, Antitrust Counseling for the 1980s, 1983. Mem.: ABA (chmn. sect. antitrust law 1976—77, ho. of dels. 1979—82), Met. Club, Chevy Chase Club. Administrative and regulatory, Antitrust. Office: Ste 1114 2801 New Mexico Ave NW Washington DC 20007-3940

ROCKETT, D. JOE, lawyer, director; b. Drumright, Okla., May 3, 1942; s. Gordon Richard and Hazel Peggy (Rigsby) R.; m. Mary Montgomery, Aug. 31, 1963; children: David Montgomery, Ann Morley. BA, U. Okla., 1964, JD, 1967. Bar: Okla. 1967, U.S. Dist. Ct. (we. dist.) Okla. 1968. Assoc. Kerr, Davis, Irvine & Burbage, Oklahoma City, 1967-69, Andrews Davis Legg Bixler Milsten & Price, Oklahoma City, 1969-73, mem., 1973—, also bd. dirs., pres., 1986-90, 96-00. Securities law advisor Oil Investment Inst., Washington, 1984-87. Bd. dirs. Myriad Gardens Conservatory, Oklahoma City, 1987—, chmn., 1991-92. Mem. ABA (fed. regulation of securities and partnership coms. of bus. law sect. 1984), Okla. Bar Assn. (securities liaison com. 1983, chmn. bus. assocs. sect. 1985, securities adminstr.'s select com. 1986—). Avocations: sailing, fishing, skiing. Corporate, general, Mergers and acquisitions, Securities. Office: Andrews Davis Legg Bixler Milsten & Price 500 W Main St Ste 500 Oklahoma City OK 73102-2275 E-mail: djrockett@andrewsdavis.com.

ROCKEY, ARLAINE, lawyer, writer; b. Parma, Ohio, Apr. 18, 1962; d. Arthur G. and Elaine D. R. BA, U. N.C., 1984; JD, U. Miami, 1989. Bar: Fla. 1989, N.C. 1991, D.C. 1992. Atty. Legal Svcs. of Gtr. Miami, Fla., 1989-91; ptnr. Rockey & Collias, Charlotte, NC, 1991—93, Legal Svcs. of So. Piedmont, Charlotte, 1993—99; assoc. Weaver, Bennett & Bland, Charlotte, 2001—02; pvt. practice Charlotte, 1999—2001, 2002—. Author: Ocean Court, 1999, Protecting Children from Sexual Abuse in Custody Cases, 2003. Mem. ACLU (bd. dirs. N.C. chpt. 1994-97), Assn. Reform of N.C. Marital Rape Laws (founder, co-chair 1991-93), N.C. Assn. Women Attys. (bd. dirs., edn. chair 1994). Avocations: music, travel. Civil rights, Family and matrimonial, Juvenile. Office: 4736 Sharon Rd Ste W-125 Charlotte NC 28210-3328 E-mail: arockey@aol.com.

ROCKLEN, KATHY HELLENBRAND, lawyer; b. N.Y.C., June 30, 1951; BA, Barnard Coll., 1973; JD magna cum laude, New England Sch. Law, 1977. Bar: N.Y. 1978, U.S. Dist. Ct. (so. and ea. dists.) N.Y. 1982, U.S. Dist. Ct. (no. dist.) Calif. 1985. Interpretive counsel N.Y. Stock Exchange, N.Y.C.; 1st v.p. E.F. Hutton & Co. Inc., N.Y.C.; v.p., gen. counsel and sec. S.G Warburg (U.S.A.) Inc., N.Y.C.; mem. Proskauer Rose LLP, N.Y.C. Adj. prof. Fordham Sch. Law. Mem. exec. com. lawyers divsn. Am. Friends Hebrew U.; mem. lawyers' divsn. exec. com. ADL. Mem. N.Y. State Bar Assn., N.Y. Women's Bar Assn., Assn. Bar City N.Y. (v.p., chmn. exec. com., chmn. drugs and law com., chmn. fed. legis. com., chmn. libr. com., securities law com., sec. 2d century com., sex and law com., young lawyers'com., corp. law com.). Banking, Corporate, general, Securities. Office: Proskauer Rose LLP 1585 Broadway New York NY 10036 E-mail: krocklen@proskauer.com.

ROCKOWITZ, NOAH EZRA, lawyer; b. N.Y.C., Apr. 11, 1949; s. Murray and Anna Rae (Cohen) R.; m. Julie Rachel Levitan, Dec. 24, 1978; children: Shira Aviva, Leora Civia, Dahlia Yaffa. BA, Queens Coll., 1969; JD, Fordham U., 1973. Bar: N.Y. 1974, U.S. Dist. Ct. (so. and ea. dists.) N.Y. 1974, U.S. Ct. Appeals (2d cir.) 1974. Tchr., chmn. social studies dept. Intermediate Sch. 74, Queens, N.Y., 1969-73; atty. Cahill Gordon & Reindel, N.Y.C., 1973-78; corp. sec., asst. gen. counsel Belco Petroleum Corp., N.Y.C., 1978—85; v.p., gen. counsel Hudson Gen. Corp., Great Neck, NY, 1985-98, sr. v.p., 1998—2001; sr. v.p., gen. counsel GlobeGround N.Am. LLC, Great Neck, NY, 2001—. Trustee, exec. com., chmn. bd. edn. The Solomon Schechter Sch. Westchester; trustee Beth El Synagogue of New Rochelle; Westchester adv. com. Bd. Jewish Edn. Greater N.Y. Mem. ABA, Am. Soc. Corp. Secs., N.Y. State Bar Assn., Assn. of Bar of City of N.Y., Am. Corp. Counsel Assn., Phi Beta Kappa. Commercial, contracts (including sales of goods; commercial financing), Corporate, general, Securities. Office: GlobeGround NAm LLC 111 Great Neck Rd PO Box 355 Great Neck NY 11022-0355

ROCKWELL, WINTHROP ADAMS, lawyer; b. Pittsfield, Mass., May 7, 1948; s. Landon Gale Rockwell and Ruth (Adams) Lonsdale; m. Barbara Washburn Wood, June 20, 1970; children: Samuel Adams, Madeleine McCord. AB, Dartmouth Coll., 1970; JD, NYU, 1975. Bar: Minn. 1975, U.S. Dist. Ct. Minn. 1975. Asst. newsman fgn. desk N.Y. Times, N.Y.C., 1970-71; asst. to pres. Dartmouth Coll., Hanover, N.H., 1971-72; assoc. Faegre & Benson, Mpls., 1975-79; assoc. chief counsel Pres.'s Commn. on Accident at Three Mile Island, Washington, 1979; assoc. Faegre & Benson, Mpls., 1979-82, ptnr., 1983—, chmn. diversity com., 1990-95, head gen. litigation group, 1995—. Bd. dirs., v.p. Children's Theatre, Mpls., 1982-83; bd. dirs. Actors Theatre St. Paul, 1975-79, Trinity Films, Mpls., 1978-82, Minn. Ctr. for Book Arts, 1996—; mem. adv. bd. Univ. Minn. Joint Degree Program in Law, Health and the Life Scis. Brit.-Am. Project fellow, 1987. Mem. ABA, Minn. Bar Assn., Hennepin County Bar Assn., Am. Agrl. Law Assn., Adirondack 46ers, Adirondack Mountain Club. Avocations: writing, tennis, mountaineering, gardening. Federal civil litigation, State civil litigation. Home: 1901 Knox Ave S Minneapolis MN 55403-2840 Office: Faegre & Benson 2200 Wells Fargo Ctr 90 S 7th St Ste 2200 Minneapolis MN 55402-3901 E-mail: wrockwell@faegre.com.

ROCKWOOD, LINDA LEE, lawyer; b. Cedar Rapids, Iowa, July 25, 1950; d. Robert Walter and Dorothy Jean (Rehberg) Sorensen; children: Holly Lynn, Christian Douglas. BA, U. Denver, 1972; JD, U. Tex., 1984. Bar: Colo. 1984, U.S. Dist. Ct. Colo., U.S. Ct. Appeals (10th cir.). Assoc. Holland & Hart, Denver, 1984-88; shareholder, dir. Parcel, Mauro & Spaanstra, Denver, 1988-98, pres., 1996-98; ptnr. Faegre & Benson, Denver, 1998—, adminstrv. ptnr., 2001—. Author: New Mines From Old Environmental Considerations in Remining and Reprocessing of Waste Materials, 1991, The Alcan Decisions: Causation Through the Back Door, 1993, RCRA Demystified: The Professional's Guide to Hazardous Waste Law, 1996, Citizen Suits: Public Interest or Private Advocacy, 2000, Institutional Controls: Brownfields Superweapon or Ultimate Trojan Horse?, 2000. Bd. dirs. Colo. Hazardous Waste Mgmt. Soc., 1986, 89-91, pres., 1987-88; mem. Mayor's Convention Ctr. Task Force, 1997-99, Ctrl. Platte Valley Devel. Coun., 1999—. Mem. Colo. Bar Assn. (exec. coun. environ. law sect. 1987-90), Environ. Law Inst., Rocky Mountain Mineral Law Found., Order of Coif, Phi Beta Kappa. Administrative and regulatory, Environmental. Office: Faegre & Benson LLP 3200 Wells Fargo Ctr 1700 Lincoln St Denver CO 80203 E-mail: lrockwood@faegre.com.

ROCQUE, VINCENT JOSEPH, lawyer; b. Franklin, N.H., Nov. 27, 1945; s. Francis Albert and Mary Helen (O'Grady) R.; m. Emily Adams Arnold, May 31, 1969; children: Amanda Adams, Peter O'Connor, Caroline Quin. BA magna cum laude, Georgetown U., 1967; JD, Columbia U., N.Y.C., 1970. Bar: D.C. 1971, U.S. Supreme Ct., 1973. Assoc. Hogan & Hartson, Washington, 1970-73; counsel, spl. asst. to Commr. Barbara Franklin, U. S. Consumer Product Safety Commn., Washington, 1973-77; asst. dir. bur. trade regulation U.S. Dept. Commerce, Washington, 1977-80; ptnr. Sullivan & Worcester, Washington, 1980-90; pvt. practice law Washington, 1990—. V.p., co-pres. Janney Pub. Elem. Sch. PTA, Washington, 1982-84; vol. coord. homeless shelters Cath. Charities, Washington and Silver Spring, Md., 1984-90. Staff sgt. USAR, 1969-75. Mem. ABA (adminstrv. law and regulatory practice sect. and internat. law and practice sect.), D.C. Bar (internat. law sect. and adminstrv. law and agy. sect.), Fed. Bar Assn. (adminstrv. law and internat. law sects.), Mid-Atlantic Literary Edification Soc., Nat. Capital YMCA, Phi Beta Kappa. Catholic. Avocations: reading, travel, American Civil War history, basketball. Administrative and regulatory, Private international, Legislative. Office: 1155 Connecticut Ave NW Ste 400 Washington DC 20036-4306

ROCUANT, PAUL A. lawyer; b. Bridgeport, Conn., Oct. 18, 1967; s. Ramiro A. and Nadejda R.; m. Kathleen M. Kearney, May 14, 1994; children: Rebecca Marie and Ryan Paul. BA, U. Conn., 1990; JD, New Eng. Sch. Law, 1993. Bar: Fla. 1993, Mass. 1993, U.S. Supreme Ct. 1998. Assoc. Bass & Chernoff, Naples, Fla., 1993-95; atty., pvt. practice Naples, Fla., 1995—. Dir. Sparks Entertainment, Inc., Naples. Pres. Divorce Support Svcs., 2002—. Mem.: Collier County Bar Assn. Family Law Sect. (pres. 1999—2000), Sigma Chi. Family and matrimonial, Personal injury (including property damage). Office: 1100 5th Ave S Ste 409 Naples FL 34102-6419

RODA, JOSEPH FRANCIS, lawyer; b. Lancaster, Pa., June 22, 1949; s. Frank Edward and Mary Virginia (Reeder) R.; m. Dianne M. Nast, Aug. 23, 1980; children: Michael, Daniel, Joseph, Joshua, Anastasia. AB, Harvard Coll., 1971; JD, U. Pa., 1974. Bar: Pa. 1974, U.S. Dist. Ct. (ea. dist.) Pa. 1975, U.S. Dist. Ct. (mid. dist.) Pa. 1981, U.S. Ct. Appeals (3d cir.) 1981, U.S. Supreme Ct. 1982. Law clk. to judge U.S. Dist. Ct. (ea. dist.) Pa., Phila., 1974-75; assoc. Kohn, Savette, Marion & Graf, P.C., Phila., 1975-80; pvt. practice Lancaster, 1980—. Mem. ABA, ATLA, Am. Coll. Trial Lawyers, Pa. Trial Lawyers Assn., Pa. Bar Assn. (ho. dels), Internat. Acad. Trial Lawyers, Lancaster Country Club, Hamilton Club (Lancaster). General civil litigation, Insurance, Personal injury (including property damage). Home: 1059 Sylvan Rd Lancaster PA 17601-1923 Office: 801 Estelle Dr Lancaster PA 17601-2130 E-mail: rodanast@aol.com.

RODEFER, JEFFREY ROBERT, lawyer, prosecutor; b. Santa Fe, Mar. 29, 1963; s. Robert Jacob and Joanne D. (Thomas) R. BS, U. Nev., 1985; JD, cert. dispute resolution, Willamette U., 1988. Bar: Calif. 1990, Nev. 1990, U.S. Dist. Ct. Nev. 1990, U.S. Dist. Ct. (ea. dist.) Calif. 1990, U.S. Ct. Appeals (9th cir.) 1990, Colo. 1991, Oreg. 1997, U.S. Supreme Ct. 1997; cert. arbitrator, Nev. Legal intern Willamette U. Legal Aid Clinic, Salem, Oreg., 1987-88; legal rschr. transp. divsn. Nev. Atty. Gen. Office, Carson City, 1989-90, dep. atty. gen. taxation divsn., 1990-93, dep. atty. gen. gaming divsn., 1993-99, sr. dep. atty. gen. gaming divsn., 1999-2001, asst. chief dep. atty. gen. gaming divsn., 2001—02; corp. compliance officer, assoc. gen. counsel and asst. sec. Boyd Gaming Corp., Las Vegas, 2002—. Author: Nevada Property Tax Manual, 1993, Nevada Gaming Law Index, 1999; contbr. articles to Nev. Lawyer. Contbg. mem. U. Nev. Coll. Bus. Adminstrn. and Athletic Dept., Reno, 1992, Willamette U. Coll. Law, Ann. Law Fund, Salem, 1992; active Nat. Parks and Recreation Assn., Washington, 1991; mem. First Christian Ch. Mem. Internat. Assn. Gaming Attys., U. Nev. Coll. Bus. Alumni Assn., Am. Inns of Ct. (Bruce R. Thompson chpt.), State Bar Nev. (functional equivalency com. 1993—, chmn. gaming law sect. 2000—), Phi Delta Phi. Republican. Office: Boyd Gaming Corp 2950 Industrial Rd Las Vegas NV 89109-1150 Office Fax: 702-696-1111. E-mail: jeffreyrodefer@boydgaming.com.

RODEMEYER, MICHAEL LEONARD, JR., lawyer; b. Balt., May 25, 1950; s. Michael Leonard and Claire Isabel (Gunther) R.; m. Dorrit Carolyn Green, June 7, 1975; children: Justin, Christoffer. AB, Princeton U., 1972; JD, Harvard U., 1975. Bar: Md. 1977, D.C. 1980, U.S. Ct. Appeals (10th cir.) 1980. Atty. Fed. Trade Commn., Washington, 1976-81, atty. advisor, 1981-84; counsel Subcom. on Natural Resources, Agr. Rsch. & Environ., Washington, 1984-88; staff dir., counsel U.S. Ho. of Reps., Washington, 1988-90, house com. on sci., chief dem. counsel, 1990-98; asst. dir. for environment White House Office of Sci. and Tech. Policy, Washington, 1998-99, dem. legis. dir., 1999-2000; exec. dir. Pew Initiative on Food and Biotech., Washington, 2000—. Democrat. Avocations: computing, bicycling. Home: 6000 Harvard Ave Glen Echo MD 20812-1114 Office: Pew Initiative on Food and Biotech 1331 H St NW Ste 900 Washington DC 20005 E-mail: mrodemeyer@pewagbiotech.org.

RODENBURG, CLIFTON GLENN, lawyer; b. Jamestown, N.D., Apr. 5, 1949; s. Clarence and Dorothy Irene (Peterman) R.; m. Donna Michele Stockman, Mar. 1, 1980. BS, N.D. State U., 1971; JD, U. N.D., 1974; M.L.I.R., Mich. State U., 1976. Bar: N.D. 1974, U.S. Dist. Ct. N.D. 1974, U.S. Ct. Appeals (8th cir.) 1974, Minn. 1980, U.S. Supreme Ct. 1980, S.D. 1983, Nebr. 1984, U.S. Dist. Ct. Minn. 1984, U.S. Dist. Ct. Nebr. 1984, Wis. 1985, U.S. Dist. Ct. Wis. 1985, Mont. 1986, U.S. Dist. Ct. Mont. 1986, bd. cert. Creditors' Rights Law, Am. Bd. Cert. Ptnr. Johnson, Rodenburg & Lauinger, Fargo, N.D., 1976—; pres., gen. counsel Rodenburg Group, Inc., Fargo, 1980—. Contbg. editor: The Developing Labor Law, 1976-80;

drafter N.D. garnishment statutes, 1982. Mem. Acad. Comml. and Bankruptcy Law Specialists. Commercial, consumer (including collections, credit), Commercial, contracts (including sales of goods; commercial financing), Labor (including EEOC, Fair Labor Standards Act, labor-management relations, NLRB, OSHA).

RODEWALD, JOERG, lawyer; b. Cologne, Germany, Mar. 21, 1963; 1st state exam, U. Cologne, 1988, 2nd state exam, 1994, diploma in bus. adminstrn., 1991. Bar: Dist. Ct. Cologne 1994, Berlin 1997. Assoc. Freihalter Krueger & Ptnr., Cologne, 1995—96; sr. assoc., mgr. Andersen Freihalter, Cologne and Berlin, 1996—2000; ptnr. Andersen Luther/Luther Menold, Berlin, 2000—. Lectr. U. Potsdam, Germany, 1997—2003. Author: Handbuch der gmbH & Co, 1997, Handbuch der Rechnungslegung, 2002; contbr. articles to profl. jours. Corporate, general, Taxation, general. Office: Luther Menold Franzoesischestrasse 48 10117 Berlin Germany

RODGERS, FREDERIC BARKER, judge; b. Albany, N.Y., Sept. 29, 1940; s. Prentice Johnson and Jane (Weed) R.; m. Valerie McNaughton, Oct. 8, 1988; 1 child: Gabriel Moore. AB, Amherst Coll., 1963; JD, Union U., 1966. Bar: N.Y. 1966, U.S. Ct. Mil. Appeals 1968, Colo. 1972, U.S. Supreme Ct. 1974, U.S. Ct. Appeals (10th cir.) 1981, U.S. Ct. Appeals (fed. cir.) 2001. Chief dep. dist. atty., Denver, 1972-73; commr. Denver Juvenile Ct., 1973-79; mem. Mulligan Reeves Teasley & Joyce, P.C., Denver, 1979-80; pres. Frederic B. Rodgers, P.C., Breckenridge, Colo., 1980-89; ptnr. McNaughton & Rodgers, Central City, Colo., 1989-91; county ct. judge Gilpin County Combined Cts., Colo., 1987—. Presiding mcpl. judge cities of Breckenridge, Blue River, Black Hawk, Central City, Edgewater, Empire, Idaho Springs, Silver Plume and Westminster, Colo., 1978-96; chmn. com. on mcpl. ct. rules of procedure Colo. Supreme Ct., 1984-96; mem. gen faculty Nat. Jud. Coll. U. Nev., Reno, 1990—, elected to faculty coun., 1993-99 (chair 1999). Author: (with Dilweg, Fretz, Murphy and Wicker) Modern Judicial Ethics, 1992; contbr. articles to profl. jours. Mem. Colo. Commn. on Children, 1982-85, Colo. Youth Devel. Coun., 1989-98, Colo. Family Peace Task Force, 1994-96. Served with JAGC, U.S. Army, 1967-72; to maj. USAR, 1972-88. Decorated Bronze Star with oak leaf cluster, Air medal. Recipient Outstanding County Judge award Colo. 17th Judicial Dist. Victim Adv. Coalition, 1991; Spl. Community Svc. award Colo. Am. Legion, 1979, Lifetime Achievement award Denver Law Club, 2003. Fellow Am. Bar Found., Colo. Bar. Found. (life); mem. ABA (jud. div. exec. coun. 1989-2000, vice-chair 1996-97, chair-elect 1997, chair 1998-99, mem. Ho. of Dels. 1993—, jud. divsn. del. to ABA nominating com. 2000-01, bd. govs. Dist. 11 2001—), Colo. Bar Assn. (bd. govs. 1986-88, 90-92, 93-99, 2002—), Continental Divide Bar Assn., Denver Bar Assn. (bd. trustees 1979-82), First Jud. dist. Bar Assn. (trustee 2000-02), Nat. Conf. Spl. Ct. Judges (chmn. 1989-90), Colo. County Judges Assn. (pres. 1995-96), Colo. Mcpl. Judges Assn. (pres. 1986-87), Colo. Trial Judges Coun. (v.p. 1994-95, sec. 1996-97), Denver Law Club (pres. 1981-82), Colo. Women's Bar Assn., Am. Judicature Soc., Nat. Coun. Juvenile and Family Ct. Judges, Federalist Soc. for Law and Pub. Policy Studies, Judge Advs. Assn., Univ. Club (Denver), Arlberg Club (Winter Park), Marines Meml. Club (San Francisco), Rotary (charter pres. Peak to Peak 2000—, Paul Harris fellow 1996). Episcopalian. Office: Gilpin County Combined Trial Cts 2960 Dory Hill Rd Golden CO 80403-8827 E-mail: frederic.rodgers@judicial.state.co.us.

RODGERS, JOHN HUNTER, lawyer; b. Lubbock, Tex., Jan. 18, 1944; s. James O'Donnell Rodgers and Dorothy (Ulin) Carpenter; m. Anne C. Smith, Nov. 29, 1969; children; Anne Elizabeth, Catherine Hunter. BA, Tex. A&M, 1966; JD, U. Tex., 1969. Bar: Tex. 1969, U.S. Supreme Ct. 1973. Atty. The Southland Corp., Dallas, 1973-79, gen. counsel, 1979-91, sec., 1987-95, sr. v.p., chief adminstrv. officer, 1991-93, exec. v.p., chief adminstrv. officer, 1993-95; pres. Clairemead Corp., Dallas, 1996-2000; sr. v.p., gen. counsel, sec. Am. Pad & Paper Co., Dallas, 1998-2000, pres., 2000—. Mem. visual arts com. Tex. A&M U., 1985-94, bd. dirs. student fund enrichment bd., 1986-94; mem. exec. com. Jr. Achievement Dallas, 1988-93; mem. Dallas Citizens Coun., 1992-95; bd. dirs. Boys and Girls Clubs of Greater Dallas, 1998—; nat. chair Tulane U. Parents Coun., 1997-98; trustee Goals for Dallas, 1991-92; nat. bd. dirs. Boys and Girls Clubs Am., 1993-98; mem. mktg. com. Dallas Mus. Art, 1994-97. Capt. JAGC, U.S. Army, 1969-73, Vietnam. Mem. ABA, Tex. Bar Assn. (coun. mem. corp. counsel sect. 1988), Dallas Bar Assn., Southwestern Legal Found. (adv. bd. Internat. and Comparative Law Ctr., rsch. fellow 1986-94), Nat. Assn. Convenience Stores (bd. dirs. 1993-95). Roman Catholic. Commercial, contracts (including sales of goods; commercial financing), Corporate, general, Mergers and acquisitions. Office: 17304 Preston Rd Ste 555 Dallas TX 75252

RODGERS, STEPHEN JOHN, lawyer, physician, consultant; b. Phila., July 10, 1943; s. Harry Edward Rodgers and Antoinette Julia Muckenfuss; m. Roberta Elaine Rhine, Sept. 21, 1974; children: Abigail Elizabeth, Rebecca Elizabeth. MD, Hahnemann U., 1969; JD, Widener U., 1989. Bar: Pa. 1990, N.J. 1990; med. lic., Pa., Del., N.J. Pvt. practice in family practice and emergency medicine Del. Pain Clinic, Wilmington, 1975-89, asst. dir., 1989-92; pvt. practice as medicolegal cons. Wilmington, 1992—. Mem. Med. Assistance and Health Svcs. Adv. Bd., N.J., 1996-98; chair Task Force on Ind. Med. Exam., Dept. Labor and Industry, Commonwealth of Pa., 1996-98. Comdr. USN, 1968-75; capt. USNR, 1975—; surgeon gen. N.J. Naval Militia Joint Command. Fellow Am. Acad. Family Physicians, Am. Acad. Disability Evaluating Physicians, Am. Acad. Emergency Medicine, Am. Coll. Legal Medicine; mem. Aerospace Med. Assn., Pa. Bar Assn. (health care com. 1991—), Del. Acad. Medicine, N.J. Acad. Family Physicians (ho. of dels. 1989, 90, 91), Vietnam Vets. of Am. Republican. Roman Catholic. Avocations: equestrian, pro bono veterans and disability advocate. Health. Home: PO Box 54 Alloway NJ 08001-0054 Office: Ste 14 1701 Augustine Wilmington DE 19803

RODMAN, JOHN SLATER, lawyer; b. Boston, June 21, 1953; s. Sumner and Helen (Morris) R.; m. Pamela Taglienti, May 30, 1976; children: Calvin, Lydia. BA, U. Pa., 1975; JD, Boston U., 1978. Bar: Mass. 1978, U.S. Dist. Ct. Mass. 1978, U.S. Ct. Appeals (1st cir.) 1979, U.S. Supreme Ct. 1982, U.S. Dist. Ct. (no. dist.) Ill. 1998. With Gargill, Sassoon & Rudolph, Boston, 1979-89; head of bankruptcy dept. Parker, Coulter, Daley & White, Boston, 1989-94; pvt. practice Boston, 1994—; of counsel Mauser & Mauser, Boston, 1999—. Chmn. Newton (Mass.) Hist. Commn.; mem. Chestnut Hill Hist. Dist. Commn., Newton. Mem. Mass. Bar Assn., Boston Bar Assn., Comml. Law League Am., Am. Bankruptcy Inst. Bankruptcy, Property, real (including real estate development, water). Office: 180 Canal St Ste 400 Boston MA 02114-1804

RODMAN, LEROY ELI, lawyer; b. N.Y.C., Feb. 22, 1914; s. Morris and Sadie (Specter) R.; m. Toby Chertcoff, Mar. 14, 1943; children: John Stephen, Lawrence Bernard. AB, CCNY, 1933; JD (James Kent scholar), Columbia, 1936. Bar: N.Y. 1937. Practiced in, N.Y.C., 1937-43, 46—; law sec. to U.S. dist. judge Bklyn., 1936; law asst. Am. Law Inst., N.Y.C., 1937; chief food enforcement unit N.Y. Regional Office, OPA, 1942-43; mem. firm Lawrence R. Condon, N.Y.C., 1937-42; ptnr. Joseph & Rodman, N.Y.C., 1946-53; sr. ptnr. Rodman, Maurer & Dansker, N.Y.C., 1964-73, Carro, Spanbock, Londin, Rodman & Fass, N.Y.C., 1973-78, Rodman & Rodman, N.Y.C., 1978-89, Teitelbaum, Hiller, Rodman, Paden & Hibsher, P.C., N.Y.C., 1990-96; of counsel Morrison, Cohen, Singer & Weinstein LLP, N.Y.C., 1996—. Sec. Ameribrom, Inc., Clearon Corp. Editorial bd.: Columbia Law Rev, 1934-36; Contbr. articles to legal jours. V.p. Ctrl. Synagogue, pres. brotherhood, 1958—60, hon. trustee; bd. dirs. Manhattan coun. Boy Scouts Am., v.p., 1961—68, pres., 1972—75, exec. bd. Greater N.Y. coun. Capt. JAGD U.S. Army, 1943—46. Recipient Certs. Svc., Silver Beaver award Boy Scouts Am., 1962, Eagle Scout. Fellow: Am. Coll. Trust and Estate Counsel; mem.: ABA, Judge Adv. Assn., Assn. of Bar of City of N.Y., N.Y. County Lawyers Assn., Metropolis Country Club (White Plains, N.Y.) (sec. 1976—77, 1980—82, v.p. 1977—78, bd. govs. 1976—82), Univ Club (N.Y.C.), Phi Beta Kappa. Jewish. Corporate, general, Probate (including wills, trusts), Estate taxation. Home: 535 E 86th St New York NY 10028-7533 Office: 750 Lexington Ave New York NY 10022-1200

RODNUNSKY, SIDNEY, lawyer, educator; b. Edmonton, Alta., Can., Feb. 3, 1946; s. B. and I. Rodnunsky; m. Teresita Asuncion; children: Naomi, Shawna, Rachel, Tevie, Claire, Donna, Sidney Jr. BEd, U. Alberta, 1966, LLB, 1973; MEd, U. Calgary, 1969, grad. diploma, 1990; BS, U. of State of N.Y., 1988; MBA, Greenwich U., 1990. Served as regional counsel to Her Majesty the Queen in Right of the Dominion of Can.; former gov. Grande Prairie Regional Coll.; now prin. legal counsel Can. Nat. exec., Alta. coord. for gifted children, ombudsman, SIG coord. Mensa Can.; past pres. Grande Prairie and Dist. Bar Assn., Alta Tchrs. Assn., Aspenview. Author: Breathalyzer Casebook; editor: The Children Speak. Decorated knight Grand Cross Sovereign and Royal Order of Piast, knight Grand Cross Order of St. John the Baptist; knight Hospitaller Order St. John of Jerusalem; Prince of Kiev, Prince of Trabzon, Prince and Duke of Rodari, Duke of Chernigov, Count of Riga, Count of St. John of Alexandria; named to Honorable Order of Ky. Colonels; named adm. State of Tex.; recipient Presdl. Legion of Merit. Mem. Law Soc. Alta., Law Soc. Sask., Can. Bar Assn., Inst. Can. Mgmt., Phi Delta Kappa. Address: PO Box 92 Whale Cove NU Canada X0C 0J0 E-mail: wonderfulschool@hotmail.com.

RODOVICH, ANDREW PAUL, magistrate; b. Hammond, Indiana, Feb. 24, 1948; s. Andrew H. and Julia (Makar) R.; m. Gail Linda (Patrick), May 27, 1972; children: Caroline Anja, Mary Katherine, James Patrick. BA, Valparaiso U., Ind., 1970, JD, 1973. Bar: Ind., 1973. Ptnr. Hand, Muenich, and Rodovich, Hammond, Ind., 1973-78; chief dep. prosecutor Lake County Prosecutor's Office, Crown Point, Ind., 1979-82; U.S. magistrate U.S. Dist. Ct., Hammond, Ind., 1982—. Referee Hammond City Ct., 1978; adj. prof. Valparaiso Law Sch.,Ind., 1985—. Fellow Ind. Bar Found.; mem. Nat. Coun. U.S. Magistrates, Delta Theta Phi. Republican. Avocation: sports. Home: 7207 Baring Pkwy Hammond IN 46324-2218 Office: US Dist Ct 5400 Federal Plz Ste 3700 Hammond IN 46320-1529

RODOWSKY, LAWRENCE FRANCIS, retired state judge; b. Balt., Nov. 10, 1930; s. Lawrence Anthony and Frances (Gardner) R.; m. Colby Fossett, Aug. 7, 1954; children: Laura Rodowsky Ramos, Alice Rodowsky-Seegers, Emily Rodowsky Savopoulos, Sarah Jones Rodowsky, Gregory, Katherine Rodowsky O'Connor. AB, Loyola Coll., Balt., 1952; LLB, U. Md., 1956. Bar: Md. 1956. Ct. crier, law clk. U.S. Dist. Ct. Md., 1954-56; asst. atty. gen. State of Md., 1960-61; assoc., ptnr. firm Frank, Bernstein, Conaway & Goldman, Balt., 1956-79; judge Ct. Appeals Md., Annapolis, 1980-2000, mem. rules com., 1969-80; sr. status judge Ct. of Spl. Appeals Md., Annapolis, 2001—. Lectr., asst. instr. U. Md. Law Sch., 1958-68, 87-91; reporter jud. dept. Md. Constl. Conv. Commn., 1966-67. Chmn. Gov. Md. Commn. Racing Reform, 1979. Fellow Am. Coll. Trial Lawyers; mem. Md. Bar Assn., Balt. Bar Assn. Roman Catholic. Home: 6614 Walnutwood Cir Baltimore MD 21212-1213 Office: 620 CM Mitchell Jr Courthse 100 N Calvert St Baltimore MD 21202 E-mail: Lawrence.Rodowsky@courts.state.md.us.

RODRIGUES, FABIANA UTRABO, lawyer; b. Londrina, Brazil, Aug. 5, 1972; d. Angelo Simeão and Marilene Utrabo Rodrigues. LLB, PUC, São Paulo, Brazil, 1997; LLM, Northwestern U., 2001. Atty. Machado Meyer Sendacz e Opce Advogados, São Paulo, 1998—2000, Souza, Cescon, Avedissian Barrieu e Flesch Advogados, São Paulo, 2001—. Commercial, contracts (including sales of goods; commercial financing), Corporate, general. Office: Souza Cescon Advogados Rua Funchal 263 11 Audar São Paulo Brazil

RODRIGUEZ, ANNABELLE, state attorney general; BA, JD, U. P.R. From asst. solicitor gen. to solicitor gen. P.R. Dept. Justice; ptnr. Martino, Odell & Calabria, Hato Rey, PR, 1993—96; judge U.S. Dist Ct (P.R. dist.), 1996; atty. gen. Commonwealth of P.R., 2001—. Office: Atty Gen PO Box 9020192 San Juan PR 00902*

RODRIGUEZ, ANTONIO JOSE, lawyer; b. New Orleans, Dec. 7, 1944; s. Anthony Joseph and Josephine Olga (Cox) R.; m. Virginia Anne Soignet, Aug. 23, 1969; children: Henry Jacob, Stephen Anthony. BS, U.S. Naval Acad., 1966; JD cum laude, Loyola U. of the South, New Orleans, 1973. Bar: La. 1973, U.S. Dist. Ct. (ea. dist.) La. 1973, U.S. Ct. Appeals (5th cir.) 1973, U.S. Dist. Ct. (mid. dist.) La. 1975, U.S. Dist. Ct. (we. dist.) La. 1977, U.S. Ct. Appeals (11th cir.) 1981, U.S. Supreme Ct. 1987, U.S. Dist. Ct. (so. dist.) Miss. 1991, U.S. Ct. Appeals (4th cir.) 1991, U.S. Ct. Appeals (1st cir.) 1997, U.S. Ct. Internat. Trade, 1991. Assoc. Phelps, Dunbar, Marks, Claverie & Sims, New Orleans, 1973-77; ptnr. Phelps Dunbar, New Orleans, 1977-92, Fowler Rodriguez Kingsmill Flint, Gray & Chalos, LLP, New Orleans, 1992—. Prof. law Tulane U., New Orleans, 1981—; mem. nat. rules of the road adv. coun. U.S. Dept. Transp., Washington, 1987-90, chmn. nat. navigation safety adv. coun., 1990-94, mem., 2000—; spkr. on admiralty and environ. Co-author: Admiralty-Limitation of Liability, 1981—, Admiralty-Law of Collision, 1990—; author: (chpt.) Benedict on Admiralty, 1995—; assoc. editor Loyola Law Rev., 1971-73; contbr. articles to profl. maritime and environ. jours. Bd. dirs. Greater New Orleans Coun. Navy League, 1988—, Propeller Club of New Orleans, 1997—. Lt. USN, 1966-70; capt. USNR, 1970-95. Decorated Navy Commendation medal; recipient Disting. Pub. Svc. award U.S. Dept. Transp., 1993. Fellow La. Bar Found.; mem. ABA, La. State Bar Assn., La. State Law Inst., Maritime Law Assn. U.S. (proctor 1975—), New Orleans Bar Assn., Southeastern Admiralty Law Inst., Assn. Average Adjusters U.S., Assn. Average Adjusters U.K., Naval Res. Assn. (chpt. pres. 1982-84), U.S. Naval Acad. Alumni Assn. (chpt. pres. 1981-83), Bienville Club, Phi Alpha Delta, Alpha Sigma Nu. Republican. Roman Catholic. Admiralty, General civil litigation, Environmental. Home: 4029 Mouton St Metairie LA 70002-1303 Office: Fowler Rodriguez Kingsmill Flint Gray & Chalos LLP 201 Saint Charles Ave Fl 36 New Orleans LA 70170-1000 E-mail: ajr@frc-law.com.

RODRIGUEZ, RAQUEL, lawyer; b. Miami Beach, Fla., 1961; JD, U. Miami, 1985. Assoc. Greenberg Traurig, P.A., Miami, Fla., 1985—97, shareholder, 1993—97, dir. global affiliations, coord internat. practice group, 1999—2002, with lit. dept. Washington, 2002; exec. dir. Multilaw Multinational Assn. Ind. Law Firms, London, 1997—99; gen. counsel to gov. Office Gov. State of Fla., Tallahassee, 2002—. Adj. prof. U. Miami. Office: Office Gov The Capital Tallahassee FL 32399*

RODRIGUEZ, VINCENT ANGEL, lawyer, director; b. Cayey, P.R., 1921; s. Vicente and Maria (Antongiorgi) R. BS, Harvard U., 1941; LLB, Yale U., 1944. Bar: N.Y. 1947. Assoc. Sullivan & Cromwell, N.Y.C., 1944-56, ptnr., 1956—. Mem. Council Fgn. Relations, ABA, Assn. Bar City N.Y., Am. Soc. Internat. Law Clubs: River (N.Y.C.). Home: 4521 Fisher Island Dr Miami FL 33109-0156 Office: Sullivan & Cromwell 125 Broad St Fl 28 New York NY 10004-2489

RODRIGUEZ, VIVIAN N. lawyer, accountant; b. Riverdale, N.Y., Dec. 16, 1969; d. Felix and Maria Rodriguez. AA in Bus., Miami Dade C.C., Miami, Fla., 1989; B of Acctg., Fla. Internat. U., Miami, 1991, M of Acctg., 1992; JD, U. Miami, 1995, LLM in Taxation, 2001. Bar: Fla.; CPA, Fla. Acct. Norman A. Eliot & Co., Miami, 1991-96; atty., acct. Managed Recovery Svcs. Corp., Miami, 1996-97; sole practitioner Miami, 1997—2001; atty. Office Chief Counsel/IRS/Dept. Treasury, 2001—. Mem. ABA, AICPA, ATLA, Am. Assn. Atty.-CPAs, Fla. Assn. Atty.-CPAs, Fla. Inst. CPAs, Dade County Bar Assn., Fla. Bar. Republican. Roman Catholic. Avocation: science fiction. Estate planning, Probate (including wills, trusts), Taxation, general.

RODRIGUEZ-DIAZ, JUAN E. lawyer; b. Ponce, P.R., Dec. 27, 1941; s. Juan and Auristela (Diaz-Alvarado) Rodriguez de Jesus; m. Sonia de Hostos-Anca, Aug. 10, 1966; children: Juan Eugenio, Jorge Eduardo, Ingrid Marie Rodriguez. BA, Yale U., 1963; LLB, Harvard U., 1966; LLM in Taxation, NYU, 1969. Bar: N.Y. 1968, P.R. 1970. Assoc. Baker & McKenzie, N.Y.C., 1966-68, McConnell, Valdes, San Juan, P.R.; undersec. Dept. Treasury P.R., 1971-73; mem. Sweeting, Pons, Gonzalez & Rodriguez, 1973-81; pvt. practice San Juan, 1981-94, Totti & Rodriguez-Diaz, 1994—. Bd. dirs. Ochoa Indsl. Sales Corp., Ensco Caribe, Inc., Industrias Vassallo, Inc., Triangle Cargo Services, Inc. Bd. govs. Aqueduct and Sewer Authority P.R., 1979-84; mem. adv. com. collective bargaining negotiation of P.R. elec. Power Authority to Gov. P.R., 1977-78; bd. govs. P.R. coun. Boy Scouts Am., mem. transition com., 1984-85; mem. adminstrv. coun. Ballajá. Mem. N.Y. State Bar Assn., P.R. Bar Assn., AFDA Club, Berwind Country Club, Palmas de Mar Country Club. Commercial, contracts (including sales of goods; commercial financing), Corporate, general, Taxation, general. Office: Suite 1200 416 Ave Ponce De Leon Hato Rey San Juan PR 00918-3418 E-mail: JERD@TRDLAW.com.

ROE, CHARLES BARNETT, lawyer; b. Tacoma, June 25, 1932; s. Charles Brown and Gladys Luvena (Harding) Roe; m. Marilyn Marie Quam, July 31, 1954; children: Sharon Lynn Roe De Groot, Jeannine Carole Roe Dellwo. AB, U. Puget Sound, 1953; postgrad., U. Calif.-Berkeley, 1957—58; JD, U. Wash., 1960. Bar: Wash. 1960, U.S. Dist. Ct. (ea. and we. dists.) Wash. 1960, U.S. Ct. Appeals (9th cir. 1963, U.S. Supreme Ct. 1963, U.S. Ct. Appeals (D.C. cir.) 1964. Asst. atty. gen. depts. natural resources, conservation, water resources and pollution control commn. State of Wash., Olympia, 1960—70, asst. dir. dept. water resources, 1967—69, sr. asst. atty. gen., 1970—90; of counsel Perkins Coie, Olympia, 1991—. Chief counsel Dept. Ecology, 1970—85, Nuclear Waste Bd., 1983—90; counsel natural resources com. Wash. Ho. of Reps., Olympia, 1970; supr. sea grant trainees U. Wash. Law Sch., 1970—72; adj. prof. Gonzaga U. Sch. Law, Spokane, 1973—76, U. Puget Sound Law Sch., 1985—90; contr. Nat. Water Commn., Washington, 1970—71; legis. aide Gov. Daniel J. Evans, 1969—77. Rep. Western States Water Coun., Salt Lake City, 1970—90; sec. Olympia Audubon Soc., 1962—63; chmn. bd. mgrs. United Chs., 1967—68. 1st lt. USAF, 1954—57. Mem.: ABA (chmn. water resources com. natural resources sect. 1981—83), Wash. Cts. Hist. Soc. (bd. dirs. 1998—), Wash. State Bar Assn. (chmn. environ. law sect. 1971—72), Rotary, Masons, Phi Delta Phi, Kappa Sigma. United Ch. Of Christ. Home: 2400 Wedgewood Dr SE Olympia WA 98501-3841 Office: 111 Market St NE Olympia WA 98501-6965 E-mail: croe@perkinscoie.com.

ROE, MARK J. law educator; b. N.Y.C., Aug. 8, 1951; m. Helen Hsu, Aug. 12, 1974; children: Andrea Hsu, Jessica Hsu. BA, Columbia U., 1972; JD, Harvard U., 1975. Bar: N.Y. 1976. Atty. Fed. Res. Bank, N.Y.C., 1975-77; assoc. Cahill Gordon & Reindel, N.Y.C., 1977-80; prof. Rutgers U. Law Sch., Newark, 1980-86, U. Pa. Law Sch., 1986-88, Columbia U. Law Sch., N.Y.C., 1988-2001, Harvard Law Sch., Cambridge, Mass., 2001—. Author: (book) Strong Managers, Weak Owners: The Political Roots of American Corporate Finance, 1994, Corporate Reorganization and Bankruptcy, 2000, Political Determinants of Corporate Governance, 2003. E-mail: mroe@law.harvard.edu.

ROE, ROGER ROLLAND, JR., lawyer; b. Mpls., Dec. 31, 1947; s. Roger Rolland Roe Jr.; m. Paula Speltz, 1974; children: Elena, Madeline. BA, Grinnell Coll., 1970; JD, U. Minn., 1973. Bar: Minn. 1973, U.S. Dist. Ct. Minn. 1974, U.S. Ct. Appeals (8th cir.) 1977, U.S. Supreme Ct. 1978, Wis. 1988, U.S. Dist. Ct. Nebr. 1995, U.S. Dist. Ct. (ea. and we. dists.) Wis. Law clk. to Hon. Judge Amdahl Hennepin County Dist. Ct., Mpls., 1973-74; from assoc. to ptnr. Rider, Bennett, Egan & Arundel, Mpls., 1974-91; mng. ptnr. Yaeger, Jungbauer, Barczak, Roe & Vucinovich, PLC, Mpls., 1992-2000; ptnr. Best & Flanagan LLP, Mpls., 2000—. Mem. nat. panel arbitrators Am. Arbitration Assn.; judge trial practice class and moot ct. competitions law sch. U. Minn.; guest lectr. Minn. Continuing Legal Edn. courses. Fellow Internat. Soc. Barristers; mem. ATLA (guest lectr.), Am. Bd. Trial Advs. (diplomat, Minn. chpt. pres. 1996-97), Million Dollar Round Table. Avocations: golfing, downhill skiing. General civil litigation, Personal injury (including property damage), Product liability. Office: Best & Flanagan LLP 225 S 6th St # 4000 Minneapolis MN 55402

ROEDDER, WILLIAM CHAPMAN, JR., lawyer; b. St. Louis, June 21, 1946; s. William Chapman and Dorothy (Reifeiss) R.; m. Gwendolyn Arnold, Sept. 13, 1968; children: William Chapman, Barcley Shane. BS, U. Ala., 1968; JD cum laude, Cumberland U., 1972. Bar: Ala. Law clk. to chief justice Ala. Supreme Ct., Montgomery, 1972; ptnr. McDowell Knight Roedder & Sledge, L.L.C., Mobile, Ala., 1997—. Comments editor Cumberland-Samford Law Rev.; contbr. articles to legal publs. Mem.: ABA (vice chair com. trial tactics, torts and ins. practice 1995—96), Def. Rsch. Inst., Ala. Def. Lawyers Assn., Fedn. Def. and Corp. Counsel (chmn. products liability sect. 1990—93, bd. dirs. 1993—2000, regional v.p. 1994—96, exec. com. 1997—, sec.-treas. 1999—2000, pres.-elect 2000—01, pres. 2001—02, chmn. bd. dirs. 2002—), Mobile County Bar Assn. (past sec., past chmn. ethics com. 1988—90, grievance com. 1994—96), Ala. State Bar Assn., Order of Barristers, Curia Honoris, Phi Alpha Delta (pres. 1971—72). Aviation, General civil litigation, Commercial, contracts (including sales of goods; commercial financing). Home: 211 Levert Ave Mobile AL 36607-3219 Office: McDowell Knight Roedder & Sledge LLC PO Box 350 Mobile AL 36601-0350 E-mail: broedder@mcdowellknight.com.

ROEGER, WILLIAM COLEY, JR., lawyer; b. Doylestown, Pa., Apr. 15, 1947; s. William Coley and Alice Virginia (McKeown) R.; m. Ellen R. Ball, Apr. 4, 1970; children: William C. III, Matthew Barton. BS in Physics, Muhlenberg Coll., 1969; JD, Dickinson U., 1973. Bar: Pa. 1973, U.S. Dist. Ct. (ea. dist.) Pa. 1981. Assoc. Pa. Power and Light Co., Allentown, 1973-75; assoc., pres. Donald B. Smith and Assoc., Perkasie, Pa., 1975-86; pres. Roeger & Walker, Perkasie, 1986, Roeger, Walker, Cassel & Holko, Perkasie, 1986—. Asst. county solicitor Bucks County, Pa. Contbr. articles to profl. jours. Mem. council Peace Luth. Ch., Perkasie, 1977-83; exec. com. Bucks County Rep. Com., Pa., 1978—. Served to capt. Pa. Air N. G., 1970-83. Mem. ABA, Pa. Bar Assn., Bucks County Bar Assn., Pa. Trial Lawyers Assn. (bd. govs. 1980—, exec. com. 1984—, chmn. dem. rels. sect. 1986-89, comptroller 1991—), Assn. Trial Lawyers Am., Jaycees (named one of Outstanding Young Men in Am.), Tau Kappa Epsilon. Lutheran. Avocations: tennis, woodworking, weight lifting. Family and matrimonial, Insurance, Personal injury (including property damage). Home: 2075 Turnberry Ct Center Valley PA 18034-8931 Office: Roeger Walker Cassel & Holko 210 W Walnut St PO Box 218 Perkasie PA 18944-0218

ROEHL, JERRALD J. lawyer; b. Austin, Tex., Dec. 6, 1945; s. Joseph E. and Jeanne Foster (Scott) R.; m. Nancy J. Meyers, Jan. 15, 1977; children: Daniel J., Katherine C., J. Ryan, J. Taylor. BA, U. N.Mex., 1968; JD, Washington and Lee U., 1971. Bar: N.Mex. 1972, U.S. Ct. Appeals (10th cir.) 1972, U.S. Supreme Ct. 1977. Practice of law, Albuquerque, 1972—; pres. Roehl Law Firm P.C. and predecessors, Albuquerque, 1976—. Lectr. to profl. groups; real estate developer, Albuquerque. Bd. advs. ABA Jour. 1981-83; bd. editors Washington and Lee Law Rev., 1970-71. Bd. dirs. Rehab. Ctr. of Albuquerque, 1974-78; mem. assocs. Presbyn. Hosp. Ctr., Albuquerque, 1974-82; incorporator, then treas. exec. com. Ctr. City Coun.,

1991-98, law coun. Washington & Lee U. Law Sch., 2002—. Recipient award of recognition State Bar N.Mex., 1975-77. Mem. ABA (award of achievement Young Lawyers div. 1975, council econs. of law practice sect. 1978-80, exec. council Young Lawyers div. 1979-81, fellow div. 1984—, council tort and ins. practice sect. 1981-83), N.Mex. Bar Assn. (pres. young lawyers sect. 1975-76), Albuquerque Bar Assn. (bd. dirs. 1976-79), N.Mex. Def. Lawyers Assn. (pres. 1983-84), Sigma Alpha Epsilon, Sigma Delta Chi, Phi Delta Phi. Clubs: Albuquerque County, Albuquerque Petroleum. Roman Catholic. Federal civil litigation, Corporate, general, Insurance. Home: 4411 Constitution Ave NE Albuquerque NM 87110-5721 Office: Roehl Law Firm PC 300 Central Ave SW Albuquerque NM 87102-3298 E-mail: jjr@roehl.com.

ROESER, RONALD O. lawyer, consultant; b. Berwyn, Ill., May 6, 1950; s. John O. and Mary Jean (Marsden) R.; m. Susan Marie Gill, July 22, 1972; children: Michelle Marie, Michael Franklin. BA, So. Ill. U., 1972; JD, DePaul U., 1975. Bar: Ill. 1975, U.S. Dist. Ct. (no. dist.) Ill. 1975, U.S.Tax. Ct. 1975, U.S. Ct. Appeals (7th cir.) 1975. Assoc. Imming & Faber, Elgin, Ill., 1975-77; ptnr. Imming, Faber & Roeser, Elgin, 1977-81, Imming & Roeser, Elgin, 1981-83, Roeser & Vucha, Elgin, 1983-84, Roeser, Vucha & Carbary, Elgin, 1984—. Mem. Fed. Trial Bar, Ill. Bar Assn., Kane County Bar Assn., Chgo. Bar Assn., Ill. Trial Lawyers Assn., Dundee Jaycees (treas., bd. dirs. 1975—, Outstanding Merit awards 1976, 78, 81), Lions. Republican. Roman Catholic. Avocations: history, reading, contact sports. General civil litigation, Commercial, contracts (including sales of goods; commercial financing). Home: 34w921 Duchesne Dr Dundee IL 60118-3101 Office: Roeser & Vucha 920 Davis Rd Elgin IL 60123-1390

ROESLER, JOHN BRUCE, lawyer; b. Portland, Oreg., Oct. 9, 1943; s. Bruce Emil and Charlotte Amanda (Naess) R.; m. Kathryne Elise Nilsen, Aug. 14, 1965; children: Paul, Mark, Nico. BA, U. Kans., 1966, JD, 1971. Bar: Mo. 1971, N.Mex. 1979, Colo. 1998, U.S. Dist. Ct. (we. dist.) Mo. 1971, U.S. Dist. Ct. N.Mex. 1979, U.S. Dist. Ct. Colo. 1998. U.S. Ct. Appeals (10th cir.) 1979, U.S. Ct. Appeals (5th cir.) 1988, U.S. Ct. Appeals (4th cir.) 1992, U.S. Supreme Ct. 1987. Assoc. The Gage Firm, Kansas City, Mo., 1971-74; civil rights advocate State of N.Mex. Human Rights, Santa Fe, 1977-78; law clk. Hon. Edwin L. Felter N.Mex. Supreme Ct., Santa Fe, 1978-79; asst. dist. atty. Taos (N.Mex.) Dist. Atty.'s Office, 1979-80; asst. spl. pros. Santa Fe Dist. Atty.'s Office, 1980-82; pvt. practice Santa Fe, 1982-97; of counsel Roth, Van Amberg, Gross, Rogers & Ortiz, 1991-94; spl. asst. atty. gen. Colo. Atty. Gen's Office, 1997-99; assoc. Jones & Keller, Denver, 1999-2000; pvt. prac. Denver, 2000—. Instr. John Marshall Law Sch., Chgo., summer, 1974; spkr. edn. law and civil rights issues U. Miami Law Sch., 2000, Nat. Com. for Prevention of Child Abuse, Chgo., 1989, Little Rock, 90. Author: (books) How To Find the Best Lawyers, In Harm's Way: Is Your Child Safe in School; mem. law rev. U. Kans. Sch. Law, 1970-71; contbr. articles to profl. jours. and treatise. Mem. Colo. Bar Assn., Denver Bar Assn., Colo. Trial Lawyers Assn. Democrat. Roman Catholic. Avocations: skiing, hiking, gardening. Civil rights, Federal civil litigation, Education and schools. Home: 2571 S Sherman St Denver CO 80210-5725 Office: 303 E 17th Ave Ste 700 Denver CO 80203

ROESSLER, P. DEE, lawyer, former judge, educator; b. McKinney, Tex., Nov. 4, 1941; d. W.D. and Eunice Marie (Medcalf) Powell; m. George L. Roessler, Jr., Nov. 16, 1963 (div. Dec. 1977); children: Laura Diane, Trey. Student, Austin Coll., 1960-61, 62-64, Wayland Bapt. Coll., 1961-62; BA, U. West Fla., 1968; postgrad., East Tex. State U., 1975, U. Tex.-Dallas, 1977; JD, So. Meth. U., 1982. Bar: Tex. 1982, U.S. Dist. Ct. (ea. dist.) Tex. 1983, U.S. Dist. Ct. (no. dist.) Tex. 1983, U.S. Supreme Ct. 2000. Tchr. Van Alstyne Ind. Sch. Dist., Tex., 1968-69; social worker Dept. Social Svcs., Fayetteville, N.C., 1971-73, Dept. Human Svcs., Sherman and McKinney, 1973-79, 81; assoc. atty. Abernathy & Roeder, McKinney, 1982-85, Ronald W. Uselton, Sherman, 1985-86; prof., program coord. for real estate Collin County C.C., McKinney, 1986-87, program coord. criminal justice, 1986—91, program coord., legal asst., 1986—99; asst. county atty. Grayson County, Tex., 1999—2000; solo practice, 2000—. Mcpl. judge City of Mckinney Mcpl. Ct., 1986-89; mem. Tex. State Bar Com. on Legal Assts., 1990-94, Tex. State Bar Com. on Child Abuse and Neglect, 1996-2001. Mem. Collin County Shelter for Battered Women, 1984-86, chmn., 1984-85; v.p. Collin County Child Welfare Bd., 1986, pres., 1987-88, 96-97, treas., 1989, mem., 1985-89, 94-98; Rep. jud. candidate Collin County, 1986; chmn. bd. Tri County Consortium Mental Health Mental Retardation, 1984-85; mem. Tex. Area 5 Health System Agy., 1979, Collin County Mental Health Adv. Bd., 1978-79; trustee Willow Park Hosp., HCA, 1987-88; chair Collin County Criminal Justice Sub-com., 1987-88; mem. Collin County Pub. Responsibility Com., 1991-96, chair, 1994-95; bd. dirs. Ct. Apptd. Spl. Advocates, 1991-95. Mem. Collin County Bar Assn., Plano Bar Assn. Baptist. Avocations: gardening, reading, writing, traveling. Alternative dispute resolution, Estate planning, Government contracts and claims. Home: 5 Shadybrook Cir Melissa TX 75454-8912 Office: 1600 1st Ave Mc Kinney TX 75069

ROETHE, JAMES NORTON, lawyer; b. Milw., Jan. 27, 1942; s. Arthur Frantz and Bess Irma (Norton) R.; m. Nita May Dorris, July 15, 1967; children: Melissa Dorris, Sarah Rebacca. BBA, U. Wis., Madison, 1964, JD, 1967. Bar: Wis. 1967, Calif. 1968, U.S. Dist. Ct. (we. dist.) Wis. 1967, U.S. Dist. Ct. (no. dist.) Calif. 1972, U.S. Ct. Claims 1975, U.S. Ct. Appeals (9th cir.) 1980, U.S. Dist. Ct. (ea. dist.) Calif. 1982, U.S. Dist. Ct. (ctrl. dist.) Calif. 1986). U.S. Ct. Appeals (4th cir.) 1988, U.S. Ct. Appeals (2d cir.) 1989. Assoc. Pillsbury, Madison & Sutro, San Francisco, 1971-77, ptnr., 1978-92; sr. v.p., dir. litigation Bank of Am., San Francisco, 1992-96, exec. v.p., gen. counsel, 1996-98, dep. gen. counsel, 1998-99; ptnr. Pillsbury Winthrop LLP, 2000—. Staff atty. Commn. on CIA Activities within U.S., Washington, 1975. Editor: Africa, 1967; editor-in-chief Wis. Law Rev., 1966-67. Bd. dirs. Orinda (Calif.) Assn., 1984-85, pres., 1986; mem. City of Orinda Planning Commn., 1988-94, chmn., 1990, 93; bd. dirs. Calif. Shakespeare Festival, 1993—, pres., 2001; bd. visitors U. Wis. Law Sch., 1994-99. Served to lt. USNR, 1967-71. Fellow Am. Bar Found.; mem. ABA, Wis. Bar Assn., Calif. Bar Assn., Bar Assn. San Francisco, Wis. Law Alumni Assn. (bd. dirs. 2000—), Orinda Country Club, Order of Coif, Phi Kappa Phi. Federal civil litigation, General civil litigation, Utilities, public. E-mail: jimroethe@aol.com., jn@pillsburywinthrop.com.*

ROFF, ALAN LEE, lawyer, consultant; b. Winfield, Kans., July 2, 1936; s. Roy Darlis and Mildred Marie (Goodaile) R.; m. Sonyia Ruth Anderson, Feb. 8, 1954; 1 child, Cynthia Lee Roff Edwards; m. Molly Gek Neo Tan, July 21, 1980. BA with honors and distinction, U. Kans., 1964, JD with distinction, 1966. Bar: Okla. 1967. Staff atty. Phillips Petroleum Co., Bartlesville, Okla., 1966-75, sr. atty., 1976-85, sr. counsel, 1986-94; cons. in Asia, 1995—. Mem. editl. bd. Kans. Law Rev., 1965-66. Precinct com. man Rep. Party, Lawrence, Kans., 1963-64; assoc. justice Kans. U. Chancery Club; mem. Kans. U. Young Reps. Elizabeth Reeder scholar U. Kans., 1965-66, Eldon Wallingford award, 1964-66. Mem. ABA, Okla. Bar Assn., Washington County Bar Assn., Phoenix Club (Bartlesville) (bd. dirs. 1985-86, gen. counsel 1986-91), Order of the Coif, Masons, Hon. Order Ky. Cols., Phi Alpha Delta, Pi Sigma Alpha. Mem. First Christian Ch. Avocation: travel. Commercial, contracts (including sales of goods; commercial financing), Corporate, general, Private international. Home and Office: 2247 Mountain Dr Bartlesville OK 74003-6954

ROGAN, JAMES E. federal agency administrator, former congressman; m. Christine Apffel. BA in Polit. Sci., U. Calif., Berkeley, 1979; JD, UCLA, 1983. Past atty. Lillick McHose and Charles (now Pillsbury, Madison and Sutro), L.A.; past dep. dist. atty. L.A. County; judge Glendale (Calif.) Mcpl. Ct., 1990—93, presiding judge, 1993—94; past mem. Calif. Assembly, 1994—96, assembly majority leader, 1996; mem. U.S. Congress from 27th Calif. dist., 1996—2001; mem. house jud. com., mem. commerce com., asst. minority whip; ptnr. Venable, Baetjer, Howard & Civiletti, Washington, 2001; under sec. of commerce for intellectual property, 2001—; dir. US Patent & Trademark Office, 2001—. Adj. prof. trial advocacy Sch. Law Southwestern U.; adj. prof. criminal law Coll. Law Glendale U.; past adj. prof. criminal law Glendale C.C.; mem. Selective Svc. Sys. U.S. Govt., 1981—. Republican. Office: US Patent & Trademark Office Crystal Plaza 3 Rm 2C02 Washington DC 20231 Fax: 202-225-5828.*

ROGERS, ARTHUR HAMILTON, III, lawyer; b. Florence, S.C., Apr. 19, 1945; s. Arthur Hamilton Jr. and Suzanne (Wilson) R.; m. Karen Lyn Hess, June 22, 1968; children: Sarah Elizabeth, Thomas Hess. BA, Rice U., 1967; JD, Harvard U., 1970. Bar: Tex. 1970. Assoc. Fulbright & Jaworski LLP, Houston, 1970-74; participating assoc. Fulbright & Jaworski L.L.P., Houston, 1974-77; ptnr. Fulbright & Jaworski, L.L.P., Houston, 1977—; gen. counsel Lifemark Corp., Houston, 1981-82. Sec. Mosher, Inc., Houston, 1984-97. Bd. dirs. Alley Theatre, Houston, 1990—, v.p. fin., 2001—, mem. exec. com., 2001—; bd. dirs. Autry House, 1994-97; mem. exec. com. Rice U. Fund Coun., Houston, 1993-99, vice chmn., 1996-97, chmn., 1997-98. Mem. ABA, State Bar Tex., Assn. of Rice Alumni (treas. 1995-97), Petroleum Club of Houston, The Forest Club. Episcopalian. Corporate, general, Health, Securities. Home: 5309 Bordley Dr Houston TX 77056-2323 Office: Fulbright & Jaworski LLP 1301 Mckinney St Fl 51 Houston TX 77010-3031 E-mail: arogers@fulbright.com.

ROGERS, CHARLES MYERS, lawyer; b. Monticello, Utah, Nov. 21, 1947; s. Milton David and Wanda (Myers) R.; m. Jean Evelyn Rankin, Dec. 12, 1970 (div. June, 1983); m. Christine Theresa Sill, Apr. 14, 1984; children: Christopher Thales, Fiona Eleanor. BA in Philosophy, U. Mo., Kansas City, 1973, JD, 1976. Bar: Mo. 1976, U.S. Dist. Ct. (we. dist.) Mo. 1976, U.S. Ct. Appeals (8th cir.) 1997, U.S. Ct. Appeals (9th cir.) 1999, U.S. Dist. Ct. Kans. 1999., U.S. Dist. Ct. (ea. dist.) Mo. 2001, U.S. Supreme Ct. 1994. From asst. pub. defender to 1st asst. pub. defender Jackson County Pub. Defender's Office, Kansas City, Mo., 1976-89; regional defender Mo. State Pub. Defender Sys., Kansas City, 1989-94; staff atty. Mo. Capital Punishment Resource Ctr., Kansas City, 1994-95; shareholder Wyrsch Hobbs & Mirakian , Kansas City, 1995—. Sole practice law, Kansas City, 1982-86. Served in U.S. Army, 1968-70. Mem.: ABA, Kansas City Metro Bar Assn. (chair criminal law com. 2000), Mo. Assn. Criminal Def. Lawyers (bd. dirs. 1988—2001, v.p. 2002—03, pres. 2003—), Mo. Bar Assn., Nat. Assn. Criminal Def. Lawyers. Democrat. Avocations: cycling, oenology. Criminal. Home: 11403 Holly Ct Kansas City MO 64114-1506 Office: Wyrsch Hobbs et al 1101 Walnut St Ste 1300 Kansas City MO 64106-2180 E-mail: acquit@whmlaw.net.

ROGERS, DAVID JOHN, lawyer; b. Lawrence, Mass., Aug. 13, 1960; s. James Martin and Eleanor Elizabeth (Jones) R. BA, Coll. William and Mary, 1982; JD, U. Pitts., 1988. Bar: N.H. 1988, Mass. 1989. Contract adminstr. Sanders Assocs., Inc., Nashua, N.H., 1983-85; assoc. Devine, Millimet, Stahl & Branch, Manchester, N.H., 1988-89; ptnr. Carpenito & Rogers, PA, Salem, N.H., 1989-90; asst. corp. counsel City of Nashua, 1991; pvt. practice Londonderry, N.H., 1991-98; atty. Landmark Title, Inc., Manchester, N.H., 1998-2000. Mem. Worker's Compensation Appeals Bd., State of N.H., 1993—. Active Salem Youth Com., 1989-95; fin. com. West Congl. Ch., Haverhill, Mass., 1990-95. U. scholar U. Pitts., 1988. Mem. Mass. Bar Assn., N.H. Bar Assn., Young Lawyers Com. Republican. Avocations: golf, running, reading, community theater. Estate planning, General practice, Workers' compensation. Home: 20 Cindy Dr Hooksett NH 03106-2003 Office: 1244 Hooksett Rd Ste 7 Hooksett NH 03106

ROGERS, GARTH WINFIELD, lawyer; b. Fort Collins, Colo., Nov. 4, 1938; s. Harlan Winfield and Helen Marie (Orr) R.; m. Joanne Kathleen Rapp, June 16, 1962; children: Todd Winfield, Christopher Jay, Gregory Lynn, Clay Charles. BS, U. Colo., 1958, LLB, 1962. Bar: Colo. 1962; U.S. Dist. Ct. Colo. 1962. Law clk. to presiding justice U.S. Dist. Ct., Denver, 1962-63; assoc. Allen, Stover & Mitchell, Ft. Collins, 1963-68; ptnr. Allen, Rogers & Vahrenwald, Ft. Collins, 1968-97; ret., 1997. Articles editor Rocky Mountain Law Rev., 1961-62. Past bd. dirs. Salvation Army, Ft. Collins, Ft. Collins C. of C., United Way of Ft. Collins, Trinity Luth. Ch., Ft. Collins, others; bd. dirs. Poudre Sch. Dist. Bd. Edn. Mem. ABA, Colo. Bar Assn., Larimer County Bar Assn. Avocations: nicaragua projects, participative sports, amateur writing, reading. Banking, Property, real (including real estate development, water). Office: 215 W Oak St Ste 777 Fort Collins CO 80521-2734

ROGERS, HARVEY DELANO, lawyer; b. Krosniewice, Poland, Jan. 2, 1946; s. Bernard and Rose (Zaltztrager) R.; m. Maria Cimitiere, Dec. 22, 1978; children: Daniel, Randall, Rachel, Amanda. BA, CCNY, 1968, MA, 1970; JD, U. Miami, 1974. Bar: Fla. 1975, U.S. Dist. Ct. (no. and so. dists.) Fla. 1975, U.S. Ct. Appeals (5th cir.) 1975, U.S. Ct. Appeals (11 cir.) 1981, Supreme Ct. Fla. 1975, U.S. Supreme Ct.1980. Sole practice, Miami, Fla., 1974—. Arbitrator Am. Arbitration, Miami, 1975—. Fellow Fla. Criminal Defense Attys.; mem. ABA, Lawyers Title, Fla. Trial Lawyers Assn., Phi Alpha Delta. Avocations: history, sports, fishing. State civil litigation, Criminal, General practice. Home: 6401 SW 123rd Ter Miami FL 33156-5560

ROGERS, JAMES DEVITT, judge; b. Mpls., May 5, 1929; s. Harold Neil and Dorothy (Devitt) R.; m. Leanna Morrison, Oct. 19, 1968. AB, Dartmouth Coll., 1951; JD, U. Minn., 1954. Bar: Minn. 1954, U.S. Supreme Ct. 1983. Assoc. Johnson & Sands, Mpls., 1956-60; sole practice Mpls., 1960-62; judge Mpls. Municipal and Dist. Ct., 1959-91. Mem. faculty Nat. Judicial Coll. Bd. dirs. Mpls. chpt. Am. Red Cross, chmn. service to mil. families and vets. com.; bd. dirs. Minn. Safety Coun., St. Paul, 1988-91; founding dir., sec. Forest Landowners Tax Coun. Served sgt. U.S. Army, 1954-56. Mem. ABA (chmn. nat. conf. spl. ct. judge, spl. com. housing and urban devel. law, traffic ct. program com., chmn. criminal justice sect., jud. adminstrn. div.), Nat. Jud. Coll. (bd. dirs.), Nat. Christmas Tree Grower's Assn. (pres. 1976-78), Mpls. Athletic Club. Congregationalist. Office: 14110 Prince Pl Minnetonka MN 55345-3027

ROGERS, JOHN MARSHALL, judge, law educator; b. Rochester, N.Y., June 26, 1948; s. Harry Lovejoy III and Virginia Kathryn (Meyers) R.; m. Ying Juan Xiong, 1990. BA, Stanford U., 1970; JD, U. Mich., 1974. Bar: D.C. 1975, Ky. 1980, U.S. Ct. Appeals, U.S. Supreme Ct. Commd. USAR, 1970; appellate atty. civil div. U.S. Dept. Justice, Washington, 1974-78; asst. prof. U. Ky., Lexington, 1978-81, assoc. prof., 1981-86, prof., 1986—. Vis. prof. Civil Divsn. U.S. Dept. Justice, Washington, 1983-85; Fulbright lectr. Fgn. Affairs Coll., Beijing, 1987-88, Zhongshan U., Guangzhou, People's Republic of China, 1994-95; spl. counsel impeachment com. Ky. Ho. of Reps., 1991. Contbr. articles to profl. jours. Mem. Am. Soc. Internat. Law, Order of Coif, Phi Beta Kappa. Republican. Office: 532 Potter Stewart US Courthouse 100 E 5th St Cincinnati OH 45202-3988*

ROGERS, JOHN TORREY, JR., lawyer; b. Saint Louis, Mo., Apr. 2, 1955; BS with distinction, Stanford U., Calif., 1978; JD, UCLA , L.A., 1981. Bar: Calif. 1981, U.S. Dist. Ct., (ctrl. dist.) Calif. 1982, cert.: State Bar of Calif. Bd. of Legal Specialization (Specialist, Estate Planning, Trust and Probate Law) 1995. Assoc. Zobrist, Vienna & McCullough, L.A., 1981—85; ptnr. Parker, Milliken, Clark, O'Hara & Samuelian, L.A., 1985—96, Ross, Sacks & Glazier LLP, L.A., 1996—2001, Holland & Knight LLP, L.A., 2001—. Mem., probate mediation panel LA County Superior Ct., L.A., 1996—. Fellow: Am. Coll. of Trust and Estate Counsel; mem.: L.A. Estate Planning Coun. (pres. 1993—94), L.A. County Bar Trusts and Estates Sect. (chair 1995—96). Probate (including wills, trusts), Alternative dispute resolution, Estate taxation. Office: Holland & Knight LLP 633 West Fifth St 21st Fl Los Angeles CA 90071

ROGERS, LAURENCE STEVEN, lawyer; b. N.Y.C., Jan. 19, 1950; s. Henry and Frances (Kanarek) R.; m. Iris S. Rosen, July 2, 1977; children: Matthew Benjamin, Heather Aimee. BSEE with distinction, Cornell U., 1972; JD, NYU, 1975. Bar: N.Y. 1976, U.S. Dist. Ct. (ea. and so. dists.) N.Y. 1976, U.S. Ct. Appeals (Fed. cir.) 1983, U.S. Supreme Ct. 1999, U.S. Patent and Trademark Office. Ptnr. Fish & Neave, N.Y.C., 1986—. Mem. ABA, N.Y.C. Bar Assn., N.Y. Intellectual Propert Law Assn., Fed. Cir. Bar Assn., Phi Kappa Phi, Eta Kappa Nu, Tau Beta Pi. Federal civil litigation, Patent, Trademark and copyright. Home: 15 Aspen Rd Scarsdale NY 10583-7346 Office: Fish & Neave 1251 Avenue Of The Americas Fl 50 New York NY 10020-1105

ROGERS, LEONARD DAVID, lawyer; b. Norton, Va., Oct. 13, 1962; s. Jack D. and Marylou (Sturgill) R.; m. Donna Geneva Salyers, Oct. 11, 1991. BA in History, U. Va., Wise, 1985; JD, U. Tenn., 1988. Bar: Va. 1988, U.S. Dist. Ct. (we. dist.) Va. 1989, U.S. Dist. Ct. (we. dist.) Va. 1989, U.S. Ct. Appeals (4th cir.) 1989, U.S. Bankruptcy Ct. 1989. Assoc. Mullins, Thomason & Harris, Norton, 1988-90; ptnr. Cline, Adkins, Cline & Rogers, Norton, 1990-95; pvt. practice, 1996—. Mem. Forward Wise County, 1989. Mem. ABA, Va. Bar Assn., Va. State Bar, Va. Trial Lawyers Assn., Wise County C. of C. Avocations: golf, mountain biking, travel. General civil litigation, Pension, profit-sharing, and employee benefits, Property, real (including real estate development, water). Office: Leonard D Rogers PC PO Box 1097 Wise VA 24293-1097

ROGERS, NANCY HARDIN, dean, law educator; b. Lansing, Mich., Sept. 18, 1948; d. Clifford Morris and Martha (Wood) Hardin; m. Douglas Langston Rogers, Jan. 30, 1970; children: Lynne, Jill, Kim. BA with highest distinction, U. Kans., 1969; JD, Yale U., 1972. Bar: D.C. 1975, Ohio 1972, U.S. Ct. Appeals (6th cir.) 1973, U.S. Dist. Ct. (no. dist.) Ohio 1974, U.S. Dist. Ct. (so. dist.) Ohio 1975. Law clk. U.S. Dist. Judge Thomas D. Lambros, Cleve., 1972-74; staff atty. Cleve. Legal Aid Soc., 1974-75; vis. asst. prof. Coll. of Law Ohio State U., Columbus, 1975-76, asst. prof., 1976-78, 83-89, assoc. prof., 1989-92, prof., assoc. dean acad. affairs, 1992-97, prof., 1992—, Joseph S. Platt, Porter, Wright, Morris & Arthur prof. law, 1995—2001, vice provost acad. adminstrn., 1999—2001, dean, Michael E. Moritz chair in alternative dispute resolution Michael E. Moritz Coll. Law, 2001—. Adj. prof. Ohio State U., Columbus, 1982-83; adj. prof. Ohio State Coll., 1981-83; vis. prof. law Harvard Law Sch., 2000. Author (with Frank E.A. Sander, Sarah R. Cole, Stephen B. Goldberg): (Book) Dispute Resolution: Negotiation, Mediation and Other Processes), 1992; author: (with Frank E.A. Sander and Stephen B. Goldberg) 4th edit., 2003; author: (book with Craig A. McEwen and Sarah R. Cole) Mediation: Law, Policy, Practice, 2nd edit., 1994, (book with Frank E. Sander and Stephen B. Goldberg) Teacher's Manual to Dispute Resolution, 3d edit., 1999, (book supplement with Craig A. McEwen) Supplement to Mediation: Law, Policy, Practice, 2d. edit., 1995, 1996, (book supplement) Supplement to Mediation: Law, Policy, Practice, 2d edit., 1998; contbr. articles and book chpts.; mem. (adv. bd.) World Arbitration and Mediation Report, 1991—, Alternatives, 1992—, co-chair (editl. bd. with Frank E.A. Sander) Dispute Resolution mag., 1994—2002. Bd. dirs. Assn. for Developmentally Disabled, Columbus, 1980-85; Legal Svcs. Corp. 1995-2003. Named Outstanding Prof., Ohio State U. Coll. Law Alumni Assn., 1996; recipient Book prize, Ctr. Pub. Resources for A Student's Guide to Mediation and the Law, 1987, Ctr. Pub. Resources for Mediation: Law, Policy, Practice, 1989, Peacemaker of Yr. award, Comty. Mediation Svcs. Ctrl. Ohio, 1990, Disting. Svc. Recognition, Soc. Profls. in Dispute Resolution, 1990, Whitney North Seymour sr. medal, Am. Arbitration Assn., 1990, Svc. Recognition award, Legal Aid Soc. Columbus, 1996, Ritter award, Ohio State Bar Found for outstanding contbns. to adminstrn. of justice, 1998; grantee Exxon Edn. Found., 1986, William and Flora Hewlett Found., 1990, Ohio State U. Interdisciplinary Seed, 1990, Ohio State U. Symposium, 1992, William and Flora Hewlett Found., 1992—96, Nat. Sci. Found., 1993—95, State Justice Instn., 1994, Fund for Improvement Post-Secondary Edn., U. Mo., 1996—97, William and Flora Hewlett Found., 1997—2003. Mem. ABA (chair, standing com. dispute resolution 1988-91), Phi Beta Kappa. Office: Ohio State U Coll Law 55 W 12th Ave Columbus OH 43210-1306 Business E-Mail: rogers.23@osu.edu .

ROGERS, PAUL GRANT, lawyer, former congressman; b. Ocilla, Ga., June 4, 1921; s. Dwight L. and Florence (Roberts) R.; m. Rebecca Bell, Dec. 15, 1962; 1 child, Rebecca Laing. BA, U. Fla., 1942, JD, 1948, LLD; LLD (hon.), Fla. Atlantic U., U. Md., Duke U., L.I. U.; DSc (hon.), George Washington U., U. Miami, Albany Med. Coll. of Union U.; D.Sc. (hon.), Commonwealth U. Va.; HHD (hon.), Nova U.; LHD (hon.), N.Y. Med. Coll., N.Y. Coll. Podiatric Medicine, Hahnemann Med. Coll.; DMedSci (hon.), Med. U. S.C. Bar: Fla. 1948. Partner Burns, Middleton, Rogers, Farrell & Faust, 1952-69; mem. 84th-95th congresses from 11th Dist. Fla., 1955-79; chmn. house subcom. on health and environ. Hogan & Hartson, Washington, 1979—, ptnr., 1979—. Trustee Cleve. Clinic Found.; bd. dirs. Am. Cancer Soc., Scripps Rsch. Inst.; co-chmn. Nat. Coalition on Health Care; chmn. Nat. Osteoporosis Found., Friends of Nat. Libr. Medicine, Rsch! Am.; mem. nat. coun. Washington U. Sch. Medicine; mem. dean's coun. Harvard Sch. Pub. Health. Recipient Pub. Welfare medal, Nat. Acad. Scis., 1982, Sea Grant award, 1985, Yr. 2000 award, Nat. Cancer Inst., 1987, award for pub. svc., Albert and Mary Lasker Found., 1993, Hugo Schaefer award, APHA, 1994, Leadership award, NOF, 1995, Maxwell Finland award, Disting. Svc. award, Am. Cancer Soc., 1997, Disitng. Am. award, Nat. Cmty. Pharmacists Assn., 1998, Environment Golden Eagle award, Nat. Assn. Physicians, 1999, Paul G. Rogers award, Physicians for the Environment, 1999, Paul G. Rogers Plz. at NIH named in his honor, U.S. Congress, 2001. Mem. ABA, Fla. Bar Assn. (gov. jr. sect. 1952-53), Palm Beach County Bar Assn., D.C. Bar Assn., Inst. Medicine of NAS, Phi Delta Phi, Phi Delta Theta. Methodist (steward). Office: Hogan & Hartson 555 13th St NW Ste 1200 Washington DC 20004-1109

ROGERS, RANDALL LEE, judge; b. Ft. Worth, May 2, 1949; s. Raymond Lee and Shirley G. R.; m. Lois Ruth Jackson; children: Angelique, Randall Jr., Rebel, Niki, Scott. BBA in Internat. Econs., Tex. Tech. U., 1971, JD, 1974. Bar: Tex. 1974, U.S. Dist. Ct. (ea. dist.) Tex. 1974, U.S. Dist. Ct. (no. and so. dists.) Tex. 1976, U.S. Ct. Appeals (5th and 11th cirs.) 1976. Assoc. Crumley, Murphy, Shrull, Ft. Worth, 1974-76; felony prosecutor McLennan County Dist. Atty., Waco, Tex., 1976-83, Smith County Dist. Atty., Tyler, Tex., 1983-87; judge Smith County Ct., Tyler, 1987, Smith County Ct. Law 2, Tyler, 1987—. Instr. advanced juvenile law Jud. Coll. Tex., Austin, 1996. Mem. city coun. City of Forest Hill, Tex., 1975-76; treas. Youth Alternatives, Smith County, Tyler, Tex., 1990-97. Mem. Internat. Order Odd Fellows (noble, grand 1995). Republican. Methodist. Avocation: camping. Office: Smith County Ct Law 2 Smith County Courthouse Tyler TX 75702 E-mail: ccl2@co.smith.tx.us.

ROGERS, RICHARD DEAN, federal judge; b. Oberlin, Kans., Dec. 29, 1921; s. William Clark and Evelyn May (Christian) R.; m. Helen Elizabeth Stewart, June 6, 1947; children— Letitia Ann, Cappi Christian, Richard Kurt. BS, Kans. State U., 1943; JD, Kans. U., 1947. Bar: Kans. 1947. Ptnr. firm Springer and Rogers (Attys.), Manhattan, Kans., 1947-58; instr. bus. law Kans. State U., 1948-52; partner firm Rogers, Stites & Hill, Manhattan, 1959-75; gen. counsel Kans. Farm Bur. & Service Cos., Manhattan, 1960-75; judge U.S. Dist. Ct., Topeka, Kans., 1975—. City commr., Manhattan, 1950-52, 60-64, mayor, 1952, 64, county atty., Riley County, Kans., 1954-58, state rep., 1964-68, state senator, 1968-75; pres. Kans. Senate, 1975. Served with USAAF, 1943-45. Decorated Air medal, Dfc. Mem. Kans., Am. bar assns., Beta Theta Pi. Clubs: Masons. Republican. Presbyterian. Office: US Dist Ct 444 SE Quincy St Topeka KS 66683

ROGERS, RICHARD HUNTER, lawyer, business executive; b. Flushing, N.Y., Sept. 11, 1939; s. Royden Harrison and Frances Wilma (Hunter) R.; children: Gregory P., Lynne A., Reade H. BS in Bus. Adminstrn, Miami U., 1961; JD, Duke, 1964. Bar: Ill. 1964, Ohio 1973. Atty. Continental Ill. Nat. Bank, Chgo., 1964-65; sr. atty. Brunswick Corp., Chgo., 1965-70; corporate counsel The A. Epstein Cos., Inc. (real estate developers), Chgo., 1970-73; v.p., gen. counsel, sec. Price Bros. Co., Dayton, Ohio, 1973-82; v.p., divsn. mgr. Water Systems Tech. div. Price Bros. Co., Dayton, Ohio, 1982-85; pres. Internat. divsn. Price Bros. Co., Dayton, Ohio, 1986—88; pvt. practice law Dayton, 1988—; pres. Richard H. Rogers & Assocs. LPA. Pres. adv. coun. Miami U. Bus. Sch.; bd. dirs. Red and White Club, Miami U.; mem. Washington Twp. Task Force on Future Govt.; trustee Woodhaven, Inc.; mem. Washington Twp. Zoning Commn., 1990—, chmn., 1999—. Mem. ABA (forum com. on constrn.), Ill. Bar Assn., Ohio Bar Assn., Dayton Bar Assn. (chmn. corp. law dept. com. 1983-84, exec. com. 1986-87, editor Bar Briefs 1990-91), Miami U. Alumni Assn. (pres.), Miami U. Pres.'s Club. State civil litigation, Construction, Private international. Office: 7333 Paragon Rd Ste 200 Dayton OH 45459-4157 Address: PO Box 751144 Dayton OH 45475-1144 E-mail: rhrlawoffice@aol.com.

ROGERS, RICHARD MICHAEL, judge; b. Lorain, Ohio, Dec. 8, 1944; s. Paul M. and Lillie (Morris) R.; m. Sophia Lydia Wagner, Dec. 23, 1967; children: L. Danielle, David K., Marisa D., Matthew D. BA, Ohio No. U., 1966, JD, 1972. Bar: Ohio 1972, U.S. Dist. Ct. (no. dist.) Ohio 1973. Assoc. Martin, Hall & Rogers, Marion, Ohio, 1972-76; ptnr. Rogers & Rogers, Marion, 1976-81; asst. law dir., police prosecutor City of Marion, 1973-74; pub. defender, 1975; asst. county prosecutor Marion County, 1976-81; village solicitor La Rue, Ohio, 1976-81; judge Marion Mcpl. Ct., 1982-88, Common Pleas Ct., 1989—; mem. traffic rules rev. commn. Ohio Supreme Ct., 1989—. Judge dist. competition Nat. Bicentennial Competition on Constitution and Bill of Rights, 1988, judge state competition, 1988—, judge nat. competition, 1989, 93, 95; instr. faculty Ohio Jud. Coll. Mem. Marion Active 20/40 Svc. Club, 1973-84, treas., 1976-80, bd. dirs., 1976-84, pres., 1980-81; chmn. bd. dirs., pres., co-founder Marion Area Driver Re-edn. Project, 1974-81; pres. Big Bros./Big Sisters Marion County, 1986-87, bd. dirs., 1984-88; mem. sch. bd. St. Mary's Elem. Sch., 1985-88, v.p., 1986, bd. dirs. Marion Cath. High Sch. Endowment Fund, 1986—, v.p., 1991—; mem. Marion Cath. Jr./Sr. High Sch. Bd., 1988-94, pres., 1990-91; mem. fellow in criminal justice steering com. Marion campus Ohio State U., 1996—; mem. paralegal adv. com. Marion Tech. Coll., 1994-96; trustee Ohio State Bar Found., 1997-99. With U.S. Army, 1968-69. Mem. Ohio State Bar Assn. (modern cts. com. 1982-85, jud. adminstrn. and legal reform com. 1982-93, legis. subcom. of jud. adminstrn. and legal reform com. 1989-93, coun. dels. 1991-93, bd. govs. 1996-99, chmn. govt. affairs com. 1998-99, vice-chair criminal justice com. 2001-02, chmn. jury instrn. com. 2002-), Marion County Bar Assn. (pres. 1985-86), Ohio Jud. Conf. (gen. adminstrn. 1984-85, vice chair family matters video com. 1991—, chmn. subcom. legal matters video, civil law and procedure com. 1991-95, editl. bd. Ohio Jury Instrn. 1995—), Ohio Bar Coll., Marion County Law Libr. Assn. (trustee 1982—, pres. 1991-93), Ohio Common Pleas Judges Assn., Delta Theta Phi, Sigma Pi. Republican. Methodist. Avocations: golf, scuba diving. Home: 310 Edgefield Blvd Marion OH 43302-5802 Office: Common Pleas Ct Marion County Courthouse 100 N Main St Marion OH 43302-3089

ROGERS, THEODORE OTTO, JR., lawyer; b. West Chester, Pa., Nov. 17, 1953; s. Theodore Otto and Gladys (Bond) R.; m. Hope Tyler Scott, Nov. 7, 1981; children: Helen Elliot, Theodore Scott, Robert Montgomery Bond. AB magna cum laude, Harvard U., 1976, JD cum laude, 1979. Bar: N.Y. 1980, U.S Ct. Appeals (2nd cir.) 1984, U.S. Dist. Ct. (so. and ea. dists.) N.Y. 1980, D.C. 1981, U.S. Ct. Claims, 1982, U.S. Supreme Ct. 1983, U.S. Ct. Appeals (6th and 10th cirs.) 1983, U.S. Ct. Appeals (1st cir.) 1984, U.S. Ct. Appeals (fed. cir.) 1986. From assoc. to ptnr. Sullivan & Cromwell, N.Y.C., 1979—. Co-author: (books) Employment Litigation in New York, 1996, Employment Law DeskBook for Human Resources Professionals, 2001. Mem. U.S. Presdl. Transition Team, 1980. Fellow Coll. Labor and Employment Lawyers; mem. N.Y. State Bar Assn. (co-chair individual rights and responsibilities com. labor and employment law sect.), Assn. of Bar of City of N.Y. (labor and employment law). Republican. General civil litigation, Labor (including EEOC, Fair Labor Standards Act, labor-management relations, NLRB, OSHA), Probate (including wills, trusts). Home: 535 E 86th St New York NY 10028-7533 Office: Sullivan & Cromwell 125 Broad St Fl 28 New York NY 10004-2489 E-mail: rogerst@sullcrom.com.

ROGERS, THOMAS SYDNEY, communications executive; b. New Rochelle, N.Y., Aug. 19, 1954; s. Sydney Michael Rogers Jr. and Alice Steinhardt; m. Sylvia Texon, Oct. 9, 1983; children: Robert, Jessica, Jason. BA, Wesleyan U., 1975; JD, Columbia U., 1979. Bar: N.Y. 1980, U.S. Dist. Ct. (so. and ea. dists.) N.Y. 1980, U.S. Ct. Appeals (D.C. cir.) 1981. Legis. aide to Congressman Richard Ottinger U.S. Ho. Reps., Washington, 1975-76, sr. counsel subcom. telecommunications, 1981-86; assoc. Lord, Day & Lord, N.Y.C., 1979-81; v.p. policy planning and bus. devel. Nat. Broadcasting Co., Inc., N.Y.C., 1987-88; pres. NBC Cable, 1988-89, NBC Cable & Bus. Devel., 1989-99; exec. v.p. NBC, N.Y.C., 1992-99; vice chmn. NBC Internet, 1999; chmn., CEO Primedia, Inc., 1999—. Pres., CEO internat. coun. Nat. Acad. TV Arts and Scis., 1994-97, chmn., 1998-99; lectr. in field. Named one of Outstanding Young Men in Am., 1985. Mem. N.Y. State Bar Assn., Internat. Radio and TV Soc. Office: Primedia Inc 745 5th Ave Fl 23D New York NY 10151-0099

ROGERS, WILLIAM DILL, lawyer; b. Wilmington, Del., May 12, 1927; m. Suzanne Rochford, Sept. 7, 1926; children: William Rogers, Daniel. BA, Princeton U., 1948; LL.B., Yale U., 1951. Bar: D.C. 1952, U.S. Supreme Ct. 1954. Ptnr. Arnold & Porter, Washington, intermittently 1953—; dep. U.S. coordinator Alliance for Progress, AID, 1962-65; pres. N.Y. Ctr. Inter.-Am. Relations, 1965-72; asst. sec. of state inter-Am. relations Dept. State, 1974-76, undersec. of state for econ. affairs, 1976-77; mem. law faculty Cambridge U., Eng., 1982-83. Sr. counselor Bipartisan Commn. on Central Am., 1983-84; vice chmn. Kissinger Assocs. Inc. Author: The Twilight Struggle: The Alliance for Progress and U.S.-Latin-American Relations, 1967. Co-chmn. U.S.-Mexico Binat. Commn.; bd. dirs. Coun. Fgn. Rels., 1981-90. Mem. Am. Soc. Internat. Law (pres. 1971-73), ABA. Office: Arnold & Porter 555 12th St NW Washington DC 20004-1206

ROGOFF, JEFFREY SCOTT, lawyer; b. Manhasset, N.Y., May 11, 1968; s. Arnold Steven and Paula Rogoff. BA, Binghamton U., 1990; JD, NYU, 1993. Bar: N.J. 1993, U.S. Dist. Ct. N.J. 1993, U.S. Dist. Ct. (so. and ea. dists.) N.Y. 1994, U.S. Dist. Ct. (no. and we. dists.) N.Y. 2000, U.S. Ct. Appeals (3d cir.) 1998. Law clk. Magistrate Judge Michael Dolinger U.S. Dist. Ct. (so. dist.) N.Y., N.Y.C., 1993-94; assoc. Kronish, Lieb, Weiner & Hellman, N.Y.C., 1994-95, Schindel, Farman & Lipsius LLP, N.Y.C., 1995-2000; solicitor U.S. Dept. Labor, N.Y.C., 2000—. Mem. Phi Beta Kappa. Jewish. Appellate, General civil litigation, Insurance. Home: 11 Furman Dr Wayne NJ 07470-5304 Office: US Dept Labor Office of Solicitor 201 Varick St Room 983 New York NY 10014 E-mail: Rogoff.Jeffrey@dol.gov.

ROGOVIN, LAWRENCE H. lawyer; b. NYC, June 10, 1932; s. Abraham and Laura R.; m. Saundra Schwartz, Aug. 11, 1957; children: Jayne Lina, Wendy Renee, Evan Lewis. BS in Econ., U. Pa., 1953; LLB cum laude, NYU, 1956. Bar: N.Y. 1956, Fla. 1971. Dep. asst. atty. gen. State of N.Y., 1956-57, asst. atty. gen., 1960-61; assoc. Squadron, Gartenberg, Ellenoff & Plesent and predecessors, N.Y.C., 1962-67, ptnr., 1967-72; pvt. practice Miami, Fla., 1972—74, 1983—98, 2002—; ptnr. Squadron, Ellenoff, Plesent & Lehrer, N.Y.C., 1974-75, Cohen, Angel & Rogovin, North Miami, Fla., 1978-82, Cohen, Rogovin, Reed & Ivans, Miami, 1982-83; v.p., gen. counsel Rare, Inc., Miami, 1998—2002. 1st lt. JAGC, USAFR, 1957-60. Recipient Founders Day award, NYU Law Sch., 1956. Mem.: ABA, Fed. Bar Assn., Fla. Bar Assn. General practice, Property, real (including real estate development, water). Fax: 305-932-9583.

ROHLFING, FREDERICK WILLIAM, lawyer, political consultant, retired judge; b. Honolulu, Nov. 2, 1928; s. Romayne Raymond and Kathryn (Coe) R.; m. Joan Halford, July 15, 1952 (div. Sept. 1982); children: Frederick W., Karl A., Brad (dec.); m. Patricia Ann Santos, Aug. 23, 1983. BA, Yale U., 1950; JD, George Washington U., 1955. Bar: Hawaii 1955, Am. Samoa 1978. Assoc. Moore, Torkildson & Rice, Honolulu, 1955-60; ptnr. Rohlfing, Nakamura & Low, Honolulu, 1963-68, Hughes, Steiner & Rohlfing, Honolulu, 1968-71, Rohlfing, Smith & Coates, Honolulu, 1981-84; pvt. practice Honolulu, 1960-63, 71-81, Maui County, 1988—; dep. corp. counsel County of Maui, Wailuku, Hawaii, 1984-87, corp. counsel, 1987-88; land and legal counsel Maui Open Space Trust, 1992-97, also bd. dirs. Polit. cons., 1996, 98, 2002; magistrate judge U.S. Dist. Ct. Hawaii, 1991-96. Active Hawaii Ho. Reps., 1959-65, 80-84, Hawaii State Senate, 1966-75; US alt. rep. So. Pacific Commn., Noumea, New Caledonia, 1975-77, 1982-84; Maui adv. coun. State Reapportionment Commn., 2001; hon. chmn. Maui coms. George W. Bush for Pres., 2000. Capt. USN, 1951-54, ret. USNR. Mem. Hawaii Bar Assn., Maui Country Club, Naval Intelligence Profls. Avocations: ocean swimming, golf, skiing. Administrative and regulatory, Land use and zoning (including planning), Legislative. Home and Office: 2807 Kekaulike Ave Kula HI 96790

ROHNER, RALPH JOHN, lawyer, educator, university dean; b. East Orange, N.J., Aug. 10, 1938; AB, Cath. U. Am., 1960, JD, 1963. Bar: Md. 1964. Teaching fellow Stanford (Calif.) U., 1963-64; atty. pub. health div. HEW, 1964-65; prof. law Cath. U. Am. Sch. Law, Washington, 1965—, acting dean, 1968-69, assoc. dean, 1969-71, dean, 1987-95; staff counsel consumer affairs subcom. U.S. Senate Banking Com., 1975-76; cons. Fed. Res. Bd., 1976-83, chmn. consumer adv. council, 1981; cons. FDIC, 1978-80; spl. counsel Consumer Bankers Assn., 1984—. Cons. U.S. Regulatory Coun., 1979-80. Co-author: Consumer Law: Cases and Materials, 1979, 2d edit., 1991; co-author, editor The Law of Truth in Lending, 1984, republished, 2000. Bd. dirs. Migrant Legal Action Program, Inc., Washington, Automobile Owners Action Coun., Washington, Credit Rsch. Ctr., Georgetown U., Am. Fin. Svcs. Assn. Edn. Found. Conf. on Consumer Fin. Law. Mem. ABA, Am. Law Inst., Coll. of Consumer Fin. Svcs. Lawyers. Home: 10909 Forestgate Pl Glenn Dale MD 20769-2047 Office: Cath U Sch Law 620 Michigan Ave NE Washington DC 20064-0001 E-mail: rohner@law.edu.

ROHR, RICHARD DAVID, lawyer; b. Toledo, Ohio, Aug. 31, 1926; s. Lewis Walter and Marie Janet (Pilliod) R.; m. Ann Casey, Aug. 25, 1951; children: Martha, Elizabeth, Matthew, Sarah, Margaret, Thomas. BA magna cum laude, Harvard U., 1950; JD, U. Mich., 1953. Bar: Mich. 1954, U.S. Dist. Ct. (so. dist.) Mich. 1954, U.S. Ct. Appeals (6th cir.) 1960, U.S. Supreme Ct. 1961. Assoc. Bodman, Longley & Dahling, L.L.P., Detroit, 1954-58, ptnr., 1958-75, mng. ptnr., 1975-2000. Adj. prof. U. Mich., Ann Arbor, 1976-82. With U.S. Army, 1945-46. Mem. ABA, Detroit Bar Assn., Mich. Bar Assn., Detroit Athletic Club, Order of Coif, Phi Beta Kappa. Roman Catholic. Banking, Corporate, general, Finance. Home: 441 Rivard Blvd Grosse Pointe MI 48230-1627 Office: Bodman Longley Dahling LLP 100 Renaissance Ctr Ste 34 Detroit MI 48243-1001

ROHRMAN, DOUGLASS FREDERICK, lawyer; b. Chgo., Aug. 10, 1941; s. Frederick Alvin and Velma Elizabeth (Birdwell) R.; m. Susan Vitullo; children: Kathryn Anne, Elizabeth Clelia, Alessandra Claire. AB, Duke U., 1963; JD, Northwestern U., 1966. Bar: Ill. 1966. Legal coord. Nat. Communicable Disease Ctr., Atlanta, 1966-68; assoc. Keck, Mahin & Cate, Chgo., 1968-73, ptnr., 1973-97, Lord, Bissell and Brook, Chgo., 1997—. Exec. v.p., dir. Kerogen Oil Co., 1967—; chmn. bd. visitors Nicholas Sch. of Environment Duke U., 1993-2001. Co-author: Commercial Liability Risk Management and Insurance, 2 vols., 1978, 86, Lenders Guide to Environmental Law: Risk and Liability, 1993; mem. editl. bd., columnist Ecol. Soc. Am., 2001—; contbr. articles on law to profl. jours. Vice chmn., commr. Ill. Food and Drug Commn., 1970-72. Lt. USPHS, 1966-68. Fellow: Am. Numismatic Soc. (life; chmn. adv. com.); mem.: ABA, William Preston Few Assn. (mem. pres. coun.), Duke U. Alumni Assn., James B. Duke Soc., Selden Soc., Am. Soc. Law and Medicine, Environ. Law Inst., 7th Cir. Bar Assn., Chgo. Bar Assn. (chmn. com. food & drug law 1972—73), Am. Numismatic Assn. (life), Wigmore Club (fellow), Mich. Shores Club, Legal Club. Democrat. Episcopalian. Commercial, contracts (including sales of goods; commercial financing), Environmental, Product liability. Home: 520 Brier St Kenilworth IL 60043-1064 Office: Lord Bissell & Brook 115 S La Salle St Ste 3200 Chicago IL 60603-3902

ROKOSZ, GREGORY JOSEPH, emergency medicine physician, lawyer, educator; b. Passaic, N.J., Mar. 27, 1955; s. Ferdinand and Stella D. (Wirkowski) R.; m. Christine M. Muller, Oct. 1, 1983; 1 child, Stefanie Lee. BA in Biol. Scis. with honors, Rutgers U., 1977; DO, Des Moines U., 1980; JD magna cum laude, Seton Hall U., 1999. Diplomate Am. Bd. Emergency Medicine, Am. Bd. Osteo. Emergency Medicine, Am. Osteo. Bd. Family Physicians. Intern Met. Hosp., Phila., 1980-81; resident in family practice Union (N.J.) Hosp., 1981-82, emergency dept. physician, 1982-94, 98, dir. med. edn., 1993-2001, v.p. med. affairs, 1994-2000, sr. v.p. med. and acad. affairs, 2001—, dir. transitional yr. residency program, 2000—02, v.p. med. edn., 2000—; med. dir. N.J. Paramedic Registry Exam., 1990-94; mobile ICU insp. N.J. Dept. Health, Office EMS, Newark, 1990-94; med. dir. St. Barnabas Outpatient Ctrs., 2003—. Mem. N.J. Bd. Med. Examiners, Trenton, 1994—, v.p., 1997—99, pres., 1999—2001; clin. instr. dept. emergency medicine U. Medicine and Dentistry Sch. Osteo. Medicine, Stratford, 1992—93, asst. clin. prof., 1993—; asst. prof. emergency medicine N.Y. Coll. Osteo. Medicine/N.Y. Inst. Tech., Old Westbury, 1994—96, assoc. prof., 1996—, clin. asst. dean, 1997—; assoc. prof. dept. medicine St. George's U. Sch. Medicine, 2001—; assoc. mem. PRO of N.J., 1991—; dir. emergency medicine residency program Newark (N.J.) Beth Israel Med. Ctr., 1998—99; expert witness in emergency medicine; vice-chmn. N.Y. Coll. Osteo. Medicine Ednl. Consortium, 1999—; mem. accreditation rev. com. Accreditation Coun. for Continuing Med. Edn., 2000—. Contbg. author: Continuous Quality Improvement for Emergency Departments, 1994; mem. Seton Hall Law Rev., 1997-99. Fellow Am. Coll. Emergency Physicians, Am. Coll. Osteo. Emergency Physicians; mem. ABA, Am. Osteo. Assn., Am. Coll. Osteo. Family Physicians, Assn. Osteo. Dirs. and Med. Educators, Am. Coll. Physician Execs., Assn. for Hosp. Med. Edn., Grad. Med. Edn. Coun. N.J. (mem. adv. bd. 1997—). Republican. Roman Catholic. Avocations: skiing, sports, cultural events, music, family activities. Home: 8 Wildlife Run Boonton NJ 07005-9043 Office: St Barnabas Med Ctr 95 Old Short Hills Rd Livingston NJ 07039

ROLAND, RAYMOND WILLIAM, lawyer, mediator, arbitrator; b. Ocala, Fla., Jan. 3, 1947; s. Raymond W. and Hazel (Dunn) R.; m. Jane Allen, Dec. 28, 1968; children: John Allen, Jason William. BA, Fla. State U., 1969, JD, 1972. Bar: Fla. 1972, U.S. Dist. Ct. (no. dist.) Fla. 1973, U.S. Dist. Ct. (mid. dist.) Fla. 1985, U.S. Ct. Appeals (5th cir.) 1974, U.S. Ct. Appeals (11th cir.) 1983, U.S. Supreme Ct. 1985; cert. cir. ct. mediator. Assoc. Keen, O'Kelley & Spitz, Tallahassee, 1972-74, ptnr., 1974-77; ptnr., v.p. McConnaughhay, Roland, Maida & Cherr, P.A., Tallahassee, 1978-97; owner Roland Mediation Svcs., Tallahassee, 1997—2002; cir. mediator U.S. Ct. Appeals 11th Cir., 2002—. Diplomate mem. Fla. Acad. of Profl. Mediators, Inc.; adj. prof. Bapt. Coll. Fla. Bd. dirs. So. Scholarship Found., Tallahassee, 1985-89, 98-99, v.p. 1989; bd. visitors Bapt. Coll. Fla. Mem. Internat. Assn. Def. Coun., Def. Rsch. Inst., Fla. Bar, Kiwanis (life, lt. gov. 1984-85), Capital City Kiwanis Club (Kiwanian of Yr. 1978, pres. 1979), Fla. Kiwanis Found. (life fellow). Republican. Baptist. Avocations: reading, hiking, camping, golf. General practice, Insurance, Personal injury (including property damage). Home: 800 Freedom Ln Roswell GA 30075 E-mail: BRoland487@aol.com.

ROLES, FORREST HANSBURY, lawyer; b. Balt., Aug. 19, 1942; s. Forrest and Agnes (Campbell) R.; m. Emily Lynn McPhail, Feb. 25, 1967; children: Margaret Jean, Elizabeth Jane. BA, Davidson Coll., 1964; LLB, W.Va. U., 1967. Bar: U.S. Dist. Ct. (so. dist.) W.Va. 1967, U.S. Ct. Appelas (4th cir.) 1971, U.S. Supreme Ct. 1978. Assoc. Jackson & Kelley, Charleston, W.Va., 1967-72, ptnr., 1972-82, Smith, Heenan & Althen, Charleston, 1983-97, Hennan, Althen & Roles, Charleston, 1997—2002, Dinsmore & Sholid, Charleston, 2003—. Bd. dirs. Concord Coll. Found., 1996—, chmn. 1999—; bd. dirs. Kanawha County Pub. Defender, Charleston, 1986—. Named among Best Lawyers in Am. Woodward/White, Inc., 1995—. Republican. Labor (including EEOC, Fair Labor Standards Act, labor-management relations, NLRB, OSHA). Home: 904 Bird Rd Charleston WV 25314-1401 Office: Box 2549 1380 BB&T Sq Charleston WV 25329 E-mail: froles@harlaw.com.

ROLFE, RONALD STUART, lawyer; b. N.Y.C., Sept. 5, 1945; s. Nat and Florence I. (Roth) R.; m. Yvonne S. Quinn, Sept. 1, 1979 (div. Apr. 2002); m. Sara Darehshori; 1 child, Andrew. AB, Harvard U., 1966; JD, Columbia U., 1969. Bar: N.Y. 1969, U.S. Ct. Appeals (2d cir.) 1970, U.S. Dist. Ct. (so. and ea. dists.) N.Y. 1971, U.S. Supreme Ct. 1973, U.S. Dist. Ct. (no. dist.) Calif. 1982, U.S. Ct. Appeals (6th and 5th cirs.) 1982, U.S. Ct. Appeals (9th cir.) 1983, U.S. Dist. Ct. (ea. dist.) Ky. 1984, U.S. Ct. Appeals (7th and 10th cirs.) 1989, U.S. Ct. Appeals (fed. cir.) 1991, U.S. Ct. Appeals (3d cir.) 1992, U.S. Ct. Appeals (4th cir.) 1991. Law clk. to judge U.S. Dist. Ct. (so. dist.) N.Y., 1969-70; assoc. Cravath, Swaine & Moore, 1970-77, ptnr., 1977—. Sec. bd. trustees Allen-Stevenson Sch., 1981—91, pres., 1992—; trustee Lawrenceville Sch., 1987—, v.p., 2001—. Trustee DeLaSalle Acad., 2002—. Fellow: Am. Bar Found.; mem.: ABA, Am. Law Inst., Fed. Bar Coun. (trustee 1989—94), Assn. Bar City NY, NY State Bar Assn., Turf and Field Club (N.Y.C.), Stanwich Club (Greenwich, Conn.), Univ. Club, Union Club. Antitrust, General civil litigation, Securities. Office: Cravath Swaine & Moore Worldwide Plz 825 8th Ave 40th Fl New York NY 10019-7475 E-mail: rrolfe@cravath.com.

ROLFES, JAMES WALTER, SR., lawyer; b. Providence, May 21, 1942; s. George Henry and Mary Helen (Clark) R.; m. Dorothy Patricia Robison, Sept. 10, 1966; children: John George, James Walter Jr. BS, U. Cin., 1975; JD, No. Ky. State Coll., 1975. Bar: Ohio 1975, U.S. Supreme Ct. 1985. Asst. sec. Eagle Savings and Loan, Cin., 1967-70; acct. Kings Island, Kings Mill, Ohio, 1970-73, Bode-Finn, Cin., 1973-76; asst. prosecutor Madison County, London, Ohio, 1976-79, acting mcpl. ct. judge, 1982-90; pvt. practice London, 1975—. Tchr. Madison County Alcohol Diversion Program, London, 1982-90, Ohio Peace Officers Tng. Acad., London, 1976-79. Chmn. Madison County Heart Assn., London, 1977, Madison County Mental Health Adv. Bd., London, 1980-84; pres. Fairfield Youth Assn. Recipient Millard W. Mack scholarship U. Cin., 1970. Mem. Ohio Bar Assn., Madison County Bar Assn. (pres. 1986), London Merchants Assn., Inc. (chmn. 1983-86), Rotary, K.C. (grand knight 1985-87). Republican. Roman Catholic. General practice. Office: 17 S Main St PO Box 0024 London OH 43140-0024

ROLFS, CRAIG ALAN, lawyer; b. Waterloo, Iowa, May 3, 1940; s. Floyd Otto and Jean (Rawlins) R.; m. Marilyn Jean Holland, June 9, 1962 (div. Aug. 1980); children: Robert David, Scott Andrew, Matthew Stuart; m. Monica Jean Crandall, May 1, 2002. Student, Grinnell Coll., 1958-60; BA, U. S.D., 1962; JD, Drake U., 1965. Ba: Iowa 1965, Mich. 1973. Ptnr. Van Eman, Mulder, Klinkenborg & Rolfs, Parkersburg, Iowa, 1965-73, Anuta, Minerman & Rolfs, Menominee, Mich., 1973-75; county atty. Butler County, Allison, Iowa, 1967-73; city atty. City of Parkersburg, Iowa, 1965-72; pros. atty. Menominee County, Mich., 1975-79, judge probate, 1979-88; pvt. practice Menominee, 1989—. Chmn. Menominee Zoning Bd.; bd. dirs. Rainbow House; mem. ethics com. BAMC. Mem. Menominee Bar Assn. (pres. 1986-92), Elks, Twi-Cees (pres. 1989). Estate planning, Probate (including wills, trusts), Property, real (including real estate development, water). Office: 721 10th Ave Menominee MI 49858-3308

ROLL, DAVID LEE, lawyer; b. Pontiac, Mich., May 1, 1940; s. Everett Edgar and Garnette (Houts) R.; m. Nancy E. Spindle, Aug. 17, 1963; children: Richard, Molly. BA cum laude, Amherst Coll., 1962; JD, U. Mich., 1964. Bar: Mich. 1965, U.S. Dist. Ct. (ea. dist.) Mich. 1965, U.S. Ct. Appeals (6th cir.) 1969, D.C. 1974, U.S. Dist. Ct. D.C. 1975, U.S. Supreme Ct. 1975, U.S. Ct. Appeals (4th cir.) 1976, U.S. Ct. Appeals (D.C. cir.) 1983, U.S. Ct. Appeals (3rd and 11th cirs.) 1985, U.S. Ct. Appeals (9th cir.) 1992, U.S. Ct. Appeals (fed. cir.) 1993. Assoc. Hill, Lewis, Detroit, 1965-70, ptnr., 1970-72; asst. dir. gen. litigation Bur. of Competition Fed. Trade Commn., Washington, 1972-75; ptnr. Steptoe & Johnson, Washington, 1975—, chmn., 1993—98. V.p. bus. devel., bd. dirs. eLawForum, 2000—. Mem. ABA (chair Robinson Patman Act com., antitrust sect. 1984-86, Clayton Act com., antitrust sect. 1986-88, Energy Litigation com., litigation sect. 1992-93, mem. task force on indsl. competitiveness 1987, coun., antitrust sect. 1988-91, author, editor antitrust sect.), Lex Mundi (bd. dirs., chair competition com.). Administrative and regulatory, Antitrust, Federal civil litigation. Office: 1330 Connecticut Ave NW Washington DC 20036-1704 E-mail: droll@steptoe.com.

ROLL, JOHN MCCARTHY, judge; b. Pitts., Feb. 8, 1947; s. Paul Herbert and Esther Marie (McCarthy) R.; m. Maureen O'Connor, Jan. 24, 1970; children: Robert McCarthy, Patrick Michael, Christopher John. BA, U. Ariz., 1969, JD, 1972; LLM, U. Va., 1990. Bar: Ariz. 1972, U.S. Dist. Ct. Ariz. 1974, U.S. Ct. Appeals (9th cir.) 1980, U.S. Supreme Ct. 1977. Asst. pros. atty. City of Tucson, 1973; dep. county atty. Pima County (Ariz.), 1973-80; asst. U.S. Atty. U.S. Attys. Office, Tucson, 1980-87; judge Ariz. Ct. Appeals, 1987-91, U.S. Dist. Ct. Ariz., 1991—. Mem. criminal justice mental health standards project ABA, 1980—83, mem. com. model jury instrns. 9th circ., 1994—2001, chair com. model jury instrns. 9th circ., 1998—2001; mem. panel workshop criminal law CEELI Program, Moscow, 1997; mem. U.S. Jud. Conf. Adv. Com. Criminal Rules, 1997—. Contbr. Merit Selection: the Arizona Experience, Ariz. State Law Jour., 1991, The Rules Have Changed: Amendments ot the Rules of Civil procedure, Defense Law Jour., 1994, Ninth Cir. Judges' Benchbook on Pretrial Proceedings, 1998, 2000, 2002. Recipient Disting. Faculty award Nat. Coll. Dist. Attys., U. Houston, 1979, Outstanding Alumnus award U. Ariz. Coll. Law, 1992. Mem. Fed. Judges Assn., KC (adv. coun. 1991). Republican. Office: US Dist Ct 405 W Congress Tucson AZ 85701

ROLLMANN, DIETER JOSEF, consultant, lawyer, energy executive; b. Dettingen, Bavaria, Germany, Oct. 31, 1951; s. Alfred and Theresia R.; m. Madeleine Kaiser, June 3, 1979; children: Dominique, Frederik. Student internat. law, Sorbonne U., Paris, 1977; degree in bus. mgmt., U. Frankfurt, Germany, 1978; degree in business, London Sch. Econs., 1979; studies in Internat. Trade Law, U. London, U. Frankfurt, 1980's. Atty. at law and barrister, Germany. Deputy head of leagal dept. Urangesellschaft & Affiliates, Frankfurt, 1981-85, internat. lawyer, 1981—; dep. head of legal dept. Nukem Gmbh and Nukem, Inc., Frankfurt, Atlanta, 1985-88; head legal and contract dept. Landis & Gyr. Cie., Zug, Switzerland, 1988-91; head of comml. dept. Rieter AG, Winterthur, Switzerland, 1991-93; comml. mgr. Brochier-SRB Energy Plant & Pipeline Cie, Germany, 1993-97; cons., dir. internat. affairs SIEPE AG, Germany, 1997—; chmn. Maacs Consultancy Bd., Malaysia, 1997—. Cons. Tng. of Sales and Project Mgrs. Cie, Frankfurt, 1985—. Co-author: Software License Contracts, 1991. Dep. mgr. headquarters German Red Cross for Greater Offenbach area, 1977-93 Mem. Greater Frankfurt Lawyers Assn. Roman Catholic. Avocations: skiing, mountain climbing, travel in 3rd world countries. Home and Office: Postfach 1228 Muehlheim am Main D-63152 Germany E-mail: didirollmann@hotmail.com.

ROMANDER, CLAS GUSTAV JOHANNES, lawyer; b. Stockholm, July 18, 1955; s. Nils and Gudrun (Ekeskog) R.; m. Catharina Elisabeth Gyllencreutz; children: Andrea, Lovisa. LLM, U. Stockholm, 1981. Bar: Sweden 1987. Legal officer EFTA, Geneva, 1981-82; jr. judge City Ct. Gothenburg, Sweden, 1982-83; assoc. Wesslau, Holm & Co., Stockholm, 1983-85, White & Case, LLP, Stockholm, 1985-88, ptnr., 1995—, Verum, Stockholm, 1989-95, White & Case, LLP, Stockholm, 1995—. Bd. dirs. Global MediTech Investment, Stockholm, Adera Venture Zone, Stockholm. Contbr. articles to profl. jours. Mem. ABA, Internat. Bar Assn., Swedish Bar Assn., Am. C. of C. in Sweden, Swiss Arbitration Assn., London Inst. Internat. Arbitration, Am. Club Sweden. Avocations: art, architecture, history, hunting, literature. Banking, Corporate, general, Securities. Office: White & Case PO Box 5573 S-11485 Stockholm Sweden

ROMANELLO, NICHOLAS WILLIAMS, lawyer; b. Port Chester, N.Y., Jan. 6, 1968; s. William Nicholas and Loretta Anita Romanello. B, Fla. State U., 1990; JD, St. Thomas U., 1993. Bar: Fla. 1998, U.S. Dist. Ct. (so. dist.) Fla. 2000. Assoc. Conrad & Scherer, Ft. Lauderdale, Fla., 1998—. Personal injury (including property damage). Office: Conrad & Scherer 633 S Federal Hwy Fort Lauderdale FL 33301

ROMAN PALACIOS, HUMBERTO, judge; b. Veracruz, Mexico, Apr. 15, 1936; Grad., U. Nacional Autonoma Mexico, 1965. Min. Supreme Ct. Justice, Mexico City, 1995—; gov. Guerrero State, 1963—69; prof. U. Autonoma de Guerrero, 1966—69, U. Panamericana, Inst. de Especializacion Jud. de la Suprema Corte de Justicia de la Nacion; min. Supreme Ct. Justice, 1995—, pres., 1998—99. Office: Suprema Corte de la Nacion Pino Suarez No 2 Col Centro 06065 Mexico City Mexico*

ROMANS, JOHN NIEBRUGGE, lawyer; b. Bklyn., May 23, 1942; s. John McDowell and Helen Pond (Niebrugge) R.; m. Caroline Ward; children: John A., Andrew C. BA, Williams Coll., 1964; LLB, Columbia U., 1967. Bar: N.Y. 1967, U.S. Dist. Ct. (so. and ea. dist.) N.Y. 1971, U.S. Ct. Appeals (2d cir.) 1971, U.S. Ct. Appeals (3rd cir.) 1976, U.S. Ct. Appeals (4th and 7th cirs.) 1987, U.S. Ct. Appeals (9th cir.) 1992, U.S. Ct. Appeals (11th cir.) 1996, U.S. Supreme Ct. 1971. Ptnr. Curtis, Mallet-Prevost, Colt & Mosle, N.Y.C., Katten Muchin & Zavis, N.Y.C., Rosen Weinhaus, LLP, N.Y.C. Lectr. on air law topics at various seminars. Contbr. articles to profl. jours. Trustee Summit (N.J.) Unitarian-Universalist Ch., 1978, Mamaroneck Pub. Libr. Dist., 1990-99; mem. budget com. Village of Mamaroneck, 2001—, chmn, 2002; dir. The Univ. Glee Club NYC, 1993—. Lt. USNR, 1968-71. Mem. Assn. Bar City N.Y. (aero. com. 1983-85, chmn. 1986-89, 92-94, 2000, products liability com. 1989-91), Larchmont (N.Y.) Yacht Club. Avocation: sailing. Aviation, Product liability. Office: Rosen Weinhaus LLP 40 Wall St 32d Fl New York NY 10005-1304

ROMARE, CARL, maritime lawyer; b. Stockholm, Oct. 28, 1950; s. Goran and Marika (Holm) R.; m. Eva Gustafsson, Aug. 9, 1980; children: Jacob, David. LLM, Stockholm U., 1981. Asst. claims mgr. Salén Reefer Svcs., Stockholm, 1979-82; legal advisor Blue Water Law Firm, Stockholm, 1982-85; claims exec. Skuld AB, Stockholm, 1985-90, asst. dir., 1990-92, dir. legal & claims, 1992—2001; atty. Advokatfirman IHRE AB, 2001—. Lectr. maritime law Maritime Acad., Stockholm, 1981-84. Mem. Swedish Maritime Law Assn. Office: Advokatfirman IHRE AB PO Box 13004 10301 Stockholm Sweden E-mail: carl@ihrelawfirm.se.

ROMARY, PETER JOHN MICHAEL, lawyer; b. Leeds, Eng. came to U.S., 1992; s. John Gerald Robert and Joy (Linley) R.; m. Marcia Wiggs; 1 child, Elizabeth Grace. LLB, U. Reading, Eng., 1992; JD, U. N.C., 1994. Bar: N.C. 1994, D.C. 1996, U.S. Dist. Ct. (ea. dist.) N.C., U.S. Ct. Appeals (4th cir.) 1996, U.S. Supreme Ct. 1997. Law clk. Pethybridges Solicitors, Bodmin, Eng., 1988-92; assoc. Harrington, Edwards & Braddy LLP, Greenville, N.C., 1994-96; ptnr. Harrington, Braddy & Romary, LLP, Greenville, 1996—2000, Tanner & Romary, P.A., Greenville, 2000—. Adj. prof. U. N.C. Sch. Law, Chapel Hill, 1995; supervising atty. New Directions Domestic Violence Shelter, Greenville, 1996—. Recipient Pro Bono Atty. of Yr. award, N.C. Bar Assn., 1999, Champion of Justice award, Nat. Crime Victims Bar Assn., 2001, 40 Under 40 award, Nat. Law Jour., 2002, Pro Bono award, 2002. Mem. ABA, N.C. Acad. Trial Lawyers, Million Dollar Advocates Forum (life), Masons. Democrat. Episcopalian. Avocations: running, reading, current affairs. State civil litigation, Criminal, Personal injury (including property damage). Office: Tanner & Romary PA 600 Lynndale Ct Ste C Greenville NC 27858-1030

ROMERO, ANTHONY D. legal association administrator; b. N.Y.C. Grad., Princeton U., Stanford U. With Rockefeller found.; program officer for civil rights and racial justice Ford Founds. Human Rights and Internat. Cooperation Program; exec. dir. ACLU, N.Y.C., 2001—. Dinkelspiel scholar, Stanford U., Cane scholar, Princeton U., Nat. Hispanic scholar, Stanford U., Princeton U. Mem.: Coun. on Fgn. Rels., N.Y. State Bar Assn. Office: ACLU 18th Fl 125 Broad St New York NY 10004*

ROMERO, JUAN DIAZ, judge; b. Mexico, Nov. 5, 1930; Grad., U. Nacional Autonoma de Mexico, 1965. Former dist. ct. judge; former magistrate Collegiate Cir. Ct.; min. Supreme Ct. Justice, Mexico City, 1995—, pres. adminstrv. and labor affairs, 1995—. Office: Suprema Corte de Justicia de la Nacion Pino Suarez No 2 Col Centro 06065 Mexico City Mexico*

ROMERO, VICTOR CARREON, law educator; b. Manila, Philippines, Jan. 28, 1965; Student, U. Philippines, Quezon City, 1983-84; BA, Swarthmore (Pa.), 1987; JD, U. So. Calif., L.A., 1992. Bar. Calif. 1992, Mass. 1995. Assoc. Folger, Levin & Kahn, L.A., 1992-93; law clk. to U.S. Dist. Judge David Kenyon L.A., 1993-95; asst. prof. law Penn State Dickenson Sch. Law, Carlisle, Pa., 1995-98, assoc. prof. law, 1998-2000, prof., 2000—. Mem. Pa. State U. Faculty Senate, 1997-2000. Co-editor: (with Chin and Scaperlanda) Immigration and the Constitution, 2000. V.p. Am. Civil Liberties Union So. Ctrl. Pa. Chpt., 1996—, pres. NAACP Greater Carlisle area, 2001-2002. Named Nat. Finalist Am. Soc. Writers on Legal Subjects, 1992. Mem. Pa. State U. Faculty Senate. Office: Penn State Dickinson Sch Law 150 S College St Carlisle PA 17013-2861 E-mail: VCR1@psu.edu.

ROMINGER, M. KYLE, lawyer; b. Indpls., Mar. 5, 1968; s. Roger Kyle and Phyllis Rae Rominger; m. Jennifer Lynn Gist, July 16, 1994. BS in Ecology, Ethology and Evolution, U. Ill., 1990; JD, U. Louisville, 1997. Bar: Ill. 1997, U.S. Dist. Ct. (ctrl. dist.) Ill. 1997. Intern Office of Gov., Office of Dept. of Transp., State of Ill., Springfield, 1989; rsch. asst. U. Ill., Champaign, 1989; project mgr. Ill. EPA, Springfield, 1991-94; assoc. Giffin, Winning, Cohen & Bodewes, Springfield, 1997-99; asst. counsel Ill. EPA, Springfield, 1999—. Mem. ABA, Ill. Bar Assn., Sangamon County Bar Assn. Administrative and regulatory, Environmental, Legislative. Office: 1021 N Grand Ave E Springfield IL 62702-4059 E-mail: kyle.rominger@epa.state.il.us.

ROMNEY, RICHARD BRUCE, lawyer; b. Kingston, Jamaica, Dec. 29, 1942; came to U.S., 1945, naturalized, 1956; s. Frank Oswald and Mary Ellen (Burton) R.; m. Beverly Cochran, Sept. 11, 1965 (dec. 1984); children: Richard Bruce, Jr., Stephanie Cochran; m. Lynthia H. Walker, Aug. 14, 1988; children: Alisa Dawn, Kristen Elizabeth. BA, U. Pa., 1964; JD, U. Va., 1972. Bar: N.Y. 1973, U.S. Ct. Appeals (2d cir.) 1975. Assoc. Dewey, Ballantine, Bushby, Palmer & Wood, N.Y.C., 1972—80, ptnr., 1981—. Mem. editl. bd. U. Va. Law Rev., 1970-72. Lt. USN, 1964—68. Mem. ABA, N.Y. State Bar Assn., Assn. Bar City N.Y., Order of Coif. Corporate, general, Mergers and acquisitions, Securities. Home: 35 Deerfield Rd Chappaqua NY 10514-1604 Office: Dewey Ballantine LLP 1301 Ave Americas New York NY 10019-6022 E-mail: rromney@dbllp.com.

RONDEPIERRE, EDMOND FRANCOIS, insurance executive; b. N.Y.C., Jan. 15, 1930; s. Jules Gilbert and Margaret Murray (Moore) R.; m. M. Anne Lerch, July 5, 1952; children: Aimee S., Stephen C., Peter E., Anne W. BS, U.S. Mcht. Marine Acad., 1952; JD, Temple U., 1959. Bar: D.C. 1959, Conn. 1988, U.S. Supreme Ct. 1992. Third mate Nat. Bulk Carriers, 1952-53; field rep. Ins. Co. N.Am., Phila., 1955-59, br. mgr., 1959-61, asst. sec. underwriting, 1965-67, asst. gen. counsel, 1967-70, sr. v.p., gen. counsel, 1970-76; v.p., dep. chief legal affairs INA Corp., Phila., 1976-77; v.p., gen. counsel Gen. Reins. Corp., Stamford, Conn., 1977-79, sr. v.p., corp. sec., gen. counsel, 1979-94, sr. v.p., 1994-95; pres., dir. ARIAS-US, 1994-99, dir. emeritus, 1999—. Bd. dirs. Arias-US. Lt. USN, 1953-55. Mem. ABA, Conn. Bar Assn., D.C. Bar Assn., Inter-Am. Bar Assn., Soc. CPCU, Internat. Assn. Def. Counsel (past bd. dirs.), AIDA Reins. and Ins. Arbitration Soc. (dir., pres.), Stamford Yacht Club, Wee Burn Country Club. Roman Catholic.

RONDON, EDANIA CECILIA, lawyer; b. Santiago, Cuba, Oct. 22, 1960; came to U.S., 1965; d. Edalio Marcelino and Ylia Nayda (Jacas) R.; m. Antonio Omar Maldonado, Sept. 5, 1987. BA, Syracuse U., 1982; JD, Boston U., 1985. Bar: N.J. 1985, U.S. Ct. Appeals (3d cir.) 1985. Assoc. Thomas A. Declemente, P.C., Union City, N.J., 1985-88; pub. defender City of Union City, 1985—; assoc. ins. def. James D. Butler, P.A., Jersey City, 1988-93; assoc. Edania C. Rondon, P.A., Union City, 1993—. Mem. ABA, Hudson County Bar Assn. Democrat. Roman Catholic. Home: 630 Slocum Ave Ridgefield NJ 07657-1837 Office: Edania C Rondon PA 3700 Bergenline Ave Ste 201 Union City NJ 07087-4847

RONEY, JOHN M. lawyer; b. Wash., D.C., Sept. 21, 1939; m. Barbara Kennedy; children: Christopher, Carley, Kristina. BA, Providence Coll.; JD, Cath. U. Am. Atty. Roney & Labinger, Providence; senator R.I. State Senate, 1994—. Dep. majority leader, vice chair fin., health, edn. welfare R.I. State Senate. Mem. Lawyers for the Arts; bd. dirs. R.I. Legal Svcs.; mem. Leadership R.I., R.I. Coun. on Alcoholism. Mem.: R.I. Bar Assn. (exec. com.). Democrat. Office: Roney and Labinger 344 Wickenden St Providence RI 02903*

RONEY, PAUL H(ITCH), federal judge; b. Olney, Ill., Sept. 5, 1921; m. Sarah E. Eustis; children: Susan M., Paul Hitch Jr., Timothy Eustis. Student, St. Petersburg Jr. Coll., 1938—40; BS in Econs., U. Pa., 1942; LLB, Harvard U., 1948; LLD, Stetson U., 1977; LLM, U. Va., 1984. Bar: N.Y. 1949, Fla. 1950. Assoc. Root, Ballantine, Harlan, Bushby & Palmer, N.Y.C., 1948—50; ptnr. Mann, Harrison, Roney, Mann & Masterson (and predecessors), St. Petersburg, Fla., 1950—57; pvt. practice, 1957—63; ptnr. Roney & Beach, St. Petersburg, 1963—69, Roney, Ulmer, Woodworth & Jacobs, St. Petersburg, 1969—70; judge U.S. Ct. Appeals (5th cir.), St. Petersburg, 1970—81, U.S. Ct. Appeals (11th cir.), St. Petersburg, 1981—86, chief judge, 1986—89, sr. cir. judge, 1989—. Adv. com. on adminstrv. law judges U.S. CSC, 1976—77; pres. judge U.S. Fgn. Intelligence Surveillance Ct. of Rev., 1994—2001; lectr. Stetson U. Coll. of Law. With U.S. Army, 1942—46. Fellow: Am. Bar Found.; mem.: ABA (chmn. legal adv. com. Fair Trial-Free Press 1973—76, task force on cts. and public 1973—76, jud. adminstrn. divsn., chmn. appellate judges conf. 1978—79, Gavel Awards com. 1980—83), Jud. Conf. U.S. (subcom. on jud. improvements 1978—84, exec. com. 1986—89, com. to review circuit coun. conduct and disability orders 1991—93), Nat. Jud. Coll. (faculty 1974—75), St. Peterburg Bar Assn. (pres. 1964—65), Fla. Bar Assn., Am. Law Inst., Am. Judicature Soc. (bd. dirs. 1972—76). Office: US Ct Appeals Bank of Am One Progress Plz 200 Central Ave Saint Petersburg FL 33701-3326 Fax: 727-893-3851.

RONGEY, ROBERT WILLIAM, II, lawyer; b. Granite City, Ill., Jan. 20, 1960; s. Robert William and Marilyn Louise Rongey; m. Ann Elizabeth Callis, Sept. 12, 1992 (div. Mar. 1998); 1 child, Caroline JoAnna. BA, So. Ill. U., 1986, JD, 1992. Bar: Ill. 1987, U.S. Dist. Ct. (so. dist.) Ill. 1988, U.S. Ct. Appeals (7th cir.) 1995, U.S. Supreme Ct. 2001. Atty. Dunham, Boman and Leskera, Belleville, Ill., 1986-96, Callis Law Firm, Granite City, 1996—, MetroEast Sanitary Dist., 2000—. Mem. ABA, Ill. State Bar Assn., Tri-City Bar Assn., St. Clair County Bar Assn. (arbitrator 1992—), Madison County Bar Assn., Am. Trial Lawyer's Assn., Ill. Trial Lawyers Assn., Phi Alpha Delta Democrat. Presbyterian. Avocations: golf, motorcycles, travel, sports. Office: Callis Law Firm 1326 Niedringhaus Ave Granite City IL 62040-4626

RONZETTI, THOMAS A. TUCKER, lawyer, law educator; b. Ft. Meade, Md., Oct. 15, 1964; s. Thomas Anthony and Anna Susan (Arcieri) R.; m. Nancy Ellen Dennebaum, June 23, 1990; children: Michael Hogan, Cara Grace, Emma Faith. BA in Econs., Duke U., 1987; JD, U. Miami, 1992. Bar: Fla. 1992, U.S. Dist. Ct. (so. dist.) Fla. 1993, U.S. Ct. Appeals (11th cir.) 1996, U.S. Supreme Ct. 1998. Law clk. Judge Edward B. Davis, Miami, Fla., 1992-93; assoc. Valdez-Fauli, Cobb, et al, Miami, 1993-94; asst. county atty. Dade County Atty., Miami, 1994—2001; of counsel Kozyak, Tropin & Throckmorton, P.A., Miami, 2001—. Instr. U. Miami Sch. Law, 1992—. Editor-in-chief: U. Miami Law Rev., 1991—92. Mem. Order of the Coif. Avocations: guitar, boating, fishing. Office: Kozyak Tropin & Throckmorton PA 200 S Biscayne Blvd Ste 2800 Miami FL 33131-

ROOKS, JOHN NEWTON, lawyer; b. Evanston, Ill., Jan. 7, 1948; s. R. Newton and Ruth Dunlop (Darling) R.; m. Mary Preston Noell, Sept. 15, 1973; children: John Newton, Thomas N. BA, DePauw U., 1970; JD, Washington U., 1973. Bar: Ill. 1973, U.S. Dist. Ct. (no. dist.) Ill. 1973. Corp. atty. No. Trust Co., Chgo., 1973-76; ptnr. Hynds, Rooks, Yoknka Mattingly & Bzdill, Morris, Ill., 1976—. Chmn. bd. dirs. ARC, Morris, 1980-82, adv. com., 1996-97; adminstrv. coun. 1st United Meth. Ch., Morris, 1985-86; trustee, 1982-84; citizens adv. com. Morris Cmty. H.S., 1984-87; bd. dirs. Morris Elem. Sch. Dist. 54, 1987-91, 95; v.p., Morris Downtown Devel. Partnership, Inc., 1996—2000, v.p., 1996—, pres., 2000-03. Mem. ABA, Ill. Bar Assn., Chgo. Bar Assn., Grundy County Bar Assn. (pres. 1983-84), Grundy County C. of C. (chmn. bd. 1982). Republican. Methodist. Corporate, general, General practice, Probate (including wills, trusts). Home: 102 Briar Ln Morris IL 60450-1611 Office: Hynds Rooks Yohnka Mattingly & Bzdill PO Box 685 Morris IL 60450-0685 E-mail: rooksjn@uti.com.

ROONEY, GEORGE WILLARD, lawyer; b. Appleton, Wis., Nov. 16, 1915; s. Francis John and Margaret Ellen (O'Connell) R.; m. Doris I. Maxon, Sept. 20, 1941; children: Catherine Ann, Thomas Dudley, George Willard. BS, U. Wis., 1938; JD, Ohio State U., 1948. Bar: Ohio 1949, U.S. Supreme Ct. 1956, U.S. Ct. Appeals 1956. Assoc. Wise, Roetzel, Maxon, Kelly & Andress, Akron, Ohio, 1949-54; ptnr. Roetzel & Andress, and predecessor, Akron, 1954—; dir. Duracote Corp. Nat. bd. govs. ARC, 1972-78; trustee, mem. exec. bd. Summit County chpt. ARC, 1968, 1975—; v.p. Akron coun. Boy Scouts Am., 1975—; pres. Akron Automobile Assn., 1980-83, trustee, 1983—; chmn. bd. Akron Gen. Med. Ctr., 1981-86, trustee, mem. exec. com., 1986—; trustee Mobile Meals Found., Bluecoats, Inc. Maj. USAAF, 1942-46. Decorated D.F.C. with 2 oak leaf clusters, Air medal with 3 oak leaf clusters; recipient Disting. Community Svc. award Akron Labor Coun.; Disting. Svc. award Summit County chpt. ARC, 1978. Mem. ABA, Ohio Bar Assn. Akron Bar Assn. Am. Judicature Soc., Rotary (past pres.), Portage Country Club (past pres.), Cascade Club (past chmn., bd. govs.), KC. Republican. Roman Catholic. Avocations: golf, travel, gardening. Corporate, general, Labor (including EEOC, Fair Labor Standards Act, labor-management relations, NLRB, OSHA). Home: 2863 Walnut Ridge Rd Akron OH 44333-2262 Office: Roetzel & Andress 222 S Main St Akron OH 44308-1533

ROONEY, JOHN PHILIP, law educator; b. Evanston, Ill., May 1, 1932; s. John McCaffery and Bernadette Marie (O'Brien) R.; m. Jean Marie Kliss, Feb. 16, 1974 (div. Oct. 1988); 1 child, Caitlin Mairin. BA, U. Ill, 1953; JD, Harvard U., 1958. Bar: Ill. 1958, Calif. 1961, Mich. 1975, U.S. Tax Ct. 1973. Assoc. lawyer Chapman & Cutler, Chgo., 1958-60, Wilson, Morton, San Mateo, Calif., 1961-63; pvt. practice San Francisco, 1963-74; prof. law Cooley Law Sch., Lansing, Mich., 1975—. Author: Selected Cases (Property), 1985; contbr. articles to profl. jours. Pres. San Francisco coun. Dem. Clubs, 1970. 1st lt. U.S. Army, 1953-55. Recipient Beattie Teaching award Cooley Law Sch. Grads., 1979, 90, 92. Fellow Mich. Bar Found.; mem. ABA (real estate fed. tax problems com., title ins. com.), Ingham County Bar Assn., Univ. Club. Democrat. Unitarian Universalist. Office: Cooley Law Sch 300 S Capitol Ave Lansing MI 48933-1586 E-mail: rooneyj@cooley.edu.

ROONEY, MATTHEW A. lawyer; b. Jersey City, May 19, 1949; s. Charles John and Eileen (Dunphy) R.; m. Jean M. Alletag, June 20, 1973 (div. Dec. 1979); 1 child, Jessica Margaret; m. Diane S. Kaplan, July 6, 1981; children: Kathryn Olivia, S. Benjamin. AB magna cum laude, Georgetown U., 1971; JD with honors, U. Chgo., 1974. Bar: Ill. 1975, U.S. Dist. Ct. (no. dist.) Ill. 1975, U.S. Ct. Appeals (7th cir.). 1990. Law clk. to cir. judge U.S. Ct. Appeals (7th cir.), Chgo., 1974-75; assoc. Mayer, Brown, Rowe & Maw, Chgo., 1975-80, ptnr., 1981—. Assoc. editor U. Chgo. Law Rev., 1973. Fellow Am. Coll. Trial Lawyers; mem. ABA, 7th Cir. Bar Assn., Order of Coif, Phi Beta Kappa. Democrat. Roman Catholic. Avocations: jogging, golfing. Federal civil litigation, Communications, Nuclear power. Home: 2718 Sheridan Rd Evanston IL 60201-1754 Office: Mayer Brown Rowe & Maw 190 S La Salle St Ste 3100 Chicago IL 60603-3441 E-mail: mrooney@mayerbrownrowe.com.

ROONEY, PAUL C., JR., lawyer, retired; b. Winnetka, Ill., Oct. 23, 1943; s. Paul C. and Mary K. (Brennan) R.; m. Maria Elena Del Canto, Sept. 6, 1980. BA, Harvard U., 1963, LLB, 1966. Bar: Mass. 1968, N.Y. 1972, Fla. 1980, U.S. Dist. Ct. (ea. and so. dists.) N.Y., U.S. Ct. Appeals (2d cir.). Ptnr. White & Case, N.Y.C., 1983-98, ret., 1998. Served to lt. USNR, 1966-69. Mem. N.Y. State Bar Assn., Univ. Club (N.Y.C.), Mashomack Preserve (N.Y.), Sharon Country Club (Conn.). Finance, Corporate taxation, Taxation, general. Home: 11 Lilac Ln PO Box 271 Sharon CT 06069-0271 Office: White & Case 1155 Avenue Of The Americas New York NY 10036-2787

ROONEY, ROBERT GERARD, lawyer; b. Kansas City, Mo., Sept. 28, 1965; s. William Donald and Marie Joan Rooney. BA in Polit. Philosophy, U. Dallas, 1988; JD, Georgetown U., 1992. Bar: Mo., Kans., U.S. Dist. Ct. Kans., U.S. Dist. Ct. (we. dist.) Mo., U.S. Supreme Ct. Assoc. Armstrong Teasdale, Kansas City, 1992—94, Blackwell Sanders LLC, Kansas City, 1994—97; ptnr. Wagstaff & Cartmell LLP, Kansas City, 1997—. Legal advisor Healthwide Solutions, Boston, 2000—. Mem. ball com. Leukemia Lymphoma Soc. of Kansas City, 2002—. Mem.: Kansas City Mo. Bar Assn. (mem. torts, med. and legal coms. 2001—02), Kans. Bar Assn., Mo. Bar (mem. health law and torts com. 2000—02). Avocations: travel, climbing, running, tennis, hiking. Personal injury (including property damage), Product liability, Toxic tort. Office: Wagstaff & Cartmell LLP 4740 Grand Ave Ste 300 Kansas City MO 64113 E-mail: rrooney@wcllp.com.

ROOSEVELT, JAMES, JR., health plan executive, lawyer; b. L.A., Nov. 9, 1945; s. James and Romelle (Schneider) R.; m. Ann M. Conlon, June 15, 1968; children: Kathy, Tracy, Maura. AB, Harvard U., 1968, JD, 1971. Bar. Mass. 1971, D.C. 1973, U.S. Ct. Appeals (D.C. cir.) 1973, U.S. Ct. Appeals (1st cir.) 1976, U.S. Supreme Ct. 1975. Assoc. Winthrop, Stimson, Putnam & Roberts, N.Y.C., 1971, Herrick & Smith, Boston, 1975-80, ptnr., 1981-86, Nutter, McClennen & Fish, Boston, 1986-88, Choate, Hall & Stewart, Boston, 1988-98; assoc. commr. for retirement policy Social Security Adminstrn., Washington, 1998-99; sr. v.p., gen. counsel Tufts Health Plan, Waltham, Mass., 1999—. Mem. Dem. Nat. Com., Washington, 1980—, Dem. State Com., Boston, 1980—; trustee Emmanuel Coll., Boston, 1982-92, 95—; trustee Care Group, Inc., Boston, 1996-00, Mt. Auburn Hosp., Cambridge, Mass., 1984-2000, chmn., 1988-92, chmn. bd. overseers, 2000—. Lt. JAGC, USN, 1972-75. Mem. ABA, Boston Bar Assn., Mass. Bar Assn., Am. Health Lawyers Assn. (pres. 2002-03), Mass. Hosp. Assn. (trustee 1987-99, chmn. 1996-97), Harvard Club. Roman Catholic. Avocation: public policy. Office: Tufts Health Plan 333 Wyman St Waltham MA 02451-1282 E-mail: james_roosevelt@tufts-health.com.

ROOT, GERALD EDWARD, legal administrator; b. Gridley, Calif., May 5, 1948; s. Loris Leo Root and Mary Helen (Wheeler) Murrell; m. Tricia Ann Caywood, Feb. 13, 1982 (widowed); children: Jason Alexander, Melinda Ann. AA in Bus., Yuba C.C., Marysville, Calif., 1968; BA in Psychology, Calif. State U., Sonoma, 1974; MA in Social Sci., Calif. State U., Chico, 1977; postgrad., U. San Francisco, 1999—2001. Gen. mgr. Do-It Leisure Therapeutic Recreation, Chico, 1977-79; CETA projects coord. City of Chico, 1980-81; exec. dir. Voluntary Action Ctr., Inc., South Lake Tahoe, Calif., 1981-83; devel. dir. Work Tng. Ctr., Inc., Chico, 1983-92; exec. dir. North Valley Rehab. Found., Chico, 1986-92; adminstrn. officer Superior Ct. of Calif., County of Sacramento, 1992—2002, project mgr. self-represented litigants action plan initiative, 2000—03, project mgr. virtual courthouse tour--distance learning, 2001—02, project mgr. lang. aides pilot program, 2002—03, legis. coord., 2003—. Project mgr. Juvenile Detention Alternatives Initiative, 1992-98, Feather River Industries Vocat. Tng., 1991, Creative Learning Ctr. Constrn., 1988-89, Correctional Options-Drug Ct., 1994, Violence Prevention Resource Ctr., 1995-96, Communities That Care-Juvenile Delinquency Prevention Initiative, 1995, Securing the Health and Safety of Urban Children Initiative, 1995-97, Joint Cabinets Youth Work Group/Child Welfare League Am., 1996-97, Task Force on Fairness-The Juvenile Justice Initiative, 1994-97, SacraMentor, Inc., CA Wellness Found., 1994-95, Violent Injury Prevention Coalition/Calif. Dept. Health and Human Svcs., 1995—, Domestic Violence Coord. Coun., Sacramento County, 1995-98, Family Violence Summit, 1997, Ptnrs. in Protection Conf. 1997 Child Abuse Prevention Coun., The Drug Store, Calif. N.G. drug demand reduction program, 1996-97, disporportionate minority confinement rsch. com. Criminal Justice Cabinet, 1997-99, Court Cmty.-Focused Strategic Plan, 1998—, Sunrise Recreation and Park Dist. 10 Yr. Master Plan, 1999-2000; steering com. Multicultural Family Violence Prevention Conf., 1996-2001; presenter in field. Bd. dirs. Cmty. Action Agy., Butte County, Calif., 1990-92, ARC, Butte County, 1989-90, Sunrise Recreation and Park Dist., 1996-2001; adv. bd. Butte C.C. Dist., 1987-92, Cmty. Svcs. Planning Coun., 1994-96; blue ribbon task force for strategic plan Calif. Found. for Parks and Recreation, 2000. Grantee Annie E. Casey Found., USDA, U.S. Dept. Justice, Robert Wood Johnson Found., Calif. Office Criminal Justice Planning, U.S. Dept. Labor, Office Juvenile Justice and Delinquency Prevention, Sacramento Criminal Justice Cabinet, Calif. Wellness Found., Calif. Endowment, Adminstrv. Office of the Cts., 1998-03; recipient Ralph N. Kleps award Calif. Judicial Coun., 2000. Office: Superior Ct Calif County of Sacramento 720 9th St Sacramento CA 95814-1302 E-mail: rootg@saccourt.com.

ROOT, STANLEY WILLIAM, JR., lawyer, retired; b. Honolulu, Mar. 2, 1923; s. Stanley William and Henrietta E. (Brown) R.; m. Joan Louise Schimpf, Sept. 3, 1949; children: Henry, Louise. AB, Princeton U., 1947; LLB, U. Pa., 1950. Bar: Pa. 1950, U.S. Ct. Mil. Appeals 1951, U.S. Supreme Ct. 1971. Ptnr. Foley, Schimpf & Steeley, Phila., 1952-69, Ballard,

Spahr, Andrews & Ingersoll, Phila., 1970-91, of counsel, 1992-97; ret., 1998. Lectr. Pa. Bar Assn., 1970-80; bd. dirs. Boardman-Hamilton Co., sec. 1980-98. Exec. v.p. Chestnut Hill Cmty. Assn., Phila., 1978; with Whitpain Farm Assn., Blue Bell, Pa., 1987, 90, pres., 1992-94; with St. Paul's Ch. Vestry, Phila., 1969-75; bd. dirs. Lansdale (Pa.) Med. Group, 1972-95, E.B. Spaeth Found. Wills Hosp., Phila., 1975-88, Chevalier Jackson Clinic, Phila., 1965-88; trustee Civil War Libr. and Mus., 1985-93, v.p., 1989, sec., 1992-93, mem. adv. bd., 1993-95; trustee Soc. Protestant Episc. Ch., Pa. Diocese, 1955-95. Lt. col. U.S. Army, 1942-45, ETO, 1950-52, Korea. Decorated Bronze Star; recipient Pa. Commendation medal State of Pa., 1962; named Comdr. Phila. chpt. Mil. Order Fgn. Wars, 1972. Mem. Union League (pres. 1983-85), Sunnybrook Golf Club, Royal Poinciana Golf Club, Brit. Officers Club, Mil. Order Loyal Legion. Republican. Episcopalian. Avocations: golf, tennis, fishing. Home: 16 Hounds Run Ln Blue Bell PA 19422-2456 Office: Ballard Spahr Andrews & Ingersoll 51st Fl 1735 Market St Fl 51 Philadelphia PA 19103-7599 E-mail: stanislaw16@aol.com.

ROOX, KRISTOF, lawyer, educator; b. Maaseik, Belgium, Aug. 21, 1971; m. Astrid van Daele, Nov. 25, 1975. LicJur, Free U. Brussels, 1994; M in Intellectual Property Law, U. London, 1996. Bar: Brussels 1994. Atty. Crowell & Moring, Brussels, 1996—; asst. prof. conflicts of law U. Ghent, Belgium, 1998—2002. Contbr. articles to profl. jours. Office: Crowell & Moring 71 Rue Royale Brussels B-1000 Belgium Fax: 32 0 2 230 6399. E-mail: kroox@crowell.com.

ROPER, HARRY JOSEPH, lawyer; b. Bridgeport, Conn., Apr. 15, 1940; BEE, Rensselaer Poly. Inst., 1962; LLB, NYU, 1966. Assoc. Neuman, Williams, Anderson & Olson, Chgo., 1966-70, ptnr., 1970-90, Roper & Quigg, Chgo., 1990—. Federal civil litigation, Intellectual property, Patent. Home: 611 W Fullerton Pky Chicago IL 60614-2613 Office: Roper & Quigg 200 S Michigan Ave Chicago IL 60604-2402 E-mail: hroper@roperandquigg.com.

RORSCHACH, RICHARD GORDON, lawyer; b. Tulsa, Aug. 9, 1928; s. Harold Emil and Margaret (Hermes) R.; m. Martha Kay King, Dec. 23, 1979; children by previous marriage: Richard Helm, Reagan Cartwright, Andrew Maxwell. BS, MIT, 1950; MS, U. Okla., 1952; JD, U. Houston, 1961. Bar: Tex. 1961; lic. prof. engr., Tex. Cons. civil engr. Freese & Nichols, Ft. Worth, 1955; cons. engr. Freese, Nichols & Turner, Houston, 1955-56; petroleum engr. Marathon Oil Co., Bay City, Tex., 1956-57, Houston, 1957-61, atty., 1961-64; ptnr. Broady, Kells & Rorschsch, Houston, 1964-68, Ragan, Russell & Rorschach, Houston, 1968-80, Kilgore, Tex., 1980—. Mem. exec. com. Colonial Royalties Co., Tulsa, 1970-77; officer Little River Oil & Gas Co., 1980-88; mng. ptnr. Pentagon Oil Co., 1988—; pres. Nat. Assn. Royalty Owners-Tex., 1993-96; chmn. Nat. Assn. Royalty Owners, Inc., 1996-99, bd. dirs., 1999-2000; mem. exec. com. Nat. Assn. Royalty Owners, Inc.; owner, breeder, exhibitor Arabian Horses Shadowbrook Farm, Kilgore, Tex., 1980—. Author: How to Protect Your Royalty Interests: Texas Perspectives, Vols. 1 & 2, 2002. Served to 1st lt. C.E., AUS, 1952-54, Korea. Mem. ASME, ASCE, Tex. Bar Assn., Rotary Club (pres. Kilgore chpt. 1984-85), Sigma Xi, Sigma Alpha Epsilon. Republican. Presbyterian. Oil, gas, and mineral. Home: RR 4 Box 210 Kilgore TX 75662-9023 Office: 1100 Stone Rd PO Box 1934 Kilgore TX 75663-1934

ROSCH, JOHN THOMAS, lawyer; b. Council Bluffs, Iowa, Oct. 4, 1939; s. H.P. and Phebe Florence (Jamison) R.; m. Carolyn Lee, Aug. 18, 1961; children: Thomas Lee, Laura Lee. BA, Harvard U., 1961, LLB, 1965. Bar: Calif. 1966, U.S. Dist. Ct. (no. dist.) Calif. 1966, U.S. Dist. Ct. (ea. dist.) Calif. 1967, U.S. Ct. Appeals (9th cir.) 1966. Assoc. McCutchen, Doyle, Brown & Enersen, San Francisco, 1965-72, ptnr., 1972-73, 75-93, Latham & Watkins, San Francisco, 1994—, office mng. ptnr., 1994—99. Dir. Bur. Consumer Protection, FTC, Washington, 1973-75, The Eisenhower Inst. Contbr. articles profl. jours. Fellow Am. Bar Found., Am. Coll. Trial Lawyers; mem. ABA (past chmn. antitrust sect.), State Bar Calif., San Francisco Bar Assn., Calif. State and Antitrust and Trade Regulation Sect. (past sect. chair, Calif. Antitrust Lawyer of Yr. 2003). Republican. Episcopalian. Antitrust, Federal civil litigation, State civil litigation. Office: Latham & Watkins 505 Montgomery St Fl 19th San Francisco CA 94111-2552

ROSCOPF, CHARLES BUFORD, lawyer; b. Marvell, Ark., Apr. 21, 1928; s. Emmett Lee and Sally Virginia (King) R.; m. Mary Anne Maddox, Aug. 22, 1954; children— Charles David; Ann Karen. Student, Hendrix Coll., 1948-50; JD, U. Ark., 1954. Bar: Ark. bar 1954, U.S. Dist. Cts 1955, 64, U.S. Supreme Ct. bar 1965. Pvt. practice, Helena, Ark., 1954—; assoc. firm Burke, Moore & Burke, 1954-58; ptnr. firm Burke & Roscopf, 1958-64; sr. ptnr. Roscopf and Roscopf, P.A., 1964—. Mem. Ark. Ho. of Reps., 1953-58; del. Ark. Constl. Conv., 1968; mem. Ark. Probate Drafting Com.; mem. Ark. State Bd. Law Examiners, 1973-79; spl. justice Ark. Supreme Ct. Served with USN, 1946-48; served with USAFR, 1962-68. Fellow Am. Bar Found., Ark. Bar Found. (pres. 1995-96); mem. ABA, Ark. Bar Assn. (pres. 1990-91), Am. Law Inst., Rotary (Paul Harris fellow), Masons, Shriners, Kappa Sigma. Methodist. Home: 117 Avalon Pl Helena AR 72342-1715 Office: Helena Nat Bank Bldg PO Box 610 Helena AR 72342-0610

ROSE, ALBERT SCHOENBURG, lawyer, educator; b. Nov. 9, 1945; s. Albert Schoenberg Sr. and Karleen (Klein) Rose; m. Nancy K. Rose; children: Claudia, Micah Daniel. BSBA, U. Ala., 1967; JD, Washington U., St. Louis, 1970; LLM in Taxation, George Washington U., 1974. Bar: Mo. 1970, U.S. Dist. Ct. (ea. dist.) Mo. 1970, U.S. Tax Ct. 1970, U.S. Ct. Mil. Appeals 1970, U.S. Supreme Ct. 1970. Ptnr. Lewis Rice & Fingersh, St. Louis, 2001—. Adj. prof. law Washington U., 1979-98, Fontbonne Coll., 1993-96. Co-author: Missouri Taxation Law and Practice, 1986, supplement, 1989. Capt. U.S. Army, 1970-74, Korea. Mem.: Civic Entrepreneurs Orgn. (Bd. dirs., sec.), Tax Lawyers Club (pres.), Mid.Am. Tax Conf. (chmn.). Corporate, general, Estate planning, Corporate taxation. Office: Lewis Rice & Fingersh 500 North Broadway Ste 2000 Saint Louis MO 63102 E-mail: arose@lewisrice.com.

ROSE, DAVID L. lawyer; b. Ft. Monmouth, NJ, Feb. 18, 1955; s. Llewellyn Paterson and Bebe (Faulk) R.; m. Laura Marie Jarvis, Sept. 3, 1989; children: Allison Michelle, Jessica Morgan, Ashley Elizabeth. BA in Comm., U. Colo., 1980; JD, Ariz. State U., 1991. Bar: Ariz. 1991, U.S. Dist. Ct. Ariz. 1991, U.S. Ct. Appeals (9th cir.) 1993, U.S. Supreme Ct. 1997. Law clk. Bonn & Anderson, Phoenix, 1988-91, Maricopa County Superior Ct., Phoenix, 1990-91; lawyer Anderson, Brody, Levinson, Weiser & Horwitz, Phoenix, 1991-92, Brandes, Lane & Joffe, Phoenix, 1992-93; pvt. practice Phoenix, 1993—; lawyer Rose & Hildebrand, P.C., 1997—. Judge pro-tem Maricopa County Superior Ct. Editor: Missive, 1992. Bd. dirs. Maricopa County Family Support Adv. Com., Phoenix; adv. coun. Washington Sch. Dist., Phoenix; mem. Ariz. State Legis., Domestic Rels. Reform Com., Phoenix. Mem. Maricopa County Bar Assn. (adv. family law com.), ABA (adv. family law sect.), Nat. Congress for Men (pres.), Father's for Equal Rights of Colo. (pres.). Avocations: aviation, computer systems. General civil litigation, Criminal, Family and matrimonial. Office: 1440 E Washington St Phoenix AZ 85034-1109

ROSE, DONALD MCGREGOR, retired lawyer; b. Cin., Feb. 6, 1933; s. John Kreimer and Helen (Morris) R.; m. Constance Ruth Lanner, Nov. 29, 1958; children: Barbara Rose Mead, Ann Rose Weston. AB in Econs., U. Cin., 1955; JD, Harvard U., 1958. Bar: Ohio 1958, U.S. Supreme Ct. 1962. Asst. legal officer USNR, Subic Bay, The Philippines, 1959-62, with Office of JAG The Pentagon, Va., 1962-63; assoc. Frost & Jacobs, LLP, Cin., 1963-70, ptnr., 1970-93, sr. ptnr., 1993-97, ret. ptnr., 1997. Co-chmn. 6th Cir. Appellate Practice Inst., Cin., 1983, 90, mem. 6th Cir. adv. com., 1990-98, chmn. subcom. on rules, 1990-94, chmn., 1994-96. Trustee Friends of Cin. Pks., Inc., 1980-89, 93-98, pres. 1980-86; trustee Am. Music Scholarship Assn., Cin., 1985-88; pres. Social Health Assn. Greater Cin. Area Inc., 1969-72; co-chmn. Harvard Law Sch. Fund for So. Ohio, Cin., 1985-87; pres. Meth. Union, Cin., 1983-85; chmn. trustees Hyde Pk. Cmty. United Meth. Ch., Cin., 1974-76, chmn. coun. on ministries, 1979-81, chmn. adminstrv. bd., 1982-84, chmn. mem. canvass, 1985, chmn. staff parish rels. com., 1988-90, chmn. commn. missions, 1993-95; trustee Meth. Theol. Sch. Ohio, vice chmn. devel. com., 1990-94, sec. 1992-94, chmn. devel. com., 1994-98, vice chmn., 1998, chmn., 1999—; loaned exec. United Way, Cin., 1999. Lt. USNR, 1959-63. Mem. Cin. Citizens Police Assn., On Air Reader, Cin. Assn. for Blind, Univ. Club (Cin.), Cin. Country Club, Boothbay Harbor Yacht Club. Republican. Avocations: sailing, golf. General civil litigation. Home: 8 Walsh Ln Cincinnati OH 45208-3435 also: 11 Blackstone Rd Boothbay Harbor ME 04538-1943 E-mail: dmrose@fbtlaw.com.

ROSE, DONNA, lawyer, educator; b. Chgo., Aug. 19; d. James R. and Dorothy L. Johnson; 1 child, Yvonne. AA, St. Peter Jr. Coll., Clearwater, Fla., 1990, AS, 2000; B, U. S. Fla., 1995; JD, Stetson U., 1998. Bar: Fla. 1998, U.S. Dist. Ct. (mid. dist.) Fla. 1999. Pvt. practice, Clearwater, 1998—; prof. St. Peter Jr. Coll., Clearwater, 2002—. Rschr. for other attys., 1998—. Editor: Lobbying for Nonprofits: The New Environment, 1998. Treas. Clearwater Bar Found., 2001—. Mem.: Clearwater Bar Assn. (Young Lawyers Divsn. bd. dirs. 2001—03, sec. 2002—03), Fla. Assn. Women Lawyers (pres.-elect 2001—02, pres. 2002—03). Baptist. Family and matrimonial, Criminal, Probate (including wills, trusts). Office: PO Box 365 Clearwater FL 33757 Office Fax: 727-467-0840. Business E-Mail: vonall4him@aol.com.

ROSE, ELIHU ISAAC, lawyer; b. Bklyn., Nov. 27, 1941; s. Aaron Henry and Frances (Klinger) R.; m. Gail Roberta Cohen, Aug. 22, 1964; children: Melissa Kaye, Heidi Jill. AB, Columbia U., 1963, MBA, 1965; JD, St. John's U., Bklyn., 1968. Bar: N.Y.; CPA, N.Y. Sr. tax acct. Price Waterhouse & Co., N.Y.C., 1967-71; dir. taxes Exec. Monetary Mgmt., Inc., N.Y.C., 1971-79; pres. Elihu I. Rose, P.C., Lake Success, N.Y., 1979—; of counsel Sahn & Ward PLLC, Garden City, NY, 2003—. Mem. ABA, AICPA, N.Y. State Bar Assn., N.Y. State Soc. CPAs, Bar Assn. Nassau County, Estate Planning Coun. L.I. Estate taxation, Personal income taxation, Probate (including wills, trusts). Office: 1983 Marcus Ave Ste 129 New Hyde Park NY 11042-1016 E-mail: roselaw@sprintmail.com.

ROSE, JOEL ALAN, legal consultant; b. Bklyn., Dec. 26, 1936; s. Edward Isadore and Adele R. Rose; m. Isadora Fenig, Apr. 12, 1964; children: Susan, Terri Angstriech. BS in Econs., NYU, 1958; MBA, Wharton Grad. Sch., U. Pa., 1960. Asst. purchasing agt. Maidenform Inc., N.Y.C., 1960-62; personnel dir. E.J. Korvette Inc., N.Y.C., 1962-66; mgmt. cons. Daniel J. Cantor & Co. Inc., Phila., 1966—, sr. v.p., 1987—; mgmt. cons. to legal profession. Coord. Ann. Conf. on Law Firm Mgmt. and Econs. Author: Managing the Law Office; mem. adv. bd. Law Office Economics and Management, 1987; contbg. columnist N.Y. Law Jour., 1984—, Nat. Law Jour. Extra, 1996—, Phila. Legal Intelligencer, 1995—, L.A. Daily Times, 1999—, Legal Times of Washington, 1998—, N.J. Law Jour., 2000-, The Barrister, 1995-; contbr. articles to profl. jours.; bd. editors Acctg. for Law Firms, Law Firm Partnership and Benefits Report, 2001—; editl. adv. bd. Corp. Counsel's Guide to Law Dept. Mgmt. With U.S. Army, 1960, Res., 1960-66. Fellow Coll. of Law Practice Mgmt.; mem. ABA (chmn. acquisition and mergers com., practice mgmt. sect., large law firm interest group), Inst. Mgmt. Cons., Am. Arbitration Assn. (nat. panel), Adminstrv. Mgmt. Soc. (past chpt. pres.), Am. Mgmt. Assn., Assn. Legal Adminstrs. Office: Joel A Rose & Assoc Inc PO Box 162 Cherry Hill NJ 08003-0162

ROSE, JONATHAN CHAPMAN, lawyer; b. Cleve., June 8, 1941; s. Horace Chapman and Katherine Virginia (Cast) R.; m. Susan Anne Porter, Jan. 26, 1980; 1 son, Benjamin Chapman. AB, Yale U., 1963; LL.B. cum laude, Harvard U., 1967. Bar: Mass. 1968, D.C. 1972, U.S. Supreme Ct. 1976, Circuit Ct. Appeals 1977, Ohio 1978. Law clk. Justice R. Ammi Cutter, Mass. Supreme Jud. Ct., 1967-68; spl. asst. to U.S. pres., 1971-73; gen. counsel Coun. on Internat. Econ. Policy, 1973-74; assoc. dept. atty. gen. U.S. Dept. Justice, 1974-75; dept. asst. atty. gen. U.S. Dept. Justice (Antitrust Div.), 1975-77, asst. atty. gen. Office of Legal Policy, 1981-84; ptnr. firm Jones, Day, Reavis & Pogue, Washington, 1977-81, 84—. Prin. Ctr. for Excellence in Govt.; pres. Yale Daily News Found.; bd. govs. Yale Alumni Assn., 1996-99. 1st lt. U.S. Army, 1969-71. Mem. ABA, D.C. Bar Assn., Mass. Bar Assn., Ohio Bar Assn., Fed. Bar Assn., Am. Law Inst. Clubs: Met, Chevy Chase, Union, Yale, Harvard. Republican. Episcopalian. Administrative and regulatory, Federal civil litigation, Environmental. Office: Jones Day Reavis & Pogue 51 Louisiana Ave NW Washington DC 20001-2113 E-mail: jcrose@jonesday.com.

ROSE, KIM MATTHEW, lawyer, educator; b. Gallipolis, Ohio, Mar. 21, 1956; s. Dave and Lois Ann R.; m. Pamela Carol Sims, Aug. 11, 1990. Student, USMA, 1974—76; BBA, Ohio U., 1977; JD, Capital U. Law, 1981; MBA, Ashland Coll., 1988. Bar: Ohio 1981, U.S. Dist. Ct. (so. dist.) Ohio 1981, U.S. Ct. Appeals (6th cir.) 1987, U.S. Supreme Ct. 1988. Asst. prosecutor Knox County Prosecutor, Mt. Vernon, Ohio, 1982-90; with Critchfield, Critchfield & Johnston, Mt. Vernon, 1982—. Adj. prof. Mt. Vernon Nazarene Coll., 1982-2002. Active Met. Housing Authority, Knox County, 1990-2002; adv. bd. Salvation Army, Mt. Vernon, 1991—; bd. dirs. Knox Cmty. Hosp., Mt. Vernon, Ohio, 2000. Maj. USAR, 1974-95. Mem. Ohio State Bar Assn., Knox County Bar Assn. (past pres.), Mt. Vernon Nazarene Coll. Found. (rec. sec. bd. 1995—), Mt. Vernon-Knox County C. of C., Masons. Avocations: flying, skiing, fishing, golfing, biking. Corporate, general, General practice, Probate (including wills, trusts). Home: 1413 Greenbrier Dr Mount Vernon OH 43050-9101 Office: Critchfield Critchfield & Johnston 10 S Gay St Mount Vernon OH 43050-3546 E-mail: rose@core.com., kimr@ccj.com.

ROSE, NORMAN, retired lawyer, retired accountant; b. N.Y.C., July 7, 1923; s. Edward J. and Frances (Ludwig) R.; div.; children: Ellen, Michael; m. Judith Rose; stepchildren: Dwight, Audrey, Jason. BBA, CCNY, 1947; JD, N.Y. Law Sch., 1953. Bar: N.Y. 1954, U.S. Dist. Ct. (ea. dist.) N.Y. 1956, U.S. Tax Ct. 1956, U.S. Dist. Ct. (so. dist.) N.Y. 1960, U.S. Supreme Ct. 1961, U.S. Ct. Appeals (2d cir.) 1967, Fla. 1979. Pvt. practice, N.Y.C., 1954-69, Ft. Lauderdale, Fla., 1979-91; ptnr. Dean, Falanga & Rose, Carle Pl., N.Y., 1979-81. Referee Small Claims Ct., N.Y.C., 1959-69; arbitrator Accident Claims Tribunal, Am. Arbitration Assn., 1960-65; C.P.A., N.Y.C., 1951-57; lectr. in field. Author law note Liability of Golfer to Person Struck by Ball, 1959 (Hon. Mention 1960). Pres. Nassau South Shore Little League, Lawrence, N.Y., 1966-68; treas. 5 Towns Dem. Club, Woodmere, N.Y., 1966-67; chmn. United Fund, Village of Lawrence, 1967. Capt. USAF, 1943-45, ETO. Decorated DFC, Air medal with 5 oak leaf clusters, Silver Star, Purple Heart. Mem. ATLA (sustaining), Acad. Fla. Trial Lawyers (sustaining), N.Y. State Assn. Plaintiffs Trial Lawyers, N.Y. State Bar Assn., Fla. Bar, Nassau County Bar Assn. (chmn. med-legal com. 1975-77), Lawyer/Pilots Bar Assn., Pompano Beach Power Squadron (safety officer), Masons, Shriners. State civil litigation, Insurance, Personal injury (including property damage). Home: 6508 Via Primo St Lake Worth FL 33467 E-mail: normierose@aol.com.

ROSE, RICHARD LOOMIS, lawyer; b. Long Branch, N.J., Oct. 21, 1936; s. Charles Frederick Perrott and Jane Mary (Crotta) R.; m. Marian Frances Irons, Apr. 1, 1960; children: Linda, Cynthia, Bonnie. BA, Cornell U., 1958; JD, Washington and Lee U., 1963. Bar: N.Y. 1963, Conn. 1966, U.S. Dist. Ct. (so. dist.) N.Y. 1964, U.S. Dist. Ct. Conn. 1966, U.S. Ct. Appeals (2d cir.) 1965, U.S. Supreme Ct. 1970. Assoc. Cummings & Lockwood, Stamford, Conn., 1965-71, ptnr., 1971-91, Kleban & Samor, P.C., Southport, 1991-93; of counsel Whitman Breed Abbott & Morgan, Greenwich, Conn., 1993-95; prin. Roberts, Rose & Bates, P.C., Stamford, Conn., 1995—. Bd. dirs. and sec. Index Corp.; mem. adv. com. Conn. Banking Commr. on Conn. Securities Laws, 1982—; dir. Conn. World Trade Assn. Editor: Washington and Lee Law Rev. Chmn. Fgn. Trade Zone Com. to Mayor of City of Bridgeport, Conn., 1988-90; mem. fgn. trade awareness com. S.W. Area Industry and Commerce Assn., Task Force, 1987-88; bd. dirs. German Sch. of Conn., Inc., 1992—. 1st lt. U.S. Army, 1958-60, Korea. Mem. ABA, Conn. Bar Assn. (exec. com. corp. sect.), Internat. Bar Assn., New Canaan Country Club, Phi Delta Phi, Omicron Delta Kappa, Phi Delta Theta. Republican. Banking, Commercial, contracts (including sales of goods; commercial financing), Public international. Office: Roberts Rose & Bates PC PO Box 3610 17 Hoyt St Stamford CT 06905

ROSE, ROBERT E(DGAR), state supreme court justice; b. Orange, N.J., Oct. 7, 1939; BA, Juniata Coll., Huntingdon, Pa., 1961; LL.B., NYU, 1964. Bar: Nev. 1965. Dist. atty. Washoe County, 1971-75; lt. gov. State of Nev., 1975-79; judge Nev. Dist. Ct., 8th Jud. Dist., Las Vegas, 1986-88; justice Nev. Supreme Ct., Carson City, 1989—, chief justice, 1993-94, 1999—2000. Office: Nev Supreme Ct Capitol Complex 201 S Carson St Carson City NV 89701-4702

ROSE, ROBERT GORDON, lawyer; b. Newark, June 25, 1943; s. Harry and Ann Shirley (Gordon) R.; m. Ellen Nadley Berkowitz, July 2, 1966; children: Lisa Pauline, Michael Allan. BA, SUNY, Buffalo, 1965; MA, Columbia U., 1969; JD, Seton Hall U., 1974. Bar: N.J. 1974, U.S. Dist. Ct. N.J. 1974, U.S. Ct. Appeals (3rd cir.) 1974, U.S. Ct. Appeals (2nd cir.) 1975. Law clk. to Hon. John J. Gibbons U.S. Ct. Appeals (3rd cir.), Newark, 1974-75; assoc. Pitney, Hardin, Kipp & Szuch, Morristown, N.J., 1975-80, ptnr., 1980—. Mem. com. on unauthorized practice of law N.J. Supreme Ct., 1989-2001, apptd. com. chair, 2000-2001; apptd. lawyers adv. com. U.S. Dist. Ct., Dist. N.J., 2002—; trustee Legal Svcs. N.J., 2001—. Contbr. articles to profl. jours. Recipient Disting. Grad. award Seton Hall U. Law Sch., 2000. Mem. ABA, N.J. Bar Assn., Morris County Bar Assn. (trustee 1989-90). Avocations: travel, philately. General civil litigation, Construction, Environmental. Office: Pitney Hardin Kipp & Szuch Park Ave at Morris County PO Box 1945 Morristown NJ 07962-1945 E-mail: rrose@pitneyhardin.com.

ROSE, TODD ALAN, lawyer; b. Merced, Calif., Oct. 26, 1962; s. William Arthur and Mary (Brooks) R.; m. Teresa Gail Suiter, June 1, 1991; children: Miranda Brooke, Savannah Leigh, Emily Jane, Thomas Pierce. BS, Murray State U., 1988; JD, Vanderbilt U. Law Sch., 1991. Bar: Tenn. 1991, U.S. Dist. Ct. (we. dist.) Tenn. 1992. Asst. dist. atty. State of Tenn., Paris, 1994-97; mem. Burch, Porter & Johnson, P.L.L.C., Paris, 1991-94, 97—. General civil litigation, Personal injury (including property damage), Product liability. Office: Burch Porter & Johnson PLLC 107 W Blythe St Paris TN 38242-4150

ROSE, WILLIAM SHEPARD, JR., lawyer; b. Columbia, S.C., Mar. 9, 1948; s. William Shepard and Meta Cantey (Boykin) R.; m. Frances John Hobbs, Aug. 11, 1973; children: Katherine Cummings, William Shepard, III, Whitaker Boykin. BA in English, U. South, 1970; JD, U. S.C., 1973; LLM in Taxation, Georgetown U., 1976. Bar: S.C. 1973, Ohio 1977, D.C. 1974, U.S. Dist. Ct. D.C. 1976, U.S. Tax Ct. 1976, U.S. Supreme Ct. 1976, U.S. Ct. Claims Ct. 1978, U.S. Ct. Appeals (10th cir., 5th cir., 4th cir.) 1987, U.S. Ct. Appeals (3d, 6th, 7th, 8th, 9th and 11th cirs.) 1988. Trial atty. Office of Chief Counsel IRS, Washington, 1973-77; assoc. Frost & Jacobs, Cin., 1977-80, McNair Law Firm PA, Hilton Head Island, S.C., Washington, 1980-83, ptnr., 1983-87, 89—. Asst. atty. gen., tax divsn. U.S. Dept. Justice, Washington, 1987-89; chmn., dir. Sea Pines Montessori Sch., 1983-86, Hilton Head Broadcasting, 1983-87, MBR Corp., Adwell Corp., Links Group, Inc., The Dye Preserve, LLC, Hilton Head Prep. Sch., 1986-87, 89-93, dir. Boys & Girls Club of Hilton Head Island, 1992—, Hilton Head Humane Soc., 1985, Nickel Plate Properties, Inc., Lima Lake Inc., Lakeside Corp., The Nickel Plate Line, Inc. Contbr. articles to profl. jours. Asst to chmn. bus. fundraising Beaufort County United Way, Hilton Head Island, 1984; vice chmn. Beaufort County Rep. Party, 1991-92, 93, chmn., 1992-93, vice chmn., 1993-95; mem. Beaufort County Transp. Com., 1994-95; commr. Sea Pines Pub. Svc. Dist., South Island Pub. Svc. Dist. Mem. ABA (past co-chmn. subcom. tax sect.), Am. Coll. Tax Counsel, Ohio Bar Assn., D.C. Bar Assn., S.C. Bar Assn., Beaufort County Bar Assn., Hilton Head Bar Assn., S.C. Yacht Club (bd. govs. 1989-94, exec. com. 1993-94, rear commodore 1993-94), Caroliniana Ball. Republican. Episcopalian. Corporate, general, Taxation, general. Home: 11 Jessamine Pl Hilton Head Island SC 29928-4255 Office: PO Drawer 7787 52 New Orleans Rd Ste 204 Hilton Head Island SC 29928-4780 E-mail: rrose@mcnair.net.

ROSE-ACKERMAN, SUSAN, law and political economy educator; b. Mineola, N.Y., Apr. 23, 1942; d. R. William and Rosalie Rose; m. Bruce A. Ackerman, May 29, 1967; children: Sybil, John BA, Wellesley Coll., 1964; PhD, Yale U., 1970. Asst. prof. U. Pa., Phila, 1970-74; lectr. Yale U., New Haven, Conn., 1974-75, asst. prof., 1975-78, assoc. prof., 1978-82; prof. law and polit. economy Columbia U., N.Y.C., 1982-87; Ely prof. of law and polit. econ. Yale U., New Haven, 1987-92, co-dir. Ctr. Law, Econ. and Pub. Policy, 1988—, Luce prof. jurisprudence law and polit. sci., 1992—. Panelist Am. studies program Am. Coun. Learned Socs., 1987-90; review panelist, faculty Fulbright Commn., 1993-96; vis. rsch. fellow World Bank, 1995-96. Author: (with Ackerman, Sawyer and Henderson) Uncertain Search for Environmental Quality, 1974 (Henderson prize 1982); Corruption: A Study in Political Economy, 1978; (with E. James) The Nonprofit Enterprise in Market Economies, 1986; editor: The Economics of Nonprofit Institutions, 1986; (with J. Coffee and L. Lowenstein) Knights, Raiders, and Targets: The Impact of the Hostile Takeover, 1988, Rethinking the Progressive Agenda: The Reform of the American Regulatory State, 1992, Controlling Environmental Policy: The Limits of Public Law in Germany and the United States, 1995, Corruption and Government: Causes, Consequences and Reform, 1999 (Levine Prize 2000); contbr. articles to profl. jours.; bd. editors: Jour. Law, Econs. and Orgn., 1984—, Internat. Rev. Law and Econs., 1986—, Jour. Policy Analysis and Mgmt., 1989—, Polit. Sci. Quar., 1988—. Guggenheim fellow 1991-92, Fulbright fellow, Free U. Berlin, 1991-92; fellow Ctr. for Advanced Study in the Behavioral Scis., Stanford, Calif., 2002, Collegium Budapest, 2002. Mem. Am. Law and Econs. Assn. (bd. dirs. 1993-96, 2002-), Am. Econ. Assn. (mem. exec. com. 1990-93), Am. Polit. Sci. Assn., Assn. Am. Law Schs., Assn. Pub. Policy and Mgmt. (policy coun. 1984-88, treas. 1998-2000). Democrat. Office: Yale U Law Sch PO Box 208215 New Haven CT 06520-8215

ROSELLI, RICHARD JOSEPH, lawyer; b. Chgo., Mar. 2, 1954; s. H. Joseph and Dolores Roselli; m. Lisa McNelis; children: Nicholas Joseph, Christiana Elise, Alexandra Grace, Michaela Luciana, Anthony Santino. BA, Tulane U., 1976, JD, 1980. Bar: Fla. 1981, U.S. Dist. Ct. (so. dist.) Fla. 1981, U.S. Ct. Appeals (5th and 11th cirs.); bd. cert. civil trial lawyer. Ptnr. Krupnick, Campbell, Malone, Roselli et al, Ft. Lauderdale, 1981—2001, Roselli & Roselli Trial Lawyers, 2001—. Mem. bd. advisors physician asst. program Nova Southeastern U., adj. asst. prof. Trustee Fla. Dem. Party, 1992-95. Mem. ATLA (pres.' coun. 1996-97), Am. Bd. Trial Advocates, Am. Soc. Law and Medicine, So. Trial Lawyers Assn. (founder), Acad. Fla. Trial Lawyers (bd. dirs. 1987—, exec. com. 1990-97, sec. 1993, treas. 1994, pres. elect. 1995, pres. 1996, chmn. Fla. lawyers action group-PAC 1996, Golden Eagle award, 1989, 1996, 98, Silver Eagle award, 1990, Crystal Eagle award 1995), Broward County Trial Lawyers (bd. dirs.), Trial

Lawyers for Pub. Justice, Lawyer Pilots Bar Assn., St. Jude Catholic Ch. Personal injury (including property damage), Product liability. Office: Ste 600 3471 N Federal Hwy Fort Lauderdale FL 33306

ROSEMAN, ARNOLD DAVID, lawyer; b. N.Y.C., Apr. 10, 1917; s. Samuel Victor and Pauline (Kaplan) R.; m. Rose L. Mirkin, June 20, 1948 (dec. 1991); children: Paula Saler, Robert L. BS, CCNY, 1938; JD, Harvard U., 1941. Bar: N.Y. 1941, J.S. Dist. Ct. (so. and ea. dists.) N.Y. 1946, U.S. Ct. Appeals (2d cir.) 1948, U.S. Supreme Ct. 1960. Sole practice, N.Y.C. and Westchester, 1941—. N.Y. State commr. of investigation, 1974-75; acting city judge New Rochelle (N.Y.), 1972; spl. dist. atty. Westchester County, N.Y., 1977-78; lectr. N.Y. State Bar, 1979-82. Author: (with others) Basic Criminal Practice, 1979-8[9]6. Whip and minority leader Westchester Bd. Suprs., 1957-67; chmn. Cmty. Chest, 1956-57. Served to capt. USAAF, 1941-46, PTO. Mem. ABA, N.Y. State Bar Assn., Westchester County Bar Assn., New Rochelle Bar Assn., Lions (pres. 1974), VFW, Am. Legion, Elks. Criminal, General practice. Address: 416 Grand Blvd Scarsdale NY 10583-6552 Fax: 914-725-2479.

ROSEMAN, CHARLES SANFORD, lawyer; b. Jersey City, Feb. 26, 1945; s. Leon and Edith (Neidorf) R.; children: Rochelle Lynn, Loren Scott. BA, Calif. State U., 1968; JD, U. San Diego, 1971. Bar: Calif. 1972, U.S. Dist. Ct. (so. dist.) Calif. 1972, U.S. Dist. Ct. (cen. dist.) Calif. 1975, U.S. Supreme Ct. 1980, U.S. Claim Ct. 1990. Assoc. Greer, Popko, Nickoloff & Miller, San Diego, 1972-73; ptnr. Roseman & Roseman, San Diego, 1973-78, Roseman & Small, San Diego, 1978-82, Frank, Roseman, Freedus & Mann, San Diego, 1982-86, Roseman and Mann, 1986-92; pvt. practice San Diego, 1992—; judge pro tem San Diego County Superior Ct., 1975—; also arbitrator, mediator, 1977—. Bd. dirs. Glenn Aire Cmty. Devel. Assn., San Diego, 1972-73, Big Bros. San Diego County, 1973-81,; bd. dirs. San Diego County Anti-Defamation League, 1985—; chmn. exec. com. 1984-85, assoc. nat. commr., 1995—; bd. dirs. San Diego County Legal Aid Soc., 1988-89, Tifereth Israel Synagogue, pres. 1982-84, Homeys Youth Found., 2002--. Mem. ABA, ATLA, Consumer Attys. of Calif. (Recognition of Experience award 1985), Calif. Bar Assn., Am. Arbitration Assn. (arbitrator, panel 1985—), San Diego Bar Assn., Consumer Attys. of San Diego (bd. dirs. 1982-84), U. San Diego Sch. Law Alumni Assn. (bd. dirs. 1972-73), B'nai B'rith (pres. 1978). Democrat. State civil litigation, Insurance, Personal injury (including property damage). Office: Law Offices Charles S Roseman & Assocs 170 Laurel St San Diego CA 92101-1419 E-mail: csr1@flash.net.

ROSEN, CHARLES, II, lawyer; b. New Orleans, Jan. 29, 1925; s. Louis Leucht and Nita (Silverstein) R.; m. Mary Alice Waldauer (div. 1976); children: Charles III, Virginia, Jane, James Louis; m. Sandra Reed (div. 1995); m. Emily Hart, 1995. BA, Tulane U., 1948, LLB, 1951. Bar: La. 1951. Assoc. Rosen, Kammer, Wolff, Hopkins & Burke, New Orleans, 1951-55, Jones, Walker, Waechter, Poitevent, Carrere & Denegre, New Orleans, 1955-58, ptnr., 1958-90; spl. counsel Locke, Purnell, Rain, Harrell (now Locke Liddell & Sapp), New Orleans, 1990-97; of counsel Sullivan Stolier & Resor, New Orleans, 1997—. Past chmn. and mem. exec. com. Golf & Sports Attractions, Inc., ret. mem. fore kids Found. Past trustee Touro Synagogue; hon. trustee Touro Infirmary; chmn. lawyers div. Jewish Fedn. Greater New Orleans, 1969; past chmn. lawyers div. United Fund. 1st lt. U.S. Army, 1944-46, PTO. Mem. ABA, La. Bar Assn., New Orleans Bar Assn., Am. Coll. Real Estate Attys., Anglo Am. Real Property Inst., So. Golf Assn. (past bd. dirs.), New Orleans Golf Assn. (past pres., past bd. dirs.), Tulane Green Wave Club (past bd. dirs.), Lakewood Country Club (past pres., bd. dirs.). Republican. Avocation: golf. Home: 410 Northline Metairie LA 70005-4452 Office: Sullivan Stolier & Resor 909 Poydras St Ste 2600 New Orleans LA 70112-4022 E-mail: attorney@ssrlawfirm.com.

ROSEN, CHARLES ARTHUR, lawyer; b. N.Y.C., May 28, 1940; s. David H. and Mildred R.; m. Suzanne M. Diamond, Aug. 17, 1963; children— Laurence, Caroline. B.S., Cornell U., 1962; J.D., NYU, 1965. Bar: N.Y. 1966, N.J. 1967. Labor relations specialist N.J. Mfrs. Assn., Newark, 1965-71; counsel N.J. Dept. Labor and Industry, Trenton, 1971-73; ptnr., shareholder Irwin, Post & Rosen, Roseland, N.J., 1973—8, ptnr. Law Office of Charles A. Rosen, NJ, 1987- , also N.Y.C. Mem. cons. com. Inst. Mgmt. and Labor Relations, Rutgers U., 1965-71; mem. State Bd. Cert. Shorthand Reporters, 1973-73; mem. N.J. Vocat. Edn. Adv. Council, 1970-80, chmn., 1977-79. Mem. ABA, N.J. State Bar Assn., N.Y. State Bar Assn., Atty. Roseland NJ Planning Bd., 1987-, Essex County Bar Assn. Republican. Jewish. Clubs: Roseland Rep. (pres.), Masons. Contbr. articles to legal publs. Commercial, contracts (including sales of goods; commercial financing), Corporate, general, Land use and zoning (including planning). Office: 5 Becker Farm Rd Roseland NJ 07068-1741

ROSEN, GERALD ELLIS, federal judge; b. Chandler, Ariz., Oct. 26, 1951; s. Stanley Rosen and Marjorie (Sherman) Cahn; m. Laurie DeMond; 1 child, Jacob DeMond. BA, Kalamazoo Coll., 1973; JD, George Washington U., 1979. Researchist Swedish Inst., Stockholm, 1973; legis. asst. U.S. Senator Robert P. Griffin, Washington, 1974-79; law clk. Seyfarth, Shaw, Fairweather & Gerardson, Wash., 1979; from assoc. to sr. ptnr. Miller, Canfield, Paddock and Stone, Detroit, 1979-90; judge U.S. Dist Ct. (ea. dist.) Mich., Detroit, 1990—. Mem. Jud. Evaluation Com. (co-chmn. 1983-88), Detroit; adj. prof. law Wayne State U., 1992—, U. Detroit Law Sch., 1994—; mem. U.S. Jud. Conf. Com. on Criminal Law; lectr. CLE confs., others. Co-author: Federal Civil Trials and Evidence, 1999, Michigan Civil Trials and Evidence, 2001; contbr. articles to profl. jours. Rep. candidate for U.S. Congress, Mich., 1982; chmn. 17th Congl. Dist. Rep. Com., 1983-85; mem. Mich. Criminal Justice Commn., 1985-87; mem. Birmingham Athletic Club; bd. visitors George Washington U. Law Sch., 2000—; bd. dirs. Focus Hope, 2000—. Fellow Kalamazoo Coll. (sr. 1972); recipient Career Achievement award Rolex/Intercollegiate Tennis Assn. Mem. Fed. Judges Assn. (bd. dirs.). Jewish. Office: US Courthouse 231 W Lafayette Blvd Rm 802 Detroit MI 48226-2707

ROSEN, JON HOWARD, lawyer; b. Bklyn., May 20, 1943; s. Eli and Vera Horowitz Rosen; children: Jason Marc, Hope Terry. BA, Hobart Coll., 1965; JD, St. John's U., 1968; postgrad. in bus., CCNY, 1969—71. Bar: N.Y. 1969, Calif. 1975, Wash. 1977. Atty. FAA, N.Y.C., 1968-71; regional atty., contract adminstr. Air Line Pilots Assn., N.Y.C., Chgo., L.A., San Francisco, 1971-77; pvt. practice Seattle, 1977-80; ptnr. Frank and Rosen, Seattle, 1981-98, Frank Rosen Freed Roberts LLP, Seattle, 1999—2002, The Rosen Law Firm, 2002—. Instr. labor studies Shoreline C.C., 1978-90. Trustee Temple DeHirsch Sinai, 1991-98, v.p., 1998-2000, pres.-elect 2000-01, pres., 2001-03; chair Ward Springs Pk. Steering Com.; trustee French-Am. Sch. of Puget Sound, 2003—; mem. African-Am./Jewish Coalition for Justice, Interfaith Alliance. Fellow: Coll. Labor and Employment Lawyers; mem.: ABA (union co-chmn. com. on employee rights and responsibilities 1992—96, union co-chmn. regional programs subcom. 1998—2000, union co-chmn. nat. programs. subcom. 2000—02, union co-chmn. ADR in labor and employment law com. 2002—, co-regional EEOC liaison), Wash. State Trial Lawyers Assn. (past chair employment law com.), Nat. Employment Lawyers Assn. (state steering com. 1990—95, founding state chair), King County Bar Assn. (past chmn. aviation and space law sect., past chmn. Pacific Coast Labor and Employment Law Conf., past chmn. labor law sect.). Administrative and regulatory, Civil rights, Labor (including EEOC, Fair Labor Standards Act, labor-management relations, NLRB, OSHA). Office: Rosen Law Firm 705 2nd Ave Ste 1200 Seattle WA 98104-1729 E-mail: jhr@jonrosenlaw.com.

ROSEN, LEON, lawyer; b. N.Y.C., May 21, 1924; s. Irving and Kate (Woronoff) R. BA, Coll. of William and Mary, 1949; JD, NYU, 1953. Bar: N.Y. 1954, U.S. Supreme Ct. 1960, U.S. Ct. Appeals (2d, 3d and 9th cirs.). Investigator, atty. U.S. Immigration and Naturalization Svc., Dept. Justice, N.Y.C., 1951-55; pvt. practice N.Y.C., 1955-87; spl. counsel Clifton, Budd & DeMaria, N.Y.C., 1987—. With USAAC, 1943-46. Decorated Air medal, 2 oak leaf clusters; recipient Presdl. Citation award. Mem. Am. Immigration Lawyers Assn. (past. nat. pres.). Democrat. Jewish. Avocation: golf. Home: 10701 Dover Creek Ave Las Vegas NV 89134 Office: Amesbury & Schutt 703 S 8th St Las Vegas NV 89101

ROSEN, MARTIN JACK, lawyer; b. L.A., Sept. 9, 1931; s. Irving and Sylvia (Savad) R.; m. Joan D. Meyersieck, Oct. 22, 1954; children: Dirk Rosen, Marika. BA, UCLA, 1953; JD, U. Calif., Berkeley, 1956. Pvt. practice, Merced, Calif., 1960-62, San Francisco, 1962-82; mem. Silver, Rosen, Fischer & Stecher, P.C., San Francisco, 1964-79. Lectr. Haas Sch. Bus., U. Calif., Berkeley, 1998. Author: Oral Histor, 2000. Past pres. Trust for Pub. Land, 1979-97. With USAF, 1958-60. Fellow internat. legal studies U. Calif. Law Sch./Inst. Social Studies, The Hague, 1956-57; conservation fellow Yale Sch. Forestry, 1999. Administrative and regulatory, Environmental, Property, real (including real estate development, water). Fax: 415-4594816. E-mail: kentwilds1@cs.com.

ROSEN, MARVIN SHELBY, lawyer; b. Detroit, Aug. 8, 1947; s. Joseph P. and Rachel K. (Kaplan) R.; m. Sandra Mira Levy, Nov. 22, 1970; children: Joseph H., Bradley J. BA, Columbia U., 1970, JD, MBA, 1973; B in Hebrew Lit., Jewish Theol. Sem., N.Y.C., 1970. Bar: Mich. 1974, Fla. 1984. Assoc. Honigman Miller Schwartz and Cohn, Detroit, 1974-78, ptnr., 1978-84, mng. ptnr., 1984-97; shareholder Ruden, McClosky, Smith, Schuster & Russell, P.A., West Palm Beach, 1997—. Contbr. articles to profl. jours. Mem. bd. overseers List Coll., N.Y.C.; v.p. Pres. Country Club, 1995-99, Jewish Fedn. Palm Beach County, 1992-99; pres. Jewish Cmty. Day Sch., 1987-88; founding chmn. Commn. for Jewish Edn., 1990-93; pres. Temple Emanu-El, Palm Beach, 2000—. Named one of Best Lawyers in Am., 1989—. Mem. Mich. State Bar (chmn. com. on mortgages, land contracts and related security devices real property sect. 1982-84), Detroit Bar Assn. (chmn. real property sect. 1982-83). Finance, Property, real (including real estate development, water). Office: Ruden McClosky Smith Schuster & Russell PA 222 Lakeview Ave Ste 800 West Palm Beach FL 33401-6148 Fax: 561-832-3036. E-mail: msr@ruden.com.

ROSEN, MICHAEL JAMES, lawyer; b. Miami, Fla., Oct. 25, 1949; s. E. David and Muriel G. (Gerstein) R.; children: Jason, Lauren. BA, U. South Fla., 1971; JD, U. Miami, 1974. Bar: Fla. 1974, U.S. Dist. Ct. (so. dist.) Fla. 1974, U.S. Ct. Appeals (5th cir.) 1975, U.S. Ct. Appeals (6th cir.) 1979, U.S. Dist. Ct. (mid. dist.) Fla. 1980, U.S. Ct. Appeals (11th cir.) 1981, U.S. Ct. Appeals (2d cir.) 1983, U.S. Tax Ct., U.S. Supreme Ct. 1979. Asst. fed. pub. defender Fed. Pub. Defender, Miami, 1974-76; ptnr. Rosen & Rosen PA, Miami, 1976-87; pvt. practice Miami, 1987—. Adj. prof. RICO fed. criminal law U. Miami Sch. Law; counselor Peter T. Fay Am. Inn. Ct., St. Thomas Sch. Law. Mem. ABA, FBA (chmn. criminal discovery com. 1983), ACLU, Nat. Assn. Criminal Def. Lawyers. Federal civil litigation, Criminal. Office: Michael J Rosen PA 2400 S Dixie Hwy Ste 105 Miami FL 33133-3141 E-mail: mjrpalaw@aol.com.

ROSEN, MURRAY HILARY, lawyer; b. London, Aug. 26, 1953; s. Joseph and Mercia (Herman) R.; m. Lesley Samuels, Dec. 9, 1975; 4 children. MA with honors, Cambridge U., 1975; postgrad., Brussels Free U., 1976. Called to Bar, Eng. 1976; apptd. Queen's Counsel 1993. Pvt. practice, London, 1976—; recorder, 2000—. Chmn. Bar Sports Law Group, 1997-2001. Fellow Chartered Inst. Arbitrators; Sports Dispute Resolution Panel (panel chair). Avocations: music, sports, books, real tennis. Office: 11 Stone Bldgs Lincolns Inn London WC2A 3TG England E-mail: rosen@11stonebuildings.com.

ROSEN, PAUL MAYNARD, lawyer; b. Queens, N.Y., Sept. 29, 1943; s. Lewis L. and Leanore (Frant) R.; m. Clare E. Rosenberg, June 17, 1967; children: Rebecca K., Chad D. BS, Rensselaer Poly. Inst., 1965; JD, Cornell U., 1968. Bar: N.Y. 1969, U.S. Supreme Ct. 1980, U.S. Dist. Ct. (so. and ea. dist.) N.Y. 1981. Asst. dist. atty. Westchester County, White Plains, N.Y., 1970-72; law sec. Westchester County Ct. Judge, White Plains, N.Y., 1972-74; ptnr. Natale & Rosen, Yonkers, N.Y., 1974-80; pvt. practice law Briarcliff, N.Y., 1980—. Impartial hearing officer State Edn. Dept., 1986—. Town chmn. Ossining Rep. Party, 1982-94; v.p. congregation Sons of Israel, 1982-84. With U.S. Army, 1968-70. Paul Harris fellow Rotary, 1985. Mem. Ossining Bar Assn., Rotary (pres. 1984), Masons. Criminal, Education and schools, Property, real (including real estate development, water). Home and Office: 130 Marlborough Rd Briarcliff Manor NY 10510-2013

ROSEN, RICHARD DAVID, lawyer; b. Pitts., June 24, 1940; s. Benjamin H. and Bertha B. (Broff) R.; m. Ellaine H. Heller, June 23, 1963; children: Deborah H. Fidel, Jaime M. Cohen. BA, Yale U., 1962; JD, Harvard U., 1965. Bar: Pa. 1966, Fla. 1979. Mgr. Bachrach, Sanderbeck & Co., Pitts., 1965-70; mng. ptnr. Grant Thornton, Pitts., 1970-76; chmn. tax dept. Baskin & Sears, Pitts., 1977-78; pres. Gas Transmission, Inc., Pitts., 1979—2000; dir., shareholder Cohen & Grigsby, Pitts., 1989—. Dir. UPMC Presbyn./UPMC Shadyside Hosps., 2003—. Contbr. articles to profl. jours. Trustee Jewish Healthcare Found., 1995—, chmn. investment com., 2001—. Fellow: Am. Coll. Trust and Estate Counsel; mem.: ABA, Pa. Bar Assn. (mem. estate planning com. 1996—, com.chmn. 1998—2000), Westmoreland Country Club, United Jewish Fedn. Greater Pitts. (chmn. profl. adv. com. 1997—). Avocations: golf, tennis. Home: 1198 Beechwood Ct Pittsburgh PA 15206-4522 Office: Cohen & Grigsby PC 11 Stanwix St 15 Fl Pittsburgh PA 15222-1312 E-mail: rrosen@cohenlaw.com.

ROSEN, RICHARD LEWIS, lawyer, real estate developer; b. N.Y.C., Mar. 6, 1943; s. Morris and Lorraine (Levy) R.; m. Doris Ellen Bloom, Aug. 28, 1983. BA, Cornell U., 1965; JD, N.Y. Law Sch., 1968; cert., NYU Real Estate Inst., 1980. Bar: N.Y. 1968, U.S. Dist. Ct. (so. and ea. dists.) N.Y. 1972; lic. real estate broker. Pvt. practice, N.Y.C., 1971-73; ptnr. Rosen, Wise, Felzen & Salomon, N.Y.C., 1973-79, Rosen & Felzen, N.Y.C., 1979-84, Rosen, Rudd, Kera, Graubard & Hollender, N.Y.C., 1985-88, Bell, Kalnick, Klee and Green, N.Y.C., 1989-90; shareholder Rosen, Einbinder & Dunn, P.C., N.Y.C., 1990—. Contbg. author: Franchising 101, The Complete Guide to Evaluating, Buying and Growing Your Franchise Business; author: Renewal of Your Franchise: Some Solutions, Franchise Times. Named Ea. States Lightweight Weightlifting Champion, 1968; N.Y. State Regents scholar. Mem. ABA (mem. Forum Com. on Franchising), Am. Assn. Franchises and Dealers (former chmn. legal steering com., chmn. fair franchising stds. com., chmn. alternate dispute resolution com., bd. dirs.), Franchise Lawyers Assn., Am. Franchise Assn., N.Y. State Bar Assn. (founding mem. franchise law com., chmn. mission statement com. of franchise law com.), Nat. Franchise Mediation Program (mem. steering com.), Assn. Bar City N.Y. (panel mem. com. on franchising, panel mem. com. on corp. law), Red Key Hon. Soc., Cornell U., Sphinx Head Hon. Soc., Cornell U., Spiked Shoe Soc., Cornell U., Ea. Intercollegiate Athletic Assn. (named Lightweight Football All Ea. Selection 1963, 64). Avocations: guitar, reading, coaching youth soccer and track, masters track competition. Corporate, general, Franchising, Property, real (including real estate development, water). Home: 1 Old Jericho Tpke Jericho NY 11753-1205 Office: Rosen Einbinder & Dunn PC 641 Lexington Ave New York NY 10022-4503 E-mail: RLR@redlawfirm.com.

ROSEN, RICHARD S. lawyer; b. Charleston, S.C., Aug. 15, 1949; BA, Tulane U., 1971; JD, U. S.C., 1975. Bar: S.C. 1975, U.S. Dist. Ct. S.C. 1975, U.S. Ct. Appeals (4th cir.) 1993, U.S. Supreme Ct. 1993. Mem.: ABA, Am. Bd. Trial Advs., Assn. Trial Lawyers Am., S.C. Trial Lawyers Assn., S.C. Bar (bd. govs. 1991—94, Ho. of Dels. 1984, chmn. 1996, nominating com. 1986—89, continuing legal edn. com. 1995, law practice mgmt. com. 1995, sec. 1999, treas. 2000, pres.-elect 2001, pres. 2002), Charleston County Bar Assn. (exec. com. 1982—83), Soc. Wig and Robe, Charleston Lawyer's Club (pres. 1982). Office: Rosen Rosen & Hagood LLC PO Box 893 134 Meeting St Ste 200 Charleston SC 29402*

ROSEN, SANFORD JAY, lawyer; b. N.Y.C., Dec. 19, 1937; s. Alexander Charles and Viola S. (Grad) R.; m. Catherine Picard, June 22, 1958; children: Caren E. Andrews, R. Durelle Schacter, Ian D., Melissa S. AB, Cornell U., 1959; LLB, Yale U., 1962. Bar: Conn. 1962, Calif. 1974, D.C. 1974, U.S. Supreme Ct. 1966. Law clk. to Hon. Simon E. Sobeloff U.S. Ct. Appeals, Balt., 1962-63; prof. sch. law U. Md., Balt., 1963-71; assoc. dir. Coun. on Legal Edn. Opportunity, Atlanta, 1969-70; vis. prof. law U. Tex., Austin, 1970-71; asst. legal dir. Nat. ACLU, N.Y.C., 1971-73; legal dir. Mex.-Am. Legal Def. Fund, San Francisco, 1973-75; ptnr. Rosen, Remcho & Henderson, San Francisco, 1976-80, Rosen & Remcho, San Francisco, 1980-82; prin. Law Offices of Sanford Jay Rosen, San Francisco, 1982-86; sr. ptnr. Rosen & Phillips, San Francisco, 1986-89; prin. Rosen & Assocs., San Francisco, 1990; sr. ptnr. Rosen, Bien & Asaro, San Francisco, 1991—. Mem. Balt. Cmty. Rels. Commn., 1966-69; mem. com. Patuxent Instn., Md., 1967-69; ad hoc adminstrv. law judge Calif. Agrl. Labor Rels. Bd., San Francisco, 1975-80; interim monitor U.S. Dist. Ct. for no. dist. Calif., San Francisco, 1989, early neutral evaluator, 1987—, mediator, 1993—; judge pro tem San Francisco Superior Ct., 1991—; perm. atty. del. Jud. Conf. U.S. Ct. Appeal for 4th Cir.; atty. del. Jud. Conf. U.S. Ct. Appeals 9th cir., 1996-98. Contbr. articles to profl. jours. Mem. Com. on Adminstrn. of Criminal Justice, Balt., 1968; mem. adv. com. HEW, Washington, 1974-75. Mem. ABA, Assn. Trial Lawyers Am. (chair civil rights sect. 1993-94), D.C. Bar Assn., Calif. Bar Assn., Bar Assn. San Francisco. Avocations: reading, travel, movies. Civil rights, State civil litigation, Corporate, general. Office: Rosen Bien & Asaro 155 Montgomery St Fl 8 San Francisco CA 94104-4113 E-mail: srosen@rbalaw.com.

ROSEN, WILLIAM WARREN, lawyer; b. New Orleans, July 22, 1936; s. Warren Leucht and Erma (Stich) R.; m. Eddy Kahn, Nov. 26, 1965; children: Elizabeth K., Victoria A. BA, Tulane U., 1958, JD, 1964. Bar: La. 1964, U.S. Dist. Ct. (ea. dist.) La. 1965, U.S. Ct. Appeals (5th cir.) 1965, U.S. Supreme Ct. 1984, U.S. Dist. Ct. (mid. dist.) La. 1985, Colo. 1989. Assoc. Dodge & Friend, New Orleans, 1965-68, Law Office of J.R. Martzell, New Orleans, 1968-70; pvt. practice New Orleans, 1970-79, 89-90; ptnr. Lucas & Rosen (and predecessor firms), New Orleans, 1979-87, Herman, Herman, Katz & Cotlar, New Orleans, 1987-88, Rosen and Samuel, New Orleans, 1990-95; of counsel Rittenberg & Samuel, New Orleans, 1996-99; founder & dir. Litigation Consultation Svcs., New Orleans, 1996—; ptnr. Rosen & Lundeen, L.L.P., New Orleans, 1999—2002; pvt. practice New Orleans, 2002—. Adj. prof. trial advocacy Law Sch. Tulane U., 1988—, mem. adv. com. paralegal studies program, 1977-86, instr. bus. orgns., 1978, instr. legal interviewing, 1980-81; mem. adv. com. Paralegal Inst. U. New Orleans, 1990—, instr. legal interviewing and investigations, 1986-87; lectr. legal and paralegal fields; lectr. real and demonstrative evidence Nat. Edn. Network, 1993; lectr. new judges seminar La. Jud. Coll., 2000, 01, 02, 03. Author: (with others) Trial Techniques publ. La. Trial Lawyers Assn., 1981; columnist Briefly Speaking publ. New Orleans Bar Assn., 1993-2000. Mem. budget and planning com. Jewish Welfare Fedn., 1970-73; mem. adv. coun. on drug edn. La. Dept. Edn., 1973; mem. profl. adv. com. Jewish Endowment Found., 1982—; mem. exec. com. U.S. Olympic Com., La., 1982-84; bd. dirs. Planned Parenthood La., 1994-2001, Hillel Found. N.O. 2003-; pres. Dad's Club, Isidore Newman Sch., 1984-85, Uptown Flood Assn., 1982-85; bd. dirs. Jewish Children's Home Svc., 1973-76, Met. Crime Commn. New Orleans, 1976-82; spl. agt. Office Spl. Investigations USAF, 1958-61. Fellow, Inst. of Politics. Loyola U. Mem. ABA, ATLA (keyperson com. 1986-89, vice chmn. paralegal com. 1986-89, mem. family law adv. com. 1989-90, sec. family law sect. 1990-91, lectr. legal edn. 1979, 81, 83, 86, 88); mem. La. Bar Assn. (vice chmn. pub. rels. com. 1970-73, 88-89, past chmn. state youth drug abuse edn. program, vol. lawyers for arts 1986-96, chmn. sr. counsel com. 1995-96), Am. Arbitration Assn., Nat. Fedn. Paralegal Assn. (adv. coun. 1989-1998), Assn. Atty. Mediators (pres. La. chpt. 1995), Nat. Choice in Dying (legal adv. com. 1992-96), Nat. Edn. Network (lectr. legal edn. 1993), New Orleans Bar Assn. (CLE com. 1990-91, chmn. 1991-92, mem. alternative dispute resolution com. 1996-2000, panel moderator 1997), Inn of Ct. (master 1992—), Rotary Club New Orleans (bd. dirs. 1996-98, 2003—, chmn. legal com. 1996—). Avocation: photography. Personal injury (including property damage). Office: 210 Baronne St 18th Flr New Orleans LA 70112-4132 Fax: 504-525-4380. E-mail: lcsno@aol.com.

ROSENBAUM, JACOB I. lawyer; b. Cleve., Oct. 4, 1927; s. Lionel C. and Dora (Heldman) R.; m. Marjorie Jean Arnold, Apr. 20, 1952; children: Laura Rosenbaum, Alexander, Judith Bartell. JD, U. N.Mex., 1951. Bar: N.Mex. 1951, Ohio 1952. Pres. Ohio Savs. Assn., Cleve., 1955-60, sr. v.p., 1960-92, also dir.; ptnr. Burke, Haber & Berick, Cleve., 1955-79, Arter & Hadden, Cleve., 1979-94, of counsel, 1994—. Mem., bd. of vis. U.N. Mex. Coll. Law, 2000—. Pres. Kiwanis Found. of Cleve., 1994—; active Judson Retirement Cmty., Cleveland Heights, Ohio, 1990—, trustee, 1994, pres., 1992; trustee Cleve. Zool. Soc., 1983—, Cleve. Nat. Air Show, 1981—, pres., 1987—90, 1994—, pres. Found., 1995—2003; trustee Golden Age Ctrs. of Cleve., 1996—; pres. Temple Emanu El, University Heights, Ohio, 1965—67, 1995—; bd. visitors U. N.Mex. Law Sch. Mem.: Cleve. Execs. Assn. (pres. 1989—2003, chmn. 1990), Greater Cleve. Bar Assn., Ohio Bar Assn. (chmn. aviation law com. 1981—84), Lawyer-Pilots Bar Assn. (pres. 1981—82, editor jour. 1982—97), Kiwanis Club of Cleve. (pres. 1970—71). Democrat. Jewish. Aviation, Property, real (including real estate development, water), State and local taxation. Home: 28050 N Woodland Rd Cleveland OH 44124-4521 Office: Arter & Hadden 1100 Huntington Bldg 925 Euclid Ave Cleveland OH 44115-1475

ROSENBAUM, LOIS OMENN, lawyer; b. Newark, Apr. 10, 1950; d. Edward and Ruth (Peretz) Omenn; m. Richard B. Rosenbaum, Apr. 4, 1971; children: Steven, Laura. AB, Wellesley Coll., 1971; JD, Stanford U., 1974. Bar: Calif. 1974, Oreg. 1977, D.C. 1974, U.S. Supreme Ct. 1990, Wash. 2001. Assoc. Fried, Frank, Harris, Shriver & Kampelman, Washington, 1974-75, Orrick, Herrington, Rowley & Sutcliffe, San Francisco, 1975-77, Stoel Rives LLP (formerly Stoel, Rives, Boley, Jones & Grey), Portland, Oreg., 1977-81, ptnr., 1981—. Mem. U.S. Dist. Ct. Mediation Panel. Bd. dirs. Providence Med. Found., 1990-95, Robison Jewish Home, 1994-97, Jewish Family & Child Svc., 1997-2000, Am. Jewish Commn., 2000—; past mem. Nat. Legal Com. Am. Jewish Com. Wellesley Coll. scholar, 1971. Mem. ABA, Multnomah County Bar Assn. (arbitration panel), Wellesley Club (pres. 1987-88). Federal civil litigation, General civil litigation. Office: Stoel Rives LLP 900 SW 5th Ave Ste 2600 Portland OR 97204-1268 E-mail: lorosenbaum@stoel.com.

ROSENBERG, A. IRVING, lawyer; b. Newark, Aug. 4, 1921; s. Sam and Dora Rosenberg; m. Toby Kalb, Dec. 12, 1943; children: Jeffrey, Elliot. Stenographic ct. reporting cert., Ct. Reporting Sch., Newark, 1940; Law Degree, Rutgers U., Newark, 1948. Bar: N.J. 1948. Office staf U.S. Secret Svc. Treasury Dept., Newark and N.Y.C., 1940-42; pvt. practice law, 1948—. Pres., dir. Psychic Studies Inst., Union, N.J., 1978—; lectr. in field. Author: Autobiography of the Unconscious, 1978; law rev. staff Rutgers Law Rev. Jour., 1941; contbr. articles to profl. jours. Comdr. Jewish War Vets. Post, Union, 1971-72; dir. C. of C., Union, 1975-85; chancellor comdr. Knights of Pythias, Union, 1985-86. With USN, 1942-45. Mem. Internat. Soc. for the Study of Multiple Personality and Dissociation (also N.J. chpt.), Am. Soc. for Psychical Rsch. Avocations: tennis, boating, antique collecting, trance mediumship and hypnosis. General practice, Probate (including wills, trusts), Property, real (including real estate development, water). Office: 1227 Morris Ave Union NJ 07083-3307

ROSENBERG, ALAN STEWART, lawyer; b. N.Y.C., Mar. 29, 1930; s. Louis and Sadye (Knobler) R.; m. Ilse Rosenberg/Klein, Aug. 15, 1963; children: Gary, Robert. BA, Stanford U., 1949; LLB, Columbia U., 1952; LLM, NYU, 1960. Bar: N.Y. 1955. Assoc. Wolf Haldenstein Adler & Freeman, N.Y.C., 1955-56; ptnr., chmn. tax dept. Proskauer Rose Goetz & Mendelsohn, N.Y.C., 1957—92. Contbr. articles to profl. jours. Mem. exec. com., bd. visitors Stanford (Calif.) U. Law Sch., 1982-85, Jewish studies program, 1986—; chmn. bd. N.Y. Alliance for the Pub. Sch., 1988-91; mem. adv. com. on pub. issues Advt. Coun., 1991-94; bd. dirs., sec. Univ.-Urban Schs. Nat. Task Force Inc., 1981-96; mem. bd. visitors Columbia U. Law Sch., 1991-96; bd. dirs. Ctr. Ednl. Innovation, 2000—; bd. dirs., treas. Justice Resource Ctr., 1994-97; bd. dirs. The Abraham Fund; chmn. bd. dirs. Richalan Found. Lt. (j.g.) USN, 1952-55. Avocations: amateur opera singer, tennis. Taxation, general, State and local taxation, International taxation. Home: 115 Central Park W New York NY 10023-4153 E-mail: aandi98@aol.com.

ROSENBERG, DANIEL P. lawyer; b. London, May 8, 1962; s. Leonard Jack and Susanna (Sternfeld) R.; m. Helena Rudie, Aug. 11, 1985; children: David, Liana. BA in Law, U. Cambridge, 1984, LLM, 1986. Bar: High Ct. England and Wales. Articled clk. Slaughter & May, London, 1985-87; asst. solicitor Berwin Leighton, London, 1987-92, ptnr., 1992-2001, Taylor Wessing, London, 2001—. Co-author, gen. editor: Practical Commercial Precedents, 1991; co-author: Tolley's Financial Management Handbook, 1996, Commercial Transaction Checklists, 1997. Trustee Awards for Young Musicians, London, 1999—. Mem. ABA, Law Soc. England and Wales (company law com. 1998—), Confedn. Brit. Industry (corp. law panel 1999—), London First Ctr. (N.Am. adv. task force 1998—) Avocations: music, theatre, cycling, family. Corporate, general, Private international, Mergers and acquisitions. Office: Taylor Wessing Carmelite 50 Victoria Embk London EC4Y ODX England Office Fax: 44-207-300-7100. E-mail: d.rosenberg@taylorwessing.com.

ROSENBERG, GERALD ALAN, lawyer; b. N.Y.C., Aug. 5, 1944; s. Irwin H. and Doris (Lowinger) R.; m. Rosalind Navin, Aug. 13, 1971; children: Clifford D., Nicholas D. BA cum laude, Yale U., 1966; JD, Harvard U., 1969. Bar: N.Y. 1970, U.S. Dist. Ct. (so. dist.) N.Y. 1971, U.S. Ct. Appeals (2d cir.) 1974, U.S. Dist. Ct. (we. dist.) N.Y. 1977, U.S. Dist. Ct. (cen. dist.) Calif. 1978, U.S. Supreme Ct. 1979, U.S. Dist. Ct. (ea. dist.) N.Y. 1981, U.S. Tax Ct. 1984. Atty. Legal Aid Soc. San Mateo/VISTA, Redwood, Calif., 1969-70; asst. atty. U.S. Dept. Justice, N.Y.C., 1971-75; assoc. Rosenman & Colin, N.Y.C., 1975-77, ptnr., 1978—2002, mem. mgmt. com., 1991—94; counsel KMZ Rosenman, N.Y.C., 2002—. Arbitrator U.S. Dist. Ct. (ea. dist.) N.Y.; mem. faculty Ctr. Internat. Legal Studies, Salzburg, Austria, 1999—. Bd. dirs. Non Profit Coord. Com. Inc., N.Y.C., 1983—, N.Y. Lawyers for the Pub. Interest Inc., 1988—; bd. dirs. The Parks Coun., 1988—, pres., 1991-95; trustee Central Park Conservancy, 1995—. Mem. Am. Law Inst. Federal civil litigation, State civil litigation, Property, real (including real estate development, water). Office: KMZ Rosenman 575 Madison Ave Fl 22 New York NY 10022-2585 E-mail: gerald.rosenberg@kmzr.com.

ROSENBERG, HOWELL K. lawyer; b. Phila., June 30, 1950; s. Martin and Thelma Rosenberg; m. Sondra Kramer, Dec. 25, 1971; children: Sydney, Carrie, Jake. BA in Polit. Sci., Pa. State U., 1971; JD cum laude, Villanova U., 1974. Bar: Pa. 1974, U.S. Dist. Ct. (ea. dist.) Pa. 1976, U.S. Ct. Appeals (4th cir.) 1993, U.S. Ct. Appeals (3d cir.) 1994, U.S. Surpeme Ct. 1997. Asst. dist. atty. Phila. Dist. Attys. Office, 1974—80, asst. dist. atty. chief spl. investigations, 1980—82; assoc. Shein & Brookman, 1982—84; founding ptnr. Brookman, Rosenberg, Brown & Sandler, 1984—. Clin. prof. law Widener Law Sch., Del., 1985—91. Assoc. editor: Villanova U. Law Rev., 1973—74. Bd. dirs. Libr. Co. of Phila. Mem.: ATLA, Phila. Trial Lawyers Assn. (bd. dirs. 2001—), Order of Coif. General civil litigation, Personal injury (including property damage), Product liability. Office: Brookman Rosenberg Brown & Sandler 305 15th St 17th Fl Philadelphia PA 19102 Fax: 215-569-2222.

ROSENBERG, JEROME ROY, lawyer, accountant; b. N.Y.C., Oct. 5, 1926; s. Louis and May (Schack) R.; m. Julia Daniels, Apr. 21, 1968; children: Louise I., Daniel M. BS, NYU, 1949, JD, 1953, LLM in Taxation, 1972; postgrad., Oxford U., 1949. Bar: N.Y. 1956, U.S. Dist. Ct. (so. dist.) N.Y. 1985, U.S. Dist. Ct. (ea. dist.) N.Y. 1985, U.S. Claims Ct. 1977, U.S. Tax Ct. 1965, U.S. Supreme Ct. 1968. Acct. Apfel & Englander, CPAs, N.Y.C., 1950-52; with Abraham J. Briloff, CPA, N.Y.C., 1952-54, Samuel Aronowitz & Co., CPAs, N.Y.C., 1955-57, David Berdon & Co., CPAs, N.Y.C., 1957-63; sole practice N.Y.C., 1964—; spl. tax counsel Jackson & Nash, N.Y.C., 1964-70, Seward & Kissel, N.Y.C., 1968—. Lectr. NYU, 1972; co-founder N.Y. Tax Study Group, Inc. Author: Managing Your Own Money, 1979; asst. tech. editor Jour. Taxation, 1964; mem. editl. bd. Practical Acct., 1968-85; sr. tech. editor Income Tax Workbook, 1970-75. Served with USAF, 1943-45. Mem. ABA, AICPA, Assn. Bar City N.Y. (sr. lawyers com. 2001—, chair pub. affairs luncheon program 2002—), N.Y. Soc. CPAs (mem. exec. tax com. 1983-92, Disting. Svc. award 1993). Probate (including wills, trusts), Personal income taxation, State and local taxation. Home: 50 Park Ave New York NY 10016-3075

ROSENBERG, MARK LOUIS, lawyer; b. Lexington, Ky., Sept. 21, 1947; s. Edward George and Shirley Lee (Berkin) R.; m. Betty Adler, May 16, 1982; stepchildren: Aaron, Sarah Claxton; children: Eli, Daniel. BA, U. Mich., 1969; JD, harvard U., 1973; LLM in Taxation, Georgetown U., 1985. Bar: D.C. 1973, Md. 1991, U.S. Dist. Ct. D.C. 1973, U.S. Ct. Appeals (D.C. cir.) 1973. Asst. to v.p. George Washington U., 1973-75; counsel U.S. Ho. of Reps., Washington, 1975-77; sr. atty. FTC, Washington, 1977-85; ptnr. Gordon, Feinblatt et al, Washington, 1989-91; prin. Law Offices of Mark L. Rosenberg, 1991—; of counsel The Jacobovitz Law Firm, 1994-97. Mem. Fed. Bar Assn. (dep. sect. coord., Disting. Svc. award 1982, 83, 87). Democrat. Jewish. Property, real (including real estate development, water), Commercial, contracts (including sales of goods; commercial financing), Taxation, general. Home: 6101 Shady Oak Ln Bethesda MD 20817-6027 Office: Law Offices of Mark L Rosenberg 6917 Arlington Rd Ste 301 Bethesda MD 20814-5211

ROSENBERG, MICHAEL, lawyer; b. N.Y.C., Oct. 13, 1937; s. Walter and Eva (Bernstein) Rosenberg; m. Jacqueline Raymonde Combe, Apr. 29, 1966; children: Andrew James, Suzanne Jennifer. AB in Econs. with honors, Ind. U., 1959; LLB, Columbia U., 1962. Bar: NY 1963, US Ct Appeals (2d cir) 1975, US Dist Ct (ea dist so div) Mich 1989. From. dep. asst. atty. gen. to asst. atty. gen. N.Y. State Dept. Law, N.Y.C., 1963-66; assoc. Hellerstein, Rosier & Rembar, N.Y.C., 1966-73; assoc. gen. counsel Gen. Instrument Corp., N.Y.C., 1973-78; from assoc. gen. counsel to dep. gen. counsel U.S. Filter Corp., N.Y.C., 1978-82; v.p., gen. counsel, sec. Alfa-Laval Inc., Ft. Lee, N.J., 1982-88; counsel Becker Ross Stone De Stefano & Klein, N.Y.C., 1988-89; ptnr. Rosenberg & Rich, White Plains, N.Y., 1989-95, Quinn, Marantis & Rosenberg, LLP, White Plains, N.Y., 1995-97, Marantis, Rosenberg & van Nes, LLP, White Plains, 1997-2001; atty. Law Offices of Michael Rosenberg, White Plains, 2001—. Mem Zoning Bd Appeals Town of North Castle, NY, 1995—. Mem.: ABA, Westchester County Bar Assn., NY State Bar Assn. Commercial, contracts (including sales of goods; commercial financing), Property, real (including real estate development, water), Estate planning. Office: Law Offices of Michael Rosenberg 120 Bloomingdale Rd White Plains NY 10605

ROSENBERG, PAUL I. lawyer; b. Newark, N.J., Feb. 26, 1937; BS in Econs., U. Pa. Wharton Sch., 1959; MBA, NYU, 1964, JD, 1970, LLM, 1975. Bar: N.J. 1970, U.S. Dist. Ct. N.J. 1970, N.Y. 1982, U.S. Dist. Ct. (3rd dist.) N.Y. 1982, U.S. Tax Ct. 1983, U.S. Supreme Ct. Ptnr. Fox and Fox LLP, Livingston, 1974—. Mem. Essex Co. Probate Early Settlement panel. Fellow Am. Coll. Trust and Estate Counsel (mem. nat. employee benefits in estate-planning, estate and gift tax com.); mem. ABA (vice chmn. real property probate sect. com. on estate and gift taxes), Essex County Bar Assn., N.J. State Bar Assn. Probate (including wills, trusts), Corporate taxation, Estate taxation. Home: One Belgrade Terr West Orange NJ 07052 Office: Fox and Fox LLP 70 S Orange Ave Livingston NJ 07039-4994

ROSENBERG, RUTH HELEN BORSUK, lawyer; b. Plainfield, N.J., Feb. 23, 1935; d. Irwin and Pauline (Rudich) Borsuk; children— Joshua Cohen, Sarah, Rebecca, Daniel, Miriam, Tziporah, Isaac AB, Douglass Coll., 1956; JD, U. Pa., 1963. Bar: Pa. 1964, N.Y. 1967, D.C. 1986, Md. 1987, Va. 1994, Mass. 1995, U.S. Ct. Appeals (3d cir.) 1969, U.S. Supreme Ct. 1969, U.S. Ct. Appeals (4th cir.) 1994. Law clk. Ct. Common Pleas, Phila., 1963-64; assoc. Blank, Rudenko, Klaus & Rome, Phila., 1964-67; atty. Office Corp. Counsel, City of Rochester, 1967-68; assoc. Nixon, Hargrave, Devans & Doyle, Washington, 1968-74, ptnr., 1975-99, Nixon Peabody LLP, Washington, 1999—. Vice chairperson character and fitness com. Appellate divsn. 4th dept. 7th Jud. Dist. N.Y. Supreme Ct., 1976-80, mem. grievance com., 1981-84. Bd. dirs. Soc. Prevention Cruelty to Children, 1976-77, N.Y. Civil Liberties Union, 1972-85, v.p. 1976-85; bd. dirs. Jewish Home and Infirmary, 1978-83, pres., 1980-83; v.p. Jewish Fedn. Rochester, 1983, Yachad, Inc., Jewish Cmty. Housing Devel. Corp., 1990-94; bd. dirs. Jewish Cmty. Coun., Greater Washington, 1989-93, Leadership Washington, 1990-91, Libr. Theatre, 1994-97, Op. Understanding, D.C., 1994-95. Mem. ABA, D.C. Bar Assn., Md. Bar Assn., Va. Bar Assn., Phi Beta Kappa. Land use and zoning (including planning), Property, real (including real estate development, water). Office: Nixon Peabody LLP 401 9th St NW Ste 900 Washington DC 20004-2128 E-mail: rrosenberg@nixonpeabody.com.

ROSENBERG, SHELI ZYSMAN, lawyer, financial management executive; b. N.Y.C., Feb. 2, 1942; d. Stephen B. and Charlotte (Laufer) Zysman; m. Burton X. Rosenberg, Aug. 30, 1964; children: Leonard, Marcy. BA, Tufts U., 1963; JD, Northwestern U., 1966. Bar: Ill. 1966. Ptnr. Schiff, Hardin & Waite, Chgo., 1973-80; exec. v.p., gen. counsel Equity Fin. Mgmt., Chgo., 1980-90, Equity Group Investments, Inc., Chgo., 1988-94, pres., CEO, 1994—, Equity Fin. and Mgmt. Co., Chgo., 1994—; prin. Rosenberg & Liebentritt, P.C., Chgo., 1995—. Bd. dirs. Gt. Am. Mgmt. & Investment, Chgo., 1984—, v.p., gen. counsel, 1985-90, sec., 1983-90; bd. dirs. CVS Corp. Ill.; trustee Equity Residential Properties Trust, Manufactured Home Cmtys., Inc.; mem. bd. trust Equity Office Properties. Bd. dirs., pres. Chgo. Network. Corporate, general, Property, real (including real estate development, water), Securities.

ROSENBERRY, WILLIAM KENNETH, lawyer, educator; b. St. Louis, Aug. 14, 1946; s. William Hugh and Shirley Anne (Love) Rosenberry; m. Linda Lou Lang, Aug. 24, 1968 (div. Jan. 1985); children: Ashlie Anne, Allison Renee; m. Donna L. Pruitt; stepchildren: Corey David Pruitt, Lindsey Lee Pruitt. BBA, U. Tex., Arlington, 1967; JD, Baylor U., 1970. Bar: Tex. 1970, Colo. 1991, U.S. Dist. Ct. (no. dist.) Tex. 1971, cert.: (specialist in comml. real estate law), Tex. (residential real estate law). Assoc. Hinds & Chambers, Arlington, 1970-71; ptnr. Duke, Rosenberry, Duke & Jelinek, Arlington, 1971-76; pvt. practice, Arlington, 1976—. Mem. faculty U. Tex., 1991—; bd. dirs. Equitable Bank, NA, Arlington, Equitable Bankshares, Dallas; gen. mgr. Triple R. Properties; escrow officer Am. Title Co., 1984—; assoc. bd. dirs. First Savs. Bank, Arlington. Pres. Pantego Christian Acad. Boosters, Arlington, 1990—92; mem. Arlington City Zoning Bd., 1989—92; bd. dirs. Baylor Bear Found. of Baylor U., Childrens Charities Ft. Worth, v.p., 1999—; bd. dirs. Ft. Worth Charities, Inc. Named, Outstanding Young Men in Am., 1980; recipient Outstanding Part-Time Faculty Tchg. award, U. Tex. Dept. Real Estate and Fin., 1992. Mem.: Arlington Bar Assn. (bd. dirs. 1987), Arlington Rep. Club, Arlington Sportsmans Club. Mem. Pantego Bible Ch. Avocation: Avocations: fishing, hunting, jogging.. State civil litigation, Family and matrimonial, Property, real (including real estate development, water). Office: 3010 W Park Row Dr Arlington TX 76013-2048

ROSENBLATT, ALBERT MARTIN, state appeals court judge; b. N.Y.C., Jan. 17, 1936; s. Isaac and Fannie (Dachs) R.; m. Julia Carlson, Aug. 23, 1970; 1 child, Elizabeth. BA, U. Pa., 1957; LLB (JD), Harvard U., 1960. Bar: N.Y. 1961.. Dist. atty. Dutchess County, N.Y., 1969-75, county judge, 1976-81; justice N.Y. State Supreme Ct., 1982-89, chief adminstrv. judge, 1987—89, justice, appellate divsn., 1989-98; judge N.Y. Ct. Appeals, 1999—. Instr. judge N.Y. State, 1987-89; vis. prof. Vassar Coll., 1993; moderator N.Y. State Fair Trial Free Press Conf., 2000-03; creator Dutchess County 1st consumer protection bur., 1973; instr. newly elected state supreme ct. judges and county judges; asst. dist. attys., 1974, 75; instr. law tng. N.Y. State Police Acad., 1997; lectr. Nat. Dist. Attys. Assn., 1968-74; mem. vis. faculty trial advocacy workshop Harvard Law Sch., 1998, 99. Mem. bd. editors N.Y. State Bar Jour., 1992-99; contbr. articles on law to profl. jours. and popular mags. Bd. dirs. United Way Cmty. Chest, 1970; bd. dirs. Bardavon 1869 Opera House, Dutchess County Hist. Soc.; mem. adv. bd. Jewish Cmty. Ctr., 1987—; pres. Hist. Soc. Cts. of State of N.Y., 2002—; mem. State-Fed. Jud. Coun., 2003—. With USAR, 1960-66. Mem. N.Y. State Bar Assn. (named Outstanding Prosecutor 1974, Outstanding Jud. Svcs. award 1994), N.Y. State Dist. Attys. Assn. (pres. 1974, Frank S. Hogan award 1987, Jud. Svcs. award 1994), Profl. Ski Instrs. Am. (cert. 1984—), Baker St. Irregulars Club (former assoc. editor Baker St. Jour.). Republican. Jewish. Home: 300 Freedom Rd Pleasant Valley NY 12569-5431 Office: 10 Market St Poughkeepsie NY 12601-3228

ROSENBLATT, PAUL GERHARDT, judge; b. 1928; AB, U. Ariz., 1958, JD, 1963. Asst. atty. gen. State of Ariz., 1963-66; adminstrv. asst. to U.S. Rep., 1967-72; soel practice, 1971-73; judge Yavapi County Superior Ct., Prescott, Ariz., 1973-84, U.S. Dist. Ct. Ariz., Phoenix, 1984—. Office: US Dist Ct Sandra Day O'Connor Ct Ste 621 401 W Washington St SPC 56 Phoenix AZ 85003-2156

ROSENBLATT, PETER RONALD, lawyer, former ambassador; b. N.Y.C., Sept. 4, 1933; s. William and Therese Amalia (Steinhardt) Rosenblatt; m. Naomi Henriette Harris; children: Therese Sarah Sonenshine, Daniel Harris, David Steinhardt. BA, Yale U., 1954, LL.B., 1957; postgrad. fellow, Tel-Aviv U., 1971. Bar: N.Y. 1959, D.C. 1969. Teaching asst. history Yale U., New Haven, 1954-55; asst. dist. atty. N.Y. County, 1959-62; asso. Stroock & Stroock & Lavan, N.Y.C., 1962-66; dep. asst. gen. counsel AID, Washington, 1966; mem. White House staff, Washington, 1966-68; jud. officer, chmn. bd. contract appeals U.S. Post Office Dept., Washington, 1968-69; v.p., dir. EDP Technology, Inc., Washington, 1969-71; chmn. bd. Internat. Devel. Services, Washington, 1969-71; spl. cons. to Senator Edmund S. Muskie, 1970-72; practice law Washington, 1972-77, 81-91; founding ptnr. Heller & Rosenblatt, Washington, 1991—. Personal rep. of Pres. with rank amb. to conduct negotiations on future polit. status of Trust Ter. of Pacific Islands, Washington, 1977-81; mem. Mid. East study group Dem. Adv. Coun. Elected Ofcls., 1974-76; bd. dirs. MediSense, Inc., 1983-96. Sec., chmn. exec. com. Coalition for a Dem. Majority, 1973-77, pres., 1983-93; bd. dirs. Com. on Present Danger, 1976-77, 82-93; mem. U.S. Nat. Com. Pacific Econ. Cooperation, 1986, sec., 1987—; bd. govs. Haifa (Israel) U., 1990-94, 98—; sec.-treas. Fund for Democracy and Devel., 1991-94, pres., 1994—; mem. adv. coun. Nixon Ctr., 1994—; mem. task force on fgn. policy Dem. Policy Comm., 1986; bd. govs. Am. Jewish Com., 1998—, pres. D.C. chpt. 2003—, bd. dirs. UN Watch, 2000—, chmn., bd. govs. Koppelman Inst. on Am. Jewish-Israeli Rels., 1999-2002; bd. advisors Jewish Inst. for Nat. Security Affairs, 2000—; mem. The Alliance for Am. Leadership, 2001—. Mem. ABA, N.Y., D.C. Bar, Coun. Fgn. Rels. Jewish. Private international, Public international, Government. Office: Heller & Rosenblatt 1101 15th St NW Ste 205 Washington DC 20005-5002 E-mail: ffdd@erols.com.

ROSENBLEETH, RICHARD M. lawyer; b. Phila., Mar. 20, 1932; s. Morris B. and Henrietta (Friedman) R.; m. Judith A. Alesker, June 20, 1954; children— Dori, Lyn BS in Econs., U. Pa., 1954, JD, 1957. Bar: Pa. 1958, U.S. Supreme Ct. 1961. Asst. dist. atty. City of Phila., 1957-62; assoc. Richman, Price & Jamieson, 1962-65; ptnr. Blank, Rome, Comisky & McCauley, Phila., 1965-97; gen. coun. MBIA Muni Svcs. Co., 1998-2001, Arbitration and Mediation Svcs., Phila., 2001—. Mem. Civil Justice Reform Act Adv. Group, U.S. Dist. Ct. (ea. dist.) Pa., 1991—; co-chair Mayor Rendell's Transition Task Force on the Law Dept., 1991; judge pro tem Phila. Ct. Common Pleas, 1992—. Pres. Merion Park Civic Assn., Pa., 1967; mem. Citizens Crime Commn., Phila., 1979-87; commr. Youth Svcs. Coordinating Commn., Phila., 1979-85; Pa. state mem. chair U.S. Supreme Ct. Hist. Soc., 1994-95; pres., Corp. Alliance for Drug Edn., 1998-2000, chmn. Pa. Conv. Ctr. Authority, 1996-2000. Fellow Am. Coll. Trial Lawyers (chmn. Pa. state com. 1993-94), Internat. Acad. Trial Lawyers, Am. Bar Found.; mem. ABA, Pa. Bar Assn., Phila. Bar Assn., Phila. Bar Found. (pres. 1994). Avocations: golf, art collecting. Office: One Logan Sq 8th Fl Philadelphia PA 19103-6998 E-mail: rosenbleeth@hotmail.com.

ROSENBLOOM, H. DAVID, lawyer; b. NYC, May 26, 1941; s. Milton M. and Rose Gold R.; m. Carla L. Peterson, June 23, 1968; children: Sarah Alix, Julia Micol. AB, Princeton U., 1962; postgrad. (Fulbright scholar), U. Florence, Italy, 1962-63; JD, Harvard U., 1966. Bar: N.Y. 1967, D.C. 1968. Spl. asst. to Arthur J. Goldberg U.S. amb. to UN, 1966-67; law clk. to Abe Fortas U.S. Supreme Ct., 1967-68; assoc. Caplin & Drysdale, Washington, 1968-72, ptnr., 1972-77, 81—. Spl. asst. to dep. asst. sec. for tax policy Dept. Treasury, Washington, 1977, internat. tax counsel, 1978—81; lectr. Harvard U. Law Sch., 1984—87, 1990—93, 1995—96, 1999, Pub. Fin. Tng. Inst., Taipei, 1985—86, 1989, Stanford U. Law Sch., 1988, Inst. Tecnologico Autonomo d' Mex., 1993, 95, 97, Columbia U. Law Sch., 1997, U. Pa. Law Sch., 1998, NYU Law Sch., 2000—, U. Commerciale Luigi Bocconi, Milan, 2001; faculty of law U. Sydney, 2001; lectr. South African Tax Inst., U. Pretoria South, 2002; dir. internat. tax program NYU Law Sch., 2002—. Home: 2948 Garfield Ter NW Washington DC 20008-3507 Office: 1 Thomas Cir NW Washington DC 20005-5802

ROSENBLOOM, LEWIS STANLEY, lawyer; b. Fort Riley, Kans., Feb. 28, 1953; s. Donald and Sally Ann (Warsawsky) R.; m. Rochelle Leavitt, Dec. 16, 1973; children: Micah, Shaina. BA, Lake Forest Coll., 1974; JD with high honors, DePaul U., 1977. Bar: Ill. 1977, U.S. Dist. Ct. (no. dist.) Ill, 1977, U.S. Ct. Appeals (7th cir.) 1979, U.S. Supreme Ct. 1983, U.S. Ct. Appeals (9th cir.) 1987, U.S. Ct. Appeals (3rd cir.) 1993. Sr. acct. Gale, Takahasi & Channon, Chgo., 1973-74; law clk. to Hon. Robert L. Eisen U.S. Dist. Ct. (no. dist.) Ill., Chgo., 1976; assoc. Nachman, Munitz & Sweig, Ltd., Chgo., 1976-82, prin., 1982-87; ptnr., co-chmn. involvency, bankruptcy & bus. reorgn. dept. Winston & Strawn, Chgo., 1987-93; ptnr., sr. corp. reorgn. counsel McDermott, Will & Emery, Chgo., 1994—; chmn. distressed transactions SBU. Mem. bd. advisors to bankruptcy, comml. law advisor Bus. Laws, Inc., 1988—; lectr. in field. Contbr. articles to profl. jours. Mem. adv. com. and fin. subcom. Ill. Bd. Higher Edn., Springfield; mem. state edn. and legal aid subcom. Ill. Coun. on Children and Youth Welfare, Chgo. Coll. scholar Lake Forest Coll., 1973-74. Fellow Am. Coll. Bankruptcy; mem. ABA (bus. bankruptcy com. 1982—, chmn. new and pending bankruptcy legis. com. 1982-85, chmn. transp. reorganizations com. 1985-88), Chgo. Bar Assn. (bankrupcy reorganization com., co-chmn. subcom. on retention and fees 1987-88). Bankruptcy, Commercial, contracts (including sales of goods; commercial financing), Mergers and acquisitions. Office: McDermott Will & Emery 227 W Monroe St Ste 3100 Chicago IL 60606-5096 E-mail: lrosenbloom@mwe.com.

ROSENBLOOM, NORMA FRISCH, lawyer; b. N.Y.C., Dec. 2, 1925; d. Jacob Frisch and Anna (Fox) Frisch Schwartz; m. Philip Rosenbloom, Oct. 31, 1946; children: David, James, Eric. BA, New Sch. Social Rsch., 1951; JD, Rutgers U., Newark, 1979. Bar: N.J. 1979, N.Y. 1980. Mem. faculty, head dept. music Ranney Sch., Tinton Falls, N.J., 1962-74; chief law clk. Monmouth County (N.J.) Prosecutor's Office, 1979-80; assoc. Karasic & Karasic, P.C., Oakhurst, N.J., 1980-82; ptnr. Abrams, Gatta, Rosen & Rosenbloom, Ocean Twp., N.J., 1982-90, Abrams, Gatta, Rosen, Rosenbloom & Sevrin, P.C., 1990-92; of counsel Abrams, Gatta, Falvo & Sevrin, P.A., 1992-99, Abrams Gatta Falvo LLP; legal adv. Epiphany House Inc., Asbury Park, N.J., 1999—. Asst. county counsel Monmouth County, 1987-88; mem. N.J. Supreme Ct. Family Part Practice Com., 1997-98. Sec., mem. exec. bd. Temple Beth Miriam, Elberon, N.J., 1969-74; mcpl. leader Monmouth Beach (N.J.) Dem. Com., 1973—; del. Dem. Nat. Conv., 1976; freeholder rep. to Monmouth County Cmty. Action Program, poverty program, 1975-76; bd. dirs. Cen. Jersey Regional Health Planning Bd., 1973-75; trustee search com. Brookdale C.c., Lincroft, N.J., 1984-85; trustee Planned Parenthood Monmouth County, 1981-88. Recipient award for cmty. involvement Asbury Park-Neptune Youth Coun., 1970. Fellow Am. Acad. Matrimonial Lawyers; mem. ABA, N.J. Women Lawyers Assn. (pres. 1994-95), N.J. State Bar Assn. (dispute resolution sec., trustee women in the profession sect.), Women Lawyers Monmouth County. Democrat. Jewish. Avocation: classical pianist. Family and matrimonial. Home: Channel Club Towers Monmouth Beach NJ 07750 Office: Epiphany House 300 4th Ave Asbury Park NJ 07712-6006

ROSENBLOOM, THOMAS ADAM, lawyer; b. N.Y.C., Mar. 17, 1963; s. Robert I. and Pauline W. R.; m. Jessica E. Bussgang, Aug. 18, 1990; children: Raquel J., Alana S., Michael D. BA, U. Wis., 1985; JD, Boston U., 1988. Bar: N.Y. 1988, Mass. 1990. Assoc. Wormser, Keily, Galef & Jacobs, White Plains, N.Y., 1988-89, O'Connor, Broude & Aronson, Waltham, Mass., 1989-96; ptnr. Epstein, Becker & Green, Boston, 1996—. Vol. tchr. Jr. Achievement, Boston, 1995-96; vol. Taft Sch./Harvard Bus. Sch., Boston, 1989-90. Mem. ABA, N.Y. State Bar Assn., Mass. Bar Assn. Avocations: basketball, exercise, theater, art, travel. Corporate, general, Mergers and acquisitions, Securities. Office: Epstein Becker & Green 111 Huntington Ave 26th Fl Boston MA 02199

ROSENBLUM, EDWARD G. lawyer; b. Union City, N.J., Aug. 2, 1944; s. Milton and Frances (Nardi) R.; m. Charis Ann Schlatter, Dec. 1, 1971; children: Deborah, Michelle. BA, Rutgers U., 1966, JD, 1969. Bar: N.J. 1969. Ptnr. Rosenblum & Rosenblum, P.A., Jersey City, 1971-79, Secaucus, N.J., 1979-93, Rosenblum Wolf & Lloyd, P.A., Secaucus, 1994—, Teaneck, 1998—. Lectr. in field. Author: N.J. Lawyer, 1980, N.J. Municipalities, 1987. Active Table to Table, Englewood, N.J. Mem. N.J. State Bar Assn. (vice chmn. tax ct. rules com. taxation sect. 1984—, chmn. real property tax com. 1984—, vice chmn. taxation sect. 1987—, chmn.-elect 1987, chmn. 1988-89, Supreme Ct. com. on tax ct. 1982-92). Condemnation (eminent domain), State and local taxation. Office: 115 W Allendale Ave Allendale NJ 07401

ROSENBLUM, ELLEN F. judge; b. 1951; m. Richard Meeker. BS, U. Oreg., 1971, JD, 1975. Bar: Oreg. 1975. Cir. ct. judge Multnomah County Ct., Portland, Oreg. Trustee Nat. Jud. Coll. Mem.: ABA (bd. govs., sec. 2002—). Office: Multnomah County Courthouse Rm 512 1021 SW 4th Ave Portland OR 97204*

ROSENBLUM, WILLIAM F., JR., lawyer; b. N.Y.C., May 11, 1935; AB cum laude, Princeton U., 1957; JD, Columbia U., 1960. Bar: N.Y. 1961, U.S. Dist. Ct. (so. dist.) N.Y. 1965. Gen. atty. Stanley Warner Corp., 1964-66; assoc. Leon, Weill & Mahony, 1967-70, Finley, Kumble, Wagner & Heine, 1970-74; pvt. practice, 1975; v.p. legal affairs Rep. Nat. Bank

N.Y., 1976-82; sr. v.p., dep. gen. counsel, corp. sec. Rep. N.Y. Corp., 1987—2001; sr. v.p., dep. gen. counsel HSBC USA Inc., 2000—01; mng. dir., gen. counsel NuVerse Advisors LLC, N.Y.C., 2001—. Mem.: ABA (mem. bus. law sect., mem. futures and investors regulation com.), Assn. of Bar of City of N.Y. (fgn. and comparative law com. 2000—, futures and derivatives regulation com.), N.Y. State Bar Assn. (mem. sect. bus. law, commodities and derivatives regulation 1990—). Banking, Corporate, general, Securities. Office: Nuverse Advisors LLC 645 Fifth Ave New York NY 10022

ROSENFELD, ARTHUR H. lawyer, publisher; b. Bklyn., May 24, 1930; s. Abraham and Sadie (Albert) R.; m. Lois E. Glantz, Apr. 15, 1956; children: Felicia Ann, Carolyn Jane, Sara Ellen. Student, St. Andrew's U., 1950-51; AB, Union Coll., Schenectady, 1952; JD, Harvard U., 1955; postgrad., CCNY, 1962-63. Bar: N.Y. 1955. Pres. Warren, Gorham & Lamont, Inc., N.Y.C., 1970-81, Internat. Thomson Profl. Pub., N.Y.C., 1981-84; chmn. bd. Rosenfeld, Emanuel Inc., Larchmont, N.Y., 1984-88; pres. Prentice Hall Tax & Profl. Ref., N.Y.C., 1988-89, Maxwell Macmillan Profl. and Bus. Reference Div., Englewood Cliffs, N.J., 1989-92; chmn. Arthur H. Rosenfeld Assocs., 1991—; Civic Rsch. Inst., Inc., 1992—. Mem. ABA, N.Y. State Bar Assn., Am. Assn. Pubs. (exec. coun. 1991), Harvard Club. Democrat. Office: 2067 Broadway Ste 50 New York NY 10023 E-mail: ahrcri@aol.com.

ROSENFELD, MARTIN JEROME, management consultant to law firms, educator; b. Flint, Mich., Oct. 3, 1944; s. Israel Edward and Lillian Edith (Natchez) R.; m. Marcy Tucker Colman; 1 child, Joshua; stepchildren: Jessica Colman, Zachary Colman. BA, Mich. State U., 1968, MHA, 1978; MBA with high honors, Ind. No. U., 1979. Adminstr. Care Corp., Grand Rapids, Mich., 1969-70, Chandler Convalescent Ctr., Detroit, 1970-71, Grand Community Hosp., Detroit, 1971-73; exec. v.p., chief exec. officer Msgr. Clement Kern Hosp. Spl. Surgery, Warren, Mich., 1973-84; pres. M.J. Rosenfeld Assocs., 1984-85; COO Dickinson, Wright, Moon, Van Dusen & Freeman, 1985-88; acting COO New Ctr. Hosp., Detroit, 1995-96; prin. Rosenfeld Partners LLP, Farmington Hills, Mich., 1988—; instr. U. Phoenix, 2001—. Instr. Marygrove Coll., 1975-80; assoc. prof. Mercy Coll., Detroit, 1978-80; mem. faculty Inst. on Continuing Legal Edn., Ann Arbor, Mich., Inst. Law Firm Mgmt., Ann Arbor; instr. Legal Tech '87, Chgo. Author papers in field. Mem. editl. bd. The Human-Size Hosp.; mem. panel of experts The Health Care News. V.p. Detroit chpt. Jewish Nat. Fund, 1978—; pres. Cranbrook Village Homeowners Assn., 1977; chmn. Community Hosps. of Southeastern Mich., 1981-84; mem. tech. work group Comprehensive Health Planning Coun. of Southeastern Mich., 1981-84; mem. fin. mgmt. com., mem. hosp. affairs bd. Greater Detroit Area Hosp. Coun., 1981-84; bd. dirs., com. chmn. Detroit Symphony Orch., 1984-90; bd. dirs., mem. fund raising com. Detroit Met. Orch., 1984-87. Mem. ABA, Assn. Legal Adminstrs., Am. Assn. Health Care Cons., Royal Soc. Health, Am. Podiatry Assn. (com. hosps. 1981-84), Warren C. of C. (com. chmn. 1975), Nat. Assn. Legal Search Cons., Nat. Assn. Pers. Svcs., Mich. Assn. Pers. Svcs., Sanford Rose Assocs. Dirs. Assn. (pres. 1993-95, treas. 1995-97). Office: Rosenfeld Partners LLP 31420 Northwestern highway Suite L-100 Farmington Hills MI 48334-1770 E-mail: mjr@rosenfeldllc.com.

ROSENFELD, ROBERT THOMAS, lawyer; b. Cleve., July 2, 1933; AB, Brown U., 1954; LLB, Case Western Res. U., 1958. Bar: Ohio 1958, U.S. Supreme Ct. 1966. Field atty. NLRB, Seattle and Cleve., 1958—62; various partnerships Cleve., 1983—95; solo practitioner, 1995—. Instr. collective bargaining Cleve. State U. Indsl. Rels. Ctr.; pres. Indsl. Rels. Rsch. Assn., N.E. Ohio chpt., 2000—03. Pres. Suburban Temple; bd. dirs. Friends of Crawford Mus., Cleve., 1983—84. Served to comdr. U.S. C.G. Res., 1956—57. Mem.: Am. Arbitration Assn. (labor panel), Cleve. Bar Assn. (chmn. labor sect. 1993—94), Ohio Bar Assn., Mayfield Curling Club, Classic Car Rolls Royce Owners Club. Avocations: collecting cars, curling. Administrative and regulatory, Labor (including EEOC, Fair Labor Standards Act, labor-management relations, NLRB, OSHA), Alternative dispute resolution. Home and Office: 31853 Cedar Rd Mayfield Hts OH 44124-4445 E-mail: robertrosenfeld@ameritech.net.

ROSENFELD, STEVEN B. lawyer; b. N.Y.C., Apr. 12, 1943; s. Eugene David and Laura (Sipin) R.; m. Naomi Eve Winkler, Aug. 21, 1965; children: Kathryn Anne, Elizabeth Jane. BA, Columbia Coll., 1964; LLB, Columbia U., 1967. Bar: N.Y. 1967, D.C. 1984, U.S. Dist. Ct. (so. dist.) N.Y. 1969, U.S. Dist. Ct. (ea. dist.) N.Y. 1970, U.S. Ct. Appeals (2d cir.) 1971, U.S. Ct. Appeals (3d cir.) 1974, U.S. Ct. Appeals (Fed. cir.) 1978, D.C. 1979, U.S. Supreme Ct. 1979, U.S. Ct. Appeals (5th cir.) 1982, U.S. Ct. Appeals (6th and D.C. cirs.) 1984, U.S. Ct. Appeals (4th and 9th cirs.) 1987, U.S. Ct. Appeals (1st cir.) 1989, U.S. Ct. Appeals (10th cir.) 1991. Law clk. to Hon. Charles M. Metzner U.S. Dist. Ct. (so. dist.) N.Y., 1967-68; assoc. Rosenman & Colin, N.Y.C., 1968-71; dep. gen. counsel N.Y. State Commn. on Attica, N.Y.C., Batavia, N.Y., 1971-72; assoc. Paul, Weiss, Rifkind, Wharton & Garrison, N.Y.C., 1972-75, ptnr., 1976—. Lectr. Columbia U. Sch. Law, 1995—; chmn. N.Y.C. Conflict of Interest Bd., 2002—. Contbr. articles to profl. jours. Bd. dirs. N.Y. Assn. New Ams., N.Y.C., 1973-95; trustee Dalton Sch., N.Y.C., 1988-94; trustee Putney Sch. Putney, Vt., 1995-2001, N.Y. Theatre Workshop, 1996—. Mem. N.Y. State Bar Assn. (ho. of dels. 1996-98), Assn. Bar City N.Y. (exec. com. 1992-96, v.p. 1998-99, past mem. various coms.), Legal Aid Soc. (pres. 1989-91, bd. dirs., exec. com. 1978-95). Democrat. Jewish. Avocations: opera and chamber music, theatre, tennis. E-mail: srosenfeld.paulweiss.com. Federal civil litigation, State civil litigation, Trademark and copyright. Office: Paul Weiss Rifkind Et Al 1285 Ave of Americas New York NY 10019-6028

ROSENGREN, DAVID E. lawyer; b. NYC, July 30, 1951; m. Sally S. Shulman; children: Samuel Noah, Anna Rebecca. BA, Randolph-Macon Woman's Coll., 1978; JD, U. of Va., 1981. Bar: Conn. 1981, U.S. Dist. Ct. 1982, Mass. 2002, U.S. Ct. of Fed. Claims 1990, U.S. Ct. Appeals (2nd cir.) 1991. Assoc. Ried & Riege, P.C., Hartford, Conn., 1981—83; ptnr. Pepe & Hazard LLP, Hartford, Conn., 1983. Contbr. articles to profl. jour. Master: Nat. Inst. for Trial Advocacy (master 1998—99); fellow: Conn. Bar Found.; mem.: ABA, Conn. Bar Assn., constrn. law sect. (exec. com. 1989, sec. 1989—91, vice chmn. 1992—94, chmn. 1994—96), Am. Arbitration Assn. (mem. 1986—2002), U. Hartford Constrn. Inst. (dir. of publications 1989—91, edn. com 1999), Conn. Bar Assn., Fed. Judiciary Com., Phi Beta Kappa. General civil litigation, Commercial, contracts (including sales of goods; commercial financing), Construction. Home: 14 Fulton Place West Hartford CT 06107 Office: Pepe & Hazard LLP 225 Asylum Street Hartford CT 06103-4302 Office Fax: 860-522-2796. E-mail: drosengren@pepehazard.com.

ROSENHOUSE, HOWARD, retired lawyer; b. Bklyn., Oct. 15, 1939; s. Barnet and Sonia Rosenhouse. BA, Bklyn. Coll., 1960, MA, 1969; JD, Bklyn. Law Sch., 1963, LLM, 1965; MS, Pace U., 1975. Bar: N.Y. 1963, N.J. 1985, U.S. Dist. Ct. (so. and ea. dists.) N.Y. 1985, U.S. Dist. Ct. N.J. 1985, U.S. Supreme Ct. 1980. Tchr. social studies, guidance counselor, acting asst. prin. N.Y.C. Bd. Edn., 1963-79, counsel to bd. examiners, 1979-90, atty. at bd. edn., 1991-94. Mem. N.Y. State Bar Assn., Bklyn. Law Sch. Alumni Assn. Jewish.

ROSENHOUSE, MICHAEL ALLAN, lawyer, editorial consultant; b. Chgo., Nov. 8, 1946; s. Seymour Samuel and Jeanne Mozette (Rosenthal) R. BA, Yale U., 1968; JD, U. Chgo., 1974. Bar: Ill. 1974, N.Y. 1982. Atty. in pvt. practice, Rochester, N.Y. Mng. editor: Am. Jurisprudence, 2d edit., 1991—93, Am. Law Reports (Fed.), 1991—93; editor: (newsletter) Bank Employment Law Report, 1998—99; author: Recent Court. of Appeals Decisions Reflect Strict Interpretation of Procedure Requirements, 2003, Employment Law (Syracuse Law Rev.), 1998; columnist: The Daily Record, 2001—03. Mem.: ABA, N.Y. State Bar Assn., Monroe County Bar Assn. (co-chair Disability Labor and Employment Law Commn. 1998—99), U. Chgo. Club of Rochester (bd. dirs. 1999—2001), Yale Alumni Assn. (schs. com. 1997—), U. Chgo. Law Sch. Alumni Assn. (bd. dirs. 1977—80). Avocations: squash, tennis, golf. Appellate, Labor (including EEOC, Fair Labor Standards Act, labor-management relations, NLRB, OSHA). Office: 70 Linden Oaks Rochester NY 14625 E-mail: mike@rosenhouse.com.

ROSENKRANZ, STANLEY WILLIAM, lawyer; b. N.Y.C., Aug. 20, 1933; s. Jacob and Adele R.; m. Judith Ossinsky, Aug. 14, 1960; children: Jack Michael, Andrew Lawrence. BS in Acctg, U. Fla., 1955, JD with honors, 1960; LLM (Kenneson fellow), NYU, 1961. Bar: Fla. 1960, Ga. 1970, cert.: (tax lawyer). Mem. firm Macfarlane, Ferguson, Allison & Kelly, Tampa, Fla., 1961-68, 71-79; with King & Spalding, Atlanta, 1969-71, Holland & Knight, Tampa, 1979-86, Shear, Newman, Rosenkranz, Burton & Lamb, Tampa, 1986-2000, Ruden McClosky Smith Schuster & Russell, Tampa, 2000—03, Akerman Sentor, 2003—. Adj. prof. Grad. Sch. Law, U. Fla., 1975-79, Grad. Coll. Bus. Adminstrn., U. Tampa, 1989, 97-99, Stetson U. Coll. Law. Pres. Congregation Schaarai Zedek, Tampa, 1981-83; bd. dirs. Union Am. Hebrew Congregations, 1990—, v.p. S.E. region, 1988-90, pres., 1992-96. With U.S. Army, 1955-57. Named Young Man of Year Tampa Jaycees, Fla., 1967 Mem. ABA, Am. Coll. Tax Counsel, Am. Law Inst., Fla. Bar Assn., Ga. Bar Assn., Greater Tampa C. of C. (bd. govs., chmn. anti-drug task force). Corporate, general, Health, Corporate taxation. Home: 1125 Shipwatch Cir Tampa FL 33602-5785 Office: 401 E Jackson St Fl 27 Tampa FL 33602-5233 E-mail: swr@ruden.com., srosenkranz@akerma.com.

ROSENN, HAROLD, lawyer; b. Plains, Pa., Nov. 4, 1917; s. Joseph and Jennie (Wohl) R.; m. Sallyanne Frank, Sept. 19, 1948; 1 child, Frank Scott. BA, U. Mich., 1939, JD, 1941; LLD, Coll. Misericordia, 1991. Bar: Pa. 1942, U.S. Supreme Ct. 1957. Ptnr. Rosenn & Rosenn, Wilkes Barre, Pa., 1948-54, Rosenn, Jenkins & Greenwald, Wilkes Barre, 1954-87, of counsel, 1988—. Mem. Pa. State Bd. Law Examiners, 1983-93, Pa. Gov.'s Justice Commn., 1968-73, Pa. Crime Commn., 1968-73, Fed. Jud. Nominating Com., Pa., 1977-79, Appellate Ct. Nominating Com., Pa., 1979-81; asst. dist. atty. Luzerne County, Pa., 1952-54. Chmn. United Jewish Appeal Campaign of Wyoming Valley, 1956, 84, ARC, Wilkes-Barre, 1959-77, chair, 1963-65, life bd. dirs., 1991—; pres. Pa. Coun. on Crime and Delinquency, Harrisburg, 1969-71; bd. dirs. Coll. Misericordia, Dallas, Pa., 1976-86, emeritus, 1986—, Hoyt Libr., Kingston, Pa., 1971-78, Nat. Coun. on Crime and Delinquency, N.Y.C., 1969-71, Jewish Cmty. Ctr. Wilkes-Barre, Pa., 1964-66; chmn. United Way Campaign of Wyoming Valley, 1975, chmn. bd., 78-80; pres. Temple Israel of Wilkes Barre, 1972-74, chmn. bd. 1974-84, life bd. dirs.; comdr. post 395 Am. Legion, Kingston, 1948; bd. dirs. Keystone State Games, Jewish Fedn. Bd. of Greater Wilkes-Barre, St. Vincent de Paul Soup Kitchen, 1987-2000. Capt. USAAF, 1942-45, ETO. Decorated medal with 6 bronze stars, European combatant cross French Govt.; named Golden Key Vol. of Yr., United Way of Pa., 1989; recipient Erasmus medal, Dutch Govt., Disting. Svc. award in Trusteeship, Assn. Governing Bds., Univs. and Colls., 1990, Disting. Cmty. Svc. award, Greater Wilkes-Barre Soc. Fellows Anti-Defamation League, 1991, Clara Barton honor award, Wyoming Valley chpt. ARC, 1992, Lifetime Achievement award, United Way of Wyoming VAlley, 1992, Outstanding Vol. Fundraiser award, Greater Pocono chpt. Nat. Soc. of Fundraising Execs., 1995, honoree, Wyoming Valley Interfaith Coun., 1986, Ethics Inst. N.E. Pa., 2001, inductee, Jr. Achievement Hall of Fame for N.E. Pa., 1997. Mem. ABA, Pa. Bar Assn., Am. Judicature Soc., The Pa. Soc., B'nai B'rith (pres. Wilkes Barre 1952-53, Cmty. Svc. award 1976), U. Mich. Club N.E. Pa. (pres. 1946-76), Westmoreland Club (Wilkes-Barre), Huntsville Golf Club (Lehman, Pa.). Republican. Jewish. Corporate, general, Family and matrimonial, General practice, Estate planning, Probate (including wills, trusts). E-mail: hr@rjglaw.com.

ROSENN, JONATHAN RUDGE, lawyer; b. Rio de Janeiro, Sept. 21, 1970; arrived in U.S., 1970; s. Keith Samuel and Silvia Rudge Rosenn; m. Debora D'Angelo Rosenn, Aug. 17, 2001. BA in English, Oberlin Coll., 1992; JD magna cum laude, U. Miami, 1996. Bar: Fla. 1996, U.S. Dist. Ct. (so. dist.) Fla. 1998. Assoc. Freeman, Butterman & Haber, LLP, Miami, 1996—97; fgn. legal cons. Wald e Associado's Advogados, São Paulo, Brazil, 1997—98; assoc. Fine & Martinez, P.A., Miami, 1998—2001, Stanley M. Rosenblatt, P.A., Miami, 2001—. Mem.: Dade County Bar Assn. Product liability, Personal injury (including property damage), Appellate. Office: Stanley M Rosenblatt PA 12th Fl 66 W Flagler St Miami FL 33130

ROSENNE, MEIR, lawyer, government agency administrator; b. Iasi, Romania, Feb. 19, 1931; arrived in Israel, 1944; s. Jacob and Mina Rosenhaupt; m. Vera Ayai, June 9, 1959; children: Mihal, Dafna. MA in Polit. Sci., Inst. Polit. Sci., Paris, 1953; LLB, Sorbonne, U. Paris, 1955, PhD in Internat. Law with honors, 1957; grad., Inst. Internat. Studies, Paris, 1953. In govt. service, Israel, 1953—; consul Israel Consulate, N.Y.C., 1967-69; sr. lectr. in polit. sci. U. Haifa, Israel, 1969-71; coordinator Atomic Energy Commn. Israel, 1969-71; chief legal adviser Fgn. Office Israel, Jerusalem, 1971-79; Israeli amb. to France, Paris, 1979-83; Israeli amb. to U.S. Washington, 1983-87; pres. State of Israel Bonds, N.Y., 1989-93; ptnr. Balter, Guth, Aloni & Co., Jerusalem, 1994—. Chmn. overseas com. Jerusalem Bank; bd. dirs. Israel Discount Bank Holding, Ltd. Contbr. Chmn. internat. bd. govs. Share-Zedek Hosp., Jerusalem, 1989—94. Sgt. Israeli Air Force, 1948—50. Named comdr., Nat. Order French Legion of Honor; recipient Harold Weil medal, NYU Sch. Law, Elie Wiesel award. Mem.: French Assn. Internat. Law, Am. Soc. Internat. Law, Israeli Bar Assn., Soc. Internat. Law, Internat. Law Soc. France, Internat. Club Washington. Avocations: volleyball, swimming. Office: Balter Guth & Aloni 23 Hillel St Jerusalem Israel E-mail: mrosenne@bgalaw.co.il.

ROSENSAFT, MENACHEM ZWI, lawyer, author, foundation executive, community activist; b. Bergen-Belsen, Germany, May 1, 1948; came to U.S., 1958, naturalized, 1962; s. Josef and Hadassah (Bimko) R.; m. Jean Bloch, Jan. 13, 1974; 1 child, Joana Deborah. BA, MA, Johns Hopkins U., 1971; MA, Columbia U., 1975, JD, 1979. Bar: N.Y. 1980. Adj. lectr. dept. Jewish studies CCNY, 1972-74, professorial fellow, 1974-75; rsch. fellow Am. Law Inst., 1977-78; law clk. to judge U.S. Dist. Ct. (so. dist.) N.Y., N.Y.C., 1979-81; assoc. Proskauer, Rose, Goetz & Mendelsohn, N.Y.C., 1981-82, Kaye, Scholer, Fierman, Hays & Handler, N.Y.C., 1982-89; v.p., sr. assoc. counsel Chase Manhattan Bank, N.Y.C., 1989-93; spl. counsel Hahn & Hessen, N.Y.C., 1994-95; sr. internat. counsel Ronald S. Lauder Found., N.Y.C., 1995-97; exec. v.p. Jewish Renaissance Found., Inc., N.Y.C., 1996-2000; ptnr. Ross & Hardies, N.Y.C., 2000—. Author: Moshe Sharett, Statesman of Israel, 1966, Fragments, Past and Future (poetry), 1968, Not Backward to Belligerency, 1969; editor: Bergen Belsen Youth mag., 1965, Life Reborn, Jewish Displaced Persons 1945-1951, 2001; book rev. editor Columbia Jour. Transnat. Law, 1978-79; co-editor (with Yehuda Bauer) Antisemitism: Threat to Western Civilization, 1988; contbg. editor: Reform Judaism, 1993—; contbr. to various publs. including N.Y. Times, Nat. Law Jour., N.Y. Law Jour., Washington Post, Newsweek, N.Y. Post, L.A. Times, N.Y. Daily News, Phila. Inquirer, Miami Herald, Internat. Herald Tribune, Nat. Law Jour., Forward, Jerusalem Post, Liberation, Paris, Davar, Tel Aviv, El Diario, Santiago de Chile, (with Joana D. Rosensaft) Fordham Internat. Law Jour., Columbia Human Rights Law Rev., Jewish Social Studies, Leo Baeck Inst. Year Book XXI, Columbia Jour. Environ. Law, (with Michael I. Saltzman) Tax Planning Internat. Rev., Fellowship, Reform Judaism, United Synagogue Rev., Midstream, N.Y. Jewish Week; dir., editor-in-chief Holocaust Survivors' Memoirs Project of World Jewish Congress, 2000—. Chmn. Internat. Network Children Jewish Holocaust Survivors, 1981—84, founding chmn., 1984—; nat. pres. Labor Zionist Alliance, 1988—91; chmn. commn. human rights World Jewish Congress, 1986—91, chmn. exec. com. Am. sect., 1986—90; mem. Gen. Coun. World Zionist Orgn., 1987—92; mem. U.S. Holocaust Meml. Coun., 1994—2000, chmn. content com., 1994—2000, chmn. collections and acquisitions com., 1996—2000, chmn. task force on procs. for com. on conscience, 1996, mem. exec. com., 1996—2003, chmn. governance com., 2001—02; bd. dirs., exec. com. Nat. Com. for Labor Israel, 1988—91, 1995—2001; mem. Am. Zionist Tribunal, 1988—90, chmn., 1990; sec. Am. Zionist Fedn., 1990—93; bd. dirs. Am. Jewish Joint Distbn. Com., 1988—91, Mercaz, 1991—97; mem. exec. com. Nat. Jewish Cmty. Rels. Adv. Coun., 1994—97; organizer, leader demonstration in Germany against Pres. Reagan's visit to Bitburg Cemetery and Bergen-Belsen concentration camp, 1985; del. meeting on recognition of Israel between five Am. Jews and leaders of Palestine Liberation Orgn., 1988; mem. N.Y.C. Holocaust Meml. Commn., 1982—96, chmn. collections com., 1987—89; mem. N.Y. County Dem. Com., 1981—85; mem. nat. adv. bd. United Synagogue Conservative Judaism, 1995—, also chmn. United Synagogue del. to Nat. Jewish Cmty. Rels. Adv. Coun., 1994—97; pres. Park Ave. Synagogue, 2003—, sec., 1988—2003, trustee, 1994—; chmn. Sherr Inst. Adult Jewish Studies, 1993—2002. Recipient Abraham Joshua Heschel Peace award, 1989, Parker Sch. recognition of achievement with honors in internat. and fgn. law, 1979, 400th Anniversary medal City of Warsaw, 1999, commendation Jewish Heritage Week, Comptroller of N.Y.C., 1999; Harlan Fiske Stone scholar, 1977-79. Mem. ABA, Phi Beta Kappa. Federal civil litigation, Private international, Securities. Home: 179 E 70th St New York NY 10021-5109 Office: Ross & Hardies 65 E 55th St New York NY 10022-3219 E-mail: menachem.rosensaft@rosshardies.com.

ROSENSTEIN, JAMES ALFRED, lawyer, mediator, negotiation facilitator; b. Phila., Jan. 4, 1939; s. Louis Charles and Natalie Selma (Stern) R.; m. Linda Merle Lederman, Sept. 7, 1969; 1 child, Judith Esther AB, Harvard U., 1961, JD, 1968. Bar: Pa. 1968. Assoc. Wolf, Block, Schorr and Solis-Cohen, Phila., 1968-76, ptnr., 1976-97; prin. Rosenstein Assocs., Phila., 1997—. Mem. adv. com. task force on condominiums Joint State Govt Commn., Pa. Gen. Assembly, 1977-79; mem. condominium-coop. steering com. Phila. City Planning Commn., 1980-81 Contbr. articles to profl. jours. Trustee Jewish Fedn. of Greater Phila., 1977—, mem. exec. com., 1989-97, 98-2002, chmn. com. on local svcs., 1986-89, sec., 1987-88, v.p., 1988-94, chmn. com. on allocations and planning, 1989-92; v.p. jewish Cmty. Rels. Coun., 1982-85, 89-90, 96-2000, pres., 2000-2002; trustee United Way of Greater Phila., 1979-84, bd. dirs., 1982-85, 91-97; pres. Hillel Greater Phila., 1981-83; vice chmn. Synagogue-Fedn. Coun. Greater Phila., 1995-97, chmn., 1997-99. Lt. USN, 1961-64. Mem. ABA (chmn. devel. and financing of condominium projects 1993-97), Pa. Bar Assn. (chmn. common interest ownership com. 1980-93, chmn. real property divsn. 1993-95, chmn. real property, probate and trust law sect. 1995-96), Phila. Bar Assn. (co-chmn. legis. rels. com. 1996-97, co-chmn. ADR com. 2003—), Am. Coll. Real Estate Lawyers, Coll. Cmty. Assn. Lawyers, Soc. Profls. in Dispute Resolution (co-chmn. comml. sect. 1998-2000), Coun. Jewish Fedns. (bd. dirs. 1986-98, chmn. com. on svcs. to aging 1991-94, chair nat. funding coun. 1996-98, exec. com. 1997-98), United Jewish Cmtys. Fedn. N.Am. (chmn. N.E. region 1998-2001). Environmental, Property, real (including real estate development, water), Alternative dispute resolution. Office: Rosenstein Assocs 1650 Arch St 22nd Fl Philadelphia PA 19103-2097 E-mail: jrosenstein@earthlink.net.

ROSENSTOCK, LOUIS ANTHONY, III, lawyer; b. Petersburg, Va., July 27, 1941; BA, Washington and Lee U., 1963; JD, LLB, U. Richmond, 1966. Bar: Va. 1966. Judge 11th Jud. Dist., Petersburg, 1973-75; sole practice, 1975-98; purchasing agt., risk mgr., code enforcement support mgr. City of Petersburg, 1999—. Special asst. city atty., Petersburg. Capt. JAGC, U.S. Army, 1966-71. Mem. Va. State Bar, Petersburg Bar Assn. (pres. 1984-85). Government contracts and claims. Office: City of Petersburg City Hall Annex 103 W Tabb St Petersburg VA 23803-3211 E-mail: labuy@earthlink.net.

ROSENTHAL, ALAN, lawyer; b. Newark, N.J., Apr. 19, 1948; s. Robert Rosenthal; children: Keith Michael Rosenthal, Greg Jason Rosenthal. BA, Syracuse U., 1970, JD, 1974. Bar: N.Y. 1975, U.S. Dist. Ct. (no. and we. dists.) N.Y. 1975. Lawyer Ctr. Cmty. Alternatives, Inc., N.Y. Mem. N.Y. State Bar Assn., Nat. Lawyers Guild, Onondaga County Bar Assn., Nat. Legal Aid and Defender Assn., Assn. Trial Lawyers Am., N.Y. State Trial Lawyers Assn. Civil rights, Criminal, Personal injury (including property damage). Home: 340 Kensington Pl Syracuse NY 13210-3310 Office: 115 E Jefferson St Ste 300 Syracuse NY 13202-2480

ROSENTHAL, ALAN D. lawyer; b. Dallas, Apr. 28, 1949; s. Harry and Esther P. (Moskowitz) R.; m. Sondra Elise Aron, May 19, 1985; children: Adam Caplan, Kenneth Caplan, Jennifer. BSEE, Princeton U., 1971; JD, U. Tex., 1974. Ptnr. Baker & Botts, Houston, 1974-92, Fish & Richardson, Houston, 1992-98, Rosenthal & Osha, Houston, 1998—. Avocations: fishing, cooking, travel. Patent, Trademark and copyright. Home: 6614 Wakeforest St Houston TX 77005-3956 Office: Rosenthal & Osha 700 Louisiana St Ste 4550 Houston TX 77002-2793

ROSENTHAL, CHARLES A., JR., prosecutor; Dist. atty. Harris County, Houston. Office: Ste 600 1201 Franklin St Houston TX 77002-1923*

ROSENTHAL, DEBORAH GAIL, lawyer; b. Manhasset, N.Y. d. Jay S. and Gladys Rosenthal. AB in Econs. cum laude, Wellesley Coll., 1984; JD magna cum laude, Cornell U., 1987; LLM in Taxation, NYU, 1991. Bar: Mass. 1987, N.Y. 1988, Mass. 1988. Jud. law clk. to Chief Justice John Greaney Mass. Ct. Appeals, Boston, 1987—88; assoc. Dewey Ballantine, N.Y.C., 1988—91, Squadron Ellenoff et al, N.Y.C., 1992—95, Hertzog, Calamari & Gleason, N.Y.C., 1995—97; asst. gen. counsel The BOC Group, Murray Hill, NJ, 1997—2002; ptnr. Rosenthal, Attys. at Law, P.C., Great Neck, NY, 2002—. Bd. dirs. Sarci's Ctr., Great Neck. Mem.: Order of Coif. Office: Rosenthal Attys at Law PC 336 Northern Blvd Great Neck NY 11021 Office Fax: 516-487-1659. E-mail: drosenthal4@nyc.rr.com.

ROSENTHAL, HERBERT MARSHALL, lawyer; BA, UCLA; JD, Hasting Coll. Law, U. Calif., San Francisco. Bar: Calif. 1962. Formerly exec. dir. State Bar Calif., San Francisco; pvt. practice Millbrae, Calif.; pres. Found. State Bar Calif., San Francisco. Administrative and regulatory. Office: PO Box 507 Millbrae CA 94030-0507

ROSENTHAL, LEE H. federal judge; b. Nov. 30, 1952; m. Gary L. Rosenthal; children: Rebecca, Hannah, Jessica, Rachel. BA in Philosophy with honors, U. Chgo., 1974, JD with honors, 1977. Bar: Tex. 1979. Law clk. to Hon. John R. Brown U.S. Ct. Appeals (5th cir.), 1977-78; assoc. Baker & Botts, 1978-86, ptnr., 1986-92; judge U.S. Dist. Ct. (so. dist.) Tex., 1992—. Vis. com. Law Sch. U. Chgo., 1983-86, 94-97, 99-2001; mem. Fed. Jud. Conf. Adv. Com. for Fed. Rules of Civil Procedure, 1996—; chair 1999 Fifth Cir. Jud. Conf. Mem. bd. editors Manual for Complex Litigation, 1999—. Mem. adv. com. Tex. Children's Hosp., 1988-92; pres. Epilepsy Assn. Houston/Gulf Coast, 1989-91; trustee Briarwood Sch. Endowment Found., 1991-92; bd. dirs. Epilepsy Found. Am., 1993-98, DePelchin Children's Ctr., 2000—. Fellow Tex. Bar Found.; Mem. ABA, Am. Law Inst. (consultative group for transnat. rules of civil procedure), Texas Bar Assn., Houston Bar Assn. Office: US Dist Ct US Courthouse Rm 11535 515 Rusk St Houston TX 77002-2600

ROSENTHAL, MEYER L(OUIS), lawyer; b. Wilkes-Barre, Pa., May 27, 1944; s. Samuel J. and Lottie G. (Goncher) R.; m. Susan M., Aug. 19, 1967; children: Norman, Bonnie. BA, Rutgers Coll., 1966, JD, 1969. Bar: N.J. 1969, U.S. Dist. Ct. N.J. 1969, Calif. 1975, U.S. Dist. Ct. (cen. dist.) Calif.

1981, U.S. Dist. Ct. (ea. dist.) N.Y. 1980, U.S. Dist. Ct. (so. dist.) N.Y. 1981, U.S. Ct. Appeals (9th cir.) 1981. Law sec. Hon. Leon Milmed N.J. Superior Ct., Newark, 1969-70; assoc. Kaufman & Kaufman, Elizabeth, N.J., 1970-76; ptnr. Trueger & Rosenthal, Morristown, N.J., 1976-82; atty. pvt. practice, Morristown, N.J., 1982—. Editor Rutgers Law Rev. Cub scout leader Morris Area Boy Scouts Am., Randolph, N.J., 1980; chmn. Morris City Human Rels. Commn., Morristown, 1992-95, chmn. emeritus, 1999; trustee United Jewish Comtys. of Metrowest N.J., 2002—; mem. cmty. adv. com. County Coll. of Morris, 2002—. Recipient Comty. Hero award Morris County Orgn. Hispanic Affairs, 1996. Mem. Comml. Law League Am., Calif. Bar Assn., N.J. Bar Assn., B'nai B'rith (bd. govs. 1975—, pres. dist. 3 1988-89, Internat. Young Leadership award 1982, Internat. Founders award 1985, nat. commn. anti-defamation league 1992—), United Jewish Communities of MetroWest N.J. (trustee 2002—), County Coll. of Morris Cmty. (adv. com. 2002—). State civil litigation, Commercial, contracts (including sales of goods; commercial financing), Property, real (including real estate development, water). Office: 161 Washington St Morristown NJ 07960-3753 E-mail: meyer@therosenthals.net.

ROSENTHAL, SOL, lawyer; b. Balt., Oct. 17, 1934; s. Louis and Hattie (Getz) R.; m. Diane Myra Sackler, June 11, 1961; children: Karen Abby, Pamela Margaret, Robert Joel. AB, Princeton U., 1956; JD, Harvard U., 1959. Bar: Md. 1959, Calif. 1961. Law clk. to chief judge U.S. Ct. Appeals, 4th cir., Balt., 1959-60; assoc. Kaplan, Livingston, Goodwin, Berkowitz & Selvin, Beverly Hills, Calif., 1960-66, ptnr., 1966-74, Buchalter, Nemer, Fields & Younger, L.A., 1974-96; of counsel Blanc, Williams, Johnston & Kronstadt, L.A., 1996-2000, Arnold & Porter, 2000—. Bd. dirs. Playboy Enterprises, Inc., Chgo.; arbitrator Dirs. Guild Am., L.A., 1976—, Writers Guild Am., L.A., 1976—, Am. Film Mktg. Assn., 1989—, SAG, L.A., 1992—; negotiator Writers Guild-Assn. Talent Agts., L.A., 1978—; mem. entertainment and large complex case panels Am. Arbitration Assn., 1997—. Founder Camp Ronald McDonald for Good Times, L.A., 1985; charter founder Mus. Contemporary Art, L.A., 1988. Fellow: Coll. Comml. Arbitrators, Am. Bar Found.; mem.: ABA, Beverly Hills Bar Assn. (pres. 1982—83), Acad. TV Arts and Scis. (bd. govs. 1990—92), L.A. Copyright Soc. (pres. 1973—74), Los Angeles County Bar Assn. (trustee 1981—82), Calif. Bar Assn., Phi Beta Kappa. Alternative dispute resolution, Entertainment. Office: Arnold & Porter 1900 Ave Of Stars Ste 1700 Los Angeles CA 90067-4408

ROSENTHAL, WILLIAM J. lawyer; b. Balt., Nov. 4, 1920; s. Justin J. and Ray Marian (Stern) R.; m. Margaret Irwin Parker, July 4, 1956; children—Adriane Leigh, Jacqueline Rae, John Justin. AB, Johns Hopkins U., 1941; LL.B., U. Balt., 1950. Bar: Md. 1950. Adminstrv. asst. Office Price Adminstrn., Washington, 1941-42; assoc. firm Earle K. Shawe (name changed to Shawe & Rosenthal 1967), Balt., 1951-67; ptnr. Shawe & Rosenthal, Balt., 1967—. Lectr. U. Balt., 1952-56; mem. regional adv. council NLRB; vets. rep. Md. Constrn. Adv. Council, 1946-49; lectr. NYU Conf. Labor Relations, Boston U. Labor Law Seminar, 1985; expert witness on labor law, legis. and congl. coms. Contbg. author: The Developing Labor Law; contbr. articles to profl. jours. Served to lt. USNR, 1942-46, ETO. Mem. ABA, Md. Bar Assn., Balt. Bar Assn., Spiked Shoe Soc., Omicron Delta Kappa, Pi Delta Epsilon. Clubs: Suburban of Baltimore County (bd. govs., pres.). Labor (including EEOC, Fair Labor Standards Act, labor-management relations, NLRB, OSHA). Home: 8207 Cranwood Ct Baltimore MD 21208-1823 Office: Shawe & Rosenthal Sun Life Bldg Charles Center Baltimore MD 21201 E-mail: rosenthal@shawe.com.

ROSENZWEIG, CHARLES LEONARD, lawyer; b. N.Y.C., Apr. 12, 1952; s. William and Frieda (Dechner) R.; m. Rya R. Mehler, June 14, 1975; children: Jessica Sara, Erica Danielle. AB cum laude, Princeton U., 1974; JD, NYU, 1977. Bar: N.Y. 1978, U.S. Dist. Ct. (ea. and so. dists.) N.Y. 1978, U.S. Ct. Appeals (7th cir.) 1980, U.S. Ct. Internat. Trade 1981, U.S. Ct. Appeals (2d cir.) 1985. Assoc. Graubard, Moskovitz et al, N.Y.C., 1977-85; ptnr. Rand, Rosenzweig, Smith, Radley, Gordon & Burstein LLP, N.Y.C., 1987—. Mem. panel of neutrals comml. divsn. Supreme Ct. State N.Y. Editor NYU Jour. Internat. Law. and Politics. Chmn. of bd. Jewish Cmty. Ctr., Harrison, 1998-2000. Mem. ABA (internat. law sect.), N.Y. State Bar Assn. (co-chair internat. litigation com. 1995-98, mem. exec. com. comml. and fed. litigation sect.), Am. Arbitration Assn., NYU Alumni Assn. (chmn. jour. internat. law and politics alumni 1985-87), Assn. of Commercial Fin. Attys. Avocations: skiing, cycling, tennis, scuba diving. Federal civil litigation, Corporate, general, Private international. Office: Rand Rosenzweig et al 605 3rd Ave New York NY 10158-0180 Home: 9 Hadley Rd Armonk NY 10504-2417

ROSINEK, JEFFREY, judge; b. N.Y.C., Sept. 13, 1941; s. Isidore and Etta (Kramer) R.; m. Sandra Gwen Rosen, Aug. 7, 1977; 1 child, Ian David. BA in History, U. Miami, 1963; postgrad. in polit. sci., JD, 1974. Bar: Fla. 1974. Tchr. Coral Gables (Fla.) High Sch., 1963-78; sole practice Miami, 1974-76; assoc. Tendrich and Todd, Miami, 1976-77; ptnr. Todd, Rosinek & Blake, Miami, 1984-86; judge Dade County Ct., Miami, 1986-89, 11th Jud. Cir., Fla., 1990—, assoc. adminstr. appeal divsn., 1999—; judge Miami Dade County Drug Ct., 1999—. Instr. Boston U., 1975; mem. faculty Fla. Coll. Advanced Jud. Studies, 1992—, Nat. Jud. Coll., 2000—; lectr., presenter in field of juvenile justice and substance abuse. Contbr. articles to profl. jours. Chmn. Miami Environ. Rsch. Adv. Com., 1969-73; mem. Miami Beach Tranportation commn., Nat. Bicentennial Competiion on the Constitution and Bill of Rights com., Dade County Youth Adv. Bd., 1973-75; bd. dirs. U. Miami Law Sch., treas., 1973-75; bd. dirs. U. Miami Law Sch., treas. alumni, jud. dir.; past pres. Dade County Young Dems.; mem. Congl. Civilian Rev. Bd., 1975-90, chmn., 1976-78; bd. dirs., treas. fla. Congl. Com., Legal Svcs. Greater Miami; chmn., 1976-78; chmn. Dade County adv. Coun. Close-Up Found.; Fla. chmn. Project Concern Internat.; internat. state chmn. Fla. Walk for Mankind, Project Concern, legal adv. com., Kiwanis, 1982-86; v.p. Beth David Congregation, 1982-86; bd. trustees Haven Ctr.; bd. dirs., treas., organizer South Miami-Kendall pro bono project Legal Svc. of Greater Miami, 1983-86; traffic rev. com. Dade County, 1987-92; bd. dirs. Fla. Law Related Edn., 1988—, Adv. Program, 1988—; mem. Miami-Dade County task force for homeless, 1992-94; active Dade Coalition for the Homeless, 1992—, Dade County Homeless Trust, 1993-2001, 2003-, chmn. criminal justice com.; chmn. Beck Mus. Judaica, 1988—; ednl. dir. Tempel Judea; jud. cir. rep. Dept. corrections "Boot Camp" program, 1994-98; 11th jud. cir. organizer, rep. Homeless Alt. Rehab. Tracking Program, 1994—, rep. Comprehensive Homeless Integration Program (CHIP), 1992-94, chair Fla. 1st Annual Edn. Seminar/Retreat, 1995, Eugent P. Spellman Am. Inn of Ct., 1996—, bd. dirs., 2002--, South Fla. Super Bowl XXXIII Host Com.; 1st v.p. Coral Gables High Sch. Parent-Tchr.-Students Assn., 1995-96, pres., 1996-98; mem. adv. bd. Coconut Grove Art Festival, 2002—. Recipient award Jewish Theol. Sem., 1978, Outstanding Law Student award Merit award Profl. Law Enforcement Assn., appreciation award Liberty City Christian Assn., Dade County Chief of Police Svc. award, 2001. Mem.: ABA (task force reduction of litig. cost and delay 1995—), Fla. Assn. Drug Ct. Profls. (inaugural chair), Nat. Ct. Reporters Assn. (strategic com. 1993—), Am. Judges Assn. (bd. govs. 1988—92, domestic violence com. 1990—96, chair 32d Ann. Edn. Conf., Miami Beach 1992, sec. 1992—93, 2d v.p. 1993—94, 1st v.p. 1994—95, chair fed.-state rels. com. 1994—96, pres. 1996—97, exec. com. 1997, chair nominations com. 1997, coord. Close-UP Found. project 1997—, chair 38th Ann. Edn. Conf., Orlando 1998, edn. com. 1998—, exec. com. 2000—01, Image of Judiciary com.), Bar and Gavel Soc., Wig and Robe (chancellor 1973—74), Fla. Conf. Cir. Ct. Judges (criminal justice com. 1995—), Cuban Am. Bar Assn., Miami Beach Bar Assn. (bd. dirs.), Fla. Bar Assn. (rules com. family law sect. 1984—87, jud. nominating procedures com.), Coral Gables Bar Assn., South Miami-Kendall Bar Assn. (past pres.), Dade County Bar Assn. (criminal cts. com. 1994—), Greater Miami C. of C. (v.p. permanent housing 1996—98, pres. 1999—2000, Carrefour Housing Corp. for homeless), U. Miami Law Sch. Alumni Assn. (sec.-treas. 1985—87, jud. dir. 1987—), Chabad of Dade (bd. dirs. 1999—), Dade Ptnrs., Miami-Dade Lions Club (charter), Key Internat. (pres. 1980—81, 1994—95, sec. 1995—, counselor Fla. dist., Key of Honor 1979, honoree 1984), Biscayne Bay Kiwanis (pres. 1994—, disting. past pres., Major Emphasis chmn., lt. gov. Fla. Dist., Kiwanian of Yr. 1983—84), Kiwanis Internat. (life). Home: 535 Bird Rd Coral Gables FL 33146-1307 Office: 1351 NW 12th St Miami FL 33125-1644 E-mail: jefaroz@aol.com.

ROSNER, JONATHAN LEVI, lawyer; b. N.Y.C., Sept. 4, 1932; s. Oscar S. and Miriam (Reinhardt) R.; m. Lydia Sokol, Dec. 23, 1956; children: Beth, Marianne, Josh. BA, Wesleyan U., Middletown, Conn., 1954; JD, NYU, 1959. Bar: N.Y. 1959, U.S. Dist. Ct. (so. dist.) N.Y. 1962, U.S. Dist. Ct. (ea. dist.) N.Y. 1964, U.S. Ct. Appeals (2d cir.) 1964, U.S. Supreme Ct. 1964, U.S. Dist. Ct. Md. 1969, U.S. Dist. Ct. P.R. 1972, U.S. Ct. Appeals (D.C. cir.) 1976, U.S. Dist. Ct. (ea. dist.) Mich. 1984, U.S. Ct. Appeals (11th cir.) 1984. Law clk. to judge U.S. Dist. Ct. (so. dist.) N.Y., N.Y.C., 1959-60, asst. U.S. atty., 1960-63; ptnr. Rosner, Rosner & McEvoy, N.Y.C., 1963-79; pvt. practice N.Y.C., 1979-85; ptnr. Rosner & Murray, N.Y.C., 1985—. Adj. prof. law NYU, 1970-83, Pace U., White Plains, N.Y., 1984-86; chief counsel N.Y.C. Spl. Commn. on Power Failure, 1977, dep. commr., gen. counsel N.Y. State Commn. on Criminal Justice and Use of Force, 1985-87. Co-author: How to Prepare Witnesses for Trial, 1985, Cross-Examination of Witnesses, 1989, Impeachment of Witnesses, 1990. Bd. dirs. Westchester Jewish Community Services, 1970-73; trustee Woodlands Community Temple, 1971-76; mem. Wesleyan U. Alumni Assn. (adv. council 1972-79, schs. com. 1964-78, alumni fund class agt. 1954-2000). Mem. ABA, N.Y. State Bar Assn. (com. on grievances 1974-76), Assn. Bar of City of N.Y. (coms. on profl. discipline 1983-87, grievances 1970-74, entertainment 1964-68, 78-82, 93—, ABA-CLE panelist 1976-78), N.Y. County Lawyers Assn., NYU Law Alumni Assn. (bd. dirs. 1965-69, 84-88, 93—), N.Y. County Dist. Attys. Ann. Trial Advocacy Program (faculty 1978-2002). State civil litigation, Criminal, General civil litigation, Public international. Home: 10 Westhaven Ln White Plains NY 10605-5458 Office: Rosner & Murray 1140 Ave of the Ams New York NY 10036 E-mail: jlrosner@aol.com.

ROSNER, LEONARD ALLEN, lawyer; b. N.Y.C., Apr. 13, 1967; s. Arnold and Betty (Zimmerman) R.; m. Rachel Stein, Nov. 19, 1994; children: Andrew N., Leah Rose. AB in Polit. Sci., AB in Pub. Rels., Syracuse U., 1989, JD cum laude, 1992. Bar: N.Y. 1993. With Harter, Secrest & Emery LLP, Rochester, NY. Fin. editor Syracuse Jour. Internat. Law and Commerce, 1991-92. Assigned coun. Monroe County Assigned Coun., Rochester, 1993-94. Mem.: Monroe County Bar Assn., N.Y. Bar Assn. Avocations: golfing, reading, television sports, nautilus. Property, real (including real estate development, water), Landlord-tenant, General practice. Office: 1600 Bausch & Lomb Pl Rochester NY 14604-2711

ROSNER, SETH, lawyer, educator; b. N.Y.C., Jan. 6, 1931; s. Oscar S. and Miriam (Reinhardt) R.; m. Sara Jane Sheldon, Dec. 4, 1970 (div. Mar. 1978); m. Ann E. Del Toro, June 23, 1983; 1 child, Rachel Ferrer. AB, Wesleyan U., Middletown, Conn., 1952; JD, Columbia U., 1955; LLM in Comparative Law, NYU, 1960; postgrad., U. Paris, 1960-61. Bar: N.Y. 1955, U.S. Dist. Ct. (so. and ea. dists.) N.Y. 1956, U.S. Supreme Ct. 1967. Ptnr. Rosner & Rosner, N.Y.C., 1955-80; sr. ptnr. Marchi Jaffe Cohen Crystal Rosner & Katz, N.Y.C., 1981-88; pvt. practice N.Y.C., 1989-97, 2001—; counsel Jacobs Persinger & Parker, N.Y.C., 1997-2001. Adj. prof. NYU Sch. of Law, 1961—89. Trustee, v.p. exec. com. Fedn. Jewish Philanthropies, N.Y.C., 1977-86; pres., chmn. Jewish Home and Hosp. for Aged, N.Y.C., 1978-82; bd. trustees Wesleyan U. Middletown, Conn., 1982-86; bd. govs. Josephson Inst. of Ethics, Marina Del Rey, Calif., 1986-99, 2000—, chmn. bd., 2000-03; bd. dirs. Saratoga Automobile Mus., Saratoga Springs, N.Y., 1999—, N.Y. State Judicial Inst. on Professionalism in the Law, 2001-. Lt. USN, 1956-59. Fellow Am. Bar Found. (life); mem. ABA (chmn. gen. practice sect. 1980-81, ethics and profl. responsibility com. 1983-89, chmn. professionalism com. 1992-95, chmn. com. on scope, chmn. com. on lawyer competence 1995-97, bd. govs. 1997-2000, chmn. coord. counc. Ctr. Profl. Responsibility), Assn. Profl. Responsibility Lawyers (bd. dirs. 1990-96, pres.-elect 1993-94, pres. 1994-95), Assn. of Bar of City of N.Y. (ethics com. 1970-73), N.Y. State Bar Assn. (chmn. gen. practice sect. 1982-83). Avocations: writing, photography, Ferrari automobiles. Corporate, general, General practice, Professional liability. E-mail: sethrosner1@msn.com.

ROSOFF, WILLIAM A. lawyer, executive; b. Phila., June 21, 1943; s. Herbert and Estelle (Finkel) R.; m. Beverly Rae Rifkin, Feb. 7, 1970; children: Catherine D., Andrew M. BS with honors, Temple U., 1964; LLB magna cum laude, U. Pa., 1967. Bar: Pa. 1968, U.S. Dist. Ct. (ea. dist.) Pa. 1968. Law clk. U.S. Ct. Appeals (3d cir.), 1967-68; instr. U. Pa. Law Sch., Phila., 1968-69; assoc. Wolf, Block, Schorr & Solis-Cohen, Phila., 1969-75, ptnr., 1975-96, chmn. exec. com., 1987-88; also vice chmn. bd. dirs. Advanta Corp., Spring House, Pa., 1996—, pres., 1999—. Trustee RPS Realty Trust, 1990-96, Atlantic Realty Trust, 1996—; guest lectr. confs. and seminars on tax law; mem. tax adv. bd. Commerce Clearing House, 1983-94; mem. legal activities policy bd. Tax Analysts, 1978—; mem. Little, Brown Tax Adv. Bd., 1994-96; chmn. bd. dirs. RMH Telesvcs., Inc., 1997-99. Editor U. Pa. Law Rev., 1965-67; mem. bd. contbg. editors and advisors Jour. Partnership Taxation, 1983-2000; contbr. articles to profl. jours. Bd. dirs., past mem. com. on law and social action Phila. coun. Am. Jewish Congress. Fellow Am. Coll. Tax Counsel; mem. Am. Law Inst. (cons. taxation of partnerships 1976-78, assoc. reporter taxation of partnerships, 1978-82, mem. adv. group on fed. income tax project 1982-2000, cons. taxation of pass-through entities 1995-2000, past bd. dirs.), Order of Coif, Beta Gamma Sigma, Beta Alpha Psi. Corporate taxation, Personal income taxation. Office: Advanta Corp Welsh and McKean Rd Spring House PA 19477

ROSOW, STUART L. lawyer; b. N.Y.C., Mar. 28, 1950; s. Bernard and Lillian (Bonime) R.; m. Amy Berk Kuhn. AB cum laude, Yale U., 1972; JD cum laude, Harvard U., 1975. Law clk. to presiding justice U.S. Ct. Appeals (7th cir.), Chgo., 1975-76; assoc. Paul, Weiss et al, N.Y.C., 1976-79, Kaye, Scholer, Fierman, Hays & Handler, N.Y.C., 1979-84, ptnr., 1984-97, Proskauer Rose LLP, N.Y.C., 1997—. Adj. prof. Columbia Law Sch., N.Y.C., 1998—. Mem. ABA, N.Y. State Bar Assn., Assn. of Bar of City of N.Y. Corporate taxation, Personal income taxation. Office: Proskauer Rose LLP 1585 Broadway Fl 27 New York NY 10036-8299

ROSS, CHRISTOPHER T.W. lawyer; b. Denver, Oct. 19, 1925; s. Michael Peter and Martha (Stockhausen) R.; m. Luise Maria Reile, June 11, 1952 (div.); children: Mark Alexander, Katherine Luise, Sonya Catherine (dec.). LLB, U. Buffalo, 1950; JD, SUNY, Buffalo, 1968. Bar: N.Y. 1961, U.S. Dist. Ct. (we. dist.) N.Y. 1952, U.S. Ct. Mil. Appeals 1953, U.S. Supreme Ct. 1970, U.S. Ct. Appeals (2d cir.) 1971. Assoc. Lutwak, Parrino & Maurin, Buffalo, 1959-63; atty. pvt. practice, Buffalo, 1963—. Pres. N.Y. State Assn. Bds. Visitors Dept. Mental Hygiene, 1874-78; pres. West Seneca (N.Y.) Devle. Ctr., 1968-70, 72-74; trustee Buffalo Boy's & Girls Clubs. With USN, 1943-46, 52-59; comdr. USNR, ret.; capt. N.Y. NAval Militia, ret. Mem. N.Y. Bar Assn., N.Y. State Assn. Criminal Def. Lawyers, Erie County Bar Assn., Erie County Trial Lawyers Assn., Lawyer-Pilots Assn., Naval Res. Assn. (vp. legis., v.p. ret. persons), NAval order of U.S., U.S. Navy League, Royual Can. Mil. Inst. (bd. dirs. 1994-97, hon. officer, internat. affairs), Sovereign Mil. Order of Jerusalem, Naval Officers Assn. Can., Buffalo Athletic Club, Quiet Birdmen Club, Saints and Sinners Club, Silver Wings Club, Aero Club, Toronto Naval Club. Republican. Roman Catholic. Aviation, Criminal, Personal injury (including property damage). Office: Ste 233 2330 Maple Rd Williamsville NY 14221-4058 E-mail: ctwross@aol.com.

ROSS, DENNIS E. automotive executive; b. 1951; Bachelors, Law Degree, U. Mich. Tax legis. counsel, dep. asst. sec. Office Tax Policy U.S. Treasury Dept., 1986—89; tax ptnr. Davis Polk and Wardwell, NY, 1989—95; chief tax officer Ford Motor Co., Dearborn, Mich., 1995—2000, v.p., gen. counsel, 2000—. Office: Ford Motor 10th Fl Rm 1060a The American Rd Whq Dearborn MI 48121*

ROSS, DONALD ROE, federal judge; b. Orleans, Nebr., June 8, 1922; s. Roe M. and Leila H. (Reed) Ross; m. Janice S. Cook, Aug. 29, 1943; children: Susan Jane, Sharon Kay, Rebecca Lynn, Joan Christine, Donald Dean. JD, U. Nebr., 1948, LLD (hon.) , 1990. Bar: Nebr. 1948. Practice law, Lexington, Nebr., 1948—53; mayor City of Lexington, 1953; assoc. Swarr, May, Royce, Smith, Andersen & Ross, 1956—70; U.S. atty. Dist. Nebr., 1953—56; gen. counsel Rep. party, Nebr., 1956—58; mem. Rep. Exec. Com. for Nebr., 1952—53; com. mem. Rep. Nat. Com., 1958—70, vice-chmn., 1965—70; sr. judge U.S. Ct. Appeals (8th cir.), 1971—.

ROSS, DONALD HENRY, lawyer; b. Modesto, Calif., Oct. 14, 1923; s. Guy Walden Ross and Dolly Mae Brewer; m. Ruth Lorene Kitching, May 13, 1946; children: Genie Ann Kuehne, Robin Mae. BS in Indsl. Mgmt., U. So. Calif., 1953; MS in Internat. Affairs, George Washington U., 1965; JD, U. Pacific, 1982. Bar: (Nev.) 1982. Sgt. pilot RAF, 1941-42; commd. 2d. lt. USAF, 1942, advanced through grades to maj. gen., retired, 1974; atty. pvt. practice, Carson City, Nev., 1982—. Republican. Avocations: flying, old car restoration, shooting. Home and Office: 4350 Meadow Wood Rd Carson City NV 89703-9493

ROSS, DONALD RAE, judge; b. Henderson, Tex., Mar. 8, 1939; s. Monnie Manning Ross and Maud Gertrude Findley; m. Kaye Diane Owen, Aug. 3, 1968; children: John Ryan, Owen K. AA, Kilgore Coll., 1959; BA, Gaylor U., 1961; MA, Taylor U., 1963; JD, So. Meth. U., 1970. Bar: Tex. Instr. Kilgore (Tex.) Coll., 1965—67; county/dist. atty. Rusk County, Henderson, Tex., 1972—82; dist. judge 4th Dist. Tex., Henderson, 1982—96; justice 6th Ct. Appeals Tex., Texarkana, 1996—. Mem. Texarkana Civic Chorale, 2000—02; vol. Peace Corp, Thailand, 1963—65. Named Outstanding Alumnus, Henderson H.S., 1998, Outstanding Ex-student, Kilgore Coll., 2000; recipient Lifetime Achievement award, Rusk County Bar Assn., 1996. Mem.: Texarkana Kiwanis Club (bd. dirs. 2000—01), N.E. Tex. Bar Assn., Texarkana Bar Assn. (pres. 2002—). Democrat. Methodist. Avocation: shaped note a capella singing. Office: 6th Ct Appeals 100 N State Line Ave #20 Texarkana TX 75501

ROSS, HAROLD ANTHONY, lawyer; b. Kent, Ohio, June 2, 1931; s. Jules and Helen Assumpta (Ferrara) R.; m. Elaine Louise Hunt, July 1, 1961; children: Leslie Ann, Gregory Edward, Jonathan Harold. BA magna cum laude, Case Western Res. U., 1953; JD, Harvard U., 1956. Bar: Ohio 1956. Assoc. Marshman, Hornbeck, Hollington, Steadman & McLaughlin, Cleve., 1961-64; pres. Ross & Kraushaar Co., Cleve., 1964—. Gen. counsel Brotherhood of Locomotive Engrs., Cleve., 1966—; adv. bd. mem. Ctr. for Advanced Study of Law and Dispute Resolution Procedures, George Mason U. Sch. Law, 2000—. Trustee Citizens League Greater Cleve., 1969-75, 76-82, pres., 1981-82; active Charter Rev. Com. North Olmsted, 1970, 75. With AUS, 1956-58. Fellow Coll. Labor and Employment Lawyers; mem. ABA (co-chair rwy. and airline labor law sect. 1976-78), Ohio State Bar Assn., Cleve. Bar Assn., Phi Beta Kappa, Delta Sigma Rho, Omicron Delta Kappa. Roman Catholic. Labor (including EEOC, Fair Labor Standards Act, labor-management relations, NLRB, OSHA). Office: 1548 Standard Bldg 1370 Ontario St Cleveland OH 44113-1701

ROSS, HOWARD PHILIP, lawyer; b. May 10, 1939; s. Bernard and Estelle (Maremont) R.; m. Loretta Teresa Benquil, 1962 (div.); children: Glen Joseph, Cynthia Ann, Ryan Reeve; m. Jennifer Kay Shirley, 1984. BS, U. Ill., 1961; JD, Stetson Coll. Law, 1964. Bar: Fla. 1964, U.S. Ct. Appeals (5th cir.) 1965, U.S. Supreme Ct. 1969, U.S. Ct. Appeals (11th cir.) 1981; cert. civil trial lawyer, bus. litigator. Assoc. Parker & Battaglia and predecessor firm, St. Petersburg, Fla., 1964-67; ptnr. Battaglia, Ross, Dicus & Wein, P.A., St. Petersburg, 1967-87, 1987—, pres., CEO, 1992-99, chmn. bd. dirs., 2000—. Lectr. Stetson Coll. Law, St. Petersburg, 1971-72, adj. prof., 1987. Author: Florida Corporations, 1979; co-author: Managing Discovery in Commercial and Business Litigation, 1993; contbr. articles to profl. jours. Hon. chair St. Petersburg br. Awards Banquet NAACP, 1995; bd. dirs. St. Petersburg Neighborhood Housing Svcs., Inc., 1997, legal counsel, 1997—, pres., 2000—; bd. dirs. Cmty. Alliance, 1997—. Recipient Woman's Svc. League Best Groomed award, 1979, Fla. Bar Merit citation, 1974, Cmty. Svc. award, NAACP, 1998, Humanitarian award, YMCA of Tampa Bay, 1999, C.W. Bill Young Pinellas Pinnacle award, 2002. Mem. ABA, Fla. Bar Assn. (chmn. civil trial certification com. 1993-94), St. Petersburg Bar Assn., St. Petersburg Area C. of C. (bd. govs. 1990-95, 2000—, v.p. pub. affairs 1992-93, v.p. membership 1993-94, exec. com. 1992-95, counsel 1994-95, dean entrepreneurial acad. 1996—, treas. 2000-2002, chair-elect 2002-2003, chmn. 2003—, Mem. of Yr. 1993-94), Citizen Rev. Com. City of St. Petersburg (chmn. subcom. 1992-94, co-chair 1994-97). Republican. Jewish. General civil litigation, Commercial, contracts (including sales of goods; commercial financing), Corporate, general. Office: Battaglia Ross Dicus & Wein PA PO Box 41100 980 Tyrone Blvd N Saint Petersburg FL 33710-6382 E-mail: hross@brdwlaw.com.

ROSS, JAMES ULRIC, lawyer, accountant, educator; b. Del Rio, Tex., Sept. 14, 1941; s. Stephen Mabrey and Beatrice Jessie (Hyslop) R.; m. Janet S. Calabro, Dec. 28, 1986; children: James Ulric Jr., Ashley Meredith. BA, U. Tex., 1963, JD, 1965. Bar: Tex. 1965, U.S. Tax Ct. 1969; CPA, Tex. Estate tax examiner IRS, Houston, 1965-66; tax acct. Holmes, Raquet, Harris & Shaw, San Antonio, 1966-67; pvt. practice law and acctg. Del Rio and San Antonio, Tex., 1968—. Instr. St. Mary's U., San Antonio, 1973-75; assoc. prof. U. Tex., San Antonio, 1975-99, ret. Contbr. articles on U.S. and Internat. Estate Planning and Taxation to legal and profl. jours. Active Am. Cancer Soc., Residential Mgmt., Inc., Am. Heart Assn. Mem. ABA, Tex. Bar Assn., Tex. Soc. CPAs, San Antonio Bar Assn., San Antonio Estate Planners Coun. Probate (including wills, trusts), Corporate taxation, Personal income taxation. Home: 3047 Orchard Hl San Antonio TX 78230-3078 Office: 760 Tex Commerce Bank Bldg 7550 IH 10 W San Antonio TX 78229-5803

ROSS, JULIA, lawyer; 1 child, Jennifer. BA, San Francisco State Coll., 1964; MA, Calif. State U., 1971; MPH, U. Calif., Berkeley, 1972; JD, Golden Gate U., 1977. Bar: Calif. 1977, U.S. Dist. Ct. (no. dist.) Calif. 1977. Realtor Mason McDuffee, Berkeley, Calif., 1973-77; educator health Mission Mental Health Svcs., San Francisco, 1973; counselor, coord. teen clinics Planned Parenthood, San Francisco, 1969-71; judge pro tem Berkeley-Albany Mcpl. Ct., 1982—; atty. pvt. practice, Berkeley, 1977—. Contbr. articles to mags. Mem. Calif. State Bar Assn., Alameda County Bar Assn., Berkeley-Albany Bar Assn. (pres. 1991). Personal injury (including property damage), Probate (including wills, trusts), Property, real (including real estate development, water). Office: 1442 Walnut St # 301 Berkeley CA 94709-1405 E-mail: juliar@attylad.com.

ROSS, KENNETH L. lawyer; b. Orange, Tex., Dec. 2, 1944; s. Albert LeVergene Ross and Noreen Belle Welch; m. Lorinda Foltmer Ross, June 4, 1967 (div. 1976); 1 child, Ashley Nicole; m. Linda Cooper, May 27, 1978; children: Dixie Lee, Megan Mae. BA, Southeastern La. U., 1967; JD, La. State U., 1971. Bar: La. 1972, U.S. Dist. Ct. (ea. dist.) La. 1981, U.S. Supreme Ct. 1992, U.S. Dist. Ct. (mid. dist.) La. 1998. Ptnr. Seale Sledge & Ross, Hammond, La., 1972-79, Seale Macaluso Daigle & Ross, Hammond, 1979-96, Seale Daigle & Ross, Hammond, 1997—2002, Seale & Ross, Hammond, 2003—. Bd. dirs Ross & Wallace Paper Products, Inc., Hammond, One Mass. Ave. Corp., Washington; chmn. S.E. Region Airspace Conf. for Air Nat. Guard, Washington, 1996-98. Mem. Hammond Airport Bd., 1995; chmn. Leadership Tangipahoa, Hammond, 1996. Brig. gen. USAF Air Nat. Guard, 1969-98. Decorated DSM; recipient Leion of Merit State of La., 1998. Mem. Nat. Guard Assn. of the U.S. (exec. coun. 1992-2000, Disting. Svc. medal 1996, treas. 2000—), Nat. Guard Assn. of La. (pres. 1988), La. Dist. and State Bar Assn., La. Regional Airport Authority. Republican. Southern Baptist. Avocations: flying, boating, scuba diving. General civil litigation, Corporate, general, Probate (including wills, trusts). Home: 610 W Thomas St Hammond LA 70401-3164 Office: Seale & Ross PLC 200 N Cate St Hammond LA 70401-3301

ROSS, MARK SAMUEL, lawyer, educator, funeral director, writer; b. Newark, June 6, 1957; s. Herbert and Selma Ruth (Feldman) R.; m. Robin Liebman, May 19, 1984; children: Adam Micah, Danielle Leah. BA with honors, Rutgers U., 1979; JD, Benjamin Cardozo Law Sch., 1982; diploma, McAllister Inst. Funeral Svc., 1984. Bar: N.J. 1983, U.S. Dist. Ct. N.J. 1983, N.Y. 1989. V.p. Art/Craft Monuments-Shalom Memls., Union, N.J., 1980—; sec., treas., counsel Menorah Chapels at Millburn, Union, NJ, 1983—, funeral dir., 1984—; atty. pvt. practice, Union, N.J., 1983—. Counsel Com. for Consumer Protection, Union, 1985—; adj. prof. law Am. Acad.-McAllister Inst., N.Y.C., 1984-85; instr. Jewish law Emanu-El Religious Sch., Westfield, N.J., 1985. Author: (newspaper column) Through My Father's Eyes, 1995—. V.p. Temple Beth Am, Springfield, N.J., 1986-92, pres., 1992-94; counsel Found. Jewish Arts and Heritage, Inc., Union, 1986—. Named Man of Yr., Springfield B'nai B'rith, 1995, Temple Beth Ahm, Springfield, 2001; recipient Internat. Cmty. Svc. award, B'nai B'rith Internat., 1995. Mem. ABA, N.J. Bar Assn., Union County Bar Assn., B'nai B'rith (pres. 1980-83, Nat. Founders award 1982). Avocations: art, music, photography, golf. Administrative and regulatory, General practice, Probate (including wills, trusts). Office: 2950 Vauxhall Rd Vauxhall NJ 07088-1246 also: PO Box 641 Millburn NJ 07041-0641

ROSS, MATTHEW, lawyer; b. N.Y.C., Dec. 28, 1953; s. Harvey and Cecile (Shelsky) R.; m. Susan Ruth Goldfarb, Apr. 20, 1986; children: Melissa Danielle, Henry Max, Thomas Frank. BS in Econs., U. Pa., 1975; JD, U. Va., 1978. Bar: N.Y. 1979, U.S. Dist. Ct. (so. dist.) N.Y. 1979. Assoc. Cravath, Swaine & Moore, N.Y.C., 1978-84; prin., assoc. gen. counsel KPMG LLP, N.Y.C., 1984-90; prin., deputy gen. counsel Deloitte & Touche USA, LLP, N.Y.C, 1990—. Mem. ABA (corp. law sect.), N.Y. State Bar Assn. (corp. banking and bus. law sect.), Assn. of Bar of City of N.Y. (corp. law com.), Beta Gamma Sigma. Avocations: basketball, golf, tennis, skiing. Home: 5 Barker Ln Scarsdale NY 10583-7507 Office: Deloitte & Touche USA LLP 1633 Broadway New York NY 10019-6708

ROSS, MICHAEL AARON, lawyer; b. Newark, N.J., Sept. 15, 1941; s. Alexander Ash and Matilda (Blumenthal) R.; m. Leslie Gordon, June 26, 1976; children— Christopher Gordon, Alan Gordon. BA, Franklin and Marshall Coll., 1963; JD, Columbia U., 1966; MS in Econs., U. London, 1967. Bar: N.Y. 1968. Assoc., then ptnr. Shearman & Sterling, N.Y.C., 1967-93; dep. gen. counsel Citigroup, N.Y.C., 1993—2001; gen. counsel Citigroup Internat., 2002. Mem. ABA, Am. Law Inst., New York County Lawyers Assn., Assn. of Bar of City of N.Y., University Club. Banking, Finance. Office: Citigroup 399 Park Ave 10th Flr New York NY 10043-0001

ROSS, RICHARD C. lawyer; b. N.Y.C., May 5, 1927; s. Louis H. and Mollie S. (Silverman) Rosoff; m. Joan A. Flug, Sept. 7, 1952; children: Marcia S., William N., Andrew D. BA, NYU, 1949, LLB, 1950, LLM, 1953. Bar: N.Y. 1950, U.S. Dist. Ct. (so. dist.) N.Y., U.S Supreme Ct. Assoc. Engleman & Hart, N.Y.C., 1950, Leon London, Esq., N.Y.C., 1952-53; pvt. practice Mt. Vernon, N.Y., 1953—. Supr. Westchester County, White Plains, N.Y., 1964-65; city councilman Mt. Vernon, N.Y., 1966-72; assemblyman N.Y. State Assembly, 1973-80; active B'nai B'rith. With USN, 1945-46. Mem. Elks, Lions, Masons. Republican. Jewish. Estate planning, Family and matrimonial, Property, real (including real estate development, water). Home: 24 Palmer Ave Mount Vernon NY 10552-1217 Office: 22 W 1st St Mount Vernon NY 10550-3000

ROSS, ROBERT DWAIN, lawyer; b. Hope, Ark., Dec. 3, 1932; s. George Raymond and Alma Lillian (Putman) R.; m. Frances Roots Mitchell, June 15, 1963; children: Robert Mitchell, Virginia Frances, Mary Starr. Student So. State Coll., 1951-53; BSL, U. Ark., 1962, JD, 1962. Bar: Ark. 1961, U.S. Dist. Ct. (ea. dist.) Ark. 1962, U.S. Supreme Ct. 1966. Law clk. Ark. Supreme Ct., 1961-62, 63; assoc. Pope, Shamburger, Buffalo & Ross, Little Rock, 1963-65, ptnr., 1965-94, sr. mem. Pope, Ross, Dendy & Cazort, PLC, 1994—; sec., exec. dir. Ark. Constl. Conv., 1980. Bd. dirs. Elizabeth Mitchell Children's Ctr. (now Ctrs. for Youth and Families, Inc.), 1972-78, 83-96, treas., 1974, pres., 1978, 84-85, v.p. and treas., 1983; bd. dirs. Quapaw Quarter Assn., 1977-80, pres., 1979. Served with U.S. Army, 1956-58. Recipient Disting. Svc. award Mental Health Coun. Ark., 1993. Fellow Ark. Bar Found. (bd. dirs. 1982-85); mem. ABA, Ark. Bar Assn. (sec.-treas. 1969-72, ho. of dels. 1973-76, 78-81, mem. exec. coun. 1973, 75-78, chmn. 1981-82, chmn. judicial nominations com. 1989-94, mem. jud. nominations health law and web oversite coms.), Pulaski County Bar Assn. (dir. 1978-79). Democrat. Episcopalian. Commercial, contracts (including sales of goods; commercial financing), Insurance, Labor (including EEOC, Fair Labor Standards Act, labor-management relations, NLRB, OSHA). Office: Ste 210 620 W 3rd St Little Rock AR 72201-2223

ROSS, STANFORD G. lawyer, government official; b. St. Louis, Oct. 9, 1931; m. Dorothy Rabin, June 9, 1958; children: John, Ellen. AB with honors, Washington U., 1953; JD magna cum laude, Harvard U., 1956. Bar: D.C. 1969, Calif. 1956, N.Y. 1959. Assoc. Irell & Manella, L.A., 1956-57; tchg. fellow, rsch. asst. Harvard Law Sch., 1957-58; assoc. Dewey, Ballantine, Bushby, Palmer & Wood, N.Y.C., 1958-61; asst. tax legis. counsel U.S. Dept. Treasury, 1961-63; prof. law N.Y. U., 1963-67; White House staff asst. to Pres. Johnson, 1967-68; gen. counsel U.S. Dept. Transp., 1968-69; ptnr. Caplin & Drysdale, Washington, 1969-78; commr. Social Security Adminstrn., Washington, 1978-79; ptnr. Califano, Ross & Heineman, Washington, 1980-82, Arnold & Porter, Washington, 1983—2002. Pub. trustee Social Security Trust Funds, Washington, 1990-95; chmn. Social Security Adv. Bd., 1997-2002. Editor: Harvard Law Rev, 1954-56. Mem. ABA, Fed. Bar Assn., Internat. Fiscal Assn., Nat. Acad. Social Ins. Administrative and regulatory, Private international, Taxation, general. Office: Arnold & Porter 555 12th St NW Washington DC 20004-1206

ROSS, WAYNE ANTHONY, lawyer; b. Milw., Feb. 25, 1943; s. Ray E. and Lillian (Steiner) R.; m. Barbara L. Ross, June 22, 1968; children: Gregory, Brian, Timothy, Amy. BA, Marquette U., 1965, JD, 1968. Bar: Wis. 1968, Alaska 1969. Asst. atty. gen. State Alaska, 1968-69; trustee, standing master Superior Ct. Alaska, 1969-73; assoc. Edward J. Reasor & Assocs., Anchorage, 1973-77; prin. Wayne Anthony Ross & Assocs., Anchorage, 1977-83; ptnr. Ross, Gingras & Frenz, Anchorage and Cordova, Alaska, 1983-84, Ross & Gingras, Anchorage and Cordova, 1985; pres. Ross, Gingras and Miner, P.C., Anchorage, 1986-93, Ross and Miner, P.C., Anchorage, 1993—. Col. area def. counsel Alaska State Def. Force; pres. Tyone Mountain Syndicate, Inc. Alaska Rep. Nat. Committeeman, 1992-98; Republican candidate for Gov. of Alaska, 1998, 2002. Decorated knight comdr. Order of Polonia Resituta (Poland), knight Equestrian Order of the Holy Sepulchure of Jerusalem (Vatican). Mem. NRA (bd. dirs. 1980-92, 94—, benefactor), Alaska Bar Assn. (Stanley award), Anchorage Bar Assn., Alaska Gun Collectors Assn. (pres. emeritus), Ohio Gun Colllectors Assn. (hon. life), Smith and Wesson Collectors Assn., 49th Territorial Guard Regiment (pres. 1987-94, 95-96), Alaska Territorial Cavalry (sec. 1991-97, 2001—), Mil. Vehicle Preservation Assn. (v.p. 1994-96), Alaska Peace Officers Assn. Roman Catholic. Criminal, Family and matrimonial, Personal injury (including property damage). Home: PO Box 101522 Anchorage AK 99510-1522 Office: Ross & Miner 327 E Fireweed Ln Ste 201 Anchorage AK 99503-2110 E-mail: waralaska@alaska.com.

ROSS, WILLIAM JARBOE, lawyer, director; b. Oklahoma City, May 9, 1930; s. Walter John and Bertha (Jarboe) R.; m. Mary Lillian Ryan, May 19, 1962; children: Rebecca Anne Roten, Robert Joseph, Molly Kathleen. BBA, U. Okla., 1952, LLB, 1954. Bar: Okla. 1954. Since practiced in, Oklahoma City; asst. municipal counselor Oklahoma City, 1955-60; mem. firm Rainey, Ross, Rice & Binns, 1960—, ptnr., 1965-99, of counsel, 2000—. Mem. admissions and grievences com. U.S. Dist. Ct. (we. dist.) Okla. Bd. visitors Coll. of Law U. Okla., St. Anthony's Hosp. Found., Harn Homestead; dir. Ethics and Excellence in Journalism Found., Inasmuch Found. Mem. Okla. Bar Assn., Okla. Heritage Assn. (vice chmn. edn. com.), The Newcomen Soc., Okla. City Golf and Country Club, Econ. Club, Rotary, Phi Alpha Delta, Beta Theta Pi, KC. Estate planning, General practice, Probate (including wills, trusts). Home: 6923 Avondale Ct Oklahoma City OK 73116-5008

ROSS, WILLIAM ROBERT, lawyer; b. Sundance, Wyo., Aug. 10, 1929; s. James Thomas and Kathryn Melvina (Ormsby) R.; m. Dorothy Evelyn Spencer, Mar. 19, 1951 (dec. July 1980); children: James Bradley, Keith Spencer, Rebecca Ann Ross Duncan; m. Kathleen Riggin Worthington, July 30, 1983. BS in Law, U. Nebr., 1958; LLB, U. Md., 1958. Bar: Wyo. 1958, Colo. 1967. Atty., spl. asst. to solicitor U.S. Dept. of Interior, Washington, 1958-61; atty. Am. Sugar Co., N.Y.C., 1961-64; internat. counsel Gates Rubber Co., Denver, 1964-69; pres. Wexco Internat. Corp., Denver, 1969-70; atty., shareholder Lohf & Barnhill, PC, Denver, 1970-87; pres., shareholder Lohf, Shaiman & Ross, PC, Denver, 1987-93; pvt. practice Littleton, Colo., 1993—. Instr. Law Sch., U. Denver, 1967-73, instr. Bus. Sch., 1970-72. Contbr. articles to profl. law jours. Founding dir., exec. com. World Trade Ctr., Denver, 1989-94. With USAF, 1950-54. Mem. Wyo. State Bar, Colo. Bar Assn., Denver Bar Assn. Corporate, general, General practice, Mergers and acquisitions. Office: 9425 S Desert Willow Way Littleton CO 80129-5744 E-mail: wrross@pcisys.net.

ROSS, WILLIAM WARFIELD, lawyer; b. Washington, Oct. 3, 1926; s. W. Warfield and Vera Elfleda (Payne) R.; m. Jennie Fitch, Jan. 30, 1963; children— James, Mary, Billy; m. Nan Robertson, Sept. 25, 1999. AB, St. John's Coll., Annapolis, Md., 1948; LL.B., Yale U., 1951. Bar: D.C. 1951. Legal asst. Exec. Office Pres. Harry S. Truman, 1952-53, Pres. Dwight D. Eisenhower, 1953; atty. appellate sect. civil div. Dept. Justice, Washington, 1954-57; asst. to solicitor FPC, Washington, 1957-59; ptnr. Wald, Harkrader & Ross, Washington, 1963-87, Pepper, Hamilton & Scheetz, Washington, 1987-91. Adj. prof. Cornell U. Grad. Sch. Bus. and Pub. Adminstrn., 1977-80; chmn. D.C. Council Commn. on Bd. Appeals and Rev. of D.C. Govt., 1972 Chmn. Nat. Capital area ACLU, 1966-68; chmn. audit hearing panel Title I ESEA of 1965, 1976-80. Served with USN, 1945-46 Mem. ABA (chmn. sect. adminstrv. law 1978-79), Bar Assn. D.C. (chmn. adminstrv. law sect. 1968-69, gov. 1969-70), D.C. Bar, Fed. Bar Assn., Fed. Energy Bar Assn. (contbr. articles to jour.). Administrative and regulatory, Antitrust, Utilities, public. Home: 4978 Sentinel Dr Apt 303 Bethesda MD 20816-3573

ROSSEEL-JONES, MARY LOUISE, lawyer; b. Detroit, Apr. 19, 1951; d. Rene Octave and Marie Ann (Metcko) Rosseel; m. Mark Christopher Jones, Mar. 16, 1984; 1 child, Kathleen Marie. BA in French with honors, U. Mich., 1973, MA in French, 1976; JD, U. Detroit, 1981. Bar: Mich. 1982, U.S. Ct. Appeals (6th cir.) 1982, U.S. Dist Ct. (ea. dist.) Mich. 1982, U.S. Dist. Ct. (we. dist.) Mich. 1983. Tchg. fellow Wayne State U., Detroit, 1973—74; teaching asst. French U. Mich., Ann Arbor, 1974-76; law clk. Johnson, Auld & Valentine, Detroit, 1979-80; assoc. Monaghan, Campbell et al, Bloomfield Hills, Mich., 1981-82; lectr. law U. Clermont, Clermont-Ferrand, France, 1981-82; staff atty. Mich. Nat. Corp., Bloomfield Hills, 1983-85; litigation atty. Am. Motors Corp., Southfield, Mich., 1985-87; staff counsel Chrysler Corp., Auburn Hills, Mich., 1987-98; freelance designer, pvt. lang. and piano tutor, editor, writer; pvt. law counselor, 1998—; jr. h.s. homesch. tchr., 2002—. Editor: sequel One Life to Give. Recipient Mich. Competitive scholarship, 1969-70, Julia Emanuel scholarship, 1974-75, Henderson House scholarship, 1973; Wayne State U. fellow, 1973-74, U. Mich. fellow, 1974-76, U. Detroit fellow, 1981-82. Republican. Roman Catholic. Avocations: classical pianist, interior design. Corporate, general, Public international, Product liability.

ROSSEN, JORDAN, lawyer; b. Detroit, June 13, 1934; s. Nathan Paul and Rebecca (Rizy) R.; m. Susan Friebert, Mar. 24, 1963 (div. June 1972); 1 child, Rebecca; m. M. Elizabeth Bunn, Jan. 3, 1981; children— N. Paul, Jordan David. BA, U. Mich., 1956; JD, Harvard U., 1959. Bar: Mich. 1960, N.Y. 1998, U.S. Dist. Ct. (ea. dist.) Mich. 1960, U.S. Ct. Appeals (6th cir.) 1966, U.S. Supreme Ct. 1966, U.S. Ct. Appeals (7th cir.) 1974, U.S. Ct. Appeals (D.C. cir.) 1984, U.S. Ct. Appeals (3rd cir.) 1987, U.S. Dist. Ct. (ea. and so. dists.) N.Y. 1999. Assoc. Sullivan, Elmer, Eames & Moody, Detroit, 1960-62; assoc. Sugar & Schwartz, Detroit, 1962-64; asst. gen. counsel UAW, Detroit, 1964-74, assoc. gen. counsel, 1974-83, gen. counsel, 1983-98; of counsel Meyer, Suozzi, English and Klein, N.Y.C., N.Y., 1998—; prof. labor studies Wayne State U., 2000—. Vice pres. N.P. Rossen Agy., Inc., Detroit, 1960-83; gen. counsel Mich. Health & Social Security Research Inst., Inc., Detroit, 1965-83; dir. UAW Job Devel. & Tng. Corp., Detroit, 1984-90. Editor: Mich. Bar Labor Section Publication, 1961-64. Contbr. articles to profl. jours. Pres. Young Democrats, Mich., 1963-65; chmn. Americans for Democratic Action, Mich., 1966-68; chmn. Voter Registration Dem. Party, Mich., 1967. Recipient Human Rights award, City of Detroit, 1978. Mem.: Fed. Bar Assn., N.Y. Bar Assn., Mich. Bar Assn. Jewish. Administrative and regulatory, Civil rights, Labor (including EEOC, Fair Labor Standards Act, labor-management relations, NLRB, OSHA). Office: 1350 Broadway Ste 501 New York NY 10018-7705 Fax: 212-239-1311. E-mail: jrossen@msek.com.

ROSSI, CARLOS ALBERTO DE SOUZA, lawyer; b. São Paulo, Brazil, Apr. 19, 1942; s. Eduardo Garcia and Maria Stella (Galvão Souza) Rossi; m. Vera Regina Pachelo Borges, June 14, 1966; children: Felide de Souza Rossi, Fernando de Souza Rossi. Law Degree, IUC, São Paulo; LLM, So. Meth. U. Bar: Brazil, Portuguese. Assoc. Baker & McKenzie, São Paulo, 1967—72, ptnr., 1972—90, chmn., 1990—. Officer Comml. Assn., São Paulo, 1978. Mem.: Brazil-Can. C. of C. (legal com.), Brasil-Am. C. of C. (legal com.). Mergers and acquisitions, Corporate taxation, Corporate, general. Office: Baker & McKenzie Av Dr Chucri Zaidan 920-13 04583-904 São Paulo Brazil

ROSSI, DEAN CHRISTOPHER, lawyer; b. San Mateo, Calif., Mar. 26, 1969; s. Ronald Raymond and Dawne Diane Rossi. BA in Philosophy, U. San Diego, 1991; JD, Whittier U., 1997. Bar: Calif. 1997. Assoc. Cotchett, Pitre & Simon, Burlingame, Calif., 1997—2000, Liccardo, Rossi, Sturges and McNeil, San Jose, Calif., 2000—01, Rossi, Hamerslough, Reischl and Chuck, San Jose, 2001—. Named one of San Jose's Top Lawyers, San Jose Mag., 2001—02. Mem.: ABA (co-chair 2000—), Santa Clara County Trial Lawyers Assn. (v.p. elect 2001—). Avocations: running, skiing, bicycling. Property, real (including real estate development, water). Office: Rossi Hamerslough Reischl & Chuck Ste 200 1960 The Alameda San Jose CA 95126

ROSSI, FAUST F. lawyer, educator; b. 1932; BA, U. Tornoto, 1953; JD, Cornell U., 1960. Bar: N.Y. 1960. Tax trialy atty. Dept. Justice, Washington, 1960-61; sole practice Rochester, N.Y., 1961-66; assoc. prof. Cornell U., Ithaca, N.Y., 1966-69, prof., 1970—, assoc. dean, 1973-75, Samuel S. Leibowitz prof. trial techniques, 1982—. Vis. prof. Emory U., 1990; cons. report of fed. class actions Am. Coll. of Trial Lawyers, 1971-72; cons. com. on proposed fed. rules of evidence N.Y. Trial Lawyers Assn., 1970; cons., instr. annual seminar N.Y. State Trial Judges, 1970-78; cons., instr. Nat. Inst. for Trial Advocacy, 1974-75, 80-84, 88; cons. N.Y. Law Revision Commn. Project for N.Y. Code of Evidence, 1978-80. Author: Study of the Proposed Federal Rules of Evidence, 1979, Report on Rule 23 Class Actions, 1972, The Federal Rules of Evidence, 1970, Expert Witnesses, 1991; co-author: New York Evidence, 1997; contbr. articles to profl. jours. Lt. j.g. USN. Recipient Jacobsen prize for tchg. trail advocacy, 1992. Mem. Order of Coif. Office: Cornell U Law Sch Myron Taylor Hall Ithaca NY 14853 E-mail: ffr1@cornell.edu.

ROSSI, WILLIAM MATTHEW, lawyer; b. Coldwater, Ohio, June 11, 1954; s. Hugh Dominic and Patricia Jean (Putts) R.; m. Constance Sue Streacker, July 21, 1973; children: Bryan Thomas, Lauren Michelle, Alexandria Marie. BA cum laude, Miami U., Oxford, Ohio, 1977; JD magna cum laude, U. Dayton, 1981. Bar: Ohio 1981, U.S. Dist. Ct. (so. dist.) Ohio 1982, U.S. Supreme Ct. 1986, U.S. Ct. Appeals (6th cir.) 1987, Fla. 1991, U.S. Dist. Ct. (so. and mid. dists.) Fla. 1992, U.S. Ct. Appeals (11th cir.) 1992. Assoc. Milliken & Fitton, Hamilton, Ohio, 1981-83; dep. law dir., chief city negotiator City of Middletown, Ohio, 1984-89; pvt. practice, 1989-92; assoc. Jackson, Lewis, Schnitzler and Krupman, Orlando, Fla., 1992-93; dep. county atty. Sarasota County, Fla., 1993—. Bd. dirs. Columbia Inst. Bus., Middletown, 1977-78; lectr. Sawyer Coll., Dayton, 1982-83; small claims referee, 1984-92. Asst. coach Knothole Baseball, Middletown, 1981; bd. dirs. Butler County Mental Health Ctr., Hamilton, 1983-85, Summer Youth Theatre, Middletown, 1985-86; mem. bd. rev. Troop 20 Boy Scouts Am., 1986-87; mem. Sch. Adv. Coun., 1996—; mem. adv. bd. St. Joseph's Coll.; chmn. allocations panel United Way, 2001—. Recipient Am. Jurisprudence award Lawyers Coop. Pub. Co., 1979, 81, Internat. Youth Achievement award Internat. Biog. Ctr. and Am. Biog. Inst., 1982. Mem. ABA, Fla. Bar Assn. (co-chmn. labor rels. com. 2002), Nat. Pub. Employer Labor Rels. Assn., Phi Beta Kappa, Phi Delta Phi (bd. dirs., historian 1979-80). Republican. Roman Catholic. Avocations: golf, travel, writing. State civil litigation, Labor (including EEOC, Fair Labor Standards Act, labor-management relations, NLRB, OSHA). Home: 6215 Aventura Dr Sarasota FL 34241-9448

ROSSKOPF, GABRIELE, lawyer; b. Marbach, Germany, Mar. 19, 1969; 1st state examination, U. Tübingen, Germany, 1993; Doctorate, U. Tübingen, 1999; 2nd state examination, Dist. Ct. Tübingen, 1995; LLM, King's Coll., London, 1996. Bar: Germany 1998. Assoc. Gleiss Lutz, Stuttgart, Germany, 1998—2000, ptnr., 2001—. Office: Gleiss Lutz Maybachstr 6 70469 Stuttgart Germany

ROSSMANN, ANTONIO, lawyer, educator; b. San Francisco, Apr. 25, 1941; s. Herbert Edward and Yolanda (Sonsini) R.; m. Kathryn A. Burns, Oct. 6, 1991; children: Alice Sonsini, Maria McHale. Grad., Harvard Coll., 1963, JD, 1971. Bar: Calif. 1972, D.C. 1979, N.Y. 1980, U.S. Supreme Ct. 1980. Law clk. to Justice Mathew Tobriner Calif. Supreme Ct., 1971-72; assoc. Tuttle & Taylor, L.A., 1972-75; pub. advisor Calif. Energy Commn., 1975-76; sole practice San Francisco, 1976-82, 85—; exec. dir. Nat. Ctr. for Preservation Law, 1979-80; mem. McCutchen, Doyle, Brown & Enersen, San Francisco, 1982—85. Adj. prof. law Hastings Coll. Law, 1981-84; vis. prof. UCLA Sch. Law, 1985-87; Fulbright lectr. U. Tokyo, 1987-88; adj. prof. Stanford Law Sch., 1989-90, U. Calif. Sch. Law, Boalt Hall, 1991—. Editor Harvard Law Rev., 1969-71; contbr. articles to legal jours. Bd. dirs. Planning and Conservation League, 1984—, Calif. Water Protection Coun., 1982-83, San Francisco Marathon, 1982-90; pres. Western State Endurance Run, 1991-96, counselor, 1996—; pres., bd. dirs. Toward Utility Rate Normalization, 1976-79. Served to lt. comdr. USN, 1963-68. Mem. Calif. State Bar (chmn. com. on environment 1978-82), U.S. Rowing Assn., U.S. Soccer Fedn. (state referee) L.A. Athletic Club, Harvard Club (San Francisco, N.Y.C.), Harvard Law Sch. Assn. No. Calif. (pres. 1997-2002). Constitutional, Environmental, Land use and zoning (including planning). Office: 380 Hayes St San Francisco CA 94102-4421 E-mail: ar@landwater.com.

ROSSTON, RICHARD MARK, lawyer; b. San Francisco, June 29, 1951; s. Edward William and Maxine G. (Aaron) R.; children: Ryan, Matthew, Jean. BA, Dartmouth Coll., 1973; JD, U. Calif., Berkeley, 1977. Bar: Calif. 1977, Alaska 1978. Shareholder Guess & Rudd, Anchorage, 1977—98; mem. Bogle & Gates, PLLC, Anchorage, 1998—99; ptnr. Dorsey & Whitney, LLP, Anchorage, 1999—. Mem.: ABA, Alaska Bar Assn., Calif. Bar Assn. Corporate, general, Finance, Property, real (including real estate development, water). Office: Dorsey & Whitney LLP 1031 w 4TH Ave # 600 Anchorage AK 99501-1964

ROSZKOWSKI, JOSEPH JOHN, lawyer; b. Pawtucket, R.I., Aug. 11, 1938; s. Joseph J. and Anna T. Roszkowski; m. Geraldine J. Szpila, July 2, 1966. BA, Alliance Coll., 1960; JD, Marquette U., 1964. Bar: Wis. 1964, U.S. Dist. Ct. (ea. dist.) Wis. 1964, R.I. 1965. Ptnr. Zimmerman, Roszkowski & Brenner, Woonsocket, R.I., 1965—. Corporator Fogarty Hosp., North Smithfield, RI, 1976—88; counsel Landmark Med. Ctr., 1989—90. Mem. Nat. Ski Patrol, RI, 1974—83; legal counsel R.I. Tuna Tournament, 1975—; bd. dirs. R.I. Legal Svcs., Providence, 1974—87, Legal Aid Soc., Providence, 1985—. Mem. ABA (ho. of dels. 1996-2003, state del. 2000-2001, 2003—, bd. govs. 2001, 2002, commr. Interest on Lawyers' Trust Accounts 1986-90, 2002—), R.I. Bar Found. (pres. 1990-95), R.I. Bar Assn. (pres. 1985-86), Am. Law Inst., Am. Judicature Soc., Fed. Tax Inst. New England (adv. com. 1985-86), R.I. Med. Examiners, U.S. Jaycees (nat. dir. 1968), Am. Acad. Hosp. Attys. Lodges: Rotary (pres. Cumberland, R.I. 1987). Avocations: skiing, sailing, gardening, tennis. Probate (including wills, trusts), Property, real (including real estate development, water). Home: 1o Little St Cumberland RI 02864-1101 Office: Zimmerman Roszkowski & Brenner 1625 Diamond Hill Rd Woonsocket RI 02895-1541 E-mail: jroskow@aol.com.

ROSZKOWSKI, STANLEY JULIAN, retired federal judge; b. Boonville, N.Y., Jan. 27, 1923; s. Joseph and Anna (Christkowski) R.; m. Catherine Mary Claeys, June 19, 1948; children: Mark, Gregory, Dan, John. BS, U. Ill., 1949, JD, 1954. Bar: Ill. 1954. Sales mgr. Warren Petroleum Co., Rockford, Ill., 1954; ptnr. Roszkowski, Paddock, McGreevy & Johnson, Rockford, 1955-77; judge U.S. Dist. Ct. (we. dist.), Rockford, Ill., 1977-98; pres. First State Bank, Rockford, 1963-75, chmn. bd., 1977—; mediator-arbitrator JAMS/ENDISPUTE, Chgo., 1998—. Chmn. Fire and Police Commn., Rockford, 1967-74, commr., 1974— ; chmn. Paul Simon Com., 1972; active Adlai Stevenson III campaign, 1968-71, Winnebago County Citizens for John F. Kennedy, 1962, Winnebago County Dem. Cen. Com., 1962-64; bd. dirs. Sch. of Hope, 1960— ; mem. Ill. Capital Devel. Bd., 1974— . With USAAF, 1943-45. Decorated Air medal with 2 oak leaf clusters.; recipient Pulaski Nat. Heritage award Polish Am. Congress, Chgo., 1982 Mem. ABA, Ill. Bar Assn., Fla. Bar Assn., Winnebago County Bar Assn., Am. Coll. Trial Lawyers, Am. Judicature Soc., Assn. Trial Lawyers Am., Ill. Trial Lawyers Assns., Am. Arbitration Assn. (arbitrator), Fed. Judges Assn. (bd. dirs. 1988—).

ROTCH, JAMES E. lawyer; b. Auburn, Ala., Mar. 26, 1945; s. Elroy B. and Martha (Ellisor) R.; m. Darlene Edwards; children: Jamison B., Susannah R., Amie L. Vaughn. BS, Auburn U., 1967, postgrad., 1967-68; JD, U. Va., 1971. Bar: Ala. 1971, U.S. Dist. Ct. (no. dist.) Ala. 1973. Rsch. asst. Office Instl. Rsch. Auburn (Ala.) U., 1967-68; clk. U.S. Judiciary System, Birmingham, Ala., 1971-72; assoc. Bradley Arant Rose & White LLP, Birmingham, 1971-76; ptnr. Bradley, Arant, Rose & White LLP, Birmingham, 1976—, administrv. ptnr., 1990-93. Mem. adv. com. Bioelastics Rsch. Ltd., Birmingham, 1992—, Gov.'s Task Force on Biotechnology, Ala., 1993. Author: The Birmingham Pledge. Pres. adv. com. Birmingham

Mus. Art, 1989-92; bd. dirs. Operation New Birmingham, 1990-91, 95—, co-chmn. cmty. affairs com., mem. exec. com.; Coalition for Better Edn., Birmingham, 1990—; active Boy Scouts Am.; bd. dirs. Birmingham Com. for Olympic Soccer, 1994-96, Ala. Sports Found., 1994-98, Entrepreneurial Ctr. Inc., 1996—, chmn., 2002; mem. adminstrv. bd. Canterbury United Meth. Ch., 1991-93; chmn. Birmingham Pledge Found., 2000—. Capt. USAR, 1972-78. Mem. ALA, Auburn U. Bar Assn., Birmingham Bar Assn., Internat. Bar Assn., Ala. State Bar Assn., Leadership Birmingham, Leadership Ala. (bd. dirs. 1998--), , Auburn Coll. Liberal Arts (adv. coun.), U. Va. Alumni Assn., Newcomen Soc., Birmingham Area C. of C. (bd. dirs. 2001, vice chmn. for tech. devel. 2002), Auburn U. Alumni Assn., Birmingham Venture Club (bd. dirs. 2001), Country Club of Birmingham, Jockey Club, Summit Club (charter), Kiwanis (sec. 1998-99). Methodist. Avocations: horses, bird hunting, cattle farming, golf. Corporate, general, Mergers and acquisitions, Securities. Office: Bradley Arant Rose & White LLP One Federal Pl 1819 5th Ave N Birmingham AL 35203

ROTCHFORD, PATRICIA KATHLEEN, lawyer, mediator; b. Chgo., Nov. 17, 1945; d. Charles E. Sr. and Mary (Rodde) R.; 1 child, John. BA with honors, Rosary Coll., River Forest, Ill., 1966; JD, No. Ill. U., 1979. Bar: Ill. 1979; cert. mediator/arbitrator, Mich., Ill. Tchr. pub. schs., Schiller Park, Ill., 1966-76; sole practice Elmhurst, Ill., 1977-79; assoc. Shand, Morahan, Evanston, Ill., 1979-83; corp. counsel CNA Fin., Chgo., 1983-86; gen. counsel, v.p. and corp. sec. MMI Cos., Bannockburn, Ill., 1986-87; gen. counsel, v.p., corp. sec. Inland Group, Northbrook, Ill., 1987-90; pvt. practice fin. and ins. legal counsel, Northbrook, 1990—. Bd. dirs. Notre Dame Corp., Chgo.; U.S. rep. ins. claims Lloyds of London; mediator. Author: (pamphlet) Handle Your Own Claims, 1983, (book) Women's Resource Guide, 1988, Women's Insurance and Financial Resource Guide, 1988. Counselor for battered women. Mem. ABA (mem. dispute resolution sect.), Mich. Bar, Womens Bar Assn. Ill. (active coms. and activities), Corp. Councils Am., Womens Exec. Network, Nat. Assn. for Women in Careers (nat. bd. dirs.), Spider. General practice, Insurance. Office: PO Box 4422 Northbrook IL 60065-4422

ROTH, DANIEL BENJAMIN, lawyer, business executive; b. Youngstown, Ohio, Sept. 17, 1929; s. Benjamin F. and Marion (Benjamin) R.; m. Joann M. Roth; children: William M., Jennifer A., Rochelle. BS in Fin., Miami U., Oxford, Ohio, 1951; JD, Case-Western Res. U., 1956. Bar: Ohio 1956, U.S. Supreme Ct. 1960, D.C. 1983. Chmn. Roth, Blair, Roberts, Strasfeld & Lodge, LPA, Youngstown, 1969—; co-founder, vice chmn. Nat. Data Processing Corp., Cin., 1961-69; chmn., pres., CEO Torent, Inc., Youngstown, 1971—, Morrison Metalweld Process Corp., 1979—; vice chmn. McDonald Steel Corp., 1980—, Torent Oil & Gas Co., 1979—2002, Vaughn Indsl. Car & Equipment Co., 1988—. Bd. dirs. Morrison Metalweld Process Corp., Gasser Chair Co. Profl. singer: appearances including Steve Allen Show, 1952. Bd. dirs. Youngstown Symphony, Stambaugh Auditorium; bd. dirs. Youngstown Playhouse, v.p., 1991-93; pres. Rodef Sholom Temple, Youngstown, 1982-84. 1st lt. USAF, 1951-53, lt. col. Res., ret. Recipient Mgr. of Yr. award Mahoning Valley Mgmt. Assn., 1989, Man of Yr. award Youngstown YWCA, 1995. Mem. ABA, D.C. Bar Assn., Ohio Bar Assn., Mahoning County Bar Assn., Lawyer-Pilots Bar Assn., Soc. Benchers of Case Western Res. U. Law Sch., Youngstown Club, Pelican Marsh Club (Naples, Fla.), Pelican Isle Yacht Club (Naples), Zeta Beta Tau (nat. v.p. 1964-66), Omicron Delta Kappa, Phi Eta Sigma, Tau Epsilon Rho. Jewish. Corporate, general, Estate planning, Family and matrimonial. Office: Roth Blair Roberts Strasfeld & Lodge 600 City Centre One Youngstown OH 44503-1514

ROTH, EUGENE, lawyer; b. Wilkes-Barre, Pa., June 28, 1935; s. Max and Rae (Klein) R.; m. Constance D. Smulyan, June 16, 1957; children: Joan Roth Kleinman, Steven P., Jeffrey H., Lawrence W. BS, Wilkes U., 1957; LLB, Pa. State U., 1960. Bar: Pa. 1960, U.S. Dist. Ct. (mid. dist.) Pa. 1961. Assoc. Rosenn, Jenkins & Greenwald LLP, Walkes-Barre, 1960-64, ptnr., 1964—. Mem. Northeastern Pa. Regional bd. 1st Union Bank; bd. dirs. RCN Corp., Commonwealth Telephone Enterprises, Inc.; chmn. Greater Wilkes-Barre Partnership, Inc., 1991-93. Trustee Wilkes U., 1979—, chmn. 1993-98; chmn. United Way of Wyoming Valley, 1983; chmn. annual campaign Osterhout Free Libr. Campaign, 1999; Northeastern Pa. regional bd. dirs. Geiseinger-Wyoming Valley Hosp. Recipient Disting. Pennsylvanian award Phila. C. of C., 1980, Cmty. Svc. award B'nai B'rith, 1994, Disting. Citizen award N.E. Pa. Boy Scouts Am., 1998, Shofar award United Hebrew Inst., 2001; named Outstanding Vol. Fund Raiser Nat. Soc. Fund Raising Exec., 1993. Mem. ABA, Pa. Bar Assn., Luzerne County Law and Libr. Assn., Wilkes-Barre C. of C. (chmn. 1980, vice com. for econ. growth), Wyo. Valley United Jewish Campaign (chmn. 1978 and 1993), B'nai B'rith. Republican. Jewish. Avocations: reading, community svc. Commercial, contracts (including sales of goods; commercial financing), Corporate, general, Mergers and acquisitions. Office: Rosenn Jenkins & Greenwald LLP 15 S Franklin St Wilkes Barre PA 18711-0076 E-mail: er@rjglaw.com.

ROTH, HADDEN WING, lawyer; b. Oakland, Calif., Feb. 10, 1930; s. Mark and Jane (Haley) R.; m. Alice Becker, Aug., 1987; 1 child, Elizabeth Wing. AA, Coll. Marin, 1949; BA, U. Calif., Berkeley, 1951; JD, U. Calif., San Francisco, 1957. Bar: Calif. 1958, U.S. Dist. Ct. (no. dist.) Calif. 1958, U.S. Ct. Appeals (9th cir.) 1958, U.S. Supreme Ct. 1966. Pvt. practice, San Rafael, 1970—. Judge Marin County Mcpl. Ct., 1966-70; spl. cons. Marin Muni Water Dist., Corte Madera, Calif., County of Marin; atty. Bolinas Pub. Utility Dist., Ross Valley Fire Svc., Tiburon Fire Protection Dist., Town of Ross and San Anselmo, Calif.; hearing officer dist. hosps., 1981—; lectr. law Golden Gate Coll. Law, San Francisco, 1971-73. Chmn. Marin County prison task force, 1973; bd. dirs. Marin Gen. Hosp., 1964-66. Named Outstanding Citizen of Yr., Coll. Marin, 1972. Mem. ABA, Am. Trial Lawyers Assn., Calif. Bar Assn., Marin County Bar Assn., San Francisco Trial Lawyers Assn., Am. Assn. Ind. Investors, Assn. Bus. Trial Lawyers. Avocations: running, weightlifting, reading. Alternative dispute resolution, Appellate, General civil litigation. Office: PO Box 151567 San Rafael CA 94915

ROTH, JANE RICHARDS, federal judge; b. Philadelphia, Pa., June 16, 1935; d. Robert Henry Jr. and Harriett (Kellond) Richards; m. William V. Roth Jr., Oct. 9, 1965; children: William V. III, Katharine K. BA, Smith Coll., 1956; LLB, Harvard U., 1965; LLD (hon.), Widener U., 1986, U. Del., 1994. Bar: Del. 1965, U.S. Dist. Ct. Del. 1966, U.S. Ct. Appeals (3d cir.) 1974. Adminstrv. asst. various fgn. service posts U.S. State Dept., 1956-62; assoc. Richards, Layton & Finger, Wilmington, Del., 1965-73, ptnr., 1973-85; judge U.S. Dist. Ct. Del., Wilmington, 1985-91, U.S. Ct. Appeals (3d cir.), Wilmington, 1991—. Adj. faculty Villanova U. Sch. Law. Hon. chmn. Del. chpt. Arthritis Found., Wilmington; bd. overseers Widener U. Sch. Law; bd. consultors Villanova U. Sch. Law; trustee Hist. Soc. Del. Recipient Nat. Vol. Service citiation Athritis Found., 1982. Fellow Am. Bar Found.; mem. ABA, Fed. Judges Assn., Del. State Bar Assn. Republican. Episcopalian. Office: US Court of Appeals 3rd Circuit 844 King St Lock Box 12 Wilmington DE 19801-1790

ROTH, MICHAEL, lawyer; b. N.Y.C., July 22, 1931; s. Philip Arthur and Mollie (Breitenbach) R.; m. Jeanny Macoir, Nov. 24, 1957; 3 children BA, Yale Coll., 1953; JD, Columbia U., 1956, M. Internat. Affairs, 1964. Bar: N.Y. 1956. Law assoc. Stroock & Stroock & Lavan, N.Y.C., 1956-63; ptnr. Roth, Carlson, Kwit & Spengler, N.Y.C., 1964-74; chmn. N.Y. State Liquor Authority, N.Y.C., 1974-77; ptnr. Shea & Gould, N.Y.C., 1979-89; of counsel Katten, Muchin, Zavis, Rosenman, N.Y.C., 1989—. Mem. U.S. del. to UN Population Commn., 1969; Rep.-Conservative candidate for N.Y. State atty. gen., 1978; mem. Pres.' Task Force on Internat. Pvt. Enterprise, 1983-84, Pres.' Commn. on Mgmt. AID Programs, 1991-92. Mem. Sunningdale Country Club (Scarsdale, N.Y.). Republican.

ROTH, MICHAEL B. law librarian; b. Norfolk, Va., Nov. 27, 1955; s. David and Rhoda Roth; m. Aldona Kudlinski. AB, Vassar Coll., 1985; MLIS, Queens Coll., 1988. Reference libr. NY Pub. Libr., N.Y.C., 1984—88; head legal reference Cravath, Swaine & Moore, N.Y.C., 1988—98; assoc. dir. libr. svcs. Chadbourne & Parke, N.Y.C., 1998—. Mem.: Am. Assn. Law Librs., Law Libr. Assn. Greater NY. Democrat. Avocations: swimming, books, paranormal research. Office: Chadbourne & Parke LLP 30 Rockefeller Plz Fl 33 New York NY 10112-0002

ROTH, PHILLIP JOSEPH, retired judge; b. Portland, Oreg., Feb. 29, 1920; s. Harry William and Minnie Alice (Segel) R.; m. Ida Lorraine Thomas, Feb. 22, 1957 (div. 1977); children: Phillip Joseph, David Harry; m. Allison Blake Ramsey, Feb. 14, 1978 (div. 1994). BA cum laude, U. Portland, 1943; JD, Lewis and Clark Coll., 1948. Bar: Oreg. 1948, U.S. Dist. Ct. Oreg. 1949, U.S. Ct. Appeals (9th cir.) 1959, U.S. Supreme Ct. 1962. Dep. atty. City of Portland, 1948-50; dep. dist. atty. Multnomah County, Portland, 1950-52; pvt. practice Portland, 1952-64; cir. judge Multnomah County State of Oreg., Portland, 1964-94, presiding cir. judge, 1970-71, 76-78. Adj. prof. Lewis & Clark U. Law Sch., Portland, 1978-80, standing com., 1972-90; exec. com. Nat. Conf. State Trial Judges, 1980-91. Author: Sentencing: A View From the Bench, 1973; co-author: The Judicial Immunity Doctrine Today: Between the Bench and a Hard Place, 1984, The Brief Jour.; The Dangerous Erosion of Judicial Immunity, 1989. Mem. Oreg. Legislature, 1952-54; Rep. nominee for Congress, 1956; chmn. Oreg. Rep. Ctrl. Com., 1962-64; adv. bd. Portland Salvation Army, 1976—; mem. bd. overseers Lewis and Clark Coll., 1972-90. Named Alumnus of Yr. U. Portland, 1963, Lewis & Clark Law Sch., 1973. Fellow Am. Bar Found.; mem. ABA (chmn. jud. immunity com. jud. adminstrn. divsn. 1982-90, mem. commn. on standards jud. adminstrn. divsn. 1973-77, chmn. conf. state trial judges 1990-91, HBH Comm. on State Justice Initiatives 1994-98, chmn. jud. adminstrn. divsn. 1994-95), Oreg. Bar Assn. (bd. govs. 1961-64), Multnomah County Bar Assn. (pres. 1959), Am. Judicature Soc., Oreg. Cir. Judges Assn. (pres. 1988-89), U. Portland Alumni Assn. (pres. 1967), Lewis and Clark Coll. Alumni Assn. (pres. 1974-76, 80-81), Multnomah Law Libr. Assn. (bd. dirs.), City Club, Univ. Club, Masons, Shriners, Rotary, B'nai B'rith, Delta Theta Phi. Jewish. Home: 2495 SW 73rd Ave Portland OR 97225-3274

ROTH, RICHARD ALAN, lawyer; b. Endicott, N.Y., Dec. 6, 1958; s. David Manuel and Nelida (Ortner) R.; m. Mara Orentreich, Apr. 11, 1987. BA cum laude, Union Coll., 1981; JD, Hofstra U., 1984. Bar: N.Y. 1985, U.S. Dist. Ct. (so. dist.) N.Y. 1985, U.S. Dist. Ct. (ea. dist.) N.Y. 1985, U.S. Dist. Ct. (no. dist.) N.Y. 1985, U.S. Dist. Ct. (we. dist.) N.Y. 1988, U.S. Ct. Appeals (2d cir.), 1988, U.S. Ct. Appeals (3d cir.) 2000, U.S. Supreme Ct. 2000. Atty. Wilson, Elser Law Firm, N.Y.C., 1984-86, Solin & Breindel Law Firm, N.Y.C., 1986-87, Gordon Hurwitz Law Firm, N.Y.C., 1987-92, Littman, Krooks & Roth, N.Y.C., 1992—2003; pvt. practice Roth Law Firm, N.Y.C., 2003—. Rep. 20th Century Fox, Warner Bros. Records, Actors Guild, IMG, Steiner Sports, Nat. Football League, Grad. Sch. N.Y. Acad. Art, City Light Prodns., Giant Records, Azoff Entertainment, Revolution, Robert Edward Auctions, Tin Pan Apple Records, Tomandandy, Eclipse Records, Discart. Contbr. to law revs. Mem. ABA (entertaiment sect. 1988—, fed. litigation sect. 1988—), N.Y. State Bar Assn. (litigation sect. 1986—). Office: The Roth Law Firm 90 Park Ave 38th Fl New York NY 10016 also: 81 Main St White Plains NY 10601

ROTH, ROBERT CHARLES, lawyer; b. Racine, Wis., Feb. 6, 1945; s. Robert Charles and Lucille (Holy) R.; m. Karen Trombley, May 18, 1974; children: David, Michael. BBA, St. Norbert Coll., 1967; JD, Marquette U., 1970; postgrad. course in law, George Washington U., 1972. Bar: Wis. 1970, U.S. Dist. Ct. (ea. dist.) Wis. 1970, U.S. CT. Mil. Appeals 1970, U.S. Army Ct. Mil Rev. 1971, Colo. 1974, U.S. Dist. Ct. Colo. 1974, U.S. Ct. Appeals (10th cir.) 1974, U.S. Ct. Appeals (5th cir.) 1979, U.S. Ct. Claims 1980. Atty. Shaw & Coghill, Denver, 1974-76; ptnr. Shaw, Spangler & Roth, Denver, 1976-96, Kutak Rock, Denver, 1996—. Pub. arbitrator Nat. Assn. Securities Dealers. Served as capt. U.S. Army, 1970-74. Mem. ABA, Colo. Bar Assn., Denver Bar Assn., Wis. Bar Assn. Avocations: basketball, golf. Federal civil litigation, State civil litigation, Oil, gas, and mineral. Office: Kutak Rock LLP 1801 California St Denver CO 80202

ROTHBAUM, SANDRA LAZARUS, lawyer; b. Indpls., Aug. 29, 1944; d. Kiefer and Sara (Lisker) L.; m. Donald Alan Rothbaum, June 18, 1967; children: Daniel, Anne, Michael, Lia, Mark, Jonathan, Aaron, Jessica. BA cum laude, Harvard U., 1966; MA, U. Wis., 1967; JD summa cum laude, Ind. U., 1984. Bar: Ind. 1984, U.S. Dist. Ct. (no. and so. dists.) Ind. 1984. Assoc. Rubin & Levin, Indpls., 1984-87, Garelick, Cohen & Fishman, Indpls., 1987-88; pvt. practice Carmel, Ind., 1988-90; ptnr. Atlas & Rothbaum, Indpls., 1990-94, Cohen Garelick & Glazier, Indpls., 1994—. Co-pres., sec. Nat. Coun. Jewish Women, Indpls., Ind., 1988-89; chmn. women's div. Jewish Fedn. Greater Indpls., 1989—. Recipient Wall St. Jour. award, 1984. Mem. ABA, Ind. Bar Assn., Indpls. Bar Assn., Harvard Club Ind. (v.p. 1989-91). Estate planning, General practice, Probate (including wills, trusts). Office: Cohen Garelick & Glazier 8888 Keystone Xing Ste 800 Indianapolis IN 46240-4616 E-mail: srothbaum@cgglawfirm.com.

ROTHBERG, GLENDA FAY MORRIS, lawyer; b. Rome, Ga., Aug. 7, 1946; d. Glenn Howell and Fay (Givens) Morris; m. Gerald Rothberg, June 18, 1970 (div. Jan. 1989); children: Laura, Abigail. AB, Randolph-Macon Woman's Coll., 1968; JD, Benjamin Cardozo Law Sch., 1985. Bar: N.Y. 1986, U.S. Dist. Ct. (so. and ea. dists.) N.Y. 1987, U.S. Supreme Ct. 1990. Law guardian juvenile rights divsn. Legal Aid Soc., N.Y.C., 1988-91; pvt. practice N.Y.C., 1992—. Faculty dir. Inst. for not-for-profit Mgmt. Columbia Bus. Sch., N.Y.C., 1994-98. Vol. Manhattan Mediation Ctr., N.Y.C., 1996-99; chair legal com. N.Y.C. Comptr. Task Force on Open Adoption, 1999—. Fellow Am. Bar Found.; mem. ABA, Assn. of Bar of City of N.Y. (com. chair 1996-99, mem. coun. on children 1999—). Family and matrimonial, Juvenile. Office: 386 Park Ave S Ste 904 New York NY 10016-1001 E-mail: gmrlaw@aol.com.

ROTHENBERG, ALAN I. lawyer, professional sports association executive; b. Detroit, Apr. 10, 1939; m. Georgina Rothenberg; 3 children. BA, U. Mich., 1960, JD, 1963. Bar: Calif. 1964. Assoc. O'Melveny & Myers, LA, 1963—66; ptnr. Manatt Phelps Rothenberg & Phillips, LA, 1968—90, Latham & Watkins, LA, 1990—; instr. sports law U. So. Calif., 1969, 1976, 1984, Whittier Coll. Law, 1980, 1984; pres., gen. counsel LA Lakers and LA Kings, 1967—79, LA Clippers Basketball Team, 1982—89; pres. U.S. Soccer Fedn., Chgo., 1990—98; chmn., founder Maj. League Soccer, N.Y.C., 1995. Bd. dirs., pres. Constl. Rights Found., 1987—90; soccer commr. 1984 Olympic Games; chmn., pres., CEO 1994 World Cup Organizing Com., 1990—94; founder, chmn. Major League Soccer, 1994—. Mem.: NBA (bd. govs. 1971—79, 1982—89), ABA, N.Am. Soccer League (bd. govs. 1977—80, Major League Soccer mgmt. com. 1994—), LA Bar Assn., LA County Bar Assn., State Bar Calif. (pres. 1989—90), Order of Coif. General practice. Office: Latham & Watkins 633 W 5th St Ste 4000 Los Angeles CA 90071-2005

ROTHENBERG, ELLIOT CALVIN, lawyer, author; b. Mpls., Nov. 12, 1939; s. Sam S. and Claire Sylvia (Feller) R.; m. Sally Smalying; children: Sarah, Rebecca, Sam. BA summa cum laude, U. Minn., 1961; JD, Harvard U. (Fulbright fellow), 1964. Bar: Minn. 1966, U.S. Dist. Ct. Minn. 1966, D.C. 1968, U.S. Supreme Ct. 1972, N.Y. 1974, U.S. Ct. Appeals (2d cir.) 1974, U.S. Ct. Appeals (8th cir.) 1975. Assoc. project dir. Brookings Inst., Washington, 1966-67; fgn. svc. officer, legal advisor U.S. Dept. State, Washington, 1968-73; Am. Embassy, Saigon; U.S. Mission to the UN; nat. law dir. Anti-Defamation League, N.Y.C., 1973-74; legal dir. Minn. Pub. Interest Rsch. Group, Mpls., 1974-77; pvt. practice law Mpls., 1977—. Adj. prof. William Mitchell Coll. Law, St. Paul, 1983—; faculty mem. several nat. comm. law and First Amendment seminars. Author: (with Zelman Cowen) Sir John Latham and Other Papers, 1965, The Taming of the Press: Cohen v. Cowles Media Co., 1999, The Taming of the Press, 1999; contbr. articles to profl. and scholarly jours. and books, newspapers, popular mags. State bd. dirs. YMCA Youth in Govt. Program, 1981-84; v.p. Twin Cities chpt. Am. Jewish Com., 1980-84; mem. Minn. Ho. of Reps., 1978-82, asst. floor leader (whip), 1981-82; pres., dir. North Star Legal Found., 1983—; legal affairs editor Pub. Rsch. Syndicated, 1986—; briefs and oral arguments published in full Landmark Briefs and Arguments of the Supreme Ct. of the U.S., Vol. 200, 1992; mem. citizens adv. com. Voyageurs Nat. Pk., 1979-81. Recipient Legis. Evaluation Assembly Legis. Excellence award, 1980, Vietnam Civilian Svc. medal U.S. Dept. State, 1970, North Star award U. Minn., 1961; Fulbright fellow, 1964-65. Mem. ABA, Minn. Bar Assn., Harvard Law Sch. Assn., Am. Legion, Mensa, Phi Beta Kappa. Jewish. General civil litigation, Communications, Constitutional. Home: 3901 W 25th St Minneapolis MN 55416-3803 Office: 3010 Hennepin Ave S Ste 231 Minneapolis MN 55408-2614 E-mail: srothenbe@aol.com.

ROTHENBERG, KAREN H. dean, law educator; BA, Princeton U., 1973, MPA, 1974; JD, U. Va., 1979. Dean law sch.'s law and health care program U. Md., 2001—, law educator, 2001—. Formerly practiced with Washington D.C. Law firm of Covington and Burling; worked with a variety of health and med. orgns. ; pres. Am. Soc. Law, Medicine and Ethics; lectr. on legal issues in health care; dir. law sch.'s law and health care program U. Md.; spl. asst. to dir. , 1995—96. Co-editor-in-chief (jours.) Jour. Law, Medicine, and Ethics; co-editor: (book with Elizabeth Thompson) Women and Prenatal Testing: Facing the Challenges of Genetic Technology ; contbr. articles on AIDS, women's health, genetics, right to forego treament. Recipient Joseph Healey Health Law Tchr.'s award, Am. Soc. Law, Medicine and Ethics. Mem.: NIH (sect. on prenatal care, recruitment & ret. of women in clin studies, sect. on ethical, legal and social implications of genetics), Nat. Inst. Child & Human Develop. (adv. coun.), ABA (coordinating group on bioethics and the law), Nat. Action Plan Breast Cancer, Ethics in Reproduction (nat. adv. bd.), Inst. Medicine's Com. (sect. legal and ethical issues for inclusion of women in clin. stud.). Office: U Md Law Sch 515 West Lombard St Baltimore MD 21201 Fax: 410-706-0407. Business E-Mail: krothenberg@law.umaryland.edu.

ROTHENBERGER, DOLORES JANE, legal association administrator, actress, singer; b. Blue Island, Ill., July 19, 1932; d. Ervin Louis and Emily Lorraine (Karafa) R. Grad. h.s., Chgo. Sec. claims dept. Continental Casualty Co., Chgo., 1950-51; legal sec. Rlwy. Express Agy., Chgo., 1951-59, Slovacek and Galliani, Chgo., 1959-69; actress, singer various theaters, 1967—; asst. to exec. dir. Internat. Assn. of Def. Counsel, Chgo., 1982-98. Mng. editor company newsletter, 1985-98. Active campaign Gov. Otto Kerner, Ill.; dir. ch. choir, writer, prodr., choreographer ch. shows. Recipient 1st Joseph Jefferson award for Best Chgo. Actress, Joseph Jefferson Com., 1970, Svc. award Village of Calumet Park, 1983. Mem. Actors' Equity Assn. Roman Catholic.

ROTHENBERG-WILLIAMS, MICHELLE M. lawyer; b. Colchesk, England, Jan. 20, 1974; arrived in U.S., 1976; d. Simon Jeremy and Wheila Yolisa Rothenberg; m. Kisten Paul St. Jae Williams, Sept. 2, 2001. BA in Sociology, Vanderbilt U., 1995; JD, Duke U., 1999. Bar: Ga. Assoc. Nelson, Mullins, Riley & Scarbaugh, Atlanta, 1997, Walston, Wells, Anderson & Burns, Birmingham, Ala., 1997, Cleary, Gottlieb, Staurt & Hamilton, N.Y.C., 1998, Hunter & Williams, Atlanta, 1998, King & Spalding, 1999—2000, Meadows, Ichter & Bowers, 2001—. Mem.: ABA, Gate City Bar Assn., Atlanta Bar Assn., Ga. Bar Assn. Office: Meadows Ichter & Bowers 8 Peidmont Ctr 3525 Piedmont Rd Ste 300 Atlanta GA 30305 Fax: 404-261-3656. E-mail: mrw@miblaw.com.

ROTHMAN, BERNARD, lawyer; b. N.Y.C., Aug. 11, 1932; s. Harry and Rebecca (Fritz) R.; m. Barbara Joan Schaeffer, Aug. 1953; children: Brian, Adam, Helene. BA cum laude, CCNY, 1953; JD, NYU, 1959. Bar: N.Y. 1959, U.S. Dist. Ct. (ea. and so. dists.) N.Y. 1962, U.S. Ct. Appeals (2d cir.) 1965, U.S. Supreme Ct. 1966, U.S. Tax Ct. 1971. Assoc. Held, Telchin & Held, 1961-62; asst. U.S. atty. Dept. Justice, 1962-66; assoc. Edward Gettinger & Peter Gettinger, 1966-68; ptnr. Schwartz, Rothman & Abrams, P.C., 1968-78, Ferster, Bruckman, Wohl, Most & Rothman, LLP, N.Y.C., 1978-98, Law Offices of Bernard Rothman, N.Y.C., 1999—. Acting judge Village of Larchmont, 1982-88, dep. Village atty., 1974-81, former arbitrator Civil Ct., N.Y.C., family disputes panel Am. Arbitration Assn.; guest lectr. domestic rels. and family law on radio and TV, also numerous legal and mental health orgns. Author: Loving and Leaving-Winning at the Business of Divorce, 1998; co-author: Family Law Syracuse Law Rev. of N.Y. Law, 1992, Leaving Home, Family Law Review, 1987, Put Your Kids First, Am. Bar Assn. Family Adv. Quar., 2000; contbr. articles to profl. jours. Mem. exec. bd., past v.p. Westchester Putnam coun. Boy Scouts Am., 1975—; past mem. nat. coun., 1977-81; mem. adv. com. N.Y. State PEACE, 1994—; pres. Congregation B'nai Israel, 1961-63, B'nai Brith, Larchmont chpt., 1981-83. Recipient Silver Beaver award Boy Scouts Am., Wood Badge award. Fellow Am. Acad. Matrimonial Lawyers (bd. govs. N.Y. chpt. 1986-87, 91-93), Interdisciplinary Forum on Mental Health and Family Law (co-chair 1986-97); mem. ABA (family law sect., contbr. Family Advocate Quar.), N.Y. State Bar Assn. (exec. com. family law sect. 1982—, co-chmn. com. on mediation and arbitration 1982-88, 93—, com. on legis. 1978-88, com. on child custody 1985-88, com. alt. dispute resolution), Assn. of Bar of City of N.Y. (women in the cts. com. 1996-99), N.Y. State Magistrate Assn., Westchester Magistrate Assn., N.Y. Rd. Runners Club, Limousine 6 Track Club. Democrat. State civil litigation, Family and matrimonial. Office: 750 3rd Ave Fl 29 New York NY 10017-2703 E-mail: divorcelawyer@worldnet.att.net.

ROTHMAN, DAVID BILL, lawyer; b. N.Y.C., Apr. 25, 1952; s. Julius and Lillian (Halpern) R.; m. Jeanne Marie Hickey, July 7, 1974; children: Jessica Suzanne, Gregory Kozak. BA, U. Fla., 1974, JD, 1977. Bar: Fla. 1977, U.S. Dist. Ct. (so. dist.) Fla. 1980, U.S. Ct. Appeals (5th cir.) 1980, U.S. Supreme Ct. 1981, U.S. Ct. Appeals (11th cir.) 1982, U.S. Dist. Ct. (ea. dist.) Ky. 1985, U.S. Dist. Ct. (mid. dist.) Fla. 1986, cert.: Fla. Bd. , Nat. Bd. Trial Advocacy (criminal trial law). Asst. state atty. Dade County State Atty.'s Office, Miami, Fla., 1977-80; ptnr. Thornton Rothman, P.A., Miami, 1980—. Adj. prof. U. Miami Sch. Law, 1995—; com. mem. Fla. Rules Criminal Procedures, 1990-93, metro Dade Ind. Rev. Panel, 1989-97, co-chmn., 1990-91, chmn., 1991-92, 95-97; panel mem. fee arbitration 11th Cir. Ct., 1994-96, co-chair, 1995-96. Mem. ABA, Fla. Bar Assn. (bd. govs. 1999—), Dade County Bar Assn. (criminal ct. com. 1984—, chmn. 1987-90, bd. dirs. 1990-93, treas. 1993-94, sec. 1994-95, v.p. 1995-96, pres. 1997-98), Nat. Assn. Criminal Def. Lawyers, Fla. Assn. Criminal Def. Lawyers (bd. dirs. Miami chpt. 1991—, pres. Miami chpt. 1993-94, statewide sec. 1996-97, treas. 1997-98, v.p. 1998-99, pres.-elect 1999-2000, pres. 2001), Eugene Spellman Inns of Ct. Democrat. Jewish. Avocations: running, weightlifting, reading. Criminal. Home: 9951 SW 127th Ter Miami FL 33176-4833 Office: Thornton & Rothman PA 200 S Biscayne Blvd Ste 2690 Miami FL 33131-5331 E-mail: DBR@ThorntonRothmanLaw.com.

ROTHMAN, DENNIS MICHAEL, lawyer; BA, Yale U., 1974; JD, St. John's U., 1977. Bar: N.Y. 1978, N.J. 1997, U.S. Dist. Ct. (ea. and so. dists.) N.Y. 1978, U.S. Ct. Appeals (2d cir.) 1978, U.S. Dist. Ct. N.J. 1998, U.S. Tax Ct. 1984, U.S. Supreme Ct. 1986. Ptnr. Lester Schwab Katz & Dwyer LLP, N.Y.C., 1991—. Federal civil litigation, State civil litigation, Intellectual property. Office: Lester Schwab Katz & Dwyer LLP 120 Broadway Fl 38 New York NY 10271-0071 E-mail: drothman@lskdnylaw.com.

ROTHMAN, HENRY ISAAC, lawyer; b. Rochester, N.Y., Mar. 29, 1943; s. Maurice M. and Golde (Nusbaum) R.; m. Golda R. Shatz, July 3, 1966; children: Alan, Miriam, Cheryl, Suri. BA, Yeshiva U., 1964; JD, Cornell U.,

1967. Bar: N.Y. 1967. Trial atty. SEC, N.Y.C., 1967-69; ptnr. Booth, Lipton & Lipton, N.Y.C., 1969-87, Parker, Chapin, Flattau & Klimpl, N.Y.C., 1987-2000, Jenkens & Gilchrist Parker Chapin LLP, N.Y.C., 2001—. Bd. dirs. Camp Morasha, Lake Como, Pa., 1982—, vice chmn., 1992—; bd. dirs. Assn. of Jewish Sponsored Camps, Inc., 1986-2001; bd. dirs. Yeshiva U. High Schs., N.Y.C., 1984-99, vice chmn. bd., 1990-91, chmn. bd., 1992-95; v.p. Manhattan Day Sch., N.Y.C., 1985-96, bd. dirs.; assoc. v.p. Orthodox Union, N.Y.C., 1990-2000, v.p., 2001—; vice chmn. bd. dirs. Azrieli Grad. Sch. Jewish Edn. and Adminstrn., 2000—. Mem. ABA (com. on fed. regulation of securities), N.Y. State Bar Assn., Assn. of Bar of City of N.Y., Yeshiva U. Alumni Assn. (pres. 1986-88, hon. pres. 1988-90). Corporate, general, Private international, Securities. Office: Jenkens & Gilchrist Parker Chapin LLP The Chrysler Bldg 405 Lexington Ave New York NY 10174-0002 E-mail: hrothman@jenkens.com.

ROTHSCHILD, DONALD PHILLIP, lawyer, arbitrator; b. Mar. 31, 1927; s. Leo and Anne (Office) R.; m. Ruth Eckstein, July 7, 1950; children: Nancy Lee, Judy Lynn Hoffman, James Alex. AB, U. Mich., 1950; JD summa cum laude, U. Toledo, 1965; LLM, Harvard U., 1966. Bar: Ohio 1966, D.C. 1970, U.S. Supreme Ct. 1975, R.I. 1989. Tchg. fellow Harvard U. Law Sch., Cambridge, Mass., 1965—66; instr. solicitor's office U.S. Dept. Labor, Washington, 1966—67; prof. law George Washington U. Nat. Law Ctr., Washington, 1966—89, prof. emeritus, 1989; prof. law N.Y. Law Sch., 1989—96. Vis. prof. U. Mich. Law Sch., Ann Arbor, 1976; dir. Consumer Protection Ctr., 1971—, Inst. Law and Aging, Washington, 1973—89, Ctr. for Cmty. Justice, Washington, 1974—78, Nat. Consumers League, Washington, 1981—87; v.p. Regulatory Alternatives Devel. Corp., Washington, 1982—; cons. Washington Met. Coun. Govt., 1979—82; counsel Tillinghast, Collins & Graham, Providence, 1989—95, chair human resource group. Author: From the Cockpit of the Rubaiyat, 2002; co-author: Consumer Protection Text and Materials, 1973, Collective Bargaining and Labor Arbitration, 1979, Fundamentals of Administrative Practice and Procedure, 1981; contbr. articles to profl. jours. Chmn. bd. dirs. D.C. Citizens Complaint Ctr., Washington, 1980; mayoral appointee Adv. Com. on Consumer Protection, Washington, 1979—80. Recipient Cmty. Svc. award, Television Acad., Washington, 1981. Mem.: ABA, D.C. Bar Assn., Am. Arbitration Assn., Fed. Mediation and Conciliation Svc., Nat. Acad. Arbitrators, Nat. Assn. Coll. and Univ. Attys. (Brown U.), Fed. Trade Commn. Adv. Coun., Phi Kappa Phi. Jewish. Office: Shadow Farm Way Unit 4 Wakefield RI 02879-3631

ROTHSCHILD, STEVEN JAMES, lawyer; b. Worcester, Mass., Mar. 23, 1944; s. Alfred and Ilse (Blumenfeld) R. BA, U. Vt., 1965; JD, Georgetown U., 1968. Bar: D.C. 1968, Del. 1969, N.Y. 1992. Ptnr. Skadden Arps Slate Meagher & Flom, Wilmington. Mem. Del. Bd. on Profl. Responsibility, 1992-98, vice chmn., 1993, chmn., 1994-98; vice chmn. rules com. Del. Supreme Ct., 1991-94; chmn. Del. Gov.'s Commn. on Major Comml. Litigation Reform, 1993-94; adj. prof. law Georgetown U. Law Ctr., 2000—; lectr. in law U. Pa. Law Sch., 2001—. Bd. dirs. United Way Del., 93-99, v.p., 1981-84, chmn. 1994-95; bd. dirs. Milton and Hattie Kutz Home, 1972—, pres., 1982-84; pres., Del. Art Mus., 1990-92; bd. trustees U. Del., 1998—. Mem. ABA, Bar Assn. D.C., Assn. of Bar of City of N.Y., Del. Bar Assn. Federal civil litigation, State civil litigation, Corporate, general. Office: Skadden Arps Slate Meagher & Flom One Rodney Sq PO Box 636 Wilmington DE 19899-0636 E-mail: srothsch@skadden.com.

ROTHSTEIN, BARBARA JACOBS, federal judge; b. Bklyn., Feb. 3, 1939; d. Solomon and Pauline Jacobs; m. Ted L. Rothstein, Dec. 28, 1968; 1 child, Daniel. BA, Cornell U., 1960; LL.B., Harvard U., 1966. Bar: Mass. 1966, Wash. 1969, U.S. Ct. Appeals (9th cir.) 1977, U.S. Dist. Ct. (we. dist.) Wash. 1971, U.S. Supreme Ct. 1975. Pvt. practice law, Boston, 1966-68; asst. atty. gen. State of Wash., 1968-77; judge Superior Ct., Seattle, 1977-80, Fed. Dist. Ct. Western Wash., Seattle, 1980—, chief judge, 1987-94, dir. Fed. Jud. Ctr., 2003—. Faculty Law Sch. U. Wash., 1975-77, Hastings Inst. Trial Advocacy, 1977, N.W. Inst. Trial Advocacy, 1979—; mem. state-fed. com. U.S. Jud. Conf., chair subcom. on health reform. Recipient Matrix Table Women of Yr. award Women in Communication, Judge of the Yr. award Fed. Bar Assn., 1989; King County Wash. Women Lawyers Vanguard Honor, 1995. Mem. ABA (jud. sect.), Am. Judicature Soc., Nat. Assn. Women Judges, Fellows of the Am. Bar, Wash. State Bar Assn., U.S. Jud. Conf. (state-fed. com., health reform subcom.), Phi Beta Kappa, Phi Kappa Phi. Office: US Dist Ct 705 US Courthouse 1010 5th Ave Ste 215 Seattle WA 98104-1189

ROTHSTEIN, DAVID ALAN, lawyer; b. Yonkers, N.Y., Sept. 28, 1970; s. Ron and Olivia Rothstein; m. Patricia Florez, Feb. 3, 2001. JD, U. Miami, 1995. Bar: Fla. 1995, U.S. Dist. Ct. (so. dist.) Fla. 1996. Jud. intern U.S. Dist. Ct. - Magistrate Ct., Judge William Turnoff, Miami, 1993—93; cert. legal intern Office Of The State Atty., 1994; assoc. atty. Stearns, Weaver, Miller, Weissler, , Alhadeff & Sitterson, P.a., 1995—99, Hanzman, Criden, Chaykin & Rolnick, P.a., Coral Gables, 2000—01; atty. mem. Hanzman & Criden, P.a., 2002—. Author: (law review article) Entertainment And Sports Law Review. Commercial, consumer (including collections, credit), Securities. Office: Hanzman & Criden PA 220 Alhambra Circle Coral Gables FL 33134 Personal E-mail: drothstein@hanzmancriden.com. E-mail: drothstein@hanzmancriden.com.

ROTI, THOMAS DAVID, judge; b. Evanston, Ill., Jan. 20, 1945; s. Sam N. and Theresa S. (Salerno) R.; m. Donna Sumichrast, July 22, 1972; children: Thomas S., Kyle D., Rebecca D., Gregory J. BS, Loyola U., Chgo., 1967, JD cum laude, 1970. Bar: Ill. 1970, U.S. Dist. Ct. (no. dist.) Ill. 1971, U.S. Ct. Appeals (7th cir.) 1971. Sr. law clk. to Judge Frank McGarr, U.S. Dist. Ct. No. Dist. Ill., 1971-72; assoc. Arnstein, Gluck & Lehr, Chgo., 1972-73, Boodell, Sears et al, Chgo., 1973-75; asst. gen. counsel Dominick's Finer Foods, Inc., Northlake, Ill., 1975-77, v.p., gen. counsel, 1977-97; judge Cir. Ct. Cook County, 2000—. Mem. nat. conf. lawyers and econs. com. Food Mktg. Inst., Washington, 1987-97, legis. com. Ill. Retail Mchts. Assn., Chgo., 1987-97; dir. NCCJ. Trustee Joint Civic Com. Italian Ams., Chgo., 1986-95; mem. Chgo. Coun. EDU-CARE Scholarship Program, 1988. Recipient Am. Jurisprudence award, 1970, Alumni Assn. award Loyola U., 1970. Mem. ABA, Ill. Bar Assn., Ill. Judges Assn., Chgo. Bar Assn., Justinian Soc. Lawyers, Cath. Lawyers Guild Chgo., Phi Alpha Delta, Alpha Signa Nu. Roman Catholic. Office: 1401C Richard J Daley Ctr Chicago IL 60602 Home: 5002 Sunset Ct Palatine IL 60067-9047 E-mail: tdroti@attbi.com.

ROUGH, LISA M, lawyer; b. Teaneck, N.J., Aug. 5, 1975; d. Dr. William A and Catherine E Rough. BSBA, Bucknell U., Lewisburg, Pa., 1997; JD, Villanova U., Pa., 2000. Bar: N.J. 2000, Pa. 2000. Assoc. Raffaele & Puppio, LLP, Media, Pa., 2000—01, Stark & Stark, P.C., Princeton, NJ, 2001—. Sec. of bd. of dirs. Parents Anonymous of N.J., Princeton, 2002. Mem.: ABA, Mercer County Bar Assn. (Young Lawyer's divsn. 2001—02, mem. women's caucus), Bucks County Bar Assn., N.J. State Bar Assn., Pa. State Bar Assn. Family and matrimonial. Office: Stark & Stark PC PO Box 5315 Princeton NJ 08543 Office Fax: 609-896-0629. E-mail: lrough@stark-stark.com.

ROUNICK, JACK A. lawyer, company executive; b. Phila., June 5, 1935; s. Philip and Nettie (Brownstein) R.; m. Noreen A. Garrigan, Sept. 4, 1970; children: Ellen, Eric, Amy, Michelle. BBA, U. Mich., 1956; JD, U. Pa., 1959. Bar: Pa. 1960, U.S. Dist. Ct. (ea. dist.) Pa. 1960; diplomate Am. Coll. Family Trial Lawyers. Spl. asst. atty. gen., 1963-71; ptnr. Israelit & Rounick, 1960-67, Moss & Rounick, 1968-69, Moss, Rounick & Hurowitz, Norristown, Pa., 1969-72, Moss & Rounick, Norristown, 1972-73, Pechner, Dorfman, Wolffe, Rounick and Cabot, Norristown, 1973-87; v.p., gen. counsel Martin Lawrence Ltd. Edits., Inc., 1987-93, dir., 1984—95, Deb Shops, Inc., 1974—; counsel to firm Wolf Block, Schorr & Solis-Cohen LLP, 1997—. Author: Pennsylvania Matrimonial Practice, 6, vols., 1982; editor Pa. Family Lawyer, 1980-87; mem. bd. editors Family Advocate. Fin. chmn. Pa. Young Reps., 1964-66, treas., 1966-68, chmn., 1968-70. Recipient Boss of Yr. award Montgomery County Legal Secs. Assn., 1970, Cert of Appreciation, Pa. Bar Inst., 1980. Fellow: Am. Acad. Matrimonial Lawyers (pres. Pa. chpt. 1982—84, gov. 1983—85, v.p. 1985—87, chmn. bd. rev. 1997—), Internat. Acad. Matrimonial Lawyers; mem.: FLS, ABA (coun. family law sect. 1982—87, coun. 2000—03, bd. editors Family Advocate), Friends of Hebrew U. (bd. dirs. 1987—93, nat. coun. trustees 1987—93, pres. Phila. chpt. 1988—91, v.p. 1990—91), Montgomery Bar Assn., Pa. Bar Assn. (past chmn. family law sect., Spl. Achievement award 1979—80). Republican. Jewish. Family and matrimonial. Office: 325 Swede St Norristown PA 19401-4801 E-mail: JRounick@WolfBlock.com.

ROUNTREE, ASA, lawyer; b. Birmingham, Ala., Aug. 9, 1927; s. John Asa and Cherokee Jemison (Van de Graaff) R.; m. Elizabeth Rhodes Blue, Aug. 11, 1951 (dec.); children— Robert B., John A.; m. Helen Hill Updike, Oct. 10, 1998. AB, U. Ala., 1949; LL.B., Harvard U., 1954. Bar: Ala. 1954, U.S. Dist. Ct. (no. dist.) Ala. 1954, U.S. Ct. Appeals (5th cir.) 1955, N.Y. 1962, U.S. Dist. Ct. (so. dist.) N.Y. 1963, U.S. Ct. Appeals (2d cir.) 1963, U.S. Supreme Ct. 1972. Assoc. Cabaniss & Johnston, Birmingham, Ala., 1954-60, ptnr., 1960-62; assoc. Debevoise & Plimpton, N.Y.C., 1962-63, ptnr., 1963-91; mem. Maynard, Cooper, & Gale, P.C., Birmingham, 1991—. Bd. dirs. U. Ala. Law Sch. Found. Served with U.S. Army, 1945-46, to lt., 1951-53. Mem. ABA (chmn. litigation sect. 1980-81), Ala. Bar Assn., N.Y. State Bar Assn., Assn. Bar City N.Y., Am. Law Inst., Am. Coll. Trial Lawyers, Am. Bar Found. Clubs: River (N.Y.C.); Mountain Brook (Birmingham). Episcopalian. Federal civil litigation, State civil litigation. Office: Maynard Cooper Gale PC 2400 AmSouth/Harbert Plz 1901 6th Ave N Birmingham AL 35203-2618

ROUSE, ROBERT KELLY, JR., judge; b. Lexington, Ky. s. Robert Kelly and Luane (Adams) R.; m. Donna R. Walker, Dec. 21, 1969; children: Kelly B., Erin E. Smith. AA, Daytona Beach (Fla.) C.C., 1966; BS, Fla. State U., 1968; JD, U. Fla., 1974. Bar: Fla. 1975. Ptnr. Regency Talent, Daytona Beach, 1968-69; supr. food divsn. Walt Disney Co., Anaheim, Calif., 1969-70; mgr. restaurants Walt Disney World Co., Orlando, Fla., 1970-71; from assoc. to ptnr. Smalbein, Eubank, Johnson, Rosier & Bussey, P.A., Daytona Beach, 1974-81; ptnr. Smith, Schoder, Rouse & Bouck, P.A., Daytona Beach, 1981-95; circuit judge State of Fla., Daytona Beach, 1995—; chief judge Seventh Jud. Cir., Daytona Beach, 1999—2003. With USAR, 1969—75. Mem. Am. Bd. Trial Advs., Volusia County Bar Assn. (pres. 1989-90), Volusia Civil Trial Attys. Assn. (pres. 1993-95). Office: Volusia County Courthouse 101 N Alabama Ave Deland FL 32724 Office Fax: 386-943-7076.

ROUSTAN, YVON DOMINIQUE, lawyer, real estate broker; b. Managua, Nicaragua, June 22, 1944; came to U.S., 1962; s. Pierre Dominique and Concepcion (Reyes) R.; m. Estela Maria Fiol, Apr. 1, 1967; children: Estela, Pierre, Paul. BA, St. Mary's Coll., Winona, Minn., 1966; MBA, U. Chgo., 1969; JD, DePaul U., 1976. Bar: Ill. 1976, U.S. Supreme Ct. 1987. Chief chemist Bird and Son Inc., Chgo., 1967-69; mgr. Grasas S.A., Chinandega, Nicaragua, 1969-72; assoc. Vincent Lopez, Chgo., 1976-77; sole practice Chgo., 1977—. Mem. Chgo. Bar Assn., Coun. of Trial Lawyers. Lodges: Lions (Chgo.) (v.p. 1983, pres.). Avocations: computers, reading. Criminal, Personal injury (including property damage), Property, real (including real estate development, water). Office: 2911 N Cicero Ave Chicago IL 60641-5131

ROUT, ROBERT HOWARD, lawyer; b. Bklyn., Apr. 14, 1927; s. David S. and Shirley (Rosenthal) R.; m. Valerie Marrow, Jan. 27, 1958; children: Robert Howard Jr., W. Christopher, Romanie O'Neill. Grad., N.Y. State Maritime Acad., 1947; BA, U. Wis., 1949; JD, Harvard U., 1952. Bar: N.Y. 1953, U.S. Ct. Mil. Appeals 1953, P.R. 1958, U.S. Dist. Ct. P.R. 1958, Conn. 1976, U.S. Ct. Appeals (1st cir.) 1983, U.S. Supreme Ct. 1983. Pvt. practice, N.Y.C., 1955-58, San Juan, P.R., 1958-75; ptnr. Aller & Rout, Lakeville, Conn., 1975—2002; pvt. practice Lakeville, 2002—. Chmn. Zoning Bd. Appeals, Salisbury, Conn., 1984-93. Lt. USNR, 1953-55. Mem.: Assn. of Bar of City of N.Y., Harvard Club (N.Y.). General practice, Probate (including wills, trusts), Property, real (including real estate development, water). Home and Office: 160 Wells Hill Rd Lakeville CT 06039-2200 Office Fax: 860-435-0394. E-mail: therouts@webtv.net.

ROUTH, JOHN WILLIAM, lawyer; b. Knoxville, Tenn., Dec. 3, 1957; s. John C. and Mary (Parker) R.; m. Martha Carol Carter, Aug. 6, 1983; children: John Carter, Carol Ann. BA, U. Tenn., 1979, JD, 1983. Bar: Tenn. 1983, U.S. Dist. Ct. (ea. dist.) Tenn. 1983. Assoc. Francis W. Headman, Knoxville, 1983-87, Wm. R. Banks and Assocs., Knoxville, 1987-97; judicial commr. Knox County Gen. Sessions Ct., Knoxville, 1992-94; sole practice law Knoxville, 1997—. Bd. dirs. Cerebral Palsy Ctr. for Handicapped Adults, Knoxville, 1985-88; chmn. adminstv. bd. Emerald Ave. United Meth. Ch., Knoxville, 1988-90, 1998-2000. Mem. Tenn. Bar Assn., Knoxville Bar Assn., Tenn. Assn. Criminal Def. Lawyers, City Salesman Club (v.p. 1988, sec. 1987, pres. 1998). Methodist. Criminal, General practice, Personal injury (including property damage). Office: 4611 Old Broadway St Knoxville TN 37918-1784

ROVER, EDWARD FRANK, lawyer; b. Oct. 4, 1938; s. Frederick James and Wanda (Charkowski) R.; m. Maureen Wyer, June 15, 1968; children: Elizabeth, Emily, William. AB, Fordham U., 1961; JD, Harvard U., 1964. Bar: N.Y. 1964, U.S. Tax Ct. 1968, U.S. Dist. Ct. (so. dist.) N.Y. 1975, U.S. Supreme Ct. 1994. Assoc. White & Case, N.Y.C., 1964-71, ptnr., 1972—. Bd. dirs. Cranshaw Corp., N.Y.C., Harvard-Mahoney Neurosci. Inst., Boston, Waterford Sch., Sandy, Utah, Dana-Farber, Boston, Norton Simon Art Mus., L.A., Rumsey-Carter Found., Geneva, Charles A. Dana Found., N.Y.C.; pres. Dana Found.; sec. Solomon R. Guggenheim Found. Mem. ABA, N.Y. Bar Assn., N.Y. County Lawyers Assn., Assn. Bar City N.Y., Century Assn., Scarsdale Golf Club, Harvard Club, Univ. Club. Avocations: sailing, skiing. Pension, profit-sharing, and employee benefits, Corporate taxation, Estate taxation. Home: 1111 Park Ave New York NY 10128-1234 Office: White & Case Bldg Ll 1155 Avenue Of The Americas New York NY 10036-2787 E-mail: erover@whitecase.com.

ROVINE, ARTHUR WILLIAM, lawyer; b. Phila., Apr. 29, 1937; s. George Isaac and Rosanna (Lipsitz) R.; m. Phyllis Ellen Hamburger, Apr. 7, 1963; children: Joshua, Deborah. AB, U. Pa., 1958; LLB, Harvard U., 1961; PhD, Columbia U., 1966. Bar: D.C. 1964, N.Y. 1984. Assoc. Curtis, Mallet-Prevost, Colt & Mosle, N.Y.C., 1964—66; asst. prof. Cornell U., Ithaca, NY, 1966—72; editor Digest of U.S. Practice in International Law U.S. Dept. State, Washington, 1972—75, asst. legal adviser, 1975—81, agt. of U.S. Govt. to Iran-U.S. Claims Tribunal The Hague, Netherlands, 1981—83; of counsel Baker & McKenzie, N.Y.C., 1983—85, ptnr., then sr. ptnr., 1985—. Adj. prof. law Georgetown U., Washington, 1977-81; vis. lectr. law Yale U., 1998. Author: The First Fifty Years: The Secretary-General in World Politics, 1920-1970, 1970; editor: Digest of U.S. Practice in International Law, 1973, 74; co-editor: The Case Law of the International Court of Justice, 1968, 1972, 1974, 1976; bd. editors Am. Jour. Internat. Law, 1977-87; also articles on internat. law. Mem. panel on settlement of transnat. bus. disputes, N.Y. panel Ctr. for Pub. Resources; chmn. law subcom. of internat. adv. coun. on profl. edn. Coun. on Internat. Ednl. Exch.; mem. Coun. on Fgn. Rels. Mem. ABA (chmn. internat. law sect. 1985-86, del. to Ho. of Dels. 1988-90), Am. Soc. Internat. Law (cert. of merit 1974, exec. coun. 1975-77, v.p. 1998-99, pres. 2000-02), U.S. Coun. for Internat. Bus. (arbitration com.), Am. Arbitration Assn. (panel of arbitrators), Assn. Bar City N.Y. (coun. on internat. affairs). Alternative dispute resolution, Federal civil litigation, Private international. Home: 215 East 68th St New York NY 10021 Office: Baker & McKenzie 805 3rd Ave New York NY 10022-7513 E-mail: arthur.w.rovine@bakernet.com.

ROVIRA, LUIS DARIO, state supreme court justice; b. San Juan, P.R., Sept. 8, 1923; s. Peter S. and Mae (Morris) R.; m. Lois Ann Thau, June 25, 1966; children— Douglas, Merilyn. BA, U. Colo., 1948, LL.B., 1950. Bar: Colo. 1950. Justice Colo. Supreme Ct., Denver, 1979-95, chief justice, 1990-95, ret., 1995. Mem. Pres.'s Com. on Mental Retardation, 1970-71; chmn. State Health Facilities Council, 1967-76; arbiter and mediator Jud. Arbiter Group, Denver. Bd. dirs Children's Hosp.; trustee Temple Buell Found. With AUS, 1943-46. Mem. ABA, Colo. Bar Assn., Denver Bar Assn. (pres. 1970-71), Colo. Assn. Retarded Children (pres. 1968-70), Alpha Tau Omega, Phi Alpha Delta. Clubs: Athletic (Denver), Country (Denver). Home: 4810 E 6th Ave Denver CO 80220-5137 Office: Judicial Arbiter Group 1601 Blake St Denver CO 80202

ROVNER, ILANA KARA DIAMOND, federal judge; b. Riga, Latvia, 1938; arrived in U.S., 1939; d. Stanley and Ronny (Medalje) Diamond. AB, Bryn Mawr Coll., 1960; postgrad., U. London King's Coll., 1961, Georgetown U., 1961—63; JD, Ill. Inst. Tech., 1966; LittD (hon.) , Rosary Coll., 1989, Mundelein Coll., 1989; DHL (hon.) , Spertus Coll. of Judaica, 1992. Bar: Ill. 1972, U.S. Dist. . (no. dist.) Ill. 1972, U.S. Ct. Appeals (7th cir.) 1977, U.S. Supreme Ct. 1981, Fed. Trial Bar (no. dist.) Ill. 1982. Jud. clk. U.S. Dist. Ct. (no. dist.) Ill., Chgo., 1972—73; asst. U.S. atty. U.S. Atty.'s Office, Chgo., 1973—77; dep. chief of pub. protection, 1975—76; chief pub. protection, 1976—77; dep. gov., legal counsel Gov. James R. Thompson, Chgo., 1977—84; dist. judge U.S. Dist. Ct. (no. dist.) Ill., Chgo., 1984—92; cir. judge U.S. Ct. Appeals (7th cir.), Chgo., 1992—. Mem. Gannon-Proctor Commn. on the Status of Women in Ill., 1982—84; mem. civil justice reform act adv. com. 7th Cir. Ct., Chgo., 1991—95, mem. race and gender fairness com., 1993—; mem. fairness com. U.S. Ct. Appeals (7th cir.), 1996—, mem. gender study task force, 1995—96; mem. jud. conf. U.S. Com. Ct. Adminstrn. Case Mgmt., 2000—. Ctrl. and East European law initiative vol. ABA, 1997—; trustee Bryn Mawr Coll, Pa., 1983—89; mem. bd. overseers Ill. Inst. Tech./Kent Coll. Law, 1983—; trustee Ill. Inst. Tech., 1989—; mem. adv. coun. Rush Ctr. for Sports Medicine, Chgo., 1991—96; bd. dirs. Rehab. Inst. Chgo., 1998—; bd. visitors No. Ill. U. Coll. Law, 1992—94; vis. com. Northwestern U. Sch. Law, 1993—98, U. Chgo. Law Sch., 1993—96, 2000—; chair Ill. state selection com. Rhodes Scholarship Trust, 1998—2000. Named Today's Chgo. Woman of the Yr., 1985, Woman of Achievement, Chgo. Women's Club, 1986; named one of 15 Chgo. Women of the Century, Chgo. Sun Times, 1999; named to Today's Chgo. Women Hall Fame, 2002; recipient Spl. Commendation award, U.S. Dept. Justice, 1975, Spl. Achievement award, 1976, Ann. Nat. Law and Social Justice Leadership award, League to Improve the Cmty., 1975, Ann. Guardian Police award, 1977, Profl. Achievement award, Ill. Inst. Tech., 1986, Louis Dembitz Brandeis medal for Disting. Legal Svc., Brandeis U., 1993, 1st Woman award, Valparaiso U. Sch. Law, 1993, ORT Women's Am. Cmty. Svc. award, 1987—88, commendation def. of prisoners com., Chgo. Bar Assn., 1987, Svc. award, Spertus Coll. of Judaica, 1987, Ann. award, Chgo. Found. for Women, 1990, Arabella Babb Mansfield award, Nat. Assn. Women Lawyers, 1998, award, Chgo. Attys. Coun. of Hadassah, 1999, 1st Woman award, Georgetown U. Law Ctr., 2001, Today's Chicago Women Hall of Fame, 2002, Hebrew Immigrant Aid Soc. Chgo. 85th Anniversary honoree, 1996, Chicago Historical Soc. Trailblazers Award, 2003, Trailblazers award, Chgo. Hist. Soc., 2003, Vanguard award, Chgo. Bar Assn. and Lesbian and Gay Bar Assn. Chgo., 2003, First Woman award, Chgo. Bar Assn. Alliance for Women and Women's Bar Assn. Ill., 2000. Mem.: Decalogue Soc. of Lawyers (citation of honor 1991, Merit award 1997), Chgo. Coun. Lawyers, Women's Bar Assn. Ill. (ann. award 1989, 1st Myra Bradwell Woman of Achievement award 1994, 1st Woman Award (in conjunction with Chicago Bar Assn. Alliance for Women) 2000), Fed. Judges Assn., Fed. Bar Assn. (mem. selection com. Chgo. chpt. 1977—80, treas. 1978—79, sec. 1979—80, 2d v.p. 1980—81, 1st v.p. 1981—82, pres. 1982—83, 2d v.p. 7th cir. 1983—84, v.p. 7th cir. 1984—85), Kappa Beta Pi, Phi Alpha Delta (hon.). Office: 219 S Dearborn St Ste 2774 Chicago IL 60604-1803

ROWDEN, MARCUS AUBREY, lawyer, former government official; b. Detroit, Mar. 13, 1928; s. Louis and Gertrude (Lifsitz) Rosenzweig; m. Justine Leslie Bessman, July 21, 1950; children: Gwen, Stephanie. BA in Econs, U. Mich., Ann Arbor, 1950, JD with distinction, 1953. Bar: Mich. 1953, D.C. 1978. Trial atty. Dept. Justice, 1953-58; legal advisor U.S. Mission to European Communities, 1959-62; solicitor, assoc. gen. counsel, gen. counsel AEC, 1965-74; commr., chmn. U.S. NRC, Washington, 1975-77; 2tnr. Fried, Frank, Harris, Shriver and Jacobson, Washington, 1977—. Served with AUS, 1946-47. Decorated officer Order Legion of Honor Republic of France; Recipient Disting. Service award AEC, 1972 Mem. Am., Fed., Mich., D.C. bar assns., Internat. Nuclear Law Assn., Order of Coif. Home: 7937 Deepwell Dr Bethesda MD 20817-1927 Office: Fried Frank Harris Shriver and Jacobson 1001 Pennsylvania Ave NW Washington DC 20004-2505

ROWE, AUDREY, paralegal; b. Albuquerque, June 26, 1958; d. James Franklin Ringold and Geneva Doris (Jennings) Robinson. A in Specialized Bus. in Acctg., ICS Ctr. for Degrees, Scranton, Pa., 1988, A in Specialized Bus. in Fin., 1989; BSBA, Century U., 1991, MBA, 1995, cert. paralegal studies, 1996, A in Specialized Bus. in Paralegal Studies, 1999. Svc. rep. Mountain and Southwestern Bell Telephone Co., Albuquerque, Houston, 1978-83; clk., carrier U.S. Postal Svc. PS05, Bellaire, Sugar Land, Tex., 1983-86; supr. mails U.S. Postal Svc. EAS15, Sugar Land, 1986-87; officer-in-charge U.S. Postal Svc. EAS 18, Rosharon, Tex., 1987; from supr. mails EAS 15 to gen. supr. mails EAS 17 U.S. Postal Svc., Houston, 1987-89; relief tour supt. U.S. Postal Svc. EAS 21 (Detail Assignment), Houston, 1989; mgr. gen. mail facility U.S. Postal Svc. EAS22 (Detail Assignment), Capitol Heights, Md., 1989-90; mgr. mail processing U.S. Postal Svc. EAS21, Charlottesville, Va., 1990-91; MSC dir. city ops. U.S. Postal Svc. EAS23 (Detail Assignment), Roanoke, Va., 1991; mgr. gen. mail facility U.S. Postal Svc. EAS24, Washington, 1991-96; plant mgr. U.S. Postal Svc. EAS25, Dulles, Va., 1992; pvt. contractor, paralegal, 1996-98; paralegal Lenox, Biddinger & Conrad, P.C., Woodbridge, Va., 1997-99, Wilson Strickland & Benson P.C., Atlanta, 1999-2000, Chamberlain, Hrdlicka, White, Williams & Martin, 2000—03, Holland & Knight, LLP, 2003—. Mem. Am. Soc. Notaries, Nat. Capital Area Paralegal Assn., Nat. Fedn. Paralegal Assn., Nat. Assn. Legal Assts. Avocations: piano, violin, reading.

ROWE, DAVID WINFIELD, lawyer; b. Chgo., Nov. 7, 1954; s. Bernard John and Gertrude Katherine (Johnson) R.; m. Martha Lynn Plott, June 12, 1977; children: Daniel, Peter. BA, Davidson Coll., 1976; PhD in Psychology, U. Tenn., 1981; JD, U. Mich., 1987. Bar: Colo. 1987, U.S. Dist. Ct. Colo. 1987, U.S. Ct. Appeals (10th cir.) 1987, Nebr. 1989, U.S. Dist. Ct. Nebr. 1989. Vis. asst. prof. Davidson (N.C.) Coll., 1981-82; mental health worker Peninsula Psychiat. Hosp., Louisville, 1982-84; asst. prof. dept. psychology U. Tenn., Knoxville, 1982-84; assoc. Gorsuch, Kirgis, Campbell, Walker & Grover, Denver, 1987-89; NIMH postdoctoral fellow in law and psychology U. Nebr., Lincoln, 1989-91; ptnr. Kinsey, Ridenour, Becker & Kistler, Lincoln, Nebr., 1991—. Mem. interim study group on foster care Health and Human Svcs. com. Nebr. State Legislature, 1990-91; adj. prof. psychology U. Nebr., Lincoln, 1992-94; bd. dirs., past treas. Lincoln Attention Ctr. for Youth; mem. The Mediation Ctr. Author: (with others) Dimensions of Child Advocacy: Advocating for the Child in Protection Proceedings, 1990, Children Under Three in Foster Care, 1991. Exec. com. Lancaster County Rep. Com., 1991-97, chmn., 1993-95; mem. adv. bd. Juvenile Detention Ctr.; bd. dirs. Lincoln-Lancaster Mental Health Found., 1993—, v.p., 1995-96, pres., 1996-97; mem. Ctrl. Com. Nebr. Rep. Com.,

1993-97; mem. adv. bd. Juvenile Detention Ctr., 2003—; deacon Westminster Prebyn. Ch., 1996-99. Mem. ABA, Nebr. Bar Assn. (alternative dispute resolution com. 1990—), Kiwanis (pres. Lincoln 1997-98). Bankruptcy, General civil litigation, Family and matrimonial. Office: Kinsey Ridenour Becker & Kistler 121 S 13th St#601 PO Box 85778 Lincoln NE 68501-5778 E-mail: drowe@krbklaw.com.

ROWE, G. STEVEN, state attorney general; BS, U.S. Mil. Acad.; MBA, U. Utah; JD, U. Maine. Mem. Dist. 30 Maine Ho. of Reps. , 1993-95; mem. Dist. 35 Maine Ho. of Reps., 1995—2001; atty. gen. State of Maine, 2001—. Democrat. Office: State House Station 6 Augusta ME 04333*

ROWE, LARRY JORDAN, lawyer; b. Boston, May 24, 1958; s. Benson and Marcia Rowe; m. Nancy Ellen Cardinal; children; Jonathan B., Elizabeth J., David C. AB, Dartmouth Coll., 1980; MPP, JD, Harvard U., 1984. Bar: Mass. 1985, U.S. Dist. Ct. Mass. Assoc. Ropes & Gray, Boston, 1984-93, ptnr., 1993—. Mem. Sudbury (Mass.) Fin. Com., 1998—; pres. Hillel Found. New Eng., 1991-94, bd. dirs., 1986—. Mem. ABA, Mass. Bar Assn., Boston Bar Assn. Corporate, general, Non-profit and tax-exempt organizations, Securities. Home: 10 Spiller Cir Sudbury MA 01776-2681 Office: Ropes & Gray 1 International Pl Fl 4 Boston MA 02110-2624 E-mail: lrowe@ropesgray.com.

ROWE, LARRY LINWELL, lawyer; b. Bluefield, W.Va. m. Julia; 3 children. BA, W.Va. U., 1970, MPA, JD, W.Va. U., 1976. Bar: W.Va. 1976, U.S. Dist. Ct. (so. dist.) W.Va. 1976, U.S. Ct. Appeals (4th cir.) 1978, U.S. Supreme Ct. 1992. Staff counsel W.Va. Housing Devel. Fund, Charleston, W.Va., 1976-77; sr. law clk. for U.S. Cir. Judge K.K. Hall U.S. 4th Cir. Ct. Appeals, Charleston, 1978-79; pvt. practice Charleston, 1980—. Mem. W.Va. Senate 2000—, House of Del., 1997-00; hearing examiner W.Va. Bd. Regents, Charleston, 1985-89, W.Va. Bd. Medicine, Charleston, 1987-88; adj. law prof. U. Charleston, 1980-81. Bd. mem. W.Va. Artists & Craftsmen's Guild, Charleston, 1980-84, Cedar Lakes' Mountain State Arts & Crafts Fair, Ripley, 1981-82; chmn., mem. Legal Aid Soc. of Charleston, 1981-84; pres. W.Va. Dance Theatre, Charleston, 1981-82. Recipient W.Va. Bd. of Regents scholarship W.Va. Univ. Coll. Law, Morgantown, 1974-76, Cato scholarship, 1974-76. Mem. Midland Trail Scenic Hwy. Assn., W.Va. U. Alumni Assn., Order of Coif, Phi Beta Kappa. Democrat. Insurance, Personal injury (including property damage), Workers' compensation. Office: 4200A Malden Dr Charleston WV 25306-6442

ROWE, MAX L. lawyer, corporate executive, management and political consultant, writer, judge; b. Dallas City, Ill., Aug. 14, 1921; s. Samuel Guy and Nellie (Moyes) R.; m. Maxine Marilyn Gladson, May 23, 1944; children: Melody Ann (Mrs. Gunn), Susan Elaine, Joyce Lynn, Andrew Blair. Student, Knox Coll., Galesburg, Ill., 1939-40; AB, U. Ill., 1943, JD, 1946; MBA, U. Chgo., 1952. Bar: Ill. 1947, Ind. 1954, also U.S. Supreme Ct. 1964. Pvt. practice in Aurora and Urbana, 1947; asst. to sec., asst. treas. Elgin Nat. Watch Co., 1948-50; gen. atty., asst. to pres.-treas. Rival Packing Co., 1950- 51; gen. counsel, asst. sec.-treas. Victor Mfg. & Gasket Co., Chgo., 1951-54; sec. Mead Johnson & Co., Evansville, Ind., 1954-55; assoc. counsel Caterpillar Tractor Co., 1955-62; assoc. gen. counsel, sec., asst. treas. Thomas J. Lipton, Inc. and subs., 1962-68; v.p., treas. Seeburg Corp., Chgo., 1968-69; v.p. fin., law and adminstrn. Nightingale Conant Corp., Chgo., 1970-71; pvt. legal practice, also mgmt. and polit. cons., 1968—; v.p. law, sec. Ward Foods, Inc., Wilmette, Ill., 1972-76; mem. firm Kirkland & Ellis, Chgo., 1978-87; pres., CEO Rowe Enterprises, 1987—; atty. Ill. Dept. Profl. Regulation, Chgo. and Springfield, 1987-92; adminstrv. law judge State of Ill., 1993—. Dir. Ward-Johnston, Inc., Ward Internat., Inc., Superior Potato Chips, Inc., Quinlan Pretzel Co., Honiron-Philippines, Inc.; instr. extension div. U. Ill., 1960-61, eve. div. Fairleigh Dickinson U., 1966-68; leader Am. Mgmt. Assn., other corp. seminars, 1966-87. Actor various TV, radio and print commercials, 1992—. Treas. Peoria County (Ill.) Republican Ctrl. Com., 1958-62, Rep. precinct committeeman, Peoria County, 1958-62, Bergen County, N.J., 1966-68, del., Rep. Nat. Conv., 1980; elder Presbyn. Ch., 1975—; mem. Pres. Carter's nat. adv. coun. SBA, 1976-78; chmn., mem. adv. bd. Ill. Dept. Pers., 1979-82; mem. Ill. Compensation Rev. Bd., 1984-87; mem. Pres. Reagan's Nat. Commn. for Employment Policy, 1984-88; mem. U. Ill. Found. and Pres.'s Coun., 1979—, bd. visitors Coll. of Law, 1993—; dir., mem. exec. com., chmn. Outreach and Devel., World Heritage Mus., 1992-98; dir., Spurlock Mus. of World Culture, 1998—; mem. bd. dirs. Oak Ridge Cemetary, 1994—. Served to 2d lt. AUS, 1943-45, newspaper columnist, 1994—, producer, writer, host of closed circuit TV programs, 1998—. Named Alumni of Month, U. Ill. Coll. Law, 1982; inductee Sr. Illinoisans Hall of Fame, 1995. Mem. Am. Mgmt. Assn., Conf. Bd., Am., Ill, Chgo., Sangamon County bar assns., Am. Soc. Corp. Secs., Phi Gamma Delta. Clubs: Union League (Chgo.), Execs. (Chgo.). Republican. Corporate, general, Property, real (including real estate development, water). Office: 49 Inverness Rd Springfield IL 62704-3110

ROWE, PAUL ANDREW, lawyer; b. Budapest, Hungary, June 9, 1936; came to U.S., 1939; s. Bela and Mary (Laszlo) Rosenberg; children—Jacqueline, Douglas. A.B., Tufts U., 1958; LL.B., Columbia U., 1961. Bar: N.Y. 1961, U.S. Dist. Ct. (so. dist.) N.Y. 1961, N.J. 1962, U.S. Dist. Ct. N.J. 1962, U.S. Ct. Appeals (3d cir.) 1979, U.S. Dist. Ct. (ea. dist.) N.Y. 1981, U.S. Tax Ct. 1983; cert. civil trial atty. Ptnr., Greenbaum, Rowe, Smith, Ravin, Davis & Himmel LLP, and predecessors firms, Newark, 1962-73, Woodbridge, N.J., 1973—; lectr. Inst. Continuing Legal Edn. Served with USAR, 1961-67. Author: New Jersey Business Litigation, 2000; co-author: Guidebook to Chancery Practice in New Jersey. Recipient lifetime achievement award Trial Attys. of N.J., 1993. Pres. Legal Svcs. Found., Essex County, N.J., 1997-98. Fellow Am. Coll. Trial Lawyers, Am. Bar Found.; mem. ABA, N.J. State Bar Assn., Essex County Bar Assn. (trustee 1981-85, pres. 1988-89), Internat. Acad. Trial Lawyers. Federal civil litigation, State civil litigation. Office: 99 Wood Ave S Iselin NJ 08830-2715 also: 6 Becker Farm Rd Roseland NJ 07068-1735

ROWE, STEPHEN ASHFORD, lawyer; b. Courtland, Ala., Mar. 20, 1953; s. Alvah Leo and Jane (Ashford) R.; m. Julia Bradley, May 26, 1984. Student, U. of the South, 1971-72; BA, U. Ala., 1975, JD, 1978. Bar: Ala. 1978, U.S. Dist. Ct. (no. and so. dists.) Ala. 1980, U.S. Ct. Appeals (5th, 6th and 11th cirs.) 1983, U.S. Supreme Ct. 1985. Assoc. Lange, Simpson, Robinson & Somerville, Birmingham, Ala., 1978-83, ptnr., 1983—. Mem. ABA, Am. Judicature Soc., Birmingham Bar Assn. (pres. young lawyers' sect. 1986, exec. com. 1995—), Ala. Bar Assn. (exec. com. Young Lawyers sect. 1986-88, bd. bar commrs. 1996—), Nat. Assn. R.R. Trial Lawyers, Ala. Def. Lawyers Assn., Mountain Brook Club, Rotary. Episcopalian. General civil litigation, Health, Product liability. Office: 2100 3d Ave N Ste 1100 Birmingham AL 35203-3367 E-mail: steve.rowe@arlaw.com.

ROWE, WILLIAM L. S. lawyer; b. Martinsville, Va., Mar. 31, 1948; s. Mason Cole Rowe and Catherine (Thomas) Showalter; m. Carol Lawhorne, June 6, 1970 (div. 1991); children: William L. S. Rowe, Jr., Benjamin C., Susannah B.; m. Pamela-Jean Love, Feb. 29, 1992. BA, Washington & Lee Univ., Va., 1970; JD, Univ. Va., 1973. Bar: Va. 1973, U.S. Dist. Ct. E.D. Va., U.S. Ct. Appeals (4th cir.), U.S. Claims Ct., U.S. Tax Ct. Assoc. Hunton & Williams, Richmond, Va., 1973-1980, ptnr., 1980—. Special tax counsel, Va. Mfg. Assn.; general counsel Greater Richmond Community Found. 1990—; speaker in the field. Contbr. articles to profl. jours. Bd. gov., trustee, Greater Richmond Community Found., 1979-91, bd. dirs. REB Found., Massey Found., 1980-89. Fellow Am. Coll. of Tax Counsel; mem. ABA, Va. State Bar (bd. trustees sect. on taxation 1988-90), Va. Bar Assn. (chmn. com. on taxation 1985-87), Richmond Bar Assn., Va. State C. of C. (chmn. tax com. 1994—). Avocations: fly fishing, wild flowers, gardening. Estate planning, Estate taxation, State and local taxation. Office: Hunton & Williams Riverfront Plz East Tower PO Box 1535 Richmond VA 23218-1535

ROWLAND, ROBERT ALEXANDER, III, lawyer; b. McAllen, Tex., Apr. 27, 1943; s. Robert Alexander Jr and Marguerite (Gerry) Rowland; m. Victoria Nalle, Apr. 2, 1977; children: Julia Marie, Emily Nalle. BS, Tex. A&M U., 1966; JD, George Washington U., 1972. Bar: Tex 1972, US Dist Ct (so dist) Tex 1973, US Ct Appeals (5th cir) 1973, US Supreme Ct 1976, US Dist Ct (no dist) Tex 1979, US Dist Ct (we dist) Tex 1982, US Dist Ct (ea dist) Tex 1983. Law clk. U.S. Ct. Appeals (5th cir.), Houston, 1973-74; assoc. Vinson & Elkins, Houston, 1975-81; ptnr. susman, Godfrey & McGowan, Houston, 1982-88; mng. dir. Johnson and Gibbs, Houston, 1988-91; ptnr. Hutcheson & Grundy, LLP, Houston, 1992-94; chmn., CEO Associated Counsel of Am., 1995—; ptnr. Roach & Rowland, Houston, 2003—. Bd. dirs. Vol. Ctr., Houston, 1975—84, pres., 1982—83; founding mem., bd. dirs. Tex. Accts. and Lawyers for Arts, 1979—92, pres., 1989—91; mem. devel. com. Sch. Liberal Arts Tex. A&M U., 1992—; co-chmn. Mayor's Transition Com., City of Houston, 1992—94; candidate for State Rep., Tex. Legis. Dist. 134, Rep. Primary, 2002; mem. fin. com. Harris County Rep. Party, 2002—; bd. dirs. United Reps. of Harris County, 2002—; mem. Mission Outreach coun. Christ Ch. Cathedral, 2002—; bd. dirs. Contemporary Art Mus. Houston, 1974—80, 1991—94; bd. dirs. Sarah Campbell Blaffer Gallery of Art U. Houston, 1989—94; bd. dirs. Tex. Opera Theater, 1988—89, Houston Pks. Bd., 1993—, chmn., 2003—; bd. dirs. Nat. Recreation and Pk. Assn., 1992—95, Cultural Arts Coun., Houston, 1981—86, Pk. People Inc., 1979—2001, pres., 1991—92, chmn. Endowment Com., 1994. Capt U.S. Army, 1966—69, Vietnam. Fellow: Tex Bar Found., Houston Bar Found.; mem.: Houston Young Lawyers Assn. (bd dirs 1975—79, pres 1978—79), State Bar Tex., Houston Bar Assn. (dir 1979—88, secy 1984—85, 2d vpres 1985—86, chmn law and art comt 1984—85), Coronado Club, River Oaks Country Club, Phi Delta Phi. Episcopalian. Federal civil litigation, State civil litigation. Home: 2010 Chilton Rd Houston TX 77019-1502 Office: Associated Counsel Am Inc Ste 125 4605 Post Oak Pl Houston TX 77027-9744 E-mail: wickr@swbell.net., rob@associatedcounsel.com.

ROWLETT, ROBERT DUANE, lawyer; BSME, U. Calif., Santa Barbara, 1985, MS in Engring., 1987; JD, U. San Diego, 1994. Bar: Calif. 1995; registered profl. engr., Calif.; registered patent atty. Project engr. Bardex Corp., Goleta, Calif., 1985-87; sr. engr. Gen. Atomics, Inc., La Jolla, Calif., 1987-92; patent counsel 3D Systems, Inc., Valencia, Calif., 1995-96; patent atty. Howard, Rice, Nemerovski, et al, Newport Beach, Calif., 1998-2000; gen. counsel Wink Comm., Inc., Alameda, Calif., 2000—. Trustee Capistrano Unified Sch. Bd. Republican. Roman Catholic. Intellectual property, Corporate, general, Trademark and copyright.

ROWLEY, GLENN HARRY, lawyer; b. Hyannis, Mass., May 16, 1948; s. Harold Frederick and Olive Nellie (Jones) R.; 1 child, Brewster Westgate. BBA, U. Mass., 1970; JD with cum laude, Western New Eng. Coll., 1980. Bar: Mass. 1980, U.S. Dist. Ct. Mass. 1981, U.S. Tax Ct. 1981; cert. elder law atty. Nat. Elder Law Found./ABA. Staff mem. Cape Cod Planning and Econ. Devel. Commn., Barnstable, Mass., 1975-76; staff, estate planning tax dept. Coopers and Lybrand, Springfield, Mass., 1980-81; legal assoc. Roberts and Farrell, West Chatham, Mass., 1982-84; ptnr. Roberts, Farrell & Rowley, West Chatham, 1984-97; pvt. practice Chatham, Mass., 1997—. Cons. Local Citizen Scholarship Trusts, Harwich and Chatham, Mass., 1985—. Contbr. (weekly news column) The Enterprise, others; contbr. articles to profl. jours. Founding mem. Brewster (Mass.) Conservation Trust, 1984; elected mem. Brewster Hist. Dist. Com., 1975; adv. bd. The May Inst., The Cape Cod Writers Ctr., Inc. With USN, 1971-74, Iceland. Recipient Am. Jurisprudence awards Lawyers Co-op. Pub. Co., 1978, 79. Mem. Mass. Bar Assn., Ocean Edge Exec. Club, Profl. Writers of Cape Cod, Cape Cod Estate Planning Coun., Nat. Acad. Elder Law Attys., Phi Delta Phi. Avocations: travel, writing. Estate planning, Probate (including wills, trusts), Estate taxation. Home: Annaniases Knoll/Sheep Pond Brewster MA 02631 Office: The Marketplace PO Box 1489 26 George Ryder Rd S West Chatham MA 02669

ROY, ARTHUR PUTNAM, lawyer; b. Baton Rouge, Nov. 23, 1940; s. Chalmer John and Elizabeth Putnam (Richards) R.; m. Sara Hinrichsen, Mar. 16, 1963; children: Mary Louise Manchadi, Christine Elizabeth Roy Yoder, Sara Katherine Allex. BS, Iowa State U., 1962; JD, U. Colo., 1969. Bar: Colo. 1969, U.S. Dist. Ct. Colo. 1969, U.S. Ct. Appeals (10th cir.) 1972, U.S. Supreme Ct. 1973. Pvt. practice, Ft. Collins, Colo., 1969-70; assoc. counsel State Bd. Agriculture, Ft. Collins, Colo., 1970-73; dep. dist. atty. Office of Dist. Atty., Greeley, Colo., 1973-74; pvt. practice Greeley, Colo., 1974-94; judge Colo. Ct. Appeals, Denver, 1994—. Capt. USAR, 1963-74, Vietnam, 1965-66. Mem. ABA, Colo. Bar Assn. (v.p. 1984-85), Denver Bar Assn. Republican. Presbyterian. Home: 2800 S University Blvd Denver CO 80210-6070 Office: Colo Ct Appeals 2 E 14th Ave Denver CO 80203-2115 E-mail: Arthur.Roy@judicial.state.co.us.

ROY, EMMANUEL, lawyer; b. Port-Au-Prince, Haiti, Feb. 8, 1967; s. Joseph Victor and Marie Sylvie Roy(Stepmother). JD, Fla. Coastal Sch. Law, 2000. Bar: N.Y. 2000. Legal assoc. Merrill Lynch Credit Corp., Jacksonville, Fla., 1998—2000; asst. dist. atty. Kings County Dist. Atty., Bklyn., 2000—02; mng. ptnr. Roy & Roper, LLP, Hempstead, NY, 2002—. Pres. of the bd. HCCC, Bklyn., 2001. Recipient Best Oralist, Fla. Coastal Sch. Law, 1998. Mem.: Haitian Bar Assn. (assoc.; pres. 2002). Democrat. Roman Catholic. Civil rights, Intellectual property, Immigration, naturalization, and customs. Office: Roy & Roper LLP 292 Fulton Ave Ste 204 Hempstead NY 11550 Office Fax: 516-489-6442. Personal E-mail: royroperlaw@aol.com.

ROY, MATTHEW LANSING, lawyer; b. Gainesville, Fla., May 5, 1968; s. Lansing John and JoAnn Ruth R.; m. Melinda Iresta Leaver, Aug. 15, 1993. BS in Acctg., Oral Roberts U., 1990; JD, U. Fla., 1993. Bar: S.C. 1994, Oreg. 1994. Atty. Drose, Davidson & Bennett, Greenville, S.C., 1993-94, Vick & Conroyd, Salem, Oreg., 1994—. Recipient Family Law Book award, U. Fla., 1993. Mem. ABA, Oreg. State Bar Assn. (mem. exec. com. workers' compensation sect., mem. exec. com. new lawyers div., med. legal com.), Marion County Bar Assn. Republican. Avocations: hunting, fishing, skiing, golf, basketball. Personal injury (including property damage), Product liability, Workers' compensation. Home: 1476 St Helens St NW Salem OR 97304 Office: Vick & Conroyd 698 12th St SE Ste 200 Salem OR 97301-4010 E-mail: mroy@vickronroydlaw.com.

ROYCE, JAMES RICHARD, lawyer; b. Gravette, Ark., Jan. 10, 1956; s. James Jackson and Ann Rudisill Royce; m. Kathy Dean Brooks, Apr. 29, 1983 (div. May 1989); m. Margaret Ruth Yuckers, Apr. 14, 1990; children: Patricia Ann, James Jackson II, Conor Patrick. BA in History, Northwestern U., 1978; JD, Vanderbilt U., 1982. Bar: Mo. 1982, U.S. Dist. Ct. (we. dist.) Mo. 1992, Ct. Appeals of Armed Forces 1995, Ct. Vet. Appeals 1993, U.S. Supreme Ct. 2000. Judge adv. USMC, Jacksonville, NC, 1983—86, 1990—92, Memphis, 1986—90; assoc. Woolsey, Fisher, Whiteaker & McDonald, Springfield, Mo., 1992—95; prin. shareholder William H. McDonald & Assocs., Springfield, Mo., 1995—. Maj. USMC, 1983—92. Mem.: Springfield Met. Bar Assn., ABA. Republican. Methodist. Avocations: scouting, Masonic activities. Family and matrimonial, Criminal, Military. Office: William H McDonald & Assocs PC 300 S Jefferson Springfield MO 65806 Office Fax: 417-831-7852. E-mail: whmassoc@swbell.net.

ROYCE, RAYMOND WATSON, lawyer, rancher, citrus grower; b. West Palm Beach, Fla., Mar. 5, 1936; s. Wilbur E. and Veda (Watson) R.; m. Catherine L. Setzer, Apr. 21, 1979; children: Raymond, Steven, Nancy, Kathryn, Ryan. BCE, U. Fla., 1958, JD, 1961. Bar: Fla. 1961, U.S. Dist. Ct. (so. dist.) Fla. 1961, U.S. Ct. Appeals (5th cir.) 1961, U.S. Ct. Appeals (11th cir.) 1981. With Scott, Royce, Harris & Bryan P.A., Palm Beach, Fla., 1962-99; pres. Scott, Royce, Harris, Bryan, Barra and Jorgensen, P.A., Palm Beach Gardens, Fla., 1982-99; ptnr. Holland & Knight LLP, West Palm Beach, 1999—. Bd. suprs. No. Palm Beach Improvement Dist., 1995-99. Mem. Fla. Bar (bd. govs. 1974-78), Fla. Blue Key, Phi Delta Phi. Democrat. Presbyterian. Administrative and regulatory, Corporate, general, Property, real (including real estate development, water). Home: 5550 Whirlaway Rd Palm Beach Gardens FL 33418-7735 Office: Holland and Knight LLP 222 Lakeview Ste 1000 West Palm Beach FL 33401-4027

ROZANSKI, STANLEY HOWARD, lawyer; b. N.Y.C., July 19, 1952; s. Israel and Frida (Huber) R.; 1 child, Justin. BA, Hunter Coll., 1974; JD, San Fernando Coll. Law, 1977. Bar: Calif. 1978, U.S. Dist. Ct. (cen. dist.) Calif. 1978, U.S. Ct. Appeals (9th cir.) 1982. Ptnr. Rozanski & Friedland, L.A., 1980—, San Jose, Calif., 1983—, L.A., San Jose. Judge pro tem L.A. County Cts., 1985—. Recipient Outstanding Contributions award State Bar Calif., 1985. Mem. Calif. Bar Assn., Assn. Trial Lawyers Am., Calif. Trial Lawyers Assn., L.A. Trial Lawyers Assn., ABA, L.A. County Bar Assn., Beverly Hills Bar Assn. Jewish. Avocations: skiing, swimming, golf. Criminal, Insurance, Personal injury (including property damage). Office: Ste 650 12400 Wilshire Blvd Los Angeles CA 90025-1055

ROZZELL, SCOTT ELLIS, lawyer; b. Texarkana, Tex., Apr. 12, 1949; s. George M. and Dora Mae (Boyett) Rozzell; m. Michelle Miller Rozzell; children from previous marriage: Stacey Elizabeth Murphree, Kimberly Marie Murphree. BA, So. Meth. U., 1971; JD, U. Tex., 1975. Bar: Tex. 1975, U.S. Dist. Ct. (so. dist.) Tex. 1975, U.S. Dist. Ct. (no. dist.) Tex. 1977, U.S. Ct. Appeals (1st, 3d, 9th cirs.) 1977, U.S. Ct. Appeals (5th and D.C. cirs.) 1976. Assoc. BakerBotts, LLP, Houston, 1975-82, ptnr., 1983-94, sr. ptnr., 1995-2000; exec. v.p., gen. counsel CenterPoint Energy, Inc., Houston, 2001—. Mem. State of Tex. Aircraft Pooling Bd., 1997-2002; devel. bd. U. of Tex. Health Sci. Ctr. Houston, 1992—; mem. Tex. Commn. for Lawyer Discipline, 2001-2003, chair 2002-2003. Bd. dirs. Manned Space Flight Edn. Found., Inc., 1997—, vice chair 2000-, Tex. Aviation Hall of Fame, 2001—; vice-chmn. Cancer Counseling Inc., Houston, 1991-92; mem. so. regional adv. bd. Inst. Internat. Edn. Fellow Tex. Bar Found. (sustaining life), Houston Bar Found. (sustaining life, bd. dirs. 1991-93, chair 1993), Am. Bar Found.; mem. ABA, State Bar Tex. (bd. dirs. 1997-2000), Houston Bar Assn. (bd. dirs. 1991-95, pres. 1996-97), Fed. Energy Bar Assn., Houston Young Lawyers Assn. (bd. dirs. 1978-82, pres. 1983-84), Coronado Club, Houstonian. Republican. Presbyterian. Avocation: flying vintage airplanes. Administrative and regulatory, Utilities, public. Home: 1229 Post Oak Park Houston TX 77027 Office: CenterPoint Energy Inc PO Box 4567 Houston TX 77210-4567 E-mail: scott.rozzell@centerpointenergy.com.

RUBACK, ALAN STEVEN, lawyer; b. Bklyn., June 9, 1949; s. Isidore and Shirley Ruback; m. Carol Maselli, Jan. 24, 1976; children: Joshua, Jenna. BA, SUNY, Stony Brook, 1971; JD, New Eng. Sch. of Law, 1974. Bar: Mass. 1974, Fla. 1978, U.S. Dist. Ct. (so. dist.) Fla. 1978. Staff atty. Office of Hearings and Appeals Social Security Adminstrn., Raleigh, N.C., 1976-77, Miami, Fla., 1977-82, Ft. Lauderdale, Fla., 1982-83; ptnr. Connors Ruback & Koster P.A., Ft. Lauderdale, 1983-96; sole practice Ft. Lauderdale, 1996—. Mem. Nat. Orgn. Social Security Claimant's Reps. (sustaining), Mass. Bar Assn., Fla. Bar Assn., B'nai B'rith Justice League. Pension, profit-sharing, and employee benefits. Office: PO Box 1659 440 S Andrews Ave Fort Lauderdale FL 33302-1659 E-mail: aruback171@aol.com.

RUBEN, ALAN MILES, law educator; b. Phila., May 13, 1931; s. Maurice Robert and Ruth (Blatt) R.; m. Betty Jane Willis, May 23, 1965. AB, U. Pa., 1953, MA, JD, U. Pa., 1956. Bar: Pa. 1957, Ohio 1972. Law clk. Supreme Ct. Pa., 1956-58; pvt. practice Phila., 1958-65; assoc. counsel Aetna Life & Casualty Co., Hartford, Conn., 1965-69; corp. counsel Lubrizol Corp., Cleve., 1969-70; prof. Cleve.-Marshall Coll. Law, Cleve. State U., 1970—; adv. prof. law Fudan U., Shanghai, People's Republic of China, 1993—; dep. to city solicitor Phila., 1958-61; dep. atty. gen. State of Pa., 1961-65; spl. counsel to U.S. Senate Subcom. on Nat. Stockpile, 1962; commentator Higher Edn. Issues Sta. WCLV-FM, Cleve., 1975-87. Mem. nat. panel labor arbitrators Nat. Acad. Arbitrators, Fed. Mediation and Conciliation Svc. and Am. Arbitration Assn., Ohio State Employment Rels. Bd.; lectr. law U. Conn. Law Sch., 1968; vis. prof. law FuDan U., Shanghai, Peoples Republic of China, 1988-89; cons. Shanghai Law Office for Fgn. Economy and Trade, Peoples Republic of China, 1991-94. Author: The Constitutionality of Basic Protection for the Automobile Accident Victim, 1968, Unauthorized Insurance: The Regulation of the Unregulated, 1968, Arbitration in Public Employee Labor Disputes: Myth, Shibboleth and Reality, 1971, Illicit Sex of Campus: Federal Remedies for Employment Discrimination, 1971, Model Public Employees Labor Relations Act, 1972, Sentencing the Corporate Criminal, 1972, Modern Corporation Law, supp. edit., 1978, An American Lawyer's Observations on the Inauguration of the Shanghai Stock Exchange, 1989, Ohio Limited Partnership Law, 1992—, Practice Guides, Ohio Limited Liability Company, Law, 1995—; co-editor: How Arbitration Works, 1997; contbr.: With an Eye to Tomorrow: The Future Outlook of the Life Insurance Industry, 1968, The Urban Transportation Crisis: The Philadelphia Plan, 1961, Philadelphia's Union Shop Contract, 1961, The Administrative Agency Law: Reform of Adjudicative Procedure and the Revised Model Act, 1963, The Computer in Court: Computer Simulation and the robinson Patman Act, 1964. Bd. dirs. U.S. Olympic Com., 1968-73; chmn. U.S. Olympic Fencing Sport Com., 1969-73; pres. U.S. Fencing Assn., 1968-73; capt. U.S. Pan-Am. Fencing Team, 1971, U.S. Olympic Fencing Team, 1972; bd. dirs. Legal Aid Soc. Cleve., 1973-77; trustee Cleve.-San Jose Ballet, 1999-2001. Winner Internat. Inst. Edn. Internat. Debate Championship, 1953; recipient Harrison Tweed Bowl and Am. Law Inst. prizes Nat. Moot Ct. Competition, 1955; named Guggenheim scholar, 1949-53, Fulbright scholar FuDan U., Shanghai, 1993-94. Mem. ABA, Ohio Bar Assn. (corp. law and profl. responsibility com.), Cleve. Bar Assn. (Securities Law Inst.), Assn. Am. Law Schs. (chmn. sect. law and edn. 1976-78), Internat. Indsl. Rels. Rsch. Assn., Internat. Soc. Labor Law, Internat. Bar Assn., Union Internat. Des Avocats, Internat. Law Assn., AAUP (pres. Ohio conf. 1974-75), Rowfant Club, Phi Beta Kappa, Pi Gamma Mu. Home: 9925 Lake Shore Blvd Bratenahl OH 44108-1052 Office: Contact Am Arbitration Assn Ste 200 25050 Country Club Blvd North Olmsted OH 44070

RUBEN, AUDREY H. ZWEIG, lawyer, arbitrator, actress; m. Robert J. Ruben; children: Pamela, James B. BA, NYU, 1948; MA, Columbia U., 1953; JD, St. John's U., 1976. Bar: N.Y. 1977, U.S. Dist. Ct. (so. and ea. dists.) N.Y. 1977, U.S. Supreme Ct. 1982. Law intern Westchester Dist. Atty.'s Office, White Plains, NY, 1975, Westchester Legal Svcs., White Plains, 1976-77; assoc. Pierro, Colangelo & Killea, Port Chester, N.Y., 1979-84; legal adminstr. Poloron Products, Harrison, N.Y., 1984-86; pvt. practice Rye, N.Y., 1986-90. Arbitrator N.Y. State Office of Ct. Adminstrn., 1979-90, Am. Arbitration Assn., 1980—, Better Bus. Bur., 1980—, N.Y. Stock Exch., 1991—, Nat. Assn. Securities Dealers, 1991—, Pacific Stock Exch., 1993—; mediator Westchester Med. Ctr. Cluster, Westchester County, N.Y., 1984-90; law guardian Family Ct., Westchester County, 1979-84; guardian ad litem Surrogates Ct., Westchester, 1978-84. Theatre critic (newspaper) L.I. Herald; movie reviewer Saddleback Valley News; freelance children's book reviewer; actress cmty. and summer theatre; actress Readers Repertory Theatre. Commr. Human Rights Commn., Rye, 1984-89, Rye Cable TV Commn., 1989-90; pres. LWV of Rye, 1971-73; bd. dirs. pub. rels. com. Community Media Orgns.; bd. dirs. Rye Youth Coun.,

1974-80; mem. Mission Viejo Cultural Arts com.; MME Modjeska chpt. Orange County Performing Arts Ctr. Mem. ABA, AAUW, Am. Arbitration Assn., N.Y. State Bar Assn., N.Y. Women's Bar Assn., Westchester County Bar Assn., Portchester/Rye Bar Assn., Internat. Fedn. Women Lawyers, Am. Judges Assn., Columbia U. Club of So. Calif., Rye Woman's Club. Avocations: theatre, swimming, aerobics, skiing, dancing. Administrative and regulatory, Alternative dispute resolution. Home and Office: 21285 Amora Mission Viejo CA 92692-4930

RUBEN, ROBERT JOSEPH, lawyer; b. N.Y.C., Apr. 9, 1923; m. Audrey H. Zweig, Nov. 20, 1949; children: Pamela Joan, James Bradford. BS, Columbia U., 1943; MA, Harvard U., 1948; LL.B., Fordham U., 1953. Bar: N.Y. 1954. Exec. trainee Chase Nat. Bank, N.Y.C., 1948-49; economist, 1949-53; assoc. Milbank, Tweed, Hope & Hadley, N.Y.C., 1953-55; assoc., then ptnr. Shea & Gould, N.Y.C., 1955-90; sec. Gen. Battery Corp., Reading, Pa., 1963-73, Fiat Metal Mfg. Co., Inc., Plainview, N.Y., 1961-64, Filtors, Inc., East Northport, N.Y., 1961-64, Trans-Industries, Inc., 1969-2001, dir., 2001—; asst. sec. Elgin Nat. Industries, 1975-88. Asst. judge City Ct., Rye, N.Y., 1977-90; arbitrator Nat. Assn. Securities Dealers, 1990—, Pacific Stock Exch., 1992—, Am. Arbitration Assn., 1990—, N.Y. Stock Exch., 1994—. Trustee Rye Hist. Soc.; bd. dirs. Carver Center, Port Chester, N.Y., 1972-90. Served with AUS, 1943-46. Decorated Combat Inf. medal. Mem. ABA, N.Y. State Bar Assn., Assn. Bar of City of N.Y., Harvard Club (N.Y.C.), Harvard-Radcliffe Club So. Calif., Columbia U. Club So. Calif., Beta Gamma Sigma, Zeta Beta Tau. Home: 21285 Amora Mission Viejo CA 92692-4930

RUBENFELD, STANLEY IRWIN, lawyer, director, mediator, arbitrator; b. N.Y.C., Dec. 7, 1930; s. George and Mildred (Rose) R.; children: Lise Susan, Kenneth Michael; m. Madeleine Conway, Nov. 5, 2000. BA, Columbia U., 1952, JD, 1956. Bar: N.Y. 1956. Practice law, N.Y.C., 1956-65, 68—, 1965-68; assoc. Shearman & Sterling, 1956-65, ptnr., 1965-68, N.Y.C., 1968-93, of counsel, 1994—. Arbitrator and mediator NASD; mediator U.S. Fed. Ct., IRS Panel, CPR Panel; arbitrator NYSE, Internat. C. of C.; bd. dirs. Brit. Gas US Holdings, Inc., BG Energy Fin. Inc., South ?Shore Music, Inc., BGLNG Svcs., Inc. Editor-in-chief Columbia Law Rev., 1955-56; contbr. articles to profl. jours. Past pres. Port Washington (N.Y.) Cmty. Chest; former bd. dirs. Residents for a More Beautiful Port Washington. Lt. (j.g.) USNR, 1952-54. Stone scholar, 1951-52, 54-55, 55-56; Rockefeller Found. grantee, 1955 Mem. ABA, N.Y. State Bar Assn. (tax sec., past chmn. fgn. activities com., reorgn. corp.), Assn. Bar City N.Y. (past chmn. com. on recruitment lawyers), Nat. Assn. Law Placement (past bd. dirs., exec. com.), Columbia U. Law Sch. Alumni Assn. (bd. visitors, adviser, past bd. dirs.), Columbia Coll. Alumni Assn., Tax Club (past chmn.), Phi Delta Phi, Tau Epsilon Phi (past pres.). Corporate, general, Corporate taxation, Personal income taxation.

RUBENSTEIN, ALAN MORRIS, county judge; b. Phila., Mar. 13, 1946; s. Philip and Lilyian Ruth (Eveloff) R.; m. Marilynn Z. Rubenstein, Mar. 31, 1973; children: Samuel Alex, Justin Simon. BA in History, Temple U., 1967; JD, U. Toledo, 1970. Bar: Pa. 1971, U.S. Dist. Ct. (ea. dist.) Pa. 1971, U.S. Ct. Appeals (3d cir.) 1985, U.S. Supreme Ct. 1980. Pvt. practice, Phila., 1970-73; asst. dist. atty. Bucks County Dist. Atty.'s Office, Doylestown, Pa., 1973-75, dep. dist. atty., 1975-79, chief dep. dist. atty., chief trials, 1979-83, 1st asst. dist. atty., 1983-86, dist. atty., 1986-2000; judge Ct. of Common Pleas of Bucks County, 2000—. Law enforcement coordinating com. for ea. dist. Pa., U.S. Dept. Justice Drug task force adv. com. Office Atty. Gen., Commonwealth of Pa.; mem. Bucks County Prison Adv. Bd.; bd. dirs. Bucks County Hero Scholarship Fund; advisor, bd. dirs. for Southea. Pa., Joe Frazier's Golden Gloves; judge Pa. Athletic Commn., Del. Boxing Commn., N.J. Athletic Control Bd., Conn. State Athletic Commn. Recipient award for outstanding performance and svc. to cmty. Fraternal Order Police, Phila., 1987, Disting. Pub. Svc. award County and State Detectives Assn. Pa., 1989, award for outstanding svc. in field law enforcement Delaware Valley Assn. Profl. Police Ofcls., 1991, Law Enforcement commendation medal Valley Forge chpt. Nat. Soc. SAR, 1992, award in appreciation for svc. for drug and alcohol prevention through edn. Nat. Awareness Found., 1996, N.E. Cmty. Svc. award, 1996, Diamond Achievement award in social scis. Temple U. Coll. Arts and Scis., 1997 Mem. ATLA, Am. Coll. Pros. Attys., Assn. Govt. Attys. in Capital-Death Penalty Litigation, Am. Judicature Soc., Pa. Dist. Attys. Assn. (mem. exec. com. 1985-97, sec.-treas. 1989-90, v.p. 1990-91, pres. 1991-92, Pa. Dist. Attys. Inst. (bd. dirs. 1986-97, pres. 1993-94, 96-97), Order Ky. Cols., Phi Alpha Delta. Republican. Jewish. Office: Ct of Common Pleas Bucks County Main and Court Sts Doylestown PA 18901

RUBENSTEIN, ALLEN IRA, lawyer; b. N.Y.C., Apr. 1, 1942; s. Nathan and Ida (Yankowitz) R.; m. Carole Toby Ballin, Aug. 24, 1963; children: Daniel Stuart, Samuel Philip. BS in Physics, CCNY, 1962; PhD in Physics, MIT, 1967; JD, Boston U., 1974. Bar: N.Y., U.S. Dist. Ct. (so. and ea. dists.) N.Y. 1975, U.S. Ct. Appeals (2d cir.) 1975, U.S. Ct. Appeals (1st and fed. cirs.) 1982, U.S. Supreme Ct. 2000. Physicist Stanford (Calif.) U., 1967-69; fellow Weizmann Inst., Rehovoth, Israel, 1969-71; assoc. Kenyon & Kenyon, N.Y.C., 1974-82; ptnr. Gottlieb, Rackman & Reisman, P.C., N.Y.C., 1982—. Trustee Beth Israel Anshei Emet, Bklyn. 1981—. Recipient Ward medal CCNY, 1962. Mem. ABA, Am. Phys. Soc., Phi Beta Kappa. Intellectual property, Patent, Trademark and copyright. Home: 59 Livingston St Brooklyn NY 11201-4834 E-mail: arubenstein@grr.com., AllenR@alum.mit.edu.

RUBENSTEIN, JEROME MAX, lawyer; b. St. Louis, Feb. 16, 1927; s. Jacob J. and Anne (Frankel) R.; m. Judith Hope Grand, July 31, 1954; children— Edward J., Emily Rubenstein Muslin, Daniel H. AB, Harvard U., 1950, LLB, 1955. Bar: Mo. 1956, U.S. Dist. Ct. (ea. dist.) Mo. 1956, U.S. Ct. Appeals (8th cir.) 1956. Mem. English lit. faculty U. So. Philippines, Cebu, 1950-51; law clk U.S. Dist. Ct., St. Louis, 1955-56; assoc. Lewis, Rice, Tucker, Allen & Chubb, St. Louis, 1956-64, Grand, Peper & Martin, St. Louis, 1964-65, ptnr., 1965-66; jr. ptnr. Bryan Cave, St. Louis, 1966-67, ptnr., 1968-97, of counsel, 1998—. Dir. Commerce Bank, N.A. Bd. dirs. Independence Ctr., St. Louis, 1985-88, The Arts and Edn. Coun. Greater St. Louis, 1991-99. Served with USN, 1945-46. Bd. dirs. Independence Ctr., St. Louis, 1985. Served with USN, 1945-46 Mem. ABA, Mo. Bar Assn., St. Louis Bar Assn., Mo. Athletic Club, Harvard Club of St. Louis (pres. 1982-83, bd. dirs. 1983-90). Jewish. Avocations: jogging; tennis. Banking, Corporate, general, Property, real (including real estate development, water). Home: 7394 Westmoreland Dr Saint Louis MO 63130-4240 Office: Bryan Cave 1 Metropolitan Sq Ste 3600 Saint Louis MO 63102-2750

RUBIN, ALIX R. lawyer; BA magna cum laude, Tufts U., Medford, Mass., 1977; MA in Journalism, Temple U., Phila., 1981; JD, U. Pa., Phila., 1996. Bar: NJ. (Admission) 1996, Pa, 1996, U.S. Dist. Ct., NJ 1996, U.S. Ct. of Appeals (3d cir.) 2001, U.S. Dist. Ct. (so. and ea dists..) NY 2002. Asst. dir. of pub. rels./publs. editor Pa, Hosp., Phila., 1981—86; sr. comm. assoc. Jewish Fedn. of Greater Phila., 1987—90; news editor Jewish Times, Huntingdon Valley, Pa., 1990—93; law clk. Wapner, Newman and Associates, Phila., 1994; summer assoc. Hannoch Weisman, A PC, Roseland, NJ, 1995, assoc., 1996—99, Lowenstein Sandler PC, Roseland, NJ, 1999—2002, counsel, 2003—. Presenter workshop "Exploring the Real World of Employee Relations". Editor: (journal) Comparative Labor Law Jour., 1994—96; contbr. articles to legal jours. Facilitator NJ. World Trade Ctr. Disaster Legal Response Team, NJ. Legal Rsch. Fellow, U. Pa, Law Sch., 1995-1996. Mem.: ABA, Essex County Bar Assp., NJ. State Bar Assn. Avocations: hiking, poetry writing, travel. General civil litigation, Labor (including EEOC, Fair Labor Standards Act, labor-management relations, NLRB, OSHA), Trademark and copyright. Office: Lowenstein Sandler PC 65 Livingston Ave Roseland NJ 07068

RUBIN, ARNOLD E. lawyer; b. Phila., Dec. 8, 1935; s. Harry and Nettie Rubin. BS, Drexel Univ., 1958; JD, Temple Univ., 1961. Bar: Pa. 1962, U.S. Supreme Ct. 1965, Ct. of Common Pleas Del. County, Pa. 1962. Atty. Public Defender, Delaware Co., Pa., 1965-69, first. asst., 1970-74; pvt. practice Delaware Co., Pa., 1974—. Author, lectr., instr. Dist. Justice Sch., 1974, 75, 76, 77; mem. election bd. 2d Precinct Upper Providence, 2002. With U.S. Army, 1961-75. Mem. Masonic Lodge (floor worker 1979-87). Democrat. Jewish. Criminal, Family and matrimonial, Probate (including wills, trusts). Office: Arnold E Rubin 211 W State St Media PA 19063-3139

RUBIN, BLAKE DOUGLAS, lawyer; b. Phila., Jan. 11, 1955; s. Alan and Helen (Metz) R.; m. Deborah F. McIlroy, Oct. 30, 1982; children; Bret Andrew, Keith Michael. BA, Haverford Coll., 1976; MBA with distinction, JD cum laude, U. Pa., 1980. Bar: Pa. 1980, D.C. 1988, U.S. Dist. Ct. (ea. dist.) Pa. 1980, U.S. Ct. Appeals (3d cir.) 1980. Assoc. Wolf, Block, Schorr & Solis-Cohen, Phila., 1980-84; atty., Office of Tax Legis. Counsel U.S. Dept. Treasury, Washington, 1984-87; ptnr. Steptoe & Johnson, Washington, 1987—2000, Arnold & Porter, Washington, 2000—. Adj. prof. grad. tax program Villanova (Pa.) U., 1982-84; mem. adv. bd. Nat. Inst. on Real Estate Taxation; frequent speaker in field. Mem. adv. coun. Washington Tax Rev., Tax Mgmt. Real Estate Jour., Jour. Real Estate Taxation; contbr. articles to profl. jours. Mem. ABA (taxation sect.), Order of Coif, Beta Gamma Sigma, Beta Alpha Psi. Republican. Avocations: tennis, swimming, sailing. Corporate taxation, Taxation, general, Personal income taxation. Home: 5120 Sangamore Rd Bethesda MD 20816-2326 Office: 555 12th St NW # 816 Washington DC 20004-1200

RUBIN, E(RWIN) LEONARD, lawyer; b. Chgo., Jan. 11, 1933; s. Samuel and Frances Birdie (Rabin) R.; m. Stephanie Siegel, Mar. 4, 1961 (div. Dec. 1981); children: Matthew, Suzanne; m. Audrey Gay Holzer, May 8, 1983; children: Margot, Bette. Student, U. Ill., Urbana, 1948-51; AB, U. Miami, 1956, JD, 1959. s. N.Y. 1960, Ill. 1962, U.S. Dist. Ct. (no. dist.) Ill. 1962, U.S. Ct. Appeals (7th cir.) 1990, U.S. Ct. Appeals (5th cir.) 1998. Assoc. Hays, St. John A&H, N.Y.C., 1960-62, Devoe, Shadur, Mikva & P., Chgo., 1962-65; gen. counsel Playboy Enterprises, Inc., Chgo., 1965-78; ptnr. E. Leonard Rubin Law Offices, Chgo., 1978-81, Epton, Mullin & Druth Ltd., Chgo., 1981-86, Brinks, Hofer, Gilson & Lione, Chgo., 1986-96, Gordon & Glickson, LLC, Chgo., 1996—2002, Sachnoff & Weaver, Ltd., Chgo., 2002—. Adj. prof. U. Ill., Northwestern U. Law Sch., Loyola U. Sch. Law, John Marshall Law Sch. Pres. Lawyers for Creative Arts, Chgo., 1983-85; bd. dirs. Wisdom Bridge Theatre, Chgo., 1983-85; mem., bd. dirs. Appletree Theater of Highland Park. Cpl. U.S. Army, 1953-5, ETO. Mem. ABA, Ill. Bar Assn., Chgo. Bar Assn. (bd. mgrs. 1983-85, chmn. various coms., dir. Christmas Spirits Satire Show 1965-99), Union Internat. Des Avocats (pres. intellectual property commn. 1997-2000), Copyright Soc. Am. (trustee, past pres. midwest chpt.). Jewish. Entertainment, Libel, Trademark and copyright. Home: 270 Sunset Dr Northfield IL 60093-1047 Office: Sachnoff & Weaver Ltd 30 S Wacker Dr Ste 2900 Chicago IL 60606 E-mail: elrubin@sachnoff.com.

RUBIN, HERBERT, lawyer; b. Lisbon, Conn., June 4, 1918; s. Simon and Rose (Berko) R.; m. Rose Luttan, July 6, 1941; children: Barbara, Caroline, Donald. AB, CCNY, 1938; JD, NYU, 1942. Bar: N.Y. 1942, U.S. Dist. Ct. (so. and ea. dists.) N.Y. 1951, U.S. Supreme Ct. 1956, U.S. Ct. Appeals (2d, 3d, 4th, 6th, 9th, 10th, 11th and D.C. cirs.). Assoc. Newman & Bisco, 1942; faculty NYU Law Sch., 1946-50, 57-62; prof. creditors' rights Rutgers U. Law Sch., 1949-57; pvt. practice, 1946-56; ptnr. Sereni, Herzfeld & Rubin, and successor Herzfeld & Rubin, N.Y.C., 1956—, sr. ptnr., 1968—. Instr. mil. law, 1944-46; prof. constl. law L.I. U., 1963-68; trustee North Shore L.I. Jewish Hosp. Editor-in-chief NYU Law Rev., 1940-41; bd. editors N.Y. Law Jour., 1971—; contbr. articles to profl. jours. Mem. N.Y. State Banking Bd., 1975-85, N.Y. State Jud. Selection Com., 1975-83, Sen. Moynihan's Jud. Selection Com., 1982-2000, Sen. Schumer's Jud. Selection Com., 1999—, City Charter Revision Commn., 1998-2001; trustee Am. Assn. Jewish Lawyers and Jurists. 1st lt. Signal Corps, AUS, 1942-46. Recipient award NCCJ, 1967, United Jewish Appeal, 1968, 97, Israel Bonds, 1973, NYU Law Assn. award 1987, Judge Weinfeld award, 1992. Fellow Am. Bar Found.; mem. ABA (mem. coun. N.Y. state), N.Y. State Bar Assn., Queens County Bar Assn. (pres. 1970), Assn. Bar City Of N.Y., Fed. Bar Coun., Jewish Lawyers Guild (award 2001). General civil litigation, Corporate, general, Private international. Office: Herzfeld & Rubin 40 Wall St Fl 54 New York NY 10005-2301

RUBIN, JEFFREY MARK, lawyer, insurance company executive; b. N.Y.C., Apr. 26, 1956; s. Irwin S. and Tamara (Benenson) R.; m. Susan L. Rubin, Aug. 4, 1990; children: Leigh, Kate, Tess, Abe. BA in Polit. Sci., SUNY, Oneonta, 1978; JD, Cornell U., 1981. Bar: Ill. 1981. Assoc. Abramson & Fox, Chgo., 1981-84; from assoc. to ptnr. Phelan, Pope & John, Ltd., Chgo., 1984-96; of counsel Lovell White Durrant, Chgo., 1996-97; sr. v.p., sec., gen. counsel, bd. dirs. Internat. Ins. Co., Chgo., 1997-99, v.p., dir. claims litigation, 1999-2001; v.p. reins. work-out, 2001—. Mem. ABA (chair tort and ins. sect. corporate counsel com. 1995-96), Chgo. Bar Assn. (chair jud. evaluation com. 1995-96, bd. mgrs. 1997-99), Law Club of Chgo., Abraham Marovitz Inn of Ct. General civil litigation, Corporate, general, Insurance. Office: RiverStone Reins Svcs LLC 250 Commercial St Ste 5000 Manchester NH 03101-1143 E-mail: JeffRubinNH@attbi.com., Jeff_Rubin@trg.com.

RUBIN, MICHAEL, lawyer; b. Boston, July 19, 1952; m. Andrea L. Peterson, May 29, 1983; children: Peter, Eric, Emily. AB, Brandeis U., 1973; JD, Georgetown U., 1977. Bar: Calif. 1978, U.S. Dist. Ct. (no. dist.) Calif. 1978, U.S. Ct. Appeals (9th cir.) 1978, U.S. Ct. Appeals (5th, 7th, 10th cirs.) 1982, U.S. Supreme Ct. 1984, U.S. Ct. Appeals (D.C. cir.) 1984, U.S. Ct. Appeals (11th cir.) 1987. Teaching fellow Law Sch. Stanford (Calif.) U., 1977-78; law clerk to Hon. Charles B. Renfrew U.S. Dist. Ct. (no. dist.) Calif., San Francisco, 1978-79; law clerk to Hon. James R. Browning U.S. Ct. Appeals (9th cir.), San Francisco, 1979-80; law clerk to Hon. William J. Brennan, Jr. U.S. Supreme Ct., Washington, 1980-81; assoc. Altshuler & Berzon, San Francisco, 1981-85, ptnr., 1985-89, Altshuler, Berzon, Nussbaum, Berzon & Rubin, San Francisco, 1989-2000, Altshuler, Berzon, Nussbaum, Rubin & Demain, San Francisco, 2000—. Civil rights, Federal civil litigation, Labor (including EEOC, Fair Labor Standards Act, labor-management relations, NLRB, OSHA). Office: Altshuler Berzon Nussbaum Rubin & Demain 177 Post St Ste 300 San Francisco CA 94108-4700 E-mail: mrubin@altshulerberzon.com.

RUBIN, MICHAEL HARRY, lawyer, educator; b. Baton Rouge, Jan. 13, 1950; s. Alvin B. and Janice (Ginsberg) R.; m. Ayan J. (Liss), June 11, 1972; children: Bethany, Gillian. BA(hon.) , Amherst Coll., 1972; JD, La. State U., 1975. Bar: La., 1975; U.S. Ct. Appeals (5th cir.) 1975; U.S. Dist. Ct. (mid., ea. and we. dists.) La., 1976; U.S. Supreme Ct., 1982. Ptnr. Sanders, Downing, Kean, and Cazedessus, Baton Rouge, 1983-93, McGlinchey and Stafford, Baton Rouge, 1993—. Adj. prof. La. State U. Law Sch., 1976. Author: Louisiana Security Devices, Cases, 2003; contbr. articles to law jour. Mem.: La. Bankers Assn., Baton Rouge Bar Assn., So. Conf. Bar Pres., past pres. of La. State Bar Assn. Appellate, Federal civil litigation, Property, real (including real estate development, water). Office: McGlinchey & Stafford One American Pl 9th Fl Baton Rouge LA 70825

RUBIN, RICHARD ALLAN, lawyer; b. N.Y.C., June 19, 1942; s. Louis Max and Ruth Ann (Goldman) R.; m. Susan Deborah Levitt, June 18, 1966; children: Karen, Jill. BS, Queens Coll., 1964; JD, Bklyn. Law Sch., 1967; LLM, NYU, 1968. Bar: N.Y. 1967. Assoc. Schwartz and Frank, N.Y.C., 1968-69, Javits and Javits, N.Y.C., 1969-71; ptnr. Wolf Haldenstein Adler Freeman Herz & Frank, N.Y.C., 1972-76, Parker Chapin LLP, N.Y.C., 1977-2000, Jenkens & Gilchrist, Parker Chapin LLP, N.Y.C., 2001—. Lectr. Am. Mgmt. Assn., N.Y. Bar Assn. Mem. ABA. Corporate, general, Finance, Securities. Office: Jenkens & Gilchrist Parker Chapin LLP Chrysler Bldg 405 Lexington Ave New York NY 10174-0002

RUBINE, ROBERT SAMUEL, lawyer; b. Rockaway, N.Y., Feb. 28, 1947; s. George and Beatrice (Simon) R.; m. Marilyn Goldberg Rubine, Aug. 15, 1970; children: Seth B., Marisa H. BA, Queens Coll., 1968; JD, Syracuse U., 1971. Bar: N.Y. 1972, Fla. 1975; U.S. Dist. Ct. (ea. and so. dists.) N.Y., 1976; U.S. Supreme Ct. 1976. Trial atty. Legal Aid Soc. Nassau County, Mineola, N.Y., 1971-77; atty. Reifman and Rubine, Jericho, N.Y., 1977-79; ptnr. Stein, Rubine and Stein, Mineola, 1979-94, Rubine and Rubine, Mineola, 1995—. Adj. prof. C.W. Post Coll., Greenvale, N.Y., 1979-82. Author: (chpt.) Criminal and Civil Investigation Handbook, 1981. Dir. Legal Aid Soc. Nassau County, 1989—, pres., 1994-95, treas., 1996—. Mem. N.Y. State Bar Assn., N.Y. State Assn. Criminal Def. Lawyers, N.Y. State Defenders Assn., Nassau County Bar Assn. Avocation: golf. Criminal, Family and matrimonial, Personal injury (including property damage). Home: 5 Woodland Rd Oyster Bay NY 11771-3910 Office: Rubine and Rubine PLLC 114 Old Country Rd Mineola NY 11501-4400

RUBINO, VICTOR JOSEPH, academic administrator, lawyer; b. N.Y.C., Dec. 25, 1940; s. Joseph V. and Olympia (Gayda) R.; 1 child, Victor Gayda. BA in Govt., Cornell U., 1962, LLB, 1965. Bar: N.Y. 1965, U.S. Dist. Ct. (so. dist.) N.Y. 1969. Staff atty. Westchester Legal Svcs., White Plains, N.Y., 1968-71; assoc. Squadron Ellenoff Plesent & Lehrer, N.Y.C., 1971; treas., program officer Council on Legal Edn., N.Y.C., 1971-79; assoc. dir. Practising Law Inst., N.Y.C., 1979-83, exec. dir., 1983—. Democratic candidate for N.Y. State Assembly, 1970; chmn. Rye (N.Y.) Human Rights Commn., 1975-76. Served to capt. U.S. Army, 1966-68. Mem. ABA, Assn. Bar City N.Y. Office: Practising Law Inst 810 7th Ave Fl 26 New York NY 10019-5818

RUBINSTEIN, ALAN JAY, lawyer; BA, U. Miami, 1963; JD, U. Fla., 1965. Bar: Fla. 1965, U.S. Supreme Ct. 1971; cert. marital & family lawyer Fla. Bar. 1985. Ptnr. Goldberg, Rubenstein & Buckley, 1965-88; pvt. practice Ft. Myers, Fla., 1988—. Lectr. in field. Contbr. articles to profl. jours. Fellow Am. Acad. Matrimonial Lawyers (chair-person sub bd. examiners Fla. chpt.); mem. ABA (family & econs. law sects.), Am. Arbitration Assn., Fla. Bar Assn. (bd. examiners, exec. com. 1980-88), Lee County Bar Assn., Family and matrimonial. Office: PO Box 368 Fort Myers FL 33902-0368

RUBINSTEIN, ESTA, paralegal; b. Jacksonville, Fla., Oct. 18; m. Alan J. Rubinstein. BS in Advt., U. Fla., 1965. Cert. legal asst.; cert. small claims ct. mediator. Legal asst. R&B, Ft. Myers, Fla., 1979-89; office mgr. R&H, Ft. Myers, 1989-2000, Goldburg, Rubinstein & Buckley, 1979—89. Dir., cmty. adv. bd. Riverside Bank, N. Ft. Myers; mem. foster care Task Force for Lee County. Chair N. Ft. Myers LRPC, 1997-99; mediator, Small Claims Ct., 1999—. Avocations: reading, travel.

RUBINSTEIN, FREDERIC ARMAND, lawyer; b. Antwerp, Belgium, Apr. 20, 1931; came to U.S., 1942; s. Samuel N. and Steffa (Warrenreich) R.; m. Susan August, Dec. 24, 1968; 1 child, Nicolas Eric August Rubinstein. BA, Cornell U., 1953, JD, 1955. Bar: N.Y. 1955. Assoc. Law Offices of I. Robert Feinberg, N.Y.C., 1955-60, Guggenheimer & Untermyer, N.Y.C., 1960-65, ptnr., 1965-85, Kelley Drye & Warren LLP, N.Y.C., 1985—. Vice chmn. zoning & planning com. Local Community Bd. # 6, N.Y.C., 1980-86. Mem. ABA (bus. law sect., emerging growth ventures subcom., chmn. 1988-96), Cornell Club of N.Y. Corporate, general, Mergers and acquisitions, Securities. Office: Kelley Drye & Warren LLP 101 Park Ave New York NY 10178-0002

RUBRIGHT, JAMES ALFRED, paper company executive; b. Phila., Dec. 17, 1946; s. James Alfred and Helen Lucille (Evans) R. (deceased); m. Mary Elizabeth Angelich, Dec. 30, 1987; children: Noah Michael, Benjamin James, Jami Anne, Nathaniel Drew, James McCurdy, William Angelich. BA, Yale U., 1969; JD, U. Va., 1972. Bar: Ga. 1972. Ptnr. King & Spalding, Atlanta, 1972-94; sr. v.p., gen. counsel Sonat Inc., Birmingham, 1994-97; pres. So. Natural Gas Co. subs. Sonat Inc., Birmingham, 1997-98; exec. v.p. Sonat Inc., Birmingham, 1998-99; CEO Rock-Tenn Co., Norcross, Ga., 1999—. Office: Rock-Tenn Co 504 Thrasher St Norcross GA 30071-1914

RUBY, STANLEY L. lawyer; b. Louisville, Feb. 23, 1937; s. David and Dorothy (Kantrovitz) R.; m. Sara A. Brown, Aug. 18, 1963; children: Jill M., Allison D. BA, Vanderbilt U., 1959, LLB, 1961; LLM in Taxation, NYU, 1964. Bar: Ky. 1962, D.C. 1966, Ohio 1971, U.S. Tax Ct. 1985. Atty. advisor U.S. Tax Ct., Washington, 1964-66; assoc. Surrey, Karasik, Gould & Greene, Washington, 1966-68; atty. U.S. Dept. of Justice, Washington, 1968-70; assoc. Paxton & Seasongood, Cin., 1970-76; shareholder Schwartz, Manes & Ruby, Cin., 1976—. Contbr. articles to profl. jours. Corporate, general, Estate planning, Taxation, general. Office: Schwartz Manes & Ruby 441 Vine St Cincinnati OH 45202

RUCKER, DOUGLAS PENDLETON, JR., lawyer; b. Richmond, Va., Dec. 26, 1945; s. Douglas Pendleton and Margaret (Williams) R.; m. Marian F. Copeland; 1 child, Louise Meredith. BA, Hampden-Sydney Coll., 1968; JD, U. Va., 1972. Bar: Va. 1972, D.C. 1986, U.S. Dist. Ct. (ea. and we. dists.) Va. 1972, U.S. Ct. Appeals (4th cir.) 1982, U.S. Supreme Ct. 1982, U.S. Ct. Claims 1995. Assoc. Sands, Anderson, Marks & Miller, Richmond, Va., 1972-76, mem., 1977—, also bd. dirs. Active Lewis Ginter Bot. Garden; mem. adv. com. Richmond Renaissance; active St. John's Episcopal Ch., mem. vestry, 1994—98, register, 1996, jr. warden, 1997, sr. warden, 1998, trustee, 1994—; bd. dirs., treas. Va. Ctr. for the Book Capital chpt. ARC; bd. dirs., vice chmn. James River Devel. Corp. With Va. Army N.G., 1968—74. Mem.: SAR, ABA, Met. Richmond C. of C., Bar Assn. D.C., Soc. Colonial Wars in the State of Va. (dep. gov. gen.), Richmond Bar Assn. (real estate sect., bd. dirs. 1994—97), Va. Bar Assn. (constrn. law chmn. 1992, real estate and bus. law sects., exec. com. 1992—97, pres. 1996), Va. Law Found. (bd. dirs. 1998—), Am. Bar Found., The Twenty-Three Hundred Club, The Country Club Va., The Commonwealth Club. Property, real (including real estate development, water), General civil litigation, Professional liability. Office: Sands Anderson Marks & Miller PO Box 1998 Richmond VA 23218-1998 E-mail: DRucker@sandsanderson.com.

RUCKER, R.D. lawyer; b. Swifton, Ark., Jan. 14, 1950; s. Curtis and Demora (Tidwell) R. BA, U. Ark., 1971; MA, U. Iowa, 1972, PhD, 1981; JD, U. Tex., 1985. Bar: Tex. 1985, U.S. Dist. Ct. (no. dist.) Tex. 1988, U.S. Ct. Appeals (5th cir.) 1989. Asst. atty. gen. Atty. Gen.'s Office, Austin, Tex., 1985-86; asst. dist. atty. Dist. Atty.'s Office, Waco, Tex., 1986-87; 1st asst. pub. defender Pub. Defender's Office, Wichita Falls, Tex., 1987-88; atty. R.D. Rucker's Law Office, Dallas, 1988—. Author: Eros and the Sexual Revolution: Studies in the Psychology of the Human Mind, 1991, Drugs, Drug Addiction and Drug Dealing: The Origin and Nature of, and the Solution to, the American Drug Problem, 1991, Abraham Lincoln's Social and Political Thought, 1992, Jesus Christ and the Origin of Christianity, 1993, Marriage, Love, and the Family: An Investigation into the Role of the Black Woman in the African-American Family, 1998, Sweet Land of Liberty: A Poetical Journey Through America, 1996-1998, 1998, The Nature, Evolution and Structure of the Universe: A Twenty First Century Theory, 1999. Avocations: poetry, track, calisthenics. Appellate, Criminal. Office: PO Box 222167 Dallas TX 75222-2167 E-mail: RDRUCK@aol.com.

RUCKER, ROBERT D. judge; b. Canton, Ga. married; 3 children. BA, Ind. U.; JD, Valparaiso Sch. of Law; LLM, U. Va. Dep. prosecuting atty., Lake County, Ind.; city atty. City of Gary, Ind.; pvt. practice East Chicago; justice Ind. State Supreme Ct., Indpls., 1999—. Former vice chmn. Ind. Commn. for Continuing Legal Edn. Bd. dirs. Legal Svcs. of N.W. Ind. Decorated Vietnam Vet. Office: State House Rm 312 200 W Washington St Indianapolis IN 46204-2798

RUDDY, FRANK, lawyer, former ambassador; b. N.Y.C., Sept. 15, 1937; s. Francis Stephen and Teresa (O'Neil) Ruddy; children: Neil, David, Stephen. AB, Holy Cross Coll., 1959; MA, NYU, 1962, LLM, 1967; LLB, Loyola U., New Orleans, 1965; PhD, Cambridge U., Eng., 1969. Bar: D.C., N.Y., Tex., U.S. Supreme Ct. Faculty Cambridge U., 1967-69; asst. gen. counsel USIA, Washington, 1969-72; sr. atty. Office of Telecomm. Policy, White House, Washington, 1972-73; dep. gen. counsel USIA, Washington, 1973-74; counsel Exxon Corp., Houston, 1974-81; asst. adminstr. AID (with rank asst. sec. state) Dept. State, Washington, 1981-84; U.S. ambassador to Equatorial Guinea, 1984-88; gen. counsel U.S. Dept. Energy, Washington, 1988-89; v.p. Sierra Blanca Devel. Corp., Washington, 1989-92; ptnr. Ruddy & Muir, Washington, 1998—. Vis. scholar Johns Hopkins Sch. Advanced Internat. Studies, 1990—94; dep. chmn. UN Referendum for Western Sahara, 1994. Author: International Law in the Enlightenment, 1975; editor: American International Law Cases (series); editor in chief Internat. Lawyer; contbr. articles to legal jours. Bd. dirs. African Devel. Found., Washington, 1983-84, Human Life Internat., 1999—; mem. Coun. of Am. Ambs., Washington, 1988—. Served with USMCR, 1956-61 Mem.: ABA (chmn. treaty compliance sect. 1991—93), Hague Acad. Internat. Law Alumni Assn., Internat. Law Assn., Am. Soc. Internat. Law, Dacor House, Cosmos Club (Washington). Republican. Roman Catholic. Nuclear power, Environmental, Private international. Home: 5600 Western Ave Chevy Chase MD 20815-3406 Office: Ruddy and Muir 1717 K Street NW Ste 600 Washington DC 20036 E-mail: global@globalltd.com.

RUDEBUSCH, ALICE ANN, lawyer; b. Milw., July 9, 1966; d. Leroy George and Maryann Grace (Carlson) Rudebusch; m. Todd William Nejedlo, May 25, 1991 (div. 1999). BA, Northwestern U., 1988; JD, U. Wis., 1991; Certificat De Langue, Université De Paris, 1986. Bar: Wis. 1991, U.S. Dist. Ct. (we. dist.) Wis. 1991, U.S. Dist. Ct. (ea. dist.) Wis. 1995, U.S. Dist. Ct. (no. dist.) Ill. 1995. Assoc. Hanson Gasiorkiewicz & Weber, S.C., Racine, Wis., 1991-96; ptnr. Hanson & Gasiorkiewicz, S.C., Racine, Wis., 1997—. Alderperson City of Oak Creek Common Coun.; bd. dirs. YWCA, Racine, 1995—2001, sec., 1996—98, pres., 1999—2001; vol. Legal Action of Wis., Kenosha, 1996—97. Mem. State Bar Wis., Wis. Acad. Trial Lawyers, Racine County Bar Assn. General civil litigation, Personal injury (including property damage), Workers' compensation. Office: Hanson & Gasiorkiewicz SC 2932 Northwestern Ave Racine WI 53404-2249 E-mail: info@lawracine.com.

RUDER, DAVID STURTEVANT, lawyer, educator, government official; b. Wausau, Wis., May 25, 1929; s. George Louis and Josephine (Sturtevant) R.; m. Susan M. Small; children: Victoria Chesley, Julia Larson, David Sturtevant II, John Coulter; m stepchildren: Elizabeth Frankel, Rebecca Wilkinson. BA cum laude, Williams Coll., 1951; JD with honors, U. Wis., 1957, LLD, 2002. Bar: Wis. 1957, Ill. 1962. Of counsel Schiff Hardin & Waite, Chgo., 1971-76; assoc. Quarles & Brady, Milw., 1957-61; asst. prof. law Northwestern U., Chgo., 1961-63, assoc. prof., 1963-65, prof., 1965—, William W. Gurley meml. prof. of law, 1994—, assoc. dean Law Sch., 1965-66, dean Law Sch., 1977-85; chmn. Securities and Exch. Commn., Washington, 1987-89; ptnr. Baker & McKenzie, Chgo., 1990-94, sr. counsel, 1994-99. Cons. Am. Law Inst. Fed. Securities Code; planning dir. Corp. Counsel Inst., 1962-66, 76-77, com. mem., 1962-87, 90—; adv. bd. Ray Garrett Jr. Corp. and Securities Law Inst., 1980-87, 90—; vis. lectr. U. de Liege, 1967; vis. prof. law U. Pa., Phila., 1971; faculty Salzburg Seminar, 1976; mem. legal adv. com. bd. dirs. N.Y. Stock Exch., 1978-82; mem. com. profl. responsibility Ill. Supreme Ct., 1978-87; adv. bd. Securities Regulation Inst., 1978—, chmn., 1994-97; bd. govs. Nat. Assn. Securities Dealers, 1990-93, chmn. Legal Adv. Bd., 1993-96, Arbitration Policy Task Force, 1994-97; trustee Fin. Acctg. Found., 1996-2002, Internat. Acctg. Stds. Com. Found., 2000—; mem. Internat. Acctg. Stds. Com. Strategy Working Party, 1997-99; chmn. Securities and Exch. Commn. Hist. Soc., 1999—; chmn. Mut. Fund Dirs. Forum, 1999—. Editor-in-chief: Williams Coll. Record, 1950-51, U. Wis. Law Rev, 1957; editor: Proc. Corp. Counsel Inst, 1962-66; contbr. articles to legal periodicals. 1st lt. AUS, 1951-54. Fellow Am. Bar Found.; ABA (sec. bus. law 1970—, coun. 1970-94, com. chmn., mem. various coms.), Chgo. Bar Assn., Wis. Bar Assn., Am. Law Inst., Order of Coif, Comml. Club of Chgo., Lawyers Club Chgo., Gargoyle Soc., Phi Beta Kappa, Phi Delta Pi, Zeta Psi. Home: 325 Orchard Ln Highland Park IL 60035-1939 E-mail: d-ruder@law.northwestern.edu.

RUDLOFF, WILLIAM JOSEPH, lawyer; b. Bonne Terre, Mo., Feb. 19, 1941; s. Leslie W. and Alta M. (Hogenmiller) R.; m. Rita Howton, Aug. 5, 1965; children: Daniel, Andrea, Leslie, Susan. AB, Western Ky. U., 1961; JD, Vanderbilt U., 1965. Bar: Ky. 1965, Tenn. 1965, U.S. Supreme Ct. 1975, U.S. Ct. Appeals (sixth cir.) 1981. U.S. magistrate Western Dist. Ky., 1971-75. NDEA fellow U. Nebr., 1961-62, U. Ky. fellow. Fellow: Ky. Bar Found. (life; charter); mem.: Internat. Acad. Litigators (diplomate), Ky. Acad. Trial Attys., Am. Coll. Legal Medicine, Trial Attys. Am., Def. Rsch. Inst., Am. Counsel Assn., Am. Bd. Trial Advocates. Federal civil litigation, State civil litigation, Insurance. Home: 126 Broadway St Smiths Grove KY 42171-8258 Office: 553 E Main St Bowling Green KY 42101-2256 E-mail: rudloff@aol.com.

RUDMAN, PAUL LEWIS, judge; b. Bangor, Maine, Mar. 26, 1935; s. Abraham Moses and Irene (Epstein) R.; m. Inez Lee Kolonel, Oct. 8, 1961; Andrew Isaac, Carole Sue. AB, Yale Coll., 1957; JD, George Washington U. Sch. Law, 1960. Bar: Maine 1960, D.C. 1960; U.S. Dist. Ct. Maine, 1961. Ptnr. Rudman & Winchell, Bangor, 1960-92; justice Maine Supreme Jud. Ct., Bangor, 1992—. Capt. Maine Air NG, 1960-66. Office: Maine Supreme Jud Ct Penobscot County Courthouse 97 Hammond St Bangor ME 04401

RUDNICK, IRENE KRUGMAN, lawyer, former state legislator, educator; b. Columbia, S.C., Dec. 27, 1929; d. Jack and Jean (Getter) Krugman; m. Harold Rudnick, Nov. 7, 1954 (dec.); children: Morris, Helen Gail. AB cum laude, U. S.C., 1949, JD, 1952. Bar: S.C. 1952. Individual practice law, Aiken, S.C., 1952—; now ptnr. Rudnick & Rudnick; instr. bus. law, criminal law U. S.C., Aiken, 1962—; tchr. Warrenville Elem. Sch., 1965-70; supt. edn. Aiken County, 1970-72; mem. S.C. Ho. of Reps., 1972-78, 80-84, 86-94. Pres. Adath Yeshurun Synagogue; active Aiken County Dem. Party, S.C. Dem. Party; hon. mem. Aiken Able-Disabled. Recipient Citizen of Yr. award, 1976-77, Bus. and Profl. Women's Career Woman of Yr., 1978, 94, Aiken County Friend of Edn. award, 1985, 93, Outstanding Legis. award Disabled Vets., 1991, Citizen of the Yr. award Planned Parenthood, 1994, Sertoma Svc. to Mankind award, 1996. Mem. NEA, S.C. Tchrs. Assn., Aiken County Tchrs. Assn., Am. Bar Assn., Aiken County Bar Assn., Nat. Order Women Legislators, AAUW, Aiken Able-Disabled (hon.), Aiken Hist. Soc., Alpha Delta Kappa, Order Eastern Star, Hadassah Sisterhood, Am. Legion Aux. Office: PO Box 544 135 Pendleton St NW Aiken SC 29801-3859

RUDNICK, PAUL DAVID, lawyer; b. Chgo., May 15, 1940; s. Harry Louis and Cele (Gordon) R.; m. Hope Korshak, June 13, 1963; children: William A., Carolyn. BS, Tulane U., 1962; JD cum laude, Northwestern U., 1965. Bar: Ill. 1965, Colo. 1994, U.S. Dist. Ct. (no. dist.) Ill. Assoc. Schiff, Hardin & Waite, Chgo., 1965-66; ptnr. Piper Rudnick, Chgo., 1966-99, sr. counsel, 2000—. Editor Northwestern U. Law Rev., 1964-65; co-editor, author: Illinois Real Estate Forms, 1989. Mem. Pitkin County Colo. Planning and Zoning Commn. Mem. Order of Coif. Corporate, general, Landlord-tenant, Property, real (including real estate development, water). Office: Piper Rudnick 203 N La Salle St Ste 1800 Chicago IL 60601-1210 E-mail: paul.rudnick@piperrudnick.com.

RUDO, SAUL E. tax lawyer; b. Balt., Aug. 2, 1958; m. Gail Rudo, June 12; children: Victor, Sarah. BS in Acctg., U. Ill., 1980; JD, Harvard U., 1983. Bar: Ill. 1983. Ptnr. Katten Muchin Zavis Rosenman, Chgo., 1983—. Bd. dirs. First Bank Highland Park, 2002—. Bd. dirs. Bernard Weinger Jewish Cmty. Ctr., Deerfield, Ill., 1997-2002. Mem. Chgo. Bar Assn., U. Ill. Commerce Alumni Assn. (bd. dirs.). Public international, Mergers and acquisitions, Taxation, general. Home: 510 Susan Ln Deerfield IL 60015-3951 Office: Katten Muchin Zavis Rosenman 525 W Monroe St Ste 1600 Chicago IL 60661-3693 E-mail: saul.rudo@kmzr.com.

RUDOLPH, GEORGE COOPER, lawyer; b. Butte, Mont., June 29, 1951; Student, Mont. Coll. Mineral, Sci. and Tech., 1969-71; BA in Psychology magna cum laude, U. S.C., 1973; JD, U. Calif., San Francisco, 1976. Bar: Calif. 1976, U.S. Dist. Ct. (cen. dist.) Calif. 1977, U.S. Dist. Ct. (no. dist.) Calif. 1977, U.S. Ct. Appeals (9th cir.) 1977, U.S. Dist. Ct. (so. dist.) Calif. 1983, U.S. Supreme Ct. 1985. Assoc. Fulop, Rolston, Burns & McKittrick, Beverly Hills and Newport Beach, Calif., 1976-81, Fulop & Hardee, Newport Beach, 1981-82, ptnr., 1982, McKittrick, Jackson, DeMarco & Peckenpaugh, Newport Beach, 1983-87, The Rudolph Law Group, Costa Mesa, Calif., 1988-99, Buchalter Nemer Fields & Younger, Newport Beach, 1999—. Lectr. Calif. Continuing Edn. of The Bar, 1985-97, UCLA, U. Calif., Irvine, San Diego, Santa Barbara, 1985-89. Mem. ABA, Assn. Trial Lawyers Am., Assn. Bus. Trial Lawyers, Orange County Bar Assn., B'nai B'rith. Democrat. Jewish. Federal civil litigation, State civil litigation, Intellectual property. Office: Buchalter Nemer Fields & Younger 895 Dove St Ste 400 Newport Beach CA 92660 E-mail: grudolph@buchalter.com.

RUDOLPH, GILBERT LAWRENCE, lawyer; b. L.A., Aug. 23, 1946; s. Martin and Marion R.; Susan Ilene Fellenbaum, Sept. 18, 1983; children: Samara Lisa, Felicia Beth. BA, Ariz. State U., 1967; postgrad., Am. U., Washington, 1967-69; JD, U. Cin., 1973. Bar: D.C. 1973, U.S. Dist. Ct. D.C. 1974, U.S. Ct. Appeals (D.C. cir.) 1974, Ariz. 1975, U.S. Dist. Ct. Ariz. 1975, Calif. 1979. Assoc. Streich, Lang, Weeks & Cardon, P.A., Phoenix, 1975-78; ptnr. Gilbert L. Rudolph, P.C., Phoenix, 1978-87; sr. mem. O'Connor, Cavanagh, Anderson, Killingsworth & Beshears, P.A., Phoenix, 1987-99; shareholder Greenberg Traurig LLP, Phoenix, 1999—. Lectr. on lending issues. Bd. dirs. Temple Chai, 2002—, Make-A-Wish Found. of Am., 1984—89, Aid to Adoption of Spl. Kids, Ariz., 1995—. Fellow Am. Coll. Consumer Fin. Svcs. Lawyers; mem. ABA (com. on consumer fin. svcs. bus. law sect. 1981—, com. on comml. fin. svcs. 1989—, mem. com. on uniform comml. code 1992—), Conf. on Consumer Fin. Law (governing com. 1986—). Republican. Jewish. Banking, Commercial, consumer (including collections, credit), Commercial, contracts (including sales of goods; commercial financing). Office: Greenberg Traurig LLP Ste 700 2375 E Camelback Rd Phoenix AZ 85016 E-mail: rudolphg@gtlaw.com.

RUDOLPH, JAMES LEONARD, lawyer; b. Beverly, Mass., Sept. 26, 1950; s. Robert P. and Joyce B. (Yoffa) R.; m. Susan B. Gouchberg, Oct. 31, 1981. B.A., U. Denver, 1972; J.D., Boston Coll., 1975. Bar: Mass. 1975, U.S. Dist. Ct. Mass. 1976, U.S. Ct. Appeals (1st cir.) 1978, U.S. Supreme Ct. 1984. Ptnr. Gargill, Sassoon & Rudolph, Boston, from 1976; now ptnr. Rudolph Friedmann LLP, Boston; trustee Eastern Bank. Chmn. Swampscott Zoning Bd. Appeals (Mass.), 1984—89, mem., 1983—89; pres. Jewish Rehab. Ctr., Swampscott, 1984-89; pres. Camp Kingswood, Bridgton, Maine, 1987—89; chmn. North Shore adv. group, mem. nat. exec. com. Anti-Defamation League; trustee Gov. Dummer Acad.; past pres. JRC Charitable Found. Mem. ATLA, ABA, Boston Bar Assn., Mass. Bar Assn., Mass. Conveyancers Assn., Mass. Assoc. Builders and Contractors (gen. counsel, past pres.), Belmont Country Club, Boston Yacht (Marblehead, Mass.), Mt. Scopus Lodge (Malden, Mass.). Commercial, contracts (including sales of goods; commercial financing), Corporate, general, Property, real (including real estate development, water). Office: Rudolph Friedmann LLP 92 State St Boston MA 02109-2004

RUEDA, PEDRO ANTONIO, lawyer; b. Madrid, July 25, 1962; JD, U. Complutense de Madrid, 1985; LLM, U. Pa., 1987. From assoc. to ptnr. Gomez-Acebo & Pombo, Madrid, 1987-94; fgn. assoc. Skadden Arps Slate Meagher & Flom, N.Y.C., 1989-90; ptnr. Araoz & Rueda, Madrid, 1994—. Fulbright scholar, 1986. Mem. Madrid Bar Assn. (scholar 1987). Mergers and acquisitions. Office: Araoz & Rueda Castellana 164 Madrid 28046 Spain E-mail: rueda@araozyruedaabogados.es.

RUEGGER, PHILIP T., III, lawyer; b. Plainfield, N.J., Oct. 14, 1949; s. Philip T. Jr. and Gloria Marie (McLaughlin) R.; m. Rebecca Lee Huffman, Aug. 3, 1974; children: Sarah, Britt, Michael. AB, Dartmouth Coll., 1971; JD, U. Va., 1974. Bar: N.Y. 1975. Assoc. Simpson Thacher & Bartlett, N.Y.C., 1974-81, ptnr., 1981—, head corp. dept. Mem. Assn. Bar City N.Y., Phi Beta Kappa. Clubs: Manursing Island (Rye, N.Y.), Apawamis (Rye). Corporate, general, Mergers and acquisitions. Home: 275 Grace Church St Rye NY 10580-4201 Office: Simpson Thacher & Bartlett 425 Lexington Ave Fl 15 New York NY 10017-3954 E-mail: pruegger@stblaw.com.

RUFE, CYNTHIA MARIE, judge; b. Phila., Oct. 30, 1948; d. Lucien Russell and Antoinette Marie (Galizia) Favata; m. John J. Rufe, Jan. 2, 1999; children: Tiffany Marie, Meredith Anne. BA, Adelphi U., 1970; secondary edn. cert., Bloomsburg State Coll., 1972; JD, SUNY, Buffalo, 1977. Bar: Pa. 1977, U.S. Dist. Ct. (ea. dist.) Pa. 1983, U.S. Ct. Appeals (3d cir.) 1987, U.S. Supreme Ct. 1984. Tchr. Bristol (Pa.) Jr./Sr. H.S., 1970-72; law clk. Div. of Claims, State of N.Y., Buffalo, 1976; asst. pub. defender Bucks County, Doylestown, Pa., 1977-79, dep. pub. defender, 1979-81; pvt. practice Newtown, Pa., 1982-93; judge Ct. of Common Pleas, Bucks County, 1994—2002; judge ea. dist. U.S. Dist. Ct., Pa., 2002—. Appellate ct. rules com. Supreme Ct. of Pa. Appellate Ct., 1999-2002; solicitor Children and Youth Agy., Bucks County, 1984-88; spkr., panelist on various law related issues, Bucks County; mem. Conf. State Trial Judges, 1994-2002, jud. edn., correction and nominating com. juvenile ct. sect. Pres. bd. dirs. Preventive Rehab. Youth and Devel., Bristol, 1978-81; bd. dirs. Reaching-at-Problems Group Home, Chalfont, Pa., 1981-84, Three Arches, Inc., Falls Twp., Pa., 1985, Orgn. to Prevent Teenage Suicide, 1984-93, Youth Svcs., Inc., 1984-93, Today, Inc., 1987-93, Schofield Ford Bridge Reconstrn. Com., 1990-93. Recipient Trial Lawyer's award Erie County Bar Assn., 1977, Four Chaplains Legion of Honor, 1987, M.J. Kirkpatrick Leadership award A Woman's Place, 1999, award Commn. for Social Justice, Sons of Italy, 2000. Mem. Nat. Coun. Juvenile and Family Ct. Judges, Bucks County Bar Assn. (dir. 1983-85, chair criminal law sect. 1987-88, chair bench-bar com. 1988-89, chair membership com. 1983-85, lawyer reaching lawyer com. 1996-2002), Pa. Bar Assn., Pa. Trial Lawyers Assn., Pa. Coll. Criminal Def. Lawyers, Ill. Bar Assn., Temple Inn of Ct., Fed. Judges Assn., Soroptimists (past pres.). Republican. Roman Catholic. Office: Judges Chambers 601 Market St US Courthouse Rm 4000 Philadelphia PA 19106

RUFFNER, CHARLES LOUIS, lawyer; b. Cin., Nov. 7, 1936; s. Joseph H. and Edith (Solomon) R.; m. Mary Ann Kaufman, Jan. 30, 1966 (div. 1993); children: Robin Sue, David Robert; m. Nanette Diemer, Feb. 26, 1995. BSBA in Acctg., U. Fla., 1958; JD cum laude, U. Miami, 1964. Bar: Fla. 1964, U.S. Dist. Ct. (so. and Mid. dists.) Fla. 1964, U.S. Ct. Appeals (5th cir.) 1964, U. S. Ct. Appeals (11th cir.) 1984, U.S. Claims Ct. 1966, U.S. Tax Ct. 1966, U.S. Supreme Ct. 1969; cert. in taxation. Trial atty. tax divsn. Dept. Justice, Washington, 1964-67; pres. Forrest, Ruffner, Traum & Hagen, P.A., Miami, Fla., 1967-78, Ruffner, Hagen & Rifkin, P.A., Miami, 1978-81; tax ptnr. Myers, Kenin, Levinson, Ruffner, Frank & Richards, Miami, 1982-84; pres. Charles L. Ruffner, P.A., 1984—. Lectr. Fla. Internat. U., Miami. Author: A Practical Approach to Professional Corporations and Associations, 4 edits., 1970, (column) Tax Talk, Miami Law Rev.; editor Miami Law Rev., 1963-64; contbr. numerous articles on taxation to law jours. Named One of Best Lawyers in Am., 1999—. Mem. ABA, Fed. Bar Assn., Fla. Bar (exec. coun. tax sect. 1967-92, 95—, amicus curiae in test case of validity profl. corps.), Dade County Bar Assn., South Fla. Tax Litigation Assn. (chmn. 1986-00), Phi Alpha Delta, Phi Kappa Phi. Estate planning, Corporate, general, Taxation, general. Office: 8830 SW 67th Ct Miami FL 33156-1700 Fax: 305-668-6672. E-mail: cruff7117@aol.com.

RUGGERI, ROBERT EDWARD, lawyer; b. N.Y.C., Sept. 16, 1952; s. Mario Philip and Margaret Gloria (Pascale) R.; m. Mary Beth Thackeray, June 6, 1981. BA, Union Coll., 1974; JD, Antioch U., 1980. Bar: D.C. 1981, N.Y. 1993, U.S. Dist. Ct. D.C. 1982, U.S. Ct. Internat. Trade 1982, U.S. Ct. Appeals (fed. and D.C. cirs.) 1982, U.S. Supreme Ct. 1984. Trainee Commn. European Communities, Brussels, Belgium, 1980-81; legal cons. Secretariat, OECD, Paris, France, 1981-82; assoc. Stewart & Stewart, Washington, 1982-83, Graham and James, Washington, 1984-85, Rogers & Wells, Washington, 1985-92; dep. dir. legal affairs N.Y. State Dept. Environ. Conservation, 1993-94; assoc. counsel SUNY System, Albany, 1994—. Arbitrator NAFTA panels apptd. by U.S., Can., and Mex. govts., 1992—; adj. prof. Georgetown U. Law Ctr., 1988-92. Editor comments Antioch Law Jour., 1979-80. Trustee Schenectady County C.C., 1999—. Fulbright scholar, 1980-81. Mem. ABA, D.C. Bar Assn., Washington Fgn. Law Soc. (sec., treas. 1985-87, bd. govs. 1987-88), Am. Soc. Internat. Law. Roman Catholic. Legislative. Home: 1846 Union St Niskayuna NY 12309-4502 Office: SUNY Office U Counsel Univ Plz Rm S315 Albany NY 12246-0001

RUHM, THOMAS FRANCIS, retired lawyer, investor; b. Bridgeport, Conn., June 8, 1935; s. Herman David and Martica (Sturges) R.; m. Michele Wood, Oct. 5, 1974; children: Wendy Sturges, Thomas Wood. BA, Yale U., 1957; JD, Havard U., 1962. Bar: N.Y. 1963, U.S. Dist. Ct. (so. and ea. dists.) N.Y. 1964, U.S. Ct. Appeals (2d cir.) 1969. Assoc. Shearman & Sterling, N.Y.C., 1962-70; asst. gen. counsel Bessemer Securities Corp., N.Y.C., 1970-96, v.p., 1981-96; ret., 1996. Chmn. legal aspects venture capital investing Practicing Law Inst., N.Y. and San Francisco, 1979-81; lectr. on venture capital NYU Grad. Sch., 1986-90, Concordia Coll., Bronxville, N.Y., 1999-2001; expert on fed. securities law, venture capital legal matters, investment tax policy, Fed. Res. monetary policy; witness during 1980s fed. tax hearings; adj. prof. fin. St. John's U., 2000—. Contbg. author: Technology and Economic Policy, 1986; contbr. articles to profl. jours. Commr. upper divsn. Eastchester (N.Y.) Youth Soccer League, 1990-91, coach, 1985-91, dir. coaching 1995-96; sr. warden Christ Ch., Bronxville, N.Y., 1991-94; past v.p. and treas. Bronxville Sch. PTA; treas., bd. dirs. Friends of Bronxville Pub. Libr., 1997-2000; mem. Quogue (N.Y.) Cultural Com., 1998—; mem. Blue Hill Troupe, Ltd., 1972—. Lt. (j.g.) USNR, 1957-59, Res., 1961. Mem. Univ. Club (mem. coun. 2001—), Bronxville Field Club, Quogue Field Club, Quogue Beach Club. Republican. Corporate, general, Finance, Securities.

RUIZ, MICHELE ILENE, lawyer; b. Washington, Nov. 3, 1969; BS, Cornell U., 1991; JD, U. Chgo., 1994. Bar: U.S. Dist. Ct. (no. dist.) Ill. 1994. Assoc. McDermott, Will & Emery, Chgo., 1994—96, Sidley Austin Brown & Wood, Chgo., 1996—. Corporate, general, Securities. Office: Sidley Austin Brown & Wood Bank One Plz 10 S Dearborn Chicago IL 60603 Office Fax: 312-853-7036. E-mail: mruiz@sidley.com.

RUIZ, VANESSA, judge; b. San Jaun, P.R., Mar. 22, 1950; d. Fernando and Irma (Bosch) Ruiz-Suria; married; m. David E. Birenbaum, Oct. 22, 1983; stepchildren: Tracy, Matthew. BA, Wellesley Coll., 1972; JD, Georgetown U., 1975. Bar: D.C. 1972. Assoc. Fried, Frank, Harris, Shrives & Kampelman, Washington, 1975—83; sr. mgr., counsel Sears World Trade Inc., Washington, 1983—94; assoc. judge D.C. Ct. of Appeals, 1994—. Spkr. in field. Mem.: ABA, Inter-Am. Bar Assn. Office: DC Ct of Appeals 500 Indiana Ave NW Fl 6 Washington DC 20001-2131

RUIZ-VALERA, PHOEBE LUCILE, law librarian; b. Barranquilla, Colombia, Jan. 27, 1950; d. Ramon and Marion (Mehlman) Ruiz-Valera; m. Thomas Patrick Winkler, Mar. 27, 1981. BA cum laude, Westminster Coll., 1971; MLS, Rutgers U., 1974; MA, NYU, 1978. Libr. trainee Passaic (N.J.) Pub. Libr., 1973-74, reference libr., 1974; libr. assoc. cataloger NYU Law Libr., N.Y.C., 1974-79, asst. curator, cataloger, 1979-81; libr. III, cataloger Rutgers U. Libr., New Brunswick, N.J., 1981-82; chief cataloger Assn. Bar City N.Y., 1982-85, head tech. svcs., 1985-99; tech. svcs. libr. Cleary, Gottlieb, Steen and Hamilton, N.Y.C., 1999—. Mem. Am. Assn. Law Librs., Am. Translators Assn. (cert. translator English to Spanish), Law Libr. Assn. Greater N.Y., Reforma, Salalm. Democrat. Presbyterian. Office: 1 Liberty Plz Fl 43 New York NY 10006-1404 E-mail: pruiz-valera@cgsh.com.

RULE, CHARLES FREDERICK (RICK RULE), lawyer; b. Nashville, Apr. 28, 1955; s. Frederick Charles and Mary Elizabeth (Malone) R.; m. Ellen Friedland, May 13, 1976 BA, Vanderbilt U., 1978; JD, U. Chgo., 1981. Bar: U.S. Ct. Appeals. (D.C. cir.) 1983. Law clk. U.S. Ct. Appeals (fed. cir.), Washington, 1981-82; spl. asst. to asst. atty. gen. Antitrust div. Dept. Justice, Washington, 1982-83, dep. asst. atty. gen. policy planning, 1984-85, acting asst. atty. gen., then dep. asst. atty. gen. regulatory affairs, 1985-86, asst. atty. gen., 1986-89; ptnr. Covington & Burling, Washington, 1989-2001, Fried, Frank, Harris, Shriver & Jacobson, Washington, 2001—. Legal, econ. analyst Lexecon, Inc., Chgo., 1979-80 Mem. Bar of D.C. Ct. Appeals, Phi Beta Kappa, Phi Eta Sigma. Republican. Presbyterian. Office: Fried Frank Harris Shriver & Jacobson 1001 Pennsylvania Ave Nw Washington DC 20004-2505

RUMAN, SAUL I. lawyer; b. Chgo., May 12, 1925; s. James A. and Pauline (Scharfer) R.; m. Beverlee Mahan, June 17; children: Loral Ruman Conrad, Melissa Ruman Stewart, Elizabeth Ruman Plumlee. BS, Ind. U., 1949, JD with distinction, 1952. Bar: Ind. 1952, U.S. Supreme Ct. 1963, U.S. Dist. Ct. Ind. 1952, U.S. Ct. Appeals (7th cir.) 1962. Atty. pvt. practice, Hammond, Ind., 1952—; mng. ptnr. Ruman, Clements & Holub, P.C., 1990. Former lectr. bus. law Ind. U. N.W.; mem. faculty numerous insts. on law; mem. com. on rules of practice and procedure Supreme Ct. Ind., 1983-92, Ind. Jud. Nominating Commn., 1990; mem. Ind. Supreme Ct. character and fitness com., 1975—. Pres. Ind. U. Sch. Law Alumni Assn., 1972-73, bd. visitors, 1973; bd. advisors N.W. Campus Ind. U., 1973-85, class rep., 1983; faculty Nat. Inst. Trial Advocacy, 1984-86; trustee Ind. Legal Svcs. Fund, 1978, 84. With usn, 1942-45. Fellow Internat. Acad. Trial Lawyers (dir. 1980-86); mem. Ill. Trial Lawyers Assn., Ind. Bar Assn. (chmn. trial lawyers sect. 1970-71), Ind. Trial Lawyers Assn. (emeritus dir., pres. 1980-81, lifetime achievement award 1997), Coll. Fellows, Assn. Trial Lawyers Am., Am. Bd. Trial Advocates, Order of Coif. Federal civil litigation, State civil litigation, Personal injury (including property damage). Office: 5261 Hohman Ave Hammond IN 46320-1721

RUMBAUGH, CHARLES EARL, arbitrator, mediator, educator, lawyer, speaker, judge; b. San Bernardino, Calif., Mar. 11, 1943; s. Max Elden and Gertrude Maude (Gulker) R.; m. Christina Carol Pinder, Mar. 2, 1968; children: Eckwood, Cynthia, Aaron, Heather. BS, UCLA, 1966; JD, Calif. Western Sch. Law, 1971; cert. in advanced mgmt., U. So. Calif., 1993. Bar: Calif. 1972, U.S. Dist. Ct. (cen. dist.) Calif. U.S. Ct. Appeals (9th cir.), U.S. Supreme Ct. Engr. Westinghouse Electric Corp., Balt., 1966-68; legal counsel Calif. Dept. of Corps., L.A., 1971-77, Hughes Aircraft Co., L.A.,

1977-84, asst. to corp. dir. contracts, 1984-89, asst. to corp. v.p. contracts, 1989-95; corp. dir. contracts/pricing Lear Astronics Corp., 1995-97; pres. Ctr. for Conflict Resolution, 1998-99. Arbitrator, mediator, comml., govt. contracts, internat. law, franchise, securities, torts, personal injury, real estate and constrn. panels Am. Arbitration Assn., L.A., San Francisco; former EEOC mediator, adminstrv. law judge; mem. arbitration and mediation panels ArbitrationWorks, 1994—2002, Nat. Assn. Security Dealers, Franchise Arbitration & Mediation, Inc., L.A. County Superior Ct., Santa Barbara County Superior Ct.; mem. panel pvt. alt. dispute resolution neutrals U.S. Ct. Fed. Claims; armed svcs. bd. of contract appeals panel of pvt. alt. dispute resolution neutrals, DLA panel of dispute neutrals, also settlement officer U.S. Dist. Ct.; alternative dispute resolution panel World Bank; adj. faculty Calif. State U.; spkr. in field. Mem. editl. bd. Nat. Contract Mgmt. Jour., 1996-00; contbr. articles to profl. jours. Counselor Boy Scouts Am., L.A., 1976—; mem. City of Palos Verdes Estates (Calif.) Citizen's Planning Com., 1986—90; judge pro tem L.A. County Superior Ct. , L.A., 1991—2000. Fellow: Nat. Contract Mgmt. Assn. (pres. L.A./South Bay chpt. 1991—92, nat. dir. 1992—93, nat. v.p. southwestern region 1993—95, founder, chmn. alt. dispute resolution com., cert. profl. contracts mgr., nat. bd. advisors, Fellow of Yr. award 1994, Nat. Achievement award 2001); mem.: FBA (pres. Beverly Hills chpt. 1992—93), ABA (founder fed. contracts dispute resolution com. dispute resolution sect, forum on franchising, forum on constrn. industry, pub. contract law sect., vice chair strategic alliance com.), Christian Legal Soc., Aerospace Industries Assn. (chmn. procurement techniques com. 1987—88, 1993—94), Soc. Profls. in Dispute Resolution (chmn. internat. sector com. 1996—2000, past bd. dirs. L.A. chpt.), State Bar Calif. (chmn. franchise law com. 2002—03, Wiley W. Manual pro bono award 1992), Nat. Def. Indsl. Assn. (vice-chmn. west coast legal subcom. 1994—2000, procurement planning com. 1994—), Calif. Dispute Resolution Coun. (cons. to qualifications com. 1997—99), Nat. Assn. Purchasing Mgmt. (chair acquisition info.). Avocations: camping, skiing, jogging, equestrian. Office: PO Box 2636 Rolling Hills CA 90274 E-mail: adroffice@ieee.org.

RUMMAGE, STEPHEN MICHAEL, lawyer; b. Massillon, Ohio, Dec. 27, 1955; s. Robert Everett and Kathleen Patricia (Newman) R.; m. Elizabeth Anne Seivert, Mar. 24, 1979; children: Everett Martin, Carter Kevin. BA in History and English, Stanford U., 1977; JD, U. Calif., Berkeley, 1980. Bar: Wash. 1980, U.S. Dist. Ct. (we. dist.) 1980, U.S. Ct. Appeals (9th cir.) 1983, U.S. Supreme Ct. 1985. Assoc. Davis, Wright et al, Seattle, 1980-85; ptnr. Davis Wright Tremaine, Seattle, 1986—. Co-author: Employer's Guide to Strike Planning and Prevention, 1985. Mem. Wash. Athletic Club. Democrat. Roman Catholic. Appellate, General civil litigation, Securities. Office: Davis Wright Tremaine 1501 4th Ave Ste 2600 Seattle WA 98101-1688 E-mail: steverummage@dwt.com.

RUMMEL, EDGAR FERRAND, retired lawyer; b. New Bern, N.C., June 29, 1929; s. Robert French and Reba Jeanette (Burgess) R.; m. Lillian Hildebrandt, Dec. 28, 1954. BA, Ohio State U., 1955; JD, DePaul U., 1965; LLB, U. London, Eng., 1973; LLM, George Washington U., 1978. Bar: U.S. Dist. Ct. D.C. 1967, U.S. Ct. Appeals (D.C. cir.) 1968, U.S. Supreme Ct. 1971, Md. 1980. Atty.-adviser Dept. Army, Washington, 1971-74, 78, counsel U.S. Army Real Estate Agy., Frankfurt, W.Ger., 1975-77, supervisory atty.-adviser, asst. div. chief Office of Chief of Engrs., Dept. Army, Washington, 1977-83; sr. atty. advisor Office of Judge Advocate Gen., Dept. Army, Washington, 1983-85, trial atty., 1987; spl. asst. U.S. Atty. Dist. Colo., 1985-87, ret. 1987; chmn. mineral leasing com. Dept. Def., 1981-84; mem. Oreg. Nat. Trial Adv. Council, 1983-84. With AUS, 1947-51. Mem. Md. State Bar Assn. Democrat. Episcopalian (vestryman 1981-84). Home: 7812 Adelphi Ct Hyattsville MD 20783-1848

RUNDIO, LOUIS MICHAEL, JR., lawyer; b. Chgo., Sept. 13, 1943; s. Louis Michael Sr. and Germaine Matilda (Pasternack) R.; m. Ann Marie Bartlett, July 10, 1971; children: Matthew, Melissa. BS in Physics, Loyola U., Chgo., 1965, JD, 1972. Bar: Ill. 1972, U.S. Dist. Ct. (no. dist.) Ill. 1972, U.S. Ct. Appeals (7th cir.) 1974, U.S. Dist. Ct. (ea. dist.) Mich. 1983. Assoc. McDermott, Will & Emery, Chgo., 1972-77, ptnr., 1978—. Served to 1st lt. U.S. Army, 1965-68, Vietnam. Mem. ABA, Chgo. Bar Assn. Federal civil litigation, State civil litigation, Environmental. Home: 676 Skye Ln Barrington IL 60010-5506 Office: McDermott Will & Emery 227 W Monroe St Ste 3100 Chicago IL 60606-5096

RUNDLETT, ELLSWORTH TURNER, III, lawyer; b. Portland, Maine, Jan. 12, 1946; s. Ellsworth Turner II and Esther (Stevens) R.; m. Lisa Warren, Oct. 25, 1964 (div. June 1967); 1 child, Ellsworth Turner IV; m. Jamie Donnelly, June 7, 1982 (div. 1986); m. Marilyn DeJenzano, Aug. 17, 1994. AB cum laude, Bowdoin Coll., 1968; JD, U. Maine, 1973. Bar: Maine 1973, U.S. Dist. Ct. Maine 1973, U.S. Ct. Appeals (1st cir.) 1973; cert. civil trial specialist, Nat. Bd. Trial Advocacy; diplomate Nat. Coll. Advocacy. Bodwoin Coll. intern U.S. Senate, Washington, 1967; law clk. Superior Ct. Maine, Portland, 1972-73; asst. corp. counsel City of Portland, 1973-76; ptnr. Childs, Rundlett, Fifield & Childs, Portland, 1980—. Author: Maximizing Damages in Small Personal Injury Cases, 1991; contbr. legal articles to Maine Bus. Digest, 1978-84. Pres. Pine Tree Alcohol Treatment Ctr., Windham, Maine, 1978-80; trustee Portland Players, Inc., South Portland, Maine, 1977-84, pres., 1985-87. Mem. ATLA, Cumberland County Bar (trustee 1983-84, 86-87, v.p. 1988-90, pres. 1990), Maine Bar Assn. (bd. govs. 1991—), Maine Trial Lawyers Assn. (pres. 2000-01), U. Maine Law Alumni (bd. dirs. 1984-87, v.p. 1988, pres. 1989, bd. govs. 1991—), Cumberland Club, Portland Club (gov. 1983-86), Bowdoin Club of Portland (pres. 1978). State civil litigation, General practice, Personal injury (including property damage). Office: Childs Rundlett & Fifield 257 Deering Ave Portland ME 04103-4858 E-mail: derry@maine.rr.com.

RUNGE, PATRICK RICHARD, lawyer; b. Iowa City, Iowa, Oct. 25, 1969; s. Richard Gary and Sally Louise (Cozzolino) R. BSBA in Econs., U. Nebr., Omaha, 1991; JD, Creighton U., 1994. Bar: Nebr. 1994, U.S. Dist. Ct. Nebr. 1994. Prodn. editor U.N.O. Gateway, Omaha, 1990-91; graphic designer Omaha Pub. Power Dist., 1991-97; intern U.S. Dist. Ct., Omaha, 1993; rsch. asst. Creighton U., Omaha, 1993; sr. cert. law student Creighton Legal Clinic, Omaha, 1994; atty. Runge Law Office, Omaha, 1994-95, Runge & Chase, Omaha, 1995—. Pub. defender Winnebago Tribe Nebr., 1996—, Omaha Tribe Nebr., 2000-01. Disting. scholar Omaha (Nebr.) World-Herald, 1987-91; Merit scholar Creighton Law Sch., Omaha, 1991-94. Mem. ABA, Winnebago Bar Assn., Omaha Tribal Bar Assn. Democrat. Lutheran. Constitutional, Criminal, Family and matrimonial. Office: Runge & Chase 7701 Pacific St Ste 323 Omaha NE 68114-5480 E-mail: runge@rungeandchase.com.

RUNQUIST, LISA A. lawyer; b. Mpls., Sept. 22, 1952; d. Ralf E. and Violet R. BA, Hamline U., 1973; JD, U. Minn., 1976. Bar: Minn. 1977, Calif. 1978, U.S. Dist. Ct. (ctrl. dist.) Calif. 1985, U.S. Supreme Ct. 1995. Assoc. Caldwell & Toms, L.A., 1978-82; ptnr. Runquist & Flagg, L.A., 1982-85; pvt. practice Runquist & Assocs., L.A., 1985-99, Runquist & Zybach LLP, L.A., 1999—. Mem. adv. bd. Exempt Orgn. Tax Rev., 1990—, Calif. State U. L.A. Continuing Edn. Acctg. and Tax Program, 1995—. Mem. editl. bd.: ABA Bus. Law Today, 1994—2002. Mem. ABA (com. on nonprofit corps. 1986—, chair 1991-95, subcom. current devels. in nonprofit corp. law 1989—, chair 1989-91, subcom. rels. orgns. 1989—, chair 1987-91, 95-98, subcom. legal guidebook for dirs. 1986—, ad hoc com. on info. tech., 1997—, chair 1997-98, co-chair, 1998—2002, sect. liaison to ABA tech. coun. 1997-2000, subcom. model nonprofit corp. act, partnerships and unincorp. bus. orgns. com. 1987—, state regulation of securities com. 1988-99, corp. laws com. 1999-, subcom. guidebook for dirs. of closely held corps. chair 2000—), Calif. Bar Assn. (bus. law sect., nonprofit and unincorp. orgns. com. 1985-92, 93-96, 97—, chair 1989-91), Christian Legal Soc., Ctr. Law and Religious Freedom, Christian Mgmt. Assn. (dir. 1983-89). Corporate, general, Non-profit and tax-exempt organizations, Securities. Office: 10618 Woodbridge St Toluca Lake CA 91602-2717 E-mail: lisa@runquist.com.

RUNYON, BRETT L. lawyer; b. Fresno, Calif., Oct. 20, 1959; AA, Fresno City Coll., 1981; BS, Calif. State U., Fresno, 1982; JD, San Joaquin Coll. Law, 1986; MS, Syracuse U. Bar: Calif. 1988, D.C., U.S. Dist. Ct. (ea. dist.), U.S. Ct. Appeals (Fed. cir.) 1998. Arbitrator Fresno County Superior Ct., Fresno County Farm Bur. Mem. ABA, ATLA, Fed. Bar Assn., No. Calif. Assn. Def. Counsel, Fresno County Bar Assn., Delta Theta Phi (meritorious svc. award 1986). Insurance, Product liability, Toxic tort. Office: Mardersian Runyon Cercone & Lehman 1260 Fulton Mall Fresno CA 93721-1916

RUPORT, SCOTT HENDRICKS, lawyer; b. Nov. 22, 1949; s. Fred Hendricks and Juyne (Kennedy) R.; m. Linda Darlene Smith, Sept. 12, 1970. BSBA, Bowling Green U., 1971; JD, U. Akron, 1974. Bar: Ohio 1974, U.S. Dist. Ct. (no. dist.) Ohio 1974, U.S. Ct. Appeals (6th cir.) 1975, U.S. Supreme Ct. 1978, Pa. 1984, Fla. 2002, Mass. 2002; cert. civil trial specialist Nat. Bd. Trial Advocacy. Assoc. Schwab, Sager, Growenburgh, Rothal, Fort, Skidmore & Nukes, Akron, Ohio, 1974-76, Skidmore & George Co. LPA, Akron, 1976-79. Skidmore, Ruport & Haskings, Akron, 1979-83; ptnr. Roderick, Myers & Linton, Akron, 1983-85, Ruport Co. LPA, Akron, 1985—. Instr. real estate law U. Akron, 1976-77, adj. asst. prof. constrn. tech. Coll. Engring., 1983—. Capt. Fin. Corps. USAR, 1971-79. Mem. ABA, ATLA, Ohio Bar Assn., Ohio Acad. Trial Lawyers (chmn. civil and bus. litigation sect. 1989), Akron Bar Assn., Beta Gamma Sigma, Sigma Chi. Federal civil litigation, State civil litigation, Construction. Office: Ruport Co LPA 3700 Embassy Pkwy Ste 440 Akron OH 44333-8367

RUPPE, ARTHUR MAXWELL, lawyer; b. Boone, N.C., Dec. 15, 1928; s. Arthur Monroe and Floye (Robinson) R.; m. Ruth Marie Ledford; children: Ruth Carol, Sharon Marie, Arthur Maxwell Jr., Susan Lunette. AA, Gardner Webb Coll., 1947; AB, U. N.C. Law Sch., 1950, JD, 1952. Bar: N.C. 1952, U.S. Dist. Ct. (ea. dist.) N.C. 1955, U.S. Ct. Mil. Appeals 1968; cert mediator. Asst. staff, judge advocate U.S. Army, Ft. Bragg, N.C., 1952-55; sole practice Fayetteville, N.C., 1955-98; mediator, 1997—. Served to 1st lt. U.S. Army, 1952—55. Mem. ABA, N.C. Bar Assn. (patron), Cumberland County Bar Assn. (pres. 1982-83), K.P. Democrat. Baptist. Avocations: snow skiing, tennis. Alternative dispute resolution. Home: 336 Summertime Rd Fayetteville NC 28303-4658

RUPPERT, JOHN LAWRENCE, lawyer; b. Chgo., Oct. 7, 1953; s. Merle Arvin and Loretta Marie (Ford) R.; m. Katharine Marie Tarbox, June 5, 1976. BA, Northwestern U., 1975; JD, U. Denver, 1978; LLM in Taxation, NYU, 1979. Bar: Colo. 1978, U.S. Dist. Ct. Colo. 1978, Ill. 1979, U.S. Tax Ct. 1981. Assoc. Kirkland & Ellis, Denver, 1979-84, ptnr., 1984-88, Ballard, Spahr, Andrews & Ingersoll, Denver, 1988-96; shareholder Brownstein Hyatt Farber & Strickland, P.C., Denver, 1996—. Lectr. U. Denver Coll. Law, fall 1984-92; adj. prof. law grad. tax program, 1993-94; sec. Capital Assocs., Inc., 1989-96; sec. Brothers Gourmet Coffees, Inc., 1995-2000; asst. sec. Renaissance Cosmetics, Inc., 1996-98; sec. Skillset Software, Inc., 2000-01; asst. sec. Rhythms NetConnections Inc., 2000-01. Contbr. articles to profl. jours. Mem. ABA, Colo. Bar Assn. (mem. exec. coun. tax sect. 1985-89), Denver Bar Assn. Mergers and acquisitions, Corporate taxation, Personal income taxation. Office: Brownstein Hyatt Farber & Strickland PC 410 17th St Fl 22D Denver CO 80202-4402 E-mail: jruppert@bhfs.com., jruppert53@aol.com.

RUPPERT, RUPERT EARL, lawyer, political consultant; b. Nov. 22, 1943; s. Paul Edward and Sarah Elizabeth (Morgan) R.; children: Jason, Ryan, Bradley. BA, Ohio State U., 1968; JD, Capital U., 1976. Bar: Ohio 1976. Asst. to gov. State of Ohio, Columbus, 1971—74, asst. to atty. gen., 1974—77, spl. counsel to atty. gen. and to asst. atty. gen., 1977—93; ptnr. Ruppert, Bronson & Ruppert, Franklin, Ohio, 1977—. Dir., atty. Miami Valley Bank of S.W. Ohio, Franklin, 1979—89. Mem. Franklin City Charter Commn., 1978, Franklin CSC, 1978—79; v.p. Franklin City Schs. Bd. Edn., 1980—95, pres., 1983, 1992, 1994, Franklin City Planning Commn., 1990—92; trustee Franklin Twp., 1995—; mem. Warren County Dem. Com., 1978—80, chmn., 1978—80, Warren County Brown for Atty. Gen., 1978; dep. campaign mgr. William J. Brown for Gov., Ohio, 1982; state campaign mgr. U.S. Sen. John Glenn, 1986. With U.S. Army, 1968—70, Vietnam. Decorated Bronze Star; named Citizen of Yr., City of Franklin, 1992, Franklin C. of C., 1993; named to, Ohio Vets. Hall of Fame, 2002; recipient Presdl. award for outstanding civic achievment among Vietnam vets, 1979. Mem.: VFW, Ohio Trial Lawyers, Warren County Bar Assn. (pres. 2002—03), Ohio Bar Assn., Am. Legion. State civil litigation, Personal injury (including property damage), Probate (including wills, trusts). Home: 11 Kentwood Dr Franklin OH 45005-1657 Office: PO Box 369 Franklin OH 45005-0369

RUSCH, JONATHAN JAY, lawyer; b. Nyack, N.Y., Oct. 16, 1952; s. Thaddeus David and Alice Marjorie Rusch; m. Doreen Evelyn Lacovara, Aug. 10, 1974; children: Rachel Madeline, Catherine Elizabeth. AB in Pub. Affairs with honors, Princeton U., 1974; MA, U. Va., 1978, JD, 1980. Bar: D.C. 1981, U.S. Dist. Ct. D.C. 1981, U.S. Ct. Appeals (D.C. cir.) 1981, U.S. Ct. Appeals (7th cir.) 1985, U.S. Ct. Appeals (9th cir.) 1990, U.S. Ct. Appeals (5th cir.) 1992, U.S. Supreme Ct. 1992. Assoc. Cleary, Gottlieb, Steen & Hamilton, Washington, 1980-83; spl. asst. to atty. gen. U.S. Dept. Justice, Washington, 1983-84; counsel Pres. Commn. on Organized Crime, Washington, 1984-86; acting dir., then dir. office of fin. enforcement U.S. Dept. Treasury, Washington, 1986-88; trial atty. fraud sect., criminal divsn. U.S. Dept. Justice, Washington, 1988-93, asst. spl. counsel House banking facility, 1992, sr. litigation counsel fraud sect., criminal divsn., 1993—, spl. counsel for fraud prevention, criminal divsn., 1998—. Adj. prof. Georgetown U. Law Ctr., 1996—. Recipient Atty. Gen.'s Disting. Svc. award, 1995. Mem. ABA (chmn. regulatory initiatives com. 1998—, sec. 2002--), Tower Club. Home: 4600 Connecticut Ave NW Apt 207 Washington DC 20008-5702 Office: US Dept Justice Bond Bldg Rm 4300 10th and Constitution Ave NW Washington DC 20530 E-mail: jonathan.rusch@worldnet.att.net., Jonathan.Rusch2@usdoj.gov.

RUSCHKY, ERIC WILLIAM, prosecutor; b. Wareham, Mass., June 28, 1948; s. Harold William and Viola Emma R.; m. Mary Lenwood Dixon, Apr. 1, 1972; 1 child, Jane Spencer. BA, Wheaton (Ill.) Coll., 1970; JD, U. Va., 1973. Bar: Va 1973, S.C. 1974. Asst. U.S. atty. U.S. Dept. Justice, Columbia, S.C., 1974—. Active child support enforcement divsn. S.C. Dept. Social Svcs., Friends of Child Support.

RUSKEY, JOHN A. lawyer; b. Feb. 6, 1939; Ptnr. Gibson, Dunn & Crutcher, L.A. Mem. bd. editors Annual Survey of Am. Law, 1965-66. Mem. L.A. County Bar Assn., Order of the Coif. Estate planning, Family and matrimonial, Probate (including wills, trusts). Office: Gibson Dunn & Crutcher 333 S Grand Ave Ste 4400 Los Angeles CA 90071-3197

RUSMISEL, STEPHEN R. lawyer; b. N.Y.C., Jan. 27, 1946; s. R. Raymond and Esther Florence (Kutz) R.; m. Beirne Donaldson, Sept. 6, 1980 (div. Jan. 1984); 1 child, Margo Alexander; m. Melissa J. MacLeod, Aug. 24, 1985 (div. Oct. 1996); children: Benjamin William, Eric Scot Kunze, Erin Lea Kunze; m. Teresa R. Paterniti, June 28, 1997; 1 child, Sarah J. Lamendola. AB, Yale U., 1968; JD, U. Va., 1971. Bar: N.Y. 1972, U.S. Ct. Appeals (2d cir.) 1974, U.S. Dist. Ct. (so. dist.) N.Y. 1975. Assoc. Winthrop, Stimson, Putnam & Roberts, N.Y.C., 1971-80, ptnr., 1980-2000, Pillsbury Winthrop LLP, N.Y.C., 2001—. Aux. officer Bedminster Twp. (N.J.) Police, 1976—. Mem. Practicing Law Inst., Am. Arbitration Assn. (arbitrator 1976—), Far Hills Polo Club (Annandale, N.J.), Ausable Club (St. Huberts, N.Y.), Essex Hunt Club (Peapack, N.J.), Phi Delta Phi. Republican. Avocations: polo, flying, carpentry, gardening, poetry. Corporate, general, Mergers and acquisitions, Securities. Home: Shadowline Farm Bedminster NJ 07921 Office: Pillsbury Winthrop LLP One Battery Park Plz New York NY 10004-1490 E-mail: srusmisel@pillsburywinthrop.com.

RUSS, JAMES MATTHIAS, lawyer; b. Duluth, Minn., Sept. 20, 1929; s. Matthias James and Agnes Margaret (Jerina) R.; m. Nanelle Davis, June 27, 1953; children: Tanya, Robin, Sarah, Claudia, Janine, Monica, Matthias James, Kateri. AB cum laude, Spring Hill Coll., 1955; JD, Georgetown U., 1957. Bar: D.C., 1957, Fla., 1958, U.S. Dist. Ct. (no., so. and mid. dists.) Fla., U.S. Ct. Appeals (5th and 11th cirs.), U.S. Supreme Ct.; cert. criminal trial lawyer 1987, criminal appellate lawyer 1992. County solicitor Orange County, Fla., 1961-65. Lectr. criminal law and legal ethics seminars. Contbr. articles to profl. jours. Trustee Orange County Legal Aid Soc.; chmn. The Chester Bedell Meml. Found., 1997-98. Recipient Tobias Simon Pro Bono Svc. award Fla. Supreme Ct., 1997. Master, Am. Inns of Ct.; fellow Am. Coll. Trial Lawyers, Am. Bd. Criminal Lawyers; mem. ABA (criminal justice sect.-speedy trial com. 1976-77, com. on privacy 1982-83, def. function com. 1983-89, chmn. 1987-89), The Fla. Bar (chmn. criminal law com. 1964-65, 66-67, exec. coun. trial lawyers sect., 1967-68, mem. criminal law cert. com. 1988-91, recipient President's Pro Bono Svc. award, 9th jud. cir. 1993), Orange County Bar Assn. (exec. coun. 1967-70, sec. 1984-88), Nat. Assn. Criminal Def. Lawyers (2d v.p. 1992-93, 1st v.p. 1993-94, dir. 1984—, chmn. Lawyers' Assistance Strike Force 1987-89, Robert C. Heeney Meml. award 1988), Fla. Assn. Criminal Def. Lawyers (chmn. Lawyers' Assistance Strike Force 1988-89, Steven M. Goldstein Criminal Justice award 2002), Nat. Bd. Trial Advocacy (cert. 1982). Appellate, Criminal. Office: Tinker Bldg 18 W Pine St Orlando FL 32801-2612

RUSSELL, ANTONETTE PATRICE, lawyer; b. Belfield, Saint Mary, Jamaica, June 3, 1971; d. Leleith Lemour and Rainford Augustus Kelly(Stepfather); children: N/A N/A None, N/A N/A N/A. JD, U. Nebr. Lincoln, 1997; BSBA, Nova Southeastern U., 1994; AA in Bus. Adminstrn., Broward C.C., Fort Lauderdale, Florida, 1993. Bar: Supreme Ct. Fla. 1997, Ct. Appeals D.C. 1999. Staff atty. Cath. Charities Legal Svcs., Miami, Fla., 1998—2000; supervising atty. Cath. Charities Legal Svcs.-Broward, Lauderdale Lakes, Fla., 2001—. Mem.: ABA, Broward County Bar Assn., Am. Immigration Lawyers Assn., Nat. Notary Assn. Avocations: reading, travel, sports. Immigration, naturalization, and customs, Juvenile, Family and matrimonial. Office: Catholic Charities Legal Services Inc 3661 West Oakland Park Blvd Suite 305 Lauderdale Lakes FL 33311 Office Fax: 954-486-5090. Personal E-mail: arussell71@yahoo.com. E-mail: arussell@cclsmiami.org.

RUSSELL, C. EDWARD, JR., lawyer; b. Portsmouth, Va., Aug. 19, 1942; BA, Hampden-Sydney Coll., 1964; LLB, Washington & Lee U., 1967. Bar: Va. 1967. Law clk. to Hon. John A. MacKenzie U.S. Dist. Ct. (ea. dist.) Va., 1967-68; atty. Kaufman & Canoles, Norfolk. Mem. ABA (bus. law sect., real property, probate and trust law sect.), Va. State Bar (bus. law sect., real property sect., health law sect.), Va. Bar Assn. (bus. law sect., real estate sect., chmn. young lawyers sect. 1977), Omicron Delta Kappa, Phi Alpha Delta. Commercial, contracts (including sales of goods; commercial financing), Corporate, general, Property, real (including real estate development, water). Office: PO Box 13368 Norfolk VA 23506-0368 E-mail: cerussell@kaufcan.com.

RUSSELL, CHARLES STEVENS, judge, educator; b. Richmond, Va., Feb. 23, 1926; s. Charles Herbert and Nita M. (Stevens) R.; m. Carolyn Elizabeth Abrams, Mar. 18, 1951; children: Charles Stevens Jr., David Tyler. BA, U. Va., 1946, LL.B., 1948. Bar: Va. 1949, U.S. Dist. Ct. (ea. dist.) Va. 1952, U.S. Ct. Appeals (4th cir.) 1955, U.S. Supreme Ct. 1958. Assoc. Jesse, Phillips, Klinge & Kendrick, Arlington, Va., 1951-57, ptnr., 1957-60, Phillips, Kendrick, Gearheart and Aylor, Arlington, 1960-67; judge 17th Jud. Ct. Va., Arlington, 1967-82, Supreme Ct. Va., Richmond, 1982-91, ret. Mem. jud. coun. Va., 1977-82; adj. prof. law George Mason U., Arlington, 1977-86, T.C. Williams Sch. Law U. Richmond, 1987-90; mem. exec. com. Va. State Bar, Richmond, 1964-67; mem. faculty Nat. Jud. Coll., Reno, 1980—, Appellate Judges Inst., NYU, 1986—. Mem. Adv. Com. on Youth, Arlington; mem. nat. council of trustees Freedoms Found., Valley Forge, Pa., 1986-91. Served to lt. comdr. USNR, 1944-51. Fellow Am. Bar Found.; mem. ABA, Arlington County Bar Assn., Va. Bar Assn., Richmond Bar Assn., Va. Trial Lawyers Assn., Am. Judicature Soc., Am. Law Inst. (adv. com. on complex litigation 1989-91). Episcopalian. Home: 11 James Falls Dr Richmond VA 23221-3942 Office: PO Box 1315 Richmond VA 23218-1315

RUSSELL, DAN M., JR., federal judge; b. Magee, Miss., Mar. 15, 1913; s. Dan M. and Beulah (Watkins) R.; m. Dorothy Tudury, Dec. 27, 1942; children— Ronald Truett, Dorothy Dale, Richard Brian. BA, U. Miss., 1935, LL.B., 1937. Bar: Miss. bar 1937. Practice in, Gulfport and Bay St. Louis, Miss.; U.S. judge So. Dist. Miss., 1965—; now sr. judge. Lt. comdr. U.S. Naval Intelligence, 1941-45. Recipient U.S. Supreme Ct. Justice Scalia award, 2000. Founder's Day award Gulfport Rotary Club, 2001. Mem. Miss. Bar Assn., Hancock County Bar Assn., Hancock and Harrison Counties Bar Assn., Bay St. Louis Rotary Club (hon.), Gulfport Rotary Club (hon.), Am. Inns Ct. (hon. Russell-Blass-Walker chpt.), Federalist Soc. (adv. bd. Miss. chpt.), Hancock County C. of C., Tau Kappa Alpha. Clubs: Rotarian (pres. Bay St. Louis, Miss. 1946). Office: US Dist Ct PO Box 1930 Gulfport MS 39502-1930

RUSSELL, DAVID BRENT, lawyer; b. Portage, Wis., Aug. 13, 1948; s. Donald Eugene and Jean (Cuff) R.; m. Nancy Jean Senior, June 7, 1975; children: Angela, Christopher. BBA, U. Wis., 1974, JD, 1979. Bar: Wis. 1979, U.S. Dist. Ct. (we. dist.) Wis. 1979. Assoc. Hale, Skemp, Hanson & Skemp, LaCrosse, Wis., 1979-83, mng. ptnr., 1993—. Bd. dirs. Western Wis. Legal Services, 1988-94; vis. lectr., bus. law, U. Wis., LaCrosse, 2001-. Dir. Discovery Child Care Ctrs., LaCrosse, 1980-83; bd. dirs. Boys & Girls Clubs of LaCrosse, 1997-, sec. 1999-; mem. Youth Adv. Com., 1998-; bd. dirs. LaCrosse Pub. Edn., v.p. 2002-. Mem. State Bar of Wis., LaCrosse County Bar Assn. (sec., treas. 1986-87), U.S. Curling Assn. (bd. dirs. 1984-96, v.p. 1988-92, pres. 1992-93), Wis. State Curling Assn. (bd. dirs. 1977—, v.p. 1982-84, pres. 1984-86). Avocations: curling, golf, tennis, running. Bankruptcy, General practice. Office: Hale Skemp Hanson Skemp & Sleik 505 King St Ste 300 La Crosse WI 54601

RUSSELL, DAVID L. federal judge; b. Sapulpa, Okla., July 7, 1942; s. Lynn and Florence E. (Brown) R.; m. Dana J. Wilson, Apr. 16, 1971; 1 child, Sarah Elizabeth BS, Okla. Bapt. U., 1963; JD, Okla. U., 1965. Bar: Okla. 1965. Asst. atty. gen. State of Okla., Oklahoma City, 1968-69, legal adviser to gov., 1969-70; legal adviser Senator Dewey Bartlett, Washington, 1973-75; U.S. atty. for Western dist. Okla. Dept. Justice, 1975-77, 81-82; ptnr. Benefield & Russell, Oklahoma City, 1977-81; judge U.S. Dist. Ct. (we. dist.) Okla., Oklahoma City, 1982—, chief judge, 1994—2002. Lt. comdr. JAGC, USN, 1965-68. Selected Outstanding Fed. Ct. Trial judge Okla. Trial Lawyers Assn., 1988. Mem. Okla. Bar Assn., Fed. Bar Assn. (pres. Oklahoma City chpt. 1981), Order of Coif (alumnus mem.). Republican. Methodist. Office: US Dist Ct US Courthouse 200 NW 4th St Oklahoma City OK 73102-3026

RUSSELL, DAVID WILLIAMS, lawyer; b. Lockport, NY, Apr. 5, 1945; s. David Lawson and Jean Graves (Williams) R.; m. Frances Yung Chung Chen, May 23, 1970; children: Bayard Chen, Ming Rennick. AB, Dartmouth Coll., 1967, MBA, 1969; JD cum laude, Northwestern U., 1976. Bar: Ill. 1976, Ind. 1983. English tchr. Talledega (Ala.) Coll., summer 1967; math. tchr. Lyndon Inst., Lyndonville, Vt., 1967-68; asst. to pres. for planning Tougaloo (Miss.) Coll., 1969-71, bus. mgr., 1971-73; law clk. Montgomery, McCracken, Walker & Rhoads, Phila., summer 1975; with Winston & Strawn, Chgo., 1976-83; ptnr. Klineman, Rose, Wolf & Wallack, Indpls., 1983-87, Johnson, Smith, Pence, Densborn, Wright & Heath, Indpls., 1987-99, Bose McKinney & Evans, Indpls., 1999—. Cons. Alfred P. Sloan Found., 1972-73; dir. Forum for Internat. Profl. Svcs., 1985—, sec., 1985-88, pres. 1988-89; U.S. Dept. Justice del. to U.S. China Joint Session on Trade, Investment & Econ. Law, Beijing, 1987; leader Ind. Products Trade Fair, Kawachinagano, Japan, 1996; lectr. Ind. law Ind. Gov.'s Trade Mission to Japan, 1986, internat. law Ind. Continuing Legal Edn. Forum, 1986-96, 2000-02, chmn., 1987, 89, 91, 2001-02; adj. prof. internat. bus. law Ind. U., 1993-95; nat. selection com. Woodrow Wilson Found. Adminstrv. Fellowship Program, 1973-76; vol. Lawyers for Creative Arts, Chgo., 1977-83; dir. World Trade Club of Ind., 1987-93, v.p., 1987-91, pres., 1991-92; dir. Ind. Swiss Found., 1991—; dir. Writer's Ctr., Indpls., 1999—, treas., 2001-; dir. Asian Am. Alliance, 1999—, Friends of Taiwan Assn., Inc., 2001-; dir. Ind. Soviet Trade Consortium, 1991-99, sec., 1991-92; v.p., bd. dirs. Ind. Sister Cities, 1988—; dir. Internat. Ctr. Indpls., 1988-92, v.p. 1988-89; Ind. dist. enrollment dir. Dartmouth Coll., 1990-99; dir. Carmel Sister Cities, 1993—, v.p. 1995-96, pres. 1997-99, chmn., 1999—; v.p., gen. coun. Lawrence Durrell Soc., 1993—; internat. affairs adv. bd. Kelley Sch. Bus., Ind. U., 2001-; bd. advisors Ctr. for Internat. Bus. Edn. and Rsch. Krannert Grad. Sch. Mgmt. Purdue U., 1995—; dir., v.p., gen. coun. Global Crossroads Found., Inc., 1995—; mem. bd. arbitrators NASD, 1999—; mem. Ind. Dist. Export Coun., 1999—. Named Hon. fellow, Ctr. for Internat. Legal Studies, 2002—, Internat. Bus. Person of Yr., World Trade Club of Ind., 2002, Sagamore of the Wabash, 2002, Jan. 15, 2002 David Williams Russell Day in his honor, Indpls.; Adminstrv. fellow, Woodrow Wilson Found., 1969—72. Mem. ABA, ACLU, Ill. Bar Assn., Ind. Bar Assn. (vice chmn. internat. law sect., 1988-90, treas. 2002—, chmn. 1990-92, 2002—, co-chmn. written publs. com. 1997-99), Indpls. Bar Assn., Dartmouth Lawyers Assn., Indpls. Assn. Chinese Ams., Chinese Music Soc., Dartmouth Club of Ind. (sec. 1986-87, pres. 1987-88), Internat. Bar Assn., Zeta Psi. Presbyterian. Corporate, general, Private international, Property, real (including real estate development, water). Home: 10926 Lakeview Dr Carmel IN 46033-3937 Office: Bose McKinney & Evans LLP 2700 First Ind Plz 135 N Pennsylvania St Indianapolis IN 46204-2400

RUSSELL, JAMES FRANKLIN, lawyer; b. Memphis, Mar. 21, 1945; s. Frank Hall and Helen (Brunson) R.; m. Marilyn Land, June 1, 1968 (div. May 1976); children: Mary Helen, Myles Edward; m. Linda Hatcher, July 9, 1977; 1 child, Maggie Abele. BA, Rhodes Coll., 1967; JD, Memphis State U., 1970. Bar: Tenn. 1971, U.S. Dist. Ct. (we. dist.) Tenn. 1971, U.S. Ct. Appeals (6th cir.) 1971, U.S. Dist. Ct. (no. dist.) Miss. 1976, U.S. Ct. Appeals (5th cir.) 1977, U.S. Ct. Appeals (8th cir.) 1987. Assoc. Nelson, Norvell, Wilson, McRae, Ivy & Sevier, Memphis, 1971-75; ptnr. Stanton, Russell & Challen, Memphis, 1975-78, Russell, Price, Weatherford & Warlick, Memphis, 1978-82, Price, Vance & Criss, Memphis, 1982-85, Apperson, Crump, Duzane & Maxwell, Memphis, 1985-97, 1985-97; cir. ct. judge Divsn. II 30th Jud. Dist., 1997—. V.p. mid-south chpt. Am. Red Cross, Memphis, 1992-94; treas. Epilepsy Found. West Tenn., Memphis, 1992-94. Mem. ABA, Nat. Assn. R.R. Trial Counsel, Internat. Assn. Def. Counsel, Tenn. Bar Assn., Tenn. Def. Lawyers Assn., Memphis Bar Assn. (pres. 1992). Episcopalian. Avocations: golf, snow skiing. Insurance, Transportation, Workers' compensation. Home: 1045 Reed Hooker N Eads TN 38028-6958 Office: Shelby County Courthouse 140 Adams Ave Memphis TN 38103-2000

RUSSELL, MICHAEL JAMES, lawyer; Cert. in German, U. Vienna, 1979; BA summa cum laude, Gettysburg Coll., 1980; MA, JD, Vanderbilt U., 1984. Bar: Pa. 1984, D.C. 1985, U.S. Supreme Ct. 1995. Atty. USDA, Washington, 1984-85; majority counsel subcom. on juvenile justice senate judiciary com. U.S. Senate, Washington, 1985-86, minority gen. counsel subcom. on constn., 1987, legis. dir. to Senator Arlen Specter, 1987-90; senate staff mem. Congrl. Crime Caucus, 1987-90; dep. dir. Nat. Inst. Justice U.S. Dept. Justice, Washington, 1990-93, acting dir., 1993-94; pres. Russell & Assocs., Washington, 1994-96; sr. pub. safety advisor Corp. Nat. Svc., Washington, 1994-96; dep. chief of staff to Senator Ben Nighthorse Campbell, Washington, 1996—2001; dep. asst. sec. for policy and budget (enforcement) U.S. Dept. Treasury, Washington, 2001—. Office: Treasury Dept Rm 4308 1500 Pennsylvania Ave NW Washington DC 20220

RUSSELL, PATRICK, lawyer; b. Milw., Dec. 26, 1967; s. Michael H. and Susan K. Russell. BA, Marquette U., 1990; JD, U. Miami, 1993. Bar: Fla. 1994. Gen. counsel Insta-Check Sys., Inc., Miami, Fla., 1994-95; pvt. practice Miami, 1995—. Adj. prof. Fla. Internat. U., North Miami, 1996. Mem. ATLA, ABA, Fla. Bar Assn., Dade County Bar Assn. General civil litigation, Commercial, consumer (including collections, credit), Insurance. Office: Russell Law Offices 201 W Flagler St Miami FL 33130-1510

RUSSELL, RICHARD LLOYD, lawyer; b. Kokomo, Ind., Dec. 13, 1946; s. James E. and Doris R. R.; m. Cynthia L. Hamilton, May 29, 1999; children from previous marriage: Ryan, Rachel, Casey, Ryun. BA in Polit. Sci., Purdue U., 1970; JD, Ind. U., 1975. Bar: Ind. 1975. Chief dep. prosecutor Howard County, Kokomo, 1978-86; city atty. City of Kokomo, 1978-80; atty. Russell, McIntyre, Hilligoss & Welke, Kokomo, 1980—. Chmn. bd. Kokomo Devel. Corp., 1996-98 Named Sagamore of Wabash, State Ind., 1991. Mem. Am. Trial Lawyers, Ind. Trial Lawyers (sustaining mem.), Kokomo Howard County C. of C. (chmn. bd. 1997-98). State civil litigation, Family and matrimonial, Personal injury (including property damage). Office: Russell McIntyre Hilligoss & Welke 116 N Main St Kokomo IN 46901-4625

RUSSELL, TERRENCE JOSEPH, lawyer; b. Jacksonville, Fla., Sept. 26, 1944; AA, St. Leo Coll., 1964; BA, U. Fla., 1966; JD, Fla. State U., 1968. Bar: Fla. 1969. Law clk. to Hon. W.O. Mehrtens U.S. Dist. Ct. (so. dist.) Fla., 1969; atty. Ruden, McClosky, Smith, Schuster & Russell, P.A., Ft. Lauderdale, Fla. Mem. appellate restructure commn. Fla. Supreme Ct., 1985—86, mem. nominating com., 1994—, chmn. nominating com., 1997, 98; mem. Fed. Magistrate's merit selection panel, 1985; vice-chmn. 17th Jud. Cir. Nominating Commn., 1982—84, chmn., 1985—86; mem. spl. com. representation of death sentenced inmates Fla. Bar, 1984—85, bd. govs., 1987—91, pres., 2001—02. Bd. govs. Nova U. Law Sch., 1981, chmn., 1993, 1997; bd. dirs. Broward County Legal Aid Svcs., 1985—86. Mem.: ATLA, ABA (ho. of dels. 2000—, sects. litigation, legal edn.), Fla. Bar Found. (bd. dirs. 1992—98, pres. elect 2003—), Assn. Trial Lawyers Am., Fla. State U. Law Sch. Alumni Assn. (pres. 1985), Am. Bd. Trial Advs., Am. Bar Found., Acad. Fla. Trial Lawyers (coll. diplomates), Broward County Trial Lawyers Assn., No. Broward Bar Assn., Broward County Bar Assn. (chmn. spl. com. legal malpractice ins. 1978, bar-bench liaison com. 1978, jud. selection and tenure com. 1978—79, exec. com. 1980, 1981, pres. 1984—85), Gold Key, Delta Theta Phi. Office: Ruden McClosky et al PO Box 1900 Fort Lauderdale FL 33302-1900

RUSSELL, THOMAS ARTHUR, lawyer; b. Corona, Calif., Aug. 2, 1953; s. Larry Arthur Russell and Patricia Helena (Collins) Heath; m. Mary Ellen Leach, June 20, 1992; children: Trevor James, Elizabeth Mary, John Thomas. BS, U. Calif., Berkeley, 1976; JD, U. So. Calif., 1982. Bar: Calif. 1983, U.S. Dist. Ct. (cen. dist.) Calif. 1983, U.S. Ct. Appeals (9th cir.) 1986, U.S. Supreme Ct. 1988. Law clk. Calif. Ct. Appeals, L.A., 1981; assoc. Graham & James, Long Beach, Calif., 1982-88; ptnr. Wooley & Russell, Long Beach, 1988—2002; gen. counsel Port of L.A., 2002—. Spkr., panelist Nat. Marine Bankers Assn., Chgo., 1987—, Conf. on Consumer Fin. Law, 1995—; bd. dirs. Internat. Bus. Assn. So. Calif., 1989-96, pres., 1994-95. Contbg. author Benedict on Admiralty, 1995—, Recreational Boating Law, 1992, Moore's Federal Practice, Admiralty Vol., 1997—; editor Boating Briefs, 1991-96. Bd. dirs. World Trade Ctr. Assn., L.A.-Long Beach, 1996—, Long Beach Area C. of C., 1994—; hon. mem. Am. Vessel Documentation Assn., 1995. Mem. ABA (Bronze Key award 1982, maritime fin. subcom., chmn. 1994—), Maritime Law Assn. U.S. (proctor 1988—, recreational boating com. chmn. 2002—), Maritime Arbitration Assn. U.S. (pres. 1999—), Calif. Bar Assn., L.A. County Bar Assn., Calif. Yacht Brokers Assn. (Merle Parke award 1996, 2002). Republican. Roman Catholic. Avocations: tennis, skiing. Admiralty, Construction, Government contracts and claims. Home: 2339 Port Lerwick Pl Newport Beach CA 92660 Office: 425 S Palos Verdes St San Pedro CA 90731

RUSSO, ROY R. lawyer; b. Utica, N.Y., July 26, 1936; BA, Columbia U., 1956; LLB cum laude, Syracuse U., 1959. Bar: N.Y. 1959, D.C. 1967, U.S. Supreme Ct. 1969. Atty. FCC, 1959—66; ptnr. Cohn and Marks LLP, Washington, 1966—. Mem. Order of Coif, Phi Alpha Delta. Democrat. Communications. Home: 6528 Bowie Dr Springfield VA 22150-1309 Office: Cohn and Marks LLP 1920 N St NW Ste 300 Washington DC 20036-1622

RUSSO, THOMAS ANTHONY, lawyer; b. N.Y.C., Nov. 6, 1943; s. Lucio F. and Tina (Iarossi) R.: m. Nancy Felipe, June 18, 1966 (div. 1974); m. Janice Davis, June 10, 1977 (div. 1979); m. Marcy C. Appelbaum, June 16, 1985; children: Morgan Danielle and Alexa Anne (twins), Tyler James. BA, Fordham U., 1965; MBA, JD, Cornell U., 1969. Bar: N.Y., 1970, U.S. Ct. Appeals (2d cir.) 1971, U.S. Dist. Ct. (so. and ea. dists.) N.Y. 1971, U.S. Ct. Appeals (7th cir.) 1982. Staff atty. SEC, Washington, 1969-71; assoc. Cadwalader, Wickersham & Taft, N.Y.C., 1971-75; dir. divsn. trading and markets Commodity Futures Trading Commn., Washington, 1975—77; ptnr., mem. mgmt. com. Cadwalader, Wickersham & Taft, N.Y.C., 1977-92; vice chmn., chief legal officer, mng. dir. Lehman Bros., N.Y.C., 1993—. Vice chmn. bd. trustees, chmn. exec. com. Inst. for Fin. Markets; bd. dirs. Rev. Securities and Commodities Regulation, N.Y.C.; trustee, chmn. exec. com., chmn. devel. com. Inst. Internat. Edn.; trustee NYU Downtown Hosp.; mem. adv. com. SEC Hist. Soc.; mem. nat. bd. trustees, exec. com. and nominating com., chmn. pension investments com., vice chmn. fin. and audit com. March of Dimes; mem. Econ. Club N.Y., Fgn. Policy Assn. Author: Regulation of the Commodities Futures and Options Markets; co-author: Regulation of Brokers, Dealers and Securities Markets, Supplement Markets; editorial bd. mem. Internat. Jour. Regulatory Law and Practice; practitioner bd. advisors Stanford Jour. of Law.; mem. editl. bd. Futures and Derivatives Law Report. Mem. ABA (mem. subcom. on exec. coun., fed. regulation of securities, derivative instruments subcom., regulation of futures and derivative instruments), Assn. of Bar of City of N.Y. (chmn. internat. law sub com. of the com. on commodities regulation 1984-85, chmn. com. commodities regulations 1981-82), D.C. Bar Assn. Banking, Corporate, general, Securities. Office: Lehman Bros Inc 745 7th Ave 31st Fl New York NY 10019-6801 E-mail: trusso1@lehman.com.

RUSSON, LEONARD H. state supreme court justice; b. Salt Lake City, May 15, 1933; JD, Utah Coll., 1962. Pvt. practice, Salt Lake City, 1962-84; judge Utah Dist. Ct. (3d dist.), Utah Ct. Appeals; justice Utah Supreme Ct., Salt Lake City, 1995—. Vice chair Utah Bd. Dist. Ct. Judges; mem. Jud. Conduct Commn., Utah Supreme Ct. Adv. Com. on Code of Profl. Conduct. Office: Utah Supreme Ct PO Box 140210 450 S State St Salt Lake City UT 84114-0210

RUSSONIELLO, JOSEPH PASCAL, lawyer; b. Jersey City, Oct. 12, 1941; s. Sabin G. and Justine B. (Terraciano) R.; m. Moira F. Ward, Aug. 29, 1969. B in Social Sci., Fairfield U., 1963; JD, NYU, 1966. Bar: N.J. 1967, Calif. 1969. Spl. agt. FBI, Washington, 1966-67; dep. dist. atty. City and County San Francisco (Calif.) Dist. Atty. Offices, 1969-75; assoc. Cooley Godward Castro Huddleson & Tatum, San Francisco, 1975-78; U.S. atty. U.S. Dept. Justice (no. dist.) Calif., San Francisco, 1982-90; ptnr. Cooley Godward L.L.P., San Francisco, 1978-82, 90—. Pres., bd. dirs. San Francisco (Calif.) Law Sch., 1996—; analyst KTVU-Ch. 2, Oakland, Calif., 1994—. Pres. Northgate Cottages, Napa, Calif., 1988—; chmn. Catholics for Truth and Justice, San Francisco, 1991—; v.p. Mid-Pacific region Nat. Italian Am. Fedn., 1996-99. Recipient Man of Yr. award NIAF, 1986, Man of Yr. award St. Thomas More Soc., San Francisco, 2000, Assumpta award Trustees St. Mary's Cathedral, 2000, Papal Pro Ecclesia medal, 2000; named Alumni of Yr.-Pub. Sector, NYU Law Sch., 1991. Fellow Am. Coll. Trial Lawyers; mem. Am. bd. Trial Lawyers (adv.), McFetridge Inn of Ct. (barrister). Republican. Avocations: tennis, golf, reading, playing the saxophone. Criminal, Government contracts and claims. Home: 2850 Jackson St San Francisco CA 94115-1146 Office: Cooley Godward LLP 1 Maritime Plz San Francisco CA 94111-3404 E-mail: Russonielloj@cooley.com.

RUSTAY, JENNIFER B. lawyer; b. Kansas City, Mo., Jan. 30, 1973; m. Allen Harrington Rustay, Sept. 29, 2001. BA, Baylor U., 1995, JD, 1997. Bar: Tex. 1997, U.S. Dist. Ct. (no., so., ea. and we. dists.) Tex., Dist. of Colo., U.S. Ct. Appeals (5th cir.). Law clk. Hon. Sam Johnson U.S. Ct. Appeals (5th cir.), Austin, Tex., 1997—98; atty. Bracewell & Patterson, Houston, 1998—2001, Hagans, Bobb & Burdine, 2001—. Commercial, consumer (including collections, credit), General civil litigation, Criminal. Office: Hagans Bobb & Burdine 3200 Travis 4th Fl Houston TX 77006

RUTH, BRYCE CLINTON, JR., lawyer; b. Greenwood, Miss., Dec. 19, 1948; s. Bryce Clinton and Kathryn (Arant) R.; m. Martha M. Ruth; children: Lauren Elizabeth, Bryce Clinton III. BS, Delta State U., 1970; JD, Memphis State U., 1979. Bar: Tenn., 1979, U.S. Dist. Ct. (mid. dist.) Tenn. 1979, U.S. Ct. Mil. Appeals 1991, U.S. Ct. Appeals (6th cir.), 1994. Criminal investigation spl. agt. IRS, Memphis and Nashville, 1971-82; asst. dist. atty. Dist. Atty. Office, Gallatin, Tenn., 1982-89; asst. pub. defender Pub. Defender's Office, Gallatin, Tenn., 1989-90; pvt. practice White House, Tenn., 1989—2003; judge City of Cross Plains, Tenn., Tenn., 1992—; juvenile ct. referee judge Robertson County, Tenn., 1995-98. Mem. dist. investigating com. dist. VI Tenn. Bd. Law Examiners, 1989—; mem. child enforcement steering com. Asst. Dist. Atty. Office, 1983-84, chmn. legis. subcom., 1985; lectr. in field. Chmn. fin. com. White House First United Meth. Ch., 1983-88, trustee, 1988-90, chmn., 1990; trustee Vol. State Coll. Found., 1993-2000, chmn., 1998-99; bd. dirs. Crime Stoppers of Sumner County, 1989-94; bd. dirs. White House Youth Soccer, 1992-93, coach, 1987-91; bd. dirs. White House Soccer Booster Club, 1996-2000, pres., 1998; bd. dirs. Sumner County CASA, 1992-93; coach Jr. Pro Football, 1980-85; video cameraman for football team White House H.S., 1991—; mem. Leadership Sumner, 1989; bd. dirs. White House Men's Club, 1981-83, 85-88, v.p., 1984, 88, pres., 1985. Lt. col. JAGC, USAR, 1983—. Recipient Disting. Expert award for pistol marksmanship U.S. Treasury, Disting. Svc. award City of White House. Mem. NRA, Tenn. Bar Assn. (del. 1993—, mem. family law code revision commn. 1996—), Sumner County Bar Assn. (chmn. domestic rels. com. 1984-85, v.p. 1998-99, pres. 1999-2000), White House Area C. of C. (bd. dirs. 1990-95, pres. 1993-94), United C. of C. of Sumner County (pres. 1995). Avocations: scuba diving, skiing, golf, hunting, pistol shooting. Military. Office: Office of the Staff Judge Adv Bldg 127 Forrest Rd Fort Campbell KY 42223 Mailing: PO Box 507 Fort Campbell KY 42223 E-mail: bryce.ruth@us.army.mil.

RUTH, HENRY SWARTLEY, retired lawyer; b. Phila., Apr. 16, 1931; s. Henry Swartley and Lola Althouse (Zendt) R.; m. Christine Mallet-Prevost Polk, Dec. 4, 1955 (div. Oct. 1989); children: Laura Ruth-Davis, Diana, Tenley; m. Deborah Ruth Mathieu, Feb. 28, 1991. BA, Yale U., 1952; LLB, U. Pa., 1955. Bar: Pa. 1957, U.S. Dist. Ct. Pa. 1957, U.S. Ct. Appeals (3rd cir.) 1957, D.C. 1964, U.S. Dist. Ct. D.C. 1975, U.S. Supreme Ct. 1975, U.S. Ct. Appeals (4th cir.) 1978. Watergate dep. spl. prosecutor, 1973—74; spl. prosecutor, 1974—75; chief criminal justice rsch. Urban Inst., Washington, 1975—76; gen. counsel UMWA Health and Retirement Funds, Washington, 1976—79; litigation ptnr. Shea & Gardner, Washington, 1979—81; chief litigation divsn. Saul, Ewing, Remick, & Saul, Phila., 1981—87; ethics and spl. litigation counsel Unisys Corp., Blue Bell, Pa., 1987—91; of counsel Crowell & Moring, Washington, 1991—94; ret., 1994. Cons. Joint Legis. Com. on Crime, Trenton, N.J., 1967-68, Violence Commn., Washington, 1968, Nat. Legal Svcs. Orgn., Washington, 1975; Waco ind. reviewer Office Sec. Treasury, Washington, 1993. Co-author: The Challenge of Crime: Rethinking Our Response, 2003; contbr. articles to profl. jours. With U.S. Army, 1955-57. Avocations: hiking, piano, golf. E-mail. Home: 6251 N Camino Santa Valera Tucson AZ 85718 E-mail: hruth@dakotacom.net.

RUTHERFORD, JAY K. lawyer; b. Seymour, Tex., Dec. 2, 1962; s. Jesse Boggs and Sharon Marlene Rutherford; m. Kay Ann Howell, June 25, 1983; children: Anne, Audrey, Ross. BS in Agrl. Econs., Tex. Tech. U., 1985; JD, U. Tex., 1988. Bar: Tex. 1988, U.S. Dist. Ct. (no. and ea. dists.) Tex., U.S. Ct. Appeals (5th cir.). Atty. Law, Snakard & Gambill, Ft. Worth, 1988-92, Jackson Walker LLP, Ft. Worth, 1992—. Bd. dirs. Jr. Achievement, Ft. Worth, 1996-98. Mem. ABA, State Bar Tex., Tex. Assn. Bus./C. of C. (chmn. 1995-98). Federal civil litigation, State civil litigation, Labor (including EEOC, Fair Labor Standards Act, labor-management relations, NLRB, OSHA). Office: Jackson Walker LLP 301 Commerce St Ste 2400 Fort Worth TX 76102-4124

RUTKOFF, ALAN STUART, lawyer; b. Chgo., May 31, 1952; s. Roy and Harriet (Ruskin) R.; m. Mally Zoberman, Dec. 22, 1974; children: Aaron Samuel, Jordana Michal, Robert Nathaniel. BA with high distinction, U. Mich., 1973; JD magna cum laude, Northwestern U., 1976. Bar: Ill. 1976, U.S. Dist. Ct. (no. dist.) Ill. 1976, U.S. Ct. Appeals (7th cir.) 1977, U.S. Ct. Appeals (3d cir.) 1978, U.S. Supreme Ct. 1981, U.S. Ct. Appeals (5th cir.) 1983, U.S. Ct. Appeals (8th cir.) 1990, U.S. Dist. Ct. (we. dist.) Wis. 1996, U.S. Ct. Appeals (6th cir.) 2003. Assoc. Altheimer & Gray, Chgo., 1976-80; ptnr. Kastel & Rutkoff, Chgo., 1980-83, Holleb & Coff Ltd., Chgo., 1983-84, McDermott, Will & Emery, Chgo., 1984—. Pres. N. Suburban Synagogue Beth El, Highland Pk., Ill., 1999-2001.. Mem. ABA, Chgo. Bar Assn., Order of Coif. General civil litigation, Appellate, Professional liability. Home: 801 Timberhill Rd Highland Park IL 60035-5148 Office: McDermott Will & Emery 227 W Monroe St Ste 4400 Chicago IL 60606-5096 E-mail: arutkoff@mwe.com.

RUTLEDGE, JOHN PAUL, lawyer; s. Robert George and Mary June Rutledge; m. Fabiola Alves; 1 child, Raphael Augusto. BA in Philosophy, Loyola Marymount U., 1994; JD cum laude, Howard U., 1997; LLM in Real Property Devel., U. Miami, 1998. Bar: Calif. 1999. Summer law clk. US Dist. Ct., St. Thomas, 1995; intern Bilzin, Sumberg, Dunn, Baena, Price & Axelrod, LLP, Maimi, Fla., 1998; instr. U. Calgary, 1997; assoc. atty. Donahue, Gallagher, Woods & Wood, LLP, Mill Valley, Calif., 2000—02; ceo, gen. counsel Dead End St., LLC, Hoquiam, Wash., 1997—. Advisor GameBubbles.com, Los Angeles, 2002—; legal counsel Koror State Govt. (Republic of Palau); pres. Spot-Hoquiam, LLC; panelist Nat. Inst. Stds. and Technology's Changing the Fundamentals of Reading Conf., Washington, 2000; featured spkr. Bay Area Ind. Pub. Assn., Mill Valley, Calif., 2002; interviewee Sundry television and radio programs and print publications. Editor: (novels) Frosted Glass, The Legendary Barons, A Little Lower Than the Angels, Gabriella's Voice; contbr. articles to profl. jours. including L.A. Daily Jour., Jour. Criminal Law, Calif. Real Estate Jour., Devels. in the Law, 20 Whittier Law Rev.; profiled (book) The Harbor: A Culture of Success. Recipient Excellence for the Future Award, 1998; Bishop Found. Scholar, 1994, 1995, 1996 and 1997, Merit Scholar, Howard U. Sch. Law, 1994, 1995 and 1996, U. Miami, 1998. Mem.: Calif. Bar Assn., Phi Sigma Tau. Intellectual property, Corporate, general, Property, real (including real estate development, water). Office: Dead End Street LLC 813 Third St Hoquiam WA 98550 E-mail: jrutledge@deadendstreet.com.

RUTLEDGE, ROGER KEITH, lawyer; b. Knoxville, Tenn., Dec. 27, 1946; s. Joseph P. and Jean Mae (Karnes) R.; m. Lily Mee Kin Hee, June 6, 1970; children: Amelia Leilani, Sarah Elizabeth. BA in History with honors, U. N.C., 1968; JD cum laude, Am. U., 1977. Bar: Tenn. 1977, U.S. Dist. Ct. (we. dist.) Tenn. 1978, U.S. Supreme Ct. 1982. Served in U.S. Peace Corps, Nepal, 1968-70; fgn. service officer U.S. Dept. State, Washington and Italy, 1971-76; ptnr. Rutledge & Rutledge, Memphis, 1977—. Pres. Jabez Burns, Inc., 1998-99. Editor fiction Carolina Quar., 1967-68; assoc. editor Am. U. Law Rev., 1976-77. Mem. campaign com. Albert Gore Jr. U.S. Senate, Shelby County, 1984, for pres. campaign, 1988, 2000; bd. chmn. United Meth. Neighborhood Ctrs., Inc., 1992. Mem. ABA, Tenn. Bar Assn., Memphis Bar Assn. (editor Bar Forum 1986, asst. editor 1987). Democrat. Methodist. General civil litigation, Corporate, general, General practice. Office: Rutledge & Rutledge 1053 W Rex Rd Memphis TN 38119-3819

RUTSTEIN, DAVID W. lawyer, food products executive; b. N.Y.C., July 7, 1944; s. David and Mazie (Weissman) R.; m. Rena E. Bergsmann, July 19, 1967; children: Sara E., Charles B. BA, U. Pa., 1966; JD with honors, George Washington U., 1969. Bar: Pa. 1969, D.C. 1969. Dep. atty. gen., Pa., 1969-70; ptnr. firm Danzansky, Dickey, Tydings, Quint & Gordon, Washington, 1970-78; sr. v.p., gen. counsel Giant Food, Inc., Washington, 1978—; of counsel Venable Law Firm, Washington, 2001—. Bd. dirs., chmn., treas. Washington Met. Bd. Trade, Fed. City Coun. Bd. dirs., pres. Washington Hebrew Home for Aged, 1989-91; mem. exec. com. Fed. City Coun.; chmn. Agnes and Eugene Meyer Found., Wash. Met. Bd. Trade; trustee Greater Washington Rsch. Ctr. Mem. D.C. Bar Assn., Washington Met. Area Corp. Counsel Assn. (pres. 1986). Jewish. Commercial, contracts (including sales of goods; commercial financing), Corporate, general. Home: 9 Greentree Ct Bethesda MD 20817-1440 Office: Venable Law Firm 1201 New York Ave NW Washington DC 20005

RUTTENBERG, CHARLES BYRON, lawyer; b. Reading, Pa., Nov. 16, 1922; s. Abraham David and Mollie Belle (Rabinowitz) Ruttenberg; m. Arden Honore Suk, July 29, 1955; children: Victoria Arden, Valerie Honore, Alexandra Anne. BA, U. Va., 1946; LLB, U. Pa., 1949. Bar: D.C. With Covington & Burling, Washington; gen. counsel NSF, Washington, Nat. Found. Arts and Humanities, Washington, 1949-69; ptnr. Arent, Fox, Kintner, Plotkin & Kahn, Washington, 1969—; fed. mediator U.S. Dist. Ct., 1998—, D.C. Superior Ct., 2000—. Chmn. legis. bur., mem. exec. com., bd. dirs., gen. counsel Greater Washington Bd. Trade, 1983—92, Nat. Assn. Recording Merchandisers, Video Software Dealers Assn., 1980—95. Editor, mem. mng. bd.: U. Pa. Law Rev., 1947—49. Gen. counsel Nat. Opera Inst., 1985—95; co-chmn. U. Pa. Law Sch. Alumni Fund, Washington, 1983—91; chmn. lawyers com. D.C. Commn. Arts, 1972—75; gen. counsel People to People Music Program, Washington, 1970—91; trustee, gen. counsel Wolf Trap Found. Performing Arts, Vienna, Va., 1981—91, Nat. Inst. Music Theatre, Washington, 1969—90; gen. counsel, bd. dirs. Am. Film Inst., 1969—91; trustee U. D.C., 1990—94; bd. dirs., pres. Cosmos Club Hist. Preservation Found., 1987—; bd. dirs., v.p., exec. com. Iona Sr. Svcs., 1997—; bd. dirs. Washington Area Lawyers for Arts, 1984—95, Greater Washington Rsch. Ctr., 1980—95; mem. adv. bd. D.C. Lottery, 2002—. With USAF, 1942—46, capt. USAFR, 1946—55. Recipient Outstanding Svc. awards, U.S. Govt., 1967, 1968. Mem.: ABA, Arts Internat. (gen. counsel), U. Pa. Law Alumni Assn. (pres. 1967—71, bd. dirs. 1967—78), Washington Athletic Club (bd. govs. 1969—74), Mitchell Law Club, St. Alban's Club, Cosmos Club (bd. mgmt. 2000—03, gen. counsel 2003—), Phi Beta Kappa. Home: 4735 Butterworth Pl NW Washington DC

20016-4459 Office: Arent Fox Kintner Plotkin & Kahn 1050 Connecticut Ave NW Ste 500 Washington DC 20036-5303 E-mail: ruttenbc@arentfox.com., cbruttenberg@aol.com.

RUTTER, MARSHALL ANTHONY, lawyer; b. Pottstown, Pa., Oct. 18, 1931; s. Carroll Lennox and Dorothy (Tagert) R.; m. Winifred Hitz, June 6, 1953 (div. 1970); m. Virginia Ann Hardy, Jan. 30, 1971 (div. 1992); children: Deborah Frances, Gregory Russell, Theodore Thomas; m. Terry Susan Knowles, Dec. 19, 1992. BA, Amherst (Mass.) Coll., 1954; JD, U. Pa., 1959. Bar: Calif 1960. Assoc. O'Melveny & Myers, Los Angeles, 1959-64, Flint & MacKay, Los Angeles, 1964-67, ptnr., 1967-72, Rutter Hobbs & Davidoff, Los Angeles, 1973—. Bd. dirs. Ojai Festivals Ltd., 2001. Gov. The Music Ctr. of L.A. County, 1978-86, 89-92; bd. dirs. Music Ctr. Operating Co., 1992-96; bd. dirs. Chorus Am., Washington, 1987-96, pres., 1993-95; bd. dirs. L.A. Master Chorale Assn., 1964—, pres., 1980-92, chmn. 1992-96, vice chmn., 1996-2001; vestryman All Saints Ch., Beverly Hills, Calif., 1983-86, 88-90. Mem. ABA, Assn. Bus. Trial Lawyers (bd. dirs. 1980-82), L.A. County Bar Assn., Beverly Hills Bar Assn., Century City Bar Assn., English-Speaking Union (various offices L.A. chpt. 1963-91), L.A. Jr. C. of C. (bd. dirs. 1964-67). Democrat. Episcopalian. Avocations: classical and choral music, golf, philately. General civil litigation, Environmental, Family and matrimonial. Home: 1045 S Orange Grove Blvd Apt 10 Pasadena CA 91105-1795 Office: Rutter Hobbs & Davidoff Ste 2700 1900 Ave of Stars Los Angeles CA 90067-4508 Fax: 310-286-1728. E-mail: mrutter@rutterhobbs.com.

RYAN, J. RICHARD, lawyer; b. N.Y.C., Oct. 23, 1929; s. Peter Leon and Mary Martha (Franklin) R.; m. Diana Louise Gambarelli, Nov. 6, 1954 (dec. Feb. 1988); children: Christopher, Claudia; m. Joan Frances Revelle, Jan. 21, 1995. BA, Georgetown U., 1951; JD, Fordham U., 1954. Bar: N.Y. 1956, U.S. Dist. Ct. (so. dist.) N.Y. 1957, U.S. Supreme Ct. 1987. Assoc. Engel, Judge, Miller, Sterling & Reddy, N.Y.C., 1956-63, ptnr., 1963-66, Kantor, Shaw & Ryan, N.Y.C., 1966-71, Ryan & Silberberg, N.Y.C., 1971-84, Ryan & Fogerty, 1984-88, Ryan, Botway, Reddy & Mesrop, 1988-90; sole practitioner, 1990-99; ptnr. Ryan & Stanton LLP, N.Y.C., 1999—. Bd. dirs. Am. Health Capital Ins. Co. Bd. dirs. Guiding Eyes for the Blind, Inc., pres., 1973-77; trustee Cooper Inst. for Advanced Studies in Medicine and Humanities; Copyright Soc. candidate for Mayor of Pelham, N.Y., 1963. Served with AUS, 1954-56. Mem. ABA, N.Y. State Bar Assn., Assn. Bar City N.Y. (sports law com. 2000—), Soc. Friendly Sons of St. Patrick, Pelham Country Club (past pres.), Union League, Winged Foot Golf Club. Corporate, general, Entertainment, Trademark and copyright. Office: 516 5th Ave Ste 805 New York NY 10036-7511 E-mail: lojrrlaw@aol.com.

RYAN, JAMES LEO, federal judge; b. Detroit, Mich., Nov. 19, 1932; s. Leo Francis and Irene Agnes Ryan; m. Mary Elizabeth Rogers, Oct. 12, 1957; children: Daniel P., James R., Colleen M. Hansen, Kathleen A. LLB, U. Detroit, 1956, LLD (hon.) , 1986, BA, 1992; LLD (hon.) , Madonna Coll., 1976, Detroit Coll., 1978, Thomas M. Cooley Law Sch., Lansing, Mich., 1986. Justice of peace, Redford Twp., Mich., 1963—66; judge 3d Cir. Ct. of Mich., 1966—75; justice Mich. Supreme Ct., 1975—86; judge U.S. Ct. Appeals (6th cir.), 1986—. Faculty Nat. Jud. Coll., Reno; adj. faculty, bd. dirs. Ave Maria Sch. Law. Contbr. articles to profl. jours. Capt. JAGC USNR, 1957—92, ret. mil. judge USNR. Mem.: Fed. Bar Assn., State Bar Mich., Fed. Judges Assn., K.M., K.C. Office: US Ct Appeals US Courthouse 231 W Lafayette Blvd Detroit MI 48226-2700

RYAN, JAMES E. former state attorney general; b. Chgo., Feb. 21, 1946; m. Marie Ryan; children: John, Jim, Matt, Amy, Patrick, Anne Marie(dec.). BA in Polit. Sci., Ill. Benedictine Coll., 1968; JD, Ill. Inst. Tech., 1971. Bar: Ill. 1971. Asst. state's atty. criminal divsn. DuPage County State's Atty.'s Office, 1971—74, 1st. asst. state's atty., 1974—76; founder Ryan & Darrah; state's atty. DuPage County State's Atty.'s Office, 1984—94; atty. gen. State of Ill., 1994—2002. Disting. fellow Benedictine U., Lisle, Ill., 2003—. Named Lawyer of Yr., DuPage County Bar Assn., 1997; recipient numerous awards from various orgns. including, Nat. Assn. Counties, Alliance Against Intoxicated Motorists. Mem.: Ill. State's Attys. Assn. (past pres., Ezzard Charles award). Republican. Roman Catholic.*

RYAN, JOHN DUNCAN, lawyer; b. Portland, Oreg., Dec. 20, 1920; s. Thomas Gough and Virginia Abigail (Hadley) R.; m. Florence A. Ryan, Jan. 30, 1970 (dec. 1987); m. Virginia Kane Wilson, June 15, 1996. BS, Fordham U., 1943; JD, Lewis & Clark Coll., Portland, 1950. Bar: Oreg. 1950. Pvt. practice, Portland, 1950—. Adj. instr. Northwestern Sch. Law Lewis & Clark Coll., 1953-70. Author: (poems) Expressions, 1993, Expressions II, 1995, (book) Expressions, 1988, 1999, Cooking with John Ryan, 2002. Sgt. Air Corps, U.S. Army, 1942-46, ETO. Recipient St. Thomas More award Catholic Lawyers for Social Justice, 1993. Mem. ABA (Oreg. delegate 1985-93, chmn. spl. com. on law & literacy 1991-93), Am. Coll. Trial Lawyers, Am. Trial Lawyers Assn., Oreg. State Bar (bd. govs. 1963-67), Oreg. Trial Lawyers Assn. (Trial Lawyer of Yr. 1993), Multnomah County Bar Assn. (Professionalism award 1997), Washington County Bar Assn. Personal injury (including property damage), Probate (including wills, trusts), General civil litigation. Home and Office: 1206 Circulo Aguilar Rio Rico AZ 85648-3355 and: 503 SW Colony Dr Portland OR 97219-7763 E-mail: ryan98@theriver.com.

RYAN, JOHN M. lawyer; b. Glen Ridge, N.J., May 18, 1936; AB, Dartmouth Coll., 1958; LLB, U. Va., 1963. Bar: Va. 1964. Lectr. at law Marshall-Wythe Sch. Law Coll. William and Mary, 1976-86; ptnr. Vandeventer Black LLP, Norfolk, Va.; gen. counsel Va. Internat. Terminals, Inc. Trustee John Marshall Found., Contemporary Art Ctr. Va.; commr. Arts and Humanities Commn., City of Virginia Beach; bd. dirs. Children's Health Sys., Inc., Greater Norfolk Corp. Fellow: Va. Law Found., Am. Bar Found., Am. Coll. Trial Lawyers; mem.: ABA (labor rels., litigation sect.), So. Conf. Bar Pres., Nat. Conf. Bar Pres., Va. State Bar, Norfolk-Portsmouth Bar Assn., Maritime Law Assn. U.S. (chmn. stevedore and maritime terminals com.), Va. Bar Assn. (pres. 1988), S.E. Admiralty Law Inst., James Kent Am. Inn of Ct. (past pres.), 4th Cir. Jud. Conf. Admiralty, General civil litigation, Labor (including EEOC, Fair Labor Standards Act, labor-management relations, NLRB, OSHA). Office: Vandeventer Black LLP 500 World Trade Ctr Norfolk VA 23510-1679 E-mail: jryan@vanblk.com.

RYAN, JOSEPH W., JR., lawyer; b. Phila., June 24, 1948; s. Joseph W. Sr. and Marie R. (Hillgrube) R.; m. Mary Pat Law, Sept. 11, 1971; children: Caitlin, Joseph W. III. BA, St. Joseph's U., Phila., 1970; MA, Villanova U., 1971; JD, U. Va., 1978. Bar: Ohio 1978, U.S. Supreme Ct. 1982. Ptnr. Porter, Wright, Morris & Arthur, Columbus, Ohio, 1978—. Lectr. Sch. Dentistry Ohio State U., Columbus, 1982-89, Continuing Legal Edn. Inst., 1984—; mem. trial acad. faculty Internat. Assn. Def. Counsel, Boulder, Colo., 1994. Author: Use of Demonstrative Evidence, 1985; assoc. editor Litigation News, 1986—, editor in chief, 2000-02. Trustee Columbus Zool. Assn., 1980-90; bd. dirs. Columbus Speech and Hearing Ctr., 1988-99, pres., 1995-96. Mem. ABA, Ohio State Bar Assn., Columbus Bar Assn., Internat. Assn. Def. Counsel, Am. Arbitration Assn. (panel of arbitrators). Republican. Roman Catholic. General civil litigation, Insurance, Utilities, public. Office: Porter Wright Morris & Arthur 41 S High St Ste 30 Columbus OH 43215-6101 E-mail: jryan@porterwright.com.

RYAN, KELLY, lawyer; b. N.Y.C., July 18, 1963; d. Robert Gerard and Edith Shaffer Ryan. BA, Tulane U., New Orleans, 1985; JD, Georgetown U., Washington, 1988; LLM, Cambridge U., Eng., 1989. Bar: N.Y. 1990, Wash. 1992. Assoc. gen. counsel Office of Gen. Counsel, INS, Washington, 1992—98, chief refugee and asylum law divsn., 1998—2002; dep. asst. sec. state Bur. Population, Refugees and Migration, 2002—. Recipient Commrs. award for meritorious svc., INS, 1998, 2000. Roman Catholic.

RYAN, KEVIN V. lawyer; married; 2 children. BA in History, Dartmouth Coll.; JD, U. San Francisco. Prosecutor Alameda County Dist. Atty.'s Office; judge San Francisco Mcpl. Ct., 1996—98; mem. San Francisco Superior Ct., 1999, presiding judge criminal divsn.; U.S. atty. No. Dist. Calif., 2002—. Bd. dirs. No. Calif. High Intensity Drug Trafficking Area Working Group; mem. Pres. Bush's Corp. Fraud Task Force; apptd. mem. subcom. Controlled Substances and Terrorism and Nat. Security, appointed to Jud. Coun.'s Exec. Legis. Action Network, Chief Justice of Calif. Supreme Ct.; appointed to Criminal Law Planning Com. of Calif. Continuing Jud. Studies Program, Governing Com. of Calif. Ctr. for Jud. Edn. and Rsch.; appointed to Adult Probation Dept.'s Oversight Com., Presiding Judge for Cts.; mem. exec. com. San Francisco Superior Ct.; mem. exec. com. Am. Inn of Cts., U. San Francisco Sch. Law; bd. govs. U. San Francisco Law Soc.; bd. trustees Schs. of Sacred Heart, San Francisco; mem. faculty Intensive Trial Advocacy Program, U. San Francisco Sch. Law; lectr. in field. Recipient Mcpl. Ct. Trial Judge of Yr., San Francisco Trial Lawyers' Assn., 1998. Office: No Dist Calif 450 Golden Gate Ave San Francisco CA 94102*

RYAN, LEONARD EAMES, judge; b. Albion, N.Y., July 8, 1930; s. Bernard and Harriet Earle (Fitts) R.; m. Ann Allen, June 18, 1973; 1 child, Thomas Eames Allen-Ryan. Grad., Kent Sch., 1948; AB, U. Pa., 1954; JD, NYU, 1962. Bar: D.C. 1963, N.Y. 1963, U.S. Ct. Appeals (D.C. cir.) 1963, U.S. Dist. Ct. (so. and ea. dists.) N.Y. 1965, U.S. Ct. Appeals (2nd cir.) 1966, U.S. Supreme Ct. 1967. Field engr. constrn. U.S. Steel Fairless Works, Morrisville, Pa., 1951-52; reporter Upper Darby (Pa.) News, 1954; newsman AP, Pitts., Phila., Harrisburg, N.Y.C., 1955-62; reporter, spl. writer on law N.Y. Times, 1962-63; info. adviser corp. hdqrs. IBM, N.Y.C., 1963; trial atty. firm Perrell, Nielsen & Stephens, N.Y.C., 1964-66; trial atty. civil rights div. Dept. Justice, Washington, 1966-68; asst. to dir. bus. affairs CBS News, N.Y.C., 1968; program officer Office Govt. and Law, Ford Found., N.Y.C., 1968-74; pvt. practice law, cons. pub. affairs, N.Y.C., 1974-91; v.p., sec. W. P. Carey & Co., Inc., N.Y.C., 1977—82; impartial hearing officer Edn. for All Handicapped Children Act of 1975, 1976-91; per diem adminstrv. law judge N.Y. State Agys., 1976-91; hearing examiner N.Y. State Family Ct., 1980-81; apptd. U.S. adminstv. law judge, 1991; adminstv. law judge Office Hearings and Appeals, San Rafael, Calif., 1991—93, Phila., 1993-94, N.Y.C., 1994—. Arbitrator Small Claims Ct., N.Y.C., 1974-84; bd. dirs. Community Action for Legal Svcs. Inc., N.Y.C., 1971-77, vice-chmn., 1975-77; co-chmn. Citizens Com. to Save Legal Svcs., N.Y.C., 1975-76; bd. dirs. Lower East Side Svc. Ctr., N.Y.C., 1977-89. Author: (with Bernard Ryan Jr.) So You Want to Go Into Journalism, 1963; contbr. articles to profl. jours. Served with USAR, 1950-57. Mem. Am. Judicature Soc., Assn. of Bar of City of N.Y., N.Y. State Bar Assn., St. Elmo Club (Phila.), Heights Casino (Bklyn.). Home: 32 Orange St Brooklyn NY 11201-1634 Office: 111 Livingston St Brooklyn NY 11201-5078

RYAN, MARILYNNE R. lawyer; d. Elizabeth Barnes and David H. Regan, Jr.; m. Edward P. Ryan, Jr.; children: Suzanne Bryant, Erin Bryant. BA cum laude in Psychology, Stonehill Coll., 1981; JD magna cum laude, Mass. State Ct., 1986. Hearing officer Bd. of Bar Overseers, Boston, 1996—2002; faculty mem. for MCLE's and Mass. Bar Assn., Boston, 2002; com. mem. Norfolk County Bench Bar Com., Boston, 1995—2003, co-chairperson, 1996—98. Co-author: Massachusetts Domestic Relations Volumes. Mem.: ABA, Mass. Bar Assn. (chair child support guidelines com. 2001—03). Family and matrimonial, Probate (including wills, trusts). Office: 825 Main St Walpole MA 02081 Office Fax: 508-668-1285.

RYAN, MICHAEL D. state supreme court justice; BA, St. John's U., Collegeville, Minn., 1967; JD, Ariz. State U., 1977. Dep. county atty. Maricopa County Atty.'s Office, 1977—85; judge pro tempore Superior Ct. State of Ariz., 1985—86, judge, 1986—96; vice chief judge Ariz. Ct. Appeals, Divsn. 1, 2001—02, judge, 1996—2002; justice Ariz. Supreme Ct., 2002—. Chair Ariz. Supreme Ct. Com. Appointment Counsel for Indigent Defendants in Capital Cases; mem. Ariz. Atty. Gen. Capital Case Commn. Mem. Maricopa County Resource Site Team Ctr. for Sex Offender Mgmt., 1995—; mem. x-tattoo adv. com. At Risk Youth Divsn. City of Phoenix Parks, Recreation and Libr. Dept., 1996—. Infantry platoon comdr. USMC, 1968, Vietnam. Mem.: Maricopa County Bar Assn. (bd. dirs. 1987—91, 1998—, chair task force recruitment & retention of women and minority lawyers, Bd. Mem. of Yr. 1999—2000). Office: Ariz Supreme Ct 1501 W Washington Phoenix AZ 85007-3231*

RYAN, PATRICK MICHAEL, lawyer; b. Chgo., May 26, 1944; s. Edward Michael and Kathleen Teresa (Crimmins) R.; m. Holly Ann Daleske, Aug. 31, 1968; children: Rebecca Eileen, Brendan Patrick, Abigail Christine, Lucas Christopher. BA, St. Mary's Coll., Winona, Minn., 1966; JD, Marquette U., 1969. Bar: Wis. 1969. Law clk. Wis. Supreme Ct., Madison, 1969-70; ptnr. Quarles & Brady LLP, Milw., 1970—2001, chmn., mng. ptnr., 2002—. Dir. and officer several pvt. bus. corps. Mem. ABA, Wis. Bar Assn., Milw. Bar Assn., University Club. Avocations: reading, sports. Commercial, contracts (including sales of goods; commercial financing), Corporate, general, Mergers and acquisitions. Home: 363 Huntington Dr Cedarburg WI 53012-9507 Office: Quarles & Brady LLP 411 E Wisconsin Ave Ste 2550 Milwaukee WI 53202-4497 E-mail: pmr@quarles.com.

RYAN, ROBERT COLLINS, lawyer; b. Evanston, Ill., Sept. 15, 1953; s. Donald Thomas and Patricia J. (Collins) R.; m. Joanne Kay Holata, Nov. 5, 1983. BA in Econs., BS in Indsl. Engring. with high honors, U. Ill., 1976; JD, Northwestern U., 1979. Bar: Ill. 1979, Nev. 1999, US Dist. Ct. (no. dist.) Ill. 1980, US Dist. Ct. Nev. 2001, US Ct. Appeals (Fed. cir.) 1982, US Patent Office, 1979, US Supreme Ct. 1984. Assoc. Allegretti, Newitt, Witcoff & McAndrews, Ltd., Chgo., 1979-83, ptnr., 1983-88; founding ptnr. McAndrews, Held & Malloy, Ltd., Chgo., 1988-96, of counsel, 1998—2000; v.p. digital gen. sys., Inc. CNASDAQ DGIT, 2001—. Chief legal and intellectual property officer, exec. v.p. StarGuide Digital Networks, Inc., Reno, 1996-; ; mem. Ian Burns & Assocs., P.C., Reno, 1998—; of counsel Pauley, Petersen, Kinne & Fejer, Hoffman Estates, Ill., 1998-2002; lectr. engring. law Northwestern U. Tech. Inst., Evanston, Ill., 1981-85, adj. prof. engring. law, 1985-90; lectr. patent law and appellate practice John Marshall Law Sch., 1991-93, adj. prof. patent law and appellate advocacy, 1993-2000; mem. faculty Nat. Jud. Coll., Reno, Nev., 1998-2000; mem. alumni bd. mech. and indsl. engring. dept. U. Ill., Urbana, 1996—. Exec. editor Northwestern Jour. Internat. Law & Bus., 1978-79; contbr. articles to profl. jours. Bd. dirs. Washoe Assn. Retarded Citizens, Reno, 1997—, sec., 2001, 1st v.p., 2002-03. James scholar U. Ill., 1976. Mem. ABA, Fed. Cir. Bar Assn., Intellectual Property Law Assn. Chgo., Licensing Execs. Soc., Tau Beta Pi, Phi Eta Sigma, Alpha Pi Mu, Phi Kappa Phi. Computer, Patent, Trademark and copyright. Home: 95 Rimfire Cir Reno NV 89509-2989 Office: StarGuide Digital Networks 300 E 2nd St Ste 1510 Reno NV 89501-1591

RYAN, ROBERT DAVIS, lawyer; b. Lynbrook, N.Y., Aug. 14, 1941; s. Thomas Francis and Agnes Frances (Davis) R.; children: John, Daniel, Carolyn. BBA, St. John's U., 1962; JD, Fordham U., 1972. Bar: N.Y. 1973, U.S. Dist. Ct. (so. and ea. dists.) N.Y. 1973, U.S. Ct. Appeals (2d cir.) 1975, U.S. Supreme Ct. 1984. Asst. dist. atty. Westchester County, White Plains, N.Y., 1972-77; assoc. Clark, Gagliardi & Miller, White Plains, 1977-82; ptnr. Rende, Ryan & Downes, White Plains, 1982—. Adj. prof. law St. John's U., 1992-95, 99—. Chmn. Cable TV Adv. Com., Lewisboro, N.Y., 1983-99. Mem. Assn. Trial Lawyers Am., N.Y. State Trial Lawyers Assn., Westchester County Bar Assn., N.Y. State Bar Assn. (continuing legal edn. com. trial lawyers sect.), No. Westchester Bar Assn. (bd. govs. 1987-92, pres. 1986-87), White Plains Bar Assn. Republican. Roman Catholic. General civil litigation, Personal injury (including property damage), Product liability. Home: PO Box 113 Bedford NY 10506-0113 Office: Rende Ryan & Downes 202 Mamaroneck Ave Ste 600 White Plains NY 10601-5312

RYAN, ROBERT JEFFERS, lawyer; b. Evanston, Ill., Dec. 26, 1947; BBA in Fin., U. Notre Dame, 1970; JD, Loyola U., Chgo., 1973. Bar: Ill. 1973, U.S. Dist. Ct. (no. dist.) Ill. 1973. Pvt. practice, Winnetka, Ill., 1979—. Corporate, general, General practice, Probate (including wills, trusts). Office: 560 Green Bay Rd Ste 303 Winnetka IL 60093-2242

RYAN, STEPHEN MICHAEL, lawyer, educator; b. N.Y.C., Apr. 19, 1955; s. John J. and Madeline Ryan; m. Lisa Frasco, Apr. 17, 1982; children: John, Matthew, William. BS, Cornell U., 1977; JD cum laude, Notre Dame U., 1980. Bar: Pa. 1981, U.S. Dist. Ct. D.C. 1982, U.S. Supreme Ct. 1994, U.S. Ct. Appeals (7th cir.) 1982. Law clk. Hon. R. A. Grant, U.S. Dist. Ct., South Bend, Ind., 1979—81; assoc. Howrey & Simon, Washington, 1981—84; dep. counsel Pres.'s Commn. on Organized Crime, Washington, 1984—86; asst. U.S. atty. U.S. Dept. Justice, Washington, 1986—87; gen. counsel U.S. Senate Com. on Govtl. Affairs, Washington, 1987—91; ptnr. Brand, Lowell & Ryan, Washington, 1992—99, Manatt, Phelps & Phillips LLP, Washington, 1999—. Adj. prof. Georgetown U. Law Sch., Washington, 1994—; advisor post communist criminal law and govt. ethics reforms Govt. of Latvia, 1993, Govt. of Poland, 1993—96, Govt. of Lithuania, 1995. Columnist Govt. Computer News, prin. author The Edge: Organized Crime, Business and Unions, President's Commission on Organized Crime, 1986; co-author: The Revised Procurement Integrity Rule, NCMA, 1989, 1991. Mem. ea. regional bd. Operation Hope, Calif., 2000—; legal counsel Nat. Christ Child Soc., Md., 2002—. Roman Catholic. Avocations: soccer, collecting autograph books. Government contracts and claims, Criminal, Antitrust. Office: Manatt Phelps & Phillips 1501 M St NW Washington DC 20005 Office Fax: 202-463-4394 .

RYAN, THOMAS WILLIAM, lawyer; b. Tulsa, Feb. 16, 1953; s. Dean Lawrence and Helen Ladeen Ryan; m. Mary Ellen Poxon, Jan. 30, 1973; children: Matthew Alan, Jennifer Erin. BA, U. Houston, 1975, JD, 1978. Bar: Tex. 1978. Ptnr. Hart, Ryan & Pfeffer, Houston, 1978-80; contracts adminstr. Texaco Inc., Houston, 1980-85; asst. gen. counsel Total Minatome Corp., Houston, 1985-99; gen. counsel, corp. sec. Total Exploration Prodn. USA, Inc., Houston, 1999-2001; v.p., gen. counsel, corp. sec. Total E&P USA, Inc., Houston, 2001—. Adv. bd. Inst. for Energy Law. Coach youth sports YMCA, Houston, 1990-94. Mem. KC (adv. 1985-87), State Bar Tex. Avocations: golf, bowling. FERC practice, Oil, gas, and mineral, Labor (including EEOC, Fair Labor Standards Act, labor-management relations, NLRB, OSHA). Office: Total E&P USA Inc One Memorial City Plz 800 Gessner Ste 700 Houston TX 77024

RYCE, DONALD THEODORE, lawyer; b. New Orleans, Dec. 15, 1943; s. Donald Theodore and Martha (Herndon) R.; m. Claudine Dianne Walker, July 8, 1984; children: Ted, Martha, Jimmy. BA, U. Fla., 1966, JD, 1968. Bar: Fla. 1968, U.S. Dist. Ct. (so. dist.) Fla. 1972, U.S. Ct. Appeals (5th and 11th cirs.) 1973. Jud. law clk. Fla. Dist. Ct. Appeals (4th cir.), West Palm Beach, 1968-70; ptnr. Hogg, Allen, Ryce, Norton & Blue, Miami, Fla., 1970-89, Donald T. Ryce, P.A., Miami, 1989—. Co-chmn. liaison com. labor and employment sect. NLRB, Fla., 1990-92, mem. publs. com., 1990-91, exec. coun. labor and employment sect., 1994-98; apptd. missing children adv. bd. Fla. Dept. Law Enforcement, 1996—. Active Fla. Police Chiefs Edn. Rsch. Found.; dir. Jimmy Ryce Ctr. for Victims of Predatory Abduction. Named to Policeman Hall of Fame, 1996, Grand Knight of Order of Michael the Archangel; recipient Leadership award Fla. Police Chiefs Edn. Rsch. Found., 1993. Mem. Microcomputer Edn. for Employment of the Disabled (bus. adv. coun.), Winter Haven C. of C. (Cmty. Leadership award 1994), Miami Rotary. Episcopalian. Avocations: tennis, gourmet cooking, biking. General civil litigation, Labor (including EEOC, Fair Labor Standards Act, labor-management relations, NLRB, OSHA). Office: Ste 305 1111 Kane Concourse Bay Harbor Islands FL 33154-2041 Fax: 305-864-7008. E-mail: employerlawyer@yahoo.com.

RYDER, DAVID R. lawyer; b. Hinsdale, Ill., Oct. 8, 1946; BA, DePauw U., 1968; JD, U. Mich., 1971. Bar: Ill. 1971, Fla. 1977. Ptnr. McDermott, Will & Emery, Chgo. Mem. Ill. State Bar Assn., Fla. Bar. Taxation, general. Office: McDermott Will & Emery 227 W Monroe St Fl 57 Chicago IL 60606-5016

RYDER, HENRY C(LAY), lawyer; b. Lafayette, Ind., Feb. 18, 1928; s. Raymond Robert and Mina Elizabeth (Arnold) R.; m. Ann Sater Clay, Nov. 29, 1952 (dec.); children: David C., Sarah Paige Hugon, Anne Ryder O'Keefe; m. Velma Iris Dean, Aug. 27, 1976 BS, Purdue U., 1948; LLB, U. Mich., 1951; LLD, Hanover Coll., 1998. Bar: Mich. 1951, Ind. 1952, U.S. Dist. Ct. (so. dist.) Ind. 1953, U.S. Ct. Appeals (7th cir.) 1957, U.S. Supreme Ct. 1981. Assoc. Buschmann, Krieg, DeVault & Alexander, Indpls., 1953-57, ptnr., 1957-60, Roberts & Ryder and successor firms, Indpls., 1960-86, Barnes & Thornburg (merger), Indpls., 1987-95, of counsel, 1996—. Pres. Ind. State Symphony Soc. Inc., 1979-82, bd. dirs., 1972-91, trustee, 1991—; chmn. United Way of Greater Indpls., 1984; vice chmn. Greater Indpls. Progress Com., 1979-86, chmn., 1987-89, mem. exec. com., 1979-2000; trustee Purdue U., 1983-89, Hanover Coll., 1979—, chmn., 1988-98; bd. dirs. Hist. Landmark Found. of Ind., 1985-96, chmn., 1992-95; bd. dirs. Purdue Rsch. Found., 1992—; hon. v.p. Ind. Soc. Chgo.; com. bd. IUPUI U. Libr., 1998—, chmn. 2003—; bd. govs. Heartland Film Festival, 2000—. Lt. U.S. Army, 1951-53. Recipient Jefferson award Indpls. Star, 1983, Whistler award Greater Indpls. Progress Com., 1989; Sagamore of the Wabash, 1984; named Man of Yr., B'nai B'rith Soc., 1984, Ind. Acad., 1992, Lifetime Achievement award Nat. Soc. Fund Raising Execs., 1999. Fellow: Ind. Bar Found., Am. Bar Found.; mem.: ABA, Indpls. Bar Assn., Ind. Bar Assn., Ind. C. of C. (bd. dirs. 1991—94), Purdue U. Alumni Assn. (pres. 1975—77, Alumni Svc. award 1982, Citizenship award 1989), Indpls. Lit. Club, Kiwanis (Downtown Indpls. pres. 1983, Civic award 1981), Columbia Club (bd. dirs. 1987—90, sec. 1988, pres. Found. 1990—95, trustee 1990—, Benjamin Harrison award 1983, Columbian of Yr. award 2002), USAC Benevolent Found. (bd. dirs., pres. 1999—), USAC Properties (sec., bd. dirs.), U.S. Auto Club (sec., bd. dirs., Pres.'s award 1989, Eddie Edenburn award 2000), Lawyers Club (pres. Indpls. 1966). Republican. Presbyterian. Federal civil litigation, Labor (including EEOC, Fair Labor Standards Act, labor-management relations, NLRB, OSHA). Office: Barnes & Thornburg 11 S Meridian St Indianapolis IN 46204-3535

RYESKY, KENNETH H. lawyer; b. Phila., July 30, 1954; s. A. and Helene (Silbermann) R.; m. Tamara E. Weiss, Mar. 11, 1983; children: H.Z., Damilola. BBA, Temple U., 1977, JD, 1986; MBA, La Salle U., 1982; MLS, CUNY, 1999. Bar: Pa. 1986, N.J. 1987, N.Y. 1988, U.S. Supreme Ct. 1996. Procurement specialist Def. Logistics Agy., Phila., 1979-87; atty. IRS, N.Y.C., 1987-91; pvt. practice East Northport, N.Y., 1991—. Adj. asst. prof. Queens Coll./CUNY, Flushing, N.Y., 1993—; ct. arbitrator N.Y.C. Civil Ct., 1995—. Co-author: Federal Government Intelligence Property Guide, 1995; contbr. articles to profl. jours. Jewish. Avocations: cooking, gardening, collecting. E-mail: 'khresq@sprintmail.com. Commercial, consumer (including collections, credit), Taxation, general. Office: PO Box 926 East Northport NY 11731-0529 Fax: 631-266-3198.

RYLAND, WALTER H. lawyer; b. Richmond, Va., Jan. 23, 1943; s. John William and Evelyn (Quillin) R.; m. Madelaine Aerni, July 10, 1976; children: Mark Vanley, Caroline Aerni. BA, Washington & Lee U., 1965,

LLB, 1967. Chief dep. atty. gen. Office of the Atty. Gen. of Va., Richmond, 1978-82; ptnr. Williams, Mullen, Christian & Dobbins, Richmond, 1983—. Counselor, Va. Mus. Fine Arts, Richmond, 1983—; pres. J. Sargeant Reynolds Found., Richmond, 1990; legal adv., Southeastern Legal Found., Atlanta, Ga., 1989—. Co-editor: Racial Preferences in Government Contracting (Nat. Legal Ctr. for the Pub. Interest), 1993. Sec. bd. trustees Washington Internat. U. Va., 1989-91; bd. dirs. Coun. for Am. First Freedom, Richmond, 1988-92; pres. Theatre Va., Richmond, 1987-88; sec. Communication Disorders Found., Richmond, 1986-88, Cultural Art Ctr. and Glen Allen. Mem. ABA, Va. Bar Assn., Richmond Bar Assn. Constitutional, Education and schools, Government contracts and claims. Office: Williams Mullen Clark & Dobbins 2 James Ctr 1021 E Cary St Richmond VA 23219-4000

RYMER, PAMELA ANN, federal judge; b. Knoxville, Tenn., Jan. 6, 1941; AB, Vassar Coll., 1961; LLB, Stanford U., 1964; LLD (hon.) , Pepperdine U., 1988. Bar: Calif. 1966, U.S. Ct. Appeals (9th cir.) 1966, U.S. Ct. Appeals (10th cir.), U.S. Supreme Ct. Dir., polit. rsch. and analysis Goldwater for President Com., 1964; v.p. Rus Walton & Assoc., Los Altos, Calif., 1965—66; assoc. Lillick McHose & Charles, L.A., 1966—75, ptnr., 1973—75, Toy and Rymer, L.A., 1975—83; judge U.S. Dist. Ct. (cen. dist.) Calif., L.A., 1983—89, U.S. Ct. Appeals (9th cir.), L.A., 1989—. Faculty The Nat. Jud. Coll., 1986-88; mem. com. summer ednl. programs Fed. Jud. Ctr., 1987-88, mem. com. appellate judge edn., 1996-99; chair exec. com. 9th Cir. Jud. Conf., 1990; mem. com. criminal law Jud. Conf. U.S., 1988-93, Ad Hoc com. gender-based violence, 1991-94, fed.-state jurisdiction com., 1993-96; mem. commn. on structural alternatives Fed. Cts. Appeals, 1997-98. Mem. editorial bd. The Judges' jour., 1989-91; contbr. articles to profl. jours. and newsletters. Mem. Calif. Postsecondary Edn. Commn., 1974-84, chmn., 1980-84; mem. L.A. Olympic Citizens Adv. Commn.; bd. visitors Stanford U. Law Sch., 1986-99, trustee, 1991-2001, chair, 1993-96, exec. com., chmn. bd. trustees com. acad. policy, planning and mgmt. and its ad. hoc. com. athletics., chmn. bd. visitors Sch. Law, 1987—; bd. visitors Pepperdine U. Law Sch., 1987—; mem. Edn. Commn. of States Task Force on State Policy and Ind. Higher Edn., 1987-89, Carnegie Commn. Task Force Sci. and Tech. Jud. and Regulatory Decisionmaking, 1990-93, Commn. Substance Abuse Coll. and Univ. Campuses, 1992-94, commn. substance abuse high schs. Ctr. Addiction and Substance Abube Columbia U.; bd. dirs. Constnl. Rights Found., 1985-97, Pacific Coun. Internat. Policy, 1995—, Calif. Higher Edn. Policy Ctr., 1992-97; Jud. Conf. U.S. Com. Fed.-State Jurisdiction, 1993, Com. Criminal Law, 1988-93, ad hoc com. gender based violence, 1991-94; chair exec. com. 9th cir. jud. conf., 1990-94. Recipient Outstanding Trial Jurist award L.A. County Bar Assn., 1988; named David T. Lewis Disting. Jurist-in-Residence U. Utah, 1992. Mem. ABA (task force on civil justice reform 1991-93, mem. coord. com. agenda civil justice reform in Am. 1991), State Bar Calif. (antitrust and trade regulation sect., exec. com. 1990-92), L.A. County Bar Assn. (chmn. antitrust sect. 1981-82, mem. editl. bd. The Judges Jour. 1989-91, mem. com. professionalism 1988—, numerous other coms.), Assn. of Bus. Trial Lawyers (bd. govs. 1990-92), Stanford Alumni Assn., Stanford Law Soc. Soc. Calif., Vassar Club So. Calif. (past pres.). Office: US Ct Appeals 9th Cir US Court of Appeals Bldg 125 S Grand Ave Rm 600 Pasadena CA 91105-1621*

RYMILL, THOMAS MARK, lawyer; b. Penola, Australia, Feb. 19, 1950; s. Robert Riddoch and Gladys Edith (Hood) R.; m. Catherine Margaret Walters, March 10, 1979. LLB, U. Adelaide, South Australia, 1974. Enrolled legal practitioner, 1975; notary pub., 1984. Prin. Rymills Law Office, Mt. Gambier, SA, 1975—. Brigade capt. Country Fire Svc., Penola, 1977-82; v.p. Mt. Gambier C. of C., 1992-96; pres. Mt. Gambier br. Liberal Party, 2001-02. Recipient Nat. medal Country Fire Svc., 1986. Mem. Law Soc. of South Australia (councillor 1997), Australia Inst. Family Law Arbitrators and Mediators. General practice, Family and matrimonial, Property, real (including real estate development, water). Office: Rymills Law Office 39 Bay Rd Mount Gambier 5290 Australia

RYNEARSON, ARTHUR JOHN, lawyer; b. Caracas, Venezuela, Apr. 18, 1949; s. Arthur Preston and Kathryn Loraine Rynearson; m. Mary Linda Patteson, Oct. 26, 1996. BA, Hamilton Coll., 1971; cert. in internat. and comparative law, U. San Diego, 1975; JD, Cornell U., 1976. Bar: D.C. 1976. Fgn. affairs analyst Congl. Rsch. Svc., Libr. of Congress, Washington, 1971—73; asst. counsel Legis. Counsel's Office U.S. Senate, Washington, 1976—91, sr. counsel, 1991—99, dep. legis. counsel, 1999—2003. Lectr. Legis. Studies Inst., Washington, 1990—93, Meridian Internat. Ctr., Washington, 1999—2002, Internat. Law Inst., Washington, 1999—2002. Mem. ch. coun. United Meth. Ch., Washington, 2000—, Met. Meml., Washington. Mem.: ABA, D.C. Bar (internat. law sect., co-chair nat. security subcom. 1990—91), Am. Soc. Internat. Law, Phi Beta Kappa. Achievements include assisting in drafting of every major foreign relations and immigration legislative measure considered by the U.S. Senate from 1977 to 2003. Avocations: Native American cultures, tennis. Home and Office: 6213 N 19th St Arlington VA 22205

SAARI, JOHN WILLIAM, JR., lawyer; b. Jersey City, Oct. 12, 1937; s. John William Sr. and Ina Marie (Bain) S.; m. Susan Jo Olson, Aug. 27, 1967 (div. June 1971); m. Marjorie Ann Palm, Nov. 16, 1973. Student, Duke U., 1955-58, U. N.C., 1962-63; JD with honors, Ill. Inst. Tech., Chgo., 1972. Bar: Ill. 1972, U.S. Dist. Ct. (no. dist.) Ill. 1972, Wis. 1980, U.S. Dist. Ct. (ea. and we. dists.) Wis. 1980, U.S. Ct. Appeals (7th cir.) 1972, U.S. Supreme Ct. 1997. Assoc. Yates, Goff, Gustafson & Been, Chgo., 1972-76, Hubbard, Hubbard, O'Brien & Hall, Chgo., 1976-78; atty. Ill. Bell Telephone Co., Chgo., 1978-79; assoc. Cirilli Law Office, Rhinelander, Wis., 1979-83; pvt. practice Rhinelander, 1983-90; ptnr. Mouw, Saari, Krueger, Paulson & Smith, Rhinelander, 1990—2002; atty. pvt. practice, 2002—. Bd. dirs. Northwoods United Way, 1980-88, pres., 1983-84. With U.S. Army, 1958-61, ETO. Mem. ABA, Ill. Bar Assn., Wis. Bar Assn., Oneida-Vilas-Forest Bar Assn. (pres. 1996-97), Lions (pres. Sugarcamp 1983-84). Avocations: hunting, fishing, baseball, reading, golf. General civil litigation, Insurance, Personal injury (including property damage). Home and Office: 6998 Wildwood Ln Rhinelander WI 54501

SABADIE, FRANCISCA ALEJANDRA, lawyer, interpreter, translator; b. New Orleans, July 7, 1947; d. Alfonso and Margaret Gibbons (Burke) S.; m. Robert Thomas Dwyer, Jan. 6, 1973. BA, Newton Coll., 1968; JD, Loyola U., 1975. Bar: N.Y. 1976, U.S. Dist. Ct. (so. and ea. dists.) N.Y. 1976, U.S. Ct. Appeals (2nd cir.) 1977. Clk. Sessions, Fishman, Rosenson, Snelling, Boisfontaine, New Orleans, 1973-75; assoc. Shearman-Sterling, N.Y.C. and Paris, 1975-84; real estate developer London, 1985-87; pvt. practice Scarsdale, N.Y., 1987—. Mem. pub. affairs com. Jr. League Ctrl. Westchester (N.Y.); freedom writer Amnesty Internat.; bd. trustees Nativity Mission Ctr. Mem. Assn. Bar City of N.Y. (mem. entertainment com. 1998—). Roman Catholic. Avocations: music, cycling, cooking, reading, theatre, travel. General civil litigation, Commercial, consumer (including collections, credit), Property, real (including real estate development, water). Office: One Walworth Ave Scarsdale NY 10583-1417 Fax: 914-723-6679.

SABATINI, FRANK CARMINE, lawyer, bank executive; b. Chgo., May 24, 1932; s. Carmine and Lisetta (Arguilla) S.; m. Alice C. Chandler, Dec. 28, 1955; m. Judith Sabatini, Oct. 23, 1998 (dec.); children: Marcus, Matthew, Michael, Daniel; m. Judith Lennox, 1998. BS, Kan. U., 1954, LLB, 1957. Bar: Wis. 1958, Kans. 1957. Atty. Allis Chalmers Mfg. Co., Milw., 1958-59; mem. Lillard, Eideson, Lewis & Porter, Topeka, 1959-61; partner firm Colmerry, Davis, Bennett & McCure, 1968-69, Sabatini, Waggener, Vincent, Afterborn, & Hannah, 1969-94, Sabatini & Assocs., 1984—. Mem. Kans. Ho. of Reps., 1969; chmn. bd. Capital City State Bank, 1979—; Workmen's compensation examiner, 1967; chmn. Legal Aid Soc., 1966-68; instr. Kans. Bankers Assn., 1959-61; dir. sec. Benefit Assn., 1990-2002; fin. council Kans. Archdiocese, 1995-2000; hon. chair, Meals on Wheels, 2002-03. Chmn. Topeka chpt. March of Dimes, 1961; pres. Hayden Father and Friends, 1974; mem. sch. bd. St. Matthews Grade Sch., Topeka; bd. dirs. St. Francis Hosp.; mem. exec. bd. Boy Scouts Am. 1st lt. U.S. Army, 1957-58. Named Boss Yr., Legal Sec. Assn. Kans., 1972; recipient Silver Beaver award, Boy Scouts Am., 1990, Man Yr., 1997, St. Lawrence Student Ctr. award, 1990, Exec. Yr., 1999, Martin Luther King award, 2003. Mem. Topeka Bar Assn. (exec. com., chmn. ethics com.), Kans. Bd. Regents (chair 1996), Phi Kappa Theta. Office: Sabatini & Assoc 1205 W 6th St Topeka KS 66609-1230

SABEL, BRADLEY KENT, lawyer; b. Charleston, Ill., Oct. 6, 1948; s. Walter Bernard and Charlotte (Ahlstrom) S.; m. Nancy Jean Parker, Apr. 4, 1984 BA, Vanderbilt U., 1970; JD, Cornell U., 1975; MS in Bus. Policy, Columbia U., 1983. Bar: N.Y. 1976. Atty. Fed. Reserve Bank of N.Y., N.Y.C., 1975-80, asst. counsel, 1980, sec., asst. counsel, 1981-85, assoc. counsel, 1985-87, counsel, 1988-93, counsel, v.p., 1993-94; counsel Shearman & Sterling, N.Y.C., 1994-97, ptnr., 1997—. Contbr. numerous articles to profl. jours. Bd. dirs., treas. N.Y. Chamber Orch., N.Y.C., 1985-87; Served with U.S. Army, 1970-72 Home: 2 Midland Gdns Apt 4E Bronxville NY 10708-4727 Office: 599 Lexington Ave Fl C2 New York NY 10022-6030 E-mail: bsabel@shearman.com.

SABERS, RICHARD WAYNE, state supreme court justice; b. Salem, S.D., Feb. 12, 1938; s. Emil William and Elrena Veronica (Godfrey) S.; m. Colleen D. Kelley, Aug. 28, 1965 (dec. Feb., 1998); children: Steven Richard, Susan Michelle, Michael Kelley; m. Ellie Schmitz, June 9, 2000. BA in English, St. John's U., Collegeville, Minn., 1960; JD, U. S.D., 1966. Bar: S.D. 1966, U.S. Dist. Ct. S.D. 1966, U.S. Ct. Appeals (8th cir.) 1983. From assoc. to ptnr. Moore, Rasmussen, Sabers & Kading, Sioux Falls, S.D., 1966-86; justice Supreme Ct. S.D., Pierre and Sioux Falls, 1986—. Mem. editorial bd. U. S.D. Law Rev., 1965-66. State rep. March of Dimes, Bismarck, N.D., 1963; bd. dirs. St. Joseph Cathedral, Sioux Falls, 1971-86; trustee, bd. dirs. O'Gorman Found., Sioux Falls, 1978-86; active sch. bd. O'Gorman High Sch., Sioux Falls, 1985-86. Lt. U.S. Army, 1960-63. Named Outstanding Young Religious Leader, Jaycees, Sioux Falls, 1971. Mem. ABA, S.D. Bar Assn., Inst. Jud. Adminstrn., St. John's Alumni Assn. (pres. Sioux Falls chpt. 1975-91). Republican. Roman Catholic. Avocations: tennis, skiing, sailing, sports, wood carving. Office: SD Supreme Ct 500 E Capitol Ave Pierre SD 57501-5070 Home: 5218 S Sweetbriar Ct Sioux Falls SD 57108-2855

SABINO, WILLIAM, lawyer, consultant; b. N.Y.C., Apr. 22, 1955; s. Albert Joseph and Mildred (Smoll) S. BA, CCNY, 1976; JD, U. N.C., 1979; LLM, Washington U., St. Louis, 1984. Bar: Ill. 1980, U.S. Tax Ct. 1984. Capt. U.S. Army, 1980-85. Mem. Phi Beta Kappa, Phi Alpha Theta. Avocations: sports, exercise, travel, reading, museums. Taxation, general.

SACASAS, RENE, lawyer; b. N.Y.C., July 10, 1947; s. Anselmo and Orlanda (Soto) S.; m. Cathy Lee Van Natta, Jan. 24, 1970. BA, Am. U., 1969; JD, Emory U., 1975. Bar: Fla. 1976, U.S. Dist. Ct. (so. dist.) Fla. 1976, U.S. Ct. Appeals (5th cir.) 1976, U.S. Supreme Ct. 1980, U.S. Ct. Appeals (11th cir.) 1983. Law clk. McLarty and Aiken, Atlanta, 1974-76; assoc. Welbaum, Zook, Jones, Williams, Miami, Fla., 1976-79; ptnr. Darrach, Merkin and Sacasas, Miami, 1979-83, Merkin & Sacasas, Miami, 1984-86; of counsel Welbaum, Zook & Jones, Miami, 1986-95; Welbaum, Guernsey, Hingston, Greenleaf & Gregory, Miami, 1996—; asst. prof. bus. law U. Miami, 1985-91, assoc. prof., 1991-2002, prof., 2002—, chmn. bus. law dept., 1992—; head master Hecht Residential Coll., 1995-97. Mem. ABA, Fla. Bar Assn. (vice chmn. grievance com. 1981-84), Dade County Bar Assn., Latin Am. C. of C., U.S. Jaycees, Cuban Am. Bar Assn., Iron Arrow, Leadership Fla., Phi Sigma Kappa (ET chpt. pres. 1968), Omicron Delta Kappa, Phi Kappa Phi. Contbr. articles profl. jours. Banking, Private international, Property, real (including real estate development, water). Home: 3790 Kent Ct Miami FL 33133-6137 Office: Welbaum Zook & Jones 901 Ponce De Leon Blvd Coral Gables FL 33134-3073

SACHER, BARTON STUART, lawyer; b. Birmingham, Ala., Apr. 9, 1948; s. Martin R. and Inez (Zuckerman) S.; 1 child, Joseph Alan; m. Susan Angela Anton, Sept. 30, 1976. BS, U. Ala., 1970, JD, 1973. Law clk. to judge S. Pointer U.S. Dist. Ct., Birmingham, 1973-74; assoc. Berkowitz, Lefkowitz & Patrick, Birmingham, 1974-77; atty. investigations, trial counsel SEC, Washington, 1977-79, chief of investigations and enforcement Atlanta Region, 1979-85; ptnr. Tew, Jorden, Schulte & Beasley, Miami, 1986-90; pres., dir., ptnr. Sacher, Zelman, Van Sant, Paul, Beiley, Hartman, Terzo & Waldman PA, Miami, 1990—. V.p., trustee Temple Israel of Greater Miami, Inc.; v.p., dir. Alex Muss H.S., Israel; regional dir. ADL, Nat. Fin. Com., Dem. Party, Dem. Leadership Coun.; mem. S.E. regional coun. Union Am. Hebrew Congregations. Mem. ABA, Fed. Bar Assn., Fla. Bar Assn., D.C. Bar Assn., Ala. State Bar Assn., Greater Miami C. of C. (trustee), Grove Isle Club. Jewish. Administrative and regulatory, Federal civil litigation, Securities. Office: Sacher Zelman Van Sant Paul Beiley Hartman Terzo & Waldman P 1401 Brickell Ave 7th Fl Miami FL 33131-3506

SACHER, STEVEN JAY, lawyer; b. Cleve., Jan. 28, 1942; s. Albert N. and Cecil P. (Chessin) S.; m. Colleen Marie Gibbons, Nov. 28, 1970; children— Alexander Jerome, Barry Elizabeth, William Paul. BS, U. Wis., 1964; JD, U. Chgo., 1967. Bar: D.C. 1968. Assoc. solicitor Employee Retirement Income Security Act U.S. Dept. Labor, Washington, 1974-77; spl. counsel com. on labor and human resources U.S. Senate, Washington, 1977-79, gen. counsel, 1980-81; ptnr. Pepper, Hamilton & Scheetz, Washington, 1982-88; shareholder Johnson & Gibbs, Washington, 1988-94; ptnr. Kilpatrick Stockton LLP, Washington, 1994—. Adj. prof. law Georgetown U. Law Ctr., 1977; co-chair sr. editors Employee Benefits Law and Annual Supplements, Bur. Nat. Affairs, Washington, 1991-2000. Mem. adv. bd. BNA Pension and Benefits Reporter; mem. editorial bd. Benefits Law Jour., Jour. Pension Planning and Compliance. Founding mem. ERISA Roundtable, Washington. Fellow Coll. Labor and Employment Lawyers, Am. Coll. Employee Benefits Counsel (charter); mem. ABA (mgmt. co-chmn. com. on employee benefits, sect. on labor and employment law 1988-91, chmn. prohibited trans. subcom., com. on employee benefits, sect. on taxation 1986-91), D.C. Bar Assn. Labor (including EEOC, Fair Labor Standards Act, labor-management relations, NLRB, OSHA), Legislative, Pension, profit-sharing, and employee benefits. Office: Kilpatrick Stockton LLP 607 14th St NW Ste 900 Washington DC 20005 E-mail: ssacher@kilpatrickstockton.com.

SACHS, DAVID, lawyer; b. N.Y.C., Aug. 4, 1933; s. Morris and Fannie R. Sachs; m. Frumet P. Lome, July 7, 1957; children: Diane R., Daniel L., Francine E. BS, U. Pa., 1954; JD, Harvard U., 1957. Bar: N.Y. 1958, U.S. Tax Ct. 1959, U.S. Ct. Fed. Claims 1960, U.S. Ct. Appeals (2d cir.) 1960, U.S. Supreme Ct. 1967. Assoc. White & Case, N.Y.C., 1957-68, ptnr., 1968-88, ret. ptnr., 1988—. Fellow Am Coll. Tax Counsel, N.Y. Bar Found.; mem. N.Y. Bar Assn. (chmn. tax sect. 1980, ho. dels. 1981-82, tax sect. exec. com. 1977-), N.Y.C. Bar Assn. (chmn. com. on taxation 1986-89, mem. coun. on taxation 1990-96). Corporate taxation, Taxation, general, State and local taxation. Office: White & Case 1155 Avenue of the Americas New York NY 10036-2787

SACHS, HOWARD F(REDERIC), federal judge; b. Kansas City, Mo., Sept. 13, 1925; s. Alex F. and Rose (Lyon) S.; m. Susanne Wilson, 1960; children: Alex Wilson, Adam Phinney. BA summa cum laude, Williams Coll., 1947; JD, Harvard U., 1950. Bar: Mo. 1950. Law clk. U.S. Dist. Ct., Kansas City, Mo., 1950-51; pvt. practice law Phineas Rosenberg, Kansas City, 1951-56; with Spencer, Fane, Britt & Browne, 1956-79; U.S. dist. judge Western Dist. Mo., Kansas City, 1979—, chief dist. judge, 1990-92, now sr. judge. Contbr. articles to various publs.; contbr. chpt. to Mid-America's Promise, 1982. Mem. Kansas City Commn. Human Rels., 1967-73; chmn. Jewish Community Rels. Bur., 1968-71, Kansas City chpt. Am. Jewish Com., 1963-65; mem. exec. com. Nat. Jewish Community Rels. Adv. Coun., 1968-71; pres. Urban League Kansas City, 1957-58, Kansas City chpt. Am. Jewish Congress, 1974-77; co-chmn. Kansas City chpt. NCCJ, 1958-60; mem. Kansas City Sch. Dist. Desegregation Task Force, 1976-77; pres. Jackson County Young Democrats, 1959-60; treas. Kennedy-Johnson Club, Jackson County, 1960. Served with USNR, 1944-46. Mem. ABA, Mo. Bar, Kansas City Bar Assn., Am. Judicature Soc., Lawyers Assn. Kansas City, Dist. Judges Assn. (8th cir., pres. 1992-94), Phi Beta Kappa. Office: US Dist Ct US Courthouse 400 E 9th St Kansas City MO 64106-2607

SACK, ROBERT DAVID, judge, educator; b. Phila., Oct. 4, 1939; s. Eugene J. and Sylvia I. (Rivlin) Sack; children: Deborah Gail, Suzanne Michelle, David Rivlin. BA, U. Rochester, 1960; LLB, Columbia U., 1963. Bar: N.Y. 1963. Law clk. to judge Fed. Dist. Ct. of N.J., 1963—64; assoc. Patterson, Belknap & Webb, N.Y.C., 1964—70; ptnr. Patterson, Belknap, Webb & Tyler, N.Y.C., 1970—86, Gibson, Dunn & Crutcher, N.Y.C., 1986-98; sr. assoc. spl. counsel U.S. Ho. of Reps. Impeachment Inquiry, 1974; judge U.S. Ct. Appeals (2d cir.), 1998—. Lectr. Practising Law Inst., 1973—97, Columbia U. Law Sch., 2001—02, bd. vis.; adv. bd. Media Law Reporter. Author: Libel, Slander, and Related Problems, 1980, 2d edit., 1994, CD-ROM edit., 1995, Sack on Defamation-Libel, Slander, and Related Problems, 3d edit., 1999; co-author: Advertising and Commercial Speech, a First Amendment Guide, 1999; contbr. articles to profl. jours. Chmn. bd. dirs. Nat. Council on Crime and Delinquency, 1982—83; trustee seminars on media and society Columbia U. Sch. Journalism, 1985—92, N.Y.C. Commn. on Pub. Info. and Comm., 1995—98; v.p., bd. dirs. William F. Kerby and Robert S. Potter Fund. Fellow: Am. Bar Found.; mem.: ABA (bd. govs. forum com. on comm. law 1980—88), Assn. Bar City N.Y. (chmn. comm. law com. 1986—89). Office: US Circuit Ct for 2d Circuit 40 Foley Sq New York NY 10007-1502

SACK, SYLVAN HANAN, lawyer; b. Phila., Dec. 26, 1932; s. Isidore F. and Mollye (Bellmore) S.; m. Ellen L. Foreman, Aug. 13, 1972; children: Reuben H., Sara I. MS in Bus. Adminstrn, Pa. State U., 1956; JD, U. Balt., 1964. Bar: Md. 1964, U.S. Tax Ct. 1967, U.S. Supreme Ct. 1970; C.P.A., Md. Pvt. practice, Balt., 1967—; assoc. counsel Safety First Club of Md., 1975-78, spl. counsel, 1979—. Gov. Md. chpt. Retinitis Pigmentosa Found., 1974-75 Contbr. articles to profl. jours. Chmn. Indsl. Toxicology NIOSH Function, 1977, Occupational Disease Forum, 1979, OSHA and Diseases in Workplace Seminar, 1981. Mem. Fed. Bar Assn. (gov. chpt. 1968— , chmn. bd. govs. 1969-70, chmn. environ. law program 1984), ABA (chmn. subcom. sect. taxation 1972-75), Md. Bar Assn., Assn. Trial Lawyers Am.; mem. Md. Trial Lawyers Assn. (lectr. toxic torts 1983 conv.) Environmental, Personal injury (including property damage), Toxic tort. Home: 27 Brightside Ave Baltimore MD 21208-4802

SADER, NEIL STEVEN, lawyer; b. Torrington, Conn., Oct. 10, 1958; s. Harold M. and Carol Hope (Shimkin) S.; m. Elizabeth Napshin, Jan. 3, 1988; children: Samantha Isabel, Daniel Scott, Lani Eden. AB, Columbia U., 1980; JD, U. Kans., 1984. Bar: Mo. 1984, U.S. Ct. Appeals (10th cir.) 1988, U.S. Supreme Ct. 1993, Kans. 1994, U.S. Dist. Ct. (ea. dist.) Mich. 1995; bd. cert. consumer bankruptcy law Am. Bd. Certification, 2000. Asst. White House Domestic Policy Staff, Washington, 1980-81; assoc. Wasserstrom & Wasserstrom, 1984-86, Brown, Nachman & Sader, P.C., Kansas City, Mo., 1986-90, shareholder, 1990-97; mng. mem. Sader & Garvin LLC, Kansas City, Mo., 1997—. Planning commr. Johnson County, Kans., 1983—85; mem. Overland Pk. City Coun., 1990—, pres., 2000—01; del. Dem. Nat. Conv., 1996; precinct committeeman Johnson County Dem. Party, 1983—, mem. exec. com., 1984—90, vice chmn., 1988—90; mem. Kans. State Dem. Party Com., 2003—05; bd. dirs. Mid-Am. Regional Coun., 1993—, Jewish Family and Children's Svcs., Kans. City, 1986—90, Overland Pk. Conv. and Visitors Bur., 1995—98. Mem. Am. Bankruptcy Inst., Mo. Bar Assn., Columbia U. Club Kansas City (bd. dirs.), Kansas City Met. Bar Assn. Jewish. Avocations: travel, sports, coaching youth baseball. Administrative and regulatory, Constitutional, Criminal. Home: 11736 W 102nd St Overland Park KS 66214-2686 Office: Sader & Garvin LLC Ste 300 4739 Belleview Avenue Kansas City MO 64112-1364 E-mail: nsader@sadergarvin.com., nbsader@aol.com.

SADLER, RICHARD LAWRENCE, food company executive, lawyer; b. St. Louis, Nov. 1, 1944; s. Lawrence Fredrick and Mary Jane Sadler; m. Lynne Wangsgard, June 20, 1971; children: Jane W., Benjamin. BA in History, Carleton Coll., 1967; JD, Harvard U., 1974. Bar: Oreg. 1974, U.S. Dist. Ct. Oreg., U.S. Ct. Appeals, U.S. Supreme Ct. Ptnr. Copeland, Landye, Bennett & Wolf, Portland, Oreg., 1974—2000; now owner, pres. Dundee (Oreg.) Fruit Co. Mem. Metro-TPHC Com., Portland, 1997-98; mem. Mid Valley Initiatives, Salem, Oreg., 1998; chmn. Yamhill County Planning, McMinnville, Oreg., 1979-85. Avocations: farming, skiing, antique sports cars, jewelry making. E-mail: sadler@dundeefruit, com. Home and Office: 20189 NE Trunk Rd Dundee OR 97115-9032 Fax: 503-538=8559.

SAEGAERT, ELLEN C. lawyer; b. Iowa City, Feb. 2, 1946; d. Hugh and Ellen M. (McColl) Clark. BA, U. N.H., 1968; JD, Thomas M. Cooley Law Sch., 1981. Flight attendant Trans World Airlines, N.Y.C., 1968-72; pvt. practice Lansing, Mich., 1982-94, West Hartford, Conn., 1994—. Mem. Leadership Greater Hartford, 1996. Mem. Conn. Bar Assn., Mich. State Bar Found., Mich. Bar Assn., Hartford County Bar Assn. Juvenile, General practice, Probate (including wills, trusts). Office: 65 Lasalle Rd Ste 301 West Hartford CT 06107-2374

SAEKS, ALLEN IRVING, lawyer; b. Bemidji, Minn., July 14, 1932; m. Linda J. Levin; 1 child, Adam Charles. BS in Law, U. Minn., 1954, JD, 1956. Bar: Minn. 1956, U.S. Dist. Ct. Minn. 1956, U.S. Ct. Appeals (8th cir.) 1957, U.S. Ct. Appeals (fed. cir.) 1959, U.S. Supreme Ct. 1959, U.S. Ct. Appeals (11th cir.) 1997; cert. civil trial specialist. Asst. U.S. atty. Dept. Justice, St. Paul, 1956-57; assoc. Leonard Street and Deinard, Mpls., 1960-63, ptnr., 1964—. Adj. prof. law U. Minn. Law Sch., 1960-65; chmn. Lawyer Trust Account Bd., Interest on Lawyers Trust Accounts, 1984-87; nat. bd. dir. Equal Justice Works. Chmn. Property Tax Com., 1986—87; bd. dirs. Citizens League, Mpls., 1984—87; pres. Jewish Cmty. Rels. Coun of Minn. and the Dakotas, 1994—96. 1st lt. JAGC U.S. Army, 1957—60. Recipient City of Mpls. award, 1996, Lifetime Commitment award Cardozo Soc., 2001. Fellow Am. Bar Found. (life); mem. ABA (commn. on interest on lawyers trust accts. 1990-93), Minn. State Bar Assn., Fund for the Legal Aid Soc. (chmn. 1997-98, Law Day Testimonial award 1996), Hennepin County Bar Assn. (pres. 1983-84), Order of Coif, Phi Delta Phi. Federal civil litigation, Probate (including wills, trusts), Professional liability. Office: Leonard Street and Deinard 150 S 5th St Ste 2300 Minneapolis MN 55402-4238

SAFLEY, JAMES ROBERT, lawyer; b. Cedar Rapids, Iowa, Sept. 19, 1943; s. Robert Starr and Jean (Engelman) S.; m. Dianne Lee McInnis; children: Anne Michele, Jamie Leigh. BA, U. Iowa, 1965; JD, Duke U., 1968. Bar: Minn. 1968, U.S. Ct. Appeals (4th, 5th, 6th, 8th, 9th and 11th cirs.), U.S. Supreme Ct. Law clk. U.S. Dist. Ct. Minn., Mpls., 1968-69; assoc. Robins, Kaplan, Miller & Ciresi, Mpls., 1969-74, ptnr., 1974—. Mem. adv. coun. Women's Intercollegiate Athletics, U. Minn., 1988-94; mem. Minn. Fed. Bar Assn. Commn. on ADR, 1995—. Mem. ABA, Minn. State Bar Assn. (antitrust sect. chmn. 1985-87), Hennepin County Bar

Assn., Duke Law Alumni Assn. (bd. dirs. 2001--), Phi Beta Kappa. Antitrust, Federal civil litigation, State civil litigation. Office: Robins Kaplan Miller & Ciresi 2800 LaSalle Pla 800 Lasalle Ave Ste 2800 Minneapolis MN 55402-2015

SAFT, STUART MARK, lawyer; b. NYC, Feb. 17, 1947; s. Stanley and Dorothy (Ligerman) S.; m. Stephanie C. Optekman, June 6, 1970; children: Bradley S., Gordon D. BA, Hofstra U., 1968; JD, Columbia U., 1971. Bar: N.Y. 1972, Fla. 1975, U.S. Dist. Ct. (so. dist.) N.Y. 1975, U.S. Supreme Ct. 1990. Ptnr. Wolf Haldenstern Adler Freeman & Herz, N.Y.C., 1988—. Chmn., bd. dirs. Coun. of N.Y. Coops., N.Y.C., 1981—; vice-chmn. bd. dirs. Nat. Coop. Bank; chmn. N.Y.C. Workforce Investment Bd.; chmn. bd. dirs., CEO Pvt. Industry Coun. N.Y.C., 1994-2000; bd. dirs. Am. Women's Econ. Devel. Corp., Nat. Assn. Housing Coops., S.L.E. Lupus Found.; adj. asst. prof. NYU, Real Estate Inst. Author: Commercial Real Estate Forms, 3 vols., 1987, Commercial Real Estate Transactions, 1989, Commercial Real Estate Workouts, 1991, Real Estate Development: Strategies for a Changing Market, 1990, Commercial Real Estate Leasing, 1992, Real Estate Investor's Survival Guide, 1992, Commercial Real Estate Financing, 1993, Commercial Real Estate Forms, 3d edit., 8 vols., 2001, Commercial Real Estate Transactions, 2d edit., 1995, Commercial Real Estate Workouts, 2d edit., 1996; contbg. editor: The Real Estate Finance Jour., 1989—; contbr. articles to profl. jours. Capt USAR, 1968—76. Mem. ABA, Am. Coll. Real Estate Lawyers, N.Y. Bar Assn., Fla. Bar Assn. Property, real (including real estate development, water). Office: Wolf Haldenstein Adler Freeman & Herz 270 Madison Ave New York NY 10016-0601

SAGALKIN, SANFORD, lawyer; b. NYC, June 24, 1942; s. Nathan and Blanche (Hoffner) Sagalkin; m. Monda E. Fifield, Aug. 25, 1969; children: Nicholas, Amy. BA, Queens Coll., 1964; LLB, Columbia U., 1967. Bar: DC 1980, Md. 1986. Staff atty. NY Mental Health Info. Svc., NYC, 1967-69; mem. firm Faulkner, Banfield, Doogan, Gross and Holmes, Juneau, Alaska, 1969-74; firm Ely, Guess & Rudd, Juneau, 1974-75, mem. firm Washington, 1980-82; asst. atty. gen. Atty. Gen.'s Office, State of Alaska, 1975-77; dep. asst. atty. gen. Dept. Justice, Washington, 1977-80; pvt. practice Sharpsburg, Md., 1982-86; assoc. gen. counsel CIA, Washington, 1986—. Mem. Juneau Pks. and Recreation Com., 1972—74; bd. dirs. Tifereth Israel Congregation, 2000—01, Defenders of Wildlife, 1986—90. Mem.: Md. Bar Assn. Democrat. Jewish. Office: CIA Washington DC 20505-0001

SAGARIN, J. DANIEL, lawyer; b. Bridgeport, Conn., Feb. 15, 1941; s. Philip H. Sagarin; m. Mary Demotses; children: Joshua, Mark, Raphael. BA magna cum laude, Lehigh U., 1962; JD, Yale U., 1965. Bar: Conn. 1965, U.S. Dist. Ct. Conn. 1965, Mass. 1966, U.S. Dist. Ct. Mass. 1966, U.S. Ctp Appeals (2d cir.) 1967, U.S. Supreme Ct. 1972, U.S. Claims Ct. Law clk. to Hon. Robert C. Zampano, U.S. Dist. Ct. for Conn., Hartford, 1965-66, asst. U.S. atty., 1967-70, spl. master spl. masters program, 1988—; ptnr. Hurwitz & Sagarin, LLC, Milford, Conn., 1970—. Tutor Yale Law Sch., New Haven, 1965-66, lectr. trial practice, 1976-84. Fellow Am. Coll. Trial Lawyers (state chair 2001--), Conn. Bar Found.; mem. ABA, ATLA, Conn. Bar Assn. (exec. com. criminal law sect. 1970—, mem. fed. practice com. 1985—), Conn. Trial Lawyers Assn. Federal civil litigation, State civil litigation, Securities. Home: 72 Vineyard Pl Guilford CT 06437-3237 Office: Hurwitz & Sagarin LLC 147 Broad St Milford CT 06460-4742

SAGER, MADELINE DEAN, lawyer; b. Turlock, Calif., Feb. 9, 1946; d. Paul Kenton and Jean Madeline (Ferguson) Dean; m. Gregory Warren Sager, June, 1970; children: Jeannette Carolyn, Robert Dean. BA, Sacramento State U., 1967; JD, U. Calif., Davis, 1970. Bar: Calif. 1971, U.S. Dist. Ct. (ea. dist.) Calif. 1971, U.S. Dist. Ct. (no. dist.) Calif. 1973. Atty. Blackmon, Isenberg, Moulds & Blicker, Sacramento, 1971-72, Redwood Legal Assistance, Ukiah, Calif., 1972-77, Sager & Sager, Ukiah, Willits, Calif., 1977-87, Leonard J. LaCasse, Ukiah, Calif., 1990—2002, Nelson & Riemenscheider, Ukiah, Calif., 2002—. Dir. Law Libr. Bd., Ukiah, 1985. Sec. PTA, Calpella, Calif., 1989-90; mem. sch. site coun. Redwood Valley (Calif.) Mid. Sch., 1992-93; treas., dir. Ukiah Dolphin Swim, 1994-97; meet dir. Soroptimist Swim Meet, Ukiah, 1996. Mem. Mendocino County Bar Assn. (pres. 1986), Pacific Swimming (ofcl. 1995-98), Music Boosters Ukiah H.S. Democrat. Presbyterian. Avocations: hiking, camping, music, travel. Insurance, Probate (including wills, trusts), Property, real (including real estate development, water). Home: PO Box 72 Redwood Valley CA 95470-0072 Office: Nelson and Riemenscheider 106 N School St Ukiah CA 95482

SAHID, JOSEPH ROBERT, lawyer; b. Paterson, N.J., Feb. 14, 1944; s. Joseph James and Helen (Vitale) Sahid; m. Serra Yavuz; children: Annunziata, Joseph, Olivia. BS, Rutgers U., 1965; LLB, U. Va., 1968. Bar: N.Y. 1973, U.S. Dist. Ct. N.Y., U.S. Ct. Appeals (2d and 3d cirs.), U.S. Supreme Ct. Staff mem. Nat. Commn. on Causes and Prevention of Violence, Washington, 1968-69; cons. Pres.'s Commn. on Campus Unrest, Washington, 1970; assoc. Cravath, Swaine & Moore, N.Y.C., 1972-77, ptnr., 1977-93, cons., 1994-97; ptnr. Barrack, Rodos & Bacine, N.Y.C., 1994-96; pvt. practice N.Y.C., 1996—. Mediator U.S. Dist. Ct. (so. dist.) N.Y., N.Y. Civil Ct.; arbitrator N.Y. cts. Author: (book) Rights in Concord, 1969; co-author: Law and Order Reconsidered, 1969; contbr. articles to profl. jours. Lt. USCG, 1968—72. Mem.: ABA, Assn. of the Bar of the City of N.Y. (profl. discipline com.), N.Y. State Bar Assn. (profl. discipline com.). General civil litigation. Address: 845 3rd Ave Fl 20 New York NY 10022-6601 E-mail: sahid@att.net.

SAHLSTROM, E(LMER) BERNARD, retired lawyer; b. Seattle, Feb. 25, 1918; s. August Waldimer and Alma Carolyn (Ostrom) S.; m. Phyllis May Horstman, June 18, 1946; children: Gary Bernard, Cheryl Linn Sahlstrom Monohan, Gregory Lane. BS, U. Oreg., 1945, JD, 1947. Bar: Oreg. 1947, U.S. Dist. Ct. Oreg. 1948, U.S. Dist. Ct. Hawaii, 1961, U.S. Ct. Appeals (9th cir.), 1950, U.S. Supreme Ct. 1977; CPA, Oreg. Acct. Haskins & Sells, N.Y.C., 1941-44; mem. Thompson & Sahlstrom, Eugene, Oreg., 1947-57, Sahlstrom, Lombard, Starr & Vinson, and predecessor, Eugene, 1957-76, Sahlstrom & Lombard, Eugene, 1976-78; sole practice Eugene, 1978-80; ptnr. Sahlstrom & Dugdale, Eugene, 1980—86. Bd. visitors U. Oreg. Law Sch., 1977-79, 92—. Mem. ATLA (1st v.p. western regional conf. 1954, 4th v.p. conf. 1956, dir. 1955-56, v.p. Oreg. chpt. 1970-71, pres. So. Oreg. chpt. 1972-74), ABA, Oreg. State Bar (com. taxations, unauthorized practice of law, procedure and practice, CLE, coun. on ct. procedures), Am. Judicature Soc., Assn. Attys. and CPA's, U. Oreg. Sch. Law Alumni Assn. (bd. dirs., pres.), C. of C., Country Club, Town Club (dir. 1970-71, pres. 1978) (Eugene), Multnomah Club (Portland), Elks, Sister Theodore Marie Soc., Order of the Antelope, Order of the Buggy Ride, Phi Alpha Delta, Beta Alpha Psi. State civil litigation, Family and matrimonial, Personal injury (including property damage). Home: 745 Sand Ave Eugene OR 97401-6032

SAIED, ROBERT MACK, lawyer; b. Wellington, Tex., Mar. 21, 1953; s. Mack and Mary Lamartine (McKay) S.; m. Jane Anne Begley, June 15, 1996. BA in Psychology, U. Tex., 1976; JD, Tex. Tech U., 1980. Bar: Tex. 1980, N.Mex. 2001. Pvt. practice, Lubbock, Tex., 1982—. Oil, gas, and mineral, Entertainment, Personal injury (including property damage). Office: PO Box 16819 Lubbock TX 79490-6819

ST. ANTOINE, THEODORE JOSEPH, retired law educator, arbitrator; b. St. Albans, Vt., May 29, 1929; s. Arthur Joseph and Mary Beatrice (Callery) S.; m. Elizabeth Lloyd Frier, Jan. 2, 1960; children: Arthur, Claire, Paul, Sara. AB, Fordham Coll., 1951; JD, U. Mich., 1954; postgrad., U. London, 1957-58. Bar: Mich. 1954, Ohio 1954, D.C. 1959. Assoc. Squire, Sanders & Dempsey, Cleve., 1954; assoc., ptnr. Woll, Mayer & St. Antoine, Washington, 1958-65; assoc. prof. law U. Mich. Law Sch., Ann Arbor, 1965-69, prof., 1969—, Degan prof., 1981-98, Degan prof. emeritus, 1998—, dean, 1971-78. Pres. Nat. Resource Ctr. for Consumers of Legal Svcs., 1974—78; mem. pub. rev. bd. UAW, 1973—, chmn., 2002—, UAW-GM Legal Svcs. Plan, 1983—95; spl. counselor on workers' compensation Gov. of Mich., 1983—85; reporter Uniform Law Commrs., 1987—92; mem. Mich. Atty. Discipline Bd., 1999—, vice-chmn., 2000—02, chmn., 2002—; life mem. Clare Hall, Cambridge (Eng.) U. Co-author: (with R. Smith, L. Merrifield and C. Craver) Labor Relations Law: Cases and Materials, 4th edit., 1968, 10th edit., 1999; editor: The Common Law of the Workplace: The Views of Arbitrators, 1998; contbr. articles to profl. jours. 1st lt. JAGC U.S. Army, 1955—57. Fulbright grantee, London, 1957-58. Mem. ABA (past sec. labor law sect., coun. 1984-92), Am. Bar Found., State Bar Mich. (chmn. labor rels. law sect. 1979-80), Nat. Acad. Arbitrators (bd. govs. 1985-88, v.p. 1994-96, pres. 1999-2000), Internat. Soc. Labor Law and Social Security (U.S. br. exec. bd. 1983—, vice chmn. 1989-95), Am. Arbitration Assn. (bd. dirs. 2000—), Indsl. Rels. Rsch. Assn., Coll. Labor and Employment Lawyers, Order of Coif (life). Democrat. Roman Catholic. Home: 1421 Roxbury Rd Ann Arbor MI 48104-4047 Office: U Mich Law Sch 625 S State St Ann Arbor MI 48109-1215 E-mail: tstanton@umich.edu.

ST. CLAIR, DONALD DAVID, lawyer; b. Hammond, Ind., Dec. 30, 1932; s. Victor Peter and Wanda (Rubinska) Small; m. Sergine Anne Oliver, June 6, 1970 (dec. June 1974); m. Beverly Joyce Tipton, Dec. 28, 1987. BS, Ind. U., 1955, MS, 1963, EdD, 1967; JD, U. Toledo, 1992. Bar: Ohio 1992, U.S. Dist. Ct. (no. dist.) Ohio 1993, U.S. Supreme Ct., 1996. Assoc. prof. Western Ky. U. Coll. Edn., Bowling Green, 1967-68, U. Toledo, 1968-77, prof., 1977-92; atty., ptnr. Garand, Bollinger, & St. Clair, Oregon, Ohio, 1992-97; pvt. practice Law Offices Donald D. St. Clair, Toledo, 1997—. Mem. Ohio Coun. Mental Health Ctrs., Columbus, 1978-79; dir. honors programs U. Toledo. Author: (poetry) Daymarks and Beacons, 1983, Impressions from an Afternoon in a Paris Courtroom, 1998; contbr. articles to profl. jours. Organizer Students Toledo Organized for Peace, 1970-71; mem. Lucas County Dem. Party, 1990—. With U.S. Army, 1955-57. Mem. ABA, AAU (nat. bd. dirs. 1973-74), Am. Inns of Ct., Ohio Bar Assn., Toledo Bar Assn., Ohio Acad. Trial Lawyers, Toledo Power Squadron (comdg. officer 1981), Bay View Yacht Club, Ohio Criminal Def. Lawyers Assn., Lucas County Bar Assn., Maumee Valley Criminal Def. Lawyers Assn., Ottawa County Bar Assn., Masons (32 degree), Shriners, Ancient Order Friars, Phi Alpha Delta. Criminal, General practice, Personal injury (including property damage). Home: 3836 Wheatlands Rd Sylvania OH 43560-3552 Office: PO Box 23185 Toledo OH 43623-0185 E-mail: stclairlaw@attglobal.net.

ST. JOHN, JAMES BERRY, JR., lawyer; b. Sanford, Fla., Dec. 14, 1940; s. James Berry and Marion Kistler (Appleby) St. J.; m. Mary Ann Newman, Dec. 28, 1963; children: James, Matthew. AB, U. S.C., 1962; JD, Tulane U., 1970. Bar: La. 1971, U.S. Dist. Ct. (ea. dist.) La. 1971, Fla. 1971, U.S. Dist. Ct. (ea., we., and mid. dists.) La. 1971, U.S. Ct. Appeals (5th cir.) 1971, U.S. Ct. Appeals (1st cir.) 1978, U.S. Ct. Appeals (4th cir.) 1980, U.S. Ct. Appeals (11th cir.) 1981, U.S. Ct. Appeals (9th and D.C. cirs.) 1986. Assoc. Liskow & Lewis, New Orleans, 1970-73, ptnr., 1973—. Served to lt. comdr. USN, 1962-67. Mem. ABA (chmn. natural resources law 1985—), New Orleans Bar Assn. (pres. 1999-2000). Clubs: Pickwick (New Orleans). Republican. Episcopalian. Natural resources, Environmental. Office: Liskow & Lewis One Shell Sq 50th Floor New Orleans LA 70139

ST. PAUL, ALEXANDRA DE LA VERGNE, lawyer; b. New Orleans, Apr. 12, 1955; d. Hugh De La Vergne and Laurie (Monte) St. P.; m. David K. Deitrich, Nov. 2, 1990. BS in Econs., U. Pa., 1977; JD, Loyola U., New Orleans, 1984. Bar: Fla. 1985, U.S. Dist. Ct. (ctrl. dist.) Fla. 1988, La. 1989; cert. cir. ct. mediator, Fla. Atty. Dye, Scott & Deitrich, P.A., Bradenton, Fla., 1985-89, Phelps, Dunbar, Marks, Claverie & Sims, New Orleans, 1989-90, Deitrich & St. Paul, P.A., Bradenton, 1990-98, Dye, Deitrich, Prather, Petruff & St. Paul, P.L., Bradenton, 1998—. Dir. Sarasota-Manatee (Fla.) Lawyer Referral Svc., Inc., 1991-95, v.p., 1991-93, pres., 1993-95; dir. Gulf Coast Legal Svcs., Inc., 1991-95; mem. 12th Judicial Cir. pro bono com., 1993-94. Dir. Women's Resource Ctr. Manatee, 1994-95, v.p., 1995; bd. trustees Loyola U., Law Sch. vis. com., 1993-98; dir. Manatee Players, Inc., 1986-88, v.p., 1987-88; sec. Manatee County Head Start Adv. Coun., 1993-98, chmn., 1998-99; v.p. Tidy Island Condominium Assn., Inc., 1998-01. Recipient Tobias Simon Pro Bono Svc. award, Chief Justice of Fla. Supreme Ct., 1991. Mem. Fla. Bar Assn. (mem. grievance com. 1991-94, vice chair 1992-93, chair 1994-95; mem. family law, real property, and probate sects.), Manatee County Bar Asns. (dir. 1987-89, 90-91, treas. 1988-89; mem. family law, real property, and probate sects.), Fla. Assn. Women Lawyers (dir. Manatee County chpt. 1987-88, 91-98, 1st v.p. 1995-96, pres. 1992-93, 2d v.p. 1987-88), Bar Assn. Legal Aid Soc., Inc. (dir. 1991-94, v.p. 1992-93), Jr. League Manatee County, Inc. (dir. 1991-94, League atty. 1988-90, asst. treas. 1991-92, treas. 1992-93, chair pub. affairs com. 1993-94, nom. com. 1994-95), Leadership Manatee (class of 1993-94). Republican. Estate planning, Family and matrimonial, Property, real (including real estate development, water). Office: Dye Deitrich Prather Petruff & St Paul PL 1111 3d Ave West Ste 300 Bradenton FL 34205 E-mail: astpaul@dyefirm.com.

ST. PE, PHILIPPI PIERRE, lawyer; b. New Orleans, Oct. 2, 1939; s. Oliver William and Lucie Marie (Philippi) St P.; b. Margaret Ursula Maher, Aug. 7, 1965; children— Kenneth, Simonne, Philippi. LL.B., Loyola U., New Orleans, 1963. Bar: La. 1964; cert. mediator. Assoc. Stringer, Manning, Metairie, La., 1961-68; ptnr. Stringer, Manning & St. Pé, Metairie, 1968-71, Francipane, Regan & St. Pé, Metairie, 1971— ; judge ad hoc First Parish Ct., 1973; state dist. judge pro tem 24th Jud. Dist. Ct. Jefferson Parish, 1987—. Bd. govs. Cystic Fibrosis Found., 1972; mem. Jefferson Parish Personnel Bd., 1974-82; mem. exec. com. Loyola U. Sch. Law, 1976-78. Recipient Monte Lemann award La. Civl Service League, 1981. Mem. Jefferson Parish Bar Assn. (sec. 1971, v.p. 1972, pres. 1973), La. Trial Lawyers Assn. (bd. govs. 1980-81), La. State Bar (ho. of dels. 1975— , bd. govs. 1979-80, ethics and grievance com. 1981—), Christian Bros. Found. (New Orleans). Club: St. Matthew Action (St. Matthew Ch., River Ridge, La.). Insurance, Personal injury (including property damage). Office: 3324 N Causeway Blvd Metairie LA 70002-3532 E-mail: pstpe@cox.net.

ST. PIERRE, MICHAEL A. lawyer; b. Great Falls, Mont., May 29, 1955; BA magna cum laude, Boston Coll., 1977; JD, Suffolk U., 1980. Bar: R.I. 1980, Mass. 1980, U.S. Dist. Ct. R.I. 1981, U.S. Ct. Appeals (1st cir.) 2001, U.S. Supreme Ct. 1988. Law clk. to Chief Justice, R.I. Supreme Ct., 1980—81; asst. town solicitor Town of North Kingstown, 1980—84; atty. Revens, Revens & St. Pierre, Warwick, RI. Mem. Workers Compensation Bench Bar Com., 1991—, chmn., 1994—97; mem. disciplinary bd. R.I. Supreme Ct., 1997—. Mem.: ABA, R.I. Bar Assn. (Ho. of Dels. 1993—, meetings com. 1993—, exec. com. 1997—, pres. 2002—03), R.I. Trial Lawyers Assn. (young lawyers adv./clerkship com. 1987—92), Assn. Trial Lawyers Am., Fed. Bar Assn. Workers' compensation, Personal injury (including property damage), Corporate, general. Office: Revens REvens and St Pierre 946 Centerville Rd Warwick RI 02886*

SAITO, OSAMU, law educator; b. Kobe, Hyogo-ken, Japan, Feb. 18, 1950; s. Hiromi and Yoshiko (Ishihara) S.; m. Eiko Yano, Mar. 19, 1984; children: Takashi, Makoto, Yutaka. LLB, Kansai U., Osaka, Japan, 1972; LLD, Kobe U., Japan, 1977. Full time lectr. Kobe U. Commerce, 1978-80, asst. prof. civil law, 1980-88, prof. civil law, 1988—, head dept. bus. adminstrn., 1989-91, head Grad. Sch. Bus. Adminstrn., 1989-91, chmn., pres. of faculty meeting, 1991-92. Author: Gendai Minpo Soron, 2001, 3rd edit. 1999; co-editor Theory of Modern Civil Law (2 vol.), 2001, 2002, Study on Prevention of Corruption, 1996; contbr. articles to profl. jours. Mem. Internat. Bar Assn., Japan Bar Assn., Japan Pvt. Law Soc., Japan Comparative Law Soc., Japan Assn. Traffic Law, dir. Japan Assn. Computer Law, Japan Assn. Law Fin. Buddhism. Avocations: calligraphy, pottery, horticulture. Home: 15-3 3 chome Tsukushigaoka Kita-ku Kobe 651-1212 Japan Office: Kobe U Commerce 2-1 8-chome Gakuennishimachi Nishi-ku Kobe 651-2197 Japan E-mail: dr-saito@sannet.ne.jp., saito@kobeac.ac.jp.

SAKAI, HIDEYUKI, lawyer; b. Sakai-Gun, Fukui-ken, Japan, Dec. 9, 1949; s. Hidemasa and Reiko (Shigematsu) S.; m. Mieko Okamoto, Nov. 8, 1975; children: Daisuke, Chiharu, Haruka. BL, U. Tokyo, 1974; LLM, Duke U., 1982. Ptnr. Blakemore & Mitsuki, Tokyo, 1990-94; pvt. practice Tokyo, 1995—. Contbr. articles to profl. jours. Mem. Tokyo Bar Assn. (pres. com. on bankruptcy and creditor's rights 1998), Internat. Bar Assn. (mem. com. J 1985—), Inter Pacific Bar Assn., Japan Alumni Club of Duke U. Sch. Law (pres.). Avocations: rugby, music composition, books on sociology and cultural anthropology. Office: 9th Fl Otemachi Tatemono Toranomon Bldg 6-12 Toranomon 1-Chome Minato-ku Tokyo 105-0001 Japan Fax: 81-3-3519-8322. E-mail: sakai.h@sakailaw.com.

SAKAI, PETER A. lawyer; b. McAllen, Tex., Oct. 21, 1954; s. Pete Y. and Rose Marie (Kawahata) S.; m. Raquel M. Dias, Mar. 10, 1982; children: George Y., Elizabeth K. BA, U. Tex., Austin, 1976, JD, 1979. Bar: Tex. 1979. Asst. dist. atty. County of Bexar, San Antonio, 1980-82; pvt. practice San Antonio, 1983-94; assoc. judge Bexar County Dist. Ct., San Antonio, 1994—. Hearings arbitrator City of San Antonio, 1983-93; judge Mcpl. Ct., City of Elmendorf, Tex., 1985; juvenile assoc. judge 289th Dist. Ct., San Antonio, 1989-94; city atty. City of Leon Valley, Tex., 1986-90. Contbr. to profl. publs. Bd. dirs. Bexar County Juvenile Vols. in Probation, San Antonio, 1983-93; Japan Am. Soc. San Antonio, 1987-89, Cmty. Cultural Arts Orgn., San Antonio, 1987-92, Bexar County Local Devel. Corp., San Antonio, 1989-94. Mem. ABA, State Bar Tex., San Antonio Bar Assn. Avocation: sports. Office: Bexar County Courthouse 100 Dolorosa Rm 205 San Antonio TX 78205-3038

SALACUSE, JESWALD WILLIAM, lawyer, educator; b. Niagara Falls, N.Y., Jan. 28, 1938; s. William L. and Bessie B. (Buzzelli) S.; m. Donna Booth, Oct. 1, 1966; children: William, Maria. Diploma, U. Paris, 1959; AB, Hamilton Coll., 1960; JD, Harvard U., 1963. Bar: N.Y. 1965, Tex. 1980. Lectr. law Ahmadu Bello U., Nigeria, 1963-65; assoc. Conboy, Hewitt, O'Brien & Boardman, N.Y.C., 1965-67; assoc. dir. African Law Ctr., Columbia U., N.Y.C., 1967-68; prof., dir. Rsch. Ctr., Nat. Sch. Adminstrn., Zaire, 1968-71; Mid. East regional advisor on law and devel. Ford Found., Beirut, 1971-74, rep. in Sudan, 1974-77; vis. prof. U. Khartoum, Sudan, 1974-77; vis. scholar Harvard Law Sch., 1977-78; prof. law So. Meth. U., Dallas, 1978-86, dean, 1980-86; dean, prof. internat. law Fletcher Sch. Law and Diplomacy, Tufts U., Medford, Mass., 1986-94, Henry J. Braker prof. comml. law, 1994—. Fellow Inst. Advanced Legal Studies, U. London, 1995; vis. prof. Ecole Nat. Ponts et Chaussées, Paris, 1990-95, Inst. Empressa, Madrid, 1995, U. Bristol, U. London Sch. Oriental and African Studies, 1995—; cons. Ford Found., 1978-82, 93, U.S. Dept. State, 1978-80, UN Ctr. on Transnat. Corps., 1988—, Harvard Inst. Internat. Devel., 1990—, Asia Found., 1992, Harvard Law Sch./World Bank Laos Project, 1991-93; with Sri Lanka fin. sector project ISTI/U.S. AID, 1993-94; lectr. Georgetown U. Internat. Law Inst., 1978-94, Panam. U., Mexico City, 1981; chmn. com. on Mid. Ea. law Social Sci. Rsch. Coun., 1978-84; chmn. Coun. Internat. Exch. Scholars, 1987-91; bd. dirs. Boston World Affairs Coun., 1988-95, Emerging Markets Income Funds. I & II, Inc., Global Ptnrs. Income Fund, Inc., Salomon Bros. Worldwide Income Fund, Inc., Asia Tigers Fund, Inc., India Fund, Inc., Emerging Markets Floating Rate Fund, Inc., Mcpl. Ptnrs. Funds I & II, Salomon Bros. High Income Funds I & II, Salomon Bros. 2008 Worldwide Dollar Govt. Term Trust, Mcpl. Ptnrs. Funds I & II; trustee Southwestern Legal Found., 1992—, Am. U. Paris, 1993-97; pres. Internat. Third World Legal Studies Assn., 1987-91; chmn. Inst. Transnat. Arbitration, 1991-93; pres. Assn. Profl. Schs. Internat. Affairs, 1988-89; Fulbright disting. chair in comparative law, Italy, 2000. Author: (with Kasunmu) Nigerian Family Law, 1966, An Introduction to Law in French-Speaking Africa, Vol. I, 1969, Vol. II, 1976, (with Steng) International Business Planning, 1982, Making Global Deals-Negotiating in the International Marketplace, 1991, The Art of Advice, 1994, (video course) Negotiating in Today's World, 1995, The Wise Advisor, 2000, The Global Negotiator, 2003; contbr. articles to profl. jours. Mem. ABA, Dallas Bar Found. (trustee 1983-86), Coun. on Fgn. Rels., Am. Law Inst., Am. Soc. Internat. Law, Cosmos Club (Washington). Home: 220 Stone Root Ln Concord MA 01742-4755 Office: Tufts U Fletcher Sch Law-Diplomacy Medford MA 02155 E-mail: jeswald.salacuse@tufts.edu.

SALANGO, C. BENJAMIN, lawyer; b. Cleveland, Ohio, BA, W.Va. U., 1994, JD, 1998. Bar: W.Va. 1998, U.S. Dist. Ct. (so. dist.) W.Va. 1998, U.S. Dist. Ct. (no. dist.) W.Va. 1998, U.S. Ct. of Appeals (4th cir.) 1998, U.S. Supreme Ct. 2001. Assoc. File, Payne, Scherer & File, Beckley, W.Va., 1998—99, Flaherty, Sensabaugh & Bonasso, P.L.L.C., Charleston, W.Va., 1999—. Contbr. Recipient Frasier Singleton award, W. Va. U., 1994, Nathan Burkan award, ASCAP, 1997. Mem.: W.Va. Def. Trial Counsel, Def. Rsch. Inst. Personal injury (including property damage), Insurance, Appellate. Office: Flaherty Sensabaugh & Bonasso PLLC 200 Capitol St Charleston WV 25301

SALANS, CARL FREDRIC, lawyer; b. Chicago Heights, Ill., Mar. 13, 1933; arrived in France, 1972; s. Leon and Jean (Rudnick) Salans; m. Edith Motel, Sept. 26, 1956; children: Eric Lee, Marc Robert, Christopher John. AB, Harvard U., 1954; BA, Cambridge (Eng.) U., 1956, MA, 1958, LLB, 1958; JD, U. Chgo., 1957. Bar: Ill. 1958, D.C. 1973, U.S. Supreme Ct. 1972, (admitted in France as conseil juridique) 1972, (admitted in France as avocat) 1992. With State Dept., 1959-72, dep. legal adviser, 1966-72; practice law Paris, 1972—; ret. ptnr. Salans & Assocs., Paris, 1978—. Legal adviser U.S. del. Vietnam Peace Talk, Paris, 1968—71; vice-chmn. ICC Internat. Ct. Arbitration; arbitrator internat. cases; arbitrator U.S.-Iran Claims Tribunal, The Hague; mem. editl. bd. ICC Arbitration Bulletin. Mem.: ABA (chmn. com. East-West trade and investment 1975—82), Chartered Inst. of Arbitrators (U.K), Am. Arbitration Assn. (panel arbitrators), Am. Soc. Internat. Law, Am. C. of C. in France (bd. dirs. 1977—87, chmn. laws and pub. affairs com. 1980—85). Alternative dispute resolution, Private international, Public international. Home: 18 Ave Raphael 75016 Paris France Office: Salans & Assocs 9 Rue Boissy d'Anglas 75008 Paris France E-mail: csalans@salans.com.

SALAZAR, JOHN PAUL, lawyer; b. Albuquerque, N.Mex., Feb. 6, 1943; s. Henry Houghton and Anita (Chavez) Salazar; m. Terri J. Bestgen, June 12, 1967; children: Monique Michelle, John Paul, Stephen Houghton. BA, U. N.Mex., 1965; JD, Stanford U., 1968. Bar: N.Mex. 1968, U.S. Dist. Ct. N.Mex. 1968, U.S. Ct. Appeals (10th cir.) 1968, U.S. Supreme Ct. 1979. Dir. Rodey, Dickason, Sloan, Akin & Robb, P.A., Albuquerque, 1968—, mem. exec. com., 1984—86, mng. dir., west side office, 1985—88, chmn., environ. law sect., 1989—92, mem. exec. com., 1992—93, chair, environ. and natural resources dept., 1992—95, mem. exec. com., 1999—, chair, bus. dept., 2000—. Bd. visitors Stanford U. Law Sch., Calif., 1973—76; state campaign chmn. Jeff Bingaman for Atty. Gen., 1978, Jeff Bingaman for U.S. Sen., 1982, 84, 94; mem. presdl. search com. U. N.Mex., 1989—90; mem. Albuquerque Econ. Forum, past mem. bd. dirs., past chair, gov. affairs com., past vice chair; former hon. Cmdr. Field Command Def. Nuc. Agy., Kirtland AFB. Sr. editor N.Mex. Environ. Law Handbook, 1990, 2d edit., 1991, 3d edit., 1993. Former bd. dirs. N.Mex. Symphony Orch.; mem. Easter Seal Soc.; vice chmn. City of Albuquerque Charter Revision com., 1970—71; mem. Albuquerque Unity, 1971—73; chmn. N.Mex. Disting. Pub. Svc. Awards Coun., 1986, 1987; chmn. city affairs com. Albuquerque C. of C., 1972, v.p. govtl. affairs, 1973, pres.-elect, 1974, pres., 1975, chmn. nominating com., 1977; mem. Presbyn. Hosp. Ctr. Assocs.; bd. dirs. Albuquerque Hispano C. of C., 2000—. Mem.: ABA (environ. aspects of real estate transactions com., land use regulation com., Real Property, Probate & Trust Law sect., land use com., Urban, State and Local Govt. sect.), Albuquerque Armed Forces Adv. Assn., U. N.Mex. Alumni Assn. (pres. 1983—84, exec. com. 1982—85, bd. dirs. 1979—85), N.Mex. Chpt. Nat. Assn. Indsl. and Office Parks (past mem. N.Mex. border commn., past chair com. border devel. and internat. trade, mem. exec. com., Gov.'s Bus. Adv. Coun.), N.Mex. State Bar Assn. (former mem. jud. selection com., former sec.-treas. Young Lawyers sect., mem. Real Property, Probate and Trust sect., mem. Pub. Law sect., mem. Natural Resources, Energy and Environ. Law sect.), Albuquerque Bar Assn. (former mem. jud. selection com., former dir.), Nat. Resources, Energy & Environ. Law Sect. Roman Catholic. Condemnation (eminent domain), Land use and zoning (including planning), Property, real (including real estate development, water). Office: PO Box 1888 Albuquerque NM 87103-1888

SALAZAR, KENNETH L. state attorney general; b. Mar. 2, 1955; s. Henry and Emma Salazar; m. Hope Hernandez; children: Melinda, Andrea. BA in Polit. Sci., Colo. Coll., 1977, LLD (hon.) , 1993; JD, U. Mich., 1981. Bar: Colo. 1981, U.S. Dist. Ct. Colo. 1981, U.S. Ct. Appeals (10th cir.) 1981, U.S. Supreme Ct. 1999. Farmer, rancher, Conejos County, Colo.; law clk. Colo. Atty. Gen., 1979; assoc. Sherman & Howard, Denver, 1981—86; chief legal counsel Office of Gov., Denver, 1986—90; exec. dir. Colo. Dept. Natural Resources, Denver, 1990—94; dir. Parcel, Mauro, Hultin & Spaanstra, Denver, 1994—98; atty. gen. State of Colo., 1999—. Gov.'s rep. State Bd. Equalization, Denver, 1990. Mem. Israel Friendship League, 1986—89; chair Great Outdoors Colo., Denver, 1993—94, Rio Grande Compact Commn., 1995—97, Sangre de Cristo Land Grant Commn., 1993—95; mem. Colo. Water Conservation Bd., Denver, 1990—, City and County of Denver Ethics Panel, 1993; gov.'s rep. State Bd. on Property Tax Equalization, 1987—91; del. Soviet-Am. Young Leadership Dialogue, 1984; mem. adv. com. Colo. U. Sch. Law Natural Resources Law Ctr., 1989—92; mem. Western Water Policy Rev. Adv. Commn., 1995—97; bd. dirs. Denver Cmty. Leadership Forum, 1988, Servicios de la Raza HUD 202 Project, 1985—89, chair, 1986. Scholar Juan Tienda. Mem.: ABA, Am. Judicature Soc., Hispanic Bar Assn. (ABA task force on opportunities for minorities in legal profession, bd. dirs. 1986—87), Denver Bar Assn. (2d v.p. 1989, chair policy-cmty. rels. subcoms. 1982—84), Colo. Bar Assn. (bd. govs. 1989—90, task force to assess the legal profession 1986). Democrat. Avocations: basketball, outdoor activities, politics. Office: State Colo Dept Law 1525 Sherman St 7th Floor Denver CO 80203-1700 E-mail: attorney.general@state.co.us.*

SALCH, STEVEN CHARLES, lawyer; b. Palm Beach, Fla., Oct. 25, 1943; s. Charles Henry and Helen Louise (Alverson) S.; m. Mary Ann Prim, Oct. 7, 1967; children— Susan Elizabeth, Stuart Trenton BBA, So. Meth. U., 1965, JD, 1968. Bar: Tex. 1968, U.S. Tax Ct. 1969, U.S. Dist. Ct. (so. dist.) Tex. 1969, U.S. Dist. Ct. (ea. dist.) Tex. 1972, U.S. Ct. Appeals (5th cir.) 1969, U.S. Ct. Appeals (fed. cir.) 1982, U.S. Ct. Fed. Claims, 1982. Assoc. Fulbright & Jaworski, Houston, 1968-71, participating assoc., 1971-75, ptnr., 1975—. Co-author: Tax Practice Before the IRS, 1994; contbr. articles to legal jours. Pres. Tealwood Owners Assn., 1982—83, Meml. H.S. PTA, 1985—86; hon. life mem. Tex. PTA, 1986—; mem. devel. bd. U. Tex. Med. Br., Galveston, 2002—; adv. dir. 1894 Grand Opera House Soc., 2002—. Mem.: ABA (coun. dir. 1985—88, vice chair tax sect. 1988—91, chair tax sect. 1996—97), Houston Bar Found., Am. Bar Found., Internat. Fiscal Assn., Am. Coll. Tax Counsel (regent 5th cir. 1999—), Am. Law Inst., Fed. Bar Assn., Houston Bar Assn., State Bar Tex., Theodore Tannenwald Foundation (trustee 2000—), Colonial Williamsburg Found., Menard Soc., Pelican Club Galveston, Yacht Club, Houston Ctr. Club, Galveston Country Club, Order of Coif, Phi Delta Phi, Phi Eta Sigma, Beta Alpha Psi. Presbyterian. Administrative and regulatory, Corporate taxation, Alternative dispute resolution. Office: Fulbright & Jaworski 1301 Mckinney St Fl 51 Houston TX 77010-3031 Home: 4600 Caduceus Pl Galveston TX 77551-5719 E-mail: ssalch@fulbright.com.

SALE, DAVID TODD, lawyer; b. L.I., N.Y., July 3, 1968; s. Jon A. and Beth K. Sale. B of Polit. Sci., Gettysburg Coll., 1990; JD, Nova Southeastern U., 1993. Bar: Fla. 1994, U.S. Dist. Ct. (so. dist.) Fla. 1994. Intern to spkr of house U.S. Ho. of Reps., Washington, 1988; asst. atty. gen. Fla. Atty. Gen.'s Office, Hollywood, 1994-95; asst. state atty. Broward County State Atty., Ft. Lauderdale, Fla., 1994-97; sole practitioner Ft. Lauderdale, Fla., 1997—. Mem. Com. to Re-elect Atty. Gen. Butterworth, 1992, Com. to Re-elect Judge Gary Cowart, 1997. Mem. Broward County Bar Assn., Broward Assn. Criminal Def. Lawyers (treas. 2001-02). Avocations: politics, history, basketball, golf, tennis. Criminal, Personal injury (including property damage). Office: 400 SE 9th St Fort Lauderdale FL 33316 E-mail: DefendingD@aol.com.

SALEH, DAVID JOHN, lawyer; b. Buffalo, Apr. 24, 1953; s. Donald Thomas and Joan Barbara (Labaki) S.; m. Elizabeth Catherine Abdella, July 2, 1976; children: Anthony Donald, Amy Madeline, Anne Teresa, Andrew David. BA, SUNY, Buffalo, 1975, JD, 1978. Bar: N.Y. 1979, U.S. Dist. Ct. (we. dist.) N.Y. 1980. Assoc. Jeffrey D. Oshlag, Esq., Batavia, N.Y., 1978-82; ptnr. Oshlag, Saleh & Earl, L.L.P., Batavia, 1982—; chief counsel, sec. Am. Real Time Svcs., Inc., N.Y.C., 1988-91; atty. Town of Stafford, NY, 1994—2003; town atty. Town of Darien, NY, 2000—03, Town of Batavia, NY, 2002—03; corp. counsel, v.p. bus. support ventures Inlighten, Inc., 2003—. Prosecutor Village of Corfu, NY, 1997—; legal counsel City of Batavia Housing Authority, 1982—; atty. Village of Corfu, NY, 1981-2003, Pembroke Ctrl. Sch. Dist., 1985-90; chief counsel Intelligent Quotation Sys. Inc., Norwalk, Conn., 1987-93, Network Two Comm. Group, Inc., 1997-99; prosecutor Town of Pembroke, 1988-2003; chief counsel, dir., treas. GB's Country Corners Inc., 1991-93; v.p., chief counsel Marine Ptnrs. Funding, Inc., 1994-2002; counsel Corfu Fire Dist., 1995-2003, Weston Info. Techs. Inc., others. Mem. staff Buffalo Law Rev., 1976-78. Active Pembroke Vol. Fire Dept., 1976-79, Corfu Vol. Fire Dept., 1979—; bd. dirs. Corfu Area Bus. Assn., 1986-87; del. Rep. Caucus; trustee Corfu Free Libr. Assn., 1991-2002, pres., 1993-96; bd. dirs. St. Jerome Hosp. Found., 1992-98, treas., 1994-98; treas. Genesee Mercy Healthcare Found., Inc., 1996-98; parliamentarian Genesee County Rep. Com., 2000—. Mem. ABA, ATLA, N.Y. Defenders Assn., N.Y. State Bar Assn., Genesee County Bar Assn. (treas., mem. jud. nominations com. for 8th jud. dist. N.Y., chmn. criminal def. com. 1995-2003), Erie County Bar Assn., N.Y. State Housing Renewal Ofcls., U. Buffalo Alumni Assn. (bd. dirs., v.p. fin. 1997-99, exec. v.p., pres.-elect 1999-2000, pres. 2000-02), Lions. Republican. Roman Catholic. Corporate, general. Home: 54 E Main St Corfu NY 14036-9601 Office: Oshlag Saleh & Earl LLP 432 E Main St Batavia NY 14020-2519 E-mail: dsaleh@rochester.rr.com.

SALEH, JOHN, lawyer; b. O'Donnell, Tex., June 29, 1928; s. Nahum and Arslie S. BBA, U. Tex., 1950, JD with honors, 1952; cert. U.S. Army Judge Advocate Sch., U. Va., 1953. Bar: Tex. 1952, U.S. Ct. Mil. Appeals, 1953, U.S. Tax Ct. 1954, U.S. Dist. Ct. (no. dist.) Tex. 1956, U.S. Ct. Appeals (5th cir.) 1960, U.S. Supreme Ct. 1961, D.C. 1982. Pvt. practice, Lamesa, Tex., 1954—. Tchg. instr. legal rsch. writing U. Tex. Sch. Law, 1950-52. Mem. editl. bd. Tex. Law Rev., 1951-52. Mem. ABA, ATLA, Tex. Law Rev. Assn. (life), Tex. Bar Assn. (spl. com. to study rev. code criminal procedure 1969-71), D.C. Bar Assn., Tex. Trial Lawyers Assn., Tex. Bar Found., Order of the Coif, The Million Dollar Advocates Forum, Phi Delta Phi. General civil litigation, Personal injury (including property damage), Probate (including wills, trusts). Home: 605 Doak Odonnell TX 79351 Office: 502 N 1st St Lamesa TX 79331-5406 E-mail: bigjohn@pics.net.

SALES, JAMES BOHUS, lawyer; b. Weimar, Tex., Aug. 24, 1934; s. Henry B. and Agnes Mary (Pesek) Sales; m. Beuna M. Vornsand, June 3, 1956; children: Mark Keith, Debra Lynn, Travis James. BS, U. Tex., 1956, LLB with honors, 1960. Bar: Tex. 1960. Practiced in, Houston, 1960—; sr. ptnr. Fulbright & Jaworski, 1960—2000, head litig. dept., 1979—99; ret., 2000. Author: Products Liability in Texas, 1985; co-author: Texas Torts and Remedies, 6 vols., 1986; assoc. editor: Tex. Law Rev., 1960; contbr. articles to profl. jours. Trustee South Tex. Coll. Law, 1982—88, 1990—, A.A. White Dispute Resolution Ctr., 1991—94; cir. chair for membership The Supreme Ct. Hist. Soc., 1998—2001; bd. dirs. Tex. Resource Ctr., 1990—97, Tex. Bar Hist. Found., 1990—2001. Named among Best Lawyers in Am., 1989—. Fellow: Houston Bar Found. (chmn. bd. 1982—83, sustaining life), Tex. Bar Found. (trustee 1991—95, vice-chmn. 1992—93, chmn. 1993—94, chair adv. bd. for planned giving 1994—, sustaining life mem.), Am. Bd. Trial Advocates, Am. Bar Found. (state chmn. 1993—98, sustaining life), Internat. Acad. Trial Lawyers, Am. Coll. Trial Lawyers (state chmn. 1993—96); mem.: FBA, ABA (ho. of dels. 1984—, mem. Commn. on IOLTA 1995—97), Bar Assn. 5th Fed. Cir., Gulf Coast Legal Found. (bd. dirs. 1982—85), Houston Bar Assn. (bd. dirs. 1970—79, pres.-elect 1979—80, pres. 1980—81), Tex. Law Rev. Assn. (bd. dirs. 1996—, pres. 1999—2000), Tex. Assn. Def. Counsel (v.p. 1977—79), State Bar Tex. (bd. dirs. 1983—88, chmn. bd. 1985—86, pres. 1988—89), So. Tex. Coll. Trial Advocacy (dir. 1983—87), So. Conf. Bar, Nat. Conf. Bar Pres. (coun. 1989—92), Internat. Assn. Def. Counsel, The Forum, Order of Coif, Inns of Ct. (bd. dirs. 1981—84), Westlake Club (bd. govs. 1980—85). Roman Catholic. Home: 10803 Oak Creek St Houston TX 77024-3016 Office: Fulbright & Jaworski 1301 Mckinney St Houston TX 77010-3031 E-mail: jsales@fulbright.com.

SALINGER, FRANK MAX, lawyer; b. Landau, Isar, Germany, Dec. 4, 1951; s. Karl and Ingeborg F. (Herold) S.; m. Susan Ann Wagner, May 20, 1978. Student, Columbia Union Coll., Takoma Park, Md., 1969-72; JD, U. Balt., 1975. Bar: Md. 1975, U.S. Dist. Ct. Md. 1975, U.S. Ct. Appeals (4h cir.) 1978, U.S. Tax Ct. 1978, U.S. Ct. Mil. Appeals 1978, U.S. Ct. Appeals (5th cir.) 1982, U.S. Supreme Ct. 1983, U.S. Ct. Appeals (11th cir.) 1984, U.S. Ct. Appeals (9th cir.) 1986, D.C. 1986, U.S. Ct. Appeals (3d cir.) 1989. Pvt. practice, Balt., 1975-77; counsel Md. State Senate, Annapolis, 1975-76; assoc. counsel Am. Fin. Corp., Silver Spring, Md., 1977-78; govt. rels. counsel Truck Trailer Mfrs. Assn., Washington, 1978-80; v.p., gen. counsel, dir. govt. affairs Am. Fin. Svcs. Assocs., Washington, 1980-92; v.p. govt. rels. Advanta Corp., Wilmington, Del., 1992—. Co-author: (with Alvin O. Wiese and Robert E. McKew) A Guide to the Consumer Bankruptcy Code, 1989; (with Robert W. Green) State Regulations and Statutes on Consumer Credit, 1989, Federal Consumer Credit Regulations and Statutes, 1989. City councilman, Laurel, Md., 1976-78, zoning commr., 1976-78; chmn. Md. State Young Reps., 1977-78; bd. dirs. Am. Bankruptcy Inst., Washington, 1986-88. Mem. ABA (mem. com. on consumer fin. svcs., subcoms. on interest rate regulation and state regulation), Am. League Lobbyists (chair fin. svcs. sect. 1995-97), Federalist Soc. Law and Pub. Policy, Capitol Hill Club, Ford's Theatre Soc. Republican. Lutheran. Banking, Commercial, consumer (including collections, credit), Legislative. Office: Advanta Corp One Righter Pkwy Wilmington DE 19803

SALISBURY, EUGENE W. lawyer, justice; b. Blasdell, N.Y., Mar. 20, 1933; s. W. Dean and Mary I. (Burns) S.; m. Joanne M. Salisbury, July 14, 1950; children: Mark, Ellen, Susan, David, Scott. BA in History and Govt. cum laude, U. Buffalo, 1959, JD cum laude, 1968. Bar: N.Y. 1960, D.C. 1973, U.S. Dist. Ct. (we. and no. dists.) 1961, U.S. Ct. Appeals (2d cir.) 1970, U.S. Ct. Appeals (D.C. cir.) 1973, U.S. Supreme Ct. 1973. Ptnr. Lipsitz, Green, Fahringer, Roll, Salisbury and Cambria, Buffalo, 1960—. Justice Village of Blasdell, 1961-2001; lectr. N.Y. Office Ct. Adminstrn., N.Y.C., 1961—; mem. N.Y. State Commn. on Jud. Conduct, 1989-2001, chmn., 2000-2001. Author: Manual for N.Y. Courts, 1973, Forms for N.Y. Courts, 1977. Capt. U.S. Army, 1949-54, Korea. Decorated Bronze Star, Purple Heart; recipient Citizen of Yr. award Indsl. Rels. Rsch. Assn., 2000; named Jurist of Yr., Erie County Judges and Police Conf., 2001, Magistrate of Yr., Erie County Magistrates Assn., 2001. Mem. ABA (del. spl. ct. sect. 1988-2001), D.C. Bar Assn., Erie County Bar Assn., N.Y. State Bar Assn., World Judges Assn., N.Y. State Magistrates Assn. (pres. 1973, Man of Yr. 1974), N.Y. State Jud. Conf., Upstate N.Y. Labor Adv. Coun., 1995—. Labor (including EEOC, Fair Labor Standards Act, labor-management relations, NLRB, OSHA). Office: Lipsitz Green Fahringer Roll Salisbury and Cambria 42 Delaware Ave Ste 300 Buffalo NY 14202-3857 E-mail: esalisbury@lipsitzgreen.

SALITERMAN, RICHARD ARLEN, lawyer; b. Aug. 3, 1946; s. Leonard Slitz and Dorothy (Sloan) S.; m. Laura Shrager, June 15, 1975; 1 child, Robert Warren. BA summa cum laude, U. Minn., 1968; JD, Columbia U., 1971; LLM, NYU, 1974. Bar: Minn. 1972, D.C. 1974. Legal staff subcom. on antitrust and monopoly U.S. Senate, Washington, 1971-72; acting dir., dep. dir. compliance and enforcement divsn. Fed. Energy Office, N.Y.C., 1974; mil. atty. Presdl. Clemency Bd., White House, Washington, 1975; pres. Saliterman & Siefferman, PC, Mpls., 1975—. Adj. prof. law Hamline U., 1976-81. Author: Advising Minnesota Corporations and Other Business Organizations, 4 vols., 1975; chmn. Hennepin County Bar Jour., 1985-87. Trustee, sec. Hopkins Edn. Found.; trustee W. Harry Davis Found., 1990-96; pres. Twin Cities Coun.; mem. nat. bd. dirs. Navy League U.S., Washington, 1997—, nat. judge adv., 2001-02; bd. dirs., sec. The Pavek Mus., 1992—. State civil litigation, Corporate, general, General practice.

SALMAN, BARRY, judge; b. Bronx, N.Y., May 20, 1940; BA, CUNY, 1962; JD, St. Johns U., 1965. Bar: NY 1965, Fed. Dist. Ct. (so. and ea. dists.), U.S. Supreme Ct. Pvt. practice, 1965—67; law sec. Judge Alvin F. Klein, N.Y.C. Civil Ct., 1967—70; pvt. practice, 1970—78; judge Civil Ct. N.Y.C., 1977—90; acting justice Surpeme Ct. 12th Jud. Dist., 1981—90, justice, 1990—. Instr. Inst. for Legal Asst. and Paralegal Tng., 1980—81; adj. assoc. prof. polit. sci. Lehman Coll., CUNY, 1980—, instr. paralegal program, 1985—; adj. assoc. prof. torts and criminal law Bronx C.C. CUNY, 1988—; adj. prof. polit. sci. Coll. New Rochelle. Contbr. articles to profl. jours. Bd. dirs. N.Y.C. divsn. Am. Cancer Soc., chmn. emeritus; mem. univ. coun. St. John's U.; founder, chairperson paralegal program Lehman Coll. CUNY; city councilman N.Y.C., Bronx, 1970—78. Maj. N.Y. Guard, 1962, with USAR. Named to, The Hunter Coll. Hall of Fame; recipient Lincoln Citation and award, N.Y.C. Divsn. Am. Cancer Soc. Mem.: ATLA, Jewish Lawyers Guild, Bronx County Bar Assn. (former dir.), Supreme Ct. Justices Assn. 12th Jud. Dist. (pres.), Supreme Ct. Justices Assn. City N.Y. (v.p.), N.Y. State Trial Lawyers Assn., N.Y. State Bar Assn. (ad hoc com. of the jury sys.), St. John's U. Sch. Law Alumni Assn. (bd. dirs.), Delta Theta Pi. Avocations: pets, sports. Office: Twelfth Jud Dist Supreme Ct 851 Grand Concourse Bronx NY 10451

SALO, ANN SEXTON DISTLER, lawyer; b. Indpls., Sept. 2, 1947; d. Harry W. and Ann (Malloy) Distler; m. Donald R. Salo, June 3, 1972 (div. Feb. 1983); 1 child, Eric V. Salo; m. Phillip G. Clark, May 5, 1990; children: Ann Potter Clark, Philip Gray Clark. BA, Purdue U., 1969; JD, George Washington U., 1972; LLM in Taxation, Emory U., 1976. Bar: Ga. 1973, U.S. Dist. Ct. (no. dist.) Ga. 1974. Assoc. Hansell & Post, Atlanta, 1972-78, mng. ptnr., 1978-89; ptnr. Grenwald and Salo, Atlanta, 1989-92, Long, Aldridge & Norman, Atlanta, 1992-95, Salo & Walker, Atlanta, 1995—. Adj. prof. law Emory U., 1983-86; mem. fin. planning adv. bd. Warren Gorham & Lamont, 1988-2000. Author: Estate Planning, 1988. Bd. dirs. Auditory Edn. Ctr., Atlanta, 1987-93, 98-2001; pres. Planned Parenthood of Atlanta, 1984-86; pres. Atlanta Humane Soc., 1990-93. Fellow Am. Coll. Trust and Estate Counsel (state chair 2001—); mem. Atlanta Estate Planning Coun., Atlanta Tax Forum. Estate planning, Probate (including wills, trusts). Office: Salo & Walker 2968 Lookout Pl NE Atlanta GA 30305-3272 E-mail: adsalo@bellsouth.net.

SALOMON, DARRELL JOSEPH, lawyer; b. Feb. 16, 1939; s. Joseph and Rosalie Rita (Pool) S.; m. Christine Mariscal, Apr. 25, 1992; 1 child, Camilla Lind Mariscal. Student, Georgetown U., 1957-59; BS, U. San Francisco, 1964, JD, 1966. Bar: Calif. 1970, U.S. Dist. Ct. (cen. and no. dists.) Calif. 1970, U.S. Supreme Ct. 1971. Assoc. Offices of Joseph L. Alioto, San Francisco, 1970, 72, 73; dep. city atty. City of San Francisco, 1972; pvt. prac., 1973—84; ptnr. Hill, Farrer & Burrill, L.A., 1984-87, Arter & Hadden, L.A., 1987-94; dir. of litigation Keck, Mahin & Cate, San Francisco, 1994-96; chmn. Commerce Law Group A Profl. Corp., 1996-99; chief asst. dist. atty. City of San Francisco, 2000; gen. counsel San Francisco Examiner, 2000—03; chmn. Salomon & Assoc., 2003—. Lectr. law Santa Clara U. Mem. Human Rights Commn. City and County of San Francisco, 1975; mem., past pres. Civil Svc. Commn., San Francisco, 1976-84; trustee San Francisco War Meml. and Performing Arts Ctr., 1984-88; bd. dirs. L.A. Symphony Master Chorale, 1985-87, Marin Symphony Assn., 1995-97. Recipient Disting. Svc. citation United Negro Coll. Fund, 1975; D'alton-Power scholar Georgetown U., 1957. Mem. ABA, Consumer Attys. of Calif. (bd. govs. 1977), Soc. Calif. Pioneers, Chit Chat Club, San Francisco Lawyers Club. Antitrust, Intellectual property. Office: 591 Redwood Hwy #4000 Mill Valley CA 94941 E-mail: salomon@salomonlegal.com.

SALOMON, PHILIPPE M. lawyer; b. N.Y.C., Feb. 4, 1949; BA, Wesleyan U., 1970; JD, Temple U., 1974. Bar: N.Y. 1975, U.S. Supreme Ct. 1978. Mem. Willkie Farr & Gallagher, N.Y.C. Mem. ABA, N.Y. State Bar Assn., Assn. Bar City of N.Y. Federal civil litigation, General civil litigation, State civil litigation. Office: Willkie Farr & Gallagher 787 7th Ave New York NY 10019-6018 E-mail: psalomon@willkie.com.

SALOMONE, WILLIAM GERALD, lawyer; b. Flushing, N.Y., Apr. 14, 1948; s. Harry and Mary (Tartaro) S.; m. Mary Jo Piano, July 22, 1978; children: Jennifer Ann, Julie Marie, Joseph William. BCE, Manhattan Coll., 1970; MSCE, UCLA, 1971; PhD in Civil Engring., Purdue U., 1978; JD, U. Fla., 1985. Bar: Fla., U.S. Dist. Ct. (mid. dist.) Fla.; registered profl. engr., N.Y., N.J., Ill., Fla., Md., Ga., Ala. Rsch. fellow UCLA, 1970-71; project engr. Dames & Moore, Cranford, N.J., 1971-75; rsch. asst. Purdue U., West Lafayette, Ind., 1975-78; project mgr. Woodward-Clyde Cons., Chgo., 1978-80; prin. geotech. engr. Fluor Power Svcs., Chgo., 1980-81; v.p., dir. geotech. engring. Bromwell Engring, Inc., Lakeland, Fla., 1981-82; atty. Sarsota, Fla., 1986—. Cons. William G. Salomone, Lakeland, 1982—86; pvt. practice cons., 1986; adj. prof. bus. law U. Fla., 1985—86; adj. prof. U. South Fla., 1985, 1990—97, St. Leo U., 2000—01, 2001—02; pvt. mediator, Sarasota, 1987—; mediator Fla. Cir. Ct., 1991—, U.S. Dist. Ct. (mid. dist.) Fla., 1996—; spl. master code enforcement Sarasota County, Fla., 1991—92; water and wastewater regulation, 1999; spl. master stormwater, Cape Coral, Fla., 97; hearing officer Water and Wastewater Franchise Regulation, Hillsborough County, Fla., 1999—2003; gen. counsel Code Enforcement Bd., City of Northport, 1999—2001. Author: Salomone on Mediation: A Practice and Procedure Handbook, 1992, Earth and Its People: How We Can Prosper, 1994, Madam President, 2000, The Presidential Papers, 2000. Judge Lakeland Regional H.S. Sci. Fair, 1993, NFL Sunshine Debate Tournament Nat. Forensic League, Sarasota, 1991, Incarnation Sch. Sci. Fair, 1996, 98; chmn. citizens adv. com. Sarasota-Manatee Met. Planning Orgn., 1991-92; vice chmn. citizens adv. com. Sarasota Bay Nat. Estuary Program, 1992-93. NDEA Title IV fellow UCLA, 1970-71; recipient Letters of Commendation, Mayor of Lakeland, Sheriff of Bartow, Fla., Dept. Army C.E. Mem. ASCE (Young Civil Engr. of Yr 1982, letter of commendation, bd. county commrs.), NSPE (coll. scholarship com. 1983), Am. Arbitration Assn., Inc. (panel arbitrators and mediators), Fla. Engring. Soc. (Young Engr. of Yr. 1983, Journalism award 1992), Fla. Conflict Resolution Consortium (Excellence in Conflict Resolution award 2002) Chi Epsilon, Tau Beta Pi. Alternative dispute resolution, Environmental, Land use and zoning (including planning). Office: PO Box 15 Sarasota FL 34230-0015

SALPIETRO, FRANK GUGLIOTTA, lawyer; b. Raccuia, Italy, May 3, 1962; came to U.S., 1964; s. Vincent G. and Tina A. Salpietro; m. Janice Marie Golacinski, Aug. 8, 1987; children: Vincent, Francesco, Nicholas, Isabella. BA in Polit. Sci., Emory U., 1983; JD magna cum laude, U. Pitts., 1986. Bar: Pa. 1986. Ptnr. Meyer, Unkovic & Scott LLP, Pitts., 1986—. Mem. ABA, Pa. Bar Assn., Allegheny County Bar Assn., Rivers Club (Pitts.), Italian Sons and Daus. Am., Lions, Moose, Order of Coif, Mensa, Phi Beta Kappa. Roman Catholic. General civil litigation, Computer, Insurance. Office: Meyer Unkovic & Scott LLP 1300 Oliver Bldg Pittsburgh PA 15222 E-mail: fgs@muslaw.com.

SALSBURY, MICHAEL H. lawyer; b. 1949; BA, Dartmouth Coll.; JD, U. Va. Bar: D.C. 1975. Gen. counsel MCI Comm. Corp., Washington; exec. v.p & gen. coun. MCI; ptnr. Jenner & Block Law Firm. General civil litigation, Communications, Criminal. Office: MCI Comms Corp 1801 Pennsylvania Ave NW Washington DC 20006-3606*

SALTER, LESTER HERBERT, lawyer; b. Waterbury, Conn., Apr. 26, 1918; s. Nathan M. and Eva G. (Levy) S.; m. Nina P. Scheftel, Sept. 15, 1951; 1 child, Ellen Lee. BS in Econs, U. Pa., 1940, LLB, 1948. Bar: R.I. 1948. Trial atty. Office of Chief Counsel, IRS, Newark and Boston, 1949-53; pvt. practice Providence, 1953-57; partner Salter & McGowan, Providence, 1957-70, Salter, McGowan, Arcaro & Swartz, Providence, 1970-74; pres. Salter, McGowan, Swartz & Holden, Inc., Providence, 1974-95, Salter, McGowan & Swartz, Inc., Providence, 1995-97, Salter, McGowan, Swartz & Sylvia, Inc., Providence, 1997-99, Salter, McGowan, Sylvia & Leonard, Inc., Providence, 2000—. Lectr. Northeastern U., 1955-56; chmn. U. R.I. Fed. Tax Inst., 1972-77; chmn. disciplinary bd. Supreme Ct., R.I., 1975-81; mem. R.I. Adv. Commn. Jud. Appts., 1978-82, ethics adv. panel Supreme Ct., R.I., 1987-92. Assoc. editor: R.I. Bar Jour, 1961-68. Served with F.A. AUS, 1941-46. Decorated Bronze Star. Fellow: ABA, Am. Bar Found; mem.: Am. Law Inst., Am. Judicature Soc., New Eng. Bar Assn. (pres. 1996—97), R.I. Bar Assn. (pres. 1986—87), ABA (ho. of dels. 1987—2000, bd. govs. 1999—2000). Probate (including wills, trusts), Taxation, general, State and local taxation. Home: 75 Blackstone Blvd Providence RI 02906-5413 Office: 321 S Main St Providence RI 02903-7108

SALTIEL, DAVID MICHAEL, lawyer; b. Boston; s. Abraham M. and Anna L. S.; m. Rhoda B., Sept. 3, 1961; 1 child, Marjorie Weinberger. BA, U. Mass., 1959; JD, Harvard U., 1962. Bar: Mass., U.S. Dist. Ct. Mass., U.S. Supreme Ct. Atty. Posternak, Blankstein & Lund, Boston, 1989—. Corporate, general, Landlord-tenant, Property, real (including real estate development, water). Home: 95 Cynthia Rd Newton MA 02459-2836 Office: Posternak Blankstein & Lund 100 Charles River Plz Fl 9 Boston MA 02114-2794

SALTMAN, STUART IVAN, lawyer; b. Holyoke, Mass., Mar. 16, 1940; s. Abraham and Syd Eva (Schultz) S.; m. Sandra Lee, Sept. 19, 1964; children: Jason, Michael, Laura. BS in Polit. Sci., U. Mass., 1961; JD, Case Western Res. U., 1964. Bar: Mass. 1965, Ohio 1965, Pa. 1975. Assoc. gen. counsel Internat. Chem. Workers, Akron, Ohio, 1965; assoc. Metzenbaum, Gaines, Krupansky, Finley & Stern, Cleve., 1965-67; staff U.S. Dept. Labor, Cleve., 1967-69, NLRB, Cleve., 1969-70; regional atty. EEOC, Cleve., 1970-75; chief labor counsel Westinghouse Electric Corp., Pitts., 1975-88; chmn. labor law sect. Grigsby, Gaca & Davies, Pitts., 1988-90; asst. gen. counsel Asea Brown Boveri Power T & D Inc., Coral Springs, Fla., 1990—. Recipient Excellence Hon. award in labor law Case Western Res. U., 1965. Mem. ABA, Allegheny County Bar Assn. (chmn. 1986-88), Masons. Labor (including EEOC, Fair Labor Standards Act, labor-management relations, NLRB, OSHA). Home: 9045 Lucca St Boynton Beach FL 33437 Office: 4300 Coral Ridge Dr Coral Springs FL 33065 E-mail: stuart.i.saltman@us.abb.com.

SALTMARSH, SARA ELIZABETH, lawyer; b. Jacksonville, Fla., Nov. 15, 1956; d. Ernest Olmstead and Anne (Frankenberg) S. Student, Randolph-Macon Woman's Coll., 1974-76; BA in English with honors magna cum laude, Fla. State U., 1978; postgrad., Iowa State U., 1980-81; JD, U. Tex., 1986. Bar: Tex. 1987; cert. family law. Assoc. Ausley & Slaikeu, P.C., Austin, Tex., 1987-90, Law Offices of Edwin J. Terry, Jr., Austin, 1990-92; pvt. practice law Austin, 1992—. Mem. security com. Travis County Commr.'s Ct., 1991-93; mem. Ctrl. Tex. Collaborative Law Family Practice Group, Inc., 2002-. Editor: Reference Guide to Travis County Practice, 1991, 92, 93, 95, 96, 97. Bd. dirs. Faith Home for Children with AIDS, 1997-98. Givens Disting. scholar, 1974, Lyndon Baines Johnson Meml. scholar, 1976; recipient Am. Jur. award Wills and Estates, 1986, Marital Relations and Divorce, 1986. Fellow: Austin Young Lawyers' Assn. Found., Tex. Bar Found.; mem.: Austin Young Lawyers' Assn. (co-chmn. It's the Law com. 1990—91), Tex. Ctr. Legal Ethics Professionalism, Travis County Women Lawyers' Assn., Williamson County Bar Assn., Travis County Bar Assn. (sec.-treas. family law sect. 1989—90, v.p. 1990—91, pres. 1991—92, bd. dirs. 1991—92, chair mentor program com. 1993—94, chair mentor program com. 1996—98), Tex. Exes, Tex. Acad. Family Law Specialists, Am. Inns of Ct. (barrister 1996—99), ABA, Sierra Club, Fla. State Univ. Alumni Assn. (life), Lambda Iota Tau, Phi Beta Kappa. Democrat. Avocations: irish dance, skiing, ice skating, in-line skating, windsurfing, basketry. Alternative dispute resolution, Family and matrimonial. Office: 2700 Bee Caves Rd Ste 106 Austin TX 78746

SALTZBURG, STEPHEN ALLAN, law educator, consultant; b. Phila., Sept. 10, 1945; s. Jack Leonard and Mildred (Osgood) Adelman; m. Susan Lee, March 10, 1990; children: Mark Winston, Lisa Marie, Diane Elizabeth, David Lee Mussehl. AB, Dickinson Coll., 1967; JD, U. Pa., 1970. Bar: Calif. 1971, D.C. 1972, Va. 1976. Law clk. U.S. Dist. Ct. (no. dist.) Calif., San Francisco, 1970-71, U.S. Supreme Ct., 1971-72; asst. prof. law sch. U. Va., Charlottesville, 1972-74, assoc. prof., 1974-77, prof., 1977-87, Class of 1962 prof., 1987-90; Howrey prof. trial advocacy, litigation and profl. responsibility George Washington U. Sch. Law, Washington, 1990—. Reporter Alaska Rules of Evidence, 1976-77, Alaska Civil Jury Instrns., 1979-81, Adv. Com. on Rules of Criminal Procedure, 1984-89, Va. Rules on Evidence, 1984-85, Civil Justice Act Adv. Group, U.S. Dist. Ct. D.C., 1992-93, chmn., 1994-99; dep. asst. atty. gen. criminal divsn. U.S. Dept. Justice, 1988-89; mem. adv. com. on Fed. Rules of Criminal Procedure, 1989-95, on Fed. Rules of Evidence, 1992-95; mediator dispute resolution program U.S. Ct. Appeals, 1993—. Author: Evidence in America, 1987, American Criminal Procedure, 6th edit., 2000, Criminal Law: Cases and Materials, 1994, 2d edit., 2000, Evidence: The Objection Method, 1997, 2d edit., 2000, Federal Rules of Evidence Manual, 1975, 8th edit., 2002, Federal Rules of Evidence Trial Book, 1998, A Modern Approach to Evidence, 2d edit., 1982, Military Rules of Evidence Manual, 4th edit., 1997, Basic Criminal Procedure, 1994, 3d edit., 2003, Military Evidentiary Foundations, 1994, 2d edit., 2000, Trying Cases to Win: Anatomy of a Trial, 1999, Trying Cases to Win: Evidence: Weapons for Winning, Vol. 1, 2000, Vol. 2, 2002, California Federal Evidence Trial Book, 1999, Ohio Rules of Evidence Trial Book, 1999, Washington Evidence Trial Book, 1999. Mem.: ABA (chmn. com. on trial advocacy criminal justice sect. 1992—96, co-chmn. task force on civil trial stds. litig. sect. 1996—97, task force on Ind. Counsel Act litig. sect. 1997—99, mem. criminal justice sect. coun. 2000—01, task force on terrorism and the law 2001—02, litigation sect. coun. 2001—, ho. of dels. 2001—, task force on gatekeeper regulation and the profession 2002—, task force on terrorism and the law 2002—, task force on enemy combatants 2002—), Am. Law Inst. Office: George Washington U Law Sch 2000 H St NW Washington DC 20052

SALVADORE, GUIDO RICHARD, lawyer; b. Norton, Mass., Oct. 14, 1927; s. Michele Salvadore and Maria Grazia Costantino; m. Barbara Ann Camparone, Oct. 25, 1958; children: Peter, Richard, Susan, Stephen, Marisa. AB, Brown U., 1951; LLB, Harvard U., 1954. Bar: R.I. 1954, U.S. Dist. Ct. R.I. 1955, U.S. Ct. Appeals (1st cir.) 1996. Atty. Salvadore & Salvadore, Providence, R.I.; ptnr. Higgins, Cavanagh & Cooney, 1960-90. Dir., pres. Great Am. Nursing Ctrs., Inc., Warwick, R.I., 1969-90. Dir., v.p. R.I. Grand Opera Co., Providence, 1985—. With USN, 1946-48. Mem. ABA, Am. Trial Lawyers Assn., R.I. Bar Assn., Univ. Club, Metacomet Country Club, Brown Faculty Club. Republican. Roman Catholic. Avocations: golfing, basketball, dancing, reading. Commercial, contracts (including sales of goods; commercial financing), Corporate, general, Estate planning. Home: 38 Sunset Dr East Greenwich RI 02818-1915 Office: Salvadore & Salvadore 10 Weybosset St Providence RI 02903-2393 Office Fax: 401-751-1825.

SALVAN, SHERWOOD ALLEN, lawyer; b. N.Y.C., Dec. 2, 1942; s. Harry and Marie Ann (Deramo) S. BBA, St. Francis Coll., N.Y.C.; MBA, Pace U.; JD, postgrad., NYU. Bar: N.Y. 1969, U.S. Ct. Appeals (2d dist.) 1971, U.S. Dist. Cts. (so. and ea. dist.) N.Y. 1971, U.S. Cir. Ct. (2d cir.) 1972, U.S. Supreme Ct. 1980, D.C. 1981. Tax specialist Haskins & Sells, N.Y.C., 1969-71; sole practice N.Y.C., 1972—. Mem. cen. screening com. first dept. N.Y. Appellate Div., 1977-82; spl. master N.Y. County Supreme Ct., 1977-85; arbitrator Am. Arbitration Assn., 1976-89, N.Y. County and Bronx County Civil Cts., 1976-89; adminstrv. law judge Environ. Control Bd. City of N.Y., 1975-77. Contbr. articles to profl. jours. V.p. N.Y. County Dem. Club, 1980—; jud. del. N.Y. County dems., 1983—. Mem. N.Y. County Lawyers Assn. (chairperson com. word processing 1978-86), Am. Judge Assn., NY Law Sch. Alumni Assn. (bd. dirs. 1984—). Criminal, General practice, Personal injury (including property damage). Home: 526 E 83rd St New York NY 10028-7249 E-mail: woodmanlaw@aol.com.

SALVATY, BENJAMIN BENEDICT, lawyer; b. Chgo., Dec. 22, 1940; s. Benjamin Benedict and Marion Therese (Ryan) S.; m. Patricia Louise Recor, Aug. 29, 1964; children: Paul Benedict, Kathleen Anne. BBA, U. Notre Dame, 1962; JD, U. So. Calif., 1965. Bar: Calif. 1966, U.S. Dist. Ct. (no., cen., ea. and so. dists.) Calif., U.S. Ct. Appeals (9th cir.), U.S. Tax Ct., U.S. Supreme Ct. Sr. trial atty. Calif. Dept. Transp., 1966-79; gen. atty. The Atchison, Topeka and Santa Fe Railway Co., 1980-89; sr. ptnr. Hill, Farrer & Burrill, Los Angeles, 1990—. Mem. ABA (litigation sect. urban, state and local govt. law com. on condemnation, zoning and planning com.), Am. Bd. Trial Advs., Am. Judicature Soc., Internat. Right Way Assn., Irish Am. Bar Assn. (bd. dirs. 1985—, treas. 1991, sec. 1992, v.p. 1992-93, pres. 1993-94), Italian Am. Lawyers Assn., State Trial Attys. Assn. (pres. 1975-79), Calif. State Bar (chmn. condemnation com. 1987-88, vice chmn. 1986-87), Pasadena Bar Assn., L.A. County Bar Assn. (condemnation and land valuation com.). Condemnation (eminent domain), Land use and zoning (including planning). Office: Hill Farrer & Burrill LLP One California Plz 37th Fl 300 S Grand Ave Los Angeles CA 90071-3109 Fax: 213-624-4840.

SALVO, JOSEPH ALDO, lawyer; b. N.Y.C., Feb. 20, 1933; s. Charles A. and Marietta (Mancuso) S.; m. Joan Del Vecchio, May 30, 1959; children: Joseph C., John, Joanne. BBA, St. John's U., 1960, LLB, 1962. Bar: N.Y. 1962, U.S. Dist. Ct. (ea. and so. dists.) N.Y., U.S. Supreme Ct. Spl. agt. U.S. Treasury Dept.; pvt. practice Douglaston, N.Y., 1962—; counsel Italian Charities Am., Inc., Elmhurst, N.Y., 1975—. Chmn. Columbian Lawyers Scholarship Corp. With U.S. Army, 1954-56. Mem. Queens County Bar Assn. (chmn. law office mgmt. com. 1983—), Columbian Lawyers Assn. (pres. 1978-79, historian), Nat. Italian Am. Bar Assn. Democrat. Roman Catholic. Avocations: music, sports, arts. General practice, Probate (including wills, trusts), Property, real (including real estate development, water). Home: 1333 137th St College Point NY 11356-2006 Office: 42-24 Douglaston Pky Douglaston NY 11363-1528

SALYER, JOHN CLARK, IV, lawyer; b. Washington, Apr. 30, 1969; s. Pat Wadsworth and John Clark Salyer III; m. Paige West, Feb. 14, 1999. AB in Anthropology, U. of Ga., Athens, 1993; JD, Ga. State U., Atlanta, 1997. Bar: Ga. 1997, U.S. Dist. Ct., No. Dist. Ga. 1998, U.S. Ct. of Appeals (3d cir.) 1999, NJ. 2000, U.S. Dist. Ct., NJ. 2000, U.S. Ct. of Appeals (2d cir.) 2002, N.Y. 2003. Assoc. The Law Office of Drew Findling, Atlanta, 1997—98; Brennan fellow ACLU, Nat. Legal Dept., N.Y.C., NY, 1998—99; staff atty. ACLU of NJ., Newark, 1999—. Constitutional, Civil rights, General civil litigation. Office: Am Civil Liberties Union NJ PO Box 750 Newark NJ 07101

SALZETTA, PAUL LOUIS, lawyer; b. Rochester, N.Y., July 9, 1958; s. Remo Gino and Lina Salzetta; m. Margaret Michelle Salzetta, July 4, 1992; children: Nicolas, Anthony, Marco. BS, St. John Fisher Coll., Rochester, 1980; JD, John Marshall Law Sch., 1984. Bar: Ill. 1984, N.Y. 1986, U.S. Dist. Ct. (no. dist.) Ill. 1984, U.S. Ct. Appeals (7th cir.) 1986, U.S. Dist. Ct. (ea. dist.) Wis. 1989; cert. pvt. pilot. Assoc. Clifford & Henely, Ltd., Chgo., 1984—85, John J. Henely, Ltd., Chgo., 1986—89, Power, Rogers & Smith, Chgo., 1989—2000; ptnr. Winters, Enright, Salzetta & O'Brien, Chgo., 2000—. Mem.: ATLA, Chicago Bar Assn., Lawyer Pilot Bar Assn., N.Y. Trial Lawyers Assn., Ill. Bar Assn., Ill. Trial Lawyers Assn. Avocations: skiing, windsurfing, kite boarding. Personal injury (including property damage), Aviation, Professional liability. Home: 5282 N Lawler Ave Chicago IL 60630 Office: Winters Enright Salzetta and O'Brien 111 W Washington St Ste 1200 Chicago IL 60602-3470 Office Fax: 312-236-6426. Personal E-mail: psalzetta@wesolaw.com.

SALZMAN, GARY SCOTT, lawyer; b. Portchester, N.Y., May 26, 1963; s. David Stuart and Francine (Selenow) S.; m. Suzanne Sansone, Apr. 2, 1990. BBA, U. Miami, 1985, JD, 1988. Bar: Fla. 1988, U.S. Dist. Ct. (so. dist.) 1989, Colo. 1991, U.S. Dist. Ct. (mid. dist.) Fla. 1992, U.S. Ct. Appeals (11th cir.) 1992, U.S. Supreme Ct. 1992; cert. arbitrator and mediator; cert. in bus. litigation, Fla. Assoc. Robinson & Greenberg, PA, Coral Gables, Fla., 1988-89, Buchbinder & Elegant, PA, Miami, Fla., 1989, Mishan, Sloto, Hoffman and Greenberg, PA, Miami, 1989-91, Dempsey & Assocs., Winter Park, Fla., 1991-92; pvt. practice, Orlando and Winter Park, Fla., 1992-95; ptnr. Marlowe, Appleton, Weatherford & Salzman, Winter Park, 1996-98, Brown, Salzman, Weiss & Garganese, P.A., Orlando, 1998—. Comml.,employment and fin. arbitration panelist Am. Arbitration Assn. Mem. ABA, Fla. Bar Assn. (Fla. Bar BLSE, bus. litig. cert. com. 1995—), Bus. Exec. Network, Orange County Bar Assn. Finance, Property, real (including real estate development, water). Office: 225 E Robinson St Ste 660 Orlando FL 32801 Fax: 407-425-9596. E-mail: gssalzman@orlandolaw.net.

SALZMAN, STANLEY P. lawyer; b. N.Y.C., Jan. 30, 1931; s. George D. and Fanny M. (Pugach) S.; m. Leona Schames, June 18, 1958 (dec. Nov. 1967); m. Marilyn J. Bzura, Feb. 3, 1974; children: Ira J., Mark B., Debra G., Jeffrey M. David, Steven B. David. BA, Bklyn. Coll., 1952; JD, Bklyn. Law Sch., 1955. Bar: N.Y. 1956, U.S. Dist. Ct. (so. and ea. dists.) N.Y. 1960, U.S. Supreme Ct. 1964, U.S. Ct. Appeals (2d cir.) 1966. Assoc. Otterbourg, Steindler, Houston & Rosen, N.Y.C., 1957; ptnr. Venitt, Adler & Salzman, N.Y.C., 1958-66, Friesner & Salzman, LLP, Great Neck, N.Y., 1966—. Bd. dirs. Colora Printing Inks Inc., Linden, N.J. State civil litigation, Commercial, consumer (including collections, credit). Office: PO Box 220700 11 Grace Ave Great Neck NY 11021-2417 E-mail: legalsps@aol.com.

SAM, DAVID, federal judge; b. Hobart, Ind., Aug. 12, 1933; s. Andrew and Flora (Toma) S.; m. Betty Jean Brennan, Feb. 1, 1957; children: Betty Jean, David Dwight, Daniel Scott, Tamara Lynn, Pamela Rae, Daryl Paul, Angie, Sheyla. BS, Brigham Young U., 1957; JD, Utah U., 1960. Bar: Utah 1960, U.S. Dist. Ct. Utah 1966. Sole practice and ptnr., Duchesne, Utah, 1963-76; dist. judge State of Utah, 1976-85; judge U.S. Dist. Ct. Utah, Salt Lake City, 1985-97; chief judge U.S. Dist. Ct., Salt Lake City, 1997—99, sr. judge, 1999—. Atty. City of Duchesne, 1963-72; Duchesne County atty., 1966-72; commr. Duchesne, 1972-74; adv. com. Codes of Conduct of Jud. Conf. US, 1987-91, Jud. Coun. of 10th Cir., 1991-93; mem. US Del. to Romania, Aug. 1991. Chmn. Jud. Nomination Com. for Cir. Ct. Judge, Provo, Utah, 1983; bd. dirs. Water Resources, Salt Lake City, 1973-76. Served to capt. JAGC, USAF, 1961-63. Named Judge of Yr., Utah State Bar, 1999. Mem. Utah Bar Assn., Supreme Ct. Hist. Soc., Am. Inns of Ct. VII (counselor 1986-89), A. Sherman Christensen Am. Inn of Ct. I (counselor 1989-98), Utah Jud. Conf. (chmn. 1982), Utah Dist. Judges Assn. (pres. 1982-83), Order of Coif (hon. Brigham Young U. chpt.); bd. dirs. J. Ruben Clark Law Soc. Salt Lake Chpt., 2002—. Mem. Lds Ch. Avocations: beekeeping, reading, sports. Office: US Dist Ct US Courthouse 350 S Main St Ste 441 Salt Lake City UT 84101-2180 E-mail: davidsam@utd.uscourts.gov.

SAMET, DEE-DEE, lawyer; b. Greensboro, N.C., Sept. 18, 1940; BA, U. Ariz., 1962, JD, 1963. Bar: Ariz. 1964. Ptnr. Samet & Gage, P.C., Tucson, 2001; pvt. practice Tucson, 2001—. Arbitrator U.S. Dist. Ct. Ariz., Gender Equality Task Force, 1993; judge pro tem Pima County Superior Ct., 1985—; Ninth Cir. Lawyer rep., 1990-93; mem. Jud. Performance Rev. Commn., 1996-99. Mem. State Bar Ariz. (family law sect., workers compensation sect., trial law sect., co-chair worker's compensation sect. 1988-89, gender bias task force, bd. govs. 1994-97, pres.-elect, pres. 1999-2000), Nat. Panel Arbitrators, Am. Arbitration Assn. (com. on exams., supreme ct. state Ariz. 1984-91), Pima County Bar Assn. (bd. dirs. 1994—), Nat. Assn. Coun. for Children, Ariz. Assn. Coun. for Children, So. Ariz. Fed. Bar Assn. (exec. com. 1995—), So. Ariz. Women Lawyers Assn. (bd. dirs. 1990, pres. 1994-95), Nat. Orgn. Social Security Claimants' Reps. Family and matrimonial, Personal injury (including property damage), Workers' compensation. Office: Dee-Dee Samet PC 717 N 6th Ave Tucson AZ 85705-8304

SAMET, JACK I. lawyer; b. N.Y.C., Aug. 6, 1940; s. William and Tillie (Katz) S.; m. Helen Ray, Feb. 12, 1967; 1 son, Peter Lawrence. BA, Columbia U., 1961; JD, Harvard U., 1964. Bar: N.Y. 1964, Calif. 1973. Assoc. Whitman & Ransom, N.Y.C., 1966-69, Hall, Casey, Dickler & Howley, N.Y.C., 1969-73; ptnr. Ball, Hunt, Hart, Brown & Baerwitz, L.A., 1973-81, Buchalter, Nemer, Fields & Younger, L.A., 1981-94, Baker & Hostetler, L.A., 1994—, mem. policy com., 1997-98; ptnr.-in-charge L.A., 1997-98. Arbitrator Nat. Assn. Securities Dealers, L.A., 1976—; speaker, panelist Calif. Continuing Edn. of Bar, 1988. Mem. ABA, Sports Club/L.A., Million Dollar Advocates Forum, Am. Bd. Trial Advocates. Avocations: exercise, reading. Home: 2741 Aqua Verde Cir Los Angeles CA 90077-1502 Office: 333 S Grand Ave Los Angeles CA 90071-1504 E-mail: jsamet@bakerlaw.com.

SAMFORD, THOMAS DRAKE, III, lawyer; b. Opelika, Ala., Mar. 4, 1934; s. Thomas Drake and Aileen (Maxwell) S., Jr.; m. Jacqueline Screws, June 7, 1955; children: Thomas Drake IV, Jacquelyn, Robert Maxwell, Richard Drake. AB magna cum laude, Princeton U., 1955; JD, U. Ala., 1961. Bar: Ala. 1961. Owner firm Samford & Samford, 1961-88; judge Mcpl. Ct., Opelika, 1961-88; mem. Ala. Permanent Jud. Commn., 1979-83; gen. counsel Auburn U., 1965-95, gen. counsel emeritus, 1995—. Lectr. Ala. Law Inst., 1969, Am. Judicature Soc., 1969—. Editor-in-chief: Ala. Law Rev., 1960-61. Dir., bd. trustees Opelika Comty. Chest, 1965-68, pres., 1966-67; bd. dirs. U. Ala. Law Sch. Found., Jr. Achievement Chattahoochee-Lee; elder Presbyn. ch., 1974-94, Meth. ch., 1994—. Recipient John G. Buchanan prize politics, 1955, Jaycee Disting. Svc. award, 1996; Farrah, Order Jurisprudence U. Ala., 1956; named one of four Outstanding Young Men in Ala. Jr. C. of C., 1967. Mem. ABA, Lee County Bar Assn. (pres. 1965, Wright Jurisprudential award), Ala. State Bar, U. Ala. Nat. Alumni Assn. (pres. 1966-67), Opelika C. of C. (dir. 1967, pres. 1968), Phi Beta Kappa, Alpha Tau Omega, Phi Delta Phi, Omicron Delta Kappa. Lodges: Kiwanis (bd. dirs. 1966-67, pres. 1969-70). Home: PO Box 550 Opelika AL 36803-0550 Office: Auburn U Office Gen Counsel 101 Samford Hall Auburn AL 36849-5163

SAMFORD, YETTA GLENN, JR., lawyer, director; b. Opelika, Ala., June 8, 1923; s. Yetta Glenn and Mary Elizabeth (Denson) S.; m. Mary Austill, Sept. 6, 1949; children: Mary Austill Lott, Katherine Park Alford, Yetta Glenn III (dec.). BS, Ala. Poly. Inst., 1947; LLB, U. Ala., 1949, LLD (hon.), 1995; DHL (hon.), U. Mobile, 2001. Bar: Ala. 1949, U.S. Dist. Ct. (mid. dist.) Ala. 1950, U.S. Ct. Appeals (5th cir.) 1961, U.S. Ct. Appeals (11th cir.) 1981. Since practiced in, Opelika; ptnr. Samford, Denson, Horsley, Pettey, Bridges & Hughes (& predecessors), 1949—. Mem. Ala. Senate from Lee and Russell counties, 1958-62; mem. State of Ala. Bd. of Corrections, 1969-75; mem. adv. bd. State Docks, 1987-2000. Trustee U. Mobile, 1963-92, life trustee, 1992—, trustee U. Ala., 1972-93, trustee emeritus, 1993—. Mem. Ala. Law Inst. Coun., Ala. Acad. of Honor, Masons, Phi Delta Phi, Omicron Delta Kappa, Alpha Tau Omega. Republican. Baptist. Corporate, general, General practice, Probate (including wills, trusts). Home: 615 Terracewood Dr Opelika AL 36801-3850 Office: Samford Denson Horsley Pettey Bridges & Hughes PO Box 2345 Opelika AL 36803-2345 E-mail: pettey.sdhpb@mindspring.com.

SAMOLE, MYRON MICHAEL, lawyer, management consultant; b. Nov. 29, 1943; s. Harry Lionel and Bess Miriam (Siegel) Samole; m. Sandra Rita Port, Feb. 2, 1967; children: Stacey Ann, Karen Lynn, Rena Marie, David Aaron. Student, U. Ill., 1962—65; JD, DePaul U., 1967. Bar: Ill. 1967, U.S. Dist. Ct. (no. dist.) 1968, U.S. Ct. Appeals (7th cir.) 1968, Fla. 1981, U.S. Dist. Ct. (so. dist.) 1989, U.S. Ct. Appeals (11th cir.) 2001. Sole practice, Chgo., 1967—79, Miami, 1981—. Bd. dirs. The Sports Collection, Inc., pres. Samole Enterprises, Inc. 1986-, Carcand, Inc. 1986-. Mem.: Trial Lawyers Assn., Fla. Bar Assn., Ill. State Bar Assn., Chgo. Bar Assn., ABA, Phi Alpha Delta. Corporate, general, Family and matrimonial, General practice. Office: Samole & Berger PA 9700 S Dixie Hwy Ste 1030 Miami FL 33156-2865

SAMPSON, WILLIAM ROTH, lawyer; b. Teaneck, NJ, Dec. 11, 1946; s. James and Amelia (Roth) S.; 1 child, Lara; m. Drucilla Jean Mort, Apr. 23, 1988; stepchildren: Andy, Seth. BA History(hon.) , U. Kans., 1968, JD, 1971. Bar: Kans. 1971, US Dist. Ct. Kans. 1971, US Ct. Appeals (10th cir.) 1982, US Ct. Claims 1985, US Ct. Appeals (8th cir.) 1992. Assoc. Turner & Balloun, Gt. Bend, Kans., 1971; ptnr. Foulston & Siefkin, Wichita, Kans., 1975-86, Shook, Hardy & Bacon, Overland Pk., Kans., 1987—. Listed in The Best Lawyers in Am., adj. prof. advanced litig. U. Kans., 1994; mem. faculty trial tactics inst. Emory U. Sch. Law, 1994-97; mem. merit selection panel US Dist. Ct. Kans., 1999; lectr., presenter in field. Author: Kansas Trial Handbook, 1997; mem. Kans. Law Rev., 1969-71, editor, 1970-71; contbr. articles to profl. jour. Chmn. stewardship com. Univ. Friends Ch., Wichita, 1984-86; bd. dir. Friends U. Retirement Corp., Wichita, 1985-87; chmn. capital fund drives Trinity Luth. Ch., Lawrence, Kans., 1990-93, mem. ch. coun., 1990-92, stewardship com. Trinity Episcopal Ch., 2002-; bd. dir. Lied Ctr. of Kans., 1994-97. Lt. USNR, 1971-75. Fellow: Kans. Bar Found., Am. Bar Found.; mem.: ABA, Am. Inn Ct. (Judge Hugh Means chpt. Master of Bench), Kans. U. Law Soc. (bd. govs. 1993—96), Kans. Assn. Def. Counsel (pres. 1989—90, legis. coun. 1991, 1993, William H. Kahrs Disting. Achievement award 1994), Def. Rsch. Inst. (Kans. state rep. 1990—98, nat. bd. dirs. 1998—2000, pres. elect 2002, Exceptional Performance citation 1990), Internat. Assn. Def. Coun. (faculty mem. trial acad. 1994), Am. Bd. Trial Advs. (pres. Kans. chpt. 1990—91, nat. bd. dir. 1990—91), Wichita Bar Assn. (bd. dir. 1985—86), Johnson County Bar Assn. (bench-bar com. 1989—, Boss of Yr. award 1990), Douglas County Bar Assn., Kans. Bar Assn. (chmn. Kans. coll. advocacy 1986, CLE com. 1987—88, long-range planning), Assn. Def. Trial Attys., Lawrence Country Club, Order of Coif, Omicron Delta Kappa, Phi Alpha Theta, Delta Sigma Rho. Republican. Episcopalian. Avocations: jogging, golf, snow skiing, travel, reading. Federal civil litigation, Intellectual property, Product liability. Office: Shook Hardy & Bacon 10801 Mastin Ste 1000 Overland Park KS 66210-1669 E-mail: wsampson@shb.com.

SAMS, KATIE ELIZABETH, lawyer; b. Louisville, Ky., Dec. 12, 1969; d. David E. and Betsy B. Sams; m. Matthew Gower Johnson, May 4, 2002. BA, Dartmouth Coll., 1991; JD, Georgetown U., 1994; M in Internat. Rels., Grad. Inst. Internat. Studies, Geneva, 1997. Bar: N.Y. 1996. Law clk. Judge Boyce F. Martin U.S. Ct. Appeals (6th cir.), Louisville, 1994—95; rsch. fellow UN Inst. Disarmament Rsch., Geneva, 1998—2000; del. protection Internat. Com. Red Cross, Dili, 2000—01, del. to acad. cir. Geneva, 2001—. Author: Peachkeeping in Africa: Capabilities and Culpabilities, 2000; contbr. Office: Internat Com Red Cross 19 Ave de la Paix 1202 Geneva Switzerland

SAMSON, DAVID, lawyer; BA, Rutgers Univ., 1961; LLB, U. Pa. Law Sch., 1965. Law sec. Hon. Nathan L. Jacobs, NJ Supreme Court, 1965—66; founding prin. Wolff & Samson, 1972; gen. counsel NJ Turnpike Authority, 1982—90; atty. gen. State of NJ, 2002—03; sr. ptnr. Wolff & Samson, 2003—. Mem. Gov. Commn., 1990—91; chmn. Gov. Task Force, 1987—89; legal cons. Ethics Com., 1981—85, N.J. Supreme Court Com., 1973—77; legal cons. to atty. gen. Adv. com. on Governmental Immunity, 1967—68. Mem.: U.S. Supreme Court, N.Y. Bar Assn., Am. Bar Found., Am. Bar Assn., N.J. State Bar Assn., Essex County Bar Assn. Office: Wolff & Samson One Boland Dr West Orange NJ 07052*

SAMUEL, RAPHAEL, lawyer; b. N.Y.C., Oct. 11, 1946; s. Sam and Sarah R. (Hollenberg) S. BS in Math. magna cum laude, L.I. U., 1968; JD, NYU, 1971. Bar: N.Y. 1972, U.S. Dist. Ct. (so. and ea. dists.) N.Y. 1973, U.S. Ct. Appeals (2d cir.) 1973. Staff atty. N.Y.C. Housing Authority, 1972-78, asst. chief litigation, 1978-83, chief research, opinions and spl. assignments, 1983-87, asst. gen. counse. for spl. projects, 1987-93, assoc. gen. counsel for regulatory affairs, 1993—2002. Sec. Waterside Tenants Assn., N.Y.C., 1976-78; pres. 130 Water St. Tenants Assn., N.Y.C., 1978-80; sec. 50 8th Ave. Tenants Corp., Bklyn., 1980-83. Served with USNG, 1969-75. Mem. ABA, N.Y. State Bar Assn., Fed. Bar Coun., N.Y. County Lawyers Assn., Nat. Assn. Housing Redevel. Ofcls. Avocations: computer databases, opera, sporting events. E-mail: section8maven@prodigy.net.

SAMUELS, DONALD L. lawyer; b. Washington, May 8, 1961; s. Jack Donald Samuels and Francis Diane (Katcher) Yeoman. AB, Brown U., 1983; JD, Columbia U., 1986. Bar: Calif. 1986, U.S. Dist. Ct. (cen., no., ea. and so. dists.) Calif. 1988, U.S. Ct. Appeals (9th cir.) 1989, Colo. 1996, U.S. Ct. Appeals (7th cir.) 1996, U.S. Dist. Ct. Colo. 1997, U.S. Ct. Appeals (10th cir.) 1997, Tex. 1998. Law clk. Hon. William D. Keller, L.A., 1986-87; assoc. Sidley & Austin, L.A., 1987-94, ptnr., 1994-95, Samuels & Samuels, L.A., 1995-97; officer, dir., shareholder Ireland & Stapleton, Denver, 1997—2002; ptnr. Holme, Roberts & Owen, LLP, Denver, 2002—. Mem. ABA, Calif. Bar Assn., Colo. Bar Assn., Phi Beta Kappa. Federal civil litigation, State civil litigation, Trademark and copyright. Home: 5692 S Florence St Greenwood Village CO 80111-3713 Office: Holme Roberts & Owen LLP Ste 4100 1700 Lincoln St Denver CO 80203-4541 E-mail: samueld@hro.com.

SAMUELS, JANET LEE, lawyer; b. Pitts., July 18, 1953; d. Emerson and Jeanne (Kalish) S.; m. David Arthur Kalow, June 18, 1978; children; Margaret Emily Samuels-Kalow, Jacob Richard Samuels-Kalow, Benjamin Charles Samuels-Kalow. BA with honors, Beloit Coll., 1974; JD, NYU, 1977. Bar: N.Y. 1978, D.C. 1980. Staff atty. SCM Corp., N.Y.C., 1977-80, corp. atty., 1980-83, sr. corp. atty., 1983-85, assoc. gen. counsel Allied Paper div., 1983-86, corp. counsel, 1986, Holtzmann, Wise & Shepard, 1986-88. Mem. N.Y. State Bar Assn., Mortar Board, Phi Beta Kappa. Commercial, contracts (including sales of goods; commercial financing), Corporate, general, Securities. E-mail: JanetLSamuels@yahoo.com.

SAMUELS, JOHN STOCKWELL, III, mining company executive, financier; b. Galveston, Tex., Sept. 15, 1933; s. John Stockwell and Helen Yvonne (Poole) S.; children: Evelyn Kathleen, John Stockwell, Ainlay Leontine, Peter Ashton Hayes. AB, SM, Tex. A&M U., 1954; JD, Harvard U., 1960. Bar: N.Y. 1961. Assoc. Chadbourne, Parke, Whiteside & Wolff, N.Y.C., 1960-73; pres. Internat. Carbon & Minerals, N.Y.C., 1973-78, Carbomin Group, Inc., N.Y.C., 1978—, U.S. Reduction Inc., 1996—. Chmn. bd. J.S. Samuels & Co. Bd. dirs. City Center Music and Drama, Inc., N.Y.C.; chmn. bd. dirs. N.Y.C. Ballet, N.Y.C. Opera, 1976-81, Lincoln Ctr. Theatre, N.Y.C., 1979-81, Lincoln Ctr., N.Y.C. With U.S. Army, 1954-57. Mem. Inst. Petroleum, Century Assn. Democrat. Episcopalian. E-mail: jss@usr-inc.com.

SAMUELS, LESLIE B. lawyer; b. St. Louis, Nov. 10, 1942; s. Joseph E. and Dorothy J. (Bernstein) S.; m. Judith B. Thorn, June 19, 1966 (div. Aug. 1976); children: Colin T., Polly B.; m. Augusta H. Gross, Nov. 8, 1980. BS in Econs., U. Pa., 1963; LLB magna cum laude, Harvard U., 1966; postgrad., London Sch. Econs., 1966-67. Bar: N.Y., 1969, U.S. Dist. Ct. (so. dist.) N.Y. 1973, U.S. Tax Ct., 1980, U.S. Supreme Ct. 1994; CPA. Tax analyst Gulf Oil Co., London, 1967-68; assoc. Cleary, Gottlieb, Steen & Hamilton, N.Y.C., 1968-75, ptnr., 1975-93, 96—; asst. sec. for tax policy U.S. Dept. Treasury, Washington, 1993-96; vice-chair com. fiscal affairs OECD, 1994-96. Mem. Pres.'s Com. on the Arts and the Humanities, Washington, 1994-96. Editor Law Rev.; contbr. articles to profl. jours. Dir. Lower Manhattan Cultural Coun., N.Y.C., 1981-93, Roy Lichtenstein Found., N.Y.C., 1999—; active Carter-Mondale Transition Planning Group, Washington, 1976-77. Fulbright fellow London Sch. Econs., 1966-67. Mem. N.Y. State Bar Assn., Assn. of Bar of City of N.Y., Harvard Club (N.Y.C.). Democrat. Corporate taxation, Taxation, general. Office: Cleary Gottlieb Steen & Hamilton One Liberty Plaza New York NY 10006 E-mail: lsamuels@cgsh.com.

SAMUELSON, KENNETH LEE, lawyer; b. Natrona Heights, Pa., Aug. 22, 1946; s. Sam and Frances Bernice (Robbins) S.; m. Marlene Ina Rabinowitz, Jan. 1, 1980; children: Heather, Cheryl. BA magna cum laude, U. Pitts., 1968; JD, U. Mich., 1971. Bar: Md. 1972, D.C. 1980, U.S. Dist. Ct. (trial bar) Md. 1984. Assoc. Weinberg & Green, Balt., 1971-73, Dickerson, Nice, Sokol & Horn, 1973; asst. atty. gen. State of Md., 1973-77; pvt. practice Balt., 1978; ptnr. Linowes and Blocher, Silver Spring, 1979-93, Semmes, Bowen & Semmes, Balt., 1993-95, Washington, 1993—95, Wilkes Artis, Chartered, 1995-2001, Deckelbaum Ogens & Raftery, 2001—, Bethesda, 2001—. Spkr. in field of telecomms., fin. and real estate. Bd. govs. Wash. Bldg. Congress, 1998—2001; bd. dirs. D.C. Assn. Retarded Citizens, Inc., 1986—2001. Mem. ABA (coun. mem. sect. real property, probate and trust law 2000—, moderator various programs), Am. Coll. Real Estate Lawyers (moderator various programs), D.C. Bar (comml. real estate com., chmn. legal opinions project), Md. Bar Assn. (real property, planning and zoning sect., chmn. environ. subcom. legal opinions project 1987-89, litigation sect. 1982-84, chmn. comml. trans. com.), Md. Inst. Continuing Profl. Edn. Lawyers, Am. Arbitration Assn. (arbitrator and mediator, 1995-2003), D.C. Bldg. Industry Assn., Washington Assn Realtors, Inc., Nat. Assn. of Corp. Real Estate Execs., Civil Code Drafting Com. of the Russian Legis., Apt. and Office Bldg. Assn. Met. Washington, East Coast Builders Conf., Internat. Coun. Shopping Ctrs. (organized, co-faculty program "univ." 1988, NAFTA 1992, condemnations 1994, leasing 1997, high tech. effects 1998, pub./pvt. partnerships 1999), Montgomery County Bar Assn. (jud. selections com. 1988-90), Phi Beta Kappa, Lambda Alpha. Bankruptcy, Private international, Property, real (including real estate development, water). Office: Deckelbaum Ogens & Raftery Chartered # 165 2020 Pennsylvania Ave NW Washington DC 20006 E-mail: ksamuelson@bigfoot.com.

SAMUELSON, PAMELA ANN, law educator; b. Seattle, Aug. 4, 1948; d. Peter David and Margaret Susanne (Green) S.; m. Robert J. Glushko, May 7, 1988; 1 child, Robert M. BA in History, U. Hawaii, 1971, MA in Polit. Sci., 1972; JD, Yale U., 1976. Bar: N.Y. 1977, U.S. Dist. Ct. (so. dist.) N.Y. 1977. Rsch. assoc. Vera Inst. of Justice, N.Y.C., 1976-77; assoc. Willkie Farr & Gallagher, N.Y.C., 1977-81; prin. investigator Software Engring. Inst., Pitts., 1985-86; asst. prof. Law Sch. U. Pitts., 1981-84, assoc. prof. Law Sch., 1984-87, prof. Law Sch., 1987-96; prof. law and info. mgmt. U. Calif. Law Sch./Sch. Info. Mgmt. and Sys., Berkeley, 1996—. Bd. dirs. Berkeley Ctr. for Law and Tech./U. Calif., Berkeley; vis. prof. Emory Law Sch., Atlanta, 1989-90, Cornell Law Sch., Ithaca, 1995-96; mem. Nat. Rsch. Coun. Study Com. on Intellectual Property Rights and Info. Infrastructure, 1998-2000. Contbr. articles to profl. jours. Bd. dirs. ACLU Greater Pitts., 1983-88, Electronic Frontier Found., 2000—. John D. and Catherine T. MacArthur Found. fellow, 1997, Pub. Policy fellow Electronic Frontier Found., 1997—; recipient Disting. Alumni award U. Hawaii, 2000. Mem. ABA (sci. and tech. sect.), Am. Intellectual Property Law Assn. (subcom. chair 1988-89), Assn. Am. Law Schs. (intellectual property sect.). Democrat. Avocations: gardening, reading. Office: U Calif Berkeley Sch Info Mgmt and Sys 102 South Hall #4600 Berkeley CA 94720-4600 E-mail: pam@sims.berkeley.edu.

SAMUELSON, SUSAN STOBAUGH, law educator; b. Greenwich, Conn., May 26, 1953; d. Robert Blair and Beverly (Parker) Stobaugh; m. William F. Samuelson, Dec. 29, 1972; children: William Couper, Marion Crawford, Kendall Parker. AB cum laude, Harvard U., 1974, JD, 1977. Bar: Mass. 1977. Assoc. Choate, Hall & Stewart, Boston, 1977—83; assoc. prof. Boston U., 1992—. Editor: Law Firm Management, 1990; co-author: Business Law for a New Century, 1994, Legal Environment for a New Century, 2002, Essentials of Business Law, 2002, Business Law, Std. Edit., 3d edit. Office: Boston U Sch Mgmt 595 Commonwealth Ave Boston MA 02215

SAMUELSSON, MORTEN, lawyer; b. Copenhagen, Jan. 27, 1960; s. Paul Richard and Ritha Inge (Wennerwald) S.; m. Susan Lykke, Sept., 1992. Degree in law, U. Copenhagen, 1985, PhD, 1990. Admitted to Danish Bar and Supreme Ct. Denmark. Trainee European Parliament, Luxembourg, 1984; assoc. Advokaterne Bredgade 3, Copenhagen, 1985-88; ptnr. Lett & Co., Copenhagen, 1988-98. Lectr. Ins. Acad., Rungsted, Denmark, 1987—93; with Philip & Ptnrs., Copenhagen, 1998—2001, Samuelson Neugebauer, Copenhagen, 2001—; counsel Copenhagen Prosecution, 1994—; intern Haight, Gardner, Poor & Havens, N.Y.C., 1992. Author: Real Estate Agent Liability, 1989, Professional Liability, 1993, Directors and Officers Liability, 1997, Insurance Brokers, 2000. Mem.: Denmark-Am. Found., Brit.-Nordic Lawyers' Assn., Internat. Bar Assn., Danish Bar Assn. (litigation com. 1996—2001, ethics com. 2001—). Office: Kromann Reumert 5 Sundkrogsgade 2100 Ø Copenhagen Denmark E-mail: mos@kromannreumert.com.

SANCHEZ, CHRISTOPHER BENJAMIN, lawyer; b. Albuquerque, Jan. 15, 1974; s. Robert Ray Sanchez and Stephanie Marie Montoya. BA cum laude, U. N.Mex., 1996; JD, DePaul U., 2000. Bar: Ill. 00, U.S. Dist. Ct. (no. dist.) Ill. 00, U.S. Ct. Appeals (7th cir.) 01. Assoc. Miller Faucher and Caffety, LLP, Chgo., 1998—. Field dir. N.Mex. Pub. Interest Rsch. Group, Albuquerque, 1996; canvasser Ill. Pub. Interest Rsch. Group, Chgo., 1996. Mem.: ATLA, Ill. State Bar Assn. Avocations: snowboarding, road and mountain biking. Antitrust, Securities, General civil litigation. Office: Miller Faucher and Cafferty 30 N LaSalle Ste 3200 Chicago IL 60602 Office Fax: 312-782-4485. E-mail: csanchez@millerfaucher.com.

SANCHEZ, WALTER MARSHALL, lawyer; b. Lake Charles, La., July 3, 1959; s. John Augustine Sanchez and Louise Page Dugas Meyer; m. Frances E. Morgan, Oct. 18, 1986; children: Clare, Madeline, Kate, John. BS, La. State U., Baton Rouge, 1981, JD, 1984. Bar: La. 1984, U.S. Supreme Ct. 1984; bd. cert. family law specialist, La. Bd. of Legal Specialization. Assoc. Godwin, Painter, Roddy, Lorenzi & Watson, Lake Charles, 1985-86; ptnr. Godwin, Roddy, Lorenzi Watson & Sanchez, Lake Charles, 1986-90, Lorenzi, Sanchez & Palay, LLP, Lake Charles, 1990—. Vice chmn. La. Indigent Defender Bd., New Orleans, 1994-96; chmn. 14th Jud. Dist. Indigent Defender Bd., Lake Charles, 1987-96; mem. faculty trial advocacy tng. program La. State U. Law Ctr., 1993—; mem. Joint Legis. Com. for Study Indigent Def. Sys., 1996-97; mem. spl. com. to study reinstatement of fault in divorce La. State Law Inst., 1998-2001; apptd. judge pro tempore City Ct. of Sulphur, 1999—. Mem. La. Assn. Criminal Def. Attys. (bd. dirs. 1990—, pres. 1997-98), Am. Mensa, Order of St. Charles. Democrat. Roman Catholic. General civil litigation, Criminal, Family and matrimonial. Office: Lorenzi Sanchez & Palay LLP PO Box 3305 Lake Charles LA 70602-3305

SAND, LEONARD B. federal judge; b. N.Y.C., May 24, 1928; BS, NYU, 1947; LL.B., Harvard, 1951. Bar: N.Y. 1953, U.S. Supreme Ct. 1956, D.C. 1969. Clk. to dist. ct. judge, N.Y., 1952-53; asst. U.S. atty. So. Dist. N.Y., 1953-54; asst. to U.S. Solictor Gen., 1956-59; mem. firm Robinson, Silverman, Pearce, Aronsohn Sand and Berman, N.Y.C., 1960-78; judge U.S. Dist. Ct. So. Dist. N.Y., 1978—, now sr. judge. Adj. prof. law NYU. Note editor: Harvard Law Rev, 1950-51. Del. N.Y. State Constl. Conv., 1967; v.p., treas. Legal Aid Soc. Fellow Am. Coll. Trial Lawyers; mem. ABA, Assn. Bar City N.Y. (v.p.), N.Y. State Bar Assn., Fed. Bar Coun. Office: US Dist Ct US Courthouse 500 Pearl St New York NY 10007-1316

SAND, THOMAS CHARLES, lawyer; b. Portland, Oreg., June 4, 1952; s. Harold Eugene and Marian Anette (Thomas) S.; m. Rhonda Diane Laycoe, June 15, 1974; children: Kendall, Taylor, Justin. Student, Centro des Artes y Lenguas, Cuernavaca, Mex., 1972; BA in English, U. Oreg., 1974; JD, Lewis and Clark Coll., 1977. Bar: Oreg. 1977, U.S. Dist. Ct. Oreg. 1977, U.S. Ct. Appeals (9th cir.) 1984. Assoc. Miller, Nash, LLP, Portland, 1977-84, ptnr., 1984—, mng. ptnr., 1999—. Mem. Oreg. State Bar Com. on Professionalism, 1989, chmn., 1990; dir. young lawyers divsn. Multnomah County Bar Assn., 1980; spl. asst. atty. gen. Wasco County 1983 Gen. Election; speaker in field. Contbr. articles to legal jours. Mem. U.S. Dist. Ct. of Oreg. Hist. Soc., 1990—; bd. dirs. Portland Area coun. Camp Fire, Inc., 1978-90,pres., 1984-86; bd. dirs. Oreg. Indoor Invitational Track Meet, Inc., 1982-84. Recipient Boss of the Yr. award Portland Legal Secs. Assn., 1989. Mem. ABA (securities litigation com., subcom. on broker-dealer litigation), Oreg. Bar Assn., Multnomah Bar Assn. (bd. dirs. task force on structure and orgn. 1989, chmn. com. on professionalism 1988, nominating com. 1986, participating atty. in N.E. legal clin. Vol Lawyers project, award of merit for svc. to profession 1988), Securities Industry Assn. (compliance and legal divsn.), Northwestern Sch. of Law, Lewis and Clark Coll. Alumni Assn. (bd. dirs. 1992, pres. 1997), Valley Comm. Presbyterian Ch., Multnomah Athletic Club, Portland Golf Club. Avocations: golf, guitar, camping, river rafting, children's sports. General civil litigation, Securities. Office: Miller Nash LLP 111 SW 5th Ave Ste 3500 Portland OR 97204-3699

SANDBACK, WILLIAM ARTHUR, lawyer; b. N.Y.C., Aug. 2, 1945; s. William A. and Gertrude E. (Ryan) S.; married; children: Lauren, Adam. BA, Villanova U., 1967; postgrad. in English, L.I. U., 1968; JD, N.Y. Law Sch., 1971; LLM in Labor Law, NYU, 1974. Bar: N.Y. 1972, Fla. 1973, U.S. Dist. Ct. (ea. and so. dists.) N.Y. 1973. Fin. planner Aims Group, N.Y.C., 1971-72; asst. dist. atty. Nassau County, N.Y., 1972-73; law sec. to presiding justice Nassau County Ct., 1973-77; ptnr. Sandback, Birnbaum & Michelen, Mineola, N.Y., 1977—. Committeeman Nassau County Rep. Com., 1979-86. Mem. ABA, Nassau County Bar Assn. (com. mem.), Lions (pres. 1983-84). Roman Catholic. Avocation: golf. State civil litigation, Criminal, Labor (including EEOC, Fair Labor Standards Act, labor-management relations, NLRB, OSHA). Office: Sandback Birnbaum Michelen 200 Old Country Rd Mineola NY 11501-4235 also: 2 Penn Plz Rm 1996 New York NY 10121-1999

SANDBLOM, STEVEN KIRK, lawyer; b. Des Moines, Nov. 26, 1951; s. Donald Dean and Jane (Moffet) S.; m. Sally Anne McKlveen, June 24, 1972; children: Sarah J., Scott T. BA, Drake U., 1973, JD, 1975. Bar: Iowa 1976, U.S. Dist. Ct. (no. and so. dists.) Iowa 1976, U.S. Tax Ct. 1976, U.S. Ct. Appeals 8th cir.) 1976. Ptnr. Baker, Johnsen & Sandblom, Humboldt, Iowa, 1976—. Asst. atty. gen. State of Iowa, Des Moines, 1976; rsch. asst. Supreme Ct. Adminstr., Des Moines, 1972-75; Humboldt County magistrate Iowa Dist. Ct., Humboldt, Iowa, 1977-83, 85-96 ; juvenile ct. referee Iowa Dist. Ct., Humboldt, Wright and Pocahontas counties, 1982-89. Bd. dirs., chmn. Congregational Ch., Humboldt, 1978-82; bd. dirs. Humboldt Homes Ltd., 1982-88, Humboldt Workshop, 1984-99, Humboldt County Meml. Hosp. Found., 1997—. Mem. ABA, Iowa State Bar Assn. (mem. juvenile law com. 1983-90, bd. govs. 1990-2000, chair Gen. Practice Sect., 2001-), Humboldt County Bar Assn. (pres. 1984-85), Jud. Dist. 2B Bar Assn. (sec. 1979-84, pres. 1986-87), Kiwanis (pres. 1986-87). General practice, Personal injury (including property damage), Probate (including wills, trusts). Home: 13 Woodland Dr Humboldt IA 50548-8703 Office: Baker Johnsen & Sandblom PO Box 337 Humboldt IA 50548-0337 E-mail: ssandblom@humboldtlaw.com.

SANDERS, BARRY R. lawyer; b. Oak Park, Ill., July 21, 1957; s. Eugene Haze and Muriel Efty Sanders; m. Diane Gaffney Sanders, Dec. 28, 1985; 1 child, Mattie Maria Murielle. BA, U. Va., 1979, Cambridge U., 1981; LLM, U. Tex., 1983; MA, Cambridge U., 1986. Bar: Calif. 1984, Ariz. 1985, U.S. Dist. Ct. (no. dist.) Calif. 1984, U.S. Dist. Ct. (ea. dist.) Calif. 1985, U.S. Dist. Ct. Ariz. 1987, U.S. Ct. Appeals (9th cir.) 1989, U.S. Supreme Ct. 1996, U.S. Ct. Appeals (8th cir.) 2001. Shareholder Allen, Price & Padden, P.C., Phoenix, 1999—, Ryley, Carlock & Applewhite, P.A., 1991—99, Pohlman & Sanders, P.A., 1989—91. Recipient Henry prize in Moral Philosophy, U. of Aberdeen, Scotland, 1978. Mem.: State Bar Ariz. (chair antitrust sect. 1998—99, 2002—03). Avocation: golf. General civil litigation, Intellectual property, Antitrust. Office: Allen Price & Padden PC 3131 E Camelback Rd Ste 110 Phoenix AZ 85016

SANDERS, BRYAN HOWARD, law educator, department chair, consultant; b. Cleve., Sept. 2, 1960; s. Howard William and Marian Sanders; m. Virginia Sanders, July 31, 1982. BS in Govt., Evangel U., 1982; JD, Oral Roberts U., 1985, Regent U., 1991. Atty. W. Owen Fields and Assocs., Tulsa, Okla., 1985—87; v.p. and gen. counsel Logos Devel. Corp., Elyria, Ohio, 1987—90; pres. Reconciliation Ministries, Elyria, Ohio, 1987—90; prof. legal studies Evangel U., Springfield, Mo., 1990—, dept. chair, 1998—. V.p. Conflict Mgmt. Cons., Louisville, 1991—; instr. Springfield Police Acad., 1998—; bd. dirs. legal affairs Assn. Christian Tchrs. and Schs., Springfield. Co-author: A Legal Primer for Church Discipline, 1992; contbr. articles to mags. Mem.: Christian Legal Soc., Fellowship of Cos. for Christ Internat. (area coord. 1997—2002), Assn. for Conflict Resolution. Mem. Assemblies Of God. Avocations: golf, reading. Office: Evangel Univ 1111 N Glenstone Ave Springfield MO 65802

SANDERS, DALE R. lawyer; b. N.Y.C., Feb. 1, 1946; m. Jo-Ann Sanders, Dec. 25, 1967; 1 child. Bar: Fla. 1970, Wyo. 1991, U.S. Dist. Ct. (so. dist.) Fla. 1971, U.S. Tax Ct. 1972. Atty. Kirsch & Druck, P.A., Ft. Lauderdale, Fla., 1970-71, Kirsch, Digiulian, Druck et al, Ft. Lauderdale, Fla., 1971-72, Digiulian, Spellacy, Lyons, Ft. Lauderdale, Fla., 1972-77, Lyons & Sanders, Chartered, Ft. Lauderdale, Fla., 1977—. With USAR, 1969-75. Mem.: Broward County Trial Lawyers Assn. (pres. 1980), Broward County Bar Assn. (pres. 1990), Fla. Bar (bd. govs. 1991—95, mem. 17th cir. jud. nominating commn. 1992—96, vice chair 1996—2002, mem. State of Fla. jud. qualifications commn.). Family and matrimonial. Office: Lyons and Sanders Chartered 600 NE 3rd Ave Fort Lauderdale FL 33304-2618

SANDERS, EDWIN PERRY BARTLEY, judge; b. Madisonville, Ky., July 12, 1940; s. Virgil Perry and Eunice Jane (Denton) S.; m. Kathryn Walker, Jan. 28, 1967; children: Christopher Charles, Carroll Denton. BS in Bus., Stetson U., 1965, JD, 1968. Bar: Fla. 1968. Ptnr. Ford, Wren and Sanders, 1968-69; mem. Landis, Graham, French, Husfeld and Ford, PA, DeLand, Fla., 1970-83; prof. real estate Stetson U. Sch. Bus. Adminstrn., 1980-83; judge 7th Jud. Cir. Ct. Volusia County, DeLand, Fla., 1983—. With U.S. Army. Mem. Fla. Bar Assn., Volusia County Bar Assn., Lake Beresford Yacht Club, Rotary. Democrat. Episcopalian. Home: 340 Washington Oaks Dr Deland FL 32720-2760 Office: Volusia County Courthouse 101 N Alabama Ave Ste D443 Deland FL 32724 also: PO Box 611 Deland FL 32721-0611

SANDERS, HAROLD BAREFOOT, JR., judge; b. Dallas, Tex., Feb. 5, 1925; s. Harold Barefoot and May Elizabeth (Forrester) S.; m. Jan Scurlock, June 6, 1952; children— Janet Lea, Martha Kay, Mary Frances, Harold Barefoot III. BA, U. Tex., 1949, LLB, 1950. Bar: Tex. bar 1950. U.S. atty. No. Dist. Tex., 1961-65; asst. dep. atty. gen. U.S., 1965-66; asst. atty. gen., 1966-67; legis. counsel to President U.S., 1967-69; partner firm Clark, West, Keller, Sanders & Butler, Dallas, 1969-79; U.S. dist. judge for No. Dist. Tex., Dallas, 1979—, chief judge, 1989-95. Mem. Tex. Ho. of Reps., 1952-58; Dem. nominee U.S. Senate, 1972. Lt. (j.g.) USNR, World War II. Mem. ABA (chmn. nat. conf. fed. trial judges 1988-89), Fed. Bar Assn. (Disting. Svc. award Dallas 1964), Dallas Bar Assn., State Bar Tex. (jud. conf. U.S. 1989-92, jud. panel on multidistrict litigation 1992-2000, jud. conf. com. to rev. cir. coun. conduct and disability orders 2001—), Blue Key, Phi Delta Phi, Phi Delta Theta. Methodist. Office: US Courthouse 1100 Commerce St Ste 15 Dallas TX 75242-1016

SANDERS, RICHARD BROWNING, judge; b. Tacoma, Wash. 1 child: Laura. BA, U. Wash., 1966, JD, 1969. Assoc. Murray, Scott, McGavick & Graves, Tacoma, Wash., 1969, Caplinger & Munn, Seattle, 1971; hearing examiner State Wash., Olympia, 1970; pvt. practice Wash., 1971-95; justice Wash. Supreme Ct., Olympia, 1995—. Adj. prof. U. Wash. Sch. Law; lectr. in field. Contbr. articles to profl. jours. Office: Supreme Court of Washington Temple of Justice PO Box 40929 Olympia WA 98504-0929 Fax: (360) 357-2092. E-mail: j_r.sanders@courts.wa.gov.

SANDERS, RICHARD HENRY, lawyer; b. Chgo., Apr. 10, 1944; s. Walter J. and Marian (Snyder) Sikorski; m. Sharon A. Marciniak, July 8, 1967 (div. Oct. 1979); 1 child, Douglas Bennett. BS, Loyola U., Chgo., 1967; JD, Northwestern U., 1969. Bar: Ill. 1969, Ind. 1990, D.C. 1990, U.S. Dist. Ct. (no. dist.) Ill. 1970, U.S. Dist. Ct. (no. and so. dists.) Ind. 1990, U.S. Ct. Appeals (7th cir.) 1990, U.S. Supreme Ct. 1990. Assoc. Vedder, Price, Kaufman & Kammholz, Chgo., 1969-76, ptnr., 1976—, mem. exec. com., 1991-93, health law area leader, 1989-91, 93-95, 2001—. Adj. prof. Sch. of Law Northwestern U., 1994—; mem. svc. dispute resolver panel Am. Health Lawyers Assn. Alt. Dispute Resolution, 2000—. Mem. ABA, Ill. Bar Assn. (chmn. health sect. 1989-90), Chgo. Bar Assn., Ind. Bar Assn., D.C. Bar Assn., Am. Health Lawyers Assn., Ill. Assn. Health Attys., Univ. Club, Evanston Golf Club (Skokie). Avocations: skiing, diving, photography, golf. Corporate, general, Non-profit and tax-exempt organizations, Health. Office: Vedder Price Kaufman & Kammholz 222 N La Salle St Ste 2600 Chicago IL 60601-1100 E-mail: rsanders@vedderprice.com.

SANDERS-COCHRAN, RACHEL DEANNA, lawyer; b. Heflin, Ala., Aug. 4, 1962; children: William G., S. Sanders. BS magna cum laude, Auburn U., 1988; JD cum laude, Samford U., 1991. Bar: Ala. 1991, U.S. Dist. Ct. (mid. dist.) Ala. 1991, U.S. Dist. Ct. (no. and so. dist.) Ala. 1994, U.S. Ct. Appeals (11th cir.) 1994. Atty. Capell, Howard, Knabe & Cobbs, Montgomery, Ala., 1991-94, Pierce, Carr, Alford, Mobile, Ala., 1994-96, Carr, Alford, Clausen, Mobile, 1996, Rushton, Stakely, Johnston & Garrett, Montgomery, 1997—2002, Ala. Supreme Ct., 2001—. Mem. ABA, Def. Rsch. Inst., Ala. Bar Assn. (mem. exec. com. young lawyers divsn.), Ala. Def. Lawyers Assn. Appellate, Federal civil litigation, Commercial, consumer (including collections, credit).

SANDERSON, DOUGLAS JAY, lawyer; b. Boston, Apr. 21, 1953; s. Warren and Edith S. Sanderson; m. Audrey S. Goldstein, June 6, 1982; children: Scott M.G., Phoebe H.G. BA, Trinity Coll., Hartford, Conn., 1974; JD, George Washington U., 1977. Bar: Va. 1977, D.C. 1978, U.S. Dist. Ct. (ea. dist.) Va. 1978, U.S. Ct. Appeals (4th cir.) 1978. Assoc. Bettius, Rosenberger & Carter, P.C., Fairfax, Va., 1977-82; ptnr. Bettius & Sanderson, P.C. and predecessor firms, Fairfax, 1982-86; prin. Miles & Stockbridge P.C., Fairfax, 1986-95; br. head Miles & Stockbridge, Fairfax, 1989-91; co-owner McCandlish & Lillard, P.C., Fairfax, 1995—. Trustee Cambridge Ctr. Behavioral Studies, Cambridge, 1981-90. Editor: Consumer Protection Reporting Svc., 1976-77. Bd. dirs. Legal Svcs. No. Va., Inc., 1991-97, pres., 1993-95; vol. counsel Arts Coun. of Fairfax County, Inc., 1991--. Mem. ABA, Va. Bar Assn., Fairfax Bar Assn., Ctrl. Fairfax C. of C. (bd. dirs. 1988-93). Avocations: sports, reading. Corporate, general, Family and matrimonial, Property, real (including real estate development, water). Office: McCandlish & Lillard 11350 Random Hills Rd Ste 500 Fairfax VA 22030-6044

SANDLER, MICHAEL DAVID, lawyer; b. Los Angeles, Feb. 27, 1946; AB, Stanford U., 1967; JD, Yale U., 1972. Bar: Calif. 1973, D.C. 1973, Wash. 1985. Assoc. Steptoe & Johnson, Washington, 1972-75, 77-79, ptnr., 1980-85; spl. asst. to legal adviser Dept. of State, Washington, 1975-77; ptnr. Foster, Pepper & Shefelman, Seattle, 1985-97, Sandler Ahern & McConaughy PLLC, Seattle, 1997—. Adj. prof. law Georgetown U., Washington, 1979, 81-82, U. Wash., Seattle, 1985-92. Vol. Peace Corps, Ethiopia and Ghana, 1968-70. Mem. ABA (chair 1995-96 sect. internat. law and practice). Antitrust, General civil litigation, Private international. Office: Sandler Ahern & McConaughy PLLC 1200 5th Ave Ste 1900 Seattle WA 98101-3135 E-mail: mike@sandlaw.com.

SANDLER, ROSS, law educator; b. Milw., Jan. 31, 1939; s. Theodore T. and Laurette (Simons) S.; m. Alice R. Mintzer, Sept. 15, 1968; children: Josephine, Jenny, Dorothy. AB, Dartmouth Coll., 1961; LLB, NYU, 1965. Bar: N.Y. 1965, Fla. 1965. Assoc. atty. Cahill Gordon Reindel & Ohl, N.Y.C., 1965-68; asst. U.S. atty. So. Dist. N.Y., 1968-72; assoc. atty. Trubin Sillcocks Edelman & Knapp, N.Y.C., 1972-75; sr. staff atty. Natural Resources Def. Coun., N.Y.C., 1975-81, 83-86; spl. advisor to mayor City of N.Y., 1981-82; exec. dir. Hudson River Found., N.Y.C., 1983-86; commr. N.Y.C. Dept. Transp., 1986-90; ptnr. Jones Day Reavis & Pogue, N.Y.C., 1991-93; law prof. N.Y. Law Sch., 1993—, dir. Ctr. for N.Y.C. law, 1993—; pres. N.Y. Legis. Svc., 1998—. Mem. N.Y.C. Procurement Policy Bd., 1994—; vis. lectr. Yale Law Sch., New Haven, 1977; adj. prof. law NYU Law Sch., 1976-94; chair, mem. N.Y.C. Taxi and Limousine Commn., 1980-90. Co-author: A New Dirction in Transit, 1978, Democracy by Decree, 2003; columnist Environ. Mag., 1976—80; editor: (jour.) City Law; contbr. chapters to books, articles. Trustee Woods Hole (Mass.) Rsch. Ctr., 1983—; mem. exec. com. Hudson River Found., 1986-96; mem. adv. coun. Ctr. Biodiversity and Conservation Am. Mus. Nat. History, 1996—. Recipient Pub. Interest award NYU Law Alumni, 1987, Louis J. Lefkowitz award Fordham Law Sch. Urban Law Jour., 1989, Lifetime Achievement award N.Y. State Bar Assn., 1998. Mem. City Club of N.Y. (chair 1992-93, trustee). Office: NY Law Sch 57 Worth St New York NY 10013-2959

SANDMAN, IRVIN W(ILLIS), lawyer; b. Seattle, Mar. 19, 1954; BA summa cum laude, U. Wash., 1976; JD, UCLA, 1980. Bar: U.S. Dist. Ct. (we. and ea. dists.) Wash. 1980. Prin. Graham & Dunn, Seattle, 1980—. Staff mem. UCLA Law Review. Mem. ABA (hotel resorts and tourism com. 1996-2001, co-chair 2001—), Acad. Hospitality Attys. (charter), Wash. State Bar Assn. (chmn. creditor/debtor sect. 1988-90, editor newsletter

1984—, spkr. continuing legal edn.). Bankruptcy, Commercial, contracts (including sales of goods; commercial financing). Office: Graham & Dunn 1420 5th Ave Fl 33 Seattle WA 98101-4087

SANDMAN, JAMES JOSEPH, lawyer; b. Albany, N.Y., June 16, 1951; s. Edgar A. and Margaret M. (Dugan) S.; m. Elizabeth D. Mullin, June 2, 1985; children: Joseph M., Elizabeth D. AB summa cum laude, Boston Coll., 1973; JD cum laude, U. Pa., 1976. Bar: Pa. 1976, D.C. 1977, U.S. Supreme Ct. 1980, Colo. 1982. Law clk. to judge U.S. Ct. Appeals (3d cir.), Wilkes-Barre, Pa., 1976-77; assoc. Arnold & Porter, Washington, 1977-82, ptnr., 1991—, mng. ptnr., 1996—, assoc. Denver, 1982-83, ptnr., 1984-91. Exec. editor U. Pa. Law Rev., 1975-76. Mem. ABA, D.C. Bar Assn., Order of Coif, Phi Beta Kappa. Democrat. Roman Catholic. Federal civil litigation, State civil litigation. Office: Arnold & Porter 555 12th St NW Washington DC 20004-1206*

SANDOVAL, BRIAN, state attorney general; m. Kathleen Sandoval; 2 children. Grad., U. Nev.; law degree, Ohio State U., 1989. Mem. Assembly, 1995—97; chmn. Nev. State Gaming Commn.; atty. gen. Nev., 2002—. Republican. Office: Old Supreme Ct Bldg 100 N Carson St Carson City NV 89701*

SANDRIDGE, WILLIAM PENDLETON, JR., lawyer; b. Winston-Salem, N.C., Jan. 27, 1934; m. Jane Carolyn Yeager, Dec. 10, 1966; children: Jane, William. AB, U. N.C., 1956; LLB, U. Va., 1961. Bar: N.C. 1961. Mem.. Womble Carlyle Sandridge & Rice, PLLC, Winston-Salem, 1962—. Chmn., bd. dirs. Horizons Residential Care Ctr., 1980, Food Bank N.W. N.C., Inc., 1988-89, Data Max Corp., 1996. Banking, Commercial, contracts (including sales of goods; commercial financing), Finance. Office: Womble Carlyle Et Al One W Fourth St Winston Salem NC 27101

SANDS, DARRY GENE, lawyer; b. Charleston, Ark., Jan. 4, 1947; s. Anthony Wayne and Marjorie (Elkins) S.; m. Charlotte Moore, Dec. 28, 1968; 1 child, Spencer Justin. BS, U. Ark., 1969; JD, U. Kans., 1974. Bar: Mo. 1974, U.S. Dist. Ct. (we. dist.) Mo. 1974. Dir. Dicus, Davis, Sands & Collins, P.C., Kansas City, Mo., 1991—. Spkr. in field. Contbr. articles to profl. jours. Bd. dirs. Hope House. Mem. ABA, Nat. Assn. Coll. and Univ. Attys., Mo. Bar, Kansas City Met. Bar Assn. (chmn., past chair coll. and univ. law com., local govt. com.), Order of Coif, Lake Quivira Country Club. Democrat. General civil litigation, Education and schools, Labor (including EEOC, Fair Labor Standards Act, labor-management relations, NLRB, OSHA). Home: 5341 Canterbury Rd Shawnee Mission KS 66205-2612 Office: Dicus Davis Sands & Collins PC 1930 City Center Sq 1100 Main St Kansas City MO 64105-2105 E-mail: dsands@ddsc-law.com.

SANDS, VELMA AHDA, lawyer; d. John T. and Thelma Jane (Davis) Carlisle. BS, Calif. State U., Dominguez Hills, 1976; JD, Southwestern U., 1985. CPA. Cons. KPMG Peat Marwick Main, L.A., 1980-81; v.p. Security Pacific Bank, L.A., 1981-86; contr. L.A. Investors, 1986; mgr. IRC div. FN Realty Svcs., Pasadena, Calif., 1986-88; mgr. fin. reporting Luz Internat. Ltd., L.A., 1988-89; pvt. practice law L.A., 1990—; temporary judge L.A. Mcpl. Ct., 1996—. Instr. Fame Entrepreneurial Tng. Program; co-pres. Multicultural Bar Alliance, 2001-02. Participant career day programs for local high schs.; mem. United We Stand. Nat. Assn. Black Women Lawyers scholar, 1982; Appreciation award John M. Langston Bar Assn., 2000, recipient Commendation City of L.A., 2001, Gov. Gray Davis, 2001, Sen. Barbara Boxer, 2001, Cert. of Recognition, Calif. State Assembly, 2001, Cert. Spl. Recognition, U.S. Rep. Maxine Waters, 2001, Cert. Achievement, Law Offices of Stephenson, Acquisto & Colman, 2002, Cert. Congratulations, Black Women's Lawyers Assn. and John M. Langston Bar Assn., 2002, Cert. Appreciation, Superior Ct. of Calif., Recycling Black Dollars award - 1st Ann. Samuel L. Williams Spirit of Law award for outstanding contbn. in field of law, 2001. Mem. ABA, NAFE, Bd. Black Women Lawyers (bd. dirs.), Nat. Assn. Bank Women (chair ways and means com. of scholarship fund 1986, scholar 1984), So. Calif. Chinese Lawyers Assn., Am. Bridge Assn., L.A. County Bar Assn., Langston Bar Assn. (pres. 2000), L.A. Bench and Bar Affiliates (scholarship com., meeting host, scholar 1983, Pres.' Spl. Recognition award 1997, Appreciation award 2002, Pres.' award 2001), Am. Bridge Assn., Phi Alpha Delta. Administrative and regulatory, Bankruptcy, Personal injury (including property damage). Home and Office: 3435 Wilshire Blvd Ste 2700 Los Angeles CA 90010-2013 Address: 14122 Friar St Van Nuys CA 91401-2105

SANDSTROM, DALE VERNON, judge; b. Grand Forks, ND, Mar. 9, 1950; s. Ellis Vernon and Hilde Geneva (Williams) S.; m. Gail Hagerty, Mar. 27, 1993; children: Jack, Carrie, Anne. BA, N.D. State U., 1972; JD, U. N.D., 1975. Bar: N.D. 1975, U.S. Dist. Ct. N.D. 1975, U.S. Ct. Appeals (8th cir.) 1976. Asst. atty. gen., chief consumer fraud and antitrust div. State of N.D., Bismarck, 1975-81, securities commr., 1981-83, pub. svc. commr., 1983-92, pres. commn., 1987-91, justice Supreme Ct., 1992—. Chair N.D. Commn. on Cameras in the Courtroom, 1993—, Joint Procedure Com., 1996—; mem. exec. com. N.D. Jud. Conf., 1995—, chair-elect, 1997-99, chair, 1999-2001; mem. Gov.'s Com. on Security and Privacy, Bismarck, 1975-76, Gov.'s Com. on Refugees, Bismarck, 1976; chmn. Gov's Com. on Comml. Air Transp., Bismarck, 1983-84. Mem. platform com. N.D. Reps., 1972, 76, exec. com., 1972-73, 85-88, dist. chmn., 1981-82; former chmn. bd. deacons Luth. Ch.; mem. ch. coun., exec. com., chmn. legal and constl. rev. com. Evang. Luth Ch. Am., 1993—; mem. exec. bd. dirs., No. Lights Coun., dist. chair Boy Scouts Am., 1998-2000. Named Disting. Eagle Scout, Boy Scouts Am., 1997. Mem. ABA, N.D. Bar Assn., Big Muddy Bar Assn., Nat. Assn. Regulatory Utility Commrs. (electricity com.), N.A. Assn. Securities Adminstrs., Order of De Molay (grand master 1994-95, mem. Internat. Supreme coun., Legion of Honor award), Nat. Eagle Scouts Assn. (regent for life), Shriners, Elks, Eagles, Masons (33d degree, chmn. grand youth com. 1979-87, Youth Leadership award 1986), Bruce M. VanSickle Am. Inn of Court (pres. 1999-2001). Office: State ND Supreme Ct Judicial Wing 1st Fl 600 E Boulevard Ave Bismarck ND 58505*

SANDY, ROBERT EDWARD, JR., lawyer; b. Libertyville, Ill., Feb. 16, 1943; s. Robert Edward and Elizabeth Ann (Carroll) S.; m. Joan Mary Phillips, Apr. 19, 1969; children: Mary Rosanne Phillips-Sandy, John Robert Phillips-Sandy. AB, Harvard U., 1965; JD, U. Chgo., 1968. Bar: Mass. 1969, Maine 1972, U.S. Dist. Ct. Mass. 1970, U.S. Dist. Ct. Maine 1972, U.S. Ct. Appeals (1st cir.) 1994, U.S. Supreme Ct. 1980. Atty. Boston Redevel. Authority, 1969-72; ptnr. Sandy and Sandy, Waterville, Maine, 1972-83, Sherman and Sandy, Waterville, 1983-87; sr. ptnr. Sherman & Sandy, Waterville, 1987—. Mem. Waterville Bar Assn., Maine Bar Assn., Maine Trial Lawyers Assn., ABA. Avocations: boating, skiing, community theater, Maine Internat. Film Festival. Criminal, Family and matrimonial, General practice. Home: 9 Cleveland Pl Waterville ME 04901 Office: Sherman & Sandy 74 Silver St Waterville ME 04901-6524 E-mail: info@shermanandsandy.com.

SANETTI, STEPHEN LOUIS, lawyer; b. Flushing, N.Y., June 25, 1949; s. Alfred Julius Sanetti and Yolanda Marie (DiGioia) Boyes; m. Carole Leighton Koller, Sept. 21, 1974; children: Christopher Edward, Dana Harrison. BA in History with honors, Va. Mil. Inst., 1971; JD, Washington and Lee U., 1974. Bar: Conn. 1975, U.S. Ct. Mil. Appeals 1975, U.S. Dist. Ct. Conn. 1978, U.S. Ct. Appeals (2d cir.) 1979, U. S. Supreme Ct. 1980. Litigation atty. Marsh, Day & Calhoun, Bridgeport, Conn., 1978-80; gen. counsel Sturm, Ruger & Co., Southport, Conn., 1980—, v.p., 1993-2000, also bd. dirs., 1998-2000, vice chmn., sr. exec. v.p., 2000—. Dir. Product Liability Adv. Coun., 1988-2002; tech. advisor Assn. Firearm and Toolmark Examiners; chmn. legis. and legal affairs com. Sporting Arms and Ammunition Mfrs. Inst., 1993-2001; bd. govs. Nat. Shooting Sports Found., 2002-. Served to capt., chief criminal law 1st Cavalry Div. Staff Judge Advocate, U.S. Army, 1975-78. Mem. Am. Acad. Forensic Sci., Def. Rsch. Inst. Republican. Roman Catholic. General civil litigation, Corporate, general, Product liability. Office: Sturm Ruger & Co Inc 1 Lacey Pl Southport CT 06490-1241

SANFILIPPO, JON WALTER, lawyer; b. Milw., Nov. 10, 1950; s. Joseph Salvator and Jeanne Catherine (Lisinski) S.; m. Pamela Joy Jaeger, July 8, 1972; children: Kerri, Jessica, Jennifer. AS, U. Wis., West Bend, 1972; BS, U. Wis., Milw., 1974, MS, 1978; JD, Marquette U., 1988; postgrad., Nat. Jud. Coll., 1996. Bar: Wis. 1988, U.S. Dist. Ct. (ea. dist.) Wis. 1988, U.S. Ct. Appeals (7th cir.) 1988, U.S. Dist. Ct. (we. dist.) Wis 1989. U.S. Supreme Ct. 1994; cert. elem. tchr., ednl. adminstr., Wis. Collection agt. West Bend Co., 1970-72; educator, athletic dir., coach St. Francis Cabrini, West Bend, 1974-77; clk. of cir. ct. Washington County, West Bend, 1976-89; ptnr. Schowalter, Edwards & Sanfilippo, S.C., West Bend, 1989-94; sch. prin.K-8 Campbellsport (Wis.) Sch. Dist., 1994-95; chief dep. clk. Cir. Ct. Milw. County, Milw., 1995—, acting clk., 1997-98; jud. ct. commr. Milw. County, 1997—. Judo tchr. City of West Bend, 1967—; phys. edn. instr., judo coach U. Wis., West Bend, 1992—; fellow ct. exec. devel. program Inst. Ct. Mgmt. Nat. Ctr. State Cts., 1999. Author: Judo for the Physical Educator, 1981, Proper Falling for Education Classes, 1981. Mem. sch. bd. West Bend Sch. Dist., 1979-80; dist. chmn. Wis. Clk. of Cts. Assn., 1976-79, 95—, mem. exec. com., 1976-82, 97-98, mem. legis. com., 1982-84, 97-98. Recipient cert. study internat. and Chinese law East Chinese Inst. Politics and Law, Willamette U. Law Sch., Shanghai, People's Republic China, 1988. Mem.: ABA, Assn. Wis. Sch. Adminstrs., Washington County Bar Assn., Milw. Bar Assn. (cts. com. 1995—, criminal bench/bar com. 1997—, family bench/bar com. 1997—, civil bench/bar com. 2000—), Wis. Bar Assn. (bench/bar com. 1986—88, 1997—), Nat. Assn. for Ct. Adminstrn., Nat. Jud. Coll., Justinian Soc., U. Wis.-Washington County Found. Inc. (bd. dirs. 1993—94), U.S. Martial Arts Assn. (8th degree Black Belt Judo 2003, inductee Martial Arts Hall of Fame 2002, 2003), Universal Tae Kwon Do Assn. (3d degree Black Belt 1988), U.S. Judo Assn. (6th degree Black Belt 1995), Rotary (bd. dirs. West Bend Sunrise Club 1990—91, Paul Harris fellow). Roman Catholic. Avocations: Tae Kwon Do, Judo, photography, model railroading, Tai Chi. Office: Milw County Ct House Rm 104 901 N 9th St Milwaukee WI 53233-1425 E-mail: jon.sanfilippo@milwaukee.courts.state.wi.us.

SANFORD, BRUCE WILLIAM, lawyer; b. Massena, N.Y., Aug. 5, 1945; s. Doris (Suhrland) Sanford; m. Marilou Green, May 17, 1980; children: Ashley Anne, Barrett William. BA, Hamilton Coll., 1967; JD, NYU, 1970. Bar: N.Y. 1970, Ohio 1971, D.C. 1981, Md. 1985. Staff reporter Wall St. Jour., 1966-67; assoc. Baker and Hostetler, Washington, 1971-79, ptnr., 1979—. Author: Sanford's Synopsis Law of Libel and Privacy, rev. edit., 1991, Libel and Privacy, 2nd edit., 1991, Don't Shoot the Messenger: How Our Growing Hatred of the Media Threatens Free Speech for All of Us, 1999. Trustee Nat. Symphony Orch. Assn.; bd. dirs. Thomas Jefferson 1st Amendment Ctr., U. Va., Charlottesville; pres. Washington Nat. Cathedral Assn., 2002--. Mem. ABA (governing bd., forum com. on communication law, chmn. defamation torts com. 1985-86). Communications. Office: Baker & Hostetler LLP 1050 Connecticut Ave NW Washington DC 20036-5304

SANFORD, JOHN JOSEPH, lawyer, director; b. Providence, Sept. 24, 1944; s. Albert C. and Helen (Regan) S.; m. Claire Louise Hosinski, July 19, 1969; children: Ellen, Mary, Martha, Anna. BS, USAF, 1966; JD cum laude, Suffolk U., 1973. Bar: Maine 1973, Mass. 1973, U.S. Dist. Ct. Maine 1973. Ptnr. Harmon, Jones, Sanford & Elliott, Camden, Maine, 1973—. Vis. lectr. Law Sch., Harvard U., Cambridge, Mass., 1978— ; dir. Wayfarer Marine Corp., Camden, Maine, 1997—. Chmn. bd. trustees Camden Cmty. Hosp., 1983-84, N.E. Health, Rockport, Maine, 1984-86; trustee Camden Area YMCA, 1975-78, Camden Pub. Libr., pres., 1996-2001. Capt. USAF, 1966-70, Vietnam. Mem. ABA, ATLA, Maine Bar Assn., Maine Trial Lawyers Assn., Camden Squash Club. Roman Catholic. Federal civil litigation, State civil litigation, General practice. Home: Harbor Rd Camden ME 04843 Office: Harmon Jones Sanford & Elliott 20 Mechanic St Camden ME 04843-1707 E-mail: jsanford@mint.net.

SANG, PETER BENNETT, lawyer; b. N.Y.C., July 28, 1941; m. Penelope M. Keenan, Aug. 24, 1996. BA in Econs., Bucknell U., 1962; LLB, Boston U., 1965, LLM in Taxation, 1967. Bar: Mass. 1965, U.S. Ct. Claims 1970, U.S. Tax Ct. 1970, Maine 1971. Tax acct. Coopers & Lybrand, Boston, 1965-68; assoc. Gadsby & Hannah, Boston, 1968-71; pvt. practice Peter B. Sang, P.A., Portland, Maine, 1971-99, Trenton, Maine, 1999—. Commr. Maine Lottery, Augusta, 1973-77. Mem. Maine Bar Assn. (chmn. IRS tax liaison com. 1984—). Corporate taxation, Estate taxation, Personal income taxation. Office: 32 Dayton Pt Ln Trenton ME 04605

SANGERMAIN, LYZETTE, lawyer, mediator; b. San Juan, P.R., Nov. 28, 1959; d. Manuel M. and Elsa S. Fernandez; m. Larry W. Glover. BS, Fla. State U., 1980; JD, U. Fla., 1985. Bar: Fla., U.S. Dist. Ct. (mid. dist.) Fla. Assoc. Kuvin and Denman, Ft. Lauderdale, 1987—90, Lawrence, Landis and Morgan, Orlando, 1990—93; mng. atty. Geico Ins. Co., Orlando, 1993—95; atty., mediator Cobe, Cole and Bell, Maitland, Fla., Watson, White, Upchurch and Fraxadas, Maitland, 1995—2000, Fraxadas Mediation Firm, Maitland, 2000—03. Pres. A Civilized Divorce, Inc., Winter Park, Fla., 1999—2003. Author: (book) Parenting Notebook, 2002. Pres. Richard Hainan Nat. Park Found., Orlando, 1995—2003; bd. dirs. Planned Parenthood Greater Orlando, 1998—2003. Mem.: ABA (cert.), Acad. Profl. Mediation, Fla. Exec. Women, Assn. Conflict Resolution. Alternative dispute resolution. Office: Fraxades Mediation Firm 1051 Winderly Pl Ste 201 Maitland FL 32751 Fax: 407-661-9006. E-mail: lyzettesg@aol.com.

SANGMEISTER, GEORGE EDWARD, lawyer, consultant, former congressman; b. Joliet, Ill., Feb. 16, 1931; s. George Conrad and Rose Engaborg (Johnson) S.; m. Doris Marie Hinspeter, Dec. 1, 1951; children: George Kurt, Kimberley Ann. BA, Elmhurst Coll., 1957; LLB, John Marshall Law Sch., 1960, JD, 1970. Bar: Ill. 1960. Ptnr. McKeown, Fitzgerald, Zollner, Buck, Sangmeister & Hutchison, 1969-89; justice of peace, 1961-63; states atty. Will County, 1964-68; mem. Ill. Ho. of Reps., 1972-76, Ill. Senate, 1977-87, 101st-103rd Congresses from 4th (now 11th) Dist. Ill., 1989-95; ret., 1995; cons. McKeown, Fitzgerald, Zollner, Buck, Hutchison, Ruttle and Assocs., 1990—. Chmn. Frankfort Twp. unit Am. Cancer Soc., Will County Emergency Housing Devel. Corp.; past trustee Will County Family Svc. Agy.; past bd. dirs. Joliet Jr. Coll. Found., Joliet Will County Ctr. for Econ. Devel., Silver Cross Found., Silver Cross Hosp. With inf. AUS, 1951-53. Mem. ABA, Ill. Bar Assn., Assn. Trial Lawyers Am., Am. Legion, Frankfort (past pres.), Mokena C. of C., Old Timers Baseball Assn., Lions. Home: 20735 Wolf Rd Mokena IL 60448-8927

SANISLO, PAUL STEVE, lawyer; b. Cleve., Feb. 8, 1927; s. Paul and Bertha (Kasa) S.; m. Mary Ellen P. Conroy, May 7, 1949; 1 child, Susan J. BA, Baldwin-Wallace Coll., 1948; JD, Cleve. State U., 1961. Bar: Ohio 1961, U.S. Dist. Ct. (no. dist.) Ohio 1964. Order clk. Am. Agrl. Chem. Co., Cleve., 1948-52; safety engr. Park Drop Forge Co., Cleve., 1952-62, personnel mgr., 1954-62; assoc. then ptnr. Spohn & Sanislo, L.P.A., Cleve., 1962-81; pres., 1981-86; ptnr., pres. Sanislo, Bacevice & Assocs. LPA, Cleve., 1987-98; pres. Sanislo & Assocs. Co. LPA, 1998-2000; of counsel Stewart & Dechant, Cleve., 2000—. Spl. counsel Atty. Gen. Ohio, 1971; arbitrator Am. Arbitration Assn., 1972-78. Mem. Cleve. City Coun., 1964-67; trustee Cleve.-Marshall Law Sch., 1962-63; trustee Cleve.-Marshall Ednl. Found., 1963-68, pres., 1980-83; mem. Solon city Bd. Edn., Ohio, 1972-83, pres., 1974-83; chmn. Solon Charter Rev. Commn., 1971, mem., 2000—; past mem., organizer, legal adv. Solon Drug Abuse Ctr.; mem. Cuyahoga County Dem. Exec. Com.; ward leader 29th Ward Dem. Club, 1965-71, also past pres.; trustee Solon Dem. Ward Club, 1972-75. Recipient Disting. Svc. award City of Solon, 1984, Solon Bd. Edn., 1984, Solon Edn. Assn., 1984. Mem. Bar Assn. Greater Cleve. (Merit Svc. award 1978-79, chmn. workers compensation sect. 1975-96), Ohio Bar Assn., Cuyahoga County Bar Assn., Assn. Trial Lawyers Am., Cleve.-Marshall Law Sch. Alumni Assn. (pres. 1967-68), Hungarian Bus. and Tradesmen's Club (pres. 1967-68), Cleve. Assn. Compensation Attys. (pres. 1973-86). Democrat. Roman Catholic. Avocations: golf, travel. General practice, Personal injury (including property damage), Workers' compensation. Office: Stewart & DeChant 1440 Standard Bldg Cleveland OH 44113 E-mail: psanislo@stewartdechant.com.

SANNER, ROYCE NORMAN, lawyer; b. Lancaster, Minn., Mar. 9, 1931; s. Oscar N. and Clara Sanner; m. Janice L. Sterne, Dec. 27, 1972; children— Michelle Joy, Craig Allen. BS, Minn. State U., Moorhead, 1953; LLB cum laude, U. Minn., 1961. Bar: Minn. 1961, U.S. Dist. Ct. Minn. 1961, U.S. Supreme Ct. 1981. Tchr. English Karlstad (Minn.) High Sch., 1955-57; counsel IDS Life Ins. Co., Mpls., 1961-68, v.p., gen. counsel, 1969-72, exec. v.p., gen. counsel, 1972-77; dir. corp. devel. Am. Express Fin. Advisors, Mpls., 1968-69, v.p., gen. counsel, 1975-78, v.p., 1978-80, v.p., gen. counsel, 1980-82; v.p. law Northwestern Nat. Life Ins. Co., Mpls., 1982-83, sr. v.p., gen. counsel, sec., 1983-96, ReliaStar Fin. Corp. (formerly known as NWNL Cos., Inc.), Mpls., 1988-96; of counsel Maslon Edelman Borman & Brand, Mpls., 1996—. Bd. dirs. Fairview Univ. Med. Ctr., Friendship Found., Inc., Fraser Cmty. Svcs. Served with U.S. Army, 1953-55. Mem. ABA, Minn. Bar Assn., Hennepin County Bar Assn., Fed. Bar Assn., Assn. of Life Ins. Counsel, Minn. Corp. Counsel Assn., Rotary. Corporate, general, Insurance, Securities. Home: 734 Widsten Cir Wayzata MN 55391-1784 Office: Maslon Edelman Borman & Brand 3300 Wells Fargo Ctr 90 S 7th St Ste 3300 Minneapolis MN 55402-4140 E-mail: rsampls@aol.com.

SANO, JEANNINE YOO, lawyer; b. Seoul, Republic of Korea; m. Kazuhiko Sano. AB with honors, Stanford U.; JD, U. Calif., San Francisco. Mng. ptnr. Dewey Ballantine LLP, Palo Alto, Calif. Mem.: AIPLA, ITC Trial Lawyers Assn., Stanford Alumni Assn. Intellectual property. Office: Dewey Ballantine LLP 2300 Geng Rd Palo Alto CA 94303

SANSEVERINO, RAYMOND ANTHONY, lawyer; b. Bklyn., Feb. 16, 1947; s. Raphael and Alice Ann (Camerano) S.; m. Karen Marie Mooney, Aug. 24, 1968 (dec. 1980); children: Deirdre Ann, Stacy Lee; m. Victoria Vent, June 6, 1982 (div. 1995); m. Kimberley Frank, May 11, 2002. AB in English Lit., Franklin & Marshall Coll., 1968; JD cum laude, Fordham U., 1972. Bar: N.Y. 1973, U.S. Dist. Ct. (so. and ea. dists.) N.Y. 1973, U.S. Ct. Appeals (2d cir.) 1974, U.S. Supreme Ct. 1986. Assoc. Rogers & Wells, N.Y.C., 1972-75, Corbin & Gordon, N.Y.C., 1975-77; ptnr. Corbin Silverman & Sanseverino LLP, N.Y.C., 1978—2001, mng. ptnr., 1985—2001; ptnr. Brown Raysman Millstein Felder & Steiner LLP, 2001—, chair comml. real estate leasing group, 2001—. Contbr. articles to profl. jours.; articles editor Fordham Law Rev., 1971-72. Recipient West Pub. Co. prize, 1972. Mem. ABA, Assn. Bar City of N.Y., N.Y. State Bar Assn., Twin Oaks Swim and Tennis Club (bd. dirs. 1981-2002, pres. 1993-2001), Alumni Assn. Franklin and Marshall Coll. (bd. dirs. 2001—) Republican. Roman Catholic. Landlord-tenant, Property, real (including real estate development, water). Office: Brown Raysman et al 900 3d Ave New York NY 10022 E-mail: rsanseverino@brownraysman.com.

SANTAPIETRO, LISA, lawyer; b. Newark, Oct. 21, 1969; d. John Joseph and Linda. BA, NYU, 1991; JD, Seton Hall U., 1994. Bar: N.J., Pa., U.S. Dist. Ct. N.J. Jud. law clk. Superior Ct. N.J., Newark, 1994-95; atty. Riker, Danzig, Scherer, Hyland & Peretti, Morristown, N.J., 1995—. Cert. Family Mediator. Vol. domestic violence crisis response team Morris County Prosecutors Office, N.J. Family and matrimonial. Office: Riker Danzig et al Headquarters Plz 1 Speedwell Ave Ste 2 Morristown NJ 07960-6823

SANTELLE, JAMES LEWIS, prosecutor; b. Milw., Sept. 10, 1958; s. James Nathaniel and Carol Jean (Hasley) S. BA, Marquette Univ., 1980; JD, Univ. Chgo., 1983. Bar: Wis. 1983, U.S. Dist. Ct. (ea. and we. dist.) 1983, U.S. Ct. Appeals (7th cir.) 1983. Clerk Hon. Judge Robert W. Warren, Milw., 1983-85; asst. U.S. atty. Ea. Dist. Wis., Milw., 1985—, civil divsn. chief, 1993—99, interim U.S. atty., 2001—02; prin. dep. dir. Exec. Office U.S. Attys., U.S. Dept. Justice, Washington, 1999—2001, exec. asst. U.S. atty., 2002—. Profl. responsibility com., investigator Wis. Bd. of Attys., 1993-99, Ea. dist. of Wis. Bar Assn. (sec. 2001-). Editor: The Milw. Lawyer, 1986-92. Bd. dirs. Waukesha County Coun. Alcoholism and Other Drug Abuse, 1993-99; citizen counselor Badger Boys State, 1986—; coach Wis. Bar Found. High Sch. Mock Trial Tournament, 1986-99. Avocations: running, swimming. Office: US Atty Office 517 E Wisconsin Ave Rm 530 Milwaukee WI 53202-4580

SANTMAN, LEON DUANE, lawyer, former federal government executive; b. Phila., July 29, 1930; s. Elmer William and Anna Mary (Moffitt) S.; m. Juliet Gloria Peacock, June 16, 1952; 1 dau., Lorri Leigh Santman Myers. BS, U. S., COAST Guard Acad., 1952; LLB, U. Houston, 1953; LLM, George Washington U., 1968. Bar: Tex. 1963, Md. 1974. Commd. ensign U.S. Coast Guard, 1952, advanced through grades to comdr., 1967, ret., 1972; assoc. gen. counsel Cost of Living Council, Washington, 1972-74; asst. gen. counsel U.S. Dept. Transp., Washington, 1974-77, dir. Materials Transp. Bur., 1977-85; dir. ship ops. Maritime Adminstrn., 1985-88. Episcopalian.

SANTOPIETRO, ALBERT ROBERT, lawyer; b. Providence, R.I., Oct. 18, 1948; s. Alfred and Marie (Epifanio) Santopietro; m. Linda Stuart, 1994; children: Hope, Spencer, Anna. BA, Brown U., 1969; JD, U. Va., 1972. Bar: R.I. 1973, Conn. 1983, Mass. 1997, U.S. Dist. Ct. R.I. 1973, Ill. 1974, U.S. Dist. Ct. Mass. 1997. Atty. Met. Life Ins. Co., Oak Brook, Ill., 1974—75, Seligman Group, N.Y.C., 1975—76, Mut. Benefit Life Ins. Co., Newark, 1976—78, asst. counsel, 1978—81, counsel, 1982—; assoc. counsel Conn. Mutual Life Ins. Co., Hartford, 1981—82, counsel, 1995—; 2d v.p. and assoc. gen. counsel Mass. Mutual. Finance, Property, real (including real estate development, water). Home: 142 Pond Brook Rd Huntington MA 01050-9620 Office: 1500 Main St Ste 2800 Springfield MA 01115 Office Fax: 413-226-2068. E-mail: asantopietro@massmutual.com.

SANTORO, FRANK ANTHONY, lawyer; b. Plainfield, N.J., Dec. 14, 1941; s. Frank V. and Nancy M. (Scavuzzo) S.; m. Patricia Ferrante, Oct. 10, 1964; children— Frank, Jennifer. B.S. in Chemistry, Seton Hall U., 1963, J.D., 1970. Patent atty. Exxon Corp., Linden, N.J., 1970-73; sole practice, South Plainfield, N.J., 1973— ; atty. Planning Bd. Borough South Plainfield, 1971-73; mcpl. prosecutor Borough South Plainfield, 1972. Councilman Borough South Plainfield, 1977-79, mcpl. atty., 1985-93; mcpl. chmn. South Plainfield Republican Orgn., 1981-84. Mem. Middlesex County Bar Assn., UNICO Nat. Roman Catholic. General practice, Probate (including wills, trusts), Property, real (including real estate development, water). Office: 129 S Plainfield Ave PO Box 272 South Plainfield NJ 07080-0272

SANTORO, THOMAS MEAD, lawyer; b. Glens Falls, N.Y., Feb. 16, 1946; m. Corinne Collins, Mar. 27, 1981. AB, Colgate U., 1967; JD, Union U., Albany, N.Y., 1972. Bar: N.Y., Fla., U.S. Dist. Ct. (no., so., ea. and we. dists.) N.Y., U.S. Dist. Ct. (so. dist.) Fla., U.S. Ct. Appeals (2d and 11th cirs.), U.S. Supreme Ct. Atty. Legal Aid, N.Y.C., 1972-73, Cmty. Legal Rights Found., Inc., Albany, N.Y., 1973-74; asst. atty. gen. N.Y. State Dept. Law, Albany, 1974-76; asst. counsel SUNY, Albany, 1976-79; assoc. Bouck, Holloway & Kiernan, Albany, 1979-81; dep. univ. counsel Cornell U., Ithaca, N.Y., 1981-97; gen. counsel Fla. Internat. U., Miami, 1997—2002; of counsel Jackson Lewis LLP, Miami, 2003—. Contbr. chpt. to book. Trustee Albany Law Sch. of Union U., 1992—. Mem. N.Y. State Bar Assn.,

Fla. Bar Assn., Dade County Bar Assn., Nat. Assn. Coll. and Univ. Attys. Avocations: boating, skiing, bicycling. General civil litigation, Education and schools, Labor (including EEOC, Fair Labor Standards Act, labor-management relations, NLRB, OSHA). Home: 4161 Malaga Ave Coconut Grove FL 33133-6324 Office: 11200 SW 8th St Miami FL 33199-0001 E-mail: santorot@jacksonlewis.com.

SANTOS, ERIC CHIONG, lawyer; b. Manila, Philippines, Sept. 1, 1959; s. Francisco Lopez and Evangelina Chiong Santos; m. Elizabeth Garcia Inton, Jan. 6, 2000; children: Hans, Katrina, Francis. BS in Bus. Econ., U. of the Philippines, Quezon City, 1980, MBA, 1982, law, 1984. Lectr. U. of the Philippines, 1982—90; assoc. lawyer. Ponce Enrile Cayetano & Reyes, 1989—90; sr. assoc. Bengzon Zarraga Narciso, 1990—95; ptnr. Castillo Laman Tan Pantaleon & San Jose, 1995—2002; founder, mng. ptnr. De Borja Santos Torcuator & Santos Law Offices, 2002—. Editor articles to profl. jour. Mem.: Telecom. and Broadcast Atty., Maritime Lawyers Assn., Philippine Bar Assn., Intergrated Bar Philippines, Rotary Club of Commonwealth. Roman Catholic. Office: De Borja Santos Torcuator & Santos Unit 3201-B East Tower Philippine Stock Exchange Ortigas Ctr Pasig City Philippines 1605

SANTOS, LEONARD ERNEST, lawyer; b. Caracas, Venezuela, Aug. 5, 1946; s. Paul Joseph and Frieda (Epstein) S.; m. Jeannie Bernadette Niedermeyer, Oct. 28, 1978; children: Jonathan, Matthew, Andrew. BA cum laude, Tufts U., 1967; JD, NYU, 1971. Bar: Ariz. 1972, D.C. 1972, U.S. Dist. Ct. D.C. 1972, U.S. Ct. Appeals (9th and 5th cirs.) 1972, U.S. Supreme Ct. 1972. Law clk. to cir. judge U.S. Ct. Appeals (9th cir.), San Francisco, 1971-72; assoc. Hogan & Hartson, Washington, 1972-76; sr. atty. internat. affairs U.S. Dept. Treasury, Washington, 1976-83; internat. trade counsel U.S. Senate Fin. Com., Washington, 1983-87; ptnr. Verner, Liipfert, Bernhard, McPherson & Hand, Washington, 1987-89, Perkins Coie, Washington, 1989-98, World Mae, Washington, 1998-99, Santos Family Found., Washington, 2000—; pres. Martin Santos Properties, LLC, 2001—. Note and comment editor NYU Law Jour., 1970; contbr. legal publs.; editor ABA Compendium of Foreign Trade Remedy Laws, 1998. Exec. dir. Dole for Pres. campaign, Washington, 1988, 96. Mem. NAFTA (chpt. 19 dispute settlement panels) Republican. Roman Catholic. Avocations: architecture, economics. Private international. Office: Santos Family Found Ste 400 1775 Pennsylvania Ave NW Washington DC 20006 E-mail: santlen@aol.com.

SAPORITO, STEVEN, lawyer; b. Bklyn., Nov. 1, 1965; s. Rudolph Saporito. AB, U. Mich., 1987; JD, NYU, 1991. Bar: N.Y. Solo practitioner law, Bklyn., 1991—. Commercial, consumer (including collections, credit), General practice, Personal injury (including property damage).

SAPP, JOHN RAYMOND, lawyer; b. Lawrence, Kans., June 18, 1944; s. Raymond Olen and Amy (Kerr) S.; m. Linda Lee Tebbe, July 3, 1965; children: Jeffrey, Jennifer, John. BA, U. Kans., 1966; JD, Duke U., 1969. Bar: Wis. 1969, U.S. Dist. Ct. (ea. dist.) Wis. 1969, U.S. Ct. Appeals (7th cir.) 1974, U.S. Ct. Appeals (4th cir.) 1984, U.S. Supreme Ct. 1974. Assoc. Michael, Best & Friedrich, Milw., 1969-76, ptnr., 1976-90, mng. ptnr., 1990—. Dir. Roadrunner Freight Systems, Milw., 1992—. Bd. dirs. Milw. Symphony, 1981-95, mem. exec. com., 1993-95; bd. dirs. Boy Scouts Am., Milw., 1986—, pres. 1990-92; mem. Milw. Arts Bd., 1990, Greater Milw. Com.; bd. dirs. Zool. Soc., 1995—, v.p., 2000—; bd. dirs. Lex Mundi, 1997-2000, mem. exec. com., 1997-2001; bd. dirs. Jr. Achievement Greater Milw., 2001—. Avocations: golf, curling, print collecting. Labor (including EEOC, Fair Labor Standards Act, labor-management relations, NLRB, OSHA). E-mail: jrsapp@mbf-law.com.

SAPP, SUSAN KUBERT, lawyer; b. Lincoln, Nebr., June 12, 1965; d. Wayne William and Carole Grace (Burt) Kubert; m. Willie Leon Sapp, Mar. 26, 1988; children: Joshua A., Jared R., Jamison C. BS in Criminal Justice, U. Nebr., Lincoln, 1986, JD, 1989. Bar: Nebr. 1989; U.S. Dist. Ct.; Am. Acad. Adoption Lawyers, 1991; cert. fed. ct. mediator Fed. Ct. Dist. of Nebr., Lincoln, 1996—. Lawyer, ptnr. Cline Williams law Firm, Lincoln, Nebr., 1989—; adj. prof. U. Nebr. Lincoln Coll. Law, 1992—99. Contbr. articles to profl. jours. Southern Baptist. General civil litigation, Education and schools, Labor (including EEOC, Fair Labor Standards Act, labor-management relations, NLRB, OSHA). Office: Cline Williams Wright Johnson & Oldfatner 233 S 13th St 1900 US Bank Bldg Lincoln NE 68508

SAPP, WALTER WILLIAM, lawyer, energy company executive; b. Linton, Ind., Apr. 21, 1930; s. Walter J. and Nona (Stalcup) S.; m. Eva Kaschner, July 10, 1957 (dec.); children: Karen Elisabeth, Christoph Walter. AB magna cum laude, Harvard, 1951; JD summa cum laude, Ind. U., 1957. Bar: Ind. 1957, N.Y. 1959, Colo. 1966, U.S. Supreme Ct. 1972, Tex. 1977. Pvt. practice, N.Y.C., 1957-60, 63-66; practice in Paris, 1960—63; assoc. atty. Cahill, Gordon, Reindel & Ohl, Paris, 1960-63, N.Y.C., 1957-60, 63-65, partner, 1966; gen. counsel Colo. Interstate Corp., 1966-76, v.p., 1968-76, sec., 1971-76, sr. v.p., dir., exec. com., 1973-75, exec. v.p., 1975-76; v.p. Coastal States Gas Corp., 1973-76; sr. v.p., gen. counsel Tenneco, Inc., Houston, 1976-92, sec., 1984-86; pvt. practice Houston, 1992—. Editor-in-chief Ind. U. Law Jour., 1956-57. Trustee Houston Ballet, 1982-85, Awty Internat. Sch., 1989-98, 99—, vice-chmn., 1994-97, pres. 1997-98, chmn., 1999-2002, pres., 2002—; bd. dirs. Harris County Met. Transit Authority, 1982-84, Houston Internat. Protocol Alliance, 1992-94, Houston Symphony, 1989—, v.p., 1991-94, 2001-; adv. bd. Inst. for Internat. Edn. S.W. region, 1987—, chmn., 1992-94, Internat. and Comparative Law Ctr. Southwestern Legal Found., 1976-92. Lt. USNR, 1951-54. Recipient Chevalier, Ordre Nat. du Mérit, France. Mem.: ABA, Houston Bar Assn., Assn. Bar City of N.Y., Tex. Bar Assn., N.Y. State Bar Assn., Alliance Française Houston (bd. dirs. 1989—2001, v.p. 1991—94, 1998—2001), French-Am. C. of C. (bd. dirs. 1987—92), Order of Coif. Mem. United Ch. of Christ. Corporate, general, Private international, Securities. Office: 1111 Hermann Dr Unit 8B Houston TX 77004-6928

SARGEANT, ERNEST JAMES, lawyer, educator; b. Spokane, Wash., Sept. 26, 1918; s. Ernest Edward and Louise (McWhinnie) S.; m. Helene Sophie Kazanjian, Jan. 29, 1944 BA cum laude, Harvard U., 1940, LL.B. magna cum laude, 1947. Bar: Mass. 1947. Assoc. Ropes & Gray, Boston, 1947, 52-56, ptnr., 1956-90, of counsel, 1991—. Lectr. law Harvard U. Law Sch., Cambridge, Mass., 1961-62, 65-92; adj. prof. Boston Coll. Law Sch., 1990-98. Grad. treas. Harvard Law Rev., Cambridge, 1971-98. Capt. U.S. Army, 1942-46, 51-52. Mem. Am. Law Inst. (council), ABA, Boston Bar Assn. Clubs: Union (Boston); Country (Brookline, Mass.). Corporate, general, Mergers and acquisitions. Home: 24 Highgate Wellesley Hills MA 02481-1420 Office: Ropes & Gray 1 International Pl Boston MA 02110-2624

SARGUS, EDMUND A., JR., judge; b. Wheeling, W.Va., July 2, 1953; s. Edmund A. Sr. and Ann Elizabeth (Kearney) S.; m. Jennifer L. Smart, Jan. 7, 1978; 2 children. AB with honors, Brown U., 1975; JD, Case Western Res. U., 1978. Bar: Ohio 1978, U.S. Dist. Ct. (so. dist.) Ohio 1979, U.S. Dist. Ct. (no. dist.) Ohio 1981, U.S. Ct. Appeals (6th cir.) 1985, U.S. Dist. Ct. (no. dist.) W.Va. 1988, U.S. Ct. Appeals (4th cir.) 1988. Assoc. Cinque, Banker, Linch & White, Bellaire, Ohio, 1978-79, Stanley C. Burech, St. Clairsville, Ohio, 1980-82; ptnr. Burech & Sargus, St. Clairsville, 1983-93; U.S. Atty. Dept. of Justice, Columbus, Ohio, 1993-96; dist. judge U.S. Dist. Ct. (so. dist.) Ohio, Columbus, 1996—. Spl. counsel Ohio Atty. Gen., Columbus, 1979-93. Solicitor Village of Powhattan Point, Ohio, 1979-93; councilman City of St. Clairsville, 1987-91. Mem. ABA, Ohio Bar Assn. Office: US Dist Ct 85 Marconi Blvd Columbus OH 43215-2823

SARNER, RICHARD ALAN, lawyer; b. Stamford, Conn., Aug. 6, 1955; s. George and Patricia (Sloman) S.; m. Sharyn Frank, Apr. 5, 1986; children: Bryan, Lauren. BA, Dartmouth Coll., 1977; JD, Hofstra U., 1980. Bar: N.Y. 1982, U.S. Dist. Ct. (so. and ea. dists.) N.Y. 1982, U.S. Ct. Appeals (2d cir.) 1985, U.S. Dist. Ct. (no. dist.) N.Y. 1989, Conn. 1990, U.S. Dist. Ct. Conn. 1991, U.S. Supreme Ct. 1991. Assoc. Shea & Gould, N.Y.C., 1980-82, D'Amato & Lynch, N.Y.C., 1982-84, Lowenthal, Landau, Fischer & Ziegler, P.C., N.Y.C., 1984-90; sole practice Stamford, Conn., N.Y.C., Conn., 1990—. Bd. dirs. The Stamford Mus. and Nature Ctr., 1993-99; trustee King & Low-Heywood Thomas Sch., 1994—. Mem. ABA, N.Y. State Bar Assn., Conn. Bar Assn., Stamford/Norwalk Regional Bar Assn., Nat. Network Estate Planning Attys. Democrat. Estate planning, Probate (including wills, trusts), Estate taxation. Home: 122 Frost Pond Rd Stamford CT 06903-3031 Office: 184 Atlantic St Stamford CT 06901-3518 also: 465 Park Ave Ste 10C New York NY 10022 E-mail: rsarner@sarnerlaw.com.

SARNO, MARIA ERLINDA, lawyer, scientist; b. Manila, Philippines, July 26, 1944; BS in Chemistry magna cum laude, U. Santo Tomas, Philippines, 1967; MS in Chemistry summa cum laude, Calif. State U., Long Beach, 1975; JD cum laude, Western State U., 1993. Bar: Calif. 1994, U.S. Patent Office, 1993. Instr. U. Santo Tomas, Philippines, 1967-68; sr. chemist, analytical rsch. and quality assurance Rachelle Labs., Long Beach, Calif., 1969-74; teaching/rsch. asst. Calif. State U., Long beach, 1971-73; mgr. in charge of radioisotope section Curtis Nuclear Lab., L.A., 1974; assoc. chemist, asst. to dir. quality control Nichols Inst., San Pedro, Calif., 1974-75; mgr. rsch. and devel. Baxter Healthcare, Hyland, Calif., 1975-91; legal coord. sci. affairs Immunotherapy div. Baxter Biotech, Irvine, Calif., 1991-93, mgr. regulatory affairs, 1994-95; pvt. law practice, 1994—; bd. dirs. Small Bus. Fin. Devel. Corp. Editorial bd: (tech. editor) Western State U. Law Review; Contbr. articles to profl. jours.; patentee in field. Pres. Asian Bus. Assn. Orange County, 2001. Mem. ABA, Los Angeles County Bar Assn., Am. Chem. Soc., Am. Intellectual Property Law Assn., Filipino Am. C. of C. Orange County (bd. dirs., v.p.). Estate planning, Intellectual property, Patent. Home: 12541 Kenobi Ct Cerritos CA 90703-7756 E-mail: lindasarno@aol.com.

SARTAIN, JAMES EDWARD, lawyer; b. Ft. Worth, Feb. 9, 1941; s. James F. and May Belle (Boaz) S.; m. Barbara Hardy, Aug. 17, 1962; 1 child, Bethany Sartain Hughes. BA, Tex. A&M U., 1963; LLB, Baylor U., 1966. Bar: Tex. 1966, U.S. Ct. Mil. Appeals, 1971, U.S. Dist. Ct. (no. dist.) Tex. 1974. Staff atty. Dept. Justice, Washington, 1970-72; staff atty. to U.S. Sen. William L. Scott Fairfax, Va., 1972; pvt. practice Ft. Worth, 1973—2001, Abilene, Tex., 2001—. Bd. dirs. Ft. Worth Boys Club, 1980-89, Oakwood Cemetery, Ft. Worth, 1979-84; adv. dir. Grady McWhinney Rsch. Found., Abilene, Tex., CAP Initiatives, LLC, Austin, Tex. Capt. arty. U.S. Army, Vietnam. Fellow Coll. State Bar Tex.; mem. ABA, NRA, VFW, Abilene Bar Assn., Baylor Law Alumni Assn., Masons, Phi Delta Phi. Republican. Presbyterian. Commercial, consumer (including collections, credit), Commercial, contracts (including sales of goods; commercial financing), Corporate, general. Home: PO Box 450 Abilene TX 79604-0450

SARTOR, DANIEL RYAN, JR., lawyer; b. Vicksburg, Miss., June 2, 1932; s. Daniel Ryan and Lucy Leigh (Hubbs) S.; m. Olive Guthrie Moss, Oct. 12, 1957; children— Clara M., Daniel Ryan, Walter M. BA, Tulane U., 1952, LL.B., 1955. Bar: La. 1955. Instr. Tulane U., New Orleans, 1955-56, asst. prof., 1956-57; ptnr. Snellings, Breard, Sartor, Inabnett & Trascher, Monroe, La., 1957—. Contbr. articles to profl. jours. Fellow Am. Coll. Trust and Estate Counsel, Am. Bar Found., La. Bar Found.; mem. La. State Law Inst. (mem. council 1969— , sec. civil law sect. 1969-97, sr. officer 1997—), La. State Bar Assn. (chmn. sect. on trust estate, probate and immovable property 1973-74, bd. govs. 1974-75), Lotus Club, Bayou DeSaird Country Club. Democrat. Methodist. Banking, Corporate, general, Oil, gas, and mineral. Home: 2405 Pargoud Blvd Monroe LA 71201-2326 Office: Snellings Breard Sartor 1503 N 19th St Monroe LA 71201-4960

SARTORIUS, PETER S. lawyer; b. Jan. 15, 1947; BA, Williams Coll., 1968; JD, U. Va., 1974. Bar: Pa. 1975. Law clk to Hon. Leonard P. Moore U.S. Ct. Appeals (2nd cir.), 1974-75; ptnr. Morgan, Lewis & Bockius, LLP, Phila. Corporate, general, Mergers and acquisitions, Securities. Office: Morgan Lewis & Bockius LLP 1701 Market St Philadelphia PA 19103-2903 E-mail: psartorius@morganlewis.com.

SASSAN, DENNIS DONALD, lawyer; b. Chgo., Apr. 16, 1942; s. John Joseph and Grace Elizabeth (Gendusa) S.; m. Carol Jo Krejci, Aug. 22, 1964 (div. Oct. 1994); children: Anthony J., Dino J. JD, DePaul U., 1965. Bar: Ill. 1965, U.S. Dist. Ct. (no. dist.) Ill. 1965. Trust adminstr. Ctrl. Nat. Bank, Chgo., 1964-65; estate tax atty. U.S. Dept. Treasury, Chgo., 1965-70; pvt. practice Chgo., Oakbrook Terrace and Niles, Ill., 1970—. Mem. FBA, Ill. State Bar Assn., Chgo. Bar Assn. Family and matrimonial, Probate (including wills, trusts), Property, real (including real estate development, water). Home: 9042 N Cumberland Ave Niles IL 60714 Office: Sassan and Sassan 7788 N Milwaukee Ave Niles IL 60714 E-mail: legal@callero.com.

SASSOON, ANDRE GABRIEL, lawyer; b. Cairo, Apr. 13, 1936; came to U.S., 1959; s. Gabriel and Sarine (Tawil) S.; m. Barbara Dee Freedman, Aug. 15, 1965 (div. 2001); children: Daniel, Gabriel, Sarina. GCE, Oxford & Cambridge, England, 1953; JD, Villanova U., 1969; LLM, Harvard U., 1970. Bar: Pa. 1969, N.Y. 1970. Product mgr. Rohm & Haas Co., Phila., 1960-66; law clk. Dist. Atty.'s Office, Phila., 1968; assoc. Weil, Gotshal & Manges, N.Y.C., 1970-73; pvt. practice N.Y.C., 1973—; pres., CEO Sterimed Internat., Inc., 1999—. Dir. elem. Youth in Distress, N.Y.C., 1982—; v.p., dir. internat. Anti-Drug Abuse Found., N.Y.C., 1987—; v.p., dir., mem. exec. com. Hebrew Immigrant Aid Soc., N.Y.C., 1977—; internat. sec., gov. bd. internat. govs. World Sephardi Fedn., N.Y.C., 1988—; co-pres., chmn., U.S. com., dir. internat. Jewish Com. for Sephardi '92, N.Y.C., 1989—; mem. N.Y. State Christopher Columbus Quincetenary Commn., Statewide Outreach Com., 1991—. Editor Villanova Law Rev.; contbr. articles to profl. jours. Chmn. bd. Sloan's Auctioneers & Appraisers, 2001—03, chmn., 1953—, Sloans and Kenyon, 2003—. With USAR, 1960—66. Recipient Israel Trade award Govt. of Israel, 1985. Mem. ABA, Am. Arbitration Assn. (panel mem. 1971—), Am. Soc. Internat. Law, Order of the Coif, 0840 Internat. Pvt., 0860 Internat. Pub. Private international, Public international. Home: 641 Fifth Ave Apt 30H New York NY 10022 Office: 600 Madison Ave New York NY 10022-1615 E-mail: AndreSassoon@aol.com.

SATINSKY, BARNETT, lawyer; b. Phila., June 17, 1947; s. Alex and Florence (Talsky) S.; m. Fredda Andrea Wagner, June 17, 1973; children: Meagen, Sara Beth, Jonathan. AB, Brown U., 1969; JD, Villanova U., 1972. Bar: Pa. 1972, U.S. Dist. Ct. (ea. dist) Pa. 1975, U.S. Dist. Ct. (mid. dist.) Pa. 1975, U.S. Ct. Appeals (3d cir.) 1981. Law clk. Phila. Ct. Common Pleas, 1972-73; dep. atty. gen. Pa. Dept. Justice, Harrisburg, 1973-75; 1st asst. counsel Pa. Pub. Utility Commn., Harrisburg, 1975-77, chief counsel, 1977; assoc. Fox, Rothschild, O'Brien & Frankel, LLP, Phila., 1978-81; ptnr. Fox Rothschild, Phila., 1981—. Children Svcs. Rev. com., United Way Southeast Pa., 1984-86; bd. dirs. ACLU, Harrisburg, 1973-74, Voyage House, Inc., 1994-96. Mem. ABA (pub. utility, labor and employment law sects., employee benefits com. 1984—), Pa. Bar Assn. (labor rels., pub. utility law sects. 1980—, pub. utility law com., governing coun. 1991-93), Phila. Bar Assn. (labor law com. 1980—, chmn. pub. utility law com. 1988-91), Nat. Assn. Coll. and Univ. Attys., Nat. Assn. Regulatory Commrs. (staff subcom. law 1977), Soc. for Human Resource Mgmt., Tau Epsilon Law Soc. Democrat. Jewish. Civil rights, Labor (including EEOC, Fair Labor Standards Act, labor-management relations, NLRB, OSHA), Utilities, public. Office: Fox Rothschild 2000 Market St Philadelphia PA 19103-3291 E-mail: bsatinsky@frof.com.

SATO, GLENN KENJI, lawyer; b. Honolulu, Jan. 6, 1952; s. Nihei and Katherine (Miwa) S.; m. Donna Mae Shiroma, Apr. 4, 1980 (dec. Aug. 1985); m. Nan Sun Oh, Mar. 27, 1987 (dec. Nov. 1997); children: Gavan, Allison, Garrett; m. Sandra K. Kumagai, Nov. 21, 1999. BBA, U. Hawaii, 1975; JD, U. Calif., San Francisco, 1977. Bar: Hawaii 1978, U.S. Dist. Ct. Hawaii, 1978, U.S. Ct. Claims 1990. Assoc. Fujiyama, Duffy & Fujiyama, Honolulu, 1978-80, 83-87, ptnr., 1987-95; stockholder Law Offices of Glenn K. Sato, Honolulu, 1980-82; pres. ISL Svcs., Inc., Honolulu, 1983; ptnr. Sato & Thomas, Honolulu, 1995-98; pvt. practice Honolulu, 1998—. Vice chmn. Pattern Jury Instrn. Com., State of Hawaii, Honolulu, 1993. Treas. Polit. Action Com., Honolulu, 1993. Mem. Platform Assn., Beta Gamma Sigma. Avocations: golf, hunting, target shooting, surfing. General civil litigation, Commercial, consumer (including collections, credit), Commercial, contracts (including sales of goods; commercial financing). Office: Ste 1020 1001 Bishop St Honolulu HI 96813-3481

SATO, GREG Y. lawyer; BSEE, U. Tex.; MSEE, UCLA; JD, U. Calif., Hastings. Bar: Calif., Hawaii. Assoc. Fenwick & West LLP, Palo Alto, Calif. Intellectual property. Office: Fenwick and West LLP 2 Palo Alto Sq Palo Alto CA 94306

SATORIUS, DANIEL MARK, lawyer, film producer, television producer; b. Normal, Ill., July 13, 1951; s. Richard Ben and Erma Satorius; m. Tonda Lu Mattie, Aug. 10, 1974; children: Ashley Mattie, Taylor Mattie, Perry Mattie. BA, U. Iowa, 1973, MA, 1976; JD, So. Ill. U., 1978. Bar: Ill. 1978, Minn. 1979, U.S. Dist. Ct. Minn. 1979. Shareholder Satorius and Mattie P.A., St. Paul, 1981-89; of counsel Leonard, Street & Deinard, Mpls., 1989-94; shareholder, officer Abdo Abdo Broady & Satorius PA, Mpls., 1994—. Adj. prof. law William Mitchell Law Sch., St. Paul, 1997—; adj. faculty, lectr. Mpls. Cmty. & Tech. Coll., Mpls., 1989—, Music Tech., Mpls., 1995-98; nat. spkr., writer on entertainment law topics. Editor, prin. author: The Practical Musician, 1993; filmmaker (motion picture) Fear and Trembling, 1976 (Acad. award nomination student film award competition), assoc. prodr. Varian and Putzi, 2003, assoc. editor Entertainment and Sport Lawyer. Officer, bd. dirs. IFP/Mpls.-St. Paul, 1987—, pres., 2002—; bd. dirs. Resources and Counseling for Arts, St. Paul, 1991-97; mem. adv. bd. Minn. Chorale, Mpls., 1994—; mem. Gov.'s Task Force on Music and Recording Arts, St. Paul, 1984. Mem. ABA (Entertainment and Sports Forum 1981—, assoc. editor., Entertainment and Sports Law Lawyer, 1999—), NARAS, Minn. State Bar Assn. (mem., past chair art and entertainment law sect. 1985—). Entertainment, Intellectual property, Securities.

SATOVSKY, ABRAHAM, lawyer; b. Detroit, Oct. 15, 1907; s. Samuel and Stella (Benenson) S.; m. Toby Nayer, Sept. 4, 1938 (dec.); children: Sheldon Baer, James Bennett. BA, U. Mich., 1928, JD, 1930. Bar: Mich. 1930, U.S. Supreme Ct. 1930. Assoc. William Henry Gallagher, Detroit, 1930-65. Bldg. chmn. lawyers com. United Found. and Torch Dr. Co-chmn. profl. divsn. Allied Jewish Campaign; adv. coun. United Synagogue Am.; del. Jewish Cmty. Coun. Detroit; v.p. Mosies Chetim Orgn. Detroit; bd. dirs. Detroit Svc. Group, past chmn. fgn. mission; active fund raiser Greater Miami United Jewish Appeal; mem. fund dr. com. U. Mich. Law Sch.; trustee Clover Hill Park Cemetery, 1978-81, trustee emeritus, 1982—; bd. dirs. Congregation Shaarey Zedek, Southfield, Mich., past pres., 1959-62. Recipient Sem. award Jewish Theol. Sem. Am., 1952; citation of merit Jewish Welfare Fedn., Detroit; Jerusalem award State of Israel Bond Orgn.; numerous other awards. Mem. ABA, Mich. Bar Assn., Detroit Bar Assn., Oakland County Bar, Nat. Fedn. Jewish Men's Clubs (founder, past pres., hon. life pres., Gt. Lakes regional award 1977, Ma'Asim Tovim (Good Deeds) award 1989), Am. Arbitration Assn., Jewish Hist. Soc. Mich. (mem. adv. bd.), Am. Jewish Hist. Soc., Am. Judicature Soc., Men's Club Congregation Shaarey Zedek (past pres., hon. life pres.), Standard Club, B'nai B'rith (past pres. Detroit), Hadassah (life), Phi Beta Delta (merged with Pi Lambda Phi). Home and Office: 28455 Northwestern Hwy Southfield MI 48034-1823

SATOVSKY, STACEY YAEL, lawyer; b. Huntington, N.Y., Nov. 9, 1970; d. Gerald and Nili Finger; m. Jonathan Matthew Satovsky, May 26, 1996. AB, U. Mich., 1992; JD, Fordham U., 1995. Bar: N.Y. 1996. Assoc. Skadden, Arps, Slate, Meagher & Flom, N.Y.C., 1995-97; atty. Instinet Corp., N.Y.C., 1997-99. Mem. Order of Coif. Commercial, contracts (including sales of goods; commercial financing), Corporate, general. Home: 137 Sands Point Rd Port Washington NY 11050

SATTER, RAYMOND NATHAN, judge; b. Denver, Oct. 19, 1948; s. Charles Herbert and Muriel Vera (Tuller); m. Suzanne Elizabeth Ehlers, May 28, 1977. BA, U. Denver, 1970; JD, Cath. U., 1973. Bar: Colo. 1973, U.S. Dist. Ct. Colo. 1973, U.S. Ct. Appeals (10th cir.) 1973, U.S. Supreme Ct. 1976, U.S. Tax Ct. 1981. Assoc. Wallace, Armatas & Hahn, Denver, 1973-75; ptnr. Tallmadge, Wallace & Hahn, Denver, 1975-77; pvt. practice Denver, 1978-87; Denver County judge, 1987—; presiding judge Denver County Ct., 2001—. Gen. counsel Satter Dist., Denver, 1977-78; assoc. mcpl. judge City of Englewood, Colo., 1985-86; mem. Colo. Supreme Ct. Com. on Civil Rules, 1988—. Pres. Young Artists Orch. Denver, 1985-87; sec. Denver Symphony Assn., 1985-86. Mem. Colo. Bar Assn. (ethics com.), Denver Bar Assn. (bd. trustees 1998-2001, Jud. Excellence award 1992, 95). Avocations: sailing, opera, classical music, fishing, bridge. Office: Denver County Ct 108 City & County Bldg 1437 Bannock St Denver CO 80202-5337 E-mail: rsatter@ci.denver.co.us.

SATTERLEE, TERRY JEAN, lawyer; b. Kansas City, Mo., Aug. 28, 1948; d. Charles Woodbury and Francis Jean (Shriver) S.; m. William W. Rice, Jan. 9, 1982; children: Cassandra Jean Rice, Mary Shannon Rice. BA, Kans. U., 1970; JD, U. Mo., 1974. Bar: Mo. 1974. Lawyer Arthur Benson Assocs., Kansas City, Mo., 1974-77, Freilich & Leitner, Kansas City, 1977-78, U.S. Environ. Protection Agy., Kansas City, 1978-83; of counsel Lathrop & Norquist, Kansas City, 1985-87, ptnr., 1987—, mem. exec. com., 1997-2001. Contbr. articles to profl. jours. Chmn. Bd. Zoning Adjustment, Kansas City, 1983-87, Mo. State Parks Adv. Bd., 1997-2002; Kansas City Hazardous Materials com; steering com. COMPASS Met. Planning, Kansas City, 1990-93. Mem. Mo. Bar Assn. (chair environ. com. 1990-93), Kansas City Bar Assn. (environ. com. chmn. 1986-90, chair 2001), Mo. C. of C. (natural resource coun. 1990-2002, bd. dirs. 1999-2002, chair 1998-2002), Kansas City C. of C. (environ. com. chmn. 1992), Women's Pub. Svc. Network (named Top 25 US Women in Bus. 2000), Am. Met. Sewerage Assn. (legal affairs com. 1992—). Democrat. Episcopalian. Administrative and regulatory, Environmental, Property, real (including real estate development, water). Office: Lathrop & Gage 2345 Grand Blvd Kansas City MO 64108-2612

SAUFER, ISAAC AARON, lawyer; b. Bronx, N.Y., June 16, 1953; s. Solomon and Beatrice (Kanofsky) S.; m. Debra Edith Goldberg, June 26, 1977; children: Suzanne, Nancy, Scott, Daniel, Jonathan. BA, Yeshiva U., N.Y.C., 1975; JD, Bklyn. Law Sch., 1978; LLM in Taxation, NYU, 1982. Bar: N.Y. 1979, N.J. 1986, Fla. 1986, Conn. 1987. Summer intern N.Y. County Dist. Attys. Office, N.Y.C., 1976; legal editor Prentice-Hall, Inc., Englewood Cliffs, N.Y., 1979-80; assoc. Kurzman Karelsen & Frank, LLP, N.Y.C., 1980-85, ptnr., 1986—. Adj. assoc. prof. NYU Sch. Continuing and Profl. Studies, N.Y.C., 1988—; lectr. seminars, 1991, 93, 95, 97, 98, 2000, 2001. Co-author: (N.Y. real property forms) Bergerman & Roth, 1986-87. Estate planning, Probate (including wills, trusts), Estate taxation. Office: Kurzman Karelsen & Frank LLP 230 Park Ave Rm 2300 New York NY 10169-2399

SAUFLEY, LEIGH INGALLS, judge; m. William Saufley; 2 children. Grad., Maine Sch. Law. Pvt. practice, Ellsworth; asst. counsel U.S. VA; asst., then dep. atty. gen. Maine, 1981-90; judge Maine Dist. Ct., 1990—93; justice Maine Superior Ct, 1993—97; assoc. justice Maine Supreme Judicial Ct., 1997—2001, chief justice, 2001—. Office: Cumberland County Courthouse PO Box 368 142 Federal St Portland ME 04112-0368

SAUL, IRVING ISAAC, lawyer; b. July 9, 1929; s. Israel Jacob and Jennie (Green) S.; m. Lita Brown, Dec. 29, 1950; children: Joanne Ilene, Sandra Lynn. BA, Washington and Jefferson Coll., 1949; LLB, U. Pitts., 1952; postgrad., Georgetown U., 1949, Ohio State U., 1951. Bar: Ohio 1952, U.S. Dist. Ct. (so. dist.) Ohio 1954, U.S. Supreme Ct. 1961, U.S. Ct. Appeals (6th cir.) 1966, U.S. Dist. Ct. (no. dist.) Ohio 1967, U.S. Dist. Ct. (ea. dist.) Wis. 1973, U.S. Ct. Appeals (7th cir.) 1978, U.S. Ct. Appeals (4th cir.) 1978, U.S. Ct. Appeals (fed. cir.) 1991. Pvt. practice, Dayton, Ohio, 1952—. Cons. in antitrust litigation; bd. advs. Fed. Civil Practice Abstracts, 1986-88, Ohio Dist. Ct. Rev., 1988—; adj. prof. complex litigation Sch. of Law U. Dayton, 1996-98; lectr. in field. Contbr. articles to profl. jours. James Gillespie Blaine scholar, 1948. Mem. Ohio Bar Assn. (chmn. fed. cts. and practice com. 1977-79, chmn. pvt. enforcement com. 1979-92, bd. govs. antitrust sect. 1982-94), Dayton Bar Assn. (chmn. fed. ct. practice com. 1976-77, 78-80, chmn. com. on judiciary 1987-88), Am. Judicature Soc., Masons (Shriner), Phi Beta Kappa. Jewish. Antitrust, Federal civil litigation, State civil litigation. Office: 113 Bethpolamy Ct Dayton OH 45415-2512

SAUNDERS, BRYAN LESLIE, lawyer; b. Newport News, Va., Apr. 18, 1945; s. Raymond Hayes and Lois Mae (Pair) S.; divorced; children: Kelly Brooke, Justin Lee; m. Anne Mason Dunbar, July 15, 1995. BS, East Tenn. State U., 1967; JD, U. Tenn., 1973. Bar: Va. 1973, U.S. Dist. Ct. (ea. dist.) Va. 1973, U.S. Ct. Appeals (4th cir.) 1991. Lawyer Cogdill & Assocs., Newport News, Va., 1973—76; pvt. practice Newport News, 1976—; ptnr. Saunders & Lawrence, 2002—. Commr. in chancery Cir. Ct. of Newport News, 1990-97. Sgt. U.S. Army, 1968-71. Decorated Bronze star, 1971; recipient Outstanding Svc. to Law Enforcement Newport News and Police Dept., 1986. Mem. Va. Bar Assn., Nat. Assn. Criminal Def. Lawyers, Va. Coll. Criminal Def. Attys., Pi Kappa Phi, Pi Gamma Mu. Avocations: chess, bridge, bowling. Criminal, General practice, Juvenile. Office: 728 Thimble Shoals Blvd Ste C Newport News VA 23606-4546 E-mail: bryansaund@aol.com.

SAUNDERS, CHARLES ALBERT, lawyer; b. Boulder, Colo., Jan. 18, 1922; s. Charles and Anna (Crouse) S.; m. Betti Friedel, Oct. 18, 1946; children— Melanie, Stephen, Cynthia, Shelley. BA, U. Houston, 1942; LLB, U. Tex., 1945. Bar: Tex. bar 1945. Since practiced in, Houston; partner firm Fulbright & Jaworski, L.L.P., 1959—. Editor: How To Live-and Die-With Texas Probate, 8 vols., 1968, Texas Estate Administration, 1975. Bd. dirs. Houston Symphony Soc., 1964— ; bd. dirs. Am. Lung Assn., San Jacinto, 1965— , pres., 1972-73; past mem. bd. govs. U. Houston. Recipient Leon Jaworski award for cmty. svc. Houston Bar Assn., 1997, U. Tex. Law Sch. Disting. Alumnus award in Cmty. Svc., 1999. Mem. ABA, State Bar Assn., Houston Bar Assn., Am. Coll. Trust and Estate Coun. (regent 1972-80, pres. 1978-79), Internat. Acad. of Estate and Trust Law, Assn. Cmty. TV (bd. dirs. 1970—). Republican. Presbyterian. Corporate, general, Probate (including wills, trusts). Home: 19 Willowron Dr Houston TX 77024-7618 Office: Fulbright & Jaworski 1301 Mckinney St Ste 5100 Houston TX 77010-3031 E-mail: csaunders@fulbright.com.

SAUNDERS, GEORGE LAWTON, JR., lawyer; b. Mulga, Ala., Nov. 8, 1931; s. George Lawton and Ethel Estell (York) S.; children: Kenneth, Ralph, Victoria; m. Terry M. Rose. BA, U. Ala., 1956; JD, U. Chgo., 1959. Bar: Ill. 1960. Law clk. to chief judge U.S. Ct. Appeals (5th cir.), Montgomery, Ala., 1959-60; law clk to Justice Hugo L. Black U.S. Supreme Ct., Washington, 1960-62; assoc. Sidley & Austin, Chgo., 1962-67, ptnr., 1967-90; founding ptnr. Saunders & Monroe, Chgo., 1990—. With USAF, 1951-54. Fellow: Am. Coll. Trial Lawyers; mem.: Law Club, Quadrangle Club, Point-O-Woods Club, Chgo. Club, Order of the Coif, Phi Beta Kappa. Democrat. Baptist. Administrative and regulatory, Antitrust, General practice. Home: 179 E Lake Shore Dr Chicago IL 60611-1306 Office: Saunders & Monroe Ste 1302 33 N Dearborn St Chicago IL 60602

SAUNDERS, MARK A. lawyer; b. N.Y.C., July 9, 1946; s. Phillip George and Florence (Schell) S.; m. Paula Squillante, Sept. 2, 1972; children: David Prescott, Christina Joy. BA cum laude, Fordham U., 1968; JD, U. Va., 1972. Bar: N.Y. 1973, U.S. Dist. Ct. (so. dist.) N.Y.) 1973, U.S. Ct. Appeals (2d cir.) 1974, U.S. Ct. Appeals (D.C. cir.) 1987, U.S. Supreme Ct. 1987. Sr. ptnr. Holland & Knight, N.Y.C.; counsel to corp. fin. and mergers acquisitions depts. Morgan Stanley & Co. Inc., 1975-80; mem. faculty Internat. Law Inst., Washington, 1985—. Mem. comparative law delegation to govt. of People's Rep. of China, 1986; gen. counsel Softstrip Internat. Ltd. subs. Eastman Kodak Co., 1987; mem. adv. bd. Southwestern Legal Found.; bd. vis. Ave MAria Sch. Law, Ann Arbor, Mich., 2003—. Author: Amrican Depositary Receipts: An Introduction to U.S. Capital Markets For Foreign Companies, 1993, Fordham Internat. Law Jour., 1993; mng. bd. editors Va. Jour. Internat. Law, 1971-72; cons. editor China Banking and Fin., 1988-92. Chmn. charity benefit Ann. Good Counsel Awards Celebration, 1999, 2000; apptd. fed. adv. bd. nat. polit. action com., 1999; mem. fed. adv. bd. Ann Arbor Polit. Action Com. Jervey fellow in fgn. and comparative law Columbia U. Parker Sch. Internat. Law, 1972. Fellow Am. Coll. Investment Counsel; mem. ABA (coms. fed. securities, regulation and internat. securities matters and fgn. investment in U.S.), Assn. Bar City N.Y., Internat. Bar Assn., Legatus (pres. N.Y.C. chpt. 1998-2000), Phi Beta Kappa. Roman Catholic. Corporate, general, Private international, Securities. Home: 3 Nutmeg Dr Greenwich CT 06831-3211 Office: Holland & Knight 195 Broadway New York NY 10007-3100 E-mail: msaunders@hklaw.com.

SAUNDERS, MYRA KATHLEEN, dean, law librarian, educator; b. San Francisco, 1950; BA, U. Calif., Berkeley, 1972; MLS, U. So. Calif., 1973; JD, U. San Diego, 1979. Law libr. U. San Diego, Whittier Coll. Sch. Law, U. Calif., Berkeley; assoc. law libr. for pub. svcs. UCLA, 1983—89, law libr., prof. law in residence, 1989—, assoc. dean Hugh and Hazel Darling Law Libr., 1989—. Contbr. articles to profl. jours. Office: 1112 Law Bldg 405 Hilgard Ave Los Angeles CA 90095-1458*

SAUNDERS, PAUL CHRISTOPHER, lawyer; b. NYC, May 21, 1941; s. John Richard and Agnes Grace (Kelly) Saunders; m. Patricia Newman, Aug. 14, 1968; children: Dr. Paul Christopher, Michael Eagan. AB, Fordham Coll., 1963; JD, Georgetown U., 1966; Certificat d'Études Politiques, Institut d'Études Politiques, Paris, 1962. Bar: NY 1966, DC 1967, US Supreme Ct 1969. Assoc. Cravath, Swaine & Moore, NYC, 1971-77, ptnr., 1977—; dist. vis. prof. Georgetown U Law Ctr., 2003. Mem ed bd: Georgetown Law Jour, 1965—66; editor (editor-in-chief): The Adv., 1969—70. Trustee Fordham Univ, 1991—96; bd regents Georgetown Univ; chmn. bd. visitors Law Ctr. Georgetown Univ., 1996—97; trustee, vice-chmn Fordham Prep Sch, 1986—94; v.p., bd. dirs. Legal Aid Soc., 1983—88; bd dirs, trustee Lawyers Comt Civil Rights Under Law, 1985—, co-chair, 1995—97; v.p., trustee Vols. Legal Svc., Inc., 1999—; bd. dirs. Office of the Appellate Defender, 1999—; mem. N.Y. State Judicial Inst. on Professionalism in the Law, 2000—; mem Cardinal's Comt Laity, 1982—90; chmn bd dirs Const Project, 2000—. Capt JAGC U.S. Army, 1967—71. Decorated Meritorious Svc. medal; recipient John Carroll medal, Georgetown U., 1995, Whitney N. Seymour award, Lawyers Com. Civil Rights Under Law, 2000. Fellow: Am. Bar Found., Am. Coll. Trial Lawyers; mem.: ABA, London Ct. Internat. Arbitration, Assn. Bar City N.Y., NY State Bar Assn., Westchester Country Club (Rye, NY), Apawamis Club (Rye, NY), Knights Malta, Phi Beta Kappa, Pi Sigma Alpha. Democrat. Roman Catholic. Antitrust, Federal civil litigation, State civil litigation. Home: 1220 Park Ave New York NY 10128-1733 also: 455 Polly Pk Rd Rye NY 10580-1960 Office: Cravath Swaine & Moore, LLP Worldwide Plz 825 8th Ave Fl 39 New York NY 10019-7475 E-mail: psaunders@cravath.com.

SAUNDERS, RICHARD R. lawyer; b. Washington, May 15, 1951; s. Richard R. and Audrey H. Saunders; m. E. Dianne Moxon, Sept. 11, 1976; children: Tyler R., Daniel H., Jesse H. BA, Princeton U., 1973; JD, U. Richmond, 1976. Bar: Va. 1976. Assoc. Kuykendall, Whiting, Costello & Hanes, Leesburg, Va., 1976-82; ptnr. Hanes, Sevila, Saunders & McCahill, Leesburg, 1982—96, Sevila, Saunders & McCahill, Leesburg, 1996—98, Sevila, Saunders, Huddleston & White, Leesburg, 1998—. Mem. ethics com. Va. State Bar, 1985-87; pres. Loudoun County Bar Assn., Leesburg, 1988. Mem. Va. Trial Lawyers Assn. General civil litigation, Family and matrimonial. Office: Sevila Saunders Huddleston & White PC 30 N King St Leesburg VA 20176-2818

SAUNDERS, TERRY ROSE, lawyer; b. Phila., July 13, 1942; d. Morton M. and Esther (Hauptman) Rose; m. George Lawton Saunders Jr., Sept. 21, 1975. BA, Barnard Coll., 1964; JD, NYU, 1973. Bar: D.C. 1973, Ill. 1976, U.S. Dist. Ct. (no. dist.) Ill. 1976, U.S. Ct. Appeals (7th cir.) 1976, U.S. Supreme Ct. 1983. Assoc. Williams & Connolly, Washington, 1973-75, Jenner & Block, Chgo., 1975-80, ptnr., 1981-86, Susman, Saunders & Buehler, Chgo., 1987-94; pvt. practice Law Offices of Terry Rose Saunders, Chgo., 1995—2002; ptnr. Saunders & Doyle, Chgo., 2002—. Author: (with others) Securities Fraud: Litigating Under Rule 10b-5, 1989. Recipient Robert B. McKay award NYU Sch. Law. Mem. ABA (co-chair class actions and derivative suits com. sect. litig. 1992-95, task force on merit selection of judges, co-chair consumer and personal rights litig. com. sect. litig.), Chgo. Bar Assn., Order of Coif, Union League Club. Federal civil litigation, General civil litigation. Office: 33 N Dearborn St Chicago IL 60602 E-mail: trsaunders@saundersdoyle.com.

SAUSSER, GAIL DIANNE, lawyer; b. Richland, Wash., May 8, 1952; d. Lenard Merl and Julia Esther (Saxerud) Oathes; m. Harvey Wilson Sausser III, 1979 (div. 1982). BA in Humanities, Heritage Coll., Spokane, Wash., 1974; MA in Psychology, Antioch West, Vancouver, B.C., Can., 1977; postgrad., Seattle U., 1996-97; JD magna cum laude, Am. U., 1999. Cert. assoc. risk mgmt., Ins. Inst. Am. Counselor Chem. Dependency Program, Seattle, 1982-84; acctg. asst. Newdata Corp., Seattle, 1986-87; adminstrv. ins. broker Johnson & Higgins, Seattle, 1987-96, Ctr. Health Policy Rsch., George Washington U., 1998-99; assoc. Vinson & Elkins, Washington, 1999—2002; HIPAA compliance program mgr. Virginia Mason Med. Ctr., 2002—. Author: Transactions and Code Sets, 2000, HIPAA Facility Desk Reference, 2002, HIPAA Transaction Companion, 2003. Counselor Cmty. Mental Health Inst., Spokane, Wash., 1972-75, Seattle Mental Health Inst., 1975-77; pres. Acupuncture Rsch. Treatment Assn., Seattle, 1992-96; mem. rsch. roundtable King County Natural Health Clinic, Seattle, 1993-95, adv. bd., 1996-97; mem., co-chmn. evaluation com., managed care com. King County HIPAA Planning Coun., Seattle, 1996-97. Fellow, Ctrs. for Medicare and Medicaid Svcs., 1998. Mem.: Healthcare Fin. Mgmt. Assn. Avocation: writing. Administrative and regulatory, Health. Home: 933 Lake Washington Blvd S Seattle WA 98144

SAVAGE, DAVID WILLIAM, lawyer; b. Seattle, Nov. 14, 1944; s. Kenneth and Mary Savage; m. Sally Savage, Aug. 1, 1982; children: Jesse, Erin, Kathryn. BA in Polit. Sci., Wash. State U.; JD, U. Idaho. Bar: Wash. 1973, U.S. Dist. Ct. (ea. dist.) Wash. 1977, Idaho 1991, U.S. Dist. Ct. Idaho 1991, Mont. 1996, U.S. Ct. Appeals (9th cir.) 1997, U.S. Supreme Ct. 1999. Shareholder, pres. Irwin, Myklebust, Savage & Brown, P.S., Pullman, Wash., 1973—. Mem.: ABA, Wash. State Bar Assn. (pres.-elect 2002—), Idaho State Bar Assn. Personal injury (including property damage), Product liability, Alternative dispute resolution. Office: Irwin Myklebust Savage & Brown PS 1230 Bishop Blvd Pullman WA 99163 Office Fax: 509-332-6565.

SAVAGE, JOHN WILLIAM, lawyer; b. Seattle, Oct. 11, 1951; s. Stanley and Jennie Sabina (Siggstedt) S.; m. Rebecca Lee Abraham, Oct. 1, 1983; children: Bennett William, James Oliver. Student, Lewis and Clark Coll., 1969-71, JD Northwestern Sch. Law, 1977; BA, U. Wash., 1973. Bar: Oreg. 1977, Wash. 2002, U.S. Dist. Ct. Oreg. 1977, U.S. Ct. Appeals (9th cir.) 1977, U.S. Supreme Ct., 1985. Pvt. practice law, Portland, Oreg., 1977-79; ptnr. Bailey, Olstad, Rieke, Geil & Savage, P.C., Portland, 1979-80; ptnr., shareholder Rieke, Geil & Savage, P.C., Portland, 1980-95; shareholder Rieke & Savage, P.C., Portland, 1995—. Mem. Oreg. Literacy Inc., Portland, 1979-85; mem. standing com. City Club, Portland, 1984-88, chmn. law and pub. safety standing com. 1986-87. Recipient award of merit, Gerry Spence's Trial Lawyers Coll., 1999. Mem. ABA (chairperson young lawyers sect. Nat. Cmty. Law Week 1983-84, inmate grievance com. 1984-88), Assn. Trial Lawyers Am., Trial Lawyers for Pub. Justice, Oreg. Trial Lawyers Assn. (edn. com. 2002—), Oreg. Bar Assn. (def. of indigent accused com. 1985-89), Oreg. Criminal Def. Lawyers Assn. (bd. dirs. 1984-86), Multnomah Bar Assn. (v.p. young lawyers sect. 1980, pres.-elect 1981, pres. 1982, Disting. Svc. award, bd. dirs. 1989-92, task force chair 1992-93, jud. selection com. 1998-99, cir. ct. liaison com. 2002—, Award of Merit 1994). General civil litigation, Personal injury (including property damage), Professional liability. Home: 397 Furnace St Lake Oswego OR 97034-3957 Office: Rieke & Savage PC 140 SW Yamhill St Portland OR 97204-3007 E-mail: jwsavage@rieke-savage.com.

SAVAGE, JOSEPH FRANCIS, lawyer; b. Montague, Mass., Mar. 8, 1956; s. Joseph F. and Alice B. Savage; 1 child, Megan. BA, Harvard U., 1978; JD, U. Va., 1981. Law clk. to Hon. A. David Mazzone, Boston, 1981—82; assoc. Hale & Dorr, Boston, 1982—83; asst. U.S. atty. Office U.S. Atty., 1983—96; ptnr. Testa, Hurwitz & Thibeault, LLP, Boston, 1996—. Criminal, Intellectual property. Office: Testa Hurwitz and Thibeault LLP 125 High St Boston MA 02110 Office Fax: 617-248-7100. Business E-Mail: savage@tht.com.

SAVELA, ARI JUHANI, lawyer; MS in Econs., Turku (Finland) Sch. Econs. and Bus. Adminstrn., 1992; LLM, U. Turku, 1995, LLD, 1999. Rschr. U. Turku, 1995—99; lawyer Peltonen, Ruokonen & Itäinen Attys.-at-Law, Helsinki, Finland, 1999—2002, ptnr., 2002—. Docent in comml. law U. Turku, 1999—; expert concerning the reform of the companies act Dept. Justice, Helsinki, 2001—01. Contbr. articles to profl. jours.; author: Hostile Takeovers and Directors, 1999, Vahingonkorvaus Osakey Htiossa (Damages in Limited Companies), 1999. Mem.: Finnish Bar Assn. Corporate, general, Mergers and acquisitions, Securities. Office: Peltonen Ruokonen & Itäinen Fredrikinkatu 48 A 00100 Helsinki Finland E-mail: ari.savela@peltonenlaw.fi.

SAVELKOUL, DONALD CHARLES, retired lawyer; b. Mpls., July 29, 1917; s. Theodore Charles and Edith (Lindgren) S.; m. Mary Joan Holland, May 17, 1941; children: Jeffrey Charles, Jean Marie, Edward Joseph. BA magna cum laude, U. Minn., 1939; JD cum laude, William Mitchell Coll. Law, 1951. Bar: Minn. 1951, U.S. Dist. Ct. Minn. 1952, U.S. Ct. Appeals (8th cir.) 1960, U.S. Supreme Ct. 1971. Adminstrv. work various U.S. govt. depts., including Commerce, War, Labor, Wage Stblzn. Bd., 1940-51; mcpl. judge Fridley, Minn., 1952-53; pvt. practice law Mpls., St. Paul, Fridley, 1951-96; ret., 1997. Chmn. bd. Fridley State Bank, 1962-95; pres. Banrein, Inc., 1962-95, Babbscha Co., 1962-95; mem. faculty William Mitchell Coll. Law, 1952-59, corp. mem., 1956-99; sec. Fridley Recreation and Svc. Co., 1955-97; mem. Minn. Legislature, 1967-69. Mem. Gov.'s Com. Workers Compensation, 1965-67, Gov.'s Adv. Coun. on Employment Security, 1957-60, 62-63; gen. counsel Minn. AFL-CIO Fedn. Labor, 1952-71. 1st lt. AUS, 1943-46. Decorated Bronze Star; recipient Disting. Alumni award, Coll. Liberal Arts U. Minn., 1995, Hon. Ronald E. Hachey Outstanding Alumna/us award, Wm. Mitchell Coll. of Law Alumni Assn., 1997. Mem. ABA, Minn. Bar Assn. (chmn. 1957-58, bd. dirs. 1958-62, 68-69, labor law sect.), Justice William Mitchell Soc., Am. Legion, U. Minn. Pres.'s Club, Phi Beta Kappa. Roman Catholic. Banking, Corporate, general. Office: 916 Moore Lake Dr W Fridley MN 55432-5148

SAVELL, EDWARD LUPO, lawyer; b. Atlanta, Apr. 29, 1921; s. Leon M. and Lillian (Lupo) S.; m. Bettie Patterson Hoyt, Oct. 11, 1944; 1 dau., Mary Lillian Savell Clarke. BBA, Emory U., 1947, LL.B., 1949. Bar: Ga. 1948, U.S. Dist. Ct. (mid. and no. dist.) Ga.; cert. mediator and arbitrator, Ga. Assoc. A.C. Latimer, Atlanta, 1948-53; ptnr. Carter, Latimer & Savell, Atlanta, 1953-56, Woodruff, Latimer & Savell (and successor firms), Atlanta, 1956-87; of counsel Savell & Williams, Atlanta, 1987—. Instr. John Marshall Law Sch., 1951-55; dir. Legal Aid Soc., 1955-58; arbitrator Am. Arbitration Assn. and Fulton Superior Ct. Contbr. articles to legal jours. With USAF, 1942-45, CBI. Fellow Internat. Acad. Trial Lawyers (pres. 1978-79, Dean of Acad. 1976); mem. Atlanta Bar Assn. (sec.-treas. 1953-54), ABA, State Bar Ga., Ga. Def. Lawyers Assn. (founder, v.p.), Internat. Assn. Ins. Counsel, Atlanta Claims Assn., Lawyers Club Atlanta, Cherokee Town and Country Club, Commerce Club, Univ. Yacht Club (past commodore), Chi Phi, Phi Delta Phi (past pres.). Presbyterian. General civil litigation, Insurance, Securities. Office: Savell and Williams 1500 Equitable Bldg 100 Peachtree Atlanta GA 30303

SAVELL, POLLY CAROLYN, lawyer; b. N.Y.C., Oct. 24, 1960; d. Joel Morton and Elsie Rhea (Crane) S. BA, U. Md., 1982; diploma, Internat. Comp. Law Inst., Paris, 1983; JD, NYU, 1985. Bar: N.Y. 1986. Assoc. corp. and entertainment divsn. Battle Fowler, N.Y.C., 1986-87; atty. Columbia Pictures Entertainment Inc., N.Y.C., 1987-89; counsel Turner Broadcasting Sys. Inc., Atlanta, 1989-91; sole practice Atlanta, 1991-93; asst. gen. counsel WorldCom Inc., N.Y.C., 1993—2001; pvt. practice N.Y.C., 2001—. Bd. dirs. Eviction Intervention Svcs., Homeless Prevention, Inc. Mem. ABA, Fed. Comm. Bar Assn., Am. Corp. Counsel Assn., Assn. of Bar of City of N.Y. (telecom. law com.), Task Force Internat. Legal Studies. Democrat. Methodist. Commercial, contracts (including sales of goods; commercial financing), Communications, Private international. Office: 410 Park Ave Ste 1530 New York NY 10022

SAVETT, STUART HUBERT, lawyer; b. Phila., Jan. 9, 1939; s. Alan and Lee Savett; m. Sherrie Raiken, 1974 (div. 1992); children: Stacy L., Scott David, Lauren S.; m. Maxine Metzger Denker, Apr. 6, 2002. BA, Temple U., 1960; JD, Villanova U., 1963. Assoc. Dilworth Paxson LLP, Phila., 1963—69, of counsel, 2002—; ptnr. Kohn, Savett, Klein & Graf, Phila., 1969—91; mng. ptnr. Savett, Frutkin, Podell & Ryan, Phila., 1991—2002. Cons. Villanova (Pa.) Law Sch., 1998—. Dir. Jewish Cmty. Ctr., Phila., 1979—88. Mem.: Order of Coif, Fedn. Jewish Attys. (trustee 1982—86, 1995—99, 2000—). Securities, State civil litigation, General practice. Home: 404 Spring Graden Ln West Conshohocken PA 19428 Office: Dilworth Paxson LLP 3200 Mellon Bank Ctr 1735 Market ST Philadelphia PA 19103-7595 Office Fax: 215-575-7200. Business E-Mail: ssavett@dilworthlaw.com.

SAVILLE, DERRIC JAMES, lawyer; b. Ft. Madison, Iowa, Oct. 2, 1964; s. Jacob Abraham and Brenda K. (Lawrence) S.; m. Jeannene Irene Abbott, Mar. 21, 1987. BS, U. Iowa, 1987; M of Studies in Law, JD cum laude, Vt. Law Sch., 1991. Bar: Minn. 1991, U.S. Dist. Ct. Minn. 1995, Upper Sioux Cmty. Tribal Ct. 1996. Atty. Saville Law Office, Mpls., 1991—98; with Saville Title Svcs., Inc., Plymouth, Minn. Chair subcom. Dist. Planning Adv. Commn. #279, Maple Grove, Minn., 1994-96. Articles editor Ferae Naturae, 1991. State del. Reform Party, Maple Grove, 1996; chair mental health adv. bd. Hennepin County Commitment Def. Project, 1998-2002. Mem.: Brain Injury Assn. Minn. (bd. dirs., chair-elect 1996—, chair 1998—99), Minn. Head Injury Assn. (bd. dirs. 1995—96). Avocations: fishing, hiking, orienteering. Environmental, Personal injury (including property damage), Property, real (including real estate development, water). Home: 10835 101st Pl N Maple Grove MN 55369-3419 Office: Saville Title Svcs Inc 505 Hwy 169 N Ste 230 Plymouth MN 55441

SAVILLE, ROYCE BLAIR, lawyer; b. Cumberland, Md., Aug. 5, 1948; s. E. Blair and Audrey (Cosner) S.; m. Sharon Ann Brinkman, Apr. 3, 1981; children: Melissa Anne, Lauren Ashley, Meagan Elizabeth, Philip Clarke. BA, W.Va. U., 1970, JD, 1974. Bar: W.Va. 1974, U.S. Dist. Ct. (so. and no. dists.) W.Va. 1974. Assoc. William J. Oates, Jr. Atty. at Law, Romney, W.Va., 1974-75; ptnr. Oates & Saville Attys. at Law, Romney, 1975-78; pvt. practice Romney, 1978-99; mng. ptnr. Saville and Davis, PLLC, 1999-2001, Saville and Stewart, PLLC, 2001—. Pres. Potomac Land Co., 1975—; mental hygiene commr. Hampshire County, Romney, 1976—; mcpl. judge City of Romney, 1980-90. Mem. W.Va. Jud. Hearing Bd., Hampshire County Devel. Authority, Romney, Hampshire County Farm Bur., Nat. Trust for Hist. Preservation; dir. Potomac Highlands Travel Coun., Elkins, W.Va., 1984-88; mem. adv. bd. Peterkin Conf. Ctr. of Renewal, Romney, 1988-90; del. W.Va. Dem. Conv., Charleston, 1984; vestryman St. Stephen's Episcopal Ch., Romney, 1984-86, Bd. of Trustees, Indian Mound Cemetery 2003-. Mem. ABA, ATLA, NRA (life), W.Va. Bar Assn., South Br. Valley Bar Assn. (pres. 1996-97), W.Va. Trial Lawyers Assn., Waterfowl U.S.A. (life), N.Am. Hunting Club (life), Hampshire Camp 284 SCV (judge adv.), Civil War Preservation Trust, W.Va. Law Sch. Assn. (life), W.Va. U. Alumni Assn. (life), Masons (Clinton Lodge #86), Scottish Rite of Freemasonry, USA Valley of Martinsburg, Orient of W.Va., Osiris Temple AAONMS, Romney chpt. #84 OES, Rotary (Paul Harris fellow), Phi Alpha Delta (life). Democrat. Episcopalian. Avocations: gun collecting, antique collecting, local history. State civil litigation, General practice, Property, real (including real estate development, water), Criminal. Home: Liberty Hall 276 E Main St Romney WV 26757-1821 also: Mill Island Moorefield WV 26836 Office: 95 W Main St PO Box 2000 Romney WV 26757-2000 also: 113 Winchester Ave Moorefield WV 26836

SAVITT, SUSAN SCHENKEL, lawyer; b. Bklyn., Aug. 21, 1943; d. Edward Charles and Sylvia (Dlugatch) S.; m. Harvey Savitt, July 2, 1969 (div. 1978); children: Andrew Todd, Daniel Cory. BA magna cum laude, Pa. State U., 1964; JD, Columbia U., 1968. Bar: N.Y. 1968, U.S. Dist. Ct. (so. and ea. dists.) N.Y. 1973, U.S. Tax Ct. 1973, U.S. Ct. Appeals (2d cir.) 1981, U.S. Supreme Ct. 1980, U.S. Dist. Ct. (we. dist.) N.Y. 1996. Atty. Nassau County Legal Svcs., Freeport, N.Y., 1973-74; asst. corp. counsel City of Yonkers, 1977-78; from assoc. to ptnr. Epstein, Becker & Green, P.C., N.Y.C., 1978-94; ptnr. Winston & Strawn, N.Y.C., 1994—. Adj. prof. Elizabeth Seton Coll., Yonkers, 1982-83; mem. NYU exec. coun. Met. Ctr. for Ednl. Rsch. Devel. and Tng., 1987-90; mediator Vol. Mediation Panel, U.S. Dist. Ct. (so. dist.) N.Y., 1997—, U.S. Dist. Ct. (ea. dist.) N.Y., 1999—. Mem. Hastings-on-Hudson (N.Y.) Sch. Bd., 1984-93, v.p., 1986, 87-88, pres., 1989-90, 92-93; bd. dirs. Associated Blind, 1993-95, Nat. Child Labor Com., 2001—, Liberal Arts Alumni Coun., Pa. State U., 2001—; bd. dirs. Search for Change, 1996—2002, sec., 1998—2002; bd. dirs. Pa. State Profl. Women's Network of N.Y., 1996—, pres., 1998-2000. Mem. ABA (internat. law sect., litigation and labor law sect.), N.Y. State Bar Assn. (labor law sect., comml. litigation sect.), Women's Bar Assn., Fed. Bar Coun., Pa. State Alumni Club (v.p. Westchester County 1985-87), Phi Beta Kappa, Alpha Kappa Delta, Phi Gamma Mu, Pi Kappa Phi. Alternative dispute resolution, Federal civil litigation, Labor (including EEOC, Fair Labor Standards Act, labor-management relations, NLRB, OSHA). Office: Winston & Strawn 200 Park Ave New York NY 10166-0005

SAVRIN, LOUIS, lawyer; b. Phila., Jan. 20, 1927; s. William Philip and Anna (Sass) S.; m. Barbara J. Schwimmer, Jan. 16, 1954; children: Jonathan Eric, Philip Wade, Daniel Scott. BS, N.Y. U., 1948; JD, U. Pa., 1951. Bar: N.Y. 1952. Atty. tax dept. Arthur Young & Co. (C.P.A.'s), N.Y.C., 1951-55;

pvt. practice N.Y.C., 1955—. Gen. counsel, sec. Pickwick Internat., Inc., N.Y.C., 1965-77 Assoc. editor: U. Pa. Law Rev, 1949-51. Mem. sch. bd. Dist. 21, Bklyn., 1962-68; docent Whitney Mus. Am. Art. With AUS, 1945-46. Mem. N.Y. State Bar Assn., N.Y. County Lawyers Assn., Real Estate Tax Rev. Bar Assn.; mem. B'nai B'rith (pres. lodge 1957-59, named to lodge Hall of Fame 1967, Torch of Freedom award Anti-Defamation League 1982). Property, real (including real estate development, water), Probate (including wills, trusts), Estate planning. Home: 50 Park Ave Apt 17H New York NY 10016-3082 Office: 60 E 42nd St New York NY 10165-0006

SAWDEY, RICHARD MARSHALL, lawyer; b. Buffalo, Jan. 8, 1943; s. Marshall Douglas and Eleanor Katherine (Reichman) S.; m. Judith Hollister Helgeson, Aug. 12, 1967; children: David Marshall, Karin Ballard. BS, Mich. State U., 1965; JD, U. Mich., 1968. Bar: Ill. 1968. Assoc. McBride, Baker, Wienke & Schlosser, Chgo., 1968-73; atty. R.R. Donnelley & Sons, Chgo., 1974-75, asst. sec., 1975-83, sec., 1983-85; v.p., sec., 1985-88; of counsel Hoogendoorn & Talbot, Chgo., 1988—97, ptnr., 1998—. Mem. ABA, Ill. State Bar Assn., Chgo. Bar Assn. (chmn. fin. and investment svcs. com. 1994-95), Chgo. Estate Planning Coun. Corporate, general, Estate planning. Office: Hoogendoorn & Talbot 122 S Michigan Ave Ste 1220 Chicago IL 60603-6126

SAWICKI, DANIEL, judge; b. Dearborn, Mich., Nov. 30, 1938; s. Anthony Sawicki and Hattie Zdrodowski; m. Kathleen Rose Wozniak, Feb. 28, 1975 (div. June 1991); children: Mark, Michael, Kimberly, Nicole, James, Matthew; m. Mary Christine Hayes, July 11, 1998. BS, U. Detroit, 1962, JD, 1967. Bar: U.S. Dist. Ct. (ea. dist.) Mich. 1976, U.S. Ct. Appeals (6th cir.) 1977. Asst. city counsel City of Royal Oak, Mich., 1969—73, city counsel, 1973—80; dist. judge 44th Dist. Ct., Royal Oak, 1980—. Bd. dirs. South Oakland Boys and Girls Club, Royal Oak. Named Citizen of Yr., Met. Club Am., 1976. Mem.: Oakland County Dist. Judges Assn. (past pres. 1986), S. Oakland County Bar Assn. (past. pres.), Mich. Dist. Judges Assn., State Bar Mich. Roman Catholic. Avocations: golf, reading. Home: 1704 Woodsboro Royal Oak MI 48067 Office: 44th District Court 400 E Eleven Mile Rd Royal Oak MI 48068

SAWICKI, ZBIGNIEW PETER, lawyer; b. Hohenfels, Germany, Apr. 13, 1949; came to U.S., 1951; s. Witold and Marianna (Tukiendorf) S.; m. Katheryn Marie Loman, Aug. 19, 1972; children: James, Jeffrey, Jessica, Jason. BSChemE, Purdue U., 1972; MBA, Coll. St. Thomas, St. Paul, 1977; JD, Hamline U., 1980. Bar: Minn. 1980, U.S. Dist. Ct. Minn. 1981, U.S. Ct. Appeals (8th cir.) 1981, U.S. Patent and Trademark Office 1981, U.S. Ct. Appeals (fed. cir.) 1982, Can. Patent Office 1994, Can. Trademark Office 1995. Process engr. 3-M Co., St. Paul, 1973-75; process engrng. supr. Conwed Corp., St. Paul, 1975-77; shareholder, bd. dirs. Kinney & Lange, Mpls., 1980—. Bd. dirs. Orono (Minn.) Hockey Boosters, 1992—. With USAF, 1970-72. Mem. ABA, Am. Intellectual Property Assn., Internat. Trademark Assn., Minn. Intellectual Property Assn. (past treas.), Am. Legion. Intellectual property, Patent, Trademark and copyright. Home: 4510 N Shore Dr Mound MN 55364-9602 Office: Kinney & Lange 312 S 3d St Minneapolis MN 55415-1624 E-mail: zpsawicki@kinney.com.

SAWYER, CHRISTY CARLSON, lawyer; b. Memphis, Feb. 15, 1972; d. William Samuel and Dianne Carlson Sawyer. BA, U. Tenn., 1994, MS, 1995, JD, 1998. Bar: Tenn. 1998. Atty. Waller Lansden Dortch & Davis, PLLC, Nashville, 1998—. Health, Corporate, general, Mergers and acquisitions. Office: Waller Landsen Dortch & Davis PLLC 51 Union St Ste 2100 Nashville TN 37219 Office Fax: 615-244-6304. E-mail: csawyer@wallerlaw.com.

SAWYER, JAMES, lawyer; b. N.Y.C., Feb. 18, 1946; s. Jules and Florence Barbara (Wishnew) S.; m. Margot Peretz, June 8, 1995; children: Kim, Caryn. BA, Adelphi U., 1967; JD, St. Johns U., 1969. Bar: N.Y. 1970, U.S. Dist. Ct. (so. and ea. dist.) N.Y. 1971, U.S. Tax Ct. 1972, U.S. Ct. Appeals (2d cir.) 1972, U.S. Ct. Appeals (1st cir.) 1975, Fla. 1981, U.S. Supreme Ct. 1981. Ptnr. Martin, Van De Walle & Sawyer, Great Neck, N.Y., 1970-81, Hession, Halpern, Bekoff & Sawyer, Mineola, N.Y., 1982-87, Sawyer, Davis, Halpern and Demetri, Garden City, N.Y., 1987—. Pres. Temple Or-Elohim, Jericho, N.Y., 1987-89; active Nassau County Med. Malpractice Panel, 1982-86. Mem. ABA, N.Y. State Bar Assn., Nassau County Bar Assn. Jewish. General civil litigation, Personal injury (including property damage), Probate (including wills, trusts). Address: Sawyer Davis & Halpern and Demetri Esq 600 Old Country Rd Rm 330 Garden City NY 11530-2010. E-mail: jsawyer@sawyerlaw.com.

SAWYER, LEONARD SYLVESTER, retired lawyer; b. Lincoln, N.H., June 14, 1925; s. Howard Symmes and Rose Veronica (Eagan) S.; m. Caroline Eldora Smith, Sept. 7, 1960; children: Edward M., Charles L. BA, U. N.H., 1947; LLB, Boston U., 1950. Bar: N.H. 1950. Ptnr. Edes & Sawyer, Woodsville, N.H., 1954-56; pvt. practice Plymouth, N.H., 1956-94; ret., 1994. Justice Plymouth Dist. Ct., 1965-85. Selectman Town of Plymouth, 1963-65; moderator Plymouth Water and Sewer Dist., 1971—; del. N.H. Constl. Conv., 1984; mem. N.H. Audubon Soc., Plymouth Hist. Soc., New Hampton Hist. Soc., Upper Pemi Valley Hist. Soc.; local coord. FISH program, 1994—; vol. Plymouth Regional Sr. Ctr., Quincy Bog Natural Area. Served with U.S. Army, 1950-54. Mem. N.H. Bar Assn., Am. Judicature Soc., Lions (past pres. Plymouth chpt.), Grange (master, treas.), Am. Legion. Democrat. Roman Catholic. Avocations: hiking, swimming, reading. Family and matrimonial, Probate (including wills, trusts), Property, real (including real estate development, water). Home: 13 Cummings St Plymouth NH 03264-1106

SAWYER, RAYMOND TERRY, lawyer, consultant; b. Cleve., Oct. 1, 1943; s. R. Terry and Fanny Katherine (Young) S.; m. Katherine Margaret Schneider, Aug. 5, 1972; children: Margaret Young, John Terry. BA, Yale U., 1965; LLB, Harvard U., 1968. Bar: Ohio 1969, U.S. Dist. Ct. (no. dist.) Ohio 1970, prin., Sawyer LLC, 2002-. Assoc. Thompson Hine LLP, Cleve., 1968-76, ptnr., 1976—83, 1986—2001, chmn. bus. transactions and org. dept., 1998—2001, of counsel, 2002—; exec. dir. Ohio Housing Fin. Agy., Columbus, 1983-84; counsel to gov. State of Ohio, Columbus, 1984, chief of staff, 1985-86, chmn. Gov.'s commn. on housing, 1989-90; prin. Sawyer LLC, Cleve., 2002—. Bd. dirs. Premix, Inc., North Kingsville, Ohio. Assoc. prodr. : Frankie and Johnny in the Clair de Lune, 2002—03. Vol. VISTA, East Palo Alto, Calif., 1968—69; mem. Tech. Leadership Coun., 1987—95, Leadership Cleve., 1986—87, Cleve. Found. Study Commn. on Med. Rsch. Edn., 1991—92; chmn. George W. Codrington Charitable Found., 1989—; mem. Ohio Bd. Regents, Columbus, 1987—96, chmn., 1992—93; trustee Cleve. Ballet, 1987—2000, Cleve. Orch., 1993—, sec., exec. com., 1997—; mem. exec. com. MetroHealth Sys., 1998—; mem. Juilliard Coun. Juilliard Sch.; mem. pres.'s adv. coun. Case Western Res. U. Named Man of Yr. Womanspace, 1982. Mem. ABA, Ohio State Bar Assn. (chair corp. law com. 1993-95), Clevel. Bar Assn., Yale U. Alumni Assn. (pres. Cleve. chpt. 1980-81), Assn. Yale Alumni (del. 1996-99). Democrat. Presbyterian. Corporate, general, Finance. Office: Sawyer LLC 3900 Key Ctr Cleveland OH 44114-1216

SAWYER, SEAN JEFFREY, lawyer; b. Wheeling, W.Va., Mar. 27, 1971; s. Walter Kenneth and Shirley Joan Sawyer; m. Beth Ann Lowther, Sept. 20, 1997; children: Zechariah Matthew Turner, Ryan Michael, Nicholas Stanton. JD, W.Va. U., 1997. Bar: W.Va. 1998. Litigation assoc. Higinbotham & Higinbotham, PLLC, Fairmont, W.Va., 1996—. Mem.: ABA, W.Va. Trial Lawyers Assn., ATLA Nat. Coll. Advocacy, Phi Delta Phi. Personal injury (including property damage), Insurance, State civil litigation. Home: Rt 1 Box 189A Independence WV 26374 Office: Higinbotham & Higinbotham PLLC 201 Adams St Fairmont WV 26554 Office Fax: 304-366-2909. Personal E-mail: sawyer71@aol.com. E-mail: seanhiginbotham@wvdsl.net.

SAXBE, WILLIAM BART, lawyer, former government official; b. Mechanicsburg, Ohio, June 24, 1916; s. Bart Rockwell and Faye Henry (Carey) S.; m. Ardath Louise Kleinhans, Sept. 14, 1940; children: William Bart, Juliet Louise Saxbe Blackburn, Charles Rockwell. AB, Ohio State U., 1940; LL.B., 1948; hon. degrees, Central State U., Findlay Coll., Ohio Wesleyan U., Walsh Coll., Capital U., Wilmington Coll., Ohio State U., Bowling Green State U. Bar: Ohio 1948. Practiced in, Mechanicsburg, 1948-55; partner Saxbe, Boyd & Prine, 1955-58; mem. Ohio Gen. Assembly, 1947-48, 49-50; majority leader Ho. Reps., 1951-52, speaker, 1953-54; atty. gen. Ohio, 1957-58, 63-68; partner Dargusch, Saxbe & Dargusch, 1960-63; mem. U.S. Senate from, Ohio, 1969-74; atty. gen. U.S., 1974; ambassador to, 1975-77; partner firm Chester, Saxbe, Hoffman & Wilcox, Columbus, Ohio, 1977-81; of counsel firm Jones, Day, Reavis & Pogue, Cleve., 1981-84, Pearson, Ball & Dowd (merger Pearson, Ball & Dowd and Reed, Smith & McClay), Washington, 1984-93; ind. spl. counsel Central States Teamsters Pension Fund, 1982—; of counsel Chester Willcox & Saxbe, Columbus, Ohio, 1994—. Served with 107th Cav. AUS, 1940-42; Served with 107th Cav. USAAF, 1942-45; col. Res. Mem. Am., Ohio bar assns., Am. Judicature Soc., Chi Phi, Phi Delta Phi. Clubs: Mason (33d degree) (Columbus), University (Columbus), Columbus Athletic (Columbus), Columbus (Columbus), Scioto Country (Columbus); Urbana (Ohio) Country; Burning Tree Country (Bethesda, Md.); Country of Fla. (Boynton Beach). Republican. Episcopalian. Home: 1171 N Ocean Blvd Gulf Stream FL 33483-7273 Office: 16 S Main Mechanicsburg OH 43044

SAXL, RICHARD HILDRETH, lawyer; b. Boston, June 3, 1948; BA, U. Pa., 1970; JD, Rutgers U., Camden, N.J., 1975. Bar: Conn. 1976, U.S. Dist. Ct. Conn. 1976, U.S. Ct. Appeals (2d cir.) 1977. Assoc. Jerry Davidoff, Westport, Conn., 1976-78; ptnr. Davidoff & Saxl, Westport, 1979-94; pvt. practice law offices Richard H. Saxl, Westport, 1994—; town atty. Fairfield, Conn., 1997—99, 2001—. Mem. Fairfield Town Plan and Zoning Commn., 1981-93, chmn., 1991-93; chair Fairfield Land Acquisition com., 1997; mem. Fairfield Charter Revision Commn., 1984-85, 92. Recipient Svc. award, Conn. Fedn. Planning and Zoning Agys., 1993, cert. of commendation, Conn. Jud. Dept. Mem. Conn. Bar Assn., Westport Bar Assn., Pequot Yacht Club. Democrat. Avocations: squash, astronomy. Municipal (including bonds), Probate (including wills, trusts), Property, real (including real estate development, water). Home: 753 Sasco Hill Rd Fairfield CT 06824 Office: 5 Imperial Ave Westport CT 06880-4302 E-mail: rhsaxl@aol.com.

SAXMAN, ANNA ESTHER, lawyer; b. Latrobe, Pa., May 14, 1949; d. Harry Suydam and Eleanor Ruth S.; m. Robert Halpert, Feb. 18, 1989. BS magna cum laude, U. Vt., 1978, JD magna cum laude, 1985. Clk. to presiding justice Vt. Supreme Ct., Montpelier, 1985-86; assoc. Langrock, Sperry, Parker & Wool, Burlington, Vt., 1986—; atty. Vermont Def. Gen. Mem. Task Force on Gender Bias in the Legal System, Montpelier, 1988—. Editor U. Vt. Law Rev. Pres., bd. trustees Vt. Assn. for Mental Health, Montpelier, 1989—. Mem. ABA, Vt. Bar Assn. (chmn. women's sect. 1989—, chmn. com. on rights of the mentally and physically handicapped, 1988-89, pres.-elect 2002-03), Assn. Trial Lawyers Am. Office: Vermont Def Gen Office 120 State St Montpelier VT 05620-3301*

SAXTON, WILLIAM MARVIN, lawyer; b. Joplin, Mo., Feb. 14, 1927; s. Clyde Marvin and Lea Ann (Farnan) S.; m. Helen Grace Klinefelter, June 1, 1974; children: Sherry Lynn, Patricia Ann Painter, William Daniel, Michael Lawrence. AB, U. Mich., 1949, JD, 1952. Bar: Mich. Mem. firm Love, Snyder & Lewis, Detroit, 1952-53, Butzel, Long, Detroit, 1953—, dir., chmn., CEO, 1989-96, dir. emeritus, 1997—. Lectr. Inst. Continuing Legal Edn.; sec., bd. dirs. Fritz Broadcasting, Inc., 1983-97; mem. mediation tribunal hearing panel for 3d Jud. Dist. Mich., 1989—, 6th Jud. Dist., 1994—. Trustee Detroit Music Hall Ctr. Soc. for the Performing Arts, 1984-99; trustee Hist. Soc. U.S. Dist. Ct. (ea. dist.) Mich., 1992-95, pres., 1993-95. Recipient Distinguished award Mich. Road Builders Assn., 1987. Master of Bench Emeritus Am. Inn of Court; fellow Am. Coll. Trial Lawyers, Am. Bar Found., Am. Coll. Labor and Employment Lawyers, Mich. Bar Found.; mem. ABA, FBA, Detroit Bar Assn. (dir. 1974-79, Goodnow Pres.'s award 1996), Mich. Bar Assn. (atty. discipline panel, Disting. Svc. award 1998), Detroit Indsl. Rels. Rsch. Assn. (treas. 1980—, v.p. 1982, pres. 1984-85), Mich. Young Lawyers (pres. 1954-55), Am. Law Inst., Indsl. Rels. Rsch. Assn. Am. Arbitration Assn., U.S. 6th Cir. Ct. Appeals (life, mem. jud. conf., mem. bicentennial com.), Am. Inn Ct., Cooley Club, Renaissance Club, Detroit Golf Club (dir. 1983-89), Detroit Athletic Club. Federal civil litigation, State civil litigation, Labor (including EEOC, Fair Labor Standards Act, labor-management relations, NLRB, OSHA). Office: Butzel Long 150 W Jefferson Ave Ste 900 Detroit MI 48226-4416

SAYLOR, CHARLES HORACE, lawyer, judge; b. Bethlehem, Pa., Jan. 6, 1950; s. Howard James and Florence M. (Glasser) S.; m. Martha Louise Weaver, July 10, 1971; children: Amy Louise, Matthew Charles. BA, Pa. State U., 1971; JD, Dickinson Sch. Law, 1974. Bar: Pa. 1974, U.S. Dist. Ct. (mid. dist.) Pa. 1979. Law clk. Northumberland County Ct. Common Pleas, Sunbury, Pa., 1974-76; assoc. Wiest & Wiest, Sunbury, 1976-79; ptnr. Wiest, Wiest & Saylor, Sunbury, 1979-85, Wiest, Wiest, Saylor & Muolo, Sunbury, 1985-97, Wiest, Saylor, Muolo, Noon and Swinehart, Sunbury, 1998—2001; judge Court of Common Pleas, Northumberland County, Pa., 2002—. Solicitor Twp. of Rush, Pa., 1979-2001, Twp. of Point, Pa., 1983-2001, County of Northumberland, 1993-95; instr. Pa. State U., Schuylkill Haven, 1986. Asst. editor: Dickinson Law Rev., 1973, Northumberland (Pa.) Legal Jour., 1987—2001. Trustee Northumberland County Law Libr., 1986-2001, Priestley-Forsyth Meml. Libr., Northumberland, 1988-93, v.p., 1990-93; coach Am. Youth Soccer Assn., Northumberland, 1988-90; mem. com. YMCA, Sunbury, 1987-98, bd. dirs., 1991—, pres. of bd. dirs., 1997-98, chmn. sustaining campaign, 1992; asst. coach Girls Track and Field, Shikellamy H.S., 1992-93; profls. co-chair United Way, 2000-01. Mem. Pa. Bar Assn., Northumberland County Bar Assn. (sec.-treas. 1985-2000, pres. 2001), Pa. Trial Lawyers Assn. Republican. Roman Catholic. Avocations: running, golf. Home: 233 Honey Locust Ln Northumberland PA 17857-9679 Office: Northumberland County Courthouse 201 Market St Sunbury PA 17801

SAYLOR, THOMAS G. state supreme court justice; b. Meyersdale, Pa., Dec. 14, 1946; BA in Govt., U. Va., 1969; JD, Columbia U., 1972. Pvt. practice, 1972-82, 87-93; 1st asst. dist. atty. Somerset County, 1973-76; dir. Pa. Bur. Consumer Protection, 1982-83; 1st dep. atty. gen. Commonwealth of Pa., 1983-87; elected judge Superior Ct. Pa., 1993; elected justice Supreme Ct. Pa., 1997—. Contbr. articles to legal publications. Bd. overseers Widener U. Sch. Law. Mem. ABA, Am. Law Inst., Pa. Bar Assn., Cumberland County Bar Assn., Dauphin County Bar Assn., Appellate Judges Conf. Office: Fulton Bldg 16th Fl 200 N 3d St Harrisburg PA 17101

SAYRE, JOHN MARSHALL, lawyer, former government official; b. Boulder, Colo., Nov. 9, 1921; s. Henry Marshall and Lulu M. (Cooper) S.; m. Jean Miller, Aug. 22, 1943; children: Henry M., Charles Franklin, John Marshall Jr., Ann Elizabeth Sayre Taggart (dec.). BA, U. Colo., 1943, JD, 1948. Bar: Colo. 1948, U.S. Dist. Ct. Colo. 1952, U.S. Ct. Appeals (10th cir.) 1964. Law clk. trust dept. Denver Nat. Bank, 1948-49; asst. cashier, trust officer Nat. State Bank of Boulder, 1949-50; ptnr. Ryan, Sayre, Martin, Brotzman, Boulder, 1950-66, Davis, Graham & Stubbs, Denver, 1966-89, of counsel, 1993—; asst. sec. of the Interior for Water and Sci., 1989-93. Bd. dirs. Boulder Sch. Dist. 3, 1951-57; city atty. City of Boulder, 1952-55; gen. counsel Colo. Mcpl. League, 1959-63; prin. counsel No. Colo. Water Conservancy Dist. and mcpl. subdist., 1964-87, spl. counsel, 1987, bd. dirs. dist., 1960-64; former legal counsel Colo. Assn. Commerce and Industry. Lt. (j.g.) USNR, 1943-46, ret. Decorated Purple Heart; recipient William Lee Knous award U. Colo. Law Sch., 1999. Fellow Am. Bar Found. (life), Colo. Bar Found. (life); mem. ABA, Colo. Bar Assn., Boulder County Bar Assn. (pres. 1959), Denver Bar Assn., Nat. Water Resources Assn. (Colo. dir. 1980-89, 93-95, pres. 1984-86), Denver Country Club, Univ. Club, Phi Beta Kappa, Phi Gamma Delta, Phi Delta Phi. Environmental, Property, real (including real estate development, water). Home: 355 Ivanhoe St Denver CO 80220-5841 Office: Davis Graham & Stubbs 1550-17th St Ste 500 Denver CO 80202 E-mail: john.sayre@dgslaw.com.

SAYRE, MATT MELVIN MATHIAS, lawyer; b. Seattle, Sept. 5, 1934; s. Melvin Edward and Ethyl Elizabeth (Mathias) S.; m. Sheri Teagle, Oct. 21, 1956; children: Jeffrey Mathias, Steven Michael, David Matthew. BA, U. Wash., 1956; JD, Gonzaga U., 1964. Bar: Wash. 1964, D.C. 1981, U.S. Dist. Ct. (we. dist.) Wash. 1964, U.S. Ct. Appeals (9th cir.) 1972, U.S. Supreme Ct. 1980. Law clk. Justice Robert T. Hunter, Olympia, Wash., 1964-65; asst. counsel Pacific Car & Foundry Co., Renton, Wash., 1965-66; ptnr. Mullavey, Hageman, Treece & Sayre, Seattle, 1966-69, McBride & Sayre, 1969-71; sole practice Seattle, 1971-94; sr. ptnr. Sayre Law Offices, 1994—. Judge pro tem King County Superior Ct., 1973-83, 89—; trustee King County Bar Found., 1985-88, 92-98. Bd. visitors Seattle U. Sch. Law, 1991-2002. Served to 1st lt. USAFR, 1957-60. Recipient Pro Bono Svc. award, 1988. Mem. Wash. Bar Assn. (spl. dist. counsel 1982-88, editorial adv. bd. 1986-89, chair BAR-PAC 1991-94, chair pub. rels. com. 1992-93), King County Bar Assn. (treas. 1982-85, trustee 1985-88, bench-bar delay reduction task force 1987-89, 2d v.p. 1988-89, 1st v.p. 1989-90, pres. 1990-91, Geisness award 1997), South King County Bar Assn., Rainier C. of C. (pres. 1977-78), Lions, Wash. Athletic Club, Useless Bay Golf and Country Club, Seattle Yacht Club (staff judge advocate 2000-2001), Beta Theta Pi, Phi Delta Phi. State civil litigation, General practice, Probate (including wills, trusts). Office: Boren & Jefferson Bldg 1016 Jefferson St Seattle WA 98104-2435

SAYRE, RICHARD LAYTON, lawyer; b. Spokane, Wash., May 21, 1953; s. Charles Layton and Elizabeth Jane (Ward) S.; m. Karen Linda Sayre, Mar. 8, 1979; children: Wendi Sue Stoken, Tracey Lynn Turner. BA, U. Wash., 1976; JD, Gonzaga U., 1979. Bar: Wash. 1979, U.S. Dist. Ct. (ea. and we. dist.) Wash. 1979, U.S. Ct. Appeals (9th cir.) 1986; cert. elder law atty. Nat. Elder Law Found. Deputy prosecuting atty. Spokane County, Spokane, 1979-84; shareholder Underwood, Campbell, Brock & Cerutti, Spokane, 1984-92, Sayre & Sayre P.S., Spokane, 1992—. Pres. Nat. Acad. Elder Law Attys., Washington, 1995-96; apptd. by Wash. Supreme Ct., Washington Profl. Guardian Cert. Bd.; adj. prof. law Gonzaga U. Potentate, trustee El Katif Shrine Temple, Spokane, 1997; bd. govs. Shriner's Hosp. for Children, Spokane, 1993-96; exec. officer Order of DeMolay, Washington, 1993—, internat. supreme coun. Order DeMolay. Recipient Pro Bono award Spokane County Bar Assn., 1991, 99, Recognition of Achievement & Contribution award Lutheran Social Svcs. of Washington, Idaho, 1992, 97, Achievement award Spokane Sexual Assault Ctr., 1997, Disting. Svc. award Gonzaga U., 1997; named Super Lawyer, Washington Law & Politics, 2000, 2001, 2002, 2003. Mem. Nat. Acad. Elder Law Attys., Spokane Estate Planning Coun. Democrat. Episcopal. Avocations: sailing, skiing. Estate planning, Probate (including wills, trusts), Legislative. Office: Sayre & Sayre 201 W North River Dr Ste 460 Spokane WA 99201-3203 E-mail: dick@sayrelaw.com.

SCACCHETTI, DAVID J. lawyer; b. Newark, July 13, 1956; s. Edmond and Evelyn Scacchetti; m. Marcia Ellen Gessiness, Aug. 31, 1985; children: Gabriella Elise, Olivia Beth. BA in Polit. Sci. with honors, U. Cin., 1978, JD, 1981. Bar: Ohio 1982, U.S. Dist. Ct. (so. dist.) Ohio 1982, U.S. Dist. Ct. (ea. dist.) Ky. 1986, U.S. Dist. Ct. Ariz. 1997. Sole practitioner, Cin., 1982-98; atty. Scacchetti & Scacchetti, Cin., 1998—. Mem. ATLA, Nat. Assn. Criminal Def. Lawyers, Greater Cin. Criminal Def. Lawyer Assn., Ohio Acad. Trial Lawyers, Ham. County Trial Lawyers Assn., Phi Beta Kappa. Avocations: writing, tennis, tribal art, guitar, travel. General civil litigation, Criminal, Personal injury (including property damage). Office: Scacchetti & Scacchetti 601 Main St Fl 3D Cincinnati OH 45202-2519

SCACCIA, DANTE M. lawyer; b. Rome, Oct. 11, 1925; s. Giovanni Battista and Ines (Biagioni) Scaccia; m. Dorothea B. Koch, June 6, 1954 (dec. Mar. 31, 1982); children: Victoria Marie, Ronald Allen; m. Antonia Pizzari, Jan. 9, 1991. AB, Union Coll., 1945; LLB, Columbia U., 1949. Bar: N.Y. 1949. U.S. atty. U.S. Dept. Justice, Syracuse, 1961-65; pvt. practice Syracuse, 1965—. Lt. comdr. USN, 1943-52. Decorated Bronze star. Mem. ABA, N.Y. State Bar Assn., Onondaga Bar Assn. Democrat. Roman Catholic. Avocations: hunting, fly-fishing, hiking, mountain climbing, canoeing. Home: 159 Brookside Ln Fayetteville NY 13066-1543 Office: Scaccia Law Firm 109 S Warren St Ste 402 Syracuse NY 13202-1758

SCAFETTA, JOSEPH, JR., lawyer; b. Chester, Pa., May 10, 1947; s. Giuseppe and Mary (Koslosky) S.; m. Teresa M. Talierco, July 4, 1986; 1 child, Joseph III. BS in Aero. Engring., Pa. State U., 1969; JD, U. Pitts., 1972; M in Patent Law, Georgetown U., 1973; MBA, George Washington U., 1983. Bar: Pa. 1972, U.S. Patent and Trademark Office 1973, D.C. 1978, Va. 1979, U.S. Supreme Ct. 1980, U.S. Ct. Appeals (fed. cir.) 1982. Legal rschr. Arent, Fox, Kintner, Plotkin et al, Washington, 1973; law clk. to presiding judge U.S. Dist. Ct. S.C., Columbia, 1973-74; assoc. Colton & Stone, Arlington, Va., 1975-77, Craig & Antonelli, Washington, 1977-78, Wigman & Cohen, Arlington, 1978-83, Wenderoth, Lind & Ponack, Washington, 1983-86, Cushman, Darby & Cushman, Washington, 1986-87; counsel Russell, Georges & Breneman, Arlington, 1987-91, Young & Thompson, Arlington, 1991-96; pvt. practice Arlington, 1996-98; counsel Oblon, Spivak, McClelland, Maier & Neustadt, Arlington, 1999—. Voting mem. Nat. Commn. for Social Justice, 1995-97. Author: Book Review Copyright Handbook, 1979, The Constitutionality/Unconstitutionality of the Patent Infringement Statute, 1979, (with others) Patents on Microorganisms, 1980; editor: An Intellectual Property Law Primer, 1975; contbr. articles to profl. jours. Mem. Consumer Affairs Commn., Alexandria, Va., 1985-87; charter mem. Christopher Columbus Quincentenary Jubilee Com., 1990-93; chair Va. chpt. Commn. for Social Justice, 1987—; mem. Fairfax County Dem. Com., Falls Church, 1987-89; parliamentarian City Dem. Com., Alexandria, 1985-87. Recipient Robert C. Watson award Am. Patent Law Assn., 1975. Mem.: Patent and Trademark Office Soc., D.C. Bar Assn., Am. Intellectual Property Law Assn. (mem. pub. info. com. 1983—2001), Va. Bar Assn., Am. Arbitration Assn. (mem. comml. panel), ABA, Avanti Italiani (pres. Alexandria chpt. 1981—83), Grand Lodge Va. (state pres. 1993—95), Sons of Italy. Patent, Trademark and copyright. Office: 1755 Jeff Davis Hwy Ste 400 Arlington VA 22202-3530

SCAGLIONE, CYNTHIA M. lawyer, consultant; b. Tampa, Fla. BA magna cum laude, U. S. Fla., 1977; JD with distinction, St. Mary's U., San Antonio, 1980; LLM in Internat. Legal Studies, NYU, 1998. Bar: Tex. 1980, U.S. Dist. Ct. (no., ea. and we. dists.) Tex. 1980. Jud. clk. to Hon. Fred Shannon U.S. Dist. Ct. (we. dist.) Tex., San Antonio, 1980—81; trial atty. Law Offices Patricia A. Hill, Dallas, 1981—83; asst. atty. gen. Tex. Office Atty. Gen., Austin, 1983—86; litig. coord. Tex. Dept. Mental Health and Mental Retardation, Austin, 1986—90; asst. regional counsel Region 6 U.S. EPA, Dallas, 1990—95, asst. enforcement counsel, 1995; internat. cons., 1996—. Atty. gen.'s rep. Gov.'s Coun. Disabilities, Austin, 1985; mem. exec. com., bd. dirs. Citizens United Rehab. Errants, Washington, 1988—91, adviser, 1998—; bd. advisors A. A. White Dispute Resolution Inst. S. Tex. Coll. Law, Houston, 1989—92. Co-author: (book) Tex. Courtroom Evidence, 1980; mem. bd. editors Law & Medicine, Terre Haute, Ind., 1999—. Mem. Soviet Am. Peace Conf., Moscow, Leningrad, Russia, 1985; mem. global forum Hague (The Netherlands) Appeal Peace,

1999; mem. Dallas Com. Fgn. Visitors, 1981—83; mem. internat. hospitality com. U. Tex., 1984—90; human rights com. UN Assn., Dallas, bd. dirs., 1991—96, founding chair environment com., 1994—95, mem. govt. rels. com., 1995, v.p. adminstrn., 1995, bd. dirs. Tampa, Fla., 1996, Peacemakers, Inc., Dallas, 1992—94; mem. planning com. Russian Heritage, Inc., St. Petersburg, Fla. Mem.: ABA (mem. internat. sect.), Tex. Bar Assn. Office: 2303 S Cameron Ave Tampa FL 33629 Office Fax: 813-258-0272.

SCALETTA, PHILLIP JASPER, lawyer, educator; b. Sioux City, Iowa, Aug. 20, 1925; s. Phillip and Louise (Pelmulder) S.; m. Helen M. Beedle; children: Phillip R., Cheryl D. Kesler. BS, Morningside Coll., Sioux City, Iowa, 1948; JD, U. Iowa, 1950. Bar: Iowa 1950, U.S. Dist. Ct. Iowa 1950, Ind. 1966, U.S. Supreme Ct. 1968. Ptnr. McKnight and Scaletta, Sioux City, 1950-51; field rep. Farmers Ins. Group, Sioux City, 1951-54, sr. liability examiner, Aurora, Ill., 1954-60; br. claims mgr., Ft. Wayne, Ind., 1960-66; prof. law Purdue U., West Lafayette, Ind., 1966—; dir. profl. masters programs of the Krannet Grad. Sch. of Mgmt. Purdue U., 1987-90; of counsel with Mayfield & Brooks Attys. at Law, 1967—; arbitrator Panel of Arbitrators Am. Arbitration Assn. Co-author: Business Law and Regulatory Environments, 5th edit., 1996, Business Law Workbook, 5th edit., 1996, Foundations of Business Law and Legal Environment, 1986, 4th edit., 1997, Student Workbook and Study Guide, 1986, 4th edit., 1997; contbr. numerous articles to profl. jours. Mem. Ind. Gov's Commn. Individual Privacy, 1975. Recipient Best Tchr. of Yr. award Standard Oil Ind. Found., 1972, Outstanding Tchr. award Purdue U. Alumni Assn., 1974, Most Effective Tchr. award Krannert Grad. Sch. Mgmt. Purdue U., 1991. Mem. Am. Bus. Law Assn. (pres., Sr. Faculty Excellence award 1989), Tippecanoe County Bar Assn., Tri State Bus Law Assn. (past pres.), Midwest Bus. Adminstrn. Assn., Beta Gamma Sigma (bd. govs.). Office: Purdue U 511 Krannert Bldg West Lafayette IN 47907

SCALETTA, PHILLIP RALPH, III, lawyer; b. Iowa City, Iowa, Dec. 18, 1949; s. Phillip Jasper and Helen M. (Beedle) S.; m. Karen Lynn Scaletta, May 13, 1973; children: Phillip, Anthony, Alexander. BSIM, MS, Purdue U., 1972; JD, Ind. U., 1975. Bar: Ind. 1975, U.S. Dist. Ct. Ind. 1975, Ill. 1993. Assoc. Ice Miller Donadio & Ryan, Indpls., 1975-81, ptnr., 1981—. Contbr. articles to profl. jours. Chmn. Ind. Continuing Legal Edn. Found., Indpls., 1989; mem. Environ. Quality Control Water Com., 1988-98. Mem. Ind. Bar Assn., Indpls. Bar Assn., Def. Rsch. Inst., Internat. Assn. Def. Counsel, Gyro Club Indpls. (v.p. 1992-93, pres. 1993-94, bd. dirs. 1990—). Avocations: golf, skiing, tennis. General civil litigation, Environmental. Home: 7256 Tuliptree Trl Indianapolis IN 46256-2136 Office: Ice Miller 1 American Sq Indianapolis IN 46282-0020

SCALIA, ANTONIN, judge; b. Trenton, N.J., Mar. 11, 1936; s. S. Eugene and Catherine Louise (Panaro) Scalia; m. Maureen McCarthy, Sept. 10, 1960; children: Ann Forrest, Eugene, John Francis, Catherine Elisabeth, Mary Clare, Paul David, Matthew, Christopher James, Margaret Jane. AB, Georgetown U., 1957; student, U. Fribourg, Switzerland, 1955—56; LLB, Harvard U., 1960. Bar: Ohio 1962, Va. 1970. Assoc. Jones Day Cockley & Reavis, Cleve., 1961—67; assoc. prof. U. Va. Law Sch., 1967—70, prof., 1970—74; gen. counsel Office Telecomm. Policy, Exec. Office of Pres., 1971—72; chmn. Adminstrv. Conf. U.S., Washington, 1972—74; asst. atty. gen. U.S. Office Legal Counsel, Justice Dept., 1974—77; prof. law U. Chgo., 1977—82; judge U.S. Ct. Appeals (D.C. cir.), 1982—86; justice U.S. Supreme Ct., Washington, 1986—. Vis. prof. Georgetown Law Ctr., 1977, Stanford Law Sch., 1980—81; vis. scholar Am. Enterprise Inst. , 1977. Editor: Regulation mag., 1979—82. Fellow Sheldon fellow, Harvard U., 1960—61. Office: US Supreme Ct Supreme Ct Bldg 1 1st St NE Washington DC 20543-0001

SCANLAN, KEVIN J. lawyer; b. L.A., Mar. 28, 1970; s. James Thomas and Helen Marie Scanlan; m. Katie Scanlan, July 8, 1995. BA in Bus. Adminstrn., Carroll Coll., Helena, Mont., 1992; JD cum laude, Seattle U., 1996. Bar: Idaho, 1996, U.S. Dist. Ct. Idaho 1996. Atty. Hall, Farley, Oberrecht & Blanton, P.A., Boise, Idaho, 1996—. Editor Seattle Law Rev., 1994-96. Bd. dirs. Ronald McDonald House, Boise, 1997—. Mem. ABA, Idaho State Bar Assn. Roman Catholic. Avocations: fly fishing, skiing. General civil litigation, Intellectual property, Professional liability. Office: Hall Farley et al 702 W Idaho St Ste 700 Boise ID 83702-8908

SCANLON, PAT H. lawyer; b. Houma, La., Aug. 4, 1936; s. Leo Joseph and Mary (Ezell) S.; m. Carlene Myers, June 10, 1961; children: Margaret, Pat, Jr., Cissy, John. BS in Geology, La. State U., 1957; LLB with distinction, U. Miss., 1960. Assoc. Satterfield, Shell, Williams & Buford, Jackson, Miss., 1960-62; ptnr. Young, Scanlon & Sessums, Jackson, 1962—; chmn., commnr. Miss. Jud. Performance Commn., Jackson, 1980-83; instr. Jackson Sch. Law, 1963-66; chmn. Miss. Law Inst., Jackson, 1970. Mem. editorial bd. Miss. Law Jour., 1959-60; contbr. articles to profl. jours. Mem. vestry St. James Episcopal Ch., Jackson, 1972-75, 79-82). Served to capt. USAR. Fellow Am. Coll. Trial Lawyers, Internat. Soc. Barristers, Am. Bar Found., Miss. Bar Found. (pres. 1986-87, trustee 1980-83); mem. Miss. Bankruptcy Conf. (pres. 1984-85), Miss. Young Lawyers Assn. (pres. 1969-70), Miss. State Bar Assn. (2d v.p. 1970-71, pres. 1988-89), Hinds County Bar Assn. (pres. 1974-75), Fed. Bar Assn. (pres. Miss. chpt. 1972-73). Bankruptcy, General civil litigation, Construction. Office: 2000 Deposit Guaranty Plz Jackson MS 39201

SCANLON, ROBERT CHARLES, lawyer; b. Orange, N.J., May 25, 1950; s. Robert Alfred and Joyce (Fennimore) S.; m. Kathleen Marie Maginnis, Apr. 7, 1973; children: Elizabeth, Margaret, Marianne. BS, St. Peters Coll., 1972; JD, Gonzaga U., 1976. Bar: Wash. 1977, U.S. Dist. Ct. (ea. dist.) Wash. 1977, U.S. Dist. Ct. (we. dist.) Wash. 1979, U.S. Ct. Appeals (9th cir.) 1980. Assoc. Cooper & Roberts, Spokane, Wash., 1977-81; ptnr. Roberts, DiLuzio & Scanlon, Spokane, Wash., 1981-84; prin. Dellwo, Rudolf & Schroeder PS, Spokane, Wash., 1984-90; with Dellwo, Roberts and Scanlon PS, Spokane, Wash., 1990—. Mem. ABA, Wash. State Bar Assn. (exec. com. family law sect. 1997—, chmn. 1999-2000), Spokane County Bar Assn. (trustee 1981-82, pres. young lawyers sect. 1981-82), Comml. Law League Am. Republican. Roman Catholic. Commercial, consumer (including collections, credit), Family and matrimonial, General practice. Home: 3729 W Woodside Ave Spokane WA 99208-4860 Office: Dellwo Roberts Scanlon PS 1124 W Riverside Ave Ste 310 Spokane WA 99201-1109

SCANLON, VERA MARY, lawyer; b. Bklyn., June 23, 1968; d. Dennis P. and Alice (Keelty) S. AB summa cum laude, Columbia U., 1990; JD, Yale U., 1995. Bar: N.Y., N.J., U.S. Dist. Ct. (ea. and so. dists.) N.Y., U.S. Dist. Ct. N.J., Washington. Assoc. Hughes Hubbard & Reed LLP, N.Y.C., 1995-98; clk. to Hon. D. Dominguez U.S. Dist. Ct. Dist. P.R., San Juan, 1998; clk. to Hon. F. Block U.S. Dist. Ct. (ea. dist.) N.Y., Bklyn., 1998-2000; clk. to Hon. R. Katzmann U.S. Ct. Appeals (2d cir.), 2000—01; assoc. Beldock Levine & Hoffman LLP, 2001—. Mem. Assn. Bar City N.Y., Alumni Assn. Jesuit Vol. Corps South, Marymount Sch. Alumnae Assn. Home: 224 89th St Brooklyn NY 11209-5612 E-mail: verascanlon@aya.yale.edu.

SCARBARY, OTIS LEE, lawyer; b. Macon, Ga., Feb. 4, 1952; s. Otis Thomas Jr. and Shirley (Tucker) S.; m. Donna Lynne Hughes, June 11, 1981; 1 child, Amanda Leigh. BA, Mercer U., 1974, JD, 1977. Bar: Ga., U.S. Dist. Ct. (mid. dist.) Ga. 1977, U.S. Ct. Appeals (11th cir.) 1981. Pvt. practice, Macon, 1977-83; asst. solicitor Bibb County, Office of Solicitor, Macon, 1983-96, solicitor-gen., 1996—. Mem. Ga. Assn. of Solicitors-Gen. (exec. bd. 1997-2003, pres.-elect 2003), Macon Bar Assn., State Bar of Ga. (govt. atty. involvement com.), W.A. Bootle Inn of Ct., Lions (exec. bd. Macon Evening Lions Club 1997-99), Order of Police. Democrat. Avocations: jogging, diving, reading. Home: 110 Fredricksted Pl Macon GA 31204-1463 Office: Office of Solicitor-Gen Bibb County Cthouse Rm #504 Macon GA 31201 E-mail: odscarbary@cox.net., oscarbary@co.bibb.ga.us.

SCARINGI, MELANIE WALZ, lawyer; b. Harrisburg, Pa., July 14, 1976; d. Shaubut C. Walz III and Judith T. Walz; m. Marc A. Scaringi, July 1, 2000. BA, Dickinson Coll., 1998; JD, Pa. State U., 2001. Bar: Pa. 2001, U.S. Dist. (mid. dist.) Pa. 2001. Ptnr. Walz, Walz, Scaringi and Scaringi, Newport, Pa., 2001—. Mem. Highland United Presbyn. Ch. Mem.: Venture Club of Harrisburg, Newport Lions Club. General practice, Family and matrimonial, Estate planning. Office: Walz Walz Scaringi & Scaringi 341 Market St Newport PA 17074

SCARMINACH, CHARLES ANTHONY, lawyer; b. Syracuse, N.Y., Feb. 19, 1944; s. John Louis and Lucy (Egnoto) S.; children: John, Catherine, Karen, Charles, Robert. MA, U. Buffalo, 1965; JD, Syracuse U., 1968. Bar: N.Y. 1968, S.C. 1974. Gen. counsel Sea Pines Co., Hilton Head Island, S.C., 1973-78; sole practice Hilton Head Island, 1978-83; ptnr. Novit & Scarminach, P.A., Hilton Head Island, 1983-93, Novit Scarminach & Williams P.A., Hilton Head Island, 1993—2002, Novit, Scarminach & Akins, P.A., Hilton Head Island, 2003—. Bd. dirs. Nations Bank, Hilton Head Island. Chmn. bd. Sea Pines Montessori Sch., Hilton Head Island, 1979-83; bd. dirs. Hilton Head Preparatory Sch., 1984-93, chmn. bd. trustees 1986-93. Maj. U.S. Army, 1968-73. Mem. ABA, S.C. Bar Assn., N.Y. State Bar Assn., Hilton Head Island C. of C. (bd. dirs. 1996-99), Sea Pines Club. Roman Catholic. Corporate, general, General practice, Property, real (including real estate development, water). Home: 10 Wood Duck Ct Hilton Head Island SC 29928-3010 Office: Novit Scarminach & Akins PA PO Drawer 14 Hilton Head Island SC 29938-0014 E-mail: cscarminach@nswlaw.com.

SCAROLA, JOHN, lawyer; b. Bklyn., July 24, 1947; s. John Anthony and Grace Ellen (Turnbull) S.; m. Anita Helene Kargauer, Jan. 4, 1969; children: Kristen, John Michael, Janna, David, Cara. BA, Georgetown U., 1969, JD, 1973. Bar: Fla. 1973, U.S. Dist. Ct. (so. dist.) Fla. 1974, U.S. Ct. Appeals (5th cir.) 1976. Chief felony prosecutor State Atty.'s Office, 15th Jud. Cir., West Palm Beach, Fla., 1973-78; ptnr., dir., officer Searcy, Denney, Scarola, Barnhart & Shipley, P.A., West Palm Beach, 1978—. Spl. counsel Fla. Jud. Qualifications Commn., Tallahassee, 1981—; asst. spl. prosecutor Statewide Grand Jury, Fla., 1977-78; instr. Palm Beach Jr. Coll., Lake Worth, Fla., 1974-78. Candidate Fla. State Senate, Dist. 84, 1978; chmn. bd. The Lord's Place Inc., West Palm Beach, 1981—; bd. dirs. Children's Genetic Disease Found., Miami, Fla., 1982-87; pres. Serra Club of the Palm Beaches, West Palm Beach, 1980; bd. dirs. Fla. Rural Legal Svcs., 1997—. Served with USAR, 1966-72. Mem. ABA, Fla. Bar (bd. cert. civil trial practice and comml. and bus. litigation 1984, pres.'s pro bono award 1984), Acad. Fla. Trial Lawyers, Palm Beach County Bar Assn. (Cmty. Svc. award 1994), Palm Beach County Trial Lawyers Assn. (pres. 1989-92). Roman Catholic. General civil litigation, Personal injury (including property damage), Product liability. Home: 572 Cocoplum Dr E Jupiter FL 33458-8344 Office: Searcy Denney Scarola Barnhart & Shipley PA 2139 Palm Beach Lakes Blvd West Palm Beach FL 33409-6601

SCEPER, DUANE HAROLD, lawyer; b. Norfolk, Va., Nov. 16, 1946; s. Robert George and Marion Eudora (Hynes) S.; m. Sharon Diane Cramer, July 4, 1981; stepchildren: Karin Stevenson, Diane Stevenson. BS in Law, Western State U., 1979, JD, 1980. Bar: Calif. 1982, U.S. Dist. Ct. (so. dist.) Calif. 1982. Field engr. Memorex/Tex. Instruments, San Diego, 1968-70; computer programmer San Diego, 1970-81; atty. Allied Ins. Group, San Diego, 1981-85; sole practice San Diego, 1985-87; ptnr. Paluso & Sceper, San Diego, 1987—. Cons. computers 1980—; lectr. estate planning various orgns. Patentee in field. Active Com. to Elect King Golden to Congress, San Diego, 1978. Served with USAF, 1965-68. Recipient Am. Jurisprudence award, 1979. Mem. ABA, San Diego County Bar Assn., Assn. Trial Lawyers of Am., Calif. Trial Lawyers Assn., San Diego Trial Lawyers Assn., Am. Subrogation Attys., Assn. of Ins. Def. Counsel, So. Calif. Def. Counsel, Air Commando Assn. (life), Delta Theta Phi. Democrat. State civil litigation, Estate planning, Insurance. Home: 2641 Massachusetts Ave Lemon Grove CA 91945-3149 Office: Paluso & Sceper 1010 2d Ave Ste 1350 San Diego CA 92101

SCHAAB, ARNOLD J. lawyer; b. Newark, N.J., 1939; s. Robert George and Pauline Schaab; m. Marcia Stecker, 1964 (div. 1978); children: Emily Diana, Genevieve; m. Patricia Caesar, 1981 (div. 1996); m. Susan McGlamery, 2000. BA, New Sch. U., 1962; LLB, Harvard U., 1965. Bar: N.Y. 1967, U.S. Dist. Ct. (so. and ea. dists.) N.Y. 1967. Assoc. Chadbourne & Parke, N.Y.C., 1966-69; ptnr. Anderson, Kill & Olick, N.Y.C., 1969-78; sr. ptnr. Pryor, Cashman, Sherman & Flynn LLP, N.Y.C., 1978—. Chmn. Literacy Ptnrs., Inc. Fulbright scholar Law Faculty U. Paris. Fellow N.Y. Bar Found., Am. Bar Found.; mem. ABA (vice chair internat. fin. transactions com.), N.Y. State Bar Assn. (chmn. internat. law and practice sect., chmn. spl. com. free trade in the Ams., ho. of dels., fin. com., long range planning com., by-laws com.), Assn. Bar City N.Y. (com. internat. trade, com. fgn. and comparative law), Computer Law Assn., Univ. Club (treas., chmn. fin. com., chmn. audit com.), Doubles, Nat. Arts Club, Archaeol. Inst. Am., Bibl. Archaeology Soc. Commercial, contracts (including sales of goods; commercial financing), Corporate, general, Private international. Office: Pryor Cashman Sherman & Flynn 410 Park Ave New York NY 10022-4441

SCHAAF, DOUGLAS ALLAN, lawyer; b. Green Bay, Wis., Nov. 18, 1955; s. Carlton Otto and Fern (Brunette) S.; m. Kathlyn T. Bielke, Feb. 23, 1988. BBA magna cum laude in Internat. Bus., St. Norbert Coll., DePere, Wis., 1978; JD, U. Notre Dame, 1981. Bar: Ill. 1981, Calif. 1987. Assoc. McDermott, Will & Emery, Chgo., 1981-84, Skadden, Arps, Slate, Meagher & Flom, 1984-89; ptnr. Paul Hastings, Janofsky & Walker, L.A., 1989—. Adj. faculty mem. John Marshall Law Sch., 1984-87. Atty. Chgo. Vol. Legal Services, 1984-87; bd. dirs. Orange County Alzheimer's Assn. Mem. Orange County Bar Assn. (chair tax sect. 1994-96). Corporate, general, Corporate taxation, Personal income taxation. Office: Paul Hastings Janofsky & Walker 695 Town Center Dr Ste 1700 Costa Mesa CA 92626-7191 E-mail: dougschaaf@paalhastings.com.

SCHAAP, JACQUELINE, lawyer; b. Haarlem, Netherlands, June 27, 1961; d. Lex and Truus S. Law degree, U. Amsterdam, 1984. Trademark agt. Markgraaf, Netherlands, 1985-88; ptnr. Boekel de Neree, Netherlands, 1988—, Klos, Morel, Vos & Schaap, Amsterdam, 2003—. Author: Promotional Actions, 1997, Trademark Law, 1996; co-author: Intellectual Property, 2000; co-author, editor: Legal Questions on Marketing and Advertising, 1995; contbr. articles to profl. jours. Bd. dirs. theatre group Toneelgroep, Amsterdam. Mem. Dutch Advt. Assn., INTA, ECTA, BMM. Avocation: sports. Communications, Intellectual property, Trademark and copyright. Office: Klos Morel Vos & Schaap Albert Hahnplantsoen 23 1077 BM Amsterda PO Box 75988 1070 AZ Amsterdam Netherlands Office Fax: +31 20 577 3578. Business E-Mail: jacqueline.schaap@kmvs.nl.

SCHAEFER, JOHN FREDERICK, lawyer, educator; b. Detroit, Apr. 10, 1943; s. Gilbert Frederick and Mary Cathryn (Henderson) S.; m. Sharon Kathleen Chalmers, May 22, 1976; children: Kimberly Megan, Kelly Leigh, John Frederick, Charles Frederick. Student, U. Notre Dame, 1961-63; BA, Mich. State U., 1965, LLD, 1996; JD, Detroit Coll. Law, 1968. Bar: Mich. 1969. Ptnr. Buesser, Buesser, Snyder & Blank, Detroit, 1968-73, Williams, Schaefer, Ruby & Williams, Birmingham, Mich., 1973-89; propr. Law Firm of John F. Schaefer, Birmingham, 1989—. Adj. prof. domestic rels. Detroit Coll. Law, 1971—; instr. domestic rels. Mich. Jud. Inst., 1980-81; lectr. in field. Contbr. articles to legal jours. Trustee Detroit Coll. Law, Mich. State U., 1985—, William Beaumont Hosp., 2000; chair Detroit Coll. Law at Mich. State U. Found., 1995—; mem. ICLE Legal Edn. Inst. Fellow: Oakland Bar Found., Mich. State Bar Found. (jed. rev. com. 1997—), Am. Acad. Matrimonial Lawyers (pres. Mich. chpt. 1986—87), State Bar Mich. (family law com. 1972—73, com. on character and fitness 1972—75, coun. family law sect. 1974—, mem. fee abritration grievance bd. 1976—, chmn. 1978—79); mem.: Oakland County Bar Assn. (mem. character and fitness com. 1973, familyt law com. 1973—, chmn. com. 1974—77, cir. ct. com. 1985—88, bd. dirs. 1995—), Detroit Bar Assn. (friend of ct. and domestic rels. com. 1972—, chmn. com. 1975—76, mem. pub. adv. com. 1976—), ABA (family law sect. 1969—, jud. rev. com. 1997—). Roman Catholic. Commercial, contracts (including sales of goods; commercial financing), Family and matrimonial. Office: Ste 320 380 N Old Woodward Ave Birmingham MI 48009-5347

SCHAEFFER, MATTHEW THOMAS, lawyer; b. Troy, Ohio, July 28, 1970; s. Robert K. and Kathy L. Schaeffer; m. Johnna A. Schaeffer. BA in Polit. Sci., Ohio State U., 1993; JD cum laude, Capital U., 1996. Bar: Ohio 1996, U.S. Dist. Ct. (so. and no. dists.) Ohio 1997. Legal extern Ohio Atty. Gen., Columbus, Ohio, 1994; mng. editor Capital Law Rev., Columbus, 1995-96; assoc. Arter & Hadden, Columbus, 1997—. Co-author: Bankruptcy Law and Procedure in Ohio, 1998, Judgment Enforcement in Ohio, 2001. Lectr. Street Law, Columbus, 1994; tutor Read-to-Me, Columbus, 1994. J. Andrew Fulker Meml. scholar, 1995. Mem. Columbus Bar Assn. (bankruptcy com. mem. 1997—. Bankruptcy, General civil litigation, Commercial, contracts (including sales of goods; commercial financing). Home: 835 S Pearl St Columbus OH 43206-2036 Office: Arter & Hadden 10 W Broad St Ste 2100 Columbus OH 43215

SCHAFER, GERARD THOMAS ROGER, lawyer; b. Pitts., Mar. 20, 1956; s. Francis John Schafer and Lucille L. Davis; m. Marie Teres Paulick, Dec. 18, 1982; children: Michael, Brett, Rachael, Matthew. BS, Pa. State U., 1978; JD magna cum laude, U. Pitts., 1982. Bar: Pa. 1982, Va. 1984; U.S. Dist. Ct. (ea. dist.) Pa. 1982, U.S. Dist. Ct. (ea. dist.) Va. 1984. Assoc. Tucker Arensberg P.C., Pitts., 1982-84, Clark & Stant, P.C., Virginia Beach, 1984-85; asst. atty. Office of the Commonwealth's Atty., Virginia Beach, 1985-88; assoc. John W. Brown, P.C., Chesapeake, Va., 1988; sole practice law Virginia Beach, 1989-95; ptnr. Schafer & Russo, Virginia Beach, 1996—. Mem. Va. Trial Lawyers Assn., Allegheny County Bar Assn. (award 1982), Order of the Coif. Avocations: sports, music. Criminal, Personal injury (including property damage). Office: Schafer & Russo 4455 South Blvd Ste 310 Virginia Beach VA 23452-1159

SCHAFF, MICHAEL FREDERICK, lawyer; b. Queens, N.Y., Nov. 14, 1957; s. Raymond and Norma S.; m. Robin Barbara Rose, Mar. 17, 1985; children: Rachel Lindsay, Aaron Jacob. BA, Rutgers Coll., New Brunswick, N.J., 1979; MBA, CUNY, 1982; JD, N.Y. Law Sch., N.Y.C., 1982; LLM, Boston U., 1983. Bar: N.Y. and N.J. 1982, Md. 1983, U.S. Dist. Ct. N.J. 1983, U.S. Dist. Ct. Md. 1983, U.S. Tax Ct. 1983. Assoc. Ober, Kaler, Grimes & Shriver, Balt., 1983-84, Greenberg, Dauber & Epstein, Newark, 1984-86, Wilentz, Goldman & Spitzer, Woodbridge, N.J., 1986-91, ptnr., 1991—. Mem. N.J. Legis. Com. for the Study of Pain Mgmt. Contbr. articles to profl. jours. Masters Rsch. fellow, Bernard M. Baruch Coll., 1980. Mem. Am. Health Lawyers Assn. (chair 2001—, vice chmn. physician's orgn. com. 1997-2001, newsletter editor 1997—), N.J. Bar Assn. (chair computer related law com. 1991-93, dir. health and hosp. law sect. 1996—, vice chair 1997-98, chair elect 1998-99, chair 1999-2000), Middlesex County Bar Assn. (chair health and hosp. law com. 1995—), Med. Group Mgmt. Assn., N.J. Med. Group Mgmt. Assn., N.J. Venture Club, Omicron Delta Epsilon. Computer, Corporate, general, Health. Office: Wilentz Goldman & Spitzer 90 Woodbridge Ctr Dr Woodbridge NJ 07095-1146 E-mail: Schafm@Wilentz.com.

SCHAFFER, DAVID IRVING, lawyer; b. N.Y.C., Oct. 17, 1935; s. Frank and Edith (Montlack) S.; m. Lois Ann Warshauer, June 16, 1957; children: Susan Edith, Eric Michael. BA, U. Pa., 1956; LL.B., Harvard U., 1959. Bar: N.Y. 1960. Assoc. Shearman & Sterling, N.Y.C., 1960-65; sec., counsel Yale Express System, Inc., N.Y.C., 1965-66; sr. v.p., gen. counsel, sec. Avis, Inc., Garden City, N.Y., 1966-83; v.p., gen. counsel U.S. Surgical Corp., Norwalk, Conn., 1983-86; of counsel Meltzer, Lippe, Goldstein & Schlissel, LLP, Mineola, NY, 1986-89; ptnr. Meltzer, Lippe & Goldstein LLP, Mineola, 1989—. Past pres. Nassau County Legal Aid Soc., 1984-86. Bd. dirs. United Cmty. Fund, Great Neck, N.Y., 1980, Great Neck Estates Civic Assn., 1998—, L.I. Venture Group, 1988—. With USAR, 1960. Mem. ABA, N.Y. State Bar Assn., Nassau County Bar Assn., L.I. Software Assn., Harvard Club. Democrat. Corporate, general, Franchising, Securities. Home: 31 Amherst Rd Great Neck NY 11021-2910 Office: Meltzer Lippe Et Al 190 Willis Ave Mineola NY 11501-2693 E-mail: dlefty35@aol.com., dschaffer@mlg.com.

SCHAFRICK, FREDERICK CRAIG, lawyer; b. Sept. 20, 1948; s. Rudolph Henry and Patricia Eleanor (Zemer) Schafrick; m. Sharon Lee Halpin, May 23, 1981; children: Michael Nile, Nathaniel Henry. AB, U. Mich., 1970, JD , 1973. Bar: D.C. 1973, U.S. Ct. Appeals (D.C. cir.) 1975, U.S. Supreme Ct. 1977. Law clk. U.S. Ct. Appeals (2d cir.), N.Y.C., NY, 1973—74; assoc., then ptnr. Shea & Gardner, Washington, 1974—. Editor (adminstrv.): (law rev.) Mich. Law Rev., 1973. Mem.: ABA, Order of Coif, Phi Beta Kappa. Democrat. Presbyterian. Administrative and regulatory, Appellate, Aviation. Home: 5416 Nebraska Ave NW Washington DC 20015-1350 Office: Shea & Gardner Ste 800 1800 Massachusetts Ave NW Washington DC 20036-1872

SCHAINK, PAUL REINIER WILLEM, lawyer; b. Amsterdam, The Netherlands, June 23, 1950; children: Daniel, Marieke. LLM, Free U., Amsterdam, 1974. Bar: Dist. Ct. Amsterdam 1977. Assoc. of ombudsman, Netherlands, 1972—77; lawyer, 1977—; with Van Doorne, Law Firm, Amsterdam. Chmn., extraordinary chair for asylum law U. Amsterdam, 1992—. Mem.: Insolvency Advs. Bankruptcy, Labor (including EEOC, Fair Labor Standards Act, labor-management relations, NLRB, OSHA). Office: Van Doorne Law Firm Yachthavenweg 121 1081KM Amsterdam Netherlands

SCHALK, ROBERT PARTRIDGE, lawyer; b. Pueblo, Colo., June 20, 1931; s. Robert Louis and Elizabeth (Partridge) S.; m. Carolyn Ruthina Shoun, June 7, 1957; children: Steven Douglas, David Allen, Julie Dawn, Jeffrey Scott. BBA, U. Colo., 1953; JD, U. So. Calif., 1961; BBA, U. Colo., 1963. Bar: Calif. 1962; CPA, Calif., 1960; lic. real estate broker, Calif.; securities lic. Assoc. Millikan & Montgomery, L.A., 1961-63; tax lawyer L.H. Penney & Co., CPAs, San Francisco, 1963-67; pvt. practice law Santa Cruz, Calif., 1967—. Lt. USN, 1953-55. Corporate taxation, Taxation, general, Personal income taxation. Office: 550 Water St Bldg F-3 Santa Cruz CA 95060-4131 Fax: 831-423-5419. E-mail: rbtschalk@aol.com.

SCHALL, ALVIN ANTHONY, federal judge; b. N.Y.C., Apr. 4, 1944; s. Gordon William and Helen Schall; m. Sharon Frances LeBlanc, Apr. 25, 1970; children: Amanda Lanford, Anthony Davis. BA, Princeton U., 1966; JD, Tulane U., 1969. Bar: N.Y. 1970, U.S. Dist. Ct. (so. and ea. dists.) N.Y. 1973, U.S. Ct. Appeals (2d crct.) 1974, D.C. 1980, U.S. Dist. Ct. D.C. 1991, U.S. Ct. Appeals (D.C. crct.) 1991, U.S. Ct. Fed. Claims 1982, U.S. Ct. Appeals (fed. crct.) 1987, U.S. Supreme Ct. 1989. Assoc. Shearman & Sterling, N.Y.C., 1969—73; asst. U.S. atty. ea. dist. N.Y. Borough of Bklyn., 1973—78, chief appeals divsn., 1977—78; trial atty. civil divsn. U.S. Dept. Justice, Washington, 1978—87, sr. trial counsel, 1986—87, asst. to atty. gen., 1988—92; ptnr. Perlman & Ptnrs., Washington, 1987—88; judge U.S. Ct. Appeals (fed. cir.), Washington, 1992—. Office: 717 Madison Pl NW Washington DC 20439-0002

SCHALLER, BARRY R. judge; BA, Yale U., 1960, JD, 1963. Bar: Conn. 1963, US Dist. Ct. Conn. 1963, US Ct. Appeals (2nd cir.) 1964, US Supreme Ct. 1966. Ptnr. Bronson & Rice, Atty., New Haven, 1963-74; judge Ct. of Common Pleas, Cir., Conn., 1974-78, Superior Ct., Conn., 1978-92, Appellate Ct., Conn., 1992—. Counsel to Ho. of Reps., 1969; mem. bd. pardons State of Conn., 1971-74, chair, 1973-74; mem. exec. com. Conn. Planning Com. on Criminal Adminstrn., 1972-74; chair Superior Ct. Benchbook Com., 1985-92; vis. lectr. Yale Coll., 1986, 88; clin. instr. evidence and trial practice Yale Law Sch., 1989—; adj. prof., Quinnipiac Law Sch., 2002, vis. lectr., 2003, Wesleyan (Conn.) U., 2003; vis. lectr. Trinity Coll., Vt. Law Sch., 2003; lectr. W.Va. Magistrates Conf., 1990, Vt. Jud. Coll., 1992, Fla. Jud. Coll., 1993, 94, 96, 99, 2002, Ohio Jud. Coll., 1999, 2002, Mo. Jud. Coll., 2002, others; faculty Conn. Judges Inst., 1987-90; mem. Superior Ct. Jury Instrn. Com., 1989-92; mem. exec. com. Conn. Ctr. for Jud. Edn., 1989-92; active Superior Ct. Civil Case Mgmt. Task Force; mem. jud. evidence code drafting com. Author: A Vision of American Law: Judging Law, Literature, and the Stories We Tell, 1997, A Legal Prescription for Bioethical Ills, Quinnipiac Law Review, 2002; contbr. articles to profl. jours. Assoc. fellow Branford Coll.; adminstrv. co-sec. Yale Class of 1960; mem. adv. com. Fair Haven Mediation Bd., 19980-82; bd. dir. Russian-Am. Rule of Law Project; mem. working groups Yale Bioethics Project; vestry mem., tchr. Trinity Ch., Branford, St. Andrew's Ch., Madison. Recipient book award Quinnipic Law Sch., 1997; Guggenheim fellow Yale Law Sch., 1975-76, 84, 85-86. Fellow Conn. Bar Found. (charter life, fellows adv. com.); mem. ABA (CEELI adv.), Conn. Bar Assn., Hartford County Bar Assn., New Haven County Bar Assn., Conn. Judges Assn. (dir. 1990-92), Am. Judges Assn., Am. Judicature Soc., Am. Law Inst., Yale Law Sch. Assn. (exec. com. 1990-92), Am. Inns of Ct. (bencher 1989-90), Conn. Russian-Am. Rule of Law Program (founder, co-chair), Phi Delta Phi. Office: Appellate Ct State Conn 95 Washington St Hartford CT 06106-4431

SCHANES, CHRISTINE, lawyer; b. Jersey City, Apr. 9, 1948; d. Steven Eli and Christine (Marra) S.; m. Ron Taylor; children: Christine Elizabeth, Patrick Steven. BA, U. San Diego, 1970; JD, Am. U., 1973; PhD, U. Notre Dame, 1975. Bar: calif. 1973, U.S. Dist. Ct. (cen., no. and so. dists.) Calif. 1973. Dep. atty. gen. Calif. Dept. Justice, Los Angeles, 1975-78; sr. atty. Atlantic Richfield Co., Los Angeles, 1978-83; sole practice Santa Monica, Calif., 1983—. V.p., bd. dirs. Labor of Love Prodns., inc., 2001—. Co-dir. Nos Amis/Our Friends, Inc., Children Helping Poor and Homeless People, 1987—. Recipient Outstanding Achievement award Urban League, 1969. Mem. Calif. Bar Assn. Civil rights, Commercial, contracts (including sales of goods; commercial financing), Public international. Office: Children Helping Poor and Homeless People 2554 Lincoln Blvd Ste 522 Venice CA 90291-5082 E-mail: chphp@earthlink.net.

SCHAPIRO, DONALD, lawyer; b. N.Y.C., Aug. 8, 1925; s. John Max and Lydia (Chaitkin) S.; m. Ruth Ellen Goldman, June 29, 1952 (dec. Aug. 1991); m. Linda N. Solomon, Oct. 10, 1993; children: Jane G., Robert A. AB, Yale U., 1944, LL.B., 1949. Bar: N.Y. 1949. Assoc. Paul, Weiss, Rifkind, Wharton & Garrison, N.Y.C., 1949-51; asst. chief counsel subcom. ways and means com. on adminstrn. revenue laws U.S. Ho. of Reps., Washington, 1951-52; assoc. Barrett, Smith, Schapiro, Simon & Armstrong, N.Y.C., 1952-55, partner, 1955-88; ptnr. Chadbourne & Parke, 1988—. Vis. lectr. law Yale U. Law Sch., 1949-78, 94-95, instr. law and econs., 1945-49. Mem. Order of Coif, Phi Beta Kappa, Phi Delta Phi. Home: 1035 5th Ave New York NY 10028-0135 Office: Chadbourne & Parke 30 Rockefeller Plz Fl 32 New York NY 10112-0129 E-mail: dschapiro@chadbourne.com.

SCHAR, STEPHEN L. lawyer; b. Chgo., Oct. 19, 1945; s. Sidney and Lillian (Lieberman) Schar; m. Jessica S. Feit, Aug. 17, 1980; children: Scott Andrew, Elizabeth Loren. BA, U. Chgo., 1967; JD, DePaul U., 1970. Bar: Ill. 1970, U.S. Dist. Ct. (no. dist.) Ill. 1970. Assoc. Aaron, Aaron, Schimberg & Hess, Chgo., 1970-77, ptnr., 1977-80, Aaron, Schimberg, Hess, Rusnak, Deutsch & Gilbert, Chgo., 1980-84, Aaron, Schimberg, Hess & Gilbert, Chgo., 1984, Aaron, Schimberg & Hess, Chgo., 1984, D'Ancona & Pflaum, Chgo., 1985-98; mem. D'Ancona & Pflaum LLC, Chgo., 1999—. Instr. estate planning Loyola U., Chgo., 1978—79. Bd. dirs. Jewish Children's Bur. Chgo., 1982—2001, pres., 1996—98, hon. dir., 2001—; pres. Faulkner Condominium Assn., Chgo., 1980—82, Carl Sandburg Village Homeowners Assn., Chgo., 1981—82. Mem.: Chgo. Estate Planning Coun., Chgo. Bar Assn. (pres. probate practice divsn. III 1979), Ill. Bar Assn. Estate planning, Probate (including wills, trusts), Estate taxation. Home: 2155 Tanglewood Ct Highland Park IL 60035-4231 Office: D'Ancona & Pflaum LLC 111 E Wacker Dr Ste 2800 Chicago IL 60601-4209 E-mail: sschar@dancona.com.

SCHARFF, JOSEPH LAURENT, lawyer; b. New Orleans, Oct. 2, 1935; s. Joseph Roy and Celia Ray (Rosenhein) S.; m. Mary Susan Greulach, June 29, 1963; children: Catherine Elizabeth, Robert Laurent, Anne Victoria. BS in Journalism, Northwestern U., 1957; JD, Harvard U., 1964. Bar: D.C. 1965, U.S. Supreme Ct. 1970, U.S. Ct. Appeals (D.C. cir.) 1965, U.S. Ct. Appeals (2nd cir.) 1980, U.S. Ct. Appeals (5th cir.) 1973, U.S. Ct. Appeals (10th cir.); U.S. Ct. Claims 1965. From assoc. to ptnr. Pierson, Ball & Dowd, Washington, 1964-89; ptnr. Reed Smith Shaw & McClay, Washington, 1989-95, counsel, 1996. Mem. ABA (fair trial-free press com. 1973-76, com. reps. media 1985-95, co-chmn. 1989-92), Fed. Comm. Bar Assn., Soc. Profl. Journalists, Radio-TV News Dirs. Assn. (counsel 1965-95, Disting. Svc. award 1987, J. Laurent Scharff Legal Internship established 1996), Media Inst. First Amendment Adv. Coun. Administrative and regulatory, Communications, Corporate, general. Home and Office: 12000 Turf Ln Reston VA 20191-2123

SCHARIOTH, ULRIKE, lawyer; b. Hameln, Germany, Oct. 20, 1949; d. Rudolf and Irma Schmidt; m. Klaus Scharioth, Nov. 29, 1976; children: Nicolas, Maya, Claudia. First state exam in law, Freiburg Univ., Germany, 1973; diploma in law, Oxford Univ., Oxford, Eng., 1974; second state exam in law, Oberlandesgericht Hamburg, Germany, 1978; JD, Freiburg Univ., 1983; cert. family counseling, Iona Coll., NY, 1989. Bar: Amtsgericht and Landgericht, Bonn 1983, Landgericht and Kammergericht, Berlin 2001, specialist for family law: 1998. Lectr. Verwaltungsleiterlehrgang, Quito, Ecuador, 1980—82; lawyer Dr. Ambrosch & Ptnr., Bonn, Germany, 1984—86, Brussels, 1993—96, Düsing & Ptnr., Bonn, Germany, 1996—2001, Buse Herberer Fromm, Berlin, 2001—. Legal cons. Kath. Ehe-Familien-und Lebensberatungsstelle, Bonn, Germany, 1990—, Fruleun-und Familiendienst im AA, Bonn, Germany, 1990—. Vol. Camphill Village, Aberdeen, Scotland, 1970, Camphill Villiage, Copake, NY, 1973; legal counselor Legal Aid Soc., White Plains, NY, 1987—90. Mem.: Deutscher and Berliner Anwaltverein, Frauen und Familiendienst im AA (adv.coun. 1990—93, 1996—), Arbeitsgemeinschaft Familienrecht. Family and matrimonial, Private international. Office: Buse Heberer Fromm Kurfürstendamm 217 Berlin 10719 Germany

SCHATKIN, ANDREW JAMES, lawyer; b. N.Y.C., Aug. 19, 1948; s. Sidney Bernhard and Amy Wheeler (White) S. AB in Classical Langs. cum laude, CUNY, 1969; MDiv, Princeton Theol. Sem., 1973; JD, Villanova U., 1976; Diploma, U. Strasbourg, France, 1984; Cert. in Internat. Law, Acad. Internat. Law, The Hague, The Netherlands, 1985. Bar: NY 1977, US Dist. Ct. (so. and ea. dists.) NY 1978, US Dist. Ct. (no. dist.) NY 1998, US Ct. Claims 1991, US Ct. Mil. Appeals 1991, US Ct. Appeals (2d cir.) 1979, US Ct. Appeals (fed. cir.) 1991, US Supreme Ct. 1991. Dep. county atty. Nassau County Atty., Mineola, NY, 1977-81; Assoc. Rivkin, Leff, Sherman and Radler, Garden City, NY, 1981-82; pvt. practice Bayside, NY, 1982-86; Atty. Office of Hearings and Appeals, Social Security Adminstrn., New Haven, 1986-87; staff atty. Criminal Def. Divsn. Legal Aid Soc., NYC, 1987-94; pvt. practice Jericho, NY, 1994—. Author books and chpts. to books; contbr. over 130 articles to profl. jour. Named one of Outstanding Young Men of Am., 1979. Who's Who in the World, 2002; Mem. ABA (criminal justice sect., family law sect., internat. law and practice sect., labor and employment law sect.), Nat. Assn. Criminal Def. Lawyers (scholarship 1994, 95), NY State Assn. Criminal Def. Lawyers, NY State Defenders Assn., NY State Bar Assn., Suffolk County Bar Assn., Queens County Bar Assn., Nassau County Bar Assn. Republican. Lutheran. Avocations: reading, writing, classical music, travel, languages. Home: 21050 41st Ave Bayside NY 11361-1965 Office: 350 Jericho Tpke Jericho NY 11753-1317

SCHATKIN, SIDNEY BERNHARD, lawyer; b. N.Y.C., Oct. 29, 1903; s. Bernhard and Leah (Solin) S.; m. Amy White, June 21, 1939; children: Jane, Margaret, Andrew. LLB, N.Y. Law Sch., 1924. Bar: N.Y. Asst. corp. counsel City of N.Y., 1931-60. Lectr. paternity proceedings and blood tests bar assns., Yale U., Columbia U., NYU, N.Y. Acad. Medicine, Soc. Med. Jurisprudence, others; cons. in law; trial and appellate counsel. Author: Disputed Paternity Proceedings, 1949, 4th rev. edit., 1975; former editor Criminal Law Rev.; contbr. numberous articles to law revs. and med. jours. Scholar N.Y. Law Sch. Home: 210 Lake Shore Rd Apt 1 Brighton MA 02135-6390

SCHATZ, WILLIAM BONSALL, lawyer; b. McKeesport, Pa., Jan. 18, 1946; s. Carl Frederick and Florence Raye (Hopkins) S.; m. Betty Hurley, Aug. 2, 1970; children: Amanda Raye, Megan Hurley, Michael Hoyt. BBA, Case Western Reserve U., 1968, JD, 1973. Bar: Ohio 1973, U.S. Dist. (no. dist.) Ohio 1973, U.S. Supreme Ct. 1977, U.S. Ct. Appeals (6th cir.) 1984. Asst. dir. law City of Cleve., 1973-77; asst. gen. counsel Northeast Ohio Regional Sewer Dist., Cleve., 1977-78, gen. counsel, 1978—. Speaker on constrn., liability ins., and environ. law. Contbr. articles on constrn., ins., and environ. law to profl. jours. Mem. ABA, Ohio Bar Assn., Assn. Met. Sewerage Agys. (chmn. ins. com. 1985-88, chmn. legal affairs com. 1988-99, bd. dirs. 1999—), Water Environ. Fedn., Cuyahoga County Law Dirs. Assn., Chagrin Valley Athletic Club (Chagrin Falls, Ohio), Union Club. Home: 40 Park Ln Chagrin Falls OH 44022-2427 Office: NE Ohio Regional Sewer Dist 3826 Euclid Ave Cleveland OH 44115-2504 E-mail: schatzw@neorsd.org.

SCHAUB, HARRY CARL, lawyer; b. Hazleton, Pa., Feb. 3, 1929; s. Harry J. and Lida M. (Fisher) S.; m. Kathryn Klindt Deans, Aug. 14, 1982; children: Lisa A., Irene Cannon, Christian K. BA, U. Pa., 1950; JD, Yale U., 1955; postgrad., Columbia U., 1962. Bar: Pa. 1955. Assoc. Montgomery, McCracken, Walker & Rhoads, Phila., 1955-62, ptnr., 1963-99, of counsel, 1999—. Consul Republic of Austria to State of Pa., 1978-84, consul gen., 1984—. Dir. Concerto Soloista Phila., 1997-99, Franklin Inn, 1998-2001; contbr. articles to profl. jours. V.p., bd. dirs. Luth. Ch. of Holy Communion, Phila., 1975-88; bd. dirs. YMCA Cen., Phila., 1986-91. Capt. U.S. Army, 1951-53. Decorated Golden Medal of Honor 1st Class (Austria), Grand Cross of Honor 1st class Austria; recipient Johann Strauss award, City of Vienna, 1979. Mem.: John Peter Zenger Law Soc. (founder, bd. dirs., pres. 1994—96), Mil. Order Fgn. Wars, Austrian Soc. Pa. (v.p., bd. dirs. 1981—97), Am. Coun. on Germany, Athenaeum of Phila., The Penn Club, Rittenhouse Club, Union League of Phila., Pi Gamma Mu, Phi Beta Kappa. Lutheran. Immigration, naturalization, and customs, Private international, Securities. Home: 1420 Locust St Apt 7K Philadelphia PA 19102-4205 Office: Montgomery McCracken 123 S Broad St Fl 24 Philadelphia PA 19109-1099 E-mail: hschaub@mmwr.com.

SCHAUER, FREDERICK FRANKLIN, law educator; b. Newark, Jan. 15, 1946; s. John Adolph and Clara (Balayti) S.; m. Margery Clare Stone, Aug. 25, 1968 (div. June, 1982); m. Virginia Jo Wise, May 25, 1985. AB, Dartmouth Coll., 1967, MBA, 1968; JD, Harvard U., 1972. Bar: Mass. 1972, U.S. Supreme Ct. 1976. Assoc. Fine & Ambrogne, Boston, 1972-74; asst. prof. law W.Va. U., Morgantown, 1974-76, assoc. prof., 1976-78, Coll. William and Mary, Williamsburg, Va., 1978-80, Cutler prof., 1980-83; prof. of law U. Mich., Ann Arbor, 1983-90; Frank Stanton prof. of 1st Amendment Kennedy Sch. of Govt., Harvard U., Cambridge, Mass., 1990—, acad. dean, 1997—2002, acting dean, 2001. Vis. scholar, mem. faculty law Wolfson Coll. Cambridge (Eng.) U., 1977-78; vis. prof. Law Sch., U. Chgo., 1990; vis. fellow Australian Nat. U., 1993, 98; William Morton Disting. Sr. fellow in humanities Dartmouth Coll., 1991; vis. prof. law Harvard Law Sch., 1996, 97, 2000; Ewald Disting. vis. prof. law U. Va., 1996, vis. prof. govt. Dartmouth Coll., 1997; disting. vis. prof. law U. Toronto, 2000. Author: The Law of Obscenity, 1976, Free Speech: A Philosophical Enquiry, 1982 (ABA cert. merit 1983), Supplements to Gunther Constitutional Law, 1983-96, Playing by the Rules: A Philosophical Examination of Rule Based Decision-Making in Law and Life, 1991, The First Amendment: A Reader, 1992, 2d edit., 1995, The Philosophy of Law, 1995, Profiles, Probabilities and Sterotypes, 2003; editor: Legal Theory, 1995, 2000; contbr. articles to profl. jours. Mem. Atty. Gen.'s Commn. on Pornography, 1985-86. Served with Mass. Army N.G., 1970-71. NEH fellow, summer 1980, Guggenheim fellow, 2001-02. Fellow Am. Acad. Arts and Scis. Radcliffe Inst. for Adv. Studies, 2002—; mem. Am. Philos. Assn., Am. Soc. for Polit. and Legal Philosophy (v.p. 1996-99), Assn. Am. Law Schs. (chmn. sect. constl. law 1984-86). Office: Kennedy Sch of Govt Harvard U Cambridge MA 02138 E-mail: fred_schauer@harvard.edu.

SCHAUF, CAROLYN JANE, lawyer; b. Visalia, Calif., Sept. 30, 1946; d. William Powell and Mildred (Hudiburgh) Gateley; m. Jack Eldon Schuaf, Apr. 24, 1971; children: Christie, Jeffrey. JD, Western State Coll. Law, Fullerton, Calif., 1985. Bar: Calif. 1986. Pvt. practice, Downey, Calif., 1986—. Mem. SE Bar Assn., Los Angeles County Bar Assn. Bankruptcy, Family and matrimonial, Probate (including wills, trusts). Office: 8301 Florence Ave Downey CA 90240-3936 E-mail: cjsattorney@yahoo.com.

SCHECHTER, ARTHUR LOUIS, lawyer; b. Rosenberg, Tex., Dec. 6, 1939; s. Morris and Helen (Brilling) S.; m. Joyce Proler, Aug. 26, 1965; children: Leslie Schechter Karpas, Jennifer Schechter Rosen. BA, U. Tex., 1962, JD, 1964; postgrad., U. Houston, 1964-65. Bar: Tex. 1964, U.S. Dist. Ct. (ea. and so. dists.) Tex. 1966, U.S. Ct. Appeals (5th cir.), U.S. Supreme Ct. 1976; cert. Tex. Bd. Legal Specialization to Personal Injury Trial Law, 1964-. Pres. Arthur L. Schechter P.C., Houston, 1992-94, Schechter & Marshall, Houston, 1994-96; amb. U.S. to Commonwealth Bahamas, 1998-2000; atty. Schechter, McElwee & Shaffer, LLP, Houston, 2001—. Spkr. Marine Law Sem., 1983; spkr. in field. Contbr. to Law Rev., 1984. Bd. dirs. Theatre Under the Stars, Houston, 1972—78, Congregation Beth Israel, Houston, 1972—84, pres., 1982—84; bd. mem. Inst. Internat. Edn., 1996—98, S.E.A.R.C.H., 1996—98; pres. Am. Jewish Com., Houston, 1982—84, chmn. fgn. rels. com., chmn. United Jewish Campaign exec. com., chmn., 1993—94; pres. Jewish Fedn. Ctr. Houston, 1994—96; mem. Deans Coun. U. Tex. Law Sch.; mem. Houston Metro Bd., 2002; mng. trustee mem. fin. com. Dem. Nat. Com., 1992, fin. chmn. Tex. Clinton/Gore '96; vice chmn. Clinton/Gore Jewish Leadership Coun., 1996; v.p. exec. com. Nat. Jewish Dem. Coun., 1992; mem. Leadership Ctr. Dem. Senatorial Campaign Com.; mem. fin. coun. Nat. Dem. Orgn., 1979; chmn. of the bd. Met. Transit Autority of Harris County, 2002—. Admiralty, Personal injury (including property damage). Home: 19A West Ln Houston TX 77019-1007

SCHECHTER, DONALD ROBERT, lawyer; b. N.Y.C., Feb. 24, 1946; s. Joseph and Katherine (Beer) S.; m. Roberta Sharon Horowitz, July 3, 1968; children: Elizabeth Anne, Sarah Marilyn. BA, Queens Coll., 1967; JD, Bklyn Law Sch., 1971. Asst. dist. atty. Queens County, Kew Gardens, N.Y., 1971-73; asst. atty. gen. organized crime task force City of N.Y., 1973-74; sole practice Forest Hills, N.Y., 1974—. Legal counsel Centro Civico Colombiano, Jackson Heights, N.Y., 1978—, Fedn. of Merchants and Profls. of Queens, Spanish Orgn., Jackson Heights, 1978—; hearing officer Family Ct., Queens County, Jamaica, N.Y., 1977; consumer counsel Civil Ct., Queens County, 1980. Mem. ABA, N.Y. State Bar Assn., Queens County Bar Assn. (chmn. lawyer placement), Nassau County Bar Assn., Audobon Soc., Sierra Club. Clubs: Glass Soc. Corvette, N.Y. Mets Dream Week. Lodges: KP. Democrat. Jewish. Avocations: antique automobiles, baseball, history, antiques. Criminal, Entertainment, General practice. Office: Ste 1030 80-02 Kew Gardens Rd Kew Gardens NY 11415-3600

SCHECHTER, MARK CLIFFORD, lawyer; b. Pitts., Sept. 3, 1951; BA, Pa. State U., 1973, MA in Economics, 1975; JD, Antioch Sch. of Law, 1978. Bar: Pa. 1978, D.C. 1995, membership: U.S. Supreme Ct., U.S. Ct. of Appeals Third Cir., U.S. Dist. Ct. for Ea. Dist. Md., U.S. Dist. Ct. for D.C. Trial atty. U.S. Dept. of Justice, Office of Planning and Legis., DC, 1978—79, U.S. Dept. of Justice, Intellectual Property Sect., 1979; spec. asst. to dir. of ops. U.S. Dept. of Justice, 1979—82; trial atty. U.S. Dept. of Justice, Trial Sect., 1983—84; asst. chief U.S. Dept. of Justice, Intellectual Property Sect., 1985, U.S. Dept of Justice, Litig. Sect., 1985—88; chief U.S. Dept. of Justice, Transp., Energy and Agriculture Sect., 1988—93; dep. dir., ops. U.S. Dept. of Justice, Antitrust Divsn., 1993—95. Contbr. numerous articles to various jours. and periodicals; spkr. (numerous meetings and conferences). Grantee EU Law and Economics, U. of Amsterdam, 1983. Mem.: The Swedish-Am. C. of C. of Washington, D.C., ABA, Antitrust Sect. Office: Howrey Simon Arnold and White LLP 1229 Pennsylvania Ave NW Washington DC 20004-2400

SCHECHTMAN, STEVEN LAWRENCE, lawyer; b. Carroll, Iowa, Oct. 12, 1959; s. Ronald H. and Maribeth (James) S.; m. Pamela J. Schechtman. BA, U. Iowa, 1982; JD, Creighton U., 1986. Assoc. Houger, Miller & Stein P.A., Seattle, Adolph & Smythe, P.A., Seattle, Siegel, Brill, Groupner & Duffy, Mpls.; pvt. practice Schechtman Law Offices, Minnetonka, Minn. Contbr. articles to Star Carrier, 1986-88; mem. Creighton Law Rev. Atty.-advisor Crysallis Found., Mpls., 1992—, Vol. Lawyers Network, Mpls., 1992—. 010Mem. Hennepin County Bar Assn., Comml. Law League, Twin West C. of C. Avocation: fly fishing. General civil litigation, Commercial, consumer (including collections, credit), Family and matrimonial. Office: 5101 Thimsen Ave Ste 200 Minnetonka MN 55345-4116

SCHECTER, BENJAMIN SETH, lawyer; b. Lexington, Ky., June 11, 1971; BA in English, SUNY, Geneseo, 1993; JD, U. Louisville, 1996. Bar: Ky. 1996, U.S. Dist. Ct. (we. dist.) Ky. 1997, U.S. Dist. Ct. (ea. dist.) Ky. 1999, U.S. Ct. Appeals (6th cir.) 2000. Assoc. Pike Legal Group, Shepardsville, Ky., 1996-97, Pedley Zielke & Gordinier, PLLC, Louisville, 1997—2002; asst. U.S. Atty., Louisville, 2002—. Moot ct. negotiations team U. Louisville, 1996. Editor-in-chief Brandeis Brief Legal Mag., 1994-96; editor Jour. Law & Edn., 1994-96. General civil litigation, Condemnation (eminent domain), Construction. Office: US Dept Justice US Atty Office We Dist Ky 510 W Broadway 10th Fl Louisville KY 40202

SCHEER, MARK JEFFREY, lawyer; b. N.Y.C., Jan. 6, 1962; s. Morton Herbert and Joan Sylvia (Weiss) S.; m. Sheryl Lynn Weinberg, Oct. 24, 1987; children: Matthew Jordan, Danielle Nicole, Lindsay Gayle. BS in Acctg., U. Fla., 1983, M in Acctg., 1984, JD, 1987. Bar: Fla. 1987, U.S. Tax Ct. 1988, U.S. Dist. Ct. (so. dist.) Fla. 1991. Ptnr. Gunster, Yoakley, & Stewart, P.A., Miami, Fla., 1987—. Mem. ABA, AICPA, Fla. Bar Assn., Fla. Isnt. CPAs. Jewish. Bankruptcy, Estate planning, Corporate taxation. Office: 2 S Biscayne Blvd Miami FL 33131-1806 E-mail: mscheer@gunster.com.

SCHEIBER, HARRY N. law educator; b. 1935; BA, Columbia U., 1955; MA, Cornell U., 1957, PhD, 1961; MA (hon.), Dartmouth Coll., 1965; D.Jur.Hon., Uppsala U., Sweden, 1998. Instr. to assoc. prof. history Dartmouth Coll., 1960-68, prof., 1968-71; prof. Am. history U. Calif., San Diego, 1971-80; prof. law Boalt Hall, U. Calif., Berkeley, 1980—. Chmn. jurisprudence and social policy program, 1982-84, 90-93, assoc. dean, 1990-93, 96-99; The Stefan Riesenfeld prof., 1991—; vice chair Univ. Academic Senate, 1993-94, chair 1994-95; dir. Earl Warren Legal Inst., 2002-; Fulbright disting. sr. lectr., Australia, 1983, marine affairs coord. Calif. Sea Grant Coll. Program, 1989-2000; vis. rsch. prof. Law Inst. U. Uppsala, Sweden, 1995, hon. prof. DiTella U., Buenos Aires, 1999; cons. Calif. Jud. Coun., 1992-93; acting dir. Ctr. for Study of Law and Soc., 1999-2001; co-dir. Law of the Sea Inst., 2002—; Cassel lectr., Stockholm U., 2003—. Co-author: American Law and the Constitutional Order, 1988, The State and Freedom of Contract, 1998; author: Inter-Allied Conflicts and Ocean Law (1945-1953), 2001; co-author: American Law and the Constitutional Order, 1978, Law of the Sea: The Common Heritage and Emerging Challenges, 2000, numerous others; editor: Yearbook of the California Supreme Court Historical Society, 1994—; contbr. articles to law revs. and social sci. jours. Chmn. Littleton Griswold Prize Legal History, 1985-88; pres. N.H. Civil Liberties Union, 1969-70; chmn. Project '87 Task Force on Pub. Programs, Washington, 1982-85; dir. Berkeley Seminar on Federalism, 1986-95; cons. judiciary study U.S. Adv. Commn. Intergovernmental Rels., 1985-88; dir. NEH Inst. on Constitutionalism, U. Calif., Berkeley, 1986-87, 88-91. Recipient Sea Grant Colls. award, 1981-83, 84-85, 86-2002; fellow Ctr. Advanced Study in Behavioral Scis., Stanford Calif., 1967, 71; Guggenheim fellow, 1971, 88; Rockefeller Found. humanities fellow, 1979, NEH fellow, 1985-86; NSF grantee 1979, 80, 88-89. Fellow U. Calif. Humanities Rsch. Inst., Am. Soc. for Legal History (hon., pres.-elect 2001—), Japan Soc. for Promotion of Sci. (invitational fellow); mem. Am. Hist. Assn., Orgn. Am. Historians, Agrl. History Soc. (pres. 1978), Econ. History Assn. (trustee 1978-80), Law and Soc. Assn. (trustee 1979-81, 96-99), Nat. Assessment History and Citizenship Edn. (chmn. nat. acad. bd. 1986-87), Marine Affairs and Policy Assn. (bd. dirs. 1991-96), Ocean Governance Study Group (steering com. 1991—), Internat. Coun. Environ. Law, Calif. Supreme Ct. Hist. Soc. (bd. dirs. 1993—, v.p. 1997-98). Office: U Calif Berkeley Law Sch Boalt Hall Berkeley CA 94720-2150 E-mail: scheiber@law.berkeley.edu.

SCHEICH, JOHN F. lawyer; b. Bklyn., Aug. 6, 1942; s. Frank A. and Dorothy (O'Hara) S. BA, St. John's U., N.Y.C., 1963, JD, 1966; postgrad., John Marshall Law Sch., Chgo., 1968. Bar: N.Y. 1967, U.S. Ct. Internat. Trade Admission 1969, U.S. Dist. Ct. (ea. and so. dists.) N.Y. 1971, U.S. Ct. Appeals (2nd cir.) 1971, U.S. Supreme Ct. 1975, Pa. 1980. Spl. agt. FBI, U.S. Dept. Justice, Washington, 1966-69; asst. dist. atty. Queens County, Kew Gardens, N.Y., 1969-72; pvt. law practice, Richmond Hill, N.Y., 1970-76, 79-91; ptnr. Raia & Scheich, P.C., Richmond Hill, 1976-79; sr. ptnr. Scheich & Goldsmith, P.C., Richmond Hill, Hicksville, N.Y., 1991-95, Scheich, Goldsmith & Dreishpoon, P.C, Richmond Hill, Hicksville, 1996—; mortgage settlement atty. GMAC, N.Y., 1996—. Lectr. estate planning Nat. Bus. Inst., 1994; mem. assigned counsel panel for indigent defendants in major felony and murder cases 9th and 11th jud. dists. N.Y. State Supreme Ct., Queens County, 1972—94; lectr. Lawyers in the Classroom, 1979—91; chmn. arbitration panel Civil Ct. City of N.Y., 1981—90; bd. dirs. Ra-Li Brokerage Corp., v.p., 1975—; mem. adv. bd. 1st Am. Title Ins. Co. Am., 1995—; mortgage settlement atty. Gen. Motors Acceptance Corp. N.Y. State, 1996—; trial judge student competition St. John's U. Sch. Law Civil Trial Inst. Student Competition, 1992—. Editor: Conashaugh Courier, 1989-92; mem. editorial bd., 1988-92; contbg. columnist, 1981-89. Mem. Com. for Beautification of East Norwich, Nassau County, L.I., N.Y., 1983—, bd. dirs., 1993-96, pres. 1996—; mem. Holy Name Soc. of Our Lady of Perpetual Help Ch., 1963—, sec., 1965-67, v.p., 1969-71, pres., 1971-73; bd. dirs. Conashaugh Lakes Cmty. Assn., Milford, Pa., 1981-90, organizing mem. Conashaugh Lakes Lot Owners interim com., 1977-81, sec. 1981-82, v.p. 1982-84, pres. 1984-86, past pres. 1986-88; mem. St. Edward the Confessor Sch. Bd., Syosset, N.Y., 1986-90; parish coun. Our Lady of Perpetual Help Roman Cath. Ch., 1976-82, pres. 1978-80, fin. com., adv. to pastor, 1970-82, chmn. fin. com., 1979-82; bd. dirs. Northslope II Homeowners Assn., Shawnee-on-Delaware, Pa., 1988-90, 92-94, 2000-02, East Norwich Civic Assn., 2000—; mem. East Norwich

Rep. Club, 1982—, bd. dirs. 1984-87, 93—, v.p. 1987-89, pres. 1989-93; nat. trust and estate assoc. Meml. Sloane Kettering Cancer Ctr., N.Y.C., 1994—; active Internat. Wine Ctr., 1985-96, St. Edward the Confessor Ch., Syosset, 1982—, St. Vincent Ch., Dingman Hills, Pa., 1977—, St. Dominic's Ch., Oyster Bay, N.Y., 1982— (apptd. pastor's adv. coun. on estate planning 1998, 99, 2000, 01, 02, 03 mem. Legacy Soc. 1998—, Lincoln Ctr. Performing Arts, Inc., 1985—, Nat. Rep. Senatorial Com., 1988—, Bravo Soc., 1994—, Concern for Dying, 1984—, Sea Cliff Chamber Players, 1992-99; mem. Nassau County Rep. Com., Town of Oyster Bay, 1993—, St. John Vianney Roman Cath. Ch., St. Petersburg Beach, Fla., 1994—, Non-Resident Fellow, James Beard Found., NYC, 1995—, Performing Arts Ctr. Pinellas County, St. Petersburg, 1994—, Rep. Nat. Senate Adv. Coun., 1997—, Rep. Nat. Com. Chmn.'s Honor Roll, 1997 (cert. Achievement 1998), Pact, Inc. Ruth Eckerd Hall-Richard B. Baumgardner Ctr. for Performing Arts, Clearwater, Fla., 1995-2001; chmn. tri-centennial celebration com. Village of East Norwich, 1996-97; mem. Fransiscan Ctr. Guild, Tampa, Fla., 1996—, Tilles Ctr. Performing Arts, Inc., Long Island U., Brookville, N.Y., 1997—, adv. coun. estate planning St. Dominic's Ch., 1998—, St. Dominic's Legacy Soc., 1998—, appointed to Bus. Advisory Coun. by Nat. Repub. Congressional Comm.; bd. dirs. Northslope II Homeowners Assn., Shawnee-on-Del., Pa., 2000-2002; mem. Friends of the Arts, Locust Valley, L.I., N.Y., 1985—. Recipient J. Edgar Hoover award, 1967, award of appreciation, Civil Trial Inst., St. John's U. Sch. of Law, 1991, 95, Disting. Svc. award, 1992, cert. of appreciaiton Conashaugh Lakes Cmty. Assn., 1990, Dist. Svc. award Kiwanis Club, 1992, Cert. of Merit for Disting. Svc. award Nassau County Exec. Hon. Thomas Gulotta, 1989, Presdl. Order of Merit award Pres. George Bush, 1991, Order of Merit award Nat. Rep. Senatorial Com., 1994, Cert. Achievement, Rep. Nat. Com., 1998; named one of Best Trial Lawyers in the U.S., Town and Country Mag., 1985; non-resident fellow James Beard Found., N.Y.C., 1995—, Blue Ribbon Survey Commn. cert. of recognition, 2002. Mem. ABA (cert. of appreciation Am. Bar Endowment 1992), ATLA, Pa. State Bar Assn., N.Y. State Bar Assn., Queens County Bar Assn., Nassau County Bar Assn., N.Y. State Trial Lawyers Assn., Ciminal Cts. Bar Assn., Internat. Platform Assn., John Marshall Lawyers Assn. (bd. dirs. 1992—, pres. 1992-97, treas. 1997—), Soc. Former Spl. Agts. of FBI (nat. chpt., L.I. chpt.), N.Y. State Assn. Criminal Def. Lawyers, Legal Lawyers Assn. (bd. dirs. 2001—, bd. dirs. found. 1995-98, 2001—, sec. 2003), St. John's Coll. Alumni Assn., Asst. Dist. Attys. Assn. Queens County, St. John's U. Sch. of Law Alumni Assn., St. John's Prep. Sch. Alumni Assn., Friends of the Arts of Nassau County, Inc., Cath. Lawyers Guild of Queens County, N.Y., KC, Brookhaven Wine Lovers Soc., East Norwich Civic Assn., Sun Island Assn. (bd. dirs. 2001-02), St. John's U. McCallen Soc., 1999-. Business Advisory Coun., Phi Alpha Delta. Avocation: collecting fine wines. Probate (including wills, trusts), Personal injury (including property damage), Criminal. Home: 170 Sugar Toms Ln East Norwich NY 11732-1153 Office: Scheich Goldsmith & Dreishpoon PC 103-42 Lefferts Blvd South Richmond Hill NY 11419-2012 also: 109 Newbridge Rd Hicksville NY 11801-3908 also: 210 Conashaugh Trl Box 4042 Conashaugh Lakes Milford PA 18337

SCHEINE, EDWARD ROBERT, lawyer; b. Bklyn., Sept. 12, 1949; s. David Louis and Ruth (Peck) Scheine; m. Ora Rosen, Aug. 19, 1972; children: David, Michael, Jonathan, Amanda. BA with honors, Northeastern U., 1972; JD, Bklyn. Law Sch., 1975. Bar: NY 1976, U.S. Dist. Ct. (ea. and so. dists.) NY 1976, U.S. Supreme Ct. 1982. Atty. VA, N.Y.C., 1975—76; assoc. Jacowitz & Severance, Bklyn., 1976—77; pvt. practice Bklyn., 1977—78; ptnr. Scheine, Fusco, Brandenstein, P.C., 1978—2001, Scheine, Furey & Assocs., LLP, 2001—. Past pres. NY Workers' Compensation Bar Assn. Author: Workers Compensation for the Health Care Provider. Mem.: ABA, NY Social Security Bar Assn. Trial Lawyers Am., Suffolk County Bar Assn., NY County Lawyers Assn., NY State Bar Assn. Personal injury (including property damage), Workers' compensation. Home: 2 Carriage Ct Huntington Station NY 11746-5842 Office: Scheine Furey & Assocs LLP 200 Motor Pky Hauppauge NY 11788 also: 175 Fulton Ave Hempstead NY also: 2014 Williamsbridge Rd Bronx NY

SCHEINHOLTZ, LEONARD LOUIS, lawyer; b. Pitts., June 2, 1927; s. Bernard A. and Marie (Getzel) S.; m. Joan R. Libenson, Aug. 16, 1953; children: Stuart, Nancy, Barry. BA, U. Pa., 1948, MA, 1949; LLB, Columbia U., 1953. Bar: Pa. 1954, U.S. Ct. Appeals (3d cir.) 1959, U.S. Ct. Appeals (6th cir.) 1968, U.S. Supreme Ct. 1972, U.S. Ct. Appeals (4th cir.) 1973, U.S. Ct. Appeals (5th cir.) 1981, U.S. Ct. Appeals (11th cir.) 1991, U.S. Ct. Appeals (2d cir.) 1993. Assoc. Reed, Smith, LLP, Pitts., 1953—62, spl. ptnr., 1962—64, gen. ptnr., 1964—97, head labor dept., 1980—86, of counsel, 1997—. Dir. Am. Arbitration Assn., N.Y.C., 1980-96. Author: Exemption Under the Anti-Trust Laws for Joint Employer Activity, 1982, The Arbitrator as Judge and Jury: Another Look at Statutory Law in Arbitration, 1985. Vice chmn. Pa. AAA Fedn., Harrisburg, 1982-85 ; chmn. W. Pa. AAA Motor Club, 1979-82; trustee Montefiore Hosp., Pitts., 1976-79; bd. dirs. Nat. Aviary, 1999—; bd. dirs. United Jewish Fedn. Pitts., 1997-2000, Jewish Chronicle, Pitts., 1997-. Served with USN, 1945-46. Mem. ABA, Pa. Bar Assn., Allegheny County Bar Assn. Republican. Jewish. Labor (including EEOC, Fair Labor Standards Act, labor-management relations, NLRB, OSHA). Home: 746 Pinoak Rd Pittsburgh PA 15243-1153 Office: Reed Smith LLP Mellon Sq 435 6th Ave Pittsburgh PA 15219-1886

SCHELER, BRAD ERIC, lawyer; b. Bklyn., Oct. 11, 1953; s. Bernard and Rita Regina (Miller) S.; m. Amy Ruth Frolick, Mar. 30, 1980; children: Ali M., Maddie H., Zoey B. BA with high honors, Lehigh U., 1974; JD, Hofstra U., 1977. Bar: N.Y. 1978, U.S. Dist. Ct. (so. and ea. dists.) N.Y. 1978. Assoc. Weil, Gotshal & Manges, N.Y.C., 1977-81; sr. ptnr., chmn. bankruptcy and restructuring practice Fried, Frank, Harris, Shriver & Jacobson, N.Y.C., 1981—. Contbg. author: Collier on Bankruptcy, 15th edit. revised; rsch. editor Hofstra U. Law Rev., 1975-77. Treas., bus. mgr. Trustees of Gramercy Park, N.Y.C., 1979-87. Fellow Am. Coll. Bankruptcy; mem. ABA (bus. bankruptcy com. corp. banking and bus. law sect., creditors' rights com. litig. sect.), N.Y. State Bar Assn., Assn. Bar City of N.Y. (com. on bankruptcy and corp. reorgn. 1991-94), Sigma Alpha Mu (v.p. 1973). Jewish. Bankruptcy, Commercial, contracts (including sales of goods; commercial financing), Finance. Home: 94 Larchmont Ave Larchmont NY 10538-3723 Office: Fried Frank Harris 1 New York Plz Fl 23 New York NY 10004-1901 E-mail: Schelbr@ffhsj.com.

SCHELL, BRAXTON, lawyer; b. Raleigh, N.C., Feb. 24, 1924; s. Marshall H. and Margaret (Newsom) S.; m. Ann Cooper Knight, Mar. 30, 1951 (div. 1982); children: Braxton, Richard Knight, James Gray (dec.); m. Mary Rehill, Apr. 16, 1983. Student, N.C. State Coll., 1942-43; BS, U. N.C., 1948, JD with honors, 1951. Bar: N.C. 1951. Since practiced in, Greensboro; assoc. Smith, Moore, Smith & Pope, Greensboro, 1951-56; ptnr. Smith Moore Smith Schell & Hunter, Greensboro, 1956-85, Smith, Helms, Mullis, and Moore, 1986-87, Schell, Bray, Aycock, Abel & Livingston, 1987—. Gen. counsel, dir. Flagler Sys. and The Breakers Palm Beach, Inc. Assoc. editor: N.C. Law Rev. 1950-51. Chmn. Special Liason Tax Com. Southeastern Region, 1960-61; bd. dirs. N.C. Outward Bound Sch., 1975-88, chmn., 1977-80; trustee Outward Bound, Inc., 1978-81; bd. dirs. William R. Kenan Funds for Pvt. Enterprise, Arts and Engring., Tech. and Sci. and Ethics. Pilot USAAF, 1943-45. Fellow Am. Bar Found.; mem. ABA, N.C. Bar Assn., Greensboro Bar Assn., Order of Coif, Figure Eight Island Yacht Club, Greensboro Country Club (pres. 1971-72), Greensboro City Club (dir. 1980—), Phi Beta Kappa. Presbyterian. Home: 422B Fisher Park Cir Greensboro NC 27401-1615 Office: Schell Bray Aycock Abel & Living 1500 Renaissance Pla Greensboro NC 27420 E-mail: bschell@sbaal.com.

SCHELL, GEORGE AARON, lawyer; b. Waco, Tex., May 11, 1939; s. George Alvin and Jessie Lee S.; m. Anne, 1960 (div. 1973); 1 child, Michael. BA, Baylor U., 1961, MA, 1963; JD, Loyola U., 1977; MS, Calif. State U., 1990. Bar: Calif. Prof. speech, comm. & debate Loyola Marymount U., L.A., 1963-77; pub. defender Plumas County, Quincy, Calif., 1978-80; deputy city atty. City of L.A., 1977-78, 81—. Office: LA City Atty 6262 Van Nuys Blvd Ste 160 Van Nuys CA 91401-2647 E-mail: gschell@atty.lacity.org.

SCHENDEL, WILLIAM BURNETT, lawyer; b. 1948; BA, Swarthmore Coll., 1970; JD, Boston U., 1974. Bar: Alaska 1976, U.S. Dist Ct. Alaska (9th cir.), U.S. Supreme Ct. Ptnr. Schendel & Callahan, Fairbanks, Alaska, 1981—2002; of counsel Winfree Law Office, Fairbanks, 2002—. Pres. Alaska Bar Assn. Mem. ABA, Alaska Bar Assn. (pres. 1998-99). Civil rights, Labor (including EEOC, Fair Labor Standards Act, labor-management relations, NLRB, OSHA). Office: Winfree Law Office 301 Cushman St Ste 200 Fairbanks AK 99701-4629

SCHENECK, CAROL ANN, lawyer, educator; b. Eatontown, N.J., May 13, 1952; d. Harold Matthew and Lenora Marie (Spidaliere) S. BA in Math., Montclair State U., 1974; JD, Seton Hall U., 1980. Bar: N.J. 1980. Sys. analyst N.J. Bell, Newark, 1974-82; assoc. Dolan & Dolan, Esqs., Newton, 1982-85; legal/computer cons. Crum and Forster Inc., Basking Ridge, 1985-86; sr. trial atty. Crum & Forster-Paul Seligman, Basking Ridge, 1986-87; assoc. McGuire & Wilson, Denville, 1987-94; pvt. practice, Randolph, 1994—. Adj. prof. computer sci. County Coll. Morris, Randolph, 1983—. Past leader Brownies, Girl Scouts USA, 1970-71; past confrat. Christian doctrine tchr., St. Therese Ch., Roxbury, 1976; pres., bd. dirs. Drakesville at Roxbury Condo Assn., Roxbury Twp., 1991—; co-chair Cable TV Com., Roxbury Twp., 1994-95; mem. Bd. Adjustment, Roxbury Twp., 1997-2000, vice chair, 1998-99; active Dem. Orgn., 1995, 97, 99; elected councilwoman Ward 2, Roxbury Twp., 2000—. Roman Catholic. Avocations: computer science, exhibiting purebred american curl cats. State civil litigation, Family and matrimonial, Personal injury (including property damage). Home: 37 Drake Ln Ledgewood NJ 07852-9646 Office: 431 State Route 10 Randolph NJ 07869-2126

SCHENKLER, BERNARD, lawyer; b. Trani, Italy, Aug. 25, 1948; s. Wolf and Nettie Schenkler; m. Ellen Haberman, Sept. 25, 1977; children: Alan, Sarah. BA, U. Pa., 1970; JD, Columbia U., 1973; diploma in mcpl. law, Rutgers U., 1991. Bar: N.Y. 1974, N.J. 1977, D.C. 1979, U.S. Ct. Appeals (2d cir.) 1975, U.S. Dist. Ct. (so. and ea. dists.) N.Y. 1975, U.S. Tax Ct. 1978, U.S. Ct. Mil. Appeals 1978, U.S. Ct. Appeals (3rd cir.), U.S. Dist. Ct. (no. and we. dists.) N.Y. 1980, U.S. Ct. Claims 1985, U.S. Ct. Internat. Trade 1985, U.S. Ct. Appeals (fed. cir.) 1990, U.S. Ct. Appeals (D.C. cir.) 1990, U.S. Ct. Appeals (4th cir.) 1991, U.S. Ct. Vets. Appeals 1990, U.S. Supreme Ct. 1980. Atty bus. law unit N.Y.C. Human Resources Adminstrn., 1973-76, exec. asst. to gen. counsel, 1977; assoc. Ravin, Sarasohn, Cook, Baumgarten & Fisch, West Orange, N.J., 1978-85; ptnr. Ravin, Sarasohn, Cook, Baumgarten, Fisch & Rosen, Roseland, N.J., 1986-2000; of counsel Orloff, Lowenbach, Stifelman & Siegal, P.A., Roseland, N.J., 2000—. Author: Bankruptcy Aspects of Municipal Real Estate Taxation, 1991, Death and Bankruptcy, How the Probate and Bankruptcy Processes Interact, 1994, Close Encounters With the Bankruptcy Code, 1997. Mem. Randolph Twp. (N.J.) Bd. of Ethics, 1978-80. Mem. ABA, N.Y. State Bar Assn., N.J. State Bar Assn., Supreme Ct. N.J. (mem. dist. ethics com. Essex County 2001—), Essex County Bar Assn., D.C. Bar. Clubs: White Meadow Temple Men's Club (Rockaway, N.J.). Jewish. Avocations: Karate (black belt), golf, astronomy. Bankruptcy, General civil litigation. Office: Orloff Lowenbach Stifelman & Siegal PA 101 Eisenhower Pkwy Ste 29 Roseland NJ 07068-1082 E-mail: bs@olss.com.

SCHER, IRVING, lawyer; b. N.Y.C., July 22, 1933; s. Charles and Tillie (Ballenberg) S.; m. Amy Lynn Katz, June 8, 1985; 1 child, Sara Katz-Scher. BA, City Coll. N.Y., 1955; JD, Columbia U., 1962. Bar: N.Y. 1963. Assoc. Weil, Gotshal & Manges, N.Y.C., 1962-69, ptnr., 1969—. Adj. prof. NYU Sch. Law, 1972—; co-chmn. ann. anti-trust law inst. Practicing Law Inst., N.Y.C., 1976—; adv. bd. Antitrust and Trade Regulation Reports, 1980—. Author: Living With the Robinson-Patman Act, 2002; editor: Columbia Law Rev., 1960—61; revs. editor: , 1961—62, editor, co-author: Antitrust Advisor, 4th edit., 2001. Served as lt. USNR, 1955-59. Recipient Nat. Scholarship award, Columbia Law Sch., 1961—62; scholar Harlan Fiske Stone scholar, 1960—62, Gluck scholar, 1960—61. Mem.: ABA (mem. antitrust law sect. 1988—89), N.Y. State Bar Assn. (chmn. antitrust law sect. 1980—81, Lifetime Achievement award 1998). Office: Weil Gotshal & Manges 767 5th Ave New York NY 10153-0119 E-mail: Irving.scher@weil.com.

SCHERF, JOHN GEORGE, IV, lawyer; b. Tuscaloosa, Ala., Oct. 12, 1962; s. John G. III and Roberta Cannon (Timmons) S.; m. Lorie Lankford, Feb. 12, 1994; 1 child, Austin Tyler. AA, Okaloosa Walton Jr. Coll., Niceville, Fla., 1983; BA in Psychology, U. West Fla., 1987; JD, Samford U., 1991. Bar: Ala. 1992, U.S. Dist. Ct. (no. dist.) Ala. 1994, U.S. Dist. Ct. (mid. dist.) Ala. 1997, U.S. Dist. Ct. (so. dist.) Ala., 1999. Clk., assoc. Taylor & Taylor, Birmingham, Ala., 1992-93; assoc. Frank S. Buck, P.C., Birmingham, 1993-95; pvt. practice Birmingham, 1995—. Mem. ATLA, Ala. Bar Assn., Ala. Trial Lawyers Assn., Birmingham Bar Assn. Democrat. Methodist. General civil litigation, Insurance, Personal injury (including property damage). Home: 1324 Springs Ave Birmingham AL 35242-4862 Office: 1812 28th Ave S # B Birmingham AL 35209-2602 E-mail: smurflaw@aol.com.

SCHERMER, JUDITH KAHN, lawyer; b. N.Y.C., Feb. 28, 1949; d. Robert and Barbara Kahn; m. Daniel Woodrough Schermer; 1 child, Sarah Nicole. BA, U. Chgo., 1971; JD, William Mitchell Coll. Law, 1987. Bar: Minn. 1987, U.S. Dist. Ct. Minn. 1987. Advt. and promotion specialist U. Chgo. Press, 1971-75; systems analyst Allstate Ins. Co., Northbrook, Ill., 1975-78, Lutheran Brotherhood, Mpls., 1980-83; polit. aide Mpls. City Coun., 1986-87; ptnr. Schermer & Schermer, Mpls., 1987-99, Schermer & Guy, Mpls., 1999—2001, Judith K. Schermer PLC, 2001—. Assoc chair 5th Congl. dist., state exec. com. Dem. Farm Labor Party. Mem. ATLA, Minn. Trial Lawyers Assn. (bd. govs., chair legis. com., employment com. 1999—), Minn. State Bar Assn., Minn. Women Lawyers, Nat. Employment Law Assn. Civil rights, General civil litigation, Labor (including EEOC, Fair Labor Standards Act, labor-management relations, NLRB, OSHA). Home: 4624 Washburn Ave S Minneapolis MN 55410-1846 Office: Lumber Exch Bldg 10 S 5th St Ste 950 Minneapolis MN 55402-1006

SCHIAVO, PASCO LOUIS, lawyer; b. Hazleton, Pa., June 21, 1937; s. Louis and Josephine (Cortese) S. BA, Lafayette Coll., 1958; JD, U. Pa., 1962. Bar: Pa. 1962, U.S. Dist. Ct. (mid. dist.) Pa. 1965, U.S. Ct. Appeals (3d cir.) 1972, U.S. Supreme Ct. 1970. Assoc. Laputka, Bayless, Ecker & Cohn, Hazleton, 1963-65; asst. dist. atty. Luzerne County, Wilkes-Barre, Pa., 1963-65; pvt. practice Hazleton, 1965—. Mem. disciplinary bd. Supreme Ct. Pa., Harrisburg, 1977-83. Contbr. articles to profl. jours. Pres. Luzerne County Commn. Econ. Opportunity, Wilkes-Barre, 1966-68. Mem. ABA, ATLA, Pa. Bar Assn., Luzerne County Bar Assn., Pa. Trial Lawyers Assn., Am. Judicature Soc., Nat. Bd. Trial Advocacy (diplomate, cert. civil trial advocate). State civil litigation, General practice, Personal injury (including property damage). Office: 199 N Church St Hazleton PA 18201-5874

SCHIESSL, MAXIMILIAN, lawyer; b. Cologne, Germany, Oct. 28, 1960; s. Paul and Anny Schiessl. JD, Munich Law Sch., 1982, Dr.iur., 1985; LLM, Harvard U., 1986. Bar: Germany 1986. Ct. clk. Bavarian Ct. Appeals, Munich, 1982—85; cons. McKinsey & Co., Dusseldorf, Germany, 1985; assoc. Gleiss Lutz, Stuttgart, Germany, 1986—87, 1989, LeBoeuf Lamb, N.Y.C., 1987—88; ptnr. Hengeler Mueller, Dusseldorf, 1990—. Author: Due Diligence and Warranties, 1992, Munich Corporate Law Manual, 1996. Mem.: Internat. Bar Assn. (chmn. corp. 1996—2002, chmn. CMF 2002). Cdu. Roman Catholic. Avocations: tennis, skiing, literature, art. Mergers and acquisitions, Corporate, general. Office: Hengeler Mueller Trinkausstr 7 D40213 Düsseldorf Germany

SCHIESSWOHL, CYNTHIA RAE SCHLEGEL, lawyer; b. Colorado Springs, Colo., July 7, 1955; d. Leslie H. and Maime (Kascak) Schlegel; m. Scott Jay Schiesswohl, Aug. 6, 1977; children: Leslie Michelle, Kristen Elizabeth. BA cum laude, So. Meth. U., 1976; JD, U. Colo., 1978; postgrad., U. Denver, 1984. Bar: Colo. 1979, Wyo. 1986, Ind. 1988, Utah 2001, U.S. Dist. Ct. Colo. 1979, U.S. Ct. Appeals (10th cir.) 1984, U.S. Supreme Ct. 2000, U.S. Dist. Ct. Utah 2001, cert.: (family mediator) 1992, (civil mediator) 1994. Rsch. clk. City Atty.'s Office, Colorado Springs, Colo., 1976; investigator Pub. Defender's Office, Colorado Springs, 1976; dep. dist. atty. 4th Jud. Dist. Colo., 1979-81; pvt. practice law Grand Junction, Colo., 1981-82, Denver, 1983-84; assoc. Law Offices of John G. Salmon P.C., 1984-85; pvt. practice Laramie, Wyo., 1985-88, Indpls., 1988-90; of counsel Rund & Wunsch, Indpls., 1990—2000; dep. pros. atty. 53d Jud. Cir. Ind., 2000; pvt. practice Park City, Utah, 2001—; judge pro tempore 3d Dist. Ct. Small Claims, Park City, Utah, 2002. Guest lectr. Pikes Peak C.C., 1980; adj. prof. polit. sci. and speech Butler U., Indpls., 1993-99, spl. asst. to dean for pre-law, 1993-95, asst. dean for pre-profl. svcs., 1995-99. Advisor Explorer Law Post Boy Scouts Am., 1980—81; vol. Girl Scouts Am., 1993—94, Park City Mountain Resort, 2000—01, Canyons Resort, 2000—01, Leadership Park City, 2000; mem. Park City Singers, 2000—; hearing officer Wyo. Dept. Edn., 1987—88; vol. Project Motivation, Dallas, 1974; chairperson Wyo. Med. Rev. Panel, 1987; lectr. Ind. Pastor's Conf., Rethinking Prisons Conf., 1990, Econ. Edn. for Clergy Conf., 1991; trustee New Castle Cmty. Sch. Corp., 1998—2000, sec., 1999—2000, legis. liaison, 1999—2000; mem. exec. panel Henry County YMCA, 2000; ex officio mem. ch. devel. com. Ctrl. Rocky Mt. region Christian Ch. (Disciples of Christ), 1986—88; mem. evangelism commn. United Meth. Ch., 1987—88, fin. com. youth and music depts., 1979—81, lay del. Rocky Mountain Ann. Conf., 1986—87, acad. tutor youth programs, 1989—, Sunday sch. tchr., 1995—2000; mem. ch. and soc. com. Meridian St. United Meth. Ch., 1989—93, mem. refugee resettlement com., 1990—93; hon. pres. United Meth. Women, 1996—2000, mem. ch. choir, 1997—; bd. dirs. Art Ctr. and Art Assn. Henry County, 1997—2000, Arts-Kids, 2002—03, Multicultural Alliance, 2002—. Named U. scholar So. Meth. U., 1973. Mem.: ABA (internat. law com.), Park City Bar Assn., Indpls. Bar Assn. (internat. law sect. ethics com. 1990—93), Am. Immigration Lawyers Assn. (sec. Ind. chpt. 1991—92, 1993—94, chpt. vice chair 1992—93, asylum liaison 1990—99, chpt. chair 1994—95, bd. govs. 1994—95, Utah chpt. vice chair 2002—), Colo. Bar Assn. (ethics com. 1984—85, long range planning com. 1985—88, chairperson 1986—87), Wyo. State Bar, Alpha Delta Pi, Alpha Lambda Delta, Pi Sigma Alpha (awards com. 1999—2000). Republican. General practice, Immigration, naturalization, and customs, Estate planning. Office: PO Box 981114 Park City UT 84098-1114

SCHIFF, GUNTHER HANS, lawyer; b. Cologne, Germany, Aug. 19, 1927; came to U.S., 1936; s. Hans and Alice (Goldstein) S.; m. Katharine MacMillan, Jan. 27, 1950 (div. 1957); children: Eric Alan, Mary Alice; m. JoAnn R. Schiff; children: Jage, Hans Judson. BSFS., Georgetown U., 1949, JD, 1952. Bar: D.C. 1952, Calif. 1953. Assoc., ptnr., of counsel various firms, Beverly Hills, Calif., 1954-94; pvt. practice Beverly Hills, Calif., 1994—. Sec. Los Angeles Copyright Soc., Beverly Hills, 1975-76 Contbr. articles to profl. jours. Pres. Beverly Hills Civil Svc. Commn., 1984-85, 88-89; pres. Free Arts for Abused Children, 1993-94, dir.; chmn. Rent Control Rev. Bd., Beverly Hills, 1980-84; trustee Young Musicians Found. With USNR, 1945-46. Mem. ABA, Beverly Hills Bar Assn. (chmn. Resolutions Com. 1977-78), Los Angeles County Bar Assn., Los Angeles Copyright Soc., USCG Aux., Calif. Yacht Club. Avocations: sailing, skiing, golfing. Corporate, general, Entertainment, Property, real (including real estate development, water). Office: 9430 W Olympic Blvd Beverly Hills CA 90212-4552 E-mail: hgschiff@pacbell.net.

SCHIFF, LAURIE, lawyer; b. Newark, Apr. 24, 1960; d. Norman Nathan and Claire Jane (Schott) S. BS in Law, Western State U., Fullerton, Calif., 1987, JD, 1988. Bar: Calif. 1989. Ptnr. Schiff Mgmt., Newport Beach, Calif., 1983-89; pvt. practice Schiff & Assocs., Irvine, Calif., 1989-91; ptnr. Schiff & Shelton, 1991—. Probation monitor State Bar Ct. Calif., 1991-97, spl. prosecutor, 1997—. Producer: (record album) Boys Just Want to Have Sex, 1984. Bd. dirs. Jewish Family Svcs. of Orange County, 1994—99. Mem. Orange County Bar Assn. (arbitrator 1995—), Am. Mensa, Am. Polocrosse Assn., Saddlebrook Polocrosse (treas. 1991), Am. Quarterhorse Assn., Internat. Cat Assn. (chair legis. com. 1995-97, 98-99, legal counsel 1999—, lic. splty. judge 2001—), Tonks West (v.p. 1994-96, pres. 1996-97), Tonkinese Breed Assn., Online Feline Fanciers (v.p. 1995-97, bd. dirs. 1997—), Intern. Politically Incorrect Cat Club (v.p. 1996—). Democrat. Jewish. General civil litigation, Entertainment, Family and matrimonial. Office: Schiff & Shelton 3700 Campus Dr Ste 202 Newport Beach CA 92660-2603 E-mail: lschiff@schiff-shelton.com.

SCHIFFER, LARRY PHILIP, lawyer; b. N.Y.C. s. Jerry and Alma Schiffer; m. Gail Beverly Wachtelkonig, Aug. 19, 1978; children: Jessica, Jamie. BA magna cum laude, CUNY, Bklyn., 1976; JD, Union U., 1979. Bar: N.Y. 1980, U.S. Dist. Ct. (so. and ea. dists.) N.Y. 1980. Law asst. N.Y. Supreme Ct.-Appellate Divsn., Bklyn., 1979-81; assoc. Werner, Kennedy & French, N.Y.C., 1982-89; ptnr. Werner & Kennedy, N.Y.C., 1989-99, LeBoeuf, Lamb, Greene & MacRae, LLP, N.Y.C., 1999—. Expert commentator on reins. IRMI.com; spkr. in field. Contbr. articles to profl. jours. Mem. exec. com. Wings Over Wall Street. Mem. ABA (mem. tort and ins. practice sect., chmn. excess surplus lines and reins. com. 1994-95, editor ESLR com. newsletter 1991-93, vice chair, webmaster, listserv moderator 1997—, coord. regional meetings, mem. CLE bd. 1998-2001, chair tech. com. 1997-99, comms. coordinating group com. 1997-99, chair-elect electronic media coordinating group 1998-99, mem. litigation sect.), N.Y. State Bar Assn. (chair com. assn. ins. programs, mem. comml. and fed. litigation sect., mem. torts, ins. and compensation law sect.), Fedn. Def. and Corp. Counsel (vice chair and hot cases editor reins. sect.). Alternative dispute resolution, General civil litigation, Insurance. Home: 295 Waverly Ave East Rockaway NY 11518 Office: LeBoeuf Lamb et al 125 W 55th St New York NY 10019-5369 Fax: 212-649-9493. E-mail: lschiffe@llgm.com., lpschiffer@yahoo.com.

SCHIFFMAN, HOWARD SCOTT, law educator; b. Phila., May 17, 1964; s. Gerald and Lillian Schiffman. BA, Boston U., 1985; JD, Suffolk U., 1988; LLM, George Washington U., 1996. Bar: Mass. 88, NY 89, U.S. Dist. Ct. (ea. and so. dists.) NY 89, U.S. Supreme Ct. 00. Staff atty. Legal Aid Soc. NY, Bklyn., 1988—93, 1996—99; adj. lectr. NYU Sch. Continuing and Profl. Studies, N.Y.C., 1996—98, adj. asst. prof., 1998—. Corr. editor: Jour. Internat. Wildlife Law and Policy, 1998—; contbr. articles to profl. jours. Mem.: Internat. Law Assn., Am. Soc. Internat. Law. Jewish. E-mail: howard.schiffman@nyu.edu.

SCHIFTER, RICHARD, lawyer; b. Vienna, July 31, 1923; came to U.S., 1938; s. Paul and Balbina (Blass) S.; m. Lilo Krueger, July 3, 1948; children: Judith, Deborah, Richard P., Barbara, Karen BS in Social Sci. summa cum laude, CCNY, 1943; LLB, Yale U., 1951; DHL (hon.), Hebrew Union Coll., 1992. Bar: Conn. 1951, D.C. 1952, U.S. Supreme Ct. 1954, Md., 1958. Assoc. Fried, Frank, Harris, Shriver & Jacobson, Washington, 1951-57, ptnr., 1957-84; dep. U.S. rep. with rank of ambassador UN Security Council, N.Y.C., 1984-85; asst. sec. of state for human rights and humanitarian affairs Dept. State, Washington, 1985-92; U.S. rep. UN Human Rights Commn., Geneva, 1983-86, 93; spl. asst. to pres., counselor Nat. Security Coun., Washington, 1993-97, spl. adviser to Sec. of State, 1997-2001. Head U.S. del. Conf. on Security and Cooperation in Europe Experts Meeting on Human Rights, Ottawa, Ont., Can., 1985, Dem. Insts., Oslo, 1991; bd. dirs. U.S. Inst. Peace, 1986-92; mem. Congl. Commn. on Security and Cooperation in Europe, 1986-92. V.p., pres. Md. Bd. Edn., Balt., 1959-79; chmn. Md. Gov.'s Commn. on Funding Edn. of Handicapped Children, 1975-77, Md. Values Edn. Commn., 1979-83, Montgomery County Dem. Cen. Com., Md., 1966-70; del. Dem. Nat. Conv., 1968; bd. govs. Am. Jewish Com., 1992-93, 2001—, mem. exec. com., 2001—; chmn. Internat. Rels. Commn., 2001—; chmn. bd. dirs. Ctr. for Democracy and Reconciliation in Southeastern Europe, 2002—; bd. dirs. Inst. for Christian and Jewish Studies, 2002—. With U.S. Army, 1943-46, ETO. Decorated Austrian Gt. Golden Decoration with star, comdr. Order of the Romanian Star, Bulgarian Madarski Konnik Order 1st class; recipient Disting. Svc. award, Sec. of State, 1992. Mem. Phi Beta Kappa. Democrat. Jewish. Home: 6907 Crail Dr Bethesda MD 20817-4723 E-mail: rschifter@aol.com.

SCHILD, RAYMOND DOUGLAS, lawyer; b. Chgo., Dec. 20, 1952; s. Stanley Martin and Cassoundra Lee (McArdle) S.; m. Ellen Arthea Carstensen, Oct. 24, 1987; children: Brian Christopher, Melissa Nicole. Student, U.S. Mil. Acad., 1970; BA summa cum laude, De Paul U., 1974, JD magna cum laude, 1982; M in Life Scis., Order of Essenes, 1996. Bar: Ill. 1982, U.S. Dist. Ct. (no. dist.) Ill. 1982, U.S. Ct. Appeals (7th cir.) 1982, Idaho 1989, U.S. Dist. Ct. Idaho 1989, U.S. Ct. Appeals (9th cir.) 1989, U.S. Supreme Ct. 1990. Assoc. Clausen, Miller, Gorman, Caffrey & Witous, Chgo., 1982-84; law clk. to chief judge law divsn. Cir. Ct. Cook County, Chgo., 1984-85; assoc. John G. Phillips & Assocs., Chgo., 1985-87, Martin, Chapman, Park & Burkett, Boise, Idaho, 1988-89; pvt. practice Boise, 1989-90; pres. Martin, Chapman, Schild & Lassaw, Chartered, Boise, 1990-96; mng. assoc. prelitigation divsn. Litster Law Offices, Boise, 2001—. Dir. Behavioral Mgmt. Ctrs.; bd. dirs. Image Concepts Internat., Inc., Boise; lectr. on legal edn. ICLE and NBI, 1993-98. Co-host legal radio talk show KFXD, 1994; legal columnist Idaho Bus. Rev., 1988-96. Mem. adv. bd. Alliance for the Mentally Ill, Boise, 1991—, Parents and Youth Against Drug Abuse, Boise, 1991-92, Bethel Ministries; fair housing adminstr. Sauk Village (Ill.) Govt., 1987-88; instr. Ada County Youth Ct., Boise, 1992—. Schmitt fellow DePaul U., 1974; recipient award of merit Chgo. Law Coalition, 1987. Mem. ATLA, Idaho Trial Lawyers' Assn., Ill. State Bar Assn., Idaho State Bar Assn., Boise Estate Planning Counsel, Shriners (temple atty. 1994—, liaison Crippled Children's Hosp.), Masons (jr. steward 1992). Avocations: tennis, trombone, writing, music. General civil litigation, Corporate, general, Probate (including wills, trusts). Office: 6550 W Emerald Ste 108 Boise ID 83704

SCHILLARI, TARA ANN, lawyer; b. Teaneck, NJ, Oct. 22, 1975; d. Frank and Theresa Schillari. BA, Cath. U. Am., 1997; JD, Seton Hall U., 1999. Bar: NJ 1999, U.S. Dist. Ct. (fed. dist.) NJ 1999. Law clk. Judge Lyons-Union County, Elizabeth, NJ, 1999—2000; assoc. Shapiro & Croland, Hackensack, 2000—. Mem.: ABA, Bergen County Bar Assn., Inn of Ct., N.J. State Bar Assn. Roman Catholic. Avocations: reading, travel, fitness, home decorating. Family and matrimonial. Office: Shapiro & Croland 411 Hackensack Ave Hackensack NJ 07601 Fax: 201-262-6055. E-mail: tschillari@shapiro-croland.com.

SCHILLER, HOWARD BARRY, lawyer; b. Apr. 3, 1949; s. Charles Lawrence and Estelle (Saltzman) S.; m. Bonnie Lee York, June 11, 1972; children: Joshua Garry, Elizabeth. BA in Religion and History, Wesleyan U., 1971; JD with honors, U. Conn., 1975. Bar: Conn. 1975, U.S. Dist. Ct. Conn. 1975, U.S. Ct. Appeals (2d cir.) 1975, U.S. Supreme Ct. 1980. Staff atty. Conn. Legal Svcs., Willimantic, 1975—79; pvt. practice Willimantic, 1979—84, 1991—93; ptnr. Shepard & Schiller, Willimantic, 1984—92; prin. Howard B. Schiller, Willimantic, 1992—. Atty. Town of Windham, Conn., 1981—84. Pres. B'nai Israel, Willimantic, 1989—91; active Windham Area Interfaith Ministries, 1995—, pres., 2003; bd. dirs. Willimantic YMCA, 1976—82, Windham-Willimantic Cmty. Fed. Credit Union, 1977—79, Natchaug Valley Vis. Nurses Assn., 1985—89, pres., 1986—88. Mem.: ATLA, Nat. Orgn. Social Security Claimants Reps., Conn. Trial Lawyers Assn., Conn. Bar Assn., Masons (master 1980, 1994, sec. 1981—93, 1995—). Democrat. Jewish. State civil litigation, Personal injury (including property damage), Workers' compensation. Home: 303 North St Willimantic CT 06226-1642 Office: 55 Church St Willimantic CT 06226-2601

SCHILLER, JAMES JOSEPH, lawyer; b. Cleve., July 1, 1933; s. Jacob Peter and Helen Elizabeth (Tosh) S.; m. Sara Brooke Wilson, Oct. 24, 1964; children: Charles A., Brooke V.G., Kristan W. BS, Case Inst. Tech., 1955; JD, U. Mich., 1961. Bar: Ohio 1962. Assoc. Marshman, Hornbeck & Hollington, Cleve., 1961-68; ptnr. Marshman, Snyder & Seeley, Cleve., 1968-73, Zellmer & Gruber, Cleve., 1973-80, Weston, Hurd, Fallon, Paisley & Howley, Cleve., 1980-88, Porter, Wright, Morris & Arthur, Cleve., 1989-95, James J. Schiller & Assocs., Cleve., 1995—. Campaign mgr. John J. Gilligan for Gov. of Ohio, Cuyahoga County, 1970; campaign dir. U.S. Senator Howard M. Metzenbaum, Cleve., 1973; mem. Ohio Dem. Com., 1970-73; dep. registrar motor vehicles Dept. Hwy. Safety, Cuyahoga County, 1971-74; trustee Greater Cleve. Regional Transit Authority, 1985-87; vestryman Christ Episcopal Ch., Shaker Heights, Ohio, 1974-76, 90-93, clk., 1974-76, sr. warden, 1992-93; chmn. bd. suprs. ChristCh. Found., 1995—; trustee Recovery Resources, 1988—, chmn. bd. dirs., exec. com., 1994-96; trustee Ohio Ch. Orch., exec. com., 1996—; trustee Cleve. Ballet, 1997-98. Lt. j.g. USNR, 1955-58. Recipient Cert. Commendation Bd. County Commrs., 1987. Mem. ABA, Ohio State Bar Assn. (ethics com. 1986-88), Cleve. Bar Assn., Rowfant Club (fin. com. 1988, coun. Fellowes 1990-91, 95—, advocate 1992-95, 2002—, v.p. 1998-99, pres. 1999-2000), Union Club, Cleve. Skating Club. Avocations: sailing, skiing, restoring furniture. Federal civil litigation, General civil litigation, Corporate, general. Home: 13415 Shaker Blvd Cleveland OH 44120-1586 Office: James J Schiller & Assocs 13224 Shaker Sq Ste 210 Cleveland OH 44120-2349

SCHILLING, JOHN RUSSELL, lawyer, retail executive; b. Huntington Park, Calif., Nov. 27, 1942; s. Alice S.; m. Susan Foster, Aug. 25, 1962 (div. Jan. 1976); children: Jennifer Susan, Lisa Ann, John Payton; m. Caroline Schilling, Aug. 20, 1976 (div. Dec. 1985); 1 child, Brice David; m. Sabrina Celeste August, Aug. 21, 1993; children: Elissia Jeanne, Chanel Marie, Chloe Celeste, Arianna Rachelle. BA, U. Calif., Santa Barbara, 1964; JD, UCLA, 1967. Bar: Calif. 1968; cert. family law, Nat. Bd. Trial Advocacy. Chief rsch. atty., 4th dist., divsn. II Ct. Appeals, San Bernardino, Calif., 1967-69; pvt. practice Orange County, Calif., 1969—. Lectr. in field; mem. Nat. Bd. Trial Advocacy, 2001. Trustee Santa Ana (Calif.) Unified Sch. Dist., 1971-75. Fellow Am. Acad. Matrimonial Lawyers (v.p. 1985—); mem. ABA (sect. child custody com. 1968—), Calif. State Bar Assn., Orange County Bar Assn. (sect. treas. 1984—), Robert A. Banyard Inn of Ct. (master bencher 1996—), Internat. Acad. of Matrimonial Lawyers. Family and matrimonial. Office: 4675 MacArthur Ct Ste 590 Newport Beach CA 92660-8800 Fax: (949) 833-3883. E-mail: JRSchillingfamilylaw@earthlink.net.

SCHILT, MARGARET ANNE, lawyer; b. Buffalo, June 5, 1950; d. Earl Alfred and Mary Margaret (Belk) Schilt; children: Emily Jean, Nathan Earl, John Robert, Michael Peter. AB, U. Mich., 1972, JD, 1979; MA, Northwestern U., 1973; MLIS, Dominican U., 2000. Bar: Mich. 1979, Ill. 1991. Ptnr. Dobson, Griffin, Austin and Berman, Ann Arbor, Mich., 1979-88; faculty svcs. libr. D'Angelo Law Libr./U. Chgo. Law Sch., 2000—. Mem.: Ill. Bar, Mich. Bar Assn., Am. Assn. Law Librs. Corporate, general, Family and matrimonial. Office: D'Angelo Low Libr 1121 E 60th St Chicago IL 60637 Home: Apt 603 2626 N Lakeview Ave Chicago IL 60614 E-mail: schilt@uchicago.edu.

SCHIMMENTI, JOHN JOSEPH, lawyer; b. N.Y.C., Mar. 21, 1938; s. John Marcus and Mae M. (Miranti) S.; m. Mary Elizabeth Sleep, Apr. 18, 1964. B.A., Columbia Coll., 1959; J.D., Georgetown U., 1962, LL.M., 1964. Bar: D.C. 1962, N.Y. 1964, Calif. 1965, U.S. Dist. Ct. (cen. dist.) Calif. 1965, U.S. Ct. Appeals (9th cir.) 1966, U.S. Supreme Ct. 1971. Trial atty. Anti-Trust div. U.S. Dept. Justice, Washington, 1962-64, Lands div., Los Angeles, 1965-67; trial atty. Santa Fe R.R., Los Angeles, 1968-70; ptnr. Schimmenti, Mullins & Berberian, El Segundo, Calif., 1971— . Mem. S.W. Dist. Bar Assn. (pres. 1983), Los Angeles Bar Assn. (condemnation com. 1983), Columbia U. Alumni of So. Calif. (pres. 1978). Republican. Roman Catholic. Club: El Segundo Rotary (pres. 1977). Condemnation (eminent domain). Office: 426 Main St El Segundo CA 90245-3002

SCHINDEL, DONALD MARVIN, retired lawyer; b. Chgo., Jan. 5, 1932; s. Harry L. and Ann (Schiff) S.; m. Alice Martha Andrews, Apr. 24, 1960; children: Susan Yost, Judith Harris, Andrea Glickman. BS in Acctg., U. Ill., 1953; JD, U. Chgo., 1956. Ptnr. Sonnenschein, Nath & Rosenthal, Chgo., 1956-2000, ret., 2000. Author: Estate Administration and Tax Planning for Survivors, 1987, supplements, 1988-1996. Pres. United Way Highland Park-Highwood, Ill., 2000—, Congregation Beth Or, Deefield, Ill., 1983—85. Fellow Am. Coll. Trust and Estate Counsel; mem. Chgo. Estate Planning Coun. (Austin Fleming Disting. Svc. award 1999), ABA, Ill. Bar Assn., Chgo. Bar Assn. (chmn. probate practice com. 1981-82). Clubs: East Bank (Chgo.). Avocations: tennis, travel, bridge, carpentry, running. Estate planning, Probate (including wills, trusts), Estate taxation. Home: 636 Rice St Highland Park IL 60035-5012

SCHINK, JAMES HARVEY, lawyer; b. Oak Park, Ill., Oct. 2, 1943; s. Norbert F. and Gwendolyn H. (Hummel) S.; m. Lisa Wilder Haskell, Jan. 1, 1972 (div. 1980); children— David, Caroline, Elizabeth; m. April Townley, Aug. 14, 1982. BA, Yale U., 1965, JD, 1968. Bar: Ill. 1968, Colo. 1982. Assoc. Sidley & Austin, Chgo., 1968; law clk. to judge U.S. Ct. Appeals, Chgo., 1968-69; assoc. Kirkland & Ellis, Chgo., 1969-72, ptnr., 1972—. Sustaining fellow Art Inst. Chgo. Mem. ABA, Ill. Bar Assn., Chgo. Bar Assn., Chgo. Club, Saddle and Cycle Club, Mid-Am. Club, Econ. Club of Chgo., Sonnealp Golf Club, Vail Racquet Club, Yale Club of Chgo., Racquet Club Chgo., Game Creek Club. Republican. Presbyterian. Federal civil litigation, Environmental, Private international. Home: 1530 N State Pkwy Chicago IL 60610-1614 Office: Kirkland & Ellis 200 E Randolph St Ste 6100 Chicago IL 60601-6436

SCHLACKS, STEPHEN MARK, lawyer, educator; b. Pittsburg, Kans., Oct. 13, 1955; BA, Austin Coll., Sherman, Tex., 1978; MBA, U. Dallas, 1982; JD, Baylor U., 1986. Bar: Tex. 1987, U.S. Dist. Ct. (so. dist.) Tex. 1987, (no., ea. and we. dists.) Tex. 1988, U.S. Ct. Appeals (5th cir.) 1987, (8th cir.) 1989, U.S. Supreme Ct. 1990. In mgmt. Johnson & Johnson Products, Inc., Sherman, 1978-84; assoc. atty. Wetzel & Assocs., The Woodlands, Tex., 1986-92; ptnr. Hope, Causey & Schlacks, P.C., Conroe, Tex., 1992-96, Law Office of Stephen M. Schlacks, The Woodlands, Tex., 1996-99, Schlacks, Harrison & Cox PLLC, The Woodlands, 1999—. Adj. faculty North Harris County C.C., Houston, 1990—. Leon Jaworski scholar, 1984, Harcourt Brace Jovanovich scholar, 1986. Mem. Fed. Bar Assn., Montgomery County Bar Assn., Sigma Iota Epsilon, Pi Gamma Mu. Republican. Presbyterian. General civil litigation, Insurance. Home: 66 Racing Cloud Ct The Woodlands TX 77381-5203 Office: 2202 Timberloch Pl Ste 107 The Woodlands TX 77380-1163

SCHLAIN, BARBARA ELLEN, lawyer; b. N.Y.C., May 28, 1948; d. William and Evelyn (Youdelman) S. BA, Wellesley Coll., 1969; MA, Columbia U., 1970; JD, Yale U., 1973. Bar: N.Y. 1974, U.S. Dist. Ct. (so. dist.) N.Y. 1974, U.S. Ct. Appeals (2d cir.) 1975, U.S. Dist. Ct. (ea. dist.) N.Y. 1977. Assoc. firm Donovan Leisure Newton & Irvine, N.Y.C., 1973-76, Graubard Moskovitz McGoldrick Dannett & Horowitz, N.Y.C., 1976-79; atty. McGraw-Hill, Inc., N.Y.C., 1979-80, asst. gen. counsel, 1980-86, v.p., assoc. gen. counsel, asst. sec., 1986—. Sec. proprietary rights com. Info. Industry Assn., 1982-83. Author: outlines Practicing Law Inst., 1983, 84, 85, 86, 88; contbr. numerous articles to profl. jours. Bd. dirs., v.p., sec. Dance Rsch. Found., N.Y.C., 1983-86, chmn., 1986-98. Phi Beta Kappa scholar, Durant scholar Wellesley Coll., 1967-69. Mem. ABA, Assn. Am. Pubs. (lawyers com. 1979—), Assn. Bar City N.Y. (comm. law com. 1985-88). General civil litigation, Libel, Trademark and copyright. Office: The McGraw-Hill Companies Inc 1221 Avenue Of The Americas New York NY 10020-1095

SCHLANG, DAVID, real estate executive, lawyer; b. N.Y.C., May 2, 1912; s. Alexander and Blanche (Cohen) S.; m. Arlene Roth, May 9, 1948. LLB, NYU, 1933. Bar: N.Y. 1935, U.S. Dist. Ct. (so. dist.) N.Y. 1940. Individual practice law, 1935-42; sec., pres. Schlang Bros. & Co., Inc., N.Y.C., 1945—. Trustee Brookdale Hosp., Bklyn., 1980—, vice chmn., 1983—, Linroc Nursing Home, 1993—; founding mem. U.S. Congl. Adv. Bd.; bd. dirs., vice chmn. Samuel Schulman Inst. Nursing and Rehab. of Brookdale Hosp., 1973—; bd. dirs. Legion Meml. Sq., Inc., 1983—. With AUS, 1942—45. Decorated Croix de Guerre with palm (France); recipient Conspicious Svc. award State of N.Y., 1965. Mem.: ABA, Real Estate Bd. N.Y., N.Y. County Lawyers Assn., N.Y. State Bar Assn., Criminal Investigation Divsn. Agts. Assn., Met. Club, U.S. Senatorial Club. Home: 737 Park Ave New York NY 10021-4256 Office: 67 Wall St New York NY 10005-3101 E-mail: david@schlang.xohost.com.

SCHLEGEL, FRED EUGENE, lawyer; b. Indpls., July 24, 1941; s. Fred George and Dorothy (Bruce) S.; m. Jane Wessels, Aug. 14, 1965; children: Julia, Charles, Alexandra. BA, Northwestern U., 1963; JD with distinction, U. Mich., 1966. Bar: Ind. 1966. Assoc. lawyer Baker & Daniels, Indpls., 1966-72, ptnr., 1972—; vice chmn. Meridian St. Preservation Commn., Indpls., 1975-90. Contbr. articles to profl. jours. Chmn. Indpls. Pub. Schs. Edn. Found., 1988-90; pres. Festival Music Soc., 1974-75, 79, 86-87; bd. dirs. Indpls. Symphony Orch., 1991—, pres., 2002—; chmn. bd. dirs. Arts Coun. Indpls., 2002—. Mem. ABA, Ind. Bar Assn., Energy Bar Assn., Northwestern U. Alumni Club Indpls. (pres. 1992-94). Republican. Episcopalian. Utilities, public. Office: Baker and Daniels 300 N Meridian St Ste 2700 Indianapolis IN 46204-1782 E-mail: feschleg@bakerd.com.

SCHLEI, NORBERT ANTHONY, lawyer; b. Dayton, Ohio, June 14, 1929; s. William Frank and Norma (Lindsley) S.; m. Jane Moore, Aug. 26, 1950 (div. 1963); children: Anne C. Buczynski, William K., Andrew M.; m. Barbara Lindemann, Mar. 7, 1965 (div. 1981); children: Bradford L., Graham L. (dec. 1995), Norbert L. (dec. 1996), Blake Lindsley, Elizabeth Eldridge; m. Joan Masson, Dec. 29, 1995. BA, Ohio State U., 1950; LLB magna cum laude, Yale U., 1956. Bar: Ohio 1956, Calif. 1958, D.C. 1963, U.S. Supreme Ct. 1963. Law clk. to Justice Harlan U.S. Supreme Ct., 1956-57; assoc. atty. O'Melveny & Myers, L.A., 1957-59; ptnr. Greenberg, Shafton & Schlei, L.A., 1959-62; asst. atty. gen. U.S. Dept. Justice, Washington, 1962-66; ptnr. Munger, Tolles, Hills & Rickershauser, 1968-70, Kane, Shulman & Schlei, Washington, 1968-70; ptnr.-in-charge Hughes Hubbard & Reed, L.A., 1972-89; pres., CEO Kahala Capital Corp., Santa Monica, Calif., from 1983; pvt. practice Santa Monica, 1989—2003. Author: (with M.S. McDougal and others) Studies in World Public Order, 1961 (Am. Soc. Internat. Law ann. book award); State Regulation of Corporate Financial Practices, 1962; editor-in-chief Yale Law Jour., 1955-56. Dem. nominee for Calif. Assembly, 1962, for sec. of state Calif., 1966. Mem. Riviera Country Club (Pacific Palisades, Calif.). Avocations: tennis, golf, skiing, sailing. Federal civil litigation, Corporate, general, Private international. Died Apr. 17, 2003.

SCHLEIFENBAUM, ECKHART JOHANNES, lawyer; b. Munich, Sept. 17, 1966; s. Henrich and Dagmar S. Cert., U. Sorbonne, Paris, 1988; Cert. in Polit. Sci. and Internat. Rels., I.E.P., Strasbourg, France, 1991; 1st and 2nd State Exam, U. Regensburg, Germany, 1994, 96, PhD, 1999. Bar: Munich 1999. Rechtsreferender Superior Ct., Regensburg, 1994-96; asst. to prof. Becker Law Faculty, Regensburg, 1994-97; rechtsreferender German Embassy, New Delhi, 1996; ptnr. Nörr Stiefenhofer Lutz, Munich, 1999—. Author: Die Auseinandersetzung der Erbengemeinschaft in Italien, 1999. Communications, Corporate, general, Mergers and acquisitions. Office: Nörr Stiefenhofer Lutz Brienner Str 28 80333 Munich Germany

SCHLESINGER, HARVEY ERWIN, judge; b. June 4, 1940; BA, The Citadel, 1962; JD, U. Richmond, 1965. Bar: Va. 1965, Fla. 1965, U.S. Supreme Ct. 1968. Corp. counsel Seabord Coast Line R.R. Co., Jacksonville, Fla., 1968-70; chief asst. U.S. atty. Mid. Dist. Fla., Jacksonville, 1970-75, U.S. magistrage judge, 1975-91, U.S. Dist. judge, 1991—. Adj. prof. U. N. Fla., 1984-91; mem. adv. com. on Fed. Rules of Criminal Procedure to U.S. Supreme Ct., 1986-93; mem. Jud. Conf. Adv. Com. on Adminstrn. of Magistrate Judges Sys., 1996—, chmn., 1998—; chmn. U.S. Dist. Ct. Forms Working Group, Washington, 1983—, Jud. Ct. Ad hoc Com. on Long Range Planning, 1998—, Jud. Conf. Jud. Officers Resources Working Group, 1998-99, 11th Cir. Dist. Judges Assn., 1991—, sec.-treas. 1996- 97, v.p. 1997-98, pres.-elect. 1999-2001, pres. 2001-02. Bd. dirs. Pine Castle Ctr. for Mentally Retarded, Jacksonville, 1970-87, pres., 1972-74, chmn. bd. dirs., 1973-74; trustee Pine Castle Found., 1972-76; trustee Congregation Ahavath Chesed, Jacksonville, 1970—, v.p., 1975-80, pres., 1980-82; v.p. S.E. Coun. Union Am. Hebrew Congregations, 1984-88; asst. commr. for exploring N. Fla. Coun. Boy Scouts Am., 1983-86, exec. com., 1986-98, adv. bd., 1998—; mem. Boy Scouts Am. Nat. Jewish Com. on Scouting, Irving, Tex., 1986-93; mem. Fla. Sesquicentennial Commn., 1995-96; trustee River Garden Home for Aged, 1982—, sec., 1985—; co-chmn. bd. govs. Jacksonville chpt. NCCJ, 1983—, presiding co-chmn. 1984-89, nat. bd. trustees, N.Y.C., 1986-93; trustee Jacksonville Cmty. Found., 2000—. Capt. JAGC U.S. Army, 1965-68. Recipient Silver Beaver award Boy Scouts Am., 1986, George Washington Medal Honor, Freedoms Found., Valley Forge, Pa., 1987, Silver Medallion Humanitarian award NCCJ, 1992, Founders award, Fed. Magistrate Judges Assn., 1999, William Green award for profl. excellence U. Richmond Law Sch., 2000, Jurist of Yr. award Am. Bd. Trial Advs., 2001. Mem. ABA (fed. rules of evidence and criminal procedure com. 1979-98, Nat. Conf. Spl. Ct. Judges, 1975-90, conf. newsletter editor, 1988-90, Nat. Conf. Fed. Trial Judges, 1990—, chmn. legislation com., 1996-97, Flascher award 1989), Va. Bar Assn., Fla. Bar Assn., Fed. Judges Assn., Jacksonville Bar Assn., Fed. Bar Assn. (pres. Jacksonville chpt. 1974, 75, 81-82), Am. Judicature Soc., Chester Bedell Am. Inns of Ct. (pres. 1992-96), Rotary (Paul Harris fellow, pres. S. Jacksonville club), Masons (past master, past venerable master, knights comdr. of Ct. Honour, 33 degree Scottish Rite bodies), Shrine. Office: 300 N Hogan St PO Box 1740 Jacksonville FL 32201-1740

SCHLESINGER, NORMAN E. lawyer; b. N.J., Mar. 12, 1920; s. Ike and Rena Schlesinger; m. Carol Schlesinger, Nov. 27, 1948; children: Robert, John. BS in Econs., U. Pa., 1941; JD, Rutgers U., 1950; M of Taxation, NYU, 1953. Bar: U.S. Dist. Ct. N.J., U.S. Ct. Appeals (3d cir.), U.S. Supreme Ct. Ptnr. Saiber Schlesinger Satz Goldstein, Newark, 1954—90, of counsel, 1990—. With U.S. Army, 1941—44. Avocations: golf, bridge, reading. Estate planning. Office: Saiber Schlesinger Sats & Goldstein 1 Gateway Ctr Newark NJ 07102 E-mail: nes@saiber.com.

SCHLESINGER, SANFORD JOEL, lawyer; b. N.Y.C., Feb. 8, 1943; s. Irving and Ruth (Rubin) Schlesinger; children: Merideth, Jarrod, Alexandra. BS in Govt. with hons., Columbia U., 1963; JD, Fordham U., 1966. Bar: N.Y. 1966, U.S. Dist. Ct. (so. and ea. dists.) N.Y. 1967, U.S. Ct. Appeals (2d cir.) 1968, U.S. Ct. Internat. Trade 1969, U.S. Tax Ct. 1993, U.S. Supreme Ct. 1978. Assoc. Frankenthaler & Kohn, NYC, 1966—67; asst. atty. gen. trusts and estates bur. charitable found. div. State of N.Y., NYC, 1967—69; ptnr. Rose & Schlesinger, NYC, 1969—81, Goldshmidt, Oshatz, Powsner & Saft, NYC, 1981—85; ptnr., head trusts and estates dept. Shea & Gould, NYC, 1985—93; ptnr., head wills and estates dept. Kaye Scholer LLP, NYC, 1993—, ptnr. co-chair family owned bus. practice group, 1993—. Adj. faculty Columbia U. Sch. Law, 1989-94; adj. prof. N.Y. Law Sch., 1978—; adj. prof. grad. program in estate planning U. Miami Grad. Sch. Law, 1995—; mem. estate planning adv. com. Practising Law Inst., 1990—; bd. advisors and contbrs. Jour. of S Corp. Taxation, 1989-96; lectr. in field; condr. workshops in field. Author: Estate Planning for the Elderly Client, 1984, Planning for the Elderly or Incapacitated Client, 1993; columnist, mem. editl. bd. Estate Planning mag., 1995—; contbr. articles to profl. jours. Mem. adv. bd. Inst. Fed. Taxation NYU, 1988-96, chmn., 1993-94; mem. legis adv. com. Scarsdale (N.Y.) Sch. Bd., 1981-83, mem. nominating com., 1979-82; pres. dist. 17 N.Y.C. Cmty. Sch. Bd., 1970-71; mem. fin. and estate planning adv. bd. Commerce Clearing House, 1988—; mem. adv. bd. Tax Hotline, 1997—. Fellow Am. Coll. Trust and Estate Counsel (chmn. Downstate N.Y. 2001—); mem. ABA (chmn. social security and other govt. entitlements com. 1990-91, chmn. probate and trust com.-estate planning, drafting charitable giving coms., 1992-94), Internat. Acad. Estate & Trust Law (Academician 1992—), Nat. Acad. Elder Law Attys., Bklyn. Bar Assn., Assn. of Bar of City of N.Y., N.Y. State Bar Assn. (treas. trusts and estates sect. 1991-92, sec. trusts and estates sect. 1992-93, chmn. trusts and estates sect. 1994-95, chmn. exec. com. 1st jud. dist. 1987-91, jour. bd. editors 1995—). Avocations: baseball, writing. Estate planning, Probate (including wills, trusts), Estate taxation. Office: Kaye Scholer LLP 425 Park Ave New York NY 10022-3506

SCHLICHTING, WILLIAM HENRY, lawyer, writer; b. Austin, Minn., Jan. 24, 1944; s. John Frederick and Frances Amelia (Garbisch) Schlichting. BA, St. Olaf Coll., 1966; MS, U. Chgo., 1970; JD, Columbia U., 1973; LLM in Taxation, NYU, 1979. Bar: NY 1974, Minn. 1981, US Tax Ct. 1982. Assoc. Shea & Gould, NYC, 1973—76; editor Law Jour. Pub. Co., NYC, 1976—79; tax dept. Matthew Bender & Co., Inc., NYC, 1979—81; assoc. Peterson, Hanson, Schlichting & Davies, Albert Lea, Minn., 1981—83; gen. counsel, sec. Med. Venture, Inc., Mpls., 1983—89; writer Matthew Bender & Co., Inc., NYC, 1989—91; acquisitions editor, classifier West Group, Eagan, Minn., 1991—2002. Writer Butterworth Legal Pub., Mason divsn., St. Paul, 1983—84. Author, editor Banking Law, 1981, Clark's Digest-Annotator, 1976—79; contbr. articles to profl. jours. Mem.: Minn. Bar Assn., NY State Bar Assn., Sigma Pi Sigma, Phi Beta Kappa. Lutheran. Banking, Securities, Corporate taxation. Home: 5901 Laurel Ave #325 Golden Valley MN 55416-1075

SCHLICHTMANN, JAN R. lawyer; b. Framingham, Mass., Mar. 16, 1951; BA, U. Mass., 1973; JD, Cornell U., 1977. Bar: DC 1977, Mass. 1978, N.H. 1978, U.S. Dist. Ct. Mass. 1978, U.S. Ct. Appeals (1st cir.) 1978, U.S. Supreme Ct. 1990. Pvt. practice, Boston, 1978—. Staff atty. U.S. Ho. Reps., 1978—79; lectr. U. Wis., Nat. Judiciary Coll., 1990. Mem. com. revise Mass. hazardous waste statute Commonwealth of Mass., 1990—92. Mem.: ATLA, Mass. Acad. Trial Attys., Mass. Bar Assn., Phi Beta Kappa. General civil litigation, Toxic tort. Office: 175 Federal St Boston MA 02110 Business E-Mail: jschlichtmann@levinlaw.com.*

SCHLIEMANN, WALTER CHARLES, lawyer; b. N.Y.C., Nov. 28, 1939; BA, Dartmouth Coll., 1961; JD, George Washington U., 1969. Bar: Calif. 1970, N.Mex. 1989, U.S. Dist. Ct. (no. dist.) Calif. 1970, U.S. Ct. Appeals (9th cir.) 1970. Atty. Pillsbury, Madison & Sutro, San Francisco,

1969-73, Schuer & Engle, Santa Fe, 1988-91; pvt. practice San Francisco, 1974—87, Santa Fe, 1992—. Estate planning, General practice, Property, real (including real estate development, water). Office: 86A Sunlit Dr W Santa Fe NM 87508-9373 Fax: (505) 988-1531.

SCHLOSBERG, JONATHAN HARRY, lawyer; b. Johannesburg, Feb. 25, 1953; m. Sheli Hoppenstein, Jan. 10, 1985; children: Tammy, Adam, Gaby. B of Commerce, U. Witwatersrand, Johannesburg, 1974, LLB, 1976, higher diploma income tax, 1979. Dir. Bowman Gilfillan Inc., Johannesburg, 1979—. Mem. Internat. Assn. of Commerce and Econs. Students (trustee), Northern Provinces Law Soc., Gautens Law Soc., Transvaal Automobile Club. Avocations: tennis, theatre, films, reading. Securities, Corporate, general, Mergers and acquisitions. Office: Bowman Gilfillan Inc PO Box 785812 Sandton 2146 South Africa Home: 13 Disa Dr Gallo Manor Sandfor South Africa Fax: 2711-883-4505.

SCHLUETER, DAVID ARNOLD, law educator; b. Sioux City, Iowa, Apr. 29, 1946; s. Arnold E. and Helen A. (Dettmann) S.; m. Linda L. Boston, Apr. 22, 1972; children: Jennifer, Jonathan. BA, Tex. A&M U., 1969; JD, Baylor U., 1971; LLM, U. Va., 1981. Bar: Tex. 1971, D.C. 1973, U.S. Ct. Mil. Appeals 1972, U.S. Supreme Ct. 1976. Legal counsel U.S. Supreme Ct., Washington, 1981—83; assoc. dean St. Mary's U., San Antonio, 1984—89, prof. law, 1986—, Hardy prof. trial advocacy, dir. advocacy programs, 2000—; reporter Fed. Adv. Com. on Criminal Rules, 1988—. Chmn. JAG adv. coun., 1974-75. Author: Military Criminal Justice: Practice and Procedure, 1982, 5th edit., 1999; (with others) Military Rules of Evidence Manual, 1981, 4th edit., 1997, Texas Rules of Evidence Manual, 1983, 6th edit., 2002, Texas Evidentiary Foundations, 1992, 2d edit., 1998, Military Evidentiary Foundations, 1994, 2d edit., 2000, Military Criminal Procedure Forms, 1997, Federal Evidence Tactics, 1997, Texas Rules of Evidence Trial Book, 2000; editor-in-chief: Emerging Problems Under the Federal Rules of Evidence, 3d edit., 1998; contbr. articles to legal publs. Maj. JAGC, U.S. Army, 1972-81. Fellow Am. Law Inst., Tex. Bar Found. (life), Am. Bar Found. (life); mem. ABA (vice-chmn. criminal justice sect. coun. 1991-94, vice-chmn. com. on criminal justice and mil. 1983-84, chmn. standing com. on mil. law 1991-92, mem. standing com. on armed forces law, chmn. editl. adv. bd., Criminal Justice Mag., 1989-91, 2000-), Tex. Bar Assn. Republican. Lutheran. Office: St Marys U Sch Law 1 Camino Santa Maria St San Antonio TX 78228-8603

SCHLUETER, JAMES WILLIAM, lawyer; b. Cin., June 5, 1947; s. Franklin Charles and Kathryn Elizabeth (Moore) S.; m. Diane Marilynn Vickery Schlueter, Apr. 7, 1977. BA, U. Cin., 1970; JD, Chase Coll. Law, Ky., 1974. Bar: Ohio 1974, U.S. Dist. Ct. (so. dist.) 1974, U.S. Supreme Ct. 1978. Ct. constable Common Pleas Ct. Hamilton County, Cin., 1970-74; atty. pvt. practice, Cin., 1975-93, West Union, Ohio, 1993—; magistrate Common Pleas Ct. Adams County, West Union, Ohio, 1996—. Contbr. articles to profl. jours. Mem. Adams County Bar Assn., Cin. Bar Assn. Home: 505 Walt Allsgood Rd West Union OH 45693-9419 Office: Common Pleas Court PO Box 305 West Union OH 45693-0305

SCHLUETER, LINDA LEE, law educator; b. L.A., May 12, 1947; d. Dick G. Dulgarian and Lucille J. Boston; m. David A. Schlueter, Apr. 22, 1972; children: Jennifer, Jonathan. BA, U. So. Calif., 1969; JD, Baylor U., 1971. Bar: D.C. 1973, U.S. Supreme Ct. 1976, Ct. Mil. Appeals, 1990, Tex. 1997. Govt. rels. specialist hdqrs. U.S. Postal Svc., Washington, 1973-75; staff atty. Rsch. Group, Inc., Charlottesville, Va., 1979-81; pvt. practice Washington, 1981-83; asst. prof. law Sch. Law St. Mary's U., San Antonio, 1983-87, assoc. prof., 1987-90, prof., 1990-94. Presenter law Tex. Women Scholars Program, Austin, 1986, 87; bd. dirs Inst. for Comparative and Internat. Legal Rsch. Author: Punitive Damages, 1981-89, 4th edit., 2000, ann. suppls., Legal Research Guide: Patterns and Practice, 1986, 4th edit., 2000; editor Cmty. Property Jour., 1986-88, Cmty. Property Alert, 1989-90; editor Modern Legal Sys. Cyclopedia, 20 vols., 1990, ann. suppls. Mem. ABA, Bexar County Women's Bar Assn., San Antonio Conservation Soc., Order of Barristers, Phi Alpha Delta. Republican. Lutheran.

SCHMELZ, BRENDA LEA, legal assistant; b. Washington, Mo., June 13, 1958; d. Edward G. and Wilma D. (Hektor) R.; m. Jan M. Schmelz, Oct. 7, 1978; children: Edward L., Brent T. Secretarial sci. cert. with honors, East Ctrl. Coll., Union, Mo., 1977. Sec., paralegal Mittendorf & Mittendorf, Union, 1976-83, Eckelkamp, Eckelkamp, Wood & Kuenzel, Washington, 1983—2002. Mem. legal secretarial adv. bd. East Ctrl. Coll., 1978, chmn., 1987; mem. legal secretarial adv. bd. State Fair C.C., 1995. Mem. Nat. Assn. Ct. Reporters, Nat. Assn. Legal Secs. (mem. certifying bd. 1997-2000, chmn. 1998-2000, Jett award 1999), Mo. Ct. Reporters Assn., Mo. Assn. Legal Secs. (pres. 1994-96, pres-elect 1992-94, v.p. 1986, 89-91, sec. 1984-86, 89-90, dir. pub. rels. 1987-89, parliamentarian 1998-99, Legal Sec. of Yr. 1987), Franklin County Legal Secs. (pres. 1989-92, Legal Sec. of Yr. 1986, 95), Ill. Ct. Reporters Assn., Union of Women Today, Phi Beta Kappa. Republican. Roman Catholic. Home: 1792 Oak Parc Union MO 63084-3607 Office: Eckelkamp Eckelkamp Wood & Kuenzel Bank of Washington Bldg Main & Oak Union MO 63084

SCHMERTZ, ERIC JOSEPH, lawyer, educator; b. N.Y.C., Dec. 24, 1925; married; 4 children. AB, Union Coll., 1948, LL.D. (hon.), 1978; cert., Alliance Francaise, Paris, 1948; JD, NYU, 1954. Bar: N.Y. 1955. Internat. rep. Am. Fedn. State, County and Mcpl. Employees, AFL-CIO, N.Y.C., 1950-52; asst. v.p., dir. labor tribunals Am. Arbitration Assn., N.Y.C., 1952-57, 59-60; indsl. relations dir. Metal Textile Corp. subs. Gen. Cable Corp., Roselle, N.J., 1957-59; exec. dir. N.Y. State Bd. Mediation, 1960-62, corp. dir., 1962-68; labor-mgmt. arbitrator, N.Y.C., 1962—; mem. faculty Hofstra U. Sch. Bus., 1962-70; prof. Hofstra U. Sch. Law, 1970—, Edward F. Carlough disting. prof. labor law, 1981-98, dean Sch. Law, 1982-89, disting. prof. emeritus of law, 1998—; of counsel The Dweck Law Firm, N.Y.C., 1999—; commr. labor rels. City of N.Y., 1990-91. Scholar-in-residence Pace U. Sch. Law, 1998—; 1st Beckley lectr. in bus. U. Vt., 1981; bd. dirs. Wilshire Oil Co.; mem. N.Y. State Pub. Employment Rels. Bd., 1991-97; cons. and lectr. in field. Co-author: (with R.L. Greenman) Personnel Administration and the Law, 1978; contbr. chpts. to books, articles to profl. jours., to profl. law confs., seminars and workshops. Mem. numerous civic orgns. Served to lt. USN, 1943-46. Recipient Testimonial award Southeast Republican Club, 1969; Alexander Hamilton award Rep. Law Students Assn.; Eric J. Schmertz Disting. Professorship Pub. Law and Pub. Svc. established Hofstra Law Sch., 1993. Mem. Nat. Acad. Arbitrators, Am. Arbitration Assn. (law com., Whitney North Seymour Sr. medal 1984), Fed. Mediation and Conciliation Svc., N.Y. Mediation Bd., N.J. Mediation Bd., N.J. Pub. Employment Rels. Bd., Hofstra U. Club, Princeton Club. Office: The Dweck Law Firm 230 Park Ave Rm 416 New York NY 10169-0422 E-mail: schmertz@dwecklaw.com.

SCHMID, JOHN HENRY, JR., lawyer; b. Erie, Pa., May 11, 1944; s. John Henry Sr. and Margery (St. Lawrence) S.; m. Carol Christine Imig, July 1, 1967; children: Christine Catherine, Heidi Imig. BA, Beloit Coll., 1966; JD, U. Wis., 1969. Bar: Wis. 1969, U.S. Dist. Ct. (we. dist.) Wis. 1969, U.S. Ct. Appeals (7th cir.) 1993, U.S. Supreme Ct. 1993. Sr. ptnr. Axley Brynelson, Madison, Wis., 1969—. Emergency med. technician Village of Maple Bluff, Madison, 1977-84, trustee, 1985-89. Mem. Assn. Def. Trial Attys., Civil Trial Counsel Wis. Avocations: fishing, golf, travel. General civil litigation, Insurance, Workers' compensation. Home: 802 Farwell Dr Madison WI 53704-6034 Office: Axley Brynelson 2 E Mifflin St Madison WI 53703-2889

SCHMIDT, CHARLES EDWARD, lawyer; b. N.Y.C., Oct. 6, 1951; s. Donald J. and Yanina S. (Giera) S.; children: John Charles, Michael Joseph. AB cum laude, Boston Coll., 1972; JD, Fordham U., 1975. Bar: N.Y. 1976, U.S. Supreme Ct. 1982. Law clk. Lilly Sullivan & Purcell, P.C., N.Y.C., 1973-76, assoc., 1976-84, Donovan Maloof Walsh & Kennedy, N.Y.C., 1984-86; ptnr. Kennedy & Lillis, N.Y.C., 1986-93, Kennedy Lillis Schmidt & English, 1993—. Mem. N.Y. State Bar Assn., Maritime Law Assn., Assn. Average Adjusters U.S. (assoc.). Roman Catholic. Admiralty, Federal civil litigation, Insurance. Home: 255 W 108th St Apt 8D1 New York NY 10025-2926 Office: Kennedy Lillis Schmidt & English 75 Maiden Ln Ste 402 New York NY 10038-4816 E-mail: cschmidt@klselaw.com.

SCHMIDT, EDWARD CRAIG, lawyer; b. Pitts., Nov. 26, 1947; s. Harold Robert and Bernice (Williams) S.; m. Elizabeth Lowry Rial, Aug. 18, 1973; children: Harold Robert II, Robert Rial. BA, U. Mich., 1969; JD, U. Pitts., 1972. Bar: Pa. 1972, U.S. Dist. Ct. (we. dist.) Pa. 1972, U.S. Ct. Appeals (3d cir.) 1972, U.S. Ct. Appeals (D.C. cir.) 1975, U.S. Supreme Ct. 1981, U.S. Ct. Appeals (9th cir.) 1982, U.S. Ct. Appeals (4th cir.) 1982, U.S. Ct. Appeals (6th cir.) 1987, U.S. Ct. Appeals (2d cir.) 1992, U.S. Ct. Appeals (4th cir.) 1994. Assoc. Rose, Schmidt, Hasley & Di Salle, Pitts., 1972-77, ptnr., 1977-90, Jones, Day, Reavis & Pogue, Pitts., 1990—2001, Thompson Coburn LLP, Washington, 2002—. Mem. adv. com. Superior Ct. Pa., 1978-80; NITA instr. Duquesne U., 1998-99. Co-editor: Antitrust Discovery Handbook-Supplement, 1982; asst. editor: Antitrust Discovery Handbook, 1980; contbr. articles to profl. jours. Bd. dirs. Urban League, Pitts., 1974-77, NITA instr., Duquesne U., 1998, 99. Mem. Supreme Ct. Hist. Soc., Pa. Bar Assn., D.C. Bar Assn., Allegheny County Bar Assn. (pub. rels. com. coun. civil litigation sect. 1977-80), Internat. Acad. Trials Lawyers, Acad. Trial Lawyers Allegheny County (bd. govs. 1980), Western Res. Acad. Alumni Assn. (trustee 1998-2000), Rolling Rock Club (Ligonier, Pa.), Duquesne Club (Pitts.), Longue Vue Club (Pitts.), Country Club at Woodmore (Md.). Republican. Antitrust, Federal civil litigation, Personal injury (including property damage). Office: Thompson Coburn LLP 6th Fl 1909 K St NW Washington DC 20006-1167 Home: 110 Duke St Alexandria VA 22314

SCHMIDT, JOSEPH W. lawyer; b. Jeffersontown, Ky., July 6, 1946; s. A. W. and Olivia Ann Schmidt; m. Angela Petchara Apiradee, Dec. 20, 1969; children: Narissa Ann, Suriya Christine. BA in Psychology, Bellarmine Coll., 1969; AB in Commerce, U. Md., Bangkok, 1972; JD, Columbia U., 1975. Bar: N.Y. 1976. Law clk. to presiding judge U.S. Dist. Ct. (so. dist.) N.Y., 1975-76; assoc. Breed, Abbott & Morgan, N.Y.C., 1976-83, ptnr., 1983-93, Whitman Breed Abbott & Morgan, N.Y.C., 1993-96, Coudert Bros., N.Y.C., 1996—2002; v.p., gen. counsel, sec. Dover Corp., N.Y.C., 2003—. Adminstrv. editor: Columbia Jour. Law and Social Problems, 1974—75. Woodrow Wilson fellow, 1968, Harlan Fiske Stone scholar, 1975. Mem.: ABA, Assn. Bar City N.Y. Avocations: skiing, reading. Corporate, general, Finance, Mergers and acquisitions. Office: Dover Corp 280 Park Ave 34W New York NY 10017-1292 Business E-Mail: jws@dovercorp.com.

SCHMIDT, KATHLEEN MARIE, lawyer; b. Des Moines, June 17, 1953; d. Raymond Driscoll and Hazel Isabelle (Rogers) Poage; m. Dean Everett Johnson, Dec. 21, 1974 (div. Nov. 1983); children: Aaron Dean, Gina Marie; m. Ronald Robert Schmidt, Feb. 7, 1987. BS in Home Econs., U. Nebr., 1974; JD, Creighton U., 1987. Bar: Nebr. 1987, U.S. Dist. Ct. Nebr. 1987, U.S. Ct. Appeals (8th cir.) 1989, U.S. Supreme Ct. 1991. Apprentice printer, journeyman Rochester (Minn.) Post Bull., 1978-82; dir. customer info. Cornhusker Pub. Power Dist., Columbus, Nebr., 1982-83; artist Pamida, Omaha, 1983; offset artist Cornhusker Motor Club, Omaha, 1983-84; assoc. Lindahl O. Johnson Law Office, Omaha, 1987-88; pvt. practice Omaha, 1988-90; ptnr. Emery, Penke, Blazek & Schmidt, Omaha, 1990-91; pvt. practice, Omaha, 1992—. Atty. in condemnation procs. Douglas County Bd. Appraisers, Omaha, 1988-99, Sarpy County Bd. Appraisers, Omaha, 1999—; presenter Nebr. Sch. Bd. Assn., 1991, 92. Mem. Millard Sch. Bd., Omaha, 1989-96, treas. 1991, 92; mem. strategic planning com. Millard Sch. Dist., 1990; mem. Omaha Mayor's Master Plan Com., 1991-94. Named hon. mem. Anderson Mid. Sch., Omaha, 1991; recipient Award of Achievement, Nebr. Sch. Bd. Assn., 1991, 94. Mem. Nebr. Bar Assn., Omaha Bar Assn. (spkrs. bur. 1992—), Nat. Sch. Bd. Assn. (del. federal rels. network 1991-96, cert. recognition 1991). Republican. Lutheran. Family and matrimonial, Juvenile, Probate (including wills, trusts).

SCHMIDT, L(AIL) WILLIAM, JR., lawyer; b. Thomas, Okla., Nov. 22, 1936; s. Lail William and Violet Kathleen (Kuper) S.; m. Diana Gail (div. May 1986); children: Kimberly Ann, Andrea Michelle; m. Marilyn Sue, Aug. 11, 1990; stepchildren: Leland Darrell Mosby, Jr., Crystal Rachelle Mosby. BA in Psychology, U. Colo., 1959; JD, U. Mich., 1962. Bar: Colo. 1962, U.S. Dist. Ct. Colo. 1964, U.S. Tax Ct. 1971, U.S. Ct. Appeals (10th cir.) 1964. Ptnr. Holland & Hart, Denver, 1962-77, Schmidt, Elrod & Wills, Denver, 1977-85, Moye, Giles, O'Keefe, Vermeire & Gorrell, Denver, 1985-90; of counsel Hill, Held, Metzger, Lofgren & Peele, Dallas, 1989-94; pvt. practice law Denver, 1990-2001; ptnr. Schmidt & Horen LLP, Denver, 2001—. Lectr. in field. Author: How To Live-and Die-with Colorado Probate, 1985, A Practical Guide to the Revocable Living Trust, 1990, Preserving Your Wealth, 2003; contbr. articles to profl. jours. Pres. Luth. Med. Ctr. Found., Wheat Ridge, Colo., 1985-89; pres. Rocky Mountain Prison and Drug Found., Denver, 1986-2002; bd. dirs. Luth. Hosp., Wheat Ridge, 1988-92, Bonfils Blood Ctr. Found., 1995—, Planned Giving Adv. Group of Nat. Jewish Hosp., Denver, 1996-98, St. Joseph Hosp. Found., 1999—; planned giving adv. Aspen Valley Med. Found., 1997-98; mktg. and gifts adv. com. The Denver Found., 1998—. Fellow Am. Coll. Trust and Estate Counsel (Colo. chmn. 1981-86); mem. ABA, Am. Judicature Soc., Denver Estate Planning Coun., Rocky Mtn. Estate Planning Coun. (founder, pres. 1970-71), Greater Denver Tax Counsel Assn., Am. Soc. Magicians, Denver Athletic Club, 2% Club, Phi Delta Phi. Republican. Baptist. Avocation: magic. Estate planning, Probate (including wills, trusts), Estate taxation. Office: 1050 17th St Ste 1700 Denver CO 80265-2077 also: Law Offices Robert L Bolick Ltd 6060 Elton Ave Ste A Las Vegas NV 89107-0100 E-mail: estpln@aol.com.

SCHMIDT, LAJOS, lawyer; b. Budapest, Hungary, Apr. 23, 1920; arrived in U.S., 1954; s. Lajos Schmidt and Gisella Adorjan; m. Shirley M. Formell, Feb. 21, 1961 (dec. Aug. 1978); children: Anne, Christina, Catherine; m. Maria Bartakovics Rudolf-Schmidt, Aug. 4, 1999. PhD, Ludwig Maximilian U., Munich, 1942; JD, St. Elizebeth U., Pécs, Hungary, 1943; 2d JD, Ill. Inst. Tech., 1954. Bar: Budapest, 1947, readmitted 1992; cert. officer Supreme Ct. Ill., 1954. Supr. Armeria del Exercito Ciudad Trujillo, Dominican Republic, 1948-51; ptnr. Baker & McKenzie, Chgo., 1952-93, chmn. policy com., 1979, 82; mng. dir. Internat. Strategic Cons., Budapest, 1993-2000. Chmn. bd. Messer Hungarogaz Kft, 1989—; mem. exec. com. Hungarian sect. Internat. C.of C. Author: Munchener Volkswirtschaftliche Studien, 1943; contbr. articles to profl. jours. Bd. dirs. Am. Hungarian Found., New Brunswick, N.J., 1990—; chmn. emeritus bd. overseers Ill. Inst. Tech. Chgo./Kent Coll. Law, 1974—; trustee Ill. Inst. Tech., Chgo., 1974-90, life trustee, 1990—; mem. bd. Found. for the Support of the Internat. Exbhns. of the Mus. Fine Arts, Budapest, 1996—; pres. Friends of the Mus. of Fine Arts, 1996. Recipient German Merit of Honor 1st class, 1988, Hungarian Merit of Honor with Swords and Diamonds, 1992, George Washington award Am.-Hungarian Found., 1999. Mem.: Internat. C. of C. (mem. exec. com. Hungarian sect. 2000—). Roman Catholic. Avocation: collecting art. Home: Petofi Ter 3 B/II 6 H-1052 Budapest Hungary Address: Calle Major 30 E-17722 Darnius Spain Fax: (34) 972 535-652.

SCHMIDT, MATTHEW MARTIN, lawyer; b. Buffalo, Apr. 13, 1975; s. Douglas Martin and Christine Ann Schmidt. BS in Psychology, Pa. State U., 1997; JD, U. Dayton, 2000. Bar: Ohio 2000, U.S. Dist. Ct. (so. dist.) Ohio 2002. Rsch. atty. Lexis Nexis, Miamisburg, Ohio, 2000—01; assoc. atty. Rieser & Marx, Dayton, Ohio, 2001—03, Law Offices Nicholas E. Subashi, Oakwood, Ohio, 2003—. Instr. Sinclair Cmty. Coll., Dayton, 2000—. Insurance, General practice, Education and schools. Office: Law Offices Nicholas E Subashi 2305 Far Hills Ave Dayton OH 45419 Office Fax: 937-534-0505. Personal E-mail: mmslaw2000@yahoo.com.

SCHMIDT, RICHARD MARTEN, JR., lawyer; b. Winfield, Kans., Aug. 2, 1924; s. Richard M. and Ida (Marten) S.; m. Ann Downing, Jan. 2, 1948; children: Eric, Gregory, Rolf (dec.), Heidi. AB, U. Denver, 1945, JD, 1948. Bar: Colo. 1948, D.C. 1968. Dep. dist. atty., City and County of Denver, 1949-50; mem. firm McComb, Zarlengo, Mott & Schmidt, Denver, 1950-54; ptnr. Schmidt & Van Cise (and predecessor), Denver, 1954-65; gen. counsel USIA, 1965-68; of counsel Cohn and Marks, Washington, 1969—. Counsel spl. agrl. investigating subcom. Counsel Am. Soc. Newspaper Editors, 1968—; mem. Gov.'s Coun. Local Govt., Colo., 1963-64; chmn. Mayor's Jud. Adv. Com., Denver, 1963-64, Gov.'s Supreme Ct. Nominating Com., 1964-65; mem. Gov.'s Oil Shale Adv. Com., 1963-65, Colo. Commn. on Higher Edn., 1965; mem. bd. Nat. Press Found., 1993—. Trustee U. Denver (life). Mem. ABA (chmn. standing com. on assn. comms. 1969-73, chmn. forum com. on comms. 1979-81, co-chmn. nat. conf. lawyers and reps. of media 1984-89, mem. commn. on lawyer advt. 1964-68), Colo. Bar Assn. (gov.), Denver Bar Assn. (pres. 1963-64), D.C. Bar Assn., Cosmos Club (Washington). Episcopalian. Home: 1920 N St NW Ste 300 Washington DC 20036-1622 Office: Cohn and Marks 1920 N St NW Ste 300 Washington DC 20036-1622 E-mail: rms@cohnmarks.com.

SCHMIDT, WILLIAM ARTHUR, JR., lawyer; b. Cleve., Oct. 2, 1939; s. William Arthur and Caroline (Jäger) S.; m. Gerilyn Pearl Smith, Sept. 30, 1967; children: Deborah, Dawn, Jennifer. BSBA, Kent State U., 1962; JD, Cleve. State U., 1968. Bar: Ohio 1968, Ill. 1990. Contract specialist NASA-Lewis, Cleve., 1962-66, procurement analyst, 1967-68; atty. Def. Logistics Agy., Alexandria, Va., 1968-73; assoc. counsel Naval Sea Sys. Command, Arlington, Va., 1973-75; procurement policy analyst Energy R & D Adminstrn., Germantown, Md., 1975-76; sr. atty. U.S. Dept. Energy, Germantown, 1976-78, counsel spl. projects Oak Ridge, Tenn., 1978-83; judge Agr. Bd. Contract Appeals, Washington, 1983-87; judge Bd. Contract Appeals HUD, Washington, 1987; chief legal counsel Fermilab, Batavia, Ill., 1987-92; gen. counsel Univ. Rsch. Assn., Inc., Washington, 1992—. Co-author: (NASA handbook) R & D Business Practices, 1968. Founder/dir. DOE Contractor Attys. Assn.; dir. Spotsylvania Crime Solvers. Mem. Fed. Bar Assn. (past pres. East Tenn. 1978-83, 25 Yr. Svc. award 1994), Ill. Bar Assn., Bd. Contract Appeals Judges Assn. (dir.-sec. 1986-88), Sr. Execs. Assn., Delta Theta Phi (dist. chancellor 1978-83), Sigma Chi. Republican. Lutheran. Avocations: classic cars, m-1 carbines. Corporate, general, Government contracts and claims, Non-profit and tax-exempt organizations. Home: 10611 King Elder Ct Spotsylvania VA 22553-3666 Office: Univ Rsch Assn Inc 1111 19th St NW Ste 400 Washington DC 20036-3627

SCHMITT, WILLIAM ALLEN, lawyer; b. Louisville, Aug. 29, 1909; s. Michael Joseph and Naoma Katherine Schmitt; m. Dorothy S. Turner, June 12, 1936 (dec. Feb. 1998); 1 child, Selene S. Kaelin. Student, U. Louisville, 1933. Bar: Ky. 1936, U.S. Dist. Ct. (we. dist.) Ky. 1936, N.C. 1997. Pvt. practice law, Louisville, 1936—; assoc. atty. Schmitt & Schmitt, Louisville, 1936-60; judge Jefferson County Probate Ct., Louisville, 1962-70; alcohol beverage control adminstr. Jefferson County Govt., Louisville, 1962-70; law ptnr. Schmitt & Sandmann, Louisville, 1968-74; pvt. practice law Louisville, 1974—, Jamestown, N.C., 1997—. Author: Kentucky Probate, 1980, 2nd edit., 1997; contbr. articles to profl. jours. Election poll judge various gen. elections, Louisville; active Muir Chapel United Meth. Ch.; pres. Wildwood Country Club, 1964, Legal Aid Soc., Louisville, 1968. Lt. USN, 1944-46. Inductee Ky. Tennis Hall of Fame, 1993. Mem. ABA, ATLA, Am. Arbitration Assn. (arbitration panelist 1983—, cert. mediator 1985—), Nat. Assn. Securities Dealers (arbitration panelist 1990—, cert. mediator 1994—), Am. Coll. Trust and Estate Counsel (state chmn. 1978-83), Ky. Bar Assn. (life, spkr. at seminars and convs. 1960-80, pres. 1970-71, probate com. 1970-86, chmn. 1977-81, trustee 1971-86, chmn. 1978-86, clients indemnity fund), N.C. State Bar Assn., N.C. State Bar, Louisville Bar Assn. (spkr. at seminars 1960-80, pres. 1966, chmn. probate com. 1974-79, various meritorious svc. awards 1966-75). Avocation: tennis. Estate planning, Personal injury (including property damage), Probate (including wills, trusts). Home: 109 Sagewood Rd Jamestown NC 27282-9489 Office: PO Box 997 Jamestown NC 27282-0997 also: 500 Ky Home Life Bldg 239 S 5th St Louisville KY 40202-3213

SCHMOLL, HARRY F., JR., lawyer, educator; b. Somers Point, N.J., Jan. 20, 1939; s. Harry F. Sr. and Margaret E. S.; m. Rita L. Miescier, Aug. 29, 1977. BS, Rider Coll., 1960; JD, Temple U., 1967. Bar: Pa., D.C. 1969, N.J. 1975. With claims dept. Social Security Adminstrn., Phila., 1960-67; staff atty. Pa. State U., State College, 1968-69, instr. criminal justice University Park, 1969-74; regional dir. Pa. Crime Commn., State College, 1969-70; campaign aide U.S. Senator Hugh Scott, Harrisburg, Pa., 1970; pvt. practice law State College, 1970-74, Manahawkin, NJ, 1975-96; prof. criminal justice, bus. law Burlington County Coll., Pemberton, NJ, 1974—2002; of counsel Mattleman, Weinroth & Miller, P.C., Cherry Hill, NJ, 2003—. Judge mcpl. ct., Stafford Twp., 1982-85. Author: New Jersey Criminal Law Workbook, 1976, 2nd edit., 1979, Absecon Diary of Margie Roth, 1933-37, 2000. Former gen. counsel German Heritage Coun. N.J., Inc.; mem. Barnegat Twp. Rent Control Bd., 1991, Barnegat Twp. Zoning Bd., 1994; mem. fund distbn. com. United Way of Burlington County, N.J., 1987—; trustee H.B. Smith Indsl. Village Conservancy, 1988—; bd. trustees Holiday Village East Cmty. Svcs. Assn., 2003—; mem. Stafford Twp. Com., 1979-81; dep. mayor, 1979. Mem. Pa. Bar assn., N.J. Bar Assn., German-Am. Club So. Ocean County (past pres.), Tri-State Jazz Soc. (bd. dirs.). General practice, Personal injury (including property damage), Probate (including wills, trusts). E-mail: HarrySchmoll2@comcast.net.

SCHMUDDE, LEE GENE, corporate lawyer; b. Harvey, Ill., Apr. 13, 1950; s. Kenneth H. and Jean E. (Alexander) S.; m. Mariann Verscharen, June 25, 1976; 1 child, Leighanne K. BA summa cum laude, Cornell Coll., Mount Vernon, Iowa, 1972; JD, Duke U., 1975. Bar: Fla. 1975, U.S. Dist. Ct. (ctrl. dist.) Fla. 1975. Law clk. to Chief Judge Joseph P. McNulty 2d Dist. Ct. Appeals, Lakeland, Fla., 1975-76; atty. Peterson, Myers, Lake Wales, Fla., 1976-78; v.p. legal and environ. affairs Walt Disney World Co., Orlando, Fla. Lectr. ABA, Fla. Bar, Orange County Bar Assn., Def. Lawyers Assn. Contbr. articles to Fla. Bar Jour. Bd. dirs., treas. Fla. Symphony Orch., Orlando, 1997; bd. dirs. Children's Home Soc., 1981-85; mem. adv. bd. Jr. Achievement, 1995—; chmn. Fla. Self-Ins. Guaranty Assn., 1985, 93, bd. dirs., 1985—. Mem. Fla. Bar Assn. (lectr.), Am. Zoo and Aquarium Assn., U.S. C. of C. (Outstanding Young Man of Am. 1975), Fla. C. of C. (jud. and tort reform adv. bd. 2000—), Fla. Assn. Self-Insurers (bd. dirs. 1984-85), Ctrl. Fla. Hist. Soc. (bd. dirs. 2000—), Phi Beta Kappa. Avocations: tennis, basketball, sport fishing. Administrative and regulatory, Corporate, general, Environmental. Office: Walt Disney World Co PO Box 10 000 Lake Buena Vista FL 32830-1000

SCHMULTS, EDWARD CHARLES, lawyer, corporate and philanthropic administrator; b. Paterson, N.J., Feb. 6, 1931; s. Edward M. and Mildred (Moore) S.; m. Diane E. Beers, Apr. 23, 1960; children: Alison C., Edward M., Robert C. BS, Yale U., 1953; JD, Harvard U., 1958. Bar: N.Y. 1959, D.C. 1974. Assoc. White & Case, N.Y.C., 1958-65, ptnr., 1965-73, 77-81; gen. counsel Treasury Dept., Washington, 1973-74, undersec., 1974-75; dep. counsel to Pres. U.S., 1975-76; dep. atty. gen. of U.S. Dept. Justice, Washington, 1981-84; sr. v.p. external rels., gen. counsel GTE Corp., Stamford, Conn., 1984-94. Lectr. securities laws. Bd. dirs. GreenPoint Fin. Corp., Germany Fund, Ctrl. European Equity Fund. Served to 1st lt. USMC, 1953-55; capt. USMCR. Mem. Am. Bar Assn., Assn. Bar City N.Y., Adminstrv. Conf. U.S. (council 1977-84), Sakonnet Golf Club, Met. Club.

SCHNACK, HAROLD CLIFFORD, retired lawyer; b. Honolulu, Sept. 27, 1918; s. Ferdinand J. H. and Mary (Pearson) S.; m. Gayle Hemingway Jepson, Mar. 22, 1947 (dec. Feb. 24, 1998); children: Jerrald Jay, Georgina Schnack Hankinson, Roberta Schnack Poulin, Michael Clifford. BA, Stanford U., 1940, LLB, 1947. Bar: Hawaii 1947. Dep. prosecutor City and County Honolulu, 1947-48; gen. practice with father F. Schnack, 1948-60; pvt. practice, 1960—2001. Pres. Harcliff Corp., 1961—, Cedar Corp., 1964—, Schnack Indsl. Corp., 1969-73, Instant Printers, Inc., 1971-81, Koa Corp., 1964—, Nutmeg Corp., 1963-89, Global Answer System, Inc., 1972-78; pres., treas. Golden Rainbow, Inc. (Pasta Chef), Reno, 2001—. Pres. Goodwill Industries of Honolulu, 1971-72. Mem. Outrigger Canoe Club, Phi Alpha Delta, Alpha Sigma Phi. Office: 817 A Cedar St PO Box 3077 Honolulu HI 96802-3077

SCHNAPP, MARK PAUL, lawyer; b. N.Y.C., Sept. 29, 1951; s. Ben and Sally Schnapp. B in Elec. Engring., NYU, 1972; JD, Hofstra U., 1976. Bar: N.Y. 1977, U.S. Dist. Ct. (ea. and so. dists.) N.Y. 1977, U.S. Ct. Appeals (9th cir.) 1980, Fla. 1985, D.C. 1987, U.S. Ct. Appeals (11th cir.) 1988, U.S. Dist. Ct. (so. dist.) Fla. 1989. Assoc. Cravath Swaine & Moore, N.Y.C., 1976—81; asst. U.S. atty. U.S. Attys. Office So. Dist. Fla., Miami, 1982—89, chief pub. corp. sect., 1985—87, chief criminal divsn., 1987—89; prin. shareholder Greenberg Traurig P.A., Miami, 1989—. Bd. mem. Arts for Learning, Miami, 2001—. Mem.: ABA, Asst. U.S. Attys. Assn. (pres. so. dist. Fla.). General civil litigation. Office: Greenberg Traurig PA 1221 Brickell Ave Miami FL 33139

SCHNEBLE, ALFRED WILLIAM, III, lawyer; b. Dayton, Ohio, Nov. 4, 1956; s. A. William and Marijane (Spitler) S. BS, Marquette U., 1978; JD, Ohio No. U., 1981. Bar: Ohio 1981, Fla. 1983. Staff atty. James W. Knisley Co., Dayton, 1981-83; pvt. practice Dayton, 1983-85; prin. Alfred W. Schneble III Co. LPA, Dayton, 1986-2000; shareholder, pres. Schneble, Cass & Assoc. Co., LPA, Dayton, 2000—. Mem. Ohio Bar Assn., Fla. Bar Assn., Dayton Bar Assn., Ohio Acad. Trial Lawyers. Republican. Roman Catholic. State civil litigation, Corporate, general, Personal injury (including property damage). Office: 11 W Monument Ave #402 Dayton OH 45402

SCHNEEBALG, AVI, lawyer, mediator; b. Antwerp, Belgium, Feb. 10, 1955; s. Moshe and Sophie (Perelman) s.; m. Donatella G. Soria, June 30, 1989; 1 child, Marco G. BA in Econs., Univ. Libre de Bruxelle, Brussels, 1974, LLM, 1979. Bar: Brussels 1981. Assoc. Berenboom, Sukennik, Schneebalg, Gilles & DuFrene, Brussels, 1984—; rschr. Ctr. Legal Philosophy ULB, Brussels, 1979-81. Bus. mediator Brussels, 1998—; bd. dirs., co-founder Brussels Bus. Mediation Ctr., 1998—, Ctr. de Mediation et d'Arlitiege de Paris, 1993—; mem. Nederlands Mediation Inst,. Rotterdam, 2000—, WIPO Mediation Ctr., Geneva, 1998—, Internat. Ctr. for Dispute Resolution; mem. panel of disting. neutrals CPR Internat., 2002. Author textbook, 2002; contbr. articles to profl. jours. Mem. Brussels Bar Assn., Am. C. of C. Home: Av Louise 105/14 1050 Brussels Belgium Office: Berenboom Sukennik et al Rue de Florence 13 B-1000 Brussels Belgium

SCHNEIDER, CARL WILLIAM, lawyer; b. Phila., Apr. 27, 1932; s. Nathan J. and Eleanor M. (Milgram) S.; m. Mary Ellen Baylinson; children: Eric, Mark, Adam, Cara BA, Cornell U., 1953; LLB magna cum laude, U. Pa., 1956. Bar: Pa. 1957. Law clk. U.S. Ct. Appeals (3d cir.), Phila., 1956-57; sr. law clk. U.S. Supreme Ct., Washington, 1957-58; assoc. Wolf, Block, Schorr and Solis-Cohen LLP, Phila., 1958-65; ptnr. Wolf, Block, Schorr and Solis-Cohen, Phila., 1965-2000, of counsel, 2000—. Spl. advisor divsn. corp. fin. SEC, Washington, 1964; lectr. securities law U. Pa., 1968-70, vis. assoc. prof., 1978-81, acting dir. Ctr. for Study Fin. Instns.; bd. editors and advisors Rev. Securities and Commodities Regulations. Author: SEC Consequences of Corporate Acquisitions, 1971, Pennsylvania Corporate Practice and Forms: The Wolf, Block, Schorr and Solis-Cohen Manual, 1997; also numerous articles. Bd. dirs. Found. of Jewish Families and Children's Svc., Abramson Ctr. for Jewish Life; chmn. bd. dirs. Jewish Family and Children's Svc. of Greater Phila.; trustee Long Beach Island Found. of the Arts and Scis., Loveladies, NJ. Mem. ABA, Pa. Bar Assn., Phila. Bar Assn. (chmn. sect. corp. banking and bus. law 1972), Am. Law Inst. (life). Corporate, general, Securities. Home: 235 Linden Dr Elkins Park PA 19027-1341

SCHNEIDER, ELAINE CAROL, lawyer, researcher, writer; b. Mpls., Aug. 28, 1957; d. Allan William and Deborah G. Schneider; m. William Mack Olivé, Oct. 10, 1987 (div. July 1996); 1 child, Vanessa Inez Olivè; m. G.R. Smith, Jan. 2, 2002. BA, U. Minn., 1979; JD, William Mitchell Coll. Law, St. Paul, 1982. Bar: N.Mex. 1984, Minn. 1998, D.C. 1999. Assoc. Settles, Kalamarides & Assocs., Anchorage, 1982, Dickson, Evans & Esch, Anchorage, 1982; legal rschr. John Hanson, Anchorage, 1983, Anchorage, 1983; acct. rep. Westlaw Svcs., Inc., Albuquerque, 1984, sales rep. New Orleans, 1985-86; libr. sales rep. West Pub. Co., Spokane, Wash., 1986-87, reference atty. St. Paul, 1988-97, product mgr., 1997-2001; pvt. practice Mpls., Minn. Ethics adv. bd. N.Mex. Bar, Albuquerque, 1984-85; midwest regional conf. com. Am. Immigration Lawyers Assn., 2000. Author: Substantive Judicial Law Outline of Habeas Corpus, 1984, What They Don't Teach You in the Bar Review Course, 1991, Challenging an Incredibility Finding on Appeal, An Incredibility Paradigm, 2001; mem. law rev. staff : William Mitchell Coll. Law, 1980—81. Atty. immigration and naturalization law Minn. Advocates for Human Rights, Refugee and Immigrant Project. Recipient Vol. Pro Bono Atty. award, 15th Ann. Minn. Advocates for Human Rights, 1999. Mem. Phi Beta Kappa. Avocations: ventriloquism, skiing, swimming, travel, languages. Immigration, naturalization, and customs. Office: 701 4th Ave S Ste 500 Minneapolis MN 55415-1810 E-mail: avocatecs@aol.com.

SCHNEIDER, ELIZABETH KELLEY, law librarian; b. Bloomington, Ill., July 10, 1946; d. George Raymond and Lucille Genvieve (Sutter) Kelley; m. John James Schneider, Aug. 21, 1982. BA in History, Wesleyan U., Ill., 1968; MLS, U. Minn., 1969; JD, William Mitchell Coll. of Law, 1973; LLM in Health Law, St. Louis U., 1997. Bar: Minn. 1974, U.S. Dist. Ct. Minn. 1995. Librarian Ramsy County Law Library, St. Paul, 1971-73; asst. law librarian U. of Akron (Ohio) Coll. of Law, 1973-74; prof. law, librarian Hamline U. Sch. Law, St. Paul, 1974-81; dir. Maricopa County Law Library, Phoenix, 1981-91; assoc. dir. law libr., asst. prof. Tex. Tech. Sch. Law, 1992-2000. Instr. legal research Ariz. Legal Secs. Assn., 1982, Phoenix Coll., 1982-85, Ariz. State Library Assn., 1984. Mem. ABA, Am. Assn. Law Libraries, Ariz. Assn. Law Libraries (pres. 1985-86), Ariz. Women Lawyers Assn., Desert Sun Aux., Nat. Assistance League (sec. 1985-86, chmn. 1986-87), Southwestern Assn. of Law Libr. (sec. 1987-90, v.p. 1990-91), Legal Info. Svcs. to the Pub. (chair 1988-89), Alpha Gamma Delta (pres. 1985-86). Office: Plattner Schneidman & Schneider 4201 North 24th St Ste 100 Phoenix AZ 85016 E-mail: eksphx@yahoo.com.

SCHNEIDER, HOWARD, lawyer; b. N.Y.C., Mar. 21, 1935; s. Abraham and Lena (Pincus) S.; m. Anne Evelyn Gorfinkle; children— Andrea Rose, Jeffrey Winston AB, Cornell U., 1956, JD with distinction, 1959. Bar: N.Y. 1960, D.C. 1976. Assoc., then ptnr. Stroock & Stroock, N.Y.C., 1959—75; gen. counsel Commodity Futures Trading Commn., Washington, 1975—77, Rosenman & Colin (now Katten Muchin Zavis Rosenman), N.Y.C., 1977—. Contbr. articles to profl. jours. Served to capt. USAR, 1956-66 Mem.: Assn. Bar of City of N.Y. (chmn. com. 1982—86), ABA (chmn., com. on regulation of futures and derivative insts. 1997—2001). Republican. Jewish. Corporate, general, Securities. Home: 830 Park Ave New York NY 10021-2757 Office: Katten Muchin Zavis Rosenman 575 Madison Ave New York NY 10022-2585 E-mail: Howard.Schneider@kmzr.com.

SCHNEIDER, KAREN BUSH, lawyer, educator; b. Lansing, Mich., Mar. 17, 1951; d. Gerard Joseph and Emily Virginia (Szoka) Bush; 1 child, Emily Margaret. BA magna cum laude, U. Notre Dame, 1973, JD, 1976. Bar: Mich. 1976, U.S. Dist. Ct. (we. dist.) Mich. 1976, U.S. Dist. Ct. (ea. dist.) Mich. 1981. From assoc. to ptnr. Foster, Swift, Collins & Smith P.C., Lansing, 1976-88; ptnr. White, Schneider, Young & Chiodini, P.C., Okemos, Mich., 1988—, pres., 1994—97, 1999—2001. Adj. prof. Thomas M. Cooley Law Sch., Lansing, 1985—, vis. prof., 1988-89; mem. jud. qualifications com. State Bar Mich., 1987-91; arbitrator, Mich. Employment Rels. Commn., 1990—. Contbr. legal briefs to profl jours., quarterly articles to Greater Lansing Bus. Monthly mag., Lansing. Mem. Wharton Ctr. Adv. Coun., 2001—; bd. dirs. Am. Lung Assn. Mich., 1985—89, chmn. pers. com., 1986—89; bd. dirs. Capital Area Humane Soc., 1984—90, corr. sec., 1984, rec. sec., 1985, fundraising chmn., 1985—90, pres., 1986. Recipient Frederick Griffiths award for Tchg. Excellence, Thomas M. Cooley Law Sch., 2000. Fellow: Mich. State Bar Found.; mem.: State Bar of Mich. (continuing edn. com. 1997—, Biennial Diana award for profl. and cmty. svc. 1999), Ingham County Bar Assn. (bd. dirs., sec. 1982—83, pubs. com. 1983—85, chmn. pubs. com. 1984—85, facilitative mediator selection com. 2002—), Am. Arbitration Assn. (labor arbitrator 1985—), U. Notre Dame Alumni Assn. of Lansing (sec. 1979—80, pres. 1980—81, pub. rels. officer 1981—82, v.p. 1983—85). Roman Catholic. Avocations: fitness swimming, gourmet cooking. Civil rights, Labor (including EEOC, Fair Labor Standards Act, labor-management relations, NLRB, OSHA). Home: 16717 Thorngate Rd East Lansing MI 48823-9772 Office: White Schneider Young & Chiodini PC 2300 Jolly Oak Rd Okemos MI 48864-3546 E-mail: Kschneider@wsbyc.com.

SCHNEIDER, KARL HERBERT, lawyer; b. Columbus, Ohio, May 10, 1957; s. Herbert Henry and Betty Ramona (List) S.; m. Jennifer Furash, Mar. 27, 1982; children: Jason Edward, Kristen Allison, Kevin Wilson. BA, Denison U., 1979; JD, Capital U., 1982. Bar: Ohio 1982, U.S. Dist. Ct. (so. dist.) Ohio 1983. Exec. v.p. W. Saxbe Enterprises, Columbus, 1980-82; sole practice Columbus, 1982—; gen. counsel HER Inc., Columbus, 1984—. Lectr. real estate groups, Columbus, 1980—, Columbus Tech. Inst., 1985—; commr. Ohio Ct. of Claims. Bd. dirs. Franklin County Forum, Columbus, 1983-85. Mem. Pi Sigma Alpha, Omicron Delta Epsilon. Clubs: Columbus Athletic, Agonis. Republican. Presbyterian. Avocations: marathon running, triatholon. Administrative and regulatory, State civil litigation, Property, real (including real estate development, water). Office: Maguire & Schneider LLP 250 Civic Ctr Dr Columbus OH 43215

SCHNEIDER, LAZ LEVKOFF, lawyer; b. Columbia, S.C., Mar. 15, 1939; s. Philip L. and Dorothy Harriet (Levkoff) S.; m. Ellen Linda Shiffrin, Dec. 12, 1968; 1 child, David Allen. BA, Yale U., 1961, LLB, 1964; LLM, NYU, 1965. Bar: D.C. 1965, N.Y. 1965, Fla. 1970. Assoc. Fulton, Walter & Duncombe, N.Y.C., 1965-67, Roseman, Colin Kaye Petschek Freund & Emil, N.Y.C., 1967-69, Kronish, Lieb, Weiner, Shainswit & Hellman, N.Y.C., 1969-70; ptnr. Ruden Barnett McClosky & Schuster, Ft. Lauderdale, Fla., 1970-80, Sherr, Tiballi, Fayne & Schneider, Ft. Lauderdale, 1986-91, Berger Singerman, Ft. Lauderdale, 1991—; pvt. practice Ft. Lauderdale, 1980-86. Bd. dirs. Ocean Biochem. Inc. Grad. editor Tax Law Rev., 1964-65. Exec. com. Fla. regional bd. Anti Defamation League, 1972—. Mem. Fla. Bar Assn., Broward County Bar Assn. (chmn. sect. corp. bus. and banking law 1978-80), Yale Club (pres. 1977-79). Jewish. Corporate, general, Securities. Office: 350 E Las Olas Blvd Ste 1000 Fort Lauderdale FL 33301-4215 E-mail: Lschneider@bergersingerman.com., lazsch@att.net.

SCHNEIDER, MAHLON C. lawyer; b. 1939; BA, U. Minn., 1962, LLB, 1964. Bar: Minn. 1965. Atty. Green Giant Co., 1968—80, Pillsbury, 1980-84, v.p., gen. counsel foods divsn., 1984-89; corp. atty. Geo. A. Hormel & Co., Austin, Minn., 1989-90, v.p., gen. counsel, 1990-99, sr. v.p. external affairs, gen. counsel, 1999—. Commercial, contracts (including sales of goods; commercial financing), Product liability. Office: Hormel Foods Corp 1 Hormel Pl Austin MN 55912-3680

SCHNEIDER, MATTHEW ROGER, lawyer; b. N.Y.C., Nov. 7, 1948; s. Theodore David Schneider and Rosalind (Schwartz) Werner; m. Marjorie Ann Friedlander, Mar. 6, 1976; children: Adam Benjamin, Emily Beth. BA, Cornell U., 1970; student, Georgetown U., 1971; JD, Cath. U., Washington, 1974. Bar: D.C. 1976, U.S. Dist. Ct. D.C., 1994. Staff asst. U.S. Senate Jud. Com., Washington, 1973-74; counsel U.S. Senate Govt. Ops. Com., Washington, 1974-77; spl. asst. Office of Sec. Def., Washington, 1977-79; dir. legis. affairs SEC, Washington, 1979-81, sr. counsel, divsn. corp. fin., 1981-82; chief of staff U.S. Senator Jeff Bingaman, Washington, 1983-85; prin. Law Office Matthew Schneider, Washington, 1985-87; ptnr. Willkie, Farr & Gallagher, Washington, 1987-95, Garvey Shubert Barer, Washington, 1996—98, mng. dir. D.C. office, 1998—. Bd. dirs. Nat. Epilepsy Found., 2000—, mem. exec. com., 2001—; Bd. dirs Capitol Hill Hosp., Washington, 1987—95, chmn. govt. and legal affairs com., 1997—. Avocations: physical fitness training, singing, guitar. Administrative and regulatory, Legislative, Government Relations. Office: Garvey Schubert Barer 5th Fl 1000 Potomac St NW Ste 5 Washington DC 20007-3501

SCHNEIDER, MICHAEL H. judge; b. San Antonio, Jan. 6, 1943; BS, Stephen F. Austin State U.; JD, U. Houston; LLM, U. Va. Asst. dist. atty. Harris County; pvt. practice; mcpl. judge City of West University Place; presiding judge 157th Civil Dist. Ct. Harris County; dist. judge 1st Ct. Appeals, 1996, chief justice; justice Pa. Supreme Ct., 2002—. Tchr. Ball HS, Galveston, Tex. Named Trial Judge of the Yr., Tex. Assn. Civil Trial and Appellate Specialists, 1994, 2001. Mem.: ABA, Tex. Bar Found., Houston Bar Found., Houston Bar Assn., State Bar Tex. Methodist. Office: Tex Supreme Ct PO Box 12248 Austin TX 78711 Office Fax: 512-463-1365.*

SCHNEIDER, MICHAEL J. lawyer; b. Jasper, Ind., July 9, 1952; s. Ralph F. and Ruth L. Schneider. BS with highest distinction, Ind. U., 1974, JD, 1977. Bar: Ind. 1977, Ohio 1977, U.S. Tax Ct. 1978. Assoc. Amerman, Burt & Jones (now Buckingham, Doolittle & Burroughs), Canton, Ohio, 1977—80, Murphy, Young & Smith (now Squire, Sanders & Dempsey), Columbus, Ohio, 1980—81; ptnr. Locke, Reynolds LLP, Indpls., 1981—2000, Bose, McKinney & Evans, LLP, Indpls., 2000—. Former bd. dirs. Cmty. Orgns. Legal Assistance Project. Mem.: ABA (mem. bus. law sect., mem. negotiated acquisition com.), Indpls. Bar Assn. (mem. bus. law sect., former mem. exec. coun.), Ind. Bar Assn. (mem. bus. law sect.), Venture Club Ind., Phi Eta Sigma, Beta Gamma Sigma. Avocations: golf, fishing, travel, sports. Mergers and acquisitions, Corporate, general, Estate planning. Office: Bose McKinney and Evans LLP 2700 First Indiana Plz 135 N Pennsylvania St Indianapolis IN 46204 Office Fax: 317-223-0128. Business E-Mail: mschneider@boselaw.com.

SCHNEIDER, PAM HORVITZ, lawyer; b. Cleve., Nov. 29, 1951; m. Milton S. Schneider, June 30, 1973; 1 child, Sarah Anne. BA, U. Pa., 1973; JD, Columbia U., 1976. Bar: N.Y. 1977, Pa. 1979. Assoc. White & Case, N.Y.C., 1976-78, Drinker Biddle & Reath LLP, Phila., 1978-84, ptnr., 1984-2001; founding ptnr. Gadsden Schneider & Woodward LLP, King of Prussia, Pa., 2001—. Contbr. articles to profl. jours. Fellow Am. Coll. Trust and Estate Counsel (past regent); mem. ABA (past chair, real property probate and trust law sect.), Internat. Acad. Estate and Trust Law (academician). Estate planning, Probate (including wills, trusts), Estate taxation. Office: Gadsden Schneider & Woodward LLP The Merion Bldg 700 S Henderson Rd Ste 345 King Of Prussia PA 19406 E-mail: pschneider@gsw-llp.com.

SCHNEIDER, RICHARD GRAHAM, lawyer; b. Bryn Mawr, Pa., Aug. 2, 1930; s. Vincent Bernard and Marion Scott (Graham) S.; m. Margaret Peter Fritz, Feb. 15, 1958; children: Margaret W., Richard Graham Jr., John F. BA, Yale U., 1952; JD, U. Pa., 1957, MLA, 2001. Bar: Pa. 1958. Assoc. Dechert Price & Rhoads, Phila., 1957-66, ptnr., 1966-95; of counsel, 1995—. Case editor U. Pa. Law Rev., 1956-57. Trustee Baldwin Sch., Bryn Mawr, 1971-79; trustee Episcopal Acad., Merion, Pa., 1976-83. 1st lt. USAF, 1952-54, PTO. Mem. ABA, Pa. Bar Assn., Phila. Bar Assn., Order of Coif, Merion Cricket Club, Merion Golf Club (sec. 1997-2002), Yale Club (pres. 1966-68). Republican. Presbyterian. Antitrust, General civil litigation. Office: Dechert LLP 4000 Bell Atlantic Tower 1717 Arch St Lbby 3 Philadelphia PA 19103-2713 E-mail: gladwyne@aol.com.

SCHNEIDER, ROBERT JEROME, lawyer; b. Cin., June 22, 1947; s. Jerome William and Agnes (Moehringer) S.; m. Janice Loraine Eckhoff, Dec. 13, 1968; children: Aaron Haisley, Jared Alan, Margot Laraine. BSME, U. Cin., 1970, JD, 1973. Bar: Ill. 1973, U.S. Dist. Ct. (no. dist.) Ill. 1973, U.S. Ct. Appeals (7th cir.) 1973, U.S. Ct. Appeals (fed. cir.) 1973. Ptnr. Mason, Kolehmainen, Rathburn & Wyss, Chgo., 1973-82; ptnr., asst. chmn. patents, chmn. intellect. property dept. McDermott, Will & Emery, Chgo., 1982-94; chmn. intellectual property dept. Chapman & Cutler, Chgo., 1995—. Mem. ABA, ASME, Ill. Bar Assn., Chgo. Bar Assn., Licensing Execs. Soc., Intellectual Property Law Assn. Chgo. (sec. 1981-83), Fedn. Internat. des Conseils en Proriete Industrielle, Assn. Internationale pour la Protection de la Propertiètè Industrielle, Internat. Trademark Assn., Internat. Trade Commn. Trial Lawyers Assn., Am. Intellectual Property Law Assn., Tower Club (bd. govs. 1988—, v.p. 1994-95, pres. 1995—), Univ. Club Chgo. Republican. Roman Catholic. Federal civil litigation, Patent, Trademark and copyright. Home: 1609 Asbury Ave Winnetka IL 60093-1303 Office: Chapman & Cutler Chicago IL 60601 Fax: 530-464-2529. E-mail: iplaw@chapman.com.

SCHNEIDER, THOMAS PAUL, non-profit agency administrator; b. June 5, 1947; s. Milton and Gloria (Bocaner) S.; m. Susan G. Stein, May 31, 1987; children: Rachel Jenny, Daniel Joshua. BA with honors, JD, U. Wis., 1972. U.S. atty. U.S. Dist. Dist. Ct. (ea. dist.) Wis., Milw., 1993-2001; exec. dir. youth svcs. COA Youth & Family Ctrs., Milw., 2001—. Mem. Wis. Bar Assn. Democrat. Jewish. Office: COA Youth & Family Ctrs 909 E North Ave Milwaukee WI 53212 E-mail: tomcoa@execpc.com.

SCHNEIDER, WILLYS HOPE, lawyer; b. N.Y.C., Sept. 27, 1952; d. Leon and Lillian (Friedman) S.; m. Stephen Andrew Kals, Jan. 21, 1979; children: Peter, Josefine. AB, Princeton U., 1974; JD, Columbia U., 1977. Bar: N.Y. 1978, U.S. Dist. Ct. (ea. and so. dists.) N.Y. 1978, U.S. Tax Ct. 1979. Law clk. to hon. Jack B. Weinstein U.S. Dist. Ct. (ea. dist.) N.Y., Bklyn., 1977-78; assoc. Paul, Weiss, Rifkind, Wharton & Garrison, N.Y.C., 1978-83, Kaye Scholer LLP, N.Y.C., 1983-87, 1987—. Contbr. articles to profl. jours. Mem. ABA, N.Y. State Bar Assn., Assn. of Bar of City of N.Y. Corporate taxation, Taxation, general, Personal income taxation. Home: 320 W End Ave New York NY 10023-8110 Office: Kaye Scholer LLP 425 Park Ave New York NY 10022-3506

SCHNEIDERMAN, IRWIN, lawyer; b. N.Y.C., May 28, 1923; s. Meyer and Bessie (Klein) S.; m. Roberta Haig, Nov. 28, 1966; 1 child, Eric T. BA, Bklyn. Coll., 1943; LLB cum laude, Harvard U., 1948; DHL (hon.), Bklyn. Coll., 1993. Bar: N.Y. 1949, D.C. 1952. Assoc. Cahill Gordon & Reindel, N.Y.C., 1948-59, ptnr., 1959-89, sr. counsel, 1990—. Spl. cons. to chmn. SEC, 1981-82, mem. adv. com. on tender offers, 1983. Trustee Bklyn. Coll. Found., 1983—; chmn. N.Y.C. Opera, 1993—; bd. dirs. WNYC Radio, 1989—, City Ctr. Music and Drama, Inc., 1990—, N.Y.C. NARAL, 1990—, Lincoln Ctr. for Performing Arts, Inc., 1994—; pres. N.Y.C. NARAL Found., 1998--. Lt. (j.g.) USNR, 1943-46. Mem. Harvard Club. Corporate, general, Securities. Home: 203 E 72nd St New York NY 10021-4568 Office: Cahill Gordon & Reindel 80 Pine St Fl 17 New York NY 10005-1790

SCHNEIDLER, JON GORDON, lawyer; b. Seattle, Oct. 22, 1938; s. J. Gordon and Mary Louise (Bartholomew) S.; m. Linda Gilmore White, June 27, 1964 (div. June 1988); children: Kristina Richards, Jolie Wolcott, Andrew Schneidler, Peter Schneidler; m. Elizabeth Ann Nairn, Apr. 2, 1989; 1 stepdaughter: Jessica Albright. BA, U. Wash., 1962, JD, 1968. Bar: Wash.; U.S. Ct. Appeals (9th Cir.), U.S. Dist. Ct. (we. dist.) Wash. CEO Schneidler Industries, Inc., Seattle, 1968-70; ptnr. Cartano, Botzer & Chapman, Seattle, 1970-86. Sec. Transiplex Internat., Inc., Seattle; mem. adv. bd. Pacific Legal Found., Sacramento; trustee Ehrlich Donnan Found., Seattle. Co-author: (book) Real Property Deskbook, 1981, 2d edit. 1986; patentee Air Structure Systems, 1969. Bd. dirs. North Kitsap Sch. Bd., Poulsbo, Wash., 1984, Friends of Youth, Renton, Wash., 1974; founder, dir. Tchr. of Yr. Found., Poulsbo, 1988—. 1st lt. USAF, 1962-66. Decorated Air Force Commendation medal; recipient Baker scholar George F. Baker Foun., 1957-60. Fellow Paul Harris Found.; mem. ABA (bus. law sect., comml. lease com.), Wash. State Bar Assn., King County Bar Assn., Coll. Club (trustee, treas. 1998-2002), Rotary. Avocations: fly fishing, competitive bridge, sailing, gardening. Property, real (including real estate development, water), Corporate, general. Office: 600 University St Ste 1928 Seattle WA 98101-4115

SCHNELL, CARLTON BRYCE, lawyer; b. Youngstown, Ohio, Jan. 1, 1932; s. Carlton Wilhelm and Helen Jean (Alexander) S.; m. Dorothy Stewart Apple, Aug. 15, 1953; children— Laura, Margaret, Heidi BA, Yale U., 1953, LL.B., 1956. Bar: Ohio 1956. Assoc. Arter & Hadden, Cleve., 1956-65, ptnr., 1966-96, mng. ptnr., 1977-82, Washington, 1982-84. Exec. comm. mem. Greater Cleve. Growth Assn., Cleve., 1983-97; chmn. Build Up Cleve., 1981-89; profl. chmn. United Way, Cleve., 1983; co-chmn. Charter Rev. Commn., Cleve., 1983-84; pres. Citizen's League Rsch. Inst., 1992-95. Named Vol. of Yr., Leadership Cleve., 1985. Mem. Tex. Club Cleve. (pres. 1972-73), Cleve. Tax Inst. (chmn. 1978), Ohio C. of C. (trustee 1977-80) Clubs: Tavern, Pepper Pike. Republican. Presbyterian. Avocations: golf, tennis. Home: 31450 Shaker Blvd Pepper Pike OH 44124-5153

SCHNIPPER, DON MARTIN, lawyer; b. Little Rock, Jan. 17, 1939; m. Mary Ann Evans, June 3, 1961; children: Caroline, Elizabeth. AB, U. Ark., 1963, JD, 1964. Bar: Ark. 1964, U.S. Supreme Ct. 1971. Ptnr. Wood, Smith, Schnipper & Clay, Hot Springs, Ark., 1964—. Spl. assoc. justice Ark. Supreme Ct., 1976-88. V.p. 1st United Meth. Ch., 1976-77, pres. 1977, vice chmn. bd. dirs. 1975-76; chmn. Ouachita Regional Counseling and Mental Health Ctr., 1977, pres. bd. dirs. 1970l bd. dirs. Hot Springs Childrens Home. Fellow Am. Bar Found.; mem. ABA, Ark. Bar Assn. (chmn. young lawyers sect. 1969-70, ho. of dels. 1973-76, exec. council 1976-79, chmn. exec. council 1980-81, pres. 1985-86), Garland County Bar Assn. (pres.), Hot Springs C. of C. (bd. dirs. 1966—, pres. 1977, Disting. Svc. award 1970), U. Ark. Alumni Assn. (bd. dirs. 1978-84, nat. pres. 1982-83). General civil litigation, General practice, Probate (including wills, trusts). Home: 850 Quapaw Ave Hot Springs National Park AR 71901-3926 Office: Wood Smith Schnipper & Clay 123 Market St Hot Springs National Park AR 71901-5398

SCHNUR, ROBERT ARNOLD, lawyer; b. White Plains, N.Y., Oct. 25, 1938; s. Conrad Edward and Ruth (Mehr) S.; children: Daniel, Jonathan. BA, Cornell U., 1960; JD, Harvard U., 1963. Bar: Wis. 1965, Ill. 1966. Assoc. Michael, Best & Friedrich, Milw., 1966-73, ptnr., 1973—. Chmn. Wis. Tax News, 1983-90; adj. prof. tax law U. Wis. Law Sch., 1988—. Capt. U.S. Army, 1963-65. Fellow Am. Coll. Tax Counsel; mem. ABA, Wis. Bar Assn. (chmn. tax sect. 1986-88), Milw. Bar Assn. Corporate taxation, Taxation, general, State and local taxation. Home: 3093 Timber Ln Verona WI 53593 Office: Michael Best Friedrich 100 E Wisconsin Ave Ste 3300 Milwaukee WI 53202-4108 E-mail: raschnur@mbf-law.com.

SCHNYDER, BERNHARD, educator; b. Brig, Switzerland, Nov. 30, 1930; s. Oskar and Anny (Gentinetta) S.; m. Trudy Koenig, Mar. 30, 1974; children: Matthias, Franziska. Lizentiat, Law Sch., Fribourg, Switzerland, 1954, D, 1960, habilitation, 1970; JD, Canton Valais, Switzerland, 1957. Atty., Canton Valais, Switzerland, 1958-65; prof. Law Sch., Fribourg, Switzerland, 1965-97, dean, 1973-77; rector Univ., Fribourg, Switzerland, 1979-83. Author: Vertragsfreiheit Als Privatrechtsbergriff, 1960; co-author: Das Schweizerische Zivilgesetzbuch, 1965, 68, 75, 79, 86, 95, 2002, Kommentar Vormundschaftsrecht, 1982, 84; editor: Familie Herausforderung Der Zukunft, 1982; contbr. articles to profl. jours. Pres. Swiss Cath. Students, 1954-55, Swiss Sci. Coun., 1983-87. Col. Swiss Army, 1979-88. Recipient Walter Naef prize Swiss Nat. Sci. Found., 1967, Ruenzi prize Gov. of Valais, 1980. Roman Catholic. Avocations: music, swimming, hiking. Home: 1 Impasse des Eglantines Fribourg 1700 Switzerland

SCHOBER, THOMAS GREGORY, lawyer; b. Waukesha, Wis., Aug. 17, 1948; s. Theodore Michael and Rosalie (Blando) S.; m. Patricia Ann Farrell, Jan. 17, 1981; children: Wendy, Sara, Sarah, Sonya, Christy, Marc. BS, Marquette U., 1970, JD, 1972. Bar: Wis. 1973, U.S. Dist. Ct. (ea. and we. dists.) Wis. 1973, U.S. Tax Ct. 1976. Mng. ptnr., atty. Schober & Radtke, S.C., New Berlin, Wis., 1973-96, Schober Schober & Mitchell, S.C., New Berlin, Wis., 1996—. Prof. acctg. U. Wis., Waukesha, 1975-77; prof. law Marquette Law Sch., Milw., 1977-81; mem. adv. bd. Luth. Social Svcs., Milw., 1983-86; bd. dirs. Stepping Stones Child Devel. Ctr., New Berlin, 1998-99. Airport commr. Waukesha County Airport Commn., 1994—. With Wis. N.G., 1970-76. Republican. Lutheran. Avocation: pilot. Corporate, general, Mergers and acquisitions, Property, real (including real estate development, water). Office: Schober Schober & Mitchell SC 16845 W Cleveland Ave New Berlin WI 53151-3532 E-mail: tgs@schoberlaw.com.

SCHOBER, THOMAS LEONARD, lawyer; b. Green Bay, Wis., Jan. 5, 1946; s. Leonard M. and Ruth (Christoph) S.; m. Suzan C. Murray, Sept. 5, 1981. BA, Northwestern U., 1968; JD, U. Wis., 1973. Bar: Wis. 1973; cert. civil advocate Nat. Bd. Trial Advocacy; cert. mediator. Assoc. Trowbridge Law Firm, Green Bay, 1973-81; ptnr. Schober & Ulatowski, Green Bay, 1981—. Chmn. bd. atty.'s profl. responsibility com. Dist. 14, Supreme Ct. Wis., 1985-96. Pres. YMCA, Green Bay, 1984-85. Served as sgt. U.S. Army, 1968-70, Vietnam. Mem. ABA, Wis. Bar Assn., Def. Research Inst., Trucking Industry Def. Assn. State civil litigation, Insurance, Transportation. Office: PO Box 1780 Green Bay WI 54305-1780 E-mail: tomLS@sulaw.com.

SCHOCHET, P(AULA) RIVKA, lawyer, mediator; b. Mpls., Dec. 26, 1946; d. George E. and J. Beulah Johnson Schochet; m. Claude L. Schochet, Dec. 27, 1992; children: Bentzion, Chaya Batya, Menachem Mendel, Sara Chana, Shany, Ariel, Elisha, Shoshana, Esther. BA summa cum laude, U. Minn., 1984; JD, Columbia U., 1988. Bar: NY 1989, Mich. 1995, U.S. Ct. Appeals (6th cir.) 1996. Litigation assoc. Coudert Bros., N.Y.C., 1988—94; sr. assoc. Kemp, Klein, Umphrey & Edelman, Troy, Mich., 1995—98; assoc. Miller, Canfield, Paddock & Stone, PLC, Detroit, 2000—. Contbr. articles to profl. jours. Mediator Oakland Mediation Ctr., Southfield, Mich., Resolution Ctr., Warren, Mich. Mem.: ABA, NY State Bar Assn., N.Y.C. Bar Assn., Mich. Bar Assn. Chabad Lubavitch. Alternative dispute resolution, Appellate, Constitutional. Office: Miller Canfield Paddock & Stone Ste 2500 150 W Jefferson Ave Detroit MI 48226-4415 Fax: 313-496-8454. E-mail: schochet@millercanfield.com.

SCHOCHOR, JONATHAN, lawyer, educator; b. Suffern, N.Y., Sept. 9, 1946; s. Abraham and Betty (Hechtor) S.; m. Joan Elaine Brown, May 31, 1970; children: Lauren Aimee, Daniel Ross. BA, Pa. State U., 1968; JD, Am. U., 1971. Bar: D.C. 1971, U.S. Dist. Ct. D.C. 1971, U.S. Ct. Appeals (D.C. cir.) 1971, Md. 1974, U.S. Dist. Ct. Md. 1974, U.S. Supreme Ct. 1986. Assoc. McKenna, Wilkinson & Kittner, Washington, 1970-74, Ellin & Baker, Balt., 1974-84; ptnr. Schochor, Federico & Staton, Balt., 1984—. Lectr. in law; expert witness to state legis. Editor-in-chief: Am. U. Law Rev., 1970—71. Mem. ABA, ATLA (state del. 1991, state gov. 1992-95), Am. Bd. Trial Advs. (membership com. 1994—), Am. Bd. Trial Advs., Am. Judicature Soc., Md. State Bar Assn. (spl. com. on health claims arbitration 1983), Md. Trial Lawyers Assn. (bd. govs. 1986-87, mem. legis. com. 1985-88, chmn. legis. com. 1986-87, sec. 1987-88, exec. com. 1987-92, v.p. 1987-88, pres.-elect 1989, pres. 1990-91), Balt. City Bar Assn. (legis com. 1986-87, spl. com. on tort reform 1986, medicolegal com. 1989-90, cir. ct. for Balt. City task force-civil document mgmt. sys. 1994-95), Bar Assn. D.C., Internat. Platform Assn., Phi Alpha Delta. Federal civil litigation, State civil litigation, Personal injury (including property damage). Office: Schochor Federico & Staton PA 1211 Saint Paul St Baltimore MD 21202-2783

SCHOCK, ROBERT CHRISTOPHER, lawyer; b. New Rochelle, N.Y., Apr. 12, 1948; s. Carl Frederick and Elizabeth Woodbury (Slocomb) S. BA cum laude, Wake Forest U., 1970; JD, U. Tenn., 1973. Bar: Tenn. 1974, Ga. 1978, U.S. Dist. Ct. (no. dist.) Ga. 1978, U.S. Ct. Appeals (5th cir.) 1978, U.S. Ct. Appeals (11th cir.) 1982. Gen. atty. U.S. Dept. Justice Immigration Svc., Atlanta, 1974-80; sole practitioner Atlanta, 1980—. Contbg. author: Immigration Law, 1996, 2000, 2001. Mem. Am. Immigration Lawyers Assn. (Atlanta chpt. treas. 1992-93, sec. 1993-94, INS liaison chair 1995-96), Phi Alpha Theta. Presbyterian. Avocations: exercise, travel, gardening. Immigration, naturalization, and customs, Private international, Public international. Office: 235 Peachtree St NE Ste 400 Atlanta GA 30303-1400

SCHOEM, ALAN HOWARD, lawyer; b. Washington, Dec. 18, 1946; s. David and Lillian S.; m. Hazel Schoem, Jan. 4, 1970; children: Cara Beth, Scott Robert. BA, U. Md., 1968; JD, Am. U., 1972. Bar: D.C. 1972, Md. 1973, U.S. Ct. Appeals D.C. 1973, U.S. Supreme Ct. 1980. Atty. GAO, Washington, 1972-73; atty. Office of Gen. Counsel, Consumer Product Safety Commn., Washington, 1973-79, asst. gen. counsel Bethesda, Md., 1979-87, dir. div. adminstrv. litigation, 1987-94. Legis. fellow to U.S. Senator Paul Wellstone, Washington, 1992; atty., advisor to chmn. Ann Brown Consumer Product Safety Commn., 1994-96; exec. asst. Office of Compliance, 1996-97, dir., 1997—. Pres. Stonebridge Homeowners Assn., North Potomac, Md., 1985-86, Lakewood Elem. Sch. PTA, Rockville, Md., 1986-88; v.p. T.S. Wooton High Sch. PTSA, Rockville, 1988-91, cluster coord., 1989-91. Democrat. Jewish. Avocation: reading. Home: 14809 Rolling Green Way North Potomac MD 20878-4202 Office: Consumer Product Safety Com 4330 E West Hwy Bethesda MD 20814-4408 E-mail: aschoem@cpsc.gov.

SCHOEN, STEVAN JAY, lawyer; b. N.Y.C., May 19, 1944; s. Al and Ann (Spevack) S.; m. Cynthia Lukens; children: Andrew Adams, Anna Kim. BS, U. Pa., 1966; JD, Cornell U., 1969; MPhil, Cambridge U. (Eng.), 1980. Bar: N.Mex. 1970, N.Y. 1970, U.S. Supreme Ct. 1976, U.S. Tax Ct. 1973, U.S. Ct. Internat. Trade 1982. Dir. Vista law recruitment OEO, Washington, 1970-71; atty. Legal Aid Soc. of Albuquerque, 1971-73; chief atty. N.Mex. Dept. Health and Social Svcs., Albuquerque, 1973-77; ptnr. Brennan, Schoen & Eisenstadt, 1979-88, Stevan J. Schoen PA, 1989-2001, Bingham, Hurst, Apodaca, Wile & Schoen, P.C., 2001—03; prin. Stevan J. Schoen, P.A., Placitas, N.Mex., 2003—; probate judge Sandoval County, 1990-98. Arbitrator NYSE; mem. N.Mex. Supreme Ct. Appellate Rules Com., 1982-92; chmn. rules com. Com. on Fgn. Legal Cons., 1993; chmn. N.Mex. Supreme Ct. Com., Probate Ct. Rules and Forms, 1998-2002, Jud. Edn. Planning com.; mem. Children's Code Rules Com., 1976-78. Mem. Mayor's Albuquerque Abd. Com. on Fgn. Trade Zone, 1992-94; v.p. Placitas Vol. Fir Dept., 1974-86; bd. edn. Bernalillo Pub. Sch. Dist., 1996-97. Recipient Cert. for Outstanding Svc. to Judiciary, N.Mex. Supreme Ct., 1982, Outstanding Svc. award N. Mex. Supreme Ct., 1992, 2003, Cert. of Appreciation, N.Mex. Sec. of State, 1980, Pro Bono Pub. Svc. award, 1989, Cert. of Recognition Legal Aid, 1994, award Las Placitas Assn., 1996; named Outstanding Probate Judge, N.Mex State Senate, 1998. Mem. Am. Judges Assn. (ho. of dels. 1999-2002), Nat. Coll. Probate Judges, State Bar N.Mex. (past chmn. real property, probate and trust sect. 1989, Outstanding Contbn. award 1989, task force on regulation of advt. 1990-91, past chmn. appellate practice sect. 1991, past chmn. internat. law sect. 1991-92, commn. on professionalism 1992-95, organizing com. U.S.-Mex. law inst. 1992), N.Mex. Probate Judges Assn. (chmn. 1993-99, award 1998, N.Mex. state bar bench and bar rels. com. chair 2002, chair sr. lawyers sect. 2003), Benchard Bar Com. (co-chair 2001-2002, chair sr. lawyers sect. 2003), Oxford-Cambridge Soc. N.Mex. (sec.), M.Mex. Assn. Counties (adv. bd. 1995-98). Private international, Probate (including wills, trusts), Property, real (including real estate development, water). Home and Office: 4 Hillside Dr Placitas NM 87043 Fax: 505-867-2805. Business E-Mail: schoenlaw@comcast.net.

SCHOENE, FRIEDRICH TOBIAS, lawyer; b. Goettingen, Germany, May 20, 1966; s. Albrecht and Dagmar (Haver) S.; m. Louisa Gräfin zu Innhausen und Knyphausen, Aug. 11, 2000. Degree in law, U. Heidelberg, Muenster and Goettingen, Germany. Bar: Berlin 1996. Assoc. Oppenhoff & Raedler, Berlin, Germany, 1996-99; jr. ptnr. Oppenhoff & Raedler Linklaters & Alliance, Berlin, Germany, 1999-2000; ptnr. Hogan & Hartson Raue LLP, Berlin, Germany, 2001—. Vis. lawyer S. Horowitz & Co., Tel Aviv, 1998—99. Mem.: Order St. John (knight 1998—), German-Israeli Lawyers' Assn. (bd. dirs. 1998—2001). Appellate, General civil litigation, Corporate, general. Office: Hogan & Hartson Raue LLP Potsdamer Platz 1 Berlin 10785 Germany E-mail: FTSchoene@hhlaw.com.

SCHOENE, KATHLEEN SNYDER, lawyer; b. Glen Ridge, N.J., July 24, 1953; d. John Kent and Margaret Ann (Bronder) Snyder. BA, Grinnell Coll., 1974; MS, So. Conn. State Coll., 1976; JD, Washington U., St. Louis, 1982. Bar: Mo. 1982, Ill. 1983. Head libr. Mo. Hist. Soc., St. Louis, 1976-79; assoc. Peper, Martin, Jensen, Maichel & Hetlage, St. Louis, 1982-88, ptnr., 1989-98, Armstrong Teasdale LLP, St. Louis, 1998—. Bd. dirs. Legal Svcs. of Eastern Mo. Author: (with others) Missouri Corporation Law and Practice, 1985, Missouri Business Organizations, 1998; contbr. articles to profl. jours. Trustee Grinnell (Iowa) Coll., ex officio voting mem., 1991-93; bd. dirs. Jr. League St. Louis, 1995-96, Leadership Ctr. Greater St. Louis, 1995-96, FOCUS St. Louis, 1996-2001, exec. com., 1997-99; active St. Louis Forum, 1997—, Herbert Hoover Boys and Girls Club, St. Louis, 1999—. Mem. ABA, Nat. Conf. Bar Founds. (trustee 1996-2000, pres. elect 1997-98, pres. 1998-99), The Mo. Bar (bd. govs. 1997-99, chair bus. law com. 2000—), Ill. State Bar Assn., Bar Assn. Met. St. Louis (treas. 1991-92, sec. 1992-93, v.p. 1993-94, pres.-elect 1994-95, pres. 1995-96, chair small bus. com. 1987-88, exec. com. 1988-96, chair bus. law sect. 1988-89, mem. exec. com. young lawyers sect. 1988-90), St. Louis Bar Found. (bd. dirs. 1994-2000, v.p. 1995-96, pres. 1996-98). Corporate, general, Health, Securities. Home: 7824 Cornell Ave Saint Louis MO 63130-3701 Office: Armstrong Teasdale One Metropolitan Sq Saint Louis MO 63102 E-mail: kschoene@armstrongteasdale.com.

SCHOENER, GEORGE FRANCIS, JR., lawyer; b. Phila., Oct. 17, 1954; s. George Francis Sr. and Irene Louise (Nocito) S.; m. Patrice Irene Cipressi, Nov. 24, 1984; children: Michael James, Kristin Elizabeth, Stephen Christopher. BS, Rensselaer Poly. Inst., 1975; JD, Villanova U., 1978. Bar: Pa. 1978, U.S. Dist. Ct. (ea. dist.) Pa. 1978, U.S. Ct. Appeals (3d cir.) 1983, U.S. Supreme Ct. 1987; bd. cert. civil trial advocate Nat. Bd. Trial Advocacy. Assoc. Kessler & Sorin P.C., Phila., 1978-81, M. Mark Mendel Ltd., Phila., 1981-86, shareholder, 1986-95; atty. George F. Schoener Jr., P.C., Phila., 1995—. Seminar presenter in the field. Author: (with M.D. Zingarini and R.B. Goss) Civil Trial Procedures in Pennsylvania, 1992; co-author: Two New Products Liability Courses, 1995, Products Liability Practice Update, 1996, Products Liability Update, 1997, 99, 4th edit., 2001. Mem. ABA, FBA, Assn. Trial Lawyers Am., Pa. Bar Assn., Phila. Bar Assn., Pa. Trial Lawyers Assn., Phila. Trial Lawyers Assn., Justinian Soc., Nat. Italian-Am. Bar Assn. Avocation: long distance running. State civil litigation, Personal injury (including property damage), Product liability. Office: Eight Penn Center Ste 1301 1628 John F Kennedy Blvd Philadelphia PA 19103-2199 Fax: (215) 564-9187. E-mail: gfs@schoenerlaw.com.

SCHOENFELD, BARBARA BRAUN, lawyer, investment executive; b. Phila., Apr. 17, 1953; d. Irving Leon Braun and Virginia (Parker) Sand; m. Larry Jay Schoenfeld, June 29, 1975; children: Alexander, Gordon, Max. BA cum laude, U. Pa., 1974, M in City Planning, Social Work, 1977; JD, Boston U., 1982. Bar: R.I. 1982, U.S. Dist. Ct. R.I. 1982. Assoc. planner Del. Valley Hosp. Council, Phila., 1978-79; summer assoc. Tillinghast, Collins & Graham, Providence, 1980, 81; assoc. Edwards & Angell, Providence, 1982-86, Ropes & Gray, Providence, 1986-92; dep. treas., gen. counsel State of R.I., 1993-99; v.p. Brown Bros. Harriman & Co., Boston, 1999—. Chmn., bd. dirs. Com. Women's Health Concerns, Phila., 1978-79; bd. dirs. Jewish Family Svc., Providence, 1982-88, Jewish Fedn. of R.I., 1989-91; assoc. treas. Jewish Cmty. Ctr. of R.I.; bd. dirs. Alumni Trustees U. Pa.; chmn. admissions com. U. Pa. Alumni Club, Providence, 1982-95; trustee The Wheeler Sch., 1994-2002. Mem. R.I. Bar Assn., Ledgemont Country Club (Seekonk, Mass.). Democrat. Jewish. Avocations: skiing, travel, french. Office: Brown Bros Harriman & Co 40 Water St Boston MA 02109-3661 E-mail: bbsprov@aol.com.

SCHOENFELD, MICHAEL P. lawyer; b. Oct. 17, 1935; s. Jack and Anne Schoenfield; m. Helen Schorr, Apr. 3, 1960; childrne: Daniel, Steven, Tracy. BS in Acctg., NYU, 1955; LLB, LLD, Fordham U., 1958. Bar: N.Y. 1959, U.S. Supreme Ct. 1963. Coun. Am. Home Assurance Co., N.Y.C., 1958-62; ptnr. Schoenfeld & Schoenfeld, Melville, N.Y., 1959—. V.p. Interstate Brokerage Corp., 1965-84, pres., 1984-90; ptnr. Melville Realty Co., 1977-90; legal adv. various bus. orgns. V.p., trustee Temple Beth David, Commack, N.Y., 1972-75; chmn. Cmty. Action Com. of Dix Hills and Commack, 1970-72, Dix Hills Planning Bd., 1972-74; treas. Dix Hills Rep. Club, 1976-80; mem. Huntington (N.Y.) Zoning Bd. Appeals, 1980-91, chmn., 1986-89. Recipient United Jerusalem award Israel Bond Drive, 1977, City of Hope Svc. award, George Bacon award Fordham Law Sch. Mem. N.Y. State Bar Assn., Suffolk County Bar Assn. Insurance, Personal injury (including property damage), Product liability. Home: 14 Clayton Dr Dix Hills NY 11746-5517 Office: 999 Walt Whitman Rd Melville NY 11747-3007

SCHOENFIELD, RICK MERRILL, lawyer; b. Chgo., July 21, 1951; s. Herbert and Bernice (Krichilsky) S. BA, Northwestern U., 1973, JD cum laude, 1976; cert., Nat. Inst. Trial Advocacy, Chgo., 1979. Bar: Ill. 1976, U.S. Dist. Ct. (no. dist.) Ill. 1977, U.S. Ct. Appeals (7th cir.) 1979, U.S. Ct. Appeals (4th cir.) 1984, U.S. Supreme Ct. 1984, U.S. Dist. Ct. (ea. dist.) Wis. 1987. Assoc. Ettinger & Lake, Chgo., 1976-79, Ettinger & Assocs., Ltd., Chgo., 1979-81; ptnr. Ettinger & Schoenfield, Chgo., 1981-92, Schoenfield, Swartzman & Massin, Chgo., 1992—2002, DiVincenzo Schoenfield Swartzman, Chgo., 2002—. Instr. De Paul Law Sch., Chgo., 1977-78, Chgo.-Kent Coll. Law, 1989—, U. Ill. Chgo., 1991-94. Co-author Legal Negotiations: Gettin Maximum Results, 1988, The McGraw Hill 26 Hour Negotiation Course, 1991. Recipient award for Pro Bono Litigation, Operation Lakewatch, Chgo., 1983. Mem. Nat. Resources Def. Council. Environmental, Personal injury (including property damage), Toxic tort. Office: Di Vincenzo Schoenfield Swartzman & Massin 33 N LaSalle 29th Fl Chicago IL 60602 E-mail: rschoenfield@aol.com.

SCHOFIELD, ANTHONY WAYNE, judge; b. Farmington, N.Mex., Mar. 5, 1949; s. Aldred Edward and Margueriete (Knudsen) S.; m. Rebecca Ann Rosecrans, May 11, 1971; children: Josie, Matthew Paul, Peter Christian, Addie, Joshua James, M. Thomas, Jacob L., Daniel Z. BA, Brigham Young U., 1973, JD, 1976. Bar: Utah 1976, U.S. Dist. Ct. Utah 1976, U.S. Ct. Appeals (7th and 10th cirs.) 1977. Law clk. to hon. judge A. Sherman Christansen U.S. Dist. Ct. Utah, Salt Lake City, 1976-77; assoc. Ferenz, Bramhall, Williams & Gruskin, Agana, Guam, 1977-79; pvt. practice American Fork, Utah, 1979-80; assoc. Jardine, Linebaugh, Brown & Dunn, Salt Lake City, 1980-81; mem., dir. Ray, Quinney & Nebeker, Provo, Utah; judge 4th Jud. Dist. Ct., Provo, Utah, 1993—. Bishop Mormon Ch., American Fork, 1985-88; commr. American Fork City Planning Commn., 1980-85; trustee American Fork Hosp., 1984-93. Mem. Cen. Utah Bar Assn. (pres. 1987, 91). Avocations: photography, music. Office: 125 N 100 W Provo UT 84601-2849

SCHOLL, DAVID ALLEN, former federal judge, lawyer; b. Bethlehem, Pa., Aug. 20, 1944; s. George Raymond and Beatrice Roberta (Weaver) S.; m. Cynthia Ann Schuler Vetere, June, 1966 (div. 1972); m. Portia Elizabeth White, May 26, 1973; children: Tracy, Xavier; 1 stepchild, Sierra Milan. AB, Franklin & Marshall Coll., 1966; JD, Villanova U., 1969. Bar: Pa. 1969, U.S. Dist. Ct. (ea. dist.) 1970, U.S. Ct. Appeals (3d cir.) 1971, U.S. Tax Ct. 1975, U.S. Supreme Ct. 1975. Staff atty. Community Legal Services, Inc., Phila., 1969-73, 77-80; exec. dir. Delaware County Legal Assistance Assn., Chester, Pa., 1973-76; mng. atty. Lehigh Valley Legal Services, Bethelehem, Allentown, Pa., 1980-86; judge U.S. Bankruptcy Ct., Phila., 1986-94, chief judge, 1994-99, judge, 1999-2000. Bd. dirs. Phila. Vols. for Indigent Program, 1988—94, Consumer Bankruptcy Assistance Project, 1992—98, 2000—. Recipient Joseph Harris award Ba'Hais of Lehigh Valley, Bethelehem, 1984, Vol. of Yr. award Temple LEAP Program, 1997. Mem. Pa. Bar Assn. (chairperson consumer law commn., 1983-86), Northampton County Bar Assn. Avocations: baseball, rock music. Office: 6 St Albans Ave Newtown Square PA 19073 Fax: 610-353-7542. E-mail: judgescholl@redemptionlawcenter.com.

SCHOLLANDER, WENDELL LESLIE, JR., lawyer; BS, U. Pa., 1966, MBA, 1968; postgrad., Stetson U., 1969-70; JD, Duke U., 1972. Bar: N.C. 1977, Tenn. 1972, Fla. 1987. With Container Corp. Am., Fernandina, Fla., 1968-69; assoc. Miller, Martin, Chattanooga, 1972-75; asst. counsel R.J. Reynolds Industries, Inc., 1975-78, assoc. counsel, 1978-79, sr. assoc. counsel, 1979-82, sr. counsel, 1982-85; gen. counsel RJR Archer, Inc., Winston-Salem, N.C., 1979-85; of counsel Finger, Parker & Avram, Winston-Salem, 1985-87; ptnr. Schollander, Winston-Salem, 1987—. Gen. counsel Splty. Tobacco Council, 1985-87. Mem. ABA, N.C. Bar Assn., Forsyth County Bar Assn., Mensa, SAR, Phi Delta Phi, Kappa Sigma. Presbyterian. Bankruptcy, Corporate, general, Franchising. Office: 2000 W 1st St Ste 509 Winston Salem NC 27104-4225

SCHOLLER, THOMAS PETER, lawyer, accountant; b. Big Rapids, Mich., Aug. 15, 1937; s. Clarence Leo and Ruth Winona (Williams) S.; m. Marcia Kay Harman, June 25, 1960; children: Susan, Mark, Katrina, Laura, Emily. BS in Acctg., Ferris State U., 1959, LLD (hon.), 1984; LLB, U. Mich., 1962. CPA, Mich. Staff acct. Arthur Andersen & Co., Detroit, 1962-63, sr. acct., 1963-66, tax mgr., 1966-72, tax ptnr., 1972-91, dir. tax div. Grand Rapids, Mich., 1982-85, 88-91; of counsel Smith, Haughey, Rice & Roegge, Grand Rapids, 1992-97; dir. planned giving Archdiocese Detroit, 1997—. Contbr. articles to profl. jours. Taxation adv. com. Walsh Coll., 1972—92; trustee Ferris State U., Big Rapids, 1978—83, chmn., 1981; trustee Grand Rapids Art Mus., 1989—95, Ferris Found., 1999—; bd. dirs. Planned Giving Roundtable S.E. Mich., 2002—. Republican. Roman Catholic. Avocations: golf, swimming. Office: Archdiocese Detroit 1234 Washington Blvd Detroit MI 48226-1825 E-mail: scholler.tom@aod.org.

SCHOLTZ, KENNETH P. lawyer; b. L.A., Mar. 24, 1938; s. Walter and Sylvia (Flax) S.; m. Marion G. Bloom, Nov. 12, 1966; children: Matthew M., Brian A., Wendy D. BS, Calif. Inst. Tech., 1960; LLB, U. Calif., Berkeley, 1963. Dep. atty. gen. Calif. Atty. Gen., L.A., 1964-68; atty. Joseph Lucas Enterprises, London, 1969-70; pvt. practice L.A., 1970; assoc. Berrien & Moore, Gardena and Torrance, Calif., 1971-73; pvt. practice Beverly Hills, Calif., 1973-79; ptnr. Quan, Cohen et al, L.A., 1979-2000; of counsel Kohrs & Fiske, L.A., 2001—. Settlement officer Ct. of Appeal, L.A., 1996—; mem. arbitration and mediation panel L.A. Superior Ct., 1999—, pilot project panel, 2001; mem. mediation panel Arbitration, Mediation and Conciliation Ctr. Algorithms for Tuning Diatonic Keyboard Scales, Music Theory Online, 1998. Pres. L.A. Gifted Children's Assn., 1975-76; bd. dirs. L.A. Alzheimers Assn., 1994-2001, co-chmn. Adult Day Svcs. Inst., 2001—. Ford Found. fellow, 1963-64. Mem. Red Ribbon Squares (pres. 1985-86), Santa Monica Oceanaires (sect. 2000-01, pres. 2002-03). Avocations: dancing, music, hiking. E-mail: kscholtz@medi8.com.

SCHON, ALAN WALLACE, lawyer, actor; b. Mpls., Nov. 27, 1946; s. Hubert Adelbert and Jennie (Jamieson) S.; m. Linda Kay Long, June 14, 1969; 1 child, Cynthia Anne. BA, U. Minn., 1969; JD, William and Mary Coll., 1973; grad. Command & Gen. Staff Coll., U.S. Army, 1984. Bar: Minn. 1973, U.S. Dist. Ct. Minn., Alaska 1986, U.S. Dist. Ct. Alaska, U.S. Ct. Appeals (9th cir.) 1988, Va. 1995. Prin. Schon Law Office, Fairbanks, Alaska, 1986-94; owner, pub. Nordland Pub. Co., Hampton, Va., 1991-94; dep. city atty. mcpl. bonds, environ. law, pub.-pvt. econ. devel. funding environ. law City of Hampton, Va., 1994-99. Nationwide environ. group mgr. Delphi Info. Network, Gen. Videotex Corp., Cambridge, Mass., 1991-94; ind. assoc. Pre-Paid Legal Svcs. Inc., 1999—. Author, pub. EnvironLaw, 1991-94; editor William and Mary Law Rev., 1970-73; stage, film and TV actor; screenwriter: Operation Desert Fire, 1997, Operation Firestorm, 1998. Dir. Alaska State Fair, Fairbanks, 1987-91, Fairbanks Light Opera Theater, Fairbanks, 1991-94, Theatre of Virginia Beach, Va., 2002—; dir., v.p. bus. and fin. Williamsburg (Va.) Players Theater, 2000-01, dir. Little Theatre of Virginia Beach, Va., 2002—; dir., sec. Riding for Am., Inc., 1993-97; dir. Interior Alaska Econ. Devel. Ctr., 1993-94. Maj. U.S. Army, 1974-86. Mem. Fairbanks C. of C. (chmn. environ. concerns com. 1992-94). Avocations: outdoor sports, arts. Home and Office: 389 River Forest Rd Virginia Beach VA 23454-3288

SCHONBERG, BRUCE A. lawyer; b. Columbia, S.C., Jan. 22, 1958; s. Arnold and Myrna Schonberg; m. Tami Schonberg, June 25, 1984. BA in Polit. Sci., SUNY, Oneonta, 1980; JD, U. Buffalo, 1984. Bar: N.Y. 1985, U.S. Dist. Ct. (no. dist.) N.Y. 1990. Intern U.S. Dist. Ct. (we. dist.) N.Y., Buffalo, 1984; asst. dist. atty. Orange County N.Y. Dist. Atty., Goshen, 1985—90; ptnr. Grogen, Souto and Schonberg, Goshen, 1990—2000, Barraco and Schonberg, Highland, NY, 2000—. Zoning bd. mem. Town of Woodbury, Highland Mills, NY, 1998—; youth league soccer coach, 1991—. Mem.: ATLA, N.Y. State Bar Assn. Personal injury (including property damage), Criminal. Home: 1 Morgan Ct Central Valley NY 10917 Office: Barraco and Schonberg PO Box 1545 Highland NY 12528

SCHONFELD, ESTHER MIRIAM, lawyer; b. N.Y.C., Mar. 2, 1960; m. Alan Seth Schonfeld (div. 1994); children: Jeremy Adam, Alexandra; m. Benjamin Farkas, Oct. 10, 1999; stepchildren: Esti Farkas, David Farkas, Paul Farkas. BBA, CUNY, 1981; JD summa cum laude, Touro Law Sch., 1999. Bar: NY 2000, U.S. Supreme Ct. 2003, U.S. Ct. Appeals Armed Forces 2003, U.S. Ct. Appeals (D.C. Cir.) 2003, U.S. Ct. Fed. Claims 2003. Assoc. Koopersmith & Brown, LLP, Lake Success, NY, 1999—2002; founding ptnr. Kaplan, Mosery & Schonfeld, PLLC, N.Y.C. and Cedarhurst, NY, 2002—. Editor: Touro Law Rev., 1998—99. Scholarship, award, Jewish Lawyers Assn. of Nassau County, 1997. Mem.: ABA (mem. family law div.), Queens County Bar Assn. (mem. family law com.), Nassau County Bar Assn. (mem. matrimonial law com.), NY State Bar Assn. Avocations: travel, piano, cello, literature, art. Appellate, Family and matrimonial. Office: Kaplan Mosery & Schonfeld PLLC 112 Spruce St Ste A Cedarhurst NY 11516

SCHOOLER, STEVEN JAMES, lawyer; b. Pullman, Wash., Apr. 30, 1955; s. Arnold and Iris S.; m. Marsha Mae Mansfield, June 9, 1955; 1 child, Sarah. BA in Econs., George Washington U., 1973; JD, U. Mich., 1981. Bar: Wis. 1981, U.S. Dist. Ct. (ea. and we. dists.) Wis. 1981, U.S. Ct. Appeals (7th cir.) 1981. Atty. Axley Brynelson, Madison, Wis., 1981-89, Lawton & Cates, S.C., Madison, 1989-2000; exec. dir. Transitional Housing Inc., Madison, 2001—. Chair individual rights sect. Wis. State, Madison, 1994-96; pres., bd. dirs. Ctr. Pub. Representation, Madison, 1998-2003. Co-author: Law of Damages, 1988, Wisconsin Civil Procedures Before Trial, 1996; co-editor: Wisconsin Civil Forms Manual, 1995. Mem. adminstrv. coun. First United Meth. Ch., pres., 1993-96; bd. dirs. U. Wis. Madison Campus Ministries, sec., 1986-87; bd. dirs. Transitional Housing, Inc., Madison, 1991-99. Recipient Service to Man award, Sertoma, 2003. Mem. Order of Coif, Phi Beta Kappa. Civil rights, General civil litigation, Personal injury (including property damage). Office: Transitional Housing Inc 1490 Martin St Madison WI 53713-1140

SCHOONHOVEN, RAY JAMES, retired lawyer; b. Elgin, Ill., May 24, 1921; s. Ray Covey and Rosina Madeline (Schram) (White) S.; m. Marie Theresa Dunn, Dec. 11, 1943; children: Marie Kathleen "Kamie", Ray James, Jr., Pamela Suzanne, John Philip, Rose Lynn. BSC., U. Notre Dame, 1943; JD, Northwestern U., 1948. Bar: Ill. 1949, U.S. Supreme Ct. 1954, D.C. 1973, U.S. Ct. Mil. Appeals 1954. Assoc. Seyfarth, Shaw Fairweather & Geraldson, Chgo., 1949-57; ptnr. Seyfarth, Shaw Fairweather & Geraldson now Seyfarth Shaw, Chgo., 1957-92; ret. Chief rulings and ops. br. Wage Stabilization Bd. Region VII, Chgo., 1951-52 Book rev. editor: Ill. Law Rev., 1948. Served to lt.comdr. USNR, 1942-62. Mem. ABA, Ill. State Bar Assn., Chgo. Bar Assn., D.C. Bar Assn., Chgo. Athletic Assn., Univ. Club. Chgo., Fed. Bar Assn., Order of Coif. Republican. Roman Catholic. Administrative and regulatory, Labor (including EEOC, Fair Labor Standards Act, labor-management relations, NLRB, OSHA), Alternative dispute resolution. Home: 1182 Lynette Dr Lake Forest IL 60045-4601 Office: Seyfarth Shaw 55 E Monroe St Ste 4200 Chicago IL 60603-5863

SCHOONMAKER, SAMUEL VAIL, III, lawyer; b. Newburgh, N.Y., Sept. 1, 1935; s. Samuel V. Jr. and Catherine (Wilson) S.; m. Carolyn Peters, Sept. 18, 1965; children: Samuel V. IV, Frederick P. BA magna cum laude, Yale U., 1958, JD, 1961. Bar: Conn. 1961, U.S. Dist. Ct. Conn. 1961, U.S. Dist. Ct. (so. and ea. dist.) N.Y. 1964, U.S. Ct. Appeals (2d cir.) 1964, U.S. Supreme Ct. 1965. Assoc. Cummings & Lockwood, Stamford, Conn., 1961-70, co-mng. ptnr., 1987-90, mng. ptnr., 1990-94, chmn. exec. com., 1987-96; founder, pres. Schoonmaker George & Colin, P.C., Greenwich, Conn., 1996—. State trial referee Conn. Superior Ct., 1989; pres. Schoonmaker Family Assn., New Paltz, N.Y., 1975-77. Sr. topical editor Conn. Bar Jour., 1977-81; mem. editl. bd. Fairshare and Am. Jour. Family Law, 1992—; contbr. articles to profl. jours. Chmn. Conn. Child Support Commn., 1984-86; mem. Conn. Family Support Com., 1986-90; mem. Darien (Conn.) Rep. Town Com., 1974-76, rep. town meeting, 1990-98; pres. Youth Tennis Found. New Eng., Needham, Mass., 1975-77; pres. New Eng. Lawn Tennis Assn., 1977-79 (Man of Yr. award 1979); pres., trustee Huegenot Hist. Soc., 1999—. Fellow Am. Acad. Matrimonial Lawyers Conn. (bd. mgrs., Disting. Svc. award 1988), Internat. Acad. Matrimonial Lawyers, Am. Bar Found.; mem. ABA (chmn. family law sect. 1982-83), Conn. Bar Assn. (chmn. family law sect. 1971-74), Conn. Bus. and Industry Assn. (bd. dirs. 1993-98), S.W. Conn. Bus. and Industry Assn. (bd. dirs. 1990-97), Pub. Defenders Assn. (chmn.), Wee Burn Country Club (Darien, Conn., asst. sec.), Yale Club (N.Y.C.), Phi Beta Kappa. Avocations: tennis, platform tennis. Family and matrimonial. Home: 231 Old Kings Hwy S Darien CT 06820-5931 Office: Schoonmaker George & Colin PC PO Box 5059 81 Holly Hill Ln Greenwich CT 06831-5059

SCHOR, LAURENCE, lawyer; b. Bklyn., May 3, 1942; s. Julius and Ruth (Zackowitz) S.; m. Susan Leslie Gurevitz, Dec. 26, 1965; children: Meredith Nan, Joseph Sanford, Wendy Claire, Samuel Julius. BBA, So. Meth. U., 1963; JD, U. Tex., 1966; LLM, George Washington U., 1972. Bar: Tex. 1966, D.C. 1971, Md. 1993.; U.S. Ct. Appeals (D.C., 4th, 5th, 11th cirs.). Atty. NASA, Huntsville, Ala., 1966-68; asst. gen. counsel NASA support U.S. Army C.E., Washington, 1968-70; assoc. Sellers, Conner & Cuneo, Washington, 1970-73; from assoc. to ptnr. Max E. Greenberg, Trayman, Cantor, Reiss & Blasky, Washington, 1974-80; ptnr. Schnader, Harrison, Segal & Lewis, Washington, 1981-91, ptnr.-in-charge, 1986-88; mem. Miller & Chevalier, Washington, 1991-93; ptnr. Smith, Somerville & Case, LLC, Washington, 1993-96, McManus, Schor, Asmar & Darden, LLP, Washington, 1997—. Lectr. George Washington U., others. Author: The Right to Stop Work, 1991; author: (manual) Delays, Suspensions and Acceleration, Workplace Safety and Health in the 1990's, 1992; author: Claims Against Bonding Companys, Construction Contractors' Handbook of Business and Law, 1992, How to File a Federal Contract Claim, 1998; co-author: Suing a Government: Special Considerations for Book Construction Disputes: Representing the Contractor, 3d edit., 2001; author, editor 50 State Lien and Bond Laws, 1993—2003, Vol. 3 Form Book rewrite, 2000, editor update, 2001—03; contbr. chapters to books, articles to profl. jours. Founder, pres. Manor Lake Civic Assn., Montgomery County, 1969-71; precinct chmn. Montgomery County Dems., 1972-76; mem. D.C. City Coun. Procurement Reform Task Force, 1995-96. Mem. ABA (chmn. region III pub. contract law sect., 1982-88, chmn. constrn. com. 1986-90, sect. budget and fin. 1990-95), D.C. Bar Assn. (chmn. divsn. 10 govt. contracts and litigation, 1981-85), Fed. Bar Assn., Am. Coll. Constrn. Lawyers (founder, bd. govs., treas. 1996-2000, pres. elect 2000, pres. 2001-02), B'nai B'rith Youth Orgn (adult adv. bd. 2001-02), Phi Alpha Delta (pres. T.C. Clark chpt. 1965-66). Jewish. Avocations: reading, travel. Federal civil litigation, Construction, Government contracts and claims. Home: 7021 Mountain Gate Dr Bethesda MD 20817-3913 Office: McManus Schor Asmar & Darden LLP 1301 Connecticut Ave NW Fl 6 Washington DC 20036-1815 Business E-Mail: lschor@msadlaw.com.

SCHORLING, WILLIAM HARRISON, lawyer; b. Ann Arbor, Mich., Jan. 7, 1949; s. Otis William Schorling and Ruthann (Bales) Schorling Moorehead; m. Lynne Ann Newcomb, June 1, 1974; children: Katherine Pearce, Ann Oury, John Roberts. BA cum laude, Denison U., 1971; JD cum laude, U. Mich., 1975. Bar: Pa. 1975, U.S. Ct. Appeals (3d cir.) 1977, N.J. 1998, Del. 2001. Ptnr. Eckert, Seamans, Cherin & Mellott, Pitts., 1984-89, Klett Rooney Lieber & Schorling, PC, Pitts., 1989—. Lectr. Pa. Bar Inst., Harrisburg, 1983—, Comml. Law League, N.Y.C., 1984—, Profl. Edn. Systems, Inc., Eau Claire, Wis., 1986—, Southwest Legal Found., Dallas, 1994—; founders' coun. Comml. Fin. Assn. Edn. Found., 1991—; bd. dirs. Consumer Bankruptcy Assistance Project. Contbr. articles to profl. jours. Trustee Pa. Acad. Fine Arts. Fellow Am. Coll. Bankruptcy, Am. Bar Found.; mem. ABA (bus. law section coun. 2000—, chmn. bus. bankruptcy com. 1996-99, lectr. 1988—), Am. Banker Inst. (lectr. 1994—), Phila. Bar Assn. (lectr. 1996—), E. Dist. Bankruptcy Conf., Pa. Bar Assn. (lectr. 1983—), Allegheny County Bar Assn. (chmn. bankruptcy and comml. law sect. 1991), The Com. of Seventy (chmn. 2003—), Longue Vue Club, Duquesne Club, Pyramid Club, Pa. Soc., Bedens Brook Club. Presbyterian. Bankruptcy, Commercial, contracts (including sales of goods; commercial financing). Home: 12 Scudder Ct Pennington NJ 08534-2325 Office: Klett Rooney Lieber & Schorling 2 Logan Sq Fl 12 Philadelphia PA 19103-2707

SCHORR, BRIAN LEWIS, lawyer, business executive; b. N.Y.C., Oct. 5, 1958; s. Philip I. and Hannah Schorr; m. Amy B. Horowitz; 2 children. BA magna cum laude, MA, Wesleyan U., Middletown, Conn., 1979; JD, NYU, 1982. Bar: N.Y. 1983, D.C. 1985, U.S. Supreme Ct. 1988. Assoc. Paul, Weiss, Rifkind, Wharton & Garrison, N.Y.C., 1982-90, ptnr., 1991-94; exec. v.p., gen. counsel Triarc Cos., Inc., N.Y.C., 1994—. Mem. bd. advisors Jour. Ltd. Liability Cos., 1994-98; lectr. CLE programs. Author: Schorr on New York Limited Liability Companies and Partnerships, 1994; contbr. articles to legal jours. Bd. dirs. Bronx (N.Y.) HS Sci. Endowment Fund, Inc. Mem. ABA, N.Y. State Bar Assn., Assn. Bar City N.Y. (chmn. com. on corp. law 1993-96, co-chmn. joint drafting com. N.Y. ltd. liability co. law, mem. spl. com. on mergers, acquisitions and corp. control contests 1996—), Tri Bar Opinion Com., Bronx H.S. Sci. Alumni Assn. (trustee). Finance, Mergers and acquisitions, Securities. Office: Triarc Cos Inc 280 Park Ave New York NY 10017-1216

SCHOUMACHER, BRUCE HERBERT, lawyer; b. Chicago, May 23, 1940; s. Herbert Edward and Mildred Helen (Wagner) S.; m. Alicia Wesley (Sanchez), Nov. 4, 1967; children: Liana Cristina, Janina Maria. BS, U. Ill., Northwestern, 1961; MBA, U. Ill., Chgo., 1963, JD, 1966. Bar: Nebr. 1966, U.S. Dist. Ct. Nebr. 1966, Ill. 1971, U.S. Dist. Ct. (no. dist.) Ill. 1971, U.S. Ct. Appeals (7th cir.) 1979, U.S. Supreme Ct. 1982, U.S. Ct. Fed. Claims 1986. Assoc. Luebs, Tracy, and Huebner, Grand Island, Nebr., 1966-67, McDermott, Will, and Emery, Chgo., 1971-76; ptnr. McDermott, Will ,and Emery, Chgo., 1976-89, Querrey and Harrow, Ltd., Chgo., 1989—. Instr. bus. adminstrn., Bellevue Coll., Nebr., 1967-70; lectr., U. Md. Overseas Program, 1970. Author: Engineers and the Law: An Overview, 1986; contbg. author: Construction Law, 1986, Construction Law Handbook, 1999; co-author: Successful Business Plans for Architects, 1992; contbr. articles to profl. jour. Capt., USAF, 1967-71, Vietnam. Decorated, Bronze Star, 1971. Fellow Am. Coll. Constrn. Lawyers; mem. ABA, AIA (profl. affiliate), Nebr. Bar Assn., Ill. State Bar Assn. (ad hoc com. large law firms 1992-98), chmn. membership and bar activities com. 1988-89, coun. ins. law sect., 1986-91, mem. spl. com. on computerized legal rsch. 1986-87, Chgo. Bar Assn. (chmn. fed. civil procedure com. 1982-83), Def. Rsch. Inst., Ill. Assn. Def. Trial Counsel, Chgo. Bldg. Congress (bd. dirs. 1985—, sec. 1987-89, 95—, v.p. 1989-91), Soc. Ill. Constrn. Attys., Western Soc. Engr. (assoc.), The Lawyers Club of Chgo., Tower Club, Chgo., Univ. Club Chgo., Pi Kappa Alpha, Phi Delta Phi. Republican. Methodist. Federal civil litigation, State civil litigation, Construction. Office: Querrey & Harrow Ltd 175 W Jackson Blvd Ste 1600 Chicago IL 60604-2827

SCHOWALTER, DEBORAH, arbitrator, mediator; b. Milw., Feb. 12, 1948; d. Gilbert T. and Valerie H. (Krapfel-Kann) S. BA with honors, San Diego State U., 1970; postgrad., UCLA, 1972; JD, U. San Diego, 1975. Bar: Calif. 1975, U.S. Dist. Ct. (so. dist.) Calif. 1975. Pvt. practice, San Diego, 1975-81; commr. L.A. Superior Ct., 1981-84; adj. prof. U. Md., Rimini, Italy, 1984-87; interpreter/housing officer USAF, Rimini, 1986-87; chief purchasing and contracting U.S. Army SETAF, Vicenza, Italy, 1992; spl. prof. John Marshall Law Sch., Atlanta, 1995-97; dispute resolver, pres. Problem Solvers, Dispute Resolution, Atlanta and San Diego, 1995—; pvt. practice San Diego, 2001—. Adj. prof. U. San Diego Sch. Law, 1979-80; journalist, photographer, artist, 1988—; lectr. in field. Contbr. articles to profl. publs. Elected ofcl. Organized Nieghbors of Edgewood, Atlanta, 1997-98; bd. dirs. Mid-City Cmty. Clinic, San Diego, 1979-81. NEH fellow. Mem. Club Boccacio (Italian). Avocations: photography, painting, French horn, gardening, remodelling houses. Office: 1218 W Thorn St San Diego CA 92103-5334

SCHRADER, ALFRED EUGENE, lawyer; b. Nov. 1, 1953; s. Louis Clement and Helen Mae (Eberz) S.; m. Debra Susanne Britt-Garrett, Aug. 12, 1997. BA in Polit. Sci. magna cum laude, Kent State U., 1975; JD, Ohio State U., 1978. Bar: Ohio 1978, U.S. Dist. Ct. (no. dist.) Ohio 1978, U.S. Ct. Appeals (6th cir.) 1985, U.S. Supreme Ct. 1985. Dep. clk. Summit County Clk. of Cts., Akron, 1972-74; pvt. practice law Akron, 1978—; spl. counsel Bath Twp., Ohio, 1980-92, 95-98. Spkr. Akron Bar Assn. Akron Univ. Sch. Law CLE Seminars. Trustee Springfield Twp., Ohio, 1973-2001, pres., 1975, 79, 82, 88, 90, 95-96, 2000-01; v.p. Springfield-Akron Joint Econ. Devel. Dist., 1995-97, pres., 1997-2000; mem. adv. com. Cmty. Devel. Block, Summit County, 1985-97, Twinsburg Twp. tax abatement counsel, 1994—, Summit County Annexation Com., 1981-85; mem. Summit County Jail Study Commn., 1983, 84; mem. adv. bd. Springfield Schs., 1975; acting law dir. City of Streetsboro, Portage County, Ohio, 1997; rep. numerous twps. State of Ohio on land use planning, annexation, revenue sharing, zoning and local govt. law matters. Mem. ATLA, Akron Bar Assn. (v.p. legis. com. 1981-82, v.p. local govt. sect. 1992-93, chair local govt. sect. 1993-95, v.p. continuing legal edn. com. 2001--), Ohio Acad. Trial Lawyers, Ohio Bar Assn., Summit County Twp. Assn. (exec. com. 1983-2001), Ohio Twp. Assn., Risk Mgmt. Authority (bd. dirs. 1996-2001, sec. 1997-2000, pres. 2000-01), Nat. Assn. Town and Twp. Attys. (bd. dirs. Ohio chpt. 1986, sec. 1987-93, v.p. 1993-97). Democrat. Roman Catholic. Fax: 330 762 2255. Land use and zoning (including planning), Appellate, Personal injury (including property damage). Home: 3344 Brunk Rd Akron OH 44312-3710 Office: Schrader Romanoski Stevenson and Grant 441 Wolf Ledges Pky Ste 400 Akron OH 44311-1039 Fax: (330) 762-2255. E-mail: attysrsg@aol.com.

SCHRAG, EDWARD A., JR., lawyer; b. Milw., Mar. 27, 1932; s. Edward A. and Mabel Lena (Baumbach) S.; m. Leslie Jean Israel, June 19, 1954; children: Amelia Marie Schrag Prack, Katherine Allison Schrag Roberts, Edward A. III (dec.). BS in Econs, U. Pa., 1954; JD, Harvard, 1960. Bar: Ohio 1961. Assoc., then firm partner, now of counsel Vorys, Sater, Seymour and Pease, Columbus, 1960—. Sec. Ranco Inc., 1972-87; trustee Lake of Woods Water Co., 1972-91; mem. Ohio div. Securities Adv. Com. Mem. Downtown Area Com., 1970-74. Served to lt. (j.g.) USNR, 1954-57. Mem. ABA, Ohio Bar Assn. (chmn. corp. law com. 1986-88, chmn. securities regulation subcom., spl. com. bus. cts., bd. govs., corp. counsel sect., chmn. 1991-93), Columbus Bar Assn., Columbus Area C. of C., Navy League, Alpha Tau Omega, Beta Gamma Sigma, Phi Sigma Alpha, Pi Gamma Mu. Clubs: Capital, Crichton, Ohio State U. Pres.'s. Episcopalian. Home: 9400 White Oak Ln Westerville OH 43082-9606 Office: Vorys Sater Seymour & Pease PO Box 1008 52 E Gay St Columbus OH 43216-1008

SCHRAG, PHILIP GORDON, law educator; b. Chgo., Apr. 12, 1943; s. Louis Phillip and Lala D. (Fineman) S.; m. Emily Shiling, June 7, 1964 (div. Aug. 1985); children: David, Zachary; m. Lisa Gabrielle Lerman, Dec. 29, 1985; children: Samuel Lerman, Sarah. AB, Harvard U., 1964; LLB, Yale U., 1967. Bar: N.Y. 1967, D.C. 1981. Asst. counsel NAACP Legal Def. & Edn. Fund Inc., N.Y.C., 1967-70; consumer adv. City of N.Y., 1970-71; assoc. prof. law Columbia U., N.Y.C., 1971-73, prof. law, 1973-77; dep. gen. counsel ACDA, Washington, 1977-81; prof. law Georgetown U., Washington, 1981—. Cons. Consumer Protection Bd., N.Y., 1975, Carter-Mondale Transition Planning, 1976, Gov.'s Adv. Coun., P.R., 1970. Author: Counsel for the Deceived, 1972, Behind the Scenes: The Politics of a Constitutional Convention, 1985, A Well-Founded Fear: The Congressional Battle to Save Political Asylum in America, 2000. Del. Statehood Constnl. Conv., D.C., 1982; chair Consumer's Adv. Coun., N.Y.C., 1968-70.

SCHRAMM, PAUL HOWARD, lawyer; b. St. Louis, Oct. 6, 1933; s. Benjamin Jacob and Frieda Sylvia (Goruch) S.; m. Sue-Ann Batson; children: Scott Lyon, Dean Andrew, Thomas Edward, Jeremy Arthur Savran. AB, U. Mo., 1955, JD, 1958. Bar: Mo. 1958, U.S. Dist. Ct. (ea. dist.) Mo. 1963, U.S. Ct. Appeals (8th cir.) 1967, U.S. Tax Ct. 1970, U.S. Supreme Ct. 1972, U.S. Dist. Ct. (ea. dist.) Wis., 1988, U.S. Dist. Ct. (we.dist.) Md. 2003. Ptnr. Schramm & Schramm, St. Louis, 1959-61, Schramm & Morganstern, St. Louis, 1970-76, Schramm, Pines & Marshall, St. Louis, 1977-79, Schramm, Newman, Pines & Freyman, St. Louis, 1979-82, Schramm, Pines & Spewak, St. Louis, 1983-85, Schramm & Pines, L.L.C., St. Louis, 1985-2000, Edwards, Singer, Schramm, Watkins, Spoeneman & Waltrip, L.L.P., St. Louis, 2000—. Pros. atty. City of Ellisville, Mo., 1973-77; judge Ellisville mcpl. div. St. Louis County Cir. Ct., 1977-83; teaching faculty trial advocacy Harvard Law Sch., 1991. Mem. Bar Assn. Met. St. Louis (exec. com. 1976-77, chmn. county sect. 1976-77), St. Louis County Bar Assn. (chmn. lawyers reference service 1971, cir. ct. jud. com. 1970), Phi Delta Phi. Clubs: University (St. Louis). Avocations: music, sports, reading. General civil litigation, Corporate, general, Family and matrimonial. Home: 7507 Byron Pl Saint Louis MO 63105-2703 Office: Edwards Singer Schramm Watkins Spoeneman & Waltrip LLP 1600 Clayton Ctr 120 S Central Ave Ste 1600 Saint Louis MO 63105-1798

SCHRAUFF, CHRISTOPHER WESLEY, lawyer; b. Houston, July 18, 1968; m. Paula Leigh Barnes. BA, U. Tex., 1992, JD, 1996. Bar: Tex. 1996. V.p., counsel FIC Ins. Group, Austin, Tex., 1996—2000; assoc. Locke, Liddell, & Sapp LLP, 2000—. Avocation: guitar. Corporate, general, Insurance, Property, real (including real estate development, water). Office: Locke Liddell & Sapp 2200 Ross Ave Dallas TX 75201

SCHRECK, ROBERT A., JR., lawyer; b. Buffalo; BS in Bus. Adminstrn., Georgetown U., 1974; MBA, Northwestern U., 1975, JD, 1978. Bar: Ill. 1978. Ptnr. McDermott, Will & Emery, Chgo., 1978—. Mem. ABA. Mergers and acquisitions, Securities, Corporate, general. Office: McDermott Will & Emery 227 W Monroe St Ste 4400 Chicago IL 60606-5096 E-mail: rschreck@mwe.com.

SCHRECKENGAST, WILLIAM OWEN, lawyer; b. Greenwood, Ind., Oct. 14, 1926; s. Vernon Edward and Marthena O. (Mullinix) S.; m. Helen Margaret Sheppard, Nov. 11, 1949 (div.); children: Pamela, Sandra, James, John; m. Virginia Thompson, Mar. 14, 1990. LLB, Ind. U., 1956. Bar: Ind. 1956, U.S. Ct. Appeals (7th cir.) 1956, U.S. Dist. Ct. (so. dist.) Ind. 1956, U.S. Supreme Ct. 1967. Ptnr. Kitley, Pontius & Schreckengast, Beech Grove, Ind., 1957-59, Kitley & Schreckengast, Beech Grove, 1959-63, 78-82, Kitley, Schreckengast & Davis, Beech Grove, 1963-78, Schreckengast & Lovern, Indpls., 1982-88, Schreckengast Lovern & Helm, Indpls., 1988—. Chmn. Ind. campaign John Walsh for Sec. of State, Indls., 1958; chmn. ward Beech Grove Dems., 1958-60. Served to 1st sgt. U.S. Army, 1944-46, PTO. Mem. ABA, Ind. Bar Assn. (bd. mgrs. 1973-74, pres. citation 1974, pres. trial lawyer sect. 1977-78), Ind. Def. Lawyers Assn. (diplomat), Am. Judicature Soc., Nat. Inst. Trial Advocacy (teaching faculty 1980-85), Platform Soc. Clubs: Hillview Country (Franklin, Ind.). Lodges: Masons. Republican. Avocations: golf, flying. State civil litigation, Insurance, Personal injury (including property damage). Home: 8026 Singleton St Indianapolis IN 46227-2568 Office: Schreckengast Lovern & Helm 8007 S Meridian St Ste 1 Indianapolis IN 46217-2922

SCHREIBER, ALAN HICKMAN, lawyer; b. Muncie, Ind., Apr. 4, 1944; s. Ephriam and Clarrisa (Hickman) S.; m. Phyllis Jean Chamberlain, Dec. 22, 1972; children: Jennifer Aline, Brett Justin. Student, DePauw U., 1962-64; BS in Bus., Ind. U., 1966, JD, 1969. Bar: Fla. 1971, U.S. Dist. Ct. (so. dist.) Fla. Asst. State Atty.'s Office, Ft. Lauderdale, Fla., 1971-76; pub. defender 17th Jud. Cir., Ft. Lauderdale, 1976—. Cons. Fla. Bar News on Criminal Law, 1982; lobbyist for indigent funding, Fla., 1980—; apptd. to Supreme Ct. Com. on Racial and Ethic Bias; co-chair Chiles-MacKay task force on criminal justice. Contbr. articles to profl. jours. Mem. Dem. Exec. Com., Ft. Lauderdale, 1980; mem. Plantation Dem. Club, 1983; campaign chmn. Goldstein for Atty. Gen. Fla., 1982. Named Young Dem. of Yr., Broward County Young Dems., 1980; Man of Yr., Jewish War Vets., 1982; recipient B'nai B'rith Pub. Servant award, 1990, Dem. of Yr. award 2000, Harry Galkin Meml. award 2002. Mem. Fla. Bar Assn., Broward County Bar Assn., ABA, Nat. Legal Aid Defenders Assn., Phi Alpha Delta. Criminal. Home: 885 Orchid Dr Fort Lauderdale FL 33317-1221 Office: 201 SE 6th St Fort Lauderdale FL 33301-3303

SCHREIBER, JOHN T. lawyer; b. N.Y.C., Mar. 30, 1960; s. Toby Schreiber and Morley Ann (Perrish) Clark; children: Zoe Cassandra Bloch Schreiber, Alana Nichole Perrish Schreiber. BA Politics, Brandeis U., 1982; JD, Santa Clara U., 1986. Bar: Calif. 1987(cert. specialist appellate law); U.S. Dist. Ct. (no. dist.) Calif. 1987; U.S. Dist. Ct. (ea. dist.) Calif. 1990; U.S. Ct. Appeals (9th cir.) 1989, U.S. Supreme Ct. 1998. Assoc. Law Offices of Wm. D. McHugh, San Jose, Calif., 1987-88, Hallgrimson, McNichols, McCann & Inderbitzen, Pleasanton, Calif., 1989-92; pvt. practice Walnut Creek, Calif., 1993—. Bd. dirs. East Bay Depot for Creative Re-use, Oakland. Field coord. Cen. Contra Costa County, Tom Bradley Campaign for Govs., Concord, Calif., 1982, Clinton-Gore Campaign, Walnut Creek, Calif., 1992; mem. Ask-A-Lawyer Program Contra Costa Legal Svcs. Found., Richmond, Calif., 1992-96; co-chair Clinton-Gore Contra Costa County, 1996. Mem. ABA, Contra Costa Bar Assn. (program dir. appellate sect. 1993-95, 2000—, pres. appellate sect. 1995-96, MCLE com. 1995—), Santa Clara Bar Assn., Am. Israeli Pub. Affairs Com. Avocations: reading, golf, softball, movies, exercising. General civil litigation. Office: 961 Ygnacio Valley Rd Walnut Creek CA 94596-3825

SCHREIBER, KURT GILBERT, lawyer; b. Milw., Aug. 22, 1946; s. Raymond R. and Mildred L. (Kleist) S.; m. Nelda Beth Van Buren, May 3, 1974; children— Katharine Anne, Matthew Edward AB in Econs., Cornell U., 1968; JD, U. Mich., 1971. Bar: Wis. 1971, Tex. 1979, Tenn. 1997. Internat. atty. Tenneco Internat. Holdings Co., London, 1974-78; atty. Tenneco Inc., Houston, 1978-80; 2d v.p., asst. gen. counsel Am. Gen. Corp., Houston, 1980-83, v.p., gen. counsel, 1983-84, sr. v.p., gen. counsel, 1984-93, sr. v.p., corp. sec., 1993-94; pvt. practice Houston, 1994-96; exec. v.p., gen. counsel Direct Gen. Corp., Nashville, 1996-98, pres., 1998—2001. Fellow Tex. Bar Found.; mem. ABA, Wis. Bar Assn., Tex. Bar Assn., Tenn. Bar Assn. Corporate, general, Private international. Home: 524 Turtle Creek Dr Brentwood TN 37027-5617

SCHREIBER, MARTIN HAROLD, II, lawyer; b. Balt., Md., 1965; s. Ronald L. and Faith (Feingold) Schreiber; m. Nancy Kauder, 1993; 1 child, Camilla Lawrence. JD, U. Md., 1992; BA, Columbia U., 1987; Baccalaureat, Lycee Jean Perrin, 1984. Bar: Md. 1993. Ptnr. Brown, Goldstein & Levy, LLP, Baltimore, Md., 1994—. Asst. editor Md. Law Rev., 1990—92; law clk. Judge Thomas A. Higgins U.S. Dist. (mid. dist.) Tenn., Nashville, 1992—94; adj. prof. U. Md. Law Sch., Balt., 2000—. Recipient Bridewater M. Arnold Prize, U. of Md. Sch. of Law, John S. Strahorn, Jr. Prize. Mem.: Selden Soc., Md. State Bar Assn., Barristers, Phi Beta Kappa. General civil litigation, Criminal. Office: Brown Goldstein & Levy LLP 120 E Baltimore St Ste 1700 Baltimore MD 21202 Office Fax: 410-385-0869. E-mail: mhs@browngold.com.

SCHRIER-POLAK, CAROL, lawyer; BA, Brandeis U., 1967; postgrad., Wayne State U., 1967-68; MSW, SUNY, Buffalo, 1969; JD, Temple U., 1977. Bar: Va. 1983, Pa. 1977. Exec. dir. Coun. for Children, Inc., Atlanta, 1972-74, Support Ctr. for Child Advocates Inc., Phila., 1977-83; legal cons. ABA/Nat. Resource Ctr. for Child Advocacy and Protection, Washington, 1983-84; assoc. Sharon Lieblich, PC, Alexandria, Va., 1984-88; atty. Bean, Kinney & Korman, P.C., Arlington, Va., 1988—, ptnr., 1990—. Mediator, 1994—; faculty Va. State Bar, Va. Trial Lawyers and local bar assns.; mem. child support quadrenneal rev. panel Commonwealth of Va., 1999. Co-editor: Making Financial Decisions when Divorce Occurs: A Virginia Guide, 1993; editor legal manuals; contbr. articles to profl. jours. Bd. dirs. Legal Svcs. No. Va., 1991-97; bd. dirs. Mental Health Assn. No. Va., 1989-92; mem. Leadershihp Fairfax, Inc., 1999; mem. adv. coun. Health Families, 2000—, chair-elect, 2002-03. Fellow Am. Acad. Matrimonial Lawyers (sec.-treas. Va. chpt. 1999-2001, v.p. 2001—); mem. ABA, D.C. Bar Assn., Va. Bar Assn. (mem. family law bd. govs. 1990-94, mem. faculty professionalism course 1999-2002), Fairfax Bar Assn. (bd. dirs. 1993—, sec. 1995-96, pres. 1997-98). Office: Bean Kinney & Korman 2000 14th St N Ste 100 Arlington VA 22201-2552

SCHRIVER, JOHN T., III, lawyer; b. Evanston, Ill., May 18, 1945; AB, Coll. of Holy Cross, 1967; JD, Georgetown U., 1970. Bar: Ill. 1971, Fla. 1972. Ptnr. Duane Morris LLC, Chgo. Mem. ABA, Chgo. Bar Assn., Fla. Bar. Office: Duane Morris LLC 227 W Monroe St Ste 3400 Chicago IL 60606-5096

SCHRODER, JACK SPALDING , JR., lawyer; b. Atlanta, July 10, 1948; s. Jack Spalding Sr. and Van (Spalding) S.; m. Karen Keyworth, Sept. 1, 1973; children: Jack Spalding III, James Edward. BA, Emory U., 1970; JD, U. Ga., 1973. Bar: Ga. 1973, U.S. Dist. Ct. (no. dist.) Ga. 1973, U.S. Ct. Appeals (11th cir.) 1982. Assoc. Alston & Bird, Atlanta, 1973-78, ptnr., 1978—. Author: Credentialing: Strategies for a Changing Environment/BNA's Health Law and Business Series, 1996; co-editor, contbg. author: Georgia Hospital Law manual, 1979, 84,92. Bd. dirs. Rsch. Atlanta, 1996-2000, pres., 1999; participant Leadership Ga., Atlanta, 1986. United Way (chmn. legal divsn.), Atlanta, 1980. Mem. ABA (vice chmn. medicine and law com. 1989-90), Am. Health Lawyers Assn. (bd. dirs. 1994-99, chmn. med. staff and physician rels. com. 1991-94, vice chair hosps. and health systems law inst. 2001--), Ga. Acad. Healthcare Attys. (pres. 1981-82), State Bar Ga. (bd. govs. 1987-89), Atlanta Coun. Younger Lawyers (pres. 1977-78), Atlanta Bar Assn. (pres. 1982-83), Atlanta Bar Found. (pres. 1991-95). Health. Office: Alston & Bird 1 Atlantic Ctr 1201 W Peachtree St NW Atlanta GA 30309-3424

SCHROEDER, EDWARD JAMES, lawyer; b. Abilene, Tex., June 29, 1947; s. Edward and Alice (Dufour) S. BA, McMurry Coll., 1970; MA, Hardin-Simmons U., 1973; postgrad., U. Louvain, Belgium, 1973; JD, St. Mary's U., San Antonio, 1979. Bar: Tex. 1979, U.S. Dist. Ct. (no. dist.) Tex. 1980, U.S. Ct. Appeals (5th cir.) 1981, U.S. Dist. Ct. (we. dist.) Tex. 1981, U.S. Tax Ct. 1997. Assoc. Trueheart McMillan, San Antonio, 1979-80, Westbrook & Goldston, San Antonio, 1980-81; ptnr. Westbrook Schroeder, San Antonio, 1981-83; pvt. practice San Antonio, 1983—. Pres. Kidney Found., San Antonio, 1983-85. Mem. San Antonio Bar Assn., Club Giraud (bd. dirs.), Friends of the McNay. General civil litigation, Estate planning, General practice.

SCHROEDER, EDWIN MAHER, law educator; b. New Orleans, June 25, 1937; s. Edwin Charles and Lucille Mary (Maher) S.; m. Marietta Louise DeFazio, Aug. 1, 1936; children: Edwin Charles II, Jonathan David, Margaret Louise. AA, St. Joseph Sem., St. Benedict, La., 1957; PhB, Gregorian U., Rome, 1959; JD, Tulane U., 1964; MS, Fla. State U., 1970. Bar: Mass. 1964. Asst. prof. law U. Conn., 1965-68; asst. prof., asst. law libr. U. Tex., 1968-69; asst. prof. Fla. State U., 1969-71, assoc. prof., 1971-75, prof., 1975—, dir. Law Libr., 1969—, asst. dean Coll. Law, 1979-83, assoc. dean Coll. Law, 1983-93. Mem. ABA, Am. Assn. Law Librs. (v.p. Southwestern chpt. 1983-84, pres. 1984-85), Order of Coif, Beta Phi Mu. Roman Catholic. Home: 806 Middlebrooks Cir Tallahassee FL 32312-2439 Office: Fla State U Coll Law Law Libr Tallahassee FL 32306-1600 E-mail: eschroed@law.fsu.edu.

SCHROEDER, ERIC PETER, lawyer; b. Floral Park, N.Y., July 21, 1970; s. Fredric G. and Linda M. Schroeder. BA, Duke U., 1992; JD, Vanderbilt U., 1996. Bar: Ga. 1997, U.S. Dist. Ct. (no. dist.) Ga. 1997, U.S. Ct. Appeals (11th cir.) 1998. Law clk. Hon. William C. O'Kelley, U.S. Dist. Ct. (no. dist.) Ga., Atlanta, 1996-97; atty. Powell, Goldstein, Frazer & Murphy, Atlanta, 1997—. Mem. planning com. Ga. Bar Media Jud. Conf., 1999-2002. Articles editor Vanderbilt Law Rev., 1995-96; mem. editl. bd. INTA The Trademark Reporter, 2000-01. Vol. Ga. Vol. Lawyers for the Arts, Atlanta, 1998--; lawyer Anti-Defamation League, Atlanta, 1998. Mem. Atlanta Bar Assn., (chair election com. 2002-03), Internat. Trademark Assn., Order of Coif, Lamar Inn of Ct. Constitutional, Libel, Trademark and copyright. Home: 977 North Ave Atlanta GA 30306-4701 Office: Powell Goldstein Frazer & Murphy 191 Peachtree St Atlanta GA 30303 E-mail: eschroeder@pgfm.com.

SCHROEDER, GERALD FRANK, state supreme court vice chief justice; b. Boise, Idaho, Sept. 13, 1939; s. Frank Frederick and Josephine Ivy (Lucas) S.; children: Karl Casteel, Erich Frank. BA magna cum laude, Coll. of Idaho (now Albertson Coll. of Idaho), 1961; JD, Harvard U., 1964. Bar: Idaho 1965. Assoc. Moffatt, Thomas, Barrett & Blanton, Boise, 1965—66; pvt. practice Boise, 1966—67; asst. U.S. atty. Dept. Justice, Boise, 1967—69; judge Ada County Probate Ct., Boise, 1969—71; magistrate State of Idaho, Boise, 1971—75; dist. judge U.S. Dist. Ct. (4th dist.) Idaho, 1975—95; justice Idaho Supreme Ct., 1995—. Instr.Boise Bar Rev. Boise Bar Rev., 1973—; adj. faculty law Boise State U., 1986—95; former mem. Gov. Coun. on Crime and Delinquency. Author: Idaho Probate Procedure, 1971, (Novel) Triangle of the Sons-Phenomena, 1983; contbr. Adminstrv. and dist. judge 4th dist. State of Idaho, 1985—95; Bd. dirs. Boise Philharm. Assn., 1979—81. Fellow Toll fellow, Nat. Coun. State Govt., 1990. Mem.: Idaho Bar Assn., Boise Racquet and Swim Club (pres. bd. dirs. 1991—93).

SCHROEDER, JAMES WHITE, lawyer; b. Elmhurst, Ill., Apr. 19, 1936; s. Paul W. and Thelma C. (White) S.; m. Patricia N. Scott, Aug. 18, 1962; children: Scott W. and Jamie C. BA, Princeton U., 1958; JD, Harvard U., 1964. Bar: Colo. 1964, U.S. Dist. Ct. Colo. 1964, U.S. Ct. Appeals (10th cir.) 1965, U.S. Supreme Ct. 1972, U.S. Dist. Ct. D.C. 1973, U.S. Ct. Appeals (D.C. cir.) 1974, U.S. Ct. Appeals (8th cir.) 1977, U.S. Ct. Appeals (3d cir.) 1981, U.S. Claims Ct. 1983, U.S. Ct. Appeals (fed. cir.) 1983. Ptnr. Moseley, Wells & Schroeder, Denver, 1965-72, Kaplan Russin & Vecchi, Washington, 1973-92; counsel Whitman & Ransom, Washington, 1992-93; dep. under sec. U.S. Dept. Agr., 1993-2001. Arbitrator Am. Arbitration Assn. Active Ams. for Democratic Action, Smithsonian Instn. Lt. USNR, 1958-64. Am. Field Svc. scholar 1953, NROTC scholar, 1954. Mem. ABA, Fed. Bar Assn., Denver Bar Assn., Colo. Bar Assn., D.C. Bar Assn., Cap and Gown Club, Lincoln's Inn Club, City Club Denver (pres. 1972), Princeton Club Washington (pres. 1982-84). Democrat. Home: 4102 Lester Ct Alexandria VA 22311-1121

SCHROEDER, LEILA OBIER, retired law educator; b. Plaquemine, La., July 11, 1925; d. William Prentiss and Daisy Lavinia (Mays) Obier; divorced; 1 child, James Michael Cutshaw; m. Martin Charles Schroeder Jr., Sept. 19, 1969. BA, Newcomb Coll., 1946; MSW, La. State U., 1953, JD, 1965. Bar: La. 1965. Exec. dir. Evangeline Area Guidance Ctr. La. Dept. Hosps., Lafayette, 1955-57, dir. social services dept. East La. State Hosp. Jackson, 1957-60, cons. psychiat. social work Baton Rouge, 1960-61; research assoc. La. State U., Baton Rouge, 1965-68, asst. prof., 1968-73, assoc. prof., 1973-80, prof., 1980-96; ret., 1996. Author: The Legal Environment of Social Work, 1982, The Legal Environment of Social Work, 1995; contbr. articles to profl. jours. Fellow Am. Orthopsychiat. Assn.; mem. ABA, Nat. Assn. Social Workers, Acad. Cert. Social Workers, La. State Bar Assn., Baton Rouge Bar Assn. Home: 4336 Oxford Ave Baton Rouge LA 70808-4651

SCHROEDER, MARY MURPHY, federal judge; b. Boulder, Colo., Dec. 4, 1940; d. Richard and Theresa (Kahn) Murphy; m. Milton R. Schroeder, Oct. 15, 1965; children: Caroline Theresa, Katherine Emily. BA, Swarthmore Coll., 1962; JD, U. Chgo., 1965. Bar: Ill. 1966, D.C. 1966, Ariz. 1970. Trial atty. Dept. Justice, Washington, 1965—69; law clk. to Hon. Jesse Udall Ariz. Supreme Ct., 1970; mem. Lewis and Roca, Phoenix, 1971—75; judge Ariz. Ct. Appeals, Phoenix, 1975—79, U.S. Ct. Appeals (9th cir.), Phoenix, 1979—2000, chief judge, 2000—. Vis. instr. Ariz. State U. Coll. Law, 1976—78. Contbr. articles to profl. jours. Mem.: ABA (Margaret Brent award 2001), Am. Judicature Soc., Am. Law Inst. (coun. mem.), Fed. Bar Assn., Ariz. Bar Assn., Soroptimists. Office: US Ct Appeals 9th Cir US Courthouse Ste 610 401 W Washington St SPC-54 Phoenix AZ 85003-2156 Fax: (602) 322-7329. E-mail: mary_schroeder@ca9.uscourts.gov.

SCHROEDER, OLIVER MARCUS, lawyer; b. Darmstadt, Hessen, Germany, Dec. 16, 1969; s. Dierk Schroeder and Eva Meyer-Burg. German Bar Exam, U. Heidelberg, Germany, 1995, LLD, 2001; LLM, NYU, 1998. Bar: State Cts. Hessen 1998. Law clk. County Ct. Heidelberg, 1997, Adminstrv. Ct. Appeals, Mannheim, Germany, 1998; lawyers asst. Fed. Surpeme Ct. Germany, Karlsruhe, 1998—99; lawyer Haarmann Hemmelrath, Frankfurt, 1999—2001, mem., ptnr., lawyer, 2001—. Author: Corporate Disclosure in U.S. and Germany; contbr. articles to profl. jours.; co-author: leading commentary on takeover law. Hauser Global scholar, NYU, 1997—98. Mem.: German Brazilian Lawyers Assn., German-Am. Lawyers Assn. Avocations: travel, music, photography, cooking, sports. Corporate, general, Securities, Mergers and acquisitions. Office: Haarmann Hemmelrath Neue Mainzer Str 75 60311 Frankfurt Germany Office Fax: 69 92059133. E-mail: oliver.schroeder@haarmannhemmelrath.com.

SCHROEDER, WILLIAM WAYNE, lawyer; b. Appleton, Wis., Mar. 17, 1953; s. Donald Wayne and Mary Enneking S.; m. Wendy Hadwen, June 25, 1977; children: John Henry, Susan Hadwen. BA, Middlebury Coll., 1975; MBA, U. Calif., Berkeley, 1977; JD, Cornell U., 1980. Bar: Vt. 1981, U.S. Dist. Ct. Vt. 1981, Calif. 1983, U.S. Dist. Ct. (no. dist.) Calif. 1983, U.S. Tax Ct. 1987. Lawyer Downs Rachlin & Martin, Burlington, Vt., 1981-83, 84—, Pillsbury Madison & Sutro, San Francisco, 1983-84. Regent Am. Coll. Mortgage Attys., 2000—. Chair Charlotte (Vt.) Planning Commn., 1995-96. Environmental, Property, real (including real estate development, water), Corporate taxation. Office: Downs Rachlin Martin PLLC PO Box 190 Burlington VT 05402-0190 E-mail: bschroeder@drm.com.

SCHROER, GENE ELDON, lawyer; b. Randolph, Kans., Aug. 29, 1927; s. Harry Edward and Florence Lillian (Schwartz) S.; m. Edith Grace Kintner, Apr. 7, 1956 (div.); children: Kenneth G., Rebecca J., Sonya J., Connie J.; m. Anne Oliver; 1 child, Edward G. AB, LLB, Washburn U., 1957. Bar: Kans. 1957, U.S. Dist. Ct. Kans. 1957, U.S. Ct. Appeals (10th cir.) 1970, U.S. Supreme Ct. 1983. Pvt. practice, Topeka, 1957-68; ptnr. Schroer, Rice, P.A., Topeka, 1968—, pres., 1970—, also bd. dirs. Contbr. articles to profl. jours. and chpts. to books. Supr. Shawnee County Soil Conservation Dist., Topeka, 1968-84. With U.S. Army, 1951-53. Mem. ABA, Kans. Bar Assn., Assn. Trial Lawyers Am. (gov. 1976-79, seminar lectr. 1973—, chmn. tort sect. 1974-75, instr. Nat. Coll. Adv. 1978, 81-88), Kans. Trial Lawyers Assn. (gov. 1972—, seminar lectr. 1974—, pres. 1974-75), Nat. Bd. Trial Advocacy (sustaining founder), N.Y. Acad. Sci., Am. Bd. Trial Advs. (sec., treas. Kans. chpt. 1990-91, pres. 1991-92), Civil Justice Found. (founding sponsor), Trial Lawyers for Pub. Justice (bd. dirs. 1982-96). Democrat. Methodist. Federal civil litigation, State civil litigation, Personal injury (including property damage). Office: Schroer Rice PA 115 SE 7th St Topeka KS 66603-3901 E-mail: gschroer@schroerrice.com.

SCHROPP, JAMES HOWARD, lawyer; b. Lebanon, Pa., June 20, 1943; Work e-mail: schroja@ffhsj.com. s. Howard J. and Maud E. (Parker) S.; m. Jo Ann Simpson, Sept. 4, 1965; children: James A., John C., Jeffrey M., Jeremy M. BA, U. Richmond, 1965; JD, Georgetown U., 1973. Bar: D.C. 1973, U.S. Supreme Ct. 1980. Asst. gen. counsel SEC, Washington, 1973-79; ptnr. Fried, Frank, Harris, Shriver & Jacobson, Washington, 1979—. Adj. prof. Georgetown U., Washington, 1982-86; mem. faculty Na.t Inst. for Trial Advocacy. Mem. ABA (discovery com. litigation sect. 1984-86, tender offer litigation subcom. corp. banking and bus. law sect. 1985-86, task force on broker-dealer compliance supervisory procedures 1987-89). Federal civil litigation, Corporate, general, Securities. Office: Fried Frank Harris Shriver & Jacobson 1001 Pennsylvania Ave NW Washington DC 20004-2505

SCHUDER, RAYMOND FRANCIS, lawyer; b. Wickford, R.I., Dec. 27, 1926; s. Rollie Milton and Selma (Ball) S.; m. Betty Jo Williams, Mar. 14, 1948; children: Gregg Williams, Glen Arva. AB, Emory U., 1949, JD, 1951. Bar: Ga. 1951. With Trust Co. Ga., Atlanta, 1951-54; assoc. firm Wheeler Robinson & Thurmond, Gainesville, Ga., 1954-59; pvt. practice law Gainesville, 1959-70, 76-96; ptnr. Schuder & Brown, Gainesville, 1971-76. Mcpl. ct. judge Gainesville, 1956-60, 73-75; magistrate ct. judge, 1985—, sr. magistrate, 2001—. Supr. Upper Chattahoochee Soil and Water Conservation Dist., 1971-74; CEO, bd. dirs. Charles Thompson Estes Found., Inc., Gainesville. Cpl. USMCR, 1944-50; 1st lt. USAR, 1950-56, ret. Mem. State Bar Ga. (gov. 1966-70), Gainesville-Northeastern Bar Assn. (pres. 1969-70), Am. Legion, VFW, Elks. Methodist. Home: 2224 Riverside Dr Gainesville GA 30501-1232 Office: 2224 Riverside Dr Gainesville GA 30501-1232 E-mail: xrfs@charter.net.

SCHUELLER, THOMAS GEORGE, lawyer; b. Budapest, Hungary, Oct. 4, 1936; came to U.S., 1938; s. Herbert H. and Edith (Geiringer) S.; m. Sandra Burke, Sept. 3, 1960 (div. Apr. 1982); children: Katherine, Matthew, John. AB cum laude, Amherst Coll., 1958; LLB, Harvard U., 1962. Bar: N.Y. 1963. Salesman Gen. Mills. Inc., Utica, N.Y., 1958-59; assoc. Hughes Hubbard & Reed, N.Y.C., 1962-69, ptnr., 1969—. Bd. dirs., sec. Ballet Hispanico, N.Y.C., 1987-2001. Mem. ABA, Assn. of Bar of City of N.Y., Phi Beta Kappa. Private international, Mergers and acquisitions, Securities. Home: 335 W 70th St New York NY 10023-3525 Office: Hughes Hubbard & Reed LLP 1 Battery Park Plz New York NY 10004-1482 also: 108 Fairchild Rd Sharon CT 06069-2440 E-mail: schuelle@hugheshubbard.com.

SCHUESSLER, CINDY SANDLIN, lawyer, judge; b. Florence, Ala., Feb. 19, 1951; d. James Harold Sr. and Sarah Nell Sandlin; m. John M. Schuessler, Mar. 14, 1971; 1 child, Christopher Warren. BA, U. North Ala., 1975; JD, Cumberland Sch. Law, 1978. Bar: Ala. 1978, U.S. Dist. Ct. (no. dist.) Ala. 1978. Assoc. Engel, Hairston, Birmingham, Ala., 1978-79, Peck & Slusher, Florence, 1980—; ptnr. Schuessler & Sandlin, Florence, 1983—. Instr. Faulkner U., Florence, 1985-88; mcpl. prosecutor, Town of Killen, Ala., 1983-94, city atty., 1989—; mcpl. judge Town of Rogersville, Ala., 1988—. Pres. Harlan Sch. PTA, Florence, 1988-90; chmn. bd. trustees Highland Bapt. Ch., Florence, 1989—; mem. grant com. United Way, florence, 1989-91. Mem. Ala. State Bar Assn., Ala. Mcpl. Judges Assn. (pres. 1992-93), Lauderdale County Bar Assn., Ala. Mcpl. Attys. Assn., Phi Kappa Phi, Phi Alpha Delta. Avocations: travel, swimming, reading. Family and matrimonial, General practice, Probate (including wills, trusts). Office: Schuessler & Sandlin 225 W Alabama St Florence AL 35630-5515

SCHUETTE, CHARLES A. lawyer; b. Columbus, Ind., Feb. 24, 1942; BBA, U. Okla., 1964, JD, 1967. Bar: Okla. 1967, Fla. 1970, U.S. Supreme Ct. 1979, U.S. Dist. Ct. (so. dist.) Fla. 1982, U.S. Dist. Ct. (mid. dist.) Fla. 1982. With Akerman & Senterfitt. Fellow Am. Bar Found.; mem. ABA, Fla. Bar, Okla. Bar Assn., Dade County Bar Assn. Commercial, contracts (including sales of goods; commercial financing), Public international, Property, real (including real estate development, water). Office: Akerman & Senterfitt 1 SE 3rd Ave Fl Miami FL 33131-1700

SCHUK, LINDA LEE, legal assistant, business educator; b. Scott Field, Ill., July 19, 1946; d. Frank A. Schuk and Jessie (Bumpass) Stearns; divorced; 1 child, Earl Wade. BBA, U. Tex., El Paso, 1968. Lic. life and health ins. agt., Tex. Acct., traffic mgr. Farah Mfg. Co., El Paso, 1970-71; adminstrv. asst. Horizon Corp., El Paso, 1971-76; adminstrv. asst. in charge office ops. Foster-Scwartz Devel. Corp., El Paso, 1976-78; legal sec. Howell and Fields, El Paso, 1978-80; supr. Southland Corp., San Antonio, Waco, El Paso, 1980-83, sales mgr. San Antonio, 1983-84, dist. mgr., 1984-87; dist. supr. E-Z Mart Convenience Stores, San Antonio, 1987-89; legal asst. Brock & Brock, San Antonio, 1989—. Instr. San Antonio C.C., 1989—. Mem. NAFE. Democrat. Baptist. Avocation: music. Home: 11903 Parliament St Apt 324 San Antonio TX 78216-2451 Office: Brock & Brock 803 E Mistletoe Ave San Antonio TX 78212-3524 E-mail: ischuk@yahoo.com.

SCHULER, ALISON KAY, lawyer; b. West Point, N.Y., Oct. 1, 1948; d. Richard Hamilton and Irma (Sanken) S.; m. Lyman Gage Sandy, Mar. 30, 1974; 1 child, Theodore. AB cum laude, Radcliffe Coll., 1969; JD, Harvard U., 1972. Bar: Va. 1973, D.C. 1974, N.Mex. 1975. Assoc. Hunton & Williams, Richmond, Va., 1972-75; asst. U.S. atty. U.S. Atty.'s Office, Albuquerque, 1975-78; adj. prof. law U. N.Mex., 1983-85, 90, 98—; ptnr. Sutin, Thayer & Browne, Albuquerque, 1978-85, Montgomery & Andrews, P.A., Albuquerque, 1985-88; sole practice Albuquerque, 1988—. Bd. dirs. Am. Diabetes Assn., Albuquerque, 1980—85, chmn. bd. dirs., 1984—85; bd. dirs. June Music Festival, 1980—95, pres., 1983—85, 1993—94; bd. dirs. Albuquerque Conservation Trust, 1986—90, N.Mex. Osteo. Found., 1993—96; chairperson Albuquerque Com. Fgn. Rels., 1984—85; mem. N.Mex. Internat. Trade and Investment Coun., Inc., 1986—; chartered org. rep. troop 444 Boy Scouts Am., 1997—, mem. nominating com., mem.-at-large dist. com. Sandia dist., 1998—, dist. vice chmn., 1999—2002, v.p. Great S.W. coun., 2001—; mem. adv. bd. Care Net Pregnancy Ctr. Albuquerque, 2003—; adv. bd. Care Net Pregnancy Ctr. of Albuquerque, 2003—; mem. coun. St. Lukes Luth. Ch., 1976—80, 1982—84, 1991—96, v.p., 1978—80, 1982—84, pres., 1994—95. Recipient Award of Merit, Sandia Dist., 2000, Svc. award, Albuquerque Astron. Soc., 2002. Mem. Fed. Bar Assn. (coord.), ABA, Va. Bar Assn., N.Mex. Bar Assn. (chmn. corp., banking and bus. law 1982-83, bd. dirs. internat. and immigration law sect. 1987-95, chmn. 1993-94), Albuquerque Astron. Soc. (Svc. award 2002), Harvard U. Alumni Assn. (mem. fund campaign, regional dir. 1984-86, v.p. 1986-89, chmn. clubs com. 1985-88, chmn. communications com. 1988-91), Radcliffe Coll. Alumnae Assn. Bd. Mgmt. (regional dir. 1984-87, chmn. comms. com. 1988-91), Harvard-Radcliffe Club (pres. 1980-84). Corporate, general, Private international, Securities. Home: 632 Cougar Loop NE Albuquerque NM 87122-1808 Office: 4300 San Mateo Blvd NE Ste B380 Albuquerque NM 87110-8401 E-mail: akschuler@aol.com.

SCHULMAN, ROBERT S. lawyer; b. N.Y.C., July 9, 1941; s. Donald Benedict and Edythe (Smythe) S.; m. Susan Jan Von Helbig, Sept. 18, 1974; children: Elizabeth Jane, Jennifer Lynn. BA, Rutgers U., New Brunswick, 1963; JD cum laude, Rutgers U., Newark, 1966. Bar: N.J. 1967, Calif. 1976, U.S. Dist. Ct. N.J. 1967, U.S. Supreme Ct. 1970, U.S. Dist. Cts. (ctrl., no., so., ea., dists.) Calif. 1976, U.S. Ct. Appeals (9th cir.) Calif. 1976. With Pitney, Hardin & Kipp, Newark, N.J., 1966-74; dept. atty. gen. Office of N.J. Atty. Gen., Trenton, N.J., 1974-75; assoc. Cox, Castle & Nicholson, L.A., 1976-80; ptnr. Zobrist, Garner & Garrett, L.A., 1980-83, Stephens, Berg, Lasater & Schulman, L.A., 1984-91, Crosby, Heafey, Roach & May, L.A., 1991—. Atty. Bd. of Edn., Fairview, N.J., 1972, Bd. of Adjustment, Fairview, N.J., 1971-73. Contbr. articles to profl. jours. Dir. Deafwest Theatre, L.A., Calif., 1991-97. Mem. State Bar of Calif., Calif. Club. Republican. Congregationalist. General civil litigation, Insurance. Home: 905 Wiladonda Dr La Canada Flintridge CA 91011-3825 Office: Crosby Heafey Roach & May 355 S Grand Ave 29th Fl Los Angeles CA 90071

SCHULTE, BRUCE JOHN, lawyer; b. Burlington, Iowa, June 27, 1953; s. James Andrew and Julia Germaine S.; m. Mary E. Guest, July 1984 (div. Feb. 1995); children: James, John; m. Catherine Tobben, 2001. BA in Am. Studies, U. Notre Dame, 1975; JD, U. Iowa, 1978. Bar: Iowa 1978, U.S. Dist. Ct. (so. dist.) Iowa 1979, U.S. Ct. Appeals (8th cir.) 1982, Minn. 1988, U.S. Dist. Ct. Minn. 1988, Ill. 1989. Law clk. Justice K. David Harris Supreme Ct. Iowa, Des Moines, 1978-79; ptnr. Dailey, Ruther, Bauer, Schulte & Hahn, Burlington, Iowa, 1979-87; atty. Bennett, Ingvaldson & McInerny, Mpls., 1988; gen. counsel Blackwood Corp., St. Paul, 1988-89; publs. editor Nat. Inst. for Trial Advocacy-U. Notre Dame, Ind., 1989-91; asst. dean pub. affairs Chgo. (Ill.) Kent Coll. Law, 1991-94; dep. dir. assoc. rels. West Pub., Eagan, Minn., 1995-97; dir. mktg., v.p. acad. consulting Performance Comm. Group, Chgo., 1997-2001. Key person com. ATLA, 1984-88; mem. commn. on jud. dists. Supreme Ct. Iowa, 1987-88; publs. com. Nat. Law Firm Mktg. Assn., 1993-94. Author: Persuasive Expert Testimony, 1990, Laser Disc Technology in the Courtroom, 1990; editor: Cases and Materials on Evidence, 1991, Modern State and Federal Evidence, 1991, Problems and Cases for Legal Writing, 1991. Mem. state ctrl. com. Iowa Dem. party, 1984-88; devel. com. Frances Xavier Ward Sch., Chgo., 1993-95; mem. cmty. task force Chgo. (Ill.) Downtown Circulator Project, 1994-96; v.p. pub. affairs U. Notre Dame Alumni Class of 1975. Notre Dame scholar U. Notre Dame, Ind., 1971-72; recipient Spectra award Internat. Assn. Bus. Communicators, 1993, Silver Trumpet, Publicity Club Chgo., 1994. Mem. ABA (mem. tech. com. lawyers conf. jud. adminstrn. divsn. 1995-2000, vice chair task force on image of judiciary 2000-01), Ill. Bar Assn. (mem. standing com. legal edn. and admission to bar 1993-97), Chgo. Bar Assn. (mem. law office tech. com. 1995-97), Assn. Am. Law Schs., Chgo. Pub. Rels. Forum (treas. 1997), Notre Dame Club Chgo. (co-chair Hesburgh Forum com. 1993-98, trustee 1995-98, sec. 1997-98), Nat. Soc. Fundraising Profls. (cert. fundraising profl., Midwest conf. steering com. 1997-99), Execs. Club of Chgo. (co-chair standing com. on edn. and pub. svc.). Avocations: sailing, choir, gardening, skiing. State civil litigation. Home: 816 Main St Evanston IL 60202-1706 E-mail: brucejschulte@aol.com.

SCHULTE, JEFFREY LEWIS, lawyer; b. N.Y.C., July 24, 1949; s. Irving and Ruth (Stein) S.; m. Elizabeth Ewan Kaiser, Aug. 13, 1977; children: Andrew Riggs, Ian Garretson, Elizabeth Alexandra. BA, Williams Coll., 1971; postgrad., Harvard U., 1971-72; JD, Yale U., 1976. Bar: Pa. 1978, Ga. 1993. Law clk. to hon. John J. Gibbons U.S. Ct. Appeals (3d cir.), Newark, 1976-77; assoc. Schnader, Harrison, Segal & Lewis, Phila., 1977-84, ptnr., 1985-92, founding ptnr. Atlanta, 1992-98, exec. com., 1994-98; ptnr. Morris, Manning & Martin, Atlanta, 1998—. Nat. steering com. lawyers com. to end "Pay-to-Play."; bd. adv. Cole Sch. Bus. Kennesaw State U. Contbr. articles to profl. jours. Trustee Ga. Shakespeare Festival, 1997-99; bd. dirs. North Ardmore (Pa.) Civic Assn., pres., 1990; bd. dirs. Main Line YMCA, chmn., 1989-91; bd. advisors Terry Coll. Bus., Kennesaw State U. Mem.: ABA, Bus. and Tech. Alliance, Atlanta Venture Forum, Atlanta Bar Assn. (chmn. comm. and media rels. com.), Phila. Bar Assn., State Bar Ga., Pa. Bar Assn., Weekapaug Tennis Club, Yale Club of Ga. (bd. dirs. 1996—2002, pres. 2000—01, chmn. of bd. 2001—02), Weekapaug Yacht Club R.I., Williams Club N.Y.C., Williams Club Atlanta, Merion Cricket Club, Phi Beta Kappa. Finance, Mergers and acquisitions, Securities. Office: Morris Manning & Martin Atlanta Financial Center 3343 Peachtree Rd NE Ste 1600 Atlanta GA 30326-1044 E-mail: jls@mmmlaw.com.

SCHULTE, JOSEF L. lawyer; b. Scheda, Nordrhein-Westfalen, Germany, Dec. 31, 1953; 1st exam, U. Munster, 1983; 2d exam, Ct. Appeal Hamm, 1983; LLD (hon.) , U. Munster, 1983. Cert. Chartered acct., Min. Econ. Affairs, 1992; bar: Ct. Appeals Frankfurt 1983. Legal expert German Monopolies Commn., Cologne, Germany, 1986—91; mng. ptnr. Feddersen Laule Scherzberg Ohle Hansen Ewerwahn, Frankfurt/Main, Germany, 1991—2000, Schulte Lawyers, Frankfurt/Main, 2000—. Antitrust. Office: Schulte Lawyers Hochstrasse 49 60313 Frankfurt/Main Hessen Germany

SCHULTZ, DENNIS BERNARD, lawyer; b. Detroit, Oct. 15, 1946; s. Bernard George and Madeline Laverne (Riffenberg) Schultz; m. Andi Lynn Leslie, Apr. 18, 1967; 1 child, Karanne Anne. BS, Wayne State U., 1970; JD, Mich. State U., 1977. Bar: Mich. 1977, U.S. dist. Ct. (ea. and we. dists.) Mich., U.S. Ct. Appeals (6th cir.), U.S. Dist. Ct. (we. dist.) Pa. V.p. Barkay Bldg. Co., Ferndale, Mich., to 1976; law clk. Hon. George N. Bashara, Mich. Ct. Appeals, Detroit, 1977; shareholder Butzel Long, Detroit, 1978—. Editor: Detroit Coll. Law Rev., 1977. Scholar Detroit Coll. Law Alumni Assn., 1976, Mich. Consol. Gas Co., 1977. Mem.: Mich. Bar Assn., Detroit Bar Assn. Republican. Roman Catholic. Avocations: boating, bicycling, golf. General civil litigation, Commercial, contracts (including sales of goods; commercial financing), Construction.

SCHULTZ, LOUIS WILLIAM, retired judge; b. Deep River, Iowa, Mar. 24, 1927; s. M. Louis and Esther Louise (Behrens) S.; m. D. Jean Stephen, Nov. 6, 1949; children: Marcia, Mark, Paul. Student, Central Coll., Pella, Iowa, 1944-45, 46-47; LLB, Drake U., Des Moines, 1949. Bar: Iowa. Claims supr. Iowa Farm Mut. Ins. Co., Des Moines, 1949-55; partner firm Harned, Schultz & McMeen, Marengo, Iowa, 1955-71; judge Iowa Dist. Ct. (6th dist.), 1971-80; justice Iowa Supreme Ct., 1980-93; county atty. Iowa County, 1960-68; ret., 1993. Served with USNR, 1945-46. Mem. Am. Bar Assn., Iowa Bar Assn. (bd. govs.), Iowa Judges Assn. (pres.)

SCHULTZ, RICHARD ALLEN, lawyer, farmer; b. Emporia, Kans., Jan. 3, 1939; s. Ebur Samuel and Opal Mae (Porter) S.; m. Esther Marie Strafuss, May 8, 1971; children: William Allen, Bryan Lee. BS in Indsl. Mgmt., U. Kans., 1961; JD, Washburn U. Topeka, 1970. Bar: Kans. 1971. Sole practice law, Topeka, 1970—. Dep. dir. Kans. Govs. Com. Criminal Adminstrn., 1971-73; asst. jud. adminstr. Kans. Supreme Ct., 1973-76; ct. adminstr. 3d Jud. Dist., Kans., 1976-83; dep. sec. Dept. Corrections State of Kans., Topeka, 1983-88. Exec. bd. Topeka YMCA; dist. officer Jayhawk Area Boy Scouts Am., Nat. Eagle Scout Assn.; dir. Kans. Vets. Found., Inc. Lt. USN, 1961-67. Decorated commendation award USN. Mem. ABA, Topeka Bar Assn. (Liberty Bell award 1983), Kans. Bar Assn., Am. Legion, Vietnam Vets Am., Phi Alpha Delta, Alpha Tau Omega. Democrat. Methodist. Criminal, General practice. Office: 3109 SW Stone Ave Topeka KS 66614-2821

SCHULTZE, PASCAL, lawyer; b. Strasbourg, France, Jan. 24, 1966; s. Heinz and Marguerite Schultze; m. Sybile Girard, Sept. 2, 2000. Lic. AES, U. Strasbourg, 1987, Maitrise de Droit des Affaires, 1988; DESS de Droit Fiscal, U. Dijon, France, 1989. Tax cons. Arthur Andersen, Luxembourg, 1989-91; tax lawyer Price Waterhouse, Paris, 1991-95; tax specialist Hewlett Packard, Böblingen, Germany, 1995-98; jr. ptnr. Haarmann Hemmelrath, Paris, 1998—. Property, real (including real estate development, water), Corporate taxation, Mergers and acquisitions. Office: Haarmann Hemmelrath 23 Rue Balzac F 75406 Paris Cedex 8 France Fax: 01.53.53.02.81. E-mail: pascal_schultze@hhp.de.

SCHULZ, BRADLEY NICHOLAS, lawyer; b. Staten Island, N.Y., July 1, 1959; s. George Robert Jr. and Mary Jane (Fazakerley) S. BA, Wake Forest U., 1981; JD, N.Y. Law Sch., 1984. Bar: N.Y. 1985, N.C. 1985, N.J. 1985, U.S. Dist. Ct. (ea. dist.) N.C. 1985, U.S. Dist. Ct. (so. dist.) N.Y. 1985. Assoc. Mast, Tew, Armstrong & Morris, P.A., Smithfield, N.C., 1984-85; ptnr. Mast, Schulz Mast Mills & Stem, P.A., Smithfield, 1986—97, mng. ptnr., 1998—2001; ptnr. Mast Schulz Mast Mills Stem & Johnson, Smithfield, 1998—. Chmn. Young Republicans, Johnston County, Smithfield, 1988. Hankins scholar Wake Forest U., 1977-81, N.Y. Law Sch. scholar, 1981-84. Mem. ABA, N.C. Bar Assn., N.Y. Bar Assn., N.J. Bar Assn., N.C. Acad. Trial Lawyers, Johnston County Bar Assn., Theta Chi Fraternity. Republican. Episcopalian. Avocations: yachting, hunting, skiing. General civil litigation, Insurance, Personal injury (including property damage). Home: 946 Debro Rd Kenly NC 27542-9725 Office: Mast Schulz Mast Mills Stem & Johnson PO Box 119 Smithfield NC 27577-0119 E-mail: Brad@mastschulz.com.

SCHULZ, GEORGE E., JR., lawyer; b. Lakehurst, N.J., Oct. 9, 1945; s. George E. and Helen W. Schulz; m. Mary Lou Wiley, Sept. 1, 1973; 1 child, Kathryn Helen. BA, Vanderbilt U., 1968; JD, U. Fla., 1973. Bar: Fla., U.S. Dist. Ct. (no., mid. and so. dists.) Fla., U.S. Ct. Appeals (5th and 11th cirs.), U.S. Supreme Ct. Atty. Frates, Floyd, Deason, Miami, 1973—76, Beckham, McAliley & Schulz, Jacksonville, Fla., 1976—88, Holland & Knight, Jacksonville, 1989—, past chmn. litig. dept. Gen. counsel PACE Ctr. Girls, Jacksonville; mem. City of Jacksonville Juvenile Justice Comprehensive Strategy Bd.; bd. dirs. Jacksonville Area Legal Aid; vice chmn. Gator Bowl Assn.; trustee U. Fla. Coll. Law; mem. City of Jacksonville Ethics Commn. Lt. USN, 1968—72, Vietnam. Fellow: Am. Coll. Trial Lawyers, Am. Bar Found.; mem.: ABA, Chester Bedell Am. Inn Ct., Fla. Bar. Assn. (Pro Bono Svc. award), Am. Bd. Trial Advocacy. Democrat. Episcopalian. General civil litigation, Product liability. Home: 7738 Hollyrdge Cir Jacksonville FL 32256 Office: Holland and Knight 50 N Laura St Jacksonville FL 32202 Office Fax: 904-358-1872. Business E-Mail: bschulz@hklaw.com.

SCHULZ, KEITH DONALD, corporate lawyer, writer; b. Burlington, Iowa, Dec. 20, 1938; s. Henry Carl and Laura Iral (Bowlin) S.; m. Emily Brook Roane, Apr. 19, 1985; children: Keith Jr., Sarah, Christine, Stefan. BA, U. Iowa, 1960, JD, 1963. Bar: Iowa 1963, Ill. 1966, Wis. 1990. Dep. Sec. of State, State of Iowa, Des Moines, 1965-66; atty. AT&T, Chgo., 1966-67; sec., gen. counsel Borg-Warner Acceptance Corp., Chgo., 1967-74; asst. gen. counsel Borg-Warner Corp., Chgo., 1974-84, v.p., gen. counsel, 1984-88; of counsel Bell, Boyd & Lloyd, Chgo., 1988—. Chmn., CEO Downtown Ptnrs., Inc., 1995-96. Author: (novel) Keepers of the River, 2001; contbr. articles to Harvard Bus. Rev., Jour. for Corp. Growth. Chmn. bd. dirs. Vol. Legal Svcs. Found., Chgo., 1984-91; bd. dirs. Southeast Iowa Symphony Orch., pres., 1998-2000, 03—, Heritage Trust Found. Mem. Iowa Bar Assn., Chgo. Bar Assn. (chmn. corp. law depts. com. 1983-84), Wis. Bar Assn., Assn. of Gen. Counsel, Am. Soc. Corp. Secs., Law Club of Chgo. Clubs: University, Economic (Chgo.). Avocations: tennis, bicycling, skiing. Corporate, general, Finance, Mergers and acquisitions. Office: Bell Boyd & Lloyd 70 W Madison St Ste 3300 Chicago IL 60602-4284 E-mail: KDons@aol.com.

SCHULZE, ERIC WILLIAM, lawyer, legal publications editor, publisher; b. Libertyville, Ill., July 8, 1952; s. Robert Carl and Barbara (Mayo) S. BA, U. Tex., 1973, JD, 1977. Bar: Tex. 1977, U.S. Dist. Ct. (we. dist.) Tex. 1987, U.S. Ct. Appeals (5th cir.) 1987, U.S. Dist. Ct. (ea. and so. dists.) Tex. 1988, U.S. Dist. Ct. (no. dist.) Tex. 1989, U.S. Supreme Ct. 1989; bd. cert. civil appellate law Tex. Bd. Legal Specialization, 1990—. Rsch. asst. U. Tex., Austin, 1978; legis. aide Tex. Ho. of Reps., Austin, 1979-81; editor Tex. Sch. Law News, Austin, 1982-85; assoc. Hairston, Walsh & Anderson, Austin, 1986-87; ptnr. Walsh, Anderson, Brown, Schulze & Aldridge, Austin, 1988—, mng. ptnr., 1993—; editor Tex. Sch. Adminstrs. Legal Digest, Austin, 1986-92, co-pub., 1991—, mng. editor, 1992—. Editor: (legal reference books) Texas Education Code Annotated, 1982-85; editl. adv. com. West's Edn. Law Reporter, 1996—. Del. Tex. State Democratic Conv., 1982, Travis County Dem. Conv., 1982, 84, 86. Recipient Merit award for pubs. Internat. Assn. Bus. Communicators-Austin br., 1983, Merit award for authorship Coll. of State Bar Tex., 1992. Mem. Fed. Bar Assn., Am. Bar Assn., Tex. Bar Assn., Travis County Bar Assn., Bar Assn. of 5th Cir., Defense Rsch. Inst., Nat. Council Sch. Attys., Tex. Council Sch. Attys., Edn. Law Assn., Toastmasters (pres. Capital City chpt. 1995). Appellate, Civil rights, Education and schools. Home: 3416 Mount Bonnell Cir Austin TX 78731-5745 Office: Walsh Anderson Brown Schulze & Aldridge PO Box 2156 Austin TX 78768-2156

SCHUMACHER, HARRY RICHARD, lawyer; b. June 21, 1930; s. Henry Richard and Martha (Hagenbucher) S.; m. Katherine E. Ware, June 8, 1991; children: Richard, Garry. BA, Yale U., 1951; JD magna cum laude, Harvard U., 1958. Bar: N.Y. 1959, U.S. Supreme Ct. 1964. Assoc. firm Cahill Gordon & Reindel and predecessor firms, N.Y.C., 1958—67, ptnr., 1968—97. Chmn. Legal Svcs. for N.Y.C., Inc., 1994—2003; dir. New York Legis. Svcs., 2000—. Mem. Manhattan Borough Pres.'s Cmty. Planning Bd. 6, 1962—66; Dem. candidate N.Y. State Assembly, 1962, 1963; warden Episcopalian Ch.; bd. dirs. Incarnation Camp, Ivoryton, Conn., 1961—72. Lt. (j.g.) USNR, 1951—54. Mem.: ABA, Am. Judicature Soc., N.Y. County Lawyers Assn. (bd. dirs. 1987—93, 1996—99), Fed. Comms. Bar Assn., Assn. Bar City of N.Y., N.Y. State Bar Assn. (mem. ho. dels. 1990—94, 2001—), Yale (N.Y.C.), Union. Administrative and regulatory, Federal civil litigation. Home: 47 E 88th St New York NY 10128-1152 Office: Cahill Gordon & Reindel 80 Pine St Fl 16 New York NY 10005-1790

SCHUMACHER, JON LEE, lawyer; b. Rochester, N.Y., Feb. 28, 1937; s. Howard Alexander and Ruth S.; m. Katherine Truesdell, Apr. 22, 1967; children: Sara Wolff, Howard Alexander II. AB, Princeton U., 1959; JD, U. Va., 1964. Bar: N.Y. 1964. With Nixon Peabody LLP and predecessor firms, Rochester, 1964—; mem. mgmt. com. Nixon, Hargrave, Devans & Doyle, Rochester, 1986-90, mng. ptnr., 1988-90. Co-author Charitable Giving and Solicitation. Bd. dirs., officer Rochester Area Found., Inc., 1987-94, United Way, 1986—; pres. estate planning Coun. Rochester, 1986-87. Fellow Am. Coll. Trusts and Estate Counsel; mem. N.Y. State Bar Assn. (exec. com. trusts and estates law sect. 1985-88, 94—, chmn. 1997, chmn. estate planning com. 1992-94), Monroe County Bar Assn. (found. pres. 1995-97), Country Club of Rochester, Genesee Valley Club. Republican. Presbyterian. Avocations: walking, opera. Estate planning, Probate (including wills, trusts), Estate taxation. Home: 550 Allens Creek Rd Rochester NY 14618-3406 Office: Nixon Peabody LLP Clinton Sq PO Box 31051 Rochester NY 14603-1051 E-mail: jschumacher@nixonpeabody.com.

SCHUMACHER, PAUL MAYNARD, lawyer; b. Columbus, Nebr., Apr. 4, 1951; s. Maynard Mathew and Rita Bell (Jarosz) S.; m. Michele Suzanne Gassé, June 26, 1976; children: Nicole Suzanne, Kristen Paulette. AA, Platte Coll., 1971; BS, Fort Hays U., 1973; JD, Georgetown U., 1976. Bar: Fla. 1976, Nebr. 1977, U.S. Dist. Ct. Nebr. 1977. Mem. staff U.S. Senate, Washington, 1974-76; sole practice Miami, Fla. and Columbus, 1976—; v.p. Community Lottery Systems, Inc., Columbus, 1990-92, pres., 1992—. V.p. Megavision Corp., Columbus, 1976—. Treas. prin. Rep. campaign com. U.S. Senate Candidate, Lincoln, Nebr., 1978-79; atty. Platte County, Columbus, 1979-87; chmn. Platte county Reps., 1988-94; mem. Nebr. Rep. State Ctrl. Com., 1994-96, 2000—; CEO Lotto Nebr., 1992—; CEO Cmty. Internet Sys., Inc., 1995-98, bd. dirs., 1995—. Mem. Nebr. Bar Assn., Fla. Bar Assn., Platte County Bar Assn. (pres. 1992-93), N.Am. Gaming Regulators Assn. (internat. gaming com.), Nat. Republican small bus. adv. council, Rotary, Elks. Roman Catholic. Avocation: physics. Home: 6255 Meyer Rd Columbus NE 68601-8044 Office: PO Box 122 Columbus NE 68602-0122 E-mail: pschumac@megavision.com.

SCHUPP, ANASTASIA LUKA, retired lawyer; b. Chgo. d. Joseph Anthony and Anastasia Maria (Romel) Luka; m. William Schupp, Apr. 20, 1968 (div. June 1994); 1 child, William Joseph. BS in Social Sci., Loyola U., 1966, JD, 1977; MA, U. Mich., 1968; Jagellonian, U. Sum., Poland, 1993. Bar: Ill. 1982, U.S. Supreme Ct. 1994. Law libr. Seyfarth, Shaw, Fairweather & Geraldson, Chgo., 1979-82; ptnr. Flader & Haces, Chgo., 1982-85; pvt. practice Chgo., 1986—2001; assoc. Hyatt Legal Svcs., Chgo., 1985—86, ret., 2001. Lectr. Chgo. Bd. Realtors, 1988—89, Robert Morris Coll., Orland Park, Ill., 1992, East West U. Chgo., 1992, Montay Coll., Chgo., 1994—95, acad. coun., 1994—95; adminstrv. asst. William Joseph Schupp, 2003. Editor: An Ethnic Christmas, 1982; (newsletter) The Overture, 1980-81; contbr. articles to profl. jours. Vol. Chgo. Vol. Legal Svcs., 1991—95; arbitrator Chgo. Archdiocese, 1994—2000; atty. coord. Com. to Elect Richard J. Owens for Judge, Chgo., 1993—94. Recipient Hon. Mention, Polish Arts Club, 1996. Mem.: Advs. Soc. (historian 1985—87), Chgo. Bar Assn., Womens Bar Assn. Ill. (chair com. 1982—95), First Cath. Slovak Ladies Assn., Chgo. Artists Coalition, Polish Arts Club of Chgo. (bd. dirs. 1999—2002). Democrat. Roman Catholic. Avocations: writing, exhibiting artist. Family and matrimonial, Probate (including wills, trusts), Property, real (including real estate development, water). Home: 5425 S Richmond St Chicago IL 60632

SCHUPP, ROBERT WARREN, law educator; b. Miami Beach, Fla., Jan. 21, 1947; s. Frederick Anthony Schupp and Mary June (Barefoot) Schupp Goodall. B.S. in Mgmt., U. Fla., 1969, J.D., 1973. Bar: Fla. 1973, U.S. Dist. Ct. (mid. dist.) Fla. 1974. Instr. Fla. Jr. Coll., Jacksonville, 1972-73; assoc. prof. U. N. Fla., Jacksonville, 1973—; cons. Sears, Roebuck & Co., Inc., 1974. Contbr. articles to legal jours. Participant Leadership Jacksonville, 1979. Recipient Fla. Disting. Service medal Fla. N.G., 1981. Mem. Fla. Bar Assn., Beta Gamma Sigma, Delta Sigma Pi. Republican. Office: U N Fla 4567 Saint Johns Bluff Rd S Jacksonville FL 32224-2646

SCHURR, FRANCESCO ARMANDO, lawyer, educator; s. Adolf Anselm and Annamaria (Lorusso) Schurr. JD , Law Sch., Regensburg, 1995; PhD , Law Sch., Innsbruck, 1997. Attorney at Law/Rechtsanwalt: Bavarian Ministry of Justice 1998. Clerk Higher Dist. Ct., Munich, 1996—98; lawyer Czernich Hofstädter Guggenberger, Innsbruck, Austria, 1999—. Lectr. law sch. U. Innsbruck, Austria, 1998—. Author: (books) Commercial Law in Germany, Austria and Italy. Master: Euregio Consult European Econ. Interest Group (life). Commercial, consumer (including collections, credit), Franchising, Non-profit and tax-exempt organizations, Probate (including wills, trusts). Office: Czernich Hofstädter Guggenberger 4 Bozner Platz Tyrol Innsbruck 6020 Austria Office Fax: +43-512-56737315. E-mail: francesco.schurr@web.de.

SCHUSSLER, THEODORE, lawyer, physician, educator, consultant; b. July 27, 1934; s. Jack and Fannie (Blank) Schussler; m. Barbara Ann Gordon, June 18, 1961; children: Deborah, Jonathan, Rebecca. BA in Polit. Sci., Bklyn. Coll., 1955; LLB, Bklyn. Law Sch., 1958, JD, 1967; MD, U. Lausanne, Switzerland, 1974. Bar: N.Y. 1959, U.S. Dist. Ct. (so. and ea. dists.) N.Y. 1975, U.S. Tax Ct. 1961, U.S. Ct. Appeals (2nd cir.) 1962, U.S. Supreme Ct. 1975. Clerkship and practice, N.Y.C., 1956, 1958—59; legal editor tax divsn. Prentice-Hall, Inc., Englewood Cliffs, NJ, 1956; vol. criminal law divsn. Legal Aid Soc., N.Y.C., 1959; atty. legal dept. N.Y.C. Dept. Welfare, 1959—60; sole practice N.Y.C., 1960—. Sr. staff asst. IBM-Indsl. Medicine Program, 1969—70, 1974—76; intern in medicine St. Vincent's Med. Ctr. of Richmond, S.I., NY, 1976—77, resident emergency medicine, 1977—79; resident in gerontology, chief house physician Carmel Richmond Nursing Home, S.I., 1978—80; surg. rotation emergency dept. Met. Hosp. Ctr., 1979; house physician dept. medicine Richmond Meml. Hosp. and Health Ctr., 1979—80; gen. practice medicine, 1980—; attending physician, former chief dept. family practice, former chmn. med. care evaluation, med. records and by-laws coms., former physician Cmty. Hosp. Bklyn., 1980—94, advisor emergency dept., former mem. blood transfusion, credential's, emergency dept. coms., 1980—94, mem. med. staff, 1980—94; attending physician Meth. Hosp., Bklyn., 1984—92, supervising emergency dept. physician, dept. ambulatory care, 1980—83; attending physician Kings Hwy. Hosp., 1981—88, coord. emergency dept., 1981; clin. instr. dept. preventive medicine and cmty. health Downstate Med. Ctr. SUNY, Bklyn., 1981—88, clin. asst. prof., 1988—95, SUNY Health Sci. Ctr.; med. dir. divsn. devel. disabilities Mishkon-Jewish Bd. Family & Children's Svc., Bklyn., 1982—2000; primary care physician Jewish Home and Hosp. for Aged, N.Y.C., 1993—94; cons. in gerontology Palm Beach Home for Adults, Bklyn., 1980—92; cons. indsl. medicine IBM, 1990—92; tchr., instr., lectr., prof., 1954—95; med.-legal cons. to professions of medicine and law. Author: Torts, 1961, 1965, 1974, Jurisdiction and Practice in Federal Courts, 1967, Constitutional Law, 1973; contbr. articles to profl. jours. Recipient Pub. and Cmty. Svc. award, United Ind. Dems. 44th Assembly Dist., Bklyn. Fellow: Am. Coll. Legal Medicine; mem.: United Univ. Professions, Assn. Arbitrators of Civil Ct. of N.Y. (small claims divsn., arbitrator), Bklyn. Law Sch. Alumni Assn. (past bd. dirs.), Delta Sigma Rho. General practice, Health, Personal injury (including property damage). Home and Office: 760 E 10th St Apt 6H Brooklyn NY 11230-2352

SCHUSTER, E. ELAINE, lawyer; b. Oklahoma City, June 8, 1936; d. John Otto and Eula Delone (Campbell) Schuster. AB, Sweet Briar Coll., 1958; MA in Econs. and Fin., U. Okla., 1962, JD, 1968. Bar: Okla. 1968, U.S. Dist. Ct. (we. dist.) Okla. 1969, U.S. Dist. Ct. (no. dist.) Okla. 1981, U.S. Dist. Ct. (ea. dist.) Okla. 1991, U.S. Ct. Appeals (10th cir.) 1969. Prof. econs. Southeastern State U., Durant, Okla., 1961-65; assoc. Whitten & Whitten, Oklahoma City, 1968-71; asst. dist. atty. Oklahoma County, 7th Dist., 1972-78; ptnr. Jones, Schuster & Flaugher, Oklahoma City, 1978-82; prin. E. Elaine Schuster, P.C., Oklahoma City, 1982—. Lectr. in field. Mem. Oklahoma County Bd. Adjustment, 1978-97, chmn., 1984-97; citizen mem. profl. liaison com. City of Oklahoma City, 1980—; mem. bd. edn. Metro Area Career Tech. Sch. Dist., 1982—, Oklahoma City, pres., 1984-85, 91-93, 98-2000; mem. ch. bd. University Pl. Christian Ch., 1982-86, 89-92, elder, 1989-92, trustee, 1992; deacon, bd. dirs. Crown Heights Christian Ch., 2001—; bd. overseers Sweet Briar Coll., 1986-90; founding bd. dirs. Nat. Kidney Found. Okla., 1969-82. Named Outstanding Bus. Woman of Okla., Town Club of Bus. and Profl. women, 1986, Hon. All State Sch. Bd., Okla. State Sch. Bds. Assn., 1999, One of Fifty Women Making a Difference, Okla. Jour. Record, 1997, 2001; grantee GE, U. Va., 1963. Mem. Okla. Bar Assn. (del. 1996-97, 2000-01, alt. del. 1998-99, 2002-03, mem. budget com. 2002-03), Oklahoma County Bar Assn. (bench and bar com. 1994-95, long range planning com. 1995-97, CLE com. 1999-2003, bd. dirs. 1997-2000), AAUW (br. pres. 1978-80, Okla. divsn. bd. 1969-75, 81-83, 85-87, Polished Diamond award S.W. Ctrl. Region 1987), Sweet Briar Coll. Alumnae Assn. (bd. dirs. 1986-90, 96-2001, region IX dir. 1996-2001), Okla. Assn. of Career Tech Education, Okla. Assn. of Technical Centers (fiscal officer 2001-2003, pres. elect 2002-2003, pres. 2003—), Okla. County Historical Soc., Okla. Career Tech Adminstrv. Coun. Kappa Beta Pi, Delta Kappa Gamma (hon.). Avocations: hiking, photography, travel, history of Oklahoma and Oklahoma City. General civil litigation, Probate (including wills, trusts), Property, real (including real estate development, water). Office: Heritage Law Ctr 515 NW 13th St Oklahoma City OK 73103-2203 E-mail: eschuster@icnet.net.

SCHUSTER, PHILIP FREDERICK , II, lawyer, writer, law educator; b. Denver, Aug. 26, 1945; s. Philip Frederick and Ruth Elizabeth (Robar) S.; m. Barbara Lynn Nordquist, June 7, 1975; children: Philip Christian, Matthew Dale. BA, U. Wash., 1967; JD, Willamette U., 1972. Bar: Oreg. 1972, Wash. 2002, U.S. Dist. Ct. Oreg. 1974, U.S. Ct. Appeals (9th cir.) 1986, U.S. Ct. Appeals (D.C. cir.) 2001, U.S. Supreme Ct. 1986. Dep. dist. atty. Multnomah County, Portland, Oreg., 1972; title examiner Pioneer Nat. Title Co., Portland, 1973-74; assoc. Buss, Leichner et al, Portland, 1975-76; from assoc. to ptnr. Kitson & Bond, Portland, 1976-77; pvt. practice Portland, 1977-95; ptnr. Dierking and Schuster, Portland, 1996—; adj. prof. law Lewis & Clark Coll., 2002. Arbitrator Multnomah County Arbitration Program, 1985—; student mentor Portland Pub. Schs., 1988—. Author: The Indian Water Slide, 1999; contbg. author OSB CLE Publ., Family Law; contbr. articles to profl. jours. Organizer Legal Aid Svcs. for Community Clinics, Salem, Oreg. and Seattle, 1969-73; Dem. committeeman, Seattle, 1965-70; judge Oreg. State Bar and Classroom Law Project, H.S. Mock Trial Competition, 1988—. Mem. ABA, ATLA, NAACP (exec. bd. Portland, Oreg. chpt. 1979-98), ACLU, Multnomah Bar Assn. (Vol. Lawyers Project), Internat. Platform Assn., Alpha Phi Alpha. Avocations: river drifting, camping, swimming, walking, writing. Personal injury (including property damage), Appellate, Probate (including wills, trusts). Office: 3565 NE Broadway St Portland OR 97232-1820 E-mail: schuster@pcez.com.

SCHUSTER, ROBERT PARKS, lawyer; b. St. Louis, Oct. 25, 1945; s. William Thomas Schuster and Carolyn Cornforth (Daugherty) Hathaway; 1 child, Susan Michele. AB, Yale U., 1967; JD with honors, U. Wyo., 1970; LLM, Harvard U., 1971. Bar: Wyo. 1971, U.S. Ct. Appeals (10th cir.) 1979, U.S. Supreme Ct. 1984, Utah 1990. Dep. county atty. County of Natrona, Casper, Wyo., 1971-73; pvt. practice Casper, 1973—76; assoc. Spence & Moriarity, Casper, 1976-78; ptnr. Spence, Moriarity & Schuster, Jackson, Wyo., 1978—2002; pvt. practice Jackson, Wyo., 2002—. Trustee U. Wyo., 1985-89; Wyo. Dem. nominee for U.S. Ho. of Reps., 1994; polit. columnist Casper Star Tribune, 1987-94; pres. United Way Natrona County, 1974; bd. dirs. Dancers Workshop, 1981-83; chair Wyo. selection com. Rhodes Scholarship, 1989-98; mem. bd. visitors Coll. Arts and Scis., U. Wyo., 1991-2000; mem. Dem. Nat. Com., 1992-2000; chair Wyo. Pub. Policy Forum, 1992-98; mem. Wind River Reservation Econ. Adv. Coun., 1998-99. Ford Found. Urban Law fellow, 1970-71. Mem. ABA, ATLA, Wyo. Trial Lawyers Assn. Federal civil litigation, State civil litigation. Home: PO Box 13160 Jackson WY 83002 Office: Robert P Schuster PC 250 Veronica Ln Ste 204 PO Box 13160 Jackson WY 83002

SCHUTT, WALTER EUGENE, lawyer; b. Cleve., July 27, 1917; s. Erle Minchin and Elizabeth (Eastman) S.; m. Dorothy Louise Gilbert, Apr. 18, 1942 (dec. Mar. 2000); children: Gretchen Sue, Stephen David, Elizabeth Ann, Robert Barclay; m. Virginia Varley, Nov. 2, 2001. AB, Miami U., Oxford, Ohio, 1939; JD, U. Cin., 1948. Bar: Ohio 1948, U.S. Dist. Ct. (so. dist.) Ohio 1953, U.S. Supreme Ct. 1962, U.S. Tax Ct. 1983, U.S. Ct. Appeals (6th cir.) 1986. Pvt. practice, Wilmington, Ohio, 1948—; city solicitor, 1950-53. Mem. Wilmington Bd. Edn., 1958-65; chmn. Clinton County chpt. ARC, 1951-53; Wilmington chmn. Cin. Symphony Orch. Area Artists Series, 1969-71; trustee Wilmington Coll., 1962-74, sec. 1966-74; trustee Quaker Hill Found., Richmond, Ind., 1970-75, Friends Fellowship Cmty. Inc., 1986-93; rep. U.S. preparations com. 6th Internat. Assembly World Coun. of Chs., 1982. 1st lt. USAAF, 1943-46. Decorated DFC; recipient Disting. Svc. award Wilmington Jr. C. of C., 1953. Mem. Am. Bar Assn. (arms control and disarmament com. 1977-80), Ohio State Bar Assn., Clinton County Bar Assn. (past pres.), World Peace Through Law Ctr. Mem. Soc. of Friends (presiding clk. Friends United Meeting 1978-81, rep. to bd. Nat. Coun. Chs. of Christ 1985-96, presiding clk. Friends com. on nat. legis. 1984-87), Rotary. General practice, Non-profit and tax-exempt organizations, Probate (including wills, trusts). Home: 3043 W State Route 73 Wilmington OH 45177-9287

SCHUURMAN, WILLEM GERHARD, lawyer; b. June 21, 1940; s. William B. and Rina (Du Preez) S.; m. Karla Arnold, Feb. 15, 2001; children: Greg W., Bruce J., Angus D., D. Geordie. BS, U. Cape Town, South Africa, 1962, LLB, 1964; JD magna cum laude, South Tex. Coll. Law, 1981. Bar: Tex. 1981, U.S. Dist. Ct. (so. dist.) Tex. 1982, U.S. Dist. Ct. (we. dist.) Tex. 1985. Ptnr. Adams & Adams, Pretoria, South Africa, 1967—79; assoc. Arnold, White & Durkee, Houston, 1979—83, ptnr., 1983—98, Vinson & Elkins LLP, Austin, Tex., 1999—. Mem.: ABA, Internat. Assn. for the Protection of Indsl. Property, Travis County Bar Assn., Internat. Fedn. Indsl. Property Attys. U.S., Am. Intellectual Property Law Assn., Westwood Country Club. Federal civil litigation, Patent. Office: Vinson & Elkins LLP Terrace 7 2801 Via Fortuna Ste 100 Austin TX 78746-7568 E-mail: bschuurman@velaw.com.

SCHWAB, EILEEN CAULFIELD, lawyer, educator; b. N.Y.C., Feb. 11, 1944; d. James and Mary (Fay) Caulfield; m. Terrance W. Schwab, Jan. 4, 1969; children: Matthew Caulfield, Catherine Grimley Welykoridko, Claire Gillespie. BA, Hunter Coll., 1965; JD, Columbia U., 1971; BA magna cum laude. Bar: N.Y. 1972, U.S. Dist. Ct. (so. and ea. dists.) N.Y. 1975, U.S. Ct. Appeals (2d cir.) 1975, U.S. Tax Ct. 1980, U.S. Ct. Appeals (10th cir.) 1993. Assoc. Poletti Friedin, N.Y.C., 1971-72, Hughes Hubbard & Reed, N.Y.C., 1972-75, Davis Polk & Wardwell, N.Y.C., 1975-81; dep. bur. chief Charities Bur., Atty. Gen. of N.Y., 1981-82; counsel Brown & Wood, N.Y.C., 1983—, ptnr., 1984. Adj. prof. N.Y. Law Sch. Trustee Cath. Communal Fund; chair planned gifts, bequests and endowment com. Archdiocese of N.Y.; mem. profl. adv. com. Mus. of Modern Art, Met. Mus. Art, Cen. Park Conservancy, Calvary Hosp., Mus. of Arts and Design, N.Y. Pub. Libr.Ascension Sch.; trustee Cooke Ctr. Learning and Devel. Fellow Am. Coll. Trust and Estate Counsel; mem. N.Y. State Bar Assn., Phi Beta Kappa. Democrat. Roman Catholic. E-mail: eschwab@sidley.com.

SCHWAB, HAROLD LEE, lawyer; b. N.Y.C., Feb. 5, 1932; s. Harold Walter and Beatrice (Braverman) S.; m. Rowena Vivian Strauss, June 12, 1953; children: Andrew, Lisa, James. BA, Harvard Coll., 1953; LLB, Boston Coll., 1956. Bar: N.Y. 1957, U.S. Ct. Mil. Appeals 1958, U.S. Dist. Cts. (so. and ea. dists.) N.Y. 1967, U.S. Dist. Ct. (no. dist.) N.Y. 1974, U.S.

Dist. Ct. (we. dist.) N.Y. 1988, U.S. Dist. Ct. Conn. 1995, U.S. Dist. Ct. (ea. and we. dists.) Ark. 2000, U.S. Ct. Appeals (2d cir.) 1971, U.S. Ct. Appeals (D.C. cir.) 1986, U.S. Ct. Appelas (11th cir.) 1988, U.S. Ct. Appeals (5th cir.) 1991, U.S. Supreme Ct. 1971. V.p. H.W. Schwab Textile Corp., N.Y.C., 1959-60; assoc. Emile Z. Berman & A. Harold Frost, N.Y.C., 1960-67, ptnr., 1967-74; sr. ptnr. Lester Schwab Katz & Dwyer, N.Y.C., 1974—. Lectr. N.Y. Jud. Seminars, N.Y. State Bar Assn., N.Y. County Lawyers Assn. Contbr. articles to legal jours.; mem. editl. bd. Jour. Products and Toxics Liability, 1976-96. Served to lt. col. USAFR. Fellow Internat. Acad. Trial Lawyers; mem. ABA, ASTM, SAE, Assn. Advancement of Automotive Medicine, Product Liability Adv. Coun., N.Y. State Bar Assn. (chmn. trial lawyers sect. 1980-81, editor sect. newsletter 1981-84), Am. Bd. Trial Advs. (pres. N.Y. chpt. 1982-83), Fedn. Ins. and Corp. Counsel (v.p. 1979-80), N.Y. State Trial Lawyers Assn., Def. Assn. N.Y., Harvard Club N.Y., Downtown Assn., Ft. Hamilton Officers Club. Federal civil litigation, State civil litigation, Product liability. Home: 205 Beach 142 St Neponsit NY 11694 Office: Lester Schwab Katz & Dwyer 120 Broadway Fl 38 New York NY 10271-0071

SCHWAB, HOWARD JOEL, judge; b. Charleston, W.Va., Feb. 13, 1943; s. Joseph Simon and Gertrude (Hadas) S.; m. Michelle Roberts, July 4, 1970; children: Joshua Raphael, Bethany Alexis. BA in History with honors, UCLA, 1964, JD, 1967. Bar: Calif. 1968, U.S. Dist. Ct. (cen. dist.) Calif. 1968, U.S. Ct. Appeals (9th cir.) 1970, U.S. Supreme Ct. 1972. Clk. legal adminstrn. Litton Industries, L.A., 1967-68; dep. city atty. L.A., 1968-69; dep. atty. gen. State of Calif., L.A., 1969-84; judge Mcpl. Ct. L.A. Jud. Dist., 1984-85; judge Superior Ct. Superior Ct. L.A. County, L.A., 1985—. Mem. faculty Berkeley (Calif.) Judicial Coll., 1987—. Contbr. articles to profl. jours. Recipient CDAA William E. James award Calif. Dist. Atty.'s Assn., 1981. Mem. San Fernando Valley Bar Assn. (Appreciation award as Judge of Yr. 2002_, Inn. of Ct., Phi Alpha Delta. Democrat. Jewish. Avocations: history, book collecting. Office: 9425 Penfield Ave Chatsworth CA 91311

SCHWAB, NELSON, JR., lawyer; b. Cin., July 19, 1918; s. Nelson Sr. and Frances Marie (Carlile) S.; m. Elizabeth Bakhaus (div.); m. Sylvia Lambert; children: Nelson III, Richard O. BA, Yale U., 1940; LLB, Harvard U., 1943. Bar: Ohio 1947. Ptnr. Graydon Head & Ritchey, Cin., 1947-95; sr. counsel, 1995—. Bd. dirs. Rotex, Inc., Ralph J. Stolle co., Security Rug Cleaning Co., Yoder Die Casting Corp. Grants Review Com. The Greater Cin. Found.; mem. Cin. Pub. Schs. Degration Task Force; former chmn. bd. Vol. Lawyers for the Poor Found.; trustee Cin. Scholarship Found., FISC; adv. bd. Cin. Playhouse in the Park; ; past mem., sec. Cin. Bus. Com., 1977-88, mm. Schs. Task Force; past mem. Cin. City Mgr.'s Working Rev. Com. 2000 Plan, chmn. Reconstituted 2000 Plan Rev. Com., 1990; pres. Greater Cin. C. of C., 1973; chmn. Greater Cin. Ednl. TV, 1965-70, hon. trustee; chmn. Cincinnati and Hamilton County Am. Red Cross, 1955-57, hon. trustee; incorporator United Appeal, 1955; mem. Cin. Sch. Bd., 1959-64. Honoree Greater Cin. Region NCCJ, 1990; Great Living Cincinnatian Grater Cin. C. of C., 1991 Mem. 6th Cir. Jud. Conf., Cin. Country Club (past bd. dirs., sec.), Commonwealth Club (past pres.), Comml. Club, Recess Club (past pres.), Gyro Club (past pres.), Queen City Club, Queen City Optimists (past pres.), Cin. Yale Club (past pres.), Lincoln's Inn Soc., Delta Kappa Epsilon. Corporate, general, Estate planning, General practice. Home: 2470 W Rookwood Ct Cincinnati OH 45208-3321 Office: Graydon Head & Ritchey 2471 W Rookwood Ct Cincinnati OH 45208

SCHWAB, TERRANCE W. lawyer; b. Pitts., May 19, 1940; m. Eileen Caulfield, Jan. 4, 1969; children: Matthew Caulfield, Catherine Grimley, Claire Gillespie. BA magna cum laude, Harvard U., 1962; LLB cum laude, Columbia U., 1966. Assoc. Milbank, Tweed, Hadley & McCloy, N.Y.C., 1966-70, Kelley, Drye & Warren, N.Y.C., 1970-74, ptnr., 1975-96; sr. v.p., gen. counsel global fin. and investment banking The Sanwa Bank Ltd. (now UFJ Bank Ltd.), N.Y.C., 1996—. Lectr. various profl. orgns. Assoc. editor: Law Practice of Alexander Hamilton, 1964-1980; contbr. articles to profl. jours. Trustee, sec. Caramoor Ctr. for Music and Arts, Katonah, N.Y., 1971—; trustee Sch. of Convent of Sacred Heart, N.Y.C., 1987-93, chmn., 1990-93. Mem. ABA, N.Y. State Bar Assn., Assn. of Bar of City of N.Y., Harvard Club. Banking, Commercial, contracts (including sales of goods; commercial financing), Private international. Office: UFJ Bank Ltd 55 E 52nd St Fl 24 New York NY 10055

SCHWABE, GEORGE BLAINE, III, lawyer; b. Tulsa, Oct. 10, 1947; s. George Blaine Jr. and Marguerite Irene (Williams) S.; m. Jann Lee Schoonover, July 28, 1972; 1 child, George Blaine IV. BBA, U. Okla., 1970, JD, 1974. Bar: Maine 2001, U.S. Ct. Appeals (10th cir.) 1974, Okla. 1974, U.S. Dist. Ct. (we. dist.) Okla. 1974, U.S. Dist. Ct. (no. dist.) Okla. 1985, U.S. Dist. Ct. (ea. dist.) 1998, U.S. Supreme Ct. 1991, Maine 2001. From assoc. to ptnr. Crowe & Dunlevy, Oklahoma City, 1974-82; ptnr., dir. Mock, Schwabe, Waldo, Elder, Reeves & Bryant, Oklahoma City, 1982-96; shareholder, dir. Gable Gotwals Mock Schwabe, Oklahoma City, 1996-98; member Mock, Schwabe, Waldo, Elder, Reeves & Bryant, Oklahoma City, 1998—. Adj. prof. law Oklahome City U.; lectr. in field. Mem. Leadership Oklahoma City. Capt. USAR. Fellow Am. Coll. Bankruptcy; mem. ABA (bus. bankruptcy com. sect. bus. law), Okla. Bar Assn., Bankruptcy and Reorganization Sect. (pres. 1987-88, bd. dirs. 1985—), Leadership Oklahoma City, Okla. City Golf & Country Club, Rotary. Republican. Mem. Christian Ch. Avocation: golf, snow and water skiing, tennis.. Bankruptcy, Commercial, consumer (including collections, credit), Commercial, contracts (including sales of goods; commercial financing). Office: Mock Schwabe et al 2 Leadership Sq 14th Fl 211 N Robinson Ave Oklahoma City OK 73102-7109 E-mail: gschwabe@mswerb.com.

SCHWABE, JOHN BENNETT, II, lawyer; b. June 14, 1946; s. Leonard Wesley and Hazel Fern (Crouch) Schwabe. AB, U. Mo., Columbia; JD, U. Mo., Columbia, 1970. Bar: Mo. 1970, U.S. Dist. Ct. (we. dist.) Mo. 1970, U.S. Ct. Mil. Appeals 1971, U.S. Supreme Ct. 1973; ordained minister. Pvt. practice, Columbia, Mo., 1974—96, St. Louis, 1984—96. Mem. N. Am. Boxing Fedn., 1997—; minister, founder John Schwabe Ministries. Capt. JAGC USAF, 1970—74. Mem.: Lawyers Assn. St. Louis, Boone County Bar Assn. (sec. 1977—79), Am. Legion, Phi Delta Phi. Methodist. State civil litigation, Personal injury (including property damage), Workers' compensation. Office: John B Schwabe II Law Firm Schwabe Bldg 2 E Walnut St Columbia MO 65203-4163

SCHWARCZ, STEVEN LANCE, law educator, lawyer; b. N.Y.C., Nov. 10, 1949; s. Charles and Elinor Schwarcz; m. Susan Beth Kolodny, Aug. 24, 1975; children: Daniel Benjamin, Rebekah Mara. BS summa cum laude in Aero. Engring., NYU, 1971; JD, Columbia U., 1974. Bar: N.Y. 1971, U.S. Dist. Ct. (so. dist.) N.Y. 1975. Assoc. Shearman & Sterling, N.Y.C., 1974-82, ptnr., 1983-89; ptnr., chmn. structured fin. Kaye, Scholer, Fierman, Hays & Handler, 1996—; prof. Duke U. Sch. Law, Durham, N.C., 1996—; spl. counsel Kaye, Scholer, Fierman, Hays & Handler, 1996—; faculty dir. Duke Global Capital Markets Ctr. Adj. prof. law Yeshiva U., Benjamin N. Cardozo Sch. Law, N.Y.C., 1983-92; vis. lectr. Yale Law Sch., 1992-96; lectr. Columbia Law Sch., 1992-96. Contbr. articles to profl. jours. Chmn. Friends of the Eldridge St. Synagogue, N.Y.C., 1979-96, Legis. Drafting Rsch. Fund. George Granger Brown scholar, 1971; NSF grantee in Math., 1969. Fellow Am. Coll. Coml. Fin. Lawyers; mem. Am. Law Inst., Assn. of Bar of City of N.Y. (environ. law com. 1975-78, nuc. tech. com. 1979-81, sci. and law com. 1985—, chmn. 1987-90), Am. Law and Econs. Assn., Tau Beta Pi, Sigma Gamma Tau. Jewish. Office: Duke U Sch Law Box 90360 Science Dr & Towerview Rd Durham NC 27708 E-mail: schwarcz@law.duke.edu.

SCHWARK, EBERHARD, lawyer, educator; b. Hagen, Germany, Apr. 4, 1939; s. Bernhard and Maria (Quast) S.; m. Brigitte H. Reichelt, Sept. 3, 1965; 1 child, Christian. Student, U. Berlin, U. Freiburg; LLD, U. Bonn. Counsel Fed. Ministry of Econs., Bonn, 1969-72, Internat. Monetary Fund, Washington, 1972, Fed. Ministry of Justice, Bonn, 1975-80; prof. German and European pvt. and comml. law U. Heidelberg, Germany, 1980-81, U. Bochum, Germany, 1981-93, U. Berlin, 1993—. Dir. Inst. for Bank and Capital Mkt. Law, Berlin, 1993—. Author: Commentary to German Stock Exchange Law, 1994, Protection of Investors by Law, 1979, Economic Order and Social State, 1996; contbr. articles to profl. jours. Home: Im Haselnbusch 18 53343 Wachtberg Germany

SCHWARTZ, AARON ROBERT, lawyer, former state legislator; b. Galveston, Tex., July 17, 1926; s. Joseph and Clara (Bulbe) S.; m. Marilyn Cohn, July 14, 1951; children: Richard Austin, Robert Allen, John Reed, Thomas Lee. Pre-law student, Tex. A&M U., 1948; JD, U. Tex., 1951. Bar: Tex. 1951. Mem. Tex. Ho. of Reps., 1955-59, Tex. Senate, 1960-81, past chmn. rules, jurisprudence and natural resources coms. Chmn. Tex. Coastal & Marine Coun., U.S. Coastal States Orgn.; adj. prof., legis. and costal mgmt. law, Bates Law Sch., U. Houston. Contbr. articles to profl. jours. Mem. emeritus exec. com. Galveston Bay Fond.; apptd. to Tex. Oil Spill Oversight Commn., 1993. Served with USN, 1944-46, 2d lt. USAFR, 1948-53. Recipient conservation and legis. awards, Outstanding Citizen award Galveston Jr. C. of C., 1981, Man of Yr., People of Vision award Galveston chpt. Soc. for Prevention of Blindness, 1986, Disting. Service award Nat. Hurricane Conf., Tex. Coastal Mgmt. Adv. Com., 1987, Lifetime Coastal Achievement award, 1997. Mem. Tex. State Bar Assn., Galveston County Bar Assn. Democrat. Jewish. Address: 1122 Colorado St Apt 2102 Austin TX 78701-2142 E-mail: ars71726@aol.com.

SCHWARTZ, ALAN E. lawyer, director; b. Detroit, Dec. 21, 1925; s. Maurice H. and Sophia (Welkowitz) S.; m. Marianne Shapero, Aug. 24, 1950; children: Marc Alan, Kurt Nathan, Ruth Anne. Student, Western Mich. Coll., 1944-45; BA with distinction, U. Mich., 1947; LLB magna cum laude, Harvard U., 1950; LLD, Wayne State U., 1983, U. Detroit, 1985. Bar: N.Y. 1951, Mich. 1952. Assoc. Kelley, Drye & Warren, N.Y.C., 1950-52; mem. Honigman, Miller, Schwartz & Cohn, Detroit, 1952—. Spl. asst. counsel N.Y. State Crime Commn., 1951; bd. dirs. Pulte Corp. Editor: Harvard Law Rev., 1950. Dir. Detroit Symphony Orch.; v.p., bd. dirs. United Found.; bd. dirs. Detroit Renaissance, New Detroit, Jewish Welfare Fedn. Detroit, Wayne State Univ. Found.; trustee Cmty. Found. for Southeastern Mich., Interlochen Arts Acad.; adv. mem. Arts Commn., City of Detroit; mem. investment com. Krespe Found. Served as ensign Supply Corps, USNR, 1945-46. Recipient Mich. Heritage Hall of Fame award, 1984, George W. Romney award for lifetime achievement in volunteerism, 1994, Max M. Fisher Cmty. Svc. award, 1997. Mem. Mich. Bar Assns. Clubs: Franklin Hills Country; Detroit, Economic (dir.). Office: Honigman Miller Schwartz & Cohn 2290 1st National Bldg Detroit MI 48226

SCHWARTZ, ARTHUR JAY, lawyer; b. Atlanta, May 28, 1947; s. William B. Jr. and Sonia (Weinberg) S.; m. Joyce Straus, Aug. 12, 1972; children: Tracy Jill, Allison Jaye. BA, U. N.C., 1969; JD, Emory U., 1972. Bar: Ga. 1972, U.S. Dist. Ct. (no. dist.) Ga. 1972, U.S. Ct. Appeals (5th and 11th cirs.) 1972. Ptnr. Smith, Gambrell & Russell L.L.P., Atlanta, 1972—, chmn. exec. com., mng. ptnr., 1988-89, 92-93, 96-97, fin. ptnr., 1998—. Sec. Lamin Art, Inc., Chgo., 1984—, also bd. dirs. Mem. Emory Law Sch. Coun., 1997—2001; bd. dirs. Am. Jewish Com., Atlanta, 1982—84, The Temple, Atlanta, 1983—85, 1994—, treas., 1998—2000, v.p., 2000—02, pres., 2002—. With USAR, 1970—72. Mem. Am. Technion Soc. Atlanta (v.p., bd. dirs. 1980-87), Soc. Internat. Bus. Fellows, Buckhead Club (bd. dirs. 1987-97). Avocations: hunting, running, golf, boating. Commercial, contracts (including sales of goods; commercial financing), Corporate, general, Securities. E-mail: JSchwartz@sgrlaw.com.

SCHWARTZ, ARTHUR ZACHARY, lawyer; b. N.Y.C., Feb. 11, 1953; s. Herman and Roselind Schwartz; m. Claire Basescu, Dec. 28, 1985; children: Jacob, Rebecca. BA, Columbia Coll., 1974; JD, Hofstra U., 1978. Bar: Pa. 1978, N.Y. 1979. Ptnr. Hall, Clifton & Schwartz, N.Y.C., 1979-84, Clifton & Schwartz, N.Y.C., 1984-89, Lewis, Greenwald & Kennedy, N.Y.C., 1989-95, Kennedy, Schwartz & Cure, N.Y.C., 1995—. Gen. counsel Utility Workers Union, Washington, 1990-92, Transport Workers Union, Forester, N.Y., UNITE Allied Svcs. Joint Bd., DC1707, AFSCME, Profl. Staff Congress-CUNY, others. Chair West Village Alliance for Parks, 1994—; Dem. Party Dist. Leader, Greenwich Village, N.Y.C., 1995—; waterfront chair Cmty. Bd. 2 Manhattan, 1998—; mem. adv. bd. Assn. Union Democracy, 1985—; chair Lower Manhattan Alliance for Progressive Polit. Action; chair Hudson River Park Trust adv. coun. Labor (including EEOC, Fair Labor Standards Act, labor-management relations, NLRB, OSHA), Non-profit and tax-exempt organizations. Home: 269 W 11th St New York NY 10014-2493 Office: Kennedy Schwartz & Cure 113 University Pl New York NY 10003-4527 E-mail: aschwartz@ksclaborlawyers.com.

SCHWARTZ, BARRY FREDRIC, lawyer, diversified holding company executive; b. Phila., Apr. 16, 1949; s. Albert and Evelyn (Strauss) S.; m. Sherry L. Handsman, Mar. 21, 1985; children: Fanny Rose, Abraham David. AB cum laude, Kenyon Coll., 1970; JD, Georgetown U., 1974. Bar: Pa. 1974, Ill. 1974, N.Y. 1992, U.S. Dist. Ct. (ea. dist.) Pa. 1974, U.S. Dist. Ct. (no. dist.) Ill. 1975, U.S. Dist. Ct. (so. dist.) N.Y. 1992, U.S. Ct. Appeals (7th cir.) 1977, U.S. Ct. Appeals (3d cir.) 1978, U.S. Ct. Appeals (4th cir.) 1979, U.S. Ct. Appeals (6th cir.) 1981, U.S. Supreme Ct. 1981, N.Y. 1992. Assoc. Sachnoff, Schrager, Jones & Weaver, Chgo., 1974-76; ptnr. Wolf, Block, Schorr & Solis-Cohen, Phila., 1976-89; exec. v.p. gen. counsel MacAndrews & Forbes Holdings, Inc., N.Y.C., 1989—. Trustee Kenyon Coll.; mem. adv. coun. Westchester Holocaust Commn., 2000--; mem. Adv. Com. for Justices of the Comml. divsn. Supreme Ct., New York County, 1999--. Federal civil litigation, Mergers and acquisitions, Securities. Home: 16 Brookside Park Greenwich CT 06831-5316 Office: MacAndrews & Forbes Holdings Inc 35 E 62nd St New York NY 10021-8032

SCHWARTZ, CHARLES, JR., federal judge; b. New Orleans, Aug. 20, 1922; s. Charles and Sophie (Hess) S.; m. Patricia May, Aug. 31, 1950 (dec.); children: Priscilla May, John Putney. BA, Tulane U., 1943, JD, 1947. Bar: La. 1947. Ptnr. Guste, Barnett & Little, 1947-70; practiced in New Orleans, until 1976; ptnr. firm Little, Schwartz & Dussom, 1970-76; dist. counsel Gulf Coast dist. U.S. Maritime Adminstrn., 1953-62; judge U.S. Dist. Ct. (ea. dist.) La., New Orleans, 1976-91, sr. judge, 1991—. Mem. Fgn. Itelligence Surveillance Ct., 1992-98; prof. Tulane U. Law Sch., 1977-99; lectr. continuing law insts., 1974-75; mem. Jud. Conf. Com. U.S. on implementation of jury system, 1981-85; mem. permanent adv. bd. Tulane Admiralty Law Inst., 1984—. Bd. editors Tulane Law Rev. Pres. New Orleans unit Am. Cancer Soc., 1956-57; v.p., chmn. budget com. United Fund Greater New Orleans Area, 1959-61, trustee, 1953-65; bd. dirs. Cancer Assn. Greater New Orleans, 1958— , pres., 1958-59, 72-73; bd. dirs. United Cancer Council, 1963-85, pres., 1971-73; mem. com. on grants to agencies Community Chest, 1965-87; men's adv. com. League Women Voters, 1966-68; chmn. com. admissions of program devel. and coordination com. United Way Greater New Orleans, 1974-77; mem. comml. panel Am. Arbitration Assn., 1974-76; bd. dirs. Willow Wood Home, 1979-85, 1989-92; bd. mgrs. Touro Infirmary, 1992—; trustee Metairie Park Country Day Sch., 1977-83; mem. La. Republican Central Com., 1961-76; mem. Orleans Parish Rep. Exec. Com., 1960-75, chmn., 1964-75; mem. Jefferson Parish Rep. Exec. Com., 1975-76; del. Rep. Nat. Conv., 1960, 64, 68; mem. nat. budget and consultation com. United Community Funds and Coun. of Am., 1961; bd. dirs. Community Svcs. Coun., 1971-73. Served to 2d lt. AUS, 1943-46; maj. U.S. Army Res.; ret. Mem. La. Bar Assn. New Orleans Bar Assn. (legis. com. 1970-75), Fed. Bar Assn., Fgn. Rels. Assn. New Orleans (bd. dirs. 1957-61), 5th Cir. Dist. Judges Assn. (pres. 1984-85), Lakewood Country Club (bd. dirs. 1967-68, pres. 1975-77). Office: 219 Northline Metairie LA 70005-4447*

SCHWARTZ, CHARLES WALTER, lawyer; b. Brenham, Tex., Dec. 27, 1953; s. Walter C. and Annie (Kuehn) S.; m. Kay Anne Kern, Sept. 24, 1996. BS, U. Tex., 1975, MA, 1980, JD, 1977; LLM, Harvard U., 1980. Bar: Tex. 1977; bd. cert. civil appellate law Tex. Bd. Legal Specialization. Law clk. U.S. Ct. Appeals (5th cir.), Austin, Tex., 1977-79; assoc. Vinson & Elkins L.L.P., Houston, 1980-86, ptnr., 1996—2003, Skadden, Arps, Seate, Meagher & Flom, 2003—. Contbr. articles to law revs. Fellow: Coll. State Bar Tex., Tex. Bar Found. (sustaining life), Houston Bar Found. (life), Am. Bar Found.; mem.: ABA, Tex. Law Rev. Assn., Am. Law Inst., Bar Assn. of 5th Cir., State Bar Tex. (former chmn. griveance com. 1993—99, bd. dirs. 2000—, mem. exec. com. 2001—, chmn. 2002—). Appellate, Federal civil litigation, Securities. Home: 2154 Chilton Rd Houston TX 77019 Office: Skadden Arps Slate Meagher & Flom 1600 Smith Ste 4400 Houston TX 77002 E-mail: schwartz@sskadden.com.

SCHWARTZ, DONALD LEE, lawyer; b. Milw., Dec. 8, 1948; s. Bernard L. and Ruth M. (Marshall) S.; m. Susan J. Dunst, June 5, 1971; children: Stephanie Jane, Cheryl Ruth. BA, Macalester Coll., 1971; JD, U. Chgo., 1974. Bar: Ill. 1974. Assoc. Sidley & Austin, Chgo., 1974-80, ptnr., 1980-88, Latham & Watkins, Chgo., 1988—. Chmn. Ill. Conservative Union, 1979-81, bd. dirs. 1977-85. Served with U.S. Army, 1971-77. Mem. ABA (uniform comml. code com., comml. fin. svcs. commn.), Ill. Bar Assn. (sec. coun. banking and bankuprtcy sect. 1982-83), Chgo. Bar Assn. (chmn. comml. law com. 1980-81, fin. insts. com. 1982-83), Ivanhoe Country Club, Sea Pines Country Club, Colleton River Country Club, Met. Club. Republican. Episcopalian. Avocation: golf. Banking, Bankruptcy, Finance. Home: 191 Park Ave Glencoe IL 60022-1351 Office: Latham & Watkins Ste 5800 Sears Tower Chicago IL 60606 E-mail: Donald.schwartz@lw.com.

SCHWARTZ, EDWARD ARTHUR, lawyer; b. Boston, Sept. 27, 1937; s. Abe and Sophie (Gottheim) S.; m. Sheila Kauffman, Apr. 5, 1997; children: Eric Allen, Jeffrey Michael. AB, Oberlin Coll., 1959; LLB, Boston Coll., 1962; postgrad., Am. U., 1958-59, Northeastern U., 1970; postgrad. exec. program, Stanford U., 1979. Bar: Conn. 1962, Mass. 1965. Legal intern Office Atty. Gen. Commonwealth of Mass., 1961; assoc. Schatz & Schatz, Hartford, Conn., 1962-65, Cohn, Reimer & Pollack, Boston, 1965-67; v.p., gen. coun., sec. Digital Equipment Corp., Maynard, Mass., 1967-88; pres. New Eng. Legal Found., Boston, 1990-98. Vis. prof. law Boston Coll., 1986, adj. prof., 1987-89 bd. dirs. SatelLife Corp. Editor Boston Coll. Indsl. and Comml. Law Rev, 1960-62, Ann. Survey Mass. Law, 1960-62. Trustee Rural Land Found. Corporate, general. Home: 62 Todd Pond Rd Lincoln MA 01773-3808

SCHWARTZ, EDWARD LESTER, retired lawyer; b. N.Y.C., July 13, 1910; s. Alexander and Serene (Brown) S.; m. Edna B. Smith, July 31, 1941 (dec.); 1 child, Andrea Helen Saiet. BA, CCNY, 1931; JD, Harvard U., 1934. Bar: N.Y. 1935, Mass. 1939. Pvt. practice, N.Y.C., 1935-39, Boston, 1939-90. Lectr. law Boston U., Northeastern U., Suffolk U., New Eng. Law Inst., Mass. Continuing Legal Edn. Inst.; asst. atty. gen. State of Mass., 1970-75; commr. Nat. Conf. Commrs. on Uniform Laws (life); chmn. spl. com. Uniform Securities Act, spl. com. Landlord/Tenant Relationship Act; Mass. commr. Interstate Coop., 1949-74. Author: Lease Drafting in Massachusetts, 1961, updated 1996; contbr. articles to profl. jours. Mem. ABA, Am. Law Inst. (life), Am. Judicature Soc., Boston Bar Assn., Mass. Bar Assn. (lectr.), Scribes, New Eng. Law Inst. (exec. com.), Mass. Continuing Legal Edn. (bd. dirs.). Home: 17 Ledgewood Rd Weston MA 02493-1423

SCHWARTZ, ESTAR ALMA, lawyer; b. Bklyn., June 29, 1950; d. Henry Israel and Elaine Florence (Scheiner) Sutel; m. Lawrence Gerald Schwartz, June 28, 1976 (div. Dec. 1977); 1 child, Joshua (dec.); m. James Frances Edward Stuart, Sept. 25, 1999 (div. Aug. 2001). JD, NYU, 1980. Mgr., ptnr. Scheiner, Scheiner, DeVito & Wytte, N.Y.C., 1966-81; fed. govt., social security fraud specialist DHHS, OI, OIG, SSFIS, N.Y.C., 1982-83; pensions Todtman, Epstein, et al, N.Y.C., 1983-85; office mgr., sec. Sills, Beck, Cummis, N.Y.C., 1985-86; office mgr., bookkeeper Philip, Birnbaum & Assocs., N.Y.C., 1986-87; office mgr., sec. Stanley Posses, Esq., Queens, N.Y., 1989-90. Owner Estaris Paralegal Svc., Flushing, N.Y., 1992—, Sutel Creative Mgmt. Agy., Flushing, 1999—. Democrat. Jewish. Avocations: needlepoint, horseback riding, tennis, bowling, writing children's and other books. Pension, profit-sharing, and employee benefits, Personal injury (including property damage), Product liability. Home and Office: 67-20 Parsons Blvd Apt 2A Flushing NY 11365-2960 E-mail: Sutel@email.com., Sutelmmgmt@aol.com.

SCHWARTZ, HARALD JOSEF, lawyer; b. Koetzting, Bavaria, Germany, Jan. 31, 1969; M in Bus. Law, U. Bayreuth, Germany, 1994; staatsexamen, U. Bayreuth, 1995, Munich, 1998. Refrendar Dist. Ct. Regensburg, Germany, 1995—98; intern Law Offices of Fredericks & von der Horst, L.A., 1998; cons. KPMG, Nuremberg, Germany, 1999; lawyer Neuhof Law Offices, Nuremberg, 1999—. Mem. supervisory bd. Sparkasse Amberg-Sulzbach, Amberg, 2002—. Author: International Law of Economic Loss, 2001. Local rep. Regions Counsel, Amberg, 1996—. 1st lt. Germany Infantry, 1988—90. Avocation: sports. Banking, Bankruptcy, Entertainment. Office: Neuhof Law Offices Leipziger Platz 21 90491 Nuremberg Germany

SCHWARTZ, HERBERT FREDERICK, lawyer; b. Bklyn., Aug. 23, 1935; s. Henry and Blanche Theodora (goldberg) S.; m. Gail Lubets, Jan. 23, 1960; children: Wendy Helene, Karen Anne, Peter Andrew; m. Nan Budde Chequer, Mar. 13, 1987; stepchildren: Elizabeth Guthrie, Anne Hamilton, Laura Dunham. BSEE, MIT, 1957; MA in Applied Econs., LLB, U. Pa., 1964. Assoc. Fish & Neave, N.Y.C., 1964-70, jr. ptnr., 1970-71, ptnr., 1972—, mng. ptnr., 1985-91. Lectr. law U. Pa., Phila., 1980-89, adj. prof., 1990—. Mem. adv. bd. PTC Jour., Washington, 1983; author: Patent Law and Practice, Federal Judicial Center, 1988, 2d edit., 1995, Bureau of National Affairs, 2d edit., 1996, 3d edit., 2001; co-author: Principles of Patent Law, 1998, 2d edit., 2001; contbr. articles to profl. jours. Vice-chmn. Jr. Yacht Racing Assn. of L.I. Sound, 1985-88. 1st lt. U.S. Army, Signal Corps, 1957-59. Mem. U.S. Trademark Assn., Assn. of Bar of City of N.Y., Am. Intellectual Property Lawyers Assn., N.Y. Intellectual Property Lawyers Assn. (pres. 1999-2000), Am. Coll. Trial Lawyers, Am. Bar Found., Am. Law Inst., Order of Coif, N.Y. Yacht Club, Riverside Yacht Club, Cruising Club of Am. Avocation: racing and cruising sailboats. Federal civil litigation, Patent, Trademark and copyright. Home: 24 Cherry Tree Ln Riverside CT 06878-2629 Office: Fish & Neave 1251 Avenue Of The Americas Fl 50 New York NY 10020-1105

SCHWARTZ, IRWIN H. lawyer; b. Bklyn., Mar. 25, 1948; s. Julius and Sylvia (Holzman) S.; m. Barbara T. Granett, July 3, 1971; 1 child, Matthew Lane. BA, Bklyn. Coll., 1968; JD, Stanford U., 1971. Bar: Calif. 1972, Washington 1972, U.S. Ct. Appeals (9th cir.) 1972, U.S. Supreme Ct. 1977. Asst. U.S. atty. U.S. Dist. Ct. (we. dist.) Wash., Seattle, 1972-74, exec. asst. U.S. atty., 1974-75, fed. pub. defender, 1975-81; pvt. practice Seattle, 1981—. Fellow Am. Coll. Trial Lawyers, Am. Bd. Criminal Lawyers; mem. ABA (criminal justice sect. coun. 1991-94. 2002--), Nat. Assn. Criminal Def. Lawyers (pres. 2001-02), Wash. Athletic Club (Seattle). Avocations: photography, woodworking. Federal civil litigation, Criminal. Office: 710 Cherry St Seattle WA 98104-1925 E-mail: ischwartz@compuserve.com.

SCHWARTZ, JEFFREY SCOTT, lawyer; b. N.Y.C., Aug. 2, 1959; s. Philip Harold and Carolyn Annette (Stern) S.; m. Lynette Pam Vigdor, Dec. 23, 1984; children: Michelle Renee, Joel Benjamin. BA, SUNY, Oneonta, 1981; JD, Thomas Jefferson U., San Diego, 1984. Bar: Calif. 1987, U.S. Dist. Ct. (so. dist.) Calif. 1987, U.S. Supreme Ct. 1997, D.C. 1998. Legal asst. Law Office William O'Connell, San Diego, 1983-87, assoc., 1987-88; pvt. practice, San Diego, 1988—; CEO, pres. ionUS.com Corp., San Diego, 1999—2001; CEO, gen. counsel ion Media, 2001—. Chmn. legal clinic San Diego State U., San Diego City Coll., San Diego County Bar Assn., 1987—, vice chmn. Pub. Info. and Rels. com., 1991. Mem. ABA, State Bar Calif. (advisor gen. practice sect., author Criminal Justice Jour. 1983), San Diego County Bar Assn. (chmn. call for action 1989, 91-97), ATLA, Calif. Trial Lawyers Assn., San Diego Trial Lawyers Assn., Delta Theta Phi (supreme ct. justice 1987-95, Percy J. Power award 1987, Wiley W. Manuel award for legal svcs. 1990, Gold Medallion award 2002). Democrat. Jewish. General civil litigation, General practice, Corporate, general. Office: 8304 Clairemont Mesa Blvd Ste 213 San Diego CA 92111 E-mail: jschwartz@ionus.com.

SCHWARTZ, JEFFREY TODD, lawyer; b. Bklyn., June 16, 1962; s. Abraham and Marilyn (Friedman) S.; 1 child, Jennifer Brooke. BA, Yeshiva U., 1984, JD, 1987. Bar: N.Y. 1987, N.J. 1987, U.S. Dist. Ct. (ea. and so. dists.) N.Y. 1988, U.S. Supreme Ct. 1991. Asst. dist. atty. Queens (N.Y.) Dist. Attys. Office, 1987-93; atty. pvt. practice, N.Y.C., 1993—. Staff atty. 18B Indigent Def. Panel, N.Y.C., 1993, 35(b) Capital Defenders Panel. Mem. ATLA, Nassau Bar Assn., Manhattan Bar Assn., N.Y. County Criminal Lawyers Assn., Queens County Bar Assn., Kings County Bar Assn., Brandies Assn. Jewish. Criminal. Office: Schwartz & Klein LLP 225 Broadway Rm 2100 New York NY 10007-3001

SCHWARTZ, MARVIN, lawyer; b. Phila., Nov. 3, 1922; s. Abe and Freda (Newman) S.; m. Joyce Ellen Sidner, Sept. 7, 1947; children: Daniel Bruce, Pamela Louise Pier. LL.B., U. Pa., 1949. Bar: Pa. 1950, N.Y. 1951, D.C. 1955. Law sec. to judge U.S. Ct. Appeals, 3d Circuit, Phila., 1949-50; law sec. to Justice Burton U.S. Supreme Ct., Washington, 1950-51; assoc. Sullivan & Cromwell, N.Y.C., 1951-60, ptnr., 1960-92, sr. counsel, 1993—. Mediator U.S. Dist. (so. dist.) N.Y., N.Y. Supreme Ct. Comml. Divsn.; arbitrator Am. Arbitration Assn., N.Y. Stock Exch., Nat. Assn. Securities Dealers. Spl. master appellate divsn. 1st dept. Supreme Ct. N.Y.; chmn. Zoning Bd. of Adjustment, Alpine, N.J., 1966-74; mem. Planning Bd., Alpine, 1966-67; bd. overseers emeritus U. Pa. Law Sch.; bd. dirs. Waterbury Found. With Signal Corps U.S. Army, 1943-46. Mem. ABA, N.Y. Bar Assn., D.C. Bar Assn., Am. Coll. Trial Lawyers (sec. 1986-88, bd. regents 1981-86, chmn. Downstate N.Y. com. 1976-78), Am. Law Inst. (adviser complex litigation project), Univ. Club (N.Y.C.), Litchfield (Conn.) Country Club. Democrat. Jewish. Office: Sullivan & Cromwell 125 Broad St Fl 28 New York NY 10004-2489

SCHWARTZ, MILTON LEWIS, federal judge; b. Oakland, Calif., Jan. 20, 1920; s. Colman and Selma (Lavenson) S.; m. Barbara Ann Moore, May 15, 1942; children: Dirk L., Tracy Ann, Damon M., Brooke. AB, U. Calif. at Berkeley, 1941, JD, 1948. Bar: Calif. bar 1949. Rsch. asst. 3d Dist. Ct. Appeal, Sacramento, 1948; dep. dist. atty., 1949-51; practice in, 1951-79; partner McDonough, Holland, Schwartz & Allen, 1953-79; U.S. dist. judge Eastern Dist. Calif., U.S. Dist. Ct., Calif., 1979-90, sr. judge, 1990—2002. Prof. law McGeorge Coll. Law, Sacramento, 1952-55; mem. Com. Bar Examiners Calif., 1971-75 Pres. Bd. Edn. Sacramento City Sch. Dist., 1961; v.p. Calif. Bd. Edn., 1967-68; trustee Sutterville Heights Sch. Dist. Served to maj. 40th Inf. Divsn. AUS, 1942-46, PTO. Named Sacramento County Judge of Yr., 1990; Milton L. Schwartz Am. Inn of Court named in his honor, Davis, Calif. Fellow Am. Coll. Trial Lawyers; mem. State Bar Calif., Am. Bar Assn., Am. Bd. Trial Advocates, Anthony M. Kennedy Am. Inn of Ct. (pres. 1988-90, pres. emeritus 1990—). Office: US Dist Ct Rm 15 200 501 I St Sacramento CA 95814

SCHWARTZ, PHILIP, lawyer; b. June 7, 1930; s. Louis and Kate (Brodsky) S.; m. Iris M. Ballin, Nov. 28, 1953 (div. 1979); children: David, Elyse, Donna; m. Monique W. Wagner, July 26, 1982 (div. 1991); m. Carol J. Pruett, Aug. 14, 1992. BA, George Washington U., 1952, JD, 1959; LLM in Taxation, Georgetown U., 1961; postgrad., U. Paris, London Sch. Econs., Harvard U. Bar: Va. 1959, D.C. 1966, U.S. Tax Ct. 1966, U.S. Ct. Appeals (D.C. cir.) 1966, U.S. Ct. Mil. Appeals 1966, U.S. Supreme Ct. 1966, U.S. Ct. Appeals (4th cir.) 1982, U.S. Ct. Internat. Trade 1988, N.Am. Coun. London Ct. Internat. Arbitration 1988. Sr. intelligence analyst Nat. Security Agy., Washington, 1952-54, 56-63; assoc. Varoutsos, Koutoulakos & Arthur, Arlington, Va., 1963—68; ptnr. Schwartz & Ellis, Ltd., Arlington, 1968—2002, Schwartz & Assocs., PLLC, 2002—; of counsel Odin, Feldman & Pittleman PC, 2002—. Instr. No. Va. Life Underwriters Trng. Coun., 1974, No. Va. Paralegal Inst., Arlington, 1976; moot ct. judge George Washington U., Washington, Georgetown U., Washington, Jessup Internat. Law Competition; commr. Chancery Arlington Cir. Ct., judge Pro Tempo; spkr. in field. Contbr. articles to profl. jours. Mem. U.S. Sec. of State Adv. Com. on Pvt. Internat. Law; mem. Arlington County Bd. Zoning Appeals, 1972-85, Arlington County Coun. Human Rels., 1973; del. to Hague Conf. Pvt. Internat. Law; bd. dirs. Jewish Cmty. Ctr. Greater Washington, 975. With M.I., U.S. Army, 1954-56. Master Barrister Am. Inns of Ct.; fellow Internat. Acad. Matrimonial Lawyers (pres. 1996-97), Am. Acad. Matrimonial Lawyers (bd. govs., v.p.); mem. ABA (chmn. family law sect. com. internat. laws 1983-86, chmn. internat. law sect. com. enforcement fgn. judgments), Internat. Bar Assn. (chmn. family law divsn. 1988-92, governing coun. gen. practice sect., liaison officer to IMF), Va. Trial Lawyers Assn. (instr. 1984), Assn. Trial Lawyers Am. (vice chmn. internat. practice sect.), Va. State Bar (bd. govs. internat. law sect., liaison to ABA internat. law sect., spl. com. reducing litigation delay and costs, com. on bench/bar rels.), Calif. Bar Assn. (internat. law sect.), N.Y. State Bar Assn. (internat. law, family law sect.), D.C. Bar (internat. law, family law sect.), Arlington County Bar Assn. (cts. com., legis. com., jud. selection com.), Fairfax County Bar Assn. (family law and internat. law sects.), Brit. Inst. Internat. and Comparative Law, Am. Soc. Internat. Law, World Assn. Lawyers, Union Internationale des Avocats, Inter-Am. Bar Assn., Internat. Soc. Family Law, Solicitors Family Law Assn. Eng. and Wales, Soc. English and Am. Lawyers, Am. Fgn. Law Assn., Internat. Law Assn., Asia-Pacific Lawyers Assn., Arlington Jaycees, Kiwanis, Phi Epsilon Pi, Delta Phi Epsilon, Phi Delta Phi. Corporate, general, Family and matrimonial, Private international. Office: Schwartz & Assocs PLLC 9302 Lee Hwy 11th Fl Fairfax VA 22031 Office Fax: 703-218-2160. E-mail: philip.schwrtz@ofplaw.com.

SCHWARTZ, RENEE GERSTLER, lawyer; b. Bklyn., June 18, 1933; d. Samuel and Lillian (Neulander) Gerstler; m. Alfred L. Schwartz, July 30, 1955; children: Carolyn Susan, Deborah Jane. AB, Bklyn. Coll., 1953; LLB, Columbia U., 1955. Bar: N.Y. 1956, U.S. Dist. Ct. (so. and ea. dists.) N.Y. 1956, U.S. Ct. Appeals (2d cir.) 1956, U.S. Dist. Ct. D.C. 1983, U.S. Supreme Ct. 1986. Assoc. Botein, Hays & Sklar, N.Y.C., 1955-64, ptnr., 1965-89, Kronish, Lieb, Weiner & Hellman, N.Y.C., 1990—. Bd. dirs. New Land Found., N.Y.C., 1965—. Mem. Bar Assn. City of N.Y. Family and matrimonial, Libel, Utilities, public. Home: 115 Central Park W New York NY 10023-4153 Office: Kronish Lieb Weiner & Hellman 1114 Avenue Of The Americas New York NY 10036-7703 E-mail: rschwartz@kronishlieb.com.

SCHWARTZ, ROBERT M. lawyer; b. Phila., Aug. 6, 1940; s. Nathan and Miriam (Albus) S.; m. Karen Leaf, Feb. 11, 1966; children: Eric, Lauren. BS, Pa. State U., 1962; JD, Villanova U., 1965. Bar: Pa. 1965, U.S. Ct. Appeals (3rd cir.) 1965. Law clk. to presiding justice Common Pleas Ct. Montgomery County, Norristown, Pa., 1965; v.p., assoc. counsel Commonwealth Land Title Ins. Co., Phila., 1969—73; ptnr. in bus. dept. White and Williams, LLP, Phila., 1973—. Spkr. in field. Mem. regional exec., chmn. com. civil rights com., regional bd. trustees Anti-Defamation League, vice chmn., 1997-99; bd. dirs., mem. facilities and legal coms. Police Athletic League. Named one of Am.'s Top Lawyers, 2001—. Mem. Phila. Bar Assn. (chmn. real property com. 1981, exec. bd. real property sect. 1983-89, 91, 2002, chmn. real property sect. 1986), Am. Coll. Real Estate Lawyers (Best Lawyers in Am. award 1989-2003), Am. Coll. Mortgage Attys., Am. Land Title Assn. (lenders counsel group 1993—), Order of Coif. Republican. Jewish. Avocations: bridge, golf. Property, real (including real estate development, water). Office: White and Williams 1650 Market St Fl 18 Philadelphia PA 19103-7395

SCHWARTZ, ROGER ALAN, judge; b. N.Y.C., May 2, 1945; s. George Martin Ronald and Claire Marie (Dorsch) Schwartz; 1 child, Julia Claire. BA, Muhlenberg Coll., 1967; JD, Temple U., 1973, M in Labor Law, 1976, MPA, 1979; disting. grad., U.S. Army Command and Gen. Staff Coll.; MA in History summa cum laude, U. Scranton, 1997; postgrad., Marywood U., 1997—. Bar: Pa. 1973, N.Y. 1982, D.C. 1976, U.S. Dist. Ct. (ea. dist.) Pa. 1973, U.S. Ct. Appeals (3d cir.) 1976, U.S. Mil. Appeals 1981, U.S. Ct. Appeals (Fed cir.) 1986, U.S. Supreme Ct, 1976. Personnel mgmt. specialist CSC, Phila., 1973-74, asst. appeals officer, 1974-78; sr. adminstrv. judge U.S. Merit Systems Protection Bd., Phila., 1979-89; adminstrv. law judge Social Security Adminstrn., Wilkes-Barre, Pa., 1989—. Arbitrator Phila. Ct. Common Pleas, 1973-89; asst. prof. Inst. for Paralegal Tng., Phila., 1976-77; adj. prof. history Keystone Coll., La Plume, Pa. With U.S. Army, 1968-70, Vietnam, Persian Gulf War, 1990; col. JAGC Res., ret. Decorated Legion of Merit, Bronze Star, Purple Heart, Nat. Svc. medal with svc. star, Meritorious Svc. medal with one oak leaf cluster, Meritorious Achievement medal with 1 oak leaf cluster, Army Commendation medal with 4 oak leaf clusters. Mem. ABA, Phila. Bar Assn., Am. Judicature Soc., Am. Arbitration Assn., Res. Officers Assn. (Pa. state sec. 1996-97), Assn. Adminstrv. Law Judges (v.p. region III), Rotary (bd. dirs. Wilkes Barre chpt. 1999-2000). Avocations: piano, computers, billiards. Office: Social Security Adminstrn Office Hearings & Appeals 7 N Wilkes Barre Blvd Wilkes Barre PA 18702-5249 E-mail: rogschwartz@aol.com.

SCHWARTZ, STEVEN NORMAN, lawyer; b. Washington, Nov. 27, 1945; s. George and Sylvia (Ritzenberg) S.; m. Deborah Slobin, Apr. 6, 1972; children— Adam, Jennifer. A.B., Dartmouth Coll., 1967; LL.B., Yale U., 1970. Bar: Calif. 1970, U.S. Dist. Ct. (so. dist.) Calif. 1971, U.S. Ct. Appeals (9th cir.) 1971, U.S. Supreme Ct. 1976. Atty., Defenders, Inc., San Diego, 1970-73; ptnr. Brav & Schwartz, A.P.C., San Diego, 1973— ; adj. prof. Calif. Western Sch. Law, San Diego, 1972-73. Democrat. Jewish. Clubs: Dartmouth of San Diego; Coronado Men's Golf (Calif.). Corporate, general, Property, real (including real estate development, water). Office: Brav & Schwartz A P C 4026 Dove St San Diego CA 92103-1914

SCHWARTZ, THEODORE FRANK, lawyer; b. Clayton, Mo., Aug. 14, 1935; s. Ben and Mary (Roufa) S.; m. Barbara Jean Rader, Aug. 30, 1959; children: Michael D., Kenneth R. JD, Washington U., St. Louis, 1962. Bar: Mo. 1967, D.C. 1972, Calif. 1974, N.Y. 1981, Fla. 1994; U.S. Dist. Ct. (ea. dist.) Mo. 1962, U.S. Ct. Appeals (8th cir.) 1963, U.S. Dist. Ct. (so. dist.) Ind. 1968, U.S. Dist. Ct. (so. dist.) Tex. 1971, U.S. Ct. Appeals (5th cir.) 1971, U.S. Ct. (cen. dist.) Calif. 1978, U.S. Ct. Appeals (7th cir.) 1979, U.S. Ct. Appeals (2d, 10th and 11th cirs.) 1980, U.S. Ct. Appeals (9th cir.) 1981, U.S. Supreme Ct. 1981. Assoc. Charles M. Shaw, Clayton, 1962-64; ptnr. Ackerman, Schiller & Schwartz, Clayton, 1964-74; sole practice Clayton, 1975—. Mem. ABA, Assn. Trial Lawyer Am., Mo. Assn. Trial Lawyers, Am. Judicature Soc., Nat. Assn. Criminal Def. Lawyers. Antitrust, Federal civil litigation, State civil litigation. Home: 597 Purdue Ave Saint Louis MO 63130-4136 Office: 130 S Bemiston Ave Ste 700 Clayton MO 63105-1928 E-mail: theodore@gtw.net.

SCHWARTZ, VICTOR ELLIOT, lawyer, educator; b. N.Y.C., July 3, 1940; AB summa cum laude, Boston U., 1962; JD magna cum laude, Columbia U., 1965. Bar: N.Y. 1965, Ohio 1974. Law clk. to judge So. Dist. N.Y., 1965-67; from asst. to assoc. prof. law U. Cin., 1967-72, prof., 1972-79, acting dean, 1973-74; vis. prof. U. Va. Law Sch., 1970-71; dist. vis. scholar U. Cin., 2002—; ptnr. firm Crowell & Moring, Washington, 1980—2001; sr. ptnr. firm Fed. Interagy. task Force on Products Liability, 1976; ptnr., chair firm's pub. policy group Shook Hardy & Bacon, Washington, 2001—. Bd. visitors U. Cin. Sch., 1998—; disting. vis. scholar U. Cin., 2003—; gen. counsel, bd. dirs. Am. Tort Reform Assn.; chmn. Civil Justice Task Force, Am. Legis. Exch. Coun.; chmn. Dept. of Commerce Task Force on Product Liability and Accident Compensation, 1977-80. Author: Comparative Negligence, 1974, 4th edit., 2002; (with Prosser and Wade) Cases and Materials on Torts, 1976, 10th edit., 2000, How to Prepare for the Multi-State Bar Examination, 1977, Products Liability: Cases and Trends, 1987, Products Liability: Asset Trends, 1988, (with Lee and Kelly) Multistate Legislation, 1985; editor: Columbia Law Rev., 1965; prin. draftsman: Model Uniform Product Liability Act. Recipient Sec. of Commerce award for disting. svc., Burton award for best law rev. writing in U.S., Tort Summit award, Am. Tort Reform Assn., 2002; named One of 100 Most Influential Attys. in U.S., Nat. Law 3, 1994, 97. Mem. ABA (chmn. products liability com. 1979, uniform laws com. 1981, torts and ins. practice sect.), Am. Law Inst. (life, adv. com. Restatement Third of Torts), Phi Beta Kappa. Insurance, Personal injury (including property damage). Office: Shook Hardy & Bacon LLP 600 14th St NW Ste 800 Washington DC 20005-2004

SCHWARTZ, WILLIAM, lawyer, educator; b. Providence, May 6, 1933; s. Morris Victor and Martha (Glassman) S.; m. Bernice Konigsberg, Jan. 13, 1957; children: Alan Gershon, Robin Libby. AA, Boston U., 1952, JD magna cum laude, 1955, MA, 1960; postgrad., Harvard Law Sch., 1955-56; LHD (hon.), Hebrew Coll., 1996, Yeshiva U., 1998. Bar: D.C. 1956, Mass. 1962, N.Y. 1989. Prof. law Boston U., 1955-91, Fletcher prof. law, 1968-70, Roscoe Pound prof. law, 1970-73, dean Sch. of Law, 1980-88, dir. Ctr. for Estate Planning, 1988-91; univ. prof. Yeshiva U., N.Y.C., 1991—; of counsel Swartz & Swartz, 1973-80; v.p. for acad. affairs, chief acad. officer Yeshiva U., N.Y.C., 1993-98; counsel Cadwalader, Wickersham and Taft, N.Y.C., Washington, Charlotte, London, 1988—; mem. faculty Frances Glessner Lee Inst., Harvard Med. Sch., Nat. Coll. Probate Judges, 1970, 77, 78, 79, 88; gen. dir. Assn. Trial Lawyers Am., 1968-73; reporter New Eng. Trial Judges Conf., 1965-67; participant Nat. Met. Cts. Conf., 1968; dir. Mass. Probate Study, 1976—; chmn. spl. com. on police procedures City of Boston, 1989, 91. Bd. dirs. UST Corp., chmn. of co., 1993-94, chmn. bd. dirs., 1996-2000; bd. dirs. Viacom Inc., Viacom Internat. Inc.; chmn. compensation com., mem. adv. com. WCI Steel, Inc.; mem. legal adv. bd. N.Y. Stock Exch. Author: Future Interests and Estate Planning, 1965, 77, 81, 86, Comparative Negligence, 1970, A Products Liability Primer, 1970, Civil Trial Practice Manual, 1972, New Vistas in Litigation, 1973, Massachusetts Pleading and Practice, 7 vols., 1974-80, Estate Planning and Living Trusts, 1990, The Convention Method: The Unused Amending Superhighway, 1995, Jewish Law and Contemporary Dilemmas and Problems, 1997, Does Time Heal All Wrongs?, 1999, Amending Irrevocable Trusts, 2003, others; note editor: Boston U. Law Rev., 1954-55; property editor: Annual Survey of Mass. Law, 1960—; contbr. articles to legal jours. Rep. Office of Pub. Info., UN, 1968—73; chmn. legal adv. panel Nat. Commn. Med. Practice, 1972—73; examiner of titles Commonwealth of Mass., 1964—; spl. counsel Mass. Bay Transp. Authority, 1979; pres. Fifth Ave. Synagogue, N.Y.C., 1997—2001, hon. pres., 2001—; bd. dirs. Kerry Found.; trustee Hebrew Coll., 1975—, Salve Regina U., Yeshiva U. Recipient Homer Albers award Boston U., 1955, John Ordronaux prize, 1955; Disting. Service award Religious Zionists Am., 1977; William W. Treat award; William O. Douglas award. Fellow Am. Coll. Probate Counsel; mem. ABA, Am. Law Inst., Mass. Bar Assn. (chmn. task force tort liability), N.Y. State Bar Assn., Assn. Bar City N.Y., Nat. Coll. Probate Judges (hon. mem.), Phi Beta Kappa. Office: 100 Maiden Ln New York NY 10038-4818

SCHWARTZEL, CHARLES BOONE, lawyer; b. Louisville, Jan. 4, 1950; s. Charles Joseph and Rosemary Jane (Redens) S.; m. Rose Marie Carlisi, June 20, 1980; children: Sally Ann, Charles Gerard. BA, Vanderbilt U., 1972; JD, U. Tex., 1975. Bar: Tex. 1975. Atty. Vinson & Elkins L.L.P., Houston, 1975-98, ptnr., 1983-98; pvt. practice Houston, 1998—. Contbr. articles to profl. jours. Councilman City of West University Place, Tex., 1985-89. Fellow Am. Coll. Trust and Estate Counsel; mem. Tex. Bar Assn. Roman Catholic. Estate planning, Probate (including wills, trusts), Estate taxation. Office: Attorney at Law 1010 Lamar St Ste 1520 Houston TX 77002-6315

SCHWARTZMAN, ANDREW JAY, lawyer; b. N.Y.C., Oct. 4, 1946; s. Joel Jay and Theresa (Greenhauff) S.; m. Linda Lazarus, June 8, 1986. AB, U. Pa., 1968, JD, 1971. Bar: N.Y. 1972, D.C. 1974, Temporary Emergency Ct. Appeals 1977, U.S. Dist. Ct. D.C. 1978, U.S. Ct. Appeals (D.C. cir.) 1981, U.S. Ct. Appeals (2d cir.) 1987, U.S. Ct. Appeals (4th, 7th, 8th, 9th cirs.) 1991, U.S. Supreme Ct. 1980. Staff counsel United Ch. of Christ Office of Comm., N.Y.C., 1971-74; atty. adviser Fed. Energy Office, Washington, 1974-77; sr. atty. adviser U.S. Dept. Energy, Washington, 1977-78; bd. dirs. Safe Energy Comms. Coun., pres. bd. dirs., 1989—2003; dir. Media Access Project, Washington, 1978-96, pres., CEO, 1996—. Mem. adv. panel Study on Comms. Systems for an Info. Age; mem. adv. bd. Ctr. for Democracy and Tech., 1996—; lectr. Fairleigh Dickinson U., 1972-73; instr. Johns Hopkins U., 2003—; mem. comms. coun. forum Aspen Inst. on Comms. and Soc., 1992—; bd. dirs. Min. Media and Telecomms. Coalition, 1994—; mem. adv. bd. Nat. Inst. Entertainment and Media Law, Southwestern U. Sch. Law, 2000—. Contbg. author: Les Brown's Dictionary of Television, 3d edit., Ency. of the Consumer Movement, 1997; contbr. articles to legal jours. Recipient Everett Parker award United Ch. of Christ, 1994. Mem. ABA, Fed. Comms. Bar Assn., U. Pa. Alumni Assn. Home: 3624 Military Rd NW Washington DC 20015-1724 Office: Media Access Project # 1118 1625 K St NW Washington DC 20006-1604

SCHWARZ, MICHAEL, lawyer; b. Brookline, Mass., Oct. 19, 1952; s. Jules Lewis and Estelle (Kosberg) S.; m. Rebecca Handy; 1 child, Patrick Joshua Charles. BA magna cum laude, U. No. Colo., 1975; postgrad., U. N.Mex., 1977, JD, 1980; reader in Negligence Law, Oxford U., 1978; diploma in Legal Studies, Cambridge U., 1981. Bar: N.Mex. 1980, U.S. Dist. Ct. N.Mex. 1980, U.S. Ct. Appeals (10th, D.C. and Fed. cirs.) 1982, U.S. Ct. Internat. Trade 1982, U.S. Tax Ct. 1982, N.Y. 1987, U.S. Supreme Ct. 1983; cert. U.S.A. hockey coach, advanced level. Vol. VISTA, Albuquerque, 1975-77; rsch. fellow N.Mex. Legal Support Project, Albuquerque, 1978-79; supr. law Cambridge (Eng.) U., 1980-81; law clk. to chief justice Supreme Ct. N.Mex., Santa Fe, 1981-82; pvt. practice Santa Fe, 1982—. Spl. pros. City of Santa Fe, 1985, spl. asst. atty. gen., 1986-88; mem. west editl. adv. com. Social Security Reporting Svc., 1983-95; mem. N.Mex. Supreme Ct. Com. Profl. Responsibility, 1990—, chmn., 1998—. Author: New Mexico Appellate Manual, 1990, 2d edit., 1996; contbr. articles to profl. jours. Vice-dir. Colo. Pub. Interest Rsch. Group, 1974; scoutmaster Great S.W. Area coun. Boy Scouts Am., 1977—79; mem. N.Mex. Acupuncture Lic. Bd., 1983; level 2 referee, head coach Squirt Gold Trailrunners; advanced coaching level USA Hockey. Recipient Cert. of Appreciation Cambridge U., 1981, Nathan Burke Meml. award, 1980, N.Mex. Supreme Ct. Cert. Recognition, 1992, 93, 95, N.Mex. Supreme Ct. Cert. Appreciation Outstanding Svc. to Legal Sys., 2001. Mem.: ATLA, ABA (10th cir. editor 1998, litigation com. on profl. responsibility, mem. Ctr. Profl. Responsibility, litigation com. on pretrial practice and discovery), Am. Law Inst., N.Mex. State Bar (chmn. 1990—91, bd. dirs. employment law sect. 1990—96, family law sect. bd. 1999—2001), Bar Assn. U.S. Dist. Ct. Dist. N.Mex. (1st judical dis. bar assoc. pres. 1990—91), Santa Fe Trailrunners Hockey Assn. (bd. dirs. 2001—02). Civil rights, Federal civil litigation, State civil litigation. Home and Office: PO Box 1656 Santa Fe NM 87504-1656 E-mail: barristr@nm.net.

SCHWARZER, WILLIAM W, federal judge; b. Berlin, Apr. 30, 1925; came to U.S., 1938, naturalized, 1944; s. John F. and Edith M. (Daniel) S.; m. Anne Halbersleben, Feb. 2, 1951; children: Jane Elizabeth, Andrew William. AB cum laude, U. So. Calif., 1948; LLB cum laude, Harvard U., 1951. Bar: Calif. 1953, U.S. Supreme Ct. 1967. Teaching fellow Harvard U. Law Sch., 1951-52; asso. firm McCutchen, Doyle, Brown & Enersen, San Francisco, 1952-60, ptnr., 1960-76; judge U.S. Dist. Ct (no. dist.) Calif., San Francisco, 1976—; dir. Fed. Jud. Ctr., Washington, 1990-95. Sr. counsel Pres.'s Commn. on CIA Activities Within the U.S., 1975; chmn. U.S. Jud. Conf. Com. Fed.-State Jurisdiction, 1987-90; mem. faculty Nat. Inst. Trial Advocacy, Fed. Jud. Ctr., All-ABA, U.S.-Can. Legal Exch., 1987, Anglo-U.S. Jud. Exch., 1994-95, Salzburg Seminar on Am. Studies; disting. prof. Hastings Coll. Law U. Calif. Author: Managing Antitrust and Other Complex Litigation, 1982, Civil Discovery and Mandatory Disclosure, 1994, Federal Civil Procedure Before Trial, 1994; contbr. articles to legal publs., aviation jours. Trustee World Affairs Coun. No. Calif., 1961-88; chmn. bd. trustees Marin Country Day Sch., 1963-66; mem. Marin County Aviation Commn., 1969-76; mem. vis. com. Harvard Law Sch., 1981-86. Served with Intelligence, U.S. Army, 1943-46. Fellow Am. Coll. Trial Lawyers (S. Gates award 1992), Am. Bar Found.; mem. ABA (Meador Rosenberg award 1995), Am. Law Inst., San Francisco Bar Assn., State Bar Calif., Coun. Fgn. Rels. Office: 450 Golden Gate Ave San Francisco CA 94102-3661

SCHWEIGERT, JACK, lawyer; b. July 26, 1947; s. Charles Arthur and Alma Mae S.; m. Valerie Bavero, 1981; children: Carly, Scott. BS in Econs., U. Gannon, 1969; JD, U. Akron, 1974. Bar: Hawaii 1975, U.S. Ct. Appeals (9th cir.) 1975, U.S. Supreme Ct. 1978. Pvt. practice, Honolulu, 1975—. With U.S. Army, 1969-71. Mem. Honolulu Lions Club (dist. 50 legal counsel, Melvin Jones award 1997-98). Civil rights, Criminal. Office: The Lawyers Bldg 550 Halekauwila St Ste 309 Honolulu HI 96813-5035 Fax: 808-533-7490. E-mail: conlawjack@cs.com.

SCHWEITZER, SANDRA LYNN, lawyer, nurse; b. San Jose, Calif., Nov. 16, 1952; d. Raymond Oliver and Joanne Rae (Gale) McLean; children: Brian, Laura, Christopher. BSN, Cornell U., 1974; JD, Georgetown U., 1979. Bar: Md. 1980, D.C. 1980, U.S. Dist. Ct. Md. 1980, U.S. Ct. Appeals (D.C., fed. and 4th cirs.) 1987, U.S. Supreme Ct. 1987, Calif. 1994, U.S. Dist. Ct. (no. dist.) Calif. 1994, U.S. Ct. Appeals (9th cir.) 1994; RN, Md., Calif.; cert. family law specialist. Assoc. Shulman, Rogers, Gandal et al, Silver Spring, Md., 1978-81; pvt. practice Potomac, Md., 1981-86; assoc. Miller & Chevalier, Washington, 1987; pvt. practice Bethesda, Md., 1988-89; ptnr. Johnston & Schweitzer, P.A., Washington, 1990-93; pvt. practice Bethesda, Md., 1993—94, Oakland, Calif., 1994—. Adj. prof. George Washington U. Med. Sch., 1988—. Mem. bus. and profl. women's coun. Nat. Mus. of Women in the Arts, 1991-94. Served to capt. U.S. Army Nurse Corps, 1974-76. Fellow Am. Acad. Matrimonial Lawyers; mem. ABA, D.C. Bar Assn., State Bar Assn. Calif, Md. State Bar Assn., Calif. Women Lawyers, Butte County Bar Assn., Nat. Assn. Counsel for Children, Assn. of Family and Conciliation Cts., Assn. Cert. Family Law Specialists, Sigma Theta Tau. Family and matrimonial. Office: Law Office Sandra L Schweitzer 2725 The Esplanade Chico CA 95973

SCHWELB, FRANK ERNEST, appellate judge; b. Prague, Czechoslovakia, June 24, 1932; came to U.S., 1947; s. Egon and Caroline (Redisch) S.; m. Taffy Wurzburg, Apr. 9, 1988. BA, Yale U., 1949-53; LLB, Harvard U., 1958. Bar: N.Y. Ct. Appeals 1958, U.S. Dist. Ct. (so. and ea. dists.) N.Y. 1960, U.S. Ct. Appeals (2d cir.) 1961, U.S. Supreme Ct. 1965, U.S. Ct.

Appeals (4th cir.) 1968, D.C., D.C. Ct. Appeals, U.S. Dist. Ct. D.C. 1972. Assoc. Mudge, Stern, Baldwin & Todd, N.Y.C., 1958-62; trial atty. Civil Rights Div. U.S. Dept. Justice, Washington, 1962-79, chief eastern sect., 1969, chief housing sect., 1969-79, spl. counsel for litigation, 1979; spl. counsel rev. panel on new drug regulation HEW, Washington, 1976-77; assoc. judge Superior Ct. D.C., Washington, 1979-88, D.C. Ct. Appeals, Washington, 1988—. Instr. various legal edn. activities. Contbr. articles to profl. jours. With U.S. Army, 1955-57. Recipient Younger Fed. Lawyer award, Fed. Bar Assn., 1967. Mem. Bar Assn. D.C., World Peace Through Law Ctr., World Assn. Judges, Czechoslovak-Am. Orgns., De Tocqueville Soc., Order of the Battered Boot. Avocations: tennis, table tennis, sports, gilbert and sullivan operettas, shakespeare. Home: 4879 Potomac Ave NW Washington DC 20007-1539 Office: DC Ct Appeals 500 Indiana Ave NW Washington DC 20001-2138 E-mail: fschwelb@dcca.state.dc.us.

SCHWENCKE, JUAN PABLO, lawyer; b. P. Varas, Chile, Apr. 28, 1970; s. Jorge Schwencke and Carmen Saint-Jean; m. Barbara Larrain, Jan. 3, 1998; 1 child, Tomas. Student, Colegio Aleman, Chile, 1976—87; JD, U. Chile, 1993; LLM, U. Columbia, 1997. Assoc. Barros, Court and Correa, Santiago, Chile, 1991—95, Cleary, Gottlieb, Steen and Hamilton, N.Y.C., 1997—98; ptnr. Barros, Court and Correa, Santiago, 2001—. Advisor Ministry of Fin., Santiago, 1997; dir. Red Television, Santiago, 2000—01; prof. U. Chile Sch. Law, Santiago, 1999—2000; dir. Cranberries Austral Chile, Santiago, 2001—. Co-author: Revista Derecho y Humanidades, 1995. Scholar hon. scholar, Pres. of the Republic, 1996. Mem.: Club de Polo y Equitecion Sou Cristobal, Internat. Bar Assn. Avocations: tennis, skiing, literature. Office: Barros Court and Correa 3d Fl Av Isidora Goyemechea # 3120 Santiago Chile

SCHWENKE, ROGER DEAN, lawyer; b. Washington, Oct. 18, 1944; s. Clarence Raymond and Virginia Ruth (Gould) S.; m. Carol Lynne Flenniken, Nov. 29, 1980; 1 child: Matthew Robert; stepchildren: Tracy L. Wolf Dickey, Mary M. Wolf. BA, Ohio State U., 1966; JD with honors, U. Fla., 1969. Bar: Fla. 1970. Instr. Coll. Law U. Fla., Gainesville, 1969-70; assoc. Carlton Fields, P.A., Tampa, Fla., 1970-74, ptnr., 1975—; adminstr., dept. head Real Estate, Environ. and Land Use Dept., 1978—99. Adj. prof. Coll. Law, Stetson U., St. Petersburg, Fla., 1979-80; mem. faculty U. Miami Coll. of Law Master of Law's in Real Estate Devel. Program, 1994-96. Author chpt. in Environmental Regulation and Litigation in Florida, 1987, chpt. in Florida Real Property Complex Transactions, 1997, 2000; contbr. articles to profl. jours., chpt. to book. Mem. diocesan coun. Episc. Diocese SW Fla., 1978-86, mem. standing com., 1989-92, chief judge Eccles. Ct., 1996—. Recipient Gertrude Brick Law Rev. prize U. Fla., 1969. Fellow Am. Coll. Real Estate Lawyers (bd. govs. 1985-88), Am. Law Inst.; mem. ABA (liaison to standing com. on environ. law 1980-87, liason to com. sect. on real property 1988-95), Fla. Bar Assn., Air & Waste Mgmt. Assn., Order of Coif, Greater Tampa C. of C. (chmn. environ. coun. 1980-81), Tampa Club. Democrat. Commercial, contracts (including sales of goods; commercial financing), Environmental, Property, real (including real estate development, water). Office: Carlton Fields PO Box 3239 Tampa FL 33601-3239 Fax: 813-229-4133. E-mail: rschwenke@carltonfields.com.

SCHWIETZKE, JOACHIM, law librarian; b. Berlin, Nov. 8, 1940; Abitur, Zeppelin-Gymnasium, Stuttgart, 1959; 1st Juristische Staatsprufung, U. Freiburg, 1965; 2nd Juristische Staatsprufung, Stuttgart, 1969. Assoc. law librarian Preussischer Kulturbesitz, Berlin, 1972—75; dep. law librarian Max Planck Inst., Heidelberg, 1975—80, law librarian, 1980—. Mem.: Internat. Assn. of Law Libraries (sec., bd. dirs. 1983—95). Office: Max Planck Inst Im Neuenheimer Feld 535 Heidelberg 69120 Germany

SCHWIND, WILLIAM F., JR., lawyer, oil industry executive; b. Chgo., 1944; BS, JD, Loyola U., Chgo. Bar: Tex. 1969. With Marathon Oil Corp., Findlay, Ohio, 1974—83, gen. atty. Houston, 1984—91, gen. counsel, sec., 1992—; comml. contract mgr. Jakarta, Indonesia, 1983—84; sr. v.p. adminstrn., gen. counsel, sec. Dehli Gas Pipeline Corp., Dallas, 1991—92. Mem.: ABA, Am. Petroleum Inst. (chmn. gen. com. law), Am. Corp. Counsel Assn. Office: Marathon Oil Co PO Box 4813 5555 San Felipe Rd Houston TX 77210-4813 Office Fax: 713-296-2581.*

SCIOCCHETTI, NANCY, lawyer; b. Schenectady, N.Y., May 20, 1962; d. Andrew Sr. and Lina (DeLeonardis) S.; m. Scott K. Townsend, Dec. 8, 1990 (div. Nov. 1997); 1 child, Emma. BA cum laude, Siena Coll., 1983; JD, Union U., 1986. Bar: N.Y. 1987, U.S. Dist. Ct. (no. dist.) N.Y. 1987. Assoc. Sherrin & Glasel LLP, Albany, N.Y., 1987-91, ptnr., 1991-99, O'Connell & Aronowitz, PC, Albany, N.Y., 1999—. Trustee The Brown Sch., 1999—. Recipient Disting. Svc. award Legal Aid Soc. Northeastern N.Y., 1992. Mem. Jr. League of Albany (grants chair 1998-99, parliamentarian 1999-2000), Italian Am. Bar Assn. (bd. dirs. 1998—). Avocations: travel, reading, entertaining. Health. Office: O'Connell & Aronowitz PC 54 State St Albany NY 12207-1897

SCIPIONE, RICHARD STEPHEN, insurance company executive, lawyer, retired; b. Newton, Mass., Aug. 27, 1937; BA, Harvard U., 1959; LLB, Boston U., 1962. Bar: Mass. 1962. Atty. John Hancock Mut. Life Ins. Co., Boston, 1965-69, asst. counsel, 1969-74, assoc. counsel, 1975-79, sr. assoc. counsel, 1980-82, 2d v.p., counsel, 1982-84, v.p. gen. solicitor, 1984-85, sr. v.p. and gen. solicitor, 1986-87, gen. counsel, 1987-2000, ret., 2000. Bd. dirs. New England Legal Found., John Hancock Advisers/Distbrs. Capt. U.S. Army, 1962-65. Mem. ABA (dir. New Eng. coun.), Assn. Life Ins. Counsel (gov. 1994-98), Chatham Yacht Club, South Shore Country Club.*

SCIRICA, ANTHONY JOSEPH, federal judge; b. Norristown, Pa., Dec. 16, 1940; s. A. Benjamin and Anna (Sclafani) Scirica; m. Susan Morgan, May 6, 1966; children: Benjamin, Sarah. BA, Wesleyan U., 1962; JD, U. Mich., 1965; postgrad. Fulbright Scholar, Central U., Caracas, Venezuela, 1966. Bar: Pa. 1966, U.S. Dist. Ct. (ea. dist.) Pa. 1984, U.S. Ct. Appeals (3d cir.) 1987. Ptnr. McGrory, Scirica, Wentz & Fernandez, Norristown, Pa., 1966—80; asst. dist. atty. Montgomery County, Pa., 1967—69; mem. Pa. Ho. of Reps, Harrisburg, 1971—79; judge Montgomery County Ct. Common Pleas, Pa., 1980—84, U.S. Dist. Ct. (ea. dist.) Pa., Phila., 1984—87, U.S. Ct. Appeals (3d cir.), 1987—. Chmn. Pa. Sentencing Commn., 1980—85. Scholar Fulbright scholar, Ctrl. U., Caracas, Venezuela, 1966. Mem.: ABA, Montgomery Bar Assn., Pa. Bar Assn. Roman Catholic. Office: James A Byrne Courthouse 601 Market St Rm 2100 Philadelphia PA 19106-1715

SCISM, DANIEL REED, lawyer; b. Evansville, Ind., Aug. 27, 1936; s. Daniel William and Ardath Josephine (Gibbs) S.; m. Paula Anne Sedgwick, June 21, 1958; children: Darby Claire, Joshua Reed. BA, DePauw U., 1958; JD, Ind. U., 1965. Bar: Ind. 1965, U.S. Dist. Ct. (so. dist.) Ind. 1965, U.S. Ct. Appeals (7th cir.) 1967, U.S. Supreme Ct. 1976. Reporter Dayton (Ohio) Jour.-Herald, 1958-59; editor Mead Johnson & Co., Evansville, 1961; first assoc., then ptnr. Roberts, Ryder, Rogers & Scism and predecessor firms, Indpls., 1965—86; ptnr. Barnes & Thornburg, Indpls., 1987—. Cons. Ind. Pers. Assn., 1984-2002. Treas. Marion County chpt. Myasthenia Gravis Found., Indpls., 1970; v.p. Marion County Mental Health Assn., Indpls., 1970-71; pres. The Suemma Coleman Agy., Indpls., 1973-74; bd. dirs. Ind. Humanities Coun., 1995-2000, chmn. bd., 1997-98; trustee Indpls. Mus. Art, 2001—; bd. dirs. Westminster Village North, Inc., 2003—; pres. Persimmon Woods Homeowners Assn., 2001—. With U.S. Army, 1959—62. Edwards fellow Ind. U., 1964. Mem. ABA, Ind. Bar Assn., Indpls. Bar Assn., Ind. State C. of C. (social legis. com. 1970-80). Clubs: Indpls. Athletic; Woodland Country (bd. dirs. 1984-88, sec. 1998-99) (Carmel, Ind.). Methodist. Labor (including EEOC, Fair Labor Standards Act, labor-management relations, NLRB, OSHA). Home: 10909 300 Yard Dr Fishers IN 46038-9306 Office: Barnes & Thornburg 11 S Meridian St Indianapolis IN 46204-3535

SCOFIELD, DAVID WILLSON, lawyer; b. Hartford, Conn., Oct. 17, 1957; s. Leslie Willson and Daphne Winifred (York) S. AB, Cornell U., 1979; JD, U. Utah, 1983. Bar: Utah 1983, U.S. Dist. Ct. Utah 1983, U.S. Dist. Ct. Ariz. 1993, U.S. Dist. Ct. Hawaii 1995, U.S. Ct. Appeals (10th cir.) 1990, U.S. Ct. Appeals (9th cir.) 1995, U.S. Supreme Ct. 1996, U.S. Ct. Claims, 1997. Assoc. Parsons & Crowther, Salt Lake City, 1983-87, Callister, Duncan & Nebeker, Salt Lake City, 1987-89, ptnr., 1989-92; founding ptnr. Parsons Kinghorn Peters, A Professional Corporation (formerly Parsons, Davies, Kinghorn & Peters), Salt Lake City, 1992—, pres., 1996-97. Mem. adv. com. on Utah rules of civil procedure Utah Supreme Ct., 2002—. Author: Trial Handbook for Utah Lawyers, 1994; mem. Utah Law Rev., 1981-83; contbr. articles to legal jours. Bd. dirs. Westminster Coll. Found., 1994-96, chmn. cultivation com., 1995-96. Named to Outstanding Young Men of Am., 1986. Mem. ABA, Assn. Trial Lawyers Am., Utah Trial Lawyers Assn., Salt Lake County Bar Assn., Zeta Psi. Congregationalist. Avocations: american history, writing, sports. Federal civil litigation, General civil litigation, General practice. Home: 2331 Scenic Dr Salt Lake City UT 84109-1432 Office: Parsons Davies Kinghorn & Peters 111 East Broadway 11th FL Salt Lake City UT 84111-5225 E-mail: dws@pdkplaw.com.

SCOFIELD, LOUIS M., JR., lawyer; b. Brownsville, Tex., Jan. 14, 1952; s. Louis M. and Betsy Lee (Aiken) S.; children: Christopher, Nicholas, Emma. BS in Geology with highest honors and high distinction, U. Mich., 1974; JD with honors, U. Tex., 1977. Bar: Tex. 1977, U.S. Dist. Ct. (ea. and so. dists.) Tex., U.S. Ct. Appeals (5th cir.) 1981, U.S. Supreme Ct. 1984. Ptnr. Mehaffy & Weber, Beaumont, Tex., 1982—. Spkr. CNA Ins., Dallas, Jefferson County Ins. Adjusters, S.E. Tex. Ind. Ins. Agts., Gulf Ins. Co., Dallas, Employers Casualty Co., Beaumont, Tex. Employment Commn., Jefferson County Young Lawyers Assn., Jefferson County Bar Assn., South Tex. Coll. of Law, John Gray Inst., Lamar U., 1991, Tex. Assn. Def. Counsel, 1991; cert. arbitrator Nat. Panel of Consumer Arbitrators; arbitrator BBB; presenter Forest Park H.S., Martin Elem. Sch., St. Anne's Sch. Contbr. columns in newspapers, articles to profl. jours. Patron Beaumont Heritage Soc., John J. French Mus.; bd. dirs. Beaumont Heritage Soc., 1983-84, mem. endowment fund com., 1988; chmn. lawyers divsn. United Appeals Campaign, 1984; grand patron Jr. League of Beaumont, 1989, 90. Fellow: State Bar of Tex. (mentors com. 1995), Tex. Bar Found. (life); mem.: ABA (contbg. editor newsletter products, vice chmn.gen liability and consumer laws com.), Jefferson County Bar Assn. (disaster relief project 1979, outstanding young lawyer's com. 1980), Def. Rsch. Inst., Tex. Assn. Defense Counsel (dir. at large 1986—87, v.p. 1987—89, program chmn. San Diego 1989, adminstrv. v.p. 1989—90), Assn. Defense Trial Attys. (exec. coun. 1999—2002, chmn. Ctrl. U.S. region 2000—02, chmn. Tex. membership com.), Beaumont County Country Club, Phi Beta Kappa. Democrat. Episcopalian. Avocations: golf, reading, fishing. General civil litigation, Insurance, Personal injury (including property damage). Home: 4790 Littlefield St Beaumont TX 77706-7748 Office: Mehaffy & Weber PO Box 16 Beaumont TX 77704-0016

SCOGLAND, WILLIAM LEE, lawyer; b. Moline, Ill., Apr. 2, 1949; s. Maurice William and Harriet Rebecca S.; m. Victoria Lynn Whitham, Oct. 9, 1976; 1 child, Thomas. BA magna cum laude, Augustana Coll., 1971; JD cum laude, Harvard U., 1975. Bar: Ill. 1975, U.S. Dist. Ct. (no. dist.) Ill. 1975. Assoc. Wildman, Harrold, Allen & Dixon, Chgo., 1975-77, Hughes Hubbard & Reed, Milw., 1977-81; from assoc. to ptnr. Jenner & Block, Chgo., 1981—. Lectr. in law U. Chgo. Law Sch., 2000—. Author: Fiduciary Duty: What Does It Mean?, 1989; co-author Employee Benefits Law, 1987; contr. Tort and Ins. Law Jour., 1989, and others. Mem. Phi Beta Kappa, Omicron Delta Kappa. Republican. Mergers and acquisitions, Pension, profit-sharing, and employee benefits. Office: Jenner & Block One IBM Plz Fl 4000 Chicago IL 60611-7603

SCORSINE, JOHN MAGNUS, lawyer; b. Rochester, N.Y., Dec. 3, 1957; s. Frank and Karin (Frennby) S.; m. Susan Nauss, May 31, 1980 (div.); m. Theresa A. Burke, Dec. 17, 1988; 1 child, Jennifer E. BS, Rochester Inst. Tech., 1980; JD, U. Wyo., 1984. Bar: Wyo. 1984, U.S. Dist. Ct. Wyo. 1984, U.S. Ct. Appeals (10th cir.) 1989, U.S. Army Ct. Criminal Appeals 1995; qualified mil. trial judge 2003. Part-time deputy sheriff Monroe County (N.Y.), 1978-80; police officer Casper (Wyo.) Police Dept., 1980-81; intern U.S. Atty. Office, Cheyenne, Wyo., 1983-84; pvt. practice Rock Springs, Wyo., 1984-85; ptnr. Scorsine and Flynn, Rock Springs, 1986; prin. Scorsine Law Office, Rock Springs, 1986-95; commr. Dist. and County Court, 1986-95; dep. chief of staff for mil. support Wyo. Nat. Guard, 1995—. Ptnr. Sunset Advt., 1987-89; chmn. bd. dirs. Youth Home Inc., Rock Springs, 1987-88; treas. Sweetwater County Cmty. Corrections Bd., 1990-95; mem. Nat. Ski Patrol, 1976-97, Wyo. Bd. of Parole, 1998—. Leader Medicine Bow Ski Patrol, Laramie, Wyo., 1983; legal advisor Rocky Mountain divsn. Nat. Ski Patrol, 1984; asst. patrol leader White Pine Ski Area, Pinedale, Wyo., 1986; avalanche advisor Jackson Hole Snow King Ski Patrol, 1987—96; avalanche instr., 1993—96; sect. chief Teton sect. Nat. Ski Patrol, 1991—94; mem. Eldore Ski Patrol, 1996—97, Sweetwater County Search and Rescue, 1989—95, tng. officer, 1993—95; mem. Sweetwater County Emergency Dive Team, 1990—95, Sweetwater County Fire Dept., 1992—94, Reliance Vol. Fire Dept., 1994—95; lt.k, tng. officer Laramie Cmty. Fire Dist. #6 and Burns Ambulance Svc., 1995—98, treas., sec., bd. dirs., 1997—98; mem. Am. N. Peary Land expdn., 1989; scoutmaster Boy Scouts Am., 1987—93, 1996—98; 4H leader, 1997—; pres. Sweetwater County Vol. Fire Assn., 1993—94; mem. Laramie County Sch. Dist. #2 accreditation panel, 1998—2000; dir. emergency svcs. Wyo. Civil Air Patrol, 1998—; comdr. Wyo. wing, 1999—2002; bd. dirs., sec. Burns Cmty. Ambulance, 1997—99; bd. dirs. Liberation Prison Project, 2003—. Lt. col. JAG USAR, 1991—. Recipient Yellow Merit star Nat. Ski Patrol, 1993, Fritch Volunteerism award, 1993, Armed Forces Outstanding Vol. Svc. medal, Gibb Wilson award CAP, 2002. Mem. ABA, Wyo. State Bar, Wyo. Trial Lawyers Assn., Assn. Am. Trial Lawyers, Rock Springs C. of C., Res. Officers Assn. (nat. councilman 1993-2000, state pres. 1994), Rotary. Democrat. Buddhist. Avocations: rock climbing, backpacking, hunting, scuba, Karate. Appellate, Criminal, General practice. Office: Wyo Nat Guard 5500 Bishop Blvd Cheyenne WY 82009-3320 E-mail: john.scorsine@wy.ngb.army.mil.

SCOTT, A. TIMOTHY, lawyer, business executive; b. Natchez, Miss., Feb. 16, 1952; s. John William and Patricia (O'Reilly) S.; m. Nancy E. Howard, June 7, 1976; children: Kevin Howard, Brian Howard. BA in Psychology, Stanford U., 1974, JD, 1977. Bar: Calif. 1977, U.S. Tax Ct. 1978. Assoc. then ptnr. Agnew, Miller & Carlson, L.A., 1977-83; assoc. Greenberg, Glusker, Fields, Claman & Machtinger, L.A., 1983; ptnr. Sachs & Phelps, L.A., 1983-91; mem. Heller, Ehrman White & McAuliffe, L.A., 1991-96, of counsel, 1996-99; sr. v.p., tax counsel Pub. Storage, Inc., Glendale, Calif., 1996—. Speaker in field. Note editor Stanford Law Rev., 1976-77; contbr. article to profl. publs., chpt. to book. Mem. ABA, L.A. County Bar Assn. (chmn. real estate taxation com. 1988-91, exec. com., taxation sect. 1989-91), Order of Coif. Democrat. Avocations: volleyball, gardening, Calif. wine, contemporary art, skiing. Property, real (including real estate development, water), Taxation, general, Personal income taxation. Office: Pub Storage Inc 701 Western Ave Glendale CA 91201-2349 E-mail: tscott@publicstorage.com.

SCOTT, BEVERLY J. lawyer, consultant; b. Denver, Wyo., Oct. 28, 1941; d. Charles Grant Wilson and Lyla Amelia Mattila; m. Richard Walter Scott, Sept. 9, 1961; children: Suzanne Elaine, Kevin Richard. BS, U. Wyo., 1979, JD, 1997. Bar: Wyo. 1997, U.S. Dist. Ct. Wyo. 1997. Ptnr. James and Scott, P.C., Riverton, Wyo., 1998—. Avocations: hiking, reading. Family and matrimonial, Estate planning, Bankruptcy. Office: James and Scott PC 105 S 6th E Riverton WY 82501 Office Fax: 307-856-8501. Business E-Mail: bescott@wyoming.com.

SCOTT, BRIAN DAVID, lawyer; b. Spokane, Wash., Sept. 30, 1946; s. Dick E. and Helene L. (Johnson) S.; m. Lynita G. Muzzall, Sept. 9, 1972; children: D. Alexander, Rachel E., S. Andrew. BA, U. Wash., 1968; JD, U. Wis., 1972. Bar: Wis. 1972, Wash. 1972, U.S. Dist. Ct. (we. dist.) Wash. 1972, U.S. Dist. Ct. (we. dist.) Wis. 1972. Asst. atty. gen. Wash. State Atty. Gen.'s Office, Seattle, 1972-74; assoc. Jackson, Ulvestad, Goodwin, Grutz, Seattle, 1974-81; ptnr. Goodwin, Grutz & Scott, Seattle, 1981-96, Grutz, Scott & Kinney, Seattle, 1996-99, Grutz, Scott, Kinney & Fjelstad, Seattle, 1999—. Mem. ATLA, Wash. Trial Lawyers Assn., Wash. Athletic Club. Democrat. Avocations: boating, skiing, travel. Personal injury (including property damage), Product liability, Workers' compensation. Home: 158 Prospect St Seattle WA 98109-3750 Office: Grutz Scott Kinney & Fjelstad 600 University St Ste 1928 Seattle WA 98101-4178 E-mail: scott@gskf-law.com.

SCOTT, DAVID RODICK, lawyer, legal educator; b. Phila., Dec. 30, 1938; s. Ernest and Lydia Wister (tunis) S.; m. Ruth Erskine Wardle, Aug. 20, 1966; children: Cintra W., D. Rodman. AB magna cum laude, Harvard U., 1960, JD, 1965; MA, Cambridge U., 1962. Bar: Pa. 1966, D.C. 1977, U.S. Dist. Ct. (ea. dist.) Pa. 1966, U.S. Ct. Appeals (3rd cir.) 1966, U.S. Ct. Appeals (D.C. cir.) 1977, U.S. Supreme Ct. 1977. Law clk. to assoc. justice Supreme Ct. Pa., Phila., 1965-66; assoc. Pepper, Hamilton & Scheetz, Phila., 1966-69, 72-76; asst. dist. atty. City of Phila., 1970-72; sr. trial atty. criminal divsn. U.S. Dept. Justice, Washington, 1976-80; chief counsel, acting dir. Office Govt. Ethics, Washington, 1980-84; univ. counsel Rutgers U., New Brunswick, N.J., 1984—. Acting dir. U.S. Office Govt. Ethics, 1982-83; tchr., lectr. in law Cath. U. Am., Washington, 1977-81, Inst. Paralegal Tng., Phila., 1970-74; instr. faculty of arts and scis. Rutgers U.; lectr. in field. Contbr. chpts. to textbooks, articles to profl. jours. Trustee United Way Greater Mercer County, 1990—, Princeton Area Cmty. Found., Inc., 1991-2002; bd. mgrs. Episc. Acad., Merion, Pa., 1970-74. Keasbey Found. fellow, 1960-62. Mem ABA, Pa. Bar Assn., Nat. Assn. Coll. and Univ. Attys. (bd. dirs. 1993-96), Am. Friends Cambridge U. (head N.J. chpt. 1987-93). Corporate, general, Education and schools. Home: 255 Russell Rd Princeton NJ 08540-6733 Office: Rutgers U Office of Univ Counsel Winants Hall New Brunswick NJ 08901 E-mail: scott@oldqueens.rutgers.edu.

SCOTT, DAVID W. legal association administrator; b. Ottawa, Ont., Can., Jan. 27, 1936; BA, U. Montreal, Can., 1957; LLB, U. Ottawa, 1960, D (hon.). Bar: Ont. 1962. Fellow Am. Coll. Trial Lawyers, Ottawa, 1983, Ont. provincial chair, 1993—94, regent, 1996—2000, sec., 2000—02, pres.-elect, 2002—. Instr. U. Ottawa, 1974—82; Milvain chair advocacy U. Calgary (Can.) Law Sch., 1988; mem. Ottawa Gen. Litig. Profl. Group. Chair Triennial Rev. Commn., Canada, 1996; rep. of chief justice Ont.'s Com. Bench and Bar; bd. govs. Carleton U. Recipient medal, Advs. Soc., 1999. Fellow: Patent and Trademark Inst. Can.; mem.: Law Soc. Upper Can. (instr. 1976—88, bencher 1991, 1995, hon. doctorate). Office: Am Coll Trial Lawyers World Exch Plz 100 Queen St Ste 1100 Ottawa ON Canada K1P 1J9 Office Fax: 613-230-8842.*

SCOTT, G. JUDSON, JR., lawyer; b. Phila., Nov. 16, 1945; s. Gerald Judson and Jean Louise S.; m. Ildiko Kalman, Mar. 21, 1971; children: Nathan Emory, Lauren Jean. AA, Foothill Jr. Coll., Los Altos, Calif., 1965; BA, U. Calif., Santa Barbara, 1968; JD cum laude, U. Santa Clara, 1975. Bar: Calif. 1975, U.S. Dist. Ct. (no. dist.) Calif. 1975, U.S. Ct. Appeals (9th cir.) 1975, U.S. Supreme Ct. 1981. Assoc. Feldman, Waldman & Kline, San Francisco, 1975-76, Law Offices John Wynne Herron, San Francisco, 1976-80; of counsel firm Haines & Walker, Livermore, Calif., 1980; ptnr. Haines Walker & Scott, Livermore, 1980-84; officer, dir., shareholder firm Smith, Etnire, Polson and Scott, Pleasanton, Calif., 1984-88; pvt. practice, 1988—. Judge pro tem Livermore-Pleasanton Mcpl. Ct., 1981-83; settlement commr. Alameda County Superior Ct., 1994—, judge pro tem, 2001—; lectr. Calif. Continuing Edn. of Bar. Contbg. author: Attorney's Guide to Restitution, 1976; editor: The Bottom Line, 1989-91. Pres. Walnut Creek Open Space Found., Calif., 1981-83. Rear adm. USNR, 1968-2001. Fellow Am. Bar Found.; mem. ATLA (sustaining), Consumer Attys. Calif. (reviewer of pending Calif. legis.), The Coll. Master Advocates and Barristers (sr. counsel), Ea. Alameda County Bar Assn. (v.p. 1981-82), Calif. State Bar (mem. standing com. on lawyer referral svcs. 1985-88, mem. exec. com. law practice mgmt. sec. 1988-93, chair 1992-93), Alameda County Bar Assn. (chmn. law office econs. com. 1986-87, mem. jud. nomination evaluation com. 1996-97, chair task force 1997, bd. dirs. 1997-98, v.p. 1999, pres.-elect 2000, pres. 2001), Alameda-Contra Costa County Trial Lawyers Assn., Livermore C. of C. (past chmn. growth study 1983), Pleasanton C. of C., Million Dollar Advs. Forum. Republican. Episcopalian. General civil litigation, Insurance, Personal injury (including property damage). Office: 6140 Stoneridge Mall Rd Ste 125 Pleasanton CA 94588-3233

SCOTT, JOHN ROLAND, business law educator; b. Wichita Falls, Tex, May 13, 1937; s. John and Margaret S.; m. Joan Carol Redding, Sept. 5, 1959; 1 child, John Howard. LLB, Baylor Sch. Law, Waco, Tex., 1962. Bar: Tex. 1962, Alaska 1970, Tex., 1965, U.S. Dist. Ct. (we. dist.), U.S. Dist. Ct. Alaska 1975. Assoc. litigation sect. Lynch & Chappell, Midland, Tex., 1962-65; regional atty. Atlantic Richfield Co., Midland, 1965-79; sr. atty. Anchorage, 1969-77, Dallas, 1977-80; v.p., assoc. gen. counsel Mitchell Energy & Devel. Corp., Houston, 1980-82; asst. gen. counsel Hunt Oil Co., Dallas, 1982-84, v.p., chief counsel, 1984-91, sr. v.p. gen. counsel, 1994-2001; adj. prof. bus. law Dallas Bapt. U., Dallas, 2001—. Bar examiner in Alaska, 1974-77 Mem. State Bar Tex. (lectr.), Dallas Bar Assn., ABA, Phi Alpha Delta. Republican. Office: 3801 Hanover Ave Dallas TX 75225-7117 E-mail: joroscl3@aol.com.

SCOTT, JOHN EDWARD SMITH, lawyer; b. St. Louis, Aug. 6, 1936; s. Gordon Hatler and Luella Margarite (Smith) S.; m. Beverly Joan Phillips, Dec. 17, 1960; 1 dau., Pamela Anne. AB, Albion Coll., 1958; JD, Wayne State U., 1961. Bar: Mich. 1961, U.S. Dist. Ct. (ea. dist.) Mich. 1962, U.S. Dist. Ct. (we. dist.) Mich. 1970, U.S. Tax. Ct. 1979, U.S. Ct. Appeals (6th cir.) 1964, U.S. Supreme Ct. 1966. Law clk. Supreme Ct. Mich., Lansing, 1961-62; assoc. Dickinson, Wright, Moon, Van Dusen & Freeman, Detroit, 1962-69, ptnr., 1970—. Adj. prof. U. Detroit Law Sch., 1967-71. Supreme Ct. appointee State Bar Rep. Assembly, Detroit, 1972-77; mayor City of Pleasant Ridge, Mich., 1973-81; commr. Mich. Appellate Defender Commn., Detroit, 1979—, chmn., 1992—; hearing referee Mich. Civil Rights Commn., Detroit, 1974-80; chmn. Detroit Legal Aid & Defender Commn., 1972-77; chmn. case flow mgmt. com. Mich. Supreme Ct., 1989-90. Fellow Am. Coll. Trial Lawyers, Internat. Soc. Barristers, Internat. Acad. Trial Lawyers; mem. ABA (chmn. trial evidence com. sect. litigation 1988-91), Am. Bar Found., Mich. Bar Found., Detroit Golf Club, Order of Coif (hon.). Office: Dickinson Wright PLLC 500 Woodward Ave Ste 4000 Detroit MI 48226-3416

SCOTT, JOHN JOSEPH, lawyer; b. Chgo., Dec. 30, 1950; s. John Joseph and Alice (Pierzhala) S.; m. Maria Crawford, Aug. 17, 1974. BA, Yale U., 1972; JD, U. Chgo., 1975. Bar: Ill. 1975, U.S. Dist. Ct. (no. dist.) Ill. 1976. Assoc. Kirkland & Ellis, Chgo., 1975-82, ptnr., 1982-91; asst. gen. counsel CF Industries, Inc., Long Grove, Ill., 1991—. Mem. ABA, Chgo. Bar Assn.,

Am. Soc. Corp. Secs., Order of Coif. Roman Catholic. Avocations: reading, swimming, bike riding, playing tennis. Corporate, general, Finance, Securities. Office: CF Industries Inc One Salem Lake Dr Lake Zurich IL 60047-8401

SCOTT, KATHRYN FENDERSON, lawyer; b. Augusta, Ga., June 6, 1970; d. Robert Thomas Fenderson and Christine (Cunningham) Cormier; m. Charles Dean Scott. BA, Eckerd Coll., St. Petersburg, Fla., 1992; JD, Stetson U., St. Petersburg, 1995. Bar: Fla. 1995, U.S. Dist. Ct. (mid. dist.) Fla. 1995, U.S. Ct. Appeals (11th cir.) 1997. Assoc. Govan, Burns & Jones, St. Petersburg, 1995-97; ptnr. Scott & Fenderson, St. Petersburg, 1997—. Editl. bd. Paraclete, St. Petersburg Bar Assn., 1996-99; mentor program Stetson U. Coll. Law, St. Petersburg, 1996—. Recipient Am. Jurisprudence award Lawyer's Coop. Pub., 1992. Mem. ABA, Assn. Trial Lawyers Am., Assn. Fla. Trial Lawyers, St. Petersburg Bar Assn., Clearwater Bar Assn. Personal injury (including property damage). Office: Scott and Fenderson 4755 Central Ave Saint Petersburg FL 33713 Fax: 727-321-4499. E-mail: fenderlaw@aol.com.

SCOTT, MCGREGOR W. lawyer; b. 1962; married; 2 children. BA History, Santa Clara Univ.; JD, Hastings Coll. of Law, Univ. of Calif. Dep. dist. atty. Contra Costa County, 1989—97; Dist. atty. Shasta County, 1997—2003; interim pending State Confirm. Dist. of Calif., 2003; US Atty. for Ea. Calif. nomination by Pres. Bush, 2003—. Office: Sacramento Fed Cthse 501 1 St Ste 10-100 Sacramento CA 95814*

SCOTT, MICHAEL DENNIS, lawyer; b. Mpls., Nov. 6, 1945; s. Frank Walton and Donna Julia (Howard) S.; m. Blanca Josefina Palacios, Dec. 12, 1981; children: Michael Dennis, Cindal Marie, Derek Walton. BS, MIT, 1967; JD, UCLA, 1974. Bar: Calif. 1974, U.S. Dist. Ct. (no., so. and cen. dists.) Calif. 1974, U.S. Patent Office 1974, U.S. Ct. Appeals (9th cir.) 1974, U.S. Supreme Ct. 1978, U.S. Ct. Appeals (fed. cir.) 1989. Systems programmer NASA Electronics Research Lab., Cambridge, Mass., 1967-69, Computer Sciences Corp., El Segundo, Calif., 1969-71, Univac, Valencia, Calif., 1971; from assoc. to ptnr. Smaltz & Neelley, Los Angeles, 1974-81; exec. dir. Ctr. for Computer/Law, Los Angeles, 1977-94; pvt. practice Los Angeles, 1981-86, 88-89; pres. Law and Tech. Press, 1981-94; ptnr. Scott & Roxborough, Los Angeles, 1986-88, Graham & James, 1989-93; v.p., gen. counsel Sanctuary Woods Multimedia, Inc., San Mateo, Calif., 1993-94; of counsel Steinhart & Falconer, San Francisco, 1995-97; ptnr. Hosie Wes Sacks & Brelsford, Menlo Park, Calif., 1997-98, Perkins Coie LLP, 1998—2003. Adj. assoc. prof. law Southwestern U., L.A., 1975-80, 2001-03, prof. 2003—, Loyola U., L.A., 1997-99, 2002--, Pepperdine U., L.A., 2001—; chmn. World Computer Law Congress, L.A., 1991, 93. Author: (with David S. Yen) Computer Law Bibliography, 1979, The Scott Report, 1981-86, Computer Law, 1984, Scott on Computer Law, 1991, Multimedia: Law and Practice, 1993, Scott on Multimedia Law, 1996, (with Warren S. Reid) Year 2000 Computer Crisis: Law Business Technology, 1998, Internet and Technology Law Desk Reference, 1999—, Intellectual Property and Licensing Law Desk Reference, 2001—, Telecommunications Law Desk Reference, 2003—; editor in chief: Computer/Law Jour., 1978-94, Software Protection, 1982-92, Software Law Jour., 1985-94, Internat. Computer Law Adviser, 1986-92, Cyberspace Lawyer, 1996—, E-Commerce Law Report, 1998—. Mem. Computer Law Assn. (bd. dirs. 1994-99), Calif. State Bar Assn. Computer, Private international, Trademark and copyright. Office: 1620 26th St Santa Monica CA 90404-4013

SCOTT, ROBERT EDWIN, dean, law educator; b. Nagpur, India, Feb. 25, 1944; came to U.S., 1955; s. Roland Waldeck and Carol (Culver) S.; m. Elizabeth (Loch) Shumaker, Aug. 14, 1965; children: Christina Elaine, Robert Adam. BA, Oberlin (Ohio) Coll., 1965; JD, Coll. of William and Mary, 1968; LLM, U. Mich., 1969, SJD, 1973. Bar: Va. 1968. From asst. to prof. Law Sch. Coll. of William and Mary, Williamsburg, Va., 1969-74; prof. law Sch. of Law U. Va., Charlottesville, 1974-82, Lewis F. Powell, Jr. prof. Sch. of Law, 1982—2003, dean and Arnold H. Leon prof., 1991—2001; Justin W. D'Atri Prof. Law, Bus. & Soc. Columbia Law Sch., 2001—02; David & Mary Harrison Dist. Prof. U. Va., Charlottesville, Va., 2003—. Author: Commercial Transactions, 1982, 91, Sales Law and the Contracting Process, 1982, 91, Contract Law and Theory, 1988, 93, Payment Systems and Credit Instruments, 1996. Fellow Am. Bar Found., Am. Acad. Arts and Scis.; mem. Va. Bar. Democrat. Methodist. Home: 1109 Hilltop Rd Charlottesville VA 22903-1220 Office: U Va Rm WB179e Sch of Law Charlottesville VA 22903 Personal E-mail: res8f@virginia.edu.*

SCOTT, ROBERT GENE, lawyer; b. Montague, Mass., Aug. 29, 1951; s. Edwin Ray and Barbara Agnes (Painchaud) S.; m. Laura Beth Williams, May 27, 1978; children: Jason Robert, Amanda Marie, Leah Beth. BS, U. Notre Dame, 1973, MS, 1975; postgrad., U. Tex., 1975-76; JD, U. Notre Dame, 1980. Bar: Ind. 1980, U.S. Dist. Ct. (no. dist.) Ind. 1980, U.S. Patent Office 1980, Mo. 1981, U.S. Dist. Ct. (we. dist.) Mo. 1981, U.S. Ct. Appeals (11th cir.) 1986, U.S. Ct. Appeals (8th cir.) 1987, U.S. Ct. Appeals (10th cir.) 1987, Kans. 1989, U.S. Dist. Ct. Kans. 1989, U.S. Supreme Ct. 1999. Asst. women's basketball coach U. Notre Dame, Ind., 1977-80; assoc. atty. Oltsch, Knoblock & Hall, South Bend, Ind., 1980-81; atty. Swanson, Midgley et al, Kansas City, Mo., 1981-82; exec. adminstr. Coun. of Fleet Specialists, Shawnee Mission, Kans., 1982-83; atty. Levy and Craig, Kansas City, Mo., 1983-89, Turner, Vader & Koch, Chartered, 1989-93; pvt. practice, 1993-95, 98; atty. Neill, Scott, Terrill & Embree, LLC, Lenexa, Kans., 1996-98; pvt. practice, 1998—. Mem. Equilaw panel arbitrators Panel Arbitrators, U.S. Dist. Ct. (we. dist.) Mo. Precinct committeeman Johnson County Rep. Party, Kans., 1983-84. Mem. ABA, Ind. Bar Assn., Mo. Bar Assn., Kansas City Bar Assn., Kans. Bar Assn., Johnson County Bar Assn., Am. Arbitration Assn. (mem. panel of arbitrators, constrn. arbitrator adv. bd.), Nat. Assn. Security Dealers (panel arbitrators, complex litigation panel), Nat. Arbitration Forum (panel of arbitrators), Notre Dame Club of Kansas City (pres. 1985-86), S.W. United Soccer Club of Kans. (pres. 1994-96), Heartland Soccer Assn. (v.p. 1997-2003). Republican. Roman Catholic. General civil litigation, General practice, Workers' compensation. Office: 303 E Poplar Olathe KS 66061 E-mail: bob@rscottlaw.com.

SCOTT, ROBERT HAYWOOD, JR., lawyer; b. Hazelton, Pa., Mar. 27, 1941; s. Robert Haywood and Marjorie Jane (Briggs) S.; m. Sandra Lou Carroll, June 6, 1966; children: Paige Carroll, Robert Haywood. AB magna cum laude, Kenyon Coll., 1963; JD with distinction, Duke U., 1966. Bar: Mo. 1969, Kans. 1966, Ohio 1972. Assoc. Hoskins King Springer McGannon and Hahn, Kansas City, Mo., 1970-72; operating v.p., sr. counsel Federated Dept. Stores, Cin., 1972-83; ptnr. Roberts Fleischaker & Scott, Joplin, Mo., 1983-88; chief exec. officer W&S Mfg., Inc., Joplin, 1988-92, also chmn. bd. dirs.; CEO Robert Scott Investment Banking, 1988—. Chmn. Deep Sea Archaeology Rsch. Coun., 1994—. Contbr. articles to profl. jours. Served to capt. USAF, 1966-70. Mem. Mo. Bar Assn., Order of the Coif, Phi Beta Kappa. Republican. Episcopalian. Corporate, general, Finance, Property, real (including real estate development, water). Home: 1330 Valle Dr Joplin MO 64801-1074

SCOTT, ROGER ROY, lawyer; b. Oklahoma City, Aug. 11, 1935; s. Norvell K. and Carol Elaine (Smith) S.; m. Lucille D. Scott, Aug. 9, 1958; children: Brian Davidson, Linda Anne. BA, U. Tulsa, 1957, JD, 1960; LLM, So. Meth. U., 1965. Bar: Okla. 1960, U.S. Dist. Ct. (no., ea., we. dists.) Okla. 1960, U.S. Supreme Ct. 1971, U.S. Ct. Appeals (10th cir.) 1967, U.S. Tax Ct. 2000. Assoc. Conner, Winters et al, Tulsa, 1961-62, David M. Thornton, Tulsa, 1962-63, John S. Carlson, Tulsa, 1963-68; ptnr. Schuman, Pray, Levy & Scott, Tulsa, 1968-69, Pray, Scott & Livingston, Tulsa, 1969-71, Pray, Scott, Williamson et al, Tulsa, 1971-79, Lawrence & Scott, Tulsa, 1979-86; pvt. practice Tulsa, 1986—. Presiding judge Temporary Ct. Appeals, Tulsa, 1979-82. V.p. Boy Scouts Am., Tulsa. Recipient Ethics award, Okla. Bar Assn., 2003. Mem. Tulsa County Bar Assn. (profl. responsibility com.), Masons (master), Shrine of N.Am. (potentate). Republican. Methodist. General civil litigation, General practice, Probate (including wills, trusts). Office: 525 S Main St Ste 1111 Tulsa OK 74103-4512

SCOTT, RONALD CHARLES, lawyer; b. Greenville, S.C., Jan. 8, 1948; s. Robert Claude and Louise Helen (Tinsley) S.; m. Debra Whaley, Aug. 11, 1973; children: Robert Marion, Jordan Whaley, Carter Whaley. BBA cum laude, The Citadel, 1970; MBA, U. S.C., 1972, M in Acctg., JD, 1976. Bar: S.C. 1976, U.S. Dist. Ct. S.C. 1977, U.S. Tax Ct. 1977. Pres. Scott & Mathews P.A., Columbia, S.C., 1978-92, Scott Law Firm, P.A., Columbia, S.C., 1993—. Pres. Heritage Title, Columbia, 1980—. Mem. bd. visitors, pres.'s adv. coun. Med. U. S.C.; past state pres. Nat. Soc. to Prevent Blindness, past state sec.; state fundraising chmn. Arthritis Found. Served to capt. (adj. gen. corps.) USAR, 1970-76. Named Outstanding Young Man of Columbia Jaycees, 1982; recipient State Dist. Svc. award U.S. Jaycees, 1982, Leadership S.C. award Office of the Gov., 1986; recipient Fellowship Regional Finalist award White House, 1984. Fellow S.C. Bar Found.; mem. ABA (past state rep., significant legis. com., real property com.), S.C. Bar Assn. (sec. subcom. model corp. act panel), Columbia C. of C. (com. of 100, Leadership Columbia award 1981), Summit Club, Palmetto Club (Columbia), Wildwood Country Club, Woodcreek Country Club. Administrative and regulatory, Health, Property, real (including real estate development, water). Office: Scott Law Firm PA 1331 Laurel St # 2065 Columbia SC 29201-2513 E-mail: rons@scottlaw.com.

SCOTT, THOMAS EMERSON, JR., lawyer, former prosecutor; b. Pittsburg, Penn., Apr. 27, 1948; s. Thomas Emerson Sr. and Marie (Ebel) S.; m. Ginger Claud, Mar. 1978 (div. Aug. 1980); m. Joyce Newman, Aug. 6, 1983. BA in Econs. cum laude, U. Miami, 1969, JD cum laude, 1972; LLM, U. Va., 1989. Bar: Fla. 1972, U.S. Dist. Ct. (so. dist.) Fla. 1972, U.S. Ct. Appeals (5th and 11th cirs.) 1972. Law clk. to cir. judge 11th jud. cir. ct., State of Fla., Dade County, 1970-71; assoc. Bradford, Williams, McKay, Kimbrell, Hamann & Jennings, P.A., Miami, Fla., 1972-76, mem. firm, 1977-79; assoc. Huebner, Shaw & Burrell, Ft. Lauderdale, Fla., 1976-77; cir. judge 11th jud. cir. State of Fla., Miami, 1979-84; ptnr. Kimbrell, Hamann, Jennings, Womack, Carlson & Kniskern P.A., Miami, 1984-85, Steel Hector & Davis, Miami, Fla., 1990—; judge U.S. Dist. Ct. (so. dist.) Fla., Miami, 1985-90; U.S. atty U.S. So. Dist., Fla., 1997-99; ptnr. Shook Hardy & Bacon, Miami, Fla., 1999—. Chmn. security com. U.S. Dist. Ct., so. dist. Fla.; instr. litigation skills U. Miami, Coral Gables, 1984-86; instr. Nita program U. Fla.; instr. trial advocacy program Nova U.; instr. profl. responsibility and product liability St. Thomas U. Contbr. articles to profl. jours. Served to 1st lt. USAR, 1969—. Mem. ABA (co-chmn. com. on discovery litigation sect.), Fla. Bar Assn. (chmn. standing com. on professionalism, past chmn. CLE trial advocacy program), Dade County Bar Assn. (Outstanding Jurist award Young Lawyers' sect.), U.S. Dist. Judges' Assn., Product Liability Adv. Coun. Found. Republican. Roman Catholic. Avocations: running, collectibles. State civil litigation, Criminal, Product liability. Office: Shook Hardy & Bacon 201 S Biscayne Blvd Ste 2400 Miami FL 33131-4313 E-mail: tscott@shb.com.

SCOULAR, ROBERT FRANK, lawyer; b. Del Norte, Colo., July 9, 1942; s. Duane William and Marie Josephine (Moloney) S.; m. Donna V. Scoular, June 3, 1967; children— Bryan T., Sean D., Bradley R. BS in Aero. Engring., St. Louis U., 1964, JD, 1968. Bar: Mo. 1968, Colo. 1968, N.D. 1968, U.S. Supreme Ct. 1972, Calif. 1979. Law clk. to chief judge U.S. Ct. Appeals (8th cir.), 1968-69; ptnr. Bryan, Cave, McPheeters & McRoberts, St. Louis, 1969-89, mng. ptnr. Los Angeles, 1979-84, exec. com., 1984-85, sect. leader tech., computer and intellectual property law, 1985-89; ptnr. Sonnenschein, Nath, Rosenthal, Chgo., 1990—, mng. ptnr. L.A., 1990—, mem. policy and planning com., 1995—. Co-leader intellectual property practice, 1990-98; dir. Mo. Lawyers Credit Union, 1978-79. Contbr. articles to profl. jours. Bd. dirs. St. Louis Bar Found., 1975-76, 79; bd. dirs., vice chmn., gen. counsel L.A. Area Coun. Boy Scouts Am.; league commr. Am. Youth Soccer Orgn.; mem. alumni coun. St. Louis U., 1979-82, dean's coun. Sch. Law, 2000—; hon. dean Dubourg Soc. Recipient Nat. Disting. Eagle Scout award. Mem. ABA (nat. dir. young lawyers div. 1977-78), Bar Assn. Met. St. Louis (v.p. 1978-79, sec. 1979, chmn. young lawyers sect. 1975-76), Los Angeles County Bar Assn., Assn. Bus. Trial Lawyers, Calif. Bar. Assn., Mo. Bar (chmn. young lawyers sect. 1976-77, disting. svc. award), Fed. Bar Assn., Chancery Club. Appellate, General civil litigation, Intellectual property. Home: 1505 Lower Paseo La Cresta Palos Verdes Peninsula CA 90274-2066 Office: Sonnenschein Nath & Rosenthal 601 S Figueroa St Ste 1500 Los Angeles CA 90017-5720

SCRAIRE, JEAN-CLAUDE, lawyer, investment management executive; b. Montreal, Que., Can., Aug. 25, 1946; s. Paul and Constance (Beaulac) S.; children: Louis-Marrin, Jean-François, Valérie. Diploma, Coll. St. Laurent, 1966; Law Degree, U. Montreal, 1969. Bar: Que. 1970. Assoc. in comml. law Beaulé et Assocs., Montreal, 1970-74; various mgmt. positions Govt. of Quebec, pub. adminstrn., Quebec City, 1974-81; legal advisor Caisse de dépôt et placement du Que., Montreal, 1981-82, legal affairs dir. Montréal, 1982-83, sr. v.p. legal and corp. affairs, 1983-86, sr. v.p. legal, corp. affairs, real estate investments, 1986-93, sr. v.p. Caisse Real Estate Group, 1993-95, CEO, 1995, chmn. bd., CEO, 1995—2002; ind. adv., 2002—. Co-author: L'Éthique au Quotidien, Éditions Qué./Amérique, Mont., 1990. Mem. Bd. of Trade of Met. Montréal, World Econ. Forum; mem. Montreal Coun. for Internat. Rels.; mem . Leaders' Networking group of Que.; participant Que.-Japan Bus. Forum; gov. Jr. Chamber and Jr. Bd. of Trade of Que. Mem. French C. of C. in Can., Amnesty Internat., Laval C. of C., Mount Stephen Club (Montréal). Office: 355 des Recollects Montreal QC Canada H2Y 1V9 E-mail: jcs@scraire.com.

SCRIGGINS, LARRY PALMER, lawyer, director; b. Englewood, N.J., Nov. 27, 1936; s. Thomas Dalby and M. Patricia (Fowler) S.; m. Victoria Jackola, Feb. 17, 1979; children: Elizabeth J., Thomas P. AB, Middlebury Coll., 1958; JD, U. Chgo., 1961. Bar: Md. 1962. Law clk. to chief judge Md. Ct. Appeals, 1962; assoc. Piper & Marbury, L.L.P., Balt., 1962-69, ptnr., 1969-98, vice chmn., 1988-93, mem. exec. com., CFO, 1993-98; sr. counsel Piper Rudnick, LLP, Balt., 1999-2001, ptnr. emeritus, 2001—. Mem. legal adv. com. N.Y. Stock Exch., 1992-96; bd. dirs. USF & G Corp., 1979-98, Center Stage Assocs., 1979-89, Balt. Choral Arts Soc., 1979-96, Balt. Conv. Bur., 1982-95, YMCA of Greater Balt., 1987-94, Fund for Ednl. Excellence, 1990-98, chmn. bd. trustees, 1993-98; bd. dirs. Nat. Aquarium in Balt., bd. govs. 1987-93; bd. dirs. Balt. Symphony Orchestra, 1996-2001. Contbr. articles to profl. jours. Fellow: Am. Bar Found.; mem.: ABA (sect. on bus. law coun. 1972—76, chmn. law and acctg. com. 1985—88, vice chair and editor-in-chief The Bus. Lawyer 1989—90, chair 1991—92, chmn. com. corp. laws 1996—2000, chmn. ad hoc com. on ethics 2000 1999—2002), AICPA (planning com. 1989—92), Fin. Acctg. Stds. Bd., Task Force in Fin. Instruments, Am. Law Inst., Am. Judicature Soc., Md. Bar Assn. (coun. 1976—78, chmn. 1977—78, mem. com. on corp. laws 1981—84). Corporate, general, Finance, Securities. Home: 13663 E Columbine Dr Scottsdale AZ 85259-3752 Office: Piper Rudnick LLP 6225 Smith Ave Baltimore MD 21209-3600 E-mail: larry.scriggins@piperrudnick.com.

SCRIVEN, WAYNE MARCUS, lawyer; b. Sumter, S.C., Aug. 31, 1953; s. Philip Roosevelt and Sarah Ella (Pringle) S. BA in History Edn. cum laude, Va. Union U., 1975; JD, Golden Gate U. Sch. of Law, 1979. Bar: Va. 1980, U.S. Dist. Ct. (ea. dist.) Va. 1980, U.S. Ct. Appeals (4th cir.) 1980, S.C. 1982, U.S. Dist. Ct. S.C. 1982, U.S. Supreme Ct. 1984, Calif. 1987, U.S. Dist. Ct. (no. dist.) Calif. 1986, U.S. Ct. Appeals (9th cir.) 1986, D.C. 1993, U.S. Dist. Ct. D.C. 1994, U.S. Dist. Ct. Md. 1994, U.S. Ct. Appeals (fed. cir.) 1994, D.C. Directing atty. Petersburg (Va.) Legal Aid Soc., 1980-81; staff atty. Carolina Regional Legal Svcs. Corp., Florence, S.C., 1981-82; solo practice atty. Florence, S.C., 1982-85, Richmond, Va., 1985-86, San Francisco, 1986-93, Washington, 1993—. Contract atty. Neighborhood Legal Asst. Program, Marion, S.C., 1982-83, pro bonocontract atty., 1983-85, Carolina Regional Legal Svcs. Corp., Florence, 1983-85, Bar Assn. of San Francisco, 1987-93; notary public, S.C., 1981-91, Va., 1986-91. Bd. dirs. Young Men's Christian Assn., Florence, 1982-83, Pee Dee Crisis Ctr., Florence, 1983-84, San Francisco Neighborhood Legal Asst. Program, 1992-93. Named one of Outstanding Young Men of Am., U.S. Jaycees, 1982; recipient Outstanding Lawyer in Pub. Svc., Bar Assn. San Francisco, 1988-91. Mem. ABA, Washington Bar Assn., Assn. Trial Lawyers of Am., U.S. Supreme Ct. Hist. Soc. Baptist. Avocations: fishing, guitar playing, nature trail walking. General practice, Labor (including EEOC, Fair Labor Standards Act, labor-management relations, NLRB, OSHA), Personal injury (including property damage). Office: Scriven & Assocs 7900 Sudley Rd Ste 420 Manassas VA 20109 also: Scriven & Assocs 1225 Eye St NW Ste 500 Washington DC 20005-3914 Fax: (703) 369-7158. E-mail: Wayne-Marcus-Scriven@abanet.org.

SCRIVNER, THOMAS WILLIAM, lawyer; b. Madison, Wis., Sept. 10, 1948; s. William H. and Jane (Gehrz) S.; m. Meredith Burke, Aug. 16, 1980; children: Allison, David. AB, Duke U., 1970, MAT, 1972; JD, U. Wis., 1977. Assoc. Michael, Best & Friedrich LLP, Milw., 1978-85, ptnr., 1985—. Mem. ABA, Wis. Bar Assn., Milw. Bar Assn. (labor sect.), Corp. Practice Inst. (pres. 1989-92). Episcopalian. Administrative and regulatory, Labor (including EEOC, Fair Labor Standards Act, labor-management relations, NLRB, OSHA). Home: 4626 N Cramer St Milwaukee WI 53211-1203 Office: Michael Best & Friedrich LLP 100 E Wisconsin Ave Ste 3300 Milwaukee WI 53202-4108

SCROGGS, LARRY KENNETH, lawyer, state legislator; b. Beebe, Ark., Oct. 8, 1941; s. Kenneth Chalmers and Mildred Lorene (McDonald) S.; m. Mary Patricia Rushing, Aug. 25, 1967; children: Larry Kenneth Jr., James Kevin, Michael Kyle. BA, Harding U., 1963; JD, Vanderbilt U., 1971. Bar: Tenn. 1971, U.S. Dist. Ct. (we. dist.) Tenn. 1971, U.S. Ct. Appeals (8th cir.) 1982, U.S. Ct. Appeals (6th cir.) 1989, U.S. Supreme Ct. 1981. Assoc. Law Firm of Leo Bearman, Memphis, 1971-72, Holt, Batchelor, Spicer, Memphis, 1972-76, ptnr., 1976-80, Less & Scroggs, Memphis, 1980-92; pvt. practice, Germantown, Tenn., 1992-96; ptnr. Scroggs & Rogers, Collierville, Tenn., 1997—2003, Burch, Porter & Johnson, Memphis, 2003; mem. Tenn. Ho. of Reps., Nashville, 1996—2002. Mcpl. ct. judge City of Germantown, 1980-86; atty. for County Trustee, Shelby County, Memphis, 1990—. Mem. campaign steering com. George Bush for Pres., Memphis, 1987-92; vol. Ed Bryant for Congress campaign, Memphis, 1994, Don Sundquist for Gov. campaign, Memphis, 1994. Lt. U.S. Navy, 1964-67, Vietnam. Mem. ABA, Tenn. Bar Assn., Memphis Bar Assn. (bd. dirs. 1990-91). Republican. Mem. Ch. of Christ. Avocations: photography, boating, tennis. Federal civil litigation, State civil litigation, Construction. Office: Burch Porter & Johnson 130 N Court Ave Collierville TN 38103

SCUDDAY, ROY GEORGE, lawyer; b. Odessa, Tex., Sept. 29, 1946; s. Roy Sheppard and Letitia Roselyn (Keith) S.; children— Roy Keith, John Andrew; m. Linda R. Reed, Jan. 16, 1999. BA in History, Rice U., 1968; JD, U. Tex., 1971; MA in History, S.W. Tex. U., 2001. Bar: Tex. 1971, U.S. Dist. Ct. (so. dist.) Tex. 1979, U.S. Dist. Ct. (we. dist.) Tex. 1980, U.S. Ct. Appeals (5th cir.) 1980. Hearing examiner Tex. Water Quality Bd., Austin, 1971-73; staff atty. Gulf Coast Waste Disposal Authority, Houston, 1973-79; ptnr. Fielder & Scudday, Lockhart, Tex., 1979—88; hearings atty., comptroller of pub. accounts, 1988-96; adminstrv. law judge, comptr., 1996—. Oil, gas, and mineral, General practice, Property, real (including real estate development, water). Home: 502 W Prairie Lea St Lockhart TX 78644-2623

SCUDDER, CHARLES SEELYE KELLGREN, lawyer; b. London, Feb. 20, 1947; came to U.S., 1964; s. Evarts Seelye and Henrica Antonina (Kellgren) S.; m. Jannette Harris Ericson, June 20, 1970; children: John Whitney, Jocelyn Seelye, Ansley Harris. BA, Yale U., 1968; BA in Law with 2d class honors, Oxford U., 1973; JD with honors, U. Conn., 1975; MA (hon.), Oxford U., 1980. Bar: N.Y. 1976, U.S. Dist. Ct. N.Y. 1976. Assoc., Winthrop Stimson Putnam & Roberts, N.Y.C., 1975-81; sr. counsel Conoco Inc., E.I. DuPont De Nerrours & Co., Wilmington, Del., 1981-87; v.p. and assoc. gen. counsel Unisys Corp., Blue Bell, Pa., 1987-1991; sr. v.p., gen. counsel Carnaudmetalbox, Inc., Cin., 1995-96; ptnr. Obermayer Rebmann Maxwell & Hippel, LLP, Phila.,1991-1994, 1996-2001; asst. gen. counsel Akzo Nobel Inc., Dobbs Ferry, N.Y., 2001-. With U.S. Army, 1968-71. Editor Conn. Law Review, 1974. Mem. ABA (subcom. on multinat. corps.), N.Y. State Bar Assn., Am. Corp. Counsel Assn., George W. Bush Campaign Com. mem., 1997-, Republican. Corporate, general, Private international, Securities. Office: 7 Livinstone Ave Dobbs Ferry NY 10522

SCUDERI, JOSEPH, lawyer, architect; b. Westwood, NJ, Nov. 27, 1962; s. Thomas and Joann Scuderi; m. Suzanne Gobb, Aug. 2, 1996; children: Zoe, Aidan. BArch, NJ Inst. Tech., 1986; JD, Lewis and Clark Coll., 1996. Arch. Lindeman, Winckelmann, Martin & Dupree, AIA, Jersey City, 1985—89; field engr. Varick Constrn./Morris Cos., Secaucus, NJ, 1989—90; field engr., scheduler Perini Internat., Framingham, Mass., Egypt, 1991—93; atty. Klemm Blair Sterling & Johnson, Hagatra, 1996—2000, Cushman Law Office, Olympia, Wash., 2000—. Mem. legal affairs com. Associated Gen. Contractors Am., Seattle, 2001—. Vol. Oreg. Trout, Portland, 1995—96, Salvation Army, Portland, 1995—96. Mem.: Rotary Internat. Avocations: scuba diving, fishing, outdoor activities. Construction, Commercial, contracts (including sales of goods; commercial financing). Office: Cushman Law Offices 924 Capital Way S Olympia WA 98501 Office Fax: 360-956-9795. Business E-Mail: joescuderi@cushmanlaw.com.

SCULLIN, FREDERICK JAMES, JR., federal judge; b. Syracuse, N.Y., Nov. 5, 1939; s. Frederick James and Cleora M. (Fellows) S.; m. Veronica Terek Sauro, Aug. 31, 1984; children: Mary Margaret, Kathleen Susan, Kellie Anne, Rebecca Rose; 1 stepchild, Angel Jenette Sauro. BS in Econs., Niagara U., 1961; LL.B., Syracuse U., 1964. Bar: N.Y. 1964, Fla. 1976, U.S. Dist. Ct. (no. dist.) N.Y. 1967, U.S. Supreme Ct. 1971. Assoc. Germain & Germain, Syracuse, 1967-68; asst. dist. atty. Onondaga County, Syracuse, 1968-71; asst. atty. gen. N.Y. State Organized Crime Task Force, 1971-78, dir. regional office, 1974-78; chief prosecutor, dir. Gov.'s Council on Organized Crime State of Fla., Tallahassee, 1978—; sole practice Syracuse, 1979-82; U.S. atty. for No. Dist. N.Y., 1982-92; judge U.S. Dist. Ct. (no. dist.) N.Y., 1992—, chief judge. With U.S. Army, 1964-67, Vietnam; col. USAR. Decorated Air medal, Bronze Star; Cross of Gallantry (Vietnam); recipient Meritorious Svc. Cross, UN svc. medal, UN Campaign medal, 5 stars; Nat. Def. medal, N.Y. State Dist Svc. medal, various others. Mem. Am. Judicature Soc., Fla. Bar Assn., Fed. Bar Assn., Fed. Bar Coun., Onon City Bar Assn., Jud. Conf. U.S. Office: US Dist Ct US Courthouse 100 S Clinton St Syracuse NY 13261-6100 E-mail: fscullin@nynd.uscourts.gov.

SCULLIN, MICHAEL E. lawyer; m. Patricia S. Schindler, Feb. 5, 1999. BA in History, U. of Pa., Philadelphia, 1975—79; JD, Dickinson Sch. of Law, Penn State, Carlisle, PA, 1980—83. Bar: Pa. 1983. Of counsel Monteverde, McAlee & Hurd, Philadelphia, Pa., 2003—; ceo Breast Health Inst., Philadelphia, Pa., 2003—; exec. dir. Multilaw, London, United Kingdom, 2000—02; shareholder Monteverde, McAlee, Fitzpatrick, Tanker & Hurd, Philadelphia, Pa., 1983—2000. Dir. French Am. Chamber of Commerce, Philadelphia, 1999—. Mem. Inst. of Contemporary Art, Philadelphia, Pa., 1995—98; pres. Dickinson Law Phila. Alumni Assoc., Philadelphia, Pa., 1994—98; mem. Reading Terminal Market Merchants Catering Co., Philadelphia, Pa., 1996—98; founder Lyon Phila. Bar Exch.

Program, Philadelphia, Pa., 1997—2003. Recipient Hon. Citizen, Chollabuk-do, Korea, 1997, Cert. of Recognition, Volunteers for Indigent People, 1995, 1996. Mem.: ABA (assoc.), Am. Soc. of Assn. Executives (assoc.), Internat. Bar Assn. (assoc.), Union Internationale des Avocat (assoc.). Non-profit and tax-exempt organizations, Private international, Corporate, general. Office: 1616 Walnut St Philadelphia PA 19103 E-mail: mescullin@aol.com.

SCULLION, ANNETTE MURPHY, lawyer, educator; b. Chgo., Apr. 6, 1926; d. Edmund Patrick and Anna (Nugent) Murphy; 1 child, Kevin. BEd, Chgo. Tchrs. Coll., 1960; JD, DePaul U., 1964, MEd, 1966, Loyola U., Chgo., 1970; EdD, No. Ill. U., 1974. Bar: Ill. 1964, U.S. Dist. Ct. (no. dist.) Ill. 1965, U.S. Ct. Appeals (D.C. cir.) 1978. Lectr. Chgo. C.C., 1964-68; pvt. practice Chgo., 1964—; from asst. prof. bus. edn. to prof. Chgo. State U., 1966-98. Founder, adviser Bus. Edn. Students Assn., Chgo. State U., 1976—; sch. law workshop coord. Ill. Divsn. Vocat. and Tech. Edn., 1981, coord. edn. workshops, 1990—. Mem. ABA, Nat. Bus. Edn. Assn., Womens Bar Assn. Ill., Am. Tchr. Edn., Beta Gamma Sigma. Home: 386 Muskegon Ave Calumet City IL 60409-2347

SCULLION, KEVIN PETER, lawyer; b. Chgo., June 9, 1952; s. Peter and Annette (Murphy) S. Student, Purdue U., 1970-72; BA, Northwestern U., 1974; postgrad., Tulane U. Law Sch., Grenoble, France, 1976; JD, DePaul U., 1977, LLM in Taxation, 1986; MBA, U. Chgo., 1979; student, U. Edinburgh, Scotland, 1979. Bar: Ill. 1977, U.S. Dist. Ct. (no. dist.) Ill. 1977, Ind. 1978, Fla. 1978, U.S. Dist. Ct. (so. dist.) Ind. 1978, D.C. 1980, U.S. Dist. Ct. (ea. dist.) Mich. 1991, U.S. Dist. Ct. Ariz. 1992; CPA, Ill.; series 65 lic. NASD. In-house counsel Fin. Fed. Savs. & Loan Assn., Olympia Fields, Ill., 1977-79; assoc. firm Quinn, Jacobs & Barry, Chgo., 1979-83; tax mgr. Price Waterhouse, Chgo., 1983-86; sr. v.p. Graves Reich & Co., Inc., Northfield, Ill., 1986-91; ltd. ptnr. Graver, Bokhof & Goodwin, Chgo., 1991-2000; mng. dir., co-founder Aberdeen Wealth Mgmt. LLC, 2000—. Mem. ABA, AICPA, Chgo. Bar Assn., Ill. State Bar Assn., Ind. State Bar Assn., Ill. CPA Soc., Internat. Assn. Fin. Planners. Roman Catholic. Avocations: running, reading, travel. Home: 386 Muskegon Ave Calumet City IL 60409-2347

SCULLY, ROGER TEHAN, II, lawyer; b. Washington, Jan. 10, 1948; s. James Henry and Marietta (Maguire) S.; m. Martha Anne Seebach, Dec. 29, 1979. BS, U. Md., 1977; JD, Cath. U., 1980. Bar: Md. 1980, D.C. 1981, U.S. Tax Ct. 1982, U.S. Supreme Ct. 1988. V.p. Bogley Related Cos., Rockville, Md., 1971-75; law clk. to presiding justice Superior Ct. of D.C., Washington, 1979-81; assoc. Lerch, Early & Roseman, Bethesda, Md., 1981-82; gen. counsel Laszlo N. Tauber, M.D. & Assocs., Bethesda, 1982-94, Jefferson Meml. Hosp., Alexandria, Va., 1982-94; spl. counsel Venable, Baetjer, Howard & Civiletti, Washington, 1991-96. Cons. in real estate Order of Friar Minor, N.Y.C., 1977—; lectr. Mortgage Bankers Assn., Washington, 1984—; bd. dirs. Nozzoli Constrn. Co., Washington; exec. com., spl. counsel to bd. dirs., bd. dirs. Chromachron Technology Corp., Toronto; bd. dirs. MusicWorks, N.Y.C.; vice chair Sayett Tech., Inc., Rochester, N.Y.; vice chair, bd. dirs., exec. com. MediaShow, Inc., Rochester. Author: (with Quarles & Howard) Summary Adjudication Dispositive Motions and Summary Trials, 1991. Mem. pres.'s coun. St. Bonaventure U., Olean, N.Y., 1995—, chmn. pres.'s coun., 1986-96; trustee Belmont Abbey Coll., Charlotte, N.C., 1993-95; bd. trustees Edmund Burke Sch., Washington, 1984-2001, trustees emeritus, 2001-; bd. dirs. Nat. Children's Choir, Washington, 1980-94. Recipient First Order Affiliation Order of Friars Minor, 1985; named one of Outstanding Young Men in Am., 1982. Fellow D.C. Bar Assn.; mem. ABA, ATLA, FBA, Md. Bar Assn. (chmn. corp. counsel sect.), Am. Judicature Soc., Assn. Governing Bd. of Univs. and Colls., Am. Inns of Ct., Irish Legal Soc., Selden Soc., U.S. Jud. Conf. of 4th Cir. (permanent mem.), U.S. Jud. Conf. Fed. Cir. (del.), Jud. Conf. of D.C. (del.). Republican. Roman Catholic. Commercial, contracts (including sales of goods; commercial financing), Private international, Property, real (including real estate development, water). Home: 10923 Wickshire Way North Bethesda MD 20852-3220 Office: 7712 Greentree Rd West Bethesda MD 20817-1428

SCZUDLO, WALTER JOSEPH, lawyer; b. Fairbanks, Alaska; s. Walter and Dolores J. Sczudlo; children: Lauren Hall, Elizabeth Fairbanks, Walter Christopher; m. Rebecca Grey Tucker. AB, Middlebury Coll., 1975; JD, Golden Gate U., 1979; LLM, Georgetown U., 1987; postgrad., U. Calif., Santa Barbara, 1972, Tulane U., 1971-72, Vt. Law Sch., 1976-77. Bar: Alaska 1979, Calif. 1980, D.C. 1986, U.S. Ct. Appeals (9th cir.) 1980, U.S. Ct. Appeals (D.C. cir.) 1986, U.S. Dist. Cts. (no., cen., ea. and so. dists.) Calif., U.S. Dist. Ct. Alaska, U.S. Ct. Claims, U.S. Tax Ct. Law clk. to presiding justice Alaska Supreme Ct., 1978-79; assoc. atty. Merdes, Schaible, Staley and Delisio, Anchorage, 1979-82; legis. dir., gen. counsel U.S. Senator Murkowski, Washington, 1982-84; sr. tax assoc. Schramm and Raddue, Santa Barbara, Calif., 1984-85; dir. congl. rels., counsel Natural Gas Supply Assn., Washington, 1985-88; Washington counsel Shell Oil Co., 1988-96; v.p., Washington counsel Intercontinental Energy Corp., 1996-99; gen. counsel, exec. v.p. pub. affairs and comms. Assn. Fundraising Profls., Washington, 1999—; prin. ptnr. WEBK Broadcasting 105.3 FM, Killington, Vt., 1985—. Dir. Sun's Edge, Inc., Santa Barbara, 1987—, Natural Gas Roundtable, Washington, 1987—. Author: (with other) Washington Legal Foundation, 1988. Com. chmn. Steve Cowper for Gov., Anchorage, 1982. Recipient Am. Jurisprudence award Bancroft-Whitney Pub. Co., 1978. Roman Catholic. FERC practice, Legislative, Corporate taxation. Home: 8305 Whittier Blvd Bethesda MD 20817-3148 Office: AFP 1101 King St Ste 700 Alexandria VA 22314-2944 E-mail: wsczudlo@AFPNET.org.

SEABOLT, RICHARD L. lawyer; b. Chgo., Aug. 28, 1949; BGS with distinction, U. Mich., 1971; JD, U. Calif., Hastings, 1975. Bar: Calif. 1975. With Hancock, Rothert & Bunshoft, San Francisco, 1975—, ptnr., 1981—. Frequent speaker and author profl. jours. Mem. State Bar Calif. (exec. com. litigation sect., jury instr. subcom.), Bar Assn. San Francisco, Assn. Bus. Trial Lawyers (bd. dirs.). Appellate, General civil litigation, Commercial, contracts (including sales of goods; commercial financing). Office: Hancock Rothert & Bunshoft LLP Four Embarcadero Ctr San Francisco CA 94111-4106 E-mail: rlseabolt@HRBLaw.com.

SEAGLE, J. HAROLD, lawyer; b. Marion, N.C., May 9, 1947; s. Rufus James and Alma Rhoda (McMahan) S.; m. Linda Jean Cranford, June 3, 1967; 1 child, James Mark. BA, U. N.C., 1973, JD, 1977. Bar: N.C. 1977; U.S. Dist. Ct. (ea., middle, we. dists.) N.C. 1977, 88, 92; U.S. Ct Appeals (4th cir.) 1982; U.S. Supreme Ct. 1982. Assoc. atty. Rountree & Newton, Wilmington, N.C., 1977-79; ptnr. Rountree & Seagle, L.L.P., Wilmington, 1979—2001. Past pres. Fifth Jud. Dist. Bar. Bd. trustees and bd. deacons Winter Park Baptist Ch.; past moderator Wilmington Baptist Assn.; bd. dirs. Rescue Mission of Cape Fear; past adv. Bd. Coastal Bioethics Network; past chmn. annual fund drive Am. Cancer Soc.; past sect. chmn. Cape Fear United Way. Mem.: N.C. Bar Coun. of Pres. Wilmington Inns of Ct. (exec. com., master), Maritime Law Assn. of U.S. (proctor), Southeastern Admiralty Law Inst. (past chmn., chmn. adv. coun.), N.C. Coll. of Advocacy, N.C. Acad. Trial Lawyers, N.C. State Bar, N.C. Bar Assn., New Hanover County Bar Assn. (co-chair grievance com.). Avocations: acoustic guitar, motorcycle racing. Admiralty, General civil litigation, Environmental. Office: Rountree & Seagle LLP 2419 Market St Wilmington NC 28403-1135 Address: 19 Treetop Dr Arden NC 28704 E-mail: haroldseagle@charter.net.

SEAGULL, KEITH ALLEN, lawyer; b. Milw., Apr. 19, 1957; s. Louis and Helen Ann S.; m. Asma Parveen, Nov. 20, 1994; 1 stepchild, Samia; 1 child, Sasha Y. BS, U. Wis., Milw., 1977; JD, Southwestern U., L.A., 1981; cert. atendance, Cambridge U., 1981. Bar: Calif. 1990; cert. specialist workers' compensation State Bar Calif. Bd. Legal Specialization. Law clerk Law Offices Steven M. Hanna, Fullerton, Calif., 1981-85; asst. office mgr. Joe Kay Design & Constrn., Fullerton, Calif., 1985-89; adjuster Wausau Ins., Pasadena, Calif., 1989-90; atty., adjuster Springfield Ins., Covina, Calif., 1990-91; atty. Law Offices Rose, Klein & Marias, L.A., 1991, Stephen G. Krutzsch & Assocs., ITT Hartford Ins., Brea, Calif., 1991-94, Law Office James Max Stewart, Temecula, Calif., 1994-95; prin. Law Offices Keith A. Seagull, Pomona, Calif., 1995—. Mem. ABA, Calif. Applicants' Attys. Assn., Eastern Bar Assn. L.A. County, Masons. Avocations: sailing, world religions, walking, music, politics. Workers' compensation.

SEALE, ROBERT ARTHUR, JR., lawyer; b. Shreveport, La., July 17, 1942; s. Robert Arthur Sr. and Lucille (Frank) S.; m. Chalon Fontaine, Feb. 24, 2001; children: Robert A. III, John Meyers. BBA, La. State U., 1964, JD, 1967. Bar: La. 1967, Tex. 1969. Rsch. asst. La. Law Inst., Baton Rouge, 1967; law clk. U.S. Dist. Ct. (we. dist.) La., Shreveport, 1967-68; atty./ptnr. Vinson & Elkins, Houston, 1968—97; sr. ptnr. Phelps Dunbar LLP, Houston, 2002—. Trustee, legal counsel The Mus. of Fine Arts, Houston, 1981-89, The Creel Found., Augusta, Ga., 1989-97; pres., trustee The Lyons Found., Houston, 1986—, M.A. and J.A. Elkins, Jr. Found. Mem. La. Law Rev., 1965-67. Sr. Warden St. Martin's Episcopal Ch., Houston, 1990; pres. Pine Shadows Civic Assn., Houston, 1991; trustee Episcopal High Sch., Houston, 1985-88; bd. dir. Boys' and Girls' Country, Houston, 1990-94; mem. U. Tex. Houston Health Sci. Ctr. Devel. Bd. Fellow Houston Bar Found.; mem. ABA, Tex. Bar Assn., Houston Bar Assn., Corondo Club (pres. 1991), Omicron Delta Kappa, U. Tex. Health Sci. Ctr. Developement Bd; pres, trustee Vivian Smith Found. For Neurologic Rsch. Avocations: civic and charitable activities, golf. Estate planning, Probate (including wills, trusts), Estate taxation. Office: 3040 Post Oak Blvd Ste 900 Houston TX 77056

SEALL, STEPHEN ALBERT, lawyer; b. South Bend, Ind., Oct. 24, 1940; s. Stephen Henry and Mildred Rita (MacDonald) S.; m. Barbara Ann Halloran, June 25, 1966; children: John Paul, Edward Andrew, Ann Marie. BA, Purdue U., 1963; postgrad., Cornell U. Grad. Sch. Bus. Adminstrn., 1963; LLB, U. Notre Dame, 1966. Bar: Ind. 1966, U.S. Claims Ct. 1973, U.S. Tax Ct. 1968, U.S. Ct. Appeals (6th cir.) 1980, U.S. Ct. Appeals (7th cir.) 1969, U.S. Supreme Ct. 1973. Assoc. Thornburg, McGill, Deahl, Harman, Carey & Murray, South Bend, 1966-71; ptnr. Barnes & Thornburg and predecessor firm Thornburg, McGill, Deahl, Harman, Carey & Murray, 1972—, vice chmn. and mgmt. com., mng. ptnr. South Bend office, 1985—2001. Spkr. in field. (Mem. editl. bd.) Notre Dame Law Rev., 1964—66. Mem. Mayor's Com. on Downtown Devel., South Bend, 1975-77, Mayor's Com. on Utilization of Downtown Bldgs., South Bend, 1988-96; trustee Project Future, South Bend, 1986-2002; exec. com. Meml. Hosp. South Bend, Inc., 1999-2003; dir. Meml. Health Found., 1992-98, Meml. Health Sys., 1997-2003, United Way of St. Joseph County, Inc., 1992-98, Conv. and Tourism Industry Coun., 1994-2000. Fellow Am. Coll. Tax Counsel, Am. Bar Found., Ind. Bar Found.; mem. ABA (taxation sect.), Ind. State Bar Assn. (chmn. taxation sect. 1977-78), Summit Club (chmn. 1976-77), Morris Park Country Club (bd. dirs., sec. 1998-2001). Democrat. Roman Catholic. Avocations: golf, softball, weightlifting. Corporate, general, Property, real (including real estate development, water), Taxation, general. Home: 17705 Waxwing Ln South Bend IN 46635-1328 Office: Barnes & Thornburg 600 1st Source Bank Ctr 100 N Michigan St Ste 600 South Bend IN 46601-1632

SEAR, MOREY LEONARD, federal judge, educator; b. New Orleans, Feb. 26, 1929; s. William and Yetty (Streiffer) S.; m. Lee Edrehi, May 26, 1951; children: William Sear II, Jane Lee. JD, Tulane U., 1950, LLD (hon.), 1999. Bar: La. 1950. Asst. dist. atty., Parish Orleans, 1952-55; individual practice law Stahl & Sear, New Orleans, 1955-71; spl. counsel New Orleans Aviation Bd., 1956-60; magistrate U.S. Dist. Ct. (ea. dist.) La., 1971-76, judge, 1976—, chief judge, 1992-99; judge Temp. Emergency Ct. of Appeals, 1982-87. Adj. prof. Tulane U. Coll. Law; former chmn. com. on adminstrn. of bankruptcy sys., former chmn. adv. com. on bankruptcy rules, former mem. com. on adminstrn. of fed. magistrate sys. Jud. Conf. U.S., mem. jud. panel on multidist. litigation; former mem. Jud. Conf. of U.S. and Its Exec. Com.; former mem. cir. coun. 5th Cir. of U.S.; founding dir. River Oaks Pvt. Psychiat. Hosp., 1968. Pres. Congregation Temple Sinai, 1977-79; bd. govs. Tulane Med. Ctr., 1977—; former chmn. Tulane Med. Ctr. Hosp. and Clinic, 1980-85. Decorated Order of Vasco Nunez de Balboa (Panama) with grade of grand ofcl. Mem. ABA, La. Bar Assn., New Orleans Bar Assn., Order of Barristers, Order of the Coif (hon.). Office: US Dist Ct C-256 US Courthouse 500 Camp St New Orleans LA 70130-3313*

SEARBY, RICHARD HENRY, university chancellor, lawyer; b. July 23, 1931; s. Henry and Mary Searby; m. Caroline McAdam, 1962; 3 sons. MA (hons.), U. Oxford. Bar: London 1956, Victoria, Australia 1957. Assoc. to Chief Justice of Australia Rt. Hon. Sir Owen Dixon, 1956-59; ind. lectr. law relating to executors and trustees U. Melbourne, 1961-72; bd. dirs. News Corp. Ltd., Australia, 1977-92, chmn., 1981-91; bd. dirs. News Internat. plc, U.K., 1981-92, dep. chmn., 1987-92; chancellor Deakin U., 1997—. Bd. dirs. Times Newspapers Holdings Ltd., 1981—, dep. chmn., 1981-91; bd. dirs., chmn. S. China Morning Post, 1987-92, Equity Trustees Executors and Agy. Co. Ltd., 1975-2000; bd. dirs. BRL Hardy Ltd., Woodside Petroleum Ltd. Chmn. Geelong Grammar Sch., 1983-89; mem. coun. Nat. Libr. Australia, 1992-95, Mus. of Victoria, 1993-97 Decorated QC (Australia) 1971. Mem.: Melbourne, Australian (Melbourne). Avocations: reading, music, tennis, fishing. Office: 23A Hampden Armadale 3143 Victoria Australia also: 1 Spring St Melbourne 2010 Victoria Australia

SEARCY, WILLIAM NELSON, lawyer, director; b. Moultire, Ga., June 26, 1942; s. Floyd Hartsfield and Anna (Pidcock) S.; m. Camille Heery, June 17, 1967; 1 child, Amelia Ashburn. AB, U. Ga., 1964, JD, 1967; LLM in Taxation, Washington U., St. Louis, 1968. Bar: Ga. 1967, U.S. Dist. Ct. (so. dist.) Ga. 1970, U.S. Ct. Appeals (5th and 11th cirs.) 1976, U.S. Tax Ct. Assoc. Bouhan, Williams & Levy, Savannah, Ga., 1970-73; ptnr. Brannen, Searcy & Smith LLP, Savannah, 1973—. Chmn. bd. dirs. Citizens Bank, Cairo, Ga., 1993—; sec. Am. Fed. Savs. and Loan Assn., 1978-81; mem. adv. bd. Liberty Svgs. Bank, 1984-88. Pres. Chatham-Savannah Voluntary Action Ctr., Inc., 1978—80. Served to maj. gen. Ga. ANG, 1967—, comdr. Ga. ANG, 2000—. Mem. ABA (sec. spl. liaison tax com. S.E. region 1983-84, chmn. 1984-85), NG Assn. U.S. (chmn. air resolution com. 2001-03, bd. dirs. 2002-, chmn. resolutions com., 2003-), State Bar Ga. (chmn. sect. taxation 1983-84, mem.-at-large exec. coun. Young Lawyers sect. 1975-78, chmn. conf. with Ga. Soc. CPA's 1979-81, Ga. commn. on continuing lawyer competency 1989-95, vice chmn. 1995), Savannah Bar Assn. (pres. Younger Lawyers sect. 1975-76), Am. Judicature Soc., Savannah Estate Planning Coun., Inst. Continuing Legal Edn., Rotary, Oglethorpe Club, Savannah Golf Club, Georgian Club. Banking, Corporate, general, Estate planning. Office: PO Box 8002 Savannah GA 31412-8002

SEARLS, EILEEN HAUGHEY, retired lawyer, librarian, educator; b. Madison, Wis., Apr. 27, 1925; d. Edward M. and Anna Mary (Haughey) S. BA, U. Wis., 1948, JD, 1950, MS in LS, 1951. Bar: Wis. 1950. Cataloger Yale U., 1951-52; instr. law St. Louis U., 1952-53, asst. prof., 1953-56, assoc. prof., 1956-64, prof., 1964-2000, law libr., 1952-2000. Chmn. Coun. Law Libr. Consortia, 1984-90; sec. Bd. of Conciliaton and Arbitration, Archdiocese of St. Louis, 1986-98. Named Woman of Yr. Women's Commn., St. Louis U., 1986. Mem. ABA, ALA, Wis. Bar Assn., Bar Assn. Met. St. Louis, Am. Assn. Law Librs. (Marian Gould Gallagher Disting. Svc. award 1999), Mid Am. Assn. Law Librs. (pres. 1984-86), Mid Am. Law Sch. Libr. Consortium (chmn. 1980-84), Southwestern Assn. Law Librs., Altrusa Club. Office: 3700 Lindell Blvd Saint Louis MO 63108-3412

SEARS, JOHN PATRICK, lawyer; b. Syracuse, N.Y., July 3, 1940; s. James Louis and Helen Mary (Fitzgerald) S.; m. Carol Jean Osborne, Aug. 25, 1962; children: James Louis, Ellen Margaret, Amy Elizabeth. BS, Notre Dame U., 1960; LL.B., JD, Georgetown U., 1963. Bar: N.Y. bar 1963. Clk. N.Y. Ct. Appeals, 1963-65; asso. firm Nixon, Mudge, Rose, Guthrie, Alexander & Mitchell, 1965-66; mem. staff Richard M. Nixon, 1966-69; dep. counsel to Pres. Nixon, 1969-70; ptnr. Gadsby & Hannah, Washington, 1970-75, Baskin & Sears, Washington, 1977-84; pvt. practice Washington, 1984—. Mgr. Ronald Regan's Presdl. Campaign, 1975-76, 79-80; polit. analyst NBC Today Show, 1984-89; mem. Wall Street Jour. bd. of polit. experts, 1984—; columnist LA Times, Newsday, 1992—. Sr. advisor Jack Kemp for V.P. Campaign, 1996. Fellow Kennedy Inst. Politics, Harvard, 1970 Home: 2801 New Mexico Ave NW Washington DC 20007-3921 Office: 2021 K St NW Washington DC 20006-1003

SEARS, JOHN WINTHROP, lawyer; b. Boston, Dec. 18, 1930; s. Richard Dudley and Frederica Fulton (Leser) S.; m. Catherine Coolidge, 1965 (div. 1970). AB magna cum laude, Harvard U., 1952, JD, 1959; MLitt, Oxford U., 1957. Bar: Mass. 1959, U.S. Dist. Ct. Mass. 1982. Rep. Brown Bros. Harriman, N.Y.C., 1959-63, Boston, 1963-66; mem. Mass. Ho. Reps., 1965-68; sheriff Suffolk County, Mass., 1968-69; chmn. Boston Fin. Commn., 1969-70, Met. Dist. Commn., 1970-75; councilor-at-large Boston City Coun., 1980-82; trustee Sears Office, Boston, 1975—. Contbr. articles to profl. jours. Apptd. bd. dirs. Fulbright Scholarship, 1991-93; trustee Christ's Ch., Longwood, Brookline, Mass., 1965—, Sears Trusts, Boston, 1975—; hon. trustee J. F. Kennedy Libr., 1991—; bd. dirs. Am. Mus. Textile Heritage, 1987-97, Shirley-Eustis Assoc., Environ. League, Mass., 1994-97; Rep. candidate Sec. State, Mass., 1978, Gov. of Mass., 1982; vice chmn. Ward 5 Rep. Com., 1965-69, 75-85; chmn. Rep. State Com., 1975-76, mem., 1980-85; del. Rep. Nat. Conv., 1968, 76, State Conv., 1966-92; mem. U.S. Electoral Coll., 1984; bd. dirs. United South End Settlements, 1966—, chmn., 1977-78. Lt. comdr. USNR, 1952-54, 61-62. Recipient Outstanding Pub. Servant award Mass. Legis. Assn., 1975; Rhodes scholar, 1955 Mem. Mass. Bar Assn., New Eng. Hist. and Geneal. Soc. (bd. dirs., councillor 1977-82), Mass. Hist. Soc., Handel and Haydn Soc. (gov. 1982-87), Signet Soc., Boston Atheneum, Tennis and Racquet Club, Somerset Club, The Country Club (Brookline), St. Botolph Club, Club of Odd Vols., Wednesday Evening Club of 1777, Thursday Evening Club of 1846 (pres. 1999), Spee Club (Cambridge chpt., pres., trustee), Phi Beta Kappa. Republican. Home: 7 Acorn St Boston MA 02108-3501

SEARS, LEAH J. state supreme court justice; b. June 13, 1955; d. Thomas E. and Onnye J. Sears; married; children: Addison, Brennan. BA, Cornell U.; JD, Emory U.; M in Apellate Jud. Process, U. Va.; JD (hon.), Morehouse Coll., 1993. Judge City Ct. Atlanta; atty. Alston & Bird, Atlanta; trial judge Superior Ct. Fulton County; justice Supreme Ct. Ga., Atlanta, 1992—. Contbr. articles to profl. jours. Bd. dirs. Sadie G. Mays Nursing Home, Ga. chpt. Nat. Coun. Christians & Jews; mem. adv. bd. United Way Drug Abuse Action Ctr., Outdoor Activity Nature Ctr.; mem. Cornell U. Women's Coun.; mem. steering com. Ga. Women's History Month, Children's Def. Fund Black Cmty. Crusade Children; founder Battered Women's Project, Columbus, Ga. Recipient Outstanding Young Alumna award Emory U., One of 100 Most Influential Georgians Ga. Trend mag., Excellence in Pub. Svc. award Ga. Coalition Black Women, 1992, Outstanding Woman of Achievement YWCA Greater Atlanta, One of Under Forty & On the Fast Track, 1993. Mem. ABA (chair bd. elections), Nat. Assn. Women Judges, Ga. Bar Assn., Women's Forum Ga., Gate City Bar Assn., Atlanta Bar Assn. (past chair jud. sect.), Ga. Assn. Black Women Attys. (founder, pres.), Fourth Tuesday Group, Jack & Jill Am. (Atlanta chpt.), Links Inc. (Atlanta chpt.), Alpha Kappa Alpha. Office: Ga Supreme Ct 244 Washington Street Atlanta GA 30334-9007

SEARS, MARY HELEN, lawyer; b. Syracuse, N.Y. d. James Louis and Helen Mary (Fitzgerald) Sears. AB, Cornell U., 1950; JD with honors, George Washington U., 1960. Bar: Va. 1960, D.C. 1961, U.S. Supreme Ct. 1963. Chemist Allied Chem. and Dye Corp., Syracuse, 1950-52, Hercules Powder Co., Wilmington, Del., 1952-55; patent examiner U.S. Patent Office, Washington, 1955-60; pvt. practice Washington, 1960-61; assoc. Irons, Birch, Swindler & McKie, Washington, 1961-69; mem. firm Irons and Sears, Washington, 1969-84; chmn. trade regulation practice dept. Memel, Jacobs, Pierno, Gersh & Ellsworth, Washington, 1984-87; ptnr., chmn. intellectual property and unfair competition practice dept. Ginsburg, Feldman & Bress, Washington, 1987-91; ptnr., chmn. intellectual property and telecomm. practice group Reid & Priest, Washington, 1991-94; founder, chmn. M. H. Sears Law Firm, 1994—. Mem. adv. bd. Boardroom Reports, Inc., N.Y.C., 1980-85; mem. Cornell U. Coun., 1981-87, 89-93, life mem., 1995—, mem. adminstrv. bd., 1984-86. Contbr. articles to various publs. Recipient Outstanding Performance award U.S. Dept. Commerce, 1957; named to Guide to the World's Leading Patent Law Experts Euromoney Publs., PLC, 1995, 97. Mem.: ABA (co-chmn. appellate practice com., litigation sect. 1989—92), D.C. Bar Assn., Va. State Bar Assn., Internat. Trademark Assn., Licensing Execs. Soc., Am. Soc. Internat. Law, Am. Intellectual Property Law Assn., George Washington U. Law Alumnae Assn. (bd. dirs. 1995—2001), Order of Coif, Phi Alpha Delta. Republican. Federal civil litigation, Patent, Trademark and copyright. Office: MH Sears Law Firm Chartered 910 17th St NW Ste 800 Washington DC 20006-2606 E-mail: Mhsears@mhsears.com.

SEAVEY, WILLIAM ARTHUR, lawyer, vintner; b. Los Angeles, Aug. 28, 1930; s. Arthur Jones and Dorothy (Keyes) S.; m. Mary van Beuren, June 25, 1955; children: Dorothy K., Arthur V.B., William G., Frederic A., Charles K. AB, Princeton U., 1952; LLB, Harvard U., 1955; grad. Inst. Internat. Studies, U. Geneva, Switzerland, 1956, D in Polit. Sci., 1970. Bar: Calif. 1957, U.S. Dist. Ct. (so. and no. dist.) Calif. 1957, U.S. Ct. Appeals (9th cir.) 1957. Assoc. Luce, Forward, Kunzel & Scripps, San Diego, 1956-57; asst. U.S. atty. U.S. Dist. Ct. (so. dist.) Calif., 1957-59; with Noon & Seavey, San Diego, 1959-65; lectr. in internat. law and econ., asst. to pres. Mills Coll., Oakland, Calif., 1968-74; ptnr. Richards & Seavey, San Francisco, 1974-76, Davis, Stafford, Kellman & Fenwick, San Francisco, 1976-78; of counsel Friedman, Olive, McCubbin, Spalding, Bilter, Roosevelt etal, San Francisco, 1987—. Proprietor Seavey Vineyard, Napa County, 1981—. Author: Dumping Since the War: The Gatt and National Laws, 1970. Councilman City of Coronado, Calif., 1960-62, mayor 1962-64; trustee French-Am. Internat. Sch., San Francisco, 1968-96; pres. English Speaking Union, San Francisco, 1982-85, Alliance Francaise, San Francisco, 1979-81; chair Javits Fellowship Bd., Washington, 1989-92; mem. Columbus Fellowship Found. Bd., Washington, 1993-99; dir. San Francisco Com. on Fgn. Rels., 1995-98, chmn., 1998—. Mem. ABA, Calif. Bar Assn., San Francisco Bar Assn., Am. Soc. Internat. Law. Clubs: Pacific Union, Cercle de l'Union, World Trade (San Francisco), The Met. (Washington). Republican. Avocations: skiing, jazz piano. Corporate, general, Private international, Probate (including wills, trusts). Home: 90 Hazel Ln Piedmont CA 94611-4033 Office: 425 California St Fl 22 San Francisco CA 94104-2102 also: 1310 Conn Valley Rd Saint Helena CA 94574-9624 E-mail: waseavey@pacbell.net., waseavey@earthlink.net.

SEAWELL, DONALD RAY, lawyer, publisher, arts center executive, producer; b. Jonesboro, NC, Aug. 1, 1912; s. A.A.F. and Bertha (Smith) S.; m. Eugenia Rawls, Apr. 5, 1941; children: Brook Ashley, Donald Brockman. AB, U. N.C., 1933, JD, 1936, DLitt, 1980; LHD, U. No. Colo., 1978. Bar: N.C. 1936, N.Y. 1947. With SEC, 1939-41, 45-47, Dept. Justice, 1942-43; chmn. bd., dir., pub., pres. Denver Post, 1966-81; chmn. bd., dir. Gravure West, L.A., 1966-81; dir. Swan Prodns., London; of counsel firm Bernstein, Seawell, Kove & Maltin, N.Y.C., 1979—; chmn. bd., chief exec. officer Denver Ctr. for Performing Arts, 1972—. Ptnr. Bonfils-Seawell Enterprises, N.Y.C.; bd. vis. U. N.C. Chmn. bd. ANTA, 1965—; theatre panel Nat. Coun. Arts, 1970-74; bd. govs. Royal Shakespeare Theatre, Eng.;

trustee Am. Acad. Dramatic Arts, 1967—, Hofstra U., 1968-69, Cen. City Opera Assn., Denver Symphony; bd. dirs., Air Force Acad. Found., Nat. Ints. Outdoor Drama, Walter Hampden Meml. Library, Hammond Mus.; pres. Helen G. Bonfils Found., 1972-97, pres. emeritus, 1997—, chmn. fin. com., 1997—, Denver Opera Found.; Population Crisis Com., 1982-91; bd. dirs. Family Health Internat., Found. for Internat. Family Health; bd. visitors N.C. Sch. Arts, 1992-98; pres. Frederick G. Bonfils Found., 1972-92; chmn. Civilian Mil. Inst. Named Officer, Most Excellent Order of the Brit. Empire, 2002; recipient Am. Acad. Achievement award, 1980, Tony award for producing, On Your Toes, 1983, Vocie Rsch. and Awareness award, Voice Found., 1983, Arts and Entertainement Cable Network award, 1987, Third Millennium Leadership award, Am. Diabetes Assn., 1996, Colo. Tourism Hall of Fame award, 1999, Thomas Degaetani award, U.S. Inst. for Theatre Tech., 2000, Benjamin F. Stapleton, Jr. award, 2000, Disting. Svc. award, U. Colo., 2000, Downtown Denver award for Tantalus, 2001, AWARD Honoree award, 2001. Mem. Bucks Club (London), Dutch Treat Club (N.Y.C.), Denver Country Club, Denver Club, Cherry Hills Country Club, Mile High Club (Denver), Garden of Gods Club (Colorado Springs, Colo.), Order of Brit. Empire (officer). Office: Denver Ctr for Performing Arts 1050 13th St Denver CO 80204-2157 E-mail: geary@dcpa.org.

SEAWORTH, MARY ELLEN, lawyer; b. Bismarck, N.D., Oct. 28, 1947; d. George H. and Margaret M. (Fortune) S.; m. Henry H. Howe, Dec. 4, 1976; children: Oren, Deborah, Tavia, Christopher. Student, Coll. St. Teresa, 1965-68; BA in Speech and Theatre, U. N.D., 1971, BS in Edn., 1973, JD, 1983. Bar: Minn. 1983, N.D. 1984, U.S. Dist. Ct. N.D. 1984, U.S. Dist.Ct. Minn. 1992. Ptnr. Howe and Seaworth, Grand Forks, N.D., 1983—; adv. bd. Family Ct., NE Judicial Dist., 2002—. Instr. (part time) legal assistance program Northland Community Coll., Thief River Falls, Minn., 1988, 89. Editorial staff N.D. Law Review, 1982-83. LWV, 1991—; mem. com. Gov.'s Commn. Children Adolescents at Risk, 1985-86; commr. for Commn. Uniform State Laws, 1985-95; Dem. com. person. Recipient Women Who Care award U. N.D. Women's Ctr., 1986; named one of Oustanding Young Women Am., 1984.. Mem. N.D. Bar Assn. (chmn. family law sect. 1988, 96, Minn. Bar Assn., ABA (family law sect. 1995-), Am. Acad. Matrimonial Lawyers (family ct. adv. com. 2003). Criminal, Family and matrimonial, Personal injury (including property damage). Office: Howe and Seaworth Law Offices 421 Demers Ave Grand Forks ND 58201-4507 E-mail: seaworthm@hotmail.com.

SEBASTIAN, ARI-BEN CALLEJA, lawyer; b. Manila, Feb. 23, 1961; s. Florante and Celia (Calleja) S.; m. Pilar Juliana Schramm Cayetano, July 14, 1994; children: Maxine Selina, Nadine Sandra, Gabriel Rene (dec.). AB, U. Philippines, 1982, LLB, 1986. Bar: The Philippines 1987. Confidential assoc. Office Justice, Pronove, The Philippines, 1986-87; assoc. Siguion Reyna Montecillo & Ongsiako, The Philippines, 1987-95; mng. ptnr. Cayetano Sebastian Ata Dado & Cruz, Manila, The Philippines, 1995—. Bd. dirs. Bases Conversion Devel. Authority, sec., 1998-99, Elcom Internat. Resources Inc., sec., 1999—.asst. gen. counsel Ayala Alabang Country Club, The Philippines, 1996-98. Office: Cayetano Sebastian Ata Dado & Cruz 12th Fl 116 Tordesillas St Salcedo Village Makati City 1227 Philippines

SEBRIS, ROBERT, JR., lawyer; b. N.Y.C., May 20, 1950; s. Robert and Ruth (Kagis) Sebris; m. S. Lawson Hollweg, Sept. 8, 1973; children: Jared Matthew, Bryan Taylor. BS in Indsl. Labor Rels., Cornell U., 1972; JD, George Washington U., 1978. Bar: DC 1978, Wash. 1980. Labor rels. specialist Onondaya County Office labor rels., Syracuse, NY, 1973-74, U.S. Dept. Labor, Washington, 1972-75; labor rels. mgr. U.S. Treasury Dept., Washington, 1975-78, employee rels. mgr., 1978-80; assoc. Davis, Wright, Todd, Riese & Jones, Seattle, 1980-84; ptnr. Davis, Wright, Tremain, Bellevue, Wash., 1985-92, Sebris Busto James, Bellevue, 1992—. Expert witness T.E.A.M. Act Amendments NLRA U.S. Senate hearing, 1997. Co-author: (book) Employer's Guide to Strike Planning, 1985; contbr. articles to profl. jours. Mem. Bellevue CC Found., 1988—95, pres., 1995—96; chair employment law cert. program U. Wash. Law Sch., 1996—97. Mem.: ABA (health law forum, labo and employment law sect., mem. com. employee rights), Soc. Human Resource Mgmt., Am. Health Lawyers Assn., Pacific Coast Labor Law Conf. (planning com. 1980—93, chmn. 1991—92), Seattle/King County Bar Assn. (chmn. labor law sect. 1991—92), DC Bar Assn., Wash. Bar Assn. Avocations: golf, soccer, coaching youth sports. Alternative dispute resolution, Labor (including EEOC, Fair Labor Standards Act, labor-management relations, NLRB, OSHA). Home: 16301 Mink Rd NE Woodinville WA 98072-9463 Office: Sebris Busto James Ste 325 14205 SE 36th St Bellevue WA 98006 E-mail: rsebris@sebrisbusto.com.

SEDIA, JOHN MICHAEL, lawyer; b. Buffalo, Aug. 29, 1954; s. Pasquale Joseph and Anne Marie (Delollis) S.; m. Rosemary Piccirilli, Sept. 24, 1983. A.B. in Journalism and Spanish, Ind. U., 1976; J.D., 1979. Bar: Ind. 1979, U.S. Dist. Ct. (no. dist.) Ind. 1979. Assoc. Saul I. Ruman & Assocs., Hammond, Ind., 1979-80, Bainbridge & Tweedle, Highland, Ind., 1980-83; ptnr. Tweedle & Sedia, Highland, 1983—99; atty. John W. Sedia, Atty. at Law, 1999- ; referee juvenile divsn. Lake Superior Ct., 1994—; adj. prof. In. U. N.W., 2002—. Ind. U. Alumni Assn. scholar U. Ind., Bloomington, 1976. Mem. Justinian Soc. Lawyers (treas. N.W. Ind. chpt. 1983—), Ind. U. Alumni Assn., Ind. State Bar Assn., Blue Key, Pi Kappa Alpha. Roman Catholic. Home: 120 Pine St Schererville IN 46375-1016 Office: Highland Office Ctr 2646 Highway Ave Ste 106 Highland IN 46322

SEDLAK, ERIC WILLIAM, lawyer; b. Pitts., 1958; s. William John and Rita Katherine Sedlak. BA, Haverford Coll., 1980; JD, NYU, 1984. Bar: Ill. 1984, U.S. Dist. Ct. (no. dist) Ill. 1984, Calif. 1986, U.S. Dist. Ct. Calif (no. dist.) 1986, U.S. Ct. Appeals (9th cir.) 1986. Budget analyst food safety and quality service USDA, Washington, 1980-81; atty. The First Nat. Bank of Chgo., 1984-85; assoc. Graham & James, San Francisco, 1985-88, Tokyo, 1988-92, sr. counsel, 1993-94; ptnr. Deacons Graham & James, Ho Chi Minh City, Vietnam, 1994—98, mng. ptnr., 1997—2000; ptnr. Squire Saders & Dempsey, Tokyo, 2000—. Articles editor Jour. Internat. Law and Politics; supervising editor, Law Rev. Developing Nations, 1983-84. Mem. ACLU, Interpacific Bar Assn., Am. C. of C. (bd. dirs. legal affairs com., Ho Chi Minh City chpt., 1995-, chair, 1997-98, chair regional affairs com. Singapore chpt. 1999-, bd. govs. 1999-2000, chair legal affairs com. Tokyo chpt., 2003-), Commonwealth Club. Democrat. Mem. Soc. Of Friends. Avocation: tennis. Banking, Private international, Mergers and acquisitions. Office: Squire Saders & Dempsey LLP 1-1-39 Hiroo Shibuya-ku Tokyo 150 Japan

SEDLER, ROBERT ALLEN, law educator; b. Pitts., Sept. 11, 1935; s. Jerome and Esther (Rosenberg) S.; m. Rozanne Friedlander, Jan. 24, 1960; children: Eric, Beth. BA, U. Pitts., 1956, JD, 1959. Bar: D.C. 1959, Ky. 1968, Mich. 1979; U.S. Supreme Ct. 1969. Asst. prof., assoc. prof. law St. Louis U., 1961-65; assoc. prof. law, asst. dean Addis Ababa U., Ethiopia, 1963-66; assoc. prof. to prof. law U. Ky., Lexington, 1966-77; prof. law Wayne State U., Detroit, 1977—, disting. prof. law, Gibbs chair civil rights & civil liberty, 2000—. Author: American Constitutional Law, 2000, Across State Lines, 1989: Applying the Conflict of Law to Your Practice, 1989 (with R. Cramton) The Sum and Substance of Conflict of Laws, 1987, Ethiopian Civil Procedure, 1968; contbr. articles to profl. jours. Gen. counsel ACLU Ky., 1971-76. Gershenson Disting. Faculty fellow, Wayne State Univ., 1985-87. Mem. ABA, AAUP, Phi Beta Kappa, Order of the Coif. Democrat. Jewish. Home: 18851 Capitol Dr Southfield MI 48075-2680 Office: Wayne State U 468 Ferry Mall Detroit MI 48202-3620 E-mail: rsedler@aol.com., rsedler@wayne.edu.

SEE, EDMUND M. lawyer; b. Marietta, Ohio, Oct. 9, 1943; s. Edgar Thorpe and Katherine M. (Merriam) S.; m. Ellen Engler, June 5, 1976; children: Kevin, Gregory, Tyler. BA, Wesleyan U., Middletown, Conn., 1965; JD, Harvard U., 1971. Bar: Conn. 1971. Assoc. Day, Berry & Howard LLP, Hartford, Conn., 1971-77, ptnr., 1978—. Chmn. Mcpl. Fin. Practice Group. Vol. Peace Corps, Gabon, 1965-67, Vista, 1968-69; pres. bd. dirs. Legal Aid Soc., 1977-85, Hartford Arch. Conservancy, 1983-86; trustee St. Joseph Coll., 1991—; dir. Conn. Bar Found., 1994—; corporator Hartford Sem., 1994—. Mem. ABA, Conn. Bar Assn., Hartford County Bar Assn., Nat. Assn. Bond Lawyers, Conn. Govtl. Fin. Officers Assn., U.S. Govtl. Fin. Officers Assn., Phi Beta Kappa. Finance, Municipal (including bonds). Office: Day Berry & Howard LLP Cityplace 25th Fl Hartford CT 06103-3499 E-mail: emsee@dbh.com.

SEE, HAROLD FREND, judge, law educator; b. Chgo., Ill., Nov. 7, 1943; s. Harold Frend and Corinne Louise (Rachau) S.; m. Brenda Jane Childs, Dec. 2, 1978; children: Callie Suzanne, Garrett Brittain; children by previous marriage: Mary Elisabeth, Eric Palmer. Student, U. Chgo., 1962-63; BA, Emporia State U., 1966; MS, Iowa State U., 1969; JD, U. Iowa, 1973. Bar: Ill. 1973, U.S. Dist. Ct. (no. dist.) Ill. 1973, Ala. 1981, U.S. Ct. Appeals (fed. cir.) 1991; U.S. Supreme Ct. Instr. econs. Iowa State U., Ames, 1967-69; asst. prof. econs. Ill. State U., Normal, 1969-70; assoc. Sidley & Austin, Chgo., 1973-76; assoc. prof. law U. Ala., Tuscaloosa, 1976-78, prof., 1978-97; justice Supreme Ct. Ala., 1997—. Contbr. to books, also articles and book reviews. Mem. ABA, Ala. Bar Assn., Am. Econ. Assn., Am. Law and Econs. Assn., Soc. Profls. in Dispute Resolution, Am. Law Inst., Ala. Law Inst. Baptist. Office: Supreme Ct Ala 300 Dexter Ave Montgomery AL 36104-3741

SEGAL, PHYLLIS NICHAMOFF, mediator; b. Apr. 18, 1945; d. Sidney and Theresa Helen (Uroff) Nichamoff; m. Eli J. Segal, June 13, 1965; children: Jonathan, Mora. Student, Brandeis U., 1962-65; BA, U. Mich., 1966; JD, Georgetown U., 1973. Bar: N.Y. 1974, U.S. Dist. Ct. (so. and ea. dists.) N.Y. 1975, Mass. 1983, U.S. Supreme Ct. 1979. Deputy atty. gen. Commonwealth Mass., 1986—88; assoc. Weil, Gotshal and Manges, N.Y.C., 1973-77; legal dir. NOW Legal Def. and Edn. Fund., N.Y.C., 1977-82, gen. counsel, 1986—94; mediator ADR Assoc., L.L.C., Boston, 2001—. Chmn. Fed. Labor Rels. Auth., Washington, 1994-2000; gen. counsel Exec. office Transp. and Constrn., Commonwealth of Mass., 1984-86; adj. asst. prof. law NYU, 1980-82; fellow Bunting Inst. Radcliffe Coll., 1982-83; cons. U.S. Commn. Civil Rights. Contbr. articles to profl. jours. Mem. Commn. on Party Reform Nat. Dem. Party, 1972-73, mem. Compliance Rev. Commn., 1974-76; mem. adv. bd. Mass. Commn. Against Discrimination, 1983—. Mem. ABA, Fedn. Women Lawyers Jud. Screening Panel, Mass. Bar Assn. Home: 314 Dartmouth St Ph Boston MA 02116-1809 Office: ADR Assoc LLC 1 Huntington Ave Boston MA 02116

SEGAL, ROBERT MARTIN, lawyer; b. Atlantic City, N.J., Apr. 7, 1935; s. Nathan Albert and Edna (Dutkin) S.; m. Rhoda Sue Luber, June 8, 1958; children— Deborah Ann, William Nathan, Elizabeth Ann Student, Cornell U., 1953-54; BS in Econs., U. Pa., 1957; LLB cum laude, Harvard Law Sch., 1960. Bar: Pa. 1961. Assoc. Wolf, Block, Schorr & Solis-Cohen LLP, Phila., 1960-69, ptnr., 1969—, chmn., exec. com., 1978-79, 82-83, 86-87, 89-98. Hon. pres. Jewish Employment and Vocat. Svc. Contbr. articles to profl. jours. and mags. Constable of elections Lower Merion Twp., Pa., 1970-72; bd. dirs. Jewish Family and Children's Agy., Am. Jewish Com., Feinstein Ctr. for Am. Jewish History at Temple U., Greater Phila. Urban Affairs Coalition; bd. govs. Rep. Jewish Coalition; former trustee Hahnemann U., Fedn. Jewish Agys., Phila. Rehab. Plan, Inc., Rosenbach Mus. and Libr. Mem. ABA, Pa. Bar Assn., Phila. Bar Assn., Internat. Coun. Shopping Ctrs., Urban Land Inst. (assoc.), Am. Coll. Real Estate Lawyers, Phila. Bar Found. (trustee 1981-87), Am. Law Inst., Harvard Law Sch. Assn. Phila., The Federalist Soc., Wharton Club, Chaine des Rotisseurs, L'Ordre Mondial, Sunday Breakfast Club, La Coquille Club, Harvard Club, Beta Gamma Sigma; bd. dirs. Orleans Homebuilders, Inc. Avocations: golf, swimming. Construction, Landlord-tenant, Property, real (including real estate development, water). Office: Wolf Block Schorr & Solis-Cohen LLP 1650 Arch St Fl 22 Philadelphia PA 19103-2097 E-mail: rsegal@wolfblock.com.

SEGAL, STEVEN E. lawyer; b. Norfolk, Va., May 19, 1941; AB, Coll. William & Mary, 1963; MBA, U. Miami, 1965; JD, U. Houston, 1971. Bar: Tex. 1971. Mem. Fulbright & Jaworski L.L.P., Houston. Mem. ABA, State Bar Tex., Houston Bar Assn., Phi Delta Phi, Omicron Delta Kappa. Pension, profit-sharing, and employee benefits, Taxation, general. Office: Fulbright & Jaworski 1301 Mckinney St Ste 5100 Houston TX 77010-3031

SEGALL, JAMES ARNOLD, lawyer; b. Columbus, Ohio, Aug. 19, 1956; s. Arthur and Greta Helene (Cohen) S.; m. Janice Faye Wiesen, Mar. 14, 1981; children: Gayle Helene, Aryn Michelle, Craig Lawrence. BA, Coll. of William and Mary, 1978; JD, Washington and Lee U., 1981. Bar: Va. 1981, U.S. Dist. Ct. (ea. dist.) Va. 1981. Assoc. Phelps & King P.C., Newport News, Va., 1981-84, Buxton & Lasris P.C., Yorktown, Va., 1984-85; sole practice Newport News, 1985-89; pres. James A. Segall & Assocs., 1990-91, James A. Segall & Assocs., P.C., 1991-92, Segall & Moody, Newport News, 1992-98; ptnr. Krinick, Segall, Moody & Lewis, Newport News, Va., 1998-2000, Krinick, Segall, Moody, Lewis & Allen, Newport News, Va., 2001—. Lectr. Hampton Roads Regional Acad. Criminal Justice, 1986-89. Bd. dirs. ct.-apptd. Spl. Adv. Program, Newport News, 1986-87, Hamton-Newport News Cmty. Svcs. Bd., 1993-2002, treas., 1995-96, 99-2002, vice-chair, 1996-97, chair 1997-99; participant coop. office edn. program Newport News Pub. Schs., 1987-90; lectr. vol. programs 7th Dist. Ct. Svc. Unit, 1986-89; active City Newport News Cable TV Adv. Commn., 1990-93, Newport News Dem. City Com., 1990-91; bd. dirs. Rodef Sholom Temple, 1992-94, United Jewish Cmty., the Va. Peninsula, Inc., 1990—, chmn. spl. activities and fundraising com., 1990-91, chmn. bylaws com., 1992-93, 95—, campaign coun., 1995—, cmty. rels. coun., 1995-98, v.p. human svcs., 1998-2000, v.p. fin. and adminstrn., 2002—; Sunday sch. tchr. Rodef Sholom Temple, 2001—. Mem. Newport News Bar Assn., Va. Trial Lawyers Assn., Va. Coll. Criminal Def., B'nai B'rith (pres. 1989-91), Ruritan (sec. 1985-87), Moose. Avocations: computers, history, philosophy. Corporate, general, Family and matrimonial, Personal injury (including property damage). Home: 306 Dogwood Dr Newport News VA 23606-3728 Office: Krinick Segall Moody Lewis & Allen 525 Oyster Point Rd Ste B Newport News VA 23602-6014

SEGEL, KAREN LYNN JOSEPH, lawyer, taxation specialist; b. Youngstown, Ohio, Jan. 15, 1947; d. Samuel Dennis and Helen Anita Joseph; m. Alvin Gerald Segel, June 9, 1968 (div. Sept. 1976); 1 child, Adam James. BA in Soviet and East European Studies, Boston U., 1968; JD, Southwestern U., 1975. Bar: Calif., 1996, U.S. Tax Ct., 1996, U.S. Dist. Ct. (cen. dist.) Calif., 1996, U.S. Ct. Appeals (9th cir.), 1997. Adminstrv. asst. Olds Brunel & Co., N.Y.C., 1968-69, U.S. Banknote Corp., N.Y.C., 1969-70; tax acct. S.N. Chilkov & Co. CPA's, Beverly Hills, Calif., 1971-74; intern Calif. Corps. Commr., 1975; tax. sr. Oppenheim Appel & Dixon CPA's, L.A., 1978, Fox, Westheimer & Co. CPA's, L.A., 1978, Zebrak, Levine & Mepos CPA's, L.A., 1979; ind. cons. acctg., taxation specialist Beverly Hills, 1980—. Settlement officer L.A. County Superior Ct., 2000; law student mentor Southwestern U., 1996-2002, tax moot ct. judge, 1997. High sch. amb. to Europe People-to-People Orgn., 1963. Mem. Calif. State Bar, Women's Inner Circle of Achievement, Complex Litig. Inns of Ct., L.A. County Bar Assn, Beverly Hills Tinseltown Rose Soc. Avocations: collecting seashells, lhasa apso dog breeding, art, travel, music. E-mail: kjslaw@earthlink.net.

SEGERSTEN, ROBERT HAGY, lawyer, investment banker; b. Boston, June 24, 1941; s. Wendell C. and Claire H. S.; m. Marie E. Makinen, Feb. 13, 1965; children: Amanda Beth, Vanessa Bryce. AB, Bates Coll., 1963; JD, Boston U., 1970. Bar: Mass. 1970. Assoc. Nessen & Csaplar, Boston, 1970-75; v.p. March Co., Boston, 1975-77; pres. March-Eton Corp., Concord, Mass., 1977-82; ptnr. Nessen, Goodwin & Segersten, Concord, 1977-82, Kane & Segersten, Dedham, Mass., 1983-85; pres. Woodbine Optical Corp., Easton, Mass., 1990—. Adj. prof. Sch. Am. Studies, Boston U.; adj. prof. real estate law Bentley Coll. Officer, bd. dirs. Friends of The Jimmy Fund, Boston. Served to lt. USN, 1963-67. Mem. ACLU, Mass. Bar Assn. Democrat. Episcopalian. Home: 64 Folsom Ave Hyannis MA 02601-4823 Office: 14 Norfolk Ave Easton MA 07375

SEGLUND, BRUCE RICHARD, lawyer; b. Lansing, Mich., June 3, 1950; s. Richard Oswald and Josephine Ann (Kraus) S.; m. Connie Sue Roberts, June 19, 1970; children: Jennifer Lynne, Nicole Marie. BS, Mich. State U., 1973; JD, Thomas M. Cooley Law Sch., 1979. Bar: Mich. 1981, U.S. DIst. Ct. (ea. dist.) Mich. 1981. Assoc. Michael W. Reeds, P.C., Walled Lake, Mich., 1981-82; sole practice Walled Lake, 1982-85; ptnr. Mick and Seglund, Walled Lake, 1985-89, Connelly, Crowley, Groth and Seglund, Walled Lake, 1989—. Mem. Mich. Bar Assn. (mem. character and fitness com. dist. J 1988-2000), Oakland County Bar Assn. (lectr. 1984), Mich. Jaycees (pres. Walled Lake 1982-83, execllence award 1982-83, pres. of yr. 1982-83), Walled Lake C. of C. (bd. dirs. scholarship fund 1985-88). Lodges: KC (adv. 1982-94). Roman Catholic. Corporate, general, Labor (including EEOC, Fair Labor Standards Act, labor-management relations, NLRB, OSHA), Municipal (including bonds). Home: 8618 Buffalo Dr Commerce Township MI 48382-3408 Office: Connelly Crowley Groth & Seglund 2410 S Commerce Rd Walled Lake MI 48390-2129 E-mail: ccgs@ismi.net.

SEIDEL, ARTHUR HARRIS, lawyer; b. N.Y.C., May 25, 1923; s. Philip and Pearl (Geller) S.; m. Raquel Eliovich, Aug. 21, 1949; children: Stephen A., Paul B., Mary Beth Sharp. BS, CCNY, 1942; A.M., U. Mich., 1943; JD with honors, George Washington U., 1949. Bar: D.C. 1949, Pa. 1956, N.Y. 1957. Atty. patent dept. Gulf Oil Corp., Washington and Pitts., 1947-52; individual practice law, 1952-64; sr. ptnr. firm Seidel & Gonda, 1964-68, Seidel, Gonda & Goldhammer (P.C.), Phila., 1968-72, pres., 1972-84, Seidel, Gonda, Goldhammer & Abbott, P.C., Phila., 1984-88, Seidel, Gonda, Lavorgna & Monaco, Phila., 1988-2001; of counsel Drinker, Biddle & Reath, Phila., 2001—. Lectr. in Intellectual Property Temple U. Law Sch., 1973-86, Am. Law Inst. Editor: George Washington Law Rev, 1949; author: (with others) Trademark Practice, 2 vols, 1963, Monographs on Patent Law and Practice, 5th edit., 1993, Trademarks and Copyrights, 6th edit., 1992, Trade Secrets and Employment Agreements 3d edit, 1995; also articles. Mem. Adv. Com. for Restatement of Law of Unfair Competition. Mem. ABA, Am. Law Inst., Pa. Bar Assn., Phila. Bar Assn., Am. Intellectual Property Law Assn., Phila. Intellectual Property Law Assn., Order of Coif. Patent, Trademark and copyright. Home: 904 Centennial Rd Narberth PA 19072-1408 Office: Drinker Biddle & Reath LLP One Logan Sq Philadelphia PA 19103 E-mail: seidelah@dbr.com.

SEIDEL, SELVYN, lawyer, educator; b. Long Branch, N.J., Nov. 6, 1942; s. Abraham and Anita (Stoller) S.; m. Deborah Lew, June 21, 1970; 1 child, Emily. BA, U. Chgo., 1964; JD, U. Calif., Berkeley, 1967; diploma in law, Oxford U., 1968. Bar: N.Y. 1970, D.C. Ct. Appeals 1982. Ptnr. Latham & Watkins, N.Y.C., 1985—. Adj. prof. Sch. Law, NYU, 1974-84; instr. Practicing Law Inst., 1980-81, 84. Contbr. articles to profl. jours. Bd. dirs. Citizen Scholarship Fund Am., 1995-2000. Mem. ABA, N.Y. County Bar Assn., N.Y.C. Bar Assn. (mem. fed. cts. com. 1982-85, internat. law com. 1989-92, 95-96, art law com. 1997-2000), Boalt Hall Alumni Assn. (bd. dirs. 1980-82). Federal civil litigation, Private international. Office: Latham & Watkins 885 3rd Ave New York NY 10022-4802 E-mail: selvyn.seidel@lw.com.

SEIDEN, MARK, lawyer; b. N.Y.C., June 1, 1948; AB, U. Miami, 1970, JD, 1982. Bar: Fla. 1983, U.S. Dist. Ct. (so. dist.) Fla. 1984, U.S. Ct. Appeals (11th cir.) 1984. Police officer Met. Dade Police Dept., Miami, Fla., 1970-74, sgt., 1974-76, detective sgt., 1976-81; ptnr. Black & Seiden, Miami, Fla., 1983-95; atty. pvt. practice, Miami, Fla., 1995—. Mem. Am. Acad. Forensic Sci., Nat. Assn. Criminal Defense Attys., Internat. Assn. Blood Stain Pattern Analysts. Avocations: automobile racing driving, flying. Criminal. Office: 777 Brickell Ave Ste 100 Miami FL 33131-2812

SEIDEN, STEVEN JAY, lawyer; b. N.Y.C., June 21, 1960; s. Martin S. and Rita (Glazer) S.; m. Kathryn LaRussa, Sept. 30, 1984; children: Robert B., Daniel M., Michael J. BA, SUNY, Oneonta, 1981; JD, Hofstra U., 1984. Bar: N.Y. 1985, U.S. Dist. Ct. (ea. and so. dists.) N.Y. 1985, U.S. Supreme Ct. 1995, U.S. Ct. Appeals (fed. cir.) 1995, U.S. Ct. Fed. Claims 1995, U.S. Ct. Appeals for the Armed Forces, 1995. Assoc. Shapiro, Baines,Saasto & Shainwald, Mineola, N.Y., 1984-88; ptnr. Seiden & Kaufman, Carle Place, N.Y., 1988-93, 95—, Seiden, Kaufman, & Bosek, Carle Place, N.Y., 1993-95. Mem. ABA, N.Y. State Bar Assn., N.Y. State Trial Lawyers Assn., Assn. Trial Lawyers Am., Nassau County Bar Assn., L.I. Trial Lawyers Assn. (bd. dirs.), Civil Justice Found. (founding sponsor). Jewish. Personal injury (including property damage). Office: Seiden & Kaufman 1 Old Country Rd Ste 114 Carle Place NY 11514-1821

SEIDLER, B(ERNARD) ALAN, lawyer; b. N.Y.C., Nov. 26, 1946; s. Aaron H. and Ethel T. (Berkowitz) S.; m. Lynne Aubrey, Jan. 21, 1978; children: Jacob A., Morgan H., Lily R. BA, Colgate U., 1968; JD, Seton Hall U., 1972. Bar: N.Y. 1973, U.S. Dist. Ct. (ea., no. and so. dists.) N.Y. 1975, U.S. Ct. Appeals (2d cir.) 1976, U.S. Ct Appeals (3d cir.) 1984, U.S. Supreme Ct. 1977. Staff atty. N.Y. Legal Aid Soc., N.Y.C., 1972-75; sole practitioner N.Y.C. and Nyack, N.Y., 1975—. Mem. Snedens Landing Tennis Assn. (Palisades, N.Y.), Palisades Swim Club. General civil litigation, Criminal, Probate (including wills, trusts). Office: 127 S Broadway Nyack NY 10960-4433

SEIDLER, ROBERT LESLIE, lawyer; b. Bratislava, Slovakia, Sept. 14, 1948; s. Rudolph John and Elizabeth Seidler; m. Elaine E. Seidler; children: Katie, Kim, Solana. LLB, Sydney (Australia) U., 1973. With W.P. McElhone & Co., 1972—74, Abbott Tout Creer & Wilkinson, 1974—76, Moore & Bevins, 1976—78, ptnr., 1978—86; with Coudert Bros., Sydney, 1986—89, ptnr., 1989—91; pvt. practice The Seidler Law Firm, Sydney, 1993—. Bd. dirs. Hunter Phillip Ltd., Property Investment Capital (Holdings) Ltd.; mem. banking com. Law Coun. Australia, 1986—91; mem. representing Australia and New Zealand MITI Import Bd., 1992; mem. exec. com. Australian and New Zealand C. of C. in Japan, 1992; mem. investment adv. bd. Australian Prime Property Fund, 2000—; mem. corps. and markets adv. com. Australian Govt., 2001—. Banking, Commercial, contracts (including sales of goods; commercial financing), Corporate, general. Office: The Seidler Law Firm Level 40 Chipley Tower Sydney NSW 2000 Australia

SEIDMAN, JENNIFER L. lawyer; b. West Palm Beach, Fla., Oct. 15, 1970; d. Alfred Joseph and Dorothy Dolce. BS, Fla. State U., 1991; JD, Stetson Coll. Law, 1995. Assoc. Gunster, Yoakley, Valdes-Fauli & Stewart, West Palm Beach, 1995-97, Foley & Lardner, West Palm Beach, 1997-99; asst. gen. counsel Catalfumo Constrn. & Devel., Palm Beach Gardens, Fla., 1999—. Property, real (including real estate development, water), Construction. Office: Catalfumo Constrn & Devel 4300 Catalfumo Way Palm Beach Gardens FL 33410-4248 E-mail: jseidman@catalfumo.com.

SEIFERT, STEPHEN WAYNE, lawyer, performing arts executive; b. Washington, May 25, 1957; s. Arthur John and Frances E. (Smith) S. BA summa cum laude, Yale U., 1979; JD, Stanford U., 1982. Bar: Colo. 1982, U.S. Dist. Ct. Colo. 1982, U.S. Ct. Appeals (10th cir.) 1982, U.S. Ct.

Appeals (5th cir.) 1987, U.S. Supreme Ct. 1988. Ptnr.. Fairfield and Woods P.C., Denver, 1982-98; mng. dir. Fairfield & Woods P.C., Denver, 1990-92, 95-96; chmn. bd. dirs. Opera Colo., Denver, 1989-92, pres., exec. dir., 1997-2001; exec. dir. Newman Ctr. for Performing Arts U. Denver, 2002—. Author: Colorado Creditors' Remedies--Debtors' Relief, 1990; contbg. author: Colorado Methods of Practice; contbr. articles to profl. jours. Trustee Denver Metro C. of C., Denver Pub. Libr. Friends Found., Yale-Harvard Regatta Com., Allied Arts Inc., Rocky Mt. Region Inst. Internat. Edn.; mem. adv. bd. bioethics and humanities U. Colo. Health Scis. Ctr.; mem. chancellor's scholars and leaders coun. U. Colo., Denver. Mem. Law Club Denver (v.p. 1992-93, pres. 1993-94), Univ. Club, Phi Beta Kappa. Bankruptcy, General civil litigation, Commercial, contracts (including sales of goods; commercial financing).

SEIFERT, THOMAS LLOYD, lawyer; b. Boston, June 6, 1940; s. Ralph Frederick and Hazel Bell (Harrington) S.; m. Ann Cecelia Berg, June 19, 1965. BS cum laude, Ind. U., 1962, JD cum laude, 1965. Bar: Ill. 1965, Ind. 1965, N.Y. 1979. Assoc. law firm Keck, Mahin & Cate, Chgo., 1965-67; atty. Essex Group, Inc., Ft. Wayne, Ind., 1967-70, Amoco Corp., Chgo., 1970-73; assoc. gen. counsel, asst. sec. Canteen Corp., Chgo., 1973-75; sec., gen. counsel The Marmon Group, Inc. (and predecessor cos.), Chgo., 1975-78; v.p., gen. counsel, sec. Hanson Industries, Inc., N.Y.C., 1978-82; sr. v.p. law, chief fin. officer Petrie Stores Corp., N.Y.C., 1982-83; mem. Finley, Kumble, Wagner, Heine, Underberg, Manley, Myerson & Casey, N.Y.C., 1983-87, Paul, Weiss, Rifkind, Wharton & Garrison, N.Y.C., 1987-91; gen. counsel, chief legal officer Sterling Grace Capital Mgmt., L.P. and affiliated cos., N.Y.C., 1991—. Note editor Ind. Law Jour., 1964-65. Named to Ind. Track and Cross Country Hall of Fame, 1993. Mem. ABA, N.Y. State Bar Assn., Order of Coif, The Creek, Beta Gamma Sigma. Corporate, general, Mergers and acquisitions, Property, real (including real estate development, water). Home: Museum Tower 15 W 53d St Apt 31 E New York NY 10019-5401 Office: Sterling Grace Capital Mgmt 405 Park Ave Ste 1202 New York NY 10022 E-mail: tlseifert@msn.com.

SEIFF, ERIC A. lawyer; b. Mt. Vernon, N.Y., Apr. 25, 1933; s. Arthur N. and Mathilde (Cohen) S.; m. Sari Ginsburg, June 26, 1960 (div. Oct. 1983); children: Judith C., E. Kenneth, Dean A.; m. Meredith Feinman, Jan. 15, 1984; children: Abigail, Sarah. BA, Yale U., 1955; LLB, Columbia U., 1958. Bar: N.Y. 1958, U.S. Dist. Ct. (so. dist.) N.Y. 1960, U.S. Dist. Ct. (ea. dist.) N.Y. 1981, U.S. Ct. Appeals (2d cir.) 1965, U.S. Supreme Ct. 1967. Assoc. Bower and O'Connor, N.Y.C., 1959-60, Yellin, Kramer & Levy, N.Y.C., 1961; asst. dist. atty. N.Y.C. Dist. Atty.'s Office, 1962-67; asst. counsel Agy. for Internat. Devel., Washington, 1967-70, counsel Rio de Janeiro, 1970-72; gen. counsel N.Y. State Divsn. Criminal Justice Svcs., 1972-74; dep. chief atty. Legal Aid Soc. Criminal Def., N.Y.C., 1974-75; first dep. commr. N.Y. State Investigation Commn., 1975-77, chmn., 1977-79; ptnr. Seiff, Kretz & Abercrombie (formerly Scoppetta & Seiff), N.Y.C., 1981—; spl. dist. atty. Bronx County, 1986-89. Spl. asst. atty. gen. State of N.Y., Gov.'s Task Force Investigating Conduct of Attica Prosecutions, 1975. Bd. dirs. Legal Aid Soc., N.Y.C., 1994-2000; Prisoners' Legal Svcs., N.Y.C., 1989—, Lawyers Fund for Client Protection, N.Y., 1980—. Recipient Frank S. Hogan Meml. award Frank S. Hogan Assn., 1994. Mem.: N.Y. State Assn. Criminal Def. Lawyers (bd. dirs. 2001—), Bar Assn. City N.Y. (chmn. project on the homeless 1999—), N.Y. Criminal Bar Assn. (bd. dirs. 1980—, past pres.). General civil litigation, Criminal, Family and matrimonial. Office: Seiff Kretz & Abercrombie 645 Madison Ave New York NY 10022-1010

SEIGEL, JAN KEARNEY, lawyer; b. Bayonne, N.J., Feb. 7, 1947; s. Max and Margaret (Kearney) S.; m. Judy L. Mascuch, Aug. 29, 1971; children: Margaret, Emily, Jonas, Luke. BSBA, Georgetown U., 1968, JD, 1971; LLM in Taxation, NYU, 1974. Bar: N.J. 1971, D.C. 1972, Ga. 1972, U.S. Ct. Appeals (3d cir.) 1979, U.S. Supreme Ct. 1979. Law sec. to Hon. Theodore Rosenberg Superior Ct. of N.J., Paterson, NJ, 1971—72; asst. prosecutor Passaic County Pros.'s Office, Paterson, NJ, 1972—76; ptnr. Seigel & Assocs., Ridgewood, NJ, 1976—. Mem. faculty William Paterson Coll., 1974-79; lectr. N.J. Inst. for Continuing Edn., 1981—, N.J. State Bar and various county bar assns. Recipient Police Hon. Legion award Police Chiefs Assn. of N.J., 1980. Mem. ABA (rep. of N.J. young lawyers divsn. 1980-82), N.J. State Bar Assn. (Young Lawyer of Yr. award 1983, bd. trustees 1978-79), Passaic County Bar Assn. (bd. trustees 1973-81), Bergen County Bar Assn. Criminal, Personal injury (including property damage). Office: Seigel & Assocs 505 Goffle Rd Ridgewood NJ 07450-4027

SEIGLER, MICHAEL EDWARD, lawyer, librarian; b. Tallahassee, Oct. 14, 1948; s. Claude Milo and Roberta Bradford (Whitfield) S.; m. Janet Cummings, Feb. 19, 1971; children: Kelly Elizabeth, Megan Whitfield. AA, Lake Sumter C.C., 1968; BS, Fla. State Univ., 1970; MS, 1974; JD, Atlanta Law Sch., 1980. Bar: Ga. 1980, U.S. Ct. Appelas (5th cir.) 1980, U.S. Ct. Appeals (11th cir.) 1980, U.S. tax Ct. 1985, U.S. Supreme Ct. 1985, Cert. tchr. Libr. tchr. Sumter Correctional Inst., Bushnell, Fla., 1970-73; asst. libr. dir. Leesburg Pub. Libr. (Fla.), 1974-75, libr. dir., 1975-77, Atlanta Law Sch., 1979-81; atty. Brooks & Brock, Marietta, Ga., 1981-83; libr. Port Charlotte Pub. Libr., 1983-84; assoc. Brooks & Brock, Marietta, Ga., 1985, Brock & Barr, Marietta, 1985-86, Brock & Clay, 1987; judge pro hoc vice State Ct. of Cobb County, 1986; pvt. practice, 1986—. Asst. dir. Pine Mountain Regional Libr., 1988-95; libr. dir. Smyrna Pub. Libr.; design judge Ben Franklin Awards, 2001, 03. Columnist Smyrna Vinings Living, 2000-02; contbr. articles to jours. Vol. worker ACLU, Atlanta, 1979; mem. Fla. State U. Libr. Com., Tallahassee, 1974, Children's Program Com., Port Charlotte, 1983, Port Charlotte Cultural Ctr. Adv. Com., 1984, Pine Mountain Arts Coun., past bd. dirs.; mem. Cobb County Dem. Exec. Com., 1986-87; exec. com. Cobb Christmas, 1986-87; com. mem. Smyrna Cmty. Culture, 2000-2002, bd. dirs. 2003—; sec. program com. WRFG Cmty. Radio, 2002, bd. dirs., 2003--, chair fin. com., 2003--. Named Tchr. of Yr., Sumter Correctional Inst., 1973. Mem. Nat. Libr. Assn. (com. chmn. 1975-76), Fla. Libr. Assn. (caucus chmn. 1976-77), Ga. Libr. Assn. (mem. com. chmn. 1992—, sec. 1993-94, parliamentarian 1997, 1st v.p. 1999, pres. 2000), Metro Atlanta Libr. Assn. (v.p. 1997, pres. 1998), Southeastern Libr. Assn. (mem. com. 1988—, convention chair 2000, com. chair 2001—), ALA (con. spkr.), Atlanta Law Sch. Alumni Assn. (treas. 1986-90), Fla. State U. Alumni Assn. (life), Ga. Libr. Video Assn. (pres. 1991-92), Mensa (sec. 1987, 89, pres. Ga. chpt. 1988, mediator Ga. chpt. 2000-02, trustee Mensa Edn. and Rsch. Found. (v.p. 1993), Ga. Coun. Media Orgn. (chair steering com. 2000), Leadership Meriwether (pres. 1993). Condemnation (eminent domain), Insurance, Taxation, general. Home: 3023 Bay Berry Dr SW Marietta GA 30008-5674 Office: 100 Village Green Cir SE Smyrna GA 30080-3478

SEILER, JAMES ELMER, judge; b. LaCrosse, Wis., Sept. 2, 1946; s. Elmer Bernard and Margaret Theresa (Mader) S.; m. Sonia Gonzales, Feb. 9, 1968; children: Rebecca, Cristina. BA, U. Wis., LaCrosse, 1968; JD, U. Wis., 1973. Bar: Wis. 1973, Minn. 1981, U.S. Supreme Ct. 1985, Mo. 1986. Pvt. practice, Balsam Lake, Wis., 1973-81; in-house counsel Farm Credit Banks, St. Paul, 1981-85; corp. counsel Hussmann Corp., St. Louis, 1985-94; adminstrv. law judge Social Security, Evansville, Ind., 1994-95, Office of Hearings and Appeals, Creve Coeur, Mo., 1995—; chief adminstrv. law judge Hearing Office, Creve Coeur, Mo., 1997—. Candidate Dist. Atty., Polk County, Wis., 1980. With U.S. Army, 1969-71. Avocations: soccer coach, swimming, water skiing, running. Home: 18 Harbor Point Ct Lake Saint Louis MO 63367-1336 Office: 11475 Olde Cabin Rd Saint Louis MO 63141-7130

SEILS, WILLIAM GEORGE, lawyer; b. Chgo., Aug. 9, 1935; s. Harry H. and Hazel C. (Sullivan) S.; m. Evelyn E. Oliver, Sept. 8, 1956; children: Elizabeth Ann, Ellen Carol, Eileen Alison. AB, JD, U. Mich., 1959. Bar: Ill. bar 1959. Since practiced in, Chgo.; ptnr. Arvey, Hodes & Costello & Burman, 1968-87; gen. counsel, sec., sr. v.p. Richardson Electronics, Ltd., LaFox, Ill., 1986—. Contbr. articles to profl. jours.; asst. editor: Mich. Law Rev, 1958-59. Mem. Ill. Bar Assn., Order of Coif. Commercial, contracts (including sales of goods; commercial financing), Corporate, general, Securities. Office: Richardson Electronics Ltd PO Box 393 40w267 Keslinger Rd Lafox IL 60147-0393 E-mail: wgs@rell.com.

SEINIGER, WILLIAM BRECK, JR., lawyer; b. Richmond, Va., Oct. 28, 1947; s. William Breck and Margaret Crissy Seiniger; m. Julie Marsh, Feb. 14, 1991. BA, U. Mass., 1972; JD, U. Idaho, 1978. Founding ptnr. Seiniger, Nevin, Kofoed & Herzfeld, Boise, 1982-91, pvt. practice, 1992—. Mem. Idaho State Bar Assn. (chmn. solo and small firm sect. 1994-96, past chair 1997, Idaho civil rules com., Outstanding Svc. award 1996), Idaho Brain Injury Assn. (bd. dirs.), Idaho Lawyer's Assistance Com., Idaho Trial Lawyers Assn., Assn. Trial Lawyers Am. Avocation: computer science. Labor (including EEOC, Fair Labor Standards Act, labor-management relations, NLRB, OSHA), Personal injury (including property damage), Workers' compensation. Office: 942 W Myrtle St Boise ID 83702-7060

SEITMAN, JOHN MICHAEL, lawyer, arbitrator, mediator; b. Bloomington, Ill., Feb. 9, 1942; BS, U. Ill., 1964, JD, 1966. Bar: Calif., U.S. Dist. Ct. (so., cen., no. and ea. dists.) Calif., U.S. Ct. Appeals (9th cir.). Prin. Lindley, Lazar & Scales, San Diego, 1966-97; full-time neutral affiliated with JAMS, 1997—. Lectr. in continuing legal edn. Bd. dirs. San Diego County Bar Found., 1983-89, treas., 1983-84, pres., 1988-89; del. to 9th Cir. Jud. Conf., 1986, 88. Fellow Am. Bar Found.; mem. ABA, State Bar Calif. (pres. 1991-92), San Diego County Bar Assn. (pres. 1986). General civil litigation, Commercial, consumer (including collections, credit), General practice. Office: PO Box 2156 Del Mar CA 92014-1456 Personal E-mail: jseitman@pacbell.net.

SEITZ, PATRICIA ANN, judge; b. Washington, Sept. 2, 1946; d. Richard J. and Bettie Jean (Merrill) S.; m. Alan Graham Greer, Aug. 14, 1981. BA in History cum laude, Kans. State U., 1968; JD, Georgetown U., 1973. Bar: Fla. 1973, D.C. 1975, U.S. Dist. Ct. (no., mid., so. dists., trial bar) Fla., U.S. Ct. Appeals (5th and 11th cirs.), U.S. Supreme Ct. Reporter Dallas Times Herald, Washington, 1970-73; law clk. to Hon. Charles R. Richey U.S. Dist. Ct., Washington, 1973-74; assoc. Steel, Hector & Davis, Miami, Fla., 1974-79, ptnr., 1980-96; dir. office legal counsel Office of Nat. Drug Control Policy, Exec. Office of Pres., Washington, 1996-97; judge U.S. Dist. Ct. (so. dist.) Fla., 1998—. Adj. faculty U. Miami Law Sch., Coral Gables, Fla., 1984-88; faculty Nat. Inst. Trial Advocacy, Boulder, Colo., 1982, 83, 95, Chapel Hill, N.C., 1984, 87. Fla. region, 1989; lectr. in field. Contbr. numerous articles to law jours. Mem. Dade Munroe Mental Health Bd., Miami, 1982-84, United Way of Greater Miami comty. devel. com., 1984-87; chmn. family abuse task force United Way of Greater Miami, 1986; chmn. devel. com. Miami City Ballet, 1986-87, bd. dirs., 1986-90. Fellow Am. Bar Found., Am. Bd. Trial Advocacy, Internat. Soc. Barristers; mem. ABA (chmn. various coms. 1979-85, Ho. Dels. 1992-96), Am. Arbitration Assn. (nat. bd. dirs. 1995-97, complex case panel arbitrator), The Fla. Bar (bd. govs. young lawyer divsn. 1981-82, bd. govs. 1986-92, pres. 1993-94, bd. cert. civil trial), Fla. Assn. Women Lawyers, Dade County Bar Assn. (pub. interest law bank). Roman Catholic. Avocations: travel, art. Office: Fed Courthouse Square 301 N Miami Ave Fl 5 Miami FL 33128-7702

SEKINE, OSAMU, lawyer; b. Saitama Prefecture, Japan, June 14, 1942; s. Takeshi and Haru (Kojima) S.; m. Michiko (Ishikawa) Sekine, Apr. 27, 1969; 1 child, Akira. LLB, U. Tokyo, 1967; LLM, Harvard U., 1974. Ptnr. Blakemore & Mitsuki, Tokyo, 1980-86, Tsunematsu Yanase & Sekine, Tokyo, 1987—2000, Nagashima Ohmo & Tsunematsu, Tokyo, 2000—. Co-author: Commentary on Insider Trading Regulations, 1989, Commentary on the Financial Futures Trading Law, 1991. Commercial, contracts (including sales of goods; commercial financing), Franchising, Securities. Home: 624 Ishida Isehara-shi Kanagawa 259-1116 Japan Office: Nagashima Ohmo & Tsunematsu Kioicho Bldg 3-12 Kioicho Chiyoda-ku Tokyo 102-0094 Japan

SELBY, LELAND CLAY, lawyer; b. Granite City, Ill., July 4, 1944; s. William Edward and Agnes (Newell) S.; m. Diane Schryver, Aug. 20, 1966; children: Leland Clay, Timothy Schryver, Amanda Elizabeth. BA, U. Richmond, 1966; LLB, U. Va., 1969. Bar: Conn. 1969, N.Y. 1989. Assoc. Hirschberg, Pettengill & Strong, Greenwich, Conn., 1969-74; ptnr. Hirschberg, Pettengill, Strong & Nagle, Greenwich, 1974-78, Whitman & Ransom, Greenwich, 1978-93, Whitman Breed Abbott & Morgan, Greenwich, 1993-95; mem. Fogarty Cohen Selby & Nemiroff LLC, Greenwich, 1995—. Bd. dirs., v.p. Stamford (Conn.) Ctr. for Arts, 1989—; chmn. bd. govs. Greenwich Found. for Cmty. Gifts, 1980-90; pres. United Way of Greenwich, 1978-80; bd. dirs. Retirement Sys., Town of Greenwich, 1993-2001, Greenwich Symphony Orch., 1986-95; co-pres. Greenwich chpt. English-Speaking Union; bd. dirs. English-Speaking Union U.S. Named Greenwich Young Man of Yr., Greenwich Jaycees, 1974. Fellow Am. Coll. Trust and Estate Counsel; mem. ABA, Conn. Bar Assn., N.Y. State Bar Assn., Greenwich Bar Assn., Preston Mountain Club (sec. 1999—), Riverside Yacht Club, Va. Club of N.Y.C., Harpoon Club of Greenwich. Episcopalian. Avocations: fly fishing, sporting clays, hiking, reading, travel. Estate planning, Probate (including wills, trusts), Estate taxation. Home: One Pinecrest Rd Riverside CT 06878 Office: Fogarty Cohen Selby & Nemiroff 88 Field Point Rd Greenwich CT 06836-2508

SELCER, DAVID MARK, lawyer; b. Cleve., Feb. 12, 1943; s. Lester and Sylvia (Esral) S.; m. Belinda Weine, Aug. 8, 1968 (div. 1986); children: Daniel, Anne, Emily; m. Susan Merwin, Mar. 22, 1993. BA, Northwestern U., 1965; JD, Ohio State U., 1968. Bar: Ohio, 1968, Ill. 1969, U.S. Dist. Ct. (so. dist.) Ohio 1971, U.S. Dist. Ct. (no. dist.) Ohio 1973. Ptnr. Porter, Wright, Morris & Arthur, Columbus, Ohio, 1973-78, Krupman, Fromson & Selcer, Columbus, 1979-81, Baker & Hostetler, Columbus, 1981—. Adj. prof. Capitol U. Law Sch., Columbus, 1973-74; bd. dirs. Consolidated Stores Corp., 1990-91. Trustee Temple Israel, Columbus, 1987-94; v.p. Jewish Family Svc., 1987-94. Recipient Disting. Service award Columbus Symphony Orch., 1986-87. Mem. ABA (equal employment opportunity subcom. of labor com 1978—), Nat. Labor Relations Bd (asst. bd. mem. 1967-68), Ohio Bar Assn., Columbus Bar Assn. State civil litigation, Corporate, general, Labor (including EEOC, Fair Labor Standards Act, labor-management relations, NLRB, OSHA). Office: Baker & Hostetler 65 E State St Ste 2100 Columbus OH 43215-4260

SELCHICK, JEFFREY MARK, arbitrator, judge; b. N.Y.C., July 22, 1951; s. Bernard and Irene Selchick; m. Cathy Lynn Persans, Jan. 26, 1974; children: Lauren Anne, Brian Bernard, Karen Ruth, Alyson Hope. BA, SUNY, Plattsburgh, 1971; JD, Union U., Albany, N.Y., 1975. Bar: N.Y. 1976, U.S. Dist. Ct. (no. dist.) N.Y. 1976, U.S. Supreme Ct. 1979. Asst. counsel SUNY, Albany, 1975-76, N.Y. State Gov.'s Office of Employee Rels., Albany, 1976-78, dep. counsel, dir. litigation, 1978-82; arbitrator Albany, 1982—. Adj. prof. law Union U., Albany, 1989-92; instr. Cornell U., Ithaca, N.Y., 1982-85; cons. N.Y. State Labor-Mgmt. Inst., Albany, 1985—; judge Village of Menands, N.Y., 1986—. Mem. Am. Arbitration Assn., Nat. Acad. Arbitrators, N.Y. State Magistrate's Assn., N.Y. State Bar Assn. Avocations: jogging, competitive pistol shooting, writing. Home and Office: PO Box 11-280 Albany NY 12211-0280 E-mail: selchick@nycap.rr.com.

SELCUK, GALIP MURAT, lawyer; s. Yuksel and Yldz Selcuk. Grad., Ankara U., 1997. Bar: Ankara 1998, Istanbul 2000, cert.: Münich (European patent atty.) 2001. Lawyer Cakmak Ortak Avukat Burosu, Ankara, 1998—2000, Derman Ortak Avukat Burosu, Istanbul, Turkey, 2000—. Trademark atty. Turkish Patent Inst., Ankara, 1999—, patent atty., 1999—. Mem.: The Econ. and Social History Found. Turkey, Amateur Photographers and Cinematographers Assn. Istanbul. Mergers and acquisitions, Corporate, general, Intellectual property. Office: Derman Ortak Avukat Burosu Buyukdere Cad Maya Akar Center 100/17 34394 Istanbul Turkey Office Fax: +90 (212) 355 13 01. E-mail: gselcuk@doab.com.

SELFE, EDWARD MILTON, lawyer; b. St. Paul, Sept. 26, 1921; s. Edward Milton and Eleanor (Moen) S.; m. Rena Hill McMurry, July 10, 1950 (div. Oct. 1979); children: Murry, Edward, James; m. Jane Comer Bowron, Dec. 31, 1979. BA, Presbyn. Coll., Clinton, S.C., 1943; LLB, U. Va., 1950. Bar: N.Y., Va., Ala. Asst. prof. law Law Sch., U. Va., Charlottesville, 1950-51; assoc. Shearman & Sterling, N.Y.C., 1951-52, Bradley Arant Rose White, Birmingham, Ala., 1952-57, ptnr., 1957-2000, of counsel, 2000—; vice chmn. Secor Bank, Birmingham, 1988-91, gen. counsel, 1991-93. Lectr. Law Sch., U. Ala., Tuscaloosa, 1968—90. Chmn. Birmingham-Jefferson County Transit Authority, 1972-82. Served to capt., inf. U.S. Army, 1943-47, ETO. Decorated Silver Star, Bronze Star (V), Purple Heart. Fellow Am. Coll. Tax Counsel; mem. ABA, Ala. Bar Assn., Birmingham Bar Assn. Democrat. Avocation: tennis (ranked 4th nationally in men's singles-age 80, 2002). Securities, Federal civil litigation, Corporate taxation. Home: 84 Arlington Crest 2600 Arlington Ave S Birmingham AL 35205-4167 Office: Bradley Arant Rose & White One Federal Pl 1819 Fifth Ave N Birmingham AL 35203-2104

SELIGMAN, DELICE, lawyer; b. Worcester, Mass. m. Frederick Seligman. AB, MA, Clark U.; JD, NYU, 1971. Bar: N.Y. 1972, U.S. Dist. Ct. (so. and ea. dists.) N.Y. 1973, U.S. Supreme Ct. 1979. Assoc. Legal Aid Soc. Nassau County, Mineola, N.Y., 1972-76; ptnr. Seligman, Stein & Abromowitz, Garden City, 1976-86, Seligman & Seligman, N.Y.C., N.Y., 1986—. Legal counsel Contemporary Sculptors, Roslyn, N.Y., 1987-90, Artists Network Great Neck, N.Y., 1987-90, Woodstock Animal Rights Movement, Legal Action for Animals, Stop Graffiti Now, Inc.; pres. Wildlife Legal Action, Inc. Bd. dirs. For Our Children and Us, Hicksville, N.Y., 1985—; pres. Vol. Lawyers for Animal Rights, 2001—, Animal Advocates, Inc., 1999—. Mem. N.Y. State Bar Assn., Nassau Women's Bar Assn. (pres. 1982-83), Bar Assn. Nassau County (chair arts com. 1984-85), Phi Alpha Delta. General civil litigation, Criminal, General practice. Home: Runge Rd Shokan NY 12481 Office: 26 Broadway New York NY 10004-1703 also: Seligman & Seligman 70 Main St Kingston NY 12401-3802

SELIGMAN, FREDERICK, lawyer; b. Bklyn. s. Martin and Florence (Alperin) S.; m. Delice Felice. AB, Clark U., 1957; JD, N.Y. Law Sch., 1972. Bar: N.Y. 1973, U.S. Dist. Ct. (so. and ea. dists.) N.Y. 1974, U.S. Tax Ct. 1974, U.S. Ct. Appeals (2d cir.) 1975, U.S. Supreme Ct. 1979. Atty. N.Y.C. (N.Y.) Police Dept., 1972-73; asst. dist. atty. N.Y. County, N.Y.C., 1973-79; pvt. practice N.Y.C., 1980-85; ptnr. Seligman & Seligman, N.Y.C., 1986—. Mem. N.Y. Criminal Bar Assn., N.Y. State Defenders Assn. Criminal, General practice. Home: Runge Rd Shokan NY 12481 Office: Seligman & Seligman 26 Broadway New York NY 10004-1703

SELIGMAN, JOEL, dean; b. N.Y.C., Jan. 11, 1950; s. Selig Jacob and Muriel (Bienstock) S.; m. Friederike Felber, July 30, 1981; children: Andrea, Peter. AB magna cum laude, UCLA, 1971; JD, Harvard U., 1974. Bar: Calif. 1975. Atty., writer Corp. Accountability Rsch. Group, Washington, 1974-77; prof. law Northeastern U. Law Sch., 1977-83, George Washington U., 1983-86, U. Mich., Ann Arbor, 1986-95; dean law U. Ariz., Tucson, 1995-99; dean sch. law Washington U., St. Louis, 1999—. Cons. Fed. Trade Commn., 1979-82, Dept. Transp., 1983, Office Tech. Assessment, 1988-89; chair adv. com. on mkt. info. SEC, 2000-2001; reporter Nat. Conf. of Commrs. on Uniform State Laws, Uniform Securities Act, 2002. Author (with others) Constitutionalizing the Corporation: The Case for the Federal Chartering of Giant Corporations, 1976, The High Citadel: The Influence of Harvard Law School, 1978, The Transformation of Wall Street: A History of the Securities and Exchange Commission and Modern Corporate Finance, 1982, 3d edit., 2003, The SEC and the Future of Finance, 1985, (multi-volume) Securities Regulation, The Near Uniform Securites Act, 2003; contbr. articles to profl. jours. Mem. State Bar Calif., Am. Law Inst. (adv. com., advisor corp. governance project), AICPAs (profl. ethics exec. com. 2000—). Office: Wash U Sch Law CB 1120 1 Brookings Dr Saint Louis MO 63130-4862

SELIGMANN, WILLIAM ROBERT, lawyer, author; b. Davenport, Iowa, Oct. 10, 1956; s. William Albert and Barbara Joyce (Carmichael) S.; m. Carole Lee Francis; children: D Anna, Matthew. BA, U. Calif., Santa Barbara, 1979; JD, Santa Clara U., 1982. Bar: Calif. 1983, U.S. Dist. Ct. (no. dist.) Calif. 1983. Assoc. Office of J.R. Dempster, Cupertino, Calif., 1983-85; city atty. City of Campbell, Calif., 1985—; ptnr. Dempster, Seligmann & Raineri, Los Gatos, Calif., 1985—2001, pvt. practice, 2001—. Judge pro tem, Santa Clara County, 1992—. Bd. dirs. Los Gatos C. of C. Mem. Santa Clara County Bar Assn. (civil practice com., judiciary com.), State Bar of Calif. (exec. bd. pub. law sect. 2001—). Avocations: cross country skiing, scuba diving, swimming, writing, Aikido. General civil litigation, Land use and zoning (including planning), Property, real (including real estate development, water). Office: 333 Church St Santa Cruz CA 95060 also: Ste 206 236 N Santa Cruz Ave Los Gatos CA 95030 E-mail: bill@soutbaylaw.com.

SELINGER, JERRY ROBIN, lawyer; b. Peekskill, NY, Nov. 3, 1947; s. Philip R. and Helen D. (Klein) S.; m. Barbara D. Wax, Aug. 2, 1969; children: Elise, Scott. BS in Engring. Sci., SUNY, Buffalo, 1969; MS, Columbia U., 1971; JD, George Washington U., 1975. Bar: Md. 1975, D.C. 1976, U.S. Ct. Appeals (fed. cir.) 1977, U.S. Supreme Ct. 1978, Tex. 1980, U.S. Ct. Appeals (5th and 11th cirs.) 1981, U.S. Ct. Appeals (3d cir.) 1982. Atty. Arent, Fox, Kintner, Plotkin & Kahn, Washington, 1975-79, Richards, Harris & Medlock, Dallas, 1979-82; mem., dir. Baker, Mills & Glast, Dallas, 1982-90; ptnr. Vinson & Elkins LLP, Dallas, 1990-97; shareholder Jenkens & Gilchrist, Dallas, 1997—. Contbr. articles to profl. jours. Bd. trustees Dallas Bar Found., 2001—. Mem. ABA, Tex. Bar Assn. (chair intellectual property law sect. 1996-97, bd. dirs. 1998-2001), Dallas Bar Assn. (bd. dirs. 1995-96), Tex. Young Lawyers Assn. (bd. dirs. 1984-86, Pres. award 1986), Am. Intellectual Property Law Assn. (bd. dirs. 2002—), Dallas (Tex.) Bar Found. (bd. trustees, 2001—), Dallas Assn. Young Lawyers (sec. 1983, treas. 1984), Order of Coif, Phi Delta Phi. Federal civil litigation, State civil litigation, Trademark and copyright. Home: 10414 Woodford Dr Dallas TX 75229-6317 Office: Jenkens & Gilchrist 1445 Ross Ave Ste 3200 Dallas TX 75202-2785 E-mail: jselinger@jenkens.com.

SELLERS, BARBARA JACKSON, federal judge; b. Richmond, Va., Oct. 3, 1940; m. Richard F. Sellers; children: Elizabeth M., Anne W., Catherine A. Attended, Baldwin-Wallace Coll., 1958-60; BA cum laude, Ohio State U., 1962; JD magna cum laude, Capital U. Law Sch., Columbus, Ohio, 1979. Bar: Ohio 1979, U.S. Dist. Ct. (so. dist.) Ohio 1981, U.S. Ct. Appeals (6th cir.), 1986. Jud. law clk. Hon. Robert J. Sidman, U.S. Bankruptcy Judge, Columbus, Ohio, 1979-81; assoc. Lasky & Semons, Columbus, 1981-82; jud. law clk. to Hon. Thomas M. Herbert, U.S. Bankrupcty Ct., Columbus, 1982-84; assoc. Baker & Hostetler, Columbus, 1984-86; U.S. bankruptcy judge So. Dist. Ohio, Columbus, 1986—. Lectr. on bankruptcy univs., insts., assns. Recipient Am. Jurisprudence prize contracts and criminal law, 1975-76, evidence and property, 1976-77, Corpus Juris Secundum awards, 1975-76, 76-77. Mem. Columbus Bar Assn., Am. Bankruptcy Inst., Nat. Conf. Bankruptcy Judges, Order of Curia, Phi Beta Kappa. Office: US Bankruptcy Ct 170 N High St Columbus OH 43215-2403 E-mail: barbara_sellers@ohsb.uscourts.gov.

SELLERS, ELIZABETH MARTIN, lawyer; b. Columbus, Ohio, May 30, 1966; d. Richard Franklin and Barbara Jackson Sellers; m. Marc David Keffer, Sept. 12, 1992; children: Althea Louise, Paul Forrest Keffer. AB in Philosophy, Yale U., 1988; JD, Vanderbilt U., 1991; ML, Georgetown U., 1995. Bar: Pa. 1993, DC 1995, Maine 2000. Law clk. to Hon. Keith M. Lundin U.S. Bankruptcy Ct. (mid. dist.) Tenn., Nashville, 1991—92; assoc. atty. Sherman, Meehan, Curtis & Air, Washington, 1992—94; assoc., of counsel Caplin & Drysdale, chartered, Washington, 1994—2000; of counsel Bernstein, Shur, Sawyer & Nelson, Portland, Maine, 2000—. Mem. planned giving com. Maine Med. Ctr., Portland, 2001—. Mem. endowment com. Children's Mus. Maine, Portland, 2002—; dir. Crossroads Women, Portland, 2002—. Mem.: ABA, Yale Club Western Maine (interviewer Yale Shepard 2000—). Democrat. Avocations: reading, hiking, camping, kayaking. Taxation, general, Estate taxation, Corporate taxation. Office: Bernstein Shur Sawyer and Nelson 100 Middle St Portland ME 04104 Business E-Mail: esellers@mainelaw.com.

SELMI, WILLIAM, JR., lawyer; b. Phila., June 18, 1937; s. William and Eleanor (Mishler) S.; m. Joan H. Silver, Dec. 4, 1966 (div. 1976); children: William III, Richard Kern; m. Karen Ladd Wheeler, Sept. 19, 1998. AB, U. Miami, Coral Gables, Fla., 1969, JD, 1972. Bar: Fla. 1972, U.S. Dist. Ct. (so. dist.) Fla. 1973, U.S. Supreme Ct., 1976. Ptnr. Peer & Selmi, Jensen Beach, Fla., 1972-79; pvt. practice law Okeechobee, Fla., 1979—. Pres. Kiwanis Club, Jensen Beach, 1978; bd. dirs. Jensen Beach C. of C., 1977-78, Martin County Dem. Com., Stuart, Fla., 1977, Okeechobee br. ARC, 1990-95, Okeechobee United Way, 1993-97. Avocations: military history, fishing. Home: 136 SW 85th Ave Okeechobee FL 34974-1554 Office: 306 NW 5th St Okeechobee FL 34972-2565

SELTZER, JEFFREY LLOYD, diversified financial services company executive; b. Bklyn., July 27, 1956; s. Bernard and Sue (Harris) S.; m. Ana Isabel Sifre, Sept. 2, 1985; children: Ian Alexander, Pamela Allison. BS in Econ. cum laude, U. Pa., 1978; JD, Georgetown U., 1981. Bar: N.Y. 1982. Assoc. Austrian, Lance & Stewart, N.Y.C., 1981-85; assoc. gen. counsel, asst. v.p. Shearson Lehman Bros., N.Y.C., 1986; mng. dir. Lehman Bros., N.Y.C., 1986-94; dep. chmn., mng. dir. CIBC Oppenheimer Corp., N.Y.C., 1994-99; exec. v.p., COO Adirondack Trading Ptnrs., N.Y.C., 1999—; faculty assoc. Merrill Lynch Ctr. for Study of Internat. Fin. Mkts. and Svcs., Zarb Sch. Bus., Hofstra U. , 2001—. Spl. prof. law Hofstra U., 1999. Author: The U.S. Greeting Card Market, 1977, Starting and Organizing a Business, 1984, Swap Risk Management: A Primer, 1988, A View for the Top: The Role of the Board of Directors and Senior Management in the Derivatives Business, 1995, Financial Strategy Roundtable: Derivatives, 1995. Mem. Nat. Policy Forum, 1994—97; mem. U.S. Trade Adv. Com. on Svc. Industries, Washington, 1990—94; mem. local adv. bd. County of Nassau, 1997—99; mem. adv. bd. Huntsman Program in Internat. Studies and Bus. U. Pa., Phila., 1997—; mem. securities industry coalition Bush-Quayle campaign, 1992; mem. small bus. adv. coun. Rep. Nat. Com., Washington, 1984—90; mem. nat. adv. coun. U.S. SBA; policy analyst Reagan-Bush Com., Arlington, Va., 1980; advisor Friends of Giuliani, N.Y.C., 1989, New Yorkers for Lew Lehrman, N.Y.C., 1981—82; dir. Nassau County Sports Commn., 1997—, mem. exec. com.; vice chmn., trustee Inst. Internat. Bankers, 1998—99; chmn. Class of 1978 reunion com. U. Pa., 1997—. Recipient Disting. Alumnus award W. C. Mepham H.S., 1994. Mem. ABA, Re. Nat. Lawyers Assn., Federalist Soc., Ctr. for Study of Presidency, Securities Industry Assn. (chmn. swap and derivative products com. 1990-94). Office: 120 W 45th St New York NY 10036

SELTZER, RICHARD C. lawyer; b. N.Y.C., Sept. 3, 1943; s. Edward and Beatrice (Fishman) S.; m. Carol Reische, Aug. 31, 1969; children: Wendy, Mark. BA, Harvard U., 1965; JD, Columbia U., 1968. Bar: N.Y. 1969, U.S. Dist. Ct. (so. and ea. dists.) N.Y. 1969, U.S. Ct. Appeals (5th cir.) 1978, U.S. Ct. Appeals (2nd cir.) 1987, U.S. Supreme Ct. 1995. Ptnr. Kaye Scholer LLP, N.Y.C., 1969—. Mem. ABA, Assn. of Bar of City of N.Y. Commercial, contracts (including sales of goods; commercial financing), Patent, Property, real (including real estate development, water). Office: Kaye Scholer 425 Park Ave New York NY 10022-3506

SELZER, JAMES OTTO, lawyer; b. Lawrence, Kans., Sept. 26, 1948; s. Otto William and Ilene May Selzer; m. Barbara Lynn Phillips, Aug. 25, 1973; children: Bryan James, Kevin Andrew. BS, Baker U., Baldwin, Kans., 1970; MA, U. Oreg., 1974; JD, U. Kans., 1977. Bar: Mo. 1977. Assoc. Linde Thomson Langworthy Kolm & Van Dyke, Kans. City, Mo., 1977—79, ptnr., 1980—91, Selzer & Frerking, P.C., Mo., 1991, Morrison & Heckler, LLP, Mo., 1991—2002, Stinson Morrison Hecker LLP, Mo., 2002—. Bd. dir. Variety Club of Greater Kans. City, 1983—, Nat. Kidney Found. of Kans. and Western Mo., Kans. City, 1996—. Fulbright Scholar, Albert Ludwig U., Freiburg, Germany, 1970—71. Mem.: Met. Bar Assn. of Kans. City, Nat. Assn. Bond Lawyers. Avocations: skiing, fishing. Finance, Corporate, general, Securities. Home: 604 NE Silverleaf Pl Lees Summit MO 64064 Office: Stinson Morrison Hecker LLP 2600 Grand Ave Kansas City MO 64108

SEMAYA, FRANCINE LEVITT, lawyer; b. N.Y.C., Mar. 26, 1951; d. Julie and Ann (Tannenbaum) Levitt; m. Richard Semaya, Aug. 3, 1975; children: Stefanie Rachel, David Steven, Scott Brian. BA magna cum laude, Bklyn. Coll., 1973, MS magna cum laude, 1975; JD cum laude, N.Y. Law Sch., 1982. Bar: N.Y. 1983, U.S. Dist. Ct. (ea. and so. dists.) N.Y. 1983, U.S. Supreme Ct. 2000. Sr. legal analyst, atty. Am. Internat. Group, Inc., N.Y.C., 1977-83; assoc. counsel, asst. v.p. Beneficial Ins. Group, Inc. (formerly Benico, Inc.), Peapack, N.J., 1983-87; v.p., counsel Am. Centennial Ins. Co., Peapack, 1985-87; legal/reins. cons. Peapack, 1987; counsel reins. Integrity Ins. Co. in Liquidation, Paramus, N.J., 1988-91; ptnr. Werner & Kennedy, N.Y.C., 1991-99; sr. ptnr. Cozen O'Connor, N.Y.C., 1999—. Spkr. in field. Author: Insurance Insolvency--A New Generation, 2001, Insurance Insolvencies 2002-2003: Is the Industry Prepared?, 2002; editor: Law and Practice of Insurance Insolvency Revisited, 1999, State of Insurance Regulation: Today and Tomorrow, 1991; contbg. editor: Reference Handbook Ins. Co. Insolvency, 4th edit., 1999; contbr. articles to profl. jours. Mem. ABA (sect. del. to ho. dels. 1998—, tort, trial and ins. practice sect. coun. 1994-97, chmn. task force on ins. insolvency 1995-2000, chmn. professionalism com. 1997-98, chmn. pub. regulation of ins. law com. 1990-91, chair pub. rels. com. 1993-94, co-editor State Regulation Ins. 1991), Internat. Assn. Ins. Receivers, N.Y. State Bar Assn., Practicing Law Inst. (ins. law adv. com. 1995—), Assn. Bar City N.Y. (ins. law com.), Fedn. Regulatory Counsel, Phi Beta Kappa. Avocations: reading, travel. Administrative and regulatory, Corporate, general, Insurance. Office: Cozen O'Connor 16 Fl 45 Broadway Atrium New York NY 10006-3007 E-mail: fsemaya@cozen.com.

SEMPLE, JAMES WILLIAM, lawyer; b. Phila., Nov. 18, 1943; s. Calvin James and Marie (Robinson) S.; m. Ellen Burns, Nov. 26, 1966; children: Megan Semple Greenberg, Luke Robinson. AB, St. Josephs U., Phila., 1965; JD, Villanova U., 1974. Bar: Del. 1974, U.S. Dist. Ct. Del. 1974, D.C. 1975, U.S. Ct. Appeals (3d cir.) 1982, U.S. Tax Ct. 1996. Ptnr. Morris, James, Hitchens & Williams, Wilmington, 1983—. Lectr. numerous seminars; mediator Superior Ct. Voluntary Mediation Program. Mem.: ABA, Am. Judicature Soc., Fedn. Defense and Corp. Counsel, Am. Bd. Trial Advs. General civil litigation, Commercial, contracts (including sales of goods; commercial financing), Insurance. Office: Morris James Hitchens & Williams, LLP PO Box 2306 Wilmington DE 19899-2306 E-mail: jsemple@morrisjames.com.

SEMPLE, LLOYD ASHBY, lawyer; b. St. Louis, June 7, 1939; s. Robert B. and Isabelle A. S.; m. Cynthia T. Semple, Aug. 26, 1961; children: Whitney, Sarah, Lloyd Jr., Terrell. BA, Yale U., 1961; JD, U. Mich, 1964. Bar: Mich. 1964. Assoc. Dykema Gossett, Detroit, 1964-70, ptnr., 1971—, chmn., 1994—2002. Bd. dirs. SenSystech, Inc., 2003—. Councilman, mayor pro tem City of Grosse Pointe Farms, Mich., 1975—83; chmn. exec. com. Detroit Zool. Soc.; dir., trustee, sec. Karmanos Cancer Inst.; chmn. bd. trustees Detroit Med. Ctr. Corp. Mem. ABA, Mich. Bar Assn., Detroit Bar Assn., Country Club Detroit, Yondotega Club, Detroit Athletic Club, Yale Club (N.Y.C.), Bohemian Club (San Francisco). Episcopalian. Corporate, general, Mergers and acquisitions, Securities. Home: 57 Cambridge Rd Grosse Pointe Farms MI 48236-3004 Office: Dykema Gossett 400 Renaissance Ctr Ste 3500 Detroit MI 48243-1602 E-mail: lsemple@dykema.com.

SENEKER, CARL JAMES, II, (KIM SENEKER), lawyer; b. San Jose, Calif., Oct. 12, 1942; s. Carl James and Beth D. (Hearn) S.; m. Julie Marie Pardee, June 17, 1967; children: Mark Gwynn, Todd Christian. AB, Stanford U., 1964; JD, U. Calif., Berkeley, 1967. Bar: Calif. 1969, U.S. Dist. Ct. (no. dist.) Calif. 1973. Law clk. to Hon. William O. Douglas U.S. Supreme Ct., Washington, 1967-68; ptnr. Morrison & Foerster, San Francisco, 1971-84, 96—, L.A., 1984-96. Adj. prof. law, lectr. law sch. Stanford U., Palo Alto, Calif., 1982-83. Co-editor: California Real Estate Law and Practice, Vols. 12 & 13, 1983-96; contbr. articles to profl. jours. Bd. dirs. L.A. Hdqs. City Assn., 1988-93. Capt. USAF, 1968-71. Mem. Am. Coll. Real Estate Lawyers (bd. govs. 1989-97, pres.-elect 1996-97, pres. 1997-98), State Bar Calif. (real property law sect., vice-chair exec. com. 1987-90). Roman Catholic. Avocations: golf, travel, music. Environmental, Land use and zoning (including planning), Property, real (including real estate development, water). Office: Morrison & Foerster 425 Market St Fl 32 San Francisco CA 94105-2467

SENGEN, RYUICHIRO, law educator; b. Kyoto, Nov. 15, 1932; s. Toshio and Shizuko Sengen; m. Junko Nagao, May 17, 1970. LLB, Kyoto U., 1955, LLM, LLD, Kyoto U., 1957. Cert. advocate, arbitrator. Lectr., asst. prof. Wakayama (Japan) U., 1957-66; asst. prof., prof. Doshisha U., Kyoto, Japan, 1966—. Guest rsch. prof. Rsch. Ctr. Advanced Sci. and Tech. U. Tokyo, 1995, advocate, 2001—; lectr. on copyright law, 2000. Author: The Know-How Contract in Germany, Japan and the United States, 1984, Traite du Droit du Brevet Francais, 1997, Case Studies on Intellectual Property II, 1998, Lecture on Patent Law, 3d edit., 2000; editor: Caes Studies on Intellectual Property (jour.) Tizai Kanri, Intellectual Property Management, 1978—. Pres. Inst. Indsl. Property Law, Kyoto, 1973—; bd. dirs. Japan Assn. Indsl. Property Law, Kyoto, Japan Trademark Assn., Tokyo, Japan Internat. Econ. Law Assn., Tokyo; auditor Inamori Found., 1984—, mem. Kyoto Prizes Exec. com., 1987—. Fellow La Soc. Franco-Japanese des Techniques Indsl.; mem. Internat. Assn. for Advancement of Tchg. and Rsch. in Intellectual Property, Assn. Internat. Pour la Protection Property Indsl. Avocations: swimming, sailing, climbing, painting, travel. Home: 11 Jurakumawari-Higashimachi Nakagyoku Kyoto 604-8404 Japan Office: Doshisha U Faculty of Law Karasumadori Imadegawa Kyoto 602-8580 Japan

SENNET, CHARLES JOSEPH, lawyer; b. Buffalo, Aug. 7, 1952; s. Saunders M. and Muriel S. (Rotenberg) S. AB magna cum laude, Cornell U., 1974; JD with high honors, George Washington U., 1979. Bar: Ill. 1979, U.S. Dist. Ct. (no. dist.) Ill. 1979, U.S. Ct. Appeals (7th cir.) 1982, U.S. Ct. Appeals (D.C. cir.) 1993. Assoc. Reuben & Proctor, Chgo., 1979-83; assoc. counsel Tribune Co., Chgo., 1984-91, sr. counsel, 1991—. Adj. faculty Medill Sch. Journalism, Northwestern U., 1991-94; chmn. Television Music Lic. Com., 1995—. Contbr. articles to profl. jours. Mem. ABA (spkr. 1984-88, 91-97, 2000—, mem. gov. bd. Forum on Comms. Law 1995-98), NATAS, Ill. Bar Assn. (chmn. media law com. 1989-91), Chgo. Bar Assn., Fed. Comms. Bar Assn. Communications, Entertainment, Libel. Office: Tribune Co 435 N Michigan Ave Chicago IL 60611-4066

SENSENBRENNER, F(RANK) JAMES, JR., congressman; b. Chgo., June 14, 1943; s. F. James and Margaret Sensenbrenner; m. Cheryl Warren, Mar. 26, 1977; children: F. James III, Robert Alan. AB, Stanford U., 1965; JD, U. Wis., 1968. Bar: Wis. 1968, U.S. Supreme Ct. 1972. State rep. Wis. Assembly, Madison, 1969-75; state sen. Wis. Senate, Madison, 1975-79; asst. minority leader, 1976-79; mem. U.S Ho. of Reps., Washington, 1979—, chmn. jud. com., 2001—, chmn. sci. com., 1997-2001. Mem. Friends of Milw. Mus., Riveredge Nature Ctr. Mem. Am. Philatelic Soc., Chenequa Country Club, Capitol Hill Club. Republican. Episcopalian. Office: 2449 Rayburn House Office Bldg Washington DC 20515-4905

SENSENICH, ILA JEANNE, judge; b. Pitts., Mar. 6, 1939; d. Louis E. and Evelyn Margaret S. BA, Westminster Coll., 1961; JD, Dickinson Sch. Law, 1964, JD (hon.), 1994. Bar: Pa. 1964. Assoc. Stewart, Belden, Sensenich and Harrington, Greensburg, Pa., 1964-70; asst. pub. defender Westmoreland (Pa.) County, 1970-71; U.S. magistrate judge We. Dist. Pa., Pitts., 1971—. Adj. prof. law Duquesne U., 1982-87. Author: Compendium of the Law of Prisinor's Rights, 1979; contbr. articles to profl. jour. Trustee emeritus Dickinson Sch. Law. Vis. fellow Daniel & Florence Guggenheim program in criminal justice Yale Law Sch., 1976-77. Mem. ABA, Fed. Magistrate Judges Assn. (sec. 1979-81, 88-89, treas. 1989-90, 2d v.p. 1990-91, pres.-elect 1992-93, pres. 1993-94), Pa. Bar Assn. (comn. on women in the profession 1998—), Nat. Assn. Women Judges, Westmoreland County Bar Assn., Allegheny County Bar Assn. (fed. ct. sect., com. women in law), Womens Bar Assn. We. Pa., Am. Judicature Soc. Democrat. Presbyterian. Avocations: skiing, sailing, bicycling, classical music, cooking. Office: 518B US PO And Courthouse Pittsburgh PA 15219

SENTELLE, DAVID BRYAN, federal judge; b. Canton, N.C., Feb. 12, 1943; s. Horace Richard Jr. and Maude (Ray) Sentelle; m. Jane LaRue Oldham, June 19, 1965; children: Sharon Lewis, Regan Herman, Rebecca Acheson. AB, U. N.C., 1965, JD with honors, 1968. Bar: N.C. 1968, N.C. (U.S. Dist. Ct. (we. dist.)) 1969, (U.S. Ct. Appeals (4th cir.)) 1970. Assoc. Uzzell & Dumont, Asheville, NC, 1968—70; asst. U.S. atty. City of Charlotte, NC, 1970—74, dist. judge, 1974—77; ptnr. Tucker, Hicks, Sentelle, Moon & Hodge, P.A., Charlotte, 1977—85; judge U.S. Dist. Ct. (we. dist.) N.C., Charlotte, 1985—87, U.S. Ct. Appeals D.C., 1987—. Adj. prof. Fla. State U. Coll. Law; presiding judge Spl. Divsn. for Appointment of Ind. Counsels, 1992—; Disting. adj. prof. Geroge Mason U. Sch. Law. Contbr. articles. Chmn. Mecklenburg County Rep. Com., 1978—80, N.C. State Rep. Conv., 1979—80. Fellow, Dameron Found., 1967. Mem.: Mecklenburg County Bar Assn., Shriners, Masons (Scottish Rite), Am. Inn of Ct. Found., Edward Bennett Williams Inn of Ct. (pres.). Baptist. Office: US Court of Appeals 333 Constitution Ave NW Washington DC 20001-2866

SENTER, LYONEL THOMAS, JR., federal judge; b. Fulton, Miss., July 30, 1933; s. L. T. and Eva Lee (Jetton) S. BS, U. So. Miss., 1956; LL.B., U. Miss., 1959. Bar: Miss. 1959. County pros. atty., 1960-64; U.S. commr., 1966-68; judge Miss. Circuit Ct., Circuit 1, 1968-80, U.S. Dist. Ct. (no. dist.) Miss., 1980-82, chief judge, 1982-98, sr. judge, 1998—. Mem. Miss. State Bar Office: US Dist Ct Ste 229 725 Dr Martin Luther King Jr Blvd Biloxi MS 39530

SENTERFITT, REUBEN, lawyer, rancher; b. San Saba, Tex., June 18, 1917; s. Reuben Elby and Allie (Beck) S.; m. Patricia Gray Farley, Oct. 3, 1959; children— Shirley, Linda, Ronald, James, Melinda, Barry, Diane. J.D., U. Tex., 1940. Bar: Tex. 1940. Pvt. practice, San Saba, 1940—; city atty. City of San Saba; county atty. San Saba County. Chmn. fin. com. Comanche Trail council Boy Scouts Am.; mem. Tex. Ho. of Reps. 1940-55, speaker 1951-55; elder, trustee 1st Presbyn. Ch. Served to lt. (j.g.) USN. Mem. ABA, Tex. Bar Assn., Tex. Bar Found., San Saba C. of C. (pres. 1964-65), Order of Coif. Clubs: Rotary (pres.), Masons. General practice, Legislative, Probate (including wills, trusts). Home: 1403 W Dry St San Saba TX 76877-5407

SENZEL, MARTIN LEE, lawyer; b. Rochester, N.Y., June 21, 1944; s. Albert Benjamin and Besse (Lipson) S.; m. Dagni Maren Belgum, Feb. 17, 1979; 1 child, Whitney. BA, Yale U., 1966, LLB, 1969. Bar: N.Y. 1971, U.S. Dist. Ct. (so. dist.) N.Y., U.S. Ct. Appeals (2nd cir.) 1973. Assoc. Cravath, Swaine & Moore LLP, N.Y.C., 1969—77, ptnr., 1977—2000. Mem. ABA, N.Y. State Bar Assn., Assn. Bar City N.Y. Corporate, general, Finance, Securities. Home: 101 Central Park W New York NY 10023-4204 Office: Cravath Swaine & Moore LLP Worldwide Plz 825 8th Ave Fl 38 New York NY 10019-7475 E-mail: msenzel@cravath.com.

SEPULVEDA, EDWIN, mediator, arbitrator, educator; b. Mayabuez, P.R., Dec. 30, 1955; s. Edwin Sepulveda and Hilda Millan; m. Norma Sepulveda, Nov. 10, 1979; children: Liz Marie, Erick M. JD, La Salle U., 1994, PhD, 2001; LLM, Washington Sch. Law, Salt Lake City, 1998. Bar: P.R., Ga. Owner, adminstr. NORED Pharmacy, Sabana Grande, PR, 1985—2000; exec. dir. Ctr. Cmty. Justice, Sabana Grande, 2000—. Adj. prof. Coll. Profl. Mediation, Aguadilla, PR, 2000—. Capt. U.S. Army, 1978—90. Named to, Internat. Assn. Bus. Leaders, 2002. Mem.: ABA, Assn. Neutrals P.R. (sec. 2001—), Internat. Bar Assn., Nat. Lawyers Assn., Lions. Avocations: reading, martial arts. Office: Ctr Cmty Justice PO Box 1109 Sabana Grande PR 00637 Office Fax: 787-804-0950. E-mail: edjd@hotmail.com.

SEQUEIRA, MANUEL ALEXANDRE, JR., lawyer; b. Oct. 31, 1931; came to U.S., 1946, naturalized, 1954; s. Manuel Alexandre and Cecilia Maria (Xavier) S.; m. Angela Maria Lopes, Feb. 15, 1958; children: Joseph, Michael, Peter, Robert. BA, U. Notre Dame, 1955, JD, 1956. Bar: N.Y. 1957, U.S. Dist. Ct. (so. and ea. dists.) N.Y. 1958, U.S. Ct. Appeals (2d cir.) 1967, U.S. Supreme Ct. 1971. Assoc. atty. Hill Rivkins & Hayden LLP, N.Y.C., 1956-67; litigation house counsel Am. Internat. Group (Sequeira, Rienzo & Gillies), N.Y.C., 1967-82; pvt. practice Mahopac, N.Y., 1983—. Mem. Christian Legal Soc. Roman Catholic. General practice, Personal injury (including property damage), Property, real (including real estate development, water). Office: PO Box 563 Mahopac NY 10541-0563 E-mail: sequeira.law.office@rcn.com.

SERBIN, RICHARD MARTIN, lawyer; b. Pitts., Dec. 21, 1947; m. Francie M. Buncher, June 2, 1974; children: Lawrence B., Haley E., Joshua H. BA, U. Pitts., 1970; JD, Duquesne U., 1974. Bar: Pa. 1974, N.C. 1996, U.S. Dist. Ct. (mid. dist.) Pa. 1974, U.S. Dist. Ct. (we. dist.) Pa. 1980, U.S. Ct. Appeals (3d cir.) 1981, U.S. Supreme Ct. 1985; cert. Nat. Bd. Trial Advocacy (civil). Assoc. Barron & Zimmerman, Lewistown, Pa., 1974-77; ptnr. Mullen, Casanave, Carpenter & Serbin, Altoona, Pa., 1977-81, Levine, Reese & Serbin, Altoona, 1982-97, Reese, Serbin, Kovacs & Nypaver, Altoona, 1997—2003, Serbin, Kovacs & Nypaver, 2003—. Asst. dist. atty. Juniata County, Mifflintown, Pa., 1976-77; instr. Pa. State U., Altoona, 1979-83, 89; adj. settlement judge for Western Dist. Ct., Pa. Bd. dirs. Jewish Fedn., Altoona, 1980-89, Temple Beth Israel, Altoona, 1983-86, Pleasant Valley Community Living, 1982-86, Big Brothers/Sisters of Blair County, 1987-95; mem. Big Brothers and Friends of Boys, 1978-80. Mem. ABA, ATLA, Pa. Trial Lawyers Assn. (bd. govs. 1988-90), Blair County Bar Assn., Million Dollar Advocates Forum. Democrat. Jewish. Avocations: tennis, hiking. Personal injury (including property damage), Professional liability. Office: Serbin Kovacs & Nypaver 85 Logan Blvd Altoona PA 16602-3123

SERCHUK, IVAN, lawyer; b. N.Y.C., Oct. 13, 1935; s. Israel and Freda (Davis) S.; children: Camille, Bruce Mead, Vance Foster. BA, Columbia U., 1957, LLB, 1960. Bar: N.Y. 1961, U.S. Dist. Ct. (so. dist.) N.Y. 1963, U.S. Ct. Appeals (2d cir.) 1964, U.S. Tax Ct. 1966. Law clk. to judge U.S. Dist. Ct. (so. dist.) N.Y., N.Y., 1961-63; assoc. Kaye, Scholer, Fierman, Hays & Handler, 1963-68; dep. supt., counsel N.Y. State Banking Dept., N.Y.C., Albany, 1968-71; mem. Berle & Berle, 1972-73; spl. counsel N.Y. State Senate Banks Com., 1972; mem. Serchuk & Zelermyer LLP, White Plains, NY, 1976—2003, Todtman, Nachamie, Spizz & Johns, PC, 2003—. Lectr. Practising Law Inst., 1968-71. Mem. N.Y. State Bar Assn., Assn. of Bar of City of N.Y. Banking, Corporate, general, Mergers and acquisitions. Home: Mead St Waccabuc NY 10597 Office: Todtman Nachamie Spizz & Johns 425 Park Ave New York NY 10022 E-mail: iserchuk@tnsj-law.com.

SERGENT, BIRG EUGENE, judge; b. Jonesville, Va., May 27, 1937; s. Bascom Birg and Willie Olli (Neff) Sergent; m. Lana Kay Turner, Aug. 17, 1963; 1 child, Monica Jayne Sergent McElyea. AB, Union Coll., Barbourville, Ky., 1957; LLB, U. Richmond, 1959. Judge Lee County Cir. Ct., Jonesville, 1989—. Office: Lee County Cir Ct PO Box 426 Pennington Gap VA 24277-0426

SERNA, PATRICIO, state supreme court justice; b. Reserve, N.Mex., Aug. 26, 1939; m. Eloise Serna; children: Elena Patricia, Anna Alicia 1 stepchild, John Herrera. BSBA with honors, U. Albuquerque, 1962; JD, U. Denver, 1970; LLM, Harvard U., 1971; postgrad., Nat. Jud. Coll., 1985, postgrad., 1990, postgrad., 1992, postgrad., 1994; LLD (hon.) , U. Denver, 2002. Bar: N.Mex. 1970, Colo. 1971, U.S. Dist. Ct. N.Mex. 1970. Probation and parole officer State of N.Mex., Santa Fe, Las Cruces, 1966—67; spl. asst. to commn. mem. Equal Opportunity Commn., Washington, 1971—75; asst. atty. gen. State of N.Mex., Santa Fe, 1975—79; pvt. practice Santa Fe, 1979—85; dist. judge First Jud. Dist., Santa Fe, 1985—96; supreme ct. justice N.Mex. Supreme Ct., Santa Fe, 1996—2001, chief justice, 2001—02. Adj. prof. law Georgetown U., Washington, 1973, Cath. U., Washington, 1974—75; faculty advisor Nat. Jud. Coll., Reno, 1987. Bd. dirs. Santa Fe Group Homes Inc. With U.S. Army, 1963—65. Mem.: Santa Fe Bar Assn., No. N.Mex. Am. Inns of Ct., Nat. Hispanic Bar Assn. (HNBA Judge of Yr. award 2002, Judge of Yr. 2002), N.Mex. Hispanic Bar Assn., N.Mex. Bar Assn., Elks, Phi Alpha Delta. Avocations: hiking, fishing, Ping Pong, chess, painting. Office: NMex Supreme Ct PO Box 848 Santa Fe NM 87504-0848

SERNETT, RICHARD PATRICK, lawyer; b. Mason City, Iowa, Sept. 8, 1938; s. Edward Frank and Loretta M. (Cavanaugh) S.; m. Janet Ellen Ward, Apr. 20, 1963; children: Susan Ellen, Thomas Ward, Stephen Edward, Katherine Anne. BBA, U. Iowa, 1960, JD, 1963. Bar: Iowa 1963, Ill. 1965, U.S. Dist. Ct. (no. dist.) Ill. 1965, U.S. Supreme Ct. 1971. House counsel, asst. sec. Scott, Foresman & Co., Glenview, Ill., 1963-70, sec., legal officer, 1970-80; v.p., law sec. SFN Cos., Inc., Glenview, 1980-83, sr. v.p., sec., gen. counsel, 1983-85, exec. v.p., gen. counsel, 1985-87; pvt. practice Northbrook, Ill., 1988-90; v.p., sec., gen. counsel Macmillan/McGraw-Hill Sch. Pub. Co., 1990-92; v.p. Bert Early Assoc., Chgo., 1992-93; ptnr. Sernett & Blake, Northfield, Ill., 1993-95; ret., 1995. Mem. U.S. Dept. State Adv. Panel on Internat. Copyright, 1972-75. Chmn. bd. dirs. Iowa State U., Broadcasting Co., 1987-94. Mem. ABA (chmn. copyright divsn. 1972-73, com. on copyright legis. 1967-68, 69-70, com. on copyright office affairs 1966-67, 79-81, com. on program for revision copyright law 1971-72), Am. Intellectual Property Law Assn., Am. Soc. Corp. Secs., Ill. Bar Assn. (chmn. copyright com. 1971-72), Chgo. Bar Assn., Patent Law Assn. Chgo. (bd. mgrs. 1979-82, chmn. copyright law com. 1972-73, 77-78), Copyright Soc. U.S.A. (trustee 1972-75, 77-80), North Shore Country Club (Glenview, Ill.), Wyndemere Country Club (Naples, Fla.). Corporate, general, Mergers and acquisitions, Trademark and copyright. Home: 2579 Fairford Ln Northbrook IL 60062-8101

SEROTA, JAMES IAN, lawyer; b. Chgo., Ill., Oct. 20, 1946; s. Louis Henry and Phyllis Estelle (Horner) S.; m. Susan Perlstadt, May 7, 1972; children: Daniel Louis, Jonathan Mark. AB, Washington U., St. Louis, 1968; JD cum laude, Northwestern U., 1971. Bar: Ill. 1971, U.S. Dist. Ct. (no. dist.) Ill. 1972, D.C. 1978, U.S. Supreme Ct. 1978, U.S. Ct. Appeals (D.C. cir.) 1978, U.S. Dist. Ct. (D.C. dist.), U.S. Ct. Claims 1980, N.Y. 1981, U.S. Dist. Ct. (so. and ea. dists.) N.Y. 1981, U.S. Ct. Appeals (2d cir.)

1983. Trial atty. Antitrust div. US Dept. Justice, Washington, 1971—77; assoc. Bell, Boyd & Lloyd, Washington, 1977—81; ptnr. Werner, Kennedy & French, NYC, 1982—85, Levitsky & Serota, 1985-86, Huber, Lawrence & Abell, NYC, 1987—98, Vinson & Elkins, NYC, 1998—2002; shareholder Greenberg Traurig, NYC, 2003—. Contbr. articles to profl. jours.; editor Law Rev., Law bd., Northwestern U.; ed bd., antitrust columnist CCH Power and Telecom Law jour. Recipient Spl. Achievement award U.S. Dept. Justice, 1976. Mem. ABA (chmn. ins. industry com. 1987-90, vice chair program com. 1990-91, chair annual mtg. program 1991-94, chair fuel & energy com. 1994-97, coun. 1997-2000), N.Y. State Bar Assn., Assn. of Bar of City of N.Y. (antitrust and trade regulation com. 1988-91), Fed. Bar Council. Antitrust, Federal civil litigation. Office: Greenberg Traurig LLP 885 Third Ave New York NY 10022-4834 Office Fax: 212-224-6155. Business E-Mail: serotaj@gtlaw.com.

SEROTA, SUSAN PERLSTADT, lawyer, educator; b. Chgo., Sept. 10, 1945; d. Sidney Morris and Mildred (Penn) Perlstadt; m. James Ian Serota, May 7, 1972; children: Daniel Louis, Jonathan Mark. AB, U. Mich., 1967; JD, NYU, 1971. Bar: Ill. 1971, D.C. 1972, N.Y. 1981, U.S. Dist. Ct. (no. dist.) Ill. 1971, U.S. Dist. Ct. (so. dist.) N.Y. 1981, U.S. Dist. Ct. (ea. dist.) N.Y. 1985, U.S. Ct. Claims 1972, U.S. Tax Ct. 1972, U.S. Ct. Appeals (D.C. cir.) 1972. Ptnr. Pillsbury Winthrop LLP, N.Y.C., 1982—. Adj. prof. Sch. Law, Georgetown U., Washington, 1974-75; mem. faculty Practicing Law Inst., N.Y.C., 1983—. Editor: ERISA Fiduciary Law, 1995, Supplement, 2000; assoc. editor Exec. Compensation Jour., 1973—75, dep. editor Tax Mgmt., Estate and Gift Taxation and Exec. Compensation, 1973—75, mem. editl. adv. bd. Benefits Law Jour., 1973—, Tax Mgmt. Compensation Jour., 1993—, mem. bd. editors ERISA and Benefits Law Jour., 1992—, contbr. articles to profl. jours., —. Fellow: Am. Coll. of Employee Benefits Counsel (dir., charter fellow), Am. Coll. Tax Counsel; mem.: ABA (chmn. joint com. employee benefits 1987—88, chmn. com. employee benefits, taxation sect. 1991—92, vice-chair taxation sect. 1999—2001), Am. Bar Retirement Assn. (dir. 1994—, pres. 1999—2000), N.Y. State Bar Assn. (exec. com. tax sect. 1988—92), Internat. Pension and Employee Benefit Lawyers Assn. (co-chair 1993—95). Democrat. Mergers and acquisitions, Pension, profit-sharing, and employee benefits, Taxation, general. Office: Pillsbury Winthrop LLP One Battery Park Pla New York NY 10004-1490 E-mail: sserota@pillsburywinthrop.com.

SERRES, GREGORY A. prosecutor; BBA, Texas A&M U.; JD, Baylor U., 1986. Prosecutor Harris Co. Dist. Atty. Office, Tex., 1987—92; asst. US atty. US Dept. Justice, Southern Dist., Tex., 1992—95, chief, Special Prosecutions Div., 1995—98, first asst. US atty., 1998—, interim US atty., 2001. Grantee Nat. Merit Scholar, Lechner Fellowship. Office: US Attorney Southern Dist of Tex PO Box 61129 Houston TX 77208 Fax: 713-567-3389.*

SERUMGARD, JOHN R. lawyer; b. Rolla, N.D., June 11, 1944; s. John R. and Antoinette R. (Bedard) S.; m. K. Laura Wippich, June 9, 1969; children: Jennie Lynn, John Matthew, Kristen Leigh. AB, Georgetown U., 1966, JD, 1969, LLM, 1974. Bar: Ill. 1969, D.C. 1980, U.S. Supreme Ct. 1975. Staff asst. Office U.S. Rep. Fred Schwengel, 1967-68; legal editor labor svcs. Bur. Nat. Affairs, Inc., Washington, 1968-70; labor atty. U.S. C. of C., Washington, 1972-75; v.p. labor rels. Rubber Mfrs. Assn., Washington, 1975—2001, sr. v.p., 1998-99, exec. v.p., 1999—2001. Treas. Rubber Mfrs. Assn., Washington, 1981-89; treas. Natural Rubber Shippers Assn., Inc., 1981-89; chmn. Scrap Tire Mgmt. Coun., 1990-2001. Bd. dirs. Riverside Manor Civic Assn., 1979-80, mediator 2002-. Capt. U.S. Army, 1970-72. Mem. ABA, D.C. Bar Assn, Indsl. Rels. Rsch. Assn., River Bend Golf and Country Club (Great Falls, Va.), Farragut Square Club (Washington). Labor (including EEOC, Fair Labor Standards Act, labor-management relations, NLRB, OSHA), Corporate taxation.

SERVIS, WILLIAM GEORGE, lawyer; b. Rochester, N.Y., July 1, 1922; s. Harry Hall and Lois Ellen Servis; m. Valentine Agnes Reynouard, June 24, 1947; children: Ronald, Terry, Kim Powell. LLD, N.Y. Law Sch., 1957. Bar: N.Y., U.S. Dist. Ct. N.Y. Counsel Hon. John J. Conway, Rochester, 1958-60; asst. dist. atty. Dist. Atty.'s Office, Rochester, 1960-71; pvt. practice Rochester, 1971—. Lectr. Police and Fire Acad., Rochester, 1960-71, Monroe County Magistrates Assn., 1966-70; counsel Western Monroe Hist. Soc., Brockport, N.Y., 1960-70, Clarkson Town, 1965-75, Spencerport Vol. Ambulance, Spencerport, N.Y., 1965-97. With USN, 1942—46. Mem. ABA, N.Y. State Bar Assn., Monroe County Bar Assn. Republican. Mem. United Ch. Of Christ. Avocations: sailing, swimming. State civil litigation, Probate (including wills, trusts), Property, real (including real estate development, water). Home: 60 Laurelcrest Dr Spencerport NY 14559-2304 Office: 1379 Long Pond Rd Rochester NY 14626

SERWER, ALAN MICHAEL, lawyer; b. Detroit, Aug. 31, 1944; s. Bernard Jacob and Marian (Borin) S.; m. Laurel Kathryn Robbert, June 6, 1968; children: David Matthew, Karen Anne. BA in Econs., U. Mich., 1966; JD, Northwestern U., 1969. Bar: Ill. 1969, D.C. 1980, U.S. Dist. Ct. (no. dist.) Ill. 1970, U.S. Ct. Appeals (7th cir.) 1979, U.S. Supreme Ct. 1979, U.S. Ct. Appeals (6th cir.) 1982, U.S. Ct. Appeals (5th cir.) 1983, U.S. Ct. Appeals (11th cir.) 1984, U.S. Ct. Appeals (9th cir.) 1986. Trial atty. U.S. Dept. Labor, Chgo., 1969-78, counsel safety and health, 1978-79; assoc. Haley, Bader & Potts, Chgo., 1979-82, ptnr., 1983-87; mem. Bell, Boyd & Lloyd, Chgo., 1987—. Ill. Bar Assn., Chgo. Bar Assn. Federal civil litigation, Labor (including EEOC, Fair Labor Standards Act, labor-management relations, NLRB, OSHA), Pension, profit-sharing, and employee benefits. Home: 233 Woodland Rd Highland Park IL 60035-5052 Office: Bell Boyd & Lloyd 70 W Madison St Ste 3200 Chicago IL 60602-4244

SESSER, GARY DOUGLAS, lawyer; b. Malden, Mass., June 4, 1950; s. Ralph and Esther Anne (Chalfen) S.; m. Rachel Wolkin, June 22, 1979; children: Michael, Benjamin, Anne. BA, Cornell U., 1972; JD, U. Mich., 1975. Bar: Mass. 1975, U.S. Dist. Ct. Mass. 1976, N.Y. 1977, U.S. Dist. Ct. (so. and ea. dists.) N.Y. 1977, U.S. Ct. Appeals (2d cir.) 1978, D.C. 1980, U.S. Supreme Ct. 1980, U.S. Ct. Appeals (D.C. cir.) 1987, U.S. Ct. Appeals (11th cir.) 1990, U.S. Ct. Appeals (3d cir.) 1999. Assoc. H.M. Kaufman, Boston, 1976, Haight, Gardner, Poor & Havens, N.Y.C., 1976-84, ptnr., 1984-97, Carter, Ledyard & Milburn, N.Y.C., 1997—. Fellow Am. Bar Found.; mem. ABA, Assn. of Bar of City of N.Y., Maritime Law Assn., Fed. Bar Coun. Admiralty, Antitrust, Federal civil litigation. Home: 520 Upper Mountain Ave Montclair NJ 07043-1507 Office: Carter Ledyard & Milburn 2 Wall St Fl 13 New York NY 10005-2072

SESSIONS, JEFFERSON BEAUREGARD, III, senator; b. Hybart, Ala., Dec. 24, 1946; s. Jefferson Beauregard and Abbie (Powe) S.; m. Mary Montgomery Blackshear, Aug. 9, 1969; children: Mary Abigail, Ruth Blackshear, Samuel Turner BA, Huntingdon Coll., Montgomery, Ala., 1969; JD, U. Ala., 1973. Bar: Ala. 1973. Assoc. Guin, Bouldin & Porch, Russellville, Ala., 1973-75; asst. U.S. atty. U.S. Dept. Justice, Mobile, Ala., 1975-77, U.S. atty., 1981-93; assoc., ptnr. Stockman & Bedsole Attys., Mobile, Ala., 1977-81; ptnr. Stockman, Bedsole & Sessions, Mobile, 1993-94; atty. gen. State of Ala., 1996; U.S. senator from Ala., 1997—. Mem. U.S. atty. gen.'s adv. com., 1987-89, vice-chmn. 1989; mem. judiciary, health, edn., labor & pensions armed svcs. coms. Presdl. elector State of Ala., 1972; trustee, mem. exec. com. Mobile Bay Area Partnership for Youth, 1981-95; chmn. adminstrv. bd. Ashland Pl. United Meth. Ch., Mobile, 1982; 1st v.p. Mobile Lions Club, 1993-94. Capt. USAR, 1975-85 Recipient U.S. Atty. Gen.'s award for significant achievements in the war against drug trafficking U.S. Atty. Gen. William P. Barr, 1992. Mem. ABA, Ala. Bar Assn., Mobile Bar Assn. Republican. Home: 1119 Hillcrest Xing E Mobile AL 36695-4505 Office: 335 Senate Russell Office Bldg Washington DC 20510-0001 E-mail: senator@sessions.senate.gov.

SESSIONS, WILLIAM STEELE, former government official, lawyer; b. Ft. Smith, Ark., May 27, 1930; s. Will Anderson and Edith A. (Steele) S.; m. Alice Lewis, Oct. 5, 1952; children: William Lewis, Mark Gregory, Peter Anderson, Sara Anne. BA, Baylor U., 1956, LLB, 1958; hon. degree, John C. Marshall Law Sch., St. Mary's U., 1989; LLD (hon.), Dickinson Coll., 1988, Flager Coll., 1990, Davis & Elkins Coll., 1992, McMurry U., 1997. Bar: Tex. 1959; U.S. Dist Ct. (Western Dist.) Tex.; Ct. Appeals (5th Cir.). Ptnr. McGregor & Sessions, Waco, Tex., 1959-61; assoc. Tirey, McLaughlin, Gorin & Tirey, Waco, 1961-63; ptnr. Haley, Fulbright, Winniford, Sessions & Bice, Waco, 1963-69; sect. chief, govt. ops sect. criminal divsn. U.S. Dept. Justice, Washington, 1969-71; U.S. atty. U.S. Dept Justice, U.S. Dist. Ct., (we. dist), San Antonio, 1971-74; dist. judge U.S. Dist. Ct. (we. dist.) Tex., San Antonio, 1974-87, chief judge, 1980-87; dir. FBI, Washington, 1987-93; ptnr. Sessions & Sessions, San Antonio and Washington, 1995-2000, Holland & Knight, LLP, San Antonio and Washington, 2000—. Bd. dirs., chmn. book com. Fed. Jud. Ctr., Washington, 1981—; mem. Tex. Commn. on Judicial Efficiency, 1995, Tex. Commn. on a Representative Student Body, 1998, Gov.'s Task Force on Homeland Security, Gov.'s Anti-Crime Commn., Tex., 2002. Contbr. articles to profl. jours. Active Dr. Martin Luther King Jr. Fed. Holiday Commn., 1991-96, hon. bd. dirs., 1993-94; bd. trustees Nat. Environ. Edn. & Tng. Found., Inc., 2001—. Lt. USAF, 1951-55; capt. USAFR, Recipient Rosewood Gavel award St. Mary's U. Sch. Law, San Antonio, 1982, Disting. Alumni award Baylor U., Golden Plate award Am. Acad. Achievement, 1988, Law Enforcement Leadership award Assn. Fed. Investigators, 1989, medal of honor DAR, 1989, Disting. Eagle Scout award Boy Scouts Am., 1990, Person of Yr. award Am. Soc. for Indsl. Security, 1990, Magna Charta award Baronial Order of Magna Charta, 1990, Price Daniel Disting. Pub. Svc. award Baylor U., 2002; named Lawyer of Yr., Baylor Law Sch., 1988, Father of Yr., Nat. Fathers Day Com., 1988, Ellis Island Congl. Medal of Honor, 1992; inducted into Eagle Scout Hall of Fame, 1998. Fellow ABA (chmn. spl. com. on judicial independence 1997—, Nat. Law Day chmn. 2000-02, hon. co chmn., pres. commn. on the 21st Century Judiciary, 2002-); mem. Jud. Conf. U.S. (com. on ct. adminstrn., chmn. jud. improvements subcom. 1983-85, ad hoc com. on automation to subcom. 1984-87, mem. ad hoc ct. reporter com. 1984-87), San Antonio Bar Assn. (bd. dirs. 1973-74), Fed. Bar Assn. (pres. San Antonio sect. 1974), Am. Judicature Soc. (exec. com. 1982-84), Dist. Judges Assn. of 5th Cir. (pres. 1982-83), State Bar of Tex. (chmn. com. to develop procedures for cert. state law questions to Supreme Ct. by Fed. Cts. 1983-85), Waco McLennan County Bar Assn. (pres. 1968), San Antonio Inns of Ct. (pres. 1986), William S. Sessions Inns of Ct. Republican. Methodist. Avocations: hiking, climbing, canoeing. Office: Holland & Knight LLP Ste 100 2099 Pennsylvania Ave NW Washington DC 20006 Fax: (202) 955-5564. E-mail: wsessions@hklaw.com.

SESTRIC, ANTHONY JAMES, lawyer; b. St. Louis, June 27, 1940; s. Anton and Marie (Gasparovic) S.; m. Carol F. Bowman, Nov. 24, 1966; children: Laura Antonette, Holly Nicole, Michael Anthony. Student, Georgetown U., 1958-62; JD, Mo. U., 1965. Bar: Mo. 1965, Minn. 1996, U.S. Ct. Appeals (8th cir.) 1965, U.S. Ct. Appeals (7th cir.) 1984, U.S. Dist. Ct. Mo. 1966, U.S. Dist. Ct. (no dist.) Tex. 1985, U.S. Dist. Ct. Ill. 1994, U.S. Tax Ct. 1969, U.S. Supreme Ct. 1970, U.S. Claims Ct. 1986. Law clk. U.S. Dist. Ct., St. Louis, 1965-66; ptnr. Sestric, McGhee & Miller, St. Louis, 1966-77, Fordyce and Mayne, 1977-78, Sestric & Garvey, 1978-96, Sestric Law Firm, St. Louis, 1996—. Spl. asst. to Mo. atty. gen., St. Louis, 1968, spl. asst. circuit atty., 2001—; mem. Fed. Jud. Selection Commn., 1993, U.S. Jud. Selection Commn., 1993-94; gen. chmn. 22nd jud. cir. bar com., 1995, mem. Region XI disciplinary com., 2001—. Contbr. articles to profl. jours. Hearing officer St. Louis Met. Police Dept.; active St. Louis Air Pollution Bd. Appeals and Varience Rev., 1966-73, chmn., 1968-73; active St. Louis Airport Commn., 1975-76; dist. vice-chmn. Boy Scouts Am., 1970-76; bd. dirs. Full Achievement, Inc., 1970-77, Legal Aid Soc. St. Louis, 1976-77, Law Libr. Assn. St. Louis, 1976-78, Thomas Dunn Memls., 1995-98, Marquette Learning Ctr., 1995-98; v.p. bd. St. Elizabeth Acad., 1985-86 Mem. ABA (state chmn. judiciary com. 1973-75, cir. chmn. com. condemnation, zoning and property use 1975-77, standing com. bar activities 1982-88), Nat. Conf. Bar Pres.'s (exec. coun. 1987-90), Mo. Bar Assn. (vice-chmn. young lawyers sect. 1973-76, bd. govs. 1974-77, chmn. law practice mgmt. com. 1997-99), Bar Assn. Met. St. Louis (chmn. young lawyers sect. 1974-75, exec. com. 1974-83, 94-95, pres. 1981-82, bd. govs. 1995-98, chmn. survey com. 1999). Federal civil litigation, State civil litigation, Estate planning. Home: 3967 Holly Hills Blvd Saint Louis MO 63116-3135 E-mail: ajsestric@juno.com.

SETH, J. CABOT, lawyer; b. Ft. Ord, Calif., Apr. 17, 1953; s. Richard George and Rita Barbara (McCooey) S.; m. Tonia Marie Martin, Dec. 20, 1975; children: Hilary, Elissa, Lauren, John, Jacob. AB, U. Notre Dame, 1975; JD, U. S.C., 1977. Bar: S.C. 1978, U.S. Dist. Ct. S.C. 1983, U.S. Ct. Mil. Appeals 1986. Commd. 2d lt. USAF, 1975, advanced through grades to capt., 1978, resigned, 1983; lt. col. USAFR, 1983—; ptnr. Jones, Seth, Shuler & Killen L.L.P., Sumter, SC, 1983—. County prosecutor Sumter County, 1983; mcpl. judge City of Sumter, 1984-85. Bd. mem. Sumter Christian Charities, 1983-86; bd. dirs. office of natural family planning Diocese of Charleston, Sumter, 1983-96, mem. Cath. Charities, 1992; founding pres. Family Ho., Inc. (formerly DEPPA of S.C.), 1987—; mem. found. bd. St. Francis Xavier H.S., 1997—. Named Outstanding Young Man of S.C., S.C. Jaycees, 1984. Mem. ABA (legal econs. sect.), Sumter County Bar Assn., Sumter C. of C. (com. chmn. leadership devel. 1985-86, com. chmn. legis. affairs 1986-87, bd. dirs. 1990-96, v.p. 1992-93, chmn. bd. dirs. 1995-96), Sumter Jaycees (pres. 1985-86, Outstanding Young Man of S.C. State Divsn. 1984). Lodges: Rotary (sec. Palmetto-Sumter chpt. 1987, pres. 1988-89), K.C. (dep. grand knight 1982-83). Roman Catholic. State civil litigation, General practice, Personal injury (including property damage). Office: Jones Seth Shuler & Killen LLP 5 Law Range PO Box 1268 Sumter SC 29151-1268

SETTLE, ERIC LAWRENCE, lawyer; b. N.Y.C., July 28, 1961; s. Elliott Titus and Thelma (Radzvill) S.; m. Robin Marks, Aug. 23, 1986; children: Adam Harrison, Alexander Howard. AB cum laude, Colgate U., 1983; JD with honors, George Washington U., 1986. Bar: Pa. 1986, U.S. Dist. Ct. (ea. dist.) Pa. 1987, U.S. Dist. Ct. (mid. dist.) Pa. 1995, U.S. Ct. Appeals (3d cir.) 1992, U.S. Supreme Ct. 1995. Assoc. Wolf, Block, Schorr & Solis-Cohen, Phila., 1986-90, Fox, Rothschild, O'Brien & Frankel, Phila., 1990-95; dep. gen. counsel to gov. Commonwealth of Pa., 1995-97; regional gen. counsel Aetna U.S. Healthcare(now Aetna Inc.), Blue Bell, Pa., 1997—2002; sr. v.p., gen. counsel Americhoice Health Svcs. Inc., Vienna, Va., 2002; sr. v.p., chief counsel Americhoice a United Health Group Co., 2003—. Trustee Colgate U., Hamilton, N.Y., 1983-86, Bryn Mawr Rehab. Hosp., 1993-94; pres. Riverview Condominium Assn., Phila., 1991-93; counsel Craig Snyder for U.S. Congress, Phila., 1992. George Cobb fellow Colgate U., 1981, 82. Mem. ABA (young lawyers divsn., career issues com. 1992-93), Pa. Bar Assn. (exec. com. young lawyers divsn. 1992-93), Phila. Bar Assn. (young lawyers sect. exec. com. 1990-92, dir. bar edn. ctr. 1993-95, trustee Phila. Bar Found., 1994), Phi Alpha Delta (marshal 1984-85), Lowes Island Club. Education and schools, Government contracts and claims. Office: Americhoice Corp 8045 Leesburg Pike Ste 650 Vienna VA 22182 Home: 1105 Amanda Dr Great Falls VA 22066 E-mail: esettle@americhoice.com.

SETZLER, EDWARD ALLAN, lawyer; b. Kansas City, Mo., Nov. 3, 1933; s. Edward A. and Margaret (Parshall) S.; m. Helga E. Friedemann, May 20, 1972; children: Christina, Ingrid, Kirstin. BA, U. Kans., 1955; JD, U. Wis., 1962. Bar: Mo. 1962, U.S. Tax Ct. 1962. Assoc. Spencer, Fane, Britt & Browne, Kansas City, 1962-67, ptnr., 1968-2000, mng. ptnr., 1974-77, 78-82, chmn. trust and estate sect., 1974-2000; ptnr. Husch & Eppenberger, LLC, 2000—. Co-author: Missouri Estate Administration, 1984, supplements, 1987—2001; contbg. editor: Understanding Living Trusts, 1990, 2001; co-author, co-editor, reviewer: Missouri Estate Planning, 1986; co-author, co-editor, reviewer Missouri Estate Planning, supplements, 1987—2001; contbg. editor: A Will is Not the Way--The Living Trust Alternative, 1988; bd. editors: Wis. Law Rev., 1961—62. Amb., bd. govs., bd. dirs., chmn. found. com. Am. Royal, 1982—; mem. planning giving com., bus. coun. Nelson Atkins Mus. Art, 1984—; mem. deferred giving com. Children's Mercy Hosp., 1991—; mem. Kansas City Estate Planning Symposium Com., 1984—92, chmn., 1991; mem. adv. com. Greater Kansas City Cmty. Found., 2000—; trustee Zoo Learning Fund, 2002—; mem. adv. bd. Children's Svc. League, 2003—. Fellow: Am. Coll. Trust and Estate Counsel (state chmn. 1992—97, mem. state membership com. 1986—2001); mem.: Estate Planning Soc. Kansas City (co-founder 1965, pres. 1983—84, dir. 1984—85, mem. social com. 1968—), Kansas City Met. Bar Assn. (lectr., chmn. probate and trust 1979, 1992, vice chmn. 1983—85, 1991, legis. rev. com. 1991—95), Mo. Bar Assn. (lectr., vice chmn. probate and estate planning com. 1994—97), Sigma Xi, Order of the Coif, Phi Delta Phi. Estate planning, Probate (including wills, trusts), Estate taxation. Office: 1200 Main St Ste 1700 Kansas City MO 64105-2100 Fax: 816-421-0596. E-mail: edward.setzler@husch.com.

SEVART, DANIEL JOSEPH, lawyer; b. Oswego, Kans., June 25, 1944; s. Vernon Joseph and Alma Bridget (Carland) S.; m. Shoko Kato, Apr. 17, 1968; 1 child, Eric J. AA, Parsons Jr. Coll., 1964; BA, Washburn U., 1973, JD with honors, 1975. Bar: Kans. 1976, U.S. Dist. Ct. Kans. 1976, U.S. Ct. Appeals (10th cir.) 1976. Assoc. Render & Kamas, Wichita, Kans., 1976-78, ptnr., 1978-82, Schartz & Sevart, Wichita, 1982-83, Sevart & Sevart, Wichita, 1983—. Bd. dirs. Wichita Symphony Soc., Inc., 1989—. Served to staff sgt. USAF, 1965-72. Mem. Assn. Trial Lawyers Am., Kans. Bar Assn. (bd. govs. 1995-98, 2000-01, sec.-treas. 1998-99, v.p. 2001-02, pres.-elect 2002-03, Kans. Trial Lawyers Assn. (bd. govs. 1989—), Wichita Bar Assn. (bd. govs. 1988-90, sec.-treas. 1990-91, v.p. 1991-92, pres.-elect 1992-93, pres. 1993-94), Wichita C. of C. Democrat. Roman Catholic. Avocations: classical music, gardening, fishing, camping, traveling. Federal civil litigation, General practice, Personal injury (including property damage). Office: Sevart & Sevart 100 S Main St Ste 400 Wichita KS 67202-3208 also: 1900 L St NW Ste 500 Washington DC 20036-5031 Office Fax: 316-269-4236.*

SEVERS, CHARLES A., III, lawyer; b. N.Y.C., Sept. 16, 1942; s. Charles A. and Gertrude (O'Neill) S.; m. Regina Ferrone, Sept. 4, 1965; children: Charles A. IV, Cornelius Forsythe, Rudyard Pierrepont, Olivia Consuelo. BA, Georgetown U., 1964, JD, 1967. Bar: N.Y. 1968, D.C. 1985. Ptnr. Dewey Ballantine, N.Y.C., 1967-96; gen. counsel, exec. v.p. Nat. Madison Group, N.Y.C., 1996-97. Lectr. various continuing legal edn. programs. Contbr. articles to profl. jours. Dir., trustee various orgns. Fellow Am. Coll. Trust and Estate Counsel; mem. ABA, N.Y. State Bar Assn., Assn. of Bar of City of N.Y., D.C. Bar Assn., Union Club. Probate (including wills, trusts), Estate taxation, Personal income taxation. Address: High Meadow Old Chatham NY 12136

SEWARD, GEORGE CHESTER, lawyer; b. Omaha, Aug. 4, 1910; s. George Francis and Ada Leona (Rugh) S.; m. Carroll Frances McKay, Dec. 12, 1936 (dec. 1991); children: Gordon Day, Patricia McKay (Mrs. Dryden G. Liddle), James Pickett, Deborah Carroll (Mrs. R. Thomas Coleman). BA, U. Va., 1933, LLB, 1936. Bar: Va. 1935, N.Y., Ky., D.C., U.S. Supreme Ct. With Shearman & Sterling, N.Y.C., 1936-53, Seward & Kissel LLP, N.Y.C., 1953—. Dir. Witherbee Sherman Corp., 1952-66, pres. 1964-66, Howmet Corp., 1955-75, Chas. P. Young Co., 1965-72, Howmedica Inc., 1970-72, Benson Mines, Inc., 1980-85; trustee Benson Iron Ore Trust, 1969-80. Author: Basic Corporate Practice, 1977, Seward and Related Families, 1994; co-author: Model Business Corporation Act Annotated, 1960, We Remember Carroll, 1992. Trustee Arts and Scis. Coun. U. Va., 1983-93, pres., 1991-93; trustee Edwin Gould Found. for Children, 1955-96, Nature Conservancy of Ea. L.I., 1969-80, N.Y. Geneal. and Biog. Soc. Named to Louisville Male H.S. Alumni Assn. Hall of Fame, 1991; commd. Ky. Col., 1993. Fellow: N.Y. State Bar Found., Am. Bar Found. (chmn. model corp. acts com. 1956—65); mem.: Internat. Bar Assn. (hon. life pres., hon. pres., founder-pres. sect. on bus. law, lectr. series by heads of state named in his honor, New Delhi 1988, Lisbon 1992, Budapest 1993, Geneva 1994), Downtown Assn. (N.Y.C.), Athenaeum Lit. Assn. (Louisville), ABA (chmn. bus. law sect. 1958—59, chmn. sect. com. corp. laws 1952—58, chmn. sect. banking com. 1960—61, ho. of dels. 1959—60, 1963—74, joint com. with Am. Law Inst. on continuing legal edn. 1965—74), Greencroft Club (Charlottesville, Va.), Univ. Club (Chgo.), Met. Club (Washington), Bohemian Club (San Francisco), Gardiner's Bay Country Club (Shelter Island, N.Y.), N.Y. Yacht Club, Knickerbocker Club, Delta Sigma Rho, Theta Chi, Phi Beta Kappa, Phi Beta Kappa Fellows (pres. 1969—75), Order of Coif, Raven Soc., Cum Laude Soc. Corporate, general, Finance, Private international. Home: 48 Greenacres Ave Scarsdale NY 10583-1436 Office: Seward & Kissel LLP One Battery Park Plz New York NY 10004 also: Internat Bar Assn 271 Regent St London W1R 7PA England

SEWARD, JEFFREY JAMES, lawyer, protective services official, educator, administrator; b. Rochester, Pa., Aug. 21, 1953; s. Kelson Charles and Virginia Emma (McConnell) S. BA, Ohio No. U., 1975, JD, 1986; MS, U. Nebr., 1979. Bar: Iowa 1990, Mich. 1998. Security cons. North Hills Passavant Hosp., Pitts., 1975-77; state trooper Nebr. State Patrol, Omaha, 1977-84; pvt. practice law Omaha and Council Bluffs, 1986—. Cons. Overland Corp., 1988-89, Fire Photo Corp., Omaha, 1980-91; instr. law enforcement State Nebr., 1979; instr. environ. law and hazardous materials Nebr. State Patrol, 1979-92, technician hazardous material, 1979-84, investigator accidents, 1978-84; adj. faculty U. Nebr., Omaha, Lincoln, Southwestern Community Coll., Iowa, Lakeland Coll., West Allis, Wis.; corp. counsel Farmers Telephone Co., 1990-93, S&M Oil Co., 1990—, Environ. Protection Instrn. Cons. Corp., 1991-2000, GSI-Environ. Cons. Corp., 1991-2000, Environ. Assessment Group, 1990-2000, Firstier Bank, 1990-92, Bank One Trust Co., 1992-95, Merrill Lynch Trust Co., 1995-96, Comerica Bank, 1996-2001, So. Mich. Bank & Trust, 2001-02, Bank of Am., 2002—. Law Enforcement Assistance Adminstrn. scholar, 1978-79; recipient Life Saving award Am. Heart Assn., 1982, Am. Jurisprudence award Bancroft-Whitney Co., 1986, 87. Mem ABA, ATLA, Nat. Assn. Chiefs of Police, State Troopers Assn. Nebr., Peace Officers Assn. Nebr., Mich. State Bar Assn., Kalamazoo County Bar Assn., Environ. Assessment Assn., Am. Bankers Assn., Iowa State Bar Assn., Omaha Bar Assn., Fla. Bankers Assn., Delta Theta Phi. Republican. Lutheran. Avocation: car collecting. Corporate, general, Environmental, Probate (including wills, trusts). Home and Office: 3825 Emerald Estates Cir Apopka FL 32703

SEWARD, RICHARD BEVIN, lawyer; b. Bartlesville, Okla., May 27, 1932; s. Fredrick W. and Kittie Lea (Hudson) S.; m. Loydell E. Nash, Aug. 1, 1954; children: Ann M., Elizabeth, Amy M. BS, Okla. State U., 1954; postgrad., Tulsa U., 1959-62; JD, So. Methodist U., 1971. Bar: Tex. 1968. Personnel mgr. Unit Rig and Equipment Co., Tulsa, 1958-62, Gifford-Hill Cos., Dallas, 1962-66; labor cons. Dallas, 1966-68; partner firm Stanfield & Seward, Dallas, 1978-83; sole practice law Farmersville, Tex., 1983—. Served with AUS, 1955-57. Mem. Order of Coif. State civil litigation, Corporate, general, General practice. Home and Office: 14340 County Road 550 Farmersville TX 75442-7034 E-mail: sewfolly@aol.com.

SEXTON, JOHN EDWARD, academic administrator, law educator; b. Bklyn., Sept. 29, 1942; s. John Edward and Catherine (Humann) S.; m. Lisa Ellen Goldberg; children: Jed, Katherine. BA, Fordham U., 1963, PhD, 1978; JD, Harvard U., 1979. Bar: NY 1981, US Supreme Ct. 1984. Prof. religion St. Francis Coll., Bklyn., 1965-75; law clk. U.S. Ct. Appeals, Wash., 1979, 80, U.S. Supreme Ct., Wash., DC, 1980-81; prof. law NYU, NYC, 1981—, dean law sch., 1988—2002, pres., 2002—. Dir. Washington Sq. Legal Services, NYC, 1983-2002, Pub. Interest Law Found., N.Y.C., 1983-85. Author: A Managerial Model of the Supreme Court, 1985, Federal

Jury Instructions-Civil, 1985, How Free Are We? A Study of the Constitution, 1985, Cases and Materials in Civil Procedure, 1988. Dir. Root-Tilden Scholarship Program, 1984-88. Mem. Assn. of Am. Law Schs. (pres. 1997-98). Home: 29 Washington Sq W New York NY 10011-9180 Office: NYU Sch Law 70 Wash Sq S Rm 1216 New York NY 10012-1385*

SEYBERT, JOANNA, federal judge; b. Bklyn., Sept. 18, 1946; BA, U. Cin., 1967; JD, St. John's U., 1971. Bar: N.Y. 1972, U.S. Dist. Ct. (ea. and so. dists.) N.Y. 1973. Trial staff atty. Legal Aid Soc., N.Y.C., 1971-73, sr. staff atty. Mineola, N.Y., 1976-80; sr. trial atty. Fed. Defender Svc., Bklyn., 1973-75; bur. chief Nassau County Atty's Office, Mineola, 1980-87; judge Nassau County Dist. Ct., Hempstead, N.Y., 1987-92, Nassau County Ct., Mineola, 1992-94, U.S. Dist. Ct. (ea. dist.) N.Y., Uniondale, 1994—. Mem.: Nassau Lawyers Assn. (past pres.), Fed. Judges Assn. (v.p.), Theodore Roosevelt A. Inns of Ct. (past pres.), Suffolk County Bar Assn., Internat. Assn. Judges (del.). Office: 1034 Federal Plz Central Islip NY 11722-4443

SEYMOUR, BARBARA LAVERNE, lawyer; b. Columbia, S.C., July 9, 1953; d. Leroy Semon and Barbara Lucile (Youngblood) Seymour. BS, S.C. State Coll., 1975; JD, Georgetown U., 1979; MBA, Harvard U., 1985. Bar: S.C. 1979, Tex. 1984, U.S. Dist. Ct. (ea. dist.) Tex. 1983, U.S. Dist. Ct. (so. dist.) Tex. 1985, U.S. Tax Ct. 1986, U.S. Claims Ct. 1991. Tax atty. Texaco Inc., White Plains, N.Y., 1979-80, Houston, 1980-98; exec. asst. Office of the CFO-Gen. Counsel, Equilon Enterprises LLC, Houston, 1998-99, asst. sec., counsel, 1999—. Mem. IRS Commr.'s Adv. Group, 1995-97; mem. Simplified Tax and Wage Reporting Sys. Working Group, 1994-97; loaned exec. for task force to audit Tex. Employment Commn. by Gov. of Tex., 1987-88. Troop leader Girl Scouts U.S., White Plains, 1979-80, asst. troop leader, Houston, 1981-82; bd. dirs. Sickle Cell Assn. of the Tex. Gulf Coast, Houston, 1986-92, treas., 1986-88, pres., 1988-90, chair 25th ann. gala, 1996; vol. allocation panel United Way of the Tex. Gulf Coast; bd. dirs. Fund for Main St., The Assistance Fund, v.p., 2002—; bd. dirs. Sandra Organ Dance Co., v.p., 2000—; mem. Black Exec. Exch. program Nat. Urban League 1980-; bd. dirs., exec. com. Houston Area Urban League, 1995-2001, 3d v.p., 1998-2000, 2001—, treas. 2002—, 1st v.p., 2000-2001, chair 1997 Equal Opportunity Day Dinner, co-chair Host Com., Nat. Urban League Conf., 99; bd. dirs., asst. treas. Sheila Jackson Lee for Congress, 1995-97. Named one of 50 Outstanding Young Leaders of the Future, Ebony Mag., 1983; recipient Disting. Bus. Alumnus award S.C. State Coll., 1991, Eagle award Nat. Eagle Leadership Inst., 1995; selected for Leadership Houston, Leadership Am., 1990; finalist Five Outstanding Young Houstonians award Jaycees, 1988, one of 10 Foremost Fashionables in Houston, Alpha Kappa Alpha, 1994; named 2001's ABC channel 13 Woman of Distinction. Mem. ABA (environ. tax com., employment tax com.), Houston Black Women Lawyers Assn. (sec. 1981-82, treas. 1982-83), Houston Bus. Forum (bd. dirs. 1983, 87-90, treas. 1988-89, sec. 1989-90), Nat. Bar Assn. (com. chmn. 1982-83), S.C. Bar Assn., Tex. Bar Assn., Harvard U. Bus. Sch. Black Alumni Assn. (historian 1985-86), Black Law Alumni Coun. of Georgetown U. Law Ctr., W.J. Durham Soc., The Links, Inc. (v.p. Houston chpt. 1996-2000, pres. 2000—, chair 1995 Cotillion), Alpha Kappa Alpha. Democrat. Roman Catholic. Pension, profit-sharing, and employee benefits, Corporate taxation, State and local taxation. Office: Equilon Enterprises LLC 1100 Louisiana St Ste 1066 Houston TX 77002-5220 E-mail: blseymour@equilon.com.

SEYMOUR, EVERETT HEDDEN, JR., lawyer; b. Tuxedo Park, N.Y., Apr. 16, 1958; s. Everett Hedden and Deborah (Robinson) S. BA, Yale U., 1980; JD, U. Va., 1986. Bar: N.Y. 1988, U.S. Dist. Ct. (so. and ea. dists.) N.Y. 1988, Conn. 1988, U.S. Dist. Ct. Conn. 1988. Law clk. to justice U.S. Dist. Ct., New Haven, 1986-87; assoc. Davis Polk & Wardwell, N.Y.C., 1987-97; v.p., asst. gen. counsel J.P. Morgan Chase & Co., N.Y.C., 1997—. Articles rev. editor U. Va. Law Rev., 1984-86. Corporate, general, Environmental. Office: JP Morgan Chase & Co 270 Park Ave 39th Fl New York NY 10017-2014

SEYMOUR, MARY FRANCES, lawyer; b. Durand, Wis., Oct. 20, 1948; d. Marshall Willard and Alice Roberta (Smith) Thompson; m. Marshall Warren Seymour, June 6, 1970; 1 foster child, Nghia Pham. BS, U. Wis., LaCrosse, 1970; JD, William Mitchell Coll., 1979. Bar: Minn. 1979, U.S. Dist. Ct. Minn. 1979, U.S. Ct. Appeals (8th cir.) 1979, U.S. Supreme Ct. 1986. With Cochrane and Bresnahan, P.A., St. Paul, 1979-94, Loper & Seymour, P.A., 1994—2003; pvt. practice Pepin, Wis., 2003—, Mary F. Seymour Atty. At Law. Mem.: ABA, Ramsey County Bar Assn., Minn. Bar Assn. Federal civil litigation, General civil litigation, State civil litigation. Home and Office: PO Box 146 511 2nd St Pepin WI 54759 E-mail: maryfseymour@msn.com.

SEYMOUR, STEPHANIE KULP, federal judge; b. Battle Creek, Mich., Oct. 16, 1940; d. Francis Bruce and Frances Cecelia (Bria) Kulp; m. R. Thomas Seymour, June 10, 1972; children: Bart, Bria, Sara, Anna. BA magna cum laude, Smith Coll., 1962; JD, Harvard U., 1965. Bar: Okla. 1965. Practice, Boston, 1965—66, Tulsa, 1966—67, Houston, 1968—69; assoc. Doerner, Stuart, Saunders, Daniel & Anderson, Tulsa, 1971—75, ptnr., 1975—79; judge U.S. Ct. Appeals (10th cir.) Okla., Tulsa, 1979—94, 2000—, chief judge, 1994—2000. Mem. U.S. Jud. Conf., 1994—, com. defender svcs., 1985—90, chmn., 1987—90, com. to review cir. council conduct and disability, 1996—; joint fed. tribal rels. com. 9th and 10th cirs., 1993—; mem. Okla. State Fed. Tribal Judicial Coun., 1993—94. Task force Tulsa Human Rights Commn., 1972—76; legal adv. panel Tulsa Task Force Battered Women, 1971—77; trustee Tulsa County Law Libr., 1977—78. Mem.: ABA, Am. Inns of Ct. (Council Oak chpt.), Nat. Assn. Women Judges, Fed. Judges Assn., Tulsa County Bar Assn., Okla. Bar Assn. (assoc. bar examiner 1973—79), Phi Beta Kappa. Office: US Courthouse 333 W 4th St Ste 4-562 Tulsa OK 74103-3819*

SFEKAS, STEPHEN JAMES, lawyer, educator; b. Balt., Feb. 12, 1947; s. James Stephen and Lee (Mesologites) S.; m. Joanne Lorraine Murphy, May 27, 1973; children: James Stephen, Andrew Edward Stephen, Christina Marie; m. Elizabeth Ruff, Nov. 1, 1997. BS in Fgn. Svc., Georgetown U., 1968, JD, 1973; MA, Yale U., 1972. Bar: Md. 1973, U.S. Dist. Ct. Md. 1974, U.S. Ct. Appeals (4th cir.) 1974. Law clk. U.S. Dist. Ct., Balt., 1973-74; assoc. firm Frank, Bernstein, Conaway & Goldman, Balt., 1974-75; asst. atty. gen. State of Md., Balt., 1975-81; assoc. firm Tydings & Rosenberg, Balt., 1981-82, ptnr., 1983-86; with firm Miles & Stockbridge, Balt., 1986-90; ptnr. Weinberg & Green, Balt., 1991-98, Saul, Ewing, LLP, Balt., 1998—2001; counsel Cook & Di Franco, LLC, 2001—. Instr. legal writing C.C. Balt., 1976-79; instr. legal ethics Goucher Coll., Balt., 1979; adj. prof. adminstrv. law U. Md., Balt., 1981-93, health, 1993—, law sch. U. Balt., 1993—. Editor Georgetown Law Jour., 1972-73; contbr. articles to legal publs. Bd. dirs. Md. region NCCJ, 1981-89, co-chmn. Md. region, 1986-89, Orthodox Christian Laity, 1990—98, Ctrl. Md. Ecumenical Coun., 1991—93, Balt. Assn. for Retarded Citizens Vol. for Med. Engring., 2001-; mem. Piraeus Sister City Com., City of Balt., 1983-89; mem. parish coun. Greek Orthodox Cathedral of Annunciation, Balt., 1981-84; mem. internat. com. Balt. region ARC, 1984-85; mem. adv. com. on bread for the world Dept. Ch. and Soc., Greek Orthodox Archdiocese North & S.Am., 1984—; pres. Greek Orthodox Counseling and Social Svcs. of Balt., 1984-88; ; mem. bylaw com. Girl Scouts Ctrl. Md., 1989-91, Md. Leadership Program, 1997; mem. pres.'s adv. coun. U. Md., Baltimore County. Danforth fellow, Woodrow Wilson fellow, WHO fellow, London, 1979. Fellow: Md. Bar Found., Soc. for Values in Higher Edn. (bd. dir. 2002—); mem.: ABA (forum com. on health law, Grant Morris fellow 1979), Am. Health Lawyers Assn., Bar Assn. Balt. City, Md. Bar Assn. Democrat. Administrative and regulatory, Federal civil litigation, Health. Office: Cook & Di Franco LLC Ste 1810 120 E Baltimore St Baltimore MD 21202 E-mail: ssfekas@cookanddifranco.com.

SFIKAS, PETER MICHAEL, lawyer, educator; b. Gary, Ind., Aug. 9, 1937; s. Michael E. and Helen (Thureanos) S.; m. Freida Platon, Apr. 24, 1966; children— Ellen M., Pamela C., Sandra N. BS, Ind. U., 1959; JD, Northwestern U., 1962. Bar: Ill. 1962, U.S. Dist. Ct. (no. dist.) Ill. 1963, U.S. Ct. Appeals (7th cir.) 1963, U.S. Supreme Ct. 1970, U.S. Ct. Appeals (9th cir.) 1976, U.S. Ct. Appeals (3d cir.) 1981, U.S. Ct. Appeals (D.C. cir.) 1984, U.S. Dist. Ct. (cen. dist.) Ill. 1988. Atty. Legal Aid Bur., United Charities Chgo., 1962-63; sr. ptnr. Peterson & Ross, Chgo., 1970-95; chief counsel, assoc. exec. dir. div. legal affairs ADA, Chgo., 1995—; sr. ptnr. Bell, Boyd & Lloyd, Chgo., 1996—. Prosecutor Village of LaGrange Park, Ill., 1969-74; mem. rules com. Ill. Supreme Ct., 1975-95, mem. spl. joint com. on discovery rules, 1995; arbitrator Nat. Panel Arbitrators, 1972—; adj. prof. Loyola U. Sch. Law, 1978—; guest lectr. U. Ill. Coll. Dentistry, 1988-95; lectr. corp. counsel inst. Northwestern U. Sch. Law, 1984, lectr. Ray Garret Jr. Corp. and Securities Law Inst., 1996. Co-author: Antitrust and Unfair Competition Practice Handbook, 1996; contbr. articles to profl. jours. Mem. Ill. steering com. Ct. Watching Project, LWV, 1975-77; pres. Holy Apostles Greek Orthodox Ch. Parish Coun., 1987-89; co-pres. Oak Sch. PTO, 1989-90; mem. com. to select sch. supr., dist. 86, DuPage County, Ill., 1993-94. Recipient Maurice Weigle award, Chgo. Bar Found., 1973, Fones award and hon. membership, Conn. Dental Assn., 1998. Fellow Am. Bar Found., Am. Coll. Trial Lawyers, Chgo. Bar Found. (life); mem. ABA (editor in chief Forum Law Jour. sect. ins., negligence and compensation law 1972-76), Ill. Bar Found. (bd. dirs.), Northwestern U. Law Alumni Assn. (1st v.p. 1985-86, pres. 1986-87, Svc. award 1990), Ill. State Bar Assn. (bd. govs. 1970-76, chmn. antitrust law sect. coun. 1986-87), Chgo. Bar Assn. (editl. bd. Chgo. Bar Record 1973-84), Bar Assn. 7th Fed. Cir., Ill. Inst. Continuing Legal Edn. (chmn. profl. antitrust problems program 1976, author program on counseling corps., antitrust and trade regulation), Legal Club Chgo. (sec.-treas, 1984-86, v.p. 1989-90, pres. 1990-91). Antitrust, Federal civil litigation, State civil litigation. Office: Bell Boyd & Lloyd 70 W Madison St Ste 3300 Chicago IL 60602-4284 E-mail: P.Sfikas@BellBoyd.com.

SGARRO, DOUGLAS A. legal association administrator; b. NY, 1959; m. Breda Sgarro; 3 children. Grad, Hamilton Coll., 1981; law degree, Univ. of Va. Sch. of Law, 1984. Assoc. Brown & Wood LLP, New York, NY, 1984—93, ptnr., 1993—97; sr. v.p. and chief legal officer CVS Pharmacy, Woonsocket, RI, 1997—; pres. CVS Realty Co., Woonsocket, RI, 1999—; sr. v.p. and chief legal officer CVS Corp., Woonsocket, RI, 2000—; dir. Econ. Devel. Corp., Woonsocket, RI, 2000—. Dir. Providence Children's Mus., United Way, Rye, NY. Mem.: Am. Bar Assoc. Bus. Law Sect., Internat. Assoc. of Atty. Exec. in Corp. Real Estate. Avocations: reading, watch CNN on TV, exercise. Office: Office Chief Legal Officer CVS Corp One CVS Dr Woonsocket RI 02895*

SHABAZ, JOHN C. judge; b. West Allis, Wis., June 25, 1931; s. Cyrus D. and Harriet T. Shabaz; children: Scott J., Jeffrey J., Emily D., John D. LLB, Marquette U., 1957; BS in Polit. Sci., U. Wis., 1999. Comd. 2d. lt. U.S. Army, 1954, assigned to inactive reserves, 1964; pvt. practice law West Allis, Wis., 1957—82; mem. Wis. Assembly, 1965—81; judge U.S. Dist. Ct. (we. dist.) Wis., 1982—96, chief judge, 1996—2001. Office: US Dist Ct PO Box 591 Madison WI 53701-0591

SHACKLETON, RICHARD JAMES, lawyer, director; b. Orange, N.J., May 24, 1933; s. S. Paul and Mildred W. (Welsh) S.; m. Katharine L. Richards, June 16, 1956; children: Katharine Margaret, Julia Anne, Forrest Maxwell. Student, Kalamazoo Coll., 1957; JD, Rutgers U., 1961. Bar: N.J. 1961, U.S. Dist. Ct. N.J. 1967, U.S. Dist. Ct. (ea. dist.) N.Y. 1987, U.S. Dist. Ct. (so. dist.) N.Y. 1986, U.S. Dist. Ct. (we. and no. dists.) N.Y. 1997, U.S. Ct. Appeals (3rd cir.) 1983, U.S. Ct. Appeals (4th cir.) 1986 , U.S. Supreme Ct. 1969, Fed. Bar Coun. N.J. 1988. Ltd. atty. Berry Whitson & Berry, 1961; practice Ship Bottom, N.J., 1961—; sr. ptnr. Shackleton, Hazeltine & Dasti, Ship Bottom, N.J., 1965-84, Shackleton, Hazeltine & Bishop, Ship Bottom, N.J., 1984—. Pres. Beach Haven Inlet Taxpayers Assn., 1958—68, Ocean County Vis. Homemakers Assn., 1966—72, Brodhead Watershed Assn., 1997—98; mem. U.S. Dist. Ct. N.J. Hist. Soc.; bd. dirs., v.p. Brodhead Protective Assn. Mem. ABA (litigation sect., product liability com.), Am. Judicature Soc., Fed. Bar Coun. N.Y., N.J. Bar Assn., N.Y. Bar Assn., Ocean County Bar Assn., Def. Rsch. Inst. (mem. med. device and products sect.), Ocean County Lawyers Club, Henryville Conservation Club (chmn. bd.), Henryville Flyfishers Club (pres., bd. dirs., chmn.), The Anglers' Club Phila., Phila. Gun Club (bd. dirs.), Sandy Island Gun Club (life, bd. dirs., pres.), NRA (life), Gun Owners Am. (life), Brodhead Protective Assn. (bd. dirs.), Brodhead Watershed Assn. (bd. dirs., pres. 1997-98, 2001-02), Ancient Inc. Order of the Beefeater. Federal civil litigation, State civil litigation, Product liability. Home: 5614 West Ave Beach Haven NJ 08008-1059 Office: 22d St at Long Beach Blvd Ship Bottom NJ 08008 E-mail: shblaw@aol.com.

SHACKMAN, BEVERLY ANNE, lawyer; b. Winnipeg, Man., Can., Apr. 24, 1945; came to U.S., 1966; d. Louis and Fannie (Packer) Sisskind; m. Carl Shackman, June 26, 1966 (div. Apr. 1989); children: Megan, Dina; m. Lawrence J. Cohn, Jan. 4, 1992. BA, Bklyn. Coll., 1971; JD, Rutgers U., 1981; LLM in Taxation, NYU, 1987. Bar: N.J., 1981, N.Y. 1982. Law clk. Organized Crime Strike Force U.S. Dept. Justice, Newark, 1980-81; law clk. to Hon. Michael A. Andrew, Jr. Tax Ct. N.J., New Brunswick, 1981-82; assoc. Paul, Weiss, Rifkind, Wharton & Garrison, N.Y.C., 1982-85, Kronish, Lieb, Weiner & Hellman, N.Y.C., 1985-89, LeBoeuf, Lamb, Leiby & MacRae, N.Y.C., 1989-93; pvt. practice N.Y.C., 1993—. Of counsel Stein, Bliablias, McGuire, Pantages & Gigl, Livingston, N.J., 1996-98; staff reporter Women's Rights Reporter Newark Law Sch., 1980-81. Mem. ABA (real property and probate sect.), N.Y. Bar Assn. (trusts and estates sect.), Assn. Bar City N.Y. Avocations: reading, writing poetry, cooking, music, film. Office: 2353 St Georges Ave Rahway NJ 07065 Fax: 212-362-7230. Business E-Mail: .

SHACTER, DAVID MERVYN, lawyer; b. Toronto, Ont., Can., Jan. 17, 1941; s. Nathan and Tillie Anne (Schwartz) S. BA, U. Toronto, 1963; JD, Southwestern U., 1967. Bar: Calif. 1968, U.S. Ct. Appeals (9th cir.) 1969, U.S. Supreme Ct. 1982. Law clk., staff atty. Legal Aid Found., Long Beach, Calif., 1967-70; asst. city atty. City of Beverly Hills, Calif., 1970; ptnr. Shacter & Berg, Beverly Hills, 1971-83, Selwyn, Capalbo, Lowenthal & Shacter Profl. Law Corp., 1984-99; pvt. practice, 1999—. Del. State Bar Conf. Dels., 1976—; lectr. Calif. Continuing Edn. of Bar, 1977, 82, 83, 86; judge pro tem L.A. and Beverly Hills mcpl. cts.; arbitrator L.A. Superior Ct., 1983—, also judge pro tem; disciplinary examiner Calif. State Bar, 1986. Bd. dirs. and pres. Los Angeles Soc. Prevention Cruelty to Animals, 1979-89. Mem.: City of Hope Med. Ctr. Aux., Am. Arbitration Assn. (nat. panel arbitrators, neutral arbitrator, panel chmn.), Beverly Hills Bar Found. (pres. 1995—97, bd. govs. 1998—2001), Beverly Hills Bar Assn. (bd. govs. 1985—, sec. 1987—88, treas. 1988—89, v.p. 1989—90, pres.-elect 1990—91, pres. 1991—92, editor-in-chief jour.), Nat. Assn. Securities Dealers (arbitrator 1998—), West Los Angeles C. of C., Wilshire C. of C. (bd. dir. 1985—87, gen. counsel 1985—87). General civil litigation, Estate planning, Personal injury (including property damage). Office: 10801 National Blvd Ste 608 Los Angeles CA 90064 E-mail: david@shacter.org.

SHADOAN, WILLIAM LEWIS, judge; b. Galesburg, Ill., July 12, 1931; s. William Parker and Hortense (Lewis) S.; m. Katherine E. Thomson, 1961; children: Ann-Wayne Harlan, Kate, Tom. BS, U. Ky., 1955; JD, U. Louisville, 1961. Bar: Ky. 1961, U.S. Dist. Ct. (we. dist.) Ky. 1961. City atty., Wickliffe, Ky., 1963; county atty. Ballard County, Ky., 1963-76; chief regional judge 1st cir. Wickliffe, Ky., 1983—. Chmn. Ballard County Dem. Party, 1963; trustee Meth. Ch., Wickliffe, 1961-84; advisor Selective Svc., Peducah, Ky., 1968; chmn. Wickliffe C. of C., 1967-71; mem. exec. com. Ky. Hist. Soc., Frankfort; vice chmn. Ky. Cert. of Need and Lic. Bd., 1973-84; named assoc. justice Ky. Surpeme Ct., 1984. Capt. U.S. Army, 1955-59. Mem. ABA, Ky. Health Systems Assn. (vice chmn. 1976-82), Ky. Bar Assn. (Outstanding Judge 1997), Assn. Trial Lawyers Am., Ky. County Ofcls. Bd. (chmn. 1976-80), Miss. River Commn. (chmn. 1976-83), Ky. County Attys. Assn. (pres. 1966-77), First Dist. Bar Assn. (pres.), Masons (Wickliffe, 32 degree), Shriners (Madisonville, Ky.), Orer Ea Star, Elks. Home: RR 2 Wickliffe KY 42087-9804 Office: Ballard Courthouse 4th St Wickliffe KY 42087

SHADUR, MILTON IRVING, judge; b. St. Paul, June 25, 1924; s. Harris and Mary Shadur; m. Eleanor Pilka, Mar. 30, 1946; children: Robert, Karen, Beth. BS, U. Chgo., 1943, JD cum laude, 1949. Bar: Ill. 1949, U.S. Supreme Ct. 1957. Pvt. practice , Chgo., 1949-80; assoc. Goldberg, Devoe & Brussell, 1949-51; ptnr. Shadur, Krupp & Miller and predecessor firms, 1951-80; judge U.S. Dist. Ct. (no. dist.) Ill., Chgo., 1980-92, sr. judge, 1992—. Commr. Ill. Supreme Ct. Character and Fitness, 1961-72, chmn., 1971; gen. counsel Ill. Jud. Inquiry Bd., 1975-80; chmn. adv. com. on evidence rules to Jud. Conf. of U.S., 1999-2002, mem. adv. com., 1992-99. Editor-in-chief: U. Chgo. Law Rev., 1948-49. Chmn. visiting com. U. Chgo. Law Sch., 1971-76, mem. vis. com., 1989-92, 99-2002; bd. dirs. Legal Assistance Found. Chgo., 1972-78; trustee Village of Glencoe, 1969-74, Ravinia Festival Assn., 1976-93, exec. com. 1983-93, vice chmn. 1989-93, life trustee, 1994—. Lt. (j.g.) USNR, 1943-46. Fellow Am. Bar Found.; mem. ABA (spl. com. on youth edn. for citizenship 1975-79), Ill. State Bar Assn. (joint com. on rules of jud. conduct 1974), Chgo. Bar Assn. (chmn. legis. com. 1963-65, jud. com. 1970-71, profl. ethics com. 1975-76, sec. 1967-69), Chgo. Council Lawyers, Order of Coif Office: US Dist Ct 219 S Dearborn St Ste 2388 Chicago IL 60604-1800

SHAEVSKY, MARK, lawyer; b. Harbin, Manchuria, China, Dec. 2, 1935; came to U.S., 1938, naturalized, 1944; s. Tolio and Rae (Weinstein) S.; m. Lois Ann Levi, Aug. 2, 1964; children: Thomas Lyle, Lawrence Keith. Student, Wayne State U., 1952-53; BA with highest distinction, U. Mich., 1956, JD with highest distinction, 1959. Bar: Mich. 1959. Law clerk to presiding judge U.S. Dist. Ct., Detroit, 1960-61; assoc. Honigman Miller Schwartz & Cohn, Detroit, 1961-64; ptnr. Honigman, Miller, Schwartz & Cohn, Detroit, 1965-69, sr. ptnr., 1969—2001, of counsel, 2001—. Instr. law Wayne State U. Law Sch., Detroit, 1961-64; comml. arbitrator Am. Arbitration Assn., Detroit; bd. dirs. Charter One Fin. Inc., Charter One Bank, H.W. Kaufman Group, Inc. Contbr. Wayne State U. Law Rev., U. Mich. Law Rev., 1957-59, asst. editor, 1958-59. Dir. Detroit Mens Orgn. of Rehab. through Tng., 1969-79; mem. exec. bd. Am. Jewish Com., Detroit, 1965-74; trustee Jewish Vocat. Svcs., Detroit, 1973-76; sec., dir. Am. Friends Hebrew Univ., Detroit, 1976-84; mem. capital needs com. Jewish Welfare Fedn., Detroit, 1986-97; trustee William Beaumont Hosp., 1997—, bd. dirs., 2002—; trustee Beaumont Found., 1997—; bd. dirs. Shaevsky Family Found., 2000—. With U.S. Army, 1959-60. Burton Abstract fellow, 1959. Mem. ABA, Mich. Bar Assn., Franklin Hills Country Club, Detroit Athletic Club, Order of the Coif, Phi Beta Kappa. Corporate, general, Property, real (including real estate development, water), Securities. Home: The Hills of Lone Pine 4750 N Chipping Gln Bloomfield Hills MI 48302-2390 Office: Honigman Miller Schwartz & Cohn 2290 First National Bldg Detroit MI 48226 E-mail: mzs@honigman.com.

SHAFFER, RICHARD JAMES, lawyer, former manufacturing company executive; b. Pe Ell, Wash., Jan. 26, 1931; s. Richard Humphrys and Laura Rose (Faas) S.; m. Donna M. Smith, May 13, 1956; children: Leslie Lauren Shaffer Litsinger, Stephanie Jane Athenton. BA, U. Wash.; LL.B., Southwestern U. Bar: Calif. Vice pres., gen. counsel, sec. NI, Inc., Long Beach, Calif., 1974-89; gen. counsel Masco Bldg. Products Corp., Long Beach, 1985-89; pvt. practice, Huntington Beach, Calif., 1989—. Mem. ltd. liability co. drafting com. and task force Calif. State Bar, 1992-94; lectr. on ltd. liability cos. Trustee Ocean View Sch. Dist., 1965-73, pres., 1966, 73; mem. fin. adv. com. Orange Coast Coll., 1966; mem. Long Beach Local Devel. Corp., 1978-89, Calif. Senate Commn. on Corp. Governance, Shareholders' Rights and Securities Transactions, 1986-97, chmn. drafting com. ltd. liability co. act for senate com., 1991-93; mem. City of Huntington Beach Pers. Commn., 1996-98; mem. Huntington Beach Clean Water Sub Com. for Huntington Harbour, bd. dirs. Huntington Beach Libr. Patrons, 1996-98. Mem. ABA, Nat. Assn. Securities Dealers (bd. arbitrators), Calif. Bar Assn. (exec. com. corp. law dept. com. bus. sect. 1981-88), Orange County Bar Assn., Huntington Harbour Yacht Club, Wanderlust Skiers of Huntington Harbour (pres.). Corporate, general, Finance, Property, real (including real estate development, water).

SHAFFER, WAYNE ALAN, lawyer; b. Reno, Oct. 15, 1954; s. William V. and Shirley Joy (Perry) S.; m. Robin E. Sprung, Jan. 7, 1978. BA, U. Nev., 1977; JD magna cum laude, Calif. Western Sch. Law, 1981. Bar: Nev. 1981, U.S. Dist. Ct. Nev. 1981, Calif. 1982. Dep. dist. atty. Washoe County, Reno, 1981-82; assoc. Lionel, Sawyer & Collins, Reno, 1982-84, Law Office Eugene J. Wait Jr., Reno, 1985-89; ptnr. Wait & Shaffer, Reno, 1989—99, Bible Hoy & Trachok, Reno, 1999—2002, Law Offices of Wayne A. Shaffer, Reno, 2002—. Instr. Old Coll. Sch. Law, Reno, 1982. Mem. ABA, Nev. Bar Assn., Calif. Bar Assn., Assn. Def. Counsel No. Nev., Assn. Def. Counsel No. Calif. Republican. General civil litigation, Personal injury (including property damage), Product liability. Office: Law Office of Wayne A Shaffer 419 Flint St Reno NV 89501

SHAFFERT, KURT, retired lawyer, chemical engineer; b. Vienna, July 20, 1929; s. Rudolph nee Schafranik and Irma (Altar) S.; m. Judith Pytel, June 12, 1955; children: Elona Ruth, Robin Laurette. BChemE, CCNY, 1951; LLB cum laude, NYU, 1963. Bar: N.Y. 1963, D.C. 1965, U.S. Supreme Ct. 1967, U.S. Patent and Trademark Office 1964. Chem. engr. Diamond Alkali Co., Newark, 1951-54; process devel. engr. Am. Cyanamid Co., Stamford, Conn., 1957-59; patent liaison engr. Uniroyal Inc., 1959-63; assoc. Arthur, Dry & Kalish, N.Y.C., 1963-66, Office of Robert F. Conrad, Washington, 1966-69; sr. ptrn. Shaffert, Miller & Browne, Washington, 1970-74; sr. trial atty. intellectual property sect. Antitrust divsn. Dept. of Justice, Washington, 1974-85, professions and intellectual property sect., 1985-94, intellectual property guidelines task force, 1994, civil task force, 1994-2000; ret., 2000. Mem. Bethesda-Chevy Chase Jewish Comm. Group, 1965, pres., 1973-74, v.p. 1972-73, treas. 1971-72; mem. Jewish Comm. Ctr. of Greater Wash., 1970-78, bd. dirs., 1973-78; provided tape recorded Holocaust recollections for Stephen Spielberg Holocaust Archive Survivors of the Shoa Visual History Found., 1998. With U.S. Army, 1955-56. Mem. ABA (antitrust sect., patent, trademark and copyright sect.), Profl. Assn. Antitrust Divsn. Dept. of Justice (pres. 1978-79), Bar Assn. D.C. (council del. 1972-74), D.C. Bar Assn.

SHAHAM, SHIRI, lawyer; b. Holon, Israel, July 8, 1967; d. Uri and Nili Praiz; m. Oded Shaham, July 22, 1991; children: Yuval, Noga. LLB cum laude, Hebrew U., Jerusalem, 1990; LLM, Cambridge (Eng.) U., 1992. Lawyer, ptnr. Yigal Arnon & Co., Tel-Aviv, 1992—. Sgt. Israeli Def. Force, 1984—86. Mem.: Israel Bar Assn. (mem. 1991—). Corporate, general, Finance, Securities. Office: Yigal Arnon & Co 1 AzrieliCtr 67021 Tel Aviv Israel

SHAIKUN, MICHAEL GARY, lawyer; b. Ky., Mar. 17, 1942; s. Leon J. and Cleo (Taub) S.; m. Phyllis Miriam Cohen, Aug. 21, 1964; children: Benjamin, Stephanie, Alissa. BS in Econs. with highest honors, U. Pa., 1963; JD, Harvard U., 1966. Bar: Ky. 1966, U.S. Dist. Ct. (we. dist.) Ky. 1966. Assoc. Greenebaum Doll & McDonald PLLC, Louisville, 1966-69, mem., 1970—. Contbr. articles to profl. jours. Bd. dirs. Jewish Cmty. Fedn. Louisville, 1971—, past pres.; past chmn. Found. for Planned Giving, Jewish Cmty. Fedn., Louisville; bd. dirs., chmn. fin. devel. YMCA Safe Place Svcs., 1995—. Mem. ABA, Ky. Bar Assn., Louisville Bar Assn. Democrat. Jewish. Avocation: computers. Bankruptcy, Commercial, contracts (including sales of goods; commercial financing), Property, real (including real estate development, water). Home: 5907 Burlington Ave Louisville KY 40222-6118 Office: Greenebaum Doll & McDonald PLLC 3300 National City Tower Louisville KY 40202 E-mail: MGS@gdm.com.

SHAINES, ROBERT ARTHUR, lawyer; b. Newburyport, Mass., Nov. 24, 1929; s. Edward I. and Ruth Helena (Diamond) Shaines; m. Gladys Breger, Dec. 1954 (div. Sept. 1984); children: Stephanie, Pamela, Kate; m. Denise Kelly, Dec. 30, 1984. Student, U. N.H., 1949; JD cum laude, Boston U., 1951. Assoc. Lobel & Lobel, Boston, 1954; ptnr. Reinhart & Shaines, Portsmouth, N.H., 1954-56, Shaines Brown, Portsmouth, 1956-66, Robert A. Shaines & Assocs., Portsmouth, 1966-70, Shaines, Madrigan & McEachern, Portsmouth, 1970-85, Shaines & McEachern, Portsmouth, 1985—. Pres. Strawberry Banke, Inc., Portsmouth, 1977-80. Mayor City of Portsmouth, 1960-61; councilman City of Portsmouth, 1958-67; police commr. City of Portsmouth, 1980-81. Served as capt. USAF, 1950-54, Korea. Mem. N.H. Bar Assn. (sec. 1973-75, gov. at large 1976-79, chmn. prepaid legal services com. 1976-79), Portsmouth Bar Assn. (pres. 1963), Rockingham Bar Assn. (pres. 1972). Federal civil litigation, State civil litigation, Corporate, general. Home: 81 Garland Rd Rye NH 03870-2505 Office: Shaines & McEachern 25 Maplewood Ave Portsmouth NH 03801-3707 E-mail: rsha8125@cs.com.

SHAINWALD, SYBIL, lawyer; b. N.Y.C., Apr. 27, 1928; d. Samuel and Anne; m. Sidney Shainwald; children: Robert, Louise, Laurie, Marsha. BA, Coll. William and Mary, 1948; MA, Columbia U., 1972; JD, N.Y. Law Sch., 1976, LLD (hon.) , 2000. Bar: N.Y. 1976. Legal advisor Am. Found. for Maternal Child and Health; adj. prof. dept. law Baruch Coll., 1981—82. Co-editor: Jour. Women and Health; contbr. articles to profl. jours. Active Abortion Rights Action; co-founder, bd. mem. Trial Lawyers for Pub. Justice, 1982—88; bd. mem. Hysterectomy Edn. Resources and Svcs., 1985—, Dalkon Shield INfo. Network, Nat. Network to Prevent Birth Defects, No. Ariz. Sch. Midwifery, 1989—; bd. advisors Med. Legal Aspects of Breast Implants; bd. dirs. Consumer Interest Rsch. Inst.; fellow Roscoe Pound Inst., Morgan Libr.; trustee Civil Justice Found., 1998—99; bd. dirs. Am. Friends of Tel Aviv Mus., 2000, Friends of Tel Aviv Mus., 2000-; trustee N.Y. Law Sch., 2000—; adv. bd. Southampton The Hamptons Shakespeare Festival, 2000—; co-chair Take Home a Nude N.Y. Acad. Art, 2001; active Sybil Shainwald Charitable Found., N.Y.C. Comptrs. Health Task Force. Recipient Susan B. Anthony award, NOW; grantee, Nat. Endowment for the Humanities, Rockefeller Found., Gov. W. Averell Harriman; scholar Pres. Bryan scholar, Coll. of William and Mary, Edward Coles scholar. Mem.: ATLA (chair environ. and toxic tort sect. 1988—89, co-chair breast implant litigation group 1992—2000, mem. Dalkon shield litigation group 1995, mem. contraceptive implant litigation group 1995, co-chair DES litigation group, environ. law adv. com.), N.Y. State Trial Lawyers (bd. govs.), Assn. of the Bar of the City of N.Y. (judge nat. moot ct. competition 1988—2003), Soc. Med. Jurisprudence, Health Action Internat.-U.S. (co-founder, mem. steering com.), Lawyers Com. for Human Rights, Am. Soc. Law, Medicine and Ethics, Nat. Women's Health Alliance (pres.), Nat. Women's Health Network (bd. mem. 1980—86, chair litigation svc. 1980—86, chair health law and regulation 1981—88, chmn. bd. dirs. 1982—86, chair N.Y. state affiliate), Phi Beta Kappa. Avocation: art. Home: 25 Sutton Pl New York NY 10022-2445 Office: 950 Third Ave 10th Fl New York NY 10022

SHAKUSHO, RIN, civil law educator; b. Taipei, Taiwan, July 23, 1935; s. Rin Shi an Rin Chang Pizhl; m. Rin Shi Alen, Mar. 9, 1966; children: Yoshiho Rin, Masatoshi Rin. B in Law, Chung Shing U., 1958; MA, Nagoya (Japan) U., 1967. Asst. Nagoya U., 1971-73; asst. prof. Momoyama Gakuin U., Osaka, Japan, 1974-80, prof., 1980—, dean econs. faculty, 1982-84, councilor, 1986-92, human rights com., 1987-89, dean, law faculty, 2002—. Avocations: tennis, music, travel. Home: 8-284-7 Otori Nakamati Sakai Osaka 593-8327 Japan Office: Momoyama Gakuin U 1-1 Manabino Izumi Osaka 594-1198 Japan E-mail: kenji@andrew.ac.jp.

SHALOWITZ, HOWARD A. lawyer; b. Chgo., June 23, 1961; s. Mervin and Aileen (Goldstein) S. BA, U. Pa., 1983; JD, Washington U., 1987. Bar: Mo. 1987, Ill. 1988, U.S. Dist. Ct. (ea. dist.) Mo. 1988, U.S. Ct. Appeals (8th cir.) 1991, U.S. Ct. Appeals (7th cir.) 1993, U.S. Supreme Ct. 1994. Pvt. practice, St. Louis, 1987—. Legis. asst. Office of U.S. Senator Howard Metzenbaum, Washington, 1987; rsch. analyst Ill. Law Enforcement Commn., Chgo., 1981; mem. faculty Ctrl. Agy. for Jewish Edn., 1989-98; Dem. candidate Mo. state senate 24th dist., 1998; instr. St. Louis C.C. Lead tenor Gilbert and Sullivan operettas, 1979-84. Cantor; pres. St. Louis Circle Jewish Music, 1993-96, bd. dirs., 1987—. Bessie Bodek Miller scholar U. Pa., Phila., 1981-82; Glendy Burke Oratory medal Tulane U., New Orleans, 1981. Mem. ABA, Mo. Bar, Bar Assn. Met. St. Louis (chmn. lawyer referral and info. svc. com., pres., mem. exec. bd. govs.), St. Louis Bar Found. (pres.-elect 2003-), Cantors Assembly (chmn. amb. com., Mitzvah Star award 1994. General civil litigation, Criminal, General practice. Office: 7108 Northmoor Dr Saint Louis MO 63105-2108 E-mail: howard@shalowitz.org.

SHAMBAUGH, STEPHEN WARD, lawyer; b. South Bend, Ind., Aug. 4, 1920; s. Marion Clyde and Anna Violet (Stephens) S.; m. Marilyn Louise Pyle (dec. 1993); children: Susan Wynne Shambaugh Hinkle (dec. 1998), Kathleen Louise Shambaugh Thompson. Student, San Jose State Tchrs. Coll., 1938-40, U. Ark., 1951; LLB, U. Tulsa, 1954. Bar: Okla. 1954, Colo. 1964. Mem. staff Reading & Bates, Inc., Tulsa, 1951-54; v.p., gen. mgr., legal counsel Reading & Bates Drilling Co. Ltd., Calgary, Alta., Can., 1954-61; sr. ptnr. Bowman, Shambaugh, Geissinger & Wright, Denver, 1964-81; sole practice Denver, 1981-97; now ret. Dir., fin. counsel various corps. Col. USAF ret. Mem. Colo. Bar Assn., Okla. Bar Assn., P-51 Mustang Pilots Assn., Masons, Elks, Phi Alpha Delta. Banking, Corporate, general, Oil, gas, and mineral.

SHAMIS, EDWARD ANTHONY, JR., lawyer; b. Pensacola, Fla., Dec. 12, 1949; s. Edward Anthony Sr. and Mona Kathryn (McLaughlin) S.; m. Elizabeth Handley, Jan. 24, 1971. BS, La. State U., 1972, JD, 1974. Bar: La. 1974, U.S. Dist. Ct. (ea. dist.) La. 1975, U.S. Tax Ct. 1981, U.S. Ct. Appeals (5th cir.) 1982, U.S. Supreme Ct. 1983. Pvt. practice, Slidell, La., 1974—. Spl. counsel to Slidell City Coun., 1984—. Bd. dirs. Pope John H.S., Slidell, 1988-90, Children's Wish Endowment Fund, Inc. (formerly Northshore Children's Endowment Fund) 1991—; mem., pres. St. Tammany Assn. for Children with Learning Disabilities, Slidell, 1976-81; chmn. Slidell Bd. Zoning Adjustments, 1976-81; past mem. Boys Club; past mem. and chmn. St. Tammany Parish Ethics Commn. Mem. ATLA, La. Bar Assn. (hos. of dels. 1985-86, 88-89, 89-90, 94-97), Slidell Bar Assn. (pres. 1978-79), La. Trial Lawyers Assn. (pres.'s adv. coun. 1980-81, 84-85, 89-90, 95-96). Republican. Avocations: hunting, fishing, computers. Federal civil litigation, State civil litigation, Personal injury (including property damage). Office: 486 Brownswitch Rd Slidell LA 70458-1102 E-mail: EShamisjr@aol.com.

SHANAHAN, THOMAS M. judge; b. Omaha, May 5, 1934; m. Jane Estelle Lodge, Aug. 4, 1956; children: Catherine Shanahan Trofholz, Thomas M. II, Mary Elizabeth, Timothy F. AB magna cum laude, U. Notre Dame, 1956; JD, Georgetown U., 1959. Bar: Nebr., Wyo. Mem. McGinley, Lane, Mueller, Shanahan, O'Donnell & Merritt, Ogallala, Nebr.; assoc. justice Nebr. Supreme Ct., Lincoln, 1983-93; judge U.S. Dist. Ct. Nebr., Omaha, 1993—. Office: US Dist Ct 111 S 18th Plz Ste 3141 Omaha NE 68102

SHANDELL, RICHARD ELLIOT, lawyer; b. N.Y.C., Dec. 23, 1932; s. Edward and Dorothy (Glass) S.; m. Helene Hicken, Aug. 28, 1954; children: Andrea, Thomas, Deborah. BS in Econs., U. Pa., 1953; JD, Columbia U., 1956. Bar: N.Y. 1957. Ptnr. Katz, Shandell, Katz & Erasmous, N.Y.C, Glaser, Shandell & Blitz, N.Y.C, 1981—, Shandell Blitz Blitz & Bookson, LLP, N.Y.C. Author: The Preparation and Trial of Medical Malpractice Cases, 1981; contbg. author: Medical Malpractice: Strategic and Practical Principles 1986. Mem. Assn. Trial Lawyers Am. (gov.), N.Y. State Trial Lawyers Assn. (past pres.). Personal injury (including property damage), Product liability. Home: 325 W 86th St New York NY 10024 Office: Shandell Blitz Blitz & Bookson LLP 150 Broadway New York NY 10038-4401 Office Fax: 212-385-1916.

SHANDS, WILLIAM RIDLEY, JR., lawyer; b. Richmond, Va., Nov. 23, 1929; s. William Ridley and Josephine (Winston) S.; m. Lynneth Williams, May 31, 1958; children: William Tyler, Laura Sawyer. BA, Hampden-Sydney Coll., 1952; LLB, U. Va., 1958. Bar: Va. 1958. Atty., assoc. Christian, Barton, Epps, Brent & Chappell, Richmond, 1958-61; counsel The Life Ins. Co. of Va., Richmond, 1961-66, asst. gen. counsel, 1966-68, assoc. gen. counsel, 1968-71, gen. counsel, 1971-73, v.p., gen. counsel, 1973-78, sr. v.p., gen. counsel, 1978-79; sr. v.p. law and public affairs Continental Fin. Services Co., Richmond, 1980-85; sr. v.p., sec. Life Ins. Co. Va., Richmond, 1985-88; sr. counsel Sands, Anderson, Marks & Miller, Richmond, 1988-98; ret., 1998. Chmn. Eastern Appeal Bd. Selective Svc. System, 1969; pres., chmn. bd. dirs. Trinity Episcopal High Sch., 1971-72; bd. dirs. Richmond Area Heart Assn., 1965-71, Southampton Cotillion, 1970-72; vestryman St. Michael's Episc. Ch., 1965-68, sr. warden, 1968. Served with AUS, 1952-55, Philippines. Mem. Va. Bar Assn., Richmond Bar Assn., Assn. Life Ins. Counsel (pres. 1987-88), Am. Coun. Life Ins. (chmn. legal sect. 1982-83), Commonwealth Club, Country Club Va. Home: 3811 Darby Dr Midlothian VA 23113-1318

SHANE, RICHARD J. lawyer; b. Chgo., Dec. 12, 1953; m. Karen Rice, Sept. 16, 1979; children: Kelly, Eric, Caitlin. BA, U. Ill., Chgo., 1976; JD, No. Ill. U., 1980. Bar: N.Mex. 1980, U.S. Dist. Ct. N. Mex. 1980, U.S. Ct. Appeals (10th cir.) 1980. Atty. Dist. Atty.'s Office, Albuquerque, 1981-84; ptnr. Padilla, Riley & Shane, PA, Albuquerque, 1984-97, Riley, Shane & Hale, PA, Albuquerque, 1997—. Contbr. articles to profl. jours. Mem. Met. Parks and Adv. Bd., Albuquerque, 1995-98; founder, past pres., Vineyard Estates Neighborhood Assn. Recipient Outstanding Tchg. award N.Mex. State Bar-Lawyers With Class, 1995, Outstanding Individual award Vinyard Estates Neighborhood Assn., 1993, Honor Roll award, 1995. Mem. N.Mex. State Bar Assn. (trial practice sect.), N.Mex. Def. Lawyers Assn., Def. Rsch. Inst. Avocations: managing youth baseball, biking, hiking. General civil litigation, Insurance. Office: Riley Shane & Hale PA Ste 420 4101 Indian School Rd NE Albuquerque NM 87110-3993 Fax: (505) 883-4362. E-mail: Rshane@rshabqlaw.com.

SHANK, SUZANNE ADAMS, lawyer; b. Kansas City, Mo., Nov. 13, 1946; d. Howard Howe and Bettie Ann (Winkler) Hettick; m. Martin Smoler, May 18, 1991. BJ, U. Mo., 1972; MPA in Health Adminstrn., JD, U. Mo., Kansas City, 1982. Bar: Mo. 1982, U.S. Dist. Ct. (we. dist.) Mo. 1982. Journalist U. Kans. Med. Ctr., Kansas City, 1972-73; asst. editor Am. Family Physician, Kansas City, Mo., 1973-75; exec. dir. Lambert Med. Clinic, Kansas City, Mo., 1975-80; assoc. Shughart, Thomson & Kilroy, Kansas City, 1982-85; v.p. GE/Employers Reins. Corp., Overland Park, Kans., 1985-2000; sr. v.p. Attys. Liability Assurance Soc., Chgo., 2000—. Mem. Friends of Zoo, Kansas City, Mo., 1981—, Menorah Med. Ctr. Aux., Kansas City, 1982—, Women's Vision Internat., Kansas City, Mo., 1999—; mem. Internat. Rels. Coun., 1999—; bd. dirs. Friends Conservatory Music, 2002-, Found. Aging, Kansas City, 2003-. Mem. ABA, Mo. Bar Assn., Kansas City Bar Assn. (chmn. ins. law com.), Soc. Profl. Journalists, Soc. CPCU (rsch. com.), Com. to Protect Journalists, Kappa Tau alpha. Commercial, contracts (including sales of goods; commercial financing), Corporate, general, Insurance. Home: 2703 W 66th Ter Shawnee Mission KS 66208-1810 Office: Attorneys Liability Assurance Soc 311 S Wacker 5700 Chicago IL 60606

SHANK, WILLIAM O. lawyer; b. Hamilton, Ohio, Jan. 11, 1924; s. Horace Cooper and Bonnie (Winn) S.; m. Shirleen Allison, June 25, 1949; children— Allison Kay, Kristin Elizabeth. BA, Miami U., Oxford, O., 1947; JD, Yale, 1950. Bar: Ohio, Ill., U.S. Supreme Ct. Pvt. practice, Hamilton, Ohio, 1951-55, Chgo., 1955—; mem. firm Shank, Briede & Spoerl, Hamilton, Ohio, 1951-55; assoc. Lord, Bissell & Brook, Chgo., 1955-58; atty. Chemetron Corp., 1958-60, sr. atty., 1960-61, gen. atty., asst. sec., 1961-71, sec., gen. counsel, 1971-78; v.p., gen. counsel, sec. Walgreen Co., Deerfield, Ill., 1978-89; ptnr. Burditt & Radzius, Chartered, Chgo., 1989-98; exec. v.p. Internat. Bus. Resources, Inc., Chgo., 1993—; ptnr. Williams Montgomery & John Ltd., Chgo., 1998—. Mem. bus. adv. coun. Miami U., Oxford, Ohio, 1975—; arbitrator 19th Jud. Cir., Ill., 1995—; adv. bd. eLawForum, Washington, 1999—. Bd. dirs. Coun. for Cmty. Svcs. Met. Chgo., 1973-77; trustee Libr. Internat. Rels., 1971-78; bd. dirs. Chgo. Civic Fedn., 1984-89, Walgreen Drug Stores Hist. Found., 1990—; mem. Chgo. Crime Commn., 1985-89. 1st lt., pilot 8th Air Force, USAAF, World War II, ETO. Fellow Am. Bar Found. (life); mem. ABA (com. corp. gen. counsel), Ill. State Bar Assn., Chgo. Bar Assn. (chmn. com. on corp. law depts. 1971-72, 89-90), Am. Soc. Corp. Secs. (pres. Chgo. regional group 1983-84, nat. bd. dirs. 1984-87), Yale U. Law Sch. Assn. (past pres. Ill. Alumni, exec. com. New Haven), Walgreen Alumni Assn. (pres. 1992-94), Legal Club (pres. 1979-80), Law Club, Lawyers Club (Chgo.), Univ. Club, Econ. Club, Yale Club of Chgo., Omicron Delta Kappa, Phi Delta Phi, Sigma Chi. General civil litigation, Corporate, general, Estate planning. Home: 755 S Shore Dr Crystal Lake IL 60014-5530 Office: Williams Montgomery & John Ltd 20 N Wacker Dr Ste 2100 Chicago IL 60606 E-mail: wos@willmont.com.

SHANKS, HERSHEL, editor, writer; b. Sharon, Pa., Mar. 8, 1930; s. Martin and Mildred (Freedman) S.; m. Judith Alexander Weil, Feb. 20, 1966; children: Elizabeth Jean, Julia Emily. BA, Haverford (Pa.) Coll., 1952; MA, Columbia, 1953; LLB, Harvard, 1956. Bar: D.C. 1956. Trial atty. Dept. Justice, 1956-59; pvt. practice Washington, 1959-88; ptnr. Glassie, Pewett, Beebe & Shanks, 1964-88; editor Bibl. Archaeology Rev., Washington, 1975—. Pres. Bibl. Archaeology Soc., 1974—, Jewish Ednl. Ventures Inc., 1987—. Author: The Art and Craft of Judging, 1968, The City of David, 1973, Judaism in Stone, 1979, Jerusalem--An Archaeological Biography, 1995, The Mystery and Meaning of the Dead Sea Scolls, 1998, also articles; co-author: (with Ben Witherington III) The Brother of Jesus, 2003; co-editor: Recent Archaeology in the Land of Israel, 1984; editor: Ancient Israel, A Short History, 1988, revised edit., 1999, Christianity and Rabbinic Judaism, 1992, Understanding the Dead Sea Scrolls, 1992; editor Bible Rev., 1985—, Moment mag., 1987—, Archaeology Odyssey, 1998—; contbr. articles to profl. jours. Fellow Royal Asiatic Soc.; mem. ABA, D.C. Bar Assn., Am. Schs. Oriental Rsch., Soc. Bibl. Lit., Cosmos Club, Phi Beta Kappa. Home: 5208 38th St NW Washington DC 20015-1812 Office: Bibl Archaeology Soc 4710 41st St NW Washington DC 20016-1706 E-mail: hshanks@bib-arch.org.

SHANMAN, JAMES ALAN, lawyer; b. Cin., Aug. 1, 1942; s. Jerome D. and Mildred Louise (Bloch) S.; m. Marilyn Louise Glassman, June 11, 1972; 1 child, Ellen Joan. BS, U. Pa., 1963; JD, Yale U., 1966. Bar: N.Y. 1967, U.S. Ct. Mil. Appeals 1971, U.S. Supreme Ct. 1971, U.S. Ct. Appeals (2d cir.) 1972, U.S. Dist. Ct. (so. and ea. dists.) N.Y. 1972, U.S. Ct. Internat. Trade 1976, U.S. Ct. Appeals (fed. cir.) 1987, U.S. Dist. Ct. (ea. dist.) Mich. 1989, U.S. Ct. Appeals (7th cir.) 1999. Assoc. Cahill Gordon & Reindel, N.Y.C., 1971-74, Freeman, Meade, Wasserman, Sharfman & Schneider, N.Y.C., 1974-76; mem. firm Sharfman, Shanman, Poret & Siviglia, P.C., N.Y.C., 1976-95; ptnr. Camhy Karlinsky & Stein LLP, N.Y.C., 1995-96; mem. firm Sharfman, Siviglia, Poret, Kook, Ross & Shanman, P.C., N.Y.C., 1996-98; ptnr. Edwards & Angell, LLP, N.Y.C., 1998—. Speaker on reins. law topics. Capt. USAF, 1966-71. Mem.: ABA, ARIAS.US (cert. arbitrator), Bailliage de Conn., Confrérie de la Chaine des Rôtisseurs, Am. Arbitration Assn. (comml. panel arbitrators 1980—), Assn. of Bar of City of N.Y. (com. ins. law 1985—88, 1990—92, 1998—2001, com. profl. liability ins. 1988—92, com. on assn. ins. plans 1989—), N.Y. State Bar Assn. Federal civil litigation, State civil litigation, Insurance. Office: Edwards & Angell LLP Three Stamford Plz 301 Tresser Blvd Stamford CT 06901 E-mail: jshanman@ealaw.com.

SHANMUGAM, KANNON KUMAR, lawyer; b. Lawrence, Kans., Nov. 15, 1972; s. Sam and Radha Shanmugam. AB, Harvard U., 1993, JD, 1998; MLitt, Oxford U., 1995. Intern to Hon. Deanell Reece Tacha U.S. Ct. Appeals 10th Cir., Lawrence, 1990; intern to Hon. Robert Dole U.S. Senate, Washington, 1991; intern The Kansas City (Mo.) Star, 1992-93; summer assoc. Sidley & Austin, Chgo., 1996, Cravath Swaine & Moore, N.Y.C., 1997; law clk. to Hon. J. Michael Luttig U.S. Ct. Appeals 4th Cir., Alexandria, Va., 1998-99; law clk. to Hon. Antonin Scalia U.S. Supreme Ct., Washington, 1999-2000; assoc. Kirkland & Ellis, Washington, 2000—. Mem.: ABA (ad hoc com. on appellate rules Coun. Appellate Lawyers 2002—), Am. Inns of Ct. (assoc. trustee 2003—), Kans. Bar Assn., Federalist Soc. (exec. com. federalism and separation of powers group 2001—). Appellate. Office: Kirkland & Ellis 655 15th St NW Washington DC 20005

SHANNAHAN, WILLIAM PAUL, lawyer; b. Detroit, Mich., Nov. 21, 1934; s. William and Jean (Boyle) S.; m. Saracia L. Price, Sept. 24, 1983; children: MeglynAnne, Michael-Padraic. AB, U. Detroit, 1956; JD, Georgetown U., 1958. Bar: D.C. 1958, Mich. 1958, Calif. 1962. Ptnr. Higgs, Fletcher & Mack, La Jolla, Calif., 1967-81, Aylward, Kintz, et al, La Jolla, Calif., 1981-87, pvt. practice, La Jolla, Calif., 1987—. With U.S. Army, 1959-60. Democrat. Roman Catholic. Probate (including wills, trusts), Taxation, general. Office: 1200 Prospect St Ste 425 La Jolla CA 92037-3660

SHANNON, JOE, JR., lawyer; b. Nov. 9, 1940; s. Joe and Juanita Elizabeth (Milliorn) S.; children: Kelley Jane, Joseph Patrick, Shelley Carol. BA, U. Tex., 1962, LLB, 1963. Bar: Tex. 1963, U.S. Supreme Ct. 1977, U.S. Dist. Ct. (no. dist.) Tex. 1970, U.S. Ct. Appeals (5th cir.) 1977, U.S. Dist. Ct. (we. dist.) 1998; cert. family law Tex. Bd. Legal Specialization, matrimonial arbitrator. Ptnr. Shannon & Shannon, Ft. Worth, 1963-72; adminstrv. asst. to spkr. Tex. Ho. of Reps., Austin, 1970; chief criminal div. Tarrant County Dist. Atty., Ft. Worth, 1972-78; pvt. practice Ft. Worth, 1978-99; ptnr. Snakard & Gambill, Ft. Worth, 1986-90; chief econ. crimes Tarrant County Dist. Atty., 1999—. Adj. prof. Tex. Weslyan Sch. Law. Mem. Tex. Ho. of Reps., 1964-70. Fellow Tex. Bar Found., Am. Acad. Matrimonial Lawyers (cert.); mem. ABA, State Bar of Tex. (adv. com. family law, state bd. legal specialization 1985-99, dist. grievance com. 1973-76, chmn. 1975-76, 95—, sec. 2d ct. appeals adv. com. 1995—), Tarrant County Family Law Bar Assn. (pres. 1998), Tarrant County Bar Assn. (dir. 1999-2001, sec. treas. 2002, 2d v.p. 2003), Phi Alpha Delta, Masons, Shriners. Alternative dispute resolution, Family and matrimonial, Insurance. Office: 1701 River Run Fort Worth TX 76107-6579 E-mail: jshannon@tarrantcounty.com.

SHANNON, JOHN SANFORD, lawyer, retired railway executive; b. Tampa, Fla., Feb. 8, 1931; s. George Thomas and Ruth Evangeline (Garrett) S.; m. Elizabeth Howe, Sept. 22, 1962; children: Scott Howe, Elizabeth Garrett, Sandra Denison. AB, Roanoke Coll., 1952; JD, U. Va., 1955. Bar: Va. 1955. Assoc. Hunton Williams Gay Powell & Gibson, Richmond, Va., 1955-56; solicitor Norfolk & Western Ry., Roanoke, Va., 1956-60, asst. gen. solicitor, 1960-64, gen. atty., 1964-65, gen. solicitor, 1965-68, gen. counsel, 1968-69, v.p. law, 1969-80, sr. v.p. law, 1980-82; exec. v.p. law Norfolk (Va.) So. Corp., 1982-96, ret., 1996. Bd. dirs. Norfolk So. Ry. Co., Pocahontas Land Corp., Va. Holding Corp., Norfolk and Western Ry. Co. Editor-in-chief: Va. Law Rev, 1954-55. Chancellor Episcopal Diocese Southwestern Va., 1974-82; pres. bd. trustees North Cross Sch., Roanoke, 1973-82; trustee, past chmn. exec. com. Roanoke Coll., Salem, Va.; bd. dirs. Legal Aid Soc., Roanoke Valley, 1969-80, pres., 1970-79; trustee Chrysler Mus., Norfolk, 1982-94, Norfolk Acad., 1987-99. Mem. Va. Bar Assn., Norfolk and Portsmouth Bar Assn., Shenandoah Club, Roanoke Country Club, Norfolk Yacht and Country Club, Harbor Club, Order of Coif, Sigma Xi, Omicron Delta Kappa, Phi Delta Phi. Home: 7633 Argyle Ave Norfolk VA 23505-1701

SHANNON, PETER MICHAEL, JR., lawyer; b. Chgo., Oct. 13, 1928; s. Peter Michael Sr. and Marian (Burke) S.; m. Anne M. Mueller, April 3, 1969; children: Peter III, Stephen, Heather, Eamon. BA, St. Mary of the Lake, Mundelein, Ill., 1949, MA, 1952, STL, 1953; JCL, Gregorian U., Rome, 1958; JD, U. Calif., Berkeley, 1971. Bar: Calif. 1972, D.C. 1972, Ill. 1988, U.S. Dist. Ct. Md. 1972, U.S. Dist. Ct. D.C. 1972, U.S. Dist. Ct. (no. dist.) Ill. 1988, U.S. Ct. Appeals (1st, 2d, 3d, 4th, 5th, 6th, 7th, 8th, 9th, 10th and D.C. cirs.) 1972-75, U.S. Supreme Ct. 1975. Supervisory atty. litigation U.S. Dept. of Justice, Washington, 1971-75; sr. appellate atty. ICC, Washington, 1975-77, dir. enforcement, 1977-80; ptnr. Shannon, et al, Washington, 1980-82, Keck, Mahin & Cate, Chgo., 1982-96, Arnstein & Lehr, Chgo., 1996—2001; pvt. practice Western Springs, Ill., 2001—. Author: Energy and Transportation Implications of Ratemaking Policy Concerning Sources of Energy, 1980, Disposition of Real Estate by Religious Institutions, 1987, The Dual Approach of Civil Law Courts to Ecclestical Related Disputes, 1988. Mem. ABA (chmn. transp. com., adminstrv. law and regulatory practice sect. 1984-87, coun. mem. 1988-91), Ill. Bar Assn., Chgo. Bar Assn., Am. Acad. Hosp. Attys., Assn. Transp. Law, Logistics and Policy, Canon Law Soc. (pres. 1965-66), Ctr. for Disability and Elder Law (pres. 1997-99). Administrative and regulatory, Health, Transportation. Office: 4546 Wolf Road Western Springs IL 60558-1562

SHAPIRO, ALEENA RIEGER, lawyer; b. Poland; m. Richard A. Shapiro; children: Randi, Deborah. JD, NYU, 1981, LLM in Taxation, 1985. Bar: N.Y. 1982, U.S. Dist. Ct. (so. and ea. dists.) N.Y. 1982, U.S. Tax Ct. 1982. Assoc. Willkie Farr & Gallagher, N.Y.C., 1981-84, Battle Fowler, N.Y.C., 1984-87, Patterson, Belknap Webb & Tyler, N.Y.C., 1987-89; prin. Aleena R. Shapiro, Atty., N.Y.C., 1989-97; ptnr. Shapiro and Wender, L.L.P., N.Y.C., 1997—. Mem.: ABA, Assn. Bar City. N.Y., N.Y. State Bar Assn. (tax sect.). Corporate, general, Estate planning, Taxation, general. Office: 230 Park Ave Fl 26 New York NY 10169-2699

SHAPIRO, BENJAMIN LOUIS, lawyer, law association administrator; b. NYC, June 5, 1943; s. Leonard and Henrietta (Cohen) S. BA, L.I. U., 1966; JD, New Eng. Law Sch., 1972; LLM, NYU, 1973. Bar: Mass. 1975, U.S. Dist. Ct. Mass. 1975, U.S. Ct. Appeals (1st cir.) 1975. Ct. planner Govs. Commn. on Adminstrn. Justice, Montpelier, Vt., 1973-74; staff atty. Nat. Ctr. for State Cts., Boston, 1974-76; regional counsel U.S. Dept. Justice Law Enforcement Assistance Adminstrn., Boston, 1976-77, ct. specialist, 1977-80, exec. asst. to adminstr., 1980-81; atty. advisor U.S. Dept. Justice/Office Justice Assistance, Boston, 1981-82; program mgr., dep. asst. adminstr. Office Juvenile Justice and Delinquency Prevention, Boston, 1982-89; exec. dir. Mass. Dist. Atty. Assn., Boston, 1989-95; sr. justice cons. Capital Assocs., Reno, 1995—97; sr. cons. justice programs Dyncorp LLC, Reston, Va., 1996; gen. counsel house post audit and oversight com. Ho. of Reps., Boston, 1997—; sr. cons. Pub. Cons. Group, 2001—03, contractor, 2003—. Chmn. host com. Nat. Salute to Vietnam Vets., v.p. D.C. Chpt. Vietnam Vets. Am., 1982; presenter Internat. Symposium on Seriously Troubled Youth, Princeton U., 1986. Asst. editor-in-chief New Eng. Law Rev. Pres. Nat. Assn. Justice info. Sys. With U.S. Army, 1966-69.

Mem. Nat. Dist. Attys. Assn. (bd. dirs.). Democrat. Jewish. Home: 2001 Marina Dr Apt 610 North Quincy MA 02171-1544 Office: House of Reps Rm 146 Boston MA 02133 E-mail: benjamin.shapiro@hou.state.ma.us.

SHAPIRO, DAVID L. lawyer; b. Corsicana, Tex., May 19, 1936; s. Harry and Alice (Laibovitz) S. BA, U. Tex., 1967; JD, St. Mary's U., 1970. Bar: Tex. 1970, U.S. Dist. Ct. (we. dist.) Tex. 1972, U.S. Supreme Ct. 1975, U.S. Ct. Appeals (5th cir.) 1981. Assoc. Law Office Jim S. Phelps, Houston, 1971; pvt. practice, Austin, 1972—. Spl. counsel com. human resources Tex. Ho. Reps., Austin, 1973-74; counsel subcom. health svcs. Tex. Senate, Austin, 1983-87. With U.S. Army, 1959-61. Mem.: Travis County Bar Assn., Austin Criminal Def. Lawyers Assn., Coll. of State Bar of Tex., Travis County Bar Assn. (sec.-treas. 1977—78, dir. 1979, pres. family law sect. 1980—81), State Bar Tex. (chmn. lawyer referral svc. com. 1980—82, adminstrn. of justice com. 1990—93, jury svc. com. 1998—2001, contbr. Media Law Handbook supplement 1986). Democrat. Avocations: automobiles, reading. Criminal, Family and matrimonial, General civil litigation. Office: 1200 San Antonio St Austin TX 78701-1834

SHAPIRO, DAVID W. prosecutor; Graduate, State U. NY, Binghamton; JD, State U. NY, Buffalo. Fed. Prosecutor Eastern Dist., NY, 1986—92, chief organized crime unit; Fed. Prosecutor Dist. of Ariz., 1992—94; chief Appellate Div. Northern Dist., Calif., 1994—2001, chief Criminal Div., 1994—2001, U.S. Atty., 2001—02; partner Boies, Schiller & Flexner, 2002—. Office: Boies, Schiller & Flexner 1999 Harrison Street Ste 900 Oakland CA 94612 Fax: 415-436-7234.*

SHAPIRO, EDWIN HENRY, lawyer; b. Chgo., Mar. 12, 1938; s. Irving and Esther (Mikell) S.; m. Lesley Dahlin, Dec. 27, 1959; children: Craig, Cori. BS in Acctg., U. Ill., 1959; JD, Northwestern U., 1963. Bar: Ill. 1963, U.S. Dist. Ct. (no. dist.) Ill. 1970, U.S. Supreme Ct. 1979. Tax acct. Arthur Andersen & Co., Chgo., 1962-67; ptnr. Rosenfeld, Rotenberg, Hafron & Shapiro, Schaumburg, Ill., 1967—. Mem. ABA, Ill. Bar Assn., N.W. Suburban Bar Assn. (pres. 1985-86), Tau Epsilon Phi. Avocations: swimming, travel. State civil litigation, Property, real (including real estate development, water). Office: 1111 N Plaza Dr Ste 570 Schaumburg IL 60173-4992 E-mail: rrhs2@aol.com.

SHAPIRO, EDWIN STANLEY, lawyer, judge; b. Bklyn., Jan. 14, 1931; s. Harry I. and Ann (Safanie) S.; m. Sandra I. Bernstein, Sept. 15, 1957; children: James A., Sarah E. BA, Trinity Coll., Hartford, Conn., 1952; LLB, JD, Harvard Law Sch., 1955. Bar: N.Y. 1956, U.S. Dist. Ct. (so. and ea. dist.) N.Y. 1956, U.S. Ct. Appeals 1957. Atty. Levin & Weintraub, N.Y.C., 1956-57; pvt. practice N.Y.C., 1957-59; ptnr. Smith, Shapiro & Scheier, N.Y.C., 1959-62, Basch, Seits & Shapiro, N.Y.C., 1970-74, Seits & Shapiro, N.Y.C., 1974-81; town justice Ossining, N.Y., 1980—; pvt. practice N.Y.C., 1981-95, Briarcliff Manor, N.Y., 1996—. Lawyer Staten Island Open Lands Found., 1965-67. Mem. Assn. of Bar of City of N.Y. (environ. law com. 1970-73, com. on state cts. 1982-83, corrections com. 1996-98), Ossining Area Bar Assn. (pres. 2003—). General civil litigation, Probate (including wills, trusts). E-mail: shaplaw@bestweb.net.

SHAPIRO, FRED DAVID, lawyer; b. Cleve., Nov. 10, 1926; s. Isadore R. and Lottie (Turetsky) S.; m. Helen Solomon, Sept. 5, 1948; children— Gary N., Ira R., Diane S. BA cum laude, Ohio State U., 1949; LL.B., Harvard U., 1954. Bar: Ohio 1954. Since practiced in, Cleve.; sr. atnr. Shapiro and Lodwick, Co., L.P.A, 1994—. Served with USNR, 1945-46. Mem. Ohio Bar Assn., Greater Cleve. Bar Assn., Cuyahoga County Bar Assn., The Rowfant Club, Phi Beta Kappa. Jewish. Estate planning, Personal injury (including property damage), Probate (including wills, trusts). Home: 29226 S Woodland Rd Cleveland OH 44124-5737

SHAPIRO, GAIL J. mediator; b. Ramapo, N.Y., July 2, 1965; d. Leonard S. and Helen S. Beier. BA in Art Adminstrn., George Washington U., 1986; MA in Legal Studies, Montclair State U., 2000. Trainer Family and Divorce Mediation Conn. Mediation, Wilton, 1998—, mediator Family and Divorce, 1998—. Instr. On-line True Colors Internat., 2002. Author: Peaceful Colors-How to Use Personality Assessment to Reduce Most Conflicts, 2002. Mem.: Conn. Coun. Divorce Mediation, Assn. Conflict Resolution. Office: Connecticut Mediation PO Box 7381 Wilton CT 06897-7381

SHAPIRO, GEORGE HOWARD, retired lawyer; b. St. Louis, Nov. 10, 1936; s. Isadore T. and Alice (Schucart) S.; m. Mary Kenney Leonard, 1977 (div. 1994); m. Ray Ann Kremer, 1999; 1 child, Ellen. BA, Harvard U., 1958, LLB, 1961; postgrad., London Sch. Econs., 1961-62. Bar: Ga. 1960, D.C. 1963. Atty. U.S. Dept. Labor, Washington, 1962-63; assoc. Arent Fox Kintner Plotkin & Kahn, Washington, 1963-69, ptnr., 1970-99; ret., 2000. Co-author: 'Cable Speech' The Case for First Amendment Protection, 1983; editor: New Program Opportunities in the Electronic Media, 1983, Current Developments in CATV, 1981. With USAR, 1962-68. Frank Knox Meml. fellow Harvard U., 1961-62. Mem. D.C. Bar Assn., Fed. Communications Bar Assn. Democrat. Jewish. Avocation: skiing. Federal civil litigation, Communications, Constitutional. Home: Apt 906 3180 Mathieson Dr NE Atlanta GA 30305-1871 E-mail: GHSinATL@aol.com.

SHAPIRO, HAROLD DAVID, lawyer, educator; b. Chgo., Apr. 15, 1927; s. Charles B. and Celia (Nierenberg) S.; m. Beatrice Cahn, June 6, 1950; children: Matthew D., Michael Ann, Nicholas J. BS, Northwestern U., Chgo., 1949, JD, 1952. Adminstrv. asst. State of Ill. Dept. Fin., Springfield, 1952; assoc. Sonnenschein Nath & Rosenthal, Chgo., 1953-59, ptnr., 1959—; Edward A. Harriman adj. prof. law Northwestern U., Chgo., 1970—. Sec., bd. dirs. West Side Affordable Housing, Inc., West Side Village, Inc. Trustee, mem. exec. com., sec. Jr. Achievement of Chgo.; bd. dirs. Schwab Rehab. Ctr., Chgo.; pres. Homan & Arthington Found., 1995—96, The Ringer Found., 2000—, Northwestern U. Law Sch. Alumni Assn., Chgo., 1984—85, chmn. dean's adv. coun., 1997—99. Served with Seabees USNR, 1945—50, PTO. Recipient Merit award Northwestern U., 1988. Mem. Ill. Bar Assn., ABA, Chgo. Bar Assn., Chgo. Council Lawyers, Legal Club of Chgo. (pres.), Law Club of Chgo., Order of Coif, Wigmore Key, Standard Club, Met. Club, Cliff Dwellers, Chicago Club, Lake Shore Country Club. Democrat. Jewish. Corporate, general, Private international. Home: 34 Linden Ave Wilmette IL 60091-2837 Office: Sonnenschein Nath & Rosenthal 8000 Sears Tower 233 S Wacker Dr Ste 8000 Chicago IL 60606-6491

SHAPIRO, HARRY DEAN, lawyer; b. Louisville, June 21, 1940; s. Herman Shapiro and Toby (Spector) Levy; m. Linda Siegel, Dec. 19, 1970; 1 child, Deborah Anne. BS, U. Louisville, 1962, JD, 1964. Bar: Ky. 1964, D.C. 1968, Md. 1970. Trial and appellate atty. U.S. Dept. Justice, Washington, 1964-70; assoc. Venable, Baetjer & Howard, Balt., 1970-74, ptnr., 1975-87; sr. ptnr., head of tax practice Weinberg & Green, Balt., 1987—98, chmn. corp. dept., 1993-95; transaction group coord., 1995-98; head tax practice Saul Ewing LLP (formerly Saul, Ewing, Remick & Saul LLP), 1998-99; chmn. tax dept. Saul Ewing LLP (formerly Saul, Ewing, Remick & Saul LLP), 1999—. Author: Federal Tax Liens, 1981; contbr. articles to profl. jours. Mem. Md. State Bd. Edn., 1990-97; v.p. Assoc. Jewish Charities of Balt., Inc. 1991-94; vice chmn. The Assoc. Jewish Cmty. Fedn. Balt. 1987-89, asst. treas., 1989-91, mem. exec. com., 1993-97; trustee Sinai Hosp., Balt., 1987-90; counsel Balt. Mus. Art, 1984-97, trustee, 1984-96, sec., 1985-92, v.p., sec., 1992-94, v.p., 1994-96; dir., 1989-96; chmn. Joint Budgeting Coun., 1993-96, Coun. Jewish Fedns.; trustee Acad. Art Mus., Easton, 1998—. Capt. USAR, 1967-70. Recipient Disting. Alumni award Brandeis Sch. of Law, 1996, Chmn.'s award Balt. Mus. Art, 1996. Mem. ABA (tax sect.), Md. State Bar Assn., Ky. Bar Assn., D.C. Bar Assn., Md. Club, Center Club. Corporate taxation, Taxation, general, State and local taxation. Home: 7903 7 Mile Ln Baltimore MD 21208-4306 Office: Saul Ewing LLP 100 S Charles St Ste 1500 Baltimore MD 21201-2771 E-mail: hshapiro@saul.com.

SHAPIRO, ISAAC, lawyer; b. Tokyo, Jan. 5, 1931; s. Constantine and Lydia (Chernetzky) S.; m. Jacqueline M. Weiss, Sept. 16, 1956; children: Tobias, Alexandra, Natasha. AB, Columbia U., 1954, LLB, 1956; postgrad., U. Paris, 1956—57. Bar: N.Y. 1957, U.S. Supreme Ct. 1971, Paris 1991. Assoc. Milbank, Tweed, Hadley & McCloy, N.Y.C., 1956-65, ptnr., 1966-86, resident ptnr. Tokyo, 1977-79; ptnr. Skadden Arps Slate Meagher & Flom LLP, N.Y.C., 1986—2001; resident ptnr. Skadden Arps Slate Meagher & Flom, Hong Kong, 1989-90, Paris, 1990—2001; of counsel Skadden Arps Slate Meagher & Flom LLP, N.Y.C., 2001—; tchg. fellow comparative law NYU, 1959-61. Lectr. Soviet law, 1961-67; adj. asst. prof. NYU, 1967-69, adj. assoc. prof., 1969-71, 74-75; adj. prof. and dir. Russian Legal Studies, Columbia Law School, 1999-2000; bd. dirs. Bank of Tokyo Mitsubishi Trust Co., N.Y.C., 1975-77, 80-2001, Enherent, Inc., Windsor, Conn., 1981-. Author: (with Hazard and Maggs) The Soviet Legal System, 1969; author: Japan: The Risen Sun (in Japanese), 1982; editor: The Middle East Crisis-Prospects for Peace, 1969; contbr. articles to profl. jours. Mem. Joint Com. U.S.-Japan Cultural and Ednl. Cooperation, Washington, 1972-78; mem. Japan-U.S. Friendship Commn., 1975-78; mem. svcs. policy adv. com. to U.S. Trade Rep., 1981-91; trustee Nat. Humanities Ctr., Triangle Park, N.C., 1976-89, Bank of Tokyo Mitsubishi Found., 1996—; trustee, v.p. Chamber Music Soc. Lincoln Ctr., 1980-86, Isamu Noguchi Zaidan, Japan, 1999—; trustee, pres. Isamu Noguchi Found., N.Y., 1985—; trustee, chmn. Ise Cultural Found., 1984-90; bd. dirs. Bus. Coun. for Internat. Understanding, 1989-95, Nat. Com. for U.S.-China Rels., 1989-95, Asian Cultural Coun., 1980—; bd. adv. Trust for Mutual Understanding, N.Y.C., N.Y., 1985-. With U.S. Army, 1950-52. Fulbright scholar, 1956-57. Mem.: ABA, Barristers Chambers London, N.Y. State Bar Assn., Coun. Fgn. Rels., Japan Soc., Century Assn. (N.Y.C.), Cercle de l'Union Interalliee (Paris), Royal Automobile Club (London). Private international. Office: Skadden Arps Slate Meagher & Flom LLP 4 Times Sq New York NY 10036-6522

SHAPIRO, JAMES EDWARD, judge; b. Chgo., May 28, 1930; BS, U. Wis., 1951; JD, Harvard U., 1954. Bar: Wis. 1956, U.S. Dist. Ct. (ea. dist.) Wis. 1956, U.S. Ct. Appeals (7th cir.) 1962, U.S. Supreme Ct. 1971. Sole practice, Milw., 1956-57; resident house counsel Nat. Presto Industries, Eau Claire, Wis., 1957-60; ptnr. Bratt & Shapiro, Milw., 1960-64; sole practice Milw., 1964-74; ptnr. Frank, Hiller & Shapiro, Milw., 1974-82; judge U.S. Bankruptcy Ct., Milw., 1982—, chief judge, 1996-2000. Mem. Bayside Bd. Appeals, Wis., 1969-77; Milw. county ct. commr., 1969-78; dir. Milw. Legal Aid Soc., 1969-77. Served to 1st lt. U.S. Army, 1954-56. Jewish. Office: US Courthouse 140 Fed Bldg 517 E Wisconsin Ave Milwaukee WI 53202-4500 E-mail: james_e_shapiro@wieb.uscourts.gov.

SHAPIRO, LARRY, lawyer, Internet company executive; B, U. Pa.; JD, U. Mich. Assoc. Weil, Gotshal & Manges, L.A., O'Melveny & Myers, L.A.; v.p., counsel corp. legal dept. Walt Disney Co.; exec. v.p. bus. devel. and ops. Buena Vista Internat Group subs. Walt Disney Co., sr. v.p. bus. and legal affairs; exec. v.p. bus. devel. and ops., gen. counsel Walt Disney Internet Group, North Hollywood, Calif., 1999—. Office: Walt Disney Internet Group 5161 Lankershim Blvd North Hollywood CA 91601 Office Fax: 818-623-3577.*

SHAPIRO, MARVIN SEYMOUR, lawyer; b. N.Y.C., Oct. 26, 1936; s. Benjamin and Sally (Book) S.; m. Natalie Kover, July 12, 1959; children: Donna, Meryl. AB, Columbia U., 1957, LLB, 1959. Bar: D.C. 1959, Calif. 1962. Atty. appellate sect. Civil Div. U.S. Dept. Justice, Washington, 1959-61; ptnr. Irell & Manella, L.A., 1962-99, mng. ptnr., 1992-97. Lectr. U. So. Calif. Tax Inst., Calif. Continuing Edn. of the Bar, Practising Law Inst. Articles editor Columbia Law Rev., 1958-59. V.p., bd. dirs. Jewish Fedn. Coun., L.A., 1985-95; treas. Alan Cranston Campaign, 1974, 80, 86; chmn. credentials com. Dem. Nat. Com., 1972-76; bd. dirs. L.A. Opera Co., 1997—. Mem. Beverly Hills Barristers (pres. 1970). Avocations: travel, golf. Corporate, general, Property, real (including real estate development, water), Taxation, general. Home: 432 N Cliffwood Ave Los Angeles CA 90049-2620

SHAPIRO, MICHAEL HENRY, government executive; b. Bayonne, N.J., Sept. 23, 1948; s. William and Sophie (Slotkin) S. BS, Lehigh U., 1970; MS, Harvard U., 1972, PhD, 1976. Assoc. prof. Harvard U., Cambridge, Mass., 1976-82, analyst, 1980-81, br. chief, 1981-83, dir. econs. and tech. divsn., 1983-89; dep. asst. adminstr., air and radiation U.S. EPA, Washington, 1989-93, dir. office of solid waste, 1993-99, dep. asst. adminstr., solid waste and emergency response, 1999—2002, dep. asst. adminstr., water, 2002—. Office: EPA # 5101 1200 Pennsylvania Ave NW Washington DC 20460-0002

SHAPIRO, NELSON HIRSH, lawyer; b. Feb. 3, 1928; s. Arthur and Anna (Zenitz) S.; m. Helen Lenora Sykes, June 27, 1948; children: Ronald Evan, Mitchell Wayne, Jeffrey Mark, Julie Beth. BEE, Johns Hopkins U., 1948; JD, George Washington U., 1952. Bar: D.C. 1952, Va. 1981. Patent examiner U.S. Patent Office, 1948-50; patent advisor U.S. Signal Corps, 1950-52; mem. Shapiro & Shapiro, Arlington, Va., 1952-98, Vorys, Sater, Seymour and Pease LLP, Washington, 1998-2001, Miles & Stockbridge, McLean, Va., 2001—. Patentee; contbr. articles to legal publs. and Ency. of Patent Practice and Invention Mgmt., 1964. Mem. ABA, Am. Patent Law Assn., Bar Assn. D.C., Order of Coif, Tau Beta Pi. Patent, Trademark and copyright. Home: 7001 Old Cabin Ln Rockville MD 20852-4531 Office: 1751 Pinnacle Dr Ste 500 Mc Lean VA 22102-3833 E-mail: nshapiro@milesstockbridge.com.

SHAPIRO, PETER A. lawyer; b. Miami, Fla., Mar. 21, 1967; s. Barry E. and Claire S. Shapiro. BSE, Va. Inst. Tech., 1988; JD, U. Fla., 1992. Bar: Fla. 93, U.S. Dist. Ct. (mid. dist.) Fla. 93. Engr. GE, Charlottesville, Va., 1988—90; law clk. Fine, Furhash & Parlapiano, P.A., Gainesville, Fla., 1990—92; assoc. Morgan, Colling & Gilbert, P.A., Orlando, Fla., 1992—96; pvt. practice Law Offices of Peter A. Shapiro, P.A., Orlando, 1996—. Bd. dirs. Sr. Resource Alliance, Orlando, 1993—2001; mem. Young Reps., Orlando, 1996—. Mem.: ABA, Downtown Orlando Partnership, Acad. Fla. Trial Lawyers. Avocations: tennis, water-skiing, coins, surfing, stamps. Personal injury (including property damage), Insurance, Professional liability. Office: Law Offices of Peter A Shapiro 211 E Livingston St Orlando FL 32801 Fax: 407-420-1039. E-mail: pshapirolawofc@bellsouth.net.

SHAPIRO, PHILIP ALAN, lawyer; b. Chgo., May 14, 1940; s. Joe and Nettie (Costin) Shapiro; m. Joyce Barbara Chapnick, May 29, 1966; children: David Ian, Russell Scott, Mindi Jennifer. AA, Wilson Coll., 1960; BS in Fin., So. Ill. U., 1965; MBA, Nat. Univ., San Diego, Calif., 1975; MBA in Mktg. with distinction, San Diego State U., San Diego, 1977; JD, JD, Western State U., 1985. Bar: Calif. 1988. Spl. agt. U.S. Secret Svc., Washington, 1965-67, Chgo., 1967-77; mgr. divsn. sales Roche Labs. divsn. Hoffman-La Roche, Inc., Chgo.; account exec. Cellular Comm., Inc., San Diego, 1985; with Complete Comm., San Diego, 1983—; assoc. Law Office Jeffrey S. Schwartz, 1988-91; pvt. practice, 1991—. Chair gen. and solo practice sect. State Bar of Calif. Editor (law rev.): We. State U. Coll. Law. Mem. adv. bd. Spreckes Elem. Sch., San Diego, 1976—77; mem. Univ. City Town Coun., San Diego, 1977; pres. Congregation Beth El, La Jolla, Calif., 1976—79. With USMC, 1958—60. Recipient Merit award, U.S. Treasury Dept., 1965, Israel Solidarity award, 1977, U. Of Judaism award, 1978. Mem.: ABA (vice chmn. gen. practice sect.), Assn. Former Agts. of U.S. Secret Svc., San Diego Bus. Referrals (pres. 1998—99), San Diego County Bar Assn., State Bar Calif. (Wiley W. Manuel award 1990, 1991, exec. com. gen. practice sect.), Calif. Trial Lawyers Assn., Assn. Ret. Spl. Agents US Secret Svc., Thomas Jefferson Sch. of Law Alumni Assn. (bd. dirs.). Bankruptcy, Criminal, Personal injury (including property damage). Office: PO Box 178475 San Diego CA 92177-8475 Fax: 858-483-4639. E-mail: pshaplaw@san.rr.com.

SHAPIRO, RAYMOND L. lawyer; b. N.Y.C., Aug. 1, 1934; s. Alexander and Sadye (Morrison) S.; m. Judith Manis, Dec. 23, 1956; children: Joel, Todd, Lisa. BS, Temple U., 1956, LLB, 1959. Ptnr. Wexler, Weisman, Forman & Shapiro, Phila., 1959-84, Blank, Rome, Comisky & McCauley, Phila., 1984—. Author: Dunlap-Hanna Pa. Forms, 1963-83, Pa. Civil Practice Handbook, 1973-83; contbg.-author: Business Workouts Manual. Trustee Phila. Fedn. Jewish Agys., 1979—, treas., 1984-87, v.p., 1987-90; pres. Jewish Pub. Group, 1992-95. Fellow Am. Coll. Bankruptcy (v.p., chmn. bd. dirs. 1997-2001); mem. ABA, Nat. Bankruptcy Conf., Pa. Bar Assn., Phila. Bar Assn. Office: Blank Rome LLP One Logan Sq Philadelphia PA 19103-6998

SHAPIRO, RICHARD ALLEN, lawyer; b. Phila., Feb. 27, 1958; s. A. Morton and Sandra Shapiro; m. Judith L. Dickert, May 30, 1982; children: Sara, Sharon. BA in Politics, Brandeis U., 1980; JD, Rutgers U., 1983. Bar: N.J. 1983, Pa. 1983, U.S. Dist. Ct. N.J. 1983, U.S. Dist. Ct. (ea. dist.) Pa., 1984, U.S. Ct. Appeals (3rd cir.) 1985. Prin. Shapiro & Shapiro, P.C., Cherry Hill, N.J., 1983—; solicitor Camden County Coll., Blackwood, N.J., 1987—. Mem. Camden County Workforce Investment Bd., 1995—; del. Dem. Nat. Conv., N.Y.C., 1992; chmn. Cherry Hill Dem. Party, 1991—; vice chmn. Camden County Dem. Party, 1997—2000; bd. dirs. Jewish Nat. Fund So. N.J. Region, Cherry Hill, 1996—. Construction, Corporate, general, General practice. Office: Shapiro and Shapiro PC 1415 Route 70 E Ste 508 Cherry Hill NJ 08034-2238

SHAPIRO, ROBERT, lawyer; b. Plainfield, N.J., Sept. 2, 1942; BS in Fin., UCLA, 1965; JD, Loyola U., L.A., 1968. Bar: Calif. 1969, U.S. Ct. Appeals (9th cir.) 1972, U.S. Dist. Ct. (cen., no. & so. dists.) Calif. 1982. Dep. dist. atty. Office of Dist. Atty., L.A., 1969-72; sole practice L.A., 1972-87, 88—; of counsel Bushkin, Gaims, Gaines, Jonas, L.A., 1987-88; Christensen, Miller, Fink & Jacobs, L.A., 1988-95; ptnr. Christensen, Miller, Fink, Jacobs, Glaser, Weil & Shapiro, L.A., 1995—. Author: Search for Justice, 1996, Misconception, 2001. Recipient Am. Jurisprudence award Bancroft Whitney, 1969. Mem. Nat. Assn. Criminal Def. Lawyers, Calif. Attys. for Criminal Justice, Trial Lawyers for Pub. Justice (founder 1982), Century City Bar Assn. (Best Criminal Def. Atty. 1993). General civil litigation, Criminal. Office: 2121 Avenue Of The Stars Fl 19 Los Angeles CA 90067-5010

SHAPIRO, ROBYN SUE, lawyer, educator; b. Mpls., July 19, 1952; d. Walter David and Judith Rae (Sweet) S.; m. Charles Howard Barr, June 27, 1976; children: Tania Shapiro-Barr, Jeremy Shapiro-Barr, Michael Shapiro-Barr. BA summa cum laude, U. Mich., 1974; JD, Harvard U., 1977. Bar: D.C., 1977, Wis., 1979, U.S. Supreme Ct., 1990. Assoc. Foley & Lardner, Washington, 1977-79; ptnr. Barr & Shapiro, Menomonee Falls, Wis., 1980-87; assoc. Quarles & Brady, Milw., 1987-92; ptnr. Michael Best & Friedrich, Milw., 1992—. Adj. asst. prof. law Marquette U., Milw., 1979-83; assoc. dir. bioethics ctr. Med. Coll. Wis., Milw., 1982-85, dir., 1985—; asst. prof. bioethics Med. Coll. Wis., 1984-89, assoc. prof. bioethics, 1989-97, prof. bioethics, 1997—, Ursula Von der Ruhr prof. bioethics, 2000—; dir. Wis. Ethics Com. Network, 1987-98, Midwest Ethics Com. Network, 1998—; bd. dirs. Wis. Health Decisions, 1990-93. Mem. editl. bd. Cambridge Quar., 1991—, HEC Forum, 1988-91, Human Rights, 1998—; contbr. articles to profl. jours. Mem. ethics com. St. Luke's Med. Ctr., Milw., 1983—, Elmbrook Meml. Hosp., Milw., 1983-86, Cmty. Meml. Hosp., Menomonee Falls, 1984—, Aurora Sinai Hosp., Milw., 1986—, Milw. County Mental Health Complex, 1984—, Froedtert Meml. Luth. Hosp., 1985—; mem. subcom. organ transplantation Wis. Health Policy Coun., Madison, 1984, bioethics com., 1986-89; mem. com. study on bioethics Wis. Legis. Coun., Madison, 1984-85; bd. dirs. Jewish Home and Care Ctr., 1994—, chair ethics com., 1994—; chair Bayside Ethics Bd., 1994—; bd. dirs. Milw. area chpt. Girl Scouts U.S., Am. Bioethics Assn., 1995-97, Wis. Perinatal Found., 1996-99, Am. Soc. Bioethics and Humanities, 1997-2000, Manor Park Found., 2002—; mem. sec.'s adv. com. on xenotransplantation U.S. Dept. Health and Human Svcs., 2001—; mem. sci. adv. com. Alzheimer's Assn. Southeastern Wis., 1997—; mem. data and safety monitoring bd. GlaxoWellcome, 1995—. James B. Angell scholar, 1971-72. Mem. ABA (health law sec., vice chair clin. ethics group 1998-2001, individual rights and responsibilities sec., health rights com. chair 1994-99, coun. 1999—, coordinating com. on bioethics and law, chair 1995-99, adv. nat. conf. of commrs. on uniform state laws, misuse of genetic info. study group 2002—, mem. working group on health info. privacy 2000-02), Nat. Health Lawyers Assn., Am. Hosp. Assn. (bioethics tech. panel 1991-94, spl. com. HIV & practitioners 1991-93), Wis. Bar Assn. (chair Wis. health law sect. 1988-89, individual rights sect. coun. 1987-90), Assn. Women Lawyers, ACLU, Wis. Found. (Atty. of Yr. 1988), Assn. Post-Doctoral Programs in Clin. Neurophysiology (bd. dirs.), Am. Soc. Law, Medicine, and Ethics, Milw. Acad. Medicine (coun. 1992-98, chair bioethics com. 1992-98), Milw. AIDS Coalition (steering com. 1988-91), Am. Soc. Transplant Surgeons (ethics com. 1999—), Internat. Bioethics Assn. (chair task force on ethics coms.), Profl. Dimensions (Golden Compass award 1994), Phi Beta Kappa (Wis. chpt. scholarship com. chair 1990-93), others. Health. Home: 9474 N Broadmoor Rd Milwaukee WI 53217-1309 Office: Med Coll Wis Bioethics Ctr 8701 W Watertown Plank Rd Milwaukee WI 53226-3548 E-mail: rshapiro@mcw.edu.

SHAPIRO, SANDER WOLF, retired lawyer; b. St. Louis, Sept. 24, 1929; s. Robert and Bess (Fisher) S.; m. Lottie F. Frankel, Aug. 14, 1955; children: Julie A. Shapiro Schechter, Susan B. Shapiro Schmitz. BA, Rice U., 1951; postgrad., Columbia U., 1951-52; JD, U. Tex., 1954. Atty. tax div. Dept. Justice, Washington, 1955-57; atty. advisor U.S. Tax Ct., Washington, 1957-58; ptnr. Clark, Thomas, Winters & Shapiro, Austin, Tex., 1958-84; sr. prtnr. Shapiro, Edens & Cook, Austin, 1984-91; of counsel Jenkens & Gilchrist, P.C., Austin, 1991-2000; ret. Adj. prof. law U. Tex., 1975-2000; lectr. in tax field. Author, editor Tex. Franchise Earned Surplus and Tax, 1985, Family Solutions to Family Concerns, 1991, A Walk Through Form 706, 1991; co-editor Tex. Tax Svc., 1986-94. Bd. dirs. Austin Symphony Orch. Soc., 1974-97, dir. emeritus, 1997—, fin. v.p., 1980-95; bd. dirs. U. Tex. Coll. Fine Arts Adv. Coun., 1987-95, hon. bd. dirs., 1995—, pres., 1991-94; bd. dirs. Capital of Tex. Pub. Telecomm. Coun., 1988-97, pres., 1994-95; bd. dirs. Ronald McDonald House of Ctrl. Tex., Austin, 1990-98, pres., 1994-95; bd. dirs. Capital Met. Transit Authority, 1988-91, chair, 1990; bd. dirs. Austin Cmty. Found., 1985-92, pres., 1991; adv. coun. U. Tex. Press, 1998—, vice chmn. 1999, chmn. 2000. Sander W. Shapiro Presdl. Scholarship in Law at U. Tex. endowed in his honor by Jenkens & Gilchrist, 1992; recipient Disting. Lawyer award Travis County, 1999. Fellow Am. Bar Found. (life), Am. Coll. Tax Counsel, Tex. Bar Found. (sustaining life); mem. ABA, State Bar of Tex., Am. Law Inst., Nat. Assn. State Bar Tax Sects. (bd. dirs., chair 1997, dir. emeritus 2002—), Tex. Law Rev. Assn. (pres. 1992-93). Avocations: reading, music, golf. E-mail: sws@austin.rr.com.

SHAPIRO, SANDRA, lawyer; b. Providence, Oct. 17, 1944; d. Emil and Sarah (Cohen) S. AB magna cum laude, Bryn Mawr Coll., Pa., 1966; LLB magna cum laude, U. Pa., 1969. Bar: Mass. 1970, U.S. Dist. Ct. Mass. 1971, U.S. Ct. Appeals (1st cir.) 1972, U.S. Supreme Ct. 1980. Law clk. U.S. Ct. Appeals (1st cir.), Boston, 1969-70; assoc. Foley, Hoag & Eliot LLP, Boston, 1970-75, ptnr., 1976—. Mem. bd. bar overseers Mass. Supreme Judicial Ct., 1988-92, mem. gender bias study com., 1986-89; dir. Mass. Govt. Land Bank, 1994-96. Contbr. articles to profl. jours. Bd. dirs. Patriots'

Trail coun. Girl Scouts U.S., 1994-97; mem. bd. overseers Boston Lyric Opera, 1993-99, New England Conservatory of Music, 1995-2001, Celebrity Series of Boston, 1997—. Woodrow Wilson fellow, 1966. Mem.: ABA (ethics, profl. and pub. edn. com. 1994—), U. Pa. Law Sch. Alumni Assn. (bd. mgrs. 1990—94), Boston Bar Assn. (mem. coun.), Mass. Bar Assn. (chmn. real property sect. coun., com. on profl. ethics), Nat. Women's Law Ctr. Network, New Eng. Women in Real Estate, Women's Bar Assn. Mass. (pres. 1985—86), Boston Club, Order of Coif. Commercial, contracts (including sales of goods; commercial financing), Land use and zoning (including planning), Property, real (including real estate development, water). Office: Foley Hoag LLP 155 Seaport Blvd Boston MA 02210-2600 E-mail: sshapiro@foleyhoag.com.

SHAPIRO, STEVEN ANDY, lawyer; b. Bklyn., Sept. 29, 1956; s. Arthur F. and Eleanore Shapiro; m. Mona; children: Lauren, Preston. BA in Pre-Law, Pa. State, 1979; JD, Thomas M. Cooley Law Sch., 1982. Bar: Colo. 1983, U.S. Dist. Ct. Colo., U.S. Ct. Claims, U.S. Ct. Appeals (10th cir.), U.S. Supreme Ct. Shareholder Fleishman & Shapiro P.C. (formerly Gelt, Fleishman & Sterling P.C.), Denver. Writer Colo. Chiropractic Assn. Mag., Riders for Justice, A.B.A.T.E., Ala. State Chiropractic Assn. Newsletter, Homebuilder Mag.; speaker in field. Bd. trustees Nat. Sports Ctr. for Disabled; bd. dirs. Trauma-Care IPA, LLC, 1997—. Mem. ABA, ATLA, Colo. Trial Lawyers Assn. (auto litigation task force 1992—, trial tactics chair auto litigation task force 1995-99, membership com. 1991-92), Colo. Bar Assn. (intra/inter profl. com. 1989-2000, Colo. Supreme Ct. grievance com. 1996—), Denver Bar Assn. (intra/inter profl. com. 1989—), Douglas Bar Assn., Brain Injury Assn. Colo. (bd.dirs. 2000-02), Anti-Defamation League (ptnrs.-in leadership coun.). Avocations: basketball, tennis, softball, racquetball. Commercial, contracts (including sales of goods; commercial financing), Personal injury (including property damage), Transportation. Office: 1600 Broadway Ste 2600 Denver CO 80202-4989

SHARE, RICHARD HUDSON, lawyer; b. Mpls., Sept. 6, 1938; s. Jerome and Millicent S.; m. Carolee Martin, 1970; children: Mark Lowell, Gregory Martin, Jennifer Hillary, Ashley. BS, UCLA, 1960; JD, U. So. Calif., 1963. Bar: Calif. Sup. Ct. 1964, U.S. Dist. Ct. (cen. and so. dists.) Calif., U.S. Supreme Ct. 1974. Field agt. IRS, 1960-63; mem. law divsn., asst. sec. Avco Fin. Svcs., 1963-72; founder Frandzel and Share, A Law Corp., L.A., 1972-99, Richard Hudson Share & Assocs., 1999—. Lectr. Nat. Bus. Inst., Creditor's Rights; adj. prof. Loloya Law Sch., 1999. Mem. Calif. Bankers Assn. Banking, Commercial, consumer (including collections, credit), Commercial, contracts (including sales of goods; commercial financing). Office: PO Box 1003 Pacific Palisades CA 90272-1003 also: 150 N Santa Anita Ave Ste 530 Arcadia CA 91006-3127 E-mail: sharelaw@aol.com.

SHARETT, ALAN RICHARD, lawyer, environmental and disability litigator, mediator and arbitrator, law educator; b. Hammond, Ind., Apr. 15, 1943; children: Lauren Ruth, Charles Daniel; m. Cherie Ann Vick, Oct. 15, 1993. Student, Ind. U., 1962-65; JD, DePaul U., 1968; advanced postgrad. legal edn., U. Mich. and U. Chgo., 1970-71; postgrad. in human resource law, Fla. Internat. U., 1999-2000; cert. mediator, Am. Arbitration Assn., 1994; cert. tng. and human resource devel., Fla. Internat. U., 2000. Bar: Ind. 1969, N.Y. 1975, U. S. Ct. Appeals (2d cir.) 1975, U.S. Ct. Appeals (7th cir.) 1974, U.S. Supreme Ct. 1973. Assoc. World Peace Through Law Ctr., Washington, 1967-68, Call, Call, Borns and Theodoros, Gary, Ind., 1969-71; judge protem Gary City Ct., 1970-71; environ. dist. atty. 31st Jud. Cir., Lake County, Ind., 1971-75; counsel Dunes Nat. Lakeshore Group, Ind., 1971-75; mem. Cohan, Cohan and Smulevitz, 1971-75; town atty. Independence Hill, Ind., 1974-75; judge pro tem Superior Ct. (31st cir.), Lake County, Ind., 1971-75; pvt. practice Flushing, N.Y., 1980-82, Miami Beach, Fla., 1988—; lead trial counsel, chmn. lawyers panel No. Ind. ACLU, 1969-71; liaison trial counsel Lake County and Ind. State Health Depts., and Atty. Gen., 1971-75. Professorial dir. NYU Pub. Liability Inst., N.Y.C., 1975-76; adj. faculty prof. constl. law Union Inst., Miami, Cin., 1990-92; adj. prof. environ. litigation and alternative dispute resolution Ward Stone Coll., Miami, 1994; guest prof. internat. environ. law Dept. Internat. and Comparative Law, U. Miami, 1992—; mem. adv. panel internat. environ. law Hemispheric Interam. Dialogue on Water Mgmt.(U.N. Agenda 21), 1993; mem. Nat. Dist. Attys. Assn., 1972-75, mem. environ. protection com.; pres. ESI Group, Nat. Environ. Responsibility Cons. Inc.; spkr. in field. Editor-in-chief DePaul U. The Summons, 1967-68; mem. staff DePaul Law Rev., 1968; contbr. articles to profl. jours. Gen. counsel Marjory Stoneman Douglas Friends of Everglades, 1992-93; asst. atty. gen., chair fed. and constnl. practice litigation group N.Y. State, N.Y.C., 1976-78; mem. Coalition Fla. Save Our Everglades Program; diplomate, vice chancellor Law-Sci. Acad. Am., 1967. Recipient Honors award in forensic litigation Law-Sci. Acad. Am., 1967. Mem. ABA (nat. article editor law student divsn. 1967-68, nat. com. environ. litigation, com. fed. procedures, com. toxic torts, hazardous substances and environ. law, com. energy resources law, com. internat. environ. law, com. internat. litigation, environ. interest group, sect. natural resources, energy and environ. law, judge negotiation competition championship round, law student divsn., midyr. meeting 1995, sect. sci. and tech., biotech. com., environ. law and pub. health com., standing com. sci. evidence, spl. com. legal edn., nat. toxic and hazardous substances and environ. law com., sect. tort and ins. practice, corp. gen. counsel com., non-profit orgns. com., media law and defamation torts com., tort and hazardous substances and environ. law com., govt. and pub. sector lawyers divsn.), Judicature Soc., Soc. Am. Arbitration Assn. (cert. program in mediation 1993), N.Y. County Lawyers Assn. (com. on fed. cts., insurance and health law, arbitration and alternative dispute resolution, labor relations and employment law, tech. and automation), ATLA (nat. coms. toxic, environ. and pharm. torts, environ. litigation), Ill. State Bar Assn. (staff editor 1967-68), N.Y. State Bar Assn. (environ. law sect., family law sect.), Ind. State Bar Assn. (environ. law sect., internat. law sect., trial practice sect.), Greater Miami C. of C. (trustee 1993-94, com. environ. awareness, environ. econs., biomed. exch., planning and growth mgmt., internat. econ. devel., bus. and industry econs. devel., govtl. affairs, ins., internat. banking, Europe/Pacific), The Planetary Soc. Environmental, Health, Labor (including EEOC, Fair Labor Standards Act, labor-management relations, NLRB, OSHA). Office: ESI Group Nat Environ Responsibility Cons Inc 14630 Bull Run Rd Ste 213 Miami Lakes FL 33014-2017

SHARFMAN, STEPHEN L. lawyer; b. 1944; AB, George Washington U., 1966; JD, Georgetown U., 1969. Bar: D.C. 1970. Asst. gen. coun. Met. Area Transit Comn., Washington; gen. counsel Postal Rate Commn., Washington. Bd dir. Danbury Forest Civic Assn.; Lakeside Village Cmty. Assn; Oak Marr Homeowners Assn. Office: Office Gen Counsel 1333 H St NW Washington DC 20268-0001 E-mail: sharfman@prc.gov.

SHARGEL, GERALD L. lawyer; b. New Brunswick, N.J., Oct. 5, 1944; BA, Rutgers U., 1966; JD, Bklyn. Law Sch., 1969. Bar: N.Y. 1969, U.S. Dist. Ct. (ea. and so. dists.) N.Y. 1969, U.S. Ct. Appeals (2nd, 3rd, 5th and 9th cirs.) 1969. Pvt. practice, N.Y.C., 1970—. Faculty mem. Practising Law Inst., 1976—77; adj. assoc. prof. law NYU, 1977—82; adj. prof. law Bklyn. Law Sch.; mem. adv. bd. NYU Sch. Law, Ctr. for Rsch. in Crime and Justice, 1984—88. Mem.: ABA, Fed. Bar Coun., N.Y. State Trial Lawyers Assn., N.Y. County Lawyers Assn., Assn. Bar City N.Y., N.Y. State Bar Assn., Criminal Bar Assn. Office: 16th Fl 570 Lexington Ave New York NY 10022*

SHARP, ALLEN, federal judge; b. Washington, D.C., Feb. 11, 1932; s. Robert Lee and Frances Louise (Williams) S.; children: Crystal Catholyn Sharp Bauer, Scarlet Frances Thomas. Student, Ind. State U., 1950-53; AB, George Washington U., 1954; JD, Ind. U., 1957; MA, Butler U., 1986. Bar: Ind. 1957. Practiced in, Williamsport, 1957-68; judge Ct. of Appeals Ind., 1969-73, U.S. Dist. Ct. (no. dist.) Ind., South Bend, 1973—. Served to JAG USAF, Res. Mem. Ind. Judges Assn., Blue Key, Phi Delta Kappa, Pi Gamma Mu, Tau Kappa Alpha. Republican. Mem. Christian Ch. Club: Mason. Office: US Dist Ct 124 Fed Bldg 204 S Main St South Bend IN 46601-2122

SHARP, KEVIN HUNTER, lawyer; b. Memphis, Tenn., Jan. 22, 1963; s. Harmon Thomas and Annette Gray Sharp; m. Holland Ashley Conner, Feb. 9, 2002; 1 child, Sydney Marie. A, Mesa C.C., 1988; BS summa cum laude, Christian Bros. Coll., 1990; JD, Vanderbilt U., 1993. Bar: U.S. Dist. Ct. (mid. dist. and we. dist.) Tenn. 1993, U.S. Ct. Appeals (6th cir.) 1994, U.S. Supreme Ct. Tenn. 1993. Assoc. Stokes & Bartholomew, P.A., Nashville, 1993—96; atty. Office of Compliance U.S. Congress, Washington, 1996—97, dep. gen. counsel Office of Compliance, 1997; assoc. Stokes Bartholomew Evans & Petree, P.A., Nashville, 1997—2000, ptnr., 2000—02; prin. Preston & Sharp, P.C., Nashville, 2003—. Mem. Cumberland Valley Girl Scout Coun., Nashville, 2002. Mem.: ABA, Nashville Bar Assn., Tenn. Bar Assn., Am. Legion. Labor (including EEOC, Fair Labor Standards Act, labor-management relations, NLRB, OSHA), Civil rights, General civil litigation. Office: Preston & Sharp PC 216 19th Ave N Nashville TN 37203 Office Fax: 615-321-4607.

SHARP, REX ARTHUR, lawyer; b. Liberal, Kans., Jan. 1, 1960; s. Gene Hugh and Jo Ann (King) S.; m. Lori Renee Lewis, May 23, 1987; children: Lori Alexandra, Lewis Arthur, William Hugh. Student, U. Okla., 1978-79; AB in Econs. with honors & distinction, Stanford U., 1982; JD cum laude, U. Mich., 1985. Bar: Tex. 1985, Kans. 1985, Okla. 1986, Colo. 1988, Mo. 2000, U.S. Dist. Ct. (so. and no. dists.) Tex., U.S. Dist. Ct. (we. and no. dists.) Okla., U.S. Dist. Ct. Kans., U.S. Dist Ct. (we. dist.) Mo. , U.S. Ct. Appeals (10th cir.), U.S. Supreme Ct.; civil trial cert. N.B.T.A. Litigation assoc. Fulbright & Jaworski, Houston, 1985-87; assoc. Neubauer, Sharp, McQueen, Dreiling & Morain, Liberal, 1987-89; ptnr. McKinley, Sharp, McQueen, Dreiling, Morain & Tate, P.A., Liberal, 1989-97, Husch & Eppenberger, Kansas City, Mo., 1997-2000, Sharp Law LLC, Prairie Village, Kans., 2000; stockholder Gunderson, Sharp, & Walke, P.C., Prairie Village, 2000—. Asst. city atty. City of Liberal, 1988-93, city atty., 1993-97. Avocation: golf. General civil litigation, General practice, Personal injury (including property damage). Office: Gunderson Sharp & Walke PC 4121 W 83d St Ste 256 Prairie Village KS 66208 Fax: 913-901-0419. E-mail: rsharp@midwest-law.com.

SHARPE, JAMES SHELBY, lawyer; b. Ft. Worth, Sept. 11, 1940; s. James Henry and Wanzel (Vanderbilt) S.; m. Martha Moudy Holland, June 9, 1962; children: Marthanne Freeman, Caren Sharp, Stephen. BA, U. Tex., 1962, JD, 1965. Bar: Tex. 1965, U.S. Dist. Ct. (no. dist.) Tex. 1966, U.S. Dist. Ct. (ea. dist.) Tex. 1993, U.S. Dist. Ct. (ea. and we. dists.) Ark. 1997, U.S. Ct. Appeals (5th and 6th cirs.) 1982, U.S. Ct. Appeals (fed. cir.) 1983, U.S. Ct. Appeals (10th cir.) 1992, U.S. Supreme Ct. 1972. Briefing atty. for chief justice Supreme Ct. of Tex., Austin, 1965-66; ptnr. Brown, Herman, Scott, Dean & Miles, Ft. Worth, 1966-84, Gandy Michener Swindle Whitaker & Pratt, Ft. Worth, 1984-87; shareholder Sharpe & Tillman, Ft. Worth, 1988—. Adj. prof. polit. sci. Tex. Christian U., Ft. Worth, 1969-79, Dallas Bapt. U., 1987, 1992-94; gen. counsel U.S.A. Radio Network, Internat. Christian Media, Denton Pub. Co. Pres. Ft. Worth-Tarrant County Jr. Bar, 1969-70, bd. dirs., 1968, sec., 1968, v.p., 1968-69; head marshal USA-USSR Track and Field Championships, Ft. Worth, USA-USSR Jr. Track and Field Championships, Austin, Tex., Relays, Austin, 1963—, NCAA Nat. Track and Field Championships, 1976, 80, 85, 92, 95, S.W. Conf. Indoor Track and Field Championships, 1987-96, Olympic Festival, San Antonio, 1993, Colorado Springs, 1995; 12 time head marshal S.W. Conf. Track and Field Championships, Big 12 Outdoor Conf. Track and Field Championship, 1997, 98, 99, 2001, 2002, 2003, head marshall 2000 Olympic Trials in Track and Field. USA/Mobil Track Championship, 1994, 95; USA Nat. Jr. Track Championship, 1994, 95, 98, 99, USA Track and Field Track Championship, 1997, 2001, 2002, 2003, Master's Nat. Track and Field Nat. Championship, 1996, 98, 2002. Mem. ABA, State Bar of Tex. (dist. 7-A grievance com. 1983-85, com. adminstrn. of justice 1985-92, com. on ct. rules 1992—, chmn. 1992-93, 93-94). Baptist. General civil litigation, Constitutional, Libel. Office: Sharpe & Tillman 6100 Western Pl Ste 901 Fort Worth TX 76107-4679 E-mail: utlawman@aol.com.

SHARPE, KEITH YOUNT, retired lawyer; b. Hiddenite, N.C., July 11, 1930; s. Ruel Yount and Eileen Lois (Lackey) S.; m. Margaret Joyce Land, Aug. 27, 1955 (div.); children: Jonathan, Matthew, Leonora, Felicia. AB, Duke U., 1952; JD, Wake Forest U., 1957, MBA, 1982. Bar: N.C. 1957. Practiced law, Winston-Salem, N.C., 1957-62, 82-94; asst. solicitor Mcpl. Ct. of Winston-Salem, 1958-60; with Pilot Freight Carriers Inc., Winston-Salem, 1962-82, sr. v.p., 1967-76, v.p., 1976-82; also dir.; v.p., dir. Comml. Automotive Co., 1967-76, Terminal Warehouse Corp., 1967-82. Bd. govs. So. Motor Carriers Rate Conf., 1977-81 Served with inf. U.S. Army, 1952-54. Mem. Assn. Transp. Practitioners, Phi Alpha Delta, Theta Chi. Democrat. Episcopalian. State civil litigation, Criminal, Personal injury (including property damage). Home: PO Box 19633 Asheville NC 28815-1633

SHARPE, ROBERT FRANCIS, JR., lawyer; b. Long Branch, N.J., Mar. 9, 1952; s. Robert Francis and Audrey Carolyn (Rembe) S.; 1 child, Robert Francis III; m. Maria S. Renna, Sept. 9, 2000. BA, DePauw U., 1975; BSE, Purdue U., 1975; JD, Wake Forest U., 1978. Bar: N.C. 1978. Atty. Capital Synergistics Corp., Winston-Salem, N.C., 1977-80; asst. counsel R.J. Reynolds Industries, Winston-Salem, 1980-82, assoc. counsel, 1983-85, counsel, 1985-86; corp. and comml. counsel R.J. Reynolds Tobacco Co., Winston-Salem, 1986-87; sr. counsel, asst. sec. R.J. Reynolds Nabisco, Inc., Atlanta, 1987-88, asst. gen. counsel, asst sec., 1989-93, v.p., sec., gen. counsel, 1996-97; v.p. mergers and acquisitions Tyco Internat., 1994-95; sr. v.p. pub. affairs & gen. coun. PepsiCo, Inc., Purchase, NY, 1998—2002; ptnr., Brunswick Grp., Inc., 2002—. Bd. dirs. Whitman Corp., Pepsi Bottling Group. Active Jr. Achievement, U.S. C. of C. Bd. dirs. Whitman Corp., Pepsi Bottling Group. Mem. ABA, N.C. Bar Assn., Am. Corp. Counsel Assn. Republican. Episcopalian. Avocations: golf, fishing. Commercial, contracts (including sales of goods; commercial financing), Corporate, general, Securities. Office: Brunswick Group 135 E 57th St New York NY 10022*

SHATTUCK, CATHIE ANN, lawyer, former government official; b. Salt Lake City, July 18, 1945; d. Robert Ashley S. and Lillian Culp (Shattuck). BA, U. Nebr., 1967, JD, 1970. Bar: Nebr. 1970, U.S. Dist. Ct. Nebr. 1970, Colo. 1971, U.S. Dist. Ct. Colo. 1971, U.S. Supreme Ct. 1974, U.S. Ct. Appeals (10th cir.) 1977, U.S. Dist. Ct. D.C. 1984, U.S. Ct. Appeals (D.C. cir.) 1984. V.p., gen. mgr. Shattuck Farms, Hastings, Nebr., 1967-70; asst. project dir. atty. Colo. Civil Rights Commn., Denver, 1970-72; trial atty. Equal Employment Opportunity Commn., Denver, 1973-77, vice chmn. Washington, 1982-84; pvt. practice law Denver, 1977-81; mem. Fgn. Svc. Bd., Washington, 1982-84, Presdl. Personnel Task Force, Washington, 1982-84; ptnr. Epstein, Becker & Green, L.A. and Washington, 1984—. Lectr. Colo. Continuing Legal Edn. Author: Employer's Guide to Controlling Sexual Harrassment, 1992; mem. editorial bd. The Practical Litigator, 1988—. Bd. dirs. KGNU Pub. Radio, Boulder, Colo., 1979, Denver Exchange, 1980-81, YWCA Met. Denver, 1979-81. Recipient Nebr. Young Career Woman Bus. and Profl. Women, 1967; recipient Outstanding Nebraskan Daily Nebraskan, Lincoln, 1967 Fellow Am. Coll. of Labor and Employment Lawyers; mem. ABA (mgmt. chair labor and employment law sect. com. on immigration law 1988-90, mgmt. chair com. on legis. devels. 1990-93), Nebr. Bar Assn., Colo. Bar Assn., Colo. Women's Bar Assn., D.C. Bar Assn., Nat. Women's Coalition, Delta Sigma Rho, Tau Kappa Alpha, Pi Sigma Alpha, Alpha Xi Delta, Denver Club. Administrative and regulatory, Civil rights, Juvenile.

SHATTUCK, GARY G. lawyer; b. Nashua, N.H., 1950; m. Katherine H. Catlin, 1972. BA, U. Colo., 1972; JD magna cum laude, Vt. Law Sch., 1987. Bar: Vt. 1987, U.S. Dist. Ct. Vt. 1987, U.S. Ct. Appeals (2d cir.) 1992. Dep. sheriff Boulder County Sheriff's Dept., Boulder, Colo., 1973-75; patrol comdr. Vt. State Police, Waterbury, 1975-87; litigation assoc. Reiber, Kenlan, Schweibert & Hall, P.C., Rutland, Vt., 1987-89; asst. atty. gen. Office of Atty. Gen., Montpelier, Vt., 1989-91; suprvising atty. Vt. Drug Task Force, Montpelier, 1989-91; asst. U.S. atty. Organized Crime Drug Enforcement Task Force, U.S. Dept. Justice, Burlington, Vt., 1991—. Adj. prof. Castleton (Vt.) State Coll., 1997-98; U.S. Dept. Justice legal advisor to UN Mission in Kosovo, Pristina, 2000, Sarajevo, Bosnia-Herzegovina, 2001; anti-terrorism coord. Dist. Vt., 2002—; appointee Gov.'s Homeland Security Adv. Coun., 2003—. Bd. dirs. Rutland Mental Health, 1991; citizen's adv. com. Rutland Solid Waste Dist., 1987; del. Nat. Assn. Asst. U.S. Attys., 1994-99; bd. dirs. Vt. Archeol. Soc., 1998-99; appointee gov.'s homeland security adv. coun., 2003-. Recipient Atty. Gen. Janet Reno Spl. Achievement award, 1993, award Dept. Justice for svc. in Kosovo. Office: Office of US Atty PO Box 570 Burlington VT 05402-0570 E-mail: garyshattuck@hotmail.com.

SHATZ, PHILLIP, lawyer, banker, insurance executive; b. White Plains, N.Y., Sept. 1, 1926; s. Hyman and Ruth (Futoran) S.; m. Bettie Dorsey, Oct. 18, 1957 (dec.); children: Phillip Dorsey, Sallie Dean; m. Natalie Marshall, May 27, 1988. BS, Syracuse U., 1948; LLB, Columbia U., 1954. Bar: N.Y. 1954, U.S. Dist. Ct. (so. dist.) N.Y. 1955, U.S. Supreme Ct. 1960. Pres., chmn. bd. Rich, Shatz and Duncan, Inc., Mahopac, N.Y., 1948-75; v.p. Putnam County Fed. Savs. and Loan Assn., 1953-63, pres., chmn. bd., 1933-78; sole practice Mahopac, 1954-70; ptnr. Shatz & Braatz, Mahopac, 1970-74, Shatz & Thomsen, Mahopac, 1974-77, Shatz, Thomsen & Mace, Mahopac, 1977-80; sr. ptnr. McCabe & Mack, Poughkeepsie, NY, 1980—2000, of counsel, 2000—. Spl. prosecutor Putnam County; dir. Mid-Hudson Legal Svcs. Chmn. Putnam County Young Republicans. With USNR, 1943-46. Mem. ABA, N.Y. State Bar Assn., Dutchess County Bar Assn., Assn. Bar City of N.Y., Univ. Club (N.Y.C.). State civil litigation, Corporate, general, Family and matrimonial. Home: 157 Skidmore Rd Pleasant Valley NY 12569-5001 Office: McCabe & Mack Esqs 63 Washington St Poughkeepsie NY 12601-2313 E-mail: pshatz@mccm.com.

SHAUGHNESSY, ROXANNE C. lawyer; b. Apr. 5, 1955; AA in Liberal Arts, Normandale Coll., 1983; BA in Sociology, Hamline U., 1989; JD, William Mitchell Coll. Law, 1992. Bar: Minn. 1992, U.S. Claims Ct. 1993. Assoc. Shaughnessy, Warren & Shaughnessy, P.A., Mpls., 1992-93, ptnr., 1993-97, pres., 1997—. Bd. dirs. Uppermidwest Golden Gloves, 1983-91; chief judge Uppermidwest Region, 1985-91; nat. amateur boxing judge USA Boxing and Golden Gloves, 1977—; profl. boxing judge, 1997—; mem. Internat. Boxing Coun., 1998—. Mem. ABA, Minn. State Bar Assn., Hennepin County Bar Assn., Minn. Trial Lawyers Assn., Assn. of Trial Lawyers of Am. Office: 5212 W 62d St Edina MN 55436

SHAVER, PHILIP ALCOTT, lawyer; b. Oberlin, Ohio, Mar. 17, 1938; s. Chester Linn and Alice Louise (Crafts) S.; m. Viola Golod, July 29, 1961 (div. 1980); children: Peter Vaughan, Emily Anne, Andrew Alcott; stepchild, Michele Lynn Cooke Andresen; m. Barbara King, Mar. 14, 1981. Student, Harvard Coll., Cambridge, 1954-55; AB, Oberlin Coll., 1959; LLB, Yale U., 1962. Bar: Ohio 1963, Mass. 1965, N.J. 1977, U.S. Ct. Appeals (3d cir.) 1995. Assoc. Allen Hull, Cleve., 1962-65; atty., sec. Fed. Res. Bank Boston, 1965-69; assoc. coun. 1st Nat. Bank, Boston, 1969-77; sec., legal coun. City Fed. Savs. & Loan, Somerville, N.J., 1977-80; assoc. coun. United Jersey Banks, Princeton, N.J., 1980-81; pvt. practice, Princeton, 1981—. Editor: Federal Banking Laws, 1969, ann. supplements, 1967-72. Trustee Princeton Cemetery, 1988—; mem. allocations com. United Way, Princeton, 1986-96; deacon Nassau Presbyn. Ch., 1996-99, elder, 1985-88; trustee Rockingham Assn., 1997—. Mem. Am. Honky Tonk Bar Assn., Princeton Bar Assn. (trustee 1993-97, pres. 1996-97), Hist. Soc. Princeton (trustee 1987-94, Outstanding Vol. Svc. 1995). Avocation: leading walking tours of historic princeton and princeton cemetery. General civil litigation, Estate planning, Property, real (including real estate development, water). Home: 25A Chestnut Ct Princeton NJ 08540-1716 Office: 33 Witherspoon St Princeton NJ 08542-3207

SHAVIT, ILAN, lawyer; b. London, July 31, 1958; LLB, Hebrew U., Jerusalem, 1984. Bar: Israel Bar Assn. Legal intern, Jerusalem, 1983—84; intern, assoc. lawyer Raven Abramson & Co., Jerusalem, 1984—86; assoc., ptnr. Dan Cohen, Spigelman & Co., Tel Aviv, 1986—92; sr. ptnr. Shavit Bar-On Inbar, Tel Aviv, 1992—. Dir. Ruby-Butonia Group, Hong Kong, Bangalore. Maj. Israeli Inf., 1977—. Corporate, general, Communications, Private international. Office: Shavit Bar-On Inber Law Offices 2 Kremnitzky St 67899 Tel Aviv Israel

SHAW, BARRY N. lawyer; b. Newark, July 31, 1940; s. Harry G. and Evelyn (Kruger) S.; m. Cheryl Lynn Rosen, Mar. 24, 1963; children: Jennifer B., Jonathan M. BS in Acctg., Rutgers U., 1962, LLB, 1965. U.S. Supreme Ct. 1988, Oreg. 1996. Tax supr. Coopers & Lybrand, Phila., 1965—68; corp. counsel Lincoln Bank, Phila., 1968—72, Waste Resources Corp., Phila., 1972—74; ptnr. Spivack, Dranoff & Shaw, Phila., 1974—75, Dranoff & Shaw, Phila., 1975—79, Jubanyik, Varbalow Tedesco Shaw & Shaffer, Cherry Hill, NJ, 1979—95, Dilworth, Paxson, Kalish & Kauffman (successor firm), Cherry Hill, NJ, 1995—97, Davis, Gilstrap, Hearn & Shaw PC, Ashland, Oreg., 1997—2000, Grantland, Blodgett & Shaw, LLP, Medford, Oreg., 2000—. Lectr. in banking and real estate law. Author: Selected Decisions in Lender Liability Law, 1990, Environmental Lender Liability, 1992. Chmn. Shamong Twp. (N.J.) Planning Bd., 1990-93, Local Civic Assn.; active Shamong Twp. Com., 1993-97; mayor Shamong Twp., 1995; sec. Pinelands Mcpl. (Mayors') Coun., 1996-97. Mem. Oreg. State Bar, Jackson County Bar Assn., Rotary (pres. 2001-2002). Republican. Avocations: farming, writing. Commercial, contracts (including sales of goods; commercial financing), Corporate, general, Probate (including wills, trusts). Office: Grantland Blodgett & Shaw LLP 1818 E McAndrew Rd Medford OR 97504 Fax: 541-770-1290. E-mail: bshaw@mighty.net.

SHAW, CHARLES ALEXANDER, judge; b. Jackson, Tenn., Dec. 31, 1944; s. Alvis and Sarah S.; m. Kathleen Ingram, Aug. 17, 1969; 1 child, Bryan Ingram. BA, Harris Stowe State Coll., 1966; MBA, U. Mo., 1971; JD, Cath. U. Am., 1974. Bar: D.C. 1975, Mo. 1975, U.S. Ct. Appeals (8th and D.C. cirs.) 1975, U.S. Dist. Ct. (ea. dist.) Mo. 1976, U.S. Ct. Appeals (6th and 7th cirs.) 1976. Tchr. St. Louis Pub. Schs., 1966-69, D.C. Pub. Schs., Washington, 1969-71; law clk. U.S. Dept. Justice, Washington, 1972-73, NLRB, Washington, 1973-74, atty., 1974-76; assoc. Lashly, Caruthers, Theis, Rava & Hamel, St. Louis, 1976-80, asst. U.S. atty., 1980-87; judge Mo. Cir. Ct., St. Louis, 1987-94, asst. presiding judge, 1993-94; judge U.S. Dist. Ct., St. Louis, 1994—. Hearing officer Office of the Mayor, Washington, 1973-74; instr. U. Mo., St. Louis, 1980-81. State bd. dirs. United Negro Coll. Fund, St. Louis, 1979-83; trustee St. Louis Art Mus., 1979-82, 89-96; bd. dirs. Arts and Edn. Coun., 1992-96, Metro Golf Assn., 1993-2000, Landmarks Assn., St. Louis, 1980-82. Danforth Found. fellow, 1978-79; Cath. U. Am. scholar, 1971-74. Mem. D.C. Bar Assn., Mo. Bar Assn., Mound City Bar Assn., Bar Assn. Metro. St. Louis, Harris-Stowe State Coll. Alumni Assn. (bd. dirs., Disting. Alumni 1988), Nat. Assn. Guardsmen (sec. St. Louis chpt. 1999-2001), Phi Alpha Delta (svc. award 1973-74), Sigma Pi Phi (pres. St. Louis chpt. 1999-2001). Avocation: golf. Office: 111 S 10th St Saint Louis MO 63102

SHAW, CURT, lawyer, communications executive; B with honors, Trinity Coll.; JD, Columbia U. Assoc. gen. counsel Occidental Chem. Corp., 1983—88, v.p., gen. counsel, 1986—88; counsel NYNEX, 1988—97; sr., v.p., gen. counsel Charter Comm., St. Louis, 1997—, also sec. bd. dirs. Office: Charter Comm Legal Dept 12405 Powerscourt Saint Louis MO 63131*

SHAW, DONALD HARDY, lawyer; b. Oelwein, Iowa, June 1, 1922; s. John Hardy and Minnie (Brown) S.; m. Elizabeth Jean Orr, Aug. 16, 1946; children: Elizabeth Ann, Andrew Hardy, Anthony Orr. BS, Harvard U., 1942; JD, U. Iowa, 1948. Bar: Ill. 1949, Iowa 1948, cert. fin. planner 1983. With firm Sidley & Austin, Chgo., 1948-55; with Iowa-Ill. Gas & Electric Co., Davenport, Iowa, 1956-87, treas., 1960-72, v.p. finance, 1973-87, also dir.; of counsel Walton, Creen, Curry and Robertson, Davenport, Iowa, 1987-88, Newpor, Bell, Leon & Martinez, Davenport, 1989-98. Mem. Iowa State Bd. Regents, 1969-81, Iowa State TV-Radio Com., 1976-81; trustee St. Luke's Hosp., Davenport, 1966-91. Served to capt. USAAF, 1942-45. Recipient Philo Sherman Bennett award, 1942 Mem. Rock Island Arsenal Club, Outing Club, Harvard Club N.Y.C., Order of Coif, Duck Creek Tennis Club, Delta Theta Phi. Congregationalist. Home: 29 Hillcrest Ave Davenport IA 52803-3726

SHAW, ELIZABETH ORR, lawyer; b. Monona, Iowa, Oct. 2, 1923; d. Harold Topliff and Hazel (Kean) Orr; m. Donald Hardy Shaw, Aug. 16, 1946; children: Elizabeth Ann, Andrew Hardy, Anthony Orr. AB, Drake U., 1945; postgrad., U. Minn., 1945-46; JD, U. Iowa, 1948. Bar: Ill. 1949, Iowa 1956. Assoc. Lord Bissell & Brook, Chgo., 1949-52; pvt. practice law Arlington Heights, Ill., 1952-56; ptnr. Wood & Shaw, Davenport, Iowa, 1968-72; mem. Iowa Ho. of Reps., Des Moines, 1967-72, Iowa Senate, Des Moines, 1972-77; county atty. Scott County, Davenport, 1977-78; corp. atty. Deere & Co., Moline, Ill., 1979-89; pvt. practice Davenport, 1990-98; ret., 1999. Mem. Scott County Bar Assn. (com. chmn. 1970-72), Iowa State Bar Assn. (chmn. family law com. 1970-76), Order of Coif, Phi Beta Kappa, Kappa Kappa Gamma, PEO. Republican. Mem. United Ch. of Christ. Administrative and regulatory, Corporate, general, Environmental. Home and Office: 29 Hillcrest Ave Davenport IA 52803-3726

SHAW, L. EDWARD, JR., lawyer; b. Elmira, N.Y., July 30, 1944; s. L. Edward and Virginia Anne (O'Leary) S.; m. Irene Ryan; children: Christopher, Hope, Hillary, Julia, Rory BA in Econs., Georgetown U., Washington, 1966; JD, Yale U., New Haven, 1969. Bar: N.Y. 1969. Assoc. Milbank, Tweed, Hadley & McCloy, N.Y.C., 1969-77, ptnr., 1977-83; sr. v.p., gen. counsel Chase Manhattan Corp., N.Y.C., 1983-85, exec. v.p., gen. counsel, 1985-96; vice chmn., gen. counsel Natwest Markets, N.Y.C., 1996-97, pres., 1997-99; gen. counsel Aetna Inc., 1999—. Mem. Assn. Bar City N.Y., Winged Foot Golf Club, Phi Beta Kappa. Roman Catholic. Avocations: youth athletics, golf. Office: Aetna Inc RC4B 151 Farmington Ave Hartford CT 06156-3124 E-mail: ShawJL@aetna.com.

SHAW, LEANDER JERRY, JR., state supreme court justice; b. Salem, Va., Sept. 6, 1930; s. Leander J. and Margaret S. BA, W.Va. State Coll., 1952, LLD (hon.), 1986; JD, Howard U., 1957; PhD (hon.) in Pub. Affairs, Fla. Internat. U., 1990; LLD (hon.), Nova Law Sch., 1991, Washington & Lee Law Sch., 1991. Asst. prof. law Fla. A&M U., 1957-60; sole practice Jacksonville, Fla., 1960-69, 72-74; asst. pub. defender, 1965-69; asst. state's atty., 1969-72; judge Fla. Indsl. Relations Commn., 1974-79, Fla. Ct. Appeals (1st dist.), 1979-83; justice Fla. Supreme Ct., Tallahassee, 1983—2003, chief justice, 1990-92. Office: Fla Supreme Ct Supreme Ct Bldg 500 S Duval St Tallahassee FL 32399-6556 E-mail: SupremeCourt@FLCOURTS.ORG.*

SHAW, MELVIN ROBERT, lawyer; b. Bklyn., Nov. 23, 1948; s. Arthur and Pearl (Gutterman) S. BA in Polit. Sci., L.I. U., 1970; MPA, U. Ill., 1973; LLD (hon.), Roman Coll., Rome, 1974; BS in Law, Western State U., San Diego, 1984; JD, Thomas Jefferson Sch. of Law, 1984; MA in Human Behavior, Nat. U., 1985; MS in Mgmt., NYU, 1988; LLM in Health Law, DePaul U., 1989; postgrad., Golden Gate U., 1989; PhD in Pub. Health, NYU, 1993. Bar: Ind. 1985, U.S. Dist. Ct. (no. and so. dists.) Ind. 1985, U.S. Dist. Ct. (no. dist.) Calif. 1985, U.S. Dist. Ct. (ea. dist.) Wis. 1985, U.S. Dist. Ct. Hawaii 1985, U.S. Ct. Appeals (3d, 5th, 7th, 9th, D.C., fed. cirs.) 1985, U.S. Ct. Internat. Trade 1985, U.S. Ct. Mil. Appeals 1985, U.S. Ct. Fed. Claims 1985, U.S. Tax Ct. 1985, U.S. Supreme Ct. 1988, U.S. Dist. Ct. (no. dist.) Ill. 1989, U.S. Ct. Appeals for Vets. Claims 1990, U.S. Dist. Ct. (ea., so., and no. dists.) N.Y. 1992, USAF Ct. Criminal Appeals, 2001, USN/Marine Corp. Ct. Criminal Appeals, 2001. Exec. asst. N.Y. State Senate, Albany, 1969-71; polit. cons. Kirson & Shaw, Ltd., N.Y.C., 1972-76; pres. Master Pubs., Inc., Chgo., 1976-80; lectr. Inst. for Internat. Affairs, Washington, 1978—; sr. ptnr. Littlejohn & Shaw Assocs., N.Y.C., Chgo., San Diego, 1980-85; pvt. practice South Bend, Ind. and N.Y.C., South Bend, Ind., 1985-99; sr. ptnr. Shaw and Dessureau, NYC and South Bend, Ind., 1999—. Instr. law Calif. C.C.'s, 1985—; dir. Hudson Industries, San Diego, Master Commn., N.Y.C., Inst. for Internat. Affairs, 1979—. Editor Internat. Rels. Jour., 1982; contbr. articles to profl. jours. Active Am. Jewish Com., Dem. Nat. Com.; chmn., bd. govs. Mental Health and Criminal Justice Policy Inst. Am.; v.p. Shorefront Mental Health Bd. Mem. ABA, ACLU, ATLA, Fed. Bar Assn., Ind. State Bar Assn., N.Y. State Bar Assn., Chgo. Bar Assn., Am. Soc. Internat. Law (chpt. pres. 1983-84), Am. Judicature Soc., Am. Arbitration Assn., Nat. Health Lawyers Assn., Am. Soc. Commns. and Media Execs., Am. Soc. Law, Medicine, and Ethics, Nat. Assn. Mgmt. Execs., Amnesty Internat., Odd Fellows, Delta Theta Phi. Democrat. Jewish. Immigration, naturalization, and customs, Labor (including EEOC, Fair Labor Standards Act, labor-management relations, NLRB, OSHA), Military. Office: Shaw and Dessureau 82 Wall St Ste 1105 New York NY 10005-3600 E-mail: shawdessureau@lawyer.com.

SHAW, RICHARD ALLAN, lawyer; b. Portland, Oreg., Oct. 14, 1937; s. Leland B. and Vena (Gaskill) S.; m. Jo-Ann O. Shaw, Mar. 23, 1959; 1 child, Kevin A. BS, U. Oreg., 1959, JD, 1962; LLM in Taxation, NYU, 1963. Bar: Oreg. 1962, Ariz. 1967, Calif. 1969. Assoc. Kramer, Roche, Burch, Streich & Cracchiolo, Phoenix, 1966-68, Hewitt & Greaves, San Diego, 1968-71; ptnr. Hewitt & Shaw, San Diego, 1972-77; pres. Shenas, Shaw & Spievak A.P.C., San Diego, 1978-96; ptnr. Shaw & O'Brien, LLP, San Diego, 1996-2000, Higgs, Fletcher & Mack, LLP, San Diego, 2000—. Teaching fellow NYU Sch. Law, N.Y.C., 1962-63; disting. adj. prof. advanced bus. planning and advanced corporate tax problems U. San Diego Sch. Law, 1978—; founding incorporator, dir. San Diego County Bar Found., 1979; lectr. insts. and programs nationally; chair Taxation Taskforce White House Conf. on Small Bus. Editor Oreg. Law Rev., 1961-62, The Fed. Bar Jour., 1964-68, The Tax Lawyer, 1973-74, Jour. of S Corp. Taxation, 1988-98, Jour. of Bus. Entities, 1998—; contbr. articles in field to profl. jours. Pres. San Diego County Boy Scouts, 1982-84; chmn. Washington-Lincoln Laurels for Leaders, San Diego, 1986-87; chmn. Corp. Fin. Coun., 1993-94; chmn. Eagle Scout Alumni Assn., 1978. Capt. JAGC, U.S. Army, 1963-66. Recipient Silver Beaver award Boy Scouts Am., San Diego, 1979, Silver Antelope award, 1982, Disting. Eagle Scout award, 1988. Fellow ABA (chmn. tax. com. on S corps. 1974-76, coun. dir. taxation sect. 1988-94, vice-chmn. taxation sect. 1991-94, chair taxation sect. 2003—); mem. Am. Coll. Tax Counsel (regent 9th cir.), Oreg. State Bar, Ariz. State Bar, Calif. State Bar (chmn. taxation sect. 1981-82, V. Judson Klien award 1985), Western Region Tax Bar Assn. (chmn. 1988), San Diego County Bar Assn. (chmn. bus. law sect. 1974), Am. Bar Retirement Assn. (chmn. bd. dirs. 2002-03), Kiwanis (disting. past pres. 1985-86). Republican. Avocations: golf, painting, stained glass. Corporate taxation, Estate taxation, Taxation, general. Office: Higgs Fletcher & Mack LLP 401 West A S-2600 San Diego CA 92101

SHAW, RUSSELL CLYDE, lawyer; b. Cleve., Mar. 19, 1940; s. Clyde Leland and Ruth Arminta (Williams) S.; BS, Ohio State U., 1962; JD, Ohio State U., 1965; m. Jane Ann Mohler, Feb. 15, 1969 (div. 1988); children: Christopher Scott, Robin Nicole, Curtis Russell; m. Lynn Baird Breuer, Oct. 21, 1989; stepchildren: Heather Shaw, Matthew Breuer, Russell Breuer. Bar: Ohio 1965, U.S. Supreme Ct. 1968. Assoc., Thompson, Hine & Flory, Cleve., 1965, 69-74, ptnr., 1979-93, chmn. area specialty group, 1988-90; ptnr. Walter & Haverfield LLP (formerly Walter, Haverfield, Buescher & Chockley), Cleve., 1993—, chmn. area specialty group, 1993—. Adj. assoc. prof. law Case Western Res. U. Coll. of Law, 2002--. Mem. Geauga United Way Svcs. Council, 1980-87, officer, 1982-87, chmn. (chief vol. officer), 1984-87; trustee United Way Svcs. of Cleve., 1983-88, assoc. v.p., 1986-88; trustee Cleve. Community Fund, 1986-88, Ohio Citizen's Council; trustee Ohio United Way, 1986—, v.p., 1987-90, chmn., 1990-92, mem. exec. com., 1990-94; chmn. Ohio Citizen's Council Welfare Reform Task Force, 1987-90, mem. United Way of Am. Welfare Reform Task Force; mem. Ohio Adv. Coun. for the Aging, 1990-99, vice chmn., 1992-93, chmn., 1993-99; mem. Gov. Ohio's Ops. Improvement Task Force, 1991-93; Nat. Inst. for Responsible Fatherhood and Family Devel., 1990-95; mem. Cleve. adv. bd. Inst. for Responsible Fatherhood and Family Revitalization, trustee, exec. com. mem. 1995-98; del. White House Conf. on Aging, Washington, 1995; trustee, exec. com. mem. Univ. Settlement, 1996-2001. Served to capt. AUS, 1965-69. Recipient Harvey H. Hebert Meml. award Delta Sigma Phi, 1989, Mr. Delta Sigma award, 1999; named to Honorable Order of Ky. Cols. Commonwealth of Ky. Mem. ABA (employee benefits com. taxation sect.), Def. Rsch. Inst. (employee benefits com.), Fed. Bar Assn., Ohio Bar Assn., Nat. Lawyers Club, Internat. Found. Employee Benefit Plans, Employee Benefits Attys. Forum Cleve., Old English Sheepdog Club Am. (nat. officer 1972-74), Fedn. Ohio Dog Clubs (pres. 1978-82), Sugarbush Kennel Club (pres. 1975-78, 81—), Midwest Pension Conf., Delta Sigma Phi (nat. officer 1975—, nat. officer Found. 1978—, trustee Found. 1983-95, Herbet Meml. award), Pres.'s (Ohio State U.). Presbyterian. Pension, profit-sharing, and employee benefits. Office: Walter & Haverfield 50 Public Sq 1300 Terminal Tower Cleveland OH 44113 E-mail: rshaw@walterhav.com.

SHAY-BYRNE, OLIVIA, lawyer; b. Trenton, N.J., Aug. 14, 1957; d. Stewart and Elizabeth (Sherrill) B. Student, Vanderbilt U., 1975-76; BA, Bowdoin Coll., 1979; JD, U. Toledo, 1982; LLM in Taxation, Georgetown U., 1987. Bar: Tex. 1982, Ohio 1984, Md. 1985. Assoc. Whiteford, Taylor & Preston, Balt., 1984-87, Linowes & Blocher, Silver Spring, Md., 1987-90; ptnr. Sutherland Asbill & Brenna LLP, Washington, 1996—2000, ReedSmith LLP, Washington, 2000—. Bd. dir. D.C. Mktg. Ctr.; bd. dirs. D.C. Mktg. Ctr., Inc. Author: The At-Risk Rules Under the Tax Reform Act of 1986, The Door Closes on Tax Motivated Investments, IRS Issues New Guidelines for Management Contracts Used for Facilities Financed with Tax Exempt Bonds, 1993, RRA '93 Loosens Real Estate Rules for Exempt Organizations, 1993; editor Nat. Mcpl. Fin. Jour.; contbr. articles to profl. jours. Mem. Tax Coun. for State of Md., Leadership Montgomery, 1996; bd. dirs. Bethesda Acad. Performing Arts, Inc.; chair GULC Nat. Tax Exempt Bond Conf., 1997. Mem. ABA (exempt orgn. com. taxation sect. 1991—), Md. Bar Assn. (coun. taxation sect.), Balt. City Bar Assn. (chmn. speakers bur. young lawyers sect.), Lawyers for Arts Washington, Comml. Real Estate Woman (bd. dirs., pres.), Profls. for Strathmore Hall (co-chmn.), D.C. Bowdoin Coll. Alumni Assn. (pres. 1992—), Howard County C. of C. (legis. com. 1989), Rotary. Corporate, general, Corporate taxation, Taxation, general. Home: 1083 Mill Field Ct Great Falls VA 22066 Office: Reed Smith LLP East Tower Fl 11 1301 K St NW Washington DC 20005

SHAYNE, STANLEY H. lawyer; Mng. ptnr. Shayne & Greenwald, 1994—. Corporate, general, Mergers and acquisitions, Taxation, general. Office: Shayne & Greenwald 221 High St Columbus OH 43215

SHEA, DAVID MICHAEL, state supreme court justice; b. Hartford, July 1, 1922; s. Michael Peter and Margaret (Agnes) S.; m. Rosemary Anne Sasseen, Apr. 28, 1956; children: Susan, Kathleen, Margaret, Rosemary, Christina, Michael, Maura, Julie BA, Wesleyan U., 1944; LLB, Yale U., 1948. Bar: Conn. 1948. Assoc. Tunick & Ferris, Greenwich, Conn., 1948-49; assoc. Bailey & Wechsler, Hartford, 1949-57; ptnr. Bailey, Wechsler & Shea, Hartford, 1957-65; judge Conn. Superior Ct., Hartford, 1966-81; justice Conn. Supreme Ct., Hartford, 1981-92, state judge referee, 1992—. Served with U.S. Army, 1943-46 Democrat. Roman Catholic. Office: Conn Superior Ct 95 Washington St Hartford CT 06106-4431

SHEA, EDWARD EMMETT, lawyer, educator, author; b. Detroit, May 29, 1932; s. Edward Francis and Margaret Kathleen (Downey) S.; m. Ann Marie Conley, Aug. 28, 1957; children: Michael, Maura, Ellen. AB, U. Detroit, 1954; JD, U. Mich., 1957. Bar: Mich. 1957, Fla. 1959, N.Y. 1961. Assoc. Simpson Thacher & Bartlett, N.Y.C., 1960-63, Dykema, Wheat, Spencer, Detroit, 1963-69, Cadwalader Wickersham & Taft, N.Y.C., 1969-71; v.p., gen. counsel, chmn. Reichhold Chems., White Plains, N.Y., 1971-81; adj. prof. Pace U. Grad. Sch. Bus., N.Y.C., 1982—; counsel, ptnr. Windels, Marx, Davies & Ives, N.Y.C., 1982-84; ptnr. Windels, Marx, Lane & Mittendorf, N.Y.C., 1986—; sr. v.p., gen. counsel GAF Corp., 1984-86. Sec. Peridot Chems., 1988-97; lectr. N.Y. Inst. Fin., 1995—. Author: An Introduction to the U.S. Environmental Laws, 1995, The Lead Regulation Handbook, 1996, The McGraw-Hill Guidebook to Acquiring and Divesting Businesses, 1998, Environmental Law and Compliance Methods, 2002; editor: The Acquisitions Yearbook, 1991-93; contbr. articles to profl. jours. Mem. adv. bd. N.Y. State Small Bus. Ct. Program, 1988-93. 1st lt. JAGC, USAF, 1957-60. Mem. N.Y. Athletic Club. Environmental, Finance, Private international. Office: Windels Marx Lane & Mittendorf 156 W 56th St Fl 23 New York NY 10019-3867 E-mail: eshea@windelsmarx.com.

SHEA, JAMES WILLIAM, lawyer; b. N.Y.C., July 10, 1936; s. William P. and Mildred E. (McCaffrey) S.; m. Ann Marie Byrne, June 6, 1964; children: James T., Kathleen A., Tracy A. BS, St. Peters Coll., 1957; JD, Fordham U., 1962; LLM in Taxation, NYU, 1965. Bar: N.Y. 1962, U.S. Dist. Ct. (so. and ea. dists.) N.Y. 1966, U.S. Supreme Ct. 1967. Revenue agent U.S. Treasury Dept., N.Y.C., 1961-63; tax atty. Kennecott Copper Corp., N.Y.C., 1963-67; tax counsel CBS Inc., N.Y.C., 1968-71; ptnr. Hunton & Williams and predecessor firm Conboy, Hewitt, O'Brien & Boardman, N.Y.C., 1971—2001, sr. counsel, 2001—. Rep. committeeman, Staten Island, N.Y., 1980; mem. adv. com. tax and fin. N.Y. State Charter Commn. City of S.I. Served to 1st lt. U.S. Army, 1957-61, to capt. USAR, 1962-72. Mem. N.Y. State Bar Assn., Richmond County Country Club S.I. (sec. 1993-96, v.p. 1996-98, pres. 1998-2000, bd. dirs. 1993—). Republican. Roman Catholic. Probate (including wills, trusts), Personal income taxation, State and local taxation. Home: 399 Tysens Ln Staten Island NY 10306-2844 Office: Hunton & Williams 200 Park Ave Rm 4300 New York NY 10166-0091 E-mail: jws@si.rr.com.

SHEA, JOSEPH WILLIAM, III, lawyer; b. Cin., Jan. 3, 1947; s. Joseph W. Jr. and Gertrude Mary (Reardon) S.; m. Elaine N. Miller, May 29, 1971; children: J. Blane, Doyle Reardon, C. Lauer. BA, U. Cin., 1969; JD, No. Ky. U., 1974. Bar: Ohio 1974, Ky. 1990, U.S. Dist. Ct. Ohio 1974, U.S. Ct. Appeals (6th cir.) 1980, U.S. Supreme Ct. 1981; diplomate Nat. Bd. Trial Advocacy. Prin. Shea & Assocs., Cin., 1974—. Founder Lawriter Corp., Cin., 1983—; mem. Ohio Supreme Ct. Bd. Bar Examiners, 1983-90, chair 1988-89. Author: Shea's Forms for Ohio Trial Practice, 1983, Shea Civil Practice, 1985; contbg. author: Personal Injury in Ohio, CLE Inst., 1984, Civil Litigation in Ohio, 1991, 93, 95, 98, 2000, CLE Inst.; editor Ohio Verdict Reporter, vols. 1-310, 1976—; contbr. articles to profl. jours. Mem. Supreme Ct. Bd. Bar Examiners, 1982-89, chmn., 1988-89; diplomate Nat. Bd. Trial Advocacy, 1985—. Recipient Profl. Achievement award, No. Ky. U., 1998. Fellow Am. Coll. Trial Lawyers, Ohio Acad. Trial Lawyers (pres. 1981-82), Internat. Soc. Barristers; mem. Am. Bd. Trial Advocacy (adv. 1989—, nat. rep. 1990—), Ohio State Bar Assn., Ky. Bar Assn., Cin. Bar Assn., Nat. Bar Examiners (bd. examiners 1984-89, chmn.), Nat. Bd. Trial Advocacy (cert. trial specialist 1985—, nat. cert. bar examiner 1984-87, 91, 94, 2001, 03). Roman Catholic. Avocations: sailing, snow skiing. Federal civil litigation, General civil litigation, State civil litigation. Home: 510 Baum St Cincinnati OH 45202 Office: Shea & Assocs 444 Chiquita Ctr 250 E Fifth St Cincinnati OH 45202-4119

SHEACH, ANDREW JONATHAN, lawyer; b. Ilford, Essex, Eng., Apr. 7, 1963; BA in Law with honors, Cambridge U., Eng., 1984. Trainee solicitor Cameron Markby, London, 1985-87, solicitor, 1987-93; ptnr. CMS Cameron McKenna, London, 1993—. Corporate, general, Mergers and acquisitions. Office: CMS Cameron McKenna 160 Aldersgate St EC1A 4DD London England Fax: 00 44 207 367 2000. E-mail: ajs@cmck.com.

SHEAHAN, MICHAEL JOHN, lawyer; b. St. Paul, Minn., Jan. 27, 1934; s. Louis Patrick and Evelyn Sylvia (Frediani) S.; m. Charlene Ruth Schermerhorn, Nov. 5, 1960; children: John M., Mark W., Stephen P. BS, U. Minn.-Mpls., 1960, LL.B., 1961. Bar: Minn. 1961, U.S. Dist. Ct. Minn. 1964. Assoc. T. O. Kachelmacher, Mpls., 1961; ptnr. Cummins, Gislason, & Sheahan, Ltd., St. Paul, 1973-76, Peterson, Gray & Sheahan, Ltd., St. Paul, 1976-85; prin. Michael J. Sheahan, P.A., St. Paul, 1985—. Chmn. Ramsey County Bar Fund, St. Paul, 1983-84. Mem., sec. St. Paul City Charter Commn., 1976-80; dean Acad. Cert. Trial Lawyers Minn., 1995-96. Trustee, St. Thomas Acad., St. Paul, 1983-95. Served with U.S. Army, 1955-57. Named Minn. Super Lawyer, Minn. Law and Politics mag., 1998. Mem. Minn. Trial Lawyers Assn. (dir.), Ramsey County Bar Assn., ABA, Minn. State Bar Assn., Nat. Bd. Trial Advocacy, Phi Delta Phi. Roman Catholic. Clubs: St. Paul Athletic (past. sec., dir.), Pool & Yacht, Optimists (past pres.), Gyro. Corporate, general, Personal injury (including property damage), Probate (including wills, trusts). Home: 8160 Emerald Ln Saint Paul MN 55125-3325

SHEAHAN, ROBERT EMMETT, lawyer, consultant; b. Chgo., May 20, 1942; s. Robert Emmett and Lola Jean (Moore) S.; m. Pati Smith, Mar. 20, 1991. BA, Ill. Wesleyan U., 1964; JD, Duke U., 1967; MBA, U. Chgo., 1970. Bar: Ill. 1967, La. 1975, N.C. 1978. Vol. VISTA, N.Y.C., 1967-68; trial atty. NLRB, Milw., New Orleans, 1970-75; ptnr. Jones, Walker, Waechter, Poitevent, Carrere & Denegre, New Orleans, 1975-78; pvt. practice High Point, N.C., 1978—. Bd. dirs. Inst. for Effective Mgmt., Bus. Pubis. Inst. Author: Employees and Drug Abuse: An Employer's Handbook, 1994, The Encyclopedia of Drugs in the Workplace, Labor and Employment Law in North Carolina, 1991, Personnel and Employment Law in North Carolina, 1992, Desk Book of Labor and Employment Law for Healthcare Employers' Desk Manual, 1995, North Carolina Lawyers' Desk Book; contbg. author: The Developing Labor Law, 1975—; editor: The World of Personnel; contbg. editor: Employee Testing and the Law; contbr. periodic supplements N.C. Gen. Practice Deskbook, 1992—. Bd. dirs. High Point United Way, 1979-83; mem. congl. action com. High Point C. of C., chmn., 1991—, bd. dirs., 1996—. Mem. ABA, N.C. Bar Assn., High Point Bar Assn., Ill. Bar Assn., La. Bar Assn., Sedgefield (N.C.) Country Club, String and Splinter Club, Bald Head Island Club. Republican. Roman Catholic. Labor (including EEOC, Fair Labor Standards Act, labor-management relations, NLRB, OSHA). Home: 101 Bellwood Ct Jamestown NC 27282 Office: Robert E Sheahan & Assocs 603 Eastchester Dr Ste B High Point NC 27262-7647

SHEARER, WILLIAM KENNEDY, lawyer, publisher; b. Marysville, Calif., Jan. 21, 1931; s. William and Eva (Kennedy) S.; m. Eileen Mary Knowland; Nov. 25, 1956; 1 child, Nancy Lorena; stepchildren: David, Douglas, Dianne. BA, San Diego State U., 1955; JD, Western State U., 1975. Bar: Calif. 1975, U.S. Dist. Ct. (so. dist.) Calif. 1975, U.S. Ct. Claims 1976, U.S. Supreme Ct. 1982, U.S. Ct. Appeals (fed. cir.) 1982, U.S. Ct. Appeals (9th cir.) 1983. Legis. asst. to Congressman James Utt, 1953, 55-56; exec. dir. San Diego County Rep. Cen. Com., 1956-58; pub. Oceanside-Carlsbad Banner, Oceanside, Calif., 1958-63; adminstrv. asst. Assemblyman E.R. Barnes, Sacramento, Calif., 1963-65; polit. campaign cons. Banner Advt., San Diego, Los Angeles, 1964-75; atty. Duke, Gerstel, Shearer LLP, San Diego, 1975—. Pub. newsletters Calif. Statesman, 1962—, Legis. Survey, 1963—, Fgn. Policy Rev., 1972—, Am. Ind., 1974—. Rep. nominee for State Assembly, San Diego County, 1956, 58; state chmn. Am. Ind. Party, Calif., 1967-70, nat. chmn. 1968-71, 73-77; nat. vice chmn. U.S. Taxpayers Party, 1992-96, chmn. 1996-99; Am. Ind. nominee for Gov., 1970; adv. com. Elections Com., Calif. Legislature, Sacramento, 1971-76; mem. Blue Ribbon Task Force on Calif.'s Home Constrn. Industry, 1996-97; bd. dirs. San Diego Gilbert & Sullivan Co., 1984-90, pres. 1986-88, v.p., 1985-86, 88-90. With U.S. Army, 1953-55. Mem. Calif. Bar Assn., San Diego County Bar Assn. Avocations: ancient near eastern history, gardening, music. Home: 8160 Palm St Lemon Grove CA 91945-3028 Office: Duke Gerstel Shearer LLP WKS 101 W Broadway Ste 1120 San Diego CA 92101-8296

SHEARING, MIRIAM, state supreme court justice; b. Waverly, NY, Feb. 24, 1935; BA, Cornell U., 1956; JD, Boston Coll., 1964. Bar: Calif. 1965, Nev. 1969. Justice of peace Las Vegas Justice Ct., 1977-81; judge Nev. Dist. Ct., 1983-92, chief judge, 1986; justice Nevada Supreme Ct., Carson City, 1993-97, chief justice, 1997—. Mem. ABA, Am. Judicature Soc. (chair 2001-), Nev. Judges Assn. (sec. 1978), Nev. Dist. Ct. Judges Assn. (sec. 1984-85, pres. 1986-87), State Bar Nev., State Bar Calif., Clark County Bar Assn. Democrat. E-mail: shearing@nvcourts.state.nv.us.*

SHEARN, MICHAEL JOSEPH, lawyer, mediator, arbitrator; BA with honors, U. Tex., 1973, JD, 1976; Cert. Internat. Law, London Sch. Econs., 1974. Bar: D.C. 1976, Tex. 1976, U.S. Supreme Ct. 1980. Assoc. Surrey & Morse, Washington, 1976-80; shareholder Law, Snakard, Gambill, Ft. Worth, 1981-84, Cox & Smith, San Antonio, 1984-90; gen. counsel Tex. Nat. Rsch. Lab. Commn., De Soto and Waxahachie, Tex., 1991; counsel Don McManus Law Offices, San Antonio, 1992-94; pvt. practice San Antonio, 1994—2000; assoc. gen. counsel Ilex Oncology Inc., San Antonio, 2000—. Troop com. mem. Boy Scouts Am., San Antonio, 1993—97; trustee Univ. Meth. Ch., San Antonio, 1995—97. Fellow: Tex. Bus. Law Found.; mem.: Phi Delta Phi, Phi Beta Kappa. General civil litigation, Commercial, contracts (including sales of goods; commercial financing), Corporate, general. Office: PO Box 781466 San Antonio TX 78278

SHEBLE, WALTER FRANKLIN, retired lawyer; b. Chestnut Hill, Pa., Sept. 14, 1926; s. Franklin and Harriett Elizabeth (Smith) S.; m. Nancy Altemus, July 7, 1956; 3 children. AB, Princeton U., 1948; JD, George Washington U., 1952, LLM, 1953. Bar: U.S. Dist. Ct. D.C. 1952, U.S. Ct. Appeals D.C. 1952, U.S. Supreme Ct. 1953, U.S. Ct. Appeals Md. 1960. Assoc. Hudson & Creyke, Washington, 1953-56, H. William Tanaka, Washington, 1956-61, 63-66; cons. Office of Pres., Washington, 1961-63; spl. asst. to postmaster gen., U.S. rep. Univ. Postal Union, Bern, Switzerland, 1966-70; spl. asst. to gen. counsel Interam. Devel. Bank, Washington, 1970-88. Trustee New Eng. Coll. Mem. bd. mgrs. Chevy Chase Village, 1985-89; pres. Parents Assn. Nat. Cathedral Sch., 1969-70, mem. governing bd. 1970. Mem. ABA (exec. coun. gen. practice sect. 1982-87), Bar Assn. D.C., Colonial Club, Barristers Club, Met. Club, Chevy Chase Club. Avocations: gardening, surf fishing. General practice, Public international, Legislative.

SHEDD, DENNIS W. federal judge; b. 1953; BA, Wofford Coll., 1975; JD, U. S.C., 1978; LLM, Georgetown U., 1980. Bar: S.C. Mem. staff U.S. Senator Strom Thurmond, 1978-88; chief counsel U.S. Senate Jud. Com., Washington, 1985-86; of counsel Bethea, Jordan & Griffin, Columbia, S.C.,

1988-90; pvt. practice, 1989-90; judge U.S. Dist. Ct. S.C., Greenville, 1991—. Adj. prof. U. S.C., 1989-90. Mem. S.C. Bar Assn., Richland County Bar Assn., Phi Beta Kappa. Office: US Courthouse 100 Laurel St Columbia SC 29201-2431*

SHEEDY, KATHLEEN ANN, lawyer; b. June 18, 1956; d. Patrick Thomas Sheedy and Margaret Pelkey Mulvaney; m. Mark Louis Pedriani, Sept. 25, 1982; children: Gabrielle, Katherine, Jennifer. BS in Bus. Adminstrn., Georgetown U., 1978; JD, Marquette U., 1981. Bar: Wis. 1981, Ill. 1981, U.S. Dist. Ct. (no. dist.) Ill. 1981, U.S. Dist. Ct. (ea. dist.) Wis. 1981. Assoc. Chapman & Cutler, Chgo., 1981-83; mgr. Peat Marwick, Paris, 1983-84; assoc. Quarles & Brady, Milw., 1984-86; sr. mgr. KPMG Peat Marwick, Paris, 1986-90; sr. atty. Kohler (Wis.) Co., 1991—. Commercial, contracts (including sales of goods; commercial financing), Corporate, general, Property, real (including real estate development, water). Office: Kohler Co Legal Dept 444 Highland Dr Kohler WI 53044-1500

SHEEHAN, LAWRENCE JAMES, lawyer; b. San Francisco, July 23, 1932; AB, Stanford U., 1957, LLB, 1959. Bar: Calif. 1960. Law clk. to chief judge U.S. Ct. Appeals 2d Cir., N.Y.C., 1959-60; assoc. O'Melveny & Myers, L.A., 1960-68, ptnr., 1969-94, of counsel, 1995—. D. dirs. FPA Mut. Funds, Source Capital, Inc. Mem. ABA, Los Angeles County Bar Assn., Calif. Bar Assn., Order of Coif. Corporate, general, Securities. Office: O Melveny & Myers 1999 Avenue Of The Stars Los Angeles CA 90067-6035 also: 400 S Hope St Los Angeles CA 90071-2801 E-mail: lsheehan@omm.com.

SHEEHAN, ROBERT C. lawyer; b. N.Y.C., Oct. 12, 1944; s. John Edward and Mary Elizabeth (Trede) Sheehan; m. Elizabeth Mary Mammen, Aug. 17, 1968; children: Elizabeth, Robert, William. BA, Boston Coll., 1966; LLB, Univ. Pa., Phila., 1969. Bar: NY 1970. Ptnr. Skadden, Arps, Slate, Meagher & Flom LLP, N.Y.C., 1978—, exec. ptnr., 1994—. Banking, Corporate, general, Mergers and acquisitions. Office: Skadden Arps Slate Meagher Flom LLP 4 Times Sq New York NY 10036-6595

SHEEHY, BARBARA, lawyer; b. Kalamazoo, Mich., Mar. 26, 1974; d. Francis Edmund and Florence Lois Sheehy. BA, Kalamazoo Coll., 1995; JD with high honors, U. Conn., 2000. Bar: Conn. 2000, U.S. Dist. Ct. Conn. 2001, N.Y. 2002, Ill. 2001. Law clk. Horton Shields & Cormier, Hartford, Conn., 2000; judical law clk. Appellate Ct. Conn., Hartford, 2000—01; assoc. Cummings & Lockwood, Hartford, 2001—03; nat. negotiator Nat. Treasury Employers Union, Washington, 2003—. Participant Lawyers for Children. Mem.: ABA, Ill. Bar Assn., N.Y. State Bar Assn., Conn. Bar Assn. Democrat. Avocations: travel, soccer, languages, rowing. Labor (including EEOC, Fair Labor Standards Act, labor-management relations, NLRB, OSHA), Civil rights, Education and schools. Office: NTEU Nat Office 1750 H St NW Ste 1000 Washington DC 20006 Business E-Mail: bsheehy@nteu.org.

SHEEHY, FRANCES DIANE, lawyer; b. Mason City, Iowa, Jan. 1, 1947; d. M. ARthur and Adeline K. (Huizel) McCoid; m. Michael J. Sheehy, DEc. 17, 1967 (div. June 1989); children: D. Michael, Peter J. BS in Acctg., Bus. adminstrn., U. Ariz., 1984, JD, 1987. Bar: Ariz. 1987, Fla. 1988, U.S. Tax Ct. 1987, U.S. Dist. Ct. (so. dist.) Fla. 1992. Spl. asst. U.S. atty. Chief Counsel IRS, Miami, 1987-92; assoc. Patricia A. Redmond, Miami, 1992; pvt. practice Ft. Lauderdale, Fla., 1992-94; ptnr. Gutter, Josepher, Ruffin & Sheehy, P.A., Ft. Lauderdale, 1994-96; pvt. practice Coconut Creek, Fla., 1996—. Adv. group IRS Commrs., 1996-98. Mem. Fla. Bar Assn. (govt. lawyers sect., exec. coun. 1990—), Fla. Assn. Women Lawyers, Dade County Bar Assn. Roman Catholic. Avocations: golf, reading, dancing. Bankruptcy, Taxation, general. Office: 1367 Lyons Rd Coconut Creek FL 33063-3908

SHEFFIELD, ALDEN DANIEL, JR., lawyer; b. St. Paul, Sept. 10, 1947; s. Alden Daniel Sheffield and Martha Terrell Yaeger; m. Pamela Roesner, Oct. 8, 1983; children: Charles Alden Sheffield, Elliot Alden Sheffield. BA, Colo. Coll., 1969; JD, U. Minn., 1974. Bar: Min. 1974, Ariz. 1975, Colo. 1991. Atty. Ryley Carlock & Applewhite, Phoenix, 1975-92; sole practice Colorado Springs, 1992—. With U.S. Army, 1970-72. General civil litigation, Condemnation (eminent domain), Property, real (including real estate development, water). Home: 1624 Culebra Pl Colorado Springs CO 80907-7333 Office: 24 South Weber St Ste 300 Colorado Springs CO 80903-1914

SHEFFIELD, FRANK ELWYN, lawyer; b. Tallahassee, Jan. 4, 1946; s. Byron Elmer and Essie Faustine (West) S.; m. Judith Elizabeth Powell, July 26, 1968 (div. July 1971); m. Janice Alicia Gentry, Feb. 22, 1975; stepchildren: Lorimer H. Blitch, Richard S. Noles; children: Brett Elwyn, Jennifer Alicia. BS in Mktg., Fla. State U., 1968, JD, 1972. Bar: Fla. 1972, U.S. Dist. Ct. (no. dist.) Fla. 1972, U.S. Ct. Appeals (5th cir.) 1975, U.S. Tax Ct. 1978, U.S. Ct. Appeals (11th cir.) 1982, U.S. Dist. Ct. (mid. dist.) Fla. 1983. Sole practice, Tallahassee, 1972, 73-78, 80—; assoc. Dye & Conner, Tallahassee, 1973; ptnr. Michaels, Sheffield, Perkins & Collins, Tallahassee, 1978-80; sole practice Tallahassee, 1980—. Mem. ABA, Fla. Bar Assn., Assn. Trial Lawyers Am., Acad. Fla. Trial Lawyers, Fla. Assn. Criminal Def. Lawyers, Delta Sigma Pi. Democrat. Mem. Assembly of God Ch. Avocations: woodworking, scuba diving, automobile restoration. General civil litigation, Criminal, Personal injury (including property damage). Home: 4028 Old Bainbridge Rd Tallahassee FL 32303-2110 Office: 906 Thomasville Rd Tallahassee FL 32303-6220 E-mail: fesattrny@aol.com.

SHEFMAN, DAUCIE ELANA, lawyer; b. Denver, Nov. 24, 1972; d. Michael Henry and Sue Ann Shefman. BA, U. Tex., 1994; JD, U. Houston, 1999. Bar: Tex. 2000, U.S. Dist. Ct. (so. dist.) Tex. 2000, U.S. Ct. Appeals (5th cir.) 2000. Intern Andersen Consulting, Austin, 1992—94; assoc. Columbus Realty Trust, Dallas, 1994—96; law clk. Schneider & McKinney, PC, Houston, 1997—99; pvt. practice Houston, 2000—. Found. Harris County Public Defender Law Ctr., 2003. Editor: Defender Mag., 2002—. Mem. civil rights com. Anti-Defamation League, Houston, 2002; mem. polit. leadership initiative Am. Israel Pub. Affairs Commn., Houston, 2001. Mem.: ACLU, Houston Young Lawyers Assn., So. Povertly Law Ctr. Jewish. Avocations: travel, running, water-skiing, reading. Criminal. Office: 1301 McKinney St #3100 Houston TX 77010 Office Fax: 713-951-9854. E-mail: daucie@aol.com.

SHEFTMAN, HOWARD STEPHEN, lawyer; b. Columbia, S.C., May 20, 1949; s. Nathan and Rena Mae (Kantor) S.; children from a previous marriage: Amanda Elaine, Emily Catherine; m. Karyn L. Jenkins. BS in Bus. Adminstrn., U. S.C., 1971, JD, 1974. Bar: S.C. 1974, U.S. Dist. Ct. 1975, U.S. Ct. Appeals (4th cir.) 1982. Assoc. Kirkland, Taylor & Wilson, West Columbia, S.C., 1974-75; ptnr. Sheftman, Oswald & Holland, West Columbia, 1975-77, Finkel & Altman, LLC, Columbia, 1977—. Pres. Met. Sertoma Club, 1986—87. Mem. S.C. Bar Assn. (chmn. practice and procedure com. 1999-2001), S.C. Trial Lawyers Assn. (chmn. domestic rels. sect. 1982-83, bd. govs. 1987-93, 94-98), Richland Bar Assn. Jewish. Federal civil litigation, State civil litigation, Family and matrimonial, Personal injury (including property damage). Office: Finkel & Altman LLC PO Box 1799 Columbia SC 29202-1799 E-mail: hsheftman@finkellaw.com.

SHEIKH, KEMAL A. lawyer; b. Aberdeen, Md., Jan. 14, 1956; s. Ramsey U. and Betty J. Nelson Sheikh. BA, Colby Coll., 1977; LLB magna cum laude, U. Edinburgh, Scotland, 1983; JD, U. Pa., 1985. Bar: N.Y. 1987. Assoc. Curtis, Mallet-Prevost Colt & Mosle, N.Y.C., 1985-97, spl. counsel, 1997—. Commercial, contracts (including sales of goods; commercial financing), Private international, Mergers and acquisitions. Office: Curtis Mallet-Prevost Colt & Mosle 101 Park Ave Fl 34 New York NY 10178-0061

SHEILS, DENIS FRANCIS, lawyer; b. Ridgewood, N.J., Apr. 7, 1961; s. Denis Francis and Anna Marie (Clifford) Sheils; m. Harriet A. Bonawitz, Sept. 17, 1988; children: Denis F., Dylan I., Matthew D. BA, La Salle Coll., 1983; JD, Fordham U., 1986. Bar: N.Y. 1987, Pa. 1987, U.S. Dist. Ct. (ea. dist.) Pa. 1987, U.S. Ct. Appeals (3d cir.) 1987, U.S. Dist. Ct. (so. and ea. dists.) N.Y. 1992, U.S. Supreme Ct. 1994, U.S. Dist. Ct. (no. dist.) N.Y. 1997, U.S. Ct. Appeals (2d cir.) 1999. Assoc. Kohn, Swift & Graf, PC, Phila., 1987-97, shareholder, 1997—. Active Lower Makefield Twp. Cable TV Adv. Bd. Mem. AAAS, ABA, Phila. Bar Assn. Roman Catholic. Federal civil litigation, General civil litigation, State civil litigation. Home: 2124 Ashley Rd Newtown PA 18940-3737 Office: Kohn Swift & Graf PC 21st Fl One South Broad St Philadelphia PA 19107 E-mail: dsheils@kohnswift.com.

SHEIMAN, RONALD LEE, lawyer; b. Bridgeport, Conn., Apr. 26, 1948; s. Samuel Charles and Rita Doris Sheiman; m. Deborah Joy Lovitky, Oct. 16, 1971; children: Jill, Laura. BA, U. Mich., 1970; JD, U. Conn., 1973; LLM in Taxation, NYU, 1974. Bar: Conn. 1973, U.S. Ct. Appeals (2d cir.) 1975, U.S. Supreme Ct. 1977, D.C. 1978, N.Y. 1981. Tax atty. Office of Regional Counsel IRS, Phila., 1974-78; pvt. practice Westport, Conn., 1978—. Mem. adv. bd. Early Childhood Resource and Info. Ctr., N.Y. Pub. Libr., N.Y.C. Mem.: ABA, Conn. Bar Assn., Fed. Bar Assn. Corporate taxation, Estate taxation, Personal income taxation. Home: 128 Random Rd Fairfield CT 06432-1408 Office: 1804 Post Rd E Westport CT 06880-5607

SHEINFELD, MYRON M. lawyer, educator; b. Mass., Mar. 18, 1930; s. Robert and Sadye (Rosenberg) S.; m. Christina Trzcinski, Mar. 30, 1985; children: Scott, Tom. BA, Tulane U., 1951; JD, U. Mich., 1954. Bar: Mich. 1954, Tex. 1956. Rschr. Legis. Rsch. Inst., U. Mich., 1954; asst. U. S. atty. So. Dist. Tex., 1958-60; law clk. U.S. Dist. Judge, 1960-61; ptnr. Strickland, Gordon & Sheinfeld, Houston, 1961-68; shareholder, of counsel Sheinfeld, Maley & Kay, P.C., Houston, 1968-96, counsel to firm, 1006—. Adj. prof. law U. Tex.; mem. Nat. Bankruptcy Conf.; former chmn. Tex. Bankruptcy Adv. Commn.; bd. dirs. Nabors Industries; mem. Tex. Bd. Legal Specialization. Bd. editors Practical Lawyer, Collier On Bankruptcy (15th edit.); contbr. articles to profl. jours. With JAG U.S. Army, 1955-58. Fellow Am. Coll. Bankruptcy; mem. State Bar Tex., Houston Ctr. Club (bd. dirs.), Phi Beta Kappa, Phi Sigma Alpha. Bankruptcy, Mergers and acquisitions, Taxation, general. Office: Akin Gump Strauss Hauer & Feld LLP Pennzoil Place-South Tower 711 Louisiana StreetSte 1900 Houston TX 77002 E-mail: msheinfeld@akingump.com.

SHELBY, MICHAEL T. lawyer; b. Nov. 1958; BS, Tex. A&M U., 1981; JD, U. Tex., 1984. Asst. U.S. atty. So. Dist. Tex., 1989—91, 1992—97, Dist. Ariz., 1997—2001; U.S. atty. So. Dist. Tex., 2002—. Office: PO Box 61129 910 Travis St Houston TX 77208*

SHELBY, RICHARD CRAIG, senator, former congressman; b. Birmingham, Ala., May 6, 1934; s. O.H. and Alice L. (Skinner) S.; m. Annette Nevin, June 11, 1960; children: Richard Craig, Claude Nevin. AB, U. Ala., 1957, LLB, 1963. Bar: Ala. 1961, D.C. 1979. Law clk. Supreme Ct. of Ala., 1961-62; practice law Tuscaloosa, Ala., 1963-79; prosecutor City of Tuscaloosa, 1964-70; spl. asst. atty. gen. State of Ala., 1969-70; U.S. magistrate No. Dist. of Ala., 1966-70; mem. Ala. State Senate, 1970-78, 96th-99th Congresses from 7th Ala. dist., 1979-87; mem. energy and commerce com.; mem. vets. affairs com.; U.S. senator from Ala., 1987—; mem. com. on appropriations, com. on banking, housing, and urban affairs, chmn. com. on govtl. affairs, spl. com. on aging. Active Boy Scouts Am.; pres. Tuscaloosa County Mental Health Assn., 1969-70; bd. govs. Nat. Legis. Conf., 1975-78. Mem. ABA, Ala. Bar Assn., Tuscaloosa County Bar Assn., D.C. Bar Assn., Exch. Club. Republican. Presbyterian. Home: 1414 High Forest Dr N Tuscaloosa AL 35406-2152 Office: US Senate 110 Hart Senate Bldg Washington DC 20510-0001

SHELDON, J. MICHAEL, lawyer, educator; b. Mt. Carmel, Pa., Sept. 1, 1951; s. Lloyd Loomis and Helen Roberta (Sosnoski) S. AA, Harrisburg (Pa.) Community Coll., 1978; BS, Pa. State U., 1980; M in Journalism, Temple U., 1991; JD, Widener U. Sch. Law, 1996. News announcer Sta. WNUE-AM, Ft. Walton Beach, Fla., 1974-76, Sta. WFEC-AM, Harrisburg, 1977-78; announcer Sta. WCMB-AM, Wormleysburg, Pa., 1979-80; writer newspaper Pa. Beacon, Harrisburg, 1982-85; media specialist Commonwealth Media Svcs., Harrisburg, 1982-86; dir. communications Pa. Poultry Fedn., Harrisburg, 1986-89; news anchor Sta. WGAL-TV, Lancaster, Pa., 1989-90; dir. pub. rels. Profl. Ins. Agts. - Pa., Md., Del., Mechanicsburg, Pa., 1990-92; v.p. comm. and mktg. United Way of the Capital Region, Harrisburg, Pa., 1992-93, Widener U. Sch. of Law, 1994-96; pres. Open Mike Comm., Harrisburg, 1994—. Mem. adj. faculty dept. journalism Temple U., 1992; mem. faculty dept. humanities Pa. State U., 1995-97, 99—. Contbg. author: Pa. 12th Annual Civil Litigation Update, Spoliation of Evidence: Why You Can't Have Your Cake and Eat it Too, 1999; contbg. editor: A Practical Guidebook to Massachusetts Aviation Law, 1999; Contbr. articles to profl. jours. Pub. rels. advisor Cen. Pa. Leukemia Soc., Harrisburg, 1989-90; media advisor Polit. Campaign, Hershey, Pa., 1990. With USAF, 1969-73. Mem. U.S. Fed. Mid. Dist. Bar, Pa. Bar, Dauphin County Bar, VFW (life), Am. Legion, Knights of Columbus (4th degree Knight), Chi Gamma Iota, Delta Tau Kappa. Republican. Roman Catholic. Avocations: motorcycles, music, electronics, martial arts. Office: 6059 Allentown Blvd Harrisburg PA 17112-2672

SHELDON, TERRY EDWIN, lawyer, business consultant, advisor; b. Sacramento, June 22, 1945; s. Earl M. and Christine M. S.; m. Jan L. Winters, Aug. 26, 1966; children: Jeffrey, Tiffini, Melissa. BS magna cum laude, Abilene Christian U., 1967; JD, So. Meth. U., 1970. Bar: Calif. 1970. Assoc. Bronson, Bronson & McKinnon, San Francisco, 1970-74; gen. counsel, also dir. Consol. Capital Cos., Emeryville, Calif., 1974-83, exec. v.p., chief oper. officer, 1984-85, cons., advisor, 1986-87; pres., trustee Consol. Capital Spl. Trust, 1980-85; exec. v.p., trustee Consol. Capital Realty Investors, 1975-85, Consol. Capital Income Trust, 1978-85, Consol. Capital Income Opportunity Trust, 1983-85, Consol. Capital Income Opportunity Trust 2, 1985; chmn. Nat. Syndication Forum (a div. of RESSI), 1981-82; real estate securities specialist RESSI. V.p., prin. Alpha Venture Corp., Walnut Creek, Calif., 1987; bus. cons., 1988—. Chmn. bd. visitors adv. com. Coll. of Bus. Adminstrn. Abilene Christian U., 1990. Mem. ABA, Calif. Bar Assn., Nat. Assn. Securities Dealers (direct participation programs com., real estate com., standing adv. com. to bd. govs. 1980-83), Nat. Syndication Forum. Republican. Mem. Ch. of Christ.

SHELL, LOUIS CALVIN, lawyer; b. Dinwiddie County, Va., Dec. 8, 1925; s. Roger LaFayette and Susie Ann (Hill) S.; m. Barbara Marie Pamplin, Aug. 5, 1950; children: Pamela Shell Baskervill, Patricia Shell Caulkins. BA, U. Va., 1946, LLB, 1947. Bar: Va. 1947. Sr. trial atty. Shell, Johnson, Andrews Baskervill & Petersburg. Va. chmn. Petersburg Electoral Bd., 1952, vice mayor city coun., 1957-60; trustee Petersburg Dist. United Meth. Ch. Named Outstanding Young Man, Petersburg Jr. C. of C., 1956. Fellow Am. Coll. Trial Lawyers; mem. Petersburg Bar Assn., Va. State Bar Assn. (coun. 1972-75), Kiwanis. State civil litigation, Personal injury (including property damage). Home: 10813 Lakeview Dr Petersburg VA 23805-7152 Office: Shell Johnson Andrews & Baskervill PO Box 3090 Petersburg VA 23805-3090

SHELLER, JOHN WILLARD, lawyer; b. L.A., Oct. 29, 1950; s. Willard Newton and Barbara (Tremaine) S.; m. Mary Elizabeth Hodor, Aug. 9, 1975; children: Matthew John, James Henry. BA, Stanford U., 1972; JD, Loyola U., L.A., 1975. Bar: Calif. 1975. Ptnr. Haight, Brown & Bonesteel, Santa Monica, Calif., 1975—; pub. Melville Press, Pacific Palisades, Calif., 1996—. Mem. Am. Bd. Trial Advs. Contbr. articles to profl. jours. Mem. Calif. State Bar Assn., Los Angeles County Bar Assn., So. Calif. Assn. Def. Counsel, Fedn. Ins. and Corp. Counsel, L.A. Country Club. Avocation: golf. General civil litigation. Home: 15461 De Pauw St Pacific Palisades CA 90272-4370 Office: Haight Brown & Bonesteel 6080 Center Dr Ste 800 Los Angeles CA 90045-1574 E-mail: jsheller@hbblaw.com.

SHELLER, PATRICK MICHAEL, lawyer; b. Altoona, Pa., Apr. 21, 1961; s. Francis Xavier and Gertrude Ann (Johnson) S. BA, St. Lawrence U., 1983; JD, Union U., 1986. Bar: N.Y. 1987, D.C. 1993. Staff atty. Bur. of Competition FTC, Washington, 1986-88, atty. advisor to chmn., 1988-89; assoc. McKenna & Cuneo, Washington, 1989-93; atty. Eastman Kodak Co., Rochester, NY, 1993—99, chief antitrust counsel, 1999—. Mem. ABA, D.C. Bar Assn. Avocations: golf, photography, jogging, travel. Antitrust, Private international, Commercial, contracts (including sales of goods; commercial financing). Office: Eastman Kodak Co PO Box 92988 Rochester NY 14692-9088

SHELTON, DOROTHY DIEHL REES, lawyer; b. Manila, Sept. 16; d. William Walter John and Hedwig Diehl; m. Charles W. Rees, Jr., June 15; children: Jane Rees Stebbins, John B., Anne Rees Slack, David C.,; m. Thomas C. Shelton, Mar. 4, 1977. BA in Music, Stanford Univ.; JD, Western State Univ. Coll. Law. Bar: Calif. U.S. Dist. Ct. (so. dist.) Calif. Pvt. practice, San Diego, 1977—. Mem. ABA, Calif. State Bar, San Diego County Bar Assn., Consumer Attys. San Diego, Stanford U. Alumni Assn., Jr. League San Diego, Gt. Pyrenees Club Am., Dachshund Club Am., Nu Beta Epsilon. Avocations: gardening, reading, great pyrenees dogs. General civil litigation, Criminal, General practice. Office: 110 W C St Ste 711 San Diego CA 92101-3906

SHEN, MICHAEL, lawyer; b. Nanking, Jiangsu, Peoples Republic of China, Aug. 15, 1948; came to U.S. 1951; s. James Cheng Yee and Grace (Pai) S.; m. Marina Manese (div.); m. Pamela Nan Bradford, Aug. 12, 1983; 1 child, Jessica Li. BA, U. Chgo., 1969; MA, U. Pa., 1970; JD, Rutgers U., 1979. Bar: U.S. Dist. Ct. N.J. 1979, N.Y. 1980, U.S. Dist. Ct. (so., no. and ea. dists.) N.Y. 1980, N.J. 1981, U.S. Ct. Appeals (2d cir.) 1987, U.S. Supreme Ct. 1988, U.S. Ct. Appeals (3rd cir.) 1996. Staff atty. Bedford Stuyvesant Legal Svcs., Bklyn., 1979-80, Com. for Interns and Residents, N.Y.C., 1980-81; ptnr. Shneyer & Shen, P.C., N.Y.C. 1981—. Pres. bd. dirs. Asian Am. Legal Def. and Edn. Fund, N.Y.c.; of counsel 318 Restaurant Workers Union, N.Y.C., 1984—. Bd. dirs. Nat. Asian Pacific Am. Legal Consortium, N.Y.C., Nat. Employment Law Project; past bd. dirs. N.Y. Civil Liberties Union, N.Y.C., 1987-98. Mem. Internat. Platform Assn., Nat. Employees Lawyers Assn., N.Y. State Bar Assn., N.Y. County Bar Assn., Nat. Lawyers Guild. Avocations: arts, reading. Civil rights, Labor (including EEOC, Fair Labor Standards Act, labor-management relations, NLRB, OSHA), Workers' compensation. Office: Shneyer & Shen PC 2109 Broadway Ste 206 New York NY 10023-2106 also: 1085 Cambridge Rd Teaneck NJ 07666-1901 E-mail: shenlaw@compuserve.com.

SHENKER, JOSEPH C. lawyer; b. N.Y.C., Nov. 6, 1956; BS in Acctg., CUNY, 1977; JD, Columbia U., 1980. Bar: N.Y. 1981, U.S. Dist. Ct. (ea. and so. dists.) N.Y 1981, U.S. Claims Ct. 1982, U.S. Tax Ct. 1982, U.S. Supreme Ct. 1988. Assoc. Sullivan & Cromwell, N.Y.C., 1980-86, ptnr., 1986—. Contbr. articles to profl. jours. Bd. dirs. Am. Friends of Yeshivat Kerem B'yavneh, Inc., Rabbinical Sem. of Am.; pres. Met. N.Y. Coordinating Coun. on Jewish Poverty, Inc. Fellow Am. Bar Found.; mem. ABA, N.Y. State Bar Assn., Assn. Bar City N.Y. Corporate, general, Property, real (including real estate development, water), Securities. Office: Sullivan & Cromwell 125 Broad St Fl 33 New York NY 10004-2400 E-mail: shenkerj@sullcrom.com.

SHENTOV, OGNJAN V. lawyer, researcher; b. Sofia, Bulgaria, Aug. 22, 1958; came to U.S., 1986; s. Varban and Lalka Shentov; m. Lubima Kalinkova, Feb. 14, 1994. BS, Tech. U., Sofia, 1984; MS, U. Calif., Santa Barbara, 1988, PhD, 1991; JD, N.Y. Law Sch., 1997. Bar: N.Y. 1998, U.S. Dist. Ct. (ea. and so. dists.) N.Y. 1998, U.S. Ct. Appeals (fed. cir.) 1998. Tchg. and rsch. asst. U. Calif., 1986-91; postdoctoral rsch. asst. SUNY, Stony Brook, 1991—92; assoc. Pennie & Edmonds LLP, N.Y.C., 1992—. Co-author: Handbook for Dig. Sig. Proc., 1991; contbr. articles to profl. jours. Me. IEEE. Federal civil litigation, Intellectual property, Patent. Office: Pennie & Edmonds LLP 1155 Ave of Americas New York NY 10036

SHEPARD, JULIAN LEIGH, lawyer, humanitarian; b. St. Paul, Feb. 17, 1957; s. Frank and Beatrice (Getsug) S. BS, Ind. U., 1980, JD, 1983; postgrad., Am. U., 1995-98. Bar: Pa. 1985, Ind. 1984, D.C. 1987; U.S. Ct. Appeals (D.C. cir.) 1984; U.S. Dist. Ct. (so. dist.) Ind. 1984. Atty. Nat. Assn. Broadcasters, Washington, 1984-86, asst. gen. counsel, 1986-87; counselor at law Heron, Burchette, Ruckert & Rothwell, Washington, 1987-88; sr. policy adv. mass media Nat. Telecommunications & Info. Adminstrn./U.S. Dept. Comm., Washington, 1988-90; v.p., gen. counsel Assn. for Maximum Svc. TV, Inc., Washington, 1990-95; atty., shareholder Verner, Liipfert, Bernhard, McPherson & Hand, Washington, 1995—2001; ptnr. Venable, Baetjer, Howard and Civiletti, L.L.P., 2001—. Mem. fed. spectrum planning and policy adv. com., U.S. Dept. Commerce, Washington, 1992—. Co-chmn. editorial adv. bd. Fed. Comms. Law Jour., Washington, 1992-94; contbr. articles to profl. jours. Bd. vis. Georgetown U. Inst. on Comparative Polit. and Econ. Systems, 1984-95; prin. Coun. for Excellence in Govt., Washington, 1990-. Bd. Regents Fund for Am. Studies, Washington, 1999—; mem. ABA (law practice mgmt. sect. leadership activities bd. 1995-96), Fed. Comms. Bar Assn. (law jour. com. 1992—), Ind. State Bar Assn., Phi Delta Phi (Nat. Balfour scholar 1983). Avocations: visual arts, scuba diving, photography, boating. Administrative and regulatory, Communications, Legislative. Home: PO Box 6643 Mc Lean VA 22106-6643 Office: Venable Baetjer Howard & Civiletti LLP 1201 New York Ave NW Ste 1000 Washington DC 20005-3917

SHEPARD, RANDALL TERRY, state supreme court chief justice; b. Lafayette, Ind., Dec. 24, 1946; s. Richard Schilling and Dorothy Ione (Donlen) S.; m. Amy Wynne MacDonell, May 7, 1988; one child, Martha MacDonell. AB cum laude, Princeton U., 1969; JD, Yale U., 1972; LLM, U. Va., 1995; LLD (hon.), U. So. Ind., 1995. Bar: Ind. 1972, U.S. Dist. Ct. (so. dist.) Ind. 1972. Spl. asst. to under sec. U.S. Dept. Transp., Washington, 1972-74; exec. asst. to mayor City of Evansville, Ind., 1974-79; judge Vanderburgh Superior Ct., Evansville, 1980-85; assoc. justice Ind. Supreme Ct., Indpls., 1985-87, chief justice, 1987—. Instr. U. Evansville, 1975-78, Indiana U., 1995, 99 Author: Preservation Rules and Regulations, 1980; contbr. articles to profl. publs. Bd. advisors Nat. Trust for Hist. Preservation, 1980-87, chmn. bd. advisors, 1983-85, trustee, 1987-96; dir. Hist. Landmarks Found. Ind., 1983—, chmn., 1989-92, hon. chmn., 1992—; chmn. State Student Assistance Commn. on Ind., 1981-85; chmn. Ind. Commn. on Bicentennial of U.S. Constn., 1986-91; vice chmn. Vanderburgh County Rep. Ctrl. Com., 1977-80. Recipient Friend of Media award Cardinal States chpt. Sigma Delta Chi, 1979, Disting. Svc. award Evansville Jaycees, 1982, Herbert Harley award Am. Judicature Soc., 1992. Mem. ABA (coun. mem. sect. on legal edn. 1991—, chair sect. on legal edn. 1997—, immediate past chair appellate judges conf. 1997-98), Ind. Bar Assn., Ind. Judges Assn., Princeton Club (N.Y.), Capitol Hill Club (Washington), Columbia Club (Indpls.). Republican. Methodist. Home: 3644 Totem Ln Indianapolis IN 46208-4171 Office: Ind Supreme Ct 304 State House Indianapolis IN 46204-2213

SHEPARD, ROBERT M. lawyer, investment banker, engineer; b. Amityville, N.Y., Feb. 15, 1932; s. Sidney M. and Undine L. (Lehmann) Shapiro; m. Barbara S. Stannard, June 25, 1955 (div. 1980); children: Karen Michele Shepard Sweer, Daniel Robert; m. Joanne E. Devlin, May 16, 1981 (div. 1993); m. Martha Kothe, Nov. 24, 1999. B.C.E., Cornell U., 1954; MBA, Hofstra Coll., 1960; LL.B., Yale U., 1963; LLM, NYU, 1988. Bar: N.Y. 1964; registered profl. engr., N.Y., Conn. Project engr. Lockwood Kessler & Bartlett, Syosset, N.Y., 1956-60; assoc. atty. Cravath, Swaine & Moore, N.Y.C. and Paris, 1963-70; gen. ptnr. Kuhn, Loeb & Co., N.Y.C., 1970-77; sr. v.p. Donaldson, Lufkin & Jenrette, N.Y.C., 1977-83; gen. ptnr. Donovan Leisure Newton & Irvine, N.Y.C., 1983-89, Adler & Shepard, N.Y.C., 1989-91, Shepard & van Essche, N.Y.C., 1991, Ballon Stoll Bader & Nadler, P.C., N.Y.C., 1992—. Note and comment editor: Yale Law Jour., 1962-63. Bd. dirs. N.Y. Grand Opera, Regency Whist Club. Recipient Fuertes Medal Cornell U., 1953 Mem. ABA, Am. N.Y. State Bar Assn., Pub. Power Assn., Nat. Assn. Bond Lawyers, Order of Coif, Union League Club, Regency Whist Club, Inc., Tau Beta Pi, Chi Epsilon. Municipal (including bonds), Securities, Corporate taxation. Home: 750 Park Ave Apt 2C New York NY 10021-4252 Office: Ballon Stoll Bader & Nadler 1450 Broadway New York NY 10018-2201

SHEPHERD, JOHN FREDERIC, lawyer; b. Oak Park, Ill., May 22, 1954; s. James Frederic Shepherd and Margaret Joanne (Crotchett) Woollen; children: Eliza Marion, Justine Catherine. AB magna cum laude, Dartmouth Coll., Hanover, N.H., 1976; JD, U. Denver, 1979. Bar: Colo. 1979, U.S. Dist. Ct. Colo. 1979, D.C. 1981, U.S. Dist. Ct. D.C. 1981, U.S. Ct. Appeals (10th cir.) 1981, U.S. Ct. Appeals (D.C. cir.) 1982, U.S. Ct. Appeals (9th cir.) 1990, U.S. Supreme Ct. 1984. Assoc. Holland & Hart, Denver, 1979-81, Washington, 1981-85, ptnr., 1985-87, Denver, 1987—; natural resources disting. practitioner in residence U. Denver Coll. Law, 1998. Reporter Mineral Law Newsletter, 1985-92. Mem. 50 for Colo., Denver, 1989. Mem. ABA (chmn. pub. lands and land use com. 1991-93, mem. coun. for sect. of natural resources energy and environ. law 1993-96), Rocky Mountain Mineral Law Found. (mem. long-range planning com. 1988-2001, trustee 1993-95), Dartmouth Alumni Club (pres. Washington chpt. 1985-86, trustee Rocky Mt. chpt., 1998-2001), Denver Athletic Club. Avocations: flyfishing, basketball, running. Oil, gas, and mineral, Environmental, Natural resources. Home: 320 Clermont St Pkwy Denver CO 80220-5642 Office: Holland & Hart 555 17th St Ste 3200 Denver CO 80202-3950 E-mail: JShepherd@Hollandhart.com.

SHEPPARD, BEN H., JR., lawyer; b. Amarillo, Tex., Jan. 18, 1943; BA, U. North Tex., 1965; LLB, U. Tex., 1968. Bar: Tex. 1968. Mem. Vinson & Elkins L.L.P., Houston. Adj. prof. U. Houston Law Ctr. Editor-in-chief: Internat. Arbitration News. Adv. bd. Inst. Transnat. Arbitration. Mem. Chancellors, Order of Coif, Phi Delta Phi. Oil, gas, and mineral. Office: Vinson & Elkins 3300 First City Tower 1001 Fannin St Ste 3300 Houston TX 77002-6706

SHEPPARD, BERTON SCOTT, lawyer; b. Zanesville, Ohio, Aug. 6, 1936; s. Isaac and Ruth (Scott) S.; m. Regina Polka, Oct. 6, 1962; children: Kristina M., Cynthia A. BS in Agr. Engring., Mich. State U., 1958; JD, Northwestern U., 1961. Bar: Ill. 1962, U.S. Dist. Ct. (no. dist.) Ill. 1962, U.S. Dist. Ct. Md. 1965, U.S. Ct. Appeals (4th cir.) 1970, U.S. Ct. Appeals (7th cir.) 1974, U.S. Ct. Appeals (fed. cir.) 1982, U.S. Ct. Customs and Patent Appeals 1976, U.S. Supreme Ct. 1976. With Leydig, Voit & Mayer, Ltd. and predecessor firms, Chgo., 1959-62, assoc., 1962-70, ptnr., 1971-2000, of counsel, 2001—. Mem. editl. bd. Northwestern Law Rev., 1960-61. With USAR, 1961. Mich. State U. scholar, 1954-58, Hardy scholar Northwestern U., 1958-61. Mem. ABA, Am. Intellectual Property Law Assn., Fed. Cir. Bar Assn., Fed. Bar Assn., Intellectual Property Law Assn. Chgo., Lawyers Club Chgo. Republican. Federal civil litigation, Patent, Trademark and copyright. Office: Leydig Voit & Mayer 2 Prudential Plz Ste 4900 Chicago IL 60601 E-mail: bertons202@earthlink.net.

SHEPPARD, LAURA E. lawyer; b. Newton, Mass., Oct. 11, 1963; d. Leonard Edward and Alice L. Sheppard; m. Kevin R. Bathalon, Sept. 30, 2000. BA in Legal Studies, U. Mass., 1987; JD, Mass. Sch. Law, 1996. Bar: Mass. 96, U.S. Dist. Ct. Mass. 97, U.S. Ct. Appeals (1st cir.) 97, NH 98. Assoc. Joel H. Schwartz, P.C., Boston, 1996—2000, Hamblett & Kerrigan, P.A., Nashua, NH, 2000—. Mem.: Nashua C. of C. (mem. Leadership Greater Nashua 2000—01). Personal income taxation. Office: Hamblett & Kerrigan 146 Main St Nashua NH 03060 Fax: 603-880-0458. E-mail: lsheppard@hamker.com.

SHER, DENISE LINDA, judge; b. Oct. 26, 1954; d. Leonard and Ruth Harvey; m. Robert G. Sher, June 26, 1976; children: Noah, Sarah, Janelle. BA, Queens Coll., 1975; JD, Hofstra U., 1978. Bar: NY 79, U.S. Supreme Ct., U.S. Dist. Ct. (ea. and so. dists.) NY, U.S. Tax Ct. Contbr. articles to profl. jours. Bd. dirs. sisterhood Hewlett-East Rockaway Jewish Ctr.; mem. Peninsula Counseling Ctr., Ctrl. Coun. PTA, Hewlett; former bd. dirs. Woodmere Sch. Dist.; mem. Five Towns Cmty. Chest; life mem. Hewlett Hadassah; mem. Yashar, Hewlett-East Rockaway ORT; former pub. works chmn. Village of Hewlett Harbor, Hewlett Harbor; bd. dirs. Family and Children's Assn. L.I.; former bd. dirs. Ctr. for Family Resources, Child Care Coun. Nassau County; former coun. Island Park C. of C., Nassau County Coun. Chambers; former mem. planned giving com. Am. Cancer Soc.; former mem. bd. dirs. Friedberg South Shore YJCC; mem. Tilles Cmty. Com.; former mem. legis. com. L.I. Com. for Soviet Jewry. Named Woman of Yr., Island Park Jewish Ctr., 1988, Alumnus of Yr., Phi Alpha Delta, 1998; named one of Top 50 Women, L.I. Bus. News, 2002, Top 90 Women, Girl Scouts of Nassau County, 2002; named to L.I. Ctr. Hall of Fame; recipient Pathfinder award, Town of Hempstead, 1992, Martin Luther King Jr. Living the Dream award, 1994, Woman of Yr. award, Ct. Officers Benevolent Assn. Nassau County, 1999, Pub. Svcs. award, Indian Kerala Ctr., 2000, Woman of Distinction award, Soroptimist of Nassau County Inc., 2001. Mem.: ABA, L.I. Ctr. for Bus. and Profl. Women (Achievers award), Nassau County Dist. Ct. Judges Assn., NY Dist. Ct. Judge's Assn., Nassau Lawyers' Assn. L.I., Inc., Nat. Assn. Women Judges, Jewish Lawyer's Assn. of Nassau County, NY State Bar Assn., NY State Women's Bar Assn., Nassau-Suffolk Women's Bar Assn. (bd. dirs., mem. jud. screening com.), Nassau County Bar Assn. (dir. Acad. of Law, mem. matrimonial com., mem. estates and trusts com., mem. young lawyers com., mem. cmty .edn. and pub. rels. com., mem. mentor program, active mock trial, mock jury selection, moot ct. competition, Vol. Lawyer award 1991), Columbian Lawyers Assn. (assoc.), Kiwanis. Office: Nassau County Dist Ct 99 Main St Hempstead NY 11550

SHER, MICHAEL LEE, lawyer; b. N.Y.C., Oct. 20, 1938; s. David and Mae Phyllis (Tulin) S.; m. JoAnn Veronica Giffuni, Feb. 2, 1970 (div.). AB, Johns Hopkins U., 1961; JD, Fordham U., 1968. Bar: N.Y. 1969, D.C. 1974, U.S. Dist. Ct. (ea., no, so, we. dists.) N.Y., U.S. Cir. Ct. (fed. cir.), U.S. Cir. Ct. (2d cir.), U.S. Supreme Ct. Spl. asst. to dir. pub. affairs Peace Corps, Washington, 1964-65; dep. dir., acting dir. exec. secretariat OEO Office of the Pres., Washington, 1965-66; assoc. Phillips, Nizer, Benjamin, Krim & Ballon, N.Y.C., 1969-70; dir., exec. secretariat, spl. asst., spl. counsel, sec. mgmt. rev. com. N.Y.C. Health and Hosps.. Corp., 1971-72; v.p. Wertheim Asst. Mgmt. Svcs., Inc., 1972-76; assoc. Finley, Kumble, Wagner, Heine, Underberg, Manley & Casey, N.Y.C., 1976-79; dep. chmn., exec. dir., spl. counsel State of N.Y. Mortgage Agy., N.Y.C., 1979-82; pvt. practice N.Y.C., 1982—. Lect. Practising Law Inst., U. Nanjing, China; rapporteur Task Force on Internat. Legal Svcs.; founder UNCITRAL Internat. Moot Arbitration Competition, Willem C. Vis Internat. Comml. Arbitration Moot; judge internat. final rounds Jessup Internat. Moot Ct. Competition. Trustee Dalton Sch., N.Y.C., 1962-66, Endl. Alliance, N.Y.C., 1970-88, mem. exec. com., 1974-75; mem. Gov.'s Com. Scholastic Achievement, N.Y.C., 1976-86; aux. mem. housing adv. sounding bd. Young Pres.'s Orgn.; bd. dirs. United Neighborhood Houses of N.Y., N.Y.C., 1983-88; initiator, chmn. Ad Hoc Com. of the Am. Community of Higher Edn.; mem. Nat. Com. on U.S.-China Rels.; aux. mem. sounding bd. young pres's. orgn. Boys Choir of Harlem, 1990—, Fr. Flanagan's Boys Home Boys Town USA, 1990—. Mem. ABA (coord. liaisons internat. law sect., liaison with coun. of Bars of the European union., dispute resolution sect.), Am. Bar Assn. Fellows (life), D.C. Bar Assn., Assn. Bar City N.Y. com. sustaining mem. (mem. coun. on internat. affairs, co-chair UN group, mem. and rapporteur task force on internat. legal svcs., former mem. com. on aeronautics, chmn. sub-com. on econs., founding mem. spl. com. on lawyers in transition and sub-com. on lectrs. and cont. edn., various others), Canadian Bar Assn. hon. mem., Union Internat. des Avocats, dep. sec. gen. Internat. Org., former Am. C. of C. in France 1970-2000. Commercial, contracts (including sales of goods; commercial financing), Corporate, general, Private international. Home: 166 E 61st St New York NY 10021-8509

SHERBY, KATHLEEN REILLY, lawyer; b. St. Louis, Apr. 5, 1947; d. John Victor and Florian Sylvia (Frederick) Reilly; m. James Wilson Sherby, May 17, 1975; children: Michael R.R., William J.R., David J.R. AB magna cum laude, St. Louis U., 1969, JD magna cum laude, 1976. Bar: Mo. 1976. Assoc. Bryan Cave, St. Louis, 1976-85; ptnr. Bryan Cave LLP, St. Louis, 1985—. Contbr. articles to profl. jours. Bd. dirs Jr. League, St. Louis, 1989-90, St. Louis Forum, 1992-99, pres., 1995-97; chmn. Bequest and Gift Coun. of St. Louis U., 1997-99; jr. warden Ch. of St. Michael and St. George, 1998-2000; bd. dirs. Bistate chpt. ARC, 2000—; bd. trustees St. Louis Sci. Ctr., 2000—. Fellow Am. Coll. Trust and Estate Coun. (regent 1997—), Estate Planning Coun. of St. Louis (pres. 1986-87), Bar Assn. Met. St. Louis (chmn. probate sect. 1986-87), Mo. Bar Assn. (chmn. probate and trust com. 1996-98, chmn. probate law revision subcom. 1988-96). Episcopalian. Estate planning, Probate (including wills, trusts), Estate taxation. Home: 47 Crestwood Dr Saint Louis MO 63105-3032 Office: Bryan Cave LLP 1 Metropolitan Sq Ste 3600 Saint Louis MO 63102-2733

SHERER, SAMUEL AYERS, lawyer, urban planning consultant; b. Warwick, N.Y., June 17, 1944; s. Ernest Thompson and Helen (Ayers) S.; m. Dewi Sudewinahidah, June 28, 1980 (dec. Dec. 2000). AB magna cum laude, Oberlin Coll., 1966; JD, Harvard U., 1970; M in City Planning, MIT, 1970. Bar: D.C. 1972, U.S. Supreme Ct. 1979. Atty., advisor HUD, Boston, 1970; sr. cons. McClaughry Assoc., Washington, 1970-71, 74-76; cons. Urban Inst., Washington, 1971-72; atty., urban planner IBRD Jakarta (Indonesia) Urban Devel. Study, 1972-74; atty., advisor Office Minority Bus. U.S. Dept. Commerce, Washington, 1976-77; ptnr. Topping & Sherer, Washington, 1977-90; pres. Sherer-Axelrod-Monacelli, Inc., Cambridge, Mass., 1978-99; prin. The Washington Team, Inc., 1992—2002, Richardson & Sherer, LLC, 2000—. Bd. dirs. EnviroClean Solutions, Inc., The Urban Agr. Network; rep. Internat. Devel. Law Inst., Washington, 1983-90; sr. fellow Climate Inst., 1988—; cons. in field. Co-author: Urban Land Use in Egypt, 1977; editor: Important Laws and Regulations Regarding Land, Housing and Urban Development in the Arab Republic of Egypt, 1977, Important Laws and Regulations Regarding Land, Housing and Urban Development in the Hashemite Kingdom of Jordan, 1981. Bd. dirs. MIT Enterprise Forum of Washington-Balt., 1980-82; mem. D.C. Rep. Cent. Com., 1984-88; mem. nat. governing bd. Ripon Soc., Washington, 1977-83. Urban Studies fellow HUD, 1969-70. Mem. ABA, D.C. Bar Assn., Am. Planning Assn., The Am. Soc. of Internat. Law, Asia Soc., Phi Beta Kappa. Avocations: tennis, reading. Environmental, Public international, Land use and zoning (including planning). Home: 4600 Connecticut Ave NW Apt 205 Washington DC 20008-5702 Office: 7 Brookes Ave Gaithersburg MD 20877-2754 E-mail: washteam@aol.com.

SHERESKY, NORMAN M. lawyer; b. Detroit, June 22, 1928; s. Harry and Rose (Lieberman) S.; m. Elaine B. Lewis, Oct. 30, 1977; 1 child, from previous marriage, Brooke Hillary. A.B., Syracuse U., 1950; LL.B., Harvard U., 1953. Bar: N.Y. 1953. Assoc. Gold & Pollack, N.Y.C., 1954-60; sole practice, N.Y.C., 1960-72; ptnr. Sheresky & Kalman, N.Y.C., 1972-77; ptnr. Colton, Hartnick, Yamin & Sheresky, N.Y.C., 1977-93; ptnr. Baer, Marks & Upham, N.Y.C., 1993-95; ptnr. Sheresky, Aronson & Mayefsky, 1995—. adj. prof. matrimonial litigation N.Y. Law Sch., 1979-86; mem. judiciary com. N.Y.C. Bar Assn.; pres.-elect Am. Coll. Family Trial Lawyers. Mem. Internat. Acad. Matrimonial Lawyers (past treas., gov. N.Y. chpt.), Am. Acad. Matrimonial Lawyers (gov., past pres. N.Y. chpt., pres. elect.), N.Y. State Bar Assn., Assn. Trial Lawyers Am., Met. Trial Lawyers Assn., Internat. Acad. Matrimonial Lawyers (bd. govs. 1986—, com. to examine lawyer conduct in matrimonial actions 1992-95). Author: (with Marya Mannes) Uncoupling, 1972; On Trial, 1977; contbr. editor: Fairshare mag. Family and matrimonial. Office: Sheresky Aronson & Mayefsky LLP 750 Lexington Ave New York NY 10022-1200 E-mail: sheresky@samllp.com.

SHERIDAN, PETER LOUIS, solicitor; b. Singapore, Mar. 19, 1958; s. Lee and Margaret S.; m. Helen Frances Dudley, Feb. 9, 1993; children: Anna, Katherine. BA with honors, Oxford U., Eng., 1980. Cert. solicitor Eng., Wales, 1994. Articled clk. Loosemores, Cardiff, Wales, 1981-84; solicitor Phillips & Buck, Cardiff, Wales, 1984-85, Cameron Markby, London, 1985-93; solicitor, ptnr. Shadbolt & Co., Reigate, Eng., 1992—. Author: Construction and Engineering Arbitration, 1999 (Brit. Constrn. Industry Lit. award 1999); contbr. articles to profl. jours. Mem. Soc. Constrn. Law, Law Soc., Arbitration Club. Construction, Arbitration. Office: Shadbolt & Co Chatham Ct Leibourne Rd Surrey Reigate RH2 7LD England

SHERIFF, SEYMOUR, retired lawyer; b. Rye, N.Y., Aug. 22, 1917; s. Michael and Anna (Rosenfeld) S.; m. Selene Gloria Wolf, Oct. 15, 1950; children: Steven, Susan, Ellen, Carol. BSS cum laude, CCNY, 1935; JD cum laude, Yale U., 1938. Bar: D.C. 1938, N.Y. 1938, Md. 1957. Pvt. practice, Washington, 1938-58; sr. ptnr. Gardner, Morrison, Sheriff & Beddow, Washington, 1958-2000; ret., 2000. With AUS, 1942-45. Decorated Legion of Merit. Mem. Order of Coif, Phi Beta Kappa. Corporate, general.

SHERK, GEORGE WILLIAM, lawyer; b. Washington, Mo., June 23, 1949; s. George William and Lorraine Martha (Meyer) Sherk; m. Patricia F. Sherk, Oct. 27, 2001. AA, St. Louis C.C., 1970; BA, Colo. State U., 1972, MA, 1974; JD, U. Denver, 1978; DSc, George Washington U., 2002. Bar: Am. Samoa 1978, Colo. 1979, U.S. Dist. Ct. Colo. 1979, U.S. Ct. Claims 1984, U.S. Supreme Ct. 1985. Cons. office of legis. counsel Govt. of Am. Samoa, Pago Pago, 1978-79; atty. advisor western area power adminstrn. U.S. Dept. Energy, Colo., 1979—80; pvt. practice law Denver, 1980-82; staff assoc. Nat. Conf. State Legis., Denver, 1980-82; spl. asst. office of water policy U.S. Dept. Interior, Washington, 1982-83; atty. land and natural resources div. U.S. Dept. Justice, Washington, 1984-90; of counsel Will & Muys, Washington, 1990-93; pvt. practice, 1993—. Vis. scholar U. Wyo. Coll. Law, 1993; vis. prof. Ga. State U. Coll. Law, 1994-95, Ga. State U. Policy Rsch. Ctr., 1995-96; assoc. professorial lectr. George Washington U. Sch. Engring. and Applied Sci., Washington, 1997-2002; hon. assoc. Internat. Water Law Rsch. Inst., U. Dundee, Scotland, 1998—; lectr. various colls. and univs.; mem. assoc. faculty Va. Inst. Marine Sci., Coll. of William and Mary, Gloucester Pt., Va., 1989-94; dep. dir. Ctr. Risk Sci. and Pub. Health Sch. Pub. Health & Health Svcs. George Washington U., 2000-01. Author, co-author or editor numerous books and articles on water law and alternative energy law; book review editor Rivers: Studies in the Science, Environmental Policy and Law of Instream Flow, 1989-2000. Mem. ABA, ASCE, Water Environ. Fedn., State Bar Colo. Avocations: automobile racing and rallying, sports, reading, outdoor activites, sailing. Federal civil litigation, Environmental, Property, real (including real estate development, water). Home and Office: 4033 E 130th Ct Thornton CO 80241

SHERK, KENNETH JOHN, lawyer; b. Ida Grove, Iowa, Feb. 27, 1933; s. John and Dorothy (Myers) Sherk; children: Karin Fulton, Katrina, Keith, Kyle. BSC, U. Iowa, 1955; JD, George Washington U., 1961. Bar: Ariz. 1962, U.S. Dist. Ct. Ariz. 1962, U.S. Ct. Appeals (9th cir.) 1966, U.S. Supreme Ct. 1974. Assoc. Moore & Romley, Phoenix, 1962-67, ptnr., 1967-79, Romley & Sherk, Phoenix, 1979-85; dir. Fennemore Craig, Phoenix, 1985—. 1st lt. U.S. Army, 1955-58, Korea. Recipient Profl. Achievement Svcs. award George Washington Law Assn., 1986, Ariz. Judges Assn., 1989, Disting. Svc. award Phoenix Assn. Def. Counsel, 1990; named Mem. of Yr. State Bar of Ariz., 1994. Fellow Am. Coll. Trial Lawyers, Am. Acad. Appellate Lawyers, Am. Bar Found., Ariz. Bar Found. (Walter E. Craig award 1999); mem. ABA (ho. of dels. 1990-93), Ariz. Bar Assn. (pres. 1985-86), Maricopa County Bar Assn. (pres. 1978-79). Republican. Congregationalist. Avocations: fishing, hiking, bicycling. General civil litigation, Personal injury (including property damage). Home: 1554 W Las Palmaritas Dr Phoenix AZ 85021-5429 Office: Fennemore Craig 3003 N Central Ave Ste 2600 Phoenix AZ 85012-2913

SHERLAND, BARBARA C. lawyer; married; 3 children. BA magna cum laude, Hood Coll., 1974; JD, U. Wash., 1984. Bar: Wash., U.S. Dist. Ct. (we. dist.) Wash. Law clk. to Hon. Eugene Wright U.S. Ct. Appeals (9th cir.), 1984; with Stoel River LLP, Seattle. Mem. adv. bd. Stat. KCTS-TV. Vice chmn. bd. dirs. Puget Sound Blood Ctr.; mem. adv. bd. Fred Hutchinson Cancer Rsch. Ctr., Am. Lung Assn.; mem. endowment bd. United Way King County. Named one of Wash.'s Super Lawyers, Wash. Law & Politics, 1999, 2000, 2002, Seattle's Top 100 Lawyers, Seattle Mag., 2001. Fellow: Am. Coll. Trust and Estate Counsel; mem.: Wash. Plannned Giving Coun. (mem. exec. com.), Wash. State Bar Assn. (chair real property, probate and trust sect.). Office: 600 University St Ste 3600 Seattle WA 98101 Office Fax: 206-386-7500. Business E-Mail: bcsherland@stoel.com.*

SHERLING, FRED W. lawyer; b. Dec. 22, 1933; s. Weaver V. and Ruth M. (Bowen) S.; m. Camille Margaret Brochetto, Nov. 29, 1969; children: Charlotte, Sharon, Cheryl. BS in Chem. Engring., U. Tenn., 1957; LLB, George Washington U., 1961. Bar: U.S. Ct. Appeals (D.C. cir.) 1963, U.S. Ct. Customs and Patent Appeals 1963, U.S. Ct. Appeals (fed. cir.), 1982, U.S. Supreme Ct. 1982. Patent examiner U.S. Patent Office, Washington, 1957-63; assoc. solicitor, 1963-86; sole practice, 1986—. Mem. patent Office Soc. Baptist. E-mail: charlotte2002c@aol.com., fred-weaver@excite.com.

SHERLOCK, E. TODD, lawyer; b. St. Francis, Kans., July 16, 1957; s. Frederick Earl and Ruth Alice Sherlock. BS in Journalism, Kans. State U., 1979; JD, Washburn U., 1983. Bar: Kans. 1983. Dir. govtl. affairs Kans. Assn. Rels., Topeka, 1983—84; real estate mgr. Payless Caseways, Inc., Kansas City, Mo., 1984—90; dir. real estate Western Auto Supply Co., Kansas City, 1990—93, assoc. counsel, 1993—96; gen. ptnr. Sherlock & Huffman LLC, Overland Park, Kans., 1996—2000; area market atty. Nextel Comm., Overland Park, 2000—01; atty. Applebee's Internat., Inc., Overland Park, 2002—. Property, real (including real estate development, water), Corporate, general, Environmental. Home: 9640 Manor Rd Leawood KS 66206 Office: Applebees Internat Inc 4551 W 107th Overland Park KS 66207 Office Fax: 913-341-1696. Business E-Mail: todd.scherlock@applebees.com.

SHERLOCK, MARY EVA, lawyer; b. N.Y.C., May 26, 1958; d. Leonard Joseph and Joan Ann (Lang) Schnappauf; m. Michael Paul Sherlock, July 10, 1982; children: Christina Lynn, Stephen Michael. BA, Lemoyne Coll., 1980; JD, Widener U., 1983. Bar: Del. 1983, U.S. Dist. Ct. Del. 1984, U.S. Ct. Appeals (3d cir.) 1986. Assoc. Doroshow & Pasquale, Dover, 1983-84, Robert B. Young, Dover, 1984—92; ptnr. Young & Sherlock, Dover, Del., 1985-92; assoc. White & Williams, Wilmington, Del., 1992-94, Brown Shiels Beauregard & Chasanov, Dover, 1994—. Mem. ABA, AAUW (br. pres.), Del. Bar Found. (bd. dirs. 1987-88), Del. Bar Assn. (exec. com. 1988-90, jud. nominating com. 1997—), Del. Trial Lawyers Assn. (preliminary rev. com., Supreme Ct. com. 1998—), Am. Bd. Trial Advocates, Terry-Carey Inn of Ct. Democrat. Roman Catholic. Avocations: tennis, swimming, gardening. General civil litigation, Insurance, Personal injury (including property damage). Office: Brown Shiels Beauregard & Chasanov 104 E Water St Dover DE 19901-3614

SHERMAN, EDWARD FRANCIS, dean, law educator; b. El Paso, Tex., July 5, 1937; s. Raphael Eugene and Mary (Stedmond) S.; m. Alice Theresa hammer, Feb. 23, 1963; children: Edward F. Jr., Paul. BA, Georgetown U., 1959; MA, U. Tex., El Paso, 1962, 67; LLB, Harvard U., 1962, SJD, 1981. Bar: Tex. 1962, Ind. 1976. Aide to gov. Nev., state govt. fellow, Carson City, 1962; law clk. judge U.S. Dist. Ct. (we. dist.) El Paso, Tex., 1963; ptnr. Mayfield, Broaddus & Perrenot, El Paso, 1963-65; tchg. fellow Law Sch. Harvard U., Cambridge, Mass., 1967-69; prof. Sch. Law Ind. U., Bloomington, 1969-77; Edward Clark Centennial prof. U. Tex., Austin, 1977-96; prof., dean Tulane U. Law Sch., 1996—. Fulbright prof. Trinity Coll., Dublin, 1973-74; vis. prof. Stanford Law Sch., 1977, U. London, 1989, Sch. Pub. Adminstrn., Warsaw, Poland, 1995, Chuo U., Tokyo, 1995, U. New South Wales, Australia, 2002; counsel Tex. County Jail Litigation, 1978-85; bd. dirs., officer Travis County Dispute Resolution, 1993—; mem. arbitrtor panel, course dir. Internat. Ctrs. Arbitration. Co-author: The Military in American Society, 1979, Complex Litigation, 1985, 3d edit., 1998, Processes of Dispute Resolution, 1989, 3d edit., 2002, Civil Procedure: A Modern Approach, 1989, 3d edit., 2000, Rau & Sherman & Shannon's Texas ADR and Arbitration Statutes, 1994, 3d edit., 1999. Capt. U.S. Army, 1965-67, lt. col. Res., 1970-90. Fellow Tex. Bar Found.; mem. ABA (reporter civil justice improvements project 1993, offer of judgement task force 1995, com. on pro bono and pub. svc. 1997—, chmn. task force class action legis. 2002-03), Am. Arbitration Assn. (arbitrator panel), AAUP (gen. counsel 1986-88), Am. Law Inst., Tex. State Bar Assn. (alternative dispute resolution com. 1985-96, chair pattern jury charge com. 1983-94, Evans award for excellence in dispute resolution 1998), Tex. Civil Liberties Union (gen. counsel 1985-91), La. Law Inst., La. State Bar (bd. govs. 1997-99, com. on codes of lawyer and jud. conduct 1999—, com. on multi-juris. practice 2000—); La. Bar Found. (jud. liason com. 1999—), Assn. Am. Law Schs. (chmn. Sect. Litigation 1999, chmn. Sect. ADR 1995, com. on clin. legal edn. 1999—. Office: Tulane Law Sch 6329 Freret St New Orleans LA 70118-6231 Home: 21 Newcomb Blvd New Orleans LA 70118

SHERMAN, FREDERICK HOOD, lawyer; b. Deming, N.Mex., Aug. 9, 1947; s. Benjamin and Helen (Hood) S.; m. Janie Carol Jontz, Oct. 23, 1973; children: Jerah Elizabeth, Frederick Jakub. BBA, Southern Meth. U., 1970, JD, 1972. Bar: Tex. 1972, N.Mex. 1973, U.S. Dist. Ct. N.Mex. 1973, U.S. Dist. Ct. (we. dist.) Tex. 1974, U.S. Supreme Ct. 1979; cert. mediator. Assoc. Sherman & Sherman, Deming, 1973-74, ptnr., 1974-78, prin., 1978—, owner, 1998—. Mem. spacialization com. N.Mex. Supreme Ct., 1986—94; liaison N.Mex. Supreme Ct. and Workers Compensation Bd., 1991—94; apptd. guardian Assets State Fiscal Acctg. State N.Mex., 1992—; state coord. Nat. Bd. Trial Advocates for Bd. Cert. Trial Specialist, 1994—98. Contbr. articles to profl. jours. Chmn. Luna County Planning Commn., Deming, 1976-78; apptd. visitor to U. N.Mex. Law Sch., 1983—; treas. Luna County Econ. Devel. PSS, 1987-88, also bd. dirs.; bd. dirs. Luna County Hosp., 1991-94; bd. mem. Deming Pub. Sch., 1991-94, pres., 1991-92, elected bd. mem. 1991-95; chmn. bd. dirs. Luna County Charitable Found., 1991—; hon. dir. Deming Art Coun., 1989—; pres. Luna County Sch. Bd., 1991-92; pres., chmn. of the bd. Sherman Family Charitable Found., 1991—; mem. N. Mex. High Sch. Task Force, 1993-94. Recipient Svc. award, N.Mex. Bd. Legal Specialization, 1994, Cert. Advocacy, Nat. Coll. Advocacy, 2001. Mem.: Supreme Ct. Com. Professionalism, Col. Albert Fountain Inns of Ct. (charter), Coll. State Bar Tex. (pro bono 1995—), Am. Inns of Ct. (master atty. 1995—, officer 1997—),

6th Jud. Bar Assn., Tex. Bar Assn., State Bar N.Mex. (commr. 1978—86, alternative dispute resolution com. 1980—91, jud. selection com. 1985—88, mem. jud. selection com. 1985—88, co-chair 1986—87, legal retreat com. 1986—89, med. rev. com. 2000, arbitration com. 2000, Outstanding Svc. award 1986, Dedication award 1986), N.Mex. Bar Assn., N.Mex. Trial Lawyers Assn. (bd. dirs. 1986—, sec. 1989, 1997, officer 1997—98, desingated mentor in personal injury/auto and social security 1998—, Notably Large award 1983, 1984, 1985, Amicus Curiae award 1991), ATLA (del. 2000—, state del. 2000—, pub. edn. com. 2001—, lectr. winter convention 2003, mem. jud. selection com. 6th jud. selection 2003). Democrat. Roman Catholic. Avocations: skiing, investments, camping, farming, wine making. General civil litigation, Pension, profit-sharing, and employee benefits, Personal injury (including property damage). Office: Sherman & Sherman PO Box 850 Deming NM 88031-0850

SHERMAN, HAROLD, lawyer; b. Newark, Oct. 19, 1921; s. Myron H. and Mollie (Zell) S.; m. Sylvia Selikowsky, Feb. 20, 1943; children: Ralph, Neal. AB, Bklyn. Coll., 1942; PhD, NYU, 1956; JD, Pace U., 1986. Bar: Conn. 1987, U.S. Dist. Ct. Conn. 1988. Physicist Premier Crystal Labs., N.Y.C., 1944-47, Schlumberger-Doll Rsch., Ridgefield, Conn., 1956-83; instr. physics St. Peter's Coll., Jersey City, 1949-51; rsch. assoc. NYU, 1952-56; pvt. practice Ridgefield, 1987--. Cons. Teleco Oilfield Svcs., Meriden, Conn., 1985-92. Patentee (5) in field. Vol., Conn. Legal Svcs., 1988-97. Mem. Conn. Bar Assn., Am. Phys. Soc., Soc. Profl. Well Log Analysts, Sigma Xi. Avocations: gardening, photography. Commercial, contracts (including sales of goods; commercial financing), Juvenile, Probate (including wills, trusts). Home and Office: 24 Webster Rd Ridgefield CT 06877-4308 Fax: 203-438-6870. E-mail: attyharoldsherman@msn.com.

SHERMAN, LAWRENCE JAY, lawyer; b. Pitts., May 20, 1942; s. Ben E. and Leonora C. (Weill) S.; m. Iris Shapiro, Aug. 19, 1967; children: Rachel L., Jessica S. BA in Polit. Sci. with honors, U. Pitts., 1963; JD, U. Mich., 1966. Bar: D.C. 1967, Calif. 1967, Md. 1984, U.S. Dist. Ct. D.C., U.S. Dist. Ct. Md., U.S. Claims Ct., U.S. Ct. Appeals (D.C., 1st, 3rd, 4th, 5th and 6th cir.). Appellate atty. NLRB, Washington, 1966-69; assoc. Cohen & Berfield, Washington, 1969-70; exec. dir. Migrant Legal Action Program, Washington, 1970-75; assoc. Lichtman, Abeles, Anker & Nagle, P.C., Washington, 1975-77; pvt. practice Washington, 1977-81; ptnr. Sherman & Lapidus, Washington, 1981-86; counsel Deso, Thomas, Spevack, Weitzman & Rost PC, Washington, 1991-2000; ptnr. Brown & Sherman, LLP, Washington, 2001—02; prin. Law Offices of Lawrence J. Sherman, P.C., Washington, 2002—. Adj. prof. George Meany Ctr. for Labor Studies, Silver Spring, Md. 1988-2000; prin. Mng. Human Resources For 21st Century, Washington, 1990-99. Contbr. articles to profl. jours. Fellow Am. Bd. Trial Advocates; mem. D.C. Bar (labor and employment law sect., litig. sect., co-chmn. steering com., 1981-85, labor law sect. 1978-84, co-chmn. labor law sect. 1983-84, lawyers coord. com.), Met. Washington Employment Lawyers Assn., Md. Employment Lawyers Assn., Nat. Employment Lawyers Assn. Democrat. Avocations: tennis, racquetball, photography, travel, reading. Civil rights, General civil litigation. Office: Lawrence J Sherman PC 1400 K St NW Washington DC 20005-2403 E-mail: jdlarry@aol.com.

SHERMAN, LESTER IVAN, retired lawyer; b. Flagler, Colo., June 1, 1936; s. Lester B. and Helen E. S.; m. Lois E. Hafling, July 19, 1958 (div. Mar. 1986); children: Kathi, Scott, Brett; m. Kay A. Swanson, Dec. 21, 1993. Student, Colo. State U., 1954-55; BSBA, U. Denver, 1958, JD, 1961. Bar: Colo. 1961, U.S. Dist. Ct. Colo. 1961. Pvt. practice, Durango, Colo., 1965-67, 79-81, 1986-97; ret., 1997; ptnr. Hamilton, Sherman, Hamilton & Shand, P.C., Durango, 1967-78, Sherman, Rhodes & Wright, P.C., Durango, 1981-86; judge La Plata County (Colo.) Ct., 1966-76. Cons. in field; mem. Colo. Commn. on Jud. Qualifications, 1974-76. Mem. La Plata County Bd. for Mentally Retarded and Seriously Handicapped, Inc., 1968-75, pres., 1970-73; bd. dirs. Colo. County Judges Assn., 1973-74. Mem. S.W. Colo. Bar (pres. 1969-70), Colo. Bar Assn. (gov. 1970-72, 74-76), ABA, Petroleum Club, Elks, Phi Delta Phi, Sigma Chi. Republican. Corporate, general, Estate planning, Property, real (including real estate development, water). Home: 320 N Skylane Dr Durango CO 81303-6040

SHERMAN, MICHAEL, lawyer; b. 1946; AB, U. Conn., JD, 1971. Bar: Conn. 1971. Asst. pub. def. Stamford Superior Ct., asst. pros.; asst. town atty. Town of Greenwich; ptnr. Sherman & Richichi, Stamford, Conn., 1971—. Mem.: ATLA, Conn. Trial Lawyers Assn., Nat. Assn. Criminal Def. Lawyers, Conn. Criminal Def. Lawyers Assn. (founding mem., officer, bd. mem., lectr.). Office: Sherman & Richichi 27 5th St Stamford CT 06905*

SHERMAN, PETER R. lawyer, educator; b. South Bend, Ind., Apr. 14, 1939; BS with distinction, Ind. U., 1961; JD, Georgetown U., 1964, ML in Trail Advocacy, 1966. Bar: DC. Law clk. to Hon. L. W. Youngdahl U.S. Dist. Ct. DC, 1965—66; ptnr. Sherman, Meehan, Curtin & Ain, P.C., Washington. Adj. prof. Washington Coll. Law Am. U., 1977—80, 1993—; pvt. bar rep. rules com. family divsn. Superior Ct. DC, mem. rules revision com., 1991—96. Bd. editors Georgetown Law Jour., 1963—64. Mem. Task Force Race and Ethnic Bias in DC Cts., 1990—91. Prettyman fellow, Georgetown U., 1965—66. Fellow: Am. Acad. Matrimonial Lawyers. Office: 1900 M St NW Ste 600 Washington DC 20036-3565 Office Fax: 202-530-4411.*

SHERMAN, SANDRA BROWN, lawyer; b. Galesburg, Ill., May 14, 1953; d. Charles Lewis and Lois Maria (Nelson) Brown; m. Robert Sherman, June 10, 1979; children: Michael Wesley, Stephen Averill, Alexander Joseph. B of Music Edn., Ind. U., 1975; JD, U. Ill., 1979, LLM, 1981. Bar: Ill. 1979, Tex. 1982, N.J. 1984, U.S. Tax Ct. 1988, N.Y. 1997. Instr. law U. Ill., Champaign, 1979-81; assoc. Law Offices of William E. Remy, San Antonio, 1984, Gutkin Miller Shapiro & Selesner, Millburn, N.J., 1985-88, ptnr., 1989-91; counsel Riker Danzig Scherer Hyland & Perretti LLP, Morristown, N.J., 1991-95; ptnr. Riker Danzig Scherer Hyland & Perretti, LLP, Morristown, N.J., 1996—. Contbr. articles to profl. jours. Trustee, sec. Found. U. Medicine and Dentistry N.J., 1998—; trustee Jersey Battered Women's Svc., 1999—. Scholar Ind. U., 1971-75, U. Ill., 1977-79. Mem. ABA (probate and trust law divsn.), N.J. Bar Assn., Estate Planning Coun. No. N.J., Estate Planning Coun. N.Y.C., Park Ave. Club. Avocation: music. Corporate, general, Estate planning, Taxation, general. Home: 15 Hawthorne Dr New Providence NJ 07974-1111 Office: Riker Danzig Scherer Hyland & Perretti LLP Headquarters Plz 1 Speedwell Ave Morristown NJ 07961-1981 E-mail: ssherman@riker.com.

SHERWIN, JAMES TERRY, lawyer; b. N.Y.C., Oct. 25, 1933; s. Oscar and Stella (Zins) S.; m. Judith Johnson, June 21, 1955 (div. Apr. 1984); children— Miranda, Alison, Galen; m. Hiroko Inouye, June 15, 1985. BA, Columbia U., 1953, LLB (Stone scholar), 1956. Bar: N.Y. 1956, U.S. Supreme Ct. 1963. Assoc. Kaye, Scholer, Fierman, Hays & Handler, N.Y.C., 1957-60; with GAF Corp., N.Y.C., 1960-83, 84-90, assoc. counsel, gen. mgr. European ops., 1969-71, group v.p. photography, 1971-74, exec. v.p. fin. and adminstrn., legal and investment svcs., 1974-83, vice chmn., chief adminstrv. officer Wayne, N.J., 1984-90; exec. v.p., CFO Triangle Industries, Inc., 1983-84, Hunter-Douglas N.V., 1991-99, bd. dirs., 1999—. Bd. dirs. Internat. Rescue Com., chmn. exec. com., v.p. to 1990; mem. coun. U. Bath, 2001--. Lt. comdr. USCGR, 1956-57. U.S. intercollegiate chess champion, 1951-53, N.Y. State champion, 1951, U.S. speed champion, 1956-57, 59-60, internat. master. Mem. Am. Chess Found. (pres., bd. dirs. to 1990), Marshall (N.Y.) Chess Club (pres. 1967-69, gov. to 1990), Phi Beta Kappa. Home: The Chase Winsley Nr Bradford-on-Avon Wiltshire BA15 2LX England E-mail: jsherwin@thechase99.freeserve.co.uk.

SHERWOOD, ARTHUR LAWRENCE, lawyer; b. L.A., Jan. 25, 1943; s. Allen Joseph and Edith (Ziff) S.; m. Frances Merele, May 1, 1970; children: David, Chester. BA magna cum laude, U. Calif., Berkeley, 1964; MS, U. Chgo., 1965; JD cum laude, Harvard U., 1968. Bar: Calif. 1969, US. dist. cts. (cen. dist.) Calif. 1968 (no. dist.) Calif. 1971 (so. dist.) Calif. 1973 (ea. dist.) Calif. 1973, U.S. Ct. Appeals (9th cir.) 1973, U.S. Ct. Appeals (D.C. cir.) 1991, U.S. Supreme Ct., 1980. Instr. UCLA Law Sch., 1968-69; assoc. Gibson, Dunn & Crutcher, L.A., 1968-75, ptnr., 1975-98; of counsel, 1998-; judge pro tem., L.A. Mcpl. and Superior Ct., 1980-98; instr. law, UCLA, 1968-69, arbitrator N.Y. Stock Exchange., Nat. Futures Assn. Co-author: Civil Procedure During Trial, 1995, Civil Procedure Before Trial, 1990; contbr articles to profl. jours. NASA fellow U. Chgo., 1964-65; chmn. Far Ea. Art Coun., L.A. County Mus. Art, 1992-97. Mem. Calif. Bar Assn., Phi Beta Kappa. Republican. Avocations: art, 18th century Am. history. Antitrust, General civil litigation, Securities. Home: 300 N Swall Dr Unit 305 Beverly Hills CA 90211 Office: 300 N Swall Dr Beverly Hills CA 90211-4733

SHERWOOD, DEVON FREDRICK, lawyer; b. Hanibal, Mo., June 20, 1943; s. Malcolm and Virginia Dolores (Gresham) S.; m. Stephanie Jan Wanner, Dec. 26, 1963 (div. Feb. 1976); children: Leslie, Jennifer, Stuart; m. Wanda Lee Mullins, May 17, 1977. AB, U. Mo., 1965, JD, 1968. Bar: Mo. 1968, U.S. Dist. Ct. (we. dist.) Mo. Assoc. Lilley & Cowan, Springfield, Mo., 1968-69, Donald Bonacker, Springfield, 1969-72; sr. ptnr. Sherwood & Bruer, Springfield, 1972-77; sole practice, Springfield, 1977-80; sr. ptnr. Sherwood, Honecker & Bender, Springfield, 1980— ; city atty. Fair Grove, Mo., 1973-76. Bd. editors Mo. Law Rev., 1967-68. Elder deacon National Avenue Christian Ch., Springfield, 1969-74; del. Springfield Area Council Chs., 1971-74. Recipient Lon O. Hocker Outstanding Trial Lawyers award Mo. Bar Found. Mem. ATLA, Mo. Bar Assn., Springfield Met. Bar Assn., Mo. Assn. Trial Lawyers, Phi Delta Phi. Republican. General civil litigation, Criminal, Family and matrimonial. Office: Sherwood Honecker & Bender 155 Park Central Sq Springfield MO 65806-1322 Home: 2101 E Wornall Pl Springfield MO 65804-8007 E-mail: shb@pcis.net.

SHESTACK, JEROME JOSEPH, lawyer; b. Atlantic City, N.J., Feb. 11, 1925; s. Isidore and Olga (Shankman) Shestack; m. Marciarose Schleifer, Jan. 28, 1951; children: Jonathan Michael, Jennifer. AB, U. Pa., 1944; LLB, Harvard U., 1949; LLD (hon.) , Dickinson Coll. Law, 1997, Stetson Sch. of Law, 1998, Whittier Coll. Law, 1998. Bar: Ill. 1950, Pa. 1952. Tchg. fellow Northwestern U. Law Sch., Chgo., 1949—50; asst. prof. law, faculty editor La. State Law Sch., Baton Rouge, 1950—52; dep. city solicitor City of Phila., 1952, 1st dep. solicitor, 1952—55; ptnr. Schnader, Harrison, Segal & Lewis, Phila. and Washington, 1956—91, Wolf, Block, Schorr & Solis-Cohen, Phila., 1991—. Adj. prof. law U. Pa., 1956; U.S. amb. to UN Human Rights Commn., 1979—80; U.S. del. to ECOSOC, UN, 1980; sr. U.S. del. to Helsinki Accords Conf., 1979—80; mem. U.S. Commn. on Improving Effectiveness of UN, 1989—; chmn. Internat. League Human Rights, 1973—94, hon. chmn., 1994—; U.S. del. to CSCE Conf., Moscow, 1991; founder, chmn. Lawyers Com. Internat. Human Rights, 1978—80, Jacob Blaustein Inst. Human Rights, 1988—92; mem. nat. adv. com. legal svcs. OEO, 1965—72; bd. dirs., exec. com. Lawyers Com. Civil Rights; mem. coun. Holocaust Mus., 1999—, exec. com., chair com. on conscience. Editor (with others): Rights of Americans, 1971, Human Rights, 1979, International Human Rights, 1985, Bill of Rights: A Bicentennial View, 1991, Understanding Human Rights, 1992, Thomas Jefferson: Lawyer, 1993, Francis Scott Key, 1994, Abraham Lincoln, Circuit Lawyer, 1994, The Holocaust, 1997, Moral Foundations of Human Rights, 1997, The Philosophy of Human Rights, 1997, W.B. Yeats, Poet of Passionate Intensity, 1997. Mem. exec. com. Nat. Legal Aid and Defender Assn., 1970—80; trustee Eleanor and Franklin Roosevelt Inst., 1986—; bd. govs. Tel Aviv U., 1983—, Hebrew U., 1969—; chmn. bd. dirs. Am. Poetry Ctr., 1976—91; trustee Free Libr. Phila., vice chmn., 1989—96; v.p. Am. Jewish Com., 1984—89. With USNR, 1943—46. Fellow Rubin, Columbia U. Law Sch., 1984, hon., U. Pa. Law Sch., 1980. Mem.: ABA (ho. of dels. 1971—73, 1977—, mem. jud. com. 1985—90, bd. govs. 1992—95, exec. com. 1994—95, pres.-elect 1996, pres. 1997—98, pres. ALI-ABA 1997—98), Nat. Conf. Bar Found. (bd. dirs. 1998—, pres.-elect 2003), Am. Soc. Internat. Law, Internat. Assn. Jewish Lawyers and Jurists (Am. Soc. pres. 2000—02), Am. Acad. Appellate Lawyers, Am. Coll. Trial Lawyers, Am. Arbitration Assn. (bd. dirs. 1999—2003), Am. Law Inst., Am. Soc. Internat. Law (exec. com. 1993—95, internat. com. jurists exec. com. 1998—2001, counsellor 1999—), Internat. Acad. Trial Lawyers, Internat. Bar Assn. (chmn. com. on human rights 1990—94, chmn. com. profl. ethics 2000—), Order of Coif. Appellate, Federal civil litigation, Insurance. Home: Parkway House 2201 Pennsylvania Ave Philadelphia PA 19130-3513 Office: Wolf Block Schorr & Solis-Cohen 1650 Arch St Fl 20 Philadelphia PA 19103-2029 E-mail: jshestack@wolfblock.com.

SHEVLIN, GEORGE FELIX, IV, legislative staff member; b. Glens Falls, N.Y., Dec. 24, 1961; s. George Felix Shevlin III and Linda Owens Shevlin. BA, U. Notre Dame, 1984; JD, U. Balt., 1988; LLM, London U., 1989. Bar: Md. Counsel U.S. Ho. Reps., Washington, 1990—. Home: PO Box 33661 Washington DC 20033

SHIDELER, SHIRLEY ANN WILLIAMS, lawyer; b. Mishawaka, Ind., July 9, 1930; d. William Harmon and Lois Wilma (Koch) Williams; 1 dau., Gail Shideler Frye. LLB, Ind. U., 1964. Bar: Ind. 1964. Legal sec. Barnes, Hickam, Pantzer & Boyd, Indpls., 1953-63; assoc. Barnes & Thornburg, 1964-70, ptnr., 1971-92, of counsel, 1993—. Participant fund drives Indpls. Symphony, 1968-81, Indpls. Mus. Art, 1969-79, Marion County Libr. Restoration, 1985-88, Goodwill Industries, 1988-89; bd. dirs. Bus. Unit Gals Indpls. Mus. Art, 1973-80; bd. dirs. Indpls. Legal Aid Soc., 1982-93, Cmty. Hosp. Found., 1986-94, Ctrl. Newspapers Found., 1979-99. Fellow Am. Coll. Trust and Estate Counsel, 1981-96; mem. Ind. Bar Assn. (sec. 1975-76, chmn. probate, trust and real property sect. 1982), Nat. Conf. Bar. Founds. (trustee 1988-94), Indpls. Bar Assn. (bd. mgrs. 1968-72, v.p. charge affairs 1972), Ind. Bar Found. (bd. mgrs. 1980-92, sec. 1981-82, treas. 1981-86, v.p. 1986-88, pres. 1988-90), Indpls. Bar Found. (bd. mgrs. 1970-82, sec. 1972-77), Women's Rotary (pres. Indpls. club 1969-71, dir. 1968-79). Home: 2224 Boston Ct Apt C Indianapolis IN 46228-3257 Office: Barnes & Thornburg 11 S Meridian St Ste 1313 Indianapolis IN 46204-3535

SHIELDS, CRAIG M. lawyer; b. Oceanside, N.Y., Nov. 28, 1941; s. John Anderson and Lillian Ethel (Hagen) S.; m. Candia Atwater Shields, July 13, 1963 (div. 1985); children: Mark, Christopher, Evan; m. Norma Magor Peters, Apr. 25, 1998. Bar: N.Y. 1967, U.S. Dist. Ct. (so. and ea. dists.) N.Y. 1967, U.S. Ct. Appeals (2d cir.) 1967, U.S. Supreme Ct. 1976. Assoc. Clark, Carr & Ellis, N.Y.C., 1966-69; ptnr. Borden & Ball, N.Y.C., 1969-76, Sage, Gray, Todd & Sims, N.Y.C., 1976-80; counsel Conboy, Hewitt, O'Brien & Boardman, N.Y.C., 1980-83; ptnr. Collier, Cohen, Shields & Bock, N.Y.C., 1983-92, Quinn & Suhr, White Plains, N.Y., 1992-95; v.p., gen. counsel United Vanguard Homes, Inc., Glen Cove, N.Y., 1992—. Contbr. articles to profl. jours. Bd. dirs. Group House of Port Washington (N.Y.) Inc., 1973-85, Children's House, Inc., Mineola, N.Y., 1985-89, Resources for Program Devel., Inc., Port Washington, 1982—; pres. Port Washington Community Action Coun., 1968-69; committeeman Dem. Party, Port Washington, 1967-71. Mem. ABA, Assn. of Bar of City of New York, N.Y.State Bar Assn. Democrat. Methodist. Corporate, general, Securities. Home: 103 E 86th St Apt 7A New York NY 10028-1058 Office: United Vanguard Homes Inc 4 Cedar Swamp Rd Glen Cove NY 11542-3744 E-mail: afeck@uvhco.com.

SHIELDS, PETER D. lawyer; BA with honors, SUNY; JD, Syracuse U. Bar: D.C., N.Y., U.S. Ct. Appeals (D.C. cir.), U.S. Supreme Ct. Ptnr. Wiley Rein Fielding, LLP, Washington. Named Pro Bono Atty. of the Yr., D.C. Bar, 1993—94. Mem.: Fed. Comm. Bar Assn. (pres. 2002—03, Disting. Svc. award 1997—98). Office: Wiley Rein & Fielding 1776 K St NW Washington DC 20006*

SHIELDS, THOMAS CHARLES, lawyer; b. Evergreen Park, Ill., Apr. 26, 1941; s. Thomas James and Adelaide (McElligott) S.; m. Nicoline M. Murphy, Sept. 14, 1974; children: Thomas James II, Nicoline M.E., Suzanne Adelaide, Kerry Anne. AB, Georgetown U., 1963; JD cum laude, Northwestern U., 1966. Bar: Ill. 1966, U.S. Dist. Ct. (no. dist.) Ill. 1966, U.S. Ct. Appeals (7th cir.) 1966, U.S. Tax Ct. 1968, U.S. Supreme Ct. 1977. Assoc. Hopkins & Sutter, Chgo., 1966-73, ptnr., 1973-93; ptnr., chair health law dept. Bell, Boyd & Lloyd, Chgo., 1994—; chief counsel Cath. Health Assn. U.S., St. Louis, 1994—. Adv. bd. Health Law Inst. Loyola U. Sch. Law, Chgo., 1984-89, Health Law Inst. DePaul U. Sch. Law, Chgo., 1985-96; lectr. Ill. Inst. Continuing Legal Edn., 1973; bd. dirs. Ill. Health Facilities Authority; trustee Village of Riverside, Ill., 2001--. Contbr. articles to profl. pubs., chpt. to book; mng. editor Northwestern Law Rev., 1965-66. Bd. dir. Cancer Rsch. Found., Chgo., 1987—, Brother Louie and Fannie Roncoli Found., 1994—, Chgo. Zool. Soc., Cath. Charities Chgo.; trustee Village of Riverside, 2001—. Mem.: Chgo. Bar Assn., Ill. Assn. Healthcare Attys. (bd. dir. 1983—89, pres. 1987—88), Ill. Bar Assn., Am. Hosp. Assn. (tax adv. group 1987—90), Am. Health Lawyers Assn. (bd. dir. 1983—91, pres. 1989—90), Mid-Am. Club Chgo., Order of Coif. Avocations: skiing, bicycling, golf, tennis. General practice, Health, Probate (including wills, trusts). Office: Bell Boyd & Lloyd 3 First Nat Plz Ste 3200 Chicago IL 60602

SHIENTAG, FLORENCE PERLOW, lawyer; b. N.Y.C. d. David and Ester (Germane) Perlow; m. Bernard L. Shientag, June 8, 1938. BS, NYU, 1940, LLB, 1933, JD, 1940. Bar: Fla. 1976, N.Y. Law aide Thomas E. Dewey, 1937; law sec. Mayor La Guardia, 1939-42; justice Domestic Relations Ct., 1941-42; mem. Tchrs. Retirement Bd., N.Y.C., 1942-46; asst. U.S. atty. So. dist. N.Y., 1943-53; cir. ct. mediator Fla. Supreme Ct., 1992; pvt. practice N.Y.C., 1960—, Palm Beach, Fla., 1976—. Lectr. on internat. divorce; mem. Nat. Commn. on Wiretapping and Electronic Surveillance, 1973—, Task Force on Women in Cts., 1985-86. Contbr. articles to profl. jours. Candidate N.Y. State Senate, 1954; bd. dirs. UN Devel. Corp., 1972-95, Franklin and Eleanor Roosevelt Inst., 1985—; bd. dirs., assoc. treas. YM and YWHA; hon. commr. commerce, N.Y.C. Mem. ABA, Fed. Bar Assn. (exec. com.), Internat. Bar Assn., N.Y. Women's Bar Assn. (pres., dir., Life Time Achievement award 1994, special award 2002), N.Y. State Bar Assn., N.Y.C. Bar Assn. (chmn. law and art sect.), N.Y. County Lawyers Assn. (dir.), Nat. Assn. Women LAwyers (sec.). Home: 737 Park Ave New York NY 10021-4256 Address: 44 Cocoanut Row Palm Beach FL 33480

SHILLING, MONICA JILL, lawyer; b. Kansas City, Kans., Dec. 17, 1969; d. David Randall Shilling and Shelia Jan Brown. BA in Creative Writing and French, U. Redlands, 1992; JD magna cum laude, Georgetown U., 1995. Bar: Calif. 1995. Assoc. Skadden, Arps, Slate, Meagher & Flom LLP, L.A., 1995—. Mem.: ABA, L.A. County Bar Assn., Calif. Bar Assn., Order of Coif, Phi Beta Kappa. Corporate, general, Finance, Mergers and acquisitions. Office: Skadden Arps Slate Meagher & Flom LLP 300 S Grand Ave Los Angeles CA 90071-3109 E-mail: mshillin@skadden.com.

SHIMM, MELVIN GERALD, law educator; b. N.Y.C., Jan. 30, 1926; s. Joseph George and Sadie Rosalie (Rosenblatt) Shimm; m. Cynia Brown, Aug. 15, 1948; children: David Stuart, Jonathan Evan. AB, Columbia U., 1947; LLB, Yale U., 1950. Bar: NY 50. Assoc. Cahill, Gordon, Zachry & Reindel, N.Y.C., 1950—51; atty. Wage Stblzn. Bd., Washington, 1951—52; Bigelow fellow U. Chgo., 1952—53; asst. prof. Duke U. Law Sch., Durham, NC, 1953—56, assoc. prof., 1956—59, prof., 1959—96, prof. emeritus, 1996—, assoc. dean, 1978—83. Vis. prof. NYU, 1957, U. So. Calif., 1965, U. Mich., Ann Arbor, 1973, U. Tex., Austin, 1976; chmn. Durham (NC) Bd. Adjustment, 1966—70; dir. Assn. Am. Law Schs. Orientation Program in Am. Law, 1968—70, Duke Inst. in Transnat. Law, 1987—92; cons. The Brookings Instn., 1965—67; mem. NC Gen. Statutes Commn., 1984—88. Editor-in-chief: Law & Contemporary Problems, Jour. Legal Edn., Am. Editor Jour. Bus. Law; editor: Yale Law Jour. Bd. dirs., vice-chmn. Lucy Daniels Found., 1989—; bd. advisors Ctr. for Law, Ethics and Nat. Security, 1993—; pres. Beth El Congregation, Durham, NC, 1967—70, 1975—78; chmn. Jewish Fedn. Durham/Chapel Hill, 1967—69. Lt. U.S. Army, 1943—46. Mem.: Order of Coif, Phi Beta Kappa. Office: Duke U Sch Law PO Box 90360 Durham NC 27708-0360 E-mail: shimms@earthlink.net., shimm@law.duke.edu.

SHIMOFF, PAUL MARTIN, lawyer; b. San Francisco, Nov. 1, 1947; s. Marcus and Louise Barbara (Jacobs) S.; m. Susan Louise Richmond, Aug. 27, 1972; children: Aaron, Jared. BA, UCLA, 1969; JD, U. Calif. Hastings Coll. Law, 1972. Bar: Calif. 1972, U.S. Dist. Ct. (so. and cen. dists.) Calif. 1972, U.S. Ct. Appeals (9th cir.) 1972, U.S. Tax Ct. 1973, U.S. Ct. Claims 1973, U.S. Supreme Ct. 2001; cert. specialist in taxation law, Calif. Shareholder McPeters, McAlearney Shimoff & Hatt, A Profl. Corp., Redlands, Calif., 1985—98. Bd. dirs. San Bernardino Legal Aid Soc., 1985-86; advisor San Bernardino Community Law-Related Edn., 1985; bd. dirs. Inland Empire Symphony, San Bernadino, 1981, bd. dir., v.p. Inland Action Cmty. Hosp. San Bernardino; trustees, U. Calif., Riverside; trustee, Found. State Bar Calif. Fellow Am. Coll. Trusts and Estates Counsel; mem. San Bernardino County Bar Assn. (pres. 1985-86), Estate Planning Council for San Bernardino County (pres. 1985-86), Calif. Bd. Legal Specialization (cert.). Corporate taxation, Estate taxation, Personal income taxation. Home: 12912 Hilary Way Redlands CA 92373-7466 Office: 4 W Redlands Blvd Fl 2 Redlands CA 92373-4702

SHIMPOCK, KATHY ELIZABETH, lawyer, writer; b. Mooresville, N.C., July 20, 1952; d. Charles Walter and Minna Ethel (McLean) S.; m. David Edward Vieweg, Sept. 3, 1983 (div. Mar. 1997); children: Jessica Kim Vieweg, Jayme Elise Kyung Vieweg. BA, Colo. Coll., 1973; JD, U. Wyo., 1977; MLL, U. Denver, 1979; MBA, Ariz. State U., 1992. Bar: Ariz. 1977. Asst. librarian Stanford (Calif.) U. Coll. Law, 1979—82; law librarian, asst. prof. law U. Bridgeport (Conn.) Coll. Law, 1982—83; dir. Law Libr. Adminstrv. Svcs., Mountain View, Calif., 1983—85; exec. asst. to dean Ariz. State U. Coll. Law, Tempe, 1985—87; dir. Law Libr. Adminstrv. Svcs., Mesa, Ariz., 1987—95; dir. libr. svcs. Jennings, Strouss & Salmon, Phoenix, 1988—89; dir. rsch. svcs. O'Connor, Cavanagh et al, Phoenix, 1989—95; pres. Juris Rsch., Mesa, 1998—; counsel Muchmore & Wallwork, Phoenix, 1995—98; pres. Juris Rsch., Tempe, 1998—; rsch. and legal info. mgr. Bryan Cave LLP, 2000—. Adv. bd. West Pub. Co., St. Paul, 1991-94; bd. dir. Dillon S.W., Scottsdale, Ariz.; mediator Alternative Dispute Resolution Program, Maricopa County, Ariz. Author: Business Research Handbook: Methods and Sources for Lawyers and Business Professionals, 1996—; co-author: Arizona Legal Research Guide, 1992; contbr. chpts. to books, articles to profl. jours.; bi-monthly columnist AzALL News, 1996-97, Legal Assistant Today, 1993-96; contbr. book revs. to Libr. Jour., Legal Info. Alert, 1993-98; editor Southwest Assn. Law Librs. Bull., 1990, Ariz. State U. Coll. Law Law Forum, 1986, Juris Rsch. E-line, 1999—. Rsch. atty. Comml. Law Project for the Ukraine, Phoenix, 1995-96. Mem. ABA (co-chair law practice mgmt. environ. divsn. 1996-99), Am. Assn. Law Librs. (chair 1994-95), Ariz. Assn. Law Librs. (pres. 1996-97, pres.'s award 1997, Disting. Mem. award 1998), State Bar of Ariz. (chair 1996-98, Cont. Legal Edn. award 1998), Ariz. Women Lawyers Assn. (steering com. 1998-2000). Democrat. United Meth. Avocations: reading, yoga, painting, drawing. Environmental, Intellectual property, Labor (including EEOC, Fair Labor Standards Act, labor-management relations, NLRB, OSHA). Office: Juris Rsch PO Box 2157 Tempe AZ 85280-2157 E-mail: kshimpock@jurisresearch.com.

SHINDLER, DONALD A. lawyer; b. New Orleans, Oct. 15, 1946; s. Alan and Isolene (Levy) S.; m. Laura Epstein, 1969; children: Jay, Susan. BSBA, Washington U., St. Louis, 1968; JD, Tulane U., 1971. Bar: La. 1971, U.S. Dist. Ct. (ea. dist.) La. 1971, U.S. Tax Ct. 1974, Ill. 1975, U.S. Dist. Ct. (no. dist.) Ill. 1975; CPA, La.; lic. real estate broker, Ill. Assoc. Pope, Ballard, Shepard & Fowle, Chgo., 1975-78, Rudnick & Wolfe, Chgo., 1978-81, ptnr., 1981-99; gen. counsel America's Second Harvest Nat. Food Bank Network, 1998-2000; ptnr. Piper Marbury Rudnick & Wolfe, Chgo., 1999—2002, Piper Rudnick, Chgo., 2002—. Seminar lectr. ABA, Chgo. Bar Assn., Ill. Inst. CLE, Profl. Edn. Sys., Inc., Internat. Assn. Corp. Real Estate Execs., Urban Land Inst., Am. Corp. Counsel Assn., Bldg. Owners and Mgrs. Assn., Internat. Assn. of Attys. and Execs. in Corp. Real Estate, others. Contbr. articles on real estate to legal jours. Trustee Glencoe (Ill.) Pub. Libr., 1981-87, pres., 1986-87; alumni bd. govs. Washington U., 1992-93; mem. Glencoe Zoning Commn./Bd. Appeals, 1994-2000. Lt. JAGC, USNR, 1971-75. Mem. ABA, La. State Bar Assn., Chgo. Bar Assn. (com. chmn. 1979-80, 83-84, 90-94, 96-99, editor land trust seminars 1984-96), Urban Land Inst. (mem. steering com. Chgo. dist. coun.), CoreNet Global (pres. Chgo. chpt. 1997-98, dir. 1991—), Internat. Assn. Attys. and Execs. in Corp. Real Estate, Union League Club (chair real estate group 1993-96), Order of Coif, Beta Gamma Sigma, Omicron Delta Kappa. Corporate, general, Environmental, Property, real (including real estate development, water). Office: Piper Rudnick Ste 1800 203 N La Salle St Ste 1800 Chicago IL 60601-1210 E-mail: donald.shindler@piperrudnick.com.

SHINDURLING, JON J. judge; b. Idaho Falls, Idaho, Apr. 13, 1947; s. Boyd Thomas and Donna Marie (Fullmer) S.; m. Christine Moss, May 24, 1974; children: Melissa, Marianne, Amanda, Alison. BA in English, Ariz. State U., 1972; JD, U. Idaho, 1977. Bar: Idaho. Ptnr. May & May Law Offices, Twin Falls, Idaho, 1977-88, Wright Law Offices, Idaho Falls, 1990-93; field dir. Sch. of Urban and Wilderness Survival, Shoshone, Idaho, 1988-90; dep. prosecuting atty. Bonneville County, Idaho Falls, 1994-2000, chief dep., 1995-2000; dist. judge 7th Jud. Dist., 2000—. Mem. continuing legal edn. com. Idaho Law Found., Boise, 1985-88; mem. civil jury instns. com. Idaho Supreme Ct., Boise, 1987-89, 96—. Mem. coun. exec. bd. Boy Scouts Am.-Snake River Area, Twin Falls, 1979-90; bd. dirs. Magic Valley YFCA, Twin Falls, 1988-90, Idaho Falls Opera Theatre, 1993-99. Mem. Idaho State Bar (mem. bar examination com. 1979-82, chmn. com. 1980-82, mem. fee disputes resolution com. 1991—). Mem. Lds Ch. Avocations: reading, fishing, scouting. Office: Office Dist Ct 605 N Capital Ave Idaho Falls ID 83402-3582 E-mail: jshindurling@co.bonneville.id.us.

SHINE, DAVID BRUCE, lawyer; b. Boston, Aug. 11, 1938; s. Thomas Foss and Alice Matilda (Hudgins) S.; m. Elizabeth Magoffin, May 31, 1969; children: James Vincent, Edward Magoffin, David Bruce Jr. BSBA, Tusculum Coll., 1960; JD, Vanderbilt U., 1964; postgrad., Columbia U., 1964-65; LLD (hon.), Tusculum Coll., 1984; LLM, U. Leicester, Eng., 1999. Bar: Tenn. 1964, N.Y. 1966, D.C. 1975. Mem. legal dept. Broadcast Music, Inc., 1964-66; legis. asst. to U.S. Sen. Ross Bass, 1966; mem. Office of Spl. Counsel V.P. U.S., 1966-67; assoc. McLellan, Thatcher & Donoahue, Washington and Kingsport, Tenn., 1967-69; ptnr. Ferguson & Shine, Kingsport, 1969-83; pvt. practice Kingsport, 1983-88; ptnr. Shine & Mason, Kingsport, 1988—. Gen. counsel United Textile Workers Am., AFL-CIO, 1978—; adj. prof. law Appalachian Sch. Law, 2000; vis. fellow Internat. Maritime Low Inst., Malta, 2000—. Contbr. articles to profl. jours. Chmn. bd. trustees Tusculum Coll., 1977-88; bd. trustees Hiwassee Coll., 1994-98; mem. Dem. Nat. Com., 1972-76; commr. ADR, Supreme Ct. of Tenn., 1996—. Decorated Order of Merit (Italy). Fellow ABA, Tenn. Bar Assn.; mem. Nat. Lawyers Club. Anglican Catholic. Avocations: canoeing, collecting toy soldiers. Federal civil litigation, Labor (including EEOC, Fair Labor Standards Act, labor-management relations, NLRB, OSHA), Pension, profit-sharing, and employee benefits. Home: 548A Fleetwood St Kingsport TN 37660-3493 Office: 433 E Center St Kingsport TN 37660-4803 E-mail: bruceshine@chartertn.net.

SHINKLE, JOHN THOMAS, lawyer; b. Albany, N.Y., May 9, 1946; s. Robert Thomas and Margery Joan (Kneip) S.; m. Csilla Elizabeth Bekasy, Sept. 2, 1967; children: Reka, Ildiko. BA, Yale U., 1967; JD, Harvard U., 1970. Bar: D.C. 1971, N.Y. 1983, U.S. Supreme Ct. 1974. Law clk. U.S. Ct. Appeals for D.C. Circuit, Washington, 1970-71; assoc. Caplin & Drysdale, Washington, 1971-77, ptnr., 1977-80; assoc. dir. divsn. corp. fin. SEC, Washington, 1980-81, dep. gen. counsel, 1981-82; gen. counsel Salomon Bros. Inc., N.Y.C., 1982-94, v.p., 1982-87, dir., 1988-94, Asia Pacific legal and compliance dir., 1995; mng. dir. Salomon Bros., Hong Kong, 1996-97, Salomon Smith Barney, Hong Kong, 1997—. Contbr. articles to profl. jours. Mem. ABA, Assn. Bar City N.Y., Securities Industry Assn. (chmn. fed. regulation com. 1989-91), Futures Industry Assn. (dir. 1989-97), Downtown Athletic Club (N.Y.C.). Corporate, general, Private international, Securities. Home: 2703B Queen's Garden 9 Old Peak Rd Hong Kong Hong Kong Office: Salomon Smith Barney 3 Exchange Sq Fl 20 Hong Kong Hong Kong

SHINN, CLINTON WESLEY, lawyer; b. Haworth, Okla., Mar. 7, 1947; s. Clinton Elmo and Mary Lucille (Dowdy) Shinn; m. Catherine Borne; children: Laura Kathryn, Clinton Wesley, Timothy Daniel. BS, McNeese State U., 1969; JD, Tulane U., 1972; LLM, Harvard U., 1973. Bar: La. 1972, U.S. Dist. Ct. (ea. dist.) La. 1975, U.S. Dist. Ct. (we. dist.) La. 1980, U.S. Ct. Appeals (5th cir.) 1981, U.S. Ct. Appeals (11th cir.) 1982, U.S. Tax Ct. 1982. Asst. prof. law Tulane U., New Orleans, 1973—75; assoc. Stone, Pigman et al, New Orleans, 1975—78, ptnr., 1979—97, Gill & Shinn, LLC, Covington, La., 1998—2000, of counsel, 2000—; assoc. prof. law Appalachian Sch. Law, 1999—2002, Miss. Coll. Sch. Law, 2002—. Co-founder, bd. dirs. Childhood Ctr. Families Network, 1987—90; co-founder Camp Challenge, 1988; team leader Campaign for Caring, Children's Hosp., New Orleans, 1989—91; bd. dirs. Greater New Orleans YMCA, 1989—98, 1999—2000, exec. com., 1991—98, asst. sec., 1994—95, sec., 1996—98, mem. fin. com., 1994—98, exec. dir. search com., 1996, 2d vice-chair, 1998; mem. Leadership Coun., 1997—98; active Indian Guides/Princesses; bd. dirs. West ST. Tammany YMCA, 1987—95, exec. com., 1988—95, chmn. bd. dirs., 1989—90, 1992—93; bd. dirs. La. Air & Waste Mgmt. Assn., 1993—99, chmn. corp. rels. com., 1992—93, vice chmn., 1996—97, chair, 1997—98, past chair, 1998—99; bd. dirs. Christ Episcopal Sch., Covington, 1988—91, chmn. long-range planning, 1990—91, mem. exec. com., 1989—91, chmn. legal com., 1989—91, chmn. admissions/recruitment com., 1988—90, mem. headmaster search com., 1993; bd. dirs. Christwood, 1992—2001, v.p. bd. dirs., 1997—99. Co-recipient Pals of the Yr. award, Greater New Orleans YMCA Indian Guides/Princesses, 1987—88; named Vol. of the Yr., West St. Tammany YMCA, 1990, 1992. Fellow: La. Bar Found., Am. Coll. Trust and Estate Counsel; mem.: ABA, Air and Waste Mgmt. Assn., New Orleans Estate Planning Coun., Nat. Wildlife Fedn. (life), La. Forestry Assn., La. Bar Assn., Nat. Assn. Securities Dealers (bd. arbitrators), Order Coif. Avocations: backpacking, gardening. Corporate, general, Environmental, Probate (including wills, trusts). Home: 101 Aspen Dr Madison MS 39110 Office: Miss Coll Law Sch 151 E Griffith Jackson MS

SHINN, MICHAEL ROBERT, lawyer; b. Salem, Oreg., June 25, 1947; s. William Robert and Miriam Jean (Becke) S. BA, Willamette U., 1969, JD, 1973. Bar: Oreg. 1973, U.S. Dist. Ct. Oreg. 1973, U.S. Ct. Appeals (9th cir.) 1973. Law clk. to judge U.S. Dist. Ct., Portland, Oreg., 1974-75; pvt. practice Portland, 1975—. Lectr. Masters at Trial Oreg., We. Trial Lawyers Assn., Oreg. State Bar, Mont. State Bar, Oreg. Law Inst., Nat. Bus. Inst. Editor Trial Lawyer Quar., 1988; dir., editor, producer: (videotape) (with Gerry Spence) Spence in Trial, 1989-90; co-producer, dir.: (videotape) Spence in Trial, Series for Trial Lawyers; cons. NBC mini-series Dead By Sunset, 1995. Pres. W. Hills and Island Neighbors Assn., Portland, 1983-84; del. Citizen to Citizen Legal Amb. Dels. to China, 1988; mem., bd. dirs. adv. coun. Oreg. Hearing Rsch. Ctr., 1992; bd. dirs. Portland Civic Theater. Inducted Willamette U. Athletic Hall of Fame, 1998. Mem. Oreg. Trial Lawyers Assn., (pres. 1980-81, edn. dir. 1984-89, svc. award 1986, 87), Am. Inns. of Ct. (master barrister 1988). Avocations: writing, wind surfing, skiing, water skiing, tennis, rugby. Civil rights, General civil litigation, Personal injury (including property damage). Office: 621 SW Morrison St Ste 1000 Portland OR 97205-3821 E-mail: michaelshinn@aol.com.

SHIPLEY, DAVID ELLIOTT, dean, lawyer; b. Urbana, Ill., Oct. 3, 1950; s. James Ross and Dorothy Jean (Elliott) S.; m. Virginia Florence Coleman, May 24, 1980; 1 child, Shannon C. BA, Oberlin Coll., 1972; JD, U. Chgo., 1975. Bar: R.I. 1975. Assoc. Tillinghast, Collins & Graham, Providence, 1975-77; asst. prof. U. S.C. Sch. Law, Columbia, 1977-81, assoc. prof., 1981-85, prof., 1985-90, assoc. dean, 1989-90; dean U. Miss. Sch. Law, University, 1990-93, U. Ky. Coll. Law, Lexington, 1993-98; prof., dean Sch. Law U. Ga., Athens, 1998—. Vis. prof. Coll. William and Mary, Williamsburg, Va., 1983-84, Ohio State U. Coll. Law, Columbus, 1986-87. Author: South Carolina Administrative Law, 1983, 2d edit., 1989; co-author Copyright Law, 1992. Pres. Shandon Neighborhood Assn., Columbia, 1988-90. Named Prof. of Yr., U. S.C. Sch. Law, 1990, faculty scholar, 1989-90. Mem. ABA, R.I. Bar Assn., S.C. Bar Assn. (assoc.). Methodist. Avocations: running, yardwork, gardening, reading. Home: 475 River Bottom Rd Athens GA 30606-6430 Office: U Ga Sch Law Dean Office Athens GA 30602-6012*

SHIPP, DAN SHACKELFORD, lawyer; b. Yazoo City, Miss., Jan. 6, 1946; s. Dan Hugh and Anora Nona (Shackelford) A.; m. Carolyn Julie Perry, Nov. 30, 1974; children: Perry Lee, Clay Alexander. AA, Holmes Jr. Coll., 1966; BA, Miss. State U., 1968; JD, U. Miss., 1971. Bar: Miss. 1971, U.S. Dist. Ct. (no. dist.) Miss. 1971, U.S. Dist. Ct. (so. dist.) Miss. 1976, Colo. 1986, U.S. Ct. Appeals (5th cir.) 1982, U.S. Ct. Appeals (10th cir.) 1986, U.S. Dist. Ct. Colo. 1986. Pvt. practice, Yazoo City, Miss., 1974-83, Aspen, 1986—2001, Basalt, Colo., 2002—. Speaker in field. Recipient Master Advocate Cert. award Nat. Inst. Trial Advocacy Notre Dame Law Sch., 1993. Mem. ABA, Colo. Trial Lawyers Assn. (bd. dirs. 1986-88), Assn. Trial Lawyers Am., Colo. Bar Assn., Toastmasters Internat. Avocations: hunting, archery, traveling. General civil litigation, General practice, Personal injury (including property damage). Home: 0300 Vagneur Ln Basalt CO 81621-9103 Fax: 970-927-6633. E-mail: danshipplaw@comcast.net.

SHIPPER, DAVID W. lawyer; b. N.Y.C., Oct. 30, 1958; s. Herbert K. and Judith S. (Sigall) S. BA, NYU, 1979; JD, N.Y. Law Sch., 1982. Bar: N.Y. 1983, N.J. 1983, Fla. 1984; U.S. Dist. Ct. N.J. 1983, U.S. Dist. Ct. (so. and ea. dists.) N.Y. 1983; U.S. Tax Ct. 1989. Pvt. practice, N.Y.C., 1983—. Trustee N.Y. Law Sch., 1999—2002. Mem. ABA, N.Y. State Bar Assn., N.Y. Law Sch. Alumni Assn. (dir. 1983—, treas. 1991-95, v.p. 1995-99, pres. 1999-2002), Phi Delta Phi. Probate (including wills, trusts), Property, real (including real estate development, water), Taxation, general. Home: 201 E 69th St New York NY 10021-5471 Office: 567 3d Ave New York NY 10016

SHIPPEY, SANDRA LEE, lawyer; b. Casper, Wyo., June 24, 1957; d. Virgil Carr and Doris Louise (Conklin) McClintock; m. Ojars Herberts Ozols, Sept. 2, 1978 (div.); children: Michael Ojars, Sara Ann, Brian Christopher; m. James Robert Shippey, Jan. 13, 1991; 1 child, Matthew James. BA with distinction, U. Colo., 1978; JD magna cum laude, Boston U., 1982. Bar: Colo. 1982, U.S. Dist. Ct. Colo. 1985. Assoc. Cohen, Brame & Smith, Denver, 1983-84, Parcel, Meyer, Schwartz, Ruttum & Mauro, Denver, 1984-85, Mayer, Brown & Platt, Denver, 1985-87; counsel western ops. GE Capital Corp., San Diego, 1987-94; assoc. Page, Polin, Busch & Boatwright, San Diego, 1994-95; v.p., gen. counsel First Comml. Corp., San Diego, 1995-96; legal counsel NextWave Telecom Inc., San Diego, 1996-98; ptnr. Procopio, Cory, Hargreaves and Savitch, LLP, 1998—. Spkr. in field. Contbr. articles to profl. jours. Active Pop Warner football and cheerleading; bd. dirs. Southwestern Christian Schs., Inc., 2002—, San Diego Christian Found., 2001—. Mem. Calif. State Bar (uniform comml. code com.), Phi Beta Kappa, Phi Delta Phi. Republican. Mem. Ch. of Christ. Avocations: tennis, golf, photography. Banking, Corporate, general, Finance. Home: 15839 Big Springs Way San Diego CA 92127-2034 Office: Procopio Cory Et Al 530 B St Ste 2100 San Diego CA 92101-4496 E-mail: sls@procopio.com.

SHIRAI, SHUN, law educator, lawyer; b. Tokyo, June 18, 1942; s. Kyo and Tomi Shirai; m. Junko Matsushita, Apr. 10, 1969; children: Akiko, Yuko, Jin. LLB, Hitotsubashi U., Tokyo, 1966, LLM, 1969. Cert. atty. at law. Asst. prof. criminal law Kokugakuin U., Tokyo, 1974-81, prof., 1981—, dean Grad. Sch., 1999-2001. Atty. Tokyo 2nd Bar Assn., 1992—. Author: Phenomenology of Crime, 1984, rev. edit., 1998, Thought on Criminal Law of Ancient India, 1985, Legal History on Criminal Law of Ancient India, 1990, Philosophy of Criminal Law in Ancient India, 1995, Phenomenology and Indian Philosophy for the Study on Ancient Indian Criminal Law, 1997, Prof. Shirai's Lectures on the Law of Criminal Procedure, 1998, Philosophy of Criminal Law in Bhagavad-gītā at Ancient India, 1998, Crime and Sorrowness of Human Being, 1999, Defence Lawyer's Statements in Criminal Court, 2000, Thoughts on Death Penalty in Ancient India, 2000, The Sanskrit, as a Legal Language, appearing in Judicial Documents of British India and Non-Violent Theory of Punishment, originated in Ancient India, 2000, Thought on Righteousness in Criminal Law, handed down by Tradition from Ancient India, 2002, On Basic Principles of Hindu Criminology, derived from Ancient Indian Criminal Law, 2002, Introduction to Study on Practice of Japanese Criminal Jurisdiction, 2003, Philosophy of Crime of Contemporary Indian Thought on Human Being, 2003—. Mem. Indian History Congress. Buddhist. Home: 703 Kinsen Bldg 2-16-1 Hanakawado Taito-ku Tokyo 111-0033 Japan Office: Kokugakuin U 4-10-28 Higashi Shibuya-Ku Tokyo 150-8440 Japan

SHIRE, HAROLD RAYMOND, law educator, writer, scientist; b. Denver, Nov. 23, 1910; s. Samuel Newport and Rose Betty (Herman) S.; m. Cecilia Goldhaar, May 9, 1973; children: David, Darcy, Esti, Donna, Margaret. MBA, Pepperdine U., 1972, LLD (hon.), 1975; JD, Southwestern U., L.A., 1974; M in Liberal Arts, U. So. Calif., 1977; PhD in Human Behavior, U.S. Internat. U., San Diego, 1980. Bar: Calif. 1937, U.S. Dist. Ct. (so. dist.) Calif. 1939, U.S. Supreme Ct. 1978. Dep. dist. atty. L.A. County, Calif., 1937-38; asst. U.S. atty. So. Dist. Calif., L.A. and San Diego, 1939-42; pvt. practice L.A., 1946-56; pres., chmn. bd. Gen. Connectors Corp., U.S. and Eng., 1956-73; prof. mgmt. and law Pepperdine U., Malibu, Calif., 1974-75, U.S. Internat. U., San Diego, 1980-83; dir. Bestobell Aviation, Eng., 1970-74. Author: Cha No Yu and Symbolic Interactionism: Method of Predicting Japanese Behavior, 1980, The Tea Ceremony, 1984. Patentee aerospace pneumatics; invented flexible connectors; designed, manufactured flexible integrity systems. Advisor U.S.C. Gerontology Andrus Ctr., pre-retirement tng., 1976-80; bd. dirs. Pepperdine U., 1974-80; nat. bd. govs. Union Orthodox Jewish Congregations Am., 1973—; mem. Rep. Nat. Com.; pres. Jewish Nat. Fund Legion of Honor, 1991—; mem. Presdl. Roundtable, Washington, 1989-97; mem. Inner Cir., Pres. Regan and Bush, 1989-92; life mem. Rep. Nat. Com. With U.S. Army, 1942-46. Decorated chevalier du vieux moulin (France); companion Royal Aero. Soc. (U.K.); recipient Tea Name Grand Master Soshitsu Sen XV Urasenke Sch., Kyoto, Japan, 1976, Medal of Honor Jewish Nat. Fund, Legion of Honor, 1991, U.S. Senate Medal of Freedom. Mem. ABA, Am. Welding Soc., Soc. Material and Process Engrs., Am. Legion (svc. officer China #1 Shanghai), Calif. Symphony Soc. (pres. 1998—), Masons (32 degree, Hiram award 1994), Royal Arch, Shrine, Legion of Honor Jewish Nat. Fund (nat. chmn. bd. 1999). Achievements include design and manufacture of fluidic systems flexible integrity for Saturn IV and welding in Apollo XI landing on moon, 1969. Office: PO Box 1352 Beverly Hills CA 90213-1352

SHIRK, KENELM LAWRENCE, JR., lawyer; b. Lancaster, Pa., June 26, 1922; s. Kenelm Lawrence and Beatrice Marie (Wertz) S.; m. Romaine Sensenig, Nov. 10, 1945; children— Kenelm Lawrence III, Kathie R. Shirk Gonick, Kraig Leofric. B.A., Washington and Lee U., 1943; J.D., Dickinson Sch. Law, 1948. Bar: Pa. 1949, U.S. Supreme Ct. 1954. Sole practice, Lancaster, 1949, 56-67; ptnr. Shirk and Shirk, Lancaster, 1950-56; ptnr. Shirk, Reist, Wagenseller & Shirk and predecessors and successors, Lancaster, 1967— ; charter pres. Lancaster Mediation Ctr. Chmn. Rep. Com. Lancaster County, 1964-71; bd. dirs. Urban League Lancaster County (Pa.), 1985-91, 98-, Community Hosp. Lancaster, Spanish-Am. Civic Assn. Devel. Corp.; charter mem. bd. dirs. Jr. Achievement Lancaster County, Inc.; co-chmn. Bi-partisan Com. for study Lancaster County Govt.; chmn. Shade Tree Meml. Com., Lancaster County; res. elder First Presbyn. Ch., Lancaster. Served to capt. USAAF, 1943-45, with USAF, 1951-53. Decorated Air medal, Presdl. citation; named Jaycee of World, Jr. Chamber Internat., 1960, Boss of Yr., Legal Secs. Assn., 1981; recipient Disting. Service award Lancaster Jr. C. of C., 1954, Good Govt. award, 1970, Humanitarian award Lancaster City-County Human Relations Commn., 1981, Adult Human Relations award Lancaster Chpt. NCCJ, 1986, Exemplar award, Lancaster C. of C. and Industry, 2001, Svc. to Mankind award, Sertoma, 2001, Cmty. Svc. award, Rotary, 1999. Fellow Am. Bar Found.; mem. Am. Coll. Trust and Estate Counsel, Am. Coll. Real Estate Lawyers (charter mem.), Pa. Bar Assn. (ho. of dels. 1979-88, bd. govs. 1985-88, Spl. Achievement award 1979-80, chmn. sect. mcpl. law 1980-81, chmn. sect. real property, probate and trust law 1981-82), Lancaster Bar Assn. (pres. 1980), Inst. for Land Info. (past pres.), World Peace Through Law Ctr. (past chmn. com. resolutions), ABA (chmn. sect. coms.), Am. Judicature Soc., Nat. Sojourners (Lancaster chpt.), Lancaster Rifles (Heroes of '76). Clubs: Hamilton, Tucquan (past pres.). Lodge: Elks (lodge exalted ruler Lancaster chpt. 1952-53, Elk of Yr. 1956, pres. South Cen. dist. Pa. 1956-57). Estate planning, Property, real (including real estate development, water), Land use and zoning (including planning). Home and Office: PO Box 1552 Lancaster PA 17608-1552

SHKLAR, MICHAEL CHARLES, lawyer; b. Boston, Sept. 28, 1960; s. Gerald and Judith (Nisse) S.; m. Carol Marie Stamatakis, Mar. 23, 1985; children: Rachel, Abraham. BA, Carleton Coll., 1982; JD, Case Western Res. U., 1985. Bar: N.H. 1985, U.S. Dist. Ct. N.H. 1985, U.S. Ct. Appeals 1990, U.S. Ct. Vet. Appeals 1990, U.S. Supreme Ct. 1992, U.S. Tax Ct. 1993. Assoc. Feeney & Kraeger, Newport, N.H., 1985, Elliott & Jasper, Newport, 1986-87; pvt. practice Newport, 1987-2000; ptnr. Elliott Jasper, Auten & Shklar, 2000—. Pres. bd. Orion House, Inc., Newport, 1986-95; bd. dirs. Women's Supportive Svcs., Claremont, N.H., 1987-94, gen. counsel, 1994—; mem. Goshen Lempster (N.H.) Sch. Bd., 1988-93, chair, 1990-91; moderator Lempster (N.H.) Sch. Dist., 1998—, Town of Lempster (N.H.) 1998—. Mem. ATLA, N.H. Bar Assn. (mem. fee dispute resolution com. 1988-90, bd. govs. 1992-94, Pro Bono Atty. of Yr. 1987, 89, 91, 92, 2001), Sullivan County Bar Assn. (sec.-treas. 1998-99, pres. 2000-01), N.H. Trial Lawyers Assn. (bd. govs. 1994-96). Democrat. Avocations: reading, cooking. Bankruptcy, General practice, Juvenile. Office: PO Box 297 Newport NH 03773-0297

SHMUKLER, STANFORD, lawyer; b. Phila., June 16, 1930; s. Samuel and Tessye (Dounne) S.; m. Anita Golove, Mar. 21, 1951; children: Jodie Lynne Shmukler Girsh, Joel Mark, Steven David. BS in Econs., U. Pa., 1951, JD, 1954. Bar: D.C. 1954, Pa. 1955, U.S. Ct. Appeals (2d cir.) 1959, U.S. Supreme Ct. 1959, U.S. Ct. Appeals (3d cir.) 1960, U.S. Ct. Mil. Appeals 1966. Atty. U.S. Bur. Pub. Roads, 1954-55, cons., 1955-57; sole practice Phila., 1955—. Lectr. Temple U. Law Sch., 1975-78; mem., past sec., exec. dir. criminal procedural rules com. Pa. Supreme Ct., 1971-87; mem. lawyers adv. com. Ct. Appeals for 3d cir., 1977-80, selection com. Criminal Justice Act Panel, 1979-84; chmn. selection com. Phila. Bar Ct. Appointments, 1988-91. Contbr. articles to profl. jours. Bd. dirs. Ecumenical Halfway House, 1967-71; bd. mgrs. Alumni Assn., Ctrl. High Sch., Phila. Served to col. JAGC, USAR, from 1955 (ret.). Recipient Phila. Bar Assn. Criminal Justice Sect. award, 1977, Justice Thurgood Marshall award, 1992; Legion of Honor, Chapel of the Four Chaplains, 1983. Mem. ABA, Pa. Bar Assn., Phila. Bar Assn. (bd. govs. 1971-73, past chmn. criminal justice com. and mil. justice com.), Fed. Bar Assn. (past chmn. criminal law com. adminstrn. justice sect., co-chmn. criminal law com. Phila. chpt., Leadership award Phila. 1991, 94), Pa. Assn. Criminal Def. Lawyers, Nat. Assn. Criminal Def. Lawyers. Democrat. Jewish. Appellate, Criminal, Military. Home: 1400 Melrose Ave Elkins Park PA 19027-3155 E-mail: SSESQ1@aol.com.

SHNIDER, BRUCE JAY, lawyer; b. Lansing, Mich., Oct. 16, 1950; s. Harold A. and Raynor (Seidner) Shnider; m. Patricia Lynn Strandness, Dec. 28, 1973; 1 child, Ruth Strandness. AB magna cum laude, Dartmouth Coll., 1972; MPP, JD magna cum laude, Harvard U., 1977. Bar: Minn. 1977, U.S. Dist. Ct. Minn. 1977, U.S. Tax Ct. 1978, U.S. Ct. Appeals (8th cir.) 1980, U.S. Supreme Ct. 1981. Asst. to dir. Mich. Dept. Commerce, Lansing, 1972-73; law clk. United Mineworkers Am. Health/Retirement Funds, 1975; summer assoc. Robins, Davis & Lyon, Mpls., 1976; assoc. Dorsey & Whitney, Mpls., 1977-82, ptnr., 1983—; chmn. diversity com., 1990-93; chmn. tax practice group, 1994-98. Bd. dirs. Minn. Justice Found., Mpls., 1989—91. Mem.: ABA, Hennepin County Bar Assn., Minn. State Bar Assn. Corporate taxation, Taxation, general, Pension, profit-sharing, and employee benefits. Home: 1908 James Ave S Minneapolis MN 55403-2831 Office: Dorsey & Whitney 50 S 6th St Ste 1500 Minneapolis MN 55402-1498 E-mail: shnider.bruce@dorseylaw.com.

SHOAFF, THOMAS MITCHELL, lawyer; b. Ft. Wayne, Ind., Aug. 21, 1941; s. John D. and Agnes H. (Hanna) S.; m. Eunice Swedberg, Feb. 7, 1970; children: Andrew, Nathaniel, Matthew-John. BA, Williams Coll., 1964; JD, Vanderbilt U., 1967. Bar: Ind. 1968. Assoc. Isham, Lincoln & Beale, Chgo., 1967-68; ptnr. Baker & Daniels, Ft. Wayne, Ind., 1968—. Bd. dirs. Weaver Popcorn Co., Inc., Ft. Wayne, Dreibelbiss Title Co., Inc., Ft. Wayne, Am. Steel Investment Corp., Ft. Wayne. Bd. dirs. McMillen Found., Ft. Wayne, Wilson Found., Ft. Wayne. Mem. ABA, Allen County Bar Assn., Ind. State Bar Assn. Presbyterian. Avocations: golf, sailing. Corporate, general. Office: Baker & Daniels 111 E Wayne St Ste 800 Fort Wayne IN 46802-2603

SHOCKEY, GARY LEE, lawyer; b. Casper, Wyo., Sept. 25, 1950; s. Bernis L. and Shirley E. (Diehl) Shockey; m. Dona K. Galles, June 1, 1979; children: Amber, Jeremy, Kimberly. AB in Polit. Sci. and Sociology, Yale U., 1973; JD, U. Wyo., 1976. Bar: Wyo. 1976, U.S. Dist. Ct. Wyo. 1976, U.S. Ct. Appeals (10th cir.) 1984, U.S. Ct. Appeals (9th cir.) 1988, U.S. Claims Ct. 1989, U.S. Supreme Ct. 1989, U.S. Ct. Appeals (fed. cir.) 1993, U.S. Dist. Ct. Ariz. 1994. Pub. defender State of Wyo. and City of Casper, 1976-78; pvt. practice Casper, 1976-79; assoc. Spence, Moriarity & Shockey, Casper and Jackson, Wyo., 1978-82, ptnr. Jackson, 1982—. Mem.: ATLA, ABA, Wyo. Trial Lawyers Assn. (bd. dirs. 1984—90), Wyo. State Bar (continuing legal edn. com. 1984—85, law and legis. reform com. 1986—88). Federal civil litigation, State civil litigation, Personal injury (including property damage). Office: Spence Moriarity & Shockey PO Box 548 Jackson WY 83001-0548 E-mail: garyshockey@smswy.com.

SHOEMAKER, BOBBY LYNN, lawyer; b. Bay Springs, Miss., Jan. 1, 1952; s. Dewey O'Farrell and Doris Ann (Evans) S.; m. Lillous Faye Alexander, Jan. 1, 1971; children: Megan Leigh, Lillous An, Bobby Barr, Joanna Ophelia. BA in History and Polit. Sci., U. So. Miss., 1974; JD, U.

Miss., 1977. Bar: Miss. 1977, U.S. Dist. Ct. (no. and so. dists.) Miss. 1977. Pvt. practice, Bay Springs, 1977—. Mem. adv. bd. First United Bank, Bay Springs, 1983-89; referee Jasper County Youth Ct., Bay Springs, 1984— , Jasper County Lunancy Ct., Bay Springs, 1984— . Mem. ABA, ATLA, Miss. Bar Assn., Miss. Trial Lawyers Assn., Miss. Prosecutors Assn. (bd. dirs. 1980-83), Bay Springs C. of C. (pres. 1984-85), Rotary (sec. Bay Springs 1977, v.p. 1978, pres. 1979). Methodist. Commercial, consumer (including collections, credit), Criminal, General practice. Office: 44 S 5th St # 258 Bay Springs MS 39422-5114

SHOEMAKER, JAMES MARSHALL, JR., lawyer; b. La Jolla, Calif., Aug., 1932; s. James M. and Frances (Little) S.; m. Mary Hunter Sloan, Jan. 3, 1959; children— James M. III, Edward Sloan, Jonathan Evans. B.A., U. Va., 1955, J.D., 1965. Bar: S.C. 1965. Fgn. service officer U.S. Dept. State, 1958-62; with Bur. Cultural Affairs, Washington, 1958-60; vice consul Am. Embassy, Tokyo, 1960-62; mem. Wyche, Burgess, Freeman & Parham, Greenville, S.C., 1965— ; dir. Palmetto Bank, Ryan's Family Steak Houses, Inc., Span Am. Med. Systems, Inc. Served with USMC, 1955-58, to maj., USMCR. Bd. dirs. Greater Greenville YMCA, 1980-82; bd. dirs. Greenville Urban League, 1980-84, pres., 1983-84; chmn. City of Greenville Civil Service Commn., 1977-78; mem. Greenville City Council, 1971-73; pres. Family and Children Service, Greenville County, 1969; mem. Little Theatre Council, 1967-71; United Fund. Div. chmn. Mem. ABA, Am. Judicature Soc., S.C. Bar Assn., Greenville County Bar Assn., Greater Greenville C. of C. (bd. dirs. 1977-82, pres. 1979), S.C. C. of C. (bd. dirs. 1983-85, 87—, pres. 1988). Republican. Episcopalian. Clubs: Greenville Country, Poinsett, Commerce, Cotillion, St. Andrews Soc. Federal civil litigation, State civil litigation, Corporate, general. Home: 109 Pine Forest Dr Greenville SC 29601-4421 Office: PO Box 728 Greenville SC 29602-0728

SHOOK, ANN JONES, lawyer; b. Canton, Ohio, Apr. 18, 1925; d. William M. and Lura (Pontius) Jones; m. Gene E. Shook Sr., Nov. 30, 1956; children: Scott, William, Gene Edwin Jr. AB, Wittenberg U., 1947; LLB, William McKinley Law Sch., 1955. Bar: Ohio 1956, U.S. Dist. Ct. (no. dist.) Ohio 1961, U.S. Ct. Appeals (6th cir.) 1981. Cost acct. Hoover Co., North Canton, Ohio, 1947-51; asst. sec. Stark County Prosecutor's Office, Canton, Ohio, 1951-53; ins. adjuster Traveler's Ins. Co., Canton, 1953-56; ptnr. Shook & Shook, Toledo, 1958-62, North Olmsted, Ohio, 1962—. Mem. at large coun. Olmsted Community Ch., Olmsted Falls, Ohio, 1987-90; chmn. ways and means com. North Olmsted PTA, 1968; area chmn. United Way Appeal, North Olmsted, 1963; v.p. LWV, Toledo, 1960-62. Mem. Cleve. Bar Assn. Avocations: reading, boating, dancing, fitness. Estate planning, Probate (including wills, trusts), Personal income taxation. E-mail: shooklaw@worldnet.att.net.

SHORE, ERIC EUGENE, internist, consultant, lawyer; b. Phila., Feb. 12, 1948; s. Reuben and Mary (Osinoff) S.; m. Mona Diane Cherry, Oct. 23, 1977 (div. Dec. 1991); children: Brett Ian, Matthew Adam. Student, Temple U., 1965—67; BS in Biology, Widener U., 1969; DO, Phila. Coll. Osteo. Med., 1973; MBA, St. Joseph's U., 1997; postgrad in law, Widener U., 1999—2000; JD, Rutgers U., 2003. Med. diplomate Nat. Bd. Examiners, diplomate Am. Bd. Utilization Rev. and Quality Assurance. Intern Botsford Gen. Hosp., Farmington, Mich., 1973-74; resident Phila. (Pa.) Gen. Hosp., 1974; instr. in medicine Hahnemann Med. Coll., Phila., 1975-78; treas. med. staff West Park Hosp., Phila., 1986-87, chief of geriatrics, 1986-88; sec. of med. staff Jefferson Park Hosp., Phila., 1987-91, chief of family medicine, 1988-96; pres. Gen. Medicine Assocs., Ltd., Phila., 1987—, Bala Clin. Assocs., P.C., 1989—; asst. prof. medicine Phila. Coll. Osteopathic Medicine, Phila., 1987—; clin. asst. prof. medicine Med. Coll. Pa., Phila., 1991—2001, Drexel Coll. Medicine, Phila., 2002—. Med. dir. Fairmount Geriatric Ctr., Phila., 1985-88, Bala Nursing & Retirement Ctr., Phila., 1990-95; chmn. bd. UniMed Systems, Inc., Phila., 1989—, Am. Medigroup, Inc., 1997—; CEO, Am. MediGroup, Inc., 1996—; cons. medicine and geriatrics Phila. Psychiat. Ctr., Phila., 1987—. Med. officer Civil Air Patrol, Phila., 1976-78. Recipient Legion of Honor, Chapel of Four Chaplains, Phila., 1981. Fellow: Am. Coll. Legal Medicine, Am. Coll. Utilization Rev. Physicians, Am. Acad. Family Physicians; mem.: ATLA, AMA (physician's recognition award 1990, 1994, 1997, 1999, 2003), ABA, AAAS, Pa. Bar Assn. (Phila. chpt.), N.Y. Acad. Scis., Am. Coll. Physician Execs., Am. Health Lawyers Assn., Am. Geriatrics Soc., Royal Soc. Medicine. Avocations: music, flying, computers, sculpting, tennis. Home: 19 W Dartmouth Rd Bala Cynwyd PA 19004-2520 Office: Am MediGroup Inc Ste B 1100 N 63rd St Philadelphia PA 19151-2102 Business E-Mail: eshore@shoremedlaw.com.

SHORE, HEATHER FIELD, lawyer; b. Greenville, S.C., July 23, 1968; d. Kenneth M. Shore and Nelda C. Leon. BS in Mktg., U. Colo., 1990; JD, Loyola U., Chgo., 1996. Bar: Colo. 1996. Sales exec. WNOK FM 100, Columbia, S.C., 1991-93; extern judge Rebecca R. Pallmeyer Chgo., 1994, 95; atty. Kennedy & Christopher, P.C., Denver, 1996-97, Tilly & Graves, P.C., Denver, 1997-2000, Shughart, Thomson & Kilroy, P.C., 2000—. Vol. Law Line Ch. 9, Denver, 1998—. Mem. ABA, Colo. Bar Assn., Denver Bar Assn. General civil litigation, Corporate, general. Office: Shughart Thomson & Kilroy PC 17th St Ste 2300 Denver CO 80265 E-mail: hshore@stklaw.com.

SHORE, THOMAS SPENCER, JR., retired lawyer; b. Akron, Ohio, Jan. 1, 1939; s. T. Spencer and Harriet G. (Delicate) S.; m. Margaret F. Kudzma, Aug. 12, 1961; children— Thomas Spencer III, John Christopher, Daniel Andrew, Mary Margaret. BA, Brown U., 1961; JD, Northwestern U., 1964. Bar: Ohio 1964. Assoc. Taft, Stettinius and Hollister, Cin., 1964-69, Rendigs, Fry, Kiely & Dennis, Cin., 1969-71, ptnr., 1972—2003; ret., 2003. Adj. asst. prof. Chase Law Sch., U. No. Ky. Bd. dirs. United Cerebral Palsy of Cin., 1978— ; bd. dirs., sec. Boys Club Am., Cin.; trustee emeritus Family Svc. of Cin. Area; past pres. Vis. Nurse Assn. of Cin., hon. trustee. Mem. Cin. Bar Assn., Ohio Bar Assn., Am. Bar Assn. Clubs: Cin. Country, Cin. Tennis, Queen City, Webhanet. Home: 3224 Columbia Pkwy Cincinnati OH 45226-1042 Office: 900 4th and Vine Tower 1 W 4th St Cincinnati OH 45202 E-mail: t.shore@rendigs.com.

SHORR, SCOTT ALDEN, lawyer; b. N.Y.C., July 5, 1968; s. Ronald Philip and Jean Fishack Shorr. AB, Vassar Coll., 1990; JD, U. Calif., Berkeley, 1995. Bar: Oreg. 1996, U.S. Dist. Ct. Oreg. 1997, U.S. Ct. Appeals (9th cir.) 1998. Law clk. to Hon. Richard L. Unis Oreg. Supreme Ct., Salem, 1995-96; assoc. Stoll Stoll Berne Lokting & Shlachter, Portland, Oreg., 1996—. Contbr. articles to profl. jours. Pres. bd. dirs. Hands On Portland, 1998-2000; bd. dirs. Oreg. Pub. Affairs Network, 2000—. Mem. Oreg. Trial Lawyers Assn., Multnomah Bar Assn., Fed. Bar Assn. Democrat. Avocations: soccer, music, politics. Appellate, Federal civil litigation, Securities. Office: Stoll Stoll Berne Lokting & Shlachter 209 SW Oak St Ste 500 Portland OR 97204-2798 E-mail: sshorr@ssbls.com.

SHORS, JOHN D. lawyer; b. Ft. Dodge, Iowa, July 21, 1937; s. George A. and Catherine (Shaw) S.; m. Patricia Ann Percival, Oct. 7, 1967; children: John, Tom, Matt, Luke. BSEE, Iowa State U., 1959; JD, U. Iowa, 1964. Bar: Iowa, U.S. Supreme Ct. Assoc. then shareholder Davis, Brown, Koehn, Shors & Roberts, P.C., Des Moines, 1964—. Co-author: Closely Held Corporations in Business and Estate Planning, 1982. Pres. Mercy Hosp. Found., Des Moines, 1981-84; chair Iowa State U. Found., Ames, 1989-92; bd. dirs. Mercy Housing, Denver, 1992—. Cpl. U.S. Army, 1960-61. Recipient Iowa State U. Alumni medal, YLS Merit award Iowa State Bar Assn. Mem. Iowa State Bar Assn. (pres. 1992) Iowa Women Profl. Corp. (Good Guy award 1987), Iowa Rsch. Coun. (bd. dirs. 1994—), Am. Judicature Soc. (bd. dirs. 1974-79), Polk County Bar Assn. (pres. 1986), Rotary (Des Moines chpt.), DM Club, Glenoaks C.C. Republican. Roman Catholic. Office: Davis Brown Koehn Shors & Roberts PC 666 Walnut St Ste 2500 Des Moines IA 50309-3904 E-mail: johnshors@lawiowa.com.

SHORT, J. LINDSEY, JR., lawyer; b. Houston, Oct. 22, 1943; s. J. Lindsey and Roberta (Prince) S.; m. Agnes G. May, July 22, 1967; children: Ashley K., Shelley F., Sidney F. AB, Washington and Lee U., 1965; JD, U. Tex., 1967. Bar: Tex. 1967, U.S. Dist. Ct. (so. dist.) Tex. 1979, U.S. Ct. Appeals (5th and 11th cirs.) 1981, U.S. Supreme Ct., 2000. Assoc. Barrow, Bland and Rehmet, Houston, 1969-71; pvt. practice Houston, 1971-76; ptnr. Lilly and Short, 1976-80; pres. J. Lindsey Short Jr. and Assoc., Houston, 1980-87, Short and Little, P.L.C., Houston, 1987-88, J. Lindsey Short Jr. & Assocs., Houston, 1988—2000, Short & Jenkins, 2000—. Lectr. in field. Contbr. articles to profl. jours. Lt. (j.g.) USNR, 1967-70. Fellow Am. Acad. Matrimonial Lawyers (editor 1987-90, pres.2001-02); mem. Tex. Bar Assn., Tex. Acad. Family Lawyers (past pres.), Internat. Acad. Matrimonial Lawyers, Family Law Adv. Commn., Tex. Bar Found. (life fellow), State Bar Tex. (bd. dirs. 1990—), Forest Club, Houston Club, Pres. Club. Family and matrimonial. Office: Short & Jenkins LLP 700 One Greenway Plz Houston TX 77027-7528

SHORT, JOEL BRADLEY, lawyer, software publisher; b. Birmingham, Ala., Dec. 27, 1941; s. Forrest Edwin and Laura Elizabeth (Bradley) S.; m. Georgianna Pohl, June 5, 1965 (div. Apr. 1973); m. Nancy Ann Harty, Dec. 17, 1977; children: Christopher Bradley, Matthew Douglas. BA, U. Colo., 1963, LLB, 1966, JD, 1968. Bar: Kans. 1966, U.S. Dist. Ct. Kans. 1966, U.S. Ct. Appeals (10th cir.) 1975, U.S. Supreme Ct. 1976. Ptnr. Short & Short, Attys., Fort Scott, Kans., 1966-77, Nugent & Short, Overland Park, Kans., 1977-83; pvt. practice J. Bradley Short & Assoc., Overland Park, Kans., 1983-91; ptnr. Short & Borth, Overland Park, Kans., 1991—; owner Bradley Software. Mem. tech. adv. com. Kans. Jud. Coun., Topeka, 1991-95. Contbg. author: Practitioner's Guide to Kansas Family Law, 1997-2002. 1st lt. U.S. Army, 1967-73. Fellow Am. Acad. Matrimonial Lawyers; mem. Johnson County Bar Assn. (ethics com. 1983-98, family law com. 1983—). Avocation: sailing. Family and matrimonial. Office: Short and Borth 55/500 Corporate Woods 9300 W 110th St Overland Park KS 66210-1405 E-mail: brad@shortandborth.com.

SHORT, TIMOTHY ALLEN, lawyer; b. Russell, Kans., July 17, 1952; d. H. Francis and Ruth (Teeter) Short; m. Barbara Diane Phillips, June 30, 1979; children: Justin Corey, Kisha Erin. BA in Speech Communication, Kans. U., 1974, JD, 1977. Bar: Kans. 1977. Atty. Fred Spigarelli, P.A., Pittsburg, Kans., 1976-82; ptnr. Spigarelli, McLane & Short, Pittsburg, Kans., 1882—2002, Short & Kennard, Pittsburg, Kans., 2002—. Mem. ABA, Assn. Trial Lawyers Am., Kans. Bar Assn., Kans. Trial Lawyers Assn. (bd. govs. 1987—, exec. bd. 1990—, parliamentarian 1991-92), Southeast Kans. Bar Assn., Crawford County Bar Assn. (sec. 1979). Democrat. Presbyterian. Avocations: canoeing, softball, computers, basketball. State civil litigation, Personal injury (including property damage), Workers' compensation. Home: 601 W Kansas St Pittsburg KS 66762-4923 Office: Short & Kennard 705 N Locust PO Box 1506 Pittsburg KS 66762 Business E-Mail: tashort@shortandkennard.com.

SHORTRIDGE, JUDY BETH, lawyer; b. Johnson City, Tenn., Feb. 17, 1954; d. George Edd and Anna Louise (Salmon) Copenhaver; m. Michael L. Shortridge, July 27, 1984; children: Sarah Elizabeth, Alexander Blake. BA, Va. Poly. Inst. and State U., 1976; MEd, U. Va., 1982; JD, U. Tenn., 1989. Bar: Va. 1990, U.S. Dist. Ct. (we. dist.) Va. 1990, Ea. Dist. Tenn., 1995. Tchr. Stafford County (Va.) Sch. System, 1976-84, Wise County (Va.) Sch. System, 1984-86; ptnr. Shortridge & Shortridge, P.C., Norton and Abingdon, Va., 1990—. Recipient Am. Jurisprudence award U. Tenn., 1989. Mem. Va. Bar Assn. Administrative and regulatory, Insurance, Personal injury (including property damage). Home: 340 Winterham Dr Abingdon VA 24211-3800 Office: Shortridge & Shortridge PC 170 Valley St NW Abingdon VA 24210-2836

SHOSS, CYNTHIA RENÉE, lawyer; b. Cape Girardeau, Mo., Nov. 29, 1950; d. Milton and Carroll Jane (Duncan) S.; m. David Goodwin Watson, Apr. 13, 1986; 1 child, Lucy J. Watson. BA cum laude, Newcomb Coll., 1971; JD, Tulane U., 1974; LLM in Taxation, NYU, 1980. Bar: La. 1974, Mo. 1977, Ill. 1978, N.Y. 1990. Law clk. to assoc. and chief justices La. Supreme Ct., New Orleans, 1974-76; assoc. Stone, Pigman et al, New Orleans, 1976-77, Lewis & Rice, St. Louis, 1977-79, Curtis, Mallet-Prevost, et al, N.Y.C., 1980-82; ptnr. LeBoeuf, Lamb, Greene & MacRae, L.L.P., N.Y.C., 1982—; mng. ptnr. London office LeBoeuf, Lamb, Leiby & MacRae, 1987-89. Assoc. editor Tulane Law Rev., 1972-74; frequent speaker before profl. orgns. and assns. Contbr. articles to profl. jours. Mem.: ABA, Assn. Life Ins. Counsels, Power of Atty., Inc. (chair bd. dirs.), Am. Mgmt. Assn. (ins. and risk mgmt. coun.). Insurance, Corporate taxation, Administrative and regulatory. Office: LeBoeuf Lamb Greene Et Al 125 W 55th St New York NY 10019-5369

SHOUP, TINA LOUISE, lawyer; b. Takoma Park, Md., Aug. 10, 1956; d. Max Wallace and Carrie Irene Shoup; m. Gordon C. Gebauer Jr., Oct. 4, 1997; 1 child, Bryan Christopher Johns. ASN, So. Adventist U., 1976; BS in Health Care Adminstrn., Johnson State Coll., 1990. Bar: Vt. 95, U.S. Dist. Ct. Vt. 95. Assoc. Manchester Law Offices, Burlington, Vt., 1995—2000; ptnr. Gebauer & Shoup PC, Burlington, 2000—. Recipient Disting. Alumni awrd, JOhnson State Coll., 2002. Mem.: ATLA, Vt. Bar Assn., Am. Assn. Nurse Attys., Vt. Trial Lawyers Assn. Avocations: Alpine skiing, hiking, raising llamas, gardening. Product liability, Professional liability, Personal injury (including property damage). Office: Gebauer & Shoup PC 3 Main St Burlington VT 05401 Office Fax: 802-862-9977 . E-mail: tshoup@sover.net.

SHOUSE, AUGUST EDWARD, lawyer; b. Houston, Aug. 12, 1949; s. Earl Edward Shouse and Mary Ann (Myers) Carrico; m. Deborah Lee Symonds; children: William Bundy, Edwrd Booth, Tucker Clayton. BS, Stanford U., 1971; JD, U. Tex., 1974. Bar: Tex. 1974. From assoc. to ptnr. Vinson & Elkins, Houston, 1974—. Bd. dirs. Greater Houston area chpt. ARC. Mem. Order of Coif, Phi Beta Kappa, Tau Beta Pi. Episcopalian. Corporate, general, Landlord-tenant, Property, real (including real estate development, water). Home: 3645 Ella Lee Ln Houston TX 77027-4104 Office: Vinson & Elkins 2300 First City Tower 1001 Fannin St Houston TX 77002-6706

SHOWALTER-JOHNSON, DEBORAH K. law librarian; b. St. Joseph, Mo., Oct. 29, 1948; d. Ralph Abraham and Johnnie Belle (Veazey) Showalter; m. G. Brad Johnson, Nov. 1, 1982; children: James Alexander Johnson, Anne Hillary Johnson. AA, Mo. Western Jr. Coll., 1968; BS, S.W. Mo. State Coll., 1970; MLS, U. Mo., 1980. Sch. libr. Cameron (Mo.) Sch. Dist., 1970—73; libr. asst. Kansas City (Mo.) Pub. Libr., 1973—76, reference libr., 1976—80, reference specialist, 1980—85, govt. document specialist, 1986—87; asst. libr. U.S. Ct. Appeals (8th cir.), Kansas City, 1990—2002, acting br. libr., 2002—03, br. libr., 2003—. Mem.: Kansas City Assn. Law Librs., Mid-Am. Assn. Law Librs., Am. Assn. Law Librs. Office: US Ct Appeals (8th cir) Libr 9440 Charles Evans Whitaker US Ct House 400 E 9th St Kansas City MO 64106

SHPIECE, MICHAEL RONALD, lawyer, educator; b. Detroit, Nov. 13, 1956; s. Harold Edwin and Rose Marie (Wheeler) S.; m. Tracy B. Schwartz; children: David E. Schwartz, Daniel E. Schwartz. PhB, Wayne State U., 1977; JD, U. Mich., 1984. Bar: Mich. 1985. Com. adminstr. Joint Legis. Com. on Aging, Lansing, Mich., 1979-81; policy analyst to commr. Mich. Ins. Bur., Lansing, 1981; legis. cons Cmty. Action Program Mich. UAW, Lansing, 1981-82; dep. dir. Mich. Dept. Licensing and Regulation, Lansing, 1983-85; assoc., ptnr. Honigman Miller Schwartz & Cohn, Detroit, 1985-93; adj. prof. law Wayne State U. Law Sch., Detroit, 1996—; of counsel Shapack, McCullough & Kanter, Bloomfield Hills, Mich., 1994-98; prin. Miller, Shpiece & Tischler, Southfield, Mich., 1998—. Pres. Friends of Child Abuse Prevention, Southfield, Mich., 1994—; bd. dirs. chmn. Mich. Freedom of Info. Com., Detroit, 1996-98. Contbr. articles to profl. jours. Pres. and trustee Farmington (Mich.) Bd. Edn., 1975-83; chairperson Farmington Hills Ad Hoc Com. on Ethics, 1990-96. Mem.: ABA (liaison to joint com. on employee benefits), Oakland County Bar Assn., Am. Statis. Assn., Econ. Club Detroit. Democrat. Jewish. Home: 39372 Plumbrook Dr Farmington Hills MI 48331-2976 Office: Ste 200 26711 Northwestern Hwy Southfield MI 48034-2159 E-mail: mshpiece@msapc.net.

SHREVE, GENE RUSSELL, law educator; b. San Diego, Aug. 6, 1943; s. Ronald D. and Hazel (Shepherd) S.; m. Marguerite Russell, May 26, 1973. AB with honors, U. Okla., 1965; LLB, Harvard U., 1968, LLM, 1975. Bar: Mass. 1969, Vt. 1981. Appellate atty. and state extradition hearing examiner Office of Mass. Atty Gen., 1968-69; law clk. U.S. Dist. Ct., Dallas, 1969-70; staff and supervising atty. Boston Legal Assistance Project, 1970-73; assoc. prof. Vt. Law Sch., Royalton, 1975-81; vis. assoc. prof. George Washington U., Washington, 1981-83; assoc. prof. law N.Y. Law Sch., N.Y.C., 1983-84, prof., 1984-87; vis. prof. law Ind. U., Bloomington, 1986, prof., 1987-94, Richard S. Melvin Prof. Law, 1994—. Author: A Conflict of Laws Anthology, 1997; co-author: Understanding Civil Procedure, 2d edit., 1994; mem. editl. bd. Am. Jour. Comparative Law, 1994—, Jour. Legal Edn., 1998-2001; contbr. numerous articles to legal jours. Mem. Am. Law Inst., Am. Soc. for Pol. and Legal Phil., Assn. Am. Law Schs. (civil procedure sect. chair 1997, conflict of laws sect. chair 1998). Democrat. Episcopalian. Office: Ind U Sch Law Bloomington IN 47405

SHRINER, THOMAS L., JR., lawyer; b. Lafayette, Ind., Dec. 15, 1947; s. Thomas L. Sr. and Margaret (Kamstra); m. Donna L. Galchick, June 5, 1971; children: Thomas L. III, John H. , Joseph P., James A. AB, Ind. U., 1969, JD, 1972. Bar: Wis. 1972, U.S. Ct. Appeals (7th cir.) 1972, U.S. Dist. Ct. (ea. dist.) Wis. 1973, U.S. Dist. Ct. (we. dist.) Wis. 1977, U.S. Supreme Ct. 1978, U.S. Ct. Appeals (8th cir.) 1989, U.S. Ct. Appeals (fed. cir.) 1990. Law clk to Hon. John S. Hastings U.S. Ct. Appeals (7th cir.), Chgo., 1972-73; assoc. Foley & Lardner, Milwaukee, Wis., 1973-79, ptnr., 1979—. Chmn. bd. trustees Cath. Charities of Archdiocese of Milw., 2001—02. Fellow Am. Coll. Trial Lawyers; mem. 7th Cir. Bar Assn. (pres. 1993-94), Phi Beta Kappa. Republican. Roman Catholic. Appellate, General civil litigation, Constitutional. Office: Foley & Lardner 777 E Wisconsin Ave Ste 3800 Milwaukee WI 53202-5367 E-mail: tshriner@foleylaw.com.

SHRIVER, ROBERT SARGENT, JR., lawyer; b. Westminster, Md., Nov. 9, 1915; s. Robert Sargent and Hilda Shriver; m. Eunice Mary Kennedy, May 23, 1953; children: Robert Sargent III, Maria, Timothy, Mark Kennedy, Anthony Paul Kennedy. Student, Canterbury Sch.; BA cum laude, Yale U., 1938, LLB, 1941; LLD, St. Procopius Coll., 1959, Notre Dame U., DePaul U., Seton Hall Coll., 1961, St. Louis U., Kansas State U., Brandeis U., 1962, St. Michael's Coll., Vt., Fordham U., Boston Coll., Yale U., Duquesne U., N.Y.U., Wesleyan U.; DCL, U. Liberia, 1963; HHD, Salem Coll., 1963, Bowling Green State U.; LHD, Springfield (Mass.) Coll., 1963, U. Scranton, Providence Coll.; D in Polit. Sci., Chulalongkorn U., Bangkok, Thailand, The Am. U. of Paris, 2002. Bar: N.Y. 1941, Ill. 1959, U.S. Supreme Ct. 1969, D.C. 1971. With Winthrop, Stimson, Putnam & Roberts, 1940—41; asst. editor Newsweek, 1945—46; assoc. Joseph P. Kennedy Enterprises, 1947—48; asst. gen. mgr. Merchandise Mart, Chgo., 1948—61; dir. Peace Corps., Washington, 1961—66, Office Econ. Opportunity, 1964—68; U.S. ambassador to France, 1968—70; spl. asst. to the Pres., 1965—68; sr. ptnr. law firm Fried, Frank, Harris, Shriver & Jacobson, N.Y.C., Washington, L.A., London, Eng., 1971—86, of counsel, 1986—; pres. Spl. Olympics, Washington, 1986—90, chmn., CEO, 1990—96, chmn. bd. dirs., 1996—. Mem. Am. Com. on East-West Accord, 1978—, Ams. for SALT, 1979—. Author: Point of the Lance, 1964. Pres. Chgo. Bd. Edn., 1955—60; mem.-at-large Nat. Coun. Boy Scouts Am.; chmn. Internat. Orgn. Patrons on Israel Mus., 1972—75; bd. dirs. The Arms Control Assn., 1983—; Dem. candidate for v.p., 1972; ran for Dem. presdl. election, 1976; pres. Cath. Interracial Coun. Chgo., 1955—60. Lt. comdr. USNR, 1940—45. Named Lay Churchman of Yr., Religious Heritage Am., 1963; recipient Yale U. medal, 1957, Chgo. medal of merit, 1957, James H. Hoey award, Cath. Interracial Coun. N.Y., 1958, Golden Heart Presdl. award, Philippines, 1964, Laetare medal, U. Notre Dame, 1968, Franklin D. Roosevelt Freedom from Want award, 1993, Presdl. Medal of Freedom, 1994, Equal Justice award, Nat. Ctr. on Poverty Law, 1999, William O. Douglas award, Pub. Counsel Law Ctr., 1999. Mem.: Chgo. Coun. Fgn. Rels. (dir.), Yale U. Law Sch. Assn. (exec. com.), Navy League (life), Yale Club (N.Y.C.), Onwentsia Club (Lake Forest, Ill.), Execs. Club (Chgo.), Econ. Club, Serra Club, Racquet Club, Delta Kappa Epsilon. Roman Catholic. Achievements include extensive world travel to visit Peace Corps projects, 1961-1966. Office: Spl Olympics Internat 1325 G St NW Ste 500 Washington DC 20005-3104

SHUBB, WILLIAM BARNET, judge; b. Oakland, Calif., May 28, 1938; s. Ben and Nellie Bernice (Fruechtenicht) S.; m. Sandra Ann Talarico, July 29, 1962; children: Alisa Marie, Carissa Ann, Victoria Ann. AB, U. Calif., Berkeley, 1960, JD, 1963. Bar: Calif., 1964, U.S. Ct. Internat. Trade 1981, U.S. Customs Ct. 1980, U.S. Ct. Appeals (9th cir.) 1964, U.S. Supreme Ct. 1972. Law clk. U.S. Dist. Ct., Sacramento, 1963-65; asst. U.S. atty., Sacramento, 1965-71; chief asst. U.S. atty. (ea. dist.) Calif., 1971-74; assoc. Diepenbrock, Wulff, Plant & Hannegan, Sacramento, 1974-77, ptnr., 1977-80, 81-90; U.S. atty. Eastern Dist. Calif., 1980-81; judge U.S. Dist. Ct. (ea. dist.) Calif., 1990-96, chief judge, 1996—; chmn. com. drafting of local criminal rules U.S. Dist. Ct. (ea. dist.) Calif., 1974, mem. speedy trial planning com., 1974-80; lawyer rep. 9th Cir. U.S. Jud. Conf., 1975-78; mem. faculty Fed. Practice Inst., 1978-80; instr. McGeorge Sch. Law, U. Pacific, 1964-66. Mem. ABA, Fed. Bar Assn. (pres. Sacramento chpt. 1977), Calif. Bar Assn., Assn. Def. Counsel, Am. Bd. Trial Advs., Sacramento County Bar Council.

SHUGHART, DONALD LOUIS, lawyer; b. Kansas City, Mo., Aug. 12, 1926; s. Henry M. and Dora M. (O'Leary) Shughart; m. Mary I. Shughart, July 25, 1953; children: Susan C. Hogsett, Nancy J. Goede. AB, U. Mo., Columbia, 1949, JD, 1951. Bar: Mo. 1951, U.S. Dist. Ct. (we. dist.) Mo. 1951, U.S. Tax Ct. 1979. With Shughart, Thompson & Kilroy, PC, Kansas City, Mo., 1951—. With AC, U.S. Army, 1944-47. Mem. Kansas City Bar Assn. (chmn. bus. orgns. com. 1990-91), Mo. Bar Assn. (chmn. corp. com. 1980-81, 82-83), Lawyers Assn. Kansas City, Am. Judicature Soc., Mo. Orgn. Def. Lawyers (pres. 1971-72), U. Mo. Law Soc., Phi Delta Phi, Sigma Chi. Republican. Roman Catholic. Corporate, general, Estate planning. Home: 1242 W 67th Ter Kansas City MO 64113-1941 Office: Shug Thom Kilroy 12 Wyandotte Pla 120 W 12th St Kansas City MO 64105-1917

SHULA, ROBERT JOSEPH, lawyer; b. South Bend, Ind., Dec. 10, 1936; s. Joseph Edward and Bertha Mona (Buckner) S.; m. Gaye Ann Martin, Oct. 8, 1978; children: Deirdre Regina, Robert Joseph II, Elizabeth Martin. BS in Mktg., Ind. U., 1958, JD, 1961. Bar: Ind. 1961. Ptnr. Bingham Summers Welsh & Spilman, Indpls., 1965-82, sr. ptnr., 1982-89; ptnr. Price & Shula, Indpls., 1989-91, Lowe Gray Steele & Darko, Indpls., 1991—2003; of counsel Norris Choplin and Schroeder, Indpls., 2003—. Mem. faculty Nat. Inst. Trial Advocacy; guest lectr. Brit. Medicine and Law Soc., 1979, Ind. U. Sch. Law; medico-legal lectr. Ind. U. Schs. Medicine, Dentistry, and Nursing. Bd. dirs. Arts Ind., Indpls., 1995-99; pres. Oriental Arts Soc., Indpls., 1975-79, Meridian Women's Clinic, Inc., Indpls.; trustee Indpls. Mus. Art, 1975-78, life trustee, 1984—; bd. dirs. Ind. Repertory Theatre, Indpls., 1982-92, chmn. bd. dirs., pres., 1985-89; pres. Repertory Soc., 1993-96; v.p., bd. dirs. Flanner House of Indpls., Inc., 1977-88, chmn., 1988-99; pres. Internat. Ctr. of Indpls., Inc., 1993-96. Maj. JAGC, USAFR, 1961—65. Recipient Gov.'s award of Sagamore of the Wabash, 1998. Master Am. Inns of Ct.; fellow Internat. Soc. Barristers; mem. ABA, FBA,

Ind. Bar Assn., Indpls. Bar Assn., Am. Bd. Trial Advs. (pres. 2000), Am. Law Inst., Am. Coll. Legal Medicine, Def. Trial Counsel Ind. (diplomate), Confrerie Chevaliers du Tastevin, Woodstock Country Club. Democrat. Episcopalian. Alternative dispute resolution, Health, Professional liability. Home: 7924 Beaumont Green Pl Indianapolis IN 46250-1663 Office: 101 W Ohio St 9th Flr Indianapolis IN 46204-4213 E-mail: RShula@ncs.com.

SHULER, SAMUEL PETER, III, legal consultant; b. Carmel, Calif., Mar. 2, 1943; arrived in Thailand, 1998; s. Samuel Peter Shuler Jr. and Ruth Ann Shuler; m. Pakinee Amarapitak Shuler, Aug. 15, 1984; m. Alison Livingston Early Shuler, 1974 (div. 1977). AB with honors in history, Ind. U., 1965; MBA, JD, Columbia U., 1970. Bar: N.Y. 1971. Atty. Fed. Res. Bank N.Y., N.Y.C., 1970—73; counsel Am. Express Co., London, 1973—80, N.Y.C., 1973—80; legal counsel Arab Banking Corp., Manama, Bahrain, 1980—97; exec. v.p. support svcs. Internat. Bank Asia, Hong Kong, 1997—98; sr. cons. Siam Premier Internat. Law Office, Bangkok, 1998—. Bd. dirs. NEP Realty and Industry Pub. Co. Ltd., chmn. dirs. audit com., 1999—. Pres., dir., mem. Am. Assn. Bahrain, Manama, 1982—97; mem. U.S. Ambs. Roundtable, Manama, 1995—97; vice chmn., dir. English Speaking Union, Bangkok, 1999—. Mem.: ABA, N.Y. State Bar Assn., Internat. Bar Assn., Kiarti Thanee Country Club, Thai Country Club. Avocation: golf. Office: Siam Premier Internat Law Office 21/147-150 S Sathorn Rd 24/26F Thai Wah Bangkok 10120 Thailand

SHULMAN, ADLEY M. lawyer, educator; b. L.A., Aug. 28, 1931; s. Reuben and Dee (Rosenbaum) S.; m. Corinne S. Shulman, June 22, 1952; children: Gail Denise Feinberg, Susan Linda, Ogden, Nancy Ann Pullen, Barton Alan. BA with highest honors, UCLA, 1953, JD, 1958. Bar: Calif. 1958, U.S. Dist. Ct. (ctrl. dist.) Calif. 1958, U.S. Ct. Appeals (9th cir.) 1958, U.S. Supreme Ct. 1967. Ptnr. firm Shulman & Shulman, Beverly Hills, Calif., 1958-84, Shulman, Shulman & Siegel, 1984-2000, Shulman & Shulman, Hydesville, Calif., 2000—. Tchr. adult sch. L.A. Area Cmty. Schs., 1971-82; mem. faculty Humboldt State U., 1984-91. Mem. editl. staff UCLA Law Rev., 1956-58; contbr. articles to profl. publs. Bd. dirs. Hospice of Humboldt, 1988-95; mem. joint commn. on social action United Synagogue of Am., L.A., 1963-66; mem. L.A. 5th Councilmanic Adv. Commn., 1968-73; mem. com. on law and legis. Jewish Fed. Coun., L.A., 1971-78; mem. Humboldt County Human Rights Commn., 1997-2001. Recipient 1st ann. Human Rels. award L.A. City Human Rels. Bur., 1970. Mem. Calif. State Bar Assn., Los Angeles County Bar Assn. (trustee 1982-83), Beverly Hills Bar Assn. (pres. 1983-84), Order of Coif, Phi Beta Kappa. Democrat. Jewish. Administrative and regulatory, General practice, Property, real (including real estate development, water). Office: Shulman & Shulman PO Box 642 Hydesville CA 95547-0642

SHULMAN, MADELYN R. SPATT, lawyer; b. NYC, Apr. 11, 1948; d. Max and Sarah (Rivin) Spatt; m. Michael Joel Shulman, Mar. 7, 1970; children: Jonathan, Jeremy. BA in Polit Sci., U. Mich., 1968; MA in Communications, Stanford U., 1976; JD, NYU, 1979, LLM in Tax Law, 1987. Bar: NY 1980. Assoc. Stroock & Stroock & Lavan, NYC, 1979-83, Hayt, Hayt & Landau, Great Neck, NY, 1984-87, Parker, Chapin, Flattau & Klimpl, Jericho, NY, 1987-89, Law Offices of Madelyn Spatt Shulman, Great Neck, NY, 1989-91; ptnr. Soberman, Shulman & Rosenberg, Lake Success, NY, 1991-99; of counsel Meltzer, Lippe, Goldstein, Wolf & Schissel P.C., Mineola, NY, 1999—2000; prin. Madelyn Spatt Shulman PC, Jericho, NY, 2000—. Bd. dir. Women Econ. Developers L.I., 1996—. Mem. ABA, Nassau County Bar Assn. (chmn. corp. law com. 2002—), NY State Bar Assn., Order of Coif. Democrat. Jewish. Corporate, general, Securities, Taxation, general. Office: Madelyn Spatt Shulman PC 350 Jericho Tpke Ste 101 Jericho NY 11753-1317

SHULMISTER, M(ORRIS) ROSS, lawyer; b. Atlanta, Jan. 6, 1940; s. Morris and Kathryn Sybella (Baker) S.; m. Benita Vee Rosin, Dec. 16, 1974. BEE, U. Fla., 1962, JD, 1973. Bar: Fla. 1973, U.S. Dist. Ct. (so. dist.) Fla. 1974, U.S. Dist. Ct. (mid. dist.) Fla. 1985, U.S. Ct. Appeals (5th and 11th cirs.) 1981. Pvt. practice, Broward County, Fla., Ft. Lauderdale, Fla., 1974—. Spl. master for code enforcement, Pompano Beach, Fla., 1991-92. Mem. Broward County Consumer Protection Bd., 1983-2001, chmn., 1999-2000; chmn. Charter Review Bd., Pompano Beach, Fla., 1994-97; dir. South Pompano Civic Assn., 1989-2000, v.p., 1989, pres., 1992-98. Lt. col. USAF, 1964-70, ret., USAFR, 1970-93. Mem. Fla. Bar (mem. constrn. law subcom., civil trial cert. 1984-99), Broward County Bar Assn. (bd. dirs. 2003—). General civil litigation, Construction, Probate (including wills, trusts). Office: 590 SE 12th St Pompano Beach FL 33060-9409

SHUMAKER, ROBERT E. lawyer; b. Sheboygan, Wis., May 9, 1954; s. Ernest Glen and Lucille Rose Shumaker; m. Janet Kilde Shumaker, Oct. 15, 1983; 1 child, John Kilde. BS with distinction, U. Wis., 1976, MS in Edn., 1983, JD cum laude, 1986. Bar: Wis., U.S. Dist. Ct. (ea. dist.) Wis., U.S. Dist. Ct. (we. dist.) Wis., U.S. Ct. Appeals (7th cir.), U.S. Supreme Ct. Tchr. social studies Beaver Dam Unified Sch. Dist., Wis., 1976—83; atty. Foley & Lardrer, Milw., 1986—90, DeWitt Ross & Stevens, Madison, 1990—. Mem.: Rotary. Avocations: sports, photography. General civil litigation, Appellate, Labor (including EEOC, Fair Labor Standards Act, labor-management relations, NLRB, OSHA). Home: 222 Lakewood Blvd Madison WI 53704 Office: DeWitt Ross & Stevens 2 E Mifflin St Ste 600 Madison WI 53703 Fax: 608-252-9243. E-mail: res@dewittross.com.

SHURN, PETER JOSEPH, III, lawyer; b. Queens, N.Y., Aug. 30, 1946; s. Peter J. Jr. and Vivienne M. (Tagliarino) Shurn; m. Ingrid Kelbert; children: Steven Douglas, Vanessa Leigh, David Michael. BSEE magna cum laude, Poly. Inst. Bklyn., 1974; JD magna cum laude, New Eng. Sch. Law, 1977; LLM in Patent and Trade Regulation Law, George Washington U., 1981. Bar: N.C. 1977, Va. 1979, Tex. 1982. Rsch. scientist GTE Labs., 1965—77; pvt. practice Raleigh, NC, 1977—78; assoc. Burns, Doane, Swecker & Mathis, Alexandria, Va., 1978—80; tech. advisor to judge U.S. Ct. Appeals (fed. cir.), 1980—81; ptnr. Arnold, White & Durkee, Houston, 1981—2000, Howrey, Simon, Arnold and White LLP, Houston, 2000—01. Adj. prof. S. Tex. Coll. Law, 1984—88, 2000—; invited mem. nat. panel neutrals Am. Arbitration Assn., 1993—; arbitrator Nat. Patent Bd., 1999—. Contbr. articles to profl. jours. With U.S. Army, 1966—68. Fellow: Coll. State Bar Tex., Houston Bar Found. (life); mem.: IEEE, ABA, ATLA, Houston Patent Law Assn., Am. Patent Law Assn. (Robert C. Watson award 1981), Houston Patent Law Assn., Sigma Xi. Alternative dispute resolution, Patent, Intellectual property. Office: 14138 Heatherfield Dr Houston TX 77079-6805 E-mail: pjshurn@ieee.org.

SHURTLEFF, MARK L. state attorney general; BA, Brigham Young U.; JD, U. Utah. Officer, atty. JAG USN, 1985—90; pvt. practice in law Calif., 1990—93; asst. atty. gen. State of Utah, 1993—97; dep. county atty. Salt Lake County, 1997—98; commr. Salt Lake County Commn., 1999—2000, chmn., 2000; atty. gen. State of Utah, 2001—. Leader Boy Scout troops, 1980—; anti-drug lectr., at-risk youth mentor. Republican. Office: State Capitol Bldg Rm 236 Salt Lake City UT 84114

SHURTLIFF, MARVIN KARL, lawyer; b. Idaho Falls, Idaho, Nov. 6, 1939; s. Noah Leon and Melba Dorothy (Hunting) S.; m. Peggy J. Griffin, Nov. 23, 1963; 1 dau., Jennifer Karyl. BA, Idaho State Coll., 1962; JD, U. Idaho, 1968. Bar: Idaho 1968. Tchr. pub. schs., Jefferson County, Idaho, 1964-65; atty. U.S. Dept. Justice, Washington, 1968-74; commr. Idaho Pub. Utilities Commn., 1974-75, pres., 1975-76; spl. asst., legal counsel Gov. of Idaho, Boise, 1977; U.S. atty. for Dist. of Idaho, Boise, 1977-81; practice law Boise, 1981—. Mem. Idaho Ho. of Reps., 1962-64 Mem. Idaho State Bd. Edn., 1990—95, Idaho Commn. on Redistricting, 2001. Mem. Idaho Bar Assn. Democrat. Administrative and regulatory, General civil litigation, Criminal. Home: 62 Horizon Dr Boise ID 83702-4419 Office: PO Box 1652 Boise ID 83701-1652

SHURTZ, STEVEN PARK, lawyer; b. Panquitch, Utah, Jan. 23, 1956; s. Doyle Park and Loree (Munson) S.; m. Jane Wanee Welch, Dec. 29, 1978; children: Thomas Park, Melissa Jane, Amy Marie, Timothy Evan, Stephanie Ann, Richard Steven, Kimberly Rae, Nathan Samuel. BS in Chem. Engring., U. Utah, 1980, JD, 1983. Bar: Ill. 1983, Utah 1997, U.S. Dist. Ct. (no. dist.) Ill. 1983, U.S. Dist. Ct. Utah 1997, U.S. Patent & Trademark Office 1984, U.S. Ct. Appeals (fed. cir.) 1989. Assoc. Brinks Hofer Gilson & Lione, Chgo., 1983-88, shareholder, 1989—. Mem. ABA, Am. Intellectual Property Law Assn., Chgo. Bar Assn. Mem. Lds Ch. Intellectual property. Home: 1040 W Austin Ln Palatine IL 60067-5802 Office: Brinks Hofer Gilson & Lione Ste 3600 455 N City Front Plaza Dr Chicago IL 60611 E-mail: sshurtz@brinkshofer.com.

SIBLEY, HORACE HOLDEN, lawyer; b. Phila., Oct. 13, 1939; s. John Adams and Barbara (Thayer) S.; m. Beverly Bryan, Mar. 18, 1961; children: Clare, Holden, Eve. BA, Vanderbilt U., 1961; LLD, U. Ga., 1964; MBA, Ga. State U., 1971. Bar: Ga. 1964, U.S. Supreme Ct. 1975. Assoc. King and Spalding, Atlanta, 1968-72, ptnr., 1972—2001. Chmn. Ga. Ctr. for Advanced Telecom. Tech., 1994-2000, So. Ctr. for Internat. Studies; bd. dirs. Woodruff Arts Ctr., Glenayre Technologies, Inc.; bd. advisors Carter Ctr., 1996-2001; bd. trustees Callaway Gardens Found.; hon. consul Dominican Republic. Trustee, mem. exec. com. Agnes Scott Coll., Atlanta, 1977; trustee Henrietta Egleston Hosp. for Children, Atlanta, 1974-77, trustee, mem. exec. com., 1977-90, chmn. bd. dirs., 1983-90; mem. exec. com. Atlanta Organizing Com. Summer Olympics, 1989-90; bd. dirs. Atlanta Com. for Olympic Games, 1991-99; chmn. bd. dirs. Butler St. YMCA, Atlanta, 1981, Atlanta Commn. on Homelessness, 2003; past bd. dirs. United Way, Nat. Assn. of Childrens' Hosp. and various other charitable orgns.; participant Leadership Ga., 1978, Leadership Atlanta, 1973, Soc. Internat. Bus. Fellows, 1982—; elder Trinity Presbyn. Ch., 1969-73. Capt. inf. U.S. Army, 1965-68, Germany. Mem. ABA, Ga. Bar Assn., Atlanta Bar Assn., World Trade Club Atlanta (bd. dirs. 1988-92), Japan-Am. Soc. (bd. dirs. 1981-87), Rotary, Blue Key Svc. Soc., Phi Kappa Phi, Omicron Delta Kappa. Democrat. Presbyterian. Avocations: tennis, golf, fishing. Construction, Corporate, general, Mergers and acquisitions. Office: King & Spalding 191 Peachtree St NE Ste 40 Atlanta GA 30303-1740 E-mail: hsib@aol.com.

SIBLEY, JAMES MALCOLM, retired lawyer; b. Atlanta, Aug. 5, 1919; s. John Adams and Nettie Whitaker (Cone) S.; m. Karen Norris, Apr. 6, 1942; children: Karen Mariea, James Malcolm Jr., Jack Norris, Elsa Alexandria Victoria, Quintus Whitaker. AB, Princeton U., 1941; student, Woodrow Wilson Sch. Law, 1942, Harvard Law Sch., 1945-46. Bar: Ga. 1942. Assoc. King & Spalding, Atlanta, 1942-47, ptnr., 1947-91. Bd. dirs. Summit Industries, Inc.; exec. com., mem. pub. affairs com. Coca-Cola Co., 1979-91; chmn. exec. com. John H. Harland Co., 1963-91; chmn. exec. com., mem. compensation com. Trust Co. of Ga., 1975-92; mem. exec. com., mem. compensation com. SunTrust Banks, Inc., 1985-92. Trustee Joseph B. Whitehead Found., Lettie Pate Evans Found., A.G. Rhodes Home, Inc., Robert W. Woodruff Found., Inc. (formerly Trebor Found.), John H. and Wilhelmina D. Harland Charitable Found., Inc.; trustee emeritus Berry Coll., The Lovett Sch., Callaway Gardens Found., Emory U. With USAF, 1942—45. Mem. ABA, Ga. Bar Assn., Atlanta Bar Assn., Am. Coll. Probate Counsel, Am. Bar Found., Am. Law Inst. Clubs: Piedmont Driving, Commerce. Episcopalian. Banking, Corporate, general, Probate (including wills, trusts). also: King & Spalding 191 Peachtree St NE Ste 40 Atlanta GA 30303-1740 Home: 3045 Slaton Dr NW Atlanta GA 30305-2006

SICA, JOHN, lawyer; b. Scranton, Pa., Jan. 23, 1962; s. John Anthony and Betty May (Sherbourne) S. BS, U. Md., Princess Anne, 1987; JD, No. Ill. U., 1989. Bar: Md. 1990. Mng. lawyer Sentinel Title Corp., Frederick, Md., 1989-90; pvt. practice Frederick, 1990—. Mem. Am. Agrl. Law Assn., Md. Bar Assn. (pub. svc. com.). General practice, Land use and zoning (including planning), Agriculture. Home: 9099 Ridgefield Drive Ste 103 Frederick MD 21701 E-mail: jsica80730@aol.com.

SICHERMAN, MARVIN ALLEN, lawyer; b. Cleve., Dec. 27, 1934; s. Harry and Malvina (Friedman) S.; m. Sue Kovacs, Aug. 18, 1957; children: Heidi Joyce, Steven Eric. BA, Case Western Res. U., 1957, LLB, 1960, JD, 1968. Bar: Ohio 1960. Mng. prin. Dettelbach, Sicherman & Baumgart, Cleve., 1971—. Editorial bd.: Case-Western Res. Law Rev, 1958-60; Contbr. articles to legal jours. Mem. Beachwood (Ohio) Civic League, 1972-92; mem. Beachwood Bd. Edn., 1978-86, pres., 1981, 85, v.p., 1984; trustee Beachwood Arts Council, 1977-84. Mem. Ohio Bar Assn. (lectr. truth in lending 1969, lectr. bankruptcy 1972, 81, 84, 99, 2000, Meritorious Service awards 1971, 77, 78, 79, 83, 84, 85, 86, 87), Cleve. Bar Assn. (lectr. practice and procedure clinic 1960-80, 82-87, chmn. bankruptcy ct. com. 1971-73), Jewish Chautauqua Soc., Tau Epsilon Rho, Zeta Beta Tau. Jewish (trustee Temple brotherhood 1968-76, sec. 1971-73). Bankruptcy, Federal civil litigation, Commercial, contracts (including sales of goods; commercial financing). Home: 24500 Albert Ln Cleveland OH 44122-2302 Office: Dettelbach Sicherman & Baumgart 1100 Ohio Savings Plz Cleveland OH 44114 E-mail: msicherman@dsb-law.com.

SIDAMON-ERISTOFF, CONSTANTINE, lawyer; b. N.Y.C., June 28, 1930; s. Simon C. and Anne Huntington (Tracy) Sidamon-E.; m. Anne Phipps, June 29, 1957; children: Simon, Elizabeth, Andrew. BSE. in Geol. Engring, Princeton U., 1952; LL.B., Columbia U., 1957. Clk., then assoc. firm Kelley Drye Newhall Maginnes & Warren, N.Y.C., 1957-64; individual practice law N.Y.C., 1964-65, 74-77; exec. asst. to Congressman John V. Lindsay, 1964-65; city coordinator Lindsay Mayoral Campaign, N.Y.C., 1965; asst. to mayor City of N.Y., 1966, commr. hwys., 1967-68, transp. adminstr., 1968-73; prin. Sidamon-Eristoff, Morrison, Warren, & Ecker, N.Y.C., 1978-83; counsel Morrison & de Roos, 1984-88; pvt. practice N.Y.C., 1988-89; regional adminstr. Region II EPA, N.Y.C., 1989-93; of counsel Patterson, Belknap, Webb & Tyler, N.Y.C., 1993-99, Lacher & Lovell-Taylor P.C., N.Y.C., 1999—. Mem. N.Y. State Met. Transp. Authority Bd., 1974—89; commr. N.Y. State Jud. Commn. on Minorities, 1987—91; mem. Gov.'s Coun. on Hudson River Valley Greenway, 1989; trustee United Mut. Savs. Bank, N.Y.C., 1979—82, Phipps Houses, N.Y.C., 1974—, chmn., 1986—2001, chmn. emeritus, 2001—. Trustee Am. the Beautiful Fund, Washington, 1985—97; chmn. Audubon N.Y. , 1999—; trustee Allaverdy Found., N.Y.C., 1962—, Am. Farm Sch., Thessaloniki, Greece, 1973—79, Carnegie Hall, N.Y.C., 1967—92, Millbrook (N.Y.) Sch., 1971—89, hon. trustee, 1989—, Orange County (N.Y.) Citizens Found., 1974—81; bd. dirs., mem. exec. com. Mid-Hudson Pattern for Progress, Poughkeepsie, NY, 1975—89, chmn., 1981—85; bd. dirs. Coun. on Mcpl. Performance, N.Y.C., 1979—87, chmn., 1981—85, vice chmn., 1986—87; mem. Orange County (N.Y.) Planning Bd., 1997—; N.Y. State Rep. committeeman, 1980—89; chmn. emeritus Tolstoy Found., N.Y.C., 2001—, bd. dirs., 1975—2002, chmn., bd. dirs., 1979—89, 1994—2001; bd. dirs. Caramoor Ctr. Music and Arts, Katonah, NY, 1961—80, Boyce Thompson Inst. for Plant Rsch., Ithaca, NY, 1994—; emeritus Tolstoy Found., N.Y.C., 2001—. 1st lt. arty. AUS, 1952—54, Korea. Decorated Bronze Star; co-recipient Civic Leadership award (with wife), Citizens Union, 1997, Force for Nature award (with wife), Natural Resources Def. Coun., 1999, Environ. Leadership award (with wife), Nat. Audubon Soc., 2001; recipient Honor award, Kings County chpt. N.Y. State Soc. Profl. Engrs., 1969, Greater N.Y. coun. Girls Scouts U.S., 1973, Bd. Leadership award, Coun. Mcpl. Performance, 1984, Transp. Man of Yr. award, Greater N.Y. March of Dimes, 1985, award of excellence, Mid-Hudson Pattern for Progress, 1990, Honor award, Nat. and N.Y. Parks and Conservation Assn., 1992, Bronze medal, USEPA, 1993. Mem. ABA, N.Y. State Bar Assn., Assn. of Bar of City of N.Y., N.Y. County Lawyers Assn., Kent Moot Ct., AIME, Phi Delta Phi, Delta Psi. Clubs: Century Assn. (N.Y.C.), Knickerbocker (N.Y.C.), Racquet and Tennis (N.Y.C.). Eastern Orthodox. Office: Lacher & Lovell-Taylor PC 4th Fl 750 Lexington Ave New York NY 10022-8165 E-mail: cseristoff@lltlaw.com., ananouri@aol.com.

SIDES, JACK DAVIS, JR., lawyer; b. Dallas, Sept. 18, 1939; s. Jack Davis Sr. and Edith Eugenia (Lowrie) S.; m. Nancy Pauline Cantwell, July 22, 1967 (div. Sept. 1976); children: Mary Katharine, Jack Davis III; m. Laura Gail Miller, Aug. 2, 1979; children: Susan Ashley, Stacy Anne. BBA, U. Tex., 1962, JD with honors, 1963. Bar: Tex. 1963. Assoc. Jackson, Walker, et al, Dallas, 1963-67, White, McElroy, White, Sides & Rector, Dallas, 1968-78; sole practice Dallas, 1978—. Editor: U. Tex. Law Review, 1963. With USAFNG, 1963-69. Fellow Dallas Bar Found., Tex. Bar Found. (life); mem. ABA, Tex. Bar Assn. (grievance subcom. 1979-86), Dallas Bar Assn. (ethics com. 1973-77, jud. com. 1988—), Tex. Assn. Def. Counsel, Dallas Assn. Def. Counsel (sec. 1973-74). Clubs: Brook Hollow Golf (Dallas). Republican. Methodist. Avocations: reading, tennis, exercising. Federal civil litigation, State civil litigation. Office: 2301 Cedar Springs Rd Ste 350 Dallas TX 75201-7803

SIDMAN, ROBERT JOHN, lawyer; b. Cleve., Aug. 4, 1943; s. Charles Frances and Louise (Eckert) S.; m. Mary Mato, July 29, 1967; children: Christa Mary, Alicia Mary. BA, Benedictine Coll., 1965; JD, U. Notre Dame, 1968. Bar: Ohio 1968, U.S. Dist. Ct. (so. dist.) Ohio 1970, U.S. Ct. Appeals (6th cir.) 1971, U.S. Supreme Ct. 1971. Law clk. U.S. Dist. Ct. (so. dist.) Ohio, Columbus, 1968-70; assoc. Mayer, Tingley & Hurd, Columbus, 1970-75; judge Bankruptcy Ct. U.S. Dist. Ct. (so. dists.) Ohio, Columbus, 1975-82; ptnr. Vorys, Sater, Seymour & Pease, Columbus, 1982—. Prof. Ohio State U. Law Sch., Columbus, 1984, 85, 86. Mem. Nat. Conf. Bankruptcy Judges (bd. dirs. 1981-82), Assn. Former Bankruptcy Judges (bd. dirs. 1983-89, treas. 1986-87, pres. 1988-89). Bankruptcy, Federal civil litigation, Commercial, contracts (including sales of goods; commercial financing). Office: Vorys Sater Seymour & Pease PO Box 1008 52 E Gay St Columbus OH 43215-3161 E-mail: rjsidman@vssp.com., rsidman843@aol.com.

SIEBERT, WILLIAM ALAN, lawyer; b. Royal Oak, Mich., Jan. 25, 1955; s. William Edward and Mary Elizabeth (Northrup) S. BA, Albion Coll., 1977; JD, U. Detroit, 1980. Bar: Mich. 1980, U.S. Dist. Ct. (ea. dist.) Mich. 1981, U.S. Dist. Ct. (we. dist.) Mich. 1995. Gen. counsel RARE Realty, Beaverton, Mich., 1983-85; sole practice Gladwin, Mich., 1985—. Exec. com. Gladwin County Reps., 1983-92; candidate for Gladwin County Prosecuting Atty., 1984, 88. Mem. Mich. Bar Assn. (real property sect. title ins. com. 1984-2002), Clare-Gladwin Trial Lawyers, Masons (v.p. Gladwin Temple Assn. 1988-92, worshipful master 1992), Albion Coll. Alumni Bd., Phi Alpha Delta (chpt. clk. 1980). Commercial, consumer (including collections, credit), Criminal, Property, real (including real estate development, water). E-mail: wsiebert@chartermi.net.

SIEDLECKI, NANCY THERESE, lawyer, funeral director; b. Chgo., May 30, 1954; d. LeRoy John and Dorothy Josephine (Wilczynski) Schielka; m. Jonathan Francis Siedlecki, June 18, 1977; children: Samantha Ann, Abigail Marie. Student Triton Jr. Coll., 1971-73; grad. funeral dir., Worsham Coll., 1974; student Loyola U., Chgo., 1974-76., U. Ill.-Chgo., 1976-77; JD with honors, Chgo.-Kent Coll. Law, 1980. Bar: Ill. 1980. Paralegal in real estate Rosenberg, Savner & Unikel, Chgo., 1974-77; pvt. practice law, Burr Ridge, Ill., 1980—; cons. probate and various small bus. corps., Chgo., 1980—. Mem. ABA, Ill. State Bar Assn., Chgo. Bar Assn. Roman Catholic. General practice, Probate (including wills, trusts), Property, real (including real estate development, water). Office: 5300 Main St Downers Grove IL 60515-4846

SIEDZIKOWSKI, HENRY FRANCIS, lawyer; b. Chester, Pa., Dec. 27, 1953; s. Henry W. and Virginia (Szymanski) S. BA cum laude, Juniata Coll., 1975; JD magna cum laude, Villanova U., 1979. Bar: Pa. 1979, U.S. Dist. Ct. (ea. dist.) Pa. 1979, U.S. Ct. Appeals (3d cir.) 1979, U.S. Ct. Appeals (8th cir.) 1981, U.S. Dist. Ct. (we. dist.) Pa. 1986. Assoc. Dilworth, Paxson, Kalish & Kauffman, Phila., 1979-86; ptnr. Baskin Flaherty Elliott & Mannino P.C., Phila., 1986-90, Elliott Bray & Riley, Phila., 1990-92, Elliott, Vanaskie & Riley, 1992-94, Elliott, Reihner, Siedzikowski & Egan, 1994—. Mem. hearing com. disciplinary bd. Supreme Ct. Pa., 1985—91. Mem. ABA (chmn. Lanham act subcom. of bus. torts com. of litigation sect. 1986—, rotating editor newsletter of antitrust sect. franchisee com.), Pa. Bar Assn., Phila. Bar Assn. (chmn. subcom. disciplinary rules for profl. responsibility com. 1984-90). Democrat. Roman Catholic. Bankruptcy, Federal civil litigation, Franchising. Office: Elliott Reihner et al 925 Harvest Dr Blue Bell PA 19422-1956 E-mail: hfs@erse.com.

SIEFERT, JOHN, judge; b. Racine, Wis., Apr. 14, 1949; s. Robert Siefert and Ann Dugas; children: Amanda, Elizabeth, Regina. BA, U. Chgo., 1971; JD, U. Wis., 1974. Bar: Wis. 1974. Newspaper reporter Chgo.'s Am., 1967—71; police officer Milw. Police Dept., 1976—89; asst. v.p. Golden Rule Ins., Indpls., 1989—90; treas. County of Milwaukee, Milw., 1990—93; mcpl. judge City of Milw., 1993—99. Home: 2951 N Marietta Milwaukee WI 53211 Office: Courthouse 901 N 9th St Milwaukee WI 53211 Business E-Mail: jsiefert@wi.rr.com.

SIEFKIN, SUSAN DEEBLE, judge; b. Long Beach, Calif., June 12, 1943; d. Roy Edgar and Cora Elizabeth (Cotant) Deeble; m. Randolph R. Siefkin, Aug. 21, 1965; children: Nelson R., Kristen M. BA, U. Calif., Santa Barbara, 1965; MA, Rutgers U., 1966; JD, Humphreys Coll., Stockton, Calif., 1983; student, U. Bordeaux, France, 1963=64. Bar: Calif. 1983, U.S. Dist. Ct. (ea. and no. dists.) Calif. 1983. Intermittent instr. polit. sci. Modesto (Calif.) Jr. Coll., 1970-79; assoc., shareholder Law Offices Gianelli & Israels, Modesto, 1983-89; assoc., ptnr. Damrell, Nelson, Schrimp, Pallios & Ladine, Modesto, 1991-95; judge Stanislaus County Mclp. Ct., Modesto, 1995-98, Stanislaus County Superior Ct., Modesto, 1998—. Vis. lectr. polit. sci. Calif. State U. Stanislaus, Turlock, 1977-79. Mem. Modesto City Coun., 1975-83. Named Outstanding Woman, Stanislaus County Commn. for Women, 1982. Mem. Stanislaus County Bar Assn. (pres. 1989), Calif. Women Lawyers (bd. dirs., bd. govs. 1993-95), Modesto Rotary Club. Avocations: quilting, antiques, travel. Office: Stanislaus County Superior Ct 1100 I St Modesto CA 95354-2325

SIEGAL, JOEL DAVIS, lawyer; b. Plainfield, N.J., Feb. 9, 1937; s. Samuel and Florence (Ravitz) S.; m. Ronny J. Greenwald, Oct. 14, 1972; children: Samuel Jesse, Evan Charles. BA in Polit. Sci., U. Pa., 1958; JD, Yale U., 1961; MA in Internat. Rels., U. Stockholm, 1963. Bar: N.J., 1962, N.Y., 1965; U.S. Dist. Ct. N.J., 1962, U.S. Ct. Appeals (3rd cir.), 1963, U.S. Supreme Ct., N.Y., 1969, U.S. Dist. Ct. (so. and ea. dist.) N.Y., 1975. Law clk. to Hon. Arthur S. Lane, Newark, N.J., 1961-62; law clk. to Hon. Phillip Forman, 1963-64; assoc. Hellring Lindeman Goldstein & Siegal, Newark, 1967-70, ptnr., 1970—. Commr. Nat. Conf. Commrs. on Uniform Laws, 1991-98; mem. U.S. Dist. Ct. Adv. Bd., Newark, 1991-92. Contbr. articles to profl. jours. Mcpl. chmn. Dem. Party, Borough of Alpine, N.J., 1983-86. Fellow Am. Bar Found.; mem. ABA, N.J. Bar Assn., Essex County Bar Assn., Bergen Bar Assn., Assn. Fed. Bar N.J. (nat. del. N.J. 1974, pres. 1990-92, adv. bd. 1993—), Harmonie Club of N.Y.C. Democrat. Jewish. General civil litigation, Family and matrimonial. Office: Hellring Lindeman Goldstein Siegal 1 Gateway Ctr Fl 8 Newark NJ 07102-5386 Home: 32-40 N Dawn St Englewood NJ 07631 Fax: 973-621-7406. E-mail: jdsiegal@hlgslaw.com.

SIEGAN, BERNARD HERBERT, lawyer, educator; b. Chgo., July 28, 1924; s. David and Jeannette S.; m. Sharon Goldberg, June 15, 1952 (dec. Feb. 1985); m. Shelley Zifferblatt, Nov. 19, 1995. AA, Herzl. Jr. Coll., Chgo., 1943, 46; Student, Roosevelt Coll., Chgo., 1946-47; JD, U. Chgo., 1949. Bar: Ill. 1950. Practiced in, Chgo.; partner firm Siegan & Karlin, 1952-73; pres., sec. various small corps. and gen. partner in partnerships engaged in real estate ownership and devel., 1955-70; weekly columnist Freedom newspaper chain, other papers, 1974-79. Cons. law and econs. program U. Chgo. Law Sch., 1970-73; adj. prof. law U. San Diego Law Sch., 1973-74, Disting. prof., 1975—; adj. scholar Cato Inst., Washington, 1991—, Heritage Found., 1992—; cons. windfalls and wipeouts project HUD, 1973-74; cons. FTC, 1985-86, U.S. Justice Dept., dir. constl. bibliog. project, 1986-88; keynote speaker 5th Internat. Conf. on Urbanism, Porto Alegre, Brazil, 1989; nominated by Pres. Reagan to U.S. Ct. Appeals (9th cir.) Feb. 2, 1987, confirmation denied July 14, 1988 by party line vote Senate Judiciary Com. Author: Land Use Without Zoning, 1972, Spanish edit., 1995, Other People's Property, 1976, Economic Liberties and the Constitution, 1980, The Supreme Court's Constitution: An Inquiry Into Judicial Review and Its Impact on Society, 1987, Drafting a Constitution for a Nation or Republic Emerging into Freedom, 1992, 2d edit., 1994, Portuguese, Ukrainian, Polish and Spanish edits., 1993, Property and Freedom: The Constitution, Supreme Court and Land Use Regulation, 1997, Adapting a Constitution to Protect Freedom and Provide Abundance (in Bulgarian), 1998, Property Rights: From Magna Carta to the Fourteenth Amendment, 2001; editor: Planning without Prices, 1977, The Interaction of Economics and the Law, 1977, Regulation, Economics and the Law, 1979, Government, Regulation and the Economy, 1980. Mem. pres.-elect's Task Force on Housing, 1980-81; mem. Pres.'s Commn. on Housing, 1981-82; mem. Nat. Commn. on bicentannial of U.S. Constn., 1985-91; chmn. adv. com. Affordable Housing Conf., San Diego, 1985, Rights of Regulated Conf., Coronado, Calif., 1976; chmn. Conf. on the Taking Issue, 1976; mem. Houston Regional Urban Design Team, Study of Houston, 1990; mem. U.S. team Bulgarian Econ. Growth and Transition Project, 1990; mem. devel. bd. Mingei Internat. Mus. World Folk Art, 1981-84. Served with AUS, 1943-46. Research fellow law and econs. U. Chgo. Law Sch., 1968-69; Urban Land Inst. research fellow, 1976-86; recipient Leander J. Monks Meml. Fund award Inst. Humane Studies, 1972, George Washington medal Freedom Founds. at Valley Forge, 1981, Spl. award Liberal Inst. of Rio Grande do Sul, Porto Alegre, Brazil, 1989, Thorsnes award for outstanding legal scholarship, 1998; named Univ. Prof., U. San Diego, 1997-98.

SIEGEL, BERNARD LOUIS, lawyer; b. Pitts., Sept. 15, 1938; s. Ralph Robert and Frieda Sara (Stein) S.; m. Marcia Margolis, Sept. 3, 1961 (div. Aug. 1983); children: Jonathan, Sharon; m. Susan Erickson, Aug. 31, 1997 (div. June 2001). BA, Brandeis U., 1960; JD, Harvard U., 1963. Bar: Pa. 1964, U.S. Dist. Ct. (we. dist.) Pa. 1964, U.S. Dist. Ct. (ea. dist.) Pa. 1985, U.S. Ct. Appeals (3d cir.) 1985, U.S. Supreme Ct. 1985. Assoc. Silin, Eckert & Burke, Erie, Pa., 1963-66; ptnr. Silin, Eckert, Burke & Siegel, Erie, Pa., 1966-73; 1st asst. dist. atty. Erie County, 1972-76; dep. atty. gen. Pa. Dept. Justice, Phila., 1976-78; dep. dist. atty. Dist. Atty. of Phila., 1978-86; pvt. practice Phila., 1986—. Adj. prof. La Salle U., Phila., 1986-98; lectr. Fed. Law Enforcement Tng. Ctr., Glynco, Ga., 1986-97, Mercyhurst Coll., Erie, 1974-76, Nat. Coll. Dist. Attys., Houston, 1978-85; adj. prof. Temple U. law sch., 1995—; mem. criminal rules com. Pa. Supreme Ct., Phila., 1976-85; commr. Pa. Crime Commn., Harrisburg, 1976-79. Author: (with others) Pennsylvania Grand Jury Practice, 1983, By No Extraordinary Means, 1986. Mem. ABA, Nat. Assn. Criminal Def. Lawyers, Pa. Assn. Criminal Def. Lawyers (bd. dirs. 1988—, treas. 2002-), Pa. Bar Assn. (chmn. criminal law sect. 1988-91), Phila. Bar Assn. (chmn. criminal justice sect. 1990-91). Democrat. Jewish. Avocations: bicycling, reading, hiking. Criminal. Office: 1515 Market St Ste 1915 Philadelphia PA 19102-1920 E-mail: blsesq@snip.net.

SIEGEL, EDWARD, lawyer; b. Asbury Park, N.J., Jan. 15, 1931; s. Nathan Albert and Fannie Siegel; m. Helen Dorothy Haber, Aug. 29, 1954; children: Sharon, Frances. BA, U. Fla., 1952, JD, 1955. Bar: Fla. 1955. Spl. asst. atty. gen. Office Atty. Gen. Fla., Tallahassee, 1955; ptnr. Adams, Rothstein & Siegel, Jacksonville, Fla., 1957-90. Author: How to Avoid Lawyers, 1969, Defend Yourself! The Moneysworth Legal Advisor, 1972, Just Like a Lawyer, 1993; mem. editorial bd. Fla. Bar Jour., 1979-86. Bd. dirs. Jacksonville Jewish Ctr., 1968-70; bd. dirs., v.p. Jewish Family and Children's Svcs., 1970-75; trustee Jacksonville Libr. Bd., 1978-82. Served as 1st lt. USAF, 1955-57. Mem. ABA, Fla. Bar Assn., Jacksonville Bar Assn. (chmn. fee arbitration com. 1976-77), Blue Key, Order of Coif, Phi Beta Kappa. Democrat. Commercial, consumer (including collections, credit), Family and matrimonial, Property, real (including real estate development, water). Home: 6855 San Sabastian Ave Jacksonville FL 32217-2731

SIEGEL, EDWARD M. lawyer; b. N.Y.C., Apr. 14, 1934; s. Charles and Rose (Fritzhand) S.; m. Elyse R. Roth, Mar. 9, 1969; children: Eric, Eve-Lynn. BA, Columbia Coll., 1955; MA, Columbia U., 1957, JD, 1960. Bar: N.Y. 1961. Legal asst. to dean Columbia U. Law Sch., N.Y.C., 1960-65; gen. counsel Transp. Displays, Inc., N.Y.C., 1965-75, corp. sec., 1968-75, v.p., 1972-73, sr. v.p., 1973-75; pub. affairs mgr. J.C. Penney Co., N.Y.C., 1975-77; gen. counsel, corp. sec. Electro Audio Dynamics, Inc., Great Neck, N.Y., 1977-85, v.p., 1981-85; v.p. legal affairs East View Co., N.Y.C., 1985-87; ptnr. Bangser Klein Rocca & Blum (formerly Bangser & Weiss), N.Y.C., 1988-92; sr. v.p., gen. coun., corp. sec. Nat. Med. Funding Corp., N.Y.C., 1992-94; atty pvt. practice N.Y.C., 1994—. Mem. N.Y. State Bar Assn., Columbia Law Sch. Alumni Assn. (dir. 1966-70). General practice, Probate (including wills, trusts), Property, real (including real estate development, water). Home: 1036 Park Ave Apt 6D New York NY 10028-0971 Office: 7 Penn Plz Ste 505 New York NY 10001-3900

SIEGEL, HOWARD JEROME, lawyer; b. Chgo., July 29, 1942; s. Leonard and Idele (Lehrner) S.; m. Diane L. Gerber; children: Sari D., Allison J., James G. BS, U. Ill., 1963; JD, Northwestern U., 1966. Bar: Ill. 1966, U.S. Dist. Ct. (no. dist.) Ill. 1967. Assoc. Ancel, Stonesifer & Glink, Chgo., 1966-70; ptnr. Goldstine & Siegel, Summit, Ill., 1970-75; sole practice Chgo., 1975-77; pres. Wexler, Siegel & Shaw, Ltd., Chgo., 1978-82; ptnr. Keck, Mahin & Cate, Chgo., 1982-95, Neal Gerber & Eisenberg, Chgo., 1995-99; counsel Fagel & Haber, Chgo., 1999—. Bd. dirs. various corps. Mem.: ABA, Chgo. Bar Assn., Ill. Bar Assn., Twin Orchard Country Club (Long Grove. Ill.). Corporate, general, Property, real (including real estate development, water). Office: FabelHaberLLC 55 E Monroe 40th Fl Chicago IL 60603 E-mail: hsiegel@fagelhaber.com.

SIEGEL, JEFFREY NORTON, lawyer; b. N.Y.C., Nov. 27, 1942; s. George Siegel and Rose (Friedman) Gerber; m. Judith Sharon Chused, June 11, 1966; children: Daniel, Linda. AB, Brown U., 1964; LLB, Harvard U., 1967. Bar: N.Y. 1968. Assoc., ptnr. Golenbock & Barell, N.Y.C., 1967—89; ptnr. Whitman & Ransom, N.Y.C., 1990—93, Shack Siegel Katz & Flaherty, P.C., N.Y.C., 1993—. Mem. bus. com. The Jewish Mus. Mem. ABA, Assn. Bar City N.Y. (com. securities regulation 1987-90, com. profl. responsibility 1979-84), Phi Beta Kappa. Corporate, general, Mergers and acquisitions, Securities. Home: 975 Park Ave New York NY 10028-0323 Office: Shack Siegel Katz & Flaherty PC 530 5th Ave New York NY 10036-5101

SIEGEL, SARAH ANN, lawyer; b. Providence, Aug. 29, 1956; BA in History cum laude, Brandeis U., 1978; JD, Washington U., St. Louis, 1981. Bar: Mo. 1982, U.S. Dist. Ct. (ea. dist.) Mo. 1983. Assoc. atty., St. Louis, 1982-83; staff atty. Land Clearance for Redevel. Authority, St. Louis, 1983-85, gen. counsel, 1985-88, Econ. Devel. Corp., St. Louis, 1988-90, St. Louis Devel. Corp., 1990-91; spl. counsel for devel. City of St. Louis, 1991-92; assoc. Suelthaus & Walsh, P.C., St. Louis, 1992-95, prin., 1995-99; v.p., gen. counsel Dierbergs Mkts. Inc., St. Louis, 1999—. Exec. com. Friends of the Sheldon Concert Hall, 2001—; pres. Ctrl. Reform Congregation, St. Louis, 1991—93, v.p., 1989—91, bd. dir., 1987—89, St. Louis Art Fair, 2001—03, Friends of the Sheldon Concert Hall, 1997—. Mem. ABA, Mo. Bar Assn. (vice chair com. on eminent domain 1990-91, steering com. 1987-89, 95-96), Women's Lawyer Assn. (bd. dirs. 1985-90, v.p. 1989-90), Am. Corp. Counsel Assn. (mem. St. Louis chpt., bd. dirs. 2000-, v.p. 2000-). Avocations: hiking, swimming. Corporate, general, Property, real (including real estate development, water), Alternative dispute resolution. E-mail: siegels@dierbergs.com.

SIEGEL, STANLEY, lawyer, educator; b. N.Y.C., Mar. 2, 1941; s. David Aaron and Rose (Minsky) S. BS summa cum laude, NYU, 1960; JD magna cum laude, Harvard U., 1963. Bar: N.Y. 1963, D.C. 1964, Mich. 1970, Calif. 1976; CPA, Md. Atty. Office Sec. of Air Force, 1963-66; asst. prof. law U. Mich., Ann Arbor, 1966-69, assoc. prof., 1969-71, prof., 1971-74; ptnr. Honigman, Miller, Schwartz & Cohn, Detroit, 1974-76; prof. law UCLA, 1976-86, NYU, 1986—, assoc. dean, 1987-89. Vis. prof. Stanford Law Sch., 1973, Ctrl. European U., Budapest, 1993—2001, U. Konstanz, Germany, 1996, Tel Aviv U., 1998; fellow Max-Planck Inst., Hamburg, 1988; cons. reorgn. U.S. Postal Svc., 1969—71; exec. sec. Mich. Law Revision Commn., 1973; mem. bd. examiners AICPA, 1980—83. Author: (with Schulman and Moscow) Michigan Business Corporations, 1979, (with Conard and Knauss) Enterprise Organization, 4th edit., 1987, (with D. Siegel) Accounting and Financial Disclosure: A Guide to Basic Concepts, 1983, (with others) Swiss Company Law, 1996; mem. editl. bd. Lexis Electronic Author's Press, 1996-98. Served to capt. USAF, 1963-66. Mem. ABA, D.C. Bar Assn., Calif. Bar Assn., Assn. of Bar of City of N.Y., Am. Law Inst., AICPA. Office: NYU Law Sch 40 Washington Sq S New York NY 10012-1099 E-mail: ss3@nyu.edu.

SIEGFRIED, DAVID CHARLES, retired lawyer; b. New York, Feb. 15, 1942; s. Charles Albert and Marjorie Claire (Young) S.; m. Meri Stephanie (Smith); children: Karin Elisabeth, Christine Elise. BA(hon.) , Princeton U., 1964; JD, Harvard U., 1967. Bar: N.Y., 1970. Assoc. Milbank, Tweed, Hadley, and McCloy, N.Y.C., 1968-76, ptnr., 1977—98, resident ptnr. Hong Kong and Singapore, 1979-83, 85-88. Speaker in field. Bd. dir. Cmty. Agy. Corp. N.J., Inc.; v.p. found. 1st lt. USAR, 1967-74. Mem.: ABA, Princeton U. (exec. com. alumni coun.), Millburn Short Hills Hist. Soc. (pres.), Millburn N.J. Hist. Preservation Commn. (vice chmn.), Assn. of Bar City of N.Y., N.Y. State Bar Assn., Princeton (New York); Short Hills (N.J.); Am. (Hong Kong and Singapore); Tanglin (Singapore),;Cricket. Congregationalist. Avocations: running, tennis, historic reading. Banking, Commercial, contracts (including sales of goods; commercial financing), Private international. Home: 30 Western Dr Short Hills NJ 07078-3230

SIEKMAN, THOMAS CLEMENT, lawyer; b. Somerville, Mass., Sept. 22, 1941; s. Aloysius C. and Estelle M. (Forte) S.; children: Michael T., James T., Amy K. BS in Engring., Merrimack Coll., 1963; JD, Villanova U., 1966. Bar: Mass. 1966, U.S. Dist. Ct. Mass. 1969. Patent atty. Bethlehem (Pa.) Steel, 1966-68, Mohawk Data Scis., Stoneham, Mass., 1968-72, Chittick, Thompson & Pfund, Boston, 1972-73; from patent atty. to v.p. and gen. counsel Digital Equipment Corp., Maynard, Mass., 1973-98; Sr. v.p., gen. coun., sec. Compaq Computer Corp., 1998—2002; of counsel Skadden, Arps, Slate, Meagher & Flom LLP. Bd. dirs., chmn. N.E. Legal Found. Trustee Mass. Taxpayers Found., Merrimack Coll.; mem. New Eng. Legal Found.; mem. Houston cmty. adv. bd. Teach Am.; bd. dirs. Houston African-Am. Mus. Mem. ABA, Am. Corp. Counsel Assn., Assn. Gen. Counsel. Avocations: squash, skiing. Office: Skadden, Arps, Meagher & Flom LLP 1440 New York Ave, NW Washington DC 20005*

SIEMER, DEANNE CLEMENCE, lawyer; b. Buffalo, Dec. 25, 1940; d. Edward D. and Dorothy J. (Helsdon) S.; m. Howard P. Willens; 1 child, Jason L. BA, George Washington U., 1962; LLB, Harvard U., 1968. Bar: N.Y. 1968, D.C. 1969, Md. 1972. Economist Office of Mgmt. and Budget, Washington, 1964-67; assoc., then ptnr. Wilmer, Cutler & Pickering, Washington, 1968-77, 80-90; ptnr. Pillsbury, Madison & Sutro, Washington, 1990-95; mng. dir. Wilsie Co., Washington and Saipan, M.P., 1995—. Gen. counsel U.S. Dept. of Def., Washington, 1977—79; spl. asst. to sec. U.S. Dept. of Energy, Washington, 1979—80. Author: Tangible Evidence, 1996, National Security and Self-Determination: United States Policy in Micronesia, 1999, Corel Presentations for Litigators, 2000, PowerPoint for Litigators, 2000, Effective Use of Courtroom Technology: A Judge's Guide to Pretrial and Trial, 2001, An Honorable Accord: The Covenant Between the Northern Mariana Islands and the United States, 2001, Effective Use of Courtroom Technology: A Lawyer's Guide to Pretrial and Trial, 2002, Easy Tech: Cases and Materials on Courtroom Technology, 2002, The Patronus Technique: A Practical Proposal In Asbestos-Driven Bankruptcies, 2002, Power Point 2002 for Litigators, 2003. Mem. Lawyers Com. for Civil Rights, Washington, 1973—; mediator D.C. Superior Ct., Washington, 1986—, U.S. Ct. Appeals, Washington, 1988—; trustee Nat. Inst. Trial Advocacy, 1989—, Am. Law Inst., 1990—; arbitrator Atty. Client Arbitration Bd., NASD. Recipient Citation Air Force Assn., 1977, Dist. Pub. Service medal Sec. of Def., 1979, Commendation Pres. of U.S. 1981. Mem. ABA, D.C. Bar Assn., No. Marianas Bar Assn. Episcopalian. Administrative and regulatory, Federal civil litigation, State civil litigation.

SIEMON, JOYCE MARILYN, lawyer, writer; b. Bridgeport, Conn., Dec. 4, 1944; d. George Lewis and Rita (Siegel) Nissenson; m. Robert G. Cash, Oct. 7, 2001; 1 child, Alyssa Karen. BA in English, Carnegie Inst. Tech., 1966; JD with high honors, Fla. State U., 1980. Bar: Fla. 1981. Tech. writer Computer Sci. Rsch. Ctr. Carnegie Inst. Tech., Pitts., 1966-67; tchr. Leesville (La.) Jr. HS, 1967-68; mag. editor VanTrump, Zeigler and Shane, Pitts., 1969; news editor Pitts. Press, 1970; staff writer Dade County Pub. Safety Dept., Miami, Fla., 1971-75; reporter North Dade Jour., Miami, 1977; freelance writer, 1977—; instr. legal writing and rsch. Coll. Law Fla. State U., Tallahassee, 1979-80; intern Fla. Supreme Ct., 1980; law clk. Office Gen. Counsel Fla. Dept. Gen. Svcs., Tallahassee, 1980; assoc. Young, Stern & Tannenbaum, P.A., North Miami Beach, Fla., 1981, Greenberg, Traurig, Askew, Hoffman, Lipoff, Quentel & Wolff, Miami, 1981—82, Hornsby & Whisenand, Miami, 1982-85; pvt. practice North Miami Beach, 1985-92, Boca Raton, Fla., 1992—. Author: employee manual, advtsg. brochures, newspaper articles and ads, book revs.; editor: (book) Lawrenceville: A Short History, 1969; columnist: Siemon Says North Dade Jour., 1977; contbr. Mem. Dade County Coord. Network, 1983. Mem.: ABA, Dade County Bar Assn., Fla. Bar Assn., Internat. Platform Assn., Am. Jewish Congress (v.p. S.E. region), Am. Judicature Soc., Kiwanis Internat., West Boca Toastmasters Club, Order of the Coif, Phi Alpha Delta. Alternative dispute resolution, Appellate.

SIENKO, LEONARD EDWARD, JR., lawyer; b. Hancock, N.Y., Aug. 24, 1946; s. Leonard Edward and Louise Albina (Gaudor) S. BA, Boston Coll., 1968, JD, 1977; MDiv, Andover-Newton Theol., 1971. Bar: N.Y. 1978, U.S. Dist. Ct. (no. dist.) N.Y. 1980, U.S. Supreme Ct. 1982. Estate tax atty. Del. County N.Y. State Dept. Taxation & Fin., Delhi, NY, 1983-93; ct. atty. trial part Del. County Ct., Delhi, 1993—2002; town atty. Town of Hancock, 1990—. County chair Del. County Dem. Com., N.Y., 1987-93. Mem. Del. County Bar Assn. (pres. 1993-95), N.Y. State Bar Assn. (Ho. Dels. 1993-97, N.Y. Law Net com. 1995—, mem. President's Task Force on Electronic Comm. 1996—). Democrat. Unitarian Universalist. Avocation: computers. Office: PO Box 579 12 E Main St Hancock NY 13783-1126 Home: PO Box 425 Hancock NY 13783-0425 E-mail: lennyesq@hancock.net., sienkolawoffice@yahoo.com.

SIEPELT-BABILON, STEFAN, lawyer; b. Cologne, Germany, Aug. 22, 1964; s. Horst-Guenter and Marlene Siepelt; m. Karin Babilon, Aug. 31, 2002; 1 child, Alexander Babilon. JD, U. Cologne, 1991, LLD, 1993. Bar: Regional Ct. 1993, Appelate Ct. 2002. Sci. asst. Inst. Comml. and Labour Law, U. Cologne, 1989—93; assoc. CBH-Rechtsanwaelte, Cologne, 1993—99, ptnr., 1999—. Mem. supervisory bd. Bruder Mannesmann AG, Remscheid, 1998—2001; chmn. bd. WKM Terrain-und- Beteiligung AG, Munich, 2000—. Author: Shareholder's Right to Speech in a General Meeting of Shareholders, 1991. Pres. and mem. bd. Round Table Cologne, 1996—2002. Mem.: Assn. for Comml. Law. Corporate, general, Commercial, contracts (including sales of goods; commercial financing), Mergers and acquisitions. Office: CBH-Rechtsanwaelte Bismarkstr 11-13 50672 Cologne Germany

SIFF, ANDREW, lawyer; Chief counsel to Rep. majority U.S. Senate Com. Rules and Adminstrn., Washington, 2001—02; counselor to sec. labor U.S. Dept. of Labor, Washington, 2002—. Office: US Dept Labor Frances Perkins Bldg 200 Constitution Ave NW Washington DC 20210 Business E-Mail: siff-andrew@dol.gov.*

SIFTON, CHARLES PROCTOR, federal judge; b. N.Y.C., Mar. 18, 1935; s. Paul F. and Claire G. S.; m. Susan Scott Rowland, May 20, 1986; children: Samuel, Tobias, John. AB, Harvard U., 1957; LL.B., Columbia U., 1961. Bar: N.Y. 1961. Assoc. Cadwalader, Wickersham & Taft, 1961-62, 64-66; staff atty. U.S. Senate Fgn. Rels. Com., 1962-63; asst. U.S. atty. N.Y.C., 1966-69; ptnr. LeBoeuf, Lamb, Leiby and MacRae, N.Y.C., 1969-77; judge U.S. Dist. Ct. (ea. dist.) N.Y., Bklyn., 1977—, chief judge, 1995-2000, sr. judge, 2000—. Mem.: Bar Assn. City of NY. Office: US Dist Ct US Courthouse 225 Cadman Plz E Rm 244 Brooklyn NY 11201-1818

SIGETY, CHARLES EDWARD, lawyer, family business consultant; b. N.Y.C., Oct. 10, 1922; s. Charles and Anna (Toth) S.; m. Katharine K. Snell, July 17, 1948; children: Charles, Katharine, Robert, Cornelius, Elizabeth. BS, Columbia U., 1944; MBA, Harvard U., 1947; LLB, Yale U., 1951; LHD (hon.), Cazenovia Coll., 1994. Bar: N.Y. 1952, D.C. 1958. With Bankers Trust Co., 1939-42; instr. adminstrv. engring. Pratt Inst., 1948; instr. econs. Yale U., 1948-50; vis. lectr. acctg. Sch. Gen. Studies Columbia U., N.Y.C., 1948-50, 52; rapporteur com. fed. taxation for U.S. coun. Internat. C. of C., 1952-53; asst. to com. fed. taxation Am. Inst. Accts., 1950-53; with Compton Advt. Agy., N.Y.C., 1954; vis. lectr. law Yale U., 1952; pvt. practice law N.Y.C., 1952-67; pres., dir. Video Vittles, Inc., N.Y.C., 1953-67; dep. commr. FHA, 1955-57; of counsel Javits and Javits, 1959-60; 1st asst. atty. gen. N.Y., 1958-59; dir., mem. exec. com. Gotham Bank, N.Y.C., 1961-63; dir. N.Y. State Housing Fin. Agy., 1962-63; chmn. Met. Ski Slopes, Inc., N.Y.C., 1962-65; pres., exec. adminstr. Florence Nightingale Health Ctr., N.Y.C., 1965-85; dir. Schaerer AG, Wabern, Switzerland, 1982-88; chmn. Kenbar Group, N.Y.C., 1997—, Internat. Bioimmune Sys., Inc., Great Neck, NY, 1999—2002. Professorial lectr. Sch. Architecture, Pratt Inst., N.Y.C., 1962-66; mem. Sigety Assocs., cons. in housing mortgage financing and urban renewal, 1957-67; ho. cons. Govt. of Peru, 1956; mem. missions to Hungary, Poland, Fed. Republic Germany, Malta, Czechoslovakia, Russia, Israel, Overseas Pvt. Investment Corp., 1990-92; owner, operator Peppermill Farms, Pipersville, Pa., 1956—. Bd. dirs., sec., v.p., treas. Nat. Coun. Health Ctrs., 1969-85; bd. dirs. Am.-Hungarian Found., 1974-76, Pritikin Rsch. Found., 1991—, Stratford Arms Condo Assn., 1992-93, 2002--, Global Leadership Inst., 1993—; founding mem., bd. dirs., Natl. Assn. for Continence, 1982, trustee Cazenovia (N.Y.) Coll., 1981-2002, Delaware Valley Coll. Sci. and Agr., Doylestown, Pa., 1998—; trustee, v.p. Woodmere Art Mus. Phila., 2000—, Navy Supply Corps Found., Athens, Ga., 2000—; del. White House Conf. on Aging, 1971, White House Conf. on Mgmt. Tng. and Market Econs. Edn. in Ctrl. and Ea. Europe, 1991; bd. visitors Lander Coll., U. S.C., Greenwood, 1982-84; mem. fin. com. World Games, Santa Clara, 1981, London, 1985, Karlsruhe, 1989, The Hague, 1993, Confrerie des Chevaliers du Tastevin, Confrerie de la Chaine des Rotisseurs, Wine and Food Soc., Wednesday 10. Lt. (j.g.) Supply Corps, USNR, 1942-46. Recipient President's medal Cazenovia Coll., 1990, George Washington laureate Am. Hungarian Found., 1996; named Prin. for Day, Townsend Harris H.S. N.Y.C. Bd. Edn., 1997-2001, Disting. Alumnus U.S. Navy Supply Corps Sch., Athens, Ga., 1998; Baker scholar Harvard U., 1947. Mem. DOCA (Defense Orientation Conf. Assn.). Presbyterian. Office: 7155 Old Easton Rd Box 156 Pipersville PA 18947-9701 E-mail: sigety@msn.com.

SIGMOND, CAROL ANN, lawyer; b. Phila., Jan. 9, 1951; d. Irwin and Mary Florence (Vollmer) S. BA, Grinnell Coll., 1972; JD, Cath. U., 1975. Bar: Va. 1975, D.C. 1980, Md. 1988, N.Y. 1990, U.S. Dist. Ct. (ea. dist.) Va. 1975, U.S. Dist. Ct. (so. and ea. dist.) N.Y. 1991, U.S. Ct. Appeals (4th cir.) 1976, U.S. Ct. Appeals (fed. cir.) 1987, U.S. Ct. Appeals (2d cir.) 2000. Asst. gen. counsel Washington Met. Area Transit Authority, 1978-85; acting assoc. gen. counsel for appeals and gen. law, 1985-86; assoc. Patterson, Belknap, Webb & Tyler, Washington, 1986-89, Berman, Paley, Goldstein & Kannry, N.Y.C., 1991-93; prin. Law Offices of Carol A. Sigmond, N.Y.C., 1993-97; of counsel Pollack & Greene, LLP, N.Y.C., 1998-2000; pvt. practice N.Y.C., 2000—. Mem. Women's Nat. Dem. Club. Active Womens Nat. Dem. Club. Mem. ABA, D.C. Bar Assn., Arlington County Bar Assn., Va. State Bar Assn., Md. State Bar Assn., Assn. of Bar of City of N.Y. Democrat. Mem. Lds Ch. Avocations: piano, bridge. Construction, Government contracts and claims. Office: 733 3d Ave Fl7 New York NY 10017 E-mail: csigmond@attglobal.net.

SIGMOND, RICHARD BRIAN, lawyer; b. Phila., Dec. 7, 1944; s. Joseph and Jean (Nissman) S.; children: Michael, Catherine, Alina; m. Susan Helen Peteraf, Dec. 24, 1984. BS, Phila. Coll. Textiles & Sci., 1966; JD, Temple U., 1969. Bar: Pa. 1969, U.S. Supreme Ct. 1973, U.S. Dist. Ct. (ea. dist.) Pa. 1975, U.S. Ct. Appeals (3d cir.) 1975, N.Y. 1982, D.C. 1995. Atty. Pub. Defender Assn., Phila., 1969-70; ptnr. Meranze, Katz, Spear & Wilderman, Phila., 1970-84; sr. ptnr. Spear, Wilderman, Sigmond, Borish & Endy, Phila., 1985-89, Jennings Sigmond, Phila., 1989—; gen. counsel Internat. Brotherhood Painters and Allied Trades, 1997-2000. Chmn., bd. dirs. Gatehouse Phila., 1972-83; lectr. Pvt. Industry Coun., Phila., 1985—, labor studies div., Pa. State U., 1978-82, 85-86; gen. counsel Stabilization Agreement, Sheet Metal Industry Trust Fund, 1994—, Internat. Painters and Allied Trades Industry Pension Fund, 1997—. Mem. ABA (labor law com., litigation com.), AFL-CIO (lawyers coordinating com.), Pa. Bar Assn. (labor law com.), Phila. Bar Assn. (labor com.), Phi Alpha Delta. Avocations: sailing, writing. Federal civil litigation, Labor (including EEOC, Fair Labor Standards Act, labor-management relations, NLRB, OSHA), Pension, profit-sharing, and employee benefits. Office: Penn Mutual Towers 510 Walnut St Fl 16 Philadelphia PA 19106-3601

SIGNER, GREGORY RICHARD, lawyer; b. Denver, June 28, 1951; s. Merton Ira and Dorothy Marie (Richards) S.; m. Nancy L. Sangster, Apr. 19, 1980; children: Benjamin, Timothy. BS, U. Colo., 1974, JD, 1977. Bar: Colo. 1977, U.S. Dist. Ct. Colo. 1977, U.S. Ct. Appeals (D.C. cir.) 1980, (6th cir.) 1982, (11th cir.) 2000, Tenn. 1988. Staff atty. Office of Gen. Counsel TVA, Knoxville, Tenn., 1977-90, sr. environ. atty., 1990—. Chmn. permitting and compliance com. Utility Air Regulatory Group, Washington, 1991—; adj. assoc. prof. Coll. Law, U. Tenn., Knoxville, 1992-95; editor ABA Nat. Rsch. Environ., 2001—. Contbr. articles to profl. jours. Mem. ABA (natural resources sect.). Home: 230 Woodland Trace Dr Knoxville TN 37922-1720 Office: TVA Office Gen Counsel 400 E Summit Hill Dr Knoxville TN 37915-1027

SIGNORILE, VINCENT ANTHONY, lawyer; b. Jersey City, Mar. 22, 1959; s. Ralph R. and Rita (DeRosa) S. BS, St. Peter's Coll., Jersey City, 1981; JD, Seton Hall U., 1985. Bar: N.J. 1985, Pa. 1985. Aide Jersey City Mcpl. Coun., 1980-81, Office of Mayor, City of Jersey City, 1981; law clk. Corp. Counsel Jersey City, 1981-85; law sec. Superior Ct. N.J. for Hudson County, Jersey City, 1985-86; assoc. atty. Jersey City, 1986-89; ptnr.

Signorile & Saminski, Jersey City, 1989-97; atty. Jersey City Zoning Bd. Adjustment, 1994-97, Bayonne City Ethics Bd., 1995-97; judge Jersey City Mcpl. Ct., 1996—99, chief judge, 1999—. Judge Jersey City Mcpl. Ct., 1996-97, chief judge 1997—. Mem. Hudson County Dem. Com., 1977-81, Jersey City Environ. Com., 1989-93, Jersey City Planning Bd. Com., 1991-93, Jersey City Ins. Fund Com., 1989-93; co-chmn. Hudson County Columbus Parade, 1984-85; elected to Mcpl. Coun. Jersey City, 1989-93. Mem. ABA, N.J. Bar Assn., Pa. Bar Assn., Hudson County Bar Assn. (treas. Young Lawyer's Assn. 1987-88, scholar 1984-85), Assn. Trial Lawyers Am. Roman Catholic. General practice. Home: 1691 John F Kennedy Blvd Jersey City NJ 07305-1841 Office: Jersey City Municipal Ct 365 Summit Ave Jersey City NJ 07306

SIGUENZA, PETER CHARLES, JR., territory supreme court justice; b. Guam, July 1, 1951; s. Peter C. and Barbara L. (Bordallo) S.; m. Joleen Taitano Rios, Dec. 6, 1969; 1 child, Dawn. BA, Calif. State U., 1976; JD, U. of the Pacific, 1980. Bar: Calif. 1981, Guam 1981, U.S. Ct. Appeals (9th cir.), Commonwealth No. Marianas 1983. Pvt. practice Klemm, Blair & Barusch; staff atty. Guam Legal Svcs. Corp.; clk. Superior Ct. Guam; libr. Calif. Ct. Appeal; judge Guam Superior Ct., Agana, 1984-96; justice Supreme Ct. Guam, Agana, 1999—2001; chief justice Guam Supreme Ct., 1996—99, 2001—. Designated judge Dist. Ct. Guam, Supreme Ct. Federated States Micronesia; chair bd. trustees Father Duenas Meml. Sch., 1991; chair rules commn. Supreme Ct. Guam, 1993. Mem. ABA, Am. Judges Assn. Office: Supreme Ct Guam Judiciary Bldg Ste 300 120 W O'Brien Dr Hagatna GU 96910-5174*

SIGUION-REYNA, LEONARDO, lawyer, business executive; b. Dagupan City, The Philippines, Apr. 18, 1921; s. Lamberto and Felisa (Tiongson) S.; m. Armida Ponce-Enrile, Nov. 24, 1952; children: Monica, Leonardo, Carlos. LLB, U. Santo Tomas, Manila, 1946-48. Bar: Philippines, 1948. Sr. ptnr. Siguion Reyna, Montecillo, and Ongsiako, Makati Metro Manila. Chmn. bd. Phimco Industries, Inc., Manila, Sandvick Philippines, Inc.; pres. Electronic Tele. Systems Industries, Inc., Manila Meml. Park Cemetary, Inc., Valmora Investment & Mgmt. Corp.; dir. ABB (Phils) Inc., Crismida Realty Corp., Dole Philippines, Inc., Filflex Indsl. & Mfg. Corp., Goodyear Philippines, Inc., Indsl. Realties, Inc., Investment & Capital Corp. of the Philippines, Unilever (Phil) Inc., Ionics Circuits., Inc., Petronas (Phil) Inc. Mem. Philippine Bar Assn., Casino Español de Manila. Roman Catholic. CLubs: Manila Yacht, Manila Polo, Rotary. Commercial, contracts (including sales of goods; commercial financing), Corporate, general, Labor (including EEOC, Fair Labor Standards Act, labor-management relations, NLRB, OSHA). Home: 7 Tangile Rd/North Forbes Manila Philippines

SIHNHOLD, ROBERT H. lawyer; b. St. Louis, June 26, 1943; s. Robert H. and Paulina L. (Hayo) S.; m. Dianne B., Sept. 6, 1942; children: Robert, Brett. BS, Westminster Coll., 1964; JD, Washington U., 1967. Bar: Mo. Atty. Firemen's Fund Ins., St. Louis, 1969; assoc. Evans & Dixon, St. Louis, 1969-70; atty. Employers' of Nausau, St. Louis, 1970-75; adminstrv. law judge Workers' Comp. - Mo., St. Louis, 1975-89; pvt. practice St. Louis, 1989—. Instr. continuing edn., St. Louis C.C., 1975—. Contbr. articles to profl. jours. Mem. Gov.'s Com. to Hire Handicapped, 1979. Mem. Am. Trial Lawyers Assn., Mo. Assn. Trial Lawyers, Bar Assn. of St. Louis, St. Louis Metro Bar Assn. (bd. dirs. work place litigation group). Workers' compensation. Office: 906 Olive St Ste 510 Saint Louis MO 63101-1435

SIKOROVSKY, EUGENE FRANK, retired lawyer; b. Jackson, Mich., Nov. 27, 1927; s. Frank Joseph and Betty Dorothy (Malik) S.; m. Patricia O'Byrne, July 11, 1953; children: Paul, Charles, Catherine, Elizabeth, Emily. BSEE, U. Mich., 1948; LLB, Harvard U., 1951. Bar: N.Y. 1952, Va. 1970, Ill. 1978. Assoc. predecessor firms Cahill, Gordon & Reindel, 1954-63, ptnr., 1964-68; v.p., gen. counsel, dir. Reynolds Metals Co., Richmond, Va., 1969-76; gen. counsel Gould Inc., Rolling Meadows, Ill., 1977-79, v.p., 1977-81; dep. gen. counsel Bell & Howell Co., Skokie, Ill., 1981-83, v.p. Chgo., 1983-88, gen. counsel, 1983-92, sec., 1984-92, sr. v.p., dir., 1988-92. Lt. USNR, 1951-54. Mem. Ill. State Bar Assn., Tau Beta Pi, Eta Kappa Nu, Phi Eta Sigma, Phi Delta Theta. Episcopalian. Home: 720 Grandview Ln Lake Forest IL 60045-3953 E-mail: genesik@aol.com.

SILAK, CATHY R. former state supreme court justice; b. Astoria, N.Y., May 25, 1950; d. Michael John and Rose Marie (Janor) S.; m. Nicholas G. Miller, Aug. 9, 1980; 3 children. BA, NYU, 1971; M in City Planning, Harvard U., 1973; JD, U. Calif., 1976. Bar: Calif. 1977, U.S. Dist. Ct. (no. dist.) Calif. 1977, D.C. 1979, U.S. Ct. Appeals (D.C. cir.) 1979, U.S. Dist. Ct. (so. dist.) N.Y. 1980, Idaho 1983, U.S. Dist. Ct. Idaho 1983, U.S. Ct. Appeals (2nd cir.) 1983, U.S. Ct. Appeals (9th cir.) 1985. Law clk. to Hon. William W. Schwarzer U.S. Dist. Ct. (no dist.), Calif., 1976-77; pvt. practice San Francisco, 1977-79, Washington, 1979-80; asst. U.S. atty. So. Dist. of N.Y., 1980-83; spl. asst. U.S. atty. Dist. of Idaho, 1983-84; pvt. practice Boise, Idaho, 1984-90; judge Idaho Ct. Appeals, 1990-93; justice Idaho Supreme Ct., Boise, 1993—2000; ptnr. Hawley, Troxell, Ennis, and Hawley. Assoc. gen. counsel Morrison Knudsen Corp., 1989-90; mem. fairness com. Idaho Supreme Ct. and Gov.'s Task Force on Alternative Dispute Resolution; instr. and lectr. in field. Assoc. note and comment editor Calif. Law Rev., 1975-76. Land use planner Mass. Dept. Natural Resources, 1973; founder Idaho Coalition for Adult Literacy; bd. dirs. Literacy Lab., Inc.; mem. adv. bd. Boise State U. Legal Asst. Program. Recipient Jouce Stein award Boise YWCA, 1992, Women Helping Women award Soroptimist, Boise, 1993. Fellow Idaho Law Found (ann., lectr.); mem. ABA (nat. conf. state trial judges jud. adminstrn. divsn.), Nat. Assn. Women Judges, Idaho State Bar (corp./securities sect., instr.), Am. Law Inst., Fellows of the Am. Bar Found, Am. Judicature Soc. (bd. dirs.). Office: Hawley Troxell Ennis & Hawley PO Box 1617 Boise ID 83702-1617

SILBER, ALBERT J. lawyer; b. Detroit, Mar. 15, 1912; s. Ben Baruch Silber and Ida (Kogut) S.; m. Merry J. Kurtz, June 9, 1935; children: Michael D., Marc S., Julie E. BA, Wayne State U., 1930; JD magna cum laude, U. Mich., 1932. Bar: Mich. 1933, U.S. Dist. Ct. Mich. 1933. Sec., gen. counsel, dir. Barley Earhart Co., Portland, Mich., 1938, 2B Systems Inc., Sterling Heights, Mich., 1976-96; mng. ptnr. Venoy Palmer Ctr., Westland, Mich., 1958—, King Investment Co., Dearborn, Mich., 1979—. Del. World Jewish Congress, Montreux, Switzerland, 1948; pres. Mich. coun. Am. Jewish Congress, 1949. Inductee Mich. Jewish Sports Hall of Fame, 1993. Fellow: The Order of the Coif; mem.: Mich. Bridge Assn. (pres. 1953—54), Am. Contract Bridge League (Gold Life master), Tau Epsilon Rho Legal Soc. (nat. pres. 1950—51). Achievements include first to Youngest graduate at age 20 yrs, 3 mos. with BA and JD degrees; Youngest person ever to earn a coll. varsity sport letter at age 14 at Wayne State U (track). Avocations: playing bridge, writing poetry and song lyrics. Corporate, general, Probate (including wills, trusts), Property, real (including real estate development, water). Office: Silber and Silber Ste 920 21700 Northwestern Hwy Southfield MI 48075-4985 Fax: 248-552-8616.

SILBER, NORMAN JULES, lawyer; b. Tampa, Fla., Apr. 18, 1945; s. Abe and Mildred (Hirsch) Silber; m. Linda Geraldine Hirsch, June 10, 1979; 1 child, Michael Hirsch. BA, Tulane U., 1967, JD, 1969; postgrad. in bus. adminstrn., NYU, 1970—72. Bar: Fla. 1970, U.S. Dist. Ct. (so. dist.) Fla. 1975, U.S. Tax Ct. 1975, U.S. Ct. Appeals (5th cir.) 1975, U.S. Ct. Appeals (11th cir.) 1981. With legal dept. Fiduciary Trust Co. N.Y., N.Y.C., 1969—72, asst. trust officer, 1971—72; exec. v.p. I.R.E. Fin. Corp., Miami, Fla., 1972—76; mng. atty. Norman J. Silber, P.A., Miami, 1973—85; ptnr. McDermott, Will & Emery, 1985—2001, Ruden, McClosky, Smith, Schuster & Russell, P.A., 2001—. Mem.: Fla. Bar (chmn. 11th jud. cir. grievance com. 1982—84). Republican. Jewish. Corporate, general, General practice, Property, real (including real estate development, water). Home: 1232 Palermo Ave Miami FL 33134-6327 Office: Ruden McClosky Smith Schuster & Russell PA 701 Brickell Ave Fl 19 Miami FL 33131 Business E-Mail: norman.silber@ruden.com.

SILBERGELD, ARTHUR F. lawyer; b. St. Louis, June 1, 1942; s. David and Sabina (Silbergeld) S.; m. Carol Ann Schwartz, may 1, 1970; children: Diana Lauren, Julia Kay. BA, U. Mich., 1968; M in City Planning, U. Pa., 1971; JD, Temple U., 1975. Bar: N.Y. 1976, Calif. 1978, D.C. 1983, U.S. Ct. Appeals (2nd cir.), U.S. Ct. Appeals (9th cir.), U.S. Ct. Appeals (D.C. cir.), U.S. Supreme Ct. 1999. Assoc. Vladeck, Elias, Vladeck & Lewis, N.Y.C., 1975-77; field atty. NLRB, L.A., 1977-78; ptnr., head employment law practice group McKenna, Conner & Cuneo, L.A., 1978-89; ptnr. Graham & James, L.A., 1990-96; labor ptnr. Sonnenschein Nath & Rosenthal, L.A., 1996-99; ptnr. Proskauer Rose LLP, L.A., 1999—. Instr. extension divsn. UCLA, 1981-89. Author: Doing Business in California: An Employment Law Handbook, 2nd edit., 1997, Advising California Employers, 1990-95 supplements; contbr. articles to profl. jours. Founding mem. L.A. Mus. Contemporary Art; bd. dirs. Bay Cities unit Am. Cancer Soc., Calif., 1981-85, Jewish Family Svc., L.A., 1981-85, So. Calif. Employers Roundtable, Leadership coun., So. Poverty Law Ctr., Leadership Task Force, Drs. Without Borders; pres. Mo. Valley Fedn. of Temple Youth, 1959-60; mem. Calif. com. south Human Rights Watch, 2003—; treas. L.A. Child Devel. Ctr., 2001—. Mem. L.A. County Bar Assn. (chair labor and employment law sect. 1999-2000, trustee 2000-01), Mus. Modern Art (N.Y.C.), Coll. of Labor and Employment Lawyers. Labor (including EEOC, Fair Labor Standards Act, labor-management relations, NLRB, OSHA). Office: Proskauer Rose LLP 2049 Century Park E Fl 32 Los Angeles CA 90067-3101

SILBERMAN, ALAN HARVEY, lawyer; b. Chgo., Oct. 22, 1940; s. Milton J. and Mollie E. (Hymanson) S.; m. Margaret Judith Auslander, Nov. 17, 1968; children: Elena, Mark. BA with distinction, Northwestern U., 1961; LLB, Yale U., 1964. Bar: Ill. 1964, U.S. Dist. Ct. (no. dist.) Ill. 1966, U.S. Ct. Appeals (7th cir.) 1970, (5th and 9th cir.) 1977, (D.C. cir.) 1979, (4th cir.) 1980, (11th cir.) 1981, (3rd cir.) 1982, (8th and 10th cirs.) 1993, U.S. Supreme Ct. 1978. Law clk. U.S. Dist. Ct., Chgo., 1964-66; assoc. Sonneschein Nath & Rosenthal, Chgo., 1964-71, ptnr., 1972—. Mem. antitrust adv. bd. Bur. Nat. Affairs, Washington, 1985—; mem. Ill. Atty. Gen. Franchise Adv. Bd., 1996—; bd. dirs., mem. exec. com. Mercaz, USA.. Contbr. articles to profl. jours. Bd. dirs., v.p., sec. Camp Ramah in Wis., Inc., Chgo., 1966-86, pres., 1986-94; bd. dirs. Nat. Ramah Commn., Inc. of Jewish Theol. Sem. Am., N.Y.C., 1970—, v.p., 1986-94, pres., 1994-99, sr. v.p., 1999—; mem. U.S. del. 33d World Zionist Congress, Jerusalem, 1997, 34th World Zionist Congress, Jerusalem, 2002; bd. dirs., mem. exec. com. Masorti/Olami/World Coun. of Synagogues, 2002—. Mem. ABA (chmn. antitrust sect. FTC com. 1981-83, chmn. nat. insts. 1983-85, mem. coun. antitrust sect. 1985-88, fin. officer 1988-90, sect. del. ho. of dels. 1990-92, chmn.-elect 1992-93, chmn. 1993-94), Ill. Bar Assn. (chmn. antitrust sect. 1975-76), Northwestern U. 1851 Soc. (chair 1994-97), regional vice-chair Lex Mundi, Competition and Antitrust (1999-2003, internat. chair elect 2003-). Antitrust. Home: 430 Oakdale Ave Glencoe IL 60022-2113 Office: Sonnenschein Nath 233 S Wacker Dr Ste 8000 Chicago IL 60606-6491

SILBERMAN, CURT C. lawyer; b. Wuerzburg, Fed. Republic Germany, May 23, 1908; came to the U.S., 1938, naturalized, 1944; s. Adolf and Ida (Rosenbusch) S.; m. Else Kleemann, 1935. Student, U. Berlin, U. Munich; JD summa cum laude, Wuerzburg U., 1931, Rutgers U., 1947; Dr. (hon.), Middlebury Coll., 1997. Bar: N.J. 1948, U.S. Supreme Ct. 1957. Pvt. practice internat. pvt. law, West Orange, N.J., 1948—. Lectr. internat. pvt. law, 1954, 81, 82, 87, 91, 95; prin. guest lectr. at Univ.'s 400th anniversary U. Wuerzburg, 1982. Contbr. articles to legal jours. Pres. Am. Fedn. Jews from Ctrl. Europe, N.Y., 1962-86, chmn. bd., 1986—; past pres. Jewish Philanthropic Fund of 1933, Inc., N.Y., 1971-87, chmn. bd., 1987—; hon. trustee Leo Baeck Inst., N.Y., 1962—, N.Y. Found. Nursing Homes, Inc., Jewish Family Svc. of Metro-West, N.J.; past co-chmn. Coun. Jews from Germany, 1974-98; chmn. Rsch. Found. for Jewish Immigration, Inc., N.Y.; past bd. dirs. Conf. on Jewish Material Claims Against Germany. Recipient Golden Doctoral Diploma, U. Wuerzburg Law Faculty, 1982, Festschrift dedicated to him by Am. Fedn. Jews from Ctrl. Europe in N.Y., 1969; recipient Pub. Svc. medal. Mem. N.J. Bar Assn. (chmn. com. comparative jurisprudence 1966-73, chmn. com. internat. trade 1974-78), Essex County Bar Assn., Am. Coun. on Germany, Internat. Biographical Dictionary of Ctrl. European Emigres (adv. bd.). Private international.

SILBERMAN, LAURENCE HIRSCH, federal judge; b. York, Pa., Oct. 12, 1935; s. William and Anna (Hirsch) S.; m. Rosalie G. Gaull, Apr. 28, 1957; children: Robert Stephen, Katherine DeBoer Balaban, Anne Gaull Otis. BA, Dartmouth Coll., 1957; LLB, Harvard U., 1961. Bar: Hawaii 1962, D.C. 1973. Assoc. Moore, Torkildson & Rice and Quinn & Moore, Honolulu, 1961-64; ptnr. Moore, Silberman & Schulze, Honolulu, 1964-67; atty. appellate divsn. gen. counsel's office NLRB, Washington, 1967-69; solicitor of labor U.S. Dept. Labor, Washington, 1969-70, undersec. labor, 1970-73; ptnr. Steptoe & Johnson, Washington, 1973-74; dep. atty. gen. U.S. Washington, 1974-75; amb. to Yugoslavia, 1975-77; mng. ptnr. Morrison & Foerster, Washington, 1978-79, 83-85; exec. v.p. Crocker Nat. Bank, San Francisco, 1979-83; judge U.S. Ct. Appeals (D.C. cir.), Washington, 1985—. Lectr. labor law and legis. U. Hawaii, 1962—63; adj. prof. adminstrv. law Georgetown U., Washington, 1987—94, Washington, 1997, Washington, 1999—2001, NYU, 1995, 96, Harvard U., 1998; lectr. labor law Georgetown U., Washington, 2001; Pres.' spl. envoy on ILO affairs, 1976; gen. adv. com. on Arms Control and Disarmament, 1981—85; mem. Def. Policy Bd., 1981—85; vice-chmn. State Dept.'s Commn. on Security and Econ. Assistance, 1983—84. Bd. dirs. Com. on Present Danger, 1978-85, Inst. for Ednl. Affairs, 1981-85; vice chmn. adv. coun. on gen. govt. Rep. Nat. Com., 1977-80. With AUS, 1957-58. Am. Enterprise Inst. sr. fellow, 1977-78, vis. fellow 1978-85. Mem. U.S. Fgn. Intelligence Surveillance Act Ct. of Rev., Coun. on Fgn. Rels.

SILBERMAN, RALPH MICHAEL, lawyer, editor; b. Bourne, Mass., Sept. 16, 1951; s. Henry Kurt and Janine (Jonas) S.; m. Margaret M. Clark, Apr. 25, 1987; children: Evan Jonas, Magdalen Anna. BA, Oberlin Coll., 1973; JD, U. Va., 1976; MA, George Washington U., 1982. Bar: Va. 1976, D.C. 1979. Editor, Lawyers Coop. Publishing Co., Washington, 1977-82; project editor Research Inst. Am., Washington, 1982-86, sr. editor, 1987-89, mng. editor RIA Group, Alexandria, Va., 1991-97, Director, Project Management, AlignMark Information Publishing, 1997-2000, propr., Neathridge Content Solutions, 2001—; editor loose leaf service Social Security Coordinator, 1984, Employment Coordinator, 1985, Pension Coordinator, 1987. Mem. Am. Soc. Internat. Law. Avocations: bicycling, bookbinding. Home: 1107 20th St S Arlington VA 22202-2109

SILBERMAN, ROBERT A. S. lawyer; b. Lebanon, Pa., Mar. 4, 1945; s. Henry T. and Genevieve (Mensh) S.; m. Nancy D. Netzer, Nov. 10, 1974. BA magna cum laude, Yale U., 1967; JD, Harvard U., 1970. Bar: Mass. 1970, Pa. 1984. Assoc. Csaplar & Bok, Boston, 1970—78, ptnr., 1978—90, Gaston & Snow, Boston, 1990—91, Edwards & Angell, Boston, 1991—2000, Erickson Israel Schaffer Silberman PC, Wellesley, Mass., 2000—. Mem. editl. bd. Managed Care Law Strategist, Am. Lawyer Media newsletter, 1999-2001. Citizens rev. com. United Way Mass. Bay, Boston, 1981-89; bd. dirs. All Newton (Mass.) Music Sch., 1994-96, v.p., 1995-96; bd. overseers Boston Baroque, 1998-2000, bd. dirs., chmn. bd. overseers, 2000-02, chmn. bd. dirs., 2003—. Mem. ABA (vice chmn. health law com. sect. bus. law 1992-95, chmn., 1995-99), Internat. Bar Assn., Boston Bar Assn., Nat. Health Lawyers Assn., Phi Beta Kappa. Office: Erickson Israel Schaffer Silberman PC Ste 150 20 William St Wellesley MA 02481 Office Fax: 781-235-1571. E-mail: rsilberman@ericksonisrael.com.

SILER, EUGENE EDWARD, JR., federal judge; b. Williamsburg, Ky., Oct. 19, 1936; s. Eugene Edward and Lowell (Jones) Siler; m. Christy Dyanne Minnich, Oct. 18, 1969; children: Eugene Edward, Adam Troy. BA cum laude, Vanderbilt U., 1958; LLB, U. Va., 1963; LLM, Georgetown U., 1964; LLM, U. Va., 1995. Bar: Ky. 1963, Va. 1963, D.C. 1963. Pvt. practice, Williamsburg, 1964—65; county atty. Whitley County, Ky., 1965—70; atty. U.S. Atty., Ea. Dist., Lexington, 1970—75; judge U.S. Dist. Ct., Ea. and We. Dists., Ky., 1975—91; chief judge U.S. Dist. Ct., Ea. Dist., Ky., 1984—91; judge U.S. Ct. Appeals (6th cir.), 1991—. Trustee Cumberland Coll., Williamsburg, 1965—73, 1980—88; campaign co-chmn. Congressman Tim L. Carter, 1966, 5th Congl. Dist., U.S. Senator J.S. Cooper, 1966; 1st v.p. Ky. Bapt. Convention, 1986—87; bd. dirs. Bapt. Healthcare System Inc., 1990—. With USN, 1958—60, with USNR, 1960—83. Recipient Freedom's Found. medal, 1968; E. Barrett Prettyman fellow, 1963—64. Mem.: Va. State Bar, D.C. Bar Assn., Ky. Bar Assn. (Judge of Yr. 1992), Fed. Bar Assn. Republican. Baptist. Home: PO Box 129 Williamsburg KY 40769-0129 Office: US Ct Appeals 310 S Main Street Room 333 London KY 40741

SILETS, HARVEY MARVIN, lawyer; b. Chgo., Aug. 25, 1931; s. Joseph Lazarus and Sylvia Silets; m. Elaine L. Gordon, June 25, 1961; children: Hayden Leigh, Jonathan Lazarus (dec.), Alexandra Rose. BS cum laude, DePaul U., 1952; JD (Frederick Leicke scholar), U. Mich., 1955. Bar: Ill. 1955, U.S. Dist. Ct. (no. dist.) Ill. 1955, N.Y. 1956, U.S. Tax Ct. 1957, U.S. Ct. Mil. Appeals 1957, U.S. Ct. Appeals (7th cir.) 1958, U.S. Supreme Ct. 1959, U.S. Ct. Appeals (6th cir.) 1965, U.S. Ct. Appeals (2d cir.) 1971, U.S. Ct. Appeals (5th cir.) 1972, U.S. Ct. Appeals (11th cir.). Assoc. Paul, Weiss, Rifkind, Wharton & Garrison, N.Y.C., 1955-56; asst. atty. U.S. Dist. Ct. (no. dist.) Ill., 1958-60; chief tax atty. U.S. atty. No. Dist. Ill., Chgo., 1960-62; ptnr. Harris, Burman & Silets, Chgo., 1962-79, Silets & Martin, Ltd., Chgo., 1979-92, Katten Muchin Zavis Rosenman, Chgo., 1992—. Asst. advance tng. program IRS, U. Mich., 1952-53; law lectr. advance fed. taxation John Marshall Law Sch., 1962-66; adj. prof. taxation Chgo.-Kent Coll. Law, 1985—; gen. counsel Nat. Treasury Employees Union, 1968-92; mem. adv. com. tax litigation U.S. Dept. Justice, 1979-82; mem. Tax Reform Com., State of Ill., 1982-83; mem. Speedy Trial Act Planning Group U.S. Dist. Ct. (no. dist.) Ill., 1976-79; mem. civil justice reform act adv. com. U.S. Dist. Ct. (no. dist.) Ill., 1991-94; lectr. in field. Contbr. articles to profl. jours. Trustee Latin Sch., Chgo., 1970-76; active Chgo. Crime Commn., 1975-93, Govv.'s Commn. Reform Tax Laws, Ill., 1982-83. With AUS, 1956-58. Fellow Am. Coll. Trial Lawyers (chmn. com. on fed. rules of criminal procedure 1982-91, fed. rules of evidence com. 1988-93, jud. com., fed. criminal procedures com., Upstate Ill. com. chmn. 1990-91), Am. Coll. Tax Counsel, Internat. Acad. Trial Lawyers, Soc. Advanced Legal Studies (London); mem. ABA (active various coms.), Bar Assn. 7th Fed. Cir. (chmn. com. criminal law and procedure 1972-82, bd. govs. 1983-86, sec. 1986-88, v.p. 1989-90, pres. 1990-91), NACDL, FBA (bd. dirs. 1971—, pres. 1977-78, v.p. 1976-77, sec. 1975-76, treas. 1974-75, active various coms.), Chgo. Bar Assn. (tax com. 1958-66, com. devel. law 1966-72, 78-88, com. fed. taxation 1968—, com. evaluation candidates 1978-80, exec. com. tax sect. 1994—), Am. Bd. Criminal Def. Lawyers, Decalogue Soc. Lawyers, Bar Assn. N.Y. City, Standard Club, Cliff Dwellers Club, Chgo. Club, Phi Alpha delta, Pi Gamma Mu. Corporate, general, Criminal, Taxation, general. Office: Katten Muchin Zavis Rosenman 525 W Monroe St Ste 1600 Chicago IL 60661-3693 E-mail: harvey.silets@kmzr.com.

SILK, THOMAS, lawyer; b. Beaver, Pa., Dec. 12, 1937; s. Thomas and Alice Genevieve (Beck) S.; m. Arlene Schlaifer, Sept., 1959 (div.); 1 child, Nicole Amory; m. Susan Clark, 1979 (div.); m. Suzanne Vinson, Mar. 1996. AB, U. Calif., Berkeley, 1959, LLB, 1963. Bar: Calif. 1964, U.S. Dist. Ct. (no. dist.) Calif. 1964, U.S. Ct. Appeals (D.C., 2-10th cirs.) 1966-68, U.S. Supreme Ct. 1967. Appellate atty. tax divsn. U.S. Dept. Justice, Washington, 1964-66, spl. asst. to asst. atty. gen. tax divsn., 1966-68; assoc. Brobeck, Phleger & Harrison, San Francisco, 1968-71; founder, chmn. Silk, Adler & Colvin, San Francisco, 1972—. Lectr. in field. Editor: Philanthropy and Law in Asia; author: Corporate Philanthropy and Tax Choices. Trustee Jenifer Altman Found., U. San Francisco Inst. for Nonprofit and Orgn. Mgmt.. Corporate, general, Probate (including wills, trusts), Corporate taxation. Office: Silk Adler & Colvin Ste 1220 235 Montgomery St San Francisco CA 94104-2902

SILKENAT, JAMES ROBERT, lawyer; b. Salina, Kans., Aug. 2, 1947; s. Ernest E. and Mildred R. (Iman) S.; children: David Andrew, Katherine Anne. BA, Drury Coll., 1969; JD, U. Chgo., 1972; LLM, NYU, 1978. Bar: N.Y. 1973, D.C. 1980. Assoc. Cravath, Swaine & Moore, N.Y.C., 1972-80; counsel Internat. Fin. Corp., Washington, 1980-86; ptnr. Morgan, Lewis & Bockius, N.Y.C., 1986-89, Morrison & Foerster, N.Y.C., 1989-92, Pillsbury, Winthrop, N.Y.C., 1992—2002, Arent Fox, N.Y.C., 2002—. Chmn. Council N.Y. Law Assocs., 1978-79, Lawyers Com. Internat. Human Rights, 1978-80. Editor ABA Guide to Fng. Law Firms, Moscow Conf. on Law Bilateral Econ. Rels., ABA Guide to Internat. Bus. Negotiations; contbr. articles to profl. jours. Capt. U.S. Army, 1972-73. Fellow NEH, 1977, U.S. Dept. State, 1981. Fellow Am. Bar Found.; mem. ABA (chmn. internat. law and practice sect. 1989-90, chmn. sect. officer's conf. 1990-92, mem. ho. of dels. 1989—, bd. govs. 1994-97). Corporate, general, Finance, Private international. Office: Arent Fox 1675 Broadway New York NY 10019

SILLER, STEPHEN I. lawyer; b. May 8, 1949; m. Helen Seewald, June 6, 1971. BA, Bklyn. Coll., 1970, JD cum laude, 1973; LLM, NYU, 1978. Bar: N.Y. 1974, U.S. Dist. Ct. (so. and ea. dists.) N.Y. 1974, U.S. Ct. Appeals (2d cir.) 1974. Assoc. Fried, Frank, Harris, Shriver & Jacobson, N.Y.C., 1973-78, Feit & Ahrens, N.Y.C., 1978-80, ptnr., 1981-87; founder, sr. ptnr. Siller Wilk LLP, N.Y.C., 1987—. Mem. ABA (partnership law com., negotiated acquisitions com.), Internat. Bar Assn., Assn. Bar City of N.Y. (transp. com. 1978—, U.S. in global economy com. 1996-97). Corporate, general, Mergers and acquisitions, Securities. Office: Siller Wilk LLP 675 3rd Ave Fl 9 New York NY 10017-5704 E-mail: ssiller@sillerwilk.com.

SILSBY, PAULA, prosecutor; U.S. atty. U.S. Dept. Justice, Maine, 2001—. Office: PO Box 9718 Portland ME 04104*

SILVA, EUGENE JOSEPH, lawyer; b. Gloucester, Mass., May 23, 1942; s. Edward Joseph and Rose (Lebre) S.; m. Nancy Blue-Pearson, Jan. 8, 1972; children: Eugene Joseph II, Michael Joseph. BS with honors, Maine Maritime Acad., 1964; JD, U. Notre Dame, 1972. Bar: Calif. 1972, U.S. Dist. Ct. (so. and cen. dists.) Calif. 1972, Tex. 1977, U.S. Dist. Ct. (so. and ea. dists.) Tex. 1978, U.S. Ct. Appeals (5th, 9th, 2d and 11th cirs.) 1978, U.S. Supreme Ct. 1981; lic. Master Mariner. Assoc. Luce, Forward, Hamilton & Scripps, San Diego, 1972-77, Vinson & Elkins, Houston, 1977-79, ptnr., 1980—2003. Bd. dirs. Cabrillo Festival Inc., San Diego, 1974-77, San Jose Clinic, Inc., 1990-97, pres. 1993-95; bd. dirs. Portuguese Heritage Scholarship Found., 1995-2000, St. Joseph Hosp. Found., 1996—; mem. adv. bd. Admiralty Law Inst., 1999—. Decorated knight comdr. with star Equestrian Order of Holy Sepulchre of Jerusalem; recipient Outstanding Alumni award Maine Maritime Acad., 1990. Mem. Houston Bar Assn., Calif. Bar Assn., Tex. Bar Assn., Internat. Bar Assn., Grays Inn U. Notre Dame Sch. Law (pres. 1970-72), Maritime Law Assn. U.S. (proctor in admiralty 1974—), Portuguese Union Calif. (bd. dirs. 1973-74), Portuguese Am. League San Diego (pres. 1974-75), Portuguese Am. Leadership Coun. U.S., Asia-Pacific Lawyers Assn., Notre Dame Club (pres. San Diego chpt. 1976-77), The Naval Club (London). Roman Catholic. Admiralty, Private international, Insurance. Home: 8 Smithdale Estates Dr Houston TX 77024-6600 Office: Vinson & Elkins 2300 First City Tower 1001 Fannin St Ste 3300 Houston TX 77002-6706

SILVA MEZA, JUAN N. judge; b. Mexico, Sept. 13, 1944; Grad., U. Nacional Autonoma de Mexico, 1970. Former magistrate Unitary Cir. Ct.;

former judge Dist. Ct.; prof. law U. Nacional Autonoma de Mexico, 1972; min. Supreme Ct. Justice, Mexico City, 1995—. Office: Suprema Corte de Justicia de la Nacion Pino Suarez No 2 Col Centro 06065 Mexico City Mexico*

SILVER, ALAN IRVING, lawyer; b. St. Paul, Sept. 17, 1949; s. Sherman J. Silver and Muriel (Bernstein) Brawerman; m. Janice Lynn Gleekel, July 8, 1973; children: Stephen, Amy. BA cum laude, U. Minn., 1971, JD cum laude, 1975. Bar: Minn. 1975, U.S. Dist. Ct. Minn. 1975, U.S. Dist. Ct. (ea. dist.) Wis. 1975, U.S. Ct. Appeals 8th and 10th cirs.) 1975. Assoc. Doherty, Rumble & Butler, P.A., St. Paul, 1975-80, ptnr. Mpls., 1980-99, Bassford, Remele (formerly called Bassford, Lockhart, Truesdell & Briggs, P.A.), Mpls., 1999—. Mem. 2d Jud. Dist. Ethics Com., St. Paul, 1985-88, 4th Jud. Dist. Ethics Com., Mpls., 1990-97. Author: Building a New Foundation: Torts, Contracts and the Economic Class Doctrine, 2000, other numerous continuing edn. seminar material. Vol. atty. Legal Assistance Ramsey County, St. Paul, 1975-82; mem. St. Louis Park (Minn.) Sch. Bd., 1993-99, chair, 1995-97; mem. St. Louis Park Human Rights Commn., 1987-91; chmn. site mgmt. coun. Susan Lindgren Sch., St. Louis Park, 1986-93; bd. dirs. Jewish Cmty. Rels. Coun., Anti-Defamation League Minn. and Dakotas, 1987-93, 97—, treas., 1992-93, v.p., 2003-. Mem. ABA, Minn. Bar Assn. (exec. bd. antitrust sect. 1984, litigation chair probate and trust sect.), Hennepin County Bar Assn. Avocations: running, guitar, reading. Antitrust, Federal civil litigation, General civil litigation. Home: 4320 W 25th St Minneapolis MN 55416-3841 Office: Bassford Remele Ste 3800 33 S 6th St Minneapolis MN 55402-1501 E-mail: alans@bassford.com.

SILVER, BARRY MORRIS, lawyer; b. Mt. Vernon, N.Y., Nov. 18, 1956; s. Samuel Manuel and Elaine Martha (Shapiro) S. BA, Fla. Atlantic U., 1979; JD, Nova U., 1983. Bar: Fla. 1983. Atty. pvt. practice, Boca Raton, 1986—. Asst. rabbi Congregation L'Dor Va-Dor, Boynton Beach. Fla.; tchr. bilingual edn. Palm Beach County Schs., Delray Beach, Fla., 1981-83; faculty Palm Beach Jr. Coll., Boca Raton, 1990—; atty. NOW, South Palm Beach County; mem. Fla. Ho. Reps., 1997-98. Vol. Haitian Refugee Ctr., Miami, 1982. Mem. Fla. Bar Assn., Palm Beach County Bar Assn., Sierra Club. Democrat. Jewish. Avocations: languages, tennis, frisbee, chess. Civil rights, General civil litigation, Personal injury (including property damage). Office: 1200 S Rogers Cir Ste 8 Boca Raton FL 33487- Home: 18624 Cape Sable Dr Boca Raton FL 33498-6374 E-mail: barryboca@aol.com.

SILVER, CAROL RUTH, lawyer; b. Boston, Oct. 1, 1938; d. Nathan and Mildred S.; children: Steven Chao Silver, Jefferson Chao Frensley Silver; m. Stanley Mayerson, 1990 (div. 1994). BA, U. Chgo., 1960, JD, 1964. Bar: Calif. 1964, U.S. Supreme Ct. 1970, U.S. Dist. Ct. (so. dist.) La., U.S. Dist. (no. and cen. dists.) Calif. Dir. atty. Calif. Rural Legal Assistance, Delano, 1965-68; exec. dir. Berkeley (Calif.) Neighborhood Legal Svcs., 1968-71; tchr. Golden Gate Law Sch., San Francisco, 1970-73; legal counsel to sheriff City of San Francisco, 1972-75; elected ofcl. Bd. of Suprs., City and County of San Francisco, 1978-89; real estate broker San Francisco, 1985—, Carol Ruth Silver Real Estate, San Francisco, 1990—; pvt. practice law San Francisco, 1976—. Spl. counsel ABRH Cons., Washington, 1988-90; cons. Nat. Legal Aid & Defender Assn., Washington, 1968-75; del. to ho. dels. Calif. Bar, Sacramento, 1972-74. Founder, editor, pub. Myers Flat News, 1996—; contbr. articles to profl. jours.; initial bd. editors Tikun. Pres. Golden Gate Bridge Dist., San Francisco, 1988, San Francisco Bay Area Air Pollution Control Dist., 1987, Friends of San Francisco Inmates and Deps., 1982, Golden Gate Dem. Club, San Francisco, 1976; founder Chinese Am. Internat. Sch., San Francisco, bd. dirs., 1980-2000; pres., co-founder Every Child A Wanted Child, San Francisco, 1989-95; bd. dirs. UN World Ctr., San Francisco, 1981—; chmn. bd. dirs. Jewish Ednl. Ctr., 1997-98; candidate for Dem. nomination U.S. Congress, 1996; bd. dirs. WildAid, 2001-02; chair 1961 Freedom Riders 40th Reunion, Jackson, Miss.; co-chair San Francisco Friends of Afghanistan, 2002—; gen. counsel Green Aid Med. Marijuana Legal Def. and Edn. Fund, Inc., 2002-. Fellow Sch. Govt., Harvard U., 1973-74; recipient Cable Car award Tavern Guild, 1985, Award of Merit, Lawyers Constl. Def. Com., 1965. Mem. NOW, ACLU, Nat. Abortion Rights Action League. Jewish. Avocations: opera, family activities, travel, writing, hiking. Alternative dispute resolution, Estate planning, Property, real (including real estate development, water). E-mail: myersflat@aol.com.

SILVER, DAVID, lawyer; b. N.Y.C., Jan. 27, 1931; s. Sol and Fannie (Stein) S.; m. Meryl Young, Sept. 14, 1952 (dec.); children: Daniel, Matthew, Joshua; m. Ann Schwartz, June 4, 1993. BA, CCNY, 1953; LL.B. cum laude, Harvard U., 1958. Bar: N.Y. 1958, D.C. 1979. Pvt. practice law, N.Y.C., 1960-61; spl. counsel SEC, Washington, 1961-65; gen. counsel Investors Planning Corp., N.Y.C., 1965-66; asst. counsel Investment Co. Inst., Washington, 1966-69, gen. counsel, 1969-77, pres., 1977-91, ICI Mut. Ins. Co., Bethesda, Md., 1987-2001. Cons. securities regulation Govt. of India, 1964; mutual fund regulation Govt. of China, 1999; lectr. Law Sch. Boston U., 1995—98; mem. individual investor adv. com. N.Y. Stock Exch., 1994—99; dir. PGAM, Milan, 2001—. Served with U.S. Army, 1953-55. Mem. Fed. Bar Assn. (exec. council securities com., past chmn. investment co. com.). Home and Office: 9410 Brooke Dr Bethesda MD 20817-2110 E-mail: anndave@verizon.net.

SILVER, GREGORY K. lawyer; b. Indpls., Oct. 16, 1946; s. David Mayer and Anita (Cohen) S.; m. Florence Ruekberg, Aug. 7, 1971; children: Sara Jennifer, Scott Henry. BA in Govt., Miami U., Oxford, Ohio, 1968; JD, Ind. U., 1972. Bar: Ind. 1972, D.C. 1975. Assoc. Eskenazi, Yosha & Hurst, Indpls., 1968-74; pvt. practice Indpls., 1974—. Cons. U.S. State Dept. Task Force on Population, 1994. Chmn. Indpls. Greenways Bd., 1996-2003; dir. Indpls. Clean City Com., 1975—; candidate Ind. State Senate, 1986, Indpls. City Coun., 1991; active Nat. Dem. Platform Com., Washington, 1984-8, Underground Storage Tank Bd., Ind., 1996-2003; bd. dirs. Indpls. Hebrew Cong. Recipient Sagamore of Wabash award, 1998. Mem. Sertoma, Indpls. Athletic Club, pres. Country Club of Palm Beach, Broadmoor Country Club Indpls. Avocations: travel, basketball, children. Bankruptcy, Environmental, Family and matrimonial. Home: 8442 Oakwood Ct Indianapolis IN 46260-2355 Office: 342 Massachusetts Ave Ste 400 Indianapolis IN 46204-2132

SILVER, HARRY R. lawyer; b. Phila., Aug. 8, 1946; s. Jerome Benjamin Silver and Josephine Sandler (Steinberg) Furr; m. Jessica Dunsay, Nov. 23, 1972; children: Gregory, Alexander. BA, Temple U., 1968; JD, Columbia U., 1971. Bar: N.Y. 1972, D.C. 1973, U.S. Dist. Ct. D.C., U.S. Ct. Claims, U.S. Ct. Appeals (1st, 4th, 5th, 7th, 8th, 9th, 10th, fed. and D.C. cirs.), U.S. Supreme Ct. Law clk. to Hon. Harold R. Medina, U.S. Ct. Appeals (2d cir.), N.Y.C., 1971-72; assoc. Arent, Fox, Kintner, Plotkin & Kahn, Washington, 1972-74; atty. U.S. Dept. Justice, Washington, 1974-77, U.S. Dept. Energy, Washington, 1977-78; assoc. Akin, Gump, Strauss, Hauer & Feld, Washington, 1978-81, ptnr., 1981-88, Oppenheimer, Wolff & Donelly, Washington, 1988-91, Davis Wright Tremaine, Washington, 1991-94, Ober, Kaler, Grimes & Shriver, Washington, 1994—. Mem. ABA, Fed. Bar Assn. Avocations: running, music, travel. Administrative and regulatory, Health, Government contracts and claims. Home: 6829 Wilson Ln Bethesda MD 20817-4948 Office: Ober Kaler Grimes & Shriver 1401 H St NW Ste 500 Washington DC 20005-2175 E-mail: hrsilver@ober.com.

SILVER, MARVIN S. lawyer; b. Portland, Maine, Nov. 21, 1951; BS, Syracuse U., 1974; JD, Boston U., 1977, LLM, 1981. Bar: Mass. 1977, U.S. Dist. Ct. Mass. 1978, U.S. Tax Ct. 1983. Atty. Seder & Seder, Worcester, Mass., 1977-82, Seder & Chandler, Worcester, 1983—. Bd. dirs. Jewish Cmty. Ctr. of Worcester, Inc., Mass., 1982-84; mem. fin. com. Town of Shrewsbury, Mass., 1986-93, vice chmn., 1987-88, chmn. 1988-89; bd. dirs. Children's Friend Inc., 1990-99; bd. dirs. Westborough Edn. Found., Inc., 1996--, pres. 1999-2002, treas. 1996-99. Fellow Am. Coll. Trust and Estate Counsel; mem. Mass. Bar Assn. (chmn. estate planning com. tax sect. 1982-84, mem. tax sect. coun. 1983-86, mem. bus. law sect., probate law sect., taxation sect.), Worcester County Bar Assn. (co-chmn. tax law sect. 1981-84, 86-87, 97-98, bankruptcy and comml. law sect. 1987-88), Estate and Bus. Planning Coun. Worcester County (pres. 1990-91), Exch. Club of Tri-Towns, Inc. (pres. 1984-85) (Shrewsbury). Corporate, general, Estate planning, Estate taxation. Office: Seder & Chandler 339 Main St Ste 300 Worcester MA 01608-1585

SILVER, PAUL ALLEN, lawyer; b. Providence, R.I., Mar. 1, 1950; s. Carroll M. and Gail (Arkin) Silver; m. Katherine C. Haspel, June 22, 1975; children: Andrew Haspel, Nathaniel Haspel. AB, Harvard U., 1972; JD, Boston U., 1975. Bar: R.I. 1975, U.S. Dist. Ct. R.I. 1975, Mass. 1985. Assoc. Hinckley, Allen, Salisbury & Parsons, Providence, 1975—81; ptnr. Hinckley, Allen & Snyder, Providence, 1981—. Faculty mem. MS in Taxation Program Bryant Coll., North Smithfield, RI, 1982. Author: (Book) Cheap Eats, 1972, 3d rev. edit., 1975. Bd. dirs. Traveler's Aid Soc. R.I., Providence, 1983—89, 1995—99, pres., 1986—89, Ronald McDonald House, 1987—95; bd. dirs. Camp Ruggles, 1991—; bd. trustees Providence Athenaeum, 1995—2001; bd. dirs. Planned Giving Coun. R.I., 2002—. Mem.: ABA, Internat. Assn. Fin. Planning (bd. dirs. R.I. chpt. 1986—95), Estate Planning Coun. R.I., R.I. Bar Assn., Moses Brown Sch. Alumni Assn. (bd. dirs. 1984—). Jewish. Avocations: business, finance. Estate planning, Probate (including wills, trusts), Personal income taxation. Home: 310 Olney St Providence RI 02906-2326 Office: Hinckley Allen & Snyder 1500 Fleet Ctr Providence RI 02903-2319 E-mail: psilver@haslaw.com.

SILVER, SIDNEY J. lawyer; b. Hartford, Conn., Mar. 30, 1934; s. Daniel B. and Sara F. Silver; m. Margaret Ann McKewen; children: Patricia, David, Lisa, Beth, Daniel. BS, Lehigh U., 1957, MBA, 1959; JD, Georgetown U., 1962. Bar: Va. 1962, D.C. 1963, U.S. Tax Ct. 1965, U.S. Ct. Appeals (D.C. cir.) 1965, U.S. Supreme Ct. 1996. Mng. ptnr. Silver, Freedman & Taff, Washington, 1972—. With U.S. Army, 1953-55. Corporate, general, Estate planning, Corporate taxation. Home: 6605 Kenhill Rd Bethesda MD 20817 Office: Silver Freedman & Taff 1700 Wisconsin Ave NW Washington DC 20007-2313 E-mail: sjs@sftlaw.com.

SILVERBERG, JAY LLOYD, lawyer; b. N.Y., Oct. 1, 1961; s. Sheldon and Elissa (Nenner) S.; children: Jennifer, Rebecca, Sabrina. BA, Brandeis U., 1983; JD, Boston U., 1986. Bar: N.Y. 1987, N.J. 1987, U.S. Dist. Ct. (so. dist.) N.Y. 1990, U.S. Dist. Ct. (ea. dist.) N.Y. 1991. Assoc. McCarter & English, Newark, 1986-87, Proskauer Rose, N.Y.C., 1987-91; mem. Silverberg, Stonehill & Goldsmith, P.C., N.Y.C., 1991—. Lectr. Nat. Assn. Credit Mgmt., Columbia U. Sch. Bus., 1996. Editor: Annual Review of Banking Law, 1986. Paul J. Liacos scholar Boston U. Sch. Law, 1985, G. Joseph Tauro scholar, 1984. Mem. N.Y. Inst. Credit, Manhattan Credit Club (pres. 1998), Turnaround Mgmt. Assn. Bankruptcy, Commercial, contracts (including sales of goods; commercial financing), Corporate, general. Office: Silverberg Stonehill & Goldsmith PC 111 W 40th St New York NY 10018-0968 E-mail: JLSilverberg@SSGPC.com.

SILVERBERG, MARK VICTOR, lawyer, educator; b. Akron, Ohio, Sept. 26, 1957; s. Alvin Harold and Marilyn (Bierman) S.; m. Marsha Phyllis Mermelstein, Aug. 11, 1979; childern: Samantha Michele, Marissa Jill. BS, Rider Coll., 1979; JD, Pace U., 1983. Bar: N.J. 1983, N.Y. 1984, U.S. Dist. Ct. (so. dist.) N.Y., U.S. Dist. Ct. N.J. Atty. Met. Life Ins. Co., N.Y.C., 1983-84; corp. counsel H & N Chem. Co., Totowa, N.J., 1984-85; pvt. practice East Brunswick, N.J., 1985-90; gen. coun. East Coast Title Ins., 1990-91; CEO New Century Mortgage Corp., 1991—. Prof. law Middlesex County Coll., Edison, N.J., 1985—, Mercer County Coll., Trenton, N.J., 1985—, Upsala Coll., East Orange, N.J., 1991—. Mem. ABA (real estate, probate and property law sect., corp. law sect.), N.Y. State Bar Assn., N.J. Bar Assn. (real estate, probate and property law sect., corp. law sect.), Middlesex County Bar Assn., Rotary. Republican. Jewish. Avocations: basketball, golf, hockey, woodworking, gardening. Corporate, general, Probate (including wills, trusts), Property, real (including real estate development, water).

SILVERBERG, MICHAEL JOEL, lawyer; b. Rochester, N.Y., Aug. 12, 1932; s. Goodman and Minnie (Krovetz) S.; m. Charlotte Goldman, June 19, 1955; children: Mark (dec. 1999), Daniel. BA, U. Rochester, 1954; JD, Columbia U., 1957. Bar: N.Y. 1958, U.S. Dist. Ct. (so. dist.) N.Y. 1965, U.S. Dist. Ct. (ea. dist.) N.Y. 1990, U.S. Ct. Appeals (2d cir.) 1975, U.S. Supreme Ct. 1967. Instr. Columbia U. Law Sch., N.Y.C., 1957—58; assoc. Phillips Nizer LLP (formerly Phillips, Nizer, Benjamin, Krim & Ballon), N.Y.C., 1960—67, ptnr., 1967—. Pres. Nat. Alliance Mentally Ill N.Y.C., Inc., 1997—; cons. sci. program com. Am. Psychiat. Assn., 2000—01. Bd. editors Columbia Law Rev., 1955—57. Mem. exec. bd. N.Y. chpt. Am. Jewish Com.; bd. dirs. Nat. Alliance for Mentally Ill of N.Y. State, 1998—, pres., 1999—; mem. adv. bd. dept. psychiatry Columbia U.; mem. adv. bd. N.Y.C. Vis. Nurse Svc., mem. bd of editors, Columbia Law Review, 1955-57. Fulbright scholar U. Strasbourg, France, 1958-59. Mem. ABA, N.Y. State Bar Assn. (com. on internat. litigation), Assn. Bar City N.Y. Federal civil litigation, General civil litigation, State civil litigation. Home: 205 W End Ave New York NY 10023-4804 E-mail: MSILVERBERG@PHILLIPSNIZER.COM.

SILVERBERG, STEVEN MARK, lawyer; b. Bklyn., June 7, 1947; m. Arlene Leopold, July 4, 1971; 2 children. BA, Bklyn. Coll., 1969; JD, NYU, 1972. Bar: N.Y. 1973, U.S. Dist. Ct. (so. and ea. dists.) N.Y. 1974, U.S. Supreme Ct. 1976, U.S. Ct. Appeals (2nd cir.) 1978. Asst. dist. atty. Kings County Dist. Atty., Bklyn., 1972-75; dep. town. atty. Town of Greenburgh, N.Y., 1975-79; ptnr. Stowell, Kelly & Silverberg, White Plains, N.Y., 1979-83, Hoffman, Silverberg & Wachtell, Elmsford, N.Y., 1983-86, Hoffman, Silverberg, Wachtell & Koster, White Plains, N.Y., 1986-89; pvt. practice White Plains, 1989-92; ptnr. Kirkpatrick & Silverberg LLP, White Plains, 1993—2000, Wilson, Elser, Moskowitz, Edelman & Dicker LLP, White Plains, 2001—. Adj. assoc. prof. N.Y. Law Sch., 1990—93. Co-author: Wetlands and Coastal Zone Regulations and Compliance, 1993; contbr. to profl. publs. Counsel Greenburgh Housing Authority, 1979-84, Town of Mamaroneck, N.Y., 1984-96, Village of Mamaroneck, 1999—, planning and zoning bd. Town of Haverstraw, 2001—; bd. dirs. Temple Beth Torah, Upper Nyack, N.Y., 1977-89, 2000-03, pres. 1984-86; bd. dirs. N.J. West Hudson Valley Region Union of Am. Hebrew Congregations, 1986-88, Westchester Mcpl. Planning Fedn. Mem. ABA, N.Y. State Bar Assn., Westchester County Bar Assn. (chair environtl. law com. 1997—). Corporate, general, Environmental, Property, real (including real estate development, water). Office: Wilson Elser Moskowitz Edelman & Dicker LLP 3 Gannett Dr White Plains NY 10604

SILVERMAN, ALAN HENRY, lawyer; b. N.Y.C., Feb. 18, 1954; s. Melvin H. and Florence (Green) S.; m. Gretchen E. Freeman, May 25, 1986; children: Willa C.F., Gordon H.F. BA summa cum laude, Hamilton Coll., 1976; MBA, JD, U. Pa., 1980. Bar: N.Y. 1981, U.S. Dist. Ct. (so. and ea. dist.) N.Y. 1981, U.S. Ct. Internat. Trade 1981, D.C. 1986, U.S. Supreme Ct. 1990. Assoc. Hughes, Hubbard & Reed, N.Y.C., 1980-84; asst. counsel Newsweek, Inc., N.Y.C., 1984-86; v.p., gen. counsel, sec., dir. adminstrn. Cable One, Inc., Phoenix, 1986—. Contbr. articles to profl. jours. Mem. prevention adv. com. Gov. Pa. Justice Commn., 1975-79; bd. dirs. Lawyers' Alliance for N.Y., 1982-85, N.Y. Lawyers Pub. Interest, 1983-85, Nat. Assn. JD-MBA Profls., 1983-85, Bus. Vols. for Arts, Inc., Phoenix, 1989-93, Ariz. Vol. Lawyers for the Arts, Inc., 1994-97, First Amendment Coalition Ariz., Inc., 1991—; mem. Maricopa County Citizens Jud. Adv. Coun., 1990-93; mem. citizens' bond com. City of Phoenix, 2000. Mem. ABA, Assn. of Bar of City of N.Y., D.C. Bar Assn., Phi Beta Kappa. Communications, Entertainment, Libel. Home: 5833 N 30th St Phoenix AZ 85016-2401 Office: Cable One Inc 1314 N 3d St Phoenix AZ 85004 E-mail: alan.silverman@cableone.net.

SILVERMAN, ARNOLD BARRY, lawyer; b. Sept. 1, 1937; s. Frank and Lillian Lena (Linder) S.; m. Susan L. Levin, Aug. 7, 1960; children: Michael Eric, Lee Oren. B of Engring. Sci., Johns Hopkins U., 1959; JD cum laude, U. Pitts., 1962. Bar: U.S. Dist. Ct. (we. dist.) Pa. 1963, Pa. 1964, U.S. Patent and Trademark Office 1965, U.S. Supreme Ct. 1967, Can. Patent Office 1968, U.S. Ct. Claims 1975, U.S. Ct. Appeals (3d cir.) 1982, U.S. Ct. Appeals (fed. cir.) 1985. Patent atty. Alcoa, New Kensington, Pa., 1962-67, 68-72, sr. patent atty., 1972-76; ptnr. Price and Silverman, Pitts., 1967-68; v.p., gen. patent counsel Joy Mfg. Co., Pitts., 1976-80; ptnr. Murray Silverman & Keck, Pitts., 1980-81, Buell, Blenko, Ziesenheim & Beck, Pitts., 1984; ptnr. intellectual property dept. Eckert, Seamans, Cherin & Mellott, Pitts., 1984—, chmn., 1992—, chmn. info. tech. practice group, 1992-97; spl. asst. atty. gen. State of W.Va., 1985—; spl. counsel patents U. Pitts., 1975—. Spkr. on patents, trademarks, copyright, computer law; nat. panel of arbiters Am. Arbitration Assn., 1987—. Contbr. articles to profl. jours. Mem. Churchill CSC (Pa.), 1967-90, chmn., 1975-90; mem. Pitts. law com. Anti-Defamation League, 1981—, regional adv. bd., 1982—, ch-chmn. Pitts. region ann. dinner, 1983, mem. chmn. by-laws com., 1983; bd. govs. Slippery Rock U. Found., 1985-91; Pitts. steering com. MIT Enterprise Forum, 1986-87. With U.S. Army, 1963-64. Recipient Am. Spirit Honor medal, Ft. Knox, 1963, Fellow: Mensa (lawyers in Mensa 1978—, nat. assoc. counsel patents and trademarks copyrights 1980—82, inventors' spl. interest group 1980—86); mem.: ASME, ABA, Assn. Corp. Patent Counsel (emeritus mem.), Intertel (treas. Pitts. Forum 1983—), Stratford Cmty. Assn. (v.p. 1966—67, gov. 1966—70, pres. 1967—68), Golden Panthers, U. Pitts. Law Alumni Assn. (bd. dirs. 1992—, treas. 1997—98, v.p. 1998—99, pres.-elect 1999—2000, pres. 2001—02), Johns Hopkins Soc. Engring. Alumni, Johns Hopkins U. Alumni Assn. (chmn. publicity com. 1963—66, exec. com. 1966—87, v.p. 1969—70, pres. 1971—72, nat. alumni coun. 1989—92, coun. mem. 2000—), Brit. Inst. Chartered Patent Agts. (fgn. mem.), Licensing Execs. Soc. (co-chmn. Pitts. chpt. 1994—96), Am. Chem. Soc. (chemistry and the law sect.), Nat. Assn. Coll. and Univ. Attys., Pa. Bar Assn. (co-chmn. sports/entertainment arts law com. 2001—), D.C. Bar Assn., U.S. Trademark Assn. (chmn. task force on advt. agys. 1981, membership com. 1987—89), Am. Intellectual Property Law Assn. (membership com. 1985—88, pub. rels. com. 1994—), Pitts. Patent Law Assn. (chmn. pub. rels. com. 1968—69, chmn. patent laws com. 1970—72, chmn. legis. action com. 1972—75, chmn. nominating com. 1973, bd. mgrs. 1974—88, newsletter editor 1974—88, sec.-treas. 1976—84, v.p. 1984—85, pres. 1985—86, pub. rels. com. 1994—95, program com. 1995—96), Allegheny County Bar Assn. (chmn. pub. rels. com. 1978—80, vice-chmn. intellectual property sect. 1981—83, chmn. 1984—85), Robert Bruce Assn. Law Fellows (life), U. Pitts. Gen. Alumni Assn. (life; bd. dirs. 2001—), Duquesne Club, Order of Coif, Psi Chi, Tau Epsilon Rho. Republican. Jewish. Computer, Patent, Trademark and copyright. Home: 2019 High Pointe Ct Murrysville PA 15668-8515 Office: 600 Grant St 44th Fl Pittsburgh PA 15219-2703 E-mail: arnie@telerama.com., abs@escm.com.

SILVERMAN, ARTHUR CHARLES, lawyer; b. Lewiston, Maine, June 13, 1938; s. Louis A. and Frances Edith (Brownstone) S.; BS in Elec. Engring., BS in Indsl. Mgmt., MIT, 1961; JD, Columbia U., 1964; m. Donna Linda Zolov, June 18, 1961; children: Leonard Stephen, Daniel Edward. Bar: N.Y. 1965, U.S. Supreme Ct. 1971. Engr., engring. asst. Gen. Electric Co., Pittsfield, Mass. and Phila., 1958-62; assoc. Baer & Marks, N.Y.C., 1965-68; assoc. Golenbock and Barell, N.Y.C., 1968-72, ptnr., 1972-89; ptnr. Reid & Priest LLP, N.Y.C., 1989-98, dep. chair, 1996-98; ptnr. Thelen Reid & Priest LLP, N.Y.C., 1998—. Treas., trustee Ramaz Sch., 1977-84, vice chmn., 1984-85, 86-88, chmn., 1988-92, hon. chmn., 1992—; bd. govs. MIT Hillel Found., 1979-84; mem. Bd. Jewish Edn. of City of N.Y., 1981-84; mem. exec. com. Nat. Jewish Ctr. for Learning and Leadership, 1984-90. Mem. IEEE, ABA, NSPE, N.Y. State Bar Assn., Fed. Bar Council, Assn. Bar City N.Y., N.Y. Soc. Architects, Internat. Bar Assn., Inter-Pacific Bar Assn., Constrn. Mgmt. Inst., Constrn. Specifications Inst. General civil litigation, Construction, Property, real (including real estate development, water). Home: 200 E 74th St New York NY 10021-3618 Office: Thelen Reid & Priest LLP 875 Third Ave New York NY 10022

SILVERMAN, BARRY G. federal judge; b. N.Y.C., Oct. 11, 1951; 1 child, Bagel Ann. BA summa cum laude, Ariz. State U., 1973, JD, 1976. Bar: Ariz. 1976, U.S. Dist. Ct. Ariz. 1976, U.S. Ct. Appeals (9th cir.) 1976, U.S. Supreme Ct. 1980. Asst. city prosecutor, Phoenix, 1976—77; dep. atty. Maricopa County, 1977—79; ct. commr., 1979—84; judge Superior Ct. Ariz. Maricopa County, 1984—95; apptd. magistrate judge U.S. Dist. Ct. Ariz., 1995—98; judge U.S. Ct. Appeals 9th cir., 1998—. Instr. constnl. law Coll. Law, Ariz. State U., 1983, adj. prof. advanced criminal procedure, 89; lectr. cmty. property BAR/BRI Ariz., Idaho and Nev. Bar Rev. Courses, 1989—. Recipient Exel award, Soc. Nat. Assn. Publs., 1992. Mem.: ABA, Maricopa County Bar Assn. (Henry Stevens award 1991), State Bar Ariz. Avocations: magic, beagles, baseball, wine tasting. Office: US Ct of Appeals 401 W Washington St SPC 78 Phoenix AZ 85003

SILVERMAN, BRADLEY ALLAN, lawyer; b. Windsor, Can., Dec. 22, 1968; arrived in U.S., 1993; s. Thomas Andrew and Susan Silverman. BA, York U., 1991; JD, U. Miami, 1996. Bar: Fla. 1997, U.S. Dist. Ct. (so. dist.) Fla. 1997, U.S. Ct. Appeals (11th cir.) 1997, U.S. Supreme Ct. 2000. Assoc. Andrew J. Anthony, Miami, Fla., 1997—. Personal injury (including property damage), Insurance, Product liability. Office: Andrew J Anthony 866 S Dixie Hwy Miami FL 33146 E-mail: bsilverman@ajalaw.com.

SILVERMAN, DONALD N. lawyer; b. N.Y.C., Nov. 28, 1947; s. Mortoh and Estelle Silverman; m. Robin A. Bikkal, Apr. 5, 1987; children: Miranda, Douglas. BS, Boston U., 1969; JD, George Washington U., 1972. Bar: N.Y. 1973. Co-dir. Jackson Co. Legal Svcs., Medford, Oreg., 1972—73; staff counsel Legal Aid Soc. West Co., White Plains, NY, 1973—76; pvt. practice White Plains, NY, 1976—83; West County ct. judge N.Y. State Judiciary, White Plains, 1988—92, Supreme ct. justice, 1992—98; ptnr. Silverman & Bikkal, LLP, White Plains, 1998—. Dean N.Y. State Trial Lawyers Inst., N.Y.C., 1999—2002. Chair YMCA, White Plains, 2000—01, Cardozo Soc., White Plains, 2000—01, West County Human Rights Com., White Plains, 2000—01. Avocations: reading, fishing, golf. Product liability, Personal injury (including property damage). Office: Silverman & Bikkal LLP 81 Main St White Plains NY 10601

SILVERMAN, LEON, lawyer; b. N.Y.C., June 9, 1921; BA, Bklyn. Coll., 1942; LL.B., Yale U., 1948; postgrad., London Sch. Econs., 1948-49. Bar: N.Y. 1949. Assoc. firm Riegelman, Strasser, Schwartz & Spiegelberg, N.Y.C., 1949-53; asst. U.S. atty. So. Dist. N.Y., 1953-55; asst. dep. atty. gen. Dept. Justice, Washington, 1958-59, spl. prosecutor, 1981-82, ind. counsel investigating Sec. Labor, 1987; co-chmn. firm Fried, Frank, Harris, Shriver & Jacobson, N.Y.C., 1960—80, counsel to, 1980—. Counsel N.Y. Gov.'s Com. to Rev. N.Y. Laws and Procedure in the Area of Human Rights, 1967-68, Com. to Rev. Legis. and Jud. Salaries, 1972-73; mem. adv. com. on criminal rules to com. on rules of practice and procedure Jud. Conf. U.S.; mem. joint com. to monitor N.Y. drug laws; pres. N.Y. Legal Aid Soc., 1970-72, dir., 1966—; pres U.S. Supreme Ct. Hist. Soc., 1980-92, chmn. 1992-; spl. master Appellatte divsn. 1st dept. N.Y. Supreme Ct., 1984—. Trustee William Nelson Cromwell Found., 1983—; chmn. Legal Council for Soviet Jewery, 1987—. Recipient Judge Learned Hand Human Relations award, 1981, Emory Buckner Pub. Service medal, 1982, Judge Joseph M. Proskauer award, 1982. Mem. ABA, N.Y. State Bar Assn., Fed. Bar Assn., Am. Coll. Trial Lawyers (regent 1979— , pres. 1982-83), Am. Law

Inst., Am. Judicature Soc., Practising Law Inst. (trustee), Assn. Bar City N.Y., Fed. Bar Council. Federal civil litigation, State civil litigation. Home: 16 Oak Dr Great Neck NY 11021-1810 Office: Fried Frank Harris Shriver & Jacobson 1 New York Plz 25th Fl New York NY 10004-1980

SILVERMAN, MOSES, lawyer; b. Bklyn., Mar. 3, 1948; s. Bernard and Anne Silverman; m. Betty B. Robbins, Jan. 19, 1980; children: Benjamin, Rachel. AB, Colby Coll., 1969; JD, NYU, 1973. Bar: N.Y. 1974, U.S. Dist. Ct. (so. and ea. dists.) N.Y. 1974, U.S. Ct. Appeals (2d cir.) 1974, U.S. Ct. Appeals (D.C. cir.) 1977, U.S. Supreme Ct. 1977, D.C. 1982, U.S. Ct. Appeals (fed. cir.) 1985, U.S. Ct. Appeals (11th cir.) 2001, U.S. Dist. Ct. (D.C.) 2001, U.S. Ct. Appeals (9th cir.) 2002. Assoc. Paul, Weiss, Rifkind, Wharton & Garrison, NYC, 1973-81, ptnr., 1981—. Vol. U.S. Peace Corps., Istanbul, Turkey, 1969-70; bd. dirs. Legal Aid Soc., 1998-, Am. Sephardi Fedn., 2002; mem. bd. overseers Colby Coll., 2002—. Mem. ABA, NY State Bar Assn., Assn. of Bar of City of NY Antitrust, Federal civil litigation, State civil litigation. Home: 7 Gracie Sq New York NY 10028-8001 Office: Paul Weiss Rifkind Wharton & Garrison 1285 Ave of Americas New York NY 10019-6028 E-mail: msilverman@paulweiss.com.

SILVERMAN, SAM MENDEL, physicist, lawyer; b. N.Y.C., Nov. 16, 1925; s. Moshe Aaron and Gitel (Korenbaum) S.; m. Jacqueline Greenberg, Sept. 12, 1948 (div. Apr. 1965); children: Ann, William, Nancy; m. Phyllis Rolfe, June 26, 1966; children: Gila, Aaron. BChE, CCNY, 1945; PhD, Ohio State U., 1952; JD, Suffolk U., 1982. Bar: Mass. 1982, U.S. Dist. Ct. Mass. 1982, U.S. Ct. Appeals (1st cir.) 1982, N.Y. 1983, U.S. Supreme Ct. 1986. Assoc. Ohio State U., Columbus, 1952-55; asst. prof. chem. physics U. Toledo, 1955-57; rsch. physicist Air Force Cambridge Rsch. Labs., Bedford, Mass., 1957-80, chief polar atmospheric processes br. and dir. geopole obs., 1963-74, cons., 1980—. Vis. rsch. assoc. Queens U., Belfast, 1963-64; vis. prof. Osmania U., Hyderabad, India, 1965-66; mem. adv. bd. Inst. Space and Atmospheric Studies, U. Sask. (Can.), 1965-69; sr. rsch. physicist Boston Coll., 1981-97; co-chmn. interdivisional commn. history Internat. Assn. Geomagnetism and Aeronomy, 1987-91; lectr. palliative care courses, Poland, 1993, 94, 2000. Contbr. articles to profl. jours. Mem. Town Meeting Lexington, Mass., 1973-79, 84—; elected mem. Lexington Dem. Town Com., 1996—; legal counsel Internat. Work Group on Death, Dying and Bereavement. With USAAF, 1945-46. Recipient Thurgood Marshall award, com. pub. counsel svcs. Mass. Pub. Defender's Agy., 2002. Fellow Am. Phys. Soc., Explorers Club; mem. Am. Geophys. Union (editor History of Geophysics newsletter 1983-91), Internat. Work Group on Death, Dying and Bereavement. Home: 18 Ingleside Rd Lexington MA 02420-2522 E-mail: smpr@rcn.com.

SILVERMAN, STEVEN D. lawyer; b. N.Y.C., Dec. 4, 1947; s. Hyman A. and Phyllis (Helfand) S.; m. Freddye Lynn Kaufman, June 24, 1971; children: Matthew Craig, Zachary Neal. BA, Adelphi U., 1969; JD, U. Md., 1972. Bar: Md. 1972, U.S. Dist. Ct. Md. 1979, U.S. Ct. Appeals (4th cir.) 1979, U.S. Supreme Ct. 1978. Asst. state's atty. Baltimore County State's Atty.'s Office, Towson, Md., 1971-75; assoc. Friedman, Pachino & Friedman, Dundalk, Md., 1975-81; pvt. practice law Dundalk, 1981-85; ptnr. Rosolio & Silverman, Towson, 1985-96; pvt. practice law Owings Mills, Md., 1996—. Presenter, lectr. in field. Bd. dirs. Beth El Congregation, 2001—, Md. Vol. Lawyers Svcs., Balt., 1995—, v.p., 1997—, pres. 1998—; pres. Greengate Homeowners Assn., Balt., 1993—; founder Greengate Security Corp., Balt., 1994. Mem. Md. State Bar Assn., Balt. County Bar Assn., Suburban Country Club. Democrat. Jewish. Avocations: sports, movies, foreign travel. Family and matrimonial, General practice. Home: 6 Mandel Ct Baltimore MD 21209-1016 Office: 9505 Reisterstown Rd Owings Mills MD 21117-4451

SILVERMAN, STEVEN DONALD, lawyer; b. Balt., Oct. 28, 1966; s. Joseph A. and Sydna R. Silverman; m. Paula Bridges Silverman, June 12, 1993; children: Samantha, Ryan. BA, U. Richmond, 1988; JD, U. Balt., 1991. Bar: Md. 1991, U.S. Dist. Ct. Md. 1994, D.C. 2002. Law clk. Md. Atty. Gen.-Civil Litigation, Balt., 1989—91; asst. pub. defender felony narcotics Office of the Pub. Defender, Balt., 1991—94; pvt. practice, mng. ptnr. Silverman & Thompson, Balt., 1995—. Lectr. in field. Fellow, Roscoe-Pound Inst., Washington, 2001—02. Mem.: ATLA, Balt. City Bar (jud. selection com. 2001—02), Md. Criminal Def. Attys. Assn., Md. Bar Assn., Million Dollar Advs. Forum. Criminal. Office: Silverman & Thompson 26th Fl 201 N Charles St Baltimore MD 21201

SILVERSHEIN, JOEL MICHAEL, lawyer; b. Bklyn., Aug. 3, 1961; s. Milton and Joyce (Pullman) S. BA in History, Tulane U., 1983; JD, Nova U., 1986. Bar: Fla. 1986, U.S. Tax Ct. 1987, U.S. Claims Ct. 1987, U.S. Ct. Appeals (11th cir.) 1987. Asst. state atty. Broward County, Ft. Lauderdale, Fla., 1986—. Author: (with others) Florida Juvenile Law and Practice, 3d edit., 1992, 4th edit., 1995, 5th edit., 1997, 6th edit., 1999, 7th edit., 2001; rschr. The Law of Life and Health Insurance, 1988. Mem. ABA, Fla. Bar Assn. (juvenile rules com. 1987-2002, criminal rules com. 2002-). Office: Broward County State Attys Office 201 SE 6th St Ste 660 Fort Lauderdale FL 33301-3304

SILVERSTEIN, LEONARD A. lawyer; b. Mobile, Ala., Apr. 18, 1958; s. Burton Howard and Fannye Mitchell Silverstein; m. Ellen Sue Frauenthal, May 25, 1986; children: Andrew, Laura, Anna. BA magna cum laude, Vanderbilt U., Nashville, 1980; JD, Vanderbilt U., 1983. Bar: Ga. 1983. Assoc./ptnr. Powell Goldstein Frazer & Murphy LLP, Atlanta, 1983—94; ptnr. McKenna Long & Aldridge LLP, Atlanta, 1994—. Mem. Ga. Biomed. Partnership, Atlanta, 2002—; mem., biosciences exec. com. Met. Atlanta C. of C., 2002—. Contbr. ; assoc. mng. editor, Vanderbilt Law Rev., 1982—83. Pres. Vanderbilt U. Alumni Club, Atlanta, 1991; co-pres. Bach n' Rollers, Divsn. of The Atlanta Symphony Assocs., 1992—93; bd. mem. and exec. com. mem. Zoo Atlanta, 1996—2001, bd. mem., 2003, Am.-Israel C. of C., S.E. Region, Atlanta, 1995—; bd. mem. and exec. com. mem. Am. Jewish Com., Atlanta, 1999—; bd. of trustees The Atlanta Symphony Assocs., 1992—93. Recipient IPO Rainmaker, IPO Counsel - The Corp. Fin. Inst., 1996. Mem.: Vanderbilt U. Alumni Assn. (bd. dirs. 1992—96), Ga. Bar Assn. (vice chair/chair elect of securities subcom. 2001—02), Atlanta Bar Assn. Achievements include patents pending for Reloadable Rights Plan for Preferred and Common Stock Rights Plans. Avocations: triathlons, golf. Securities, Mergers and acquisitions, Biotech. Office: McKenna Long & Aldridge LLP 303 Peachtree St Ste 5300 Atlanta GA 30308 Office Fax: 404-527-4198. E-mail: lsilverstein@mckennalong.com.

SIMANDLE, JEROME B. federal judge; b. Binghamton, N.Y., 1949; s. Paul R. Sr. and Mary F. Simandle; married; children: Roy C., Liza Jane. BSE magna cum laude, Princeton U., 1971; JD, U. Pa., 1976; diploma in Social Scis., U. Stockholm, 1974-75. Bar: Pa. 1977, N.J. 1978. Law clk. to Hon. John F. Gerry U.S. Dist. Ct., N.J., 1976-78; asst. U.S. atty. Dist. N.J., 1978-83; U.S. magistrate judge U.S. Dist. Ct., N.J., 1983-92, judge, 1992—. Mem. lawyers adv. com. U.S. Dist. Ct., NJ, 1984—95; mem. ct. adminstrn. case mgmt. com. Jud. Conf. U.S., 1991—97; mem. joint adv. coun. of Adminstrv. Office of U.S. Cts., 2002—; mem. CPR Inst. for Dispute Resolution Commn. on Ethics and Stds. in Alternative Dispute Resolution, 1996—. Internat. grad. fellow Rotary Found., 1974-75. Master: Camden Inn of Ct. (program chmn. 1990—93, vice chmn. 1996—); fellow: Am. Bar Found.; mem.: Camden County Bar Assn., Am. Judicature Soc., Fed. Judges Assn. (bd. dirs. 1997—, nat. treas. 2003—). Office: 1 John F Gerry Pl Camden NJ 08101-0888

SIMKANICH, JOHN JOSEPH, lawyer, engineer; b. Clairton, Pa., 1941; BSEE, Drexel Inst. Tech., 1964; MSEE, Purdue U., 1966; JD, George Washington U., 1972. Bar: U.S. Patent Office 1970, Pa. 1973, U.S. dist. Ct. (ea. dist.) Pa. 1977, U.S. Supreme Ct. 1977, U.S. Ct. Appeals (Fed. cir.) 1982, U.S. Ct. Appeals (3d cir.) 1992. Elec. engr. U.S. Steel Co., 1963-65; engr. Westinghouse Aerospace, Balt., 1966-69; sys. developer TRW Sys. Inc., Washington, 1969-70; patent atty. Burroughs Corp., Paoli, Pa., 1970-74, Johnson & Johnson, New Brunswick, N.J., 1974-77; pvt. practice intellectual property law Newtown, Pa., 1977—. Adv. Soup, Inc., Washington, 1970-72; introduted to FTC truth-in-advt. law; presenter in field. Patentee in field; product developer and licensing; analog and digital computer designer, programmer. Mem. IEEE (sr.), Pa. Bar Assn., Bucks County Bar Assn., Phila. Intellectual Property Law Assn., Am. Intellectual Property Law Assn., Delta Theta Phi, Eta Kappa Nu. Roman Catholic. Republican. Computer, Patent, Trademark and copyright. Office: Paul & Paul 2900 Two-Thousand Market St Philadelphia PA 19103

SIMMONS, CHARLES BEDFORD, JR., lawyer; b. Greenville, S.C., Dec. 4, 1956; s. Charles Bedford and Mary Margaret (Mason) S.; children: Charles B. III, Elizabeth S., Mason W. AA magna cum laude, Spartanburg Meth. Coll., 1977; BS magna cum laude, E. Tenn. State U., 1979; JD, U. S.C., 1982. Bar: S.C. 1982, U.S. Dist. Ct. S.C. 1983, U.S. Ct. Appeals (4th cir.) 1986. Law clk. to presiding justice S.C. Cir. Ct., Greenville, 1982-83; with Carter Law Firm, Greenville, 1983-86; ptnr. Wilkins, Nelson, Kittredge & Simmons, Greenville, 1986-89; civil ct. judge Greenville, 1989—; presiding judge 13th Circuit Drug Ct. Mem. bench-bar com. S.C. Supreme Ct., 1992-97; presiding judge 13th cir. Drug Ct. Mem. adv. com. paralegal program Greenville Tech. Coll., 1989-97, chmn., 1990-91; mem. Friends of 200 Adv. Bd., 1991-99. Named Big Brother of Yr., Big Bros.-Big Sisters, 1988; recipient Svc. to Manking award Rotary Club, 1989, Outstanding Young Disting. Svc. award Greenville Jaycees, 1990-91. Mem. S.C. Bar Assn. (young lawyer liason 1985-89, named Outstanding Young Lawyer of Yr. 1989), Greenville Bar Assn., Assn. Trial Lawyers Am., S.C. Trial Lawyers Assn., Greenville Young Lawyers (pres. 1988—1990), Gamma Beta Phi, Pi Gamma Mu, Phi Delta Phi. Clubs: Greenville City, Textile (v.p. 1985-87), Revelers (Greenville). Republican. Presbyterian. Home: 11 W Hillcrest Dr Greenville SC 29609-4615 Office: Ste 313 County Courthouse Greenville SC 29601

SIMMONS, DAVID NORMAN, lawyer; b. Denver, Aug. 29, 1957; s. David Lee and Janet Thelma (Meseroll) S.; m. Neri Alcocer Argáez, Mar. 15, 1986; children: Chester Rolando, Laura Victoria. BA, U. Denver, 1980, JD, 1985. Bar: Colo. 1986, U.S. Dist. Colo. 1987, U.S. Ct. Appeals (10th cir.) 1993. Pvt. practice, Denver, 1986—. Hon. legal counsel Mex. Consulate Gen., Denver, 1987—99; adj. prof. U. Denver Coll. Law, 2002—. Bd. dirs. Justice Info. Ctr., Denver, 1997-2002, Mexican Cultural Ctr., Denver, 1992-95; elder Presbyn. Ch. U.S.A., Denver, 1986--; with CAP Aux. USAF, 1971—, Colo. Wing legal officer, 1992-96, nat. legal officer, 1998-2001. Mem. Colo. Bar Assn. (diversity com. 1997—), Denver Bar Assn., Am. Immigration Lawyers Assn. (exec. com. Colo. chpt. 1993-97, pres. 1996-97), Denver Law Club (asst. sec. 1997-98, co-sec. 1998-99, treas. 1999-2000, v.p. 2001-2002, pres. 2002-03). Democrat. Avocations: pilot, choral singing, bicycling. Immigration, naturalization, and customs. Office: 333 W Hampden Ave Ste 703 Englewood CO 80110-2337 E-mail: dnsimmons@uswest.net.

SIMMONS, MYRIAM MICHELE SIDO, lawyer; b. Albuquerque, July 14, 1967; d. Abdulcadir and Kyra Sido; m. Haywood Simmons, Sept. 4, 1998; 1 child, Tatjana Ariel Sido. BA in Sociology, U. Wis., 1993; JD, Rutgers U., Camden, N.J., 1998; LLM, John Marshall Law Sch., 2003. Bar: Ill. Cons. Deloitte & Touche, LLP, Chgo., 1998—2001; counsel Sears, Roebuck and Co., Hoffman Estates, Ill., 2001—. Mem. Corp. Funding Solutions, LLC, 2002—. Mem.: ABA, Am. Corp. Counsel Assn. State and local taxation, Corporate taxation. Office: Sears Roebuck and Co 3333 Beverly Rd B2-161B Hoffman Estates IL 60179 Office Fax: 847-286-4908. Personal E-mail: mysimmons@msn.com. E-mail: msimm18@sears.com.

SIMMONS, PETER, law and urban planning educator; b. N.Y.C., July 19, 1931; s. Michael L. and Mary A. S.; m. Ruth J. Tanfield, Jan. 28, 1951; children: Sam, Lizzard. AB, U. Calif., Berkeley, 1953, LL.B., 1956; postgrad. (Alvord fellow), U. Wis., 1956-58. Prof. SUNY, Buffalo, 1963-67; mem. faculty Ohio State U., 1967-75, U. Ill., 1972, Case Western Res. U., 1974-75; prof. law and urban planning Rutgers U. Coll. Law, Newark, 1975—, dean, 1975-93; university prof. Rutgers U., 1993—. Contbr. articles to profl. jours. Mem. Ohio Housing Commn., 1972-74; commr. Ohio Reclamation Rev. Bd., 1974-75; chmn. N.J. Criminal Disposition Commn., 1983-84; mem. N.J. Law Revision Commn., 1987—. Mem. Am. Planning Assn., Urban Land Inst., Am. Law Inst., AAUP (nat. council 1973-76). Office: Rutgers U Law Sch 15 Washington St Newark NJ 07102-3192 E-mail: psimmons@andromeda.rutgers.edu.

SIMMONS, PETER LAWRENCE, lawyer; b. N.Y.C., May 1, 1965; s. John Derek and Rosalind (Wellish) S. AB magna cum laude, Columbia U., 1985, JD, 1987. Bar: N.Y. 1987, U.S. Dist. Ct. (so. and ea. dists.) N.Y. 1988, U.S. Ct. Internat. Trade 1991, U.S. Spreme Ct. 1991, U.S. Ct. Appeals (2d cir.) 1992, U.S. Ct. Appeals (1st cir.) 1993, U.S. Ct. Appeals (6th cir.) 2001. Law clk. to Hon. Lawrence W. Pierce U.S. Ct. Appeals (2d cir.), N.Y.C., 1987-88; assoc. Fried, Frank, Harris, Shriver & Jacobson, N.Y.C., 1988-94, ptnr., 1994—. Treas., sr. editor Columbia Law Rev., 1985-87. Harlan Fiske Stone scholar, 1985-87. Mem.: ABA, Assn. Bar City NY (profl. responsibility com. 1998—2001, civil rights com. 1989—92), NY Bar Assn., Fed. Bar Coun., Phi Beta Kappa. General civil litigation. Home: 91 West Rd Short Hills NJ 07078 Office: Fried Frank Harris Shriver & Jacobson 1 New York Plz Fl 22 New York NY 10004-1980 E-mail: peter.simmons@ffhsj.com.

SIMMONS, RAYMOND HEDELIUS, lawyer; b. Salinas, Calif., May 27, 1958; s. Raymond Hedelius and Antoinette (Lynch) S. BA magna cum laude, U. Calif., San Diego, 1979; JD magna cum laude, U. Calif., San Francisco, 1982. Bar: Calif. 1982, U.S. Dist. Ct. (no. dist.) Calif. 1982, Ga. 1987. Assoc. Farella, Braun & Martel, San Francisco, 1982-85; atty., v.p. Barnett-Range Corp., Atlanta, 1985-86; counsel Nationwide Capital Corp. subs. HomeFed. Bank, Atlanta, 1986, HomeFed. Bank, San Diego, 1987-90; gen. counsel, sr. v.p., sec. ITT Fed. Bank, San Francisco, 1990-95; also ITT Residential Capital Corp., ITT Residential Capital Servicing Corp., San Francisco; pvt. practice, Newport Beach, Calif., 1995—. Mem.: ABA, Calif. Bar Assn., Calif. Scholarship Fedn. (life), Thurston Soc., Order of Coif. Commercial, contracts (including sales of goods; commercial financing), Corporate, general, Property, real (including real estate development, water). E-mail: rsimmons@simmonslawoffices.com.

SIMMONS, SHERWIN PALMER, lawyer; b. Bowling Green, Ky., Jan. 19, 1931; AB, Columbia U., 1952, LLB, 1954, JD, 1969. Bar: Tenn. 1954, Fla. 1957. Assoc. Fowler, White, Collins, Gillen, Humkey & Trenam, Tampa, Fla., 1956-60, ptnr., 1960-70, Trenam, Simmons, Kemker, Scharf & Barkin, Tampa, 1970-77; stockholder, pres. Trenam, Simmons, Kemker, Scharf, Barkin, Frye & O'Neill, PA, Tampa, 1977-94; ptnr., chair tax group Steel Hector & Davis, LLP, Miami, Fla., 1994—. Atty. adv. U.S. Tax Ct., Washington, 1954-56, mem. nominating commn., 1978-81; mem. adv. group Commr. of IRS, 1978-79, 89-90, U.S. Dept. Justice, 1979-80; adj. prof. U. Miami, 1995—. Contbr. articles to legal jours. Trustee Hillsborough County Soc. Crippled Children & Adults, 1956-65, pres., 1960-61; treas., chmn. Hillsborough County Pub. Edn. Study Commn., 1965-66; mem. adv. bd. Salvation Army, 1959-62, 64-66, sec., 1960-61; chmn., bd. dirs. The Fla. Orch., 1987-89; founding trustee, pres. Am. Tax Policy Inst., 1996-99; trustee Tampa Bay Performing Arts Ctr., Inc., 1984-93, program adv. com., 1985-89, investment com., 1986-91. Fellow Am. Coll. Trust and Estate Counsel (bd. regents 1982-88), Am. Bar Found. (fellow 1969—, devel. com. 1992-94), Am. Coll. Tax Counsel (regent 1987-93, vice chmn. 1989-91, chmn. 1991-93); mem. ABA (vice chmn. adminstrn. taxation sect. 1972-75, chmn. 1975-76, ho. of dels. 1985-90, bd. govs. 1990-93, chmn. bd. govs. fin. com. 1992-93, chmn. commn. on multidisciplinary practice 1998-2000), Am. Bar Retirement Assn. (bd. dirs. 1984-90, v.p. 1987-88, pres. 1988-89), Am. Law Network ABA-Am. Law Inst. (com. continuing profl. edn. 1973—), FBA, Fla. Bar Assn. (chmn. taxation sect. 1964-65), Am. Judicature Soc., So. Fed. Tax Inst. (trustee, pres. 1974, chmn. 1975 trustee emeritus 1999—), Internat. Acad. Estate and Trust Law, Internat. Fiscal Assn., Am. Law Inst. (mem. coun. 1985—, exec. com. 1994-97, 99—, mem. com. 1997—, chmn. 1999—). Corporate taxation, Estate taxation, Taxation, general. Office: 200 S Biscayne Blvd Ste 4100 Miami FL 33131-2362 Personal E-mail: spshome@msn.com. Business E-Mail: spstax@steelhector.com.

SIMMONS, STEPHEN JUDSON, lawyer; b. Columbus, Ohio, Feb. 19, 1946; s. Samuel A. and Jane A. (McGrath) S.; m. Claire Maxine Schriber, Aug. 15, 1970; children: Darren, Judson. BA, Ohio State U., 1968; JD, U. Cin., 1972. Bar: Ohio 1973, Tex. 1982. Sr. law clk. U.S. Dist. Ct. (ea. dist.) Tenn., Knoxville, 1972-74; asst. atty. gen. Office of Atty. of Ohio, Columbus, 1974-75; assoc. McGrath & Shirey, Columbus, 1975; corp. counsel Wendys, Inc., Columbus, 1975-79; sr. v.p., gen. counsel Precision Tune, Inc., Beaumont, Tex., 1979-87, also dir.; sr. v.p. adminstrn., dir. Kwik-Kopy Corp., Cypress, Tex., 1988-90; v.p. Deli Mgmt., Inc., 1990-94; pvt. practice Houston, 1994—. Bd. editors U. Cin. Law Rev., 1971-72. Mem. Tex. Bar Assn. Roman Catholic. Corporate, general, Franchising, Property, real (including real estate development, water). Home: 13603 Balmore Cir Houston TX 77069-2703 Office: 3845 Fm 1960 Rd W Ste 250 Houston TX 77068-3548 Fax: 281-586-0088. E-mail: sjsimmons@aol.com.

SIMON, H(UEY) PAUL, lawyer; b. Lafayette, La., Oct. 19, 1923; s. Jules and Ida (Rogére) S.; m. Carolyn Perkins, Aug. 6, 1949 (dec. Dec. 1999); 1 child, John Clark. BS, U. Southwestern La., 1943; JD, Tulane U., 1947. Bar: La. 1947; CPA, La. 1947. Pvt. practice, New Orleans, 1947—; asst. prof. advanced acctg. and taxation U. Southwestern La., 1944-45; staff acct. Haskins & Sells (now Deloitte & Touche), New Orleans, 1945-53, prin., 1953-57; ptnr. Deutsch, Kerrigan & Stiles, 1957-79; sr. founding ptnr. Simon, Peragine, Smith & Redfearn, 1979—. Mem. New Orleans Bd. Trade. Author: Community Property and Liability for Funeral Expenses of Deceased Spouse, 1946, Income Tax Deductibility of Attorney's Fees in Action in Boundary, 1946, Fair Labor Standards Act and Employee's Waiver of Liquidated Damages, 1946, Louisiana Income Tax Law, 1956, Changes Effected by the Louisiana Trust Code, 1965, Gifts to Minors and the Parent's Obligation of Support, 1968; co-author: Deductions—Business or Hobby, 1975, Role of Attorney in IRS Tax Return Examination, 1978; assoc. editor: The Louisiana CPA, 1956-60; mem. bd. editors Tulane Law Rev., 1945-46, adv. bd. editors, 1992—; estates, gifts and trusts editor The Tax Times, 1986-87. Bd. dirs., mem. fin. com. World Trade Ctr., 1985-86; mem. New Orleans Met. Crime Commn., Coun. for a Better La., New Orleans Met. Area Com., Bur. Govtl. Rsch., Pub. Affairs Rsch. Coun.; co-chmn. NYU Tax Conf., New Orleans, 1976; mem. dean's coun. Tulane U. Law Sch. Fellow Am. Coll. Tax Counsel; mem. ABA (com. ct. procedure tax sect. 1958—), AICPA, La. Bar Assn. (com. on legis. and adminstrv. practice 1966-70, bd. cert. tax atty.), New Orleans Bar Assn., Internat. Bar Assn. (com. on securities issues and trading 1970-88), Am. Judicature Soc., Soc. La. CPAs, New Orleans Assn. Notaries, Tulane U. Alumni Assn., New Orleans C. of C. (coun. 1952-66), Tulane Tax Inst. (program com. 1960-96, emeritus 1997--), Internat. House (bd. dirs. 1976-79, 82-85), Internat. Platform Assn., City Energy Club, Press Club, New Orleans Country Club, Phi Delta Phi (past pres. New Orleans chpt.), Sigma Pi Alpha. Roman Catholic. Corporate, general, Estate planning, Corporate taxation. Home: 6075 Canal Blvd New Orleans LA 70124-2936 Office: 30th Fl Energy Ctr New Orleans LA 70163 E-mail: hpsimon@aol.com., hpsimon@spsr-law.com.

SIMON, JAMES LOWELL, lawyer; b. Nov. 8, 1944; s. K. Lowell and Elizabeth Ann (Unholz) S.; m. RuthAnn Beck, July 4, 1997; children: Heather Lyn Small, Brandon James; stepchildren: Gary G. Mower, Richard M. Nazareth II, Juliet A. Nazareth. Student, U. Ill., 1962-63, JD with honors, 1975; BSEE magna cum laude, Bradley U., 1967. Bar: Fla. 1975, Utah 1999, Calif. 2002, U.S. Dist. Ct. (mid. dist.) Fla. 1976, U.S. Dist. Ct. Utah 1999, U.S. Dist. Ct. (no. dist.) Calif. 2002, U.S. Ct. Appeals (11th cir.) 1981, U.S. Patent Office 1983. Engr. Pan Am. World Airways, Cape Kennedy, Fla., 1967-68; assoc. Akerman, Senterfitt & Eidson, Orlando, Fla., 1975-80; ptnr. Bogin, Munns, Munns & Simon, Orlando, 1980-87, Holland & Knight, LLP, 1987-99; corp. counsel Agilent Technologies Inc., Palo Alto, Calif., 2000—. With Seminole County Sch. Adv. Coun., Fla., 1981-88, chmn., 1982, 83; with Forest City Local Sch. Adv. Com., Altamonte Springs, Fla., 1981-84, Code Enforcement Bd., Altamonte Springs, 1983-84, Cen. Bus. Dist. Study com., Altamonte Springs, 1983-85, Rep. Coun. of '76, Seminole County, 1982-87; mem. Seminole County Libr. Adv. Bd., 1989-92, sec., 1990, pres., 1991, Seminole County Citizens for Quality Edn., 1990-92; mem. Seminole County Sch. Dist. Strategic Planning Com., 1991-99, Leadership Orlando Alumni, 1992-99; bd. dirs. Found. for Seminole County Pub. Schs., Inc., 1992-95, chmn., 1993-94; bd. dirs. Greater Seminole C. of C., 1993; active Lake Brantley H.S. Band Boosters, 1995-2000, Lake Brantley H.S. PTSA, 1995-2000, Chorus Boosters, 1997, Leadership Club-Heart of Fla. United Way, 1997; sponsor concerts Orlando Philharm. Orch. for Boys and Girls Clubs. Cen. Fla., 1996-97; regional dir. region 5 Holocaust Remembrance Project, 1997-99. Capt. USAF, 1968-72. Mem. ABA, Am. Corp. Counsel Assn., Am. Intellectual Property Law Assn., Intellectual Property Owners Assn. (chair copyright law com. 2003—), U. Ill. Alumni Club, Phi Kappa Phi, Tau Beta Pi, Sigma Tau, Eta Kappa Nu. Republican. Intellectual property, Patent, Trademark and copyright. Home: 1675 Tupolo Dr San Jose CA 95124-4754 Office: M/S 26U-25 3500 Deer Creek Rd Palo Alto CA 94304-1317 E-mail: jim_simon@agilent.com., JimandRuthann@earthlink.net.

SIMON, JOEL MARK, lawyer; b. Bronx, NY, June 12, 1961; s. Gilbert and Shirley S.; m. Beth Ann Spinola, Aug. 23, 1992. BS in Indsl. and Labor Rels., Cornell U., 1982, JD, 1985. Bar: N.Y. 1986. Assoc. atty. Cahill Gordon & Reindel, N.Y.C., 1985-94; ptnr. Dorsey & Whitney, N.Y.C., 1994—95, Paul, Hastings, Janofsky & Walker LLP, N.Y.C., 1995—98, London, 1998—. Contbr. articles in law jours. Mem. ABA. Avocations: astronomy, music, camping, hiking. Office: Paul Hastings 88 Wood St London EC2V 7AJ England

SIMON, JOHN BERN, lawyer; b. Cleve., Aug. 8, 1942; s. Seymour Frank and Roslyn (Schultz) S.; children: Lindsey Helaine, Douglas Banning. BS, U. Wis., 1964; JD, DePaul U., 1967. Bar: Ill. 1967. Asst. U.S. atty. U.S. Justice Dept., Chgo., 1967-70, dep. chief civil div., 1970-71, chief civil div., 1971-74; spl. counsel to dir. Ill. Dept. Pub. Aid, Chgo., 1974-75; legal cons. to Commn. on Rev. of Nat. Policy Toward Gambling, Chgo., 1975-76; ptnr. firm Friedman & Koven, 1975-85, mem. exec. com., 1983-85; ptnr. firm Jenner & Block, 1986—. Spl. cons. to adminstr. DEA Dept. Justice, 1976-77; counsel to Gov.'s Revenue Study Commn. on Legalized Gambling, 1977-78; spl. counsel Ill. Racing Bd., 1979-80; lectr. tng. seminars and confs.; instr. U.S. Atty. Gen.'s Advocacy Inst., Washington, 1974; lectr. Nat. Conf. Organized Crime, Washington, 1975, Dade County Inst. Organized Crime, Ft. Lauderdale, Fla., 1976; faculty Cornell Inst. Organized Crime, Ithaca, N.Y., 1976, judge Miner Moot Ct. competition Northwestern U., 1971-73; mem. law coun. DePaul U., 1974-83, mem. alumni assn., 1984-85, chmn., 1975-79; adj. prof. DePaul U. Coll. Law, 1977, 81; faculty Practising Law Inst., Chgo., 1984. Contbr. articles to profl. jours. Bd. dirs. Lawyer's Trust Fund of Ill., 1998—, treas., 2000-01, v.p., 2002—, Cmty. Film Workshop of Chgo., 1977-90, Friends of Glencoe Parks, 1977-78, sec., 1978-79; mem. nominating com. Glencoe Sch. Bd., 1978-81, chmn. rules com., 1980-81; pres. Glencoe Hist. Soc., 1979-82; mem. Glencoe Zoning Bd. Appeals, Zoning Commn., Sign Bd. Appeals, 1981-86, chmn., 1984-86; mem. Ill. Inaugural Com., 1979, 83, 87, 95; bd. dirs., mem. exec. com.

Chgo. World's Fair 1992 Authority, 1983-85; mem. Chancery divsn. task force Spl. Commn. on Adminstrn. of Justice in Cook County, 1985-87; trustee De Paul U., 1990, chair phys. plant and property com., 1992-94, vice chair, 1995—; commr. Ill. Racing Bd., 1990—; gen. trustee Lincoln Acad. Ill., 1993—, regent, 1999—, chancellor, 2001—; mem. Ill. Supreme Ct. Planning and Oversight Com. for Jud. Performance Evaluation Program, 1997-98, 2000—. Recipient Bancroft-Whitney Am. Jurisprudence award, 1965, 66, Judge Learned Hand Human Rels. award Am. Jewish Com., 1994, award for outstanding svc. to legal profession DePaul U. Coll. Law, 1996, Am. ORT Jurisprudence award, 1999. Mem. ABA (com. on liaison with the judiciary 1983-95), FBA (fed. civil procedure com. 1979-85, chmn. 1985-86, bd. mgrs. 1987-89, chmn. house com. 1989-90, treas. 1990-91, 2d v.p. 1991-92, 1st v.p. 1992-93, pres. 1993-94), Ill. State Bar Assn., Women's Bar Assn., Ill. Police Assn., Ill. Sheriffs Assn., U.S. Treasury Agts. Assn., Chgo. Bar Assn., DePaul U. Alumni Assn. (pres. 1985-87, chmn. spl. gifts com. campaign, chmn. Simon Commn. 1989-91, nat. chair for ann. giving 1991-94), Std. Club. General civil litigation, Corporate, general, Insurance. Office: Jenner & Block One IBM Plz 42nd Fl Chicago IL 60611

SIMON, JOHN ROGER, lawyer; b. Los Angeles, Sept. 16, 1939; s. Abram Robert and Roserna (Finsterwald) S.; m. Mary Ellen Bartlett; children: David, Gregory, Whitney, Andrew, Kate. B.S., U. Calif.-Berkeley, 1961, LL.B., 1964. Bar: Calif. 1965, U.S. Dist. Ct. (cen. dist.) Calif. 1965. Assoc. Keatinge and Sterling, Los Angeles, 1964-65; sole practice, Palm Springs, Calif., 1965-66; assoc. Schlesinger, Schlecht & McCullough, Palm Springs, 1966-68, Fine & Pope, Los Angeles, 1968-70, Cox, Castle & Nicholson, Los Angeles, 1970-72; ptnr. Cox, Castle & Nicholson, Los Angeles and Newport Beach, Calif., 1973-86; ptnr. Sheppard, Mullin, Richter & Hampton, Newport Beach, 1986—. Contbr. articles to legal jours. Property, real (including real estate development, water). Office: Sheppard Mullin Richter Hampton 650 Town Center Dr Fl 4 Costa Mesa CA 92626-1993

SIMON, M. DANIEL, lawyer; b. London, Mar. 15, 1965; s. John J. and Sarah Simon. BSc (with 1st class honors), U. Sussex, UK, 1988; grad., Coll. of Law, London, 1991. solicitor of the Supreme Court of England and Wales. Trainee Forsyte Kerman Solicitors, London, U.K, 1991-93, solicitor, 1993-98; solicitor, ptnr. Paisner & Co., London, 1999—2001; ptnr. Collyer-Bristow Solicitors, London, 2001—. Contbr. articles to profl. jours. Dir. treas. Forest Sch. Camps (Children's Charity), 1990—; trustee Juliet Gomperts Memorial Trust (Art Charity), 1990—. Mem. Charity Law Assn., Internat. Bar Assn., European Assn. Planned Giving. Avocations: cycling, camping, croquet. Estate planning, Probate (including wills, trusts), Estate taxation. Office: Collyer-Bristow 4 Bedford Row London WC1R 4DF England E-mail: daniel.simon@collyerbristow.com.

SIMON, NANCY RUTH, lawyer; b. Gary, Ind. BSEE, Iowa State U., 1985; MBA, U. Dallas, 1988; JD, So. Meth. U., 1991. Bar: Tex. 1991, Calif. 1994, U.S. Patent and Trademark. Elec. engr. Tex. Instruments, Dallas, 1986-88; law clk. to pvt. law firms Dallas, 1989-91; law clk. U.S. Attys. Office, 1991; assoc. Felsman, Bradley, Gunter & Dillon, LLP, Ft. Worth, 1991-93; patent counsel Apple Computer, Inc., Cupertino, Calif., 1993-2000; ptnr. Simon & Koerner, LLP, Cupertino, 2000—. Realtor Coldwell Banker, San Jose, Calif., 1997—98. Co-author: (legal article) Attorney's Fees in IPL Cases; mem.: So. Meth. U. Law Rev. Jour. Air Law and Commerce, 1990—91. Bd. dirs. Sunset Pk. Sunnyvale Homeowners Assn., 1998—. Mem.: ABA, Am. Inn of Ct., San Francisco Bay Area Intellectual Property, State Bar Calif., State Bar Tex., Am. Intellectual Property Law Assn., Iowa State U. Student Alumni Assn. (mem. career awareness com. 1984—85), Mensa, Phi Delta Phi, Zeta Tau Alpha (social chmn. 1982—83, ho. mgr. 1983—84, chmn. jud. bd. 1984—85), Sigma Iota Epsilon. Avocations: reading, music, scuba diving. Computer, Intellectual property, Patent. Office: Simon & Koerner LLP 10052 Pasadena Ave Ste B Cupertino CA 95014-5945

SIMON, SEYMOUR, lawyer, former state supreme court justice; b. Chgo., Aug. 10, 1915; s. Ben and Gertrude (Rusky) S.; m. Roslyn Schultz Biel, May 26, 1954; children: John B., Nancy Simon Cooper, Anthony Biel. BS, Northwestern U., 1935, JD, 1938; LLD (hon.), John Marshall Law Sch., 1982, North Park Coll., 1986, Northwestern U., 1987. Bar: Ill. 1938. Spl. atty. Dept. Justice, 1938-42; practice law Chgo., 1946-74; judge Ill. Appellate Ct., Chgo., 1974-80; presiding justice Ill. Appellate Ct. (1st Dist., 3d Div.), 1977, 79; justice Ill. Supreme Ct., 1980-88; ptnr. Piper Rudnick (formerly Piper Marbury Rudnick & Wolfe), Chgo., 1988—. Former chmn. Ill. Low-Level Radioactive Waste Disposal Facility Siting Commn.; former dir. Nat. Gen. Corp., Bantam Books, Grosset & Dunlap, Inc., Gt. Am. Ins. Corp. Mem. Cook County Bd. Commrs., 1961-66, pres., 1962-66; pres. Cook County Forest Preserve Dist., 1962-66; mem. Pub. Bldg. Commn., City Chgo., 1962-67; Alderman 40th ward, Chgo., 1955-61, 67-74; Democratic ward committeeman, 1960-74; bd. dirs. Schwab Rehab. Hosp., 1961-71, Swedish Covenant Hosp., 1969-75. With USNR, 1942-45. Decorated Legion of Merit; recipient Pub. Svc. award Tau Epsilon Rho, 1963, Hubert L. Will award Am. Vets. Com., 1983, award of merit Decalogue Soc. Lawyers, 1986, Judge Learned Hand award Am. Jewish Com., 1994, Frances Feinberg Meml. Crown award Associated Talmud Torahs of Chgo., 1995, Bill of Rights in Action award Constl. Rights Found., 1997, Civic Contbn. award LWV Chgo., 2000; named to Sr. Citizen's Hall of Fame, City of Chgo., 1989, Hall of Fame Jewish Cmty. Ctrs. Chgo., 1989, Laureate Lincoln Acad. Ill., 1997, Chgo. Coun. Lawyers and the Appleseed Fund Justice Commitment to Justice award, 1998, Lifetime Achievement award Ill. Judges Assn., 2002. Mem. ABA, Ill. Bar Assn., Chgo. Bar Assn., Chgo. Hist. Soc., Decalogue Soc. Lawyers (Merit award 1986), Izaak Walton League, Chgo. Hort. Soc., Comml. Club Chgo., Std. Club, Variety Club, Order of Coif, Phi Beta Kappa, Phi Beta Kappa Assocs. Administrative and regulatory, Antitrust, General civil litigation. Home: 1555 N Astor St Chicago IL 60610-1673 Office: Piper Marbury Rudnick & Wolfe 203 N La Salle St Ste 1800 Chicago IL 60601-1210

SIMONE, JOSEPH R. lawyer; b. N.Y.C., Jan. 7, 1949; m. Virginia E. Simone, May 29, 1971; children: Jacquelyn, Robert. BA cum laude, Queens Coll., 1971; LLM in Taxation, NYU, 1977; JD cum laude, Fordham U., 1974. Bar: N.Y. 1975, U.S. Dist. Ct. (so. dist.) N.Y. 1975, U.S. Ct. Appeals (2d cir.) 1975. Ptnr. Patterson, Belknap, Webb & Tyler, N.Y.C., 1982-88, Schulte, Roth & Zabel, N.Y.C., 1988—2002; spl. prof. law Hofstra U. Sch. Law, 1998—2003; of counsel Pitney Hardin Kipp & Szuch LLP, N.Y.C., 2003—. Author: (textbooks) Pension Answer Book, 5th edit., 1990, Essential Facts: Pension and Profit-sharing Plans, 1999; editl. advisor Jour. of Pension Planning. Mem. Am. Arbitration Assn. (panel on multiemployer pension plans), Am. Coll. Employee Benefits (counsel 2003—), Phi Beta Kappa. Pension, profit-sharing, and employee benefits. Office: Pitney Hardin Kipp & Szuch LLP 685 3d Ave 20th Fl New York NY 10017-4024 E-mail: jsimone@pitneyhardin.com.

SIMONEAUX, JERRY W. lawyer; b. Port Arthur, Tex., Apr. 20, 1966; s. Jerry W. Simoneaux and Jane A. Ferguson; life ptnr. Christopher Bown, Dec. 12, 1991. BA in French, BBA, U. of Houston, 1997; JD, South Tex. Coll. of Law, Houston, 2001. Bar: Tex. 2001; Certificat Pratique de Francais Chambre de Commerce et de l'Industrie de Paris, 1997. Asst. aux directeurs adjoints La DATAR (French Govt.), Houston, 1996—99; pvt. practice Simoneaux Law Firm, Houston, 1999—. Gen. counsel to the bd. of directors Montrose Counseling Ctr. Endowment, Houston, 2002. Contbr. Nat. bd. Nat. Lesbian and Gay Law Assn., New York, NY, 2002—. Mem.: Stonewall Law Assn. of Greater Houston (pres. and ceo 2002—). General practice. Office: The Simoneaux Law Firm 12 Greenway Plz Ste 1100 PMB 141 Houston TX 77046 Home Fax: 281-893-0960; Office Fax: 281-893-0960. E-mail: jerry@simoneaux.com.

SIMONI, CHRISTOPHER, dean, law educator; AB in English, U. Mich., 1968; MA in English Lit., Marquette U., 1970, PhD in Am. Lit., 1977; JD, Northwestern U., 1980; MLIS, U. Tex., 1989. Prof. English Instituto Universitario Pedagogico Exptl. de Barquisimeto, Venezuela, 1973—75; from instr. to assoc. prof. Coll. Law Willamette U., 1980—85; with Tarlton Law Libr. U. Tex., Austin, 1987—90; assoc. dir., head pub. svcs. Law Libr. Northwestern U., Chgo., 1990—93, acting dir., 1993, assoc. dean libr. and info. svcs., prof. Sch. Law, 1996—; dir. Law Libr., asst. prof. Marquette U., 1994—96. Cons. Addis Ababa (Ethiopia) U. Law Faculty, 1997, U. Ghana Faculty Law, Legon, 2000. Assoc. editor: Scribes Jour. Legal Writing, 1990—92; mem. editl. bd. Perspectives: Tchg. Legal Rsch. Writing, 1994—2000. Mem.: ABA (mem law librs. com. 1999—), Chgo. Assn. Law Librs. (co-chair continuing edn. com. 1991—93), Oreg. State Bar, Am. Assn. Law Librs. (chair sect. librs. 1999—2000, mem. com. librs. and techs. 1999—2002, chair 2001—02, mem. law libr. jour. adv. com. 1996—99). Office: Northwestern U Sch Law Pritzker Legal Rsch Ctr 357 E Chicago Ave Chicago IL 60611 Business E-Mail: csimoni@law.northwestern.edu.*

SIMONIAN, JOHN S. lawyer; b. Apr. 1965; s. Samuel and Mary Simonian. BA, U. R.I.; JD, Boston U. Bar: R.I., U.S. Dist. Ct. R.I. Sole practice, Cranston, RI, 1992—. State rep. R.I. Ho. of Reps., Providence, 1991-2002, dep. majority leader, 1993-2002, chmn. commn. on criminal justice, mem. house com. on fin., joint com. on veteran's affairs. Democrat. Apostolic. Home: 43 Eldridge St Cranston RI 02910-1810 Mailing: 273 Pontiac Ave Cranston RI 02910*

SIMONS, BARBARA M. lawyer; b. N.Y.C., Feb. 7, 1929; d. Samuel A. and Minnie (Mankes) Malitz; m. Morton L. Simons, Sept. 2, 1951; 1 child, Claudia. BA, U. Mich., 1950, JD, 1952. Bar: N.Y. 1953, U.S. Supreme Ct. 1963, U.S. Ct. Appeals (D.C. cir.) 1971, (5th cir.) 1992, (1st cir.) 1994. Ptnr. Simons & Simons, Washington, 1962—. Pres. Forest Hills Citizens Assn., Washington, 1998-2002; past pres. D.C. chpt. U. Mich. Alumnae, Washington. Alumnae scholar U. Mich., 1946-50. Mem. Washington Coun. Lawyers, Nat. Partnership Women & Families, Sierra Club, Nat. Symphony Orch. Assn., Phi Beta Kappa, Phi Kappa Phi, Alpha Lambda Delta. Administrative and regulatory, FERC practice, Utilities, public. Office: Simons & Simons 5025 Linnean Ave NW Washington DC 20008-2042

SIMONS, BARRY THOMAS, lawyer; b. Lynn, Mass., Dec. 14, 1946; s. Emanuel Isador and Betty (Darish) S.; m. Laurie Jean Louder, May 5, 1985; children: Britton Eugene, Brett Jacob. BS in Govt., Am. Univ., 1968; JD, NYU, 1971. Bar: Calif. 1971, U.S. Dist. Ct. (ctrl. dist.) Calif. 1972, U.S. Ct. Appeals (9th cir.) 1972, U.S. Supreme Ct. 1978, U.S. Dist. Ct. (so. and no. dists.) Calif. 1979. Pvt. practice, Laguna Beach, Calif., 1971—. Editor (law rev.) N.Y. Law Forum, 1971. Apptd. mem. gen. plan revision com. and local coastal task force City of Laguna Beach, 1980. Mem. Orange County Bar Assn. (bd. dirs. 1981), Newport/Harbor Bar Assn. (bd. dirs. 1979), South Orange County Bar Assn. (pres. 1986, bd. dirs. 1980-95), Calif. Attys. for Criminal Justice (chair misdemeanor com. 1995), Nat. Assn. Criminal Def. Attys. (vice chair D.U.I. com.), Nat. Coll. D.U.I. Def. (founding mem., regent), Assn. Calif. D.U.I. Defenders (bd. dirs.), Deuce Defenders Assn. (specialist mem.). Criminal, Juvenile. Office: 260 Saint Anns Dr Laguna Beach CA 92651-2737 Fax: 949-497-3971. E-mail: simonslaw@aol.com., info@simonslaw.com.

SIMONS, RICHARD DUNCAN, lawyer, retired judge; b. Niagara Falls, N.Y., Mar. 23, 1927; s. William Taylor and Sybil Irene (Swick) S.; m. Muriel (Penny) E. Genung, June 9, 1951 (dec. 1992); m. Esther (Esi) Turkington Tremblay, May 21, 1994; children: Ross T., Scott R., Kathryn E., Linda A. AB, Colgate U., 1949; LLB, U. Mich., 1952; LLD (hon.), Albany Law Sch., 1983. Bar: N.Y. 1952. Pvt. practice, Rome, N.Y., 1952-63; asst. corp. counsel City of Rome, 1955-58, corp. counsel, 1960-63; justice 5th jud. dist. N.Y. Supreme Ct., 1964-83, assoc. justice appellate divsn. 3d dept., 1971-72, assoc. justice appellate divsn. 4th dept., 1973-82; assoc. judge N.Y. Ct. Appeals, 1983-96, acting chief judge, 1992-93; counsel McMahon, Grow & Getty, Rome, N.Y., 1997-00; dir. N.Y. State Capital Defender Office, 1997-2000; chief appellate judge Oneida Indian Nation, 1997—. Jurist in residence Syracuse U. Law Sch., 1998; mem. Law Sch. Admission Svcs., Bar Passage Study Com. Editorial staff: N.Y. Pattern Jury Instructions, 1979-83. Chmn. Republican City Com., 1958-62; vice chmn. Oneida County Rep. Com., 1958-62; bd. mgrs. Rome Hosp. and Murphy Meml. Hosp., 1953; mem. Chief Judge's Commn. on Fiduciary Appointments, Chief Judge's Com. to Promote Trust and Confidence in the Legal Sys., N.Y. Fair Elections Project, Inc., Campaign for Effective Justice. Served with USN, World War II. NEH fellow U. Va. Law Sch., 1979 Fellow Am. Bar Found., N.Y. State Bar Found. (chmn. 1997-98); mem. ABA, N.Y. State Bar Assn. (chair task force on ct. reorganization 1999-2002, Disting. Svc. award 2000), Oneida County Bar Assn., Rome Bar Assn., Am. Law Inst., Inst. Jud. Adminstrn. Home: 6520 Pillmore Cir Rome NY 13440-7337 Office: McMahon Grow & Getty 301 N Washington St Ste 4 Rome NY 13440-5152

SIMPKINS, WILLIAM B. federal agency administrator; BS in Bus. Adminstrn., Boston Coll., 1969; AS in Law Enforcement, Northeastern U., 1972. Police officer City of Newton, Mass., 1973—74; spl. agt. Drug Enforcement Adminstrn., 1974—86, resident agt. in charge West Palm Beach Resident Office, 1986, unit chief in planning and inspection divsn., spl. asst. to asst. adminstr. for planning and inspection, spl. asst. to the asst. adminstr. for intelligence, assoc. dep. chief insp., dep. chief insp., acting chief insp., asst. adminstr. for operational support, 1999—, acting dep. adminstr., 2001. Chmn. strategic mgmt. exec. coun. Drug Enforcement Adminstrn., bd. mem. survivor's benefit fund, mem. justice wireless comm. bd., mem. justice automated booking sys. and pub. safety wireless network exec. com.; mem. adv. com. Global Criminal Justice Info. Netowkr. Mem.: Internat. Assn. Chiefs of Police. Office: Drug Enforcement Adminstrn 2401 Jefferson Davis Hwy Alexandria VA 22301*

SIMPSON, CHARLES R., III, judge; b. Cleve., July 8, 1945; s. Charles Ralph and Anne M. Simpson; married; 3 children. BA, U. Louisville, 1967, JD, 1970. Bar: Ky. 1970, U.S. Dist. Ct. (we. dist.) Ky. 1971, U.S. Cir. Ct. (6th cir.) 1985. With Rubin, Trautwein & Hays, Louisville, 1971-75, Levin, Yussman & Simpson, Louisville, 1975-77; judge U.S. Dist. Ct. (we. dist.) Ky., Louisville, 1986—; pvt. practice Louisville, 1977-86. Part-time staff counsel Jefferson County Judge/Exec., 1978-84; adminstr. Jefferson County Alcoholic Beverage Control, 1983-84; city clk. City of Rolling Fields, 1985-86. Roman Catholic. Office: We Dist Ct Ky 247 US Courthouse 601 W Broadway Louisville KY 40202-2238 E-mail: judgesimpson@kywd.vscourts.gov.

SIMPSON, DANIEL REID, lawyer, mediator; b. Glen Alpine, N.C., Feb. 20, 1927; s. James R. and Margaret Ethel (Newton) S.; m. Mary Alice Leonard, Feb. 25, 1930; children: Mary Simpson Beyer, Ethel B. Simpson Todd, James R., II. BS, Wake Forest U., 1949, LLB, 1951. Bar: N.C. 1951, U.S. Dist. Ct. (we. dist.) N.C. 1951, U.S. Ct. Appeals (4th and 5th cirs.) 1980; cert. mediator. Former ptnr. Simpson Aycock PA, Morganton, N.C.; of counsel Simpson, Kuehnert, Vinay & Bellas, P.A., Morganton. Author: American Angels, 2001. Mem. N.C. Ho. of Reps., 1959-65; mem. N.C. Senate, 1984-96; del. Rep. Nat. Conv., 1968, 76; mem. N.C. Rep. Exec. Com. Served with AUS, 1943-45, PTO. Recipient Guardian Small Bus. award Order of Longleaf Pine; named to NRA Legion of Honor; sports complex named in his honor by Town of Glen Alpine, N.C. Mem. N.C. Bar Assn., Burke County Bar Assn., Masons. Baptist. Corporate, general, Franchising. Home: 2358 E Point Rd Nebo NC 28761-9694 Office: Simpson Kuehnert Vinay & Bellas PA 216 N Sterling St Morganton NC 28655 also: PO Box 1329 Morganton NC 28680-1329

SIMPSON, JOHN M. lawyer; b. Ponca City, Okla., Sept. 26, 1950; AB, Harvard U., 1972; JD, Columbia U., 1978. Bar: D.C. 1979, N.C. 1988. Mem. Fulbright & Jaworski L.L.P., Washington. Office: Fulbright & Jaworski LLP Market Square 801 Pennsylvania Ave NW Washington DC 20004-2615 E-mail: jsimpson@fulbright.com.

SIMPSON, LARRY DEAN, lawyer; b. Jacksonville, Fla., June 10, 1949; s. Rufus McCord and Louise Smith Simpson; m. Linda Vaughan, Apr. 17, 1970; children: Louis Martin, Dean McCord. BS, Fla. State U., Tallahassee, 1971, JD, 1973. Bar: Fla. (Criminal Trial Lawyer) 1988. Asst. state atty. State Attorney's Office, Tallahassee, 1974—80; ptnr. Davis, Judkins & Simpson, Tallahassee, 1980—93, Kitchen, Judkins, Simpson & High, Tallahassee, 1993—. Master: Tallahassee Am. Inns of Ct. (charter mem. and master of the bench 1994—96); mem.: Fla. Assn. Criminal Def. Attys. (pres., tallahassee chpt. 1994—95), Am. Acad. Forensic Scis., Tallahassee Bar Assn. (pres. 1987—88), Fla. Bar (chair; grievance com. 1982—85, chair: judicial qualifications comn. 1995—98). State civil litigation, Federal civil litigation, Criminal. Office: Kitchen Judkins Simpson et al 1102 North Gadsden St Tallahassee FL 32303 Office Fax: 850-561-1471. E-mail: lsimpson@kjshlaw.com.

SIMPSON, LYLE LEE, lawyer; b. Des Moines, Oct. 15, 1937; s. R. Clair and Martha B. (Accola) S. BA, Drake U., 1960, JD, 1963. Bar: Iowa 1963, U.S. Dist. Ct. (so. and no. dists.) Iowa 1963, U.S. Ct. Appeals (8th cir.) 1963, U.S. Tax Ct. 1963, U.S. Supreme Ct. 1970, U.S. Ct. Mil. Appeals 1972. Pvt. practice, Des Moines, 1963—; mem. Beving and Swanson, Des Moines, 1964-68; sr. ptnr. Peddicord, Simpson & Sutphin, Des Moines, 1968-83; pres. Dreher, Simpson & Jensen, PC, 1984—. Gen. counsel campaign com. Gov. Iowa, 1978-98. Contbr. articles to profl. jours. Chmn. bd. trustees Broadlawns Med. Ctr., 1974-80; mem. Iowa Inaugural Com., 1983, 87, 89, 91, 95; bd. dirs. YMCA Boys Camp, 1967-86, Home, Inc., 1981-85, Project H.E.L.P.E.R., 1983-87, Batten Found.; pres., bd. dirs. Polk County Health Svcs., 1972-88; chmn. Iowa Health Facilities Coun., 1988-93; pres. First Unitarian Ch., 1958-70, Iowa Humanities Bd., 1988-94, Humanist Found., 1980—, East High Alumni Found., 1992-2000; treas. Iowa Humanities Found., 1994-99, vice-chmn., Iowa Health Found., 1993—; mem. investment com., fin. com. Iowa Health Sys., 2000—. Recipient Oren E. Scott award, Class of 1915 award in liberal arts Drake U., 1960. Mem. ABA, Iowa Bar Assn., Polk County Bar Assn., Am. Arbitration Assn., Am. Humanist Assn. (pres. 1979-89), Prairie Club (pres. 1992), Morning Club (pres. 1965), Le Chevaliers de vin Club (pres. 1976-85), YMCA Heritage Club (pres.), Masons, Scottish Rite (Shriner, 33 degree), Rotary. Republican. Congregationalist. Corporate, general, Estate planning, Property, real (including real estate development, water). Address: 222 Equitable Bldg 604 Locust St Des Moines IA 50309-3723 E-mail: lsimpson@dreherlaw.com.

SIMPSON, ROBERT GLENN, lawyer; b. Seattle, June 27, 1932; s. Harold Vernon and Anna Rondeau (McCabe) S.; m. Josephine Anne Heald, June 7, 1959; children: Jenifer Jane, Thomas Glenn, Mary Elizabeth. BS, U. Oreg., 1954; LLB, Willamette U., 1959. Bar: Oreg. 1959. Assoc. William B. Adams Law Office, Portland, Oreg., 1959-67; ptnr. Adams McLaughlin & Simpson, Portland, 1967-70, Schwabe Williamson & Wyatt, Portland, 1970—. Trustee, sec. Legacy Good Samaritan Hosp. and Med. Ctr., Portland, 1983-89, mem. cmty. bd., 1989-98; trustee, chancellor Episcopal Diocese of Oreg., Portland, 1988—. Mem. Oreg. State Bar (exec. com. health law sect. 1987-90), Am. Health Lawyers Assn. (program com. 1987-88), Oreg. Acad. Healthcare Attys. (pres. 1977-78, legis. com. 1989), Multnomah Athletic Club, Univ. Club. Corporate, general, Health, Transportation. Home: 13345 SW Iron Mountain Blvd Portland OR 97219-9306 Office: Schwabe Williamson & Wyatt 1211 SW 5th Ave Ste 1800 Portland OR 97204-3795 E-mail: rsimpson@schwabe.com.

SIMPSON, RUSSELL AVINGTON, retired law firm administrator; b. Greybull, Wyo., June 19, 1935; s. William Avington and Margaret E. (Draper) S.; m. Margarita A. del Valle, Dec. 19, 1960; children: Margaret E., Robert A., Alexandra P., Christina M. BS with honors, U. Wyo., 1957; LLB, Harvard U., 1965. Bar: Tex. 1965, Mass. 1966. Assoc. Bonilla, de Pena, Read & Bonilla, Corpus Christi, Tex., 1965-66; asst. dean, dir. admissions Harvard Law Sch., Cambridge, Mass., 1966-75, asst. dean, dir. fin. aid, 1972-78, asst. dean for fin. and gen. adminstrn., 1978-84; dir. adminstrn. Hill & Barlow, Boston, 1984-90; v.p., treas. The Archs. Collaborative, Cambridge, 1991-92, ret., 1992. Chmn. devel. com. Law Sch. Data Assembly Service, 1969; pres. bd. dirs. Law Sch. Admissions Services, Newtown, Pa., 1979-80, bd. dirs., 1989-91; trustee Law Sch. Admission Coun., 1968-70, 72-78, 81-82, chmn. svcs. com. 1972-74, chmn. test devel. and rsch. 1976-78; founder Grad. and Profl. Sch. Fin. Aid Coun. Mem. Belmont (Mass.) Town Meeting, 1975-96, Belmont Sch. Com., 1977-83. Capt. USAF, 1957-62. Mem. Tex. Bar Assn., Rotary (bd. dirs. Belmont 1978-80), Phi Kappa Phi. Democrat. Home: 49 Elizabeth Rd Belmont MA 02478-3819 E-mail: russsmpsn@earthlink,net.

SIMPSON, RUSSELL GORDON, lawyer, former mayor, not-for-profit developer, consultant; b. Springfield, Mass., May 22, 1927; s. Archer Roberts and Maude Ethel (Gordon) S.; m. Bickley F. Flower, Sept. 11, 1954; children: Barbara G., Elisabeth Pires-Fernandes, Helen Blair. BA, Yale U., 1951; JD, Boston U., 1956; postgrad., Parker Sch. Internat. Law, 1962. Bar: Mass. 1956, U.S. Dist. Ct. (fed. dist.) Mass. 1957, U.S. Ct. Appeals (2d cir.) 1958, U.S. Supreme Ct. 1980. Advt. mgr. Burden Bryant Co., Springfield, 1951-53; assoc. Goodwin, Procter & Hoar, Boston, 1956-64, ptnr., 1965-87, of counsel, 1987—. Sr. advisor to pres. World Learning, Inc., Brattleboro, Vt., 1988-89, exec. v.p., 1989-90, sr. v.p., 1990-91, trustee, 1991—, exec. com., 1994—; trustee, mem. exec. com., Save the Children Fedn., Westport, Conn., 1995-2002; mem. exec. group Internat. Save the Children Alliance, Geneva, Switzerland and London, Eng., 1996—; dir., vice chmn., mem. exec. com., Cmty. Found. Palm Beach and Martin Counties, West Palm Beach, Fla., 1994-2000; counselor to not-for-profit orgns., 1991—. Author: The Lawyer's Basic Corporate Practice Manual, 1971, rev. edit., 1978, 84, 87. Mayor Jupiter Island, Fla., 1993-99; hon. consul New Eng. of Bolivia, 1958-82, mem. spl. com. to revise Mass. Corrupt Practices Act, 1961-62; bd. govs. Jupiter Island Club, 2000-2002; mem. blue ribbon commn. Martin County Fla. Econ. Coun. Named Outstanding Young Man of Greater Boston, 1963. Fellow Am. Bar Found., Mass. Bar Found.; mem. Mass. Bar Assn. (chmn. banking and bus. law sect. 1980-83, bd. dels., exec. com. 1983-87, v.p. 1985-87), ABA (corp. banking and bus. law sect., com. on law firms, co-chmn. com. on law firm governance, panel on corp. law ednl. programs), Hobe Sound Yacht Club (gov., sec. 2001-2002). Home: 1400 Sorolla Avenue Coral Gables FL 33134-3520

SIMPSON, STEVEN DREXELL, lawyer; b. Sturgis, Mich., Sept. 20, 1953; s. Rex and Lorraine Simpson; m. Peggy Deibert, Apr. 28, 1979; children: Andrew Drexell, Christine Elizabeth, Marianne Tyner. BA, Hillsdale (Mich.) Coll., 1975; JD, Wake Forest U., 1978; LLM in Taxation, Georgetown U., 1981. Bar: Fla. 1978, D.C. 1980, N.C. 1984. Assoc. Bradford, Williams et al, Miami, Fla., 1978-80, Webster & Chamberlain, Washington, 1980-82, Fisher, Wayland et al, Washington, 1982-84, Maupin, Taylor & Ellis, P.A., Raleigh, N.C., 1984-98; ptnr. Law Offices of Steven D. Simpson P.A., 1998—. Author: Taxation of Broadcasters, 1984, Tax-Exempt Organizations: Organizational and Operational Requirements, 2000, Tax-Exempt Organizations: Reporting, Disclosure and Other Procedural Aspects, 2000, Taxable Expenditures, 2000, Tax Compliance for Tax-Exempt Organizations, 2003; contbr. articles to profl. jours. Mem. ABA (exemp orgns. com.). Republican. Methodist. Avocations: golf, running.

Health, Non-profit and tax-exempt organizations, Taxation, general. Home: 409 Hillandale Dr Raleigh NC 27609-7036 Office: Landmark Center II 4601 Six Forks Rd Ste 530 Raleigh NC 27609-5286 E-mail: s.simpsonlaw@verizon.net.

SIMS, JOHN R. food products executive; b. 1950; Bachelors, JD, U. Mo. Dep. gen. counsel Federated Dept. Stores, Inc., 1990—2002; exec. v.p., gen. counsel Albertson's Inc., Boise, Idaho, 2002—. Office: Albertsons Corp Hdqr 250 Park Center Blvd Boise ID 83706

SIMS, JOHN ROGERS, JR., lawyer; b. Red Star, W.Va., Apr. 10, 1924; s. John Rogers and Myrtle (Hutchison) S.; m. Geraldine L. Bucklew, Oct. 8, 1966; children: John Rogers III, Joyce Rebecca. BS in Commerce, U. Va., 1950, LLB, 1952. Assoc. Dow, Lohnes & Albertson, Washington, 1953-57; gen. counsel D.C. Transit Sys., Inc., Washington, 1957-65; individual practice law Washington, 1965-68; ptnr. Wrape and Hernly, Arlington, Va., 1968-71, Sims, Walker & Steinfeld (and predecessor firm), Washington, 1972-95; pvt. practice Nellysford, Va., 1995—. Chmn. bd. dirs. John Sims Assocs., Inc., 1978-2000, Purnell Bros. Transport, Ltd., 1981-91; co-founder, bd. dirs., gen. counsel A Presdl. Classroom for Young Ams., Inc., chmn. bd. dirs., 1979-83; dir., v.p., gen. counsel, sec. SunWorld Internat. Airways, Inc., 1984-88; chmn. corp. bd. adv. Omniplex World Svcs. Corp., 1997—. Vice chmn. Falls Church (Va.) Planning Commn., 1958-64; pres. Falls Church Republican Party, 1961-62; bd. dirs. Heart Assn. No. Va., Inc., pres., 1963-64; bd. dirs., v.p., gen. counsel Commonwealth Doctors Hosp., Fairfax, Va., 1967-74; bd. dirs., vice chmn. Jefferson Area Bd. for Aging. Served with Armed Forces, 1943-45. Mem. ABA, W.Va. Bar Assn., D.C. Bar Assn., Va. State Bar, Motor Carrier Lawyers Assn. (nat. pres. 1971-72), Assn. for Transp. Law, Logistics and Policy, Va. Trial Lawyers Assn., Rotary, Masons (Shriner), Washington Golf and Country Club, Farmington Country Club (Charlottesville, Va.). Presbyterian. Administrative and regulatory, Federal civil litigation, Corporate, general. Home: 31 Sawmill Creek Dr Nellysford VA 22958-9538 also: PO Box 623 Nellysford VA 22958-0623 E-mail: sims@firstva.com.

SIMS, REBECCA LITTLETON, lawyer; b. Macon, Ga., May 24, 1957; d. William Harvey and Carlan Patricia (Hammond) Littleton; m. Charles Neil Sims, Jr., Dec. 29, 1984; children: Charles Neil III, William Vickers, Caroline Greer. Student, Tex. A&M U., 1977; JD, Baylor U., 1981; BA in Polit. Sci. with honors, U. South, 1979; MPA, Valdosta State U., 2002. Bar: Ga. 1983, U.S. Dist. Ct. (so. dist.) Ga. 1984, U.S. Dist. Ct. (no. dist.) Ga. 1985, U.S. Dist. Ct. (mid. dist.) Ga. 1992, U.S. Supreme Ct. 2001. Law clk., Waco, Tex., 1981, Waycross Jud. Cir., Waycross and Douglas, Ga., 1982-83; asst. dist. atty. Waycross cir. Dist. Atty.'s Office, Douglas, 1983-84; spl. asst. to atty. gen. Dept. Family and Children's Svcs., Coffee County, 1988-90; pvt. practice Douglas, 1985-92; state ct. solicitor Coffee County, Ga., 1989-96; in-house counsel Sims Funeral Home, 1997-99; instr. polit. sci. South Ga. Coll., Douglas, 2000—. Mem Bar of United States Supreme Ct., 2001. Mem. altar guild St. Andrew's Episcopal Ch., Douglas, 1983-90, 2000—, vestryman, clk. of vestry, 1986-88, 2002—; bd. dirs. Shelter for Abused Women, Waycross, 1986-87; trustee U. South, Diocese of Ga., Savannah, 1988-91; mem. First Meth. Ch., Douglas, Ga., 1991-99, United Meth. Women Cir. # 8, 1991-98; dir. Vacation Bible Sch., 1997, 98; legis. aid Charles Neil Sims, Jr., Ga. Ho. Reps., 1997—. Mem. State Bar Ga., Acad. Boosters Club (awards chmn. 1997-98), Beta Sigma Phi (pres. 1997-98), Ga. Regent's Adv. Com. Polit. Sci. Avocations: gardening, reading, needlework, cooking, antiques. Criminal, Family and matrimonial, Probate (including wills, trusts). Office: PO Box 2352 Douglas GA 31534-2352 E-mail: rsims@sga.edu.

SIMS, ROGER W. lawyer; b. Cleve., Aug. 3, 1950; BA with high honors, U. Fla., 1972, JD, 1974. Bar: Fla. 1975. Mem. Holland & Knight, Orlando, Fla. Mem. Moot Ct. U. Fla.; contbr. to profl mags and jours. Mem. ABA (mem. standing com. on environ. law 2000—), Fla. Bar Assn. (chmn. environ., land use law sect. 1988-89), Phi Beta Kappa, Phi Kappa Phi, Omicron Delta Kappa, Phi Alpha Delta, Fla. Blue Key. Administrative and regulatory, Environmental, Property, real (including real estate development, water). Office: Holland & Knight PO Box 1526 200 S Orange Ave Ste 2600 Orlando FL 32801-3453

SIMS, WILSON, lawyer; b. Nashville, Dec. 24, 1924; s. Cecil and Grace (Wilson) S.; m. Linda Bell, Aug. 12, 1948; children: Linda Rickman, Suzanne, Wilson. BA, U. N.C., 1946; JD, Vanderbilt U., 1948. Bar: Tenn. 1948. Since practiced in, Nashville; ptnr. Bass, Berry & Sims; gen. counsel, dir. Baird Ward Printing Co., Southeastern Capital Corp., Martha White Foods, Synercon Corp., Forrest Life Ins. Co., Charter Co., The Bailey Co., Kenworth of Tenn., Inc. Chmn. Tenn. Commn. for Human Devel., Tenn. Commn. on Continuing Legal Edn.; mem. Tenn. Gen. Assembly; bd. dirs. Nashville YMCA, United Cerebal Palsy, Kidney Found., Matthew 25, McKendree Village; trustee Meharry Med. Coll., Webb Sch., Bell Buckle, Tenn.; adv. bd. Jr. League; mem. bd. visitors U. N.C. 1st lt. USMCR, 1942-45, 50-52. Fellow Am. Bar Found. (life), Nashville Bar Found.; mem. ABA, Tenn. Bar Assn. (past speaker ho. of dels., past pres.), Nashville Bar Assn. (past pres., dir., Pub. Svc. award), Tenn. Bar Found. (past chmn.), Am. Judicature Soc., Am. Acad. Polit. Sci., Vanderbilt U. Law Alumni Assn. (past pres., Disting. Svc. award), Nashville C. of C. (2 terms bd. govs.), Belle Meade Country (bd. dirs.), Wade Hampton Golf Club, High Hampton Colony Club (bd. dirs.). Methodist. Federal civil litigation, State civil litigation, Corporate, general. Home: 22 Foxhall Close Nashville TN 37215-1862 Office: Bass Berry & Sims 2700 First Am Ctr Nashville TN 37238

SIMSON, GARY JOSEPH, law educator; b. Newark, Mar. 18, 1950; s. Marvin and Mildred (Silberg) S.; m. Rosalind Slivka, Aug. 15, 1971; children: Nathaniel, Jennie Anne. BA, Yale Coll., 1971; JD, Yale U., 1974. Bar: Conn. 1974, N.Y. 1980. Law clk. to judge U.S. Ct. Appeals 2d Cir., 1974-75; from asst. prof. law to prof. law U. Tex., 1975-80; prof. law Cornell U., Ithaca, N.Y., 1980-97, prof. law, assoc. dean, 1997—. Vis. prof. law Cornell U., Ithaca, 1979-80, U. Calif., Berkeley, 1986; chmn. adv. bd. law casebook series Carolina Acad. Press. Author: Issues and Perspectives in Conflict of Laws, 1985, 3d edit., 1997; contbr. articles to profl. jours. Mem. ABA, ACLU, Phi Beta Kappa. Office: Cornell U Law Sch Myron Taylor Hall Ithaca NY 14853 E-mail: simson@law.mail.cornell.edu.

SINCLAIR, JULIE MOORES WILLIAMS, lawyer, law library consultant; b. Montgomery, Ala., May 2, 1954; d. Benjamin Buford and Marilyn Moores (Simpson) Williams; m. Winfield James Sinclair, Dec. 16, 1978. BA, U. of South, 1976; MLS, U. Ala., Tuscaloosa, 1977; JD, Washington U., St. Louis, 1987. Bar: Ala. 1989, U.S. Dist. Ct. (no. dist.) Ala. 1989. Serials libr. Ala. Dept. Archives and History, Montgomery, 1977; cataloguing libr. Ala. Pub. Libr. Svc., Montgomery, 1978; league libr. Ala. League Municipalities, Montgomery, 1978-84; asst. libr. Mo. Ct. Appeals, St. Louis, 1984-86, law clk., 1987-88; cons. Law Libr. Cons., Birmingham, Ala., 1988—; staff atty. Ct. Civil Appeals Ala., 2001—. Contbr. numerous articles to profl. jours. Mem. Ala. Bar Assn., Ala. Libr. Assn., Am. Assn. Law Librs., Law Libr. Assn. Ala. (charter, v.p. 1992-93, pres. 1993-94), Ala. Fedn. Bus. and Profl. Women (pres. 1997-98), Order of Gownsmen, Phi Alpha Theta. Episcopalian. Avocations: travel and sightseeing, reading, attending theatre, especially Shakespeare. Office: Ct Civil Appeals 300 Dexter Ave Montgomery AL 36104 E-mail: jmwsinclair@mindspring.com.

SINDER, JOAN B. lawyer; b. Willimantic, Conn., Oct. 20, 1949; d. John J. and Bernadette (Lambert) S. BA, Wheaton Coll., 1971; JD, Syracuse U., 1974. Bar: Conn. 1974, U.S. Dist. Ct. Conn. 1978. Pvt. practice, Willimantic, 1974—. Corporator Savs. Inst., Willimantic, 1978—. Mem. Conn. Bar Assn., Windham County Bar Assn. Roman Catholic. Avocation: show horses. Family and matrimonial, Probate (including wills, trusts), Property, real (including real estate development, water). Office: 756 Main St Willimantic CT 06226-2504

SINDERBRAND, DAVID I. lawyer; b. Atlantic City, June 14, 1961; s. Saul Albert and Joyce Rita Sinderbrand; m. Jennifer M. Sinderbrand, June 24, 1995. BA, Ithaca Coll., 1983; JD, Calif. Western Sch. Law, San Diego, 1987. Bar: N.J. 1988, U.S. Dist. Ct. N.J. 1988; cert. civil trial atty. N.J. Supreme Ct., 2000. Lawyer Horn, Goldberg et al, Atlantic City, 1988-90, Manchel, Lundy & Lessin, Phila., 1990-92, Westmoreland, Vesper et al, Atlantic City, 1992—. Mem. Am. Trial Lawyers Assn., Atlantic County Bar Assn. General civil litigation, Personal injury (including property damage), Product liability. Office: Westmoreland Vesper et al Bayport One Ste 500 Pleasantville NJ 08232

SINDON, GEOFFREY STUART, lawyer; b. Dec. 3, 1952; s. Arlen Earle and Rita Nathalie (Dillon) S.; children: Jennifer Lorraine, Darryl Aaron. BS cum laude, U. Utah, 1973; JD, Pepperdine U., 1976. Bar: Calif. 1976, U.S. Dist. Ct. (cen. dist.) Calif. 1977, U.S. Dist. Ct. (no. dist.) Calif. 1980, U.S. Dist. Ct. Appeals (9th cir.) 1980. Mem. Litt and Wells, L.A., 1977—78, Cohen and Steinhart, L.A., 1978—82, Trope and Trope, L.A., 1982—83, Sindon and Vogt, L.A., 1983—88; pvt. practice, 1988—. Mediator L.A. Superior Ct., 1996—2000. Mem.: State Bar Calif., L.A. County Bar Assn., San Fernando Valley Bar Assn. State civil litigation, Family and matrimonial, Probate (including wills, trusts). Office: 12145 Mission Ridge Way Granada Hills CA 91344 E-mail: GSindon@socal.rr.com.

SINE, WESLEY FRANKLIN, lawyer; b. Salt Lake City, Dec. 13, 1936; s. Ira F. and Dora Ann (Popp) S.; m. Barbara A. Belnap, June 6, 1958 (div. 1978); children: Barri Ann, Jeri Charlene, Wesley D., Anthony L.; m. Melva Carol Holmes, Dec. 30, 1978; children: Tammy Louise, Dorethea Ann, Christina Jean, Jared F., Katrina C., Joshua F., Kathryn M. JD, U. Utah, 1962. Bar: Utah 1962, U.S. Dist. Ct. Utah 1962, U.S. Ct. Appeals (10th cir.) 1962. Pvt. practice, Salt Lake City. Bd. dirs. Utah Hotel Motel Assn., Salt Lake City, 1963-79, pres. 1976; pres. Salt Lake Valley Inn, Salt Lake City, 1978, Utah Apt. Assn., 1977, Utah State Bowling Proprs., 1965, 83. Mem. Rep. Lincoln Day Club, Salt Lake City, 1985—. Mem.: Kiwanis (pres. Salt Lake City 1984—85, 1999—2000, dist. adminstr. collegiate orgn. Utah-Idaho dist. 1988—, lt. gov. divsn. 2 Utah 1989—90, George F. Hixon fellow award 2000). Mem. Lds Ch. Corporate, general, Family and matrimonial, Personal injury (including property damage). Home: 451 Northmont Way Salt Lake City UT 84103-3322

SING, WILLIAM BENDER, lawyer; b. Houston, Oct. 16, 1947; s. William Bender Sr. and Alice Irene S.; m. Doris Anne Spradley, Sept. 1, 1967; children: Erin Elaine, Emily Elizabeth. BS cum laude, U. Houston, 1968, JD magna cum laude, 1971; MLA, U. St. Thomas, 1995. Bar: Tex. 1971. Assoc. Fulbright & Jaworski, LLP, Houston, 1973-80, ptnr., 1980—. Elder, trustee St. Andrew's Presbyn. Ch., Houston; past pres., bd. dirs. St. Andrew's Presbyn. Sch., Houston; past pres. Houston C.C. Place Civic Assn. 1st lt. U.S. Army, 1971-73. Mem. ABA, Tex. Bar Assn., Houston Bar Assn., Order of the Barons Law Honor Soc., U. Houston Alumni Orgn. (life), Phi Delta Phi (life), Phi Kappa Phi, Omicron Delta Epsilon. Presbyterian. Avocation: reading history and literature. Bankruptcy, Property, real (including real estate development, water). Office: Fulbright & Jaworski LLP 1301 Mckinney St Houston TX 77010-3031

SINGER, MICHAEL HOWARD, lawyer; b. NYC, Nov. 22, 1941; s. Jack and Etta (Appelbaum) S.; m. Saundra Jean Kupperman, June 1, 1962; children: Allison Jill, Pamela Faith. BS in Econs., U. Pa., 1962; JD, NYU, 1965, LLM in Taxation, 1968. Bar: N.Y. 1965, U.S. Ct. Claims 1968, U.S. Supreme Ct. 1969, U.S. Ct. Appeals (6th cir.) 1970, D.C. 1972, U.S. Tax Ct. 1972, Nev. 1973, U.S. Ct. Appeals (9th cir.) 1973. Law asst. Appellate Term Supreme Ct., N.Y.C., 1965-68; trial lawyer Ct. Claims Tax Div., Washington, 1968-72; tax lawyer Beckley, DeLanoy & Jemison, Las Vegas, 1972-74; ptnr. Oshins, Singer, Segal & Morris, Las Vegas, 1974-87; pvt. practice Las Vegas, 1987; ptnr. Michael H. Singer Ltd., Las Vegas, 1987-96, Singer, Brown, and Barringer, LLC, Las Vegas, 1996-99, Singer & Brown, LLC, 1999—. Settlement judge Nev. Supreme Ct., 1997—. Pres. Las Vegas chpt. NCCJ, 1980-82. Mem. ABA, ABI, Nev. Bar Assn., Las Vegas Country Club (bd. dirs. 1999—, v.p. 2001-02, chmn. membership com. 2002—). Democrat. Jewish. Avocations: golf, tennis. Commercial, contracts (including sales of goods; commercial financing), Corporate, general, Property, real (including real estate development, water). Home: 4458 Los Reyes Ct Las Vegas NV 89121-5341 Office: Singer & Brown LLC 520 S 4th St Fl 2 Las Vegas NV 89101-6524 E-mail: mhsinger@lvcm.com.

SINGER, MYER R(ICHARD), lawyer; b. Everett, Mass., Oct. 24, 1938; s. Nathan and Celia (Rudin) Singer; m. Elaine Doris Ginesky, June 17, 1962; children: Andrew L., Stephen D., Jocelyn G. BSBA, Boston U., 1960, LLB, 1963. Bar: Mass. 1963, U.S. Ct. Appeals (1st cir.) 1963. Atty. Boston Legal Aid Soc., 1963—64; pvt. practice Dennis Port, Mass., 1965—2001; ptnr. Singer & Singer, LLC, 2001—. Trustee, corporator, mem. bd. investment Cape Cod Five Cents Savs. bank, Harwich Port, Mass.; trustee Cape Cod Mus. of Natural History, 2001—; faculty Mass. Continuing Legal Edn., Inc., 1985, 1990—98; program chmn. Real Estate Devel. Cape Cod-Mass. Bar Inst., 1999; spkr. in field. Co-author: (book) Creation and Care of Condominiums, 1985, Everything You Need to Know about the Cape Cod Commission Act, 1990. Pres. Dennis Yarmouth Band Parents, 1986—87; mem. adv. bd. Cape Mus. Fine Arts, Dennis, 1988—96; former trustee Cape Cod Synagogue; mem., clk. Yarmouth (Mass.) Zoning Bd. Appeals, 1980—86; former bd. dirs. Cape Cod and Island chpt. of Mass. Heart Assn.; former pres. Legal Svcs. of Cape Cod and Island, Inc. Mem.: ABA, Barnstable County Bar Assn. (mem. exec. com. 1999—), Mass. Bar Assn. (chmn. bar assn. program real estate devel. Cape Cod 1999). Avocations: boating, photography. Land use and zoning (including planning), Property, real (including real estate development, water). Home: 238 Greenland Circle East Dennis MA 02641-1302 Office: PO Box 67 26 Upper County Rd Dennis Port MA 02639-0067 E-mail: msinger.singerlaw@earthlink.net.

SINGER, PAUL MEYER, lawyer; b. Pitts., May 20, 1943; s. Sidney Morris and Doris (Lyttle) S.; m. Laurie Stern, 1989. BS in Bus., U. Minn., 1965; JD, U. Pitts., 1968; LLM, Harvard U., 1970. Law clk. to presiding justice Pa. Supreme Ct., Pitts., 1970-71; atty. Am. Express Credit Corp., N.Y.C., 1971-73; ptnr. Reed Smith LLP, Pitts., 1973—. Mem. Am. Coll. Bankruptcy (bd. dirs.), Harvard-Yale-Princeton Club, Duquesne Club. Banking, Bankruptcy, Corporate, general. Office: Reed Smith LLP 435 6th Ave Pittsburgh PA 15219-1886

SINGER, PAULA NOYES, lawyer, software company executive; b. Portsmouth, N.H., Aug. 2, 1944; d. Paul Snowman and Grace Marion (Smith) Noyes; m. Wayne Allen Goodrich, Sept. 6, 1964 (div. 1973); 1 child, Beth Ann; m. Gary Philip Singer, June 1, 1976; 1 child, Samantha Anne. BA, U. Maine, Orono, 1966; JD, U. Maine, Portland, 1978. Bar: Maine 1978, Mass. 1978, U.S. Dist. Ct. Maine 1978, U.S. Dist. Ct. Mass. 1979, U.S. Tax Ct. 1985, U.S. Ct. Appeals (1st cir.) 1996, U.S. Supreme Ct. 1986. Programmer New Eng. Mut. Life Ins. Co., Boston, 1966-67; programmer to sr. systems analyst Union Mut. Life Ins. Co., Portland, 1968-77; tax specialist Peat, Marwick, Mitchell & Co., Portland, 1977-79; internat. personnel specialist Arthur D. Little, Cambridge, Mass., 1979-85; lawyer Vacovec, Miller & Rothenberg, Brookline, Mass., 1985-88; ptnr. Vacovec, Rothenberg, Mayotte & Singer, Newton, Mass., 1988-90, Vacovec, Mayotte & Singer, Newton, Mass., 1990—; co-founder, CEO Windstar Techs., Inc., 1994—; co-founder, pres. Windstar Publ., Inc., 2000—. Contbr. articles to profl. jours. Bd. dirs. U. Maine Law Sch. Alumni, 1989-95. Mem. ABA, Mass. Bar Assn., Boston Bar Assn., Am. Assn. Immigration Lawyers, Women in World Trade (bd. dirs. 1987-89), ADL Alumni Assn. (bd. dirs. 187-95), Internat. Fiscal Assn., Phi Beta Kappa, Phi Kappa Phi. Democrat. Jewish. Avocation: boating. Private international, Estate taxation, Personal income taxation. Office: Vacovec Mayotte & Singer 255 Washington St Ste 340 Newton MA 02458-1634

SINGER-FRANKES, DEBORAH, lawyer; d. David Juris and Linda (Cohen) F.; m. Chaim Singer-Frankes, Jan. 5, 1992. BA in Govt., Cornell U., 1989; JD, U. Calif. Sch. of Law, 1994. Bar: Calif., 1996. Trial atty. Aux. Legal Svcs., Inc., L.A., 1996-99; assoc. L.A. County Counsel, Monterey Park, Calif., 1999—. Mem. L.A. County Bar Assn. Office: Office Co Counsel 201 Centre Plaza Dr Ste 1 Monterey Park CA 91754-2142

SINGH, HARBACHAN, solicitor, barrister; b. Klang, Malaysia, Mar. 11, 1939; came to U.S., 1969; s. Kishen Singh and Dhan Kaur; m. Susil Kaur, Jan. 12, 1963; children: Sukhwant, Ramesh, Praveen. Barrister-at-law, Honorable Soc. Lincoln's Inn, London, 1967; MA, St. John's U., 1981. Police interpreter Royal Malaysian Police, Malaysia, 1957-63; advocate, solicitor Allen & Gledhill Law Firm, Kuala Lumpur, Malaysia, 1967-69; chief of travel UN, N.Y.C., 1969-79, chief of transp., 1979-90, chmn. hdqrs. com. on contracts, 1995—99, chmn. hdqrs. property survey bd., 1987—99; mng. dir. Triangle Mortgage Svcs., Inc., 2000—. UN team leader Return of Property from Iraq to Kuwait, UN Security Coun. Resolution, 1994-95; sr. exec. officer UN Mission East Timor, 1999; chmn. UN Appointments and Promotion Com., 1987-89; elected mem. UN Panel of Counsel Joint Appeals bd., 1987-92; mem. U.S. Presdl. Gateway Improvement Task Force; mem. Staff Union, 1969-99. Mem. Queens Borough County Cmty. Bd. 8, 2000—; ofcl. del. Queens Borough Gen. Assembly, 2003—; bd. dirs. Annual Meml. Day March and Celebrations Com., 2003—, Hollis Park Gardens Assn., Queens, 2002—, Ea. Queens Dem. Club, 2002—. Home: 193-12 Foothill Ave Hollis NY 11423-1259 E-mail: hsingh@nyc.rr.com., Harbachan@hotmail.com.

SINGH, HARCHARAN, law librarian; b. Lahore, Pakistan, Sept. 5, 1937; came to U.S., 1970; s. Surjan Singh and Ajit Kaur; m. Surinder Kaur, May 10, 1938; children: Amardeep K., Harbinder. BA, Punjab U., Chandigarh, India, 1957, LLB, 1959, diploma in libr. sci., 1962, MA in Polit. Sci., 1969; MLS, CUNY, Flushing, 1973. Head libr. dept. law Punjab U., Chandigar, 1964-70; acquisition and serials libr. New Sch. Social Rsch., N.Y.C., 1973-79; asst. head dept. serials SUNY, Stonybrook, 1979-82; acquisition and serials libr. Bklyn. Law Sch., 1989—. Home: 14 Botany Ln Stony Brook NY 11790-2520 Office: Bklyn Law Sch Libr 250 Jora Lemon St New York NY 11790 E-mail: hcsingh@brooklaw.edu.

SINGLETARY, ALVIN D. lawyer; b. Sept. 27, 1942; s. Alvin E. and Alice (Pastoret) Singletary; m. Judy Louise Singletary, Dec. 3, 1983; children: Kimberly Dawn, Shane David, Kelly Diane. BA, La. State U., 1964; JD, Loyola U., New Orleans, 1969. Bar: La. 1969, U.S. Dist. Ct. (ea. dist.) La. 1972, U.S. Ct. Appeals (5th cir.) 1972, U.S. Ct. Appeals (11 cir.) 1981, U.S. Ct. Internat. Trade 1981, U.S. Ct. Customs and Patent Appeals 1982, U.S. Supreme Ct. 1978. Instr. Delgado Coll., New Orleans, 1976—77; sole practice Slidell, La., 1970—. Spl. asst. dist. atty 22d Judicial Dist. Ct. , Parish of St. Tammany, La.; sec., treas. St. Tammany Pub. Trust Fin. Authority, 1978—2002. Chmn. sustaining membership enrollment Cypress dist. Boy Scouts Am., 1989—; treas. Slidell Centennial commn.; councilman-at-large City of Slidell, 1978—2002, interim mayor, 1985; mem. Dem. State Ctrl. Com., 1978—82; mem. Rep. State Ctrl. Com. Dist. 76, La., 1996—2000; del. La.Constl. Conv., 1972—73; chmn. Together We Build Program First Baptist Ch. of Slidell, La.; bd. dir. St. Tammany Coun. on Aging. Mem.: Lions, Delta Theta Phi. Baptist. General practice, Probate (including wills, trusts), Property, real (including real estate development, water). Office: PO Box 1158 Slidell LA 70459-1158

SINGLETON, HARRY MICHAEL, lawyer; b. Meadville, Pa., Apr. 10, 1949; s. Getdins T. and Rose Ann (Fucci) S.; children: Harry M. Jr., Leah Rose DiFucci. BA, Johns Hopkins U., 1971; JD, Yale U., 1974. Bar: D.C. 1975, Pa. 1976, Calif. 1999, Md. 1999, U.S. Dist. Ct. D.C. 1975, U.S. Dist. Ct. Md. 2001, U.S. Ct. Appeals (D.C. cir.) 1975, U.S. Ct. Mil. Appeals 1975. Assoc. Houston & Gardner, Washington, 1974-75, Covington & Burling, Washington, 1976-77; atty. FTC, Washington, 1975-76; dep. minority counsel Com. on D.C./U.S. Ho. of Reps., Washington, 1977-79, minority chief counsel, staff dir., 1979-81; dep. asst. sec. U.S. Dept. Commerce, Washington, 1981-82; asst. sec. U.S. Dept. Edn., Washington, 1982-86; pres. Harry M. Singleton & Assocs., Washington, 1986-91; pvt. practice law Washington, 1991—; pres. Singleton Entertainment, LLC, Washington, 1999-2000; pres., gen. counsel Single Source Tech. Solutions, LLC, Washington, 2001—. Legis. cons. Am. Enterprise Inst., Washington, 1975. Pres. bd. trustees Barney Neighborhood House, Washington, 1978-80; corp. bd. dirs. Children's Hosp. Nat. Med. Ctr., Washington, 1984-88; mem. crime com. Boys and Girls Clubs of Greater Washington, 1994-97; mem. D.C. Rep. State Com., 1991—, Rep. Nat. Com., 1992-2000, R.N.C. exec. coun., 1993-95, resolutions com., 1997-2000; mem. Rep. Nat. Hispanic Assembly Washington, 1991-92. Mem. Rep. Nat. Lawyers Assn. (bd. dirs. D.C. chpt. 1990-91), Coun. of 100 Black Reps. (bd. dirs. 1991-92), D.C. Black Rep. Coun. (chmn. 1992-93), Rep. Nat. African-Am. Coun. (nat. chmn. 1993-2001), D.C. Rep. Nat. African-Am. Coun. (chmn. 1993-2001). Republican. Presbyterian. Personal injury (including property damage), Corporate, general, General civil litigation. Office: 2121 K St NW Ste 800 Washington DC 20037-1829

SINGLETON, JAMES KEITH, federal judge; b. Oakland, Calif., Jan. 27, 1939; s. James K. and Irene Elisabeth (Lilly) S.; m. Sandra Claire Hoskins, Oct. 15, 1966; children: Matthew David, Michael Keith. Student, U. Santa Clara, 1957-58; AB in Polit. Sci., U. Calif., Berkeley, 1961, LLB, 1964. Bar: Calif. 1965, Alaska, 1965. Assoc. Delaney Wiles Moore and Hayes, Anchorage, 1963, 65-68, Law Offices Roger Cremo, Anchorage, 1968-70; judge Alaska Superior Ct., Anchorage, 1970-80, Alaska Ct. Appeals, Anchorage, 1980-90, U.S. Dist. Ct. for Alaska, Anchorage, 1990—, chief judge, 1995—2002. Chmn. Alaska Local Boundary Commn., Anchorage, 1966-69. Chmn. 3d Dist. Rep. Com., Anchorage, 1969—70. Mem. ABA, Alaska Bar Assn., Phi Delta Phi, Tau Kappa Epsilon. Office: US Dist Ct 222 W 7th Ave Unit 41 Anchorage AK 99513-7504

SINGLETON, LESLIE EMILIE, prosecutor; b. Greensboro, N.C., Sept. 20, 1971; BS, U. N.C., Greensboro. Asst. dist. atty. Kings County Dist. Attys. Office, Bklyn., 1998—. Office: Kings County DAs Office 350 Jay St Brooklyn NY 11201

SINK, ROBERT C. lawyer; b. Racine, Wis., 1938; AB, Duke U., 1959, LLB, 1965. Bar: N.C. 1965. Ptnr. Robinson, Bradshaw & Hinson, P.A., Charlotte, N.C., 1965—. Assoc. editor Duke Law Jour., 1964-65. Trustee Pub. Libr. Charlotte and Mecklenburg County, 1985-90, chmn., 1989-90; bd. dirs. Mus. New South, 1991-97, chmn., 1996-97. Lt. USN, 1959-62, USNR. Mem. ABA (ho. dels. 2001—), N.C. State Bar (councilor 1988-96, pres. 1998-99), Mecklenburg County Bar (pres. 1986-87), Order of Coif, Phi Beta Kappa. Construction, Government contracts and claims, Property, real (including real estate development, water). Office: Robinson Bradshaw & Hinson PA 101 N Tryon St Ste 1900 Charlotte NC 28246-0103

SINNOTT, JOHN PATRICK, lawyer, educator; b. Bklyn., Aug. 17, 1931; s. John Patrick and Elizabeth Muriel (Zinkand) Sinnott; m. Rose Marie Yuppa, May 30, 1959; children: James Alexander, Jessica Michelle. BS, U.S. Naval Acad., 1953; MS, USAF Inst. Tech., 1956; JD, No. Ky. U., 1960. Bar: Ohio 1961, NY 1963, NJ 1970, Ga 2000, US Patent Office 1963, US

Supreme Ct 1977. Assoc. Brumbaugh, Graves, Donohue & Raymond, N.Y.C., 1961-63; patent atty. Bell Tel. Labs., Murray Hill, N.J., 1963-64, Schlumberger Ltd., N.Y.C., 1964-71; asst. chief patent counsel Babcock & Wilcox, N.Y.C., 1971-79; chief patent and trademark counsel Am. Std. Inc., N.Y.C., 1979-92; of counsel Morgan & Finnegan, N.Y.C., 1992-99, Langdale & Vallotton, Valdosta, Ga., 2000—. Adj lectr NJ Inst Technology, Newark, 1974—89; adj prof Seton Hall Univ Sch Law, Newark, 1989—98. Author: (book) Counterfeit Goods Suppression, 1998, World Patent Law and Practice, Vols 2-2P, 1999, A Practical Guide to Document Authentication, 2003; contbr. articles to profl jours. Mem. local Selective Serv Bd., Plainfield, NJ, 1971; bd dirs New Providence Community Swimming Pool, NJ, 1970. Capt. USAF, 1953—61, col. AUS ret., 1977—91. Decorated Legion of Merit, others. Mem. N.Y. Intellectual Property Law Assn. (bd. dirs. 1974-76), Squadron A Club, Cosmos Club, Valdosta Country Club. Republican. Roman Catholic. Patent, Trademark and copyright. Home: 2517 Rolling Rd Valdosta GA 31602-1244 Office: Langdale & Vallotton 1007 N Patterson St PO Box 1547 Valdosta GA 31603 Fax: (229) 244-9646. E-mail: specan23@aol.com.

SINNOTT, JOHN WILLIAM, lawyer; b. St. Louis, Jan. 5, 1966; s. John and Joan Martha Sinnott. AB, Dartmouth Coll., 1988; JD, Tulane U., 1995. Bar: La. 1995, U.S. Ct. Appeals (5th and 10th cirs.) 1995, U.S. Dist. Ct. (ea., mid., and we. dists.) La. 1995. Assoc. Phelps Dunbar, New Orleans, 1995—97, Montgomery, Barnett, Brown, Read, Hammond & Mintz, New Orleans, 1997—2000; ptnr. Irwin Fritchie Urquhart & Moore LLC, New Orleans, 2000—. Capt. USMC, 1988-92. Mem.: ABA, New Orleans Assn. Def. Counsel, La. Assn. Def. Counsel, Def. Rsch. Inst., La. State Bar Assn. Insurance, Personal injury (including property damage), Product liability. Office: Irwin Fritchie Urquhart Moore LLC 400 Poydras St Ste 2700 New Orleans LA 70130 E-mail: jsinnott@irwinllc.com.

SINOR, HOWARD EARL, JR., lawyer; b. New Orleans, Sept. 6, 1949; s. Howard E. and Beverly M. (Bourgeois) S.; children: Sally, Vera Sue, Sarah, Sadie. BA with honors, U. New Orleans, 1971; JD cum laude, Harvard U., 1975. Bar: La. 1975, U.S. Supreme Ct. 1983, U.S. Ct. Appeals (3rd, 5th and 11th cir.), U.S. Dist. Ct. (ea., middle, we.) Dist. La. Ptnr. Jones, Walker, Waechter, Poitevent, Carrere & Denegre, 1975-98, Gordon, Arata, McCollam, Duplantis & Eagan, New Orleans, 1999—. Contbg. author: La. Appellate Practice Handbook, 1990, 97; editor: CLE Manual of Recent Developments, 1985; contbr. articles to profl. jours. Recipient Pres.'s award, La. State Bar Assn., 1987. Fellow La. Bar Found.; mem. ABA, FBA, La. State Bar Assn. (chmn. antitrust sect. 1987-89). Avocations: golf, hiking. General civil litigation, Construction, Environmental. Office: Gordon Arata et al 201 Saint Charles Ave Fl 40 New Orleans LA 70170-4000

SINSHEIMER, WARREN JACK, lawyer; b. N.Y.C., May 22, 1927; s. Jerome William and Elizabeth (Berch) S.; m. Florence Dubin, Mar. 30, 1950; children: Linda Ruth, Ralph David, Alan Jay, Michael Neal. Student, Ind. U., 1943-47; JD cum laude, N.Y. Law Sch., 1950; LLM, NYU, 1957; MPhil, Columbia U., 1977; HLD (hon.) , Drew U., 2002. Bar: N.Y. bar 1950. Ptnr. Sinsheimer, Sinsheimer & Dubin, N.Y.C., 1950-78, Satterlee & Stephens, N.Y.C., 1978-86, Patterson, Belknap, Webb & Tyler, N.Y.C., 1986-91; counsel Patterson Belknap Webb & Tyler, N.Y.C., 1991-96; pres., bd. dirs. Neighborhood Bagel Corp., 1994—. Pres. Plessey, Inc., N.Y.C., 1956-70, chmn., CEO, 1970-89; dir. oversees ops. and devel. The Plessey Co., Ltd., Illford, Essex, Eng., 1969-70, dep. chief exec., dir., 1976-89; dir. Plessey, Inc.; trustee NYU Sch. Law, 1996—; pres., bd. dirs. Legal Svcs. for Children, Inc., 1998—. Chmn. Com. of 68, 1964-67; Mem Westchester County Republican Com., 1956-73; chmn. Nat. Scranton for Pres. Com., 1964; mem. N.Y. State Assembly, 1965-66; Bd. visitors Wassaic State Sch., 1962-64; trustee Sch. Law, NYU, 1996—, bd. dirs. Shalom Hartman Inst., Jerusalem, 1991—, treas., 1996—; trustee City Bar Fund, 1998—. Served with USNR, 1944-45; with USAF, 1950-52. Mem. ABA, Assn. Bar City N.Y., Torch and Scroll, Century Club (Purchase, N.Y., gov., treas. 1997—), Century Assn. N.Y.C., Univ. Club, Zeta Beta Tau. Jewish. Home: 22 Murray Hill Rd Scarsdale NY 10583-2828 Office: 271 Madison Ave New York NY 10016-1001 E-mail: Sinsheimer@kidslaw.org.

SIPORIN, SHELDON, lawyer, consultant; B, CUNY; JD, U. Calif. Bar: N.Y., U.S. Dist. Ct. (ea. and so. dist.) N.Y., U.S. Ct. Appeals (2d. cir.). Asst. counsel Ctr. for Law and Health Care Policy, N.Y.C., 1983; assoc. Morgan, Melhuish & Monaghan, N.Y.C., 1984; sole practice N.Y.C., 1985—. Cons. ADP-UCM, N.Y.C., 1986; of counsel various law firms, N.Y.C., 1985—; arbitrator Kings County Fee Dispute Panel, 2003; presenter Adult Basic Edn. Conf., N.Y.C., 2002. Vol. atty. Office of Aging, Legal Aid Soc., N.Y.C., 1985, Vol. Lawyers for Arts, 1990; arbitrator Am. Arbitration Assn., N.Y.C., 1983-86, small claims Civil Ct., N.Y.C., 1985-86, Civil Ct. Arbitration Panel, N.Y. County; trustee Lawyers Sq. N.Y., 1985. Mem. ABA (citizenship edn. com. young lawyers div. 1986-87), Am. Judges Assn., Soc. Profls. in Dispute Resolution (assoc.), N.Y. State Bar Assn. (com. fed. constn., film and video com. 1988—), N.Y. County Lawyer's Assn. (com. on entertainment law 1988—, arbitration and conciliation com. 1990-91, com. on legal tech. 1996—, com. on health and ins. law 2000—, com. on security law, 2001—), Bldg. Bar Assn. Cmty. Elder Law, Assn. Computing Machinery, Bklyn. Bar Assn. (com. on arbitration 1994—, com. on elder law 2002-), Assn. Ind. Video and Filmmakers, Phi Beta Kappa. Presenter ABE conf. Adult Literacy. General civil litigation, Constitutional, Entertainment.

SIPPEL, WILLIAM LEROY, lawyer; b. Fond du Lac, Wis., Aug. 14, 1948; s. Alfonse Aloysious and Virginia Laura (Weber) S.; m. Barbara Jean Brost, Aug. 23, 1970; children: Katharine Jean, David William. BA, JD, U. Wis. Bar: Wis. 1974, U.S. Dist. Ct. (we. dist.) Wis. 1974, Minn. 1981, U.S. Dist. Ct. Minn. 1981, U.S. Ct. Appeals (10th cir.) 1984, U.S. Ct. Appeals (8th cir.) 1985. Research assoc. dept. agrl. econs. U. Wis., Madison, 1974-75; counsel monopolies and comml. law subcom. Ho. Judiciary Com., Washington, 1975-80; spl. asst. to asst. gen. antitrust div. U.S. Dept. of Justice, Washington, 1980-81; from assoc. to ptnr. Doherty, Rumble & Butler, Mpls. and St. Paul, Minn., 1981-99; ptnr. Oppenheimer, Wolff & Donnelly, LLP, Mpls., 1999—. Bd. dirs. Music in the Park, Inc.; mem. adj. faculty antitrust William Mitchell Coll. Law, spring of 2000, 2001. Co-author: The Antitrust Health Care Handbook, 1988; contbg. author: ABA Energy Antitrust Handbook, 2002. Mem. program com. Minn. World Trade Assn., Mpls., St. Paul, 1985-86, bd. dirs., 1986, Minn.; dir. Music in the Park, Mpls.; dir. Person to Person Inc.; chmn. antitrust mktg. orders com. Nat. Coun. Farmer Coops., 2001—. With USAR, 1971-77. Mem. ABA (vice chmn. ins. industry com. 1990-91, contbr. ABA Joint Ventures in Health Care), Minn. Bar Assn. (co-chmn. antitrust sect. 1986-88, internat. law sect. coun. 1986-89, treas. 1989-90, sec. 1990-91, vice chmn. 1995-96, chmn. 1996-97), Minn. Med. Alley Assn. (co-chmn. internat. bus. com. 1990-95, Hennepin County Office Internat. Trade (bd. dirs. 1988-93), Phi Beta Kappa. Roman Catholic. Avocations: reading, photography, computers. Antitrust, Federal civil litigation, Private international. Home: 2151 Commonwealth Ave Saint Paul MN 55108-1730 Office: Oppenheimer Wolff Donnelly LLP Plaza VII 45 S Seventh St Ste 3400 Minneapolis MN 55402-1609 E-mail: bsippel@oppenheimer.com.

SIRES, NORMAN GRUBER, JR., lawyer; b. Charleston, S.C., Sept. 14, 1942; s. N. Gruber and Emily (Neese) S.; m. Ann Jackson, Oct. 3, 1964; children: N. Gruber III, David Brian. BS in Bus. Adminstrn., U. S.C., 1967, JD, 1971. Bar: S.C. 1971, U.S. Dist. Ct. S.C. 1974. Pvt. practice, Seneca, S.C., 1971—; pub. defender Oconee County, S.C., 1972—; city atty. City of Clemson (S.C.), 1981-95. Pres. Oconee County Bar, 1978; commr. S.C. Indigent Def. Commn., 1992—. Mem. House Dels., S.C. Bar Assn. With U.S. Army, 1963-66. Coxswain USCG Aux, past vice Flotilla commdr., 1996. Mem. S.C. Bar Assn., Oconee County Bar Assn. Republican. Methodist. Criminal, Family and matrimonial, General practice. Office: Commons Sq 123 PO Box 1277 Seneca SC 29679-1277

SIRLIN, ROGER H. judge; b. Mamaroneck, N.Y., Nov. 24, 1941; m. Ellen T. Sirlin; children: Clifford, Robin, Jeffrey. AB, Lafayette Coll., 1963; LLB, NYU, 1966. Bar: N.Y. 1966, U.S. Ct. Appeals (2d dist.) 1966, U.S. Dist. Ct. (ea. and so. dists.) N.Y. 1966, Ga. 1969, U.S. Supreme Ct. 1969. Asst. dist. atty. Westchester Dist. Attys. Office, NY, 1969—71; town atty. Town of Yorktown, 1972—80; ptnr. Sirlin & Sirlin, Mamaroneck, 1972—98; judge Village of Mamaroneck, 1980—. Mem. environ. moot ct. Pace U., 2000—03; mem. Criminal Justice Adv. Bd., Westchester County, 2002—. Capt. U.S. Army, 1967—69. Mem.: Mamaroneck-Harrison Larchmont Bar Assn. (pres. 1985—87), Westchester County Magistrates Assn. (pres. 2001—02). Avocations: tennis, golf, trapshooting. Office: 211 Mamaroneck Ave Mamaroneck NY 10543 Fax: 914-698-3727. E-mail: sirlin@prodigy.net.

SIRO, RIK NEAL, lawyer; b. Bklyn., Dec. 31, 1957; s. Jack N. and Beatrice Siro; m. Teresa A. Woody, Aug. 9; children: Alexander Lewis, Lia Ann Yuesong. BA, U. Mo., 1979; JD, U. Calif., San Francisco, 1982. Bar: Mo., Calif., U.S. Dist. Ct. (we. dist.) Mo., U.S. Dist. Ct. (no. dist.) Calif., U.S. Ct. Appeals (7th, 8th, 9th, 10th cirs.). Assoc. Murphy, Pearson, Bradley & Feeney, San Francisco, Calif., 1982-84, Gage & Tucker, Kansas City, Mo., 1984-86; sr. ptnr. Blumer, Nally & Siro, Kansas City, 1986—. Bd. dirs., pres.-elect, pres. Big Bros., Big Sisters of Greater Kans. City, 1987—; bd. dirs. Mattie Rhodes Counseling and Art Ctr., Kansas City, chair Art of the Mask Fundraising, 1993—. Mem. ATLA, Mo. Assn. Trial Attys. (bd. govs.), Nat. Employment Lawyers Assn., Kansas City Met. Bar Assn. Avocations: spanish, french, skiing, guitar, piano. General civil litigation, Labor (including EEOC, Fair Labor Standards Act, labor-management relations, NLRB, OSHA), Personal injury (including property damage). Home: 3654 Belleview Ave Kansas City MO 64111-3860 Office: Blumer Nally & Siro 1621 Baltimore Ave Kansas City MO 64108-1347

SISK, DANIEL ARTHUR, lawyer; b. Albuquerque, July 12, 1927; s. Arthur Henry and Myrl (Hope) S.; m. Katharine Banning, Nov. 27, 1954; children: John, Sarah, Thomas. BA, Stanford U., 1950, JD, 1954. Bar: N.Mex. 1955, Calif. 1954. Ptnr. firm Modrall, Sperling, Roehl, Harris & Sisk, Albuquerque, 1954-70, 71—; justice N.Mex. Supreme Ct., Santa Fe, 1970. Chmn. bd. Sunwest Fin. Svcs., Inc., Albuquerque, 1975-90. Pres. Legal Aid Soc., Albuquerque, 1960-61; trustee Sandia Sch., 1968-72, Albuquerque Acad., 1971-73, A.T. & S.F. Meml. Hosps., Topeka, 1966-82; bd. dirs. N.Mex. Sch. Banking Found., 1981-85. Served with USNR, 1945-46, PTO; to capt. USMCR, 1951-52, Korea. Mem. N.Mex. Bar Assn., Albuquerque Bar Assn. (dir. 1962-63), ABA, State Bar Calif. Presbyn. (elder). Office: 500 4th St NW Albuquerque NM 87102-5324

SISKE, ROGER CHARLES, lawyer; b. Starkville, Miss., Mar. 2, 1944; s. Lester L. and Helen (Cagan) S.; m. Regina Markunas, May 31, 1969; children: Kelly, Jennifer, Kimberly. BS in Fin. with honors, Ohio State U., 1966; JD magna cum laude, U. Mich., 1969. Bar: Ill. 1969. Assoc. Sonnenschein Nath & Rosenthal, Chgo., 1969-78, ptnr., 1978—. Chmn. nat. employee benefits and exec. compensation dept. Served to capt. U.S. Army, 1970-71. Decorated Bronze Star. Fellow Am. Coll. Employee Benefits Counsel (charter); mem. ABA (past chmn. tax sect. employee benefits com., past chmn. joint com. on employee benefits and exec. compensation and bus. law sect., employee benefits and exec. compensation com.), Chgo. Bar Assn. (past chmn. employee benefits com., mem. exec. coun. of tax com.), past chmn. employee benefits coun. ISBA, Order of Coif (editor law review), Phi Alpha Kappa. Republican. Pension, profit-sharing, and employee benefits, Corporate taxation, Estate taxation. Office: Sonnenschein Nath Rosenthal 233 S Wacker Dr Ste 8000 Chicago IL 60606-6491

SISKIND, DONALD HENRY, lawyer; b. Providence, Dec. 25, 1937; s. Samuel and Sadie (Wasserman) S.; m. Beth Mohel, July 15, 1962; children: Steven M., Edward M. BS, U. Pa., 1959; LLB, Columbia U., 1962. Bar: Mass. 1962, N.Y. 1963. Assoc. Marshall Bratter Greene Allison & Tucker, N.Y.C., 1962-69, ptnr., 1969-82, Katten Muchin Zavis Rosenman, N.Y.C., 1982—. Bd. dirs. Chgo. Title Ins. Co.; chmn. various seminars Practicing Law Inst., 1974—; vis. lectr. Columbia U. Sch. Law, 1993—; mem. exec. com. of adv. bd. Wharton Real Estate Ctr. Adv. bd. Real Estate Fin. Jour.; contbr. articles to profl. jours. Pres. Greenville Community Coun., 1974-76; pres. bd. edn. Union Free Sch. Dist., Scarsdale, N.Y., 1978-81 Mem. ABA, Am. Coll. Real Estate Lawyers (past pres.), Anglo Am. Real Property Inst. (pres.-elect), N.Y. State Bar Assn., Assn. of Bar of City of N.Y., Phi Alpha Psi. Property, real (including real estate development, water). Home: 876 Park Ave New York NY 10021-1832 Office: Katten Muchin Zavis Rosenman 575 Madison Ave Fl 26 New York NY 10022-2585 E-mail: donald.siskind@kmzr.com.

SISSEL, GEORGE ALLEN, manufacturing executive, lawyer; b. Chgo., July 30, 1936; s. William Worth and Hannah Ruth (Harlan) S.; m. Mary Ruth Runsvold, Oct. 5, 1968; children: Jenifer Ruth, Gregory Allen. BS in Elec. Engring., U. Colo., 1958; JD cum laude, U. Minn., 1966. Bar: Colo. 1966, Ind. 1973, U.S. Supreme Ct. 1981. Assoc. Sherman & Howard, Denver, 1966-70; with Ball Corp., Broomfield, Colo., 1970—, assoc. gen. counsel, 1974-78, gen. counsel, 1978-95, corp. sec., 1980-95, v.p., 1981-87, sr. v.p., 1987-95, pres., 1995-98, CEO, 1995-2001, chmn. bd., 1996—2002, also bd. dirs. Bd. advisors Bank One Equity Capital, 1995-2002; bd. dirs. First Merchants Corp. Assoc. editor: U. Minn. Law Rev., 1965-66. Served with USN, 1958-63. Mem. Colo. Assn. Commerce & Industry, Order of Coif, MIT Soc. Sr. Execs., (bd. govs. 1987-95), Sigma Chi, Sigma Tau, Eta Kappa Nu. Lodges: Rotary. Methodist.

SISSON, JERRY ALLAN, lawyer; b. Memphis, Oct. 13, 1956; s. Thomas E. and Jewel O. (Hipps) S.; m. Debra Elaine Martin, Aug. 13, 1977; children: Jennifer Elaine, Elizabeth Diane, Meredith Lydia, Allan Martin BBA, Memphis State U., 1977, JD, 1979. Tenn. 1980, U.S. Dist. Ct. (we. dist.) Tenn. 1980, U.S. Supreme Ct. 1992; cert. property mgr. Ptnr. Sisson & Sisson, Memphis, 1980—. Bd. dirs. Tenn. Housing Devel. Agy., 1996—, chmn. policy and programs, 1997, vice chmn. bd., 2002—. Mem. Firewise Found. Named one of Outstanding Young Men Am., 1981. Mem. Tenn. Bar Assn., Memphis-Shelby County Bar Assn., Inst. Real Estate Mgmt., Memphis Jaycees (legal counsel 1985, v.p. community action 1986-87, v.p. individual devel. 1987-88, pres. 1988-89). Republican. Mem. Ch. Christ. Corporate, general, Probate (including wills, trusts), Property, real (including real estate development, water). Home: 7919 Birnam Wood Cv Germantown TN 38138-4916 Office: Sisson & Sisson 2171 Judicial Dr Ste 215 Germantown TN 38138-3800

SITES, JAMES PHILIP, lawyer, consultant; b. Detroit, Sept. 17, 1948; s. James Neil and Inger Marie (Krogh) Sites; m. Barbara Teresa Mazurek, Apr. 9, 1978; children: Philip Erling, Teresa Elizabeth. Student, U. Oslo, Norway, 1968-69; BA, Haverford Coll., 1970; JD, Georgetown U., 1973, ML in Taxation, 1979. Bar: Md. 1973, DC 1974, U.S. Supreme Ct. 1978, Mont. 1984, U.S. Dist. Ct. Mont. 1984, U.S. Tax Ct. 1984, U.S. Ct. Appeals (9th cir.) 1988. Law clk. to Hon. James C. Morton, Jr. Ct. Spl. Appeals Md., Annapolis, 1974-75; law clk. to Hon. Orman W. Ketcham Superior Ct. DC, Washington, 1975-76; gen. atty. U.S. Immigration & Naturalization Svc., Washington, 1976-77; trial atty. tax divsn. U.S. Dept. Justice, Washington, 1977-84; ptnr. Crowley, Haughey, Hanson, Toole & Dietrich, Billings, Mont., 1984—; consul for Govt. of Norway State of Mont., Billings, 1987—. Instr. Norwegian Eastern Mont. Coll., 1987—88, Sons of Norway, 1989—; instr. polit. sci. Mont. State U., Billings, 1997—; v.p. Scandinavian Studies Found., 1989—; bd. dirs. Billings Com. Fgn. Rels., Festival Cultures; mem. Mont. Coun Internat. Visitors, Norsemen's Fedn. Chmn. local exec. bd. Mont. State U., Billings, 1993—. Decorated knight 1st class Royal Norwegian Order Merit; scholar, U. Oslo, 1969. Mem.: Am. Imigration Lawyers Assn., DC Bar Assn., Mont. State Bar (co-chmn. com. income and property taxes 1987—91, chair tax and probate sect. 1991—92), Md. Bar Assn., Billings C. of C. (bd. dirs. 1998—, chair), Norwegian-Am. C. of C., Kenwood Golf and Country Club, Hilands Golf Club. Avocations: hiking, Nordic skiing. Administrative and regulatory, Immigration, naturalization, and customs, State and local taxation. Office: Crowley Haughey Hanson Toole & Dietrich Consulate for Norway 490 N 31st St Billings MT 59101-1256

SIU, WANG-NGAI, solicitor; b. Hong Kong, Feb. 14, 1938; s. Man-Wan and Wai-Ying (Cheung) S.; m. Yuen-Ling April Lee. Grad., St. Francis Xavier's Coll., 1959, Coll. Law, London, 1967. Solicitor T.S. Tong & Co., Hong Kong, 1971-73, Chan & Ho, Hong Kong, 1973-77, Gallant Y.T. Ho & Co., Hong Kong, 1977—97. Chmn. Fedn. Hong Kong-Macau Photographic Assns., Hong Kong. Author: Chinese Opera: Images and Stories, 1997, Hong Kong Ballet, 2003. Royal Photographic Soc. Gt. Britain fellow, Bath, 1985, 89. Mem. Law Soc. Hong Kong, Soc. Notaries. Avocations: photography, classical music, Go.

SIVERD, ROBERT JOSEPH, lawyer; b. July 27, 1948; s. Clifford David and Elizabeth Ann (Klink) S.; m. Bonita Marie Shulock, Jan. 8, 1972; children: Robert J. Jr., Veronica Leigh. AB in French, Georgetown U., 1970, JD, 1973; postgrad., The Sorbonne, Paris, 1969. Bar: N.Y. 1974, U.S. Dist. Ct. (so. and ea. dists.) N.Y. 1974, U.S. Ct. Appeals (2d cir.) 1974, U.S. Supreme Ct. 1980, U.S. Dist. Ct. (ea. dist.) Pa. 1984, U.S. Ct. Appeals (3d cir.) 1984, U.S. Ct. Appeals (6th cir.) 1985, Ohio 1991, Ky. 1992. Assoc. Donovan Leisure Newton & Irvine, N.Y.C., 1973-83; staff v.p., litigation counsel Am. Fin. Group, Inc., Greenwich, Conn., 1983-85, v.p. litigation counsel, 1986-87, v.p. assoc. gen. counsel Cin., 1987-92; sr. v.p., gen. counsel and sec. Gen. Cable Corp., 1992-94, exec. v.p., gen. counsel and sec., 1994—. Mem. ABA, Ky. Bar Assn. Republican. Antitrust, Federal civil litigation, Corporate, general. Office: Gen Cable Corp 4 Tesseneer Dr Newport KY 41076-9167

SIX, FRED N. retired state supreme court justice; b. Independence, Mo., Apr. 20, 1929; AB, U. Kans., 1951, JD with honors, 1956; LLM in Judicial Process, U. Va., 1990. Bar: Kans. 1956. Asst. atty. gen. State of Kans., 1957-58; pvt. practice Lawrence, Kans., 1958-87; judge Kans. Ct. Appeals, 1987-88; justice Kans. Supreme Ct., Topeka, 1988—2003. Editor-in-chief U. Kans. Law Review, 1955-56; lectr. on law Washburn U. Sch. Law, 1957-58, U. Kans., 1975-76. Served with USMC, 1951-53; USMCR, 1957-62. Recipient Disting. Alumnus award, U. Kans. Sch. Law, 1994, Disting. Alumni Achievement award, U. Kans. Coll. Liberal Arts and Sci., 2000—01. Fellow Am. Bar Found. (chmn. Kans. chpt. 1983-87); mem. ABA (jud. adminstrn. divsn.), Am. Judicature Soc., Kans. Bar Assn., Kans. Bar Found., Kans. Law Soc. (pres. 1970-72), Kans. Inn of Ct. (pres. 1993-94), Order of Coif, Phi Delta Phi. Address: 1180 E 1400 Rd Lawrence KS 66046 E-mail: fsix@kscourts.org.

SKAFF, ANDREW JOSEPH, lawyer, public utilities, energy and transportation executive; b. Sioux Falls, S.D., Aug. 30, 1945; s. Andrew Joseph and Alice Maxine (Skaff) Skaff; m. Lois Carol Phillips, Oct. 4, 1971; 2 children. BS in Bus. Adminstrn, Miami U., Oxford, Ohio, 1967; JD, U. Toledo, 1970. Bar: Calif. 1971, U.S. Supreme Ct. 1974. Prin., sr. counsel Calif. Public Utilities Commn., 1977; gen. counsel Delta Calif. Industries, Oakland, 1977-82, sec., 1978-82; mem. Silver Rosen, Fischer & Stecher, San Francisco, 1982-84; sr. ptnr. Skaff and Anderson, San Francisco, 1984-90; pvt. practice Law Office of Andrew J. Skaff, 1990-95; ptnr. Knox Ricksen LLP, Oakland, 1995-97, Crosby, Heafey Roach & May, Oakland, 1997-99, Energy Law Group LLP, Oakland, 2000—02. Officer Delta Calif. Industries and subs. Contbr. articles to legal jours.; contbg. mem. law rev. U. Toledo, 1970. Mem. ABA, Calif. Bar Assn., Conf. Calif. Pub. Utilities Counsel, Calif. Cogeneration Coun., Assn. Transp. Practitioners, Alameda County Bar Assn. Administrative and regulatory, Corporate, general, Utilities, public. Office: Law Office of Andrew J Skaff Lake Merrit Plz 1999 Harrison St Ste 2700 Oakland CA 94612-3582 E-mail: Askaff@energy-law-group.com.

SKAGGS, SANFORD MERLE, lawyer; b. Berkeley, Calif., Oct. 24, 1939; s. Sherman G. and Barbara Jewell (Stinson) Skaggs; m. Sharon Ann Barnes, Sept. 3, 1976; children: Stephen, Paula Ferry, Barbara Gallagher, Darren Peterson. BA, U. Calif., Berkeley, 1961; JD, U. Calif., 1964. Bar: Calif. 1965. Atty. Pacific Gas and Electric Co., San Francisco, 1964-73; gen. counsel Pacific Gas Transmission Co., San Francisco, 1973-75; ptnr. Van Voorhis & Skaggs, Walnut Creek, Calif., 1975-85, McCutchen, Doyle, Brown & Enersen, San Francisco and Walnut Creek, 1985—2002, Bingham McCutchen LLP, 2002—; dir. John Muir Mt. Diablo Health Sys., 1997—. Mem. Calif. Law Revision Commn., 1990—2001, chmn., 1993. Councilman City of Walnut Creek, 1972-78, mayor 1974-75, 76-77; bd. dirs. East Bay Mcpl. Utility Dist., 1978-90, pres., 1982-90. Mem.: Contra Costa County Bar Assn., Calif. State Bar Assn., Phi Delta Phi, Alpha Delta Phi, Lambda Alpha. Republican. State civil litigation, Condemnation (eminent domain), Land use and zoning (including planning). Office: Bingham McCutchen 1333 N California Blvd Ste 210 Walnut Creek CA 94596-4585

SKALKA, DOUGLAS SCOTT, lawyer; b. N.Y.C., Sept. 28, 1960; s. Philip and Margery Skalka; m. Susan Michelle Prince, MAy 12, 1985; children: Elizabeth, Rachel, Abigail. AB, Cornell U., 1982; JD, Boston U., 1985. Bar: Conn. 1985, N.Y. 1986, U.S. Dist. Ct. Conn. 1986, U.S. Dist. Ct. (so. and ea. dists.) N.Y. 1990, U.S. Ct. Appeals (2d cir.) 2001; cert. in bus. bankruptcy. Assoc. atty. Whitman & Ransom, Greenwich, Conn., N.Y.C., 1985-93; ptnr. Whitman Breed Abbott & Morgan, Greenwich, Conn., N.Y.C., 1994-95; prin. Neubert, Pepe & Monteith, P.C., New Haven and Southport, Conn., 1995—. Mem. adv. bd. CPA/Law Forum of Fairfield County, Southport, Conn., 1996-2000. Contbg. editor: Bankruptcy, 1997, 98; editor-in-chief Probate Law Jour., 1984-85. Mem. exec. com. Southwestern Regional Planning Agy., Norwalk, Conn., 1996-2000; mem. Southwestern Corridor Action Coun., Bridgeport, Conn., 1998-2000. Recipient Bernard E. Farr Estate Planning award Boston U., 1985, Paul Liacos scholar, 1984. Mem. ABA (bus. law sect.), Conn. Bar Assn. (exec. com. of comml. law and bankruptcy sect. 1994—), Stamford/Norwalk Regional Bar Assn. (co-chair bankruptcy com. 1994-96), Am. Bankruptcy Inst., Conn. Turnaround Mgmt. Assn. (bd. dirs. 1996—, pres. 1999-2000), New Haven County Bar Assn. (chair bankruptcy com. 2002—). Bankruptcy, Commercial, consumer (including collections, credit), Commercial, contracts (including sales of goods; commercial financing). Office: Neubert Pepe & Monteith PC 195 Church St New Haven CT 06510-2009 E-mail: dss@npmlaw.com.

SKARDA, LYNELL GRIFFITH, lawyer, banker; b. Clovis, N.Mex., Aug. 28, 1915; s. Albert S. and Bertha V. (Taylor) S.; m. Kathryn Burns Skarda, Dec. 25, 1939; children— Jeffrey J., Patricia Lyn, Katrina A., Gregory A.F. BS, U. Calif., Berkeley, 1937; JD, Washington & Lee U., 1941. Bar: N.Mex. 1941. Sole practice, Clovis, 1941— ; chmn. bd. Citizens Bank of Clovis 1968— ; mem. Uniform Jury Instrn. Com., 1963-83. Served to capt. JAG Corps, U.S. Army, World War II. Fellow Am. Coll. Trust and Estate Counsel; mem. ABA, N.Mex. Bar Assn., Am. Judicature Soc. Banking, General practice, Probate (including wills, trusts). Home: PO Box 400 Clovis NM 88102-0400 Office: Citizens Bank Bldg PO Box 400 Clovis NM 88102-0400 E-mail: lskarda@3lefties.com.

SKARE, ROBERT MARTIN, lawyer, director; b. Jan. 13, 1930; s. Martin Samuel and Verna Adelle (Forseth) S.; m. Marilyn Hutchinson, Aug. 28, 1954; children: Randolph, Robertson, Rodger, Richard. Student, St. Olaf Coll., 1947-48; BS, U. Minn., 1951, JD, 1954. Bar: Minn. 1956. Clk. Minn. Supreme Ct., 1953-54; assoc. Best and Flanagan, Mpls., 1956-60, ptnr., 1960-90, sr. ptnr., 1970-90, of counsel, 1990—. Founder, dir., gen. counsel, v.p. Luth. Brotherhood Mut. Funds, Mpls., 1969—93; corp. mcpl. counsel

City of Golden Valley, Minn., 1963—88; bd. dirs. Vesper Soc. Group, San Francisco, Son of Heaven, Seattle, Aspen Inst. Cmty. Forum, Nat. Coun. Search Inst. Youth Initiative, Venture Catalysts of Calif.; nat. pres. Luth. Human Rels. Assn. Am., 1977—79; founder, dir. Episc. Found. of Aspen, Vinland Nat. Ctr.; founder Westwood Luth. Found.; adv. bd. Venture Fin. Inst. Claremont Calif. U. P.F. Drucker Grad. Sch., 2003—. Trustee Am. Luth. Ch.; mem. bd. mgmt. U. Minn. YMCA. Officer Counter-Intelligence Corps U.S. Army, 1954—56. Recipient Pres. award Luth. Human Rels. Assn. Am., 1979, Presdl. award Search Inst., 1997, Disting. Svc. award Luth. Brotherhood, 1992; named Disting. Mil. Student Res. Officers Tng. Corps., 1954. Mem. ABA, Minn. State Bar Assn., Hennepin County Bar Assn., U. Minn. Alumni Club (charter), Mpls. Club, Torske Klubben, Sigma Alpha Epsilon (Disting. Alumni Svc. award 1978). Office: 4000 US Bank Pl Minneapolis MN 55402-4331 Home: Villa Sandia de Luz 47000 Box 1390 Fallbrook CA 92088 Office: 780 Mt Laurel Aspen CO 81611

SKELTON, BYRON GEORGE, federal judge; b. Florence, Tex., Sept. 1, 1905; s. Clarence Edgar and Avis (Bowmer) Skelton; m. Ruth Alice Thomas, Nov. 28, 1931; children: Sue, Sandra. Student, Baylor U., 1923—24; AB, U. Tex., 1927, MA, 1928, LLB, 1931. Bar: Tex. 1931, U.S. Ct. Appeals 1937, U.S. Supreme Ct. 1946, FCC 1950, Tax Ct. U.S. 1952, U.S. Treasury Dept. 1952, ICC 1953. Practice of law, Temple, Tex., 1931—66; ptnr. Saulsbury & Skelton, 1934—42, Saulsbury, Skelton, Everton, Bowmer & Courtney, 1944—55, Skelton, Bowmer & Courtney, 1955—66; judge U.S. Ct. Claims, Washington, 1966—77, sr. fed. judge, 1977—82; sr. judge U.S. Ct. Appeals (fed. cir.), Washington, 1982—. County atty. Bell County, Tex., 1934—38; spl. asst. U.S. amb. to Argentina, 1942—45; atty. City of Temple, 1945—60; bd. dirs. First Nat. Bank of Temple. Past pres. Temple YMCA; pres. Temple Indsl. Found., 1966; Dem. nat. committeeman for Tex., 1956—64; del. Dem. Nat. Conv., 1948, 1956, 1960, 1964, Tex. Dem. Conv., 1946, 1948, 1950, 1952, 1954, 1956, 1960, 1962, 1964, vice-chmn., 1948, 1958; chmn. Dem. Adv. Coun. of Tex., 1955—57. Named Ky. Col. and Adm. in Tex. Navy, 1959; recipient Legion of Honor DeMolay, 1980, Temple Outstanding Citizen award, 1990. Mem.: ABA, Am. Judicature Soc., Am. Law Inst., State Bar Tex., Bell-Lampasas and Mills Counties Bar Assn. (past pres.), Ex-Students' Assn. U. Tex. (past pres., exec.coun.), Temple C. of C. (past pres., dir.), Masons (past worshipful master), Kiwanis (past pres.), Shriners, Delta Theta Phi, Sigma Delta Pi, Pi Sigma Alpha, Phi Beta Kappa. Democrat. Methodist. Home: 1101 Dakota Dr Temple TX 76504-4905 Office: US Ct Appeals 305 Fed Bldg Temple TX 76501

SKELTON, MARK ALBERT, lawyer; b. Kingsport, Tenn., Jan. 8, 1957; s. George Haskell and Mary Lucille (Berry) S.; m. Joanna Coffey, Sept. 8, 1979. BBA, U. Tenn., 1979, JD, 1982. Bar: Tenn. 1983, U.S. Dist. Ct. (ea. dist.) Tenn. 1984, U.S. Ct. Appeals (6th cir.) 1990, U.S. Supreme Ct. 1993. Sole practice, Rogersville, Tenn., 1983—. City atty. City of Surgoinsville, Tenn., 1984-98. Bd. dirs., v.p. Rogersville Heritage Assn., 1985-89; bd. trustees Surgoinsville First United Meth. Ch., 1992-96; chmn. bd. dirs. Surgoinsville Med. Ctr., Inc., 1994-99. Mem. ABA, ATLA, Tenn. Bar Assn., Tenn. Trial Lawyers Assn., Hawkins County Bar Assn., Nat. Assn. Criminal Def. Lawyers, Tenn. Assn. Criminal Def. Lawyers, Nat. Orgn. Social Security Claimants Reps., Nat. Assn. Consumer Bankruptcy Attys., Am. Bankruptcy Inst., Hawkins County C. of C., Phi Kappa Phi, Beta Gamma Sigma, Gamma Beta Phi, Pi Sigma Alpha. Methodist. Family and matrimonial, General practice, Personal injury (including property damage). Home: 903 Main St Surgoinsville TN 37873-6057 Office: 121 S Depot St Rogersville TN 37857-3303 Fax: 423-272-0712. E-mail: maslaw@usit.net.

SKEMP, WILLIAM, lawyer; b. La Crosse, Wis., Sept. 29, 1964; BA, Coll. St. Thomas, 1987; JD, U. San Diego, 1990. Bar: Wis. 1990, U.S. Dist. Ct. (we. dist.) Wis. 1990, Minn. 1992, U.S. Dist. Ct. Minn. 1992. Atty. Hale, Skemp, Hanson & Skemp, La Crosse, 1990—92; pvt. practice La Crosse, 1992—. Mem.: ABA, La Crosse County Bar Assn., State Bar Wis. Personal injury (including property damage), Workers' compensation. Office: 700 N 3d St Ste 202 La Crosse WI 54601 Office Fax: 608-791-2510. Business E-Mail: skemplaw@centurytel.net.

SKIDD, THOMAS PATRICK, JR., lawyer; s. Thomas Patrick and Anna Skidd; m. Judith Chase Roberts, Sept. 10, 1960; children: Suanne C., Sherry E., Thomas Patrick III, Jody E. BA in Econs. cum laude, Georgetown U., 1958; LLB, Yale U., 1961. Bar: Conn. 1961, U.S. Supreme Ct. 1963. Prin. Cummings & Lockwood LLC, Stamford, Conn., 1961—. Mem. Conn. Bar Assn. (real estate sect. and land use sect.), Stamford-Norwalk Regional Bar Assn., Roton Point Club (Rowayton, Conn.). Roman Catholic. Avocation: phonograph record collector. Office: Cummings & Lockwood 107 Elm St 12th Fl Stamford CT 06904-0120

SKIGEN, PATRICIA SUE, lawyer; b. Springfield, Mass., June 16, 1942; d. David P. and Gertrude H. (Hirschhaut) Skigen; m. Irwin J. Sugarman, May 1973 (div. Nov. 1994); 1 child, Alexander David Sugarman; m. Gary W. Guttman, May 2001. BA with distinction, Cornell U., 1964; LLB, Yale U., 1968. Bar: N.Y. 1968, U.S. Dist. Ct. (so. dist.) N.Y. 1969. Law clk. Anderson, Mori & Rabinowitz, Tokyo, 1966-67; assoc. Rosenman Colin Kaye Petschek Freund & Emil, N.Y.C., 1968-70, Willkie Farr & Gallagher, N.Y.C., 1970-75, ptnr., 1977-95; v.p., corp. fin. group legal dept. J.P. Morgan Chase & Co., N.Y.C., 1995—2002, mng. dir., assoc. gen. counsel, 2002—. Dep. supt., gen. counsel N.Y. State Banking Dept., N.Y.C., 1975-77, first dep. supt. banks, 1977; adj. prof. Benjamin Cardozo Law Sch. Yeshiva U., 1979. Contbr. articles to profl. jours. Cornell U. Dean's scholar, 1960-64, Regent's scholar, 1960-64, Yale Law Sch. scholar, 1964-68. Mem.: ABA (corp. banking and bus. law sect.), Assn. of Bar of City of N.Y. (chmn. com. banking 1991—94, long range planning com. 1994—96, audit com. 1995—2001), Phi Kappa Phi, Phi Beta Kappa. Banking, Corporate, general, Finance. Office: JP Morgan Chase and Co 270 Park Ave Fl 40 New York NY 10017-2014

SKILLERN, FRANK FLETCHER, law educator; b. Sept. 26, 1942; s. Will T. and Vera Catherine (Ryberg) S.; m. Susan Schlaefer, Sept. 3, 1966; children: Nathan Edward, Leah Catherine. AB, U. Chgo., 1964; JD, U. Denver, 1966; LLM, U. Mich., 1969. Bar: Colo. 1967, Tex. 1978. Pvt. practice law, Denver, 1967; gen. atty. Maritime Adminstrn., Washington, 1967-68; asst. prof. law Ohio No. U., 1969-71, Tex. Tech U., Lubbock, 1971-73, assoc. prof. law, 1973-75, prof. law, 1975—, George W. McCleskey prof. water law, 1998—. Vis. prof. U. Tex. Law Sch., summer 1979, U. Ark. Law Sch., 1979-80, U. Tulsa Coll. Law, 1981-82; cons. and speaker in field. Author: Environmental Protection: The Legal Framework, 1981, 2d edit. published as Environmental Protection Deskbook, 1995, Regulation of Water and Sewer Utilities, 1989, Texas Water Law, Vol. I, 1988, rev. edit., 1992, Vol. II, 1991; contbr. chpts. to Powell on Real Property, Zoning and Land Use Controls, others; author cong. procs. and numerous articles. Mem. ABA (mem. publs. com. Sect. Natural Resources Law 1984—, vice chair internat. environ. law com. Sect. Natural Resources Law 1987). Office: Tex Tech U Sch Law PO Box 40004 Lubbock TX 79409-0004

SKILTON, JOHN SINGLETON, lawyer; b. Washington, Apr. 13, 1944; s. Robert Henry and Margaret (Neisser) S.; m. Carmen Fisher, Jan. 28, 1967; children: Laura Anne, Susan Elizabeth, Robert John. BA, U. Wis., 1966, JD, 1969. Bar: Wis. Supreme Ct. 1969, U.S. Dist. Ct. (ea. and we. dists.) Wis. 1969, U.S. Ct. Appeals (7th cir.) 1969, U.S. Supreme Ct. 1989, U.S. Ct. Appeals (Fed. cir.) 1991. Law clk. 7th Cir. Ct. Appeals, Milw., 1969-70; assoc. Foley & Lardner, Milw., 1970-77, ptnr. Madison, Wis., 1977-2000; shareholder Heller, Ehrman, White & McAuliffer, Washington, 2000—. Bd. visitors U. Wis. Law Sch., Madison, 1982-90, chmn., 1988-89; chair Wis. Fed. Nominating Commn., 1994; mem. Gov.'s Task Force on Bus. Ct., 1994-95; pres. Wis. Law Found., 2000-02. Fellow Am. Bar Found., Am. Coll. Trial Lawyers, Internat. Acad. Trial Lawyers; mem. ABA (chmn. standing com. on delivery of legal svcs. 1996-2000, chmn. consortium legal svcs. and pub. 2000-02), Am. Law Inst., Am. Acad. Appellate Lawyers, 7th Cir. Bar Assn. (pres. 1985-86, chmn. 7th cir. adv. com. on rules 1994-2000), State Bar Wis. (pres. 1995-96, Pres.'s award of excellence 1989, Sinykin award for publ svc. 1996), Western Dist. Wis. Bar Assn. (pres. 1992-93), Western Dist. Adv. Group (chmn. 1991), Wis. Law Found. (pres. 2000-02), James E. Doyle Am. Inn of Ct. (coun. 1992-94), Am. Inns of Ct. Found. (trustee 1995-98), U. Wis. Law Alumni Assn. (bd. dirs. 1991-97, pres. 1993-95). Federal civil litigation, General civil litigation, Product liability. Home: 917 Woodward Dr Madison WI 53704 Office: 1 E Main St Madison WI 53703-5118

SKINNER, GWYNNE LYNETTE, lawyer; b. Des Moines, July 17, 1964; d. Robert Elvin Skinner, Jr. and Joy Ann Skinner; life ptnr. Elizabeth Skrypzak; 1 child, Lucy. BA, U. No. Iowa, 1986; JD, U. Iowa, 1991, MA, 1993. Bar: Iowa 1991, Wash. 1994, Oreg. 2002, U.S. Dist. Ct. (we. and ea. dists.) Wash. 2002, U.S. Ct. Appeals (4th and 8th cirs.) 2002. Atty. U.S. Dept. Justice, Washington, 1991—92; atty., investigator U.S. Dept. Labor, Seattle, 1992—94; atty. King County Prosecutor's Office, Seattle, 1994—95, Frank & Rosen LLP, Seattle, 1995—98, Littler, Mendelson LLP, Seattle, 1998—2000, Dorsey & Whitney LLP, Seattle, 2000—. Legal com. Northwest Womens Law Ctr., Seattle, 1995—; bd. dirs. Greater Seattle Bus. Assn., 2000—02. Mem.: ABA, King County Bar Assn. (pro bono panel 1995—), Wash. Bar Assn., World Coun. Wash., Wash. Dems. Lutheran. Avocations: skiing, hiking, bicycling, poetry. Labor (including EEOC, Fair Labor Standards Act, labor-management relations, NLRB, OSHA), General civil litigation, Civil rights.

SKINNER, MICHAEL DAVID, lawyer; b. Shreveport, LA, Jan. 5, 1950; s. Roger Gilman and Jerry Ann (Steed) S.; m. Janet Louise Horaist, Jan. 7, 1978. JD, La. State U., 1976. Bar: La. 1977, U.S. Dist. Ct. (we. dist.) La. 1978, U.S. Ct. Appeals (5th and 11th cirs.) 1978, U.S. Dist. Ct. (mid. dist.) La. 1982, U.S. Supreme Ct. 1982, U.S. Dist. Ct. (so. dist.) Tex. 1983. Pvt. practice, Lafayette, La., 1976-84; asst. dist. atty. Lafayette Parish, 1983—84; ptnr. Guilliot, Skinner & Everett, 1984-86; asst. parish atty. Lafayette Parish, 1988—93; ptnr. Goode, Skinner & Hawkland, 1986-93; U.S. atty. West Dist. La., 1993-2000; atty. OneBane Law Firm, Lafayette, La. Chmn. La. Democratic Party, 2003—. Bd. dirs. Greater Lafayette C. of C. Mem. La. State Bar Assn. (mem. ho. of dels.). Democrat. Corporate, general, Criminal, Property, real (including real estate development, water). Office: 102 Versailles Blvd Ste 600 Lafayette LA 70501-6700 also: La Dem Party PO Box 4385 Baton Rouge LA 70821*

SKINNER, WALTER JAY, federal judge; b. Washington, Sept. 12, 1927; s. Frederick Snowden and Mary Waterman (Comstock) S.; m. Sylvia Henderson, Aug. 12, 1950; 4 children. AB, Harvard, 1948; JD, 1952. Bar: Mass. 1952, U.S. Dist. Ct. 1954. Assoc. firm Gaston, Snow, Rice & Boyd, Boston, 1952-57; pvt. practice law Scituate, Mass., 1957-63; asst. dist. atty. Plymouth County, 1957-63; town counsel Scituate, 1957-63; asst. atty. gen., chief Criminal Div., Commonwealth of Mass., 1963-65; mem. firm Wardwell, Allen, McLaughlin & Skinner, Boston, 1965-74; judge U.S. Dist. Ct. of Mass., 1974—; sr. status, 1992—. Bd. dirs. Douglas A. Thom Clinic, 1966-70. Mem. Mass. Bar Assn., Boston Bar Assn. Office: US Dist Ct 1 Courthouse Way Boston MA 02210-3002

SKINNER, WILLIAM FRENCH COCHRAN, JR., lawyer; b. Richmond, Va., June 18, 1943; s. W. French and Emma Sue (Linkous) S.; m. Judy Bryant, Aug. 28, 1965; children: Chip, Carey. BS in Commerce, Washington & Lee U., 1965; JD, Emory U., 1968. Bar: Ga. 1967, U.S. Dist. Ct. (no. dist.) Ga. 1973, U.S. Supreme Ct. 1974, U.S. Ct. Appeals (11th cir.) 1981. Assoc. Rich, Bass, Kidd & Broome, Decatur, Ga., 1968, 71-74; ptnr. Rich, Bass, Kidd & Skinner, Decatur, 1974; pvt. practice Decatur, 1974—. Capt. U.S. Army, 1969-70, Vietnam. Mem. State Bar Ga., DeKalb Bar Assn., Inc. Episcopalian. Avocations: sports, family. State civil litigation, Family and matrimonial, Property, real (including real estate development, water). Office: 315 W Ponce De Leon Ave Ste 956 Decatur GA 30030-2471 E-mail: wmskinner@aol.com.

SKINNER, WILLIAM POLK, lawyer; b. St. Louis, Apr. 4, 1951; s. Edwin Lemoine Jr. and Grizelda Gilchrist (Polk) S.; m. Karen Kenny, Aug. 2, 1975; children: Suzanne, William. BA, Harvard U., 1972, JD, 1975. Bar: Mo. 1976, D.C. 1976. Assoc. Covington & Burling, Washington, 1976-83, ptnr., 1983—. Federal civil litigation, Insurance, Labor (including EEOC, Fair Labor Standards Act, labor-management relations, NLRB, OSHA). Office: Covington & Burling PO Box 7566 1201 Pennsylvania Ave NW Washington DC 20044

SKIPPER, WALTER JOHN, lawyer; b. Kenosha, Wis., Aug. 5, 1964; s. Walter J. Sr. and Marilyn A. Skipper; m. Irene P. Skipper, Oct. 6, 1996; 1 child, Jonathan Walter. BS in Acctg., Fin. and Econ., Marquette U., 1985; JD, U. Wis., 1990. Bar: Wis. 1990, Md. 1991. Assoc. Fried, Frank, Harris, Shriver & Jacobson, Washington, 1990-92, Quarles & Brady LLP, Milw., 1992—. Author: Wisconsin Handbook for Securities Attorneys, 1994-98. Mem. fin. com., Elm Grove, Wis., 1998—. Mem. Wis. State Bar Assn. (exec. com. bus. law sect.), Inst. Cert. Mgmt. Accts., Elm Grove Downtow Master Plan Com., Order of Coif, Alpha Sigma Nu, Beta Gamma Sigma. Corporate, general, Mergers and acquisitions, Securities. Home: 1035 Upper Ridgeway Elm Grove WI 53122-2405 Office: Quarles & Brady 411 E Wisconsin Ave Ste 2550 Milwaukee WI 53202-4497

SKIPWORTH, ROBERT ALLISON, lawyer; b. El Paso, Tex., Nov. 1, 1945; s. Ernest Thomas and Lucille Georgia Skipworth; m. Mary Ann Howrey, Aug. 30, 1965; children: Hillary Elise, Jeffrey Robert. BA, U. Tex., 1967, JD, 1970. Bar: Tex. 1970, U.S. Dist. Ct. (we. dist.) Tex. 1972, U.S. Dist. Ct. (no. dist.) Tex. 1975, U.S. Supreme Ct. 1976, N.Mex. 2001, lic.: Am. Bd. TYrial Advocates. Assoc. Owen Dudley Brewster Steinberger & Co., El Paso, 1971, Dudley, Highsmith, & Skipworth., El Paso, 1971—74, Dudley & Skipworth, 1974—77; owner Robert A. Skipworth, Atty., El Paso, 1977—79, 1997—; ptnr. Ainsa, Skipworth, Zavaleta & Butterworth, El Paso, 1979—91, Ainsa, Skipworth, Driscoll, & Martinez, 1991—96. Bd. dirs. El Paso Rehab. Ctr., 1982—. 1st lt. U.S. Army, 1970—76. Avocations: reading, golf, fly fishing. Commercial, contracts (including sales of goods; commercial financing), Product liability, Professional liability. Office: Law Offices of R A Skipworth 310 N Mesa Ste 600 El Paso TX 79901

SKLAR, WILFORD NATHANIEL, retired lawyer, real estate broker; b. Salt Lake City, Dec. 13, 1916; s. Benjamin B. Sklar and Blanche Blau; m. Sarah Cohen, Jan. 16, 1945 (dec. Dec. 2000); children: Beth-Lynn (dec.), Teri Helene. BBA, U. Pitts., 1942; JD, Southwestern Sch. Law, 1960. Bar: Calif. 1960, U.S. Dist. Ct. Calif. 1962, U.S. Supreme Ct. 1965. Pvt. practice, Riverside, Calif., 1960-98; ret., 1998. Co-pub. worker's compensation books. Co-comdr. mil. affairs com. March AFB, Calif.; active Riverside Family Svcs., 1965-85. Sgt. USAF, 1942-46. Mem. B'nai B'rith (Akiba Dist. award 1970, 74), Riverside Jewish War Vets. Democrat. Jewish. Avocations: golf, coin collecting, real estate investments. Home: 5904 Copperfield Ave Riverside CA 92506-4510

SKLAR, WILLIAM PAUL, lawyer, educator; b. N.Y.C., Sept. 10, 1958; s. Morris and Helen (Meyers) S.; m. Lori Ann Hodges, Jan. 5, 1985. BBA magna cum laude, U. Miami, 1977, JD, 1980. Bar: Fla. 1980, N.Y. 1986, U.S. Dist. Ct. (so. dist.) Fla. 1981, U.S. Tax Ct. 1980, U.S. Ct. Appeals (5th cir.) 1980, U.S. Ct. Appeals (11th cir.) 1981. Assoc. Wood, Cobb, Murphy & Craig, West Palm Beach, Fla., 1980-85, ptnr., 1985-88, Foley & Lardner, West Palm Beach, 1989—, ptnr.-in-charge, 1995—2002. Chmn. Fla. Real Estate Dept., 1991—; adj. prof. law Sch. Law, U. Miami, Coral Gables, Fla., 1980—; dir. Inst. on Condo. and Cluster Devels., Inst. on Real Property Law, 1986—. Co-author: Cases and Materials in Condominium and Cluster Developments, 1980; author, co-editor; Florida Real Estate Transactions, 1983; contbr. articles to profl. jours. Atty. adv. bd. Morse Geriatric Ctr., West Palm Beach, 1984-88. Mem. ABA (chmn. subcom. on condominium and coop. housing sect. gen. practice 1983-88), Fla. Bar (com. condominium and planned devels. 1980—, bd. cert. real estate lawyer 1994, exec. coun. mem. real property, probate and trust law sect. 1997—), Palm Beach County Bar Assn., Coll. Cmty. Assn. Lawyers, Am. Coll. Real Estate Lawyers, Phi Delta Phi, Pi Sigma Alpha. Republican. Avocations: travel, tennis. Land use and zoning (including planning), Property, real (including real estate development, water). Home: 7238 Montrico Dr Boca Raton FL 33433-6930 Office: Foley & Lardner West Tower 777 S Flagler Dr Ste 901 West Palm Beach FL 33401-6161

SKOGLUND, MARILYN, state supreme court justice; b. Chgo., Aug. 28, 1946; BA, So. Ill. U., 1971; clerkship, 1977-81. Bar: Vt. 1981, U.S. Dist. Ct. Vt. 1981, U.S. Ct. Appeals (2d cir.) 1983. Asst. atty. gen. Civil Law Divsn., 1981-88, chief, 1988-93, Pub. Protection Divsn., 1993-94; judge Vt. Dist. Ct., 1994-97; assoc. justice Vt. Supreme Ct., 1997—. Office: Vt Supreme Ct 109 State St Montpelier VT 05609-0001

SKOLNICK, S. HAROLD, lawyer; b. Woonsocket, R.I., June 17, 1915; s. David and Elsie (Silberman) S.; m. Shirley Marshall. AB cum laude, Amherst Coll., 1936; JD, Boston U., 1940. Bar: R.I. 1940, U.S. Supreme Ct. 1946, D.C. 1947, Fla. 1952, U.S. Dist. Ct. (so. dist.) Fla. 1953, U.S. Ct. Appeals (5th cir.) 1960, U.S. Ct. Appeals (11th cir.) 1981. Atty. Dept. of War, Washington, 1940-42; asst. gen. counsel, asst. chief legal dept. Office Chief Ordnance, Dept. of Army, Washington, 1947-50; assoc. Francis I. McCanna, Providence, R.I., 1951-52; ptnr. French & Skolnick, Miami, Fla., 1953-60; sole practice Miami, Fla., 1961—. Served to lt. col. U.S. Army, 1942-47. Mem. ABA, Am. Judicature Soc., Nat. Def. Indsl. Assn. (life), R.I. Bar Assn., D.C. Bar Assn., Dade County Bar Assn., Estate Planning Coun. Greater Miami, Masons, Shriners. Insurance, Probate (including wills, trusts). Home and Office: 6521 SW 122d St Miami FL 33156-5550

SKOLNIK, BARNET DAVID, retired lawyer; b. N.Y.C., Feb. 8, 1941; s. Jack and Edythe (Savitz) S.; m. Patricia L. Krohn; children: Sarah, Deborah, Daniel, Joseph, Benjamin, Rebecca, Zachary. AB in Am. Govt. cum laude, Harvard U., 1962, LLB, 1965. Bar: D.C. 1966, Md. 1984, Maine 1991. Atty. criminal div. U.S. Dept. Justice, Washington, 1966-68; asst. U.S. atty. for Dist. Md., Balt., 1968-78; chief public corruption unit U.S. Atty.'s Office, Balt., 1973-78; pvt. practice law Washington, 1978—83; pvt. practice Law Balt., 1982—91; pvt. practice law Portland, Maine, 1991—94; ret. Tchr., lectr. on trial practice, white collar criminality, public corruption. Recipient Spl. Achievement award Dept. Justice, 1972, 74, Spl. Commendation for Outstanding Svc., Dept. Justice, 1978, Younger Fed. Lawyer award Fed. Bar Assn., 1974, Atty. Gen.'s Disting. Service award, 1974, Legal award Assn. Fed. Investigators, 1977 Antitrust, General civil litigation, Criminal. E-mail: bskolnik@megalink.net.

SKOPIL, OTTO RICHARD, JR., federal judge; b. Portland, Oreg., June 3, 1919; s. Otto Richard and Freda Martha (Boetticher) Skopil; m. Jane Rae Lundy, July 27, 1956; children: Otto Richard III, Casey Robert, Shannon Ida, Molly Jo. BA in Econs., Willamette U., 1941, LLB, 1946, LLD (hon.), 1983. Bar: Oreg. 1946, U.S. Dist. Ct. Oreg., U.S. Ct. Appeals (9th cir.), U.S. Supreme Ct. 1946. Assoc. Skopil & Skopil, 1946—51; ptnr. Williams, Skopil, Miller & Beck (and predecessors), Salem, Oreg., 1951—72; judge U.S. Dist. Ct., Portland, 1972—79, chief judge, 1976—79; judge U.S. Ct. Appeals (9th cir.), Portland, 1979—85, sr. judge, 1986—. Chmn. com. adminstrn. of fed. magistrate sys. U.S. Jud. Conf., 1980—86; co-founder Oreg. chpt. Am. Leadership Forum; chmn. 9th cir. Jud. Coun. Magistrates Adv. Com., 1988—91; chmn. U.S. Jud. Conf. Long Range Planning Com., 1990—95. Hi-Y adviser Salem YMCA, 1951—52; appeal agt. SSS Marion County (Oreg.) Draft Bd., 1953—66; master of ceremonies 1st Gov.'s Prayer Breakfast for State Oreg., 1959; citizens adv. com. City of Salem, 1970—71; Gov.'s Com. on Staffing Mental Instns., 1969—70; pres., bd. dirs. Marion County Tb and Health Assn., 1958—61; bd. dirs. Willamette U., 1969—71; elder Mt. Park Ch., 1979—81; bd. dirs. Willamette Valley Camp Fire Girls, 1946—56, Internat. Christian Leadership, 1959, Fed. Jud. Ctr., 1979. Lt. USNR, 1942—46. Recipient Oreg. Legal Citizen of Yr. award, 1986, Disting. Alumni award, Willamette U. Sch. Law, 1988. Mem.: ABA, Internat. Soc. Barristers, Assn. Ins. Attys. U.S. and Can. (Oreg. rep. 1970), Def. Rsch. Inst., Oreg. Assn. Def. Counsel (bd. dirs.), Am. Judicature Soc., Marion County Bar Assn., Oreg. Bar Assn. (bd. dirs.), Prayer Breakfast Movement (fellowship coun.), Illahe Hills Country Club (pres., bd. dirs. 1964—67), Exchange Club (pres. 1947), Salem Club. Office: Sr Circuit Judge 827 US Courthouse 1000 SW 3rd Ave Portland OR 97204-2930

SKRETNY, WILLIAM MARION, federal judge; b. Buffalo, Mar. 8, 1945; s. William S. and Rita E. S.; m. Carol Ann Skretny; 3 children. AB, Canisius Coll., 1966; JD, Howard U., 1969; LLM, Northwestern U., 1972. Bar: Ill. 1969, U.S. Dist. Ct. (no. dist) Ill. 1969, N.Y. 1972, U.S. Ct. Appeals (7th cir.) 1972, U.S. Dist. Ct. (we. dist.) N.Y. 1973, U.S. Ct. Appeals (2d cir.) 1976, U.S. Supreme Ct. 1980. Asst. U.S. atty. Office of U.S. Atty. No. Dist. Ill., Chgo., 1971-73, Office of U.S. Atty. We. Dist. N.Y., Buffalo, 1973-81, 1st asst., 1975-81; gen. ptnr. Duke, Holzman, Yaeger & Radlin, Buffalo, 1981-83; 1st dep. dist. atty. Office Dist. Atty Erie County, Buffalo, 1983-88; with Gross, Shuman, Brizdle and Gillfillan, PC, Buffalo, 1988, Cox, Barrell, Buffalo, 1989-90; judge U.S. Dist. Ct. (we. dist.) N.Y., Buffalo, 1990—. Mem. jud. conf. com. on security and facilities, 1994; chair subcom. on planning and space mgmt.; com. liaison for long range planning; spl. counsel U.S. Atty. Gen.'s Advocacy Inst., 1979; staff atty., Office of Spl. Prosecutor U.S. Dept. Justice, 1980. Named Citizen of Yr. Am Pol Eagle Newspaper, 1977, 90, Disting. Grad. Nat. Cath. Edn. Assn. Dept. Elem. Sch., 1991, Disting. Alumnus Canisius Coll., 1993; named to Wall of Fame Law Sch. Northwestern U. Mem. ABA, Fed. Judges Assn., Bar Assn. of Erie County, Di Gamma, Phi Alpha Delta, Alpha Sigma Nu. Republican. Roman Catholic. Office: US District Court 68 Court St Rm 507 Buffalo NY 14202-3405

SKULINA, THOMAS RAYMOND, lawyer; b. Cleve., Sept. 14, 1933; s. John J. and Mary B. (Vesely) S. AB, John Carroll U., 1955; JD, Case Western Res. U., 1959, LLM, 1962. Bar: Ohio 1959, U.S. Supreme Ct. 1964, ICC 1965. Ptnr. Skulina & Stringer, Cleve., 1967-72, Riemer Oberdank & Skulina, Cleve., 1978-81, Skulina, Fillo, Walters & Negrelli, 1981-86, Skulina & McKeon, Cleve., 1986-90, Skulina & Hill, Cleve., 1990-97; atty. Penn Ctrl. Transp. Co., Cleve., 1960-65, asst. gen. atty., 1965-78, trial counsel, 1965-76; with Consol. Rail Corp., 1976-78; pvt. practice Cleve., 1997—. Tchr. comml. law Practicing Law Inst., N.Y.C., 1970; practicing labor arbitrator Fed. Mediation and Conciliation Svc., 1990—; arbitrator Mcpl. Securities Rulemaking Bd., 1994-98, N.Y. Stock Exch., 1995—, NASD, 1996—; mediator NASD, 1997—, AAA Comml., 1997—; mediator vol. panel EEOC, 1997-99, contract panel, 1999-2000, v.p., 2001—; arbitrator Better Bus. Bur., 2000—. Contbr. articles to legal jours. Income tax and fed. fund coord. City of Warrensville Heights, Ohio, 1970-77; spl. counsel City of North Olmstead, Ohio, 1971-75, spl. counsel to Ohio Atty. Gen., 1983-93, Cleve. Charter Rev. Commn., 1988; pres. Civil Svc. Commn., Cleve., 1977-86, referee, 1986—; fact-finder State Employees Rels. Bd., Ohio, 1986—; hearing officer Human Resource Commn., Summit County, Ohio, 2000—. With U.S. Army, 1959. Mem. ABA (R.R. and motor carrier com. 1988-96, jr. chmn. 1989-96, alt. dispute resolution com. 1998—), FBA, Assn. Conflict Resolution, Cleve. Bar Assn. (grievance com. 1987-93, chmn. 1997-98, trustee 1993-96, ADR com. 1997—), Ohio Bar Assn. (bd. govs. litigation sect. 1986-98, negligence law com. 1989-96, ethics and profl. responsibility com. 1990-91, alt. dispute resolution com. 1996—), Am. Arbitration Assn. (practicing labor arbitrator 1987—), Nat.

Assn. R.R. Trial Counsel, Internat. Assn. Law and Sci., Pub. Sector Labor Rels. Assn., Internat. Indsl. Rels. Rsch. Assn. Democrat. Roman Catholic. Alternative dispute resolution, Federal civil litigation, Transportation. Home: 3162 W 165th St Cleveland OH 44111-1016 Office: 24803 Detroit Rd Cleveland OH 44145-2553 E-mail: tskulina@msn.com.

SKUTNIK, BOLESH J. optics scientist, lay worker, lawyer; b. Passaic, N.J., Aug. 19, 1941; s. Boleslaw Stanley and Helen Marie (Dzierzynska) S.; m. Phyllis Victoria Wojciechowski, Sept. 2, 1967 (div. July 1991); children: Pam, Janeen, Todd; m. Anita Marie Bacon, Aug. 2, 1997. BS, Seton Hall U., 1962; MS, Yale U., 1964, PhD, 1967; JD, U. Conn., 1995. Bar: N.Y. 1996, Conn. 1996. Chief scientist Ensign Bickford Coating Co., Simsbury, Conn., 1979-91; prin. B.J. Assocs., New Britain, Conn., 1991-97, West Hartford, Conn., 1997—; patent atty., rsch. scientist Fiberoptic Fabrications, Inc., East Longmeadow, Mass., 1995-97; dir. rsch., dir. patents and licensing Sci. Fiberoptic Fabrications, Inc., East Longmeadow, Mass., 1997—2002; corp. counsel, dir. rsch. Ceram Optec Industries, Inc., East Longmeadow, Mass., 2003—. Lector, mem. parish coun. St. Catherine of Siena, West Simsbury, Conn., 1980-85, St. Maurice, New Britain, Conn., 1985-2000, St. Thomas Apostle, West Hartford, 2000—; chmn., del. synod Archdioces of Hartford, Conn., 1990-96; chmn. parish Holy Family Retreat League, New Britain, 1989-2000; pres. Enbic Employees Credit Union, Simsbury, 1988-91; asst. prof. chemistry Fairfield U., Conn., 1973-79. Patentees in field; contbr. articles to profl. jours. Interviewer Yale Alumni Schs. Com., L.I. and Hartford, Conn., 1969—; mem. Yale Assn. of Yale Alumni Rep., New Britain Club, 1997-2000. Mem. ABA (subcom. chair 1993, 94, 96), Conn. Bar Assn., N.Y. State Bar Assn., Conn. Patent Lawyers Assn., Am. Intellectual Property Lawyers Assn., Soc. Photo-optical Engrs., Am. Ceramic Soc., (coord. symposium 1991), Materials Rsch. Soc. (chair symposium 1987-89), Am. Chem. Soc. (alt. coun. 1988-90. sect. chair 1994, vice chair 1993, bd. dirs. 1985-2002), Porsche Club Am. (various positions Conn. Valley region), Yale Club New Britain (dir. 1994-2000), Yale Alumni (assoc.). Democrat. Roman Catholic. Home: 51 Banbury Ln West Hartford CT 06107-1102 Office: Ceram Optec Industries Inc 515 Shaker Rd East Longmeadow MA 01028-3126

SKWARYK, ROBERT FRANCIS, judge; b. Erie, Pa., Nov. 4, 1948; s. Frank and Gloria (Hinkle) S. BS, Pa. State U., 1973; JD, U. Kans., 1977. Bar: Pa. 1977, U.S. Dist. Ct. (we. dist.) Pa. 1977. Legal intern legal svcs. Clallum and Jefferson Counties, Port Angeles, Wash., 1977; assoc. Galbo, McNelis, Restifo & Held, Erie, 1977-80; instr. bus. law Behrend Coll. Pa. State U., Erie, 1978-80; appeals referee Commonwealth of Pa., Harrisburg and Pottsville, 1981, Pitts. and Erie, 1985-88, adminstrv. law judge Allentown, 1988-96, Pitts., 1996—. Contbg. author ct. opinions Pa. Liquor Control Bd., 1988—. Mem. Behrend Coll. Soccer Alumni Assn., Erie, 1974-90. Sgt. USMC, 1967-70, lt. (j.g.) USN, 1981-85, lt. USNR, 1986-92, Saudi Arabia, lt. comdr. USNR, 1992-98, comdr., 1998—. Fellow Theatre-Sciptworks, Pa. Coun. Arts, 2002. Mem. ABA, Pa. State Bar Assn., Erie County Bar Assn., Pa. Conf. Adminstrv. Law Judges, First Marine Air Wing Assn., Pa. State U. Alumni Assn. Avocations: soccer, flying, orienteering. Home: 833 Greentree Rd Apt 2-6 Pittsburgh PA 15220-3418 Office: Commonwealth Pa Office Adminstrv Law Judge 875 Greentree Rd Pittsburgh PA 15220-3508

SLABACH, STEPHEN HALL, lawyer; b. Nov. 15, 1934; s. Carl Edward and Alvine A. Slabach; m. Elizabeth Havard Cartwright, Feb. 15, 1958; children: Elizabeth Slabach Schmit, Stephen Edward, William Cartwright. BSME, Northwestern U., 1957; postgrad., George Washington U. Sch. Law, 1957—59; LLB, Stanford U, 1961. Bar: Calif., U.S. Dist. Ct. (no. dist.) Calif. 62, U.S. Ct. Appeals (9th cir.) 73, U.S. Supreme Ct. 76. Law clk. to judge Calif. First Dist. Ct. Appeal, San Francisco, 1961—62; assoc. Cooley, Corwley, Gather, Godward, Castro & Huddleson, San Francisco, 1962—65, Cushing, Cullinan, Hancock & Rothert, San Francisco, 1965—73, ptnr., 1973—75; sole practice Burlingame, Calif., 1975—88, San Mateo, Calif., 1988—. Legal aid vol. San Mateo County; trustee San Mateo County Law Libr. Com., 1993—2002, v.p., 1998—2002; pres. Pacific Locomotive Assn., 1988—90, gen. counsel, 1980—. Mem.: ABA, State Bar Calif., Kiwanis. Republican. Episcopalian. General civil litigation, Corporate, general, Estate planning. Office: 520 S El Camino Real Ste 700 San Mateo CA 94402-1720

SLACK, MARK ROBERT, lawyer; b. Amherst, Ohio, Aug. 17, 1957; s. Robert James and Lois Jean (Basl) S.; m. Diana Joan Thomas, Sept. 23, 1994. BA in Pub. Adminstrn. & History, Ohio No. U., 1979, JD, 1982. Bar: Ohio 1983, U.S. Dist. Ct. (no. dist.) Ohio 1983, U.S. Tax Ct. 1984, U.S. Ct. Appeals (6th cir.) 1984, U.S. Supreme Ct. 1986; cert. nat. and state Better Bus. Bur. arbitrator; cert. basic fireman, Ohio. New constrn. insp. Ohio Hwy. Dept., 1977—78; social worker Columbiana County Welfare Dept., Lisbon, Ohio, 1979-80; criminal intern Allen County Welfare Dept., Lima, Ohio, 1982; social security intern Blackhoff Area Legal Svcs., Lima, 1982; mem. staff for docket indexing sys. juvenile divsn. Columbiana County Common Pleas, 1983, guardian ad litem, arbitrator, 1983—98; asst. pub. defender Columbiana County Pub. Defender's Office, Lisbon, 1984; criminal idigency appointment panel Columbiana County, all county cts., 1985—98; pvt. practice law Salem, Ohio, 1983—. Regional counsel Northeast Ohio Legal Svcs., Lisbon, 1984-2000, Youngstown, Ohio, 1988-89, Warren, Ohio, 1988. Active Columbiana County Big Bros., 1985-86; chmn. profl. divsn. No. Columbiana County United Way, 1984-85; vol. fireman Franklin Twp., 1972-76; ch. elder Holy Trinity Ch., Salem, Ohio, coord. ch. finances, 1986-89; legal advisor Emmanual Luth. Ch., Salem, 2002-. Recipient 1st place cooking award Salem News, 1986; named Outstanding Young Men Am., 1980-89, 92, 96. Mem. ABA, Ohio Bar Assn., Ohio Bar Coll. 2001, Columbiana County Bar Assn. (grievence com. 1996-97, Recognition for Pro Bono Svc. 1995, 96, 97, 98, 99. 2000), Mahoning Valley Astron. Soc. (legal advisor 1985—), Canal Soc. Ohio (trustee 1996—), Salem Hist. Soc. (v.p., trustee, legal advisor 1985-87, trustee 1997-99), Youngstown Outspoken Wheelman (legal advisor 1985-93, chmn. presdl. sports award 1986-93, Outstanding Svc. award 1986-93), Mayflower Descs. Am., Descs. of the Soldiers of Valley Forge, Descs. of Ohio Civil War Soldiers, Mahoning Valley Civil War Round Table, Mahoning Valley WWII Round Table, Sandy and Beaver Canal Assn. (founder 1988), chmn. Slack Family Reunion, 1997-, Phi Alpha Delta. Avocations: long distance bicycling, astronomy, regional history, cooking, geneaology. Criminal, Family and matrimonial, General practice. Home: 370 W 9th St Salem OH 44460-1556 Office: PO Box 765 Salem OH 44460-0765

SLADE, LYNN, lawyer; b. Santa Fe, N.Mex., Jan. 29, 1948; m. Susan Zimmerman, 1 child, Benjamin, 1 child from a previous marriage, Jessica. BA in Econs., U. N.Mex., 1973, JD, 1976. Bar: N.Mex. 1976, U.S. Dist. Ct. N.Mex. 1976, U.S. Ct. Appeals (10th cir.) 1978, U.S. Ct. Appeals (D.C. cir.) 1984, U.S. Supreme Ct. 1984. Ptnr. Modrall, Sperling, Roehl, Harris & Sisk, PA, Albuquerque, 1976—. Adj. prof. U. N.Mex. Sch. Law, Albuquerque, 1990. Editor N.Mex. Law Rev., 1975-76; contbr. articles to profl. jours. Trustee-at-large Rocky Mountain Min. L. Found., 1995—97; bd. dirs. N.Mex. First, 1999—, co-chair nominating and membership com., 2001—. Fellow N.Mex. Bar Found.; mem. ABA (sect. of environ., energy and resources, membership officer 1998-2000, chair com. on Native Am. natural resources 1991-94, coun. mem. 1995-98, mem. sects. litigation, dispute resolution, internat. law, pub. utilities and comm., and transp. law), N.Mex. State Bar (chair, bd. dirs. sect. of natural resources 1983-87, bd. dirs. Indian law sect. 2002-). Federal civil litigation, Native American, Natural resources. Home: 143 Olguin Rd Corrales NM 87048-6930 Office: Modrall Sperling Roehl Harris & Sisk PA 500 4th St NW Ste 1000 Albuquerque NM 87102-2186 E-mail: lslade@modrall.com.

SLADKUS, HARVEY IRA, lawyer; b. Mar. 5, 1929; s. Samuel Harold and Charlotte Dorothy Sladkus; m. Harriet Marcia Barske, Nov. 26, 1967 (div.); children: Steven David, Jeffrey Brandon; m. Roberta Frances Pope, Oct. 24, 1986. AB, Syracuse U., 1950; JD, NYU, 1961. Bar: N.Y. 1962, U.S. Supreme Ct. 1967, Conn. 1981. Assoc. Morris Ploscowe, N.Y.C., 1961-66; pvt. practice N.Y.C., 1968-95, 97—; ptnr. Dweck & Sladkus and Feiden, Dweck & Sladkus, N.Y.C., 1968-95, Dweck & Sladkus, LLP, 1996. Small claims arbitrator Civil Ct. City of N.Y., 1977—; adj. prof. law Benjamin N. Cardozo Sch. Law, 1994—95; lectr. family and matrimonial law. Co-author: (book) Practice Under New York's Matrimonial Law, 1971—79; editor-in-chief: Family Law Practice, 1982, contbg. columnist: It's the Law, Suffolk Times, 1999—2002; contbr. articles to profl. jours. 1st lt. U.S. Army, 1952—53, Korea. Decorated Bronze Star, War Svc. medal Korean Govt.; named Arbitrator of Yr., N.Y. Civil Small Claims Ct., 2002, Civil Ct. N.Y. County, 2002; recipient George Washington Honor medal, Freedoms Found., Valley Forge, 1953. Mem.: Suffolk County Bar Assn., Am. Arbitration Assn. (nat. panel arbitrators), Am. Judges Assn., Internat. Acad. Matrimonial Lawyers, Am. Acad. Matrimonial Lawyers, Assn. Bar City N.Y., N.Y. State Bar Assn. Jewish. Federal civil litigation, State civil litigation, Family and matrimonial. Office: 425 Park Ave New York NY 10022-3506 E-mail: hisatty@nyc.rr.com.

SLAGLE, JAMES WILLIAM, lawyer; b. Marion, Ohio, Nov. 8, 1955; s. Gene and Emily Frances (Weber) S.; m. Heidi Ann Schweinfurth, Feb. 12, 1983. BA in Polit. Sci., Ohio State U., 1977, JD, 1980. Bar: Ohio 1980, U.S. Dist. Ct. (no. dist.) Ohio 1982. Pvt. practice, Marion, 1980-96. Spl. counsel Ohio Atty. Gen., Cols, 1984-88; pros. atty. Marion County, 1985—. Pres. Hardinge Area coun. Boy Scouts Am., 1991-93, v.p. coun., 1989-91, dist. chmn., 1986-87. Mem. Nat. Dist. Attys. Assn., Ohio Pros. Attys. Assn. (pres. 1995). Methodist. Criminal, Government contracts and claims. Home: 528 King Ave Marion OH 43302-5320 Office: Marion County Pros Atty 134 E Center St Marion OH 43302-3801

SLATER, CRAIG ALLYN, lawyer; b. Elmira, N.Y., Dec. 22, 1955; s. Gary B. and Nancy S.; m. Deborah F. Slater, July 29, 1978; children: Emily, Kaylin, Jared. BA, SUNY, 1978, JD, 1981. Bar: N.Y.; U.S. Ct. Appeals (2nd cir.); U.S. Dist. Ct. (we., no. and so. dist.). Sr. litigation assoc. pvt. practice, 1981-88; asst. atty. gen. N.Y. State Atty. Gen. Office, 1988-91; dir. environ. practice group Saperton & Day PC, 1991-95; ptnr. Harter, Secrest & Emery, 1995—. Contbr. articles to profl. jours. Mem. Erie County Indsl. Adv. Bd., 1993-98, City of Buffalo Med. Waste Disposal Options Task Force, 1991-93, Erie County Plastic/Recycling Task Force, 1989-91, City of Buffalo Pesticide Adv. Bd., 1989-91. Mem. Erie County Bar Assn. (chair 1994-97), N.Y. State Bar Assn., Environ. Law Inst., Erie County C.C. Environmental. Office: Harter Secrest & Emery LLP Twelve Fountain Plaza 4th Fl Buffalo NY 14202-2228

SLATER, DANIEL B. lawyer; b. La Junta, Colo., July 24, 1972; s. John F. and Karen Slater; m. Angelia M. Russell, May 25, 1994; children: Madison M., Ethan S. BA, U. Okla., 1994; JD, Am. U., 1998. Bar: Colo. 1998, U.S. Dist. Ct. Colo. 1999, U.S. Ct. Appeals (10th cir.) 1999. Media dir. Kinsella Comm., Ltd., Washington, 1996—98; assoc. McDermott Law Firm, Canon City, Colo., 1998—. Candidate Colo. State Senate Dist. 2, 2002; chair Fremont County Dem. Party, Colo., 1999—2002; del. Dem. Nat. Conv., L.A., 2000; sec. Colo. Dem. Party, 2003—. Recipient Rising Star award, Colo. Dem. Party, 2000. Mem.: Fremont/Custer Bar Assn. (rep. to Colo. Bar Assn. bd. govs. 2000—), Colo. Trial Lawyers Assn., Colo. Bar Assn. (bd. govs. 2000—, nom. com. 2001—). Personal injury (including property damage), Property, real (including real estate development, water), General practice. Office: McDermott Law Firm 303 N 7th St Ste 201 Canon City CO 81212 E-mail: dslater@mcdermottlawfirm.com.

SLATER, RALPH EVAN, lawyer; b. Bklyn., July 14, 1948; s. Ralph Groff and Silvia Helen (Montanelli) S.; m. Cynthia Elaine Mahn, Aug. 29, 1970; children: Robert Evan, Andrew Montgomery, Steven Edward. AB, Princeton U., 1970; JD, U. Pa., 1973. Bar: Conn. 1973, U.S. Dist. Ct. Conn. 1984, U.S. Tax Ct. 1984, U.S. Supreme Ct. 1987. Assoc. Gregory & Adams, Wilton, Conn., 1973-79, ptnr., 1980-93; prin. Gregory & Adams P.C., 1994—, pres., 1996—. Chmn. bd. The Wilton Bank, 1986—; atty. Planning and Zoning Commn., Zoning Bd. Appeals, Ridgefield, Conn., 1979-81. Chmn. bd. edn. 1st Congl. Ch., Ridgefield, Conn., 1982-84, chmn. bd. trustees, 1985-87. Mem. Conn. Bar Assn. (exec. com. estates and probate sect. 1984-86, 93-99), Western Conn. Estate and Tax Planning Coun. Inc. (dir. 1992-96). Republican. Mem. Ch. of Christ. Probate (including wills, trusts), Estate taxation, Personal income taxation. Home: 30 Strawberry Ridge Rd Ridgefield CT 06877-6019 Office: Gregory & Adams 190 Old Ridgefield Rd Wilton CT 06897-4023 E-mail: rslater@gregoryandadams.com.

SLATER, THOMAS GLASCOCK, JR., lawyer; b. Washington, Mar. 15, 1944; s. Thomas G. and Hylton R. S.; m. Scott Newell Brent, Aug. 31, 1996; children: Thomas Glascock, Tacie Holden, Andrew Fletcher. BA, Va. Mil. Inst., 1966; LLB, U. Va., 1969. Bar: Va. 1969, U.S. Dist. Ct. (ea. dist.) Va. 1970, U.S. Dist Ct. (we. dist.) Va. 1979, U.S. Ct. Appeals (4th cir.) 1975, U.S. Ct. Appeals D.C. 1980, U.S. Supreme Ct. 1981. Assoc. Hunton & Williams, Richmond, Va., 1969-76, ptnr., 1976—. Bd. dirs. Tredegar Industries. Pres. VMI Found., 1995—97. Fellow: ABA, Am. Coll. Trial Lawyers; mem.: Richmond Bar Assn. (pres. 1989—90), D.C. Bar Assn., Va. State Bar Coun. (exec. com.), 4th Cir. Jud. Conf., Va. Law Found., Va. Mil. Inst. Alumni Assn. (past pres.). Antitrust, Federal civil litigation. Office: Hunton & Williams Riverfrnt Plaza East Tower 951 E Byrd St Richmond VA 23219-4074

SLAUGHTER, ALEXANDER HOKE, lawyer; b. Charlottesville, Va., Nov. 24, 1937; s. Edward Ratliff and Mary (Hoke) S.; m. Virginia Borah, 1964 (div.); 1 child, David A.; m. Mary Peeples, 1971. BA, Yale U., 1960; LLB, U. Va., 1963. Ptnr. McGuire, Woods, Richmond, Va., 1969—. Episcopalian. Home: 3016 Rugby Rd Richmond VA 23221-3936 Office: McGuire Woods One James Ctr 901 E Cary St Richmond VA 23219-4030 E-mail: aslaughter@mcguirewoods.com.

SLAUGHTER, DAVID WAYNE, lawyer; b. Rexburg, Idaho, Nov. 4, 1951; s. Richard Del and Ruth Julienne (Hill) S.; m. Connie Jo Brower, July 2, 1975; children: Shad, R. Colby, Nathan. BA magna cum laude, Brigham Young U., 1975, JD magna cum laude, 1981. Bar: Utah 1981, U.S. Dist. Ct. Utah 1981, U.S. Ct. Appeals (10th cir.) 1981, U.S. Ct. Appeals (D.C. cir.) 1982. Law clk. U.S. Ct. Appeals (D.C. cir.), 1981-82; assoc. Snow, Christensen & Martineau, Salt Lake City, 1982-86, ptnr., 1986—. Served to 1st lt. U.S. Army, 1975-78. Mem.: ABA, Am. Arbitration Assn. (panel mem.), Salt Lake County Bar Assn., Utah Bar Assn. Republican. Mem. Lds Ch. Avocations: hiking, photography, raquetball. Federal civil litigation, Construction, Finance. Office: Snow Christensen & Martineau 10 Exchange Pl 11th Floor PO Box 45000 Salt Lake City UT 84145-5000

SLAUGHTER, EDWARD RATLIFF, JR., lawyer; b. Raleigh, N.C., Sept. 15, 1931; s. Edward Ratliff and Mary McBee (Hoke) S.; m. Anne Limbosch, July 25, 1957; children: Anne-Marie, Hoke, Bryan. AB, Princeton U., 1953; postgrad. (Rotary Found. fellow), U. Brussels, 1955-56; LLB, U. Va., 1959. Bar: Va. 1959, D.C. 1981. Assoc. firm McGuire, Woods & Battle (now McGuire Woods) and predecessors, Charlottesville, Va., 1959-64; ptnr. McGuire, Woods & Battle and predecessors, 1964-79, head dept. litigation, 1964-79, spl. asst. for litigation to atty. gen. U.S., 1979-81; ptnr. firm Whitman & Ransom, Washington, 1981-84; prin. Slaughter & Redinger, P.C., Charlottesville, 1984-95, Slaughter, Izakowitz, Clarke & Nunley, P.C., 1995-96, Woods, Rogers & Hazlegrove, P.L.C., 1996—2002, of counsel, 2002—. Vis. lectr. trial advocacy U. Va., 1970-77, Va. procedure, 1986-91; disting. lectr. U. Tunis, 1996; mem. standing com. on commrs. of accounts Jud. Coun. of Va., 1993—, chmn., 1995-2001. Chmn. Albemarle County (Va.) Dem. Com., 1969-73; pres. Charlottesville-Albemarle United Way, 1972; commr. accounts Albemarle County, 1986—; trustee Lime Kiln Arts, Inc., 1992-98. Served with USNR, 1953-55. Recipient William J. Brennan award U. Va. Trial Advocacy Inst., 1996. Fellow Am. Bar Found., Am. Coll. Trial Lawyers; mem. Am. Bar Assn., D.C. Bar, Charlottesville-Albemarle Bar Assn. (pres. 1976-77), Va. Bar Assn. (pres. 1978), Va. State Bar (bd. govs. internat. practice sect. 1992-2000), Va. Trial Lawyers Assn., Thomas Jefferson Inn Ct. (pres. 1995-96), Farmington Country. General civil litigation, Private international, Personal injury (including property damage). Home: 200 Tuckahoe Farm Ln Charlottesville VA 22901-5531 Office: Woods Rogers & Hazlegrove PLC PO Box 2964 250 W Main St Ste 300 Charlottesville VA 22902 E-mail: eslaught@woodsrogers.com.

SLAVIK, DONALD HARLAN, lawyer; b. Milw., June 17, 1956; s. Donald Jean and Sally Ann (Croy) S.; m. Cynthia Sue Barfknecht, Jan 5, 1980. BS in Nuclear Engring., U. Wis., 1978, JD, 1981. Bar: Wis. 1981, U.S. Dist. Ct. (ea. and we. dists.) Wis. 1981, Tex. 2002, Colo. 2002. Mem. Habush, Habush & Rottier, Milw., 1981—. Lectr. engring. extension U. Wis., Madison, 1985—95. Author: (with others) Anatomy of a Roof Crush Case, 1985, Seat Belt Handbook, 1987, Crashworthiness, 1989, 98; contbr. articles to profl. jours. Mem. Assn. Trial Lawyers Am. (co-chair exch. com. 1986-87, 91-93, chmn. computer law office tech. 1993-97, 2000—), Wis. Bar Assn., Attys. Info. Exch. Group (bd. dirs., exec. com. 1987—, lectr. 1987—, pres. 2001-2003), Assn. for Advancement of Automotive Medicine (sci. program com. 1996-2001). Personal injury (including property damage), Product liability. Office: Habush Habush Davis & Rottier Ste 2300 777 E Wisconsin Ave Milwaukee WI 53202-5381

SLAVITT, BEN J. lawyer; b. Newark, Dec. 31, 1934; s. Arthur and Berdie (Goodman) S.; children: Lauri, Julie, Donna, John. BA, Bucknell U., 1956; LLB, U. Va., 1959. Bar: N.J. 1959, U.S. Dist. Ct. N.J. 1959, U.S. Supreme Ct. 1973. Ptnr. Slavitt & Cowen PA, and predecessors, Newark, 1959—. Served with U.S. Army, 1959-60. Mem. N.J. Bar Assn. Democrat. Jewish. General civil litigation, Family and matrimonial, Property, real (including real estate development, water). Office: Slavitt & Cowen 17 Academy St Ste 415 Newark NJ 07102-2905

SLAVITT, DAVID WALTON, retired lawyer; b. Chgo., Mar. 15, 1931; s. Isaac and Fay (Goldstein) S.; m. Roberta Chelnek, July 26, 1953; children: Steven, Denise, Howard. BS, UCLA, 1952, JD, 1955. Bar: Calif. 1956; C.P.A., Calif. Since practiced in Los Angeles; pres. Slavitt & Borofsky (P.C.), 1969-87. Moderator continuing edn. programs. Author articles in field. Served with USNR, 1955. Mem. Am. Assn. Atty.-C.P.A.s (pres. 1964), ABA, State Bar Calif., Calif. Assn. Atty.-C.P.A.s (pres. 1963), Beverly Hills Bar Assn. (vice chmn. continuing edn. of bar 1970, asst. chmn. law practice mgmt. com. 1973).

SLAVITT, EARL BENTON, lawyer; b. Chgo., Sept. 12, 1939; s. Harold Hal and Rose (Hoffman) S.; m. Amy Lerner, July 12, 1987; 1 child, Gabriel Harrel; children from previous marriage: Andrew Miller, Lesley Deborah. BS in Econs., U. Pa., 1961, JD, 1964. Bar: Ill. 1964, U.S. Dist. Ct. (no. dist.) Ill. 1964, U.S. Supreme Ct. 1971. Assoc. Wisch, Crane & Kravets, Chgo., 1964-67, Ressman & Tishler, Chgo., 1967-69; assoc., then ptnr. Levy & Erens, Chgo., 1969-78; ptnr. Tash & Slavitt, Chgo., 1978-81, Katten Muchin, Rosemary, Chgo., 1981—. Contbr. articles to profl. jours.; author poems and plays. Vol. Hospice of Ill. Masonic Med. Ctr., Chgo., 1987-89, Pro bono Advocates, 1989, Chgo. Ho., 1991 (recipient Outstanding Vol. award), Lawyers for the Creative Arts, Bus. Vols. for the Arts, 1992—; bd. dirs. Playwrights Ctr., Chgo., 1987, Jewish Reconstructionist Congregation, Chgo., 1978, 91, 92, Legal Clinic for the Disabled, 1993-96, pres., 1995-96, Sarah's Circle, 1994-96. Mem. Ill. State Bar Assn. (mem. real estate com. 1976, recipient Pro Bono Cert. Accomplishment 1994), Chgo. Bar Assn. (mem. real estate com. 1976, real estate fin. com. 1982), Chgo. Coun. Lawyers (mem. jud. selection com. 1969), Lawyers in Mensa (bd. govs. 1983). Democrat. Jewish. Property, real (including real estate development, water). Office: Katten Muchin Zavis Rosenman 2029 Century Park E Ste 2600 Los Angeles CA 90067 E-mail: earl.slavitt@kmzr.com.

SLAYTON, JOHN HOWARD, lawyer, trust company executive; b. Sparta, Wis., July 6, 1955; s. Rex Gordon and Elizabeth (Ward) S.; m. Judith Hughes. BA in Polit. Sci. cum laude, Marquette U., 1977; JD cum laude, George Washington U., 1980, MBA in Fin., 1982; LLM in Taxation, Georgetown U., 1986. Bar: D.C. 1981, U.S. Ct. Appeals (D.C. cir.) 1981, U.S. Dist. Ct. (D.C. dist.) 1981, Va. 1993. Assoc. Metzger, Shadyac & Schwarz, Washington, 1980-83, Pillsbury, Madison & Sutro, Washington, 1983-87, Leland & Assocs., Inc., Washington, 1987-95; cons. Gordon Getty Family trust, Washington, 1995—96; pres., CEO The Trust Co. of the South, Burlington, 1996—. Instr. real estate syndication, Arlington (Va.) County Continuing Edn./Realty Bd., 1982; mem. Joint Commn. N.C. Bankers Assn. and N.C. Bar Assn. Contbr. articles to profl. jours. Mem.: N.C. Bar Assn. (chmn. legis. com. of estate planning com., chmn. uniform trust code subcom. of estate planning legis. com.), D.C. Bar Assn., Va. Bar Assn., ABA (chmn. trusts and investments subcom. of banking com., com. fed. regulation of securities). Roman Catholic. Corporate, general, Securities, Corporate taxation. Office: The Trust Co of the South 3041 S Church St Burlington NC 27215-5154 E-mail: jslayton@tcts.com.

SLEDGE, JAMES SCOTT, judge; b. Gadsden, Ala., July 20, 1947; s. L. Lee and Kathryn (Privott) S.; m. Joan Nichols, Dec. 27, 1969; children: Joanna Scott, Dorothy Privott. BA, Auburn U., 1969; JD, U. Ala., 1974, postgrad., 1989. Bar: Ala. 1974, U.S. Ct. Appeals (5th cir.) 1975, U.S. Ct. Appeals (11th cir.) 1981. Ptnr. Inzer, Suttle, Swann & Stivender, P.A., Gadsden, 1975-91; judge U.S. Bankruptcy Ct. No. Dist. Ala., 1991—; chair Nat. Conf. Fed. Judges, 2000—. Instr. U. Ala., Gadsden, 1975-77, Gadsden State C.C., 1989-90. Lay min., vestryman Holy Comforter Episc. Ch., Gadsden, 1976—, sr. warden, 2000; exec. com. Ala. Coun. on the Arts, 1994—, chmn. 2002-; incorporator Episc. Day Sch., Gadsden, 1976, Kyle Home for Devel. Disadvantaged, Gadsden, 1979; bd. dirs. Salvation Army, 1984-91, Etowah County Health Dept., 1975-91, Episc. Day Sch., 1992-96, Gadsden Symphony, 1993-96; active Ala. Dem. Exec. Com., 1990-91, Etowah County Dem. Exec. Com., 1984-91; founder Gadsden Cultural Arts Found., 1983, chmn., 1986-91. Capt. U.S. Army, 1969-71, Vietnam. Decorated Legion of Honor (Vietnam); recipient Gov.'s award for art Ala. Coun. of Arts, 1993. Mem. ABA (publs. chair 1997-98, chair jud. divsn. 2002), Gadsden-Etowah C. of C. (gen. counsel, v.p., bd. dirs. 1986-93), Kiwanis (bd. dirs. 1981-84), Phi Kappa Phi, Phi Eta Sigma. Home: 435 Turrentine Ave Gadsden AL 35901-4059

SLEET, GREGORY M. lawyer, judge; b. N.Y.C. m. Mary Sleet; children: Moneta, Kelsi. BA in Polit. Sci. cum laude, Hampton U., 1973; JD, Rutgers U., 1976. Bar: Del., N.Y., Pa., U.S. Dist. Ct. (ea. dist.) Pa., U.S. Dist. Ct. (ea. dist.) Del., U.S. Ct. Appeals (3d cir.). Pvt. practice, Phila.; dep. atty. gen. State of Del.; in-house counsel Hercules Inc.; dep. atty. gen. U.S. Dist. Ct., Del.; U.S. atty. U.S. Dist. Ct. (ea. dist.), Del., 1994—, judge, 1998—. Mem. Atty. Gen. Janet Reno's adv. com., 1995-97, vice-chair, 1996—. Bd. overseers Widener U. Sch. of Law. Recipient Disting. Svc. award NAACP, 1994. Office: US Courthouse Lockbox 19 844 King St Wilmington DE 19801-3519

SLEIGHT, VIRGINIA MAE, lawyer; b. Queensbury, N.Y., Mar. 10, 1932; d. Henry Jay and Helen Adelaide (Bennett) S. BA in Polit. Sci., Russell Sage Coll., 1962. Bar: N.Y. 1964, U.S. Dist. Ct. (no. dist.) N.Y. 1966, U.S. Surpeme Ct. 1981. Clk. of ct. & hearing reporter Warren County Family Ct., Queensbury, N.Y., 1954-71; law asst., reporter Warren County

Ct., Queensbury, N.Y., 1971-75, 1st asst. dist. atty., 1975-94, coord. asst. dist. atty., 1994-96; atty. pvt. practice, Queensbury, N.Y., 1996—. Adminstrv. v.p. Mohican Coun., Boy Scouts Am., Glens Falls, N.Y., 1994-98, mem. exec. bd. Twin Rivers Coun., Albany, 1998-2000. Mem. AAUW, N.Y. Bar Assn., Warren County Bar Assn., Bus. & Profl. Women, Soc. Prevention Cruelty to Animals Upstate N.Y., Chapman Hist. Mus., Hyde Mus. Republican. Avocations: swimming, skiing. Probate (including wills, trusts), Property, real (including real estate development, water). Home and Office: 369 Aviation Rd Queensbury NY 12804-2915

SLEIK, THOMAS SCOTT, lawyer; b. La Crosse, Wis., Feb. 24, 1947; s. John Thomas and Marion Gladys (Johnson) S.; m. Judith Mattson, Aug. 24, 1968; children: Jennifer, Julia, Joanna. BS, Marquette U., 1969, JD, 1971. Bar: Wis. 1971, U.S. Dist. Ct. (we. dist.) Wis. 1971. Assoc. Hale Skemp Hanson Skemp & Sleik, La Crosse, 1971-74, ptnr., 1975—. State pres. Boy Scouts Am., 1981—83, bd. dirs. Gateway Area Con., 1973—99, pres., 1980—81; trustee La Crosse Pub. Libr., 1981—; bd. dirs. Children's Mus. of La Crosse, 1997—2002, Greater La Crosse Area United Way, 1985—92, campaign chmn., 1986, pres., 1987; mem. Sch. Dist. La Crosse Bd. Edn., 1973—77, v.p., 1977; festmaster Oktoberfest (LaCross Festivals Inc.), 2001, trustee, 2001—. Fellow Am. Acad. Matrimonial Lawyers (pres. Wis. chpt. 1999-2000); mem. ABA, State Bar Wis. (bd. govs. 1987-94, pres. 1992-93, spkr. litigation sect. and family law seminars), La Crosse County Bar Assn. Roman Catholic. State civil litigation, Family and matrimonial, Labor (including EEOC, Fair Labor Standards Act, labor-management relations, NLRB, OSHA). Home: 4082 Glenhaven Dr La Crosse WI 54601-7503 Office: Hale Skemp Hanson Skemp & Sleik 505 King St Ste 300 La Crosse WI 54602-1927 E-mail: tss@haleskemp.com.

SLEMBOSKI, JAMES E. lawyer; b. Martin's Ferry, Ohio, Nov. 3, 1950; s. Edward and Lyda Mae Slemboski; m. D. Alaina Strong; children: James Scott, Aaron Thomas, Gaylene Rene, Corinne Michelle, Janelle Monet, Jared Michael, Nathan Edward, Alaina Nicole, Stephen Bryant, Shari Marie. Student, Mt. San Antonio Jr. Coll., Walnut, Calif., 1968—70; BSBA, Calif. State U., San Jose, 1973; postgrad., Brigham Young U., 1973—76; MBA, U. Utah, 1978; JD, Golden Gate U., 1982. Bar: Utah 1984, U.S. Ct. Mil. Rev. 1984, U.S. Dist. Ct. Utah 2001. Commd. 2d lt. U.S. Army, 1976, staff officer, 1977—79, staff officer 5th U.S. Army Hdqs., 1984, promoted to capt., 1984, atty., 1984—88; law clk. Atty. Gen.'s Office State Calif., Sacramento, 1982—83; pvt. practice St. George, Utah, 1988—. Pres. Rocky Mountain Dist. Exch. Club, 2000—01; bishop LDS Ch., 1985—88, 1994—99; bd. dirs. Dixie Health Care Found., 1989—97, chmn., 1992—94; bd. dirs. Dixie Regional Med. Ctr., 1992—94, Dixie Care & Share, 1998—, So. Utah Ctr. for Deaf, 2002—, Erin Kimball Found., 2003—. Recipient Nat. award for making Rocky Mountain Dist. number two in the nation for growth, Nat. Exchange Club. Mem.: St. George Noon Exchange Club (pres. 1997—98, Nat. Disting. Pres. award). Republican. Avocations: reading, hiking, bicycling. Estate planning, Family and matrimonial, Corporate, general. Office: 32 East 100 South Ste 203 Saint George UT 84770 Fax: 435-628-1489. E-mail: jslemboski@slemboski-law.com.

SLEMMER, CARL WEBER, JR., retired lawyer; b. Camden, N.J., Mar. 28, 1923; s. Carl and Annetta (Donner) S.; m. Renée Jeannette Kinsey, Oct. 11, 1952; children: Michael, John, Sandra. BS, Muhlenberg Coll., 1948; JD, Temple U., 1963. Bar: N.J. 1972, Pa. 1972, U.S. Dist. Ct. N.J. 1972, Fla. 1974. Various pers. positions RCA, Camden, 1950-55; mgr. labor rels. Allied Chem. Corp., Morristown, N.J., 1955-67; dir. employee rels. Exide Corp., Phila., 1967-82; pvt. practice Cherry Hill, N.J., 1982-83; dir. labor rels. Columbia U., N.Y.C., 1983-89; mgr. tax office H & R Block, Marlton, N.J., 1991-93; ret., 1993. Mem. labor coun. U. Pa., Phila., 1967-82. Lt. (j.g.) USN, 1943-46, PTO. Republican. Presbyterian. Avocations: tennis, reading, travel, legal research. Home: 888 Heritage Rd Moorestown NJ 08057-1330 E-mail: carlslemmer@cs.com.

SLEWETT, ROBERT DAVID, lawyer; b. N.Y.C., June 4, 1945; s. Nathan and Evelyn (Miller) S.; m. Sheila Faith Winkler, Jan. 27, 1973; children: Gregory, Danielle. BA in Pub. Affairs, George Washington U., 1967; JD, Cornell U., 1970. Bar: Fla. 1970. Mem. Smith and Mandler, Miami Beach, Fla., 1970-73; with Robert D. Slewett, Atty. at Law, Miami Beach, 1973-87; ptnr. Steinberg, Slewett & Yaffe, Miami Beach, 1987-98, Robert D. Slewett, P.A., Miami Beach, 1998—. Lectr. in probate and medicaid field. Exec. v.p., gen. counsel Nat. Parkinson Found., Miami, Fla., 1993—; bd. dirs., legal counsel Boystown of Jerusalem Found. Am., N.Y.C., 1993—; mem. Dade County Estate Planning Coun., Heritage Soc. Miami Jewish Home and Hosp. Named One of Leading Fla. Attys. in Field of Trusts and Estates. Mem. Nat. Acad. Elder Lawyers, Fla. Bar Assn. (probate litigation com., probate rules com. 2000—), Dade County Bar Assn. (chmn. spl. needs trust com., Pro Bono award 2002), Estate Planning Coun. Dade County. Estate planning, Probate (including wills, trusts), Property, real (including real estate development, water). Home: 2235 NE 204th St Miami FL 33180-1311 Office: 801 NE 167 St Fl 2 North Miami Beach FL 33162 Fax: 305-455-2049. E-mail: slewlaw@msn.com.

SLICKER, FREDERICK KENT, lawyer; b. Tulsa, Aug. 21, 1943; s. James Floyd and Lucille Geneva (Nordling) S.; children: Laura, Kipp. BA, U. Kans., 1965, JD with highest distinction, 1968; LLM, Harvard U., 1973. Bar: Kans. 1968, U.S. Ct. Mil. Appeals 1968, U.S. Supreme Ct. 1972, Tex. 1973, Okla. 1980. Prin. founder Slicker Law Firm, P.C., 2000—. Author: A Practical Guide to Church Bond Financing, 1985, Angels All Around, 1999; Ambassador with Promise Keepers. Mem. Promise Keepers. Capt. U.S. Army, 1965—72. Mem. ABA, Okla. Bar Assn., Order of Coif. Democrat. Methodist. Avocation: Christian men's ministries. Franchising, Mergers and acquisitions, Securities. Office: 4444 E 66th Ste #201 Tulsa OK 74136-4206 E-mail: fslicker@swbell.com.

SLIGER, HERBERT JACQUEMIN, JR., lawyer; b. Urbana, Ill., Nov. 21, 1948; s. Herbert Jacquemin and Marina (Mantia) S.; m. Sandra Ann Ratti, May 3, 1996; children: Lauren Christine, Matthew Ryan, Nicholas Adam, Claire Nicole, Adam Gregory. BS in Fin., U. Ill., 1970; JD, U. Ariz., 1974. Bar: Ariz. 1974, Ill. 1975, U.S. Supreme Ct. 1983, Okla. 1984, U.S. Ct. Appeals (7th cir.) 1980, U.S. Tax Ct. 1980; CPA, Okla. Lawyer Charles W. Phillips Law Offices, Harrisburg, Ill., 1974—75; trust counsel Magna Trust Co., F/K/A Millikin Nat. Bank, Decatur, Ill., 1976—80, First of America Trust Co., Springfield, Ill., 1980—83; trust counsel personal fin. svcs. group First Interstate Bank Okla. NA, Oklahoma City, 1983—86; mgr. employee benefits trust dept. First Interstate Bank of Okla., NA, Oklahoma City, 1986—89; v.p., pension counsel Star Bank, NA, Cin., Cin., 1989—90; asst. gen. counsel Bank One Ariz. Corp., Phoenix, 1990—95; asst. gen. counsel, nat. practice group head Banc One Corp., Columbus, Ohio, 1995—98, state gen. counsel Phoenix, 1996—97; sec. of bd. and cashier Bank One, Ariz. NA, 1996—97; sec. of bd. and statutory agt. Banc One Ariz. Corp., 1996—97; sec. bd. Bank One Trust Co. N.A., Columbus, 1996—; asst. gen. counsel, trust counsel practice group head law dept. Bank One Corp., Chgo., 1999—2003, sr. counsel, 2003—. Co-chmn. Nat. Conf. Lawyers and Corp. Fiduciaries, 1992-94; instr. Chaminade U. Hawaii, Hawaii Tax Inst., 1999. Contbr. articles to profl. jours. Mem. ABA (sect. bus. law, banking law com., trust and investment svcs. subcom. 1991-99, sect. real property, probate and trust law 1974—, fiduciary income taxation subcom. 1994—, fiduciary environ. problems com. 1993-99, sect. of taxation, employee benefits com. 1991-2001), State Bar of Ariz. (mem. exec. coun., probate and trust sect., chmn. ethics com., mem. subcom. uniform laws 2002—), Okla. Bar Assn., Am. Bankers Assn. (chmn. trust counsel com. 1992-94, mem. and head of fiduciary law dept. Nat./Grad. Trust Sch. Bd. of Faculty Advisors 1994-95, faculty mem. teaching "fiduciary duties under ERISA" Nat. Employee Benefit Trust Sch. 1994-96, spokesman Environ. Risk Task Force 1994-95, mem. trust and investment divsn. exec. com. 1992-94, mini-adv. bd. chairperson trusts and estates 1995-99), Nat. Conf. Lawyers and Corp. Fiduciaries (co-chmn. 1992-94), Am. Corp. Counsel Assn. Roman Catholic. Avocations: phys. fitness. Estate planning, Estate taxation, Taxation, general.

SLINGER, MICHAEL JEFFERY, law library director; b. Pitts., Apr. 12, 1956; s. Maurice and Mary Helen (Kengerski) S.; m. Cheryl Blaney, Apr. 19, 1980; children: Rebecca, Sarah. BA, U. Pitts., 1978; M Librianship, U. S.C., 1979; JD, Duquesne U., 1984. Reference libr. Duquesne U. Sch. Law, Pitts., 1983-84; rsch. libr. U. Notre Dame (Ind.) Sch. Law, 1984-85, head rsch. svcs., 1985-86, assoc. dir. pub. svcs., 1986-90; law libr. dir., assoc. prof. law Suffolk U. Sch. Law, Boston, 1990-93, law libr. dir., prof. law, 1994-95; law libr. dir., prof. law, assoc. dean Cleve. State U., 1995—. Contbr. articles to profl. jours., chpt. to book. Mem. ABA, ALA, Am. Assn. Law Librs., Am. Assn. Law Schs. (exec. bd. sect. on law librs. 1993-94), New Eng. Law Libr. Consortium (treas. 1992-95), Ohio Regional Assn. Law Librs. (v.p. 1987-88, pres. 1988-89, Pres. award 1989). Avocations: reading, sports, family. Office: Cleveland-Marshall Coll Law Law Libr 1801 Euclid Ave Cleveland OH 44115-2223 Business E-Mail: michael.slinger@law.csuohio.edu.

SLIVKA, MICHAEL ANDREW, lawyer; b. Ambridge, Pa., Jan. 14, 1955; s. Andrew and Veronica (Yanko) S. AB in Psychology, Cornell U., 1977; JD, U. Miami, 1980. Bar: Fla. 1980, U.S. Dist. Ct. (so. dist.) Fla. 1981, U.S. Ct. Appeals (5th cir.) 1981, U.S. Ct. Appeals (11th cir.) 1981, Colo. 1997, U.S. Dist. Ct. Colo. 1999, U.S. Tax Ct. 2001; cert. arbitrator Coun. Better Bus. Burs. Pvt. practice, Ft. Lauderdale, Fla., 1990-99; pvt. practice Colorado Springs, 1999. Precinct capt., exec. com. Broward County Rep. Party, 1991-92; v.p. West Broward Rep. Club, 1991-92; sec. North Dade/South Broward Estate Planning Coun., 1991-92. Albert C. Murphy scholar Cornell U., 1973. Mem. Fla. Bar Assn., Assn. for Objective Law, Weston Area Jaycees (past sec.), Colo. Sport Compact Racing (bd. dirs.). Republican. Avocations: objectivist philosophy, weightlifting, motorcycling, gardening. Bankruptcy, General civil litigation, Personal injury (including property damage). Home and Office: 225 Thames Dr Colorado Springs CO 80906-5952 Fax: 719-576-6963. E-mail: michaelslivka@msn.com.

SLOAN, DONNIE ROBERT, JR., lawyer; b. Nashville, July 24, 1946; s. Donnie R. Sr. and Mary Catharine (Willis) S. BS in Indsl. Engring., Ga. Inst. Tech, 1968; JD cum laude, U. Ga., 1971; LLM, Harvard U., 1975. Bar: Ga. 1971, U.S. Dist. Ct. (no. dist.) Ga. 1971, U.S. Ct. Appeals (11th cir.). Atty. Southwire Co., Carrollton, Ga., 1971-74; assoc., ptnr. Hyatt & Rhoads, P.C., Atlanta, 1975-89; pvt. practice, 1989-96; ptnr. Davidson, Fuller & Sloan, LLP, 1996—. Instr. legal rsch. U. Ga., Athens, 1970-71; instr. music law Ga. State U., Atlanta, 1976. Mem. editl. bd. Ga. Law Rev., 1969-71. Treas. Ga. Wheelchair Athletic Assn., Atlanta, 1981-84; pres., treas. Dixie Wheelchair Athletic Assn., Atlanta, 1984-87. Recipient Appreciation award Ga. Wheelchair Sports and Recreation Assn., 1979; named one of Outstanding Young Men of Am., 1981; named to Dixie Wheelchair Athletic Assn. Hall of Fame, 1990. Mem. Am. Judicature Soc., Phi Kappa Phi, Alpha Phi Mu, Ga. Tech. Club, Harvard Club. Presbyterian. Avocations: skiing, jogging, swimming. Corporate, general, Property, real (including real estate development, water), Franchising. Home: 820 Saddlehill Rd Roswell GA 30075 Office: 11330 Lakefield Dr Ste 250 Duluth GA 30097-1578 E-mail: drsloan@dfslaw.com.

SLOAN, F(RANK) BLAINE, law educator; b. Geneva, Nebr., Jan. 3, 1920; s. Charles Porter and Lillian Josephine (Stiefer) S.; m. Patricia Sand, Sept. 2, 1944; children: DeAnne Sloan Riddle, Michael Blaine, Charles Porter. AB with high distinction, U. Nebr., 1942, LLB cum laude, 1946; LLM in Internat. Law, Columbia U., 1947. Bar: Nebr. 1946, N.Y. 1947. Asst. to spl. counsel Intergovtl. Com. for Refugees, 1947; mem. Office Legal Affairs UN Secretariat, N.Y.C., 1948-78; gen. counsel Relief and Works Agy. Palestine Refugees, Beirut, 1958-60; dir. gen. legal divsn., dep. to the legal counsel UN Legal Office, N.Y.C., 1966-78, rep. of Sec. Gen. to UN Commn. Internat. Trade Law, 1969-78, rep. to Legal Sub-com. on Outer Space, 1966-78; rep. UN Del. Vietnam Conf., Paris, 1973; rep. UN Conf. on Carriage of Goods by Sea Hamburg, 1978; prof. internat. law orgn. and water law Pace U., 1978-87, prof. emeritus, 1987—. Law lectr. Blaine Sloan Internat., 1988—. Author: United Nations General Assembly Resolutions in Our Changing World, 1991; contbr. articles to legal jours. Cons. UN Office of Legal Affairs, 1983-84, UN Water Resources Br., 1983; supervisory com., Pace Peace Ctr.; legal advisor Korean Missions, 1951, 53, UNTSO, Jerusalem, 1952, UNEF I, Gaza, 1957-58; prin. sec.UN Commn. to investigate Sec.-Gen. Hammarskjold's crash, 1961-62. Navigator AC, U.S. Army, 1943-46 Decorated Air medal. Mem. Am. Soc. Internat. Law, Am. Acad. Polit. and Social Sci., Am. Arbitration Assn., Order of Coif, Phi Beta Kappa, Phi Alpha Delta (hon.). Republican. Roman Catholic. Home: HCR-68 Box 72 Foxwind-Forbes Park Fort Garland CO 81133 Office: 78 N Broadway White Plains NY 10603-3710 also: 375 Soubry Pl Forbes Park Fort Garland CO 81133

SLOAN, WILLIAM MARSHALL, lawyer; b. Omaha, May 30, 1930; s. William McKinley and Esther Marguarette (Marshall) S.; m. Joan Arlene Dennis, Aug. 18, 1957; children— Valerie, Michael, Bonnie, Kathryn. B.S., U. Oreg., 1952, LL.B., 1956. Bar: Oreg. 1956, U.S. Dist. Ct. Oreg. 1956. Assoc. Johnson & Telfer, Grants Pass, Oreg., 1956-58; ptnr. Johnson, Telfer & Sloan, Grants Pass, 1958-67, Johnson, Sloan & Jordan, Grants Pass, 1968-76, Sloan, Hawkins & Neufeld, Grants Pass, 1977-80. Sloan & Hull, Grants Pass, 1981-85; legal counsel Oreg. State Jaycees, 1961-62; circuit judge pro-tem, 2003—. Advisor, committeeman Trahern for State Rep., Grants Pass, 1982; pres. Josephine County Cancer Assn., Grants Pass, 1961; patrolman Nat. Ski Patrol Service, Mt. Ashland, Oreg., 1963-72; chmn. bldg. fund Bethany Presbyterian Ch., Grants Pass, 1962, Josephine County Park Bd. 1980-93, Bd. of Four Way Cmty. Found. 1994-2000 (chmn. 1996-97). Served to 1st lt. U.S. Army, 1952-54; Korea. Decorated Bronze Star; recipient Disting. Service award Jaycees, 1962. Mem. Josephine County Bar Assn. (pres. 1963-64), Jaycees (pres. 1962-63), Phi Delta Phi. Republican. Presbyterian. Club: Caveman Coin (pres. 1959-60) (Grants Pass). Lodge: Elks. Estate planning, Probate (including wills, trusts), Property, real (including real estate development, water). Home: 456 Pickett Creek Rd Grants Pass OR 97527-9617 Office: 130 NW D St PO Box 1476 Grants Pass OR 97528-0332 E-mail: williamjoan@juno.com.

SLOMAN, MARVIN SHERK, lawyer; b. Fort Worth, Apr. 17, 1925; s. Richard Jack and Lucy Janette (Sherk) S.; m. Margaret Jane Dinwiddie, Apr. 11, 1953; children: Lucy Carter, Richard Dinwiddie. BA, U. Tex., 1948; LLB with honors, 1950. Bar: Tex. 1950, N.Y. 1951. Assoc. Sullivan & Cromwell, N.Y.C., 1950-56, Carrington, Coleman, Sloman & Blumenthal LLP and predecessor, Dallas, 1956-60, ptnr., 1960-97; sr. counsel, 1998—. Appellate, General civil litigation, General practice. Office: Carrington Coleman Sloman & Blumenthal LLP 200 Crescent Ct Ste 1500 Dallas TX 75201-1848

SLONAKER, WILLIAM MARTIN, SR., business law educator; b. Dayton, Ohio, Apr. 18, 1946; BS, U. Dayton, 1968, MBA, 1969; JD, Ohio State U., 1972. Bar: Ohio 1972; lic. sr. profl. in human resources. Assoc. Allbery & Roberts, Dayton, 1972-77; ptnr. Slonaker & Laurito, Dayton, 1977-78, Cohen, Gregg, Slonaker & Laurito, Dayton, 1978-85; asst. prof. bus. law Wright State U., Dayton, 1985-89, chair dept. mgmt., 1989-90, 94, asst. prof. bus. law, 1990-92, assoc. prof., 1992—. Commr. Accrediting Commn. of Career Schs. and Colls. Tech., Washington, 1992—; labor arbitrator FMCS, Neutral Ohio SERB; mediator U.S. Dist. Ct. So. Divsn.; arbitrator AAA. Co-creator Ohio Employment Discrimination Studies; contbr. articles to profl. jours. Home: 609 Lamont Dr Kettering OH 45429-3215 Office: Wright State U Dept Mgmt Dayton OH 45435

SLOVITER, DOLORES KORMAN, federal judge; b. Phila., Sept. 5, 1932; d. David and Tillie Korman; m. Henry A. Sloviter, Apr. 3, 1969; 1 child, Vikki Amanda. AB in Econs. with distinction, Temple U., 1953, LHD (hon.) , 1986; LLB magna cum laude, U. Pa., 1956; LLD (hon.) , Dickinson Sch. Law, 1984, U. Richmond, 1992, Widener U., 1994. Bar: Pa. 1957. From assoc. to ptnr. Dilworth, Paxson, Kalish, Kohn & Levy, Phila., 1956—69; mem. Harold E. Kohn PA, Phila., 1969—72; from assoc. prof. to prof. Temple U. Law Sch., Phila., 1972—79; judge U.S. Ct. Appeals (3rd cir.), Phila., 1979—, chief judge, 1991—98. Bd. overseers U. Pa. Law Sch., 1993—99; bd. trustees Nat. Constitution Ctr., 1998—; mem. Jud. Conf. of U.S., 1991—98. Mem. S.E. region Pa. Gov.'s Conf. on Aging, 1976—79, Com. of 70, 1976—79; U.S. com. Bicentennial Constn., 1987—90; com. on Rules of Practice and Procedure, 1990—93; trustee Jewish Publ. Soc. Am., 1983—89. Recipient Juliette Low medal, Girl Scouts Greater Phila., Inc., 1990, Honor award, Girls High Alumnae Assn., 1991, Jud. award, Pa. Bar Assn., 1994, James Wilson award, U. Pa., 1996, Cert. of Honor award, Temple U., 1996; Disting. Fulbright scholar, Chile, 1990. Mem.: ABA, Phila. Bar Assn. (gov. 1976—78, Sandra Day O'Connor award 1997), Am. Judicature Soc. (bd. dirs. 1990—95), Nat. Assn. Women Judges, Am. Law Inst., Fed. Judges Assn., Fed. Bar Assn., Order of Coif (pres. U. Pa. chpt. 1975—77), Phi Beta Kappa. Office: US Ct Appeals 18614 US Courthouse 601 Market St Philadelphia PA 19106-1713

SLUTSKY, STEVEN H. human resources executive, consultant; b. Bklyn., Apr. 12, 1963; s. Myron and Arden Slutsky; m. Abby L. Goldstein, May 24, 1987; children: Jason, Ross. BS in Econs., U. Pa., 1985; MBA, JD, Boston U., 1988. Bar: Mass. 1988, NY 1989, U.S. Dist. Ct. (so. and ea. dists.) NY 1989, NJ 1990, Pa. 1992, U.S. Ct. Appeals (3d cir.), U.S. Dist. Ct. NJ, U.S. Dist. Ct. (we. dist.) Tex., U.S. Dist. Ct. (ea. and we. dists.) Pa. With Jackson Lewis, Phila., 1988—92, Wolf, Block, Schorr and Solis-Cohen, Phila., 1992—96; prin., exec. compensation cons. Mercer Human Resource Cons., Phila., 1997—. Author: Executive Compensation, 2002. Commr. Whitemarsh Twp. Planning Commn., Lafayette Hill, Pa., 1997—2001, chmn., 2001; bd. dirs. Colonial Bd. Sch. Dirs., Lafayette Hill, 2002. Avocations: reading, exercising, tennis, flying. Office: Mercer Human Resource Consulting 1717 Arch St Fl 27 Philadelphia PA 19103 E-mail: steve.slutsky@mercer.com.

SLY, JOHN T. lawyer; b. Queens, NY, Dec. 21, 1966; s. Dean and Patricia Sly; m. Shelley A. Sly, May 29, 1999; 1 child, Evan W. BA cum laude, SUNY, Albany, 1989, JD, MD, 1996. Bar: NY, Md., U.S. Dist. Ct., Alsam Law Sch., NY, U.S. Dist. Ct. Md. Atty. Carter Conboy et al, Albany, 1996—99, Miles & Stockbridge PC, Balt., 1999—. Mem.: DRI, ABA, MDC, MBA, Federalist Soc. Product liability, Personal injury (including property damage). Office: Miles & Stockbridge PC 10 Light St Baltimore MD 21202

SMAGULA, JOHN WILLIAM, lawyer; b. Waterbury, Conn., Nov. 17, 1970; BA in Internat. Rels., Pomona Coll., 1992; JD, Washington U., St. Louis, 1995. Bar: P.R. 1996, U.S. Ct. Appeals (1st cir.) 1996, N.Y. 1998, N.H. 1998. Assoc. Totti & Rodriguez Diaz, San Juan, P.R., 1995-97, Paul, Weiss, N.Y.C., 1997-2000; spl. counsel Yale-China Assn., New Haven, 2000—03; dir. Asian legal studies Temple U. Sch. Law, Phila., 2003—. Dir. St. Charles Borromeo Ch., N.Y.C., 1997—; mem. dist. com. Conn. Yankee coun. Boy Scouts Am., 2000—. Roman Catholic. Avocation: proficiency in spanish and mandarin chinese. Commercial, contracts (including sales of goods; commercial financing), Education and schools, Immigration, naturalization, and customs. E-mail: jsmagula@alum.pomona.edu.

SMAILI, JIHAD M. lawyer; b. Toledo, Aug. 25, 1971; s. Mohamed Smaili and Ibfisum Karkoukli. BA in Polit. Sci., U. Toledo, 1993; JD magna cum laude, Cleveland-Marshall Coll. Law, 1998. Bar: Ohio 1998, U.S. Ct. Appeals (6th cir.) 1999, U.S. Dist. Ct. (so. and no. dists.) Ohio 1999. Asst. atty. gen. Office of Ohio Atty. Gen., Columbus, 1998—2000; asst. pros. atty. Office of Cuyahoga County Prosecutor, Cleve., 2000—02; atty. Cleve., 2002—. Editor: Cleve. State Law Rev., 1997—98. Pro bono vol. Lawyers for Justice Program, Columbus, 1999—2000; bd. dirs., treas. Arab-Am. Anti-Discrimination Com., Cleve., 2001—. Mem.: Criminal Law Soc. (treas.), Pi Sigma Alpha. Moslem. Avocations: billiards, travel. Civil rights, Immigration, naturalization, and customs, Criminal. Office: 1133 W 9th St Ste 503 Cleveland OH 44113

SMALL, ALDEN THOMAS, judge; b. Columbia, S.C., Oct. 4, 1943; s. Alden Killin and Shirley Edna (Eldridge) Small; m. Judy Jo Worley, June 25, 1966; children: Benjamin, Jane. AB, Duke U., 1965; JD, Wake Forest U., 1969. Bar: N.C. 1969. Asst. v.p. First Union Corp., Greensboro, N.C., 1969-72; assoc. dir., gen. counsel Cmty. Enterprise Devel. Corp. Alaska, Anchorage, 1972-73; v.p., assoc. gen. counsel First Union Corp., Raleigh, N.C., 1973-82; judge U.S. Bankruptcy Ct., N.C., 1982—, chief judge, 1992-99. Bd. govs. Nat. Conf. Bankruptcy Judges, 1987—90; adj. prof. law Campbell U. Sch. Law, 1980—82; bd. dirs. Am. Bankruptcy Inst., 1989—95, Fed. Jud. Ctr., 1997—2001, Am. Coll. Bankruptcy; sec. Nat. Conf. Bankruptcy Judges, 1998—, pres.-elect, 1999, pres., 2000—01; chmn. Nat. Conf. Bankruptcy Judges Ednl. Endowment, 1993—94; mem. long range planning com. U.S. Jud. Conf., 1991—95, adv. com. bankruptcy rules, 1996—99, chair adv. com. on bankruptcy rules, 2000—; faculty mem. Nat. Comml. Lending Sch., 1981—82; cons. Nat. Coalition for Bankruptcy Reform, 1981—82. Contbg. editor: Norton Bankruptcy Law and Practice. Mem.: ABA, N.C. Bar Assn. (bankruptcy coun.), N.C. Bankers Assn. (bank counsel com. 1980—82), Am. Bankers Assn. (bankruptcy task force 1980—82), Am. Coll. Bankruptcy, Phi Alpha Delta, Kappa Sigma. Republican. Office: US Bankruptcy Ct PO Box 2747 Raleigh NC 27602-2747

SMALL, MARSHALL LEE, lawyer; b. Kansas City, Mo., Sept. 8, 1927; s. Phillip and Lillian Small; m. Mary Rogell, June 27, 1954; children: Daniel, Elizabeth. BA, Stanford U., 1949, JD, 1951. Bar: Mo. 1951, Calif. 1955, N.Y. 1990. Law clk. to Justice William O. Douglas U.S. Supreme Ct., Washington, 1951-52; assoc. Morrison & Foerster, San Francisco, 1954-60, ptnr., 1961-92, sr. of counsel, 1993—. Reporter corp. governance project Am. Law Inst., 1982-92. 1st lt. U.S. Army, 1952-54. Mem. ABA (com. corp. laws 1975-82), Phi Beta Kappa, Order of Coif Corporate, general. Office: Morrison & Foerster LLP 425 Market St San Francisco CA 94105-2482 E-mail: msmall@mofo.com.

SMALL, STEPHEN BRADLEY, lawyer; b. St. Louis, 1960; BA, U. Mo., 1981; JD, U. Mo., Kansas City, 1985; diploma, Mo. Auction Sch., Kansas City, 1994. Bar: Mo. 1985, Kans. 1986, U.S. Dist. Ct. Kans. 1986, U.S. Dist. Ct. Mo. 1985, U.S. Ct. Appeals (8th cir.) 2000, U.S. Supreme Ct. 2000. Pvt. practice Small Law Office, Kansas City, Mo., 1986—; auctioneer Kansas City, Mo., 1994—. Mem. ATLA, ABA, Mo. Bar Assn., Kans. Bar Assn., Kansas City Metro Bar Assn. (Fee Dispute com.), Mo. Trial Lawyers Assn., Am. Legal Svcs. Assn., Nat. Auctioneers Assn. Avocations: antiques, automated musical instruments. General civil litigation, Commercial, consumer (including collections, credit), Personal injury (including property damage). Office: Small Law Office PO Box 414678 Kansas City MO 64141-4678

SMART, ROY LOUIS, III, lawyer; b. Atlanta, Ga., Dec. 20, 1953; s. Roy Louis Smart, Jr. and Florence Bartleson Smart; m. Mary Davis McLendon, June 2, 1986; children: R. Louis IV, Cordon M., Mary Stuart. BA in History, Harvard U, 1976; JD, U Va., 1979. Bar: N.Y. 1980, N.C. 1983. Assoc. Winthrop, Stimson, Putnam & Roberts, N.Y.C., 1979—83, Parker Poe Adams and Bernstein Llp., Charlotte, 1983—86; ptnr. Parker Poe Adams and Bernstein Llp., 1987—. Mem., bus. sect. coun. N.C. Bar Assn., Raleigh; mem. N.C. Commn. Bus. Laws and Economy, Raleigh. Chair, Carolinas adv. coun. Trust for Pub. Land, Charlotte. Mem.: N.C. Bar Assn., Franchise

Forum, ABA, Negotiated Acquisitions Com., ABA. Corporate, general, Franchising, Mergers and acquisitions. Office: Parker Poe Adams and Bernstein Llp 401 S Tryon St Ste 3000 Charlotte NC 28202-1942

SMARTT, MICHAEL STEWART, lawyer; b. Missoula, Mont., Mar. 5, 1951; s. George Madison and Alice Marion (Haggarty) S.; m. Sheila Boetcher, Aug. 15, 1975; children: Seanna Dawn, Heather Lynn, Michael Stewart. BA, U. Mont., 1974; JD, Gonzaga U., 1977. Bar: Montana 1977. Law clk. to presiding judge Mont Dist. Ct. (8th dist.), Great Falls, 1977; assoc. Hartelius & Assocs., Great Falls, 1977; assoc. atty. pub. defenders Great Falls, 1980-84; pres. The Law Ctr., Great Falls, 1982-84; assoc. Big Sky Law Ctr., Great Falls, 1985—; County Justice of Peace, 1999—2002. Active participant Cursillo and Cum Cristo, Great Falls, 1978-85; pres., bd. dirs. Montessori Sch. Mem. ABA, Mont. Bar Assn., Cascade County Bar Assn. (bd. dirs. 1986—). Avocations: music, gardening, carpentry. Bankruptcy, Criminal, Family and matrimonial. Home: PO Box 2323 212 3rd Ave N Great Falls MT 59401-2419 Office: Big Sky Law Ctr PC 613 Strain Bldg Great Falls MT 59401

SMEDINGHOFF, THOMAS J. lawyer; b. Chgo., July 15, 1951; s. John A. and Dorothy M. Smedinghoff; m. Mary Beth Smedinghoff. BA in Math., Knox Coll., 1973; JD, U. Mich., 1978. Bar: Ill. 1978, U.S. Dist. Ct. (no. dist.) Ill. 1978. Assoc. McBride, Baker & Coles and predecessor McBride & Baker, Chgo., 1978-84, ptnr., 1985-99; ptnr. Baker & McKenzie, Chgo., 1999—. Adj. prof. computer law John Marshall Law Sch., Chgo.; chair Ill. Commn. on Electronic Commerce and Crime, 1996—; mem. U.S. Del. to UN Commn. on Internat. Trade Law. Author: Online Law, 1996. Mem. ABA (chair electronic commerce divsn. 1995—). Computer, Corporate, general, Intellectual property. Office: Baker & McKenzie 130 E Randolph St Ste 3700 Chicago IL 60601-6342 E-mail: smedinghoff@bakernet.com.

SMEGAL, THOMAS FRANK, JR., lawyer; b. Eveleth, Minn., June 15, 1935; s. Thomas Frank and Genevieve (Andreachi) S.; m. Susan Jane Stanton, May 28, 1966; children: Thomas Frank, Elizabeth Jane. BS in Chem. Engring., Mich. Technol. U., 1957; JD, George Washington U., 1961. Bar: Va. 1961, D.C. 1961, Calif. 1964, U.S. Supreme Ct. 1976. Patent examiner U.S. Patent Office, Washington, 1957-61; staff patent atty. Shell Devel. Co., San Francisco, 1962-65; patent atty. Townsend and Townsend, San Francisco, 1965-91, mng. ptnr., 1974-89; sr. ptnr. Graham and James, San Francisco, 1992-97; pres., ptnr. Knobbe, Martens, Olson & Bear, San Francisco, 1997—. Mem. U.S. del. to Paris Conv. for Protection of Indsl. Property; mem. adv. com. Ct. of Appeals for Fed. Cir., 1992-96. Contbr. articles to profl. jours. Pres. bd. dirs. Legal Aid Soc. San Francisco, 1982-84, Youth Law Ctr., 1973-84; bd. dirs. Nat. Ctr. for Youth Law, 1978-84, San Francisco Lawyers Com. for Urban Affairs, 1972—, Legal Svcs. for Children, 1980-88; bd. dirs., presdl. nominee Legal Svcs. Corp., 1984-90, 93-2003. Capt. Chem. Corps, U.S. Army, 1961-62. Recipient St. Thomas More award, 1982. Mem. ABA (chmn. PTC sect. 1990-91, ho. of dels. 1988-2000, mem. standing com. Legal Aid and Indigent Defendants 1991-94, chair sect. officer conf. 1992-94, bd. govs. 1994-97, standing com. on Pro Bono and Pub. Svc. 1997-2001, standing com. on Gavel awards 2001—), Intellectual Property Law Assn. (chmn. nat. coun. 1989), Nat. Inventors Hall of Fame (pres. 1988), Calif. Bar Assn. (v.p. bd. dirs. 1986-87), Am. Patent Law Assn. (pres. 1986), Internat. Assn. Intellectual Property Lawyers (pres. 1995-2001), Bar Assn. San Francisco (pres. 1979), Patent Law Assn. San Francisco (pres. 1974), World Trade Club, Olympic Club, Golden Gate Breakfast Club, Claremont Club (Berkeley). Republican. Roman Catholic. Patent, Trademark and copyright. Office: Knobbe Martens Olson & Bear 201 California St Ste 1150 San Francisco CA 94111-5002 Home: 107 King Ave Piedmont CA 94610 E-mail: tsmegal@kmob.com.

SMILEY, GUY IAN, lawyer; b. N.Y.C., July 30, 1938; s. Edward and Minerva June (Silverman) S.; m. Constance Ann Rodbell, July 30, 1967; children: Erica, Andrew. BA, Cornell U., 1960; JD, Columbia U., 1963. Bar: N.Y 1964, U.S. Dist. Ct. (so. dist.) N.Y. 1965, U.S. Dist. Ct. (ea. dist.) N.Y. 1965, U.S. Ct. Appeals (2d cir.) 1967, U.S. Supreme Ct. 1970. Assoc. Law Offices of Harry H. Lipsig, N.Y.C., 1964-68; ptnr. Smiley & Smiley LLP (formerly Smiley, Schwartz & Captain), N.Y.C., 1968—. Arbitrator Am. Arbitration Assn., N.Y. 1974—, Civil Ct. City of N.Y., 1974-80; co-chmn. Combined Jud. Screening Panel City of N.Y., 1983—. Contbr.: (book) The Lawyers Secretary, 1972. V.p., gen. counsel Westchester Emergency Communications Assn., White Plains, N.Y., 1979—; vol. counsel Am. Radio Relay League, 1983—. Served to lt. (JAGC) USN 1966-70. Mem. Assn. Trial Lawyers Am. (sustaining), N.Y. State Trial Lawyers Assn. (mem. legis. com., 1979-85, bd. dirs. 1982—, editor-in-chief newsletter, 1984—, dep. treas. 1986), Jewish Lawyers Guild (sec. 1984—). Avocations: amateur radio, tennis, skiing. Federal civil litigation, State civil litigation, Personal injury (including property damage). Home: 425 E 58th St New York NY 10022-2300 Office: Smiley & Smiley LLP 60 E 42nd St Rm 950 New York NY 10165-0999 E-mail: gsmiley@smileylaw.com.

SMILEY, JOHN CLINTON, lawyer; b. Chgo., Jan. 27, 1960; s. John Wallace and Kay Alice Smiley; m. Pamela Kay St. John, Aug. 12, 1983; children: Kristine M., Alison R. BS, Colo. State U., 1983; JD, U. Wyo., 1986. Bar: Colo. 1986, Wyo. 1986, U.S. Dist. Ct. Colo., U.S. Dist. Ct. Wyo., U.S. Ct. Appeals (10th cir.). Assoc. Sherman Howard, Denver, 1986—90, Lindquist & Vennum PLLP, Denver, 1991—93, ptnr., 1994—. ptnr.-in-charge, 2001—. Co-coord faculty fed. advocates Bankruptcy Pro Bono Program, Denver, 2002—. Avocations: fly fishing, skiing, reading. Bankruptcy. Office: Lindquist & Vennum PLLP 600 17th St Ste 1800-S Denver CO 80202 Fax: 303-573-1956. E-mail: jsmiley@lindquist.com.

SMILLIE, DOUGLAS JAMES, lawyer; b. Glen Ridge, N.J., Aug. 16, 1956; s. James and Nancy (Albright) S.; m. Nancy Marie McKenna, Jan. 27, 1990; children: Sara Grace, Jeffrey Douglas, Heather Patricia. BA in Polit. Sci. cum laude, Muhlenberg Coll., 1978; JD, Villanova U., 1982. Bar: Pa. 1982, U.S. Dist. Ct. (ea. dist.) Pa. 1982, U.S. Ct. Appeals (3d cir.) 1983, N.J. 1984, U.S. Dist. Ct. N.J. 1984, U.S. Dist. Ct. (mid. dist.) Pa. 1995. Assoc. Clark, Ladner, Fortenbaugh & Young, Phila., 1982-90, ptnr., 1991-96; dir., shareholder, v.p., chair litigation sect. Fitzpatrick Lentz & Bubba, P.C., Center Valley, Pa., 1996—. Lectr. bus. bankruptcy Lehigh-Carbon C.C., 1999; spkr. in field. Author: When Worlds Collide: The Impact of the Bankruptcy Stay on Environmental Clean-Up Litigation, 1989, The Absolute Priority Rule: Catch 22 for Reorganizing Closely-Held Businesses, 1992; editor (newsletter) Environ. Impact, 1985—96, Villanova Law Rev.; contbr. articles to profl. jours. Recipient Rev. Joseph Ullman award. Mem. ABA (litigation sect.), Nat. Bus. Inst., Am. Bankruptcy Inst., Turnaround Mgmt. Assn., Comml. Law League Am. (bankruptcy and insolvency sect., creditors rights sect.), Assn. Comml. Fin. Attys., Robert Morris Assocs., N.J. Bar Assn. (bankruptcy sect.), Phila. Bar Assn. (Ea. Dist. Bankruptcy Conf.), Lehigh County Bar Assn. Avocation: Second City Troop Rugby Football Club Alumni. Bankruptcy, General civil litigation, Commercial, contracts (including sales of goods; commercial financing). Office: Fitzpatrick Lentz & Bubba PC Box 219 Stabler Corp Ctr 4001 Schoolhouse Ln Center Valley PA 18034-0219 also: 301 North Church St Ste 220 Moorestown NJ 08057 Fax: 610-797-6663. E-mail: dsmillie@flblaw.com.

SMIT, ROBERT H. lawyer; b. N.Y.C., July 19, 1959; s. Hans and Beverly Smit; m. Rachel M. Margulies, Nov. 3, 1990; children: Marley, Jessie. BA, Cornell U., 1981; degree d'etudes approfondies, U. Paris I, 1986; JD, Columbia U., 1986. Ptnr. Simpson Thacher & Bartlett, N.Y.C., 1988—. Mem. ICC Internat. Ct. Arbitration. Author: A Comparison of International Commercial Arbitration Rules, 1998, The Newly Revised CPR Rules for Non-Administered Arbitration of International Arbitration, 2001; contbr. articles to profl. jours. Mem.: ABA, Assn. Bar of City of NY, Internat. Bar Assn. (vice chair internat. arbitration com.), NY State Bar Assn. International Arbitration, General practice. Office: Simpson Thacher & Bartlett 425 Lexington Ave New York NY 10017

SMITH, AL JACKSON, JR., environmental engineer, lawyer; b. Meridian, Miss., Aug. 26, 1935; s. Al Jackson and Katherine (Felker) S.; m. Patricia Scruggs, Dec. 20, 1957; children: Johnny, Vicki, Katherine. BSCE, Miss. State U., 1958; MS in Environ. Engring., Vanderbilt U., 1969; JD, Atlanta Coll. Law, 1977; LLM, Woodrow Wilson Coll., 1980. Bar: Ga. 1979, U.S. Dist. Ct. (no. dist.) Ga. 1979, U.S. Ct. Appeals (11th cir.). Engr. City of Vicksburg, Miss., 1964-66; dir. br. emergency Region IV EPA, Atlanta, 1966-86, dep. dir. div. water, 1986-90; counsel Hurt, Richardson, Todd, Garner and Caddenhead, Atlanta, 1990-93, McRae Secrest & Fox, Atlanta, 1993; pvt. cons., 1994-95; dir. engring. Kiber Environ. Svcs., Inc., Atlanta, 1995—. Solicitor City of Stockbridge, Ga., 1984-87; lectr. Nat. Emergency Tng. Ctr., Emmitsburg, Md. 1980—; city judge Locust Grove, Ga., 1988—. Author: Managing Hazardous Substance Accidents, 1981; Oil Pollution Control, 1973; contbg. author: Hazardous Materials Handbook, 1982; contbr. articles to profl. jours. Served to capt. USAR, 1958-70. Mem. Internat. Assn. Chiefs Police, Ga. Bar Assn., N.C. Assn. Fire Chiefs. Baptist. Home: 1550 S Ola Rd Locust Grove GA 30248-2239

SMITH, ALEXANDER WYLY, JR., lawyer; b. Atlanta, June 9, 1923; s. Alexander Wyly and Laura (Payne) S.; m. Betty Rawson Haverty, Aug. 31, 1946; children— Elizabeth Smith Crew, Clarence Haverty, Laura Smith Brown, James Haverty, Edward Kendrick, Anthony Marion, William Rawson. Grad., Marist Sch., 1941; student, Holy Cross Coll., 1941-42; BBA, U. Ga., 1947, LL.B. cum laude, 1949. Bar: Ga. 1948. Practiced in, Atlanta, 1948-98; ret. ptnr. Smith, Gambrell & Russell and predecessor, 1994—. Bd. dirs. Our Lady of Perpetual Help Free Cancer Home; bd. dirs., planning and devel. coun. Cath. Archdiocese Atlanta, Marist Sch., Atlanta, John and Mary Franklin Found. Served with USAAF, 1943-46. Mem. Ga. Bar Assn., Atlanta Bar Assn., Phi Delta Phi, Chi Phi, Piedmont Driving Club Atlanta, Peachtree Golf Club Atlanta (pres. 1989-91). Banking, Estate planning, Insurance. Home: 2771 Peachtree Rd #5 Atlanta GA 30305-3523 Office: 3100 Promenade II Atlanta GA 30309-3574

SMITH, ALISON LEIGH, lawyer; b. Brownsville, Tex., Sept. 24, 1952; d. Arthur Lee and June (Allen) Smith; m. Dean A. Burkhardt, Apr. 24, 1981. B in Journalism summa cum laude, U. Tex., 1974, JD cum laude, 1977. Bar: Tex. 1977, U.S. Dist. Ct. (so. dist.) Tex. (1978), U.S. Ct. Appeals (5th cir.) 1981, U.S. Dist. Ct. (no. dist.) Tex. 1987, U.S. Ct. Appeals (D.C. cir.) 1989. Assoc. Vinson & Elkins LLP, Houston, 1977-84, ptnr., 1984-89, 91—; dep. asst. atty. gen. antitrust divsn. U.S. Dept. Justice, Washington, 1989-91. Adj. prof. law U. Tex., Austin, 1992-93. Alternate del. Rep. Nat. Conv., New Orleans, 1988; mem. ethics com. City of Houston, 1988-89. Mem. ABA (antitrust law sect., chair transp. industry com., 1992-95, co-chmn. pvt. antitrust litig. com. 2001-), Am. Law Inst., Tex. Bar Found., Houston Bar Assn. Antitrust, Federal civil litigation, State civil litigation. Home: 2125 Bolsover St Houston TX 77005-1617 Office: Vinson & Elkins 3300 First City Tower 1001 Fannin St Ste 3300 Houston TX 77002-6706

SMITH, ANNE ORSI, lawyer; b. Upper Darby, Pa., July 2, 1962; d. John Francis Jr. and Anne Robinson (Nichols) O.; m. Fletcher Bodky Smith Jr., June 3, 1988; 1 child, Fletcher Bodky Smith III. BA, Colgate U., 1984; JD, U. Ark., 1988. Bar: Ark. 1988, U.S. Dist. Ct. Ark. (ea. and we. dists.) 1990. Law clk. Ark. Supreme Ct., Little Rock, 1988-89; staff atty. Office of the Prosecutor Coord., Little Rock, 1989-91; hearing officer Ark. Appeal Tribunal, Little Rock, 1991-93; pvt. practice Little Rock, 1993—. Mem. ABA, Ark. Trial Lawyers Assn. (chmn. domestic rels.com. 1997-98), Ark. Bar Assn. (chair-elect Juvenile Justice and Child Welfare Law sect. 2002-03), Pulaski County Bar Assn., Ark. Assn. of Women Lawyers (pres. 1995-96, v.p. 1994-95, paliamentarian 1993-94). Avocations: genealogy, herbs. Family and matrimonial, Juvenile. Office: PO Box 17087 Little Rock AR 72222-7087

SMITH, ARTHUR B., JR., lawyer; b. Abilene, Tex., Sept. 11, 1944; s. Arthur B. and Florence B. (Baker) S.; m. Tracey L. Truesdale, 1999; children: Arthur C., Sarah R. BS, Cornell U., 1966; JD, U. Chgo., 1969. Bar: Ill. 1969, N.Y. 1976. Assoc. Vedder, Price, Kaufman & Kammholz, Chgo., 1969-74; asst. prof. labor law N.Y. State Sch. Indls. and Labor Rels., Cornell U., 1975-77; ptnr. Vedder, Price, Kaufman & Kammholz, Chgo., 1977-86; founding mem. Murphy, Smith & Polk, Chgo., 1986-98; shareholder Ogletree, Deakins, Chgo., 1999—. Guest. lectr. Northwestern U. Grad. Sch. Mgmt., 1979, Sch. Law, spring 1980; mem. hearing bd. Ill. Atty. Registration and Disciplinary Commn. Author: Employment Discrimination Law Cases and Materials, 5th edit., 2000, supplement, 2002, Construction Labor Relations, 1984, supplement, 1993; co-editor-in-chief: 1976 Annual Supplement to Morris, The Developing Labor Law, 1977; chpt. editor: The Developing Labor Law, 4th edit., 2000, supplement, 2002; contbr. articles to profl. jours. Recipient award for highest degree of dedication and excellence in tchg. N.Y. State Sch. Indsl. and Labor Rels., Cornell U., 1977. Fellow Coll. Labor and Employment Lawyers; mem. ABA (co-chmn. com. on devel. law under Nat. Labor Rels. Act, Sect. Labor Rels. Law 1976-77), N.Y. State Bar Assn., Phi Eta Sigma, Phi Kappa Phi, Chgo. Athletic Assn., Mid-Day Club. Presbyterian. Administrative and regulatory, Federal civil litigation, Labor (including EEOC, Fair Labor Standards Act, labor-management relations, NLRB, OSHA). Office: Ogletree Deakins et al 2 First National Plz Fl 25 Chicago IL 60603 E-mail: Arthur.Smith@odnss.com.

SMITH, ARTHUR LEE, lawyer; b. Davenport, Iowa, Dec. 19, 1941; s. Harry Arthur Smith and Ethel (Hoffman) Duerre; m. Georgia Mills, June 12, 1965 (dec. Jan. 1984); m. Jean Bowler, Aug. 4, 1984; children: Juliana, Christopher, Andrew, Wendy. BA, Augustana Coll., Rock Island, Ill., 1964; MA, Am. U., 1968; JD, Washington U., St. Louis, 1971. Bar: Mo 1971, DC 1983. Telegraph editor Davenport Morning Democrat, 1962-64; ptnr. Peper Martin Jensen Maichel & Hetlage, 1971-95, Husch & Eppenberger, St. Louis, 1995—. Arbitrator Nat Asn Security Dealers, 1980—, Am Arbit Asn, 1980—. Columnist: St Louis Lawyer, syndicated columnist: Technolawyer-.com and other publications. Dir. P. Buckley Moss Found. for Children's Edn., 2001—. Lt USN, 1964—68. Mem.: ABA, Bar Assn. Met. St. Louis (chmn law mgt comt 1993—96, chair technology comt 1996—99, Pres.'s award Exceptional Service 1995, 2003), P. Buckley Moss Soc. (dir 1994—, v.p. 1998—2000, exec vpres 2001—02, pres. 2002—), Mo. Bar Assn. (vice-chair ins programs comt 1981—83, vice-chair antitrust comt 1981—83, chair admin law comt 1995—97), D.C. Bar Assn. (chmn law practice mgt 1990—91), Order of Coif. Federal civil litigation, Utilities, public, Securities. Office: Husch & Eppenberger Ste 600 190 Carondelet Plz Saint Louis MO 63105-3441 E-mail: arthur.smith@husch.com.

SMITH, BOB, lawyer, state senator, educator; b. Scranton, Pa., Mar. 25, 1947; s. Philip and Ruth (Delmar) S.; m. Ellen Theresa Foster; children: Karen Elizabeth, Lisa. BA in History, U. Scranton, 1969, MS in Chemistry, 1970; MS in Environ. Sci., Rutgers U., 1973; JD, Seton Hall U., 1981. Bar: N.J. 1981. Sci. tchr. Lourdesmont H.S., Clark Summit, Pa., 1968-70; environ. health sci. curriculum coord. Middlesex County Coll., Edison, N.J., 1972-73, adminstrv. asst. to dean sci., 1974-77, instr., 1970-74, asst. prof., 1974-76, assoc. prof., 1976-79, prof. chemistry and environ. sci., 1979-86; law clk. N.J. Dept. Environ. Protection, Trenton, 1980; prin., pvt. practice law Bob Smith and Assocs., Piscataway, N.J., 1981—. Prosecutor East Brunswick, 1997—, South Brunswick, 1998—. Contbg. author Jour. Air Pollution Control Assn., 1976, Environ. Health Sci., 1975; co-editor: New Jersey State Wastewater Treatment Operations Manual, 1979. Mayor of Piscataway Twp., 1981-86; N.J. assemblyman N.J. 17th Legis. Dist., 1986-2001, mem. appropriations com. and environ. quality com., assembly select com. on ocean pollution, 1988, assembly energy and hazardous waste com. policy and rules, 1994; mem. N.J. State Senate, 2002—, mem. jud. com. and environment com.; parliamentarian Assembly Dem. Caucus, 1988-90, chmn. task force on environment, 1987; chmn. Piscataway Dem. Orgn., 1981-90; counsel N.J. State Dem. Platform Com., 1987, 89; chmn. Middlesex County Dem. Orgn., 1991-92; Assembly Dem. Dept. Minority Leader, 1993-95; councilman-at-large Piscataway Twp., 1977-80, pres. coun., 1979, v.p., 1978; mem. Middlesex County Transp. Coordinating Com., 1980-86; chmn. Piscataway Planning Bd, 1981-86, sec., 1975, chmn., 1976; bd. dirs. N.J. Conf. Mayors, 1984-86; mem. tech. adv. com. air pollution Middlesex County Planning Bd., 1973-74; mem. Greenbrook Basin com. Area 208 Mgmt. Planning Program, 1975-76; mem. commr.'s adv. com. N.J. Dept. Environ. Protection, 1972-86; N.J. senator 17th legis. dist., 2001—; mem. judiciary com., 2001—, mem. environ. com., 2001—. Recipient Disting. Citizen award Piscataway Jewish Congregation B'nai Shalom, 1982; named Legis. of Yr. Eden Inst., N.J. State VFW, 1998, Environ. Legislator of Yr., N.J. Environ. Fedn., 1990; U. Scranton Presdl. scholar, 1965-69. Mem. Middlesex County Bar Assn. Roman Catholic. Commercial, contracts (including sales of goods; commercial financing), Land use and zoning (including planning), Property, real (including real estate development, water). Office: 216 Stelton Rd B-1 Piscataway NJ 08854-3284 also: 216 Stelton Rd E-5 Piscataway NJ 08854-2600

SMITH, BRADLEY YOULE, lawyer; b. N.Y.C., Feb. 11, 1948; s. Bradley and Christine (Brown) S.; m. Anne Barre, Dec. 31, 1986; children: Bradley McLaren, Andrew Robert, Lauren Barre, Timothy James, Lynden Eleanor, Christina McLaren. BA in History cum laude, Yale U., 1970; JD, NYU, 1974. Bar: N.Y. 1975, U.S. Dist. Ct. (so. dist.) N.Y. 1975, U.S. Ct. Appeals (2d cir.) 1975. With Davis Polk & Wardwell, N.Y.C., 1974—, ptnr., 1980—. Trustee Royal Coll. Surgeons Found., Inc. Mem. ABA (chmn. subcom. secured transactions 1983-87, moderator and panelist com. banking law and uniform comml. code), Am. Law Inst., N.Y. State Bar Assn. (mem. banking law com.). Banking, Commercial, contracts (including sales of goods; commercial financing). Office: Davis Polk & Wardwell 450 Lexington Ave New York NY 10017-3982 E-mail: bradley.smith@dpw.com.

SMITH, BRIAN WILLIAM, lawyer, former government official; b. N.Y.C., Feb. 3, 1947; s. William Francis and Dorothy Edwina (Vogel) S.; m. Donna Jean Holverson, Apr. 24, 1976; children: Mark Holverson, Lauren Elizabeth. BA, St. John's U., N.Y.C., 1968, JD, 1971; MS, Columbia U., 1981. Bar: N.Y. 1972, D.C. 1975, U.S. Dist. Ct. (ea. and so. dists.) N.Y. 1975, U.S. Supreme Ct. 1976, U.S. Dist. Ct. D.C. 1986. Atty. Am. Express Co., N.Y.C., 1970-73, CIT Fin. Corp., N.Y.C., 1973-74; assoc. counsel, mng. atty. Interbank Card Assn. (named changed to Master Card Internat., Inc.), N.Y.C., 1974-75, sr. v.p., corp. sec., gen. counsel, 1975-82; chief counsel Compt. of Currency, Washington, 1982-84; ptnr. Stroock & Stroock & Lavan, Washington, 1984-92, mng. ptnr., 1986-92; ptnr. Mayer, Brown, Rowe & Maw, Washington and N.Y.C., 1992—. Lectr. fin. industry. Editor: E-Commerce, Investment Products Deskbook, 2002, Financial Products and Services, 2003. Capt. USAR, 1970—78. Mem. ABA, N.Y. State Bar Assn., D.C. Bar Assn., Assn. Bar City N.Y., Fed. Bar Assn., N.Y. Athletic Club, Met. Club (N.Y.), Met. Club (Washington). Antitrust, Banking, Corporate, general. Home: 35 W Lenox St Chevy Chase MD 20815-4208 Office: Mayer Brown Rowe & Maw 1909 K St NW Washington DC 20006-1152 E-mail: bsmith@mayerbrownrowe.com.

SMITH, BRUCE ARTHUR, lawyer; b. Terre Haute, Ind., Jan. 4, 1952; s. Wayne Coakley and Stella Inez S.; m. Lora L. Smith, May 16, 1992; children: Ashley Nicole, Haley Marie, Nathan Wayne, Evan McKean. BS, Ind. State U., 1973; JD cum laude, Ind. U., 1976. Bar: Ind. 1976, Ill. 1984, Ky. 2002, U.S. Dist. Ct. (so. dist.) Ind. 1976, U.S. Tax Ct. 1977, U.S. Supreme Ct. 1983; cert. in bus. bankruptcy law and consumer bankruptcy law Am. Bd. Cert. Ptnr. Sturm, Smith & Parmenter, Vincennes, Ind., 1976—. Instr. paralegal edn. Vincennes U., 1977-81, mem. adv. bd. dept. small bus. edn., 1984-86; dep. pros. atty. Knox County Prosecutor's Office, Vincennes, 1976-82; instr. Ind. Continuing Legal Edn. Forum, 1995, 97, 99, 2001. Mem. Ind. Bar Assn. (chair bankruptcy law sect., 1994-95), Ill. Bar Assn., Knox County Bar Assn. (pres. 1982-83), Kiwanis (pres. 1981-82), Elks (exalted ruler 1983-84), Phi Delta Phi. Banking, Bankruptcy, Commercial, contracts (including sales of goods; commercial financing). Home: 564 N Deer Creek Dr Vincennes IN 47591-9600 Office: Sturm Smith & Parmenter 302 Main St PO Box 393 Vincennes IN 47591-0393

SMITH, CAROLE DIANNE, retired lawyer, editor, writer, product developer; b. Seattle, June 12, 1945; d. Glaude Francis and Elaine Claire (Finkenstein) S.; m. Stephen Bruce Presser, June 18, 1968 (div. June 1987); children: David Carter, Elisabeth Catherine. AB cum laude, Harvard U., Radcliffe Coll., 1968; JD, Georgetown U., 1974. Bar: Pa. 1974. Law clk. Hon. Judith Jamison, Phila., 1974—75; assoc. Gratz, Tate, Spiegel, Ervin & Ruthrouff, Phila., 1975—76; freelance editor, writer Evanston, Ill., 1983—87; editor Ill. Inst. Tech., Chgo., 1987—88; mng. editor LawLetters, Inc., Chgo., 1988—89; editor ABA, Chgo., 1989—95; product devel. dir. Gt. Lakes divsn. Lawyers Coop. Pub., Deerfield, Ill., 1995—96; product devel. mgr. Midwest Market Ctr. West Group, Deerfield, Ill., 1996—97; mgr acquisitions, bus. and fin. group CCH, Inc., Riverwoods, Ill., 1997—2002; ret. Author Jour. of Legal Medicine, 1975, Selling and the Law: Advertising and Promotion, 1987; (under pseudonym Sarah Toast) 79 children's books and stories, 1994-2002; editor The Brief, 1990-95, Criminal Justice, 1989-90, 92-95 (Gen. Excellence award Soc. Nat. Assn. Pubs. 1990, Feature Article award-bronze Soc. Nat. Assn. Pubs. 1994), Franchise Law Jour., 1995; mem. editl. bd. The Brief, ABA Tort and Ins. Practice Sect., 1995-2000, editor-in-chief, 1998-2000. Dir. Radcliffe Club of Chgo., 1990-93; mem. parents coun. Latin Sch. Chgo., 1995-96; trustee Winnetka-Northfield Libr., 2003—. Mem. ABA (tort trial and ins. practice sect. 1998-). E-mail: carole_d_smith@msn.com.

SMITH, CHARLES Z. retired state supreme court justice; b. Lakeland, Fla., Feb. 23, 1927; s. John R. and Eva (Love) S.; m. Eleanor Jane Martinez, Aug. 20, 1955; children: Carlos M., Michael O., Stephen P., Felica L. BS, Temple U., 1952; JD, U. Wash., 1955. Bar: Wash. 1955. Law clk. Wash. Supreme Ct., Olympia, 1955-56; dep. pros. atty., asst. chief criminal div. King County, Seattle, 1956-60; ptnr. Bianchi, Smith & Tobin, Seattle, 1960-61; spl. asst. to atty. gen. criminal div. U.S. Dept. Justice, Washington, 1961-64; judge criminal dept. Seattle Mcpl. Ct., 1965-66; judge Superior Ct. King County, 1966-73; former assoc. dean, prof. law U. Wash., 1973; justice Wash. Supreme Ct., Olympia. Mem. adv. bd. NAACP, Seattle Urban League, Wash. State Literacy Coun., Boys Club, Wash. Citizens for Migrant Affairs, Medina Children's Svc., Children's Home Soc. Wash., Seattle Better Bus. Bur., Seattle Foundation, Seattle Symphony Orch., Seattle Opera Assn., Community Svc. Ctr. for Deaf and Hard of Hearing, Seattle U., Seattle Sexual Assault Ctr., Seattle Psychoanalytic Inst., The Little Sch., Linfield Coll., Japanese Am. Citizens League, Kawabe Meml. Hous, Puget Counseling Ctr, Am. Cancer Soc., Hutchinson Cancer Rsch. Ctr., Robert Chinn Found.; pres. Am. Bapt. Chs. U.S.A., 1976-77, U.S. Commn. on Internat. Religious Freedom, 1999-2000. lt. col. ret. USMCR Mem. ABA, Am. Judicature Soc., Washington Bar Assn., Seattle-King County Bar Assn., Order of Coif., Phi Alpha Delta, Alpha Phi Alpha. Mailing: PO Box 146 Olympia WA 98507-0146

SMITH, CRAIG BENNETT, lawyer; b. Wilmington, Del., Oct. 16, 1943; s. Wilfred Winter and Louetta Beatrice (Bennett) S.; m. Charlotte Anne Boucheron, May 27, 1967; 1 child, Stuart Evan. BA in English, Carleton Coll., 1966; MA in Creative Writing, Syracuse U., 1969, JD summa cum laude, 1975. Bar: U.S. Dist. Ct. Del. 1975. Assoc. Morris, Nichols, Arsht & Tunnell, Wilmington, 1975-83; ptnr. Biggs & Battaglia, Wilmington, 1983-84, Lassen, Smith, Katzenstein & Furlow, Wilmington, 1984-91, Smith, Katzenstein & Furlow, L.L.P., Wilmington, 1992—. Mem. adv. bd.

Bur. Nat. Affairs Corp. Practices Series, Washington, 1988—. Co-author: State Limited Partnership Laws, 1987, Guide to the Takeover Law of Delaware, 1988, Limited Partnerships: Legal Aspects of Organization, Operation and Dissolution, 1992 (book chpts.) New York and Delaware Business Entities, 1997; mem. editorial bd. State Ltd. Partnership Laws-Prentice Hall Law & Bus., 1987—; sr. notes and comments editor Syracuse Law Rev., 1974-75; contbr. articles to profl. jours. Mem. Del. Gov's High Tech. Task Force, Wilmington, 1986, com. bus. & indsl. devel. cos. Del. Econ. Devel. Office, Wilmington, 1988. Named to Justinian Soc., 1974. Fellow ABA (litigation sect. 1985—, bus. law sect. 1975—); mem. Del. State Bar Assn. (corp. law sect. com. 1987-90, 93—, com. Del. Revised Uniform Ltd. Partnership Act 1984—, chancery ct. fiduciary rules adv. com. 1986-89), Order of Coif. Republican. Avocations: classical guitar playing, sculpturing. General civil litigation, Corporate, general, Securities. Home: 318 Spalding Rd Wilmington DE 19803-2422 Office: Smith Katzenstein & Furlow LLP The Corporate Plaza 800 Delaware Ave Wilmington DE 19801-1322

SMITH, CULLEN, lawyer; b. Waco, Tex., May 31, 1925; s. Curtis Cullen and Elizabeth (Brient) S.; m. Laura Risher Dossett, Mar. 6, 1948; children: Sallie Smith Wright, Alethea Risher Smith Gilbert, Elizabeth Brient Smith. Student, Emory U., 1943-44, Duke U., 1944; BBA, Baylor U., 1948, JD, 1950. Bar: Tex. 1950. Ptnr. firm Smith, McIlheran & Smith, Weslaco, Tex., 1950-53, Naman, Howell, Smith & Lee LLP, Waco, 1953—. Lectr. law Baylor U. Sch. Law, 1964-72 Contbr. articles to legal publs. Mem. standing com. Episcopal Diocese of Tex., 1960-63, 74-75; trustee Episcopal Theol. Sem. of S.W., 1962-67; mem. Waco City Coun., 1983-86; chmn. bd. Vanguard Sch., 1975; bd. dirs. G.H. Pape Found., 1993-94; bd. dirs., vice chmn. Tex. Ctr. for Legal Ethics and Professionalism, 1994-99; mem. adv. coun. Baylor U. Coll. Arts and Scis., 1998-2003. 1st lt. USMCR, 1943-46. Named One of 5 Outstanding Young Texans Tex. Jr. C. of C., 1957, Baylor Lawyer of Yr., 1980; recipient Disting. Alumnus award Waco Ind. Sch. Dist. Edn. Found., 2002. Fellow Am. Bar Found., Tex. Bar Found. (chmn. bd. 1973-74, 50 Yr. Lawyer award 2000), fellow Coll. of Law Practice Mgmt.; mem. ABA (chmn. standing com. econs. law practice 1965-69, chmn. spl. com. on law book pub. practices 1970-72, chmn. gen. practice sect. 1973-74, mem. house of dels. 1974-81), Am. Law Firm Assn. (chmn. 1989-90), Waco-McLennan County Bar Assn. (pres. 1956-57), Mont. Bar Assn. (hon.), State Bar Tex. (pres. jr. bar 1957-58, chmn. profl. econs. com. 1959-61, chmn. spl. com. on revision Tex. Canons Ethics 1969-71, dir. 1971-74, pres. 1978-79), Philos. Soc. Tex., Baylor U. Law Alumni Assn. (pres. 1962-63), Order of Coif, Delta Sigma Phi, Phi Delta Phi, Am. Inns Ct. (master), Ridgewood Country Club (pres. 1965), Hedonia Club (pres. 1957), Rotary. Avocation: photography. Corporate, general, General practice. Home: Oak Grove Farm 447 Meandering Way China Spring TX 76633-2905 Office: Naman Howell Smith & Lee LLP Tex Ctr PO Box 1470 Waco TX 76703-1470

SMITH, CURTIS DAVID, lawyer; b. Freeport, Ill., Oct. 16, 1951; s. David Logan and Patricia Lou (Scott) S.; m. Terrie Lee Grant, Sept. 25, 1981; children: Grant, Megan, Gavin. BA, U. Ill., 1973; JD, Wm. Mitchell Coll. of Law, St. Paul, 1979. Bar: Minn. 1979, U.S. Dist. Ct. Minn. 1979, U.S. Tax Ct. 1980. Atty. Wiese & Cox, Ltd., Mpls., 1979-85; shareholder Moss & Barnett, Mpls., 1985—. Dir. Am. Subcontractors Assn. of Minn., St. Paul, 1992—. Coach White Bear, Minn. Hockey Assn., 1989—. Mem. ABA, Minn. State Bar Assn., Hennepin County Bar Assn. General civil litigation, Government contracts and claims. Home: 6160 Woodchuck Cir White Bear Lake MN 55110-1045 Office: Moss & Barnett 4800 Wells Fargo Ctr Minneapolis MN 55402 E-mail: smithc@moss-barnett.com.

SMITH, D. BROOKS, federal judge; b. 1951; BA, Franklin and Marshall Coll., 1973; JD, Dickinson Sch. Law, 1976. Pvt. practice Jubelirer, Carothers, Krier, Halpern & Smith, Altoona, Pa., 1976-84; judge Ct. Common Pleas of Blair County, Pa., 1984-88, U.S. Dist. Ct. (we. dist.) Pa., 1988—2002, chief judge, 2001—02; judge U.S. Ct. Appeals 3d Cir., Johnstown, Pa., 2003—. Asst. dist. atty. Blair County, part-time, 1977-79, spl. prosecutor, 1981-83, dist. atty. part-time, 1983-84; instr. Pa. State U., Altoona campus, 1977—, St. Francis Coll., 1986—; adv. com. on criminal rules U.S. Jud. Conf., 1993-99. Trustee St. Francis Coll. vice chmn. of bd. of trustees U. Mem. Am. Law Inst., Pa. Bar Assn., Am. Judicature Soc., Pa. Soc., Amen Corner, Blair County Game, Fish and Forestry Assn., Fed. Judges Assn. (bd. dirs. 1993-97, 2002—), Inns of Ct., Allegheny County Bar Assn., Pi Gamma Mu. Office: US Courthouse 319 Washington St Ste 104 Johnstown PA 15901-1624

SMITH, DANIEL CLIFFORD, lawyer; b. Cin., Aug. 9, 1936; s. Clifford John and Vivian Aileen (Stone) S.; m. Carroll Cunningham; children: Edward, Andrew, Scott. BS, Ariz. State U., 1960; postgrad., George Washington U., 1961-62; JD, Am. U., 1965. Bar: D.C. 1965, U.S. Ct. Appeals (D.C. cir.) 1966, U.S. Ct. Appeals (Fed. cir.), U.S. Dist. Ct. D.C. 1966, Va. 1967, U.S. Supreme Ct. 1969, U.S. Ct. Appeals (4th cir., 5th cir., 6th cir., 7th cir., 9th cir., 11th cir.), U.S. Ct. Claims, U.S. Ct. Customs and Patent Appeals, U.S. Tax Ct. Assoc. Alpern & Feissner, Washington, 1963-66; atty. FTC, Washington, 1966-70; ptnr. Arent, Fox, Kintner, Plotkin & Kahn, Washington, 1970-93, Canfield & Smith, Washington, 1993—. Pres., dir. Country Pl. Citizens Assn., Inc., 1974-77; bd. dirs. Sea Watch Condominium, Ocean City, Md., 1978—, treas., 1982-86, pres. 1986—; active Supreme Ct. Hist. Soc., The Federalist Soc., Smithsonian Inst. Assocs., Ariz. State Soc. Served with USMC. Mem. D.C. Bar Assn. (bd. dirs. 1974-76, chmn. consumer protection com. 1972-74, chmn. D.C. affairs sect. 1975-76), Va. State Bar Assn., Fed. Bar Assn., Assn. Trial Lawyers Am., Nat. Field Selling Assn. (gen. counsel), Ariz. State U. Alumni Assn., Rotary Club (pres. 1987-88, 96-97), Optimist (pres. 1972-73), Internat. Town and Country Club (dir. 1969-73), Masons, Delta Theta Phi. Administrative and regulatory, Corporate, general, Federal civil litigation. Office: Canfield & Smith Ste 800 910 17th St NW Washington DC 20006-2606

SMITH, DANIEL LYNN, lawyer; b. Ottawa, Kans., June 22, 1952; s. Daniel H. and Mary K. (Lynn) S.; m. Alana A. Windhorst, Aug. 15, 1981; children: Tricia, Lauran, Alexa. BA, U. Kans., 1973; JD, Duke U., 1976. Bar: Kans. 1976, U.S. Dist. Ct. Kans. 1976, U.S. Ct. Appeals (10th cir.) 1977, U.S. Tax Ct. 1977. Assoc. Bronston Law Offices, Overland Park, Kans., 1976-78; ptnr. Oliver, Smith & Oliver, Overland Park, 1978-80, Bronston and Smith, Overland Park, 1981-92, Ankerholz & Smith, Overland Park, Kans., 1992—; pvt. practice Westwood, Kans., 1980-81. Mem. Kans. Bar Assn., Kans. Trial Lawyers Assn. (bd. govs. 1981—), Civil War Roundtable Kansas City, Phi Beta Kappa. General civil litigation, Personal injury (including property damage), Workers' compensation. Home: 10075 Goodman Dr Shawnee Mission KS 66212-3432 Office: Ankerholz & Smith 6900 College Blvd Overland Park KS 66211-1547

SMITH, DAVID BURNELL, lawyer; b. Charleston, W.Va., Apr. 8, 1941; s. Ernest Dayton and Nellie Dale (Tyler) S.; m. Rita J. Hughes, Sept. 25, 1967. BA, U. Charleston, 1967; JD, U. Balt., 1972; MJS, U. Nev., 1995. Bar: Colo. 1972, Md. 1972, U.S. Supreme Ct. 1980, Ariz. 1983, U.S. Dist. Ct. Md. 1972, U.S. Dist. Ct. Colo. 1972, U.S. Ct. Appeals (4th Cir.) 1972, U.S. Ct. Appeals (9th cir. 1972, U.S. Ct. Appeals (10th cir.) 1983. Sales rep. Gulf Oil, Washington, 1967-72; pvt. practice Littleton, Colo., 1972-83, Glendale, Ariz., 1983-86, Phoenix, 1986-88, Scottsdale, Ariz., 1988—. Pro-tempore judge Wickenburg Mcpl. Ct., 1986—; presiding judge Peoria (Ariz.) Mcpl. Ct., 1987-94, Cave Creek Mcpl. Ct., 1995-98. Appeared as actor in movie Dead Girls Don't Tango, 1990. V.p. South Jefferson County Reps., Lakewood, Colo., 1979, pres., 1990; candidate Dist. 6 for Congress; pres. Ariz. Rep. Assembly Dist. 28, Scottsdale (Ariz.) Constitution Commemorative com., 2002—. Served with USCG, 1959-66. Mem. ATLA, ABA (vice-chmn. family law 1983), Nat. Assn. Criminal Lawyers, Am. Judicature Soc., Nat. Assn. Criminal Def. Attys., Ariz. Magistrates Assn., Colo. Bar Assn., Ariz. Bar Assn., Scottsdale (Ariz.) Bar Assn. (pres., 2003—), Md. Bar Assn., Colo. Trial Lawyers Assn., Maricopa County Bar Assn., Scottsdale Bar Assn. (bd. dirs., sec. 1996—), Masons, Shriners, Elks. State civil litigation, Criminal, Personal injury (including property damage). Home: PO Box 5145 36418 N Wildflower Rd Carefree AZ 85377-5145 Office: 4310 N 75th St Scottsdale AZ 85251-3578 E-mail: dbsatt@earthlink.net.

SMITH, DAVID JAMES, corporate lawyer; Asst. sec. Archer Daniels Midland, Decatur, Ill., 1988-97, asst. gen. counsel, 1995-97, v.p., sec., gen. counsel, 1997—2001, sr. v.p., sec., gen. counsel, 2002—03, exec. v.p., sec. and gen. counsel, 2003—. Office: Archer Daniels Midland Co 4666 E Faries Pkwy Decatur IL 62526-5666

SMITH, DAVID SHIVERICK, lawyer, former ambassador; b. Omaha, Jan. 25, 1918; s. Floyd Monroe and Anna (Shiverick) S.; m. June Noble, Dec. 8, 1945 (div. 1968); children:Noble, David Shiverick, Jeremy T., Bradford D.; m. Mary Edson, Feb. 14, 1972. Degre Superieur, Sorbonne, Paris, 1938; BA magna cum laude, Dartmouth Coll., 1939; JD, Columbia U., 1942. Bar: N.Y. 1942, Conn. 1950, D.C. 1954. Assoc. Breed, Abbott & Morgan, N.Y.C., 1946-48; legal dept. ABC, N.Y.C., 1948-50; partner Chapman, Bryson, Walsh & O'Connell, N.Y.C. and Washington, 1950-54; spl. asst. to undersec. Dept. State, Washington, 1954; asst. sec. Air Force, 1954-59; founder, dir. internat. fellows program Columbia U., 1959-75, coordinator internat. studies, 1960-75, asso. dean sch. internat. affairs, 1960-74; cons. AEC, 1959-60; ptnr. Baker & McKenzie (and predecessor), N.Y.C. and Washington, 1960-75, Martin & Smith (and predecessors), Washington, 1975-76, 77-88, cons., 1988—; ambassador to Sweden, 1976-77. Dir. United Svcs. Life Ins. Corp., Internat. Bank, USLICO Corp., Liberian Svcs., Inc.; mem. Coun. Fgn. Rels.; dir. Fgn. Policy Assn.; mem. adv. coun. Sch. Advanced Internat. Studies, Johns Hopkins U., 1962—; pres., dir. Ctr. for Inter-Am. Rels., N.Y.C., 1969-74. Adv. and contbg. editor: Jour. Internat. Affairs, 1960-74; editor: The Next Asia, 1969, Prospects for Latin America, 1970, Concerns in World Affairs, 1973, From War to Peace, 1974. Chmn. bd. George Olmsted Found., 1977-2001; advisor emeritus Nat. Trust Hist. Preservation; active in past various charitable orgns. Lt. USNR, 1942-54; PTO; col. USAFR, 1955-75. Decorated Purple Heart. Mem. ABA, Am. Soc. Internat. Law, Am. Fgn. Law Assn., N.Y. State Bar Assn., Conn. Bar Assn., Fed. Bar Assn. (v.p. for N.Y., N.J. and Conn.), Pilgrims of U.S., France-Am. Soc., English Speaking Union, Asia Soc., Coun. on Foreign Rels., Hudson Inst., Washington Inst. Fgn. Affairs, Coun. Fgn. Rels., Coun. Am. Ambs. (founder, bd. dirs., sec.), Soc. Mayflower Descs., Soc. Cin. (hon. mem.), Brook Club (N.Y.C.), Met. Club (Washington), Chevy Chase Club, Bathing Corp. of Southampton (N.Y.), Meadow Club (Southampton), Soc. Four Arts, Bath and Tennis Club, Everglades Club (Palm Beach), The Crocodiles, Old Guard Soc. Palm Beach Golfers, Phi Beta Kappa. Home: 525 S Flagler Dr Apt 20C West Palm Beach FL 33401-5925

SMITH, DEIRDRE O'MEARA, lawyer; b. N.Y.C., June 2, 1946; d. Thomas Francis and Mary Veronica (Meehan) O'Meara; children: Thomas Brady Ahr, Andrew Travers Ahr; m. Gerald Monroe Smith, Aug. 15, 1992. BA cum laude, Trinity Coll., 1968; MEd, Va. Commonwealth U., 1976; JD, U. Mo., 1982. Bar: Mo. 1982, U.S. Dist. Ct. (we. dist.) Mo. 1982. Tchr. Prince George's County Schs., Md., 1968-70, St. Michael's Sch., Richmond, Va., 1976-78; staff lawyer Mo. Supreme Ct., Jefferson City, 1982-83; gen. counsel State of Mo. Detention Facilities Commn., Jefferson City, 1983, State of Mo. Jud. Fin. Commn., Jefferson City, 1983-85; clk. of the ct. Mo. Ct. Appeals Eastern Dist., St. Louis, 1985-98. Bd. dirs. Downtown St. Louis, 1994-95. Recipient Acad. Excellence award in environ. law U. Mo. Sch. Law, 1981; disting. fellow St. Louis Bar Found. Fellow Am. Bar Found., Mo. Bar Found.; mem. ABA (jud. divsn. lawyers conf., exec. com. 1997-2000), Nat. Conf. Bar Pres., Nat. Conf. Bar Founds., Mo. Bar Assn. (Mo. Client Security Security Trust Fund bd. dirs. 1991-95, chmn. 1995-96), St. Louis County Bar Assn., Lawyers Assn. St. Louis (Outstanding Svc. award 1998), Met. St. Louis Bar Assn. (exec. com. 1988-96, pres. 1994-95), Beaufort, S.C. Art Assn. (bd. dirs. 1999-2002), Dataw Island Owners Assn. (sec. 2001-02, v.p. 2002-03, pres. 2003—), St. Louis Bar Found. (bd. dirs. 1989-96, pres. 1995-96), St. Louis Women Lawyers Assn. (bd. dirs. 1989-94, pres. 1992-93), Am. Judicature Soc. (bd. dirs. 1990-94, bd. exec. com. 1993—, v.p. 1995-97, sec. 1997-99, treas. 1999-2001, pres. 2001—), Nat. Conf. Appellate Ct. Clks. (exec. com. 1990-92), Media Club St. Louis (bd. dirs.), Phi Delta Phi. Roman Catholic.

SMITH, DENNIS JAY, lawyer; b. Newark, Sept. 2, 1943; s. Sidney H. and Theresa K. Smith; m. Sandra Kotzen Smith, Jan. 25, 1944; children: Sheryl, Lori. BA, Brandeis U., 1961; JD, Boston Coll., 1968. Bar: N.J. 1968, U.S. Ct. Appeals (3d cir.) 1986. Sole proprietor, East Orange, N.J., 1968-77, Millburn, N.J., 1977-83; ptnr. Clancy Callahan & Smith, Newark, N.J., 1983-87, Roseland, N.J., 1987—. Mem. Am. Bar Assn., N.J. State Bar Assn. (ethics com. 1998-2002), Essex County Bar Assn. (chmn. gen. practice com. 1995-96), Mental Health Assn. Essex County (bd. dirs. 1977, pres. 1980-82, v.p. 2000—). State civil litigation, Commercial, contracts (including sales of goods; commercial financing), General practice. Office: Clancy Callahan & Smith 103 Eisenhower Pkwy Ste 10 Roseland NJ 07068-1090

SMITH, DWIGHT CHICHESTER, III, lawyer; b. Ft. Meade, Md., June 24, 1955; s. Dwight Chichester Jr. and Rachel (Stryker) S.; m. Mindy L. Kotler, Aug. 18, 1985; children: Dwight C. IV, Cornelia R. BA, Yale U., 1977, JD, 1981. Bar: D.C. 1982, N.Y. 1982. Para-legal House Ethics Com., Washington, 1977-78; law clk. to Hon. Hugh Bownes U.S. Ct. Appeals (1st cir.), Concord, N.H., 1981-82; assoc. Kaye, Scholer, Fierman, Hays & Handler, Washington, 1982-84, Covington & Burling, Washington, 1984-90; dep. chief counsel for legal policy Office of Thrift Supervision, Dept. of Treasury, Washington, 1990-94, dep. chief counsel for bus. transactions, 1995-99; counsel Alston & Bird LLP, Washington, 1999—2001; ptnr. Alston & Bird, LLP, Washington, 2002—. Article and book rev. editor Yale Law jour., 1980-81; contbr. articles to profl. jours. Mem. Potomac Boat Club, City Tavern Club. Presbyterian. Avocation: rowing. Home: 1606 32nd St NW Washington DC 20007-2930 Office: Alston & Bird LLP North Bldg 11th Fl 601 Pennsylvania Ave NW Washington DC 20004-2601 E-mail: dcsmith@alston.com.

SMITH, EDWARD REAUGH, retired lawyer, retired funeral director, consultant; b. Flora, Ill., Sept. 23, 1932; m. Jo Anne Myers, Sept. 10, 1954; children: Mark and Michael (twins), Jillian. BS, Midwestern U., 1953; LLB, So. Meth. U., 1957. Bar: Tex. 1957, U.S. Dist. Ct. (so. dist.) Tex. 1957, U.S. Dist. Ct. (no. dist.) Tex. 1961, U.S. Tax Ct. 1961, U.S. Ct. Appeals (5th cir.) 1971, U.S. Ct. Claims 1971, U.S. Supreme Ct. 1982; CPA, Tex. Atty. Vinson, Elkins, Weems & Searls, Houston, 1957-59, Nelson, McCleskey & Harringer, Lubbock, Tex., 1959-61; pvt. practice Lubbock, 1961-62; ptnr. Smith, Baker, Field & Clifford Inc. (formerly Smith & Baker Inc.), Lubbock, 1962-84; chmn., CEO Resthaven Funeral Home and Cemetery, Lubbock, 1979-93; cons. Svc. Corp. Internat., Lubbock, 1993—. Bd. dirs. Briercroft Savs. Assn., 1962-84, Tex. Cemetery Assn., 1986-87, 90-91; pres., bd. chmn. Resthaven Funeral Home, 1965-69, Resthaven of Lubbock, Inc., 1979-93, Lakeview Meml. Gardens, 1978-86; lectr. profl. meetings on taxes and estate planning; bd. visitors So. Meth. U. Law Sch., 1968-71; chmn. estate planning seminar for women Tex. Tech. Found., 1971; pres. South Plains Trust and Estate Coun., 1963-64, others. Author: The Burning Bush, 1997, The Incredible Births of Jesus, 1998, The Disciple Whom Jesus Loved, 2000, David's Question "What is man?", 2001; contbr. articles to profl. jours. Mem. Lubbock Planning and Zoning Commn., 1964-65, chmn., 1966, budget divsn. United Fund; co-chmn. profl. divsn. United Way, 1981; tchr., bd. dirs. First Meth. Ch., Lubbock, 1963-88; pres. Haynes Elem. Sch. PTA, 1968-69; past mem. pres.'s adv. bd. Lubbock Christian Coll.; bd. dirs. Tex. Tech. U. Found., 1968-89, sec., 1969-76, vice-chmn., 1976-78, chmn., 1978-81, chmn. fund raising com., 1979-81; bd. dirs. Tex. Tech. U. Med. Sch. Found., 1970-78, vice-chmn., 1972-73, chmn., 1973-74; mem. chancellor's coun. Tex. Tech. U., 1978—; mem. adv. bd. Sophia Found. of N.Am., 2000—; spkr. ann. banquet Flora Acad. Found., Flora H.S., 1991, N.Y. Open Ctr., 1999, Anthrop. Soc. Conf., 2000; bd. dirs. Lubbock Symphony Orch., 1996-. Mem. Am. Acad. Religion/Soc. Biblical Lit., Am. Anthroposophical Soc., Tex. Cemeteries Assn. (hon. life), Alpha Chi. Avocations: mountain trails, research, writing, concert pianist.

SMITH, EDWIN DUDLEY, lawyer; b. N.Y.C., Oct. 4, 1936; s. Edwin Dudley Jr. and Mary Jane (Bannigan) S.; m. Joan Joyce Mortenson, June 29, 1963; children: Edwin Dudley V, Patrick Townshend. BA, U. Kans., 1960, JD, 1963. Bar: Kans. 1963, Mo. 1992, U.S. Dist. Ct. Kans. 1963, U.S. Ct. Appeals (10th cir.) 1967, U.S. Supreme Ct. 1972, U.S. Dist. Ct. (we. dist.) Mo., 1998. Assoc. Fisher Patterson Sayler & Summers, Topeka, 1963-66; ptnr. Fisher Patterson Sayler & Smith, L.L.P., Topeka, Overland Park, 1966—. Contbg. author: Pharmacy Law Annual, 1991. Chpt. advisor Tau Kappa Epsilon Frat., 1988-93; mem. adv. bd. Florence Crittenton Svcs., Topeka, 1988-91; chmn. legis. com. U.S. Swimming, 1986-90; chmn. Missouri Valley Swimming, 1987-89. Fellow Kans. Bar Found.; mem. ABA, Kans. Bar Assn. (bd. govs. 1986-92, Outstanding Svc. award 1978), Topeka Bar Assn., Johnson County Bar Assn., Kansas City Met. Bar Assn., Internat. Assn. Def. Counsel, Am. Judicature Soc. (bd. dirs. 1984-89), Am. Bd. Trial Adv. (pres. Kans. chpt. 1989-90), Kans. Assn. Def. Counsel, Def. Rsch. Inst., Am. Soc. Pharmacy Law, Mercedes-Benz Club Am. (bd. dirs. Kansas City sect. 1998-2003). Avocation: photography. General civil litigation, Personal injury (including property damage), Professional liability. Home: 4344 W 124th Ter Leawood KS 66209-2277 Office: Fisher Patterson Sayler & Smith LLP 51 Corporate Woods Ste 300 9393 W 110th St Shawnee Mission KS 66210 also: Fisher Patterson Sayler & Smith LLP 3550 SW 5th St Topeka KS 66606-1998 E-mail: dsmith@fisherpatterson.com.

SMITH, EDWIN ERIC, lawyer; b. Louisville, Sept. 29, 1946; s. Lester Henry and Nancy Joy (Heyman) S.; m. Katharine Case Thomson, Aug. 16, 1969; children: Benjamin Clark, George Lewis, Andrew Laurence. BA, Yale U., 1968; JD, Harvard Law Sch., 1974. Bar: Mass. 1974, U.S. Dist. Ct. Mass. 1974. Assoc. BinghamMcCutchen LLP, Boston, 1974-81, ptnr., 1981—. Lectr. in field; Mass. commr. on uniform state laws; mem. uniform comml. code articles 5 and 9 drafting com.; chmn. uniform comml. code payments article divsn. drafting com.; U.S. del. to receivables assignment working group UN Commn. on Internat. Trade Law. Lt. USNR, 1969-71. Recipient Achievement Medal USN, 1971. Mem. ABA (chmn. uniform comml. code com. bus. law sect. 1995-99, advisor to the permanent editl. bd. uniform comml. code 1999—), Am. Law Inst. (Uniform Comml. Code article 9 study com.), Am. Coll. Comml. Fin. Lawyers (pres. 2002-03), Assn. Comml. Fin. Attys., Nat. Bankruptcy Conf. Banking, Bankruptcy, Commercial, contracts (including sales of goods; commercial financing). Home: 4 Chiltern Rd Weston MA 02493-2714 Office: Bingham McCutchen LLP 150 Federal St Boston MA 02110-1713 E-mail: edwin.smith@bingham.com.

SMITH, FRANCIS M. lawyer; b. Paterson, NJ, Jan. 17, 1951; s. John Francis and Mary Rose Smith; m. Gail Luria Smith, Oct. 20, 1978; children: Evan, Alison, Wyatt. BA, Seton Hall U., 1973; JD, Creighton U., 1976. Bar: NJ 76, U.S. Dist. Ct. NJ 76, U.S. Supreme Ct. 96. Staff counsel Chubb & Sons Ins. Co., Short Hills, NJ, 1977—82, Continental Ins. Co., Tinton Falls, NJ, 1982—86; sr. assoc. Joseph Dirienzo Esquire, Westfield, NJ, 1986—89; ptnr. Hoyt & Smith, P.C., Westfield; pvt. practice Westfield, 1996—. Ct. apptd. arbitrator NJ Superior Ct, 1992—, ct. apptd. mediator, 1997—. Pres. bd. dirs. Gingham Giraffe Presch., Chatham, NJ, 1990—; mem. com. Westfield Rep. Com., 2001—; mem. Westfield Zoning Bd. Adjustment, 2002—. Mem.: ATLA, Richard Hughes Inn of Ct. (barrister), NJ State Bar Assn., Union County Bar Assn., Westfield Hist. Soc. Republican. Roman Catholic. Personal injury (including property damage), Insurance. Home: 544 Forest Ave Westfield NJ 07090 Office: PO Box 99 Westfield NJ 07091 Fax: 908-233-8488. E-mail: frank@franksmithlaw.com.

SMITH, G. THOMAS, lawyer; s. Garland and Mary Cooper Smith; m. Jennie H. Harkey; children: Laura Susan, Garland Thomas Smith, Jr., Jennie H. Smith Mooney. B in Indsl. Engring., Ga. Inst. Tech.; LLM in Taxation, U. Ala.; JD, U. Fla. Bar: Fla. 1966, U.S. Dist. Ct. (mid. dist.) Fla. 1967, U.S. Dist. Ct. (no. dist.) Fla. 1973, U.S. Ct. Appeals (11th cir.) 1982. Atty., ptnr. Smith, Sauer & DeMaria, Pensacola, Fla., 1986—. Chair unauthorized practice law com. First Jud. Cir. Ct., Fla., 1978—83; exec. bd. Escambia-Santa Rosa County Bar Assn., Fla.; bd. dirs. Attys. Title Ins. Fund, Inc.; presenter in field. Contbr. articles to profl. jours. Mem. alumni coun. U. Fla. Coll. Law; exec. coun. Gulf Coast Coun. Boy Scouts Am.; asst. scout master Boy Scouts; spkr. Gulf Breeze H.S. Career Day; chmn. states issues task force Pensacola Area C. of C.; councilman City Gulf Breeze; pres., sec. standing com. Episcopal Diocese Ctrl. Gulf Coast; lay reader, chalice bearer, vestry mem., dep. gen. conv. and adult Sunday sch. tchr. St. Francis Episcopal Ch.; dir. Pensacola Symphony Orch.; participant YMCA Father and Dau. Programs. Mem.: ABA (standing com. on lawyers title guaranty funds 2001—, bd. cert.in real property law), Am. Coll. Real Estate Attys., Fla. Bar Assn. (mem. bd. legal specialization and edn., chair real property, probate and trust law sect. 1999—2000, divsn. dir. real property probate and trust law sect. 1996—99, sec. real property, probate and trust law sect. 1993—95, chair CLE com. 1994—95, chair alternative dispute resolution com., chair oil, gas and mineral law com.), Five Flags Rotary, Pensacola Rotary. Avocations: travel, fishing, boating, reading, bicycling. Property, real (including real estate development, water), Corporate, general, Environmental. Office: Smith Sauer & DeMaria 510 East Zaragoza St Pensacola FL 32502 Office Fax: 850-438-8860. E-mail: gts345@bellsouth.net.

SMITH, GEORGE ANTHONY, lawyer; b. Lexington, Ky., Feb. 4, 1948; s. Frank Enz and Anna Lois Smith; m. Martha J. Becker; children: Wesley Tyler, Benjamin Cooper. BA, U. Ky., 1970, JD, 1973. Bar: Ga. 1973, Ky. 1973, U.S. Dist. Ct. (no. dist.) Ga. 1973, U.S. Ct. Appeals (1st and 3rd cirs.) 1973. Ptnr. Smith Currie & Hancock, Atlanta, 1973—92, Sutherland Asbill & Brennan, Atlanta, 1992—. Fellow: Chartered Inst. Arbitrators; mem.: London Ct. Internat. Arbitrators, Internat. Bar Assn., Am. Coll. Constrn. Lawyers. Avocations: motorcycling, hiking, hunting, golf, cooking. Alternative dispute resolution, Construction. Office: Sutherland Asbill & Brennan LLP 999 Peachtree St NE Atlanta GA 30309

SMITH, GEORGE BUNDY, state supreme court justice; b. New Orleans, Apr. 7, 1937; m. Alene L. Smith; children: George, Jr., Beth Beatrice. Cert. Polit. Studies, Institut d'Etudes Politiques, Paris, 1958; BA, Yale U., 1959, JD, 1962; MA in Polit. Sci., NYU, 1967, PhD, 1974; M of Jud. Process, U. Va., 2001. Staff atty. NAACP, 1962-64; law sec. to Hon. Jawn Sandifer, 1964-67; law sec. to Hon. Edward Dudley, 1967-71; law sect. to Hon. Harold Stevens, 1972-74; adminstr. model cities City of N.Y., 1974-75; interim judge Civil Ct. N.Y.C., 1975-76, judge, 1976-79, N.Y. State Supreme Ct., 1980-86, assoc. justice appellate divsn., 1st dept., 1987-92; assoc. judge N.Y. State Ct. Appeals, 1992—. Apptd. mem. N.Y. State Ethics Commn. Unified Ct. System, 1989-90; adj. prof. law Fordham U., 1981—. Author: (with Alene L. Smith) You Decide: Applying the Bill of Rights to Real Cases; contbr. articles to profl. jours. Trustee Grace Congl. Ch., Harlem, N.Y., Horace Mann-Barnard Sch., Bronx, N.Y., 1977-99; bd. dirs. Harlem-Dowling Westside Ctr. for Children and Family Svcs., N.Y.C.; former alumni trustee Phillips Acad., Andover, Mass. Mem. Met. Black Bar Assn. (founding, former pres. Harlem Lawyers Assn., bd. dirs., chmn. 1984-88), Assn. of Bar of City of N.Y. (v.p. 1988-89), Judicial Friends. Office: NY Court Appeals 29th Fl 61 Broadway Rm 2900 New York NY 10006-2802 also: Ct of Appeals Hall 20 Eagle St Albany NY 12207-1009*

SMITH, GEORGE CURTIS, judge; b. Columbus, Ohio, Aug. 8, 1935; s. George B. and Dorothy R. Smith; m. Barbara Jean Wood, July 10, 1963; children: Curtis, Geoffrey, Elizabeth Ann. BA, Ohio State U., 1957, JD, 1959. Bar: Ohio 1959, U.S. Dist. Ct. (so. dist.) Ohio 1987. Asst. city atty. City of Columbus, 1959-62; exec. asst. to Mayor of Columbus, 1962-63; asst. atty. gen. State of Ohio, 1964; chief counsel to pros. atty. Franklin County, Ohio, 1965-70; pros. atty., 1971-80; judge Franklin County Mcpl. Ct., Columbus, 1980-85, Franklin County Common Pleas Ct., 1985-87. Mem. 2003 Ohio Bicentennial Com.; mem. Historical Marker com., 2003; mem. Ohio Supreme Ct. Coun. on Victims Rights; judge in residence Law Sch. U. Cin.; chair Fed. Ct. Case Settlement Svc.; faculty Ohio Jud. Coll., Litig. Practice Inst.; chmn., Fed. Bench-Bar Conf.; lectr. ABA Anti-Trust Sec.; alumni spkr. law graduation Ohio State U.; pres. Young Rep. Club; chmn. Perry Group, 2003; exec. com. Franklin County Rep. Party, 1971-80. Elder Presbyn. Ch. Recipient Superior Jud. Svc. award Supreme Ct. Ohio; recipient Outstanding Pub. Svc. award Fr. Co. Rep. Orgn., 2001. Mem. Ohio Pros. Attys. Assn. (pres., Ohio Pros. of Yr. Award of Hon. Leadership award), Columbus Bar Assn., Columbus Bar Found., Columbus Athletic Club (pres., dir.), Lawyers Club of Columbus (pres.), Masons (33d degree), Shriners. Office: 85 Marconi Blvd Columbus OH 43215-2823

SMITH, GLEE SIDNEY, JR., lawyer; b. Rozel, Kans., Apr. 29, 1921; s. Glee S. and Bernice M. (Augustine) S.; m. Geraldine B. Buhler, Dec. 14, 1943; children: Glee S., Stephen B., Susan K. AB, U. Kans., 1943, JD, 1947. Bar: Kans. 1947, U.S. Dist. Ct. 1951, U.S. Supreme Ct. 1973, U.S. Ct. Mil. Appeals 1988. Ptnr. Smith Burnett & Larson, Lanred, Kans., 1947—. Of counsel Barber, Emerson et. al., Lawrence, Kans., 1992—, Kans. state senator, 1957-73, pres. Senate, 1965-73; mem. Kans. Bd. Regents, 1975-83, pres., 1976; bd. govs. Kans. U. Law Soc., 1967—; mem. Kans. Jud. Coun., 1963-65; county atty. Pawnee County, 1949-53; mem. bd. edn. Larned, 1951-63; Kans. commr. Nat. Conf. Commn. on Uniform State Laws, 1963—; bd. dirs. Nat. Legal Svcs. Corp., 1975-79. Served to 1st lt. U.S. Army Air Corps, 1943-45. Recipient disting. svc. award U. Kans. Law Sch., 1976; disting. svc. citation U. Kans., 1984. Fellow Am. Coll. Probate Counsel, Am. Bar Found.; mem. ABA (bd. of govs. 1987-90, chmn. ops. com. 1989-90, exec. com. 1989-90, chmn. task force on solo and small firm practitioners 1990-91, chmn. com. on solo and small firm practitioners 1992-94, chmn. task force on applying fed. legis. to congress 1994-96), Kans. Bar Assn. (del. to ABA ho. of dels. 1982-92, bd. govs. 1982-92, leadership award 1973, medal of distinction 1993), Southwest Kans. Bar Assn., Am. Jud. Soc., Kiwanis, Masons, Rotary. Republican. Presbyterian. General practice, Probate (including wills, trusts), Estate taxation. Home: 4313 Quail Pointe Rd Lawrence KS 66047-1966

SMITH, GORDON HOWELL, lawyer; b. Syracuse, N.Y., Oct. 26, 1915; s. Lewis P. and Maud (Mixer) S.; m. Eunice Hale, June 28,1947; children: Lewis Peter, Susan S. Rizk, Catherine S. Maxson, Maud S. Daudon. BA, Princeton U., 1932-36; LL.B., Yale U., 1939. Bar: N.Y. 1939, Ill. 1946. Asso. Lord, Day & Lord, N.Y.C., 1939-41, Gardner, Carton & Douglas, Chgo., 1946-51; partner Mackenzie, Smith & Michell, Syracuse, 1951-53, Gardner, Carton & Douglas, 1954-57, 60-85, of counsel, 1986-96, retired ptnr., 1996—. Sec., dir. Smith-Corona, Inc., 1951-54, v.p., Syracuse, 1957-60 Bd. dirs. Rehab. Inst. Chgo., chmn., 1974-78, 83-86; bd. dirs. United Way Met. Chgo., 1962-85. Served to lt. comdr. USNR, 1941-46. Mem. Am. Soc. Corporate Secs., Am., Ill., Chgo. bar assns. Clubs: Comml., Law, Econ., Legal, Chgo., Old Elm (Chgo.). Corporate, general. Home: 1302 N Green Bay Rd Lake Forest IL 60045-1108 Office: 321 N Clark St Ste 3400 Chicago IL 60610-4717 E-mail: gsmith1302@aol.com.

SMITH, GRANT BUTLER, lawyer; b. Durham, N.C., Oct. 18, 1961; s. J. Graham and Jean Butler S.; m. Holly Harnsberger, Aug. 25, 1990; children: Caroline Grace, Sarah Elizabeth. BBA, U. Ga., 1983, MBA, 1984, JD, 1987. Assoc. Dennis, Corry Porter & Smith, Atlanta, 1987-94, ptnr., 1995—, mng. ptnr., 1996-97. Mem. ABA (vice chair comml. transp. litigation com. 1998-99, chmn. 1990-2000, newsletter editor 1998-99), Ga. Defense Lawyers Assn. (dir. 1998—, v.p. 2001—, sec.-treas. 2002-03), Def. Rsch. Inst. (mem. trucking law com. 2000—), Trucking Industry Def. Assn., Lawyers Club Atlanta, Atlanta Claims Assn. Federal civil litigation, State civil litigation, Transportation. Home: 1186 Village Cv NE Atlanta GA 30319-5308 Office: Dennis Corry Porter & Smith Piedmont Fourteen 3535 Piedmont Rd Ste 900 Atlanta GA 30305

SMITH, JACK DAVID, lawyer; b. Honolulu, Jan. 4, 1946; s. Jack David and Gloria June (Slater) S.; m. Mary Elizabeth Zasadny, Sept. 17, 1977; children: Amy Elizabeth, Amanda Marie. BA in Polit. Sci., George Washington U., 1968, JD, 1971. Bar: Va. 1971, U.S. Ct. Mil. Appeals 1971, U.S. Ct. Appeals (1st and D.C. cirs.) 1975, U.S. Ct. Appeals (2d and 7th cirs.) 1976, U.S. Supreme Ct. 1976, D.C. 1986. Atty. litig. div. FCC, Washington, 1974-81, dept. chief common carrier bur., 1981-83, chief common carrier bur., 1983-84, gen. counsel, 1984-86; dep. gen. counsel Fed. Home Loan Bank Bd., Washington, 1986-89, Fed. Deposit Ins. Corp., Washington, 1989—. Served to capt. USMC, 1971-74. Mem. Va. Bar Assn., D.C. Bar Assn. Avocations: tennis, running, skiing. Home: 7824 Telegraph Rd Alexandria VA 22315-3701 Office: Fed Deposit Ins Corp 550 17th St NW Washington DC 20429-0002 E-mail: jsmith@fdic.gov.

SMITH, JAMES BARRY, lawyer; b. N.Y.C., Feb. 28, 1947; s. Irving and Vera (Donaghy) S.; m. Kathleen O'Connor, May 28, 1977; children: Jennifer, Kelly. BA in Econs., Colgate U., 1968; JD, Boston U., 1974. Assoc. McDermott, Will & Emery, Chgo., 1974-78, Ungaretti & Harris, Chgo., 1978-80, ptnr., 1980. Lt. U.S. Navy, 1968-70. Mem. Chgo. Mortgage Atty. Assn. Avocations: sports, reading, travel. Property, real (including real estate development, water). Office: Ungaretti & Harris 3500 Three First Nat Pla Chicago IL 60602 E-mail: jbsmith@uhlaw.com.

SMITH, JAMES A. lawyer; b. Akron, Ohio, June 11, 1930; s. Barton H. and Myrna S. (Young) S.; m. Melda I. Perry, Jan. 17, 1959; children: Hugh, Sarah Louise. AB, Western Res. U., 1952; postgrad., Columbia U., 1954-56, LLB, 1961; postgrad., Yale U., 1956-58. Bar: Ohio 1961, U.S. Dist. Ct. (no. dist.) Ohio 1963, U.S. Ct. Appeals (6th cir.) 1973, U.S. Supreme Ct. 1974, U.S. Ct. Appeals (11th cir.) 1983, U.S. Ct. Appeals (D.C. cir.) 1984. Assoc. Squire, Sanders and Dempsey, Cleve., 1961-70, ptnr., 1970-91, counsel, 1991-96; adj. prof. Case Western Res. U. Sch. Law, 1997-98, ret., 1994. Mem. spl. adv. com. Nat. Conf. Commrs. on Uniform State Laws, 1972-74. Trustee Chagrin Falls Park Cmty. Ctr., 1968-78, Greater Cleve. Neighborhood Ctrs. Assn., 1973-78, Legal Aid Soc. Cleve., 1977-80, Cleve. Inst. Music, 1994—; mem. Charter Rev. Commn., Chagrin Falls, 1966. Lt. (j.g.) USNR, 1952-54. Fellow Am. Coll. Trial Lawyers; mem. ABA, Ohio Bar Assn., Cleve. Bar Assn. (trustee 1988-92), U.S. Ct. Appeals for 6th Cir. Jud. Conf. (life), Ohio Ct. Appeals for 8th Jud. Dist. Conf. (life), Ct. of Nisi Prius (clk. 1975-76, judge 1994-95), Phi Beta Kappa, Omicron Delta Kappa, Delta Sigma Rho. Democrat. Federal civil litigation, General civil litigation, State civil litigation.

SMITH, JAMES ALBERT, lawyer; b. Jackson, Mich., May 12, 1942; s. J. William and Mary Barbara (Browning) S.; m. Lucia S. Santini, Aug. 14, 1965; children: Matthew Browning, Aaron Michael, Rachel Elizabeth. BA, U. Mich., 1964, JD, 1967. Bar: Mich. 1968, U.S. Dist. Ct. (ea. dist.) Mich., U.S. Ct. Appeals (6th and D.C. cirs.), U.S. Supreme Ct. Assoc. Bodman, Longley & Dahling, Detroit, 1967-75, ptnr., 1975—. Mem. panel Atty. Discipline Bd., Wayne County, Mich., 1987—; arbitrator Am. Arbitration Assn., 1975—; mem. Banking Commrs. com. on Contested Case Adminstrn., 1978. Mem. pro bono referral group Call For Action, Detroit, 1982—. Mem. ABA, State Bar Mich., Detroit Bar Assn. Roman Catholic. Avocations: sailing, travel. Federal civil litigation, Insurance, Utilities, public. Office: Bodman Longley & Dahling 100 Renaissance Ctr Ste 34 Detroit MI 48243-1001

SMITH, JAMES RANDOLPH, JR., lawyer; b. Martinsville, Va., Mar. 7, 1945; s. James Randolph and Ruth (Boykin) S. BA, Randolph-Macon Coll., 1967; LLB, U. Va., 1970. Bar: Va. 1970, U.S. Dist. Ct. (we. dist.) Va. 1972, U.S. Supreme Ct. 1973, U.S. Ct. Appeals (4th cir.) 1976. Law clk. to judge U.S. Dist. Ct., Wilmington, Del., 1970-71; asst. commonwealth atty. City of Martinsville, 1971-81; ptnr. Smith & Penn, P.C., Martinsville, 1981-86; commonwealth atty. City of Martinsville, 1981-98; pvt. practice, Martinsville, 1998-99; exec. sec. Va. Charitable Gaming Commn., Richmond, 1999-2000; dep. dir. Va. Dept. Rail and Pub. Transp., Richmond, 2000—02; asst. commonwealth atty. County of Henry, Martinsville, Va., 2002—. Instr. Piedmont Criminal Justice Acad., 1980-97, 2002-. Vice chmn. Martinsville Rep. Com., 1986-90, chmn., 1990-94; chmn. bd. dirs. Broad Street Christian Ch., 1996. Mem. Martinsville-Henry County Bar Assn. (v.p. 1983-84, pres. 1984-85), Am. Judicature Soc., Va. Trial Lawyers Assn., Rotary (pres. 1993-94), Phi Delta Phi. Mem. Christian Ch. (Disciples Of Christ). Appellate, General practice, Juvenile. Home: 817 Mulberry Rd Martinsville VA 24112-4414 Office: 3160 Kings Mountain Rd Ste D Martinsville VA 24112-3966

SMITH, JAMES W., JR., state supreme court justice; b. Louisville, Miss., Oct. 28, 1943; BS, U. So. Miss., 1965; JD, Jackson Sch. Law, 1972; MEd with honors, Miss. Coll., 1973. Bar: Miss. 1972, U.S. Dist. Ct. (no. and so. dists.) Miss. 1973, U.S. Ct. Appeals (5th cir.) 1974. Pvt. practice, Pearl, 1972-78, 1979-80; prosecuting atty. City of Pearl, 1973-80; prosecutor Rankin County, 1976; dist. atty. 20th Jud. Dist., 1977-82; judge Rankin County, 1982-92; Supreme Ct. justice Cen. Dist., 1993—. Instr. courtroom procedure and testifying Miss. Law Enforcement Tng. Acad., 1980-91. With U.S. Army, 1966-69. Named Wildlife Conservationist of Yr. Rankin County, 1988; recipient Outstanding Positive Role Model for Today's Youth award, 1991, Child Forever award Miss. Voices of Children and Youth, 1992, You've Made a Difference award, 1995, Alumnus of Yr. award Hinds C.C., 1996. Fellow Miss. Bar Found. (bd. dirs. 1998); mem. Miss. State Bar Assn., Rankin County Bar Assn., Nat. Wildlife Fedn., Nat. Wild Turkey Fedn., Am. Legion, Rotary. Office: Carroll Gartin Justice Bldg PO Box 117 Jackson MS 39205-0117

SMITH, JEFFREY MICHAEL, lawyer; b. Mpls., July 9, 1947; s. Philip and Gertrude E. (Miller) S.; 1 son, Brandon Michael. Student, U. Malaya, 1967-68; BA cum laude, U. Minn., 1970, JD magna cum laude, 1973. Bar: Ga. 1973. Assoc. Powell, Goldstein, Frazier & Murphy, 1973-76; ptnr. Rogers & Hardin, 1976-79, Bondurant, Stephenson & Smith, 1979-85, Arnall, Golden & Gregory, 1985-92, Katz, Smith & Cohen, 1992-98; shareholder Greenberg Traurig, 1998—. Vis. lectr. Duke U., 1976-77, 79-80, 89-93; adj. prof. Emory U., 1976-79, 81-82; lectr. Vanderbilt U., 1977-82. Co-author: Preventing Legal Malpractice, 1999, Legal Malpractice, 1999. Bd. visitors Law Sch. U. Minn., 1976-82. Mem. ABA (vice-chmn. com. profl. liability 1980-82, mem. standing com. lawyer's profl. liability 1981-85, chmn. 1985-87, standing com. lawyer competency 1993-95), State Bar Ga. (chmn. profl. liability and ins. com. 1978-89, trustee Inst. Cont. Legal Edn. in Ga. 1979-80), Order of the Coif, Phi Beta Kappa. Entertainment, Professional liability. Home: 145 15th St NE Apt 811 Atlanta GA 30309-3559 Office: 3290 Northside Dr NW Ste 400 Atlanta GA 30327

SMITH, JEROME DAVID, lawyer; b. Montgomery, Ala., Nov. 1, 1936; s. Perry and Ida (Jaffe) Smith; m. Bella R. Smith, Aug. 13, 1961; children: Perry, Shelley Smith Parker, Miriam. BS, U. Ala., 1958, LLB, 1962; postgrad., George Washington U.; LLM of Taxation, NYU, 1963. Bar: Ala. 1962, Miss. 1965, Ga. 1973, U.S. Dist. Ct. (mid. dist.) Ala. 1969, U.S. Supreme Ct. 1973, U.S. Ct. Appeals (11th cir.) 1981. Assoc. Capouano, Smith, Warren and Klinner PC, Montgomery, Ala. Capt. U.S. Army, 1961—62. Mem.: Dixie Lions Club. Avocation: tennis. Estate planning, Probate (including wills, trusts), Elder law. Office: Capouano Smith Warren Klinner PC 322 Alabama St Montgomery AL 36104

SMITH, JERRY LEON, lawyer; b. Tulsa, Oct. 18, 1938; s. William Ernest and Von Ceil S.; m. Ann Clay, June 17, 1961; children: Grant, Reed. BA, U. Okla., 1960; LLB, Cornell U., 1963. Assoc. White & Case, N.Y.C., Brussels, 1964-71; from assoc. to ptnr. Fried, Frank, Harris et al, N.Y.C., London, 1971-99, ret., of counsel, 1999—. Fulbright scholar, U. Aix-en-Provence-Marseilles, France, 1963-64. Mem. ABA, Assn. Bar City of N.Y. Avocations: literature, theater, music, visual arts, food and wine. Corporate, general, Private international, Mergers and acquisitions. Office: Fried Frank et al 99 City Rd London ECIY 1AX England E-mail: jlacsmith@aol.com.

SMITH, JILL GALBREATH, lawyer; b. Kansas City, Mo., Nov. 1, 1963; d. William Lawrence and Joyce (Webb) Galbreath. BA in Polit. Sci., U. Kans., 1986, JD, 1989. Bar: Mo. 1989, Kans. 1990, U.S. Dist. Ct. (we. dist.) Mo. 1989, U.S. Dist. Ct. Kans. 1990. Assoc. Brown, James & Rabbitt, Kansas City, 1989-90, Perry, Hamill & Fillmore, Overland Park, Kans., 1990-95; of counsel Spencer, Fane, Britt & Browne, LLP, Overland Park, Kans., 1995—2002; shareholder Holman, Hansen & Colvile, P.C., Overland Park, 2002—. Sec., bd. dirs. Johnson County CASA, Olathe, Kans., 1995-2001; mem. Jr. League of Wyandotte and Johnson Counties, Kansas, 1992—. Recipient 1st place award for svc. to pub. ABA, 1995. Mem. Kans. Bar Assn., Mo. Bar Assn., Johnson County Bar Assn. (sec., pres.-elect, pres. young lawyers sect. 1992-95, bd. dirs. 1994-95, 96-2000), Kansas City Met. Bar Assn. General civil litigation, Labor (including EEOC, Fair Labor Standards Act, labor-management relations, NLRB, OSHA), Workers' compensation. Office: Holman Hansen & Colvile PC 10724 Nall Ste 200 Overland Park KS 66212

SMITH, JOHN CHURCHMAN, lawyer; BA, JD, Dickinson U. Bar: Pa. 1962, U.S. Ct. Appeals (3d cir.) 1962, U.S. Dist. Ct. (ea. dist.) Pa. 1969, U.S. Supreme Ct. 1969; cert. civil trial advocate; diplomate Am. Bd. Profl. Liability Attys. Shareholder in charge of litigation John Churchman Smith and Assocs., P.C., Media, Pa., 1997—; mediator, arbitrator. Mem. ABA, Pa. Bar Assn., Delco Bar Assn. (pres. 1985), Pa. Trial Lawyers Assn., Guy G. DeFuria Inns of Ct. (pres. 1994-95), Rolling Green Golf Club (Springfield, Pa.). General civil litigation, Personal injury (including property damage), Professional liability. Office: 117 N Olive St Media PA 19063-2809

SMITH, JOHN FRANCIS, III, lawyer; b. White Plains, N.Y., Sept. 24, 1941; s. John Francis and Mary Dake (Mairs) S.; m. Susan Brown; children: John, Stephen, Peter. AB, Princeton U., 1963; LLB, Yale U., 1970. Bar: Pa. 1970, U.S. Supreme Ct. 1985. Assoc. Dilworth, Paxson, Kalish & Kauffman, Phila., 1970-75, ptnr., 1975-86, sr. ptnr., 1986-91; sr. litigation ptnr. Reed Smith LLP, Phila., 1991—, mem. exec. com., 1993—. Mem. exec. com. Employment Discrimination Referral Project, 1971-74; pres. Society Hill Civic Assn., 1975-76, Phila. Chamber Ensemble, 1977-80; bd. govs. Pa. Economy League (ea. divsn.), 1983—, sec. 1995-97; vice chair Health Care Task Force, 1993-96; bd. dirs. World Affairs Council Phila., 1983-87, chmn. program com., 1986-87; Burn Found., 1987-95; moderator Main Line Unitarian Ch., 1986-89, 2000—; founder and pres. Found. for Individual Responsibility and Social Trust (FIRST), 1995—. Served to lt. (j.g.) USNR, 1963-67; Vietnam. Mem. ABA, Phila. Bar Assn., Yale Law Sch. Alumni Assn. (exec. com. 1982-88, sec. 1987-88), Princeton Club (Phila.). Federal civil litigation, Labor (including EEOC, Fair Labor Standards Act, labor-management relations, NLRB, OSHA). Office: Reed Smith LLP 2500 One Liberty Pl Philadelphia PA 19103

SMITH, JOHN KERWIN, lawyer; b. Oct. 18, 1926; 1 child, Cynthia. BA, Stanford U.; LLB, Hastings Coll. Law. Ptnr. Haley, Purchio, Sakai & Smith, Hayward, Calif. Bd. dirs. Berkeley Asphalt, Mission Valley Ready-Mix, Coliseum Found., Mission Valley Rock, Rowell Ranch Rodeo, Hastings Coll. Law (alumnus of yr. award 1989). Gen. ptnr. Oak Hills Apts., City Ctr. Commercial, Creekwood I and II Apts.; Road Parks commn. 1957; city coun. 1959-66, mayor 1966-70; chmn. Alameda County Mayors conf. 1968, revenue taxation com. League Calif. Cities, 1968; vice chmn. Oakland-Alameda County Coliseum; vol. Hastings 1066 Found. (pres., vol. svc. award 1990), Martin Kauffman 100 Club; bd. dirs. Hastings Coll. of Law, 1999—. Mem. ABA, Calif. Bar Assn., Alameda County Bar Assn., Am. Judicature Soc., Rotary. Probate (including wills, trusts), Property, real (including real estate development, water). Office: Haley Purchio Sakai & Smith 22320 Foothill Blvd Ste 620 Hayward CA 94541-2700 E-mail: hpssckb@aol.com.

SMITH, JOHN STUART, lawyer; b. Rochester, N.Y., Sept. 4, 1943; s. Cecil Y. and Helen M. (Van Patten) S.; m. Nancy Schauman, Aug. 28, 1965; children: Kristan, Debra Barton. AB magna cum laude, Harvard U., 1965, LLB cum laude, 1968. Bar: N.Y. 1968, D.C. 1968, Tex. 1980, U.S. Dist. Ct. (we. dist.) N.Y. 1969, U.S. Dist. Ct. (so. dist.) N.Y. 1973, U.S. Dist. Ct. (no. dist.) N.Y. 1977, U.S. Dist. Ct. (no. dist.) Tex. 1980, U.S. Ct. Appeals (5th cir.) 1971, U.S. Ct. Appeals (2d cir.) 1972, U.S. Ct. Appeals (9th cir.), 1980, U.S. Supreme Ct., 1978. Assoc. Nixon Peabody, Rochester, 1968-74, mem., 1975—92. Bd. dirs. Rochester Chamber Orch., 1970-75, Geva Theater, 1988-97. Mem. ABA, N.Y. State Bar Assn. (com. on attys. professionalism, commn. on advt.), Monroe County Bar Assn. Antitrust, Federal civil litigation, Trademark and copyright. Office: PO Box 1051 1 Clinton Sq Rochester NY 14603

SMITH, JOY KAREN TURNHEIM, lawyer; b. Jersey City, N.J., Apr. 21, 1965; d. Palmer Turnehim and Gloria Grace (Freer) Turnheim; m. Douglas Scot Smith, Oct. 31, 2001. AB, Dartmouth Coll., 1985; JD, Northwestern U., 1988; MBA with distinction, DePaul U., 1993; MPhil, NYU, 1997, PhD in Mgmt. and Orgnl. Behavior, 2002. Bar: Ill. 1988, U.S. Dist. Ct. (no. dist.) Ill. 1988. Law clk. to Hon. Sophia H. Hall Ill. Circuit Ct., Chgo., 1988-89; assoc. Nathanson & Wray, Chgo., 1989-90, Horvath & Wigoda, Chgo., 1990; pvt. practice Law Offices Joy K. Turnheim, 1991—2000; exec. dir. Chenny Troupe, Chgo., 1993; instr. Ind. U. Purdue U., Fort Wayne, 2000—02; asst. prof. IPFW, 2002—. Adj. prof. Columbia Coll., 1992-94; chpt. atty. Assn. Women in Metals Industry, 1989-91. Treas. Presbyn. Women in 4th Ch., Chgo., 1989-94; chmn. Silver Apple Ball, Chgo., 1990; moderator Kairos Fellowship, Chgo., 1990-92; deacon 4th Presbyn. Ch., 1992-95; mem. Jr. League Chgo., 1992—2002; chair Project CON:CERN, 1995-98; founding mem., women's bd. Community Support Svcs., 1992-95; mem. Friends of Red Cross, 1990-94; grant maker Seeds of Tomorrow, 2002-2003. Mem. ABA, Ill. State Bar Assn., Jr. League Ft. Wayne. Avocations: tennis, skiing, golf.

SMITH, JULES LOUIS, lawyer; b. N.Y.C., Oct. 7, 1947; s. Henry Newman and Leonora (Fuerth) S.; m. Alexandra Remington Northrop, Feb. 15, 1986. BS, Syracuse U., 1969, JD, 1971. Bar: N.Y. 1972, U.S. Dist. Ct. (no. dist.) N.Y. 1972, U.S. Dist. Ct. (we. dist.) N.Y. 1973, U.S. Ct. Appeals (2d cir.) 1975, U.S. Supreme Ct. 1982. Assoc. Blitman and King LLP, Syracuse, N.Y., 1971-77, ptnr., 1977-88, resident ptnr., 1988—. Lectr. to legal and profl. assns., confs., colls., 1980—, including AFL-CIO Union Lawyers Conf., 1991, ABA Labor and Employment Law, 1992, 25th Pacific Coast Labor Law Conf., 1992, ABA Satellite Seminar, 1992, N.Y. State Bar Assn. Labor and Employment Law Sect. Ann. Meeting, 1993; lectr. Inst. Indsl. Labor Rels.; mem. N.Y. State Bar Assn. Task Force on Adminstrv. Hearings, Albany, 1986—; bd. advisors LeMoyne Inst. Labor Rels., LeMoyne Coll., Syracuse Inst. Labor Rels.; mem. exec. bd. Greater Mem. editl. bd. Syracuse Law Rev., 1970-71; contbr. articles to legal publs. Sec. Onondaga Neighborhood Legal Svcs., 1978, pres., 1979, v.p. bd. dirs., 1983-87; chair Prevention Ptnrs., 1994-97, pres. 1994-96; co-chair legal divsn. fund raising activities Syracuse Symphony Orch., 1985-86; bd. dirs. fundraising activities Am. Heart Assn., 1985-86; bd. dirs. Greater Rochester Fights Back, 1990-92, vice chair, 1992-93, chair, 1994; pres. Prevention Ptnrs., 1994-96, bd. dirs., 1999—; bd. dirs. United Way Greater Rochester, Cmty. Legal Intake Project, 1998—; v.p. Rochester Com. on Fgn. Rels., 1990-94. Fellow N.Y. Bar Found.; mem. ABA (union chmn. EEO com. labor and employment law sect. 1985-88, co-chairperson labor and employment law sect., mem. ad hoc com. to comment on EEO com. Ams. with Disabilities Act regulations, Coll. of Labor and Employment Lawyers award 1996), FBA, N.Y. State Bar Assn. (chmn. membership and fin. com. 1980-83, mem. spl. com. on specialization 1983-85, chmn. labor and employment law sect. 1984-85, mem. ho. dels. 1989-92), Onondaga County Bar Assn., Monroe County Bar Assn., N.Y. State Trial Lawyers Assn., Am. Trial Lawyers Assn., Fed. Bar Coun., Indsl. Rels. Rsch. Assn., Assn. Ctrl. N.Y. (co-founder, v.p. 1981), Justinian Honor Soc., Order of Coif. Democrat. Jewish. Avocations: skiing, running, cooking, reading. Federal civil litigation, General civil litigation, Labor (including EEOC, Fair Labor Standards Act, labor-management relations, NLRB, OSHA). Office: Blitman and King LLP 16 Main St W Ste 207 Rochester NY 14614-1601

SMITH, KATHY RAE, judge; b. Goshen, Ind., Jan. 7, 1952; d. Charles Dean and Lucille E. Smith. BS, Ball State U., 1974; JD, Ind. U., 1980. Bar: Ind., U.S. Supreme Ct., U.S. Dist. Ct. (so. dist.) Ind. Part-time dep. prosecutor Clinton County Prosecutor's Office, Frankfort, Ind., 1980, part-time chief dep. prosecutor, 1981—83; civil atty. Campbell, Hardesty, Douglas (formerly Campbell, Hardesty, Pearson & Douglas), Frankfort, Ind., 1980—83; judge Clinton County Superior Ct., Frankfort, Ind., 1983—. Mem. domestic rels. com. Ind. Jud. Conf., Indpls., 1998—; mem. character/fitness com. Ind. Bd. Law Examiners, Indpls., 1990—. Sec., bd. dirs. Clinton County Boys and Girls Club, Frankfort, 1990—; bd. dirs. Clinton County Found. for Youth, Frankfort, 1997—, treas., 1999—2000. Mem.: Ind. Judges Assn., Zonta, Optimists. Avocations: photography, swimming, gardening. Office: Clinton Superior Ct 320 Courthouse Sq Frankfort IN 46041

SMITH, KENNETH M. lawyer; BS in Acctg., Brigham Young U., 1971, JD, 1977; MBA, U. Utah, 1973. Bar: Ariz. 1978, Utah 1978; CPA, Tex. Ptnr. Carson Messinger, Phoenix, 1978-86, Andersen & Smith, Mesa, Ariz., 1986—. Mem. AICPA. Corporate, general, Estate planning, Property, real (including real estate development, water). Office: Andersen & Smith 6053 E University Dr Mesa AZ 85205-7517

SMITH, LANGDON, lawyer; b. Cucro, Tex., Aug. 6, 1969; s. Lang Smith and Jan Blackwell; m. Selina Brand, Jan. 16, 1999; children: Brittany, Austin. BA in Econs., U. Tex., 1991; JD, South Tex. Coll. Law, 1996. Bar: Tex., U.S. Dist. Ct. (so. and we. dists.) Tex. Mng. ptnr. Hjalmerson & Smith, Houston, 1996—99, Hjalmerson, Smith & Harcock, Houston, 1999—. Insurance, Personal injury (including property damage), Professional liability. Office: Ste 275 11811 I-10 East Houston TX 77029

SMITH, LARRY FRANCIS, lawyer, internist; b. Lynchburg, Va., Dec. 8, 1949; s. Fred C. and Ruth Guill S. BS in Biology magna cum laude, Hampden-Sydney U., 1972; MD, U. Va., 1976; JD, Washington and Lee U., 1995. Bar: Tex., U.S. Dist. Ct. (ea. and we. dists.) Tex. Med. pvt. practice, Appomattox, Va., 1979—; assoc. Morgan & Weisbrod, Dallas, 1995-97, sr. equity ptnr., 1998—2001; founding ptnr. Smith & Marchand, Dallas, 2002—. Mem. bd. zoning appeals Appomatox Ct., Va., 1990-92, chmn. redistricting com., 1990. Fellow Am. Coll. Legal Medicine; mem. Phi Beta Kappa. Avocation: private pilot. Personal injury (including property damage), Product liability, Professional liability. Office: 10000 North Central Expy Ste 1043 Dallas TX 75231 Office Fax: 214-378-6399.

SMITH, LARRY IRA, lawyer, director; b. Augusta, Ga., Aug. 18, 1950; s. John Milledge and Estelle Julia (Barnard) Smith; children: Brooke Estelle, Barclay Gerlad; m. Lynne J. Owens, Mar. 27, 2002. BA, Augusta Coll., 1974; JD, U. Ga., 1977. Bar: Ga. 1977, U.S. Dist. Ct. (so. dist.) Ga. 1978,

U.S. Ct. Appeals (5th cir.) 1978, U.S. Ct. Appeals (11th cir.) 1981. Assoc. Fleming & Blanchard, Augusta, 1977—82; ptnr. Paine, Dalis, Smith & McElreath, Augusta, 1982—87, Lee, Smith, Thompson, Black, Scheer & Hart, PA, Augusta, 1987—89, Thompson & Smith PC, Augusta, 1990—. City ct. judge, Grovetown, Ga., 1982—. Active Com. to Elect Sam Sibley D.A., Augusta, 1980, Com. to Re-elect Sam Sibley, Augusta, 1984, Com. to Elect Hardy Gregory, Supreme Ct., Augusta, 1983. With USMC, 1970—74. Mem.: ABA, Augusta Area Trial Lawyers Assn., Augusta Bar Assn., Ga. Trial Lawyers Assn., State Bar Ga., Assn. Trial Lawyers Am., Augusta Country Club. Presbyterian. Federal civil litigation, Insurance, Personal injury (including property damage). Office: Thompson & Smith 2909 Professional Pkwy Ste A Augusta GA 30907-6507 Home: 74 Bristlecone Ln Augusta GA 30909

SMITH, LAURA CHALK, lawyer; b. Albuquerque, N.Mex., Sept. 22, 1970; m. Keith Alan Smith. JD, Yale Law Sch., 1995. Bar: N.C. 1995. Assoc. Robinson, Bradshaw & Hinson, P.A., Charlotte, NC, 2000—; counsel Continental Gen. Tire, Inc., Charlotte, NC, 1999—2000; assoc. Robinson, Bradshaw & Hinson, P.A., Charlotte, NC, 1996—99; law clk. to the hon. t.s. ellis, iii U.S. Dist. Ct. (ea. dist.) Va., Alexandria, Va., 1995—96. Dir. Martha Connerton/Kinetic Works, Inc., Charlotte, 2001—02. Mem. pub. info. com. Mecklenburg County Bar, Charlotte, NC, 2002, mem. professionalism com., 2000—01, vol. Lawyers Program, 1996—2002; mem. pre-law counseling com. N.C. Bar, NC, 2001—02. Mem.: ABA, Mecklenburg County Bar (professionalism com. 2000—01, vol. Lawyers Program 1996—2002, pub. info. com. 2002), N.C. Bar Assn. (pre-law counseling com. 2001—02), Charlotte Track & Triathlon Club. D-Liberal. Presbyterian. Avocations: triathlon, distance running, reading. Securities, Finance, Corporate, general. Office: Robinson Bradshaw & Hinson PA 101 North Tryon St Ste 1900 Charlotte NC 28209 Office Fax: 704-378-4000. E-mail: lsmith@rbh.com.

SMITH, LAUREN ASHLEY, lawyer, journalist, clergyman, physicist; b. Clinton, Iowa, Nov. 30, 1924; s. William Thomas Roy and Ethel (Cook) S.; m. Barbara Ann Mills, Aug. 22, 1947; children: Christopher A., Laura Nan Smith Pringle, William Thomas Roy II. BS, U. Minn., 1946, JD, 1949; postgrad., U. Chgo., 1943-49; MDiv, McCormick Theol. Sem., 1950; postgrad., U. Iowa, 1992. Bar: Colo. 1957, Iowa 1959, Ill. 1963, Minn. 1983, U.S. Supreme Ct. 1967; ordained to ministry Presbyn. Ch., 1950. Pastor Presbyn. Ch., Fredonia, Kans., 1950-52, Lamar, Colo., 1952-57, Congl. Ch., Clinton, 1975-80; editor The Comml., Pine Bluff, Ark., 1957-58; ptnr. Schoenauer Smith & Fullerton ASP, Clinton, 1995—. CEO LASCO Pub. Group, Clinton, 1995—; CEO, founder Interlink for the Internet Generation; internat. conferee Stanley Found., Warrenton, Va., 1963—72; legal observer, USSR, 1978; co-sponsor All India Renewable Energy Conf., Bangalore, 1981; law sch. conferee U. Minn., China, 1983; lectr. law, religion, physics, nat. policy U. Wis., 2001, Spl. lectr. contemporary physics and religion, 01. Author: (jurisprudence treatise) Forma Dat Esse Rel, 1975, (monograph) First Strike Option, 1983; co-author: India On to New Horizons, 1989; columnist Crow Call, 1968—; co-editor Press and News of India, 1978-82; pub. Crow Call; pseudonym Christopher Crow, 1981—; writer BBC World Svc., London; editor Asian Econ. Cmty. Jour.; contbr. articles to religious publs. Minister-at-large Presbyn. Ch. U.S.A., Iowa, 1987—; bd. dirs. Iowa divsn. UN Assn. U.S.A., Iowa City, 1970-85; fellow Molecular Nanotechnology Foresight Inst., Palo Alto, Calif.; Franciscans United Nations Non Govt. Orgn.; assoc. Westar Inst. (The Jesus Seminar), Santa Rosa, Calif., 1997; active Quad City Estate Planning Coun.; founder, CEO Interlink relating quantum mechanics and religion. Mem. Iowa Bar Assn., Ill. Bar Assn., St. Andrews Soc., Clinton County Bar Assn. (pres. 1968, Best in Iowa citation), Clinton Ministerial Assn., Samaritan Health Systems Chaplain Corps. (pres.), European Soc. for Study of Sci. and Religion, Quad City Estate Planning Coun., Quaker Internat. Yokefellow, Nat. Network for New Spiritual Formation Presbyn. Ch. USA, Franciscans Internat., City Club of Quad Cities (bd. dirs.).

SMITH, LESTER V., JR., lawyer, educator; b. Mt. Pleasant, Pa., May 10, 1940; s. Lester V. and Margaret (Kurtz) S.; m. Nadine A. Wooley; children: Julia, Ann Marie. AB, Duke U., 1962; JD, U. N.C., 1965. Bar: N.C. 1965, Ill. 1972, Oreg. 1973, U.S. Dist. Ct. Oreg. 1973, U.S. Dist. Ct. (no. dist.) Ill. 1969, U.S. Dist. Ct. (so. dist.) Ill. 1970, U.S. Ct. Appeals (9th cir.) 1975, U.S. Supreme Ct. 1981. Atty. NLRB, Peoria, Ill., 1965-66, 69-78; spl. trial counsel U.S. Army, Germany, 1966-69; assoc. Davies, Biggs, Strayer, Stoel & Boley, Portland, Oreg., 1973-77; founder, ptnr. Bullard, Korshoj, Smith & Jernstedt, Portland, Oreg., 1977-2000, Bullard, Smith, Jernstedt & Wilson, Portland, 2000—. Lectr., instr. Bus. Sch. U. Md., W.Ger., 1966-69, Lewis and Clark Sch. Law, Portland, 1983-87. Sect. editor Advising Oreg. Bus.; contbr. articles to profl. jours. Chmn. Dorchester Conf., Seaside, Oreg., 1981; event dir. Portland Marathon, 1982—; trustee Multnomeh Athletic Found., 1998—; bd. dirs. Oreg. Sports Authority, 1999—. Capt. U.S. Army, 1966-69. Mem. ABA (labor law sect.), Ill. Bar Assn., Oreg. State Bar Assn. (chmn. labor rels. sect. 1982-83), Multnomah County Bar Assn., Duke U. Alumni Assn. (chmn. Oreg. area 1980—), Multnomah Athletic Club (trustee 1984-87, pres. 1986-87). Labor (including EEOC, Fair Labor Standards Act, labor-management relations, NLRB, OSHA). Home: 2744 SW Sherwood Dr Portland OR 97201-2251 Office: Bullard Smith Jernstedt Wilson 1000 SW Broadway Ste 1900 Portland OR 97205-3062 E-mail: lsmith@bullardlaw.com.

SMITH, LOREN ALLAN, federal judge; b. Chgo., Dec. 22, 1944; m. Catherine Yore; children: Loren Jr., Adam (dec.). BA in Polit. Sci., Northwestern U., 1966, JD, 1969; LLD (hon.), John Marshall Law Sch., 1995, Capital U. Law Sch., 1996, Campbell U., 1997. Bar: Ill. 1970, U.S. Ct. Mil. Appeals 1973, U.S. Ct. Appeals (D.C. cir.) 1974, U.S. Supreme Ct. 1974, U.S. Ct. Claims, 1985, U.S. Ct. Appeals (fed. cir.) 1986, U.S. Ct. Fed. Claims. Host nightly radio talk show What's Best for America?, 1972; cons. Sidney & Austin, Chgo., 1972-73; gen. atty. FCC, 1973; asst. to spl. counsel to the pres. White House, Washington, 1973-74; spl. asst. U.S. Atty., D.C., 1974-75; chief counsel Reagan for Pres. campaigns, 1976, 80; prof. Del. Law Sch., 1976-84; dep. dir. Office Exec. Br. Mgmt. Presdl. Transition, 1980-81; chmn. Adminstrv. Conf. U.S., 1981-85; appointed judge U.S. Ct. Fed. Claims, Washington, 1985, designated chief judge, 1986-2000; sr. judge, 2000—. Prof. law Del. Law Sch., 1976-84; adj. prof. Internat. Law Sch., 1973-74, Georgetown U. Law Ctr., 1992—, Washington Coll. Law, Am. U., 1996; Disting. lectr. Columbus Sch. Law, Cath. U. Am., 1996—; Disting. adj. prof. George Mason U. Sch. Law, 1998—; past mem. Pres.'s Cabinet Coun. on Legal Policy, Pres.' Cabinet Coun. on Mgmt. and Adminstrn.; chmn. Coun. Ind. Regulatory Agys.; served as disting. jurist in residence U. Denver; Allen chair U. Richmond Sch. Law, 1995. Co-author: Black America and Organized Labor: A Fair Deal?, 1979; contbr. articles to profl. jours. Adv. bd. mem. WETA Pub. Radio Cmty. Adv. Bd. Recipient Presdl. medal Cath. U. Am. Law Sch., 1993, Romanian medal of justice Romanian Min. of Justice, 1995, Ronald Reagan Pub. Svc. award Nat. Property Rights Conf., 1997. Mem. Bar Assn. D.C. (hon. mem., judicial honoree award 1997), Univ. Club (Washington, named club mem. of the yr. 1991, chmn. entertainment com., centennial com.). Republican. Jewish. Office: US Ct of Fed Claims 717 Madison Pl NW Suite 328 Washington DC 20005

SMITH, MARK P. foundation executive; b. Charleston, W.Va., July 27, 1949; s. Bernard Henry and Josephine (Polan) S.; m. Jane Stephens, May 6, 1978; children: Stephen Noble, Allison Baxter. B.A., Princeton U., 1971; J.D., Yale U., 1978. Asst. to exec. dir. ABA, Chgo., 1976-79; exec. dir. W.Va. State Bar, Charleston, 1979-88; v.p. Ctr. Am. and Inernat. Law, Richardson, Tex., 1996— (dir. Inst. for Transnational Arbitration, 1993-98); dir. Mcpl. Legal Studies Ctr., 1998—; sec. W.Va. Legal Services Plan, Inc., Charleston, 1987-88; treas. Found. for Youth and Govt., Charleston, 1983-88; pres. Saigling Elem. Sch., PTA, 1991-92; lectr. U. Tex., Dallas, 1990-94. Pres., bd. dirs. Coalition for Homeless, Charleston, 1986-87; sec. W.Va. Coalition for the Homeless, 1986-87; pres. Volunteer Ctr. Collin County, 2001—; mem. bd. Vol. Ctr. North Tex., 2001-. Mem. Nat. Assn. Bar Execs. (chmn. continuing edn. com. 1981-82, mem. exec. com. 1984-86). Office: Ctr Am and Internat Law PO Box 799030 Richardson TX 75379-9030

SMITH, MAXWELL PAUL, lawyer; b. Elyria, Ohio, Jan. 8, 1924; s. Maxwell P. and Hilma Lillian (Holmgren) S.; m. Vaunceil Hulda Tiarks, Nov. 10, 1928; children— Mark Paul, Terri Smith Lindvall, Amy Szwabowicz, Laura Eckstein. J.D., Valparaiso U.,. 1950. Bar: Ind. 1950, U.S. Dist. Ct. (no. dist.) Ind. 1950, U.S. Dist. Ct. (so. dist.) Ind. 1950, U.S. Ct. Appeals (6th cir.) 1982. Pres. Krueckeberg and Smith, P.C., Ft. Wayne, Ind., 1982-90, M.P. Smith & Assocs., P.C., Ft. Wayne, 1990—. Pres. bd. trustees, elder First Presbyterian Ch., Ft. Wayne; pres. Neighbors, Inc., Ft. Wayne; bd. dirs. Samaritan Counseling, Inc. Served to 1st lt. JAGC, U.S. Army, 1952-53. Decorated Army Commendation medal. Mem. Allen County Bar Assn., Ind. State Bar Assn. (citation for article 1982). Club: Wildwood Racquet (Ft. Wayne). Contbg. author: Professional Corporations, 1978, Indiana Continuing Legal Edn. Forum, 1983. Corporate, general, Probate (including wills, trusts). Office: 622 S Calhoun St Fort Wayne IN 46802-1708

SMITH, MICHAEL W. lawyer; b. Detroit, Apr. 23, 1943; s. Clarence William and Mary Drane (Corbett) S.; m. Sandra Lea Bartel, Dec. 17, 1967; children: Dominick, Jordan, Sloan. BBA, U. Mich., 1965; JD, U. Wis., 1968. Bar: Wis. 1968. Staff atty. Wis. Legis. Coun., Madison, 1968-70; assoc. Sieker, Reynolds & Peckham, Madison, 1970-72; pvt. practice Lodi, Wis., 1973—. City atty. City of Lodi, 1973—. Pres. Lodi Sch. Bd., 1983-89, Lodi Optimist Club, 1973. Mem. State Bar of Wis., Columbia County Bar Assn. Avocations: reading, skiing, bicycling, kayaking. Estate planning, Municipal (including bonds), Property, real (including real estate development, water). Office: Law Offices Michael W Smith 154 S Main St Lodi WI 53555-1119

SMITH, MORTON ALAN, lawyer; b. N.Y.C., Mar. 13, 1931; s. David and Augusta S.; m. Nancy, July 2, 1954 (div. July 1974); children: Robynn, Jeffrey, Richard; m. Jane Saffir, June 10, 1979; children: Michael, Richard. BA, U. Fla., 1953; LLD with honors, U. N.C., 1956. Bar: N.Y. 1957, D.C. 1957. Spl. trial atty. Office Chief Counsel IRS, Phila., 1956-58; spl. asst. U.S. Atty. Dist. N.J., 1957; law clk. to judge U.S. Tax Ct., Washington, 1958-60; assoc. Kaye Scholer, N.Y.C., 1960-62, Saul Silverman, N.Y.C., 1962-67; sr. ptnr. Hall, Dickler, Lawler, Kent & Friedman, N.Y.C., 1967—. Bd. dirs. Eden Park Health Corp., Albany, N.Y. Contbr. articles to profl. jours. V.p. Rye Brook (N.Y.) Bd. Edn., 1968-73; organizer of incorporation of Village of Rye Brook, 1982, now spl. counsel; bd. dirs. Herbert Birch Sch. for Exceptional Children, N.Y.C., Westchester County United Way, 1991; leadership chmn. United Way Campaign, Rye Brook, 1989-91; mem. Westchester County Housing Implementation Commn.; bd. dirs. Eden Park Health Svcs., Albany, N.Y.; pres. Bocaire Home Owners Assn., Boca Raton, Fla. Mem. ABA (tax sec.). Avocations: golf, skiing, tennis, gardening, reading. Criminal, Taxation, general. Office: Hall Dickler Lawler Kent & Friedman 909 3rd Ave New York NY 10022-4731 E-mail: msmith@halldickler.com.

SMITH, NUMA LAMAR, JR., lawyer; b. Rock Hill, S.C., Nov. 22, 1915; s. Numa Lamar and Grace (Hanes) S.; m. Mary Catherine Gray, Mar. 24, 1941; children: Patricia Gray (dec.), Elizabeth Hanes, Lamar Douglas. AB, Furman U., 1938; LL.B. with distinction, Duke U., 1941. Bar: N.Y. 1942, D.C. 1946. Assoc. firm White & Case, N.Y.C., 1941-42, Miller & Chevalier, Washington, 1946-49, partner, 1949-83, counsel, 1983—; bd. visitors, 1973-83. Sr. fellow Duke U. Law Sch., 1979-80 Assoc. editor: Duke Law Jour, 1940-41. Served with U.S. Army, 1942-46; with Judge Adv. Gen. Corps 1944-46. Recipient Gen. Excellence award Furman U., 1938 Fellow Am. Bar Found.; mem. ABA, D.C. Bar Assn., Am. Law Inst., Duke Law Alumni Assn. (pres. 1967-69), Order of Coif, Met. Club (Washington), Burning Tree Club (Bethesda, Md.), Washington Golf Club (Arlington, Va.), The Club at Pelican Bay, Sigma Alpha Epsilon. Baptist. Home: 7515 Pelican Bay Blvd Naples FL 34108-6520

SMITH, PATTI, lawyer; b. Mount Clemens, Mich., Mar. 17, 1972; d. Timothy Nelson and Judith Margaret Smith. BA summa cum laude, Adrian Coll., 1994; JD, U. Wis., 1996. Bar: Mich. 1997. Spl. asst. prosecuting atty. Wayne County Prosecutor's Office, Detroit, 1997—98; atty. Law Offices of Robert Beardslee, Birmingham, Mich., 1998—2001; jr. ptnr. Ronin Legal Svcs., P.C., Southgate, Mich., 2001—03; atty. VAW legal svcs., Dearborn, Mich., 2003—. Co-chair Huron Valley Greens. Mem.: ACLU, Mich. Abortion Rights Action League, Inc. Assn. Irish-Am. Lawyers, Washtenaw County Bar Assn., Downriver Bar Assn., Sierra Club, Jaycees. Green Party. Avocations: writing, science fiction, reading, music. Bankruptcy, Family and matrimonial, Probate (including wills, trusts). Office: Law Offices of Robert Beardslee 5220 Oakman Blvd Birmingham MI 48126

SMITH, PERRY MARSHALL, lawyer; b. Worcester, Mass., Apr. 28, 1958; s. Russell Howard and Frances Mary (Gullberg) S.; m. Eva Margaret Ribarits, Apr. 9, 1988. AB, Dartmouth Coll., 1980; JD, Am. U., 1984; LLM in Taxation, Boston U., 1987. Bar: N.Y. 1985, Mass. 1985, U.S. Dist. Ct. Mass. 1985, U.S. Tax Ct. 1986, U.S. Supreme Ct. 1989. Asst. counsel State Mut. Life Assurance Co., Worcester, 1984-87; atty. New Eng. Mut. Life Ins. Co., Boston, 1987-90; dir. estate and bus. planning Commonwealth Fin. Group, Waltham, Mass., 1990-97; dir. of fin. svcs. Carlin, Charron & Rosen LLP, Worcester, Mass., 1997—2000, Baystate Fin. Svcs., LLC, 2000—. Lectr. Met. Coll. Boston U., 1991—. Mem. ABA, Mass. Bar Assn., Am. CLU and Chartered Fin. Cons. Republican. Avocations: numismatics, tennis, swimming, hiking. Estate planning, Probate (including wills, trusts), Estate taxation. Home: 42 Beechwood Rd Wellesley MA 02482-2333 Office: Baystae Fin Svcs LLC One Exeter Plz Fl 14 Boston MA 02116 E-mail: psmith@baystatefinancial.com.

SMITH, PEYTON NOBLE, lawyer; b. Austin, Tex., Feb. 19, 1964; s. Ralph Morgan and Bess (Noble) S.; m. Elizabeth Barrington Nance, June 23, 1990; children: Lincoln David, Scarlett Elizabeth. BBA in Mktg. and Fin., Baylor U., 1986, JD, 1989. Bar: Tex. 1990, U.S. Dist. Ct. (we. dist.) Tex., U.S. Dist. Ct. (so. dist.) Tex. Assoc. Small Craig & Werkenthin PC, Austin, 1989-94; ptnr. Law Office of Jeffrey Jones, Austin, 1994-96, Jackson & Walker, L.L.P., Austin, 1997-99; shareholder Winstead Sechrest & Minick, P.C., Austin, 2000—. Cons. Rooster Andrews Sporting Goods, Austin, 1998, Weiner's Stores, Inc., 1994—, Randall's Food Stores, Houston, 1995—, The Home Depot, U.S.A., 2000—. Author, seminar spkr., cons. handbook for employees, 1997—. Chmn., trustee Hyde Park Bapt. Ch., Austin, 1997-98. Fellow Tex. Bar Found.; mem. Tex. Assn. Def. Counsel, Assn. Corp. Growth, Tex. Young Lawyers Assn. (pub. rels. com. 1996). Baptist. State civil litigation, Labor (including EEOC, Fair Labor Standards Act, labor-management relations, NLRB, OSHA), Personal injury (including property damage). Office: Winstead Sechrest & Minick PC 100 Congress Ave Ste 809 Austin TX 78701-4042 E-mail: psmith@winstead.com.

SMITH, R. GORDON, lawyer; b. Roanoke, Va., May 28, 1938; BA with highest honors, U. Va., 1960; LLB magna cum laude, Harvard U., 1964. Bar: Va. 1964. Law clk. to judge U.S. Ct. Appeals (5th cir.), 1964-65; ptnr. McGuire, Woods, Battle & Boothe, Richmond, Va., 1969—. Exec., legislation editor Harvard Law Rev., 1963-64; bd. dirs. Scott & Stringfellow Fin., Inc., Trigon Healthcare, Inc., Va. C. of C. Fellow Am. Bar Found.; mem. Va. Bar Assn. (pres. 1987-88), Am. Law Inst., Phi Beta Kappa, Omicron Delta Kappa. Office: McGuire Woods 901 E Cary St Richmond VA 23219-4057

SMITH, RALPH WESLEY, JR., retired federal judge; b. Ghent, N.Y., July 16, 1936; s. Ralph Wesley and Kathleen S. (Callahan) S.; m. Nancy Ann Fetzer, Dec. 30, 1961 (div. 1981); children: Mark Owen, Tara Denise, Todd Kendall; m. Barbara Anne Milian, Nov. 8, 1982; stepchildren: Kim Highter, Jeffrey Highter, Eric Highter. Student, Sorbonne, U. Paris, Paris, 1954-55; BA, Yale U., 1956; LLB, Albany Law Sch., 1966. Bar: N.Y. 1966, U.S. Dist. Ct. (no. dist.) N.Y. 1966. Assoc. Hinman, Straub Law Firm, Albany, N.Y., 1966-69; chief asst. dist. atty. Albany County, N.Y., 1969-73, dist. atty., 1974; regional dir. state nursing home investigation Asst. Atty. Gen., Albany, 1975-77; dir. State Organized Crime Task Force, 1978-82; U.S. magistrate judge U.S. Dist. Ct. (no. dist.) N.Y., Albany, 1982-2001. Judge moot ct. Albany Law Sch., 1983-2001; lectr. N.Y. State Bar Assn., 1985—, Am. Inns of Ct., 1994-99. Capt. (ret.) USNR, 1957-82. Mem. Fed. Magistrate Judges Assn. (dir. 2d cir. 1992-99), Columbia County Magistrates Assn. Republican. Roman Catholic. Avocations: fishing, bicycling, skiing, sailing, camping. Home: 40 Wequasset Rd Harwich Port MA 02646

SMITH, RICHARD MULDROW, lawyer; b. Jefferson City, Mo., Sept. 2, 1939; s. Elmer Clyde and Mary (Muldrow) S.; children: Stephen, Michael. JD, U. Ark., 1963; postgrad., U. Ill., 1963-64. Bar: Ark. 1963, D.C. 1980, U.S. Ct. Appeals (D.C. cir.) 1980, U.S. Supreme Ct. 1980. Asst. prof. U. N.C., Chapel Hill, 1964-67, assoc. prof., 1967-73, prof., 1973-79; spl. counsel FPC, Washington, 1976-77; mem. White House Energy Policy Staff, Washington, 1978-79; dir. Office of Policy Coordination, Dept. of Energy, Washington, 1978-79; ptnr. Mayer, Brown & Platt, Washington, 1979-91; pres. Little Creek Marina Inc., Norfolk, Va., 1992—. Author: (with others) North Carolina Uniform Commercial Code Forms Annotated, 2 vols., 1967. Mem. ABA (pub. utility law sect., coun. mem. 1985-88, chmn. gas com. 1988-89, chmn. publ. com. 1989-91). Commercial, contracts (including sales of goods; commercial financing), FERC practice, Utilities, public. Home: 4725 Bradston Rd Virginia Beach VA 23455 Office: 4801 Pretty Lake Ave Norfolk VA 23518-2005

SMITH, ROBERT BLAKEMAN, lawyer; b. Mt. Vernon, N.Y., June 18, 1949; s. William Blakeman and Helen Theresa (Curley) S.; m. Laura Lindley Brock, July 18, 1987; children: Morgan Lindley, Justin Pierce. BS, Rensselaer Poly. Inst., 1971, ME, 1973; JD, Boston U., 1976. Bar: N.Y. 1977, U.S. Dist. Ct. (so. and ea. dists.) N.Y. 1977, U.S. Dist. Ct. (no. dist.) N.Y. 1981, U.S. Dist. Ct. Ariz. 1992, U.S. Patent and Trademark Office 1977, U.S. Ct. Appeals (7th cir.) 1979, U.S. Ct. Appeals (fed. cir.) 1982, U.S. Supreme Ct. 1981. Assoc. Brumbaugh, Graves, Donohue & Raymond, N.Y.C., 1976-84, ptnr., 1984-89; of counsel White & Case, N.Y.C., 1989-99, Skadden, Arps, Slate, Meagher & Flom, N.Y.C., 1999—. Lectr. IEEE, N.Y.C., 1983-88, Practising Law Inst., 1990-99. Trustee Delta Phi Found., Ithaca, N.Y., 1978-86, St. Elmo Found., Pearl River, N.Y., 1986—. Mem. N.Y. Intellectual Property Law Assn., Am. Intellectual Property Law Assn. Patent, Trademark and copyright. Home: 100 Riverside Dr New York NY 10024-4822 Office: Skadden Arps Slate Meagher & Flom Four Times Sq New York NY 10036-6522 E-mail: Robsmith@SKadden.com.

SMITH, ROBERT ELLIS, lawyer, journalist; b. Providence, Sept. 6, 1940; s. Ronald Bancroft and Clarice (Evans) S.; children: Mark O., David E., Benjamin E., Gregor E. BA, Harvard U., 1962; JD, Georgetown U., 1975. Bar: D.C. 1976, R.I. 1987. News reporter Detroit Free Press, 1962-65, Newsday, Garden City, N.Y., 1966-70; asst. dir. Office for Civil Rights HEW, Washington, 1970-73; pub. Privacy Jour., Washington and Providence, 1974—; pvt. practice Block Island, RI, 1978—; spl. asst. atty. gen. State of R.I., Providence, 1991-92; vice-chmn. R.I. Coastal Resources Mgmt. Coun., 1996—2002. Mem. D.C. Commn. Human Rights, 1983-85. Author: Privacy: How to Protect What's Left of It, 1979, Compilation of State and Federal Privacy Laws, 1976, 78, 81, 84, 88, 92, 97, 2002, Workrights, 1983, Celebrities and Privacy, 1985, The Law of Privacy Explained, 1993, Our Vanishing Privacy, 1993, Ben Franklin's Web Site, 2000. Pres. Block Island Conservancy, 1990-94; arbitrator R.I. Superior Ct.; chair Harvard Crimson Grad. Bd., 1999-2002. With U.S. Army, 1963-65. Mem. ABA, R.I. Bar Assn., Harvard Club. Avocation: writing. Civil rights, Land use and zoning (including planning), Libel. Office: Privacy Jour PO Box 28577 Providence RI 02908-0577 also: PO Box 984 Block Island RI 02807-0984 E-mail: orders@privacyjournal.net.

SMITH, ROBERT EVERETT, lawyer; b. N.Y.C., Mar. 15, 1936; s. Arthur L. and Augusta (Cohen) S.; m. Emily Lucille Lehman, July 17, 1960; children: Amy, Karen, Victoria. BA, Dartmouth Coll., 1957; LLB, Harvard U., 1960. Bar: N.Y. 1960, U.S. Dist. Ct. (so. dist.) N.Y. 1962, U.S. Ct. Appeals (2d cir.) 1963, U.S. Supreme Ct. 1967, U.S. Dist. Ct. (ea. dist.) N.Y. 1969, U.S. Ct. Appeals (3d cir.) 1982, U.S. Ct. Appeals (9th cir.) 1988. Assoc. Paul, Weiss, Rifkind, Wharton & Garrison, N.Y.C., 1960-65; from assoc. to ptnr. Baar, Bennett & Fullen, N.Y.C., 1965-74; ptnr. Guggenheimer & Untermyer, N.Y.C., 1974-85, Rosenman & Colin LLP, N.Y.C., 1985-98, chmn., 1994-97, counsel, 1998—2002, KMZ Rosenman, N.Y.C., 2002—. With U.S. Army, 1961-64. Mem. ABA, N.Y. State Bar Assn., Assn. of Bar of City of N.Y., Fed. Bar Coun., N.Y. County Lawyers Assn., Am. Arbitration Assn. (nat. panel arbitrators), The Am. Law Inst. Federal civil litigation, State civil litigation, Corporate, general. Office: KMZ Rosenman 575 Madison Ave Fl 26 New York NY 10022-2585 E-mail: Robert.Smith@kmzr.com..

SMITH, R(OBERT) MICHAEL, lawyer; b. Cin., Nov. 25, 1951; s. Barney and Jean (Maloney) S.; m. Leslie Y. Straub. BA in Polit. Sci., U. Cin., 1982; JD, Ohio State U., 1985; MDiv in Bibl. and Theol. Studiees, So. Bapt. Theol. Sem., 2002. Bar: Ohio 1985, U.S. Dist. Ct. (so. dist.) Ohio 1992, U.S. Supreme Ct. 1992; ordained minister So. Bapt. Ch., 1999. Law clk. to Justice Holmes Ohio Supreme Ct., Columbus, 1985-89; sr. staff atty., referee, editor Ohio Ct. Claims, Columbus, 1989-94. Instr. law Ohio State U., 1985—, instr. continuing edn. courses, 1990—. Incorporator, trustee various non-profit orgns., Cin. and Columbus; pres. So. Bapt. Messianic Fellowship, 1994-97; 2d v.p. Ohio So. Bapt. Conv. Republican. Avocations: target shooting, writing, running, construction. Home: 4325 Kinloch Rd Louisville KY 40207-2853 Office: 4325 Kinloch Rd Louisville KY 40207-2853

SMITH, ROBERT MICHAEL, lawyer, mediator, arbitrator; b. Boston, Nov. 4, 1940; s. Sydney and Minnie (Appel) S.; m. Catherine Kersey, Apr. 14, 1981 (dec. 1983); m. Clarissa Redmond, Feb. 11, 1999 (dec. 2001). AB cum laude, Harvard Coll., 1962; diploma, Centro de Estudos de Espanol, Barcelona, 1963; MA in Internat. Affairs, Columbia U., 1964, MS in Journalism with high honors, 1965; JD, Yale U., 1975. Bar: Calif., N.Y., D.C., U.S. Supreme Ct.; barrister Inner Temple, London; solicitor Supreme Ct. of Eng. and Wales; accredited mediator Hong Kong Internat. Arbitration Ctr.; chartered arbitrator, Eng.; registered mediator Ctr. Mediation d'Arbitrage Paris. Intern in econ. devel. UN, Geneva, 1964; corr. Time Mag., N.Y.C., 1965-66, The N.Y. Times, Washington, 1968-72, 75-76; atty. Heller, Ehrman, White & McAuliffe, San Francisco, 1976-78; spl. asst. Office of Atty. Gen. of U.S., Washington, 1979-80; dir. Office Pub. Affairs U.S. Dept. Justice, Washington, 1979-80; mem. U.S. delegation U.S. v. Iran Internat. Ct. of Justice, The Hague, 1980; asst. U.S. atty. No. Dist. Calif., San Francisco, 1981-82; counsel, sr. counsel to sr. litigation counsel Bank of Am. NT & SA, San Francisco, 1982-86. Lectr. FBI Acad., Quantico, Va., 1980, Internat. Bankers Assn. Calif., 1994, Calif. Bankers Assn., 1994, Cmty. Bankers No. Calif., 1994, 95; judge Golden Medallion Broadcast Media awards State Bar of Calif., 1985; judge pro tem Mcpl. Ct. City and County of San Francisco, 1989—; conciliator Peninsula Conflict Resolution

Ctr.; panelist World Intellectual Property Orgn., Geneva; arbitrator internat. Commercial arbitration ctrs., Vancouver, Cairo, Singapore, Kuala Lumpur, India; CPR Panel of Disting. Neutrals; mem. panel Nat. Assn. for Dispute Resolution. Author: Alternative Dispute Resolution for Financial Institutions, 1995, revised, 1996, 97, 98; bd. editors Yale Law Jour., 1974-75; editor Litigation, jour. ABA litigation sect., 1978-81; mem. editl. adv. bd. Bancroft-Whitney, 1991-94; contbr. articles to profl. jours. Bd. dirs. Neighborhood Legal Assistance Found., San Francisco, 1985-87, Nob Hill Assn., San Francisco, 1985-93; bd. dirs., fin. com. St. Francis Found., San Francisco, 1993-94. 1st lt. inf., USAR, 1965-71. Recipient UPI Award for Newswriting, 1958; Harvard Coll. scholar, 1958-62, Fulbright scholar, 1962-63; Columbia U. Internat. fellow, 1964-65. Fellow Internat. Acad. Mediators, Am. Coll. Civil Trial Mediators, Hong Kong Inst. Arbitrators, Chartered Inst. Arbitrators (London); mem. ABA (corp. counsel com. 1986-96, alternative dispute resolution sect. 1994-98), Assn. Atty. Mediators (v.p. No. Calif. chpt. 1995), State Bar of Calif. (pub. affairs com. 1982-85, litigation sect. 1990-96), Bar Assn. of San Francisco (bench-bar media com. 1985-96, alternative dispute resolution com. 1994-98), Assn. Bus. Trial Lawyers No. Calif., Assn. of Former U.S. Attys. No. Dist. Calif., Am. Arbitration Assn. (mem. comml. arbitration panel, No. Calif. adv. coun., mediator Am. Arbitration Ctr. for Mediation), Nat. Assn. Dispute Resolution, The Mediation Soc. (chmn. bd., pres.), Profl. Atty. Mediators, Cmty. Bds. of San Francisco (conciliator), French-Am. C. of C., German-Am. C. of C. West U.S., Harvard Club of San Francisco (bd. dirs. 1986-94, pres. 1992-94), Yale Club of San Francisco (bd. dirs. 1989-94), Soc. Profls. in Dispute Resolution, Columbia U. Alumni Club of No. Calif. (exec. com. 1978-92). Alternative dispute resolution, Banking, General civil litigation. Office: 120 Montgomery St Ste 1790 San Francisco CA 94104-4320 E-mail: rms@robertmsmith.com.

SMITH, ROBERT SHERLOCK, lawyer, educator; b. N.Y.C., Aug. 31, 1944; s. Robert and Janet W. (Welt) S.; m. Dian Goldston Smith, Aug. 31, 1969; children: Benjamin Eli, Emlen Matthew, Rosemary Friedman. BA, Stanford U., 1965; LLB, Columbia U., 1968. Bar: N.Y. 1968, U.S. Dist. Ct. (so. dist.) N.Y. 1969, U.S. Dist. Ct. (ea. dist.) N.Y. 1977, U.S. Ct. Appeals (2d cir.) 1970, U.S. Ct. Appeals (4th cir.) 1986, U.S. Ct. Appeals (1st cir.) 1988, U.S. Ct. Appeals (7th cir.) 1989, U.S. Ct. Appeals (6th cir.) 1995, U.S. Ct. Appeals (D.C. and 8th cirs.) 1997, U.S. Ct. Appeals (5th cir.) 1999, U.S. Tax Ct. 1974, U.S. Supreme Ct. 1979. Assoc. Paul, Weiss, Rifkind, Wharton & Garrison, N.Y.C., 1968-76, ptnr., 1976—2003; spl. counsel Kornstein, Veisz, Wexler & Pollard, 2003—. Vis. prof. Columbia Law Sch., N.Y.C., 1980-81, lectr. law, 1981-90. Mem. ABA (sect. litigation 1977—), N.Y. State Bar Assn. (vice chair com. on jud. adminstrn. 2001—), Assn. Bar City N.Y. (com. fed. legis. 1981-84, com. on judiciary 1984-87, com. on bicentennial of U.S. Constitution 1988-91), Federalist Soc. N.Y. (pres. lawyers chpt. 1994—). Republican. Mem. Reformed Ch. Federal civil litigation, State civil litigation. Office: 757 1d Ave 18th Fl New York NY 10017 E-mail: rsmith@robertssmithfirm.com.

SMITH, RONALD CHARLES, lawyer, educator; b. Chgo., Dec. 9, 1933; s. Riley C. Smith and Rita Elizabeth (Thompson) De Vito; m. Mary Ann Scherer, June 27, 1971; children: Michael Charles, Matthew James. BS, Loyola U., 1955, JD, 1965. Bar: Ill. 1965, U.S. Dist. Ct. (no. dist.) Ill., 1967, U.S. Ct. Appeals (7th cir.) 1977, U.S. Supreme Ct. 1992. Lectr. Loyola U., Chgo., 1955-56; clk. Justice John McCormick Ill. Appellate Ct. Cook County, Chgo., 1965-66; atty. law dept. Santa Fe R.R., Chgo., 1966-68; mem. faculty John Marshall Law Sch., Chgo., 1966-68, prof., 1968—. Mem. Ill. Constitutional Conv., Springfield, 1969-70; asst. state's atty. Cook County, 1975-76, 1979-80; spl. hearing officer Ill. Civil Svc. Commn., 1977-78 Author: (trial books) ABA National Criminal Justice Trial Advocacy Competition, 1990—; contbr. articles on Ill. Constitution to profl. jours. Bd. dirs. Com. on Ill. Govt., Chgo., 1971-78, Ill. Bd. Ethics, 1974-77; chmn. Ind. Precinct Orgn., Chgo., 1973-74; mem. Gov.'s Transition Task Force, Ill., 1972-73; mem. Ill. Supreme Ct. Criminal Rules Com., 1992—; mem. Cook County Criminal Justice Coord. Com., 1992-96; chair edn. com. Chgo. Sisters Internat. Program, Galway, Ireland. Lt. comdr. USNAF Res., 1956-77. Recipient Alumni scholarship Loyola Law Sch., Chgo., 1962-65./ Mem. ABA (criminal justic sect., dir. Nat. Criminal Justice Trial Advocacy Competition 1990—, vice chair publs. 1996-98, vice chair planning 1999-2000, chair elect 2000-01, chair 2001-02), Internat. Bar Assn., Internat. Assn. Prosecutors, Blue Key, Pi Gamma Mu, Alpha Sigma Rho. Criminal, Public international. Home: 5400 N Wayne Ave Chicago IL 60640-1305 Office: John Marshall Law Sch 315 S Plymouth Ct Chicago IL 60604-3968 E-mail: 7smith@jmls.edu.

SMITH, RONALD EHLBERT, lawyer, educator, pastor, public speaker, writer, motivator, real estate developer; b. Atlanta, Apr. 30, 1947; s. Frank Marion and Frances Jane (Canida) S.; m. Annemarie Krumholz, Dec. 26, 1969; children: Michele, Erika, Damian. BME, Stetson U., 1970; postgrad., Hochschule Fuer Musik, Frankfurt, Fed. Republic Germany, 1971-74; Masters in German Lit., Germany & Middlebury Coll., 1975; JD, Nova U., 1981; postgrad., Gammon Sem. Sch., 2000—. Bar: Fla. 1982, U.S. Dist. Ct. (mid. dist.) Fla. 1983, U.S. Ct. Appeals (11th cir.) 1990, Ga. 1994, U.S. Dist. Ct. (no. dist.) Ga. 1994; cert. ednl. leader, Ga. Asst. state atty. 10th Jud. Cir. Ct., Bartow, Fla., 1982-85; pvt. practice Lakeland, Fla., 1985-94, Atlanta, 1994—; of counsel Mark Boychuk & Assocs., 1998—. Asst. 10th Jud. Cir. Ct., Bartow, 1981-82; instr. Broward County C.C., Ft. Lauderdale, Fla., 1976-79, 91-94, pub. and pvt. schs., Broward County, Atlanta Schs., 1998-2002, Offenbach, Germany, 1971-78; instr. Polk C.C. and Police Acad., Winter Haven, Fla., 1981-94; adj. prof. English, Ga. State U., 1996—; adj. prof. law DeKalb Coll., 1997-2002; part-time police instr. Police Acad., Forsyth, Ga., 1996—; music instr. Atlanta Pub. Schs., 1999-2002. Tchr., drama dir. Disciples I and II, United Meth. Ch., Lakeland, 1980-94, Glenn Meml. United Meth. Ch., Atlanta, 1994—, cand. to ministry, 2000—; Billy Graham counseling supr., 1994—; promoter Promise Keepers, 1995—; spkr., promoter ProNet, 1996—; min. music Scott Blvd. Bapt. Ch., Decatur, Ga., 1998, Gideon Internat., 1999-2002; cert. candidate Ordained Ministry United Meth. Ch. Freedom Bridge fellow German Acad. Exch. Svc., Mainz, 1974-75. Mem. ABA, Christian Legal Soc., Lakeland Bar Assn., Am. Immigration Lawyers Assn. General civil litigation, Education and schools, Estate planning. E-mail: smith321@bellsouth.net.

SMITH, R(ONALD) SCOTT, lawyer; b. Washington, D.C., June 30, 1947; s. Joseph Peter Smith and Roberta Ann (Bailey) George; m. Cheryle Rae Coffman, Nov. 15, 1974 (div. July 1977); m. Gloria Jean Haralson, Nov. 30, 1985. BJ, U. Mo., 1970, JD, 1973. Bar: Mo. 1973, U.S. Dist. Ct. (we. dist.) Mo. 1973, U.S. Ct. Appeals (10th cir.) 1990, U.S. Ct. Appeals (8th cir.) 1992, U.S. Dist. Ct. (ea. dist.) Mo. 1996. Field dir. The Mo. Bar, Jefferson City, 1973-75; law clk. to judge Mo. Ct. Appeals (we. dist.), 1975-76; ptnr. Shirkey, Norton & Smith, Kansas City, 1976-77, Jackson & Sherman, P.C. and predecessors, Kansas City, 1977-84, Birmingham & Furry, Kansas City, 1984, Birmingham, Furry & Smith, 1985-92, Birmingham, Furry, Smith & Stubbs, 1992-95, Furry & Smith, P.C., Kansas City, 1996—. Author: (with others) Automobile Accident Handbook, 1984, rev., 1986, Vexatious Refusal and Bad Faith, 1990, Insurance Claims, 1993; editor: The Rights & Responsibilies of Citizenship in a Free Society, 1974, Due Process of Law, 1974, News Headnotes, 1976-84, Young Lawyer, 1977-80; mem. editorial bd. Mo. Bar Jour., 1978-81; (TV series) legal script advisor Lex Singularis, 1973-75; (multimedia) producer, author Freedoms Lost, 1976; producer, playwright (musical-comedy play) Silly in Philly, 1987. Mem. ABA (mem. various coms.), Mo. Bar Assn. (dist. 12 chmn. 1979—, mem. various coms., Disting. Svc. award young lawyers sect. 1978, 79, 80), West Mo. Def. Lawyers Assn., Kansas City Met. Bar Assn. (pres. young lawyers sect. 1981-82, mem. various coms., Disting. Svc. award young lawyers sect. 1982, Leadership award sr. sect. 1985, First Ann. Pres. award sr. sect. 1987), Kansas City Claim Assn., Phi Delta Phi. Democrat. Roman Catholic. General civil litigation, Personal injury (including property damage), Product liability. Home: 3411 Shady Bend Dr Independence MO 64052-2816 Office: 200 Noland Plz Office Bldg 3675 S Noland Rd Independence MO 64055-6505 Fax: 816-252-5319. E-mail: SSmith@furrysmithlaw.com.

SMITH, ROY PHILIP, judge; b. L.I., N.Y., Dec. 29, 1933; s. Philip Aloysius and Virginia (Collins) S.; m. Elizabeth Helen Wink, Jan. 23, 1965; children: Matthew P., Jean E. BA, St. Joseph's Coll., Yonkers, N.Y., 1956; JD, Fordham U., 1965. Bar: N.Y. Asst. reg. counsel FAA, N.Y.C., 1966-79; adminstrv. law judge U.S. Dept. Labor, Washington, 1979-83; adminstrv. appeals judge Benefits Rev. Bd., Washington, 1983—, chmn., chief adminstrv. appeals judge, 1988-90. Adj. prof. aviation law Dowling Coll., Oakdale, N.Y., 1972-79; adj. prof. transp. law Adelphi U., Garden City, N.Y., 1975-79; vis. prof. Georgetown U. Law Sch., 1989—. With U.S. Army, 1957-59. Mem.: Fed. Adminstrv. Law Judges Conf. (treas. 1983—84, exec. com. 1982—83), Assn. Bar of City of N.Y. (sec.-treas. aeronautics com. 1978—79), Georgetown U. Libr. Assocs., Friendly Sons of St. Patrick, Edgemoor Club. Avocation: tennis. Home: 6700 Pawtucket Rd Bethesda MD 20817-4836 Office: Benefits Rev Bd 200 Constitution Ave NW Washington DC 20210-0001 E-mail: smith-roy@DOL.gov.

SMITH, RUSSELL BRYAN, lawyer; b. Ft. Worth, Nov. 1, 1936; s. Russell Bryan Sr. and Marie Antoinette (Hornick) S.; children: Robert B., Donna Sue. BBA, So. Meth. U., 1959, JD, 1962. Bar: Tex. 1962, U.S. Dist. Ct. (no., ea., we. and so. dists.) Tex., U.S. Ct. Appeals (5th cir.) 1962, U.S. Ct. Appeals (8th cir.) 1981, U.S. Ct. Appeals (11th cir.) 1982, U.S. Supreme Ct. 1967, U.S. Ct. Claims 1987, U.S. Ct. Appeals (fed. and D.C. cirs.). Assoc. Woodruff and Hill, Dallas, 1959-65; ptnr. Woodruff, Hill Kendall and Smith, Dallas, 1965-75; with Smith & Smith, L.L.P., Dallas, 1975—. Concession chmn. Byron Nelson Golf Classic, 1975-2001; mem. Dallas Assembly, 1973-87, Dallas Big Bros., 1967—; bd. trustees Dallas Hist. Soc., 1978-87, Dallas 40, 1967—; bd. dirs. Dallas Police Athletic Assn., 1979-86, Dallas Urban League, 1978-86, Dallas Zool. Soc., 1980—, Greater Dallas Planning Coun., 1978-92; bd. dirs., gen. counsel, vice chmn. bd. dirs. State Fair Tex., 1972—; adv. coun. St. Paul Hosp., 1974-88; mem. Dallas City Coun., 1971-75, dep. mayor pro tem, 1973-75; bd. dirs. Greater Dallas Sesquicentennial Commn., 1982-87. With USNR, 1955-62. Recipient Disting. Svc. award Dallas Jaycees, 1976, award Tex. Jaycees, 1972; named Outstanding Man in Dallas, 1975, Cy Johnston Spirit award, 1998; named Ky. col. Fellow Coll. State Bar (charter); mem. ABA, Tex. Bar Assn., Am. Bd. Trial Advs., Internat. Assn. Gaming Attys., Nat. Assn. Amusement Ride Safety Ofcls., Dallas Bar Assn., Dallas Estate Coun., Am. Judicature Soc., Dallas Bar Found., Bar Assn. Fifth Fed. Cir. (charter), U.S. Claims Ct. Bar Assn., Sports Lawyers Assn., Internat. Amusement and Leisure Def. Assn., Outdoor Amusement Bus. ASsn., Internat. Assn. Amusement Parks and Attractions, Internat. Assn. Fairs and Expns., Internat. Profl. Rodeo Assn., Salesmanship of Dallas Club (life), All Sports Assn. (pres. 1977), Dallas Athletic Club, Woodvale Fishing Club, Rock Creek Barbecue Club (life), Phi Alpha Delta. Methodist. Avocations: fishing, boating, traveling, hunting. Federal civil litigation, State civil litigation, Corporate, general. Office: Two Turtle Creek Vlg # 224 Dallas TX 75219 E-mail: attorneys@smith-firm.com.

SMITH, SCOTT A. lawyer; b. Grand Forks, N.D., July 17, 1957; married. BA, Stanford U., 1978; JD, U. Calif., Berkeley, 1981. Bar: Wash. 1981, U.S. Ct. Appeals (9th cir) 1982, U.S. Dist. Ct. (Ea. and We. dists.) Wash. Law clk. to Hon. Jerome Farris 9th Cir. U.S. Ct. of Appeals, 1981—82; ptnr. Short Cressman & Burgess, Seattle, 1988—. Chair Wash. State Access to Justice Bd., Seattle, 2002—. Recipient Pro Bono award, Wash. State Bar Assn., Allies for Justice award, LEGALS of Wash. Fellow: Am. Bar Found.; mem.: King County Bar Assn. (pres. 1996—97, trustee 1991—97, Helen Geisness award Exemplary Svc.). Property, real (including real estate development, water), General civil litigation, Product liability. Office: Short Cressman & Burgess 999 Third Ave Suite 3000 Seattle WA 98104 Office Fax: 206-230-8328.

SMITH, SELMA MOIDEL, lawyer, composer; b. Warren, Ohio, Apr. 3, 1919; d. Louis and Mary (Oyer) Moidel; 1 child, Mark Lee. Student, UCLA, 1936-39, U. So. Calif. Law School, 1939-41; JD, Pacific Coast U., 1942. Bar: Calif. 1943, U.S. Dist. Ct. 1943, U.S. Supreme Ct. 1958. Gen. practice law; mem. firm Moidel, Moidel, Moidel & Smith, 1943—. Field dir. civilian adv. com. WAC, 1943—45; mem. nat. bd. Med. Coll. Pa. (formerly Woman's Med. Coll. Pa.), 1953—, mem. exec. bd., 1976—80, pres., 1980—82, chmn, past pres. com., 1990—92. Author: A Century of Achievement: The National Association of Women Lawyers, 1998, The First Women Members of the ABA, 1999; composer: Espressivo-Four Piano Pieces (orchestral premiere, 1987, performance Nat. Mus. Women in the Arts, 1989), numerous works. Decorated La Orden del Merito Juan Pablo Duarte (Dominican Republic), 1956. Fellow: Am. Bar Found. (life); mem.: ASCAP, ABA (jr. bar conf. 1946—52, activities com. 1948—49), Calif. Supreme Ct. Hist. Soc. (bd. dirs. 2001—), ABA Sr. Lawyers Divsn. (vice-chair editl. bd. Experience mag. 1997—99, chair arts com. 1998—99, chair editl. bd. Experience mag. 1999—2001, exec. coun. 1999—, Experience mag. adv. bd. 2001—), Assn. Learning in Retirement Orgns. in West (pres. 1993—94, exec. com. 1994—95, Disting. Svc. award 1995), Plato Soc. UCLA (discussion leader UCLA Constitution Bicentennial Project 1985—87, moderator UCLA extension lecture series 1990, Toga editor 1990—93, sec. 1991—92, chmn. colloquium com. 1992—93, Exceptional Leadership award 1994), Euterpe Opera Club (chair auditions 1972, chair awards 1973—75, v.p. 1974—75), Docents LA Philharm. (press and pub. rels. 1972—75, cons. coord. 1973—75, v.p. 1973—83, chair Latin Am. cmty. rels.), Calif. Fedn. Music Clubs (chair Am. music 1971—75, conv. chair 1972), Nat. Fedn. Music Clubs (vice-chair Western region 1973—78), Nat. Assn. Composers USA (dir. 1974—79, luncheon chair 1975), Calif. Pres. Coun. (1st v.p.), LA Bus. Women's Coun. (pres. 1952), Calif. Bus. Women's Coun. (dir. 1951), Coun. Bar Assns. LA County (charter sec. 1950), So. Calif. Women Lawyers Assn. (pres. 1947, 1948), Inter-Am. Bar Assn., League of Ams. (dir.), Nat. Assn. Women Lawyers (regional dir. western states, Hawaii 1949—51, jud. adminstrn. com. 1960, nat. chair world peace through law com. 1966—67, liaison to ABA Sr. Lawyers Divsn. 1996—, chair bd. elections 1997—98, centennial com. 1997—99, chair com. unauthorized practice of law, social commn. UN, Lifetime Svc. award 1999), LA Lawyers Club (pub. defenders com. 1951), LA Bar Assn. (servicemen's legal aid com. 1944—45, psychopathic ct. com. 1948—53, Outstanding Svc. award 1993), State Bar Calif. (conf. com. on unauthorized practice of medicine 1964, Disting. Svc. award 1993), Women Lawyers Assn. LA (hon life; chair Law Day com. 1966, subject of oral hist. project 1986, 2001), Iota Tau Tau Legal Scholastic Soc. (dean LA 1947, supreme treas. 1959—62, 1st prize 1942). General practice. Home: 5272 Lindley Ave Encino CA 91316-3518

SMITH, SHARON LOUISE, lawyer, consultant; b. Williamsport, Pa., Apr. 21, 1949; d. Stuart Mallory and Phyllis Virginia (Hartzell) S. Student, Schiller Coll., Heidelberg, Fed. Republic Germany, 1969-70; AB, Grove City Coll., 1971; MA, Kent State U., 1973; JD, Temple U., 1978. Bar: Pa. 1978, U.S. Dist. Ct. (we. dist.) Pa. 1980, U.S. Ct. Appeals (3rd cir.) 1992. Assoc. Laurel Legal Services, Brookville, Pa., 1980-82; pvt. practice Brookville, 1982—. Cons. Prothonotary, Brookville, 1984-86. Mem. multidisciplinary team for child abuse Jefferson County Child Welfare Dept., Brookville, 1985; bd. dirs. Clarion-Jefferson Community Action, Brookville, 1982, Clearfield-Jefferson Drug and Alcohol Commn., DuBois, Pa., 1983-84. Mem. Pa. Bar Assn., Law Alumnae Assn. Temple U. Presbyterian. Avocations: swimming, reading. Bankruptcy, Probate (including wills, trusts), Property, real (including real estate development, water). Home: 172 Franklin Ave Brookville PA 15825-1164 Office: 197 Main St Brookville PA 15825

SMITH, SHEILA MARIE, lawyer; b. Chgo. d. Donald Thomas and Catherine Ellen (Mariga) Morrison; m. Melvin Smith, Nov. 11, 1989. BSEE, Purdue U., 1981; JD, U. Cin., 1995. Bar: Ohio 1995, U.S. Dist. Ct. (so. dist.) Ohio 1996, U.S. Ct. Appeals (6th cir.) 1996, U.S. Supreme Ct., 1999. Mfg. engr., 1981-92; assoc. Freking & Betz, Cin., 1995-99, ptnr., 2000—. Spkr. in field. Named to Order of Coif U. Cin., 1995. Mem. ABA, Am. Trial Lawyers Assn., Nat. Employment Lawyers Assn., Ohio Employment Lawyers Assn., Cin. Employment Lawyers Assn., Ohio Bar Assn., Cin. Bar Assn. Avocations: golf, traveling, cooking. Civil rights, Labor (including EEOC, Fair Labor Standards Act, labor-management relations, NLRB, OSHA). Home: 3345 Legendary Trails Dr Cincinnati OH 45245-3074 Office: Freking & Betz 215 E 9th St Fl 5 Cincinnati OH 45202-2139 E-mail: ssmith@frekingandbetz.com.

SMITH, SIDNEY OSLIN, JR., lawyer; b. Gainesville, Ga., Dec. 30, 1923; s. Sidney Oslin and Isabelle Caroline (Charters) S.; m. Patricia Irwin Horkan, Aug. 4, 1944 (dec. Oct. 19, 2001); children— Charters Smith Wilson, Ellen Smith Andersen, Sidney Oslin III. AB cum laude, Harvard Coll., 1947; LL.B. summa cum laude, U. Ga., 1949. Bar: Ga. 1948. Ptnr. Telford, Wayne & Smith, Gainesville, Ga., 1949-62; asst. solicitor Superior Cts., Northeastern Jud. Cir. Ga., 1951-61, judge, 1962-65, U.S. Dist. Ct. (no. dist.) Ga., 1965-68, chief judge, 1968-74; ptnr. Alston, Miller & Gaines, Atlanta, 1974-82, Alston & Bird, Atlanta, 1982-94, of counsel, 1994—. Chmn. Gainesville Bd. Edn., 1959-62; trustee Brenau Coll., Gainesville, 1974— , chmn., 1976-84; mem. state bd. regents Univ. System of Ga., 1980-87, chmn., 1984-85. Served to capt. U.S. Army, 1943-46, ETO. Fellow ABA, Am. Coll. Trial Lawyers; mem. Am. Law Inst., Am. Judicature Soc., Commerce Club, Chattahoochee Club, Phi Beta Kappa, Phi Kappa Phi, Phi Delta Phi, Phi Delta Theta. Democrat. Episcopalian. Federal civil litigation, Alternative dispute resolution. Home: 3206 Club Pointe Way Gainesville GA 30506-1638 Office: Alston & Bird 1 Atlantic Ctr Atlanta GA 30309-3400 E-mail: smit977@bellsouth.net.

SMITH, SIMEON CHRISTIE, IV, lawyer; b. Lake Charles, La., Oct. 21, 1969; s. Simeon Christie III and Shirley Mae (Pearce) S.; m. Christina A. Lord. BA, La. State U., 1992, JD, 1996. Bar: La. 1997, U.S. Dist. Ct. (we., ea. and mid. dists.) La. 1997, U.S. Ct. Appeals (5th cir.) 1997, U.S. Supreme Ct. 2001; cert. La. Indigent Defense Assistance Bd. 2002. Ptnr. The Smith Law Firm, L.L.P., Leesville, La., 1997—. Fellow Roscoe Pound Found.; mem. ATLA, Fed. Bar Assn., La. State Bar Assn., La. Trial Lawyers Assn. (bd. gos. 1997—), L.A. Assn. Criminal Def. Lawyers, 30th Jud. Cir. Bar Assn. (pres. 2000). Roman Catholic. General civil litigation, Criminal, Personal injury (including property damage). Office: 300 Courthouse PO Box 1528 Leesville LA 71496-1528

SMITH, SPENCER THOMAS, lawyer; b. N.Y.C., May 3, 1943; s. Spencer H. and Marie K. (Walter) S.; m. Jenny Matilda Anderson, Aug. 15, 1965; children: S. Anders, J. Kirsten. B.M.E., Cooper Union Sch. Engring., 1965; JD, Am. U., 1968. Bar: N.Y. 1969, U.S. Dist. Ct. (ea. and so. dists.) N.Y. 1971, U.S. Ct. Appeals (fed. cir.) 1983. Assoc. Nolte & Nolte, N.Y.C., 1968-70, Nims, Halliday, Whitman, Howes, Collison & Isner, 1970-72; group patent and licensing counsel Litton Industries, Inc., Hartford, 1984-85; sole practice Hartford, 1984-85; sr. group patent atty. Emhart Copr., Farmington, Conn., 1985-89, Black & Decker Corp., Towson, Md., 1989-98; legal counsel Emhart Glass, Enfield, Conn., 1998. Author: Primarily Merely, 1973, Italian System Works Well to Resolve Disputes, 1997. Coach basketball program Farmington Valley YMCA, Simsbury, Conn., 1976-80, Simsbury Youth Soccer Assn., 1976-86. Mem. Licensing Execs. Soc., Greater Hartford C. of C. (mem. high tech. continuing edn. task force 1981-89). Republican. Methodist. Federal civil litigation, Patent, Trademark and copyright. Home: 53 Silver Brook Ln North Granby CT 06060-1111 Office: Emhart Glass Rsch Inc 89 Phoenix Ave PO Box 1229 Enfield CT 06082

SMITH, STEPHEN CHADWICK, lawyer; b. Lock Haven, Pa., Aug. 24, 1950; s. James Thomas and Meta (Chadwick) S.; m. Susan Paula Bada, July 20, 1984; 1 child, Demian James. BA, U. Pa., 1972; JD, U. Del., 1981. Bar: Pa. 1982, U.S. Ct. Appeals (3d cir.) 1985, U.S. Supreme Ct. 1993, U.S.. Dist. Ct. (mid. dist.) Pa. 1994. Pvt. practice, Lock Haven, 1983—; pub. defender Clinton County, Lock Haven, 1983—. Mem. Lions, Elks. Democrat. Roman Catholic. Criminal, Probate (including wills, trusts), Property, real (including real estate development, water). Home and Office: 226 E Water St Lock Haven PA 17745-1354 E-mail: smithlaw@cub.kcnet.org.

SMITH, STEPHEN JAMES, lawyer, director; b. Milw., Feb. 16, 1949; s. James Milon and Helen Kathryn Smith; m. Jerilyn Sue Jenson, Feb. 6, 1971; children: Justin Paul, Lindsay Jeane, Erika Helen. BA magna cum laude, Luther Coll., 1971; JD cum laude, Northwestern U., 1976. Bar: Wis. 1976. Auditor Arthur Andersen & Co., Chgo., 1971-73; ptnr. Hostak, Henzl & Bichler, Ltd. (formerly Thompson & Coates), Racine, Wis., 1976—. Reporter taxation sect. Wis. State Bar; mem. adv. bd. and steering com. Sustainable Racine, Inc., 1997-99. Bd. dirs. Goodwill Industries S.E. Wis., Racine, 1980-83, Goodwill Industries Milw., 1983-2002, Racine Area United Way, 1982-88, Taylor Home, 1985-91, 1997-2001, pres., 1998-2000; bd. dirs. Racine Cmty. Found., 1991-99, pres., 1997-99; founder The Family Vision Experience, 2002. Mem. ABA, Wis. State Bar. Lutheran. Corporate, general, Estate taxation, Personal income taxation. Office: Hostak Henzl & Bichler SC 840 Lake Ave Racine WI 53403-1566 E-mail: ssmith@hhb.com.

SMITH, STEPHEN MARK, lawyer; b. Newport News, Va., July 1, 1948; s. Joseph and Marian (Sturman) S.; m. Dawn Lee Williams, Dec. 10, 1978; children: Ryan David, Miles Stephen. BA in Psychology, William & Mary, 1971, JD, 1974. Bar: Va. 1974, N.Y. 1975, D.C. 1975, U.S. Supreme Ct., U.S. Ct. Appeals (2d, D.C., 4th cirs.). Lawyer Rothblatt, Rothblatt, et al., N.Y.C., 1974-76, Joseph Smith Ltd., Hampton, Va., 1976-99; founding mem. Brain Injury Law Ctr. P.C. Bd. dirs. Enrenfried Techs. Mem. com. Va. Beach Dems., 1990—; bd. dirs., coord. Va. state Trial Lawyers Pub. Justice. Included in Best Lawyers in Am., 1997—. Mem. ATLA, Am. Bd. Trial Lawyers (diplomate), Am. Bd. Trial Advocates, Va. Trial Lawyers Assn. (bd. dirs. 1978—), Brain Injury Assn. Va. (bd. dirs. 1997—). Avocations: fishing, reading, boating, jogging, golf. Libel, Personal injury (including property damage), Product liability. Office: Brain Injury Law Center 2100 Kecoughtan Rd Hampton VA 23661

SMITH, STEVEN LEE, judge; b. San Antonio, Apr. 19, 1952; s. Bill Lee and Maxine Rose (Williams) S.; m. Rebecca Ann Brimmer, Aug. 5, 1978; children: William Christopher, Laura Charlotte. B in Music Edn. magna cum laude, Abilene Christian U., 1974; JD, U. Tex., 1977. Bar: Tex. 1977. U.S. Dist. Ct. (so. dist.) Tex. 1979, U.S. Dist. Ct. (we. dist.) Tex. 1980; cert. civil trial lawyer, Tex. Bd. Legal Specialization. Assoc. Dillon & Giesenschlag, Bryan, Tex., 1977-80, ptnr., 1980-84, Dillon, Lewis, Elmore & Smith, Bryan, 1985-88, Hoelscher, Lipsey, Elmore and Smith, College Station, Tex., 1988-94; asst. mcpl. judge City of College Station, 1988-91, presiding mcpl. judge, 1992-95; judge Brazos County Ct. at Law # 1, Bryan, 1995-98, 361st Dist. Ct., Bryan, 1999—. Chair Nat. Conf. Spl. Ct. Judges, 2001—02. Chmn. Brazos Valley chpt. March of Dimes, 1983-84; Leadership Brazos Devel. Program, Bryan/Coll. Sta. C. of C., 1984-85; pres. Meml. Student Ctr. Opera and Performing Arts Soc., College Station, 1985-86; trustee Abilene Christian U., 2001—. Recipient Charles Plum Disting. Svc. award Tex. A&M U., 1986. Mem. U. Tex. Law Sch. Alumni Assn. (dist. dir. 1986-89), U. Tex. Ex-Students Assn. Exec. Coun. (club rep. 1987-88), Optimists (pres. 1982-83). Mem. Ch. Of Christ. Avocations: golf, flying. Home: 3840 Cedar Ridge Dr College Station TX 77845-6275 Office: 361st Dist Ct 300 E 26th St Ste 305 Bryan TX 77803-5361 E-mail: ssmith@co.brazos.tx.us.

SMITH, STEVEN RAY, law educator; b. Spirit Lake, Iowa, July 8, 1946; s. Byrnard L. and Dorothy V. (Fischbeck) S.; m. Lera Baker, June 15, 1975. BA, Buena Vista Coll., 1968; JD, U. Iowa, 1971, MA, 1971. Bar: Iowa 1971, Ky. 1987, Ohio 1992. From asst. to assoc. dean Sch. Law U. Louisville, 1974-81, acting dean, 1974-75, 76, prof. law, 1971-88, assoc. in medicine Med. Sch., 1983-88; dep. dir/ Assn. Am. Law Schs., 1987-88; dean, prof. law Cleve. State U., 1988-96; pres., dean and prof. Calif. Western Sch. of Law, 1996—. Author: Law, Behavior and Mental Health: Policy and Practice, 1987; contbr. chpts. to books, articles to profl. jours. Trustee U. Louisville, 1980-82, SCRIBES, 1993—; bd. dirs. San Diego Mediation Ctr., pres. Ky. Congress of Senate Faculty Leaders, 1982-84; bd. trustees Am. Bd. Profl. Psychology, 1994-2001; bd. dirs. Nat. Register of Health Svc. Providers in Psychology, 2002—, San Diego Vol. Lawyers Program, 1998—, San Diego Mediation Ctr., 2003—; sec., bd. dirs. Assn. for Accreditation of Human Rsch. Protection Programs, 2001—. Recipient Grawemeyer award Innovative Teaching. Metroversity Consortium, 1983. Fellow Ohio State Bar Found.; mem. ABA (stds. rev. com. 1991-95, govt. rels. com. 1993-95, joint commn. ABA/Assn. Am. Law Schs. financing of legal edn. 1993-94, 97-98, coun. sect. legal edn. and admission to the bar 1997—), APA (pub. mem. ethics com.), Am. Econs. Assn., Assn. Am. Law Schs. (chmn. librs. com., dep. dir. 1987-88, mem. accreditation com. 1993-96, chair accreditation com. 1994-96), Ohio State Bar Assn. (coun. of dels. 1992-96), Order of Coif, City Club of Cleve. (pres. 1994-95). Office: Calif Western Sch Law Office of Pres 225 Cedar St San Diego CA 92101-3046

SMITH, STEVEN W. judge; b. Tex. m. Susan Smith; children: Emily, Allison. BBA in Fin., U. Tex., Arlington, 1983; JD with honors, U. Tex., 1986. Judge Tex. State Supreme Ct., Austin, 2002—. Office: Tex Supreme Ct PO Box 12248 Austin TX 78711 Office Fax: 512-463-1365.*

SMITH, TAD RANDOLPH, lawyer; b. El Paso, Tex., July 20, 1928; s. Eugene Rufus and Dorothy (Derrick) S.; m. JoAnn Wilson, Aug. 24, 1949; children: Laura Borsch, Derrick, Cameron Ann Compton. LLB, U. Tex., 1951, BBA, 1952. Bar: Tex. 1951. Assoc. firm Kemp, Smith Duncan & Hammond P.C., El Paso, Tex., 1951-52, ptnr., 1952-81, CEO, 1975—98, shareholder, 1981—99; of counsel Kemp Smith, LLP, El Paso, 1999—. Active United Way of El Paso; chmn. El Paso County Reps., 1958-61, Tex. Rep. State Exec. Com., 1961-62; alt. del. Rep. Nat. Conv., 1952, 62, del. 1964, dir. El Paso Elec. Co. , 1961-90, State Nat. Bank of El Paso, 1969-90, The Leavell Co., 1970-94; trustee Robert E. and Evelyn McKee Found., 1970-90, Property Trust of Am., 1971-91; mem. devel. bd. U. Tex., El Paso, 1973-81, v.p., 1975, chmn. 1976; dinner treas. Nat. Jewish Hosp. and Rsch. Ctr., 1977, chmn. 1978, presenter of honoree, 1985; bd. dirs. NCCJ 1965-76, chmn. 1965-78; bd. dirs. Southwestern Children's Home, El Paso, 1959-78; trustee Hervey Found., 1990-99, Lydia Patterson Inst., 1994-99. Named Outstanding Young Man, El Paso Jaycees; named to Bd. of Fellows, U. Tex., El Paso, 1997—2001; recipient Humanitarian award, El Paso chpt. NCCJ, 1983. Fellow Am. Bar Found., Tex. Bar Found.; mem. ABA, Tex. Bar Assn., El Paso Bar Assn. (pres. 1971-72), El Paso C. of C. (dir. 1979-82), Sigma Chi. Republican. Methodist. Corporate, general, Finance, Securities. Home: PO Box 831 Alto NM 88312 Office: Kemp Smith LLP Wells Fargo Plz 221 N Kansas St Ste 1700 El Paso TX 79901

SMITH, TEFFT WELDON, lawyer; b. Evanston, Ill., Nov. 18, 1946; s. Edward W. and Margery T. (Weldon) S.; m. Nancy Jo Smith, Feb. 25, 1967; children: Lara Andrea, Tefft Weldon II. BA, Brown U., 1968; JD, U. Chgo., 1971. Bar: Ill. 1971, D.C. 2000, U.S. Supreme Ct. 1977. Sr. litigation ptnr. Kirkland & Ellis, Chgo., 1971—, ptnr.-in-charge competition and antitrust practice group. Mem. adv. bd. Bur. Nat. Affairs Antitrust and Trade Regulation Reporter; instr. trial advocacy. Contbr. numerous articles on trial practice and antitrust issues to law jours. Mem. ABA (litigation sect., antitrust law sect.), Econ. Club., Univ. Club, Mid-Am. Club, Sea Pines Country Club (Hilton Head, S.C.). Avocations: squash, ferraris, sculpture. Office: Kirkland & Ellis 200 E Randolph St Fl 54 Chicago IL 60601-6636 also: 655 15th St NW Washington DC 20005-5701 Home: 700 New Hampshire Ave NW Washington DC 20037

SMITH, THOMAS A. lawyer, investment company executive; b. Springfield, Ill., Dec. 14, 1956; BA, Wabash Coll., 1978; JD, St. Louis U., 1983, MBA, 1984. Bar: Ill. 1984, Mo. 1985, N.Y. 1990; lic. series 7 Nat. Assn. Securities Dealers, series 24 Nat. Assn. Securities Dealers. Enforcement atty. Ill. Securities Dept., 1984—85; staff atty. divsn. investment mgmt. U.S. SEC, 1986—89; sr. assoc. Wilkie Farr & Gallaghar, 1989—91; asst. gen. counsel Dreyfus Corp., 1991—93, N.Y. Life Ins. Co., N.Y.C., 1994—96, assoc. gen. counsel, 1996—97, v.p., assoc. gen. counsel, 1997—99; exec. v.p., gen. counsel Van Kampen Investments, Inc., 1999—2001; mng. dir., gen. counsel U.S. investment mgmt. Morgan Stanley, N.Y.C., 2001—. Co-author: (book) Regulation of Investment Companies. Securities, Corporate, general. Office: Morgan Stanley Law Dept 1221 Ave of the Americas 5th Fl New York NY 10020 Office Fax: 212-762-5530.*

SMITH, THOMAS RAMSAUR, lawyer; b. Feb. 12, 1938; AB, Princeton U., 1960; LLB, U. Va., 1963. Assoc. Brown & Wood LLP, N.Y.C., 1963-71, ptnr., 1971-96, mng. ptnr., 1996—. Office: Sidley, Austen, Brown, & Wood 787 Seventh Avenue New York NY 10019*

SMITH, TURNER TALIAFERRO, JR., lawyer; b. Washington, Dec. 16, 1940; s. Turner Taliaferro and Lois (Fisk) S.; m. Christine H. Perdue; children: Turner T., III, John Webb Tyler. BA magna cum laude, Princeton U., 1962; LLB cum laude, Harvard U., 1968. Bar: Va. 1968, D.C. 1977. Ptnr. Hunton & Williams, Richmond, Va., 1975—; tchr. environ. law Washington and Lee U., 1978, Coll. William and Mary, 1979, 80. Mem. ABA (chmn. standing com. environ. law 1983, 84, 85, chmn. corp., banking and bus. law sect. com. on environ. controls 1973-80), Va. Bar Assn.. Administrative and regulatory, Environmental, Legislative. Office: Hunton & Williams 1900 K St NW 12 Fl Washington DC 20001

SMITH, WALTER ERNEST, lawyer; b. Cin., Jan. 1, 1947; s. Walter F. and Kathleen M. (Vickers) S.; m. Healther Williamson, Mar. 3, 1979; children: Walter Todd, Kristan Lyn, Melanie Kathleen, Jennifer Erin. BS, Ohio State U., 1968; JD, Stetson U., 1971. Bar: Ohio 1971, Fla. 1971; cert. civil trial and bus. litigation law. Ptnr. Smith & Kircher, Cin., 1971-73, Davis & Smith, West Palm Beach, Fla., 1973-78, Meros & Smith PA, St. Petersburg, Fla., 1978—. With USAR, 1969-75. Mem.: ABA, Pinellas County Trial Lawyers, Am. Assn. Trial Lawyers, St. Petersburg Bar Assn., Fla. Bar Assn., Ohio Bar Assn. Democrat. Methodist. Family and matrimonial, Property, real (including real estate development, water).

SMITH, WALTER JOHN, lawyer; b. Omaha, Apr. 19, 1948; s. Walter H. and Margaret A. (Ortman) S.; m. Mary Lou Dreves, June 20, 1970; children: Benjamin, Michael, Jeffrey. JD, Creighton U., 1972; LLM, Harvard U., 1975. Bar: Nebr. 1972, Tex. 1975. Law clk. to Judge E.A. Tamm U.S. Ct. Appeals (D.C. cir.), 1972-73; mem. Monen, Seidler, McGill, Festerson & Koley, Omaha, 1973-74; mem., then sr. ptnr. Baker & Botts, Houston, 1975—. Bd. dirs. Reprogenesis, Cambridge, Mass. Mem. Houston Club. Corporate, general, Securities. Office: Baker & Botts 3000 One Shell Plz 1200 Smith St Ste 1200 Houston TX 77002-4592

SMITH, WALTON NAPIER, lawyer; b. Macon, Georgia, Feb. 26, 1942; s. Robert Monroe and Marion Rose (Napier) S.; m. Susan Rush (Baum), Oct. 10, 1970; children: Rush Hendley, Berkeley Bosman. BA, Dartmouth Coll., 1964; JD, Harvard U., 1967. Bar: Ga., 1966; D.C., 1972; Ill., 1978; U.S. Supreme Ct., 1971. Counsel Nat. R.R. Passenger Corp., Washington, 1971-75; assoc. Lord, Bissell, and Brook, Washington and Chgo., 1975-79, ptnr. Chgo. and Atlanta, 1980—. Sec. Brit. Am. Bus. Group. Mem. bd. America's Watershed Land Keeper. Capt. JAGC U.S. Army, 1964—71. Decorated Bronze Star, Army Commendation Medal. Mem. ABA, Ill. Bar Assn., State Bar Ga., Nat. Assn. R.R. Trial Counsel, Union League Club, Chgo. Democrat. Episcopalian. Environmental, Insurance, Personal injury (including property damage). Office: The Proscenium 1170 Peachtree St Ste 1900 Atlanta GA 30309 E-mail: wsmith@lordbissell.com.

SMITH, WAYNE RICHARD, lawyer; b. Petoskey, Mich., Apr. 30, 1934; s. Wayne Anson and Frances Lynetta (Cooper) S.; m. Carrie J. Swanson, June 13, 1959; children: Stephen, Douglas (dec.), Rebecca. AB, U. Mich., 1956, JD, 1959. Bar: Mich. 1959. Asst. atty. gen. State of Mich., 1960-62; pros. atty. Emmet County (Mich.), 1963-68; dist. judge 90th Jud. Dist., Mich., 1969-72; city atty. City of Petoskey, 1976-98. Trustee North Central Mich. Coll., 1981-98, chmn., 1992-97; trustee/chmn. N. Ctrl. Mich. Coll. Found., 1999—; mem. No. Mich. Community Mental Health Bd., 1972-92, chmn., 1979-81. Mem. Emmet-Charlevoix Bar Assn. (pres. 1967), State Bar Mich., Mich. State Bar Found. Presbyterian. Land use and zoning (including planning), Probate (including wills, trusts), Property, real (including real estate development, water). Home: PO Box 4677 Harbor Springs MI 49740-4677 Address: 365 E Main St PO Box 4677 Harbor Springs MI 49740-4677

SMITH, WENDY HOPE, lawyer; b. N.Y.C., Jan. 19, 1957; d. Morton and Doris Smith. AB, Smith Coll., 1978; JD, Boston U., 1981. Bar: N.J. 1981, U.S. Dist. Ct. 1981, U.S. Ct. Appeals (3d cir.), Supreme Ct. U.S. Law sec. to judge Superior Ct. N.J., Bergen County, 1981-82; assoc. firm Sellar, Richardson, Stuart & Chisholm, Roseland, N.J., 1982-89, ptnr., 1989-97, Sellar Richardson, P.C., 1997-2000, Marshall, Dennehey, Warner, Coleman & Goggin, Roseland, N.J., 2000—. Mem. adv. com. Inst. CLE, 1983-91. Mem. ABA, N.J. Bar Assn., Bergen County Bar Assn., Essex County Bar Assn., Mensa, Smith Coll. Alumnae Assn. (fund rep. 1978-83). Insurance, Construction, Personal injury (including property damage). Home: 401 Hancock Ct Edgewater NJ 07020-1627 Office: Marshall Dennehey Warner Coleman & Goggin 425 Eagle Rock Ave Ste 302 Roseland NJ 07068

SMITH, WILLIAM CHARLES, lawyer; b. Batavia, N.Y., June 9, 1930; s. William F. and Verna B. (Busmire) S.; m. Lucia P. Pierce, July 10, 1954; children: William Charles, Leonard P., Victoria J. BA, U. Buffalo, 1952; LLB, Harvard U., 1955. Bar: Maine 1955, D.C. 1962, Fla. 1995, U.S. Dist. Ct. Maine, 1956, U.S. Tax Ct. 1960, U.S. Ct. Appeals (1st cir.) 1977, U.S. Ct. Claims 1985, U.S. Supreme Ct. 1960. Assoc., Portland, Maine, 1955-57; ptnr. Hutchinson, Pierce, Atwood & Allen, Portland, 1957-59; counsel Office Tax Legis. Counsel, U.S. Treasury Dept., Washington, 1959-61; ptnr. Pierce, Atwood, Scribner, Allen, Smith and Lancaster, Portland, 1961-96, of counsel, 1996—. Exec. com. Fed. Tax Inst., New Eng. Vice chmn. budget com. United Community Services, 1966-68, chmn., 1968-70, nat. budget and consultation com., 1969-71; bd. dirs. Portland Goodwill, Inc., 1967-69, United Way, Inc., 1968-74, 75-80, Portland Widow's Wood Soc., 1962— ; trustee Portland Regional Opportunity Program, 1967-68, Freyburg Acad., 1976-96 , Found. Blood Research, 1979-85. Mem. ABA, Maine Bar Assn., D.C. Bar, Fla. Bar, Cumberland County Bar Assn., Am. Law Inst., Am. Coll. Trust and Estate Counsel, Am. Coll. Tax Counsel, Portland Country Club, Mid-Ocean Club (Bermuda), Meadows Country Club (Fla.), Cumerland Club (Maine). Republican. Unitarian Universalist. Corporate taxation, Estate taxation, Personal income taxation. Home: 392 Spring St Portland ME 04102-3642 Office: Pierce Atwood One Monument Sq Portland ME 04101-1110 E-mail: wsmith@pierceatwood.com.

SMITH, WILLIAM DOUGLAS, lawyer; b. Spartanburg, S.C., Apr. 3, 1958; s. Milton Alfred and Suzanne (Earnhardt) S.; m. Alison Evans Smith; children: Cameron McIver, Anna Douglas. BA, Wofford Coll., 1980; JD, U. S.C., 1983. Bar: S.C. 1983, U.S. Dist. Ct. S.C., U.S. Ct. Appeals S.C. Assoc. Johnson, Smith Firm, Spartanburg, S.C., 1983-86, ptnr., 1986—. Bd. dirs. MOD, Inc., Spartanburg. Mem. S.C. Ho. of Reps., 1992—, spkr. pro tempore, 2000—. Mem. S.C. Bar Assn., Spartanburg County Bar Assn., S.C. Golf Assn. (bd. dirs. 1995). Republican. Presbyterian. Avocation: golf. General practice, Personal injury (including property damage), Workers' compensation. Home: 19 Springdale Ln Spartanburg SC 29302-3410 Office: Johnson Smith 220 N Church St Spartanburg SC 29306-5104

SMITH, WILLIAM REECE, JR., lawyer; b. Athens, Tenn., Sept. 19, 1925; s. William Reece and Gladys (Moody) S. BS, U. S.C., 1946; JD, U. Fla., 1949; Rhodes scholar, Oxford U., 1949-52; LL.D., U. So. Fla., 1973, Rollins Coll., 1980, U. Fla., 1980, U. S.C., 1981, Stetson U., 1985; D.C.L., Central Meth. Coll., 1980, New Eng. Coll., 1980; D.H.L., Calif. West Sch. Law, 1981; DBA, Tampa (Fla.) Coll., 1991; LHD, U. So. Fla., 1990. Bar: Fla. 1949. Mem. firm Carlton, Fields, Ward, Emmanuel, Smith and Cutler, Tampa, 1953—, now chmn.; emeritus, interim pres. U. So. Fla., 1976-77; city atty. Tampa, 1963-72. Asst. prof. law U. Fla., 1952-53; adj. prof. law Stetson U., 1954-59, 91—; past pres. Am. Bar Endowment, Fla. Legal Svcs., Inc. Past pres. Tampa Philharmonic Assn., Fla. Gulf Coast Symphony, Inc.; sec. Fla. Rhodes Scholar Selection Com., 1969-94. Midshipman and ensign USNR, 1943—46. Named Outstanding Young Man of Tampa, 1961; recipient Good Govt. award Fla. Jr. C. of C., 1965, Disting. Am. award Tampa Chpt. Nat. Football Found., 1977, Humanitarian award B'nai B'rith Found., 1977, Pres.'s award Fla. Assn. Retarded Citizens, 1978, Von Briesen award Nat. Legal Aid and Defender Assn., 1980, Brotherhood award NCCJ, 1980, Herbert Harley award Am. Judicature Soc., 1983, Citizen of Yr. award Civitan Club, 1986, Algernon Sydney Sullivan award, U. S.C., 1987, Pub. Svc. award Stetson U. Coll. Law, 1990, C.H.I.E.F. award Fla. Ind. Colls. and Univs., 1990, Professionalism award Am. Inns of Ct., 2002. Fellow Am. Coll. Trial Lawyers, Internat. Acad. Trial Lawyers, Am. Bar Found. (past pres.), Fla. Bar Found. (past pres.); mem. ABA (chmn. jr. bar conf. 1960-61, life, ho. dels., sec. 1967-71, pres. 1980-81, Gold medal 1989, Pro Bono Publico award 1994), Internat. Soc. Barristers, Am. Law Inst. (mem. coun.), Internat. Bar Assn. (past pres.), Inter-Am. Bar Assn. (mem. exec. coun. 1972-77), Fla. Bar Assn. (pres. 1972-73), Hillsborough County Bar Assn. (pres. 1963), Nat. Conf. Bar Pres. (pres. 1978-79), Greater Tampa C. of C. (pres. 1986-87). Methodist. Antitrust, Federal civil litigation, State civil litigation. Home: PO Box 3239 Tampa FL 33601-3239 Office: Carlton Fields Ward Emmanuel Smith & Cutler 1 Harbour Pl 777 S Harbour Island Blvd Tampa FL 33602-5729

SMITHBURN, JOHN ERIC, law educator, judge; b. Noblesville, Ind., Nov. 21, 1944; s. Charles Edward and Edna Anderson Smithburn; m. Aladean Marie DeRose, Oct. 25, 1986; 1 child, Scott Eric. BS, Ind. U., 1966; MA in History, Ind. U., 1970; JD, Ind. U., 1973. Bar: Ind. 1974, U.S. Dist. (so. dist.) Ind. 1974, U.S. Dist. Ct. (no. dist.) Ind. 1979, Eng. and Wales 1989. Atty. Feagler, Sowinski & Easterday, Plymouth, Ind., 1974—76; judge Marshall County Ct., Plymouth, 1976—78; assoc. prof. Notre Dame (Ind.) Law Sch., 1979—82, prof., 1982—. Bd. advisors Ind. Juvenile Justice Task Force, Indpls., 1975—; arbitrator Nat. Arbitration Forum, Mpls., 1997—; sr. judge appointee Ind. Supreme Ct., 2001. Author: Judicial Discretion: Successor Edition, 1991, Indiana Family Law Vol. 14 and 15, 1991, Cases and Materials in Juvenile Law, 2002, 7 other books; contbr. articles to profl. jours. Recipient Disting. Tchr. award, Nat. Jud. Coll., Reno, 1987, 1992. Mem.: Hon. Soc. Mid. Temple (London), Selden Soc., Cambridge Club, Oxford Club. Avocations: birdwatching, reading, films. Home: 1421 E Washington Ave South Bend IN 46617 Office: Notre Dame Law Sch Notre Dame IN 46556 Office Fax: 574-631-4197. E-mail: smithburn@nd.edu.

SMITHSON, LOWELL LEE, lawyer; b. Kansas City, Mo., Apr. 29, 1930; s. Spurgeon Lee and Lena Louise (Ruddy) S.; m. Rosemary Carol Leitz, Jan. 30, 1960 (div. Sept. 1985); m. Phyllis Galley Westover, June 8, 1986; children: Carol Maria Louise, Katherine Frances Lee. AB in Polit. Sci., U. Mo., 1952, JD, 1954. Bar: Mo. 1954, U.S. Dist. Ct. (we. dist.) Mo. 1955, U.S. Supreme Ct. 1986. Ptnr. Smithson & Smithson, Kansas City, 1956-59; assoc. Spencer, Fane, Britt & Browne, Kansas City, 1959-64, ptnr., 1964—. Adj. prof. law U. Mo., Kansas City, 1982. Pres. Kansas City Mental Health Assn., 1963-65; mem. bd. pres. All Souls Unitarian Ch. Kansas City, 1965-67; chmn. com. select dean for law sch. U. Mo., 1983. Btry. Comdr. U.S. Army, 1954-56, Korea. Mem. Kansas City Bar Assn., Lawyers Assn. Kansas City, Assn. Trial Lawyers Am., Western Mo. Def. Lawyers Assn., Fed. Energy Bar Assn., Phi Beta Kappa, Phi Delta Phi. Democrat. Unitarian Ch. Avocations: skiing, reading, painting, swimming, canoeing. General civil litigation, Condemnation (eminent domain), Environmental. Home: 1215 W 65th St Kansas City MO 64113-1803 Office: Spencer Fane Britt & Browne 1000 Walnut 1400 Commerce Bank Bldg Kansas City MO 64106-2140 E-mail: lsmithson@spencerfane.com.

SMOAK, EVAN L. lawyer; b. Columbia, S.C., Jan. 30, 1967; s. Lewis E. and Phyllis Anderson. BAS cum laude, U. S.C., 1989; JD, U. Va., 1992. Bar: Conn. 1992, N.Y. 1993, U.S. Dist. Ct. (so. and ea. dists.) N.Y. 1993, U.S. Ct. Appeals (2d cir.) 2000. Actor S.C. Ednl. Television, Columbia, 1977-86; atty. Werner & Kennedy, N.Y.C., 1992-97; assoc., ptnr. Barger & Wolen, N.Y.C., 1997—. Art auction co-chair Empire State Pride Agenda, N.Y.C., 1996-98, devel. com., 1999—, bd. dirs., 2000—, N100 fundraiser co-chair, 2001-02, exec. com. 2002—, bd. counsel, 2002—; vice-chair fall dinner fundraiser, 2002, co-chair, 2003—. Recipient Thomas Moore Craig award U. S.C., 1988; Carolina scholar, 1985-89, Nat. Merit scholar, 1985-89. Mem. ABA, Assn. Bar of City of N.Y., Phi Beta Kappa, Omicron Delta Kappa. Democrat. Alternative dispute resolution, Federal civil litigation, State civil litigation. Home: 445 W 23d St New York NY 10011 Office: Barger & Wolen 500 5th Ave Fl 46 New York NY 10110-4699 E-mail: esmoak@barwol.com.

SMOAK, LEWIS TYSON, lawyer; b. Orangeburg, S.C., Feb. 11, 1944; s. William B. and Louise (Dempsey) S.; m. Elizabeth Adams Babb, July 16, 1969; children— Katherine, Blair, Tyson. B.A., Furman U., 1966; J.D., U. S.C., 1969. Bar: S.C. 1969, D.C. 1982. Founder, Ogletree, Deakins, Nash, Smoak and Stewart, Greenville, S.C., 1969— . Fellow Coll. Labor and Employment Lawyers; mem. ABA, Greenville County Bar Assn., S.C. Bar Assn., D.C. Bar Assn., Poinsett Club, Greenville Country Club, Wade Hampton Golf Club (Cashiers, N.C.), Doonberg (Ireland) Golf Club. Environmental, Labor (including EEOC, Fair Labor Standards Act, labor-management relations, NLRB, OSHA). Office: 300 N Main St Greenville SC 29602

SMOLEV, TERENCE ELLIOT, lawyer, educator; b. Bklyn., Oct. 5, 1944; s. Lawrence and Shirley (Lebowitz) S.; m. Sherry Gale Rosen, Nov. 24, 1968 (div.); children: Cindy, Scott; m. Phyllis C. Rudko, Oct. 8, 1995. BBA, Hofstra U., 1966; JD, American U., 1969; LLM, NYU, 1974. Bar: N.Y. 1970. Acct. Peat Marwick & Mitchell, N.Y.C., 1969-70; dir. deferred giving Hofstra U., Hempstead, N.Y., 1971-74; editor Panel Publishers, Greenvale, N.Y., 1970-71; ptnr. Naidich & Smolev, P.C., Bellmore, N.Y., 1972-92; pvt. practice Terence E. Smolev, P.C., Mineola, N.Y., 1992-2000; ptnr. Forchelli, Curto, Schwartz, Mineo, Carlino & Cohn LLP, Mineola, N.Y., 2000—, ptnr. in charge tax, trusts and estates, 2001—. Bd. trustees Hofstra U., 1992—; adj. prof. Hofstra U., Hempstead, N.Y., 1971—; dist. counsel North Merrick (N.Y.) UFSD, 1975-99. Author of book chpt. Mem. Nassau County, N.Y. Dem. Com., 1972-80, mem. judicial screening com., 1992—; mem. IRS Small Bus. Adv. Com., Washington D.C., 1975-77; bd. dirs. Arthritis Found. L.I., 1995-97, mem Israeli Bond Cabinet Long Island, 1996—; bd. dirs. L.I. chpt. Anti-Defamation League; mem. Nassau County Micro-Econ. Commn. Recipient George M. Estabrook award Hofstra U., 1991, Alumni Achievement award Hofstra U., 1993, Cmty. Svc. award Hebrew Acad. Nassau County, 1997; named Senator of Yr., Hofstra U., 1985, Alumnus of Yr., 1996. Mem. ABA, N.Y. State Bar Assn., Nassau County Bar Assn., N.Y. State Assn. Sch. Attys. (pres. 1984), Hofstra U. Alumni Senate (pres. 1987-89), Hofstra U. Club (bd. dirs. 1981-95). Avocations: photography, golf. Estate planning, Probate (including wills, trusts), Corporate taxation. Office: PO Box 31 330 Old Country Rd Ste 301 Mineola NY 11501 E-mail: tsmolev@fcsmcc.com.

SMOLKER, GARY STEVEN, lawyer; b. L.A., Nov. 5, 1945; s. Paul and Shayndy Charolette (Sirott) S.; m. Alice Graham; children: Terra, Judy, Leah. BS, U. Calif., Berkeley, 1967; MS, Cornell U., 1968; JD cum laude, Loyola U., L.A., 1973. Bar: Calif. 1973, U.S. Dist. Ct. (ctrl. dist.) Calif. 1973, U.S. Tax Ct. 1973, U.S. Ct. Appeals (9th cir.) 1973, U.S. Supreme Ct. 1978, U.S. Dist. Ct. (so., ea. and no. dists.) Calif. 1981. Guest rschr. Lawrence Radiation Lab., U. Calif., 1967; tchg. fellow Sch. Chem. Engring., Cornell U.; mem. tech. staff Hughes Aircraft Co., Culver City, Calif., 1968-70; in advanced mktg. and tech. TRW, Redondo Beach, Calif., 1970-72; sole practice Beverly Hills, Calif., 1973-89, L.A., 1989—. Guest lectr. UCLA Extension, 1973-74, Loyola U. Law Sch., 1979; speaker, panelist in field; adv. Loyola U. Law Sch., 1973—. Columnist Heating Piping Air Conditioning Engring. Mag., 1999-2000; contbr. articles to profl. jours. Mem. Nat. Assn. Real Estate Editors, Calif. State Bar Assn., L.A. County Bar Assn., Beverly Hills Bar Assn. (sr. editor jour. 1978-79, contbg. editor jour. 1980-82, 86-90, editor-in-chief 1984-86, pub. Smolker Letter 1985—), B'nai B'rith (anti-defamation league). Jewish. Achievements include inventor self-destruct aluminium tungstic oxide films, electrolytic anticompromise process. Construction, Finance, Property, real (including real estate development, water). Office: 4720 Lincoln Blvd Ste 280 Marina Del Rey CA 90292 Home: A-321 13175 Fountain Pk Dr Playa Vista CA 90094-2023

SMOOT, OLIVER REED, JR., lawyer, trade association administrator; b. San Antonio, Aug. 24, 1940; s. Oliver Reed and Angie Frances (Watters) Smoot; m. Sandra Lee Curry, July 25, 1964; children: Stephen Reed, Sheryl Anne. BS, MIT, 1962; JD, Georgetown U., 1966. Bar: DC 1966, Va. 1967. Computer sys. mgr. Inst. Def. Analyses, Arlington, Va., 1962-69; from program mgr., v.p., to exec. v.p. and treas. Info. Tech. Industry Coun. (formerly Computer & Bus Equipment Mfrs. Assn.), Washington, 1969-2000; v.p. extrnal vol. stds. rels. Info Tech Industry Coun., Washington, 2000—. Author (with others): (book) Computers and the Law, 3d edit., 1981; chpt. editor: book Toward a Law of Global Communications Networks, 2001. Pres. Internat. Orgn. Standardization, 2003—; chmn. Am. Nat. Stds. Inst., 2001—02, 2003—. Mem.: ABA (chmn. sci. and tech. sect. 1989—90), Assn. Computing Machinery, Computer Law Assn. (pres. 1990—91). Methodist. Avocations: alpine skiing, gardening. Computer. Office: Info Tech Industry Coun 1250 I St NW Ste 200 Washington DC 20005-3922

SMOUSE, H(ERVEY) RUSSELL, lawyer; b. Oakland, Calif., Aug. 13, 1932; s. Hervey Reed and Vernie (Rush) Smouse, Hervey Reed and Vernie (Rush) Smouse; m. Creta M. Staley, June 15, 1955; children: Kristin Anne, Randall Forsyth, Gregory Russell. AB, Princeton U., 1955; LLB, U. Md., 1958. Bar: Md. 58, U.S. Tax. Ct. 79, U.S. Ct. Appeals (4th cir.) 60, U.S. Supreme Ct. 74. Atty. Atty. Gen.'s Honors Program, Dept. Justice, Washington, 1958—60; asst. U.S. atty. Dist. Md., 1960—62; assoc. Pierson and Person, Balt., 1962—64; atty. B.&O. R.R., Balt., 1964—66; mem. Pierson and Pierson, 1966—69, Clapp, Somerville, Black & Honemann, Balt., 1969—74; pvt. practice Law Offices H. Russell Smouse, 1974—81; mem. Melnicove, Kaufman, Weiner & Smouse, P.A., Balt., 1981—89, chmn. litigation, 1985—89; mem. Whiteford, Taylor & Preston, Balt., 1989—93, chmn. litigation dept., 1989—93; head gen. litigation Law Offices Peter G. Angelos, 1993—; gen. counsel Balt. Orioles, 1993—. Permanent mem. jud. conf. U.S. Ct. Appeals (4th cir.; v.p. Legal Aid Bur. Balt. City, 1972—73; bd. dirs. Md. Legal Svcs. Corp., 1987—93. Fellow: Am. Coll. Trial Lawyers; mem.: ABA, Nat. Assn. R.R. Trial Counsel (exec. com., v.p. ea. region 1986—92), Bar Assn. Balt. City (chmn. grievance com. 1969—70, chmn. judiciary com. and nominating com. 1980, mem. exec. com.

1969—70, 1980, chmn. exec. com. lawyers' com. for ind. judiciary 1989—96), Md. State Bar Assn. (gov. 1981—83). Republican. Presbyterian. Federal civil litigation, State civil litigation, Criminal.

SMUTHRANOND, ARCHAVA, lawyer, educator; b. Bangkok, Dec. 8, 1961; s. Paitoon and Suthin Smuthranond; m. Rashnee Smuthranond, Nov. 11, 1992; children: Tharm, Thai. LLB, Thammasat U., Bangkok, 1984; M Comparative Jurisprudence, Howard U., 1988; MBA, Southeastern U., 1989; LLM, So. Meth. U., 1990. Bar: Thailand 1986. Lawyer Bangkok Internat. Law Office, 1984—87, Ukrit Mongkolnavin Law Office, Bangkok, 1990—93; ptnr., exec. dir. Legal Advisory Coun. Ltd., Bangkok, 1994—. Part-time lectr. Assumption U., Bangkok, 1991—98, Ramkamhaeng U., Bangkok, 1997—, Bangkok U., 2001—. Pres. Thammasat Law Alumni, Bangkok, 1992—93. Recipient Am. Jurisprudence award, The Lawyers Cooperative Pub. Co./Bancroft-Whitney Co., 1987. Mem.: Thai-Russian Trade Assn. (mem. exec. com. 2001—), Thai Bar Assn., Law Asia, Rotary Club Bangkok. Buddhist. Avocations: tennis, reading. Mergers and acquisitions, Commercial, contracts (including sales of goods; commercial financing), Property, real (including real estate development, water). Home: 18/1 Soi Ekamai 6 Wattana Dist Bangkok 10110 Thailand Office: Legal Adv Coun Ltd 444 Olympia Thai Tower 16th Fl Bangkok 10320 Thailand

SMYTH, GERARD A. lawyer, administrator; b. N.Y.C., June 29, 1945; s. Eugene J. and Theresa Smyth; m. Janice Anderson, Aug. 1, 1987; children: Gregg Smyth, Tricia Smyth, Lindsey Hall, Thomas Hall. BA, Fairfield U., 1967; JD, U. Conn., 1975. Bar: Conn. 1975. Asst. atty. gen. State of Conn., Hartford, 1975-76; asst. pub. defender Divsn. Pub. Defender Svcs., State of Conn., Hartford, 1976-85, chief of capital def. and trial svcs., 1985-91, dep. chief pub. defender, 1991-94, chief pub. defender, 1994—. Mem. Conn. Alcohol and Drug Policy Coun., Hartford, 1996—, Gov.'s Task Force on Justice for Abused Children, Hartford, 1997—, Ct. Prison and Jail Overcrowding Commn., 1994—, Ct. Commn. on the Death Penalty, 2001--, Ct. Criminal Justice Info. Sys. Governing Bd., 2000--. Bd. dirs. Ct. Justice Edn. Ctr., Ct. Correctional Ombudsman, Cmty. Ptnrs. in Action; mem. adv. bd. Conn. Law Tribune, 2003--; mem. Zoning Bd. Appeals, Town of Granby, Conn., chmn. charter revision com. Capt. USAF, 1968-73. Mem. Nat. Assn. Criminal Def. Lawyers, Conn. Criminal Def. Lawyers Assn., Conn. Bar Assn. (exec. com. criminal justice 1994—), Hartford County Bar ASsn., Nat. Legal Aid and Defender Assn. (defender policy group 2000—), Am. Coun. Chief Defenders (exec. com.). Office: Office of Chief Pub Defender 30 Trinity St Fl 4 Hartford CT 06106-1629 E-mail: g.smyth@po.state.ct.us.

SMYTH, PAUL BURTON, lawyer; b. Phila., Aug. 15, 1949; s. Benjamin Burton and Florence Elizabeth (Tomlinson) S.; m. Denise Elaine Freeland, May 31, 1975. BA, Trinity Coll., 1971; JD, Boston Coll., 1974. Bar: Conn. 1974, D.C. 1975, U.S. Dist. Ct. D.C., 1980, U.S. Supreme Ct., 1985. With Dept. Interior, 1974—. Atty. Office of Hearings and Appeals, Arlington, Va., 1974—76, Office of Solicitor, Washington, 1976—82; asst. solicitor for land use and realty, Washington, 1982—87; deputy assoc. solicitor for energy and resources, Washington, 1987—95; acting dir. Office of Hearings and Appeals, Arlington, Va., 1993—94; deputy assoc. solicitor for land and water uses, 1995—; lectr. environ. law George Wash. U. Law Sch., Washington, 1997—. Editor: Federal Reclamation and Related Laws Annotated, Reclamation Reform Act Compilation, 1982—88; contbr. articles to legal pubs. Bd. dirs. EcoVoce, 1998—; trustee Rocky Mtn. Mineral Law Found., 1999—2001. Mem. ABA (coun. 1991-94, budget officer 1994-98, sec. natural resources, energy and environ. law, exec. editor Nat. Resources and the Environ. 1989-91). Office: Office of Solicitor Dept Interior 18th And C Sts NW Washington DC 20240-0001 E-mail: paul_smyth@ios.doi.gov.

SNAID, LEON JEFFREY, lawyer; b. Johannesburg, Transvaal, Republic of South Africa, Dec. 24, 1946; came to U.S., 1981; s. Mannie and Hene (Blume) S.; children: Jedd, Nicole. Diploma in Law, U. Witwatersrand, Johannesburg, 1969. Bar: Supreme Ct. Republic South Africa 1971, High Ct. of the Kingdom of Lesotho 1976, Calif. 1982, U.S. Dist. Ct. (so. and ctrl. dists.) Calif. 1982, U.S. Supreme Ct. 1999; cert. immigration law specialist, State Bar Calif. Bd. Legal Specialization. Assoc. Reeders, Teeger & Rosettenstein, Johannesburg, 1972; sole practice Johannesburg, 1973-76; ptnr. Snaid & Snaid, Johannesburg, 1976-81; sole practice San Diego, 1982—. Lectr. legal edn. seminars, San Diego, 1984—. Author, pub. quar. newsletter Immigration and Internat. Law, The Newcomers Guide to Living in the U.S.A. Mem. ABA, Am. Immigration Lawyers Assn. (past chmn. continuing legal edn. San Diego chpt.), San Diego County Bar Assn. (past chmn. immigration com.). Immigration, naturalization, and customs, Private international. Home: 5060 Via Papel San Diego CA 92122-3923 Office: Ste # 211 2727 Camino Del Rio S San Diego CA 92108

SNEAD, KATHLEEN MARIE, lawyer; b. Steubenville, Ohio, July 1, 1948; d. Donald Lee and Mary Alice (Hobright) O'Dell; m. John Jones Snead, Oct. 14, 1972; 1 child, Megan Marie. BA, Pa. State U., 1970; JD, U. Denver, 1979. Bar: Colo. 1979, U.S. Ct. Appeals (10th cir.) 1980, U.S. Supreme Ct. 1986. Field examiner NLRB, Pitts., 1970-72; freelance photographer Charleston, W.Va., 1973-74; labor relations examiner U.S. Dept. Labor, Denver, 1974-77, labor relations officer, 1978-79; staff atty. Denver & Rio Grande Western R.R., Denver, 1979-81, asst. gen. atty., 1981-84, gen. atty., 1984-92, Southern Pacific Lines, 1992-96, Union Pacific R.R., Denver, 1996-97; pvt. practice Golden, Colo., 1997—. Mem. ABA, Colo. Bar Assn. (adv. coun. environ. law sect.), Colo. Women's Bar Assn., Colo. R.R. Assn. (dir. 1982-84). Avocations: reading, swimming, biking, skating. General civil litigation, Environmental, Labor (including EEOC, Fair Labor Standards Act, labor-management relations, NLRB, OSHA). Home: 233 S Devinney St Golden CO 80401-5316 E-mail: skaterlaw@aol.com.

SNEED, JAMES LYNDE, lawyer; b. Tulsa, June 24, 1938; s. Earl and Cornelia (Lynde) S.; m. Jane Barnes, Sept. 5, 1959; children: David, Elizabeth, Thomas. AB cum laude, Harvard U., 1960; JD, U. Okla., 1963. Bar: Okla. 1963, U.S. Dist. Ct. (no. dist.) Okla. 1963. Ptnr. Conner, Winters, Randolph & Ballaine, Tulsa, 1962-70; chmn., pres., ptnr. Sneed, Lang, Adams & Barnett, Tulsa, 1970-86; pvt. practice Tulsa, 1986—. Bd. dirs. Grand River Dam Authority, 1974-79; trustee Hillcrest Med. Ctr., Tulsa, 1974-92; trustee Okla. Nature Conservancy, 2000—; active Salvation Army Bd., 1995—. Fellow Am. Bar Found., Okla. Bar Found. (pres. 1982—, chmn. 1985); mem. ABA, Okla. Bar Assn., Okla. Bar Assn., Tulsa County Bar Assn., Am. Judicature Soc., Summit Club, Tulsa Tennis Club (pres. 1978-81), Order of Coif, Phi Delta Phi. Democrat. Presbyterian. Corporate, general, Oil, gas, and mineral, Estate planning. Home: 1618 E 30th Pl Tulsa OK 74114-5308 Office: 309 Philtower 427 S Boston Ave Tulsa OK 74103-4141 E-mail: jlsneedlaw@sbeglobal.net.

SNEED, RICHARD DURWOOD, JR., lawyer; b. New Orleans, May 31, 1946; m. Martha Sue Trimble, Mar. 29, 1968; children: Laurie, Kellie. BA in Econs., U. South Fla., 1968; JD, Stetson U., 1971. Bar: Fla. 1971, U.S. Dist. Ct. (so. dist.) Fla. 1972, U.S. Tax Ct. 1975, U.S. ct. Appeals (5th cir.) 1975, U.S. Supreme Ct. 1975, U.S. Ct. Appeals (11th cir.) 1981, U.S. Dist. Ct. (mid. dist.) Fla. 1990. Assoc. Fee, Parker & Neil, Ft. Pierce, Fla., 1971-73; shareholder Sneed & Messer, P.A., Ft. Pierce, 1973-89; pvt. practice Richard D. Sneed, Jr., P.A., Ft. Pierce, 1989—99. Commr. Ft. Pierce Housing Authority, Ft. Pierce, 1989—; bd. dirs. Learn To Read, Inc.; vice chancellor to Bishop Ctrl. Diocese Fla. Mem.: ATLA, ABA, Ft. Pierce Bar Assn., Fla. Bar (standing com. unlicensed practice law 1986—, probate litigation com., probate law com., cert. real estate lawyer), Exch. Club (pres. Ft. Pierce 1980), Phi Alpha Delta. Episcopalian. Avocations: show horses, flying, vintage sports car racing. State civil litigation, Probate (including wills, trusts), Property, real (including real estate development, water). Office: Mardi Exec Ctr 1905 25th St S Ste 20604 Fort Pierce FL 34947

SNEERINGER, STEPHEN GEDDES, lawyer; b. Lancaster, Ohio, Mar. 27, 1949; s. Stanley Carlylle and Mary Eleanor (Fry) S.; m. Kristine Karen Serfling, Oct. 6, 1974; children: Mary Rhonda, Robyn Kathleen. BA magna cum laude, Denison U., 1971; JD, Washington U., 1974. Bar: Mo. 1974. Sr. v.p. A.G. Edwards & Sons Inc., St. Louis, 1974—. Arbitrator N.Y. Stock Exch., NASD Dispute Resolution, Inc., Nat. Futures Assn., Am. Arbitration Assn. Editor: Urban Law Ann., 1973-74; bd. editors Securities Arbitration Commentator. Am. Jurisprudence scholar, 1974. Mem. ABA (dispute resolution sect., arbitration com.), Mo. Bar Assn., Securities Industries Assn. (arbitration com.), Futures Industries Assn., Nat. Assn. Securities Dealers (mem. nat. arbitration and mediation com. 1992-94, 2001—), Securities Industry Conf. on Arbitration. Federal civil litigation, State civil litigation, Securities. Office: AG Edwards & Sons Inc 1 N Jefferson Ave Saint Louis MO 63103-2205

SNELL, BRUCE M., JR., retired judge; b. Ida Grove, Iowa, Aug. 18, 1929; s. Bruce M. and Donna (Potter) Snell; m. Anne Snell, Feb. 4, 1956; children: Rebecca, Brad. AB, Grinnell Coll., 1951; JD, U. Iowa, 1956. Bar: Iowa 1956, N.Y. 1958. Law clk. to presiding judge U.S. Dist. Ct. (no. dist.) Iowa, 1956-57; asst. atty. gen., 1961-65; judge Iowa Ct. Appeals, 1976-87; justice Iowa Supreme Ct., Des Moines, 1987—2001; ret., 2001. Comments editor: Iowa Law Rev. Mem.: ABA, Am. Judicature Soc., Iowa State Bar Assn., Order Coif. Methodist. Home: PO Box 192 Ida Grove IA 51445-0192

SNOW, CHARLES, lawyer; b. Bklyn., May 3, 1932; s. Irving S. and Bessie S.; m. Deanna Friedman, Jan. 15, 1961; children: Lisa C., Amy M. BA, U. Vt., 1954; LLB, Bklyn. Law Sch., 1959. Bar: N.Y. 1959, U.S. Dist. Ct. (ea. and so. dists.) N.Y. 1961, U.S. Ct. Appeals (2d cir.) 1961, U.S. Supreme Ct. 1965. Dep. asst. atty. gen. N.Y. Dept. Law, N.Y.C., 1959—60; asst. U.S. atty. U.S. Dist. Ct. (ea. dist.) N.Y., Bklyn., 1960—61; asst. regional adminstr. SEC, N.Y.C., 1961—68; ptnr. Wofsey Certilman Haft Snow & Becker, PC, N.Y.C., 1968—77, Snow Becker Krauss, P.C., N.Y.C., 1977—. Gen. counsel Securities Traders' Assn. N.Y. Chmn. Harrison (N.Y.) Planning Bd., 1977-88; mem. New Castle Planning Bd., 1991-97. Mem. N.Y. State Bar Assn. (mem. bus. sect., com. on securities regulation), Securities Traders Assn. N.Y. (hon.). Republican. Jewish. Federal civil litigation, Corporate, general, Securities. Office: 605 3rd Ave New York NY 10158-0180 E-mail: csnow@sbklaw.com.

SNOW, CUBBEDGE, JR., lawyer; b. Macon, Ga., May 20, 1929; AB, Emory U., 1951; JD magna cum laude, Mercer U., 1952. Bar: Ga. 1952. Ptnr. Martin, Snow, Grant, Napier, Macon. Col. JAGC, USAFR, 1952-89. Fellow Am. Coll. Trial Lawyers, Am. Bar Found. (state chmn. 1988-92), Fedn. Ins. and Corp. Counsel, Ga. Def. Lawyers Assn., Am. Prepaid Legal Svcs. Inst. (bd. dirs. 1983-89); mem. ABA (ho. of dels. 1984—, chmn. prepaid legal svcs. com. 1986-88, bd. govs. 1993-96), Macon Bar Assn. (pres. 1967), State Bar Ga. (pres. 1974-75), Am. Judicature Soc. (bd. dirs. 1978-82, Herbert Harley award 1986), Phi Beta Kappa, Phi Alpha Delta, Omicron Delta Kappa. Office: Martin Snow 240 3rd St PO Box 1606 Macon GA 31202-1606

SNOW, GARY PAUL, judge, lawyer; b. Biloxi, Miss., Sept. 3, 1943; s. David Paul and Marietta Snow; m. Linda Esther Fast, Apr. 25, 1965; children: Molly Melinda Snow Martin, Wendy Lynn Snow Wrigley, Lindsay Rebecca. BA, Okla. Christian U., Oklahoma City, 1965; MA, U. Okla., 1967, JD, 1971. Bar: Okla. 1972, U.S. Dist. Ct. (ea. dist.) Okla. 1973, U.S. Dist. Ct. (we. dist.) Okla. 1986, U.S. Ct. Appeals (10th cir.) 1976, U.S. Supreme Ct. 1978. Instr. in history U. Southwestern La., Lafayette, 1967-69; atty. Sandlin, Daugherty & Snow, Holdenville, Okla., 1972-74, Gary P. Snow Firm, Holdenville, 1974-83; mcpl. judge City of Holdenville, 1975-77; city atty. Town of Calvin, Okla., 1975-77; atty. Mattingly & Snow, Seminole, Okla., 1983—2002; mcpl. judge City of Seminole, 1994—2002. City atty. Town of Bowlegs, Okla., 1983-88; judge Ct. Appeals, Temporary Divsn. No. 126, 1982; mem. ad hoc com. on lawyer discipline Okla. Supreme Ct., 1986; dist. judge, 2002—. Bd. dirs., officer Youth and Family Svcs., Wewoka, Okla., 1978-91; officer Hughes County Dem. Party, Holdenville, 1973-83; bd. dirs., officer regional council Girl Scouts Am., McAlester, Okla., 1976-80; league dir. Kiwanis Little League Basketball, Seminole, 1993-96. Mem. Seminole Kiwanis Club (bd. dirs., officer, Disting. Svc. award 1993). Mem. Ch. of Christ (elder). Avocations: reading, running, tennis. Home: 2705 Eastgate Dr Seminole OK 74868-2403 Office: PO Box 1681 Seminole OK 74818-1681

SNOW, TOWER CHARLES, JR., lawyer; b. Boston, Oct. 28, 1947; s. Tower Charles and Margaret (Harper) S. BA in English magna cum laude, Dartmouth Coll., 1969; JD, U. Calif., Berkeley, 1973. Bar: Calif. 1973, U.S. Dist. Ct. (no. dist.) Calif. 1973, U.S. Ct. Appeals (9th cir.) 1973, U.S. Supreme Ct. 1976, U.S. Dist. Ct. (ea. dist.) Calif. 1979, U.S. Ct. Appeals (fed. cir.) 1980, U.S. Ct. Claims 1980, U.S. Ct. Appeals (2d cir.) 1987, N.Y. 1988, U.S. Dist. Ct. (ea. and so. dists.) N.Y. 1988, U.S. Dist. Ct. (ctrl. dist.) Calif. 1989, U.S. Dist. Ct. (no. dist.) Tex. 1995, U.S. Dist. Ct. (so. dist.) Calif. 1996, U.S. Dist. Ct. Ariz. 1996. Ptnr., chmn. litigation dept. Orrick, Herrington & Sutcliffe, San Francisco, 1973-89; ptnr. Shearman & Sterling, San Francisco, 1989-94; ptnr., chmn. securities litigation group, mem. policy com. Brobeck, Phleger & Harrison, LLP, San Francisco, 1995-97; chmn., CEO Brobeck, Phleger & Harrison, San Francisco, 1998—2001; ptnr., mem. Americas Mgmt. Group, Clifford Chance LLP, 2002—. Arbitrator Nat. Assn. Securities Dealers, Am. Stock Exch., N.Y. Stock Exch., Pacific Coast Stock Exch., Superior Ct. City and County San Francisco, Am. Arbitration Assn.; lectr. in field. Author numerous law handbooks and articles to prof. jours. Mem. San Francisco Mus. Soc., San Francisco Symphony, San Francisco Ballet, San Francisco Opera, Am. Conservatory Theatre. Named Best Lawyer in the U.S. in his Field, Corp. Bd. Member Mag., 2001; named one of 100 Most Influential Lawyers in Am., Nat. Law Jour., 2000, 100 Most Influential Lawyers in Calif., Calif. Law and Bus., 2000; recipient, 2002; Rufus Choate Scholar. Mem. ABA (chmn. subcom. pub. offering litig. 1984-88, co-chair task force on securities arbitration 1988-89, vice chair securities litig. com. 1986-88), Continuing Edn. Bar (bus. law inst. planning com. 1986), Securities Industry Assn., Nat. Inst. Trial Advocacy, San Francisco Bar Assn. (pres. securities litig. sect. 1995). Democrat. Avocations: travel, skiing, running, scuba diving, photography. Federal civil litigation, State civil litigation, Securities. Home: 177 Ridge Dr Napa CA 94558-9777 E-mail: tower.snow@cliffordchance.com.

SNOWBARGER, VINCE, former congressman; b. Kankakee, Ill., Sept. 16, 1949; s. Willis Edward and Wahnona Ruth (Horger) S.; m. Carolyn Ruth McMahon, Mar. 25, 1972; children: Jeffrey Edward, Matthew David. BA in History, So. Nazarene U., 1971; MA in Polit. Sci., U. Ill., 1974; JD, U. Kans., 1977. Bar: Kans. 1977, U.S. Dist. Ct. Kans. 1977, Mo. 1987. Instr. Mid-Am. Nazarene Coll., Olathe, Kans., 1973—76; ptnr. Haskin, Hinkle, Slater & Snowbarger, 1977—84, Dietrich, Davis, Dicus et al, 1984—88, Armstrong, Teasdale, Schafly & Davis, Overland Park, 1989—92, Holbrook, Heaven & Fay, P.C., Merriam, 1992—94, Snowbarger & Veatch LLP, Olathe, 1994—96; mem. 105th Congress from 3rd Kans. dist., 1997—99; exec. dir. Kans. Assn. Am. Educators, 2000—01; asst. exec. dir. legis. affairs Pension Benefit Guaranty Corps., Washington, 2002—. Mem. Kans. Legislature, Topeka, 1985-96; majority leader Ho. of Reps., 1993-96; mem. Olathe Planning Commn., 1982-84, Leadership Olathe; divsn. chmn. United Way, Olathe, 1985-88, chmn. citizen rev. com., 1991-95. Mem. Olathe Area C. of C. (bd. dirs. 1984). Republican. Nazarene. Avocation: politics. Home: 7902 Oak St Dunn Loring VA 22027-1017 Office: 1200 K St NW Washington DC 20005-4026 E-mail: vincesnowbarger@netscape.net.

SNOWISS, ALVIN L. lawyer; b. Lock Haven, Pa., June 16, 1930; s. Benjamin and Lillian (Kalin) S.; m. Jean Yarnell, Mar. 16, 1973. BA, U. Pa., Phila., 1952, JD, 1955; hon. alumnus, Pa. State U., 1998. Bar: Pa. 1956, U.S. Dist. Ct. (mid. dist.) Pa. 1958, U.S. Supreme Ct. 1972. Pvt. practice, Lock Haven, 1955-61; ptnr. Lugg & Snowiss, Lock Haven, 1961-74, Lugg, Snowiss, Steinberg & Faulkner, Lock Haven, 1974-86, Snowiss, Steinberg Faulkner, and Hall LLP, Lock Haven, 1987—. Solicitor Clinton County, Lock Haven, 1964-72. Chmn. bd. Lock Haven Hosp. Found., 1986-92; pres. Lock Haven Hosp., 1982-86; bd. govs. Clinton County Cmty. Found., Lock Haven, 1970-97; chmn. adv. bd. Palmer Mus. Art, State College; v.p. bd. trustees Ross Libr., Lock Haven, 1963-86; mem. exec. com. Pa. Rep. Com., Harrisburg, 1974-80; state committeeman Clinton County Rep. Com., 1967-80. Fellow Am. Coll. Trust and Estate Counsel, Am. Bar Found., Pa. Bar Found. (founding, bd. dirs. 1984-95); mem. Pa. Bar Assn. (zone del. 1976-82, zone gov. 1983-86, treas. 1987-90), Clinton County Bar Assn. (pres. 1975-76), Kiwanis (pres. Lock Haven 1966-67). Republican. Avocations: art history, golf, historical research. E-makl. Estate planning, Probate (including wills, trusts), Property, real (including real estate development, water). Home: 414 W Main St Lock Haven PA 17745-1107 Office: 333 N Vesper St Lock Haven PA 17745-1342 E-mail: ajsnow16@aol.com.

SNYDER, ARTHUR KRESS, lawyer, restaurant manager; b. L.A., Nov. 10, 1932; s. Arthur and Ella Ruth (Keck) S.; m. Mary Frances Neely, Mar. 5, 1953; children: Neely Arthur, Miles John; m. Michele Maggie Noval, May 14, 1973; 1 child, Erin-Marisol Michele; m. Delia Wu, Apr. 18, 1981. BA, Pepperdine U., 1953; JD, U. So. Calif., 1958; LLD, Union U., 1980. Bar: Calif. 1960, U.S. Supreme Ct. 1982. Sole practice, L.A., 1960-67; founder, pres. Arthur K. Snyder Law Corp., L.A., 1981-94; pres. Snyder & Assocs., Attys., L.A., 1994—. Pres. Marisol Corp., real estate and fgn. trade, 1978—; pres. real estate holdings Keck Investment Properties, 1990—; CFO Royal Star of Nev., Restaurateurs, 1999—; past instr. L.A. City Schs.; CEO Marisol of Nev., LLC Restaurateurs, 2002—. Mem. City Coun. L.A., 1967-85. Served to capt. USMC. Decorated La Tizona de El Cid Compeador (Spain), medal Legion of Honor (Mex.), Hwa Chao Zee You medal (Republic of China), numerous other commendations, medals, awards. Mem. ABA, ATLA, Los Angeles County Bar Assn., Calif. Bar Assn., World Film Inst. (chmn. bd. dirs. 1997-), Masons. Baptist. Administrative and regulatory, State civil litigation, Property, real (including real estate development, water). Office: 1000 W Sunset Blvd Ste 200 Los Angeles CA 90012-2105 E-mail: artsnyder@alumni.usc.edu.

SNYDER, BROCK ROBERT, lawyer; b. Topeka, Sept. 18, 1935; s. Ralph and Helen (Fritze) S.; m. Carol Lee Cunningham, June 5, 1957 (div. Nov. 1976); children: Lori, Holli, Staci; m. Sheryl Anita Clarke, Apr. 1, 1985 (div. Apr. 1997); children: Brock Robert II, Samantha. BS, U. Kans., 1957; JD, Washburn U., 1964. Bar: Kans. 1964. Ptnr. Eidson, Lewis, Porter & Haynes, Topeka, 1964-82; sole practice Topeka, 1982—. Lectr. on sch. discipline and due process, 1975-80; pres. Kans. Legal Services, Topeka, 1977-80. Served to capt. USMC, 1957-61. Fellow Kans. Bar Assn. (chmn. legal assts. com. 1983-84); mem. ABA, Kans. Trial Lawyers Assn. (bd. govs.), Topeka Bar Assn., Topeka Legal Aid Soc. (pres. 1976-78). Republican. Lutheran. Avocation: scuba. Corporate, general, General practice, Personal injury (including property damage). Office: 1401 SW Topeka Blvd Topeka KS 66612-1818 E-mail: brsnyder@inlandnet.net.

SNYDER, CHARLES AUBREY, lawyer; b. Bastrop, La., June 19, 1941; s. David and Shirley Blossom (Haas) S.; m. Sharon Rae Veta, Aug. 29, 1963; children: David Veta, Shelby Haas, Claire Frances. BBA, Tulane U., 1963; JD, La. State U., 1966. Bar: La. 1966. Assoc. firm. Milling Benson Woodward, LLP and predecessors, New Orleans, 1966-69, ptnr., 1969—. Bd. dirs. Delta Petroleum Co., Terre aux Boeufs Land Corp., Kemper and Leila Williams Found. Bd. dirs. New Orleans Speech and Hearing Ctr., pres., 1978-80; bd. dirs. City Pk. Commn., 1991-98, pres., 1995, dir. emeritus, 1999-2002; bd. dirs. New Orleans Mus. Art, 1996-2002, v.p., 1998-99, sec., 1999-2000; fellow La. Coll. Securities Counsel. Mem. ABA, La. Bar Assn. (chmn. sect. on corp. and bus. law 1982-83), New Orleans Bar Assn., Am. Law Inst., La. Law Inst. (coun. 2000—, coms. on mineral code and revision of partnership law, property law tutorship), Plimsoll Club, Bienville Club, Beta Gamma Sigma. Corporate, general, Estate planning, State and local taxation. Home: 74724 River Rd Covington LA 70435-2222 Office: Milling Benson Woodward LLP 909 Poydras St Ste 2300 New Orleans LA 70112-1010 E-mail: csnyder@millinglaw.com.

SNYDER, DAVID RICHARD, lawyer; b. Kalamazoo, Mich., Oct. 9, 1949; s. Richard E. and Margaret L. (Vanderplough) S.; m. Phyllis Alford, Aug. l4, 197l; children: Jason Richard, Carrie Lynn. BA with high honors, Mich. State U., 197l; JD with distinction, Cornell U., 1974. Bar: Calif. 1974. Assoc. Jenkins & Perry, San Diego, l974-77, ptnr., 1978-83, Aylward, Kintz & Stiska, San Diego, 1983-86, Luce, Forward, Hamilton & Scripps, San Diego, 1986-93, Pillsbury Madison & Sutro LLP, San Diego, 1993—; mng. bd. Pillsbury Winthrop LLP, San Diego, 1999—. V.p., dir. San Diego Venture Group, 1989-91; adj. prof. Calif. Western Sch. Law, San Diego, 1982-84; lectr. Calif. Continuing Edn. of Bar, 1983—. Co-author: Drafting Legal Instruments, l982; editor Cornell Law Rev., 1973-74. Bd. dirs. Boys Club Chula Vista, Calif., 1979-83; pres. Corpus Christi Parish Coun., Bonita, Calif., 1988-90; trustee Children's Hosp. Found., San Diego, 1988—, chmn., 1990-92. Mem.: ABA (fed. securities law com. 1987—, chmn. subcom. on ann. rev. fed. securities regulation, dir. corp. dirs. forum), Corp. Dirs. Forum (bd. dirs. 2001—), San Diego County Bar Assn., State Bar Calif., Am. Electronics Assn. (bd. dirs., mem. exec. com. San Diego chpt. 1991—93), Order of Coif, Phi Beta Kappa. Republican. Roman Catholic. Office: Pillsbury Winthrop 101 W Broadway Ste 1800 San Diego CA 92101-8298

SNYDER, GEORGE EDWARD, lawyer; b. Battle Creek, Mich., Feb. 7, 1934; s. Leon R. and Edith (Dullabahn) S.; m. Mary Jane Belt, July 27, 1957 (div. Sept. 23, 1982); children: Sara Lynn, Elizabeth Jane; m. Claudia Gage Brooks, Feb. 25, 1984 BS, Mich. State U., 1957; JD, U. Mich., 1960. Bar: Mich. 1961, U.S. Dist. Ct. (we. and ea. dists.) Mich. 1961. With Gen. Electric Co., 1957-58; asso. firm Miller, Johnson, Snell & Commisky, Grand Rapids, 1960-62, Goodenough & Buesser, Detroit, 1962-66; partner firm Buesser, Buesser, Snyder & Blank, Detroit and Bloomfield Hills, 1966-85, Meyer, Kirk, Snyder & Lynch PLLC, Bloomfield Hills, 1985—. Chmn. bd. dirs. Bill Knapps Mich., Inc., 1998-2000. Chmn. E. Mich. Environ. Action Council, 1974-78; pub. mem. inland lakes and streams rev. com. Mich. Dept. Natural Resources, 1975-76. Served as 2d lt. AUS, 1957. Fellow Am. Acad. Matrimonial Lawyers (pres. Mich. chpt. 1991-92), Am. Coll. Family Trial Lawyers, Am. Bar Found., Internat. Acad. Matrimonial Lawyers, Mich. Bar Found; mem. ABA, Am. Judicature Soc., Am. Arbitration Assn. (panel arbitrators), State Bar Mich. (chmn. family law com. 1968-72, mem. rep. assembly 1972-78, chmn. rules and calendar com. 1977-78, mem. family law sect. coun. 1973-76, environ. law sect. coun. 1980-85, prepaid legal svcs. com. 1973-82, com. on judicial selection 1974, com. on specialization 1976-82), Detroit Bar Assn. (chmn. family law com. 1966-68), Oakland County Bar Assn., Delta Upsilon (chmn. trustees, alumni chpt. dep. 1965-70), Tau Beta Pi, Pi Tau Sigma, Phi Eta Sigma. Clubs: Detroit Athletic, Birmingham (Mich.) Athletic. Episcopalian. General civil litigation, Family and matrimonial. Home: 32965 Outland Trl Bingham Farms MI 48025-2555 Office: Meyer Kirk Snyder & Lynch PLLC Ste 100 100 W Long Lake Rd Bloomfield Hills MI 48304-2773 E-mail: gsnyder@meyerkirk.com.

SNYDER, MARK ALLEN, lawyer; b. Balt., Nov. 20, 1951; s. Hyman William Snyder and Rhea Belle Thiman; m. Nancy Virginia Salmon, Aug. 18, 1974; children: Erin Hayley, Meredith Ann. JD, U. Baltimore Sch. Law, 1975; BS, U. Md. Coll. Park, 1973. Cert. Md. Ct. Appeals, 1976, U.S. Supreme Ct., 1981—. Pres., mng. ptnr. Cohen, Snyder, Eisenberg & Katzenberg, Balt., 1976—. Bd. trustees Fair Oaks Cmty. Assn., Severna Park, Md., 1995-97, Md. Inst. for Continuing Profl. Edn. of Lawyers,

1995-97. Mem. Md. State Bar Assn. (bd. govs. 1998-00), Md. Trial Lawyers Assn. (bd. govs. 1994-96), Anne Arundel Bar Assn. (bd. dirs. 1994—, pres. 1997-98, Pres. award 1994, trustee's award 1999), Md. Workers Compensation Ednl. Assn. (bd. govs. 1996—), U. Balt. Alumni Assn. (bd. trustees 1980-82). Democrat. Jewish. Avocations: scuba, golf, skiing. Criminal, Personal injury (including property damage), Workers' compensation. Office: Cohen Snyder Eisenberg & Katzenberg 347 N Charles St Baltimore MD 21201-4307

SNYDER, PAUL, lawyer; b. Hollywood, Calif., Jan. 18, 1943; s. Paul and Helen Jean (Trayan) S.; m. Kathy Jane Pope, Oct. 7, 1945 (div.); m. Martha Kate Frick, June 15, 1948; children: Jeffrey Randall, Suzanne Leigh. BA, U. Colo., 1965, JD, 1967. Bar: Colo. 1967. Assoc. Williams, Taussig & Trine, 1967-70; ptnr. Taussig, McCarthy & Snyder, 1970-73; of counsel Taussig & Cobb, 1974-75; pres. Snyder, Neuman & Enwall PC, 1978-81, Paul Snyder Jr. PC, Boulder, Colo., 1981-83; ptnr. Martin and Snyder, 1983-85, Brauchli-Snyder LLC, 1986-96; atty. Town of Westcliffe, Westcliffe, 1997—; ptnr. Stevens & Snyder, 1998—2002. Faculty Nat. Inst. Trial Advocacy, 1982-94. Chmn. Boulder Growth Mgmt. Task Force, 1980-81. Mem. Colo. Bar Assn., Boulder Bar Assn. (Merit award 1993). General practice, Estate taxation, Property, real (including real estate development, water). Home: 4928 County Road 125 Westcliffe CO 81252-8600 Office: 4928 County Road 125 Westcliffe CO 81252-8600

SNYDER, WILLARD BREIDENTHAL, lawyer; b. Kansas City, Kans., Dec. 18, 1940; s. N.E. and Ruth (Breidenthal) S.; m. Lieselotte Dieringer, Nov. 10, 1970 (dec. Nov. 1975); 1 child, Rolf; m. T.J. Sewall, May 17, 1996. BA, U. Kans., 1962, JD, 1965; postgrad., Hague Acad. Internat. Law, The Netherlands, 1965-66, U. Dijon, France, 1966; grad., Command and Gen. Staff Coll., Ft. Leavenworth, Kans., 1977. Bar: Kans. 1965, Mo. 1986, U.S. Tax Ct. 1977, U.S. Ct. Mil. Appeals 1981, U.S. Dist. Ct. Kans. 1965, U.S. Supreme Ct. 1977. Atty., Kansas City, 1970-80, 85—; trust officer, corp. trust officer Security Nat. Bank., Kansas City, 1980-83, corp. sec., 1983-85; pres. Real Estate Corp. Inc., Leawood, Kans., 1984—; adv. dir. United Mo. Bank, 1985-90. Bd. dirs. Blue Ridge Bank, mem. trust and investment com., 1991—; German Consul (H) for Kans., Western Mo., 1972—. Mem. Platte Woods (Mo.) City Coun., 1983-84; bd. govs., 1st v.p. Liberty Meml. Assn.; mem. nomination com. MacJannett Found., Talloires, France; chmn. Breidenthal-Snyder Found.; mem. nominating and exec. com. Hoover Pres. Libr.; bd. dirs. Unicorn Theatre, KCKs Cmty. Found.; trustee St. Mary Coll., 1998-2001; bd. dirs. Wy. Co. Kans. Cmty. Found., Kansas City Metro Crime Com, The Unicorn Theater, Navy SEAL Museums, Ft. Pierce, Fla.; vol. Kansas City Cmty. Kitchen. Col. inf. ret. USAR & KARNG. Decorated Bundensverdienst Kreuz, 1982, BVK 1KL (Germany), 1992, Bundeswehr Kreuz (silver), 1987, Ge. Abn., Legion of Merit; KARNG medal of excellence; named to Hon. Order Ky. Cols., 1988; recipient Golden Honour badge German Vet. Orgn., Bavaria, 1988, Mil. Order of WW award, OCS Hall of Fame. Mem. Mo. Bar Assn., Kansas City Bar Assn., Kansas City Hosp. Attys., Mil. Order of World Wars (chpt. comdr. 1983-84, regional comdr. 1987-91, Patrick Henry award), Nat. Eagle Scout Assn. Avocations: scuba, hunting, notgeld collections, cartridge collection. Corporate, general, Public international, Non-profit and tax-exempt organizations. Office: 8014 State Line Rd Ste 203 Shawnee Mission KS 66208-3712

SNYDER, WILLIAM HENRI, lawyer; b. West Chester, Pa., Mar. 14, 1931; s. Robert Paul and Helen Louise (Bable) S.; 1 dau., Terri Elizabeth. B.S. in Econs., Franklin and Marshall Coll., 1953; J.D., UCLA, 1958. Bar: Calif. 1959. Ptnr., Collins & Snyder, Pacific Palisades, Calif., 1959-76; sole practice, Pacific Palisades, 1976-82; ptnr. Snyder & Polin, Pacific Palisades, 1982-92, Snyder & Pecsok, Pacific Palisades, 1992—; Bd. dirs. Palisades-Malibu YMCA, 1968-76; pres. bd. trustees Pacific Palisades Presbyterian Ch., 1972. Mem. ABA, Calif. State Bar Assn. (cert. specialist estate planning, probate & trust law), Santa Monica Bar Assn. (pres. 1976-77), Los Angeles County Bar Assn., Beverly Hills Bar Assn., Pacific Palisades C. of C. (bd. dirs. 1980-82). Republican. Club: Optimist (Pacific Palisades pres. 1965-66). Served to Lt. USNR, 1953-55. Office: Snyder & Pecsok 881 Alma Real Dr Ste 308 Pacific Palisades CA 90272-3731

SOBEL, GERALD, lawyer; BEE, City Coll. N.Y., 1960; JD, NYU, 1963; MA in Econs., New Sch. Social Rsch., N.Y.C., 1967. Bar: N.Y., U.S. Ct. Appeals (2d and fed. cirs.), U.S. Dist. Ct. (so., ea. and no. dists.) N.Y., U.S. Supreme Ct. Atty. AT&T, N.Y.C., 1963-64; law clerk to Hon. Richard H. Levet U.S. Dist. Ct. (so. dist.) N.Y., N.Y.C., 1964-65; atty., ptnr., sr. litig. ptnr. Kaye, Scholer, Fierman, Hays & Handler, N.Y.C., 1965—. Adj. assoc. prof. Sch. Law NYU; lectr. Columbia Sch. Law, Stanford Sch. Law. Contbr. articles on litigation to profl. jours. Fellow: ABA, Am. Intellectual Property Law Assn., Assn. NY Intellectual Property Law. Antitrust, General civil litigation, Patent. Office: Kaye Scholer LLP 425 Park Ave New York NY 10022-3506

SOBELLE, RICHARD E. lawyer; b. Cleve., Mar. 18, 1935; BA, Stanford U., 1956, JD, 1960; LLM, U. So. Calif., 1967. Bar: Calif. 1961, U.S. Supreme Ct. 1969. Exec. Tracinda Corp. Mem. ABA (mem. corp., banking and bus. law sect. 1969-95), State Bar Calif. (del. to conf. state bar dels. 1965-77, mem. exec. com. bus. law sect. 1977-78), L.A. County Bar Assn. (mem. exec. coun., jr. barristers 1965-68, mem. exec. com. bus. and corps. sect. 1973-75). Office: Tracinda Corp 150 S Rodeo Dr Ste 250 Beverly Hills CA 90212-2417

SOBLE, MARK RICHARD, lawyer; b. San Francisco, Dec. 25, 1964; life ptnr. Leslye Soble, Nov. 2000. BA with deptl. honors, Stanford U., 1985; JD, U. Mich., 1988. Bar: Calif. 1988, U.S. Dist. Ct. (cen. dist.) Calif. 1988, U.S. Dist. Ct. (ea. dist.) Calif. 1990. Law clk. to chief judge U.S. Dist. Ct. for S.D., Pierre, 1988-89; assoc. Lewis, D'Amato, Brisbois & Bisgaard, L.A., 1989-90; counsel enforcement div. Fair Polit. Practices Commn., Sacramento, 1990-96, sr. counsel, 1996—2001; dep. atty. gen. civil div. Office of Calif. Atty. Gen., 2001—. Note editor U. Mich. Jour. Law Reform, 1987-88. Raymond K. Dykema scholar U. Mich. 1987. Mem. State Bar Calif., Sacramento County Bar Assn. (mng. editor Docket 1997, mem.-at-large bar coun. 1998-00).

SODEN, RICHARD ALLAN, lawyer; b. Feb. 16, 1945; s. Hamilton David and Clara Elaine (Seale) S.; m. Marcia LaMonte Mitchell, June 7, 1969; children: Matthew Hamilton, Mark Mitchell. AB, Hamilton Coll., 1967; JD, Boston U., 1970. Bar: Mass. 1970. Law clk. to judge U.S. Ct. Appeals (6th cir.), 1970-71; assoc. firm Goodwin, Procter & Hoar LLP, Boston, 1971-79, ptnr., 1979—. Instr. Law Sch. Boston Coll., Chestnut Hill, Mass., 1973-74. Mem. South End Project Area Com.; hon. dir. United South End Settlements, pres., 1977-79; chmn. Boston Mcpl. Rsch. Bur.; pres. Boston Minuteman coun. Boy Scouts Am.; trustee Judge Baker Children's Ctr., chmn., 1994-96, pres., 1992-94; trustee New Eng. Aquarium, Boston U.; bd. visitors Boston U. Goldman Sch. Grad. Dentistry; mem. bd. overseers WGBH; mem. Mass. Minority Bus. Devel. Commn.; mem. Adv. Task Force on Securities Regulation; mem. Adv. Com. on Legal Edn.; steering com. Lawyers Com. for Civil Rights under Law, chmn., 1992-94. Mem. ABA (chmn. standing com. on bar svcs. and activities), Commn. on Lawyer Assistance Programs Adv. Coun. on Diversity, 1998-2000, Nat. Bar Assn., Mass. Bar Assn. (past vice chmn. bus. law coun. 1990-91), Boston Bar Assn. (pres. 1994-95), Mass. Black Lawyers Assn. (pres. 1980-81). Corporate, general, Finance, Securities. Home: 42 Gray St Boston MA 02116-6210 Office: Goodwin Procter LLP Exchange Pl Boston MA 02109-2803

SODERQUIST, LARRY DEAN, law educator, lawyer, consultant, writer; b. Ypsilanti, Mich., July 20, 1944; s. Hugo E. and Emma A. (Johansen) S.; m. Ann Mangelsdorf, June 15, 1968; children: Hans, Lars. BS, Ea. Mich. U., 1966; JD, Harvard U., 1969; DMin, Trinity Sem., 1998. Bar: N.Y. 1971, Tenn. 1981. Assoc. Milbank, Tweed, Hadley & McCloy, N.Y.C., 1971—76; assoc. prof. law U. Notre Dame, South Bend, Ind., 1976—80, prof., 1980—81; vis. prof. law Vanderbilt U. Law Sch., Nashville, 1980—81, prof., 1981—. Dir. corp. and securities law inst. 1993—; of counsel Dinsmore & Shohl LLP; spl. master U.S. Dist. Ct. (no. dist.) Ohio, 1977; vis. prof. law Harvard U. Law Sch., Cambridge, Mass., 1999. Author: Corporations, 1979, 5th edit., 2001, Understanding the Securities Laws, 4th edit., 2003, Securities Law, 1998, Securities Regulation, 5th edit., 2003, Corporate Law and Practice, 2d edit., 1999, Law of Federal Estate and Gift Taxation: Code Commentary, 1978, Analysis, 1980, Investor's Rights Handbook, 1993; (novels) The Labcoat, 1998, The Iraqi Provocation, 2003; contbr. articles to profl. jours. Capt. U.S. Army, 1969-71. Decorated Army Commendation medal. Mem. ABA, Am. Law Inst. Home: 2000 Grand Ave Ste 801 Nashville TN 37212 Office: Vanderbilt U Sch Law 131 21st Ave S Nashville TN 37203-1120

SOEFKER, CURT REID, lawyer; b. Memphis, Oct. 19, 1970; married. BS, So. Meth. U., 1993; JD, U. of Memphis, 1998. Bar: US Dist. Ct. (we. dist.) Tenn. 1999, U.S. Ct. of Appeals (6th cir.) 1999. Atty. Martin, Tate, Morrow & Marston, P.C., Memphis, 1998—. Bd. dirs. Hands on Memphis, 2001. Recipient Dean's Award for Excellence/Cali Award in Civil Procedure, Decedent's Estates, Fed. Income Taxation, Land Use Law, Bus. Organizations, Evidence, U. of Memphis Sch. of Law, 1995—98, West Scholar's Award, Westlaw, 1997; fellow Cecil C. Humphreys fellow, Plow Found., 1996—98. Mem.: Am. Inns of Ct. (assoc.). Construction, General civil litigation, Transportation. Office: Martin Tate Morrow & Marston 22 N Front St Ste 1100 Memphis TN 38103

SOEHLE, TRACY MORSE, lawyer; b. Rockland, Maine, Nov. 27, 1965; d. Linda C.; m. John S Soehle, Sept. 7, 1991; children: Hayley Diane, Andrew John. JD, Tulane Law Sch., New Orleans, LA, 1993—96. Bar: Mass. 1996. Atty. Dechert LLP, Boston, 1997—, Testa Hurwitz & Thibeault, LLP, Boston, 1996—97. Mem.: Order of the Coif. Securities, Corporate, general, Financial Services. Office: Dechert LLP 200 Clarendon Street Boston MA 02116 Office Fax: 617-426-6567. E-mail: tracy.soehle@dechert.com.

SOFAER, ABRAHAM DAVID, lawyer, educator, judge, consultant; b. Bombay, May 6, 1938; came to U.S., 1948, naturalized, 1959; m. Marian Bea Scheuer, Oct. 23, 1977; children: Daniel E., Michael J., Helen R., Joseph S., Aaron R., Raphael J. BA in History magna cum laude, Yeshiva Coll., 1962; LLB cum laude, NYU, 1965. Bar: N.Y. 1965, D.C. 1988. Law clk. to Hon. J. Skelly Wright, U.S. Ct. Appeals (D.C. cir.), Washington, 1965-66; law clk. to Hon. William J. Brennan Jr. U.S. Supreme Ct., Washington, 1966-67; asst. U.S. atty. U.S. Dist Ct. (so. dist.) N.Y., N.Y.C., 1967-69; prof. law Columbia U., N.Y.C., 1969-79; judge U.S. Dist. Ct. (so. dist.) N.Y., 1979-85; legal advisor U.S. Dept. State, Washington, 1985-90; ptnr. Hughes Hubbard & Reed, Washington, 1991-94; George P. Shultz disting. scholar, sr. fellow Hoover Instn., Stanford U., 1994—. Hearing officer N.Y. Dept. Environ. Conservation, 1975-76. Author: War, Foreign Affairs and Constitutional Power: The Origins, 1976; contbr. articles to legal, polit., fgn. jours.; editor-in-chief: NYU Law Rev, 1964-65. Served with USAF, 1956-59. Root-Tilden scholar NYU, 1965. Mem. ABA, Fed. Bar Assn., N.Y.C. Bar Assn., N.Y. Bar Assn., Am. Law Inst. Jewish. Alternative dispute resolution, Bankruptcy, Public international. Office: Stanford Univ The Hoover Instn Stanford CA 94305-6010 Fax: 650-723-2103. E-mail: sofaer@hoover.stanford.edu.

SOFFAR, WILLIAM DOUGLAS, lawyer; b. Houston, Sept. 8, 1944; s. Benjamin and Esther Goldy (Garfinkel) S.; m. Nancy Elise Axelrod, Mar. 29, 1969 (div. Sept. 1989), m. Gail Shinbaum, Jan. 16, 2000; children: Pamela Beth, Stephanie Michelle, Jill Denise. BA, U. Houston, 1966, JD, 1969. Bar: Tex. 1969, U.S. Dist. Ct. (so. dist.) Tex. 1970, U.S. Ct. Appeals (5th cir.) 1974, U.S. Supreme Ct. 1974; cert. mediator in civil law and family law. Atty. examiner U.S. Interstate Commerce Commn., Washington, 1969-70; atty. Law Office of Adolph Uzick, Houston, 1970-72, Walsh & Soffar, Houston, 1972-73; lawyer, sole practice Law Offices of William D. Soffar, Houston, 1973-74; ptnr. Soffar & Levit, Houston, 1974—. Family law and civil mediator, basic mediation and family mediation trainer Atty.-Mediator's Inst. Bd. dirs. Miller Theater Adv. Coun., Houston, 1985-90, Zina Garrison Found., Houston, 1989-91. Mem. Houston Bar Assn. (bd. dirs., family law sect. mem. 1989-90), Jewish Cmty. Ctr. (health club com. 1971—), Jewish Family Svc. (bd. dirs. 1970-71), Phi Delta Phi. Jewish. Avocations: travel, reading, raquetball. Family and matrimonial, General practice, Personal injury (including property damage). Office: Soffar & Levit 6575 West Loop S Ste 630 Bellaire TX 77401-3604

SOFIANOPOULOS, DIMITRIOS, lawyer; b. Pirgos, Greece, Sept. 16, 1966; s. Fotios and Ioulia (Diamantopoulos) Sofianopoulos. LLB, Aristotelion U., Thessaloniki, Greece, 1988; LLM, Queen Mary & Westfield Coll., London, 1989; MSc, City U., London, 1990. Bar: Athens 1991. Asst. solicitor Norton Rose, London, ptnr.; asst. atty. Seward & Kissel, N.Y.C.; gen. counsel Stelmar Shipping Ltd., NY. Vis. lectr. Cass Bus. Sch., London, 1999—. Mem.: Athens Bar Assn., IBA, Greek Comml. Lawyers Assn. Avocations: football, travel. Admiralty, Finance, Transportation. Office: Norton Rose 126 Kolokotroni St 185 35 Piraeus Greece Office Fax: 3021004282427. Business E-Mail: sofianopoulosdf@nortonrose.com.

SOGAARD, KLAUS, lawyer; b. Aalborg, Denmark, Oct. 17, 1955; m: Elisabeth Rask Jorgensen, May 30, 1987; children: Christian, Henrik. JD, Aarhus, Denmark, 1980; LLM, U. Pacific, Sacramento, CA, 1985. Mem. Danish Bar. Ptnr. Gorrissen Federspiel Kierkegaard, Copenhagen, 1986—. Banking, Mergers and acquisitions, Securities. Office: Gorrissen Federspiel Kierkegaard HC Andersens Blvd 12 1553 V Copenhagen Denmark Fax: 45 33414133. E-mail: ks@gfklaw.dk.

SOGG, WILTON SHERMAN, lawyer; b. Cleve., May 28, 1935; s. Paul P. and Julia (Cahn) S.; m. Saralee Frances Krow, Aug. 12, 1962 (div. July 1975); 1 child, Stephanie; m. Linda Rocker Lehman, Dec. 22, 1979 (div. Dec. 1990); m. Nancy Rosenfield Walsh, June 2, 1991. AB, Dartmouth Coll., 1956; JD, Harvard U., 1959; postgrad., London Grad. Sch. Bus. Studies, 1974-76. Bar: (Ohio) 1960, (Fla) 1970, (U.S. Tax Ct.) 1961, (U.S. Supreme Ct.) 1969. Assoc. Gottfried, Ginsberg, Guren & Merritt, 1960-63, ptnr., 1963-70, Guren, Merritt, Feibel, Sogg & Cohen, Cleve., 1970-84; of counsel Hahn, Loeser, Freedheim, Dean and Wellman, Cleve., 1984-85; ptnr. Hahn Loeser & Parks LLP, Cleve., 1986-2000; of counsel McCarthy, Lebit, Crystal & Liffman Co., Cleve., 2001—. Trustee, pres. Cleve. Jewish News; adj. prof. Cleve. State Law Sch., 1960—; lectr. Harvard U. Law Sch., 1978-80. Author: (with Howard M. Rossen) new and rev. vols. of Smith's Review Legal Gems series, 1969—; editor: Harvard Law Rev.; contbr. articles to profl. jours. Trustee Jewish Cmty. Fedn. of Cleve., 1966-72; bd. overseers Cleveland Marshall Coll. Law, Cleve. State U., 1969—, vis. com. Coll. Bus. Adminstrn., 1996-2001, 2003-; mem. U.S. and State of Ohio Holocaust commns. Fulbright fellow U. London, 1959-60. Mem. Ohio Bar Assn., Fla. Bar Assn., Germany Philatelic Soc., Audubon Soc. (bd. dirs. 2003—), Oakwood Club, Union Club, Chagrin Valley Hunt, Phi Beta Kappa. Alternative dispute resolution, Construction, General practice. Home: PO Box 278 Gates Mills OH 44040-0278 Office: McCarthy Lebit Crystal & Liffman 1800 Midland Bldg 101 W Prospect Ave Cleveland OH 44115-1088 E-mail: wss@mccarthylebit.com.

SOHLMAN, TARA LEA, lawyer; b. Minn., Oct. 23, 1972; d. Glen and Marilyn Sohlman. BS, Coll. of St. Benedict, St. Joseph, Minn., 1995; JD, Ind. U., 1998. Assoc. Wilhite & Assocs., Evansville, Ind., 1998—99, Fine & Hatfield, Evansville, 1999—2002; atty. Stephenson Daly Morow & Semler, Indpls., 2002—. Mem.: ABA, Ind. State Bar Assn. Avocations: showing quarter horses, biking, travel. Office: Stewart & Irwin PC 251 E Ohio St Indianapolis IN 46204

SOHNEN, HARVEY, lawyer; b. Bklyn., June 20, 1947; s. Nathan M. and Shirley (Strauss) S.; m. Kathleen M. Meagher, Mar. 17, 1978; children: Eleanor, Julia. BA, Columbia U., 1968; MS in Math., MIT, 1969; JD, U. Calif., Berkeley, 1974. Bar: Calif. 1974, U.S. Dist. Ct. (no. dist.) Calif. 1974, U.S. Dist. Ct. (ea. dist.) Calif. 1975, U.S. Supreme Ct. 1981. Staff atty. Stanislaus Co. Legal Assistance, Modesto, Calif., 1975-76, Legal Aid for Alameda County, Oakland, Calif., 1977-82; assoc. Lerner & Veit, San Francisco, 1982-85; ptnr. Page & Sohnen, Walnut Creek, Calif., 1986-98, prin., 1998—. Mem. Am. Inns of Ct., Calif. Employment Lawyers Assn., Contra Costa Bar Assn. Commercial, contracts (including sales of goods; commercial financing), Labor (including EEOC, Fair Labor Standards Act, labor-management relations, NLRB, OSHA), Personal injury (including property damage). Office: 2 Theatre Sq Ste 230 Orinda CA 94563-3346 E-mail: hs@fairpaycal.com.

SOIFER, AVIAM, law educator, dean; b. Worcester, Mass., Mar. 18, 1948; married; 2 children. BA cum laude, Yale U., 1969, MA in Urban Studies, JD, Yale U., 1972. Bar: Conn. 1974, U.S. Dist. Ct. Conn. 1974, U.S. Supreme Ct. 1994. Law clk. to Judge Jon O. Newman U.S. Dist. Ct. Conn., 1972-73; asst. prof. U. Conn. Sch. Law, 1976-77, assoc. prof., 1977-78, prof., 1978-80, Boston U. Sch. Law, 1980-93, 98—; dean Boston Coll. Law Sch., 1993-98. Vis. prof. Boston U. Sch. Law, 1979-80. Author: Law the the Company We Keep, 1995; contbr. numerous articles to profl. jours. Vice chair Supreme Jud. Ct. Mass. Task Force on Jud. Edn., 1996-2001; mem. steering com. 1st Cir. Task Force on Gender, Race and Ethnicity, 1995-99; trustee New Eng. Med. Ctr., 1997—, Cambridge Health Alliance, 2002-. Recipient Disting. Sr. Rsch. award Boston Coll., 2001-02; named Disting. Scholar Legal Studies Inst., U. Wis., 2001-; Harvard Program in Law and Humanities fellow, 1976-77; Kellog Nat. fellow, 1981-84. Mem. ABA (commn. on coll. and univ. legal studies 1996-2000. Office: Boston Coll Law Sch 885 Centre St Newton Center MA 02459-1148

SOKOL, LARRY NIDES, lawyer, educator; b. Dayton, Ohio, Sept. 28, 1946; s. Boris Franklin and Kathryn (Konowitch) S.; m. Beverly Butler, Aug. 3, 1975; children: Addie Teller, Maxwell Philip. BA, U. Pa., 1968; JD, Case Western Res. U., 1971. Bar: Oreg. 1972, U.S. Dist Ct. Oreg. 1972, U.S. Ct. Appeals (9th cir.) 1973, U.S. Supreme Ct. 1980. Law clk. chief judge Oreg. Ct. Appeals, Salem, 1971-72; pvt. practice Portland, Oreg., 1972—; prof. law Lewis and Clark Law Sch., Portland. Adj. prof. law sch. environ. litigation Lewis & Clark U., 1984— Commr. planning City of Lake Oswego, Oreg., 1981-84. Sgt. USAR, 1968-74. Mem. Oreg. State Bar Assn. (chmn. litigation sect. 1983, disciplinary rev. bd. 1982-85), Oreg. Trial Lawyers Assn. Democrat. Jewish. Avocations: running, swimming, squash, model trains, scuba diving. Environmental, Personal injury (including property damage). Office: 735 SW 1st Ave Portland OR 97204-3326

SOKOL, STEPHEN M. lawyer; b. Melbourne, Australia, Jan. 14, 1945; came to U.S., 1948; s. George J. and Cynthia E. (Wilson) S.; m. Susan S. Schreiber, Jan. 23, 1973; children: Andrew, Debora. BA magna cum laude, U. Pitts., 1968; JD, Duquesne U., 1971. Bar: Pa. Staff atty. FTC, Washington, 1971-72; atty. gen. Atty.'s Gen. Office, Harrisburg, Pa., 1972-75; pvt. practice Pitts., 1975—. Bd. dirs. Keystone Printing Co., Pitts. Law rev. editor Duquesne U., 1970-71. Mem. Big. Bros. of Pa., Pitts., 1994-95, Dem. Com., Pitts., 1974-80. Fellow Pa. Bar Assn., Allegheny County Bar Assn. (adv. bd. 1978-85); mem. Lions, Rotary. Avocations: oil painting, handball, tennis, hiking, travel. Federal civil litigation, Criminal, Personal injury (including property damage). Office: SM Sokol 517 Frick Bldg Pittsburgh PA 15219

SOKOLOV, RICHARD SAUL, real estate company executive; b. Phila., Dec. 7, 1949; s. Morris and Estelle Rita (Steinberg) S.; m. Susan Barbara Saltzman, Aug. 13, 1972; children: Lisa, Anne, Kate. BA, Pa. State U., 1971; JD, Georgetown U., 1974. Assoc. Weinberg & Green, Balt., 1974-80, ptnr., 1980-82; v.p., gen. counsel The Edward J. DeBartolo Corp., Youngstown, Ohio, 1982-86, sr. v.p. devel., gen. coun., 1986-94; pres., CEO DeBartolo Realty Corp., Youngstown, Ohio, 1994-96; pres., COO Simon DeBartolo Group, Indpls., 1996-98; pres, COO Simon Property Group, Indpls., 1998—. Mem. investment com. Jewish Fedn., Youngstown, 1992—; trustee U. Wis.-Madison Ctr. for Urban Land Econs. Rsch., Youngstown/Mahoning Valley United Way. Alumni fellow Pa. State U., 2000. Mem. Internat. Coun. Shopping Ctrs. (trustee 1994—, chmn. 1998-99), Urban Land Inst. (assoc.). Office: Simon Property Group 115 W Washington St Ste 1465 Indianapolis IN 46204-3464

SOKOLOW, LLOYD BRUCE, lawyer, psychotherapist; b. N.Y.C., Nov. 3, 1949; s. Edwin Jay and Harriet (Corman) S.; m. Christina Carol Smolinski, Jan. 27, 1979; children: Joshua, Jessica. BA, U. Buffalo, 1971, MS, 1974, JD, 1978, PhD, 1979. Bar: U.S. Dist. Ct. (we. dist.) N.Y. 1979, Conn. 1985, U.S. Dist. Ct. Conn. 1986. Rsch. scientist Rsch. Inst. on Alcoholism, Buffalo, 1976—80; legal cons. N.Y. Gov.'s Task Force on Drinking and Driving, Albany, 1979—82; pvt. practice Schenectady, NY, 1986—2000; counsel, exec. dir. Conifer Park, Scotia, NY, 1981—83; counsel, dir. substance abuse svcs. Inst. of Living, Hartford, Conn., 1984—86; founder, exec. dir. Lifestart Health Svcs., 1986—2000; prin. Lloyd Sokolow & Assocs., Schenectady, 2000—. Atty. Town of Knox, NY, 1980—92; cons., 2000—. Bd. dirs. Schenectady Community Svc. Bd., 1982—89; pres. Schenectady Cmty. Svc. Bd., 1989; mem. Surrogate Decision Making Commn., 1990—2001, N.Y. Commn. on Quality of Care; dir. addictions State of Md., 1988—89; counsel Apogee, Inc., 1996—98. Regent scholar NY State, 1967; Univ. fellow U. Buffalo, 1973, Baldy Law fellow, 1979. Mem.: APA. Family and matrimonial, Health, Property, real (including real estate development, water). Home: 2183 Grand Blvd Niskayuna NY 12309-5843 E-mail: lpilotus@yahoo.com.

SOLAN, LAWRENCE MICHAEL, lawyer; b. N.Y.C., May 7, 1952; s. Harold Allen and Shirley (Smith) S.; m. Anita Lois Rush, Mar. 27, 1982; children: Renata, David. BA, Brandeis U., 1974; PhD, U. Mass., 1978; JD, Harvard U., 1982. Bar: N.J. 1982, N.Y. 1984. Law clk. to Hon. Pollock Supreme Ct. N.J., Morristown, 1982-83; assoc. Orans, Elsen & Lupert, N.Y.C., 1983-89, ptnr., 1989-96; assoc. prof. law Bklyn. Law Sch., 1996-2000, prof. law, 2000—. Bd. dirs. Internat. Acad. Law and Mental Health; vis. assoc. prof. Princeton (NJ) U., 1999—2000, vis. prof., 2002. Author: The Language of Judges, 1993, Pronominal Reference, 1983. Mem. Assn. of Bar of City of N.Y., Phi Beta Kappa. Home: 163 Ralston Ave South Orange NJ 07079-2344 Office: Bklyn Law Sch 250 Joralemon St Brooklyn NY 11201-3700

SOLANO, CARL ANTHONY, lawyer; b. Mar. 26, 1951; s. Nick D. and Catherine A. (Occhiato) S.; m. Nancy M. Solano, 1989; children: Melanie A., Carla Nicole. BS magna cum laude, U. Scranton, 1973; JD cum laude, Villanova U., 1976. Bar: Pa. 1976, U.S. Dist. Ct. (ea. dist.) Pa. 1978, U.S. Ct. Appeals (3d cir.) 1980, U.S. Ct. Appeals (5th cir.) 1981, U.S. Supreme Ct. 1982, U.S. Ct. Appeals (9th cir.) 1986, U.S. Dist. Ct. (mid. dist.) Pa. 1988, U.S. Ct. Appeals (6th cir.) 1988, U.S. Ct. Appeals (fed. cir.) 1989, U.S. Ct. Appeals (6th cir.) 1988, U.S. Ct. Appeals (7th cir.) 1996. Law clk. Hon. Alfred L. Luongo U.S. Dist. Ct. (ea. dist.) Pa., Phila., 1976—78; assoc. Schnader, Harrison, Segal & Lewis, Phila., 1978—84, ptnr., 1985—. Adj. prof. Villanova U. Sch. Law, 1999—2001. Mem.: ABA, Justinian Soc., St. Thomas More Soc., Phila. Bar Assn. (chair bar news media com. 2003—), Pa. Bar Assn. (statutory law com. 1980—95), Am. Law Inst., Order of Coif, Pi Gamma Mu. Roman Catholic. Appellate, Communications, Libel. Home: 5 Barrister Ct Haverford PA 19041-1137 Office: Schnader Harrison Segal & Lewis LLP 1600 Market St Ste 3600 Philadelphia PA 19103-7287 E-mail: CSolano@Schnader.com.

SOLANO, HENRY L. lawyer; m. Janine Solano; children: Mateo, Amalia, Guadalupe. BS in Mech. Engring., U. Denver; JD, U. Colo.; LLD (hon.), U. Denver. Asst. atty. gen. Human Resources divsn. Colo. Dept. Law, 1977-82; asst. U.S. atty. Dist. Colo., 1982-87; U.S. atty. for Colo. U.S. Dept. Justice, Denver, 1994-98; solicitor U.S. Dept. Labor, Washington, 1998-2001; ptnr. LeBoeuf, Lamb, Greene & MacRae L.L.P., Denver, 2001—. Exec. dir. Colo. Dept. Instns., 1987-91, Colo. Dept. Regulatory Agys., 1987; acting exec. dir. Colo. Dept. Corrections, 1989-90; chair Cabinet Coun. on Families and Children, 1990-91; mem. adv. com. U.S. Atty. Gen., 1994-95; lectr. Kennedy Sch. Govt. Bd. dirs. Nat. Latino Children's Inst., Mex.Am. Legal Def. Edn. Fund, Denver Housing Authority, Denver Women's Commn., Colo. Dept. Social Svcs., Colo. Transit Constrn. Authority, Regional Transit Dist. , Labor (including EEOC, Fair Labor Standards Act, labor-management relations, NLRB, OSHA), Pension, profit-sharing, and employee benefits, Legislative. Office: LeBoeuf Lamb Greene & MacRae 633 17th St Ste 2000 Denver CO 80202

SOLBERG, NORMAN ROBERT, lawyer; b. Toledo, Aug. 28, 1939; s. Archie Norman and Margaret Jane (Olsen) S.; m. Megumi; children: Eric Norman, Anne Olsen, Robert Charles Kenneth. BA, Columbia Coll., 1961; LLB, Columbia U., 1964; postgrad., Parker Sch. Law, 1969. Bar: N.Y. 1964, Mass. 1973, Mo. 1978, Ill. 1984, Japan 1992. Assoc. firm Wickes, Riddell, Bloomer, Jacobi & McGuire, N.Y.C., 1964-69; sr. atty. Gillette Co., Boston, 1969-75; asst. internat. counsel Monsanto Co., St. Louis, 1975-79; sr. staff counsel Household Internat., Inc., Prospect Heights, Ill., 1979-87; v.p., gen. counsel Alberto-Culver Co., Melrose Park, Ill., 1987-89; atty. pvt. practice, 1989—. Pvt. practice Solberg Internat. Law Office, Osaka, Japan, 1992—. Mem. Osaka Bar Assn., Am. C. of C. in Japan (v.p., chair Kansai chpt., 2002-). Republican. Lutheran. Corporate, general, Private international, Mergers and acquisitions. Mailing: Koyoen Megamiyamacho 24-23 Nishinomiya Hyogo-ken 662-0011 Japan Office: Shin Yamamoto Bldg 7F Dojima 1-chome 1-25 Kita-ku Osaka 530-0003 Japan Office Fax: 81-6-6344-1924. E-mail: solberg@gaiben.com.

SOLER, LESLIE T. lawyer; b. Havana, Cuba, Nov. 12, 1971; d. Patricia Hernandez and Hermin Soler; m. Normand Y. Rainville, Jr., July 4, 1998; 1 child, Yvan P. Rainville. BS, Trinity Coll., 1993; JD, U. Conn., 1996. Bar: Fla. 1996, Conn. 1997. Counsel The Hartford, Simsbury, Conn., 1996—. Dir. Conn. Hispanic Bar Assn., Hartford, 1998—2001. Dir. Old State Ho., Hartford, 2000—03. Recipient Spl. Achievement award, The Hartford, 1998, 2000, Honors in Polit. Sci., Trinity Coll., 1993. Mem.: ABA, Conn. Hispanic Bar Assn. (pres.-elect 1998—99, pres. 1999—2000, Recognition award 2000), Nat. Hispanic Bar Assn., Conn. Bar Assn. Mergers and acquisitions, Private international, Corporate, general. Office: The Hartford 200 Hopmeadow St Simsbury CT 06089 Office Fax: 860-392-6422. E-mail: lsoler@hartfordlife.com.

SOLET, MAXWELL DAVID, lawyer; b. Washington, May 15, 1948; s. Leo and Pearl (Rose) S.; m. Joanne Marie Tolksdorf, Sept. 27, 1970; children: David Marc, Paul Jacob. AB, Harvard U., 1970, JD, 1974. Bar: Mass. 1974, U.S. Tax Ct. 1976, U.S. Ct. Claims 1976, U.S. Supreme Ct. 1976. Assoc. Gaston Snow & Ely Bartlett, Boston, 1974-79, Mintz, Levin, Cohn, Ferris, Glovsky & Popeo, P.C., Boston, 1979-82, ptnr., 1982—. Mem. ABA, Mass. Bar Assn., Boston Bar Assn. (chmn. tax sect. 1987-89), Nat. Assn. Bond Lawyers (mem. steering com. bond atty.'s workshop 1992-95). Taxation, general, State and local taxation. Home: 15 Berkeley St Cambridge MA 02138-3409 Office: Mintz Levin Cohn Ferris Glovsky & Popeo PC One Financial Ctr Boston MA 02111 E-mail: msolet@mintz.com.

SOLKOFF, SCOTT M. lawyer; b. Rochester, NY, July 5, 1966; s. Jerome Ira and Doreen Solkoff; m. Lauren Resa Kalish, Nov. 23, 1996; children: Jacob Solomon, Lola Danielle. BA, U. Fla., 1991; JD cum laude, Nova Southeastern U., 1994. Bar: Fla. 1994, U.S. Dist. Ct. (so. dist.) Fla. 1995, U.S. Ct. Appeals (11th cir.) 1995, bd. cert. elder law atty.:. Prin. Solkoff & Zellen, PA, Boynton Beach, Fla., 1994—. Chair elder law sect. Fla. Bar, Tallahassee, 2003—; bd. dirs. Fla. State Guardianship Assn. Contbr. articles to profl. jours. Mem. adv. bd. State of Fla. Office Pub. Guardian, Tampa, 2000—01; bd. dirs. Palm Beach County, Fla., 2002. Recipient Charlotte Brayer Pub. Svc. award, Fla. Bar, 1998. Mem.: Nat. Acad. Elder Law Attys., Acad. Fla. Elder Law Attys. (faculty, pres. emeritus, past pres.). Estate planning, Probate (including wills, trusts). Office: Solkoff & Zellen PA 1901 S Congress Ave #350 Boynton Beach FL 33426

SOLL, HERBERT D. lawyer; b. 1936; BS, U. Denver, 1958, LLB, 1960. Dir. Peace Corps , Rio de Janeiro, 1967—70; chief pub. defender Alaska, 1971—75; trust territory pub. defender, 1975—79; dir. criminal prosecution, 1986—90; dir. Peace Corps, Sao Tome, 1990—93; judge Superior Ct., 1979—86; atty. gen. No. Mariana Islands, Saipan, 2000—. Office: Office Atty Gen PO Box 10007 Adminstrn Bldg Saipan MP 96950 E-mail: acsoll@gtepacifica.net.*

SOLOMON, JACK AVRUM, JR., lawyer, automotive distributor, art dealer; b. Omaha, Oct. 25, 1928; s. John A. and Matilda (Bienstok) S.; m. Josephine J. Kleiman, June 1948 (div. Mar. 1971); children: Debra, Alisa, Michael, Rena; m. Carolyn Summers, Dec. 1973. BS, U. Nebr., 1950, LL.B. cum laude, 1952; LL.M. (Cook fellow), U. Mich., 1953. Bar: Nebr. 1950, Ill. 1951. Practice law, Chgo., 1950—; with firm Stiefel, Greenberg, Burns, Baldridge & Solomon, 1953-66, ptnr., 1958-66, Solomon, Rosenfeld, Elliot & Stiefel, and predecessor, 1966—, sr. ptnr., 1966—. Dir. Amco Industries, Inc., Chgo., 1968—, chmn. bd., 1968-69, sec., gen. counsel, 1969—; sec., dir. Mogen David Wine Corp., Chgo., 1964-71; chmn. bd., dir. Arts and Leisure Corp., 1969-76; pres., chmn. bd., dir. Circle Fine Art Corp., 1968-94; chmn. bd. S2 Art Group, Ltd., 1996—, Re Society, 1997—, Art of the Movies.com, 1999—; pres. The Las Vegas Art Dist., 2002--. Mem. Ill., Nebr. bar assns.; mem. Fine Art Pubs. Assn. (pres. 1982—); Mem. Order of Coif. Jewish (pres. temple 1959-61). Club: Nat. Arts (N.Y.C.). Home: 2870 Augusta Las Vegas NV 89109 Office: 1 E Charleston Las Vegas NV 89104 E-mail: jsolomon@s2art.com.

SOLOMON, MARK RAYMOND, lawyer, educator; b. Pitts., Aug. 23, 1945; s. Louis Isadore and Fern Rhea (Josselson) S. BA, Ohio State U., 1967; MEd, Cleve. State U., 1971; JD with hons., George Washington U., 1973; LLM in Taxation, Georgetown U., 1976. Bar: Ohio, Mich., U.S. Dist. Ct. (ea. dist.) Mich., U.S. Ct. Appeals (6th cir.), U.S. Tax Ct., U.S. Ct. Fed. Claims. Tax law specialist corp. tax br. Nat. Office of IRS, 1973—75; assoc. Butzel, Long, Gust Klein & Van Zile, Detroit, 1976—78; dir., v.p. Shatzman & Solomon, P.C., Southfield, Mich., 1978—81; prof., chmn. tax/bus. law dept., dir. MS in Taxation Program Walsh Coll., Troy, Mich., 1981—; of counsel Meyer, Kirk, Snyder & Lynch, PLLC, Bloomfield Hills, Mich., 1981—. Adj. prof. law U. Detroit, 1977-81. Editor: Cases and Materials on Consolidated Tax Returns, 1978, Cases and Materials on the Application of Legal Principles and Authorities to Federal Tax Law, 1990. Mem. Mich. Bar Assn., Phi Eta Sigma. Avocation: bridge (life master). Estate planning, Corporate taxation, Taxation, general. Home: 2109 Golfview Dr Apt 102 Troy MI 48084-3926 Office: Meyer Kirk Snyder & Lynch PLLC 100 W Long Lake Rd Ste 100 Bloomfield Hills MI 48304-2773 also: Walsh Coll 3838 Livernois Rd Troy MI 48083-5066 E-mail: msolomon@walshcol.edu.

SOLOMON, RANDALL LEE, lawyer; b. Dayton, Ohio, June 8, 1948; BA summa cum laude, Wright State U., 1970; JD, Case Western Res. U., 1973. Bar: Ohio 1973, U.S. Dist. Ct. (no. dist.) Ohio 1973, U.S. Ct. Appeals (6th cir.) 1973, U.S. Ct. Appeals (fed. cir.) 1988, U.S. Supreme Ct. 2002. Ptnr. Baker & Hostetler, Cleve. Speaker in field. Fellow Am. Coll. Trial Lawyers; mem. ABA (mem. litigation, tort and ins. practice sects.), Ohio State Bar Assn., Cleve. Bar Assn. (chair litigation sect. 1991-92), Nat. Inst. Trial Advocacy (mem. nat. session 1978), Def. Rsch. Inst., Anthony J. Celebrezze Inn. of Ct. (master). General civil litigation, Construction, Toxic tort. Office: Baker & Hostetler LLP 3200 Nat City Ctr 1900 E 9th St Ste 3200 Cleveland OH 44114-3475 E-mail: rsolomon@bakerlaw.com.

SOLOMON, ROBERT H. lawyer; b. Bklyn., Aug. 23, 1958; s. Murray and Mildred (Teger) S.; m. Felicia Irene Smith, June 30, 1985; children: Zachary, Alexander. BS in Econ cum laude, U. Pa., 1979; JD, Duke U., 1982. Bar: N.Y. 1983, U.S. Supreme Ct., U.S. Ct. Internat. Trade, U.S. Dist. Ct. (ea. & so. dists.) N.Y. Assoc. LeBeouf Lamb Leiby & MacRae, N.Y.C., 1982-84, Wofsey Certilman Haft et al, N.Y.C., 1984-87, Zimmer Victor Schwartz et al, N.Y.C., 1987-89; prin. Robert H. Solomon P.C., Long Beach, 1989—. Arbitrator N.Y. Dist. Ct., Hempstead, 1989—. Trustee Long Beach Bdn. Edn., 1995; bd. dirs. Long Beach Med. Ctr., 2002; pres. Lido Home Civic Assn. David Siegal scholar Duke U., 1980-82, Regents scholar, 1980. Mem. ABA, N.Y. State Bar Assn., Bar Assn. of N.Y.C., Nassau County Bar Assn., Long Beach Lawyers Assn. (pres. 1995-2000), Wharton Club. Avocation: tennis. General civil litigation, Commercial, contracts (including sales of goods; commercial financing), Finance. Office: 24 E Park Ave Long Beach NY 11561-3504 E-mail: Pennduke@aol.com.

SOLOMON, RODNEY JEFF, lawyer; b. Hamilton, Ohio, Apr. 14, 1949; s. Julius Franklin and Justine Paula (Rodney) S.; m. Nancy Griesemer, Oct. 17, 1976; children: Julia, Justin. BA, Amherst Coll., 1971; MPA, Harvard U., 1976, JD, 1979. Bar: Mass. 1979, D.C. 1979, U.S. Dist. Ct. Mass. 1988. Legis. asst. Office of sen. Robert Taft Jr., Washington, 1971-76; legal asst. Cambridge-Somerville Legal Svcs., Cambridge, Mass., 1977-78; cons. Mayor's Office Cmty. Devel., Chelsea, Mass., 1977-78; assoc. Caplar & Bok, Boston, 1978; spl. counsel Mass. Housing Fin. Agy., Boston, 1979-80; acting asst. adminstr. planning and redevel. Boston Housing Authority, 1980-81, spl. counsel to receiver, dir. spl. projects, 1980-83, from acting gen. counsel to gen. counsel, 1983-92; from dep. exec. dir. to acting exec. dir. Housing Authority City of Atlanta, 1992-94; dir. spl. actions Office Pub. and Indian Housing/U.S. Dept. HUD, Washingon, 1994-96, sr. dir. policy and legislation, 1996-99; dep. asst. sec. for policy, program and legis. initiatives U.S. Dept. HUD, Washington, 1999—2003; atty. Hawkins, Delafield & Wood, 2003—. Mem. staff distressed properties com. Coun. Large Pub. Housing Authorities, Washington, 1990-94; mem. Housing Working Group, Pres.'s Commn. on Model State Drug Laws, 1992. Author reports, legislation in field. Bd. dirs. Midnight Basketball League of Atlanta, Inc., 1992-96. Recipient Friend of Coun. of Large Pub. Housing Authorities award (nat. legis.), 1991, Proclamation by Mayor of City of Boston of "Rod Solomon Day", June 18, 1992; citations for svc. to Boston's Pub. Housing Residents, Mass. Senate and Ho. of Reps., 1992; recognition of assistance provided on Housing and Community Devel. Act of 1992, U.S. Senate Banking, Housing and Urban Affairs Com., 1992, Coun. of Large Pub. Housing Authorities, 1999, recognition of contribution to Quality Housing and Work Responsibility Act, 1998, others. Mem. Mass. Bar Assn., D.C. Bar. Office: Hawkins Delafield & Wood 601 Thirteenth St NW Washington DC 20005 Personal E-mail: RSolomon@hdw.com.

SOLOMON, STEPHEN L. lawyer; b. N.Y.C., Aug. 15, 1942; s. Sam and Ruth (Goldblum) S.; m. Regina Fisher, Aug. 14, 1969; children: Todd, Lisa. AB, Columbia Coll., 1964; LLB, NYU, 1967. Bar: N.Y. 1967, U.S. Dist. Ct. (so. and ea. dists.) 1969, U.S. Ct. Customs 1970, U.S. Supreme Ct. 1975. Assoc. Burns, Jackson, Summit, N.Y.C., 1969-74; ptnr. Miller, Singer, Michaelson & Raives, N.Y.C., 1974-79; ptnr., pres. Jarblum, Solomon & Fornari, PC, N.Y.C., 1979-97; ptnr. Rubin Baum LLP, N.Y.C., 1997—2002, Sonnenschein Nath & Rosenthal, N.Y.C., 2002—. Contbr. articles to profl. jours. Active Com. on Philanthropic Orgns., N.Y.C., 1980-83; bd. dirs. Emanu-El Midtown YM/YWHA, N.Y.C., 1979-85, Columbia Coll. Alumni Assn., 1995—. Mem. Assn. Bar City of N.Y. Democrat. Corporate, general, Property, real (including real estate development, water), Non-profit and tax-exempt organizations. Home: 40 Fifth Ave New York NY 10011-8843 Office: Sonnenschein Nath & Rosenthal 1221 Ave of Americas New York NY 10020 Fax: 212-768-6800.

SOLOMONS, MARK ELLIOTT, lawyer, art dealer, entrepreneur; b. Buffalo, Mar. 4, 1946; s. Alvin and Trude (Salant) Solomons; m. Jill E Kent, Aug. 20, 1978. BA, U. Rochester, 1967; JD, U. Pa., 1970; LLM, George Washington U., 1973. Staff atty. U.S. Dept. Labor, Washington, 1970-73, counsel coal miners benefits, 1973-77, legis. counsel, 1977-80; prin. Kilcullen Wilson & Kilcullen, Washington, 1980-86; ptnr. Arter and Hadden, Washington, 1986-2001, mem. exec. com., 1989-98; shareholder Greenberg Traurig, Washington, 2001—. Guest lectr law and hist SUNY, Stony Brook, 1970—76, Univ Mich, 1977—78, Hobart Col, 1972—76; prin Coun for Excellence in Govt, 1991—; co-owner Frogeye Co; chmn Atlantic Threadworks, 1998—2001; del Atlantic Treaty Asn Gen Assembly, 2000—. Contbr. articles to profl jours. Trustee, secy China Found, 1997—. Master: Am Inn of Ct (counselor 1996—97); mem.: ABA (chair workers compensation and employers liability comt 1987—88, sr. vice chair 1988—, vice chair appellate advocacy comt), NY Bar Asn, DC Bar Asn, Fed Bar Asn (chair regulatory reform comt 1988—89). Republican. Federal civil litigation, Insurance, Workers' compensation. Office: Greenberg Traurig LLP 800 Connecticut Ave NW Washington DC 20006 E-mail: solomonsm@gtlaw.com.

SOLOWAY, DANIEL MARK, lawyer; b. Buffalo, Jan. 21, 1959; s. Sol Murray and Shirley (Prashker) S.; m. Natalie Ann-Marie Chin, June 10, 1989; children: Rachael Ann, Rebecca Leigh. BA cum laude, SUNY, Buffalo, 1982; JD with honors, Fla. State U., 1985. Bar: Fla. 1985, U.S. Dist. Ct. (no. dist.) Fla. 1985, (mid. dist.) Fla. 1995, (so. dist.) Ala. 1986, U.S. Ct. Appeals (11th cir.) 1985, U.S. Supreme Ct. 1989; bd. cert. in civil trial law, Fla.; cert. Nat. Bd. Trial Advocacy, 1998, civil ct. mediator, 2000. Law clk. Circuit Judge, Tallahassee, 1983-84, Douglass, Davey, Cooper & Coppins, Tallahassee, 1984-85; ptnr. McKenzie & Soloway, Pensacola, Fla., 1985-98; pvt. practice Daniel M. Soloway, P.A., Pensacola, 1998—. Author: Criminal Justice: An Analysis Toward Reform, 1981; contbr. articles to profl. jours.; editor Escambia-Santa Rosa Bar Assn. newsletter, 1989-90, Dry Shoes, Fla. Bar Jour., 1992. Profl. adv. bd. N.W. Fla. Epilepsy Soc., Pensacola, 1989—; speaker on AIDS, State of Fla. Dept. HRS, 1988—; active Escambia County Human Rels. Commn., 1996-98. Recipient Pro Bono Svc. award Escambia-Santa Rosa Bar, 1989-90, Pro Bono Svc. Pres.'s award Fla. Bar, 1990. Mem. Million Dollar Advocates Forum (diplomat), ABA, Assn. Trial Lawyers Am., Escambia-Santa Rosa Bar Assn. (editor newsletter 1989-90), Acad. Fla. Trial Lawyers (speaker 1993—), Nat. Orgn. Social Security Claimants Reps.. Democrat. Jewish. Avocation: writing. Civil rights, General civil litigation, Personal injury (including property damage). Office: 901 Scenic Hwy Pensacola FL 32503-6866

SOMER, STANLEY JEROME, lawyer; b. N.Y.C., Oct. 29, 1943; s. David Meyer and Rose (Bleifeld) S.; children: Penny Lynn, Andrew Michael; m. Batia Lebhar, Sept. 13, 1987. BBA in Acctg., Hofstra U., 1966; JD, New York Law Sch., 1969. Bar: N.Y. 1970, U.S. Dist. Ct. (ea. and so. dists.) N.Y. 1972, U.S. Tax Ct. 1983. Assoc. Halpin, Keough & St. John, N.Y.C., 1970-71, Bodenstein & Gumson, N.Y.C., 1971-73; counsel Heatherwood Comm., Hauppauge, N.Y., 1973-74; ptnr. Somer & Wand, P.C., Commack and Smithtown, N.Y., 1974-88, Somer, Wand & Farrell, Commack and Smithtown, 1989-90; sole practice Commack and Smithtown, 1990-98; ptnr. Somer & Heller LLP, Commack, 1999—. Lectr. N.Y. Law Sch., N.Y.C., 1970-73, Income Property Cons., Huntington, N.Y., 1976-85. Commiteeman Suffolk Reps., East Northport, N.Y., 1978. Mem. N.Y. State Bar Assn., Suffolk Bar Assn., Comm. Assoc. Inst., L.I. Builders Inst. Lodges: Lions (pres. East Northport chpt. 1977-78). General practice, Landlord-tenant, Property, real (including real estate development, water). Office: Somer & Heller LLP 2171 Jericho Tpke Ste 350 Commack NY 11725-2947

SOMERS, CLIFFORD LOUIS, lawyer; b. Portland, Maine, Dec. 27, 1940; s. Norman Louis and Adeline Wilhemina (Witzke) Somers; m. Jennie Sierra Somers; children from previous marriage: Alan Mark, Penelope Lee. BA, U. Fla., Gainsville, 1965, JD, 1967. Bar: Fla 1967, US Ct Mil Appeals 1968, US Dist Ct (mid dist) Fla 1972, cert.: (civil trial lawyer), (mediator). Ptnr. Burton, Somers & Reynolds, Tampa, 1975-77, Miller, McKendree & Somers, Tampa, 1977-85, McKendree & Somers, Tampa, 1985-89, Somers and Morgan, Tampa, 1989-91, Somers and Assocs., Tampa, 1991-99, Barr, Murman, Tonelli, Slother & Sleet, Tampa, 1999—. Instr law Univ Fla, Gainesville, 1967; secy, treas Chester H Ferguson-Morris S White Inn, Am Inns Ct, 1987—89, pres-elect, 1989—90, pres, 1990—91. Contbr. articles to profl jours. With U.S. Army, 1961—64, Vietnam, capt JAG U.S. Army, 1968—72, mil judge JAG U.S. Army, 1971—72. Mem.: Am Bd Trial Attys (vpres Tampa chpt 1990—91), Def Research Inst (chmn 2d dist area west coast 1985—95), Fla Bar Asn (chmn procedure rules comt 1991—92), Brandon Vets Post and Park, Am Legion (comdr Post 278 1975). Avocations: writing, aerobics, weight lifting. State civil litigation, Insurance, Personal injury (including property damage). Home: 2517 S Ysabella St Tampa FL 33629 Office: Barr Murman Tonelli Slother & Sleet Ste 1700 201 E Kennedy Blvd Tampa FL 33602-5829 E-mail: csomers@barrmurman.com.

SOMMER, JAMES KOCH, lawyer; b. Crawfordsville, Ind., June 5, 1932; s. Edwin John and Sophia Kurth (Koch) Sommer; m. Michael Jean Stewart, Feb. 23, 1964; children: John Stewart, Whitney Suzanne Sommer Gregoline. BA, Yale U., 1954; LLB, Harvard U., 1959. Bar: Ind. 1959, U.S. Supreme Ct. 1970. Assoc. Barnes, Hickam, Pantzer & Boyd, Indpls., 1959—62; founding ptnr. and dir. Sommer Barnard Ackerson (and certain predecessor firms), Indpls., 1962—2003, of counsel, 2003—. Chmn. Indpls. Regulatory Study Commn., 1992—93. Fellow: Indpls. Bar Found. (Disting.); mem.: ABA, Bar Assn. Seventh Fed. Ct., Ind. Bar Assn., Indpls. Bar Assn. Corporate, general. Home: 8170 Ecole St Indianapolis IN 46240 Office: Sommer Barnard Ackerson One Indiana Sq Ste 3500 Indianapolis IN 46240

SOMMERFELD, DAVID WILLIAM, lawyer, educator; b. Detroit, Jan. 21, 1942; s. Henry Anthony and Hilda (Diffley) S.; m. Anne Marlaine Toth, June 27, 1964; children: Catherine, David Jr., Michael, Caroline. BS, U. Detroit, 1963; JD, Detroit Coll., 1967. Trust officer Nat. Bank Detroit, 1963-68; tax supr. Ernst & Ernst, Detroit, 1968-73; ptnr. Monaghan, Campbell, LoPrete & McDonald, Detroit, 1973-77; prof. Detroit Coll., 1977-86; ptnr. Butzel Long, Detroit, 1987—. Lectr. Ind. Soc. CPAs, Indpls., 1980-93, Ohio Soc. CPAs, Columbus, 1987, W.Va. Soc. CPAs, Charleston, 1983-86, 91. Editor Mich. Probate and Trust Law Jour., 1981-83. Fellow Am. Coll. of Trust and Estate Counsel; mem. Mich. Bar Assn., Detroit Bar Assn., Am. Inst. CPA's, Mich. Assn. CPA's, Forest Lake Country Club, Detroit Athletic Club. Roman Catholic. Avocations: bowling, spectator sports, gardening. Estate planning, Estate taxation. Office: Butzel Long Ste 200 100 Bloomfield Hills Pkwy Bloomfield Hills MI 48304

SOMMERS, GEORGE R. lawyer; b. N.Y.C., Jan. 27, 1955; BA, U. So. Fla., 1975; JD, NYU, 1987. Bar: N.J. 1987, U.S. Dist. Ct. N.J. 1987, N.Y. 1988, U.S. Dist. Ct. (all dists.) N.Y. 1988, U.S. Ct. Appeals (3d cir.) 1988, U.S. Ct. Appeals (2d cir.) 1989, U.S. Supreme Ct. 1992. Assoc. Sullivan & Cromwell, N.Y.C., 1987-90; pvt. practice lawyer N.Y.C., 1990—. Pres. Bill of Rights Found., N.Y.C., 1994—. Seidler scholar NYU Sch. Law, N.Y.C., 1985. Mem. Hoboken Bar Assn. (pres. 1994). Jewish. Avocations: sailing, chess. Civil rights, General civil litigation, Personal injury (including property damage). Office: 51 Newark St Hoboken NJ 07030-4548

SOMSEN, HENRY NORTHROP, retired lawyer; b. New Ulm, Minn., Aug. 12, 1909; s. Henry N. and Meta (Koch) S.; m. Anne Elizabeth Duncan, Sept. 12, 1936 (dec.); children: Pennell Anne, Stephen Duncan. BA, U. Minn., 1932, JD, 1934. Bar: Minn. 1934. Practice law, New Ulm, 1934-85; ptnr. Somsen, Dempsey, Johnson & Somsen, 1934-40, Somen Dempsey & Somsen, 1940-46, Somsen & Somsen, 1946-55; sole practice, 1955-64; ptnr. Somsen & Dempsey, 1965-71, Somsen Dempsey & Schade, 1971-85, of counsel, 1985—. Bd. editors U. Minn. Law Rev., 1932-33. Trustee Minn. State Parks Found., 1967-77; bd. dirs. Minn. Council State Parks, 1956—, pres., 1974-75; bd. dirs., pres. New Ulm Community Concert Assn., 1947-85; bd. dirs. Union Hosp., New Ulm, 1959-77, Highland Homes, Inc., 1970-79, New Ulm Meml. Found., 1958-79; bd. dirs. New Ulm Industries Inc., 1952-85, pres., 1968-77; bd. dirs. New Ulm Industries Found., Inc., 1953-85, pres., 1968-77, bd. dirs. 1953-83, chmn., 1958-83 Farmers and Mchts. Bank, New Ulm, Minn.; bd. dirs. Klossner State Bank, Minn., 1947-84, State Bond and Mortgage Co., 1950-80, Am. Artstone Co., 1955-84, others; mem. City Charter Commns., 1940, 51, 66, pres., 1966. Served from pvt. to capt. JAGC, AUS, 1943-46. Mem. ABA, Minn. Bar Assn., Am. Judicature Soc., Am. Arbitration Assn. (panel of arbitrators 1967-85), Mpls. Club, Masons, Rotary, Shriners. Episcopalian. Home: 211 2d St NW Apt 1907 Rochester MN 55901-3101

SONDERBY, SUSAN PIERSON, federal judge; b. Chicago, May 15, 1947; d. George W. and Shirley L. (Eckstrom) Pierson; m. James A. De Witt, June 14, 1975 (dec. 1978); m. Peter R. Sonderby, Apr. 7, 1990. AA, Joliet Jr. Coll., Joliet, Ill., 1967; BA, U. Ill., 1969; JD, John Marshall Law Sch., 1973. Bar: Ill., 1973; U.S. Dist. Ct. (cen. and so. dists.) Ill., 1978,; U.S. Dist. Ct. (no. dist.) Ill., 1984; U.S. Ct. Appeals (7th Cir.), 1984. Assoc. O'Brien, Garrison, Berard, Kusta, and De Witt, Joliet, Ill., 1973-75, ptnr., 1975-77; asst. atty. gen. consumer protection div., litig. sect. Office of the Atty. Gen., Chgo., 1977-78, asst. atty. gen., chief consumer protection divsn. Springfield, Ill., 1978-83; U.S. trustee (no. dist.) Ill. Chgo., 1983-86; judge U.S. Bankruptcy Ct. (no. dist.) Ill., Chgo., 1986—, chief fed. bankruptcy judge, 1998—2002. Mem. law faculty Fed. Jud. Tng. Ctr., Ill., Practicing Law Inst., Ill., U.S. Dept. Justice, Ill., Nat. Bankruptcy Inst., Ill., Ill. Continuing Edn.; spl. asst. atty. gen., Ill., 1972—78; adj. faculty De Paul U. Coll. Law, Chgo., 1986; past mem. U.S. Trustee adv. com., Ill.; consumer adv. coun. Fed. Res. Bd., Ill.; past sec. of State Fraudulent I.D. com. Dept. of Ins. Task Force on Improper Claims Practices, Ill.; former chair pers. rev. bd., mem. task force race and gender bias, U.S. Dist. Ct.; jud. conf. planning com. 7th Cir. Jud. Conf.; former mem. Civil Justice Reform Act Adv. Com.; mem. Adminstrv. Office of the U.S. Cts. Bankruptcy Judges Adv. Group; former mem. Ct. Security com.; mem. Adminstrv. Office of the U.S. Cts. Budget and Fin. Coun. Contbr. articles to profl. jour. Mem. Fourth Presbyn. Ch., Art Inst. Chgo.; past mem. Westminster Presbyn. Ch., Chgo. Coun. of Fgn. Rels.; past bd. dirs. Land of Lincoln Coun. Girl Scouts U.S.; past mem. individual guarantors com. Goodman Theatre, Chgo.; past chair clubs and orgns. Sangamon County United Way Capital campaign; past bd. dirs., chair house rules com. and legal subcom. Lake Point Tower; past mem. Family Svc. Ctr., Aid to Retarded Citizens, Henson Robinson Zoo. Named Young Career Woman, Bus. and Profl. Women, One of Ten Outstanding Bankruptcy Judges, Turnarounds and Workouts, 2002; recipient Spl. Achievement Award, Dept. Justice, 1984, Disting. Svc. Alumni Award, Joliet Jr. Coll., 1987, Disting. Alumni Award, John Marshall Law Sch., 1988, Dir. Award, Exec. Office U.S. Trustee, Leadership Award, Internat. Orgn. Women Exec., Outstanding Svc. to Bench, Am. Bankruptcy Inst., 1990. Master: Abraham Lincoln Marovitz Inn of Ct. (former pres., membership com.); fellow: Am. Coll. Bankruptcy (circuit admissions com.); mem.: ATLA, Comml. Law League Am. (former exec. coun. mem., bankruptcy and insolvency sect., coord. with nat. conf. bankruptcy judges com.), Nat. Conf. Bankruptcy Judges (co-chair ednl. program com. conf. 2001, liaison with bankruptcy rev. commn. com.), Bar Assn. (7th cir.) (former treas., judicial conf. planning com.), Am. Bankruptcy Inst. (bd. dirs. Chgo. chpt.), Fed. Bar Assn., Chgo. Archtl. Found., John Marshall Law Sch. Alumni Assn. (bd. dirs.), Nordic Law Club (past legis. com.), Lawyers Club Chgo. (hon.). Avocations: travel, flying, interior decorating. Office: US Bankruptcy Ct 219 S Dearborn St Ste 638 Chicago IL 60604-1702

SONDOCK, RUBY KLESS, retired judge; b. Apr. 26, 1926; d. Herman Lewis and Celia (Juran) Kless; m. Melvin Adolph Sondock, Apr. 22, 1944; children: Marcia Cohen, Sandra Marcus. AA, Cottey Coll., Nevada, Mo., 1944; BS, U. Houston, 1959, LLB, 1961. Bar: Tex. 1961, U.S. Supreme Ct. 1977. Pvt. practice, Houston, 1961-73, 89—; judge Harris County Ct. Domestic Rels. (312th Dist.), 1973-77, 234th Jud. Dist. Ct., Houston, 1977-82, 83-89; justice Tex. Supreme Ct., Austin, 1982; of counsel Weil Gotshal and Manges, 1989-93, Houston Ctr., 1993—. Mem. ABA, Tex. Bar Assn., Houston Bar Assn., Houston Assn. Women Lawyers, Order of Barons, Phi Theta Phi, Kappa Beta Pi, Phi Kappa Phi, Alpha Epsilon Pi. Address: 550 Westcott #220 Houston TX 77007

SONEGO, IAN G. assistant attorney general; b. Louisville, May 27, 1954; s. Angelo and Zella Mae (Causey) S. BA in Polit. Sci. with high honors, U. Louisville, 1976, JD, 1979. Bar: Ky. 1979, U.S. Dist Ct. (ea. dist.) Ky. 1980, U.S. Dist. Ct. (we. dist.) Ky. 1989, U.S. Ct. Appeals (6th cir.) 1989, U.S. Supreme Ct. 1990. Asst. atty. Office Commonwealth's Atty. Pike County, Pikeville, Ky., 1980, sr. asst. atty., 1988-89; assoc. John Paul Runyon Law Firm, Pikeville, 1981-87; asst. atty. gen. Office Atty. Gen., Frankfort, Ky., 1989—. Lectr. criminal law Ky. Bar Assn., Jenny Wiley Park, 1981, Ky. Prosecutors Confs., 1989, 93; mem. Atty. Gen.'s task force child sexual abuse, 1992-94, Nat. Conf. on Domestic Violence, 1996. Contbg. editor Ky. Prosecuter Newsletter, 1991—. Recipient Kesslman award, U. Louisville, 1975, Bd. trustee award, 1979, Outstanding Prosecutor award, Ky. Atty., Award Outstanding Advocacy, Assn. Govt. Attys. in Capital Litigation, 2001. Mem.: Ky. Commonwealth's Attys. Assn. (hon.; lectr. 1987, 90, chmn. com. ethics 1984—86, bd. dirs. 1983—85, Spl. award 1987). Office: Office Atty Gen Criminal Appellate Divsn 1024 Capital Center Dr Frankfort KY 40601-8204 E-mail: isonego@law.state.ky.us.

SONFIELD, ROBERT LEON, JR., lawyer; b. Houston, Oct. 28, 1931; s. Robert Leon and Dorothy Harriett (Huber) S.; 1 dau., Sheree. BA, U. Houston, 1956, LL.B., JD, 1959; PhD (hon.), U. Eastern Fla., 1962; LL.D. (hon.), London Inst. Applied Research, 1973; certificate fed. taxation, NYU, 1973; certificate securities regulation, Harvard U., 1983. Bar: Tex. 1959, U.S. Supreme Ct. 1959, U.S. Dist. Ct. Tex. 1960, U.S. Tax Ct. 1960, U.S. Ct. Appeals 1960, U.S. Ct. Claims 1974. Mng. dir. Sonfield & Sonfield, Houston, 1959—. Mem. nat. adv. council Nat. Fedn. Ind. Bus. Author: Corporate Financing by Sale of Securities to the Public, 1969, Mergers and Acquisitions, 1970, Student Rights, 1971, The Limited Partnership as a Vehicle for Real Estate Investment, 1971, Integration of Partnership Offerings, 1974, The Grantor Trust Rules After The Tax Reform Act of 1986, Incentive Equity Program, Corporate Name Protection Along With Name Registration, A Guide to SEC Corporate Filing, Organizational Professionals' Residual Litigation and Investment Strategy, Comparing California, Delaware and Nevada: Corporate Laws in Light of California Corporations Code Section 2115 and Offering of Unregistered Securities Only to Accredited Investors, Disclosure Policies, Practices and Procedures For Public Companies, Regulation of Franchises, How to Become a Publicly Held Company Via the Registered Ditribution of a Percentage of Your Company's Stock to Shareholders, numerous others. Recipient St. John Garwood award, 1957, Frio-Finnegan Outstanding Alumnus award, 1970-71, citation for outstanding contbn. to legal profession, 1971 Mem. Am. Tax Lawyers Assn. (pres.), Lawyers Soc. Houson, Am. Judicature Soc., ABA, Tex. Bar Assn. (dist. com. on admission to state bar, chmn. clients security fund com.), Houston Bar Assn. (com. chmn. council, tax sect.), Tex. Equal Access to Justice Found., Houston Bar Found., Real Estate Securities and Syndication Inst., Huguenot Soc. of London, Order Stars and Bars, SAR, Sons Confederate Vets., Mil. Order World Wars, Mil. and Hospitaller Order St. Lazarus of Jerusalem, Knightly Assn. St. George the Martyr, Smithsonian Assocs., Houston Heritage Soc., Houston Mus. Fine Arts, Newcomen Soc. N.Am., Phi Delta Phi, Delta Sigma Phi. Clubs: Metropolitan (N.Y.C.); Argyle (San Antonio); Houston, Houstonian. Office: Sonfield & Sonfield 770 S Post Oak Ln Houston TX 77056-6665 E-mail: robert@sonfeld.com.

SONNENFELD, MARC JAY, lawyer; b. Bryn Mawr, Pa., Sept. 16, 1946; s. Burton David and Rochelle (Galant) S. BA, Swarthmore Coll., 1968; JD, Harvard U., 1971. Bar: Pa. 1971, Mass. 1971, D.C. 1977, Fla. 1978, U.S. Supreme Ct. 1976. Lectr. Wellesley (Mass.) Coll., 1971-72; law clk. to chief judge U.S. Dist. Ct. (ea. dist.) Pa., Phila., 1972-73; assoc. Ewing & Cohen, Phila., 1973-74, Morgan, Lewis & Bockius, Phila., 1974-78, ptnr., 1978—. Dem. committeeman, Phila., 1980-84; chmn. Pa. Lawyers for Dem. Victory, 1988; bd. mgrs. Swarthmore Coll., 1989—, gen. chmn. ann. fund, 1985-87; trustee Am. Inns of Ct. Found.; mem. bd. mgrs. Swarthmore Coll. Fellow Am. Coll. Trial Lawyers; mem. ABA, Pa. Bar Assn., Phila. Bar Assn. (exec. com. young lawyers sect. 1976-79, appellate cts. com., fed. cts. com., state civil jud. procedures com., nominating com., chmn. city policy com., chmn. profl. responsibility com. 1985, co-chmn. legis. liaison com. 1987-91, bus. banking and corp. law sect., vice chmn. bd. govs. 1986, chmn. 1987, chmn. ann. meeting 1991, asst. treas. 1996, co-chair commerce cost task force 1996-97), Harvard Law Sch. Assn. of Phila. (pres.1987-88), Swarthmore Coll. Annual Fund (bd. mgrs.). Jewish. Avocations: reading, sailing. Alternative dispute resolution, Federal civil litigation, State civil litigation. Office: Morgan Lewis & Bockius 1701 Market St Philadelphia PA 19103-2921 Home: 234 Cuylers Ln Haverford PA 19041

SONNENSCHEIN, ADAM, lawyer; b. N.Y.C., Oct. 15, 1938; s. Harry D. and Sybil (Reinus) S.; m. Phyllis Cokin, Oct. 25, 1968; children: Andrew, Michael. BA, Amherst Coll., 1960; LLB, Columbia U., 1965. Bar: N.Y. 1965, Mass. 1970. Assoc. Berlack, Israels & Liberman, N.Y.C., 1965-70; ptnr. Sprague Assocs., Boston, 1970-72, Walter & Sonnenschein, Boston, 1972-78, Hausserman, Davison & Shattuck, Boston, 1978-83, Foley, Hoag & Eliot, Boston, 1983—. Mem. ABA, Mass. Bar Assn., Boston Bar Assn., Assn. of Bar of City of N.Y. Office: Foley Hoag LLP 155 Seaport Blvd Boston MA 02210-2600

SONSINI, LARRY W. lawyer; b. Rome, N.Y., Feb. 5, 1941; AB, U. Calif., Berkeley, 1963; LLB, U. Calif., 1966. Bar: Calif. 1966. Ptnr. Wilson, Sonsini, Goodrich & Rosati, Palo Alto; prof. securities regulation Boalt Hall Sch. law U. Calif., Berkeley, 1984—. Mem. exec. com. Securities Re Mem. ABA (com. on fed. regulation securities, subcom. on registration statements), Am. Law Inst. Office: Wilson Sonsini Goodrich & Rosati 650 Page Mill Rd Palo Alto CA 94304-1050*

SORBELLO, JOSEPH CHARLES, retired lawyer; b. Redlands, Calif., Apr. 8, 1925; s. Salvatore and Maria (Gallotto) S.; m. Sharon Broome, June 3, 1945, Margaret Pillsbury, June 10, 1969 (dec. June 1995); m. Marguerite Geftakys, Apr. 23, 1997. BS in Pharmacy, Wash. State U., 1951; JD, Lincoln U., 1975. Bar: Calif. 1975; lic. pharmacist Calif., Wash. Owner Community Pharmacy, Edgemont, Calif., 1955-60; pharmacist Owens Pharmacy, Bishop, Calif., 1961-69; supervising insp. Calif. State Bd. Pharmacy, San Francisco, L.A., 1969-87; pvt. practice Westminster, Calif., 1987-95; ret., 1996. Lectr. in pharmacy law U. So. Calif., L.A., 1984, 85, 86. Bd. dirs. Moreno Valley Sch. Dist., Sunny Mead, Calif. Staff sgt. USMC, 1942-46, PTO. Mem. Masons, Nu Beta Epsilon, Rho Chi. Democrat. Avocation: amateur radio. Home: 3942 S Mission Rd Fallbrook CA 92028-9455

SORENSEN, HARVEY R. lawyer; b. Chgo., Nov. 3, 1947; s. Harvey T. and Jean Louise (Cline) S.; m. Emily Smith, May 31, 1969 (div. May 1980); children: Abigail, Jeanne, Cornelia; m. Stephanie Sorensen, Dec. 31, 1980; 1 child, Tyler. BA, Beloit Coll., 1969; MSBA, Boston U., 1972; JD cum laude, Northwestern U., 1974. Bar: Wis. 1974, U.S. DISt. Ct. (ea. dist.) Wis. 1974, U.S. Dist. Ct. Kans., U.S. Tax Ct., 1975, U.S. Ct. Claims 2002. Tax acct. Arthur, Young & Co., Chgo., 1974; assoc. Whyte & Hirschboeck, Milw., 1974-75; asst. adj. prof. Wichita (Kans.) State U. Sch. Bus., 1979; ptnr. Foulston & Siefkin, Wichita, 1975—. Dir. World Svcs. Group, Inc., 2002—; chmn. Veri Prime, Inc.; bd. dirs. Nat. Bank Andover, Wichita Greyhound Charities, 1999. Trustee, vice chmn. Kans. Pub. Telecom. Svc., 1978—97, chmn., 1997—99, Wichita Downtown Devel. Corp., 1996—2003, dir., 2003—; chmn. adv. bd. City of Wichita Self Supporting Mcpl. Improvement Dist., 2001—03; project bus. cons. Jr. Achievement, 1978—93; trustee Wichita Symphony Soc., 1986—96, Wichita Collegiate Sch., 1994—, Wichita Sedgewick County Hist. Mus., 1986—89, Wichita Arts Coun., 1979—82, Goodwill Industries/Easter Seals of Kans. Area, 2001—; bd. cmty. adv. KMUW, 1981—82; commr. City of Eastborough, Kans., 1991—93; treas. St. James Episcopal Ch., 1996—99. With U.S. Army, 1970—72. Fellow Am. Coll. Tax Counsel; mem. ABA (chair-elect agricultural com. sect. taxation 2003-, state and local tax com. Lex Mundi 2003-, Wichita Bar Assn., Kans. Bar Assn. (past sect., v.p., pres. tax. sect. 1984-88), Attys. for Family Held Enterprises, Wichita Area C. of C. (bd. dirs. 2000—, vice chmn. 2003), Rotary. Republican. Episcopalian. Corporate taxation, Estate taxation, Taxation, general. Home: 13 Colonial Ct Wichita KS 67207-1056 Office: Foulston Siefkin LLP 700 Bank of Am Ctr Wichita KS 67202-2207

SORENSEN, MURRAY JIM, lawyer; b. Blackfoot, Idaho, Feb. 10, 1948; s. Murray L. and Lona Mae (Clegg) S.; m. Gay Grimshaw, May 25, 1974; children— Benjamin Jim, Joshua John, Matthew Murray, Daniel Henry, Adam Michael. Student in Political Sci., Brigham Young U., 1965-72; J.D., U. Idaho, 1975. Bar: Idaho 1975, U.S. Dist. Ct. Idaho 1975. Asst. prosecutor Bingham County, Idaho, 1975-77, pub. defender, 1979-82; city atty. City of Blackfoot, 1978-79; ptnr. Blasen & Sorensen Chartered, Blackfoot, 1981— ; city atty. City of Basalt, Idaho, 1984—. Chmn. Eastern Idaho Fair Parade, Blackfoot, 1978-79, United Fund, Blackfoot, 1979, Ducks Unltd., Blackfoot, 1983-84; Pres., Idaho 7th Dist. Bar, 1996-97 (v.p. and gen. coun. 1992-94). Named to Outstanding Young Men Am., U.S. Jaycees, 1982. Mem. ABA, Assn. Trial Lawyers Am., Idaho Trial Lawyers Assn., Blackfoot C. of C. (bd. dirs. 1979-80). Mormon. Lodge: Kiwanis (bd. dirs. local lodge 1983-84). Bankruptcy, General practice, Personal injury (including property damage). Office: Blaser & Sorensen Chartered 265 NW Main St # 1047 Blackfoot ID 83221-2242

SOROKOFF, DAVID, lawyer; b. N.Y.C., Sept. 22, 1959; s. Sheldon A. and Nancy (Grant) S. BA, U. Pa., Phila., 1981, JD, 1985. Assoc. Shearman & Sterling, N.Y.C., 1985-96; asst. gen. counsel Deloitte & Touche LLP, N.Y.C., 1997. Recipient Thurgood Marshall award Assn. Bar N.Y., 1998. Mem. ABA, Assn. Bar City of N.Y., N.Y. City Lawyers Assn., Fed. Cts. Commn. N.Y. City Lawyers Assn. Office: Deloitte & Touche LLP 1633 Broadway New York NY 10019-6708

SORRELL, WILLIAM H. state attorney general; b. Burlington, Vt., Mar. 9, 1947; s. Marshal Thomas and Esther Sorrell; children: McKenzie, Thomas. AB, U. Notre Dame, 1970; JD, Cornell U., 1974. Dep. state's atty. Chittenden County State of Vt., 1975—77, state's atty. Chittenden County, 1977—78, 1989—92; ptnr. McNeil, Murray & Sorrell, 1978—89; sec. adminstrn., 1992—97; atty. gen. State of Vt., 1997—. Bd. dir. Am. Legacy Found. Pres. United Cerebral Palsy Vt.; sec. Vt. Coalition Handicapped; bd. dirs. Winooski Valley Pk. Dist., Am. Legacy Found. Mem.: Nat. Assn. Attys. Gen. (v.p.). Democrat. Office: Office Atty Gen 109 State St Montpelier VT 05609-0001

SORRELS, RANDALL OWEN, lawyer; b. Va., Dec. 11, 1962; s. Charles Vernon and Marjorie Elaine (Jones) S.; m. Cheryl Ann Casas, June 29, 1985; children: Ashley Michelle, Stephanie Leigh, Darby Nicole, Garrett Ryan. BA in Polit. Sci.and Speech Comm. magna cum laude, Houston Bapt. U., 1984; JD magna cum laude, South Tex. Coll. Law, 1987. Bar: Tex. 1987, U.S. Dist. Ct. (so. dist.) Tex.; bd. cert. in civil trial law and personal injury trial law tex. Bd. Legal Specialization. Assoc. Fulbright & Jaworski, Houston, 1987-90; ptnr. Abraham, Watkins, Nichols, Sorrels, Matthews & Friend, Houston, 1990—. Contbr. articles to profl. jours. Fellow Tex. Bar Found. (trustee 1997-2000, sustaining life), Houston Bar Found. , Tex. Bar Found. (sustaining life); mem. ABA, Houston Bar Assn. (v.p. 2000-2003, dir. 1998-2000), Houston Trial Lawyers Found. (pres. 2000-2001), Houston Trial Lawyers Assn. (pres. 1999-2000), Houston Lawyer's Referral Svc. (pres. 2000-2001), State Bar Tex. (dir. 1994-97), Tex. Trial Lawyers Assn. (dir. 1994—), Houston Trial Lawyers Found. (dir. 1998—), Houston Trial Lawyers Assn. (v.p. 1996-98, dir. 1993-96), Am. Bd. Trial Advs. (1997—), Nat. Bd. Trial Advs., Coll. State Bar Tex., Coll. State Bar Tex., Houston Trial Lawyers Found., Houston Bar Assn., Tex. Young Lawyers Assn., Houston Young Lawyers Assn., Assn. Civil Trial and Appellate Specialists, Am. Trial Lawyers Assn., Million Dollar Advs. Forum, Tex. Assn. Def. Counsel (former mem.), Am. Inns of Ct. Insurance, Personal injury (including property damage), Product liability. Home: 311 Terrace Dr Houston TX 77007-5046 Office: Abraham Watkins Nichols Sorrels Matthews & Friend 800 Commerce St Houston TX 77002-1776

SORTLAND, PAUL ALLAN, lawyer; b. Powers Lake, N.D., July 30, 1953; s. Allan Berdette and Eunice Elizabeth (Nystuen) S.; m. Carolyn Faye Anderson, June 23, 1979; children: Joseph Paul, Martha Marie, Nicholas John, Benjamin David. BA, St. Olaf Coll., 1975; JD, U. Minn., 1978. Bar: Minn. 1978, N.D. 1981, U.S. Dist. Ct. Minn. 1979, U.S. Dist. Ct. N.D. 1980, U.S. Ct. Appeals (8th cir.) 1987, U.S. Supreme Ct. 1991. Assoc. Alderson & Ondov, Austin, Minn., 1978-80, Qualley, Larson & Jones, Fargo, N.D., 1980-83; ptnr. Holand, Lochow & Sortland, Fargo, 1983-85; pres. Sortland Law Office, Fargo, 1985-88; ptnr. Messerli & Kramer, Mpls., 1988-92; Sortland Law Office, Mpls., 1993—. Adj. prof. bus. law Moorhead State U., 1987. Mem. ATLA, N.D. Bar Assn., Minn. Bar Assn. (cert. civil trial specialist), Kiwanis, Million Dollar Advocates Forum, Upper Lake Minnetonks Yacht Club, Gamma Eta Gamma. Lutheran. Personal injury (including property damage), General civil litigation. Home: 120 Quebec Ave S Minneapolis MN 55426-1509 Office: 33 S 6th St Ste 4100 Minneapolis MN 55402-3729

SOSENSKY, STEVEN CHARLES, lawyer; b. New Haven, Conn. BA in Polit. Sci., U. Conn., 1985; JD, We. New Eng. Sch. of Law, 1988. Bar: Conn. 1988, U.S. Dist. Ct. Conn. Summer assoc. Schatz & Schatz, Ribicoff & Kotkin, Hartford, Office of the Atty. Gen., Hartford; assoc. Joseloff & Joseloff, Wethersfield, Conn., 1989-90; pvt. practice New Haven, 1991—2001; ptnr. Shipman & Sosensky, 2001—. Cons. bus. transactions, complex civil litigation, bankruptcy, wills and trusts, collections, pub. utilities law, environ. regulation, New Haven. Mem. Conn. Bar Assn. Bankruptcy, General civil litigation, Commercial, contracts (including sales of goods; commercial financing). Office: Shipman & Sosensky LLC 363 Main St Hartford CT 06106 also: 9 Trumbull St New Haven CT 06511 E-mail: steven@shipso.com.

SOSLAND, KARL Z. lawyer; b. Springfield, Mass., Apr. 3, 1933; s. Saul and Bessie (Shub) S.; m. June L. Sosland, Mar. 31, 1975; children: Daniel, Cynthia, Jayne, Rachel, Elizabeth. BA, U. Conn., 1955; LLB, Columbia U., 1959. Bar: N.J. 1960. Assoc. Robert Gruen, Hackensack, N.J., 1960-64, Gruen & Sosland, Hackensack, N.J., 1964-65, Scangarella and Sosland, Pompton Plains, N.J., 1965-70; pvt. practice Pompton Plains, Paramus, N.J., 1970-97, Hackensack, 1997—. Atty. Bd. Adjustment Norwood (N.J.), 1965-74; mcpl. atty. Pequannock Twp., N.J., 1971-80; judge Mcpl. Ct. Pompton Lakes, 1976-78. Active Fairlawn (N.J.) Bd. Edn., 1964-66; pres. Kinnelon (N.J.) Bd. Edn., 1971. Mem. ABA, N.J. Bar Assn., Morris County Bar Assn., Bergen City Bar Assn. State civil litigation, Commercial, contracts (including sales of goods; commercial financing), Property, real (including real estate development, water). Home: 11 Tecumseh Trl Oakland NJ 07436-2802 Office: 19 Main St Hackensack NJ 07601-7023 E-mail: soslaw@aol.com.

SOSMAN, MARTHA B. judge; b. Boston, Mass., Oct. 20, 1950; BA Middlebury Coll, JD U. Mich. Assoc. Foley, Hoag & Eliot, Boston, 1979—84; with U.S. Atty.'s Office, Boston, 1984—89; founding ptnr. Kern, Sosman, Hagerty, Roach & Carpenter, Boston, 1989—93; apptd. judge Superior Ct., Concord, Mass., 1993; assoc. justice Mass. Supreme Jud. Ct., 2000—. Office: Mass Supreme Jud Ct 1300 New Ct Hse Pemberton Sq Boston MA 02108*

SOSSAMAN, WILLIAM LYNWOOD, lawyer; b. High Point, N.C., May 30, 1947; s. Robert Allison and Elizabeth Bryce (Hethcox) S.; m. Sandra Clare Ward, June 9, 1973; children: Joana Leslie, David Lynwood. AB, Davidson Coll., 1969; JD, Vanderbilt U., 1972. Bar: Fla. 1972, U.S. Ct. Mil. Appeals 1973, U.S. Dist. Ct. (mid. dist.) Fla. 1977, Tenn. 1978, U.S. Dist. Ct. (we. dist.) Tenn. 1979, U.S. Dist. Ct. (no. dist.) Miss. 1979, U.S. Dist. Ct. (ea. and we. dists.) Ark, 1980, U.S. Dist. Ct. (mid. dist.) Tenn. 1985, U.S. Dist. Ct. (ea. dist.) Mich. 1988, U.S. Ct. Appeals (6th and 8th cirs.) 1989, U.S. Ct. Appeals (11th cir.) 1991. Mktg. resch. analyst First Tenn. Bank, Memphis, 1967-70; assoc. Alley, Rock & Dinkel, Tampa, Orlando and Miami, Fla., 1972-73, Rock & Brown, Orlando, 1976-77, Young & Perl, Memphis, 1978-88; ptnr. Allen, Scruggs, Sossaman, & Thompson, Memphis, 1988—. Asst. county atty. Shelby County Govt., Memphis, 1978-79; asst. city atty. City of Memphis, 1978-79. Author: Preventing Lawsuits for Wrongful Termination, 1995. N.Am. regional sec. Project Ams., Davidson, N.C., 1967-69. Capt. U.S. Army, 1973-76. Named Hon. City Councilman City of Memphis, 1982. Mem. ABA (labor and employment sect., litigation sect., EEO com.), Fla. Bar (labor and employment law sect.), Mgmt. Counsel Roundtable (chmn. 1986-87), Def. Rsch. Inst. (employment law com.), Tenn. Bar Assn. (labor law sect.), Memphis Bar Assn., The Justice Network (bd. dirs. 1990-93), Poplar Pike Arts Guild (bd. dirs. 1998-2002). Presbyterian. Federal civil litigation, Labor (including EEOC, Fair Labor Standards Act, labor-management relations, NLRB, OSHA). Home: 8411 Beaverwood Dr Germantown TN 38138-7641 Office: Allen Scruggs Sossaman & Thompson Brinkley Plz Ste 650 80 Monroe Ave Memphis TN 38103-2481 E-mail: wls@asstlaw.com.

SOTOMAYOR, SONIA, judge; b. N.Y.C., June 25, 1954; d. Sonia and Celina (Baez) Sotomayor; m. Kevin Edward Noonan, Aug. 14, 1976 (div. 1983). AB, Princeton U., 1976; JD, Yale U., 1979; LLD honoris causa (hon.) , 1999, JD (hon.) honoris causa, 2001. Bar: N.Y. 1980, U.S. Dist. Ct. (ea. and so. dists.) N.Y. 1984. Asst. dist. atty. Office of Dist. Atty. County of N.Y., N.Y.C., 1979—84; assoc., ptnr. Pavia & Harcourt, N.Y.C., 1984—92; fed. judge U.S. Dist. Ct. (so. dist.) N.Y., N.Y.C., 1992—98; cir. judge U.S. Ct. Appeals (2d Cir.), N.Y.C., 1998—. Adj. prof. NYU Sch. Law, 1998; lectr. law Columbia Law Sch., 1999. Editor: Yale U. Law Rev., 1979. Mem. State Adv. Panel on Inter-Group Rels., N.Y.C., 1990—92, 1990—91; bd. dirs. P.R. Legal Def. and Edn. Fund, N.Y.C., 1980—92, State of N.Y. Mortgage Agy., N.Y.C., 1987—92, N.Y.C. Campaign Fin. Bd., 1988—92. Mem.: ABA, Am. Philos. Soc., N.Y. Women's Bar Assn., P.R. Bar Assn., Hispanic Bar Assn., Phi Beta Kappa. Office: US Courthouse 410 US Corthouse 40 Centre St New York NY 10007-1502

SOUDER, SUSAN, judge, lawyer; b. Washington, Sept. 20, 1956; BA, U. Md., 1978; JD, Georgetown U., 1981. Bar: Md. 1981. Trial atty. U.S. Dept. Justice, Washington, 1981-85; spl. asst. U.S. atty. Los Angeles, 1983; ptnr. Gordon, Feinblatt, Rothman, Balt., 1985-94, Ballard Spahr Andrews & Ingersoll, Balt., 1994-97; pvt. practice, Catonsville, Md., 1997—; judge Balt. (Md.) County Cir. Ct., 2002—. Mem.: Women's Bar Assn., Baltimore County Bar Assn., Md. Bar Assn., Catonsville Sunrise Rotary (pres. elect). Office: Courthouse 401 Bosley Ave Towson MD 21204

SOULATI, BEHNAZ, lawyer; b. Rezaieh, Iran, Dec. 16, 1969; arrived in U.S., 1987; d. Firooz and Mihan Soulati. BA, U. Iowa, 1993, MA, 1995, JD, 1999. Bar: Iowa 1999, U.S. Dist. Ct. (so. and no. dists.) Iowa 2000, U.S. Ct. Appeals (8th cir.) 2000. Tchg. asst. U. Iowa, Iowa City, 1993—95; lectr. U. Poitiers, Poitiers, France, 1995—96; jud. clk. Scott County Courthouse, Davenport, Iowa, 1999—2000; litigation assoc. Davis Law Firm, Des Moines, 2000—. General civil litigation. Office: Davis Brown Koehn Shors & Roberts PC 666 Walnut St Ste 2500 Des Moines IA 50309

SOULE, ROBERT GROVE, lawyer; b. Boston, Jan. 12, 1958; s. Augustus W. and Mary R. Soule; m. Maura Kelley, Aug. 21, 1982; children: Courtney K., Katherine W., Zachary A. BA, Harvard U., 1979; JD, Suffolk U., 1983. Bar: Mass. 1983, U.S. Dist. Ct. Mass. 1983. Of counsel First Am. Title Ins. Co., Boston, 1982-85, asst. regional counsel, 1985-87; New Eng. states counsel Minn. Title Ins. Co., Boston, 1987-89; N.E. regional counsel Old Republic Title Ins. Co., Boston, 1989-93; mgr. nat. divsn. Lawyers Title Ins. Corp. (LandAmerica), Boston, 1993—. Contbr. articles to profl. jours., chpts. to books. Mem. Am. Land Title Assn., New Eng. Land Title Assn. (bd. dirs. 1996-2001, pres. 1999-2000), Mass. Conveyancers Assn. (title standards com. 1987—, exec. com. 1989-92), Mass. Bar Assn., Abstract Club. Property, real (including real estate development, water). Office: LandAmerica One Washington Mall Boston MA 02108-2804 Fax: 617-619-4848. E-mail: rsoule@landam.com.

SOUTER, DAVID HACKETT, United States supreme court justice; b. Melrose, Mass., Sept. 17, 1939; s. Joseph Alexander and Helen Adams (Hackett) Souter. BA, Harvard U., 1961, LLB, 1966; Rhodes scholar, Oxford U., 1961—63, MA, 1989. Bar: N.H. Assoc. Orr & Reno, Concord, 1966—68; asst. atty. gen. N.H., 1968—71; dep. atty. gen., 1971—76; atty. gen., 1976—78; assoc. justice Superior Ct. N.H., 1978—83, N.H. Supreme Ct., 1983—90; judge U.S. Ct. Appeals (1st cir.), NH, 1990; assoc. justice U.S. Supreme Ct., Washington, 1990—. Trustee Concord Hosp., 1973—85, pres. bd. trustees, 1978—84; bd. overseers Dartmouth Med. Sch., 1981—87. Mem.: N.H. Bar Assn., N.H. Hist. Soc. (v.p. 1980—85, trustee 1976—85), Phi Beta Kappa. Republican. Episcopalian.

SOUTHERN, ROBERT ALLEN, lawyer; b. Independence, Mo., July 17, 1930; s. James Allen and Josephine (Ragland) S.; m. Cynthia Agnes Drews, May 17, 1952; children: David D., William A., James M., Kathryn S. O'Brien. BS in Polit. Sci., Northwestern U., 1952, LL.B., 1954. Bar: Ill. 1955. Assoc. Mayer, Brown & Platt (now Mayer, Brown, Rowe & Maw) , Chgo., 1954-64, ptnr., 1965-96, mng. ptnr., 1978-91, L.A., 1991-96; CEO So. Assocs., Gurnee, Ill., 1997—. Editor in chief Northwestern U. Law Rev., 1953-54. Trustee, v.p., gen. counsel LaRabida Children's Hosp. and Rsch. Ctr., Chgo., 1974-89; trustee Kenilworth (Ill.) Union Ch., 1980-88; pres. Joseph Sears Sch. Bd., 1977-79; trustee Rush-Presbyn.-St. Luke's Med. Ctr., 1983-91, life trustee, 1991—; bd. dirs. Boys and Girls Clubs Chgo., 1986-91; governing mem. Orchestral Assn. Chgo., 1988-93. With U.S. Army, 1955-57. Mem. ABA, Chgo. Bar Assn., Lawyers Club Chgo., Order of Coif, Indian Hill Club, Chgo. Club. Banking, Corporate, general, Securities. Office: 7600 Bittersweet Dr Gurnee IL 60031-5110 E-mail: rsouthern2@earthlink.net.

SOUTHGATE, RICHARD W. lawyer, director; b. Chgo., May 6, 1929; m. Anna Fisher Hart, Aug. 25, 1951; children— Richard W., Sarah B., Rebecca W. C., John P. AB cum laude, Harvard U., 1951, LL.B. cum laude, 1954. Bar: Mass. 1954. Assoc. Covington & Burling, Washington, 1956-58; assoc., then ptnr., chmn. policy com. Ropes & Gray, Boston, 1958-94; vol.

atty. Greater Boston Legal Svcs., 1995—. Mem. Mass. Commn. on Anti-Takeover Laws; adj. prof. Northeastern U. Sch. Law, Boston, 1996-97. Author: (with Donald W. Glazer) Massachusetts Corporation Law and Practice, 1991. Moderator, Town of Manchester, Mass., 1976-94. Served as sgt. U.S. Army, 1954-56 Mem. Boston Bar Assn., ABA, Mass. Bar Assn. Clubs: Essex County, Somerset; Harvard (Boston). Home: 22 School St Manchester MA 01944-1336 Office: Greater Boston Legal Svcs 197 Friend St Boston MA 02114-1802

SOUTTER, THOMAS DOUGLAS, retired lawyer; b. N.Y.C., Nov. 1, 1934; s. Thomas G. and Hildreth H. (Callanan) S.; m. Virginia Hovenden; children: Alexander D., Christopher A., Hadley H. BA, U. Va., 1955, LL.B., 1962; postgrad., Advanced Mgmt. Program, Harvard U., 1980. Bar: N.Y. 1962, R.I. 1969. Atty. Breed, Abbott & Morgan, N.Y.C., 1962-68; with Textron Inc., Providence, 1968-95, gen. counsel, 1970-95, v.p., 1971-80, sr. v.p., 1980-85, exec. v.p., gen. counsel, 1985-95; cons., 1995-97. Mem. adv. bd. Internat. and Comparative Law Ctr., 1975-95; mem. Assn. Gen. Counsel; bd. dirs. Avco Fin. Svcs., Inc., 1985-95, Paul Revere Corp. 1993-95; trustee New England Legal Found. Nat. chmn. ann. giving campaign U. Va. Law Sch., 1992-94, mem. exec. com. campaign, 1995-2000; former trustee Providence Preservation Soc., Providence Performing Arts Ctr.; mem. U. Va. Arts and Scis. Alumni Coun.; mem. Narragansett coun. Boy Scouts Am. Lt. USNR, 1955-59. Mem. ABA, N.Y. State Bar Assn., R.I. Bar Assn., Internat. Bar Assn. Antitrust, Corporate, general, Private international. Office: 2 White Birch Ln Barrington RI 02806-4932 E-mail: tdsout@aol.com.

SOUZA, JOSEPH CHARLES, lawyer; b. Pitts., Aug. 27, 1947; s. Charles Richard Souza and Frances F. Fana; m. Marcia Gembral, Mar. 30, 1984; children: Jeff, Garrett, Lizzie. BA, U. Conn., 1970; JD, U. Louisville, 1974. Bar: Ky. 1974. Lectr., various legal topics, 1996—2002; asst. county pros. atty., Louisville, 1976—80. Office: Garner Ewing & Souza Ste 1600 Meidinger Tower Louisville KY 40202

SOWALD, BEATRICE KRONICK, lawyer; b. Amsterdam, N.Y., May 29, 1927; d. Maurice and Rose (Gray) Kronick; widowed; children: Malcolm, Debra, Heather. BA, Ohio State U., 1948, JD, 1966. Bar: Ohio 1966, U.S. Supreme Ct. 1987, U.S. Dist. Ct. (so. dist.) Ohio, 1970. Supr. Legal Aid Soc., Columbus, Ohio, 1967-80; ptnr. Sowald & Sowald, Columbus, 1980-84; judge Franklin County Ct. of Common Pleas, Columbus, 1984, Franklin County Mcpl. Ct., Columbus, 1985; ptnr. Sowald, Sowald & Clouse, Columbus, 1986—. Mem. Ohio Bd. of Bar Examiners, Columbus, 1996-99. Editor: Ohio Domestic Relations Law, 1996, 2002. Trustee Legal Aid Soc., Columbus, 1989-97. Mem. Ohio State Bar Assn. (coun. of delegates 1983—), Columbus Bar Assn. (Professionalism award 1993), Franklin County Trial Lawyers. Family and matrimonial, Probate (including wills, trusts). Home: 125 Eastmoor Blvd Columbus OH 43209-2017 Office: Sowald Sowald & Clouse 400 S 5th St Ste 101 Columbus OH 43215-5430

SOWARD, JOE WELDON, II, lawyer; b. Saratoga Springs, NY, July 17, 1969; s. Joe Weldon and Marlene Reddell Soward; m. Kendra Kaye Walker, Aug. 21, 1993; children: Jacob Weldon, Joshua Walker. Student, U. Houston, 1987—91; BS, U. Tex., Tyler, 1992; JD, St. Mary's U., 1997. Bar: Tex., U.S. Dist. Ct. (ea. dist.) Tex. 99. Gen. mgr. GTJ Internat., Tyler, 1992—94; intern Hon. Harry S. McKee, Tyler, 1992; assoc. Collins, Norman & Basinger, P.C., Dallas, 1998—2000, Sucheck & Assocs., P.C., Ft. Worth, 2000, Mararhan & Assocs., P.C., Ft. Worth, 2000—01; ptnr. Staton & Taylor. P.C., Ft. Worth, 2001—. Contbr. articles to profl. jours. Bd. dirs. Boys and Girls Club Tarrant County, Ft. Worth, 2000—. Named one of Top Trial Lawyers in Tarrant County, Ft. Worth, Tex. mag., 2002. Mem.: ATLA, Tarrant County Trial Lawyers Assn., Tex. Trial Lawyers Assn. Democrat. Baptist. Avocations: hunting, martial arts, cooking. Personal injury (including property damage), Transportation, Product liability. Office: 902 S Jennings Fort Worth TX 76104 Fax: 817-870-2781. E-mail: joesoward@charter.net.

SOWERS, WESLEY HOYT, lawyer, management consultant; b. Whiting, Ind., Aug. 26, 1905; s. Samuel Walter and Bertha E. (Spurrier) S.; m. Gladys Krueger, Jan. 21, 1929; children: Penny (Mrs. David Buxton), Wesley Hoyt Jr. BS, Purdue U., 1926, MS, 1927; JD, DePaul U., 1941; grad., Advanced Mgmt. Program, Harvard, 1960. Bar: Ill. 1940; registered patent atty. and practitioner ICC. Chemist Shell Oil Co., East Chicago, Ind., 1927-29; sales engr. Nat. Lead Co., St. Louis, 1929-31; lab. supr. patent atty. Pure Oil Co., Chgo., 1932-42; v.p. Bay Chem. Co., New Orleans, 1942-50, Frontier Chem. Co., Wichita, Kans., 1950-57; pres. Frontier Chem. div. Vulcan Materials Co., 1957-65; exec. v.p., dir. Vulcan Materials Co., Birmingham, 1958-65; mgmt. counsel, 1965—. Mem. health professions vis. com. Wichita State U. Patentee in field Past chmn. Met. Planning Commn., Wichita and Sedgwick County, 1958; commr. Kans. Econ. Devel. Bd.; chmn. Kansas Com. for Constitutional Revision, Sedgwick County U.S. Savs. Bonds Sales; past chmn. Kans. Radio Free Europe; past mem. adv. com. Kans. Geol. Survey; mem. Kans. Senate, 1970-81; former mem. engring. adv. council Sch. Engring. and Architecture, Kans. State U.; regent, trustee Wichita State U., HCA/Wesley Med. Ctr., Wichita; bd. dirs. Health Systems Agy. of Southeast Kans., Bd. of Health Sedgwick County, Inst. Logopedics, Quivira council Boy Scouts Am., YMCA, Health Systems Agy. S.E. Kans.; past trustee Midwest Research Inst.; mem. adv. bd. Kans. U. Bus. Sch.; vis. com. Coll. Health Profession, Wichita State U.; chmn. Kans. Health Care Providers Malpractice Commn.; mem. Kans. Health Care Costs Commn., Kans. Health Coordinating Council, Wichita/Sedgwick County Bd. Health; mem. gov.'s adv. commn. Kans. Dept. Health and Environment. Mem. AAAS, Kans. C. of C. (past pres., past dir.), Wichita C. of C. (past pres. 1959, past dir., Uncommon Citizen award 1988), Kans. Assn. Commerce and Industry (past pres., dir.), Am. Chem. Soc., AAAS, Smithsonian Assocs., Soc. Chem. Industry, Ill. Bar Assn., Wichita Bar Assn., Phi Delta Theta. Lodges: Rotary. Home and Office: 600 W Arapaho Rd Apt 1034 Richardson TX 75080

SOYSTER, MARGARET BLAIR, lawyer; b. Washington, Aug. 5, 1951; d. Peter and Eliza (Shumaker) S. AB magna cum laude, Smith Coll., 1973; JD, U. Va., 1976. Bar: N.Y. 1977, U.S. Dist. Ct. (so. and ea. dists.) N.Y. 1977, U.S. Ct. Appeals (2nd cir.) 1979, U.S. Supreme Ct. 1981, U.S. Ct. Appeals (4th cir.) 1982, U.S. ct. Appeals (11th cir.) 1987, U.S. Ct. Appeals (7th cir.) 1991, U.S. Ct. Appeals (3d cir.) 1992. Assoc. Rogers & Wells, N.Y.C., 1976-84, ptnr., 1984-99, Clifford Chance U.S. LLP, N.Y.C., 2000—. Mem. ABA, Assn. of Bar of City of N.Y., Nat. Assn. Coll. and Univ. Attys., Phi Beta Kappa. Federal civil litigation, Labor (including EEOC, Fair Labor Standards Act, labor-management relations, NLRB, OSHA), State civil litigation. Office: Clifford Chance US LLP 200 Park Ave Ste 5200 New York NY 10166-0005

SOZANSKY, MICHAEL WILLIAM, JR., lawyer; b. Charleroi, Pa., June 17, 1949; s. Michael William and Mildred Marie (Buchta) S.; m. Deborah Ann Conti, June 15, 1985; children: Sarah Elizabeth, Alexander Michael. BA, Duquesne U., 1971; JD, Temple U., 1980. Bar: Pa. 1980, N.J. 1982, U.S. Dist. Ct. N.J. 1982, U.S. Tax Ct. 1989, U.S. Ct. Appeals (3d cir.) 1989, U.S. Supreme Ct. 1989, U.S. Dist. Ct. (ea. dist.) Pa. 1991. Legal aide N.J. Civil Svc. Commn., Trenton, 1976-80; law clk. to presiding justice N.J. Tax Ct., Trenton, 1980-81; dep. atty. gen. State of N.J., Trenton, 1981-84; assoc. Schaff, Mahon, Motiuk, Gladstone & Conley, Flemington, N.J., 1985-87; pres. Ligorano & Sozansky, P.C., Flemington, 1987—98, Archer & Greiner, P.C., 1998—2001, Norris, McLaughlin & Marcus, P.A., 2001—. Cons. N.J. Dept. Pers., Trenton, 1989-91. Mem. Hunterdon County Facilities Com., 1989-96; pres. Hunterdon County Edn. Found., 1993-2002. Mem. ATLA, ABA, N.J. Bar Assn. (trustee 2003-), Hunterdon County Bar Assn. (pres. 1998-99), Assn. Trial Lawyers N.J. Republican. Roman Catholic. Avocation: computer science. General civil litigation, Corporate, general, State and local taxation. Office: Norris Mclaughlin & Marcus PA 721 Rt 202-206 Somerville NJ 08876

SPACE, THEODORE MAXWELL, lawyer; b. Binghamton, N.Y., Apr. 3, 1938; s. Maxwell Evans and Dorothy Marie (Boone) S.; m. Susan Shultz, Aug. 18, 1962 (div. Apr. 1979); children: William Schuyler, Susanna; m. Martha Collins, Apr. 6, 1991. AB, Harvard U., 1960; LLB, Yale U., 1966. Bar: Conn., 1966, U.S. Dist. Ct. Conn. 1966, U.S. Supreme Ct. 1970, U.S. Tax Ct. 1989, U.S. Ct. Appeals (2nd cir.) 1967, U.S. Ct. Appeals (6th cir.) 1992, U.S. Ct. Appeals (11th cir.) 1994, U.S. Dist. Ct. (ea. dist.) Mich. 1997. Assoc. Shipman & Goodwin LLP, Hartford, Conn., 1966-71, ptnr., 1971—, mng. ptnr., 1984-87, adminstv. ptnr., 1988-91. Mem. Bloomfield (Conn.) Bd. Edn., 1973-85, chmn., 1975-85; treas. Citizens Scholarship Found., Bloomfield, 1971-73, bd. dirs., 1973-91; mem. Bloomfield Human Rels. Commn., 1973-75; mem. Bloomfield Town Dem. Com., 1976-83; corporator Hartford Pub. Libr., 1976—; trustee Conn. Hist. Soc., 1997—, mem. libr. com., 1990—, chair, 1993-2000; chmn. fin. com., coun. mem. Unitarian Soc. Hartford, 1988-91. Lt. (j.g.) USN, 1960-63. Mem. ABA, Conn. Bar Assn. (mem. exec. com. adminstrv. law sect. 1980—), Hartford County Bar Assn., Am. Law Inst., Am. Health Lawyers Assn., Conn. Health Lawyers Assn., Swift's Inn, Hartford Club. Democrat. Unitarian Universalist. Avocations: reading, classical music. Administrative and regulatory, General civil litigation, Health. Home: 59 Prospect St Bloomfield CT 06002-3038 Office: Shipman & Goodwin LLP One American Row Hartford CT 06103-2833

SPAEDER, ROGER CAMPBELL, lawyer; b. Cleve., Dec. 20, 1943; s. Fred N. and Luceil (Campbell) S.; m. Frances DeSales Sutherland, Sept. 7, 1968; chidlren: Michael, Matthew. BS, Bowling Green U., 1965; JD with honors, George Washington U., 1970. Bar: D.C. 1971, U.S. Dist. Ct. D.C. 1971, U.S. Ct. Appeals (D.C. cir.) 1971, U.S. Ct. Claims 1979, U.S. Dist. Ct. Md. 1984, U.S. Ct. Appeals (2d and 4th cirs.) 1985, U.S. Supreme Ct. 1976. Asst. U.S. atty. D.C., Washington, 1971-76; ptnr. Zuckerman Spaeder LLP, Washington, 1976—. Faculty Atty. Gen. Advocacy Inst., 1974-76, Nat. Inst. Trial Adv., 1978-79; adj. faculty Georgetown U. Law Ctr., 1979-80, Am. U. Ctr. Adminstrn. Justice, 1976-79; lectr. D.C. Bar Continuing Legal Edn. Programs, 1980-90; Cardozo Prize judge Yale Law Sch., 1992; master Edward Bennett Williams Inn of Ct., 1996—; mem. D.C. Cir. Jud. Conf., 1991. Contbr. articles to profl. jours. and chpts. to books. Recipient Spl. Achievement award Dept. Justice, 1971. Mem. ATLA, ABA (co-chair com. on complex crimes litigation 1989-92, divsn. co-dir. sect. litigation 1992-94), Bar Assn. D.C. (lectr. Criminal Practice Inst. 1977-80), D.C. Bar (com. criminal jury instrns. 1972, divsn. cts. lawyers, adminstrn. of justice 1976-78; adv. com. continuing legal edn. 1986), Def. Rsch. Inst., Assn. Plaintiffs' Trial Attys., Nat. Assn. Criminal Def. Lawyers, Omicron Delta Kappa. Federal civil litigation, Criminal. Home: 7624 Georgetown Pike Mc Lean VA 22102-1412 Office: Zuckerman Spaeder LLP 1201 Connecticut Ave NW Fl 12 Washington DC 20036-2605

SPAETH, EDMUND BENJAMIN, JR., retired lawyer, retired law educator, former judge; b. Washington, June 10, 1920; s. Edmund B. and Lena (Link) S. AB magna cum laude, Harvard U., 1942, LLB, 1948. Bar: Pa. 1949. Judge Ct. of Common Pleas, Phila., 1964-73, Superior Ct of Pa., 1973-86, pres. judge, 1983-86; of counsel Pepper Hamilton LLP, Phila., 1986—2002. Adj. prof. U. Pa. Law Sch., 1974-97; chair Pennsylvanians for Modern Cts., 1987-2000. Fellow Am. Bar Found. (life); mem. Am. Law Inst. (life), Am. Judicature soc., Order of Coif, Phi Beta Kappa. Home: Cathedral Village Apt L-206 600 E Cathedral Rd Philadelphia PA 19128-1933

SPAETH, NICHOLAS JOHN, lawyer, former state attorney general; b. Mahnomen, Minn., Jan. 27, 1950; AB, Stanford U., 1972, JD, 1977; BA, Oxford U., Eng., 1974. Bar: Minn. 1979, U.S. Dist. Ct. (Minn.) 1979, U.S. Ct. Appeals (8th cir.) 1979, N.D. 1980, U.S. Dist. Ct. (N.D.) 1980, U.S. Supreme Ct. 1984. Law clk. U.S. Ct. Appeals (8th cir.), Fargo, N.D., 1977-78; law clk. to Justice Byron White U.S. Supreme Ct., Washington, 1978-79; pvt. practice, 1979-84; atty. gen. State of N.D., Bismarck, 1984-93; ptnr. Dorsey & Whitney, Fargo, 1993-99, Oppenheimer, Wolff & Donnelly, Mpls., Calif., 1999, Cooley Godward, Palo Alto, Calif., 1999—. Adj. prof. law U. Minn., 1980-83. Rhodes scholar, 1972-74. Democrat. Roman Catholic. Criminal. Office: 5200 Metcalf Ave Overland Park KS 66202-1265 E-mail: nicholas.spaeth@ercgroup.com.

SPAHN, GARY JOSEPH, lawyer; b. N.Y.C., July 23, 1949; s. Harry G. and Mary (Hopkins) S.; m. Lois Luttinger, Aug. 9, 1975; children: Gary J. Jr., Lori J. BA, L.I. U., 1971, MA, 1976; JD, U. Richmond, 1975. Bar: Va. 1975, U.S. Ct. Appeals (4th cir.) 1975, U.S. Supreme Ct. 1980. Law clk. to Hon. Judge Dortch U.S. Dist. Ct. (ea. dist.) Va., Richmond, 1975—77; from assoc. to ptnr. Troutman Sanders LLP (formerly Mays & Valentine), Richmond, 1977—, now ptnr., past chmn. products liability and ins. sect. Lectr. in field, 1980—; mem. judicial conf. U.S. Ct. Appeals (4th cir.). Co-author: Virginia Law of Products Liability, 1990. Pres. Southhampton Citizens Assn., Richmond, 1982-85; bd. dirs. Southhampton Recreation Assn., Richmond. 1983, Chesterfield County Crime Solvers, 1997—; mem. coun. Southside Montessori Sch., Richmond, 1983-85. With USAF, 1967-73. Mem. ABA (litigation and tort and ins. sects.), Internat. Assn. Def. Counsel, Am. Assn. Ins. Attys., Assoc. Def. Trial Attys., Def. Rsch. Inst., Va. Assn. Def. Attys., Va. Mfrs. Assn., Products Liability Adv. Counsel, Va. Power Boat (commodore). Avocations: boating, basketball, racquetball. General civil litigation, Insurance, Personal injury (including property damage). Office: Troutman Sanders LLP PO Box 1122 1111 E Main St Richmond VA 23219-3531

SPAIN, THOMAS B. retired state supreme court justice; Justice Ky. Supreme Ct, Frankfort, 1991-95; ret., 1995; of counsel Whitfield & Cox P.S.C. Office: Whitfield & Cox PSC 29 E Center St Madisonville KY 42431-2037

SPALDING, CATHERINE, lawyer; b. Lebanon, Ky. d. Hugh C. and Bernadette (Hill) S. BS in Biology, Spalding U., Louisville, 1970; JD, U. Louisville, 1983. Bar: Ky., U.S. Ct. Appeals (6th cir.), Ct. Vets. Appeals, Fed. Dist. Ct. Pvt. practice law, Louisville, 1983—; asst. county atty. Jefferson County, 1993—2000, family ct. atty., guardian ad litem, 2000—. Editor newsletter Ky. Bar Assn. Family Law Sect.; editor book supplement: Kentucky Family Law, 1990. Past bd. dirs. LWV, Portland Mus. Louisville. Mem. ABA, Ky. Bar Assn. (chairperson family law sect. 1990-91, spkr., moderator seminars), Louisville Bar Assn. (chairperson social security sect. 1992-93), AAUW (past bd. dirs.), DAR (past bd. dirs.) Optimist Club (past bd. dirs.), LWV (past bd. dirs.). Avocation: snow skiing. Family and matrimonial, Juvenile, Personal injury (including property damage). Home: 1917 Trevilian Way Louisville KY 40205-2139 Office: Ste 3 325 W Ormsby Ave Louisville KY 40203-2907 Fax: 502-634-4488.

SPALLONE, JEANNE FIELD, retired state judge; b. N.Y.C., Jan. 18, 1928; d. Charles William and Flora (Kopp) Field; m. Daniel Francis Spallone, June 4, 1950; children: Janne Field Spallone, Niel Francis Spallone, James Field Spallone. BS, U. Conn., 1950. News and feature writer, reporter Middletown (Conn.) Press, 1952-53, 59-65; adminstrv. asst. to amb. Hon. Chester Bowles, Essex, Conn., 1953-56; mem. Conn. State Legislature, Hartford, 1959-61; columnist op-ed Middletown Press, 1993-96; judge of probate State of Conn., Dept. Judiciary, Dist. of Deep River, Hartford, 1979-95. Contbr. articles to jours., books, newspapers. Trustee, historian Deep River Hist. Soc., 1976-94; chmn. bd. dirs. Winthrop Cemetery Assn., 1978—. Mem. Conn. Order Women Legislators, Soroptimists (pres. local chpt. 1982-84), Block Island (R.I.) club (pres. 1982-84). Democrat. Avocations: family history, travel. Home and Office: 6 Westbrook Rd Deep River CT 06417-1504

SPALTY, EDWARD ROBERT, lawyer; b. New Haven, Oct. 1, 1946; s. Kermit and Elinor Turgeon; m. Suzy Clune; children: Thomas John, Kathleen Tess. AB, Emory U., 1968; JD, Columbia U., 1973. Bar: Mo. 1975, U.S. Dist. Ct. (we. dist.) Mo. 1975, U.S. Ct. Claims 1977, U.S. Ct. Appeals (8th cir.) 1984, U.S. Supreme Ct. 1994, Nebr. 1997, Kans. 1998, U.S. Ct. Appeals (10th cir.) 1999, Colo. 03. Assoc. Webster & Sheffield, N.Y.C., 1973-74; ptnr. Armstrong Teasdale LLP, Kansas City, Mo., 1991-2001. Contbr. articles to profl jours. Chmn. bd. dirs. Mo. Easter Seals, 1990—92; founding mem. Heartland Franchise Assn.; bd. dirs., vice chmn. affiliate svcs. com. Nat. Easter Seal Soc. With U.S. Army, 1968—70. Mem.: ABA (litigation sect, franchising forum comt), Int Relations Coun Kansas City, Def Research Inst, Mo Orgn Def Attys, Lawyers Asn Kansas City, Kansas City Metropolitan Bar Asn (chmn antitrust and franchise law comt, co-chair 14th and 16h ann Nat Franchise Law Inst), Mo Bar Asn (civil rules and procedures comt), German-Am CofC (vpres Kansas City chpt), Nat Golf Club Kansas City (founder), Phi Delta, Pi Sigma Alpha, Sigma Nu. Federal civil litigation, State civil litigation, Franchising. Home: 13703 NW 73rd St Parkville MO 64152-1120 Office: Armstrong Teasdale LLP 2345 Grand Blvd Ste 2000 Kansas City MO 64108-2617 Business E-Mail: espalty@armstrongteasdale.com.

SPANBOCK, MAURICE SAMUEL, lawyer; b. N.Y.C., Jan. 6, 1924; s. Benjamin and Belle (Ward) S.; m. Marion Rita Heyman, Nov. 21, 1954; children: Jonathan H., Betsy W. BA, Columbia U., N.Y.C., 1944; LLB, Harvard U., 1950. Bar: N.Y. 1950. Assoc. Goldstone and Wolff, N.Y.C., 1950-52; ptnr. Carro and Spanbock (name changed to Carro, Spanbock, Kaster et al), N.Y.C., 1952-94; of counsel Kleinberg Kaplan Wolff & Cohen, N.Y.C., 1994—. Trustee Carnegie Coun. on Ethics and Internat. Affairs, N.Y.C., 1980-86, 93-2000, hon. trustee, 2002--, chmn. bd., 1987-92; hon. pres. Lincoln Square Synagogue, N.Y.C.; sec. Ohr Torah Stone Instns. Israel. Cpl. AUS, 1943-46, ETO. Mem. ABA (chmn. com. on taxation, patent, trademark and copyright law sect. 1979-81), Assn. of Bar of City of N.Y. (com. on copyright 1965-67, art law com. 1977-80, 86-88), Fed. Bar Coun., Nat. Panel Arbitrators, Am. Abitration Assn., Practising Law Inst. (panel on copyrights, 1979). Jewish. Corporate, general, Entertainment, Estate planning. Home: 88 Central Park W New York NY 10023-5209 Office: Kleinberg Kaplan Wolff & Cohen 551 5th Ave Fl 18 New York NY 10176-1800

SPARKMAN, STEVEN LEONARD, lawyer; b. Sarasota, Fla., May 30, 1947; s. Simeon Clarence and Ursula (Wahlstrom) S.; m. Terry Jeanne Gibbs, Aug. 23, 1969; children: Joanna Jeanne, Kevin Leonard. BA, Fla. State U., 1969, JD, 1972. Bar: Fla. 1972, U.S. Dist. Ct. (mid. dist.) Fla. 1974, U.S. Ct. Appeals (5th cir.) 1975. Legal rsch. asst. Office Gen. Counsel, Fla. Dept. Revenue, Tallahassee, 1971; legis. intern com. on community affairs Fla. Ho. of Reps., Tallahassee, 1971-72; jud. rsch. aide Fla. 2d Dist. Ct. Appeals, Lakeland, 1972-73; asst. county atty. Hillsborough County, Tampa, Fla., 1973-75; assoc. Carlton, Fields, Ward, Emmanuel, Smith & Cutler, P.A., Tampa, 1975-80, sr. atty., 1980-2001; pvt. practice Plant City, Fla., 2001—. Mem. bd. visitors Fla. State U. Coll. Law, 1994-00. Deacon 1st Bapt. Ch., Plant City, 1980—; sec., bd. dirs. Bapt. Towers Plant City, Inc., 1981—84; bd. dirs. Tampa Kiwanis Found., 1997—2000. 1st lt. USAFR, 1973. Mem.: Plant City Bar Assn., Hillsborough County Bar Assn., Fla. Bar Assn. (exec. coun. local govt. law sect. 1978—79), Kiwanis (Plant City). Democrat. Land use and zoning (including planning), Property, real (including real estate development, water), Estate planning. Office: Steven L Sparkman PA 212 N Collins St Ste 1 Plant City FL 33563 E-mail: sls@sparklaw.com.

SPARKS, BILLY SCHLEY, lawyer; b. Marshall, Mo., Mar. 1, 1923; s. John and Clarinda (Schley) S.; m. Dorothy O. Stone, May 14, 1946; children: Stephen Stone, Susan Lee Sparks Raben Taylor, John David. AB, Harvard U., 1945, LLB, 1949. Bar: Mo. 1949. Ptnr. Langworthy, Matz & Linde, Kansas City, Mo., 1949-62, Linde, Thomason, Fairchild, Langworthy, Kohn & Van Dyke, Kansas City, 1962-91; ret., 1991. Mem. Mission (Kans.) Planning Coun., 1954-63; treas. Johnson County (Kans.) Dem. Ctrl. Com., 1958-64; candidate for rep. 10th Dist., Kans., 1956, 3d Dist., 1962; mem. Dist. 100 Sch. Bd., 1964-68, pres., 1967-69; mem. Dist. 512 Sch. Bd., 1969-73, pres., 1971-72; del. Dem. Nat. Conv., 1964; ; mem. Kans. Civil Svc. Commn., 1975-90. Lt. USAAF, 1944-46. Mem. ABA, Mo. Bar Assn., Kansas City Bar Assn., Law Assn. Kansas City, Harvard Law Sch. Assn. Mo. (past dir.), Nat. Assn. Sch. Bds. (mem. legis. com. 1968-73), St. Andrews Soc., Harvard Club (v.p. 1953-54), The Kansas City (Mo.) Club, Milburn Golf and Country Club, Am. Legion, Kansas City C. of C. (legis. com. 1956-82), Mem. Christian Ch. Federal civil litigation, State civil litigation, General practice. Home and Office: 8517 W 90th Ter Shawnee Mission KS 66212-3053

SPARKS, DAVID THOMAS, lawyer; b. Bowling Green, Ky., Dec. 17, 1968; s. Lee Thomas and Ann Louis S. BS, We. Ky., 1992; JD, U. Ky., 1995. Bar: Ky. 1995, U.S. Dist. Ct. (we. dist.) Ky. 1995, U.S. Dist. Ct. (ea. dist.) Ky. 1996. Assoc. atty. Bell, Orr, Ayers & Moore, Bowling Green, 1995—2000; atty. Mike Bran Attys. at Law, PSC and David T. Sparks Law Office, Bowling Green, 2000—. Deacon First Christian Ch., Bowling Green, 1988-98, elder, 1998-, mem. personnel com., 1998-2002. Mem. ABA, Ky. Bar Assn., Bowling Green Warren County Bar Assn., Future Bus. Leaders Am., Phi Beta Lambda. Republican. Mem. Christian Ch. Avocations: basketball, softball, model railroading, marine aquarium, reading. General civil litigation, Personal injury (including property damage), Insurance. Home: 2512 Thompson Dr Bowling Green KY 42104-4375 Office: 1700 Destiny Ln Bowling Green KY 42104

SPARKS, JOHN EDWARD, lawyer; b. Rochester, Ind., July 3, 1930; s. Russell Leo and Pauline Anna (Whittenberger) S.; m. Margaret Joan Snyder, Sept. 4, 1954; children: Thomas Edward, William Russell, Kathryn Chapman McCarthy. AB, Ind. U., 1952; LL.B., U. Calif., Berkeley, 1957; postgrad., London Sch. Econs., 1957-58. Bar: Calif. 1958, U.S. Supreme Ct., 1968. Assoc. Brobeck, Phleger & Harrison, San Francisco, 1958-66, ptnr., 1967-95, of counsel, 1996—2003. Adj. prof. law U. San Francisco, 1967-69; pres. Legal Aid Soc. San Francisco, 1978-79, dir., 1971-81. Editor U. Calif. Law Rev., 1956-57. Served to 1st lt. Q.M.C. U.S. Army, 1952-54, Korea. Recipient Wheeler Oak Meritorious award U. Calif., Berkeley, 1986. Fellow Am. Bar Found., Am. Coll. Trial Lawyers; mem. State Bar Calif., Bar Assn. San Francisco (bd. dirs. 1974-75), ABA, Am. Judicature Soc., Boalt Hall Alumni Assn. (pres. 1983-84), Pacific Union Club (San Francisco). Democrat. Administrative and regulatory, General civil litigation, State civil litigation. Office: 111 Southampton Ave Berkeley CA 94707

SPARKS, SAM, federal judge; b. 1939; BA, U. Tex., 1961, LLB, 1963. Aide Rep. Homer Thornberry, 1963; law clk. to Hon. Homer Thornberry U.S. Dist. Ct. (we. dist.) Tex., 1963-65; assoc. to ptnr., shareholder Hardie, Grambling, Sims & Galatzan (and successor firms), El Paso, Tex., 1965-91; dist. judge U.S. Dist. Ct. (we. dist.) Tex., 1991—. Fellow Am. Coll. Trial Lawyers, Tex. Bar Found. (life); mem. Am. Bd. Trial Advocates (advocate), State Bar Tex. Office: US Dist Ct Judge 200 W 8th St Ste 100 Austin TX 78701-2333

SPARKS, STEPHEN STONE, lawyer; b. Kansas City, Mo., June 21, 1954; s. Billy Schley and Dorothy (Stone) S.; m. Martha Nelson, Oct. 19, 1979; children: Matthew Nelson, Adam Nelson. BA, New Coll. of U. of South Fla., 1976; JD with distinction, U. Mo., Kansas City, 1979. Bar: Mo. 1979, U.S. Dist. Ct. (we. dist.) Mo. 1979, U.S. Dist. Ct. Kans. 1998. Assoc.

Linde, Thomson, Langworthy, Kohn & Van Dyke P.C., Kansas City, 1979-82, ptnr., 1982-91, Smith, Gill, Fisher & Butts, Kansas City, 1991-95, Bryan Cave LLP, Kansas City, 1995—. Mem. ABA, Kansas City Bar Assn., Lawyers Assn. K.C. Mo., Nat. Assn. Bond Lawyers, Milburn Country Club, Shadow Glen Golf Club. Democrat. Avocation: golf. Corporate, general, Municipal (including bonds), Property, real (including real estate development, water). Home: 10818 W 102nd St Overland Park KS 66214-2539 Office: Bryan Cave LLP 1200 Main St Fl 35 Kansas City MO 64105-2122 E-mail: sssparks@BryanCave.com.

SPARROW, HERBERT GEORGE, III, lawyer, educator; b. Ft. Bragg, N.C., May 26, 1936; s. Herbert George and Virginia (Monroe) S.; m. Nancy Woodruff, Mar. 4, 1962; children: Amy Winslow, Edward Harrison, Herbert G. IV, Alison Kidder. AB cum laude, Princeton U., 1958; JD, U. Mich., 1961. Bar: Mich. 1961, Calif. 1964, D.C. 1979, U.S. Ct. Claims 1982, U.S. Tax Ct. 1983, U.S. Ct. Mil. Appeals 1962, U.S. Supreme Ct. 1976. Assoc. Dickinson Wright PLLC, Detroit, 1965-70, ptnr., 1970—. Adj. prof. Detroit Coll. Law, Mich. State U., 1977-99. Author numerous articles environ. law.; speaker in field. Bd. dirs. Family Life Edn. Coun., Grosse Pointe, Mich., 1982-88, Adult Well-Being Svcs., Inc., Detroit, 1995-2001; cons. Adult Well-Being Svcs. Inc., 2001—. Capt. JAGC, U.S. Army, 1962-65. Mem. ABA, Mich. Bar Assn. (rep. assembly 1979-85, environ. law sect. coun. 1985-91), Calif. Bar Assn., D.C. Bar Assn., Detroit Bar Assn., Am. Arbitration Assn. (panel arbitrators 1975—), Mich. State Bar Found. (fellow 1989—), Environment Law Inst. (assoc.), Phi Delta Phi (pres. Kent Inn Assn., Ann Arbor 1985-97). Corporate, general, Environmental. Office: Dickinson Wright PLLC 500 Woodward Ave Ste 4000 Detroit MI 48226-3416

SPARROW, ROBERT E. lawyer; b. N.Y.C., Feb. 26, 1935; s. Sidney G. and Dorothy (Boardman) S.; m. Marcia Galler, Apr. 14, 1957; children: Laurie Joy, David Gregory. BA, Columbia U., 1955, JD, 1957. Bar: N.Y. 1957, U.S. Dist. Ct. (ea. and so. dists.) N.Y. 1961, U.S. Supreme Ct. 1962. Ptnr. firm. Sparrow, Singer & Schreiber, N.Y.C., 1957—. Mem. com. on character and fitness, appellate divsn. N.Y. Supreme Ct., 1992-2000. Pres. Eastern Queens Dem. Club, N.Y., 1971, Pub. Sch. 188 PTA, Queens, 1971. Served as sgt. USAR, 1957-63. Mem. Queens Criminal Cts. Bar Assn. (pres. 1971-72, Lawyer of Yr. 1993), Queens County Bar Assn. (vice chmn. criminal cts. com. 1973-76). Democrat. Jewish. Lodges: K.P., B'nai B'rith, Elks. Criminal, General practice, Personal injury (including property damage). Home: 21749 Stewart Rd Flushing NY 11364-3538 Office: Sparrow Singer & Schreiber 12510 Queens Blvd Kew Gardens NY 11415-1519

SPATT, ARTHUR DONALD, federal judge; b. 1925; Student, Ohio State U., 1943-44, 46-47; LLB cum laude, Bklyn. Law Sch., 1949. Assoc. Davidson & Davidson, N.Y.C., 1949, Lane, Winard, Robinson & Schorr, N.Y.C., 1950, Alfred S. Julien, N.Y.C., 1950-52, Florea & Florea, N.Y.C., 1953; pvt. practice N.Y.C., 1953-67, Spatt & Bauman, N.Y.C., 1967-78; justice 10th judicial cir. N.Y. State Supreme Ct., 1979-82; adminstrv. judge Nassau County, 1982-86; assoc. justice appellate div. Second Judicial Dept., 1986-89; dist. judge U.S. Dist. Ct. (ea. dist.) N.Y., Bklyn., 1989-90, Uniondale, N.Y., 1990-2000, Central Islip, N.Y., 2000—. Book review editor Bklyn. Law Review, 1948—49. Active Jewish War Vets. With USN, 1944—46. Mem. ABA, Assn. Supreme Ct. Justices State of N.Y., Bar Assn. Nassau County, Jewish Lawyers Assn. Nassau County, Long Beach Lawyers Assn. Office: Long Island Courthouse 1024 Federal Plaza Central Islip NY 11722-4445

SPATT, ROBERT EDWARD, lawyer; b. Bklyn., Mar. 26, 1956; s. Milton E. and Blanche S. (Bakstansky) S.; m. Lisa B. Malkin, Aug. 11, 1979; 1 child, Mark Eric. AB, Brown U., 1977; JD magna cum laude, U. Mich., 1980. Bar: N.Y. 1981. Assoc. Simpson Thacher & Bartlett, N.Y.C., 1980-87, ptnr., 1987—. Mem. ABA, N.Y. State Bar Assn., City of N.Y. Bar Assn., Order of Coif, ACLU. Avocations: photography, boating, reading. Corporate, general, Mergers and acquisitions, Securities. Office: Simpson Thacher & Bartlett 425 Lexington Ave New York NY 10017-3954 E-mail: RSpatt@stblaw.com.

SPEAKER, SUSAN JANE, lawyer; b. Dallas, Dec. 25, 1946; d. William R. and Jane E. (Aldrich) Turner; m. David C. Speaker, Dec. 21, 1968; children: David Allen, Melissa. BA, U. Ark., 1970, JD, 1985. Bar: Okla. 1985, U.S. Dist. Ct. (no., ea. and we. dists.) Okla. 1985. Assoc. Hall, Estill, Hardwick, Gable, Golden & Nelson, P.C., Tulsa, 1985-91; atty. Resolution Trust Corp., 1991-92; shareholder Speaker & Matthews, P.C., 1992-96; atty. Comml. Fin. Svcs., Inc., Tulsa, 1996-99; dir. properties and concessions Dollar Thrifty Automotive Group, Inc., 1999—. Editor U. Ark. Law Rev., 1983-85. Mem. ABA, ATLA, Okla. Bar Assn., Tulsa Bar Assn., Tulsa Title and Probate Lawyers Assn., Phi Beta Kappa, Delta Theta Phi. Corporate, general, Landlord-tenant, Property, real (including real estate development, water).

SPEAR, HARVEY M. lawyer; b. Providence, May 24, 1922; s. Alfred and Esther S.; m. Ruth Abramson, June 27, 1965; children: Jessica, Elizabeth Anne. AB, Brown U., 1942; LL.B., Harvard, 1948; MA, George Washington U., 1949, LL.M., 1952, S.JD, 1955. Bar: Mass. 1948, D.C. 1948, N.Y. 1954, U.S. Supreme Ct. 1954; CPA, Md. Asst. U.S. atty. D.C., 1948; legal asst. to chmn., asst. to vice chmn. SEC, 1948-50; spl. asst. to atty. gen. Dept. Justice, 1951-54; pvt. practice law N.Y.C. and Washington, 1956—; counsel Cadwalader Wickersham & Taft, N.Y.C., 1996—. Contbr. articles to profl. jours. Active Met. Opera Assn., 1961—2002. Mem. ABA, Assn. of Bar of City of N.Y. Home: 765 Park Ave New York NY 10021-4254 Office: 100 Maiden Ln New York NY 10038-4818 Home: 78 Hither Ln East Hampton NY 11937

SPEARS, LARRY JONELL, lawyer; b. Webb, Miss., Jan. 10, 1953; s. John Spears and Lillian Belle Embrey; m. Treycè L. Gaston, Jan. 14, 1989;children: Lyndzè Rae, Joshua Lawrence. BS, U. Ill., 1976, JD, 1979; MS, So. Ill. U., 1990. Bar: Ill. 1980. Asst. atty gen. Ill. Atty. Gen.'s Office, Murphysboro, 1980-84; asst. pub. defender Jackson County Pub. Defender's Office, Murphysboro, 1985; lectr. Crime Study Ctr., Carbondale, Ill., 1985; sole practice Carbondale, 1985-86; asst. state's atty. Peoria (Ill.) State's Atty. Office, 1986-90, Sangamon County State's Atty. Office, Springfield, Ill., 1990-94. Cons. Minority Contractors Assn., Carbondale, 1985; mem. Inmate Advocacy Group, Murphysboro, 1985-86; lectr. Sangamon State U., Springfield, 1990-96. Elijah P. Lovejoy scholar, 1972. Mem. Ill. State Bar Assn., McLean County Bar Assn., Adminstrn. of Justice Assn. (treas. 1984-85), Am. Soc. Criminology (discussant 1984-85), Midwest Criminal Justice Assn., Am. Judicature Soc., LWV, Sphinx Club (Carbondale), Phi Alpha Delta (treas. 1979), Alpha Phi Sigma. Republican. Baptist. Avocations: golf, fishing, songwriting, tennis, volleyball. Home: 1603 E Oakland Ave Bloomington IL 61701-5617 Office: Ill State U Student's Legal Svcs Normal IL 61761 E-mail: ljspear@mail.ilstu.edu.

SPEARS, ROBERT FIELDS, lawyer; b. Tulsa, Aug. 1, 1943; s. James Ward and Berneice (Fields) S.; m. Jacquelyn Castle, May 10, 1961; children: Jeff, Sally. BBA, Tex. Tech. U., 1965; JD, U. Tex., 1968. Bar: Tex. 1968. Assoc. Rain, Harrell, Emery, Young & Doke, Dallas, 1968-73, ptnr., 1974-87, Locke Purnell Rain Harrell, Dallas, 1987-91; gen. counsel Fin. Industries Corp., Austin, Tex., 1991-96; gen. counsel, sec. Lone Star Techn. Inc., Dallas, 1996—. Pres. Sr. Citizens of Greater Dallas, 1988. Mem. ABA, Tex. Bar Assn., Dallas Bar Assn., Dallas Country Club, Phi Delta Phi. Republican. Baptist. Avocation: tennis. Corporate, general, Mergers and acquisitions, Securities. Office: Lone Star Technologies Inc PO Box 803546 Dallas TX 75380-3546

SPEARS, RONALD DEAN, judge; b. Michigan City, Ind., July 30, 1951; s. Lonnie and Frances Ellen (Benad) Spears; m. Annette Jean Greffe, Dec. 22, 1973; 1 child, Donald Dean. BA, U. Ill., 1974; JD, So. Ill. U., 1977. Bar: Ill. 1977, U.S. Dist. Ct. (ctrl. and so. dists.) Ill. 1977, U.S. Ct. Appeals (7th cir.) 1977, U.S. Supreme Ct. 1983. Law clk. U.S. Dist. Ct., Springfield, Ill., 1977-79; ptnr. Miley, Meyer, Austin, Spears & Romano, P.C., Taylorville, Ill., 1979—93; judge Ill. Cir. Ct., 4th Jud. Cir., Taylorville, 1993—. Atty. City of Taylorville. Col. JAGC, Ill. Army N.G. Mem.: ABA, Lincoln-Douglas Am. Inn of Ct., Christian County Bar Assn. (pres. 1987), Ill. State Bar Assn. (bd. govs. 1997—2002), Toastmasters (pres. 1988), So. Ill. U. Law Sch. Alumni Assn. (pres. 1984), Optimists (pres. 1986, lt. gov. 1986—87). Home: 3501 Lake Dr Taylorville IL 62568-8930 Office: Ill Cir Ct 4th Jud Cir Rm 316 Christian County Courthouse Taylorville IL 62568-2245 E-mail: jspears@chipsnet.com.

SPEARS, SALLY, lawyer; b. San Antonio, Aug. 29, 1938; d. Adrian Anthony and Elizabeth (Wylie) S.; m. Tor Hultgreen, July 15, 1961 (div. Jan. 1983); children: Dagny Elizabeth, Sara Kirsten, Kara Spears. BA, U. Tex., 1960, LLB, 1965. Bar: Tex. 1961, Ill. 1971. Practice law, Stamford, Conn., 1966-67, Chgo., 1970-71, Northbrook, Ill., 1972-73, Toronto, Ont., Can., 1973-81; assoc. firm Cummings & Lockwood, Stamford, 1966-67, Kirkland & Ellis, Chgo., 1970-71; sr. atty. Allstate Ins. Co., Northbrook, Ill., 1971-73; gen. counsel, sec. Reed Paper Ltd., Reed Ltd., Toronto, 1973-78, Denison Mines Ltd., Toronto, 1978-81; pvt. practice law San Antonio, 1981—. Apptd. by Sec. of Def. to serve on Def. Adv. Com., Women in the Svcs., 1997-99. Author: Call Sign Revlon: The Life and Death of Navy Fighter Pilot Kara Hultgreen, 1998. Mem. Tex. Bar Assn., San Antonio Bar Assn., Bankruptcy Bar Assn., Bexar County Women's Bar Assn., San Antonio Country Club, The Club at Sonterra. Bankruptcy, Family and matrimonial, Probate (including wills, trusts). Home: 433 Evans Ave San Antonio TX 78209-3725 Office: Ste 106 8151 Broadway San Antonio TX 78209-1938 E-mail: sespears@swbell.net.

SPECTER, RICHARD BRUCE, lawyer; b. Phila., Sept. 6, 1952; s. Jacob E. and Marilyn B. (Kron) S.; m. Jill Ossenfort, May 30, 1981; children: Lauren Elizabeth, Lindsey Anne, Allison Lee. BA cum laude, Washington U., St. Louis, 1974; JD, George Washington U., 1977. Bar: Mo. 1977, U.S. Dist. Ct. (ea. and we. dists.) Mo. 1977, U.S. Ct. Appeals (8th cir.) 1977, Ill. 1978, Pa. 1978, U.S. Dist. Ct. (ea. dist.) Ill. 1979, U.S. Ct. Appeals (7th cir.) 1979, Calif. 1984, U.S. Dist. Ct. (cen. dist.) Calif. 1985, U.S. Ct. Appeals (9th cir.) 1986, U.S. Dist. Ct. (so. dist.) Calif. 1987, U.S. Dist. Ct. (no. dist.) Calif. 1988, U.S. Supreme Ct. 1999. Assoc. Coburn, Croft, Shepherd, Herzog & Putzell, St. Louis, 1977-79; ptnr. Herzog, Kral, Burroughs & Specter, St. Louis, 1979-82; exec. v.p. Uniqey Internat., Santa Ana, Calif., 1982-84; pvt. practice law L.A. and Irvine, Calif., 1984-87; ptnr. Corbett & Steelman, Irvine, 1987—. Instr. Nat. Law Ctr. George Washington U. 1975. Mem. ABA, Ill. Bar Assn., Mo. Bar Assn., Pa. Bar Assn., Calif. Bar Assn. Jewish. State civil litigation, Entertainment, Sports. Home: 37 Bull Run Irvine CA 92620-2510 Office: 18200 Von Karman Ave Ste 200 Irvine CA 92612-1086 E-mail: rspecter@corbsteel.com.

SPECTOR, DAVID M. lawyer; b. Rock Island, Ill., Dec. 20, 1946; s. Louis and Ruth (Vinikour) S.; m. Laraine Fingold, Jan. 15, 1972; children: Rachel, Laurence. BA, Northwestern U., 1968; JD magna cum laude, U. Mich., 1971. Bar: Ill. 1971, N.Y. 2002, U.S. Dist. Ct. (no. dist.) Ill. 1971, U.S. Ct. Appeals (7th cir.) 1977, U.S. Ct. Appeals (4th cir.) 1984, U.S. Dist. Ct. (cen. dist.) Ill. 1984, U.S. Ct. Appeals (2nd cir.) 2002, U.S. Supreme Ct. 1999. Clk. Ill. Supreme Ct., Chgo., 1971-72; ptnr., assoc. Isham, Lincoln & Beale, Chgo., 1972-87; ptnr. Mayer, Brown & Platt, Chgo., 1987-97, Hopkins & Sutter, Chgo., 1997-2001, Schiff, Hardin & Waite, Chgo., 2001—. Chmn. ABA Nat. Inst. on Ins. Co. Insolvency, Boston, 1986; co-chmn. ABA Nat. Inst. on Internat. Reins.: Collections and Insolvency, N.Y., 1988; chmn. ABA Nat. Inst. on Life Ins. Co. Insolvency, Chgo., 1993; spkr. in field. Editor: Law and Practice of Insurance Company Insolvency, 1986, Law and Practice of Life Insurer Insolvency, 1993; co-editor: Law and Practice of International Reinsurance Collections and Insolvency, 1988; contbr. articles to profl. jours. Mem. ABA (chair Nat. Inst. on Life Insurer Insolvency 1993), Chgo. Bar Assn., Lawyer's Club of Chgo. Federal civil litigation, Insurance. Office: Schiff Hardin & Waite 6600 Sears Tower Chicago IL 60606 Home: 1418 Lake Shore Dr Chicago IL 60611 E-mail: dspector@schiffhardin.com.

SPECTOR, MARTIN WOLF, lawyer, business executive; b. Phila., 1938; BA, Pa. State U., 1959; JD, U. Pa., 1962. Bar: Pa. 1962. Judge U.S. Dist. Ct., until 1967; asst. gen. counsel ARA Services, Phila., assoc. gen. counsel, 1969-76, v.p., 1976-83, gen. counsel, 1983—, formerly sr. v.p.; exec. v.p. ARAMARK, Phila., 1985—. Served to lt. USN, 1953-56. Office: ARAMARK 1101 Market St Ste 45 Philadelphia PA 19107-2988*

SPECTOR, PHILLIP LOUIS, lawyer; b. L.A., July 15, 1950; s. Everett L. Spector and Rebecca (Horn) Newman; m. Carole Sue Lebbin, May 11, 1980; children: Adam, David. Student, U. Birmingham, Eng., 1970-71; BA with highest honors, U. Calif., Santa Barbara, 1972; M in Pub. Policy, JD magna cum laude, Harvard U., 1976. Bar: Calif. 1976, D.C. 1978, U.S. Ct. Appeals (D.C. cir.) 1983, U.S. Supreme Ct. 1983, U.S. Dist. Ct. D.C. 1985. Law clk. U.S. Ct. Appeals (2d cir.), Brattleboro, Vt., 1976-77; law clk. to U.S. Supreme Ct., Washington, 1977-78; assoc. asst. to Pres. U.S., Washington, 1978-80; assoc. Verner, Liipfert, Bernhard & McPherson, Washington, 1980-83; ptnr. Goldberg & Spector, Washington, 1983-92, Paul, Weiss, Rifkind, Wharton & Garrison, Washington, 1992—, mng. ptnr. Washington office, 2001—. Cons. U.S. exec. br. Close-Up Found., Alexandria, Va., 1980—. Co-author: Communications Law and Practice, 1995, Communications and Techology Alliances: Business and Legal Issues, 1996; mem. bd. editors Multimedia & Internet Strategist; contbr. articles to profl. jours. Mem. Coun. on Fgn. Rels., N.Y.C., 1980-85; moot ct. judge Nat. Assn. Attys. Gen., Washington, 1987—; adviser Dem. caucus U.S. Ho. Reps., Washington, 1981-83; speechwriter, podium prodr. Dem. Nat. Convs., N.Y.C., 1980, Phila., 1982, San Francisco, 1984, Atlanta, 1988, N.Y.C., 1992, Chgo., 1996, L.A., 2000. Recipient Disting. Achievement in Pub. Svc. Medal U. Calif., Santa Barbara, 1981, Close-Up Found. awards Via Satellite Mag., Vol. Recognition award Nat. Assn. Attys. Gen., 1993; named Leading Satellite Specialist in Washington, European Counsel, 2000. Mem. ABA (former chair internat. comm. law com.), Fed. Comms. Bar Assn., Bethesda Country Club, Addison Res. Country Club, Wintergreen Club, Phi Beta Kappa. Jewish. Communications, Computer, Private international. Office: Paul Weiss Rifkind Wharton & Garrison 1615 L St NW Ste 1300 Washington DC 20036-5694 E-mail: pspector@paulweiss.com.

SPEED-BOST, REGINA Y. lawyer; b. Bethesda, Md, Feb. 17, 1965; d. Albert Arthur and Margaret Lucille Speed; m. Mark Bernard Bost, Aug. 6, 1988; children: Ariel Gervais Bost, Avery Alexander Bost. AB, Dartmouth Coll., Hanover, NH, 1987; JD, Georgetown U. Law Ctr., Washington D.C., 1990. Bar: MD 1990, U.S. Dist. Ct. MD 1991, U.S. Supreme Ct. 2001, U.S. Ct. Appeals (D.C. Cir.) 2003. Trial atty. Fed. Energy Regulatory Commn., DC, 1990—93, advisory atty., 1993—96; legal adv. to commissioner William L. Massey DC, 1996—98; sr. assoc. Duane, Morris & Hecksher LLP, DC, 1998—99; of counsel Verner, Liipfert, Bernhard, McPherson & Hand, DC, 1999—2001, Sullivan & Worcester LLP, DC, 2001—02, ptnr., 2003—. FERC practice. Office: Sullivan & Worcester LLP 1666 K St W Ste 700 Washington DC 20006

SPEER, JOHN ELMER, paralegal, reporter, counselor; b. Conrad, Mont., Mar. 19, 1956; s. Elmer Constant and Mildred Saphrona (LaBelle) S.; m. Sharron D. Knotts, May 23, 1982 (div. Mar. 1986); 1 child, Jeremy Keith; 1 foster child, Casey; m. Adah C. Corbett, March 10, 2000; stepchildren: Jody, Jay, Jill, Jessica. Paralegal assoc., Coll. of Great Falls, Mont., 1994; BS in paralegal studies, U. of Great Falls, Mont., 1999. Bar: Mont. 1996; cert. scuba diver. Farmer, Valier, Mont., 1956-73; janitor Shelby (Mont.) pub. schs., 1974-75; freelance news reporter Sta. KSEN, Shelby, 1980—2000, various TV stas., newspapers, Great Falls, 1980-90; office cleaner Parkdale Housing Authority, Great Falls, 1990-95; freelance paralegal Great Falls, 1993—; law clk., paralegal Mont. State Dist. Judge Thomas McKittrick, Great Falls, 1993. Rschr. line-up identification appeal binder to U.S. Supreme Ct., 1993; trial assistance atty. Chas. Joslyn, spring 1996. Contbr. victim-witness assistance program operating manual, 1992. Counselor and adv. Victim-Witness Assistance Svcs., Great Falls, 1991-93. Mem. Mont. Big Sky Paralegal Assn., Am. Counseling Assn., Brain Injury Assn. of Mont. (chpt. v.p. 1997). Jehovah'S Witness. Avocations: hiking, fishing, cooking, travel, swimming. Address: PO Box 206 Great Falls MT 59403-0206

SPEERS, ROLAND ROOT, II, lawyer; b. Jacksonville, Fla., Oct. 8, 1933; s. Roland Root and Alice (Calkins) S.; m. Florence Briscoe, Dec. 18, 1954; children: Kirsten, Guy, Gina Marie. BA cum laude, UCLA, 1955, JD, 1958. Bar: Calif. 1958, D.C. 1978. Dep. commr. corps. Calif. Dept. Corps., Los Angeles, 1958-59; sec., gen. counsel Suburban Cos., Pomona, Calif., 1959-64; sec. Amcord, Inc., Los Angeles, 1964-66, asst. to pres., 1968, v.p. corp. devel., 1969, v.p., gen. counsel, 1970, sr. v.p., 1971, exec. v.p., 1972-75, pres., 1975-94; ptnr. Speers, Dana, Teal Balfour & MacDonald, Costa Mesa, Calif., 1977-97. Dir. Logicon, Inc., Torrance, Calif., Twelve Eleven Press, Newport Beach, Calif. Trustee Pitzer Coll., Pomona, 1975-80; bd. councillors Center Pub. Affairs U. So. Calif., 1976-81; bd. dirs. Newport Harbor Art Mus., 1977-82; sr. warden St. James Episcopal Ch., 1993. Mem. D.C. Bar Assn., State Bar Assn. Calif., UCLA Alumni Assn., UCLA Law Sch. Alumni Assn., Phi Alpha Delta. Clubs: Big Canyon Country (Newport Beach).

SPEIGHT, JOHN B. lawyer; b. Cheyenne, May 29, 1949; s. Jack B. and Kathryn Elizabeth (Schmidt) S.; m. Sally Karolee Sullivan, Aug. 20, 1960; children— Sheryl, Tricia, Jackie; m. Carol Ann McBee, Sept. 16, 1979. BA, U. Wyo., 1962, JD, 1965. Bar: Wyo. 1966, U.S. Dist. Ct. Wyo. 1967, U.S. Dist. Ct. Colo. 1967, U.S. Ct. Appeals (10th cir.) 1967, U.S. Supreme Ct. 1970; diplomate Am. Bd. Trial Attys. Atty., Standard Oil Co. of Calif., 1965-67; asst. atty. gen. State of Wyo., 1967-69; adminstrv., legal asst. to Gov. Wyo., 1969-71; atty. for Reorgn. Commn., State of Wyo., 1969-71; asst. U.S. atty. Litigation divsn., 1971-72; cons. sec. interior, 1975; ptnr. Speight McCue & Assocs, Cheyenne, 1972— ; bd. dirs. First Wyo. Bank, East Cheyenne, Laramie County Legal Svc. Inc. Bd. dirs. Laramie County United Fund. Mem. Wyo. Bar Assn., ABA, Wyo. Trial Lawyers Assn., Am. Trial Lawyers Assn., Laramie County United Fund. Mem. Wyo. Bar Assn., ABA, Wyo. Trial Lawyers Assn. (bd. dirs. 1982—), Am. Trial Lawyers Assn., Laramie County Bar Assn. (pres. 1982-83), Commrs. for Uniform State Laws from the State of Wyo., Jud. Supervisory Commn., Cheyenne Kiwanis Club (bd. dirs.) Young Men's Literary Club. Republican. Roman Catholic. Federal civil litigation, State civil litigation, Personal injury (including property damage).

SPELFOGEL, SCOTT DAVID, lawyer; b. Boston, Nov. 27, 1960; s. Evan. J. and Beverly (Kolenberg) S. BS, Boston U., 1982; JD, Syracuse U., 1985; LLM, Boston U., 1990. Bar: Mass. 1985, N.Y. 1986, U.S. Dist. Ct. (no. dist.) N.Y. 1986, U.S. Dist. Ct. Mass. 1987; lic. real estate broker, Mass., 1987. Assoc. Jeffrey M. McCrone, P.C., Syracuse, N.Y., 1985-87, Tatarian Law Offices, Boston, 1987-88; asst. gen. counsel The Berkshire Group, Boston, 1988-90, v.p., asst. gen. counsel, 1990-96, v.p., gen. counsel, 1996, sr. v.p., gen. counsel, 1997—. Mem. ABA, Am. Corp. Counsel Assn., Boston Bar Assn., N.Y. Bar Assn., Mass. Bar Assn. General civil litigation, Corporate, general, Property, real (including real estate development, water). Home: 27 Sentry Hill Rd Sharon MA 02067-1521 Office: The Berkshire Group 1 Beacon St Ste 1500 Boston MA 02108-3116

SPELLMAN, THOMAS JOSEPH, JR., lawyer; b. Glen Cove, N.Y., Nov. 11, 1938; s. Thomas J. and Martha H. (Erwin) S.; m. Margaret Mary Barth, June 23, 1962; children: Thomas Joseph, Kevin M., Maura N. BS, Fordham U., 1960, JD, 1965. Bar: N.Y. 1966, U.S. Dist. Ct. (so. and ea. dist.) N.Y. 1968, U.S. Ct. Appeals (2nd cir.) 1980, U.S. Supreme Ct. 1981. Staff atty. Allstate Ins. Co., N.Y.C., 1966-69; trial atty. Hartford Ins. Co., Hauppauge, N.Y., 1969-71; ptnr. Wheller & Spellman, Farmingville, N.Y., 1971-76, Devitt, Spellman, Barrett, Callahan & Kenney, LLP, Smithtown, N.Y., 1976—. Mem. grievance com. 10th Jud. Dist., Westbury, N.Y., 1984-92. Trustee Acad. St. Joseph, Brentwood, N.Y., 2000—; bd. govs. St. Catherine of Sienna Med. Ctr., Smithtown, NY, 2002--. Capt. USAR, 1960-68. Fellow: N.Y. Bar Found., Am. Bar Found.; mem.: N.Y. Bar State Bar Assn. (ho. of dels. 1989—, nominating com. 1992—93, v.p. 1996—98), Suffolk County Bar Assn. (bd. dirs., sec.-treas. v.p. 1982—, pres. 1992—93), Swordfish Club. Westhampton Beach, N.Y. (bd. dirs., sec. 2000—01). General civil litigation, Insurance, Personal injury (including property damage). Home: 8 Highwoods Ct Saint James NY 11780-9610 Office: Devitt Spellman et al 50 Route 111 Ste 314 Smithtown NY 11787-3700

SPELTS, RICHARD JOHN, lawyer; b. Yuma, Colo., July 29, 1939; s. Richard Clark and Barbara Eve (Pletcher) S.; children: Melinda, Meghan, Richard John Jr.; m. Gayle Merves, Nov. 14, 1992. BS cum laude, U. Colo., 1961, JD, 1964. Bar: Colo. 1964, U.S. Dist. Ct. Colo. 1964, U.S. Supreme Ct. 1968, U.S. Ct. Appeals (10th cir.) 1970, U.S. Dist. Ct. (ea. dist.) Mich. 1986. With Ford Motor Internat., Cologne, Germany, 1964-65; legis. counsel to U.S. Senator, 89th and 90th Congresses, 1967-68; minority counsel U.S. Senate Subcom., 90th and 91st Congresses, 1968-70; asst. U.S. atty., 1st asst. U.S. atty. Fed. Dist. of Colo., 1970-77; pvt. practice Denver, 1977-89; risk mgr. sheriff's dept. Jefferson County, Golden, Colo., 1990-91. Selected for Leadership Denver, 1977; recipient cert. for outstanding contbns. in drug law enforcement U.S. Drug Enforcement Adminstrn., 1977, spl. commendation for criminal prosecution U.S. Dept. Justice, 1973, spl. commendation for civil prosecution U.S. Dept. Justice, 1976. Mem. Fed. Bar Assn. (chmn. govt. torts seminar 1980), Colo. Bar Assn. (bd. govs. 1976-78), Denver Bar Assn., Colo. Trial Lawyers Assn., Denver Law Club, Order of Coif. Republican. Methodist. Home and Office: 9671 Brook Hill Ct Lone Tree CO 80124-5431 Fax: 303-662-9957.

SPENCE, GERALD LEONARD, lawyer, writer; b. Laramie, Wyo., Jan. 8, 1929; s. Gerald M. and Esther Sophie (Pfleeger) S.; m. Anna Wilson, June 20, 1947; children: Kip, Kerry, Kent, Katy; m. LaNelle Hampton Peterson, Nov. 18, 1969. BSL, U. Wyo., 1949, LLB, 1952, LLD (hon.), 1990. Bar: Wyo. 1952, U.S. Ct. Claims 1952, U.S. Supreme Ct. 1982. Sole practice, Riverton, Wyo., 1952-54; county and pros. atty. Fremont County, Wyo., 1954-62; ptnr. various law firms, Riverton and Casper, Wyo., 1962-78; sr. ptnr. Spence, Moriarity & Schuster, Jackson, Wyo., 1978—2002, Spence, Moriarty & Shockey, 2002—. Lectr. legal orgns. and law schs. Author: (with others) Gunning for Justice, 1982, Of Murder and Madness, 1983, Trial by Fire, 1986, With Justice for None, 1989, From Freedom to Slavery, 1993, How To Argue and Win Every Time, 1995, The Making of a Country Lawyer, 1996, O.J.: The Last Word, 1997, Give Me Liberty, 1998, A Boy's Summer, 2000, Gerry Spence's Wyoming: The Landscapes, 2000, Half Moon and Empty Stars, 2001, Seven Simple Steps to Personal Freedom, 2001. Mem. ABA, Wyo. Bar Assn., Wyo. Trial Lawyers Assn., Assn. Trial Lawyers Am., Nat. Assn. Criminal Def. Lawyers Criminal, Personal injury (including property damage), Product liability. Office: Spence Moriarity & Shockey PO Box 548 Jackson WY 83001-0548

SPENCE, HOWARD TEE DEVON, judge, arbitrator, lawyer, consultant, insurance executive, government official; b. Corinth, Miss., Sept. 29, 1949; s. T. P. and Dorothy M.S.; m. Diane Earl Williams, Feb. 26, 1977 (div. June 1986); children: Derek, Tina, Steven. BA, Mich. State U., 1970, M in Criminal Justice Adminstrn., 1975, M in Labor-Indsl. Relations, 1981, MBA, 1983; JD, U. Mich., 1976, M in Pub. Adminstrn., 1977. Bar: Mich.

1976, U.S. Dist. Ct. (ea. dist.) Mich. 1976, U.S. Ct. Appeals (6th cir.) 1976, U.S. Supreme Ct. 1980, U.S. Dist. Ct. (we. dist.) Mich. 1986; cert. ins. examiner. Counselor State Prison of So. Mich., Jackson, 1971-76; personnel adminstr. Mich. Dept. Commerce, Lansing, 1976-77; asst. dir. Mich. Pub. Service Commn., Lansing, 1977-78; dep. ins. commr. Mich. Ins. Bur., Lansing, 1978-92; ptnr., cons. Spence & Assocs., Lansing, 1983—; adminstrv. law judge State of Mich., Lansing, 1992—2002. Arbitrator U.S. Dist. Ct. (we. dist.) Mich., Grand Rapids, 1986, Mich. Employment Rels. Commn., 1992-2002; adj. law prof. Thomas M. Cooley Law Sch., Lansing, 1977-80; adj. instr. Nat. Jud. Coll., Reno, 1993-98; instr. MBA law program West Mich. campus U. Phoenix, 2003—; presenter in field. Author short stories. Sec., v.p. Ingham County Housing Commn., Okemos, Mich., 1985-90; bd. dirs. Econ. Devel. Corp. City of Lansing, 1981-85. Mem.: NAACP (life), Ins. Regulatory Examiners Soc. (bd. dirs., nat. pres. 1990—91), Am. Judges Assn., Wolverine Bar Assn., Black Lawyers Assn., Nat. Assn. Adminstrv. Law Judges, Mich. Assn. Adminstrv. Law Judges (pres. 1998), Assn. Black Judges Mich., Nat. Bar Assn., Mich. Bar Assn. (legal edn. com., mem. adminstrv. law sect. coun.), ABA (editor in chief NCALJ newsletter 1998—99), Blue Key, Kappa Delta Lambda (pres., chmn. bd. dirs., adminstr. Project Alpha, Edn. Found. Inc.), Alpha Phi Alpha. Mem. Ch. of Christ. Club: Renaissance, Economic (Detroit). Avocations: tennis, racquetball, camping, dancing. Home: 1637 Willow Creek Dr Lansing MI 48917-9643 E-mail: htspence@spence-associates.com.

SPENCER, DAVID JAMES, lawyer; b. Altadena, Calif., June 23, 1943; s. Dorcy James and Dorothy Estelle (Pingry) S.; m. Donna Rae Blair, Aug. 22, 1965; children: Daniel, Matthew. BA, Rocky Mountain Coll., 1965; JD, Yale U., 1968. Bar: Minn. 1968, U.S. Dist. Ct. Minn. 1968, U.S. Ct. Appeals (8th cir.) 1970. Mem. firm Briggs and Morgan, P.A., Mpls. and St. Paul, 1968—. Contbg. author 10 William Mitchell Law Rev., 1984; contbr. articles to profl. jours. Trustee Rocky Mountain Coll., Billings, Mont., 1980-01; bd. dirs. Reentry Svcs., Inc., 1993—, River Valley Arts Coun., 1996-01, Stillwater Area Arts Ctr. Alliance, 1998-01, Homeward Bound, Inc., 1999—; pres., bd. dirs. St. Croix Friends of Arts, Stillwater, Minn., 1981-84; bd. dirs. Valley Chamber Chorale, Stillwater, 1989-92; v.p. Minn. Jaycees, St. Paul, 1974; elder Presbyn. Ch. Recipient Silver Key St. Paul Jaycees, 1974; Disting. Svc. award Rocky Mountain Coll., 1981, Outstanding Svc. award, 1988, Disting. Achievement award, 1992. Fellow Am. Coll. Real Estate Lawyers; mem. ABA, Minn. Bar Assn., Ramsey County Bar Assn., Stillwater Country Club, Stillwater Sunrise Rotary Club (bd. dirs. 1997-99). Presbyterian. Avocations: trout fishing, golf, singing. Condemnation (eminent domain), Landlord-tenant, Property, real (including real estate development, water). Home: 10135 Waterfront Dr Woodbury MN 55129 Office: Briggs & Morgan 2200 First Nat Bank Bldg 332 Minnesota St Ste W2200 Saint Paul MN 55101-1396 E-mail: dspencer@briggs.com.

SPENCER, RICHARD HENRY, lawyer; b. Kansas City, Mo., Nov. 29, 1926; s. Byron Spencer and Helen Elizabeth (McCune) Hockaday; m. Barbara G. Rau, Aug. 2, 1952 (div. 1955); 1 chlid, Christina G. Cuevas; m. Katherine Graham, Dec. 28, 1957; children: Elisabeth M., Katherine S. Rivard. BS in Engring., Princeton U., 1949; LLB, U. Mo., 1952. Bar: Mo. 1952, U.S. Dist. Ct (we. dist.) Mo. 1955. Assoc. Spencer, Fane, Britt & Browne, Kansas City, 1952-59, ptnr., 1959-94; ret. ptnr., 1995—. Co-author: Fiduciary Duties, Rights and Responsibilities of Directors, 1985. Sec., bd. dirs. Met. Performing Arts Fund, Kansas City, 1984—; trustee Barstow Sch., Kansas City, 2002--. Mem. ABA, Mo. Bar Assn., Lawyers Assn. Kansas City, Kansas City Club (pres. 1974), Kansas City Country Club (pres. 1986), Rotary. Republican. Episcopalian. Avocations: hunting, golf, traveling. Corporate, general, Finance, Mergers and acquisitions. Home: 77 Le Mans Ct Shawnee Mission KS 66208-5230 Office: Spencer Fane Britt & Browne 1400 Commerce Bank Bldg 1000 Walnut St Kansas City MO 64106-2140

SPERBER, DAVID SOL, lawyer; b. July 28, 1939; m. Zoila Luz Martinez, Dec. 27, 1986; children: Toby, Elliot, Joshua, Mira, Natalie, Emily, Benjamin. AB in Polit. Sci., UCLA, 1961, JD, 1964. Bar: Calif. 1965, U.S. Dist. Ct. Calif. 1965, U.S. Ct. Appeals (9th cir.) 1966, U.S. Supreme Ct. 1973, U.S. Dist. Ct. (5th cir.) 1978. Dep. atty. gen. Atty. Gen.'s Office, State of Calif., 1964-68; pvt. practice Encino, Calif., 1968—. Mem. UCLA Law Rev. Mem. County Dem. Ctrl. Com., L.A., 1968-69; mem. parole aide program Jr. Barristers, 1972-73; trustee Hillel Hebrew Acad.; assoc. chmn. met. divsn. United Jewish Welfare Fund; chmn. legal com. Yeshiva U. Holocaust Ctr.; pres. bd. trustees Hear Ctr. Haynes scholar; named Man of Yr., CHABAD, 1986. Mem. Calif. Trial Lawyers Assn. (ins. com.), L.A. Trial Lawyers Assn., San Fernando Valley Criminal Bar Assn., L.A. County Bar Assn. (criminal law and procedure sect., real property sect.), Lawyers Club (spkrs. bur.). General civil litigation, Insurance. Office: 15910 Ventura Blvd Ste 1525 Encino CA 91436-2830

SPERINGO, DAVID A. lawyer, consultant; b. New Haven, Dec. 21, 1974; s. Alphonse and Ilona Speringo. BA in Polit. Sci., History, U. Conn., 1997; JD, Roger Williams Sch. Law, 2000. Bar: R.I. 2001. Assoc., info. tech. dir. Garcia and Milas, P.C., New Haven, 2000—. Youth group adviser Pilgrim Fellowship, Guilford, Conn., 1991—. Home: 995 Boston Post Rd Apt 5 Guilford CT 06437 Office: Garcia and Milas PC 44 Trumbull St New Haven CT 06510 Business E-Mail: osperingo@garciamilas.com.

SPERLING, JOY HARMON, lawyer; b. Bklyn., Mar. 25, 1961; d. Aaron and Lenore Harmon; m. Norman Jay Sperling, July 1, 1984; 1 child, Daniel Steven. BA cum laude, Rutgers U., 1983, JD, 1986. Bar: N.J. 1986, U.S. Dist. Ct N.J. 1986, U.S. Ct. Appeals (3d cir.) 1995, U.S. Dist. Ct. (so. dist.) N.Y. 1998. Clk. to Hon W.P. Diana, Assignment and Chancery Judge Superior Ct. of N.J., Somerville, N.J., 1986-87; assoc. Pitney, Hardin, Kipp & Szuch, Morristown, N.J., 1987-95, ptnr., 1996—. Mem. ABA, N.J. State Bar Assn., Phi Beta Kappa. General civil litigation, Commercial, consumer (including collections, credit). Home: 11 Argonne Farm Dr Bridgewater NJ 08807-1480 Office: Pitney Hardin Kipp & Szuch PO Box 1945 Morristown NJ 07962-1945 E-mail: jsperling@pitneyhardin.com.

SPERLING, SHELDON J. prosecutor; BA Northeastern State Coll., JD U. Tulsa. Pvt. practice, Tulsa, 1979—82; asst. dist. atty. Okla. Dist. Atty.'s Office, 1983—85; asst. U.S. atty. Ea. Dist. Okla. U.S. Dept. Justice, 1985—89, 1st asst. U.S. atty., criminal chief, 1989—2000, U.S. atty., 2000—. Office: 1200 W Okmulgee St Muskogee OK 74401

SPERO, KEITH ERWIN, lawyer, educator; b. Cleve., Aug. 21, 1933; s. Milton D. and Yetta (Silverstein) S.; m. Carol Kohn, July 4, 1957 (div. 1974); children: Alana, Scott, Susan; m. Karen Weaver, Dec. 28, 1975. BA, Western Res. U., 1954, LLB, 1956. Bar: Ohio 1956. Assoc. Sindell, Sindell & Bourne, Cleve., 1956-57, Sindell, Sindell, Bourne, Markus, Cleve., 1960-64; ptnr. Sindell, Sindell, Bourne, Markus, Stern & Spero, Cleve., 1964-74, Spero & Rosenfield, Cleve., 1974-76, Spero, Rosenfeld & Bourne, LPA, Cleve., 1977-79, Spero & Rosenfield Co. LPA, 1979—. Tchr. bus. law U. Md. overseas div., Eng., 1958-59; lectr. Case-Western Res. U., 1965-69; instr.; nat. panel arbitrators Am. Arbitration Assn. Author: The Spero Divorce Folio, 1966, Hospital Libaiblity for Acts of Professional Negligence, 1979. Trustee Western Res. Hist. Soc., 1984—2000, exec. com., 1992—2000; v.p., chmn. libr. display and collections com. Western Res. Hist. Soc, 1992—95, chmn. history mus. com., 1995—99; commodore Dugway Creek Yacht Club, 1985—87; bd. dirs. Vail Valley Inst., 2000—. 1st lt. JAG USAF, 1957—60, capt. Res. USAF, 1960—70. Fellow Am. Acad. Matrimonial Lawyers; mem. ABA, Ohio Bar Assn., Cleve. Bar Assn., Cuyahoga County Bar Assn., Ohio Acad. Trial Lawyers (pres. 1970-71), Assn. Trial Lawyers Am. (state committeeman 1971-75, bd. govs. 1975-79, sec. family law litigation sect. 1975-76, vice-chmn. 1976-77, chmn. 1977-79), Am. Bd. Trial Advs., Order of Coif, Masons, Sonnenalp Golf Club Eedwards, Colo.), Phi Beta Kappa, Zeta Beta Tau, Tau Epsilon Rho. Jewish. (trustee, v.p. congregation 1972-78). State civil litigation, Family and matrimonial, Personal injury (including property damage). Office: 440 Leader Bldg E 6th and Superior Cleveland OH 44114-1214 E-mail: keith@vail.net.

SPERO, MORTON BERTRAM, retired lawyer; b. N.Y.C., Dec. 6, 1920; s. Adolph and Julia (Strasburger) S.; m. Louise Thacker, May 1, 1943; children: Donald S., Carol S. Flynn. BA, U. Va., 1942, LLB, 1946. Bar: Va. 1946, U.S. Supreme Ct. 1961. Mem. legal staff NLRB, Washington, 1946-48; pvt. practice Petersburg, Va., 1948—70, 1985—2001; sr. ptnr. Spero & Levinson, Petersburg, 1970-75, Spero & Diehl, Petersburg, 1975-85; ret., 2001. Chmn. The Community Bank, Petersburg, 1976-79, dir., 1976-91. Chmn. United Fund Drive, 1960, bd. dirs., 1999—; pres. Dist. IV Petersburg Coun. Social Welfare, Southside Sheltered Workshop, 1965, pres. Congregation B'rith Achim, 1973; bd. dirs. World Fund, 1999-2001. Lt. USNR, 1943-45. Recipient Outstanding Mem. award Petersburg chpt. B'nai B'rith, 1966; Svc. to Law Enforcement award Petersburg Police Dept., 1965. Fellow Am. Acad. Matrimonial Lawyers; mem. Va. Bar Assn., Petersburg Bar Assn. (pres. 1981-82), Va. State Bar (coun. 1981-84, chmn. criminal law sect. 1972, chmn. family law sect. 1979, bd. dirs. litigation sect. 1983-86, Lifetime Achievement award for family law sect. 1995), Va. Trial Lawyers Assn. (v.p. 1972), Civitan Club (hon.), Rotary, Elks (exalted ruler 1968). Democrat. Jewish. State civil litigation, Criminal, Family and matrimonial. Home: 9706 Bunker Ct Petersburg VA 23805-9125

SPERRY, MARTIN JAY, lawyer; b. Troy, N.Y., May 15, 1947; s. Raymond Leon and Selma (Jenkins) S.; m. Faith S. Sperry; children: Jana, Douglas, Jill. BSBA, U. Fla., 1969, JD, 1971. Bar: Fla. 1972, U.S. Dist. Ct. (mid. dist.) Fla. 1972, U.S. Dist. Ct. (so. dist.) Fla. 1974, U.S. Supreme Ct. 1976, N.Y. 1983. Sr. law clk. to chief judge U.S. Dist. Ct. (mid. dist.) Fla., Orlando, 1972-74; ptnr. Carey, Dwyer, Cole, Selwood & Bernard, Ft. Lauderdale, Fla., 1974-78, Krathen & Sperry, Ft. Lauderdale, Fla., 1978-84, Selwood & Sperry, Ft. Lauderdale, Fla., 1984-85, Sperry, Shapiro & Kashi, Ft. Lauderdale, Fla., 1985—. Mem. Fourth Dist. Ct. Appeals Judicial Nominating Commn., 1996-2000. Contbg. author: Casebook of Florida Constitutional Law, 1971. Served as capt. U.S. Army Reserves, 1969-77. Mem. Acad. Fla. Trial Lawyers (diplomate), Assn. Trial Lawyers Am. (sustaining), N.Y. State Bar Assn., Fla. Bar Assn. (bd. cert. civil trial lawyer), Fed. Bar Assn., Nat. Bd. Trial Advs. (cert. civil trial adv.), Am. Bd. Trial Advocates, Am. Inns of Ct. Lodges: B'nai B'rith. Democrat. Jewish. Avocations: sports, traveling. State civil litigation, Insurance, Personal injury (including property damage). Office: 1776 N Pine Island Rd Ste 324 Plantation FL 33322 E-mail: ssklaw@aol.com.

SPEZIALE, JOHN ALBERT, lawyer; b. Winsted, Conn., Nov. 21, 1922; s. Louis and Mary (Avampato) S.; m. Mary Kocsis, Aug. 12, 1944; children: John Albert, Marcia Jean. BA in Econs., Duke U., 1943, JD, 1947. Bar: Conn. 1948. Clk. Judiciary Com. of Conn. Gen. Assembly, 1949; judge Mcpl. Ct., Torrington, Conn., 1949-51; dir. CD, 1951-52; fed. atty. OPS, 1951-52; mem. Conn. State Jud. Council, 1955-59; sr. partner firm Speziale, Mettling, Lefebre & Burns, Torrington, 1958-61; city atty. Torrington, 1957-59; treas. State of Conn., 1959—61; judge Conn. Ct. Common Pleas, 1961-65, Conn. Superior Ct., 1965-77; presiding judge Conn. Superior Ct. (Appellate div.), 1975-77, chief judge, 1975-77, mem. exec. com., 1975-84, chmn. exec. com., 1977-81; justice Conn. Supreme Ct., 1977-81, chief ct. adminstr., 1978-81, chief justice, 1981-84; sr. ptnr. Cummings & Lockwood, Hartford, 1984-92; of counsel, 1992—. Atty. trial referee Conn., 1986—; mem. exec. com. Nat. Conf. State Trial Judges, 1970-74; faculty advisor grad. session Nat. Coll. State Judiciary, U. Nev., 1973; mem. Conn. Jud. Rev. Coun., 1975-77; co-chmn. planning commn. criminal adminstrn. Conn. Justice Commn., 1975-78; mem. Conn. Commn. on Adult Probation, 1976-77, Adv. Coun. on Ct. Unification, 1976-78, Conn. Bd. Pardons, 1977-78; mem. exec. com. Nat. Bd. Trial Advocacy, 1983-88, dir. 1988—; mem. mediation com. Ctr. Pub. Resources, 1985—; chmn. State-Fed. Rels. Com. Conf. of Chief Justices, 1983-84; chmn. adv. bd. Use of Vol. Lawyers to Supplement Jud. Resources, Nat. Inst. Justice and Nat. Ctr. for State Ctrs., 1983-87; mem. lawyers com. Nat. Ctr. for State Cts., 1985-88; chmn. subcom. jud. decisions Nat. Assn. Ins. Commrs. Adv. Com. Environ. Liability Ins., 1985-87; mem. Panel of Trial and Appellate Judges, Asbestos Claims Facility, 1986—; arbitrator Ins. Arbitration Forums, Inc., 1986—, others. Trustee Conn. Jr. Republic, 1975-83; bd. dirs. Newington Children's Hosp. 1983-86, corporator 1983—; chmn. awards com. Freedoms Found. at Valley Forge, 1982, trustee Nat. Council, 1986—; fellow Pvt. Adjudication Found. Duke U. Sch. Law, 1986—. Lt. (j.g.) USNR, 1942-46, PTO. Recipient Conn. Trial Lawyers Jud. award, 1977; 1st Unico Nat. Disting. Key award, 1977; Citizen of Yr. award Elks, 1982; Alva P. Loiselle lifetime achievement award, 1984; Disting. Service award Nat. Ctr. for State Cts., 1985; Significant Practical Achievement award Ctr. for Pub. Resources Legal Program, 1985; Conn. Law Rev. award, 1985. Fellow Am. Bar Found. (life), Conn. Bar Found. (charter life fellow, chmn. James W. Cooper fellows 1994-97, John A. Speziale Symposia named in his honor); mem. ABA (vice chmn. 1984-86, com. on stds. jud. adminstrn. jud. adminstrn. divsn.), Inst. Jud. Adminstrn., Am. Judicature Soc. (dir. 1978-82), Conn. Bar Assn. (com. on alternative dispute resolution 1985-87, com. on liaison with state cts. 1986-92), Hartford Bar Assn., Litchfield County Bar Assn., Supreme Ct. Hist. Soc., Am. Arbitration Assn. (comml. panel arbitrators 1987-2001, panelist large complex case program 1993-2001), Am. Fedn. Musicians (life), Sons of Italy of Am., Conn. State Srs. Golf Assn., Inc., Litchfield County Univ. Club, Torrington Country Club, Unico Club (life), Bear Lakes Country Club (Fla.), K.C., Phi Beta Kappa. Roman Catholic. Home: 278 Windtree St Torrington CT 06790-7904 Office: Cummings & Lockwood 1 Cityplace Hartford CT 06103-3408 E-mail: judgespeziale@aol.com.

SPIEGEL, HART HUNTER, retired lawyer; b. Safford, Ariz, Aug. 30, 1918; s. Jacob B. and Margaret (Hunter) S.; m. Genevieve Willson, Feb. 12, 1946; children: John Willson, Claire Margaret Spiegel Brian, Jennifer Emily Spiegel Grellman. BA, Yale U., 1940, LLB, 1946. Bar: Calif. 1946, D.C. 1960. Assoc. Brobeck, Phleger & Harrison, San Francisco, 1947-55, ptnr., 1955-90. Chief counsel IRS, Washington, 1959-61, mem. adv. group to commr., 1975. Served to lt. USMC, 1942-46, PTO. Mem. ABA (coun. mem. tax sect. 1966-68), Am. Law Inst., Bar Assn. San Francisco (pres. 1983), Pacific Union Club, Berkeley Tennis Club (pres. 1964-65). Corporate taxation, State and local taxation. Home: 3647 Washington St San Francisco CA 94118-1832 Office: Brobeck Phleger & Harrison 1 Market Pla Spear St Tower San Francisco CA 94105

SPIEGEL, JERROLD BRUCE, lawyer; b. N.Y.C., Apr. 11, 1949; s. Seymour S. and Estelle (Minsky) S.; m. Helene Susan Cohen, Mar. 3, 1972; children: Dana Sean, Amy Barrett, Evan Tyler. BS, Queens Coll., 1970; JD cum laude, NYU, 1973. Bar: N.Y. 1974. Assoc. Austrian, Lance & Stewart, N.Y.C., 1973-75, Gordon Hurwitz Butowsky Baker Weitzen & Shalov, N.Y.C., 1975-79; ptnr. Shapiro Spiegel Garfunkel & Driggin, N.Y.C., 1979-86, Frankfurt Kurnit Klein & Selz P.C., N.Y.C., 1986—. Editor Ann. Survey Am. Law, 1972-73. Mem. ABA (corp. law sect.), Order of the Coif, Omicron Delta Epsilon. Computer, Corporate, general, Intellectual property. Office: Frankfurt Kurnit Klein & Selz PC 488 Madison Ave Fl 9 New York NY 10022-5754 E-mail: jbspiegel@aol.com.

SPIEGEL, LINDA F. lawyer; b. Bronx, NY, Mar. 13, 1953; d. Rubin E. and Edna (Zucker) S.; m. Paul Duboff, June 12, 1983; 1 child, Joshua Michael. AB, Barnard Coll., Columbia U., 1974; JD, Boston U., 1978. Bar: N.J. 1978, U.S. Dist. Ct. N.J. 1978, N.Y. 1980, U.S. Dist. Ct. (so. and ea. dists.) N.Y. 1980, U.S. Supreme Ct. 1982. Tax editor Prentice Hall, Englewood, N.J., 1978; pvt. practice, Hackensack, N.J., 1978-83, 88—; assoc. Friedman, Carney & Wilson, Newark, 1983-84; pvt. practice New Milford, N.J., 1984-85; assoc. LaFianza and Strull, Hackensack, 1985-87, ptnr., 1987-88. Instr. Inst. Legal Asst. and Paralegal Tng., Mahwah, NJ, 1978-81; co-chair Bergen County Youth Svcs. Commn., 2001-03. Spkr. Boy Scouts Am., Bergen, N.J., 1980; atty.-acct. divsn. United Jewish Cmty., River Edge, N.J., 1978—; trustee Women's Am. Orgn. Rehab. through Tng., 1987-88; chmn. Jean Robertson Women Lawyers Scholarship Found., Inc., 1987-94. Mem. ABA, Am. Arbitration Assn. (comml. and constrn. arbitrator 1989—), N.J. Women Lawyers Assn., N.J. State Bar Assn., Bergen County Bar Assn. (trustee 1989-94, editor-in-chief Bergen Barrister 1991-94), Women Lawyers in Bergen County (pres. 1987-89), B'nai Brith. Democrat. Avocations: theater, tennis, swimming, square and country dancing. Alternative dispute resolution, General civil litigation, Family and matrimonial. Office: 79 Main St Ste 1 Hackensack NJ 07601-7126 E-mail: lfsesq@aol.com.

SPIEGEL, S. ARTHUR, federal judge; b. Cin., Oct. 24, 1920; s. Arthur Major and Hazel (Wise) S.; m. Louise Wachman, Oct. 31, 1945; children: Thomas, Arthur Major II, Andrew, Roger Daniel. BA, U. Cin., 1942, postgrad., 1949; LLB, Harvard U., 1948. Assoc. Kasfir & Chalfie, Cin., 1948-52; assoc. Benedict, Bartlett & Shepard, Cin., 1952-53, Gould & Gould, Cin., 1953-54; ptnr. Gould & Spiegel, Cin., 1954-59; assoc. Cohen, Baron, Druffel & Hogan, Cin., 1960; ptnr. Cohen, Todd, Kite & Spiegel, Cin., 1961-80; judge U.S. Dist Ct. Ohio, Cin., 1980—; sr. status, 1995—. Served to capt. USMC, 1942-46 Mem. ABA, FBA, Ohio Bar Assn., Cin. Bar Assn., Cin. Lawyers Club. Democrat. Jewish. Office: US Dist Ct 838 US Courthouse 5th Walnut St Cincinnati OH 45202

SPIELBERG, JOSHUA MORRIS, lawyer; b. Atlanta, July 31, 1955; s. Sol and Gisela (Meyer) S.; m. Anindita Banerji, May 31, 1977; children: Lela, Ben, Hannah. BA, Oberlin Coll., 1977; JD magna cum laude, U. Pa., 1981. Bar: Del., N.J., Pa., U.S. Ct. Appeals (3d and 6th cir.), U.S. Supreme Ct. Law clk. to Judge Walter K. Stapleton U.S. Dist. Ct. Del., Wilmington, 1981-82; Reginald Heber Smith fellow Cmty. Legal Aid, Wilmington, 1982-84; atty., ptnr. Tomar, Simonoff, Cherry Hill, NJ, 1984-2000; ptnr. Shivers, Spielberg, Gosnay & Greatrex, Cherry Hill, NJ, 2000—. Trustee Camden Regional Legal Svcs., 1993-2002, South Jersey Legal Svs., 2003-; mem. trust adv. com. DI Asbestos Disease Trust, Media, Pa., 1993-95; lectr. Rutgers Law Sch., Camden, 1993-99, adj. prof., 2000-01. Contbr. articles to law jours. Mgr. Little League baseball Haddon Twp. Athletic Assn.; trustee Congregation M'Kor Shalom, Cherry HIll, 2002--. Recipient Fordham Human Rights award U. Pa. Law Sch., 1981, Outstanding Bd. Svc. award Legal Svcs. N.J., 2000. Mem. ATLA, N.J. Bar Assn., Order of Coif, Phi Beta Kappa. Jewish. Appellate, Personal injury (including property damage), Toxic tort. Home: 337 Westmont Ave Westmont NJ 08108-3536 Office: Shivers Spielberg Gosnay & Greatrex 1415 Rte 70 E Ste 210 Cherry Hill NJ 08034 E-mail: jspielberg@ssglawfirm.com.

SPIELMAN, KIM MORGAN, lawyer, educator; b. Ft. Wayne, Ind., Jan. 1, 1953; s. George Homer and Mary Ruth (Steininger) S.; m. Susan Kay Altekruse, Apr. 15, 1972; children: Matthew Ryan, Nathan Daniel. BS, Ind. U., 1982, MPA, 1984; JD with high distinction, Ohio No. U., 1986. Bar: Ind. 1987, U.S. Dist. Ct. (no. and so. dists.) Ind. 1987, U.S. Ct. Appeals (7th cir.) 1990. Officer Ft. Wayne Police Dept., 1975-84; assoc. Barnes & Thornburg, Ft. Wayne, 1986-91; assoc. prof. Ind. U., Ft. Wayne, 1988—; chief counsel Allen County Prosecutor's Office, Ft. Wayne, 1991-92; with Beers, Mallers, Backs & Salin, Ft. Wayne, 1992-95; gen. counsel Hercules Machinery Corp., Ft. Wayne, 1995-98, Blackburn & Green, Ft. Wayne, 1999—. Instr. Ft. Wayne Police Acad. Del. Ind. State Rep. Conv., Indpls., 1982, 84, 92, 94, 96, 98; bd. dirs. Jr. Achievement of No. Ind.; ward chmn. Mayor's Police/Cmty. Rels. Task Force, 1997-98; pres. Safety and Security Svcs., LLC; judge pro tem, Allen County Superior Ct.; mem. Bd. Public Safety, City Ft. Wayne, 1998-2000. Mem. ABA, ATLA, Ind. Bar Assn., Allen County Bar Assn., Greater Ft. Wayne C. of C. Republican. Lutheran. Home: 3222 Sudbury Pl Fort Wayne IN 46815-6224 Office: 3344 Mallard Cove Ln Fort Wayne IN 46804-2884 E-mail: kspielman@blackburn-green.com.

SPIERER, HOWARD, lawyer, writer; b. Bklyn., Feb. 25, 1957; s. Seymour and Barbara Rose S.; m. Dorry G. Bless, Feb. 11, 1989; 1 child, Orli Sam. BA, NYU, 1980; JD, SUNY, 1986. Bar: Pa. 1986, U.S. Dist. Ct. (ea. dist.) Pa. 1986, N.J. 1987, U.S. Dist. Ct. N.J. 1987, N.Y. 1989, U.S. Dist. Ct. (so. and ea. dists.) N.Y. 1990. Atty. Cohen & Shapiro, Phila., 1986-89, Weil, Gotshal & Manges, N.Y.C., 1989-95, AT&T Corp., Basking Ridge, N.J., 1995—. Author: (play) Still Waiting, 1993, Confessions of a Peep Show Junkie, 1994; pub./editor-in-chief Actors' Resource, 1992-96. Vice chmn. Doe Fund, N.Y.C., 1995-96; bd. dirs. Svcs. Underserviced, N.Y.C., 1996—; co-founder Rivercenter Soul space for the Arts, Frenchtown, N.J., 1999—. Mem. ABA (editor in chief Litigation News 1995-98, co-chair electronic pub. com. 1999—). Alternative dispute resolution, General civil litigation, Communications. Home: 139 Mount Joy Rd Milford NJ 08848-1748 Office: One AT&T Way Bedminster NJ 07921

SPIES, FRANK STADLER, lawyer; b. Adrian, Mich., Aug. 7, 1939; s. Charles F. and Lucille M. (Stadler) S.; m. Lynette K. Wells, July 25, 1964; children: Anne, Jane, Charles. BBA, U. Mich., 1961, LLB, 1964. Bar: Mich. 1964, U.S. Dist. Ct. (we. dist.) Mich. 1964, U.S. Ct. Appeals (6th cir.) 1971. Assoc. Schmidt, Smith, Howlett & Halliday, Grand Rapids, Mich., 1964-66; asst. city atty. City of Grand Rapids, 1966-69, U.S. Dept. Justice, Grand Rapids, 1969-77; U.S. atty. Western Dist. Mich., Grand Rapids, 1974-77; pvt. practice Grand Rapids, 1977-81, 84-97; assoc. Kaufman, Payton & Kallas, Grand Rapids, 1981-84; ptnr. Bensinger, Cotant, Menkes & Aardema, Grand Rapids, 1997—. Instr. bus. law Davenport Coll., Grand Rapids, 1967-68, Grand Valley State U., Grand Rapids, 1978-79. Recipient Dirs. Honor award U.S. Secret Svc., 1977. Mem. ABA, Grand Rapids Bar Assn., Nat. Assn. Former U.S. Attys., Grand Rapids East Rotary, Republican. Presbyterian. Insurance, Personal injury (including property damage), Product liability. Home: 2122 Tenway Dr SE Grand Rapids MI 49506-4526 Office: 983 Spaulding Ave SE Grand Rapids MI 49546-3700 E-mail: fspies@bcma.net.

SPIES, LEON FRED, lawyer; b. Blue Grass, Iowa, Oct. 8, 1950; s. Fred William and Alma Lois (Lineburg) S.; m. Janet Rae Peterson, July 15, 1979; children: Caitlin, Allison. BBA with distinction, U. Iowa, 1972, JD with distinction, 1975. Bar: Iowa 1975, U.S. Dist. Ct. (no. and so. dists.) Iowa 1975, U.S. Ct. Appeals 1975, U.S. Supreme Ct. 1987, U.S. Dist. Ct. (cen. dist.) Ill. 2000. Assoc. Heintz & Mellon, Iowa City, 1975-76; ptnr. Mellon & Spies, Iowa City, 1976—. Magistrate jud. dept. State of Iowa, 1978-83; instr. trial advocacy U. Iowa Coll. Law, 1996—. Bd. chmn. Johnson County Red Cross, Iowa City, 1982-84; bd. dirs. Big Bros./ Big Sisters, Johnson County, Iowa, 1985-89. Master: Am. Inns of Ct. (pres. Dean Mason Ladd Inn 1995—96); fellow: Iowa Acad. Trial Lawyers; mem.: ATLA, ABA, Am. Judicature Soc., Assn. Trial Lawyers Iowa, Iowa Bar Assn., Nat. Assn. Criminal Def. Lawyers. Democrat. Methodist. State civil litigation, Criminal, Personal injury (including property damage). Home: 2349 Kent Ct NE Iowa City IA 52240-9633 Office: Mellon & Spies 102 S Clinton St Iowa City IA 52240-4024

SPIESS, F. HARRY, JR., lawyer; b. Norristown, Pa., Mar. 17, 1943; s. F. Harry and Sara E. (Jenkins) S.; m. Merrily S. Brown, Aug. 22, 1964; children: Jill, Blake, Alexandra, Ryan. AB, Lafayette Coll., Easton, Pa., 1964; JD, Villanova U., 1968. Bar: Pa. 1968. Assoc. Greenwell Porter Smaltz Royal, Wayne, Pa., 1968-72, ptnr., 1972-95, Davis Bennett Barr & Spiess, Wayne, 1995—2001, Davis Bennett Spiess & Prendergast, 2002—. Mem. Radnor Twp. Meml. Day Parade Com., 1976—, pres., 1985; pres. Wayne Jaycees, 1972-73, Rotary Club of Wayne, 1976-77, bd. dirs., counsel Radnor Hist. Soc., 1993—; charter mem. Hist. Assn. Tobyhanna Twp., 1996—; chmn. Constellation Dist. Boy Scouts Am., 1997-2001. Recipient

Robert Morris Citizenship award, 2001. Mem. Pa. Bar Assn., Delaware County Bar Assn. (sec. 1981, chmn. golf com. 1994—, dir. 2000-2002, Pres.'s award 2002), Monroe County Bar Assn., Main Line Lawyers Forum (past pres.), Wayne Bus. Assn. (pres. 1987-89), St. Davids Golf Club (counsel, sec.-treas. 1995—). Avocations: golf, reading. Commercial, contracts (including sales of goods; commercial financing), Estate planning, General practice. Home: Lansdowne Ave Wayne PA 19087 Office: Davis Bennett Spiess & Prendergast PO Box 191 130 W Lancaster Wayne PA 19087 E-mail: hspiess@davisbennett.com.

SPIGLER, KAREN JENSEN, lawyer, accountant; d. Earl E. and Kathy Jensen; m. Harvey N. Spigler, Aug. 14, 1989; children: Paul Michael Jensen, Kris Kelly. BS, U. Tex., 1984, MA in Internat. Mgmt., 1986, MBA, 1990; JD, U. Miami, 1999, LLM, 2000. CPA Tex., 1986, S.C., 1989, Fla., 1999; bar: Fla. 1999. Pvt. practice CPA, Plantation, Fla., 1986—; pvt. practice law, 1999—. Mng. editor: U. Miami Entertainment and Sports Law Rev. Office: Law Firm Karen Spigler LLC 499 NW 70th Ave #105 Plantation FL 33317 E-mail: kspigler@justice.com.

SPILLIAS, KENNETH GEORGE, lawyer; b. Steubenville, Ohio, Nov. 8, 1949; s. George and Angeline (Bouyoucas) S.; m. Monica Mary Saumweber, May 10, 1975; children: Geoffrey David, Alicia Anne, Stephanie Marie. BA, Pa. State U., 1971; JD magna cum laude, U. Pitts., 1974. Bar: Pa. 1974, Fla. 1978, U.S. Supreme Ct. 1978, U.S. Ct. Appeals (2d, 3d, 4th, 5th, 6th cirs.) 1975, (11th cir.) 1981, U.S. Dist. Ct. (mid. dist.) Fla. 1979, U.S. Dist. Ct. (so. dist.) Fla. 1978; cert. cir. ct. mediator. Trial atty. U.S. Dept. Justice, Washington, 1974-76; asst. dist. atty. Dist. Atty. of Allegheny County, Pitts., 1976-78; asst. atty. gen. Fla. Dept. Legal Affairs, West Palm Beach, Fla., 1978-79; ptnr. Spillias & Mitchell, West Palm Beach, 1979-82, Considine & Spillias, West Palm Beach, 1982-83, Schneider, Maxwell, Spillias et al, West Palm Beach, 1984-86, Wolf, Block, Schorr et al, West Palm Beach, 1986-88, Shapiro & Bregman, West Palm Beach, 1988-91; of counsel Greenberg, Traurig et al, West Palm Beach, 1991; pvt. practice West Palm Beach, 1991-97; ptnr. Lewis, Longman & Walker, P.A., West Palm Beach, 1997—. Instr. bus. law Coll. of the Palm Beaches, West Palm Beach, 1980-81; CLE lectr. Palm Beach County Bar Assn., 1983—. County commr. Bd. County Commrs., Palm Beach County, 1982-86; co-founder, mem. Children's Svcs. Coun., Palm Beach County, 1986-91; steering com. Fla. Atlantic U. Inst. of Govt., Boca Raton, 1983-94; bd. dirs. The Literacy Coalition of P.B.C., West Palm Beach, 1990-2000, health and human svcs. Fla. Dist. IX, 1995-98, Ctr. for Family Svc., West Palm Beach, 1992-96, Palm Beach County Coun. of Arts, 1987-1988; mem. West Palm Beach Planning Bd., 1997— chmn., 2001—; mem. policy coun. Fla. Inst. Govt., Tallahassee, 1985-86; fund raising chmn. United Cerebral Palsey Telethon, West Palm Beach, 1984-85; judge Palm Beach Post Pathfinders Awards, 1992-98. Recipient Cmty. Svc. award Downtown Civitan Club, West Palm Beach, 1983, Man of the Day award United Cerebral Palsey, 1986, Spl. Honoree award Palm Beach County Child Advocacy Bd., 1986, Children's Trust award Exch. Club/Dick Webber Ctr. for Prevention Child Abuse, 1991, Up and Comers Award in Law, South Fla. Bus. Jour./Price Waterhouse, 1988, Achievement award Nat. Assn. Counties, 1986; named to Outstanding Young Men of Am., U.S. Jaycees, 1975, 84, recipient Employment Law award, Palm Beach County Legal Aid Soc., 2002. Mem. ABA, Palm Beach County Bar Assn. (appellate practice com. 1990—), Am. Hellenic Ednl. Progressive Assn. (pres. 2001-02), Fla. Bar (appellate advocacy and city, county and local govt. sects.), Order of Coif, Kiwanis. Avocations: sports, writing, theater, reading, music. Appellate, General civil litigation, Municipal (including bonds). Home: 147 Gregory Rd West Palm Beach FL 33405-5029 Office: Ste 1000 1700 Palm Beach Lakes Blvd West Palm Beach FL 33401-2006 E-mail: kspillias@llw-law.com.

SPINA, ANTHONY FERDINAND, lawyer; b. Chgo., Aug. 15, 1937; s. John Dominic and Nancy Maria (Ponzio) S.; m. Anita Phyllis De Orio, Jan. 28, 1961; children: Nancy M. Spina Okal, John D., Catherine M. Spina Samatas, Maria J. Spina Samatas, Felicia M. Spina DiGiovanni. BS in Social Sci., Loyola U., Chgo., 1959; JD, DePaul U., 1962. Bar: Ill. 1962. Assoc. Epton, Scott, McCarthy & Bohling, Chgo., 1962-64; pvt. practice Elmwood Park, Ill., 1964-71; pres. Anthony & Spina, PC, 1971-84; arbitrator Circuit Ct. of Cook County, 1990—98; pres. Spina, McGuire & Okal, PC, Elmwood Park, 1985—. Codifier Rosemont Village Ordinances, 1971, Elmwood Park Bldg. Code, 1975, Leyden Twp. Codified Ordinances, 1987. Mem. Elmwood Pk. Bldg. Code Planning Commn. Bd. Appeals; bd. dirs. Sheridan Carrol Charitable Works Fund, 1994—; atty. Leyden Twp., Ill., 1969—89, Village of Rosemont, Ill., 1971; counsel for Pres. and dir. Cook County Twp. Ofcls. Ill., 1975—96; counsel for exec. dir. Ill. State Assn. Twp. Ofcls., 1975—96; counsel Elmwood Park Village Bd., 1967—89, Norwood Park St. Lighting Dist., 1988—, various Cook County Twps. including DuPage, 1980—82, Maine, 1981—97, 1982—, Wayne, 1982—84, Berwyn Twp., 1997—99, Hanover Twp., 1997, Cook County Hwy. Commrs. Traffic Fine Litigation, 1974—96, 1999—2001, Hanover Twp. Mental Health Bd., 1991—2002, Glen Edens Assn., 1994—99, Berwyn Twp. Mental Health Bd., 1997—2002. Recipient Lacodaire medal Deans Key Loyola U., Loyola U. Housing awards, 1965, 71, 76; Appreciation award Cook County Twp. Ofcls., B. Scidmore award Ill. Twp. Attys. Assn., 2002. Mem. ABA, Ill. Bar Assn., Chgo. Bar Assn., West Suburban Bar Assn. Cook County (past chmn. unauthorized practice law sect.), Am. Judicature Soc., Justinian Soc. Lawyers, Ill. State Twp. Attys. Assn. (past v.p., pres. 1982-86, dir. 1996-99, dir. emeritus 1999—,. B. Scidmore award 2002), Nat. Inst. Town and Twp. Attys. (past v.p., pres. 1993-95, Ill. del.), Montclare/Leyden C. of C., Edgebrook C. of C. (past bd. dirs.), Nat. Assn. Italian Am. Lawyers, Joint Civic Com. Chgo. (exec. com.), World Bocce Assn. (dir. 1994--), St. Rocco Soc. Simbario, KC (scribe, trustee, past Grand Knight, bldg. corp. dir. 1967-99), Calabresi in Am. Orgn. (bd. dirs. 1991—), Fra Noi Ethnic Publ. (dir. 1995—), Blue Key, Delta Theta Phi, Tau Kappa Epsilon, Pi Gamma Mu. Roman Catholic. State civil litigation, Estate planning, General practice. Office: 7610 W North Ave Elmwood Park IL 60707-4100 E-mail: spinalaw@aol.com.

SPINA, FRANCIS X. state supreme court judge; m. Sally O'Donnell; 2 children. BA, Amherst Coll.; JD, Boston Coll. Prosecutor, Berkshire County, Mass., 1979—83; pvt. law practice Pittsfield, Mass., 1983—93; judge Mass. Superior Ct., 1993-97, Appeals Ct., Pittsfield, 1997-99; assoc. justice Mass. Supreme Jud. Ct., Boston, 1999—. Office: Mass Supreme Ct New Ct House Pemberton Sq Boston MA 02108

SPINDLER, KESTER LARS, lawyer; b. Velbert, Germany, Aug. 20, 1975; s. Guenter Spindler and Birgit Schilbach-Spindler. BS, Liberty U., 1997; JD, Pepperdine U., 1999. Bar: Calif. 2000, England & Wales 2002. Assoc. Kirkland & Ellis, London, 2000—. Mem.: ABA, Calif. Bar Assn. Republican. So. Baptist. Avocations: golf, travel, scuba diving. Corporate, general, Mergers and acquisitions, Securities. Office: Kirkland & Ellis Tower 42 25 Old Broad St London EC2N 1HQ England Fax: +44 20 7816 8764. E-mail: kester_spindler@uk.kirkland.com.

SPINING, W. CARL, lawyer; b. Bowling Green, Ky., Feb. 11, 1967; s. William Parker and Carol Artis Spining; m. Erin Claire Doyle, Aug. 5, 1989; children: Molly Maureen, Patrick Ryan, Mary Caitlin, Jack Dugan. BA, U. Tenn., 1989, JD, 1993. Bar: Tenn. 1993, U.S. Dist. Ct. (mid. dist.) Tenn. 1993, U.S. Dist. Ct. (ea. dist.) 2001. Staff counsel Tenn. Dept. Revenue, Nashville, 1993-94; atty. Ortale, Kelley, Herbert & Crawford, Nashville, 1994—. Roman Catholic. General civil litigation, Corporate, general, Probate (including wills, trusts). Office: Ortale Kelley Herbert & Crawford 200 4th Ave N Fl 3 Nashville TN 37219-2114 E-mail: cspining@ortalekelley.com.

SPIRA, IMMANUEL ISAAC, lawyer, consultant; BS in Zoology cum laude, Duke U., 1985; JD, Northwestern U., 1990. Bar: Calif. 1990, U.S. Dist. Ct. (ctrl. dist.) Calif. 1990. Assoc. Wyman Bautzer Kuchel & Silbert, LA, 1989—91, Katten Muchin & Zavis, LA, 1991—98; v.p. bus. and legal affairs Motion Picture Bond Co., LA, 1998—2001; prin. IIS Consulting, LA, 2001—. Exec. com., bd. dirs. Jewish Fedn., LA, 2000—, LA Hillel Coun., 1990—. Entertainment, Intellectual property, Corporate, general. E-mail: ispira@alumni.duke.edu.

SPITZ, HUGO MAX, retired lawyer; b. Richmond, Va., Aug. 17, 1927; s. Jacob Gustav and Clara (Herzfeld) S.; m. Barbara Steinberg, June 22, 1952; children: Jack Gray, Jill Ann Levy, Sally Spitz. AA, U. Fla., 1948, BLaws, 1951, JD, 1967. Bar: Fla. 1951, S.C. 1955, U.S. Dist. Ct. (so. dist.) Fla. 1951, U.S. Dist. Ct. (ea. dist.) S.C. 1956, U.S. Ct. Appeals (4th cir.) 1957. Asst. atty. gen. State of Fla., Tallahassee, 1951; assoc. Williams, Salomon & Katz, Miami, Fla., 1951-54, Steinberg & Levkoff, Charleston, S.C., 1954-57; sr. ptnr. The Steinberg Law Firm L.L.P., Charleston, 1957-2001; ret., 2001. Lectr. S.C. Trial Lawyers Assn., Columbia, 1958—, S.C. U. Sch. Law, Columbia, 1975, S.C. Bar Assn., 1955—; assoc. mcpl. judge Charleston, 1972-74, chief mcpl. judge, 1974-76; commr. Charleston County Substance Abuse Commn., 1976-79; bd. govs. S.C. Patient's Compensation Fund, Columbia, 1978-97; adv. mem., atty. S.C. Legis. Coun. for Worker's Compensation; chmn. bd. dirs. Franklin C. Fetter Health Ctr., Charleston, 1977-78; mem. S.C. Appellate Def. Commn., 1985-86; founding sponsor Civil Justice Found., 1986—; bd. pres. Charleston Jewish Fedn., 1990-91, pres., 1991-92. Pres. Synagogue Emanu-El, 1969-71. With USN, 1945-46. Awarded Order of Silver Crescent, Gov. S.C., 2001. Fellow S.C. Bar Assn., U. S.C. Ednl. Found.; mem. ABA, Civil Justice Found., S.C. Law Inst., S.C. Trial Lawyers Assn. (founder and pres. 1985-86), S.C. Claimants' Attys. for Worker's Compensation (hon. life bd. mem., founder, exec. com. 1986), S.C. Worker's Compensation Ednl. Assn. (bd. dirs. 1978-98), S.C. Law Inst., Am. Judicature Soc., Trial Lawyers Am. (mem. pres. coun. 1986-87, stalwart 2001), Nat. Rehab. Assn., Nat. Orgn. Social Security Claimants' Reps. S.C. Bar (chmn. trial and appellate sect. 1982-83, ho. of dels. 1984-85), So. Assn. Workmen's Compensation Adminstrs., Nat. Inst. for Trial Advocacy (com. chmn. 1985), Hebrew Benevolent Soc. (life, pres. 1974-75), Jewish Cmty. Ctr. (Charleston) (v.p. 1972-74), Hebrew Orphan Soc. (life, pres. 2000-01), B'nai B'rith, Elks (life). Democrat. State civil litigation, Personal injury (including property damage), Workers' compensation. Home: 337 Confederate Cir Charleston SC 29407-7430 E-mail: hspitz@comcast.net.

SPITZBERG, IRVING JOSEPH, JR., lawyer; b. Little Rock, Feb. 9, 1942; s. Irving Joseph and Marie Bettye (Seeman) S.; m. Roberta Frances Alprin, Aug. 21, 1966 (div. 1988); children— Edward Storm, David Adam; m. Virginia V. Thorndike, Dec. 24, 1988. BA, Columbia U., 1964; B.Phil., Oxford U., 1966; JD, Yale U., 1969. Bar: Calif. 1969, D.C. 1985, Va. 1995. Asst. prof. Pitzer Coll., Claremont, Calif., 1969-71; fellow Inst. Current World Affairs, N.Y.C., 1971-74; vis. lectr. Brown U., Providence, 1973; assoc prof. SUNY, Buffalo, 1974-80, dean of coll., 1974-78; gen. sec. AAUP, Washington, 1980-84; exec. dir. Coun. for Liberal Learning of Assn. Am. Colls., Washington, 1985-89; pres. The Knowledge Co., Fairfax, Va., 1985-2001; ptnr. Spitzberg & Drew, Washington, 1990-92; of counsel Spirer & Goldberg, Washington, 1993—; pvt. practice, 1993—. Coord. Alvan Ikoku Coll., Nigeria, 1979-80; cons. Bd. Adult Edn., Kenya, 1973-74, Philander Smith Coll., Little Rock, 1978-80; co-dir. nat. study on campus life for Carnegie Found. for Advancement Teaching, 1989-90. Author and editor: Exchange of Expertise, 1978, Universities and the New International Order, 1979, Universities and the International Exchange of Knowledge, 1980; author: Campus Programs on Leadership, 1986, Racial Politics in Little Rock, 1987; co-author: (with Berdahl and Moodie), Quality and Access in Higher Education, 1991, (with Virginia Thorndike) Creating Community on College Campuses, 1992; polit. columnist Prince William Times, 2001-02. Founder Coalition for Ednl. Excellence, Western N.Y., 1978-80; founding mem. Alliance for Leadership Devel., Washington, 1985; counsel GASP, Pomona, Calif., 1969-71; Dem. Committeeman, Erie County, N.Y., 1978-80; founding pres. Internat. Found. for St. Catherine's Coll., Oxford, 1986-91; founder Coun. for Liberal Learning; mem. Ethical Culture Soc. Nat. winner Westinghouse Sci. Talent Search, 1960; Kellett scholar Trustees of Columbia U., 1964-66. Mem. Am. Immigration Lawyers Assn., Nat. Acad. Elder Law Attys., Washington Ethical Soc., Columbia Club, Yale Club (Washington), Rotary Internat.. Jewish. Avocations: kids, the internet. Estate planning, Immigration, naturalization, and customs, Probate (including wills, trusts). E-mail: ijs@aol.com.

SPITZER, ELIOT, state attorney general; m. Silda Spitzer; 3 children. Grad., Princeton U., 1981; JD, Harvard U., 1984. Clk. U.S. Judge Robert W. Sweet; assoc. Paul, Weiss, Rifkind, Wharton & Garrison, Skadden Arps Slate Meagher & Flom; ptnr. Constantine & Ptnrs., N.Y.C.; asst. dist. atty. State of N.Y., Manhattan, 1986—92, atty. gen. Albany, 1999—. Analyst, commentator on nat. news programs including NBC's Today Show, CNN's Burden of Proof, CNBC, Court TV. Editor: Harvard Law Rev.; contbr. articles in leading newspapers and legal jours. Founder Ctr. for Cmty. Interest; trustee Montifiore Med. Ctr. Democrat. Office: Dept of Law The Capitol, 2nd Fl Albany NY 12224*

SPITZER, HUGH D. lawyer; b. Seattle, Feb. 14, 1949; s. George Frederick and Dorothy Lea (Davidson) S.; m. Ann Scales, Oct. 14, 1983; children: Johanna Spitzer, Claudia Spitzer, Jenny Spitzer. BA, Yale U., 1970; JD, U. Wash., 1974; LLM, U. Calif., 1982. Bar: Wash. 1974, U.S. Dist/ Ct. (ea. and we. dists.) Wash. 1975, U.S. Ct. Appeals (9th and D.C. cirs.) 1975, U.S. Supreme Ct. 1980. Program analyst N.Y.C. Health and Hosp. Corp., 1970-71; labor lawyer Hafer, Cassidy & Price, Seattle, 1974-76; legis. asst. Seattle City Coun., 1976-77; legal counsel to mayor City of Seattle, 1977-81; mcpl. bond lawyer Foster Pepper & Shefelman, PLLC, Seattle, 1982—. Affiliate prof. sch. law U. Wash. Contbr. articles to profl. jours. Vice chair Puget Sound Water Quality Authority Wash. State, 1989-96; chair Seattle Low Income Housing Levy Oversight com., 1988-96; chair Wash. State Affordable Housing Adv. Bd., 2000—; vice chair State Tax Structure Com., 2001-02. Mem. Nat. Assn. Bond Lawyers, Pub. Legal Edn. Working Group, Am. Judicature Soc. (mem. exec. com. Coun. on Pub. Legal Edn.). Democrat. Avocations: piano, hiking, skiing. Municipal (including bonds). Office: Foster Pepper & Shefelman PLLC 1111 3rd Ave Bldg Ste 3400 Seattle WA 98101-3292 E-mail: spith@foster.com.

SPITZER, JOHN BRUMBACK, lawyer; b. Toledo, Mar. 6, 1918; s. Lyman and Blanche (Brumback) S.; m. Lucy Ohlinger, May 10, 1941 (dec. Oct. 13, 1971); children: John B., Molly (Mrs. Edmund Frost), Lyman, Adelbert L.; m. Vondah D. Thornbury, July 3, 1972 (dec. Nov. 2001); stepchildren: Vondah, Barbara, James R. Thornbury. Grad., Phillips Andover Acad., 1935; BA, Yale U., 1939, LLB, 1947. Bar: Ohio 1947. Law clk. to U.S. Supreme Ct. Justice Stanley Reed, 1947-48; ptnr. Marshall, Melhorn, Cole, Hummer & Spitzer, Toledo, 1955-86, Hummer & Spitzer, Toledo, 1986-89; with Hummer Legal Svcs. Corp., 1990—2002; ptnr. Spitzer and Hummer, 2002—. Pres. Spitzer Box Co., 1955-63; v.p. Spitzer Bldg. Co., 1960-91, pres. 1992—. Pres. Toledo Symphony Orch., 1956-58, v.p., sec., 1958-86. Maj. AUS, World War II. Mem.: Belmont Country Club. Congregationalist. Home: 29620 Gleneagles Rd Perrysburg OH 43551-3530 Office: Spitzer & Hummer 4841 Monroe St Ste 205 Toledo OH 43623-4352 E-mail: h/lsc@accessToledo.com.

SPITZER, MATTHEW LAURENCE, law educator, dean; b. L.A., June 23, 1952; s. William George and Jeanette Dorothy S.; m. Jean Fuksman, July 8, 1973; 1 child, Amanda Elizabeth. BA in Math., UCLA, 1973; JD, U. So. Calif., 1977; PhD in Social Scis., Calif. Inst. Tech., 1979. Assoc. Nossaman, Guthner, Knox & Elliott, L.A., 1977—79; asst. prof. Northwestern U., Chgo., 1979—81; William T. Dalessi prof. law U. So. Calif., L.A., 1987—2000, assoc. prof., 1981—84, prof., 1984—, dir. law and rational choice programs, 1990—2000, dir. Comms. Law and Policy Ctr., 1998—2000, dean, Carl Mason Franklin prof. law, 2000—; prof. law and social scis. Calif. Inst. Tech., Pasadena, 1992—2000. Vis. prof. law U. Chgo., 1996, Stanford (Calif.) U., 1997; mem. organizing com. Telecoms. Policy Rsch. Conf., Washington, 1991-94. Author: Seven Dirty Words and Six Other Stories, 1986; co-author: (with T. Hazlett) Public Policy Toward Cable Television, 1997. Recipient (shared with Elizabeth Hoffman) Ronald H. Coase prize U. Chgo., 1986. Mem.: Am. Law and Econs. Assn. (bd. dirs. 1997—2000). Avocations: paperweight collecting, audiophile. Office: U So Calif Law Sch Los Angeles CA 90089-0071

SPITZLI, DONALD HAWKES, JR., lawyer; b. Newark, Mar. 19, 1934; s. Donald Hawkes and Beatrice (Banister) S.; children: Donald Hawkes III, Peter Gilbert, Seth Armstrong. AB, Dartmouth Coll., 1956; LL.B., U. Va., 1963. Bar: Va. 1963. Assoc. Willcox, Savage, Lawrence, Dickson & Spindle, Norfolk, Va., 1964-67, 68-70, ptnr., 1971-77; atty. Eastman Kodak Co., Rochester, N.Y., 1967-68; pres. Marine Hydraulics Internat., Inc., Chesapeake, Va., 1978-80; sole practice Virginia Beach, Va., 1980—. Owner Chieftain Motor Inn, Hanover, N.H., 1980-87. Comdr. USNR, 1956-70. Episcopalian. Bankruptcy, Property, real (including real estate development, water), General practice. Office: 281 Independence Blvd Ste 605 Virginia Beach VA 23462-2975 E-mail: airbuzzard24@aol.com.

SPIVAK, LEONARD A. lawyer; b. N.Y.C., July 11, 1943; s. Jack and Esther (Peckolick) S.; children: Kate, Allison, Jon, Gabrielle. B.A. with honors, SUNY-Stony Brook, 1964; LL.B. cum laude, Columbia U., 1967. Bar: N.Y. 1967, U.S. Dist. Ct. (so. and ea. dists.) N.Y., U.S. Ct. Appeals (2d, 3d, 5th, 75th and cirs.), U.S. Supreme Ct. Assoc., Gilbert, Segal & Young, N.Y.C., 1967-68; assoc. Cahill, Gordon & Reindel, N.Y.C., 1968-75, ptnr., 1975— . Bd. dirs. Stony Brook Found., Raby Peck Found. Mem. Alumni Assn. SUNY-Stony Brook (past pres.). Democrat. Federal civil litigation, State civil litigation, Corporate, general. Office: Cahill Gordon & Reindel 80 Pine St Fl 17 New York NY 10005-1790 E-mail: LSpivak@cahill.com.

SPIVEY, BROADUS AUTRY, lawyer; b. Lakeview, Tex., Oct. 7, 1936; s. Claude Clifton and Mary Eddith (Stafford) S.; m. Ruth Ann King, Aug. 1, 1956; children: Danny C., Marci M. Diploma, Clarendon Jr. Coll., 1956; BA in Govt., U. Tex., 1960, JD, 1962. Bar: Tex. 1962, U.S. Dist. Ct. (no., so., we. and ea. dists.) Tex., U.S. Ct. Appeals (5th cir.) 1971, U.S. Ct. Claims (11th cir.) 1979, U.S. Supreme Ct. 1973, UTE Indian Tribal Ct. 1997; cert. in personal injury trial law Tex. Bd. Legal Specialization. Asst. county atty. Lubbock County, Lubbock, Tex., 1962-64; ptnr. West, Spivey & Brackett, Lubbock, 1964-65; assoc. Huff & Bowers, Lubbock, 1965-70; sole practitioner Lubbock, 1970-71; ptnr. Gibbins & Spivey, Austin, Tex., 1971-76; sr. ptnr. Spivey & Ainsworth and predecessor firms, Austin, 1976—. Author: The Trial of Contested Paternity Cases, 1977; co-author: Texas Pattern Jury Charges, vol. 3, 1982; contbr. articles to profl. jours. Fellow Internat. Soc. Barristers, Internat. Acad. Trial Lawyers (pres. 2002-03, bd. dirs. 1993—, editor law rev. The Advocate), Am. Coll. Trial Lawyers; mem. Travis County Bar Assn., Capital Area Trial Lawyers Assn. (pres. 1977-79), State Bar Tex. (pres. 2001-2002, chmn. tort and compensation sect. 1976-77, Supreme Ct. adv. com. 1984-90, pres. 2001-), Fed. Bar Assn., Tex. Bar Found., Am. Bd. Trial Advocates, Lawyer Pilots Bar Assn., Tex. Trial Lawyers Assn. (pres. 1981-82), Assn. Trial Lawyers Am. (cert., bd. govs. 1982-85), Trial Lawyers Pub. Justice (bd. dirs. 1982-93, treas. 1989-90), Delta Theta Phi (Outstanding Alumnus award, 1973, 1978). Democrat. Methodist. Avocations: skiing, piloting, reading, woodworking. Aviation, General civil litigation, Personal injury (including property damage). Office: Spivey & Ainsworth 48 East Ave Austin TX 78701-4317

SPIVEY, RANDALL L. lawyer; b. Toledo, Apr. 8, 1968; s. Randall L. Spivey, Sr. and Patricia Ann Spivey; m. Tricia Ann Spivey, Aug. 30, 1997; children: Randall Matthew, Ashley Morgan. BS in Mktg., U. South Fla., 1991; JD, MBA, Loyola U., New Orleans, 1995. Bar: Fla. 1995, U.S. Dist. Ct. (mid. dist.) Fla., cert.: (bd. cert. civil trial atty.). Assoc. Assocs. and Bruce L. Scheiner, Ft. Myers, Fla., 1995—. Former pres. Lee County Personal Injury Assn., Ft. Myers, 1999—2001. Avocations: fishing, weightlifting. Personal injury (including property damage), Product liability. Office: Assocs and Bruce L Scheiner 4020 Evans Ave Fort Myers FL 33906

SPIZZIRI, JOHN ANTHONY, lawyer; b. Paterson, N.J., Sept. 2, 1934; s. Louis George and Carmella (Ianacone) S.; m. Alexandra Vitale, July 15, 1972; children: John A. Jr., Victoria Jean, Miriam. BS, Georgetown U., 1957, JD, 1960. Bar: N.J. 1961, U.S. Dist. Ct. N.J. 1961; cert. mediator. Pvt. practice, Wyckoff, N.J., 1961—; pros. Ramsey (N.J.) Borough, 1964-77, Oakland (N.J.) Borough, 1969-83, Borough Upper Saddle River, N.J.; counsel Franklin Lakes Planning Bd., 1970—; atty. Borough of Elmwood Park (N.J.), 1981—; police prosecutor Township of Wyckoff, 1964-66. Condemnation commr. Meadowlands Sports and Expn. Authority, presiding condemnation commr. Rte. 287; asst. counsel Bergen County (N.J.), 1970-71; judge Mcpl. Ct., Oakland, 1986; atty. Wyckoff Ambulance Corp., 1970—, Franklin Lakes Ambulance Corp., 1994—. Mem. Wyckoff Sewer Com., Wyckoff Planning Bd.; past co-chmn. Wyckoff Heart Fund; past vice chmn. N.W. Bergen County fund drive Boy Scouts Am.; mem. N.J. Gen. Assembly, 1971—77, minority whip and asst. minority leader; mayor Twp. of Wyckoff, 1969; past pres. Wyckoff Rep. League; Rep. mem. CVom. to Study Expenditures of Casino Gambling Revenue; state trustee, nat. del. Ducks Unltd., 2000—01; bd. dirs. 36 SSS; chmn. Hudson River Ducks Unltd., 1999—2001; N.J. state chmn. Ducks Unltd. Mem. ABA, N.J. Bar Assn., Bergen County Bar Assn., Nat. Wildlife Fedn., Allendale Field and Stream Assn., Wyckoff Vol. Ambulance Corps (hon.), Lawyers Club Bergen County (past pres.), Ducks Unltd. (chmn. N.J. chpt. 2000-2001, 2002—, chmn. Hudson River chpt.), Lions (past bd. dirs., pres. Wyckoff chpt. 1989-90). Roman Catholic. General practice, Land use and zoning (including planning). Office: 356 Franklin Ave Wyckoff NJ 07481-1909

SPLITT, DAVID ALAN, lawyer, writer; b. Ripon, Wis., Nov. 28, 1945; s. Orville Sylvester and Joyce Eileen (Anson) S.; m. Martha Ann Corson, Mar. 19, 1966; children: Amy Emmeline, Sarah Daisy. BA in English, Va. Poly. Inst. and State U., 1966; JD, Am. U., 1971. Bar: D.C. 1971, U.S. Supreme Ct. 1981. Tchr. Bowie (Md.) H.S., 1966-68; freelance journalist and photographer Washington, 1968-70; ptnr. Christensen, Splitt & King, Washington, 1971-74; gen. counsel D.C. Bd. Edn., 1974-79; dir. documents, 1979—82; of counsel Stein, Miller, Brodsky & Beerman, Washington, 1983-84; pvt. practice Washington, 1985—2000; v.p., sr. corp. counsel Affiliated Computer Svc., Inc., 2001—. Gen. counsel D.C. Sch. Law, 1988-96, adj. prof. law, 1995-97, U. D.C., 1991-96; spl. asst. city adminstr. for fin. mgmt. systems, dir. city computer ctr., Washington, 1980-81. Dir., vice chmn. Choral Arts Soc. of Washington, 1974-84, chmn., 1984-85; dir., v.p. Traditional Music Documentation Project, Washington. Author: Post-Conviction Relief for Federal Prisoners, 1973, The Resolution of Detainers for Federal and State Prisoners, 1971; editor: Inquiry and Analysis, 1977-79, Becoming a Better Board Member, 1982, D.C. Rulemaking Handbook and Publications Style Manual, 1983, D.C. Produrement Regulations, 1987, A Guide to Procurement Law in the District, 1998; columnist: The Exec. Educator, 1978-96, eSch. News Law and Ethics, 1997—. Recipient Outstanding Svc. awards D.C. Govt., 1976, 78, 79, Mayor's Disting. Pub. Svc. award, 1983. Mem. ABA, Inter-Am. Bar Assn., Computer Law Assn., Aircraft Owners and Pilots Assn., Exptl. Aircraft Assn., Lawyer-Pilots Bar Assn., Am. Radio League, (licensee amateur extra class), Indian Spring Country Club. Republican. General civil litigation, Education and schools, Government contracts and claims. Home: 6111 Utah Ave NW Washington DC 20015-2461

SPOLAN, HARMON SAMUEL, lawyer; b. Phila., Dec. 12, 1935; s. Jay and Edythe (Greenberg) S.; m. Betty Jane Evnitz, Mar. 30, 1958; children: Michael, Suzanne. AB, Temple U., 1957, LLB, 1959; postgrad., Oxford U., 1966. Bar: Pa. 1960. Ptnr. Ravetz & Shuchman, Phila., 1960-68, Blair &

Co., N.Y.C., 1968-72; v.p. Butcher & Singer, Phila., 1972-74; pres. Capital First Corp., Phila., 1974-75, State Nat. Bank, Rockville, Md., 1975-78, Jefferson Bank, Phila., 1978-99; pres., bd. dirs. JeffBanks, Inc., Phila., 1986-99; sr. mem. Cozen O'Connor, Phila., 1999—. Lectr. law U. Pa., Phila., 1964-68. Author: Federal Aids to Financing, 1970; contbr. articles to profl. jours. Former chmn. bd. Huntingdon Hosp., Willow Grove, Pa., 1982—89; bd. dirs. YMHA, Phila., 1978—95, Anti-Defamation League, 1982. Named Man of Yr., Nat. Assn. Women Bus. Owners, 1978, Disting. Alumnus, Central H.S., 1975. Mem. ABA, Phila. Bar Assn. Democrat. Jewish. Banking, Corporate, general, Finance. Office: 1900 Market St Philadelphia PA 19103-3527 E-mail: hspolan@cozen.com.

SPONSLER, THOMAS CLYDE, lawyer; b. Highland Park, Ill., Aug. 4, 1944; s. Thomas Clyde and Signe Ruth (Gaines) S.; m. Virginia Marie Payne, Jan. 2, 1966; 1 child, Brian Andrew. Student, Calif. State U., Long Beach, 1962-65; BS, Willametter U., 1966, JD, 1967; LLM, U. London, 1974. Bar: Calif. 1968, Oreg. 1975. Law clk. Oreg. Legis. Counsel, Salem, 1966-67; trial atty. U.S. Dept. Justice, Washington, 1967-68; dir. litigation Legal Aid Found., Long Beach, 1968-71; assoc. Demler Perona Langer & Bergkvist, Long Beach, 1971-72; sr. assoc. Barnes Schag Johnson & Kennedy, Newport Beach, Calif., 1972-73; asst. prof. law U. of the Pacific, Sacramento, 1974-75; dir. edn. Oreg. State Bar, Portland, 1975-78; city atty. City of Gresham, Oreg., 1979-97; county atty. Multnomah County, 1997—2003; of counsel Beery & Elsner LLP, 2003—. Author, mng. editor: Oregon Government Law, 1993, Nature of Local Government, 1991; contbr. articles to profl. jours. Mem. Internat. Mcpl. Law Assn. (com. chmn. 1983-87), Oreg. State Bar, Calif. State Bar Assn. Office: Ste 380 1750 SW Harbor Way Portland OR 97201 E-mail: Tom@gov-law.com.

SPONZILLI, EDWARD GEORGE, lawyer; b. Newark, Mar. 30, 1948; s. Edward James and Dorothy Maria (Murillo) Sponzilli. BA in History with high honors, Rutgers U., 1971, JD, 1975; summer diploma, Cath. Inst. of Paris, 1971; MA, Columbia U., 1972. Bar: NJ 75, U.S. Dist. Ct. NJ 75, U.S. Ct. Appeals (3d cir.) 76, U.S. Supreme Ct. 79, DC 79, NY 81. Law clk. to judge U.S. Dist. Ct. NJ, Newark, 1975—77; assoc. Pitney, Hardin & Kipp, Morristown, NJ, 1975—81, Dunn, Pashman, Sponzilli, Swick & Finnerty (formerly Cummins, Dunn & Pashman), Hackensack, NJ, 1982—, ptnr., 1984—95, Norris, McLaughlin & Marcus, Pa., 1995—. Co-adj. prof. Rutgers U., New Brunswick, NJ, 1980—81, New Brunswick, 1994, New Brunswick, 98, mcpl. pros., 1981—, mem. Jessup Internat. Law Moot Ct. Team, 1975, coach Mock Trial Team, 1994—97; counsel Judo of NJ Inc., Cranford, 1983—; judge law sch. moot ct. competition Seton Hall, 1977—79, 1981, 81, 86; cert. civil trial atty. NJ Supreme Ct., 1997—; mem. faculty Nat. Inst. Trial Advocacy, 1995—. Active Rutgers U. Found., 1987—. Recipient Hancy Higgenson Dorr award, Rutgers U., 1971, Disting. Svc. award, Animals Need You-Kindness Corp., NJ, 1981, Client Protection award, NJ Supreme Ct. Fund for Client Protection, 1999; Henry Rutgers scholar. Master: Am. Inns of Ct (pres. 2000—01); mem.: ATLA, ABA (trial practice com. of litigation sect.), Middlesex County Bar Assn., Exxec. County Bar Assn., Bergen County Bar Assn., Trial Attys. NJ (trustee 1987—), NJ Trial Lawyers Assn., Assn. Fed. Bar NJ, Fed. Bar Assn., NJ State Bar Assn., Columbia Grad. Faculties Alumni Assn., Scarlet R Round Table Alumni Assn., Rutgers U. Law Sch. Alumni Assn. (exec. counsel, nominating com. 1982, program dir. 1982, alumni fedn. rep., treas. 1991—92, sec. 1992—93, v.p. 1993—94, pres. 1994—95), Orgn. Am. Historians, Am. Hist. Assn., So. Hist. Assn., Civil War History Assn., Phi Alpha Delta, Kappa Sigma (dist. grand master 1986—2000, alumnus advisor 1978—99, trustee Gamma Upskon chpt., sec. 1978—79, v.p. 1979—82, pres. 1982—86, 1994—, chmn. nat. legal comm. 1995—97), Phi Beta Kappa. Federal civil litigation, State civil litigation, Labor (including EEOC, Fair Labor Standards Act, labor-management relations, NLRB, OSHA). Home: 37 Brookside Ave Caldwell NJ 07006-5603 Office: Norris McLaughlin & Marcus PA 721 Rt 202-206 PO Box 1018 Somerville NJ 08876-1018 E-mail: egsponzilli@nmmlaw.com.

SPOONER, RALPH CHARLES, lawyer; b. Milw., June 12, 1946; s. Ralph C. and Sylvia M. (Troyk) S.; children: Melissa, Robin, Robert, Thomas. BA, U. Ill., 1968; JD cum laude, Ill. Inst. Tech., 1973. Bar: Oreg. 1973, Ill. 1973, U.S. Dist. Ct. Oreg. 1973. Assoc. Bruce W. Williams P.C., Salem, Oreg., 1973-75; ptnr. Williams, Spooner and Graves, Salem, 1976-80, Williams and Spooner, Salem, 1981-83, Williams Spooner and Much, Salem, 1983-84, Spooner and Much, Salem, 1984—96, Spooner, Much, & Ammann, 1996—. Contbr. articles to profl. assn. jours. Mem. civil svc. commn. Marion County Fire Dist. 1, Salem, 1975-76; chmn. fin. commn., Sun. sch. tchr. St. Marys Ch., Shaw, Oreg., 1981—. Mem. Oreg. Assn. Def. Counsels (bd. dirs. 1980-86, pres. 1986), Marion County Bar Assn. (bd. dirs. 1980-86, pres. 1986), Illahe Country Club., Intl. Assn. of Defense Counsel, Fed. of Insurance and Corporate Counsel, Council on Court Procedures (chair 2003). Republican. Roman Catholic. Avocations: river rafting, fishing, golf. Federal civil litigation, State civil litigation, Insurance. Home: 3650 Christen St S Salem OR 97302-9743 Office: Spooner Much & Ammann PC 530 Center St NE Ste 722 Salem OR 97301-3756 Office Fax: 503-588-5899. E-mail: rspooner@smapc.com.

SPOONHOUR, JAMES MICHAEL, lawyer; b. San Antonio, Mar. 24, 1946; s. Robert W. and Marie C. (Schulze) S.; m. Terri Walker; children: Taylor, Erin, Whitney, Michael. BA, U. Nebr., 1968, MA, 1970; JD, Georgetown U., 1974. Bar: Fla. 1974, U.S. Dist. Ct. (mid. dist.) Fla. 1974. Assoc. Lowndes, Piersol, Drosdick & Doster, Orlando, Fla., 1974-76; asst. prof. law Loyola U., New Orleans, 1976-77; ptnr. Lowndes, Drosdick, Doster, Kantor & Reed, P.A., Orlando, 1977—. Lectr. on eminent domain and property taxes. Contbr. articles to profl. jours. Bd. dirs. Vis. Nurse Assn., Orlando, 1979-89, Croquet Found. Am., 2001; chmn. sch. bd. The First Acad., Orlando, 1986-89. With USAF, 1970-72. Mem. ABA, Assn. Eminent Domain Profls., Fla. Bar, Orange County Bar Assn. Republican. General civil litigation, Condemnation (eminent domain), State and local taxation. Office: Lowndes Drosdick Doster Kantor & Reed PA 215 N Eola Dr Orlando FL 32801-2095 E-mail: james.spoonhour@lowndes-law.com.

SPOTO, DAVID DENNIS, lawyer; b. Rochester, N.Y., Nov. 23, 1967; s. Joseph Salvatore and Carolyn Ann Spoto; m. Stacey Merrill Couvillon, Mar. 25, 1995. BA in Polit. Sci., SUNY, Fredonia, 1989; JD, Widener U., 1992. Bar: N.Y. 1993, U.S. Dist. Ct. (we. dist.) N.Y. 2000, U.S. Ct. Appeals (2d cir.) 2000. Assoc. Tendler, Goldberg & Biggins, Washington, 1992—93; asst. dist. atty. Monroe County Dist. Atty. Office, Rochester, 1993—99; assoc. Gallo & Iacovangelo, LLP, Rochester, 1999—2000, ptnr., 2000—. Mem.: ATLA. Personal injury (including property damage), Insurance, Criminal. Office: Gallo and Iacovengelo LLP 39 State St Rochester NY 14614 Office Fax: 585-454-2102. Business E-Mail: DavidSpoto@gallolaw.com.

SPRAGUE, GARY DAVID, lawyer; b. Stockton, Calif., Aug. 4, 1955; s. Tom Harold and Patricia Anne Sprague; m. Michele Beth Freed, Sept. 5, 1991; children: Emily Lila Claire, Daria Barbara Inez. BA, Stanford U., 1977; JD, Harvard U., 1981. Bar: Calif. 1981, U.S. Tax Ct. 1990. Congl. intern U.S. Ho. of Reps., Washington, 1974; clk. Fed. Home Loan Bank Bd., Washington, 1976; legal clk. Avon Products, N.Y.C., 1978, Markbys, London, 1978; summer assoc. Coudert Bros., N.Y.C., 1980; assoc. Lillick, McHose & Charles, San Francisco, 1981—85, Baker & McKenzie, San Francisco, 1985—90, ptnr. Palo Alto, Calif., 1990—. Bus. co-chair OECD Income Characterization and Bus. Profits TAGs, Palo Alto. Commr. San Mateo Parks & Recreation Commn., San Mateo, Calif. Corporate taxation. Office: Baker & McKenzie 660 Hansen Way Palo Alto CA 94304 Office Fax: 650-856-9299. E-mail: gary.d.sprague@bakernet.com.

SPRATT, DAVID HOWARD, lawyer; b. Fairfax, Va., Nov. 10, 1969; m. Michelle Renee Roach, May 20, 2000. BA in Psychology, Govt., Coll. William and Mary, 1991; JD, Washington U., 1994. Bar: Va. 1994, DC 1996. Atty. advisor USDA, Washington, 1994—96; assoc. Law Office Betty A. Thompson, Ltd., Arlington, Va., 1996—98, Lewis Law Firm, Washington, 1999—2001; ptnr., founder Schwartz & Spratt, Fairfax, 2001—. Vol., mem. leadership team Celebrate Fairfax. Mem.: ABA, Fairfax Bar Assn., Va. Bar Assn. (vice chair domestic rels. coun. 2000—). Family and matrimonial. Office: Schwartz and Spratt PLC 3927 Old Lee Hwy Ste 102A Fairfax VA 22030

SPRINGER, BYRON EUGENE, lawyer; b. June 25, 1932; s. Charles A. and Vivian E. (Kagi) Springer; m. Marion J. Peltier, June 13, 1959; children: Byron Eugene, Allison A., Carolyn J. BA, U. Kans., 1955, JD, 1960. Bar: Kans. 1960, U.S. Dist. Ct. Kans. 1960, U.S. Ct. Appeals (10th cir.) 1981. Ptnr. Springer & Springer, Lawrence, Kans., 1960—71, Barber, Emerson, Springer, Zinn, Lawrence & Murray, Lawrence, 1971—. Instr. bus. law U. Kans., 1960. Mem. Kans. Ho. Reps., 1961—62. Served with U.S. Army, 1955—57. Fellow: Am. Bar Found., Kans. Bar Found. (trustee 1993—99, pres. 1997—98); mem.: ABA, Kans. Bar Assn. Probate (including wills, trusts), Estate taxation, Estate planning. Office: PO Box 667 Lawrence KS 66044-0667

SPRINGER, CHARLES EDWARD, retired judge; b. Reno, Feb. 20, 1928; s. Edwin and Rose Mary Cecelia (Kelly) S.; m. Jacqueline Sirkegian, Mar. 17, 1951; 1 dau., Kelli Ann. BA, U. Nev., Reno, 1950; LLB, Georgetown U., 1953; LLM, U. Va., 1984; student Grad. Program for Am. Judges, Oriel Coll., Oxford (Eng.), 1984. Bar: Nev. 1953, U.S. Dist. Ct. Nev. 1953, D.C. 1954, U.S. Supreme Ct. 1962. Pvt. practice law, Reno, 1953-80; atty. gen. State of Nev., 1962, legis. legal adv. to gov., 1958-62; legis. bill drafter Nev. Legislature, 1955-57; mem. faculty Nat. Coll. Juvenile Justice, Reno, 1978—; juvenile master 2d Jud. Dist. Nev., 1973-80; justice Nev. Suprem Ct., Carson City, 1981—; vice-chief justice Nev. Supreme Ct., Carson City, 1987, chief justice, 1998-99, ret., 1999. Mem. Jud. Selection Commn., 1981, 98, Nev. Supreme Ct. Gender Bias Task Force, 1981—; trustee Nat. Coun. Juvenile and Family Ct. Judges, 1983—; mem. faculty McGeorge Sch. Law, U. Nev., Reno, 1982—; mem. Nev. Commn. for Women, 1991-95. With AUS, 1945-47. Recipient Outstanding Contbn. to Juvenile Justice award Nat. Coun. Juvenile and Family Ct. Judges, 1989, Midby-Byron Disting. Leadership award U. Nev., 1988. Mem. ABA, Am. Judicature Soc., Am. Trial Lawyers Assn., Phi Kappa Phi. Home: 1001 Dartmouth Dr Reno NV 89509 Office: Nev Supreme Ct Capitol Complex 201 S Carson St Carson City NV 89701-4702

SPRINGER, ERIC WINSTON, lawyer; b. N.Y.C., May 17, 1929; s. Owen Winston and Maida Christina (Stewart) S.; m. Cecile Marie Kennedy, Oct. 25, 1958; children: Brian, Christina. AB, Rutgers U., 1950; LLB, NYU, 1953. Bar: N.Y. 1953, Pa. 1975, U.S. Dist. Ct. (we. dist.) Pa. 1978. Law clk. to justice N.Y. State Supreme Ct., 1955-56; research assoc. U. Pitts., 1956-58, asst. prof. law, 1958-64, assoc. prof. law, 1965-68; dir. compliance EEOC, 1967; v.p., dir. Publs. Aspen Systems Corp., Pitts., 1968-71; ptnr. Horty, Springer & Mattern, Pitts., 1971-2000, exec. v.p., 1982—, of counsel, 2000— dir. Duquesne Light Co., Pitts. Author: Group Practice and the Law, 1969. Editor Nursing and the Law, 1970; Automated Medical Records and the Law, 1971; contbg. editor monthly newsletter Action-Kit for Hosp. Law, 1973— . Bd. dirs. Presbyn. Univ. Hosp., Pitts., 1966—, Cath. Health Corp., Omaha, 1988—, Hosp. Utilization Project., Pitts., 1975-86; mem. Pitts. Commn. on Human Relations, 1963-68, chmn., 1964-68. Fellow Am. Coll. Healthcare Execs. (hon.), Am. Pub. Health Assn.; mem. ABA, Nat. Bar Assn., Allegheny County Bar Assn. (pres. 1994), Am. Acad. Hosp. Attys. (charter), Order of Coif. Democrat. Health. Office: Horty Springer & Mattern PC 4614 5th Ave Pittsburgh PA 15213-3663

SPRINGER, JAMES ELTEN, lawyer; b. Fort Wayne, Ind., Sept. 5, 1941; s. Gerald Elten and Alma May Springer; m. Janice Irene Moser, July 20, 1964 (div.); children: Keri, Heather Robin Church; m. Judy Shultz. Studied, Purdue U., 1959—61; BS, Valparaiso U., Ind., 1965, JD, 1968. Bar: Supreme Ct. Ind., U.S. Dist. Ct., No. Dist. Ind. Dep. prosecutor Allen County, Ind. Prosecutor's Office, Ft. Wayne, 1969—73; atty. Bondner and Springer, Ft. Wayne, 1969—71, O'Dowd & Orman, Ft. Wayne, 1971—76, Kean & Springer, Ft. Wayne, 1971—77; pvt. practice James Springer Law Office, Ft. Wayne, 1977—86, James E. Springer Profl. Corp., Ft. Wayne, 1983—. Co-chair, tech. com. Allen County Bar Assn., Ft. Wayne, Ind., 2001—02. Co-founder Anthony Wayne Coun., Boy Scouts Am., Ft. Wayne, Ind., 1977, exploring chmn., 1984; bd. mem. Waynedale Bus. and Profl. Assn., Waynedale, Ind., 1996; elder St. Matthews Lutheran Ch., 1990—2002. E-4 USAR, 1963—69, Ft. Wayne, Ind. Mem.: Ind. State Bar Assn. (author, editor, State Bar Section News Letter 1998—2001, chmn., vice chair, sec., GP, Solo and Small Firm Sections 2002, Presdl. Citation 2002), Waynedale Lions Club (pres., tail twister 1996), Ft. Wayne Lodge 155 Elks (exhaulted ruler 1969—2002). Republican. Lutheran. Avocations: golf, bowling, bridge. Estate planning, Family and matrimonial, General practice. Home: 7611 Aboite Ctr Rd Fort Wayne IN 46804 Office: James E Springer Profl Corp 7111 Old Trail Rd Fort Wayne IN 46809 Fax: 260-747-7577.

SPRINGER, JEFFREY ALAN, lawyer; b. Denver, Feb. 26, 1950; s. Stanley and Sylvia (Miner) S.; m. Amy Mandel, Nov. 11 1995; children: Cydney Erin, Samantha Libby, Jackson Stanley, Harrison Louis. AB, Princeton U., 1972; JD, U. Colo., 1975. Bar: Colo. 1975, U.S. Dist. Ct. Colo. 1975, U.S. Ct. Appeals (10th cir.) 1975, U.S. Supreme Ct. 1978, U.S. Ct. Appeals (8th cir.) 1986. Assoc. Gerash & Springer, Denver, 1975-79; sole practice Denver, 1979-81; pres. Springer and Steinberg, P.C., Denver, 1981—. Mem. com. on mcpl. ct. rules Supreme Ct. Colo., 1985-86; mem. standing criminal justice act com. U.S. Dist. Ct., 1994-96. Mem. ABA, Assn. Trial Lawyers Am., Colo. Trial Lawyers Assn. (bd. dirs. 1988-90), Colo. Criminal Def. Bar (bd. dirs. 1985-86, 87-88, pres. 1988-89). Criminal, Personal injury (including property damage). Office: 1600 Broadway Ste 1950 Denver CO 80202-4920 E-mail: jspringer@uswest.net.

SPRINGER, PAUL DAVID, lawyer, motion picture company executive; b. N.Y.C., Apr. 27, 1942; s. William W. and Alma (Markowitz) S.; m. Mariann Frankfurt, Aug. 16, 1964; children: Robert, William. BA, U. Bridgeport, 1963; JD, Bklyn. Law Sch., 1967. Bar: N.Y. 1968, U.S. Dist. Ct. (so. and ea. dists.) N.Y. 1968, U.S. Ct. Appeals (2d cir.) 1970, U.S. Supreme Ct. 1973, Calif. 1989. Assoc. Johnson & Tannenbaum, N.Y.C., 1968—70; assoc. counsel Columbia Pictures, N.Y.C., 1970, Paramount Pictures, N.Y.C., 1970—79, v.p., theatrical distbn. counsel, 1979—85, sr. v.p., chief resident counsel East Coast, 1985—87, sr. v.p., asst. gen. counsel L.A., 1987—. Bar: N.Y. 1968, U.S. Dist. Ct. (so. and ea. dists.) N.Y. 1968, U.S. Ct. Appeals (2d cir.) 1970, U.S. Supreme Ct. 1973, Calif. 1989. Trustee West Cunningham Park Civic Assn., Fresh Meadows, N.Y., 1978—. Mem. ABA, Assn. of Bar of City of N.Y., L.A. Copyright Soc., Acad. Motion Picture Arts and Scis., Motion Picture Pioneers. Antitrust, Entertainment, Corporate, general. E-mail: paul_springer@paramount.com.

SPRINGER, ROBERT P. lawyer; b. Bklyn., Nov. 5, 1928; s. Leo J. and Anna K. (Kasen) S.; m. Nesha E. Bass, Sept. 23, 1951; children: Nancy, Mark, Carrie, Stephen. Student, NYU, 1945; BA, U. Mich., 1948; JD, Harvard U., 1951. Bar: N.Y. 1951, U.S. Ct. Mil. Appeals 1952, Mass. 1954, U.S. Supreme Ct. 1978. Ptnr. Silk & Springer, and successors, Boston, 1955-69; pres., gen. counsel Gt. No. Land Corp., Boston, 1969-72; ptnr. Linsky, Springer & Finnegan, Boston, 1973-78; sr. ptnr. Springer, Havey & Ziemian, 1978-82; sr. mem. Law Offices Robert P. Springer, Boston, 1982-89; ret., 1989. Chmn. bd. dirs. Space Scis., Inc., Waltham, Mass., 1967-69; personal counsel to gov. Mass., 1956-60, 62-64; gen. ptnr. KSG Realty Co., Boston, 1968-81. Bd. dirs. Mass. Bay Transp. Authority, 1964-69, Greater Framingham Jewish Family Svc., 1985-89; mem. Jewish Big Bros./Sisters Assn. Greater Boston, 1987-89; vice chmn. trustee coun. Leonard Morse Hosp., Natick, 1978-89; trustee Temple Beth Am, 1985-89. 1st lt. JAGC, U.S. Army, 1951-54. Named Big Brother of Yr., 1987; recipient Lifetime Honoree, Nat. Coun. Christians and Jews, 1987, United Fund, 1987. Office: PO Box 891 Sunapee NH 03782 Home: 35 Fairway Dr Sunapee NH 03782-1300 E-mail: bobspringb@earthlink.net.

SPRINGFIELD, JAMES FRANCIS, retired lawyer, banker; b. Memphis, Nov. 5, 1929; s. C.L. and Mildred (White) S.; m. Shirley Burdick, June 1, 1951 (div.); children: Sidney, Susan, James Francis; m. Nancy Hardwick Ragan, Feb. 8, 1987 (dec. Jan. 1988); m. Donna Thomas Moore, Feb. 22, 1989. BA with distinction in econs., Southwestern at Memphis (now Rhodes Coll.), 1951; LLB, U. Memphis, 1960. Bar: Tenn. 1960. With Union Planters Nat. Bank, Memphis, 1951-94, exec. v.p., sr. trust officer, head trust dept., 1968-85, gen. counsel, sec. bd., 1985-94; sec. bd., exec. v.p., gen. counsel Union Planters Corp., 1985-94; ret., 1994. Mem. adv. bd. Memphis Alzheimer's Assn., 1999-2001; mem. president's coun. Rhodes Coll., Memphis, chmn., 1991-92, internat. chmn. ann. fund, 1995-96; chmn. bd. trustees So. Coll. Optometry, 1978-80; trustee Plough Found., Memphis Conf. United Meth. Ch. Found., 1978-85, U. Tenn. Med. Units Found., 1975-82, MidSouth Pub. Comm. Found., 1985-87, 98—; chmn. fin. com. Hutchinson Sch.; sec. bd. trustees Vision Edn. Found., 1977-78; bd. regents Tenn. Trust Sch., chmn., 1977; mem. president's adv. coun. Lambuth Coll., 1982-85; mem. exec. bd. Chickasaw coun. Boy Scouts Am., 1983-87; bd. visitors Memphis State U. Cecil C. Humphreys Sch. Law, treas. Balmoral Civic Club, 1967-68; pres., dir. Village of Bailey Station Homeowners Assn., Inc., 2000-2001. Lt. (j.g.) USNR, 1951-54. Mem. Tenn. Bar Assn. (chmn. interprofl. rels. com. 1976), Memphis and Shelby County Bar assn. (chmn. moral fitness com. 1972), Tenn. Bankers Assn. (chmn. legis.com. trust div. 1976-77, treas. 1972-73, pres. 1976-77, bd. dirs. 1976-77), Bank Adminstrn. Inst. (chmn. trust commn. 1981-82), Estate Planning Coun. Memphis (pres. 1973-74), Sigma Nu (div. comdr. 1967-68, treas., bd. dirs. House Corp. 1966-81), Omicron Delta Kappa (Rhodes Coll. chpt., pres. ODK Assocs. 2002-2003). Republican. Home: 1692 Village Ridge Rd Collierville TN 38017-9793 E-mail: jimmyspringfield@msn.com.

SPRITZER, RALPH SIMON, lawyer, educator; b. N.Y.C., Apr. 27, 1917; s. Harry and Stella (Theuman) S.; m. Lorraine Nelson, Dec. 23, 1950; children: Ronald, Pamela. BS, Columbia U., 1937, LL.B., 1940. Bar: N.Y. bar 1941, U.S. Supreme Ct. bar 1950. Atty. Office Alien Property, Dept. Justice, 1946-51; anti-trust div. Dept. Justice, 1951-54, Office Solicitor Gen., 1954-61; gen. counsel FPC, 1961-62; 1st asst. to solicitor gen. U.S., 1962-68; prof. law U. Pa., Phila., 1968-86, Ariz. State U., Tempe, 1986—; gen. counsel AAUP, 1983-84. Adj. prof. law George Wasington U., 1967; cons. Adminstrv. Conf. U.S., Ford Found., Pa. Gov.'s Justice Commn. Served with AUS, 1941-46. Recipient Superior Service award Dept. Justice, 1960; Tom C. Clark award Fed. Bar. Assn., 1968 Mem. Am. Law Inst. Home: 1024 E Gemini Dr Tempe AZ 85283-3004 Office: Ariz State Univ Coll Law Tempe AZ 85287

SPRIZZO, JOHN EMILIO, judge; b. Bklyn., Dec. 23, 1934; s. Vincent James and Esther Nancy S.; children— Ann Esther, Johna Emily, Matthew John. BA summa cum laude, St. John's U., Jamaica, N.Y., 1956; LLB summa cum laude, St. John's U., 1959. Bar: N.Y. 1960. Atty. U.S. Dept. Justice, 1959-63; asst. U.S. atty. so. dist. N.Y. Dept. Justice, N.Y.C., 1963-68, chief appellate atty., 1965-66, asst. chief criminal div., 1966-68; assoc. prof. Fordham U. Law Sch., N.Y.C., 1968-72; ptnr. Curtis, Mallet-Prevost, N.Y.C., 1972-81; dist. judge U.S. Dist. Ct. (so. dist.) N.Y., N.Y.C., 1981—. Cons. Nat. Com. for Reform of Criminal Laws, N.Y.C., 1971-72; mem. Knapp Commn., 1971-72; assoc. atty. Com. of Ct. on Judiciary, N.Y.C., 1971-72 Co-contbr. articles to profl. law revs. Mem. ABA, D.C. Bar Assn., Assn. of Bar of City of N.Y. Office: US Dist Ct US Courthouse Foley Sq New York NY 10007-1501

SPROAT, CHRISTINE A. lawyer; b. Poughkeepsie, N.Y., Feb. 6, 1952; d. John and Jean (Hayes) Morabito; m. James P. Sproat, June 29, 1984; children: Ashley E., William C. AAS in Nursery Edn. cum laude, Dutchess C.C., Poughkeepsie, 1976; BS in Psychology, SUNY, New Paltz, 1978, postgrad., 1979-80; JD, Pace U., 1983. Bar: N.Y. 1984, U.S. Dist. Ct. (so. dist.) N.Y. 1996, U.S. Dist. Ct. (ea. dist.) N.Y. 1997. Atty. Michael Haggerty, Esq., Poughkeepsie, 1983-86; law clk. to Hon. Judith A. Hillery N.Y. Supreme Ct., Poughkeepsie, 1986-96; atty. Gellert & Cutler, P.C., Poughkeepsie, 1996—2001; prin. law clk. N.Y. Supreme Ct., Poughkeepsie, 2001—03; prin. law clk. to Hon. Bruce E. Tolbert AJSC, 2003; supreme ct. justice 9th Judicial Dist., NY. Adj. lectr. law Marist Coll., Poughkeepsie, 1994-96. Editor, contbg. author Criminal Law Digest, 1987. Mem. Mid-Hudson Women's Network, Highland, NY, 1997—; founding mem. Beekman Women's Rep. Club; bd. dirs. YWCA, 1999—2002, treas., 2000—01; trustee Arlington Edn. Found., 2000—, Dutchess C.C., Poughkeepsie, 1997—. Mem.: Dutchess County Bar Assn. (asst. treas. 1998—99, treas. 1999—2000, sec. 2000—01, v.p. 2001—02, pres.-elect 2002—), Mid-Hudson Women's Bar (pres. 1986—87, 1999—2000), N.Y. State Bar Assn. Republican. Roman Catholic. Avocations: gardening, hiking. State civil litigation, Municipal (including bonds), Personal injury (including property damage). Office: Dutchess County Courthouse 10 Market St Poughkeepsie NY 12601 E-mail: csproat@courts.state.ny.us.

SPROGER, CHARLES EDMUND, retired lawyer; b. Chgo., Feb. 18, 1933; s. William and Minnette (Weiss) Sproger. BA (David Himmelblau scholar), Northwestern U., 1954, JD, 1957. Bar: Ill. 1957. Assoc. Ehrlich & Cohn, 1958-63, Ehrlich, Bundesen, Friedman & Ross, 1963-72; partner Ehrlich, Bundesen, Broecker & Sproger, 1972-77; pvt. practice, 1977—2000; ret., 2000. Mem. adv. com. curriculum Ill. Inst. Continuing Legal Edn., Chgo., 1976—90; v.p. Mediation Coun. of Ill., 1986-87; arbitration panelist for Cir. Ct. Cook County, 1990—. Editor: Family Lawyer, 1962-63; contbr. articles to legal publs. Mediator Pastoral Psychotherapy Inst., 1982-86. Fellow Am. Acad. Matrimonial Lawyers (bd. examiners 1972-86, chmn. Law Day U.S.A. 1975); mem. ABA, Ill. Bar Assn. (chmn. coun. family law 1970-71), Chgo. Bar Assn. (matrimonial law com. 1958-2000), Am. Arbitration Assn. (divorce mediation com. 1983-92), Decalogue Soc., U. Mich. Club Chgo. (pres. 1988-89), Phi Alpha Delta. Family and matrimonial. Address: 2800 W Birchwood Ave Chicago IL 60645-1218

SPROWL, CHARLES RIGGS, lawyer; b. Lansing, Mich., Aug. 22, 1910; s. Charles Orr and Hazel (Allen) S.; m. Virginia Lee Graham, Jan. 15, 1938; children: Charles R., Robert A., Susan G., Sandra D. AB, U. Mich., 1932, JD, 1934. Bar: Ill. 1935. Pvt. practice, 1934—; of counsel Taylor, Miller, Sprowl, Hoffnagle & Merletti, 1986—. Dir. Simmons Engring. Corp., Petersen Aluminum Corp. Mem. Bd. Edn., New Trier Twp. High Sch., 1959-65, pres. 1962-65; mem. Glencoe Zoning Bd. Appeals, 1956-76, chmn., 1966-76; mem Glencoe Plan Commn., 1962-65; bd. dirs. Glencoe Pub. Libr., 1953-65, pres. 1955-56; trustee Highland Park Hosp., 1959-69; bd. dirs. Cradle Soc., 1968-92. Fellow Am. Coll. Trial Lawyers; mem. Chgo. Bar Assn. (bd. mgrs. 1949-51), Ill. Bar Assn., ABA, Juvenile Protective Assn. (dir. 1943-53), Northwestern U. Settlement (pres. 1963-70, dir.), Soc. Trial Lawyers, Law Club (pres. 1969-70), Legal Club (pres. 1953-54), Univ. Chgo. Club, Skokie Country Club, Delta Theta Phi, Alpha Chi Rho. Presbyterian. Corporate, general, Probate (including wills, trusts), Estate taxation. Home: 380 Green Bay Rd Apt 2A Winnetka IL 60093-4051 Office: 33 N La Salle St Chicago IL 60602-2603

SPRUNG, ARNOLD, lawyer; b. N.Y.C., Apr. 18, 1926; s. David L. and Anna (Stork) S.; m. Audrey Ann Caire; children: Louise, John, Thomas, Doran, D'Wayne. AB, Darmuth Coll., 1947; JD, Columbia U., 1950. Bar: N.Y. 1950, U.S. Dist. Ct. (so. dist.) N.Y. 1950, U.S. Patent Office 1952, U.S. Dist. Ct. (we. dist.) N.Y. 1954, U.S. Ct. Appeals (2d cir.) 1958, U.S. Ct.

Customs and Patent Appeals 1958, U.S. Dist. Ct. (ea. dist.) N.Y. 1962, U.S. Dist. Ct. (no. dist.) Tex. 1971, U.S. Supreme Ct. 1971, and others. Sr. ptnr. Sprung, Kramer, Schaefer & Briscoe, Westchester, N.Y., 1950—. Lt. USN, 1943-46, PTO. Mem. ABA, N.Y. Intellectual Property Assn. Avocations: skiing, wind surfing, racquetball, biking, tennis. Intellectual property, Patent, Trademark and copyright. E-mail: asprung@aol.com.

SPRY, DONALD FRANCIS, II, lawyer; b. Bethlehem, Pa., Nov. 17, 1947; s. Donald Francis and Carol Annette (Bolger) S.; m. Mary Frances, June 20, 1981; stepchildren: Michael Matlaga, Michelle Fehnel. BA, Moravian Coll., 1969; JD, U. Pitts., 1972. Bar: Pa. 1972, U.S. Dist. Ct. (ea. dist.) Pa. 1975. Assoc. Law Offices of Edmund P. Turtzo, Bangor, Pa., 1973-76; ptnr. Turtzo, Spry, Powlette & Sbrocchi, P.C., Bangor, 1976-83, Turtzo, Spry, Powlette, Sbrocchi & Faul, P.C., Bangor and Stroudsburg, Pa., 1983-90, Turtzo, Spry, Sbrocchi, Faul & LaBarre, P.C., Bangor and Stroudsburg, 1990-2000; mem. King, Spry, Herman, Freund & Faul, LLC, Bethlehem, Pa., 2001—. Capt. USAR 1979-80. Mem. ABA (family law sect.), Pa. Bar Assn. (family law sect. edn. law com.), Northampton County Bar Assn. (family law com.), North County Bar Assn. (pres.-elect 1989, pres. 1990), Pa. Sch. Bds. Assn., Nat Sch. Bds. Assn., ACLU, Edn. Law Assn., Pomfret Club. Republican. Methodist. Capt. USAR, 1979-80. Mem. ABA (family law sect.), Pa. Bar Assn. (family law sect. edn. law com.) Northampton County Bar Assn. (family law com.), North County Bar Assn. (pres.-elect 1989, pres. 1990), Pa. Sch. Bds. Assn., Nat. Sch. Bds. Assn., ACLU, Edn. Law Assn., Pomfret Club. Republican. Methodist. Education and schools, Family and matrimonial. also: 930 N 9th St Stroudsburg PA 18360-1208 Office: King Spry Herman Freund & Faul LLC 1 W Broad St Bethlehem PA 18018 Office Fax: 610-332-0314. E-mail: dfs@kingspry.com.

SPURGEON, EDWARD DUTCHER, law educator, foundation administrator; b. Newton, N.J., June 2, 1939; s. Dorsett Larew and Mary (Dutcher) S.; m. Carol Jean Forbes, June 17, 1963; children: Michael Larew, Stephen Edward. AB, Princeton U., 1961; LLB, Stanford U., 1964; LLM in Taxation, NYU, 1968. Bar: Calif. 1965. Assoc. atty. Stammer McKnight et al, Fresno, Calif., 1964-67, Paul Hastings Janofsky and Walker, L.A., 1968-70, ptnr., 1971-80; prof. law U. Utah, Salt Lake City, 1980-90, Wm. H. Leary prof. law and policy, 1990-93, assoc. dean acad. affairs Coll. Law, 1982-83, dean Coll. Law, 1983-90; dean Sch. Law U. Ga., Athens, 1993-98, prof., 1993—; ptnr. Moyle & Draper, Salt Lake City, 2000—. Vis. prof. law Univ. Coll. London, fall 1990, Stanford U. Law Sch., spring 1991; ex-officio mem. Utah State Bar Commn., 1984-90. Co-author: Federal Taxation of Trusts, Grantors and Beneficiaries, 1st edit., 1978, 2d edit., 1989, 3d edit., 1997. Mem. Utah Gov.'s Task Force Officers and Dirs. Liability Ins., 1985-87, Utah Dist. Ct. Reorgn. Commn., 1986-87, Justice in 21st Century Commn., Utah, 1989-91; bd. visitors, exec. com. Stanford U. Law Sch., 1988-93; pres., dir. Albert and Elaine Borchard Found., 1983—; exec. dir. Ctr. on Law and Aging, 1998—; dir. Nat. Sr. Citizens Law Ctr., 1999—. Mem. ABA (Commn. on Legal Problems of the Elderly 1991-95, spl. advisor 1995—), Am. Bar Found. Mailing: 4486 Zarahemla Dr Salt Lake City UT 84124

SQUIRE, WALTER CHARLES, lawyer; b. NYC, Aug. 5, 1945; s. Sidney and Helen (Friedman) S.; m. Sara Jane Abamson; children: Harrison, Russell, Zachary, Andrew. BA, Yale U., 1967; JD, Columbia U., 1971. Bar: N.Y. 1971, U.S. Dist. Ct. (so. and ea. dists.) N.Y. 1975, U.S. Ct. Appeals (2d cir.) 1974, U.S. Supreme Ct. 1977. Ptnr. Jones Hirsch Connors & Bull P.C., NYC, 1986-98, Jacobson, Mermelstein & Squire, LLP, NYC, 1998—; prin. Squire & Co., LLC, NYC, 1998—. Bd. govs. Arthritis Found. N.Y., Inc., 1993-99; bd. dirs. MedicAlert Found., N.Y., 1990-99. Mem. ABA, N.Y. State Bar Assn., Assn. of Bar of City of N.Y., Internat. Bar Assn., Licensing Execs. Soc., Chartered Inst. Arbitrators (London), Am. Arbitration Assn. (arbitrator 1975-2000, mediator 1993—), Am. Acad. Hosp. Attys., Risk Ins. Mgmt. Soc. (lectr. 1983-84), AIDA Reinsurance & Ins. Arbitration Soc. (cert.). Corporate, general, Insurance, Trademark and copyright. Office: Jacobson Mermelstein et al 52 Vanderbilt Ave New York NY 10017-3808

SQUIRES, JOHN HENRY, judge; b. Oct. 21, 1946; married; five children. AB cum laude, U. Ill., 1968, JD, 1971. Bar: Ill. 1971, U.S. Dist. Ct. (cen. dist.) Ill. 1972, U.S. Tax Ct. 1978. Assoc. Brown, Hay & Stephens, Springfield, Ill., 1971-76, ptnr., 1977-87; judge U.S. Bankruptcy Ct. No. Dist. Ill. ea. divsn., 1988—2001, reappointed, 2002—. Trustee in bankruptcy, 1984-87; adj. prof. law John Marshall Law Sch., Chgo., 1994, DePaul U., Chgo., 1995-96; lectr. Am. Bankruptcy Inst., Sangamon County Bar Assn., Winnebago County Bar Assn., Chgo. Bar Assn., Ill. Inst. CLE, Comml. Law League Am., DuPage County (Ill.) Bar Assn. Mem. Nat. Conf. Bankruptcy Judges, Am. Bankruptcy Inst., Fed. Bar Assn., Am. Bus. Club, Union League Club Chgo. Office: US Bankruptcy Ct No Dist Ill Ea Div 219 S Dearborn St #676 Chicago IL 60604-1702

SQUIRES, KATHERINE LANDEY, lawyer; b. N.Y.C., Mar. 28, 1959; BA, Clark U., 1980; JD, U. Dayton, 1982; LLM in Tax, Georgetown U., 1983; MDiv, Biola U., 1994, ThM, 1996, MEd, 2001. Bar: D.C. 1983, Calif. 1986, N.Y. 1999. Assoc. Kutak, Rock & Campbell, Washington, 1983—85; pres., CEO Plan Care, Inc., Irvine, Calif., 1985—88; ptnr. Finley, Kumble, Wagner et.al., Newport Beach, Calif., 1986—88, Sheppard, Mullin, Richter & Hampton, Newport Beach, 1988—89; prin. Law Office of Katherine L. Squires, Irvine, Calif., 1989—97; pres. LawPrep, Inc., LawPrep Press, Inc., 1989—97; atty., mgr. firm-wide tech. devel. tng. and forms Akin Gump Strauss Mauer & Feld, Dallas, 1997—2000; pres., COO Legal EdNet.com., Atkin EdNet.com. and TrainEd.com, Dallas, 1999—2000; chief learning officer, pres. CLE divsn. WebCE.com., LLC, 2000—; pres., chief learning officer Edway Online; CEO Fabricon, Inc., Dallas; COO Tech. Tng. Svs. Corp., Irvine. Vis. prof. Stern Sch. Bus. NYU. Contbr. articles on taxation and comml. law to profl. jours. Rep. candidate for U.S. Senate, 1993-94; commr. Workers' Compensation Appeals Bd., 1994-96; mktg. mgr. Bowne Imaging Network, 1996. Mem. ABA (chmn. internat. law com. of gen. practice sect., 1986—), Orange County Bar Assn., Nat. Assn. Women Lawyers (chmn. bankruptcy com., 1983—), Nat. Assn. Women Execs., Newport Beach (Calif.) C. of C. Republican. Avocations: aviation, gourmet cooking, languages, architecture. Corporate, general, Private international, Securities.

SQUIRES, WILLIAM RANDOLPH, III, lawyer; b. Providence, Sept. 6, 1947; s. William Randolph and Mary Louise (Gress) S.; m. Elisabeth Dale McAnulty, June 23, 1984; children: Shannon, William R. IV, Mayre Elisabeth, James Robert. BA in Econs., Stanford U., 1969; JD, U. Tex., 1972. Bar: Wash. 1973, U.S. Dist. Ct. (we. dist.) Wash. 1973, U.S. Dist. Ct. (ea. dist.) Wash. 1976, U.S. Ct. Appeals (9th cir.) 1976, U.S. Supreme Ct. 1976, U.S. Ct. Fed. Claims 1982. Assoc. Oles, Morrison, Rinker, Stanislaw & Ashbaugh, Seattle, 1973-78; ptnr., chmn. litig. group Davis Wright Tremaine, Seattle, 1978-97; mem. Summit Law Group, Seattle, 1997—. Fellow Am. Coll. Trial Lawyers; mem. ABA, Internat. Bar Assn., Wash. State Bar Assn., King County Bar Assn., Wash. Athletic Club, Rainier Club (Seattle). Episcopalian. Federal civil litigation, Construction, Labor (including EEOC, Fair Labor Standards Act, labor-management relations, NLRB, OSHA). Home: 5554 NE Penrith Rd Seattle WA 98105-2845 Office: Summit Law Group 315 Fifth Ave S Ste 1000 Seattle WA 98104 E-mail: randys@summitlaw.com.

SQUIRES-LIND, JOAN A. lawyer; b. Berkeley, Calif., May 2, 1941; d. Robert Charles and Jayne Arline (Browning) Squires; children: Jason Mark Alexander, Vanessa Antonia Alexandra. BA in Modern European Lit., Stanford U., 1962; JD, Cornell U., 1977. Bar: N.Y. 1978, France 1988, U.S. Supreme Ct. 1990. Assoc. Thaler & Thaler, Ithaca, N.Y., 1977-79, ptnr., 1980-86; pvt. practice Paris, 1986—. Mem. Am. Immigration Lawyer Assn., Computer Law Assn., N.Y. State Bar Assn., Am. Arbitration Assn. (panel of arbitrators), Cercle Interallié. Immigration, naturalization, and customs. Office: 6 rue du Foin 75003 Paris France

SRISANIT, EKBURUS, lawyer, consultant; b. Bangkok, Oct. 10, 1974; parents Anek and Darunee Srisanit. LLB, Assumption U., Bangkok, 1997; M in Intellectual Property, Franklin Pierce, 1998. Paralegal Anek and Assocs. Co., Ltd., Bangkok, 1996—97, assoc., 1998—99, ptnr., 2003—; intern trainee, gen. dep. Whitman Breed Abbot and Morgan, L.A., 1998. Lectr. Assumption U., Bangkok, 1999—. Mem.: Thai C. of C., Internat. Bar Assn., Inter Pacific Bar Assn. Office: Anek & Assocs Co Ltd 19th Fl Wall St Tower Surawong Rd Suriyawong Bangrak Bangkok Thailand 10500 Fax: 662-236-5835. E-mail: ekburus@aneklaw.com.

SRISKANDARAJAH, ATCHUTHAN, lawyer; b. Sri Lanka, Apr. 10, 1971; s. Thiagarajah and Sundrakumari Sriskandarajah; m. Rekha Sriskandarajah, Aug. 30, 2001. BS in Acctg., George Mason U.; JD, Quinnipiac Coll. Bar: Va. 1997. Pvt. practice, Prince William, Va., 1997—99, Fairfax, Va., 1999—. Mem.: George Mason Inns Ct. (assoc.), Kiwanis (v.p. Manassas chpt. 2002). Family and matrimonial, Criminal, Immigration, naturalization, and customs. Office: 4008 Williams Ct Fairfax VA 22032 Office Fax: 703-278-0420. Business E-Mail: asris@yahoo.com.

STAAB, MICHAEL JOSEPH, lawyer; b. Hays, Kans., Oct. 12, 1955; s. Robert Joseph and Beatrice Agnes Staab; m. Kathy Lee Brock, Jan. 11, 1986; children: Colton Brock, Matthew Michael. BA magna cum laude, Ft. Hays State U., 1978; JD, Drake U., 1981; LLM in Health Law, DePaul U., 1993. Bar: Idaho 1981, U.S. Dist. Ct. Idaho 1981, Utah 1986, U.S. Dist. Ct. Utah 1986, Ill. 1990, U.S. Dist. Ct. (no. dist.) Ill. 1990. Assoc. Quane, Smith, Howard and Hull, Boise, Idaho, 1981-83, Meuleman & Miller, Boise, Idaho, 1983; pvt. practice Boise, Idaho, 1983-85; ptnr. Biele, Haslam & Hatch, Salt Lake City, 1985-89, Parsons, Behle & Latimer, Salt Lake City, 1989-90; assoc. Steinberg, Polacek & Goodman, Chgo., 1990-93, Ruff, Weldenaar and Reidy, Ltd., Chgo., 1994-96; ptnr. Gardner, Carton and Douglas, Chgo., 1996—2002, of counsel, 2002—; v.p. legal svcs., mng. counsel Caremark Inc., Northbrook, Ill., 2002—. Mem. Chgo. adv. bd. Drake U., 1996—2001; bd. counselors Drake U. Law Sch., 2001—; adv. bd. Health Law Inst., DePaul U. Coll. Law, 2002—; lectr. in field. Contbr. articles to legal publs. Bd. dirs. Winnetka Village Caucus, 1992—94, Big Bros./Big Sisters, Salt Lake City, 1985—89, Utah Head Injury Assn., Salt Lake City, 1988—90, Pediat. Brain Injury Assn., Salt Lake City, 1988—90; pack master Cub Scouts 15, 1999—. Mem. ABA, Ill. Bar Assn., Chgo. Bar Assn., Nat. Health Lawyers Assn., Nat. Order of Barristers, Order of Omega, K.C., Phi Kappa Phi, Phi Alpha Theta, Phi Eta Sigma. Roman Catholic. Avocations: bicycling, reading, basketball, baseball, antiques. Health. Home: 173 De Windt Rd Winnetka IL 60093-3708 Office: Caremark Inc 2211 Sanders Rd Northbrook IL 60062 E-mail: michael.staab@caremark.com.

STABLER, LEWIS VASTINE, JR., lawyer; b. Greenville, Ala., Nov. 5, 1936; s. Lewis Vastine and Dorothy Daisy Stabler; m. Monteray Scott, Sept. 5, 1958; children: Dorothy Monteray Scott, Andrew Vastine, Monteray Scott Smith, Margaret Langston. BA, Vanderbilt U., 1958; JD with distinction, U. Mich., 1961. Bar: Ala. 1961. Assoc. Cabaniss & Johnston, Birmingham, Ala., 1961-67; assoc. prof. law U. Ala., 1967-70; ptnr. Cabaniss, Johnston, Gardner, Dumas & O'Neal (and predecessor firms), Birmingham, 1970-91, Walston, Stabler, Wells, Anderson and Bains, Birmingham, 1991-97; pvt. practice, Birmingham, 1997—. Mem. com. of 100 Candler Sch. Theology, Emory U. Bd. editors: Mich. Law Rev, 1960-61. Fellow Am. Bar Found. (life); mem. Am. Law Inst. (life), Ala. Law Inst. (mem. coun., dir. 1968-70), ABA, Ala. Bar Assn., Birmingham Bar Assn., Am. Judicature Soc., Am. Assn. R.R. Trial Counsel, Order of Coif. Methodist (cert. lay speaker). Clubs: Country of Birmingham, Rotary. Antitrust, Federal civil litigation, State civil litigation. Home: 3538 Victoria Rd Birmingham AL 35223-1404 Office: PO Box 53-1161 Birmingham AL 35253-1161

STACEY, JAMES ALLEN, retired judge; b. Norwalk, Ohio, Dec. 26, 1925; s. James Calvin and Glenna (Cleveland) S.; m. Marlyn Frederick, Aug. 21, 1948; children: James A., Libble M. Romigh, Lorrie Stacey Singler, David F., CamAllison Shenigo, Tricia Stacey Berger. Student, Bucknell U., 1943-44, Ohio Wesleyan U., 1944, 46, 47, U. N.C., 1944-45; JD, Cleveland-Marshall Law Sch., 1951. Bar: Ohio 1952, U.S. Dist. Ct. (no. dist.) Ohio 1955. Ptnr. McGory & Stacey, Sandusky, Ohio, 1954-56; assoc. Steinemann & Zieher, Sandusky, Ohio, 1956-60; ptnr. Work, Stacey & Moyer, 1960-67; judge Sandusky Mcpl. Ct., 1967-95, ret., 1995. Mem. Ohio State Traffic Law Com., 1969-95, chmn., 1978-82. Mem. Erie-Ottawa Mental Health Bd., 1968-87; mem. Ex-Offenders for Help Bd., 1975-81; bd. dirs. Camp Fire Girls, 1956-60, L.E.A.D.S., 1984-86, Sandusky C. of C., 1984-86. Served with USNR, 1943-46. Mem. Ohio State Bar Assn., Ohio Mcpl. Judges Assn. (exec. bd. 1970-80), Am. Judicature Soc., Am. Judges Assn., Erie County Bar Assn., Amvets, Sandusky Exch. Club (bd. dirs. 1999—), Elks, Eagles Club, Italian-Am. Beneficial Club. Republican. Presbyterian. Home: 1407 Julianne Cir Sandusky OH 44870-7032

STACHOWSKI, MICHAEL JOSEPH, lawyer, consultant; b. Buffalo, Feb. 27, 1947; s. Stanley Joseph and Pearl (Wojcik) S.; children: Lisa Ann, Evan Michael, Crystal Lee; m. Deborah Ann Jakubczak, Oct. 19, 1979. BA, Canisius Coll., 1970; JD, SUNY-Buffalo, 1973; cert., Hague Acad. Internat. Law, The Netherlands, 1976. Bar: N.Y. 1974, U.s. Dist. Ct. (we. dist.) N.Y. 1974, U.S. Ct. Appeals (2d cir.) 1974. Atty. Sportservice, Inc., Buffalo, 1973-74; assoc. Siegel & McGee, Buffalo, 1974-75; confidential clk. 8th dist. N.Y. Supreme Ct., Buffalo, 1975-77; rsch. counsel N.Y. State Assembly, Albany, 1977-80; sole practice Buffalo, 1976-86; dep. atty. Town of Cheektowaga, N.Y., 1986-98, spl. prosecutor, 1996-98, litigation town atty., 1998-99, town atty., 2000—. Michael J. Stachowski P.C., 1987—. Campaign mgr. various jud. candidates, Buffalo, 1977—; fund raiser Erie County Dems., Buffalo, 1979—, vice chmn., 1988-97, chmn. jud. screening com., 1991—; bd. dirs. Buffalo Columbus Hosp., 1988-96, sec., 1991-92, treas., 1993-95, chmn. merger com. with Buffalo Gen.; bd. dirs. Buffalo Healthcare Corp.; mem. N.Y. State Dem. Com., 1988-96; chmn. pres.'s coun. Canisius Coll. 2000, mem. bd. regents, 2002; vice chmn. programs Silver Lakes dist. Greater Niagara coun. Boy Scouts Am., 2001. Mem. ATLA, N.Y. State Bar Assn., Erie County Bar Assn., East Clinton Profl. Businessmen's Assn. (v.p. 1976—, pres. 1985), Pi Gamma. Roman Catholic. State civil litigation, Family and matrimonial, Personal injury (including property damage). Home: 12 Beaverbrook Ct Depew NY 14043-4242 Office: 2025 Clinton St Buffalo NY 14206-3311 E-mail: stachlaw@aol.com.

STACKABLE, FREDERICK LAWRENCE, lawyer; b. Howell, Mich., Dec. 4, 1935; s. Lawrence Peter and Dorothea R. (Kiney) S. BA, Mich. State U., 1959; JD, Wayne State U., 1962. Bar: Mich. 1962, U.S. Dist. Ct. (ea. and we. dists.) Mich. 1964; U.S. Supreme Ct. 1968. Commr. Ingham County Cir. Ct.; sole practitioner Lansing, Mich., 1975—; pvt. practice, 1975—. V.p. Mich. Assn. Cir. Ct. Commrs., 1963, pres., 1963—70; 18th dist. rep. Ingham County Bd. Suprs.; mem. Com. on Mich. Law Revision Commn.; state rep. 58th Ho. Dist., 1971, 72, 73, 74. County del. Rep. Party, Ingham County, Mich., 1969-70, state del., Mich., 1971-74; Lansing city atty., 1975. Recipient Disting. Alumni award Wayne State U. Sch. Law, Detroit, 1987. Mem. Mich. Bar Assn., Ingham County Bar Assn., Nat. Conf. Commrs. Uniform State Laws, Mich. Trail Riders Assn. (dir., past pres.), Mich. Internat. Snowmobile Assn., Sportsman's Alliance Mich., Cycle Conservation Club, Am. Judicature Soc. Avocations: horseback riding, snowmobiling, skiing, traveling. State civil litigation, Personal injury (including property damage), Probate (including wills, trusts). Office: 300 N Grand Ave Lansing MI 48933-1214

STADNICAR, JOSEPH WILLIAM, lawyer; b. Corpus Christi, Tex., Oct. 30, 1963; s. Edward and Carrie Louise (Garris) S. BBA, John Carroll U., 1986; MBA, Ohio State U., 1989, JD, 1990. Bar: Ohio 1990. Assoc. Gerald E. Schlafman Co., Fairborn, Ohio, 1991-95; pvt. practice Beavercreek, Ohio, 1995-97. Asst. prosecuting atty. City of Fairborn, 1990-95; prosecuting atty. City of Beavercreek, 1990-2001; assoc. Hammond & Stier Law Office, Beavercreek, 1996-98, ptnr. Hammond, Stier and Stadnicar, 1998—. Trustee Family Violence Prevention Ctr. of Greene County, Xenia, Ohio, 1995—, Am. Heart Assn., Miami Valley, Ohio, 1996—. Mem. ABA, Ohio Bar Assn., Greene County Bar Assn., Rotary, Beavercreek C. of C., Fairborn C. of C. Avocations: fishing, camping. Commercial, consumer (including collections, credit), Criminal, Personal injury (including property damage). Office: 3834 Dayton Xenia Rd Beavercreek OH 45432-2833 E-mail: jstadnicar@beavercreeklaw.com.

STADTMUELLER, JOSEPH PETER, federal judge; b. Oshkosh, Wis., Jan. 28, 1942; s. Joseph Francis and Irene Mary (Kilp) S.; m. Mary Ellen Brady, Sept. 5, 1970; children: Jeremy, Sarah. BS in Bus. Adminstrn., Marquette U., 1964, JD, 1967. Bar: Wis. 1967, U.S. Supreme Ct. 1980. With Kluwin, Dunphy, Hankin and McNulty, 1968-69; asst. U.S. atty. Dept. Justice, Milw., 1969-74, 1st. asst. U.S. atty., 1974-75; with Stepke, Kossow, Trebon and Stadtmueller, Milw., 1975-76; asst. U.S. atty. Dept. Justice, 1977-78, dep. U.S. atty., 1978-81, U.S. atty., 1981-87; judge U.S. Dist. Ct. (ea. dist.) Wis., Milw., 1987—, chief judge, 1995—2002. Mem. 7th Cir. Jud. Coun., 1995—2002. Recipient Spl. Commendation award Atty. Gen. U.S., 1974, 80. Mem. ABA, State Bar Wis. (bd. govs. 1979-83, exec. com. 1982-83), Am. Law Inst., Fed. Judges Assn. (bd. dirs. 1995—, sec. 2001--). Clubs: University (Milw.). Republican. Roman Catholic. Office: 471 US Courthouse 517 E Wisconsin Ave Milwaukee WI 53202-4500

STAELIN, EARL HUDSON, lawyer; b. Toledo, Apr. 24, 1940; s. Carl Gustav and Margaret E. (Hudson) S.; m. Carol Jane Keeney, Mar. 24, 1973 (div. 1995); 1 child, Vijay Hudson. BA, Yale U., 1962; LLB, U. Mich., 1966. Bar: Ohio 1966, U.S. Dist. Ct. (no. dist.) Ohio 1967, Tex. 1982, U.S. Dist. Ct. (we. dist.) Tex. 1988, U.S. Dist. Ct. (no. dist.) Tex. 1991, U.S. Ct. Appeals (5th cir.) 1994, Colo. 1998. Assoc. atty. Marshall, Melhorn, Toledo, 1966-69; pvt. practice Toledo, 1969; lectr. law U. Toledo Coll. Law, 1971-72; staff atty. Toledo Legal Aid Soc., 1969-71, dir., 1971-76, sr. staff atty., 1977-81; pvt. practice cons. nutrition Austin, Tex., 1981—82, Denver, 2001—; staff atty. City of Austin Law Dept., 1982-86; pvt. practice Law Ofcs. of Earl H. Staelin, Austin and Aurora, Colo., 1986—. Presenter in field. Contbr. articles to profl. jours. Pres. Toledo Coun. on World Affairs, 1971-76; chmn. Mayors' com to rewrite Housing Code, Toledo, 1976; co-organizer Conferences on Nutrition and Crime, Austin, 1982, San Antonio, 1983. Mem. Colo. Bar Assn., State Bar Tex., Interfaith Alliance Colo. Democrat. Unitarian Universalist. Construction, Personal injury (including property damage), Family and matrimonial. Home: 12701 E Asbury Cir # 102 Aurora CO 80014-5317 Office: 12701 E Asbury Cir # 102 Aurora CO 80014-5317 E-mail: estaelin@attbi.com.

STAFFARONI, ROBERT J. lawyer; b. Sept. 19, 1952; BA, Yale U., 1973; JD, U. Pa., 1976. Bar: N.Y. 1978. Mem. Debevoise & Plimpton, N.Y.C. Mem. N.Y. State Bar Assn. Taxation, general, Corporate taxation. Office: Debevoise & Plimpton 919 Third Ave 45th Fl New York NY 10022

STAFFIERI, NICHOLAS J. lawyer; b. Phila., Aug. 25, 1948; BA, LaSalle U., 1970; MA, Temple U., 1972; JD, Wake Forest U., 1974. Bar: Pa. 1974, U.S. Dist. Ct. (ea. dist.) Pa. 1975, U.S. Ct. Appeals (3d cir.) 1987, U.S. Supreme Ct. 1979. Counsel Com. of Pa. State Senate, Harrisburg, 1979—82; trial atty. Southeastern Pa. Transp. Authority, Phila., 1983—2000, gen. counsel, 2000—. Corporate, general, Transportation. Office: Southeastern Pa Transp Authority 1234 Market St 5th Fl Philadelphia PA 19107-3780

STAG, MICHAEL GREGORY, lawyer; b. Tachikawa, Japan, July 15, 1967; came to U.S., 1969; s. Richard Hopkins and Paulette (Tasca) S. BBA, Loyola U., New Orleans, 1990; MBA, JD, Loyola U., 1994. Bar: La. 1994, U.S. Dist. Ct. (ea. dist.) La., U.S. Dist. Ct. (mid. dist.) La. Law clk. Capitelli & Wicker, New Orleans, 1993-94; law clk. to Hon. Ronald Sholes Civil Dist. Ct., New Orleans, 1994-95; assoc. McQuaig & Solomon, New Orleans, 1995-96, Sacks & Smith, New Orleans, 1996—. General civil litigation, Environmental. Office: Smith Stag LLC 365 Canal St # 2850 New Orleans LA 70130-1112

STAGEBERG, ROGER V. lawyer; B of Math. with distinction, U. Minn., 1963, JD cum laude, 1966. Assoc. Mackall, Crounse & Moore, Mpls., 1966-70, ptnr., 1970-86; shareholder and officer Lommen, Nelson, Cole & Stageberg, P.A., Mpls., 1986—. Co-chmn. joint legal svcs. funding com. Minn. Supreme Ct., 1995-96. Mem. U. Minn. Law Rev. Bd. dirs. Mpls. Legal Aid Soc., 1970—, treas., 1973, pres., 1977, dir. of fund, 1980—, chmn. of fund, 1998-2000; chmn. bd. trustees Colonial Ch. of Edina, 1975, chmn. congregation, 1976, pres. found., 1978; officer, trustee Mpls. Found, 1983-88. Mem. Minn. State Bar Assn. (numerous offices and coms., pres. 1994), Hennepin County Bar Assn. (chmn. securities law sect. 1979, chmn. attys. referral svc. com. 1980, sec. 1980, treas. 1981, pres. 1983), Order of Coif. Corporate, general, Mergers and acquisitions, Securities. Office: Lommen Nelson Cole & Stageberg PA 1800 IDS Center 80 S 8th St Minneapolis MN 55402-2100

STAGG, CLYDE LAWRENCE, lawyer; b. St. Petersburg, Fla., May 22, 1935; s. Milton Gurr and Clyda Montese (Lawrence) S.; m. Betsy Barron, Aug. 22, 1959; children: Sharon, Brian, Lauren, Stephen. BSJ, U. Fla., 1956, LLB, 1959. Bar: Fla. 1959, U.S. Dist. Ct. (mid. dist.) Fla. 1959, U.S. Ct. Appeals (5th cir.) 1969, U.S. Supreme Ct. 1971, U.S. Ct. Appeals (11th cir.) 1987. Assoc. Shackleford, Farrior, Tampa, Fla., 1959-60; asst. solicitor Hillsborough County Solicitor's Office, Tampa, 1960-61; chief asst. state atty. State Atty.'s Office, Tampa, 1963-64, asst. state atty., 1961-63; ptnr. Whitaker, Mann & Stagg, Tampa, Knight, Jones & Whitaker, Tampa, 1965-67, Holland & Knight, Tampa, 1968-74, 80-86, Stichter, Stagg, Hoyt, et al, Tampa, 1974-79, Stagg, Hardy, Ferguson, Murnaghan & Mathews P.A., Tampa, 1986-93, Akerman, Senterfitt & Eidson P.A., Tampa, 1993—. Bd. dirs. Fla. Lawyers Mut. Ins. Co. Mem., sec. Hillsborough Area Regional Transit Authority, Tampa, 1979—85; mem., sec., vice chmn., chmn. Tampa Sports Authority, 1985—89; spl. counsel U.S. Senator Bob Graham, 1988; mem. nat. conf. of commrs. Uniform State Laws, 1997—; bd. dirs. United Way Greater Tampa, Inc., Tampa, 1988—91, Fla. Blood Svcs., Inc., Tampa, 1989—, treas., 2001—. Mem. ABA, Am. Bar Found., Fla. Bar (bd. govs. 1974-75), Hillsborough County Bar Assn. (pres. 1970-71, Outstanding Lawyer award 1998), Fla. Bar Found., Am. Bd. Trial Advocates, Greater Tampa C. of C. (bd. dirs. 1988-91), Am. Inn Ct. (master emeritus of bench). Alternative dispute resolution, General civil litigation, Product liability. Home: 3303 W San Nicholas St Tampa FL 33629-7034 Office: Akerman Senterfitt & Eidson PA PO Box 3273 Tampa FL 33601-3273

STAHL, MADONNA, retired judge; b. Robinson, Ill., Sept. 26, 1928; d. Lawrence Joy and Inez Lucille (Kennedy) S.; children: Khushro Ghandhi, Rustom Ghandhi, Behram Ghandhi. BS, U. Ill., 1950; JD, Albany Law Sch., 1973. Bar: N.Y. 1974, U.S. Dist. Ct. (no. dist.) N.Y. 1974, U.S. Ct. Appeals (2nd cir.) 1975, U.S. Supreme Ct. 1978. Atty. trainee N.Y. State Dept. Commerce, Albany, 1973-74; atty. Legal Aid Soc., Albany, 1974-76; ptnr. Powers, Stahl & Somers (and predecessor firms), 1976-89; part-time judge Albany City Ct., 1984-89, full-time judge, 1990-97; ret., 1997. Mem. com. on character and fitness N.Y. State Supreme Ct. A.D. 3d Dept., Albany,

1980-86; jud. hearing officer State of N.Y., 1997-2000. Lobbyist Com. for Progressive Legislation, Schenectady, 1968-70. Mem. Women's Bar Assn. State N.Y. (Capital dist. pres. 1983-84). Democrat. Unitarian Universalist. E-mail: judge_stahl@yahoo.com.

STAHL, NORMAN H. judge; b. Manchester, N.H., 1931; BA, Tufts U., 1952; LLB, Harvard U., 1955. Law clk. to Hon. John V. Spalding Mass. Supreme Ct., 1955—56; assoc. Devine, Millimet, Stahl & Branch, Manchester, NH, 1956—59, ptnr., 1959—90; dist. judge U.S. Dist. Ct. (N.H. dist.), 1990—92; cir. judge U.S. Ct. Appeals (1st cir.), Concord, NH, 1992—. Del to Rep. Nat. Conv., 1988. Mem.: N.H. Bar Assn. Office: US Courthouse Ste 8730 1 Courthouse Way Boston MA 02210

STAHL, ROBERT GEORGE, lawyer; b. Newark, N.J., July 21, 1957; m. Elizabeth Scott Ferguson, Apr. 10, 1999; children: Andrew, Elizabeth. JD, Seton Hall U., Newark, 1989. Bar: N.J. 1989, US Dist. Ct. N.J. 1989, U.S. Ct. Appeals (3d cir.) 1997, US Dist. Ct. (so. dist.) N.Y. 1997, US Dist. Ct. (ea. dist.) N.Y. 1997, US Supreme Ct. 1997. Law clk. for dist. judge U.S. Dist. Ct. N.J., Newark, 1989—91; asst. U.S. atty. U.S. Atty.'s Office, Dist. of N.J., Newark, 1991—97; pvt. practice Law Office of Robert G. Stahl, Westfield, NJ, 1997—. Com. person Rep. Com., Westfield, NJ, 2000—02. Mem.: ATLA, ABA, N.J. State Bar Assn., Fed. Bar Assn., Assn. of Criminal Def. Attys. General practice, Family and matrimonial, Criminal. Office: Law Office of Robert G Stahl 220 St Paul St Westfield NJ 07090 Office Fax: 908-301-9008. E-mail: stahlesq@bellatlantic.net.

STAINE, ROSS (ROSS DONAN ALLISON STAINE JR.), lawyer; b. El Paso, Tex., July 13, 1924; s. Ross Donan Allison and Dennie Joe (Stowe) S.; m. Mary Louise Sibert, Aug. 15, 1947; children: Martha Louise, Julie Ann, Ross. BA, Tex. A&M U., 1947; LL.B., U. Tex., 1950. Bar: Tex. Assoc. Baker Botts, Houston, 1947, ptnr., 1962—. Served to 1st lt. U.S. Army, 1943-46, PTO. Mem. State Bar Tex., Houston Bar Assn., Tex. Law Rev. Assn., Chancellors, Forest Club (Houston), Order of Coif, Phi Delta Phi. Baptist. Home: 5555 Del Monte Dr Apt 807 Houston TX 77056-4117 Office: Baker & Botts 3000 One Shell Plaza Houston TX 77002 E-mail: rdall@swbell.net.

STAKER, ROBERT JACKSON, judge; b. Kermit, W.Va., Feb. 14, 1925; s. Frederick George and Nada (Frazier) S.; m. Sue Blankenship Poore, July 16, 1955; 1 child, Donald Seth; 1 stepson, John Timothy Poore. Student, Marshall U., Huntington, W.Va., W.Va. U., Morgantown, U. Ky., Lexington; LL.B, W.Va. U., 1952. Bar: W.Va. 1952. Practiced in, Williamson, 1952-68; judge Mingo County Circuit Ct., Williamson, 1969-79; U.S. dist. judge So. Dist. W.Va., Huntington, 1979-95, sr. U.S. dist. judge, 1995—. Served with USN, 1943-46. Democrat. Presbyterian. E-mail: robert_staker@wvsd.uscourts.gov.

STALCUP, JOE ALAN, lawyer, clergyman; b. Hooker, Okla., Feb. 13, 1931; s. Herbert I. and Ruby (Gantt) S.; m. Nancy Jo Vaughn, Sept. 3, 1950; children: Melinda, Sondra Jo, Cheri Ann. BBA cum laude, So. Methodist U., 1951, JD magna cum laude, 1959, M.Th. magna cum laude, 1978. Bar: Tex. 1959. Tchr. Dallas Ind. Sch. Dist., 1951-57; assoc. atty. firm Locke, Purnell, Boren, Laney & Neely, Dallas, 1959-66; assoc. atty., partner firm Geary, Brice & Lewis, Dallas, 1966-67; founder, sr. partner firm Stalcup, Johnson, Meyers & Miller (and predecessor firm), Dallas, 1968-75; dean Sch. Theology for the Laity, 1978-80, 92-96. Pres. Dallas County Young Democrats, 1952-54; Bd. dirs., mem. exec. com. N. Tex. Christian Communications Commn., 1972-78; bd. dirs., v.p. Greater Dallas Council Chs., 1972-75; bd. dirs., chmn. Christian Ch. Found., 1976-84, 86-91, Christian Bd. Publ., 1991-98. Mem. ABA, Tex. Bar Assn., Dallas Bar Assn., Am. Judicature Soc., Phi Alpha Delta. Mem. Disciples of Christ (minister). Personal income taxation, Probate (including wills, trusts), Property, real (including real estate development, water). Home: 7594 Benedict Dr Dallas TX 75214-1903 Office: 6510 Abrams Rd Dallas TX 75231-7217

STALEY, JOHN FREDRIC, lawyer; b. Sidney, Ohio, Sept. 26, 1943; s. Harry Virgil and Fredericka May (McMillin) S.; m. Sue Ann Bolin, June 11, 1966; children: Ian McMillin, Erik Bolin. AB in History, Fresno State Coll., 1965; postgrad., Calif. State U., Hayward, 1967-68; JD, U. Calif., San Francisco, 1972. Bar: Calif. 1972. Ptnr. Staley, Jobson & Wetherell, Pleasanton, Calif., 1972—. Lectr. U. Calif. Hastings Coll. Law, San Francisco, 1973-74; founding mem. Bank of Livermore (now U.S. Bank); del. U.S.-China Joint Conf. on Law, Beijing, 1987. Mem. Livermore City Coun., 1975-82, vice mayor, 1978-82; bd. dirs. Alameda County Tng. and Employment Bd., Alameda-Contra Costa Emergency Med. Svcs. Agy., Valley Vol. Ctr. With M.I., U.S. Army, 1966-67. Fellow Am. Acad. Matrimonial Lawyers; mem. ABA, Calif. State Bar, Alameda Bar Assn., Amador Valley Bar Assn., Calif. Assn. Cert. Family Law Specialists (pres. 1988-89, Hall of Fame award 1994), Hastings Coll. Law Alumni Assn. (bd. dirs.). Family and matrimonial, Property, real (including real estate development, water). Office: Staley Jobson & Ford Ste 310 5775 Stoneridge Mall Rd Pleasanton CA 94588-2838

STALL, RICHARD J., JR., lawyer; b. Covington, Ky., July 5, 1941; BS with distinction, Purdue U., Lafayette, Ind., 1963; JD, Stanford U., Calif., 1966. Bar: Calif., U.S. Supreme Ct., U.S. Dist. Ct. (ctrl. dist.), U.S. Ct. Appeals (9th cir.). Assoc. Lawler, Felix & Hall (now Arter & Hadden), L.A., 1966-70; ptnr. pvt. practice, L.A., 1971-93; prin. Law Office of Richard J. Stall, Jr., et al, L.A., 1994—. Contbg. author: Ins. Jour. Mem.: ABA, Culver-Marina Bar Assn. (past pres., dir.), Santa Monica Bar Assn., Nat. Assn. Railroad Trial Counsel, L.A. County Bar Assn., Calif. State Bar Assn. (real estate sect.), Beverly Hills Bar Assn. (real estate sect.), Assn. Bus. Trial Lawyers, Am. Arbitration Assn., Lion's Club (past pres.), Tau Beta Pi, Sigma Chi (Delta Delta Chpt. past pres.). Office: Law Office Richard J Stall Jr Ste 200 10507 W Pico Blvd Los Angeles CA 90064-2319 Fax: 310-470-3673. E-mail: rstall@picolaw.com.

STALLINGS, NORMAN (CHARLES NORMAN STALLINGS), lawyer; b. Tampa, Fla., Apr. 3, 1914; s. Otto Pyromus and Minnie Henderson (Mitchell) S.; m. Mary Phillips Powell, Feb. 6, 1943 (dec. 1999); children: Charles Norman, Jean Katherine (dec.), Mary Anne. AB, U. Fla., 1935; JD, Harvard U., 1938, LL.M., 1940. Bar: Mo. 1939, Fla. 1940, D.C. 1941, Ga. 1946. Asso. firm Ryland, Stinson, Mag & Thomson, Kansas City, Mo., 1938-39, Sutherland, Tuttle & Brennan, Washington, 1940-41, Atlanta, 1946-49; mem. firm Shackleford, Farrior, Stallings & Evans, Tampa, Fla., 1949-84, of counsel, 1984—2002. Vice chmn. Hillsborough County (Fla.) Aviation Authority, 1955-61. Served to lt. col. U.S. Army, 1941-46, ETO. Decorated Bronze Star; Croix de Guerre avec Palma, Belgium. Fellow Am. Coll. Trial Lawyers; mem. ABA, Hillsborough County Bar Assn. (past pres.), Fla. Bar (past gov.), Univ. Club (past pres.), Tampa Yacht and Country Club (past gov.), Ye Mystic Krewe of Gasparilla (past capt. and king), Phi Delta Phi, Kappa Alpha. Republican. Episcopalian. Home: 3501 Bayshore Blvd Apt 201 Tampa FL 33629 Office: PO Box 3324 Tampa FL 33601-3324

STALLINGS, RONALD DENIS, lawyer; b. Evansville, Ind., Feb. 22, 1943; s. Denis and Gertrude (Tong) S.; m. Vicki Lee Chandler, Aug. 21, 1965; children: Courtnay, Claire, Ryan. B in Indsl. Engring., Ga. Inst. Tech., 1965; LLB, U. Va., 1968. Bar: Ga. 1968. Assoc. Powell, Goldstein, Frazer & Murphy LLP, Atlanta, 1968-75, ptnr., 1976-2000, co-counsel, 2001—; sr. v.p., gen. counsel, corp. sec. Reliance Trust Co., Atlanta, 2001—. Co-author: Georgia Corporate Forms, 1988. Mem. ABA, Ga. Bar Assn., Atlanta Bar Assn., Nat. Assn. Bond Lawyers, Am. Soc. Corp. Secs., Phoenix Soc. Atlanta (trustee 1987-93). Roman Catholic. Banking, Corporate, general, Finance. Home: 4601 Polo Ln NW Atlanta GA 30339-5345 Office: Reliance Trust Co Ste 900 3384 Peachtree Rd NE Atlanta GA 30326-1106 E-mail: rstallings@relico.com.

STAMM, ALAN, lawyer; b. Galesburg, Ill., Nov. 22, 1931; s. Gustave Frederick and Miriam (Simon) S.; m. Shelley Lynn Ramage, Mar. 19, 1978; 1 child, Lucinda Anne. Student, Universidad Nacional de Mex., summer 1950; AB, Yale U., 1952; JD, Harvard U., 1957. Bar: Calif. 1957, U.S. Supreme Ct. 1963. Assoc. Thelen, Marrin, Johnson & Bridges, San Francisco, 1957-60; staff atty. Litton Industries Inc., Beverly Hills, Calif., 1960-66, asst. sec., 1963-66; sec., gen. counsel Internat. Rectifier Corp., L.A., 1966-69, v.p., 1968-69; v.p., gen. counsel Republic Corp., L.A., 1969-71, also bd. dirs., 1970-71; v.p., gen. counsel Sat. Rev. Industries, N.Y.C., 1971-72, Mattel Inc., Hawthorne, Calif., 1972-74, staff cons., 1974-75; of counsel Long & Levit, L.A., 1975-82, O'Donnell & Gordon, L.A., 1983-87, Hedges, Powe & Caldwell, L.A., 1988-90; pvt. practice L.A., 1990—. Judge pro tem Mcpl. Ct. L.A. Jud. Dist., 1977—; arbitrator L.A. Superior Ct. 1979—, judge pro tem L.A. Superior Ct. 1989—, arbitrator Nat. Assn. Securities Dealers, 1981—. Founding trustee Ctr. for Law in the Pub. Interest; trustee Marlborough Sch., L.A.; bd. govs. Century City Hosp., L.A.; counsel bus. and profl. com. L.A. Philharmonic; bd. dirs. Yale Alumni Fund. Lt. (j.g.) USNR, 1952-54; lt. comdr. Res.; ret. Mem. ABA, Calif. Bar Assn., L.A. Bar Assn., Am. Jewish Com., Harvard Law Sch. Assn., L.A. County Art Mus., Am. Arbitration Assn. (nat. panel arbitrators), NAACP, Sierra Club, Nat. Assn. Yale Alumni (former bd. govs.), Yale Club of So. Calif. (former dir.), Harvard Club of So. Calif., Phi Beta Kappa. Home: 422 Denslow Ave Los Angeles CA 90049-3507 Office: 1950 Pelham Ave Los Angeles CA 90025

STAMM, CHARLES H. lawyer; BA, Princeton Univ.; JD, Yale Univ. Exec. v.p., gen. counsel Tchrs. Ins. & Annuity Assn., N.Y.C. Office: Tchrs Ins & Annuity Assn 730 3rd Ave New York NY 10017-3206*

STAMPER, JOE ALLEN, lawyer; b. Okemah, Okla., Jan. 30, 1914; s. Horace Allen and Ann (Stephens) S.; m. Johnnie Lee Bell, June 4, 1936; 1 child, Jane Allen (Mrs. Ernest F. Godlove). BA, U. Okla., 1933, LL.B., 1935, JD, 1970. Bar: Okla. bar 1935. Practice in, Antlers, 1935-36, 46—; mem. firm Stamper, Hadley & Reasor, 1974—; atty. Pushmataha County, 1936-39; spl. justice Okla. Supreme Ct., 1948. Mem. Okla. Indsl. Commn., 1939-40; pres. Antlers Sch. Bd., 1956-67, Pushmataha Found., 1957— ; mem. Okla. Bicentennial Com., 1971— ; vice chmn. bd. U. Okla. Law Center, 1975-78; mgr. Okla. Democratic party, 1946, dist. chmn., 1946-50; alt. del. Dem. Nat. Conv., 1952. Served to col. AUS, 1935-46, E O. Decorated Bronze Star. Fellow Am. Bar Found., Am. Coll. Trial Lawyers, Am. Bd. Trial Advocates (advocate); mem. ABA (del. 1974-91, state del. 1975-86, mem. com. on law book pub. practices 1974-76, bd. govs. 1986-89, standing com. on fed. jud. improvement 1989-92), SAR, Okla. Bar Assn. (bd. govs. 1969-73, Pres.'s award 1977, 80, 93, 2001), Okla. Bar Found. (pres. 1977), Mil. Order World Wars, Pi Kappa Alpha. Baptist (deacon). Clubs: Petroleum (Oklahoma City). Lodges: Masons, Shriners, Lions. Federal civil litigation, State civil litigation, General practice. Home: 1006 NE 2nd St Antlers OK 74523-2822 Office: PO Box 100 112 N High St Antlers OK 74523-2250

STANDISH, WILLIAM LLOYD, judge; b. Pitts., Feb. 16, 1930; s. William Lloyd and Eleanor (McCargo) S.; m. Marguerite Oliver, June 12, 1963; children: Baird M., N. Graham, James H., Constance S. BA, Yale U., 1953; LLB, U. Va., 1956. Bar: Pa. 1957, U.S. Supreme Ct. 1967. Assoc. Reed, Smith, Shaw & McClay, Pitts., 1957-63; ptnr., 1963-80; judge Ct. Common Pleas Allegheny County (Pa.), 1980-87, U.S. Dist. Ct. (we. dist.) Pa., 1987—. Solicitor Edgeworth Borough Sch. Dist., 1963-66. Bd. dirs. Sewickley (Pa.) Cmty. Ctr., 1981-83, Staunton Farms Found., mem., 1984—, trustee, 1984-92; corporator Sewickley Cemetery, 1971-87; trustee Mary and Alexander Laughlin Children's Ctr., 1972-90, Leukemia Soc. Am., 1978-80, We. Pa. chpt., 1972-80, We. Pa. Sch. Deaf, 1983—, YMCA of Sewickley, 1996—; bd. dirs. Pitts. Theol. Sem., 2001—. Recipient Pres. award Leukemia Soc. Am., 1980. Mem. ABA, Pa. Bar Assn., Allegheny County Bar Assn., Am. Judicature Soc., Acad. Trial Lawyers Allegheny County (treas. 1977-78, bd. dirs. 1979-80), Am. Inn of Ct. (Pitts. chpt. 1993—). Office: US Dist Ct 605 US Post Office Ct House 700 Grant St Pittsburgh PA 15219-1906

STANHAUS, JAMES STEVEN, lawyer; b. Evergreen Park, Ill., Oct. 22, 1945; s. Wilfrid Xavier and Mary (Komanecky) S.; m. Naomi Evelyn Miller, June 27, 1971; 1 child, Heather. AB magna cum laude, Georgetown U., 1966; JD cum laude, Harvard U., 1970. Bar: Ill. 1970, U.S. Dist. Ct. (no. dist.) Ill. 1970. Assoc. Mayer, Brown, Rowe & Maw, Chgo., 1971-76, ptnr., 1977—. Mem. ABA, Ill. Bar Assn., Chgo. Bar Assn., Chgo. Coun. Lawyers, Chgo. Estate Planning Coun., Met. Club, Riverpark Club (Chgo.), Phi Beta Kappa. Avocations: computers, tennis, racquetball. Estate planning, Probate (including wills, trusts), Personal income taxation. Office: Mayer Brown Rowe & Maw 190 S La Salle St Ste 3100 Chicago IL 60603-3441

STANKEE, GLEN ALLEN, lawyer; b. Clinton, Iowa, Sept. 27, 1953; s. Glen Earl and Marilyn Jean (Clark) S.; m. Carol Ann Prowe, Feb. 19, 1984. BSBA, Drake U., 1975; MBA, Mich. State U., 1977; JD, U. Detroit, 1979; LLM in Taxation, U. Miami, 1983. Bar: Mich. 1980, U.S. Dist. Ct. (ea. dist.) Mich. 1980, U.S. Ct. Appeals (6th cir.) 1980, U.S. Tax Ct. 1980, Fla. 1981, U.S. Ct. Appeals (11th cir.) 1981, U.S. Dist. Ct. (so. dist.) Fla. 1982, U.S. Dist. Ct. (mid. dist.) 1984, U.S. Supreme Ct. 1987; CPA, Fla. Assoc. Raymond & Dillon P.C., Detroit, 1980-81, West Palm Beach, Fla., 1981-85, prin., 1985-86, Ft. Lauderdale, Fla., 1987-93; ptnr. Ruden, McClosky, Smith, Schuster & Russell, P.A., Ft. Lauderdale, 1993—. Contbr. articles to profl. jours. Mem. ABA, Fed. Bar Assn., Fla. Bar Assn., Mich. Bar Assn., Am. Inst. CPA's, Fla. Inst. CPA's, Palm Beach County Bar Assn., South Fla. Republican. Avocation: golf. Federal civil litigation, Corporate taxation, State and local taxation. Office: Ruden McClosky Smith Schuster & Russell PA PO Box 1900 Fort Lauderdale FL 33302-1900 E-mail: glen.stankee@ruden.com.

STANLEY, BRIAN JORDAN, lawyer; b. Duncan, Okla., Sept. 10, 1954; s. Elmer E. and Betty Sue Stanley; m. Ruth Anne Lynn Stanley, Apr. 6, 1979 (div. Mar. 1989); children: Lindsey Jordan, Brent Alan; m. Francine Michelle La Valle, Oct. 18, 1996. BA in Polit. Sci., U. Okla., 1979; JD with honors, Oklahoma City U., 1985. Bar: (Okla.) 1985, (U.S. Dist. Ct. (we. dist.) Okla.); cert. comml. investment mem. Sports writer The Norman (Okla.) Transcript, 1979-80; oil and gas landman Milt McCullough, Oklahoma City, 1980-81; trust officer Liberty Nat. Bank & Trust, Oklahoma City, 1981-83; atty. Michael P. Rogalin, Oklahoma City, 1985-86, William H. Mattoon, Norman, 1986-87, Fed. Deposit Ins. Corp., Oklahoma City, 1987, Reed, Shadid & Pipes, Oklahoma City, 1987-88, Mosburg, Sears, Kunzman & Bollinger, Oklahoma City, 1988; v.p., corp. gen. counsel The Hefner Co., Inc., Oklahoma City, 1989—. Bd. dirs. The Hefner Co., Inc.; trustee Dr. Brent Hisey Irrevocable Trust, Oklahoma City, 1998—. Contbr. articles to profl. jours. Mem.: ABA (cert. comml. investment mem.), Cert. Comml. Investment Member Designation, Soc. King Charles Martyr, Mensa. Republican. Episcopalian. Avocations: Italian language, theology, politics. Corporate, general, Oil, gas, and mineral, Property, real (including real estate development, water). Office: The Hefner Co Inc PO Box 2177 Oklahoma City OK 73101-2177 E-mail: vito1954@hotmail.com.

STANLEY, HUGH MONROE, JR., lawyer; b. Ft. Lewis, Wash., Oct. 25, 1944; s. Hugh Monroe Sr. and Rita (McHugh) S.; m. Patricia Page, Aug. 17, 1968; children: Allison Michelle, Matthew Monroe, Trevor Marshall. BA magna cum laude, U. Dayton, 1966; JD, Georgetown U., 1969. Bar: Ohio 1969, U.S. Ct. Appeals (6th cir.) 1983, U.S. Supreme Ct. 1979. Assoc. Arter & Hadden, Cleve., 1969-76, ptnr., 1976—, chmn. litigation dept., 1983-96. Staff editor Georgetown Law Jour., bd. editors. Fellow Am. Bar Found., Bar Assn. Greater Cleve., Am. Coll. Trial Lawyers, Internat. Acad. Trial Lawyers, Internat. Soc. Barristers, Nat. Assn. R.R. Trial Counsel; mem. ABA, Fed. Bar Assn., Def. Rsch. Inst., Cleve. Assn. Civil Trial Attys., Ohio Assn. Civil Trial Attys. Republican. Roman Catholic. Avocation: reading. Office: Arter & Hadden 1100 Huntington Bldg 925 Euclid Ave Ste 1100 Cleveland OH 44115-1475

STANSELL, LELAND EDWIN, JR., lawyer, mediator, educator; b. Central, S.C., July 13, 1934; s. Leland Edwin and Hettie Katherine (Hollis) S.; children: James Leland, Susan. BS, Fla. So. Coll., 1957; LLB, U. Miami, Fla., 1961, JD, 1968. Bar: Fla. 1961; cert. civil mediator Fla. Supreme Ct., U.S. Dist. Ct. Fla. Assoc. Wicker & Smith, Miami, 1961-62, ptnr., 1962-75; pvt. practice, Miami, 1975-99, Leland E. Stansell, Jr., P.A., Miami, 1995—. Chmn. Appellate Jud. Nominating Com., Dade County (Fla.), 1983-87; mem. adv. com. Am. Arbitration Assn., 1975-90. Served with U.S. Army, 1957. Mem. ABA (ho. of dels. 1982-86), Fla. Bar (bd. govs. 1966-70, 70-80), Dade County Bar Assn. (dir. 1969-72, exec. com. 1974-75, pres. 1975-76), U. Miami Law Alumni Assn. (dir., officer, pres. 1968-69), Fla. Criminal Def. Attys. Assn. (treas. 1964-66), Am. Judicature Soc., Am. Bd. Trial Advs., Internat. Assn. Def. Counsel, Fla. Acad. Profl. Mediators, Fedn. Ins. Counsel, Miami Beach Rod and Reel Club (pres.), Coral Reef Yacht Club, Bankers Club, Ocean Reef Yacht Club, Delta Theta Phi (pres. Miami alumni chpt. 1966, regional dir. 1968. General civil litigation, Insurance, Personal injury (including property damage). Office: 19 W Flagler St Miami FL 33130-4400

STANTON, GEORGE PATRICK, JR., lawyer; b. Fairmont, W.Va., Nov. 21, 1933; s. George Patrick and Wilma Roberta (Everson) S.; m. Shirley Jean Champ, Sept. 3, 1956; children: George Patrick, Edward Scott. BS in Bus. Adminstrn., Fairmont Coll., 1956; MBA in Fin., U. Dayton, 1969; JD, U. Balt., 1977. Bar: Md. 1978, U.s. Dist. Ct. Md. 1978, W.Va. 1979, U.S. Dist. Ct. (so. dist.) W.Va. 1979, U.S. Dist. Ct. (no. dist.) W.Va. 1980, U.S. Ct. Appeals (4th cir.) 1985. Auditor 1st Nat. Bank Fairmont, 1955-61; asst. cashier S.C. Nat. Bank, Columbia, 1961-64; sr. sys. analyst Chase Manhattan Bank, N.Y.C., 1964-65; asst. v.p. Winters Nat. Bank, Dayton, Ohio, 1965-69, Md. Nat. Bank, Balt., 1969-74; v.p. Equitable Trust Co., Balt., 1974-79; gen. ptnr. Stanton & Stanton Attys. at Law, Fairmont, 1979—. Asst. pros. atty. Marion Co., W.Va.; staff sect. leader, mem. faculty Sch. for Bank Adminstrn. U. Wis.-Madison, 1978-89. Treas. Montaineer Area coun. Boy Scouts Am., Fairmont, 1982-90; pres. Three Rivers Coal Festival, Inc., Fairmont, 1984-85, pres., 1985-86, bd. dirs., 1982-86; pres. Appalachian Coal Festival, 1985-86, bd. dirs., 1985—; mem. adv. bd. Inst. for Living, Fairmont, 1983-85; pres. Firemans' CSC, Fairmont, W.Va., 1992-96; elder Christ Cmty. Ch., 2003. Mem. W.Va. Bar Assn. (Kaufman award 1997), Marion County Bar Assn., Md. Bar Assn., W.Va. Trial Lawyers Assn., Marion County C. of C. (bd. dirs. 1983—), Fairmont State Coll. Alumni Assn. (bd. dirs. 1982—, pres. 1992-94, Alumnus of Yr. 2002), Fairmont Field Club, Rotary, Masons. Commercial, consumer (including collections, credit), Personal injury (including property damage), Property, real (including real estate development, water). Home: 2 W Hills Dr Fairmont WV 26554-5015 Office: Stanton & Stanton PO Box 968 WesBanco Bldg Ste 707 Fairmont WV 26555-0968

STANTON, LOUIS LEE, federal judge; b. N.Y.C., Oct. 1, 1927; s. Louis Lee and Helen Parsons (La Fétra) S.; m. Berit Eleonora Rask; children: L. Lee, Susan Helen Benedict, Gordon R., Fredrik S. BA, Yale U., 1950; JD, U. Va., 1955. Assoc. Davis Polk Wardwell Sunderland & Kiendl, N.Y.C., 1955-66, Carter, Ledyard & Milburn, N.Y.C., 1966-67, ptnr., 1967-85; sr. judge U.S. Dist. Ct. (so. dist.) N.Y., N.Y.C., 1985—. Served to 1st lt. USMCR, 1950-52. Fellow Am. Coll. Trial Lawyers, N.Y. Bar Found.; mem. Va. Bar Assn.

STANTON, PATRICK MICHAEL, lawyer; b. Phila., Sept. 8, 1947; s. Edward Joseph and Helen Marie (Coghlan) S.; m. Kathleen Ann Fama, Aug. 22, 1970; children: Cheryl Marie, Susan Elizabeth. BS in History, St. Joseph's U., 1969; JD, U. Va., 1972; MBA, Fairleigh Dickinson, 1984. Bar: Ohio 1972 (inactive), N.J. 1982, U.S. Dist. Ct. (so. dist.) Ohio 1972, U.S. Dist. Ct. (ea. dist.) N.J. 1982, U.S. Dist. Ct. (so. dist.) N.Y. 1984. Assoc. Taft, Stettinius & Hollister, Cin., 1972—80; labor counsel Union Camp Corp., Wayne, NJ, 1980—83; dir. labor rels., equal employment opportunity programs W.R. Grace & Co., N.Y.C., 1983—86; of counsel Shanley & Fisher, P.C., Morristown, NJ, 1986—89, ptnr., chmn. labor and employment group, 1989—95; dir. Stanton, Hughes, Diana, Cerra, Mariani & Margello, P.C., Morristown, NJ, 1995—. Adj. prof. bus. law Fairleigh Dickinson U. 1984-92; pres. Sidney Reitman employment law Am. Inn. Ct., 1997-2001. Pres., bd. dirs. N.Y. State Adv. Coun. on Employment Law, Inc., N.Y.C., 1985-86. DuPont scholar U. Va., 1970. Mem. ABA, N.J. State Bar Assn. (exec. com. labor employment law sect. 1989—, rec. sec. 1995-97, treas. 1997-99, 2d vice chair 1999-2001, 1st vice chair 2001-2003, chair 2003—), Phi Alpha Theta, Delta Mu Delta. Roman Catholic. Labor (including EEOC, Fair Labor Standards Act, labor-management relations, NLRB, OSHA). Home: 292 Forest Ave Glen Ridge NJ 07028-1808 Office: Stanton Hughes Diana Cerra Mariani & Margello PC 10 Madison Ave Ste 402 Morristown NJ 07960-7303 Fax: 973-656-1611. E-mail: pstanton@stantonhughes.com.

STANTON, ROGER D. lawyer; b. Oct. 4, 1938; s. George W. and Helen V. (Peterson) S.; m. Judith L. Duncan, Jan. 27, 1962; children: Jeffrey B., Brady D., Todd A. AB, U. Kans., 1960, JD, 1963. Bar: Kans. 1963, U.S. Dist. Ct. Kans. 1963, U.S. Ct. Appeals (10th cir.) 1972, U.S. Supreme Ct. 1973. Assoc. Stanley, Schroeder, Weeks, Thomas & Lysaught, Kansas City, 1968-72, Weeks, Thomas & Lysaught, Kansas City, 1969-80, also bd. dirs., chmn. exec. com., 1981-82, Stinson, Mag & Fizzell, Kansas City, 1983-96, chmn. products practice group, also bd. dirs., 1993-95; ptnr. Berkowitz, Stanton, Brandt, Williams & Shaw, Prairie Village, Kans., 1997—. Chmn. bd. editors Jour. Kans. Bar Assn., 1975-83; contbr. articles to profl. jours. Active Boy Scouts Am., 1973-79; pres. YMCA Youth Football Club, 1980-82; co-chmn. Civil Justice Reform Act com. Dist. of Kans., 1991-95; bd. dirs. Kans. Appleseed Found., 2000—. Fellow Am. Coll. Trial Lawyers (state chmn. 1984-86); mem. Internat. Assn. Def. Counsel, Exec. com., 1994-99 East Kansas/West Miss. Chpt., Am. Bd. Trial Adv., Def. Rsch. Inst. (state co-chmn. 1979-90, Exceptionl Performance award 1979), Kans. Bar Assn. (Pres.'s award 1982), Johnson County Bar Found. (pres., trustee), Chmn. Bench/Bar Com. of Johnson Co. Bar Assn., Kans. Assn. Def. Counsel (pres. 1977-78), Kans. Inn. Ct., U. Kans. Sch. Law Alumni Assn. (bd. dirs. 1972-75, 2001-), U. Kans. Kansas City Alumni (bd. dirs. 2001--). Federal civil litigation, Health, Securities. Office: Berkowitz Stanton Brandt Williams & Stueve 4121 W 83rd St Ste 227 Prairie Village KS 66208

STAPLES, LYLE NEWTON, lawyer; b. Radford, Va., Feb. 16, 1945; s. Lester Lyle and Velma Jean (King) S.; m. Christie Mercedes Carr, Feb. 1, 1971; children: Scott Andrew, John Randolph, Brian Matthew, Melissa Ann. BA, U. Md., 1967, JD, 1972; LLM in Taxation, Georgetown U., 1977. Bar: Md. 1973, U.S. Supreme Ct. 1978, U.S. Tax Ct. 1981, U.S. Dist. Ct. Md. 1981, U.S. Ct. Appeals (4th cir.) 1981. Tax law specialist IRS, Washington, 1972-77; assoc. Hessey & Hessey, Balt., 1978-82, Rosenstock, Burgee & Welty, Frederick, Md., 1982-84; sole practice Hampstead, Md., 1984-91; mem. firm Johnson, Parker & Hess, Westminster, Md., 1991-96; pvt. practice Westminster, 1996—. Vis. asst. prof. Towson (Md.) State U., 1981—82. Treas., bd. dirs. Literacy Coun. of Carroll County, Inc., 1993-98. Served with U.S. Army, 1968-69, Vietnam. Mem. ABA, Md. Bar Assn., Fin.

Planning Assn., Carroll County C. of C. Democrat. Methodist. Corporate, general, Estate planning, Taxation, general. Home: 813 Clearview Ave Hampstead MD 21074-2325 Office: Ste 210 79 E Main St Westminster MD 21157-5026

STAPLES, RICHARD FARNSWORTH, lawyer; b. Providence, Nov. 24, 1919; s. Harold E. and Margaret (Smith) S.; m. Mary Kingsbury, June 20, 1942; children: Richard Farnsworth, Jr., Benjamin T., Edward K. AB, Harvard U., 1941, LLB, 1949. Bar: R.I. 1949. Ptnr. Tillinghast, Collins & Graham, Providence, 1949-81, Hinckley, Allen & Snyder, Providence, 1981-87, of counsel, 1987—. Mem. commn. on jud. tenure and discipline, 1987-93; mem. ethics adv. panel R.I. Supreme Ct., 1995-97. Chmn. sch. com. Town of Barrington (R.I.), 1956-62, mem., 1957-62; mem. State Bd. Edn., Providence, 1964-69, chmn., 1968-69; pres. R.I. Hist. Soc., 1981-83. Served to 1st lt. U.S. Army, 1943-46. Decorated Bronze Star Mem. ABA, R.I. Bar Assn., Soc. Colonial Wars, Providence Art Club, Harvard Club. Home: 180 Slater Ave Providence RI 02906-5723 also: 79 Loon Lake Rd Freedom NH 03836-0298

STAPLETON, WALTER KING, federal judge; b. Cuthbert, Ga., June 2, 1934; s. Theodore Newton and Elizabeth Grantland (King) Stapleton; m. Georgianna Duross Stapleton; children: Russell K., Theodore N., Teryl J. BA, Princeton, 1956; LLB, Harvard, 1959; LLM, U. Va., 1984. Bar: Del. Assoc. Morris, Nichols, Arsht & Tunnell, Wilmington, Del., 1959—65; dep. atty. gen. State of Del., 1963; ptnr. Morris, Nichols, Arsht & Tunnell, 1966—70; judge U.S. Dist. Ct. , Wilmington, Del., 1970—85, chief judge, 1983—85; judge U.S. Ct. Appeals (3d cir.), 1985—. Dep. atty. gen., Del., 1964; mem. Jud. Conf. U.S., 1984—85. Bd. dirs. Am. Bapt. Chs., 1978. Baptist. Office: US Ct Appeals 844 N King St Wilmington DE 19801-3519

STARCHER, LARRY VICTOR, state supreme court chief justice; b. Rocksdale, W.Va., Sept. 25, 1942; AB cum laude, W.Va. U., 1964, JD, 1967. Bar: W.Va. 1967. Judge and chief judge W.Va. Ct. (17th jud. cir.), 1977-96; justice W.Va. Supreme Ct. Appeals, 1997—, chief justice, 2003—. Pvt. practice, Morgantown, 1976—; dir. North Ctrl. W.Va. Legal Aid Soc., 1969-76; former instr. law, pub. adminstrn., and history W.Va. U.; contract adminstr. W.Va. U., 1966-67, asst. to v.p., 1967-69. Editor W.Va. Law Rev.; contbr. articles to profl. jours. Mem. City Coun. Morgantown, 1971-72; mem. W.Va. Martin Luther King, Jr. Holiday Commn. Fellow Harvard U., summer 1978. Mem. ATLA, Am. Correctional Assn., W.Va. Jud. Assn., W.Va. State Bar, Monongalia County Bar Assn., Kanawha County Bar Assn., Conf. Chief Justices, Beta Theta Pi, Phi Delta Phi, Phi Alpha Theta, Pi Sigma Alpha. Avocations: carpentry, gardening, skiing. Office: Supreme Ct Appeals State Capitol Rm E 307 Charleston WV 25305

STARING, GRAYDON SHAW, lawyer; b. Deansboro, N.Y., Apr. 9, 1923; s. William Luther and Eleanor Mary (Shaw) S.; m. Joyce Lydia Allum-Poon, Sept. 1, 1949; children: Diana Hilary Agnes, Christopher Paul Norman. AB, Hamilton Coll., 1947; JD, U. Calif., Berkeley, 1951. Bar: Calif. 1952, U.S. Supreme Ct. 1958. Atty. Office Gen. Counsel, Navy Dept., San Francisco, 1952-53; atty. admiralty and shipping sect. U.S. Dept. Justice, San Francisco, 1953-60; assoc. Lillick & Charles (now Nixon Peabody), San Francisco, 1960-64, ptnr., 1965-95, of counsel, 1995—. Titulary mem. Internat. Maritime Com.; bd. dirs. Marine Exchange at San Francisco, 1984-88, pres. 1986-88; instr. pub. speaking Hamilton Coll., 1947-48; adj. prof. Hastings Coll. Law, 1996-97, Boalt Hall, U. Calif., 1999. Author: Law of Reinsurance, 1993; assoc. editor Am. Maritime Cases, 1966-92, editor, 1992—; contbr. articles to legal jours. Mem. San Francisco Lawyers Com. for Urban Affairs, 1972-90; bd. dirs. Legal Aid Soc., San Francisco, 1974-90, v.p., 1975-80, pres., 1980-82. With USN, 1943-46, comdr. USNR. Fellow Am. Bar Found., Am. Coll. Trial Lawyers; mem. ABA (chmn. maritime ins. com. 1975-76, mem. standing com. admiralty law 1976-82, 86-90, chmn. 1990, ho. dels. 1986-90), FBA (pres. San Francisco chpt. 1968), Bar Assn. San Francisco (sec. 1972, treas. 1973), Calif. Acad. Appellate Lawyers, Maritime Law Assn. U.S. (exec. com. 1977-88, v.p. 1980-84, pres. 1984-86), Brit. Ins. Law Assn., Brit.-Am. C. of C. (bd. dirs. 1987-2001), World Trade Club San Francisco, Tulane Admiralty Inst. (permanent adv. bd.), Assocs. Maritime Mus. Libr. (dir. 1990-2001, pres. 1992-94). Admiralty, Insurance. Office: 2 Embarcadero Ctr Ste 2700 San Francisco CA 94111-3900 E-mail: gstaring@nixonpeabody.com., Starlaw@aol.com.

STARK, ALBERT MAXWELL, lawyer; b. Trenton, N.J., May 3, 1939; m. Ellen Stark, Nov. 20, 1966; children: Jared, Rachel. BA, Darmouth Coll., Hanover, N.H., 1960; LLD, U. Pa., Phila., 1963. Bar: N.J. 1964. Asst. to gov. of N.J., 1964; asst. atty. City of Trenton, 1965-66; asst. prosecutor Mercer County, N.J., 1967-68. Author: Beyond the Bar - Challenges in the Life of a Lawyer, 2002; host radio programs Lawline, WHWH, 1985—95, In the Pub. Interest, WIMG, 1996. Recipient Humanitarian award Thomas A. Edison State Coll., 2000, award Trial Attys. of N.J., 2000. Mem. ABA, N.J. Bar Assn., Mercer County Bar Assn., Mercer County C. of C. (Citizen of Yr. 1994), Rotary Internat. (Fred Harris fellow 1996). Avocations: writing, tennis, skiing. Office: Stark & Stark 993 Lenox Dr Ste 301 Lawrenceville NJ 08648-2316

STARK, RICHARD ALVIN, lawyer; b. Ann Arbor, Mich., Apr. 6, 1921; s. Judson Luther and Evelyn (Briley) S.; m. Barbara Jones, Feb. 5, 1944; children: Susan S. Woglom, Sarah S. Oldham, Margaret S. Worthington, Barbara Stark Baxter, Richard J. Stark. AB, DePauw U., 1943; MBA, Harvard U., 1947; JD, Ind. u., 1948. Bar: N.Y. 1949, Ind. 1948. Assoc. Milbank, Tweed, Hadley & McCloy, N.Y.C., 1948-56, ptnr., 1957—90. Bd. dirs. Buttonwood Petroleum Corp., Tulsa; chmn. bd. dirs. Savance Corp., Evanston, Ill. Chmn. Vero Beach Mus. Art, 1996—98; mem. bd. dirs. Riverside Theatre, Vero Beach; chmn. Treasure Coast Homeless Svs. Coun., 2000—. Mem. ABA, N.Y. State Bar Assn., Assn. of Bar of City of N.Y., Am. Law Inst. Clubs: Creek (Locust Valley, N.Y.); Wall St., Downtown Athletic (N.Y.C.); John's Island (Vero Beach, Fla.). Home: 340 Palmetto Pt Vero Beach FL 32963-3356 Office: Milbank Tweed Hadley & McCloy 1 Chase Manhattan Plz Fl 47 New York NY 10005-1413

STARKE, HAROLD E., JR., lawyer; b. Richmond, Va., Aug. 1, 1944; BA, Randolph-Macon Coll., 1967; JD, U. Richmond, 1971; LLM in Taxation, NYU, 1973. Bar: Va. 1971, D.C. 1981. Mem. Troutman Sanders LLP, Richmond. Editor U. Richmond Law Rev., 1970-71. Bd. trustees Randolph-Macon Coll., 1983-85, 95-97, 99—. Fellow Am. Coll. Tax Counsel; mem. ABA (taxation sect.), Va. State Bar (chmn. taxation sect. 1985-86), D.C. Bar, Richmond Estate Planning Coun., McNeill Honor Soc., Phi Delta Phi. Corporate, general, Estate planning, Taxation, general. Office: Troutman Sanders LLP Bank of Am Center PO Box 1122 Richmond VA 23218-1122

STARKMAN, MARK T. lawyer, health care consultant; b. N.Y.C., Sept. 14, 1956; s. Stanley Keith and Suzanne Libby (Blau) S.; m. Joanne Colp Schwartz, Mar. 15, 1981; children: Jessica Anne, Emma Ariel. BA, SUNY, Stony Brook, 1978; MBA, St. John's U., Jamaica, N.Y., 1986; JD, Pace U., 1994. Bar: N.Y. 1995. Emergency med. svcs. specialist N.Y.C. Health and Hosps. Corp., 1980-87; adminstr. Albert Einstein Coll. Medicine, Bronx, N.Y., 1987-89, Montefiore Med. Ctr., Bronx, 1989-96; dir. practice mgmt. Phymatrix N.E., Inc., Ridgefield, Conn., 1996-97; cons. AmeriHealth Health Plans, Inc., White Plains, NY, 1997-98; atty. McCabe & Mack, LLP, Poughkeepsie, NY, 1998—2002, Jacobowitz & Gubits, LLP, Walden, NY, 2002—. Coach Am. Youth Soccer Orgn., Somers, N.Y., 1996—; mem. Somers Planning Bd., 1997—. N.Y.C. mayor's grad. scholar, 1984. Mem. ABA, Am. Coll. Healthcare Execs., N.Y. State Bar Assn. (managed care com. 1995—, payment issues com. 1995—), Assn. Bar City of N.Y. (health law com. 1998-2001). Republican. Jewish. Avocations: reading classics, golf, racquetball, softball. Office: Jacobowitz & Gubits LLP 158 Orange Ave PO Box 367 Walden NY 12586

STARR, ISIDORE, law educator; b. Bklyn., Nov. 24, 1911; BA, CCNY, 1932; LLB, St. John's U., Jamaica, N.Y., 1936; MA, Columbia U., 1939; JSD, Bklyn. Law Sch., 1942; PhD, New Sch. Social Rsch., 1957. Bar: N.Y. 1937. Tchr. various high schs., N.Y.C., 1934-61; from assoc. prof. to prof. edn. Queen's Coll., 1961-75, prof. emeritus, 1975—. Dir. Inst. on Law-Related Edn., Lincoln-Filene Ctr., Tufts U., 1963; dir. Law Studies Inst., N.Y.C., 1974; adv. on Our Living Bill of Rights Film Series (6 films) Ency. Brit. Ednl. Corp.; mem. Ariz. Ctr. for Law-Related Edn.; mem. coun. on pub. legal edn. State of Wash., 2001—; cons. in field. Author: The Lost Generation of Prince Edward COunty, 1968, The Gideon Case, 1968, The Feiner Case, 1968, The Mapp Case, 1968, The Supreme Court and Contemporary Issues, 1968, Human Rights in the United States, 1969, The American Judicial System, 1972, The Idea of Liberty, 1978, Justice: Due Process of Law, 1981; co-editor Living American Documents, 1971. Bd. dirs. Phi Alpha Delta Juvenile Justice Program, 1981—. 1st lt. U.S. Army, 1943-46. John Hay fellow, 1952-53; recipient Outstanding Citizen award Philip Morris Cos., 1992. Mem. ABA (hon. chair adv. commn. on Youth Edn. for Citizenship, Isidore Starr award for Spl. Achievment in Law Studies, Leon Jaworski award 1989), Am. Judicature Soc., Am. Soc. Legal History, Am. Legal Studies Assn., Nat. Coun. Social Studies (past pres.), Washington Coun. Pub. Legal Edn., Phi Beta Kappa, Phi Alpha Delta (cert. of appreciation 1981). Address: 12501 Greenwood Ave N Apt C110 Seattle WA 98133-8000

STARR, IVAR MILES, lawyer; b. N.Y.C., Sept. 19, 1950; s. Charles S. Scholnicoff and Rosalie (Paletz) Starr. AA, Nassau Community Coll., 1970; BA, Queens Coll., 1972; JD, U. Miami, 1980. Bar: Fla. 1981, U.S. Dist. Ct. (so. dist.) Fla. 1981, N.Y. 1988. Rep. securities sales Aetna Variable Life Ins. Co., Garden City, N.Y., 1973-75; freelance real estate broker New Fairfield, Conn., 1973-79; assoc. Law Offices of Peter Lopez, Miami, Fla., 1981-82, Mills & London P.A., Miami, 1982; pvt. practice Miami, 1982—. Lectr. Dade County (Fla.) Consumer Advs. Office, 1984-87; instr. paralegal courses Briarcliffe Coll., 1991. Candidate judge Dade County Ct., 1988. Recipient Outstanding Svc. award Miami Beach Bd. Realtors, 1986, 87, 88, 91, 92. Mem. The Fla. Bar (vol. bar liaison com. 1993-96), Miami Beach Bar Assn. (bd. dirs. 1984-, treas. 1991, v.p. 1993, pres.-elect 1995, pres. 1996, immediate past pres. 1997), Miami Beach C. of C. (lectr. 1985-89), Better Bus. Bur. South Fla. (arbitrator 1984-, Cert. of Appreciation 1985), Queens Coll. Alumni in South Fla. (chmn. 1986-96), Internat. Toastmasters (so. divsn. gov. dist. 47 1993-94, Able Toastmaster Bronze 1992, Able Toastmaster Silver 1993, dist. 47 pub. rels. officer 1997-98, Dist. 47 Enthusiasm award 1993-94, Disting. Toastmaster 1994, 99, Advanced Toastmaster gold and Competent Leader 1997, 2003, Advanced Toastmaster Bronze 2001, Advanced Toastmaster Silver and Advanced Leader 1999, Disting. Toastmaster, 1999, Competent Toastmaster 2000, 2003). Avocations: boating, swimming, music. State civil litigation, General practice, Property, real (including real estate development, water). Office: 350 Lincoln Rd Ste 407 Miami FL 33139-3155 Home: PO Box 414511 Miami Beach FL 33141-0511

STARR, JUDSON WILMARTH, lawyer; b. Boulder, Colo., July 18, 1945; s. Wilmarth Holt and Eva Jones Starr; 1 child, Alexander. BA, Washington and Jefferson Coll., 1968; JD, Georgetown U., 1975. Bar: D.C. 1975, Va. 1978. Staff Office of the Adminstr. U.S. EPA, Washington, 1972—73; asst. editor Environ. Law Inst., Washington, 1973—75; assoc. Price Grove, Washington, 1975—78; dir. environ. crimes unit Dept. Justice, Washington, 1982—87, chief environ. crimes sect., 1987—88; ptnr. Venable, LLP, Washington, 1988—. Adv. mem. U.S. Sentencing Commn. on Corp. Sentencing; co-chair Annual ALI-ABA Conf. on Environ. Crimes; chair Environ. Crimes Subcom. Bus. Contbr. articles to profl. jours. Founding mem., pres. Bethesda (Md.)/Chevy Chase Baseball League, 1995—99. Capt. U.S. Army, 1968—70. Decorated Bronze Star. Mem.: Barristers. Avocations: baseball, golf, sailing. Corporate, general, Criminal, Environmental. Office: Venable LLP Ste 1000 1201 New York Ave NW Washington DC 20005

STARR, KENNETH WINSTON, lawyer; b. Vernon, Tex., July 21, 1946; s. W. D. and Vannie Maude (Trimble) Starr; m. Alice Jean Mendell, Aug. 23, 1970; children: Randall Postley, Carolyn Marie, Cynthia Anne. BA, George Washington U., 1968; MA, Brown U., 1969; JD, Duke U., 1973; LLD (hon.) , Hampden Sydney Coll., Shenandoah U., Mitchell Coll. Law. Bar: Calif. 1973, D.C. 1979, Va. 1979. Law clk. to Judge David Dyer U.S. Ct. Appeals (5th cir.), Miami, Fla., 1973—74; assoc. Gibson, Dunn & Crutcher, Los Angeles, 1974—75; law clk. to Chief Justice Warren E. Burger, U.S. Supreme Ct., Washington, 1975—77; assoc., ptnr. Gibson, Dunn & Crutcher, Washington, 1977—81; counselor to atty gen. of U.S. Dept. Justice, Washington, 1981—83; judge U.S. Ct. Appeals (D.C. circuit), Washington, 1983—89; solicitor gen. Dept. Justice, Washington, 1989—93; ptnr. Kirkland & Ellis, Washington, 1993—; ind. counsel for Whitewater, 1994—. Contbr. articles to legal jours. Legal advisor CAB transition team office of pres.-elect, 1980—81, SEC transition team, 1980—81; bd. adv. Duke Law Jour. Recipient Disting. Alumni awards, George Washington U., Duke U., Atty. Gen.'s award for disting. svc., 1993, Am. Values award, U.S. Indsl. Coun. Ednl. Found., 1993. Fellow: Am. Bar Found. (jud. fellows com., jud. conf. com. on bicentennial of U.S. constn.); mem.: ABA, Va. Bar Assn., D.C. Bar Assn., Calif. Bar Assn., Supreme Ct. Hist. Soc., Inst. Jud. Adminstrn. (pres.), Am. Judicature Soc., Am. Law Inst., Phi Delta Phi (Hughes chpt. Man of Yr. 1973), Order of Coif.

STARRETT, FREDERICK KENT, lawyer; b. Lincoln, Nebr., May 23, 1947; s. Clyde Frederick and Helen Virginia (Meyers) Starrett; m. Linda Lee Jensen, Jan. 19, 1969; children: Courtney, Kathryn, Scott. BA, U. Nebr., 1969; JD, Creighton U., 1976. Bar: Nebr 1976, Kans 1977, US Dist Ct Nebr 1976, US Dist Ct Kans 1977, US Ct Appeals (8th and 10th cirs) 1983, Mo 1987, US Dist Ct (we dit) Mo 1987, US Supreme Ct 1993. Pvt. practice law, Gt. Bend, Kans., 1976-77, Topeka, 1977-86; with Miller, Bash & Starrett, P.C., Kans. City, Mo., 1986-90; ptnr. Lathrop Norquist & Miller, 1990-91, Lathrop and Norquist, Overland Pk., Kans., 1991-95, Lathrop & Gage L.C., Overland Pk., Kans., 1996—. Judicial nominating comnr 10th Judicial Dist, 2000—. Lt (jg) USNR, 1969—72. Mem.: ABA, Mo. Orgn. Def. Lawyers, Def. Rsch. Inst. (state rep. Kans. 1998—2001, bd. dirs. 2002—), Am. Bd. Trials Advs. (pres. Kans. chpt. 1997), Kans. Bar Assn. (pres. litigation sect. 1985—86, bd. dirs. 2002—), Civitan Club (pres. 1985—86, Disting. Pres. award 1985—86). Democrat. Presbyterian. Avocations: aviation, scuba diving. Personal injury (including property damage), Transportation, Product liability. Office: Lathrop & Gage LC Bldg 82 10851 Mastin Blvd Ste 1000 Shawnee Mission KS 66210-2007 E-mail: fstarrett@lathropgage.com.

STARRETT, KEITH, lawyer; b. McComb, Miss., July 15, 1951; s. Melvin and Mary (Roberts) S.; m. Barbara O'Neal, Dec. 18, 1971; children: Josh, Whit, Leah Claire. BS, Miss. State U., 1972; JD, U. Miss., 1974. Bar: Miss. 1974, U.S. Dist. Ct. (no. and so. dists.) Miss. 1974. Ptnr. Statham, Watkins & Starrett, Magnolia, Miss., 1975-79; pvt. practice Magnolia, 1980-89, McComb, 1989-92; cir. judge 14th Cir. Dist., 1992—. Baptist. Avocations: backpacking, jogging, canoeing. Admiralty, General civil litigation, General practice. Office: 299 Apache Dr Mccomb MS 39648-6307 E-mail: starrett@telapex.com.

STARRS, ELIZABETH ANNE, lawyer; b. Detroit, Jan. 1, 1954; d. John Richard and Mabel Angeline (Gilchrist) S. BA, U. Mich., 1975; JD, Suffolk U., 1980. Bar: Mass. 1980, Colo. 1983, U.S. Dist. Ct. Mass. 1981, U.S. Ct. Appeals (1st. cir.) 1981, Colo. 1983, U.S. Dist. Ct. Colo. 1983, U.S. Ct. Appeals (10th cir.) 1983. Assoc. Denner & Benjoya P.C., Boston, 1980-83, Kennedy & Christopher P.C., Denver, 1983-86, ptnr., 1986—, pres., mng. ptnr., 1994-2000. Mem. jud. nominating commn. 2d Jud. Dist., Colo., 2000-06. Troop leader Girl Scouts U.S., Denver, 1984-85; pres. Colo. Women's Bar Assn. Found., 1992-94. Fellow Am. Coll. Trial Lawyers., Colo. Bar Found.; mem. ATLA, FBA, Colo. Bar Assn. (litigation coun. 1989-96, chair 1993-94, profl. liability chair 1991-93), Denver Bar Assn. (bd. trustees 2001—, pres. 2002-03), Colo. Women's Bar Assn. (bd. dirs. 1984-85, v.p. 1989-90), US Dist. Ct. Colo. (com. conduct 1997-2003), Am. Bd. Trial Advs., Def. Rsch. Inst., Faculty Fed. Advs. Roman Catholic. Federal civil litigation, State civil litigation, Professional liability. Office: Kennedy & Christopher PC 1050 17th St Ste 2500 Denver CO 80265

STARRS, JAMES EDWARD, law and forensics educator, consultant; b. Bklyn., July 30, 1930; s. George Thomas and Mildred Agatha (Dobbins) S.; m. Barbara Alice Smyth, Sept. 6, 1954; children: Mary Alice, Monica, James, Charles, Liam, Barbara, Siobhan, Gregory. BA, LLB, St. John's U., Bklyn., 1958; LLM, NYU, 1959. Bar: N.Y. 1958, D.C. 1966, U.S. Ct. Mil. Appeals 1959, U.S. Dist. Ct. (so. and ea. dists.) N.Y. 1960. Assoc. Lawless & Lynch, N.Y.C., 1958; tchg. fellow Rutgers U., Newark, 1959-60; asst. prof. law DePaul U., Chgo., 1960-64; assoc. prof. law George Washington U., Washington, 1964-67, prof. law, 1967—, prof. forensic scis., 1975—. Cons. Nat. Commn. Reform Fed. Criminal Laws, Washington, 1968, Cellmark Diagnostics, Germantown, Md., 1987—, Time-Life Books, 1993; participant re-evaluation sci. evidence and trial of Bruno Richard Hauptmann for Lindbergh murder, 1983; participant reporting sci. re-analysis of firearms evidence in Sacco and Vanzetti trial, 1986; project dir. Alfred G. Packer Victims Exhumation Project, 1989, A Blaze of Bullets: A Sci. Investigation into the Deaths of Senator Huey Long and Dr. Carl Austin Weiss, 1991, Meriwether Lewis Exhumation Project, 1992—, Frank R. Olson Exhumation Project, 1994, Jesse W. James Exhumation Project, 1995, Samuel Washington-Harewood Excavations, 1999, The Boston Strangler Re-Investigation, 2000, The Exhumation of Carl E. Williams, Sr., 2001, The Exhumation of Samuel Swan, 2002, The Gettysburg Excavations, Pa., 2002—; Snider lectr. U. Toronto, 1999, Boston Strangler Re-Investigation, 2000, Mutter Lectr. Coll. of Physicians, Phila., 2003. Author: (with Moenssens and Inbau) Scientific Evidence in Criminal Cases, 1986; (with Moenssens, Inbau and Henderson) Scientific Evidence in Civil and Criminal Cases, 1995; editor: The Noiseless Tenor, 1982; co-editor: (review) Scientific Sleuthing, 1976—; mem. editl. bd. Jour. Forensic Sci., 1980-98, Encyclopedia of Forensic Sciences; contbr. articles to profl. jours. Sgt. U.S. Army, 1950-53, Korea. Recipient Vidocq Soc. award, 1993; Ford Found. fellow, 1963; vis. scholar in residence USMC, 1984. Fellow Am. Acad. Forensic Sci. (chmn. jurisprudence sect. 1984, 1994, 1995, bd. dirs. 1986-89, 98-2001, Jurisprudence Sect. award 1988, Disting. fellow 1996); mem. ABA , Mid-Atlantic Assn. Forensic Sci. (emeritus), Assn. Trial Lawyers Am., Internat. Soc. Forensic Sci. (chmn. jurisprudence sect. 1988), Internat. Assn. for Identification, Geol. Soc. Am. Roman Catholic. Home: 8602 Clydesdale Rd Springfield VA 22151-1301 Office: George Washington U Nat Law Ctr 720 20th St NW Washington DC 20006-4306 E-mail: jstarrs@main.nlc.gwu.edu.

STASSEN, JOHN HENRY, lawyer; b. Joliet, Ill., Mar. 22, 1943; s. John H. and Florence C. (McCarthy) S.; m. Sara A. Gaw, July 6, 1968; children: John C., David A. BS, Northwestern U., 1965, JD, Harvard U., 1968. Bar: Ill. 1968. Assoc. Kirkland & Ellis, Chgo., 1968, 73-76, ptnr. 1977—. Contbr. articles to legal jours. Mem. bd. govs. Northwestern U. Libr., chmn., 2003—; bd. dirs. Landmark Preservation Coun. Ill., chmn., 2001-03. Lt. comdr., JAGC, USNR, 1969-72. Mem. ABA (past chmn. com. on futures regulation), Ill. Bar Assn., Chgo. Bar Assn., Phila. Soc., Mid America Club. Administrative and regulatory, Federal civil litigation, Corporate, general. Home: 1310 N Astor St Chicago IL 60610-2114 Office: Kirkland & Ellis 200 E Randolph St Ste 5900 Chicago IL 60601-6436 E-mail: john_stassen@kirkland.com.

STATHIS, NICHOLAS JOHN, lawyer; b. Calchi, Greece, Feb. 27, 1924; Republican. s. John and Sylvia (Koutsonouris) S. Student, Columbia U., 1942-43, 44-48, AB, 1946, JD, 1948. Bar: N.Y. 1949. Assoc. James Maxwell Fassett, NYC, 1948—50; asst. counsel to spl. com. to investigate organized crime in interstate commerce U.S. Senate, Washington, 1951; trial atty. Fidelity & Casualty Co., NYC, 1952; law sec. to Harold R. Medina Judge U.S. Ct. Appeals (2d cir.), NYC, 1952—54; spl. dep. atty. gen. N.Y. State Election Frauds Bur., Dept. Law, N.Y.C., 1956; assoc. Watson, Leavenworth, Kelton & Taggart, NYC, 1954—60, ptnr., 1961—81, Hopgood, Calimafde, Kalil, Blaustein & Judlowe, NYC, 1981—84, Botein, Hays & Sklar, NYC, 1984—89; of counsel White & Case, NYC, 1989—93; corp. coun., dir. intellectual property Aphton Corp., NYC, 1993—. Lectr. Practising Law Inst., N.Y.C., 1968-69. Contbr. articles to profl. jours. on trademarks. Pres., exec. dir., chmn., bd. dirs. Found. Classic Theatre and Acad., 1973—; bd. dirs. Concert Artists Guild, 1974-91, Pirandello Soc., 1976—, Bklyn. Philharm. Orch., 1986-91, Orpheon, Inc., 1986-98, Friends of Young Musicians, 1998—. With AUS, 1943-44. Mem. ABA, Assn. of Bar of City of N.Y., N.Y. State Bar Assn., Fed. Bar Coun., Am. Intellectual Property Law Assn., N.Y. Intellectual Property Law Assn. Greek Orthodox. Intellectual property, Patent, Trademark and copyright. Home: 1885 John F Kennedy Blvd Jersey City NJ 07305-2113 Office: 515 Madison Ave Ste 2511 New York NY 10022-5403

STATON, ROBERT HOWARD, retired judge; b. Indpls., Apr. 7, 1925; s. William Howard and Pearl Mae (Edwards) Staton; life ptnr. Jane Ellen Cox, June 28, 1958 (dec. Feb. 15, 1985); children: Elizabeth Staton Taleman, Jennifer Staton Stoesz. BA, Ind. U., 1952; LLB, Ind. U., Indpls., 1955, JD, 1967. Chief trial dep. prosecutor 19th Jud. Cir., Indpls., 1955—59; hearings judge Ind. Pub. Svc. Commn., Indpls., 1959—62; mng. ptnr. Staton and Ward, Indpls., 1962—70; judge Ind. Ct. Appeals, Indpls., 1971—2000, sr. judge, 2000—03; ret., 2003. Chmn. Supreme Ct. Com. Legal Edn. & Competency Bar, 1980—2000. Contbr. articles to profl. jours. Chmn. Ind. Continuing Edn. Commn., Indpls.; mem. exec. coun. Ind. U., rep. Law Sch. Sgt. Spl. Forces U.S. Army, 1943—46. Recipient Maynard K. Hine medal, Ind. U. Mem.: ABA, Ind. Bar Assn. (chmn. consotium competency 1983—86), Ind. U. Sch. Law Indpls. Alumni Assn. (past pres., bd. dirs., Alumni award), Columbia Club. Democrat. Mem. Soc. Of Friends. Avocations: golf, travel, history, art, painting. Office: Ct Appeals 200 W Washington St Ste 409 Indianapolis IN 46204-2733

STAUBITZ, ARTHUR FREDERICK, lawyer, healthcare products company executive; b. Omaha, Nebr., Mar. 14, 1939; s. Herbert Frederick Staubitz and Barbara Eileen (Dallas) Alderson; m. Linda Medora Miller, Aug. 18, 1962; children: Michael, Melissa, Peter. AB cum laude, Wesleyan U., Middletown, Conn., 1961; JD cum laude, U. Pa., 1964. Bar: Ill. 1964, U.S. Dist. Ct. (no. dist.) Ill. 1964, U.S. Ct. Appeals (7th cir.) 1964, Pa. 1972. Assoc. Sidley & Austin, Chgo., 1964-71; sr. internat. atty., asst. gen. counsel, dir. Japanese ops. Sperry Univac, Blue Bell, Pa., 1971-78; from asst. to assoc. to dep. gen. counsel Baxter Internat. Inc., Deerfield, Ill., 1978-85, v.p., dep. gen. counsel, 1985-90; v.p. Baxter Diagnostics, 1990-91; sr. v.p., sec., gen. counsel Amgen, Inc., Thousand Oaks, Calif., 1991-92; v.p., gen. mgr. Ventures Group Baxter World Trade Corp., Deerfield, Ill., 1992-93; v.p., sec., gen. counsel Baxter Internat. Inc., Deerfield, Ill., 1993, sr. v.p., gen. counsel, 1993-97, sr. v.p. portfolio strategy, 1997-98. Bd. dirs. Aastrom Bioscis., Inc. Mem. Planning Commn., Springfield Twp., Montgomery County, Pa., 1973-74, mem. Zoning Hearing Bd., 1974-78; bd. dirs. Twp. H.S. Dist. 113, Deerfield and Highland Park, Ill., 1983-91, pres., 1989-91; trustee Food and Drug Law Inst., 1991-92, 93-96, Carthage Coll., Kenosha, Wis., 1996—, exec. com., 1999—; bd. dirs. Music of the Baroque,

1994-2001, vice-chmn.; mem. adv. bd. UA Presents; mem. adv. bd. Ariz. Cancer Ctr. Episcopalian. Antitrust, Corporate, general, Private international. Home: 6251 E Placita Aspecto Tucson AZ 85750 E-mail: staubitz@msn.com.

STAUDER, MICHAEL H. lawyer; b. St. Louis, Nov. 20, 1944; s. Harry W. and Mary Jane S.; m. Theresa L. Stauder; children: Michael Stauder Jr., C. Brooke Stauder, Kelly Morrison, Kristen Morrison, Marissa Lynn Stauder. BA in Bus. Adminstrn., Christian Bros. U., 1966; JD, U. Miss., 1969. Bar: Miss. 1969, Fla. 1972, cert.: U.S. Supreme Ct. 1978, U.S. District Ct. (no. dist.) 1969, U.S. District Ct. (so. dist.) 1974. Spl. agt. FBI, Washington, 1969-72; pvt. practice North Palm Beach, Fla., 1972—. Mem.: ATLA, Fla. Workers Advocates, Palm Beach County Bar Assn., Palm Beach County Trial Lawyers Assn., Acad. Fla. Trial Lawyers, Soc. Former FBI Agts. (pres. Palm Beach chpt. 1975—76), Fla. Trial Lawyers Assn. Office: 1201 US Highway One Ste 315 North Palm Beach FL 33408 E-mail: staudmike@adelphia.net.

STAUFFER, ERIC P. lawyer; b. Tucson, Feb. 1, 1948; s. Robert D. and Jeanne E. (Catlin) S.; m. Jane F. Snyder, Aug. 2, 1969; children: Curtis Austen, Marcus Elias, Laura Afton. BA, New Coll. of Fla., 1969; JD, Yale U., 1972. Bar: Ariz. 1972, Maine 1974, D.C. 1979. Spl. asst. to gov., fed. state coord. State of Maine, 1973-75; Maine alt. to New England Regional Commn., 1973-75; gen. counsel Maine State Housing Auth., 1976-77; adminstrv. asst. to chmn. Dem. Nat. Com., 1977-78; mem. Preti, Flaherty, Beliveau Pachios & Haley, LLC, Portland, Maine, 1978—. Bd. dirs. Jr. Achievement Maine, Inc., 1995-98; pres. Goodwill Industries No. New Eng., 1981-82, bd. dirs., 1979-93, 99—. Mem. Am. Health Lawyers Assn., Maine State Bar Assn., Ariz. State Bar, D.C. Bar, Maine Real Estate Devel. Assn. (bd. dirs. 1991—, Pub. Svc. award 1992, Founder's award 2002). Commercial, contracts (including sales of goods; commercial financing), Computer, Mergers and acquisitions. Office: Preti Flaherty Beliveau Pachios & Haley LLC PO Box 9546 One City Ctr Portland ME 04112-9546 E-mail: estauffe@preti.com.

STAUFFER, RONALD EUGENE, lawyer; b. Hempstead, N.Y., Jan. 22, 1949; s. Hiram Eugene and Florence Marie (Hintz) S.; m. Vicki Lynn Hartman, June 12, 1973; children: Eric Alan, Craig Aaron, Darren Adam. SB, MIT, 1970; JD magna cum laude, Harvard U., 1973. Bar: D.C. 1973, U.S. Ct. Mil. Appeals 1976, U.S. Tax Ct. 1979. Ptnr. Hogan & Hartson, Washington, 1977-87, Sonnenschein Nath & Rosenthal, Washington, 1988—. Contbr. articles to profl. publs. Capt. U.S. Army, 1970-77. Mem. ABA (chair TIPS Employee Benefits Com. 1977—), D.C. Bar Assn., Tau Beta Pi, Sigma Gamma Tau. Avocations: running, water skiing. Pension, profit-sharing, and employee benefits, Corporate taxation. Home: 10207 Woodvale Pond Dr Fairfax Station VA 22039-1658 Office: Sonnenschein Nath & Rosenthal 1301 K St NW Ste 600 Washington DC 20005-3317 E-mail: rstauffer@sonnenschein.com.

STAUFFER, SCOTT WILLIAM, lawyer, accountant; b. Oshkosh, Wis., Aug. 17, 1954; s. Robert Edward and Shirley Lydia (Wrasse) S.; m. Debralee Bowland, Nov. 14, 1987. BBA in Acctg., U. Wis., 1975; JD, U. Denver, 1979. Bar: Colo. 1979; CPA, Colo. Tax acct. Arthur Andersen & Co., Denver, 1979-82; tax mgr. Gary-Williams Oil, Englewood, Colo., 1982-85; pvt. practice Aurora, Colo., 1986—. Pres. Colo. Chorale, Denver, 1984-85, 92-93. Mem. ABA, AICPA, Colo. Bar Assn. (mem. multidisciplinary practice taskforce 2000—, ethics com. 1997-99, vice chair, exec. coun. solo and small firm sect. 2002-03), Denver Bar Assn. (chmn. law office mgmt. com. 1993-95, intraprofl. com. 1997—), Colo. Soc. CPAs (chmn. fed. tax com. 1994-96, mem. 1999-2000, bd. dirs. 2000-02), Am. Assn. Atty.-CPAs., Denver Tax Assn. (chair 2002-03), Bethany Luth. Ch. Found. (pres. 2003—). Lutheran. Avocations: singing, golf, travel, reading, computer. Corporate, general, Corporate taxation, Personal income taxation. Home: 8147 W Frost Pl Littleton CO 80128-4325 Office: 2851 S Parker Rd Ste 720 Aurora CO 80014-2728 E-mail: swstauff@ix.netcom.com.

STAVINS, RICHARD LEE, lawyer; b. Urbana, Ill., Sept. 26, 1943; s. Sidney and Joan (Shaul) S.; m. Karen Kessler, June 18, 1967; children: Eric, Randi. BS, Northwestern U., 1965, JD, 1968. Bar: Ill. 1968, U.S. Dist. Ct. (no. dist.) Ill. 1969, U.S. Ct. Appeals (7th cir.) 1969. U.S. Supreme Ct. 1972. Assoc. Dorfman, DeKoven & Cohen, Chgo., 1968-70, Blumenthal & Schwartz, Chgo., 1970-76; ptnr. Blumenthal & Stavins, Chgo., 1976-81, Keith & Greenblatt, Chgo., 1981-82, Greenblatt Yusim & Stavins, Chgo., 1982-85; assoc. Robbins, Salomon & Patt, Chgo., 1985-86, ptnr., 1986—. Ford Found. fellow, 1967. Federal civil litigation, General civil litigation, State civil litigation. Home: 155 N Harbor Dr Chicago IL 60601-7364 Office: Robbins Salomon & Patt 25 E Washington St Chicago IL 60602-1708

STAVROS, PETER JAMES, lawyer; b. N.Y.C., Sept. 16, 1966; s. James P. and Suzanne T. Stavros. BA in English, Duke U., 1988; grad. in creative writing, Harvard U., 1989; JD, U. Ky., 1995. Bar: Ky. 1995, U.S. Dist. Ct. (ea. and we. dists.) Ky. 1995, U.S. Ct. Appeals (6th cir.) 1995, U.S. Ct. Appeals (fed. cir.) 1996, U.S. Supreme Ct. 2000. Reporter AP, Louisville, 1990, Charleston, W.Va., 1990, Indpls., 1991; law clk. Supreme Ct. Ky., Frankfort, 1995-96; assoc. Frost Brown Todd LLC, Louisville, 1996—. Articles editor Ky. Law Jour., 1995. Mem. ABA, Ky. Bar Assn., Louisville Bar Assn. Avocation: triathlons. Federal civil litigation, Intellectual property, Patent. Office: Frost Brown Todd LLC 400 W Market St Fl 32 Louisville KY 40202-3346 E-mail: pstavros@fbtlaw.com.

STAYIN, RANDOLPH JOHN, lawyer; b. Cin., Oct. 30, 1942; s. Jack and Viola (Tomin) S.; children: Gregory S., Todd R., Elizabeth J. BA, Dartmouth Coll., 1964; JD, U. Cin., 1967. Bar: Ohio 1967, U.S. Dist. Ct. (so. dist.) Ohio 1968, U.S. Dist. Ct. D.C. 1977, U.S. Ct. Appeals (6th cir.) 1968, U.S. Ct. Appeals (fed. cir.) 1986, U.S. Supreme Ct. 1974, U.S. Ct. Appeals (D.C. cir.) 1976, U.S. Ct. Internat. Trade, 1985. Assoc. Frost & Jacobs, Cin., 1967-72; exec. asst., dir. of legislation U.S. Sen. Robert Taft, Jr., Washington, 1973-74, chief of staff, 1975-76; assoc. Taft, Stettinius & Hollister, Washington, 1977, ptnr., 1978-88, Barnes & Thornburg, Washington, 1988—. Mem. adv. coun. U.S. and FGN. Comml. Svc., U.S. Dept. Commerce. Chmn., mem. numerous coms., chmn., worker campaigns for local politicians Rep. Party state and local orgns.; mem. Citizens to Save WCET-TV, 1967-72, Fine Arts Fund, 1970-72, Cancer Soc., 1970-72; chmn. agy. rels. com. Hamilton County Mental Health and Mental Retardation Bd., 1969-71, vice chmn., 1971, chmn., 1971-72; v.p. Recreation Commn., City of Cin., 1970-72; mem. funds mgmt. com. Westwood 1st Presbyn. Ch., 1968, v.p., 1969, pres., 1970, trustee, 1970, elder, 1971-72; bd. dirs. Evans Mill Pond Owners Assn., v.p., 1986, pres., 1987; chmn. Washington Nat. Cathedral Fund Com., mem. devel. com. Mem.: ABA (sect. on internat. law and practice, vice chmn.com.on nat. legislation 1977—79, internat. sect., anti-trust sect.), D. C. Bar Assn. (com. on internat. law), Internat. Bar Assn., Am. Soc. Assn. Execs. (legal sect., internat. sect.). Avocations: theater, tennis, skiing, travel, boating. Administrative and regulatory, Private international, Legislative. Office: Barnes & Thornburg 750 17th St NW Ste 900 Washington DC 20006-2225

STAYTON, THOMAS GEORGE, lawyer; b. Rochester, Minn., May 1, 1948; m. Barbara Joan Feck, Aug. 8, 1970; children: Ryan, Megan. BS, Miami U., Oxford, Ohio, 1970; JD, U. Mich., 1973. Bar: Ind. 1973, U.S. Dist. Ct. (so. dist.) Ind. 1973, U.S. Ct. Appeals (7th cir.) 1977. Ptnr. Baker & Daniels, Indpls., 1973—. Sustaining mem. Product Liability Adv. Coun. Recipient Sagamore of the Wabash Gov. of Ind., 1988. Mem. ABA, Ind. State Bar Assn., Indpls. Bar Assn., Indpls. Athletic Club. Federal civil litigation, General civil litigation, Product liability. Office: Baker & Daniels 300 N Meridian St Ste 2700 Indianapolis IN 46204-1782 E-mail: tstayton@bakerd.com.

STEADMAN, JAMES ROBERT, lawyer; b. Girard, Pa., Aug. 28, 1950; s. Robert Emmet and Ruth Harriet (Blair) S.; m. Alison Terry, June 16, 1973; children: Elizabeth, Kathryn, Anne. BA in Polit. Sci., Grove City Coll., 1972; JD, Dickinson Sch. Law, 1975. Bar: Pa. 1975, U.S. Dist. Ct. (we. dist.) Pa. 1976, U.S. Supreme Ct. 1981. Atty., advisor SBA, Harrisburg, Pa., 1975-76; pvt. practice Girard, 1976—. Dir. Penn. Attys. Title Ins. Co., Erie. Councilman, Girard Borough, 1978-82; bd. dirs. Rice Ave. Cmty. Pub. Libr. (formerly Willcox Libr.), Girard, 1982—, treas., 1982-86; bd. dirs. Battles Village Sr. Citizen Housing, Girard, 1981-84, Erie Philharm., 1998—. Mem. Pa. Bar Assn. (coun. mem. small firm sect. 1993—, chmn. 1995), Erie County Bar Assn. (dir. 1983-85, 90-92, pres. 1991). Family and matrimonial, Probate (including wills, trusts), Property, real (including real estate development, water). Home: 205 Penn Ave Girard PA 16417-1543 Office: PO Box 87 24 Main St E Girard PA 16417-1703

STEADMAN, JOHN MONTAGUE, appellate court judge; b. Honolulu, Aug. 8, 1930; s. Alva Edgar and Martha (Cooke) S.; m. Alison Storer Lunt, Apr. 8, 1961; children— Catharine N., Juliette M., Eric C. Grad., Phillips Acad., Andover, Mass., 1948; BA summa cum laude, Yale U., 1952; LLB magna cum laude, Harvard U., 1955. Bar: D.C. 1955, Calif. 1956, U.S. Supreme Ct. 1964, Hawaii 1977. Assoc. Pillsbury, Madison & Sutro, San Francisco, 1956-63; atty. Dept. Justice, 1963-64; dep. under sec. army for internat. affairs, 1964-65; spl. asst. to sec. and dep. sec. def. Dept. Def., 1965-68; gen. counsel Dept. Air Force, 1968-70; vis. prof. law U. Pa. Law Sch., 1970-72; prof. law Georgetown U. Law Ctr., Washington, 1972-85, assoc. dean, 1979-84; assoc. judge D.C. Ct. Appeals, 1985—. Instr. Lincoln Law Sch., San Francisco, 1961-62, San Francisco Law Sch., 1962-63; vis. prof. U. Mich. Sch. Law, 1976, U. Hawaii Sch. Law, 1977; of counsel firm Pillsbury, Madison & Sutro, Washington, 1979-85 Editor: Harvard Law Rev, 1953-55. Sinclair-Kennedy Traveling fellow, 1955-56 Mem. Am. Law Inst., Cosmos Club, Phi Beta Kappa, Delta Sigma Rho, Zeta Psi. Episcopalian. Home: 2960 Newark St NW Washington DC 20008-3338 Office: DC Ct Appeals 500 Indiana Ave NW Washington DC 20001-2131 E-mail: jsteadman@dcca.state.dc.us.

STEANS, PHILLIP MICHAEL, lawyer; b. Oak Park, Ill., May 23, 1943; s. William B. and Evelyn A. (Leonetti) S.; m. Randi R. Solberg, Sept. 17, 1966; children: Erik, Joshua, Molly. BA summa cum laude, Ripon (Wis.) Coll., 1965; JD, U. Chgo., 1968. Bar: Wis. 1968, Ill. 1968, U.S. Dist. Ct. (we. dist.) Wis. 1968. Ptnr. Solberg & Steans, Menomonie, Wis., 1968-85; mng. ptnr. Steans, Skinner, Schofield & Higley, Menomonie, 1985-91; shareholder Bakke-Norman, S.C., Menomonie, 1991-94; pres. Phillip M. Steans, S.C., Menomonie, 1994—. Dist. atty. Dunn County, Wis., Menomonie, 1969-74; asst. city atty. City of Menomonie, 1969-86; asst. family ct. commr. Dunn County, 1993. NCAA scholar, 1965. Mem. Nat. Bd. Trial Advocacy (civil sect.). Avocations: racquetball, reading. Criminal, Personal injury (including property damage), Product liability. Home: E5745 708th Ave Menomonie WI 54751-5515 Office: 393 Red Cedar St Ste 6 Menomonie WI 54751-2267 E-mail: psteans@steanslaw.com.

STEARNS, FRANK WARREN, lawyer; b. Washington, July 20, 1949; s. Robert Maynard and Ermyntrude (Vaiden) S.; m. Judith Anne Ketcheson, Sept. 7, 1974; children: Frank W. Jr., Brian S., Joe G. BA, Washington & Lee, 1971; JD with honors, George Washington U., 1974. Bar: Washington DC 1975, Va. 1980, U.S. Supreme Ct. 1980, U.S. Dist. Ct. DC 1975, U.S. Ct. Appeals (DC cir.) 1975, U.S. Ct. Appeals (4th cir.) 1985. Law clk. Superior Ct. D.C., Washington, 1974-75; asst. corp. counsel Office of the Corp. Counsel, Washington, 1975-79; asst. county atty. County Atty's Office, Fairfax County, Va., 1979-80; mng. ptnr. Wilkes Artis P.C., Fairfax, Va., 1984-2001; ptnr. Venable, Baetjer & Howard, LLP, McLean, Va., 2001—. Bd. dirs. No. Va. Bldg. Industry Assn., 1987-94; trustee Greater Washington Bd. Trade-P.A.C., 1987-2003; chmn. tech. adv. com. NVBIA, Loudoun, Va., 1986-90. Coun. Excellence in Govt., Washington, 1989—98; Commr. Arlington County Econ. Devel. Commn., Arlington, Va., 1987—91. Mem. Barristers, Counsellors, Fairfax C. of C. (PAC trustee 2003—). Avocations: tennis, golf. Construction, Land use and zoning (including planning), Property, real (including real estate development, water). Office: Ste 300 8010 Towers Crescent Dr Vienna VA 22182 E-mail: fwstearns@venable.com.

STEARNS, RICHARD GAYLORE, judge; b. L.A., June 27, 1944; s. Gaylore Rhodes and Jeannetta Viola (Hofheinz) S.; m. Patricia Ann McElligott, Dec. 21, 1975. BA, Stanford U., 1968; MLitt, Oxford U., Eng., 1971; JD, Harvard U., 1976. Bar: Mass. Dep. campaign mgr. McGovern for Pres., Washington, 1970-72; spl. asst. U.S. Senate, Washington, 1972-73; asst. dist. atty. Norfolk County, Dedham, 1976-79, 80-82; del. dir. Kennedy for Pres., Washington, 1979-80; asst. U.S. atty. U.S. Dept. Justice, Boston, 1982-90; assoc. justice Superior Ct. Mass., Boston, 1990-94; U.S. dist. judge U.S. Dist. Ct. Mass., Boston, 1994—. Author: Massachusetts Criminal Law: A Prosecutor's Guide, 21st edit., 2001. Mem. jud. conf. com. on federal-state jurisdiction, mem. mass torts working group; trustee Vincent Meml. Hosp., Boston. Rhodes scholar, 1968. Mem. ABA, Mass. Bar Assn., Phi Beta Kappa. Office: US Courthouse 1 Courthouse Way Ste 7130 Boston MA 02210-3009

STEARNS, SUSAN TRACEY, lighting design company executive, lawyer; b. Seattle, Oct. 28, 1957; d. Arthur Thomas and Roberta Jane (Arrowood) S.; m. Ross Alan De Alessi, Aug. 11, 1990; 1 child, Chase Arthur. AA, Stephens Coll., 1977, BA, 1979; JD, U. Wash., Seattle, 1990. Bar: Calif. 1990, U.S. Ct. Appeals (9th cir.) 1990, U.S. Dist. Ct. (no. dist.) Calif 1990, U.S. Dist. Ct. (we. dist.) Wash. 1991, Wash. 1991. TV news prodr. KOMO, Seattle, 1980-86; atty. Brobeck, Phleger & Harrison, San Francisco, 1990-92; pres. Ross De Alessi Lighting Design, Seattle, 1993—. Author periodicals in field. Alumnae Assn. Coun. Stephens Coll., Columbia, Mo., 1995—. Named Nat. Order of Barristers U. Washington, Seattle, 1990. Mem. ABA (mem. state labor and employment law subcom.), Wash. State Bar Assn. (mem. bench-bar-press com.), State Bar Calif., King County Bar Assn., Bar Assn.San Francisco, Wash. Athletic Club. Avocations: travel, dance. Office: Ross De Alessi Lighting Design 3313 W McGraw Seattle WA 98199

STEBBINS, HENRY BLANCHARD, lawyer; b. Hartford, Conn., June 14, 1951; s. Herbert Bellows and Katherine (Reynolds) S.; m. Alison Finney, May 30, 1976; children: Duncan Finney, Martha Reynolds, H. Benjamin. BA cum laude, U. N.H., 1973; JD, Boston U., 1976. Bar: N.H. 1976, U.S. Dist. Ct. N.H. 1976. Assoc. Sheenan, Phinney, Bass & Green, Manchester, N.H., 1976-80, ptnr., 1980-97, mgmt. com., 1994-97; sr. ptnr. Stebbins Lazos & Van Der Beken, Manchester, N.H., 1997—. Trustee Manchester Boys and Girls Club, 1983—; chmn. Vocat. Partnership Found., 1986-91; bd. dirs. Brookside Ch. Nursery Sch., 1984-90, Leadership N.H., 1994-95; bd. dirs. United Way Greater Manchester, 1996-95, chmn., 1990-92; mem. N.H. Rep. State com., 1995-99, N.H. Rep. Fin. Com., 1995-97, N.H. legal counsel Dole for Pres. Campaign; mem. fin. com. George W. Bush Presdl. Campaign; bd. dirs., legal counsel, mem. exec. com. Manchester C. of C., 1997-2001; hon. co-chair bus. adv. coun. Rep. Nat. Com., 2002-03. Named N.H. Businessman of Yr., 2003. Mem. ABA, N.H. Bar Assn., Manchester Bar Assn. (pres. 1982-83), Assn. Bank Holding Cos. (lawyers div. 1985-93), Rissa Club. Banking, Construction, Property, real (including real estate development, water). Office: 66 Hanover St Manchester NH 03101-2230

STECHER, ESTA E. lawyer, investment company executive; b. Mpls., Apr. 3, 1957; BA summa cum laude, U. Minn., 1979; JD, Columbia U., 1982. Bar: N.Y. 1983. Ptnr. Sullivan & Cromwell, 1982—94; gen. counsel, mng. dir. Goldman, Sachs & Co., N.Y.C., 1994—. Mem.: ABA, Assn. Bar City of New York, N.Y. Bar Assn. Office: Goldman Sachs and Co Legal Dept 1 New York Plz 37th Fl New York NY 10004 Office Fax: 212-902-3876.*

STEEG, MOISE S., JR., lawyer; b. New Orleans, July 25, 1916; s. Moise S. and Carrie (Gutmann) S.; m. Marion B., Sept. 14, 1943 (dec.); children: Barbara Steeg Midlo, Marion, Robert M.; m. Melba Law, Nov. 29, 1969. LLB, Tulane U., 1937. Bar: La. 1937, U.S. Dist. Ct. (ea. dist.) La. 1939, U.S. Ct. Appeals (5th cir.) 1946, U.S. Supreme Ct. 1950, U.S. Ct. Appeals (11th cir.) 1981. Practice, New Orleans, 1937—; assoc. Rittenberg & Rittenberg, 1937-38; sole practice, 1938-46; founder Gertler & Steeg, 1946-48, Steeg & Morrison, 1948-50, Marcus & Steeg, 1950-54, Steeg & Shushan, 1954-71; sr. ptnr. Steeg & O'Connor, 1972—. Bd. dirs. Loyola U., chmn., 1979—, mem. search com. for dean Coll. Law; chmn., founder New Orleans Hist. Dist. and Landmarks Com.; bd. dirs. chmn. bd. New Orleans Mus. Art, 1980; bd. overseers Hebrew Union Coll.; bd. dirs. Delgado Jr. Coll., New Orleans Symphony; founder, dir. New Orleans Ednl. and Rsch. Corp.; bd. dirs. Louise Davis Sch. for Retarded Children, Touro Infirmary, 1963-69; mem. Ochsner Found. Hosp. Bd., 1985—; bd. visitors Trinity Episcopal Sch., 1989—; organizer, sec. New Orleans Bus. Coun., 1986; pres. Temple Sinai, 1966-67; chmn. Anti-Defamation League, Jewish Community Ctr., chmn. Acquarium Drive, Acquarium of Ams.; local counsel Nat. Dem. Party, 1966. Served to capt. USAF, 1942-46. Recipient Brotherhood Award, NCCJ, 1980, Disting. Alumnus award Tulane Law Sch., 1991, Isidore Newman Sch., Svc. award Newcomb Coll. Soc., Cmty. Svc. award New Orleans Bar Assn. Mem. Paul Tulane Honor Soc. Commercial, contracts (including sales of goods; commercial financing), Probate (including wills, trusts), Property, real (including real estate development, water). Home: One River Place 3 Poydras St New Orleans LA 70130-1665 Office: 201 Saint Charles Ave Ste 3201 New Orleans LA 70170-1032

STEEL, RICHARD D. lawyer; b. Phila., May 13, 1941; s. Philip Steel and Janet Khan; m. Laura Berman; children: Emily, Marc. BA with honors, Dickinson Coll., 1963; LLB, U. Pa., 1966. Bar: Pa., U.s. Supreme Ct., U.S. Ct. Appeals (3d and 9th cirs.), U.S. Dist. Ct. (ea. and we. dists.) Pa. Ptnr. Steel, Rudnick & Ruben, Phila., 1974—. Course planner Pa. Bar Inst., Phila. Author: (book) Steel on Immigration Law 2d, 1985. Bd. dirs. Nationalities Svc. Ctr., Phila., 1988—, chair. Capt. U.S. Army, 1967—71. Mem.: Pa. Bar Assn., Am. Immigration Lawyers Assn. (course planner, lectr. 1978—, Mentor award 1995, Edith Lowenstein award 2000). Immigration, naturalization, and customs. Office: Steel Rudnick and Ruben 1608 Walnut St Ste 1500 Philadelphia PA 19103 Office Fax: 215-546-4222. Business E-Mail: rsteel@steelrudnickruben.com.

STEELE, C. CARLYLE, lawyer; b. Lancaster, S.C., Nov. 18, 1945; s. Curtis Carlyle and Connie (Kennington) S.; m. Jennifer Smith, Nov. 17, 1979; children: Mary Kennington, Andrew J. BA, U. S.C., 1968, JD, 1974. Assoc. dir. county rec. divsn. S.C. Archives, Columbia, S.C., 1968-71; ptnr. Warder & Steele, Greenville, S.C., 1974-88; atty. pvt. practice, Greenville, S.C., 1988—. Author: History of Hopewell United Methodist Church 1870-1970, 1970. Pres. Greenville Eleven Dem. Club, 1986—. Mem. Greenville County Bar Assn. (sec.-treas. 1974-77). Methodist. Avocations: walking, reading, politics, travel. Criminal, Family and matrimonial, Personal injury (including property damage). Home: 213 Tindal Ave Greenville SC 29605-3975 Office: 16 Whitsett St Greenville SC 29601-3137

STEELE, MYRON THOMAS, lawyer; b. Taunton, Mass., July 28, 1945; s. Myron Thetus and Coleen Amelia (Polk) Steele; m. Beverly June Heaps, Feb. 4, 1967; children: Clayton Carter, Jenness Farnham. BA, U. Va., 1967, JD, 1970. Bar: Va. 1970, Del. 1970, U.S. Dist. Ct. Del. 1970, U.S. Ct. Appeals (3d cir.) 1974. Assoc. Prickett, Ward, Burt & Sanders, Dover, Del., 1970, 1973, ptnr., 1974; dep. atty. gen. State of Del., 1971—72; v.p., dir. Prickett, Jones, Elliott, Kristol & Schnee, Dover, 1974—88; assoc. judge Superior Ct., 1988—90, res. judge, 1990—94; vice chancellor Ct. Chancery, Del., 1994—2000; justice Del. Superior Ct., 2000—. Chmn. Ctrl. Del. Health Care Corp., 1990—93; mem. exec. com. Del. Democratic State Com., 1974—88; bd. dirs. Childrens Bur. Del., Del. News Coun.; chmn. Consumer Affairs Bd., 1974—88. Served to 1st. lt. U.S. Army, 1970, col. ret. Del. N.G., 1974—97. Mem.: ABA (mem. jud. liaison comml. and bus. litig. com., bus. sect.), Del-Vets, Commn. on Ct. 2000 (Del.), Kent County Bar Assn. (past pres.), Va. State Bar, Del. Bar Assn. (past v.p.), Kiwanis (past pres.), Rehoboth Beach Country Club, Wilmington Club, Masons. Episcopalian. Banking, State civil litigation, Insurance. Office: 57 The Green Dover DE 19901

STEELE, RODNEY REDFEARN, judge; b. Selma, Ala., May 22, 1930; s. C. Parker and Miriam Lera (Redfearn) S.; m. Frances Marion Blair, Aug. 1, 1964; children: Marion Scott, Claudia Redfearn, Parker Blair. AB, U. Ala., 1950, MA, 1951; LLB, U. Mich., 1954. Bar: Ala. 1954, U.S. Dist. Ct. (mid. dist.) Ala. 1959, U.S. Ct. Appeals (5th cir., now 11th cir.) 1981. Law clk. Ala. Ct. Appeals, 1956-57; assoc. Knabe & Nachman, Montgomery, Ala., 1957-61; asst. U.S. atty. Dept. Justice, Montgomery, 1961-66; staff atty. So. Bell T&T Co., Atlanta, 1966-67; judge U.S. Bankruptcy Ct., Mid. dist. Ala., Montgomery, 1967—, chief judge, 1985-99; ret., 1999—. Served with U.S. Army, 1954-56, Korea. Mem. ABA, Ala. State Bar, Montgomery County Bar Assn. Democrat. Episcopalian. Home: 1227 Magnolia Curv Montgomery AL 36106-2136

STEELE, THOMAS LEE, lawyer; b. Kearney, Nebr., Oct. 16, 1959; s. Clyde M. and L. Lorene S.; m. Sarah E. Owens, May 8, 1992; 1 child, Andrew. BA, U. Mo., 1984; JD, Creighton U., 1987. Bar: Nebr. 1987, Mo. 1988, Kans. 1989, U.S. Supreme Ct. 1993. Gen. counsel Gen. Fin. Svcs., Inc., Wichita, 1995—, Dunes Hotels and Casinos, Inc., 2000—; spec. coun. Martin & Churchill Chtd. Bd. dirs. The Inland Corp., Norwich, Kans. Precinct chmn. Wichita Rep. Com., 1996—; exec. bd. Quivira coun. Boy Scouts Am., 1993—. Mem. ABA, Am. Assn. Sales Profls. (bd. dirs. 2000—), Mo. Bar Assn., Kans. Bar Assn., Nebr. Bar Assn., Pi Omicron Sigma. Presbyterian. Corporate, general, Property, real (including real estate development, water), Securities. Home: 156 Belmont Pl Wichita KS 67208 Office: Gen Fin Svcs Inc 8441 E 32d St N Wichita KS 67226

STEER, REGINALD DAVID, lawyer; b. N.Y.C., July 16, 1945; s. Joseph D. and Rozica (Yusim) S.; m. Marianne Spizzy, July 22, 1983; children: Derek B., Trevor A. BA, U. Minn., 1966, JD, 1969. Bar: Minn. 1969, Calif. 1973, U.S. Dist. Ct. (no., ea. and cen. dists.) Calif., U.S. Ct. Mil. Appeals 1969, U.S. Ct. Appeals (9th cir.), U.S. Ct. Appeals (11th cir.), U.S. Supreme Ct. 1981, U.S. Ct. Internat. Trade, 1994. Assoc. Pillsbury, Madison & Sutro, San Francisco, 1973-79, ptnr., 1979-2000, Skjerven Morrill, LLP, San Francisco, 2000—, Pillsbury Winthrop, LLP, Palo Alto, Calif., 2003—. Capt. U.S. Army, 1969—73. Fellow Am. Coll. Trial Lawyers; mem. ABA (antitrust and litigation sects.). Avocations: piano, tennis, photography. Antitrust, Federal civil litigation, State civil litigation. Office: Pillsbury Winthrop LLP 2550 Hanover St Palo Alto CA 94304 E-mail: rsteer@pillsburywinthrop.com.

STEFANON, ANTHONY, lawyer; b. Bellefonte, Pa., Sept. 6, 1949; s. Severino and Dorothy (Albright) S.; m. Elizabeth Jo Windsor, Nov. 22, 1969; children: Dyon, Justin. BS in Aerospace Engring., Pa. State U., 1971; JD, Dickinson U., 1977. Bar: Pa. 1977, U.S. Dist. Ct. (mid. dist.) Pa. 1977, U.S. Ct. Appeals (3rd cir.) 1991. Assoc. Myers & Potteiger, Harrisburg, Pa.,

1977-79; ptnr. Myers, Potteiger & Stefanon, Harrisburg, Pa., 1979-82; assoc. Thomas & Thomas, Harrisburg, Pa., 1982-85; ptnr. Stefanon & Lappas, Harrisburg, Pa., 1985-88; pvt. practice Harrisburg, Pa., 1988—. Mem. Assn. of Trial Lawyers of Am., Pa. Trial Lawyers Assn., Pa. Bar Assn., Dauphin County Bar Assn. Avocations: squash, auto racing, restorations. General civil litigation, Personal injury (including property damage), Product liability. Office: 407 N Front St Harrisburg PA 17101-1221

STEFFEL, VERN JOHN, JR., lawyer; b. Chgo., July 10, 1950; s. Vern John and Adeline T. (Safranski) S.; m. Cynthia Louise Corkum, Aug. 4, 1973; children: Corkum L., Gabrielle M. BS, Western Mich. U., 1972; postgrad., U. Notre Dame, London, summer 1974; JD, Ohio No. U., 1975. Bar: Mich. 1975, U.S. Dist. Ct. (ea. and we. dists.) Mich. 1980. Assoc. Allen, Worth & Hatch, Battle Creek, Mich., 1975-78; sole practice Battle Creek, 1978-85; sr. ptnr. Steffel & Steffel, Battle Creek, 1985—. Bd. dirs. Steffel Design Studio, Battle Creek. Editor Ohio No. U. Law Review, 1974. Bd. dirs. Y-Ctr. Battle Creek, 1984—, pres. 1990. Mem. ABA, Assn. Trial Lawyers Am., Comml. Law League Am., Mich. Bar Assn., Mich. Trial Lawyers Assn., Calhoun County Bar Assn. (sec. 1981-84). Roman Catholic. Avocations: marathons, racquetball, skiing. Banking, Commercial, contracts (including sales of goods; commercial financing), Property, real (including real estate development, water). Home: 564 Breezy Bluff St Battle Creek MI 49015-3576 Office: 332 Columbia Ave E Ste A Battle Creek MI 49015-4411 E-mail: vsteffel@steffellaw.com.

STEFFEN, THOMAS LEE, retired judge, lawyer; b. Tremonton, Utah, July 9, 1930; s. Conrad Richard and Jewel (McGuire) S.; m. LaVona Ericksen, Mar. 20, 1953; children— Elizabeth, Catherine, Conrad, John, Jennifer Student, U. So. Calif., 1955-56; BS, U. Utah, 1957; JD with honors, George Washington U., 1964; LLM, U. Va., 1988. Bar: Nev. 1965, U.S. Dist. Ct. Nev. 1965, U.S. Tax Ct. 1966, U.S. Ct. Appeals 1967, U.S. Supreme Ct. 1977. Contracts negotiator U.S. Bur. Naval Weapons, Washington, 1961-64; private practice Las Vegas, 1965-82; justice Supreme Ct. Nev., Carson City, 1982-94, chief justice, 1995-97, ret., 1997, chmn. code of jud. conduct study com., 1991; of counsel Hutchison & Steffen, Las Vegas, also Provo, Utah, 1997—. Vice chmn. Nev. State Jud. Edn. Coun., 1983-84; chmn. Nev. State-Fed. Jud. Coun., 1986-91, mem., 1986-93. Mem. editorial staff George Washington U. Law Rev., 1963-64; contbr. articles to legal jours. Bd. dirs. So. Nev. chpt. NCCJ, 1974-75; mem. exec. bd. Boulder Dam Area coun. Boy Scouts Am., 1979-83; bd. visitors Brigham Young U., 1985-89. Recipient merit citation Utah State U., 1983 Mem. Nev. Bar Assn. (former chmn. So. Nev. med.-legal screening panel), Nev. Trial Lawyers Assn. (former dir.) Republican. Mem. Lds Ch. Avocations: reading, spectator sports. Office: Lakes Business Park 8831 W Sahara Ave Las Vegas NV 89117-5865 also: 481 E Normandy Dr Provo UT 84604-5963 E-mail: Tlsrcjnset@aol.com.

STEFFEY, FRED H. lawyer; b. Wilmington, N.C., July 8, 1931; s. Fred L. and Leila Newman Steffey; m. Betty Stimpson Steffey, Sept. 9, 1951; children: Cynthia, Eric. BA, Duke U., 1952, LLB, 1955. Instr. Duke U., Durham, NC, 1955—56; trial atty. IRS Office Chief Coun., Atlanta, 1956—62, Jacksonville, Fla., 1956—62; ptnr. Mahoney, Hadlow & Adams, Jacksonville, 1962—82; pvt. practice Jacksonville, 1982—. Dir. Hope Haven Childrens Clinic, Jacksonville, 1975—95. Mem.: ABA, Fla. Bar, N.C. State Bar, Rotary Internat. Taxation, general, Probate (including wills, trusts), Estate planning. Home: 88 San Juan Dr Ponte Vedra Beach FL 32082 Office: 6620 Southpoint Dr S #300 Jacksonville FL 32216

STEGALL, WHITNEY, retired lawyer; b. Rockvale, Tenn., Feb. 17, 1916; s. Benjamine Duggin and Nannie May (Love) Stegall; m. Orene E. Cowen, Dec. 30, 1936; children: Whitney Jr., Amy. BS, Mid. Tenn. State U.; JD, Vanderbilt U. Tchr. chemistry and biology Rutherford County Schs.; ednl. advisor Civil Coll. Corp.; solo practice atty.; chancellor, judge 16th Jud. Dist., Rutherford County, Tenn. Maj. Signal Corps U.S. Army, 1943—47, Pacific. Democrat. Mehodist. Home: 132 Park Cir Murfreesboro TN 37130-3530

STEGER, EVAN EVANS, III, retired lawyer; b. Indpls., Oct. 24, 1937; s. Charles Franklin and Alice (Hill) S.; m. Suzy Gillespie, July 18, 1964; children: Cynthia Anne, Emily McKee. AB, Wabash Coll., 1959; JD, Ind. U., 1962. Bar: Ind. 1962, U.S. Dist. Ct. (so. dist.) Ind. 1962, U.S. Ct. Appeals (7th cir.) 1972, U.S. Tax Ct. 1982, U.S. Supreme Ct. 1982. Assoc. Ice, Miller, Donadio and Ryan and predecessor firm Ross, McCord, Ice and Miller, Indpls., 1962-69, ptnr., 1970-96, mng. ptnr., 1996-99, ret., 2000. Fellow Am. Coll. Trial Lawyers. Democrat. Presbyterian. Federal civil litigation, State civil litigation. Office: Ice Miller Box 82001 1 American Sq Indianapolis IN 46282-0020 E-mail: essteger@comcast.net.

STEGER, WILLIAM MERRITT, federal judge; b. Dallas, Aug. 22, 1920; s. Merritt and Lottie (Reese) S.; m. Ann Hollandsworth, Feb. 14, 1948; 1 son, Merritt Reed (dec.). Student, Baylor U., 1938-41; LL.B., So. Meth. U., 1950. Bar: Tex. 1951. Pvt. practice, Longview, 1951-53; apptd. U.S. dist. atty. Eastern Dist. Tex., 1953-59; mem. firm Wilson, Miller, Spivey & Steger, Tyler, Tex., 1959-70; U.S. dist. judge Ea. Dist. Tex. U.S. Dist. Ct. (ea. dist.) Tex., Tyler, 1970—, sr. judge, 1988—. Republican candidate for gov. of Tex., 1960; for U.S. Ho. of Reps., 1962; mem. Tex. State Republican Exec. Com., 1966-69; chmn. Tex. State Republican Party, 1969-70. Pilot with ranks 2d lt. to capt. USAAF, 1942-47. Mem. State Bar Tex., Masons (32 degree, Shriner). Home: 801 Meadowcreek Dr Tyler TX 75703-3524 Office: US Courthouse PO Box 1109 Tyler TX 75710-1109

STEIGER, SHELDON GERALD, lawyer; b. Cleve., May 27, 1945; s. Max and Fannie (Axelrod) S.; m. Sally Blumental, Sept. 6, 1971; children: Jeremy M., Suzanna L., Melissa R. BA, Ohio State U., 1967; JD, Cleve. State U., 1971. Bar: Ohio 1972, U.S. Dist. Ct. (no. dist.) Ohio 1975. Asst. dir. law City of Cleve., 1973-74; assoc. Berger & Kirschenbaum, Cleve., 1974; pvt. practive, Cleve., 1975—. Mem. Ohio Bar Assn., Cleve. Bar Assn. Probate (including wills, trusts), Workers' compensation. Home: 4426 Silsby Rd University Heights OH 44118-3939 Office: 75 Public Sq Ste 650 Cleveland OH 44113-1901 E-mail: steiger@winstarmail.com.

STEIL, GEORGE KENNETH, SR., lawyer; b. Darlington, Wis., Dec. 16, 1924; s. George John and Laura (Donahoe) S.; m. Mavis Elaine Andrews, May 24, 1947; children: George Kenneth, John R., MIchelle Steil Bryski, Marcelaine Steil-Zimmermann. Student, Platteville State Tchrs. Coll., 1942-43; JD, U. Wis., Madison, 1950. Bar: Wis. 1950, U.S. Tax Ct. 1971, U.S. Dist. Ct. (western dist.) Wis. 1950. Assoc. J. G. McWilliams, Janesville, 1950-53; ptnr. McWilliams and Steil, Janesville, 1954-60, Brennan, Steil, Basting & MacDougall, Janesville, 1960-72; pres. Brennan, Steil & Basting (S.C., and predecessor), Janesville, 1972—. Lectr. law U. Wis., 1974; bd. dirs. Acuity Ins. Co., Sheboygan, Wis., Acuity Bank, SSB, Tomah, Wis., chmn. 2000—; trustee, bd. dirs. Roman Cath. Diocese of Madison; mem. Wis. Supreme Ct. Bd. Atty. Profl. Responsibility, 1982-87, chmn., 1984-87; chmn. gov.'s adv. coun. jud. selection State of Wis., 1987-92; chmn. Wis. Lottery Bd., 1987-90. Bd. dirs. St. Coletta Sch. for Exceptional Children, Jefferson, Wis., 1972-76, 78-84, 86-89, chmn., 1982-83; bd. regents U. Wis., 1990-97, pres., 1992-94; bd. dirs. U. Wis. Hosp. Authority, 1996—, chmn., 2002-; bd. dirs., chair U. Wis. Med. Found., 1996-99. Recipient Disting. Svc. award U. Wis. Law Alumni, 1991, Cath. Leadership awrd Diocese of Madison, 1998; named Knight of St. Gregory, Pope John Paul II, 1997. Fellow Am. Bar Found. (life), Am. Coll. Trust and Estate Counsel; mem. ABA, Jamesville Area C. of C. (pres. 1970-71), State Bar Wis. (pres. 1977-78), Wis. Bar Found. (bd. dirs. 1976-2003, Charles L. Goldberg Disting. Svc. award 1990). Roman Catholic. Construction, Corporate, general, Probate (including wills, trusts). Home: 2818 Cambridge Ct Janesville WI 53545-2797 Office: PO Box 1148 1 E Milwaukee St Janesville WI 53545 Office Fax: 608-756-9000. Business E-Mail: gsteilsr@brennansteil.com.

STEIN, ALLAN MARK, lawyer; b. Montreal, Quebec, Can., Oct. 18, 1951; came to U.S., 1977; s. Boris and Beatrice (Fishman) S. B in Commerce, Sir George Williams, 1972; BA, Loyola, Montreal, 1973; B in Civil Law, McGill U., 1976, LLB, 1977; JD, Nova U., 1979. Bar: Fla. 1979, U.S. Dist. Ct. (so. dist.) Fla. 1979, U.S. Ct. Appeals (5th cir.) 1980, U.S. Ct. Appeals (11th cir.) 1983, U.S. Dist. Ct. Ariz. 1993. Assoc. Law Offices of Paul Landy Beiley, Miami, Fla., 1980, Heitner & Rosenfeld, Miami, 1980-85, Rosenfeld & Stein, Miami, 1985-90, Rosenfeld, Stein & Sugarman, Miami, 1990-94, Rosenfeld & Stein P.A., Miami, 1994—. Mem. North Dade Bar Assn. (bd. dirs. 1985-90). Republican. Jewish. Avocations: photography, history. Bankruptcy, Commercial, consumer (including collections, credit), Commercial, contracts (including sales of goods; commercial financing). Office: 18260 NE 19th Ave Ste 202 Miami FL 33162-1632

STEIN, DANIEL ALAN, public interest lawyer; b. Washington, Mar. 9, 1955; s. Edward Seymour and Ann Rose Stein; m. Sharon McCloe, Oct. 18, 1986; children: Claire, Corrieanne. BA, Ind. U., 1977; JD, Cath. U. Am., 1984. Bar: D.C. 1984, U.S. Dist. Ct. D.C. 1985, U.S. Ct. Appeals (D.C. cir.) 1987, U.S. Tax Ct. 1987, Md. 2002, U.S. Dist. Ct. Md. 2003. Profl. staff mem. select com. on narcotics abuse and control U.S. Ho. of Reps., Washington, 1977-81; pvt. practice Washington, 1984-89; exec. dir. Immigration Reform Law Inst., Washington, 1986-88, Fedn. for Am. Immigration Reform, Washington, 1982-86, 89—. Mem. adv. bd. Social Contract periodical, Petosky, Mich., 1990—. Mem. Capitol Hill Club, Nat. Press Club. Republican. Avocations: trombone, american history, western civilization, jazz, antique books. Office: Fedn for Am Immigration Reform 1666 Connecticut Ave NW Ste 400 Washington DC 20009-1039

STEIN, GARY S. retired judge, lawyer; b. Newark, June 13, 1933; s. Morris J. and Mollie (Goldfarb) S.; married, July 1, 1956; children— Jill, Carrie, Michael, Terri, Jo; m. Et Tilchin, July 1, 1956 AB, Duke U., 1954, LL.B. with distinction, 1956; D.H.L. (hon.), N.J. Inst. Tech., 1985. Bar: D.C. 1956, Ohio 1957, N.Y. 1958, N.J. 1963. Research asst. U.S. Senate AntiTrust and Monopoly Subcom., Washington, 1955; assoc. Kramer, Marx, Greenlee & Backus, N.Y.C., 1956-65; sole practice Paramus, N.J., 1966-72; ptnr. Stein & Kurland, Esquires, Paramus, N.J., 1972-82; dir. Gov.'s Office of Policy and Planning, Trenton, N.J., 1982-85; assoc. justice Supreme Ct. N.J., Hackensack, 1985—2002, ret., 2002; counsel Pashman Stein, Hackensack, 2002—. Mcpl. atty., Paramus, 1967-71; counsel N.J. Election Law Revision Commn., 1970; atty. Bd. Adjustment, Teaneck, N.J., 1973-82 Mem. editorial bd. Duke Law Jour., 1954-56, assoc. editor, 1955-56. Mem. Dist. Ethics Com. for Bergen County, N.J., 1977-80, chmn. 1981. Served with U.S. Army, 1957-58, 61-62 Mem. ABA, N.J. State Bar Assn. (com. on state legislation 1973-79, chmn. 1973-76, jud. selection com. 1976-81, Constl. amendment com. 1977-79, court modernization com. 1976-79), Bergen County Bar Assn., Order of Coif. Jewish. Avocation: tennis. Office: Pashman Stein 45 Essex St Hackensack NJ 07601-5415

STEIN, JOHN C. lawyer; b. Flint, Mich., May 8, 1939; s. Joseph Aloyosius and Gertrude (Carlin) S.; m. Dorothea Ruel, Nov. 20, 1965; children: John Jr., Christian, Peter, Thea. BA, U. San Francisco, 1963; JD, U. Calif. Hastings, San Francisco, 1966; cert., Mil. Justice Sch., Newport, R.I., 1968. Bar: Calif. 1966, U.S. Dist. Ct. (no., ctrl. and so. dists.) Calif. 1969. Dep. city atty. City of San Francisco, Office of City Atty., 1969-71; with The Boccardo Law Firm, San Jose, Calif., 1971—, mng. ptnr., 1981-99. Judge pro tem San Francisco County Superior Ct., 1978—, Santa Clara County Superior Ct., 1981—; lectr. U. Santa Clara Law Sch., 1985—, Hastings Coll. of Law, U. C. San Francisco. Bd. dirs. Katherine Delmar Burke Sch. Girls, San Francisco, 1988-92, Planning Orgn. for The Richmond, San Francisco, 1985-88. Capt. USMC, 1966-69. Fellow Am. Coll. Trial Lawyers; mem. ATLA, Consumer Attys. of Calif. (Trial Lawyer of Yr. San Jose), Am. Bd. Trial Advocates. Democrat. Roman Catholic. Avocations: golf, skiing, scuba diving. General civil litigation, Personal injury (including property damage), Product liability. Office: Boccardo Law Firm 111 W Saint John St Ste 1100 San Jose CA 95113-1107

STEIN, JULIE LYNNE, lawyer; b. Rochester, N.Y., Nov. 9, 1970; d. Frank and JoAnn Stein. BA, U. Md., 1993; JD, Union U., Albany, N.Y., 1996. Bar: N.Y. 1997. Atty. Western Auto Supply Co., Kansas City, Mo., 1996-98, YKK Corp. Am., Marietta, Ga., 1999-2000; with Hire.com, Auston, Tex., 2000—02, Cendant Car Rental Group, Inc., Parsippany, NJ, 2002—. Mem. ABA, Am. Corp. Counsel Assn., N.Y. State Bar Assn. Antitrust, Commercial, contracts (including sales of goods; commercial financing), Advertising. Office: Cendant Car Rental Group Inc 6 Sylvan Way Parsippany NJ 07054 Home: Apt 306 1221 S Congress Ave Austin TX 78704-2404

STEIN, LAWRENCE A. lawyer; b. Balt., Mar. 18, 1965; s. Hersh and Ellen (Hart) S.; m. Diane Wells, June 23, 1991; children: Joshua A., Julie E. AB, U. Chgo., 1988; JD, No. Ill. U., 1993. Bar: Ill. 1993, U.S. Dist. Ct. (no. dist.) Ill. 1993, U.S. Ct. Appeals (7th cir.) 1993, Md. 1994, U.S. Dist. Ct. Md. 1994, U.S. Supreme Ct. 1997. Shareholder Huck, Bouma, Martin, Jones & Bradshaw, Wheaton, Ill., 1993—. Advisor Prairie State Legal Svcs., Carol Stream, Ill., 1993—. Commr. Glen Ellyn (Ill.) Architecture Review Commn., 1994-97. Recipient Am. jurisprudence award for excellence in appellate advocacy Lawyers Coop., 1991. Mem.: ABA, Am. Inns Ct., Ill. State Bar Assn., DuPage County Bar Assn., Phi Delta Phi. Republican. Jewish. Appellate, Banking, Probate (including wills, trusts). Home: 300 Lorraine St Glen Ellyn IL 60137-5632 Office: Huck Bouma Martin Jones & Bradshaw 1755 S Naperville Rd Ste 200 Wheaton IL 60187-8144 E-mail: lstein@huckbouma.com.

STEIN, MILTON MICHAEL, lawyer; b. N.Y.C., Sept. 18, 1936; s. Isidore and Sadie (Lefkowitz) S.; m. Jacqueline Martin, June 17, 1962; children: April, Alicia. AB, Columbia U., 1958, LLB, 1961. Bar: N.Y. 1962, Pa. 1971, U.S. Supreme Ct. 1971. Asst. dist. atty. N.Y. County, 1962-67; sr. counsel Nat. Commn. for Reform of Fed. Criminal Law, Washington, 1967-70; asst. dist. atty., chief of appeals City of Phila., 1970-73; asst. dir. Nat. Wire Tapping Commn., Washington, 1973-75; dir. D.C. Law Revision, Washington, 1975-77; spl. asst. HUD, Washington, 1977-79; asst. gen. counsel U.S. Commodity Futures Trading Commn., Washington, 1979-83; v.p. N.Y. Futures Exch., N.Y.C., 1983-89, N.Y. Stock Exch., N.Y.C., 1989—. Mem. ABA, N.Y. State Bar Assn., Assn. of Bar of City of N.Y. Democrat. Jewish. Administrative and regulatory, Securities. Home: Hudson House PO Box 286 Ardsley On Hudson NY 10503-0286 E-mail: m.stein@nyse.com.

STEIN, ROBERT ALLEN, legal association executive, law educator; b. Mpls., Sept. 16, 1938; s. Lawrence E. and Agnes T. (Brynildson) S.; m. Sandra H. Stein; children: Linda Stein Routh, Laura Stein Conrad, Karin Stein O'Boyle. BS in Law, U. Minn., 1960, JD summa cum laude, 1961; LLD (hon.), Uppsala U., Sweden, 1993. Bar: Wis. 1961, Minn. 1967. Assoc. Foley, Sammond & Lardner, Milw., 1961-64; prof. U. Minn. Law Sch., Mpls., 1964-77; assoc. dean U. Minn., 1976-77, v.p. adminstrn. and planning, 1978-80; dean U. Minn. Law Sch., 1979-94; faculty rep. men's intercollegiate athletics U. Minn., 1981-94; of counsel Mullin, Weinberg & Daly, PA, Mpls., 1970-80, Gray, Plant, Mooty, Mooty & Bennett, Mpls., 1980-94; exec. dir., COO ABA, Chgo., 1994—. Vis. prof. UCLA, 1969-70, U. Chgo., 1975-76; commr. Uniform State Laws Commn. Minn., 1973—; v.p. Nat. Uniform Laws Com., 1991-93, exec. comm., 1991—, sec., 1997—; acad. fellow Am. Coll. Trusts and Estates Counsel, 1975—; vis. scholar Am. Bar Found., Chgo., 1975-76; trustee Gt. No. Iron Ore Properties, 1982—, Uniform Laws Found., 1992—; advisor Restatement of Law Second, Property, 1977—, Restatement of Law Trusts (Prudent Investor Rule), 1989-90, Restatement of Law Third, Trusts, 1993—; chmn. bd. dirs. Ednl. Credit Mgmt. Corp., 1993—; bd. dirs. Fiduciary Counselling Inc. Author: Stein on Probate, 1976, 3d edit., 1995, How to Study Law and Take Law Exams, 1996, Estate Planning Under the Tax Reform Act of 1976, 2d edit, 1978, In Pursuit of Excellence: A History of the University of Minnesota Law School, 1980, contbr. articles to profl. jours. Founding bd. dirs. Park Ridge Ctr., 1985-95; co-chair Gov.'s Task Force on Ctr. for Treatment of Torture Victims, 1985, bd. dirs., 1985-87. Fellow Am. Bar Found (bd. dirs. 1987-94), Am. Coll. Tax Counsel; mem. ABA (coun. sect. of legal edn. and admission to bar 1986-91, vice chairperson 1991-92, chair-elect 1992-93, chair 1993-94), Internat. Acad. Estate and Trust Law (academician), Am. Judicature Soc. (bd. dirs. 1984-88), Am. Law Inst. (coun. mem. 1987—, exec. com. 1993—), Minn. Bar Assn. (bd. govs. 1979-94, exec. coun., probate and trust law sect. 1973-77), Hennepin County Bar Assn. Home: 990 N Lake Shore Dr Apt 7A Chicago IL 60611-1342 Office: American Bar Assn 750 N Lake Shore Dr Chicago IL 60611-4497

STEIN, SAM L. lawyer; b. Cherokee, Okla., Nov. 19, 1958; s. Leroy Clark and Rosevelyn Edith (Peterson) Stein; m. Kelly Lee Pelter, Dec. 27, 1980; children: Patrick Leroy, Kelsy Lee. BS in Agr., Okla. State U., 1981; JD, U. Okla., 1987. Bar: Okla. 1987, U.S. Dist. Ct. (we. dist.) Okla. 1987, U.S. Dist. Ct. (no. dist.) Tex. 1987, Tex. 1988, U.S. Dist. Ct. (we. dist.) Tex. 1989, U.S. Ct. Appeals (5th cir.) 1993, cert.: Tex. Bd. Legal Specialization (civil trial and consumer and comml. lawl) 1994. Assoc. Morris, Moore, Dalrymple, et. al., Amarillo, Tex., 1987—89, Templeton & Garner, PC, Amarillo, 1989—90; shareholder Garner, Stone & Lovell, Amarillo, 1990—94; mng. shareholder Garner, Lovell & Stein, PC, Amarillo, 1994—97; prin. Garner & Stein, LLP, Cherokee, Okla., 1997—2001, Garner, Stein & Dean, LLP, Cherokee, 2001—. Asst. scoutmaster Troop 335 Boy Scouts Am., Cherokee, 1997—, bd. dirs. Cimarron Coun. Enid, Okla., 1999—. Recipient Profl. Responsibility award, U. Okla., 1987. Mem.: ATLA, ABA, Okla. Bar Assn., State Bar Tex. Commercial, consumer (including collections, credit), Personal injury (including property damage), General civil litigation. Office: Garner Stein & Dean LLP 305 S Grand Cherokee OK 73728 E-mail: sstein@akslc.net.

STEIN, STEPHEN WILLIAM, lawyer; b. N.Y.C., Apr. 12, 1937; s. Melvin S. and Cornelia (Jacobowitz) S.; m. Judith N., Jan. 22, 1966. AB, Princeton U., 1959; LLB, Columbia U., 1962; LLM, NYU, 1963. Bar: N.Y. 1962, Fla. 1962. Assoc. White & Case, N.Y.C., 1963-67; atty. advisor U.S. Agy. Internat. Devel., Washington, 1967-69, regional legal advisor Mission to India New Delhi, 1969-71, asst. gen. counsel Washington, 1971-73; assoc. ptnr. Delson & Gordon, N.Y.C., 1973-87; ptnr. Kelley Drye & Warren, N.Y.C., 1987—. Mem. U.S. exec. com. Indonesian Trade, Tourism & Investment Promotion Program, 1990-92; mem. U.S.-Indonesia Trade & Investment Adv. Com., 1989-92; vis. instr. internat. Devel. Law Inst., 1993; lectr. Internat. Law Inst., Washington, 1984, 85; spkr. in field. Mem. ABA (mem. sect. internat. law, co-chair African law com. 1999-2002), Internat. Bar Assn. (mem. sect. energy resources law, sect. bus. law, mem. various coms.), Assn. Bar of City of N.Y. (mem. com. project fin. 1997—, mem. com. Asian affairs 1992—, former mem. others), Am. Indonesian C. of C. (bd. dirs. 1986—, pres. 1989-96). Oil, gas, and mineral, Finance, Private international. Home: 320 Central Park W New York NY 10025-7659 Office: Kelley Drye & Warren 101 Park Ave Fl 30 New York NY 10178-0062 E-mail: sstein@kelleydrye.com.

STEIN, WILLIAM ROBERT, lawyer; b. N.Y.C., Mar. 23, 1952; s. Norman William and Alyce Josephine (Amorosino) S.; m. Victoria Jane Griffiths May 30, 1981; 1 child, Katherine Jane. BA magna cum laude, Columbia U., 1974, JD, 1977. Bar: N.Y. 1978, U.S. Ct. Appeals (3d cir.) 1978, D.C. 1980, U.S. Dist. Ct. D.C. 1980, U.S. Ct. Appeals (D.C. cir.) 1980, U.S. Supreme Ct. 1982, U.S. Ct. Appeals (11th cir.) 1987, U.S. Dist. Ct. (so. dist.) N.Y. 1990U.S. Ct. Appeals (2d and 8th cirs.) 1990, U.S. Ct. Appeals (4th and 5th cirs.) 1991, U.S. Dist. Ct. Md 1992, U.S. Ct. Appeals (9th cir.) 2002. Law clk. to judge Leonard I. Garth U.S. Ct. Appeals (3d cir.), Newark, 1977-78; assoc. Hughes, Hubbard & Reed, Washington, 1978-85, ptnr., 1985—. Mng. editor Columbia Law Rev., 1976-77. Harlan Fiske Stone scholar Columbia U. Law Sch., 1975, 76, James Kent scholar Columbia U. Law Sch., 1977. Mem. ABA, D.C. Bar, Phi Beta Kappa. Administrative and regulatory, Appellate, Federal civil litigation. Home: 8812 Altimont Ln Bethesda MD 20815-4751 Office: Hughes Hubbard & Reed 1775 I St NW Washington DC 20006-2402

STEINBACH, HAROLD I. lawyer; b. Bronx, N.Y., Aug. 31, 1956; s. Aaron and Phyllis (Feldfeber) S.; m. Beryl Joy Schwartz, Mar. 14, 1982; children: Sarah Brandl, Rachel Beth, Avi Michael. BA, SUNY, Binghamton, 1978; JD, NYU, 1981. Bar: N.Y. 1982, N.J. 1983, U.S. Dist. Ct. (so. dist.) N.Y. 1982. Assoc. Flemming, Zulack & Williamson, N.Y.C., 1981-83; assoc., then ptnr. Kleinberg, Kaplan, Wolff & Cohen, P.C., N.Y.C., 1983-2000; ptnr. Parker Duryee Rosoff & Haft, PC, N.Y.C., 2000—01, Steinbach & Assocs., Hackensack, NJ, 2002—. Trustee Jewish Braille Inst. Am., Inc., 1992—. Mem. N.Y. State Bar Assn. (bus. law and property law sects.), Phi Beta Kappa, NJ Bar Assn., Assn. Bar N.Y.C. Jewish. Corporate, general, Property, real (including real estate development, water). Home: 665 Ogden Ave Teaneck NJ 07666-2203 Office: 1 Univ Plz One Ste 412 Hackensack NJ 07601 Office Fax: 201-584-0353. E-mail: harold@steinbachesq.com.

STEINBAUM, ROBERT S. publisher, lawyer; b. Englewood, N.J., Oct. 13, 1951; s. Paul S. and Esther R. (Rosenberg) S.; m. Rosemary Konner, May 26, 1982; children: Marshall, Elliot. BA, Yale U., 1973; JD, Georgetown U., 1976. Bar: D.C. 1976, N.J. 1980, N.Y. 1982. Atty. Cole & Groner P.C., Washington, 1976-79; asst. U.S. atty. U.S. Atty.'s Office, Newark, 1979-84; atty. Scarpone & Edelson, Newark, 1984-87; publ. N.J. Law Jour., Newark, 1987—. Trustee N.J. Jewish News, Whippany, 1990-95, 96—, pres., 2002—; trustee Blood Ctr. N.J., East Orange, 1987-93, Leadership N.J., 1990, Leadership Newark, 1997—. Office: NJ Law Jour PO Box 20081 238 Mulberry St Newark NJ 07101-6081 E-mail: rsteinbaum@amlaw.com.

STEINBERG, AVERY, lawyer, mortgage broker; b. Bklyn., Dec. 10, 1956; m. Rebecca E. Shoemaker, Nov. 25, 1992. BA, Yeshiva U., 1978, JD, 1981. Bar: N.Y. 1982. Assoc. Groman & Wolf, Mineola, N.Y., 1981-83, Gluck, Rubin & Gluckman, N.Y.C., 1983-87, Bear, Marks & Upham, N.Y.C., 1988-89, Squadron Ellenoff, N.Y.C., 1989-93; owner Avery Steinberg, Esq., Bronx, N.Y., 1993—. Pension, profit-sharing, and employee benefits. Office: Avery Steinberg Esq 50 Leighton Ave Yonkers NY 10705-3725

STEINBERG, HOWARD ELI, lawyer, financial services company executive, public official; b. N.Y.C., Nov. 19, 1944; s. Herman and Anne Rudel (Sinnreich) S.; m. Judith Ann Schucart, Jan. 28, 1968; children: Henry Robert, Kathryn Jill. AB, U. Pa., 1965; JD, Georgetown U., 1969. Bar: N.Y. 1970, U.S. Dist. Ct. (so. and ea. dists.) N.Y. 1973, U.S. Ct. Appeals (2d cir.) 1976. Assoc. Dewey, Ballantine, Bushby, Palmer & Wood, N.Y.C., 1969-76, ptnr., 1977-83; exec. v.p., gen. counsel Reliance Group Holdings, Inc., N.Y.C., 1983-2000, exec. v.p., chief corp. ops., 2000—01; exec. v.p., gen. counsel Prudential Securities Inc., N.Y.C., 2001—. Chmn. N.Y. State Thruway Authority, 1996-99; dep. chmn. L.I. Power Authority, 1999—. Editor Georgetown Law Jour., 1968-69. Bd. dir. Puerto Rican Legal Def. and Edn. Fund. Inc., 1993-95, Sheltering Arms Childrens Svc., 1997—; bd. regents Georgetown U., 1999—; bd. overseers U. Pa. Sch. Arts and Scis., 1989-2002. Capt. JAGC, USAR, 1972-74. Mem. ABA, N.Y. State Bar Assn., Assn. of Bar of City of N.Y. (com. on securities regulation 1984-87, com. on corp. law 1987-90, com. on fed. legis. 1990-93, chair ad hoc com.

on Senate Confirmation Process 1991-92), Securities Industry Assn. (mem. fed. regulation com. 2001-, mem. exec. com. compliance and legal divsn. 2001-), Univ. Club. Corporate, general, Securities, Finance. Office: Prudential Securities Inc One Seaport Plaza New York NY 10292

STEINBERG, JONATHAN ROBERT, judge; b. Phila., Jan. 3, 1939; s. Sigmund Hopkins and Hortense B. (Gottlieb) S.; m. Rochelle Helene Schwarts, May 30, 1963; children: Andrew Joshua, Amy Judith. BA, Cornell U., 1960; LLB cum laude, U. Pa., 1963. Bar: D.C. 1963, U.S. Ct. Appeals (D.C. cir.) 1964. Law clk. to judge U.S. Ct. Appeals (D.C. cir.), 1963-64; atty. advisor, then dep. gen. counsel Peace Corps, Washington, 1964-69; com. on labor and pub. welfare, counsel subcom. vets. affair U.S. Senate, 1969-71, counsel subcom. on R.R. retirement, 1971-73, counsel spl. subcom. on human resources, 1972-77, chief counsel com. on vets affairs., 1977-81, minority chief counsel and staff dir. com. on vets. affairs, 1981-87, chief counsel and staff dir. com. on vets. affairs, 1987-90; judge U.S. Ct. of Appeals for Vets. Claims, 1990—. Contbr. to legal jours. Bd. dirs. Bethany West Recreation Assn., Bethany Beach, Dels., 1973-84, 86-90. Mem. ABA, D.C. Bar Assn., Order of Coif. Democrat. Jewish. Office: US Ct of Appeals for Vets Claims 625 Indiana Ave NW Ste 900 Washington DC 20004-2917

STEINBERG, LAWRENCE EDWARD, lawyer; b. Dallas, Nov. 25, 1935; s. Oscar J. and Pearl L. (Soloman) S.; children: Adam Joseph, Ilana Sara, Oliver David. BBA, U. Tex., 1958; JD, So. Methodist U., 1960. Bar: Tex. 1960. Since practiced in, Dallas; ptnr. firm Steinberg Soloman & Meer, 1971-88, Johnson & Steinberg, Dallas, 1988-93; of counsel Jenkins & Gilchrist, Dallas, 1994-98; chmn., CEO Eagle Equity, Inc., Dallas, 1991—. Active Urban Rehab. Stds. Bd., Dallas, 1975-76; adv. com. affirmative action program Dallas Ind. Sch. Dist., 1974-76; regional bd. chmn. Anti-Defamation League of B'nai Brith, 1974-77, nat. exec. com., 1977—, nat. law com., 1974-87; trustee Edna Gladney Home, 1975-92; v.p., trustee Shelton Sch., 1987-90; trustee Temple Emanu-El, 1992-94, Dallas Jewish Cmty. Found., 1990-2001; pres. U. Tex. Hillel Found., 2001—; bd. dirs. Jewish Fedn. Greater Dallas, 1984-87, 91-94, Dallas Coun. on World Affairs, 1998—, Stephen Wise, Acad., 1998—, Dallas Holocaust Ctr., 1998—, Jewish Inst. Nat. Securities Affairs, 1999—, Am. Jewish Commn., 2003—; regional bd. chmn. Am. Israel Pub. Affairs Com., 1997-2001, nat. exec. com., 1998—. 2d lt. U.S. Army, 1959-60. Mem. Lincoln City Club, Columbian Club, Masons, Shriners, Zeta Beta Tau., Phi Delta Phi, Beta Gamma Sigma, Pi Tau Pi (nat. pres. 1964-66). Corporate, general, Mergers and acquisitions, Securities. Home: 10131 Hollow Way Rd Dallas TX 75229-6634 Office: 5430 LBJ Fwy Ste 1575 Dallas TX 75240

STEINBERG, MARK ROBERT, lawyer; b. Chgo., Aug. 23, 1945; s. Matthew and Irma (Polacek) S.; m. Marjorie Anne Scott, Sept. 3, 1966; 1 child, Matthew Martin. BA, Carleton Coll., 1966; MA, Stanford U., 1968; JD cum laude, Northwestern U., 1972. Bar: Calif. 1972, U.S. Dist. Ct. (cen. dist.) Calif. 1973, U.S. Dist. Ct. (no., ea. and so. dists.) Calif. 1980, U.S. Ct. Appeals (3d cir.) 1981, U.S. Ct. Appeals (9th cir) 1983, U.S. Ct. Appeals (fed. cir.) 1991. Ptnr. O'Melveny & Myers, L.A., 1980—93, 1997—2001; counselor to legal adviser U.S. Dept. State, Washington, 1993-94, spl. rep. for persons missing and detained in the former Yugoslavia, 1996-97; dir. exec. office for nat. security, assoc. dep. atty. gen. U.S. Dept. Justice, Washington, 1994-95; spl. counsel law and policy SAG, LA, 2002—; sr. advisor L.A. City Atty., 2003—. Sr. policy advisor Internat. Commn. on Missing Persons, 1996-97, Cyrus Vance, chmn.; sr. adv. City Atty. LA, 2003. Articles editor Northwestern U. Law Rev., 1971-72. Trustee Carleton Coll., 1990-94; bd. dirs. Legal Aid Found., LA, 1990-93, Town Hall of LA, 1998-2001; dep. gen. counsel Ind. Commn. on LA Police Dept., 1991; mem. US Presdl. Transition Team, Dept. Justice, 1992-93; chmn. LA City Atty. Transition Team, 2001. Mem. Coun. on Fgn. Rels., Carleton Coll. Alumni Assn. (pres. 1988-90).

STEINBERG, MARTY, lawyer; b. Balt., May 13, 1945; BS cum laude in Pharmacy, U. Pitts., 1968; JD cum laude, Ohio State U., 1971. Bar: Ohio 1971, Fla. 1974; U.S. Supreme Ct. 1981; Registered Pharmacist Ohio 1968. Atty. U.S. Dept. Justice, Washington, Miami, 1972-78, atty. in charge N.Y. regional offices Washington, 1978-79; chief counsel, permanent subcommittee on investigations U.S. Senate, Washington, 1979-82; ptnr. Holland & Knight, Miami, Fla.; mng. ptnr., Fla. office Hunton & Williams, Miami, 1999—. Inst. Canisius Coll. Buffalo, N.Y. 1978-79, SUNY Buffalo 1978-79, Am. U. Washington D.C. 1980-81. Contbr. articles to profl. jours. Bd. dirs. Miami Citizens Against Crime. Recipient Am. Jurisprudence award. Mem. ABA, Fla. Bar Assn., Ohio State Bar Assn., Am. Pharm. Assn., Am. Assn. Corp. Counsel, Am. Law Inst. (chmn. civic justice adv. com.). Office: Hunton & Williams Law Firm 1111 Brickell Ave Miami FL 33131

STEINBERG, SYLVAN JULIAN, lawyer; b. New Iberia, La., July 25, 1933; s. Emanuel and Myrtle (Weil) S.; m. Judith Ann Benson, Sept. 7, 1959; children: Jeanne Wyn, Susan Beth, Jonathan Michael. BBA with honors, Tulane U., 1955, JD with honors, 1957. Bar: La. 1957, U.S. Dist. Ct. (ea. dist.) La. 1958, U.S. Supreme Ct. 1963, U.S. Ct. Appeals (5th cir.) 1976, U.S. Ct. Appeals (11th cir.) 1981, U.S. Dist. Ct. (mid. dist.) La. 1984, U.S. Dist. Ct. (we. dist.) 1989. Assoc. Weinstein and Bronfin, New Orleans, 1958-62; ptnr. Bronfin & Heller, New Orleans, 1962-99; of counsel Heller, Draper, Hayden, Patrick & Horn LLC, New Orleans, 2000—. Gen. adv. bd. cont. legal edn. Tulane Law Sch. Mem. editorial staff Tulane U. Law Rev., 1955-57, book rev. editor, 1957, mem. bd. adv. editors. Mem., former pres. bd. advisors B'nai B'rith Hillel Found. Tulane U., Loyola U. and U. New Orleans; past pres. Tikvat Shalom Synagogue, New Orleans; cmty. rels. com., past trustee New Orleans Jewish Welfare Fedn., budget com.; past adv. bd. New Orleans region Anti-Defamation League; past tech. adv. com. regional econ. devel. Regional Planning Commn.; past bd. dirs. Jewish Family and Children's Svc.; profl. adv. com. Jewish Endowment Found.; past chmn. bd. commrs. Cmty. Improvement Agy. for City of New Orleans; trustee, mem. exec. com. Jewish Fedn. Greater New Orleans, chmn. budget and allocations com.; bd. dirs. New Orleans Redevel. Authority, 1994-95; past v.p. B'nai B'rith State of La. Maj. JAGC, U.S. Army, and USAR, 1957-66. Mem. ABA, New Orleans Bar Assn. (chmn. gen. practice com. 1986 mem. continuing legal edn. com., chmn. legis. com., chmn. sr. lawyers com.), Fed. Bar Assn. (Fed. Ct. Bench bar liaison com.), La. Bar Assn. (mem. task force selection, election judges 1988), La. Assn. Def. Counsel, New Orleans C. of C. (mem. com. on housing), Masons, B'nai B'rith (v.p.). General civil litigation, Commercial, contracts (including sales of goods; commercial financing), Health. Home: 2710 Chestnut St New Orleans LA 70130-5731 Office: Heller Draper Hayden Patrick & Horn LLC 650 Poydras St Ste 2500 New Orleans LA 70130-6103 E-mail: ssteinberg@hellerdraper.com.

STEINDLER, WALTER G. retired lawyer; b. N.Y.C., Dec. 2, 1927; s. Mortimer B. and Ray (Feingold) S.; m. Carol A. Halpin, June 28, 1969; children: Michael, Morty, Melissa, Amy, Ellen. BA, Queens Coll., 1950; JD, NYU, 1953. Bar: N.Y. 1953, U.S. Supreme Ct. 1965, U.S. Dist. Ct. (ea. dist.) N.Y. 1972, U.S. Dist. Ct. (so. dist.) 1974, U.S. Ct. Appeals (2d cir.) 1974. Ptnr. Borden Skidell Fleck & Steindler, Jamaica, N.Y., 1955-62; pvt. practice law Babylon, N.Y., 1962-67; town atty. Town of Babylon, 1967-69; asst. county atty. Suffolk County, N.Y., 1970-71; ptnr. Sarisohn, Carner, Steindler, Lebow, Braun & Castrovinci, Commack, N.Y., 1976-93; ret., 1993. Capt., judge adv. 2d area command N.Y. Guard, N.Y.C., 1965-70; guardian ad litem 20th Jud. Cir. Lee County, Fla., 1995-98. With U.S. Army, 1946-47. Mem. Free Sons Israel (pres. 1953), Masons. State civil litigation, Family and matrimonial. Office: 350 Veterans Memorial Hwy Commack NY 11725-4330

STEINER, DAVID MILLER, lawyer; b. Phoenix, Apr. 9, 1958; s. Paul Miller and Nan (Adamson) S. BA, Columbia U., 1980; MALD, Tufts U., 1985; JD, Cornell U., 1988; M of Internat. and Pub. Affairs, Columbia U., 1989; LLM in Taxation, NYU, 1993. Bar: N.Y. 1988. English tchr. Peace Corps, Tahoua, Niger, 1980-82; law clk. to Judge Jane Restani U.S. Ct. Internat. Trade, N.Y.C., 1989-91; law clk. to Judge Reynaldo Garza U.S. Ct. Appeals (5th cir.), Brownsville, Tex., 1991-92; assoc. Wasserman, Schneider and Babb, 1993-95; with N.Y.C. Law Dept. Office of the Corp. Counsel, 1995—2002, U.S. Dept. Justice, Washington, 2002—. Mem. ABA, Assn. Bar City N.Y. (state and local tax com.), N.Y. County Lawyers Assn. (com. on taxation), Univ. Club, Cornell Club, Meridian Soc., Linden Cir., Young New Yorkers for the Philharm, Young Friends of Save Venice. Avocations: ballroom dancing, backgammon, running. Home: 2298 17th St NW # 3 Washington DC 20009- Office: US Dept Justice Tax Divsn PO Box 55 Ben Franklin Sta Washington DC 20044- E-mail: sirius_001@yahoo.com.

STEINER, HENRY JACOB, law and human rights educator; b. Mt. Vernon, N.Y., June 14, 1930; s. Meier and Bluma (Henigson) S.; m. Pamela Pomerance, Aug. 1, 1982; stepchildren: Duff, Jacoba. BA magna cum laude, Harvard U., 1951, MA, LLB magna cum laude, Harvard U., 1955. Bar: N.Y. 1956, Mass. 1963. Law clk. to Hon. John M. Harlan U.S. Supreme Ct., 1957-58; assoc. Sullivan and Cromwell, N.Y.C., 1958-62; asst. prof. sch. law Harvard U., Cambridge, Mass., 1962-65, prof., 1965—, Jeremiah Smith Jr. prof. law, 1986—. Founder, dir. Law Sch. Human Rights Program, 1984—; chair univ. com. on human rights studies Harvard U., 1994—2002; bd. dirs. U. Middle East project, 1996—99, chair bd. dirs., 2000—; vis. prof. Yale U., 1972—73, Stanford U., 1965; cons. AID, 1962—64, Ford Found., 1966—69. Co-author: (textbook) Transnational Legal Problems, 4th edit., 1994, Tort and Accident Law, 2d edit., 1989, International Human Rights in Context: Law, Politics, Morals, 2d edit., 2000; author: Moral Argument and Social Vision in the Courts, 1987, Diverse Partners: Non-Governmental Organizations in the Human Rights Movement, 1991; former devels. editor Harvard Law Rev.; contbr. articles to profl. jours. Office: Harvard U Law Sch Cambridge MA 02138 E-mail: hsteiner@law.harvard.edu.

STEINGASS, SUSAN R. lawyer; b. Cambridge, Mass., Dec. 18, 1941; BA in English Lit., Denison U., 1963; MA in English Lit. with honors, Northwestern U., 1965; JD with honors, U. Wis., 1976. Bar: Wis. 1976, U.S. Dist. Ct. Wis. 1976. Instr. dept. English La. State U., 1965-66, Calif. State Coll., L.A., 1966-68, U. Wis., Stevens Point, 1968-72; law clk. Hon. Nathan S. Heffernan Wis. Supreme Ct., 1976-77; ptnr. Stafford, Rosenbaum, Reiser and Hansen, 1977-85; judge Dane County Cir. Ct., Wis., 1985-93; ptnr. Habush, Habush & Rottier, S.C., Madison, Wis., 1993—. Lectr. civil procedure, environ. law, evidence, trial advocacy Law Sch., U. Wis., 1981—; instr. Nat. Inst. for Trial Advocacy, 1987—, Nat. Jud. Coll., 1993—. Note and comment editor Wis. Law Rev., 1974-76; co-editor: Wisconsin Civil Procedure Before Trial, 1994, The Wisconsin Rules of Evidence: A Courtroom Handbook, 1998—. Chairperson Wis. Equal Justice Task Force, 1989-91. Named Wis. Trial Judge of Yr. Am. Bd. Trial Advocates, 1992. Fellow Wis. Bar Found.; mem. ATLA, ABA (ho. dels. 2000—), Am. Bar Found., Am. Law Inst., Am. Adjudicature Soc. (bd. dirs., v.p.), Wis. Bar Assn. (pres. 1998-99), Wis. Law Alumni Assn. (bd. dirs., v.p.), Wis. Acad. Trial Lawyers, Wis. Equal Justice Fund (pres.), Dane County Bar Assn., Order of the Coif. Personal injury (including property damage). Office: Habush Habush Davis & Rottier SC 150 E Gilman St Ste 2000 Madison WI 53703-1481 E-mail: ssteinga@habush.com.

STEINHAUER, GILLIAN, lawyer; b. Aylesbury, Bucks, Eng., Oct. 6, 1938; d. Eric Frederick and Maisie Kathleen (Yeates) Pearson; m. Bruce William Steinhauer, Jan. 2, 1960; children: Alison (Humphrey) Eric, John, Elspeth. AB cum laude, Bryn Mawr (Pa.) Coll., 1959; JD cum laude, U. Mich., 1976. Bar: Mich. 1976, Mass. 1992, Tenn. 1998, U.S. Dist. Ct. (ea. dist.) Mich. 1976, U.S. Ct. Appeals (6th cir.) 1982. From assoc. to sr. ptnr. Miller, Canfield, Paddock & Stone, Detroit, 1976-92; dir. Commonwealth of Mass. Workers' Compensation Litigation Unit, Boston, 1992—2002; atty. U.S. Postal Svc., 2002—. Chancellor Cath. Ch. St. Paul, Detroit, 1976-83, 91; pres. bd. trustees Cath. Cmty. Svcs. Inc., 1989-92; bd. dirs. Spaulding for Children, 1991-92, Davenport House, 1992-96, chair 1995-96, mem. Vestry St. Michael's Ch., Marblehead, Mass., 1994-97. Mem. Mich. State Bar Found. (life), Fed. Jud. Conf. 6th Cir. (life). Home: 505 Tennessee St #417 Memphis TN 38103

STEINHAUSER, JOHN WILLIAM, retired lawyer; b. Akron, Ohio, June 25, 1924; s. John Hugo and Francis Lillian (Pearson) S.; m. Patricia E. Mooney, Dec.1, 1956; children: John, Christian, Mark, Sharon. BSBA, Ohio State U., 1949; JD, U. Mich., 1950. Bar: Mich. 1950, Colo. 1972. Atty., dir. L.Am., dir. export sales, gen mgr. Africa-Far E. Chrysler Corp., dir. Chrysler Internat., dir. Africa-Far East, 1950-71; atty. Denver, 1971—; founder, dir., pres. Pearson Energy Corp., 1977—. Founder, chmn. Sharon Energy, Ltd., Denver, 1980, also dir., 1980-97. Active Colo. Rep. Com.; sponsor Denver Symphony; pres. John and Patricia Steinhauser Found. With USNR, 1943—46. Mem. ABA, Colo. Bar Assn., Mich. Bar Assn., Soc. Internat. Law, Rocky Mountain Mineral Law Found., Cherry Hills Country Club, Royal Poinciana Golf Club, Rotary. Home: 46 Charlou Cir Englewood CO 80111-1103 E-mail: jwsteinhauser@prodigy.com.

STEINHORN, IRWIN HARRY, lawyer, educator, corporate executive; b. Dallas, Aug. 13, 1940; s. Raymond and Libby L. (Miller) Steinhorn; m. Deborah Kelley Steinhorn, Apr. 7, 2002; 1 child, Leslie Robin. BBA, U. Tex., 1961, LLB, 1964. Bar: Tex. 1964, U.S. Dist. Ct. (no. dist.) Tex. 1965, Okla. 1970, U.S. Dist. Ct. (we. dist.) Okla. 1972. Assoc. Oster & Kaufman, Dallas, 1964-67; ptnr. Parness, McQuire & Lewis, Dallas, 1967-70; sr. v.p., gen. counsel LSB Industries, Inc., Oklahoma City, 1970-87; v.p., gen. counsel USPCI, Inc., Oklahoma City, 1987-88; ptnr. Hastie & Steinhorn, Oklahoma City, 1988-95; mem., officer, dir. Conner & Winters, Oklahoma City, 1995—. Adj. prof. law Oklahoma City U. Sch. Law, 1979—; lectr. in field. Mem. adv. com. Okla. Securities Commn., 1986—; mem. exec. adv. bd. Oklahoma City U. Sch. Law, 2000—; bd. dirs. Okla. Venture Forum, 2000—. Served to capt. USAR, 1964-70. Mem. ABA, Tex. Bar Assn., Okla. Bar Assn. (bus. assn. sect., sec.ptreas. 1986-87, chmn. 1988-89), Com. to Revise Okla. Bus. Corp. Act, Rotary, Phi Alpha Delta. Republican. Jewish. Corporate, general, Environmental, Securities. Home: 224 NW 18th St Oklahoma City OK 73103 Office: Conner & Winters One Leadership Sq 211 N Robinson Ave Ste 1700 Oklahoma City OK 73102-7136 E-mail: isteinhorn@cwlaw.com.

STEINHOUSE, CARL LEWIS, lawyer; b. N.Y.C., July 18, 1931; s. Samuel A. and Sophia (Schwartz) S.; m. Diana Joan Wasserman, Aug. 16, 1953; children: Samuel A., Jane W., Laura A. BS in Acctg., NYU, 1952; LLB, Bklyn. Law Sch., 1959. Bar: N.Y. 1959, U.S. Dist. Ct. (so. dist.) N.Y. 1960, U.S. Dist. Ct. Hawaii 1962, Ohio 1971, U.S. Dist. Ct. (no. dist.) Ohio, U.S. Dist. Ct. (no. dist.) N.Y., U.S. Ct. Appeals (fed. and 6th cirs.) 1983, U.S. Supreme Ct. 1983. Acct. D. Grossman & Co., N.Y.C., 1954-59; trial atty. anti-trust div. U.S. Dept. Justice, N.Y.C., 1959-61, 1961-65, chief Great Lakes div., 1965-73; assoc. Jones, Day, Reavis & Pogue, Cleve., 1973-75, ptnr., 1975—94, ret., 1994. Author: Wallenberg Is Here, 2002; editor: Jury Instructions in Criminal Law Antitrust Cases, 1982, Criminal Antitrust Litigation Manual, 1983, Sample Antitrust Jury Instruction Criminal, 1984, Antitrust Grand Jury Investigations, 1988, Handbook on Antitrust Grand Jury Investigations, 2d edit., 1989; contbr. articles to profl. jours. Mem. com. Soviet Jewry Jewish Community Fedn., Cleve., 1985—, older persons svcs., 1983-85; mem. Nat. Conf. on Soviet Jews, 1985—; trustee Pepper Pike Civic League, Ohio, 1979-80. Sgt. U.S. Army, 1952-54. Mem. ABA (vice chmn. antitrust sect., 1987-88, antitrust coun. 1984-88, antitrust com. Sherman Act Com. 1982-84, criminal com. 1979-82, litigation sect., chmn. antitrust computer tech. com. 1988-90). Avocations: tennis, computer science. Antitrust, Federal civil litigation, Criminal. Home: 5174 Kensington High St Naples FL 34105-5649

STEINKAMP, ROBERT THEODORE, lawyer; b. St. Louis, Sept. 11, 1945; s. William P. and Leona M. (Kraus) S.; m. Cheryl Sue Dunlop, Aug. 19, 1967; children: Theodore Bewick, Rebecca Anne. BA, William Jewell Coll., Liberty, Mo., 1967; JD, U. Mo., Kansas City, Mo., 1971; postgrad., U. Mo., Kansas City, 1971-72. Bar: Mo. 1971, U.S. Dist. Ct. (we. dist.) Mo. 1971, U.S. Tax Ct. 1971, U.S. Ct. Appeals (8th cir.) 1971. Assoc. Morris, Foust, Moudy & Beckett, Kansas City, 1971-76; ptnr. Morris, Foust & Beckett, Kansas City, 1976-78, Beckett & Steinkamp, Kansas City, 1978-90; v.p., gen. counsel, sec. Applebee's Internat., Inc., Kansas City, 1990—. Mem. Downtown, Inc., Kansas City, 1978-84, Friends of Art, Nelson Art Gallery, Kansas City, 1985—, Nat. Hist. Preservation Found., 1985—; bd. dirs., committeeman Kappa Alpha Order Nat. Fraternity Housing Corp., Lexington, Va., 1984-92; bd. dirs., pres. ADKASHA, Liberty, Mo., 1977—; bd. dirs. Liberty Symphony Orch., Inc., 1982-87, pres. 1984-86; Clay County Fine Arts Coun., 1991-93; sec. Heartland Franchising Assn., 1991-93; nat. co-chmn. William Jewell Coll., Ann. Fund. 1995-96, 96-97; mem. com. Denison Univ. Parent's Fund, 1996-2000. Mem. ABA (forum on franchising, corp. and tax sects.), Kansas City Bar Assn. (vice-chmn. bus. law com. 1996, chmn. 1997), Lawyer's Assn. Kansas City, Mo. Bar Assn., Clay County Bar Assn., Kans. City Club, Liberty Hills Country Club (bd. dirs. 1985-87). Republican. Methodist. Avocations: golf, tennis, reading, travel. Corporate, general, Property, real (including real estate development, water), Taxation, general. Office: Applebees Internat Inc 4551 W 107th St Ste 100 Overland Park KS 66207-4037

STEINMEYER, ROBERT JAY, lawyer; b. Aug. 10, 1921; s. William F. and Willie ((Davis)) Steinmeyer; m. Susie (Levicki), Dec. 23, 1948; children: William Bruce, James Jay, Sharon Sue. BS, U. Nebr., 1943; post grad., Albany Law Sch., 1947—48; LLB, George Washington U., 1949. Bar: D.C. 1950, Calif. 1958. Devel. engr. G.E. Co., Schenectady, NY, 1943—46, patent atty., 1947—53, patent counsel, 1953—57, Beckman Instruments, Inc., Fullerton, Calif., 1957—63, resident counsel, 1963—71, v.p., legal, 1971—85, dir., 1984—85; sole practice Fullerton, Calif., 1985—86; of counsel Karon, Morrison, and Savikas Ltd., Fullerton, Calif., 1986—88. Mem.: ABA, Assn. Corp. Patent Counsel (pres. 1975—76), Am. Patent Law Assn., Pi Mu Epsilon, Sigma Tau, Order of Coif. Home: 813 Morningside Dr Fullerton CA 92835

STEINWURTZEL, RICHARD A. lawyer; b. Newark, Jan. 1, 1950; BA cum laude, Union Coll., 1972; JD with honors, George Washington U., 1975. Bar: D.C. 1975. Ptnr. Fried, Frank, Harris, Shriver & Jacobson, Washington. Mem. ABA (sect. corp., banking and bus. law), N.Y. State Bar Assn., D.C. Bar, Securities Industry Assn. (mem. legal and compliance divsn. 1985—). Office: Fried Frank Harris Shriver & Jacobson 1001 Pennsylvania Ave NW Washington DC 20004-2505

STELTZLEN, JANELLE HICKS, lawyer; b. Atlanta, Sept. 18, 1937; d. William Duard and Mary Evelyn (Embrey) Hicks; divorced; children: Gerald William III, Christa Diane. BS, Okla. State U., 1958; MS, Kans. State U., 1961; JD, U. Tulsa, 1981. Bar: Okla. 1981, U.S. Dist. Ct. (no., ea. and we. dists.) Okla. 1981, U.S. Tax Ct. 1982, U.S. Ct. Claims 1982, U.S. Ct. Appeals (10th cir.) 1983, U.S. Ct. Appeals (Fed. cir.) 1984, U.S. Supreme Ct. 1986; lic. real estate broker. Pvt. practice, Tulsa, 1981-97. Lectr. Coll. of DuPage, Glen Ellyn, Ill., 1976, Tulsa Jr. Coll., 1981-88; dietitian, Tulsa; res. dep. for Tulsa County Sheriff's Office; 2d dep., legal Tulsa County Clk., 1997-2000. Christian counselor 1st United Meth. Ch., Tulsa, 1986—, coord. legal counseling ministry, 1985—, lay pastor, 1987—; mem. Tulsa County Bd. Equalization and Excise Tax Bd., 1989-90; mem. Leadership Tulsa XX, 1993—; recipient of Leadership Tulsa Paragon award, 1996; bd. dirs. Sister Cities Tulsa/San Luis Potosi, 1988—, South Peoria Neighborhood Connection Found., 1991—, pres., 1995-96; active Tulsa County Tax Oversight Com., 1994—, Tulsa Home Rule Charter Com., 1994—. Recipient Okla. Sr. Olympics medal. Mem. Okla. Bar Assn., Tulsa County Bar Assn., Vol. Lawyers Assn. (bd. dirs.), Am. Dietetic Assn., Tulsa Dist. Dietetic Assn., Kiwanis Internat., Mensa, DAR, Delta Zeta. Republican. Avocations: swimming, scuba diving, jogging, bicycling, reading, painting, needlework, photography. Family and matrimonial, Probate (including wills, trusts), Property, real (including real estate development, water). Home: 6636 S Jamestown Pl Tulsa OK 74136-2615

STENBERG, DONALD B. lawyer; b. David City, Nebr., Sept. 30, 1948; s. Eugene A. and Alice (Kasal) Stenberg; m. Susan K. Hoegemeyer, June 9, 1971; children: Julie A., Donald B. Jr., Joseph L., Abby E. BA, U. Nebr., 1970; MBA, JD cum laude, Harvard U., 1974. Bar: Nebr. 1974, U.S. Dist. Ct. Nebr. 1974, U.S. Ct. Appeals (fed. cir.) 1984, U.S. Ct. Claims 1989, U.S. Ct. Appeals (8th cir.) 1989, U.S. Supreme Ct. 1991. Assoc. Barlow, Watson & Johnson, Lincoln, Nebr., 1974—75; ptnr. Stenberg and Stenberg, Lincoln, 1976—78; legal counsel Gov. of Nebr., Lincoln, 1979—82; sr. prin. Erickson & Sederstrom, Lincoln, 1983—85, of counsel, 2003—; pvt. practice Lincoln, 1985—90; atty. gen. State of Nebr., Lincoln, 1991—2002. Bd. dirs. Translink Transmission Co. Mem.: Phi Beta Kappa. Republican. Administrative and regulatory, Appellate, Corporate, general. Office: Erickson & Sederstrom Regency Westpointe 10330 Regency Pkwy Dr Ste 100 Omaha NE 68114-3761

STENEHJEM, WAYNE KEVIN, state attorney general, lawyer; b. Mohall, N.D., Feb. 5, 1953; s. Martin Edward and Marguerite Mae (Peg) (McMaster) Stenehjem; m. Tama Lou Smith, June 16, 1978 (div. Apr. 1984); 1 child, Andrew; m. Beth D. Bakke, June 30, 1995. AA, Bismarck (N.D.) Jr. Coll., 1972; BA, U. N.D., 1974, JD, 1977. Bar: N.D. 1977. Ptnr. Kuchera & Stenehjem, Grand Forks, ND, 1977—2000; spl. asst. atty. gen. State of N.D., 1983—87, atty. gen., 2000—; mem. ND Indsl. Commn., 2001—; chair RAGA, 2001—; mem. N.D. Ho. Reps. , 1976—80, N.D. State Senate, 1980—2000, pres. pro tempore, 1998—99; bd. Univ. and Sch. Lands, 2001—. Chmn. Senate Com. on Social Svcs., 1985—86, Senate Com. on Judiciary, 1995—2000, Interim Legis. Judiciary Com., 1995—2000, Legis. Coun., 1995—2000; mem. Nat. Conf. Commrs. on Uniform State Laws, 1995—2000, Gov.'s Com. on Juvenile Justice. Bd. dirs. N.D. Spl. Olympics, 1985—89; chmn. Dist. 42 Reps., Grand Forks, 1986—88; bd. dirs. Christus Rex Luth. Ch., pres., 1985—86. Named Champion of People's Right to Know, Sigma Delta Chi, 1979, N.D. Friend of Psychology, N.D. Psychol. Assn., 1990; named one of Outstanding Young Man of N.D, Jaycees, 1985; recipient Excellence in County Govt. award, N.D. Assn. Counties, 1991, Love Without Fear award, Abused Adult Resource Ctr., 2003. Mem.: Grand Forks County Bar Assn., N.D. State Bar Assn. (Legis. Svc. award 1995). Republican. Home: 1216 Crestview Ln Bismarck ND 58501 Office: Office of the Atty Gen State Capitol Bldg 600 E Boulevard Ave Bismarck ND 58505

STENTZ, JON WILLIAM, lawyer; b. Balt., June 6, 1958; BS, Georgetown U., 1980, JD, 1983. Bar: Pa. 1983, D.C. 1985. Corp. trial counsel U.S. Army Judge Adv. Gens. Corp. U.S. Army, Republic of Korea, 1984—85, pros., 1985—87; def. appellate counsel, Supreme Ct. coord., sr. atty. Marriott Corp., Bethesda, Md., 1989—93; asst. gen. counsel Host Marriott Corp., Bethesda, Md., 1989—93; v.p., chief counsel devel. and brands HMS Host Corp., Bethesda, Md., 1996—. Bd. mem. Montgomery County (Md.) Recreation Bd., 1997—99. Mem.: ABA, D.C. Bar Assn., Pa. Bar Assn. Corporate, general, Franchising, Government contracts and claims. Office: HMS Host Corp Sixth Fl 6600 Rockledge Dr Bethesda MD 20817

STEPANIAN, STEVEN ARVID, II, lawyer, financial consultant; b. Charleroi, Pa., Apr. 15, 1935; s. Steven A. and Edithmarion M. (McElligott) S.; m. Pamela S. Abbey, Feb. 15, 1979. AB magna cum laude, U. Pitts., 1957; LLB, Harvard U., 1963. Bar: Pa. 1964, U.S. Supreme Ct. 1967. Assoc. Reed Smith, 1963-69, ptnr., 1970-78; pvt. practice law, 1978—; ptnr., gen. counsel Marine Magnesium Co., 1988—, U.S. Windforce, 1998—, dir.; NFL Alumni, 1982-89. Maj. USAF, 1957-60, 68-69. Mem.

ABA (chair sports law com.), Pa. Bar Assn. Democrat. Roman Catholic. Clubs: Duquesne, Univ. (past pres.), Nemacolin Encampment (Pitts.). Corporate, general, Entertainment, Property, real (including real estate development, water). Home: 123 Millstone Ln Pittsburgh PA 15238-1623 Office: Gateway Towers Ste 4-G 320 Fr Duquesne Blvd Pittsburgh PA 15222-1103

STEPHAN, KENNETH C. judge; b. Omaha, Oct. 8, 1946; m. Sharon Ross, Apr. 19, 1969; children: Alissa Potocnik, Karen Borchert, Charles. BA, U. Nebr., 1968, JD with high distinction, 1972. Bar: Nebr. Former pvt. practice atty., 1973-97; judge Nebr. Supreme Ct., Lincoln, 1997—. With U.S. Army, 1969—71. Mem.: Am Col Trial Lawyers (jud fellow), Lincoln Bar Asn (former trustee), Nebr State Bar Asn (former chmn young lawyers sect, former mem house delegs). Office: Nebr Supreme Ct State Capitol Bldg Rm 2211 PO Box 98910 Lincoln NE 68509-8910 E-mail: kstephan@nsc.state.ne.us.

STEPHEN, JOHN ERLE, lawyer, consultant; b. Eagle Lake, Tex., Sept. 24, 1918; s. John Earnest and Vida Thrall (Klein) S.; m. Gloria Yzaguirre, May 16, 1942; children: Vida Leslie Stephen Renzi, John Lauro Kurt. JD, U. Tex., 1941; postdoctoral, Northwestern U., 1942, U.S. Naval Acad. Postgrad. Sch., Annapolis, 1944; cert. in internat. law, U.S. Naval War Coll., Newport, R.I., 1945; cert. in advanced internat. law, U.S. Naval War Coll., 1967. Bar: Tex. 1946, U.S. Ct. Appeals (D.C. cir.) 1949, U.S. Tax Ct. 1953, U.S. Supreme Ct. 1955, U.S. Dist. Ct. D.C. 1956, U.S. Ct. Appeals (2nd cir.) 1959, U.S. Ct. Appeals (7th cir.) 1964, U.S. Dist. Ct. (so. dist.) N.Y. 1964, U.S. Dist. Ct. (so. dist.) Fla. 1969, D.C. 1972, U.S. Dist. Ct. (no. dist.) Ill. 1974, U.S. Dist. Ct. (we. dist.) Wash. 1975, Mich. 1981, U.S. Dist. Ct. (we. dist.) Mich. 1981, U.S. Dist. Ct. (so. dist.) Tex. 1981. Gen. mgr., corp. counsel Sta. KOPY, Houston, 1946; gen. atty., exec. asst. to pres. Tex. Star Broadcasting Co. and affiliated cos., Houston, 1947-50; ptnr. Hofheinz & Stephen, Houston, 1950—56; sr. v.p., gen. counsel TV Broadcasting Co., Tex. Radio Corp., Gulf Coast Network, Houston, 1953—56; spl. counsel, exec. asst. Mayor, City of Houston, 1953-57; spl. counsel Houston C. of C., 1953—57; sr. v.p., gen. counsel Air Transp. Assn. Am., Washington, 1958-70; v.p., gen. counsel Amway Corp. and affiliated cos., Ada, Mich., 1971-82; counsellor, cons. Austin, Tex., 1983—. Chief protocol City of Houston, 1953-56; advisor Consulates Gen. of Mex., San Antonio, Houston, New Orleans, Washington, 1956-66; atty. Gen. Creighton W. Abrams Jr., Comdr. U.S. Mil. Assistance Command, Vietnam, Saigon/Washington, 1970-71; mem. adv. bd. Jour. of Air Law and Commerce, 1966-72; vis. lectr. Harvard Bus. Sch., Pacific Agribus. Conf., The Southwestern Legal Found., Inter-Am. Law Conf., Inst. Aerospace Law; apptd. by Pres. of U.S. legal advisor, del. U.S. Diplomatic Dels. to Internat. Treaty Confs., Paris, London, Rome, Tokyo, Madrid, Bermuda, Guadalajara, Dakar, 1958-69, Internat. Air-Rte. Dels. to U.K., France, Spain, Portugal, Belgium, The Netherlands, Japan, Rep. of Korea, Mex., Australia, Argentina, Soviet Union, and Brazil, 1958-69; legal advisor, del. U.S. dels. to UN pecialized Orgns., Montreal, Geneva, 1964-71; U.S. rep. Internat. Conf. on Aircraft Disturbance, London, 1966; hon. faculty mem., vis. lectr. sch. of law, sch. of bus., U. Miami, 1968—; accredited corr. UN, Rep. and Dem. Nat. Convs.; exec. officer USNR Pub. Affairs Co. 8-7, 1950-57. Author, editor, media prodr. Comm. and transp. group chief Harris County/Houston CD, 1952-56; chmn. legal com. Nat. Aircraft Noise Abatement Coun., Washington; mem. adv. bd. Mus. Fine Arts Houston, 1953-57; bd. dirs. Contemporary Arts Assn. and Mus., Houston, 1952-57; mem. exec. com. Tex. Transp. Inst., 1964-72; apptd. conferee Global Strategy Conf., U.S. Naval War Coll., 1958. Comdr. USNR, 1941-46, PTO and S.E. Asia; mem. staff comdr. Supreme Allied Command Atlantic, NATO. Recipient Jesse L. Lasky award RKO Pictures-CBS, Hollywood, Calif., 1939, H.J. Lutcher Stark prize U. Tex., 1939, 40, Walter Mack award PepsiCo, U. Tex., 1941, Best U.S. Pub. Svc. Broadcasts award CCNY, 1946, First-FM (West) award Frequency Modulation Assn., Houston, 1947, Tex. State Network award mobile coverage Nat. Presdl. Convs., Phila., 1948, Chgo., 1952, Trusonic Wireless Microphone award Acad. Motion Picture Arts & Scis., Beverly Hills, 1951, Frank White award, Mutual Broadcasting Sys., N.Y., 1953, H.M.S. SHEFFIELD citation Brit. Royal Navy U.S. Cruise, 1954, C.R. Smith Aviation Devel. award, Am. Airlines, N.Y., 1955, KLM Royal Dutch Airlines award, Washington, 1956, Capt. Eddie Rickenbacker Air Transport Advancement award Eastern Air Lines, N.Y., 1956, Padre Alvarez award Boys Town Chorale Internat. Tour, Canavati Industries, Monterrey, 1957, Allied Rod & Gun Club Triple Crown trophy, Gander, Nfld., 1958, Iron Duke award No. Va. Lit. Soc., Arlington, 1962, President's Outstanding commendation internat. law, U.S. Naval War Coll., Newport, 1967, IBM Corp. Exec. Computer Concepts prize, San Jose, Calif., 1976, M.Y. ENTERPRISE award Peter Island, Brit. V.I., 1978, Glacier Bay award M.V. MALIBU, Sitka, Alaska, 1980. Mem. ABA (chmn., coun. sect. pub. utility, comms. and transp. law, standing com. on aero. law, chmn. sect. adminstrv. law aviation com.), The Am. Law Inst. (advisor Restatement (2d) of Torts), World Peace Through Law Ctr. Geneva (chmn. internat. aviation law com., advisor world air piracy treaty), The Fed. Bar Assn. (exec. com. transp. coun., comm. coun.), The D.C. Bar, State Bar Tex. (50 Yr. Meritorious Practice award 1996), State Bar Mich., Fed. Comm. Bar Assn. (frequency modulation broadcasting com.), Assn. ICC Practitioners, Am. Judicature Soc., Washington Fgn. Law Soc. (vis. lectr. 1967-68), USS ST. PAUL (CA-73) Assn., Japanese Air Law Soc. (hon.), Venezuelan Air and Space Law Soc. (hon.), SOVEDAE (hon.), USS PRESIDENT ADAMS Assn., Naval Submarine League, Naval War Coll. Found., Internat. Club (Washington), Houston Polo Club, Lake Shore Club (Chgo.), Nat. Aviation Club (Washington), Saddle and Cycle Club (Chgo.), Breakfast Club (Houston), Execs. Club (Houston), Order Ky. Cols., Tex. Navy Adm., Flying Col., Phi Eta Sigma, Delta Sigma Rho (pres. Tex. chpt. 1940). Home: 6904 Ligustrum Cv Austin TX 78750-8352

STEPHENS, GEORGE EDWARD, JR., lawyer; b. Lawrence, Kans., Mar. 26, 1936; s. George Edward and Mary Helen (Houghton) Stephens; m. Gretel Geiser, Dec. 31, 1965; children: Thaddeus Geiser, Edward Houghton, Mary Schoentgen. Student, U. Colo., Boulder, 1954-57, U. Colo., Denver, 1957-59; LLB, Stanford U., 1962. Bar: Calif. 1963, U.S. Dist. Ct. (cen. dist.) Calif. 1963, U.S. Ct. Appeals (9th cir.) 1971. Law clk. to judge U.S. Dist. Ct., L.A., 1962-64; assoc. ptnr. Pollock & Palmer, L.A., 1964-69; ptnr. Gates, Morris, Merrill & Stephens, L.A., 1969-72, Paul, Hastings, Janofsky & Walker, L.A., 1972—. Mem. Coordinating Coun. on Lawyer Competence, Conf. Chief Justices, 1983-86; chmn. probate sect. L.A. County Bar Assn., 1979-80. Nat. chmn. Stanford (Calif.) U. Law Fund Quad Program, 1980-87; mem. bd. visitors Stanford Law Sch., 1982-85; founder mus. Contemporary Art, L.A., 1982; bd. dirs. Pacific Oaks Coll., 1990-94. Recipient Stanford Assocs. award, 1982. Fellow: Fellows of Contemporary Art (bd. dirs. 1991—92), Internat. Acad. Probate and Trust Law, Am. Coll. Trust and Estates Counsel, Am. Bar Found.; mem.: Stanford Law Soc. (pres. 1972—73, chmn. 1998—99), ABA (chmn. standing com. specialization 1979—82, standing com. lawyer referral svcs. 1969—76, consortium delivery legal svcs. and the pub. 1979—82), The Athenaeum, Valley Hunt (Pasadena, Calif.), Annandale Golf (Pasadena, Calif.), Chancery (L.A.). Episcopalian. Estate planning, Probate (including wills, trusts), Estate taxation. Office: Paul Hastings Janofsky & Walker 515 S Flower St 25th Fl Los Angeles CA 90071-2300

STEPHENS, MARLA JEAN, lawyer; b. Milw., Mar. 1, 1952; m. Robert J. Dvorak. BA, U. Wis., 1978; JD, Marquette U., 1981. Bar: Wis. 1981, U.S. Dist. Ct. Wis. 1981. Asst. pub. defender, Milw., 1981-94; 1st asst. pub. defender Wis. Pub. Defender, Milw., 1994-96, dir. appellate divsn. Milw. and Madison, 1996—. Mem. Wis. Jud. Coun., Madison, 1996—, chair, 2000—. Mem. Nat. Assn. Criminal Def. Lawyers, Wis. Assn. Criminal Def. Lawyers, Assn. for Women Lawyers, Milw. Bar Assn., State Bar Wis. (appellate practice bd. 1999-2002). Office: Office Wis Pub Defender Appellate Divsn 735 N Water St Ste 912 Milwaukee WI 53202 E-mail: stephensm@mail.opd.state.wi.us.

STEPHENS, RICHARD H. retired prosecutor; Adj. prof. SMU Sch. of Law & Cox Sch. of Bus.; asst. dist. atty. under Henry Wade; military judge US Navy; private practice Dallas; US Atty., 1993, Northern Dist. , Tex. Office: US Attorney 1100 Commerce St 3rd Fl Dallas TX 75242-1699

STEPHENS, ROBERT C. lawyer; b. Charlotte, N.C., Aug. 18, 1945; s. Robert Clifton and Onita (Mitchell) Stephens; m. Claire D. Stephens, Apr. 28, 1984; children: Elizabeth D., Robert M.; m. Martha Stephens, June 11, 1966 (div. Feb. 1981); children: Ansley, Blair. BA, Wake Forest U., 1967, JD, 1970. Bar: N.C. 1970, U.S. Dist. Ct. (we., mid., and ea. dists.) N.C. 1970, U.S. Ct. Appeals (4th cir.) 1971, U.S. Supreme Ct. 1973. Assoc. Sanders, Walker and London, Charlotte, NC, 1973—75, Horack, Talley, Pharr and Lowndes, Charlotte, 1975—2000, Kilpatrick Stockton, Charlotte, 2000—01, Hamilton Gaskins Fay and Moon, Charlotte, 2001—. Gen. counsel Pub. Libr. Charlotte-Mecklenburg County, 1975—. Chmn., bd. mgrs. Uptown YMCA, Charlotte, 1998; pres. Myers Park County Club, Charlotte, 2000; chmn., bd. mgrs. Gateway YMCA, Charlotte, 2002. Lt. U.S. Army, 1970—72, Korea. Recipient George Williams award for Outstanding Vol. Yr., Charlotte Metro YMCA. Mem.: Mecklenburg County Bar Assn. (bd. dirs., pres. 2002), N.C. Bar Assn., Am. Arbitration Assn. (cert. arbitrator). Republican. Baptist. Construction, General civil litigation. Office: Hamilton Gaskins Fay and Moon PLLC 201 S College St Ste 2020 Charlotte NC 28244-2020

STEPHENS, WILLIAM THEODORE, lawyer, business executive; b. Balt., Mar. 31, 1922; s. William A. and Mildred (Griffin) S.; m. Arlene Alice Lesti, June 2, 1958; children: William Theodore Jr., Renée Adena. Grad., Balt. City Coll., 1941; student, U. Md., 1946-47; AB, JD, George Washington U., 1950, postgrad., 1951. Bar: D.C. 1951, Md. 1950, Va. 1959. Assoc. J.L. Green, Washington, 1950-51; with J.M. Cooper, Washington, 1952-54; sr. ptnr. Stephens Law Firm, Washington, 1955—. Gen. counsel Exotech, Inc., Gaithersburg, Md.; prin. owner BARBCO, Inc., Va., Fairfax Raquet Club; gen. counsel various nat. corps. and assns. Author: Rental Contracts - Contracts for the Rental of Personal Property, 2000. 1st lt. AUS, 1941-45. Mem. ABA, D.C. Bar Assn. (sect. taxation 1959—, sect. corps, banking and bus. law 1960—), Bar Assn. D.C. (sec. taxation 1959-68), XVI Corps Assn. (pres. 1967), Commonwealth Club, Univ. Club, Capitol Hill Club, Army-Navy Country Club, Regency Sport and Health Club, Jockey Club, LaCosta Country Club, Racquet Club Internat., Kappa Alpha (preceptor, ct. of honor, James Ward Wood Province 1988-91), Delta Theta Phi. Corporate, general. Home: 1800 Old Meadow Rd Mc Lean VA 22102-1819 also: 881 Ocean Dr Key Biscayne FL 33149-2609 E-mail: billstephens@cox.net.

STEPHENSON, ALAN CLEMENTS, lawyer; b. Wilmington, NC, Nov. 7, 1944; s. Abram Clements and Ruth (Smith) S.; m. Sherri Jean Miller, Dec. 19, 1970; children: Edward Taylor, Anne Baldwin. AB in Hist., U. N.C., 1967; JD, U. Va., 1970. Bar: N.Y. 1971. Assoc. Cravath, Swaine & Moore, N.Y.C., 1970-78, ptnr., 1978-88; mng. dir. Wasserstein, Perella and Co. Inc., N.Y.C., 1988-92; ptnr. Cravath, Swaine & Moore, N.Y.C., 1992—. Mem. external adv. bd. undergrad. honors program U. N.C., 1998—. Trustee Poly Prep Country Day Sch., N.Y.C., 2000—. Morehead scholar John M. Moorehead Found., 1963. Mem. NY State Bar Assn., Assn. of Bar of City of NY, Brook Club, Links Club, Tuxedo Club, Union Club, Meadow Brook Club, Farmington Country Club, Phi Beta Kappa. Corporate, general, Securities. Home: 116 Central Park S Apt 15N New York NY 10019 Office: Cravath Swaine & Moore 825 8th Ave 47th Fl New York NY 10019-7475

STEPHENSON, MASON WILLIAMS, lawyer; b. Atlanta, May 29, 1946; s. Donald Grier and Katherine Mason (Williams) S.; m. Linda Frances Partee, June 13, 1970; children: Andrew Mason, Walter Martin. AB cum laude, Davidson Coll., 1968; JD, U. Chgo., 1971. Bar: Ga. 1971, U.S. Dist. Ct. (no. dist.) Ga. 1985. Assoc. Alston, Miller & Gaines, Atlanta, 1971-76, ptnr., 1976-77, Trotter, Bondurant, Griffin, Miller & Hishon, Atlanta, 1977-82, Bondurant, Miller, Hishon & Stephenson, Atlanta, 1982-85, King & Spalding, Atlanta, 1985—, mng. ptnr. Atlanta office, 2001—. Mem. fin. com. Atlanta Olympic Organizing Com., 1988-90. Mem. ABA (sect. bus. law, real property, probate and trust sect.), Am. Coll. Real Estate Lawyers, State Bar Ga. (exec. com., real property law sect. 1989-97, chair intangible rec. tax com. 1994-97), Atlanta Bar Assn. (chair real estate sect. 1981-82), Causeway Club, Capital City Club, Phi Beta Kappa, Phi Delta Phi. Avocations: sailing, skiing, jogging. Property, real (including real estate development, water). Office: King & Spalding 191 Peachtree St NE Ste 4900 Atlanta GA 30303-1740

STEPHENSON, RICHARD ISMERT, lawyer; b. Augusta, Kans., Oct. 13, 1937; s. Paul Noble and Dorothy May (Ismert) S.; m. Mary Lynn Bryden, July 2, 1967 (div. 1973); 1 child, Richard William; m. Linda Cox, Apr. 5, 1976. BA, U. Kans., 1958; JD, U. Mich., 1965. Bar: Kans. 1965, U.S. Dist. Ct. Kans. 1965, U.S. Ct. Appeals (10th cir.) 1965. Assoc. Fleeson, Gooing, Coulson & Kitch, Wichita, Kans., 1965-72, ptnr., 1973-95; gen. counsel RAGE Inc. and Affiliated Cos., Wichita, 1995—. Lt. (j.g.) USNR, 1959-62. Recipient Hilden Gibson award U. Kans., 1958. Mem. ABA (forum on franchising), Def. Rsch. Inst., Internat. Assn. Def. Counsel, Kans. Bar Assn., Wichita Bar Assn., Wichita Country Club, Pi Sigma Alpha, Beta Theta Pi. Avocations: golf, fishing. Corporate, general, Franchising. Home: 9203 Killarney Wichita KS 67206-4027 Office: RAGE Inc 1313 N Webb Rd Ste 200 Wichita KS 67206-4077

STEPHENSON, ROSCOE BOLAR, JR., state supreme court justice; b. Covington, Va., Feb. 22, 1922; AB, Washington and Lee U., 1943, JD, 1947, LL.D. (hon.), 1983. Bar: Va. 1947. Ptnr. Stephenson & Stephenson, Covington, 1947-52; commonwealth's atty. Alleghany County, Va., 1952-64; ptnr. Stephenson, Kostel, Watson, Carson and Snyder, Covington, 1964-73; judge 25th Jud. Cir. Ct. Commonwealth Va., Covington, 1973-81; justice Va. Supreme Ct., Richmond, 1981-97, sr. justice, 1997—. Recipient Covington Citizen of Yr. award, 1973, Outstanding Alumni award Covington H.S., 1973, Disting. Alumnus award Washington and Lee U., 1997. Fellow Am. Coll. Trial Lawyers; mem. Va. State Bar (council 1969-73), Va. Bar Assn., Va. Trial Lawyers Assn., Order of Coif, Omicron Delta Kappa. Home: North Ridge Hot Springs VA 24445 Office: Va Supreme Ct 214 W Main St PO Box 198 Covington VA 24426-0198 also: Va Supreme Court Supreme Court Bldg 100 N 9th St Richmond VA 23219-2335

STEPNER, DONALD LEON, lawyer; b. Boston, Apr. 23, 1939; s. Neil and Sadie (Adelman) S.; m. Beth Klass, Aug. 14, 1965 (div. Dec. 1985); children: David, Jeff. AA, Wentworth Inst., Boston, 1958; BA, Ky. Wesleyan U., 1963; JD, U. Ky., 1966. Bar: Ky. 1966, U.S. Dist. Ct. Ky. 1966, U.S. Ct. Appeals (6th cir.) 1966, U.S. Supreme Ct. 1971. Assoc. Charles Adams, Covington, Ky., 1966-69; ptnr. Adams, Stepner, Woltermann & Dusing, Covington, 1969—. Pres. Ky. State Ethics Com. Bd. dirs. Boys Club. Recipient Human Rels. award NCCJ, 1986. Fellow Am. Coll. Trial Lawyers; mem. ABA, Ky. Bar Assn. (pres. 1999-2000), No. Ky. Bar Assn. (judiciary com., ethics and unauthorized procedure com.), Ky. Def. Rsch. Inst., Kenton County Bar Assn. (pres. 1973-74, Merit award 1973, Gavel award 1973), U.S. Soccer Fedn. (cert. referee, pres. 1980-85), Ky. High Sch. Referees Assn., No. Ky. Soccer Assn. (ofcl. pres. 1980—). Avocations: golf, jogging, biking. General civil litigation, Insurance, Personal injury (including property damage). Office: Adams Stepner Woltermann & Dusing PO Box 12861 Covington KY 41012-0861

STEPTER, CHARLES RAYMOND, JR., lawyer; b. Dallas, Aug. 29, 1945; s. Charles Raymond Sr. and Eugenia Belle (Baise) S.; m. Marie Lanneau, June 28, 1970; A.B., Mercer U., 1970; J.D., Stetson U., 1973. Bar: Fla. 1973, U.S. Dist. Ct. (mid. dist.) Fla. 1973, U.S. Supreme Ct. 1977, U.S. Dist. Ct. (no. and so. dists.) Fla. 1981, U.S. Ct. Appeals (11th cir.) 1981, U.S. Tax Ct. Dep. clerk Cir. Ct., Orange County, Fla., 1971. Assoc. Fishback, Davis, Dominick & Simonet, Orlando, Fla., 1973-74, law clerk, 1973-74; ptnr., 1974-78; ptnr. Fishback, Davis, Dominick & Bennett, Orlando, 1978-82; ptnr. Fishback, Davis, Dominick & Simonet, and Fishback, Davis, Dominick & Bennett, 1974-81; of counsel Zinkow, Kosto & Rotella and Kosto & Rotella, PA, 1982-86; bd. dirs. Fla. Legal Services, Inc.; pvt. practice, 1986-89; ptnr. Fishback, Dominick, Bennett, Stepter, Ardaman, Ahlers & Bonus, 1990-; gen. counsel Nat. Auto Auction Assn., 1986-; rsch. asst. Prof. Harry W. Haden. Exec. dir. Stetson Law Rev. Bd. dirs. Orange County Legal Aid Soc., Orlando, treas., 1979—, pres., 1982-83. Served with U.S. Army, 1968-70, 199th Light Infantry Brigade, Vietnam. Mem. ABA, Fla. Bar (chmn. delivery legal services com. 1984—, ex-officio mem. commn. access to legal system), Acad. Fla. Trial Lawyers, Orange County Bar Assn. (vice chmn. remember the kids com., student intern legal aid soc. 1972), Phi Alpha Delta (marshall). Home: 1833 Lake Grove Ln Orlando FL 32806-7838 Office: Fishback Dominick Bennett Stepter Ardaman Ahlers & Bonus 170 E Washington St Orlando FL 32801-2397 Office Fax: 407-425-2863., 407-425-3679.

STERN, BRUCE H. lawyer; b. Washington, Apr. 13, 1956; s. Harvey L. and Carol (Bash) S.; m. Linda Korsen, May 23, 1981. BA cum laude, Duke U., 1977; JD cum laude, Rutgers U., Camden, N.J., 1981. Bar: N.J. 1981, Pa. 1982, U.S. Dist. Ct. N.J. 1981, U.S. Ct. Appeals (3rd cir.) 1982, U.S. Dist. Ct. (ea. and so. dists.) N.Y. 1983. Assoc., Trenton, N.J., 1982-85, 1985-88, Stark & Stark, Lawrenceville, N.J., 1988-89, ptnr., 1989—. Mem. Supreme Ct. Com. on Spl. Civil Practice, 1987-90, Supreme Ct. Com. Model Jury Charge Civil, 1990—. Mem. editorial bd. N.J. Lawyer, 1989-91, Neurolaw Letter Trial Lawyer; assoc. editor: Nat. Trial Lawyer; state editor N.J. Trial Lawyer; contbr. articles to legal jours. Mem. Mercer County Bar Assn. (pres. 1997-98, trustee 1988-94) Trial Lawyers of N.J., N.J. State Bar Assn. (exec. bd. civil trial sect.), Assn. Trial Lawyers Am. (exec. bd. traumatic brain injury litigation group), Assn. Trial Lawyers N.J. (bd. govs., treas. 1997-98, 2d v.p. 1999—, 1st v.p. 2000-2001, pres. elect 2001-2002, pres. 2002-), Brain Injury Assn. N.J. (bd. trustees), Brain Injury Assn. Insurance, Personal injury (including property damage). Office: Stark & Stark PC 992 Lenox Dr CN 5315 Princeton NJ 08543-5315

STERN, CARL LEONARD, former news correspondent, federal official; b. N.Y.C., Aug. 7, 1937; s. Hugo and Frances (Taft) S.; m. Joy Elizabeth Nathan, Nov. 27, 1960; children: Lawrence, Theodore. AB, Columbia U., 1958, MS, 1959; JD, Cleve. State U., 1966, JD (hon.), 1975, New Eng. Coll. Law, 1977. Bar: Ohio 1966, D.C. 1968, U.S. Supreme Ct. 1969. Law corr. NBC News, Washington, 1967-93; dir. Office of Pub. Affairs U.S. Dept. Justice, Washington, 1993-96; Shapiro Prof. of Media and Pub. Affairs George Washington U., 1996—. Lectr. Nat. Jud. Coll.; adj. prof. George Washington U., Stanford U. Editorial bd.: The Dist. Lawyer. Mem. Dept. Transp. Task Force on Assistance to Families in Aviation Disasters, 1997; mem. nat. adv. coun. Cleveland-Marshall Law Sch. Recipient Peabody award, 1974, Emmy award, 1974, Gavel award, 1969, 74, Headliner Club award, 1991, Edmond J. Randloph award U.S. Dept. Justice. Mem. ABA (vice chmn. criminal justice sect. com. on criminal justice and the media, gov., forum com. on communications law, working group intelligence requirements and criminal code reform, mem. standing com. on strategic comms.), AFTRA (nat. exec. bd. 1984-86, first v.p. Washington, Balt. chpt. 1985-87). Home: 2956 Davenport St NW Washington DC 20008 Office: George Washington U #400 805 21st St NW Washington DC 20052 Personal E-mail: sterncarl@aol.com. E-mail: cstern@gwu.edu.

STERN, DONALD KENNETH, lawyer; BA, Hobart Coll., 1966; JD, Georgetown U., 1969; LLM, U. Pa., 1973. Intern Dist. Atty.'s Office, Mineola, N.Y., 1967, Citizen's Adv. Ctr., Washington, 1968; staff atty. Defender Assn. Phila., Cmty. Legal Svcs., Phila., 1969-71; adj. prof. law, supervising atty. Boston Coll. Law Sch., Boston Coll. Legal Assistance Bur., 1971-73, asst. prof. law, dir. clin. programs, supervising atty., 1973-75; asst. atty. gen., dir. atty. gen. clin. program, Mass. Atty. Gen.'s Office, Boston Coll. Law Sch., 1975-77, asst. prof. law, dir. atty. gen. clin. program, spl. asst. atty. gen., 1977-78, asst. atty. gen., dir. atty. gen. clin. program, 1978-79; chief govt. bur. Mass. Atty. Gen.'s Office, 1979-82; assoc. Hale and Dorr, Boston, 1982-85, jr. ptnr., 1985-87, sr. ptnr., 1987, 91-93, of counsel, 1990-91; chief legal counsel to Gov. Mass., 1987-90; U.S. atty. Dist. Mass., 1993—2001; ptnr. Bingham McCutchen, LLP, 2001—; lectr. Harvard Law Sch., 2002—. General civil litigation, Criminal. Office: Bingham McCutchen LLP Federal St Boston MA 02210-1726 E-mail: donald.stern@bingham.com.

STERN, DORON DANIEL, lawyer; b. Jerusalem, Feb. 18, 1958; s. Gideon Karl and Tamar S.; m. Anat Shamgar, Aug. 18, 1982; children: Gad, Tamar. LLB, Hebrew U., 1983. Fgn. atty. Willkie Farr & Gallagher, N.Y.C., 1983-86; assoc. Yossi Avraham & Co., Tel Aviv, 1986-87; assoc., ptnr. Y. Raveh & Co., Israel, 1987-94; founder, ptnr. Tulchinsky Stern & Co., Israel, 1995—. Judge in disciplinary ct. Israel Bar, 2000—; dir. IBetcha, 1999-2001; panelist IVC and UC confs., 1999—; advisor Jerusalem Venture Ptnr., 1999—. Mem. Nativ Acting Sch., Jerusalem, Tenuot Dance, Nature Preservation. Sgt. Elite Commando Unit, IDF, 1976-96. Mem. Israeli Bar Assn. Avocations: hiking, music, literature, photography. Environmental, Finance, Mergers and acquisitions. Office: Tulchinsky Stern & Co 22 Kanfey Nesharim Beit Riger Federman Givat Shaul Jerusalem Israel Office Fax: 972-2-6513133. E-mail: jer@tslaw.co.il.

STERN, EDWARD MAYER, lawyer, educator; b. Albany, N.Y., Feb. 18, 1946; s. William Barnet and Louise (Mayer) S.; m. Ann Swanson, Jan. 22, 1972; children: Jared William, Jordan Carl. BS in Civil Engring., Tufts U., 1968; JD, Boston U., 1972; diploma for a dental technician, 1969. Bar: Mass. 1972, U.S. Dist. Ct. Mass. 1973, U.S. Supreme Ct. 1980, N.Y. 1983. Civil engr. Std. Engring. Corp., Albany, N.Y., 1966-67; environ. engr. Fed. Water Pollution Control Adminstrn., Needham Heights, Mass., 1968-69; civil engr. Anderson-Nichols Engring. Co., Boston, 1970; legal aid law student Multi-Service Ctr., South Boston, Mass., 1971-72; staff atty. Boston Legal Assistance Project-Juvenile Ct. Adv. program, 1972-74; legal counsel Treatment Alternative to Street Crime-Juveniles Youth Activities Commn., Boston, 1974-75; staff atty., project dir. Action Plan for Legal Svcs., Boston, 1976; lawyer in residence U. Mass., Boston, 1976-77; pvt. practice Newton, Mass., 1976—; v.p., gen. counsel, real estate developer Triangle Devel. Corp., Newton Centre, Mass., 1987-90; pres. Mass. Funding Group, Inc., 1988-97. Asst. dean for pre-law advising Boston U., 1977—; vis. lectr. dept. sociology U. Mass., 1977—; lectr. continuing edn. Tufts-New Eng. Med. Ctr., Boston, 1973—75; bd. dirs. Pre-Law Advisors Nat. Coun., 1986—88; bd. visitors Walnut Hill Sch., 1995—97; adv. bd. paralegal studies program Boston U., 1994—2002, coach mock trial team, 1993—, coach mock mediation team, 2002—; pres. N.E. Assn. Pre-Law Advs., Inc., 1987—88, bd. dirs., 1982—84. Co-author (with Emily Soltanoff): The NAPLA Pre-Law Advisors Guide, 1982—94; author, 1987, Charting a Law School Course, 1982; mo. columnist The Mass. Psychologist, 2000—, performer Action Plan for Legal Services (Criminal), 1976—; co-author (with Gerald Wilson): The Book of Law School Lists, 1998—2002; contbr. Former mem. Gov.'s Com. Prevention of Drug Abuse; bd. dirs., pres. Citizens for Juvenile Justice, 1997—; mem. med. policy rev. com. Nat. Neurofibromatosis Found., Inc., 1987—, Pub. Svc. award, 1990; former mem. pub. affairs com. and civil rights com. Anti Defamation League, Boston. With USAR, 1968—69, with res. USAR, 1968—74. Named Outstanding Participant, Nat. Coll. Juvenile Justice, 1975; recipient Merit award Boston Mayor's Office Youth Activities Commn., 1973, Pub. Svc. award Nat. Neurofibromatosis Found., Inc., 1990, Excellence in Advising award Boston U., 2003. Mem. ABA, Mass. Bar Assn. (adminstrn. justice com., family law com.), N.E. Assn. Pre-Law Advisors, Inc. (pres. 1987-88), Nat. Neurofibromatosis Found. (med. policy com. 1987—). Jewish. General practice, Juvenile, Property, real (including real estate development, water). Home: 178 Nehoiden Rd Waban MA 02468-1344 Office: 60 Austin St Ste 210 Newton MA 02460-1857 E-mail: stern@bu.edu.

STERN, ELIZABETH ESPIN, lawyer; b. Prince Georges County, Md., June 21, 1961; d. Cesar A. and M. Cecilia (Salvador) E.; m. Michael L. Stern, May 16, 1992; 1 child, Alexander. BA magna cum laude, U. Va., 1983, JD, 1986. Bar: Va. 1986, U.S. Dist. Ct. (ea. dist.) Va., D.C. 1988. Ptnr. comml. immigration Shaw, Pittman, Potts & Trowbridge, Washington, 1986—. Past chair young lawyers sect. Vol. Bar Assn. D.C. Recipient Martin Preis award Vol. Bar Assn. D.C., 1992; named one of top 75 lawyers in Washington, Washingtonian Mag. Mem. NAFE, Am. Immigration Lawyers Assn., Va. Bar Assn., D.C. Bar Assn. (internat. sec. 1986—, del. to ABA, chair young lawyers sect. 1992-93, Young Lawyer of Yr. 1994), Immigration Tech. Assn. Am. Republican. Avocation: journalism. Immigration, naturalization, and customs, Labor (including EEOC, Fair Labor Standards Act, labor-management relations, NLRB, OSHA). Home: 8529 Century Oak Ct Fairfax Station VA 22039-3343 Office: Shaw Pittman Potts & Trowbridge 2300 N St NW Fl 5 Washington DC 20037-1172

STERN, GERALD MANN, lawyer; b. Chgo., Apr. 5, 1937; s. Lloyd and Fannye (Wener) S.; m. Linda Stone, Dec. 20, 1969; children: Eric, Jesse, Maia. BS in Econs., U. Pa., 1958; LL.B. cum laude, Harvard, 1961. Bar: D.C. 1961, Calif. 1991, U.S. Supreme Ct. 1971. Trial atty. civil rights div. U.S. Dept. Justice, 1961-64; assoc. firm Arnold & Porter, Washington, 1964-68, ptnr., 1969-76; founding ptnr. Rogovin, Stern & Huge, Washington, 1976-81; exec. v.p., sr. gen. counsel Occidental Petroleum Corp., Washington, 1981—92; spl. counsel fin. instn. fraud and health care fraud U.S. Dept. Justice, Washington, 1993-95; ind. legal cons. pvt. practice, Washington, 1995—; cons. Antitrust divsn. U.S. Dept. Justice, 1998—2001. Bd. dirs. Oceania Cruises, Inc. Author: The Buffalo Creek Disaster, 1976; co-author: Southern Justice, 1965, Outside the Law, 1997. Trustee Facing History and Ourselves, 1996—, bd. dirs., Oceania Cruises, Inc. Mem. ABA. Home and Office: 3322 Newark St NW Washington DC 20008-3330 Fax: 202-364-2595. E-mail: GMS37@aol.com.

STERN, LYNNE ROTHSCHILD, mediator, arbitrator; b. New Orleans, Feb. 1, 1947; d. Arthur Maurice and Aline Loewenberg Rothschild; m. Maurice Mayer Stern, Aug. 12, 1973; children: Maury Stern, Walter Stern. BA, U. Mich., 1968; JD, Columbia U., 1971. Bar: La. 1971; U.S. Dist. Ct. (ea. dist.) La. 1971, U.S. Ct. Appeals (5th cir.) 1971. Law clk. U.S. Dist. Ct. (ea. dist.) La., New Orleans, 1971-72; ptnr. Nelson, Nelson, Garretson, Lombard & Stern, New Orleans, 1972-74; asst. prof. Loyola Law Sch., New Orleans, 1974-76; part-time assoc. Phelps, Dunbar, New Orleans, 1981-82; cons. various attys., New Orleans, 1982-93; contract mediator The Martin Group, New Orleans, 1993-95, ADRinc., Metairie, La., 1995—. Author: (newsletter) Conflict Management, 1997. Pres. Kingsley House, New Orleans, 1988-90, Garden Dist. Assn., New Orleans, 1996-97. Mem. ABA (chmn. mediation sub-com., litigation sect. 1995-2000, award 1998), Nat. Healthcare Lawyers Panel of Mediators, NASD Panel of Mediators, JAMS panel of mediators, nat. employment mediation svcs. panel of mediators, La. Bar Assn. (program co-chmn. ADR sect. 1998—), New Orleans Bar Assn. Democrat. Jewish. Avocation: tennis. Office: ADRinc 3813 N Causeway Blvd Ste 2880 Metairie LA 70002-1724

STERN, RALPH DAVID, lawyer; b. Longview, Tex., June 20, 1943; children: Eric, Justin. AB, Bucknell U., 1963; JD, U. Chgo., 1966. Bar: D.C. 1967, Ill. 1967, Calif. 1970, U.S. Supreme Ct. 1970. Law clk. Ill. Appellate Ct., Chgo., 1966-67; assoc. Ressman & Tishler, Chgo., 1968-70; exec. asst. Orange County Bd. Suprs., Santa Ana, Calif., 1970-71; gen. counsel San Diego City Schs., 1971-83; ptnr. Whitmore, Kay & Stevens, Palo Alto, Calif., 1983-88, Stern & Keebler, San Mateo, Calif., 1988-90; gen. counsel Schs. Legal Counsel, Hayward, Calif., 1990—2001; chief sch. counsel Sch. and Coll. Legal Svcs. of Calif., 2002—. Chmn. Nat. Coun. Sch. Attys., 1982-83; pres. Leagal Aid Soc. San Diego, 1976-79, Nat. Orgn. on Legal Problems of Edn., 1981-82. Editor: Law and the School Principal, 1978; contbr. articles to profl. jours. Mem. exec. bd., county membership chair Boy Scouts Am., San Diego, 1979-81; vice chmn. Laurels for Leaders, San Diego, 1980-83; mem. ednl. adminstrn. adv. com. U. San Diego, 1981-86.; mem. adv. com. West's Ednl. Law Reporter, 1981-85. Named Outstanding Young Citizen, San Diego Jaycees, 1977. Office: Sch and Coll Legal Svcs 313 W Winton Ave Rm 372 Hayward CA 94544-1136

STERN, SAMUEL ALAN, lawyer; b. Phila., Jan. 21, 1929; AB, U. Pa., 1949; LLB, Harvard U., 1952. Bar: Mass. 1952, D.C. 1958. Ptnr. Wilmer, Cutler & Pickering, Washington, 1962-88, Dickstein, Shapiro & Morin, Washington, 1988-92; pvt. practice law and bus. Washington and St. Petersburg, Russia, 1992-94; counsel Rogers & Wells, Washington, N.Y.C., 1994-97; pvt. practice law and bus. Washington, 1997-98; gen. counsel Global Energy Investors, Inc., Washington, 1997-2000; ptnr. Hills & Stern LLP, Washington, 1999—; pres. Hills Enterprises, 1999—; counselor Hills & Co., 1999—. Vis. prof. law Harvard Law Sch., Cambridge, Mass., 1976; dir. Internat. Law Inst. Georgetown U., 1971—, adj. prof. law, 1979—92; asst. counsel Warren Commn., 1964; cons. UN, 1984—96; bd. dirs. Hills Enterprises, Ltd., Global Energy Investors Inc., Warp Broadband Corp., Verisign, Verihealth, Macrobuild.com, Lexsite.com, India, Flag Resources, Canada, Pan-Asia Media, VeriPay; lectr. profl. confs. on project fin., privatization, cross-border investment and dispute resolution; arbitrator internat. comml. arbitration. Contbr. articles to legal jours. Mem. ABA, Am. Law Inst., Internat. Bar Assn., D.C. Bar Assn. Commercial, contracts (including sales of goods; commercial financing), Corporate, general, Private international. Home: 210 Lee Ct Alexandria VA 22314 Office: 1200 19th St NW Washington DC 20036-2412 E-mail: sastern@hillsandstern.com.

STERN, STEPHEN JEFFREY, lawyer; b. L.A., Dec. 31, 1940; s. M.E. and Jane (VanDement) S.; m. Betsy Stern, June 16, 1962 (div. 1974); children: Christopher, Jeffrey; m. Sheila Duckworth, Apr. 23, 1976. BS in Econs., U. Calif., 1962; JD, U. San Francisco, 1965. Bar: Calif., N.Y. Ptnr. O'Melveny & Myers, L.A., 1966—. Lectr., chmn. N.Y. Law Jour., Calif. League of Cities, Mcpl. Fin. Officers Assn. Mem. ABA, Calif. State Bar Assn., N.Y. State Bar Assn., Nat. Assn. Bond Lawyers, Bel Air Bay Club. Office: O'Melveny & Myers 3 Finsbury Sq London EC2A 1LA England

STERNMAN, JOEL W. lawyer; b. N.Y.C., Oct. 20, 1943; s. Abraham and Sarah (Simon) S.; children: Mark S., Cheryl A.; m. Barbara E. Shiers, March 31, 1985; children: Matthew S., Julia S. AB, Dartmouth Coll., 1965; LLB, Yale U., 1968. Bar: N.Y. 1970, U.S. Dist. Ct. (so. and ea. dists.) N.Y. 1971, U.S. Ct. Appeals (2d cir.) 1972, U.S. Supreme Ct. 1984, U.S. Ct. Appeals (6th cir.) 1985, U.S. Ct. Appeals (9th cir.) 1994, U.S. Tax Ct. 1996, U.S. Dist. Ct. (e. dist.) Mich. 1997. Law clk. to judge U.S. Dist. Ct., New Haven, 1968-69; assoc. Rosenman Colin Freund Lewis & Cohen, N.Y.C., 1969-77; ptnr. Rosenman & Colin LLP, N.Y.C., 1977—2002, Katten Muchin Zavis Rosenman, 2002—. Editor Yale Law Jour., New Haven, 1966-68. Mem. Phi Beta Kappa. Federal civil litigation, State civil litigation, Appellate. Office: Katten Muchin Zavis Rosenman 575 Madison Ave New York NY 10022-2585 E-mail: j.sternman@kmzr.com.

STERRETT, SAMUEL BLACK, lawyer, former judge; b. Washington, Dec. 17, 1922; s. Henry Hatch Dent and Helen (Black) S.; m. Jeane McBride, Aug. 27, 1949; children: Samuel Black, Robin Dent, Douglas McBride. Student, St. Albans Sch., 1933-41; grad., U.S. Mcht. Marine Acad., 1945; BA, Amherst Coll., 1947; LLB, U. Va., 1950; LLM in Taxation, NYU, 1959. Bar: D.C. 1951, Va. 1950. Atty. Alvord & Alvord, Washington, 1950-56; trial atty. Office Regional Counsel, Internal Revenue Service, N.Y.C., 1956-60; ptnr. Sullivan, Shea & Kenney, Washington, 1960-68; municipal cons. to office vice pres. U.S., 1965-68; judge U.S. Tax Ct., 1968-88, chief judge, 1985-88; ptnr. Myerson, Kuhn & Sterrett, Washington, 1988-89; of counsel Vinson & Elkins, Washington, 1990—2002; pvt. practice Law Offices of Samuel B. Sterrett, Washington, 2002—. Bd. mgrs. Chevy Chase Village, 1970-74, chmn., 1972-74; 1st v.p. bd. trustees, mem. exec. com. Washington Hosp. Center, 1969-79, chmn. bd. trustees, 1979-84, mem. bd. trustees, 1999—; chmn. bd. trustees Washington Healthcare Corp., 1982-87; chmn. bd. trustees Medlantic Healthcare Group, 1987-89; mem. audit com. Medstar Health, 1990—; mem. Washington Cathedral, 1973-81, 99—, mem. fin. com., 1998—, chmn., 1999—; mem. governing bd. St. Albans Sch., 1977-81; trustee Louise Home, 1979-89. Served with AUS, 1943; Served with U.S. Mcht. Marine, 1943-46. Fellow Am. Bar Found. (life); mem. ABA, D.C. Bar Assn., Am. Coll. Tax Counsel, Soc. of the Cincinnati, Coun. for Future, Am. Inns. of Ct., Chevy Chase Club (bd. govs. 1979-84, pres. 1984), Met. Club, Lawyers Club, Alibi Club, Alfalfa Club, Ch. of N.Y. Club, Beta Theta Pi. Episcopalian. Office: Law Offices of Samuel B Sterrett Ste 600 1455 Pennsylvania Ave NW Fl 7 Washington DC 20004-1013

STERRETT, TATE KINCAID, lawyer; b. Charlottesville, Va., Dec. 6, 1946; s. S. Willson and Eleanor Miriam Sterrett; m. Theckla Donsbach, May 17, 1968; children: M. Todd, Theckla M. BA, Davidson Coll., 1969; JD, U. Va., 1972. Bar: N.C. 1973, U.S. Dist. Ct. (we. dist.) N.C. 1973, cert.: N.C. State Bar Bd. Legal Specialization (specialist in family law) 1992, N.C. State Bar Dispute Resolution Commn. (mediator) 1992. Assoc. Hicks & Harris, Charlotte, NC, 1973—76; ptnr. Hicks & Sterrett, Charlotte, NC, 1976—86, Bradley, Guthery, Turner & Curry, Charlotte, NC, 1986—89; shareholder Horack, Talley, Pharr & Lowndes, Charlotte, NC, 1989—. 1st lt. USAR, 1972—73. Mem.: ABA, N.C. Bar Assn. Family and matrimonial, Alternative dispute resolution. Office: Horack Talley Pharr & Lowndes 301 S College St Ste 2600 Charlotte NC 28202 Office Fax: 704-372-0448. E-mail: TSterrett@horacktalley.com.

STERZEL, FREDRIK ALBERT CHRISTIAN, judge, researcher; b. Stockholm, Oct. 29, 1934; s. Fredrik Julius Christian and Gisela Ella Marion (Hallberg) S. LLB, U. Stockholm, 1954; LLD, U. Uppsala, Sweden, 1961; MA, U. Lund, Sweden, 1972, PhD, 1983. Pvt. practice, 1955-63; assoc. prof. pub. law U. Uppsala, 1963-74; sec. gen. Constl. Com. Swedish Parliament, 1965-74; div. head Adminstrv. Ct. Appeal, Gothenburg, Sweden, 1974-76, Ct. Appeals, Stockholm, 1976-79; undersec. State Ministry of Local Govt., Stockholm, 1976-79; justice Supreme Ct., Sweden, 1979-80, 87-95; mem. Law Council, 1985-87, 89-91; prof. constitutional law U. Uppsala, 1995-99. Presider several pub. commns., 1976—. Author several books and numerous articles to profl. jours. Home: Norr Mälarstrand 32 11220 Stockholm Sweden Office: Kungsgatan 4B 11143 Stockholm Sweden

STEUER, RICHARD MARC, lawyer; b. Bklyn., June 19, 1948; s. Harold and Gertrude (Vengar) S.; m. Audrey P. Forchheimer, Sept. 9, 1973; children: Hilary, Jeremy. BA, Hofstra U., 1970; JD, Columbia U., 1973. Bar: N.Y. 1974, U.S. Dist. Ct. (ea. and so. dists.) N.Y. 1974, U.S. Ct. Appeals (2d cir.) 1974, U.S. Supreme Ct. 1979, U.S. Dist. Ct. (no. dist.) N.Y. 1984, U.S. Dist. Ct. (we. dist.) N.Y. 1997, U.S. Ct. Appeals (3d cir.) 1987, U.S. Ct. Appeals (5th cir.) 1995. Ptnr. Kaye Scholer LLP, N.Y.C., 1973—2002, chair antitrust practice group, 1996—2002; ptnr. Mayer, Brown, Rowe and Maw, N.Y.C., 2002—. Adj. assoc. prof. law NYU, 1985; lectr. in field; neutral evaluator U.S. Dist. Ct. Ea. Dist., N.Y, 1994-96. Author: A Guide to Marketing Law: Law and Business Inc., 1986; contbr. articles to profl. jours. Fellow: Am. Bar Found. (others); mem.: ABA (lectr. 1969, 1978, chmn. monograph com. refusals to deal and exclusive distributorships 1983, editl. bd. antitrust devel. vol. 1984—86, lectr. 1985, vice-chmn. program com. 1988—91, lectr. 1989, chmn. spring meeting program com. 1991—92, Sherman Act sect. 1 com. 1991—93, coun. sect. antitrust law 1993—96, chmn. publs. com. 1996—98, lectr. 1997, 1998, editl. chmn. Antitrust mag. 1998—2001, lectr. 1999, 2000, coun. sect. antitrust law 2001—, lectr. 2002), Assn. Bar City N.Y. (chmn. antitrust and trade regulation 1995—98, antitrust and trade regulation, internat. trade, lectures and CLE coms). Antitrust, General civil litigation, Trademark and copyright. Office: Mayer Brown Rowe and Maw 1675 Broadway New York NY 10019-5820 E-mail: rsteuer@mayerbrownrowe.com.

STEVENS, CHARLES DANIEL, lawyer; b. Richmond, Va., Nov. 10, 1940; s. Charles Robert and Alice Dixon Stevens; m. Sarah M. St. Clair, Aug. 24, 1963; children: John David, Robert Mark. BA, U. Richmond, 1962, LLB, 1966. Bar: Va. 1966. Assoc. McCaul, Grigsby & Pearsall, Richmond, 1966-70, Christian & Barton LLP, Richmond, 1970-76, ptnr., 1976—. Trustee Children's Hosp., Richmond, 1998—. Fellow Am. Coll. Trust and Estate Counsel; mem. Va. State Bar. Baptist. Avocations: golf, travel. Estate planning, Probate (including wills, trusts), Estate taxation. Home: 8004 Cameron Rd Richmond VA 23229-8402 Office: Christian & Barton LLP 909 E Main St Ste 1200 Richmond VA 23219-3013 E-mail: cdspossum@aol.com., cstevens@cblaw.com.

STEVENS, DAVID BOYETTE, law educator; b. Augusta, Ga., Jan. 31, 1923; s. Henry Boyette and Floreid Elizabeth (Miller) S.; m. Willa King Horner, July 18, 1942; children: David Boyette, Caroline Elizabeth, Paul King. BS in Bus., U. N.C., 1949, JD, 1951; LLM, Duke U., 1956. Bar: N.C. 1951, U.S. Ct. Mil. Appeals 1965, U.S. Supreme Ct. 1967. Commd. 2d lt. U.S. Army Air Force, 1944; advanced through grades to col. USAF, 1968; asst. prof. internat. law U.S. Air Force Acad., Colorado Springs, Colo., 1959-63; judge adv., acting dir. U.S. Air Force Judiciary, Washington, 1963-70; ret., 1970; asst. prof. bus. East Carolina U., Greenville, N.C., 1970-74, prof., 1984—, dir. EEO Office, 1974-81, univ. atty., 1970—. Divsn. chmn. United Fund Svc., East Carolina U., 1972; mem. Greenville Bd. Adjustments, 1983—. Recipient Meritorious Achievement award USAF, 1970, Outstanding Svc. award East Carolina U. Law Soc., 1978. Mem. Fed. Bar Assn., N.C. Bar Assn., Pitt County Bar Assn., Nat. Assn. Coll. and Univ. Attys., Kiwanis (pres. Greenville 1976-77, lt. gov. 1979-80, Disting. Lit. Gov. ward 1981), Delta Theta Phi. Democrat. Baptist. Home: 304 Francis Asbury Ln Greenville NC 27858

STEVENS, DAVID BRUCE, lawyer; b. Pontiac, Mich., Dec. 18, 1941; s. Charles How and Myrtle Louise (Cottrell) S.; m. Charlene Louise Grove, Mar. 17, 1968 (div. 1973). BS in Pharmacy, Drake U., 1964, JD, 1971. Bar: Iowa 1971, Wash. 981, Alaska 1990, U.S. Dist. Ct. (so. dist.) Iowa 1971, U.S. Ct. Appeals (8th cir.) 1974, U.S. Tax Ct. 1976, U.S. Ct. Claims 1977, U.S. Dist. Ct. (we. dist.) Wash. 1982. Pharmacist E. VonHermann Drugs, Chgo., 1964-68; staff atty. Polk County Legal Aid, Des Moines, 1971-73, Bertroche, Watson & Swanson, Des Moines, 1973-74; sr. ptnr. Stevens, Price & Fultz, Des Moines, 1974-81; pvt. practice David B. Stevens, Seattle, 1981—. Mem. Am. Soc. Pharmacy Law, Wash. State Trial Lawyers Assn. Avocations: travel, cruising, sports car racing. Personal injury (including property damage). Home and Office: 9707 35th Ave NE Seattle WA 98115-2506

STEVENS, HERBERT FRANCIS, lawyer, law educator; b. Phila., Nov. 19, 1948; s. Herbert F. and Lois Marie (Kenna) S.; m. Jane Pickard, 1994; children: Sarah, Ben. SB, MIT, 1970; JD, Catholic U. Am., 1974; ML in Tax, Georgetown U, 1983. Bar: D.C., 1975; U.S. Supreme Ct., 1980. Law clk Md. Ct. of Spl. Appeals, 1974-75; with Morgan, Lewis & Bockius, Washington, 1975-78, Lane & Edson, P.C., Washington, 1979-89, Kelley Drye & Warren, Washington, 1989-93, Nixon Peabody LLP, Washington, 1993—; adj. prof. Georgetown U. Law Ctr., 1983-98. Spkr. nat. confs., seminars, TV Editor: Real Estate Aspects of the 1984 Tax Law, 1984; author: Real Estate Taxation: A Practitioner's Guide, 1986, Developer's Guide to Low Income Housing Tax Credit, 4th edit., 2000. Bd. dirs. Ctr. for Mental Health, Inc., 1987-2000 (exec. com.); bd. dirs. Nat. Fund for U.S. Botanic Garden, 1992—, exec. com. Mem. ABA, D.C. Bar Assn. Democrat. Presbyterian. Property, real (including real estate development, water), Securities, Taxation, general. Home: 8301 Hackamore Dr Potomac MD 20854-3877 Office: Nixon Peabody LLP 401 9th St NW Washington DC 20004-2128 E-mail: hstevens@nixonpeabody.com.

STEVENS, JOHN PAUL, judge; b. Chgo., Apr. 20, 1920; s. Ernest James and Elizabeth (Street) Stevens; m. Elizabeth Jane Sheeren, June 7, 1942; children: John Joseph, Kathryn Stevens Jedlicka, Elizabeth Jane Stevens Sesemann, Susan Roberta Stevens Mullen; m. Maryan Mulholland, Dec. 1979. AB, U. Chgo., 1941; JD magna cum laude, Northwestern U., 1947. Bar: Ill. 1949. Practiced in, Chgo.; law clk. to Hon. Wiley Rutledge U.S. Supreme Ct. , 1947—48; assoc. Poppenhusen, Johnston, Thompson & Raymond, 1949—52; assoc. counsel sub-com. on study monopoly power, com. on judiciary U.S. Ho. of Reps., 1951; ptnr. Rothschild, Stevens, Barry & Myers, 1952—70; judge U.S. Cir. Ct., 1970—75; assoc. justice U.S. Supreme Ct., 1975—. Lectr. anti-trust law Northwestern U. Sch. Law, 1952—54, U. Chgo. Law Sch., 1955—58; mem. Atty. Gen.'s Nat. Com. to Study Anti-Trust Laws, 1953—55. With USNR, 1942—45. Decorated Bronze Star. Mem.: Am. Law Inst., Fed. Bar Assn., Ill. Bar Assn., Am. Bar Assn., Chgo. Bar Assn. (2d v.p. 1970), Order of Coif, Phi Delta Phi, Psi Upsilon, Phi Beta Kappa. Office: US Supreme Ct Supreme Court Bldg One 1st St NE Washington DC 20543*

STEVENS, MARK ALAN, lawyer, environmental engineer; b. Phila., July 30, 1949; BA, Brandeis U., 1971; MSc in Engring., Wash. State U., Pullman, 1976; JD, Temple U., 1987. Bar: Pa., N.J. Prof. assoc. U. Man., Winnipeg, Can., 1976-78; tech. cons. BCM Engrs., Plymouth Meeting, Pa., 1978-86; ptnr. Langsam Stevens , Phila., 1995—. Mem. ABA (litigation sect.), Pa. Bar Assn., N.J. State Bar Assn., Phila. Bar Assn. Administrative and regulatory, Environmental, Property, real (including real estate development, water). Office: 1616 Walnut St Ste 1700 Philadelphia PA 19103-5308 E-mail: mstevens@langsamstevens.com.

STEVENS, PAUL SCHOTT, lawyer; b. New Orleans, Nov. 19, 1952; s. Miles Gordon and Rosemary Louise (Schott) S.; m. Joyce Lynn Pilz, Aug. 18, 1979; Paul Schott Jr., Alexander Holmes, Andrew Colby, Carl Bernard. BA magna cum laude, Yale U., 1974; JD, U. Va., 1978. Bar: D.C. 1979, U.S. Dist. Ct. D.C. 1979, U.S. Ct. Appeals (D.C. cir.) 1979, U.S. Ct. Appeals (fed. cir.) 1983, U.S. Supreme Ct. 1982. Assoc., prin. Dickstein, Shapiro & Morin, Washington, 1978-85, ptnr., 1989-93; dep. dir., gen. counsel Pres.'s Blue Ribbon Commn. on Def. Mgmt., Washington, 1985-86; legal adviser NSC, Washington, 1987, exec. sec., 1987-89; spl. asst. to Pres. for nat. security affairs The White House, Washington, 1987-89; exec. asst. to Sec. of Defense, Washington, 1989; sr. v.p., gen. counsel Investment Co. Inst., Washington, 1993-97; sr. v.p., gen. counsel Mut. Funds and Internat. Enterprise, Charles Schwab & Co., Inc., San Francisco, 1997-99; ptnr. Dechert LLP, Washington, 1999—. Lectr. law Washington Coll. Law, Am. U., Washington, 1980-83; trustee M.G. Stevens Corp., New Orleans, 1978—; mem. quality of markets com. NASDAQ Stock Market, Inc., 1997, mem. investment cos. com. NASD Regulation, Inc., 1999; mem. adv. bd. Ctr. Banking & Fin. Law, Boston U., 1996—. Author: U.S. Armed Forces and Homeland Defense: The Legal Framework, 2001. Chmn. bd. dirs. Student Conservation Assn., Charlestown, N.H., 1986-87, bd. dirs., 1985-91, 94-96, sec., gen. counsel, 1991-93. Recipient medal for disting. pub. svc. Dept. Def., 1989; Bates fellow Yale U., 1973, Scholar of House, 1973-74; Rotary Internat. Found. grad. fellow, 1978, U.S.-Japan Leadership fellow Japan Soc., 1989-90, assoc. fellow Saybrook Coll., Yale U., 1993—. Mem.: ABA (chmn. standing com. law and nat. security 1995—98), Federalist Soc. (vice chmn. internat. and nat. security law practice group), Internat. Bar Assn., DC Bar Assn., Fed. Bar Assn., Soc. War of 1812, Coun. Fgn. Rels., Cosmos Club, Elizabethan Club, Yale Club, Met. Club. Republican. Roman Catholic. Office: Dechert 1775 Eye St NW Washington DC 20006-2402 E-mail: paul.stevens@dechert.com.

STEVENS, ROBERT BOCKING, lawyer, educator; b. U.K., June 8, 1933; naturalized, 1971; s. John Skevington and Enid Dorothy (Bocking) S.; m. Katherine Booth, Dec. 23, 1985; 1 child, Robin; children by previous marriage: Carey, Richard. BA, Oxford U., 1955, BCL, 1956, MA, 1959, DCL, 1984; LLM, Yale U., 1958; LLD (hon.), N.Y. Law Sch., 1984, Villanova U., 1985, U. Pa., 1987; D.Litt. (hon.), Haverford Coll., 1991. Grays Inn bencher, 1999. Barrister-at-law, London, 1956; tutor in law Keble Coll. Oxford U., 1958-59; asst. prof. law Yale U., 1959-61, assoc. prof., 1961-65, prof., 1965-76; provost, prof. law and history Tulane U., 1976-78; pres. Haverford Coll., 1978-87; chancellor, prof. history U. Calif., Santa Cruz, 1987-91; counsel Covington and Burling, Washington and London, 1991—; master Pembroke Coll., Oxford, 1993-2001; mem. Essex Court Chambers, 1966—; sr. rsch. fellow Univ. Coll., London, 2001—. Vis. prof. U. Tex., 1961, U. East Africa, 1962, London Sch. Econs., 1963, Stanford U., 1966, Brookings Instn., 1967-68, U. Coll. London, 1991-94; cons. UN, HEW, U.S. Dept. State; hon. fellow, Keble Coll., Oxford U., 1985, Pembroke Coll., 2001. Author: The Restrictive Practices Court, 1965, Lawyers and the Courts, 1967, In Search of Justice, 1968, Income Security, 1970, Welfare Medicine in America, 1974, Law and Politics, 1978, The Law School, 1983, The Independence of the Judiciary, 1993, The English Judges, 2002. Chair Marshall Memorial Commn., 1994—2001; mem. Nat. Humanities Coun., 1982—86. Fellow Russell Sage Found., 1967—68, NEH, 1973—74; grantee, Rockefeller Found., 1962—64, Ford Found., 1962—64, 1973—74, NEH, 1973—74, Nuffield Found., 1975, Pembrooke Coll., Oxford, 2001. Home and Office: Mill Bank Northleach GL54 3HJ England E-mail: rstevens@cov.com.

STEVENS, ROGER ROSS, lawyer; b. N.Y.C., Nov. 7, 1951; s. Stanley and Miriam S.; m. Nina Iaria, July 17, 1977; 1 child, Alexis. Student, NYU, 1969-71; BBA cum laude, Pace U., 1974, JD, 1979. Bar: N.Y. 1980, U.S. Dist. Ct. (ea. and so. dists.) N.Y. 1980. Supt. John T. Brady & Co., New Rochelle, N.Y., 1970-72, office mgr., 1973-79, corp. counsel, 1980-84; pvt. practice New Rochelle, 1985-86; asst. gen. counsel George A. Fuller Co., N.Y.C., 1986-94; gen. counsel PMS Cons. Mgmt. Corp., New Rochelle, N.Y., 1994—. Elected mem. Representative Town Meeting, Greenwich, 1980-98. Mem. N.Y. State Bar Assn., Am. Arbitration Assn. (arbitrator). Avocations: trap shooting, off road trucking, tennis. Construction, Corporate, general, Government contracts and claims. Office: PMS Cons Mgmt Corp 92 North Ave New Rochelle NY 10801-7413 E-mail: pmscm@aol.com.

STEVENS, THOMAS CHARLES, lawyer; b. Auburn, N.Y., Oct. 17, 1949; s. Alice (Kerlin) S.; m. Christine Eleanor Brown, June 2, 1973; children: Erin, Leigh, Timothy. BA, SUNY, Albany, 1971; JD, Duke U., 1974. Bar: Ohio 1974. Mng. ptnr. Thompson, Hine & Flory, Cleve., 1991-96; vice-chmn., chief adminstrv. officer, sec. KeyCorp., Cleve., 1996—. Trustee Greater Cleve. Growth Assn., 1993-96, Greater Cleve. Roundtable, 1993—,(chmn. of bd. trustees), Playhouse Sq. Found., 1998—; active Leadership Cleve., 1992-93, Young Audiences, 1999—, 1999 United Way Campaign. Mem. ABA, Cleve. Bar Assn., Am. Soc. Corp. Secs., Nisi Prius. Banking, Corporate, general, Securities. Office: KeyCorp 127 Public Sq Cleveland OH 44114-1306 E-mail: thomas_stevens@keybank.com.

STEVENS, WILLEM FRANS CASIMIR, lawyer; b. The Hague, The Netherlands, Oct. 2, 1938; s. Christiaan Hubertus Adolf Stevens and Joanna Maria (Aldegonda) Jansen; m. Marianne Stevens-Mullens; children: Willem Jeroen, Rogier Juliette. Grad., U. Leiden, The Netherlands, 1961, Rijksbelasting Acad., Rotterdam, The Netherlands, 1963; LLM, Harvard U.,

1963. Student assoc. Hale & Dorr, Boston, 1965—72; lawyer, tax advisor Caron & Van den Heuvel, Amsterdam, Netherlands, 1972—2002; sr. ptnr. Caron & Stevens, Baker & McKenzie, Amsterdam, Netherlands, 2002—; sr. counsel Baker & McKenzie, Amsterdam, Netherlands, 2002—. Mem. supervisory bd. Aegon Ins. Co., The Hague, 1997—; chmn. supervisory bd. NIB Capital NV, Bank, The Hague, 1999—. Senator Senate, The Hague, 1991—2003. 2nd lt. Huzaren van Boreel, 1963—65. Named knight in the order of the Netherlands Lion, Queen of the Netherlands, 1994; recipient knight in the order of Oranji Nassau, 1994. Roman Catholic. Avocations: golf, squash. Office: Baker & McKenzie Leidseplein 29 1017 PS Amsterdam Netherlands

STEVENS, WILLIAM J. lawyer; b. Chgo., Jan. 26, 1940; s. Richard James and Jane (Collidge) S.; m. Peggy Hess, Sept. 17, 1960; children: Mark, David. BA, U. Chgo., 1962; JD, Chgo. Kent, 1966. Bar: Ill. 1966, Ind. 1983, U.S. Dist. Ct. (no. dist.) Ill. 1966, Mich. 1996. Assoc. Tenney & Bentley, Chgo., 1966-70; ptnr. Foss Schuman & Drake, Chgo., 1970-86; pvt. practice Chgo., 1986-98; assoc. Kopka Landau & Pinkus, Crown Point, Ind., 1998-2001, Hettinger & Hettinger, Kalamazoo, Portage, Mich., 2001—03; pvt .practice, 2003—. Contbg. author: Illinois Trial Guide, 1991. Federal civil litigation, State civil litigation, Criminal. Office: 22 1/2 Whittaker New Buffalo MI Fax: 269-469-2316. E-mail: butterflypeggy@qtm.net.

STEVENS, WILLIAM KENNETH, lawyer; b. Chgo., Apr. 19, 1917; s. Ernest James and Elizabeth (Street) S.; m. Anne Hughes, Jan. 4, 1943; children: Anne Elizabeth Stevens Fishman, William Hughes Stevens, Mary Carol Stevens Williams, Martha Street Stevens Gingrich. AB cum laude, U. Calif., Berkeley, 1938; MA, U. Chgo., 1940; JD, Harvard U., 1948. Bar: Ill. 1948, Fla. 1977. With First Nat. Bank Chgo., 1948-74, asst. v.p., 1958-61, v.p., 1961-74; ptnr. McDermott, Will & Emery, Chgo., 1974-85, Myers Krause & Stevens, Naples, Fla., 1986—2001; of counsel Fowler White Boggs Banker, Naples, Fla., 2001—. Author: Illinois Estate Administration, 1968. Chmn. Ill. Inst. Continuing Legal Edn., 1971-72; pres. Hinsdale (Ill.) Pub. Libr., 1977-79. Lt. USNR, 1941-45. Recipient Disting. Svc. award Chgo. Estate Planning Coun., 1981. Fellow Am. Coll. Trust and Estate Counsel; mem. ABA, Am. Law Inst., Chgo. Bar Assn., Ill. Bar Assn., Fla. Bar Assn. (bd. cert. estate planning and probate lawyer), Internat. Acad. Estate and Trust Law. Clubs: Mid-Day, Hinsdale Golf; Chikaming Country (Lakeside, Mich.), The Club at Pelican Bay (Naples). Estate planning, Probate (including wills, trusts), Estate taxation. Home: 314 S Lincoln St Hinsdale IL 60521-4008 Office: Ste 600 5811 Pelican Bay Blvd Naples FL 34108-2711 E-mail: wstevens@fowlerwhite.com.

STEVENSON, ADLAI EWING, III, lawyer, former senator; b. Chgo., Oct. 10, 1930; s. Adlai Ewing and Ellen (Borden) S.; m. Nancy L. Anderson, June 25, 1955; children: Adlai Ewing IV, Lucy W., Katherine R., Warwick L. Grad., Milton Acad., 1948; AB, Harvard U., 1952, LL.B., 1957. Bar: Ill. 1957, D.C. 1977. Law clk. Ill. Supreme Ct., 1957-58; assoc. Mayer, Brown & Platt, Chgo., 1958-66, ptnr., 1966-67, 81-83, of counsel, 1983-91; treas. State of Ill., 1967-70; U.S. senator from Ill., 1970-81; chmn. SC&M Internat. Ltd., Chgo., 1991-95, pres., 1995-98, chmn. of bd., 1998—. Mem. Ill. Ho. of Reps., 1965-67; Dem. candidate for gov. of Ill., 1982, 86. Capt. USMCR, 1952-54. Private international. Office: 20 N Clark St Ste 750 Chicago IL 60602

STEVENSON, DOUGLAS BRUCE, lawyer; b. Port Huron, Mich., May 21, 1948; s. Glenn Edgar and Helen Elizabeth (Smeckert) S.; children: Mareika, Holly, Virginia, Margaret. BS, U.S. Coast Guard Acad., 1970; JD, U. Miami, 1977. Bar: N.Y., Fla. Ensign USCG, 1970, advanced through grades to comdr., 1984, ret., 1990; dir. Ctr. for Seafarers' Rights Seamen's Ch. Inst., N.Y.C., 1990—. Adv. bd. Jour. Maritime Law and Commerce, 1995—. Mem. adv. com. to Anglican observer to UN. Office: Seamen's Church Inst 241 Water St New York NY 10038-2016

STEVENSON, JOHN W. lawyer; b. June 19, 1947; BA, Centre Coll. Ky.; JD, U. Ky. Bar: Ky. 1947. Atty. Connor, Neal, Stevenson & Mitchell, LLP, Owensboro, Ky. Mem.: Ky. Bar Assn. (pres.-elect). Office: Connor Neal Stevenson and Mitchell Corp Ctr Bldg D Ste 102 401 Frederica St Owensboro KY 42301*

STEVENSON, PHILIP DAVIS, lawyer; b. Canton, Republic of China, Sept. 15, 1936; s. Donald Day and Lois (Davis) S.; m. Carol Rusch, June 14, 1958 (div. 1975); children: Katherine, Ross; m. Joan Ann Lukey, Oct. 8, 1976. BA, Yale U., 1958, LLB, 1961. Assoc. Robbins, Noyes & Jansen, Boston, 1961-69, Hale and Dorr, Boston, 1969-71, jr. ptnr., 1971-75, sr. ptnr., 1975—, chmn. real estate dept., 1984-90. Contbr. articles on Mass. continuing legal edn. Mem. Weston (Mass.) Planning Bd., 1968-73, chmn., 1973. Mem. ABA, Am. Coll. Real Estate Lawyers, Mass. Bar Assn., Boston Bar Assn., N.H. Bar Assn., Abstract Club. Democrat. Unitarian Universalist. Avocations: sailing, skiing. Environmental, Land use and zoning (including planning), Property, real (including real estate development, water). Office: Hale & Dorr 60 State St Boston MA 02109-1816

STEVENSON, ROBERT BRUCE, lawyer; b. Detroit, Jan. 28, 1951; s. Allan M. and Rose A. (Ferriole) S.; m. Sharon A. Buslepp, Mar. 19, 1982; children: Ruth, Kate. BA with highest honors, Mich State U., 1973; JD, U. Mich., 1976. Bar: Mich. 1976. Assoc. Hill, Lewis, Adams, Goodrich & Taft, Detroit, 1976-82, ptnr., 1982-86; assoc. Rose, Schmidt, Chapman, Duff & Hasley, Ann Arbor, Mich., 1986-87; ptnr. Stevenson Keppelman Assocs., Ann Arbor, 1987—. Author: Incorporating the Small Business - A Systems Approach, 1983. Fellow: Am. Coll. of Employee Benefits Counsel (charter); mem.: State Bar Mich. (chmn. employment benefits com., tax sect. 1987—89). Avocation: skiing. Pension, profit-sharing, and employee benefits. Office: 444 S Main St Ann Arbor MI 48104-2304

STEVER, DONALD WINFRED, lawyer; b. Altoona, Pa., Jan. 25, 1944; s. Donald Winfred and June Lily (Bargfrede) S.; m. Betsy Jean Seaman, May 28, 1968 (div. Oct. 1975); 1 child, Heather Elene; m. Margo Leaman Taft, July 30, 1976; children: David Whittaker, James Taft. BA, Lehigh U., 1965; JD, U. Pa., 1968. Bar: Conn. 1968, N.H. 1969, D.C. 1983, N.Y. 1983, U.S. Dist. Ct. N.H. 1969, U.S. Dist. Ct. Conn. 1986, U.S. Dist. Ct. (so. dist.) N.Y. 1985, U.S. Dist. Ct. (no. and we. dists.) N.Y. 1990, U.S. Ct. Appeals (1st cir.) 1974, U.S. Ct. Appeals (10th cir.) 1980, U.S. Ct. Appeals (5th, 11th and Fed. cirs.) 1982, U.S. Ct. Appeals (2d cir.) 1990, U.S. Supreme Ct. 1972. Atty. Aetna Life & Casualty co., Hartford, Conn., 1968-69, Office of N.H. Atty. Gen., Concord, 1969-72, asst. atty. gen., chief environ. protection, 1972-77; atty. pollution control sect. U.S. Dept. Justice, Washington, 1978-79, chief pollution control sect., 1979-80, chief environ. def. sect., 1980-82; prof. Pace U. Sch. Law, White Plains, N.Y., 1982-87, adj. prof. environ. law, 1987-92; ptnr. Sidley and Austin, N.Y.C., 1987-93, Dewey Ballantine, N.Y.C., 1993—. Bd. dirs. Environ. Law Inst., Washington, chmn., 1996-97, Hudson Valley Writers Ctr. Inc., Sleepy Hollow, N.Y. Author: Seabrook and The Nuclear Regulatory Commission, 1980; Law of Chemical Reation and Hazardous Waste, 1986; editor: Environmental Law & Practice, 1992; co-editor Environmental Law & Practice, 1992. Bd. dirs. Biddeford Pool (Maine) Improvement Assn., 1989-93; mem. adv. com. North Tarrytown (N.Y.) Conservation, 1989—. Mem. Biddeford Pool Yacht Club (treas. 1989-92, sec. 1992—), Sleepy Hollow Country Club, Abenakee Club, Mill Reef Club. Avocations: golf, tennis, sailboat racing, early music. Federal civil litigation, Environmental, Private international. Home: 157 Millard Ave Sleepy Hollow NY 10591-1412 Office: Dewey Ballantine 1301 Avenue Of The Americas New York NY 10019-6022

STEWARD, JAMES BRIAN, lawyer, pharmacist; b. Cleve., Mar. 25, 1946; s. Louis Fred and Helen Elaine Steward; m. Betty Kay Krans, Dec. 14, 1968; children: Christina Lynn, Brian Michael. BS in Pharmacy, Ferris State Coll., 1969; JD, U. Mich., 1973. Bar: Mich. 1973, U.S. Dist. Ct. (we. dist.) Mich. 1979, U.S. Cir. Ct. (6th cir.) 1980, U.S. Supreme Ct. 1986, cert.: Nat. Elder Law Found. (elder law atty.) 2001. Pharmacist Revco Pharmacies, Grand Rapids, Mich., 1969-70, Coll. Pharmacy, Ypsilanti, Mich., 1970-73; assoc. Bridges & Collins, Negaunee, Mich., 1973-80; ptnr. Steward, Peterson, Sheridan & Nancarrow, Ishpeming, Mich., 1980-94, Steward & Sheridan, Ishpeming, 1995—. Mem., chmn. Negaunee Commn. on Aging, 1974-86; mem., chmn., sec. Marquette County Commn. on Aging, 1976-82; trustee, v.p., pres. Negaunee Bd. Edn., 1984-88, 91-95; mem., chmn., adv. bd. trustee Greater Ishpeming Area Cmty. Fund, 1995—; mem. combined ad hoc com. Marquette County Commn. on Aging, 1996; bd. mem. Noguemanon Trails Network, 2000—. Mem.: Am. Soc. for Pharmacy Law, Marquette County Bar Assn. (sec.-treas.., v.p., pres.), Mich. Bar Assn. (mem. awards com. 1996—), Nat. Acad. Elder Law Attys., Wawonowin Country Club, Greater Ishpeming Cross County Ski Club, Superiorland Cross Country Ski Club, Rho Chi, Phi Delta Chi. Avocations: cross country ski racing, downhill and water skiing, running, biking, classic cars. Corporate, general, Probate (including wills, trusts), Property, real (including real estate development, water). Office: 205 S Main St Ishpeming MI 49849-2018

STEWART, CARL E. federal judge; b. Shreveport, LA, 1950; BA magna cum laude, Dillard U., 1971; JD, Loyola U., New Orleans, 1974. Atty. Piper & Brown, Shreveport, La., 1977—78; staff atty. La. Atty. Gen. Office, Shreveport, 1978—79; asst. U.S. atty. Office U.S. Atty. (we. dist.) La., Shreveport, 1979—83; prin. Stewart & Dixon, Shreveport, 1983—85; spl. asst. dist. atty., asst. prosecutor City of Shreveport, 1983—85; judge La. Dist. Ct., 1985—91, La. Ct. Appeals (2d cir.), 1991—94, U.S. Ct. Appeals (5th cir.), 1994—. Adj. instr. dept. mgmt. and mktg. La. State U., Shreveport, 1982—85. Mem. chancellor's adv. bd. La. State U., Shreveport, 1983—89, chmn., 1988—89; mem. black achievers program steering com. YMCA, 1990. Capt. JAGC other, 1974—77, Ft. Sam Houston, Tex. Mem.: La. State Bar Assn. (bench/bar liaison com.), La. Conf. Ct. Appeal Judges, Black Lawyers Assn. Shreveport-Bossier, Am. Inns of Ct. (Harry Booth/Henry Politz chpt. Shreveport), Nat. Bar Assn., Omega Psi Rhi (Rho Omega chpt.). Office: US Ct Appeals 5th Cir 300 Fannin St Ste 2299 Shreveport LA 71101-3124*

STEWART, DAVID PENTLAND, lawyer, educator; b. Milw., Dec. 24, 1943; s. James Pentland and Frederica (Stockwell) S.; children from previous marriage: Jason, Jonathan; m. Jennifer Kilmer, June 21, 1986; children: Daniel, Mary Elizabeth. AB, Princeton U., 1966; JD, MA, Yale U., 1971; LLM, N.Y.U., 1975. Bar: N.Y. 1972, U.S. Dist. Ct. (ea. and so. dists.) N.Y. 1973, U.S. Ct. Appeals (2d cir.) 1973, D.C. 1976. Assoc. Donovan, Leisure, Newton & Irvine, N.Y.C., 1971-76; atty. adviser, office of legal adviser U.S. Dept. State, Washington, 1976-82, asst. legal adviser, 1982—. Adj. prof. law Georgetown U., Washington, 1984—, Am. U., Washington, 1985-86, Johns Hopkins U. Sch. Advanced Internat. Studies, 2000—; vis. lectr. Sch. Law U. Va., 1993-96, Nat. Law Ctr., George Washington U., 1993—. Contbr. articles to profl. jours.; also editorial adv. bds. Mem. dean's adv. coun. internat. law Am. U., 1984-88. Served to maj. USAR, 1970-87. Mem. ABA, Fed. Bar Assn., Am. Soc. Internat. Law., Internat. Law Assn. (adv. coun. procedural aspects internat. law inst.). Office: US Dept State Office Legal Adviser Washington DC 20520-6310 E-mail: stewartdp@ms.state.gov.

STEWART, JAMES MALCOLM, lawyer; b. Aberdeen, Wash., May 8, 1915; s. Malcolm M. and Ethel Lucille (Hinman) S.; m. Dorothy Vera Gilardi, Sept. 16, 1945; children: Barbara Jane, Robert Bruce, William James. BA, U. Wash., 1939, JD, 1941. Bar: Wash., 1941, U.S. Dist. Ct. (we. dist.) Wash., 1948, U.S. Supreme Ct., 1998. Dep. prosecuting atty. Grays Harbor County, Wash., 1945-48; pvt. practice Montesano, Wash., 1952-99. Pres., dir. Gray Harbor Coll. Found., Aberdeen, 1955-95; bd. dirs. St. Joseph Hosp., Aberdeen, 1972-87; organizer Gray Harbor Cmty. Found., Aberdeen, 1993; scout leader Boy Scouts Am. Lt. USNR, 1942-45, PTO, admirality officer, 1945-46, lt. comdr., 1950-52, Korea, ret. Decorated 16 Battle Stars, 2 Silver Stars, Gold Star. Mem. Am. Judicature Soc., Wash. State Bar Assn. (hon.; 50 Yr. award 1991), Gray Harbor Bar Assn. (pres. 1953), Aberdeen Pioneers Assn. (pres., dir. 1948-98), Lions (Melvin Jones award 1997), Elks, Sigma Nu, Phi Delta Phi. Republican. Episcopalian. Avocations: tree farming, hiking, horseback riding, tennis. Corporate, general, Estate planning, General practice. Home: 711 3rd St N # D Montesano WA 98563-1625

STEWART, JOHN MITCHELL, lawyer; b. Coral Gables, Fla., Jan. 23, 1970; m. Brandy Stewart. BA, Coll. of William and Mary, Williamsburg, Va., 1992; JD, Nova Southeastern U., Ft. Lauderdale, Fla., 1997. Bar: Fla. 1997, U.S. Dist. Ct. (mid. dist.) Fla. 1997, U.S. Ct. Appeals (11th cir.) 1997, U.S. Dist. Ct. (so. dist.) Fla. 1998, cert.: mediator. Ptnr. Stewart & Evans, P.A., Vero Beach, Fla., 1997—. Bd. govs. young lawyers divsn. Fla. Bar, 1999—. Pro bono com. mem. Fla. Rural Legal Svcs., Inc, Ft. Pierce, Fla., 1999—2002. Mem.: ABA, Indian River County Bar Assn., Acad. of Fla. Trial Lawyers. State civil litigation, General civil litigation, Insurance. Office: Stewart & Evans PA 3355 Ocean Dr Vero Beach FL 32963 Office Fax: 772-231-9876. E-mail: jms@st-ev.com.

STEWART, JOSEPH GRIER, lawyer; b. Tuscaloosa, Ala., July 24, 1941; s. Jesse Grier and Kyle Vann (Pruett) S.; m. Linda Louise Hogue, Mar. 2, 1963; children: Joseph Grier Jr., Robert Byars, James Vann. BS, U. Ala., Tuscaloosa, 1963, LLB, 1966. Bar: Ala. 1966, U.S. Dist. Ct. (no. dist.) Ala. 1968, U.S. Dist. Ct. (middle Dist.of Ala.), 1996, U.S. Tax Court. Ptnr. Burr & Forman LLP, Birmingham, Ala., 1968—. Mem. ABA, Ala. State Bar, Birmingham Bar Assn. (chmn. com. 1989-90), Ala. Law Inst., Kiwanis, Birmingham Tip Off Club (pres. 1988-89). Methodist. Avocation: tennis. Commercial, contracts (including sales of goods; commercial financing), Corporate, general, Mergers and acquisitions. Office: Burr & Forman LLP 3100 S Trust Tower 420 20th St N Birmingham AL 35203-5200

STEWART, LAWRENCE EDWARD, lawyer; b. Cleve., Mar. 15, 1925; s. Samuel E. and Sarah (Gamble) S.; m. Barbara Joan Metcalfe, Aug. 19, 1950; children— Scott E., Brian P., Kerry T., Jennifer M., Bruce J. B.S.C. with honors, Ohio U., 1949; J.D., Case Western Res. U., 1950. Bar: Ohio 1950, U.S. Dist. Ct. (no. dist.) Ohio 1952, U.S. Ct. Appeals (6th cir.) 1957, U.S. Supreme Ct. 1966, U.S. Ct. Appeals (D.C. cir.) 1980, U.S. Ct. Appeals (3d and 11th cirs.) 1986. Assoc. Edward E. Lurie, 1950-56; sole practitioner, from 1956; past pres. Steward & DeChant Co., L.P.A., Cleve.; mem. nat. panel arbitrators Am. Arbitration Assn., 1961—90; mem. med.-legal com. Cleve. Acad. Medicine, 1963-75. Trustee Cleve. Law Libr., 1987-2000. Served with U.S. Army, 1943-46; ETO. Fellow Am. Coll. Trial Lawyers (Ohio state chmn. 1986-88), Internat. Acad. Trial Lawyers; mem. Am. Coll. Legal Medicine (assoc.-in-law), Am. Soc. Law and Medicine, Am. Judicature Soc. (bd. dirs. 1986—), Greater Cleve. Bar Assn. (trustee 1969-72, chmn. ct. mgmt. project 1973-75, pres. 1976-77), Cuyahoga County Bar Assn. (chmn. med.-legal com. 1962-63, co-chmn. com. 1963), Ohio Bar Assn., ABA (ho. of dels. 1978-80), ATLA, Am. Bd. Profl. Liability Attys., Cleve. Acad. Trial Attys. (trustee 1972-74, pres. 1977-78), Ohio Acad. Trial Lawyers (trustee 1973-75, v.p. 1976-77), Soc. of Benchers, Cleve. Athletic Club, Cleve. Yacht Club, Five Seasons Country Club, East Chop Beach Club, East Chop Tennis Club, Edgartown Golf Club. Federal civil litigation, State civil litigation, Personal injury (including property damage). Office: 1440 Standard Bldg 1370 Ontario Cleveland OH 44113 E-mail: les@stewardechant.com.

STEWART, MILTON ROY, lawyer; b. Clovis, N.Mex., Dec. 16, 1945; s. Virgil Maurice and E. Marie (Collins) S. BA, Ind. U., 1968, JD summa cum laude, 1971. Bar: Oreg. 1971, U.S. Ct. Appeals (9th cir.) 1971, U.S. Dist. Ct. (no. dist.) Oreg. 1971. Assoc. Davies, Biggs et al, Portland, Oreg., 1971-75; v.p., gen. counsel U.S. Datacorp, Portland, Oreg., 1975-77; pvt. practice Portland, Oreg., 1977-86; ptnr. Davis, Wright, Tremaine & predecessor firm, Portland, Oreg., 1987—. Past chmn. Oreg. chpt. Nat. Multisclerosis Soc., 1994—; bd. dirs. Nat. Multiple Sclerosis Soc.; past mem. bd. visitors Ind. U. Law Sch.; mem. Bd. Ind. Univ. Found. Capt. U.S. Army, 1968-78. State Farm Found. fellow, 1970; John H. Edwards fellow Ind. U. Found., 1971. Mem. Oreg. State Bar Assn., Wash. State Bar Assn., Multnomah Athletic Club, Astoria Golf and Country Club. Commercial, contracts (including sales of goods; commercial financing), Corporate, general. Office: Davis Wright Tremaine 1300 SW 5th Ave Ste 2200 Portland OR 97201-5667 E-mail: miltstewart@dwt.com.

STEWART, MURRAY BAKER, retired lawyer; b. Muskogee, Okla., May 16, 1931; s. Francis and Fannie Penelope (Murray) S.; m. Roseanna Furgason; children: Melinda, Jeffrey, Cheryl. BA, U. Okla., 1953, JD, 1955; postgrad., Georgetown U., 1958-59. Bar: Okla. 1955; CLU, ChFC. Judge adv. U.S. Army, 1955-59; ptnr. Stewart & Stewart, Tulsa and Muskogee, Okla., 1955, 62-72; asst. v.p. First Nat. Bank and Trust Co. of Tulsa, 1959-62, 77-78; mem. Hutchins, Stewart, Stewart & Elmore, Tulsa, 1972-77; atty. cons. advanced underwriting Metlife Ins. Co., N.Y.C., 1978-94; assoc. Metlife Securities, Inc., SEC Registered Investment Advisors, 1984-94; of counsel Brumley & Bishop, Tulsa, 1997-99; ret., 1999. Cons., lectr. in field. Contbr. articles to profl. and hist. jours.; prodr. texts and videos on history, investment and bus. Fellow Life Mgmt. Inst.; mem. Okla. Bar Assn., Okla. Indian Bar Assn., Sons Confederate Vets. (judge advocate Army of Trans-Mississippi 1998-2000, Kans. divsn. 2002—), Civil War Roundtable Tulsa. Estate planning, Insurance, Native American. Office: PO Box 1000 Broken Arrow OK 74013-1000

STEWART, RICHARD BURLESON, law educator; b. Cleve., Feb. 12, 1940; s. Richard Siegfreid and Ruth Dysert (Staten) Stewart; m. Alice Peck Fales, May 13, 1967; children: William, Paul, Elizabeth; m. Jane Laura Bloom, Sept. 20, 1992; children: Emily, Ian. AB, Yale U., 1961; MA (Rhodes scholar), Oxford (Eng.) U., 1963; LLB, Harvard U., 1966; D (hon.), Erasmus U., Rotterdam, 1993. Bar: DC 1968, U.S. Supreme Ct. 1971. Law clk. to Hon. Potter Stewart U.S. Supreme Ct., 1966-67; assoc. Covington & Burling, Washington, 1967-71; asst. prof. law Harvard U., 1971-75, prof., 1975-82, Byrne prof. adminstrv. law, 1982-89, assoc. dean, 1984-86; asst. atty. gen. environment and natural resources div. Dept. Justice, Washington, 1989-91; prof. law NYU Law Sch., N.Y.C., 1992-94, Emily Kempin prof. law, 1994—2002, John Edward Sexton prof. law, 2002—, univ. prof., 2002—; of counsel Sidley & Austin, 1992—. Spl. counsel U.S. Senate Watergate Com., 1974; vis. prof. U. Calif., Berkeley Law Sch., 1979—80, U. Chgo. Law Sch., 1986—87, Georgetown U., 1991—92, Europen U. Inst., 1995; dir. Ctr. Environ. and Land Use Law, Health Effects Inst.; mem. adv. bd. Environ. Def. Author: (book) The Reformation of American Administrative Law (in Chinese), 2002; author: (with P. Menell) Environmental Law and Policy, 1994; author: (with S. Breyer, C. Sunstein and M. Spitzer) Administrative Law and Regulation, 1979, Administrative Law and Regulation, 5th edit., 2002; author: (with E. Rehbinder) Integration Through Law: Environmental Protection Policy, 1985, Integration Through Law: Environmental Protection Policy, paper edit., 1987; author: (with R. Revesz) Markets v. Environment?, 1995; author: (with R. Revesz and P. Sands) Environment, the Economy, and Sustainable Development, 2001; author: (with J. Weaver) Reconstructing Climate Policy, 2003; editor (with R. Revesz): (book) Analyzing Superfund: Economics, Science, and Law, 1995. Fellow: Am. Acad. Arts and Scis.; mem.: ABA, Am. Law Inst. Office: NYU Law Sch 40 Washington Sq S New York NY 10012-1099 E-mail: stewartr@juris.law.nyu.edu.

STEWART, RICHARD WILLIAMS, lawyer; b. Harrisburg, Pa., Aug. 21, 1948; s. Alexander H. and M. Winifred (Williams) S.; m. Mary A. Simmonds, June 7, 1975; 1 child, Anne W. AB cum laude, Franklin and Marshall Coll., 1970; JD, Duke U., 1973. Bar: Pa. 1973, U.S. Dist. Ct. (mid. dist.) Pa. 1975, U.S. Tax Ct. 1984. Assoc. Stone & Sajer, New Cumberland, Pa., 1973-77; ptnr. Stone, Sajer & Stewart, New Cumberland, 1977-87, Johnson, Duffie, Stewart & Weidner, Lemoyne, Pa., 1987—. V.p. Secured Land Transfers, Inc., Camp Hill, Pa., 1985-2000, pres., 2000—; solicitor West Shore Sch. Dist., Lemoyne, Pa., 1977-93, No. York County Sch. Dist., Dillsburg, Pa., 1984—, Camp Hill Sch. Dist., 1986—, Fairview Twp., 1987-98; v.p. Cedar Cliff Abstract Agy., 1980-87. Chmn. Cumberland County Rep. Com., 1981-84; mem. Rep. State Com. Pa., 1990—. Mem. ABA, Pa. Bar Assn., Cumberland County Bar Assn., Supreme Ct. of Pa. (disciplinary bd. 1998—, vice chmn. 2003), Ctrl. Pa. Estate Planning Coun. (bd. dirs. 1983-85), Pa. Sch. Solicitors Assn. (pres. 1995), Rotary (bd. dirs. West Shore). Presbyterian. Commercial, consumer (including collections, credit), Probate (including wills, trusts). Home: 1811 Warren St New Cumberland PA 17070-1148 Office: 301 Market St Lemoyne PA 17043-1628

STEWART, SUE S. lawyer; b. Oct. 9, 1942; d. Fraizer McVale and Carolyn Eliabeth (Hunt) S.; m. Arthur L. Stern, III, July 31, 1965 (div.); m. children: Anne, Mark Alan; m. John A. Ciampa, Sept. 1, 1985 (div.); m. Stephen L. Raymond (dec.). BA, Wellesley Coll., 1964; postgrad., Harvard U. Law Sch., 1964-65; JD, Georgetown U., 1967. Bar: N.Y. 1968. Clk. to judges Juvenile Ct., Washington, 1967-68; mem. Nixon, Hargrave, Devans & Doyle (now Nixon Peabody LLP), Rochester, N.Y., 1968-74, ptnr., 1975—2001, mng. ptnr., 1998—2001, ret., 2001. Lectr. in field; trustee Found. of Monroe County (N.Y.) Bar, 1976-78. Author: Charitable Giving and Solicitation. Sec., dir. United Cmty. Chest of Greater Rochester, 1973-87, 92-2003; trustee, sec. Internat. Mus. Photography at George Eastman House, Rochester, 1974-97, 2000-03, Genesee Country Mus., Mumford, N.Y., 1976-2002; bd. dirs. Ctr. for Govtl. Rsch., 1990-97; trustee, chmn. United Neighborhood Ctr. of Greater Rochester Found., 1991-03; trustee, chmn. exec. com. Nat. Ctr. Edn. and Economy, 1997—. Mem. ABA (chmn. task force on charitable giving, exempt orgns. com. tax sect. 1981-2003), N.Y. State Bar (exec. com. tax sect. 1974-76, chmn. com. exempt orgns. 1975-76), Monroe County Bar Assn. (trustee 1974-75), BNA Portfolio, Pvt. Found. Distbns. (Athena award 2000, de Tocqueville award 2003). Health, Non-profit and tax-exempt organizations, Corporate taxation. Office: Nixon Peabody LLP PO Box 31051 Clinton Sq Rochester NY 14603-1051

STICK, MICHAEL ALAN, lawyer; b. Elizabeth City, N.C., June 2, 1954; s. David and Phyllis (Stapells) S.; m. Debra Joan Braselton, May 22, 1993. BA, Davidson Coll., 1976; JD, U. N.C., 1981. Bar: Ill. 1981, U.S. Dist. Ct. (no. dist.) Ill. 1982, U.S. Ct. Appeals (7th cir.) 1983, U.S. Ct. Appeals (8th cir.) 1986. Assoc. Jenner & Block, Chgo., 1981-84, Butler, Rubin, Newcomer, Saltarelli & Boyd, Chgo., 1984-87; ptnr. Butler, Rubin, Saltarelli & Boyd, Chgo., 1988—. Co-author: Environmental Law Handbook, 1988, Environmental Law in Illinois, 1993; mem. staff U. N.C. Law Rev., 1979-80. Chmn. spl. gifts divsn. United Way Crusade of Mercy, Chgo., 1993-94. Me. ABA, Chgo. Bar Assn. Democrat. Methodist. Avocations: travel, skiing, art. General civil litigation, Environmental. Home: 616 E Hickory St Hinsdale IL 60521-2413 Office: Butler Rubin Saltarelli & Boyd Three First Nat Pla # 1800 Chicago IL 60602

STICKNEY, JOHN MOORE, lawyer; b. Cleve., Apr. 8, 1926; s. Isaac Moore and Alicia Margaret (Burns) S.; m. Elfriede von Rebenstock, Oct. 4, 1958; children: Michaela B., Alicia J., Thomas M. AB, Western Res. U., 1948, LLB, 1951. Bar: Ohio 1952. Sole practice, Cleve., 1952-79; ptnr. Burgess, Steck, Andrews & Stickney, Cleve., 1979-88; of counsel Weston, Hurd, Fallon, Paisley & Howley, Cleve., 1988-90, sole practice, 1990—;

pres. Scranton-Averell, Inc., Cleve., 1979—. Trustee Cleve. Music Sch. Settlement, 1967—, Salzedo Sch. Harp, Cleve., 1962—, Bishop Brown Fund, Cleve., 1981—, Flats Oxbow Assn., Lake Erie Sci. & Nature Ctr., 1996—, also pres., 1970-72; co-trustee Margaret & Edwin Griffiths Trusts, Cleve., 1968—. Served with USNR, 1945-46. Mem. ABA, Ohio State Bar Assn., Cleve. Bar Assn., Hermit Club (Cleve.), Rowfant Club (Cleve.). Republican. Episcopalian. Corporate, general, Estate planning, Estate taxation.

STIEFEL, LINDA SHIELDS, lawyer; b. Syracuse, N.Y., Nov. 14, 1948; d. Harold F. and Ellen (Brown) Shields; m. John L. Stiefel, Sept. 20, 1969; 1 child, John L. BS, Tusculum Coll., 1988; JD, Akron Sch. Law, 1991. Bar: Ohio 1992, D.C. 1993, N.Y. 1998, U.S. Dist. Ct. (no. dist.) Ohio 1993, U.S. Supreme Ct. 1997. Judicial law clk. Stark County Common Pleas, Canton, Ohio, 1991-94; pvt. practice Louisville, Ohio, 1992-97, Cape Vincent, N.Y., 1998—. Trustee, mem. exec. com. Am. Handweaving Mus., 1997-2001. Mem. ABA, NOW, N.Y. State Bar Assn., Jefferson County Bar Assn. Methodist. Appellate, Family and matrimonial, Probate (including wills, trusts). Home and Office: 596 West Broadway Cape Vincent NY 13618

STIEFF, JOHN JOSEPH, legislative lawyer, educator; b. Indpls., Feb. 28, 1952; s. James Frederick and Mary Therese (Bisch) S.; m. Dusty Lee-Ann Warner, Apr. 21, 1989; stepchildren: Robert Franklin Russell, E.I. Annie Russell. BA with Distinction, Ind. U., 1973, JD, 1977. Bar: Ind. 1977. Sr. atty. Office of Bill Drafting & Rsch., Legislative Svcs. Agy., Indpls., 1977-86; dep. dir. and asst. revisor of statutes Office of Code Revision, Legislative Svcs. Agy., Indpls., 1986-92, dir. and revisor of statutes, 1992—. Adj. prof. law Ind. Univ., Bloomington, 1985-86; instr. continuing legal edn. Ind. Gen. Assembly, Indpls., 1987-96; faculty mem. Nat. Conf. State Legislatures, Denver, Colo., 1988-89; supervising atty. program on law and state govt. Ind. U. Sch. Law, Indpls., 2001—; assoc commr. Nat. Conf. Commrs. on Uniform State Laws, Chgo., 1993—. Editor in chief: (books) The Acts of Indiana, 1986—, The Indiana Code, 1993—; ast. editor, The Indiana Code, 1986-92. Poetry instr. Gage Inst. for Gifted Children, Indpls., 1982-86. Named Hoosier Scholar, Indiana Commn. for Higher Edn., 1970-73. Mem. Writer's Ctr. of Indpls. (founding mem.), Ind. U. Varsity Club. Avocations: travel, photgraphy, writing poetry, Am. blues music. Home: 7707 Windy Hill Way Indianapolis IN 46239-8749 Office: Legislative Svcs Agy Office Code Revision 1 N Capitol Ave Ste 420 Indianapolis IN 46204-2097

STIEGEL, MICHAEL A. lawyer; b. Greenfield, Mass., Sept. 15, 1946; s. Sid James and Ida Eleanor (Solomon) S.; m. Marsha Palmer, Sept. 10, 1983. BA, U. Ariz., 1968; JD cum laude, Loyola U., Chgo., 1971. Bar: Ill. 1971, U.S. Dist. Ct. Ill. 1971, U.S. Ct. Appeals (7th cir.) 1971, U.S. Ct. Appeals (6th cir.) 1975, U.S. Supreme Ct. 1975, Wis. 1985, Fla. 1987. Law clk. to fed. judge U.S. Dist. Ct. Ill., Chgo., 1971-72; assoc. Arnstein & Lehr, Chgo., 1972-78, ptnr., 1978-82, equity ptnr., 1982-85, dir. trial dept., 1985-87, mng. ptnr., 1985-98. Vice chmn. exec. com., 1987-98; adj. prof. law Northwestern U.; faculty Nat. Inst. Trial Advocacy Equity, La. State U. Trial Advocacy Program, 1995. Contbr. articles to profl. jours. Mem. fin. com. Lynn Martin for Senate, Ill., 1989-90. Recipient Cert. of Appreciation, Nat. Safety Coun., Chgo., 1987, Cert. of Distinction, Chgo. Bar Assn., 1975. Mem. ABA (sects. on litigation, business law, and labor and employment law, vice chmn. trial evidence com. litigation sect. 1990-91, co-chmn. trial evidence com. 1991-95, lawyers conf. standards for admissibility of technologically sophisticated evidence com., co-chair nat. CLE programs 1995-97, coun. 1997-2000, budget officer 2000-02, revenue officer, 2002—, litigation sect. advisor, uniform laws commn., drafting com. on Model Punitive Damages Act), Ill. Bar Assn., Fla. Bar Assn., Wis. Bar Assn., Chgo. Club, 410 Club, Economic Club Chgo., East Bank Club. Avocations: sports, reading, horse racing syndications. General civil litigation, Labor (including EEOC, Fair Labor Standards Act, labor-management relations, NLRB, OSHA), Product liability. Office: Michael Best & Friedrich 401 N Michigan Ave Ste 1900 Chicago IL 60601-1635

STIEGER, WERNER, lawyer; b. St. Gallen, Switzerland, Nov. 14, 1946; JD, U. of Zurich. Bar: High Ct. of the Canton of Zurich 1984, Canton of Nidwalden 1986, Canton of St. Gallen 1987, Canton of Aargau 1988, Canton of Berne 1989, Canton of Schwyz 1989, Canton of Lucerne 1991, Canton of Basle-City 1992, Canton of Zug 1997, Canton of Thurgau 1998. Ptnr. Gmür Gehrig Stieger Bachofner Schaetzle, Zurich, Switzerland, 1986—93, Homburger, Zurich, Switzerland, 1994—. Lectr. for postgraduate program Fed. Tech. U., Zurich, Switzerland, 1998—; lectr. for postgrad, program U. of Zurich, Zurich, Switzerland. Recipient Prof. Walther Hug award (Dissertation), Faculty U. Zurich, 2002. Mem.: Licensing Execs. Soc., Assn. Internat. pour la Protection de la Propriété Intellectuelle, Inst. for the Protection of Comml. Rights (bd. mem. 2001), Swiss Forum for Comm. Law (v.p. 2001). Intellectual property, Federal civil litigation, Arbitration. Office: Homburger Rechtsanwälte Weinbergstr 56/58 PO Box 338 Zürich 8035 Switzerland Office Fax: +41-43-222 1500.

STIEHL, WILLIAM D. federal judge; b. 1925; m. Celeste M. Sullivan; children: William D., Susan M. Student, U. N.C., 1943-45; LLB, St. Louis U., 1949. Pvt. practice, 1952-78; ptnrs. Stiehl & Hess, 1978-81; ptnr. Stiehl & Stiehl, 1982-86; judge, former chief judge U.S. Dist. Court, (so. dist.) Ill., East Saint Louis, 1986—96, sr. judge, 1996—. Spl. asst. atty. gen. State of Ill., 1970-73. Mem. bd. Belleville Twp. High Sch. and Jr. Coll., 1949-50, 54-56, pres., 1956-57, Clair County, Ill., county civil atty., 1956-60. Mem. Ill. State Bar Assn., St. Clair County Bar Assn. Office: US Dist Ct 750 Missouri Ave East Saint Louis IL 62201-2954*

STIER, CHARLES HERMAN, JR., lawyer; b. Dayton, Ohio, Nov. 26, 1950; s. Charles Herman and betty Jane Stier; m. Debra Jean Delk, Jan. 10, 1981; children: Adam C., Christine A., Eric D. BA, Wright State U., 1973; JD, U. Dayton, 1977, MA, 1985. Bar: Ohio 1977, U.S. Dist. Ct. Ohio, U.S. Tax Ct. 1980. Assoc. Stier Law Office, Xenia, Ohio, 1977-85, Hammond & Stier, Beavercreek, Ohio, 1985—; ptnr. Hammond, Stier & Stadnicar, Beavercreek, 1987—. Magistrate Greene County Juvenile Ct., Xenia, 1980-90; spl. asst. pros. Greene County Pros. Office, Xenia, 1984-98. Cmty. bd. mem. Med. Health Svcs., Dayton, 1982-85; bd. dirs. Greene County YMCA, 1983—, pres. bd. dirs., 1998; bd. dirs. Beavercreek Soccer Assn., 1994—; mem. exec. com. Greene County Dem. Party, 1980-82; bd. dirs. Miami Valley Juvenile Rehab. Ctr. Mem. Ohio State Bar Assn., Green County Bar Assn. (chmn. 1997-98). Avocations: coaching youth sports, running. Estate planning, Probate (including wills, trusts), Property, real (including real estate development, water). Home: 1971 N Springcrest Ct Beavercreek OH 45432-1882 Office: Hammond stier & Stadnicar 3836 Dayton Xenia Rd Beavercreek OH 45432-2845 E-mail: hsslaw@donet.com.

STILLER, SHALE DAVID, lawyer, educator; b. Rochester, N.Y., Feb. 23, 1935; s. Maurice Aaron and Dorothy (Salitan) S.; m. Ellen M. Heller; children: Lewis B., Michael J., Kenneth R.; stepchildren: William Heller, Lawrence Heller. BA, Hamilton Coll., 1954; LL.B., Yale U., 1957; M.L.A., Johns Hopkins U., 1977. Bar: Md. 1957. Ptnr. Piper & Marbury, Balt., 1992—. Lectr. U. Md. Law Sch., 1963—. Contbr. articles to profl. jours. Trustee Johns Hopkins U., Assn. Jewish Charities, Peabody Inst., Weinberg Found.; trustee, vice chmn. Johns Hopkins Medicine; mem. adv. bd. Tax Mgmt., 1972-93; chmn. Jud. Nominating Commn., Balt., 1979-83; officer, bd. dirs. Park Sch., 1973-79, pres., 1982-86; pres. Jewish Family Agy., 1972-74. Mem. ABA, Am. Law Inst., Am. Coll. Tax Counsel, Am. Coll. Trust and Estate Counsel, Order of Coif. Clubs: 14 W Hamilton St (Balt.). Democrat. Jewish. General civil litigation, Mergers and acquisitions, Taxation, general. Home: 807 St Georges Rd Baltimore MD 21210-1408 Office: Piper Marbury Rudnick & Wolfe 6225 Smith Ave Baltimore MD 21209-3600

STILLMAN, ELINOR HADLEY, retired lawyer; b. Kansas City, Mo., Oct. 12, 1938; d. Hugh Gordon and Freda (Brooks) Hadley; m. Richard C. Stillman, June 25, 1965 (div. Apr. 1975). BA, U. Kans., 1960; MA, Yale U., 1961; JD, George Washington U., 1972. Bar: D.C. 1973, U.S. Ct. Appeals (10th cir.) 1975, U.S. Ct. Appeals (9th cir.) 1976, U.S. Ct. Appeals (2d cir.) 1976, U.S. Ct. Appeals (5th cir.) 1983, U.S. Ct. Appeals (4th cir.) 1985, U.S. Supreme Ct. 1976. Lectr. in English CUNY, 1963-65; asst. editor Stanford (Calif.) U. Press., 1967-69; law clk. to judge U.S. Dist. Ct. D.C., Washington, 1972-73; appellate atty. NLRB, Washington, 1973-78; asst. to solicitor gen. U.S. Dept. Justice, Washington, 1978-82; supr. appellate atty. NLRB, Washington, 1982-86, chief counsel to mem. bd., 1986-88, 94-00, chief counsel to chmn. bd., 1988-94; ret., 2000. Mem.: D.C. Bar Assn., Order of Coif, Phi Beta Kappa. Democrat.

STINCHFIELD, JOHN EDWARD, lawyer; b. Alameda, Calif., July 31, 1947; s. John Eastwood and Pauline Finch (Acker) S.; m. Niall O'Melia, May 15, 1976; children: John Ryan, Noel O'Neil. BA, Wesleyan U., Middletown, Conn., 1969; JD, U. Calif., 1973. Bar: Calif. 1974, D.C. 1980. Atty. advisor Divsn. Corp. Fin. U.S. SEC, 1974-76, Divsn. Investment Mgmt. SEC, 1976-77; atty., advisor Bur. of Competition U.S. FTC, 1977-79; corp. counsel, sec. The Donohoe Cos., Inc., Washington, 1979—, also bd. dirs. Bd. dirs. Fed. Ctr. Plaza Corp. Bd. dirs. Christmas in April of Washington, D.C., Inc. Mem. ABA, D.C. Bar Assn., State Bar Calif., Columbia Country Club (Chevy Chase, Md.), Tenley Sport and Health Club. Construction, Pension, profit-sharing, and employee benefits, Property, real (including real estate development, water). E-mail: johns@donohoe.com.

STINE, J(AMES) LARRY, lawyer; b. Birmingham, Ala., Dec. 18, 1950; s. James O. and Helen M. Stine; m. Kathryn Stokely, June 10, 1972; children: Kathryn Anne DeLoach, Laura Elizabeth Stine, Amanda Leigh Franklin. BS cum laude, U. Ga., 1972, JD cum laude, 1975. Bar: Ga., U.S. Dist. Ct. (no. dist.) Ga. 1975, U.S. Dist. Ct. (mid. dist.) Ga. 1997, U.S. Ct. Appeals (11th cir.) 1992, U.S. Ct. Appeals (6th cir.) 1998, U.S. Dist. Ct. (ea. and we. dists.) Ark. 1999. Trial atty. U.S. Dept. of Labor, Atlanta, 1975-82, regional counsel, 1982-89; atty. Thompson, Mann & Hudson, Atlanta, 1989-92; of counsel Wimberly & Lawson, Atlanta, 1992-95; prin. Wimberly Lawson Steckel, Atlanta, 1995—. Bd. dirs. King's Bridge, Atlanta, 1992—2001. Author: Wage and Hour Law: Compliance and Practice, 1995, Family and Medial Leave Act, 2001. Mem. Decatur Kiwanis (pres. 1988-89). Labor (including EEOC, Fair Labor Standards Act, labor-management relations, NLRB, OSHA). Office: Wimberly Lawson & Steckel Ste #400 3400 Peachtree Rd NE Atlanta GA 30326-1107 E-mail: jls@wimlaw.com.

STINNETT, MARK ALLAN, lawyer; b. Jackson, Miss., Sept. 15, 1955; s. Allan J. and Joan (Mouser) S.; m. Carol Fowler, Sept. 5, 1992; children: Michelle, Michael. BA in Polit. Sci. with honors, Tex. Tech U., 1977; JD with honors, U. Tex., 1980. Bar: Tex. 1980, U.S. Dist. Ct. (no. and ea. dists.) Tex. 1981, U.S. Ct. Appeals (5th cir.) 1993. Founding ptnr., mng. ptnr. Stinnett Thiebaud & Remington L.L.P., Dallas, 2000—; shareholder Cowles & Thompson, Dallas, 1986—2000. Mem. Philmont Ranch com. Boy Scouts Am. Mem. ABA, Am. Bd. Trial Advocates, Am. Inns of Ct., Am. Coll. Legal Medicine, Am. Health Lawyers Assn., State Bar of Tex., Dallas Bar Assn., Tex. Assn. Def. Counsel, Dallas Assn. Def. Counsel, Def. Rsch. Inst., Inns Ct. (barrister Dallas chpt. 1988-91), Tex. Ctr. Legal Ethics and Professionalism, Nat. Eagle Scout Assn., Philmont Staff Assn. (pres. 1994-98). Avocations: backpacking, softball, military history. General civil litigation, Personal injury (including property damage), Health. Home: 5541 Mallard Trce Frisco TX 75034-5058 Office: Stinnett Thiebaud & Remington LLP 1445 Ross Ave Ste 4800 Dallas TX 75202-2702 E-mail: mstinnett@strlaw.net.

STINNETT, TERRANCE LLOYD, lawyer; b. Oakland, Calif., July 22, 1940; s. Lloyd Monroe and Gertrude (Hyman) S. BS, Stanford U., 1962; JD magna cum laude, U. Santa Clara, 1969. Bar: Calif. 1970, U.S. Dist. Ct. (no. dist.) Calif. 1970, U.S. Dist. Ct. (ea. ctrl. and so. dists) Calif. 1975, U.S. Ct. Appeals (9th cir.) 1970, U.S. Supreme Ct. 1975. Law clk. to judge Calif. Ct. Appeals, San Francisco, 1969-70; assoc. Hyman, Rhodes & Aylward, Fremont, Calif., 1970-71, Glicksberg, Kushner & Goldberg, San Francisco, 1972-77; mem. Goldberg, Stinnett Meyers & Davis, San Francisco, 1977—. Bd. dirs. Fremont Bancorp, Fremont Bank, vice-chmn. bd., 1998-2000. Mem. ABA, Bar Assn. San Francisco (chmn. bench bar liaison com. for U.S. Bankruptcy Ct., No. Dist. of Calif. 1997). Republican. Roman Catholic. Bankruptcy. Home: 131 Alamo Hills Ct Alamo CA 94507-2243 Office: Goldberg Stinnett Meyers & Davis 44 Montgomery St Ste 2900 San Francisco CA 94104-4803 E-mail: tstinnett@gsmdlaw.com .

STIRLING, CLARK TILLMAN, lawyer; b. Washington, July 4, 1956; s. Edwin Tillman and Genevieve (Ruffner) S.; m. Linda Poumirau, May 30, 1986; children: Stephen Tillman, Grace Elizabeth. BS, Vanderbilt U., 1979; JD, George Washington U., 1983. Bar: D.C. 1984, Alaska 1984, Calif. 1987. Clk. to Judge Cutler, State of Alaska, Palmer, 1983-84, asst. dist. atty. Anchorage, 1984-87; assoc. Archbald & Spray, Santa Barbara, Calif., 1987-91; ptnr. Law Offices Kristofer Kallman, Santa Barbara, 1991-95; pvt. practice, Santa Barbara, 1996—2000; assoc. Snyder & Strozier, 2000; ptnr. Nye, Peabody & Stirling, LLP, Santa Barbara, 2001—. Bd. dirs. Childrens Creative Project, Santa Barbara, 1992-95, Wilderness Youth Project, 1999—; pres. bd. dirs. Transition House, Santa Barbara, 1993—; mem. centennial com. All Sts.-By-Sea, Santa Barbara, 1996—. Mem. Calif. Bar Assn., Alaska Bar Assn., D.C. Bar Assn., Santa Barbara County Bar Assn. (co-chmn. litigation sect. 1996-97, conf. of dels. 1998—), Santa Barbara Inns Ct., Soc. of Cincinnati. Republican. Avocations: writing, reading, tennis. Office: 33 W Mission St Ste 201 Santa Barbara CA 93101

STITH, LAURA DENVIR, state supreme court justice; b. St. Louis, Oct. 30, 1953; BA magna cum laude, Tufts U., 1975; JD magna cum laude, Georgetown U., 1978. Law clk. to Hon. Robert E. Seiler, Mo. Supreme Ct., 1978—79; assoc. Shook, Hardy & Bacon, Kansas City, Mo., 1979—84, ptnr., 1984—94; judge. Mo. Ct. Appeals (we. dist.), 1994—2001; judge Supreme Ct. Mo., 2001—. Office: PO Box 150 Jefferson City MO 65102

STOCK, MARGARET DEBORAH, lawyer; b. Boston, 1961; m. Neil Thomas O'Donnell, June 6, 1992. BA, Harvard-Radcliffe U., 1985; JD, Harvard U., 1992. Bar: Alaska 1993, U.S. Dist. Ct. Alaska 1993, U.S. Ct. Appeals (9th cir.) 1996. Assoc. Atkinson Conway & Gagnon, Anchorage, 1992-98; pvt. practice, Stock & Moeller, LLC, Anchorage, 1998—; asst. prof. Dept. Law U.S.M.A., West Point, NY. Editor-in-chief Harvard Jour. Law and Pub. Policy, 1991-92. Maj. USAR, 1982—. Mem. ABA, Alaska Bar Assn. (chair immigration law sect. 1995-96), Anchorage Bar Assn. (pres. young lawyers sect. 1995-96), Am. Immigration Lawyers Assn., Federalist Soc. General civil litigation, Immigration, naturalization, and customs, Labor (including EEOC, Fair Labor Standards Act, labor-management relations, NLRB, OSHA). Office: Dept Law US Military Acad West Point NY 10996 E-mail: em7396@usma.edu.

STOCK, STUART CHASE, lawyer; b. St. Louis, July 19, 1946; s. Sheldon Harry and Muriel Cecile (Lovejoy) S.; m. Judith Ann Stewart, July 18, 1970; 1 child, Frederick Chase. BS with highest distinction, Purdue U., 1968; JD magna cum laude, Harvard U., 1971. Bar: Mo. 1971, Ind. 1973, D.C. 1974. Law clk. to Chief Judge Henry J. Friendly U.S. Ct. Appeals 2d cir., New York, 1971-72; law clk. to Justice Thurgood Marshall U.S. Supreme Ct., Washington, 1972-73; assoc. Covington & Burling, Washington, 1974-78, ptnr., 1978—. Lectr. law U. Va., Charlottesville, 1987-90. Mem. Am. Law Inst. Antitrust, Banking, Mergers and acquisitions. Office: Covington & Burling PO Box 7566 1201 Pennsylvania Ave NW Washington DC 20044

STOCK, THOMAS JOHN, lawyer; b. Rockville Centre, NY, Dec. 29, 1950; s. Henry J. and Rita Kerr (Hughes) S.; m. Lea M. Bartel, Jan. 15, 1972; children: Thomas H., Martin W., Katherine L. BA, Adelphi U., 1972; JD, St. John's U., 1978. Bar: NY 1979, US Dist. Ct. (so. and ea. dists.) NY 1979, US Ct. Appeals 1985. Assoc. Flynn, Gibbons & Dowd, NYC, 1977-80, Gervais & Decicco, Garden City, NY, 1980-83; ptnr. Stock & Osborn, Mineola, NY, 1983—94, Stock & Carr, Mineola, 1994—. Sgt. USMCR, 1972-77. Mem. NY State Bar Assn., Assn. Trial Lawyers Am., NY State Trial Lawyers Assn., Nassau-Suffolk Trial Lawyers Assn., St. John's U. Alumni Assn., K.C. Democrat. Roman Catholic. Avocation: antique automobiles. Insurance, Personal injury (including property damage). Home: 6 Dalton Ln East Northport NY 11731-3909 Office: Stock & Carr 88 2nd St Mineola NY 11501-3035

STOCKARD, JAMES ALFRED, lawyer; b. Lake Dallas, Tex., Aug. 4, 1935; s. Clifford Raymond and Thelma Gladys (Gotcher) S.; m. Mary Sue Hogan, Aug. 17, 1956; children— Bruce Anthony, James Alfred, Paul Andrew. BA with honors, N. Tex. State U., Denton, 1956; LLB magna cum laude, So. Methodist U., 1959. Bar: Tex. 1959. Pvt. practice, Dallas, 1959-62; with Employers Casualty Co., Dallas, 1962-65; v.p. Southland Life Ins. Co., Dallas, 1965-77, sr. v.p., gen. counsel, dir., 1977-87; exec. v.p., gen. counsel, sec. Southland Fin. Corp., Dallas, 1978-87; dir. Tex. Life, Accident, Health and Hosp. Svc. Ins. Guaranty Assn., 1978-84, chmn. bd., 1980-84; ptnr. Butler & Binion, Dallas, 1987-2000; pvt. practice Dallas, 2000—; gen. counsel Employers Gen. Ins. Group, Inc., 1994—. Bd. dirs. Ins. Systems Am., Atlanta; pres., bd. dirs. Dallas County Mcpl. Utility Dist. 1, Irving, Tex.; gen. counsel, bd. dirs. Lone Star Life Ins. Co., 1988-99; counsel Employers General Ins. Group, 1992—. Contbr. legal jours. Mem. exec. com., precinct chmn. Dallas County Dem. Com., 1971. Mem. Am., Tex., Dallas Bar Assn., Assn. Life Ins. Counsel. Methodist. Home: 3607 Asbury St Dallas TX 75205-1848 Office: 7501 Inwood Rd Dallas TX 75209-4019 E-mail: jastockard@sbcglobal.net.

STOCKBURGER, JEAN DAWSON, lawyer; b. Scottsboro, Ala., Feb. 4, 1936; d. Joseph Mathis Scott and Mary Frances (Alley) Dawson; m. John Calvin Stockburger, Mar. 23, 1963; children: John Scott, Mary Staci, Christopher Sean. Student, Gulf Park Coll., 1954-55; BA, Auburn U., 1958; M in Social Work, Tulane U., 1962; JD, U. Ark., Little Rock, 1979. Bar: Ark. 1979, U.S. Dist. Ct. (ea. dist.) Ark. 1980. Assoc. Mitchell, Williams, Selig, Gates & Woodyard and predecessor, Little Rock, 1979-85, ptnr., 1985-94, of counsel, 1994—. Bd. dirs., sec. Cen. Ark. Estate Coun., Little Rock, 1984-85, 2d v.p., 1985-86, pres. 1987-88. Assoc. editor U. Ark. Law Rev., 1978-79. Bd. dirs. Little Rock Cmty. Mental Health Ctr., 1994—, v.p., 1996—99, pres., 1999—2001; bd. dirs. Sr. Citizens Activities Today, Little Rock, 1983—88, treas., 1986—88; bd. dirs. Vol. Orgn. for Ctrl. Ark. Legal Svcs., 1986—91, sec., 1987—88, chmn., 1989—91, H.I.R.E. Inc., 1994—2001. Mem. ABA, Ark. Bar Assn. (chmn. probate and trust law sect. 1986-88), Pulaski County Bar Assn. (bd. dirs. 1994-97), Ark. Bar Found., Am. Coll. Trust and Estate Counsel. Democrat. Methodist. Estate planning, Probate (including wills, trusts). Office: Mitchell Williams Selig Gates & Woodyard 425 W Capitol Ave Ste 1800 Little Rock AR 72201-3525

STOCKMAR, TED P. lawyer; b. Denver, May 9, 1921; s. Theodore Paul and Elda Marie (Robinson) S.; m. Suzanne Louise Harl, Feb. 14, 1947; children: Stephen Harl, John Brian, Anne Baldwin Stockmar Upton BS in Petroleum Engring., Colo. Sch. Mines, Golden, 1943; LLB, U. Denver, 1948; DEng (hon.), Colo. Sch. of Mines, Golden, 1988. Bar: Colo. 1948. Ptnr. Holme Roberts & Owen Denver, 1951-91; of counsel, 1991—. Co-author: Law of Federal Oil and Gas Leases 1964, 1984; also articles. Trustee Colo. Sch. Mines, Golden, 1948-82, bd. pres., 1970-80. 1st lt. USAF, 1943-45 Mem. Denver Bar Assn., Colo. Bar Assn., Rocky Mountain Oil and Gas Assn. (dir., exec. com. 1982-93, chmn. legal com. 1986-88), Denver Country Club, Univ. Club, Law Club. Republican. Avocations: bird watching, reading, gardening. Banking, Corporate, general, Natural resources. Home: 2552 E Alameda Ave Apt 8 Denver CO 80209-3324 Office: Holme Roberts & Owen LLP 1700 Lincoln St Ste 4100 Denver CO 80203-4541

STOCKMEYER, NORMAN OTTO, law educator, consultant; b. Detroit, May 24, 1938; s. Norman O. and Lillian R. (Hitchman) S.; m. Marcia E. Rudman, Oct. 1, 1966; children: Claire, Kathleen, Mary Frances. AB, Obelin Coll., 1960; JD, U. Mich., 1963. Bar: MIch. 1963, U.S. Ct. Appeals (6th cir.) 1964, U.S. Supreme Ct. 1974. Legis. grad. fellow Mich. State U., 1963; legal counsel Senate Judiciary Com., Mich. Legislature, 1964; law clk. Mich. Ct. Appeals, 1965, commr., 1966-68, rsch. dir., 1969-76; assoc. prof. law Thomas M. Cooley Law Sch., 1977-78, prof., 1978—. Vis. prof. Mercer U. Sch. Law, 1986, Calif. Western Sch. Law, 1993; lectr. Mich. Judicial Inst., 1995. Editor Mich. Law of Damages, 1989; contbr. numerous articles to state and nat. legal jours. Named one of 88 Greats, Lansing State Jour., 1988. Fellow Am. Bar Found. (life); mem. ABA (chmn. Mich. membership 1972-73, ho. of dels. 1988-92, editl. bd. Compleat Lawyer 1990-99), Nat. Conf. Bar Founds. (trustee 1985-90, sec. 1988-89), Mich. State Bar Found. (pres. 1982-85, trustee 1971-92), State Bar Mich. (chmn. Young Lawyers sect. 1971-72, rep. assembly 1972-79, bd. commrs. 1985-93), Ingham County Bar Assn. (bd. dirs. 1981-85), Mich. Assn. Professions (bd. dirs. 1981-84, Profl. of Yr. 1988), Thomas M. Cooley Legal Authors Soc. (pres. 1982-83), Scribes (bd. dirs. 1994—), Delta Theta Phi (dean Christiancy Senate 1962, Outstanding Prof. 1984). Address: PO Box 13038 Lansing MI 48901-3038 E-mail: stockmen@cooley.edu.

STOCKTON, RALPH MADISON, JR., lawyer; b. Winston-Salem, N.C., June 22, 1927; s. Ralph Madison and Margaret (Thompson) S.; m. Frances Bowles, July 15, 1950 (dec. Apr. 27, 1994); children: Mary Ellen Sartin, Ralph Madison III, David Anderson, James Alexander; m. Margaret Norfleet, Mar. 3, 1995. BS, U. N.C., 1948, LL.B. cum laude, 1950; LL.D. (hon.), Winston-Salem U., 1983. Bar: N.C. 1950. Assoc. firm Dwight, Royal, Harris Koeger & Caskey, Washington, 1950-51; with Petree Stockton, Winston-Salem, Charlotte, N.C. and Raleigh, N.C., 1951—, ptnr., 1956—, chmn. exec. com., 1980—. Permanent mem. jud. conf. U.S. Ct. Appeals (4th cir.), 1958—. Trustee Winston-Salem State U., 1958-84, vice chmn., 1973-84; trustee Forsyth County Legal Aid Soc., 1966-70, pres., 1969; trustee Meth. Children's Home, 1966-84, chmn. exec. com., 1969-75, pres. bd. trustees, 1975-84; bd. mgrs. Meth. Home, Charlotte, N.C., 1967-70; bd. dirs. Winston-Salem Found., 1979-86, chmn. bd., 1985-86; mem. Leadership Winston-Salem, 1984-85, alumni council, 1987-88; co-chmn. N.C. Legis. Com. on Evidence and Comparative Negligence, 1980-82; mem. Gov.'s Jud. Nominating Com., 1982-85; chmn. adminstrv. bd. local United Meth. Ch., 1984-86. Mem. ABA (Ho. of Dels. 1986-91, standing com. fed. judiciary 1989-92), N.C. Bar Assn. (bd. govs. 1957-60, chmn. comml. banking and bus. law com. 1958-60, chmn. appellate rules study com. 1973-75, pres. 1976-77, named to Hall of Fame 1993), Forsyth County Bar Assn. (pres. 1965-66), Am. Coll. Trial Lawyers (state chmn. 1984-86), regent 1987-91), Nat. Conf. Bar Presidents, Fellows of Am. Bar Found., Supreme Ct. Hist. Soc. (state chmn. 1989-91, cir. rep. nat. membership 1991-93), Law Alumni Assn. U. N.C. (pres. 1964, dir. gen. 1970-73, Disting. Alumni award 1994), Order of Coif, Phi Delta Phi. Lodges: Rotary (pres. Winston-Salem 1965-66). Democrat. Methodist. Federal civil litigation, State civil litigation, Corporate, general. Office: Kilpatrick Stockton LLP 1001 W Fourth St Winston Salem NC 27101

STOEBUCK, WILLIAM BREES, law educator; b. Wichita, Kans., Mar. 18, 1929; s. William Douglas and Donice Beth (Brees) S.; m. Mary Virginia

Fields, Dec. 24, 1951; children: Elizabeth, Catherine, Caroline. BA, Wichita State U., 1951; MA, Ind. U., 1953; JD, U. Wash., 1959; SJD, Harvard U., 1973. Bar: Wash. 1959, U.S. Supreme Ct. 1967. Pvt. practice, Seattle, 1959-64; asst. prof. law U. Denver, 1964-67; assoc. prof. U. Wash., Seattle, 1967-70, prof., 1970-95, Judson Falknor prof., 1995—; of counsel Karr, Tuttle, Campbell, Seattle, 1988—. Author: Washington Real Estate: Property Law, 1995, Washington Real Estate: Transactions, 1995, Basic Property Law, 1989, Law of Property, 1984, 3d edit., 2000, Nontrespassory Takings, 1977, Contemporary Property, 1996, 2d edit., 2002; contbr. articles to profl. jours. Bd. dirs. Cascade Symphony Orch., 1978-83, Forest Park Libr., 1975-80. 1st lt. USAF, 1951-56. Mem. Am. Coll. Real Estate Lawyers, Am. Coll. Mortgage Attys., Wash. State Bar Assn., Assn. Am. Law Schs., Order of Coif, Seattle Yacht Club. Home: 3515 NE 158th Pl Lk Forest Park WA 98155-6649 Office: U Wash Law Sch Seattle WA 98195 E-mail: stoebuck@u.washington.edu.

STOHR, DONALD J. federal judge; b. Sedalia, Mo., Mar. 9, 1934; s. Julius Leo and Margaret Elizabeth (McGaw) Stohr; m. Mary Ann Kuhlman, July 31, 1957; 5 children. BS, St. Louis U., 1956, JD, 1958. Bar: Mo. 1958, U.S. Dist. Ct. (ea. dist.) Mo. 1958, U.S. Ct. Appeals (8th cir.) 1966, U.S. Supreme Ct. 1969. Assoc. Hocker Goodwin & MacGreevy, St. Louis, 1958-63, 66-69; asst. counselor St. Louis County, 1963-65, counselor, 1965-66; U.S. atty. Ea. Dist. Mo., St. Louis, 1973-76; ptnr. Thompson & Mitchell, St. Louis, 1969-73, 76-92; judge U.S. Dist. Ct. (ea. dist.) Mo., St. Louis, 1992—. Mem. ABA, Mo. Bar Assn., Am. Judicature Soc., St. Louis Met. Bar Assn. Office: 111 S 10th St Rm 16 182 Saint Louis MO 63102

STOKES, ARCH, lawyer, writer; b. Atlanta, Sept. 2, 1946; s. Mack B. and Rose Stokes; m. Maggie Mead; children: Jennifer Jean, Austin Christopher, Susannah Rose, Travis, Emmarose. BA, Emory U., 1967, JD, 1970. Bar: Ga. 1970, U.S. Dist. Ct. (no. dist.) Ga. 1970, U.S. Ct. Appeals (5th cir.) Ga. 1970, U.S. Ct. Mil. Appeals 1971, U.S. Ct. Appeals (9th cir.) Ga. 1980, (2d cir.) Ga. 1990, U.S. Supreme Ct. 1981, U.S. Dist. Ct. (no. dist.) Calif. 1981, U.S. Ct. Appeals (11th cir.) Calif. 1982, U.S. Ct. Appeals (7th cir.) Calif. 1986, U.S. Ct. Appeals (1st cir.) Calif. 1992, U.S. Ct. Appeals (8th cir.) Calif. 1991, U.S. Dist. Ct. (no. dist.) N.Y. 1991, U.S. Dist. Ct. (ea. dist.) Mich. 1986. Ptnr. Stokes Lazarus & Carmichael, Atlanta, 1972-92, Stokes & Murphy, Atlanta, 1992—, San Diego, Pitts., 1992—, Las Vegas, Ithaca, NY, 2001—. Author: The Wage & Hour Handbook, 1978, rev. edit., 2000, The Equal Employment Opportunity Handbook, 1979, The Collective Bargaining Handbook, 1981. Founding mem. adv. bd. William F. Harrah Hotel Coll., U. Nev., Las Vegas, also vis. spkr.; vis. spkr. Cornell U., Johnson and Wales U., U. Houston, Ga. State U. Recipient Hal Holbrook award Internat. Platform Assn., 1990. Mem. ABA, ATLA, Union Internat. des Avocats, Internat. Soc. Hospitality Cons., Confrérie de la Chaîne des Rôtisseurs, Am. Hotel and Lodging. General civil litigation, Labor (including EEOC, Fair Labor Standards Act, labor-management relations, NLRB, OSHA), Labor (including EEOC, Fair Labor Standards Act, labor-management relations, NLRB, OSHA). Office: Stokes & Murphy PC 3593 Hemphill St College Park GA 30337-0468 E-mail: astokes@stokesmurphy.com.

STOKES, JAMES SEWELL, lawyer; b. Englewood, N.J., Jan. 24, 1944; s. James Sewell III and Doris Mackey (Smith) S.; m. Esther Moger, Aug. 19, 1967; children: Jessica Neale, Elizabeth Sewell BA, Davidson (N.C.) Coll., 1966; LLB, Yale U., 1969. Bar: Ga. 1969. Asst. to gen. counsel Office Gen. Counsel of the Army, Washington, 1969-72; assoc. Alston, Miller & Gaines, Atlanta, 1972-77; ptnr. Alston & Bird (previously Alston, Miller & Gaines), Atlanta, 1977—, chmn. environ. group, 1998—2001, chmn. bus. devel. com., 1983-85, 93-94, 96—; mem. ptnr.'s com. Alston & Bird, Atlanta, 1995-98; chmn., 1998. Speaker on environ. matters to various seminars and meetings; mem. Gov.'s Environ. Adv. Coun., 1991—, chmn., 1997-99; chmn. Gov.'s Conf. on Pollution Prevention and the Environment, 1997. Contbr. articles to profl. jours. Mem. Metro Atlanta Chamber Clean Water Iniative, 2000, chair, Metro Atlanta Chamber Water Com. 2002—; Co-chmn. Spotlight on Ga. Artists V, 1986; mem. City of Atlanta Zoning Rev. Bd., 1978-85, chmn., 1984-85; bd. dirs. Brookwood Hills Civic Assn., 1975-77, pres., 1977; bd. dirs. Nexus Contemporary Arts Ctr., Atlanta, 1987-92, vice chmn. capital campaign, 1989, chmn. nominating com., 1988, chmn. fundraising com., 1987-88; bd. dirs. Butler St. YMCA N.W. br., 1973-75, Dynamo Swim Club, 1988-91, Arts Festival Atlanta, 1994-98; trustee Inst. Continuing Legal Edn., Athens, 1980-81, Trinity Sch., Atlanta, 1988, 97—, Charles Loridans Found., 1994—; mem. session Trinity Presbyn. Ch., 1986-89, 97—, clk. of session, 1988-89, chmn. cmty. concerns com., 1987-88, chmn. pers. com., 1989-90, 99—, chmn. assoc. pastor search com., 1991-92; bd. dirs. The Hambidge Ctr., 2000—; bd. dirs. Park Pride, 1992; bd. dirs. Ga. C. of C., 1998—, chmn. environ. com., 1987-92, environ. legal counsel, 1981-87; mem. spl. program Leadership Atlanta, 1979-80, Leadership Ga., 1985; mem. Ga. bd. advisors Trust for Pub. Land, 1990-95. Capt. U.S. Army, 1969-72. Decorated D.S.M.; recipient Spl. award Atlanta chpt. AIA, 1988, Mayor Andrew Young, 1985. Mem. ABA (natural resources sect.), State Bar Ga. (chmn. environ. law sect. 1979-82), Atlanta Bar Assn., City of Atlanta Hist. Preservation (policy steeering com. 1989), Ga. C. of C. (bd. dirs. 1998—), Atlanta C. of C. (water resources task force 1982-87, solid waste task force 1989, air quality task force 1993-97, environ. affairs com. 1998—), Ga. Indsl. Developers Assn. (hazardous waste com. 1983-84), Phi Beta Kappa, Omicron Delta Kappa. Avocations: swimming, bird watching, community activities. Environmental, Land use and zoning (including planning). Home: 129 Palisades Rd NE Atlanta GA 30309-1532 Office: Alston & Bird One Atlantic Ctr 1201 W Peachtree St LLP Atlanta GA 30309-3424

STOKES, RICHARD FRANCIS, lawyer; b. Teaneck, N.J., Jan. 7, 1946; s. Edwin Matthew and Norma S. (Bonn) S.; m. Sally Scott, Mar. 28, 1970; children— Sarah S., Richard Hunter. B.A., Colgate U., 1967; J.D., Duke U., 1970. Bar: Del. 1970, U.S. Dist. Ct. Del. 1970., Del. Superior Ct. 1999. Law clk. Superior Ct., Wilmington, Del., 1970; ptnr. Tunnell & Raysor, Georgetown, Del., 1978— ; counsel Beebe Hosp., Lewes, Del., 1983— ; dir. Seaside Med. Assoc., Lewes. Bd. dirs. Community Legal Aid, Georgetown, Del., 1978-82; elder Rehoboth Beach Presbyterian Ch., Del., 1983— ; chmn. Sussex County Dem. Exec. Com. 1986-88. Served to capt. USAF, 1971-75. Mem. Bd. Profl. Responsibility. Lodge: Rotary (sec. 1983). Home: 137 E Side Dr Rehoboth Beach DE 19971-1311

STOKES, RON, lawyer; b. Springfield, Mo., Dec. 2, 1950; s. Joe Alfred Stokes and MaryLee (Bennett) Marsh; m. Christine Monteleone, Nov. 9, 1986. BA, U. Ill., 1973; JD, St. John's U., Jamaica, N.Y., 1976. Bar: N.Y. 1977, U.S. Dist. Ct. (so. dist.) N.Y. 1987. Assoc. Francis J. Young, Hartsdale, N.Y., 1976-78; pvt. practice Rye Brook, N.Y., 1979-95, Yorktown, 1995—. Mem. N.Y. State Dem. Com., 1976-95, Westchester County Dem. Exec. Com., White Plains, N.Y., 1976-95; mem. bd. mgrs. Rye Ridge Condominium, 1989-95, pres., 1995. Mem. Westchester County Bar Assn. (sec. criminal justice sect. 1989-91, chair 1991-92), Sierra Club, Adirondack Mountain Club. Lutheran. Avocations: hiking, mountain climbing, sailing. State civil litigation, Criminal, Probate (including wills, trusts). Home and Office: 3224 S Shelly St Mohegan Lake NY 10547-1908 E-mail: r.j.stokes@att.net.

STOLKER, RICHARD SAMUEL, lawyer; AB, Dickinson Coll., Carlisle, Pa., 1966; JD, Temple U., 1969. Bar: Pa. 1969, Md. 1972, D.C. 1974, Va. 1989. Atty. U.S. Dept. of Justice, Washington, 1969-80; pvt. practice Bethesda, Md., 1980-85, Rockville, Md., 1985-90, 92—; atty. Joseph, Greenwald & Laake, P.A., Greenbelt, 1990-92.—. Mem. Md. State Bar Assn., Bankruptcy Bar Assn. Md., No. Va. Bankruptcy Bar Assn., Montgomery County Bar Assn., Montgomery County C. of C. Bankruptcy, General civil litigation, Corporate, general. Office: 110 N Washington St Ste 320 Rockville MD 20850

STOLL, NEAL RICHARD, lawyer; b. Phila., Nov. 7, 1948; s. Mervin Stoll and Goldie Louise (Serody) Stoll Wilf; m. Linda G. Seligman, May 25, 1972; children: Meredith Anne, Alexis Blythe. BA in History with distinction, Pa. State U., 1970; JD, Fordham U., 1973. Bar: N.Y. 1974, U.S. Dist. Ct. (ea. dist.) N.Y. 1974, U.S. Ct. Appeals (2d cir.) 1974, U.S. Ct. Appeals (11th cir.) 1982, U.S. Dist. Ct. (ea. dist.) Mich. 1983, U.S. Dist. Ct. (so. dist.) N.Y. 1974, U.S. Supreme Ct. 1986. Assoc. Skadden, Arps, Slate, Meagher & Flom, LLP, N.Y.C., 1973-81, mem., 1981—. Lectr. Practicing Law-Inst., N.Y.C. Author: (with others) Aquisitions Under the Hart Scott Rodino Antitrust Improvements Act, 1980; contbr. articles to profl. pubs. Mem. Assn. Bar City of N.Y. (mem. trade regulation com. 1983-85), ABA, N.Y. State Bar Assn. Democrat. Antitrust, Federal civil litigation. Office: Skadden Arps Slate Four Times Sq New York NY 10036-6522 E-mail: nstoll@skadden.com.

STOLL, RICHARD G(ILES), lawyer; b. Phila., Oct. 2, 1946; s. Richard Giles and Mary Margaret (Zeigler) S.; m. Susan Jane Nicewonger, June 15, 1968; children: Richard Giles III, Christian Hayes. BA magna cum laude, Westminster Coll., 1968; JD, Georgetown U., 1971. Bar: D.C. 1971, U.S. Dist. Ct. D.C. 1971, U.S. Ct. Appeals D.C. 1971, U.S. Ct. Appeals (4th cir.) 1977. Assoc. Arent, Fox, Kintner, Plotkin & Kahn, Washington, 1971-73; atty. Office of Gen. Counsel EPA, Washington, 1973-77, asst. gen. counsel, 1977-81; dep. gen. counsel Chem. Mfrs. Assn., Washington, 1981-84; ptnr. Freedman, Levy, Kroll & Simonds, Washington, 1984-2001, Foley & Lardner, Washington, 2001—. Instr. environ. law and policy U. Va., Charlottesville, 1981-90. Co-author: Handbook on Environmental Law, 1987, 88, 89, 91, Practical Guide to Environment Law, 1987; contbr. articles to profl. jours.; moderator, panelist legal ednl. TV broadcasts and tapes ABA and Am. Law Inst. Elder Georgetown Presbyn. Ch. Capt., USAR, 1968-76. Recipient Alumni Achievement award Westminster Coll., 1998. Mem. ABA (sect. environment, energy and resources; chmn. water quality com. 1980-82, hazardous waste com. 1983-85, coun. mem. 1985-88, sect. chmn. 1990-91), Washington Golf and Country Club, Cosmos Club. Avocations: piano, golf, music composition. Administrative and regulatory, Environmental. Office: Foley & Lardner 3000 K St NW Washington DC 20007 E-mail: rstoll@foleylaw.com.

STOLPMAN, THOMAS GERARD, lawyer; b. Cleve., June 2, 1949; s. Joseph Eugene and Katherine Ann (Berry) S.; m. Marilyn Heise, Aug. 17, 1974; children: Jennifer, Peter. BA, UCLA, 1972; JD, Los Angeles, 1976. Bar: Calif. 1976, U.S. Dist. Ct. (ctrl. dist.) Calif. 1976, U.S. Dist. Ct (ea. dist.) Calif. 1985, U.S. Dist. Ct. (so. dist.) Calif. 1995, U.S. Ct. Appeals (9th cir.) 1993, U.S. Supreme Ct. 1994. Ptnr. Stolpman Krissman Elber & Silver LLP, Long Beach, Calif., 1976—. Editor The Forum, 1978-84; editor-in-chief The Advocate, 1984-87; contbr. articles to profl. jours. Bd. dirs. Miraleste Recreation and Park Dist., Rancho Palos Verdes, Calif., 1982-96. Named Trial Lawyer of Yr. So. Calif., Verdictum Juris, 1984. Fellow: Internat. Acad. Trial Lawyers, Am. Coll. Trial Lawyers; mem.: ATLA, Long Beach Bar Assn., South Bar Bar Assn., Nat. Bd. Trial Advocacy, Am. Bd. Trial Advocates (bd. govs. 1998—, pres. L.A. chpt. 2003), L.A. County Bar Assn. (bd. trustees 1986—87, exec. com. litigation sect. 1990—94), Calif. Trial Lawyers Assn. (bd. govs. 1987—90, exec. com. 1989—90, 2001, fin. sec. 2001, bd. govs. 2001—02), L.A. Trial Lawyers Assn. (bd. govs. 1979—93, pres. 1989), State Bar of Calif. (bd. govs. 1993—97, v.p. 1995—96, pres. 1996—97). Democrat. Roman Catholic. Admiralty, Federal civil litigation, Personal injury (including property damage). Office: Stolpman Krissman Elber & Silver LLP PO Box 22609 111 W Ocean Blvd Fl 19 Long Beach CA 90801-5609 E-mail: stolpman@stolpman.com.

STOMPOLY, JOHN GEORGE, lawyer; b. New Brunswick, NJ, Apr. 6, 1935; s. Albert and Ethel Stompoly; children: Pamela, Christopher, John Amos. Student, Notre Dame U., 1953—54; BA, U. Mo., 1957; LLB, Rutgers U., 1962. Bar: NJ 1963, U.S. Dist. Ct. NJ 1963, Ariz. 1966, U.S. Dist. Ct. Ariz. 1967, U.S. Supreme Ct. 1971, U.S. Ct. Appeals (9th cir.) 1972, Calif. 1976, Hawaii 1983, NY 1984, Tex. 1987, D.C. 1988, Mont. 1990, Wyo. 1991, Nev. 1993, Colo. 1994. Law clk. NJ Appellate Ct., Trenton, 1962—63; atty. Ewart, Lommell, Muccifori & Adler, Toms River, NJ, 1963—65; law clk. Ariz. Supreme Ct., Phoenix; ptnr. Johnson, Hayes, Morales & Stompoly, Tucson, 1966—73, Johnson, Hayes & Dowdall, Tucson, 1973—75, Stompoly & Stroud, PC, Tucson, 1975—93, Stompoly, Stroud, Glicksman & Erickson, PC, Tucson, 1993—. With Army NG, 1957. Mem.: Am. Coll. Legal Medicine. Personal injury (including property damage). Office: Stompoly Stroud Glicksman & Erickson PC 1 S Church Ave #1640 Tucson AZ 85701

STONE, ANDREW GROVER, lawyer; b. L.A., Oct. 2, 1942; s. Frank B. and Meryl (Pickering) S.; divorced; 1 child, John Blair; m. Susan Anselma, Feb. 14, 2003. BA, Yale U., 1965; JD, U. Mich., 1969. Bar: D.C. 1970, U.S. Dist. Ct. D.C. 1970, U.S. Ct. Appeals (D.C. cir.) 1972, Mass. 1981. Assoc. Rogers & Wells, Washington, 1969-71; atty. Bur. Competition, FTC, Washington, 1971-80; antitrust counsel Digital Equipment Corp., Maynard, Mass., 1980-83, mgr. N.E. law group, 1983-86, mgr. headquarters sales law group, 1986-88; asst. general counsel U.S. (acting), 1987, 88; corp counsel, 1988-90; corp. counsel, pub. sect. mktg. Thinking Machines Corp., Cambridge, Mass., 1990-91, corp. counsel, 1992-95; pvt. practice on-site legal svcs. Marblehead, Mass., 1995—. Corp. mem. Tenacre Country Day Sch., Wellesley, Mass., 1981-88. Mem. ABA (bus. law sect.), Mass. Bar Assn. (internat. law steering com. 1993-94), Boston Bar Assn. (membership com. 1998-2000, chair corp. counsel com. 1995-98, gen. counsel forum 1995—), Am. Arbitration Assn. (comml. arbitrator), New Eng. Corp. Counsel Assn., Assn. Ind. Gen. Counsel. Commercial, contracts (including sales of goods; commercial financing), Computer, Government contracts and claims.

STONE, DAVID PHILIP, lawyer; b. N.Y.C., Sept. 11, 1944; s. Robert and Laura Stone; m. Arlene R. Stone, June 11, 1966; children: Aaron J., Rachel E. AB, Columbia U., 1967; JD, Harvard U., 1970. Bar: N.Y. 1971. Assoc. Cahill, Gordon & Reindel, N.Y.C., 1970-74, Baer & McGoldrick, N.Y.C., 1974-76, Weil, Gotshal & Manges, L.L.P., N.Y.C., 1976-79, ptnr., 1979—. Private international, Mergers and acquisitions, Securities. Office: Weil Gotshal & Manges LLP 767 5th Ave New York NY 10153-0119 Business E-Mail: david.stone@weil.com.

STONE, DONALD GENE, lawyer; b. Berkeley, Calif., Aug. 18, 1947; s. James Sherman and Rachel M. (Loomis) S.; m. Carole Jean Barrett, Aug. 23, 1969; children— Nathan Andrew, Suzanne Michelle. B.A., U. Idaho, 1969, J.D., 1972. Bar: Wash. 1972, Idaho 1972, U.S. Dist. Ct. Idaho 1972, U.S. Ct. Mil. Appeals 1973, U.S. Dist. Ct. (ea. dist.) Wash. 1976. Assoc., Paine, Lowe, Coffin, Herman & O'Kelly, Spokane, 1976-79; ptnr. Paine, Hamblen, Coffin & Brooke, Spokane, 1979— ; local counsel Avista Corp., Avista Energy, Honda N.Am., Wayne-Dalton Corp., Aegis Ins., Federated Rural Elec. Ins. Assn., Employers of Wasau, Assoc. Electric Gas Ins. Svcs., others. Mem. editl. bd. Idaho Law Rev., 1971-72. Pres. Fire Safe Spokane; v.p. Spokane Valley Baseball League. Served to capt. USAF, 1972-76. Decorated Air Force commendation medal; recipient McLean scholarship award U. Idaho, 1969; Gen. Dynamics AFROTC award U. Idaho, 1969. Mem. ABA, Spokane County Bar Assn., Washington Bar Assn., Idaho Bar Assn., Def. Rsch. Inst., Wash. Def. Trial Lawyers Assn., Idaho Assn. Def. Trial Lawyers, Spokane Club, Order of Barristers, Blue Key, Phi Beta Kappa, Phi Kappa Phi. Republican. Roman Catholic. General civil litigation, Utilities, public, Personal injury (including property damage). Home: 1812 S Vera Crest Dr Veradale WA 99037-9035 Office: Paine Hamblen Coffin Brooke and Miller LLP 1200 N Washington St Spokane WA 99201-2434

STONE, DONALD P. lawyer; b. Ironwood, Mich., July 31, 1937; s. Paul Clarence and Ethel (Moore) S.; m. Barbara Ann Schneider, Nov. 24, 1962 (dec.); children: Kimberly Ann, Paul Christian, Sandra Jane; m. Stephanie L. Brooks, Jan. 31, 1997. BA, Tchrs. cert., U. Mich., 1959, JD, 1962. Bar: Mich. 1962, U.S. Dist. Ct. (we. dist.) Mich. 1963. Ptnr. Stone, Campbell & Hoffelder, P.L.C., Niles, Mich., 1963—. Mem. ABA, Mich. Bar Assn., Berrien County Bar Assn. (pres. 1973-74), Elks. Presbyterian. Estate planning, General practice, Probate (including wills, trusts). Office: Stone Campbell & Hoffelder 223 N 4th St # 249 Niles MI 49120-2301

STONE, EDWARD HERMAN, lawyer; b. July 20, 1939; s. Sidney and Ruth Stone; m. Paul G. Gray (dec. 1990); children: Andrew, Matthew; m. Elaine Ornitz, Dec. 22, 1995. BS in Acctg., U. Ill., 1961; JD, John Marshall Law Sch., 1967. Bar: Ill. 1967, Calif. 1970, cert.: Calif. (specialist probate, estate planning, and trust law). With IRS, 1963-71; assoc. Eilers, Baranger, Myers & Smith, 1971-72; pvt. practice Newport Beach, Calif., 1972-2001, Santa Ana, 1988-89; mem. Davis, Samuelson, Goldberg & Blakely (formerly Cohen, Stokke & Davis), Santa Ana, 1984-88; ptnr. Edward H. Stone A Law Corp., 1990—. Instr. income and estate taxes Western States U. Sch. Law, 1971—72; mem. CEB Joint Adv. Com.; judge pro tem, jud. arbitrator Orange County Superior Ct.; moderator, spkr. Calif. Trust and Probate Litig. CEB, 1999; moderator, spkr. postmortem trust adminstrn. CEB, Calif., 2002—03; moderator, spkr. Calif. Trust and Probate Litig. CEB, 2001; mediator IRS ADR tax cases in appeals, 2000—. Contbr. articles to profl. jours. Pres. Jewish Family Svcs. Orange County, 1975; v.p., bd. dirs. Jewish Fedn. Orange County, 1985—88; bd. dirs. Heritage Points Orange County, 1992—95, Eastbluff Homeowners Cmty. Assn., Newport Beach, 1980—82, pres., 1981—82. Mem.: Orange County Bar Assn. (vice-chmn. estate planning probate and trust law sect. 1976—77, chmn. sect. 1977—78, instr. Probate Clinic 1980, chairperson ADR com. 1996, spkr. in substantive law, dir. 1977—82, past chmn. profl. edn. coun., chmn.del. real property and probate sect, chmn. del. real property and probate sect. state bar conv. 1992—), Phi Alpha Delta (pres. alumni chpt. 1975—76). Corporate, general, Estate planning, Probate (including wills, trusts).

STONE, FRANK BUSH, lawyer; b. Houghton, Mich., Dec. 18, 1913; s. John Grover and Helen Grace (Ball) S.; m. Meryl A. Pickering, Aug. 26, 1939 (dec. 1991); children: Andrew G., William D.; m. Patricia A. Fath, Jan. 25, 1993. (dec. 2002). AB, Yale U., 1935; JD, U. Mich., 1938. Bar: Mich. 1939, N.Y. 1941, D.C. 1942, Calif. 1943. Assoc. Chadbourne, Wallace, Parke & Whiteside, Washington, L.A., N.Y.C., 1938-43; resident counsel N.Am. Aviation, L.A., 1943-45; assoc. Chadbourne, Parke, Whiteside, Wolff & Brophy, N.Y.C., 1945-55, ptnr., 1955-83; of counsel Chadbourne & Parke, LLP, N.Y.C., 1983—. Vestryman, sr. warden St. Andrew's Episcopal Ch., Murray Hill, N.J., 1976-79. Mem. Old Guard of Summit (dir. 1991). Avocation: genealogy. Home: 24 Ramsey Dr Summit NJ 07901-3015

STONE, GEOFFREY RICHARD, law educator, lawyer; b. Nov. 20, 1946; s. Robert R. and Shirley (Weliky) S.; m. Nancy Spector, Oct. 8, 1977; children: Julie, Mollie. BS, U. Pa., 1968; JD, U. Chgo., 1971. Bar: N.Y. 1972. Law clk. to Hon. J.S. Kelly Wright U.S. Ct. Appeals (D.C. cir.), 1971-72; law clk. to Hon. William J. Brennan, Jr. U.S. Supreme Ct., 1972-73; asst. prof. U. Chgo., 1973-77, assoc. prof., 1977-79, prof., 1979-84, Harry Kalven Jr. disting. svc. prof., 1984—, dean Law Sch., 1987-93, provost, 1994—2002. Author: Constitutional Law, 1986, 4th edit., 2001, The Bill of Rights in the Modern State, 1992, The First Amendment, 1999, Eternally Vigilent: Free Speech in the Modern Era, 2001; editor The Supreme Ct. Rev., 1991—; contbr. articles to profl. jours. Bd. dirs. Ill. divsn. ACLU, 1978-84; bd. advisors Pub. Svc. Challenge, 1989; bd. govs. Argonne Nat. Lab., 1994—. Fellow AAAS; mem. Chgo. Coun. Lawyers (bd. govs. 1976-77), Am. Law Inst. Assn. Am. Law Schs. (exec. com. 1990-93), Legal Aid Soc. (bd. dirs. 1988), Order of Coif. Office: U Chgo 1111 E 60th St Chicago IL 60637-5418

STONE, LAWRENCE MAURICE, lawyer, educator; b. Malden, Mass., Mar. 25, 1931; s. Abraham Jacob and Pauline (Bernstein) S.; m. Anna Jane Clark, June 15, 1963; children: Abraham Dean, Ethan Goldthwaite, Katharine Elisheva. AB magna cum laude, Harvard U., 1953, JD magna cum laude, 1956. Bar: Mass. 1956, Calif. 1958. Rsch. asst. Am. Law Inst., Cambridge, Mass., 1956-57; assoc. Irell and Manella, L.A., 1957-61, ptnr., 1963, 79-96, of counsel, 1997—; internat. tax coordinator U.S. Treasury Dept., Washington, 1961-62, tax. legis. counsel, 1964-66; prof. law U. Calif., Berkeley, 1966-78. Vis. prof. law Yale U., New Haven, 1969, Hebrew U. Jerusalem, 1973-74, U. So. Calif., L.A., 1984; mem. adv. group to commr. IRS, Washington, 1973-74; mem. President's Adv. Commn. on Tax Ct. Appointments, Washington, 1976-80; tax advisory bd. Little Brown Co., 1994-96. Author: (with Doernberg) Federal Income Taxation of Corporations and Partnerships, (with Klein, Bankman and Bittker) Federal Income Taxation; bd. editors Harvard Law Rev., 1955-56. Fellow Am. Coll. Tax Counsel; mem. ABA, Am. Law Inst., Internat. Fiscal Inst., Am. Arbitration Assn., L.A. County Bar Assn. (recipient Dana Latham award 1995), Phi Beta Kappa. Corporate taxation, Taxation, general, Personal income taxation. Office: Irell & Manella 1800 Avenue Of The Stars Los Angeles CA 90067-4276

STONE, RALPH KENNY, lawyer; b. Bainbridge, Ga., Aug. 7, 1952; s. Ralph Patrick and Joyce (Mitchell) S.; m. Julie Ann Waldren, Aug. 24, 1974; children: Laura Lee, Rebecca, Michael. BBA magna cum laude, U. Ga., 1974, JD cum laude, 1977. Bar: Ga. 1977, U.S. Dist. Ct. (so. dist.) Ga. 1977, U.S. Supreme Ct. 1980, U.S. Ct. Appeals (11th cir.) 1981. Staff acct. Price Waterhouse & Co., Columbia, S.C., 1974; assoc. Calhoun & Donaldson, Savannah, Ga., 1977; ptnr. Franklin & Stone, Statesboro, Ga., 1977-88, Edenfield, Stone & Cox, Statesboro, Ga., 1988-94; pres. R. Kenny Stone, P.C., 1994—. Instr. taxation Ga. So. Coll., Stateboro, 1979-80. Sect. chmn. United Way S.E. Ga., campaign chmn., 1989, pres. 1991; charter pres. Leadership Bulloch, Inc., 1984; chmn. Bulloch County Dem. Com., 1984-90, Bulloch 2000 Com., 1986-88; alt. del. Dem. Nat. Conv., 1988; sec. Ga. Assn. Dem. County Chairs, 1985-89, pres. 1989-91; dist. chmn. Boy Scouts Am., 1985; pres. Forward Bulloch Inc., 1986; participant Leadership Ga., 1986; mem. Ga. Bd. Industry Trade & Tourism, 1991-96. Mem. ABA, State Bar Ga., Bulloch County Bar Assn. (pres. 1982-83), Statesboro-Bulloch C. of C. (pres. 1986, chmn. bd. dirs. 1987, chmn. devel. authority Bulloch County 1991-2001), Rotary (Statesboro), Optimist Club (pres. 1980-81, dist. lt. gov. 1981-82), Phi Kappa Phi, Beta Alpha Psi. Baptist. Bankruptcy, State civil litigation, General practice. Home: 319 Dogwood Trl Statesboro GA 30461-4253 Office: R Kenny Stone PC PO Box 681 Statesboro GA 30459-0681

STONE, SAMUEL BECKNER, lawyer; b. Martinsville, Va., Feb. 4, 1934; s. Paul Raymond and Mildred (Beckner) S.; m. Shirley Ann Gregory, June 18, 1955; children: Paul Gregory, Daniel Taylor. BSEE, Va. Polytech. Inst. & State U., 1955; JD, George Wash. U., 1960. Bar: Md. 1960, Calif. 1963, Patent and Trademark Office. Patent examiner, 1955-58; patent adv. Naval Ordinance Lab., Silver Spring, Md., 1958-59; assoc. Thomas & Crickenberger, Washington, 1959-61, Beckman Instruments Inc., Fullerton, Calif., 1961-65, Lyon & Lyon, L.A., 1965-72, ptnr., 1972, mng. ptnr. Irvine, Calif., 1982-2000. Judge Disneyland Com. Svc. Awards, Anaheim, Calif., 1987. Mem. Orange County Bar Assn. (bd. dirs. 1988-91, travel seminar chair 1986-92), Orange County Patent Law Assn. (pres. 1987, bd. exec. com. 1987-90), Calif. Bar Assn. (intellectual property sect. bd. 1987-90), Am. Arbitration Assn. (intellectual property panel neutral arbitrators 1997-2000), Am. Electronics Assn. (lawyers com. 1988-99, co-chair 1996-97), Orange County Venture Group (dir. 1985-99, pres. 1996-97), Rams Booster Club (dir. 1984-90), Pacific Club (mem. legal adv. com., chair 1989-92, bd. dirs. 1999-2002). Republican. Avocations: tennis, waterskiing, music. Intellectual property, Patent, Trademark and copyright. Home: 1612 Antigua Way Newport Beach CA 92660-4344 Office: Orrick Herrington & Sutcliffe LLP 4 Park Plz Ste 1600 Irvine CA 92614 E-mail: sstone@orrick.com.

STONE, VICTOR J. law educator; b. Chgo., Mar. 11, 1921; s. Maurice Albert and Ida (Baskin) S.; m. Susan Abby Cane, July 14, 1951; children: Mary Jessica, Jennifer Abby, Andrew Hugh William. AB, Oberlin Coll., 1942; JD, Columbia U., 1948; LLD, Oberlin Coll., 1983. Bar: N.Y. 1949, Ill. 1950. Assoc. Columbia U., N.Y.C., 1948-49, Sonnenschein, Chgo., 1949-53; rsch. assoc. U. Chgo., 1953-55; asst. prof. law U. Ill., Champaign, 1955-57, assoc. prof. law, 1957-59, prof. law, 1959-91, prof. law emeritus, 1991—, assoc. v.p. acad. affairs, 1975-78. Mem. jud. adv. coun. State Ill., 1959-61; mem. com. jury instrns. Ill. Supreme Ct., 1963-79, reporter, 1973-79; mem. Ill. State Appellate Defender Commn., 1973-83, vice-chmn., 1973-77, 79-83; bd. dirs. Champaign County Ct.-Apptd. Spl. Advocate Program, 1995-99, pres., 1998-99. Co-editor: Ill. Pattern Jury Instructions, 1965, 71, 77; Civil Liberties and Civil Rights, 1977. Trustee Oberlin Coll., 1982-97, AAUP Found., 1983-90. Lt. USNR, 1942-46. Ford Found. fellow, 1962-63. Fellow Ill. Bar Found. (charter 1986—); mem. ABA, CASA (bd. dirs. 1994-98, pres. 1998-99), Ill. Bar Assn. (chmn. individual rights and responsibilities 1971-72, mem. coun. civil practice and procedure 1978-82), Chgo. Bar Assn., AAUP (gen. counsel 1978-80, pres. 1982-84 , pres. Ill. conf. 1968-70, pres. Ill. chpt. 1964-65, mem. coun. 1982-90), ACLU (bd. dirs. Ill. div. 1986-96, exec. com. 1991-96, Roger Baldwin award for lifetime achievement 2002), Am. Bar Found. (life 1986), State Univs. Annitants Assn. (pres. 1994-95, mem. state exec. com. 1995-97). Office: U Ill Coll Law 504 E Pennsylvania Ave Champaign IL 61820-6909 E-mail: v-stone@uiuc.edu.

STONEHOUSE, JAMES ADAM, lawyer; b. Alameda, Calif., Nov. 10, 1937; s. Maurice Adam and Edna Sigrid (Thuesen) S.; m. Marilyn Jean Kotkas, Aug. 6, 1966; children: Julie Aileen, Stephen Adam. AB, U. Calif., Berkeley, 1961; JD, U. Calif., San Francisco, 1965. Bar: Calif. 1966; cert. specialist probate, estate planning and trust law. Assoc. Hall, Henry, Oliver & McReavy, San Francisco, 1966-71; ptnr. Whitney Hanson & Stonehouse, Alameda, 1971-77; pvt. practice Alameda, 1977-79; ptnr. Stonehouse & Silva, Alameda, 1979—. Judge adv. Alameda coun. Navy League, 1978-98. Founding dir. Alameda Clara Barton Found., 1977-80; mem. Oakland (Calif.) Marathon-Exec. Com., 1979; mem. exec. bd. Alameda coun. Boy Scouts Am., 1979—, pres., 1986-88, endowment chair area III, 1996—; trustee Golden Gate Scouting, 1986-95, treas., 1989-91, v.p., 1991-92, pres., 1993-95, v.p. area III western region, 1990-95, bd. dirs. western region, 1991—; bd. dirs. Lincoln Child Ctr. Found., 1981-87, 94-98, pres., 1983-85; pres. Robert L. Lippert Found., 1990—; mem. sch. bd. St. Joseph Notre Dame, 1994-2000, pres., 1997-2000. Recipient Lord Baden-Powell Merit award Boy Scouts Am., 1988, Silver Beaver award, 1991, Silver Antelope award, 1999, Citizen of Yr. award City of Alameda, 1999; named Boss of Yr., Alameda Jaycees, 1977; Coro Found. fellow, 1961-62. Mem. ABA, Alameda County Bar Assn. (vice chmn. com. office econs. 1977-78), Commonwealth Club, Rotary (dir. 1976-78, trustee Alameda Rotary Found. 1991—, treas. 1994-98, pres. 1998-2000), Elks (past exalted ruler, all state officer 1975-76, all dist. officer 1975-77, 78-79). Republican. Roman Catholic. Estate planning, Probate (including wills, trusts), Estate taxation. Home: 2990 Northwood Dr Alameda CA 94501-1606 Office: Stonehouse & Silva 512 Westline Dr Ste 300 Alameda CA 94501-5870

STONER, WILLIAM EDWARD, lawyer; b. Elgin, Ill., May 16, 1956; m. Nancy Kay Stoner. JD, Duke U., Durham, NC, 1981. Bar: Calif. 1981, Ill. 1981, U.S. Dist. Ct. Calif. 1981. Assoc. Pillsbury Winthrop, L.A., 1981—2000, Hennigan Bennett & Dorman LLP, L.A., Alaska, 2000—. Bd. dirs. LCF Ednl. Found., La Canada, Calif., 1995—2000. State civil litigation, Federal civil litigation, Securities. Office: Hennigan Bennett & Dorman LLP 601 S Figueroa #3300 Los Angeles CA 90017 Personal E-mail: stoner_we@yahoo.com.

STOOPS, DANIEL J. lawyer; b. Wichita, Kans., May 27, 1934; s. Elmer F. and Margaret J. (Pickrell) S.; m. Kathryn Ann Piepmeier, Aug. 28, 1954; children: Sharon, Janet. BA, Washburn U., 1956, JD, 1958. Bar: Kans. 1958, Ariz. 1959, U.S. Dist. Ct. Kans. 1958, U.S. Dist. Ct. Ariz. 1960, U.S. Ct. Appeals (9th cir.) 1975, U.S. Supreme Ct. 1971. Assoc. Wilson, Compton, & Wilson, Flagstaff, Ariz., 1959-64; ptnr. Wilson, Compton & Stoops, Flagstaff, 1964-67, Mangum, Wall & Stoops, Flagstaff, 1967-77, Mangum, Wall, Stoops & Warden, Flagstaff, 1977—. Editor Washburn Law Rev., 1958. Pres. Flagstaff Festival of the Arts, 1988-89, Flagstaff Sch. Bd., 1961-73, Ariz. Sch. Bd. Assn., 1971 Fellow Ariz. Bar Found., Am. Bar Found., Am. Coll. Trial Lawyers (state chmn. 1984-85), Internat. Soc. Barristers; mem. Ariz. Bar Assn. (pres. 1980-81), Masons. Republican. Methodist. Avocations: golf, political and historical reading and research. Product liability, Insurance, Personal injury (including property damage). Office: Mangum Wall Stoops & Warden 100 N Elden St Flagstaff AZ 86001-5295 E-mail: flagstaffattys@quest.net.

STORER, MARYRUTH, law librarian; b. Portland, Oreg., 1953; d. Joseph William and Carol Virginia Storer; m. David Bruce Bailey, 1981; children: Sarah, Allison. BA in History, Portland State U., 1974; JD, U. Oreg., 1977; M in Law Librarianship, U. Wash., 1978. Bar: Oreg. 1978. Assoc. law libr. U. Tenn., Knoxville, 1978-79; law libr. O'Melveny & Myers, L.A., 1979-88; dir. Orange County Pub. Law Libr., Santa Ana, Calif., 1988—. Mem. Am. Assn. Law Librs. (exec. bd. 1999-2002), So. Calif. Assn. Law Librs. (pres. 1986-87), Coun. Calif. County Law Librs. (sec./treas. 1990-94, pres. 1994-96), Arroyo Sero Libr. Network (chair 2000-03). Democrat. Episcopalian. Office: Orange County Public Law Library 515 N Flower St Santa Ana CA 92703-2304

STOREY, CHARLES PORTER, lawyer; b. Austin, Tex., Dec. 4, 1922; s. Robert Gerald and Frances Hazel (Porter) S.; m. Helen Hanks Stephens, Oct. 14, 1950; children: Charles Porter, Harry Stephens, Frederick Schatz. BA, U. Tex., 1947, LLB, 1948; LLM, So. Methodist U., 1952. Bar: Tex. 1948. Pvt. practice law, Dallas, 1948—; sr. counsel Carrington Coleman Sloman & Blumenthal, LLP. Pres. Dallas Day Nursery Assn., 1958, Greater Dallas Coun. Chs., 1970-71; chmn. Internat. Com. YMCA, 1969-71; nat. bd. dirs. U.S. YMCA, 1964-75; pres. Children's Devel. Ctr., Dallas, 1959; trustee Baylor Coll. Dentistry, 1981-90, Hillcrest Found., 1994—; trustee emeritus Southwestern Legal Found., chmn. 1980-90; dir. Zale Lipshy U. Med. Ctr., 1999—. 1st lt., pilot USAAF, 1943-45, ETO. Decorated Air medal. Master emeritus Dallas Inn of Ct. (pres. 1991-93); fellow Am. Coll. Trial Lawyers, Am. Bar Found., Tex. Bar Found.; mem. ABA, Tex. Bar Assn. (bd. dirs. 1976-79), Dallas Bar Assn. (pres. 1975), Philos. Soc. Tex., Dallas Country Club, Crescent Club, Idlewild Club, Phi Delta Phi, Phi Delta Theta. Mem. Christian Ch. (Disciples Of Christ). Corporate, general, Probate (including wills, trusts). Home: 5855 Farquhar Ln Dallas TX 75209 Office: 200 Crescent Ct Ste 1500 Dallas TX 75201-7839 Fax: 214-855-1333. E-mail: cstorey@ccsb.com.

STOREY, JAMES MOORFIELD, lawyer; b. Boston, Apr. 12, 1931; s. Charles Moorfield and Susan Jameson (Sweetser) S.; m. Adair Miller, Aug. 28, 1954 (div. 1973); children: Barbara Sessums Storey McGrath, Mary Sweetser Storey Meley, Susan Adair Storey Frank, Eliza Allison Tebo Storey Anderson, Alice Leovy Storey Wille; m. Isabelle Helene Boeschenstein, May 17, 1973 AB, Harvard U., 1953, LL.B., 1956. Bar: Mass. 1956. Atty. SEC, Washington, 1956-57, legal asst. to chmn., 1957-59; assoc. Gaston, Snow, Motley & Holt, Boston, 1959-62; ptnr. Gaston, Snow, Motley & Holt (name changed to Gaston Snow & Ely Bartlett), Boston, 1962-87, Dechert Price & Rhoads, Boston, 1987-94, ret., 1994, profl. trustee, corp. dir., 1994—. Trustee Mt. Auburn Cemetery, Cambridge, Mass., 1980— Co-author: Mutual Fund Law Handbook, 1998, The Uneasy Chaperone, 2000. Mem. ABA, Boston Bar Assn., Tavern Club Boston (pres. 1985-87), Century Assn. of N.Y. Unitarian Universalist. Home: 89A Mt Vernon St Boston MA 02108-1330 Office: 5 Boylston Pl Boston MA 02116

STOREY, LEE A. lawyer; b. Ypsilanti, Mich., Nov. 28, 1959; d. Henry Perry Herold and Elsie Lorraine (Long) Wolf; m. William Storey; children: Jason Michael, Jenifer Lorraine. Student, U. Mich., 1977-79; BA, UCLA, 1982, MA, 1984; JD, U. Calif., Berkeley, 1987. Bar: Ariz. 1988, U.S. Dist. Ct. 1990. Circulations mgr. Inst. Archaeology UCLA, 1980-84; rsch. asst. John Muir Inst., Napa, Calif., 1985, Am. Indian Resources Inst., Oakland, Calif., 1985; assoc. editor Ecology Law Quarterly U. Calif., Berkeley, 1985-86; assoc. Evans, Kitchel & Jenckes, Phoenix, 1987-89, Gallagher & Kennedy, Phoenix, 1989-90, Meyer, Hendricks, Victor, Osborn & Maledon, Phoenix, 1991-95; ptnr. Meyer Hendricks Bivens & Moyes P.A., 1995-99; prin. ptnr. Moyes Storey, Ltd., 1999—. Guest lectr. water transfers Hydrological Soc. Symposium, Phoenix, 1989, environ. studies Ariz. State U., Tempe, 1990, water quality Soc. Mining Engrs., Denver, 1991, water transfers Wind River Assocs., Denver, 1991-92, Phoenix, 1992, Ctrl. Ariz. Project Utilization, Am. Water Resources Assn. Symposium, Tucson, 1992, Colo. River Basin Tribes, Coun. Energy Resource Tribes, Tucson, 1993, Indian Sovereignty, U.S. Dept. Interior, Bureau Reclamation, Phoenix, 1993; Indian Econ. Devel. Fed. Indian Bar Albuquerque, 1994, Water Rights, Ariz. Judicial Conf., Ariz. State Bar, Tucson, 1994, National Land Coun. sem., Water Rights, Rico Rico, Ariz., 1995, Ariz. Water Law, 2000, Western Water Law Conference, CLE, Denver, 2002, Recent Devels. in Ariz. Water Law, Phoenix, 2002, Recent Developments in Ariz. Water Law, 2002, Water Resources Rsch. Ctr. Annual Conf.; chair Ambs. for Change, 1996—; adj. prof. Indian water rights Sch. Law Ariz. State U., 1992, 97, mem. adv. com. on Indian law program Coll. of Law, 1999—, guest lectr. Flagstaff leadership program, 2000, 2002. Co-author: Leasing Indian Water: Choices in Colorado River Basin, 1988; contbr. articles to profl. jours.; mem. Calif. Law Rev. U. Calif. Berkeley, 1985-87. Landlord tenant clinics Vols. Lawyers Program, Phoenix, 1988-89; mem. Ariz. Ctr. for Law-Related Edn., Ariz. Bar Found., Drug Awareness Program for Schs., 1990; chmn. bd. Ambs. for Change, 1996—; mem. Ariz. Town Hall, 1997, 2000. Scholar UCLA, 1980-84; recipient Am. Jurisprudence award Lawyers Coop., 1986. Mem. ABA, Ariz. State Bar Assn. (mem. com. on minorities and women in law 1993-97, chair-elect Indian law sect. 1997-98, chair 1998—, asst. editor Environ. and Natural Resources newsletter 1990-94, editor Indian law sect. Arrow newsletter 1996—), Ariz. Women Lawyers Assn., Maricopa County Bar Assn. Environmental, Native American, Property, real (including real estate development, water). Office: Moyes Storey 3003 N Central Ave Ste 1250 Phoenix AZ 85012-2923

STORM, ROBERT WARREN, lawyer; b. Battle Creek, Mich., June 3, 1951; s. Robert Warren and Patricia Ellen Knight (Klinck) S. AB in History, William and Mary Coll., 1973, JD, 1989; MA in History, Duke U., 1977. Bar: Conn., 1989; ordained elder Collinsville (Conn.) Congl. Ch., 1997. Historian, archivist U.S. Govt., Washington and Austin, Tex., 1977—85; cons. in info. mgmt. Arlington, Williamsburg, Va., 1985—88; assoc. Robinson & Cole, Hartford, 1989—92; pvt. practice West Hartford, Conn., 1993—. Gubernatorial appointee State Hist. Records Adv. Bd., Hartford, 1993—96; hon. advisor Ethiopian Cmty. Ctr., Conn., 1996—; bd. dirs. The Children's Home, Cromwell, Conn., 1993—99, v.p., 1995—96; bd. dirs. Conn. Coalition of Mut. Assistance Assns., 1997—, v.p., 1998—99, treas., 1999—2000; bd. dirs. Lea's Found. for Leukemia Rsch., 1998—. Mem.: ABA, Mil. Order Loyal Legion of U.S. (comdr. Conn. 2001—), Conn. Bar Assn., Soc. of the Cin. in the State of Conn. (mem. standing com. 2003—), Soc. Colonial Wars in Conn. (treas. 2001—), Soc. Descs. of Founders of Hartford (councillor 2003—). Avocations: reading, writing, music, nature, the fine arts. Estate planning, General practice, Private international. Office: PO Box 271645 West Hartford CT 06127-1645

STORME, MARCEL LEON VICTOR, barrister, educator; b. Gent, Flanders, Belgium, Aug. 3, 1930; s. Jules Jacob and Maria (Bosteels) S.; m. Godelieve de Schrijver, July 11, 1956; 1 child, Matthias. JD, State U., Gent, 1952, lic. Economy, 1955; Dr. honoris causa, Curie U., Lublin, 1994. Barrister Bar of Gent, 1952—; prof. law U. Antwerp, Gent, 1958-91, Gent, 1961-95, Queen Mary Coll., London, 1985-86, Vlaamse Leergangen, Leuven, Belgium, 1986-87, U. Leiden, 1987-88; chair Leverhulme, London, 1991-92; pvt. practice Gent, 1952—. Dean Law Faculty U. Gent, 1982-84; prof. honoris causa China U., Beijing, 1988, Beijing U. Editor: Procedural Reporter, 1983—, Tydschrift Privaatrecht, 1964—, European Private Law Review, 1992—; author: The Burden of Proof, 1962, European Caselaw, 1973, 1984 and the Law, 1984, International Arbitration, 1989. Sen. Belgian Sen., Brussels, 1977-81; mem. Provincial Coun., Gent, 1958-77; v.p. Bd. Belgian Radio and TV, Brussels, 1968-77. Mem. Young Barristers Assn. (pres. 1967-69), Comparative Law Soc. (pres. 1988), Centre Arbitration Brussels (v.p. 1980), Belgian Ctr. Procedural Law, Internat. Assn. Procedural Law (sec. gen. 1983-95, pres. 1995—), Royal Acad. Scis. (pres. 1997-98), Acad. Europaea, Flemish Lawyers Assn. (pres. 1983), Internat. C. of C. (arbitrator 1970—), De Prince Club, Quglo-Belgian Club London, Commr. Order Orange Nassau, Frenico Gourico Redenti. Christian Democrat. Roman Catholic. Home: Coupure 3 9000 Gent Belgium Office: Storme, Leroy Law Firm Coupure 5 9000 Gent Belgium E-mail: m.storme@storme-law.be.

STORMER, CINDY HODGE, lawyer, educator; b. Ponca City, Okla., May 22, 1956; d. Lloyd John and Clara Louise (Reisch) Hodge; m. Kenneth John Stormer; 1 child, Julia Lauren Stormer. AA, Tarrant County Jr. Coll., Hurst, Tex., 1981; BA, U. Tex., 1983; JD, So. Tex. Coll. Law, 1986. Bar: U.S. Dist. Ct. (no. dist.) Tex. 1991, U.S. Dist. Ct. (ea. dist.) Tex. 1992. Peace officer City of Dallas, 1978-79, Tarrant County Jr. Coll., Hurst, 1979-86; asst. dist. atty. Tarrant County Dist. Atty.'s Office, Ft. Worth, 1986-89; chief atty., asst. city atty. Dallas Police Dept., 1989-90; sole practice Gainesville, Tex., 1990—; prof. North Ctrl. Tex. Coll., Gainesville, 1991—, mem. legal curriculum adv. bd., 1994-96. Mem. pro bono com. West Tex. Legal Svcs., Gainesville. Contbr. articles to profl. jours. Pres. Cooke County Child Welfare Bd., Gainesville, 1993-96. Mem. LWV, Tex. Trial Lawyers Assn., Lions Club. Office: 102 Elm Gainesville TX 76240

STORMS, CLIFFORD BEEKMAN, lawyer; b. Mount Vernon, N.Y., July 18, 1932; s. Harold Beekman and Gene (Pertak) S.; m. Barbara H. Grave, 1955 (div. 1975); m. Valeria N. Parker, July 12, 1975; children: Catherine Storms Fischer, Clifford Beekman. BA magna cum laude, Amherst Coll., 1954; LLB, Yale U., 1957. Bar: N.Y. 1957. Assoc. Breed, Abbott & Morgan, N.Y.C., 1957-64; with CPC Internat., Inc., Englewood Cliffs, N.J., 1964-97, v.p. legal affairs, 1973-75, v.p., gen. counsel, 1975-88, sr. v.p., gen. counsel, 1988-97, atty. alternate dispute resolution, corp. dir., 1997—; pvt. practice Greenwich, Conn., 1997—. Bd. dirs. Corn Products Internat., Inc., Atlantic Legal Found.; mem. Conn. Alternate Dispute Resolution panel Ctr. for Pub. Resources. Trustee emeritus Food and Drug Law Inst. Mem. ABA (com. of corp. gen. counsel), Am. Arbitration Assn. (panel arbitrators large complex case program), Assn. Gen. Counsel (pres. 1992-94), Assn. Bar City N.Y. (sec., com. on corp. law depts. 1979-81), Indian Harbor Yacht Club, Yale Law Sch. Assn. (exec. com.), Phi Beta Kappa. Alternative dispute resolution, Corporate, general. Home: 19 Burying Hill Rd Greenwich CT 06831-2604 Office: Ste 100 Two Sound View Dr Greenwich CT 06830 E-mail: cbstorms@aol.com.

STORY, MONTE ROBERT, lawyer; b. Edmore, Mich., May 18, 1931; s. Charles and Helen R. (Brown) S.; m. Barbara Brooks, June 27, 1953; children: Julie Kay Story-Wood, Bret C. BA, Mich. State U., 1953; JD, Detroit Coll. Law, 1970. Bar: Mich. 1970, U.S. Tax Ct. 1971. Ptnr. Lyle D. Hepfer & Co., CPA's, Lansing, Mich., 1953-64, Danielson, Story, Lake & Schultz, Lansing, 1964-71; chmn. bd. dirs. Farhat & Story PC, East Lansing, Mich., 1971—. Capt. USAFR, 1954-66. Mem. ABA, Am. Inst. CPA's, Mich. Assn. CPA's, Mich. State Bar Assn., Ingham County Bar Assn. Republican. Lutheran. Corporate, general, Estate planning, Probate (including wills, trusts). Office: Farhat & Story PC 4572 S Hagadorn Rd Ste 300 East Lansing MI 48823-5385

STOTLER, ALICEMARIE HUBER, judge; b. Alhambra, Calif., May 29, 1942; d. James R. and Loretta M. Huber; m. James Allen Stotler, Sept. 11, 1971. BA, U. So. Calif., 1964, JD, 1967. Bar: Calif. 1967, U.S. Dist. Ct. (no. dist.) Calif. 1967, U.S. Dist. Ct. (cen. dist.) Calif. 1973, U.S. Supreme Ct. 1976; cert. criminal law specialist. Dep. Orange County Dist. Attys. Office, 1967-73; mem. Stotler & Stotler, Santa Ana, Calif., 1973-76, 83-84; judge Orange County Mcpl. Ct., 1976-78, Orange County Superior Ct., 1978-83, U.S. Dist. Ct. (cen. dist.) Calif., L.A., 1984—. Assoc. dean Calif. Trial Judges Coll., 1982; lectr., panelist, numerous orgns.; standing com. on rules of practice and procedure U.S. Jud. Conf., 1991-98, chair, 1993-98; mem. exec. com. 9th Cir. Jud. Conf., 1989-93, Fed. State Jud. Coun., 1989-98, jury com., 1990-92, planning com. for Nat. Conf. on Fed.-State Jud. Relationships, Orlando, 1991-92, planning com. for We. Regional Conf. on State-Fed. Jud. Relationships, Stevens, Wash., 1992-93; chair dist. ct. symposium and jury utilization Ctrl. Dist. Calif., 1985, chair atty. liaison, 1989-90, chair U.S. Constn. Bicentennial com., 1986-91, chair magistrate judge com., 1992-93; mem. State Adv. Group on Juvenile Justice and Delinquency Prevention, 1983-84, Bd. Legal Specializations Criminal Law Adv. Commn., 1983-84, victim/witness adv. com. Office Criminal Justice Planning, 1980-83, U. So. Calif. Bd. Councilors, 1993-01; active team in tng. Leukemia Soc. Am., 1993, 95, 97, 2000; legion lex bd. dirs. U. So. Calif. Sch. Law Support Group, 1981-83. Winner Hale Moot Ct. Competition, State of Calif., 1967; named Judge of Yr., Orange County Trial Lawyers Assn., 1978, Most Outstanding Judge, Orange County Bus. Litigation Sect., 1990; recipient Franklin G. West award Orange County Bar Assn., 1985. Mem. ABA (jud. adminstrn. divsn. and litigation sect. 1984—, nat. conf. fed. trial judges com. on legis. affairs 1990-91), Am. Law Inst., Am. Judicature Soc., Fed. Judges Assn. (bd. dirs. 1989-92), Nat. Assn. Women Judges, U.S. Supreme Ct. Hist. Soc., Ninth Cir. Dist. Judges Assn., Calif. Supreme Ct. Hist. Soc., Orange County Bar Assn. (mem. numerous com.s, Franklin G. West award 1984), Calif. Judges Assn. (mem. com. on jud. coll. 1978-80, com. on civil law and procedure 1980-82, Dean's coll. curriculum commn. 1981), Calif. Judges Found. Office: Ronald Reagan Fed Bldg & Courthouse 411 W 4th St Santa Ana CA 92701-4500

STOTT, GRADY BERNELL, lawyer; b. Bailey, N.C., Sept. 19, 1921; s. William Willard and Zettie Harriett (Bissette) S.; m. Mays Beal, May 9, 1952; children: Sue J., Caroline Beal. AB, Duke U., 1947, JD, 1952. Bar: N.C. 1952. Dist. atty. 27th Jud. Dist., Gastonia, N.C., 1957-62; partner firm Stott, Hollowell, Palmer & Windham, Gastonia, 1960—. Served with USMC, 1943-48. Fellow Am. Bar Found., Am. Coll. Trial Lawyers; mem. N.C. State Bar (pres. 1978-79), Am. Bar Assn. (del. 1980), N.C. Bar Assn., Assn. Ins. Attys. Clubs: Masons. Democrat. Methodist. Office: 401 E Franklin Blvd Gastonia NC 28054-7152 E-mail: gbs@shpw.com.

STOTTER, JAMES, II, lawyer, legal consultant; b. Cleve., Oct. 12, 1929; s. Raymond H. and Janet H. (Stern) S.; m. Hollie McGlohn, Oct. 31, 1954; children: Raymond Judd (dec.), Hillary Feidler, James Robin, Cameron Elizabeth. BA, Yale Coll., 1951; LLB, Yale U., 1954; M in Law Studies, U. So. Calif., 1961. Bar: Calif., U.S. Supreme Ct., U.S. Ct. Mil. Appeals. Asst. U.S. atty. U.S. Dept. Justice, L.A., 1957-59, 68-89, asst. chief civil div., chief drug forfeiture unit, 1980-89; pvt. practice L.A., Beverly Hills, Calif., 1960-67; instr., adj. prof. law U.S. Atty. Gen.'s Advocacy Inst. Calif. Coll. Law, U. West L.A., 1970-87; judge pro tem Mcpl. and Small Claims Ct., L.A., 1970-88; atty. at law Cambria, Calif., 1989—. Guide hist. monument Hearst Castle, San Simeon, Calif., 1991; active civic and vol. orgns., Cambria and San Luis Obispo, Calif. Capt. USAF, 1954-57. Mem. Am. Arbitration Assn. (mediator/arbitrator 1970—). General civil litigation, General practice, Personal injury (including property damage). Home and Office: 2410 Langton St Cambria CA 93428-4722

STOTTER, LAWRENCE HENRY, lawyer; b. Cleve., Sept. 24, 1929; s. Oscar and Bertha (Lieb) S.; m. Ruth Rapoport, June 30, 1957; children: Daniel, Jennifer, Steven. BBA, Ohio State U., 1956, LLB, 1958, JD, 1967. Bar: Calif. 1960, U.S. Supreme Ct. 1973, U.S. Tax Ct. 1976. Pvt. practice, San Francisco, 1963—; ptnr. Stotter and Coats, San Francisco, 1981-97; sole practitioner, 1997—; mem. faculty Nat. Judicial Coll.; mem. Calif. Family Law Adv. Commn., 1979-80. Editor in chief: Am. Bar Family Advocate mag, 1977-82; TV appearances on Phil Donahue Show, Good Morning America. Pres. Tamalpais Conservation Club, Marin County, Calif.; U.S. State Dept. del. Hague Conf. Pvt. Internat. Law, 1979-80; legal adv. White House Conf. on Families, 1980— . Served with AUS, 1950-53. Mem. ABA (past chmn. family law sect.), Am. Acad. Matrimonial Lawyers (past nat. v.p.), Calif. State Bar (past chmn. family law sect.), San Francisco Bar Assn. (past chmn. family law sect.), Calif. Trial Lawyers Assn. (past chmn. family law sect.) Family and matrimonial. Home: 2244 Vistazo St E Belvedere Tiburon CA 94920-1970 Office: 1255 Columbus Ave # 200 San Francisco CA 94133-1326 E-mail: lhstotter@aol.com.

STOUP, ARTHUR HARRY, lawyer; b. Kansas City, Mo., Aug. 30, 1925; s. Isadore and Dorothy (Rankle) S.; m. Kathryn Jolliff, July 30, 1948; children: David C., Daniel P., Rebecca Ann, Deborah E. Student, Kansas City Jr. Coll., Mo. 1942-43; BA, U. Kansas City, 1950; JD, U. Mo., Kansas City, 1950. Bar: Mo. 1950, D.C. 1979, U.S. Dist. Ct. (we. dist.) Mo., U.S. Dist. Ct. Kans., U.S. Dist. Ct. Ariz. Pvt. practice law, Kansas City, 1950—. Chmn. U.S. Jud. Merit Selection Com. for Western Dist. Mo., 1981. Chmn. com. to rev. continuing edn. U. Mo., 1978—79; mem. dean search com. U. Mo. Law Sch., Kansas City, Mo., 1979, 1994—95; trustee U. Mo.-Kansas City Law Found., 1972—, pres., 1979—82; trustee U. Mo., Kansas City, 1979—2001, hon. trustee, 2001—. With USNR, 1942—45. Recipient Alumni Achievement award, U. Mo., Kansas City, 1975, Law Found. Svc. award, U. Mo.-Kansas City Law Found., 1987. Fellow Internat. Soc. Barristers (state mem. chmn.), Am. Bar Found. (life mem.); mem. ABA (ho. dels. 1976-80), Kansas City Met. Bar Assn. (pres. 1966-67, Dean of Trial Bar award 1991, mem. exec. com. 2003-), Mo. Bar (bd. govs. 1967-76, v.p. 1972-73, pres. elect 1973-74, pres. 1974-75), Lawyers Assn. Kansas City Mo., Mo. Assn. Trial Attys. (sustaining), Assn. Trial Lawyers Am. (sustaining), So. Conf. Bar Pres.'s (life), Mobar Research Inc. (pres. 1978-86), Phi Alpha Delta Alumni (justice Kansas City area alumni 1955-56). Lodges: Optimists (pres. Ward Pkwy. 1961-62, lt. gov. Mo. dist. internat. 1963-64), Sertoma, B'nai B'rith. Federal civil litigation, General civil litigation, Personal injury (including property damage). Home: 9002 Western Hills Dr Kansas City MO 64114-3566 Office: Palace Bldg Ste 230 1150 Grand Blvd Kansas City MO 64106-2317 Fax: 816-474-0714.

STOUPE, LOUISE, lawyer; arrived in Japan, 2001; BA, LLB with honors, U. Auckland, New Zealand, 1995, M in Comml. Law with first class honors, 1999; LLM, Duke U., 2000. Bar: High Ct. New Zealand 1996, Calif. 2000, U.S. Dist. Ct. (no. dist.) Calif. 2000, U.S. Ct. Appeals (9th cir.). 2001. Staff solicitor Russell McVeagh, Auckland, 1996—99; assoc. Morrison & Foerster, Palo Alto, Calif., 2000—01, Tokyo, 2001—. Editor: Duke Internat. and Comparative Law Jour. Recipient Ethel Benjamin award, New Zealand Law Found., 1998, Fulbright Buddle Findlay award, Fulbright, 1999; scholar, Ministry Fgn. Affairs and Trade, New Zealand, 1995. Mem.: ABA. General civil litigation, Alternative dispute resolution, Private international. Office: Morrison & Foerster 1-1-3 Marunouchi Chiyoda-ku Tokyo 100-0005 Japan

STOUT, LOWELL, lawyer; b. Tamaha, Okla., July 23, 1928; s. Charles W. and Rosetta (Easley) S.; m. Liliane Josue, Nov. 29, 1952; children: Georgianna, Mark Lowell. Student, Northeastern State Coll., Tahlequah, Okla., 1946-49, U. Okla., 1949-51; LLB, U. N.Mex., 1952. Bar: N.Mex. 1952. Ptnr. Easley, Quinn & Stout, Hobbs, N.Mex., 1954-58, Girand & Stout, Hobbs, 1958-60; pvt. practice Hobbs, 1960-80; ptnr. Stout & Stout, Hobbs, 1980—. With U.S. Army, 1952-54. Perenially listed in Best Lawyers in America. Fellow Am. Coll. Trial Lawyers; mem. Assn. Trial Lawyers Am., State Bar N.Mex., N.Mex. Trial Lawyers Assn., Lea County

Bar Assn. General civil litigation, Personal injury (including property damage), Workers' compensation. Home: 218 W Lea St Hobbs NM 88240-5110 Office: Stout & Stout PO Box 716 Hobbs NM 88241-0716

STOVALL, CARLA JO, former state attorney general; b. Hardner, Kans., Mar. 18, 1957; d. Carl E. and Juanita Joe (Ford) Stovall. BA, Pittsburg (Kans.) State U., 1979; JD, U. Kans., 1982, MPA , 1993. Bar: Kans. 1982, U.S. Dist. Ct. Kans. 1982. Pvt. practice, Pitts., 1982—85; atty. Crawford County, Pitts., 1984—88; gov. Kans. Parole Bd., Topeka, 1988—94; atty. gen. State of Kans., Topeka, 1995—2002. Lectr. law Pittsburg State U., 1982—84. Mem. bd. govs. U. Kans. Sch. Law; Nat. Ctr. Missing and Exploited Children; Am. Legacy Found.; Nat. Crime Prevention Coun.; Coun. State Govts.; mem. bd. govs. Kans. Children's Cabinet; pres. NAAG, 2001—02, chmn. exec. com. midwest region, sexually violent predator com., 1995—96; Bd. dirs., sec. Pittsburg Family YMCA, 1983—88. Named Outstanding Atty. Gen., Nat. Assn. Attys. Gen., 2001, Topeka Fraternal Order of Police's Amb. to Law Enforcement; recipient Champion award, Campaign Tobacco Free Kids, 2002, Adam Walsh Children's Fund Rainbow award, Nat. Ctr. Missing and Exploited Children, 2001, Kelley-Wyman award, Nat. Assn. Attys. Gen., 2001, Person of the Yr., Kans. Peace Officer Assn.'s Law Enforcement, Morton Baud Allied Profl. award, Nat. Orgn. Victim Assistance, Father Ken Czillinger award, Nat. Parents Murdered Children, Disting. Svc. to Kans. Children award, Kans. Children's Svc. League, Woman of Achievement award, Miss Kans. Pageant. Mem.: NAAG (pres. 2001—02), AAUW (bd. dirs. 1983—87), ABA, Bus. and Profl. Women Assn. (Young Careerist award 1984), Nat. Coll. Dist. Attys., Kans. County and Dist. Attys. Assn., Crawford County Bar Assn. (sec. 1984—85, v.p. 1985—86, pres. 1986—87), Kans. Bar Assn., Kans. Assn. Commerce and Industry (Leadership Kans. award 1983), Pittsburg Area C. of C. (bd. dirs. 1983—85, Leadership Pitts. award 1984), Pittsburg State U. Alumni Assn. (bd. dirs. 1983—88). Republican. Methodist. Avocations: travel, photography, tennis.

STOVSKY, MICHAEL DAVID, lawyer; b. Cleve., Mar. 10, 1964; s. Robert Leonard and Alyce Joan Stovsky; m. Jill Denise Simon, Oct. 31, 1993; children: Alexa, Matthew, Tyler. BA, Northwestern U., 1986; JD, U. Pa., 1991. Bar: Ohio 1991. Atty. Kahn, Kleinman, Yanowitz & Arnson Co., LPA, Cleve., 1991-96; ptnr. Ulmer & Berne LLP, Cleve., 1996—. Chair Internet and e-commerce Group. Contbr. articles to profl. jours. Mem. steering com. Northwestern U. Dance Marathon for United Cerebral Palsy, Evanston, Ill., 1984-85. Zeta Beta Tau/Jack London scholar, Evanston, 1983. Mem. ABA (mem. bus. law sect. com. on the law of commerce in cyberspace 1996—, mem. planning com. and faculty Nat. Inst. on Representing High Tech. Cos. 1998), Cleve. Bar Assn. (chmn. securities inst. panel on electronic securities practice 1998, chmn. tech. com. 1998), Phi Delta Phi, Pi Sigma Alpha, Alpha Lambda Delta. Avocations: golf, skiing, squash, running. Computer, Corporate, general, Securities. Office: Ulmer & Berne LLP 1300 E 9th St Ste 900 Cleveland OH 44114-1583 Fax: 216-621-7488.

STOWE, CHARLES ROBINSON BEECHER, management consultant, educator, lawyer; b. Seattle, July 18, 1949; s. David Beecher and Edith Beecher (Andrade) S.; m. Laura Everett, Mar. 9, 1985. BA, Vanderbilt U., 1971; MBA, U. Dallas, 1975; JD, U. Houston, 1982; PhD, U. Warsaw, Poland, 1998. Bar: Tex. 1982, U.S. Dist. Ct. (so. dist.) Tex. 1984, U.S. Tax Ct. 1984. Acct. exec. Engleman Co., Dallas, 1974-75; instr. Richland Coll., Dallas, 1976; acct. Arthur Andersen & Co., Dallas, 1976-78; part-time pub. rels. cons.; dir. Productive Capital Assocs., 1975-81; pres. Stowe & Co., Dallas, 1978—; from asst. to prof. dept. gen. bus. and fin. Coll. Bus. Adminstrn., Sam Houston State U., 1982—, dir. Office Internat. Programs, 1997-2001. Bd. dirs. Office Internat. programs, adminstrv. intern asst. to pres., 1985. Author: Bankruptcy I Micro-Mash Inc., 1989, rev. edit., 1995, The Implications of Foreign Financial Instutions on Poland's Emerging Entrepreneurial Economy, 1999; co-author: CPA rev.; co-editor: Knowledge Cafe for Intellect Product and Intellectual Entrepreneurship, 2001; editor Houston Jour. Internat. Law, 1981-82; contbr. articles to profl. jours. Trustee Stowe-Day Found., 1979-80; mem. nat. adv. bd. Young Am.'s Found., 1979—; vol. faculty State Bar Tex. Profl. Devel. Program, 1988—; vol., mediator Dispute Resolution Ctr. Montgomery County; mediator so. dist. U.S. Dist. Ct. Tex. 1993; team chief U.S. Mil. liaison Rep. Poland, 1994; pub. affairs officer George C. Marshall European Ctr. Security Studies, 1997. With USNR, 1971-74; capt. Res. Navy Achievement medal, Gold Star, Legion of Merit, Def. Meritorious Svc. medal with oak leaf cluster, Navy Meritorious Svc. award; Summer fellow Tex. Coordinating Bd., 1988, Prince-Babson fellow Entrepreneurship Symposium, 1991; recipient Freedoms Found. award. Mem. ABA, Am. Arbitration Assn., State Bar Tex. (vol. faculty profl. devel. program 1988-90, vice-chmn. profl. efficiency and econ. rsch. com. 1993, chmn. law office mgmt. com. 1993-94, bd. dirs. 2002—), Walker County Bar Assn. (pres. 1987-88), Tex. State Bar Coll. (bd. dirs. 2001—), Assn. for Computer Educators Tex. (bd. dirs. 2001-03), Pub. Rels. Soc. Am., Tex. Assn. Realtors, US Navy League, Naval Res. Assn., Res. Officers Assn., Dallas Vanderbilt Club (pres. 1977-78); bd. dirs. Assoc. Computer Educators Texas, 2000-, State Bar Coll. Tex., 2002-. Office: PO Box 2144 Huntsville TX 77341-2144

STRADER, JAMES DAVID, lawyer; b. Pitts., June 30, 1940; s. James Lowell and Tyra Fredrika (Bjorn) S.; m. Ann Wallace, Feb. 8, 1964; children: James Jacob, Robert Benjamin. BA, Mich. State U., 1962; JD, U. Pitts., 1965. Bar: Pa. 1966, U.S. Dist. Ct. (we. dist.) Pa. 1966, U.S. Dist. Ct. (ea. dist.) Pa. 1973, U.S. Dist. Ct. (mid. dist.) Pa. 1985, U.S. Ct. Appeals (4th and 5th cirs.) 1977, U.S. Ct. Appeals (3d and 11th cirs.) 1981, U.S. Supreme Ct. 1982, W.Va. 1996. Assoc. Peacock, Keller & Yohe, Washington, 1967-68; atty. U.S. Steel Corp., Pitts., 1968-77, gen. atty. worker's compensation, 1977-84; assoc. Caroselli, Spagnolli & Beachler, Pitts., 1984-87; ptnr. Dickie, McCamey & Chilcote, Pitts., 1987—. V.p. bd. trustees Mt. Lebanon Pub. Libr., 2002—; del. Dem. Mid-Yr. Conv., 1974; mem. Dem. Nat. Platform Com., 1976; commr. Mt. Lebanon, Pa., 1974—78. Capt. U.S. Army, 1965—67. Mem. ABA (sr. vice-chmn. worker's compensation com. 1978-94), Pa. Bar Assn. (chmn. worker's compensation law sect. 1994-95), Pa. Bar Inst. (bd. dirs. 2001-),State Bar W.Va., Allegheny County Bar Assn., Valley Brook Country Club. Democrat. Presbyterian. Personal injury (including property damage), Workers' compensation. Office: Dickie McCamey & Chilcote 2 PPG Pl Ste 400 Pittsburgh PA 15222-5491

STRADER, TIMOTHY RICHARDS, lawyer; b. Portland, Oreg., Jan. 17, 1956; s. Charles J. and Carol Jane (Dwyer) S.; m. Lisa M.K. Bartholomew, May 21, 1988; children: Kelly Meehan, Erin Dwyer. BBA in Mgmt., U. Notre Dame, 1978; JD, Willamette U., Salem, Oreg., 1981; LLM in Taxation, U. Fla., Gainesville, 1982. Bar: Oreg. 1981. Assoc. McEwen, Hanna, Gisvold & Rankin, Portland, 1982-85, Bullivant, Houser, Bailey, Hanna, Portland, 1985-87, Hanna, Urbigkeit, Jensen, et al., Portland, 1987-88, Hanna, Murphy, Jensen, Holloway, Portland, 1988-89; mem. Hanna Strader, P.C., Portland, 1989—. Mem. editorial bd. State Bar Estate Planning Newsletter, 1987—. Mem. alumni bd. Jesuit H.S., Portland, 1992-94, trustee, 1993-99; bd. dirs. Valley Cath. Sch., Beaverton, 1989-95; mem. Estate Planning Coun., Portland, 1990—, bd. dirs., 2000—. Mem. ABA, Multnomah Bar Assn., Multnomah Athletic Club, Waverley Country Club. Estate planning, Probate (including wills, trusts), Corporate taxation. Office: Hanna Strader PC 1300 SW 6th Ave Ste 300 Portland OR 97201-3461 E-mail: tstrader@hannastrader.com.

STRADLEY, RICHARD LEE, lawyer; b. Chula Vista, Calif., Sept. 10, 1951; s. George R. and Betty J. (Laughman) Stradley; m. Christine A. Crofts, Sept. 7, 1991; 1 child, Samuel Richard. BA, Coll. Santa Fe, 1972; JD, U. Miss., 1975. Bar: Miss. 1975, U.S. Dist. Ct. (no. dist.) Miss. 1975, U.S. Dist. Ct. Mont. 1980, U.S. Ct. Appeals (5th and 9th cirs.) 1980, U.S. Dist. Ct. (so. dist.) Miss. 1981, U.S. Ct. Appeals (10th and 11th cirs.) 1981, U.S. Tax Ct. 1981, U.S. Supreme Ct., Mont. 1982, U.S. Dist. Ct. (we. dist.) Tenn. 1982, U.S. Dist. Ct. (no. dist.) Tex. 1984, Oreg. 1985, U.S. Dist. Ct. Oreg. 1986, U.S. Dist. Ct. Nebr. 1986, Wyo. 1994. Pvt. practice, 1975—; staff atty. East Miss. Legal Svcs., Forest, 1979. Mem.: Chrisitian Legal Soc. Avocations: chess, computers, woodworking. Federal civil litigation, Probate (including wills, trusts), Estate taxation. Office: PO Box 2541 Cody WY 82414-2541 E-mail: richard_l.stradley@bigfoot.com.

STRAIN, JAMES ARTHUR, lawyer; b. Alexandria, La., Oct. 11, 1944; s. William Joseph and Louise (Moore) S.; m. Cheryl Sue Williamson, Aug. 19, 1967; children: William Joseph, Gordon Richard, Elizabeth Parks. BS in Econs., Ind. U., 1966, JD, 1969. Bar: Ind. 1969, U.S. Dist. Ct. (so. dist.) Ind. 1969, U.S. Ct. Appeals (7th cir.) 1972, U.S. Supreme Ct. 1975, U.S. Ct. Appeals (5th cir.) 1978. Instr. Law Sch. Ind. U., Indpls., 1969-70; law clk. to Hon. John S. Hastings 7th Cir. Ct. Appeals, Chgo., 1970-71; assoc. Cahill, Gordon & Reindel, N.Y.C., 1971-72; law clk. to Hon. William H. Rehnquist U.S. Supreme Ct., Washington, 1972-73; assoc. Barnes, Hickam, Pantzer & Boyd, Indpls., 1973-75; ptnr. Barnes, Hickam, Pantzer & Boyd (name changed to Barnes & Thornburg), 1976-96, Sommer & Barnard, PC, Indpls., 1996—. Adj. asst. prof. law Ind. U. Sch. Law, 1986-92. Mem., bd. dirs. The Penrod Soc., Indpls., 1976—, Indpls. Symphonic Choir, 1988-91, Festival Music Soc., Indpls., 1990-96. Mem. 7th Cir. Bar Assn. (meetings chmn. Ind. chpt. 1979-88, portraits 1988-89, bd. govs. 1989—, 1st v.p. 1995, pres. 1996). Avocations: photography, music. Corporate, general, Mergers and acquisitions, Securities. Office: Sommer Barnard Ackerson PC One Indiana Sq Ste 3500 Indianapolis IN 46204 E-mail: strain@sbalawyers.com.

STRAND, ROGER GORDON, federal judge; b. Peekskill, N.Y., Apr. 28, 1934; s. Ernest Gordon Strand and Lisabeth Laurine (Phin) Steinmetz; m. Joan Williams, Nov. 25, 1961. AB, Hamilton Coll., 1955; LLB, Cornell U., 1961; grad., Nat. Coll. State Trial Judges, 1968. Bar: Ariz. 1961, U.S. Dist. Ct. Ariz. 1961, U.S. Supreme Ct. 1980. Assoc. Fennemore, Craig, Allen & McClennen, Phoenix, 1961-67; judge Ariz. Superior Ct., Phoenix, 1967-85, U.S. Dist. Ct. Ariz., Phoenix, 1985—. Assoc. presiding judge Ariz. Superior Ct., 1971-85; lectr. Nat. Jud. Coll., Reno, 1978-87; mem. jud. conf. U.S. com. on info. tech., 1996-2002. Past pres. cen. Ariz. chpt. Arthritis Found. Lt. USN, 1955-61. Mem. ABA, Ariz. Bar Assn., Maricopa County Bar Assn., Nat. Conf. Fed. Trial Judges, Phi Delta Phi, Aircraft Owners and Pilots Assn. Lodges: Rotary. Avocations: computer applications, golf, fishing. Home: 5825 N 3rd Ave Phoenix AZ 85013-1537 Office: Sandra Day O'Connor US Courthouse SPC 57 401 W Washington Phoenix AZ 85003-2156

STRANGEWAYS, ERIK, lawyer; JD magna cum laude, N.Y. Law Sch., 1982. Bar: N.Y. 1982, N.J. 1982. Sr. atty. N.Y. State Divsn. Housing, Jamaica, 1988—. Alfred Gross scholar, N.Y. Law Sch., 1979. Avocation: computers. Office: NY State Divsn Housing 92-31 Union Hall St Jamaica NY 11433 Business E-Mail: estrangeways@dhcr.state.ny.us.

STRASBAUGH, WAYNE RALPH, lawyer; b. Lancaster, Pa., July 20, 1948; s. Wayne Veily and Jane Irene (Marzolf) S.; m. Carol Lynne Taylor, June 8, 1974; children: Susan, Wayne T., Elizabeth. AB, Bowdoin Coll., 1970; AM, Harvard U., 1971, PhD, 1976, JD, 1979. Bar: Ohio 1979, Pa. 1983, U.S. Tax Ct. 1980, U.S. Ct. Fed. Claims 1980, U.S. Ct. Appeals (fed. cir.) 1982, U.S. Dist. Ct. (no. dist.) Ohio 1979, U.S. Dist. Ct. (ea. dist.) Pa. 1983. Assoc. Jones Day Reavis & Pogue, Cleve., 1979-82, Morgan Lewis & Bockius, Phila., 1982-84, Ballard Spahr Andrews & Ingersoll, LLP, Phila., 1984-88, ptnr., 1988—, chmn. tax group, 2001—. Mem. ABA (tax sect., chmn. com. 1992-94), Am. Coll. Tax Counsel (regent 2003—)., Phila. Bar Assn. (tax sect., chmn. fed. tax com. 1992, coun. mem. 1995, sec.-treas. 1996, vice-chmn. 1997-98, chmn. 1999-2000). Episcopalian. Mergers and acquisitions, Corporate taxation, Taxation, general. Office: Ballard Spahr Andrews & Ingersoll LLP 1735 Market St Ste 5100 Philadelphia PA 19103-7599 E-mail: strasbaugh@ballardspahr.com.

STRATTON, EVELYN LUNDBERG, judge; b. Bangkok, Feb. 25, 1953; came to U.S., 1971 (parents Am. citizens); d. Elmer John and Corrine Sylvia (Henricksen) Sahlberg; children: Luke Andrew, Tyler John; m. Jack A. Lundberg. Student, LeTourneau Coll., Longview, Tex., 1971-74; AA, U. Fla., 1973; BA, U. Akron, 1976; JD, Ohio State U., 1978. Bar: Ohio 1979, U.S. Dist. Ct. (so. dist.) Ohio 1979, U.S. Ct. Appeals (6th cir.) 1983. Assoc. Hamilton, Kramer, Myers & Cheek, Columbus, 1979-85; ptnr. Wesp, Osterkamp & Stratton, 1985-88; judge Franklin County Ct. Common Pleas, 1989-96; justice Ohio State Supreme Ct., 1996—. Vis. prof. Nat. Jud. Coll., 1997—; spkr. legal seminars. Contbr. articles to profl. jours. Trustee Ohio affiliate Nat. Soc. to Prevent Blindness, 1989—, bd. dirs., trustee Columbus Coun. World Affairs, 1990-99, chmn. bd. dirs., 1999—; bd. dirs., trustee Dave Thomas Adoption Found., 1996—, ArChSafe Found., 1997—; mem. women's bd. Zephyrus League Cen. Ohio Lung Assn., 1989—; mem. Alliance Women Cmty. Corrections, 1993—. Recipient Gold Key award LeTourneau Coll., Gainesville, Fla., 1974, Svc. commendation Ohio Ho. of Reps., 1984, Scholar of Life award St. Joseph's Orphanage, 1998. Mem. ABA, ATLA, Columbus Bar Assn. (bd. govs. 1984-88, 90—, lectr.), Ohio Bar Assn. (jud. adminstrv. and legal reform com., coun. dels. 1992-96, Ohio Cmty. Corrections Orgn. (trustee 1995—), Columbus Bar Found. (trustee 1986-91, officer, sec. 1986-87, v.p. 1987-88), Am. Inns of Ct., Women Lawyers Franklin County, Phi Alpha Delta (pres. 1982-83). Office: Supreme Ct Ohio 30 E Broad St Fl 3 Columbus OH 43215

STRATTON, WALTER LOVE, lawyer; b. Greenwich, Conn., Sept. 21, 1926; s. John McKee and June (Love) S.; children: John, Michael, Peter (dec.), Lucinda; m. DeAnna Weinheimer, Oct. 1, 1994. Student, Williams Coll., 1943; AB, Yale U., 1948; LL.B., Harvard U., 1951. Bar: N.Y. 1952. Assoc. Casey, Lane & Mittendorf, N.Y.C., 1951-53; assoc. Donovan, Leisure, Newton & Irvine, N.Y.C., 1956-63, ptnr., 1963-84, Gibson, Dunn & Crutcher, 1984-93, Andrews & Kurth, N.Y.C., 1993-95, of counsel, 1996—. Asst. U.S. atty. So. Dist. N.Y., N.Y.C., 1953-56; lectr. Practising Law Inst. Served with USNR, 1945-46. Fellow: Am. Coll. Trial Lawyers; mem.: ABA, N.Y. State Bar Assn., Fed. Bar Coun., Greenwich Riding and Trails Assn. (chmn.), Colo. Arlberg Club, Indian Harbor Yacht Club. Home: 434 Round Hill Rd Greenwich CT 06831-2639 Office: Andrews & Kurth 805 3rd Ave New York NY 10022-7513 E-mail: walterstratton@akllp.com.

STRAUB, CHESTER JOHN, judge; b. Bklyn., May 12, 1937; s. Chester and Ann (Majewski) Straub; m. Patricia Morrissey; children: Chester, Michael, Christopher, Robert. AB, St. Peter's Coll., 1958; JD, U. Va., 1961. Bar: N.Y. 1962, U.S. Dist. Ct. (so. and ea. dists.) N.Y. 1963, U.S. Ct. Appeals (2d cir.) 1967, U.S. Supreme Ct. 1978. Assoc. Willkie Farr & Gallagher, N.Y.C., 1963—71, ptnr., 1971—98; mem. N.Y. State Assembly, 1967—72, N.Y. State Senate, 1973—75, Dem. Nat. Com., 1976—80; judge U.S. Ct. Appeals (2d cir.), 1998—. Past mediator U.S. Dist. Ct. (so. dist.) N.Y.; neutral evaluator U.S. Dist. Ct. (ea. dist.) N.Y.; chmn. jud. screening com. State of N.Y., 1988—94, first dept. jud. screening com., 1983—94, Senator Moynihan's jud. selection com., 1976—98. Trustee Lenox Hill Hosp.; Cardinal's com. laity Cath. Charities, NY. With U.S. Army, 1961—63. Mem.: ABA, Assn. of Bar of City of N.Y.C., N.Y. State Bar Assn., Kosciuszko Found. Office: US Ct Appeals Second Circuit 500 Pearl St New York NY 10007-1316

STRAUB, PETER THORNTON, lawyer; b. St. Louis, Mar. 27, 1939; s. Ralph H. and Mary Louise (Thornton) S.; m. Wendy B. Cubbage, Dec. 29, 1964; children: Karl Thornton, Philip Hamilton, Ellen Elizabeth. AB, Washington and Lee U., 1961, LLB, 1964. Bar: Mo. 1964, Va. 1964, U.S. Dist. Ct. (ea. dist.) Mo. 1967, U.S. Circuit Ct. Appeals (8th cir.) 1969, U.S. Supreme Ct. 1970. U.S. Circuit Ct. Appeals (D.C. cir.) 1971, Ct. Mil. Appeals 1970, U.S. Tax Ct. 1971, U.S. Bankruptcy Ct. 1991. Assoc. Evans & Dixon, St. Louis, 1966-68; asst. pub. defender St. Louis County, St. Louis, 1968-69; asst. U.S. Atty. St. Louis, 1969-71; trial atty. internal security div. Dept. Justice, Washington, 1971-72, atty.-adviser office of dep. atty. gen., 1972-73, dir. office criminal justice, spl. asst. to atty. gen., 1974; minority counsel com. on judiciary U.S. Ho. of Reps., Washington, 1973-74; gen. counsel SSS, Washington, 1974-76; pvt. practice Law Offices of Peter T. Straub, Alexandria, Va., 1976—. Pres., gov. bd. Alexandria Cmty. Mental Health Ctr., 1982—95; mem. No. Va. Estate Planning Coun., 1981—; mem. pres.'s coun. Trinity Coll., Washington, 1980—87; mem. adv. bd. Am. Heart Assn., Alexandria, 1991—92, Salvation Army, Alexandria, 1991—, v.p., 1994—96, chmn., 1997—99, Alexandria Cmty. Shelter Adv. Bd., 1995—97; Va. escheat atty. City of Alexandria, 1994—2002; dist. chmn. Boy Scouts Am., 1998—2001; mem. adv. bd. Hospice No. Va., 2000—, Friends of the Washington and Old Dominion Trail, 2002—; bd. dirs. Parc East Condominium, 1990—, sec., 1992—; bd. dirs. Sigma Nu Ednl. Found., Inc., 2000—; charter mem. bd. dirs. Alexandria Country Day Sch., 1983—90. Recipient certificate of award Dept. Justice, 1970, certificate of appreciation Law Enforcement Assistance Adminstrn. Dept. Justice, 1974, Silver Beaver award Boy Scouts Am., Washington , 1987. Mem.: FBA, ABA, Va. Trial Lawyers Assn., Alexandria Bar Assn., Mo. Bar Assn., Bar Assn. Met. St. Louis, Va. State Bar Assn., Optimists (bd. dirs., pres. Alexandria chpt. 1984, lt. gov. Nat. Capitol Va. Dist. 1987—89, treas. 1999—2001), Nat. Eagle Scout Assn., Nat. Lawyers Club, Sigma Nu. Republican. Congregationalist. Avocations: scouting, reading, bicycling. Estate taxation, Estate planning, General practice. Office: 1225 Martha Custis Dr # 103 Alexandria VA 22302-2040 Fax: 703-820-8602. E-mail: straublaw@erols.com.

STRAUSER, ROBERT WAYNE, lawyer; b. Little Rock, Aug. 28, 1943; s. Christopher Columbus and Opal (Orr) S.; m. Atha Maxine Tubbs, June 26, 1971 (div. 1991); children: Robert Benjamin, Ann Kathleen; m. Terri D. Seales, Oct. 17, 1998. BA, Davidson (N.C.) Coll., 1965; postgrad., Vanderbilt U., Nashville, 1965-66; LLB, U. Tex., 1968. Bar: Tex. 1968, U.S. Ct. Mil. Appeals 1971. Staff atty. Tex. Legis. Coun., Austin, 1969-71; counsel Jud. Com., Tex. Ho. of Reps., Austin, 1971-73; chief counsel Jud. Com., Tex. Constl. Conv., Austin, 1974; exec. v.p. and legis. counsel Tex. Assn. Taxpayers, Austin, 1974-85; assoc. Baker & Botts, Austin, 1985-87, ptnr., 1988—. Assoc. editor Tex. Internat. Law Jour., 1968. Mem. Tex. Ho. Speakers Econ. Devel. Com., Austin, 1986-87; assoc. dir. McDonald Obs. Bd. Visitors, 1988—; bd. dirs. Tex. Assn. Bus. and C. of C., 2000-2002; mem. Dean's Roundtable, U. Tex. Law Sch.; bd. dirs. Austin Symphony Orch. Soc., 1985—, v.p., 1993-94, nominating com., 1998-. Capt. USNR, ret. Named Rising Star of Tex., Tex. Bus. Mag., 1983. Fellow Tex. Bar Found.; mem. State Bar of Tex. (coun. mem. tax sect.), Travis County Bar Assn., Headliners Club (Austin). Administrative and regulatory, Legislative. Home: 3312 Gilbert St Austin TX 78703-2102 Office: Baker & Botts 1600 San Jacinto Blvd Austin TX 78701

STRAUSS, DAVID J. lawyer; b. Chgo., Jan. 26, 1943; BBA, U. Iowa, 1964, JD, 1967. Bar: Iowa 1967, Ohio 1967. Ptnr. Baker & Hostetler, Cleve. Mem. Phi Delta Phi, Order of Coif. Estate taxation. Office: Baker & Hostetler 3200 Nat City Ctr 1900 E 9th St Ste 3200 Cleveland OH 44114-3475

STRAUSS, GARY JOSEPH, lawyer; b. N.Y.C., July 6, 1953; s. Stanley Vinson and Frieda (Fischoff) S. BA magna cum laude, City Coll. of N.Y., 1974; JD, NYU, 1977. Bar: N.Y. 1978, Fla. 1980. Assoc. Finley, Kumble, Wagner, Heine & Underberg, N.Y.C., 1977—79; ptnr. Phillips, Nizer, Benjamin, Krim & Ballon, N.Y.C., 1979—87, Gaston & Snow, N.Y.C., 1987—88; pvt. practice N.Y.C., 1988—2002; ptnr. Gerstein Strauss & Rinaldi LLP, N.Y.C., 2002—. Mem. ABA (chmn. N.Y. com. current literature and real property law 1977), Fla. Bar Assn., N.Y. State Bar Assn. Property, real (including real estate development, water). Home: 57 W 38th St Fl 9 New York NY 10018-5500

STRAUSS, JEROME MANFRED, lawyer, banker; b. Milw., Nov. 7, 1934; s. Emanuel and Loraine (Goetz) S.; m. Susan Jean Kauffman, Dec. 30, 1967; children: Martha Lynn, Jared Lee, David Aaron. BA with honors, Ind. U., 1956; JD, NYU, 1959. Bar: Ind. 1959, Fla. 1996, U.S. Dist. Ct. (so. dist.) Ind. 1959, U.S. Tax Ct. 1965, U.S. Ct. Appeals (7th cir.) 1969. Lawyer Ice Miller Donadio & Ryan, Indpls., 1959—93, ptnr., 1969-93; sr. v.p. and regional trust mgr. Merrill Lynch Trust Co., 1993-95; with Mershon, Sawyer, Johnston, Dunwody & Cole, Miami, Palm Beach, Naples, 1995-96; established Wollman, Strauss & Assocs., P.A., 1997—2002; with Galbraith and McMains, Naples, Fla., 2003—; founder Midwest Tax and Estate Planning Inst., Indpls., 2003—. Co-author: Marital Deduction Trusts, 1963, Real Estate in an Estate, 1963, Durable Powers of Attorney, 1993; contbr. articles to profl. jours. Bd. dirs. Orton Soc., Indpls., 1970-72, Indpls., 1970-72, Indpls. Hebrew Congregation, 1979-85, Planned Giving Group of Ind., Indpls., 1988-95, Ind. Continuing Legal Edn. Forum, 1989-94; devel. com. Collier County, Fla. Cmty. Found., 1995—; mem. Planned Giving Com. of Lee County, Fla., 1995—, Fla. Planned Giving Coun., 1995—; planning coun. Naples, Fla. Estate, 1996—. Fellow Am. Coll Trust and Estate Counsel (charitable com., estate and gift tax com. 1996-2001), Am. Coll. Tax Counsel; mem. ABA (vice-chmn. marital deductin com. real estate property, probate and trust sect. 1988-90), Internat. Acad. Estate and Trust Law (academician 1987—), Ind. State Bar Assn. (sec. 1979-80, chmn. probate, trust and real property sect. 1970-71), Ind. Estate Planning Coun. (pres. 1970-71), Fla. State Bar Assn., Internat. Assn. of Fin. Planners of S.W. Fla., Collier County Bar Assn. Estate planning, Probate (including wills, trusts), Estate taxation. Home: 1056 Diamond Lake Cir Naples FL 34114-9211 Office: 9130 Galleria Ct Ste 301 Naples FL 34109 E-mail: rv-atty@lawyer4u.com.

STRAUSS, PETER L(ESTER), law educator; b. N.Y.C., Feb. 26, 1940; s. Simon D. and Elaine Ruth (Mandle) S.; m. Joanna Burnstine, Oct. 1, 1964; children: Benjamin, Bethany. AB magna cum laude, Harvard U., 1961; LLB magna cum laude, Yale U., 1964. Bar: D.C. 1965, U.S. Supreme Ct. 1968. Law clk. U.S. Ct. Appeals D.C. Cir., 1964-65, U.S. Supreme Ct., 1965-66; lectr. Halle Selassie U. Sch. Law, Addis Ababa, Ethiopia, 1966-68; asst. to solicitor gen. Dept. Justice, Washington, 1968-71; assoc. prof. law Columbia U., 1971-74, prof., 1974—, Betts prof., 1985—, vice-dean, 1996, 2001—02. Gen. counsel NRC, 1975-77, Adminstrv. Conf. U.S., 1984-95; Byrne vis. prof. Sch. Law Harvard U., Cambridge, Mass., 1994; bd. dirs. Ctr. for Computer Assisted Legal Instrn., 2002—. Mem. adv. bd. Lexis Electronic Author's Press, 1995-99; editor: SSRN Administrative Law Abstracts, 1997—; author: (with Abba Paulos translator) Fetha Negast: The Law of the Kings, 1968; (with others) Administrative Law Cases and Comments, 2003, Administrative Justice in the United States, 2002; contbr. articles to profl. jours. Recipient John Marshall prize Dept. Justice, 1970, Disting. Svc. award NRC, 1977. Mem. ABA (chair sect. administrv. law and regulatory practice 1992-93, Disting. Scholarship award 1988), Am. Law Inst. Office: Columbia U Law Sch 435 W 116th St New York NY 10027-7201

STRAUSS, ROBERT DAVID, lawyer; b. Cambridge, Mass., Oct. 20, 1951; s. Walter Adolf and Lilo (Teutsch) Strauss; m. Deborah Mackall, Feb. 15, 1986 (div. Dec. 1998); 1 child, Benjamin Walter; m. Ellen C. Handelsman, Apr. 6, 2002. BA, Emory U., 1973, JD, 1976. Bar: Ga. 1976. Assoc. Gambrell & Russell, Atlanta, 1976-81; ptnr. Smith, Gambrell & Russell, Atlanta, 1981-89, Trotter Smith & Jacobs, Atlanta, 1989-92, Troutman Sanders, Atlanta, 1992—. Contbr. articles to profl. jours. Mem. ABA (chmn. leasing subcom. 1988-94, uniform comml. code com.), State Bar of Ga., Equipment Leasing Assn. Am. Aviation, Commercial, contracts (including sales of goods; commercial financing), Finance. Home: 729 Amsterdam Ave NE Atlanta GA 30306 Office: Troutman Sanders 5200 Bank of Am Plz 600 Peachtree St NE Atlanta GA 30308-2216 E-mail: bo.strauss@troutmansanders.com.

STRAUSS, STANLEY ROBERT, lawyer; b. N.Y.C., June 3, 1915; s. Maurice M. and Blanche Anna (Danciger) S.; m. Margaret Inglis Forbes, Mar. 13, 1944 (div. 1950); m. Helen Anne Cummings, Dec. 31, 1975 (dec. 1980). BA cum laude, Williams Coll., 1936; LLB, Columbia U., 1940. Bar: N.Y. 1941, D.C. 1964, U.S. Ct. Appeals (1st cir.) 1977, U.S. Ct. Appeals (3d cir.) 1986, U.S. Ct. Appeals (4th cir.) 1974, U.S. Ct. Appeals (5th cir.) 1970, U.S. Ct. Appeals (6th cir.) 1977, U.S. Ct. Appeals (8th cirs.) 1975, U.S. Supreme Ct. 1965. Assoc. Howard Henig, N.Y.C., 1940-41; atty. NLRB, Washington, 1946-52, supervising atty., 1953-59, chief counsel, 1959-63; assoc. Vedder, Price, Kaufman & Kammholz, Washington, 1963-65, ptnr., 1965-90; of counsel Ogletree, Deakins, Nash, Smoak & Stewart, Washington, 1990—. Co-author: Practice and Procedure Before the National Labor Relations Board, 3d edit., 1980, 4th edit., 1987, 5th edit., 1996. Officer U.S. Army, 1941-45, PTO. Decorated Bronze Star; Horn scholar Columbia U. Law Sch., 1937-40. Mem. ABA, Fed. Bar Assn., D.C. Bar Assn., Kenwood Country Club. Avocations: golf, tennis. Home: 4956 Sentinel Dr Bethesda MD 20816-3594 Office: Ogletree Deakins Nash 2400 N St NW Fl 5 Washington DC 20037-1154 E-mail: stanleystrauss@odense.com.

STRAUSS, WILLIAM VICTOR, lawyer; b. Cin., July 5, 1942; s. William Victor and Elsa (Lovitt) S.; m. Linda Leopold, Nov. 9, 1969; children: Nancy T., Katherine S. AB cum laude, Harvard U., 1964; JD, U. Pa., 1967. Bar: Ohio 1967. Pres. Security Title and Guaranty Agy., Inc., Cin., 1982—, Strauss & Troy, Cin., 1995—. Trustee Cin. Psychoanalytic Inst., 1990—, Cin. Contemporary Arts Ctr., 1997—. Mem. ABA, Nat. Assn. Office and Indsl. Parks, Ohio State Bar Assn., Cin. Bar Assn., Ohio Land Title Assn. Commercial, contracts (including sales of goods; commercial financing), Estate planning, Property, real (including real estate development, water). Home: 40 Walnut Ave Wyoming OH 45215-4350 Office: Strauss & Troy Fed Res Bldg 150 E 4th St Fl 4 Cincinnati OH 45202-4018

STRAVALLE-SCHMIDT, ANN ROBERTA, lawyer; b. NYC, Jan. 2, 1957; Grad. cum laude, Phillips Exeter Acad., 1975; student, Occidental Coll., 1975-78, Oxford Coll., Eng., 1976-77; BS cum laude, Boston Coll., 1980; JD, Boston U., 1987; MBA, Rensselaer Polytechnic Inst., 2002; grad., Univ. of Phoenix Online, The Legal Environ. of Bus. Bar: Conn. 1987, U.S. Dist. Ct. Conn. 1988, U.S. Supreme Ct. 1993. Consulting staff Arthur Andersen, Boston, 1980-82; supr. CID ops. Aetna Life & Casualty, Hartford, Conn., 1982-84; summer intern US Atty.'s Office, Boston, 1985; jud. clk. Hon. Judge Thayer III NH Supreme Ct., 1987-88; trial lawyer Day, Berry & Howard, Hartford, Conn., 1988-91; sr. lawyer comml. litig. and appellate practice Berman & Sable, Hartford, Conn., 1991-96; dir. maj. case unit Travelers Property and Casualty Corp., Hartford, Conn., 1996-98; sr. atty. Robinson & Cole, Hartford, Conn., 1998-2000; gen. counsel Conn. Resources Recovery Authority, Hartford, Conn., 2000—. Brief judge Nat. Appellate Advocacy Competition, 1996. Mem. editorial bd. Conn. Bar Jour., 1990—; contbr. articles to profl. jours. Mem. Hebron Dem. Town Com., Hebron Bd. Fin., 1995-99, Hebron Sch. Bldg. Com., 1997-99; justice of peace, 1997-99; apptd. mem. Hebron Bldg. Com., 1997-99. Hennessey scholar Boston U., 1987. Mem. ABA, Conn. Bar Assn. (founder, chair appellate practice com. litigation sect. 1994-96, mem. exec. com. litigation sect.), Am. Registry of Outstanding Professionals, 2003-. General civil litigation, Commercial, consumer (including collections, credit). Home: 7 Don St Plainville CT 06062-1111 Office: Conn Resources Recovery Authority 100 Constitution Plz Ste 1700 Hartford CT 06103-1719 E-mail: astravalle@attbi.com.

STRAZZELLA, JAMES ANTHONY, law educator, lawyer; b. Hanover, Pa., May 18, 1939; s. Anthony F. and Teresa Ann Strazzella; m. Judith A. Coppola, Oct. 9, 1965; children: Jill M., Steven A., Tracy Ann, Michael P. AB, Villanova U., 1961; JD, U. Pa., 1964. Bar: Pa. 1964, D.C., 1965, U.S. Dist. Ct. (ea. and mid. dist.) Pa. 1969, U.S. Ct. Appeals (3rd cir.) 1964, U.S. Ct. Appeals (D.C. cir.) 1965, U.S. Ct. Appeals (4th cir.) 1983, U.S. Supreme Ct. 1969. Law clk. to Hon. Samuel Roberts Pa. Supreme Ct., 1964-65; asst. U.S. atty. D.C., 1965-69; vice dean, asst. prof. law U. Pa., Phila., 1969-73; faculty Temple U., Phila., 1973—; James G. Schmidt chair in law, 1989—; acting dean, 1987-89. Chief counsel Kent State investigation Pres.'s Commn. Campus Unrest, 1970; chmn. Atty. Gen.'s Task Force on Family Violence, Pa., 1985-89; mem., chmn. justice ops. Mayor's Criminal Justice Coordinating Commn., Phila., 1983-85; Pa. Joint Coun. Criminal Justice, 1979-82; mem. Com. to Study Pa.'s Unified Jud. Sys., 1980-82; Jud. Coun. Pa., 1972-82; chmn. criminal procedural rules com. Pa. Supreme Ct., 1972-85; mem. task force on prison overcrowding, 1983-85, rsch. adv. com., 1988, Pa. Commn. on Crime and Delinquency; chmn. U.S. Magistrate Judge Merit Selection Com., 1991, mem., 1989, 90, 91; co-chair Mayor's Transition Task Force on Pub. Safety, Phila., 1992; designate D.C. Com. on Adminstrn. of Justice Under Emergency Conditions, 1968; del. D.C. Jud. Conf., 1985, 95. Contbr. articles to profl. jours. and books. Mem. adv. bd. dirs., past pres. A Better Chance in Lower Merion; dir. Hist. Fire Mus., Phila., 1978—, 1st v.p., 2002—; bd. dirs. Lower Merion Hist. Soc., 1998—2000, Neighborhood Civic Assn., Bala-Cynwyd, Pa., 1984—87, Smith Meml. Playground in Fairmount Pk., 1997—, Coun. Legal Edn. Opportunity Bd., 1997—; bd. trustees Bala Cynwyd Pub. Libr., 1999—. Recipient award for disting. tchg. Linback Found., 1983, Advancement of Justice award Pa. Atty. Gen., 1989, Disting. Pub. Svc. award Assn. State and County Detectives, 1989, Spl. Merit award Pa. Assn. Police Chiefs, 1989, significant contbn. to legal scholarship and edn. Beccaria award Phila. Bar Assn. and Nat. IAB Assn., 1995. Fellow: Am. Bar Found.; mem.: St. Thomas More Soc. (pres. 1985—86, past dir. Phila. area, St. Thomas More award 1996), Phila. Bar Assn. (criminal justice sect., appellate cts. com.), Pa. Bar Assn. (commn. profl. stds. 1981—84, chmn. criminal law sect. 1986—88, Merit award 1987), FBA (Phila. crim. law com. adv. bd. 1988—93, chmn. nat. criminal law com. 1991—92), Am. Law Inst., ABA (faculty appellate judges seminars 1975—, various coms., acad. advisor appellate judges edn. com. 1993—, reporter task force on federalization criminal law 1998—99), Order of the Coif (exec. bd. U. Pa.). Roman Catholic. Home and Office: 100 Maple Ave Bala Cynwyd PA 19004-3017 Office: Temple U Law Sch 1719 N Broad St Philadelphia PA 19122-6002

STREAM, ARNOLD CRAGER, lawyer, writer; b. N.Y.C. s. Mervyn and Sophia (Hyams) S.; m. Barbara Bloom, Oct. 1, 1967; children by previous marriages: Jane, Abigail. BA, CCNY, 1936; LLD, St. Lawrence U., 1940. Bar: N.Y. 1940, D.C. 1942. Asst. U.S. Atty. N.Y.Dist., 1940-43; ptnr. Amen, Weisman & Butler, N.Y.C., 1948-55; exec. v.p., gen. counsel C & C TV Corp., 1955-60, Hazel Bishop, Inc., 1955-60; trial lawyer, 1960-91; sr. ptnr. Monasch, Chazen & Stream, N.Y.C., 1973-82, Blum, Gersen & Stream, N.Y.C., 1982-93; ret., 1993. Former trial counsel Gulfstream Aerospace Corp., Twentieth Century-Fox Film Corp., French Embassy, N.Y.C.; spl. counsel to TV industry; vis. lectr. Tauro Coll. Law; spkr. on lit. topics for Gt. Neck Libr.; archivist Palace of the Govs. and Mus. Fine Arts, Santa Fe; tutor lit. and bus. law Santa Fe C.C. Author: (novels) The Third Bullet, Until Proven Guilty, Nemo; (short story) Sudi, others; contbr. book revs., tax series, series on constl. law, articles to profl. jours. Served with JAGD, AUS, 1943-46. Mem. Bar of Assn. of City of N.Y. Federal civil litigation, General civil litigation, Family and matrimonial.

STREBE, GALEN GEORGE, lawyer, educator; b. Marshfield, Wis., July 11, 1948; s. Clyde Lavern and Bernice Ann (Pacourak) S.; m. Shannon Kathryn Dolan, July 30, 1988; children: Georgia D., Lydia D., Amelia D., James D. BS, U. Wis., 1975, JD, 1980. Bar: Wis. 1980, U.S. Dist. Ct. (ea. and we. dist.) Wis. Staff atty. Linehan Law Offices, Wausau, Wis., 1981; ptnr. Kaiser and Strebe, Ltd., Eau Claire, 1981-85; asst. corp. counsel Dane County, Madison, Wis., 1987—. Adj. prof. Cardinal Stritch U., Milw., 1991—, Concordia U. Wis., 1995—; chmn., organizer State Forms Com., Madison, 1993—. With U.S. Army, 1969-71. Decorated Purple Heart. Mem. Dane County Bar Assn., State Bar of Wis. Office: Dane County Corp Counsel 1202 Northport Dr Ste 437 Madison WI 53704-2020

STRECK, FREDERICK LOUIS, III, lawyer; b. St. Louis, Nov. 6, 1960; s. Frederick Louis Jr. and Joan Kathrine (Faerber) S.; m. Michelle Renee Harding; children: Frederick IV, Robert Harding, Joseph Walter, Samuel Franklin. BBA, Tex. Christian U., 1983; JD, St. Mary's U., 1986. Bar: Tex. 1986, U.S. Dist. Ct. (no. dist.) Tex. 1987, U.S. Ct. Appeals (5th cir.) 1987; bd. cert. in personal injury trial law, civil trial advocacy; diplomate Am. Bd. of Trial Advocacy. Atty. Kugle, Stewart, Dent & Frederick, Ft. Worth, 1986-89, The Dent Law Firm, 1990—. State del. Dem. Party, Tex., 1988. Fellow Tex. State Bar Coll.; mem. ABA, ATLA, Am. Coll. Barristers (sr. counsel), Tex. Trial Lawyers Assn., Million Dollar Adv. Forum, Am. Coll. Barristers (sr. counsel). Democrat. Roman Catholic. Avocations: wine collecting, golf, fishing, scuba diving. Federal civil litigation, Personal injury (including property damage), Workers' compensation. Office: The Dent Law Firm 1120 Penn St Fort Worth TX 76102-3417 Fax: 817-332-5809. E-mail: fstreck3@yahoo.com.

STRECKER, DAVID EUGENE, lawyer; b. Carthage, Mo., Nov. 29, 1950; s. Eugene Albert and Erma Freida (Wood) S.; m. Katherine Ann Pugh; children: Charles David, Carrie Christina. BA, Westminster Coll., 1972; JD, Cornell U., 1975, M in Indsl. Labor Rels., 1976. Bar: N.Y. 1976, Okla. 1981, U.S. Dist. Ct. (no. dist.) N.Y. 1976, U.S. Dist. Ct. (ea. dist.) Okla. 1984, U.S. Dist. Ct. (we. dist.) Okla. 2000, U.S. Dist. Ct. (we. and ea. dists.) Ark. 2000, U.S. Ct. Appeals (no. dist.) Okla. 1981, U.S. Ct. Appeals (10th cir.) 1982, U.S. Ct. Appeals (6th cir.) 1990, U.S. Supreme Ct. 1991. Assoc. Conner & Winters, Tulsa, 1980-85, ptnr., 1985-91, Shipley, Inhofe & Strecker, Tulsa, 1991-95, Strecker & Assocs. P.C., Tulsa, 1995—. Instr. paralegal program Tulsa Jr. Coll., 1985—, mem. adv. com., 1986-91; mem. Cornell Secondary Schs. Com., Tulsa, 1985—; adj. instr. labor rels. Okla. State U., 1995—; master Am. Inns of Ct. Bd. dirs., v.p. Tulsa Sr. Svcs., 1988-91; mem. pers. com. Philbrook Art Mus. Capt. JAGC, U.S. Army, 1976-80. Mem. ABA, Okla. Bar Assn. (chmn. labor sect. 1990-91), Tulsa County Bar Assn. (continuing legal edn. com. 1981—), Soc. for Human Resource Mgmt., Tulsa Area Human Resources Assn. (gen. counsel 1989-2000, v.p. 1994-98, bd. dirs. family and children's svcs. 2000—), Kappa Alpha. Democrat. Episcopalian. Avocations: jogging, golf. Federal civil litigation, Labor (including EEOC, Fair Labor Standards Act, labor-management relations, NLRB, OSHA), Workers' compensation. Home: 5112 E 107th St Tulsa OK 74137-7238 Office: Midcontinent Tower 401 S Boston Ste 2150 Tulsa OK 74103-4009 E-mail: destreck@juno.com.

STREET, ERICA CATHERINE, lawyer; b. Lansing, Mich., July 5, 1958; d. Cassius English and Helen Joanna (Hoesman) S.; m. Robert John Pratte, Oct. 20, 1984; 1 child, Chelsea Nicole Pratte. BA, Hillsdale Coll., 1979; JD, U. Mich., 1981. Bar: Minn. 1982, U.S. Dist. Ct. Minn. 1982, U.S. Ct. Appeals (8th cir.) 1983. Assoc. Best & Flanagan, Mpls., 1981-85; sr. counsel Fingerhut Corp., Minnetonka, Minn., 1985-89, Target Stores, Mpls., 1989-97, asst. gen. counsel, 1997-99; pres. Dayton Hudson Brands Inc., Mpls., 1999-2000, Target Brands, Inc., Mpls., 2000—. Entertainment, Intellectual property, Trademark and copyright. Office: Target Brands Inc 1000 Nicollet Mall Minneapolis MN 55403-3601 E-mail: erica.street@target.com.

STREET, JOHN BENSON, judge; b. Bad Cannstadt, Germany, May 11, 1956; arrived in U.S., 1956; s. John Scott and Madge Crawford Street; m. Janet Lynn Tilley; children: Scott Benson, John Kenneth, Emily Spencer, Kevin Michael. BA, Wake Forest U., 1978; JD, Washington Lee U., 1981. Bar: Ohio 1981, U.S. Dist. Ct. (so. dist.) Ohio 1982, U.S. Ct. Appeals (6th cir.) 1990, U.S. Supreme Ct. 1990. Ptnr. Phillips and Street, Chillicothe, Ohio, 1981—95; pres. Chillicothe City Coun., 1989—95; asst. pros. atty. Ross County Pros. Atty., Chillicothe, 1993—95; judge Chillicothe Mcpl. Ct., 1996—. Commr. bd. commrs. grievances and discipline Supreme Ct. Ohio, Columbus, 2002. Chmn. Salvation Army, Chillicothe, 1990—. Mem.: Ross County Bar Assn., Ohio State Bar Assn., Am. Judges Assn., Rotary (past pres.). Office: Chillicothe Mcpl Ct 26 S Paint St Chillicothe OH 45601

STREFF, WILLIAM ALBERT, JR., lawyer; b. Chgo., Aug. 12, 1949; s. William Albert Streff Sr. and Margaret (McKeough) Streff Fisher; m. Kathleen Myslinski, Sept. 29, 1984; children: Amanda, William III, Kimberly. BSME, Northwestern U., 1971, JD cum laude, 1974. Bar: Ill. 1974, U.S. Dist. Ct. (no. dist.) Ill. 1974, U.S. Dist. Ct. (no. dist.) N.Y. 1987, U.S. Dist. Ct. (no. dist.) Calif. 1988, U.S. Ct. Appeals (7th cir.) 1980, U.S. Ct. Appeals (9th cir.) 1988, U.S. Ct. Appeals (fed. cir.) 1982, U.S. Ct. Customs and Patent Appeals, 1978, U.S. Ct. Appeals (3rd cir.), 1992, U.S. Ct. Internat. Trade, 1996, U.S. Dist. Ct. (ea. dist.) Mich., 1999. Legal writing instr. Law Sch. Northwestern U., Chgo., 1973-74; assoc. Kirkland & Ellis, Chgo., 1974-80, ptnr., 1980—. Lectr. Ill. Inst. Continuing Legal Edn., 1984; adj. prof. Northwestern U. Law Sch., 1992-94, 97-99, Chgo. Kent-IIT Law Sch., 1998, John Marshall Law Sch., 2000-02. Contbr. articles to profl. jours. Mem. adv. bd. Ill. Inst. Tech./Chgo.-Kent, 1983-86; trustee Northwestern U., Evanston, 1984-86, mem. vis. com. Law Sch., Chgo., 1988-94. Mem. ABA. Antitrust, Computer, Intellectual property. Office: Kirkland & Ellis 200 E Randolph Dr Chicago IL 60601-6636

STREIB, VICTOR LEE, dean; b. Marion, Ind., Oct. 8, 1941; s. Albert Wolfe and Melba Janice Streib; m. Lynn C. Sametz, Mar. 29, 1978; children: Noah, Jessi. BS in Indsl. Engring., Auburn U., 1966; JD, Ind. U., Bloomington, 1970. Bar: Ind. 1970, U.S. Supreme Ct. 1987. Rsch. assoc., scientist Inst. Rsch. Pub. Safety Ind. U., Bloomington, 1970-72, asst. to assoc. prof. dept. forensic studies, 1972-78; assoc. prof. law New Eng. Sch. Law, Boston, 1978-80; prof., assoc. dean coll. of law Cleve. State U., 1980-96; prof. law Ohio No. U., Ada, 1996—, dean, 1996—2000. Vis. prof. law U. San Diego, 1983-84, Mich. State U., 2001-02; vis. fellow Assn. Am. Law Schs., Washington, 1993-94; mem. adv. bd. Ctr. Capital Punishment Studies U. Westminster, London, 1996—. Author: Juvenile Justice in America., 1978, Death Penalty for Juveniles, 1987, Death Penalty in a Nutshell, 2003; editor: Capital Punishment Anthology, 1993, Law Deanship Manual, 1993. Mem. ABA (site evaluator 1991-2000), North Ctrl. Assn. (cons. evaluator 1990-2001). Avocation: physical fitness. Office: Ohio No U Coll Law 525 S Main St Ada OH 45810-6000

STREICHER, JAMES FRANKLIN, lawyer; b. Ashtabula, Ohio, Dec. 6, 1940; s. Carl Jacob and Helen Marie (Dugan) S.; m. Sandra JoAnn Jennings, May 22, 1940; children: Cheryl Ann, Gregory Scott, Kerry Marie. BA, Ohio State U., 1962; JD, Case Western Res. U., 1966. Bar: Ohio 1966, U.S. Dist. Ct. (no. dist.) Ohio 1966. Assoc. Calfee, Halter & Griswold, Cleve., 1966-71, ptnr., 1972—. Bd. dirs. Provider Gateway, Inc., Sensir Technologies, Stamford, Conn., Mid Am. Consulting; mem. Divsn. Securities Adv. Bd., State of Ohio; lectr. Case Western Res. U., Cleve. State U.; mem. pvt. sector com. John Carroll U. Former trustee Achievement Ctr. for Children, Western Res. Hist. Soc., Make-A-Wish Found. Endowment. Mem. ABA, Fed. Bar Assn., Ohio State Bar Assn., Assn. for Corp. Growth, Ohio Venture Assn., Greater Cleve. Bar Assn. (founding chmn. corp., banking, bus. law sect.), Ohio State U. Alumni Assn., Case Western Res. U. Alumni Assn., Newcomen Soc., Bluecoats Club (Cleve.), Mayfield Country (bd. dirs. 1985-89), Union Club, The Pepper Pike Club, The Tavern Club, Beta Theta Pi, Phi Delta Phi. Roman Catholic. Republican. Securities. Fax: 216-241-0816. E-mail: j.streich@calfee.com.

STREIT, MICHAEL J. state supreme court justice; b. Sheldon, Iowa; married; 1 child. BA, U. Iowa, 1972; grad., U. San Diego Sch. Law, 1975. Cert.: (U.S. Ct. Appeals) 1996. Asst. atty. Lucas County, atty.; dist. ct. judge, 1983; Supreme Ct. justice Iowa State Supreme Ct., 2001—. Mem.: Blackstone Inn of Ct., Supreme Ct. Jud. Tech. Com., Iowa Jud. Inst., Judges Assn. Edn. Com., Supreme Ct. Edn. Adv. Com. Office: State House Des Moines IA 50319

STRELOW, MARKUS, lawyer; b. Tuebingen, Germany, July 13, 1961; s. Siegfried Strelow and Gertrud Weiss; m. Heike Laufmann Strelow, Dec. 12, 1995. Law Degree, U. Bonn, Germany, 1988. Bar: Germany 1993. Asst. Oppenhoff & Rädler, Cologne, Germany, 1993—95, Clifford Chance, Frankfurt, Germany, 1995—98; ptnr. Ashurst Morris Crisp, Frankfurt, 1998—. Mergers and acquisitions, Private equity, Joint ventures. Home: Wiesenau 34 60323 Frankfurt Germany Office: Ashurst Morris Crisp Oberlindau 76-78 60323 Frankfurt Germany

STREMMING, TROY ALAN, lawyer, recreational facility executive; b. Kansas City, Mo., Sept. 16, 1967; s. David Alan and Charlotte Ann Stremming; m. Abigail Lea Alexander, Jan. 3, 1998; children: Jackson, Sydney. BBA in Mktg. and Mgmt., Washburn U., 1991, JD with honors, 1994. Bar: Kans. 1994, Mo. 1995, U.S. Dist. Ct. (ea. dist.) Kans. 1995, U.S. Dist. Ct. (ea. and we. dists.) Mo. 1995. Atty. Rose, Brouilette & Shapiro, PC, Kansas City, 1994—96; gen. counsel midwest ops. Sta. Casinos, Inc., St. Louis, 1996—2000, Las Vegas, Nev., 1996—2000; v.p. legal and govt. affairs Ameristar Casinos, Inc., Kansas City, 2000—. Mem. problem gaming awareness com. Kansas City Port Authority, 1999—. Mem. editl. bd. Problem Gaming Quar., 2001—. Mem. Mayor's Corp Progress, Kansas City, 2000—. Mem.: ABA, Kansas City Met. Bar Assn., St. Louis Met. Bar Assn., Mo. Riverboat Gaming Assn. (pres.), Mo. Bar Assn., Kans. Bar Assn. Avocations: softball, basketball, golf. Entertainment, Corporate, general. Office: Ameristar Casinos Inc 3200 N Ameristar Dr Kansas City MO 64120 Office Fax: 816-414-7360. Business E-Mail: troy.stremming@ameristarcasinos.com.

STRICK, GERALD JAY, lawyer; b. N.Y.C., Oct. 19, 1934; s. Abraham and Esta (Schlaff) S.; children: Susan D., Daniel F. BA, Hobart Coll., 1955; JD, U. Mich., 1962; cert. Nat. Coll. State Trial Judges, 1971; cert. in correctional adminstrn. U. So. Calif., 1975. Bar: Ariz. 1963, U.S. Dist. Ct. Ariz. 1963, U.S. Ct. Appeals (9th cir) 1969, U.S. Ct. Appeals (fed. cir.) 1993. Assoc. Kramer, Roche, Burch & Streich, Phoenix, 1963-66; ptnr. Harrison, Strick, Myers & Singer, Phoenix, 1966-71; judge Superior Ct. Ariz., Phoenix, 1971-83; ptnr. Treon, Strick, Lucia & Aguirre, P.A., Phoenix, 1983—; mem. Ariz. Commn. on Jud. Conduct, 1993-2000; mem. faculty Nat. Inst. Trial Advocacy, 1977—, Ariz. Coll. Trial Advocacy, 1986—; adj. prof. Coll. Law Ariz. State U., 1995, vis. prof., 1994; master bencher Sandra Day O'Connor Inn of Ct.; cons. NAS, 1979-82. Majority counsel Ariz. Ho. Reps., 1969. State civil litigation, Personal injury (including property damage). E-mail: gerald.strick@tsla.com.

STRICKLAND, HUGH ALFRED, lawyer; b. Rockford, Ill., May 3, 1931; s. Hugh and Marie (Elmer) S.; m. Donna E. McDonald, Aug. 11, 1956; children: Amy Alice, Karen Ann. AB, Knox Coll., 1953; JD, Chgo. Kent Coll. Law, 1959. Bar: Ill. 1960. Partner firm McDonald, Strickland & Clough, Carrollton, Ill., 1961—; asst. atty. gen. Ill., 1960-67; spl. asst. gen., 1967-69; pres. McDonald Title Co. Mem. Greene County Welfare Svcs. Com., 1963—, Ill. Heart Assn., 1961-65; trustee Thomas H. Boyd Meml. Hosp., 1972-95. With AUS, 1953-55. Recipient award for meritorious service Am. Heart Assn., 1964 Fellow Ill. Bar Found. (charter); mem. ABA, Ill. Bar Assn., Greene County Bar Assn. (past pres.), Southwestern Bar Assn. (past pres.), Ill. Def. Counsel, Am. Judicature Soc., Def. Rsch. Inst., Elks Club, Westlake Country Club (v.p. 1968-70, dir.), Big Sand Lake Country Club, Phi Delta Theta, Phi Delta Phi. Methodist. General civil litigation, Estate planning, General practice. Home: 827 7th St Carrollton IL 62016-1421 Office: 524 N Main St PO Box 71 Carrollton IL 62016-1027 Fax: 217-942-3178. E-mail: has3@irtc.net., lawyers@irtc.net.

STRICKLAND, WILLIAM JESSE, lawyer; b. Newport News, Va., Mar. 21, 1942; BSBA, U. Richmond, 1964, JD, 1970. Bar: Va. 1969, U.S. Dist. Ct. (ea. and we. dists.) Va., U.S. Ct. Claims, U.S. Tax Ct., U.S. Ct. Appeals (4th cir.). Exec. com. coord. dept., mng. ptnr. McGuire Woods LLP, Richmond, Va., 1969—. Bd. dirs. Cableform Inc., Zion Crossroads, Va., Eimeldingen Corp., Indpls. Bd. dirs. Va. Found. Rsch. and Econ. Edn., Inc.; mem. coun. Va. Inst. Marine Scis.; founder Marine Corps Heritage Found. Capt. USMC 1964-67, Vietnam. Mem. ABA, Va. Bar Assn., Richmond Bar Assn., Nat. Assn. Bond Lawyers, Va. Govt. Fin. Officers Assn., Local Govt. Attys. Assn., Va. Bond Club. Corporate, general, Finance. Office: McGuire Woods LLP 901 E Cary St Richmond VA 23219-4057

STRICKON, HARVEY ALAN, lawyer; b. Bklyn., Nov. 9, 1947; s. Milton and Norma (Goodhartz) S.; m. Linda Carol Meltzer, July 2, 1972; children: Joshua Andrew, Meredith Cindy, Erica Stacey. BBA, CCNY, 1968; JD, NYU, 1971. Bar: N.Y. 1972, U.S. Dist. Ct. (so. and ea. dists.) N.Y. 1973, U.S. Ct. Appeals (2d cir.) 1973, U.S. Supreme Ct. 1975, U.S. Dist. Ct. (no. dist.) N.Y. 1980, U.S. Dist. Ct. (we. dist.) N.Y. 1981, U.S. Dist. Ct. Ariz. 1991, U.S. Dist. Ct. Conn., 1996. Law clk. U.S. Dist. Ct. (ea. dist.) N.Y., Bklyn., 1971-73; assoc. Moses & Singer, N.Y.C., 1973-80; from assoc. to ptnr. Kaye, Scholer, Fierman, Hays & Handler, N.Y.C., 1980-91; from ptnr. to counsel Paul, Hastings, Janofsky & Walker LLP, N.Y.C., 1991—. Mem. complaint mediation panel, departmental disciplinary com. appellate div., 1st dept. Supreme Ct. State N.Y.; mem. mediation panel U.S. Dist. Ct. (ea. dist.) N.Y.; mem. mediation register U.S. Bankruptcy Ct. (so. and ea. dists.) N.Y. Co-author: Enforcing Judgments and Collecting Debts in New York, 1996. Mem. Nassau County Rep. Com., Great Neck, N.Y., 1982—; chmn. bd. dirs. Flushing Community Vol. Ambulance Corps. Inc., N.Y., 1981-86, vice chmn., 1987-92. Mem. ABA, N.Y. State Bar Assn., Assn. Bar City N.Y. (chmn. complaint mediation panel com. on profl. discipline), Am. Judicature Soc., Assn. Comml. Fin. Attys., N.Y. Law Inst., Bankruptcy Lawyers Bar Assn., (bd. govs. 1987-89, corr. sec. 1989—), Am. Bankruptcy Inst. Republican. Jewish. Bankruptcy, Commercial, contracts (including sales of goods; commercial financing). Home: 11 West Brook Rd Great Neck NY 11024-1219 Office: Paul Hastings Janofsky & Walker LLP 75 E 55th St New York NY 10022-3205 E-mail: harveystrickon@paulhastings.com., hastrick@optonline.net.

STRICKSTEIN, HERBERT JERRY, lawyer; b. Detroit, Sept. 4, 1932; s. Samuel and Leah (Freedman) S.; m. Elaine Frances Cohen, Aug. 22, 1963; children: Jaynee Esther, Jill Rose. AA, UCLA, 1952; BS in Law, U. So. Calif., 1954, JD, 1956. Dep. judge adv. USAF, 1957-60; dep. city atty. L.A., 1960-61; assoc. Axelrad, Seville & Ross, 1961-65; ptnr. Iliff & Strickstein, 1965-72; pvt. practice Herbert J. Strickstein Law Corp., L.A., 1972—. Contbr. numerous articles to profl. jours. Commr. Small Craft Harbor Comm., Marina del Rey, Calif., 1983-2000. Mem. State Bar Calif. Assn. (real property sec.), Beverly Hills Bar Assn., El Caballero Country Club, Del Rey Yacht Club, Mission Hills Country Club. Avocations: racquetball, golf, tennis, sailing. Property, real (including real estate development, water). Office: Ste 1420 1801 Avenue Of The Stars Los Angeles CA 90067-5899

STRIDIRON, IVER ALLISON, attorney general; m. Priscilla Blyden; 4 children. BA Lincoln U., 1969; JD, Howard U. Sch. of Law, 1974. Atty. U.S. Nuclear Regulatory Commn., U.S. Commn. on Civil Rights, Washington, 1974—77; pvt. practice St. Thomas, 1977—99; mem. V.I. Legis., 1981—83, 1985—89; atty. gen. V.I., 1999—. Democrat. Office: Dept Justice 48B-50C Kronprindsens Gade GERS Bldg 2nd fl Charlotte Amalie VI 00802*

STRIEFSKY, LINDA A(NN), lawyer; b. Carbondale, Pa., Apr. 27, 1952; d. Leo James and Antoinette Marie (Carachilo) S.; m. James Richard Carlson, Nov. 3, 1984; children: David Carlson, Paul Carlson, Daniel Carlson. BA summa cum laude, Marywood Coll., 1974; JD, Georgetown U., 1977. Bar: Ohio 1977. Assoc. Thompson Hine LLP (formerly Thompson, Hine & Flory), Cleve., 1977-85, ptnr., 1985—. Loaned exec. United Way N.E. Ohio, Cleve., 1978; trustee ideastream, Mus. Theater Edn. Programming. Mem. ABA (real estate fin. com. 1980-87, vice chmn. leader liability com. 1993-97, mem. non-traditional real estate fin. com. 1987—), Am. Bar Found., Am. Coll. Real Estate Lawyers (bd. govs. 1994-98, treas. 1999), Internat. Coun. Shopping Ctrs., Nat. Assn. Office and Indsl. Parks, Urban Land Inst. (chmn. Cleve. dist. coun. 1996-2000), Cleve. Real Estate Women, Ohio Bar Assn. (bd. govs. real property sect. 1985-97), Greater Cleve. Bar Assn. (chmn. bar applicants com. 1983-84, exec. coun. young lawyers sect. 1982-85, chmn. 1984-85, mem. exec. coun. real property sect. 1980-84, Merit Svc. award 1983, 85), Pi Gamma Mu. Democrat. Roman Catholic. Commercial, contracts (including sales of goods; commercial financing), Property, real (including real estate development, water). Home: 2222 Delamere Dr Cleveland OH 44106-3204 Office: Thompson Hine LLP 3900 Key Ctr 127 Public Square Cleveland OH 44114-1216 E-mail: linda.striefsky@thompsonhine.com.

STRIMBU, VICTOR, JR., lawyer; b. New Philadelphia, Ohio, Nov. 25, 1932; s. Victor and Veda (Stancu) S.; m. Kathryn May Schrote, Apr. 9, 1955 (dec. 1995); children: Victor Paul, Michael, Julie, Sue; m. Marjorie Bichsel, Oct. 23, 1999. BA, Heidelberg Coll., 1954; postgrad., Western Res. U., 1956-57; JD, COlumbia U., 1960. Bar: Ohio 1960, U.S. Supreme Ct. 1972. With Baker & Hostetler LLP, Cleve., 1960—, ptnr., 1970—. Bd. dirs. North Coast Health Ministry; mem. Bay Village (Ohio) Bd. Edn., 1976-84, pres., 1978-82; mem. Bay Village Planning Commn., 1967-69; life mem. Ohio PTA; mem. Greater Cleve. Growth Assn.; trustee New Cleve. Campaign, 1987-94—, North Coast Health Ministry, 1989-2001, Heidelberg Coll., 1996—; mem. indsl. rels. adv. com. Cleve. State U., 1979—, chmn., 1982,1999, vice chmn., 1998. With AUS, 1955-56. Mem. ABA, Ohio Bar Assn., Greater Cleve. Bar Assn., Ohio Newspaper Assn. (minority affairs com. 1987-90), Ct. of Nisi Prius Club, Cleve. Athletic Club, The Club at Soc. Ctr. Republican. Presbyterian. Labor (including EEOC, Fair Labor Standards Act, labor-management relations, NLRB, OSHA). Office: Baker & Hostetler LLP 3200 National City Ctr 1900 E 9th St Ste 3200 Cleveland OH 44114-3475

STRINGER, EDWARD CHARLES, judge, lawyer; b. St. Paul, Feb. 13, 1935; s. Philip and Anne (Driscoll) S.; m. Mary Lucille Lange, June 19, 1957 (div. Mar. 1991); children: Philip, Lucille, Charles, Carolyn; m. Virginia L. Ward, Sept. 10, 1993. BA, Amherst Coll., 1957; LLD, U. Minn., 1960. Bar: Minn. Ptnr. Stringer, Donnelly & Sharood, St. Paul, 1960-69, Briggs & Morgan, St. Paul, 1969-79; sr. v.p., gen. counsel Pillsbury Co., Mpls., 1980-82, exec. v.p., gen. counsel, 1982-83, exec. v.p., gen. counsel, chief adminstrv. officer, 1983-89; gen. counsel U.S. Dept. Edn., Washington, 1989-91; chief of staff Minn. Gov. Arne H. Carlson, 1992-94; assoc. justice Minn. Supreme Ct., St. Paul, 1994—2002. Mem. ABA, Minn. State Bar Assn., Ramsey County Bar Assn. (sec. 1977-80), Order of Coif, Mpls. Club. Congregationalist. Home: 712 Linwood Ave Saint Paul MN 55105-3513 Office: W-2200 First Nat Bank Bldg Saint Paul MN 55101-

STRINGER, RONALD E. lawyer, educator; b. N.Y.C., Feb. 23, 1934; s. Irving and Mary Stringer; m. Sandra Deutsch, Oct. 30, 1986; children from previous marriage: Scott, David. AB, CCNY, 1954; LLB, Bklyn. Law Sch., 1957, JD, 1968. Bar: N.Y. 1958, U.S. Dist. Ct. (so. and ea. dists.) N.Y., U.S. Supreme Ct. Law sect. to comptroller City of N.Y., 1971-73, counsel to mayor, 1974-77; counsel Balsam Felber & Goldfield, 1977—; asst. prof. John Jay Coll. Criminal Justice, N.Y.C., 1992-99. Hon. consul Dominican Republic, N.Y.C., 1972-74. Recipient Svc. award Alianza Hispano-Am., 1975. Democrat. Commercial, contracts (including sales of goods; commercial financing), Corporate, general, Probate (including wills, trusts). Office: Balsam Felber & Goldfield 99 Wall St New York NY 10005-4301

STROBER, ERIC SAUL, lawyer; b. Bklyn., July 30, 1970; s. Charles and Debora Strober. BA, Syracuse U., 1992; JD, Bklyn. Law Sch., 1995. Bar: N.Y. 1996, U.S. Dist. Ct. (ea. and so. dist.) N.Y. 1996. Law clk. Kramer, Dillof, Tessel, Duffy & Moore, N.Y.C., 1994-95; atty. Callan, Regenstreich, Koster & Brady, N.Y.C., 1995-97, Parker, Chapin, Flattau & Klimpl, N.Y.C., 1997-99, Rivkin, Radler, LLP, N.Y.C. Mem. ABA, N.Y. State Bar Assn. Personal injury (including property damage), Product liability, Toxic tort. Office: Rivkin Radler LLP 275 Madison Ave New York NY 10016-1101

STROCK, MARCUS, lawyer; b. Boston, Jan. 4, 1941; s. Moses Soloman and Bernice (Sisisky) S.; m. Geniel Gwin, Apr. 18, 1970; children: Alden, Justin, Owen. AB, Harvard U., 1965, MA in Teaching, 1967; JD, NYU, 1971. Bar: N.Y. 1972, U.S. Ct. Appeals (1st cir.) 1972, U.S. Tax Ct. 1984. Law clk. to Hon. Edward M. McEntee U.S. Ct. Appeals, Providence, 1971-72; assoc. Debevoise & Plimpton, N.Y.C., 1972-81, ptnr., 1982—. Mem. ABA, N.Y. State Bar Assn., Assn. of Bar of City of N.Y. Municipal (including bonds), Corporate taxation, Taxation, general. Home: 234 W 101st St New York NY 10025-4905 Office: Debevoise & Plimpton 919 3rd Ave Fl 32 New York NY 10022-3902

STROCK, WILLIAM MATTHEW, lawyer; b. Dallas, May 16, 1973; s. William Conrad and Anne Turner Strock; m. Christi Ann Kopycinski, Dec. 27, 1997. BA, Washington and Lee U., 1995; JD, U. Tex., 1999. Bar: Tex. 1999. Assoc. Vinson & Elkins, LLP, Houston, 1999—. Bd. dirs. Urban Bus. Initiative, Houston, 2001—03. Mem.: Houston Young Lawyers Assn., Houston Bar Assn. Securities, Mergers and acquisitions, Corporate, general. Office: Vinson & Elkins LLP 2300 First City Tower 1001 Fannin St Houston TX 77002-6760 Home: 6162 Burgoyne Houston TX 77057

STRODE, JOSEPH ARLIN, lawyer; b. DeWitt, Ark., Mar. 5, 1946; s. Thomas Joseph and Nora (Richardson) S.; m. Carolyn Taylor, Feb. 9, 1969; children: Tanya Briana, William Joseph. BSEE with honors, U. Ark., 1969; JD, So. Meth. U., 1972. Bar: Ark. 1972. Design engr. Tex. Instruments Inc., Dallas, 1969-70; patent agent Tex. Instruments, Dallas, 1970—72; assoc. Bridges, Young, Matthews, Drake, Pine Bluff, Ark., 1972-74, ptnr., 1975—. Chmn. Pine Bluff Airport Commn., 1993; bd. dirs. United Way Jefferson County, Pine Bluff, 1975-77, campaign chmn., 1983, pres., 1986, exec. com., 1983-87; bd. dirs. Leadership Pine Bluff, 1983-85. Mem. Ark. Bar Assn., Jefferson County Bar Assn. (pres. 1995), Pine Bluff C. of C. (dir. 1981, 84, 94, 97), Ark. Wildlife Fed. (dir. 1979-81), Jefferson County Wildlife Assn. (dir. 1973-80, pres. 1974-76), Kiwanis (lt. gov. Mo.-Ark. divsn. 1983-84, chmn. lt. govs. 1983-84), Order of Coif, Tau Beta Pi, Eta Kappa Nu. Banking, Commercial, contracts (including sales of goods; commercial financing), Intellectual property. Home: 7600 Jay Lynn Ln Pine Bluff AR 71603-9387 Office: 315 E 8th Ave Pine Bluff AR 71601-5005 E-mail: joestrode@bridgesplc.com.

STRODEL, ROBERT CARL, lawyer; b. Evanston, Ill., Aug. 12, 1930; s. Carl Frederick and Imogene (Board) S.; m. Mary Alice Shonkwiler, June 17, 1956; children: Julie Ann, Linda Lee, Sally Payson. BS, Northwestern U., 1952; JD, U. Mich., 1955. Bar: Ill. 1955, U.S. Supreme Ct. 1970; diplomate Am. Bd. Profl. Liability Attys.; cert. civil trial specialist Am. Bd. Trial Advocacy. Mem. firm Davis, Morgan & Witherell, Peoria, Ill., 1957-59; pvt. practice Peoria, 1959-69; prin. Strodel, Kingery & Durree Assoc., Peoria, Ill., 1969-92, Law Offices of Robert C. Strodel, Ltd., Peoria, 1992—; asst. state's atty. Peoria, 1960-61; instr. bus. law Bradley U., Peoria, 1961-62; lectr. Belli seminars, 1969-87. Mem. U.S. Presdl. Commn. German-Am. Tricentennial, 1983; lectr. in trial practice and med.-legal litigation. Author: Securing and Using Medical Evidence in Personal Injury and Health-Care Cases, 1988; contbr. articles to profl. jours. Gov. appointee Ill. Dangerous Drugs Adv. Coun., 1970-71; gen. chmn. Peoria-Tazewell Easter Seals, 1963, Cancer Crusade, 1970; pres. Peoria Civic Ballet, 1969-70; mem. Mayor's Commn. on Human Rels., 1962-64; chmn. City of Peoria Campaign Ethics Bd., 1975; chmn., builder City of Peoria Mil. Svcs. Meml. Plaza Project, 1998; Peoria County Rep. Sec., 1970-74; campaign chmn. Gov. Richard Ogilvie, Peoria County, 1972, Sen. Ralph Smith, 1970; treas. Michel for Congress, 1977-94, campaign coord., 1982; bd. dirs. Crippled Children's Ctr., 1964-65, Peoria Symphony Orch., 1964-68. Served with AUS, 1956-64. Decorated Officer's Cross of Order of Merit (Fed. Republic Germany), 1984; named Outstanding Young Man Peoria Peoria Jr. C. of C., 1963. Mem. ATLA (bd. govs. 1987-96), ABA, Ill. Trial Lawyers Assn. (bd. mgrs. 1985—), Ill. Bar Assn. (Lincoln awards for legal writing 1961, 63, 65), Am. Inns of Ct. (charter master of bench, Lincoln Inn-Peoria, Ill.), Civil Justice Found. (pres., charter founder, trustee 1986-2002, Masons, Scottish Rite. Personal injury (including property damage), Professional liability, General practice. Office: 927 Commerce Bank Peoria IL 61602 E-mail: stro927@aol.com.

STROLLA, CORY CARSAN, lawyer; b. Omaha, Nebr., Jan. 1, 1973; s. Carmine and Susan Strolla. JD, Stetson Coll. Law, 1997. Bar: Fla. 1997. Asst. state atty. State Atty. Office, West Palm Beach, Fla., 1998—2000; assoc. Meldon and Barbarette PA, Gainesville, Fla., 2000—01; pvt. practice West Palm Beach, 2001—; adj. prof. Palm Beach Cmty. Coll. Judge youth ct. Palm Beach County, 1998—; trial team coach U. Fla., 2000. Contbr. Big Bros. program mem. Jewish Fedn. Palm Beach, 2001—, bd. dirs. Mem.: Fla. Bar Assn. (Young Lawyers divsn.), Fla. Assn. Criminal Def. Lawyers, Nat. Assn. Criminal Def. Lawyers. Criminal, Juvenile. Office: 319 Clematis St Ste 801 West Palm Beach FL 33401

STROM, DAVID J. lawyer, labor union administrator; Assoc. atty. Highsaw, Mahoney & Clarke, Washington; gen. counsel Am. Fedn. Tchrs., Washington, 1993—. Office: Am Fedn Tchrs 555 New Jersey Ave NW Washington DC 20001*

STRØM, EVALD JON, lawyer; b. Oslo, Feb. 15, 1942; s. Harald and Petra Jenny (Ødegaard) S.; m. Siri Kristiansen, June 17, 1966; children: Kjersti, Guro. JD, U. Oslo, 1970. Bar: Norway 1973. Asst. rschr. Uio, 1967-68; asst. judge Byfogden, Stavanger, Norway, 1971-72; pvt. practice Oslo, 1972—. Chmn. bd. Hillark AS, Skovly-Gruppen AS, Oslo, As Avisdrift (Fjell-Ljom), Roros, Hotel Røros (Norway) AS, Stiftelsen Det Brinner En Eld, Roros; mem. bd. Roros Kultur-og Konferansesenter AS, Stiftelsen Vinterfestspill i Bergstaden, Roros, Blue Cross Norway, Oslo, Blaa Kors Eiendom As, BL AA Kors Eiendom Øst AS, Amneus Boghandel AS, Roros Arkitektkontoret Hille & Melbye AS, Oslo. Author: Odelsloven, 1975, Husnøkkelen, 1985, Rørosloven av 1901, 1995. Mem., sec. Mcpl. Com. of Lumber to Peasantry, Røros, Norway, 1994-95. Mem. Norwegian Lawyer Assn., Norwegian Assn. Agrl. Law, Lions Internat. Mem. Blue Cross of Norway. Avocations: genealogy, local history, law history, cultural history, farming. Office: Advokatfirma Lindh Stabell Horten Haakon VII's GT 2 0114 Oslo Norway

STROM, J. PRESTON, JR., lawyer; b. May 21, 1959; s. Grace and J.P. Sr. S.; m. Donna Savoca, Oct. 5, 1985; children: Margaret, Caroline. BA, U. S.C., 1981, JD, 1984. Bar: S.C. 1984, U.S. Dist. Ct. S.C., 1984, U.S. Ct. Appeals (4th cir.) 1984. Asst. solicitor 5th Jud. Cir., S.C., 1985-86; ptnr. Leventis, Strom & Wicker, 1986-88, Strom Law Firm, 1988-90, Bolt, Popowski, McCulloch & Strom, 1990-93; acting U.S. atty. Office U.S. Atty., S.C., 1993, U.S. atty., 1993-96; atty. Strom Law Firm, LLC, Columbia, S.C., 1996—. Chmn. Law Enforcement Coord. Com.; chmn. juvenile justice and child support enforcement subcom. U.S. Dept. Justice; active Atty. Gen. Adv. Com. Mem. S.C. Bar, S.C. Trial Lawyers Assn., Richland County Bar Assn. (chmn. criminal law sect.). General civil litigation, Criminal. Office: Strom Law Firm LLC 1501 Main St Ste 700 Columbia SC 29201

STROM, LYLE ELMER, judge; b. Omaha, Nebr., Jan. 6, 1925; s. Elmer T. and Eda (Hanisch) Strom; m. Regina Ann Kelly, July 31, 1950 (dec.); children: Mary Bess, Susan Frances(dec.) , Amy Claire, Cassie A., David Kelly, Margaret Mary, Bryan Thomas. Student, U. Nebr., 1946-47; AB, Creighton U., 1950, JD cum laude, 1953. Bar: Nebr. 1953. Assoc. Fitzgerald, Brown, Leahy, Strom, Schorr & Barmettler and predecessor firm, Omaha, 1953-60, ptnr., 1960-63, gen. trial ptnr., 1963-85; judge U.S. Dist. Ct. Nebr., Omaha, 1985-87, chief judge, 1987-94, sr. judge, 1995—. Adj. prof. law Creighton U., 1959-95, clinical prof., 1996—; mem. com. pattern jury instrns. and practice and proc. Nebr. Supreme Ct., 1965-91; spl. legal counsel Omaha Charter Rev. Commn., 1973; chair gender fairness task force U.S. Ct. Appeals (8th cir.), 1993-97. Exec. com. Covered Wagon Coun. Boy Scouts Am., 1953—57, bd. trustees, exec. com. Mid-Am. Coun., 1988—; chmn. bd. trustees Marian H.S., 1969—71; mem. pres. coun. Creighton U., 1990—. With U.S. Maritime Svc., 1943—46. Fellow Am. Coll. Trial Lawyers, Internat. Acad. Trial Lawyers; mem. Nebr. Bar Assn. (ho. of dels. 1978-81, exec. coun. 1981-87, pres. 1989-90), Nebr. Bar Found. (bd. trustees 1998—), Omaha Bar Assn. (pres. 1980-81), Am. Judicature Soc., Midwestern Assn. Amateur Athletic Union (pres. 1976-78), Rotary (pres. 1993-94), Alpha Sigma Nu (pres. alumni chpt. 1970-71). Republican. Roman Catholic. Office: US Dist Ct Roman Hruska Courthouse 111 S 18th Plz Ste 3190 Omaha NE 68102

STROM, MILTON GARY, lawyer; b. Rochester, N.Y., Dec. 5, 1942; s. Harold and Dolly (Isaacson) S.; m. Barbara A. Simon, Jan. 18, 1975; children: Carolyn, Michael, Jonathan. BS in Econ., U. Pa., 1964; JD, Cornell U., 1967. Bar: N.Y. 1968, U.S. Dist. Ct. (W. dist.) N.Y. 1968, U.S. Ct. Claims 1969, U.S. Ct. Mil. Appeals 1969, U.S. Ct. Appeals (D.C. cir.) 1970, U.S. Supreme Ct. 1972, U.S. Dist. Ct. (so. dist.) N.Y. 1975. Atty. SEC, Washington, 1968-71; assoc. Skadden, Arps, Slate, Meagher & Flom, N.Y.C., 1971-76, ptnr., 1977—. Served with USCGR, 1967-73. Mem. ABA, N.Y. State Bar Assn. (corp. law sect.), Assn. of Bar of City of N.Y., Internat. Bar Assn., Beach Point Club. Republican. Jewish. Avocations: tennis, skiing, golf. Corporate, general, Securities. Office: Skadden Arps Slate Meagher & Flom 4 Times Sq Fl 42 New York NY 10036-6522 E-mail: mstrom@skadden.com.

STROMBERG, CLIFFORD DOUGLAS, lawyer; b. N.Y.C., June 1, 1949; s. George M. and Greta (Netzow) S.; m. Ava S. Feiner, June 25, 1972; children: Kimberly, Eric. BA summa cum laude, Yale U., 1971; JD, Harvard U., 1974. Bar: N.Y. 1975, D.C. 1975, U.S. Dist. Ct. (so. and ea. dists.) N.Y. 1975, U.S. Ct. Appeals (D.C. cir.) 1975, U.S. Ct. Appeals (2nd cir.) 1975, U.S. Supreme Ct. 1980. Law clk. to judge U.S. Dist. Ct. (ea. dist.) N.Y., 1974-75; assoc. Arnold & Porter, Washington, 1975-78, 80-83; dep. exec. sec. HHS, Washington, 1978-80; cons. FTC, Washington, 1980; ptnr. Dorsey & Whitney, Washington, 1983-84, Hogan & Hartson, Washington, 1984—. Adj. asst. prof. emergency medicine George Washington U. Sch. Medicine, 1991-97. Co-author: Mental Health and Law: A System in Transition, 1975, Alternatives to the Hospital: Ambulatory Surgery Centers and Emergicenters, 1984, Entrepreneurial Health Care: How to Structure Successful New Ventures, 1985, The Psychologist's Legal Handbook, 1988, Access to Hospital Information: Problems and Strategies: 4 Frontiers of Health Services Management 3-33, 1987, Healthcare Provider Networks: Antitrust Issues and Practical Considerations in Devels. in Antitrust Law, 1990, Healthcare Credentialing: Implications for Academic Medical Centers, 1991; mem. editl. bd. Harvard Law Rev., 1972-73; editor in chief Healthspan: The Report of Health Business and Law, 1984-87; cons. editor: Managed Care Law Strategist, 1999-2002; contbr. articles to profl. jours. Bd. dirs. Nat. Children's Eye Care Found., Washington, 1985-87. Teaching fellow in govt. Harvard U., 1973-74. Fellow Am. Bar Found.; mem. ABA (chair working group health care reform 1993-96, state membership chmn. 1984, bd. dirs. forum com. health law 1987-90, adv. com. govt. affairs 1993-98, governing bd., individual rights and responsibilities sect., exec. coun., 1980-90, sec. 1984-87, chair-elect 1987-88, chair 1988-89, legal aid and indigent defendants com. 1982-87), Am. Health Lawyers Assn., Nat. Assn. Coll. and Univ. Attys., Phi Beta Kappa. Antitrust, Federal civil litigation, Health. Office: Hogan & Hartson 555 13th St NW Washington DC 20004-1161 E-mail: cdstromberg@hh.law.com.

STROMBERG, JEAN WILBUR GLEASON, lawyer; b. St. Louis, Oct. 31, 1943; d. Ray Lyman and Martha (Bugbee) W.; m. Gerald Kermit Gleason, Aug. 28, 1966 (div. 1987); children: C. Blake, Peter Wilbur; m. Kurt Stromberg, Jan. 3, 1993; 1 child, Kristoffer Stromberg. BA, Wellesley Coll., 1965; LLB cum laude, Harvard U., 1968. Bar: Calif. 1969, D.C. 1978. Assoc. Brobeck, Phleger & Harrison, San Francisco, 1969-72; spl. counsel to dir. div. corp. fin. SEC, Washington, 1972-76, assoc. dir. div. investment mgmt., 1976-78; of counsel Fulbright & Jaworski, Washington, 1978-80, ptnr., 1980-96; dir. fin. instns. and market issues GAO, Washington, 1996-97; cons. Washington, 1997—. Mem. adv. panel on legal issues GAO, 1992—96; mem. NASD select com. on NASDAQ, 1994—96; trustee AARP Intestment Program and AARP Scudder Mut. Funds, 1997—2000; bd. dirs. Scudder Mut. Funds., Svc. Source, Inc., Mut. Fund Dirs. Forum. Dir. William and Flora Hewlett Found., 2000—; overseer Wellesley Ctrs. Women, 2003-. Mem. ABA (chmn. subcom. on securities and banks, corp. laws com., bus. sect. 1982-93), D.C. Bar Assn. (chmn. steering com. bus. sect. 1982-84), FBA (chair exec. coun., securities com. 1993-95), Am. Bar Retirement Assn. (bd. dirs. 1986-90, 94-96), Phi Beta Kappa. Corporate, general, Securities. Home and Office: 3816 Military Rd NW Washington DC 20015-2704

STROMBERG, ROSS ERNEST, lawyer; b. Arcata, Calif., May 5, 1940; s. Noah Anders and Anne Laura (Noyes) S.; m. Toni Nicholas, Dec. 16, 1961; m. Margaret Telonicher, Oct. 3, 1965; children: Kristin, Matthew, Gretchen, Erik. BS, Humboldt State U., 1962; JD, U. Calif., Berkeley, 1965. Bar: Calif. 1966, U.S. Dist. Ct. (no. dist.) Calif. 1966, U.S. Ct. Appeals (9th cir.) 1966. Assoc. Hanson Bridgett, San Francisco, 1965-70, ptnr., 1970-85, Epstein Becker Stromberg & Green, San Francisco, 1985-90, Jones Day, L.A., 1990—. Chmn. Jones Day's Healthcare Specialized Industry Practice; pres. Shyster Creek Vineyards, Healdsburg, Calif., 2002—. Author: Economic Joint Venturing, 1985, Acquisition and Enhancement of Physician Practices, 1988. Bd. dirs. Sutter Med. Ctr., Santa Rosa, 2001—; pres. Am. Acad. Hosp. Attys. of Am. Host. Assn., Chgo., 1978; chair Sutter Med. Ctr., Santa Rosa, 2003—; pres. East Bay AHEC, Oakland, Calif., 1984—87; bd. dirs. Am. Cancer Soc., Oakland, 1984—95, Wildflowers Inst., San Francisco. Mem. Am. Health Lawyers Assn. Democrat. Health. Office: Jones Day Reavis & Pogue 555 W 5th St Ste 4600 Los Angeles CA 90013-1025

STROMME, GARY L. law librarian; b. Willmar, Minn., July 8, 1939; s. William A. and Edla A. Stromme; m. Suzanne Readman, July 21, 1990. BA, Pacific Luth. U., 1965; BLS, U. B.C., Vancouver, Can., 1967; JD, U. Calif., San Francisco, 1973. Bar: Calif. 1973, U.S. Supreme Ct. 1977. Serials libr. U. Minn. St. Paul. Campus Libr., 1967-69; asst. libr. McCutchen, Doyle, Brown and Enerson, San Francisco, 1970-71, Graham & James, San Francisco, 1971-73, ind. contracting atty., 1973-74; law libr. Pacific Gas and Electric Co., San Francisco, 1974-95; cons., 1995—. Lectr. in field. Author: An Introduction to the use of the Law Library, 1974, 76, Basic Legal Research Techniques, 1979. With USAF, 1959-63. Mem. ABA (chmn. libr. com. of sect. econs. of law practice 1978-82), Am. Assn. Law Librs. (chmn. com. on indexing of legal periodicals 1986-88), Western Pacific Assn. Law Librs., No. Calif. Assn. Law Librs., Pvt. Law Librs., Corp. Law Librs. Home: 6106 Ocean View Dr Oakland CA 94618-1841 E-mail: stromme1@earthlink.net.

STRØMME, VIDAR, lawyer; b. Lyngdal , Norway, Nov. 17, 1958; Candidate of Jurisprudence, U. Oslo (Norway), 1983. Bar: Supreme Ct. Norway 1992. Police prosecutor, Follo, Norway, 1983-85; assoc. judge Ålesund, Norway, 1985-87; dist. atty. D Molde, Norway, 1987-88; legal counsellor Sunnmørsbanken, Norway, 1988-89; atty. gen. civil affairs Oslo, 1989-93; ptnr. Law Firm Schjødt, Oslo, 1993—. Communications, Entertainment, Libel. Office: Advokatfirmaet Schjødt Dronning Mauds GT 11 Postboks 2444 0201 Oslo Norway

STRONE, MICHAEL JONATHAN, lawyer; b. N.Y.C., Feb. 26, 1953; s. Bernard William and Judith Semel (Sogg) S.; m. Andrea Nan Acker, Jan. 27, 1979; children: Noah Gregory, Joshua Samuel. BA cum laude, Colby Coll., 1974; JD, Fordham Law Sch., 1978. Bar: N.J. 1978, N.Y. 1979, Conn. 1988, U.S. Ct. Appeals (2d and 3d cirs.) 1979, U.S. Dist. Ct. (so. and ea. dists.) N.Y. 1979, U.S. Dist. Ct. N.J. 1979). Assoc. Ratheim Hoffman et al, N.Y.C., 1978-80, Botein Hays et al, N.Y.C., 1980-84; v.p., assoc. gen. counsel, asst. sec. GE Investment Corp., Stamford, Conn., 1984-2000; v.p., gen. counsel real estate GE Asset Mgmt. Inc., 2000—02, sr. cons., 2002—; pres., CEO Oracle Investment Advisors, LLC, 2002—. Bd. dirs. N.Y. chpt. Juvenile Diabetes Found., N.Y.C., 1981-89, vice chmn., 1981-88; mem. fin. com. Juvenile Diabetes Found. Internat., 1981-86; asst. prin. bassist Westchester Symphony Orch., Scarsdale, N.Y., 1982-2000, pres., 1982-87, chmn. bd., 1982-90, exec. mng. dir., 1990-93; vice chmn. ann. dinner NCCJ, 1987; bd. dirs. Parkinson's Disease Soc. Am., 1989-96, chmn. merger com., 1991-96; bd. dirs. Parkinson's Action Network, 1994-98; trustee Jewish Cmty. Ctr. of Harrison, 1996—, mem. ritual com., 1996—, chmn., 2000—, chmn. alt. svcs. com., lay cantor, 1997—; chmn. county United Way Campaign, 1999, bd. dirs., gen. coun., Harrison Little League, 2001—; bd. dirs. Rye Youth Hockey, 2003—; mem. zoning bd. appeals, Village of Harrison, 2003—. Mem. ABA (chmn. pension plan investments 1989-91, chmn. asset mgmt. 1992-94, 95-97, significant legis. coms. 1985-92, chmn. subcom. on joint ventures 1988-90), Am. Coll. Real Estate Lawyers (com. professionalism 1994—, v. chmn. 1999-2000), Am. Polit. Items Collectors, The Corp. Bar Assn., Nat. Assn. Real Estate Investment Mgrs. (sr. legal officers adv. com. 1993—, ann. forum chair 1997), Colby Coll. Alumni Coun. (nominating com. 1994-97), Fordham Law Alumni Assn., The Internat. Netsuke Soc., Jewish Geneal. Soc. Republican. Corporate, general, Pension, profit-sharing, and employee benefits, Property, real (including real estate development, water). Home and Office: 10 Genesee Trail Harrison NY 10528-1802 E-mail: michael.strone@oracleinvestmentadvisors.com.

STRONG, CARTER, lawyer; b. Bronxville, N.Y., July 17, 1947; s. Shirley Carter and Hélène Strong; m. Helen Anne Marvel, May 17, 1980; children: Winslow C., Hilary H. BA in History, Ithaca Coll., 1969; JD, U. Miami, 1972. Bar: Fla. 1972, D.C. 1973. Assoc. Arent, Fox, Kintner, Plotkin & Kahn, PLLC, Washington, 1972-80, ptnr., 1981—. Mem. Chevy Chase Club, Siasconset Casino Assn. Avocations: tennis, golf, reading, travel. Corporate, general, Mergers and acquisitions, Securities. Office: Arent Fox Kintner Plotkin & Kahn PLLC 1050 Connecticut Ave NW Washington DC 20036-5339

STRONG, GEORGE GORDON, JR., litigation and management consultant; b. Toledo, Apr. 19, 1947; s. George Gordon and Jean Boyd (McDougall) S.; m. Annsley Palmer Chapman, Nov. 30, 1974; children: George III, Courtney, Meredith, Alexis. BA, Yale U., 1969; MBA, Harvard U., 1971; JD, U. San Diego, 1974. Bar: Calif. 1974, U.S. Dist. Ct. (cen. dist.) Calif. 1974; CPA, Calif., Hawaii, cert. mgmt. cons. Contr. Vitredent Corp., Beverly Hills, Calif., 1974-76; sr. mgr. Price Waterhouse, L.A., 1976-82, ptnr., 1987—2001, mng. ptnr. west region dispute analysis and corp. recovery, 1993—99, mem. policy bd., bd. dirs., 1995-98, combination bd., 1997-98; bd. ptnrs., prin Pricewaterhouse Coopers LLP, L.A., 1998-2001; ret., 2002; exec. v.p., COO Internat. Customs Service, Long Beach, Calif., 1982-84; CFO Uniform Software Systems, Santa Monica, Calif.,

1984-85; exec. v.p., COO Cipherlink Corp., 1986; pres. Woodleigh Lane, Inc., Flintridge, Calif., 1985-87; mng. dir., gen. counsel Cornerstone Rsch., 2002—. Chmn. bd. dirs. L.A. SPCA. Mem. ABA, AICPA, Calif. State Bar, Calif. Soc. CPAs, Andover Abbott Alumni So. Calif. (bd. dirs., treas.), Inst. Mgmt. Cons., Harvard Bus. Sch. Alumni Assn. (bd. dirs. 1996-99), Harvard Bus. Sch. Assn. So. Calif. (chmn. bd. trustees scholarship fund 1992—, pres. 1988-89, dir. 1996-99, 2001—), Harvard Club N.Y., Yale Club N.Y., Lincoln Club, Calif. Club, Jonathan Club, Olympic Club, Annandale Golf Club, Coral Beach and Tennis Club, Mid Ocean Golf Club, Royal Bermuda Yacht Club, Valley Hunt Club. Republican. Presbyterian. Avocations: golf, tennis, bridge. Federal civil litigation, State civil litigation, Computer. Home: 5455 Castle Knoll Rd La Canada Flintridge CA 91011-1319 Office: 555 S Flower St #2750 Los Angeles CA 90071-2300 E-mail: gstrong@cornerstone.com.

STRONG, SARA DOUGHERTY, psychologist, marriage and family therapist, mediator; b. Phila., May 30, 1927; d. Augustus Joseph and Orpha Elizabeth (Dock) Dougherty; m. David Mather Strong, Dec. 21, 1954. BA in Psychology, Pa. State U., 1949; MA in Clin. Psychology, Temple U., 1960, postgrad., 1968-72; cert. in family therapy, Family Inst. Phila., 1978. Lic. psychologist, Pa. Med. br. psychologist Family Ct. Phila., 1960-85, asst. chief psychologist, 1985-88, chief psychologist, 1988-92; ret., 1992; pvt. practice, 1992—. Cons. St. Joseph's Home for Girls, Phila., 1963-84, Daughters of Charity of St. Vincent De Paul, Albany, N.Y., 1965-90 Mem. APA (assoc.), Am. Assn. Marriage and Family Therapists, Pa. Psychol. Assn., Nat. Register of Health Svc. Providers in Psychology, Family Inst. Phila. Democrat. Avocations: reading, dramatic productions, writing, yoga, dance. Office: 1 Greystone Rd Carlisle PA 17013-3743

STROTHER, JODI LANE, lawyer, educator; b. Fayetteville, Ark., July 21, 1968; d. Lane Howard and Judith Louise (Cook) S.; m. Todd Gilbert, Dec. 5, 1993; children: Jake, Buck Wyatt. BA, Ouachita Bapt. U., 1990; JD, U. Ark., 1994. Bar: Ark. 1995. Pvt. practice, Mountain Home, Ark., 1994—. Mem. Jr. Aux., Mountain Home, 1996—, 1st Bapt. Ch., Mountain Home, 1979—. Democrat. Avocation: reading. Office: PO Box 1600 Mountain Home AR 72654-1600 E-mail: jodi@strotherfirm.com.

STROUD, JAMES STANLEY, retired lawyer; b. Wimbledon, N.D., Jan. 26, 1915; s. Herbert Montgomery and Amanda Getchell (Longfellow) S.; m. Marjorie Marsh Hovey, Sept. 11, 1940; children: Jay Stanley, Steven Hovey. AB, Jamestown Coll., 1936; JD, U. Chgo., 1939. Bar: Ill. 1939, U.S. Supreme Ct. 1945, D.C. 1972. Counsel Ill. Mcpl. Code Commn., Chgo., 1939-40; bill drafter Ill. Legis. Ref. Bur., Springfield, 1941; from assoc. to ptnr. Mayer, Brown & Platt, Chgo., 1941-71, ptnr.-in-charge Washington, 1972-80, ret., 1982. Bd. dirs. Chgo. Community Renewal Found., 1962-70; mem. adminstrv. bd. Nat. United Meth. Ch., Washington, 1982-84; coord. Extended Family Program, 1981-82. Capt. AUS, 1943-46. Home: Cottage 304 3300 Darby Rd Haverford PA 19041-1063

STROUD, ROBERT EDWARD, lawyer; b. Chester, S.C., July 24, 1934; s. Coy Franklin and Leila (Caldwell) S.; m. Katherine C. Stroud, Apr. 8, 1961; children: Robert Gordon, Margaret Lathan. AB, Washington and Lee U., 1956, LLB, 1958. Bar: Va. 1959, U.S. Ct. Appeals (4th cir.) 1967, U.S. Tax Ct. 1959. Assoc. McGuire Woods, LLP, Charlottesville, Va., 1959-64; ptnr. McGuire Woods, LLP, Charlottesville, Va., 1964—2002, exec. com., 1978-89. Lectr. math. Washington and Lee U., 1957-59; lectr. bus. tax Grad. Bus. Sch., U. Va., Charlottesville, 1969-87, lectr. corp. taxation law sch., 1985-91; lectr. to legal edn. insts., lectr. in corp. law Washington and Lee Law Sch., Lexington Va., 1984. Co-author: Buying, Selling and Merging Businesses, 1975; editor-in-chief Washington and Lee Law Rev., 1959; editor: Advising Small Business Clients, Vol. 1, 1978, 4th edit., 1994, Vol. 2, 1980, 3d edit., 1990; contbr. articles to profl. jours. Pres. Charlottesville Housing Found., 1968-73; mem. mgmt. coun. Montreat Conf. Ct., N.C., 1974-77; trustee Presbyn. Found., 1972-73, Union Theol. Sem., Va., 1983-91; bd. dirs. Presbyn. Outlook Found., 1968-2002, pres., 1985-88; mem. governing coun. Presbyn. Synod of the Virginias, 1973-78, moderator of coun., 1977-78, moderator of Synod, 1977-78; trustee, v.p. Va. Tax Found., 1984-95; adv. bd. Westminster Orgn. Concert Series, 1989-93; bd. dirs. Shannon Found. for Excellence in Pub. Edn., Charlottesville, 1996—; adv. bd. Ashlawn-Highland Summer Festival, 1989—2003, pres., 1994-2000;bd. dirs. Ash Lawn Opera Festival Found., 2003-, gov. coun. Presbyn. Presbytery of the James, 1993-96, moderator of coun., 1995-96; moderator of presbytery, 1997. Capt. inf. U.S. Army, 1958, with res. 1958-70. Fellow Am. Bar Found., Va. Law Found.; mem. ABA, Am. Judicature Soc., Va. State Bar, Va. Bar Assn., Washington and Lee Law Sch. Assn. (governing coun. 1974-80, pres. 1979-80), Redland Club, Phi Delta Sigma, Omicron Delta Kappa, Phi Delta Phi. Democrat. Corporate, general, Mergers and acquisitions, Corporate taxation. Home: 345 Terrell Ct Charlottesville VA 22901-2171 Office: McGuire Woods LLP PO Box 1288 Charlottesville VA 22902-1288 E-mail: rstroud@mcguirewoods.com.

STROUP, STANLEY STEPHENSON, lawyer, educator; b. LA, Mar. 7, 1944; s. Francis Edwin and Marjory (Weimer) S.; m. Sylvia Douglass, June 15, 1968; children: Stacie, Stephen, Sarah. AB, U. Ill., 1966; JD, U. Mich., 1969. Bar: Ill. 1969, Calif. 1981, Minn. 1984. Atty. First Nat. Bank Chgo., 1969-78, asst. gen. counsel, 1978-80, v.p., 1980; sr. v.p., chief legal officer Bank of Calif., San Francisco, 1980-84; sr. v.p., gen. counsel Norwest Corp., Mpls., 1984-93, exec. v.p., gen. counsel, 1993-98, Wells Fargo & Co., San Francisco, 1998—. Adj. faculty Coll. Law, William Mitchell Coll., St. Paul, 1985-98; mem. Regulatory Affairs Coun., Bank Adminstrn. Inst., 1996—. Bd. dirs. San Francisco Zool. Soc., 2000—, Legal Aid Soc. San Francisco, 1999—. Mem. ABA, Ill. Bar Assn., State Bar Calif., Minn. Bar Assn., Bar Assn. San Francisco (bd. dirs. 2000-02), Fin. Svcs. Roundtable. Banking, Commercial, contracts (including sales of goods; commercial financing). Office: Wells Fargo & Co 633 Folsom St San Francisco CA 94107-3600 E-mail: stroup@wellsfargo.com.

STROYD, ARTHUR HEISTER, lawyer; b. Pitts., Sept. 5, 1945; 1 child, Elizabeth. AB, Kenyon Coll., 1967; JD, U. Pitts., 1972. Bar: Pa. 1972, U.S. Dist. Ct. (we. dist.) Pa. 1972, U.S. Ct. Appeals (3d cir.) 1972. Law clk. to judge U.S. Ct. Appeals (3d cir.), Phila., 1972—75; with Reed, Smith, LLP, Pitts., 1975—, mng. ptnr., Allegheny Region, 1997—2001. Mem. Nat. Adv. Coun. on Child Nutrition, U.S. Dept. Agriculture, 1984-85. Mem. Mt. Lebanon Zoning Hearing Bd., 1978-81; pres. bd. dirs. Mt. Lebanon Sch. dist., 1981-87; solicitor Allegheny County Rep. Com., 1988-95; pres. bd. dirs. Ctr. for Theatre Arts, Pitts., 1984-93; grad. Leadership Pitts., 1991-92; chair bd. dirs. Mt. Lebanon Hosp. Authority, 1993-2001; bd. dirs. U. Pitts. Cancer Inst., 1993—; mem. alumni coun. Kenyon Coll., 1996-2000; bd. trustees Historical Soc. of Western Pa., 1999—; bd. dirs. Edn. Policy and Issues Ctr., 2000—. Lt. USNR, 1969-71. Fellow Am. Coll. Trial Lawyers; mem. ABA, Pa. Bar Assn., Allegheny County Bar Assn. (pres., bd. govs., past chair civil litig. sect., past chmn. judiciary com.), Acad. Trial Lawyers (treas., bd. govs.), mem. Pa. Supreme Ct. Civil Procedural Rules Com., Duquesne Club, Pitts. Golf Club, Western Pa. Hist. Soc. (bd. dirs. 1999—). Episcopalian. Avocations: skiing, motorcycling, golf. General civil litigation, Product liability, Construction. Office: Reed Smith LLP 435 6th Ave Pittsburgh PA 15219-1886 E-mail: astroyd@reedsmith.com.

STRUIF, L. JAMES, lawyer; b. Alton, Ill., Sept. 18, 1931; s. Leo John and Clara Lillie (Bauer) S.; m. Shirley Ann Spatz, Mar. 24, 1965; children: Scott B., Jamie Lynn Pehowski, Susan Marie Bazzell, Jeffrey James. BS, Northwestern U., 1953; JD, U. Ill., Champaign, 1960. Bar: Ill. 1960, U.S. Dist. Ct. (so. dist.) Ill. 1960. Gen. counsel So. Ill. U., 1960-64; pvt. practice Struif Law Offices, Alton, Ill., 1964—. Lectr. So. Ill. U., Edwardsville, 1960-65. Author: Guide to Law for Laymen, Field Guide to 150 Prairie Plants of S.W. Ill. Scoutmaster Boy Scouts Am., Alton, 1966-69; active civil rights worker, Miss., 1964; trustee The James and Aune Nelson Found. With USN, submarines 1953-57, Pacific. Recipient Chmns. award Madison County Urban League, Blazing Star award The Nature Inst. Democrat. Mem. United Ch. of Christ. Avocations: nature, gardening, science, piano, mathematics. Bankruptcy, Estate planning, Probate (including wills, trusts). Office: The Struif Law Offices 2900 Adams Pkwy Alton IL 62002-4857

STRUM, JAY GERSON, lawyer; b. N.Y.C., July 6, 1938; s. John and Dorothy (Chaikind) S.; m. Patricia Ann Burtis, Jan. 25, 1969; children: Daniel, Jennifer. BA in polit. sci. magna cum laude, CCNY, 1959; LLB, Harvard U., 1962. Bar: N.Y. 1963, U.S. Dist. Ct. (so. and ea. dists.) N.Y. 1963, U.S. Ct. Appeals (2d cir.) 1965, U.S. Supreme Ct. 1979. Trial atty. SEC, N.Y.C., 1963-65; ptnr. Coon, Dubow, Kleinberg & Strum, N.Y.C., 1965-67; assoc. Kaye, Scholer, Fierman, Hays & Handler, N.Y.C., 1967-70, ptnr., 1971—. Mem. ABA, Assn. of Bar of City of N.Y., Harvard Club (N.Y.C.), Phi Beta Kappa. Clubs: Harvard (N.Y.C.). Federal civil litigation, Securities. Office: Kaye Scholer Fierman Hays & Handler LLP 425 Park Ave New York NY 10022-3506

STRUTHERS, MARGO S. lawyer; BA, Carleton Coll., 1972; JD cum laude, U. Minn., 1976. Atty., shareholder Moss & Barnett, P.A. and predecessor firms, Mpls., 1976-93; ptnr. Oppenheimer Wolff & Donnelly, LLP, Mpls., 1993—. Mem. Am. Health Lawyers Assn., Minn. State Bar Assn (bus. law sect., former chair nonprofit com., former chair and former mem. governing coun. health law sect.). Health. Office: Oppenheimer Wolff & Donnelly LLP Plaza VII 45 S 7th St Ste 3300 Minneapolis MN 55402-1614 E-mail: mstruthers@oppenheimer.com.

STRUTIN, KENNARD REGAN, lawyer, educator, legal information consultant; b. Bklyn., Dec. 1, 1961; s. Fred and Estelle (Brodzansky) S. BA summa cum laude, St. John's U., Jamaica, N.Y., 1981; JD, Temple U. Sch. Law, Phila., 1984; MLS, St. John's U., 1994. Bar: N.Y. 1986, U.S. Dist. Ct. (ea. and so. dists.) N.Y. 1990, U.S. Dist. Ct. (no. and we. dists.) N.Y. 1991, U.S. Ct. Appeals (2d cir.) 1990, U.S. Ct. Appeals (fed. cir.) 1991, U.S. Tax Ct. 1991, U.S. Ct. Mil. Appeals 1991, U.S. Supreme Ct. 1990. Atty. pvt. practice, West Hempstead, N.Y., 1986; trial atty. Nassau County Legal Aid Soc., Hempstead, N.Y., 1987-88, Orange County Legal Aid Soc., Goshen, N.Y., 1988-90; atty. pvt. practice, West Hempstead, N.Y., 1990-91; staff atty. N.Y. State Defenders Assn., Albany, N.Y., 1991-93; adj. asst. prof. St. John's U., Jamaica, N.Y., 1993-96; small claims tax assessment hearing officer Supreme Ct., Nassau, Suffolk, N.Y., 1993-96; law libr. Syracuse U. Coll. Law, 1996-98; legal info. cons., 1998—. Spkr. lawyer in classroom Nassau County Bar Assn., Mineola, N.Y., 1987-94; spkr. pre-release program Correctional Facilities, Lower Hudson Valley, N.Y., 1989-94. Author: ALI-ABA's Checklist Manual on Representing Criminal Defendants, 1998, Insider's Guide: Criminal Justice Resources on the Web, 2002; co-author: (computer-assisted, interactive instrnl. program) Legal Research Methodology, 1997; contbr. articles to profl. jours. Recipient Orange County Exec. Recognition award, 1990, 93, 2nd place winner libr. divsn. Donald Trautman Ctr. for Computer-Assisted Legal Instrn. Lesson Writing Competition, 1996-97. Mem. Beta Phi Mu.

STRUVE, GUY MILLER, lawyer; b. Wilmington, Del., Jan. 5, 1943; s. William Scott and Elizabeth Bliss (Miller) S.; m. Marcia Mayo Hill, Sept. 20, 1986; children: Andrew Hardenbrook, Catherine Tolstoy, Frank Leroy Hill, Guy Miller, Beverly Marcia Wise Hill (dec.), Elena Wise Struve-Hill. AB summa cum laude, Yale U., 1963; LLB magna cum laude, Harvard U., 1966. Bar: N.Y. 1967, D.C. 1986, U.S. Dist. Ct. (so. dist.) N.Y. 1970, U.S. Dist. Ct. (ea. dist.) N.Y. 1973, U.S. Dist. Ct. (no. dist.) Calif. 1979, U.S. Dist. Ct. D.C. 1987, U.S. Dist. Ct. (no. dist.) N.Y. 2000, U.S. Ct. Appeals (2d cir.) 1969, U.S. Ct. Appeals (D.C. cir.) 1973, U.S. Ct. Appeals (8th cir.) 1976, U.S. Ct. Appeals (9th cir.) 1979, U.S. Supreme Ct. 1971, U.S. Dist. Ct. (we. dist.) N.Y. 1991. Law clk. Hon. J. Edward Lumbard, Chief Judge United States Ct. Appeals for 2d Circuit, 1966-67; assoc. Davis Polk & Wardwell, N.Y.C., 1967-72, ptnr., 1973—. Ind. Counsel's Office, 1987-94. Mem. ABA, N.Y. State Bar Assn., Assn. of Bar of City of N.Y. (chmn. com. antitrust and trade regulation, 1983-86, chmn. com. fed. cts. 1998-2001), Am. Law Inst. Antitrust, General civil litigation. Home: 116 E 63rd St New York NY 10021-7325 Office: Davis Polk & Wardwell 450 Lexington Ave Fl 31 New York NY 10017-3982

STRUYK, ROBERT JOHN, lawyer; b. Sanborn, Iowa, May 17, 1932; s. Arie Peter and Adriana (VerHoef) S.; m. Barbara Damon, Sept. 7, 1963; children: Arie Franklin, Damon Nicholas, Elizabeth Snow. BA, Hope Coll., 1954; MA, Columbia U., 1957; LLB, U. Minn., 1961. Bar: Minn., U.S. Dist. Ct. Minn. Secondary tchr. Indianola (Iowa) Pub. Schs., 1957-58; assoc., then ptnr. Dorsey & Whitney, Mpls., 1961—. Mem.: Mpls., Minikahda. Episcopalian. Estate planning, Probate (including wills, trusts), Estate taxation. Office: Dorsey & Whitney 50 S 6th St Ste 2200 Minneapolis MN 55402-1498

STUART, ALICE MELISSA, lawyer; b. N.Y.C., Apr. 7, 1957; d. John Marberger and Marjorie Louise (Browne) S. BA, Ohio State U., 1977; JD, U. Chgo., 1980; LLM, NYU, 1982. Bar: N.Y. 1981, Ohio 1982, N.Y. 1982, Fla. 1994, U.S. Dist. Ct. (so. dist.) Ohio, 1983, U.S. Dist. Ct. (so. and ea. dists.) N.Y. 1985. Assoc. Schwartz, Shapiro, Kelm & Warren, Columbus, Ohio, 1982-84, Paul, Weiss, Rifkind, Wharton & Garrison, N.Y.C., 1984-85, Kassel, Neuwirth & Geiger, N.Y.C., 1985-86, Phillips, Nizer, Benjamin, Krim & Ballon, N.Y.C., 1987—92; pvt. practice N.Y.C., 1992—98; atty. LeBoeuf, Lamb, Greene & MacRae, 1998—. Adj. prof. So. Coll., Orlando, Fla., 1997-98. Surrogate Speakers' Bur. Reagan-Bush Campaign, N.Y.C., 1984; mem. Lawyers for Bush-Quayle Campaign, N.Y.C., 1988; bd. dirs. Mayflower Soc. in State of NY, 1998-, counsellor, 2002-. Mem. ABA, N.Y. State Bar Assn., Winston Churchill Meml. Library Soc., Jr. League, Soc. Mayflower Descs. in State of N.Y. (bd. dirs. 1999--, counselor 2002--), Phi Beta Kappa, Phi Kappa Phi, Alpha Lambda Delta. Republican. Corporate, general, Finance, Securities. Office: LeBoeuf Lamb Greene & MacRae 125 W 55th St New York NY 10019-5369

STUART, LYN (JACQUELYN L. STUART), judge; b. Sept. 23, 1955; m. George Stuart; children: Tucker, Shepard, Kelly. BA in Sociology and Edn., Auburn U., 1977; JD, U. Ala., 1980. Asst. atty. gen. State of Ala.; exec. asst. to commr. and spl. asst. atty. gen. Ala. Dept. Corrections; asst. dist. atty. Baldwin County; dist. judge, 1988—97; judge Ala. Cir. Ct., 1997—2001; justice Ala. Supreme Ct., 2001—. Republican. Office: 300 Dexter Ave Rm 3-215 Montgomery AL 36104-3741

STUART, MICHAEL GEORGE, lawyer; b. N.Y.C., May 24, 1951; s. George Bernard and Diana (Porikos) S.; children: Jennifer, Katherine Nicholas. BBA, Pace U., 1973, JD, 1980. Bar: Oreg. 1981, U.S. Dist. Ct. Oreg. 1981, U.S. Tax Ct. 1981, U.S. Ct. Appeals (9th cir.) 1982, N.Y. 1987, U.S. Supreme Ct. 1988, Ill. 1990, U.S. Dist. Ct. (no. dist.) Ill. 1990; CPA, Vt., Ill. Acct. Cambridge Instrument Inc., Ossining, N.Y., 1973-76; fin. cons. Bronxville, N.Y., 1976-78; legal asst. Frank B. Hall & Co., Briarcliff Manor, N.Y., 1978-79; supr. tax specialist Coopers & Lybrand, Portland, Oreg., 1979-81; fed. tax specialist Tektronix, 1981-83; pvt. practice law Beaverton, Oreg., 1983-89; tax mgr. Smith, Batchelder & Rugg, Lebanon, N.H., 1989; atty. Pontikes, Porikos, Rodes & Economos, Chgo., 1989-91; pvt. practice Chgo., Ill., 1991—. Com. mem. Atty. Realtors, Beaverton, 1986, pres. Letip Arlington Heights, 1997. Pres. Young Adult League, Portland, 1983-85; sec. Portland Parish Council, 1983, treas. 1984; mem. Greek Civic Club Oreg., Portland, 1982—; bd. dirs. N.W. Sub. Plan Coun., 1989—, N.W. Boy Scouts, 1994—. Mem. Oreg. State Bar Assn. (tax bus. sect., taxation com. 1988), Ill. CPA Soc., Am. Hellenic Ednl. Progressive Assn., Hellenic Bar Assn., Masons. Democrat. Greek Orthodox. Avocations: guitar, backpacking, woodworking, racquetball. Estate planning, Estate taxation, Taxation, general.

STUART, PAMELA BRUCE, lawyer; b. N.Y.C., Feb. 13, 1949; d. J. Raymond and Marion Grace (Cotins) S. AB with distinction, Mt. Holyoke Coll., 1970; JD cum laude, U. Mich., 1973. Bar: N.Y. 1974, D.C. 1975, U.S. Dist. Ct. D.C. 1979, U.S. Ct. Appeals (D.C. cir.) 1980, U.S. Supreme Ct. 1980, U.S. Dist. Ct. Md. 1989, Md. 1992, Va. 1993, U.S. Ct. Appeals (4th cir.) 1993, Fla. 1994, U.S. Dist. Ct. (ea. dist.) Va. 1994, U.S. Dist. Ct. (no. dist.) N.Y. 1996, U.S. Dist. Ct. (so. dist.) Fla. 1998, U.S. Dist. Ct. (so. dist.) N.Y. 1999, U.S. Dist. Ct. (ea. dist.) N.Y. 1999, U.S. Dist. Ct. (mid. dist.) Fla. 2001. Trial atty., deputy asst. dir. Bur. of Consumer Protection, FTC, Washington, 1973-79; asst. U.S. atty. U.S. Atty's Office, Washington, 1979-85; sr. trial atty. Office of Internat. Affairs, U.S. Dept. Justice, Washington, 1985-87; atty. Ross, Dixon & Masback, Washington, 1987-89; mem. Lobel, Novins, Lamont & Flug, Washington, 1989-92; pvt. practice, Washington, 1992—. Instr. Nat. Inst. for Trial Advocacy, Atty. Gen.'s Advocacy Inst., Legal Edn. Inst., Fed. Practice Inst.; mem. Jud. Conf. D.C., 1985-88, 91-98; mem. Jud. Conf., D.C. Cir., 1996, 98, 2000; assoc. mem. Consular Corps Washington; legal analyst CNN, MSNBC, Fox News, other TV networks. Author: The Federal Trade Commission, 1991; contbr. articles to profl. jours. Bd. dirs. Anacostia Econ. Devel. Corp., 1993—, Anacostia Holding Co., Inc., Anacostia Mgmt. Co., Inc., 1997—. Mem. ABA (internat. criminal law com., chmn., 1993-96, chmn. fed. crime rules subcom. white collar crime com. sect. criminal justice 1997-99), Bar Assn. D.C. (bd. dirs. 1995-2001), Asst. U.S. Attys. Assn. D.C. (exec. coun. 1993-99, pres. 1998-99), Assn. Trial Lawyers Am., Women's Bar Assn. D.C., Fla. Bar (exec. coun. real property probate and trust law sect. 1999—), Alumnae Assn. Mt. Holyoke Coll. (bd. dirs. 1986-89, 92-95, Alumnae medal of honor 1990), Edward Bennett Williams Inn of Ct. (master of bench), Fed. City Club (bd. govs. 1992—), Cosmos Club. Avocations: writing, interior design, investments, piano, art. Federal civil litigation, Criminal, Private international. Home: 5115 Yuma St NW Washington DC 20016-4336 Office: The Stuart Bldg 1750 N Street NW Washington DC 20036 also: 111 Johns Island Dr Apt 7 Vero Beach FL 32963-3274 E-mail: pamstuart@aol.com.

STUART, WILLIAM CORWIN, judge; b. Knoxville, Iowa, Apr. 28, 1920; s. George Corwin and Edith (Abram) S.; m. Mary Elgin Cleaver, Oct. 20, 1946; children: William Corwin II, Robert Cullen, Melanie Rae, Valerie Jo. BA, State U. Iowa, 1941, JD, 1942. Bar: Iowa 1942. Pvt. practice, Chariton, 1946-62; city atty., 1947-49; mem. Iowa Senate from, Lucas-Wayne Counties, 1951-61; justice Supreme Ct. Iowa, 1962-71; judge U.S. Dist. Ct., So. Dist. of Iowa, Des Moines, 1971-86, sr. judge, 1986—. With USNR, 1943-45. Recipient Outstanding Svc. award Iowa Acad. Trial lawyer, 1987, Iowa Trial Lawyers Assn., 1988, Spl. award Iowa State Bar Assn., 1987, Disting. Alumni, U. Iowa Coll. Law, 1987. Mem. ABA, Iowa Bar Assn., Am. Legion, All For Iowa, Order of Coif, Omicron Delta Kappa, Phi Kappa Psi, Phi Delta Phi. Clubs: Mason (Shriner). Presbyterian. Home: 216 S Grand St Chariton IA 50049-2139

STUCKY, JEAN SEIBERT, lawyer; b. Berkeley, Calif., Feb. 9, 1951; d. Edward Raymond and Frances Selma (Berg) S.; m. Scott Wallace Stucky, Aug. 18, 1973; children: Mary-Clare, Joseph. BA in Econs., Wellesley (Mass.) Coll., 1973; JD, Cornell U., 1978; MA in Econs., Trinity U., San Antonio, 1980; postgrad., George Washington U., 1991—94. Bar: D.C. 1978. Atty.-advisor Adminstrv. Conf. U.S., Washington, 1978-79, Divsn. Advice, NLRB, Washington, 1979-94; contractor labor counsel U.S. Dept. Energy, Office Gen. Counsel, Washington, 1994—. Mem. Washington Cathedral Altar Guild, 1988—. Mem. D.C. Bar, Dames of Loyal Legion of U.S., Washington Wellesley Club (pres. 1992-94), Wellesley Coll. Alumnae Assn. (regional chmn. 1995-97). Republican. Episcopalian. Avocations: gardening, flower arranging. Home: 11004 Homeplace Ln Potomac MD 20854-1406 Office: US Dept Energy Office Gen Counsel 1000 Independence Ave SW Washington DC 20585-0001

STUCKY, SCOTT WALLACE, lawyer; b. Hutchinson, Kans., Jan. 11, 1948; s. Joe Edward and Emma Clara (Graber) S.; m. Jean Elsie Seibert, Aug. 18, 1973; children: Mary-Clare, Joseph. BA summa cum laude, Wichita State U., 1970; JD, Harvard U., 1973; MA, Trinity U., 1980; LLM with high honors, George Washington U., 1983; postgrad., Nat. War Coll., 1993. Bar: Kans. 1973, U.S. Dist. Ct. Kans. 1973, U.S. Ct. Appeals (10th cir.) 1973, U.S. Ct. Mil. Appeals 1974, U.S. Supreme Ct. 1976, D.C. 1979, U.S. Ct. Appeals (D.C. cir.) 1979. Assoc. Ginsburg, Feldman & Bress, Washington, 1978-82; chief docketing and svc. br. Nuclear Regulatory Commn., Washington, 1982-83; legis. counsel U.S. Air Force USAF, Washington, 1983-96, gen. counsel sen. com. on armed svcs., 1996—2001, 2003—, prin. minority counsel, 2001—03. Lectr. bus. law Maria Regina Coll., Syracuse, N.Y., 1977; congrl. fellow Office Senator John Warner, 1986; res. judge adv. USAF Res., Washington, 1982—; col. Appellate Mil. Judge, USAF Ct. Criminal Appeals, 1991-95, 97-98, 2001—; sr. reservist USAF Judiciary, 1995-97, Air Res. Pers. Ctr., 1998-99, Air Force Legal Svcs. Agy., 1990-2001. Contbr. articles to profl. jours. Capt. USAF, 1973-78. Decorated Air Force Meritorious Svc. medal with two oak leaf cluster. Mem. Fed. Bar Assn., Judge Advs. Assn. (bd. dirs. 1984-88), Res. Officers Assn., Wichita State U. Alumni Assn. (pres. chpt. 1981-86, nat. bd. dirs. 1986-92), Adoption Svc. Info. Agy. (bd. dirs. 1998-2002), Army and Navy Club (Washington), Mil. Order of Loyal Legion U.S. (state comdr. and recorder 1984-92, nat. treas. 1987-89, nat. vice comdr. 1989-93, nat. comdr.-in-chief 1993-95), Sons of Union Vets Civil War (chpt. vice-comdr 1986-88), Phi Delta Phi, Phi Alpha Theta, Phi Kappa Phi, Omicron Delta Kappa, Sigma Phi Epsilon. Republican. Episcopalian. Home: 11004 Homeplace Ln Potomac MD 20854-1406 Office: Sen Armed Svcs Com 228 Senate Office Bldg Washington DC 20510-0001

STUHAN, RICHARD GEORGE, lawyer; b. Braddock, Pa., July 1, 1951; s. George and Pauline Madeline (Pavlocik) S.; m. Mary Ann Cipriano, Aug. 23, 1975; children: Brendan George, Sara Katherine, Brian Christopher, Caitlin Emily. BA summa cum laude, Duquesne U., 1973; JD, U. Va., 1976. Bar: Va. 1976, D.C. 1977, U.S. Ct. Appeals (D.C. cir.) 1977, U.S. Ct. Appeals (4th cir.) 1977, U.S. Claims Ct. 1979, U.S. Supreme Ct. 1980, U.S. Ct. Appeals (3d cir.) 1981, U.S. Ct. Appeals (11th cir.) 1982, U.S. Dist. Ct. (no. dist.) Ohio 1985, Ohio 1986. Assoc. Arnold & Porter, Washington, 1976-84; of counsel Jones, Day, Reavis & Pogue, Cleve., 1984-86, ptnr., 1987—. Mem. Va. Law Review, 1974-76. Recipient Gold Medal for Gen. Excellence, Duquesne U., 1973, Mem. Order of Coif. Democrat. Roman Catholic. Avocations: tennis, swimming, basketball, home repair. General civil litigation, Product liability. Home: 2865 Falmouth Rd Shaker Heights OH 44122-2838 Office: Jones Day Reavis & Pogue 901 Lakeside Ave Cleveland OH 44114-1190 E-mail: RGSTUHAN@JONESDAY.COM.

STUKENBERG, MICHAEL WESLEY, lawyer; b. Freeport, Ill., Feb. 22, 1951; s. Wesley W. and Nancy Jack (Baker) S.; m. Amanda Reed Eggert, July 21, 1973; children: Sarah Reed, William Robinson. BA, Princeton U., 1973; JD, Vanderbilt U., 1976. Bar: Tex. 1977, U.S. Tax Ct. 1977, U.S. Dist. Ct. (so. dist.) Tex. 1982. Assoc. firm Matthews & Branscomb, Corpus Christi, Tex., 1976-81, shareholder, 1981—. Gov. Art Mus. South Tex., Copus Christi, 1990-96; dir., pres. Corpus Christi Estate Planning Coun., 1989-98; trustee, chair bd. trustees YMCA Corpus Christi, 1997-. Fellow Am. Coll. Trust and Estate Counsel; mem. ABA, Tex. Bar Assn. (tax sect.), Tex. Acad. of Probate and Trust Lawyers, Coll. of State Bar of Tex. Clubs: Corpus Christi Yacht, Causeway (Southwest Harbor, Maine). Episcopalian. Estate planning, Estate taxation, Taxation, general. Home: 3502 Aransas St Corpus Christi TX 78411-1302 E-mail: mstukenberg@mattbran.com.

STUMBO, JANET LYNN, state supreme court justice; b. Prestonsburg, Ky. d. Charles and Doris Stanley Stumbo; m. Ned Pillersdorf; children: Sarah, Nancee, Samantha. BA, Morehead State U., 1976; JD, U. Ky., 1980. Bar: Ky. 1980, W.Va. 1982. Staff atty. to Judge Harris S. Howard Ky. Ct. Appeals, 1980—82; asst. county atty. Floyd County, 1982—85; ptnr.

Turner, Hall & Stumbo, P.S.C., 1982—88; prosecutor Floyd Dist. Ct. and Juvenile Ct.; ptnr. Stumbo, DeRossett & Pillersdorf, 1989; judge Ct. Appeals, Ky., 1989—93, Supreme Ct. of Ky., 1993—. Named to Morehead State U. Alumni Assn. Hall of Fame, 1990, U. Ky. Coll. Law Alumni Hall of Fame, 1999; recipient Justice award, Ky. Women Advocates, 1991, Outstanding Just award, 1995, Bull's Eye award, Women in State Govt. Network, 1995. also: 311 N Arnold Ave Ste 502 Prestonsburg KY 41653-1279

STUMP, JOHN SUTTON, retired lawyer; b. Clarksburg, W.Va., Aug. 7, 1929; s. John Sutton and Helen (Mannix) S.; m. Elaine Claire Scammahorn, Sept. 14, 1968; children— John Sutton IV, James Felix. Student, Washington and Lee U., 1946-47, LL.B., 1957; BS in Commerce, U. N.C., 1951. Bar: W.Va. 1957, Va. 1957, D.C. 1983. Assoc. Jackson, Kelly, Holt & O'Farrell, Charleston, W.Va., 1957-58, Boothe, Dudley, Koontz & Boothe, Alexandria, Va., 1958-61, Boothe, Dudley, Koontz & Blankingship, Fairfax and Alexandria, Va., 1962-63; ptnr. Boothe, Dudley, Koontz, Blankingship & Stump, Fairfax and Alexandria, 1963-71, Boothe, Prichard & Dudley, 1971-87, McGuire, Woods, Battle & Boothe LLP, 1987-99. Served to lt. comdr. USNR, 1951-54, 61-62. Fellow Am. Coll. Trial Lawyers; mem. Am. Law Inst. General civil litigation, Construction, Finance. Home: 8329 Weller Ave Mc Lean VA 22102-1717 Office: 1750 Tysons Blvd Mc Lean VA 22102-4208

STUNTEBECK, CLINTON A. lawyer; b. Hibbing, Minn., May 25, 1938; s. Robert F. and S. Mary Stuntebeck; m. Mary Joan Carmody; children: Robin, M. Alison, Susan, John, William. BA in Psychology, U. Minn., 1960; LLB, U. Maine, 1968. Bar: Pa. 1969, U.S. Dist. Ct. (ea. dist.) Pa. 1969. Ptnr., chmn. corp. fin. and securities, mem. exec. com. Schnader, Harrison, Segal & Lewis, Phila. Bd. dirs. Markel Corp., Greater Phila. First Partnership for Econ. Devel.; lectr. corp. and securities law. Contbr. articles to profl. jours. Pres. Radnor (Pa.) Twp. Bd. Commn., 1981—83, 1992—2001; founder, bd. dirs. Radnor Enhancement Cmty. Trust; bd. visitors U. Maine Sch. Law; trustee Cabrini Coll.; bd. dirs. Am. Heart Assn. Capt. USAF, 1960—68. Mem. ABA, Am. Law Inst., Pa. Bar Assn., Phila. Bar Assn., Securities Industry Assn. (law and compliance com.), U. Maine Law Alumni Assn. (pres. 1974-76), Union League Phila., Phila. Country Club, Sunday Breakfast Club, Corinthian Yacht Club. Avocations: sailing, skiing, golf, tennis. Finance, Mergers and acquisitions, Securities. Office: Schnader Harrison Segal 1600 Market St Ste 3600 Philadelphia PA 19103-7287 E-mail: cstuntebeck@schnader.com.

STUPSKER, CHARLES A. lawyer; b. Toledo, May 1, 1940; s. Harry and Jeannette (Karp) S.; m. Sandra Stupsker, Aug. 22, 1965 (div. 1992); children: Julie, Laura, Hallie; m. Susan M., Nov. 26, 1993. BA, U. Mich., 1962; LLB, JD, Ohio State U., 1965. Bar: Ohio 1965. Asst. dir. law City of Toledo, 1967-75, chief prosecutor, 1971-75; atty. pvt. practice, Toledo, 1965—. Zoning commn. Sylvania Twp., Lucas County, Ohio, 1981-2000. Fellow Toledo Bar Assn. (pres. 1997); mem. ABA, Ohio State Bar Assn., Lucas County Bar Assn. (pres. 1983). Republican. Avocations: coin collecting, bridge, jogging. Estate planning, Family and matrimonial, Probate (including wills, trusts). Office: 626 Madison Ave Ste 711 Toledo OH 43604-1624

STURM, WILLIAM CHARLES, lawyer; b. Milw., Aug. 4, 1941; s. Charles William and Helen Ann (Niesen) S.; m. Kay F. Sturm, June 10, 1967; children: Patricia, Elizabeth, Katherine, William, Susan. BS in Bus. Adminstrn., Marquette U., 1963; JD, 1966. Bar: Wis. 1966, U.S. Dist. Ct. (ea. dist.) Wis. 1966, U.S. Supreme Ct. 1980. Sole practice, Milw., 1966—77; ptnr. Rausch, Hamell, Ehrle & Sturm, S.C., Milw., 1977—81, Rausch, Hamell, Ehrle, Sturm & Blom, Milw., 1981-83, Rausch, Hamell, Ehrle & Sturm, 1983-95, Rausch, Hamell, Sturm & Israel S.C., 1995-98, Rausch, Sturm, Israel & Hornik, S.C., 1999—. Asst. prof. Marquette U., 1982-91; lectr. U. Wis., Milw., 1991-97, sr. lectr. 1997-2002. Contbr. articles to profl. jours. Mem. adv. bd. Pallotine Order, 1985—; bd. dirs. Pius XI H.S., 2002-. Recipient Editors award Wis. Med. Credit Assn., 1980, Recipient Outstanding Alumni Pius XI H.S., 2002. Mem. ABA, Wis. Bar Assn., Comml. Law League Am. (exec. council midwestern dist. 1981-83, 86-88, chmn. state membership com. 1981-88, nat. nominating council 1984-86, 1988-89, sec., 2d v.p. midwestern dist. 1989-90, 1st v.p. midwestern dist. 1990-91, chmn. 1991-92, nat. bd. govs. 1997-2000, pres. elect, 2000-01, pres. 2001-02, past pres. 2002-). Acad. Legal Studies in Bus., Midwest Bus. Law Assn. (sec. 1988-89, v.p. 1989-90, pres. 1990-91), Healthcare Fin. Mgmt. Assn., Beta Alpha Psi (faculty v.p. Psi chpt. 1985-88, Eta Theta chpt. 1992-99), Midwest Bus. And Health Assn. (v.p. procs. 1987-88, v.p. program 1988-89, pres. 1989-90). Clubs: Westmoor Country (Milw.); Kiwanis (pres. 1979, lt. gov. div. 5, 1980) (Wauwatosa, Wis.). Bankruptcy, Commercial, consumer (including collections, credit). Office: 2448 South 102nd St Milwaukee WI 53227 E-mail: wsturm@wiscollect.com.

STURMAN, GLORIDA J. lawyer; b. Cortez, Colo., June 26, 1957; BS cum laude, Ariz. State U., 1979, JD, 1982. Bar: Ariz. 1982, Nev. 1983. Atty. Edwards, Hale, Sturman, Atkin & Cushing, Ltd., Las Vegas. Mem.: ABA, So. Nev. Assn. Women Attys. (pres. 1988—89), Clark County Bar Assn. (pres. 1994), State Bar Nev. (pres. 2002—03, bd. govs.), State Bar Ariz. Insurance, Personal injury (including property damage), Civil rights. Office: Edwards Hale Sturman et al 415 S Sixth St Ste 300 Las Vegas NV 89101-6937*

STURTEVANT, BRERETON, retired lawyer, former government official; b. Washington, Nov. 24, 1921; d. Charles Lyon and Grace (Brereton) S. BA, Wellesley Coll., 1942; JD, Temple U., 1949; postgrad., U. Del., 1969-71. Bar: D.C. 1949, Del. 1950. Research chemist E.I. duPont DeNemours & Co., 1942-50; law clk. Del. Supreme Ct., 1950; gen. practice law Wilmington, Del., 1950-57; partner Connolly, Bove & Lodge, Wilmington, 1957-71; examiner-in-chief U.S. Patent and Trademark Office Bd. Appeals, Washington, 1971-88. Adj. prof. law Georgetown U., 1974-79 Trustee Holton-Arms Sch., Bethesda, Md., 1977-96, chmn. or mem. all coms., trustee emerita, 1997—. Mem. ABA, Exec. Women in Govt. (charter mem., chmn. 1978-79) Clubs: Wellesley College, Washington-Wellesley (pres. 1982-84). Episcopalian. Achievements include first woman law clerk, Delaware Supreme Court; first woman patent examiner-in-chief. Home: 1227 Morningside Ln Alexandria VA 22308-1042

STUTTS, WILLIAM FLOYD, JR., lawyer, educator; b. El Dorado, Ark., Nov. 8, 1952; s. William Floyd and Marilyn Martin Stutts; m. Susan P. Campbell, May 16, 1992. BA, U. Tex., 1973; JD, U. Va., 1976. Bar: Tex. 1976, U.S. Dist. Ct. (we. dist.) Tex. 1992. Law clk. U.S. Ct. Appeals (5th cir.), Austin, 1976-77; assoc. Baker & Botts, Houston, 1978-85; ptnr. Baker Botts, Austin, 1987—, Clark, Thomas, Winters, Austin, 1985-87. Adj. prof. U. Tex. Law Sch., Austin, 1997—; instr., cons. Internat. Law Inst., Washington, 1998, 2001. Bd. dirs. Ballet Austin, 1988-96, Austin Oita Sister City Com., 1990—, Travis County Bar Assn., 1995-96, Capital Area Coun. Boy Scouts Am., Austin, 1996—. Fellow Am. Coll. Investment Counsel, Tex. Bar Found. (life); mem. ABA, Am. Bankruptcy Inst., Comml. Law League of Am. Lutheran. Home: 1405 Hardouin Ave Austin TX 78703 Office: Baker Botts 98 San Jacinto Blvd # 1500 Austin TX 78701

STUTZMAN, THOMAS CHASE, SR., lawyer; b. Portland, Oreg., Aug. 1, 1950; s. Leon H. and Mary L. (Chase) S.; m. Wendy Jeanne Craig, June 5, 1976; children: Sarah Ann, Thomas Chase Jr. BA with high honors, U. Calif., Santa Barbara, 1972; JD cum laude, Santa Clara U., 1975. Bar: Calif. 1976; cert. family law specialist. Pvt. practice, San Jose, Calif., 1976-79; pres., sec., CFO Thomas Chase Stutzman, PC, San Jose, Calif., 1979—. Instr. San Jose State U., 1977-78. Bd. dirs. Santa Cruz Campfire, 1978-80, Happy Hollow Park, 1978-80, 83-86, Pacific Neighbors, pres., 1991-92. Mem. Calif. Bar Assn., Santa Clara County Bar Assn. (chmn. environ. law com. 1976-78, exec. com. family law), Assn. Cert. Law Specialists, San Jose Jaycees (Dir. of Yr. 1976-77), Rotary, Lions (dir. 1979-81, 2d v.p. 1982-83, 1st v.p. 1983-84, pres. 1984-85), Scottish Rite, Masons, Phi Beta Kappa, Alameda Valley Rotary Club. Congregationalist. State civil litigation, Family and matrimonial, Property, real (including real estate development, water). Office: 1625 The Alameda Ste 626 San Jose CA 95126-2207 E-mail: stutzman@tomstutzman.com.

STYER, JANE M. computer consultant; b. Bethlehem, Pa., Apr. 14, 1957; d. LeRoy V. and Pauline M. (Diehl) S. Assoc in Gen. Edn., NCACC, 1977, Assoc in Applied Sci., 1979; BS in Computer Sci., St. Francis de Sales Coll., 1985, cert. profl. legal sec., 1986. PC technician A+ cert. 1997. Legal sec., asst. Lower Saucon Police Dept.; asst. to treas., bookkeeper Lehigh Valley Motor Club, Allentown, Pa.; real estate and probate paralegal, office mgr. various attys., Lehigh & Delaware Valleys, Pa., 1976-82; title ins. agt., owner, mgr. Abstractors' Svcs., Bingen, Pa., 1982—; quality control theory checker, tax preparer H & R Block, 1992—2002. Mem. NAFE, Nat. Assn. Legal Secs. (Continuing Legal Edn. Recognition award 1988), Lehigh-Northampton Counties (chmn. continuing legal edn. com. 1984-88, seminar chmn. 1985-88), Pa. Assn. Notaries, Single Sq. Dancers U.S.A. (nat. sec. 1986-87), Bachelors and Bachelorettes, Internat. (sec. Mid-Atlantic region 1980-84). Avocations: camping, square and round dancing, horseback riding. Office: Abstractors' Svcs 3228 Bingen Rd Bethlehem PA 18015-5707 E-mail: JMStyer@juno.com.

SUBAK, JOHN THOMAS, lawyer; b. Trebic, Czechoslovakia, Apr. 19, 1929; came to U.S., 1941, naturalized, 1946; s. William John and Gerda Maria (Subakova) S.; m. Mary Corcoran, June 4, 1955; children: Jane Kennedy, Kate, Thomas, Michael. BA summa cum laude, Yale U., 1950, LLB, 1956. Bar: Pa. 1956. From assoc. to ptnr. Dechert, Price & Rhoads, Phila., 1956-76, v.p., gen. counsel, dir., 1976-77; group v.p., gen. counsel, dir. Rohm and Haas Co., Phila., 1977-93; counsel Dechert Price & Rhoads, Phila., 1994—2001. Editor: The Bus. Lawyer, 1982-83. Bd. dirs. Am. Cancer Soc., 1982-95; trustee Smith Coll., 1991-2001; pres. Gasparilla Island Conservation and Improvement Assn., 2001-03. Lt. (j.g.) USN, 1950-53. Mem. ABA (chmn. corp. and bus. law sect. 1984-85), Am. Law Inst. (coun. mem.), Defender Assn. of Phila. (v.p., bd. dirs. 1982-95), Merion Cricket Club, Lemon Bay Club. Democrat. Roman Catholic. Corporate, general. Office: Dechert Price & Rhoads 4000 Bell Atlantic Tower Philadelphia PA 19102-2793 E-mail: johnsubak@aol.com.

SUBIN, ELI HAROLD, lawyer; b. Phila., June 25, 1935; s. Benjamin and Freda (Kalen) S.; m. Suzon Bette Rosenbluth, Oct. 21, 1962; children: Andrea Beth Craig, Ben William. BA, U. Pa., 1957; LLB, U. Miami, Coral Gables, Fla., 1961. Bar: Fla., 1961, U.S. Dist. Ct. (mid. dist.) Fla., 1961, U.S. Supreme Ct., 1964, U.S. Ct. Appeals (5th, 11th cirs.), 1966. Trial atty. antitrust divsn. U.S. Dept. Justice, Phila., 1962-63; rsch. aide Dist. Ct. Appeal (1st dist.) Fla., Tallahassee, 1963-64; atty. Roth Segal & Levine, Orlando, Fla., 1964-72, Subin Shams, et. al. P.A., Orlando, 1972-96; city atty. City of Orlando, 1980-82; atty. Maguire, Voorhis & Wells, P.A., Orlando, 1997-98, Holland & Knight LLP, Orlando, 1998—. Referee Supreme Ct. Fla., Tallahassee, 1975; mem. Fla. Bd. Bar Examiners, 1982-87, chmn., 1986-87. Mem. exec. com. Seminole County Dems., Sanford, Fla., 1970-74; mem. jud. nominating com. 9th cir. Fla., 1976-79; dir. Fla. Bar Found., Orlando, 1992-00. 1st lt. USAR, 1957-64. Mem. Am. Law Inst., Am. Bd. Trial Advs. (assoc.), Orange County Bar Assn. (dir. 1968-71). Jewish. Antitrust, General civil litigation. Office: Holland & Knight LLP PO Box 1526 Orlando FL 32802-1526 E-mail: esubin@hklaw.com.

SUBIN, FLORENCE, retired lawyer; b. N.Y.C., June 5, 1935; d. George and Beatrice (Rodam) Katroser; m. Bert W. Subin, June 6, 1953 (dec.); children: Glen D., Beth Subin Ambler, Herbert. BA, Lehman Coll., 1972; JD magna cum laude, Bklyn. Law Sch., 1975. Bar: N.Y. 1976, U.S. Dist. Ct. (so. and ea. dists.) N.Y. 1976. Pvt. practice, N.Y.C. and Scarsdale, N.Y., 1976-99; retired. Trustee Bklyn. Law Sch., 1998—. Mem. Assn. Trial Lawyers City of N.Y. (bd. dirs. 1982-86), Met. Women's Bar Assn. (pres. 1979-81, bd. dirs. 1981—), Bronx Women's Bar Assn. (pres. 1983-85), Bklyn. Law Sch. Alumni Assn. (pres. 1992-94), Phi Beta Kappa. Personal injury (including property damage), Probate (including wills, trusts).

SUCHODOLSKI, BENO, lawyer; b. São Paulo, Brazil, Nov. 4, 1943; s. Alexandre and Chana Albert Suchodolski; m. Flora Gusmão, Sept. 2, 1974 (div. Sept. 9, 1988); children: Pedro Gusmão Suchodolski, Sergio Gusmão Suchodolski; m. Maria Elvira Ramos, Apr. 26, 1991; 1 child, Mariana. LLB, U. São Paulo, 1966; LLM, Harvard U., 1968. Bar: São Paulo, Portugal, Fla. Ptnr. Suchodolski & Assoc., São Paulo, 1970—. Bd. mem. Fundação Bienal São Paulo, Inst. Fernand Braudel, São Paulo. Private international, Commercial, contracts (including sales of goods; commercial financing), Mergers and acquisitions. Office: Suchodolski Advogados Associados Rua Augusta 1819 - 24o 01413-000 São Paulo Brazil

SUDDABY, GLENN T. lawyer; b. 1956; Grad., SUNY, Syracuse U. Asst. dist. atty. Onondaga County Dist. Atty.'s Office, 1986—89; assoc. Menter, Rudin & Trivelpiece, Syracuse, NY, 1989—92; chief asst. dist. atty. Onandaga County Dist. Atty.'s Office, 1992, 1st chief asst. dist. atty.; U.S. atty. No. Dist. N.Y., 2002—. Office: PO Box 7198 100 S Clinton St Syracuse NY 13261*

SUDWEEKS, JAY DEAN, lawyer; b. Ft. Peck, Mont., June 10, 1940; s. Harold D. and Rachel N. Sudweeks; m. Isabell Murray, Feb. 25, 1966. AA, Ricks Coll., 1960; BS, Brigham Young U., 1966; JD, U. Utah, 1969. Bar: Idaho 1969, U.S. Supreme Ct. 1973. Ptnr. May, Sudweeks & Browning, Twin Falls, Idaho, 1969—. Bd. dirs. United Way, Twin Falls. Mem.: Idaho Trial Lawyers Assn. (pres. 5th jud. dist. 1975—76), Idaho Bar Assn. (bd. dirs. bankruptcy sect. 1984—90). Bankruptcy, General practice, Personal injury (including property damage). Office: 516 2d St E PO Box 1846 Twin Falls ID 83303-1846

SUENRAM, ANDY, lawyer; b. Lakeport, Calif., May 24, 1961; BA in Econs., U. Calif., Santa Cruz, 1985; JD, U. Mont., 1988. Bar: Mont. 1988, U.S. Dist. Ct. Mont. 1988. Atty. Erb & Suenram, Dillon. Mem.: ABA (econs. of law practice, natural resources law sects.), State Bar Mont. (exec. com. 1997—, pres.-elect 2001—02), Beaverhead County C. of C. (dir. 1990—91). Property, real (including real estate development, water), Personal injury (including property damage). Office: Erb and Suenram PO Box 1366 134 E Reeder St Dillon MT 59725-1366*

SUFLAS, STEVEN WILLIAM, lawyer; b. Camden, NJ, Oct. 7, 1951; s. William V. and Dorothy (Stafre) S.; m. Rochelle B. Volin, Apr. 15, 1978; children: Allison, Rebecca, Whitney. BA, Davidson Coll., 1973; JD with honors, U. N.C., 1976. Bar: N.J. 1976, Pa. 1978, U.S. Dist. Ct. N.J., U.S. Ct. Appeals (3d cir.). Field atty. NLRB, Phila., 1976-80; assoc. Archer & Greiner P.C., Haddonfield, NJ, 1980-86, ptnr., 1986—2002, Ballard, Spahr, Andrews & Ingersoll LLP, Voorhees, NJ, 2002—. Fellow Coll. of Labor and Employment Lawyers; mem. ABA, Pa. Bar Assn., Phila. Bar Assn., NJ Bar Assn. (exec. com. labor and employment law sect. 1985—, chmn. 1999-2001), Order of Coif, Omicron Delta Kappa. Labor (including EEOC, Fair Labor Standards Act, labor-management relations, NLRB, OSHA). Office: Ballard Spahr Andrews & Ingersoll Plaza 1000 Ste 500 Main St Voorhees NJ 08043-4636

SUGARMAN, MYRON GEORGE, lawyer; b. San Francisco, Nov. 7, 1942; s. Irving Carden and Jane Hortense (Weingarten) S.; m. Cheryl Ann Struble, June 8, 1968 (div. 1993); children: Andrew, Amy, Adam; m. Cynthia Wilson Woods, Apr. 16, 1994. BS, U. Calif., Berkeley, 1964, JD, 1967. Assoc. Cooley Godward LLP, San Francisco, 1972-77, ptnr., 1977—. Served to capt. U.S. Army, 1968-71. Fellow Am. Coll. Trust and Estate Counsel, Am. Coll. Tax Counsel, Am. Bar Found.; mem. U. Calif. Alumni Assn. (bd. dirs. 1985-88), San Francisco Tax Club (pres. 1990), San Francisco Grid Club, Order of Coif, Phi Beta Kappa, Beta Gamma Sigma. Avocations: skiing, tennis. Estate planning, Non-profit and tax-exempt organizations, Taxation, general. Office: Cooley Godward LLP 1 Maritime Plz San Francisco CA 94111-3404

SUGG, REED WALLER, lawyer; b. Morganfield, Ky., Dec. 1, 1952; s. Matt Waller and Iris (Omer) S. BA, Furman U., 1975; JD, Vanderbilt U., 1978. Bar: Mo. 1978, Ill. 1979, U.S. Ct. Appeals (8th, 9th and 7th cirs.), U.S. Dist. Ct. (ea. dist.) Mo., U.S. Dist. Ct. (so. dist.) Ill. Atty. Coburn, Croft, Shepherd & Herzog, St. Louis, 1978-79, Shepherd, Sandberg & Phoenix, St. Louis, 1979-90, Sandberg, Phoenix & von Gontard, St. Louis, 1990—. Mem. ABA, Bar Assn. Met. St. Louis, Christian Legal Soc., Lawyers Assn. St. Louis, Aviation Ins. Assn., Lawyer-Pilots Bar Assn., Phi Beta Kappa. Clubs: Mo. Athletic, Westborough Country (St. Louis). Republican. Presbyterian. Avocations: basketball, golf, reading. Federal civil litigation, State civil litigation, Personal injury (including property damage). Home: 12825 Brighton Woods Dr Saint Louis MO 63131-1413 Office: Sandberg Phoenix & von Gontard 1 City Ctr Ste 1500 Saint Louis MO 63101-1880

SUH, CHUNG-SYNN, lawyer; b. Seoul, Republic of Korea, Aug. 8, 1940; m. Jung-ja Ha; children: Chang-min, Yoolee, Young-in. BA, Seoul Nat. U., 1962. Passed the Nat. Judicial Examination: Korean Govt. 1961. Vice min. justice Dept. Justice, Seoul, 1988—89; chief admin. Legal Rsch. Training Inst., 1989—90; dep. prosecutor gen. Supreme Public Prosecutors Office, 1990—91; sr. chief pub. prosecutor Seoul High Public Prosecutors' Office, 1991—92; prosecutor gen. Seoul High Prosecutors Office, 1991—93; sr. ptnr. Hwang Mok Pk. P.C., Seoul, 1993—. Office: Hwang Mok Park PC Daekyung Bldg 120 2-ka Taepyungro Chung-ku, Seoul 100-724 Republic of Korea Office Fax: 02-772-2800. E-mail: jssuh8@hanmail.net.

SUH, EDWARD H. lawyer; b. Seoul, Korea, Sept. 19, 1957; arrived in U.S., 1972; s. Samuel Kyuhyun and Shirley Youngja Suh; m. Amy Youngmi Choi, Aug. 20, 1982; children: Minji, Hanah. B of Engring., Stevens Inst. Tech, 1980; JD, Bklyn. Law Sch., 1985. Bar: N.Y., N.J. Project engr. Rohm and Haas, Bristol, Pa., 1980—82; assoc. Sheldon Feinstein, Queens, NY, 1983—83; prin. atty. Edward H. Suh & Assocs., Queens, NY, 1983—. Mem.: Korean Am. Laywers Assn. N.Y. (pres. 1997), Queens Bar Assn., N.Y. State Trial Lawyers Assn., Am. Trial Lawyers Assn., Stevens Korean-Am. Club (pres. 1980). Avocation: reading. Personal injury (including property damage). Office: Edward H Suh and Assocs 163-07 Depot Rd Ste 101 Flushing NY 11358 Fax: 718-461-3092. E-mail: esuh@nycrr.com.

SUH, SUNG-HEE, lawyer; b. Seoul, Republic of Korea, Aug. 18, 1964; d. Chung Kyun and Chong Cha Suh; m. Peter Edward Dolotta, July 16, 1994. AB, Harvard/Radcliffe Coll., 1982—86; AM, Harvard Grad. Sch. of Arts & Scis., 1985—86; JD, Harvard Law Sch., 1987—90. Bar: N.Y. 1991, U.S. Dist. Ct. (so. dist.) 1993, U.S. Dist. Ct. (ea. dist.) 1993, U.S. Ct. Appeals (2d cir.) 1995. Law clk. U.S. Dist. Judge Robert L. Carter, N.Y.C., 1990—91; assoc. Davis Polk & Wardwell, N.Y.C., 1991—94; asst. U.S. atty. U.S. Attorney's Office, Bklyn., 1994—99; assoc. Schulte Roth & Zabel LLP, N.Y.C., 1999—2001, ptnr., 2002—. Dir. Asian Am. Legal Def. & Edn. Fund, N.Y.C., 2001—03. Recipient The Stimson Medal, N.Y. Bar Assn., 1999. General civil litigation, Criminal. Office: Schulte Roth & Zabel LLP 919 Third Ave New York NY 10025 Office Fax: 212-593-5955. E-mail: sung-hee.suh@srz.com.

SUHR, J. NICHOLAS, lawyer; b. N.Y.C., Nov. 14, 1942; s. Heinrich P. and Anna H. (Isenschmid) S.; m. Anne Aylett Stone, July 6, 1965; children: John Nicholas Jr., Erika Christl Efthymiou. BA, U. Va., 1964; JD, Am. U., 1967. Bar: N.Y. 1967, N.J. 1969, U.S. Supreme Ct. 1989; cert. civil trial atty. Assoc., ptnr. Topken & Farley, N.Y.C., 1967-73, Conboy, Hewitt, O'Brien & Boardman, N.Y.C., 1973-86; counsel Hunton & Williams, N.Y.C., 1986-87, Quinn, Cohen, Shields & Bock, N.Y.C., 1987-88; ptnr. Quinn & Suhr, White Plains, N.Y., 1988-95, Herzfeld & Rubin, P.C., N.Y.C., 1995-2000, Chase, Kurshan, Suhr, Weidenfeld, Herzfeld & Rubin, LLC, Newark, 1995-2000; pvt. practice N.Y.C., Holmdel, N.J., 2000—. Arbitrator U.S. Dist. Ct. N.J., Trenton, 1985—, Am. Arbitration Assn., N.Y.C., 1976—; qualified mediator N.J. Superior Ct., 2000—. Contbr. articles to profl. jours.; commentator Ct. TV network. 1st v.p. Liederkranz Found. Inc., N.Y.C., 2000—. Mem. ABA, N.Y. State Bar Assn., N.J. State Bar Assn., U.S. Supreme Ct. Bar, Internat. Law Soc., Consular Law Soc., German Soc. of N.Y.C. (v.p., treas., trustee 1976—), German-Am. Sch. Assn. (v.p., trustee 1986—), German Seamen's Mission N.Y. (pres., dir. 1972—). Lutheran. Avocations: fishing, woodworking. General civil litigation, Probate (including wills, trusts), Product liability. Office: 15 Glenn Way Holmdel NJ 07733 E-mail: jnsuhr@aol.com.

SUHR, PAUL AUGUSTINE, lawyer; b. Sonwunri, Chonbuk, Korea, Jan. 20, 1940; arrived in US, 1966; s. Chong-ju and Oksuk (Pang) So; m. Angeline M. Kang Suhr; 1 child, Christopher. BA, Campbell Coll., Buies Creek, N.C., 1968; MA, U. N.C., Greensboro, 1970; MS, U. N.C., Chapel Hill, 1975; JD, N.C. Cen. U., 1988. Bar: N.C. 1989, U.S. Dist. Ct. (ea. and mid. dist.) N.C. 1989, U.S. Ct. Appeals D.C. 1990, U.S. Ct. Appeals (4th cir.) 1992. Bibliographer N.C. Div. of State Libr., Raleigh, 1975-78; dir. Pender County Pub. Libr., Burgaw, N.C., 1978-80; libr. Tob. Lit. Svc., N.C. State U., Raleigh, 1980-85; pvt. practice law Law Offices of Paul A. Suhr, PLLC, Raleigh and Fayetteville, N.C., 1989—. Author short stories and novelettes various lit. mags., jours. and revs. Mem. Human Resources and Human Rels. Adv. Commn., City of Raleigh, 1990-95, chmn., 1994-95. N.C. Humanities Com. grantee, 1979-80; recipient Presdl. award President of Korea, 1992. Mem. ABA, ATLA, Am. Immigration Lawyers Assn., NC Bar Assn., NC Trial Lawyers Assn., Wake County Bar Assn. (bd. dirs. 1996-97, 2003—), DC Bar Assn. Democrat. Roman Catholic. Avocations: gardening, fishing, writing. Criminal, Immigration, naturalization, and customs, Personal injury (including property damage). Office: 1110 Navaho Dr Ste 502 Raleigh NC 27609-7322 E-mail: paulsuhr@bellsouth.net.

SUHRHEINRICH, RICHARD FRED, federal judge; b. Lincoln City, Ind., 1936; BS, Wayne State U., 1960; JD cum laude, Detroit Coll. Law, 1963; LLM, U. Va., 1990; LLM (hon.), Detroit Coll. Law, 1992. Bar: Mich. Law clerk Stringari, Fritz & Fiott, 1963; assoc. Moll, Desenberg, Purdy, Glover & Bayer, 1963—67; asst. prosecutor Macomb County, 1967; ptnr. Rogensues, Richard & Suhrheinrich, 1967; assoc. Moll, Desenberg, Purdy, Glover & Bayer, 1967—68; ptnr. Kitch, Suhrheinrich, Saurbier & Drutchas, 1968—84; assoc. prof. of law Detroit Coll. of law, 1975—85; judge U.S. Dist. Ct. (ea. dist.) Mich., Detroit, 1984—90, U.S. Ct. Appeals (6th Cir.), Lansing, 1990—2001, sr. judge, 2001—. Mem.: Ingham County Bar Assn., State Bar Mich. Office: US Ct Appeals 6th Cir USPO & Fed Bldg 315 W Allegan St Rm 241 Lansing MI 48933-1514*

SUKKAR, MAZEN M. lawyer; b. Beirut, Feb. 4, 1961; arrived in U.S., 1979; BS in Polit. Sci., Biscayne Coll., Miami, Fla., 1983; JD cum laude, Nova Southeastern U., 1987. Bar: Fla. 1987. Prin. Sukkar Arevalo & Assocs., Hollywood, Fla., 1987—. Lectr. in field; mem. cert. rev. com. The Fla. Bar, 1996—98; pres. Best Fla. Properties, Inc., 1986—. Contbr. Mem. atty.-realtor com. Hollywood Bd. Realtors, 1987—88; mem. Broward County Crime Commn. Recipient Award for Excellence in CLE, The Fla.

Bar. Mem.: ABA, Boca Raton Bd. Realtors, Hollywood Bd. Realtors (Cert. of Appreciation 1987—88), Miami Beach Bd. Realtors, Miami Bd. Realtors, Nova Southeastern Law Sch. Alumni Assn., Am. Immigration Law Assn. (bd. dirs. 1992—, pres. Fla. sect. 1994—95, bd. govs. 1998—99, vice chair exec. office of immigration rev. liaison com. 1995—96, co-chair INS Miami dist. liaison com. 1997—98, co-chair INS Tex. Svc. Ctr. liaison com. 1996—97, 1998—99, chair INS Miami Dist. liaison com. 2000—01, Cert. of Appreciation 1996), U.S. Chess Fedn. Avocations: backgammon, chess, tennis.

SUKO, LONNY RAY, judge; b. Spokane, Wash., Oct. 12, 1943; s. Ray R. and Leila B. (Snyder) S.; m. Marcia A. Michaelsen, Aug. 26, 1967; children: Jolynn R., David M. BA, Wash. State U., 1965; JD, U. Idaho, 1968. Bar: Wash. 1968, U.S. Dist. Ct. (ea. dist.) Wash. 1969, U.S. Dist. Ct. (we. dist.) Wash. 1978, U.S. Ct. Appeals (9th cir.) 1978. Law clk. U.S. Dist. Ct. Ea. Dist. Wash., 1968-69; assoc. Lyon, Beaulaurier & Aaron, Yakima, Wash., 1969-72; ptnr. Lyon, Beaulaurier, Weigand, Suko & Gustafson, Yakima, 1972-91, Lyon, Weigand, Suko & Gustafson, P.S., 1991-95; U.S. magistrate judge, Yakima, 1971-91, 95—. Mem. Phi Beta Kappa, Phi Kappa Phi. Office: PO Box 2726 Yakima WA 98907-2726

SUKONECK, IRA DAVID, lawyer; b. Newark, Jan. 20, 1947; s. Edward and Mae (Rosenkrantz) S.; m. Vicki Sherman, Oct. 29, 1972; children: Marc, Randi. BS in Pharmacy, Northeastern U., 1969; JD, Suffolk U., 1972. Bar: Mass. 1972, N.J. 1973, U.S. Dist. Ct. N.J. 1973, U.S. Supreme Ct. 1978; cert. workers compensation law atty. Assoc. ptnr. Braff, Harris & Sukoneck, Livingston, N.J., 1973—. Mem. ABA, N.J. Bar Assn., Assn. Trial Lawyers Am., Am. Inns of Ct., N.J. Workers Compensation Def. Assn. Personal injury (including property damage), Property, real (including real estate development, water), Workers' compensation. Office: Braff Harris Sukoneck 570 W Mount Pleasant Ave PO Box 657 Livingston NJ 07039-0657 E-mail: isukoneck@bhs-law.com.

SULLIVAN, BARRY, lawyer; b. Newburyport, Mass., Jan. 11, 1949; s. George Arnold and Dorothy Bennett (Furbush) S.; m. Winnifred Mary Fallers, June 14, 1975; children: George Arnold, Lloyd Ashton. AB cum laude, Middlebury Coll., 1970; JD, U. Chgo., 1974. Bar: Mass. 1975, Ill. 1975, U.S. Dist. Ct. (no. dist.) Ill. 1976, U.S. Ct. Appeals (7th cir.) 1976, U.S. Ct. Appeals (10th cir.) 1977, U.S. Supreme Ct. 1978, U.S. Ct. Appeals (11th cir.) 1986, U.S. Ct. Appeals (5th and 9th cirs.) 1987, U.S. Ct. Appeals (fed. cir.) 1993, U.S. Ct. Appeals (DC cir.) 1994, Va. 1995, U.S. Ct. Appeals (4th cir.) 1997, U.S. Ct. Appeals (2d cir.) 2002, U.S. Ct. Appeals (3d cir.) 2002. Law clk. to judge John Minor Wisdom U.S. Ct. Appeals (5th cir.), New Orleans, 1974-75; assoc. Jenner & Block, Chgo., 1975-80; asst. to solicitor gen. of U.S. U.S. Dept. of Justice, Washington, 1980-81; ptnr. Jenner & Block, Chgo., 1981-94, 2001—; prof. law Washington and Lee U., Lexington, Va., 1994-2001, dean, 1994-99, v.p., 1998-99; Fulbright prof. U. Warsaw, Poland, 2000—01; lectr. in law U. Chgo., 2001—02; spl. asst. state's atty. Cook County, Ill., 2002—03. Vis. fellow Queen Mary and Westfield Coll., U. London, 2001; spl. asst. atty. gen. State of Ill., 1989—90; spl. asst. State's Atty. Cook County, Ill., 2002—03; lectr. in law Loyola U., Chgo., 1978—79; adj. prof. law Northwestern U., Chgo., 1990—92, Chgo., 1993—94, vis. prof., 1992—93; vis. prof. Ctr. for Am. law studies U. Warsaw, 2002; Jessica Swift Meml. lectr. in constnl. law Middlebury Coll., 1991. Assoc. editor U. Chgo. Law Rev., 1973-74; contbr. articles to profl. jours. Trustee Cath. Theol. Union at Chgo., 1993—2003, trustee emeritus, 2003—; mem. vis. com. Irving B. Harris Grad. Sch. Public Policy Studies U., Chgo., 2001—, U. Chgo. Divinity Sch., 1987—2001; mem. adv. panel Fulbright Sr. Specialist Program, 2001—. Yeats Soc. scholar, 1968; Woodrow Wilson fellow, Woodrow Wilson Found., 1970. Mem. ABA (chmn. coord. com. on AIDS 1988-94, mem. standing com. on amicus curiae briefs 1990-97, mem. coun. of sect. of individual rights and responsibilities 1993-98, mem. sect. of legal edn. com. on law sch. adminstrn. 1994-98, chair sect. legal edn. com. on professionalism 1999-2000, co-chair sect. individual rights and responsibilities com. on amicus briefs 2002—, mem. sect. legal edn. stds. rev. com.. 2002—), Va. Bar Assn., Va. State Bar (chair sect. on edn. of lawyers 1998-99), Bar Assn. 7th Fed. Cir. (vice chmn. adminstrv. justice com. 1985-86), Am. Law Inst., Chgo. Bar Assn., Ill. State Bar Assn., Supreme Ct. Hist. Soc. (Ill. membership chair 2002—), Lawyers Club Chgo., Phi Beta Kappa. Democrat. Roman Catholic. Appellate, Federal civil litigation. Home: 5555 S Everett Apt A1-2 Chicago IL 60637 Office: Jenner & Block One IBM Plz Chicago IL 60611 E-mail: bsullivan@jenner.com.

SULLIVAN, BRENDAN V., JR., lawyer; b. Providence, Mar. 11, 1942; AB, Georgetown U., 1964, JD, 1967. Bar: R.I. 1967, D.C. 1970, U.S. Dist. Ct. D.C. 1970, U.S. Ct. Appeals (D.C. cir.) 1970, U.S. Supreme Ct. 1972, U.S. Dist. Ct. Md. 1974, U.S. Ct. Appeals (4th cir.) 1981, U.S. Ct. Appeals (3d cir.) 1979, U.S. Ct. Appeals (6th cir.) 1991, U.S. Ct. Appeals (9th cir.) 1996, U.S. Ct. Fed. Claims 1998. Mem. Williams & Connolly, Washington. Lectr. Practicing Law Inst., 1981—, Md. Inst. for Continuing Profl. Edn. of Lawyers, Inc., 1979—, D.C. Criminal Practice Inst., 1975-81. Author: Grand Jury Proceedings, 1981, Techniques for Dealing with Pending Criminal Charges or Criminal Investigations, 1983, White Collar Criminal Practice Grand Jury, 1985. Fellow Am. Coll. Trial Lawyers; mem. ABA, R.I. Bar Assn., D.C. Bar. Office: Williams & Connolly 725 12th St NW Washington DC 20005-5901

SULLIVAN, E. THOMAS, law educator; b. Amboy, Ill., Dec. 4, 1948; s. Edward McDonald and Mary Lorraine (Murphy) S.; m. Susan A. Sullivan, Oct. 2, 1971. BA, Drake U., 1970; JD, Ind. U., Indpls., 1973. Bar: Ind. 1973, Fla. 1974, D.C. 1975, Mo. 1980. Law clk. to Judge Joe Eaton, U.S. Dist. Ct. for So. Dist. Fla., Miami, 1973-75; trial atty. U.S. Dept. Justice, Washington, 1975-77; sr. assoc. Donovan, Leisure, Newton & Irvine, Washington, 1977-79; prof. law U. Mo., Columbia, 1979-84; assoc. dean, prof. Washington U., St. Louis, 1984-89; dean U. Ariz. Coll. Law, Tucson, 1989-95; William S. Pattee prof. law, dean U. Minn. Law Sch., Mpls., 1995—2002, Irving Younger prof. law, 2002—. Fellow Am. Bar Found.; mem. Am. Law Inst., Am. Econ. Assn. Home: 180 Bank St SE Minneapolis MN 55414-1042 Office: U Minn Law Sch Walter F Mondale Hall Office 381 229 19th Ave S Minneapolis MN 55455*

SULLIVAN, EDWARD JOSEPH, lawyer, educator; b. Bklyn., Apr. 24, 1945; s. Edward Joseph and Bridget (Duffy) S.; m. Patte Hancock, Aug. 7, 1982; children: Amy Brase, Molly Elsasser, Mary Christine. BA, St. John's U., 1966; JD, Willamette U., 1969; MA, cert. Urban Studies, Portland State U., 1974; LLM, Univ. Coll., London, 1978; diploma in law, Univ. Coll., Oxford, 1984; MA, U. Durham, 1999. Bar: Oreg. 1969, D.C. 1978, Wash. 2001, U.S. Dist. Ct. Oreg. 1970, U.S. Ct. Appeals (11th cir.) 1970, U.S. Supreme Ct. 1972. Counsel Washington County, Hillsboro, Oreg., 1969-75; legal counsel Gov. of Oreg., Salem, 1975-77; ptnr. O'Donnell, Sullivan & Ramis, Portland, Oreg., 1978-84, Sullivan, Josselson, Roberts, Johnson & Kloos, Portland, Salem and Eugene, Oreg., 1984-86, Mitchell, Lang & Smith, Portland, 1986-90, Preston Gates & Ellis, Portland, 1990—2003; owner Garvey Schubert Barer, Portland, Oreg., 2003—. Bd. dirs., pres. Oreg. Law Inst. Contbr. numerous articles to profl. jours. Chmn. Capitol Planning Commn., Salem, 1975-77, 78-81. Mem. ABA (local govt. sect., com. on planning and zoning, adminstrv. law sect.) Oreg. State Bar Assn., D.C. Bar Assn., Wash. State Bar Assn., Am. Judicature Soc., Am. Polit. Sci. Assn. Democrat. Roman Catholic. Administrative and regulatory, Land use and zoning (including planning). Office: Garvey Schubert Barer 121 SW Morrison Ste 1100 Portland OR 97204-3141 Business E-Mail: esulliva@gsblaw.com.

SULLIVAN, EDWARD LAWRENCE, lawyer; b. Boston, May 8, 1955; s. Edward L. and Dorothy L. (Gregory) S.; m. Susan M. Griffin, Dec. 2, 1983; children: Erica A., Brittany M. BA in Polit. Sci., St. Anselm Coll., 1977; JD, St. Louis U., 1980. Bar: Mo. 1980, Mass. 1981, Ill. 1981, D.C. 1986. Atty., Ill. divsn. Peabody Coal Co., Fairview Heights, 1980-85; legis. counsel Peabody Holding Co., Washington, 1985-88; dir., legal and pub. affairs, western divsn. Peabody Coal Co., Flagstaff, Ariz., 1988-90; sr. counsel Peabody Holding Co., St. Louis, 1990-94; gen. counsel Powder River Coal Co., Gillette, Wyo., 1994-95; gen. counsel, western region Peabody Holding Co., St. Louis, 1995—2000, sr. counsel, 2000—. Industry rep. (alt.) royalty policy com. U.S. Dept. Interior, Washington, 1995—. Mem. Bar Assn. Met. St. Louis. Administrative and regulatory, Commercial, contracts (including sales of goods; commercial financing), Natural resources. Office: Peabody Holding Co Inc 701 Market St Ste 700 Saint Louis MO 63101-1895

SULLIVAN, EDWARD MICHAEL, lawyer; b. Boston, June 2, 1929; s. Edward M. and Isabelle C. (Cassidy) S. BA, Dartmouth Coll., 1949; LLB, Harvard Coll., 1952. Bar: N.Y. 1952, Mass. 1953. Assoc. Wickes, Riddell, et al, N.Y.C., 1952-55; asst. counsel Boston & Maine R.R., 1955-57; pvt. practice Boston, 1957—. Avocations: reading, travel, squash. Federal civil litigation, General civil litigation, Probate (including wills, trusts). Office: Edward M Sullivan 150 Huntington Ave Boston MA 02115

SULLIVAN, EUGENE RAYMOND, federal judge; b. St. Louis, Aug. 2, 1941; s. Raymond Vincent and Rosemary (Kiely) S.; m. Lis Urup Johansen, June 18, 1966; children— Kim, Eugene II. BS, U.S. Mil. Acad., 1964; JD, Georgetown U., 1971. Bar: Mo. 1972, D.C. 1972. Law clk. to judge U.S. Ct. Appeals (8th cir.), St. Louis, 1971-72; assoc. Patton Boggs & Blow, Washington, 1972-74; asst. spl. counsel The White House, Washington, 1974; trial counsel U.S. Dept. of Justice, Washington, 1974-82; dep. gen. counsel U.S. Air Force, Washington, 1982-84, gen. counsel, 1984-86, Nat. Reconnaissance Office, 1982—86; gov. Wake Island, 1984—86; judge U.S. Ct. Appeals (Armed Forces), Washington, 1986-90, 95—, chief judge, 1990-95. Mem. Fed. Commn. To Study Honor Code at West Point, 1989-90. Trustee U.S. Mil. Acad., 1989—. With US Army, 1964-69. Decorated Bronze Star, Air medal, airborne badge, ranger badge, others. Republican. Roman Catholic. Home: 6307 Massachusetts Ave Bethesda MD 20816-1139 Office: US Ct Appeals (Armed Forces) 450 E St NW Washington DC 20442-0001

SULLIVAN, FRANK, JR., state supreme court justice; b. Mar. 21, 1950; s. Frank E. and Colette (Cleary) S.; m. Cheryl Gibson, June 14, 1972; children: Denis M., Douglas S., Thomas R. AB cum laude, Dartmouth Coll., 1972; JD magna cum laude, Ind. U., 1982; LLM, U. Va., 2001. Bar: Ind. 1982. Mem. staff Office of U.S. Rep. John Brademas, 1974-79, dir. staff, 1975-78; with Barnes & Thornburg, Indpls., 1982-89; budget dir. State of Ind., 1989-92; exec. asst. Office of Gov. Evan Bayh, 1993; assoc. justice Ind. Supreme Ct., 1993—. Mem. ABA, Ind. State Bar Assn., Indpls. Bar Assn. Home: 6153 N Olney St Indianapolis IN 46220-5166 Office: State House Rm 321 Indianapolis IN 46204-2728

SULLIVAN, JOHN CORNELIUS, JR., lawyer; b. Erie, Pa., Oct. 23, 1927; s. John Cornelius and Catherine J. (Carney) S.; m. Helen E. Kennedy, Feb. 3, 1951; children: John III, Timi Ann, Michael, Elizabeth. BA in Econs., Allegheny Coll., 1953; LLB, Dickinson Sch. Law, 1959. Bar: Pa. 1960, U.S. Supreme Ct. 1976. Sales rep. IBM Corp., 1953-56; mem. firm Nissley, Clecker & Fearen, Harrisburg, Pa., 1959-63; ptnr. Nauman, Smith, Shissler & Hall, Harrisburg, 1964—. Asst. city solicitor City of Harrisburg, 1964-68, city solicitor, 1968-70; gen. counsel Harrisburg Redevel. Authority, 1964-68, Harrisburg Mcpl. Authority, 1964-87; solicitor Silver-Spring Twp., 1970-81; dir. accounts and fin. City of Harrisburg, 1963; mem. Pa. House of Reps., 1963-64. Assoc. editor Dickinson Law Rev., 1958-59; editor Dauphin County Reporter, 1961-63. Chmn. bd. dirs. Harrisburg Pub. Library, 1965-73; bd. dirs., sec. Harrisburg Hosp.; bd. dirs. Harrisburg Hosp. Found., 1975-89. Mem. ABA, Pa. Bar Assn., Dauphin County Bar Assn. (past. dir.), The Pa. Soc. (N.Y.C.), Phi Gamma Delta. Commercial, contracts (including sales of goods; commercial financing), Estate planning, Libel. Home: 107 Sample Bridge Rd Mechanicsburg PA 17050-1940 Office: 200 N 3rd St Fl D18 Harrisburg PA 17101-1518

SULLIVAN, KATHLEEN MARIE, dean, law educator; BA, Cornell U., 1976, Oxford (Eng.) U., 1978; JD, Harvard U., 1981. Law clk. Hon. James L. Oakes U.S. Ct. Appeals (2d cir.), 1981-82; pvt. practice, 1982-84; asst. prof. Harvard U., Cambridge, Mass., 1984-89, prof., 1989-93, Stanford (Calif.) U., 1993—, Paradise fellow, 1995-96, Stanley Morrison prof., 1996—, dean, Richard E. Lang prof., 1999—. Vis. prov. U. So. Calif. Law Ctr., 1991, Stanford U., 1992; lectr., commentator on constnl. law. Co-editor: (with Gerald Gunther) Constitutional Law, 13th edit., 1997. Named one of 50 Top Women Lawyers Nat. Law Jour., 1998; recipient John Bingham Hurlbut award for excellence in tchg. Stanford U., 1996. Fellow Am. Acad. Arts and Scis, Am. Philosophical Soc. Office: Stanford U Law School Dean's Office, Rm 200 Stanford CA 94305-8610

SULLIVAN, KEVIN PATRICK, lawyer; b. Waterbury, Conn., June 9, 1953; s. John Holian Sullivan and Frances (McGrath) Coon; m. Peggy Hardy, June 13, 1975 (div. Jan. 1985); m. Jarnine Welker, Feb. 15, 1985; children: S. Craig Lemmon, Michael Scott Lemmon, Lindsay Michelle Lemmon. BS in Polit. Sci., BS in Police Sci. cum laude, Weber State Coll., 1979; JD, Pepperdine U., 1982. Bar: Utah 1982, U.S. Dist. Ct. Utah 1982, U.S. Ct. Appeals (10th cir.) 1986, U.S. Supreme Ct. 1986. Assoc. Farr, Kaufman & Hamilton, Ogden, Utah, 1982-87; ptnr. Farr, Kaufman, Hamilton, Sullivan, Gorman & Perkins, Ogden, 1987-91, Farr, Kaufman, Sullivan, Gorman & Perkins, Ogden, 1991—. Judge pro tem Utah 2d Cir. Ct.; city prosecutor of South Ogden, 1990-92. Mem. Eccles Community Art Ctr., Victim's Rights Com. of 2d Jud. Dist. Mem. ABA (criminal justice sect., litigation sect., justice and edn. fund lawyers' coun.), ACLU, ATLA, Utah Bar Assn. (criminal law, young lawyer, litigation sects., unauthorized practice law com.), Utah Trial Lawyers Assn., Utah Assn. Criminal Def. Lawyers, Weber County Bar Assn. (criminal law sect., pres.-elect 1993, pres. 1994), Weber County Pub. Defenders Assn. (assoc. dir. 1987), Weber State Coll. Alumni Assn., Amicus Pepperdine, Elks, Kiwanis, Phi Kappa Phi. Mem. Lds Ch. Avocations: skiing, golf, tennis, fishing. State civil litigation, Criminal, Personal injury (including property damage). Home: 2731 E 6425 S Ogden UT 84403-5461 Office: Farr Kaufman Sullivan Gorman & Perkins 205 26th St Ste 34 Ogden UT 84401-3109 E-mail: KevinSullivan@qwest.net.

SULLIVAN, MARCIA WAITE, lawyer; b. Chgo., Nov. 30, 1950; d. Robert Macke and Jacqueline (Northrop) S.; m. Steven Donald Jansen, Dec. 20, 1975; children: Eric Spurlock, Laura Macke, Brian Northrop. BA, DePauw U., 1972; JD, Ind. U., 1975. Assoc. Arnstein, Gluck, Weitzenfeld & Minow, Chgo., 1975-76; ptnr. Greenberger and Kaufmann, Chgo., 1976-86, Katten Muchin Zavis Rosenman, Chgo., 1986—. Adj. prof. Kent Coll. Law, Ill. Inst. Tech., Chgo., 1991—94; pres. Chgo. Real Estate Exec. Women, 2000—01. Mem. editl. adv. bd.: Real Estate Chgo., 2001—. Mem. ABA, Chgo. Bar Assn. Avocations: bicycling, cross country skiing, gardening, camping. Commercial, contracts (including sales of goods; commercial financing), Property, real (including real estate development, water). Office: Katten Muchin Zavis Rosenman 525 W Monroe St Ste 1600 Chicago IL 60661-3693

SULLIVAN, MARK FRANCIS, lawyer; b. May 28, 1947; s. Peter Jeremiah and Lillian Marie (Filippa) S.; m. Millicent Anne Meunier, Sept. 22, 1973; children: Patrick Mark, Matthew Francis, Mark Francis, Thomas John, John David. AB summa cum laude, Georgetown U., 1969; JD cum laude, U. Mich., 1972. Bar: Mich. 1972, N.Y. 1973, Hawaii 1973, U.S. Dist. Ct. (we. dist.) Mich. 1978, U.S. Ct. Appeals (6th cir.) 1980, U.S. Ct. Mil. Appeals, Calif. 1983, N.C. 1984, U.S. Dist. Ct. (no., so., cen., and ea. dists.) Calif. 1984, U.S. Ct. Mil. Appeals 1973, U.S. Ct. Appeals (9th cir.) 1984. Litigation atty. Landman, Hathaway, Latimer, Clink & Robb, Muskegon, Mich., 1977—79; sr. atty. Gen. Telephone Co. of Mich., Muskegon, 1979—82, Gen. Telephone Co. of S.E. Durham, NC, 1982—84; litigation atty. Gen. Telephone Calif., Santa Monica, 1984—85, Thousand Oaks, 1985—87; v.p., gen. counsel GTE Airfone Inc., Oak Brook, Ill., 1987—89; litigation atty. GTE Tel. Ops. West Area, Thousand Oaks, 1989—91; assoc. gen. counsel litigation GTE Calif. Inc., Thousand Oaks, 1991—2000; ret. legal dept. Verizon Comms., 2000. Cons. Hawaiian Telephone Co., Honolulu, 1982—83. Capt. JAGC USNR, 1972—2003. Mem.: Aircraft Owners and Pilots Assn., Judge Advs. Assn., Navy-Marine Corps, N.C. Bar Assn., Hawaii State Bar, Mich. Bar Assn., Ventura County Bar Assn., L.A. County Bar Assn., Calif. Bar Assn., Phi Beta Kappa. Roman Catholic. Avocation: aviation. Federal civil litigation, State civil litigation, Labor (including EEOC, Fair Labor Standards Act, labor-management relations, NLRB, OSHA). Home: 1686 Margate Pl Westlake Village CA 91361-1521 Office: Sullivan Sottle & Taketa LLP Attys Ste 205 31351 Via Colinas Westlake Village CA 91362 E-mail: msullivan@sstlawfirm.com .

SULLIVAN, MICHAEL D. lawyer; b. Chgo., Feb. 16, 1940; s. John J. and Tillie (Babel) S.; m. Irene A. Brandt. BBA cum laude, U. Notre Dame, 1962, JD, 1965. Bar: Ill. 1965, U.S. Dist. Ct. (no. dist.) Ill. 1966, U.S. Ct. Appeals (7th cir.) 1966, U.S. Tax Ct. 1967. Law clk. to judge U.S. Ct. Appeals (7th cir.), Chgo., 1965-66; assoc. Jenner & Block, Chgo., 1967-73; gen. atty. CMC & Chgo., Milw. R.R., 1974-78; gen. solicitor, corp. trustee property Chgo., Milw. R.R., Chgo., 1978-85; gen. solicitor Soo Line R.R., Chgo., 1985-86; pvt. practice River Forest, Ill.; atty. The Sullivan Firm, Ltd., Rolling Meadows, 1985—. Counsel, bd. dirs. various orgns., Chgo., 1980-85. Mem. ABA, Ill. Bar Assn., Chgo. Bar Assn., N.W. Suburban Bar Assn. Corporate, general, Taxation, general, Transportation. Home: 739 Park Ave River Forest IL 60305-1705 Office: The Sullivan Firm Ltd 2550 Golf Rd Rolling Meadows IL 60008-4051 E-mail: thesullivanfirm@aol.com.

SULLIVAN, MICHAEL J. prosecutor; b. Oct. 3, 1954; m. Terry Sullivan, 1975; children: Joseph, Kelly, Allyson, James. Grad., Boston Coll., 1979; JD, Suffolk U., 1983. Assoc. Bolles and Pritchard, 1983—90; ptnr. McGovern and Sullivan, 1990—95; mem. Mass. Ho. Reps., 1991—95; dist. atty. Plymouth County, Mass., 1995—2001; U.S. atty. U.S. Dept. of Justice, Mass., 2001—. Rep. dist. 7 Mass. Ho. of Reps., 1990—, mem. ways and means, post audit and oversight and steering and policy coms., spl. com. on edn. reform. Office: US Attys Office US Courthouse Ste 9200 1 Courthouse Way Boston MA 02210*

SULLIVAN, MICHELLE CORNEJO, lawyer; b. St. Louis, June 29, 1958; m. Dennis Keith Sullivan, May 18, 1985. BS, U. Calif., Berkeley, 1980; JD, U. Santa Clara, 1983. Bar: Calif., 1984; U.S. Dist. Ct. (no. dist.) Calif., 1984, (so. dist.) Calif., 1985; cert. family law specialist. Legal dept. Four-Phase Computers, Cupertino, Calif., 1984; asst. dist. atty. San Benito County, Hollister, Calif., 1984-85; assoc. Walters & Ward, Rancho Bernardo, Calif., 1986-87, Law Offices of Rebecca Prater, Carlsbad, Calif., 1987-88; pvt. practice Escondido & San Diego, Calif., 1988—. Pres. Women in Networking, San Diego, 1987; western horse show judge Calif. State Horseman's Assn., 1985; adv. com. San Diego Regional Conf. on Women, trustee, 1993-95. Law Faculty scholar U. Santa Clara, 1982-83. Mem. ABA, State Bar Assn., San Diego County Bar Assn. (cert. specialist), Bar Assn. No. San Diego County (chair family law sect. 1996-98, cert. specialist), Escondido Rotary Main Club, Rancho Bernardo C. of C. (amb. 1986-87), San Diego Trial Lawyers Assn. (family law sect.), Lawyers Club (v.p. North County chpt. 1988-89). Avocations: western horseback riding, golf, sailing, scuba diving. Alternative dispute resolution, Family and matrimonial. Office: 16516 Bernardo Center Dr Ste 330 San Diego CA 92128-2518 E-mail: michellesullivan@sbcglobal.net.

SULLIVAN, MORTIMER ALLEN, JR., lawyer; b. Buffalo, Sept. 19, 1930; s. Mortimer Allen Sr. and Gertrude (Hinkley) S.; m. Maryanne Calella, Nov. 20, 1965; children: Mark Allen, Michael John. BA, U. Buffalo, 1954. Bar: N.Y. 1964, U.S. Dist. Ct. (we. dist.) N.Y. 1966, U.S. Dist. Ct. (no. dist.) N.Y. 1967, U.S. Supreme Ct. 1970. Counsel liability claims Interstate Motor Freight System, Grand Rapids, Mich., 1964-82. V.p. J.P.M. Sullivan, Inc., Elmira, N.Y., 1959-67; govt. appeal agt. U.S. Selective Service System, 1967-71; dep. sci. div. Erie County (N.Y.) Sheriff's Office, 1971—, lt., 1986—. Inventor (with others) in field; creator, dir. video depiction JudiVision, 1969; composer High Flight, 1983. Chmn. com. on Constn. and Canons Episcopal Diocese of Western N.Y., 1975-96; bd. dirs. Erie County Law Enforcement Found., Inc., 1987—; bd. dirs. Orchard Park (N.Y.) Symphony Orch., 1975-97, v.p., 1977-79, 91-94. With USAF, 1954-57; spl. agt. Air Force Office of Spl. Investigations, 1972-87, col. res. ret. Decorated Legion of Merit. Mem. Erie County Bar Assn. (chmn. law and tech. com., 1970-81), Transp. Lawyers Assn., Kappa Alpha Soc. Clubs: Saturn (Buffalo); Wanakah (N.Y.) Country. Republican. Avocation: aviation. General practice. Home: 19 Knob Hill Rd Orchard Park NY 14127-3917 Office: 88 S Davis St PO Box 1003 Orchard Park NY 14127-8003 E-mail: masulaw@aol.com.

SULLIVAN, PATRICK ARTHUR, lawyer; b. Bellingham, Wash., July 21, 1935; s. James Edward and Maribel (Bailey) S.; m. Diane S. Zack, Feb. 27, 1960; children— Kevin Patrick, Kathleen Diane, Colleen Michelle, Meaghan Mari, Elizabeth. J.D., Gonzaga U., 1959; M.B.A. in Govt. Contracts, U. Va., 1960; Bar: Wash. 1959. Tchr. music pvt. schs., Spokane, Wash., 1949-62; performed with own jazz band, Spokane, 1959-62; mem. legal staff Boeing Corp., Seattle, 1962-63, chief contracts counsel Saturn br., New Orleans, 1963-64; assoc. Winston & Cashatt, Spokane, Wash., 1964-66, ptnr., 1966— , pres., chmn. bd., 1981— ; pres., dir. Squire Motor Inns, Grand Canyon Airlines, N.Am. Helicopter Corp., 1968-76; internat. arbitrator Geneva; lectr. on constrn. law and claims throughout U.S. Bd. dirs. Am. Heart Assn., YMCA, Spokane; adv. bd. Spokane Interplayers Ensemble. Served with JAGC, U.S. Army, 1959-62. Fellow ATLA, On Site Mediation Ltd. (pres.), Wash. State Bar Dists. and U.S. Supreme Cts.; mem. ABA (state chmn. constrn. litigation 1976-80, state chmn. pub. contracts sect. 1981-83), Wash. State Bar Assn., Assoc. Gen. Contractors, Internat. C. of C. Construction. Home: 1503 E 54th Ln Spokane WA 99223

SULLIVAN, ROBERT EDWARD, lawyer; b. San Francisco, May 18, 1936; s. Edward C. S. and Mary Jane (Sullivan); m. Maureen Lois Miles, June 14, 1958 (dec. 1972); children: Teresa Ann, Andrew Edward, Edward Braddock; m. Lynn Bryant, Aug. 28, 2002. BS, U. San Francisco, 1958; LLB, U. Calif-Berkeley, 1961. Bar: Calif. 1962. Assoc. Pillsbury, Madison & Sutro, San Francisco, 1963-70, ptnr., 1971—2000, Pillsbury, Winthrop, LLP, 2001—. Lectr. bus. law Calif. Continuing Edn. Bar and Practicing Law Inst.; v.p., treas., dir. MPC Ins., Ltd., 1986-93. Contbr. articles to profl. jours. Bd. dirs., exec. com. mem., sec. San Francisco Opera Assn., 1993—. 1st lt. U.S. Army, 1961-63. Mem. ABA, State Bar Calif. (com. corps. 1979-82, chmn. 1981-82, mem. exec. com. bus. law sect. 1982-85, vice chmn. 1983-84, chmn. 1984-85, advisor 1985-86, mem. partnership com. 1990-92, chmn. ltd. liability co. drafting com. 1992-93), San Francisco Bar Assn., Bankers Club San Francisco (bd. dirs., sec., treas.). Democrat. Roman Catholic. Corporate, general, Private international, Securities. Office: Pillsbury Winthrop LLP 50 Fremont St San Francisco CA 94105-2228

SULLIVAN, ROBERT EMMET, JR., lawyer; b. Detroit, Oct. 2, 1955; s. Robert Emmett Sr. and Gloria Marie (Lamb) S. BA in Polit. Sci. and Sociology, Wayne State U., 1977; M Urban Planning, U. Mich., 1979; JD, U. Detroit, 1983; postgrad., Oxford (Eng.) U., 1981. Bar: Mich. 1984, U.S. Dist. Ct. (we. dist.) Mich. 1984, U.S. Dist. Ct. (ea. dist.) Mich. 1984, U.S. Ct. Appeals (6th cir.) 1984, U.S. Ct. Appeal (D.C. cir.) 1984, U.S. Tax Ct. 1984, D.C. 1985, U.S. Supreme Ct. 1987. Planning commr. City of Detroit,

1982-85; shareholder Sullivan, Ward, Bone, Tyler & Asher, P.C., Detroit, 1984—; v.p., bd. dirs. Internat. Inst. Metro. Detroit. Contbr. articles to profl. jours. Active St. Scholastica Parish Ch., North Rosedale Park Civic Assn., Detroit Hist. Soc. Moffitt scholar, 1982, 83. Mem. AIA, Detroit Bar Assn., Am. Planning Assn., Am. Inst. Cert. Planners. Roman Catholic. General civil litigation, Constitutional, Land use and zoning (including planning). Home: 7464 Wilshire West Bloomfield MI 48322-2875 Office: Sullivan Ward Bone Tyler & Asher 25800 Northwestern Hwy Southfield MI 48075-1000 E-mail: rsullivanjr@swbta.com.

SULLIVAN, ROBERT JOHN, lawyer; b. Butte, Mont., Feb. 22, 1954; s. James David and Margorie (Ostoj) S.; m. Mary R. White, Feb. 18, 1984; children: Brian Robert, Patrick Leland. BA, U. Mont., 1976, JD, 1980; attended, Nat. Inst. Trial Advocacy, 1985. Bar: Mont. 1980, U.S. Dist. Ct. Mont. 1980, U.S. Ct. Appeals (9th cir.) 1980. Dep. county atty. Missoula (Mont.) County Atty.'s Office, 1980-85; assoc. Boone Karlberg & Haddon, Missoula, 1985-87, ptnr., 1987—. Mem. ABA, Western Mont. Bar Assn. (treas. 1989, v.p. 1990, pres. 1990-91), Mont. State Bar Assn. (trustee, mem. character and fitness com., 1991-, chmn. 2001-02, pres.-elect 2002-03, pres. 2003-). Avocations: biking, skiing, outdoors. Federal civil litigation, General civil litigation, State civil litigation. Office: Boone Karlberg & Haddon 201 W Main St Ste 300 PO Box 9199 Missoula MT 59807-9199*

SULLIVAN, THOMAS PATRICK, lawyer; b. Evanston, Ill., Mar. 23, 1930; s. Clarence M. and Pauline (DeHaye) S.; children: Margaret Mary, Timothy Joseph, Elizabeth Ann; m. Anne Landau. Student, Loras Coll., Dubuque, Iowa, 1947-49; LL.B. cum laude, Loyola U., Chgo., 1952. Bar: Ill. 1952, Calif. 1982, N.Mex., 1997. Asso. firm Jenner & Block, Chgo., 1954-62, partner, 1963-77, 81—; U.S. atty. for No. Dist. Ill., Chgo., 1977-81. Co-chair Ill. Gov.'s Commn. on Capital Punishment, 2000—02. Contbr. articles to profl. jours. Served with U.S. Army, 1952-54. Decorated Bronze Star.; Recipient medal of excellence Loyola U. Law Sch., 1965; Ill. Pub. Defender Assn. award, 1972, Justice John Paul Stevens award, 2000, 03. Fellow Am. Coll. Trial Lawyers; mem. ABA (John Minor Wisdom Pub. Svc. and Professionalism award 2003), Ill. Bar Assn., Fed. Seventh Circuit Bar Assn., Chgo. Bar Assn., Fed. Bar Assn., Am. Law Inst., Am. Judicature Soc., Chgo. Coun. Lawyers. Office: Jenner & Block 1 Ibm Plz Fl 4100 Chicago IL 60611-5697 E-mail: tsullivan@jenner.com.

SULLIVAN, WILLIAM FRANCIS, lawyer; b. San Francisco, May 6, 1952; s. Francis Michael and Jane Frances (Walsh) S.; children: Matthew, Meghan, Kathleen; m. Kait Sullivan. AB, U. Calif., Berkeley, 1974; JD, UCLA, 1977. Bar: Calif. 1977, U.S. Dist. Ct. (no. dist.) Calif. 1977, U.S. Ct. Appeals (9th cir.) 1977, U.S. Dist. Ct. (ea. dist.) Calif. 1978, U.S. Ct. Appeals (D.C. cir.) 1979, U.S. Ct. Appeals (fed. cir.) 1985, U.S. Dist. Ct. (so. dist.) Calif. 1986, U.S. Dist. Ct. (cen. dist.) Calif. 1990, U.S. Supreme Ct. 1986. Assoc. Chickering & Gregory, San Francisco and Washington, 1977-81, Brobeck, Phleger & Harrison, San Diego and San Francisco, 1981-84, ptnr., 1984—2002, mng. ptnr. San Diego, 1992-96, 2001—03, securities litigation group leader, 2002—, firmwide mng. ptnr., 1996-98; ptnr. Paul Hastinap Jonofsky & Walker, 2003—. Panelist Calif. Continuing Edn. Bar; instr. Fed. Practice Program, U.S. No. Dist., chair Litigation sect., 1992, U.S. Dist. Ct. (no. dist.) Calif., 1980; instr. Coll. of Advocacy, Hastings Law Sch.; adv. bd. AMICUS Info. Svcs. Mem. ABA, Assn. Bus. Trial Lawyers (bd. govs. San Diego chpt. 1993-95), Calif. Bar Assn. (litigation sect.), San Francisco Bar Assn., San Diego Bar Assn., Barristers Club San Francisco (bd. dirs. 1984-86, pres. 1985), Calif. Young Lawyers Assn. (bd. dirs. 1986-89, sec. 1987-99, 1st v.p. 1988-89). Democrat. Roman Catholic. General civil litigation, Intellectual property, Securities. Office: Paul, Hastings, Janofsky & Walker 12390 El Camino Real San Diego CA 92130-2081 E-mail: williamsullivan@paulhastings.com.

SULLIVAN, WILLIAM J. state supreme court justice; Student, St. Thomas Sem., 1958-59; BA in Polit. Sci., Providence Coll., 1962; B in Civil Law, Coll. William and Mary, 1965, JD, 1970. Judge Conn. Superior Ct., 1978-97, Conn. Appellate Ct., 1997-99; assoc. justice Conn. Supreme Ct., 1999-2001; chief justice, 2001—. Office: Conn Supreme Ct Supreme Ct Bldg 231 Capitol Ave Hartford CT 06106-1548

SULLY, IRA BENNETT, lawyer; b. Columbus, Ohio, June 3, 1947; s. Bernie and Helen Mildred (Koen) S.; m. Nancy Lee Pryor, Oct. 2, 1983. BA cum laude, Ohio State U., 1969, JD summa cum laude, 1974. Bar: Ohio 1974, U.S. Dist. Ct. (so. dist.) Ohio 1974. Assoc. Schottenstein, Garel, Swedlow & Zox, Columbus, 1974-78; atty. Borden, Inc., Columbus, 1978-80; sole practice Columbus, 1980—. Instr. Real Estate Law Columbus Tech. Inst., 1983-88; title ins. agt. Sycamore Title Agy., Columbus, 1983— . Bd. dirs. Rsch. Franklin County Celeste for Gov., Columbus, 1978; asst. treas. Pamela Conrad for City Coun., Columbus, 1979; treas. Leland for State Rep., Columbus, 1982, 84, Leland for City Atty., Columbus, 1985; active Ohio Dem. Bldg. Com., 1995-98; commentator Sta. WOSU, Columbus, 1980; trustee Ohio State U. Undergrad. Student Govt. Alumni Soc., 1997—, pres., 2000—. Mem. ABA, Ohio Bar Assn., Columbus Bar Assn., Agonis Club (Columbus). Democrat. Jewish. Avocations: running, coin collecting. Commercial, contracts (including sales of goods; commercial financing), Probate (including wills, trusts), Property, real (including real estate development, water). Home: 200 Reinhard Ave Columbus OH 43206-2616 Office: 844 S Front St Columbus OH 43206-2543

SULTAN, JAMES LEHMAN, lawyer; b. New Haven, Oct. 10, 1953; s. Stanley Ezra Sultan and Florence Lehman Nichols. BA, Yale U., 1974; JD, Harvard U., 1980. Bar: Mass. 1980, U.S. Dist. Ct. Mass. 1981, U.S. Ct. Appeals (1st cir.) 1981, U.S. Supreme Ct. 1989. Legis. asst. U.S. Rep. Robert F. Drinan, Washington, 1974-77; law clk. to William Wayne Justice U.S. Dist. Ct., Tyler, Tex., 1980-81; assoc. Silvergate, Shapiro & Gertner, Boston, 1981-82; pvt. practice Boston, 1982-86; ptnr. Rankin & Sultan, Boston, 1986—. Lectr. profl. seminars, 1987—. Contbr. (book) Massachusetts Criminal Law, 1990. Mem. Nat. Assn. Criminal Def. Lawyers. Criminal. Office: Rankin & Sultan 1 Comml Wharf North Boston MA 02110 E-mail: jsultan@rankin-sultan.com.

SULTANIK, JEFFREY TED, lawyer; b. N.Y.C., July 26, 1954; s. Solomon and Anna (Tiger) S.; m. Judith Ann Clyman, Nov. 14, 1981; children: Evan A., Sara A. BA cum laude, U. Pa., Phila., 1976; JD, Hofstra U., 1979. Bar: Pa. 1979, Fla. 1980, U.S. Dist. Ct. (ea. dist.) Pa., U.S. Ct. Appeals (3d cir.). Ptnr. Fox Rothschild, LLP, Lansdale, Pa., 1979-81; solicitor Upper Merion Sch. Dist., 1995—. Solicitor Boyertown (Pa.) Area Sch. Dist., 1981—, North Montco Vocat.-Tech. Sch., Lansdale, 1981—, Souderton (Pa.) Area Sch. Dist., 1989—, Wallingford-Swarthmore Sch. Dist., 1999—, Interboro Sch. Dist., 2002; spl. counsel Penn Delco Sch. Dist., Aston, Pa., Kennett Consol. Sch. Dist., 1999—, Norristown Sch. Dist., 1999—, West Chester Area Sch. Dist., 2002; mem. pers. com., chair mktg./admissions com., trustee, bd. sec. Germantown Acad., Ft. Washington, Pa., 1991—; chair edn. law group Fox Rothschild, LLP, Lansdale, Pa.; coun. Rock Sch. Dist., Newtown, Pa., 1998, Downingtown Area Sch. Dist., 2003; presenter in field. Regular columnist Your School and the Law, 1992. Mem. Nat. Sch. Bds. Assn., 2001. Mem. Nat. Assn. Sch. and Coll. Attys., Nat. Sch. Bds. Assn., Pa. Sch. Bds. Assn., Inc., Pa. Assn. Sch. Bus. Ofcls. (cert. of appreciation 1991), Pa. Bar Assn. (labor and edn. sects.), Montgomery County Bar Assn. (mcpl. law com. 1983—), Lehigh U. Law Forums, Assn. Del. Valley Ind. Schs. Republican. Jewish. Avocations: automobiles, travel. Education and schools, Labor (including EEOC, Fair Labor Standards Act, labor-management relations, NLRB, OSHA), Municipal (including bonds). Home: 3229 Barley Ln Lansdale PA 19446-5114 Office: Fox Rothschild LLP 1250 S Broad St Lansdale PA 19446-0431 E-mail: jsultanik@foxrothschild.com.

SULTON, ANNE THOMAS, lawyer, criminologist; b. Racine, Wis., Oct. 24, 1952; d. William Henry and Esther (Phillips) Thomas; m. James E. Sulton Jr., Aug. 1, 1981; children: James E. III, William Francis, Patrice Amandla. BA in Psychology, Wash. State U., 1973; MA in Criminal Justice, SUNY, 1975; PhD in Criminal Justice, U. Md., 1984; JD, U. Wis., 1985. Bar: Wis. 1985, U.S. Dist. Ct. (we. dist.) Wis. 1985, Colo. 1993, U.S. Dist. Ct. Colo. 1994, U.S. Ct. Appeals (7th cir.) 1995, U.S. Ct. Appeals (10th cir.) 1996. Instr. criminal justice and criminology Spelman Coll., Atlanta, 1976-78; rsch. assoc. Nat. Orgn. Black Law Enforcement Execs., Balt., 1978-80; lectr. criminal justice and criminology Howard U., Washington, 1980-84; asst. prof. criminal justice U. Wis., Oshkosh, 1984-85; project dir. Police Found., Washington, 1985-87; pvt. practice law Madison, Wis., 1985—, Englewood, Colo., 1993—. Dir. grad. criminal justice program U. Balt.; former instr. Atlanta U., Atlanta Fed. Penitentiary, Md. State Penitentiary, Balt. City Police Tng. Acad., Inst. Criminal Justice and Criminology, U. Md., Taycheeda Correctional Instn. for Women, Century 21 Sch. Real Estate; presenter, spkr., facilitator in field; numerous TV and radio appearances; assoc. prof. criminal justice N.J. City Univ., 2000—. Contbr. articles to various publs., poetry to books, mags. and newspapers. Bd. dirs. Washington Halfway Home for Women, 1983; pres. bd. dirs. Willard Thomas Scholarship Found., Inc., Racine, Wis., 1973—, South Madison Neighborhood Ctr., 1987-88; mem. allocations panel on un-and underemployment United Way Dane County, 1987-88; spokesperson Coalition African-Am. Orgns., Madison, 1987-88, legal counsel NAACP Madison chpt., 1989-90, Denver chpt., 1994-99; mem. Bessie Coleman Found., Inc. Recipient cert. Atlanta Commr. Pub. Safety, 1977, Outstanding Citizen award Fulton County Commr.'s Office, 1977, Atlanta's 1st Black Aviatrix award, 1977, cert. of appreciation Atlanta Crime Analysis Team, 1978, Spl. Friend award Atlanta Fed. Penitentiary Bd., NAACP, 1978; named to Washington Park High Sch. Hall of Fame, 1986. Mem. NAACP, ABA, ATLA, Acad. Criminal Justice Scis., Wis. Bar Assn., Nat. African-Am. Braintrust on Criminal Justice and Criminology, Police Exec. Rsch. Forum. Avocation: flying small aircraft. Civil rights, Federal civil litigation.

SUMERS, JEAN PETERSEN, lawyer; b. El Campo, Tex., May 22, 1967; d. Ralph Eugene Petersen and Marilyn Ann Knudsen; m. R. Sprague Sumers, Sept. 16, 1995; children: Hannah, Sprague. SBS, U. Houston, Victoria, 1989, MA in Psychology, 1994; JD, U. Houston, 1998. Bar: Tex. 1999, U.S. Dist. Ct. (so. dist.) Tex. 1999. Assoc. Harley & Price, PLLC, Houston, 1997—2001; pvt. practice Houston, 2002—. Mem.: ATLA, ABA, Nat. Assn. Elder Law Attys., Am. Health Lawyers Assn., Katy Bar Assn., Houston Bar Assn. Estate planning, Health, Probate (including wills, trusts). Home: 22511 Cascade Springs Katy TX 77494 Office: Ste 1750 3050 Post Oak Blvd Houston TX 77056 Fax: 713-850-8917. E-mail: jsumers@airmail.net.

SUMIDA, GERALD AQUINAS, lawyer; b. Hilo, Hawaii, June 19, 1944; s. Sadamy and Kimiyo (Miyahara) S. AB summa cum laude, Princeton U., 1966; JD, Yale U., 1969. Bar: Hawaii 1970, U.S. Dist. Ct. Hawaii 1970, U.S. Ct. Appeals (9th cir.) 1970, U.S. Supreme Ct. 1981. Rsch. assoc. Ctr. Internat. Studies, Princeton U., 1969; assoc. Carlsmith, Ball, Honolulu, 1970-76, ptnr., 1976-99; gen. counsel Asian Devel. Bank, 1999—. Mem. cameras in courtroom evaluation com. Hawaii Supreme Ct., 1984-86. Co-author: (with others) Legal, Instutional and Financial Aspects of An Inter-Island Electrical Transmission Cable, 1984, Alternative Approaches to the Legal, Instutional and Financial Aspects of Developing an Inter-Island, Electrical Transmission Cable System, 1986; editor Hawaii Bar News, 1972-73; contbr. chpts. to books. Mem. sci. and statis. com. Western Pacific Fishery Mgmt. Coun., 1979-99; mem. study group on law of armed conflict and the law of the sea Comdr. in Chief Pacific, USN, 1979-82; chmn. Pacific and Asian Affairs Coun. Hawaii, 1991, pres., 1982-91, bd. govs., 1976-96; bd. govs. ARC, 1994-2000, mem. exec. com., 1996-2000, chmn. human resources com., 1996-2000, chmn. Hawaii chpt., 1983-99, bd. dirs., 1983-99, vice chmn., 1990; chmn. Hawaii C. of C., 1997-98, bd. dirs., 1990-99; vice chmn. Honolulu Com. Fgn. Rels., 1983—; pres., dir., founding mem. Hawaii Ocean Law Assn., 1978—; mem. Hawaii Adv. Group for Law of Sea Inst., 1977-85; pres. Hawaii Inst. Continuing Legal Edn., 1979-83, dir., 1976-87; pres., founding mem. Hawaii Coun. Legal Edn. Youth, 1980-83, dir., 1983-88; chmn. Hawaii Commn. Yr. 2000, 1976-79; mem. Honolulu Cmty. Media Coun., 1976-99, exec. com., 1976-84, legal coun., 1979-83; bd. dirs. Hawaii Imin Centennial Corp., 1983-90, Hawaii Pub. Radio, 1983-88, Legal Aid Soc. Hawaii, 1984; founding gov., exec. v.p., chmn. rules and procedures Ctr. Internat. Comml. Dispute Resolution, 1987—; exec. com. Pacific Aerospace Mus., 1991—; exec. com. Pacific Islands Assn., 1988—; exec. com. Asia-Pacific Ctr. Res. Internat. Bus. Disputes, 1991-95; mem. Coun. Asia-Pacific Dispute Rsch. Ctrs., 1991-95; bd. dirs. U.S. C. of C., 1998—; mem. Pacific Basin Econ. Coun., 1993—; mem. mgmt. com. PBEC-U.S. Nat. Com., 1994-99. Recipient cert. of appreciation Gov. of Hawaii, 1979, resolutions of appreciation Hawaii Senate and Ho. of Reps., 1979; grantee Japan Found., 1979. Mem. ABA, Hawaii Bar Assn. (pres. young lawyers sect. 1974, v.p. 1984), Japan-Hawaii Lawyers Assn., Am. Soc. Internat. Law, Internat. Bar Assn., Am. Judicature Soc., Inter-Pacific Bar Assn., Internat. Law Assn., Plaza Club (Honolulu), Colonial Club (Princeton). Democrat. Administrative and regulatory, Corporate, general, Private international. Office: Office Gen Coun Asian Devel Bank 6 ADB Ave 0401 Manila Mandaluyong Philippines also: Gen Coun Asian Devel Bank PO Box 789 0980 Manila Philippines E-mail: gsumida@adb.org.

SUMIDA, KEVIN P.H. lawyer; b. Honolulu, Feb. 14, 1954; s. William H. and Dorothy A. Sumida. BA in Philosphy, Case Western Res. U., 1976; JD, U. Pa., 1979. Bar: Hawaii 1979, U.S. Ct. Appeals (9th cir.) 1981. Assoc. Fong & Miho, Honolulu, 1979-81; law clk. to hon. judge Harold M. Fong U.S. Dist. Ct., Honolulu, 1981-82; assoc. Matsui & Chung, Honolulu, 1982-89; ptnr. Matsui Chung Sumida & Tsuchiyama, Honolulu, 1989—. Bd. dirs., officer Farrington Alumni and Community Found., Honolulu, 1980—. Mem. ABA (litigation sect., tort and ins. practice sect.), Hawaii Bar Assn. Avocation: music. General civil litigation, Insurance, Personal injury (including property damage). Office: Matsui Chung Sumida & Tsuchiyama 737 Bishop St Ste 1400 Honolulu HI 96813-3205

SUMMERS, ALICIA LEHNES, lawyer; b. Trenton, N.J., July 21, 1964; d. James Valentine and Alice Elizabeth Lehnes; m. Michael Eugene Summers, Nov. 26, 1994; children: Matthew Ryan, Nicholas Andrew, Kathryn Alice. BA, Furman U., 1986; JD, Washington & Lee U., 1989. Bar: Va. 1989. Atty. Moshos & Byrd, Fairfax, Va., 1989-91, Trichilo, Bancroft et al, Fairfax, Va., 1991-96, David West & Assocs., Alexandria, Va., 1996—, Michael L. Davis & Assoc., Alexandria, Va., 2003—. Mem. Va. Assn. Def. Attys., Fairfax Bar Assn. Insurance, Personal injury (including property damage). Office: Michael L Davis & Assoc 5285 Shawnee Rd Ste 110 Alexandria VA 22312-2328

SUMMERS, CLYDE WILSON, law educator; b. Grass Range, Mont., Nov. 21, 1918; s. Carl Douglas and Anna Lois (Yontz) S.; m. Evelyn Marie Wahlgren, Aug. 30, 1947; children: Mark, Erica, Craig, Lisa. BS, U. Ill., 1939, JD, 1942, LLD, 1998; LLM, Columbia U., 1946, JSD, 1952; LL.D., U. Leuven, Belgium, 1967, U. Stockholm, 1978, U. Ill., 1998. Bar: N.Y. 1951. Mem. law faculty U. Toledo, 1942-49, U. Buffalo, 1949-56; prof. law Yale U., New Haven, Conn., 1956-66, Garver prof. law, 1966-75; Jefferson B. Fordham prof. law U. Pa., 1975-90, prof. emeritus, 1990—. Hearing examiner Conn. Commn. on Civil Rights, 1963-71 Co-author: Labor Cases and Material, 1968, 2d edit., 1982, Rights of Union Members, 1979, Legal Protection for the Individual Employee, 1989, 3d edit., 2002; co-editor: Labor Relations and the Law, 1953, Employment Relations and the Law, 1959, Comparative Labor Law Jour., 1984-97. Chmn. Gov.'s Com. on Improper Union Mgmt. Practices N.Y. State, 1957-58; chmn. Conn. Adv. Council on Unemployment Ins. and Employment Service, 1960-72; mem. Conn. Labor Relations Bd., 1966-70, Conn. Bd. Mediation and Arbitration, 1964-72. Guggenheim fellow, 1955-56; Ford fellow, 1963-64; German-Marshall fellow, 1977-78; NEH fellow, 1977-78, Fullbright fellow, 1984-85. Mem. Nat. Acad. Arbitrators (pres. elect), Internat. Soc. Labor Law and Social Legislation. Congregationalist. Home: 753 N 26th St Philadelphia PA 19130-2429 Office: U Pa Sch Law 3400 Chestnut St Philadelphia PA 19104-6204 E-mail: csummers@law.upenn.edu.

SUMMERS, HARDY, state supreme court justice; b. Muskogee, Okla., July 15, 1933; m. Marilyn Summers, Mar. 16, 1963; children: Julia Summers Muchmore, Andrew Murray. BA, U. Okla., 1955, LLB, 1957. Asst. county atty. Muskogee County, 1960-62; pvt. practice law Muskogee, 1962-76; dist. judge 15th dist. Okla. Dist. Ct., 1976-85; justice Okla. Supreme Ct., Oklahoma City, 1985—, chief justice, 1999-2000. Sec. Muskogee County Election Bd., 1965-72. Capt. JAGC, USAF, 1957-62. Recipient Disting. Alumnus award, U. Okla. Coll. Law, 2000. Mem. ABA, Okla. Bar Assn., Okla. Jud. Conf. (pres. 1984). Avocations: outdoor sports, music. Office: Okla Supreme Ct Rm 202 State Capital Bldg Oklahoma City OK 73105

SUMMERS, JOHN S. lawyer; b. New Haven, Nov. 8, 1958; s. Robert and Anita (Arrow) S.; m. Jane Marans, July 9, 1988; children: Helen, Daniel. BA, Wesleyan U., 1980; JD, U. Pa., 1984. Law clk. Hon. Thomas N. O'Neill U.S. Dist. Ct., Phila., 1984-86; atty., assoc./shareholder Hangley Connelly Epstein Chicco Foxman & Ewing, Phila., 1986-94; shareholder Hangley Aronchick Segal & Pudlin, Phila., 1994—. Bd. dirs. Reinvestment Fund. Mem.: Pa. Sq. Ct. Disciplinary Com., Hearing Com., The Reinvestment Fund (bd. dirs.), Phila. Bar Found. (trustee), Phila. Bar Edn. Ctr. (pres. 1996—97), Phila. Bar Assn. (bd. govs. 1998—2001), Nat. Health Lawyers Assn., Pa. Bar Assn., Com. of 70 (bd. dirs.). Office: Hangley Aronchick Segal & Pudlin 1 Logan Sq Fl 12 Philadelphia PA 19103-6900 E-mail: jsummers@hangley.com.

SUMMERS, PAUL, state attorney general; b. Somerville, Tenn., Mar. 28, 1950; BS, Miss. State U.; JD, U. Tenn. Dist. atty. gen. 25th Jud. Dist., Somerville, Tenn., 1982—90; judge Ct. of Criminal Appeals, Nashville, 1990—99; atty. gen. State of Tenn., Nashville, 1999—. Adj. prof. law U. Memphis; former adj. faculty Cumberland U.; pres. elect Tenn. Dist. Atty.'s Gen. Conf.; mem. Ct. Criminal Appeals, 1990—99; lectr. in field. Former mem. Tenn. Sentencing Commn.; col. Tenn. Army N.G. With USAF. Mem.: Tenn. Dist. Attys. Gen. Conf. (pres.), Tenn. Bar Assn. (former gov.). Democrat. Avocations: racquetball, rollerblading, Karate (black belt). Office: Office of the Attorney General 500 Charlotte Ave Nashville TN 37243-1401*

SUMMERS, THOMAS CAREY, lawyer; b. Frederick, Md., Feb. 9, 1956; s. Harold Thomas and Doris Jean (Culler) S.; m. Robin Ann Stalnaker, May 12, 1990; children: Kristin, Heather, Lindsay. BA, Dickinson Coll., 1978; JD, U. Balt., 1981. Bar: Md. 1981, U.S. Dist. Ct. Md. 1981, D.C. 1986. Assoc. Ellin & Baker, Balt., 1979-89, Peter G. Angelos, Balt., Md., 1989—. Adj. prof. law U. Balt. Sch. of Law. Mem. ABA, Md. State Bar Assn., Md. Trial Lawyers Assn. Democrat. Lutheran. Avocation: golf. State civil litigation, Personal injury (including property damage), Professional liability. Office: Law Offices of P G Angelos One Charles Ctr Baltimore MD 21201

SUMMERS, WILLIAM LAWRENCE, lawyer; b. Ravenna, Ohio, Mar. 6, 1942; s. Samuel Long and Harriet Cordellia (Jones) S.; m. Barbara A. Herbert; children: Melinda Ann, Shannon Lea, Heather Colleen, Kelly Lynn, Michael Patrick, Kevin James. BA in Polit. Sci. and Sociology, Kent State U., 1965; postgrad., U. Miami, 1966; JD, Cleve. State U., 1969. Bar: Ohio 1969, Ky. 1988, U.S. Dist. Ct. (no. dist.) Okla. 1971, U.S. Ct. Appeals (6th cir.) 1973, U.S. Ct. Appeals (3d and 5th cirs.) 1979, , U.S. Ct. Appeals (8th and 5th cirs.) 1981, U.S. Ct. Appeals (7th cir.) 1982, U.S. Ct. Appeals (9th and 10th cirs.) 1983, U.S. Ct. Appeals (11th cir.), 1984, U.S. Supreme Ct., 1973, U.S. Tax Ct. 1973, U.S. Dist. Ct. (so. dist.) Ala. 1984, U.S. Dist. Ct. (so. dist.) Ohio 1985, U.S. Dist. Ct. (ea. and we. dists.) Ky. 1988. Ptnr. Summers & Vargas Co. LPA, Cleve. and Lexington, Ky., 1969—. Cons. on death penalty State Pub. Defender, Santa Fe, 1980-83; lectr. various profl. orgns. Named one of Ten Outstanding Young Men of Cleve., Cleve. Jaycees, 1972, Five Outstanding Young Men of Ohio, Ohio Jaycees, 1972. Fellow Am. Acad. Trial Lawyers (Roscoe Pound award 1971); mem. ABA (criminal justice sect.), Ohio State Bar Assn. (ho. of dels. 1973-75, 2002-2004), Cuyahoga County Bar Assn. (trustee 1972-76, treas. 1976-79, pres. 1982-83, other coms.), Cuyahoga County Bar Assn., Cuyahoga County Criminal Ct. Bar Assn. (pres. 1977-79), Fed. Bar Assn., Portage County Bar Assn., Ohio Assn. Criminal Def. Lawyers (bd. dirs. 1988—), Ky. Assn. Criminal Def. Lawyer (bd. dirs. 1987-2000), Bar Assn. Greater Cleve., Nat. Assn. Criminal Def. Lawyers (trustee 1977-88, chmn. various coms. Pres.'s award 1981, 1986, 90, Robert C. Heeney award 1982), Am. Judicature Soc., Thoroughbred Club Am., Delta Theta Phi, Canterbury Golf Club, Elks. Roman Catholic. Avocation: thoroughbred horse breeding. Criminal, General civil litigation, Personal injury (including property damage). Home: 17549 Merry Oaks Trl Chagrin Falls OH 44023-5643 Office: Ste 525 23240 Chagrin Blvd Cleveland OH 44122-5486 E-mail: WLSLAWYER@aol.com.

SUMMERS-POWELL, ALAN, lawyer; BA, Yale Coll., 1985; JD, U. Pa., 1988. Bar: N.Y. 1989, N.J. 1989, U.S. Dist. Ct. (fed. dist.) N.J. 1989, D.C. 1990, Fla. 1993, U.S. Dist. Ct. (mid. dist.) Fla. 1996, U.S. Ct. Appeals (11th cir.) 1996, U.S. Tax Ct. 1997, U.S. Dist. Ct. (so. dist.) Fla. 2001. Pvt. practice, Palm Harbor, Fla. Chmn. David Leasing and Devel., Inc. Bankruptcy, Commercial, consumer (including collections, credit), Probate (including wills, trusts). Office: PO Box 6043 Palm Harbor FL 34684-0643

SUMNERS, LESTER FURR, lawyer; b. Blytheville, Ark., June 2, 1926; s. Chester L. and Bessie (Furr) S.; m. Mary Joyce Bonner, Feb. 12, 1956; children: Thomas Bonner, Melinda Watson, Leslie Elizabeth. BA, U. Miss., 1949, LLB, 1950. Bar: Miss. 1950. Staff atty. USDA, Washington, 1951-52; ptnr. Darden & Sumners, New Albany, Miss., 1952-76, Darden, Sumners, Carter & Trout, New Albany, 1976-83, Sumners, Carter, Trout & McMillin, New Albany, 1983-94, Sumners & Carter, P.A., New Albany, 1995—. Assoc. editor U. Miss. Law Rev., 1950. Scoutmaster Boy Scouts Am., New Albany, 1953-75; trustee NE Miss. Jr. Coll., Booneville, 1961-66. Recipient Silver Beaver award Boy Scouts Am., 1966. Fellow Internat. Acad. Trial Lawyers, Am. Coll. Trial Lawyers; mem. Miss. Bar Assn. (commr. 1950-63, 65-67, complaint commr. 1963, 65, pres. 1971-72), Miss. Bar Found. (pres. 1979-80), U. Miss. Law Alumni Chpt. (pres. 1976-77). Federal civil litigation, State civil litigation, General practice. Office: Sumners Carter & Mueller PA PO Box 730 New Albany MS 38652-0730

SUNDERMEYER, MICHAEL S. lawyer; b. Kansas City, Mo., Feb. 8, 1951; s. Edgar W. and Ruth (Shobe) S.; m. Susan Talarico; children: Kim Marie, Mark Shobe. BA, U. Kans., 1973; JD, U. Va., 1976. Bar: D.C., Md., Va., U.S. Dist. Ct. D.C., U.S. Dist. Ct. Md., U.S. Dist. Ct. (ea. dist.) Va., U.S. Dist. Ct. (no. dist.) Okla., U.S. Ct. Appeals (D.C. cir.), U.S. Ct. Appeals (4th cir.), U.S. Ct. Appeals (5th cir.), U.S. Ct. Appeals (3d cir.), U.S. Ct. Appeals (11th cir.). Law clk. to Hon. John Minor Wisdom U.S. Ct. Appeals (5th cir.), New Orleans, 1976-77; law clk. to Hon. Harry A. Blackmun U.S. Supreme Ct., Washington, 1977-78; assoc. Williams & Connolly, Washington, 1978-84, ptnr., 1985—. Editor-in-chief Va. Law Rev., 1975-76. Mem. ABA. Administrative and regulatory, Federal civil litigation, Professional liability. Office: Williams & Connolly LLP 725 12th St NW Washington DC 20005-5901 E-mail: msundermeyer@wc.com.

SUNIA, FITI, American Samoa attorney general; Asst. atty. gen. Am. Samoa Govt., Pago Pago, 1997—2001, acting atty. gen., 2001—02, atty. gen., 2002—. Office: PO Box 7 Pago Pago AS 96799*

SUPLEE, KATHERINE ANN, lawyer; b. Newark, Oct. 4, 1950; d. Frank Edward and Mary Teresa (Green) S. BA, Mt. Holyoke Coll., 1972; postgrad., Eagleton Inst. Politics, 1972-73; JD, Seton Hall U., 1977. Bar: N.J. 1978, U.S. Dist. Ct. N.J. 1978, U.S. Supreme Ct. 1983, N.Y. 1984. Assoc. Williams & Flynn, Westfield, N.J., 1978-80, Suplee, Clooney & Co., Elizabeth, NJ, 1978—2001. Atty. Union Twp. Planning Bd., Union, N.J., 1981; mem. trustee panel U.S. Trustee in Bankruptcy, Newark, 1982—; spl. counsel City of Elizabeth N.J., 1986-88; mem. adv. coun. Summit Bank, 1989-95, St. Elizabeth Hosp., 1991-2000. Fund raiser N.J. Opera Co., 1973-77, Save African Endangered Species Inc., 1980-82, Kosciusko Found.; counsel Summit chpt. Friends of Opera, 1979-84, Polish Assistance Inc., 1998-2000; bd. dirs. Westminster Ballet Co., Elizabeth, 1984-85, Union County Legal Svcs. Corp., Elizabeth, 1984-86. Mem. ABA, N.J. Bar Assn., Union County Bar Assn. (del. gen. coun. 1984, trustee 1997—), N.J. Women Lawyers (bd. dirs. 1980-87, sec. 1986-87, treas. 1988), Comml. Law League, N.J. Women in Fed. Practice (bd. dirs. 1985-98, treas. 1987-89, pres. 1995-97), Bath and Tennis Club (Spring Lake, N.J.), Spring Lake Golf Club, Suburban Golf Club (Union, N.J.), Phi Alpha Delta. Roman Catholic. Bankruptcy, Commercial, contracts (including sales of goods; commercial financing), Corporate, general. Office: 1767 Morris Ave Union NJ 07083

SURKIN, ELLIOT MARK, lawyer; b. Phila., Apr. 22, 1942; s. Hersh M. and Minnie (Shore) S.; m. Carol E. Foley, May 26, 1973; 1 child, Jennifer Dykema. AB, Princeton U., 1964; LLB, Harvard U., 1967. Bar: Mass. 1967. Assoc. Hill & Barlow, P.C., Boston, 1967-73, mem., 1973—2003, chmn. mgmt. com., 1988-92, chmn. real estate dept., 1996-2001; mng. ptnr. Piper Rudnick LLP, Boston, 2003—. Lectr. law Harvard U., 1975-96, MIT, Ctr. for Real Estate, 1996—. Chmn. bd. Boston Ctr. Arts, 1972-81, dir., mem. exec. com., 1981-83, hon. dir., 1983—; clk., trustee, mem. exec. com. Wang Ctr. for Performing Arts, Boston, 1980—, mem. fin. com., 1995—, vice chmn. bd., 1997—; mem. New Eng. com. Legal Def. Fund NAACP, 1976-93; chmn. standing com. Trustees of Reservations, 1997—, chmn. Chappaquiddick local com. 1986-97, trustee 1985—, mem. standing com. 1994—, mem. exec. com. 1996—; dir. Sheriff's Meadow Found., 1994-97. Mem. ABA, Am. Law Inst., Am. Coll. Real Estate Lawyers, Mass. Bar Assn., Boston Bar Assn., St. Botolph Club, Harvard Club of Boston, Edgartown Yacht Club, Country Club of Brookline, Mass., Kiawah Island Club. Land use and zoning (including planning), Landlord-tenant, Property, real (including real estate development, water). Home: 1784 Beacon St Waban MA 02468-1434 Office: Piper Rudnick LLP One International Pl Boston MA 02110-2600 E-mail: elliot.surkin@piperrudnick.com.

SURLES, RICHARD HURLBUT, JR., retired law librarian; b. Norfolk, Va., Mar. 28, 1943; s. Richard H. and Elda Florine (Belvin) S.; m. Judith Louise Coffin, May 29, 1964; children— Stephanie Anne, Richard H. BA, Tex. A&M U., 1963; JD, U.Houston, 1967; M.L.L., U.Wash., 1969. Bar: Colo. 1971. Asst. to law librarian U. Houston, 1966-68; asst. to law librarian King county Law Library, Seattle, 1968-69; dir. of law library, prof. law U. Denver, 1969-71, U. Tenn., Knoxville, 1971-76, U. Oreg., Eugene, 1976-81, U. Ill., Champaign, 1981—98; ret., 1998. Author: Legal Periodical Management Data, 1977 Mem. Am. Assn. Law Libraries Republican.

SURRATT, JOHN RICHARD, lawyer; b. Winston-Salem, N.C., Aug. 7, 1928; s. Wade Talmage and Julia (Efird) S.; m. Estella Eason, Dec. 2, 1961; children: Margaret Virginia, Estella Elizabeth, Susan Efird. BS in Commerce, U. N.C., 1948; JD, Duke U., 1951. Bar: N.C. 1951. Pvt. practice, Winston-Salem, 1951—. Judge Mcpl. Ct. Winston-Salem; lectr. law Wake Forest U., Winston-Salem, 1976-80. Mayor City of Winston-Salem 1961-63, chmn. city planning bd., 1972-78; sec., mem. Forsyth County Dem. Exec. Com., N.C.; mem. bar candidate com. N.C. Bd. Law Examiners. Served to capt. USAR, 1951-53, Korea. Mem. ABA, N.C. Bar Assn., Forsyth County Bar Assn. (pres. 1984, exec. com. 1986), Rotary (pres. local chpt. 1983), Old Town Club, Twin City Club. Clubs: Old Town, Twin City. Lodges: Rotary (pres. local chpt. 1983). Corporate, general, Probate (including wills, trusts), Estate taxation. E-mail: jsurratt@surrattpa.com.

SURRIDGE, STEPHEN ZEHRING, lawyer, writer; b. N.Y.C., Dec. 12, 1940; s. Robert George and Florence Elizabeth (Zehring) S.; m. Helen Frances McKenna, Mar. 15, 1969; children: Christopher S., Jonathan R., Matthew W., Martha H. BA magna cum laude, Yale U., 1962; MBA (with distinction), JD, U. Mich., 1969. Bar: Wis. 1969, Mich. 1969. Assoc. Quarles & Brady, Milw., 1969-76, ptnr., 1977-89; freelance writer, tchr., 1990—. Author: (monograph) Seven Thunders of Revelation, 1985, Revelation Revisited, 1995. 1st lt. U.S. Army, 1963-65. Mem. Phi Beta Kappa. Mem. Christian Ch. Home: 4480 N Ardmore Ave Milwaukee WI 53211-1418 E-mail: ssurridge@aya.yale.edu.

SUSKIN, HOWARD STEVEN, lawyer; b. Chgo., Aug. 9, 1959; BA, Northwestern U., 1980; JD, U. Mich., 1983. Bar: Ill. 1983, U.S. Dist. Ct. (no. dist.) Ill. 1983, U.S. Ct. Appeals (7th cir.) 1984, U.S. Ct. Appeals (6th cir.) 1987, U.S. Ct. Appeals (4th cir.) 1987; arbitrator Am. Arbitration Assn. Mem. staff Office Gen. Counsel, HEW, Chgo, 1978-80; mem. staff Ill. Atty. Gen. Office, Chgo, 1981; assoc. Jenner & Block, Chgo., 1983-90, ptnr., 1991—. Arbitrator Chgo Bd. Options Exch., Cir. Ct. Cook County. Editor Mich. Law Rev., 1982-83; co-author Illinois Civil Litigation Guide, 1998, 2000. Mem. ABA (arbitrator), Nat. Assn. Securities Dealers, Nat. Futures Assn., N.Y. Stock Exch., Chgo. Bar Assn. (chmn., legis. liaison mem. securities law com. 1997-98), Phi Beta Kappa. General civil litigation, Securities. Office: Jenner & Block 1 E IBM Plz Fl 4000 Chicago IL 60611-7603 E-mail: hsuskin@jenner.com.

SUSKO, CAROL LYNNE, lawyer, accountant; b. Washington, Dec. 5, 1955; d. Frank and Helen Louise (Davis) S. BS in Econs. and Acctg., George Mason U., 1979; JD, Cath. U., 1982; LLM in Taxation, Georgetown U., 1992. Bar: Pa. 1989, D.C. 1990; CPA, Va., Md. Tax acct. Reznick Fedder & Silverman, P.C., Bethesda, Md., 1984-85; sr. tax acct. Pannell Kerr Forster, Alexandria, Va., 1985; tax specialist Coopers & Lybrand, Washington, 1985-87; supervisory tax sr. Frank & Co., McLean, Va., 1987-88; mem. editl. staff Tax Notes Mag., Arlington, Va., 1989-90; adj. faculty Am. U., Washington, 1989—; tax atty. Marriott Corp., Washington, 1993-94; sr. tax mgr. Host Marriott Inc., Washington, 1994-99, KPMG LLP, McLean, Va., 1999—. Mem. ABA, AICPAs, Va. Soc. CPAs, D.C. Soc. CPAs, D.C. Bar Assn. Corporate taxation, Taxation, general, State and local taxation. Office: KPMG LLP Ste 3064 1660 International Dr Mc Lean VA 22102-4832 E-mail: csusko@kpmg.com.

SUSMAN, MORTON LEE, lawyer; b. Aug. 6, 1934; m. Nina Meyers, May 1, 1958; 1 child, Mark Lee. BBA, So. Meth. U., 1956, JD, 1958. Bar: Tex. 1958, U.S. Dist. Ct. (so. dist.) Tex. 1961, U.S. Ct. Appeals (5th cir.) 1961, U.S. Supreme Ct. 1961, U.S. Ct. Appeals (11th cir) 1981, D.C. 1988, U.S. Ct. Appeals (D.C. cir.) 1988, N.Y. 1990, Colo. 1996. Asst. U.S. atty., Houston, 1961-64; 1st asst. U.S. atty., 1965-66; U.S. atty., 1966-69; ptnr. Weil, Gotshal & Manges and predecessor firm Susman & Kessler, Houston, 1969-97; ret., 1998. Lt. USNR, 1958-61. Fellow Am. Coll. Trial Lawyers, Tex. Bar Found.; mem. ABA, FBA (dir., Younger Fed. Lawyer award 1968), Tex. Bar Assn. Democrat. Alternative dispute resolution, Federal civil litigation, State civil litigation. Home: 1000 Uptown Park Blvd Ste 151 Houston TX 77056-3247

SUSMAN, STEPHEN DAILY, lawyer; b. Houston, Jan. 20, 1941; m. Ellen Spencer, 1999; children: Stacy, Harry. BA magna cum laude, Yale U., 1962; LL.B. with highest honors, U. Tex., 1965. Bar: U.S. Supreme Ct. 1960, Tex. 1965, D.C. 1999, N.Y. 2000, Colo. 2002. Law clk. U.S. Ct. Appeals (5th cir.), New Orleans, 1965-66, U.S.Supreme Ct., Washington, 1966-67; ptnr. Fulbright & Jaworski, 1966-75; spl. counsel to atty. gen. Austin, Tex., 1975, Mandell & Wright, 1975-80; sr. ptnr. Susman Godfrey, Houston, 1980—. Vis. prof. law U. Tex., Austin, 1975; chmn. adv. com. on discovery Tex. Supreme Ct. Contbr. articles to profl. jours. Bd. dirs. Contemporary Arts Mus., 1988-94, 98—, Yale Art Gallery, 1998—, Yale Devel. Fund, Southwest Legal Found., Inns of Ct., Houston Grand Opera, 1998—, Phoenix House, 1998-2001, Lawyers Com. for Civil Rights, 1997-, Lawyers Com. for Human Rights, 1998—, ADL, 1999-; mem. U.S. Holocaust Meml. Coun., 2000-2002 (devel. comm.), Million Dollar Advocates Forum, (life), 2000—, others. Recipient ADL Jurisprudence award, 1995; named one of Best Trial Lawyers in Am., Nat. Law Jour., 1989; named Best Litigator in World, Comml. Litigation, Go To Lawyer for Plaintiff's Commercial Litigation, Tex. Lawyer, 2002. Mem. ABA (antitrust sect., mem. coun. litigation sect., chmn. task force on fast track litigation), Houston Bar Assn., Dallas Bar Assn., D.C. Bar Assn., N.Y. Bar Assn., State Bar Tex., Am. Law Inst., Assn. Trial Lawyers Am., Am. Bar Trial Advocates, Houston Bar Assn., Southwestern Legal Found. Rsch. Fellows, Yale Club (Houston, N.Y.C.), Houston Trial Lawyers Assn. (dir.), Tex. Assn. Civil Trial and Appellate Specialists (former pres., dir.), Houston Club, Houstonian Club, Petroleum Club (Dallas), Quinnipiac Club (New Haven), Order of the Coif, Friars, Phi Delta Ph). Avocations: jogging, hiking. Federal civil litigation, General civil litigation, State civil litigation. Office: Ste 5100 1000 Louisiana St Houston TX 77002-5091 E-mail: ssusman@susmangodfrey.com.

SUSSE, SANDRA SLONE, lawyer; b. Medford, Ma., June 1, 1943; d. James Robert and Georgie Coffin (Bradshaw) Slone; m. Peter Susse, May 10, 1969 (div. May 1993); 1 child, Toby. BA, U. Mass., 1981; JD, Vt. Law Sch., 1986. Bar: Mass. 1986, U.S. Dist. Ct. Mass. 1988, U.S. Ct. Appeals (1st cir.) 1995. Staff atty. Western Mass. Legal Svcs., Springfield, 1986—. Mem. ABA, Women's Bar Assn. Mass. Avocations: hiking, german literature, films, skating. Address: Western Mass Legal Serv 127 State St Fl 4 Springfield MA 01103-1905 E-mail: ssusse@wmls.org.

SUSSMAN, HOWARD S(IVIN), lawyer; b. N.Y.C., Feb. 12, 1938; s. Joseph and Dora (Sivin) S. AB cum laude, Princeton U., 1958; LLB, Columbia U., 1962. Bar: N.Y. 1964, U.S. Dist. Ct. (so. and ea. dists.) N.Y. 1967, U.S. Ct. Appeals (2d cir.) 1967, U.S. Tax Ct. 1969, U.S. Dist. Ct. (no. dist.) N.Y. 1970, U.S. Supreme Ct. 1970, Tex. 1979, U.S. Ct. Appeals (5th cir.) 1982. Assoc. Chadbourne, Parke, Whiteside & Wolff, N.Y.C., 1963-71; asst. U.S. atty. So. Dist. N.Y., 1971-77; assoc. prof. law U. Houston, 1977-82; of counsel Wood, Lucksinger & Epstein, Houston, 1982-83; pvt. practice, N.Y.C., 1983-94; ptnr. Sussman Sollis Ebin Tweedy & Wood, LLP, N.Y.C., 1995—. Instr. continuing legal edn. U. Houston, Nat. Inst. for Trial Advocacy. Editor Columbia U. Law Rev., 1960-62; contbr. articles to profl. jours. Harlan Fiske Stone scholar, 1959-61, Edvard Cassels Stiftelse vis. scholar, Stockholm, 1962-63; travelling fellow Parker Sch. Fgn. and Comparative Law Columbia U., 1962-63. Mem. ABA, N.Y. State Bar Assn., Assn. Bar City N.Y. (com. adminstrv. law 1974-76, profl. conf. 1979, com. fed. legis. 1984-87, com. criminal law 1987-90, com. lectr. and continuing edn. 1990-93, com. fgn. and comparative law 1993-96, arbitration com. 2002—), Fed. Bar Coun., Swedish Am. C. of C. (dir. N.Y. chpt. 1996—). Clubs: Princeton N.Y. Federal civil litigation, Criminal, General practice. E-mail: sstwsussman@msn.com.

SUSSMAN, MARK RICHARD, lawyer; b. Bklyn., Feb. 4, 1952; s. Vincent E. and Rhoda (Urowsky) S.; m. Lisa Rosner, June 8, 1975; children: Corey, Randi, Samuel. BS in Civil Engring., Tufts U., 1974; JD, U. Pa., 1977. Bar: Pa. 1977, D.C. 1980, Conn. 1981. Trial atty. land and natural resources div. U.S. Dept. Justice, Washington, 1977-81; assoc. Murtha, Cullina, Richter & Pinney, Hartford, Conn., 1981-86, ptnr., 1987—; chmn. environ. dept. Murtha Cullina LLP, Hartford, Conn., 1990—. Gov.'s blue ribbon panel to evaluate environtl. permit programs, 1996. Chmn. conservation commn. Windsor, Conn., 1984-2000; mem. Conn. Hazardous Waste Mgmt. Service Recycling Task Force, 1986, Legis. Task Force on Environ. Permitting, 1992, Conn. State Implementation Plan Revision Adv. Com., 1984—. Mem. ABA (natural resources sect.), Conn. Bar Assn. (chmn. conservation and environ. quality sect. 1984-87, faculty continuing legal edn.), Conn. Bus. and Industry Assn. (steering com. environ. policies coun. 1990-93, 98—) Tau Beta Pi. Federal civil litigation, State civil litigation, Environmental. Home: 62 Timothy Ter Windsor CT 06095-1652 Office: Murtha Cullina LLP City Pl 185 Asylum St Ste 29 Hartford CT 06103-3469

SUSSMAN, NANCY, lawyer, nurse; b. N.Y.C., Feb. 18, 1951; d. Henry and Freda (Luber) S.; children: Michael, Ashleigh. BSN, Calif. State U., L.A., 1974; JD, Calif. Western U., 1982. Bar: Calif. 1983. Ptnr. Hayworth and Sussman, San Diego, 1983-92, pvt. practice, 1992—. Mem. ATLA, San Diego Trial Lawyers Assn., Consumer Attys. of San Diego. Personal injury (including property damage), Professional liability. Office: Hayworth and Sussman 1901 1st Ave Ste 220 San Diego CA 92101-2382

SUSSMAN, NEIL A. lawyer; b. N.Y.C., Jan. 26, 1956; s. Herbert and Ruth S.; m. Suzanne R. Thompson, Aug. 31, 1990; children: Annabelle, Franklin. BS in Econs., U. Pa., 1978; JD, U. Wash., 1982. Bar: Wash. 1982. Pvt. practice, Seattle, 1982—. Mem. Wash. State Bar Assn. Entertainment, Taxation, general, Trademark and copyright. Office: 10727 Interlake Ave N Seattle WA 98133-8907 E-mail: neilsussman@mindspring.com.

SUTHAM, APISITH JOHN, lawyer, consultant; b. Bangkok, Oct. 3, 1960; s. Wanchai and Obchuay Suthambhitak; m. Nasra Suthipunt Sutham, Dec. 5, 1990; children: Pran Jeremy, Karam Justin. BA, St. John's U., 1987; JD, Fordham U., 1991; MBA, Free U., Brussels, 1994. Bar: N.Y. 1991, U.S. Ct. Internat. Trade 2000. Legal asst. Simpson Thacher & Bartlett, N.Y.C., 1989—90; assoc. Akin, Gump, Strauss, Haler & Feld, Brussels, 1994—96, Internat. Legal Counsellors Thailand, Bangkok, 1996—99; sr. assoc. White & Case, Bangkok, 1999—2001; counsel Pricewaterhousecoopers Legal and Tax, Bangkok, 2001—02; ptnr. Apisith & Alliance Ltd., Bangkok, 2002—. Non-tariff barrier com. Thai Fedn. Indsl., Bangkok, 2001—02. Contbr. articles to profl. jours.; author: (books) internat. trade and transactions. Avocations: tennis, golf, reading. Public international, Private international, General practice. Office: Apisith & Alliance Ltd Wave Pl 55 Wireless Rd 7th Fl Pathumwan 10330 Thailand

SUTHERLAND, DONALD GRAY, retired lawyer; b. Houston, Jan. 19, 1929; s. Robert Gray and Elizabeth (Cunningham) S.; m. Mary Reynolds Moodey, July 23, 1955; children: Stuart Gray, Elizabeth Dana. BS, Purdue U., 1954; LLB, Ind. U., Bloomington, 1954. Bar: Ind. 1954, U.S. Dist. Ct. (so. dist.) Ind. 1954, U.S. Tax Ct. 1956, U.S. Ct. Claims 1957, U.S. Ct. Appeals (7th cir.) 1981, U.S. Ct. Appeals (3d cir.) 1984, U.S. Ct. Internat. Trade 1987, U.S. Supreme Ct. 1987. Assoc. IceMiller, Indpls., 1954-64, ptnr., 1965-98, ret., 1998. Practitioner in residence Ind. U. Sch. of Law, Bloomington, 1987; trustee, pres. Pegasus Funds, Detroit, 1992-99; trustee, chmn. bd. dirs., pres. Bison Money Market Fund., Indpls., 1982-92. Contbr. articles to numerous profl. jours. Bd. dirs., v.p. Japan-Am. Soc. of Ind., Inc., Indpls., 1988-97; bd. dirs. Conner Prairie Inc., Fishers, Ind., 1988-97, v.p., 1989-90, chmn. bd., 1990-93; tennis ceremonies 10th Pan-Am. Games, Indpls., 1987; bd. dirs. The Children's Bur. Indpls., 1962-73, v.p., 1968-70, pres., 1970-72; bd. dirs. Orchard Country Day Sch., Indpls., 1970-73, Episc. Cmty. Svcs., Indpls., 1965-73, v.p., 1968, pres., 1969; trustee United Episc. Charities, Indpls., 1970-71, pres., 1971. With USMC, 1946-48. Mem.: Econ. Club (bd. dirs. Ind. chpt. 1988—94), Contemporary Club (pres. 2003), Woodstock Club. Republican. Avocations: golf, tennis, opera. Office: Ice Miller 1 American Sq Indianapolis IN 46282-0020

SUTHERS, JOHN WILLIAM, prosecutor; b. Denver, Oct. 18, 1951; s. William Dupont and Marguerite A. (Ryan) S.; m. Janet Gill, May 21, 1976; children: Alison, Catherine. BA in Govt. magna cum laude, U. Notre Dame, 1974; JD, U. Colo., 1977. Bar: Colo. 1977, U.S. Dist. Ct. Colo. 1977, U.S. Ct. Appeals (10th cir.) 1979. Dep. dist. atty. 4th jud. dist. State of Colo., Colo. Springs, 1977-79, chief dep. dist. atty. 4th jud. dist., 1979-81; assoc. Sparks, Dix, Enoch, Colo. Springs, 1981-82; ptnr. Sparks, Dix, Enoch, Suthers & Winslow, Colo. Springs, 1982-89; dist. atty. 4th Jud. Dist., Colo. Springs, 1989—97; sr. counsel Sparks, Dix, 1997—99; exec. dir. Colo. Dept. Corrections, 1999—2001; US atty. US Atty.'s Office Colo. Dist., 2001—. Mem. adv. bd. Sec. of State, Denver, 1983—89; Colo. commr. Uniform State Laws, 1993—97. Author: Fraud and Deceit, 1982, How to Liquidate a Lemon, 1983. Pres., chmn. bd. dirs. Cmty. Corrections of Pikes Peak Region, Inc., 1984—87; bd. dirs. Crimestoppers, Inc., Colorado Springs, 1985—88; mem. exec. com. Colo. Dist. Atty.'s Coun., 1992—97, pres., 1994—95, treas., 1993; El Paso County Rep. Ctrl. com. Colorado Springs, 1985—2001; Colo. State Rep. Ctrl. com., 1989—2001. Zimmerman Found. scholar, 1970-74. Mem. Colo. Bar Assn. (com. chmn.), El Paso County Bar Assn. (pres. 1990-91), Notre Dame Colorado Springs (pres. 1983-84). Roman Catholic. Avocations: baseball cards, golf. Home: 3040 Electra Dr Colorado Springs CO 80906-1089 Office: US Atty 1225 17th St Ste 700 Denver CO 80202

SUTPHIN, WILLIAM TAYLOR, lawyer; s. William Halstead and Catharine (Bonner) S.; m. Alissa L. Kramer, June 21, 1958. AB in History, Princeton U., 1957; LLB, U. Pa., 1960. Bar: N.J. 1960; U.S. Ct. Appeals (3d cir.) 1964, U.S. Supreme Ct. 1965. Assoc. Stryker, Tams & Dill, Newark, 1960-67, ptnr., 1967-73; sole practice Princeton, N.J., 1973—. Coadj. faculty mem. Rutgers U. Govt. Svcs. Tng. Program, 1973—; assoc. counsel N.J. Planning Ofcls., 1975-2003. Mem. Princeton Twp. Planning Bd., 1967-72, Regional Planning Bd. Princeton, 1970-74; atty. Green Brook Twp. Planning Bd., 1972-2001, Millstone Twp. Bd. Adjustment, 1978-98, Del. Twp. Bd. Adjustment, 1982—, Princeton Borough Bd. Adjustment, 1983—; committeeman Twp. Princeton, 1973-75, police commr., 1974-75; treas. Youth Employment Svc. Princeton Inc., 1981-84. Served with U.S. Army, 1953-56, capt. JAGC Ret. Mem. N.J. Bar Assn. (chmn. ins. com. 1979-81), Princeton Bar Assn. (pres. 1981-82), N.J. Inst. Mcpl. Attys. General civil litigation, Land use and zoning (including planning), Probate (including wills, trusts). Home: 501 Jefferson Rd Princeton NJ 08540-3418 Office: Law Offices of William T Sutphin 34 Chambers St Princeton NJ 08542-3700 E-mail: william.t.sutphin@verizon.net.

SUTTER, LAURENCE BRENER, lawyer; b. N.Y.C., Feb. 5, 1944; s. Meyer and Beatrice Sutter; m. Betty A. Satterwhite, June 9, 1979. AB, Columbia Coll., 1965; JD, N.Y.U., 1976. Bar: N.Y. 1977, U.S. Dist. Ct. (so. and ea. dists.) N.Y. 1977. Assoc. Shea & Gould, N.Y.C., 1976-80, Meyer, Suozzi, English & Klein P.C., Mineola, N.Y., 1980-82; assoc. counsel publs. Gen. Media Comm., Inc., N.Y.C., 1982-96, sr. v.p., gen. counsel, 1997—. With N.Y. Army N.G., 1966-72. Mem. Assn. of Bar of City of N.Y. (mem. com. on civil rights 1986-89, mem. com. on comm. and media law 1989-92, mem. com. on copyright and lit. property 1994-97), First Amendment Lawyers Assn., Nat. Arts Club, Orient (N.Y.) Yacht Club (dir. 1997-2000, sec. 2000-2001). Democrat. Jewish. Avocations: music, sailing. Communications. Office: Gen Media Comm Inc 11 Penn Plz 12th Fl New York NY 10001-0006

SUTTER, WILLIAM PAUL, lawyer; b. Chgo., Jan. 15, 1924; s. Harry Blair and Elsie (Paul) S.; m. Helen Yvonne Stebbins, Nov. 13, 1954; children: William Paul, Helen Blair Sutter. AB, Yale U., 1947; JD, U. Mich., 1950. Bar: Ill. 1950, Fla. 1977, U.S. Supreme Ct. 1981. Assoc. Hopkins & Sutter (and predecessors), Chgo., 1950-57, ptnr., 1957-89, of counsel, 1989—2001. Mem. Ill. Supreme Ct. Atty. Registration Commn., 1975-81 Contbr. articles on estate planning and taxation to profl. jours. Chmn. Winnetka Caucus Com., 1966-67; pres., trustee Lucille P. Markey Charitable Trust, 1983-98; precinct capt. New Trier Twp. (Ill.) Rep. party, 1960-68; asst. area chmn. New Trier Rep. Orgn., 1968-72; trustee Gads Hill Center, pres., 1962-70, chmn., 1971-80; trustee Northwestern Meml. Hosp., 1983-98, life trustee, 1998—; bd. dirs. Chgo. Hort. Soc., 1982—; mem. dean's coun. Sch. Medicine, Yale U., 1991—; bd. visitors Waisman Ctr., U. Wis., 1996-2002; corr. sec. Yale U. Class of 1945, 1990—. Served to 1st lt. AUS, 1943-46. Fellow Am. Bar Found., Am. Coll. Trust and Estate Counsel (bd. regents 1977-83, exec. com. 1981-83); mem. ABA (ho. dels. 1972-81, chmn. com. on income estates and trusts, taxation sect. 1973-75), Ill. Bar Assn. (bd. govs. 1964-75, pres. 1973-74), Chgo. Bar Assn. (chmn. probate practice com. 1963-64), Am. Law Inst., Internat. Acad. Estate and Trust Law, Am. Judicature Soc., Ill. LAWPAC (pres. 1977-83), Order of Coif, Phi Beta Kappa, Phi Delta Phi, Chi Psi, Mid-Day Club, Indian Hill Club, Gulf Stream Golf Club, Country Club Fla., Ocean Club (Fla.) (bd. govs. 1993-99, sec. 1993-97, pres. 1997-99), Lawyers Club Chgo. Episcopalian. Home: 96 Woodley Rd Winnetka IL 60093 Home (Winter): Two Par Club Cir Village Village Of Golf FL 33436 E-mail: wpsutter@aol.com.

SUTTERFIELD, JAMES RAY, lawyer; Bar: La., 1967; U.S. Dist. Ct. (ea. dist.) La., 1967; U.S. Ct. Appeals (5th cir.), 1967,; U.S. Dist. Ct. (mid. dist.) La., 1971; D.C., 1977; U.S. Supreme Ct., 1977; U.S. Dist. Ct. (we. dist.) La., 1982; U.S. Dist. Ct. (ea. dist.) Tex., 1985; Tex., 1993. Assoc. Law Offices Walter F. Marcus, New Orleans, 1967, Huddleston and Davis, New Orleans, 1968-70, ptnr., 1970-72, Sutterfield and Vickery, New Orleans, 1973-82, Carmouche, Gray, and Hoffman, New Orleans, 1982-89; sr. dir. Hoffman, Sutterfield, and Ensenat, A.P.L.C., New Orleans, 1989-97; sr. ptnr. Sutterfield and Webb, LLC, New Orleans, 1997—. Hon. consul gen. St. Vincent and The Grenadines, 1997-; faculty mem. tenth diving accident and hyperbaric oxygen treatment course Duke U.; del. Undersea and Hyperbaric Med. Soc. Nat. Oceanographic and Almospheric Adminstrn.; speaker in field. Author: (with others) Commercial Damages, 1989; mem. editl. bd. Hull Claims Analysis; contbr. articles to profl. jour. Mem. ABA (chmn. excess surplus lines and reins. com.); La. Bar Assn., (5th Cir.) Bar Assn.; D.C. Bar Assn.; La. Assn. Def. Counsel; Internat. Assn. Def. Counsel (chmn. maritime and energy law com., class action and multiparty litigation com.); Maritime Law Assn. U.S. (chmn. marine product liability com.); Def. Rsch. Inst.; The Harmonie Group of Ind. Law Firms (pres. 1999-2001). Admiralty, Insurance. Office: Sutterfield & Webb 650 Poydras St Fl 27 New Orleans LA 70130-6101

SUTTLE, STEPHEN HUNGATE, lawyer; b. Uvalde, Tex., Mar. 17, 1940; s. Dorwin Wallace and Ann Elizabeth (Barrett) Suttle; m. Rosemary Williams Davison, Aug. 3, 1963; children: Michael Barrett, David Paull, John Stewart. BA, Washington and Lee U., 1962; LLB, U. Tex., 1965. Bar: Tex. 1965, U.S. Dist. Ct. (no. and we. dists.) Tex. 1965, U.S. Ct. Appeals (5th cir.) 1967, U.S. Supreme Ct. 1970. Law clk. to Hon. Leo Brewster U.S. Dist. Ct., Ft. Worth, 1965-67; ptnr. McMahon, Surovik, Suttle, Buhrmann, Hicks & Gill, P.C., Abilene, Tex., 1970—. Pres. Abilene Boys Clubs, Inc., 1975—76; bd. dirs. Abilene Cmty. Theater, 1979—80, Abilene Fine Arts Mus., 1977—78. Fellow: State Bar Tex. (dir. 1999—2002), Tex. Bar Found., Am. Bd. Trial Advocates (pres. Tex. 2003), Am. Coll. Trial Lawyers; mem.: ABA (chmn. young lawyers sect. award of merit 1976), Tex. Bar Assn. (dir. 1999—2002), Abilene Bar Assn. (pres. 1987—88), Am. Judicature Soc. (bd. dirs. 1981—84), Tex. Young Lawyers Assn. (chmn. bd. dirs. 1976), Def. Rsch. Inst., Tex. Assn. Def. Counsel, Assn. Def. Trial Attys., Abilene Country Club. Episcopalian. Federal civil litigation, State civil litigation. Home: 1405 Woodland Trl Abilene TX 79605-4705 Office: McMahon Surovik Suttle Buhrmann Hicks & Gill PC PO Box 3679 Abilene TX 79604-3679 E-mail: ssuttle@mcmahonlawtx.com.

SUTTON, JEFFREY S. judge; b. Dhahran, Saudi Arabia, 1960; BA, Williams Coll., 1983; LLB, Ohio State Univ., 1990. Clk. Second Circuit Ct. for Judge Thomas Meskill, 1990—91, Supreme Ct. for Justice Scalia and ret. Justice Powell, 1991—92; assoc. Jones, Day, Reavis & Pogue, Columbus, Ohio, 1992—95; adj. law prof. Ohio State Univ., Ohio, 1994—; Solicitor Ohio State, Ohio, 1995—98; ptnr. Jones, Day, Reavis & Pogue, Columbus, Ohio, 1998—; Circuit judge Ct. of Appeals, 6th Circuit, Cin., 2003. Mr. Sutton's record shows him to be a leading proponent of "federalism" theories. He has written articles, given speeches and argued in several cases before the Supreme Ct. and other courts that Congress should be restricted in power to pass civil, disablility, workers' rights, and environ. laws. He also proposes that people challenging state governments to redress peoples violations of these laws should have restricted access to the courts. In other cases involving the State vs. People, Sutton argued successfully for the State supporting the federalism theory. Office: Office Clerk US Ct Appeals 6th Cir 532 Potter Stewart US Cthse 100 E 5th St Cincinnati OH 45202-3988*

SUTTON, JOHN EWING, lawyer; b. San Angelo, Oct. 7, 1950; s. John F. Jr. and Nancy (Ewing) S.; 1 son, Joshua Ewing; 1 stepson, Michael Brandon Ducote. BBA, U. Tex., 1973, JD, 1976. Bar: Tex. 1976, U.S. Tax Ct. 1977, U.S. Ct. Claims 1977, U.S. Ct. Appeals (5th cir.) 1978, U.S. Dist. Ct. (we. dist.) Tex. 1979, U.S. Supreme Ct. 1980; CPA, Tex. Tax specialist Peat, Marwick, Mitchell & Co., CPAs, Dallas, 1976-77; ptnr. Shannon, Porter, Johnson, Sutton and Greendyke Attys. at Law, San Angelo, Tex., 1977-87; judge 119th Dist. Ct. of Tex., 1987-99; pvt. practice Law Offices of John E. Sutton, 1999—. Treas. Good Shepherd Episcopal Ch., San Angelo, 1979-81; co-chmn. profl. divsn. United Way, San Angelo, 1980-82; trustee Angelo State U. Found., 1987-99, pres., 1988-91, 95-97, v.p., 1992-94, 98-99, sec.-treas., 1991-92. Fellow Tex. Bar Found.; mem. ABA, Tex. Bar Assn., Tex. Criminal Def. Lawyers Assn., Tom Green County Bar Assn. (sec.-treas. young lawyers 1977-78), AICPAs, Tex. Soc. CPAs (bd. dirs. 1980-87, pres. San Angelo chpt. 1980-81, mem. state exec. com. 1981-82, 86-87, state sec. 1986-87, chmn. profl. ethics com. 1985-86, Young CPA of Yr. 1984-85), Concho Valley Estate Planning Coun. (v.p. 1979-80, also dir.). Family and matrimonial, Criminal, Estate planning. Office: Law Office of John E Sutton 117 S Irving St San Angelo TX 76903-6419

SUTTON, JOHN F., JR., law educator, dean, lawyer; b. Alpine, Tex., Jan. 26, 1918; s. John F. and Pauline Irene (Elam) S.; m. Nancy Ewing, June 1, 1940; children: Joan Sutton Parr, John Ewing. JD, U. Tex., 1941. Bar: Tex. 1941, U.S. Dist. Ct. (we. dist.) Tex. 1947, U.S. Ct. Appeals (5th cir.) 1951, U.S. Supreme Ct. 1960. Assoc. Brooks, Napier, Brown & Matthews, San Antonio, 1941-42; spl. agt. FBI, Washington, 1942-45; assoc. Matthews, Nowlin, Macfarlane & Barrett, San Antonio, 1945-48; ptnr. Kerr, Gayer & Sutton, San Angelo, Tex., 1948-50, Sutton, Steib & Barr, San Angelo, 1951-57; prof. U. Tex.-Austin, 1957-65, William Stamps Farish prof., 1965-84, A.W. Walker centennial chair, 1984-88, emeritus, 1988—, dean Sch. Law, 1979-84. Editor: (with Wellborn) Materials on Evidence, 8th edit., 1996, (with Dzienkowski) Cases and Materials on Professional Responsibility of Lawyers, 1989, (with Schuwerk) Guideline to the Texas Disciplinary Rules of Professional Conduct, 1990, (with Dzienkowski) Cases and Materials on Professional Conduct, 2d edit., 2002; contbr. articles to profl. jours. Served to 1st lt. JAGC USAR, 1948-54. Fellow Am. Bar Found. (life), Tex. Bar Found. (life); mem. ABA (com. on ethics 1970-76), State Bar Tex. (com. on rules of profl. conduct, com. adminstrn. rules of evidence), Philos. Soc. Tex., Order of Coif, U. Tex. Club, Phi Delta Phi, San Angelo Country Club, North Austin Rotary (pres. 1969). Presbyterian. Home: 3830 Sunset Dr San Angelo TX 76904-5956 Office: U Tex Sch Law 727 E Dean Keeton St Austin TX 78705-3224

SUTTON, JOHN PAUL, lawyer; b. Youngstown, Ohio, July 24, 1934; m. Jane Williamson, Aug. 20, 1958; children— Julia, Susan, Elizabeth. BA, U. Va., 1956; JD, George Washington U., 1963. Bar: Calif. 1965. Patent examiner U.S. Patent Office, Washington, 1956, 59-62; law clk. U.S. Ct. Customs and Patent Appeals, Washington, 1962-64; assoc. Flehr, Hohbach, Test, Albritton & Herbert, San Francisco, 1964-68; ptnr. Limbach, Limbach & Sutton, San Francisco, 1969-91; spl. counsel Heller, Ehrman, White & McAuliffe, San Francisco, 1992-95; of counsel Medlin & Carroll, San Francisco, 1995, Bryan, Hinshaw & Barnet, San Francisco, 1996-99; sole practice, 2000—. Adj. instr. Practicing Law Inst., 1968-69; continuing edn. program Calif. State Bar, 1972, 75, U. Calif. Law Sch., Berkeley, 1975, 84. Contbr. articles to legal jours. Served with USNR, 1956-59. Mem. Calif. Patent Law Assn. (pres. 1975), San Francisco Patent Law Assn. (pres. 1976), State Bar Calif. (exec. com. patent sect. 1975-77), Fedn. Internationale des Consiels en Propriete Industrielle (pres. U.S. sec. 2003-). Am. Chem. Soc. Democrat. Episcopalian. Home and Office: 2421 Pierce St San Francisco CA 94115-1131

SUTTON, JOHN RICHARD, SR., lawyer; b. Front Royal, Va., Sept. 7, 1943; s. George Wilson and Edith Fox Sutton; m. Elaine Phillips, June 16, 1968; children: Nancy Elizabeth Sutton Howard, John Richard Jr., Emily Sutton Dezio. BS in Indsl. Rels., U. NC, 1966; JD, George Washington U., 1971. With state gift tax divsn. U.S. Treasury, 1971—72; ptnr. Sutton & Edmonds, Candler, NC, 1972—. Mem. Enka (NC) Adv. Coun.; deacon, trustee Hominy Bapt. Ch., Candler. Mem.: ABA, NC Bar Assn., Lions, Masons. Republican. Criminal, Family and matrimonial, General practice. Home: 20 Old Spring Dr Candler NC 28715 Office: Sutton & Edmonds PO Box 145 70 Pisgah Hwy Candler NC 28715 Office Fax: 828-667-0976. E-mail: jsutton@sutton-edmonds.com.

SUTTON, JOHNNY K. lawyer; b. June 1960; B in Internat. Bus., U. Tex., 1983, JD, 1987. Criminal trial prosecutor Harris County Dist. Atty. Office; asst. dist. atty. Harris County Dist. Atty.'s Office, 1987—95; criminal justice policy dir. Gov. George W. Bush, 1995—2000; assoc. dep. atty. gen. U.S. Dept. Justice, Washington, 2001; policy coord. Bush-Cheney Transition Team, Dept. of Justice; U.S. atty. We. Dist. Tex., 2001—. Avocation: baseball (played for the Longhorns, starting lef-fielder on 1983 Nat. Championship team). Office: 601 NW Loop 410 Ste 600 San Antonio TX 78216*

SUTTON, PAMELA DRU, lawyer; b. N.Y.C., Mar. 9, 1950; d. Marvin Laurence and Janet (Giblen) S.; m. Michel L. Stone, Feb. 13, 1988; 1 child, Elizabeth Sutton Stone. AB cum laude, Harvard U., 1972; JD, Bklyn. Law Sch., 1978. Bar: Fla., N.Y.; U.S. Dist. Ct. (no. dist.) Fla.; U.S. Tax Ct.; U.S. Ct. Appeals (11th cir.). Intern ACLU Children's Rights Project, N.Y.C., 1976-77; intern Criminal Divsn. Legal Aid Soc., Juvenile Divsn., N.Y.C., 1977-78; from intern to assoc. Greenfield & Baker, N.Y.C., 1977-78; staff atty. Legal Svcs. North Fla., Panama City, 1979-80; sole practice law Panama City, 1980-85; atty. Capital Divsn. Office of Pub. Defender, 14th Jud. Cir., Panama City, 1983-92; ptnr. Stone & Sutton, Panama City, 1985—. Mem. death penalty steering com. Fla. Pub. Defender Assn., Tallahassee, 1990-92; lectr. U.S. Navy & Marine JAG Officers Death Penalty Seminar, Camp LeJeune, N.C., 1992, Fla. Pub. Defender Assn. Death Penalty Confs., Tampa, Fla., 1992, 93, Fla. Assn. Criminal Defense Lawyers, 1993, Holy Nativity Episcopal Sch., 1995. Author: Note, Bklyn. Law Review, 1977; assoc. editor Bklyn. Law Review, 1977-78; co-author: (chpts) Florida Public Defender Association Death Penalty Manual, 1992, rev. 1993; featured on CBS-TV: 48 Hours, 1993. Pres. Bay County chpt. NOW, Panama City, 1992-94, 96-97. Recipient Guardian Ad Litem Atty. Pro Bono award State of Fla., 1993. Mem. ATLA, Fla. Acad. Trial Lawyers, Bay County Bar Assn. (pres. 1985). Democrat. Criminal, Family and matrimonial, Personal injury (including property damage). Office: Stone & Sutton 116 E 4th St Panama City FL 32401-3109

SUTTON, RICHARD LAUDER, lawyer; b. Dover, Del., July 4, 1935; s. Richard and Anna Kimber (Massey) S.; m. Violette Witwer, June 25, 1960; children: Jane Valentine Tidwell, Richard Mohler. AB with distinction, U. Del., 1957; LLB, Yale U., 1960. Bar: Del. 1961. Law clk. to Hon. Edwin D. Steel U.S. Dist. Ct., Wilmington, Del., 1960-61; assoc. Morris Nichols Arsht & Tunnell, Wilmington, 1961-65, ptnr., 1966-2000, of counsel. Antitrust and trade regulation com. U.S. C. of C., 1976-80, mem. council on governance, 1980-82. Chmn. Del. Gov.'s Higher Edn. Commn., 1976; treas., bd. dirs., mem. exec. com. Greater Wilmington Devel. Coun., 1970-82; trustee Wilmington Pub. Libr., 1974-96, Unidel Found., Inc., 2000—; bd. dirs. Grand Opera House, Inc., 1976-92, Am. Judicature Soc., 1995-99, U. Del. Libr. Assocs., 1981-99; chmn. William H. Heald Scholarship Fund. Mem. ABA, Am. Law Inst., Del. Bar Assn., Confrererie des Chevaliers du Tastevin, Soc. Colonial Wars, Wilmington Club, Wilmington Country Club, Pine Valley Golf Club, Vicmead Hunt Club, The Seminole, Royal and Ancient Golf Club, Phi Beta Kappa, Phi Kappa Phi, Omicron Delta Kappa, Phi Delta Phi. Home (Summer): 10 Barley Mill Dr Wilmington DE 19807-2218 Office: PO Box 1347 Wilmington DE 19899-1347 Home (Winter): 12378 Indian Road Seminole Landing North Palm Beach FL 33408

SUTTON, SAMUEL J. lawyer, educator, engineer; b. Chgo., July 21, 1941; s. Samuel J. and Elaine (Blossom) S.; m. Anne V. Sutton, Aug. 28, 1965; children: Paige, Jean, Leah, Jepson. BA in History and Philosophy, U. Ariz., 1964, BSEE, 1967; JD, George Washington U., 1969. Bar: Ariz. 1969, D.C. 1970, U.S. Ct. Appeals (fed. cir.) 1983. Patent atty. Gen. Electric Co., Washington, Phoenix, 1967-70; ptnr. Cahill, Sutton & Thomas, Phoenix, 1970-95, of counsel, 1995—. Prof. law Ariz. State U., Tempe, 1975—; expert witness Fed. Dist. Cts., 1983—; trial cons. to numerous lawyers, 1972—; arbitrator Am. Arbitration Assn., Phoenix, 1971—. Author: Patent Preparation, 1976, Intellectual Property, 1978, Art Law, 1988, Law, Science and Technology, 1991, Licensing Intangible Property, 1994, Commercial Torts, 1995, Patent Litigation, 1996, 120-hr. multimedia series on intellectual property, 1999—2003; pub. sculptures installed at Tanner Sq., Phoenix, Tucson Art Inst., Mobil Corp., Mesa, Ariz., Cox Devel. Co., Tempe, Ariz., Downtown Phoenix, Desert Bot. Garden, Phoenix, Gateway Ctr., Sedona Sculpture Garden, Construct Gallery, Phoenix. Chmn. air pollution hearing bd. City of Phoenix, Maracopa County, 1970-85. Recipient Patent prize Patent Resources Group, 1979, Publ. award IEEE, 1967, Genematus award U. Ariz., 1964, Disting. Achievement award Ariz. State U., 1980, Construct Sculpture prize, 1989. Avocation: large scale steel sculpture. Intellectual property, Patent, Trademark and copyright. Office: PO Box 32694 Phoenix AZ 85064-2694 E-mail: sam.sutton@asu.edu.

SUZUKI, NORMAN HITOSHI, lawyer; b. Honolulu, Dec. 5, 1935; s. Hajime and Mildred (Fujimoto) S.; m. Lois A. Tatsuguchi, Aug. 19, 1962; children: Grant T., Brandon A. BA, U. Mich., 1957; LLB, Harvard U., 1960. Bar: Hawaii 1960, U.S. Dist. Ct. Hawaii 1960, U.S. Ct. Appeals (9th cir.) 1962, U.S. Supreme Ct. 1974. Sole practice, Honolulu, 1960—; pres. Suzuki & Lee, Attys., Honolulu, 1990-93, Suzuki & Goo, Attys., Honolulu, 1993—. Served to capt. USAR, 1960-66. Mem. ABA, Hawaii Bar Assn. Corporate, general, Legislative, Probate (including wills, trusts). Home: 3517 Kahawalu Dr Honolulu HI 96817-1029 Office: Suzuki & Goo 1188 Bishop St Century Sq Suite 1805 Honolulu HI 96813

SUZUKI, YASUHIKO, law educator; b. Mishima, Japan, Sept. 6, 1936; arrived in U.S., 68; s. Heijo and Hiro Suzuki; m. Kyoko Teraizumi Suzuki, May 14, 1961; children: Iori, Anri, Claude. LLB, Chuo U., Tokyo, 1960; LLM, Georgetown U., 1972. V.p. Nissan Motor Corp., Gardena, Calif., 1968—85; chmn. bd. dirs. Pacific Trade & Investment Corp., Washington, 1985—90; prof. U. Va., Charlottesville, 1991—93, Showa Joshi U., Tokyo, 1994—96, George Mason U., Fairfax, Va., 1996—. Vice chmn. Automobile Importers Am., Washington, 1975—85. Author: Washington Lobby, 1990, The American Nation, 1999, The Constitution of the United States - The Evolving Constitution, 2000. Bd. dirs. Japanese C. of C., N.Y.C., 1978—85, Washington, 1979—85. Named to Automotive Hall of Fame, 1984; recipient cert. of recognition for outstanding contbns. and efforts, Humane Soc. of Washington, DC, 1980, Youth for Understanding, 1981. Mem.: Internat. Law Inst. Japan, Acad. Polit. Sci. Home: 31242 Avenida Terramar San Juan Capistrano CA 92675 Office: George Mason U 4400 University Dr Fairfax VA 22030-4444

SVALYA, PHILLIP GORDON, lawyer; b. Ferndale, Mich., June 28, 1943; s. John Michael and Ann Marie Svalya; children: Daniel Gordon, Karina Renee. BS, U.S. Naval Acad., Annapolis, Md., 1966; JD, U. Santa Clara, Calif., 1973. Bar: Calif. 1974, U.S. Dist. Ct. (no. dist.) Calif. 1974. Pvt. practice, Sunnyvale, Mountain View, Calif., 1974-81, Cupertino, Calif., 1981—. Officer, bd. dirs. Albanian Health Fund. Lt. USN, 1966-70, capt. USNR SEAL ret., 1970-91. Mem. ATLA, Calif. Bar Assn., Consumer Attys. of Calif., Santa Clara County Bar Assn., Sunnyvale/Cupertino Bar Assn., Underwater Demolition Team-SEAL Assn., Million Dollar Advocates Forum. Republican. Avocations: hiking, gardening. Personal injury (including property damage), Product liability. Office: Phillip G Svalya Inc 10455 Torre Ave Cupertino CA 95014-3203

SVEN, ROBERT, lawyer; b. Gjovik, Norway, June 3, 1968; s. Jan and Torill Sveen; m. Vibeke Elisabeth Ring Sveen, June 7, 1997; 1 child, Ise Helene Sveen. Can Jur, U. of Oslo, 1992. Bar: Norway 1995. Asst. Judge Adv. Gen., Oslo, 1993—94; sr. assoc. Law Firm Bahr, Oslo, 1994—2000; ptnr. Steenstrup Stordrange, 2000. Bd. mem. Findexa Group, Oslo, 2001—. Asst. JAG, 1993—94, Oslo. Avocation: travel. Mergers and acquisitions, Securities, Corporate, general. Home: Stasjons veien 35B 0772 Oslo Norway Office: Steenstrup Stordrange Stortings Gaten 22 Oslo 0123 Norway Business E-Mail: robert@steenstrup.no.

SWACKER, FRANK WARREN, lawyer; b. N.Y.C., May 18, 1922; m. Irene Maloney Michael; children: Carolyn, Frances, Michele, Ruth. BA, Union Coll., Schnectady, 1947; JD, U. Va., 1949; LLM in Internat. Law, NYU, 1961. Bar: Va. 1948, N.Y. 1950, Ohio 1962, Wis. 1969, D.C. 1977, Fla. 1991, U.S. Ct. Internat. Trade 1978, U.S. Supreme Ct. 1952. Pvt. practice, N.Y.C., 1949-54, 64-68, Washington, 1977-84, Clearwater, Fla., 1984-89, St. Petersburg, Fla., 1994—; atty. Caltex Petroleum Corp., N.Y.C., 1955-60, Marathon Oil Co., Ohio, 1961-63; counsel Shearman & Sterling, N.Y.C., 1964—67; internat. counsel Allis-Chalmers Corp., Milw., 1968-78; sr. mem. Swacker & Assocs., P.C., Springfield, Va., 1980—84, chmn., pres. firm, sr. mem. Largo, Fla., 1989-93; dir. ATM CardPay, Largo, Fla., 1993-94; vice chmn. Lasergate Sys., Inc., 1995-99. Spl. asst. dep. atty. gen. State of N.Y., 1950; govtl. adviser U.S., P.I., Algeria; lectr. Ohio No. U., 1962, N.Y. World Trade Inst., 1976; adj. prof. Stetson U. Coll. Law, St. Petersburg, Fla., 1996-2000, LLM internat. adv. coun., 1997—. Author: Business International Guide for Going Global, 1999; co-author: World Trade Without Barriers: World Trade Organization and Dispute Resolution, 1995, vol. 2, 1996; co-editor, contbr. Bus. and Legal Aspects of Latin American Trade and Investment, 1977, Reference Manual on Doing Business with Latin America, 1979; contbr. articles to legal jours. Mem. internat. bus. adv. bd. U. So. Fla., 1993-94. Lt. (j.g.) USN, 1943-46, WWII. Mem. ABA (rec. 1978, internat. comml. arbitration com. 1991—), Nat. Law Inst., Am. Arbitration Assn. (panel experts), World Intellectual Property Orgn. (arbitration panel). Corporate, general, Alternative dispute resolution, Antitrust. E-mail: integra10@aol.com.

SWAN, ALAN CHARLES, law educator; b. Kalimpong, West Bengal, India, Dec. 29, 1933; came to U.S., 1945; s. Charles Lundeen and Kathleen Vivian (Doucette) S.; m. Mary Joe Smith, Aug. 28, 1954; children—Kathleen Jeanette, Amalie Christine, Alan Charles. B.A., Albion Coll., 1954; J.D., U. Chgo., 1957. Bar: N.Y. 1958. Assoc. Milbank, Tweed, Hadley & McCloy, N.Y.C., 1957-61; asst. gen. counsel AID, Washington, 1961-66; asst. v.p. U. Chgo., professorial lectr. Grad. Sch. Bus., 1966-72; prof. law U. Miami, Coral Gables, Fla., 1972— ; mem. Nat. Lawyers Com. for Soviet Jewry, 1971-80. Author: The Regulation of International Business and Economic Relations, 2d edit., 2001; contbr. articles to profl. jours. Trustee Plymouth Congregational Ch., Miami, 1998-2001; mem. Miami Com. on Fgn. Relations, 1976— , sec. of state adv. com. on pvt. internat. law, 1995—. Mem. Am. Law Inst, ABA, Am. Soc. Internat. Law, Internat. Law Assn., Fla. Bar Assn. Democrat. Home: 14901 SW 82nd Ave Miami FL 33158-1906 Office: U Miami Sch Law Coral Gables FL 33124 E-mail: aswan@law.miami.edu.

SWAN, GEORGE STEVEN, law educator; b. St. Louis; BA, Ohio State U., 1970; JD, U. Notre Dame, 1974; LLM, U. Toronto, 1976, SJD, 1983. Bar: Ohio 1974, U.S. Dist. Ct. (so. dist.) Ohio 1975, U.S. Supreme Ct. 1987, U.S. Ct. Appeals (6th and 11th cirs.) 1993, U.S. Ct. Appeals (10th cir.) 1994, D.C. 1997, Ga. 1997, U.S. Dist. Ct. (no. dist.) Ga. 1997, Fla. 1997, Minn. 1998, Nebr. 1998, N.D. 1998, U.S. Ct. Appeals (7th cir.) 1998, La. 1999, Mass. 1999; ChFC, CLU, CFP. Asst. atty. gen. State of Ohio, Columbus, 1974-75; jud. clk. Supreme Ct. Ohio, Columbus, 1976-78; asst. prof. Del. Law Sch., Wilmington, 1980-83, assoc. prof., 1983-84; prof. law St. Thomas U. Law Sch., Miami, Fla., 1984-88; jud. clk. U.S. Ct. Appeals (7th cir.), Chgo., 1988-89; assoc. prof. N.C. Agrl. & Tech. State U., Greensboro, 1989—. Vis. prof. John Marshall Law Sch., Atlanta, 1996—97, 2000—01. Contbr. articles to law jours. Mem. Ohio State Bar Assn., D.C. Bar, State Bar Ga., Fla. Bar, Mass. Bar Assn., Nebr. State Bar Assn., La. State Bar Assn., N.D. State Bar Assn., Soc. of Fin. Svc. Profls., Fin. Planning Assn., Am. Polit. Sci. Assn. Office: Merrick Hall 1601 E Market St Greensboro NC 27411

SWANKIN, DAVID ARNOLD, lawyer, consumer advocate; b. Boston, Jan. 18, 1934; s. Max and Anne (Rotefsky) S.; m. Jeanne Phyllis Herrick; 1 dau., Sheryl. AB, Brandeis U., 1954; MS, U. Wis., 1957; JD, George Washington U., 1962. Mgmt. intern U.S. Dept. Labor, Washington, 1957-60, spl. asst. to asst. sec. labor, 1961-63, dep. asst. sec. labor, 1967; dir. Bur. Labor Standards, 1967-68; exec. sec. Pres.'s Consumer Adv. Council, Washington, 1964; exec, dir. Pres's Com. on Consumer Interests, Washington, 1965-66; Washington rep. Consumer's Union, 1969-71; exec. dir. Consumer Interests Found., 1971-73; sr. partner Swankin & Turner, 1973—. Pres. Citizen Advocacy Ctr. 1994—; cons. U.S. Dept. Labor; pres. Citizen Advocacy Ctr., 1994—. Mem. president's coun. Brandeis U., 1968-69; mem. PEW Health Profls. Commn., 1997-98. Served with AUS., 1954-56. Recipient Jump award U.S. Govt., 1969 Home: 300 N Cherry St Falls Church VA 22046-3522 Office: 1400 16th St NW Washington DC 20036-2217 Business E-Mail: davidswankin@cacenter.org.

SWANN, BARBARA, lawyer; b. N.Y., Sept. 15, 1950; d. George Arthur. BA summa cum laude, Montclair State U., 1988; JD, Rutgers Law, 1992. Bar: N.J. 1992, D.C. 1994, N.Y. 1995, Calif. 2000, U.S. Dist. Ct. N.J. 1992, U.S. Ct. Appeals (3rd cir.) 1994, U.S. Dist. Ct. N.Y. 1996, Calif. 2000. Correspondent The Associate Press, Newark, N.J., 1974-80; reporter, bureau chief The Hudson Dispatch, Union City, N.J., 1973-80; editorial page editor The Paterson (N.J.) News, 1980-81; v.p., acct. supr. Gerald Freeman, Inc., Clifton, N.J., 1981-86; pres. LePore Assoc., Inc., West Caldwell, N.J., 1986-89; law clk. to Hon. Robert N. Wilentz N.J. Supreme Ct., 1992-93; law clk. to Hon. Leonard I. Garth U.S. Ct. Appeals (3rd cir.), 1993-94; assoc. Cahill, Gordon & Reindel, N.Y., 1994-97; liaison Republic of Ga. ABA Cen. and East European Law Initiative, 1997-98, media law specialist, 1998-2000; exec. dir. Internat. Sr. Lawyers Project, N.Y.C., 2000—02; mem. adj. faculty U. N.Mex., 2003—. Editor-in-chief: Rutgers Computer & Technology Law Jour., 1991-92. Founding trustee Ctr. for Children's Advocacy, Riverdale, N.J. 1994—. Mem. ABA, Assn. of the Bar of the City of New York, N.J. State Bar Assn., N.Y. County Lawyers' Assn. Am. Inn of Ct., D.C. Bar Assn., State Bar Calif. General civil litigation, Constitutional, Libel. E-mail: swann2002@email.msn.com.

SWANSON, ARTHUR DEAN, lawyer; b. Onida, S.D., Apr. 19, 1934; s. Obert W. and Mary I. (Barnum) S.; m. Paula Swanson, Aug. 22, 1965 (div. Feb. 1984); children: Shelby, Dean, Sherry; m. Ann Swanson, Aug. 21, 1989. BA, Wash. State U., 1956; JD, U. Wash., 1963. Bar: Wash. 1963. Dep. prosecutor King County, Seattle, 1964-65; ct. commr. Renton and Issaquah Dist. Cts., Wash., 1966-68; pvt. practice law Renton, Wash., 1965—. Lectr. various orgns.; former counsel Wash. State Law Enforcement Assn., Wash. State Dep. Sheriff's Assn. Served with Fin. Corps, U.S. Army, 1956-58. Named one of Best Lawyers Am., 1991-92, 93-94, 95-96, 97-98, 99-2000, 2001—. Fellow Am. Coll. Trial Lawyers; mem. Wash. State Bar Assn. (past sec. trial sect.), Seattle-King County Bar Assn. (bd. trustees 1977-80), Assn. Trial Lawyers Am., Wash. State Trial Lawyers Assn. (past pres.), Am. Bd. Trial Advs. (bd. dirs., pres. Wash. state chpt. 1995-96), Damage Attys. Roundtable (pres. 1998-99). Democrat. Avocation: tennis. State civil litigation, Insurance, Personal injury (including property damage). Office: 4512 Talbot Rd S Renton WA 98055-6216 E-mail: adswanson@aol.com.

SWANSON, LESLIE MARTIN, JR., lawyer; b. Yakima, Wash., May 16, 1940; s. Leslie Martin and Eleanor Louise (Morris) S.; children: Mark, Carl, Todd. BA, Augustana Coll., Rock Island, Ill., 1961; MA, Claremont Grad. U., Calif., 1964; JD, U. Oreg., 1966. Bar: Oreg. 1966, Wash. 1993, U.S. Dist. Ct. Oreg. 1966, U.S. Ct. Appeals (9th cir.) 1969, U.S. Supreme Ct. 1978. Ptnr. Harrang, Swanson, Long & Watkinson, Eugene, Oreg., 1966-85; pres., shareholder Swanson & Walters, Eugene, 1985-92; pvt. practice Les Swanson Jr., Atty. at Law, Portland, Oreg., 1992—. Assoc. prof. and adj. prof. law U. Oreg., Eugene; prof. humanities Portland State U.; consul for Iceland, 2001—. Mem. Oreg. State Bd. Higher Edn., 1989-97, pres., 1994-96; mem. Oreg. Arts Commn., 1980-83; v.p. bd. visitors U. Oreg. Sch. Law, 1987-89; mem. bd. visitors arts and humanities Claremont Grad. U. Mem. Lane County Bar Assn. (pres. 1983-84), Am. Law Inst. Personal injury (including property damage), Product liability. Office: Neuberger 239 Portland State Univ PO Box 751 Portland OR 97207-0751 E-mail: lswanson@pdx.com.

SWANSON, ROBERT LEE, lawyer; b. Fond du Lac, Wis., July 15, 1942; s. Walfred S. and Edna F. (Kamp) S.; m. Mary Ruth Francis, Aug. 19, 1967; children: Leigh Alexandra, Mitchell Pearson. BS, U. Wis., 1964; JD, Valparaiso U., 1970; LLM, Boston U., 1979. Bar: Wis. 1970, U.S. Dist. Ct. (ea. dist.) Wis. 1970, U.S. Dist. Ct. (we. dist.) Wis. 1974, U.S. Dist. Ct. (we. dist.) Okla. 2002, U.S. Tax Ct. 1981, U.S. Dist. Ct. (cen.) Ill. 1988, Okla. 1999, U.S. Ct. Appeals (7th cir.) 1999. Atty. Kasdorf, Dahl, Lewis & Swietlik, Milw., 1970-73; atty., ptnr. Wartman, Wartman & Swanson, Ashland, Wis., 1973-80; city atty. City of Ashland, Wis., 1976-80; atty., ptnr. DeMark, Kolbe & Brodek, Racine, Wis., 1980-95; ptnr. Hartig, Bjelajac, Swanson & Koenen, Racine, 1995-99; contract atty. Okla. Indigent Def. Sys., Lincoln County, 2000—02; pvt. practice Robert Lee Swanson Law Office, 2000—; contract atty. Okla. Criminal Defense Lawyers Assn., 2002—. Lectr. civil rights and discrimination laws, 1980—; lectr.bus. law Cardinal Strich U., 1996—99, U. Wis.-Parkside, 1997—99; participating atty. Alliance Def. Fund, 2000—; legal columnist Burlington Std. Press, 1991—95, Wis. Restaurant Assn. Mag., 1986. Bd. trustees City of Chandler Aviation Authority; chmn. Ashland County Rep. Party, 1976—79; v.p., bd. dirs. Meml. Med. Ctr., Ashland, 1975—80; bd. trustees Kendrick Mcpl. Authority, Okla., 2001—; bd. dirs. Chandler Airport Authority, 2003—; vice comdr. USCG Aux. Bayfield (Wis.) Flotilla, 1975—81; vol. atty. ACLU Wis., 1975—90. 1st lt. U.S. Army, 1964—66. Named one of Outstanding Young Men of Am., Jaycees, 1978; recipient Disting. Achievement in Art and Sci. of Advocacy award Internat. Acad. Trial Lawyers, 1970. Mem. Racine County Bar Assn. (bd. dirs. 1985-89), Wis. Acad. Trial Lawyers, Def. Rsch. Inst., Am. Hockey Assn. U.S. (coach, referee 1983-90), Am. Legion, Okla. Limousin Assn. (parliamentarian, bd.

dirs. 2002—). Avocations: softball, volleyball, hockey. General civil litigation, Corporate, general, General practice. Home: RR 1 Box 478 Stroud OK 74079-9723 Office: 109 1/2 W 9th St Chandler OK 74834 E-mail: rswanson@brightok.net.

SWANSON, WALLACE MARTIN, lawyer; b. Fergus Falls, Minn., Aug. 22, 1941; s. Marvin Walter and Mary Louise (Lindsey) S.; children: Kristen Lindsey, Eric Munger. BA with honors, U. Minn., 1962; LL.B. with honors, So. Methodist U., 1965. Bar: Tex. 1965. Assoc. Coke & Coke, Dallas, 1965-70; ptnr. firm Johnson & Swanson, Dallas, 1970-88; prin. Wallace M. Swanson, P.C., Rice, Tex., 1988—; chmn., CEO Ace Cash Express Inc., Irving, Tex., 1987-88, State St. Capital Corp., 1990—. Served with USNR, 1960-65. Mem. Tex. Bar Found., State Bar Tex. (securities com. 1972-86, chmn. 1978-80, coun. bus. law sect. 1980-86), Crescent Club. Methodist. Corporate, general, Mergers and acquisitions, Property, real (including real estate development, water). Address: 6234 FM 879 Ennis TX 75119

SWANSTEIN, JERKER, lawyer; b. Helsingborg, Sweden, Feb. 9, 1952; s. Börje and Marianne Swanstein; m. Elisabeth Swanstein, Oct. 1, 1980; children: Filippa, Olivia, Axel, Hugo. LLM, U. Lund, Sweden, 1978, BA, 1980. Lectr. faculty law U. Lund, 1978—86; ptnr. Advokatfirman Carler, Helsingborg, Sweden, 1980—95, Holm Advokatbyrå, Helsingborg, 1996—. Bd. mem. Thomson Multimedia Scand., Helsingborg, S Reg AB, Helsingborg, Handelsbanken, Helsingborg, The C. of C., Malmö, Sweden. Author: Comparative Agency Law, 1979; co-author: Agency and Distribution Agreem in Sweden, 1991. Mayor Helsingborg City, 1991—94; chmn. The Conservative Party, Skåne, Sweden, 1999—. Mem.: Swedish Aquacultural Assn. (chmn.). Corporate, general, Mergers and acquisitions, Sports. Office: Holm & Co Advokatbyrå KB Drottninggatan 7 252 21 Helsingborg Sweden

SWARTZ, MARK LEE, lawyer; b. Amesbury, Mass., May 17, 1954; s. Bernard Jerome and Evelyn Vivian Swartz. BS, U. Mass., 1976; JD, Case Western U., 1979. Bar: Mass. 1979, Ohio 1979, U.S. Dist. Ct. Mass. 1980, U.S. Ct. Appeals (1st cir.) 1980. Pub. defender Essex County, Mass., 1980-83; pvt. practice Amesbury, Mass., 1980—. Atty. Amesbury Housing Rehab. Program, 1980-81, Merrimac Housing Authority, Merrimac, 1980-86, Amesbury Housing Authority, 1980-86. Mem. Greater Newburyport Bar Assn., Alliance for Amesbury, Phi Beta Kappa, Phi Kappa Phi. Republican. Avocations: reading, dancing, travel, chess, walking. Commercial, consumer (including collections, credit), Probate (including wills, trusts), Property, real (including real estate development, water). Home: PO Box 185 Amesbury MA 01913-0004 Office: 1 School St Amesbury MA 01913-2812

SWARTZ, MELVIN JAY, lawyer, writer; b. Boston, July 21, 1930; s. Jack M. and Rose (Rosenberg) S.; children: Julianne, Jonathan Samuel. BA, Syracuse U., 1953; LLB, Boston U., 1957. Bar: N.Y. 1959, Ariz. 1961. Assoc. Alfred S. Julian, N.Y.C., 1957-59; ptnr. Finks & Swartz, Youngtown, Sun City, Phoenix, 1961-70, Swartz & Jeckel, P.C., Sun City, Youngtown, Scottsdale, Ariz., 1971-82. Author: Don't Die Broke, A Guide to Secure Retirement, 1974, rev. edit., 2000, (book and cassettes) Keep What You Own, 1989, rev. edit., 2000, Retire Without Fear, 1995; columnist News-Sun, Sun City, 1979-83; author column Swartz on Aging. Bd. dirs. Valley of the Sun Sch. for Retarded Children, 1975-79. Mem. ABA, Ariz. Bar Assn., N.Y. Bar Assn., Maricopa County Bar Assn., Scottsdale Bar Assn., Ctrl. Ariz. Estate Planning Coun., Masons (Phoenix). Jewish. Estate planning, Probate (including wills, trusts), Estate taxation. Office: 3416 N 44th St Unit 22 Phoenix AZ 85018-6044 E-mail: swartzmj@worldnet.att.net.

SWARTZBAUGH, MARC L. lawyer; b. Urbana, Ohio, Jan. 3, 1937; s. Merrill L. and Lillian K. (Hill) S.; m. Marjory Anne Emhardt, Aug. 16, 1958 (deceased May 20, 2000); children: Marc Charles, Kathleen Marie, Laura Kay. BA magna cum laude, Wittenberg Coll., 1958; LLB magna cum laude, U. Pa., 1961. Bar: Ohio 1961, U.S. Dist. Ct. (no. dist.) Ohio 1962, U.S. Claims Ct. 1991, U.S. Ct. Appeals (6th cir.) 1970, U.S. Ct. Appeals (3d cir.) 1985, U.S. Ct. Appeals (Fed. cir.) 1995, U.S. Supreme Ct. 1973. Law clk. to judge U.S. Ct. Appeals (3d cir.), Phila., 1961-62; assoc. Jones, Day, Reavis & Pogue, Cleve., 1962-69, ptnr., 1970-98; ret., 1998; cons., 1998—. Note editor U. Pa. Law Rev., 1960-61; co-author: Ohio Legal Ethics, 2001. Co-chmn. Suburban Citizens for Open Housing, Shaker Heights, Ohio, 1966; v.p. Lomond Assn., Shaker Heights, 1965-68; trustee The Dance Ctr., Cleve., 1980-83; amb. People to People Internat., 1986; chmn. legal divsn. Cleve. campaign United Negro Coll. Fund, 1989-96; tutor Cleve. Reads, 2003—. Mem. ABA (litigation sect., sr. lawyers divsn.), Fed. Bar Assn., Ohio Bar Assn., Cleve. Bar Assn., Rowfant Club, Order of Coif, Beta Theta Pi. Democrat. Avocations: poetry, painting, music, skiing, photography. Professional liability. Office: Jones Day Reavis & Pogue N Point 901 Lakeside Ave E Cleveland OH 44114-1190

SWEARER, WILLIAM BROOKS, lawyer; b. Hays, Kans. Grad., Princeton U., 1951; law degree, U. Kans., 1955. Bar: Kans. 1955. Pvt. practice, Hutchinson, Kans., 1955—; ptnr. Martindell, Swearer & Shaffer, LLP, Hutchinson, 1955—. Mem. Kans. Bd. Discipline for Attys., 1979-92, chmn., 1987-92. With U.S. Army, 1952-53, Korea. Mem. ABA (ho. of dels. 1995-2000), Am. Bar Found. (state chair 1998-2002), Kans. Bar Assn. (pres. 1992-93, various offices, mem. coms.), Kans. Assn. Sch. Attys. (pres. 1989-90), Reno County Bar Assn. Corporate, general, Education and schools, Probate (including wills, trusts). Office: PO Box 1907 Hutchinson KS 67504-1907 E-mail: wbs@martindell-law.com.

SWEENEY, ASHER WILLIAM, state supreme court justice; b. Canfield, Ohio, Dec. 11, 1920; s. Walter William and Jessie Joan (Kidd) S.; m. Bertha M. Englert, May 21, 1945; children: Randall W., Ronald R., Garland A., Karen M. Student, Youngstown U., 1939-42; LL.B., Duke U., 1948. Bar: Ohio 1949. Practiced law, Youngstown, Ohio, 1949-51; judge adv. gen. Dept. Def., Washington, 1951-65; chief Fed. Contracting Agy., Cin., 1965-68; corp. law, 1968-77; justice Ohio Supreme Ct., Columbus, 1977—. Democratic candidate for Sec. of State Ohio, 1958. Served with U.S. Army, 1942-46; col. Res. 1951-68. Decorated Legion of Merit, Bronze Star; named to Army Hall of Fame Ft. Benning, Ga., 1981 Mem. Ohio Bar Assn., Phi Delta Phi. Democrat. Home: 6690 Drake Rd Cincinnati OH 45243-2706 Office: Ohio Supreme Ct 30 E Broad St Fl 3D Columbus OH 43215-3414

SWEENEY, CLAYTON ANTHONY, lawyer, business executive; b. Pitts., Oct. 20, 1931; s. Denis Regis and Grace Frances (Roche) S.; m. Sally Dimond, Oct. 4, 1958; children: Sharon, Lorrie, Maureen, Clayton Anthony, Tara, Megan. BS, Duquesne U., 1957, LLB, 1962. Bar: Pa. 1962, U.S. Supreme Ct. 1968. Supr. transp. claims H.J. Heinz Co., Pitts., 1955-57; mgr. market research Murray Corp. Am., Pitts., 1957-62; ptnr. Buchanan, Ingersoll, Rodewald, Kyle and Buerger, Pitts., 1962-78; sr. v.p. Allegheny Ludlum Industries, Inc., Pitts., 1978-81; exec. v.p., chief adminstrv. officer Allegheny Internat., Inc., Pitts., 1981-84, vice chmn., 1984-85; ptnr., mng. dir. Dickie, McCamey & Chilcote, Pitts., 1986-98, also bd. dirs.; pres. Sweeney Metz Fox McGrann & Schermer, 1998-2000; with Schnader Harrison Segal & Lewis, LLP, Pitts., 2000—. Bd. dirs. Wilkinson Sword Group Ltd., U.K., Landmark Savs. and Loan Assn., Liquid Air N.Am., Halbouty Energy Co., Koppers Holding Corp., Koppers Industries, Inc., Schaefer Mfg., Inc., Schaefer Marine, Inc., Schaefer Equipment, Inc.; adj. prof. Duquesne U. Sch. Law; lectr. Pa. Bar Inst.; mem. procedural rules com. Supreme Ct. Pa. Named Disting. Alumnus Sch. Law Duquesne U., 1997. Bd. dirs. Met. Pitts. Pub. Broadcasting, Inc., Diocesan Sch. Bd., Roman Cath. Diocese Pitts., Toner Inst., Christian Assocs. of Southwestern Pa., Wesley Inst., Inc., Jr. Achievement S.W. Pa., YMCA Western Pa.; chmn. Seton Hill Coll.; mem. St. Thomas More Sch. Bd., Bethel Park, Pa.; chmn. St. Francis Med. Ctr., St. Francis Health System; chmn. bd. DePaul Inst. With U.S. Army, 1953-55. Named one of 100 Most Disting. Living Alumni Duquesne U. Century Club, 1978 Mem. Acad. Trial Lawyers Allegheny County, ABA, Pa. Bar Assn., St. Thomas More Soc. Corporate, general, Finance, Health. Home: 232 Thornberry Cir Pittsburgh PA 15234-1025 Office: Schnader Harrison Segal & Lewis LLP Ste 2700 Fifth Ave Pl 120 Fifth Ave Pittsburgh PA 15222-3010 E-mail: csweeney@schnader.com.

SWEENEY, DEIDRE ANN, lawyer; b. Hackensack, N.J., Mar. 17, 1953; d. Thomas Joseph and Robin (Thwaites) S. AB cum laude, Mt. Holyoke Coll., 1975; JD, Fordham U., 1978. Assoc. Curtis, Mallet-Prevost, Colt & Mosle, N.Y.C., 1978—84, Eaton & Van Winkle, N.Y.C., 1984—86; ptnr. Jacobs, Persinger & Parker, N.Y.C., 1986—2002; of counsel McCanliss and Early, N.Y.C., 2002—. Mem. Hi-Five Scholarship com. CUNY, 2000—. Mem. Assn. of Bar of City of N.Y. (uniform state laws com. 1982-85). Estate planning, Probate (including wills, trusts), Estate taxation.

SWEENEY, EMILY MARGARET, prosecutor; b. Cleve., May 2, 1948; d. Mark Elliot and Neydra (Ginsburg) Mirsky; m. Patrick Anthony Sweeney, Dec. 30, 1983; 1 child, Margaret Anne. BA, Case Western Res. U., 1970; JD, Cleve. Marshall Coll. Law, 1981. Bar: Ohio 1981. Tchr. English Cleve. Pub. Schs., 1970; plant mgr. Union Gospel Press Pub. Co., Cleve., 1971-73; publ. specialist Cleve. State U., 1973-82; asst. U.S. atty. Dept. Justice, Cleve., 1982—; U.S. atty. Cleve., 1993—2002. Precinct committeeman, Woodmere, Ohio, 1978; mem. Atty. Gen.'s Adv. Com. U.S. Attys., 1993—96, 1998—99, chmn. office mgmt. and budget subcom., 1993—2001, mem. asset forfeiture, civil issues, controlled substances and drug demand reduction, LECC/victim witness subcoms., 1993—2001; chmn. law enforcement coord. com. No. Dist. Ohio, 1993—. Recipient Eddy award for graphic design, 1977, Spl Achievement award U.S. Dept. Justice, 1985. Mem.: Fed. Bar Assn. Democrat. Office: US Atty's Office 1800 Bank One Ctr 600 Superior Ave E Ste 1800 Cleveland OH 44114-2600

SWEENEY, FRANCIS E. state supreme court justice; b. Jan. 26, 1934; married; 4 children. BSBA, Xavier U., 1956; JD, Cleve.-Marshall Law Sch., 1963. Profl. football player Ottawa Rough Riders, Ont., Can., 1956-58; mem. legal dept. Allstate Ins. Co., Cleve., 1958-63; asst. prosecuting atty. Cuyahoga County, Cleve., 1963-70; judge Cuyahoga County Ct. of Common Pleas, Cleve., 1970-88; judge (8th cir.) U.S. Ct. Appeals, Cleve., 1988-92; justice Ohio Supreme Ct., Columbus, 1992—. With U.S. Army, 1957-58. Recipient Legion of Honor award Xavier U., 1956, Outstanding Jud. Svc. award Ohio Supreme Ct., 1972-85, Alumnus of Yr. award Xavier U., 1977. Office: Ohio Supreme Ct 30 E Broad St Fl 3 Columbus OH 43215-0001

SWEENEY, JAMES RAYMOND, lawyer; b. Chgo., Feb. 19, 1928; s. John Francis and Mae J. (McDonald) S.; m. Rhoda W. Davis, May 15, 1987; children from previous marriage: Margaret Elizabeth, John Francis, Thomas Edward. BS, U. Notre Dame, 1950; JD, Northwestern U., 1956. Bar: Ill. 1956. With firm Schroeder, Hofgren, Brady & Wegner, Chgo., 1956-61; ptnr. Hofgren, Wegner, Allen, Stellman & McCord, Chgo., 1962-71, Coffee, Wetzel, Sweeney, Chgo., 1971-72, Coffee & Sweeney, 1972-76, Mason, Kolehmainen, Rathburn & Wyss, Chgo., 1976-82, Mann, McWilliams, 1983-86, McWilliams Mann, 1986-89, Lee, Mann, Smith, McWilliams & Sweeney, 1989-91, Lee, Mann, Smith, McWilliams, Sweeney & Ohlson, 1991—2002; dir. ctr. intellectual property law John Marshall Law Sch., 1998—; ptnr. Barnes & Thornburg, 2003—. Commr. for disbarment matters Ill. Supreme Ct., 1963-73; mem. hearing div. Atty. Registration and Discipline Commn., 1974-77, chmn. commn. 1983-90; chmn. Ctr. for Intellectual Property Law adv. bd. John Marshall Law Sch., 1997-99. Bd. dirs., sec. Highland Park (Ill.) Hosp., 1972-79. Served as lt. (j.g.) USN, 1950-53; lt. comdr. Res. ret. Mem. ABA (coun. patent, trademark and copyright sect., sec. 1978-82), Ill. State Bar (assembly 1990-96), Chgo. Bar Assn. (sec. 1977-79), Bar Assn. 7th Cir., Intellectual Property Law Assn. Chgo., Patent Law Assn. Chgo. (pres. 1974), The Lawyers Club, Skokie (Ill.) Country Club, Union League Club. Patent, Trademark and copyright, Intellectual property. Home: 505 N Lake Shore Dr Chicago IL 60611-3427 Office: Barnes & Thornburg 209 S La Salle St Ste 410 Chicago IL 60604-1203 also: John Marshall Law Sch 315 S Plymouth Ct Chicago IL 60604-3969 E-mail: 7Sweeney@jmls.edu.

SWEENEY, JAMES STEPHEN, lawyer; b. N.Y.C., Aug. 7, 1951; s. James Joseph Sweeney and Helen Francis Callahan; m. Sharleen Ann Bickel, Oct. 25, 1987; children: Shannon, Colin. BS in Fgn. Svc., Georgetown U., 1972; JD, Bklyn. Law Sch., 1976. Bar: N.Y. 1977, Calif. 1977, U.S. Dist. Ct. (so. dist.) Ct. 1986. Pub. defender Orange County Pub. Defender's Office, Santa Ana, Calif., 1977—80; solo practitioner Mission Viejo, Calif., 1980—. Mem.: South Orange County Bar Assn. (bd. dirs. 1983—90). Avocations: sailing, kayaking, hiking. Office: 26300 La Alameda # 360 Mission Viejo CA 92691 Office Fax: 949-582-0030.

SWEENEY, JOHN J(OSEPH), lawyer; b. N.Y.C., Dec. 28, 1924; s. John J. and Rose H. (Galligan) S.; m. Rita V. Colleran, Aug. 27, 1955; children: Jean Maria, John J., Peter F., Thomas P., Michael J., Roseanne. LLB, St. John's U., 1951, BA, 1952. Bar: N.Y., 1951. Vol. lawyer Felony Ct. Legal Aid Soc., N.Y.C., 1951-52; asst. gen. counsel U.S. Trucking Corp., N.Y.C., 1952-55; pvt. practice N.Y.C., 1955-83; editor. N.Y. State Tax Monitor, N.Y.C., 1983-84; mortgage real estate loan officer N.Y.C., 1985-90; tchr. DeWitt Clinton H.S., N.Y.C., 1990-92; pvt. practice Scarsdale, 1992—. Spl. master Supreme Ct., N.Y. County; pre-trial master Civil Ct., N.Y. County; commr., referee, receiver and guardian ad litem Supreme and Surrogate's Ct.; arbitrator Am. Arbitration Assn., Civil Ct., N.Y. County, Better Bus. Bur.; arbitrator, mediator N.Y. State Mediation Bd.; litigator local, state, and fed. cts. Pres. Arthur Manor Assn., Scarsdale, 1970-73, Cath. Big Bros., N.Y.C., 1971-73; mem. nominating com. Village Trustee, Scarsdale, 1970-76, mem. nominating com. sch. bd., 1973-76; mem. Scarsdale Hist. Soc., 1980—. With U.S. Army, 1943-46. Decorated Silver star, two Bronze stars, two Purple Hearts and three Battle stars, Combat Infantry Badge. Mem. Guild Cath. Lawyers (pres. 1969-71), Scarsdale Antiques Running Club (pres. 1984-86). Democrat. Avocations: marathon running, tennis, platform tennis, softball, writing. General civil litigation, Product liability. Home and Office: 223 Boulevard Scarsdale NY 10583-5832

SWEENEY, JOHN LAWRENCE, lawyer; b. Staten Island, N.Y., Jan. 5, 1962; s. Lawrence Patrick and Lauretta (Kronen) S.; m. Karen Anne Hrebenak, Aug. 26, 1988; children: Conor, Lauren, Devin, Pearse. BA, Yale U., 1984; JD magna cum laude, Seton Hall U., 1990; LLM in Taxation, NYU, 1993. Bar: N.J. 1990, U.S. Dist. Ct. N.J. 1990, N.Y. 1991, U.S. Tax Ct. 1995. Assoc. Connell, Foley & Geiser, Roseland, N.J., 1990-92, Lampf, Lipkind, Prupis & Pettegrew, West Orange, N.J., 1992-93; atty. pvt. practice, Morristown, N.J., 1993-2000; pntr. Sweeney & Flanagan, LLC, 2001—. Editor, Peapack-Gladstone Gazette, 2000—. Interview supr. Yale Alumni Schs. Com., 1991—; charter mem. Seton Hall Prep Hall of Fame Com., 1984-94; councilman, Borough of Peapack-Gladstone, 2001—. Named to Seton Hall Prep Hall of Fame, 2002. Mem. N.J. Bar Assn., N.Y. Bar Assn., Morris County Bar Assn., Yale Club Ctrl. N.J. (trustee 1991-94, 1997—, sec. 1997-99, pres. 1999-2001), New Providence Lions Club Internat., KC (fin. sec. 2000—). Estate planning, Probate (including wills, trusts), Taxation, general. Home: 14 Farm Cottage Rd Gladstone NJ 07934-2007 Office: 51 Dumont Pl Morristown NJ 07960-4125 E-mail: sweenlaw@aol.com.

SWEENEY, NEAL JAMES, lawyer; b. Paterson, N.J., Nov. 1, 1957; s. Bernard Thomas and Mary Agnes (Keneally) S.; m. Mary Elizabeth Finocchiaro, Oct. 27, 1984; children: Daniel Fulton, Clare Kenneally, Moira Ann. BA in History and Polit Sci., Rutgers U., 1979; JD, George Washington U., 1982. Bar: Ga. 1982, U.S. Dist. Ct. (no. dist.) Ga. 1982, U.S. Dist. Ct. (no. dist.) Tex. 1982, U.S. Claims Ct. 1984, U.S. Ct. Appeals (5th cir.) 1987. Assoc. Smith, Currie & Hancock, Atlanta, 1982-87, ptnr., 1988-98; pntr. Kilpatrick Stockton LLP, Atlanta, 1998—. Co-author: Construction Business Handbook, 1985, Holding Subcontractors to Their Bids, 1986, Subcontractor Default, 1987, The New AIA Design and Construction Documents, 1988, Proving and Pricing Claims, 1995, Fifty State Construction Lien and Bond Law, 2000, Who Pays For Defective Design?, 1997, Design-Build Contracting Claims, 1999, Design-Build Contracting Handbook, 2001; editor: Construction Subcontracting, 1991, Common Sense Construction Law, 1997; editor Construction Law Update, 1992—; notes editor G.W.U.J. Internat. Law and Econs., 1981-82. Mem. ABA (pub. contract law sect., forum com. on constrn. industry), Atlanta Bar Assn., Am. Arbitration Assn. (panel of arbitrators), Water Environment Fedn. (editl. adv. bd. 1994-97), Design Build Inst. of Am. (exec. bd. s.e. chpt. 2002—). Roman Catholic. Federal civil litigation, Construction, Government contracts and claims. Home: 120 Forrest Lake Dr NW Atlanta GA 30327 Office: Kilpatrick Stockton LLP 1100 Peachtree St NE Ste 2800 Atlanta GA 30309-4530 E-mail: nsweeney@kilpatrickstock.com.

SWEENEY, THOMAS FREDERICK, lawyer; b. Detroit, Feb. 10, 1943; s. Harold Eugene and Marion Genevieve (Lunz) S.; m. Susan Carol Horn, Dec. 27, 1968; children: Sarah Elizabeth, Neal Thomas. AB, U. Mich., 1965, JD, 1968. Bar: Mich. 1968, U.S. Dist. Ct. (ea. dist.) Mich, 1968, U.S. Tax Ct. 1979, U.S. Supreme Ct. 1985. Assoc. Fischer, Franklin, Ford, Simon & Hogg, Detroit, 1969—73, ptnr., 1974—85, Houghton, Potter, Sweeney & Brenner, Detroit, 1986—95; mem. Clark Hill, Birmingham, Mich., 1995—2002, mem. exec. com., 1999—2002. Spkr. Inst. CLE; guest lectr. U. MIch. Law Sch., 2001-03. Contbr. articles to legal jours. Mem. Birmingham (Mich.) Charter Rev. Commn., 1977; bd. dirs. Cmty. House Assn., 1990—98, pres., 1993—95; trustee Baldwin Pub. Libr., Birmingham, 1981—, pres., 2001—03. Mem. ABA, Oakland County Bar Assn. (chmn. taxation com. 1988-89), Forest Hills Swim Club (pres. 1985-87). Roman Catholic. Probate (including wills, trusts), Estate taxation, Taxation, general. Home: 1493 Buckingham Ave Birmingham MI 48009-5866 Office: Clark Hill 255 S Old Woodward Ave Ste 301 Birmingham MI 48009-6182 E-mail: tsweeney@clarkhill.com.

SWEENY, WENDY PRESS, lawyer; b. Coral Gables, Fla., June 24, 1960; d. Samuel and Carol Sue Press; m. Kermit P. Sweeny Jr., Sept. 3, 1989; 1 child, Briana Mikel. AA in Bus., Broward C.C., 1981; BA in Bus., U. South Fla., 1983; JD, Nova U., 1987. Fla. 1987, Wyo. 1988, U.S. Dist. Ct. Wyo. 1988. Assoc. Messenger & Jurovich, Thermopolis, Wyo., 1987-91; county prosecuting atty. Waskakie County, Worland, Wyo., 1991-95; pvt. practice Worland, 1995—. Mem. Girl Scouts USA. Mem. Bus. and Profl. Women's Assn. (pres. 1998). Avocation: rock climbing. Criminal, Family and matrimonial, General practice. Office: 1116 Robertson Ave Worland WY 82401-2826 E-mail: wsweeny@trib.com.

SWEET, HOWARD A. lawyer; b. Madison, Wis., June 6, 1945; s. Harry M. and Esther (Mullin) S. BA, U. Wis., 1967; JD, Harvard U., 1970. Bar: Wis. 1970, U.S. Dist. Ct. (we. dist.) Wis. 1970. Assoc. LaFollette & Sinykin, Madison, 1970-73, ptnr., 1973-97; sr. atty. Hurley, Burish & Millikin, S.C., 1998—. Bd. dirs. Kids Fund, Inc., 1973-1998, Meriter Fdn. Inc., 1999-, Jewish Social Services of Madison, 1978-. Mem. State Bar Wis., Dane County Bar Assn. Corporate, general, Estate planning, Non-profit and tax-exempt organizations. Office: Hurley Burish & Millikin SC 1 E Main St 301 N Broom St Madison WI 53703-2010

SWEET, LOWELL ELWIN, lawyer, writer; b. Flint, Mich., Aug. 10, 1931; s. Leslie E. and Donna Mabel (Latta) S.; m. Mary Ellen Ebben, Aug. 29, 1953; children: Lawrence Edward, Diane Marie, Sara Anne. BA in Psychology, Wayne State U., 1953; LLB, U. Wis., 1955. Bar: Wis. 1955, U.S. Dist. Ct. (ea. dist.) Wis. 1955, U.S. Dist. Ct. (no. dist.) Ill. 1958. Ptnr. Morrissy, Morrissy, Sweet & Race and predecessor firms, Elkhorn, Wis., 1957—70; ptnr., pres. Law Office Lowell E. Sweet SC, Elkhorn, 1970—2001, Sweet & Maier, S.C., Elkhorn, 2002—. Instr. gen. practice sect. U. Wis. Law Sch., 1978, 79, 86, 90; lectr. real estate law Wis. Bar, Gateway Tech., Carthage Coll. Inst., 1974—. Author: Phased Condominiums for Matthew Bender, 1992; co-editor: Condominium Law Handbook, 1981, 93; mem. editl. bd. Workbook for Wis. Estate Planners, 1990. Mem. Walworth County Rep. com.; sect. Wis. Jt. Survey Commn. on Debt Mgmt. With CIC, U.S. Army, 1955-57. Named Outstanding Young Man of Am., Elkhorn Jaycees, 1966; recipient citation for svc. in drafting Wis. Condominium Law, Wis. Legislature, 1978. Fellow ABA, Wis. Law Found.; mem. Wis. Bar Assn. (gov. 1972-75, 91-93, 99-01), Walworth County Bar Assn., Am. Judicature Soc., The Best Lawyers in Am., Am. Coll. Real Estate Lawyers, Kiwanis, Lions, Moose, KC. Corporate, general, Probate (including wills, trusts), Property, real (including real estate development, water). Home: 3530 Westshire Cir Delavan WI 53115 Office: Sweet & Maier SC 114 N Church St Elkhorn WI 53121-1202

SWEET, ROBERT WORKMAN, federal judge; b. Yonkers, N.Y., Oct. 15, 1922; s. James Allen and Delia (Workman) S.; m. Adele Hall, May 12, 1973; children by previous marriage— Robert, Deborah, Ames, Eliza. BA, Yale U., 1944, LL.B., 1948. Bar: N.Y. 1949. Asso. firm Simpson, Thacher & Bartlett, 1948-53; asst. U.S. atty. So. Dist. N.Y., 1953-55; asso. firm Casey, Lane & Mittendorf, 1955-65, partner, 1957-65; counsel Interdepartmental Task Force on Youth and Juvenile Delinquency, 1958-78; dep. mayor City of N.Y., 1966-69; partner firm Skadden, Arps, Slate, Meagher & Flom, N.Y.C., 1970-77; mem. hearing office N.Y.C. Transit Authority, 1975-77; U.S. dist. judge So. Dist. N.Y., N.Y.C., 1978—. Participant USIA Rule of Law Program in Albania, 1991; observer Albanian elections, 1992. Pres. Community Service Soc., 1961-78; trustee Sch. Mgmt. Urban Policy, 1970— , Taft Sch.; vestryman St. Georges Epis. Ch., 1958-63. Served to lt. (j.g.) USNR, 1943-46. Recipient Alumni citation of merit Taft Sch., 1985, various other awards, citations for service as dept mayor N.Y.C. Mem. ABA, Assn. of Bar of City of N.Y., N.Y. Law Inst., N.Y. County Lawyers Assn., State Bar Assn., Am. Legion (comdr. Willard Straight Post) Clubs: Quaker Hill Country, Century Assn., Merchants, Indian Harbor Yacht, Mid City Rep.

SWENSON, DIANE KAY, lawyer; b. Sioux Falls, S.D., June 16, 1952; d. Clarence Donald and Mildred Ann (Meyer) S. BA magna cum laude, Augustana Coll., 1974; JD, Hamline U., 1981. Bar: Minn. 1981. Tchr. Malvern (Iowa) Pub. Schs., 1974-76, Rosemount Pub. Schs., Apple Valley, Minn., 1976-78; legis. asst. to Senator Larry Pressler, U.S. Senate, Washington, 1981-86; exec. v.p. Am. Tort Reform Assn., Washington, 1986-99, Nat. Assn. Fed. Credit Unions, Washington, 1999—. V.p. Emmanual Luth. Ch., Bethesda, Md., 1997. Mem. ABA. Republican. Lutheran. Avocation: skiing. Home: 6140 Stonehenge Place Rockville MD 20852-5807 Office: Nat Assn Fed Credit Unions 3138 10th St N Arlington VA 22201-2149 E-mail: dswenson@nafcunet.org., dks@erols.com.

SWERDLOFF, DAVID ALAN, lawyer; b. Buffalo, Sept. 19, 1948; s. John and Joan (Harris) S.; m. Shelley Ann Taylor, Oct. 6, 1974; children: Joan Taylor, Laura Taylor, Carolyn Taylor. AB, Brown U., 1970; MS, Northwestern U., 1974; JD, U. Conn., 1979. Bar: Conn. 1979, U.S. Dist. Ct. Conn. 1981. Assoc. Day, Berry & Howard, Hartford, Conn., 1979-83, Stamford, Conn., 1983-86, ptnr., 1986—. Sec., bd. dirs. Teen Life Ctr. Inc., Stamford, 1984-89. Bd. dirs. Vol. Ctr., Stamford, 1991-97, Sr. Svcs. of Stamford, 1998—, Stamford Mus. and Nature Ctr., 2000—. Mem. ABA, Conn. Bar Assn. (exec. com. sect. on corps. and other bus. ogrns. 1988—), Stamford Region Bar Assn. (chmn. bus. law com. 1989-91, treas. 1994-95, sec. 1995-96, v.p. 1996-98, pres. 1998-99). Commercial, contracts (including sales of goods; commercial financing), Corporate, general. Home: 87

Alexandra Dr Stamford CT 06903-1731 Office: Day Berry & Howard 1 Canterbury Grn Ste 7 Stamford CT 06901-2047 E-mail: dswerdloff@dbh.com.

SWERDLOFF, ILEEN POLLOCK, lawyer; b. Bronx, N.Y., July 15, 1945; d. Seymour Pollock and Selma (Goldin) Feinstein; m. Mark Harris Swerdloff, Dec. 24, 1967; 1 child, Jonathan Edward. BA, SUNY, 1967; JD, Western New Eng. Sch. of Law, 1978. Bar: Conn. 1979, U.S. Dist. Ct. Conn. 1981, U.S. Supreme Ct. 1985. Mng. ptnr. Swerdloff & Swerdloff, West Hartford, Conn., 1980—. Sec. Chrysalis Ctr., Hartford, Conn., 1988-91, pres., 1991-92. Mem.: ABA, Hartford County Bar Assn., Conn. Bar Assn. Jewish. Avocations: knitting, aerobics. Commercial, consumer (including collections, credit), Family and matrimonial, General practice. Home: 9 Beacon Heath Farmington CT 06032-1524 Office: Swerdloff & Swerdloff 61 S Main St West Hartford CT 06107-2486

SWERDLOFF, MARK HARRIS, lawyer; b. Buffalo, Sept. 7, 1945; s. John and Joan (Harris) S.; m. Ileen Pollock, Dec. 24, 1967; 1 child, Jonathan Edward. BA, SUNY, Buffalo, 1967; JD, U. Conn., 1975. Bar: Conn. 1975, U.S. Dist. Ct. Conn. 1975, U.S. Ct. Appeals (2d cir.) 1983, U.S. Supreme Ct. 1985, Fla. 1977. Assoc. Wilson, Asbel & Channin, Hartford, Conn., 1975-78; ptnr. Swerdloff & Swerdloff, West Hartford, Conn., 1978—. Pres. Arpus Enterprises, Old Saybrook Conn., 1993—; trial fact finder Superior Ct., Hartford, 1990—; arbitrator Dispute Resolution Inst., Hartford, 1990—. Mem. ABA, Conn. Bar Assn., Conn. Trial Lawyers Assn. Democrat. Jewish. Avocations: photography, travel, cooking. General civil litigation, Family and matrimonial, Personal injury (including property damage). Home: 9 Beacon Heath Farmington CT 06032-1524 Office: Swerdloff & Swerdloff 61 S Main St West Hartford CT 06107-2486 E-mail: mhsips@mindspring.com.

SWETNAM, DANIEL RICHARD, lawyer; b. Columbus, Ohio, Dec. 22, 1957; s. Joseph Neri and Audrey Marguerite (Mason) S.; m. Jeannette Deanna Dean, June 7, 1980; children: Jeremiah Daniel, Laura Janelle, Andrew Michael. BA, Ohio State U., 1979; JD, U. Cin., 1982. Bar: Ohio 1982, U.S. Dist. Ct. (so. dist.) Ohio 1982, U.S. Ct. Appeals (6th cir.) 1986, U.S. Supreme Ct. 1986. Assoc. Schwartz, Warren & Ramirez, Columbus, 1982-88, ptnr., 1989-96; prin. Schottenstein, Zox & Dunn, Columbus, 1997—. Deacon Grace Brethren Ch., Worthington, Ohio, 1989—; mem. Grace Brethren Christian Schs. Commn., 1993-98. Mem. ABA, Ohio State Bar Assn., Columbus Bar Assn., Comml. Law League Am., Order of Coif. Republican. Avocations: golf, tennis. Bankruptcy, General civil litigation. Home: 2178 Stowmont Ct Dublin OH 43016-9563 Office: Schottenstein Zox & Dunn 41 S High St Columbus OH 43215-6101

SWETT, ALBERT HERSEY, retired lawyer, business executive, consultant; b. Medina, N.Y., Feb. 18, 1923; s. Raymond Fuller and Marion (Hersey) S.; m. Mary Stewart, Oct. 10, 1944; children: Marion Hersey Swett Robinson, Margaret Stewart Swett Haskell, Albert Louis. Grad., The Hill Sch., 1941; B.Engring., Yale U., 1944; LL.B., Harvard U., 1949. Bar: N.Y. 1949. Assoc. Harris, Beach & Wilcox, Rochester, N.Y., 1949-56, ptnr., 1957-66; v.p., gen. counsel Xerox Corp., Stamford, Conn., 1966-75, Coca-Cola Co., Atlanta, 1975-78, v.p., counsel to chmn., 1978-80; ind. cons., 1980—. Trustee Practising Law Inst., 1977-83. Served with USNR, 1942-46. Mem. Assn. Gen. Counsel (emeritus), Tau Beta Pi. Lodges: Masons. Methodist. Home: Apt 615 1570 East Ave Rochester NY 14610-1640 E-mail: ahs30319@aol.com.

SWIBEL, STEVEN WARREN, lawyer; b. Chgo., July 18, 1946; s. Morris Howard and Gloria Swibel; m. Leslie Swibel; children: Deborah, Laura. BS, MIT, 1968; JD, Harvard U., 1971. Bar: Ill. 1971, U.S. Dist. Ct. (no. dist.) Ill. 1971, U.S. Tax Ct. 1973, U.S. Ct. Appeals (7th cir.) 1981. Assoc. Sonnenschein Carlin Nath & Rosenthal, Chgo., 1971-78, ptnr., 1978-84, Rudnick & Wolfe, 1984-93, Schwartz, Cooper, Greenberger, Krauss Chartered, Chgo., 1993—. Adj. prof. taxation Ill. Inst. Tech. Kent Coll. Law, Chgo., 1989-2001; lectr. in field; contbr. articles to profl. jours. Ednl. counselor MIT, 1979—; bd. dirs. MIT Alumni Fund, 1992-95, Chgo. chpt. MIT Enterprise Forum, 2002—, Ragdale Found., 1987-00, treas, 1987-92; bd. dirs. Kids In Danger, 1998—. Recipient Lobdell Disting. Svc. award MIT Alumni Assn., 1989. Mem. ABA (com. partnerships sect. taxation), Ill. Bar Assn., Chgo. Bar Assn. (fed. taxation com., exec. subcom. 1984—, chmn. subcom. on real estate and partnerships 1986-87, vice-chmn. 1988-89, chmn. 1990), MIT Enterprise Forum (dir. Chgo. chpt. 2002—), Met. Club, MIT Club (dir. Chgo. chpt. 1980-91, 96—, sec. 1980-87, pres. 1987-89), Sigma Xi, Tau Beta Pi, Eta Kappa Nu. Corporate, general, Corporate taxation, Personal income taxation. Office: Schwartz Cooper Greenberger & Krauss Chartered 180 N La Salle St Ste 2700 Chicago IL 60601-2757 E-mail: swibel@alum.mit.edu.

SWIFT, FRANK MEADOR, lawyer; b. N.Y.C., Dec. 27, 1911; s. Frank Meador and Alberta (Rankin) S.; m. Harriet Elizabeth Simpson, May 30, 1944 (dec. Jan. 2003); children: Frank Meador (dec.), Thomas Lamar. Student, Emory U., 1930-32; LL.B., U. Ga., 1935. Bar: Ga. 1935. Partner Swift, Currie, McGhee & Hiers, Atlanta, 1965-82, of counsel, 1982—. Served to comdr. USNR, 1942-46. Mem. Am., Ga. bar assns., Lawyers Club Atlanta, Clubs: Piedmont Driving. Republican. Presbyterian. Home: 201 Neptune Rd Apt 455 Saint Simons Island GA 31522-4246 Office: Swift Currie McGhee & Hiers 1355 Peachtree St NE Ste 300 Atlanta GA 30309-3238

SWIFT, STEPHEN CHRISTOPHER, lawyer; b. N.Y.C., Jan. 7, 1954; s. James Stephen and Rhoda Emma Jean (Howd) Swift. AA, Lansing CC, 1980; BA, Mich. State U., 1983; JD, Wayne State U., 1988. Bar: Mich. 1988, Hawaii 1989, U.S. Dist. Ct. Hawaii 1989, U.S. Ct. Fed. Claims 1990, U.S. Ct. Appeals (fed., DC and 9th cirs.) 1990, DC 1991, U.S. Supreme Ct. 1992, Va. 1995, U.S. Dist. Ct. (ea. and we. dists.) Va. 1995, U.S. Bankruptcy Ct. (ea. and we. dists.) Va. 1995, U.S. Ct. Appeals (4th cir.) 1995, U.S. Dist. Ct. DC 1997, U.S. Tax Ct. 1997, Md. 1998, U.S. Dist. Ct. Md. 1998, U.S. Ct. Internat. Trade 2000, U.S. Dist. Ct. (ea. dist.) Mich. 2002, registered: (patent atty.) 1994. Pvt. practice, Honolulu, 1989—94, Arlington, Va., 1995—2003, Alexandria, 2003—. Mem.: ABA, Am. Intellectual Property Law Assn., Fed. Cir. Bar Assn., Fed. Bar Assn. Intellectual property, Patent, Trademark and copyright. Office: Swift Law Office 1800 Diagonal Rd Ste 600 Alexandria VA 22314-2840 Fax: 703-418-1895. E-mail: steve@swift-law.com.

SWIFT, STEPHEN JENSEN, federal judge; b. Salt Lake City, Sept. 7, 1943; s. Edward A. and Maurine (Jensen) S.; m. Lorraine Burnell Facer, Aug. 4, 1972; children: Carter, Stephanie, Spencer, Meredith, Hunter. BS, Brigham Young U., 1967; JD, George Washington U., 1970. Trial atty. U.S. Dept. Justice, Washington, D.C., 1970-74; asst. U.S. atty. U.S. Atty.'s Office, San Francisco, 1974-77; v.p., sr. tax counsel Bank Am. N.T. & S.A., San Francisco, 1977-83; judge U.S. Tax Ct., Washington, 1983—. Adj. prof. Golden Gate U., San Francisco, 1976-83, U. Balt., 1987—. Mem. ABA, Calif. Bar Assn., D.C. Bar Assn. Office: US Tax Ct 400 2nd St NW Washington DC 20217-0002

SWIFT, THOMAS GROVER, JR., lawyer, mediator; b. Ft. Worth, July 7, 1931; BSc, Tex. Christian U., 1953; LLB, U. Tex., 1958. Bar: Tex. 1958, U.S. Ct. Appeals (5th cir.) 1970, U.S. Dist. Ct. Tex. (Northern dist.) 1958, U.S. Dist. Ct. Tex. (Western dist.) 1963, Bd. cert., Personal Injury Trial Law: Tex. Bd. of Legal Specialization 1978. Atty. Stone, Aggerton, Parker, Shakard Attys., Ft. Worth, 1958—62; ptnr. Wesch, Swift Attys., Kermit, Tex., 1962—63; atty. Wekler County, Kermit, 1964—69; ptnr. Street, Swift Attys., Ft. Worth, 1969—71, Street, Swift, Brockermeyer Attys., Ft. Worth, 1971—72, Street, Swift, et. al., Ft. Worth, 1972—79, Street, Swift, Brockermeyer, Tillman Attys., Ft. Worth, 1979—81, Swift, Brockermeyer, Bell, Ward Attys., Ft. Worth, 1981—87, Swift, Bell, Ward, Dorman Attys., Ft. Worth, 1987—95, Swift, Bell, Dorman Attys., Ft. Worth, 1995—97; county atty. Winkler County, Kermit, Tex., 1964—69; pvt. practice Ft. Worth, 1997—. Mem. state exec. com. Tex. Dems., Ft. Worth, 1992—2000. With U.S. Army, 1953—55, Korea. Master: Eldon B. Mahon Inn Ct.; fellow: Tex. Bar Found.; mem.: ABA, Tarrant County Bar Assn., Tarrant County Trial Lawyers Assn., State Bar Tex., Am. Bd. Trial Advs. (pres. Ft. Worth chpt. 1988). Democrat. Methodist. Avocation: golf. Personal injury (including property damage), Product liability, Alternative dispute resolution. Office: 749 N Main St Fort Worth TX 76106-9418 Office Fax: 817-870-2295. E-mail: swifteisen@aol.com.

SWIGERT, JAMES MACK, lawyer; b. Carthage, Ill., Sept. 25, 1907; s. James Ross and Pearl (Mack) S.; m. Alice Francis Titcomb Harrower, July 7, 1931 (dec. 1990); children: Oliver, David Ladd, Sally Harper (Mrs. Hamilton). Student, Grinnell Coll., 1925-27; SB, Harvard U., 1930, LLB, 1935. Bar: Ill. 1935, Ohio 1937. With Campbell, Clithero & Fischer, Chgo., 1935-36, Taft, Stettinius & Hollister, Cin., 1936—, ptnr., 1948-79, sr. ptnr. and chmn. exec. com., 1979-85, of counsel, 1985—. Dir., mem. exec. com. Union Cen. Life Ins. Co., 1963-79; dir., chmn. audit com. Philips Industries, 1975-82. Author articles on labor rels. and labor law. Bd. dirs. Cin. Symphony Orch., 1976-78; trustee, chmn. exec. com. Am. Music Scholarship Assn., 1987-92. Mem.: Queen City (past dir.), Cincinnati Country (past v.p., dir.), Queen City Optimists (past pres.), Tennis (past pres.), Recess (past pres.), Harvard Law (past pres.) (Cin.). Republican. Presbyterian. Labor (including EEOC, Fair Labor Standards Act, labor-management relations, NLRB, OSHA). Home: 2121 Alpine Pl Cincinnati OH 45206-2690 Office: 1800 US Bank Ctr Cincinnati OH 45202 E-mail: swigert@taftlaw.com.

SWINNEN, BENOIT M.J. lawyer, lawyer; b. Liege, Belgium, Jan. 7, 1961; arrived in U.S., 1992; s. J. Laurent Swinnen and Anne J.H. Goffin-Swinnen. Grad., Brussels U., 1984, Brussels I., 1988; JD, So. Meth. U., 1998. Bar: Kans., Mo. 2001. Assoc. Stibbe Simont, Brussels, 1984—87; in house counsel Fina Oil & Chem./Petroleum, 1987—91; atty. pvt. practice, Topeka, 1988—2001; ptnr., shareholder Schroer, Rice, 2001—. Mem.: Order of Coif. Avocation: horseback riding. Personal injury (including property damage), Corporate, general, Commercial, contracts (including sales of goods; commercial financing). Fax: 785-357-0216. E-mail: bswinne@schroerrice.com.

SWINTON, JEFFREY CHEEVER, lawyer; b. Salt Lake City, June 22, 1947; s. Kenneth Perry and Venice (Cheever) S.; m. Heidi Sorensen, Apr. 14, 1972; children: Cameron, Daniel, Jonathan, Ian. BA, U. Utah, 1971, JD, 1974. Bar: Utah 1974, U.S. Ct. Appeals (10th cir.) 1985, U.S. Supreme Ct. 1985. Ptnr. Stringham, Larsen, Mazuran & Sabin, Salt Lake City, 1974-79; sr. v.p. Ruti-Sweetwater, Inc., Salt Lake City, 1979-84; ptnr. Larsen, Mazuran & Verhaaren, Salt Lake City, 1984-85, Jensen & Swinton, Salt Lake City, 1986-87; ptnr., v.p., bd. dirs. Woodbury, Jensen, Kesler & Swinton, Salt Lake City, 1988-91; ptnr. Stoker & Swinton, Salt Lake City, 1991—. Assoc. editor Utah Bar Jour., 1973-74; editor Summation: Jour. Utah Law, 1973. Chmn., v.p., del. Salt Lake City Rep. Com., 1975-88; trustee Bus. Industry Cmty. Edn. Partnership, Salt Lake City, 1979-80; mem. panel judges Utah Pub. Employees Assn., 1980-83, 85-87; bd. dirs., pres. Work Activities Ctr. for Handicapped Adults, Salt Lake City, 1987-93; chair Utah state bd. svcs. People with Disabilities, 1993-99, govs. coun., 1996; dist. chmn. Boy Scouts Am., Salt Lake City, 1987-94; bd. dirs. Homeless Youth Resource Ctr., 1998-2000, Cmty. Devel. Corp. Utah, 2002--; exec. dir. Salt Lake Inner City Project, 1996—; chmn. Pioneer Region Welfare Com., 1998-2003; bishop Mormon Ch., 1977-85, stake pres., 1994-2003, Area Authority Seventy, 2002—. Mem. ABA, ATLA, Utah State Bar Assn. (chair franchise law sect. 1997-98, 2003-), Nat. Futures Assn. (arbitrator 1991), U. Utah Law Sch. Alumni Assn. (treas., trustee 1979-83), Young Alumni Assn. U. Utah (pres. 1981-83), Soc. Bar and Gavel (pres. 1976-78), Beehive, Owl and Key, Skull and Bones, Rotary (pres. 1993). Mem. Lds Ch. Avocations: tennis, golf, singing. Bankruptcy, General civil litigation, Franchising. Home: 121l East 100 South Salt Lake City UT 84102 Office: 311 S State St Ste 400 Salt Lake City UT 84111-2382

SWIRE, JAMES BENNETT, lawyer; b. Bklyn., July 10, 1942; AB, Princeton U., 1963; LLB, Harvard U., 1966. Bar: N.Y. 1967, D.C. 1976. Assoc. Rogers Hoge & Hills, N.Y.C., 1966-73, ptnr., 1974—82, Townley & Updike, N.Y.C., 1982-95, chmn. mgmt. com., 1990-95; ptnr. Dorsey & Whitney, LLP, N.Y.C., 1995—, office head, 1998—, mem. mgmt. com., 1999—2002, mem. exec. com., 2002—. Guest lectr. food and drug law Seton Hall Law Sch., 1977. Trustee Cancer Care, Inc., 1978—, v.p., 1982-86, chmn. exec. com., 1986-90, pres. 1990-95; trustee N.Y. Bd. Am. Liver Found., 2003—; chmn. cmty. bd. Beth Israel-St. Luke's Roosevelt Cancer Ctr., N.Y.C., 1999-2001. Mem. Assn. Bar City N.Y. (chmn. com. medicine and law 1977-80, sec. com. on trademarks and unfair competition 1985-88), N.Y. State Bar Assn., Internat. Trademark Assn. (assoc.). Federal civil litigation, Intellectual property, Trademark and copyright. Office: 250 Park Ave New York NY 10177-0001 E-mail: swire.james@dorseylaw.com.

SWITLO, JANICE GEORGINA ALICE E. barrister, solicitor, mediator, negotiator, legal and business consultant, strategist; b. Vancouver, B.C., Can., Jan. 10, 1959; d. Alexander Donald and Mary (Shutka) Switlo; married; 1 child. LLB, Osgoode Hall, Toronto, 1986; B.Commerce, U. B.C., 1981. Mgmt. cons. Control Data Can. Ltd., Vancouver, 1981-83; articled student Ladner Downs, 1986—87; barrister, solicitor Aydin & Co., Vancouver, 1987-88; legal counsel Dept. Justice of Can., Vancouver, 1989-93; gen. counsel Westbank Indian Band, Westbank, B.C., 1993-94; barrister, solicitor, cons. Switlo & Co., Peachland, B.C., 1993-97; candidate fed. election Okanagan-Coquihaila, 1997; legal advisor Ministry Aboriginal Affairs, Govt. N.W.T., 1999-2000. Mem. adv. coun. on multiculturalism, adv. coun. to Minister of Multiculturalism, B.C., 1996-98; presenter in field. Author: (book/screenplay) Sookinchute, 2001, (treatise) Trick or Treaty?, 1995, Apple Cede: First Nations Land Management Regime, 1999, In a perfect world...Modern day colonialism in Canada, 2001, The River Forks Here: Canada's attempt to execute the 1969 White Paper and Indigenous Peoples, 2002, (book) Gustafsen Lake: Under Seige, 1997. Dir. B.C. Parents in Crisis Soc., Vancouver, 1991—93, Orpheum Kids Club Soc., Vancouver, 1991, Vancouver Youth Theatre, 2001. Recipient univ. scholarships. Mem. Internat. Bar Assn., Internat. Commn. Jurists (Can. sect.), Can. Counsel on Internat. Law, York U. Alumni Assn., U. B.C. Commerce Alumni Assn., Phi Delta Phi. Office: Switlo & Co 10654 Whyte Ave Ste 170 Edmonton AB Canada T6E 2A7 E-mail: switlo@hotmail.com., janice@switlo.com.

SWITZER, FREDERICK MICHAEL, III, lawyer, arbitrator, mediator; b. St. Louis, Sept. 7, 1933; s. Frederick Michael Jr. and Viola Marie (Bardenheier) S.; m. Suzanne Elizabeth Reichardt, Aug. 28, 1970. BA cum laude, U. Notre Dame, 1956; JD, Washington U., 1959, LLM, 1972. Bar: Mo. 1959, U.S. Ct. Mil. Appeals 1960, U.S. Supreme Ct. 1962, U.S. Dist. Ct. (ea. dist.) Mo. 1993, U.S. Tax Ct. 1974, U.S. Ct. Appeals (8th cir.) 1978, U.S. Dist. Ct. (we. dist.) Mo. 1992, U.S. Ct. Appeals (4th cir.) 1994, U.S. Dist. Ct. (so. and ctrl. dist.) Ill. Assoc. Switzer, Barnes & Toney, St. Louis, 1963-65, ptnr., 1965-75, Fordyce & Mayne, St. Louis, 1975-87, Coburn Croft, St. Louis, 1987-92, Danna, McKitrick, P.C., St. Louis, 1992—. Dir. Bardenheier Wine Co., St. Louis, 1983-85; instr. St. Louis Univ., 1971-72. Pres., dir. St. Louis Industry Adv. Group, 1971-90; dir. St. Louis Abbey Sch. Soc., 1975—; mem. employee benefits adv. com. City of Ladue (Mo.), 1980—, St. Louis Indsl. Rsch. Assn., 1991—; secr., dir. Citizens for Mo.'s Children, St. Louis, 1986-91; adv. bd. Am. Youth Found., St. Louis, 1989—, pres. Friends of Am. Youth Found., 2000—. Capt. USNR, 1959-63. Recipient Mitchell award for playwriting, Univ. Notre Dame, 1959. Mem. ABA (labor employment section, equal employment opportunity law com., litig. section, gen. practice section), ATLA, Assn. Atty. Mediators, Mo. Bar Assn. (labor law com., chmn. mil. law com. 1969-71, bar jour. com.), St. Louis Bar Assn. (labor law com., anti-trust com.), Phi Delta Phi. Republican. Roman Catholic. Avocations: sailing, hiking, equestrian activities, tennis. Alternative dispute resolution, General civil litigation, Labor (including EEOC, Fair Labor Standards Act, labor-management relations, NLRB, OSHA). Office: Danna McKitrick PC 150 N Meramec Ave Fl 4 Saint Louis MO 63105-3779 E-mail: fswitzer@dmfirm.com.

SWOPE, RICHARD MCALLISTER, retired lawyer; b. West Chester, Pa., Apr. 19, 1940; s. Charles Seigel and Edna McPherson (McAllister) S.; m. Karen Diane Glass, Aug. 24, 1963 (div. 1972). BS in Edn., Bucknell U., 1962; LLB cum laude, Washington and Lee U., 1968. Bar: Va. 1968. Ret., 1998. Instr. Nat. Inst. Trial Advocacy, 1982-86. Mem. Virginia Beach Beautification Commn.; bd. dirs. Virginia Beach Orchestral Assn., 1982-88; v.p., bd. dirs. Swope Found., West Chester, Pa., 1961—; v.p. Swope Scholarship Found. Capt. USMC, 1962-65. Mem. Va. Assn. Def. Attys. (bd. dirs. 1975-78, 88-90), Va. State Bar Assn., Norfolk/Portsmouth Bar Assn., Virginia Beach Bar Assn., Virginia Beach C. of C., Rotary (pres. 1982, Paul Harris fellow). Avocation: golf. Civil rights, General civil litigation, Insurance. Home: 936 Poquoson Cir Virginia Beach VA 23452-4646 Office: 936 Poquoson Cir Virginia Beach VA 23452-4646

SWOPE, SCOTT PAUL, lawyer; b. Trenton, Mich., Nov. 9, 1968; AA, St. Petersburg Coll., 1990; BS, U. South Fla., 1994; JD, U. Fla., 1997. Bar: Fla. 1997, U.S. Dist. Ct. (mid. dist.) Fla. 1997. Dep. sheriff Pinellas County Sheriff's Office, Largo, Fla., 1988-94; atty. Tew, Zinober, Barnes, Zimmet & Unice, Clearwater, Fla., 1997-98, Gassman & Gulecas, P.A., Clearwater, Fla., 1998-2001, Swope & Assocs., P.A., Clearwater, 2001—. U. Fla. Coll. Law scholar, Gainesville, 1994-97. Mem. Pinellas County Estate Planning Coun., Clearwater Bar Assn. (civil traffic infraction hearing officer 2000-03). General civil litigation, Corporate, general, Probate (including wills, trusts). Office: Swope & Assocs PA 2450 Sunset Pt Rd Ste D Clearwater FL 33765 Office Fax: 727-797-3910. E-mail: sswope@swopelegal.com.

SWYERS, WALTER JOHN, JR., lawyer; b. Springfield, Mass., July 14, 1934; s. Walter John and Anne Gail Swyers; m. Jamie Elizabeth Wright, Oct. 8, 1970; children: John Timothy, Jennifer Brooke Elizabeth, Matthew Lindsey. BS in Commerce, U. Louisville, 1956, MBA, 1961, JD, 1971. Bar: Ky., Fla., U.S. Dist. Ct. (ea. and we. dists.) Ky., U.S. Ct. Appeals (6th cir.), U.S. Supreme Ct. Purchasing agt.-packaging Colgate Palmolive Co., Louisville, 1958-63; exec. dir. Printing Industry Trade Assn., Louisville, 1963-68; exec. asst. Jefferson County Fiscal Ct., Louisville, 1970-72; sole practitioner Louisville, 1972—. Mem. adv. bd. Salvation Army, 1985—, 2003-; bd. dirs. Derby Festival Com., Louisville, 1965-68. Served with U.S. Army, 1956-58, Germany. Recipient Citizen of the Year Award, Salvation Army, 2000, Alumni Service Award, Brandeis Sch. of Law, 2002. Mem. Ky. Trial Lawyers Assn., Mid Ky. Presbytery Judicial Commn. (sec.). Democrat. Presbyterian. General civil litigation, Construction, Property, real (including real estate development, water). Home: 203 Council Rd Louisville KY 40207-1507 Office: 2100 National City Tower Louisville KY 40202

SYDDALL, THOMAS HAROLD, patent lawyer; b. Auckland, New Zealand, Dec. 23, 1938; s. Clifford Walter and Lucy Ellen (Rolls) S.; m. Miriam Ann Antrobus, Dec. 24, 1983. BSc, U. New Zealand, 1960; LLB, Victoria U., Wellington, New Zealand, 1966. Barrister and solicitor High Ct. New Zealand, 1966; registered patent atty.; notary pub. With A.J. Park (formerly A.J. Park & Son), Wellington, 1960-65, ptnr., 1966—. Contbr. articles to profl. jours. Fellow New Zealand Inst. Patent Attys. (pres. 1980-82, exam. bd. 1991—); mem. Chartered Inst. Patent Agts. (Brit. oversea mem.), New Zealand Inst. Chemistry, New Zealand Assn. Scientists (mem. coun. 1992—), Wellington Dist. Law Soc., New Zealand Group Asian Patent Attys. Assn. (mem. of exec. 1985—), New Zealand Group Internat. Assn. for Protection of Indsl. Property, New Zealand Sect. Internat. Fedn. Indsl. Property Attys., Royal Soc. New Zealand. Avocations: the performing arts, reading, walking. Office: AJ Park Post Office Sq Wellington New Zealand E-mail: tom.syddall@ajpark.com.

SYKES, DIANE S. state supreme court justice; b. Milw. children: Jay, Alexander. B, Northwestern U., 1980; JD, Marquette U., 1984. Reporter Milw. Jour.; law clk. to Hon. Terence T. Evans; assoc. Whyte & Hirschboeck S.C.; judge Milw. County Ct., 1992, Wis. Supreme Ct., Madison, 1999—. Office: Wis Supreme Ct PO Box 1688 Madison WI 53702

SYKES, MELVIN JULIUS, lawyer; b. Balt., Jan. 9, 1924; s. Philip Louis and Sara (Klein) S.; m. Judith Janet Konowitz, Sept.24, 1950; children: David K., Rachel A. (dec.), Daniel E., Israel J. Grad., Balt. City Coll., 1940, Balt. Hebrew Coll., 1941; AB with honors, Johns Hopkins U., 1943; LLB magna cum laude, Harvard U., 1948. Bar. Md. 1949, U.S. Ct. Appeals (4th cir.) 1949, U.S. Dist. Ct. Md. 1950, U.S. Supreme Ct. 1955. Law clk. to Judge Morris A. Soper U.S. Ct. Appeals (4th cir.), 1948-49; pvt. practice Balt., 1949—. Draftsman Md. Dept. Legislative Reference, 1949—50; rsch. cons. Md. Commn. Adminstrv. Orgn., 1951—52; reporter Md. Commns. to Study Judiciary, 1953, Md. commns. to revise law relating to pub. svc. commn. , 1953—55; mem. standing com. on rules of practice, procedure Md. Ct. Appeals, 1954—72, 1978—; mem. legis. coun. Commsn. on Revision Condemnation Laws, 1961—63; mem. Balt. Charter Revision Com., 1962—63; pres. Bar Librs. Balt., 1962—63; mem. Md. Constl. Conv. Commn., 1966—67; cons. Gov. Md. Commn. to Revise Testamentary Laws, 1967—69; mem. Gov. Md. Commns. tostudy state aid to nonpub. edn., 1969—71, Md. Code Revision Commn., 1970—78. Co-author: West's Maryland Procedural Forms, 1964, Jewish Law (Mishpat Ivri), Cases and Materials, 1999; co-translator Elon, Jewish Law--History, Principles, Sources, 1994. Bd. dirs. Balt. Neighborhoods; mem. governing coun. Am. Assn. Jewish Edn., 1968—81; bd. dirs. Balt. Jewish Coun., 1970—72; bd. dirs. Balt. chpt. Am. Jewish Com.; bd. dirs. Inst. for Christian and Jewish Studies; former mem. and chmn. bd. trustees Balt. Hebrew U. With USAF, 1943—45. Fellow Am. Coll. Trial Lawyers, Am. Acad. of Appellate Lawyers, Am. Coll. Trust and Estate Counsel, Am. Bar Found., Md. Bar Found. (chmn. 1981-83); mem. ABA, Am. Law Inst., Md. Bar Assn., Balt. City Bar Assn. (lectr. continuing edn. programs), Am. Jewish Congress, Balt. Zionist Dist., B'nai B'rith, Phi Beta Kappa Fellows. Democrat. Appellate, General civil litigation, Probate (including wills, trusts). Home: 3811 Fords Ln Baltimore MD 21215-2804 Office: Ste 1701 120 E Baltimore St Baltimore MD 21202-6701

SYPOLT, DIANE GILBERT, federal judge; b. Rochester, N.Y., June 14, 1947; d. Myron Birne and Doris Isabell (Robie) Gilbert; m. Dwight Douglas Sypolt; children: Andrew, David. BA, Smith Coll., Northampton, Mass., 1969; postgrad., Stanford U., 1977-78, Georgetown U., 1978; JD, Boston U., 1979. Bar: D.C. 1979, Mass. 1979. Law clk. to judge D.C. Ct. Appeals, Washington, 1979-80; assoc. Peabody, Lambert & Meyers, Washington, 1980-83; asst. gen. counsel Office of Mgmt. and Budget, Washington, 1983-86; dep. gen. counsel U.S. Dept. Edn., Washington, 1986-88, acting gen. counsel, 1988-89; legal counselor to V.P. of U.S., White House; counsel Pres.'s Competitiveness Coun., Washington, 1989-90; judge U.S. Ct. Fed. Claims, Washington, 1990—. Bd. dirs. Democracy Devel. Inst. Recipient Young Lawyer's award Boston U. Law Sch., 1989. Mem. Fed. Am. Inn of Ct. (Master), Federalist Soc. Office: US Ct Fed Claims 717 Madison Pl NW Washington DC 20439-0002

SYVERUD, KENT DOUGLAS, dean; b. Rochester, N.Y., Oct. 23, 1956; s. Warren Lukken and Janet (Thatcher) S.; m. Ruth Chi-Fen Chen, May 22, 1982; children: Steven, Brian, David. BSFS, Georgetown U., 1977; JD, U.

Mich., 1981, MA, 1983. Bar: D.C. 1982, Mich. 1993. Law clk. to Judge Oberdorfer U.S. Dist. Ct. D.C., Washington, 1983-84; law clk. Justice O'Connor Supreme Ct. U.S., Washington, 1984-85; assoc. Wilmer, Cutler & Pickering, Washington, 1985-97; exec. sec. Mich. Law Revision Commn., Lansing, 1993-95; prof. U. Mich. Law Sch., Ann Arbor, 1987-97; dean, Garner Anthony prof. Vanderbilt U. Law Sch., Nashville, 1997—. Chair exec. com. Inst. for Continuing Legal Edn., Ann Arbor, 1995-97. Mem. Am. Law Inst., Law and Soc. Assn. Office: Vanderbilt Law Sch 21st Ave S Nashville TN 37240-0001

SZALKOWSKI, CHARLES CONRAD, lawyer; b. Amarillo, Tex., Apr. 14, 1948; s. Chester Casimer and Virginia Lee Szalkowski; m. Jane Howe, Dec. 28, 1971; children: Jennifer Lee, Stephen Claude. BA, BS in Acctg., Rice U., 1971; MBA, JD, Harvard U., 1975. Bar: Tex. 1975. Assoc. Baker Botts L.L.P., Houston, 1975-82, ptnr., 1983—. Speaker in field. Chmn. ann. fund campaign Rice U., Houston, 1991-93, chmn. Fund Coun., 1995-96; chmn. adminstrv. bd. St. Luke's United Meth. Ch., Houston, 1994, chmn. bd. trustees, 1997, 2003; chmn. DePelchin Children's Ctr., Houston, 2002—; bd. dirs. Meth. Children's Home, Waco, 1998-2001, MIT Enterprise Forum of Tex., Houston. Mem.: ABA (fed. regulation of securities com.), Assn. Corp. Growth (bd. dirs. Houston chpt.), Tex. Bus. Law Found. (mem. exec. com. 1988—, chmn. 1998—2000, bd. dirs.), Harvard Law Sch. Assn. Tex. (pres. 1983—84), Houston Bar Assn. (corp. counsel sect. 1989—90, chmn.), State Bar Tex. (chmn. bus. law sect. 1991—92), Am. Law Inst., Assn. Rice U. Alumni (bd. dirs. 1999—2002). Corporate, general, Mergers and acquisitions, Securities. Office: Baker Botts LLP 1 Shell Plz 910 Louisiana St Ste 3000 Houston TX 77002-4991

SZALLER, JAMES FRANCIS, lawyer; b. Cleve., Jan. 22, 1945; s. Frank Paul and Ellen Grace (O'Malley) S.; m. Roberta Mae Curtin, Oct. 23, 1967 (div. Aug. 1975); m. Charlene Nancy Smith, Apr. 28, 1984. AA, Cuyahoga Community Coll., 1967; BA, Cleve. State U., 1970, JD cum laude, 1975. Bar: Ohio 1975, U.S. Dist. Ct. (no. dist.) Ohio 1975, U.S. Supreme Ct. 1982, U.S. Ct. Appeals (6th cir.) 1983, U.S. Ct. Appeals (4th cir.) 1986. Assoc. Metzenbaum, Gaines & Stern, Cleve., 1975-79; sr. ptnr. Brown & Szaller Co., L.P.A., Cleve., 1979—. Lectr. law Cleve. State U., 1977-81. Mem. editorial bd. Cleve. State U. Law Rev., 1973-75.; contbr. articles to profl. jours. Mem. Ohio State Bar Assn., Greater Cleve. Bar Assn., Cleve. Acad. Trial Lawyers, Ohio Acad. Trial Lawyers (trustee, 2002—, Disting. Svc. award 1996), Assn. Trial Lawyers Am., Nat. Coll. Advocacy (advocate, co-chmn. Baycol Litigation Group, 2002—). Democrat. Roman Catholic. Avocations: gourmet cooking, automobile racing. General civil litigation, Personal injury (including property damage). Office: Brown & Szaller Co LPA 14222 Madison Ave Cleveland OH 44107-4510 E-mail: szaller@lawandhelp.com.

SZANYI, KEVIN ANDREW, lawyer; b. Buffalo, Jan. 7, 1960; s. Andrew John and Alice M. (Degenhart) Szanyi; m. Lyn Barnes Szanyi, Dec. 28, 1996; children: Colin Joseph, Lauren Elizabeth. BA, U. Dayton, 1982; JD, SUNY, Buffalo, 1985. Bar: N.Y. 1985. Assoc. Hodgson Russ Andrews Woods & Goodyear, Buffalo, 1985-92, ptnr., 1993-95, Harris Beach & Wilcox, Buffalo, 1995-99; mng. ptnr. Webster Szanyi LLP, Buffalo, 1999—. Mem. Def. Rsch. Inst., Nat. Assn. R.R. Trial Counsel. Personal injury (including property damage), Product liability, Toxic tort. Office: Webster Szanyi LLP 1400 Liberty Bldg Buffalo NY 14202 E-mail: kszanyi@websterszanyi.com.

SZILASSY, SANDOR, retired lawyer, library director, educator; b. Magyarbarnag, Hungary, Apr. 9, 1921; came to U.S., 1957; s. Sandor Sr. and Jolan (Fenyves) S.; m. Clara Ida Varkonyi, July 21, 1951; children: Peter S., Thomas S., Paul A.D. LLD, U. Budapest, Hungary, 1944, Lawyer-Judge Dipl., 1949; MA, Ind. U., 1959. Practicing atty., pres. law firm, Veszprém, Hungary, 1944-56; asst. libr. Anderson (Ind.) Coll. Libr., 1959-61; head div. sci. and tech. Auburn (Ala.) U. Libr., 1961-68; head libr., assoc. prof. Ind. State U., Evansville, 1968-69; dir. libr., prof. U. Tampa, Fla., 1969-72; dir. librs. Rowan U. of N.J., 1972-94. V.p. Ala. Acad. Sci., 1963-68; pres. Coun. N.J. Coll. and Univ. Librs., 1978-79, 89-90, Librs. Unltd., N.J., 1981-82, 88-89; cons. numerous orgns; radio commentator, Sta. WTEL, Phila., 1987-91. Author: Revolutionary Hungary, 1971 (Arpad Acad. Gold medal 1972), Ein Amerikanischer Diplomat uber Ungarn, 1974, Hungary's Road to Trianon, 1988, Hungary at the Brink of the Cliff, 1997, From Barnag to Miami, 1999, numerous others; author book chpts.; mem. editorial bd. Ency. Hungarica, 1989—; contbr. essays, studies, articles to profl. jours., newspapers, mags.; former editor Egyesült Amerikai Magyarság. Bd. elders Presbyn. Ch., Lakeland, Fla., 1970-72; 1st Hungarian United Ch. of Christ, Miami, 1996—. Recipient Legion of Honor award Chapel of Three Chaplains, 1981. Mem. N.J. Acad. Libr. Network (exec. bd. 1988—), Tri-State Coll. Libr. Coop. (pres. 1975-76, 88-89, Johanniter Order Knights (Germany), Arpad Acad. (sect. pres. 1979—), Miami Kossuth Club (pres.), Phi Alpha Theta. Mem. Reformed Ch. Avocations: research, writing, reading, swimming, hiking. Home: 133 N Pompano Beach Blvd Pompano Beach FL 33062-5720 E-mail: aracsi@webtv.net.

SZUCH, CLYDE ANDREW, lawyer; b. Bluefield, W.Va., Nov. 22, 1930; s. Nicholas and Aranka (Rubin) S.; m. Rosalie Hirschman Wulfson, Sept. 5, 1954; children: Peter Alan, Richard Coleman. BA, Rutgers, 1952; LLB, Harvard U., 1955. Bar: N.J. 1955, U.S. Dist. Ct. N.J. 1955, U.S. Ct. Appeals (3rd cir.) 1958, U.S. Supreme Ct. 1962. Law clk. to assoc. justice William J. Brennan Jr. U.S. Supreme Ct., Washington, 1956-57; asst. U.S. atty. U.S. Attys. Office, Newark, 1957-58; assoc. Pitney, Hardin & Kipp, Newark, 1958-62; ptnr. Pitney, Hardin, Kipp & Szuch, Morristown, NJ, 1962—2000, of counsel, 2001—02; coun. Office of Clyde A. Szuch, 2003—. Mem. panel Ctr. for Pub. Resources, N.J.; bd. dirs. Vt. Rlwy. Inc., Clarendon & Pittsford R.R. Co., Burlington, Vt., Brennan Ctr. for Justice; panelist AAA Large Complex Cases. Gov. N.J. region Nat. Conf. for Comty. and Justice. Fellow Am. Bar Found.; mem. ABA, Am. Law Inst., N.J. State Bar Assn., Morris County Bar Assn., Essex County Bar Assn., Fed. Bar Assn. (N.J. chpt.), N.J. C. of C. (bd. dirs.), Nat. Legal Aid Defender Assn., Hist. Soc. U.S. Ct. Appeals for 3d Cir. Federal civil litigation, General civil litigation, State civil litigation.

TA, TAI VAN, lawyer, researcher; b. Ninh Binh, Vietnam, Apr. 16, 1938; came to U.S., 1975; s. Duong Van and Loan thi (Pham) T.; m. Lien-Nhu Tran, Oct. 26, 1967; children: Becky, John, Khuong Virginia, Dora. LLB, U. Saigon, Vietnam, 1960; MA, U. Va., 1964, PhD, 1965; LLM, Harvard U., 1985. Bar: Mass. 1986, U.S. Dist. Ct. Mass. 1987. Prof. U. Saigon Law Sch., 1965-75, Nat. Sch. Adminstrn., 1965-75; ptnr. Tang thi Thanh Trai & Ta Van Tai, 1968-75; legal rschr. Reed Smith Shaw & McClay, Pitts., 1975; rsch. assoc. Harvard U. Law Sch., Cambridge, Mass., 1975—, adj. lectr., 1998—; pvt. practice, Brookline, Mass., 1986—; rsch. scholar NYU Law Sch., N.Y.C., 1990-94. Cons. Milbank Tweed Hadley & McCloy, N.Y.C., 1979, Shearman & Sterling, N.Y.C., 1979, Paul Weiss Rifkind Wharton and Garrison, N.Y.C., 1989, 90. Co-author: The Laws of Southeast Asia, 1986, The Le Code: Law in Traditional Vietnam, 1987, Investment Law in Vietnam, 1990; author: Vietnamese Tradition of Human Rights, 1988; contbr. articles to profl. jours. Commr. Mass. Govs. Asian-Am. Coun., 1992—. Fulbright scholar 1960-62; grantee Asia Found., 1972, Ford Found., 1975-76, Aspen Inst. 1993. Avocations: piano, swimming, foreign languages. Criminal, General practice, Private international. Home: 145 Naples Rd Brookline MA 02446-5748 Office: Harvard U Law Sch Pound 423 1563 Massachusetts Ave Cambridge MA 02138-2903

TABAKOV, TODOR DIMITROV, barrister; b. Sofia, Bulgaria, Oct. 18, 1955; s. Dimitar Todorov and Mina Petkova (Popova) T.; m. Milena Lubenova Georgieva, Mar. 24, 1979; children: Lubomir Todorov, Yvonne Todorov. Grad., French Sch., Sofia, 1974; LLB, Sofia Law Sch., Sofia, 1980. Lic. trade marks and patent rep. Patent Inst. Rep. Bulgaria, 1998. Judge City Ct., Sofia, Bulgaria, 1981-83, Mcpl. Ct., Sofia, 1985-86; legal adviser Ministry of Fin., Sofia, 1986-88, head div., 1989-90, head dept., 1990-91; expert Ministry of Economy, Sofia, 1988-89; pres. Interlex, Sofia, 1991-93; barrister Bulgarian Bar Assn., Sofia, 1993—. Cons. Orgn. Econ. Cooperation and Devel.; mem. Coun. on New Tax Legis., Ministry of Fin., 1997—. Author: Bulgaria Tax Treaties, 1991, Part II, 1994, Commentary of the Law on Individual Income Taxation, 1998; co-author: VAT in Bulgaria, 1994. Mem. supervisory bd. Open Soc. Fund, Sofia, 1990, chmn., 1997—; bd. dir. Internat. Found. Ciril and Metodius, Sofia, 1991; corr. Internat. Bur. Fiscal Documentation, 1992, Tax Notes Internat., 1991; bd. dir. Bulgarian br. Internat. Devel. Law Inst., 2003—. Lt. Bulgarian Air Forces, 1974—76. Mem. Internat. Fiscal Assn., European Fedn. Accts. and Tax Cons., Bulgarian C. of C. and Industry (chmn. bd. contbrs. 1991-93), bd. dirs.), Bulgarian Assn. Tax Experts and Cons. (dep. chmn. 1997—). Christian Orthodox. Home: 118 James Boucher Ave Sofia 1407 Bulgaria Office: 6th fl 116 James Boucher Ave Sofia 1407 Bulgaria E-mail: interlex@evrotur.net., todortabakov@evrotuk.net.

TABIN, SEYMOUR, retired lawyer; b. Chgo., May 6, 1918; s. Solomon and Lillian (Klingman) T.; m. Frances Greenfield, Oct. 26, 1940; 1 child, Lee Edward. BA, U. Chgo., 1938, D in Law cum laude, 1940. Bar: Ill. 1940, U.S. Dist. Ct. (no. dist.) Ill. 1940, U.S. Tax Ct. 1948, U.S. Supreme Ct. 1950. Ptnr. Froelich, Grossman, Teton & Tabin, Chgo., 1950-76; of counsel Gottlieb & Schwartz, Chgo., 1975-93; pvt. practice Highland Park, Ill., 1993—2001; ret., 2001—. Lt. USNR, 1942-45. Mem. Chgo. Bar Assn., Ill. Bar Assn., Order of Coif, Phi Beta Kappa. Republican. Jewish. Avocations: tennis, bridge, computers, travel, grandchildren. Banking, Corporate, general. Home: 1148 Lincoln Ave Highland Park IL 60035-4110

TACHA, DEANELL REECE, federal judge; b. Jan. 26, 1946; BA, U. Kans., 1968; JD, U. Mich., 1971. Spl. asst. to U.S. Sec. of Labor, Washington, 1971—72; assoc. Hogan & Hartson, Washington, 1973, Thomas J. Pitner, Concordia, Kans., 1973—74; dir. Douglas County Legal Aid Clinic, Lawrence, Kans., 1974—77; assoc. prof. law U. Kans., Lawrence, 1974—77, prof., 1977—85, assoc. dean, 1977—79, assoc. vice chancellor, 1979—81, vice chancellor, 1981—85; judge U.S. Ct. Appeals (10th cir.), Denver, 1985—; U.S. sentencing commr., 1994—98; chief judge U.S. Ct. Appeals (10th cir.), Denver, 2001—.

TACHNER, LEONARD, lawyer; b. Bklyn., Jan. 18, 1944; BEE, CCNY, 1965; MSEE, Calif. State U., Long Beach, 1969; JD, Western State U., Fullerton, Calif., 1973. Bar: Calif. 1973, US Patent Office 1972. Supr. electronic counter measures sect. Ford Aerospace Corp., Newport Beach, Calif., 1969—73; patent atty. Reed C. Lawlor, LA, 1973—76, Rockwell Internat. Corp., Anaheim, Calif., 1976—78; ptnr. Fischer, Tachner & Strauss, Newport Beach, 1978—84; pvt. practice Irvine, Calif., 1984—. Instr. intellectual property Calif. State U., Long Beach, 1979—; com. maintenance profl. competence Calif. State Bar, 1978—. Mem. editl. bd. Western State U. Law Rev., 1972—73, columnist Interface Age mag., 1979—, Bus.-to-Bus. mag., 1983—. Mem.: Orange County Patent Law Assn., Calif. Bar Assn., Greater Irvine Indsl. League, Phi Kappa Phi. Patent, Trademark and copyright. Office: 17961 Sky Park Cir Ste 38-E Irvine CA 92614 Personal E-mail: ltachner@aol.com. Business E-Mail: ltachner@pacbell.net.

TACKITT, SYLVAN WRIGHT, lawyer; b. Banta, Ind., June 12, 1909; s. Mitchell Albert Ward and Carrie Blanche (Stewart) T.; m. Elizabeth Estelle Stephenson, Sept. 6, 1934 (dec. Nov. 1970); children: Stephen Wright (dec.), Martha Anne Distler; m. Harriet Martin Cartmel, May 13, 1972 (dec. Dec. 1, 1995); m. Edith Boyer Schuman, May 14, 1997. BS in Bus., Ind. U., 1931, LLB, 1933. Bar: Ind. 1931. Pvt. practice, Bloomington, 1933—; prosecuting atty. Monroe County, Bloomington, Ind., 1942-46, county atty., 1964-65. Mem. 1st Christian Ch., Bloomington, 1934—; pres. YMCA, Bloomington, 1951-52; bd. dirs. Monroe County Pub. Libr., Monroe County Pub. Libr. Found.; govt. appeal agt. 1948-68. Recipient Sagamore of Wabash award Gov. of Ind., 1982. Mem. ABA, Ind. State Bar Assn. (bd. mgrs. 1970-72), Monroe County Bar Assn. (pres. 1960-61), Bloomington Country Club, Columbia Club (Indpls.), Masons, Lions (Melvin Jones fellow, pres. Bloomington chpt. 1947-48), Sigma Alpha Epsilon. Republican. Avocations: golf, bridge, cryptograms, collecting marbles and orientalia. Estate planning, Probate (including wills, trusts). Home: 1304 E 2d St Bloomington IN 47401-5104 Office: 103 N College Ave Ste 203 Bloomington IN 47404-3977

TAFT, NATHANIEL BELMONT, lawyer; b. Tarrytown, N.Y., Aug. 12, 1919; s. Louis Eugene and Etta Minnie (Spivak) Topp; m. Norma Rosalind Pike, May 22, 1943 (dec. Dec. 1997); children: Charles Eliot, Stephen Pike. BS in Econs., Fordham U., 1940; JD, Harvard U., 1948. Bar: N.Y. 1949. Asst. to gen. counsel N.Y. State Ins. Dept., Albany, 1948-50; law dept. N.Y. Life Ins. Co., N.Y.C., 1951-65, group dept., 1965-84, ret. as group v.p., 1984; sole practice law White Plains, N.Y., 1985—. Lectr., author on healthcare reform, 1992—. Contbr. articles to profl. jours.; author monographs on group ins. regulation. Bd. dirs. Westchester Philharm., 1991-2002, pres., 2001-02. Mem. ABA, N.Y. State Bar Assn., Nat. Assn. Physicians (sec.-treas. 1991—). Republican. Jewish. Avocations: golf, writing. Administrative and regulatory, Insurance, Pension, profit-sharing, and employee benefits. Home and Office: 16 Sparrow Cir White Plains NY 10605-4624 E-mail: nat@nattaftlaw.com.

TAFT, PERRY HAZARD, retired lawyer; b. L.A., Jan. 23, 1915; s. Milton and Sarah Taft; m. Callie S. Taft, Aug. 15, 1968; children by previous marriage: Stephen D., Sally L., Sheila R. Student, U. Calif., Berkeley, 1932-35; AB, UCLA, 1936; LLB, George Washington U., 1940. Bar: Calif. 1940. Spl. atty. Antitrust Divsn. U.S. Dept. Justice, L.A., 1941-42; dep. atty. gen. State of Calif., San Francisco, 1943-44; regional rep. Coun. State Govts., San Francisco, 1944-45; regional dir. govt. affairs Trans World Airlines, L.A., 1945—47; Pacific coast mgr. Am. Ins. Assn., San Francisco, 1948-66; gen. counsel Assn. Calif. Ins. Cos., Sacramento, 1967-73; asst. city atty. City of Stockton, Calif., 1973-79; pres. Perry H. Taft, P.C., Stockton, 1979-85; arbitrator Surps Line Assn., Calif., 1965-98. Contbr. articles to profl. jours. Bd. dirs. Stockton East Water Dist., 1979-83, pres., 1981-83; mem. San Joaquin County Water Adv. Com., 1982-85. Mem. State Bar of Calif., Elkhorn Country Club, Psi Upsilon. Corporate, general, Legislative. Home: 8615 Stonewood Dr Stockton CA 95209-2656

TAFT, SETH CHASE, retired lawyer; b. Cin., Dec. 31, 1922; s. Charles Phelps and Eleanor K. (Chase) T.; m. Frances Prindle, June 19, 1943; children: Frederick, Thomas, Cynthia, Tucker. BA, Yale U., 1943, LL.B., 1948. Bar: Ohio 1948. Assoc. Jones, Day, Reavis & Pogue, Cleve., 1948-59, ptnr., 1959-88. Mem. Cuyahoga County (Ohio) Bd. Commrs., 1971—78, pres., 1977—78; mem. Cuyahoga County Charter Commn., 1958—59; pres. Fedn. for Cmty. Planning, Cleve., 1986—89, Cleve. Internat. Program, 1990—94; chmn. Substance Abuse Initiative Greater Cleve., 1989—, Coun. Internat. Programs USA, 1999—2002, Cleve. Coun. World Affairs, 2000—02; Rep. candidate for mayor of Cleve., 1967; for gov. of Ohio, 1982. With USNR, 1943—46. Corporate, general, Mergers and acquisitions, Non-profit and tax-exempt organizations. Home: 6 Pepper Ridge Rd Cleveland OH 44124-4904 Office: Jones Day 901 Lakeside Ave E Cleveland OH 44114-1190 E-mail: sethtaft@aol.com.

TAFT, SHELDON ASHLEY, lawyer; b. Cleve., Mar. 2, 1937; s. Kingsley Arter and Louise Parsons (Dakin) T.; m. Rebecca Sue Rinehart, Dec. 26, 1962; children: Mariner R., Ashley A., Curtis N. BA, Amherst Coll., 1959; LLB, Harvard U., 1962. Bar: Ohio 1962. Assoc. Vorys, Sater, Seymour & Pease, Columbus, Ohio, 1965-69, 71-73, ptnr., 1974—2001, of counsel, 2002—; chief legal counsel Pub. Utilities Commn. Ohio, Columbus, 1969-71. Ohio bd. advisors Chgo. Title Ins. Co., 1967-98. Rep. candidate for justice Ohio Supreme Ct., 1974; trustee Opera Columbus, 1989—, pres., 1991-93, life trustee, 1995—; trustee Columbus Bach Ensemble 2002—, pres. 2002—; 1st lt. USAF, 1963-65. Mem. ABA (pub. utilities sect.), Ohio State Bar Assn. (pres. pub. utilities com. 1984-87), Columbus Bar Assn. (pub. utilities com.), Ohio Camera Collectors Soc. (pres. 1985-87), Rocky Fork Hunt and Country Club, Capital Club, 41 Club. Congregationalist. Avocation: camera collecting. Administrative and regulatory, Legislative, Utilities, public. Home: 27 Sessions Dr Columbus OH 43209-1440 Office: Vorys Sater Seymour & Pease PO Box 1008 52 E Gay St Columbus OH 43216-1008

TAHERI, MARSHALL M. lawyer, educator; b. Iran, Dec. 29, 1934; came to U.S., 1963; children: Tara, Sara, Dara Jon. BBA, U. Houston, 1968; JD, So. Tex. Coll. Law, 1973; PhD in Law, Ministry Scis. and Higher Edn., Iran, 1974. Bar: Tex. 1974, N.Y. 1999, U.S. Supreme Ct. 1981, D.C. 1982, U.S. Ct. Internat. Trade 1989, U.S. Dist. Ct. (so. dist.) 1975, U.S. Ct. Appeals (5th cir.) 1975, U.S. Ct. Appeals (11th cir.) 1981, U.S. Ct. Appeals (9th cir.) 1986, U.S. Ct. Appeals (fed. cir.) 1991. , 1974—; pvt. practice. Adj. prof. internat. civil litigation South Tex. Coll. Law, Houston, 1980—; participant internat. bus. litig. and arbitration conf., N.Y.C., 2002. Mem. ABA, ATLA, Tex. Bar Assn., State Bar Tex. (coll., vice chmn. com. on laws relating to immigration and nationality), Houston Bar Assn., Tex. Trial Lawyers Assn., Houston C. of C. (internat. bus. com., ad hoc mem. immigration task force 1982, 87), World Trade Assn., Inst. Internat. Edn., Internat. Lawyers Assn., South Tex. Coll. Law Alumni Assn. (past pres.), Iran-Am. C. of C. (founder), Forum Club. Commercial, contracts (including sales of goods; commercial financing), Immigration, naturalization, and customs, Personal injury (including property damage). Office: 1701 Hermann Dr PO Box 460165 Houston TX 77056-8165 E-mail: taheri@marshalltaheri.com.

TAIRA, DARRYL M. lawyer; b. L.A., July 1, 1959; s. Lorrin Toshiro and Shirley (Sakata) T.; m. Stephanie Koto Kometani, Aug. 18, 1984; children: Sean Katsumi, Lindsay Kaleo'onalani, Jessica Lynn Na'aualii. BS, U. So. Calif., 1981, MBT, JD, U. So. Calif., 1984. Bar: Hawaii 1985, U.S. Dist. Ct. Hawaii 1985, U.S. Tax Ct. 1985, D.C. 1989. Assoc. Case & Lynch, Honolulu, 1984-87; shareholder, dir. Tam, O'Connor, Henderson, Taira & Yamauchi, Honolulu, 1987—2000; of counsel Pacific Law Group, 2000—. Speaker Law Seminars, Inc., Honolulu, 1988—. Named U. So. Calif. Alumni Merit scholar, 1977. Mem. ABA (sect. taxation, real property, probate, trust law and bus.), Nat. Assn. Bond Lawyers, Hawaii Bar Assn. (sect. taxation, probate and estate planning), Hawaii Assn. Pub. Accts., Beta Gamma Sigma, Alpha Kappa Psi, Beta Alpha Psi, Phi Alpha Delta. Avocations: golf, running. Corporate, general, Property, real (including real estate development, water), Taxation, general. Office: The Pacific Law Group 700 Bishop St Ste 2000 Honolulu HI 96813

TAIT, JOHN REID, lawyer; b. Toledo, Apr. 7, 1946; s. Paul Reid and Lucy Richardson (Rudderow) T.; m. Christina Ruth Bjornstad, Mar. 12, 1972; children: Gretchen, Mary. BA, Columbia U., 1968; JD, Vanderbilt U., 1974. Bar: Idaho 1974, U.S. Dist. Ct. Idaho 1974, U.S. Ct. Appeals (9th cir.) U.S. Supreme Ct., Nez Perce Tribal Ct. Assoc. Keeton & Tait, Lewiston, Idaho, 1974-76, ptnr., 1976-86, 89—, Keeton, Tait & Petrie, Lewiston, 1986-88. Chmn. bd. No. Rockies Action Group, Helena, Mont., 1985-86, bd. dirs., 1981-88; mem. Lewiston Hist. Preservation Commn., 1975-94, chmn., 1988-94; bd. dirs. Idaho Legal Aid Svcs., Boise, 1975-99, Idaho Housing Agy., Boise, 1984-91, St. Joseph Regional Med. Ctr. Found., Inc., 1989-94, Lewiston Ind. Found. for Edn., Inc., 1996—; Dem. precinct committeeman, 1976-86, state committeeman, 1977-94, 2000—; del. Dem. Nat. Conv., 1980, 84; regional coord. Idaho State Dem. Party, 1996-99; treas. Larry LaRocco for Congress, 1990, 92. With U.S. Army, 1968-71. Recipient Pro Bono Svc. award Idaho State Bar, 1988, Cmty. Recognition award Lewiston Intergovtl. Coun., 1992, Spl. Recognition award Idaho Legal Aid Svcs., 1993. Mem. ABA, ATLA, Idaho Trial Lawyers Assn. (regional dir. 1976-77, 86-88, 97—), Idaho State Bar (bd. dirs. worker's compensation sect. 2002-), Clearwater Bar Assn. (sec. 1974-76, pres. 1984-86), Consumer Attys. Calif., Workplace Injury Litigation Group (bd. dirs. 2002). State civil litigation, General practice, Workers' compensation. Office: Keeton & Tait PO Drawer E 312 Miller St Lewiston ID 83501-1944 Fax: 208-746-0962. E-mail: lewlawus@lewiston.com.

TAIT, ROBERT E. lawyer; b. Lima, Ohio, Sept. 3, 1946; s. Robert and Helen (Smith) T.; m. Donna G. Dome, June 22, 1968; children: Heather, Jennifer, Robert. BA, Kenyon Coll., 1968; JD, U. Mich., 1973. Bar: Ohio 1973, U.S. Dist. Ct. (so. dist.) Ohio. 1976, U.S. Dist. Ct. (no. dist.) Ohio 1976, U.S. Dist. Ct. Md. 1980, U.S. Ct. Appeals (6th cir.) 1981, U.S. Supreme Ct. 1982. Ptnr. Vorys, Sater, Seymour & Pease, LLP, Columbus, Ohio, 1973—. Staff counsel Govs. Select Com. on Prevention Indsl. Accidents, Columbus, 1977-78. Served with U.S. Army, 1969-70. Fellow Columbus Bar Found.; mem. ABA (litigation sect., products liability com.), Ohio Bar Assn. (worker's compensation com.), Columbus Bar Assn. (workers compensation and professionalism coms.), Def. Rsch. Inst. (workers compensation com.), Columbus Def. Assn., Assn. Def. Trial Attys. (exec. com. 1991-94, treas., 2002-), Fedn. Def. and Corp. Counsel (toxic torts com). State civil litigation, Personal injury (including property damage), Workers' compensation. Home: 2045 Wickford Rd Columbus OH 43221-4223 Office: Vorys Sater Seymour & Pease PO Box 1008 52 E Gay St Columbus OH 43215-3161

TAKASUGI, ROBERT MITSUHIRO, federal judge; b. Tacoma, Sept. 12, 1930; s. Hidesaburo and Kayo (Otsuki) T.; m. Dorothy O. Takasugi; children: Jon Robert, Lesli Mari. BS, UCLA, 1953; LLB, JD, U. So. Calif., 1959. Bar: Calif. bar 1960. Practiced law, Los Angeles, 1960-73; judge East Los Angeles Municipal Ct., 1973-75, adminstrv. judge, 1974, presiding judge, 1975; judge Superior Ct., County of Los Angeles, 1975-76; U.S. dist. judge U.S. Dist. Ct. (cen. dist.) Calif., 1976—. Nat. legal counsel Japanese Am. Citizens League; guest lectr. law seminars Harvard U. Law Sch. Careers Symposium; commencement spkr.; mem. Legion Lex U. So. Calif. Law Ctr.; mem. Civil Justice Reform Act and Alt. Dispute Resolution Com., mem. Adv. Com. on Codes of Conduct of the Jud. Conf. of the U.S., 1987-92, Code of Conduct of Judges. Mem. editorial bd. U. So. Calif. Law Rev., 1959; contbr. articles to profl. jours. Calif. adv. com. Western Regional Office, U.S. Commn. on Civil Rights, 1983-85; chmn. blue ribbon com. for selection of chancellor L.A. C.C. With U.S. Army, 1953-55. Harry J. Bauer scholar, 1959; recipient U.S. Mil. Man of Yr. award for Far East Theater U.S. Army, 1954, Jud. Excellence award Criminal Cts. Bar Assn., Disting. Svc. award Asian Pacific Ctr. and Pacific Clinics, 1994, Freedom award Sertoma, 1995, Pub. Svc. award Asian Pacific Am. Legal Ctr. So. Calif., 1995, cert. of merit Japanese-Am. Bar Assn., Lifetime Achievement award, 2000, Trailblazer award So. Calif. region NAPABA, 1995, Spl. award Mex.-Am. Bar Assn., 1996, Spirit of Excellence award ABA, 1998, Pub. Svc. award Japanese Am. Citizens League, 1999, lifetime achievement award Japanese-Am. Bar Assn., 2000, Judicial Excellence award Criminal Cts. Bar Assn., 2002, Judicial Courage award, 2003, PACE-Setter award Pacific Asian Consort. in Employment, 2003; named Judge of Yr. Century City Bar Assn., 1995, Mem. U. So. Calif. Law Alumni Assn. (dir.), Criminal Ct. Bar Assn. (Jud. Courage award 2003). Office: US Dist Ct 312 N Spring St Los Angeles CA 90012-4701

TAKEUCHI, SHIGETOSHI, law educator; b. Okayama, May 10, 1933; s. Shigeo and Nobuko (Yabe) T.; married Akiko Shoji, Dec. 2, 1960; children: Shingi, Nobutaka, Nobuki. MA in Law, Waseda Univ., Tokyo, 1959; D of Law, Hokkaido (Japan) U., 1995. Rsch. fellow Inst. Social Sci. Tokyo U., 1959-62; councillor Legis. Bur., Ho. of Councillors, Tokyo, 1962-68; lectr. faculty of law Kumamoto U., 1968-69, assoc. prof., 1969-76, fellow govt. rsch. abroad, 1972—74, prof. of law, 1976—96. Instr. faculty of law Heidelberg U., Germany, 1980, Inst. of Pub. Adminstrn., U. Speyer,

Germany, 1993; prof. grad. sch. law Meiji U., Tokyo, 1996—; head Kumamoto Prefecture Environ. Com., 1991—; chmn. Kumamoto City Investigative Com. on Polit. Moral, 1991—. Author: The Framing of Japanese Constitution, 1983, Thoughts on the Constitution, 1985, Reflections on Problem of Social Reality, 1986, Lectures on Japanese Constitutional Law, 1989, Essays and Insights on Constitutional Law, 1996. Adviser Japan Polit. Confederation of the Legal Profession, 1992-. Mem. Kumamoto Prefecture Labour Rels. Commn. (head 1996-98), Japan Pub. Law Assn. (dir. 1983-98), Examiner pub. prosecutor (2001-). Home: 4-7-6 Kurokami Kumamoto 860-0862 Japan Office: Meiji Univ Grad Sch Law 1-1 Surugadai Kanda Tokyo 101 Japan

TALBERT, HUGH MATHIS, lawyer; b. Kennett, Mo., Dec. 3, 1937; s. Clifford Roscoe and Katharyn (Hoy) T.; m. Carol Sullivan, June 1, 1962 (div. Feb. 1968); m. Carol Ann Frederick, July 18, 1973; children: Katharyn Hoy, William Hugh, Geoffrey Richard. AB, Washington U., St. Louis, 1959, LlB, 1962. Bar: Mo. 1962, Ill. 1965, Ky. 2001, U.S. Dist. Ct. (ea. dist.) Mo. 1965, U.S. Dist. Ct. (so. dist.) Ill. 1966, U.S. Dist. Ct. (we. dist.) Ky. 2001, U.S. Dist. Ct. (ctrl. dist.) Ill. 2001, U.S. Ct. Appeals (7th cir.) 1971. Assoc. Strubinger, Tudor, Tombrink and Wion, St. Louis, 1962-65, Wiseman, Hallett, Mosele and Shaikewitz, Alton, Ill., 1965-67; ptnr. Chapman and Talbert, Granite City, Ill., 1967-73; pres. Talbert & Assocs., PC, Alton, 1974—. Asst. adj. prof. Trial Advocacy St. Louis U. Law Sch., 1992—. Mem. ABA, ATLA, Ill. State Bar Assn., Ill. Trial Lawyers Assn. (bd. mgrs. 1978-87), The Mo. Bar Assn., Ky. Bar Assn., Mo. Assn. Trial Lawyers, Madison County Bar Assn., Maritime Law Assn. of the U.S., Acad. of Rail Labor Attys., Internat. Acad. Litigators, Am. Coll. Barristers. Acad. Trial Lawyers, Million Dollar Advs. Forum, Coll. Masters Advs. and Barristers. Democrat. Methodist. Avocations: landscaping, hiking and mountaineering, sailing. Admiralty, Personal injury (including property damage), Product liability. Home: 1750 Liberty St Alton IL 62002-4514 Office: Talbert & Assocs PC PO Box 800 630 E Broadway Alton IL 62002-6308 E-mail: talbert@piasanet.com.

TALBOTT, BEN JOHNSON, JR., lawyer; b. Louisville, May 2, 1940; s. Ben Johnson and Elizabeth (Farnsley) T.; m. Sandra Riehl, Oct. 19, 1963; children: Elizabeth, Betty, John, Ben, Sandra. AB magna cum laude, Xavier U., Cin., 1961; LLB, Harvard U., 1964. Bar: Ky. 1965, U.S. Ct. Appeals (6th cir.) 1967. Law clk. to presiding justice U.S. Dist. Ct. Ky., Louisville, 1964-65; assoc. Middleton, Reutlinger & Baird, Louisville, 1965-68, ptnr., 1968-80, Westfall, Talbott & Woods, Louisville, 1980-2000, Talbott & Talbott, PLLC, Louisville, 2000—. Atty. Stitzel-Weller Distillery, 1970—72, Louisville Gen. Hosp., 1974—83, Louisville and Jefferson County Bd. Health, 1974—80, U. Louisville, 1980—95; bd. dirs. Strategia Corp., 2000. Mem. adv. bd. Louisville 15, Sta. WKPC-TV, bd. dirs., 1972-74, pres. 1974; past bd. dirs. U. Louisville Found., U. Louisville Med. Sch. Fund Orgn.; bd. dirs. Louisville Theatrical Assn., 1971—, pres., 1975-76, chmn., 1977-78; bd. dirs. Def. Enterprise Fund, 1994—; bd. dirs. Macauley Theatre, 1975, TARC Adv. Com., 1971, Jefferson County Capital Constrn. Com., 1971, Louisville Orch., 1976-86, pres., 1979-81; trustee U. Louisville, 1970-79, sec., 1974, vice chmn., 1975, chmn. fin. com., 1976; bd. dirs. Ky. Ctr. for the Arts, 1983—, Louisville Lung Assn., 1974-75, treas., 1975; bd. dirs. Historic Homes Found., 1972-78, 95-97, 2000-01, 2002—, v.p. 1978, 2002—, advisor, atty. 1978-98; bd. regents Whitehall, 1993-2001. Named Outstanding Young Man of Louisville, Louisville Jaycees, 1976. Mem.: SAR, ABA, Louisville Bar Assn. (past mem. exec. com.), The Def. Rsch. and Trial Lawyers Assn., Ky. Bar Assn. (chmn. 1989, Gen. Practice Session of CLE), Big Sand Lake Club, Louisville Country Club, Filson Club, Mayflower Soc., Harvard Law Sch. Assn. Ky. (sec. 1965, pres. 1989—), Soc. Colonial Wars, Pendennis Club, Louisville Boat Club, U. Louisville Club, Phi Kappa Phi (bd. dirs., treas. Louisville chpt. 1990—). Avocations: golf, tennis, skiing. General civil litigation, Corporate, general, Personal injury (including property damage). Home: 566 Blankenbaker Ln Louisville KY 40207-1167 Office: Talbott & Talbott 501 S 2nd St Louisville KY 40202-1864 E-mail: ben@talbottandtalbottlaw.com.

TALBOTT, FRANK, III, lawyer; b. Danville, Va., Mar. 26, 1929; s. Frank and Margaret (Jordan) T.; m. Mary Beverley Chewning, July 11, 1952; children: Beverley, Frank IV. BA, U. Va., 1951, LLB, 1953. Bar: Va. 1952. With firm Meade, Talbott & Tate, Danville, 1956—59, Talbott, Wheatley & Talbott, Danville, 1959—66; with Dan River Inc., 1966-76, v.p., gen. counsel, 1968-76; ptnr. firm Clement, Wheatley, Winston, Talbott & Majors, Danville, 1977-78; individual practice law Danville, 1979-92; gen. counsel Va. Mfrs. Assn. Inc., 1983-92; of counsel Woods, Rogers & Hazlegrove, Danville, Va., 1992—. Chmn. adv. bd. NationsBank, Danville, 1984-94. Vice-chmn. Danville Sch. Bd., 1964-70; trustee Va. Student Aid Found., 1963-68; bd. dirs. United Fund Danville, 1959-63, Meml. Hosp., Danville, 1977-90. Served with AUS, 1953-56. Decorated Commendation medal. Fellow Am. Bar Found. (life); mem. Va. Bar Assn. (v.p. 1965-66, exec. com. 1967-70), Danville Bar Assn. (pres. 1965-66), Am. Judicature Soc., Newcomen Soc., U. Va. Alumni Assn. (bd. mgrs.), Danville Golf Club, Farmington Country Club, Country Club Va., Country Club of North Carolina, Delta Psi, Phi Alpha Delta. Methodist. Corporate, general, Legislative. Home: 221 Salisbury Cir Danville VA 24541-5571 Office: PO Box 560 Danville VA 24543-0560

TALESNICK, STANLEY, lawyer; b. Indpls., June 4, 1927; s. Louis and Rose (Galerman) T.; m. Joan Goldstone, Mar. 16, 1952 (div. Feb. 1967); children: Jill Wilkins, Jane Talesnick, Kay Gilmore; m. Claudia Jean Ferrell, Nov. 28, 1969 (dec.). AB, Ind. U., 1948, LLB, 1950, JD, 1967. Bar: Ind. 1950, U.S. Dist. Ct. (no. and so. dists.) Ind. 1950, U.S. Dist. Ct. (ea. dist.) Wis. 1991, U.S. Ct. Appeals (7th cir.) 1961, U.S. Supreme Ct. 1980; cert. bus. bankruptcy law Am. Bd. Cert. Ptnr. Dulberger, Talesnick, Claycombe & Bagal, Indpls., 1952-57, Bagal & Talesnick, Indpls., 1957-67, Talesnick & Kleiman, Indpls., 1967-74, Dann Pecar Newman Talesnick & Kleiman, Indpls., 1974-94; bankruptcy and creditor's rights counsel Leagre, Chandler & Millard, Indpls., 1995-1999; of counsel Ancel & Dunlap, LLP, 2000—01, Sommer Barnard Ackerson PC (merger), 2002—. Asst. city atty. City of Indpls., 1959-67; instr. bus. law Butler U., Indpls., 1981-82. Chmn. Ind. bd. NCCJ, 1974-76; v.p. Jewish Fedn. Greater Indpls., 1985-89, pres. 1989-91; bd. dirs. Coun. Jewish Fedns. (now United Jewish Cmtys.), 1986-90; treas. Indpls. Hebrew Congregation, 1967-70; v.p. Indpls. Hebrew Congregation Found., 1992-96. With USN, 1945-46, USNR. Disting. fellow Ind. Bar Assn.; recipient Liebert I. Mossler Cmty. Svc. award outstanding & enduring vol. svcs. Jewish Fedn. Greater Indpls. Inc., 1997. Fellow Comml. Law Found., Internat. Bar Found.; mem. Ind. State Bar Assn. (ho. of dels. 1985—), Indpls. Bar Assn. (v.p. 1989-90, chmn. comml. and bankruptcy sect. 1985, bd. mgrs. 1994-96), Lawyers Assn. Indpls., Comml. Law League Am., Am. Bankruptcy Inst., B'nai Brith (local pres. 1957-58). Democrat. Jewish. Banking, Bankruptcy, Commercial, contracts (including sales of goods; commercial financing). Home: 140 Olde Mill Cir S Dr Indianapolis IN 46260-2373 Office: One Indiana Sq Ste 3500 Indianapolis IN 46204 E-mail: stalesnick@sbalawyers.com.

TALHÃO, LUIS, lawyer; b. Lisbon, Portugal, Nov. 2, 1968; s. Manuel Nunes Talhão and Helena Viegas Canelas. Law degree, Univ. Lusiada, Lisbon, 1999. Probationer Marques Bom e Assoc., Lisbon, Portugal, 1999—2001; assoc. Lopes Dias Costa Basto Fernandes E Assoc., Lisbon, Portugal, 2001—. Mem.: Internat. Legal Tng., Real Assoc. De Lisboa. Monarchal. Cath. Achievements include languages: Potuguese, English, Spanish. Avocation: reading. General civil litigation, Family and matrimonial, Immigration, naturalization, and customs. Office: Lopes Dias Costa Basto Fernandes E Assoc Av 24 De Julho 60-2 1200-869 Lisbon Portugal

TALLENT, STEPHEN EDISON, lawyer; b. Columbus, Nebr., Aug. 10, 1937; s. William E. and Helen Tallent; m. Martha Sutcliffe, Apr. 6, 1971; 1 child, Jennifer Diane. BA, Stanford U.; JD, U. Chgo.; LLD (hon.), Lincoln U. Bar: Calif. 1963, U.S. Dist. Ct. (so. and cen. dists.) Calif. 1965, U.S. Dist. Ct. (so. and ea. dists.) N.Y. 1989, U.S. Ct. Appeals (D.C. cir. 1981), U.S. Ct. Appeals (2d cir.) 1987, U.S. Ct. Appeals (3d. cir.) 1980, U.S. Ct. Appeals (4th cir.) 1982, U.S. Ct. Appeals (9th cir.) 1968, U.S. Ct. Mil. Appeals 1965, U.S. Supreme Ct. 1973. Ptnr. Gibson, Dunn & Crutcher, L.A., 1962-96; pvt. practice Washington, 1997—. Former adj. prof. Loyola Law Sch., L.A.; mem. vis. com. U. Chgo. Law Sch.; former mem. Calif. Atty. Gen.'s adv. com. for Evaluation of Anti-Organized Crime Programs; mem. L.A. Town Hall, L.A. World Affairs Council; mem. bd. visitors Stanford Law Sch.; founding dir. Am. Employment Law Coun., 1993—. Fellow Coll. Labor and Employment Lawyers (founding, pres. and gov. 1995—); mem. ABA (chair labor and employment law sect. 1998-99), Indsl. Rels. Rsch. Assn. Administrative and regulatory, Labor (including EEOC, Fair Labor Standards Act, labor-management relations, NLRB, OSHA), Legislative. Home: PO Box 512 Reedville VA 22539-0512 Office: 1050 Connecticut Ave NW Ste 900 Washington DC 20036-5320

TALLEY, RICHARD BATES, lawyer; b. Oklahoma City, Mar. 19, 1947; s. Olin Jack and Betty Lee (Bates) T.; m. Joan Walker, Sept. 15, 1992; children from a previous marriage: Richard Bates Jr., Samuel Logan, Bradley Dale, Rachel Alexandra. BBA, Okla. U., 1969, JD, 1972. Bar: Okla. 1972, U.S. Dist. Ct. (we. dist.) Okla. 1972, U.S. Ct. Appeals (10th cir.) 1973, U.S. Dist. Ct. (no. dist.) Tex. 1987, U.S. Tax Ct. 1987.; CPA, Okla. Atty. Talley, Crowder & Gallagher, Norman, Okla., 1995. Bd. dirs. Bacchus Enterprises, Inc., Norman, The Top of the Center, Inc. Pres. Cleveland Co. YMCA. Mem. ABA, Okla. Bar Found., Okla. Bar Assn., Okla. Trial Lawyers Assn., Okla. Soc. CPAs, Cleve. County Bar Assn., Soc. CPAs. Democrat. Methodist. Avocations: clock collecting, motorcycling, golf, boating. General civil litigation, Commercial, contracts (including sales of goods; commercial financing), Corporate, general. Home: 1819 Joe Taylor Cir Norman OK 73072-6650 Office: Talley Crowder & Gallagher 219 E Main St Norman OK 73069-1304 E-mail: rtalley@mmcable.com.

TALLMAN, RICHARD C. federal judge, lawyer; b. Oakland, Calif., Mar. 3, 1953; s. Kenneth A. and Jean M. Tallman; m. Cynthia Ostolaza, Nov. 14, 1981. BSC, U. Santa Clara, 1975; JD, Northwestern U., 1978. Bar: Calif. 1978, Wash. 1979, U.S. Dist. Ct. (no. dist.) Calif. 1979, U.S. Dist. Ct. (we. dist.) Wash. 1979, U.S. Ct. Appeals (9th cir.) 1979, U.S. Dist. Ct. Hawaii 1986, U.S. Supreme Ct. 1997, U.S. Dist. Ct. (ea. dist.) Wash. 1998. Law clk. to Hon. Morrell E. Sharp U.S. Dist. Ct. (we. dist.) Wash., Seattle, 1978—79; trial atty. U.S. Dept. Justice, Washington, 1979—80; asst. U.S. atty. (we. dist.) Wash., Seattle, 1980—83; assoc., then ptnr. Schweppe, Krug & Tausend, PS, Seattle, 1983—89; mem. Bogle & Gates, PLLC, Seattle, 1990—99; ptnr. Tallman & Severin, LLP, Seattle, 1999—2000; apptd. U.S. cir. judge U.S. Ct. Appeals (9th cir.), 2000—. Chmn. western dist. Wash. Lawyer Reps. to Ninth Cir. Jud. Conf., 1996—97. Instr. Nat. Pk. Svc. Seasonal Ranger Acad., Everett and Mt. Vernon, Wash., 1983—93; chmn. Edmonds C.C. Found., Lynnwood, Wash., 1990—92; gen. counsel Seattle-King County Crime Stoppers, 1987—99; mem. exec. bd. Chief Seattle coun. Boy Scouts Am., 1997—. Mem.: ABA, Fed. Judges Assn. (bd. dirs. 2002—), King County Bar Assn., Fed. Bar Assn. (we. dist. trustee 1992—93, v.p. 1994, pres. 1995), Wash. Athletic Club, Rainier Club. Avocations: hunting, hiking, fishing. Office: Park Place Bldg 1200 Sixth Avenue 21st FL Seattle WA 98101-3123

TALMADGE, PHILIP ALBERT, former state supreme court justice, former state senator; b. Seattle, Apr. 23, 1952; s. Judson H., Jr. and Jeanne C. Talmadge; m. Darlene L. Nelson, Sept. 6, 1970; children: Adam, Matthew, Jessica, Jonathan, Annemarie. BA magna cum laude, Yale U., 1973; JD, U. Wash., 1976. Bar: Wash. 1976. Atty. Karr Tuttle Campbell, 1976—89; pres. Talmadge & Cutler, P.S., 1989—95; senator State of Wash., 1979—94; justice Supreme Ct. Wash., 1995—2001; ptnr. Talmadge & Stockmeyer PLLC, 2001—. Author: The Nixon Doctrine and the Reaction of Three Asian Nations, 1973; editor: Law Rev., 1975—76; contbr. articles to profl. jours. Chair Senate Judiciary Com., 1981, 1983—87, Senate Health and Human Svcs. Com., 1992—95, Wash. Senate, 1978—94, ways and means com., children and family svcs. com., edn. com. Fellow: Am. Assn. Appellate Lawyers; mem.: King County Bar Assn., Wash. State Bar Assn. Office: 18010 Southcenter Pkwy Tukwila WA 98188

TALMO, RONALD VICTOR, lawyer, law educator; b. Wilmington, Del., May 16, 1951; s. Victor Rinaldo and Jessie (Rash) T.; m. Corinne J. Richardson, June 29, 1991; 1 child, Ellery. B.A. in Sociology, U. Del., 1974; J.D., Pepperdine U., 1977. Bar: Calif. 1977, U.S. Dist. Ct. (cen. dist.) Calif. 1977. Sole practice, Santa Ana, Calif., 1977-82; ptnr. firm Wallin, Roseman & Talmo, Tustin, Calif., 1982-85; prof. law, Western State U., Fullerton, Calif., 1979— . Contbr. articles to law revs. Legal dir. Orange County chp. ACLU, Costa Mesa, Calif., 1978-82. Recipient Civil Rights award ACLU, 1984. Mem. Orange County Bar Assn. (mem. faculty coll. trial advocacy 1984-88). Democrat. Civil rights, Criminal. Office: Western State U Coll of Law 1111 N State College Blvd Fullerton CA 92831-3000

TAM, RAYMOND J. lawyer; b. Honolulu, Mar. 8, 1934; m. Audrey Tyau; children— Rodney J., Russell J. B.A., U. Mich., 1955; J.D., U. Notre Dame, 1958. Bar: Hawaii 1958. Dep. corp. counsel C&C of Honolulu, 1960-62; assoc. Norman Chung, Honolulu, 1962-63; ptnr. Hong, Iwai & Tam, Honolulu, 1963-65; assoc. Ikenaga & Tam, 1965-72; ptnr. Shim, Sigal, Tam & Naito, 1973— . Pres., Tom Assn., Honolulu, 1980-82; trustee St. Louis High Sch., Honolulu, Friends U. Hawaii Law Sch., St. Louis Fine Arts Complex (all Honolulu). Fellow Internat. Acad. Trial Lawyers (bd. dirs.), Am. Coll. Trial Lawyers, Internat. Soc. Barristers.; mem. Am. Inns of Ct. IV (master bench), Hawaii Acad. Plaintiffs' Attys. (pres. 1981-83), Assn. Trial Lawyers Am. Personal injury (including property damage). Office: Tam & Stanford Am Savs Bank Tower Ste 1100 1001 Bishop St Honolulu HI 96813

TAMADDON-JAHROMI, MOHAMMAD HOSSEIN, economics educator, lawyer; b. Jahrom, Fars, Iran, Dec. 22, 1925; s. Mohammad and Monavar T.; m. Fataneh Mirkamali, Nov. 10, 1968. LLB, U. Tehran, Iran, 1948, LLM, 1956; Diploma Econs., Social Adminstrn., London Sch. Econs., 1961; Diploma in English Law, City of London Coll., 1962; PhD in Econs., U. London, 1966. Cert. Barrister of Law, Iran, Internat. Arbitrator. Lawyer pvt. practice, Tehran, Iran, 1956—; legal and social affairs advisor Iranian Ministry of Labour, Tehran, 1957-58; legal and econ. advisor Iranian Ministry Agr., Tehran, 1959-60; rschr. London Sch. Econs., 1960-66; econ. advisor Iranian Ministry Fin., Tehran, 1966-67; assoc. prof. econs. U. Tehran, 1967-88, prof. econs., 1988—. Vice dean faculty econs. Tehran U., 1975-77, head dept. polit. economy, 1981-85, mem. univ. promotion bd., 1985-94; mem. symposium on Am. law Salzburg Seminar, 1985; collaborator Ctr. for Study of Pub. Choice, Fairfax, Va., 1990-91; mem. econ. terminology bd. Iranian Acad. Scis., 1997-98, mem. Internat. Seminar on Am. Law, Salzburg, 1985; alt. mem. Paris ICC Ct., 2003-. Author: (book) International Finance, 1986; and others; also contbr. articles to profl. jours. Recipient scholarship Japan Found., Tokyo, 1979, scholarship Inst. Weltwirtschaft, Kiel, Germany, 1984; Sabatical U. Tehran to Ctr. for Pub. Choice, Fairfax, U.S., 1990-91; named Disting. Prof. U. Tehran, 1990. Fellow Salzburg Seminar; mem. Internat. Ct. of Arbitration of Internat. C. of C. (Iranian mem., Paris 1986-2002, apptd. alt. mem. 2003). Avocations: music, travel, philosophical discussion, langs. Home: 64 Ku Alemi Parvin-Etes-ami Fatemi St 14138 Tehran Iran Office: U Tehran Faculty Econs Serah-Al-Ahmad Tehran Iran Fax: 009821-80214/55.

TAMMELLEO, A. DAVID, lawyer, editor, publisher; b. Providence, Aug. 9, 1935; s. Anthony and Kathleen (Gilleran) T.; m. Marylouise Kenney, Aug. 8, 1964; children: David A., Kathy. BA cum laude, Providence Coll., 1957; JD cum laude, Boston Coll., 1961. Bar: R.I. 1962, U.S. Dist. Ct. R.I., U.S. Ct. Appeals (1st cir.), U.S. Supreme Ct. Spl. investigative legal counsel State of R.I., Providence, 1961-69; sr. ptnr. A. David Tammelleo & Assocs., Providence, 1962—; chief trial counsel Monti & Monti, Providence, 1969-78; chief legal counsel Dept. Employment Security State of R.I., Providence, 1978-82; pres., pub. and CEO Medica Press Inc., Med. -Legal Pub. Co., Providence, 1984—; pub. Medica Press Inc., Providence, 1984—, editor-in-chief, 1984—. Lectr. on hosp., med. and nursing law through U.S., 1984—; legal cons. Med. Econs. mag., 1984—. Editor: Nursing Law's Regan Report, 1984—; Hospital Law's Regan Report, 1984—, Medical Law's Regan Report, 1984—; mem. editl. bd. RN mag., 1984-94; contbg. editor RN Jour., 1984—; columnist Legally Speaking, Advice of Counsel, 1984—; contbr. articles to legal jours. Atty., mem. biomed. ethics commn. Diocese of Providence, 1984—. Fellow R.I. Bar Found. (editl. bd. R.I. Bar jour. 1975-90, R.I. Bar Assn. (med.-legal com., joint com. with R.I. Med. Soc.); mem. ABA, Am. Judicature Assn., Am. Acad. Hosp. Attys., Nat. Health Lawyers Assn., R.I. Bar Assn., Cath. Health Assn., New Eng. Conf. Cath. Health Assn., Boston Coll. Law Sch. Deans Coun., Boston Coll. Law Sch. Alumni Assn. Avocations: sailing, tennis, jogging, astronomy, aeronautics. General practice, Health, Personal injury (including property damage). Office: Crossroads Office Pk Ste 212 75 Sockanossett Cross Rd Cranston RI 02920-5558 E-mail: Adtlaw@aol.com.

TAMULONIS, FRANK LOUIS, JR., lawyer; b. Pottsville, Pa., Sept. 26, 1946; s. Frank Louis Sr. and Cecelia Florence (Hoffman) T.; m. Jane Alice Troutman, June 26, 1976; children: Kathryn Lydia, Frank Louis III. AB, Cornell U., 1968; JD, Villanova Law Sch., 1971. Bar: Pa. 1971, U.S. Supreme Ct. 1975, U.S. Ct. Appeals (3d cir.) 1981. Law clk. to dist. judge U.S. Dist. Ct. (ea. dist.), Phila., 1971—74; assoc. Kassab, Cherry & Archbold, Media, Pa., 1974—76, Zimmerman, Lieberman & Derenzo, Pottsville, 1976—2001; ptnr. Zimmerman, Lieberman, Tamulonis & Crossen, Pottsville, 2001—. Contbr. articles to profl. jours. Mem. Am. Trial Lawyers Assn., Def. Research Inst., Pa. Def. Inst., Inst. Pa. Trial Lawyers Assn., Pa. Bar Assn., Schuylkill County Bar Assn. Republican. Roman Catholic. General civil litigation, Personal injury (including property damage), Workers' compensation. Office: Zimmerman Lieberman Tamulonis & Crossen PO Box 238 111 E Market St Pottsville PA 17901-2914

TAN, EUSEBIO VALDEZ, lawyer; b. Manila, Philippines, Feb. 6, 1951; s. Remigio V. and Rosita G. Tan; m. Madeleine Sophie B., Jan. 8, 1989; children: Anna Kristina Vittoria B., Juan Carols Miguel B., Agnes Melissa Gabrielle B., Rodrigo Alfonso Javieer B. AB economics, De La Salle Univ., Manila, Philippines, 1971; LLB, Ateneo De Manila Univ., Manila, Philippines, 1975; LLM, Columbia Univ., N.Y., 1979. Bar: Philippine 1976. Assoc. , sr. assoc., ptnr., sr. ptnr. Angara Abello Cooncepcion Regala & Cruz Law Offices, Makati City, Metro Manila, Philippines, 1976—. Vis. letcr. for numerous profl. conf., world wide, 1989—. Recipient Gold Medal Summa Cum Laude, De La Salle Univ., 1971, Dr. Jose Rizal Honors Soc., 1971, Second Honors Silver Medal, Ateneo De Manila Univ., 1975. Mem.: LAWASIA, Fin. Exec. Inst. Philippines, Tax and Legal Com., Internat. Bar Assn. (sect. bus. law), Inter-Pacific Bar Assn. (vice chairperson), Cross Border Investment Com. (vice chairperson), Jurisdicitional Coun. Philippines, Philippine Bar Assn., Intergrated Bar Philippines (treas., Pasay, Makati, Maandluyoung, San Juan chpt. 1987—89, dir., Pasay, Makati, Maandluyoung, San Juan chpt. 1989—91, v.p., Makati City Chpt. 1991—93, Nat. Com. on Legal Aid 1991—93, pres., Makati City Chpt. 1993—95, ex-offical dir., Makati City Chpt. 1995—97). Avocations: golf, movies, basketball, squash, practical shooting. Mergers and acquisitions, Property, real (including real estate development, water), Corporate, general. Office: Angara Abello Concepcion Regala & Cruz 122 Gamboa St Legaspi Villiage Makati City 0770 Philippines

TAN, WILLIAM LEW, lawyer; b. West Hollywood, Calif., July 25, 1949; s. James Tan Lew and Choon Guey Louie; m. Shelly Mieko Ushio. BA, U. Pa., 1971; JD, U. Calif. Hastings Coll. Law, San Francisco, 1974. Bar: Calif. 1975, U.S. Dist. Ct. (cen. dist.) Calif. 1975, U.S. Ct. Appeals (9th cir.) 1975, U.S. Supreme Ct. 1979. Assoc. Hiram W. Kwan, Los Angeles, 1974-79; ptnr. Mock & Tan, Los Angeles, 1979-80; sole practice Los Angeles, 1980-81; ptnr. Tan & Sakiyama, L.A., 1981-86, 88—, Tan & Sakiyama, P.C., L.A., 1986-88. Bd. dirs. Am. Bus. Network, L.A.; pres. bd. dirs. Asian Rsch. Cons., L.A., 1983—85; mem. adv. bd. Cathay Bank, 1990—91; bd. dirs. Asian Pacific Am. Legal Ctr.; mem. Calif. State Bd. Psychology, 2002—, v.p., 2002—03, pres., 2003—; hearing examiner L.A. Police Commn., 2002—. Co-founder Asian Pacific Am. Roundtable, L.A., 1981; chmn. bd. dirs. Leadership Edn. for Asian-Pacifics, L.A., 1984-87; alt. del. Dem. Nat. Conv., San Francisco, 1984; mem. Calif. State Bd. Pharmacy, Sacramento, 1984-92, v.p., 1988-91, pres., 1991-92; mem. L.A. City and County Crime Crisis Task Force, 1981, L.A. Asian Pacific Heritage Week Com., 1980-85, Asian Pacific Women's Network, L.A., 1981, L.A. City Atty.'s Blue Ribbon Com. of Advisors, 1981, cmty. adv. bd. to Mayor of L.A., 1984, allocations vol. liaison team health and therapy divsn. United Way, L.A., 1986, mem. nominating com. bd. dirs. 1994-99; bd. dirs. Chinatown Svc. Ctr., L.A., 1983; conf. advisor U.S.-Asia, L.A., 1981-83; mem. L.A. city atty. Housing Adv. Com.; mem. Pacific Bell Consumer Product Adv. Panel, 1986-90; vice chair cmty. adv. bd. Sta. KCET-TV, PBA, 1993-94; mem. adv. commn. State of Calif. Com. on State Procurement Practices, 1989-90; mem. L.A. City Attys. Citizens' Task Force on Pvt. Club Discrimination, 1989-90; mem. Calif. Med. Summit, 1993; mem. Mayor's Com. Children, Youth and Families, 1993-96; mem. pub. access subcom. Mayor's Spl. adv. Com. on Tech. Implementation, 1994-96; bd. dirs. Asian Pacific Am. Legal Ctr., 1993—, vice chair, 1999-. Named one of Outstanding Young Men of Am., 1979. Mem.: Minority Bar Assn. (chmn. 1981—82, sec. 1980—81, chmn. adv. bd. 1982—83), So. Calif. Chinese Lawyers Assn. (pres. 1980—81, chmn. 1987—88, mem. various other coms.), L.A. County Bar Assn. (trustee 1984—86, vice chair human rights com. 1980—82, mem. numerous other coms.), Calif. State Bar Assn. (vice chmn. com. ethnic minority rels. 1983—85, chmn. pub. affairs com. 1981—82, mem. other coms.), Soc. Intercultural Edn. (conf. coord., advisor panelist tng. and rsch. com. 1983). Avocations: gourmet cooking, bicycling, swimming, tennis, water color painting. Administrative and regulatory, Immigration, naturalization, and customs, Property, real (including real estate development, water). Office: 201 S Figueroa St Ste 390 Los Angeles CA 90012-2543 E-mail: wltlaw@aol.com.

TANAKA, J(EANNIE) E. lawyer; b. L.A., Jan. 21, 1942; d. Togo William and Jean M. Tanaka. BA, Internat. Christian U., Tokyo, 1966; MSW, UCLA, 1968; JD, Washington Coll., 1984. Bar: Calif. 1984, U.S. Dist. Ct. (cen., no. dists.) Calif. 1985, U.S. Ct. Appeals (9th cir.) 1985, D.C. 1987. Instr. Aoyama Gakuin, Meiji Gakuin, Sophia U., Tokyo, 1968-75; with program devel. Encyclopedia Britannica Inst., Tokyo, 1976-78; instr. Honda, Mitsubishi, Ricoh Corps., Tokyo, 1975-80; with editorial dept. Simul Internat., Tokyo; assoc. Seki and Jarvis, L.A., 1984-86, Jones, Day, Reavis & Pogue, L.A., 1986-87, Fulbright, Jaworsky and Reavis, McGrath, L.A., 1987-89; asst. counsel Unocal, L.A., 1989-91; pvt. practice L.A., 1991—; counsel Calif. Dept. Corps., L.A., 1993—. Active Japan-Am. Soc., L.A., 1984-95, Japanese-Am. Citizens League, L.A., 1981, 92—, Japanese Am. Cultural and Cmty. Ctr., 1986-89; vol. Asian Pacific Am. Legal Ctr. So. Calif., 1985-86. Mem. Japanese-Am. Bar Assn., Mensa. Democrat. Mem. Foursquare Meth. Ch. Avocations: Japanese language, Chinese language, U.S.-Far East relations, martial arts. Administrative and regulatory, Corporate, general, Securities.

TANCREDI, LAURENCE RICHARD, law and psychiatry educator, physician; b. Hershey, Pa., Oct. 15, 1940; s. Samuel N. and Alvesta (Pera) T. AB in English, Franklin and Marshall Coll., 1962; MD, U. Pa., 1996; JD, Yale U., 1972. Diplomate Am. Bd. Neurology and Psychiatry; Bar: N.Y. 1982. Sr. profl. assoc. Inst. Medicine, NAS, Washington, 1972-74; fellow in psychiatry Columbia U. Coll. Physicians and Surgeons, N.Y.C., 1974-75; postdoctoral fellow in psychiatry Yale U. Med. Sch., New Haven, 1975-77, assoc. prof. psychiatry, 1977-84; Kraft Eidman prof. medicine and law U. Tex. Health Sci. Ctr., Houston, 1984-92, dir. health law program, 1983-92; clin. prof. psychiatry NYU, 1992—; clin. prof. health care scis. U. Calif., San Diego, 1993—; mem. staff Brookhaven nat. Labs. Clin. Ctr., 1994-96; pvt. practice N.Y.C., 1994—. V.p. Internat. Acad. Law and Mental Health, 1987—95, bd. dirs.; mem. adv. com. on transplantations Health Care Fin. Adminstrn., Dept. Health and Human Svcs., 1981—84; mem. nat. adv. bd. NIMH Ctr. Study of Pub. Mental Health N.Y. State Office Mental Health, 1994—99; cmty. svcs. bd. Dept. Mental Health, Mental Retardation and Alcohol Svcs., City of N.Y., 1995—2001; mem. sci. adv. com. Am. Suicide Found., 1995—; cons. Commn. on Med. Profl. Liability; co-prin., investigator study ABA, 1978—80; cons. in field. Fellow: N.Y. Acad. Med. Office: 129B E 71st St New York NY 10021-4201

TANENBAUM, ALLAN JAY, lawyer; b. Savannah, Ga., Aug. 9, 1946; s. Nathan and Gertrude Sadie (Palefsky) T.; m. Elaine Kruger, Aug. 8, 1971; children: Louis, Sharon, Stephen, Eric. BS in Econs., U. Pa., 1967; JD, U. Va., 1971. Bar: Ga. 1972. Ptnr. Frankel, Hardwick, Tanenbaum, Fink, P.C., Atlanta, 1972-96, Cohen Pollock Merlin Axelrod & Tanenbaum, 1996—; mng. dir. Lawyer Reference Svc. of Atlanta, 1977-87. Trustee Congregation B'nai Torah; sec., exec. com., bd. dirs. Jewish Family and Career Svcs., Inc. With USAR, 1968-74. Fellow Am. Bar Found.; mem. ABA (ho. of dels., Ga. Bar Assoc., chair gen. practice sect., spkr. young lawyers divsn., lawyer referral and info. svc., chair pub. edn. divsn., sec. com. on scope and correlation of work, sec. fellows 9th young lawyers divsn.), Atlanta Bar Assn. (past sec., del.), Lawyers Club Atlanta, Atlanta Council Younger Lawyers (past pres.). Corporate, general, General practice, Pension, profit-sharing, and employee benefits. Office: A7C Enterprises Inc Office of General Counsel Six Concourse Pkwy Ste 1700 Atlanta GA 30328

TANENBAUM, JAY HARVEY, lawyer; b. N.Y.C., Nov. 17, 1933; s. Leo Aaron and Regina (Stein) T.; m. Linda Goldman, May 28, 1961; children: Susan Hillary, Steven Eric. BA, Hobart and William Smith Colls., 1954; LLB, Union U., 1957, JD, 1961. Bar: N.Y. 1957, U.S. Dist. Ct. (so. dist.) N.Y. 1961, U.S. Supreme Ct. 1967. Internat. trader Associated Metals and Minerals Corp., N.Y.C., 1960-64; pvt. practice, N.Y.C., 1964—. Corp. counsel Internat. Gate Corp., Gen. Gate Corp. Mem. N.Y. State Bar Assn., N.Y. Trial Lawyers Assn., Bronx County Bar Assn. Clubs: St. James (London), Le Club (N.Y.). FERC practice, Family and matrimonial, Personal injury (including property damage).

TANENBAUM, JEFFREY L. lawyer; b. N.Y.C., Apr. 2, 1952; BA, SUNY, Binghamton, 1973; JD cum laude, SUNY, Buffalo, 1976. Bar: N.Y. 1977, U.S. Dist. Ct. (so., ea., and we. dists.) N.Y. 1977, U.S. Ct. Appeals (4th cir.) 1983, U.S. Ct. Appeals (11th cir.) 1984, U.S. Supreme Ct. 1986. Law clk. Appellate Divsn. 4th Dept., N.Y., 1976-78; mem. Weil, Gotshal & Manges, N.Y.C. Tech. editor Buffalo Law Review, 1975-76. Mem. ABA, Am. Bankruptcy Inst., N.Y. State Bar Assn. (banking, corporation, bus., bankruptcy and antitrust sects., com. on bankruptcy of the banking, corporation and bus. sect.), Phi Beta Kappa. Office: Weil Gotshal & Manges 767 5th Ave Fl Concl New York NY 10153-0119

TANENBAUM, RICHARD HUGH, lawyer; b. Washington, July 10, 1947; m. Cindy Marks, Mar. 22, 1996; children: Brian J., Drew S. BS, Bradley U., 1969; JD, Cath. U. Am. Sch. Law, 1974. Bar: Md. 1974, D.C. 1975, U.S. Ct. Claims 1975, U.S. Ct. Appeals (D.C. cir.) 1975, U.S. Ct. Appeals (4th cir.) 1982, U.S. Tax Ct. 1982, U.S. Supreme Ct. 1982. Consumer edn. developer, tchr. Peoria (Ill.) Pub. Sch. System, 1969-71; legal asst. Pay Bd., Exec. Office of Pres., Washington, 1971-72; acct. Alexander Grant & Co., Washington, 1972; assoc. Jones, Day, Reavis & Pogue, Washington, 1973-78; ptnr. Lerch, Early & Brewer, Bethesda, Md., 1978-85; atty. pvt. practice, Bethesda, Md., 1985—. Chmn. Am. Masterworks Devel. Co., 2002—. Mng. editor Cath. U. Law Rev., Washington, 1974. Recipient Superior Performance award Exec. Office of Pres., Washington, 1972. Mem. ABA, Montgomery County Bar Assn., D.C. Bar Assn., Bethesda-Chevy Chase C. of C. (bd. dirs. 1980-83), Bethesda Country Club, Rotary (charter mem., bd. dirs. 1980—). Commercial, contracts (including sales of goods; commercial financing), Corporate, general, Property, real (including real estate development, water). Office: Ste 775 N 7315 Wisconsin Ave Bethesda MD 20814-3202 E-mail: RHT775N@aol.com.

TANG, CYNTHIA YUEN-SHUN, lawyer; b. Hong Kong; LLB in English Law, U. Nottingham, Eng., 1987; LLB in Chinese Law, Beijing U., 1997; LLM in Corp. and Fin. Law, U. Hong Kong, 2001. Cert.: Hong Kong (solicitor) 1990, Eng. and Wales 1991, Australia Capital Territory solicitor and barrister 1991. Assoc. Denton Hall, Hong Kong, 1990—91, Herbert Smith, Hong Kong, 1991—92, Baker & McKenzie, Hong Kong, 1992—96; sr. govt. counsel Dept. Justice, Hong Kong, 1996—2001; ptnr. Baker & McKenzie, Hong Kong, 2001—. Working group mem. Hong Kong Securities Inst., 2002. Fellow: Hong Kong Inst. Dir. (China-appointed attesting officer 2003). Securities, Corporate, general, Alternative dispute resolution. Office: Baker & McKenzie 14/F Hutchison House 10 Harcourt Rd Hong Kong Hong Kong

TANICK, MARSHALL HOWARD, lawyer, law educator; b. Mpls., May 9, 1947; s. Jack and Esther (Kohn) T.; m. Cathy E. Gorlin, Feb. 20, 1982; children: Lauren, Ross. BA, U. Minn., 1969; JD, Stanford U., 1973. Bar: Calif. 1973, Minn. 1974. Law clk. to presiding justice U.S. Dist. Ct., Mpls., 1973-74; assoc. Robins, Davis & Lyons, Mpls., 1974-76; ptnr. Tanick & Heins, P.A., Mpls., 1976-89, Mansfield & Tanick, Mpls., 1989—. Prof. constrn., real estate and media law U. Minn., Mpls., 1983—, Hamline U., St. Paul, 1982—; prof. constl. law William Mitchell Coll. Law, 1994. Editor: Hennepin Lawyer, Bench, Bar and Litigation mag.; contbr. articles to mags. Avocation: writing. Federal civil litigation, State civil litigation, Communications. Home: 1230 Angelo Dr Minneapolis MN 55422-4710 Office: Mansfield & Tanick 900 2nd Ave S Ste 1560 Minneapolis MN 55402-3383

TANKARD, BAXLEY TROWER, lawyer; b. Franktown, Va., June 27, 1913; s. Philip William and Florence Mapp Tankard; m. Elizabeth M. Butzner; m. Ann Clark. BS, Randolph Macon Coll., Ashland, Va., 1935; LLB, U. Va., 1938. Pvt. practice, Eastville, Va., 1947—56, 1970—; atty. Commonwealth Northampton County, Eastville, 1956—70. Comdr. USNR, 1942—46. Estate taxation, Probate (including wills, trusts), Property, real (including real estate development, water). Home: 7257 Cedar Cottage Rd Franktown VA 23354 Office: Tankard & Gordon 16412 Courthouse Rd Eastville VA 23347

TANKERSLEY, REBECCA ELIZABETH GULDI, lawyer; b. Boston, Nov. 26, 1969; d. Richard L. and Sara S. (Pearce) G. BA with distinction, U. Mich., 1992, JD, 1995. Bar: Tex. 1995. Assoc. Locke Liddell & Sapp LLP, Dallas, 1995-99; asst. gen. counsel Software Spectrum, Inc., Garland, Tex., 1999—. Dir. Dallas Legal Hospice, 1996-1999. Mem. Dallas Assn. Young Lawyers (co-chair AIDS Legal Assistance com. 1996-98, mock trial com. 1998—), Dallas Bar Assn. Corporate, general, Mergers and acquisitions, Securities. Office: Software Spectrum Inc 2140 Merritt Dr Garland TX 75041

TANNA, WAYNE MITSUO, lawyer, educator; b. Chgo., July 26, 1955; s. Walter M. and Masae Tanna; m. Corinne S. Sato, Mar. 25, 1994; 1 child, Jenna Logan Qingyin. JD, Northwestern Sch. Law, 1989; LLM, U. the Pacific, 1990. Bar: Hawaii 1989, U.S. Dist. Ct. Hawaii 1989, U.S. Supreme Ct. 2002. Atty. Law offices of Wayne M. Tanna, Honolulu, 1991—; prof. acctg. Chaminade U., Honolulu, 1993—. Chmn., dir Hawaii Disability Rights Ctr., Honolulu, 1996—. Coach Spl. Olympic Hawaii, Honolulu, 1975—2002; chmn., bd. dirs. Hawaii Disability Rights Ctr., Honolulu, 1996—2002; pres., v.p., sec., and dir. Vol. Legal Svcs. Hawaii, Honolulu, 1997—2002. Recipient NIU award, Vol. Legal Svcs. Hawaii, 1995, 1999, William Reese Smith, Jr. award, ABA/Nat. Assn. Pro Bono Coord., 2001. Achievements include American Bar Association/National Association of Pro Bono Professionals William Reese Smith, Jr. Award for Special Service to Pro Bono; Volunteer Legal Services Hawaii NIU Award for Outstanding Contribution to the Delievery of Legal Services. Taxation, general, Education and schools, Non-profit and tax-exempt organizations. Office: Chaminade Univ 3140 Waialae Ave Honolulu HI 96816 Office Fax: 808-440-4249. Business E-Mail: wtanna@chaminade.edu.

TANNENBAUM, BERNARD, lawyer; b. N.Y.C., July 14, 1928; s. Jacob and Lillian (Jupiter) T.; m. Elinor Fried, June 3, 1950; children: Jody, Ilene, Carol, Jeffrey. BA in Edn., NYU, 1950, JD, 1953; MA (hon.), Internat. U. Comm., 1974. Bar: N.Y. 1954, D.C. 1980, U.s. Dist. Ct. (so. and ea. dists.) N.Y. 1961, U.S. Ct. Claims 1964, U.S. Supreme Ct. 1964. Assoc. Halperin, Natanson, Shivitz & Scholar, N.Y.C., 1952-54; sole practice Mineola, N.Y., 1954-60, N.Y.C., 1969-87; ptnr. Fried, Beck, Tannenbaum & Field, N.Y.C., 1960-69; counsel Meltzer, Lippe, Goldstein & Wolf, Mineola, 1987—. Spl. counsel U.S. Senate Subcom. on Juvenile Delinquency, Washington, 1965-70, subcom. on Panama Canal U.S. Ho. of Reps., Washington, 1970-71, com. on mcht. marine and fisheries U.S. Ho. of Reps., 1977-80; arbitrator Am. Arbitration Assn., N.Y.C., 1965— , Small Claims Divsn. Civil Ct., N.Y.C., 1975—. Contbr. NYU Law Rev., editor, pub., The Democratic Forum, 1960-73; bd. dirs., trstee, chmn. Daytop Village Inc., N.Y.C., 1983—; bd. advisors Assn. Children with Retarded Mental Devel., N.Y.C., 1984-86. Commercial, contracts (including sales of goods; commercial financing), Legislative, Property, real (including real estate development, water). Office: 190 Willis Ave Mineola NY 11501-2693 E-mail: Tanbern@aol.com.

TANNENWALD, PETER, lawyer; b. Washington, Apr. 8, 1943; s. Judge Theodore and Selma (Peterfreund) T.; m. Carol B. Baum, May 25, 1969; 1 child, Jonathan Mark. AB, Brown U., 1964; LLB, Harvard U., 1967. Bar: U.S. Dist. Ct. D.C. 1968, U.S. Ct. Appeals (D.C. cir.) 1968, U.S. Supreme Ct. 1972. Assoc. Arent, Fox, Kintner, Plotkin & Kahn, Washington, 1967-74, ptnr., 1975-94; v.p. Irwin, Campbell & Tannenwald, P.C., Washington, 1995—. Columnist The LPTV Report, 1988-92. Mem. cmty. coun. Sta. WAMU-FM, Washington, 1986-93, 94-97, 2003—; dir. Brown Broadcasting Svc., Inc., Providence, 1970—; chmn. maj. law firms divsn. Nat. Capital Area affiliate United Way, 1977-79. Mem. Harvard Law Sch. Assn. D.C. (pres. 1979-80), Harvard Law Sch. Assn. (sec. 1982-84). Avocations: electronics, photography. Communications. Office: Irwin Campbell Tannenwald PC 1730 Rhode Island Ave NW Washington DC 20036-3101

TANNER, DEE BOSHARD, retired lawyer; b. Provo, Utah, Jan. 16, 1913; s. Myron Clark and Marie (Boshard) T.; m. Jane Barwick, Dec. 26, 1936 (div. Aug. 1962); children: Barry, Diane McDowell; m. Reeta Walker, Dec. 6, 1981. BA, U. Utah, 1935; LLB, Pacific Coast U., 1940; postgrad., Harvard U., 1936, Loyola U., L.A., 1937. Bar: Calif. 1943, U.S. Dist. Ct. (so. dist.) Calif. 1944, U.S. Ct. Appeals (9th cir.) 1947, ICC 1964, U.S. Dist. Ct. (ea. dist.) Calif. 1969, U.S. Supreme Ct. 1971. Assoc. Spray, Davis & Gould, L.A., 1943-44; pvt. practice L.A., 1944; assoc. Tanner and Sievers, L.A., 1944-47, Tanner and Thornton, L.A., 1947-54, Tanner, Hanson, Meyers, L.A., 1954-64; ptnr. Tanner and Van Dyke, L.A., 1964-65, Gallagher and Tanner, L.A., 1965-70; pvt. practice Pasadena, Calif., 1970-95; retired, 1995. Mem. L.A. Bar Assn., World Affairs Assn., Harvard Law Sch. Assn., Lawyers' Club L.A. Federal civil litigation, Corporate Fraud. Home and Office: 1720 Lombardy Rd Pasadena CA 91106-4127 E-mail: rpltd@aol.com.

TANNER, DOUGLAS ALAN, lawyer; b. Palo Alto, Calif., Aug. 30, 1953; s. Bernard R. and Caroline (Orris) Tanner; m. Carol Scilacci, May 28, 1977; children: Lauren Elizabeth, Wynn Ann, Leigh Caroline. AB in History, Stanford U., 1974, MBA, JD, Stanford U., 1978. Bar: Calif. 1978, U.S. Dist. ct. (no. dist.) Calif. 1978, U.S. Ct. Appeals (9th cir.) 1979, N.Y. 1987. Law clk. to judge U.S. Ct. Appeals (9th cir.), San Francisco, 1978-79; assoc. Orrick, Herrington & Sutcliffe, San Francisco, 1979-83, ptnr. San Jose, Calif., 1984-86, N.Y.C., 1986-89, Milbank, Tweed, Hadley & McCloy, L.A., 1989-92, Hong Kong, 1992-2001, Palo Alto, Calif., 2001—. Mem.: San Francisco Barristers (chmn. corps. com. 1981—82), Order of Coif, Phi Beta Kappa. Republican. Episcopalian. Corporate, general, Securities. Office: 5 Palo Alto Sq 3000 El Camino Rd Palo Alto CA 94306-2109 E-mail: dtanner@milbank.com.

TANNER, W(ALTER) RHETT, lawyer; b. Athens, Ga., May 16, 1938; s. Johnnie Bryson and Walterette (Arwood) T.; m. Carolyn Laverne Watson, Nov. 11, 1967; 1 child, Walter Rhett (dec. 1989). AB cum laude, U. Ga., 1960, JD cum laude, 1962. Bar: Ga. 1961; cert. neutral Ga. Office of Dispute Resolution. Assoc. Hansell, Post, Bandon & Dorsey, Atlanta, 1963-66, ptnr., 1966-89, Jones, Day, Reavis & Pogue, Atlanta, 1989-95, of counsel, 1995-99, retired, 1999; mediator Resolution Resources, Atlanta, 1999—. Panelist Am. Arbitration Assn., 1995—. Bd. dirs. Atlanta Symphony Orch., 1975—95, mem. exec. com., 1977—86, v.p., 1978, chmn. maj. gifts campaign, 1980, bd. counsellors, 1996—; mem. Leadership Atlanta, 1980, Leadership Ga., 1982; mem. bd. visitors Grady Meml. Hosp., 1983—92; trustee Ga. Legal History Found., 1986—, pres., 1996—; hon. chmn. Atlanta Decorators Show House, 2002; trustee, vice chmn. Sr. Citizens Svc. Met. Atlanta, Inc., 2000—; bd. dirs. Highlands/Cashiers Chamber Music Festival, 2003—. Lt. comdr. USNR, 1964—72. Mem. Atlanta Bar Assn. (bd. dirs. 1982-87, exec. com. 1983-87), State Bar Ga. (vice chmn. bar and media com. 1979-82), Atlanta Bar Found. (trustee 1985-91), U. Ga. Alumni (pres. chpt. 1973-74, chmn. Atlanta/Met. coun. 1975, mem. state bd. mgrs., v.p. 1976-78), Rotary Club, Gridiron, Capital City Club, Peachtree Racket Club, Phi Beta Kappa, Omicron Delta Kappa, Phi Kappa Phi, Phi Delta Phi, Delta Tau Delta. General civil litigation, Commercial, consumer (including collections, credit). Home: 2097 Bohler Rd NW Atlanta GA 30318-1515 Office: Jones Day Reavis & Pogue 3500 Suntrust Plz 303 Peachtree St NE Ste 3500 Atlanta GA 30308-3263 E-mail: wtanner516@aol.com.

TANNON, JAY MIDDLETON, lawyer; b. Augusta, Ga., Feb. 24, 1956; m. Elizabeth M. Gabhart; 1 child, Katherine. BA, U. N.C., 1978; JD, U. Va., 1982; MBA, U. Louisville, 1983. Bar: Ky. 1982. Ptnr. Brown, Todd & Heyburn, Louisville, 1982-2000; exec. committee Frost, Brown, & Todd LLC, 2000—; chmn. Kentucky WorldTrade Ctr., 1999—. Chmn., founder Comml. Dispute Resolution Inc., Louisville, 1986—90; chmn. Ky. Export Coun., 2001—; svcs. adv. com. US Trade Rep., 2002—; internat. studies adv. bd. U. NC; bd. dirs. Vivao PLC; exec. com. Evermore Investments LLC. Contbg. author Ky. Bus. Orgns.; contbr. articles to profl. jours. Bd. dirs. U. Louisville Sch. Bus., 1985-88, Independent Industries, Inc. 1988-95. Hearst Found. scholar, 1974, Johnston scholar U. N.C., 1976, Phillips scholar U. N.C., 1977, du Pont scholar U. Va., 1979; named one of Best Lawyers in Am., Woodward-White, Am.'s Leading Bus. Lawyers Chambers & Ptnrs. Mem. ABA, Internat. Bar Assn., Ky. Bar Assn., Louisville Bar Assn. Alternative dispute resolution, Corporate, general, Mergers and acquisitions. Office: Frost Brown Todd LLC 400 W Market St Ste 3200 Louisville KY 40202-3363 E-mail: jrannon@fbtlaw.com.

TANNOUS, ROBERT JOSEPH, lawyer; b. Amman, Jordan, June 4, 1962; came to U.S., 1968; s. Jerry J. and Nadia Tannous; m. Marlo B. Tannous, Apr. 22, 1989; children: Mallory E., Alexander B. BSBA, Ohio State U., 1984, JD, 1987. Bar: Ohio 1987, U.S. Dist. Ct. (so. dist.) Ohio 1987. Ptnr. Porter, Wright, Morris & Arthur LLP, Columbus, Ohio, 1987—. Trustee Children First Inc., Columbus, 1996-00, Ohio Hist. Found., Columbus, 1999-02, Ohio Historical Soc. Devel. counsel, 2002-; fundraiser, com. various charitable orgns., Columbus, 1987—; team walk coord. March of Dimes, 1988-90; mem. Columbus Mus. of Art, Columbus Zoo. Recipient Forty Under 40 award Bus. First, 1997; named one of Ten Outstanding Young Citizens U.S. Jr. C. of C., 1997. Mem. ABA (bus. law sect.), Columbus Bar Assn. (corps. law com., sports and entertainment law com., securities law com.), Capital Club, Columbus Investment Interest Group, Columbus Coun. on World Affairs, Columbus Area C. of C. (capt. club 1991-92), Alpha Lambda Delta, Phi Eta Sigma, Phi Alpha Kappa, Beta Gamma Sigma (past pres.), Pace Setters. Republican. Episcopalian. Avocations: golf, travel, reading, ohio state buckeyes. Finance, Mergers and acquisitions, Securities. Office: Porter Wright Morris & Arthur LLP 41 S High St Ste 2800 Columbus OH 43215-6194 E-mail: rtannous@porterwright.com.

TANSILL, FREDERICK JOSEPH, lawyer; b. Washington, Feb. 27, 1948; s. Frederick Riker and Mary Eileen (Loftus) T.; m. Joan Louise Trefsgar, July 10, 1971; children: Brendan Frederick, Brooke Charlotte, Charlotte Trefsgar. BA with honors, Brown U., 1970; JD, Georgetown U., 1974, LLM in Taxation, 1982. Bar: D.C. 1974, U.S. Tax Ct. 1976, Va. 1983. Assoc. Cross, Murphy & Smith, Washington, 1974-77; ptnr. Bird & Tansill, Washington, 1977-79; assoc. Ober, Grimes & Shriver, Washington, 1979-81; ptnr. Lewis, Mitchell & Moore, Vienna, Va., 1981-86; counsel Boothe, Prichard & Dudley, McLean, Va., 1986-87; ptnr. McGuire, Woods, Battle & Boothe, McLean, 1987-90; shareholder Verner, Liipfert, Bernhard, McPherson & Hand, Chartered, McLean, 1990-97; owner-mgr. Frederick J. Tansill & Assocs., LLC, McLean, 1997—. Gen. counsel No. Va. Cmty. Found., 1995-98, 1st v.p., 1998-99, pres., 1999-2000. Fellow Am. Coll. Trust and Estate Counsel; mem. ABA, Va. Bar Assn. (exec. coun. taxation sect. 1989-92, coun. and legis. com. wills sect. 1993-99—, trusts and estate sect. 1983-99, bd. govs. 1988-96, chmn. bd. govs. 1991-92, co-chmn. spl. task force lawyers as fiduciaries 1993-95), D.C. Bar Assn. (steering com. estates, trusts and probate law sects. 1995-97, co-chair 1997-99), Fairfax County Bar Assn. (will sect. 1986, chmn. tax sect. 1987-88, CLE com. 1988-89), No. Va. Estate Planning Coun. (exec. com. 1987-92, pres. 1990-91), Tower Club (bd. dirs. 1988—). Estate planning, Probate (including wills, trusts), Taxation, general. Office: Frederick J Tansill & Assocs 1749 Old Meadow Rd Ste 301 Mc Lean VA 22102-4310 Fax: (703) 847-1357. E-mail: Fjtansill@aol.com.

TANZMAN, EDWARD ALAN, lawyer; b. Chgo. s. Jack and Mary (Grodman) T.; m. Ellen Louise Partridge. BA in Polit. Sci. with honors, U. Chgo., 1973; JD, Georgetown U., 1976. Bar: Ill. 1976, D.C. 1979. Legis. asst. U.S. Senator John A. Durkin, Washington, 1976-79; various rsch. and adminstrv. staff positions Argonne (Ill.) Nat. Lab., 1979—; legis. counsel Palau Nat. Congress, Koror, Palau, 1980-81; emergency preparedness group leader Argonne (Ill.) Nat. Lab., 2003—. Adv. bd. Lawyers Alliance for World Security, Washington; adv. bd. DePaul U. Internat. Human Rights Law Inst., Chgo., 1998—. Co-author: Manual for National Implementation of the Chemical Weapons Convention, 1998; contbr. articles to internat. law jours. Chairperson bd. dirs. Health Rsch. Inst., Inc., Naperville, 1996—; cmty. rep. Nettelhorst Locl Sch. Coun., Chgo., 1989-2000; bd. dirs. Friends of Nettelhorst Sch., Chgo., 1992—. Fellowship Leadership Greater Chgo., 1993-94; recipient Award of Merit Health Rsch. Inst., Inc., 1989. Office: Argonne Nat Lab 9700 Cass Ave Argonne IL 60439-4832 Fax: 630-252-5327. E-mail: tanzman@anl.gov.

TAPHORN, JOSEPH BERNARD, lawyer; b. Beckemeyer, Ill., Oct. 9, 1921; s. Herman Henry and Marie (Gasser) T.; m. Anna Marie Klinge, June 25, 1944 (dec. Dec. 1991); children: Robert J., Joanne M., John F.; m. Joan Campen Klemmer, July 13, 1996. BS in Agr., U. Ill., 1943; BS in Engring., George Washington U., 1949, LLB, 1950. Bar: N.Y. 1952, D.C. 1952, U.S. Dist. Ct. (so. and ea. dists.) N.Y. 1952, U.S. Dist. Ct. (no. dist.) N.Y. 1991, U.S. Dist. Ct. D.C., 1952, U.S. Ct. Appeals (D.C. cir.) 1961, U.S. Ct. Appeals (fed. cir.) 1996, U.S. Supreme Ct. 1961. Patent examiner U.S. Patent Office, Washington, 1946-49, patent classifier, 1949-50; patent agt. Pollard and Jonston, N.Y.C., 1950-52; patent atty. IBM Corp., N.Y.C., 1952-59, patent mgr., counsel various locations, 1959-70, copyright counsel Armonk, N.Y., 1970-78, copyright and trademark counsel, 1978-88; pvt. practice Poughkeepsie, N.Y., 1989—. Chmn. bd. U.S. Dynamics, Yonkers, N.Y. 1975-77. Contbr. articles to profl. jours. Pres. Huntley Civic Assn., Eastchester, N.Y., 1958-59; trustee Copyright Soc. USA, N.Y.C., 1985-88. Capt. U.S. Army, 1943-46, ETO. Mem. ABA (com. chmn. 1983-87), N.Y. State Bar Assn., Dutchess County Bar Assn., Am. Intellectual Property Law Assn., N.Y. Intellectual Property Law Assn. (com. chmn. 1987-89), Ea. N.Y. Intellectual Property Law Assn., Dutchess Golf and Country Club, Americana Tennis Club. Republican. Roman Catholic. Avocations: golf, hunting, fishing, tennis, skiing. Computer, Patent, Trademark and copyright. Home and Office: 8 Scenic Dr Poughkeepsie NY 12603-5521 E-mail: jbtaphorn@prodigy.net.

TAPLEY, JAMES LEROY, retired lawyer, railway corporation executive; b. Greenville, Miss., July 10, 1923; s. Lester Leroy and Lillian (Clark) T.; m. Priscilla Moore, Sept. 9, 1950. AB, U. N.C., 1947, JD with honors, 1950. Bar: N.C. 1951, D.C. 1962. With So. Ry. Co., Washington, 1953-83, gen. solicitor, 1967-74, asst. v.p. law, 1974-75, v.p. law, 1975-83; v.p. Washington counsel Norfolk So. Corp., Washington, 1983-87; ret., 1987. Mem. Phi Beta Kappa, Kappa Sigma. Clubs: Chevy Chase. Administrative and regulatory, Antitrust, Corporate, general.

TARASI, LOUIS MICHAEL, JR., lawyer; b. Cheswick, Pa., Sept. 9, 1931; s. Louis Michael and Ruth Elizabeth (Records) T.; m. Patricia Ruth Finley, June 19, 1954; children: Susan, Louis Michael III, Elizabeth, Brian, Patricia, Matthew. BA, Miami U., Ohio, 1954; JD, U. Pa., 1959. Bar: Pa. 1960, U.S. Dist. Ct. (we. dist.) Pa. 1960, U.S. Ct. Appeals (3d cir.) 1964, U.S. Supreme Ct. 1969, U.S. Dist. Ct. (we. dist.) Tex. 1988, U.S. Ct. Appeals (5th cir.) 1989, U.S. Ct. Appeals (4th cir.) 1994, U.S. Ct. Fed. Claims 1987, U.S. Dist. Ct. Colo. 1998; cert. civil trial adv. Nat. Bd. Trial Advocacy. Assoc., owner Burgwin, Ruffin, Perry & Pohl, Pitts., 1960-68; ptnr. Conte, Courtney & Tarasi, Beaver County, Pa., 1968-78, Tarasi & Tighe, Pitts., 1978-82, Tarasi & Johnson, P.C., Pitts., 1982-95, Tarasi & Assocs., P.C., Pitts., 1995-99, The Tarasi Lawfirm, P.C., Pitts., 1997-2001, Tarasi, Tarasi & Fishman, P.C., Pitts., 2001—. Mem. parish coun. St. James Ch., Sewickley, Pa.; mem. Sewickley Borough Allegheny Coun., 1978-1982. With U.S. Army, 1954-56. Fellow: Internat. Soc. Barristers; mem.: Am. Coll. Barristers (sr. counsel), Am. Bd. Trial Advs., Melvin Belli Soc., St. Thomas More Soc. (award 1991), West Pa. Trial Lawyers Assn. (pres. 1975), Pa. Bar Assn., Allegheny County Bar Assn., Acad. Trial Lawyers Allegheny County, Pa. Trial Lawyers Assn. (pres. 1979—80), Assn. Trial Lawyers Am. (gov., rep.). Democrat. Roman Catholic. Avocations: reading, golf, lecturing. General civil litigation, Personal injury (including property damage), Toxic tort. Home: 1 Way Hollow Rd Sewickley PA 15143-1192 Office: Tarasi Tarasi & Fishman 510 3d Ave Pittsburgh PA 15219-2107

TARAVELLA, CHRISTOPHER ANTHONY, lawyer; b. Pueblo, Colo., Sept. 19, 1951; s. Frank Louis and Ann Jean T.; m. Kathleen; children: Nicholas M., John L. BS in Engring. Mechanics, USAF Acad., 1973; JD, U. Colo., 1976; postgrad., Harvard U., 1996. Bar: Iowa 1976, Colo. 1976, U.S. Ct. Mil. Appeals 1976, U.S. Dist. Ct. Colo. 1976, Fla. 1977, U.S. Supreme Ct. 1982, U.S. Ct. Appeals (fed. cir.) 1983, D.C. 1984, U.S. Claims Ct. 1984, Mich. 1985. Commd. 2nd lt. USAF, 1973, legal intern Staff Judge Adv., 1973-76, advanced through grades to lt. col. Hurlburt Field, Fla., 1976-78, asst. staff judge adv. Zaragoza, Spain, 1978-81, chief cir. trial counsel Washington, 1981-83; chief Constitutional Torts Br. Civil Litigation, Washington, 1983-85; resigned USAF, 1985; asst. gen. counsel Chrysler Motors Corp., Highland Park, Mich., 1985-90; asst. gen. counsel comml. affairs, chief patent counsel Chrysler Corp., Auburn Hills, Mich., 1990-96; v.p., gen. counsel Daimler Chrysler Svcs. N.Am. LLC, Southfield,

Mich., 1997—. Mem. governing com. Conf. on Consumer Fin. Law. Staff Judge Adv. USAFR, 927 Air Refueling Group, Selfridge Air NG Base, Mich., 1985-94. Mem. Am. Fin. Svcs. Assn. (bd. dirs.). General civil litigation, Patent, Trademark and copyright. Office: Daimler Chrysler Svcs N Am LLC CIMS 405-27-16 27777 Inkster Rd Farmington Hills MI 48334 Business E-Mail: cat8@daimlerchrysler.com.

TAREN, JEFFREY LYNN, lawyer; b. Wilkes Barre, Pa., Sept. 20, 1952; s. Arnold and Ruth Taren; m. Carolyn Therese Bieszat, May 26, 1985; children: Jordan, Mariel. BA in Polit. Sci., Rutgers Coll., 1974; JD, Boston Coll., 1977. Staff atty. Legal Assistance of Chgo., 1977-80; ptnr. Kinoy, Taren, Gerraghty & Potter, Chgo., 1980-98; hearing officer Chgo. Human Rels. Commn., 1991—. Adv. bd. employment, Chgo., 1995—. Author: (with others) Civil Rights Annual Review, 1995. Bd. dirs. Chgo. Lawyers Com. for Civil Rights, 1996—; chmn. Oak Park Parking Traffic Commn., 1993—. Recipient Award Hope Fair Housing Ctr., 1987, Pro Bono award Lawyers Com. for Civil Rights, 1996. Avocations: basketball, playing banjo. Office: Kinoy Taren & Geraghty PC 224 S Michigan Ave Ste 300 Chicago IL 60604-2505

TARG, NICHOLAS WILLIAM, lawyer; m. Elise S. Feldman. BA, U. Calif, Santa Cruz, 1988; JD, Boston Coll., 1993. Bar: Calif. 1993. Atty. adviser Dept. of the Interior, Washington, 1993—99; counsel U.S. EPA, 1999—2002. Rschr. Interactive Sciences Inc., Palo Alto, Calif., 2000—02. Chair, environ. justice com. Sect. of Individual Rights, ABA, Washington, 2001—; sr. dir. Env. Sect., Bar Assn. D.C., 1994—97. Recipient Bronze medal for Superior Achievement, Us Epa, 2002, Fish Hook award, Selawick Coun., 2001, Bronze medal, Office of Gen. Counsel, EPA, Superior Achievement awards, Dept. of Interior, 1993—99; scholar, MIT, Grad. Sch. of Urban Studies, 1990—91, O'Keefe Family scholar, Boston Coll. Law Sch., 1992. Office: Environmental Protection Agency 1200 Pennsylvania Ave NW Washington DC 20460

TARGAN, HOLLI HART, lawyer; b. Detroit, Jan. 3, 1960; m. Anthony Andrew Targan, Aug. 11, 1985. BA, Mich. State U., 1982; JD cum laude, Wayne State U., 1985. Bar: Md. 1985, D.C. 1988, Mich. 1990. Staff atty. Office of Comptroller of the Currency, Washington, 1985-89; assoc. Dykema Gossett, Bloomfield Hills, Mich., 1989-91; staff counsel Mich. Nat. Corp., Farmington Hills, Mich., 1991-95; prin. Law Offices of H.H. Targan, Farmington Hills, 1995-96; ptnr. Jaffe, Raitt, Heuer & Weiss, P.C., Detroit, 1996—. Speaker on various electronic banking topics and electronic commerce, 1995—. Co-author: Guide to Smart Cards and Stored Value, 1999; contbr. articles to profl. jours. Sec., vice chair B'nai B'rith Youth Orgn., Mich., 1991-99. Mem. ABA (cyberspace law com.), Md. State Bar, State Bar Mich., D.C. Bar Assn., Nat. Assn. Women Bus. Owners, Electronic Transactions Assn. (dir.). Banking, Commercial, contracts (including sales of goods; commercial financing), Computer. Office: Jaffe Raitt Heuer & Weiss One Woodward Ave # 2400 Detroit MI 48226 E-mail: htargan@jafferaitt.com.

TARINO, GARY EDWARD, lawyer; b. Jersey City, Oct. 3, 1951; s. Edward G. and Veronica Tarino; m. Maureen Fitzpatrick, May 9, 1987. BA summa cum laude, Rutgers U., 1973, JD, 1976. Bar: N.J. 1976, U.S. Dist. Ct. N.J. 1976, D.C. Ct. Appeals 1978, U.S. Supreme Ct. 1980, N.Y. 1982, U.S. Dist. Ct. (so. dist.) N.Y. 1988, U.S. Dist. Ct. (ea. dist.) N.Y. 1990. Assoc. Winne, Banta, Rizzi & Harrington, Hackensack, N.J., 1976-79; asst. pros. Bergen County Pros. Office, Hackensack, 1979-83, chief organized crime squad, 1981-83; atty. Automatic Data Processing, Inc., Roseland, N.J., 1983—, assoc. gen. counsel, staff v.p., 1994—. Pub. defender Borough of Maywood, N.J., 1978; bd. dirs. N.J. Coun. Econ. Edn., 1990—; master Sidney Reitman Employment Law Am. Inn Ct., 1995-2000. Bd. dirs. Am. Heart Assn., N.J., 1976-81, Middlesex County (N.J.) chpt., 1973-81; trustee Integrity, Inc., 1991-97; grad. Leadership N.J., 1989; cubmaster pack III Boy Scouts Am., 2000—. Recipient cert. of appreciation U.S. Treasury Dept., 1983, letter of commondation PBA, 1983, Alumni Vol. Leadership award 1st Ann. Leadership N.J., 1991. General civil litigation, Computer, Criminal. Office: Automatic Data Processing 1 A D P Blvd Roseland NJ 07068-1786

TARNOE, RUNE, lawyer; b. Roskilde, Denmark, Feb. 27, 1967; LLM in European Bus. Law, U. Amsterdam, The Netherlands, 1993; LLM, U. Copenhagen, 1993. Bar: Danish Bar Assn./Danish Law Soc. 1996. Atty. J.P. Galmond & Co., Copenhagen, 1996—. Construction, Private international. Office: GP Galmond & Co HC Andersens Blvd 51 4tv DK-1553 Copenhagen Denmark

TARONJI, JAIME, JR., lawyer; b. NYC, Nov. 20, 1944; s. Jaime and Ruth T.; m. Mary Taronji, May 16, 1970; children: Ian A., Mark N., Nicole V. BA, George Washington U., 1972; JD, Georgetown U., 1976. Bar: Va. 1977, DC 1978, Ohio (corp. counsel) 1996. Asst. to dep. staff dir. U.S. Commn. on Civil Rights, Washington, 1972-76; trial atty. FTC, Washington, 1976-79; antitrust counsel Westinghouse Electric Corp., Pitts., 1979-81; group legal counsel Dana Corp., Toledo, 1982-88; v.p., gen. counsel Packaging Corp. Am. subs. Tenneco, Evanston, Ill., 1988-95; law v.p. NCR Corp., Dayton, 1996-99; v.p., gen. counsel, sec. Dayton Superior Corp., Dayton, 1999—. Adv. bd. mem. Corp. Counsel Inst., Georgetown U. Law Ctr. Author: The 1970 Census Undercount of Spanish Speaking Persons, 1974; editor: Puerto Ricans in the U.S., 1976. Capt. M.I., U.S. Army, 1965-70, Vietnam. Mem. ABA (antitrust sect.), Am. Corp. Counsel Assn., Minority Corp. Counsel Assn., Hispanic Nat. Bar Assn. Democrat. Roman Catholic. Antitrust, Corporate, general, Mergers and acquisitions. Home: 5 Grandon Rd Dayton OH 45419-2548 Office: Ste 130 7777 Washington Village Dr Dayton OH 45459-3976 E-mail: jtaronjijr@woh.rr.com.

TARPLEY, JOHN R. lawyer; b. Lebanon, Tenn., Aug. 18, 1954; BS, U. Tenn., 1976, JD, 1980. Bar: Tenn. 1981. Law ckl. to Hon. Lewis H. Conner, Jr., Assoc. Judge, Tenn. Ct. Appeals, Mid. Divsn., 1981—82; asst. atty. gen. State of Tenn., 1982—89; atty. Lewis, King, Krieg & Waldrop, P.C., Nashville. Mem.: ABA (Young Lawyers divsn. long range planning com. 1986—89, editor Barrister 1987—89, Young Lawyers divsn. assembly clk. 1989—90, Young Lawyers exec. coun. 1989—91, standing com. on assn. comm. 1989—92, Young Lawyers divsn. assembly spkr. 1990—91, coun. mem. 1991—93, Ho. of Dels. 1997—2001, coun. mem. 1999—2002, revenue officer 1999—2002, torts and ins. practice sect.), Nashville Bar Assn. (pres. Young Lawyers divsn. 1985, bd. dirs. Young Lawyers divsn. 1985—86, sec. 1989, bd. dirs. 1991—94, 1st v.p. 1994), Tenn. Bar Assn. (editor Young Lawyers Quar. 1984—86, bd. govs. 1984—90, moving v.p. 1986—87, pres.-elect 1987—88, bd. govs. 1987—89, pres. 1988—89, 1988—89, treas. 1997—2000, v.p. 2001—02, Young Lawyers Conf., pres.-elect 2002—03, chairperson-elect 1989—90, chairperson 1990—91, litigation coun.). Product liability, Commercial, consumer (including collections, credit). Office: Lewis King Krieg and Waldrop Suntrust Bank Bldg 201 Fourth Ave N Ste 1500 Nashville TN 37219*

TARPY, THOMAS MICHAEL, lawyer; b. Columbus, Ohio, Jan. 4, 1945; s. Thomas Michael and Catherine G. (Sharshal) T.; m. Mary Patricia Canna, Sept. 9, 1967; children: Joshua Michael, Megan Patricia, Thomas Canna, John Patrick. AB, John Carroll U., 1966; JD, Ohio State U., 1969. Bar: Ohio 1969, U.S. Dist. Ct. (so. dist.) Ohio 1972, U.S. Dist. Ct. (no. dist.) Ohio 1974, U.S. Ct. Appeals (6th cir.) 1982, U.S. Supreme Ct. 1997. Assoc. Vorys, Sater, Seymour & Pease LLP, Columbus, 1969-76, ptnr., 1977-85, 87—; v.p. Liebert Corp., Columbus, 1985-87. Chmn. Columbus Graphics Commn., 1980; mem. Columbus Area Leadership Program, 1975. With U.S. Army, 1969-75. Fellow Coll. Labor and Employment Lawyers; mem. ABA, Ohio Bar Assn., Columbus Bar Assn. Corporate, general, Labor (including EEOC, Fair Labor Standards Act, labor-management relations, NLRB, OSHA), Pension, profit-sharing, and employee benefits. Office: Vorys Sater Seymour & Pease LLP PO Box 1008 52 E Gay St Columbus OH 43215-3161

TARR, RALPH WILLIAM, lawyer, former federal government official; b. Bakersfield, Calif., Sept. 29, 1948; BA, Dartmouth Coll., 1970; MPA, Calif. State U., 1973; JD, U. Calif., Hastings, 1976. Extern to assoc. justice Calif. Supreme Ct., 1976; rsch. atty. to presiding justice Ct. Appeal (5th dist.) Calif., 1976-77; assoc. Baker, Manock & Jensen, Fresno, Calif., 1977-81, dir., mem. exec. com., 1981-82; mem. adminstrv. com. Fed. Register, Washington, 1982-85; dep. asst. atty. gen. U.S. Dept. Justice, Washington, 1982-84, acting asst. atty. gen., 1984-85; solicitor U.S. Dept. Interior, Washington, 1985-89, counselor, 1989-90; pvt. practice L.A., 1990—. General civil litigation, Environmental, Property, real (including real estate development, water). Home: 24011 Alder Pl Calabasas CA 91302-2394 Office: Andrews & Kurth LLP 601 S Figueroa St Ste 1725 Los Angeles CA 90017-5747 E-mail: rtarr@akllp.com.

TARSHES, DAVID C. lawyer; b. Indpls., Dec. 28, 1955; s. Gerald H. and Lois S. Tarshes; m. Carol Dawson, June 30, 1989 (dec. Sept. 12, 1992); m. Deborah Kerdeman, Aug. 20, 1995. BS, Ind. U. Sch. Bus., Bloomingdale, 1978; JD, Duke U. Sch. Law, 1981. Bar: Wash. 1983, cert.: U.S. Dist. Ct., Western Dist. 1983, U.S. Ct. Appeals, 9th Cir. 1983, U.S. Dist. Ct., Eastern Dist. 2002, Supreme Ct., State of Wash. 1983, U.S. Tax Ct. 1985. Law clk. to Hon. F. Sachs U.S. Dist. Ct., Western Dist., Kansas City, Mo., 1981—83; assoc. Davis Wright Tremaine LLP, Seattle, 1983—88, ptnr., 1989—. Co-author: Washington Civil Procedure Before Trial Deskbook Supplement, 1986; editor: Duke Law Jour., 12th Ann. Admin. Law Issue, 1981, May God Comfort You - A Guide for Mourners, 1995. Adv. bd. mem. Wash. Women's Employment and Edn., Seattle, 1986—88; co-chair NW Alternative Dispute Resolution Conf., Seattle, 1993—97; bd. mem. King County Sexual Assault Resource Ctr., Seattle, 1996—99; participant Leadership Tomorrow, Seattle, 2001—02; long range planning com. mem. Seattle Assn. for the Jewish Disabled, Seattle, 2001—; task force mem. League of King County: Future of King County Task Force, Seattle, 2002—; mcpl. adv. com. mem. Dispute Resolution Ctr. of King County, Seattle, 2002—; bd. mem. Congregation Beth Shalom, Seattle, 1997—99. Co-recipient Trial Lawyer of the Yr. award, Trial Lawyers for Pub. Justice, Washington, D.C., 1995. Mem.: Wash. State Bar Assn. (chair, alternative dispute resolution section 1999—2000, Award of Merit, Alternative Dispute Resolution sect. 1994, 1995, 1997). Alternative dispute resolution, Appellate, Admiralty. Office: Davis Wright Tremaine LLP 1501 Fourth Ave Ste 2600 Seattle WA 98101-1688 Fax: 206-903-3879. Business E-Mail: davetarshes@dwt.com.

TARTT, BLAKE, lawyer; b. Houston, Mar. 16, 1929; s. Herbert Blake and Bernice (Schwalm) T.; m. Barbara Jean Moore, Jan. 30, 1960; children: Blake III, Courtnay Elias. BBA, So. Methodist U., 1949, JD cum laude, 1959. Bar: Tex. 1959. Assoc. Fulbright & Jaworski, Houston, 1959-70, ptnr., 1970-2000, Beirne, Maynard & Parsons, LLP, Houston, 2000—. Mem. Tex. Commn. on Jud. Conduct, 1996-2001. Bd. dirs. Mus. Fine Arts, Houston. Served to 1st lt. USAF, 1951-55, Korea. Decorated Air medal. Fellow Am. Bar Found. (chmn. fellows 1987, life), Tex. Bar Found. (chmn. bd. 1974-75, chmn. fellows 1978-79, life), Am. Coll. Trial Lawyers; mem. ABA (ho. of dels. 1976-99, state del. 1990-99, standing com. fed. jud. 1996-99, chair 1997, bd. govs. 2001—), Am. Bd. Trial Advocates (advocate), Houston Bar Found. (life., chmn., bd. dirs. 1992), Fed. Bar Assn., Internat. Assn. Def. Counsel, Am. Judicature Soc. (bd. dirs. 1984-88), So. Conf. Bar Pres. (pres. 1984), State Bar Tex. (dir. 1972-75, exec. com. 1975-76, pres. elect 1982-83, pres. 1983-84), Houston Bar Assn., Dallas Bar Assn., Am. Law Inst., Tex. Jud. Council, Citizens Commn. on the Tex. Judiciary, Houston Philosophical Soc., Coronado Club, Forest Club, Argyle Club (San Antonio), Reform Club (London), Delta Theta Phi, Alpha Tau Omega. Episcopalian. Federal civil litigation, State civil litigation, Nuclear power. Office: Beirne Maynard & Parsons 1300 Post Oak Blvd Houston TX 77056-3028 E-mail: btartt@bmpllp.com.

TARUN, ROBERT WALTER, lawyer; b. Lake Forest, Ill., Sept. 1, 1949; s. Donald Walter and Bonnie Jean (Cruickshank) T.; m. Helen J. McSweeney, May 1, 1987; children: Abigail Esch, Tyler Vincent, Parker Donald, Aimée Dakota. AB, Stanford U., 1971; JD, DePaul U., 1974; MBA, U. Chgo., 1982. Bar: Ill. 1974, Calif. 1975, U.S. Dist. Ct. (no. dist.) Ill. 1974, U.S. Dist. Ct. (we. dist.) Ark. 1986, U.S. Dist. Ct. (so. dist.) Ind. 1995, U.S. Dist. Ct. (no. dist.) Calif. 1995, U.S. Dist. Ct. (ea. dist.) Mich. 1996, U.S. Dist. Ct. (ea. dist.) Wis. 2000, U.S. Dist. Ct. (ctrl. dist.) Ill. 2001, U.S. Ct. Appeals (7th cir.) 1975, U.S. Ct. Appeals (5th cir.) 1992, U.S. Ct. Appeals (3d cir.) 1993, U.S. Ct. Appeals (Fed. cir.) 1995, U.S. Ct. Appeals (9th and 11th cirs.) 1996, U.S. Supreme Ct. 1978. Asst. atty. gen. State of Ill., Chgo., 1974-76; asst. U.S. atty. U.S. Dept. Justice, Chgo., 1976-79, dep. chief criminal div., 1979-82, exec. asst. U.S. atty. no. dist. Ill., 1982-85; ptnr. Reuben & Proctor, Chgo., 1985-86, Isham, Lincoln & Beale, Chgo., 1986-88, Winston & Strawn, Chgo., 1988—. Lectr. in law U. Chgo. Law Sch., 2001—; adj. prof. Northwestern U. Sch. Law, 1999—2001, lectr. criminal law parctice, 2000—01; instr. Atty. Gen.'s Advocacy Inst., Washington, 1980—85, Nat. Inst. Trial Advs., 1990. Author (with Dan K. Webb): Corporate Internal Investigations, 1993—2003. Bd. dirs. Chgo. Ctrl. Area Com., 1994—. Fellow Am. Coll. Trial Lawyers (mem. fed. criminal procedure com. 1993—, admission to fellowship com. 1997-2000); mem. ABA (white collar crime inst. 1997—, planning com.), Bar Assn. San Francisco, Chgo. Bar Assn., U. Chgo. Grad. Sch. Bus. Alumni Assn. (bd. dirs. 1986), Racquet Club, Wong Sun Soc. (San Francisco), Kenilworth Club, H.O.G. (Black Hills chpt.), Chgo. Stanford Assn. Presbyterian. Avocations: architecture, screenplays, forensic science. Banking, Federal civil litigation, Criminal. Office: Winston & Strawn 35 W Wacker Dr Ste 4700 Chicago IL 60601-1614 Home: 219 Leicester Rd Kenilworth IL 60043-1244

TARVER, MARGARET LEGGETT, lawyer, forensic scientist; b. Birmingham, Ala., Mar. 7, 1942; d. Booker Thomas and Ernestine Williametta (Rutland) Leggett; divorced; children: James, Derrick. BS, Talladega (Ala.) Coll., 1962; MS, Howard U., 1966; JD, Seton Hall U., 1982. Bar: Pa., 1982, N.J., 1982, U.S. Dist. Ct. (ea. dist.) Pa., 1983, U.S. Dist. Ct. N.J., 1982, U.S. Supreme Ct. 2000. Rsch. asst.med. sch. Howard U., Washington, 1962-64; sci. cons. Bd. Edn., Washington, 1966-68; instr. Tech. Tng. Project, Newark, 1970-71; sr. learning ptnr. SUNY, Albany, 1972-74; forensic scientist N.J. State Police Lab., Hammonton, 1976—82, tech. dir., 1983—2001, acting lab. dir., 2001—02; ret., 2002. Cons., EMT, U. Medicine and Dentistry N.J., 1975, adj. faculty, 2002—. Vol. atty. Phila. Lawyers Vol. Indigent Program, 1983-2001; bd. dirs. YWCA, Paterson, N.J., 1976-81, Women's Haven Battered Women's Program, Paterson, 1976-81. Fellow Am. Acad. Forensic Scis. (jurisprudence sect. 1997, program co-chair ann. meeting 2000); mem. ABA, N.J. State Bar Assn. (bd. dirs. minorities in the profession sect. 1990-96, jud. adminstrn. com. 1999—, by-laws com. 1999—, editor-in-chief minorities in the profession sect. newsletter 1990-95), Pa. Bar Assn., Burlington County Bar Assn., Phila. Bar Assn., Northeastern Assn. Forensic Scientists, Mid-Atlantic Assn. Forensic Scientists, N.J. Assn. Forensic Scientists (bd. dirs. 1998-2002), Assn. Black Women Lawyers-South Jersey (mem.-at-large 1999-2001, pres. 2001—), Talladega Coll. Alumni Assn. (pres. Phila. chpt. 1983-85). Avocations: pianist, organist, oil painting, tennis, bicycling. Family and matrimonial, General practice, Probate (including wills, trusts). Home: 42 Garland Ln Willingboro NJ 08046-3012

TARWATER, JEREMY RYAN, lawyer, researcher; b. San Diego, May 28, 1976; s. James R. and Jerry Kay Tarwater. BA, U. Calif., Berkeley, 1998; JD cum laude, Georgetown U., 2001. Bar: Calif. 2002, U.S. Dist. Ct. (no., ctrl., so. dists.) Calif. 2002. Atty. Latham & Watkins, Costa Mesa, Calif., 2000—. Mem.: ABA, Orange County Bar Assn. Avocations: travel, writing, rowing, bicycling. Corporate, general, Immigration, naturalization, and customs. Office: Latham and Watkins 650 Town Ctr Ste 2000 Costa Mesa CA 92606 Office Fax: 714-755-8290. Business E-Mail: jeremy.tarwater@lw.com.

TASKER, JOSEPH, lawyer, educator; b. Tulsa, May 6, 1950; s. Joseph and Kathryn Lucille (Ahlstrom) T.; m. Constance Lee Sontheimer, May 28, 1971; children: Joseph III, Kathryn Holly. BA, U. Okla., 1972; JD, George Washington U., 1975. Bar: D.C. 1975, U.S. Dist. Ct. D.C. 1981, U.S. Ct. Appeals (D.C. cir.) 1981, U.S. Ct. Internat. Trade 1981, U.S. Ct. Appeals (fed. cir.) 1984. Staff atty. Bur. of Competition FTC, Washington, 1975-79, asst. to dir., 1979-81; assoc. Bishop, Cook, Purcell & Reynolds, Washington, 1981-85, ptnr., 1986-90; v.p., assoc. gen. counsel, govt. affairs Compaq Computer Corp., 1990-99; sr. v.p. gov't. affairs and gen. counsel Information Technology Assn. of Am., 2002—. Lectr. in sociology George Washington U., 1974, 77, lectr. George Washington U. Law Sch., 1982. Mem. ABA, D.C. Bar Assn., Order of Coif, Phi Beta Kappa. Democrat. Antitrust, Federal civil litigation, Private international.

TATAR, SERGE, lawyer; b. Hyeres, France, June 7, 1967; s. Philippe Tatar and Suzanne Dreyer. MBA, HEC, Paris, 1990; JD, U. Paris I, 1990. Assoc. Gede, Loyrette, Nouel, Paris, 1990—92; credit analyst Banque Indouvel, Oslo, 1992—93; assoc. Bredin, Prat, Paris, 1993—95, Gide, Loyrette, Nouel, Paris, 1995—2000, ptnr., 2000—. Office: Gide Loyrette Nouel 26 Cours Albert I 75008 Paris France Business E-Mail: tatar@gide.com.

TATE, HAROLD SIMMONS, JR., lawyer; b. Taylors, S.C., Sept. 19, 1930; s. Harold Simmons and Cleone (Clayton) T.; m. Elizabeth Anne Coker, Dec. 22, 1952; children— Mary Elizabeth Anne, Martha Coker, Virginia Clayton. Grad. cum laude, Harvard U., 1951, JD, 1956, postgrad., 1954. Bar: S.C. 1956. Ptnr. Haynsworth Sinkler Boyd, PA, Columbia, SC, 1962—. Chmn. U.S. Dist. Ct. (S.C.) Adv. Com., 1984—; lectr. Am. Law Inst.-ABA seminars; adv. com. on rules and procedures U.S. Ct. Appeals (4th cir.), 1990-95. Co-author: South Carolina Appellate Practice, 1985; bd. editors Federal Litigation Guide Reporter, 1985—; co-draftsman S.C. Rules of Evidence, 1995; contbr. articles and book revs. to profl. jours. Chmn. Richland County Mental Health Ctr., 1965-66; co-chmn. Columbia Hearing and Speech Ctr., 1962-64; mem. admission and scholarship com. Harvard U., 1961—; chmn. subcom. on legislation, legislation and fin. study commn. Gov.'s Adv. Group on Mental Health Planning, 1963-65; chmn. Columbia Bd. Supervisory of Registration, 1961-70; pres. Columbia Philharm. Orch., 1966-67, Town Theatre, 1967-70; bd. trustee Richland County Pub. Libr., 1973-78, Hist. Columbia Found., 1971-75, Caroliniana Soc., 1978—, Bostick Charitable Trust, 1968—, Archaeol. Rsch. Trust, 2000—; bd. mgrs. S.C. Hist. Soc., 1993-99, 2002—; commr. S.C. Commn. of Archives and History, 1995—. Capt. U.S. Army, 1951-53. Recipient DuRant award Disting Pub. Svc., 2001. Fellow Am. Coll. Trial Lawyers; mem. ABA, Am. Law Inst., Am. Judicature Soc., S.C. Bar Assn., Assn. Bar City N.Y., Richland County Bar Assn., Harvard Law Sch. Assn. S.C. (sec.-treas. 1968-70, pres. 1988—), Forest Lake Country Club, Columbia Drama Club (pres. 1963-64), Palmetto Club (sec. 1963-70, pres. 1973-76), The Forum Club, Harvard Club (N.Y.C.), Harvard Club S.C., Carolina Yacht Club. Episcopalian. Federal civil litigation, State civil litigation, Corporate, general. Home: 15 Gibbes Ct Columbia SC 29201-3923 Office: Haynsworth Sinkler Boyd PA Fl 22 1201 Main St Ste 2200 Columbia SC 29201-3232 Business E-Mail: state@hsblawfirm.com.

TATE, MILTON YORK, JR., lawyer; b. Giddings, Tex., May 14, 1939; s. Milton Y. and Miriam (Phillips) Tate; m. Twila Tate, June 4, 1960; children: Rebecca Lynn, Rachel Kelley. BBA, U. Tex., Austin, 1960, JD, 1963. Bar: Tex. 1963. Ptnr. Moorman, Tate, Moorman & Urquhart, Brenham, Tex., 1965—; pres. Washington County Abstract Co., 1965—. Bd. dirs. Tex. Nat. Bank Brenham. City atty. City of Brenham, 1982—; bd. dirs. Bohne Meml. Hosp., Brenham Indsl. Found., Inc. General practice. Address: PO Box 1808 Brenham TX 77834-1808

TATGENHORST, ROBERT (CHARLES TATGENHORST), lawyer, educator; b. Cin., Apr. 21, 1918; s. Charles and Clara (Strebel) T.; m. Louise Thompson, Sept. 6, 1951; children: David, John, James, Richard. AB, Dartmouth Coll., 1940; LL.B., U. Cin., 1947. Bar: Ohio 1947. Asst. atty. gen., State of Ohio, 1947-49; asso. firm Taft, Stettinius & Hollister, Cin., 1951-58; ptnr. firm Tatgenhorst & Tatgenhorst, Cin., 1958-61; prin. firm Robert Tatgenhorst & Assos., Cin., 1961-85; ptnr. Tatgenhorst & Bruestle, Cin., 1986—, 1986-95. Adj. prof. law Chase Coll. Law, No. Ky. U., 1962-86. Pres. Westwood Civic Assn., Cin., 1959, Meth. Union, 1960; chmn. dist. Boy Scouts Am., 1970; trustee Twin Towers Retirement Ctr., 1968-93, Westwood United Meth. Ch., bd. trustees 1985-88, pres., 1990-92, trustee, 1992. With CIC U.S. Army, 1942-46. Mem. Ohio State Bar Assn., Cin. Bar Assn. (sec. 1973-75), Ryland Lakes Country Club, Optimists (pres. Cin. club 1962), Dartmouth of Cin. Club (pres. 1965), Masons (33 deg.), Sigma Alpha Epsilon, Phi Alpha Delta (pres. 1946). Republican.

TATONE, KATHY, lawyer; b. Ft. Dodge, Iowa, Apr. 27, 1957; d. Peter and Maria Terranova; m. Marc Tatone, Aug. 29, 1978; children: Michael, Matthew. BA, U. Minn., 1981; JD cum laude, William Mitchell Coll. of Law, 1985. Bar: Minn. 1985, U.S. Ct. Appeals (8th cir.) 1985. Assoc. Karon Jepsen & Daly, St. Paul, 1985-90; ptnr. Rath Thue & Tatone, Mpls., 1990-92; pvt. practice Mpls., 1992—. Author, editor, columnist Minn. Trial Lawyers Mag., 1985—; mem. editl. bd. Barrister Mag., 1993-94; contbr. articles to profl. publs. Mem. Minn. Trial Lawyers (exec. com., bd. govs. 1990-94), Minn. Women Lawyers, Minn. State Bar Assn., Minn. Million Dollar Round Table. Personal injury (including property damage). Office: 3036 Kyle Ave N Minneapolis MN 55422

TAUB, CATHY ELLEN, lawyer; b. N.Y.C., July 22; d. Jesse and Shirley Jane Taub; m. Lowell Carl Freiberg, May 7, 1994; children: Oliver Emmett Freiberg, Julian Cole Freiberg. BA cum laude, Barnard Coll., 1980; JD with honors, George Washington U., 1983. Bar: N.Y. 1984, U.S. Dist. Ct. Md. 1984, U.S. Ct. Appeals (4th cir.) 1984. Law clk. Hon. Edward S. Northrop, 1983-84; assoc. Cahill Gordon & Reindel, N.Y.C., 1984-87, 97-98; asst. v.p., corp. counsel Reliance Group Holdings, Inc., N.Y.C., 1987-92; assoc. counsel Marsh & McLennan Cos. Inc., N.Y.C., 1993-97; assoc. broker Stribling & Assocs., Ltd., 2002—. Editor: Internat. Law Jour. Corporate, general. Home: Stribling & Assocs Ltd 924 Madison Ave New York NY 10021

TAUB, ELI IRWIN, arbitrator, mediator, lawyer; b. N.Y.C., July 6, 1938; s. Max and Belle (Slutsky) T.; m. Nancy Denese Bell, May 15, 1983; 1 child, Jennifer. BA, Bklyn. Coll., 1960; JD, NYU, 1963. Bar: N.Y. 1964, U.S. Dist. Ct. (no. dist.) N.Y. 1979. Ptnr. Silverman, Silverman & Taub, Schenectady, N.Y., 1971-77; pres. Eli I. Taub, P.C., Schenectady, 1978-2001; judge Schenectady County (N.Y.) Family Ct., 2001; arbitrator, mem. mediation panel Fed. Mediation & Conciliation Svc., 2001—. Arbitrator Am. Arbitration Assn., N.Y. State Pub. Employment Rels. Bd., 1966—, U.S. Postal Svc. and Nat. Letter Carriers; mediator U.S. Dist. Ct.; N.Y. State EMployment Rels. Bd., NYS/CSEA; hearing officer, paralegal adv. com. Schenectady County C.C. Chmn. trustee Joseph Egan Supreme Ct. Library, Schenectady, 1980, 81, 84; pres. Schenectady County Republican Club, 1985-86; v.p. Jewish Fedn. Schenectady, 1983-86; mem. surrogate decision making com. N.Y. State Commn. on Quality of Care for the Mentally Disabled; bd. dirs. Jewish Cmty. Ctr., Jewish Family Svcs., Schenectady, N.Y. Adolescent Pregnancy Prevention Svcs.; advocate Nat. Coll. of Advocacy; vice-chmn. Schenectady Co. Indsl. Devel. Agy.; sec., legal counsel 440 State St. Arts Ctr. Recipient Vol. of Yr. award Jewish Family Svcs., 1998, Humanitarian of Yr. award Alcohol and Substance Abuse Coun., 2001. Mem.: ATLA, Indsl. Rels. Rsch. Assn., Nat. Orgn. Social

Security Claimant Reps., Schenectady County Bar Assn., N.Y. State Trial Lawyers Assn., N.Y. State Bar Assn., Am. Judges Assn., B'nai B'rith (pres. 1976—77, Youth Svcs. award 1985). Family and matrimonial, Personal injury (including property damage), Workers' compensation. Home: 105 N Ferry St Schenectady NY 12305-1610 Office: 105 N Ferry St Schenectady NY 12305 Fax: 518-393-0719.

TAUB, STEPHEN RICHARD, lawyer; b. N.Y.C., Oct. 5, 1944; s. Irving Robert and Sylvia T.; m. Alyson Zoe Winter, Dec. 23, 1968. BA, Queens Coll., 1965; JD, NYU, 1968. Bar: N.Y. 1969, U.S. Dist. Ct. (ea. and so. dists.) N.Y. 1970, U.S. Ct. Appeals (2nd cir.) 1971, U.S. Supreme Ct. 1972. Asst. dist. atty., bur. chief Kings County Dist. Attys. Office, Bklyn., 1970—77; pvt. practice Garden City, NY, 1977—96; ptnr. Ostrow and Taub, LLP, Garden City, 1996—2000, Schlissel, Ostrow, Karabatos, Poepplein & Taub, PLLC, Mineola, NY, 2000—02; pvt. practice Stephen R. Taub, PLLC, Mineola, NY, 2002—. Matrimonial case neutral evaluator Nassau County Supreme Ct., Mineola, 1997—. Village Justice Village Kensington, Great Neck, N.Y., 1986-98; Acting Village Justice Village Old Brookville, N.Y., 1998—. Fellow Am. Acad. Matrimonial Lawyers; mem. ABA, N.Y. Family Law, Am. Inn of Ct. (master), N.Y. State Bar Assn., N.Y. State Magistrates Assn., Nassau County Bar Assn., Nassau County Magistrates Assn. (pres. 1993-94). Avocation: tennis. Office: 190 Willis Ave Mineola NY 11501

TAUB, THEODORE CALVIN, lawyer; b. Springfield, Mass., Jan. 1, 1935; s. Samuel and Sara Lee (Daum) T.; m. Roberta Mae Ginsburg, Aug. 23, 1959; children: Tracy, Andrew, Adam. AB, Duke U., 1956; JD, U. Fla., 1960. Bar: Fla., 1960, U.S. Supreme Ct. Atty. Shumaker, Loop & Kendrick, LLP, Tampa. Asst. city atty. City of Tampa, 1963-67; city atty. City of Temple Terrace, Fla., 1974—; panelist in field. Contbr. articles to profl. jours. Chmn. Tampa-Hillsborough (Fla.) County Expy. Authority, 1974-84; mem. Hillsborough County Charter Commn., 1966-69, Local Govt. Mgmt. Efficiency Com., 1979, State of Fla. Environ. Efficiency Study Commn., 1986-88; founder Tampa Bay Performing Arts Ctr. Fellow: Am. Bar Found; mem. ABA (chmn. real property litigation com. 1981-86, chmn. com. on housing and urban environ. 1989-91), Am. Coll. Real Estate Lawyers (bd. govs.), Am. Land Title Assn. (lenders' counsel group), Fla. Bar Assn. (bd. cert. real estate lawyer), Fla. Jaycees (pres.), Tau Epsilon Phi. Democrat. Jewish. General civil litigation, Land use and zoning (including planning), Property, real (including real estate development, water). Home: 4937 Lyford Cay Rd Tampa FL 33629-4828 Office: Bank of Am 101 E Kennedy Blvd Ste 2800 Tampa FL 33602-5869 E-mail: ttaub@slk-law.com.

TAUBENFELD, HARRY SAMUEL, lawyer; b. Bklyn., June 27, 1929; s. Marcus Isaac and Anna (Engelhard) T.; m. Florence Spatz, June 17, 1956; children: Anne Gail Weisbrod, Stephen Marshall. BA, Bklyn. Coll., 1951; JD, Columbia U., 1954. Bar: N.Y. 1955, U.S. Supreme Ct. 1965, U.S. Dist. Ct. (so. and ea. dists.) N.Y. 1976. Assoc. Benjamin H. Schor, Bklyn., 1955-58; ptnr. Zuckerbrod & Taubenfeld, Cedarhurst (N.Y.), N.Y.C., 1958—; bd. dirs. Cornerstone Real Estate Income Trust, 1993—, Next Generation Mktg., Inc., 1996-99. Village atty. Village of Cedarhurst, 1977-88, trustee, 1989-2001; mem. bd. Downtown Cedarhurst Bus. Improvement Dist., 1993; legis. chmn., counsel Nassau County Village Ofcls., 1979-86, v.p., 1991-93, pres., 1993-94, mem. exec. com., 1989-99, chmn. intergovtl. liaison com., 1991-93; mem. legis. com. N.Y. State Conf. Mayors, 1979-87, 92-93; mem. exec. bd. Tri-County Village Ofcls., 1991-95, pres., 1993-94; arbitrator Am. Arbitration Assn. Dist. Ct. Nassau County, 1980—, Assessment Rev. Panel, Supreme Ct., Nassau County, 1981—; mem. Constl. Bicentennial Com., 1987-89; hon. trustee Cong. Beth Shalom, Lawrence, N.Y., 1990-2001; nat. bd. dirs. Zionist Orgn. Am. Assoc. chmn. Am. Zionist Fedn., 1985-87; pres. Herut Zionists Am., 1977-79; v.p. Hartman YMHA, 1983-87; del. World Zionist Congress, 1977, 82, 87; mem. Zionist Gen. Coun., 1977-83; bd. govs. Jewish Agy., 1983-92; mem. exec. com. World Zionist Orgn., 1983-92; trustee United Jewish Appeal, 1986-91; bd. dirs. United Israel Appeal, 1986-91; hon. vice chmn., bd. dirs. Jewish Nat. Fund, 1987-89; nat. bd. dirs. Am. for a Safe Israel; hon. pres. World Coun. Herut Hatzoa, Jerusalem, Internat. Bd. Youthtown of Israel. Recipient Centenial award Jabotinsky Found. 1981, Betar Youth award World Betar 1982, award Internat. League for Repatriation of Russian Jews 1977, Youth Towns of Israel Leadership award 1973, Israel Bonds Leadership award 1976, Life Time Achievement award Israel Bonds 1991, Defender of Jerusalem award 1991, Israel Bonds Menachem Begin Leadership award, 1999. Mem.: Internat. Assn. Jewish Lawyers and Jurists, Beth El (New Rochelle, N.Y.), Zionist Orgn. of Am., Jewish War Vets., B'nai B'rith, Nordau Circle Club. Commercial, contracts (including sales of goods; commercial financing), Municipal (including bonds), Property, real (including real estate development, water). Home: 21 N Chatsworth Ave Larchmont NY 10538 Office: PO Box 488 575 Chestnut St Cedarhurst NY 11516-2223

TAURMAN, JOHN DAVID, lawyer; b. Charleston, W.Va., May 22, 1946; s. Ralph and Mikanna Elizabeth (Clark) T.; m. Donna Jill Naroff, June 13, 1981; children: Devon Elliott, Kyra Justine, Quinn Juliet. BA magna cum laude, Duke U., 1968; JD cum laude, Harvard U., 1971. Bar: D.C. 1971, U.S. Supreme Ct. 1981, Tex. 1984, U.S. Ct. Appeals (D.C., fed., 3d, 5th, 9th and 10th cirs.), U.S. Dist. Ct. D.C., U.S. Dist. Ct. (so., no. and ea. dists.) Tex., U.S. Ct. Fed. Claims. Assoc. Covington & Burling, Washington, 1971-78, Vinson & Elkins, Washington, 1979-82, ptnr. Houston, 1982-90, Washington, 1990—. Lectr. State Bar Inst. Tex., 1983. Editor Harvard Law Rev., 1969-71. Mem. ABA, State Bar Tex., D.C. Bar Assn., Phi Beta Kappa. Antitrust, Federal civil litigation. Office: Vinson & Elkins Willard Office Bldg 1455 Pennsylvania Ave NW Fl 7 Washington DC 20004-1013 E-mail: jtaurman@velaw.com.

TAURO, JOSEPH LOUIS, federal judge; b. Winchester, Mass., Sept. 26, 1931; s. G. Joseph and Helen Maria (Petrossi) T.; m. Elizabeth Mary Quinlan, Feb. 7, 1959 (dec. 1978); children— Joseph L., Elizabeth H., Christopher M.; m. Ann Lefavour Jones, July 12, 1980. AB, Brown U., 1953; LLB, Cornell U., 1956; JD (hon.), U. Mass., 1985, Suffolk U., 1986, Northeastern U., 1990, New Eng. Sch. Law, 1992, Boston U., 1997, Brown U., 1998. Bar: Mass. 1956, D.C. 1960. Assoc. Tauro & Tauro, Lynn, Mass., 1958-59; asst. U.S. atty. Dept. Justice, Boston, 1959-60; ptnr. Jaffee & Tauro, Boston and Lynn, Mass., 1960-71; chief legal counsel Gov. of Mass., Boston, 1965-68; U.S. atty. Dept. Justice, Boston, 1972; judge U.S. Dist. Ct., Boston, 1972—; chief judge U.S. Dist. Ct., Mass., 1992-99. Mem. exec. com. Cornell Law Assn., Ithaca, N.Y., 1968-71; mem. adv. coun. Cornell Law Sch., Ithaca, 1975-80; vis. prof. law Boston U. Law Sch., 1977—; mem. Jud. Conf. U.S., 1994-97, mem. com. on operation of jury sys., 1979-86, mem. adv. com. on codes of conduct, 1988-94. Trustee Brown U., 1978—, Mass. Gen. Hosp., Boston, 1968-72, Children's Hosp. Med. Ctr., Boston, 1979-94. 1st lt. U.S. Army, 1956-58. Recipient Disting. Alumnus award Cornell U. Law Sch., 1992, Brown Bear award Brown U., 1993; named one of 10 Outstanding Young Men, Greater Boston Jaycees, 1966. Fellow Am. Bar Found.; mem. Mass. Bar Assn., Boston Bar Assn. (coun. 1968-71), D.C. Bar Assn., Boston Yacht Club (Marblehead, Mass.). Republican. Roman Catholic. Avocations: sports; reading; music; films; theater. Office: 1 Courthouse Way Ste 7110 Boston MA 02210-3009

TAUSEND, FREDRIC CUTNER, lawyer, dean; b. July 6, 1933; s. Stanley and Louise (Cutner) T.; m. Sandra Adkisson, Apr. 26, 1962 (div. Sept. 1976); children: Jessica, Rachel; m. Marilyn Lewis, Jan. 20, 1979. AB magna cum laude, Harvard U., 1954, LLB, 1957. Bar: U.S. Dist. Ct. (we. dist.) Wash., U.S. Ct. Appeals (9th cir.), U.S. Supreme Ct. Asst. gen. atty. divsn. antitrust and consumer protection State of Wash., Seattle, 1963—64; assoc. Schweppe, Krug & Tausend, Seattle, 1958—62, 1965, ptnr., 1966—80; dean Sch. Law U. Puget Sound, Tacoma, 1980—86; ptnr. Preston, Gates & Ellis, Seattle, 1990—. Chmn. King County Bd. Adjustment, Seattle, 1967, Seattle Crime Prevention Adv. Commn., 1971—74. With U.S. Army, 1957—58. Fellow: ATLA, Am. Bar Found.; mem.: ABA, Wash. State Bar Assn. (chmn. antitrust divsn. 1981—82), Wash. Athletic Club, Harvard Club (N.Y.C.). Democrat. Jewish. Federal civil litigation, Alternative dispute resolution, Appellate. Office: 5000 Columbia Ctr 701 5th Ave Seattle WA 98104-7097

TAVROW, RICHARD LAWRENCE, lawyer, corporate executive; b. Syracuse, NY, Feb. 3, 1935; s. Harry and Ida Mary (Hodess) T.; m. Barbara J. Silver, Mar. 22, 1972; children— Joshua Michael, Sara Hallie. AB magna cum laude, Harvard U., 1957, LL.B., 1960, LL.M., 1961; postgrad., U. Copenhagen, 1961-62, U. Luxembourg, 1962. Bar: N.Y. bar 1961, U.S. Supreme Ct. bar 1969, Calif. bar 1978. Atty. W.R. Grace & Co., NYC, 1962-66; asst. chief counsel Gen. Dynamics Corp., NYC, 1966-68; chief counsel office of fgn. direct investments U.S. Dept. Commerce, Washington, 1969-71; ptnr. Schaeffer, Dale, Vogel & Tavrow, NYC, 1971-75; v.p., sec., gen. counsel Prudential Lines, Inc., NYC, 1975-78, also bd. dirs.; v.p., sec., gen. counsel Am. Pres. Lines, Ltd., Oakland, Calif., 1978-80, sr. v.p., sec., gen. counsel, 1980-91, also bd. dirs.; sr. v.p., sec., gen. counsel Am. Pres. Cos., Ltd., Oakland, Calif., 1983-91, also bd. dirs.; sr. ptnr. Law Offices of R.L. Tavrow, 1991—; chmn., pres., CEO Diabetes Healthcare & Life Enhancement Ltd., 2000—. Instr. Harvard Coll., 1959-61; lectr. Am. Mgmt. Assn., Practising Law Inst., other assns. Recipient Silver Medal award Dept. Commerce, 1970; Fulbright scholar, 1961-62 Mem. ABA, State Bar Calif., Internat. Bar Assn., Am. Soc. Internat. Law, Am. Corp. Counsel Assn., Am. Soc. Corp. Secs. Inc., Harvard Law Sch. Assn., Navy League, Harvard Club (N.Y.C.). Administrative and regulatory, Corporate, general, Transportation.

TAYLOR, A. JEFFRY, lawyer; b. L.A., Nov. 29, 1943; s. Henry Allen and Jane Clara (Bosco) T.; m. Kate Colemen Hanrahan, Apr. 10, 1965; children: Jennifer, Stefanie, Bryce, Zachary. BA, UCLA, 1965; JD, Loyola U., L.A., 1969. Bar: Calif. 1970, Vt. 1972, U.S. Supreme Ct. 1976, U.S. Tax Ct. 1985, U.S. Claims Ct. 1988, U.S. Ct. Appeals (D.C. cir.) 1990, U.S. Dist. Ct. (ctrl. dist.) Calif. 1970, U.S. Dist. Ct. Vt. 1972. Law clk. U.S. Dist. Judge 9th Cir. Ct. Appeals, L.A., 1969-70; trial atty. U.S. Dept. Justice Antitrust Divsn., L.A., 1970-72; corp. counsel Vt. Elec. Power Co., Rutland, 1972-79; hearing officer Vt. Dept. Edn., Montpelier, 1979-88; bar counsel Vt. Profl. Conduct Bd., Montpelier, 1979-88; adj. prof. law Vt. Law Sch., Royalton, 1978-88, 95-96; pvt. practice Rutland, 1979—. Contbr. articles Vt. Law Rev., 1997—. Vt. state counsel Clinton/Gore '92 and '96; Vt. rep. Nat. Lawyers Coun./Dem. Nat. Com., State Counsel, Gore 2000; Vt. bd. mem. UN Assn. U.S.; presdl. elector for State of Vt., 2000. Mem. Am. Soc. Internat. Law. Democrat. Unitarian Universalist. Avocations: opera, trout fishing. Corporate, general, Professional liability, Utilities, public. Home: 1415 East St North Clarendon VT 05759-9765 Office: One Justice Sq Rutland VT 05701 E-mail: jeffreyT905@yahoo.com.

TAYLOR, ALLAN BERT, lawyer; b. Cin., June 28, 1948; s. H Ralph and Henrietta Irene (Medalia) Taylor; m. Sally Ann Silverstein, June 6, 1971; children: Rachel Elizabeth, Karen Ruth. AB, Harvard U., 1970, M in Pub. Policy, JD, Harvard U., 1975. Bar: Conn 1975, US Ct Appeals (DC cir) 1977, US Dist Ct (so dist) NY 1979, US Ct Appeals (2d cir) 1979, US Supreme Ct 1979, US Ct Appeals (1st and 10th cirs) 1991. Law clk. to J. Skelly Wright D.C. Cir., Washington, 1975-76; law clk. to Thurgood Marshall U.S. Supreme Ct., Washington, 1976-77; assoc. Day, Berry & Howard, Hartford, Conn., 1977-83, ptnr., 1983—. Overseer Bushnell Meml Hall Corp, Hartford, 1992—. Bd dirs Hartford Infant Action Project, 1990—, pres, 1999; elected mem Hartford City Coun, 1981—87; mem. Hartford Bd. Edn., 1989—93, v.p., 1991—93; mem. Conn .State Bd. Edn., Hartford, 1994—; chmn. charter revision comns. City of Hartford, 1999—2002; bd dirs Conn Asn Bds Educ, Hartford, 1989—93, Hartford Stage Co, 1993—2001. Mem.: ABA, Hartford Bar Asn, Conn Bar Asn, Phi Beta Kappa. Democrat. Jewish. Avocations: astronomy, reading. Federal civil litigation, Insurance, Utilities, public. Home: 238 Whitney St Hartford CT 06105-2270 Office: Day Berry & Howard City Place Hartford CT 06103 E-mail: abtaylor@dbh.com.

TAYLOR, ANNA DIGGS, judge; b. Washington, Dec. 9, 1932; d. Virginius Douglass and Hazel (Bramlette) Johnston; m. S. Martin Taylor, May 22, 1976; children: Douglass Johnston Diggs, Carla Cecile Diggs. BA, Barnard Coll., 1954; LLB, Yale U., 1957. Bar: D.C. 1957, Mich. 1961. Atty. Office Solicitor, Dept. Labor, W, 1957-60; asst. prosecutor Wayne County, Mich., 1961-62; asst. U.S. atty. Eastern Dist. of Mich., 1966; ptnr. Zwerdling, Maurer, Diggs & Papp, Detroit, 1970-75; asst. corp. counsel City of Detroit, 1975-79; U.S. dist. judge Eastern Dist. Mich. Detroit, 1979—. Hon. chair United Way, Cmty. Found., S.E. Mich.; trustee emeritus Detroit Inst. Arts; co-chair, vol. Leadership Coun.; vice-chair Henry Ford Health Sys. Mem. Fed. Bar Assn., State Bar Mich., Wolverine Bar Assn. (v.p.), Yale Law Assn. Episcopalian. Office: US Dist Ct 740 US Courthouse 231 W Lafayette Blvd Detroit MI 48226-2700

TAYLOR, BRENT DOUGLAS, lawyer; b. New Castle, Ind., Jan. 14, 1957; s. Delmar and Judith T.; m. Rhonda Jenkins, May 26, 1979; children: Jennifer, Tamara, Emily, Brandon. BA in Econs. summa cum laude, Butler U., 1979; JD, Harvard U., 1982. Bar: Ind. 1982, U.S. Dist. Ct. (so. and no. dists.) Ind. 1982. Ptnr. Baker & Daniels, Indpls., 1982—. Trustee Earlham Coll. Mem. ABA, Ind. Bar Assn., Indpls. Bar Assn. (litigation sect.), Phi Kappa Phi. Democrat. Mem. Soc. Of Friends. Federal civil litigation, State civil litigation. Home: 3724 Shafer Cir Carmel IN 46033-4727 Office: Baker & Daniels 300 N Meridian St Ste 2700 Indianapolis IN 46204-1782

TAYLOR, CARROLL STRIBLING, lawyer; b. Port Chester, N.Y., Jan. 14, 1944; s. William H. Jr. and Anna P. (Stribling) T.; m. Nancy S. Tyson, Apr. 7, 1968; children: Heather, Kimberly, Tori, Tiffany, Tacy. AB, Yale U., 1965; JD, U. Calif., Berkeley, 1968. Bar: Hawaii 1969, Calif. 1969, U.S. Dist. Ct. Hawaii 1969, U.S. Dist. Ct. (cen. dist.) Calif. 1975, U.S. Ct. Appeals (9th cir.) 1975. Rschr. Legis. Reference Bur., Honolulu, 1968-70; reporter Jud. Coun. Probate Code Revision Project, Honolulu, 1970-71; assoc. Chun, Kerr & Dodd, Honolulu, 1971-75; ptnr. Hamilton & Taylor, Honolulu, 1975-80; officer, dir. Char, Hamilton, Taylor & Thom, Honolulu, 1980-82, Carroll S. Taylor Atty. at Law, A Law Corp., Honolulu, 1982-86; ptnr. Taylor & Leong, Honolulu, 1986-91, Taylor, Leong & Chee, Honolulu, 1991—. Adj. prof. Richardson Sch. Law U. Hawaii, Honolulu, 1981-86, 88-90, 97; mem. Disciplinary bd. of Supreme Ct. of Hawaii, 1994—, vice chair, 1997-99, chair, 2000—; dir. Am. Nat. Lawyers Ins. Reciprocal, 1997-2000; mem., bd. dirs. Hanahauoli Sch., 1992-97. Fellow Am. Coll. Trust and Estate Counsel; mem. ABA, Calif. Bar Assn., Hawaii State Bar Assn. (Pres.'s award 2002), Hawaii Inst. Continuing Legal Edn. (pres. 1986-88), Pla. Club (Honolulu). Episcopalian. State civil litigation, Probate (including wills, trusts), Estate planning. Home: 46-429 Hololio St Kaneohe HI 96744-4225 Office: 737 Bishop St Ste 2060 Honolulu HI 96813-3214 E-mail: ctaylor@hawaii.rr.com.

TAYLOR, CLIFFORD WOODWORTH, state supreme court justice; b. Delaware, Ohio, Nov. 9, 1942; s. Alexander E. and Carolyn (Clifford) T.; m. Lucille Taylor; 2 children. BA, U. Mich., 1964; JD, George Washington U., 1967. Asst. prosecuting atty. Ingham County, 1971-72; ptnr. Denfield, Timmer & Taylor, 1972-92; judge Mich. Ct. of Appeals, 1992-97, Supreme Ct. Justice, 1997—. Mem. standing com. on professionalism Mich. State Bar, 1992. Bd. dirs. Mich. Dyslexia Inst., 1991—, Friends of the Gov.'s Residence, 1991—; mem. St. Thomas Aquinas Ch. With USN, 1967-71. Fellow Mich. State Bar Found.; mem. Mich. Supreme Ct. Hist. Soc., Federalist Soc., Cath. Lawyers Guild, State Bar. Home: 9760 Sunny Point Dr Laingsburg MI 48848 Office: Mich Supreme Ct PO Box 300052 Lansing MI 48909

TAYLOR, DAVID BROOKE, lawyer, banker; b. Salt Lake City, Oct. 14, 1942; s. Lee Neff and June Taylor; m. Carolyn Kaufholz, May 29, 1965; children: Stewart, Allison. BA, U. Utah, 1964; JD, Columbia U., 1967. Bar: N.Y. 1967, N.C. 1995. Ptnr. Wickes, Riddell, Bloomer, Jacobi & McGuire, N.Y.C., 1967-79, Morgan, Lewis & Bockius, N.Y.C., 1979-89; banker, lawyer Chase Manhattan Bank, N.A., N.Y.C., 1989-92; pres. Geoenertec Corp., N.Y.C., 1992-93; ptnr. Fennebresque, Clark, Swindall & Hay, Charlotte, N.C., 1994-98, McGuire & Woods, LLP, Charlotte, N.C., 1999—. Mem. ABA, N.Y. State Bar Assn., N.C. Bar Assn. Banking, Corporate, general, Finance. Home: 3815 Beresford Rd Charlotte NC 28211-3713 Office: McGuire & Woods LLP 100 N Tryon St Ste 2900 Charlotte NC 28202-4022

TAYLOR, DAVID F. lawyer; BA summa cum laude, Middlebury Coll., 1982; JD magna cum laude, Harvard U., 1986. Bar: Wash. 1996, Calif. 1987, U.S. Dist. Ct. (we. dist.) Wash. 1996, U.S. Dist. Ct. (ea. dist.) Wash. 1998, U.S. Dist. ct. (cen. dist.) Calif. 1987, U.S. Dist. Ct. (no. dist.) Calif. 2000, U.S. Ct. Appeals (9th cir.) 2000. Law clk. U.S. Dist. Ct. Mass., Boston, 1986—87; assoc. Latham and Watkins, L.A., 1987—91; asst. atty. U.S. Dist. Ct. (cen. dist.) Calif., L.A., 1991—95, U.S. Dist. Ct. (we. dist.) Wash., Seattle, 1995—96; ptnr. Perkins Coie LLP, Seattle, 1998—. Bd. dirs. Mercer Island Boys and Girls Club, Mercer Island, Wash. Civil litigation, Federal civil litigation, General civil litigation. Office: Perkins Coie LLP 1201 Third Ave Seattle WA 98101

TAYLOR, EARL B. b. Opelousas, La., June 9, 1939; s. Herbert and Clara (Shurley) T.; m. Norma Lee Fouxs, July 25, 1965; children: Johnny Lee, Laura Leigh. JD, La. State U., 1965. Bar: La., U.S. Dist. Ct. (ea. and we. dists.) La., U.S. Ct. Appeals (5th cir.). Asst. dist. atty. St. Landry Parish, City of Opelousas, La., 1973-89, dist. atty., 1997—. V.p. Opelousas Area Assn. Retarded Citizens; past pres. Meth. Men's Club, Opelousas; laiety leader La. Meml. United Meth. Ch. With USAR, 1960-66. Recipient Outstanding Svc. award Grolee Elem. Sch. Mem. Assn. Trial Lawyers Am., La. Dist. Attys. Assn., La. Bar Assn. (mem. ho. dels. 1978—), La. Trial Lawyers Assn. (mem. bd. govs. 1978—), St. Landry Parish Bar Assn. (pres. 1978-79), Opelousas C. of C. (past pres.), Opelousas-St. Landry C. of C. (Man of Yr. 1986), Rotary (bd. dirs. Opelousas chpt. 1983, Paul Harris award), Jaycees (Opelousas chpt., Award of Honor 1981). Democrat. Avocation: politics. Home: 2239 Ledoux Cir Opelousas LA 70570-2739 Office: 424 N Court St PO Box 1149 Opelousas LA 70571-1149

TAYLOR, EDWARD MCKINLEY, JR., lawyer; b. Dayton, Ohio, Apr. 19, 1928; s. Edward McKinley and Margaret Helen (Gaessler) T.; m. Mary Joan McMahon; 1 dau., Mary Margaret Taylor Neises. J.D. with distinction, 1951. Bar: Ohio 1951, U.S. Supreme Ct. 1971, U.S. Ct. Mill. Appeals 1973, U.S. Dist. Ct. (so. dist.) Ohio 1959. Ptnr. Taylor & Taylor, Dayton, 1957—; asst. city atty. City of Dayton, 1957-77; solicitor Village of Union (Ohio), 1978-82, law dir., 1982, law dir. emeritus, 1982— . Served to col. JAGC, USAF. Mem. ABA, Ohio State Bar Assn., Dayton Bar Assn., Judge Advocate Assn. Clubs: Shriners, Racquet (Dayton). Probate (including wills, trusts), Property, real (including real estate development, water). Address: 7417 N Main St Dayton OH 45415-2545

TAYLOR, FRANCES O'CONNELL, lawyer; b. Atlanta, Ga., Oct. 24, 1951; d. James Joseph and Julia (Chesser) O'Connell; m. Simon R.H. Taylor, Apr. 25, 1987; children: Katherine, Emma. BA honors, U. Fla., 1973; JD honors, U. Ga., 1978; LLM, London Sch. Econs., 1986. Bar: Md. 1988, U.S. Ct. Appeals (D.C. cir.) 1983, U.S. Ct. Appeals (4th cir.) 1983. Law clk., counsel, trial counsel Nat. Labor Rev. Bd., Washington, 1979—88; assoc. Shawe and Rosenthal, Balt., 1988—95; counsel Gordon Feinblatt Rothman Hoffberger and Hollander LLC, Balt., 1998—. Contbr. Officer, bd. dirs. Goodwill Industries, Balt.; chair, bd. trustees Pumpkin Theatre, Balt. Recipient Top 100 Women in Md. award, Daily Rec., 2002. Mem.: ABA, Am. Immigration Lawyers Assn. Avocations: gardening, cooking, knitting, home repair. Immigration, naturalization, and customs. Office: Gordon Feinblatt Rothman Hoffberger and Hollander LLC 233 E Redwood St Baltimore MD 21202

TAYLOR, FREDERICK WILLIAM, JR., (FRITZ TAYLOR), lawyer; b. Cleve., Oct. 21, 1933; s. Frederick William Sr. and Marguerite Elizabeth (Kistler) T.; m. Mary Phyllis Osborne, June 1, 1985. BA in History, U. Fla., 1957; MA in Near East Studies, U. Mich., 1959; JD cum laude, NYU, 1967. Bar: N.Y. 1968, Calif. 1969, U.S. Dist. Ct. (cen. dist.) Calif. 1969. Govt. rels. rep. Arabian Am. Oil Co., Dhahran, Saudi Arabia, 1959-63, oil supply coord. N.Y.C., 1963-68, sr. counsel Dhahran, 1969-71, gen. mgr. govt. rels. orgn., 1971-74, v.p. indsl. rels., 1974-78; assoc. O'Melveny & Myers, L.A., 1968-69; ptnr. Burt & Taylor, Marblehead, Mass., 1978-80; pres., chief exec. officer Nat. Med. Enterprises Internat. Group, L.A., 1980-82; counsel Chadbourne, Parke & Afridi, United Arab Emirates, 1982-84; ptnr. Sidley & Austin, Cairo, 1984-87, 1987-93; spl. counsel Heller Ehrman White & McAuliffe, L.A. and Singapore, 1993-95; legal advisor, corp. counsel law divsn. Lucent Techs. Internat. Inc., Riyadh, Saudi Arabia, 1995—. Contbr. articles to profl. jours. Mem. ABA, Calif. Bar Assn., Order of Coif, Singapore Cricket Club, Tanglin Club, Changi Sailing Club, Singapore Am. Club, Dirab Golf Club. Commercial, contracts (including sales of goods; commercial financing), Corporate, general, Private international. Home: 9875 E Shadowlake Ct Claremore OK 74017-1444 Office: Lucent Techs Int Inc PO Box 4945 Khurais Rd Riyadh 11412 Saudi Arabia

TAYLOR, GAIL RICHARDSON, freelance writer, educator, civic worker, lawyer, former university official; b. Cleve., July 16, 1949; d. Allen Barnd and Margaret Christine (Thomas) Ricardson; m. William David Taylor, May 16, 1987; 1 child, William Robert. BA, Wellesley Coll., 1971; MS in Journalism, Northwestern U., 1978; JD magna cum laude, Case Western Reserve U., 1993. Bar: Ohio, 1993. Co-editor Time Sharing Today, Phila., 1972-73; reporter Today's Spirit (Montgomery Pub. Co.), Hatboro, Pa., 1973-76, The Argus Leader (Gannett Co.), Sioux Falls, S.D., 1978-82; writer, editor Case Western Res. U., Cleve., 1982-83, sr. writer, editor, 1983-84, dir. news svcs., 1984-87, coord. govt. rels., 1987-90, dir. govt. rels., 1990-97; freelance writer, 1997—. Substitute tchr. Oberlin (Ohio) City Schs., 2002—; adj. instr. Lorain County C.C., 2003—. Contbr. articles to newspapers and mags. Chmn. bd. trustees United Protestant Campus Ministries in Cleve., 1996-97; trustee Hot Meals, Oberlin, Ohio; mem. vestry Christ Episcopal Ch., 2003-; mem. Oberlin Bd. Edn., 1998-99; oblate Benedictine Sisters of Erie, Pa. Independent. Avocations: gardening, golf, ice skating, school volunteering. Home: 317 Elm St Oberlin OH 44074-1404 E-mail: gailt317@aol.com.

TAYLOR, GEORGE KIMBROUGH, JR., lawyer; b. Atlanta, Aug. 28, 1939; s. George Kimbrough and Helen Whiteside (Shepard) T.; m. Carol Ann McKinney, July 1, 1961 (div. 1976); children: George Kimbrough III, Thomas Haynes; m. Triska Ashley Drake, Oct. 2, 1981. BA, Emory U., 1961; LLB, U. Va., 1964. Bar: Ga. 1964, U.S. Dist. Ct. (no. dist.) Ga. 1964, U.S. Ct. Appeals (11th cir.) 1964. Assoc. Kilpatrick & Cody, Atlanta, 1964-70, ptnr., 1970-96, Kilpatrick Stockton LLP (formerly Kilpatrick & Cody), 1997—. Bd. dirs. Ont. Reins. Co. Ltd., Atlanta. Chmn. bd. dirs. Spl. Audiences, Inc., Atlanta, 1985-87; bd. dirs. Atlanta Symphony Orch., 1986—, treas., 1995-97; trustee Woodruff Arts Ctr., Atlanta, 1997—; bd. dirs. Atlanta Opera, 1995—, Ga. Humanities Coun., Atlanta, 1986-93, Ga. Conservancy, 1979-85, Ga. Trust for Hist. Preservation, 2002—; bd. dirs. Ga. Coun. Internat. Visitors, Atlanta, 1987-94, pres., 1993; bd. dirs. Brit.-Am. Bus. Group, 1989-95, pres., 1994; bd. visitors Emory U., Atlanta, 1993-96, Brit.-Am. Bus. Coun., 1997—, chmn. 1997-98; mem. alumni coun. U. Va. Law Sch., 1995-98; active Leadership Atlanta. Woodrow Wilson fellow, 1961. Mem. ABA, Internat. Bar Assn., Atlanta Bar Assn., Order of Coif, Soc. Internat. Bus. Fellows, Capital City Club, Phi Beta Kappa, Omicron Delta Kappa. Democrat. Avocations: sailing, skiing.

Corporate, general, Private international, Corporate taxation. Office: Kilpatrick Stockton LLP 1100 Peachtree St NE Ste 2800 Atlanta GA 30309-4530 E-mail: ktaylor@kilpatrickstockton.com.

TAYLOR, JANET DROKE, legal secretary; b. Bristol, Tenn., Feb. 26, 1961; d. Jimmie D. and Nancy Bell (Sluder) Droke; children: Leslie Ann, Laurie Elizabeth; m. Terry E. Taylor. AA, East Tenn. State U., 1980; student, Milligan Coll., Johnson City, Tenn., 1988-89. With Sullivan County Election Commn., Blountville, Tenn., 1978; legal sec. Boarman & Vaughn, Johnson City, 1980-84; legal asst. Bob McD. Green and Assocs., Johnson City, 1985-89; fed. judicial sec. to U.S. cir. judge U.S. Ct. Appeals, 4th Cir., Abingdon, Va., 1989—. Adv. bd. legal asst. program Milligan Coll., Johnson City, 1988-89. Mem. Tenn. Paralegal Assn. (treas. 1989, pub. rels. dir. 1990), Appalachian Paralegal Assn., Fed. Judicial Secs. Assn. (4th cir. rep. 1998-2000). Republican. Avocations: reading, piano, travel. Home: PO Box 727 Bluff City TN 37618-0727 Office: US Court of Appeals 4th Cir PO Box 868 Abingdon VA 24212-0868

TAYLOR, JERRY F(RANCIS), lawyer; b. Memphis, Oct. 2, 1934; s. Rex Brewster and Naomi (Robertson) T.; m. Jo(dy) Evelyn Katz, Mar. 5, 1971 (div. 1996); 1 child, Deborah Pagan (dec. 1999). BS, Memphis State U., 1956; JD, U. Tenn., 1963. Bar: U.S. Dist. Ct. Tenn. (we., mid. and ea. dists.) 1965, U.S. Dist. Ct. Miss. (mid. dist.) 1963, U.S. Ct. Appeals (6th cir.) 1970. Assoc. Krivcher & Cox, Memphis, 1963-65; sr. ptnr. Holt, Batchelor, Taylor & Spicer, 1965-80, Wilkes, McCullough & Taylor, Memphis, 1980-89, Taylor, Halliburton & Ledbetter, Memphis, 1989—. Pres. Second Chance Inc., 1988-2002. Fundraiser United Way Memphis, 1982; bd. dirs. Jeff Steinberg Ministries, 1983-98, Outreach to Youth, Inc., 1983—; pres., trustee Cen. Ch., Inc., 1988-2000. Served to capt. USAF, 1957-60. Law Sch. scholar Memphis-Shelby County Bar Assn., 1961. Mem. ABA, ATLA (state committeeman 1968), Tenn. Bar Assn., Memphis-Shelby County Bar Assn., Tenn. Trial Lawyers Assn. (bd. govs. 1984-89), Am. Bd. Trial Advocates (nat. bd. dirs. 1989—, advocate 1985—, sec. Tenn. chpt. 1985-86, pres.-elect Tenn. chpt. 1987-88, pres. 1988—), Am. Inns Ct. (founder, master Leo Beaman chpt. 1995-2001), Lawyers Involved in Tenn. (trustee 1983-89), Masons, Shriners. Personal injury (including property damage), Probate (including wills, trusts), Product liability. Home: 109 N Main St Apt 1101 Memphis TN 38103-5019 Office: Taylor Halliburton & Ledbetter 254 Court Ste 305 Memphis TN 38103

TAYLOR, JILL OLSEN, lawyer, artist; b. Logan, Utah, June 1, 1955; d. Keith Conrad and Norma Elveda (Correll) Olsen; m. Bruce T. Taylor, July 3, 1979; children: Jenny, Benjamin, Christina. BA summa cum laude, Brigham Young U., 1977, JD, 1980. Bar: Utah 1980. Dep. county atty. Emery County, Utah, 1980-81; corp. atty. Physicians Emergency Svc., Price, Utah, 1981-88; pvt. practice Provo, Utah, 1986—. Bd. dirs., pres. Covered Bridge Canyon Homeowners Assn., 1983-89; mem. Utah County Planning Commn., 1993-2002, chair planning commn., 1993-2000. Mem.: ABA, Meridian Sch. Found., Meridian Sch. Bd., Order of Barristers (headmaster Meridian Sch. 2001—02), Utah State Bar Assn., Am. Immigration Lawyers Assn. (chair Utah chpt. 1996, bd. govs.), Phi Kappa Phi. Republican. Mem. Lds Ch.

TAYLOR, JOB, III, lawyer; b. N.Y.C., Feb. 18, 1942; s. Job II and Anne Harrison (Flinchbaugh) T.; m. Mary C. August, Oct. 24, 1964 (div. 1978); children: Whitney August, Job IV; m. Sally Lawson, May 31, 1980; 1 child, Alexandra Anne. BA, Washington & Jefferson Coll., 1964; JD, Coll. William and Mary, 1971. Bar: N.Y. 1972, U.S. Dist. Ct. (no., so. ea. and we. dists.) N.Y. 1973, U.S. Ct. Appeals (2d cir.) 1973, U.S. Ct. Claims 1974, U.S. Tax Ct. 1974, U.S. Supreme Ct. 1975, U.S. Ct. Appeals (9th cir.) 1976, U.S. Ct. Mil. Appeals 1977, U.S. Ct. Appeals (D.C. and 10th cirs.) 1977, D.C. 1981, U.S. Ct. Internat. Trade 1981, U.S. Ct. Appeals (fed. cir.) 1982, U.S. Dist. Ct. (no. dist.) Calif. 1983, U.S. Ct. Appeals (6th cir.) U.S. Dist. Ct., 1987, U.S. Ct. Appeals (3d cir.) 1990, U.S. Dist. Ct. Conn. 1996. Ptnr. Olwine, Connelly, Chase, O'Donnell & Weyher, N.Y.C., 1971-85, Latham & Watkins, N.Y.C., 1985—. Served to lt. USN, 1964-68. Mem. ABA, Assn. Bar City N.Y., La Confrerie des Chevaliers du Tastevin, Racquet and Tennis Club, Wee Burn Country Club (Darien, Conn.), New Canaan Country Club.. Republican. Episcopalian. Avocations: squash, tennis, golf, reading. Antitrust, Federal civil litigation, Computer. Office: Latham & Watkins 885 3rd Ave Fl 9 New York NY 10022-4834

TAYLOR, JOE CLINTON, judge; b. Durant, Okla., Mar. 28, 1942; s. Luther Clinton and Virena (Parker) T.; m. Margaret Pearl Byers, June 8, 1963; children: Marna Joanne, Leah Alison, Jocelyn Camille. Student, Southeastern State Coll., 1960-62; BA, Okla. State U., 1965; JD, U. Okla., 1968. Bar: Okla. 1968. Pvt. practice, Norman, Okla., 1968-69; apptd. spl. dist. judge Durant, 1969-72; assoc. dist. judge Bryan County, Okla., 1972-76; dist. judge, chief judge 19th Dist. Ct., 1976-93; presiding judge Southeastern Okla. Jud. Adminstrv. Dist., 1984-92, Choctaw Tribal Ct., 1979-83; pres. Okla. Jud. Conf., 1987-88; chmn. Assembly Presiding Judges, 1989-90; presiding judge trial div. Okla. Ct. on the Judiciary, 1991-93; Okla. Ct. of Tax Rev., 1992—; judge Okla. Ct. of Civil Appeals, Tulsa, 1993—. Chmn. bd. dirs. Durant Youth Svcs., 1976-93; bd. dirs. Bryan County Youth Svcs., Inc., 1971-93. Lt. Col. USAR. Mem. Lions, Phi Sigma Epsilon, Delta Theta Phi. Mem. Ch. of Christ. Home: PO Box 329 Durant OK 74702-0329 Office: Ct Civil Appeals 601 State Bldg 440 S Houston Ave Tulsa OK 74127-8922 E-mail: joe.taylor@oscn.net.

TAYLOR, JOEL SANFORD, retired lawyer; b. Hazleton, Pa., Oct. 8, 1942; s. Robert Joseph and Alice Josephine (Sanford) T.; m. Donna Rae Caron, Mar. 26, 1967; children: Jason, Adam, Jeremy. BA, Swarthmore Coll., 1965; LLB, Columbia U., 1968. Bar: N.Y. 1969, U.S. Ct. Appeals (2d cir.) 1970, U.S. Dist. Ct. (no. dist.) Ohio 1974, U.S. Supreme Ct. 1974, U.S. Dist. Ct. (so. dist.) Ohio 1975, U.S. Ct. Appeals (6th cir.) 1975, U.S. Dist. Ct. (ea. dist.) Ky. 1979. Law clk. hon. Constance B. Motley U.S. Dist. Ct., N.Y.C., 1968-69; assoc. Paul, Weiss, Rifkind, Wharton & Garrison, N.Y.C., 1969-72; exec. asst. Ohio Office of Budget & Mgmt., Columbus, Ohio, 1972-74; asst. atty. gen. Ohio Atty. Gen., Columbus, 1974-83, chief counsel, 1983-91; ptnr. Dinsmore & Shohl, Columbus, 1991-2000; fin. dir. City of Columbus, 2000—. Pres. Ohio Sundry Claims Bd., Columbus, 1972-74, Ohio State Controlling Bd., Columbus, 1973-74; mem., bd. trustees Ohio State Tchrs. Retirement Sys., Columbus, 1986-91, Solid Waste Authority Ctrl. Ohio, 2001—. Mem. Govt. Fin. Officers Assn., Columbia Law Alumni Assn., Ohio Sierra Club, Nat. Wildlife Fedn., Nature Conservany. Administrative and regulatory, General civil litigation, Environmental. Office: City Hall 90 W Broad St Columbus OH 43215-9000 E-mail: jstaylor@columbus.gov.

TAYLOR, JOHN CHESTNUT, III, lawyer; b. N.Y.C., Jan. 7, 1928; s. John Chestnut and Jean Elizabeth (Willis) T.; m. Dolores Yvonne Sunstrom, Nov. 17, 1950; children: Jane Willis, John Sunstrom, Anne Holliday. BA, Princeton U., 1947; LL.B., Yale U., 1950. Bar: N.Y. 1950, D.C. 1972. Assoc. Paul, Weiss, Rifkind, Wharton & Garrison, N.Y.C., 1950, 52-60, ptnr., 1961-85, 87-91, of counsel, 1986-87, 92—; exec. v.p., dir. AEA Investors Inc., N.Y.C., 1985-86, pres., 1986-87. Bd. dirs. AFS Intercultural Programs, Inc., N.Y.C., 1972-80, trustee, 1973-79, chmn., 1975-79; trustee Carnegie Corp. N.Y., N.Y.C., 1975-84, chmn., 1979-84; trustee, mem. exec. com. Devereux Found., 1992-2001, vice chmn., 1994-2001. Served to capt. JAGC, AUS, 1950-52. Mem. Assn. of Bar of City of N.Y., Order of Coif, Phi Beta Kappa, Phi Delta Phi. Democrat. Home: 1 Hammock View Ln Savannah GA 31411-2603 Office: Paul Weiss Rifkind Wharton & Garrison 1285 Avenue Of The Americas New York NY 10019-6064 E-mail: budsunny@aol.com.

TAYLOR, JOHN MCKOWEN, lawyer; b. Baton Rouge, Jan. 20, 1924; s. Benjamin Brown and May (McKowen) T.; 1 child, John McKowen. BA, La. State U., 1948, JD, 1950. Bar: La. 1950, U.S. Supreme Ct. 1960. Assoc. Taylor, Porter, Brooks, Fuller & Phillips, Baton Rouge, 1950-55, Huckaby, Seale, Kelton & Hayes, Baton Rouge, 1955-58; ptnr. Kelton & Taylor, Baton Rouge, 1958-61; pvt. practice, Baton Rouge, 1961—. With AUS, 1943-46; maj. USAR, 1946—, ATO, ETO, PTO. Mem. ABA, AAAS, La. State Bar Assn., Baton Rouge Bar Assn., Mil. Order of World Wars, Am. Radio Relay League, Baton Rouge Country Club, City Club of Baton Rouge, Baton Rouge Amateur Radio Club, Camelot Club, SAR, Sigma Chi, Pi Gamma Mu, Phi Delta Phi. Republican. Presbyterian. Oil, gas, and mineral, Family and matrimonial, Property, real (including real estate development, water). Home and Office: 2150 Kleinert Ave Baton Rouge LA 70806-6712 E-mail: jmcktaylor@cox.net.

TAYLOR, JOSEPH HENRY, lawyer; b. Chgo., Mar. 2, 1934; s. Joseph Henry and Blanche (Murnane) T.; m. Marie Theresa Dietz, Feb. 20, 1960 (div. Dec. 21 1975); children: Lisa Marie Moose, Joseph John, Matthew Edward, Nicole; m. Joyce Louise Eriks, Jan. 1, 1977; children: Sean Philip, Ryan Joseph, Colin, Michael, Zachary. BS in Philosophy, Loyola U., Chgo., 1960, JD, 1965. Bar: Ill. 1965, U.S. Dist. Ct. (no. and so. dists.) Ill. 1965. Assoc. Pentis & Tourek, Chgo., 1965-66; pvt. practice Chgo. and Palos Heights, Ill., 1966—. Prosecutor City of Palos Heights, 1976—. Alderman City of Palos Heights, 1974-76. Cpl. USMC, 1951-54. Mem. ATLA, Ill. Trial Lawyers Assn., Ill. State Bar Assn., Chgo. Bar Assn., S.W. Suburban Bar Assn. (pres. 1970), DuPage County Bar Assn., Criminal Def. Lawyer. Avocations: pilot, motorcycles, marathon runner. Criminal. Office: 7330 W College Dr Palos Heights IL 60463-1157

TAYLOR, KEMBRA SEXTON, lawyer, state agency administrator; b. Whitesburg, Ky., July 15, 1956; d. Columbus and Nova Ferguson Sexton; m. Stephan Lance Taylor, Aug. 9, 1980; 1 child, Christopher Robert Sexton Taylor. BA, Centre Coll. Ky., 1978; JD, U. Ky., 1981. Bar: Ky. 1981, U.S. Ct. Appeals (6th cir.) 1988, U.S. Dist. Ct. (ea. dist.) Ky. 1991, U.S. Dist. Ct. (we. dist.) Ky. 2001. Assoc. atty. Cook, Taylor & Taylor, Whitesburg, Ky., 1981—82; staff atty. Commonwealth of Ky. Natural Resources and Environ. Protection Cabinet, Frankfort, 1982—87; sr. staff atty. Commonwealth of Ky. Labor Cabinet, Frankfort, 1987—92, dep. gen. counsel, 1992—95, gen. counsel, 1995—2002, dep. sec., gen. counsel, 2002—. Author: (chapter in book) Employment Law in Kentucky 2nd ed. Mem.: ABA (com. on OSHA), Phi Alpha Theta, Omicron Delta Kappa. Democrat. Presbyterian. Home: 2018 Edgewater Ct Lexington KY 40502 Office: Ky Labor Cabinet 1047 US 127 South Ste 4 Frankfort KY 40601 Office Fax: 502-564-5484. Personal E-mail: kembrataylor@aol.com. Business E-Mail: kembra.taylor@mail.state.ky.us.

TAYLOR, LELAND BARIDON, lawyer; b. Poughkeepsie, N.Y., July 5, 1920; s. Alexander J. and Elsie Jane (Van Wyck) T.; m. Rosemary Olcott Coon, June 24, 1945; children: Barry Eugene, Craig Cameron, Mark Alexander, Meg Olcott Taylor Casey. BS, Syracuse U., 1942, JD, 1948. Bar: N.Y. 1948, U.S. Dist. Ct. (no. dist.) N.Y. 1954, U.S. Supreme Ct. 1958. Ptnr. Fitzgerald, Taylor, Pomeroy & Armstrong and predecessor, Cortland, N.Y., 1948-2000; of counsel Pomeroy, Armstrong, Baranello & Casullo, Cortland, N.Y., 2000—. Judge City of Cortland, 1952-57; bd. dirs. First Nat. Bank of Dryden, Monroe Abstract & Title Corp. Trustee Cortland Free Libr., 1950—; bd. dirs. Coll. Devel. Found., Cortland, 1960-2000. With Supply Corps., USNR, 1942-45. Named Cortland County Jr. C. of C. Young Man of Yr., 1952, N.Y. State Young Man of Yr., N.Y. State Jaycees, 1953, Syracuse U. Letterman of Distinction, 1977. Fellow N.Y. Bar Found., Am. Bar Found.; mem. ABA, N.Y. State Bar Assn. (v.p. 1974-76, sec. 1976-79, chmn. fin. com. 1979-84), Cortland County Bar Assn., Rotary (Paul Harris fellow), Masons, Auto of Syracuse Club. Presbyterian. Property, real (including real estate development, water), Estate taxation. Address: 16 Tompkins St Cortland NY 13045-2541

TAYLOR, L(YNN) FRANKLIN, lawyer; b. Hutchinson, Kans., Sept. 25, 1945; s. Lynn Franklin and Rebecca Ellen (Jones) T.; m. Kathryn Ruth Achterberg, May 31, 1968; children: Laura Jeanne, Deborah Lynne. BA, Doane Coll., 1967; JD, U. Kans., 1975. Bar: Kans. 1975, U.S. Tax Ct. 1975, U.S. Supreme Ct. 1978, Mo. 1990. Pvt. practice Payne & Jones, Chartered, Overland Park, Kans., 1975-86, Speer, Austin, Holliday, Ruddick & Taylor, Olathe, Kans., 1986-89, Armstrong, Teasdale, Schlafly & Davis, Overland Park, 1989-92, Watson & Marshall L.C., Olathe, 1992-96, Norton, Hubbard, Ruzicka & Kreamer L.C., Olathe, 1996—; pres., CEO Olathe C. of C., 1999—. City atty. City of DeSoto, Kans., 1979-92; mcpl. judge City of Olathe, 1980-85. Contbr. to Kans. Estate Adminstrn. Handbook, 1980, 86, 93, Kans. Corp. Law Handbook, 1997. Active Kans. Commn. on Edn. Restructuring and Accountability, Topeka, 1992; edn. adv. com. Kans. City Partnership for Children, 1992-96; mem. bd. edn. Unified Sch. Dist. 233, Olathe, 1987-2003; vice chmn., then chmn. bd. dirs. Hidden Glen Arts Festival, 1992-94; bd. dirs. Olathe Region United Way, 1979-2000; vice chancellor Episcopal Diocese Kans., Topeka, 1981-94, chancellor, 1994—. Fellow Am. Coll. Trust and Estate Counsel; mem. Olathe Area C. of C. (Citizen of Yr. 1994), Rotary (Paul Harris fellow Olathe club 1994), Order of Coif. Republican. Avocations: snow skiing, boating, gardening, sports. Corporate, general, Municipal (including bonds), Probate (including wills, trusts). Home: 26391 W Cedar Niles Cir Olathe KS 66061 Office: Norton Hubbard Ruzicka & Kreamer LC 130 N Cherry St Olathe KS 66061-3401 E-mail: ftaylor@nhrk.com.

TAYLOR, MARVIN EDWARD, JR., lawyer; b. Smithfield, N.C., Oct. 15, 1937; s. Marvin Edward and Ellen Borden Broadhurst T.; m. Karin Gunilla Guggenheim, Nov. 29, 1969; 1 child, Karin Elizabeth Guggenheim. AB, U. N.C., 1960, JD with honors, 1965. Bar: N.Y. 1966, N.C. 1968, U.S. Dist. Ct. (ea. dist.) N.C. 1973, U.S. Ct. Appeals (4th cir.) 1974, Calif. 1976. Assoc. Nixon Mudge Rose Guthrie Alexander & Mitchell, N.Y.C., 1965-67, Sanford Cannon Adams & McCullough, Raleigh, N.C., 1967-71; atty. pvt. practice, Raleigh, N.C., 1972-75, 1984—; corp. counsel Memorex Corp., Santa Clara, Calif., 1975-80; atty. pvt. practice, Hickory, N.C., 1983. Dept. counsel GE Co., Hickory, NC, 1980—82; mem. staff N.C. Law Rev., 1964, rsch. editor, 65. Dir. Parents' Assn. N.C. State U., Raleigh, 1989-93, Coun. Entrepreneurial Devel, Research Triangle Park, N.C., 1985-88, chmn. pub. com., 1985-88; participant N.C. Ctr. Nonprofits Pro Bono Program, Raleigh, 1994—. With USAF, 1960-62. Mem.: Swedish-Am. C. of C. USA (sec. 1999—2000), N.C. Bar Assn. (com. comml. banking and bus. law 1970—75, subcom. securities regulation 1972—75, bus. law sect. coun. 1982—90, internat. law com. 1990—92, internat. law and practice sect. coun. 1992—95, pub. info. com. 1995—2000, lawyers in the schs. com. 1999—, comm. com. 2000—), Swedish-Am. C. of C. of N.C. (co-founder, dir., sec.-treas. 1998—), Order of Coif. Democrat. Episcopalian. Avocations: skiing, photography, reading. Commercial, contracts (including sales of goods; commercial financing), Corporate, general, Private international. Office: 119 SW Maynard Rd Cary NC 27511-4472

TAYLOR, RICHARD POWELL, lawyer; b. Phila., Sept. 13, 1928; s. Earl Howard and Helen Moore (Martin) Taylor; m. Barbara Jo Anne Harris, Dec. 19, 1959 (dec. Oct. 29, 2002); 1 child, Douglas Howard. BA, U. Va., 1950, JD, 1952. Bar: Va. 1952, D.C. 1956. Law clk. U.S. Ct. Appeals for 4th Circuit, 1951-52; assoc. Steptoe & Johnson LLP, Washington, 1956-61, ptnr., 1962—, chmn. transp. dept., 1978—; sec., corp. counsel Slick Corp., 1963-69, asst. sec., 1969-72, also bd. dirs., 1965-68; sec., corp. counsel Slick Indsl. Co., 1963-72; sec., bd. dirs. Slick Indsl. Co. Can. Ltd, 1966-72. Bd. dirs. Intercontinental Forwarders, Inc., 1969-72. Mem. Save the Children 50th Anniversary Com., 1982; gen. counsel Am. Opera Scholarship Soc., 1974—; mem. lawyer's com. Washington Performing Arts Soc., 1982—; mem. adv. com. Rock Creek Found. Mental Health, 1982—; mem. nat. adv. bd. DAR, 1980-83, chmn., 1983—; mem. men's com. Project Hope Ball, 1980—; nat. vice chmn. for fin. Reagan for Pres., 1979-80; mem. exec. fin. com. 1981 Presdl. Inauguration; mem. President's Adv. Com. for Arts, 1982—, Rep. Nat. Com., 1983—; Md. fin. chmn. Reagan-Bush '84, Bush-Quayle '88. Served to lt (j.g.), Air Intelligence USNR, 1952-56. Mem. ABA (co-chmn. aviation com. 1964-76, chmn. 1976-77), Fed. Bar Assn., D.C. Bar Assn., Va. Bar Assn., Fed. Energy Bar Assn., Am. Judicature Soc., Assn. Transp. Practitioners, Internat. Platform Assn., Raven Soc., Order of Coif, Univ. Club, Capital Hill Club, Nat. Aviation Club, Aero Club, Congl. Country Club (Washington), Potomac (Md.) Polo Club. Episcopalian. Administrative and regulatory, Corporate, general, Transportation. Home: 14914 Spring Meadows Dr Germantown MD 20874-3444 Office: 1330 Connecticut Ave NW Washington DC 20036-1704 E-mail: rtaylor@steptoe.com.

TAYLOR, RICHARD TRELORE, retired lawyer; b. Kewanee, Ill., Aug. 5, 1917; s. Earl G. and Lucile (Cully) T.; m. Maureen Hoey, Feb. 9, 1946. BS, U. Ill., 1939, JD, 1946; LL.M., Columbia U., 1947; LHD (hon.), Marlboro Coll., 2001. Bar: Ill. 1946, N.Y. 1947. Assoc. Cadwalader, Wickersham & Taft, N.Y.C., 1947-57, ptnr., 1957-87, presiding ptnr., 1977-87, of counsel, 1988-89. Hon. trustee Marlboro Coll. With U.S. Army, 1941—45. Decorated Bronze Star Mem. Univ. Club (N.Y.C.). Banking, Corporate, general. Home: 870 United Nations Plz New York NY 10017-1807

TAYLOR, RITCHIE W. lawyer; b. Greensboro, N.C. BS in Fin., Brigham Young U., 1996, JD cum laude, 1999. Bar: N.C. 1999, U.S. Tax Ct. 2000. Assoc. Manning, Fulton and Skinner PA, Raleigh, NC, 1999—. Instr. Nat. Bus. Inst., Raleigh, 2001—. Contbr. articles to profl. jours. Endowment com. Occoneechee Coun. Boy Scouts Am., Raleigh, 2002—; vice chmn. Friends of Scouting Campaign, Raleigh, 2003. Franchising, Corporate, general, Estate planning. Office: Manning Fulton and Skinner PA 3605 Glenwood Ave Ste 500 Raleigh NC 27612 E-mail: rtaylor@manningfulton.com.

TAYLOR, ROBERT LEE, lawyer, former judge; b. North Wildwood, N.J., Sept. 6, 1947; s. Louis Edward and Elizabeth (Zuccato) T.; m. Julie Ann Adams, Apr. 28, 1979; children: Tracy, Jennifer, Kathryn, Robyn. BS, James Madison U., 1969; JD, Washington and Lee U., 1974. Bar: N.J. 1974, U.S. Dist. Ct. N.J. 1974, U.S. Ct. Appeals (3d cir.) 1982, U.S. Supreme Ct. 1991. Assoc. George M. James, Wildwood, 1974-78; ptnr. Way, Way, Goodkin & Taylor, Wildwood, 1978-81, Way, Way, & Taylor, Wildwood, 1981-82; pvt. practice law Stone Harbor, N.J., 1982—; judge Mid. Twp. Mcpl. Ct., N.J., 1984-89. Organizer, dir. First so. State Bank, Avalon, N.J.; mem. dist. 1 ethics com. N.J. Supreme Ct., 1994-96; solicitor Lower Twp., N.J., 1994-96; diplomate N.J. Mcpl. Law. Advisor Law Explorers Boy Scouts Am., 1981, exec. bd. so. N.J. coun., 1995-2000; chmn. Cape May County Dem. Com., 1996-98. With U.S. Army, 1969-71. Mem. ABA, N.J. Bar Assn. (gen. coun. 1978-82), Cape May County Bar Assn. (pres. 1980-81), Cape May County Mcpl. Judges Assn. (treas. 1987-89), N.J. Jud. Conf. (del. 1978-82), Am. Legion, DAV (life), Delta Theta Phi. Democrat. Roman Catholic. Avocations: skiing, tennis, golf. General civil litigation, General practice, Property, real (including real estate development, water). Office: 9712 3rd Ave # 4 Stone Harbor NJ 08247-1931 E-mail: rltaylor@pro-usa.net.

TAYLOR, RONALD LOUIS, lawyer; b. Memphis, July 18, 1942; s. George Festus and Ina Dell (Sanderson) T.; m. Elsa Juanita Parker, Dec. 28, 1969; children: Anna-Kathryn, Benjamin Louis. BA magna cum laude, Miss. State U., 1964; JD, U. Miss., 1970. Bar: Miss. 1970, U.S. Ct. Appeals (5th cir.) 1976, U.S. Supreme Ct. 1976. Assoc. B.G. Perry, Southaven, Miss., 1970-71; ptnr. Perry & Taylor, Southaven, 1971-73, Perry, Taylor & Whitwell, Southaven, 1973-75, Taylor & Whitwell, Southaven, 1976-85, Taylor, Jones, Alexander, Seale & Ryan, Ltd., Southaven, 1985-89, Taylor, Jones Alexander & Sorrell Ltd., Southaven, 1994—. Mcpl. judge City of Horn Lake, Miss., 1975-77; city atty. City of Southaven, 1982—. Vice chmn. Southaven Libary Bd., 1973-76. Lt. col. USAR, 1964-2002. Fellow Miss. Bar Found.; mem. Assn. Trial Lawyers Am., Miss. Trial Lawyers (bd. govs. 1980), DeSoto County Bar Assn. (pres. 1978, 86), Exchange Club (pres. 1973), Lions, Masons (32d degree), Shriners (All Chymia Shrine Temple), Rotary (chmn. Southhaven Spring Fest). Republican. Baptist. Family and matrimonial, Personal injury (including property damage). Home: 5872 Rolling Hill Dr Olive Branch MS 38654-9583 Office: Taylor Jones Alexander Sorrell Ltd PO Box 188 961 Main St Southaven MS 38671-0188

TAYLOR, VARLEY H. lawyer, educator; b. Tulsa, Sept. 11, 1946; s. Varley H. and Gertrude H. Taylor; m. Sherry N. Taylor, Feb. 28, 1968; children: Ty, Ann, Rush. AB in History, Princeton U., 1968; JD, U. Mich., 1971; ML in Taxation, NYU, 1973. Bar: Okla. 1971. Atty. Dorner, Saunders, Daniel & Anderson, Tulsa, 1971—. Adj. prof. Tulsa CC, 1996—; vis. prof. U. Ark., Fayetteville, 2000—. Author: (book) Oklahoma Probate Handbook, 2002, Oklahoma Probate Law and Practice, 2002, Vernon's Oklahoma Estate Planning Forms with Commentary. Vol. counselor Sr. Health Care Info. Project, 1988—2001; vol. atty. Green Country Legal Aids Project, 1999. Mem.: Tulsa Tax Forum, Tulsa Tax Club, Okla. Bar Assn. (mem. ethics com. 2000—02), Okla. Alzheimer Assn. (policy com. 2000—02). Democrat. Unitarian. Probate (including wills, trusts), Corporate taxation, Estate taxation. Office: Doerner Saunders Daniel and Anderson LLP 320 S Boston Ste 500 Tulsa OK 74103 Office Fax: 918-591-5360. Business E-Mail: vtaylor@dsda.com.

TAYLOR, WILLARD B. lawyer; b. N.Y.C., 1940; BA, Yale U., 1962, LLB, 1965. Bar: N.Y. 1966. With firm Sullivan & Cromwell, N.Y.C. Adj. faculty NYU Law Sch. Trustee North European Oil Royalty Trust. Mem. N.Y. State Bar Assn. (chair tax sect. 1983-84), Am. Law Inst. Office: Sullivan & Cromwell 125 Broad St Fl 28 New York NY 10004-2489

TAYLOR, WILLIAM JAMES (ZAK TAYLOR), lawyer; b. Milw., Jan. 26, 1948; s. William Elmer and Elizabeth Emily (Lupinski) T.; m. Marlou Belyea, Sept. 20, 1975; children: Danielle Belyea, James Zachary Belyea. BA in Econs., Yale U., 1970; JD, Harvard U., 1976. Bar: Calif. 1976, U.S. Dist. Ct. (cen. dist.) Calif. 1976, U.S. Dist. Ct. (no. dist.) Calif. 1977, U.S. Ct. Appeals (9th cir.) 1977, U.S. Dist. Ct. (ea. dist.) Calif. 1980, U.S. Supreme Ct. 1980, U.S. Tax Ct. 1988. Law clk. to hon. Shirley M. Hufstedler U.S. Ct. Appeals (9th cir.), L.A., 1976-77; assoc. Broebeck, Phleger & Harrison, San Francisco, 1977-83; ptnr. Broebeck, Phleger and Harrison, San Francisco, 1983-95; shareholder Taylor & Jenkins, P.C., Oakland, Calif., 1995-96, Chilvers & Taylor, P.C., Oakland, 1996-99; of counsel Brobeck, Phleger & Harrison, LLP, San Francisco, 2000—03, Morgan Lewis & Bockius, LLP, San Francisco, 2003—. Bd. dirs. Berkeley (Calif.) Law Found., 1988-91, Legal Svcs. for Children (recipient Jean Waldman Child Advocacy award, San Francisco 1988), 1983-89; co-chmn. Attys. Task Force for Children, San Francisco, 1983-89. Editor-in-chief Harvard Civil Rights, Civil Liberties Law Rev., 1976; bd. editors No. Dist. Calif. Digest, 1978-83; co-author: California Antitrust Law, 1991; contbg. editor: Calif. Bus. Law Reporter, 1995—, Antitrust Law Developments, 1997, 2d edit., 2002. With U.S. Army, 1970-73. Mem. ABA, Bar Assn. San Francisco (bd. dirs. 1986-87, chair antitrust sect. 1987, chair fed. cts. sect. 1995-97), Am. Bus. Trial Lawyers Assn., Nat. Health Lawyers Assn., Calif. Soc. Healthcare Attorneys, Barristers of San Francisco (bd. dirs. 1980-82, v.p. 1982-83). Democrat. Antitrust, General civil litigation, Health. Office: Morgan Lewis & Bockius LLP 1 Market Spear Tower San Francisco CA 94105-1420 E-mail: wtaylor@morganlewis.com., william.taylor@sbcglobal.net.

TAYLOR, WILLIAM L. law librarian; b. Phila., June 21, 1962; s. William R. and Barbara E. Flinker Taylor; life ptnr. Mark C. Noble, Sept. 30, 1995. BA, Yale Univ., New Haven, 1984; MLS, Univ. of Md., 1993. Fgn. svc. officer USIA, Various, Germany, 1989—92; libr. Georgetown Law Libr., Washington, 1994—. Mem. editl. bd. CALI, Chgo., 2002—. Mem.: Friday Morning Music Club. Quaker. Avocation: amateur pianist. Office: Georgetown Law Library 111 G St NW Washington DC 20001 E-mail: taylorw@law.georgetown.edu.

TEAL, ARABELLA W. state attorney general; b. N.Y.C. Postgrad, Harvard Coll., Georgetown U. Law Ctr. Atty. gen. D.C., 2002—; acting prin. dep. corp. counsel D.C. Superior Court, 2000—; section chief General Litigation Section I, 1996; law clerk for sr. judges D.C. Superior Court, 1987—88. Office: Office Corp Coun 441 4th St NW Washington DC 20001*

TEARE, JOHN RICHARD, JR., lawyer; b. Phila., Sept. 23, 1954; m. Claire M. Batuk, Jan. 25, 1975 (div. Dec. 1981); 1 child, John III; m. Gale Angela Waters, June 5, 1982; children: Angela, Stephanie. BS in Criminal Justice summa cum laude, Wilmington Coll., 1987; JD cum laude, U. Richmond, 1990. Bar: W.Va. 1990, U.S. Dist. Ct. (so. dist.) W.Va. 1990, U.S. Dist. Ct. (no. dist.) W.Va. 1996, U.S. Ct. Appeals (4th cir.) 1991. Sec. guard U. Del., Newark, 1973-76; police officer City of Dover (Del.), 1976-85; summer assoc. Hirschler Fleischer Weinberg Cox & Allen, Richmond, 1989; ptnr. Bowles Rice McDavid Graff & Love, PLLC, Charleston, W.Va., 1990—; mem. exec. com., 2000—03. Counsel Charleston Police Civil Svc. Commn.; instr. Charleston Regional Police Acad., 1999. Cub scout leader Boy Scouts Am., Felton, Del., 1984-88, asst. scoutmaster, Richmond, 1988-89, Charleston, 1991-98; chmn. pub. safety commn. Greater Charleston C. of C., 1991; sec. United Meth. Men, 1993; dir. Charleston Leadership Coun. on Pub. Safety, 1993-97, chmn. police dept. resource task force, 1994-97; dir./sec. Kanawha County Pub. Safety Coun., 2000—. Mem. Def. Rsch. Inst. (state liaison to govtl. liability com./bus. litigation com.), Def. Trial Counsel W.Va., Nat. Manufactured Housing Atty. Network, Fraternal Order of Police, Nat. Eagle Scout Assn., McNeill Law Assn., Greater Charleston C. of C., Delta Epsilon Rho. United Methodist. Avocations: camping, fishing, stamp collecting. Civil rights, General civil litigation, Labor (including EEOC, Fair Labor Standards Act, labor-management relations, NLRB, OSHA). Home: 1565 Virginia St E Charleston WV 25311-2416 Office: Bowles Rice McDavid Graff & Love PLLC PO Box 1386 Charleston WV 25325-1386 E-mail: jteare@bowlesrice.com.

TEASDALE, KENNETH FULBRIGHT, lawyer; b. St. Louis, Nov. 8, 1934; s. Kenneth and Ann (Fulbright) T.; m. Elizabeth Driscol Langdon, June 13, 1964; children: Caroline, Doug, Cindy. AB, Amherst Coll., 1956; LLB, Washington U., St. Louis, 1961. Bar: Mo. 1961. Atty. antitrust div. U.S. Dept. Justice, Washington, 1961-62; asst. counsel Dem. Policy Com. U.S. Senate, Washington, 1962-63, gen. counsel Dem. Policy Com., asst. to majority leader, 1963-64; assoc. Armstrong, Teasdale, Kramer & Vaughan, St. Louis, 1964-67, ptnr., 1967-86; mng. ptnr. Armstrong, Teasdale, Schlafly & Davis, St. Louis, 1986-93, chmn. of firm, 1993—. Trustee United Way Greater St. Louis, Sci. Ctr. St. Louis, St. Louis Art Mus. ; trustee, chmn. bd. regents St. Louis U.; mem. nat. coun. Washington U. Law Sch., 1988—. Mem. ABA, Bar Assn. Mo., Bar Assn. St. Louis, Racquet Club, Noonday Club, Old Warson Country Club. Episcopalian. Office: Armstrong Teasdale Schlafly & Davis Metropolitan Sq Saint Louis MO 63102-2733

TEBLUM, GARY IRA, lawyer; b. Phila., Apr. 25, 1955; s. Milton and Marlene Ann (Rosenberg) T.; m. Lisa Ida Goldsmith, May 13, 1979; children: Corey Harris, Jeremy Brett. BS, U. Del., 1976; JD cum laude, U. Pa., 1979. Assoc. Trenam, Simmons, Kemker, Scharf, Barkin, Frye & O'Neill, Tampa, Fla., 1979-84; ptnr. Trenam, Kemker, Scharf, Barkin, Frye, O'Neill & Mullis, Tampa, Fla., 1984—. Editor U. Pa. Law Rev., 1978-79. Mem. ABA, Fla. Bar Assn., Hillsborough County Bar Assn. Jewish. Commercial, contracts (including sales of goods; commercial financing), Securities, Corporate taxation. Home: 14039 Shady Shores Dr Tampa FL 33613-1934 Office: Trenam Kemker Scharf et al 2700 Bank Am Plz Tampa FL 33602

TEDESCHI, EDOARDO, lawyer; b. Milan, Oct. 5, 1970; s. Giorgio Tedeschi and Wanna Murru. Grad., U. Law, Milan, 1994. Bar: Italy 1997. Ptnr. Bergmann, Milan, 1999—2000, Abbatescianni, Milan, 2000—. Vis. fgn. lawyer Francis & Co., Cardiff, Wales, 1999. Author: State Aids, 1994, Code of Energy and Gas, 2002. Nuclear power, Mergers and acquisitions, Finance. Office: Abbatescianni e Associati Porta Vittoria 28 20122 Milan Italy

TEDFORD, DEBORAH J. lawyer; b. Dec. 1950; Grad. cum laude, Yale U., 1972; grad., Boston U., 1976. Ptnr. Tedford, Gianni & Jensen, P.C., Mystic, Conn. Bd. dirs. Hospice Southeastern Conn. Fellow: Conn. Bar Found., Am. Coll. Trust and Estate Counsel; mem.: Southeastern Conn. Estate and Tax Planning Coun. (past pres.), Conn. Bar Assn. (chair legal problems of the elderly 1990—92, chair estates and probate sect. 1997—, sec. 1999—2000, pres. 2002—03, founding editor Estates and Probate Newsletter), Mystic Rotary Club (past pres.). Office: PO Box 350 30 Bank St New Britain CT 06050*

TEHAN, JOHN BASHIR, lawyer; b. Utica, N.Y., May 13, 1948; s. Louis Bashir and Frances Mary (Argenzia) T.; m. Regina Anne Callahan, Aug. 1, 1970; children— Aaron J., Lauren R., Eileen L. B.A., LeMoyne Coll., 1970; J.D., Catholic U., Washington, 1973. Bar: N.Y. 1974, U.S. Dist. Ct. (so. and ea. dists.) N.Y. 1975, U.S. Ct. Appeals (2d cir.) 1975. Assoc. Sullivan & Cromwell, N.Y.C., 1973-81; ptnr. Simpson Thacher & Bartlett, N.Y.C., 1981— . Roman Catholic. Banking, Corporate, general, Securities. Home: 33 Arrowhead Ct Manhasset NY 11030-4413 Office: Simpson Thacher & Bartlett 425 Lexington Ave Fl 15 New York NY 10017-3954 E-mail: jtehan@stblaw.com.

TEIMAN, RICHARD B. lawyer; b. Bklyn., May 19, 1938; AB, Princeton U., 1959; LLB, Harvard U., 1962. Bar: N.Y. 1963. Ptnr. Winston & Strawn and predecessor Cole & Deitz, N.Y.C., 1968—. Trustee Citizens Budget Commn., 1993—. Mem. Assn. Bar City N.Y. (com. Admiralty 1975-78, 87, chair 1988-91), Maritime Law Assn. (com. Maritime Financing 1980—, chmn. subcom. Recodification U.S. Ship Mortgage Act 1986-91, chmn. subcom. U.S. Coastguard, Citizenship and Related Matters 1988-94), Phi Beta Kappa. Admiralty, Commercial, contracts (including sales of goods; commercial financing), Corporate, general. Home: 5 Pryer Ln Larchmont NY 10538-4012 Office: Winston & Strawn 200 Park Ave Rm 4100 New York NY 10166-0005 E-mail: rteiman@winston.com.

TEITELBAUM, LEE E. dean, law educator; b. New Orleans, Nov. 4, 1941; BA magna cum laude, Harvard Coll., 1963; LLB, Harvard U., 1966; LLM, Northwestern U., 1968. Bar: Ill. Staff atty. Chgo. Lawyer Project, 1966—68; asst. prof. law U. N.D., 1968—70; assoc. prof. law SUNY, Buffalo, 1970—73; vis. assoc. prof. law U. N.Mex. Law Sch., 1972, assoc. prof. law, 1973—74, prof. law, 1974—87; prof. law, dir. Ctr. for the Study of Legal Policy Relating to Children Ind. U. Law Sch., 1980—81, vis. prof., 1987, U. Utah Coll. Law, 1985, prof. law, 1986—90, assoc. dean acad. affairs, 1987—90, acting dean, 1988, dean, 1990—98, Alfred C. Emery prof. law, 1994—99; Allan R. Tessler dean and prof. of law Cornell Law Sch., 1999—. Fellow legal history program U. Wis., Madison, 1984; mem. test audit subcom., bd. trustees Law Sch. Admissions Coun.; bd. mem. Law and Soc. Assn. Author (with W.V. Stapleton): In Defense of Youth: The Role of Counsel in American Juvenile Courts, 1972; author: (with A. Gough) Beyond Control: Status Offenders in the Juvenile Court, 1977; mem. bd. editors: Law & Soc. Rev., 1982—87, Law & Policy, Jour. Legal Edn., 1990—92; contbr. articles to profl. jours. Fellow: ABA (reporter ABA-IJA project on stds. for juvenile justices, stds. relatin 1979); mem.: Assn. Am. Law Schs. (exec. com.), Utah Minority Bar Assn. (award), Law & Soc. Assn. (trustee 1977—80). Office: Cornell U Law School 263 Myron Taylor Hall Ithaca NY 14853-4901

TEITELL, CONRAD LAURENCE, lawyer, author; b. N.Y.C., Nov. 8, 1932; s. Benson and Belle (Altman) T.; m. Adele Mary Crummins, May 26, 1957; children: Beth Mary, Mark Lewis. AB, U. Mich., 1954; LL.B., Columbia U., 1957; LL.M., N.Y. U., 1968. Bar: N.Y. 1958, D.C., 1968. Mem. Prerau & Teitell, N.Y.C. and White Plains, NY, 1964-96, Cummings & Lockwood, Stamford, Conn., 1996—. Dir. Philanthropy Tax Inst., Old Greenwich, Conn., 1964— ; adj. prof. U. Miami Law Sch., 1980—. Author: Philanthropy and Taxation, 5 vols., 1993-2003; editor, pub. Taxwise Giving, 1964—; contbr. articles to legal jours. Served with U.S. Army, 1957. Recipient Disting. Svc. to Higher Edn. award Am. Coll. Pub. Relations Assn., 1970, Disting. Svc. award Nat. Com. on Planned Giving, 1990, Harrison Tweed Spl. Merit award Am. Law Inst./ABA, 1992. Fellow Am. Coll. Trust and Estate Counsel; mem. ABA (former co-chmn. com. charitable giving, trusts, founds.), Assn. of Bar of City of N.Y. Probate (including wills, trusts), Personal income taxation. Home: 16 Marlow Ct Riverside CT 06878-2614 Office: Cummings & Lockwood 4 Stamford Plz Stamford CT 06902-3834 also: PO Box 299 Old Greenwich CT 06870-0299 E-mail: cteitell@cl-law.com.

TEITELMAN, RICHARD BERTRAM, state supreme court justice; b. Phila., Sept. 25, 1947; s. Nathan and May B. (Schreibman) T. BA in Math., U. Pa., 1969; JD, Washington U., St. Louis, 1973. Bar: Mo. 1974. Pvt. practice, St. Louis, 1974-75; staff atty. Legal Svcs. Ea. Mo., St. Louis, 1975-76, mng. atty., 1976-80, exec. dir., gen. counsel, 1980—; judge Mo. Ct. Appeals (ea. dist.), 1997—2000, Supreme Ct., 2002—. Bd. dirs., Citizens for Mo.'s Children, St. Louis, 1988—. Recipient Durward K. McDaniel award, Am. Coun. of Blind, 1986. Mem. ABA, Mo. Bar Assn (vice-pres., 2000-01, pres.elect, 2001-02). Met. St. Louis (pres. 1989-90; award of merit, young lawyers sect., 1985), Mound City Bar Assn., Lawyers Assn., St. Louis, Women Lawyers' Assn. Greater St. Louis, St. Louis County Bar Assn., Am. Blind Lawyers Assn., St. Louis Bar Found., Am. Judicature Soc. (bd. dirs. 1986—), Leadership St. Louis. Office: Legal Svcs Ea Mo 625 N Euclid Ave Saint Louis MO 63108-1660

TEKELL, DAVID GLENN, lawyer; b. Oklahoma City, Apr. 30, 1961; s. Ronald David Clark and Patricia Ann (Meeks) Canale; m. Angela Catherine Eads, Aug. 8, 1986; children: Coleman Clark, Marshall Clark. BS, U. So. Calif., 1983; JD, U. Calif., 1986. Bar: Tex. 1986, U.S. Dist. Ct. Ariz. 1996, U.S. Dist. Ct. (we. dist.) Tex. 1988, U.S. Dist. Ct. (no. dist.) Tex. 1987, U.S. Dist. Ct. (so. dist.) Tex. 1996, U.S. Ct. Appeals (5th cir.) 1987, U.S. Supreme Ct. 1993. Assoc. Naman Howell Smith & Lee, Waco, Tex., 1986-94, mem., 1994-97; ptnr. Malesovas, Martin & Tekell, LLP, Waco, 1997—2001; pvt. practice Waco, 2001—02; ptnr. Tekell & Tekell PC, Waco, 2002—. Civil rights, Insurance, Personal injury (including property damage). Office: Tekell & Tekell PC PO Box 23248 Waco TX 76702-3248

TEKLITS, JOSEPH ANTHONY, lawyer; b. Belleville, Ill., July 18, 1952; s. Frank Anthony and Mary (Bodish) T.; m. Deborah Ann Keevill, June 1, 1974; children: Jessica, Joseph, Michael. BA, Coll. St. Francis de Sales, Allentown, Pa., 1974; JD, U. Notre Dame, 1977. Bar: Ind. 1977, U.S. Dist. Ct. (so. and no. dists.) Ind. 1977, Pa. 1988, Pa. 1988, U.S. Dist. Ct. (ea. dist.) Pa. 1988, U.S. Ct. Appeals (3d cir.) 1988, U.S. Dist. Ct. (ea. dist.) Mich. 1989, U.S. Ct. Appeals (6th cir.) 1990, U.S. Ct. Appeals (11th cir.) 1993, U.S. Supreme Ct. 1995, U.S. Dist. Ct. Colo. 1999. Legal counsel CTS Corp., Elkhart, Ind., 1977-80; mng. labor counsel Sperry Corp. (name now Unisys Corp.), Blue Bell, Pa., 1980-87; asst. gen. counsel Unisys Corp., Blue Bell, 1987-95, assoc. gen. counsel, 1995—. Mem. mgmt. com. Equal Employment Opportunity Law. Mem. ABA (EEO com. labor and employment law and litigation sects.), Delta Epsilon Sigma. Republican. Roman Catholic. Administrative and regulatory, Federal civil litigation, Labor (including EEOC, Fair Labor Standards Act, labor-management relations, NLRB, OSHA). Office: Unisys Corp Hdqrs Unisys Way Blue Bell PA 19424-0001

TELEPAS, GEORGE PETER, retired lawyer; b. Kingston, N.Y., Nov. 20, 1935; s. Peter G. and Grace Telepas; m. Regina Tisiker, Sept. 6, 1969 (div.); m. Patricia Kilstofte, Apr. 30, 1995. BS, U. Fla., 1960; JD, U. Miami, 1965. Bar: Fla. 1965, Colo. 1986. Assoc. Preddy, Haddad, Kutner & Hardy, 1966-67, Williams & Jabara, 1967-68; pvt. practice Miami, Fla., 1968-98. Mem. citizens bd. U. Miami. With USMC, 1954-56. Mem. ATLA, ABA, Fla. Bar Assn., Colo. Bar Assn., Dade County Bar Assn., Fla. Trial Lawyers Assn., Dade County Trial Lawyers Assn., Delta Theta Phi, Sigma Nu. Personal injury (including property damage). Address: 13320 Marsh Landing Palm Beach Gardens FL 33418

TELESCA, MICHAEL ANTHONY, federal judge; b. Rochester, N.Y., Nov. 25, 1929; s. Michael Angelo and Agatha (Locurcio) T.; m. Ethel E. Hibbard, June 5, 1953; children: Michele, Stephen. AB, U. Rochester, 1952; JD, U. Buffalo, 1955. Bar: N.Y. 1957, U.S. Dist. Ct. (we. dist.) N.Y. 1958, U.S. Ct. Appeals (2nd cir.) 1960, U.S. Supreme Ct. 1967. Ptnr. Lamb, Webster, Walz, Telesca, Rochester, N.Y., 1957-73; surrogate ct. judge Monroe County, N.Y., 1973-82; judge U.S. Dist. Ct. (we. dist.) N.Y., Rochester, 1982—, chief judge, 1989-95. Apptd. to Alien Terrorist Removal Ct. by Chief Justice Rehnquist, U.S. Supreme Ct., 1996; bd. dirs. Fed. Jud. Ctr. Bd. govs. Genesee Hosp., Rochester; mem. adv. bd. Assn. for Retarded Citizens, Al Sigl Ctr., Rochester. Served to 1st lt. USMC, 1955-57. Recipient Civic medal Rochester C. of C., 1983, Hutchinson medal U. Rochester, 1990. Mem. ABA, Am. Judicature Soc., Am. Inns. of Ct. (founder, pres. Rochester chpt.), Justinian Soc. Jurists, N.Y. State Bar Assn., Monroe County Bar Assn. Republican. Roman Catholic. Office: US Dist Ct 272 US Courthouse 100 State St Ste 212 Rochester NY 14614-1309*

TELLERIA, ANTHONY F. lawyer; b. June 6, 1938; s. Carolos E. and Melida (Amador) Telleria; m. Dolores A. Rockney, Nov. 3, 1962; children: Matthew J., Andrea F. LLB, Southwestern U., 1964. Bar: Calif. 1964. Pvt. practice, L.A., 1964—71; sr. ptnr. Telleria, Townley & Doran, L.A., Calif., 1971—75; pvt. practice L.A., 1975—. Mem.: Consumer Attys. Assn. of L.A., Am. Arbitration Assn. (L.A. adv. coun. accident claims com.), L.A. County Bar Assn., Calif. Trial Lawyers Assn. State civil litigation, Workers' compensation, Personal injury (including property damage). Home: 1615 Rose Ave San Marino CA 91108-3001 Office: 150 E Colorado Blvd Ste 206 Pasadena CA 91105-3722

TELSEY, SUZANNE LISA, lawyer; b. N.Y.C., Mar. 18, 1958; d. Daubert and Jacqueline (Messite) T.; m. Steven C. Bennett, July 26, 1986; children: Danielle, Nicole. AB, Brown U., 1980; JD with honors, NYU, 1984. Bar: N.Y. 1985, U.S. Dist. Ct. (so. dist.) N.Y. 1985. Law clk. Hon. Pierre N. Leval U.S. Dist. Ct. (so. dist.) N.Y., N.Y.C., 1984-86; litig. assoc. Kramer, Levin, Naftalis & Frankel, N.Y.C., 1986-89; assoc. gen. counsel Bantam Doubleday Dell Pub. Group, Inc., N.Y.C., 1989-96; gen. counsel Atlas Editions, Inc., N.Y.C., 1996—2000; assoc. gen. counsel McGraw Hill Cos., Inc., N.Y.C., 2000—. Contbr. articles to profl. jours. Mem. Assn. of the Bar of the City of N.Y. (copyright law com. 1990-94, comms. and media law sect. 1994-97, 2000—), N.Y. State Bar Assn. (media law sect. 1998-2002), Order of the Coif. Jewish. Avocations: tennis, gardening, hiking, horseback riding, photography. Communications, Intellectual property, Trademark and copyright. Office: McGraw Hill Cos Inc 1221 Avenue of the Americas New York NY 10020

TEMIN, MICHAEL LEHMAN, lawyer; b. Phila., July 18, 1933; s. Henry and Annette (Lehman) T.; children: Aaron Lehman, Seth Lehman; m. Anne L. Hearn, 2000. BA magna cum laude, Yale U., 1954; LL.B. cum laude, U. Pa., 1957. Bar: Pa. 1958, Del. 2000, U.S. Ct. Appeals (3d cir.) 1958, U.S. Supreme Ct. 1969, U.S. Ct. Appeals (2d cir.) 1986, U.S. Ct. Appeals (9th cir.) 1992, U.S. Ct. Appeals (11th cir.) 2002. Asst. U.S. atty. U.S. Atty.'s Office, Phila., 1958-59; assoc. Wolf, Block, Schorr and Solis-Cohen, Phila., 1959-66, ptnr., 1966—. Lectr. Law Sch., U. Pa., Phila., 1982-90, adj. prof., 1990-93, 94-95, 2002—; Thomas A. O'Boyle vis. disting. practitioner, 1985, I. Grant Irey lectr., 1988. Editor U. Pa. Law Rev., 1955-57 Vice chmn. Ednl. Nominating Panel, Phila., 1981-83; bd. dirs. Citizens Com. in Pub. Edn., Phila., 1970-96, pres. 1980-82. Fellow Am. Coll. Bankruptcy (regent 1997-2003); mem. Phila. Bar Assn. (chmn. bankruptcy com., sect. corp., banking and bus. law 1979-86, chmn. profl. guidance com. 1985, sec. sect. corp. banking and bus. law 1985, treas. sect. corp. banking and bus. law 1986, vice chmn. sect. corp. banking and bus. law 1987, chmn. sect. corp. banking and bus. law 1988), Pa. Bar Assn. (ho. of dels. 1985-89, 90—), ABA (bus. bankruptcy com. of sect. corp. banking and bus. law chmn. rules subcom., 1985-92, vice chmn. chpt. 11 subcom. 1992-96, vice chmn. ea. dist. Pa. bankruptcy conf. 1994-95, chmn. ea. dist. Pa. bankruptcy conf., 1995-96), Order of Coif. Jewish. Bankruptcy, General civil litigation, Commercial, contracts (including sales of goods; commercial financing). Office: Wolf Block Schorr & Solis-Cohen LLP 22d Fl 1650 Arch St Philadelphia PA 19103-2097 E-mail: mtemin@wolfblock.com.

TEMKIN, HARVEY L. lawyer; b. Madison, Wis., Jan. 1, 1952; s. Joe L. and Sylvia (Libanoff) T.; m. Barbara Jean Myers, June 13, 1976; children: James, Daniel, Eli. BA, U. Wis., 1974; JD, U. Ill., 1978. Bar: Wis. 1978. Assoc. Foley & Lardner, Madison, 1978—83; prof. Tulane Law Sch., New Orleans, 1983-87; ptnr. Foley & Lardner, Madison, 1987—2002; shareholder Reinhart Boerner Van Deuren, s.c., Madison, 2002—. Lectr. U. Wis. Law Sch., 1990-93; mem. U.S. Senator Feingold's Bus. Adv. Group. 1st v.p. Hillel Found., Madison, 1982-83, bd. dirs., 1987-95; chmn. edn. com. Beth Israel Synagogue, Madison, 1980-82; chmn. Downtown Madison, Inc., 1989-91; chmn. Jewish edn. panel Madison Jewish Community Coun., 1993-98. Fellow Am. Coll. Real Estate Lawyers; mem. ABA (real property probate and trust sect., reporter significant legis. panel 1983-85, significant lit. panel 1985-87). Bankruptcy, Corporate, general, Property, real (including real estate development, water). Home: 2313 Sugar River Rd Verona WI 53593-8741 Office: Reinhart Boerner Van Deuren 22 East Mifflin St PO Box 2018 Madison WI 53701-2018 E-mail: htemkin@reinhartlaw.com.

TEMKO, STANLEY LEONARD, lawyer; b. N.Y.C., Jan. 4, 1920; s. Emanuel and Betty (Alderman) T.; m. Francine Marie Salzman, Mar. 4, 1944 (dec. Dec. 1998); children: Richard J., Edward J., William D. AB, Columbia U., 1940, LLB, 1943. Bar: N.Y. 1943, D.C. 1951. Practice in, N.Y.C., 1943, 46-47; law clk. Mr. Justice Wiley Rutledge, U.S. Supreme Ct., Washington, 1947-48; legal counsel Econ. Coop. Adminstrn., 1948-49; assoc. Covington & Burling, Washington, 1949-55, ptnr., 1955-90, sr. counsel, 1990—. Editor-in-chief: Columbia Law Rev, 1942-43. Trustee Beauvoir Sch., 1963-69; trustee Columbia U., 1980-91, trustee emeritus, 1991—, mem. bd. visitors Sch. Law, 1961-98, mem. emeritus, 1999—; mem. bd. govs. St. Albans Sch., 1967-73, chmn., 1971-73. 2nd lt. U.S. Army, 1943-46. Decorated Bronze Star; recipient medal for conspicuous alumni svc. Columbia U., 1979. Fellow Am. Bar Found. (chmn. rsch. com. 1970-72); mem. ABA, Am. Law Inst., D.C. Bar Assn., Columbia U. Sch. Law Alumni Assn. (pres. 1982-84), Met. Club, Nat. Press Club, Phi Beta Kappa. Administrative and regulatory, Antitrust, Health. Home: 4811 Dexter Ter NW Washington DC 20007-1020 Office: Covington & Burling 1201 Pennsylvania Ave NW Washington DC 20004-2401 E-mail: stemko@cov.com.

TEMPLAR, TED MAC, lawyer; b. Arkansas City, Kans., Sept. 27, 1929; s. H. George and Helen Marie (Bishop) T.; m. Maxine Bowman, Feb. 19, 1954; children: Lance Cameron, Kenton Lane, Clayton Neil. BBA, Washburn U., 1951, JD, 1954. Bar: Kans. 1954, U.S. Dist. Ct. Kans. 1954, U.S. Ct. Appeals (10th cir.) 1961. Dep. county lawyer Cowley County, Arkansas City, Kans., 1956-58, judge city ct., 1969-73; state rep. 79th dist. State of Kans., Topeka, 1973-77; pvt. practice Arkansas City, 1954—. 1st lt. USAR, 1951-59. Recipient Certificate Appreciation Kans. Bar Assn., 1973. Mem. Rotary Club Arkansas City, Midian Shrine, Wichita, Legion of Honor Order of DeMolay, Jaycee Internat. (senate). Republican. Avocations: hunting, fishing. Commercial, consumer (including collections, credit), General practice, Probate (including wills, trusts). Office: PO Box 1002 Arkansas City KS 67005-1002

TEMPLE, LARRY EUGENE, lawyer; b. Plainview, Tex., Dec. 26, 1935; s. Herman Edward and Grace Eileen (Ivey) T.; m. Laura Louann Atkins, Feb. 23, 1963; children: Laura Allison, John Lawrence. BBA, U. Tex., 1957, LLB with honors, 1959; LLD (hon.), Lamar U., 1985. Bar: Tex., U.S. Dist. Ct. (we. dist.) Tex., U.S. Ct. Appeals (5th cir.), U.S. Supreme Ct. Law clk. to justice Tom Clark U.S. Supreme Ct., Washington, 1959-60; assoc. Powell, Rauhut, McGinnis, Reavley & Lochridge, Austin, Tex., 1960-63; legal adminstrn. asst., exec. asst. Tex. Gov. John B. Connally, Austin, 1963-67; spl. counsel to pres. Lyndon Baines Johnson, Washington, 1967-69; pvt. practice Austin, 1969—. Bd. dirs. Temple-Inland, Inc., Guaranty Fed. Bank. Mem. U. Tex. Cancer Found., Houston, 1978-84, U. Tex. Devel. Bd., Austin, 1980-85, 90—, chmn., 1993-95; pres. U. Tex. Ex-Students Assn., 1997-98; mem. Tex. Higher Edn. Coordinating Bd., Austin, 1983-89, chmn., 1983-87; chmn. Select Com. for Higher Edn., Austin, 1985-87; bd. dirs. Lyndon B. Johnson Found., 1986—, vice chmn., 1989-2000, pres., 2000—; trustee U. Tex. Law Sch. Found., 1989—. Recipient Faculty award U. Tex. Law Sch., 1987, Humanitarian award Austin region NCCJ, 1988, Santa Rita award U. Tex. System, 1989, Disting. Alumnus award U. Tex., Austin, 1990, Outstanding Alumnus award U. Tex. Law Sch., 1999, Leon Green award Tex. Law Rev., 2003. Fellow Tex. Bar Found.; mem. ABA, Tex. Bar Assn. (chmn. legis. com. 1980, 83-86), Tex. Jr. Bar Assn. (chmn. bd. dirs. 1967), Austin Jr. Bar Assn. (pres. 1962-63). Democrat. Episcopalian. Administrative and regulatory, Banking, Legislative. Home: 2606 Escondido Cv Austin TX 78703-1610 Office: 400 W 15th St Ste 1510 Austin TX 78701-1648

TEN BRINK, CHARLES J. law educator; b. Shelby, Mich., Sept. 10, 1954; s. Carl K. and Kathryn Roth Ten Brink. BS, Mich. State U., 1976; JD, U. Mich., 1979, AMLS, 1985. Bar: Ill. 1979, Mich. 1980, Ind. 1983, Fla. 1984. Assoc. law libr. U. Chgo., 1985—2001; prof., dir. libr. and tech. Mich. State U., DCL Coll. Law, East Lansing, 2001—. Mem.: ABA (com. on law librs.). Office: Mich State U DCL Coll Law 122 Law Coll Bldg East Lansing MI 48824 E-mail: charles.tenbrink@law.msu.edu.

TENENBAUM, J. SAMUEL, lawyer; b. Frankfurt, Germany, Mar. 5, 1949; s. Josef and Chana Tenenbaum; m. Susan Kay Nabedrick, Nov. 11, 1973; 1 child, Benjamin. BA, Ohio State U., 1970; JD cum laude, Northwestern U., 1973. Bar: Ill. 1973, U.S. Dist. Ct. (no. dist.) Ill. 1974, U.S. Ct. Appeals (7th cir.) 1974, U.S. Ct. Appeals (10th cir.) 1975, U.S. Ct. Appeals (9th cir.) 1976, U.S. Supreme Ct. 1977. Law clk. to judge U.S. Dist. Ct. (no. dist.) Ill., Chgo., 1973-75; ptnr. Tenenbaum & Senerowitz and prior firms, Chgo., 1975-91, Schwartz, Cooper, Greenberger & Krauss, Chgo., 1991-95, Sachnoff & Weaver, Ltd., Chgo., 1995—. Instr., adj. prof. clin. trial advocacy Northwestern U. Sch. Law, Chgo., 1985—. Contbr. articles to profl. jours. Pres. Beth Hillel Congregation, 1992-94; nat. chmn. Northwestern U. Law Sch. Fund, 1990-92; golf coach Jewish Cmty. Ctr. MACABBI. Avocations: golf, rafting, travel, reading. Appellate, General civil litigation. Office: Sachnoff & Weaver Ltd 30 S Wacker Dr Fl 29 Chicago IL 60606-7429 E-mail: stenenbaum@sachnoff.com.

TENENBAUM, JOEL DAVID, lawyer; b. N.Y.C., June 20, 1940; s. Abraham and Pauline Tenenbaum; m. Leah M. Tenenbaum, Feb. 13, 1965; children: Harlan S., Nicole C. AB, Hunter Coll., 1962; JD, Bklyn. Law Sch., 1967. Bar: NY 1966, Del. 1972, Pa. 1981, diplomate: Am. Coll. Family Trial Lawyers. Exec. dir. Cmty. Legal Aid Soc., Wilmington, Del., 1971—72; dir. Woloshin, Tenenbaum, Lynch, Natalie & Gagne, Wilmington, 1972—; U.S. magistrate Dist. of Del., Wilmington, 1973—74. Lectr. Widener Law Sch., Wilmington, Villanova (Pa.) Law Sch. Contbr. articles to profl. jours. Mem. Govs. Task Force on Teen Pregnancy, Govs. Task Force Uniform Adoption Act. Recipient Disting. Legal Svcs. award, Cath. Charities, 1987, Presentation gavel, Del. Bar Assn., 1989. Fellow: Am. Acad. Adoption Attys., Am. Acad. Matrimonial Lawyers; mem.: ABA (chmn. Family Law Sect. Com. on Stepparents' Rights 1988—93, chmn. Family Law Sect. Adoption Com. 1989—99, liason Nat. Conf. Commrs. Uniform State Laws Adoption Act 1990—, exec. mem. Task Force Legislation and Lobbying 1992—, Family Law Sect. Council-at-Large 1996—99, Family Law Sect. Sec. 1999—2000, vice chair Family Law Sect. 2000—01, chair Family Law Sect. 2002—03, chair family law sect., liason U.S. State Dept. Hague Conf. Intercounty Adoptions, recorder Law in the Fifty States, presenter various CLE programs, presdl. recognition), Assn. Family Conciliation Ct., Internat. Law Assn., Internat. Bar Assn., Del. State Bar. Assn. (chmn. Adoption Com. 1981—, chmn. Family Law Sect. 1987—89, chmn. Com. on Special Needs of Children 1985—87). Family and matrimonial, Adoption. Office: Woloshin Tenenbaum Lynch Natalie & Gagne 3200 Concord Pike Wilmington DE 19803 Office Fax: 302-477-3210. E-mail: jtenenbaum@wtnlaw.com.

TENNEN, KEN, lawyer; b. Belmont Shore, Calif., June 30, 1947; s. Morris and Clair (Rose) T.; m. Diane Janet Sussman, Dec. 25, 1982; children: Sterling M, Skyler Alexander. Cert. counseling, UCLA, 1973; lic., U. Los Ams., Cholula Puebla, Mex., 1975; MA, Georgetown U., 1977; JD, LaVerne Coll. Law, 1996. Bar: Calif. 1996. Cons. Booz Allen & Hamilton, Washington, 1974-77; with Multinat. Corp., L.A., 1977-92; sole practitioner West Hills, Calif., 1996—. Bd. dirs., chief exec. officer Suntree Townhomes, Tarzana, Calif. Chmn. Happy Valley Sch. Bd., Ojai, Calif., 1991-2000; mem. Happy Valley Found., 1990—, pres., 2000—; bd. dirs. Rec. for the Blind, 1999—. Mem. Calif. State Bar (com. on legal profls. with disabilities 1999—), Calif. Conf. Dels. Avocations: gardening, photography, scuba. Office: 24372 Vanowen St Ste 202 West Hills CA 91307-2800 E-mail: ken@kentennen.com.

TENNEN, LESLIE IRWIN, lawyer, consultant, inventor; b. Toronto, Aug. 26, 1952; came to U.S., 1961; s. Edward and Elsie (Liberbaum) T. BA with distinction, U. Ariz., 1973, JD, 1976; Mount Scopus, Hebrew U., Jerusalem, 1975. Bar: Ariz. 1977, U.S. Dist. Ct. Ariz. 1979. Sole practice, Tucson, 1977—79; ptnr. Sterns and Tennen, Phoenix, 1979—. Cons. internat. law and aerospace activities; lectr. univs., colls. and law schs.; mem. Ariz. Space Commn., 1994-2000, also profl. aviation and aerospace congresses and seminars in N.Am., Europe, Asia, S.Am., Australia; judge Jessup Internat. Moot Court Competition, 1982, 83, 85, 92; dir., treas. Assn. U.S. Mems. Internat. Inst. Space Law; com. mem. U. Belarusian Culture Internat. Orgn. Mem. editl bd. Space Regulations Libr.; contbr. Ariz. Law Rev., 1975-76; contbr. articles to profl. jours. Precinct committeeman State Dem. Conv., 1972-73. Received highest score Ariz. Bar Exam., Feb. 1977. Mem. AIAA (sr.), Ariz. Bar Found., Internat. Eurasian Acad. Scis., Internat. Inst. Space Law (Appreciation award (with Patricia Margaret Sterns) 1998), Internat. Acad. Astronautics, Am. Soc. Internat. Law, Soc. Aerospace Communicators Inc., Internat. Law Assn., Planetary Soc., Fedn. Aerospace Socs. in Tucson (exec. bd.). Aviation, Commercial, contracts (including sales of goods; commercial financing), Private international. Office: 849 N 3rd Ave Phoenix AZ 85003-1408 E-mail: LTennen@astrolaw.com.

TENNEY, ROBERT CARL, lawyer; b. Walla Walla, Wash., Aug. 12, 1950; s. Robert DeMar and Mary (Schreiner) T.; m. Rhodi Elizabeth Nygaard, Dec. 23, 1977; children: Robert David, Christopher James. Student, Whitman Coll., 1968-70; BA, U. Wash., 1972; JD, U. Puget Sound, 1979. Bar: Wash. 1979, U.S. Dist. Ct. (ea. dist.) Wash. 1979, U.S. Dist. Ct. (we. dist.) Wash. 1983, U.S. Ct. Appeals (9th cir.) 1987. Ptnr., shareholder Halverson & Applegate, Yakima, Wash., 1979-87; atty., shareholder Meyer, Fluegge & Tenney, Yakima, 1987—. Bd. dirs. ARC, Yakima, 1985-91, United Way, Yakima, 1991—; mem. planning commn. Yakima City. 1981-84. Mem. Fed. Bar Assn., Wash. State Bar Assn., Yakima County Bar Assn., Def. Rsch. Inst., Wash. Def. Trial Lawyers Assn. (former trustee), Am. Bd. Trial Advocates. Republican. Presbyterian. Avocations: family, tennis. General civil litigation, Personal injury (including property damage), Product liability. Office: Meyer Fluegge & Tenney PO Box 22680 Yakima WA 98907-2680

TENUTA, LUIGIA, lawyer; b. Madison, Wis., June 4, 1954; d. Eugene P. and Nancy (Gardner) T. AB in Internat. Studies with honors, Miami U., Oxford, Ohio, 1976; JD, Capital U., 1981; postgrad., Pontifical Coll. Josephinum, 1987-88. Bar: Ohio 1981. With internat. mktg. dept. Dresser Industries, Columbus, Ohio, 1976-80, analyst strategic planning, 1980, mgr. internat bus. planning Stratford, Conn., 1981; pvt. practice law Columbus, 1981—. Former mem. devel. com. Miami U. Mem. Ohio Bar Assn., Columbus Bar Assn. Roman Catholic. General civil litigation, General practice. Office: 6400 Riverside Dr Dublin OH 43017-5197

TEPLEN, PHILIP H. lawyer; b. N.Y.C., Apr. 26, 1957; s. Martin Joseph and Pearl Faye Teplen; m. Patti Anne Teplen, Sept. 22, 1984; children: William, Amanda. BSBA in Fin., Georgetown U., 1979, Oxford U., 1979; JD, Bklyn. Law Sch., 1982. Prin. Teplen & Assocs. PLLC, N.Y.C., 1984—; founder, pres. Tepco Fin., N.Y.C., 1986—88; gen. counsel, v.p. Baron Devel., N.Y.C., 1988—91; founder, pres. Intelligent Solutions, N.Y.C., 1994—96; exec. v.p. Allarus Tech. Mgmt., Inc., 2002—. Guest lectr. Fla. Internat. U. Miami, 1999. Avocations: boating, tennis, golf. Office: 350 Fifth Ave New York NY 10118 E-mail: pteplen@teplenlaw.com.

TEPLITZ, ROBERT FORMAN, lawyer; b. Miami, Fla., Dec. 20, 1970; s. Alan Forman and Judith (Roberts) T. BA magna cum laude, Franklin and Marshall Coll., 1992; JD cum laude, Cornell U., 1995. Bar: Pa. 1995, U.S. Dist. Ct. (mid. dist.) Pa. 1997. Litigation assoc. McNees, Wallace & Nurick, Harrisburg, Pa., 1995-98; policy dir. Casey for Gov. campaign, 2001—02; dep. chief counsel Dept. Auditor Gen., Harrisburg, 1998—2001, spl. asst. to chief of staff, 2002—. Adj. prof. Widener Law Sch., 2002—. Bd. dirs. Am. Cancer Soc., Harrisburg, 1996—, Harrisburg Jewish Cmty. Ctr., 2000—. Mem. Phi Beta Kappa. Office: 224 Finance Bldg Harrisburg PA 17120 E-mail: tep911@aol.com.

TERK, GLENN THOMAS, lawyer; b. Feb. 27, 1949; s. Raymond Arthur and Marguerite Ida (Nichols) T.; m. Mary Ann Michaud, Sept. 25, 1982. BSME, Clarkson Coll. Tech., 1971; JD, U. Conn., 1976. Bar: Conn. 1976, U.S. Dist. Ct. Conn. 1976, U.S. Ct. Appeals (2d cir.) 2002. Engr. Combustion Engring. Co., Windsor, Conn., 1971-76; assoc. Francis, Kroopnick & O'Neil, Hartford, Conn., 1976-78; ptnr. Brignole & Terk, Hartford, Conn., 1993-95; pvt. practice Hartford, Conn., 1995—. Mem. Dem. Town Com., Windsor, 1978-79, Windsor Inland Wetlands Commn., 1978-79, Rep. Town com., Wethersfield, 1997—; chmn. Trinity United Meth. Ch. adminstrv. bd., Windsor, 1982-83, finance chmn. 1997-99. Mem. Conn. Bar Assn. (cmty. subcom. 1981-85, real property exec. com. 1994—, comml. law com. 1994—). Commercial, contracts (including sales of goods; commercial financing), General practice, Property, real (including real estate development, water). Home: 445 Old Reservoir Rd Wethersfield CT 06109-3956 Office: 81 Wolcott Hill Rd Wethersfield CT 06109-1242 E-mail: Gterk@cs.com.

TERMINI, ROSEANN BRIDGET, lawyer, educator; b. Phila., Feb. 2, 1953; d. Vincent James and Bridget (Marano) T. BS magna cum laude, Drexel U., 1975; MEd, Temple U., 1979, JD, 1985, grad. in food and pharmacy law, 1998. Bar: Pa. 1985, U.S. Dist. Ct. (ea. dist.) Pa. 1985, D.C. 1986. Jud. clk. Superior Ct. of Pa., Allentown, 1985-86; atty. Pa. Power & Light Co., Allentown, 1986-87; corp. counsel food and drug law Lemmon Co., Sellersville, Pa., 1987-88; sr. dep. atty. bur. consumer protection plain lang. law Office of Atty. Gen., Harrisburg, Pa., 1988-96; prof. Villanova U. Sch. Law, 1996-2000; prof. food and drug law Temple U. Sch. Pharmacy, 1998—, St. Joseph U., 2000—. Spkr. continuing legal edn.-plain lang. laws, environ. conf.; adj. prof. Widener U. Sch. Law, 1993—, Dickinson Sch. Law; specialized food, drug, cosmetic and med. device law course dir. pres.'s coun. Immaculata Coll.; mem. on-line distance learning legal issues pharmacy promotion St. Joseph U., 2002; instr. online exec. MBA program Drexel U., 2002—. Author: Food, Drug and Medical Device Law: Topics and Cases, 2001, (statutary supplement instr.'s manual) Health Law: Federal Regulation of Drugs, Biologies, Medical Drinks, Foods and Dietary Supplements, 2003; contbr. articles to profl. jours, law revs. Active in Sr. Citizens Project Outreach, Hospice, 1986—; mem. St. Thomas More Law Bd.; mem. pres.' coun. Immaculata Coll., 2002. Mem. ABA (various coms.), Bar Assn. D.C., Pa. Bar Assn. (ethics, exceptional children and environ. sects., Plain English award 1999), Temple U. Law Alumni Assn., Drexel U. Alumni Assn., Omicron Nu, Phi Alpha Delta. Avocations: tap dancing, hiking, cross-country skiing. E-mail: rtermini@attorney.com.

TERNUS, MARSHA K. state supreme court justice; b. Vinton, Iowa, May 30, 1951; BA, U. Iowa, 1972; JD, Drake U., 1977. Bar: Iowa 1977, Ariz. 1984. With Bradshaw, Fowler, Proctor & Fairgrave, Des Moines, 1977—93; justice Iowa Supreme Ct., Des Moines, 1993—. Editor-in-chief: Drake Law Rev., 1976—77. Mem.: Polk County Bar Assn. (pres. 1984—85), Order of Coif, Phi Beta Kappa. Office: Iowa Supreme Ct Jud Br Bldg 1111 E Court Ave Des Moines IA 50319-0001

TERP, THOMAS THOMSEN, lawyer; b. Fountain Hill, Pa., Aug. 12, 1947; s. Norman T. and Josephine (Uhran) T.; m. Pamela Robinson; children: Stephanie, Brian, Adam; step-children: Taylor Mefford, Grace Mefford. BA, Albion (Mich.) Coll., 1969; JD, Coll. of William and Mary, 1973. Bar: Ohio 1973, U.S. Dist. Ct. (so. dist.) Ohio 1973, U.S. Ct. Appeals (6th cir.) 1973, U.S. Supreme Ct. 1979. Assoc. Taft, Stettinius & Hollister, Cin., 1973-80, ptnr., 1981—. Bd. dirs. Starflo Corp., Orangeburg, S.C., Attorneys' Liability Assurance Soc., Ltd., Hamilton, Bermuda, ALAS, Inc., Chgo. Editor-in-chief William & Mary Law Rev., 1972-73; mem. bd. editors Jour. of Environ. Hazards, 1988—, Environ. Law Jour. of Ohio, 1989—. Mem. Cin. Athletic Club, Camargo Club, Epworth Assembly (Ludington, Mich.), Lincoln Hills Golf Club (Ludington), Queen City Club. Avocations: tennis, golf, travel. General civil litigation, Environmental. E-mail: terp@taftlaw.com.

TERRELL, G. IRVIN, lawyer; b. Houston, Sept. 28, 1946; s. George I. and Adella (Weichert) T.; m. Karen Steenberg, Jan. 8, 1984; 1 child, Katharine. BA, U. Tex., 1968, JD, 1972. Bar: Tex., U.S. Supreme Ct., U.S. Ct. Appeals (3d and 5th cirs.), U.S. Dist. Ct. (so., no. and ea. dists.) Tex., U.S. Dist. Ct. (we. dist.) Pa. Assoc. Baker & Botts, Houston, 1972-79, ptnr., 1980—. Mem. ABA, Houston Bar Assn., Internat. Soc. Barristers. Federal civil litigation, General civil litigation, State civil litigation. E-mail: irv.terrell@bakerbotts.com.

TERRELL, JAMES DANIEL, lawyer; b. Kansas City, Oct. 22, 1956; s. D. Ronald and Bobbie L. (Graham) T.; m. Lori J. McAlister, May 31, 1980; children: Justin Daniel, Christopher James, Alexander Graham. BS, Ctrl. Mo. State U., 1979; JD, U. Mo., 1982. Bar: Mo. 1982, U.S. Dist. Ct. (we. dist.) 1982, U.S. Dist. Ct. (ea. dist.) Mo. 1984. Assoc. Wasinger, Parham & Morthland, Hannibal, Mo., 1982-87; ptnr. Wasinger, Parham, Morthland Terrell & Wasinger, Hannibal, 1987—. Bd. dirs. Marion County Svcs. for the Developmentally Disabled, Hannibal, 1989—. Mem.: 10th Jud. Cir. Bar Assn. (pres. 2001—), Mo. Bar Assn. (family law sect.), U. Mo. Alumni Assn. (life), Phi Delta Phi. General civil litigation, Family and matrimonial, Insurance. Office: Wasinger Parham Morthland Terrell & Wasinger 2801 Saint Marys Ave Hannibal MO 63401-3775

TERRY, B. BRENT, lawyer; b. Louisville, Dec. 7, 1968; s. Bobby Swede and Eleanor (Foster) T.; m. Lee Ann, May 22, 1993. BA in History, William Jewell Coll., 1991; JD, Emory U., 1994. Bar: Ga. 1994. Sr. assoc. Attys. at Law Smith, Atlanta, 1994-99, Misner, Scott, and Martin, Atlanta, 1999—. Risk mgmt. com. Briarlake Bapt. Ch., Decatur, Ga., 1996-98. Mem. ABA, ATLA, Ga. Trial Lawyers Assn., Christian Legal Soc., Atlanta Bar Assn. Avocations: choral music, reading, politics, church activities, sports. Office: 3003 Summit Blvd Ste 800 Atlanta GA 30319 E-mail: b.brent.terry@Zurichna.com.

TERRY, FREDERICK ARTHUR, JR., lawyer; b. Buffalo, May 24, 1932; s. Frederick Arthur and Agnes Elizabeth (Tranter) T.; m. Barbara Anderson. BA, Williams Coll., 1953; LLB, Columbia U., 1956. Bar: N.Y. 1957, (U.S. Dist. Ct. (so., no. and ea. dists.) N.Y.), (U.S. Tax Ct.), (U.S. Supreme Ct.). Law clk. to Hon. Sterry R. Waterman, U.S. Ct. Appeals (2d cir.), 1956—57; assoc. Sullivan & Cromwell, N.Y.C., 1957-65, ptnr., 1965-99, sr. counsel, 2000—. Trustee Harold K. Hochschild Found.; chmn. Flagler Found.; bd. dirs. Eisenhower Fellowships, Natural Resources Def. Coun., Rockefeller U., McIntosh Found., Weinman Found. Mem. ABA, N.Y. State Bar Assn., Assn. of Bar of City of N.Y., Century Assn., River Club, Union Club, India House, Doubles (N.Y.C.), Maidstone Club (East Hampton, N.Y.), The Bathing Corp. (Southampton, NY), Lyford Cay Club (Bahamas). Office: Sullivan & Cromwell 125 Broad St Fl 25 New York NY 10004-2400

TERRY, GARY A. lawyer, former trade association executive; b. Ogden, Utah, Apr. 2, 1935; s. Hyrum Aceal and Viola (Sorenson) T.; m. Carole Ann Eitel, June 23, 1962; children— Stephanie Ann, Brendan Gary BA in Polit. Sci., UCLA, 1964; JD, George Washington U., 1968. Bars: Va. 1969 D.C. 1969. Mem. staff U.S. Ho. of Reps., Washington, 1964-65; Washington staff Bethlehem Steel Corp., 1965-69; atty. HUD, Washington, 1969; exec. v.p. Am. Land Devel. Assn. (now Am. Resort Devel. Assn.), Washington, 1969-82, pres., 1982-91, also dir.; with Jones, Waldo, Holbrook & McDonough, Washington, 1991-95, St. George, 1995-97. Dir. Internat. Found. for Timesharing, Washington, 1981-91, mem. consultative council Nat. Inst. Bldg. Scis., Washington, 1982-85; U.S. rep. land use and town planning com. Internat. Real Estate Fedn., Brussels, 1984-91; mem. Found. for Internat. Meetings, Washington, 1984-92; del. Lincoln Inst. Land Policy, Harvard U., 1984, 85 Contbr. articles to profl. jours. Asst. to exec. dir. Presdl. Inaugural Com., 1969-70; mem. adv. bd. NOAA, Washington, 1972; bd. dirs. Zacchaeus Free Med. and Legal Clinics, Washington, 1991-95, co-chair lawyers com., 1992-95; bd. dirs. Celebrity Concert Series, St. George, 1999—; chmn. Pioneer Ctr. for the Arts Found., St. George, 2000-02, bd. trustees, 1998-2003. Seved with USN, 1953-56. Decorated Am. Spirit of Honor medal. Mem. Va. Bar Assn., D.C. Bar Assn. Mem. Lds Ch. Avocations: music, literature, architectural design, art, travel. Home: 952 Lizzie Ln Saint George UT 84790-2255

TERRY, GUYTON OTIS, III, lawyer; b. Cheyenne, Wyo., Oct. 5, 1969; s. Guyton Otis Terry, Jr. and Patricia Ann (Helms) Terry; m. Gail L. Terry, Feb. 9, 2001; children: Emma Caroline, Samuel Luke. BA, U. Ga., 1991; JD, U. Wyo., 1998. Bar: Tenn. 1998, Ga. 2000, U.S. Dist. Ct. (ea. dist.) Tenn. 1998, U.S. Dist. Ct. (ctrl. dist.) Ga. 2000, U.S. Ct. Appeals (6th cir.) 1998, U.S. Ct. Appeals (11th cir.) 2000. Mem. Fuller, Vaughn & Gott, Kingsport, Tenn., 1998—2000, Moser & Terry, Valdosta, Ga., 2000—. Mem. Lowndes County Dem. Com., Valdosta, 2002. Mem.: Valdosta Assn. Criminal Def. Lawyers, State Bar of Ga., Tenn. Bar Assn., Azalea City Kiwanis Club. Avocations: golf, University of Georgia athletics. Criminal, Personal injury (including property damage). Office: Moser & Terry 1706 N Patterson St Valdosta GA 31602 E-mail: mosergot@bellsouth.net.

TERRY, JACK CHATTERSON, lawyer; b. Monett, Mo., Nov. 23, 1919; s. Jacob E. and Florence V. (Chatterson) T.; m. Susan W. Terry, June 7, 1941; children: Susan L. Terry Galewaler, Philip C. BA in History and Govt., U. Mo., Kansas City, 1949, JD, 1952. Bar: Mo. 1952, U.S. Supreme Ct. 1961. Sole practice, Independence, Mo., 1952—. Mem. Mo. Legislature, 1955-56; legis. liaison officer Jackson County (Mo.), 1967-68; atty. Inter-City Fire Protection Dist., 1955-74; city atty. City of Blue Summit (Mo.), 1971-76; atty. Jackson County (Mo.) Bd. Election Commrs., 1974—. Pres. Independence Good Govt. League, 1961-63, Jackson County League Better Govt., 1962-66. Served as officer USAAF, 1941-46, PTO. Decorated Purple Heart, Air medal. Mem. ABA, Mo. Bar Assn., Kansas City Bar Assn., Inter-City Kiwanis (pres. 1967), Masons, Shriners. Democrat. Mem. Christian Ch. (Disciples Of Christ). Family and matrimonial, Personal injury (including property damage), Workers' compensation. Home: 614 Bellevista Dr Independence MO 64055-1746

TERRY, JAMES JOSEPH, JR., lawyer; b. Yonkers, N.Y., July 2, 1952; s. James Joseph Sr. and Marie Catherine (O'Boyle) T.; m. Marguerite Mary O'Connor, Sept. 29, 1985; 1 child, James Daniel. BA, NYU, 1974; JD, Columbia U., 1977. Bar: N.Y. 1978, U.S. Dist. Ct. (so. and ea. dists.) N.Y. 1978, U.S. Ct. Appeals (2d cir.) 1981, U.S. Ct. Appeals (3d cir.) 1989, U.S. Supreme Ct. 2000. Assoc. Cole & Deitz, N.Y.C., 1977-89; ptnr. Winston & Strawn (formerly Cole & Deitz), N.Y.C., 1989—2002; v.p., gen. counsel F.J. Sciame Constrn. Co., Inc., N.Y.C., 2002—. Mem. ABA, N.Y. State Bar Assn., Def. Rsch. Inst., N.Y. County Lawyers Assn. Democrat. Roman Catholic. Avocations: fishing, reading. Federal civil litigation, State civil litigation, Construction. Home: 190 Kneeland Ave Yonkers NY 10705-2713 Office: Sciame Constrn Co Inc 80 South St New York NY 10038 E-mail: jterry@fjsciame.com.

TERRY, JOHN ALFRED, state supreme court judge; b. Utica, N.Y., May 6, 1933; s. Robert Samuel and Julia Berenice (Collins) T. BA magna cum laude, Yale U., 1954; JD, Georgetown U., 1960. Bar: D.C. 1960. Asst. U.S. atty. for D.C., 1962-67; staff atty. Nat. Commn. Reform of Fed. Criminal Laws, Washington, 1967-68; pvt. practice law Washington, 1968-69; chief appellate div. U.S. Atty.'s Office for D.C., 1969-82; judge D.C. Ct. Appeals, 1982—. Mem. D.C. Bar (bd. govs. 1977-82), ABA, Phi Beta Kappa Office: DC Ct Appeals 500 Indiana Ave NW Washington DC 20001-2138

TERRY, JOSEPH H. lawyer; b. Louisville, July 9, 1945; s. Wilbur H. and Reba Mae Terry; m. Donna Lynn Hogg, Apr. 21, 1967; children: Anne Griffin, Alexandra E. BA, U. Louisville, 1968; JD with distinction, U. Ky., 1971. Bar: Ky. 1971, U.S. Dist. Ct. (we. dist.) Ky. 1971, U.S. Ct. Appeals (6th cir.) 1975, U.S. Dist. Ct. (ea. dist.) Ky. 1983. Assoc., then ptnr. Middleton Reutlinger & Baird, Louisville, 1971-75; ptnr. Eldred Paxton & Terry, Princeton, Ky., 1975-79; spl. counsel Ligon Specialized Hauler Inc., Madisonville, Ky., 1979-80, pres., 1980-82; ptnr. Wyatt, Tarrant & Combs, Lexington, Ky., 1983-97, Dinsmore & Shohl, LLP, Lexington, 1997—. Contbr. articles to profl. jours. Vice chmn. Lexington Transit Authority, 1984-91; chmn. Lexington Area Sports Authority, 1998-2001, Ky. Registry of Elections, Frankfort, 1988-95. Fellow ABA (life); mem. Ky. Bar Assn., Sports Lawyers Assn. Democrat. Presbyterian. Avocation: golf. Corporate, general, Mergers and acquisitions, Sports. Home: 1805 St Ives Cir Lexington KY 40502-7714 Office: Dinsmore & Shohl LLP 250 W Main St Ste 1400 Lexington KY 40507-1735

TERRY, JOSEPH RAY, JR., lawyer; b. Vicksburg, Miss., Aug. 10, 1938; s. Joseph Ray Sr. and Alma Blanche (Smith) T.; m. Louise Caroline Beland, July 17, 1965; children: Kathleen A., Marie L., Bernard R. JD, Loyola U., 1965. Bar: D.C. 1966, Miss. 1968, U.S. Ct. Appeals (5th cir.) 1971, Ga. 1973, U.S. Dist. Ct. (no. and so. dists.) Ga. 1973, U.S. Ct. Appeals (D.C. cir.) 1973, U.S. Supreme Ct. 1973, U.S. Ct. Appeals (8th cir.) 1974, U.S. Dist. Ct. (we. dist.) Tenn. 1983, U.S. Ct. Appeals (6th cir.) 1989; cert. mediator. Trial atty. civil rights div. U.S. Dept. Justice, Washington, 1966-69; regional counsel U.S. Dept. HUD, Atlanta, 1969-70; ptnr. Crosland, Myer, Rindskopf & Terry, Atlanta, 1974-76; regional counsel EEOC, Atlanta, 1970-73, supr. trial atty. Litigation Cen., 1976-79, regional atty. Memphis, 1979-96, dep. gen. counsel Washington, 1996-99, cons., lectr., mediator, 1999—. Part-time asst. atty. City of Atlanta, 1975-76; cons. NLRB, Memphis, 1981-82; adj. prof. law Emory U., 1971-75; vis. prof. law St. Louis U., 1973-74, William C. Wefel disting. vis. prof. law, 1998—; acting program dir. EEOC, Washington, 1983, acting dist. dir., Memphis, 1984-85; bd. dirs. Fed. Credit Union, 1984-91; mem. adv. com. to U.S. Dist. Ct. for western dist. Tenn., 1990-93, chmn. case mgmt. subcom., 1991-98; mem. faculty Southwestern Legal Found., Dallas, spring 1998; cons. equal employment, 1999—; cert. gen. civil mediator Supreme Ct. Tenn., 2000. Author: (jour.) Eliminating the Plaintiff's Attorney in Equal Employment Litigation: A Shakespearean Tragedy, Labor Lawyer, 1989, Memphis and Race, The Commercial Appeal, 1987. Cons. Alaska Human Rights Commn., Anchorage, 1981; bd. dirs. Nat. Kidney Found. of West Tenn., Memphis, pres., 1984-85; bd. dirs. United Meth. Neighborhood Ctr., 1985-88; bd. dirs. St. Patrick's Parish Coun., Memphis, pres., 1986-88; mem. Leadership Memphis, 1988-99; bd. dirs. Place of Grace Ministries, Carlisle, Pa., 1997—; apptd. by Pres. for Selective Svc. Bd., Memphis, 2002-03. Named Honor Law Graduate U.S. Atty. Gen., 1965. Mem. ABA (EEOC liaison com. 1987-89), Fed. Bar Assn. (bd. dirs. 1988-89, v.p. West Tenn. chpt. 1991-92, pres. 1993-94, nat. coun. 1996-99, named Younger Fed. Lawyer of Yr. 1973), Supreme Ct. Hist. Soc., St. Thomas More Lawyers Guild, Salvation Army (bd. dirs. 1995-96, 2001-03). Roman Catholic. Avocations: tennis, golf, skiing, hiking, reading. Home: 1560 Harbert Ave Memphis TN 38104-5033

TERRY, KAREN ELIZABETH, lawyer; b. Miami, Fla., June 13, 1970; d. Edmund and Barbara Terry. AB, Duke U., 1991; JD and M in Mass Comm., U. Fla., 1994. Bar: Fla. 1995. Atty. Judge Walter Colbath, West Palm Beach, Fla., 1994, Searcy Denney, West Palm Beach, 1995—. Author, editor: Violence, Regulation, and First Amendment, 1995. Mem. ABA, Acad. Fla. Trial Lawyers (eagle mem.), Palm Beach County Bar Assn., Assn. Trial Lawyers Am., Million Dollar Adv. Avocations: running, rock climbing, scuba diving, tennis, golf. Health, Personal injury (including property damage). Home: 11337 Lost Tree Way North Palm Beach FL 33408 Office: Searcy Denney Scarola Barnhart & Shipley PA PO Brower 3626 West Palm Beach FL 33402-3626

TERRY, MICHAEL JOSEPH, legal process supervisor, court trainer; b. Mount Ayr, Iowa, Aug. 26, 1957; s. John Stanley and Kathryn Marie (Williams) T. BS in Psychology, Santa Clara U., 1979, paralegal cert., 1987. Dep. ct. clk. Santa Clara County Mcpl. Ct., San Jose, Calif., 1980-86; ct. attendant Santa Clara County Superior Ct., San Jose, Calif., 1986-87, courtroom clk., 1987—94, lead courtroom clk., 1994—2001, supr., 2001—. Mem. faculty Ct. Clk. Tng. Inst. Mem.: Assn. of Ct. Trainers (No. Calif. br.) (acting pres. 2002—), Superior Ct. Clks,. Assn. Calif. (pres.), Coalition of Trial Ct. Clks. Assn., Phi Delta Phi. Democrat. Avocations: literature, travel, theatre. Office: Superior Ct 191 N 1st St San Jose CA 95113

TERSCHAN, FRANK ROBERT, lawyer; b. Dec. 25, 1949; s. Frank Joseph and Margaret Anna (Heidt) T.; m. Barbara Elizabeth Keily, Dec. 28, 1974; 1 child, Frank Martin. BA, Syracuse U., 1972; JD, U. Wis., 1975. Bar: Wis. 1976, U.S. Dist. Ct. (ea. and we. dists.) Wis. 1976, U.S. Ct. Appeals (7th cir.) 1979, U.S. Ct. Appeals (10th cir.) 1989, U.S. Supreme Ct. 1992. From assoc. to ptnr. Frisch, Dudek & Slattery Ltd., Milw., 1975-88; ptnr. Slattery and Hausman Ltd., Milw., 1988-94, Terschan & Steinle Ltd.,

Milw., 1994-96, Terschan, Steinle & Ness, Milw., 1996—. Mem. Wis. Jud. Conduct Adv. Com., 2002—. Treas., sec. Ville du Park Homeowners Assn., Mequon, Wis., 1985-86; cub scout packmaster pack 3844 Boy Scouts Am., 1989-90, asst. scoutmaster Troop 865, 1991-93. Mem. ABA, Am. Bd. Trial Advocates, Wis. Bar Assn., Milw. Bar Assn., Assn. Trial Lawyers Am., Wis. Acad. Trial Lawyers (bd. dirs. 1996—), 7th Cir. Bar Assn., Order of Coif. Republican. Lutheran. Avocations: swimming, coin collecting, reading, outdoor activities. Federal civil litigation, General civil litigation, Personal injury (including property damage). Home: 10143 N Lake Shore Dr Mequon WI 53092-6109 Office: 2600 N Mayfair Rd Ste 700 Milwaukee WI 53226-1314 E-mail: frt@tsn-law.com.

TESCHER, DONALD R. lawyer; b. Brooklyn, N.Y., Sept. 26, 1944; s. Harry A. and Irma (Gordon) T.; m. SuAnn Leiken; children: Jennifer L., Jonathan M. BSBA in Acctg., U. Fla., 1966, JD, 1969; LLM, NYU, 1973. Bar: Fla., 1969, U.S. Dist. Ct. (so. dist.) Fla., U.S. Tax Ct. Sr. shareholder Schwartz Nash Heckerling & Tescher, Miami, 1973-84, Fine Jacobson Schwartz Nash Block & England P.A., Miami, 1984-86, Tescher & Milstein, P.A., 1986-90, Tescher Gutter Chaves Josepher Rubin Ruffin and Foreman, P.A., Miami, 1990—. Adj. prof. grad. tax programs Sch. Law U. Miami, 1974-80, 92-95; spkr. in field. Contbr. articles to profl. jours., chpts. to books. Bd. trustees Found. Jewish Philanthropies of The Gtr. Miami Jewish Fedn., 1985—, chmn. profl. adv. com., 1989-91; mem. profl. adv. com. Dade Cmty. Found., 1989—; bd. dirs. Switchboard of Miami, 1986-90, bd. trustees, 1990—95 pres. Beth David Congragation, 1981-83. Fellow Am. Coll. Trust and Estate Counsel (mem. bus. planning com. 1994—, spkr.), Am. Coll. Tax Counsel; mem. ABA (sect. taxation mem. com. fgn. tax problems 1973-74, com. partnerships 1974-75, com. income taxation estates and trusts 1975-77, estate and gift tax com. 1977—, charitable transfers subcom. 1990—, bus. planning-chpt. 14 subcom., chmn. subcom. internat. estate and gift taxation 1987-89), Fla. Bar (tax sect. chmn. 1984-85, del. tax sect. s.e. region liaison conf., bd. dirs. tax sect. exec. coun., spkr., real property, probate and trust law sect., mem. estate and trust tax planning com. 1986—, chmn. probate and trust problems study com. 1995-98, chair trust law com. 1998—), Gtr. Miami Tax Inst., Estate Planning Coun. Gtr. Miami, Dade County Planned Giving Coun., Boca Raton Tax Inst., South Palm Beach County Jewish Fed. (adv. com.), Planned Giving Coun. of Miami-Dade County. Avocations: snow skiing, tennis, reading. Estate planning, Taxation, general. Office: Tescher Gutter Chaves Josoher Rubin Ruffin & Forman PA 2101 NW Corporate Blvd Boca Raton FL 33431-7306

TESSIER, DENNIS MEDWARD, paralegal, lecturer, legal advisor, consultant, cartoonist; b. Royal Oak, Mich., Sept. 20, 1956; s. Medward James and Marilyn (Pitsos) Tessier; m. Michelle Terri Zeichick, July 28, 1990; children: Brian Jae, Carson Lee. Cert. paralegal, U. West L.A., 1987, cert. atty. practice, 1990; cert. in epidemiology, U.S. CDC, 1991. Cert.: U. West L.A. (paralegal) 1987, (atty. practice) 1990; epidermiology U.S. CDC, 1991. Reprodn. analyst Burroughs Corp., Detroit, 1975-76; mixologist Holiday Inn, Inc., Belair, Calif., 1977-83; spl. asst. office of the gen. counsel U.S. Jud. Intelligence Agy., Pacific Sta., L.A., 1981—; mixologist R.W. Grace Inc., Marina Del Rey, Calif., 1984-86; paralegal O'Melveny & Myers, L.A., 1986, Haight, Brown & Bonesteel, Santa Monica, Calif., 1987-93, Helsell & Fetterman, Seattle, 1993-94, Nintendo of Am. Inc., Redmond, Wash., 1994-96, Tousley Brain PLLC, Seattle, 1996-98, Preston Gates & Ellis, Seattle, 1998—. Family law cons. Helping Svcs., L.A., 1990—93, L.A. Clinic, 1990; rschr. Tessier & Assocs. Rsch., Topanga Canyon, Calif., 1983—; assoc. Starlight Found., Redmond, Wash., 1993—. Author: Beauty in Motion, 1983, Champerty and Barratry, 1998, Creek Rat Esquire, 1999, Federal Civil Trial Manual, 2003, Creek Rat Custom Cartoons and Animations; contbr. Mem.: ATLA, ABA (sci. and tech. law sect., jud. adminstrn. sect.), U.S. Nat. Acad. Scis. Academe Industry Program (spkr. CLE), King County Bar Assn., Judge Advs. Assn., Assn. Investigative Scis., Soc. Epidemiology Rsch., Am. Legion. Democrat. Lutheran. Avocations: music, arts. Home: 21100 Pioneer Way Edmonds WA 98026-6947 Office: Preston Gates & Ellis 701 Fifth Ave Ste 5000 Seattle WA 98104 E-mail: dtessier@justice.com., dennist@prestongates.com.

TETI, LOUIS N. lawyer; b. Bryn Mawr, Pa., May 29, 1950; BA, Dickinson Coll., 1972; JD, Temple U., 1976, LLM in Tax., 1981. Bar: Pa. 1976. Ptnr. MacElree Harvey, Ltd., West Chester and Exton, Pa. Mem. disciplinary bd. Surpeme Ct. Pa., 2000—. Fellow Am. Coll. Trust and Estate Counsel; mem. ABA (ho. dels. 1985-91, 99—), Pa. Bar Assn. (chmn. young lawyers divsn. 1982-83, bd. govs. 1982-85, 91-94, 97-2001, pres. 1999-2000), Chester County Bar Assn. (sec. 1979-82, 86-88, v.p. 1989, pres.-elect 1990, pres. 1991, chair young lawyers sect. 1977, bd. dirs. 1977-92), Chester County Estate Planning Coun. (pres. 1988-89). Banking, Property, real (including real estate development, water), Taxation, general. Office: MacElree Harvey Ltd 740 Springdale Dr Ste 110 Exton PA 19341-2865 Fax: 610 524 9857. E-mail: lteti@macelree.com.

TETTLEBAUM, HARVEY M. lawyer; m. Ann Safier; children: Marianne, Benjamin. AB, Dartmouth Coll., 1964; JD, AM in History, Washington U. Sch. Law, 1968. Asst. dean Washington U. Sch. Law, 1969-77; asst. atty. gne., chief counsel Consumer Protection and Anti-Trust Div., 1970-77; pvt. practice Jefferson City, Mo., 1977-90; former mem., chmn. health law practice group Husch & Eppenberger, LLC, Jefferson City, Mo., 1990—. Contbr. articles to profl. jours. Treas. Mo. Rep. State Com., 1976—; v.p. Moniteau County R-1 Sch. Dist. Bd., 1991-95, pres., 1995-96; mem. Calif. R-1 Sch. Bd., 1990-96, v.p., 1993-95, pres., 1995-96. Mem. Am. Health Lawyers Assn. (bd. dirs. 1993-99, co-chair long-term care and the law program 1993-2001, chair 2001—, chair long-term care and law program 2001—, former chair long term care substantive law com. 1997-2001), Mo. Bar Assn. (health and hosp. law com., chmn. adminstrv. law com., vice chair delivery of legal svc. com., Mo. statewide legal svc. com.),Best Lawyers in Am., 2003-2004, Am. Health Care Assn. (legal subcom. 1994—), Rep. Nat. Lawyers Assn. (bd. dirs. 1988—, 1st v.p. 2002—, pres. 2003). Administrative and regulatory, Health, Appellate. Home: 56295 Little Moniteau Rd California MO 65018-3069 Office: Husch & Eppenberger LLC Monroe House Ste 300 235 E High St PO Box 1251 Jefferson City MO 65102-1251

TETZLAFF, CHARLES ROBERT, lawyer; b. Oct. 15, 1938; s. Donald H. and Harriet (Ranney) T.; m. Joan Seugling, July 1, 1962; children: Julie Lynn Mulrow, Carl Lawrence. BA, U. Vt., 1960; LLB, Boston U., 1963; LLM, NYU, 1964. Bar: Vt. 1964, U.S. Supreme Ct. 1970. Judge advocate USAF, 1965-68; dep. state's atty. Chittenden County, Vt., 1968-70; ptnr. Latham, Eastman, Schweyer and Tetzlaff, 1969-93; U.S. atty. dist. Vt. Office U.S. Atty., Burlington, 1993—; gen. counsel U.S. Sentencing Commn., Washington, 2002—. Trustee Vt. Legal Aid, 1976-78; chair Dist. 4 Environ. Commn., 1979-83, Gov. Sentencing Study Commn., 1985-86; active Vt. Bd. Bar Examiners, 1980-84, State Police Adv. Commn., 1985-86, Gov. Bail Amendment Task Force. Capt. USAF, 1965-68. Mem. ABA, Vt. Bar Assn., Chittenden County Bar Assn. Office: US Sentencing Commn One Columbus Circle NE Washington DC 20002-8002

TETZLAFF, THEODORE R. lawyer; b. Saukville, Wis., Feb. 27, 1944; AB magna cum laude, Princeton U., 1966; LLB, Yale U., 1969. Bar: Ind. 1969, D.C. 1969, Ill. 1974. Legis. asst. to Congressman John Brademas, 1970; exec. dir. Nat. Conf. Police Community Rels., 1970-71; acting dir. U.S. Office Legal Svcs., Office Econ. Opportunity, Washington, 1972-73; counsel, Com. Judiciary U.S. Ho. of Reps., Washington, 1974; v.p., legal and external affairs Cummins Engine Co., 1980-82; gen. coun. Tenneco, Inc., Greenwich, Conn., 1992-99; ptnr. Jenner & Block, Chgo., 1976—80, 1982—2001; mng. ptnr. Chgo. office McGuireWoods LLP, Chgo., 2002—. Bd. dirs. Continental Materials Corp., Chgo. Pres. Chgo. area Found. Legal Svcs., 1983—; commr. Pub. Bldg. Commn. Chgo., 1990—. Reginald Heber Smith fellow, 1969-70. Mem. ABA (chair sect. litigation 1991-92), Ill. State Bar Assn., Ind. State Bar Assn., D.C. Bar. Office: McGuireWoods LLP Suite 4400 77 West Wacker Dr Chicago IL 60601

TEVRIZIAN, DICKRAN M., JR., b. Los Angeles, Aug. 4, 1940; s. Dickran and Rose Tevrizian; m. Geraldine Tevrizian, Aug. 22, 1964; children: Allyson Tracy, Leslie Sara. BS, U. So. Calif., 1962, JD, 1965. Tax acct. Arthur Andersen and Co., Los Angeles, 1965-66; atty., ptnr. Kirtland and Packard, Los Angeles, 1966-72; judge Los Angeles Mcpl. Ct., Los Angeles, 1972-78, State of Calif. Superior Ct., Los Angeles, 1978-82; ptnr. Manatt, Phelps, Rothenberg & Tunney, Los Angeles, 1982-85, Lewis, D'Amato, Brisbois & Bisgaard, Los Angeles, 1985-86; judge U.S. Dist. Ct., Los Angeles, 1986—. Adv. dir. sch. pub. policy U. Calif., L.A. Adv. dir. UCLA Sch. Pub. Policy. Named Trial Judge of the Yr., Calif. Trial Lawyers Assn., 1987, L.A. County Bar Assn., 1994-95; recipient Peter the Great Gold Medal of Honor Russian Acad. Natural Scis., 1998, Ellis Island Medal of Honor award, 1999. Mem. Calif. Trial Lawyers Assn. (trial judge of yr. 1987), L.A. County Bar Assn. (trial judge of yr. 1994-95), Malibu Bar Assn. (fed. ct. trial judge of yr. 1998, Maynard Toll award 2002). Office: US Dist Ct Royal Federal Bldg 255 E Temple St Los Angeles CA 90012-3332

TEWES, R. SCOTT, lawyer; b. Chgo., Mar. 23, 1956; s. Raymond Henry and Vivian Marie Tewes; m. Marcia Anne King, June 5, 1981; children: Benjamin Scott, Matthew Philip, Madeline Anne Marie, Carrie Elizabeth, Aimee Marie. BS, Bob Jones U., 1978, MS, 1980; JD, U. S.C., 1983. Bar: S.C. 1983, D.C. 1985, Ga. 1987, U.S. Supreme Ct. Assoc. Brown & Hagins, Greenville, S.C., 1983-86; law clk. to Hon. Jean Galloway Bissell U.S. Ct. Appeals Fed. Cir., Washington, 1986-87; assoc., ptnr. Kilpatrick Stockton, Atlanta, 1987—2002; with Tewes Law Group, 2002—. Articles editor S.C. Law Rev., 1982-83; contbr. articles to profl. jours. Active Greenville (S.C.) County Alcohol and Drug Abuse Commn., 1985-86; trustee Killian Hill Baptist Ch., Lilburn, Ga., 1994-2000. Mem. S.C. Bar (practice and procedure com., bar ethics adv. com. 1985-86), Am. Intellectual Property Law Assn., Christian Legal Soc., Federalist Soc., Order of Barristers. Avocations: tennis, biking, skiing. Federal civil litigation, Constitutional, Patent. Office: Tewes Law Group LLC Northlake Law Bldg 4921 LaVIsta Rd Tucker GA 30084 Office Fax: 770-724-1939. E-mail: STewes@TewesLaw.com.

TÉZÉ, BERNARD ANDRÉ, lawyer; b. Rouen, France, Apr. 1, 1965; s. André Guy and Madeleine Marie (Duverger) Tézé; m. Ruriko Shibata, Oct. 13, 1990; 1 child, Angélique Maya. MBA, Ecole des HEC, Paris, 1985; M in Pub. Law, U. Paris II, 1985, M in Pvt. Law, 1986; postgrad., U. Paris XI/HEC, 1986. Bar: Paris. Trainee Jeantet & Assocs., Paris, 1986, Cleary Gottlieb, Paris, 1986; tax lawyer Arthur Andersen, Paris, 1988—89; lawyer Clifford Chance, Paris, 1989—91, lawyer, counsel, 1995—2001; lawyer Nakagawa & Takashina, Tokyo, 1991—94; ptnr. White & Case, Paris, 2001—. Pres. Internal Sect. HEC Alumni, 1999. Mergers and acquisitions, Insurance, Corporate, general. Home: 7 Rue Guy de Maupassant 75016 Paris France Office: White & Case 11 Blvd de la Madeleine 75001 Paris France Office Fax: (33-1) 55041516. E-mail: bteze@whitecase.com.

THACKER, JOSEPH PHILLIP, lawyer; b. Toledo, Ohio, Sept. 15, 1953; s. Blaine Thomas and Mary Elizabeth (Martin) T.; m. Pamela Ann Sackett, June 23, 1978; children: John M., Samuel J., Katherine E. BA cum laude, U. Toledo, 1975, JD cum laude, 1978. Bar: Ohio 1978, Fla. 1979, U.S. Dist. Ct. (no. dist.) Ohio 1979, U.S. Dist. Ct. (no. dist.) Tex. 1983, U.S. Ct. Appeals (5th cir.) 1984, U.S. Supreme Ct. 1985, U.S. Ct. Appeals (6th cir.) 1986, U.S. Ct. Appeals (3d cir.) 1997. Asst. prosecutor, trial counsel Lucas County Prosecutor's Office, Toledo, 1978-81; shareholder Cooper & Walinski, Toledo, 1981—. Contbr. author: Taking Evidence Abroad, 1992, Personal Injury Litigation in Ohio, 1984, Bad Faith Litigation, 1994. Soccer coach Sylvania (Ohio) Youth Soccer Assn., 1986-95; baseball coach Sylvania Ohio Recreation, 1986-95. Mem. ABA (tort and ins. practice sect.), U.S. Fed. Bar Assn., Ohio Bar Found., Fla. Bar, Toledo Bar Assn. Roman Catholic. General civil litigation, Insurance, Mergers and acquisitions. Office: Cooper & Walinski 900 Adams St Toledo OH 43624

THACKERAY, JONATHAN E. lawyer; b. Athens, Ohio, July 30, 1936; s. Joseph Eugene and Betty Rutherford (Boright) T.; m. Sandra Ann McMahon; children: Jennifer, Sara, Amy, Jonathan. AB cum laude, Harvard U., 1958, JD, 1961. Bar: Ohio 1961, U.S. Dist. Ct. (no. dist.) Ohio 1961, U.S. Supreme Ct. 1972, U.S. Ct. Appeals (6th cir.) 1973, U.S. Ct. Appeals (9th cir.) 1982, N.Y. 1993. Assoc. Vorys, Sater, Seymour & Pease, Columbus, Ohio, 1961, Baker & Hostetler, Cleve., 1965-72, ptnr., 1973-93; v.p., gen. counsel The Hearst Corp., N.Y.C., 1993—2003; ret., 2003. Served to lt. USNR, 1961-65. Mem. ABA, Ohio Bar Assn., Cleve. Bar Assn., Am. Law Inst. Antitrust, Federal civil litigation, Communications. Office: The Hearst Corp 959 8th Ave New York NY 10019-3795

THALACKER, ARBIE ROBERT, lawyer, director; b. Marquette, Mich., Apr. 17, 1935; s. Arbie Otto and Jeanne (Emmett) T.; m. Rita Annette Skaaren, Sept. 11, 1956 (div. July 1992); children: Marc Emmett, Christopher Paul, Robert Skaaren; m. Deborah B. Garrett, Jan. 10, 1998. AB, Princeton U., 1957; JD, U. Mich., 1960. Bar: N.Y. 1961, U.S. Ct. Appeals (2d cir.) 1962. Assoc. Shearman & Sterling, N.Y.C., 1960-68, ptnr., 1968—. Dir. Detrex Corp., Detroit, 1981—, chmn. bd., 1993-96. Leader Rep. Dist. Com., 1966-68; v.p., trustee Greenwich Village Soc. for Hist. Preservation; trustee Naropa Univ.; bd. dirs. Meredith Monk House Found., Shambhala Internat. Mem. ABA, N.Y. Bar Assn., Assn. Bar City N.Y. (securities regulatory commn. 1975-78), Wine and Food Soc. (bd. dirs. 1976-78, 85-93, 94—), Chevaliers du Tastevin, Commanderie de Bordeaux, Siwanoy Country Club (bd. govs. 1976-79), Derby Club, Links Club, Verbank Hunting and Fishing Club. Private international, Mergers and acquisitions, Securities. Home: 17 Commerce St New York NY 10014-3763 Office: Shearman & Sterling 599 Lexington Ave Fl C2 New York NY 10022-6069

THALER, CRAIG H. lawyer; b. Queens, N.Y., Sept. 13, 1965; s. Michael S. and Karen A. T.; m. Diane P. Heller, Nov. 17, 1991; children: Justin, Eli. BA cum laude, Brandeis U., 1987; JD, Hofstra U., 1990. Bar: N.J. 1990, U.S. Dist. Ct. N.J. 1990, N.Y. 1991. Assoc. Milbank, Tweed, Hadley & McCloy, N.Y.C., 1990-95, Luskin, Stern & Eisler, LLP, N.Y.C., 1995-96; v.p., sr. counsel and asst. sec. IBJ Whitehall Bank & Trust Co., N.Y.C., 1996-99, dir. legal svcs., 1999—2002; sr. v.p., chief legal officer, sec. Whitehall Bus. Credit Corp. successor to IBJ Whitehall Bus. Credit Corp., N.Y.C., 1999—. Avocations: running, hiking, biking. Banking, Corporate, general, Finance. Office: Whitehall Bus Credit Corp One State St New York NY 10004 E-mail: cthaler@whitehallbcc.com.

THARP, CHRISTINE M. lawyer; 1 child, Caseyann. JD, St. Mary's Sch. Law, 1980. Bar: Tex. 1980; cert. in family law Tex. Bd. Legal Specialization, 1988. Law clk. Mex. Am. Legal Def. and Edn. Fund, San Antonio, 1979; staff atty. Law Offices Charles Campion, San Antonio, 1979-86; of counsel Nicholas and Barrera, Inc., San Antonio, 1986-89; pvt. practice San Antonio, 1989—. Bd. dirs. pro bono law project mem. Bexar County Legal Aid, 1988-89, adv. bd., 1988; vol. instr. for tng. Child Advocates fo San Antonio, 1990-91; mem. Bexar County Child Support Com., 1985; co-chair Bachelor Auction, March of Dimes. Named to Outstanding Young Women of Am., 1980; recipient Cert. of Appreciation, San Antonio Foster Parents. Fellow Coll. of State Bar Tex.; mem. ABA (family law sect., entertainment law sect.), ATLA (Nat. Coll. Advocacy), Tex. Acad. Family Specialists, Bexar County Women's Bar Assn. (charter, bd. dirs. 1986-90, 92, bd. dirs. Women's Bar Found. 1989-90, 92, pub. rels. chair 1991-92), Am. Profl. Soc. on Abuse of Children, Nat. Assn. of Counsel for Children, San Antonio Family Lawyers Bar Assn. (bd. dirs. 1994—, treas. 1995-96, v.p. 1997-98, pres. 1998-99), San Antonio Bar Assn. (family law sect., fee dispute com. 1983—, chair 1987-88, 88-89), Tex. Trial Lawyers Assn. (author/lectr.), State Bar of Tex. (family law sect., lectr., mem. Coll. of the bar 1989—), Christian Legal Soc., Delta Theta Phi. Baptist. Family and matrimonial. Office: 6217 Broadway St San Antonio TX 78209-4562

THATCHER, ANNA MARIE, lawyer, law educator; b. Shenandoah, Iowa, Apr. 24, 1948; d. Gerald Eugene and Darlene Marie Teachout; m. Graham Thatcher, Apr. 4, 1970. BA, Dakota Wesleyan U., 1970; MA, U. S.D., 1972; JD, Hamline U., 1994. Bar: Minn. Theater dir., Rapid City, S.D., 1976-87; owner Anakota Arts, Rapid City, 1982-87; arts and non-profit cons. St. Paul, 1987-94; mng. producer Periaktos Prodns., Rapid City, 1994—. Co-columnist Arts and the Law, Minn. Lawyer, 1997-98 Mem. ABA, Minn. Bar Assn. Avocations: cooking, travel. Non-profit and tax-exempt organizations. Office: Periaktos Prodns 3213 W Main St # 272 Rapid City SD 57702-2314 E-mail: productions@periaktos.com.

THAU, WILLIAM ALBERT, JR., lawyer; b. St. Louis, June 22, 1940; s. William Albert and Irene Elizabeth (Mundy) T.; m. Jane Hancock, Sept. 7, 1961; children: William Albert, Caroline Jane, Jennifer Elizabeth. BS in Indsl. Mgmt., Ga. Inst. Tech., 1962; JD, U. Tex., 1965. Bar: Tex. 1965. Ptnr., head of real estate sect. Jenkens & Gilchrist, Dallas, 1965—. Chmn. real estate developer/builder symposium S.W. Legal Found, 1975-79; bd. dirs. Southwestern Film Archives, So. Meth. U.; lectr. Practicing Law Inst. Author: Negotiating the Purchase and Sale of Real Estate, 1975; editor Tex. State Bar Assn. Newsletter on Real Estate, Probate and Trust Law, 1978-81; contbr. articles to Real Estate Rev., 1983—. Bd. dirs. St. Philips Sch., Dallas, 1988, So. Meth. U.; trustee Dallas Can. Acad., 1987-88. Mem. ABA, Tex. State Bar Assn. (chmn. real estate, probate, trust law sect.), Am. Coll. Real Estate Lawyers. Republican. Commercial, contracts (including sales of goods; commercial financing), Construction, Property, real (including real estate development, water). Office: 140 Tanglewood Rd Saint Simons Island GA 31522

THAXTON, MARVIN DELL, lawyer; b. Electra, Tex., June 1, 1925; s. Montgomery Dell and Ida (Scheurer) T.; m. Carolyn Moore Alexander, Aug. 30, 1949; children: Rebecca Thaxton Henderson, Gail Thaxton Fogleman, Marvin D. Jr. JD, U. Ark., 1949. Bar: Ark. 1949, U.S. Dist. Ct. (ea. dist.) Ark. 1952, U.S. Dist. Ct. (we. dist.) Ark. 1978, U.S. Dist. Ct. (we. dist.) Okla., U.S. Supreme Ct. 1987. Prin. Thaxton Furniture Co., Newport, Ark., 1949-50; ptnr. Thaxton, Hout & Howard, Attys., Newport, 1950-97; retired, 1997. Spl. assoc. justice Ark. Supreme Ct., 1978, 84; examiner Ark. State Bd. Law Examiners, 1968-73, chmn. 1973. Pres. Newport Sch. Dist. Bd. Edn., 1964; past pres. Ea. Ark. Young Men's Clubs; adult leader Newport area Boy Scouts Am., 1949-94; bd. dirs. Newport Hosp. and Clinic Inc., 2000-03. Officer U.S. Mcht. Marine, 1945-46, PTO. Fellow Ark. Bar Found.; mem. ABA, Ark. Bar Assn. (honor cert. 1973), Newport C. of C. (pres. 1956, bd. dirs. 1997-2003), Newport Rotary Club (past pres., Paul Harris fellow 1990), Sigma Chi. Democrat. Methodist. Avocations: hunting, fishing, boating. Corporate, general, General practice, Property, real (including real estate development, water). Home: 12 Lakeside Ln Newport AR 72112-3914 E-mail: mdtjd@ipa.net.

THEALL, SUSAN LORNA, lawyer; b. Jennings, La., Mar. 10, 1957; d. Francis Avery and Doris (Landry) T. BA in English, U. So. La., 1980; JD, Loyola U., 1985. Bar: La. 1985. Pvt. practice, Opelousas and Lafayette, La., 1985—. Counsel La. Sch. Bus Operators, Alexandria, 1992-97. Chmn. Lafayette Vol. Lawyers, Lafayette, 1997. Mem. La. Bar Assn. (Pro Bono publico 1996, bd. cert. family law specialist 1995, family law sec. treas. 2001-2003, family courts com. 1999-2003), Lafayette Parish Bar Assn. (bd. dirs. 1996-97, 2001, family law sec. pres., v.p., treas. 1999, 2000, 2001), Am. Inns of Ct. (Acadiana chpt. 1991). Republican. Roman Catholic. Avocation: reading. Family and matrimonial. Office: 1304 Lafayette St Lafayette LA 70501-6842

THEIBERT, RICHARD WILDER, lawyer, educator; b. Akron, Ohio, June 20, 1951; s. Philip Richard and Ann (Conners) T.; m. Willis Anne Burton, July 25, 1981; children: Leslie, Elizabeth, Jillian. BS, Johns Hopkins U., 1974; JD, NYU, 1978. Bar: Md. 1979, Ala. 1991. Assoc. Weinberg & Green, Balt., 1979-80, Niles, Barton & Wilmer, Balt., 1980-85, Prem and Dumler, Balt., 1985-91, Najjar Denaburg, Birmingham, Ala., 1991—. Prof. U. Balt., 1987, Birmingham Sch. Law, 1991-2001. Pres. Birmingham Housing Devel. Corp., 1992-2000. Mem. ABA, Ala. Bar Assn., Ala. Real Estate Lawyers Assn. (pres.)., Birmingham Bar Assn. Episcopalian. Avocations: teaching, coaching. Corporate, general, Landlord-tenant, Property, real (including real estate development, water). Home: 1000 31st St S Birmingham AL 35205-1108 Office: Najjar Denaburg 2125 Morris Ave Birmingham AL 35203-4274 E-mail: rtheibert@najjar.com.

THEIS, WILLIAM HAROLD, lawyer, educator; b. Chgo., Nov. 8, 1945; s. Clarence M. and Marion K. (McLendon) T.; m. Maria Luisa Belfiore, Dec. 5, 1973; children: Catherine, Elizabeth. AB, Loyola U., Chgo., 1967; JD, Northwestern U., 1970; LLM, Columbia U., 1977, JSD, 1982. Bar: Ill. 1970, D.C. 1971, Wis. 1998, U.S. Ct. Appeals (7th cir.) 1971, U.S. Supreme Ct. 1974, Wis. 1998. Assoc. prof. La. State U. Law Ctr., 1972-78, Loyola U. Law Sch., Chgo., 1978-81; practiced in Chgo., 1981-99; pvt. practice, 1999-2000; chief appellate atty. Fed. Defender Program, Chgo., 2000—. Part-time lectr. admiralty Northwestern Sch. Law, Chgo. Contbr. articles to legal jours. Lt. USNR, 1970-72. Mem. Am. Law Inst. Federal civil litigation, State civil litigation, Criminal. Office: 55 E Monroe St Ste 2800 Chicago IL 60603

THENELL, HEATHER JO, lawyer; b. Sturgeon Bay, Wis., Jan. 18, 1969; d. Roger H. and Faye A. Isaacson; m. Matthew J. Thenell, Jan. 19, 1996. BA cum laude, Carroll Coll., Waukesha, Wis., 1990; JD, U. Wis., Madison, 1993. Bar: Wis. 1993; cert. fin. planner. Atty. Quincey, Becker & Schuessler, Mayville, Wis., 1993-95, Bachman Law Firm, Appleton, Wis., 1995-98; sr. counsel Thrivent Fin., Appleton, 1998—. Sec. AAL Bank and Trust, FSB, Appleton, 1998-2000; dir., officer Midwest Mortgage Corp., Appleton, 1998-00. Mentor Clean Break Juvenile Diversion Program, Appleton, 1997-2002; mem. Outagamie County Estate Planning Coun. Mem. ABA, Outagamie County Bar Assn., Wis. Bar Assn. Administrative and regulatory, Estate planning, Insurance. Home: 2539 W Sunnyview Cir Appleton WI 54914-1147 Office: Thrivent Financial 4321 N Ballard Rd Appleton WI 54919-0001 E-mail: heather.thenell@thrivent.com.

THEROUX, EUGENE, lawyer; b. Medford, Mass., Apr. 29, 1938; s. Albert and Anne (Dittami) T.; m. Phyllis Grissim, Feb. 13, 1963 (div. 1978); children: Christian, Elizabeth, Justin; m. Colleen Marie Pankratz, Feb. 27, 1982; children: Jean-Paul, Alexandra, Sebastien. Student, Harvard U., 1959, 60; BID, Pratt Inst., 1961, LittD, 1982; JD, Georgetown U., 1968. Bar: D.C. 1969, Mass. 1982, Va. 1985. Ptnr. Baker & McKenzie, Washington, 1969—, mem. policy com., 1992-94. Spl. counsel joint econ. com. U.S. Congress, Washington, 1972; adv. prof. Fudan U., Shanghai, People's Republic China, 1986—; adv. bd. Fletcher Sch. Law and Diplomacy, 1987—; trustee Monterey Inst. Internat. Studies. Author: (book) Joint Ventures In USSR, 1989, Business Guide To Moscow, 1990, Business Guide to Mongolia, 1996. Trustee Am. Leprosy Found., Washington, 1987—; v.p. U.S.-China Bus. Coun., Washington, 1973-75, dir., vice chair of bd., 1991-95. 1st lt. inf., U.S. Army, 1962-64, MAC/V So. Vietnam, 1968. Mem. ABA (chair Soviet law com. 1989-91), Metro. Club. Roman Catholic. Avocations: drawing, painting, running. Private international. Home: Short Hill Mountain Farm Lovettsville VA 20180 Office: Baker & McKenzie 815 Connecticut Ave NW Washington DC 20006-4004 Home: Ox Pasture Sandwich MA 02563 E-mail: gene.theroux@bakernet.com.

THEROUX, WILLIAM GERARD, lawyer; b. Morristown, N.J., May 6, 1959; s. William E. and Mary T. (Conroy) T. BA magna cum laude, Montclair State Coll., 1981; JD cum laude, Seton Hall Law Sch., 1984. Bar: N.J. 1984, U.S. Dist. Ct. (N.J.) 1984; cert. civil trial atty. Corp. atty. Hannoch Weisman, Roseland, N.J., 1984-86; litigation atty. Francis & Berry, Morristown, 1986—96, Jackson & Buckley, PC, 1996—98, Buckley & Theroux, LLC, 1998—. Mem. N.J. State Bar Assn. Roman Catholic. Avocation: reading. Professional liability, Personal injury (including property damage), Insurance. Office: Buckley & Theroux LLC 932 State Rd Princeton NJ 08540

THEUT, C. PETER, lawyer; b. Center Line, Mich., July 24, 1938; s. Clarence William and Anna Marie (Martens) T.; m. Judith Fern Trombley, Aug. 4, 1962; children: Elizabeth Anne, Kristin Claire, Peter Christopher, Sarah Nicole. BA, U. Mich., 1960, LLB, 1963. Bar: Calif. 1964, Mich. 1964, U.S. Dist. Ct. (no. dist.) Ohio 1968, U.S. Dist. Ct. (ea. dist.) Mich. 1968. Assoc. Overton, Lyman & Prince, L.A., 1963-67; ptnr. Foster, Meadows and Ballard, Detroit, 1968-72, Theut & Schellig, Mt. Clemens, Mich., 1972-80, Hill, Lewis, Mt. Clemens, 1980-88, Butzel, Long, Detroit, 1988—. Stockbroker; chmn. Butzel Long Global Trade Group. Mem. ABA (internat. law sect., TIPS admiralty com.), Mich. State Bar Assn., Detroit Bar Assn., Macomb County Bar Assn., Calif. Bar Assn., Maritime Law Assn. (past chmn. recreational boating com.), Nat. Marine Bankers Assn. (gen. counsel), Mich. Boating Industry Assn. (gen. counsel) Lex Mundi, North Star Sail Club. Republican. Admiralty, Commercial, contracts (including sales of goods; commercial financing), Private international. Home: 38554 Hidden Ln Clinton Township MI 48036-1826 E-mail: theut@butzel.com.

THIBEAULT, GEORGE WALTER, lawyer; b. Cambridge, Mass., Sept. 21, 1941; s. George Walter and Josephine (Maraggia) T.; m. Antoinette Miller, June 30, 1963; children: Robin M., Holly Ann. BS, Northeastern U., 1964; MBA, Boston Coll., 1966, JD, 1969. Bar: Mass. 1969. Assoc. Gaston & Snow, Boston, 1969-73; ptnr. Testa, Hurwitz & Thibeault, Boston, 1973—. Mem. ABA, Mass. Bar Assn., Am. Arbitration Assn. Corporate, general, Private international, Securities. Home: 181 Caterina Hts Concord MA 01742-4773 Office: Testa Hurwitz & Thibeault High St Tower 125 High St 22d Fl Boston MA 02110-2704 E-mail: thibeault@tht.com.

THIBODEAU, THOMAS RAYMOND, lawyer; b. St.Paul, Feb. 5, 1942; m. Mollie Nan Mylor, Sept. 24, 1966; 1 child, Matthew Raymond. BA in Polit. Sci. cum laude, U. St. Thomas, St. Paul, 1964; JD, U. Minn., 1967. Bar: Minn. 1967, U.S. Dist. Ct. Minn. 1967, U.S. Ct. Appeals (8th cir.) 1970, U.S. Supreme Ct. 1982, Wis. 1983, U.S. Dist. Ct. Wis. 1983, N.D. 2000, U.S. Dist. Ct. N.D., 2000; solicitor Supreme Ct. Eng. and Wales, 1996; cert. civil trial specialist Nat. Bd. Trial Advocacy. Ptnr. Johnson, Killen & Thibodeau, Duluth, Minn., 1967-2000, Thibodeau, Johnson & Feriancek PLLP, Duluth, 2000—. Pres. Legal Aid Svc. N.E. Minn., Inc., 1969-74; mem. civil justice reform act adv. com. U.S. Dist. Ct. Minn., revision Civil Jury Instruction Guide IV, 1997—, Minn. jud. selection commn. 6th Dist., 2001—; mem. State of Minn. Jud. Selection Commn., 1999—. Chmn. Duluth City Charter Commn., 1976-78; vol. atty. St. Louis County Heritage and Arts Ctr., Duluth, 1980-87; pres. bd. trustees Marshall Sch., 1990-92. Recipient Disting. Alumni award, U. St. Thomas, 1985. Fellow Internat. Soc. Barristers, Am. Coll. Trial Lawyers; mem. Am. Bd. Trial Advs. (advocate), Minn. Bar Assn. (chmn. specialization com. 1974-78, co-chmn. revision Civil Injury Instrn. Guide III com. 1982-85, 96-99), Minn. Def. Lawyers Assn. (pres. 1988-89), Acad. Cert. Trial Lawyers of Minn. (pres. elect 1993, pres. 1994-95), Internat. Assn. Def. Counsel, Assn. Def. Trial Attys. Avocations: hunting, skiing, scuba diving and other water sports, reading. Federal civil litigation, State civil litigation, Personal injury (including property damage). Office: Thibodeau Johnson & Feriancek PLLP 800 Lonsdale 302 W Superior St Duluth MN 55802-1802

THIEL, ALBERT NICHOLAS, JR., lawyer; b. Trenton, N.J., Dec. 25, 1948; s. Albert Nicholas and Mildred Pearl (Goodrich) T.; m. Joyce Ann Hardiman, Jan. 28, 1978; children: Mary, Nicholas, Joseph, Alison. BS in Philosophy, St. Mary's Sem., 1970; JD, U. N.Mex., 1976, MBA, 1983. Bar: N.Mex. 1976, U.S. Supreme Ct. 1982. Divsn. head Legal Dept. City Albuquerque, 1977-83; pvt. practice Albuquerque, 1983-88, 90-97; ptnr. Bryan, Flynn-O'Brien & Thiel, Albuquerque, 1988-90, Robinson, Di Lando & Whitaker, Albuquerque, 1998-99, Will Ferguson and Assocs., 1999—. Insurance, Labor (including EEOC, Fair Labor Standards Act, labor-management relations, NLRB, OSHA), Personal injury (including property damage). Office: 1720 Louisiana Blvd NE Ste 100 Albuquerque NM 87110

THIELE, HERBERT WILLIAM ALBERT, lawyer; b. Gananoque, Ont., Can., Apr. 14, 1953; s. Herbert and Bertha (Shields) T.; m. Kathi M. Brown, May 29, 1982; children: Herbert R. R., Eric W. R., Brian A. J., Kelly M. M., Kevin M. H., Karl S. H. BA, U. Notre Dame, 1975; JD, U. Fla., 1978. Bar: Fla. 1978, U.S. Dist. Ct. (so. dist. trial and gen. bars) Fla. 1979, U.S. Ct. Appeals (5th and 11th cirs.) 1981, U.S. Supreme Ct. 1982, U.S. Tax Ct. 1983, U.S. Dist. Ct. (no. dist.) Fla. 1991. Assoc. Law Offices of Roger G. Saberson, Delray Beach, Fla., 1979-81; asst. city atty. City of Delray Beach, 1979-81, city atty., 1981-90; county atty. Leon County, Tallahassee, Fla., 1990—. Bd. dirs. Delray Beach Mcpl. Employees Credit Union, 1985-88; pres. Notre Dame Club of Tallahassee, 2002--. Recipient award of recognition Stetson U. Law Rev., 1989, Ralph A. Marsicano award for Local Govt. Law, Fla. Bar, 1991. Mem. ABA (vice-chmn. urban, state and local govt. com. of gen. practice sect. 1991-95, mem. labor and employment law, litigation, govt. lawyers, gen. practice and trial practice com. sects.), ATLA, FBA, Fla. Bar (exec. coun. local govt. law sect. 1986-87, sec./treas. 1987-88, chmn.-elect 1988-89, chmn., 1989-90, immediate past chmn. 1990-91, ex-officio officer 1991—, trial, real property, gen. practice and labor and employment law sects., bar com. on individual rights and responsibilities 1986-90, long-range planning com. 1991-93, continuing legal edn. com. 1998-99, Paul S. Buchman award local govt. law sect. 2000), Tallahassee Bar Assn., Fla. Mcpl. Attys. Assn. (steering com. 1985-86, bd. dirs. 1980-89, sec./treas. 1989-90, Fla. Mcpl. Atty. of Yr. 1987), Fla. Assn. Police Attys., Nat. Inst. Mcpl. Law Officers (pers. and labor law com., trial practices and litigation com., legal advocacy com., 11th cir. rep. 1989-90), Am. Soc. for Pub. Adminstrn., Fla. Pub. Employer Labor Rels. Assn., Fla. Assn. County Attys. (chmn. coun. county attys. 1990-91, bd. dirs. 1991-93, treas. 1993, sec. 1993-94, v.p. 1994-95, pres. 1995-96, chmn. 1996-97, bd. dirs. 1997—, Recognition award 1994, Ethics in Govt. award 1998, 2001), Notre Dame Club (pres. 2002-). Republican. Avocations: music, sports, philately. Home: 318 Milestone Dr Tallahassee FL 32312-3574 Office: Office of Leon County Atty Leon County Courthouse Tallahassee FL 32301

THIELE, HOWARD NELLIS, JR., lawyer; b. Dayton, Ohio, June 22, 1930; s. Howard Nellis and Irma Laura (Scheibe) T.; m. Alma Kuhn, Oct. 14, 1995; children: Leslie, Howard III, Craig. AB, Miami U., Oxford, Ohio, 1952; JD with distinction, U. Mich., 1955. Bar: Ohio 1955. Assoc., ptnr. Smith & Schnacke, LPA, Dayton, Ohio, 1957-89; ptnr. Thompson, Hine & Flory, Dayton, 1989-95; ret., 1995. Pres. Dayton Art Inst., 1981-85; bd. dirs. Dayton Area chpt. ARC, 1983—, 1st vice chmn., 1990-91, chmn., 1992-94. Capt. USAF, 1955-57. Mem.: Engrs. Club, Phi Beta Kappa, Order of the Coif. Republican. Lutheran. Corporate, general, Property, real (including real estate development, water).

THIEROLF, RICHARD BURTON, JR., lawyer; b. Medford, Oreg., Oct. 27, 1948; s. Richard Burton Sr. and Helen Dorothy (Rivolta) T. BA, Columbia U., N.Y.C., 1970; JD, U. Oreg., 1976. Bar: Oreg. 1976, U.S. Dist. Ct. Oreg. 1976, U.S. Ct. Appeals (9th cir.) 1977, U.S. Dist. Ct. (no. dist.) Calif. 1980, U.S. Supreme Ct. 1993, U.S. Ct. Fed. Claims 1993. Staff atty. Orgn. of the Forgotten Am., Inc., Klamath Falls, Oreg., 1976-77, exec. dir., 1977-79; ptnr. Jacobson, Thierolf & Dickey, P.C., Medford, 1980—. Mem. City of Medford Planning Commn., 1990-92; mem. Jackson County Planning Commn., 2001—; mem. Medford Sch. Dist. 549-C Budget Com., 1991-92, chmn., 1991. Mem. ABA, Fed. Bar Assn., Oreg. State Bar (local profl. responsibility com. 1987-89, mem. fed. practice and procedure com. 1994-97, sec. 1995-97, jud. adminstrn. com. 1998-2001, low income legal svcs. com. 1990-93, ho. of dels. 1999-2000), Jackson County Bar Assn. (sec. 1988), So. Oreg. Estate Planning Coun. (bd. dirs.2001—). Episcopalian. Avocation: violin. Federal civil litigation, General practice, Native American. Home: 234 Ridge Rd Ashland OR 97520-2829 Office: Jacobson Thierolf & Dickey PC Two N Oakdale Ave Medford OR 97501 E-mail: dthierolf@jacobsonthierolfdickey.com.

THIES, DAVID CHARLES, lawyer; b. Urbana, Ill., Dec. 6, 1955; s. Richard L. and Marilyn (Webber) T.; m. Johanna L. Bokenkamp, May 21, 1977; children: Stephanie, Daniel, Michael, Adam. Degre' Semestriel, Cours de Civilisation Francaises Sorbonne, Paris, 1975; AB in econs. with distinction, U. Ill., 1977, JD, 1980. Bar: Ill. 1980, U.S. Dist. Ct. (cen. dist.) Ill. 1982. Assoc. Webber & Thies P.C., Urbana, 1980-84, shareholder, 1984—. V.p. Champaign-Urbana Symphony, 1985-87, pres., 1987-90; chmn. Greater Urbana Champaign Econ. Devel. Corp., 1986-87; bd. dirs. Champaign County United Way, 1986-89; elected to Champaign County Bd., 1988-92. Mem. ABA, Champaign County Bar Assn., Ill. State Bar Assn. (sect. coun. young lawyers div., sec. 1987-88, chair 1989-90), Urbana C. of C. (chmn. 1985-86), Rotary (sec. 1986-88, pres. 1991-92). Democrat. Avocations: music, sports. General civil litigation, Commercial, contracts (including sales of goods; commercial financing), General practice. Home: 807 S Mckinley Ave Champaign IL 61821-4531 Office: Webber & Thies PC PO Box 189 Urbana IL 61803-0189

THOGERSEN, KAI, lawyer; b. Oslo; married. Candidate in Jurisprudence, U. Oslo, 1987. Bar: Norway. Legal adviser Oslo Tax Office, 1987-88; assoc. judge Skien (Norway) and Porsgrunn City Ct., 1988-89; assoc. Thommessen Krefting Greve Lund, Oslo, 1989-96, ptnr., 1996—. Mem. Norwegian Bar Assn. Corporate, general, Mergers and acquisitions, IT and Telecomms. Office: Thommessen Krefting Greve Lund AS PO Box 1484 Vlka N-0116 Oslo Norway E-mail: kai.thogersen@tkgl.no.

THOMAJAN, ROBERT, lawyer, management consultant; b. N.Y.C., May 4, 1941; s. Leon and Fay T. BS, NYU, 1962; JD, St. John's U., 1965. Bar: N.Y. 1965, Tex. 1987, U.S. Ct. Internat. Trade 1975, U.S. Supreme Ct. 1975, U.S. Ct. Appeals (9th cir.) 1976, U.S. Dist. Ct. (we. dist.) Tex. 1979. Atty. Nixon, Mudge, Rose, Guthrie, Alexander & Mitchell, N.Y.C., 1965—68; ptnr. Milgrim, Thomajan & Lee, N.Y.C., 1968-90; pres. Eterna Investments, Austin, Tex., 1995—. Arbitrator Civil Ct., N.Y., 1981-86; mem. adv. bd. Ronald McDonald House, 1988-90; bd. dirs. Big Bros./Big Sisters, 1988-90; mem. World Econ. Forum, 1990-93. Mem. Am. Soc. Internat. Law, Internat. Law Assn.

THOMAS, ALLEN LLOYD, lawyer, private investor; b. Orange, NJ, Sept. 15, 1939; s. Richard Lloyd and Dorothy (Carr) Thomas; m. Virginia Dehnert, June 24, 1961 (div. 1974); children: Sarah Ann, Anne Marjorie; m. Barbara Singer, Mar. 12, 1978 (div. 2001); 1 child, Allen Lloyd. BA, Wesleyan U., 1961; LLB, Yale U., 1964. Bar: N.Y. 1965, U.S. Ct. Appeals (D.C. cir.) 1981; solicitor, Eng. and Wales, 1996. Ptnr. Paul Weiss Rifkind Wharton & Garrison, N.Y.C., 1973—92; resident ptnr. Hong Kong, 1983-87; dir., gen. counsel Gerard Atkins & Co. Ltd., 1992-94; gen. counsel Gen. Atlantic Group Ltd, 1992-94. Bd. dirs. Penna Cons PLC, Eidos PLC, Moves Ltd. Chmn. Urban Bus. Assis. Corp., N.Y.C., 1971-82; chmn. Hong Kong Ballet, 1985-87; co-chmn. Internat. Com., N.Y.C. Ballet, 1986-91; pres. Internat. Salzburg Assn. Am., 1987-92; dir., mem. exec. com., gen. counsel Child Care Action Campaign, 1990-92. Fellow Am. Coll. Investment Counsel, Hartford, Conn. Mem. River Club (NY) Boodle's, Met. Club of Washington, Hong Kong Club, Hong Kong Jockey Club, Lenox Club, Buck's Club. Corporate, general, Finance, Private international. Home: 3 Chester St London SW1X 7BB England E-mail: allenlloydthomas@hotmail.com.

THOMAS, ANN VAN WYNEN, law educator; b. The Netherlands, May 27, 1919; came to U.S., 1921, naturalized, 1926; d. Cornelius and Cora Jacoba (Daansen) Van Wynen; m. A.J. Thomas Jr., Sept. 10, 1948. AB with distinction, U. Rochester, 1940; JD, U. Tex., 1943; post doctoral degree, So. Meth. U., 1952. U.S. fgn. svc. officer, Johannesburg, South Africa, London, The Hague, The Netherlands, 1943-47; rsch. atty. Southwestern Legal Found., Sch. Law So. Meth. U., Dallas, 1952-67; asst. prof. polit. sci. So. Meth. U. Sch. Law, Dallas, 1968-73, assoc. prof., 1973-76, prof., 1976-85, prof. emeritus, 1985—. Author: Communism versus International Law, 1953, (with A.J. Thomas Jr.) International Treaties, 1950, Non-Intervention—The Law and its Import in the Americas, 1956, OAS: The Organization of American States, 1962, International Legal Aspects of Civil War in Spain, 1936-1939, 1967, Legal Limitations on Chemical and Biological Weapons, 1970, The Concept of Aggression, 1972, Presidential War Making Power: Constitutional and International Law Aspects, 1981, An International Rule of Law—Problems and Prospects, 1974. Chmn. time capsule com. Grayson County Commn. on Tex. Sesquicentennial, 1986-88; co-chmn. Grayson County Commn. on Bicentennial U.S. Constn., 1988-93; co-chmn. com. Grayson County Sesquicentennial, 1994-97; co-chmn. Grayson County Commn. on the Millenium, 1997—. Recipient Am. medal Nat. DAR Soc., 1992. Mem. Tex. Bar Assn., Am. Soc. Internat. Law, Grayson County Bar Assn. Home: Spaniel Hall 374 Coffee Cir Pottsboro TX 75076-3164

THOMAS, ARCHIBALD JOHNS, III, lawyer; b. Jacksonville, Fla., Apr. 27, 1952; s. Archibald Johns and Jean (Snodgrass) T.; m. Martha Ann Marconi, Sept. 1, 1973. BA, U. So. Fla., 1973; JD, Stetson U., 1977. Bar: Fla. 1977, U.S. Dist. Ct. (mid. dist.) Fla. 1977, U.S. Ct. Appeals (11th cir.) 1981, U.S. Supreme Ct. 1981, U.S. Claims Ct. 1990; cert. labor and employment law, Fla. Law clk. to U.S. magistrate U.S. Dist. Ct., Tampa, Fla., 1977-78; 1st asst. fed. pub. defender U.S. dist. Ct., Jacksonville, 1978-84; sr. ptnr. Thomas & Skinner, P.A., Jacksonville, 1984-89; pvt. practice Jacksonville, 1990—. Mem. labor and employment law cert. com. Fla. Bar, 2002—. Mem.: NACDL, ATLA (employment rights sect.), Jacksonville Bar Assn., Fla. Nat. Employment Lawyers Assn. (pres. 2002), Nat. Employment Lawyers Assn. (co-chmn. Fla. chpt. 1992), Fed. Bar Assn., Fla. Bar Assn. (co-chmn. individual rights com. 2001). Democrat. Avocation: sailing. Labor (including EEOC, Fair Labor Standards Act, labor-management relations, NLRB, OSHA). Home: 708 Mccollum Cir Neptune Beach FL 32266-3789 Office: Riverplace Tower Ste 1640 Jacksonville FL 32207 E-mail: archibald@job-rights.com.

THOMAS, CHARLAN JOHNSON, mediator; b. Lexington, Ky., July 24, 1953; d. Joe Oliver and Mary Frances (Butler) Johnson; m. Preston Wayne Wilson, Oct. 4, 1970 (div. May 29, 1980); children: Dontai Wilson, Israel Wilson; m. Lamar Gene Thomas. BBA, Marygrove Coll., 1984; BA, U. Detroit, 1985; post grad., Ga. State U. Coll. Law, 1986—87. Cert.: Resolutions Resources Corp. (mediator and arbitrator) 2001, R.S. Thomas Tng. Assn. (property and casualty ins. sub-agt.) 2001. Mental health assoc. Ea. State Hosp., Lexington, 1969—76; asst. to dir., steward, negotiator child sexual assault unit Children's Aid Soc., Detroit, 1978—80; Medicaid screening clk. Detroit Pub. Health Dept. N.E. Clinic, 1986; legal rschr. Ga. State U. Coll. Law, CLE, Atlanta, 1987; dep. registrar Fulton County Elections Voter Registration, Atlanta, 1988; bookkeeper, staff acct. Martin Luther King Jr. Ctr., Atlanta, 1988—92; pres. God & I, Inc., East Point, Ga., 1992—. Facilitator summer workshop on nonviolence King Ctr., Atlanta, 1989—92; bookkeeper Atlanta Tribute to Nelson Mandela, Atlanta, 1990—91. Cons., vol. 1996 Olympics and Paralympics, Atlanta, 1996; active Tap Into Peace Carter Presdl. Ctr., Atlanta, 1994—95; active HUD Cmty. Policing Acad., 1996—99; vol. Dem. Nat. Conv., 1988, Jessie Jackson Presdl. Campaign, 1988. Named to Lexington Honor Program, U. Ky., 1978; recipient Iota Gamma Alpha award, Marygrove Coll., 1984. Mem.: Ga. Office Dispute Resolution, Assn. for Conflict Resolution. Democrat. Jewish. Avocations: travel, geo-politics, music. Home and Office: God & I Inc PO Box 90986 Atlanta GA 30364 Fax: 404-761-6997. E-mail: godaiinc@bellsouth.net.

THOMAS, CLARENCE, United States supreme court justice; b. Savannah, Ga., June 23, 1948; BA, Holy Cross Coll., 1971; JD, Yale U., 1974. Bar: Mo. Asst. atty. gen. State of Mo., Jefferson City, 1974—77; atty. Monsanto Co., St. Louis, 1977—79; legis. asst. to Sen. John C. Danforth, Washington, 1979—81; asst. sec. for civil rights Dept. Edn., Washington, 1981—82; chmn. U.S. EEOC, Washington, 1982—90; judge U.S. Ct. Appeals, Washington, 1990—91; assoc. justice U.S. Supreme Ct., Washington, 1991—. Office: US Supreme Court Supreme Ct Bldg 1 First St NE Washington DC 20543-0001

THOMAS, ELLA COOPER, lawyer; b. Ft. Totten, N.Y. d. Avery John and Ona Caroline (Gibson) C.; m. Robert Edward Lee Thomas, Nov. 22, 1938 (dec. Jan. 1985); 1 child, Robert Edward Lee Jr. Student, Vassar Coll., 1932-34, U. Hawaii, 1934-35, George Washington U., 1935-36, JD, 1940. Bar: U.S. Dist. Ct. D.C. 1942, U.S. Ct. Appeals (D.C. cir.) 1943, U.S. Supreme Ct. 1947, U.S. Tax Ct. 1973. Secret maps custodian U.S. Dist. Engrs., Honolulu, 1941-42; contbg. editor Labor Rels. Reporter, Washington, 1942; assoc. Smith, Ristig & Smith, Washington, 1942-45; law libr. George Washington Law Sch., Washington, 1946-53; reporter of decisions U.S. Tax Ct., Washington, 1953-75. Computer vol. Mote Marine Lab., 1992—98. Author: Law of Libel and Slander, 1949. Mem. Inter-Am. Bar Assn. (coun. mem. 1973-99), D.C. Bar Assn. Avocations: physical fitness, crostics. Home: 1700 3rd Ave W Apt 118 Bradenton FL 34205

THOMAS, FRANKLIN A., III, lawyer; b. Charleston, W.Va., Oct. 17, 1948; BA, U. Va., 1970, MA, 1971. Bar: Va. 1974, U.S. Tax Ct. 1974, U.S. Ct. Appeals (4th cir.) 1974. Atty. Shackelford, Thomas & Gregg, PLC, Orange, Va. Fellow: Am. Bar Found., Am. Coll. Trust and Estate Counsel; mem.: ABA, Order of Coif, Va. State Bar (bd. govs. trust and estates sect. 1983—90, chmn. 1988—89), Va. Bar Assn. (chair sect. wills, trusts and estates 1997—98, pres.-elect 2002). Taxation, general, Commercial, consumer (including collections, credit), Estate planning. Office: Shackelford Thomas and Gregg PO Box 871 149 W Main St Orange VA 22960*

THOMAS, FREDERICK BRADLEY, lawyer; b. Evanston, Ill., Aug. 13, 1949; s. Frederick Bradley and Katherine Kidder (Bingham) T.; m. Elizabeth Maxwell, Oct. 25, 1975; children: Bradley Bingham, Stephens Maxwell, Rosa Macaulay. AB, Dartmouth Coll., 1971; JD, U. Chgo., 1974. Bar: Ill. 1974. Law clk. to hon. judge John C. Godbold U.S. Ct. Appeals (5th cir.), Montgomery, Ala., 1974-75; assoc. Mayer, Brown, Rowe & Maw, Chgo., 1975—80, ptnr., 1981—. Bd. dirs. St. Gregory Episcopal Sch., 1989—; bd. trustees La Rabida Children's Hosp., 1990—; bd. mgrs. YMCA Met. Chgo., 2002--. Mem.: ABA, Chgo. Coun. Lawyers. Republican. Episcopalian. Computer, Corporate, general, Mergers and acquisitions. Office: Mayer Brown Rowe & Maw 190 S La Salle St Ste 3100 Chicago IL 60603-3441

THOMAS, GREGG DARROW, lawyer; b. Jacksonville, Fla., July 31, 1951; BA magna cum laude, Vanderbilt U., 1972; JD with honors, U. Fla., 1976. Bar: Fla. 1976, D.C. 1978. Law clk. U.S. Dist. Ct. (mid. dist.) Fla., 1976-79; mem. Holland & Knight, Tampa, Fla., 1979-; ptnr., 1983-. Exec. editor U. Fla. Law Rev., 1975-76. Bd. dirs. Vol. Lawyer's Resource Ctr., 1990-95; trustee Tampa Mus. of Art, 1993—, vice chmn., 1998, chair, 1999-2001. Mem. ABA (mem. forum com. comm. law 1983—), Am. Judicature Soc., Fla. Bar (co-chair Fla. bar media and comm. com. 1987-88, mem. grievance com. 1988, chmn. 1989-91), Fla. Bar Found. (mem. legal assistance to poor com. 1988-91), Hillsborough Bar Assn., D.C. Bar, Phi Beta Kappa. Constitutional, Intellectual property, Libel. Office: Holland & Knight PO Box 1288 400 N Ashley Dr Ste 2300 Tampa FL 33602-4322 E-mail: gthomas@khlaw.com.

THOMAS, JASON SELIG, lawyer; b. Lansing, Mich., Jan. 23, 1954; s. William Ellsworth and Esta (Berg) T.; m. Edith Madeline Gettes, Oct. 28, 1995; children: Monica, Sophia, Hannah. BMus, Oberlin Coll., 1976; MMus, SUNY, Stony Brook, 1978; JD, U. N.C., 1991; D of Mus. Arts, U. Wis., 1991. Bar: N.C. 1991, U.S. Dist. Ct. (ea. dist.) N.C. 1992, U.S. Dist. Ct. (mid. and we. dists.) N.C. 1995, U.S. Ct. Appeals (4th cir.) 1994. Prin. cellist Ark. Symphony Orch., Little Rock, 1978-81; asst. prof. U. Ky., Lexington, 1981-82; freelance cellist Ludwigshafen, West Germany, 1986-87; assoc. Moore & Van Allen, Raleigh, N.C., 1991-92, Hunton & Williams, Raleigh, 1992—. Contbg. author: Toxic Tort and Hazardous Substance Litigation, 1985. Recipient Outstanding Vol. Atty. award Wake County, N.C., 1995, 97. Mem. ABA, N.C. Bar Assn. (pro bono com. 1998). Administrative and regulatory, General civil litigation, Environmental. Office: Hunton & Williams 1 Hannover Sq Ste 1400 Raleigh NC 27601-2947 E-mail: jsthomas@hunton.com.

THOMAS, JEREMIAH LINDSAY, III, lawyer; b. Wilmington, Del., June 20, 1946; s. Jeremiah Lindsay Jr. and Dorothy Eleanor (Conway) T.; m. Clara Ewing Ruthrauff, Oct. 17, 1981; children: Catherine Ewing, Lindsay Barlow. BA, U. Va., 1968, JD, 1972. Bar: N.Y. 1973. Assoc. Simpson Thacher & Bartlett, N.Y.C., 1972-79, ptnr., 1979—. Mem.: ABA, Met. Golf Assn. (legal counsel 1984—, exec. com. 1992—98, dir. Found. 1992—98), Assn. Bar of City of N.Y., N.Y. State Bar Assn. Corporate, general, Securities, Banking. Office: Simpson Thacher & Bartlett 425 Lexington Ave Fl 15 New York NY 10017-3954 E-mail: jthomas@stblaw.com.

THOMAS, JOHN A. lawyer; b. Tulsa, Aug. 17, 1968; BS, Okla. State U., 1991; MBA, U. Houston, 1993; JD, So. Meth. U., Dallas, 1999. Bar: Tex. 1999, Okla. 2000. Assoc. Nat. Westminster Bank PLC, Houston, 1993—94; asst. treas. Credit Lyonnais, Houston, 1994—96; assoc. Vinson & Elkins LLP, Houston, 1999—. Mem.: Houston Bar Assn., Houston Young Lawyers Assn., Tex. Bar Assn., Okla. Bar Assn. Finance, Corporate, general, Mergers and acquisitions. Office: Vinson & Elkins LLP 2300 First City Twr 1001 Fannin St Houston TX 77002

THOMAS, JOHN CHARLES, lawyer, former state supreme court justice; b. Norfolk, Va., Sept. 18, 1950; s. John and Floretta V. (Sears) T.; m. Pearl Walden, Oct. 9, 1982; children: John Charles Jr., Ruby Virginia, Lewis LeGrant. BA in Am. Govt. with distinction, U. Va., 1972, JD, 1975. Bar: Va. 1975, U.S. Dist. Ct. (ea. and we. dists.) 1976, U.S. Ct. Appeals (4th cir.) 1976, U.S. Supreme Ct. 1979, U.S. Ct. Appeals (D.C. cir.) 1980, U.S. Ct. Appeals (10th cir.) 1991, U.S. Ct. Appeals (11th cir.) 1992. Assoc. Hunton & Williams, Richmond, Va., 1975-82, ptnr., 1982-83, 89—; justice Supreme Ct. of Va., Richmond, 1983-89. Former mem. adv. con. on appellate rules U.S. Jud. Conf., permanent mem. 4th cir. Hon. dir. U. Va. Law Sch. Found. Master John Marshall Inn of Ct. (exec. com.); fellow Am. Bar Found., Va. Bar Found.; mem. ABA (former co-chair nat. conf. of lawyers and reps. of media, mem. coun. appellate lawyers), Am. Arbitration Assn. (bd. dirs., exec. com.), Am. Acad. Appellate Lawyers, Va. State Bar, Va. Bar Assn., Bar Assn. City of Richmond, Old Dominion Bar Assn., Omega Psi Phi, Sigma Pi Phi. General civil litigation, General practice. Office: Hunton & Williams Riverfront Plz East Tower PO Box 1535 Richmond VA 23218-1535

THOMAS, KEITH RICHARD, lawyer; b. Oswego, N.Y., Dec. 27, 1970; s. Charles Robert and Carole Ann Thomas; m. Treena Renee Mayberry, Mar. 12, 1994; children: Bradley Keith, Brayden Nicole. BS in Polit. Sci., U. Tenn. Chattanooga, 1993; JD, U. Tenn. Knoxville, 1997. Bar: Tenn. 1997, U.S. Dist. Ct. (we. dist.) Tenn. 2000, U.S. Dist. Ct. (ea. and we. dists.) Ark. 2000, U.S. Ct. Appeals (6th cir.) 2000, U.S. Ct. Appeals (8th cir.) 2001. Assoc. Horton, Maddox and Anderson, Chattanooga, 1997—99, Weintraub, Stock and Grisham, Memphis, 1999—2002, Maiden and Bennett, Collierville, Tenn., 2002—. Mem.: Tenn. Bar Assn., Soc. Human Resources Mgmt. Republican. Baptist. Labor (including EEOC, Fair Labor Standards Act, labor-management relations, NLRB, OSHA). Office: Maiden and Bennett 875 W Poplar Ste 2 Collierville TN 38017

THOMAS, LOWELL SHUMWAY, JR., lawyer; b. Phila., Aug. 9, 1931; s. Lowell Shumway and Josephine (McVey) T.; m. Judith Evans, Aug. 27, 1955; children: Megan E., Heather McVey, Lowell S., Taylor G. BA, Dartmouth Coll., 1953; JD, U. Pa., 1960. Bar: Pa. 1961, U.S. Tax Ct. 1961, U.S. Dist. Ct. (ea. dist.) Pa. 1961, U.S. Ct. Appeals (3d cir.) 1961. Assoc. Duane, Morris & Heckscher, Phila., 1960-64, Saul, Ewing LLP, Phila., 1965-68, ptnr., 1968-96, of counsel, 1997—. Bd. dirs. Boardwalk Securities Corp., Peter Lumber Co., Chestnut Hill Acad., Phila., 1978-86; bd. dirs. Southeastern Pa. ARC, 1975-82, chmn., 1983-86, bd. govs., 1989-95; trustee Arcadia U., 1987-2000, emeritus trustee, 2001—, chmn., 1989-903. Author: Taxation of Marriage, Separation and Divorce, 1986. Trustee Barra Found., 1999—. Lt. USN, 1953-57. Fellow Am. Coll. Tax Counsel; mem. ABA, Pa. Bar Assn., Phila. Bar Assn., Phila. Bar Found. (trustee 1980-83), Am. Law Inst., Suunybrook Golf Club. Republican. Episcopalian. Pension, profit-sharing, and employee benefits, Corporate taxation, Personal income taxation. Office: Saul Ewing LLP 3800 Centre Sq W Philadelphia PA 19102 E-mail: LST8012@acadia.net.

THOMAS, MARGOT EVA, lawyer; b. Grass Valley, Calif., Apr. 28, 1943; d. Walter Frederick and Edith Louise (Clark) T.; life ptnr. Rose Maloof; children: Matthew E. Albertson Konda, Nicholas E. Albertson, Elizabeth R. Albertson. AB, Brown U., 1965; JD, Western New Eng. Coll., 1981. Bar: Mass. 1981. Field worker So. Christian Leadership Conf., Lisman, Ala., 1965-66; computer programmer Irving Trust Co., N.Y.C., 1966-67; social worker Phila. Dept. Welfare, 1968-70; field dir. Girl Scouts of Delaware County Pa., Upper Darby, 1971-73; project dir. Pioneer Valley Girl Scouts, Springfield, Mass., 1973-74; pvt. practice lawyer Northampton, Mass., 1981—. Pres. Northampton (Mass.) Girls Soccer Assn., 1985-91; chair Northampton (Mass.) City Dem. Com., 1989-91. Mem. Women's Bar Assn., Mass. Bar Assn., Hampshire County Bar Assn., Mass. Lesbian and Gay Bar Assn. Alternative dispute resolution, Probate (including wills, trusts), Property, real (including real estate development, water). Office: 2 Maple Ave Ste 22 Northampton MA 01060-4422

THOMAS, NORMAN ALLAN, judge; b. Norfolk, Va., Sept. 18, 1956; s. William Edward Jr. and Norma Elizabeth (Taylor) T.; children: Wesley Allan, Karen Paige. BA in Govt. and Econs., U. Va., 1978; JD, Coll. William and Mary, 1981. Bar: Va. 1981, U.S. Dist. Ct. (ea. dist.) Va. 1981, U.S. Ct. Appeals (4th cir.) 1981, U.S. Bankruptcy Ct. (ea. dist.) Va. 1982, U.S. Supreme Ct. 1988. Assoc. Crenshaw, Ware & Johnson, Norfolk, 1981-83; asst. atty. Commonwealth of Va., Norfolk, 1983-85; research asst. Va. Ct. Appeals, Norfolk, 1985-86; asst. atty. City of Norfolk, 1986-89, dep. atty., 1989-92; chief dep. atty. Commonwealth of Va., Norfolk, 1992—2000; judge 4th Jud. Dist. Va., 2001—. Methodist. Office: Norfolk Gen Dist Ct 811 E City Hall Ave Norfolk VA 23510-2711

THOMAS, PATRICIA ANNE, retired law librarian; b. Cleve., Aug. 21, 1927; d. Richard Joseph and Marietta Bernadette (Teevans) T. BA, Case Western Res. U., 1949, JD, 1951. Bar: Ohio, 1951, U.S. Supreme Ct., 1980. Libr. Arter & Hadden, Cleve., 1951-62; asst. libr., libr. IRS, Washington, 1962-78; libr. dir. Adminstrv. Office U.S. Cts., 1978-93; ret., 1993. Mem. Am. Assn. Law Librs., Soc. D.C. (pres. 1967-69), Soc. Benchers (Case Western Res. Law Sch.)

THOMAS, ROBERT MORTON , JR., lawyer; b. Kansas City, Kans., Jan. 1, 1941; s. Robert Morton Sr. and Arlowyne Edith (Arganbright) T.; m. Rebecca Ann Myers, Aug. 21, 1965; children: Brooke J., Austin B. BA, U. Kans., 1962; LLB, Harvard U., 1966. Bar: N.Y., U.S. Dist. Ct. (so. dist.) N.Y., U.S. Ct. Appeals (2nd cir.). Local govt. advisor Republic of Botswana, Gaborone, 1966, dist. officer Serowe, 1967, dist. commr. Maun, 1968; assoc. Sullivan & Cromwell, N.Y.C., 1969-75, ptnr., 1975—, ptnr.-in-charge London, 1979-82, mng. ptnr. gen. practice group N.Y.C., 1986-91. Mem. exec. bd. Manhattan coun. Boy Scouts Am.; trustee U. Kans. Endowment Assn. Mem. ABA, N.Y. State Bar Assn., Assn. of Bar of City of N.Y., Internat. Bar Assn., India House, Buck's Club, Harvard Club, Mill Reef Club, Verbank Hunting and Fishing Club (dir., pres.), Knickerbocker Club, Confrerie des Chevaliers de Tastevin. Republican. Presbyterian. Office: Sullivan & Cromwell 125 Broad St New York NY 10004-2498

THOMAS, ROBERT R. state supreme court justice; b. Rochester, N.Y., Aug. 7, 1952; m. Maggie Thomas; 3 children. BA in govt., U. Notre Dame, 1974; JD, Loyola U., 1981. Cir. ct. judge DuPage County, 1988, acting chief judge, 1989—94; judge Appellate Ct. Second Dist., 1994—2000; Supreme Ct. justice Ill. State Supreme Ct., 2000—. Mem.: DuPage County Bar Assn., Acad. All-Am. Hall of Fame (life NCAA Silver Ann. Award 1999). Office: Bldg A Rm 207A 1776 S Naperville Rd Wheaton IL 60187

THOMAS, ROGER MERIWETHER, lawyer; b. Hartford, Conn., Feb. 28, 1930; s. Frederick Metcalf and Helen Meriwether (Lewis) T.; m. Mary Dorothea Wyman, Dec. 4, 1965; children— Donald Wyman, Helen Dorothea AB, Princeton U., 1952; LL.B., Va. U., 1957; LL.M., Boston U., 1964. Bar: N.Y. 1958, Mass. 1960, U.S. Dist. Ct. (Mass) 1965, U.S. Tax Ct. 1965, U.S. Supreme Ct. 1967. Assoc. Angulo, Cooney, Marsh & Ouchterloney, N.Y.C., 1957-60; assoc., then ptnr. Gaston & Snow, Boston, 1960-91; counsel Condit & Assocs., P.C., Boston, 1992-94. Outline author and lectr. Mass. Continuing Legal Edn., Inc., Boston; past panelist New Eng. Law Inst. Estate Planning Forums, Boston. Trustee Buckingham Browne & Nichols Sch., Cambridge, Mass., 1967-69. Served to 1st lt. U.S. Army, 1952-54, Korea. Mem. Am. Coll. Trust and Estate Counsel, Boston Bar Assn., Mass. Bar Assn. Avocations: reading; sports; old movies. Estate planning, Probate (including wills, trusts), Estate taxation. Home: 40 Byron Rd Weston MA 02493-2229

THOMAS, ROGER WARREN, lawyer; b. South Weymouth, Mass., Sept. 17, 1937; s. Clement Rogers and Beatrice (Merritt) T.; m. Maria Sava Brenner, July 5, 1968; children: Caroline, Andrew, Phillip. BA, U. N.H., 1959; postgrad. (Rotary Internat. fellow), Free U. Berlin, 1960; LLB (Root-Tilden scholar), NYU, 1963, LLM (Ford Found. grantee), 1965; postgrad., U. Chile, Santiago, 1965. Bar: N.Y. 1964. Assoc. Cleary, Gottlieb, Steen and Hamilton, N.Y.C., 1965-66, 69-74, partner, 1974—. Mem. Harvard-Chile Tax Reform Project, 1966-68, head project in Chile, 1968-69; cons. to UN, Santiago, 1969; adj. prof. taxation NYU, 1974-96. Co-author: El Impuesto a la Renta, 1969. Bd. dirs. Spanish Repertory Theatre, Fundacion Chile; chmn. UNH Found. Mem. ABA, Am. Fgn. Lawyers Assn., N.Y. State Bar Assn., N.Am.-Chilean C. of C. (pres. 1984-96), Am. Soc., Coun. of Am., Down Town Assn. N.Y.C., Knickerbocker Club. Finance, Corporate taxation. Home: 1150 5th Ave New York NY 10128-0724 Office: 1 Liberty Plz New York NY 10006-1404

THOMAS, STEPHEN PAUL, lawyer; b. Bloomington, Ill., July 30, 1938; s. Owen Wilson and Mary Katherine (Paulsen) T.; m. Marieanne Sauer, Dec. 7, 1963 (dec. June 1984); 1 child, Catherine Marie; m. Marcia Aldrich Toomey, May 28, 1988; 1 child, Ellen Antonia. BA, U. Ill., 1959; LLB, Harvard U., 1962. Bar: Ill. 1962; cert. naturalist Morton Arboretum, 2001. Vol. Peace Corps, Malawi, Africa, 1963-65; assoc. Sidley, Austin, Brown & Wood, Chgo., 1965-70; ptnr. Sidley & Austin, Chgo., 1970-2000. Lectr. on law Malawi Inst. Pub. Adminstrn., 1963-65. Pres. Hyde Park-Kenwood Cmty. Conf., Chgo., 1988-90; trustee Chgo. Acad. for Arts, 1991—, chmn., 1992-97; bd. dirs. Union League Civic and Arts Found., Chgo., 1999—. Recipient Paul Cornell award Hyde Park Hist. Soc., 1981. Mem. ABA, Chgo. Bar Assn., Chgo. Fedn. of Musicians, Lawyers Club of Chgo., Union League Club Chgo., Chgo. Literary Club. Democrat. Roman Catholic. Avocations: jazz piano playing, naturalist studies. Corporate, general, Private international, Securities. Home: 9756 S Longwood Dr Chicago IL 60643-1610 Office: Sidley Austin Brown & Wood 55 W Monroe St Chicago IL 60603-5001 E-mail: sthomas@sidley.com.

THOMAS, STEVEN ALLEN, lawyer; b. Birmingham, Ala., Mar. 19, 1951; s. Reginald Allen and Billie Ruth (Brewer) T.; m. Rebecca Phillips, Aug. 1972; children: Jennifer Ruth, Matthew Allen. AS, Walker Coll., Jasper, Ala., 1971; BA, U. Ala., Tuscaloosa, 1973; JD, Samford U., Birmingham, Ala., 1976. Bar: Ala. 1977, U.S. Dist. Ct. (no. dist.) Ala. 1986. Law clk. Circuit Ct. Walker Co., Jasper, 1978-83; lawyer Beaird, Thomas, Higgins, Jasper, 1983-91; ptv. practice, Jasper, 1991—. Judge Mcpl. Ct., Carbon Hill, Ala., 1983—, Nauvoo, Ala., 1985-88, Arley, Ala., 1991—, Oakman, Ala., 1997—; prosecutor, Addison, Ala., 2001—; atty. City of Jasper Civil Svc. Bd., 2001—. Legal counsel Ala. Jaycees, Clanton, 1986-88; pres. Ala. Mining Mus., Dora, 1989—; treas. Jasper Band Boosters, 1993-95; advisor Explorers, 1991-98; bd. dirs. Assn. Ala. Fairs, Inc., 1998-2003, 1st v.p. 2000, pres. 2001-02. Named Jaycee of Yr., Jasper Jaycees, 1983-84, Officer of Yr., 1984, 88. Mem. ABA, Ala. Bar Assn., Walker County Bar Assn. (pres. 1990-91), Ala. Mcpl. Judges Assn., Ala. Assn. Mcpl. Attys., East Walker C. of C. (pres. 1992-94), Phi Alpha Delta. Methodist. Avocations: fishing, reading, swimming, boating, spectator sports. Family and matrimonial, Personal injury (including property damage), Probate (including wills, trusts). Home: 1401 9th Ave W Jasper AL 35501-4538 Office: PO Box 1951 Jasper AL 35502-1951 E-mail: stevenjd76@aol.com.

THOMAS, WAYNE LEE, lawyer; b. Sept. 22, 1945; s. Willard McSwain and June Frances T.; m. Patricia H. Thomas, Mar. 16, 1968; children: Brigitte Elisabeth Williams, Kate Adelaide Culpepper. BA, U. Fla., 1967, JD cum laude, 1971. Bar: Fla. 1971, U.S. Supreme Ct. 1975, U.S. Ct. Appeals (5th cir.) 1975, U.S. Ct. Appeals (11th cir.) 1981, U.S. Ct. Claims 1976, U.S. Dist. Ct. (mid. dist.) Fla. 1973, U.S. Dist. Ct. (so. dist. trial bar) Fla. 1975; cert. mediator and arbitrator. Law clk. U.S. Dist. Ct. (mid. dist.) Fla., 1971-73; assoc. Trenam, Simmons, Kemker, Scharf, Barkin, Frye & O'Neill, PA, Tampa, 1973-77, ptnr., 1978-81; founder, pres. McKay & Thomas, PA, Tampa, 1981-89; ptnr. Carlton, Fields, Ward, Emmanuel, Smith & Cutler, PA, 1989-95; pvt. practice Tampa, 1995—. Mem. ABA, Fla. Bar (chmn. sect. gen. practice 1981-83, mem. ethics com., vice chmn. unauthorized practice law com. 1994-98, 2000-, vice chmn. fed. practice com. 1995-96, chmn. 1996-97, mem. bd. bar examiners 1986-91, chmn. 1990-91, chmn. unauthorized practice law com. 13A 1998-2001), Nat. Conf. Bar Examiners (multistate profl. responsibility exam. policy com. 1994—), Hillsborough County Bar Assn. (chmn. grievance com. 1985-86), Order of Coif, Wm. Glenn Terrell Am. Inn of Ct., Fla. Blue Key, Phi Kappa Phi, Omicron Delta Kappa. Democrat. Alternative dispute resolution, Federal civil litigation, State civil litigation. Office: 707 N Franklin St Fl 10 Tampa FL 33602-4430

THOMAS, WILLIAM SCOTT, lawyer; b. Joliet, Ill., Aug. 16, 1949; AB, Stanford U., 1971; JD, U. Calif., Hastings, 1974; LLM in Taxation, Golden Gate U., 1981. Bar: Calif. 1975, U.S. Dist. Ct. (no. dist.) Calif. 1975, U.S. Tax Ct. 1982. Tax editor Internat. Bur. Fiscal Documentation, Amsterdam, Holland, 1974-75; tax atty. Chevron Corp., San Francisco, 1975-77; from assoc. to ptnr. Brobeck, Phleger & Harrison, San Francisco, 1978—2003; ptnr. Morgan Lewis & Bockius, San Francisco, 2003. Bd. dirs. Value Line Inc., N.Y.C. Mem. ABA (taxation sect.), Calif. Bar Assn. (exec. com. taxation sect. 1984-89, chmn. 1987-88). Probate (including wills, trusts), Personal income taxation, State and local taxation. Office: Morgan Lewis & Bockius 1 Market Plz Ste 2700 San Francisco CA 94105 E-mail: wthomas@brobeck.com.

THOMASCH, ROGER PAUL, lawyer; b. N.Y.C., Nov. 7, 1942; s. Gordon J. and Margaret (Molloy) T.; children: Laura Leigh, Paul Butler. BA, Coll. William and Mary, 1964; LLB, Duke U., 1967. Bar: Conn. 1967, Colo. 1974. Assoc. atty. Cummings & Lockwood, Stamford, Conn., 1967-70; trial atty. U.S. Dept. Justice, Washington, 1970-73; ptnr. Roath & Brega, Denver, 1975-87; mng. ptnr. Denver office of Ballard, Spahr, Andrews & Ingersoll LLP, 1987—. Vis. assoc. prof. of law Drake U. Sch. Law, Des Moines, 1973-74; frequent lectr. in field, U.S. and Can.; adj. faculty mem. U. Denver Coll. Law, 1976-80. Recipient Leland Forrest Outstanding Prof. award, Drake U. Sch. Law, 1973. Fellow Am. Coll. of Trial Lawyers, Colo. Bar Found.; mem. ABA, Colo. Bar Assn., Denver Country Club, Univ. Club. Antitrust, Federal civil litigation, State civil litigation. Office: Ballard Spahr Andrews & Ingersoll LLP 1225 17th St Ste 2300 Denver CO 80202-5535 E-mail: Thomasch@BallardSpahr.com.

THOME, DENNIS WESLEY, lawyer; b. Yakima, Wash., Feb. 1, 1939; s. Walter John and Vareta Lucille (Voris) T.; m. Penelope Lee Freeman, Aug. 27, 1961; children: Christopher, Geoffrey. BSBA, U. Denver, 1961, JD, 1967. Bar: Colo. 1967, U.S. Dist. Ct. Colo. 1967, Calif. 1971, U.S. Dist. Ct. (cen. dist.) Calif. 1971, U.S. Supreme Ct. 1971, U.S. Ct. Appeals (9th cir.) 1972. Assoc. Pehr & Newman, Westminster, Colo., 1967-69, Juggert, VaVerka & Wayman, Costa Mesa, Calif., 1975-77; house counsel Wycliffe Bible Translators, Inc., Huntington Beach, Calif., 1969-73; pvt. practice Newport Beach, Calif., 1973-75, Denver, 1977—. Bd. dirs. First Fruit, Inc., Newport Beach, MOPS Internat., Inc., Denver, Reach Internat., Inc., Denver; mem. Centennial Estate Planning Coun., 1977—. Treas. Gibson for Mayor Com., Denver, 1967; bd. dirs. Christian Eye Ministry, Inc., San Diego, 1983-91, World Eye Care, Inc., 1990-91, Christian Legal Soc. Metro Denver, Inc., 1994-98; chmn. Arvada (Colo.) Covenant Ch., 1993-94; bd. dirs., sec. Wycliffe Bible Translators, Inc., Huntington Beach, Calif., 1977-83. Mem. Colo. Bar Assn. (Bill of Rights com. 1977-90, 92—), State Bar Calif., Omicron Delta Kappa. Avocation: city league volleyball. Estate planning, Non-profit and tax-exempt organizations, Probate (including wills, trusts). Office: 1901 Kipling St Ste 220 Lakewood CO 80215

THOMPSON, ALVIN W. judge; b. 1953; BA, Princeton U., 1975; JD, Yale U., 1978. With Robinson & Cole, Hartford, Conn., 1978-94; dist. judge U.S. Dist. Ct., Conn., 1994—. Mem. ABA, Conn. Bar Assn., Hartford County Bar Assn. Office: US Dist Ct 450 Main St Rm 240 Hartford CT 06103-3022

THOMPSON, CHARLES AMOS, lawyer; b. Rockwood, Tenn., Sept. 30, 1945; s. Amos Carson and Helen (Holloway) T.; m.Deborah Kaye Perdue, June 30, 1973 (div. Oct. 1987). BSBA, U. Montevallo, 1972; JD, Birmingham Sch. Law, 1985. Bar: Ala. 1989, U.S. Dist. Ct. (no. dist.) Ala. 1990. Pvt. practice, Birmingham, Ala., 1989—. Olympic Torch bearer, 1996. Capt. USMC, 1966-69. Mem. Ala. State Bar Assn., Birmingham Bar Assn., Greater Birmingham Criminal Def. Lawyer's Assn., Birmingham Track Club (pub. rels. 1990—, marathon instr. 1986—, Dr. Arthur Black award 1987). Democrat. Methodist. Avocations: running, track and field, automobile-motorcycle-house maintenance. Criminal, General practice, Probate (including wills, trusts). Home and Office: 3174 Pipe Line Rd Birmingham AL 35243-5241

THOMPSON, CHARLES MURRAY, lawyer; b. Childress, Tex., Oct. 13, 1942; s. Walter Lee and Lois S. (Sheehan) T.; children: Murray McKay, McLean Ann. BS with honors, Colo. State U., 1965; JD cum laude, U. S.D., 1969, LLD (hon.), 1995. Bar: S.D. 1969, U.S. Dist. Ct. S.D. 1969, U.S. Ct. Claims 1989, U.S. Ct. Appeals (8th cir.) 1972, U.S. Supreme Ct. 1973. Ptnr. May, Adam, Gerdes & Thompson, Pierre, S.D., 1969—. Bd. dirs. Bank West, Pierre, SD; past pres. Delta Trust, Pierre; spkr. in field. Editor S.D. Law Rev., 1969 Pres. S.D. Council Sch. Attys., 1984-86. Fellow Am. Bar Found. (chmn. 1991-92, bd. dirs. 1989-92), Coll. Law Practice Mgmt., Am. Coll. Trial Lawyers; mem. ABA (ho. of dels. 1978-2002, bd. govs. 1983-86), ATLA, Am. Bd. Trial Advs., Am. Counsel Assn., Am. Judicature Soc. (bd. dirs. 1981-85), Am. Bar Endowment (bd. dirs. 1991—, pres. 2000-02), Nat. Conf. Bar Pres.'s (exec. coun. 1986-94, pres. 1992-93), State Bar S.D. (pres. young lawyers sect. 1974-75, pres. 1986-87), S.D. Bar Found. (pres. 1991), S.D. Trial Lawyers Assn. (pres. 1980-81), Jackrabbit Bar Assn. (chancellor 1981-82), Kiwanis (pres. local club 1977). Democrat. Avocations: flying, ranching. State civil litigation, General practice, Insurance. Home and Office: PO Box 160 Pierre SD 57501-0160

THOMPSON, CHARLES WILLIAM SYDNOR See THOMPSON, SYDNOR JR.

THOMPSON, CRAIG A. lawyer; b. Balt., Jan. 12, 1969; s. Brenda Thompson; m. Deborah St. Lawrence Thompson, June 2, 2002. BA in Afro-Am. Studies, BA in Polit. Sci., U. Md., 1992, JD, 1995. Bar: Md., U.S. Dist. Ct. Md., Md. 1995, U.S. Dist. Ct. Md. 2000. Asst. Balt. City Hall, 1989—94; pres. Grand Vision Comm., 1994—; intern Cmty. Law Ctr., 1994; law clk. Murphy and Gutierrez, P.A., 1994—95; assoc. Minority Bus. Enterprise Legal Def. Fund, Inc., 1995—96; counsel Coun. for Econ. and Bus. Opportunity, Inc., 1997—98; assoc. Law Offices of Peter G. Angelos, P.C., Balt., 1998—. Presenter in field. Author: (anthology) Tough Love: The Life and Death of Tupac Shakur, 1996, Atonement: The Million Man March, 1996; contbr. articles to profl. jours.; host (weekly talk radio show) WEAA, (weeklyn TV show) UPN. Adv. bd. mem. Chesapeake Ctr. for Youth Devel.; mem. circle of friends Black Mental Health Alliance; mem. Mayor's MBE/WBE Adv. Com., 1998—99, Govs. Task Force on Increasing African Am. Entrepreneurship in Balt. City, 2000—02; bd. dirs. Great Blacks in Wax Mus., Balt. Mentoring Partnership, Police Athletic League, 1999—2001, Big Bros. Big Sisters Ctrl. Md., 1995—97. Mem.: ATLA, ABA, Md. Trial Lawyers Assn., Bar Assn. Balt. City, Md. State Bar Assn., U. Md. Sch. Law Alumni Assn. (bd. dirs.), Phi Alpha Theta. General practice, Personal injury (including property damage). Office: Law Offices Peter G Angelos 100 N Charles St Baltimore MD 21201

THOMPSON, EUGENE CEBRON, III, lawyer; b. Warsaw, N.C., Feb. 15, 1936; s. Eugene Cebron and Lydia (Briscoe) T.; m. Mary Sue Kennedy, Mar. 30, 1969; children: Eugene Cebron IV, Kennedy Lee. AB in Econs., U. N.C., 1959; JD, Wake Forest U., 1966. Bar: N.C. 1966, U.S. Dist. Ct. (ea. dist.) 1967. Ptnr. Thompson & Mikitka, Warsaw, 1966—. Served to capt. USMC, 1959-63. Mem. ABA, N.C. Bar Assn. (sec., treas. 1971-72), Duplin County Bar Assn. (v.p. 1969, pres. 2003), Am. Trial Lawyers Assn., N.C. Trial Lawyers Assn., N.C. Mcpl. Attys. Assn. (bd. dirs. 1973-75, v.p. 1976, state pres. 1977). Methodist. Avocations: snow skiing, handball, tennis, swimming, coaching. Personal injury (including property damage), Estate planning, Criminal. Home: 714 Forrest Rd Warsaw NC 28398-2211 Office: Thompson & Mikitka 109 W Hill St Warsaw NC 28398-1815

THOMPSON, GORDON, JR., federal judge; b. San Diego, Dec. 28, 1929; s. Gordon and Garnet (Meese) T.; m. Jean Peters, Mar. 17, 1951; children— John M., Peter Renwick, Gordon III. Grad., U. So. Calif., 1951, Southwestern U. Sch. Law, Los Angeles, 1956. Bar: Calif. 1956. With Dist. Atty.'s Office, County of San Diego, 1957-60; partner firm Thompson & Thompson, San Diego, 1960-70; U.S. dist. judge So. Dist. Calif., San Diego, 1970—, chief judge, 1984-91, sr. judge, 1994—. Mem. ABA, Am. Bd. Trial Advocates, San Diego County Bar Assn. (v.p. 1970), San Diego Yacht Club, Delta Chi. Office: US Dist Ct 940 Front St San Diego CA 92101-8994

THOMPSON, HOLLEY MARKER, lawyer, marketing professional; b. Jamestown, NY, Jan. 30, 1947; d. Burdette James and Mary (Novitske) Marker; m. Lawrence D. Thompson; children: Jennifer Kristen Simos, Kendra Elise Blair, Jennifer Lynn, Stephanie Lynn. AAS, Jamestown C.C., 1966; BS, Ohio U., 1969; MA, W.Va. U., 1974, JD, 1980. Bar: W.Va. 1980, U.S. Dist. Ct. (so. dist.) W.Va. 1980, Pa. 1982, U.S. Dist. Ct. (we. dist.) Pa. 1982. Tchr. math. various pub. schs., Santa Ana (Calif.), Lakewood (N.Y.) and Morgantown (W.Va.), 1970-77; atty. for students W.Va. U., Morgantown, 1980; assoc. libr., lectr. W.Va. U. Coll. Law, Morgantown, 1980-83; assoc., libr. Jackson, Kelly, Holt & O'Farrell, Charleston, W.Va., 1983-86; cons. Hildebrandt, Inc., Somerville, NJ, 1986-94; sr. v.p. relationship marketing and marketing svs. LexisNexis, Dayton, Ohio, 1994—. Spkr. in field. Contbr. Mem.: ABA, Legal Mktg. Assn., N.J. Assn. Law Librs., Am. Assn. Law Librs., Spl. Libr. Assn., Phi Delta Phi. Office: LexisNexis 9443 Springboro Pike Miamisburg OH 45342 E-mail: holley.thompson@lexisnexis.com.

THOMPSON, HUGH P. state supreme court justice; b. Montezuma, Ga., July 7, 1943; married; 2 children. JD, Mercer U., 1969. Bar: Ga. 1970. Pvt. practice, Milledgeville, Ga., 1970—71; judge Recorder's Ct. of Milledgeville, 1971—79, Baldwin County Ct., 1973—78, Superior Ct. of Ga., 1979—94; chief judge Ocmulgee Jud. Cir., 1987—94; assoc. justice Supreme Ct. of Ga., Atlanta, 1994—. Instr. bus. law Ga. Coll., 1971—72; pres. Coun. Superior Ct. Judges, 1993—94. Communicant St. Stephen's Episcopal Ch. Named Outstanding Young Man of Baldwin County, 1972; recipient Disting. Svc. award, Baldwin County Jaycees, 1972, Outstanding Alumnus award, Mercer U. Law Sch., 1994, Disting. Svc. award, Ga. Coll. and State U., 2002. Mem.: ABA, Ga. Bar Found., State Bar Ga., Charles Longstreet Weltner Family Law Inn of Ct., Old War Horse Lawyers Club, Lawyers Club Atlanta. Avocations: hunting, gardening, golf, fishing. Office: Supreme Ct Ga State Judicial Bldg 244 Washington St SW Rm 572 Atlanta GA 30334-9007

THOMPSON, JAMES LEE, lawyer; b. L.I., N.Y., Sept. 9, 1941; s. Robert Luther and Marjorie Emma (Jones) T.; m. Diana Dill Stevenson, June 29, 1963; children: James C., Thomas J. BA, Yale U., 1963; JD, U. Va., 1966. Bar: Va. 1966, Md. 1966, U.S. Ct. Mil. Appeals 1968, U.S. Dist. Ct. Md. 1972, U.S. Supreme Ct. 1978. Ptnr. Miller & Canby, Rockville, Md., 1970—, head litigation, 1975—. Mem. jud. conf. U.S. Ct. Appeals (4th cir.). Mem. Thousand Acres Assn., Deep Creek Lake, Md., 1985-87. Capt. JAGC, USMC, 1966-70. Decorated D.S.M. Fellow Am. Coll. Trial Lawyers; mem. ABA, Md. State Bar Assn. (bd. govs. 1975, 78, 79, 83, 89, 94, sec. 1995, pres. 1999-00), Montgomery County Bar Assn. (pres. 1987-88, Cert. of Merit 1985), Nat. Conf. Bar Pres., Md. Bar Found., Montgomery County Bar Found. (pres. 1988-89), Loophole Club (pres. 1978-79), Phi Delta Phi. Democrat. Episcopalian. Avocations: sailing, skiing, tennis, golf, gardening. State civil litigation, General practice. Home: 419 Russell Ave Apt 110 Gaithersburg MD 20877-2836 Office: Miller & Canby 200 Monroe St Ste B Rockville MD 20850-4423

THOMPSON, JAMES ROBERT, JR., lawyer, former governor; b. Chgo., May 8, 1936; s. James Robert and Agnes Josephine (Swanson) T.; m. Jayne Carr, 1976; 1 child, Samantha Jayne. Student, U. Ill., Chgo., 1953-55, Washington U., St. Louis, 1955-56; JD, Northwestern U., 1959. Bar: Ill. 1959, U.S. Supreme Ct. 1964. Asst. state's atty., Cook County, Ill., 1959-64; assoc. prof. law Northwestern U. Law Sch., 1964-69; asst. atty. gen. State of Ill., 1969-70; chief criminal div., 1969; chief dept. law enforcement and pub. protection, 1969-70; 1st asst. U.S. atty. No. Dist. Ill., 1970-71, U.S.

atty., 1971-75; counsel firm Winston & Strawn, Chgo., 1975-77, ptnr., chmn., 1991—; gov. Ill., 1977-91. Chmn. Pres.' Intelligence Oversight Bd., 1989—93; adv. bd. Fed. Emergency Mgmt. Agy., 1991—93; bd. govs. Chgo. Bd. Trade; bd. dirs. FMC Corp., FMC Techs., Inc., Prime Retail Inc., Hollinger Internat., Inc., Navigant Consulting Inc., Maximus, Inc., Chgo. Mus. Contemporary Art, Lyric Opera Chgo., Econ. Club Chgo., Civic Com., Comml. Club Chgo. Co-author: Cases and Comments on Criminal Justice, 1974, Criminal Law and Its Adminstration. Chmn. Rep. Govs. Assn., 1982, Nat. Govs. Assn., Midwest Govs. Assn., Coun. Gt. Lakes Govs., 1985; mem. Nat. Commn. on Terrorist Attacks Upon the U.S., 2002—; mem. Abraham Lincoln Bicentennial Commn., 2000—. Mem. ABA, Ill. Bar Assn., Chgo. Bar Assn. Republican. Office: Winston & Strawn 35 W Wacker Dr Ste 4200 Chicago IL 60601-1695

THOMPSON, JAMES WILLIAM, lawyer; b. Dallas, Oct. 22, 1936; s. John Charles and Frances (Van Slyke) Thompson; m. Marie Hertz, June 26, 1965 (dec. 1965); children: Elizabeth, Margaret, John; m. Linda Ball Dozier, May 2, 1998. BS, U. Mont., 1958, JD, 1962. Bar: Mont. 1962; CPA, Mont. Acct. Arthur Young & Co., N.Y.C., summer 1959; instr. bus. adminstrn. Ea. Mont. Coll., Billings, 1959-60, U. Mont., Missoula, 1960-61; assoc. Cooke, Moulton, Bellingham & Longo, Billings, 1962-64, James R. Felt, Billings, 1964-65; asst. atty. City of Billings, 1963-64, atty., 1964-66; ptnr. Felt, Speare & Thompson, Billings, 1966-72, McNamer, Thompson & Cashmore, 1973-86, McNamer & Thompson Law Firm PC, 1986-89, McNamer, Thompson, Werner & Stanley, P.C., 1990-93, McNamer Thompson Law Firm PC, 1993-98, Wright Tolliver Guthals Law Firm PC, 1999—. Bd. dirs. Associated Employers of Mont., Inc., 1989—98; mem. adv. coun. Sch. Fine Arts, U. Mont., 1997—2001. Mem. Billings Zoning Commn., 1966—69; v.p. Billings Cmty. Action Program (now Dist. 7 Human Resources Devel. Coun.), 1968—70, pres., 1970—75, bd. trustees, 1975—; mem. Yellowstone County Legal Svcs. Bd., 1969—70, City-County Air Pollution Control Bd., 1969—70; pres. Billings Symphony Soc., 1970—71; bd. dirs. Billings Studio Theater, 1967—73, United Way Billings, 1973—81, Mont. Inst. Arts Found., 1986—89, Downtown Billings Assn., 1986—90, Billings Area Bus. Incubator, Inc., 1991—94, Found. of Mont. State U, Billings, 1992—98, Our Mont. Inc., 1997—; bd. dirs., treas. Rimrock Opera Co., 1998—; mem. Billings Transit Commn., 1971—73, City Devel. Agy., 1972—73; pres. Our Mont., Inc., 2000—; Diocesan Exec. Coun., 1972—75. Mem. ABA, Am. Acad. Estate Planning Attys., Nat. Acad. Elder Law Attys., State Bar Mont., Yellowstone County Bar Assn. (bd. dirs. 1983-87, pres. 1985-86), Elks, Kiwanis (pres. Yellowstone chpt. 1974-75), Sigma Chi (pres. Billings alumni assn. 1963-65). Episcopalian. Estate planning, Probate (including wills, trusts), Estate taxation. Home: 123 Lewis Ave Billings MT 59101-6034 Office: 10 N 27th St PO Box 1977 Billings MT 59103-1977 Personal E-mail: JWTLDT@aol.com.

THOMPSON, JAYNE CARR, public relations and communications executive, lawyer; b. Oak Park, Ill., Apr. 7, 1946; d. Robert Edward and Laurette (Rentner) Carr; m. James R. Thompson, June 19, 1976; 1 child, Samantha Jayne. BA, U. Ill., Chgo., 1967; JD, Northwestern U., 1970; degree (hon.) , Lincoln (Ill.) Coll., 1990, St. Xavier U., Chgo., 1995, Ill. Coll., 1995. Assoc. in litigation McDermott, Will & Emery, Chgo., 1970; asst. atty. gen. State of Ill., Chgo., 1970-77, chief of criminal appeals divsn., 1972-77, dep. chief prosecution assistance bur., 1975-76, dep. chief criminal divsn., 1976-77, acting chief criminal divsn., 1977; of counsel Brown, Hay & Stephens, Springfield, Ill., 1977-78, Silets & Martin, Chgo., 1983-84; house counsel and v.p. devel. Nat. Coll. Edn., Evanston, Ill., 1984-85; atty. Lydon & Griffin, Chgo., 1989-91; prin. Dilenschneider Group Inc., Chgo., 1999-2000, mng. prin., 2000—02; CEO, pres. Jayne Thompson and Assocs. Ltd., 2002—. Contbr. chpt. to book, articles to profl. jours. First Lady of Ill., Springfield, 1977-91; mem. Ill. Commn. on Status of Women, 1997-2001; pres. bd. dirs. Chgo. Pub. Libr., 1998—; mem. women's bd. Northwestern U., 1978—; bd. dirs. Chgo. Pub. Libr. Found., 1998—; mem. adv. bd. for Ill. Treas. for Women's Issues, 2002—; mem. chmn.'s adv. coun. Lincoln Pk. Zoo, 2002—; mem. Met. Planning Coun., 2002--. Mem. Ill. State Bar Assn., Execs. Club (Chgo.), Coun. on Fgn. Rels. (Chgo. com.), Econ. Club (Chgo.). Avocations: reading, cooking, tennis. Office: Jayne Thompson & Assocs Ltd 33 N Dearborn St Ste 2200 Chicago IL 60602 E-mail: jthompson@jaynethompson.com.

THOMPSON, JOEL ERIK, lawyer; b. Summit, N.J., Sept. 15, 1940; s. Maurice Eugene and Charlotte Ruth (Harrington) T.; m. Bonnie Gay Ransa, June 15, 1963 (div. Dec. 1980); m. Deborah Ann Korp, Dec. 24, 1980 (div. Jan. 1987); children: Janice Santiesteban, Amber; m. Shandae Emlow, Apr. 21, 2002. Student, Va. Poly. Inst., 1958, Carnegie Inst. Tech., 1960-61; BSME cum laude, Newark Coll. Engring., 1966; JD, Seton Hall, 1970. Bar: N.J. 1970, Ariz. 1975, U.S. Tax Ct. 1972, U.S. Ct. Claims 1972, U.S. Customs Ct., 1972, U.S. Ct. Mil. Appeals, 1972, U.S. Ct. Customs and Patent Appeals 1972, U.S. Dist. Ct. N.J. 1970, Ariz. 1975, U.S. Ct. Appeals (9th cir.) 1975, U.S. Supreme Ct. 1975; cert. specialist criminal law Ariz. Bd. Legal Specialization; lic. profl. engr., N.J. Sr. technician Bell Tel. Labs., Inc., Murray Hill, N.J., 1965-67, patent agent, 1967-70, staff atty., 1970-73; sr. trial atty. N.J. Pub. Defender's Office, Elizabeth, N.J., 1973-74; assoc. Cahill, Sutton and Thomas, Phoenix, 1974-76; trial lawyer Maricopa County Pub. Defender's Office, Phoenix, 1976-80; trial lawyer, criminal law specialist Henry J. Florence, Ltd., Phoenix, 1980-86; pvt. practice Phoenix, 1987—. Judge Superior Ct. Ariz., Phoenix, 1987-95; instr. Phoenix Regional Police Acad., 1976-80, Glendale C.C., 1977, Ariz. State U. Sch. of Law, 1978, Am. Inst., 1990; pres., CEO Eagle Master Corp., Phoenix, 1995—; pres. Joel Erik Thompson, Ltd., Phoenix, 1987—; bd. dirs. Am. Loans, Inc., San Diego, 1999-; presenter in field. Contbr. articles to profl. jours. Mem. planning com. Camelback East Village, Phoenix, 1992-98, chmn., 1993-96; mayor's select com., Phoenix, 1997, blue ribbon com. Maricopa Assn. Govs., 1996-97. Mem. Ariz. Bar Assn., Nat. Assn. Criminal Def. Lawyers, Ariz. Attys. Criminal Justice (charter), Ariz. Assn. Pvt. Investigators (hon.), Internat. Assn. Identification (hon.), Tau Beta Pi, Pi Tau Sigma. Criminal, Land use and zoning (including planning). Office: 3104 E Camelback Rd # 521 Phoenix AZ 85016-4502 E-mail: joel.thompson@azbar.org.

THOMPSON, KATHERINE GENEVIEVE, lawyer; b. Bklyn., May 11, 1945; d. George Otway and Marie (Burke) T. BS, Good Counsel Coll., 1966; JD, Bklyn. Law Sch., 1970; LLM, NYU, 1981. Bar: N.Y. 1971, U.S. Dist. Ct. (so. and ea. dists.) N.Y. 1978, U.S. Supreme Ct. 1981. Editor Matthew Bender Pub. Co., N.Y.C., 1970-71; atty. juvenile rights div. Legal Aid Soc., N.Y.C., 1971-76, asst. atty. in charge juvenile rights div. N.Y. County office, 1976-77; sole practice N.Y.C., 1977-78; ptnr. Rothenberg, Sherman, Thompson & Halpin, N.Y.C., 1978-84, Sherman, Thompson & Halpin, N.Y.C., 1984-87, Beldock, Levine & Hoffman, N.Y.C., 1987—. Mem. appellate div. 1st Dept. Screening Panel, 1981-82, appellate div. 1st Dept. Family Ct. Adv. Com., 1983-90, chmn., 1986-89. Co-author: Adoption Law and Practice, 1988; contbg. editor: Bender's Federal Practice Forms, 1971, Bender's Forms of Discovery, 1971. Bd. dirs. August Aichorn Resdl. Ctr., N.Y.C., 1979-94. Fellow Am. Bar Found., N.Y. State Bar Found.; mem. ABA (family law sect.) N.Y. State Bar Assn. (spl. com. on juvenile justice 1980-87, family law sect. 1980—), Assn. of Bar of City of N.Y. (family ct. and family law com. 1977-80, chmn. 1980-83, lectures and continuing edn. com. 1984-85, matrimonial law com. 1985-88), Womens Bar Assn., N.Y. County Lawyers Assn. (family ct. com. 1978-79). Family and matrimonial, General practice. Office: Beldock Levine & Hoffman 99 Park Ave Fl 16 New York NY 10016-1508

THOMPSON, LORAN TYSON, lawyer; b. N.Y.C., Dec. 23, 1947; s. Kenneth Webster and Mary (Tyson) T.; m. Meera Eleanora Agarwal, Apr. 2, 1976. BA magna cum laude, Amherst Coll., 1969; MA, Harvard U., 1970, JD, 1976. Bar: N.Y. 1977, U.S. Tax Ct. 1977. Assoc. Breed, Abbott & Morgan, N.Y.C., 1976-83, ptnr., 1983-93, Whitman Breed Abbott & Morgan LLP, N.Y.C., 1993-2000, Winston & Strawn, N.Y.C., 2000—. Mem. ABA, N.Y. State Bar Assn. (exec. com., tax sect. 1991-98, co-chmn. com. on nonqualified employee benefits 1991-95, co-chmn. com. on qualified plans 1995-98), Assn. Bar of City of N.Y., Phi Beta Kappa. Pension, profit-sharing, and employee benefits, Corporate taxation, Taxation, general. Home: 79 W 12th St Apt 12G New York NY 10011-8510 Office: Winston & Strawn 200 Park Ave New York NY 10166-4193 E-mail: lthompson@winston.com.

THOMPSON, MICHAEL, lawyer; b. Des Moines, Aug. 2, 1951; s. Harold L. and Carolyn Annette (Yacinich) T.; m. Barbara Ann Haafke, Oct. 29, 1977 (div. Oct. 1984). BA, U. No. Iowa, 1973; JD, U. Iowa, 1976, MA, 1977. Bar: Iowa 1976, N.Y. 1979, Mo. 1980, Tex. 1994, Ill. 1999, U.S. Ct. Appeals (2d cir.) 1980, U.S. Ct. Appeals (7th cir.) 1982, U.S. Ct. Appeals (D.C. cir.) 1981, U.S. Ct. Appeals (fed. cir.) 1988, U.S. Ct. Internat. Trade 1988, U.S. Supreme Ct. 1984. Asst. atty. gen. Iowa Dept. Justice, Des Moines, 1976; economist Iowa Commerce Commn., Des Moines, 1976-77; spl. asst. N.Y. Pub. Svc. Commn., Albany, 1977-80; commerce counsel Mo. Pacific R.R., St. Louis, 1980-83; atty. Southwestern Bell Corp., St. Louis, 1983—86; exec. v.p., gen. counsel SBC Internat. Devel. Corp., 1986—2000; pvt. practice Chgo., 2000—. Adj. instr. corp. fin. Drake U., Des Moines, 1977. Mem.: ABA, Caxton Club, Carlton Club, Arts Club Chgo., Grolier Club, Houston Yacht Club, Chgo. Yacht Club. Republican. Commercial, contracts (including sales of goods; commercial financing), Intellectual property, Private international. Office: 401 N Michigan Ave Ste 1200 Chicago IL 60611 Fax: 847-733-1807. E-mail: michaelthompsonlaw@earthlink.net.

THOMPSON, PHILIP C. lawyer, investment advisor, educator; b. Balt., Oct. 21, 1945; s. Earl Clinton and Virginia (Baugh) Thompson; m. Julie Ann Young, June 10, 1948; children: Kathryn Adair, Julia Hamilton, Philip Clinton Jr. BA, Washington and Lee U., 1967, BS, 1968, JD, 1971. Bar: Ga. 1973, U.S. Dist. Ct. (no. dist.) Ga. 1973. Ptnr. Jones, Day, Reavis & Pogue, Atlanta, 1973—86, Dow, Lohnes & Albertson, Atlanta, 1986—94, Arnall, Golden, Gregory LLP, Atlanta, 1994—. Adj. prof. Emory U., Atlanta, 2003—. Capt. U.S. Army, 1972—73. Mem.: Capital City Club. Republican. Reformed Anglican. Avocations: youth programs, gardening, running, tennis, chess. Commercial, contracts (including sales of goods; commercial financing), Private international, Mergers and acquisitions. Office: Arnall Golden Gregory LLP 1201 W Peachtree St Ste 2800 Atlanta GA 30309 Office Fax: 404-873-8673. Business E-Mail: philip.thompson@agg.com.

THOMPSON, RALPH GORDON, federal judge; b. Oklahoma City, Dec. 15, 1934; s. Lee Bennett and Elaine (Bizzell) T.; m. Barbara Irene Hencke, Sept. 5, 1964; children: Lisa, Elaine, Maria. BBA, U. Okla., 1956, JD, 1961. Bar: Okla. 1961. Ptnr. Thompson, Thompson, Harbour & Selph (and predecessors), Oklahoma City, 1961-75; judge U.S. Dist. Ct. for Western Dist. Okla., Oklahoma City, 1975—; chief judge U.S. Dist. Ct. (we. dist.) Okla., 1986-93. Mem. Okla. Ho. of Reps., 1966-70, asst. minority floor leader, 1969-70; spl. justice Supreme Ct. Okla., 1970-71; tchr. Harvard Law Sch. Trial Advocacy Workshop, 1981—; apptd. by chief justice of U.S. to U.S. Fgn. Intelligence Surveillance Ct., 1990-97; elected to jud. conf. of the U.S., 1997; apptd. to Edward J. Devitt Disting. Svc. Justice award selection com., 1997-99; apptd. by chief justice of U.S. to exec. com. of Jud. Conf. of the U.S., 1998-2000; coord. Long Range Planning for Fed. Judiciary, 1999-2000. Co-author: Bryce Harlow: Mr. Integrity, Bob Burke and Ralph G. Thompson, 2000. Rep. nominee for lt. gov., Okla., 1970; chmn. bd. ARC, Oklahoma City, 1970-72; chmn., pres. Okla. Young Lawyers Conf., 1965; mem. bd. visitors U. Okla., 1975-78. Lt. USAF, 1957-60, col. Res., ret. Decorated Legion of Merit; named Oklahoma City's Outstanding Young Man, Oklahoma City Jaycees, 1967, Outstanding Fed. Trial Judge, Okla Trial Lawyers Assn., 1980; recipient Regents Alumni award U. Okla., 1990, Disting. Svc. award, 1993, Jour. Record Pub. Co. award for Disting. Svc., 2001; inducted Okla. Hall of Fame, 1995; nominee Pulitzer Prize, 2000. Fellow Am. Bar Found.; mem. ABA, Fed. Bar Assn., Okla. Bar Assn. (chmn. sect. internat. law and gen. practice 1974-75), Oklahoma County Bar Assn. (Jud. Svc. award 1988), Jud. Conf. U.S. (com. on ct. adminstrn. 1981-89, com. on fed.-state jurisdiction 1988-91), U.S. Dist. Judges Assn. 10th Cir. (pres. 1992-94), Rotary (hon.), Order of Coif, Am. Inns of Ct. (pres. XXIII 1995-96), Phi Beta Kappa (pres. chpt. 1985-86, Phi Beta Kappa of Yr. 1991), Beta Theta Pi, Phi Alpha Delta. Episcopalian. Office: US Dist Ct 200 NW 4th St Oklahoma City OK 73102-3027

THOMPSON, RICHARD LEON, pharmaceutical company executive, lawyer; b. Rochester, N.Y., Dec. 5, 1944; s. Leslie L. and Marion (Cosad) T.; m. Catherine Jean Terry, July 6, 1974; children: Kristin Anne, Catherine Elizabeth. AB cum laude, SUNY, Albany, 1966; MA, Syracuse U., 1967; JD, Cath. U., 1975. Staff dir., counsel U.S. Ho. of Reps., Washington, 1973-78; dir. Abbott Labs., Washington, 1978-83; v.p. Squibb Corp., Washington, 1983-89, Bristol-Myers Squibb Corp., Washington, 1989—2001, sr. v.p. policy and govt. affairs, 2001—. Chmn. legis. adv. com. Proprietary Assn., Washington, 1984; bd. dirs. Bus. Govt. Rels. Coun. Mem. com. on changing enrollments Fairfax (Va.) County Pub. Sch., 1983-84, supts. adv. com., 1984-85, mem., 1988-98; mem. Fed. City Coun., 1992; chmn. legis. com. P.R.-U.S.A. Found., 1985-95; co-chair Edn. in 2010; bd. dirs. D.C. Hospice, Bryce Harlow Found., 1990-95; bd. dirs., treas. Ford Theater, 2000--; chmn. governance com. Meridian Internat. Ctr., 2000-02 1st lt. U.S. Army, 1968-69, Vietnam. Named one of Outstanding Young Men of Am., Jaycees, 1976. Mem. ABA, D.C. Bar Assn., Pharm. Mfrs. Assn. (chmn. Washington reps. com.1988), Congl. Country Club, City Club. Home: 1005 Woburn Ct Mc Lean VA 22102-2133 Office: Bristol-Myers Squibb Corp 655 15th St NW Ste 300 Washington DC 20005-5717

THOMPSON, RICHARD S. lawyer; b. Vidalia, Ga. m. Jennifer Darby; children: Loree Ann, Darby. Grad. cum laude, Mercer U., 1979, grad., 1982. Asst. dist. atty. Douglas County, Ga.; asst. atty. gen. State of Ga., 1986—88; pvt. practice Statesboro and Vidalia, 1989—95; ptnr. McNatt, Greene & Thompson, Vidalia, Ga., 1995—2001; U.S. atty. So. Dist. Ga., 2001—. Office: So Dist Ga PO Box 8999 Savannah GA 31412*

THOMPSON, RONALD EDWARD, lawyer; b. Bremerton, Wash., May 24, 1931; s. Melville Herbert and Clara Mildred (Griggs) T.; m. Marilyn Christine Woods, Dec. 15, 1956; children: Donald Jeffery, Karen, Susan, Nancy, Sally, Claire BA, U. Wash., 1953, JD, 1958. Bar: Wash. 1959. Asst. city atty. City of Tacoma, 1960-61; pres. firm Thompson, Krilich, LaPorte, West & Lockner, P.S., Tacoma, 1961-99. Judge pro tem Mcpl. Ct., City of Tacoma, Pierce County Dist., 1972—, Pierce County Superior Ct., 1972—. Chmn. housing and social welfare com. City of Tacoma, 1965-69; mem. Tacoma Bd. Adjustment, 1967-71, chmn., 1968; mem. Tacoma Com. Future Devel., 1961-64, Tacoma Planning Commn., 1971-72; bd. dirs., pres. Mcpl. League Tacoma; bd. dirs. Pres. Tacoma Rescue Mission, Tacoma Pierce County Cancer Soc., Tacoma-Pierce County Heart Assn., Tacoma Grand Cinema, Tacoma-Pierce County Coun. for Arts, Econ. Devel. Coun. Puget Sound, Tacoma Youth Symphony, Kleiner Group Home, Tacoma C.C. Found., Pierce County Econ. Devel. Corp., Wash. Transp. Policy Inst.; Coalition to Keep Wash. Moving, precinct committeeman Rep. party, 1969-73. With AUS, 1953-55; col. Res. Recipient Internat. Cmty. Svc. award Optimist Club, 1970, Patriotism award Am. Fedn. Police, 1974, citation for cmty. svc. HUD, 1974, Disting. Citizen award Mcpl. League Tacoma-Pierce County, 1985; named Lawyer of the Yr. Pierce County Legal Secs. Assn., 1992. Mem. ATLA, Am. Arbitration Assn. (panel of arbitrators), ABA, Wash. State Bar Assn. Local Hero award 2002), Tacoma-Pierce County Bar Assn. (sec. 1964, pres. 1979, mem. cts. and judiciary com. 1981-82), Wash. State Trial Lawyers Assn., Tacoma-Pierce County C. of C. (bd. dirs., exec. com., v.p., chmn.), Downtown Tacoma Assn. (com. chmn., bd. dirs. exec. com., chmn.), Variety Club (Seattle), Lawn Tennis Club, Tacoma Club, Optimist (Tacoma, internat. pres. 1973-74), Phi Delta Phi, Sigma Nu. Roman Catholic. General civil litigation, Personal injury (including property damage), Property, real (including real estate development, water). Home: 3101 E Bay Dr NW Gig Harbor WA 98335-7610 Office: Atty Law PO Box 1189 7525 Pioneer Way Ste 101 Gig Harbor WA 98335-1165 E-mail: retpllc@att.net.

THOMPSON, SYDNOR, JR., (CHARLES WILLIAM SYDNOR THOMPSON JR.), lawyer, mediator, arbitrator; b. Balt., Feb. 18, 1924; s. Charles William Sydnor Thompson and Helen Josephine Layne; m. Harriette Line, June 2, 1947; children: Darcy T. Kluttz, Charles William Sydnor III, Harriet T. Moore, Brenneman L., Mary Katherine Line T. Kelly. AB, Syracuse U., 1947; LLB, Harvard U., 1950; student, St. Andrews U., Scotland, 1945, Manchester U., Eng., 1950, London Sch. Econs., 1951. Cert.: N.C. Dispute Resolution Commn. (mediator), EEOC, Am. Arbitration Assn. (arbitrator), Nat. Assn. Securities Dealers. Assoc. Davis Polk & Wardwell, N.Y.C., 1951—54; ptnr. Parker Poe Thompson Bernstein Gage & Preston, Charlotte, NC, 1954—94; judge N.C. Ct. Appeals, Raleigh, NC, 1994; of counsel Parker, Poe, Adams & Bernstein, LLP, Charlotte, 1995—; prin. Mediation, Inc., Winston-Salem, NC, 1995—. Author: The Sydnor Family Saga, 2000, A Collection of Ad Hominem Verse, 2002; contbr. articles to law revs. Pres. Charlotte Symphony Orch., 1958—61, Charlotte Opera Assn., 1971—75; vice chair N.C. Arts Coun., Raleigh, 1981—84; pres. Mecklenburg Ministries, 1987—89, Wing Haven Found., 2001—02; chmn. Mecklenburg County Dem. Party, 1977—81. Served with U.S. Army, 1943—46, ETO. Decorated Bronze star; Fulbright scholar, 1950, 1951. Master: William H. Bobbitt Inn of Ct.; mem.: ABA (chmn. circuits subcom. 1977—95), Mecklenburg Bar Assn. (pres. 1990), N.C. Bar Assn. (chmn. appellate rules study com. 1989—91, chmn. local bar svcs. com. 1991—93), Old Catawba Soc., Horace Williams Philosophy Club, English Speaking Union, Sporadic Book Club, Charlotte Country Club, Tower Club. Avocations: genealogy, writing, tennis, acting. Office: Parker Poe Adams & Bernstein LLP Ste 3000 401 S Tryon St Charlotte NC 28202

THOMPSON, TERENCE WILLIAM, lawyer; b. Moberly, Mo., July 3, 1952; s. Donald Gene and Carolyn (Stringer) T.; m. Caryn Elizabeth Hildebrand, Aug. 30, 1975; children: Cory Elizabeth, Christopher William, Tyler Madison. BA in Govt. with honors and high distinction, U. Ariz., 1974; JD, Harvard U., 1977. Bar: Ariz. 1977, U.S. Dist. Ct. Ariz. 1977, U.S. Tax Ct. 1979. Assoc. Brown & Bain P.A., Phoenix, 1977-83, ptnr., 1983-92, Gallagher and Kennedy, P.A., Phoenix, 1992—. Legis. aide Rep. Richard Burgess, Ariz. Ho. of Reps., 1974; mem. bus. adv. bd. Citibank Ariz. (formerly Great Western Bank & Trust, Phoenix), 1985-86. Mem. staff Harvard Law Record, 1974-75; rsch. editor Harvard Internat. Law Jour. ,1976; lead author, editor-in-chief: Arizona Corporate Practice, 1996—; contbr. articles to profl. jours. Mem. Phoenix Mayor's Youth Adv. Bd. 1968-70, Phoenix Internat.; active 20-30 Club, 1978-81, sec. 1978-80, Valley Leadership, Phoenix, 1983-84, citizens task force future financing needs City of Phoenix, 1985-86; exec. coun. Boys and Girls Clubs of Met. Phoenix, 1990-2000, sr. coun. 2000—; bd. dirs. Phoenix Bach Choir, 1992-94; deacon Shepherd of Hills Congl. Ch., Phoenix, 1984-85; pres. Maricopa County Young Dems., 1982-83, Ariz. Young Dems., 1983-84, sec. 1981-82, v.p. 1982-83; exec. dir. Young Dems. Am., 1985, exec. com. 1983-85; others. Fellow Ariz. Bar Found.; mem. State Bar Ariz. (vice chmn. internt. law sect. 1978, sec. securities law sect. 1990-91, vice chmn. sect. 1991-92, chmn.-elect 1992-93, chmn. 1993-94, exec. coun. 1988-96, sec. bus. law sect. 1992-93, vice chmn. 1993-94, chmn. 1994-95, exec. coun. 1996-98), Nat. Assn. Bond Lawyers, Nat. Health Lawyers, Greater Phoenix Black C. of C. (bd. dirs. 1999-2001), Blue Key, Phi Beta Kappa, Phi Kappa Phi, Phi Eta Sigma. Corporate, general, Health, Securities. Home: 202 W Lawrence Rd Phoenix AZ 85013-1226 Office: Gallagher & Kennedy PA 2575 E Camelback Rd Phoenix AZ 85016-9225

THOMPSON, THOMAS MARTIN, lawyer; b. Albion, Pa., Jan. 7, 1943; s. Donald C. and Mabel Louise (Martin) T.; m. Judith E. Daucher; children: Reid, Chad, Matthew, Molly. AB, Grove City Coll., 1965; JD cum laude, Harvard U., 1968. Bar: Pa. 1968. Ptnr. Buchanan Ingersoll, Pitts., 1968—, chair corp. fin. group. Adj. prof. law U. Pitts.; past chairperson, dir. Pa. Lawyer Trust Acct. Bd. Past pres. Neighborhood Legal Svcs. Assn.; bd. dirs., mem. exec. com. Pitts. Pub. Theater. Mem. ABA, Pa. Bar Assn. (vice-chair bus. law coun., chair-elect bus. law sect., Pro Bono award 1989), Allegheny County Bar Assn. (past chmn. pub. svc. com., past chmn. bus. law coun., past chair PBA legal opinion steering com.), Assn. for Corp. Growth (past pres. Pitts. chpt.). Democrat. Corporate, general, Finance, Securities. Home: 1142 Dartmouth Rd Pittsburgh PA 15205-1705 Office: Buchanan Ingersoll One Oxford Ctr 301 Grant St Fl 20 Pittsburgh PA 15219-1410 E-mail: thompsontm@bipc.com.

THOMS, DAVID MOORE, lawyer; b. N.Y.C., Apr. 28, 1948; s. Theodore Clark and Elizabeth Augusta (Moore) T.; m. Susan Rebecca Stuckey, Dec. 16, 1972. BA, Kalamazoo Coll., 1970; M in Urban Planning, Wayne State U., 1975, LLM in Taxation, 1988; JD, U. Detroit, 1979. Bar: Mich. 1980, N.Y. 1995. Planner City of Detroit, 1971-75; atty. Rockwell and Kotz, P.C., Detroit, 1980-87; pvt. practice David M. Thoms & Assocs., P.C., Detroit, 1987—2002, Miller Canfield Paddock and Stone, P.L.C., 2002—. Adj. assoc. prof. Madonna U., 1993—; presenter NYU Tax Inst. Editor Case and Comment U. of Detroit Law Rev., 1978-79. Mem. program com. Fin. and Estate Planning Coun. Detroit, 1980—; mem. adv. bd., chmn. nominating com., mem. exec. com. Met. Detroit Salvation Army, 1980—, sec.-treas., vice chmn., 1994-95, chmn., 1995-96; bd. dirs. bylaws and property com., mem. nominating com., devel. com., exec. com. Mich. chpt. ARC; bd. dirs. L'Alliance Française de Grosse Pointe, 1980-, pres., 1985-88, 94-95; bd. dirs. French Festival of Detroit, Inc., 1986-89, 91-94, pres.; bd. dirs. Fedn. of Alliances Françaises, 1989-95, 97—, also past treas., v.p., chmn. fin. com., pres., 2000-01; bd. dirs. Detroit Symphony Orch. Hall, Inc., 1996-97; trustee Kalamazoo Coll., 1993-97, mem. exec. com., 1995-97; dir. vis. com. European art DIA, 1995-97. Decorated Officier dans l'Ordre des Palmes Academiques; recipient Prix Charbonnier; Burton scholar U. Detroit, 1979. Mem. ABA (chmn. subcom. on probate and estate planning, mem. charitable trust com.), Fed. Bar Assn., Oakland County Bar Assn., Detroit Bar Assn., State Bar Mich., N.Y. Bar Assn., Bar Assn. of City of N.Y., Am. Planning Assn. (Mich. chpt.), Detroit Athletic Club, Renaissance Club, The Grosse Pointe Club. Mem. United Church of Christ. Avocations: tennis, architectural history, music, travel, art history. Corporate, general, Estate planning, Corporate taxation. Office: 400 Renaissance Ctr Ste 950 Detroit MI 48243-1678 E-mail: thoms@ameritech.net.

THOMS, JEANNINE AUMOND, lawyer; b. Chgo. d. Emmett Patrick and Margaret (Gallet) Aumond; m. Richard W. Thoms; children: Catherine Thoms, Alison Thoms. AA, McHenry County Coll., 1979; BA, No. Ill. U., 1981; JD, Ill. Inst. Tech., 1984. Bar: Ill. 1984, U.S. Dist. Ct. (no. dist.) Ill. 1984, U.S. Ct. Appeals (7th cir.) 1985; cert. mediator 19th Jud. Cir. Ill. Assoc. Foss Schuman Drake & Barnard, Chgo., 1984-86, Zukowski Rogers Flood & McArdle, Crystal Lake and Chgo., 1986-92, ptnr., 1992—. Arbitrator 19th Jud. Ct. Ill., 1991—. Mem. women's adv. coun. to Gov. State of Ill.; mem. McHenry County Mental Health Bd., 1991—98, v.p., 1993—94, pres., 1995—98; mem. governing coun. Good Shepherd Hosp., Barrington, Ill., 2001—. Mem.: LWV, ABA, Acad. Family Mediators (cert.), Am. Trial Lawyers Assn., McHenry County Bar Assn., Chgo. Bar Assn., Ill. State Bar Assn. (coun. trust and estates sect. 2000—01, Ill. legis. dist. scholarship com. 2001, 2002—03), Phi Alpha Delta. Estate planning, Municipal (including bonds), Probate (including wills, trusts). Office: Zukowski Rogers Flood & McArdle 50 N Virginia St Crystal Lake IL 60014-4126 also: 100 S Wacker Dr Chicago IL 60606-4006

THOMSON, BASIL HENRY, JR., lawyer, university general counsel; b. Amarillo, Tex., Jan. 17, 1945; m. Margaret Shepard, May 4, 1985; children: Christopher, Matthew, Robert. BBA, Baylor U., 1968, JD, 1973. Bar: Tex. 1974, U.S. Ct. Mil. Appeals 1974, U.S. Supreme Ct. 1977, U.S. Dist. Ct. (we. dist.) Tex. 1988, U.S. Ct. Appeals (fed. cir.) 1990. Oil title analyst Hunt Oil Co., Dallas, 1971-73; atty., advisor Regulations and Adminstrv. Law div. Office of Chief Counsel USCG, Washington, 1973-77; dir. estate planning devel. dept. Baylor U., Waco, Tex., 1977-80, gen. counsel, 1980—2002; assoc. gen. counsel So. Meth. U., Dallas, 2002—. Adj. prof. law Baylor U.; lobbyist legis. Ind. Higher Edn., 71st Session of Tex. Legislature; mem. legis. com. Gov.'s Task Force on Drug Abuse; dir. govtl. relations Baylor U.; speaker at meetings of coll. and univ. adminstrs.; assisted in drafting legis. for Texan's War on Drugs Tex. Legislature; mem. legal adv. com. United Educators Ins. Risk Retention Group, 1994-96; mem. legal svcs. rev. panel Nat. Assn. Ind. Colls. and Univs., 1997—, pres.-elect, 2003, Nat. Assn. Coll. and Univ. Attys. Active Longhorn Coun. Boy Scouts of Am.; mem. bd. adjustment City of Woodway; bd. dirs. Heart of Tex. Coun. on Alcohol and Drug Abuse, 1987—91. Recipient Pres.'s award Ind. Colls. and Univs. of Tex., 1994, Dist. award of merit Boy Scouts Am. Fellow Coll. State Bar Tex.; mem. ABA, FBA, Nat. Assn. Coll. and Univ. Attys. (fin., nominations and elections coms. 1994-95, bd. dirs. 1988-91), Tex. Bar Assn., Waco Bar Assn., McLennan County Bar Assn., Owners Assn. of Sugar Creek, Inc. (bd. dirs. 1995-91, 2000—). Baptist. Avocations: backpacking, running, environmental concerns. Home: 100 Sugar Creek Pl Waco TX 76712-3410 Office: So Meth U PO Box 750132 Dallas TX 75275-0137 E-mail: bthomson@mail.smu.edu.

THOMSON, GEORGE RONALD, lawyer, educator; b. Wadsworth, Ohio, Aug. 25, 1959; s. John Alan and Elizabeth (Galbraith) T. BA summa cum laude, Miami U., Oxford, Ohio, 1982, MA summa cum laude, 1983; JD with honors, Ohio State U., 1986. Bar: Ill. 1986, U.S. Dist. Ct. (no. dist.) Ill. 1986. Teaching fellow Miami U., 1982-83; dir. speech activities Ohio State U.; Columbus, 1983-86; assoc. Peterson, Ross, Schloerb & Seidel, Chgo., 1986-87, Lord, Bissell & Brook, Chgo., 1987-94; asst. corp. counsel employment litig. divsn. City of Chgo., 1994—. Adj. prof. dept. comm. De Paul U., Chgo., 1988-90; presenter in field. Contbr. articles to profl. jours. Fundraiser Chgo. Hist. Soc., Steppenwolf Theater Co., AIDS Legal Counsel Chgo., Smithsonian Instn., Washington, 1988-90, U.S. Tennis Assn., 1990—; bd. dirs. Metro Sports Assn., 1992-94, Gerber-Hart Libr. and Archives, 1993-95, Gay and Lesbian Tennis Alliance Am., 1993-95, Team Chgo., 1994-96, Second City Tennis, 1999-2000, 02—; mem. coord. coun. Nat. Gay and Lesbian History Month; mem. Lawyer's Com. for Ill Human Rights; dir. Chgo. Internat. Charity Tennis Classic, 1993, 94, 95, 98. Recipient Spl. Commendation Ohio Ho. of Reps., 1984, 85, Nat. Forensics Assn. award, 1982. Mem. ABA, Chgo. Bar Assn., Lesbian and Gay Bar Assn., Speech Comm. Assn. Am., Mortar Bd., Phi Beta Kappa, Phi Kappa Phi, Omicron Delta Kappa, Delta Sigma Rho-Tau Kappa Alpha, Phi Alpha Delta. Presbyterian. Avocations: tennis, flute, antiques, folk arts and crafts, reading, travel. General civil litigation, Environmental, Insurance. Home: 2835 N Pine Grove Ave Unit 2S Chicago IL 60657-6109 Office: City of Chgo Dept of Law 30 N La Salle St Ste 1020 Chicago IL 60602-2503

THOMSON, HUGH TALBERT, lawyer; b. San Francisco, Nov. 21, 1944; s. Douglas Hugh and Margaret Rose Thomsom; children: Brian, Kimberly. BA, U. Calif., Berkeley, 1967; JD, U. Calif., Davis, 1970. Bar: Calif. 1971. Sole practice, San Jose, Calif., 1971—. Lectr. Judge's Conf. Fellow Am. Acad. Matrimonial Lawyers; mem. State Bar Calif. (writer family law specialization exam. 1981, 82, 84, author Family Law News, exec. com. family law sect. 1979-83), Calif. Bd. Legal Specialization for Family Law. Office: 941 W Hedding St San Jose CA 95126-1216 Business E-Mail: hugh@httlaw.com.

THOMSON, PAUL RICE, JR., lawyer; b. Syracuse, NY, Dec. 28, 1941; s. Paul Rice and Marcella Elizabeth (Shea) T.; m. Elizabeth Ann Cutliff, Aug. 21, 1965; children: Paul R. III, Pamela Judeth. BA in History, Va. Mil. Inst., 1963; JD, Washington and Lee U., 1966. Bar: Va. 1966, U.S. Dist. Ct. (we. dist.) Va. 1966, U.S. Ct. Mil. Appeals 1967, U.S. Ct. Appeals (4th cir.) 1972. Assoc. Clement, Wheatley, Winston & Ingram, Danville, Va., 1969-71; asst. U.S. atty. Western Dist. Va., Roanoke, 1971-75, U.S. atty., 1975-79; gen. counsel natural resources The Pittston Co., Lebanon, Va., 1980—87; dep. asst. adminstr. EPA, Washington, 1987—90; ptnr. Woods, Rogers & Awzlegrove PLC, Roanoke, Va., 1990—. Pres. Roanoke Valley Law Enforcement Coun., 1975-76; mem. Fed.-State Law Enforcement Coun., 1975-79; trustee Ea. Mineral Law Found., Pitts., 1980-82; adj. prof. Washington & Lee U., 1981-99. V.p. Danville Jr. C. of C., 1971. Capt. JAGC, USMC, 1966-69. Recipient Spl. Achievement award Dept. Justice, 1974 Mem. ABA, Va. Bar Assn., Fed. Bar Assn. (pres. local chpt. 1979), NRA, Trout Unltd. Roman Catholic. Avocations: fly fishing, bird hunting, raising labrador retreivers. Criminal, Environmental, Natural resources. Office: Woods Rogers & Hazlegrove PLC 10 S Jefferson St Roanoke VA 24011

THOREN-PEDEN, DEBORAH SUZANNE, lawyer; b. Rockford, Ill., Mar. 28, 1958; d. Robert Roy and Marguerite Natalie (Geoghegan) Thoren; m. Steven E. Peden, Aug. 10, 1985. BA in Philosophy, Polit. Sci./Psychology, U. Mich., 1978; JD, U. So. Calif., 1982. Bar: Calif. 1982. Assoc. Bushkin, Gaines & Gaims, L.A., 1982-84, Rutan & Tucker, Costa Mesa, Calif., 1984-86; sr. counsel First Interstate Bancorp, L.A., 1986-96; ptnr. Pillsbury Winthrop LLP, L.A., 1996—; asst. gen. counsel CarsDirect-.com; gen. counsel CD1 Financial.com; gen. counsel, sr. v.p., chief privacy officer PayMyBills.Com, 2000. Lectr. on e-commerce, privacy Bank Secrecy Act and Ethics, Office of Fgn. Assets Control. Supervising editor U. So. Calif. Entertainment Law Jour., 1982-83, Entertainment Publishing and the Arts Handbook, 1983-84; contbr. articles to profl. jours. Mem. ABA (past vice-chmn. compliance exec. com., money laundering task force, privacy task force, co chmn. BSA staff commentary com.), Calif. Bankers Assn. (regulatory compliance com., co-chmn. regulatory compliance conf., past ex-officio mem. state govt. rels. com., co-vice chmn., vice-chmn., Regulatory Compliance Profl. award 1997, Frandzel award for outside counsel 2001, award 2001), Calif. State Bar Assn. (chmn., consumer fin. com.). Avocations: riding, travel, reading, skiing. Banking, Labor (including EEOC, Fair Labor Standards Act, labor-management relations, NLRB, OSHA). Office: Pillsbury Winthrop LLP Ste 2800 725 S Figueroa St Los Angeles CA 90017-5443

THORENS, JUSTIN, lawyer; b. Geneva, Sept. 15, 1931; s. Paul Louis and Germaine (Falquet) T.; m. Colette Françoise Vecchio, Mar. 28, 1963; children: Aline, Xavier. Lic. en droit, U. Genève, 1956, docteur en droit, 1962; postgrad., Freie U., Berlin, 1957, U. London, 1958. Cert. to practice law, Geneva, 1958. Atty., Geneva, 1956—; mem. law faculty U. Genève, 1967—, assoc. prof., 1970-73, prof., 1973-96, dean law faculty, 1974-77, rector of univ., 1977-83; legal adviser, sec. gen. Geneva Chamber of Agriculture, 1961-72; alt. pres. Jurisdictional Ct., Geneva, 1971-79. Mem. coun. UN Univ., Tokyo, 1986-92, chmn., 1988-89; vis. scholar Stanford U./U. Calif., Berkeley, 1983-84; guest prof. U. Munich, 1984. Contbr. articles to profl. jours. Mem. Commn. Nat. Suisse pour l'UNESCO, 1989-2001; pres. Found. Latsis Internat., 1989—. Mem. Swiss Univs. Conf. (v.p. 1979-83), Conf. Swiss Rectors (v.p. 1981-83), Standing Conf. Rectors, Pres. and Vice Chancellors of European Univs. (mem. coun. 1982-84), Assn. Univ. Partiellement ou Entiérement de Langue Française (bd. dirs. 1978-81, vice chmn. 1981-83, 84-87, hon. vice chmn. 1987, Haut Conseil), European Ctr. for Higher Edn. (mem. adv. com. 1981, chmn. 1986-88), Internat. Assn. Univs. (bd. dirs. 1983, pres. 1985-90, hon. pres. 1990) Home and Office: 18 Chemin du Nant d'Aisy 1246 Corsier Geneva Switzerland E-mail: etude.jthorens@bluewin.ch.

THORME, MELISSA ANNE, lawyer; b. Stamford, Conn., Dec. 20, 1963; d. Robert X. and Sonia Thorme; m. Robert Truman Kingsley, July 15, 1995; children: Jamie Thorme Kingsley, Anika Thorme Kingsley. BS in Environ. Biology, Calif. Poly. State U., San Luis Obispo, 1985; MS in Ecology, U. Calif., Davis, 1988, JD, 1990; LLM in Energy and Environment, Tulane U., 1992. Bar: Calif. 1990, U.S. Dist. Ct. (ea., so., central dist.) Calif. 1993, 2000, 2002. Law clk. Dana, Dehart, Chaffin, Price, Shade & Stein, Sacramento, summer 1987; vol. legal intern Defenders of Wildlife, Sacramento, summer 1988; law clk. Sierra Club Legal Def. Fund, San Francisco, summer 1989; teaching asst. U. Calif., Davis, 1988-90; vol. legal intern Remy and Thomas, Sacramento, spring 1990; environ. law fellow Tulane Environ. Law Clinic, New Orleans, 1990-92; legal counsel, environ. scientist Larry Walker Assocs., Davis, 1993—99; counsel Beveridge & Diamond LLP, Sacramento, 1999—2000; counsel, ptnr. Downey Brand, Sacramento, 2000—. Com. mem. Barrataria-Terrebonne Nat. Estuary, Baton Rouge, 1992; chair clean water subcom. Assn. Calif. Water Agys., 1998—; pres. Riparian Improvement Orgn., 1994-96. Contbr. articles to profl. jours. Com. mem. La. Safe Drinking Water Task Force, Baton Rouge, 1990-92; working group mem. La. Solid Waste Regulations Com., Baton Rouge, 1991-92. Roscoe Hogan Environ. Law Essay winner Assn. Trial Lawyers Am., Toronto, 1991; recipient Martin Luther King Jr. Pub. Svc. award U. Calif.-Davis Law Sch., 1990, Lexis Excellence in Writing award, 1990. Mem. ABA, Riparian Improvement Orgn. (incorporator, pres. 1994-96), Assn. Calif. Water Agys. (legal affairs and water quality coms.). Avocations: dance, aqua aerobics, dressage. Administrative and regulatory, Environmental, Natural resources. Home: 39302 Granite Bay Pl Davis CA 95616-7000 Office: Downey Brand LLP 555 Capitol Mall 10th Fl Sacramento CA 95814

THORNBURG, LACY HERMAN, federal judge; b. Charlotte, N.C., Dec. 20, 1929; s. Jesse Lafayette and Sarah Ann (Ziegler) T.; m. Dorothy Todd, Sept. 6, 1953; children— Sara Thornburg Evans, Lacy Eugene, Jesse Todd, Alan Ziegler. AA, Mars Hill Coll., 1950; BA, U. N.C., 1951, JD, 1954. Bar: U.S. Dist. Ct. (we. dist.) N.C. Practiced law, Webster, N.C., 1954-67; superior ct. judge State of N.C., 1967-83, atty. gen, 1985-92; emergency judge N.C. Superior Ct., Webster, 1993-94; mem. Nat. Indian Gaming Commn., 1994-95; judge U.S. Dist. Ct. for N.C., Asheville, 1995—. Mem. staff Congressman Taylor, Sylva, N.C., 1960, Congressman David Hall, Sylva, 1959-60; mem. N.C. Ho. of Reps., 1961-65; mem. N.C. Cts. Commn., N.C. Criminal Code Commn., Capital Planning Commn., Raleigh. Chmn. Jackson County Bd. of Health, Sylva, 1965-84; commr. Tryon Palace, New Bern, N.C. Served with U.S. Army, 1947-48. Mem. Lions, Masons, Shriners. Democrat. Avocations: fly fishing, skeet shooting. Office: US Dist Ct 200 US Courthouse 100 Otis St Asheville NC 28801-2611

THORNBURGH, DICK (RICHARD L. THORNBURGH), lawyer, former United Nations official, former United States attorney general, former governor; b. Pitts., July 16, 1932; s. Charles Garland and Alice (Sanborn) T.; m. Virginia Walton Judson, Oct. 12, 1963; children: John, David, Peter, William. B in Engring., Yale, 1954; LLB, U. Pitts., 1957; hon. degrees, from 31 colls. and univs. Bar: Pa. 1958, U.S. Supreme Ct. 1965, D.C. 1998. Atty. Kirkpatrick & Lockhart, Pitts., 1959-69, 77-79, 87-88, 91-92, 94—; U.S. atty. for Western Pa. Pitts., 1969-75; U.S. asst. atty. gen. Dept. Justice, Washington, 1975-77; gov. State of Pa., Harrisburg, 1979-87; dir. Inst. Politics John F. Kennedy Sch. Govt., Harvard U., 1987-88; U.S. atty. gen. Washington, 1988-91; under-sec.-gen. for adminstrn. and mgmt. UN, N.Y.C., 1992-93. Del. Pa. Constl. Conv., 1967-68; vice chair World Com. on Disability; bd. dirs. Elan Corp. plc, Nat. Mus. Indsl. History, Gettysburg Nat. Battlefield Mus. Found. Mem. Coun. Fgn. Rels., Am. Law Inst.; trustee Urban Inst., U. Pitts. Fellow Am. Bar Found.; mem. Am. Judicature Soc. Republican. Office: Kirkpatrick & Lockhart LLP 1800 Massachusetts Ave NW, 2nd Flr Washington DC 20036-1800

THORNLOW, CAROLYN, law firm administrator, consultant; b. Kew Gardens, N.Y., May 25, 1954; 1 child, Johanna Louise Ramm. BBA magna cum laude, Baruch Coll., 1982. Gen. mgr. Richard A. Ramm Assocs., Levittown, N.Y., 1972-78; adminstr. Tunstead Schechter & Torre, N.Y.C., 1978-82, Cowan Liebowitz & Latman, P.C., N.Y.C., 1982-84, Rosenberg & Estis, P.C., N.Y.C., 1984-85; contr. Finkelstein, Borah, Schwartz, Altschuler & Goldstein, P.C., N.Y.C., 1986-92; pres. Concinnity Svcs., Hastings, N.Y., 1984—. Instr. introduction to law office mgmt. seminars Assn. Legal Adminstrs., N.Y.C., 1984. Editor: The ABA Guide to Professional Managers in the Law Office, 1996; contbr. numerous articles to profl. jours. Mem. ABA (bd. dirs. law practice mgmt. div. 2000-01), N.Y. Assn. Legal Adminstrs. (v.p. 1982-83), Internat. Assn. Legal Adminstrs. (asst. regional v.p. 1983-84, regional v.p. 1984-85), Nat. Soc. Tax Profls. (cert. tax profl.), Am. Mgmt. Assn., Inst. Cert. Profl. Mgrs. (cert.), ABA, Inst. Cert. Mgmt. Accts., Mensa, Beta Gamma Sigma, Sigma Iota Epsilon. Home and Office: 445 Broadway Hastings On Hudson NY 10706 E-mail: cthornlow@concinnityservices.com., lawbucks@aol.com., CRTinNY@aol.com.

THORNTON, D. WHITNEY, II, lawyer; b. Miami, Fla., Oct. 17, 1946; s. Dade Whitney and Hilda (Bryan) T.; m. Jane Collis, Nov. 27, 1971; children: Bryan Whitney, Elizabeth Jane, Virginia Anne. BA, Washington and Lee U., 1968, JD cum laude, 1970. Bar: Va. 1970, D.C. 1976, U.S. Ct. Appeals (4th cir.) 1978, U.S. Supreme Ct. 1980, Calif. 1987, U.S. Ct. Appeals (9th cir.) 1987. Atty. Naval Air Sys. Command, Dept. Navy, Washington, 1970-73; asst. counsel to comptr. Dept. Navy, 1973-74, asst. to gen. counsel, 1974-76; assoc. Sullivan & Beauregard, Washington, 1976-77, ptnr., 1977-81, Bowman, Conner, Touhey & Thornton, Washington, 1981-83; pres. Continental Maritime Industries, Inc., San Francisco, 1983-87; ptnr. Dempsey, Bastianelli, Brown & Touhey, San Francisco, 1987-91, Seyfarth Shaw, San Francisco, 1992—2003; of counsel Lockhead Martin Space and Strategic Missiles, Sunnyvale, Calif., 2003—. Contbr. articles to profl. jours. Mem. ABA (pub. contract law sect., chmn. suspension and debarment com. 1977), FBA (vice chmn. govt. contracts coun., Disting. Svc. award 1981), Washington Golf and Country Club (Arlington, Va.). Republican. Methodist. Construction, Government contracts and claims, General civil litigation. Office: Lockheed Martin Space & Strategic Missiles ORG 26-01 Bldg 157 1111 Lockheed Martin Way Sunnyvale CA 94089-3504 E-mail: whit.thornton@lmco.com.

THORNTON, J. PAT, lawyer; b. Omaha, Nov. 23, 1931; s. James Earl and Edna (Bridges) T.; m. Mary Lou Emery, Oct. 18, 1969; children: Earl Timothy, Bryan Patrick. BS in Fin., Creighton U., 1954, JD, 1959. Bar: Nebr. 1959. Law clk. Ct. Appeals, Omaha, 1961-63; assoc. Haney, Walsh & Wall, Omaha, 1963-64; pvt. practice Omaha, 1964—. Sec. Stellar Design Inc., Omaha, 1981-94, J&P Inc., Omaha, 1977-78. Lt. U.S. Infantry, 1954-56. Mem. Nebr. Bar Assn., Nebr. Trial Lawyers Assn., Jay Busters. Republican. Roman Catholic. Avocations: coaching basketball, golf, hiking, travel. General civil litigation, Corporate, general, Personal injury (including property damage). E-mail: ThorntonJP@aol.com.

THORNTON, JOHN WILLIAM, SR., lawyer; b. Toledo, July 3, 1928; s. Cletus Bernard and Mary Victoria (Carey) T.; m. Mary Feeley, Mar. 10, 1951; children: John W. Jr., Jane Thornton Mastrucci, Deborah Thornton Hasty, Michael; m. Gabriela Marin, 1994. AB magna cum laude, U. Notre Dame, 1950, LLB summa cum laude, 1956, JD, 1969; postgrad., U. Miami, Coral Gables, Fla. Bar: Fla. 1956, U.S. Dist. Ct. (no., mid. and so. dists.) Fla. 1956, U.S. Ct. Appeals (5th cir.) 1956, U.S. Ct. Appeals (11th cir.) 1982; cert. civil mediator Fla. Supreme Ct., arbitrator Fla. Supreme Ct.; cert. arbitrator AIDA-ARIAS U.S. and Reins. Assn. of Am. Assoc. area def. firm, Miami, Fla.; ptnr. Dixon, DeJarnette, et al, 1956-67, Stephens, Demos, Magill & Thornton, Miami, 1968-76; pvt. practice Thornton & Mastrucci, P.A. and predecessor firm, Miami, 1976—. Chairperson legis. com. Fla. Med. Malpractice Claims Coun., Inc., 1984—, legis. and adminstrv. code rep. on hosp. risk mgrs. qualifications, rules and liability and nursing home rules and liability, 1986—; lectr. Fla. tort ins. law hosp. and physician series on risk mgmt. Am. Inst. Med. Law, U. Miami Sch. Trial Techniques; lectr. South Fla. Hosp. Risk Mgmt. Soc.; legis. atty. Fla. Sch. Bd. Assn.; presenter legal, healthcare and ins. industry confs.; lectr. in field. Contbr. articles to profl. publs. Mem. Dade County Sch. Bd., 1967—. Lt. USN, 1950-53, Korea. Mem. ABA (vice chmn. torts and ins. practice sect., chair sr. issues law com., torts and ins. practice sect., 1999—, active sr. lawyers divsn. 2001—), ATLA, Internat. Assn. Def. Counsel (chmn. med. malpractice com. 1975-76, chmn. profl. errors and omissions com. 1987—, chair excess, surplus lines and reins. law com. 1988), Def. Rsch. Inst. (chmn. practice and procedure com. 1976-77), Fedn. Def. and Corp. Counsel (chmn. auto and casualty ins. sect. 1987—, chmn. legis. com. 1984-88, vice chmn. ethics com. 1990-94, mem. task force on nursing home liability 1998—), Fla. Def. Lawyers Assn. (bd. dirs. 1976), Internat. Assn. Ins. counsel (chmn. med. malpractice 1972-74, com. 1975—, def. counsel com. 1976-91, reins. excess and surplus lines com. 1980-99, spkr. and presenter 1966-2003), Dade County Def. Bar Assn., Fed. Ins. Corp. Counsel (casualty ins. law com. 1972—, med. malpractice com. 1974—, excess surplus and reins. com. 1976—, publs. com. 1976-87), Maritime Law Assn. U.S., Fla. Def. Lawyers Assn. (bd. dirs., chmn. legis. com. 1974-77), Internat. Law Soc., Broward County Bar Assn., Am. Judicature Soc., Am. Health Care Assn., Congress Romanian Ams., Coral Gables Club, Ocean Reef Club, Riviera Country Club, Sapphire Valley Country Club. Roman Catholic. Environmental, Insurance, Personal injury (including property damage). Office: 7898 SW 57th Terr Miami FL 33143 Fax: 305-668-0400. E-mail: J.ThorMas@aol.com.

THORNTON, RAY, state supreme court justice, former congressman; b. Conway, AR, July 16, 1928; s. R.H. and Wilma (Stephens) Thornton; m. Betty Jo Mann, Jan. 27, 1956; children: Nancy, Mary Jo, Stephanie. BA, Yale U., 1950; JD, U. Ark., 1956. Bar: Ark. 1956, U.S. Supreme Ct. 1956. Pvt. practice in, Sheridan and Little Rock, 1956—70; atty. gen., 1971—73; mem. 93d-95th Congresses from 4th Ark. dist.; exec. dir. Quachita Bapt. U./Henderson State U. Joint Ednl. Consortium, Arkadelphia, Ark., 1979—80; pres. Ark. State U., Jonesboro and Beebe, 1980—84, U. Ark. Sys., Fayetteville, Little Rock, Pine Bluff, Monticello, 1984—89; mem. 102nd-104th Congresses from 2d Ark. dist., 1991—96; assoc. justice Ark. Supreme Ct., 1997—. Chmn. Ark. Bd. Law Examiners, 1967—70; del. 7th Ark. Constl. Conv., 1969—70. Chmn. pres.'s devel. coun. Harding Coll., Searcy, Ark., 1971—73. Served with USN, 1951—54, Korea. Mem.: AAAS (chmn. com. on sci., engring. and pub. policy 1980). Office: 625 Marshall St, 120 Justice Building Little Rock AR 72201

THORNTON, WILLIAM P., JR., lawyer; b. Wilkes-Barre, Pa., June 27, 1961; s. William P. and Mary Ellen Thornton; m. Katherine Killeen Eagen; children: W. Evan, M. Emma. BA, Dickinson Coll., 1983; JD, Villanova U., 1991. Bar: Pa. 1996. Atty., shareholder Stevens & Lee, Reading, Pa., 1989—. Bd. dirs. Reading Royals Charities, 2002, Cath. Social Agy. Named to Sports Hall of Fame, Dickinson Coll., 2002. Mem.: St. Thomas More Soc. (treas., dir. 1999—). Democrat. Roman Catholic. Avocation: golf. Securities, Commercial, consumer (including collections, credit). Office: Stevens and Lee 111 N 6th St Reading PA 19603 Office Fax: 610-988-0813. Business E-Mail: fernando.casanueva@garrigues.com.

THORNTON-ERMES, LUCIE ELIZABETH, lawyer; b. Mena, Ark., Apr. 26, 1957; d. Oris Bryant and Carolyn (Cox) T.; m. Frank E. Lamothe (div.); children: Victorine Day Lamothe, Julien Guy Lamothe; m. Peter O. Thornton-Ermes, Oct. 6, 2001. BA, Centenary Coll., Shreveport, La., 1979; JD, Tulane U., 1982. Bar: La. 1983, U.S. Dist. Ct. (ea. dist.) La. 1983. Law clk. 1st Cir. Ct. Appeals, Baton Rouge, 1982-83; assoc. Law Offices of Charles E. Hamilton III, New Orleans, 1983-85; law clk. Civil Dist. Ct. New Orleans, 1985-92; pvt. practice New Orleans, 1992-2000; ptnr. Hemelt and Foshee, LLC, 2000—. Mem. editorial bd. La. Appellate Ct. Handbook, 1982—. Mem. La. Adv. Com. on Child Care Facilities and Child Placing Agys., 1994-98; active Jr. League of New Orleans, 1988-98, Greater Covington Jr. Svc. League, 1994-96; trustee La. Children's Mus., 1992-96; bd. dirs. Save Our Cemeteries, 1992-96, Youth Svc. Bd., 1997-99; vestrywoman Christ Episcopal Ch., 1996-98, dir. Christian Formation, 1999-2000; sustainer Jr. League New Orleans; bd. dirs. Lewisberg Civic Assn., 1995-2000; bd. rep. Christ Episcopal Sch. to Parent's Coun. New Orleans. Mem. ABA (litig. sect.), La. State Bar Assn. (CLE com. 1986-87, bench-bar liaison com. 1991-94, ho. of dels. 2003), Chi Omega. Republican. Insurance, Personal injury (including property damage). Home: 126 Live Oak Mandeville LA 70448 Office: Hemelt and Foshee LLC 717 W 17th Ave Covington LA 70433

THORPE, NORMAN RALPH, lawyer, automobile company executive, retired air force officer; b. Carlinville, Ill., Oct. 17, 1934; s. Edwin Everett and Imogene Midas (Hayes) T.; m. Elaine Frances Pritzman, Nov. 1, 1968; children: Sarah Elizabeth Chisholm, Carrie Rebecca Keough. AB in Econs., U. Ill., 1956, JD, 1958; LLM in Pub. Internat. Law, George Washington U., 1967. Bar: Ill. 1958, Mich. 1988, U.S. Supreme. Ct. 1969. Commd. 2d lt. USAF, 1956, advanced through grades to brig. gen., 1983; legal advisor U.S. Embassy, Manila, 1969-72; chief internat. law hdqrs. USAF, Washington, 1972-77; staff judge adv. 21st Air Force, McGuire AFB, N.J., 1977-80, USAF Europe, Ramstein AB, Fed. Republic Germany, 1980-84; comdr. Air Force Contract Law Ctr., Wright-Patterson AFB, Ohio, 1984-88; mem. legal staff, group counsel GM Def. and Power Products Gen. Motors Corp., Detroit, 1988—98; counsel GMR&D Planning and Fuel Cell Activity, 1998—2003; ret., 2003. Legal advisor Dept. of Def. Blue Ribbon Com. on Code of Conduct, 1975; USAF del. Internat. Aero. and Astronautical Fedn., Budapest, 1983; adj. prof. U. Dayton Sch. Law, 1986-87; partnership counsel U.S. Advanced Battery Consortium, Legal Advisor U.S. Coun. Automotive Rsch., Chrysler Corp., Ford Motor Co., GM, 1990-2002. Contbr. articles to profl. jours. Staff mem. Commn. on Police Policies and Procedures, Dayton, 1986; trustee Dayton Philharm. Orch., 1987-88; mem. bd. visitors U. Ill. Law Sch., 2002-. Recipient Disting. Svc. medal Legion of Merit. Mem. ABA (chmn. com. internat. law sect. 1977-80, coun. mem. pub. contract law sect. 1986-88, chmn. com. pub. contract law sect. 1988-95, sec. pub. contract law sect. 2000-01, vice chair 1999-2000, chair-elect 2000-01, chair 2001-02), Air Force Assn., Dayton Coun. on World Affairs, Army/Navy Club, Detroit Econ. Club. Republican. Avocations: music, piano, gardening. Commercial, contracts (including sales of goods; commercial financing), Government contracts and claims, Private international. Home: 498 Abbey Rd Birmingham MI 48009-5618 Office: 300 Renaissance Ctr Detroit MI 48243-1401

THORSON, STEVEN GREG, lawyer; b. Van Nuys, Calif., Feb. 7, 1948; s. Robert G. and Ruth C. T.; m. Patricia Lynn LaPointe, Aug. 3, 1974; 1 child, Kai Johannes. BA, St. Olaf Coll., 1977; JD, Hamline U., 1980. Bar: Minn. 1980, U.S. Dist. Ct. Minn. 1980, U.S. Tax Ct. 1980, U.S. Ct. Appeals (8th cir.) 1980. Pres. Thorson & Berg, Maple Grove, Minn., 1990-99; with Barna, Guzy & Steffen, Ltd. Attys. at Law, Mpls., 1999—. Lectr. continuing legal edn., 1986—; apptd. to Minn. State Bar Assn. Commn. on Unauthorized Practice of Law, 1990-92; atty. for Columbus Twp. (Anoka County), 1981-96; mem. residential real estate com. Minn. State Bar Assn., 1992—. Mem. ch. coun. Peace Luth. Ch. Named a Super Lawyer, Minn. Law and Politics Mag., 2000, 2001, 2002; named one of Minn. Super Lawyers, Mpls./St. Paul mag., 1998, 2000, 2001, 2002, 2003. Mem. ABA, Minn. State Bar Assn. (real property coun., chair publs. com. 2001—), Hennepin County Bar Assn. (chmn. purchase agreement com. 1986-88), Anoka County Bar Assn. (pres. real estate sect. 1988). Avocation: alpine and nordic skiing. Land use and zoning (including planning), Municipal (including bonds), Property, real (including real estate development, water). Home: 12071 Norway St NW Minneapolis MN 55448-2243 Office: 400 Northtown Fin Plz 200 Coon Rapids Blvd NW Ste 400 Minneapolis MN 55433-5894 E-mail: sthorson@bgslaw.com.

THOYER, JUDITH REINHARDT, lawyer; b. Mt. Vernon, N.Y., July 29, 1940; d. Edgar Allen and Florence (Mayer) Reinhardt; m. Michael E. Thoyer, June 30, 1963; children: Erinn Thoyer Rhodes, Michael John. AB with honors, U. Mich., 1961; LLB summa cum laude, Columbia U., 1965. Bar: N.Y. 1966, D.C. 1984. Law libr. U. Ghana, Accra, Africa, 1963-64; assoc. Paul, Weiss, Rifkind, Wharton & Garrison, N.Y.C., 1966-75, ptnr., 1975—. Mem. TriBar Opinion Com., 1995—. Bd. visitors Law Sch. Columbia U., N.Y.C., 1991—; bd. dirs. Women's Action Alliance, N.Y.C., 1975-89, pro bono counsel, 1975-97; mem. Women's Coun. Dem. Senatorial, campaign com., 1993-97; organizing com. Alumnae Columbia Law Sch., 1996—. Recipient medal of excellence, Columbia Law Sch., 2003. Mem. N.Y. County Lawyers Assn. (mem. securities and exchs. com. 1976-98), Assn. of Bar of City of N.Y. (mem. securities regulation com. 1976-79, mem. recruitment of lawyers com. 1980-82, mem. com. on mergers, acquisitions and corp. control contests 1996—). Home: 1115 5th Ave Apt 3B New York NY 10128-0100 Office: Paul Weiss Rifkind Et Al 1285 Ave of Americas New York NY 10019-6028

THRAILKILL, DANIEL B. lawyer; b. Sept. 21, 1957; BSBA, U. Ark., 1979; JD, Univ. Ark., 1981. Bar: Ark. 1982, Tex. 1988, U.S. Dist. Ct. (eas. and we. dists.) Ark. 1982, U.S. Dist. Ct. (ea. dist.) Okla. 1995, U.S. Ct. Appeals (8th cir.) 1983, U.S. Supreme Ct. 1985. Ptnr. Page, Thrailkill & McDaniel, P.A., Mena, Ark., 1981—. Assoc. prof., lectr. rich Mountain C.C.; assoc. justice Ark. Supreme Ct., 1996—; city atty. Cities of Mena and Hatfield. Mem.: ABA, ATLA, Ark. Trial Lawyers Assn., Ark. Bar Assn. (bd. govs., tenured del.), Lions Club, Phi Alpha Delta. Methodist. General practice, Personal injury (including property damage), Property, real (including real estate development, water). Home: 200 Craig St Mena AR 71953-2427 Office: Page Thrailkill & McDaniel 311 DeQueen St Courthouse Sq W Mena AR 71953

THRALL, GORDON FISH, publishing executive; b. Jamestown, N.Y., July 28, 1923; s. Clyde Lowell and Beulah Mae (Fish) T.; m. Betty Jane Roberts, Sept. 24, 1964; 1 dau., Jenifer Jane. A.B. in History and Polit. Sci., Alfred U., 1949; J.D., Baylor U., 1953. Bar: Tex. 1953, U.S. Supreme Ct. 1957, D.C. 1958, U.S. Ct. Appeals (D.C. cir.) 1958, U.S. Ct. Mil. Appeals 1958, U.S. Dist. Ct. (ea. dist.) Tex. 1976, U.S. Ct. Appeals (5th cir.) 1986. Law clk. U.S. Dist. Ct. (ea. dist.) Tex., 1953-54; asst. prosecutor Dallas County Dist. Atty., 1954-55; assoc. firm Phinney & Hallman, Dallas, 1955-56; asst. Tex. Atty. Gen., 1957; adviser, examiner ICC, Washington, 1957-59; asst. gen. counsel Tex. State Bar, Austin, 1959-61; county atty. Reagan County, Big Lake, Tex., 1961-72; ptnr. Norman, Thrall, Angle, Guy & Day, L.L.P., Jacksonville, Tex., 1972—2002; v.p. Heflin & Thrall Lang. Publs., Inc., 2002-- . Mem. exec. com. Tex. Baptist Gen. Conv., 1965-70, adminstrv. bd., 1991-95; deacon So. Bapt. Ch.; chmn. Permian Basin dist. Concho Valley council Boy Scouts Am., Big Lake, 1965-66; chmn. Jacksonville United Fund Drive, 1987, pres., 1989; pres. Cherokee County Health Facilities Devel. Corp., 1982—; v.p., bd. dirs. Travis Towers Retirement Facility, Jacksonville, 1980-2002; co-trustee Summers A. Norman Found., 1988-2002; vol. Nan Travis Meml. Hosp. Found. Bd., 1994—; pres. bd. visitors Jacksonville Coll., 1998—. Mem. Tex. State Bar, Tex. Bar Found. (vice chmn. UPL com. 1964), Big Lake C. of C. (pres. 1963, 67), Jacksonville C. of C. (pres. 1979), Cherokee Country Club, (dir. 1981-83), Kiwanis (pres. 1978, lt. gov. div. 34 1982), Big Lake Lions (pres. 1969), Masons (32 degree). Republican. Home: 702 Fort Worth St Jacksonville TX 75766-2610 Office: Heflin and Thrall Lang Publs Inc PO Box 1724 Jacksonville TX 75766 Office Fax: 903-589-2689. Business E-Mail: jheflin@language-publications.com.

THRO, WILLIAM EUGENE, lawyer, university administrator; b. Elizabethtown, Ky., Nov. 8, 1963; s. Ernest Guernsey and Joan (Young) T.; children: Sandra Lucinda Grace Edwards-Thro, William Thomas Daniel Edwards-Thro, Noah Christopher James Edwards-Thro. BA, Hanover Coll., 1986; MA, U. Melbourne, Australia, 1988; JD, U. Va., 1990. Bar: Ky. 1990, Colo. 1991, Va. 1998, U.S. Dist. Ct. (we. dist.) Ky. 1990, U.S. Dist. Ct. Colo. 1991, U.S. Ct. Appeals (6th and 10th cirs.) 1991, U.S. Ct. Appeals (3d cir.) 1993, U.S. Supreme Ct. 1993, U.S. Ct. Appeals (4th cir.) 1997, U.S. Dist. Ct. (ea. dist.) Va. 1998, U.S. Dist. Ct. (we. dist.) Va. 1998, U.S. Ct. Appeals (D.C. cir.) 1999, U.S. Bankruptcy Ct. (ea. and we. dists.) Va. 1999, U.S. Dist. Ct. (ea. dist.) Ky. 2003. Jud. clk. Judge Ronald E. Meredith, U.S. Dist. Ct. (we. dist.) Ky., Louisville, 1990-91; asst. atty. gen. State of Colo., Denver, 1991-97, Commonwealth of Va., Richmond, 1997-99; gen. counsel Christopher Newport U., Newport News, Va., 2000—; dep. state solicitor Commonwealth Va., 2002—. Mem. authors' com. West's Edn. Law Reporter, St. Paul, 1992—. Author: Why You Cannot Sue State U: A Guide to Sovereign Immunity, 2001; mem. editl. bd., Jour. Coll. and Univ. Law, 2000—; contbr. articles to scholarly jours. Mem. gen. counsel adv. bd. NCAA, 2001—. U.S. Senate Youth scholar Hearst Found., 1982; Harry S Truman scholar Truman Scholarship Found., 1984, Rotary Internat. Ambassadorial scholar, Melbourne, 1987. Mem. Va. Bar Assn., Ky. Bar Assn., Nat. Assn. Coll. and Univ. Attys., Federalist Soc., Nat. Eagle Scout Assn., Inst. for Justice, Human Human Action Network, Honorable Order of Ky. Cols, Rotary Club Oyster Point (Va.). Republican. Presbyterian. Federal civil litigation, Constitutional, Education and schools. Office: Christopher Newport U 1 University Pl Newport News VA 23606 E-mail: wthro@cnu.edu.

THROWER, RANDOLPH WILLIAM, lawyer; b. Tampa, Fla., Sept. 5, 1913; s. Benjamin Key and Ora (Hammond) T.; m. Margaret Munroe, Feb. 2, 1939; children: Margaret MacCary, Patricia Barmeyer, Laura (Mrs. David T. Harris, Jr.), Randolph William, Mary (Mrs. George B. Wickham). Grad., Ga. Mil. Acad., 1930; BPh, Emory U., 1934, JD, 1936. Bar: Ga. bar 1935, D.C. bar 1953. Partner Sutherland, Asbill & Brennan, Atlanta, Washington, 1947-69, 71—. Commr. internal revenue, 1969-71; Lectr. bar, legal meetings; spl. agt. FBI, 1942-43; mem. Arthur Andersen & Co. Bd. of Rev., 1974-80, Nat. Council on Organized Crime, mem. exec. com., 1970-71 Past pres. Ga., Met. Atlanta mental health assns.; chmn. City of Atlanta Bd. Ethics 1981-93; past trustee Emory U., Clark Coll.; past chmn., trustee Wesleyan Coll.; bd. govs. Woodward Acad.; past chmn. bd. visitors Emory U. Served as capt. USMCR, 1944-45. Mem. Atlanta Legal Aid Soc. (past pres.), Emory U. Alumni Assn. (past pres.), ABA (chmn. spl. com. on survey local needs 1971-78, past chmn. sect. taxation, mem. ho. of dels. 1964-66, 74-89), Ga. Bar Assn., Atlanta Bar Assn. (past pres.), Am. Bar Found. (dir. 1980-88, pres. 1986-88, medal 1993), Am. Law Inst., Atlanta Lawyers Club (past pres.), U.S. Claims Ct. Bar Assn. (pres. 1987-88), Phi Delta Phi. Clubs: Commerce (Atlanta), Capital City (Atlanta), Piedmont Driving (Atlanta). Republican. Methodist. Estate planning, Estate taxation, Taxation, general. Home: 2240 Woodward Way NW Atlanta GA 30305-4043 Office: Sutherland Asbill & Brennan Ste 2300 999 Peachtree St NE Atlanta GA 30309 E-mail: rwthrower@sablaw.com.

THURBER, JOHN ALEXANDER, lawyer; b. Detroit, Nov. 9, 1939; s. John Levington and Mary Anne (D'Agostino) T.; m. Barbara Irene Brown, June 30, 1962; children: John Levington II, Sarah Jeanne. AB in History, U. Mich., 1962, JD, 1965. Bar: Ohio 1965, Mich. 1968. Assoc. Hahn, Loeser and Parks, Cleve., 1965-67, Miller, Canfield, Paddock and Stone, Birmingham, Mich., 1967-73; sr. mem. Miller, Canfield, Paddock and Stone, P.L.C., Troy, Mich., 1974—. Treas. Birmingham Community House, 1971-73; pres. Birmingham Village Players, 1983-84; bd. dirs. Oakland Parks Found., Pontiac, Mich., 1984—, pres., 1989-92; mem. capital com. Lighthouse Found.; trustee Oakland Land Conservancy. Avocations: reading, theater, walking, sports. Office: Miller Canfield Paddock & Stone PLC 840 W Long Lake Rd Ste 200 Troy MI 48098-6358 E-mail: thurberj@millercanfield.com.

THURBER, PETER PALMS, lawyer; b. Detroit, Mar. 23, 1928; s. Cleveland and Marie Louise (Palms) T.; m. Ellen Bodley Stites, Apr. 16, 1955; children: Edith Bodley, Jane Chenoweth, Thomas, Sarah Bartlett BA, Williams Coll., 1950; JD, Harvard U., 1953. Bar: Mich., 1954. With Miller, Canfield, Paddock and Stone, Detroit, 1953-93, of counsel, 1994—. Trustee McGregor Fund, Detroit, 1979—. Bd. dirs. Detroit Symphony Orch., Inc., 1974-93; trustee Community Found. for Southeastern Mich., 1990-2000, Coun. Mich. Founds., 1991-2000. With U.S. Army, 1953-55. Fellow Am. Bar Found.; mem. ABA, Mich. Bar Assn. Clubs: Country of Detroit (Grosse Pointe Farms, Mich.). Roman Catholic. Avocations: reading; traveling; athletics. Home: 28 Provencal Rd Grosse Pointe Farms MI 48236-3038 Office: Miller Canfield Paddock & Stone 150 W Jefferson Ave Ste 2500 Detroit MI 48226-4416

THURMAN, ANDREW EDWARD, lawyer; b. Raleigh, N.C., May 11, 1954; s. William Gentry and Peggy Lou (Brown) T.; m. Patricia Thurman, May 19, 1979 (dec. 1989); children: Gentry Brown, Harrison Beauchamp, Andrew Guilford; m. Tracy Fletcher, Nov. 16, 1991; 1 child, Spencer Lee. BA, Columbia U., 1976; JD, Coll. William and Mary, 1979; MPH, U. Okla., 1984. Bar: Va. 1979, Okla. 1980, U.S. Ct. Appeals (10th cir.) 1981, U.S. Supreme Ct. 1985, Pa. 1988. Staff atty. Dept. of Human Services, Oklahoma City, 1979-80; counsel State of Okla. Teaching Hosps., Oklahoma City, 1980-84; mem. Miller, Dollarhide, Dawson & Shaw, Oklahoma City, 1984-87; ptnr. Berkman, Ruslander, Pohl, Lieber & Engel, Pitts., 1988-89; of counsel Buchanan Ingersoll, Pitts., 1989; sr. v.p. and gen. counsel Forbes Health System, Pitts., 1989-96; sr. counsel Allegheny Health Edn. & Rsch. Found., Pitts., 1997-98; dep. gen. counsel Allegheny U. Hosps. West, 1998-99; asst. gen. counsel Western Pa. Allegheny Health Sys., 1999—2002; assoc. prof. Carnegie-Mellon U., 2000—; pvt. practice, 2002—; assoc. prof. U. Pitts., 2003—. Pres. Council of Neighborhood Assns., Oklahoma City, 1984, Lincoln Terr. Neighborhood Assn., Oklahoma City, 1984; trustee Rader Trust, Oklahoma City, 1980—; treas. Bd. dirs. State Okla. Tchg. Hosps. Found., Oklahoma City, 1984-87, Newman Meml. Hosp., 1983-87, Willowview Hosp., Spencer, Okla., 1985-87, Allegheny U. Med. Ctrs., 1997—, AUMC/Cannonsburg Ambulance Svc., 1997—, Allegheny U. Hosps. West, 1998—, Diversified Health Group, 1998-99, Allegheny Med. Practices Network, 1999—, Allegheny Speciality Practice Network, 1999—; chair HCWP Ethics Task Force, 1993-2000. Fellow Am. Health Lawyers Assn.; mem. St. Anthony Hall Club of N.Y.C. (pres. 1976), Rivers Club. Democrat. Presbyterian. Avocation: reading detective novels. Health. Home: 106 Richmond Dr Pittsburgh PA 15215-1039 Office: 1151 Freeport Rd # 391 Pittsburgh PA 15238 E-mail: andy@thrumanhealthlaw.com., andy@thurmans.net.

THURMOND, GEORGE MURAT, judge; b. Del Rio, Tex., Oct. 22, 1930; s. Roger H. and Day (Hamilton) T.; m. Elsiejean Davis, June 27, 1959; children: Carolyn Day, Georganna, Sarah Gail. BA, U. of the South, 1952; JD, U. Tex., 1955. Bar: Tex. 1955. Ptnr. Montague & Thurmond, Del Rio, 1955-69; judge Tex. Dist. Ct. (63rd dist.), Del Rio, 1970-2000, sr. judge, 2000—. Presiding judge 6th Adminstrv. Region, Del Rio, 1983-87; chmn. jud. sect. State Bar Tex., 1988-89. Editor: U. Tex. Law Review, 1955. Rep. Tex. Ho. of Reps., 1955-58. Mem. ABA, Tex. Bar Assn. Democrat. Episcopalian. Avocations: jogging, traditional jazz, model railroading. Office: 243 W Strickland St Del Rio TX 78840-5729 E-mail: gmthur@delrio.com.

THURMOND, J. STROM, JR., lawyer; b. S.C., Oct. 18, 1972; BA in English, U. S.C., 1995, grad. in Law, 1998. Bar: S.C. Ptnr. Strom, Young & Thurmond, LLP, Columbia, SC, 1998—99; asst. solicitor S.C. 2d Jud. Cir., 1999—2001; U.S. atty. Dist. S.C., 2001—. Chmn. dist. law enforcement coordinating com. Dist. S.C., mem. atty. gen.'s adv. coun. violent crime subcom. Office: First Union Bldg 1441 Main St Ste 500 Columbia SC 29201*

THURSWELL, GERALD ELLIOTT, lawyer; b. Detroit, Feb. 4, 1944; s. Harry and Lilyan (Zeitlin) T.; m. Lynn Satovsky, Sept. 17, 1967 (div. Aug. 1978); children: Jennifer, Lawrence; m. Judith Linda Bendix, Sept. 2, 1978 (div. May 1999); chldren: Jeremy, Lindsey. LLB with distinction, Wayne State U., 1967. Bar: Mich. 1968, N.Y. 1984, D.C. 1985, Colo. 1990, Ill. 1992, U.S. Dist. Ct. (ea. dist.) Mich. 1968, U.S. Ct. Appeals (7th cir.) 1968, U.S. Supreme Ct. 1994. Student asst. to U.S. Atty. Eas. Dist. Mich., Detroit, 1966; assoc. Zwerdling, Miller, Klimist & Maurer, Detroit, 1967-68; st. prnt. The Thurswell Law Firm, Southfield, Mich. Arbitrator Am. Arbitration Assn., Detroit, 1969—; mediator Wayne County Cir. Ct., Mich., 1983—, Oakland County Cir. Ct. Mich., 1984—, also facilitator, 1991; twp. atty. Royal Oak Twp., Mich., 1982—; lectr. Oakland County Bar Assn. People's Law Sch., 1988. Pres. Powder Horn Estates Subdivsn. Assn., West Bloomfield, Mich., 1975, United Fund, West Bloomfield, 1976. Arthur F. Lederly scholar Wayne State U. Law Sch., 1965; Wayne State U. Law Sch. grad. profl. scholar, 1965, 66. Mem. ATLA (treas. Detroit met. chpt. 1986-87, v.p. 1989-90, pres. 1991-93), Mich. Bar Assn. (investigator/arbitrator grievance bd., atty. discipline bd., chmn. hearing panel), Mich. Trial Lawyers Assn. (legis. com. on govtl. immunity 1984), Detroit Bar Assn. (lawyer referral com., panel pub. adv. com. jud. candidates), Oakland County Bar Assn., Skyline Club (Southfield). State civil litigation, Personal injury (including property damage). Office: The Thurswell Law Firm 1000 Town Ctr Ste 500 Southfield MI 48075-1221

THYNESS, ERIK, lawyer; b. Oslo, May 30, 1961; s, Paul and Ellen Marie Thyness; m. Ingunn Almas, Dec. 30, 1989; children: Cathinka, Christian, Carl. Cand. jur., U. Oslo, 1987. Bar: Norway 1989. Inhouse counsel Norsk Hydro ASA, Oslo, 1988-93; assoc. judge Soer-Gudbrandsal Dist. Ct., Lillehammer, Norway, 1989-90; gen. counsel Hafslund Nycomed ASA, Oslo, 1993-96; ptnr. Wirsholm Mellbye & Bech, Oslo, 1996—. Contbg. author: Cross-Border Mergers in Europe, 1989; contbg. author: Mergers and Acquisitions, 1998. Lt. col. Norwegian Army, 1980—. Mem. Norwegian Bar Assn. Mergers and acquisitions, Securities, Corporate taxation. Office: Wiersholm Mellbye & Bech Ruseloekkveien 26 Oslo 0251 Norway Fax: 47 21 02 10 01. E-mail: erik.thyness@wiersholm.no.

TIBBLE, DOUGLAS CLAIR, lawyer; b. Joliet, Ill., May 26, 1952; BA, DePaul U., 1974; JD, Syracuse U., 1977, MPA, 1978. Bar: Ill., U.S. Dist. Ct. (no. dist.) Ill., U.S. Ct. Appeals (7th cir.), U.S. Supreme Ct. Ptnr. McBride, Baker & Coles, Oakbrook Terrace, Ill., 1996—. Mem. ABA, DuPage County Bar Assn., Chgo. Bar Assn. General civil litigation, Commercial, contracts (including sales of goods; commercial financing), Construction. Office: McBride Baker & Coles 1 Mid America Plz Ste 1000 Oakbrook Terrace IL 60181-4710 E-mail: tibble@mbc.com.

TICE, DOUGLAS OSCAR, JR., federal bankruptcy judge; b. Lexington, N.C., May 2, 1933; s. Douglas Oscar Sr. and Lila Clayton (Wright) T.; m. Janet N. Capps, Feb. 28, 1959 (div. Sept. 1976); children: Douglas Oscar III, Janet E.; m. Martha Murdoch Edwards, June 8, 1996. BS, U. N.C., 1955, JD, 1957. Bar: N.C. 1957, U.S. Ct. Appeals (4th cir.) 1964, Va. 1970, U.S. Dist. ct. (ea. dist.) Va. 1976, U.S. Bankruptcy Ct. (ea. dist.) Va. 1976. Exec. sec. N.C. Jud. Coun., Raleigh, 1958-59; assoc. Baucom & Adams, Raleigh, 1959-61; trial atty. Office Dist. Coun., IRS, Richmond, Va., 1961-70; corp. atty. Carlton Industries, Inc., Richmond, 1970-75; ptnr. Hubard, Tice, Marchant & Samuels, P.C., Richmond, 1975-87; judge U.S. Bankruptcy Ct. (ea. dist.), Richmond, Norfolk, Alexandria, Va., 1987-99, chief judge, 1999—. Co-author: Monument & Boulevard, Richmond's Grand Avenues, 1996; contbr. articles to profl. jours. Vice pres. Richmond Pub. Forum, 1976-80, com. chmn. Richmond Forum, Inc., 1986-2001; past pres. Richmond Civil War Roundtable, mem., 1965—; bd. dirs. Epilepsy Assn. Va., Inc., 1976-87. Capt. USAR, 1957-66. Mem. ABA, Va. Bar Assn., City of Richmond Bar Assn., Am. Bankruptcy Inst., Nat. Conf. Bankruptcy Judges, So. Hist. Assn., Va. Hist. Soc., Old Dominion Sertoma (pres. Richmond chpt. 1967), Am. Inn of Ct. Home: 5 Foxmere Drive Richmond VA 23233 Office: US Bankruptcy Ct 1100 E Main St Ste 339 Richmond VA 23219-3538 E-mail: home:dotice@aol.com., bus.douglas_tice@vaeb.uscourts.gov.

TICER, MARK ALLEN, lawyer; b. Oklahoma City, Feb. 14, 1956; s. James A. Ticer and Barbara P. Shaffer; m. Diedra Cecily Shull, Mar. 22, 1986; children: Adrienne, Aubrey. BS with honors, Okla. State U., 1979; JD, So. Meth. U., Dallas, 1985. Bar: Tex., U.S. Ct. Appeals (5th cir.), U.S. Dist. Ct. (no., so., and ea. dists.) Tex. Assoc. DeHay & Blanchard, Dallas, 1985—86, Coakley & Assocs., Dallas, 1986—89, Law Office James Barber, Dallas, 1989—90; pvt. practice Dallas, 1990—. Mem.: ATLA, Dallas Bar Assn., Dallas Trial Lawyers Assn., Tex. Trial Lawyers Assn. Avocations: running, basketball. Insurance, Personal injury (including property damage), Professional liability. Office: 3300 Oak Lawn Ave Ste 700 Dallas TX 75219

TICHENOR, PATRICIA E.M. lawyer; b. St. Paul, Mar. 29, 1970; d. Edward J. and Mary A. Tichenor. BA in English, Hofstra U., 1992; JD, Am. U., 1996. Bar: Calif. 1996, D.C. 1997, Minn. 1999, Va. 2001. Staff atty. U.S. Dept. Agr., Washington, 1996—2001; pvt. practice Leesburg, Va., 2001—. Estate planning, Family and matrimonial, Criminal. Office: Ste 212 7 E Market St Leesburg VA 20176 E-mail: tichenorlaw@aol.com.

TIERNEY, BETTY THORNE, lawyer; b. East Prairie, Mo., Apr. 26, 1965; d. Troy Mc and Shirley Jeanette Latamondeer Thorne; m. Kevin James Tierney, Jan. 14, 1995; 2 children, Timothy Nicholas, Jordan Elizabeth. BA in Polit. Sci., Ctrl. Meth. Coll., 1987; JD, Washington U., 1990. Bar: Mo. 1990, Ill. 1991, U.S. Dist. Ct. (ea. dist.) Mo. 1991, U.S. Dist. Ct. (so. dist.) Ill. 1993, U.S. Ct. Appeals (7th cir.) 1993, U.S. Ct. Appeals (5th cir.) 1995, U.S. Ct. Appeals (11th cir.) 1998, U.S. Ct. Appeals (8th cir.) 1999, U.S. Ct. Appeals (6th cir.) 2000, U.S. Ct. Appeals (3d cir.) 2002. Assoc. Suelthaus & Kaplan, Clayton, Mo., 1990-92; counsel The May Dept. Stores Co., St. Louis, 1992-2000, sr. counsel, 2000—. Mem. Bar Assn. Met. St. Louis. Democrat. Roman Catholic. Avocations: reading, crafts, sewing, movies, exercising. Federal civil litigation, General civil litigation, State civil litigation. Office: The May Dept Stores Co 611 Olive St Ste 1750 Saint Louis MO 63101-1721

TIERNEY, KEVIN JOSEPH, lawyer; b. Lowell, Mass., Dec. 13, 1951; s. Joseph Francis and Esther Rowena T. BS cum laude, Bowdoin Coll., 1973; JD, U. Maine, 1976. Bar: Maine 1976. Atty. Union Mutual Life Ins. Co., Portland, Maine, 1976-80, asst. counsel, 1980, 2d v.p., counsel, 1980-84, 2d v.p., counsel, corp. sec., 1984-86, UNUM Corp., Portland, 1986-89, v.p., corp. counsel, sec., 1989-91, gen. counsel, sr. v.p., sec., 1991-99; atty. in pvt. practice Falmouth, Maine, 1999—. Bd. dirs. Pine Tree Alcoholism Treatment Ctr., Maine, 1977-84, So. Regional Alcoholism and Drug Abuse Coun., Maine, 1982-85; mem. radiation therapy tech. adv. com. So. Me. Vocat. Tech. Inst., 1985; trustee Portland Symphony Orch., 1990-99; trustee, treas. Falmouth Med. Libr. Mem. ARIAS-U.S., Assn. Life Ins. Counsel, Maine State Bar Assn., Cumberland County (Maine) Bar Assn., Assn. of Life Ins. Counsel. Corporate, general, Insurance, Alternative dispute resolution.

TIERNEY, MICHAEL EDWARD, lawyer; b. N.Y., July 16, 1948; s. Michael Francis and Margaret Mary (Creamer) T.; m. Alicia Mary Boldt, June 6, 1981; children: Colin, Madeleine. BA, St. Louis U., 1970, MBA, JD, St. Louis U., 1978. Bar: Mo. Assoc., law clk. Wayne L. Millsap, PC, St. Louis, 1977-80; staff atty. Interco. Inc., St. Louis, 1980-83; textile divsn. counsel Chromalloy Am. Corp., St. Louis, 1984-87; v.p., sec. P.N. Hirsch & Co., St. Louis, 1983-84; sr. counsel, asst. sec. Jefferson Smurfit Corp., St. Louis, 1987-92, v.p., gen. counsel, sec., 1993-99, Kinexus Corp., St. Louis, 1999—2002. Adv. bd. St. Louis Area Food Bank, 1980—. U.S. Army Security Agy., 1970-73. Mem. Racquet Club St. Louis, Old Warson Country Club. Republican. Roman Catholic. Avocations: sailing, squash. Corporate, general, Mergers and acquisitions, Securities. Home: 10 Twin Springs Ln Saint Louis MO 63124-1139 Address: 18500 Edison Ave Chesterfield MO 63005-3629

TIETIG, EDWARD CHESTER, lawyer; b. Hollywood, Calif., Dec. 5, 1928; s. Chester and Tunis Dickerson Tietig; children: Mark, Brian, Erik, Kris. BBA, postgrad., U. Cin., 1951; JD, U. Mich., 1956. Bar: U.S. Supreme Ct. 1957, Fla., Mich. 1972, U.S. Dist. Ct. (no., ctrl., and so. dists.) Fla., U.S. Tax Ct. 1969, U.S. Ct. Appeals (5th cir.) 1972, U.S. Ct. Appeals (11th cir.) 1972. Pvt. practice, Palm Bay, Fla., 1956—; pres., broker Farm & Grove Realty, Valkaria, Fla., 1963—; pres. Tropstock Nursery, Miami, Fla., 1978-91, Eureka Field Nursery, Miami, 1979-91, Emerald Lake Devel. and Constrn. Co., Kissimmee, Fla., 1971—. Vis. lectr. U. Miami Law Sch., Coral Gables, Fla., 1972-74. Lt. s.g. USNR, 1951-63. Mem. ACLU (bd. dirs., past pres. 1991), Brevard County Bar Assn., Ad Astra Soc., Eau Gallie Yacht. Civil rights, Constitutional, Environmental. Office: 1326 Malabar Rd SE Ste 1 Palm Bay FL 32907-2502

TIFFANY, JOSEPH RAYMOND, II, lawyer; b. Dayton, Ohio, Feb. 5, 1949; s. Forrest Fraser and Margaret Watson (Clark) T.; m. Terri Robbins, Dec. 1, 1984. AB magna cum laude, Harvard U., 1971; MS in Internat. Relations, London Sch. Econs., 1972; JD, U. Calif., Berkeley, 1975. Bar: U.S. Dist. Ct. (no. dist.) 1975, U.S. Dist. Ct. (ea. dist.) 1977, U.S. Ct. Appeals (9th cir.) 1982. Assoc. Pillsbury, Madison & Sutro, San Francisco, 1975-82, ptnr., 1983-2001, Pillsbury Winthrop LLP, San Francisco, 2001—. Mem. ABA (antitrust, intellectual property, litigation sects.), Calif. Bar Assn., Harvard Club. Federal civil litigation, State civil litigation, Antitrust. Office: Pillsbury Winthrop LLP 2550 Hanover St Palo Alto CA 94304-1115 E-mail: jtiffany@pillsburywinthrop.com.

TIGANI, BRUCE WILLIAM, lawyer; b. Wilmington, Del., May 10, 1956; s. J. Vincent Jr. and Josephine C. (DeAngelis) T.; m. Janice Rowe, Sept. 25, 1982; children: Jessica Lynne, Bruce William Jr. Student, Georgetown U., 1974-75; BBS, U. Del., 1978; JD, Villanova U., 1981. Bar: Del. 1981, Pa. 1982, U.S. Dist. Ct. Del. 1982, U.S. Dist. Ct. (ea. dist.) Pa. 1982, U.S. Tax Ct. 1982. Assoc. Lord & Mulligan, Media, Pa., 1981-84, resident atty. Wilmington, 1984-87, ptnr., 1987-88; mng. ptnr. Werb, Tigani, Hood & Sullivan, Wilmington, 1988-99, Tigani & Hood LLP, Wilmington, 2000—. Del. to IRS, Mid. Atlantic Regional liason. Mem. lay adv. bd. The Little Sisters of Poor; active Rep. Com. of State Del. Mem. ABA, Del. State Bar Assn. (chmn. tax sect. 1991-92, real estate sect., chair trusts and estates sect. 1997-98, lectr. bus. and tax seminars), Wilmington Tax Group (chmn. 1994-95), Del. State C. of C. (commerce tax com.), Estate Planning Coun. Del., Inc. (bd. dirs. 1993-95), Concord Country Club, Univ. and Whist Club Wilmington, Blue and Gold Club. Avocations: golf, softball. Estate planning, Property, real (including real estate development, water), Taxation, general. Office: Tigani & Hood LLP PO Box 1471 1801 Mellon Bank Ctr 919 Market St Wilmington DE 19899-1471 E-mail: btigani@TiganihoodLaw.com.

TIGER, IRA PAUL, lawyer; b. Bklyn., Jan. 31, 1936; s. Sidney and Rebecca (Frankel) T.; m. Rosalind Silverman, July 4, 1957 (dec. Nov. 1972); children: Ruth, Lori; m. Ann Mae Gersh, May 5, 1974; stepchildren: Jimmie, Randy, Richard Riesenberg. BS in Econs., U. Pa., 1956, JD magna cum laude, 1959. Bar: Pa. 1960, U.S. Dist. Ct. (ea. dist.) Pa. 1960, U.S. Ct.

Appeals (3d cir.) 1960, U.S. Supreme Ct. 1971, U.S. Ct. Appeals (7th cir.) 1996. Law clk. 3d cir., 1959-60; assoc. Schnader, Harrison, Segal & Lewis, Phila., 1960-67, ptnr., 1968—2002, chmn. litigation dept., 1986-90, chmn. standing com. on profl. conduct, 1992—, sr. counsel, 2003—. Judge pro tem Phila. Ct. Common Pleas, 1994—; mediator U.S. Dist. Ct. (ea. dist.) Pa., 1991—. Rsch. editor U. Pa. Law Rev., 1958-59. Pres. Temple Sinai Synagogue, 1989-91, Elkins Park House Coun., 1996-98; mem. Planning Adv. Bd. Upper Dublin Twp., 1982-87, mem. ednl. adv. com., 1976-78; legal counsel Phila. Jr. C. of C., 1963-64, bd. dirs., 1962-66, sec. Jewish campus activities bd., 1971-73. Mem. ABA, Am. Judicature Soc., Inst. Jud. Adminstrn., Phila. Bar Assn. (chmn. fed. cts. com. 1985), Lawyers Club Phila., Order of Coif (exec. com. Pa. chpt. 1981-83), Beta Alpha Psi, Beta Gamma Sigma. Democrat. Antitrust, Federal civil litigation, State civil litigation. Office: Schnader Harrison 1600 Market St Ste 3600 Philadelphia PA 19103-7286 Office Fax: 215-972-7262. E-mail: itiger@schnader.com.

TIGHE, AUSTIN, lawyer; b. Jersey City, N.J., Feb. 13, 1966; m. Libby Barnard, Oct. 21, 1995; 1 child, Ethan McKinley. B. Liberal Arts, U. of Iowa, 1988; JD, U. of Houston, 1991. Bar: Tex. 1991, Ill. 1995, U.S. Dist. Ct. (so. dist.) Tex. 1991, U.S. Dist. Ct. (we. dist.) Tex. 1994, U.S. Dist. Ct. (no. dist.) Tex. 1993, U.S Dist. Ct. (ea. dist.) Tex. 1991, U.S. Dist. Ct. (no. dist.) Ill. 1995. Assoc. Fulbright & Jaworski, Houston, 1991—94; spl. counsel Katten, Muchin & Zavis, Chgo., 1994—95; sr. assoc. Weil, Gotshal & Manges, Houston, 1995—98; ptnr. Brobeck, Phleger & Harrison, Austin, Tex., 1998—2002, Feazell, Rosenthal & Watson, Austin, 2002—. Bd. of directors Justice for Children, Houston, 2000—. Contbr. Mem.: Austin Young Lawyers Assn. (co-chair of aspiring youth com. 2000—01), Travis County Bar Assn. (co-chair of people's law sch. com. 2002—), Tex. State Bar Coll. (chair people's law sch. com. 2002—). Personal injury (including property damage), Commercial, consumer (including collections, credit), General civil litigation, Consumer Class Action. Office: Feazell Rosenthal & Watson 6601 Vaught Ranch Rd Ste 200 Austin TX 78730 Office Fax: 512-474-2667. E-mail: atighe@frw-law.com.

TIKOSH, MARK AXENTE, lawyer; b. Arad, Banat, Romania, Aug. 17, 1955; arrived in U.S., 1981; s. Axente and Elena Ticosh; m. Mary Victoria Rotarescu, Sept. 10, 1979. BBA in Acctg. summa cum laude, Calif. State U., Fullerton, 1989; JD, U. of the Pacific, 1992, LLM, 1993. Bar: Calif. 1993. Acct., auditor II Orange County Probation Dept., 1984-88; pvt. practice Sacramento, Calif., 1993-94, Long Beach, Calif., 1994—. Cons. U. Banat Acad. Found., Timisoara, Romania, 1997—. Editor: The Transnational Lawyer, 1991. Mem. Town Hall L.A., 2002—. Scholarship McGeorge Legal Edn. Endowment Found., 1989-90, Dana Found., 1992-93. Mem. Calif. State Bar Assn. (estate planning trust and probate law sect.), L.A. County Bar Assn., Cato Inst., Beta Gamma Sigma. Republican. Avocations: travel, history, philosophy. Estate planning, Private international, Probate (including wills, trusts). Office: 800 E Ocean Blvd Ste 104 Long Beach CA 90802-5463

TILEWICK, ROBERT, lawyer; b. N.Y.C., Jan. 16, 1956; s. David and Helen (Fogel) T.; m. Susan Dara Tilewick; children: Naomi Seana, Benjamin Solomon. BA, Columbia U., 1977; JD, Temple U., 1985. Bar: N.Y. 1986, Ct. 1993, U.S. Dist. Ct. (so. and ea. dists.) N.Y. 1988, U.S. Ct. Appeals (2d cir.) 1989, U.S. Dist. Ct. Conn. 1991. Systems analyst, cons. Personnelmetrics, Inc., N.Y.C., 1977-80, 81-82; assoc. Cravath, Swaine & Moore, N.Y.C., 1985-87, Paul, Weiss, Rifkind, Wharton & Garrison, N.Y.C., 1987-91, 96-97, Wiggin & Dana, New Haven, Conn., 1991-96, Kalow, Springut & Bressler, N.Y.C., 1997-99, Graham & James, N.Y.C., 1999—. Co-designer race timing system for N.Y.C. Marathon, 1977-82. NIH grantee Marine Biol. Lab., Woods Hole, Mass, 1980. Mem. ABA, N.Y.C. Bar Assn., Conn. Bar Assn., New Haven Bar Assn., Supreme Ct. Hist. Soc. Avocation: music. Federal civil litigation, General civil litigation. Office: 885 3rd Ave New York NY 10022-4834

TILGHMAN, CARL LEWIS, lawyer; b. Detroit, Aug. 3, 1944; s. Clifford Raymond and Alma (Gillikin) T.; m. Nancy Ann Huff, Aug. 21, 1965; children: Jason Andrew, Amanda Carol. Student, Beaufort H.S., 1962; BA, Wake Forest U., 1966, JD, 1969. Bar: N.C. 1969. Asst. U.S. atty. U.S. Dept. Justice, Raliegh, N.C., 1973-76; U.S. atty. U.S. Dist. Ct. (ea. dist.) N.C., Raleigh, 1976-77; sole practice Beaufort, N.C., 1977-97; apptd. spl. Superior Ct. judge, 1997—2002; tax adminstr. Carteret County, 2003—. Vice chmn. Carteret County Commn., Beaufort, 1984—, vice chm. 1984-88, re-elected 1988, chmn., 1988-92. Served to capt. JAGC, U.S. Army, 1969-73. Mem. N.C. Bar Assn., Carteret County Bar Assn. (pres. 1983-84) N.C. Assn. County Commn. (bd. dirs.), Coastal Regional Solid Waste Authority (bd. dirs., chmn., 1991-92), Neuse River Coun. of Gov. (pres. 1991-92). Republican. Baptist. Avocations: playing saxaphone, singing. Bankruptcy, State civil litigation, Criminal. Home: RR 1 Box 214 Beaufort NC 28516-9801 Office: Attorney At Law PO Box 748 Beaufort NC 28516-0748

TILLER, LAUREL LEE, lawyer; b. Morton, Wash., Jan. 11, 1938; s. Edgar L. and Edna (Ball) T.; m. Priscilla Sue Prouty, Dec. 22, 1962; children: Peter B., Rachael M. BA, Willamette U., 1960; JD, U. Wash., 1963. Bar: Wash. 1963, U.S. Dist. Ct. (we. dist.) Wash. 1965, U.S. Dist. Ct. (ea. dist.) 1986, U.S. Ct. Appeals (9th cir.) 1982. Asst. atty. gen. State of Wash., Olympia, 1963-65; pvt. practice Tiller, Wheeler & Tiller, Centralia, Wash., 1965—. Mcpl. ct. judge City of Centralia, 1968-78. Mem. Wash. Bar Assn. (numerous coms. 1965—). General civil litigation, Probate (including wills, trusts), Property, real (including real estate development, water). Home: PO Box 58 Centralia WA 98531-0058 Office: Tiller Wheeler & Tiller Corner Of N Rock E Pine Centralia WA 98531

TILLEY, NORWOOD CARLTON, JR., federal judge; b. Rock Hill, S.C., 1943; s. Norwood Carlton and Rebecca (Westbrook) T. BA, Wake Forest U., 1966, JD, 1969. Bar: N.C. 1969, U.S. Dist. Ct. (middle dist.) N.C. 1971. Law clk. to Hon. Eugene A Gordon, U.S. Dist. Judge Middle Dist. N.C., 1969-71; asst. U.S. atty. Mid. Dist. N.C., Greensboro, 1971-73, U.S. atty., 1974-77, U.S. dist. judge Durham, 1988—; ptnr. Osteen, Adams, Tilley & Walker, Greensboro, 1977-88. Instr. Wake Forest U. Sch. Law, 1980. Office: US Dist Ct PO Box 3443 Greensboro NC 27402-3443

TILLINGHAST, DAVID ROLLHAUS, lawyer; b. N.Y.C., Feb. 25, 1930; s. Charles Carpenter and Josephine Dorothy (Rollhaus) T.; m. Phyllis Van Horn, Sept. 24, 1955 (div. Jan. 1984); m. Lisa Sewell, Feb. 25, 1984; children: Gregory Barrett Sewell, Lauren Alexa. AB cum laude, Brown U., 1951; LLB cum laude, Yale U., 1954. Bar: N.Y. 1955, Oreg. 1956, U.S. Supreme Ct. 1978. Assoc. Hughes, Hubbard & Reed, N.Y.C., 1954-55, 57-61, ptnr., 1961-62, 65-90; assoc. King, Miller, Anderson, Nash & Yerke, Portland, Oreg., 1955-57; spl. asst. for internat. tax affairs U.S. Dept. Treasury, Washington, 1962-65; ptnr. Chadbourne & Parke, N.Y.C., 1990-99, Baker & McKenzie, N.Y.C., 1999—. Adj. prof. Sch. Law, NYU, 1977-87; cons. UN Ctr. on Transnat. Corps., 1978-87; reporter Am. Law Inst. Project on Internat. Aspects of U.S. Income Taxation, 1982-91; cons. to reporters Am. Law Inst. Revision of Restatement of Fgn. Relations Law of U.S., 1982-83. Author: Tax Aspects of Internat. Transactions, 1978, 2d edit., 1984; contbr. articles to profl. publs. Mem. transition team Sec. of Treasury W. Michael Blumenthal, 1977. Estab. David L. Tillinghast lectr. on internat. taxation NYU Sch. Law. Mem.: Coun. Fgn. Rels., Tax Forum, Internat. Bar Assn. (vice chmn. com. on taxation bus. law sect. 1984—86), Internat. Fiscal Assn. (v.p. U.S. br. 1983—2000, permanent sci. com. 1983—2000, vice chmn. 1993—95, chmn. 1995—2000), Assn. of Bar of City of N.Y. (chmn. com. on taxation 1981—83). Democrat. Avocations: golf, tennis. Private international, Corporate taxation. Office: Baker & McKenzie 805 3rd Ave New York NY 10022-7513 E-mail: david.r.tillinghast@bakernet.com.

TILLMAN, KAREN SUE, lawyer; b. Garland, Tex., June 21, 1962; d. Franklin Willard and Mary Ruth Wright; m. Massie Tillman, July 2, 1993. BA, Baylor U., 1984, JD, 1986. Bar: U.S. Dist. Ct. (no. dist.) Tex. Law clk. U.S. Bankruptcy Ct., Ft. Worth, 1987-89; assoc. Hill & Gilstrap, Arlington, Tex., 1989-90; litigation atty. Radio Shack Corp., Ft. Worth, 1990—. Mem.: Ft. Worth Club. Republican. Baptist. Avocation: piano. Bankruptcy, General civil litigation. Office: Radio Shack Corp 100 Throckmorton St Ste 1700 Fort Worth TX 76102-2847 E-mail: karen.tillman@radioshack.com.

TILLMAN, MASSIE MONROE, mediator, arbitrator, art gallery owner, retired federal judge; b. Corpus Christi, Tex., Aug. 15, 1937; s. Clarence and Artie Lee (Stewart) T.; m. Karen Wright, July 2, 1993; children: Jeffrey Monroe, Holly. BBA, Baylor U., 1959, LLB, 1961. Bar: Tex. 1961, U.S. Dist. Ct. (no. dist.) Tex. 1961, U.S. Ct. Appeals (5th cir.) 1969, U.S. Supreme Ct. 1969; formerly bd. cert. Personal Injury Trial Law, Tex. Ptnr. Herrick & Tillman, Ft. Worth, 1961-66; pvt. practice, Ft. Worth, 1966-70, 79-87; ptnr. Brown, Herman et al, Ft. Worth, 1970-78, Street, Swift et al, Ft. Worth, 1978-79; U.S. bankruptcy judge Ft. Worth divsn. No. Dist. Tex., 1987-2001; mediator, arbitrator, 2001—. Author: Tillman's Trial Guide, 1970; comments editor, case notes editor; mem. editl. bd. Baylor Law Rev., 1960-61. Fellow Am. Bd. Trial Advocates, Tex. Bar Found.; mem. Ft. Worth/Tarrant County Bar (bd. dirs. 1969-70, v.p. 1970-71), Trial Attys.'s of Am., Nat. Conf. of Bankruptcy Judges, Coll. State Bar Tex., Am. Arbitration Assn. Republican. Baptist. Avocations: competition shotgun shooting, quail hunting. Address: PO Box 20213 Fort Worth TX 76102

TILSON, STEPHEN FREDERICK, lawyer; b. Madison, Tenn., June 18, 1949; s. Charles Everett and Mary Nola (Milburn) T.; m. Dawn Elaine Garverick, June 21, 1975; children— Andrea Linnet, Eric Stephen. B.A. cum laude, Ohio Wesleyan U., 1971; J.D. cum laude, Ohio State U., 1974. Bar: Ohio 1974, U.S. Dist. Ct. (so. and no. dists.) Ohio 1975. Sole practice, Columbus, Ohio, 1974-75; mem. Hottenroth, Garverick & Tilson Co. L.P.A., Galion, Ohio, 1975— . Bd. dirs. Crawford County Community Mental Health Bd., Bucyrus, Ohio, 1979-82, chmn. personnel, 1981-82; bd. dirs. Galion Community Ctr. YMCA, 1982— , Planned Parenthood North Ctrl. Ohio. Fellow Ohio Bar Found.; mem. Ohio State Bar Assn. (bd. govs. 2002—), Crawford County Bar Assn., Am. Bankruptcy Inst., Galion Area C. of C. Democrat. Lutheran. Lodge: Kiwanis. Avocations: Fishing, music, stamp collecting, art. Home: 725 Grove Ave Galion OH 44833-2428 Office: 126 S Market St Galion OH 44833-2626

TIMLIN, ROBERT J. judge; b. 1932; BA cum laude, Georgetown U., 1954, JD, 1959, LLM, 1964. Atty. Douglas, Obear and Campbell, 1960-61, Law Offices of A.L. Wheeler, 1961; with criminal divsn. U.S. Dept. Justice, 1961-64; atty. U.S. Atty. Office (ctrl. dist.) Calif., 1964-66, Hennigan, Ryneal and Butterwick, 1966-67; city atty. City of Corona, Calif., 1967-70; prin. Law Office of Robert J. Timlin, 1970-71, 75-76; ptnr. Hunt, Palladino and Timlin, 1971-74, Timlin and Coffin, 1974-75; judge Mcpl. Ct., Riverside, Calif., 1976-80, Calif. Superior Ct., Riverside, 1980-90; assoc. justice Calif. Ct. Appeals, 1990-94; judge U.S. Dist. Ct. (ctrl. dist.) Calif., L.A., 1994—. Part-time U.S. Magistrate judge Ctrl. Dist. Calif., 1970-74. Served U.S. Army, 1955-57. Mem. Calif. Judges Assn. Office: US Dist Ct Central District of Calif Eastern Divsn 3470 12th St Riverside CA 92501

TIMMER, BARBARA, United States Senate official, lawyer; b. Holland, Mich., Dec. 13, 1946; d. John Norman and Barbara Dee (Folensbee) T. BA, Hope Coll., Holland, Mich., 1969; JD, U. Mich., 1975. Bar: Mich. 1975, U.S. Supreme Ct., 1995. Assoc. McCrosky, Libner, VanLeuven, Muskegon, Mich., 1975-78; apptd. to Mich. Women Commn. by Gov., 1976-79; staff counsel subcom. commerce, consumer & monetary affairs Ho. Govt. Ops. Com., U.S. Ho. of Reps., 1979-82, 85-86; exec. v.p. NOW, 1982-84; legis. asst. to Rep. Geraldine Ferraro, 1984; atty. Office Gen. Counsel Fed. Home Loan Bank Bd., 1986-89; gen. counsel Com. on Banking, Fin. and Urban affairs U.S. Ho. of Reps., Washington, 1989-92; asst. gen. counsel, dir. govt. affairs ITT Corp., Washington, 1992-96; sr. v.p., dir. govt. rels. Home Savs. of Am., Irwindale, Calif., 1996-99; ptnr. Manatt, Phelps & Phillips, Washington, 1999—; gen. counsel MyPrimeTime, Inc., San Francisco, 2000-01; asst. sec. U.S. Senate, 2001—02, asst. sgt. at arms, 2003—. Editor: Compliance With Lobbying Laws and Gift Rule Guide, 1996. Bd. dirs. Women's HIgh Tech Coalition. Named to Acad. of Women Achievers, YWCA, 1993; recipient Affordable Housing award, Nat. Assn. Real Estate Brokers, 1990, Disting. Alumni award, Hope Coll., 2003. Mem. ABA (bus. law sect., electronic fin. svcs. subcom.), FBA (chair, exec. coun. banking law com.), Exchequer Club, Women in Housing and Fin. (bd. dirs. 1992-94, gen. counsel 1994-98), Supreme Ct. Bar Assn., Supreme Ct. Hist. Soc., Mich. Bar Assn., Bar of D.C. Episcopalian. Address: PO Box 21777 Washington DC 20009-9777 Fax: 202-228-4802. E-mail: btimmerdc@earthlink.net.

TIMMINS, EDWARD PATRICK, lawyer; b. Denver, June 8, 1955; s. M. Edward and Elizabeth Jean (Imhoff) T.; m. Mary Joanne Deziel, Dec. 27, 1985; children: Edward Patrick Jr., Joan Deziel. BA with honors, Harvard U., 1977; JD magna cum laude, U. Mich., 1980. Bar: Colo. 1981, U.S. Ct. Appeals (D.C. and 9th cirs.) 1982, U.S. Dist. Ct. Colo. 1984, U.S. Ct. Appeals (10th cir.) 1984. Law clk. to cir. justice U.S. Ct. Appeals (7th cir.), Chgo., 1980-81; trial atty. U.S. Dept. Justice, Washington, 1981-84; asst. U.S. atty. Denver, 1984-88; dir. Otten, Johnson, Robinson, Neff & Ragonetti P.C., Denver, 1985-96; pres. Timmins & Assocs., LLC, Denver, 1996—. Sr. editor U. Mich. Law Rev., 1979-80. Bd. dirs., vice chair Colo. Easter Seals; bd. dirs., chair Denver Pub. Schs. Found.; bd. dirs., chmn. career exploring com. Boy Scouts Am.; bd. dirs. March of Dimes, Am. Ireland Fund. Harvard Nat. scholar, 1976. Mem. ABA, Colo. Bar Assn. (exec. coun. jud. sect.), Colo. Bar Found., Denver Bar Assn., Order of Coif, Friends of Harvard Rowing. Avocations: skiing, golf. Antitrust, General civil litigation, Labor (including EEOC, Fair Labor Standards Act, labor-management relations, NLRB, OSHA). Office: Timmins & Assocs LLC 1625 Broadway Ste 300 Denver CO 80202-4739

TINAGLIA, MICHAEL LEE, lawyer; b. Chgo., Dec. 21, 1952; s. Michael Leo and Josephine (Esposito) T.; m. Lucia Yolando Guzzo, Oct. 14, 1978; children: Laura, Lisa, Elena. BA, Northwestern U., 1974; JD, DePaul U., 1977. Bar: Ill. 1977, U.S. Dist. Ct. (no. dist.) Ill. 1978, U.S. Dist. Ct. (ea. dist.) Wis. 1986. Assoc. Arnold & Kadjan, Chgo., 1977-79; ptnr. Leader & Tinaglia, Chgo., 1979-86; assoc. Laser, Schostok, Kolman & Frank, Chgo., 1987-92; prin. Law Office of Michael Lee Tinaglia Ltd., Chgo., 1992-93, 2000—; equity ptnr. DiMonte & Lizak, Park Ridge, Ill., 1994-99. V.p., corp. counsel Tiara Med. Sys., Inc., Oak Forest, Ill. Contbr. articles to profl. jours. Alderman City Coun., Park Ridge, 1997—, mem. pub. safety com., 1997—, mem. procedures and regulations com. Mem. Ill. Bar Assn., Chgo. Bar Assn. Roman Catholic. Avocations: skiing, guitar. General civil litigation, Labor (including EEOC, Fair Labor Standards Act, labor-management relations, NLRB, OSHA), Pension, profit-sharing, and employee benefits. Office: Law Offices of Michael Lee Tinaglia 161 N Clark St Ste 2550 Chicago IL 60601-3246

TINDALL, ROBERT EMMETT, lawyer, educator; b. N.Y.C., Jan. 2, 1934; s. Robert E. and Alice (McGonigle) T.; children: Robert Emmett IV, Elizabeth. BS in Marine Engring., SUNY, 1955; postgrad., Georgetown U. Law Sch., 1960-61; LLB, U. Ariz., 1963; LLM, NYU, 1967; PhD, City U., London, 1975. Bar: Ariz. 1963. Mgmt. trainee GE, Schenectady, N.Y., Lynn, Mass., Glens Falls, N.Y., 1955-56, 58-60; law clk. Haight, Gardner, Poor and Havens, N.Y.C., 1961; prin., mem. Robert Emmett Tindall & Assocs., Tucson, 1963—; assoc. prof. mgmt. U. Ariz., Tucson, 1969—. Vis. prof. Grad. Sch. of Law, Soochow U., China, 1972, Grad. Bus. Ctr., London, 1974, NYU, 1991—; dir. MBA program U. Ariz., Tucson, 1975-81, dir. entrepreneurship program, 1984-86; investment cons. Kingdom of Saudi Arabia, 1981—; lectr. USIA, Eng., India, Mid. East, 1974; lectr. bus. orgn. and regulatory laws Southwestern Legal Found., Acad. Am. and Internat. Law, 1976-80. Actor cmty. theatres, Schenectady, 1955-56, Harrisburg, Pa., 1957-58, Tucson, 1961-71; appeared in films Rage, 1971, Showdown at OK Corral, 1971, Lost Horizon, 1972; appeared in TV programs Gunsmoke, 1972, Petrocelli, 1974; author: Multinational Enterprises, 1975; contbr. articles on domestic and internat. bus. to profl. jours. Served to lt. USN, 1956-58. Fellow Ford Found., 1965-67; grantee Asia Found., 1972-73. Mem. Strategic Mgmt. Soc., State Bar of Ariz., Acad. Internat. Bus., Screen Actors Guild, Honourable Soc. of Mid. Temple (London), Phi Delta Phi, Beta Gamma Sigma, Assn. Corp. Growth, Royal Overseas League (London). Corporate, general, General practice, Private international. Home: PO Box 42196 Tucson AZ 85733-2196 Office: Coll Bus & Public Adminstrn U Ariz Dept Mgmt & Policy Tucson AZ 85721-0001

TINERO, ELLEN FRIEDMAN, lawyer; b. Santa Monica, Calif., June 16, 1960; d. Ray and Lorraine Friedman; m. Ron Tinero, June 21, 1987. BA, UCLA, 1983; JD, U. West L.A., 1988. Bar: Calif. 89. Legal asst., law clk. Pettit and Martin, L.A., 1976—81, Bet Tzedek Legal Svc., L.A., 1984—86, Levitt and Quinn, L.A., 1988—89; assoc. Law Offices of C. Dicker, L.A., 1989—91; ptnr. Tinero and Carson, L.A., 1992—94, Tinero and Rauch, L.A., 1995—. Mediator L.A. Bar/Cts. Mem.: Am. Cert. Mediators, San Fernando Valley Bar Assn. (mem. exec. com. 1994—), L.A. County Bar (judge pro tem 1992—). Democrat. Jewish. Family and matrimonial. Office: Tinero and Rauch 15915 Ventura Blvd # 203 Encino CA 91436

TINGLE, JAMES O'MALLEY, retired lawyer; b. N.Y.C., June 12, 1928; s. Thomas Jefferson and Mercedes (O'Malley) T. BS, U. Mont., 1950, BA, LL.B., U. Mont., 1952; LL.M., U. Mich., 1953, S.JD, 1958. Bar: Calif. 1959, Mont. 1952, N.Y. 1961. Asst. prof. law U. Mont., Missoula, 1955-56; atty. Shell Oil Co., N.Y.C., 1957-62; assoc. Pillsbury, Madison & Sutro, San Francisco, 1962-68, ptnr., 1969-2000. Author: The Stockholder's Remedy of Corporate Dissolution, 1959; editor: State Antitrust Laws, 1974. Served to 1st lt. USAF, 1953-55. William W. Cook fellow U. Mich. Mem. Mont. Bar Assn., Calif. Bar Assn., ABA Democrat. Antitrust, Legislative, Property licensing.

TIPPETT, JAMES ROYALL, JR., retired lawyer; b. Balt., Nov. 17, 1909; s. J. Royall Tippett and Lillian Valerie Dammann; m. Susan Randall Pincoffs, Apr. 20, 1951; children: James J., Susan Tippett, Ann Tippett Nutt. AB, Johns Hopkins U., 1932; LLB, U. Md., 1936. Assoc. Richard B. Tippett & Sons, Balt., 1936-42; ptnr. Hinkley & Singley, Balt., 1946-65, Clapp Somerville, Balt., 1965-86; of counsel Whiteford, Taylor & Preston, Balt., 1986-96; retired, 1996. With USN, 1942-46, PTO. Decorated Purple Heart, 1945, Bronze Star, 1945. Mem. Trial Table Law Club (pres. 1958). Democrat. Roman Catholic. Home: Baltimore, Md. Died Mar. 6, 2003.

TIPPING, HARRY A. lawyer; b. Bainbridge, Md., Nov. 2, 1944; s. William Richard and Ann Marie (Kelly) T.; m. Kathleen Ann Palmer, July 12, 1969; 1 child, Christopher A. B.A., Gannon U., 1966; J.D., U. Akron, 1970. Bar: Ohio. Asst. law dir. City of Akron, Ohio, 1971-72, chief asst. law dir., 1972-74; ptnr. Gillen, Miller & Tipping, Akron, 1974-77, Roderick, Myers & Linton, Akron, 1977-87; prin., COO Harry A. Tipping Co. L.P.A., Akron, 1987—. Mem. Fairlawn Charter Rev. Commn., 1990—; chmn. bd. Assessment Equalization for the City of Fairlawn, 1989, 90, 97; chmn. Bd. of Tax Appeals, City of Fairlawn, Ohio, 1979-81, mem. merger com., 1980-82. With USCGR, 1966-72. Mem. ABA, Am. Bd. Trial Advocates (advocate), Akron Bar Assn., Ohio Bar Assn., Def. Rsch. Inst., Am. Arbitration Assn., Fedn. Ins. & Corp. Counsel. Republican. Roman Catholic. Clubs: Fairlawn Country (Ohio), Catawaba Island (Ohio), Firestone County (Akron, Ohio). Federal civil litigation, State civil litigation, Labor (including EEOC, Fair Labor Standards Act, labor-management relations, NLRB, OSHA). Office: 1 Cascade Plz Ste 2200 Akron OH 44308-1135

TIPTON, SHEILA KAY, lawyer; b. Martins Ferry, Ohio, Aug. 4, 1951; d. Donald Duane and Elizabeth Julia T.; m. Orrin Frink, Nov. 2, 1973 (div.); m. William Llewellyn Dawe III, Dec. 6, 1985; children: Nicholas Albert, Alexander McNeill; stepchildren: William Llewellyn IV, Christopher Michael. BS, Ohio U., 1973; JD, Drake U., 1980. Bar: Iowa 1980, U.S. Dist. Ct. (no. and so. dists.) Iowa 1980, U.S. Ct. Appeals (8th cir.) 1980. Assoc. Bradshaw, Fowler, Proctor & Fairgrave, P.C., Des Moines, Iowa, 1980-85; ptnr., shareholder Bradshaw, Fowler, Proctor & Fairgrave, Des Moines, Iowa, 1985-99; ptnr. Dorsey & Whitney LLP, 1999—. Presenter in field. Contbr. articles to profl. jours. Pres. Polk County Legal Aid Soc., 1991-92; bd. dirs. Youth Home Mid-Am., 1990-97, sec., 1994-96, v.p., 1996-97; bd. dirs. des Moines Metro Opera Found., 1993-98, pres., 1997-98; bd. dirs. Des Moines Metro Opera, 1991-92, v.p. devel., 1994-95, pres.-elect, 1995-96, pres., 1996-97, v.p. long range planning com., 1998-99; bd. counselors Drake U. Law Sch., 1996-98. Recipient State of Iowa Govs. Vol. award, 1996. Mem. Iowa State Bar Assn. (adminstrv. law sect. coun. 1989-91, mem. bus. law sect. coun. 1993-97, co-chmn. quality life task force 1993-96, chair internat. trade com. 1992-94), Rotary (chmn. scholar com. 1994-95, bd. dirs. 1996—, sgt.-at-arms, 1997-98, sec.-treas. 1998-99, v.p. 1999-2000, pres.-elect 2000-01, pres. 2001-02). Avocations: opera, cooking, reading, golf, travel. Administrative and regulatory, Corporate, general, Utilities, public. Home: 13074 Lincoln Ave Des Moines IA 50325-7413 Office: Dorsey & Whitney LLP 801 Grand Ave Ste 3900 Des Moines IA 50309-2790 E-mail: tipton.sheila@dorseylaw.com., sheilatipton@mchsi.com.

TIRANA, BARDYL RIFAT, lawyer; b. Geneva, Dec. 16, 1937; s. Rifat and Rosamond English (Walling) T.; m. Anne Prather, June 22, 1985; children by previous marriage: Kyra, Amina. AB, Princeton U., 1959; LL.B., Columbia U., 1962. Bar: D.C. 1962, Md. 1986, N.Y. 1986, Va. 1986, Pa. 1992. Trial atty. Dept. Justice, 1962-64; assoc. Amram, Hahn & Sundlun, Washington, 1965-68, ptnr., 1969-72; dir., sec. Exec. Jet Aviation, Inc., Columbus, Ohio, 1970-77, Technics, Inc., Alexandria, Va., 1971-77; ptnr. Sundlun, Tirana & Scher, Washington, 1972-77; dir. def. civil preparedness agy. Dept. Def., Washington, 1977-79, mem. armed forces policy coun., 1977-79; chmn. bd. Technics, Inc., San Jose, Calif., 1979-85; of counsel Silverstein and Mullens, Washington, 1982-84, ptnr., 1984-90; pvt. practice law Washington, 1991—. Mem.-at-large D.C. Bd. Edn., 1970-74; trustee Jimmy Carter Inaugural Trust, Washington, 1977-87; co-chmn. 1977 Presdl. Inaugural Com., 1976-77; mem. exec. adv. coun. Calif. Commn. Indsl. Innovation, 1981-82; pres. China/USA Edn. Fund, Inc., Washington, 1981—; trustee, sec. The Waltz Group of Washington, 2000-; dir. Rocky Mountain Inst., Snowmass Colo., 1982-95. Recipient medal for disting. pub. svc. Dept. Def., 1979, Fuess award Phillips Acad., 1991, Svc. Commendation award YWCA of Nat. Capital Area, 1991. Mem. N.Y.C. Racquet and Tennis Club, D.C. Met. Club. Home: 3550 Tilden St NW Washington DC 20008-3121 E-mail: btirana@aol.com.

TITLE, PETER STEPHEN, lawyer; b. New Orleans, Nov. 24, 1950; s. Harold Benjamin and Beulah (Sterbcow) Title; m. Sheryl Gerber, June 14, 1981. BA, Columbia U., 1972; JD, Tulane U., 1975. Bar: La. 1975, U.S. Dist. Ct. (ea., we., mid. dists.) La., U.S. Ct. Appeals (5th cir.). Assoc. Session, Fishman & Nathan LLP, New Orleans, 1975—81, ptnr., 1982—. Instr. on property Tulane U., 1978; asst. examiner Com. on Admissions to Bar, 1980—88, examiner, 1988—; lectr. on real estate. Author: Louisiana Real Estate Transactions, 1991, 2000. Mem.: ABA, Am. Judicature Soc., Am. Coll. Mortgage Attys., New Orleans Bar Assn. (chmn. title examinations com. 1992—93), La. Bar Assn. (chmn. sect. on trust estates, probate and immovable property law 1983—84), B'nai B'rith, Order of Coif, Phi Delta Phi. Jewish. Bankruptcy, Corporate, general, Property, real (including real estate development, water). Home: 515 Hillary St New Orleans LA 70118-3833 Office: Sessions Fishman & Nathan 201 Saint Charles Ave Fl 35 New Orleans LA 70170-1000

TITLEBAUM, EARL STANLEY, lawyer; b. Boston, Apr. 20, 1935; s. Harry S. and Lillian F. (Payne) T.; m. Sandra R. Titlebaum, Oct. 18, 1956 (div.); children: Glenn B., Mark S., Julie L. Sakkos; m. Caryle H. Titlebaum, June 13, 1999. BS, BA, Northeastern U., Boston, 1958; MBA, Boston Coll., 1964; JD, Suffolk U., 1970. Bar: Mass. 1971. Asst. dist. atty. Suffolk County, Boston, 1972; pvt. practice Framingham, Mass., 1972—, Hopkinton, Mass., 1995—; prin. Greenbaum & Titlebaum, Framingham, 1987-92, Greenbaum, Titlebaum & Estrine, Framingham, 1992-95. Mem. South Middlesex Bar Assn. (bd. dirs. 1992—). Avocations: tennis, golf, gardening. Criminal, Family and matrimonial, General practice. Office: 210 Hayden Rowe St Hopkinton MA 01748-2808

TITLEY, LARRY J. lawyer; b. Tecumseh, Mich., Dec. 9, 1943; s. Leroy H. and Julia B. (Ruesink) T.; m. Julia Margaret Neukom, May 23, 1970; children: Sarah Catherine, John Neukom. BA, U. Mich., 1965, JD, 1972. Bar: Va. 1973, Mich. 1973. Assoc. Hunton & Williams, Richmond, Va., 1972-73, Varnum, Riddering, Schmidt & Howlett, Grand Rapids, Mich., 1973—. Trustee Friends Pub. Mus., 1985—94; bd. dirs. Pub. Mus. Found., 1988—97, pres., 1992—95; bd. dirs. Camp Optimist YMCA, 1993—98, Peninsular Club, 1994—2003, pres., 1997. Mem. ABA, Mich. Bar Assn., Grand Rapids Bar Assn. Corporate, general, Pension, profit-sharing, and employee benefits. Home: 520 Roundtree Dr NE Ada MI 49301-9707 Office: Varnum Riddering Schmidt & Howlett Bridgewater Pl PO Box 352 Grand Rapids MI 49501-0352 E-mail: ljtitley@vrsh.com.

TITLEY, ROBERT L. lawyer; b. Tecumseh, Mich., Dec. 15, 1947; AB, U. Mich., 1970; JD, Duke U., 1973. Bar: Wis. 1973, Mich. 1974. Ptnr. Quarles & Brady, Milw. Mem. editorial bd. Duke Law Jour., 1972-73. Mem. State Bar Mich., State Bar Wis., Order of Coif. Federal civil litigation, Intellectual property, Trademark and copyright. Office: Quarles & Brady LLP 411 E Wisconsin Ave Milwaukee WI 53202-4497

TITONE, VITO JOSEPH, state supreme court justice; b. Bklyn., July 5, 1929; s. Vito and Elena (Ruisi) T.; m. Margaret Anne Viola, Dec. 30, 1956; children: Stephen, Matthew, Elena Titone Hill, Elizabeth. BA, NYU, 1951; JD, St. John's U., 1956, LL.D., 1984. Bar: N.Y. 1957, U.S. Dist. Ct. (ea. and so. dists.) N.Y., 1962, U.S. Supreme Ct. 1964, U.S. Ct. Appeals N.Y. 1985. Ptnr. Maltese & Titone, N.Y.C., 1957-65, Maltese, Titone & Anastasi, N.Y.C., 1965-68; assoc. counsel to pres. pro tem N.Y. State Senate, 1965; justice N.Y. State Supreme Ct, N.Y.C., 1969-75; assoc. justice appellate div. 2d dept., 1975-85; judge N.Y. State Ct. Appeals, Albany, 1985—; of counsel Mintz & Gold LLP, N.Y.C., 1998—. Adj. prof. Coll. S.I., CUNY, 1969-72, St. John's U., Jamaica, N.Y., 1969-85. Bd. editors N.Y. Law Jour., 1999; contbr. articles to law jour. Bd. govs. Daytop Village Inc., N.Y.C.; bd. dirs. Boy Scouts Am.; bd. trustees The Am. Parkinson Disease Assn. With U.S. Army, 1951-53, to col. N.Y. State Guard. Named Citizen of Yr. Daytop Village, N.Y.C., 1969, Disting. Citizen Wagner Coll., S.I., 1983, Outstanding Contbr. Camelot Substance Abuse Network, 1983; recipient citation of merit S.I. Salvation Army Adv. Bd., 1983, Rapollo award Columbian Lawyers Assn., 1983, Disting. Judiciary award Cath. Lawyers Guild Diocese of Bklyn., 1991, Disting. Svc. award N.Y. State Lawyers Assn., Justice William Brennan award N.Y. Assn. Criminal Def. Lawyers, 1993, Life Achievement award N.Y. Conf. Italian Am. State Legislators, 1994, Ellis Island Medal of Honor, 1997, gold medal Bklyn. Bar Assn., 1997. Mem. ABA, N.Y. State Bar Assn., Richmond County Bar Assn., Supreme Ct. Justice Assn., VFW, Am. Legion (past comdr.), Charles C. Pinckney Tribute Def. Assn. of N.Y., Justinian Soc., K.C. Roman Catholic. Office: Mintz and Gold LLP 444 Park Ave S New York NY 10016-7321

TITUS, BRUCE EARL, lawyer; b. N.Y.C., June 5, 1942; BA, Coll. William and Mary, 1964, JD, 1971. Bar: Va. 1971, D.C. 1972, Md. 1984. Asst. dir. torts br., civil divsn. U.S. Dept. Justice, 1971-82; mem. Jones, Waldo, Holbrook and McDonough, Washington; ptnr. Venable, Baetjer and Howard, LLP, McLean, Va., 1986-976; prin. Rees, Broome & Diaz P.C., Vienna, Va., 1997—. Exec. editor William & Mary Law Review, 1970-71. Mem. ABA, Va. State Bar, D.C. Bar, Fairfax Bar Assn. (pres. 1999-2000), Md. State Bar, Phi Delta Phi, Omicron Delta Kappa. Alternative dispute resolution, Professional liability, Construction. Office: Rees Broome & Diaz PC 9th Fl 8133 Leesburg Pike Vienna VA 22182-2706

TITUS, DILJEET, lawyer; b. Gorakhpur, India, Jan. 17, 1966; s. Donald and Veena Titus; m. Anurita Netram (Dec. 22, 1991; children: Shekinah, Diyasannah. BA, St. Stephens Coll., Delhi, India, 1986; LLB, RDVV Coll., Jabalpur, India, 1989. Bar Coun. Delhi, 1989. Ptnr. Singhania & Co., Delhi, 1990-97; pvt. practice Titus & Co., Delhi, 1997—. Texaco India Pvt. Ltd., 1999—, Itochu Transp. Sys. India Pvt. Ltd., 1999—, Marathon Power Acquisitions Pvt. Ltd., 1999—, Fed. Mogul Automotive Products(India) Pvt. Ltd., 1998-, Rebus Software Pvt. Ltd., 1999-, Saba Software India Pvt. Ltd., 1999-. Mem. Supreme Ct. Bar Assn., Bar Coun. Delhi, Internat. Bar Assn, Inter Pacific Bar. Assn., Delhi High Ct. Bar Assn., India Legal Group (founding mem.), Soc. of Indian Law Firms, ICC India (Internat. C.of C.), Indian Coun. Arbitration, Indo Am. C. of C., Co. Law Bd. Bar Assn., India Israel Bus. Alliance, Fedn. Indian Chambers Commerce and Industry (corp. law and governance com.), others. Avocations: current affairs, politics, vintage and utility cars, driving. Office: Titus & Co Titus House R-4 Greater Kailish-I New Delhi 110 048 India E-mail: titusco@vsnl.com.

TITUS, JON ALAN, lawyer; b. Milw., Oct. 6, 1955; s. Mary Elna Irwin; m. Laura Jean Newman, Sept. 5, 1982; children: Katherine, Derek. BA, U. Ariz., 1977; JD, Ariz. State U., 1980. Bar: Ariz. 1980, U.S. Dist. Ct. Ariz. 1980; cert. real estate specialist. Pres. Titus, Brueckner & Berry, P.C., Scottsdale, Ariz., 1980—. Mem. Ariz. Kidney Found., 1984—, pres., 1991-92. Recipient Alumni Achievement award Ariz. State U., 1996. Mem. Ariz. Bar Assn. (chmn. securities regulation sect. 1986-87), Maricopa County Bar Assn., Scottsdale Bar Assn. (dir. 1993-95). Antitrust, Property, real (including real estate development, water), Securities. Office: Titus Brueckner & Berry PC 7373 N Scottsdale Rd Ste B-252 Scottsdale AZ 85253-3513

TITUS, ROGER WARREN, lawyer; b. Washington, Dec. 16, 1941; s. George R. and Margaret (Merithew) T.; m. Catherine Mary Gaughen, Aug. 16, 1961; children: Paula Titus Laboy, Richard Roger, Mark William. BA, Johns Hopkins U., 1963; JD, Georgetown U., 1966. Bar: Md. 1966, D.C. 1966, U.S. Dist. Ct. Md. 1966, D.C. Dist. 1966, U.S. Ct. Appeals (4th cir.) 1966, U.S. Supreme Ct. 1970. Ptnr. Titus & Glasgow, Rockville, Md., 1966-88, Venable, Baetjer & Howard, Rockville, 1988—. Asst. city atty. City of Rockville, 1966-69, city atty., 1970-82; spl. asst. Md. State Bd. of Law Examiners, 1969-72; adj. prof. law Georgetown U., Washington, 1972-78; mem. inquiry com. Atty. Grievance Commn., Annapolis, Md., 1975-80; mem. Trial Cts. Judicial Nominating Commn. Montgomery County, 1979-91; mem. standing com. on rules of practice and procedure Ct. of Appeals of Md., 1989—; mem. Appellate Jud. Nominating Commn., 1991-99. Trustee Suburban Hosp., Inc., Bethesda, Md., 1986-2000, chmn. bd., 1997-2000. Fellow: Am. Acad. Appellate Lawyers, Md. Bar Found. (bd. dirs. 1987—93, v.p. 1990—91, pres. 1991—93), Am. Bar Found., Am. Coll. Trial Lawyers; mem.: ABA (del. 1987—95), Montgomery County Bar Assn. (exec. com. 1983—84), Md. Mcpl. Attys. Assn. (pres. 1975), Am. Judicature Soc. (bd. dirs. 1995—2001), Md. Bar Assn. (sec. 1984—87, pres. 1988—89), Nat. Conf. Bar Pres. (mem. exec. coun. 1990—93), City Tavern Club. General civil litigation, Education and schools, Land use and zoning (including planning). Office: Venable Baetjer & Howard PO Box 1906 1 Church St Ste 500 Rockville MD 20850-4158

TITUS, VICTOR ALLEN, lawyer; b. Nevada, Mo., Sept. 2, 1956; s. Charles Allen and Viola Mae (Cliffman) T.; m. Laraine Carol Cook, Oct. 13, 1974 (div. Feb. 1982); 1 child, Matthew; m. Deborah Diane Carpenter, Apr. 10, 1984; 1 child, Jacquelynn. BS, BA, Ctrl. Mo. State U., 1978; JD, U. Mo., 1981. Bar: N.Mex. 1981, U.S. Dist. Ct. N.Mex. 1981, Mo. 1982, U.S. Ct. Appeals (10th cir. 1983), U.S. Supreme Ct. 1986, Colo. 1989, Ariz. 1995. Lawyer Jay L. Faurot, P.C., Farmington, N.Mex., 1981-83; ptnr. Faurot & Titus, P.C., Farmington, N.Mex., 1983-85; lawyer, sole proprietor Victor A. Titus, P.C., Farmington, N.Mex., 1985—. Arbitrator in civil disputes Alternative Dispute Resolution-Arbitration; liquor lic. hearing officer City of Farmington, 1989-94. Contbr. articles to profl. jours. Adult Behind Youth, Boys & Girls Club, Farmington, 1987—; mem. hosp. adv. bd. San Juan Regional Med. Ctr., Farmington, 1988-93. Recipient San Juan County Disting. Svc. award N.Mex. Bar Assn., 1984; named one of Best Lawyers in Am., 1995-96, 97—. Mem. Assn. Trial Lawyers of Am., N.Mex. Trial Lawyers (bd. dirs. 1983—, pres. 1993-94), State Bar of N.Mex. (disciplinary bd. 1997—, specialization com. 1992-98, legal advt. com. 1990), San Juan County Bar Assn. (pres. 1984), Nat. Assn. Criminal Def. Lawyers (life), Colo. Trial Lawyers. Democrat. Avocation: sports. Criminal, Personal injury (including property damage), Workers' compensation. Home: 5760 Pinehurst Farmington NM 87402-5078 Office: Victor A Titus PC 2021 E 20th St Farmington NM 87401-2516 E-mail: vtitus@advantas.com.

TIVENAN, CHARLES PATRICK, lawyer; b. Newark, Feb. 20, 1954; s. Gerard Charles and Mary Jo (Vogel) T.; m. Mary Katherine Herlihy, Aug. 2, 1980; children: Moire Kathleen, Sean Patrick, Liam Francis, Michala Maureen. BA in Govt., Seton Hall U., 1975, JD, 1980. Bar: N.J. 1982, U.S. Dist. Ct. N.J. 1982, U.S. Supreme Ct. 1995. Law clk. Essex County Prosecutor's Office, Newark, summer 1978, Dwyer Connell & Lisbona, Attys., Montclair, N.J., 1978-79; legal rsch. asst. Inst. Continuing Legal Edn., Newark, 1979; jud. law clk. to Hon. John J. Dios Superior Ct., Newark, 1980—81; assoc. Timothy J. Provost, Atty., Freehold, NJ, 1981—85, Arthur Stein & Assocs., Forked River, N.J., 1985-92; sole practice Bricktown, N.J., 1992—. Mediator, Early Settlement panelist Superior Ct. N.J/Ocean County, Toms River, N.J., 1987—, roster of N.J. Superior Ct. Approved Mediators, 2001—. Mem. juvenile conf. com. South Orange (N.J.) JCC, 1974-81; condemnation commr. Ocean County, Toms River, 1986—; conflict atty. Brick Twp., 1994—, planning bd. atty., 2002—; conflict pub. defender Brick Twp. Mcpt. Ct., Bricktown, 1994—; candidate Brick Twp. Coun., 1992; active Bricktown Dem. Club, trustee 1995-98, v.p. 1999—; commr. Brick Twp. Housing Authority, Brick, 1997-2001, Mcpl. Utilities Authority, Brick, 2001—; atty. advisor Brick Twp. Trial Moot Ct., 1998—. Recipient Cert. of Appreciation, Ocean County Superior Ct., 1987—, certs. of appreciation various orgns., 1985—. Mem. ABA, N.J. Bar Assn. (gen. practice, family law, dispute resolution, real estate/land use sects. 1985—), Am. Trial Lawyers Assn. (N.J. affiliate, lectr. 1985—), Ocean County Bar Assn. (family law, dispute resolution, land use coms. 1985—), KC (3d degree), Epiphany Coun. Roman Catholic. Avocations: reading, current events/politics, running, technology. General practice, Personal injury (including property damage), Property, real (including real estate development, water). Office: Godfrey Lake Profl Bldg 426 Herbertsville Rd Brick NJ 08724-1310 E-mail: cptesq@aol.com.

TOAL, JEAN HOEFER, state supreme court chief justice; b. Columbia, S.C., Aug. 11, 1943; d. Herbert W. and Lilla (Farrell) Hoefer; m. William Thomas Toal; children: Jean Hoefer Eisen, Lilla Patrick. BA in Philosophy, Agnes Scott Coll., 1965; JD, U. S.C., 1968; LHD (hon.) , Coll. Charleston, 1990; LLD (hon.) , Columbia Coll., 1992, The Citadel, 1999, Francis Marion U., 1999, U. S.C., 2000. Bar: S.C. Assoc. Haynsworth, Perry, Bryant, Marion & Johnstone, 1968-70; ptnr. Belser, Baker, Barwick, Ravenel, Toal & Bender, Columbia, 1970-88; assoc. justice S.C. Supreme Ct., Columbia, 1988-00, chief justice, 2000—. Mem. S.C. Human Affairs Commn., 1972-74; mem. S.C. Ho. of Reps., 1975-88, chmn. house rules com., constitutional laws subcom. house judiciary com.; mem. parish coun. and lector St. Joseph's Cath. Ch.; chair S.C. Juvenile Justice Task Force, 1992-94; chair S.C. Rhodes Scholar Selection Com., 1994. Mng. editor S.C. Law Rev., 1967-68. Bd. visitors Clemson U., 1978; trustee Columbia Mus. Art; bd. trustees Agnes Scott Coll., 1996—. Named Legislator of Yr. Greenville News, Woman of Yr., U. S.C., 1989; recipient Disting. Svc. award S.C. Mcpl. Assn., Univ. Notre Dame award, 1991, Algernon Sydney Sullivan award U. S.C., 1991, John W. Williams award, Richland County Bar Assn., 1994, Jean Galloway Bissell award, S.C. Women Lawyers Assn., 1995, Agnes Scott Coll. Outstanding Alumna award, 1991. Mem. ABA, S.C. Women Lawyers Assn., John Belton O'Neill Inn of Ct., Phi Beta Kappa, Mortar Bd., Order of the Coif. Office: Supreme Ct SC PO Box 11330 Columbia SC 29211-2456 E-mail: jtoal@scjd.state.sc.us.

TOBBE, LEONARD LEE, lawyer; b. Louisville, Oct. 4, 1955; s. Leonard T. and Rosemary (Birchler) T.; m. Debra Sue Sanders, July 13, 1985; children: Matthew, Christian, Samuel. BS in Commerce, U. Louisville, 1981, JD, 1984. Bar: Ky. 1984, U.S. Dist. Ct. (ea. dist.) Ky. 1986, U.S. Dist. Ct. (we. dist.) 1993, U.S. Ct. Appeals (6th cir.) 1993. Assoc. Bensinger & Payne, Louisville, 1984; sole practitioner Monticello, Ky., 1985—; asst. county atty. Wayne County, Monticello, Ky., 1995—. Mem. Ky. Assn. Trial Attys., Boy Scout Master. Democrat. Roman Catholic. Bankruptcy, Personal injury (including property damage), Workers' compensation. Home: 301 N Main St Monticello KY 42633-1529 Office: 201 Huffaker St Monticello KY 42633-1463

TOBER, STEPHEN LLOYD, lawyer; b. Boston, May 27, 1949; s. Benjamin Arthur Tober and Lee (Hymoff) Fruman; m. Susan V. Schwartz, Dec. 22, 1973; children: Cary, Jamie. Grad., Syracuse U., 1971, JD, 1974. Bar: N.H. 1974, U.S. Dist. Ct. N.H. 1974, U.S. Supreme Ct. 1978, N.Y. 1981. Assoc. Flynn, McGuirk & Blanchard, Portsmouth, N.H., 1974-79; sole practice Portsmouth, 1979-81; ptnr. Aeschliman & Tober, Portsmouth, 1981-91; prin. Tober Law Offices, P.A., Portsmouth, 1992—. Lectr. Franklin Pierce Law Ctr., Concord, N.H., 1978-80. Contbr. articles to law jours. Mem. Portsmouth Charter Commn., 1976, Portsmouth Planning Bd., 1977-81; del. N.H. Constl. Conv., Concord, 1984; city councilman, Portsmouth, 1977-81. Fellow: Internat. Acad. Trial Lawyers, Am. Bar Found.; mem.: ATLA (gov. 1980—86, chair ea. region 2003—), ABA (state del., chair credentials and admissions com., mem. standing com. on fed. judiciary, chmn. tech. and comms. com.), N.H. Bd. Bar Examiners, N.H. Trial Lawyers Assn. (pres. 1977), N.H. Bar Assn. (pres. 1988—89, chair com. to redraft code of profl. responsibility, Disting. Svc. award 1986, 1994), New Eng. Bar Assn. (bd.dirs. 1988—91). Democrat. Jewish. Avocations: reading, tennis. State civil litigation, General practice, Personal injury (including property damage). Home: 55 T J Gamester Ave Portsmouth NH 03801-5871 Office: Tober Law Offices PA PO Box 1377 Portsmouth NH 03802-1377 Business E-Mail: stober@toberlaw.com.

TOBIAS, CHARLES HARRISON, JR., lawyer; b. Cin., Apr. 16, 1921; s. Charles Harrison and Charlotte (Westheimer) T.; m. Mary J. Kaufman, June 15, 1946; children— Jean M., Thomas Charles, Robert Charles. BA cum laude, Harvard U., 1943, LL.B., 1949. Bar: Ohio 1949. Assoc. firm Steer, Strauss and Adair, Cin., 1949-56; ptnr. firm Steer, Strauss, White and Tobias, Cin., 1956-90; mem. Kepley MacConnell & Eyrich, Cin., 1990-93; mediator U.S. Ct. Appeals (6th crct.), Cin., 1993—. Bd. dirs. Cin. City Charter Com., 1955-75; mem. Wyoming (Ohio) City Council, 1972-77, vice mayor, 1974-77; bd. govs., past chmn. Cin. Overseers, Hebrew Union Coll.-Jewish Inst. Religion; pres. Met. Area Religious Coalition of Cin., 1977-80, Jewish Fedn. Cin., 1972-74; mem. nat. bd. govs. Am. Jewish Com., 1981-87. With USN, 1943-46. Mem. Cin. Bar Assn., Losantiville Country Club. Commercial, contracts (including sales of goods; commercial financing), Corporate, general, Probate (including wills, trusts). Office: US Ct Appeals Potter Stewart US Courthse 5th and Walnut St Cincinnati OH 45202 Home: 2115 Evergreen Ridge Dr Cincinnati OH 45215-5713

TOBIAS, MAX N., JR., judge; b. New Orleans, Sept. 9, 1947; BA, JD, Tulane U., 1971. Bar: La. 1971. Judge Civil Dist. Ct., New Orleans, 1986—2000, La. Ct. Appeal (4th cir.), New Orleans, 2000—. Office: La Ct Appeal 4th Cir 1515 Poydras St 7th Fl New Orleans LA 70112 Office Fax: 504-596-2426.

TOBIAS, PAUL HENRY, lawyer; b. Cin., Jan. 5, 1930; s. Charles H. and Charlotte (Westheimer) T.; 1 child, Eliza L. AB magna cum laude, Harvard U., 1951, LLB, 1958. Bar: Mass. 1958, Ohio 1962. Assoc. Stoneman & Chandler, Boston, 1958-61, Goldman & Putnick, Cin., 1962-75; ptnr. Tobias, Kraus and Torchia, Cin., 1976—. Instr. U. Cin. Law Sch., 1975-77. Author: Litigating Wrongful Discharge Claims, 1987; co-author: Job Rights and Survivor Strategies, a Handbook for Terminated Employees, 1997; contbr. articles to profl. jours. Mem. Cin. Bd. of Park Commrs., 1973-81, Cin. Human Rels. Commn., 1980-84, Cin. Hist. Conservation Bd., 1990-91. With U.S. Army, 1952-54. Mem. ABA, Nat. Employment Lawyers Assn. (founder), Nat. Employee Rights Inst. (chmn.; editor-in-chief Employee Rights quar. 2000-02), Ohio State Bar Assn., Cin. Bar Assn. (past chmn. legal aid com.), Phi Beta Kappa. Labor (including EEOC, Fair Labor Standards Act, labor-management relations, NLRB, OSHA). Home: 15 Hill And Hollow Ln Cincinnati OH 45208-3317 Office: Tobias Kraus Torchia 911 Mercantile Libr Bldg Cincinnati OH 45202

TOBIN, BRUCE HOWARD, lawyer; b. Detroit, July 17, 1955; s. Marshall Edward and Rhoda Maureen (Milman) Tobin; m. Kathleen Tobin; children: Benjamin Stewart, Jenna Rose, Lainie Nicole. BA in Social Sci., Mich. State U., 1978; JD, Detroit Coll. Law, 1982; LLM in Taxation, NYU, 1983. Bar: Mich. 1982, Fla. 1982, U.S. Dist. Ct. (ea. dist.) Mich. 1982, Nebr. 1983, U.S. Tax Ct. 1983. Assoc. Kutak, Rock & Campbell, Omaha, 1983-85; sole practice Bruce H. Tobin PLC, West Bloomfield, Mich., 1985—2002; pvt. practice West Bloomfield, 2002—. Pres. West Bloomfield Sch. Bd. Mem.: ABA, Nebr. Bar Assn., Mich. Bar Assn. (tax. com. 1985—), Fla. Bar Assn. Jewish. Property, real (including real estate development, water), Corporate taxation, Estate taxation. Office: 7001 Orchard Lake Rd Ste 312 West Bloomfield MI 48322-3607 Fax: (248) 851 4303. E-mail: btobin@tobinplc.com.

TOBIN, CRAIG DANIEL, lawyer; b. Chgo., Aug. 17, 1954; s. Thomas Arthur and Lois (O'Connor) T. BA with honors, U. Ill., 1976; JD with high honors, Ill. Inst. Tech., 1980. Bar: Ill. 1980, U.S. Dist. Ct. (no. dist.) Ill. 1980, U.S. Dist. Ct. (no. dist.) Ind. 1986, U.S. Ct. Appeals (7th cir.) 1986, U.S. Supreme Ct. 1987. Trial atty. Cook County Pub. Defender, Chgo., 1980-82; trial atty. homicide task force Pub. Defender, Chgo., 1982-84; ptnr. Craig D. Tobin and Assocs., Chgo., 1984—. Lectr. Ill. Inst. for Continuing Legal Edn., Cook County Pub. Defender, Chgo., 1983, 92, Ill. Pub. Defender Assn., 1987; instr. Nat. Inst. Trial Advocacy. Recipient award for legal excellence Midwest Comm. Coun., 2002; named to Outstanding Young Men in Am., 1985. Mem. ABA, Chgo. Bar Assn., Nat. Assn. Criminal Def. Lawyers. Roman Catholic. Criminal, Personal injury (including property damage). Office: Craig D Tobin & Assocs 3 First National Plz Chicago IL 60602

TOBIN, JAMES MICHAEL, lawyer; b. Santa Monica, Calif., Sept. 27, 1948; s. James Joseph and Glada Marie (Meisner) T.; m. Kathleen Marie Espy, Sept. 14, 1985. BA with honors, U. Calif., Riverside, 1970; JD, Georgetown U., 1974. Bar: Calif. 1974, Mich. 1987. From atty. to gen. atty. So. Pacific Co., San Francisco, 1975-82; v.p. regulatory affairs So. Pacific Communications Co., Washington, 1982-83; v.p., gen. counsel Lexitel Corp., Washington, 1983-85; v.p., gen. counsel, sec. ALC Communications Corp., Birmingham, Mich., 1985-87, sr. v.p., gen. counsel, sec., 1987-88; of counsel Morrison & Foerster, San Francisco, 1988-90, ptnr., 1990—. Mem. ABA, Calif. Bar Assn., Mich. Bar Assn., Fed. Communications Bar Assn. Republican. Unitarian Universalist. Avocations: carpentry, travel. Administrative and regulatory, Communications, Corporate, general. Home: 3134 Baker St San Francisco CA 94123-1805 Office: Morrison & Foerster 425 Market St Ste 3100 San Francisco CA 94105-2482 E-mail: jtobin@mofo.com.

TOBIN, RICHARD WILLIS, II, state government executive; b. Rantoul, Ill., Dec. 14, 1953; s. Richard Willis and Frances Irene (Kesler) T.; m. Deborah Lynne Grile, June 27, 1976; children: Richard Willis III, Michael L., Cathalain M. BS in History with honors, U.S. Air Force Acad., 1976; JD with honors, U. Fla., 1984; LLM with highest honors, George Washington U., 1993. Bar: Fla. 1984, U.S. Ct. Mil. Appeals 1985. Commd. 2d lt. USAF, 1976, advanced through grades to col., 1997; asst. staff Judge Advocate, USAF, Chanute AFB, Ill., 1984-85; area def. counsel USAF, Chanute AFB, 1985-86, dep. staff judge advocate Yokota Air Base, Japan, 1986-89, staff judge adv. Misawa Air Base, Japan, 1989, Altus AFB, Okla., 1989-92, regional counsel cen. region for environ. compliance Dallas, 1993-95, staff judge adv. Luke AFB, Ariz., 1995-97, chief environ. law and litig. divsn. Arlington, Va., 1997—2000, ret., 2000; dep. dir., acting dir., counselor to dir. Ariz. Dept. Environ. Quality, Phoenix, 2000—. Decorated Air Force Commendation medal (2), Air Force Meritorious Svc. medal (4), Legion of Merit. Mem. Order of the Coif. Republican. Presbyterian. Avocation: genealogy.

TOBIN, THOMAS F. lawyer; b. Chgo., Apr. 12, 1929; BSS, John Carroll U., 1951; JD, Loyola U., 1954. Bar: Ill. 1954. Ptnr. Connelly Robert and McGivney, Chgo. Office: Connelly Robert and McGivney 1 N Franklin St Ste 1200 Chicago IL 60606-3447

TOBISMAN, STUART PAUL, lawyer; b. Detroit, June 5, 1942; s. Nathan and Beverly (Porvin) T.; m. Karen Sue Tobisman, Aug. 8, 1965; children: Cynthia Elaine, Neal Jay. BA, UCLA, 1966; JD, U. Calif., Berkeley, 1969. Bar: Calif. 1969. Assoc. O'Melveny & Myers, L.A., 1969-77, ptnr., 1977—. Contbr. articles to profl. jours. Trustee L.A. County Bar Assn., 1983-84. With USN, 1961-63. Fellow Am. Coll. Trust and Estate Counsel; mem. Phi Beta Kappa, Order of Coif. Estate taxation, Estate planning, Probate (including wills, trusts). Office: O'Melveny & Myers LLP 1999 Avenue Of The Stars Los Angeles CA 90067-6035

TODARO, LAURA JEAN, lawyer, city magistrate; b. Neligh, Nebr., June 8, 1956; d. Andrew Robert and Mary Louise (Leenerts) T. BS, U. Ill., 1978; JD, Loyola U., New Orleans, 1981. Bar: La. 1981, U.S. Dist. Ct. (ea. and mid. dists.) La. 1981, U.S. Ct. Appeals (5th cir.) 1981, U.S. Supreme Ct. 1985. Assoc. Dutel & Dutel, New Orleans, 1981-85; ptnr. Todaro & Todaro, Kenner, La., 1985—; city atty. City of Kenner, 1985-87, prosecutor, 1987-88, exec. counsel to Mayor, 1987-90, regulatory prosecutor, 1990-92, city magistrate, 1992—. Mem. Mayor's Adv. Coun. on Law Enforcement and Funding; bd. dirs., treas. Kenner Conv. and Visitors Bur., Inc., 1992. Bd. dirs., sec., met. bd. rep., chmn. maj. gifts campaign Kenner YMCA, 1988; bd. dirs. Met. New Orleans Battered Womens' Program, 1987-92. Mem. La. State Bar Assn., Jefferson Parish Bar Assn., Kenner Profl. Women's Assn., Kenner Bus. Assn. (bd. dirs.), U. Ill. Alumni Assn. (local organizer), Phi Delta Phi. Republican. Roman Catholic. Avocations: sailing, water and snow skiing. State civil litigation, Family and matrimonial. Home: 75 Mckinley St Kenner LA 70065-1010 Office: City of Kenner c/o Clk of Ct 1801 Williams Blvd Kenner LA 70062-6296 also: 909 W Esplanade Ave Ste 202 Kenner LA 70065-2700

TODD, JAMES DALE, federal judge; b. Scotts Hill, Tenn., May 20, 1943; s. James P. and Jeanette Grace (Duck) T.; m. Jeanie M. Todd, June 26, 1965; 2 children. BS, Lambuth Coll., 1965; M Combined Scis., U. Miss., 1968; JD, Memphis State U., 1972. Bar: Tenn. 1972, U.S. Dist. Ct. (we. dist.) Tenn. 1972, U.S. Ct. Appeals (6th cir.) 1973, U.S. Supreme Ct. 1975. Tchr. sci., chmn. sci. dept. Lyman High Sch., Longwood, Fla., 1965-68, Memphis

U. Sch., 1968-72; ptnr. Waldrop, Farmer, Todd & Breen, P.A., 1972-83; cir. judge div. II 26th Jud. Dist., Jackson, Tenn., 1983-85; judge U.S. Dist. Ct. (we. dist.) Tenn., Jackson, 1985-2001, chief judge, 2001—. Recipient Lifetime Achievement award Lambuth U., 2001; named Alumnus of Yr. Lambuth Coll. Alumni Assn., 1985. Fellow Tenn. Bar Found.; mem. Fed. Judges Assn. (bd. dirs. 1998-2002), Fed. Bar Assn., Jackson Madison County Bar Assn. (pres. 1978-79), Dist. Judges Assn. of 6th Cir. (pres. 2000-2001). Methodist. Office: US Dist Ct 111 S Highland Ave Jackson TN 38301-6107

TODD, JOHN DICKERSON, JR., retired lawyer; b. Macon, Ga., June 30, 1912; s. J.D. and Hazel (McManus) T.; m. Mellicent McWhorter, Mar. 7, 1943; children— Rosalind (Mrs. Jack Harding Tedards, Jr.), John D. Student, Va. Mil. Inst., 1930-32; LLB, U. Ga., 1935. Bar: S.C. 1935. With firm Hingson & Todd, 1935-51; partner firm Leatherwood, Walker, Todd & Mann, Greenville, S.C., 1952-2000; sr. partner; judge Greenville City Ct., 1939; atty. County of Greenville, 1948-56; mem. bd. bar examiners State of S.C.; ret. Chmn. S.C. Judicial Study Commn., 1995. Served to maj. AUS, 1941-45. Mem. ABA, Am. Coll. Trial Lawyers, Am. Bar Found., 4th U.S. Cir. Jud. Conf., S.C. Bar Assn. (bd. govs., pres. 1978—), Greenville Jr. C. of C. (pres.), Greenville County Bar (past pres.), Greenville Kiwanis (past pres.), Greenville Country Club (past pres.), Summit Club, Poinsett Club, Phi Delta Phi, Sigma Nu. Baptist. Antitrust, Civil rights, State civil litigation. Home: 200 Riverside Dr Greenville SC 29605-1133

TODD, JOHN JOSEPH, lawyer; b. St. Paul, Mar. 16, 1927; s. John Alfred and Martha Agnes (Jagoe) T.; m. Dolores Jean Shanahan, Sept. 9, 1950; children: Richard M., Jane E., John P. Student, St. Thomas Coll., 1944, 46-47; B.Sci. and Law, U. Minn., 1949, LL.B., 1950. Bar: Minn. 1951. Practice in, South St. Paul, Minn., 1951-72; partner Thuet and Todd, 1953-72; asso. justice Minn. Supreme Ct., St. Paul, 1972-85; sole practice West St. Paul, 1985-92; of counsel Brenner & Glassman Ltd., Mpls., 1992—99, Orme & Assoc., Eagan, Minn., 1999—. Served with USNR, 1945—46. Mem. state bar assns., VFW. Home: 6689 Argenta Trl W Inver Grove Heights MN 55077-2208 Office: Orme & Associates 3140 Neil Armstrong Blvd Eagan MN 55121-2273 E-mail: jtodd@ormelaw.com., jjbtodd@comcast.net.

TODD, STEPHEN MAX, lawyer; b. Kansas City, Mo., Oct. 22, 1941; s. Louis O. and A. Maxine (Mittag); m. Carlene Harre; children: Stephanie A., Louis P. BA, Kans. State U., 1963; JD, U. Kans., 1966. Bar: Kans. 1966, U.S. Dist. Ct. Kans. 1966, U.S. Ct. Appeals (10th cir.) 1967, U.S. Supreme Ct. 1971, Mo. 1973. Assoc. Schroeder, Heeney, Groff & Spies, Topeka, 1966-72; office counsel Chgo. Title Ins. Co., Kansas City, 1973-78, regional counsel, 1978—. Author: Missouri Foreclosures of Deeds of Trust, 1983, 4th edit. 2001; contbr., editor books. Mem. Kans. Bar Assn., Mo. Bar (chmn. property law com. 1990-92), Am. Coll. Real Estate Lawyers, Kiwanis (pres. Topeka Downtown Club 1971-72, lt. gov. Mo.-Ark. dist. 1976-77, pres. Kansas City South Platte Club 1979-80), Phi Delta Phi. Insurance, Property, real (including real estate development, water). Home: 137 NW Pointe Dr Kansas City MO 64116-4616 Office: Chgo Title Ins Co PO Box 26370 Kansas City MO 64196-6370 E-mail: todds@ctt.com., stoddinkc@kc.rr.com.

TODD, STEVEN A. judge; b. Portland, Oreg., Dec. 27, 1955; s. Horace E. and Lois M. Todd; m. Sherry Poole, Jan. 30, 1987; 1 child, Andrew Poole. BA in Music and Polit. Sci., Northwestern U., 1978; JD, Lewis and Clark Coll., 1981. Bar: Oreg. 1981. Law clk. U.S. Dist. Ct., Portland, 1981-82, Multnomah County Cir. Ct., Portland, 1982-83; dep. dist. atty. Columbia County, St. Helens, Oreg., 1983-87, Multnomah County, Portland, 1987-97; cir. ct. judge pro tem Multnomah County Cir. Ct., Portland, 1997—. Office: Multnomah County Cir Ct 1021 SW 4th Ave Portland OR 97204-1123

TODD, WILLIAM MICHAEL, lawyer; b. Cleve., Dec. 13, 1952; s. William Charles and Jennie Ann (Diana) T. BA, U. Notre Dame, 1973; JD, Ohio State U., 1976. Bar: Ohio 1976, U.S. Dist. Ct. (so. dist.) Ohio 1977, U.S. Supreme Ct. 1987. Assoc. Porter, Wright, Morris & Arthur, Columbus, Ohio, 1976-82, ptnr., 1983-93, Squire, Sanders & Dempsey, Columbus, 1993—. Trustee Callvac Svcs., Columbus, 1985-91, pres., 1988. Mem. ABA (governing com. forum on health law 1988-91), Ohio Bar Assn., Columbus Bar Assn., Am. Soc. Med. Assn. Counsel, Am. Bd. Trial Advocates, Ohio Soc. Healthcare Attys. (pres. 1999-2000), Am. Health Lawyers Assn., Columbus Athletic Club. Roman Catholic. Avocations: music, recreational sports. Federal civil litigation, State civil litigation, Health. Office: Squire Sanders & Dempsey 41 S High St Columbus OH 43215-6101

TODICĂ, BIANCA NICOLETA, legal assistant; b. Bucharest, Romania, Aug. 13, 1973; arrived in Italy, 1999; d. Vasile and Nastasia Todică; m. Giorgio Ramponi, Jan. 13, 2000; 1 child, Fabrizio Ramponi. Grad., Nicolae Titulescu U., Bucharest, 1995. Comml. cons. Soc. Strike Inc. Bowling and Billiards, Bucharest, 1995—98; sec., functionary Notarial Bur. Albut Viorica, Bucharest, 1998—99; legal asst. Studio Legale Sutti, Milan, 2000—. Avocations: reading, travel. Office: Studio Legale Sutti Via Montenapoleane 8 20121 Milan Italy

TODOROVIC, ILIJA IKA, lawyer; b. Madison, Wis., Nov. 13, 1962; s. Radmilo and Lillian Todorovic. BA, Tex. A&M U., 1984; JD, Boston U., 1991; MA, Marquette U., 1995. Bar: Wis. 1993. Legal officer UN High Commn for Refugees, Belgrade, Yugoslavia, 1994—98, legal resettlement officer Amman, Jordan, 1998—99, Moscow, 1999—2000, legal probation officer Banja Uka, Bosnia-Herzegovina, 2000—02, rep. Minsk, Belarus, 2003—. Pvt. practice, Milw., 1992—93. Contbr. Recipient Hon. Citizenship of City of Knic, Knic Musical and Citizen's Group, 2002. Mem.: ABA, Milw. Bar Assn. Serbian Orthodox. Avocations: painting, travel, antiques, law guages. Public international, Immigration, naturalization, and customs, Refugee law. Home: 4825 W Howard Ave Milwaukee WI 53220 Office: UN High Commn for Refugees Partizansky Av 6A 220033 Minsk Belarus E-mail: todorov@un.minsk.by.

TOEDT, D(ELL) C(HARLES), III, lawyer; b. Maxwell AFB, Ala., Nov. 17, 1954; m. Maretta A. Comfort. BA with high honors, U. Tex., 1973, JD, 1981. Bar: Tex. 1982, U.S. Patent and Trademark Office 1983, U.S. Dist. Ct. (so. dist.) Tex. 1984, U.S. Ct. Appeals (fed. cir.) 1984, U.S. Supreme Ct. 1991. Atty. Schlanger, Cook, Cohn, Mills & Grossberg, Houston, 1982-83, Arnold, White & Durkee, Houston, 1983-99; v.p., gen. counsel BindView Corp., Houston, 1999—. Adj. prof. South Tex. Coll. Law, 1988-90. Sr. assoc. editor Tex. Law Rev., 1981-82; author, editor: Licensing Law Handbook: Computer Software Issues, 1987; editor Law and Bus. Computer Software, 1989-92; contbr. articles to profl. jours. Served to lt. USN, 1974-79. Mem. ABA (chmn. computer-related coms. 1985-96, elected mem. coun. sect. intellectual property law 1999-2000). Federal civil litigation, Computer, Patent. Office: BindView Corp 5151 San Felipe 25th Fl Houston TX 77056- E-mail: dc.toedt@bindview.com.

TOEDT, MARETTA COMFORT, arbitrator, mediator; b. Buffalo, July 22, 1951; d. Richard Arden and Margaret (McNair) Comfort; m. D.C. Toedt, Aug. 11, 1984; children: Richard Charles, Elizabeth Margaret. BA cum laude, Syracuse U., 1973; JD, Temple U., 1977, LLM in Labor Law, 1982. Bar: Pa. 77, Tex. 78, U.S. Dist. Ct. (ea. dist.) Pa. 80, U.S. Dist. Ct. (so. dist.) Tex. 90, cert.: Tex. Bd. Legal Specialization (labor law). Supr. Gulf Oil Corp., Phila. and Houston, Pa., 1977—85; dir. labor rels. Tenneco Oil Processing, Houston, 1985—88; assoc. labor and employment law sect. Vinson & Elkins, LLP, Houston, 1989—94; pvt. practice arbitrator, mediator Houston, 1994—. Contbg. editor: Developing Labor Law, 3d edit., 1990—92; contbr. articles to profl. jours. Sunday sch. tchr. Mem.: ABA (labor and employment sect.), SPIDR, Indsl. Rels. Rsch. Assn. (pres. local chpt. 1991—94, sec./treas. 1995—96, 2001—). Republican. Episcopalian. Office: 3139 W Holcombe PMB 610 Houston TX 77025 Fax: 713-665-2978. E-mail: maretta@toedt.com.

TOENSING, VICTORIA, lawyer; b. Colon, Panama, Oct. 16, 1941; d. Philip William and Victoria (Brady) Long; m. Trent David Toensing, Oct. 29, 1962 (div. 1976); children: Todd Robert, Brady Cronon, Amy Victoriana; m. Joseph E. diGenova, June 27, 1981. BS in Edn., Ind. U., 1962; JD cum laude, U. Detroit, 1975. Bar: Mich. 1976, D.C. 1978. Tchr. English, Milw., 1965-66; law clk. to presiding justice U.S. Ct. Appeals, Detroit, 1975-76; asst. U.S. atty. U.S. Atty.'s Office, Detroit, 1976-81; chief counsel U.S. Senate Intelligence Com., Washington, 1981-84; dep. asst. atty. gen. criminal div. Dept. Justice, Washington, 1984-88; spl. counsel Hughes Hubbard & Reed, Washington, 1988-90; ptnr. Cooter and Gell, Washington, 1990-91; ptnr., co-chmn. nat. white collar group Manatt, Phelps and Phillips, Washington, 1991-95; founding ptnr. diGenova & Toensing, Wasington, 1996—. Mem. working group on corp. sanctions U.S. Sentencing Commn., 1988-89; co-chairperson Coalition for Women's Appts. Justice Judiciary Task Force, 1988-92; spl. counsel for Teamsters investigation, U.S. Ho. of Reps., Subcom. on Oversight and Investigations of com. on Edn. and the Workforce, 1997-98. Author: Bringing Sanity to the Insanity Defense, 1983, Mens Rea: Insanity by Another Name, 1984; contbg. author: Fighting Back: Winning The War Against Terrorism, Desk Book on White Collar Crime, 1991; contbr. articles to profl. jours. Founder, chmn. Women's Orgn. To Meet Existing Needs, Mich., 1975-79; chmn. Republican Women's Task Force, 1979-81; bd. dirs. Project on Equal Edn. Rights, Mich., 1980-81, Nat. Hist. Intelligence Mus., 1987-95, America's Talking Legal Analyst, 1995; MSNBC legal analyst, 1998-99. Recipient spl. commendation Office U.S. Atty. Gen., 1980, agy. seal medallion CIA, 1986, award of achievement Alpha Chi Omega, 1992; featured on cover N.Y. Time Mag. for anti-terrorism work, April 1991. Mem. ABA (mem. standing com. on law and nat. security, mem. coun. criminal justice sect., mem. adv. com. complex crimes and litigation, vice chmn. white collar crime com., chmn. subcom. on corp. criminal liability). Administrative and regulatory, Criminal, Legislative.

TOFTNESS, CECIL GILLMAN, lawyer, consultant; b. Glasgow, Mont., Sept. 13, 1920; s. Anton Bernt and Nettie (Pedersen) T.; m. Chloe Catherine Vincent, Sept. 8, 1951. AA, San Diego Jr. Coll., 1943; student, Purdue U., Northwestern U.; BS, UCLA, 1947; JD cum laude, Southwestern U., 1953. Bar: Calif. 1954, U.S. Dist. Ct. (so. dist.) Calif. 1954, U.S. Tax Ct. 1974, U.S. Supreme Ct. 1979. Pvt. rpactice, palos Verdes Estates, Calif., 1954—. Chmn. bd., pres., bd. dirs. Fishermen & Mchts. Bank, San Pedro, Calif., 1963-67; v.p., bd. dirs. Palos Verdes Estates Bd. Realtors, 1964-65; participant Soc. Expdn. through the Northwest Passaage. Chmn. capital campaign fund Richstone Charity, Hawthorne, Calif., 1983; commencement spkr. Glasgow H.S., 1981. Served to lt. (j.g.) USN, 1938-46, ETO, PTO, commdg. officer USS Ptarmigan, 1941-45. Decorated Bronze Star; mem. Physicians for Prevention of Nuclear War which received Nobel Peace prize, 1987; named Man of Yr., Glasgow, 1984. Mem. South Bay Bar Assn., Southwestern Law Sch. Alumni Assn. (class rep. 1980—), Themis Soc.-Southwestern Law Sch., Schumacher Founders Cir.-Southwestern Law Sch. (charter), Kiwanis (sec.-treas. 1955-83, v.p., pres., bd. dirs.), Masons, KT. Democrat. Lutheran. Estate planning, Probate (including wills, trusts), Estate taxation. Home: 2229 Via Acalones Palos Verdes Peninsula CA 90274-1646 Office: 2516 Via Tejon Palos Verdes Estates CA 90274-6802 E-mail: cgtoftness@aol.com.

TOKARCZYK, ROMAN ANDRZEJ, law and philosophy researcher and educator; b. Gródki, Lublin, Poland, Mar. 16, 1942; s. Andrzej Jan and Karolina Rozalia (Dubiel) T.; m. Czestawa Paulina Malec, Apr. 30, 1942; 1 childe Malgorzata. LLM, Mariae Curie Sktodowska U., Lublin, 1966, PhD in Law, 1970. From asst. to prof. Mariae Curie Sktodowska U., Lublin, 1966—90, prof., 1990—. Rsch. assoc. prof. Notre Dame U., 1974; vis. assoc. prof. Harvard U., 1974, 93; dir. dept. faculty law and adminstrn. Mariae Curie Sktodowska U., Lublin, 1979—; dean faculty law and economy Studium Generale Sandomiriense, Sandomierz, Poland, 1996-2000. Author: Contemporary Political Doctrines, 1971, 12th edit., 2003, Law of Birth, Life and Death, 1984, Comparative Law, 1989, Philosophy of Law, 1993; : 7th edit., 2002, American Law, 1996, 6th edit., 2003, History Philosophy of Law, 1988, 3rd edit., 2001, Contemporary Law Cultures, 2000, 3rd edit., 2003, The History of Village of Gródki, 1992, 2nd edit., 2000, The History of Town Turobin, 2002, Commands of the Legal Ethics. Book of Thoughts, Norms and Sketches, 2003; contbr. more than 500 articles to profl. jours. Mem. Tribunale of State, Warsaw, Poland, 1994. Internat. Rsch. Exch. Bd. scholar, 1974, NATO scholar, 1993; recipeint awards Polish Min. Higher Edn., 1973, 77, 83, others. Mem. Internat. Communal Studies Assn. Israel, U.S. (bd. dirs.), Polish Acad. Medicine, Internat. Soc. Philosophy Law Social Philosophy. Roman Catholic. Avocations: skiing, dancing, photography. Home: Dudzinskiego 16 20-815 Lublin Poland Office: Pl Marii Curie Sktodowskiej 5 20-031 Lublin Poland E-mail: rtokarcz@temida.umcs.lublin.pl.

TOLAND, CLYDE WILLIAM, lawyer; b. Iola, Kans., Aug. 18, 1947; s. Stanley E. and June E. (Thompson) T.; m. Nancy Ellen Hummel, July 27, 1974; children: David Clyde, Andrew John, Elizabeth Kay. BA, U. Kans., 1969, JD, 1975; MA, U. Wis., 1971. Bar: Kans. 1975, U.S. Dist. Ct. Kans. 1975, U.S. Supreme Ct. 1980. Ptnr. Toland and Thompson LLC, Iola, 1975—. Author: Samuel Franklin Hubbard and Permelia Caroline (Spencer) Hubbard: Pioneer Settlers in 1857 of Allen County, Kansas Territory, and their Descendants, 1985, (with others) Clark and Eliza (Wright) Toland: Their Ancestors and Descendants, 1984, David Wilson and Charlotte Elizabeth (Cooper) Wilson, 1830-1961, and Their Ancestors and Descendants, 1988. Mem. exec. com. Friends of Libr., U. Kans., 1977-92, pres., 1988-91; pres. Allen County Hist. Soc., Inc., 1990-95; founder Annual Buster Keaton Celebration, Iola, Kans., co-chmn., 1993-97; leader restoration Frederick Funston Boyhood Home, 1991-95. Co-recipient with U.S. Sen. Nancy Kassebaum First Alumni Disting. Achievement award Coll. Liberal Arts and Scis. U. Kans., 1996. Fellow Kans. Bar Found.; mem. ABA, Kans. Bar Assn. (Outstanding Svc. award 1988), Allen County Bar Assn., U. Kans. Alumni Assn. (Strickland award 1969), Phi Beta Kappa, Order of Coif, Omicron Delta Kappa (presdl. plaque 1969). Republican. Prsbyterian. Avocations: speaking on estate planning and history, historical field trips. Estate planning, Probate (including wills, trusts), Estate taxation. Home: 211 S Colborn St Iola KS 66749-3405 Office: PO Box 404 Iola KS 66749-0404

TOLAND, JOHN ROBERT, lawyer; b. Iola, Kans., Oct. 7, 1944; s. Stanley E. and June Elizabeth (Thompson) T.; m. Karen Alice Jeffries, Apr. 26, 1980; children: Carol Jane, Mark Charles, Scott Robert, Kent William. BA with highest distinction, U. Kans., 1966, JD, 1969. Bar: Kans. 1969, U.S. Dist. Ct. Kans. 1969, U.S. Ct. Appeals (10th cir.) 1969, U.S. Supreme Ct. 1976. Ptnr. Toland and Thompson, LLC, Iola, 1973—. City atty., Yates Center, Kans., 1976-82; spkr. in field. Editor-in-chief Kans. Law Rev., 1968-69; mem. bd. editors Kans. Bar Assn. Jour., 1988-92. Trustee Allen County Hosp., Iola, 1979-82; bd. dirs. Iola Pub. Library, 1980-88, pres., 1983-88; bd. dirs. United Fund of Iola Inc., 1975-79, treas., 1975-77; bd. dirs. Iola Area Symphony Orch., 1994-97; ruling elder 1st Presbyn. Ch., Iola, 1983-85, 97-98; mem. Allen County Hist. Soc., Kans. State Hist. Soc., The Friends of the Eisenhower Found., U. Kans. Alumni Assn.; mem. com. on ministry John Calvin Presbytery, Presbyn Ch. (USA), 1986-88; mem. Permanent Jud. Commn., 1998—; coach Boys Basketball Youth League. Capt. JAGC, U.S. Army, 1969-73, Vietnam. Decorated Bronze Star, Army Commendation medal with oak leaf cluster; John Ise scholar in Econ., 1965-66, Summerfield scholar, U. Kans., 1962-66, Nat. Merit scholar, 1962-66. Fellow Kans. Bar Found.; mem. ABA, Kans. Bar Assn., Kans. Sch. Attys. Assn. (bd. dirs. 1989-93, spkr. at sch. law seminars), Allen County Bar Assn. (pres. 1980-81), Am. Legion, Rotary (pres. Iola chpt. 1980-81, Paul Harris fellow 1986), Order of Coif, VFW, Phi Beta Kappa, Phi Delta Phi, Beta Theta Pi, Sigma Pi Sigma. Education and schools, General practice, Probate (including wills, trusts). Home: PO Box 312 Iola KS 66749-0312 Office: Toland and Thompson LLC 103 E Madison St Iola KS 66749-3330 E-mail: jtoland@toland-thompson.kscoxmail.com.

TOLENTINO, CASIMIRO URBANO, lawyer; b. Manila, May 18, 1949; came to U.S., 1959; s. Lucio Rubio and Florence (Jose) T.; m. Jennifer Masculino, June 5, 1982; 2 children: Casimiro Masculino, Cristina Cecelia Masculino. BA in Zoology, UCLA, 1972, JD, 1975. Bar: Calif. 1976. Gen. counsel civil rights divsn. HEW, Washington, 1975-76; regional atty. Agrl. Labor Relations Bd., Fresno, Calif., 1976-78; regional dir. Sacramento and San Diego, 1978-81; regional atty. Pub. Employment Relations Bd., L.A., 1981; counsel, west divsn. Writers Guild Am., L.A., 1982-84; dir. legal affairs Embassy TV, L.A., 1984-86; pvt. practice L.A., 1986-87. Mediator Ctr. Dispute Resolution, Santa Monica, Calif., 1986-87; asst. chief counsel Dept. of Fair Employment and Housing, State of Calif., 1986-92, adminstrv. law judge dept. social svcs., 1992—. Editor: Letters in Exile, 1976; contbr. articles and revs. to Amerasia Jour. Chmn. adv. bd. UCLA Asian Am. Studies Ctr., 1983-90; chmn. bd. Asian Pacific Legal Ctr., L.A., 1983-93 (Decade award); pres. bd. civil svc. commrs. City of L.A., 1984-85, 90-93; bd. dirs. met. region United Way, 1987-95; bd. dirs. Rebuild L.A., 1992-97; mem. Asian-Pacific Am. adv. coun. L.A. Police Commn., 1995-97; adv. coun. L.A. Children's Scholarship Fund, 1998-2000; vice chair Philipino Am. Arts Bd., 1999—; chair Our Mother of Good Counsel Sch. Bd., 1999—. Mem. Nat. Asian-Am. Legal Consortium (bd. dirs. 1991—), State Bar Calif. (exec. com. labor law sect. 1985-88), Los Angeles County Bar Assn., Minority Bar Assn. (sec. 1984-85), Philippine Am. Bar Assn. (chmn. bd. 1988, award of merit 1999), Philippine Lawyers of So. Calif. (pres. 1984-87, award of merit 1982), Philippine-Am. Alumni Assn. (Cmty. Svc. award 2001). Democrat. Roman Catholic. Avocations: history, photography, travel.

TOLL, PERRY MARK, lawyer, educator; b. Kansas City, Mo., Oct. 28, 1945; s. Mark Irving and Ruth (Parker) T.; m. Mary Anne Shottenkirk, Aug. 26, 1967; children: Andrea Lynne, Hillary Anne. BS in Polit. Sci. and Econs., U. Kans., 1967, JD, 1970. Bar: Mo. 1970 1970, U.S. Dist. Ct. (we. dist.) Mo. 1970, U.S. Tax Ct. 1979, U.S. Supreme Ct. 1979. With Shughart, Thomson & Kilroy P.C., Kansas City, 1970—, pres., 1995—, chmn. bus. dept., 1999—. Asst. prof. deferred compensation U. Mo., Kansas City, 1979-83; bd. dirs., pres. Heart of Am. Tax Inst., Kansas City, 1975-87. Mem., chmn. Prairie Village (Kans.) Bd. Zoning Appeals, 1977-95. Mem. ABA, Mo. Bar Assn., Nat. Health Lawyers Assn., Am. Agr. Law Assn., Mo. Merchants and Mfrs. Assn., Greater Kansas City Med. Mgrs. Assn., Lawyers Assn. Kansas City, East Kans. Estate Planning Coun. (bd. dirs., pres.), Phi Kappa Tau (bd. dirs. Beta Theta chpt.). Estate planning, Health, Pension, profit-sharing, and employee benefits. Office: Shughart Thomson & Kilroy 12 Wyandotte Plz 120 W 12th St Ste 1500 Kansas City MO 64105-1929

TOLL, SHELDON SAMUEL, lawyer; b. Phila., June 6, 1940; s. Herman and Rose (Ornstein) T.; m. Roberta Darlene Pollack, Aug. 11, 1968; children: Candice Moore, John Maitland, Kevin Scott. Bar: Pa. 1967, Mich. 1972, Ill. 1990, Tex. 1990, U.S. Dist. Ct. (ea. dist.) Pa. 1968, U.S. Ct. Appeals (3d cir.) 1970, U.S. Supreme Ct. 1971, Mich. 1972, U.S. Dist. Ct. (ea. dist.), U.S. Ct. Appeals (6th cir.) 1973, U.S. Ct. Appeals (5th cir.) 1978, U.S. Dist. Ct. (no. dist.) Calif. 1986, U.S. Ct. Appeals (9th cir.) 1987, U.S. Dist. Ct. (ea. dist.) Wis. 1989. Assoc. Montgomery, McCracken et al, Phila., 1967-72; sr. ptnr. Honigman Miller Schwartz and Cohn, Detroit, 1972—. Panelist Bankruptcy Litigation Inst., N.Y.C., 1984-94. Author: Pennsylvania Crime Codes, 1972, Bankruptcy Litigation Manual, 1988. Bd. dirs. Southeastern Mich. chpt. ARC, Detroit. Mem. Fed. Bar Assn. (past pres. Detroit chpt.), ABA, Pa. Bar Assn., Phila. Bar Assn., Detroit Bar Assn., Franklin (Mich.) Hills Country Club, Phi Beta Kappa. Democrat. Jewish. Bankruptcy, Federal civil litigation, Commercial, contracts (including sales of goods; commercial financing). Office: Honigman Miller Schwartz & Cohn 2290 1st National Bldg Detroit MI 48226

TOLLIVER, ELKIN, JR., judge; b. Phila., Jan. 29, 1950; s. Elkin and Vernetta Tolliver; m. Toni Diane Bennett, Oct. 3, 1998; 1 child, Nia B. BA in Polit. Sci., Dickinson Coll., 1970; JD, Villanova U., 1976; LLM in Trial Advocacy, Temple U., 1994. Bar: Pa. 1976, U.S. Dist. Ct. (ea. dist.) Pa. Atty. Broujos & Andrews, Carlisle, Pa., 1976—78, U.S. Dept. HEW, Office Gen. Counsel, Phila., 1978—82, U.S. Dept. Edn., Office Civil Rights, 1982—85; trial atty. Pub. Defender Assn. Phila., 1985—88, State Workers' Ins. Fund, 1988—90, Rubinate Jacobs & Saba, 1990—2000; dist. justice Pa. Judiciary, Delaware County, 2000—. Pre-law advisor Lincoln U., Oxford, Pa., 2000—. Co-author: (legal digest) Digest & Index of Court Cases of the Pennsylvania State Civil Service Commission, 1975. Office: 821 Baltimore Pike East Lansdowne PA 19050 Fax: 610-622-1104. E-mail: etoll@bellatlantic.net.

TOM, ROSLYN, lawyer; b. N.Y.C. AB, Harvard U., 1985; JD, Yale U., 1989. Bar: N.Y. 1991, DC 1993. Law clk. to Hon. John T. Noonan, Jr. U.S. Ct. Appeals (9th cir.), San Francisco, 1989—90; assoc. Sullivan & Cromwell, N.Y.C., 1990—96, Dewey Ballantine LLP, N.Y.C., 1996—98, ptnr., 1999—. Mem.: ABA, Assn. Bar City N.Y. Securities, Mergers and acquisitions, Corporate, general. Office: Dewey Ballantine LLP 1301 Ave of the Americas New York NY 10019

TOMAIN, JOSEPH PATRICK, dean, law educator; b. Long Branch, New Jersey, Sept. 3, 1948; s. Joseph Pasquale and Bernice M. (Krzan) T.; m. Kathleen (Corcione), Aug. 1, 1971; children: Joseph Anthony, John Fiore. BA, U. Notre Dame, 1970; JD, George Washington U., 1974. Bar: NJ, Iowa. Assoc. Giordano and Halleran, Middletown, NJ, 1974-76; asst. to prof. law Drake U. Sch. Law, Des Moines, 1976-83; prof. law U. Cin., Cin., 1983—, acting dean, 1989-90, dean, 1990—, nippert prof. law, 1990—. Vis. prof. law, U. Tex., Austin, Tex., 1986-87. Author: Energy Law in a Nutshell, 1981, Nuclear Power Transformation, 1987; co-author: Energy Decision Making, 1983, Energy Law and Policy, 1989, Energy and Natural Resources Law, 1992, Regulatory Law and Policy, 1993, 2d edit., 1998, 3rd edit., 2003, Energy, The Environment and the Global Economy, 2000. Bd. trustees Ctr. for Chem. Addictions Treatment, Cin.; Vol. Lawyers for Poor, Cin.; mem. steering com. BLAC/CBA Round Table, Cin.; chair Knowledge Works Found. Served in USAR, 1970-76. Mem. ABA; Am. Law Inst.; Ohio State Bar Assn.(del.); Cin. Bar Assn. (bd. trustees). Roman Catholic. Home: 3009 Springer Ave Cincinnati OH 45208-2440 Office: U Cin Coll Law Office Dean PO Box 210040 Cincinnati OH 45221-0040 E-mail: joseph.tomain@uc.edu.

TOMAR, RICHARD THOMAS, lawyer; b. Camden, N.J., Mar. 4, 1945; s. William and Bette (Brown) T.; m. Adele Tomar; children: Lindsay, Leanne Meryl, Daniel Gregory. BA, Columbia U., 1967; JD, U. Pa., 1970. Bar: D.C. 1971, N.J. 1971, Md. 1976. Pvt. practice, Washington, 1971-73; assoc. Philipson, Mallios & Tomar, P.C., Washington, 1973-89, Margolius, Mallios, Davis, Rider & Tomar, LLP, Washington, 1989—2002; chair comml. litigation Karp, Frosh, Lapidus, Wigodsky & Norwind, PA, Rockville, Md., 2002—. Chmn. comml. litig. Margolius, Mallios, Davis, Rider & Tomar LLP. Mem. D.C. Trial Lawyers Assn. (bd. dirs. 1980-89). General civil litigation, Family and matrimonial. Office: Karp Frosh Lapidus Wigodsky & Norwind PA 1370 Piccard Dr Ste 290 Rockville MD 20850 Business E-Mail: rtomar@karpfrosh.com.

TOMAR, WILLIAM, lawyer; b. Camden, N.J., Oct. 10, 1916; s. Morris and Katie (Sadinsky) T.; m. Bette Brown, Nov. 28, 1942; children: Richard T., Dean Jonathon. LLB cum laude, Rutgers U., 1939. Bar: N.J. 1940, U.S. Ct. Appeals (3d cir.) 1953, U.S. Supreme Ct. 1953, Fla. 1975, D.C. 1978. Sr. ptnr. Tomar, O'Brien, Kaplan, Jacobi & Graziano, Haddonfield, N.J., 1958—. Mem. faculty Ctr. Trial and Appellate Advocacy, Hastings Coll. Law, U. Calif., 1971-86, Nat. Coll. Advocacy, Harvard U. Law Sch., 1973-75. Mem. UN Speakers Bur., UNICEF, 1960—; mem. adv. bd. Salvation Army, 1967-84, Inst. Med. Rsch., 1967—, N.J. Capital Punishment Study Commn., 1972-73, Touro Law Sch., 1981; mem. adv. bd. N.J. Student Assistance Bd., 1987-98, vice chmn., 1992-98; bd. dirs. South Jersey Assn. Performing Arts, Haddonfield Symphony Soc., 1985—; bd. dirs., pres. 1992-99; mem. exec. bd. So. N.J. Coun. Boy Scouts Am., 1985—, pres. 1992—, Disting. Citizen award, 2001; vice chmn., mem. bd. trustees Cooper Hosp., Univ. Med. Ctr. 1979-97, bd. mem. emeritus 1998; mem. planning com. World Peace Through Law Ctr., 1970—; trustee Cooper Med. Ctr., 1979—. Recipient Disting. Alumni award Rutgers U. Sch. Law, 1996, Neighbor of Yr. award N.J. chpt. ARC, 1999; honored at Juvenile Diabetes Found. South Jersey ann. gala, 2000. Fellow Am. Coll. Trial Lawyers; mem. ABA, Assn. Trial Lawyers Am. (assoc. editor jour. 1962-68, gov. 1963-64, nat. parliamentarian 1964-70, nat. exec. com. 1964-70, chmn. seminars 1965 lectr. student adv. program 1968—), World Jurist Assn. (founding mem. 1974—), N.J. Bar Assn. (fee arbitration com. 1972-74, 75-77), Trial Lawyers of N.J. (cert. by Supreme Ct. of N.J. as civil trial atty, Trial Bar award 1977), N.J. Workers Compensation Assn. (trustee 1958-83), N.Y. Trial Attys. Assn., Phila. Trial Lawyers Assn., Camden County Bar Found. (bd. trustees 1986—), Camden County Bar Assn., (com. on rels. of bench and bar 1964—, adult edn. com. 1975—). General civil litigation, Environmental, Personal injury (including property damage). Office: 20 Brace Rd Cherry Hill NJ 08034-2634

TOMBACK, JAY LOREN, lawyer; b. Chgo., Aug. 4, 1953; s. Seymour and Marilyn Lee (Klein) T.; m. Nancy Jo Corey, July 8, 1984; 1 child, Jarrett. BS in Acctg., U. Ill., 1976; JD, John Marshall Sch. Law, 1979. Bar: Ill. 1979, Ariz. 1980, U.S. Dist. Ct. Ariz. 1980, U.S. Tax Ct. 1980. Assoc. Robert L. Lane, Ltd., Phoenix, 1980-82; prin., bd. dirs. Lane & Tomback, Ltd., Phoenix, 1982-84, Lane, Tomback & Ehrlich, Ltd., Phoenix, 1984-89, Jay L. Tomback Ltd., Phoenix, 1989—. Mem. Western Pension Conf., Phoenix, 1982-92. Mem. Valley Estate Planners, Phoenix, 1980-82. Fellow Ariz. Bar Found.; mem. ABA, Internat. Assn. Fin. Planning, Am. Judicature Soc., Ill. Bar Assn., State Bar Ariz., Maricopa County Bar Assn. Corporate, general, Estate planning, Taxation, general. Office: Jay L Tomback Ltd 4000 N Central Ave Ste 1430 Phoenix AZ 85012-3506 Fax: (602) 274-1090.

TOMBET, ANDRE, lawyer; b. Mar. 2, 1927; s. Adolphe and Alice-Helene Meyer Tombet; m. Lysiane Ronchietto, Apr. 26, 2001; children: Ariane, Alain. LLB, U. Geneva, 1950; postgrad. Sch. Law, London U., 1951; LLM, Yale U., 1954. Admitted to Geneva bar, 1952. Assoc. firm White & Case, N.Y.C., 1954-56; pvt. practice Geneva, 1961-93; ptnr. Law Office of Perreard, De Boccard, Kohler, Ador & Ptnrs., Geneva, 1993—. Legal adv. permanent dels. to UN, Geneva and fgn. cos.; dir. Swiss Deposit and Creditbank, 1984-91; vice-chmn. bd. Hotel and Country Club Le Mirador, 1971-88; v.p. Martin Bodmer Found., 1980—; pres. Igor Carl Faberge Found., 1983. Capt., mil. justice, 1968-80. Mem. Swiss Fedn. Lawyers, Geneva Law Soc., Geneva Bar Assn. (mem. coun. 1984-90), Internat. Assn. for Protection Indsl. Property, Swiss Soc. Bibliophiles, Internat. Assn. Bibliophiles (mem. coun. 1986), Soc. Geneva State Archives (v.p. 1983—), Cercle De La Terrasse, Golf Club of Geneva (v.p. 1990-98), Am. Internat. (v.p. 1983-84, mem. exec. com. 1983—), Le Mirador Country (former gov.), Yale Club (N.Y.C.). Office: 44 Ave Krieg 1211 Geneva 17 Switzerland E-mail: tombet@pbka.ch.

TOMEI, ALBERT, county supreme court justice; b. N.Y.C., Jan. 30, 1940; s. Robert and Rita Tomei; m. Lynda Sumner; 1 child, Lisa Delgado. BA in History, Bklyn. Coll., 1961; JD, Bklyn. Law Sch., 1964, LLM, 1966. Bar: NY 1965, U.S. Dist. Ct. (ea. and so. dists.) NY 1966. Judge civil ct. 1st Jud. Dist., Bklyn., 1978; acting justice Supreme Ct. Kings County, Bklyn., 1981—93, justice, 1993—. Named Person of Yr., Kings County Criminal Def. Bar, Bklyn., 2000; recipient Disting. Svc. award, Bd. Judges, City of NY, 1994. Democrat. Avocations: tennis, reading, stand-up comedy, bird-watching. Office: Supreme Ct Justice 360 Adams St Brooklyn NY 11201-3712

TOMICH, LILLIAN, lawyer; b. L.A. d. Peter S. and Yovanka P. (Ivanovic) T. AA, Pasadena City Coll., 1954; BA in Polit. Sci., UCLA, 1956, cert. secondary tchg., 1957, MA, 1958; JD, U. So. Calif., 1961. Bar: Calif., U.S. Ct. Appeals (9th Cir.) 1978, 2002. Sole practice, 1961-66; house counsel Mfrs. Bank, L.A., 1966; assoc. Hurley, Shaw & Tomich, San Marino, Calif., 1968-76, Driscoll & Tomich, San Marino, 1976—. Dir. Continental Culture Specialists Inc., Glendale, Calif. Trustee St. Sava Serbian Orthodox Ch., San Gabriel, Calif. Recipient Episcopal Gramata award Serbian Orthodox Met. of Midwestern Am., 1993, Episcopal Gramata award Serbian Orthodox Bishop of Western Am., 1996, 2002; Charles Fletcher Scott fellow, 1957; U. So. Calif. Law Sch. scholar, 1958. Mem. ABA, Calif. Bar Assn., Los Angeles County Bar Assn., Women Lawyers Assn., San Marino C. of C., UCLA Alumni Assn., Town Hall and World Affairs Coun., Order Mast and Dagger, Iota Tau Tau, Alpha Gamma Sigma, Pi Kappa Delta. General practice, Personal injury (including property damage), Probate (including wills, trusts). Office: 2460 Huntington Dr San Marino CA 91108-2643

TOMLIN, JAMES MILTON, lawyer; b. Springfield, Ill., July 16, 1942; s. Bernard A. and Iona M. T.; m. Carol L. Wandell, Dec. 23, 1966 (div. Mar. 1994); children: Brian, Brad, Mitch; m. Barbara Soldwedel, Aug. 24, 1998. BS, U. Ill., 1964, JD, 1967. Bar: Ill. 1968, U.S. Dist. Ct. (no. dist.) Ill. 1973. Judge adv. gen. corps. USN, 1968-71, USNR, 1971-91; atty. Westervest, Johnson, Nicol & Keller, Peoria, Ill., 1971-73; asst. corp. counsel City of Peoria, 1973-74; pvt. practice Peoria, 1974—. Mem. law adv. bd. Ctrl. Ill. C.C., Peoria, 1990-94. Bd. dirs. Neighborhood House Assn., Peoria, 1985—, former pres., Tower Pk., Peoria Heights, 1974-84; former pres. Forest Pk. Found., Peoria, bd. dirs. Lt. USN, 1968-71, capt. USNR, 1971-92, ret. Recipient Cmty. Svc. award, Ill. State Bar Assn., 2001. Avocations: skiing, golfing, bicycling. Estate planning, General practice, Probate (including wills, trusts). Office: 5823 N Forest Park Dr Peoria IL 61614-3559 Fax: 309-688-7581. E-mail: jtomlinlaw@aol.com.

TOMLINSON, HERBERT WESTON, lawyer; b. Upland, Pa., Feb. 11, 1930; s. Herbert Elmer and Hilda Josephine (Schlosbon) T.; m. Mary Jean Litwhiler, Oct. 27, 1961. BS, Pa. State U., 1952, postgrad., 1956-57; JD, Dickinson Sch. Law, 1960; postgrad., Temple U. Law Sch., 1969-73; BA with highest distinction, Pa. State U., 1994. Bar: Pa. 1961, U.S. Supreme Ct. 1968; lic. pilot. Law clk., pres. Delaware County Bar Assn., 1960-61; assoc. DeFuria Larkin Defuria, Chester, Pa., 1960-62, Hodge & Balderston, Chester, Pa., 1962-65, Edward McLaughlin, Chester, Pa., 1965-67; exec. dir. Legal Svcs. Program, Deleware County, 1967-69; atty. pvt. practice, Media, Pa., 1969—; sr. staff atty. Delaware County Pub. Defender's Office, 1969—. Prof. bus. law Pa. State U., 1969-75, Widener U., 1971-76, 78-80, Delaware County C.C., 1971-75; arbitrator Am. Arbitration Assn. Actor in TV commercials, 1998—. Legal counsel Disabled Vets Am.; county dir. Delaware County March of Dimes, 1966-71; rep. candidate U.S. Ho. Reps., 1976; rep. committeeman, 1966—, treas. 168th Legis. Dist., 1975-81; chmn. Media Rep. Com., 1975-76, Media Borough Auditor, 1975-79; nat. dir. Jaycees, 1965-66. Capt. USMCR, 1952-56. Named Outstanding Young Men Am. U.S. Jaycees, 1966. Mem. AAUP, ABA, Am. Assn. Trial Lawyers, Nat. Assn. Securities Dealers, Am. Arbitration Assn., Pa. Bar Assn., Pa. Trial Lawyers Assn., Delaware County Bar Assn., Delaware County Real Estate Bd., Delaware County Med. Soc. (dir. pub. health fund 1967—), Aircraft Owners and Pilots Assn., Screen Actors Guild, Kiwanis, Masons, Shriners, Rotary, Phi Theta Kappa (past pres.), Phi Kappa Phi, Alpha Sigma Lambda), Beta Gamma Sigma. Republican. Presbyterian. Family and matrimonial, Personal injury (including property damage), Probate (including wills, trusts). Home: 103 Kershaw Rd Wallingford PA 19086-6311 Office: Rm 20 247 N Middletown Rd Media PA 19063-4535 E-mail: westontomlinson@msn.com.

TOMLINSON, JOHN RANDOLPH, lawyer; b. Seattle, Jan. 11, 1931; s. Charles Lawrence and Irma (Schnauffer) T.; m. Susan Jo Weaver, June 15, 1953; children: John R. Jr., Lynn M., James L., Anne E. BBA, U. Wash., 1953, JD, 1955. Bar: Wash. 1955, U.S. Dist. Ct. (we. and ea. dists.) Wash. 1955, U.S. Ct. Appeals (9th cir.) 1957, U.S. Supreme Ct. 1975. Assoc. Jones, Grey & Bayley, Seattle, 1957-61, ptnr., 1962-78, Lane Powell Spears Lubersky, Seattle, 1979—. Lectr. on continuing legal edn. Editorial bd. U. Wash. Law Rev., 1953. Served to 1st lt. USAFR, 1955-77. Fellow Am. Coll. Trial Lawyers; mem. ABA (chmn. litigation sect. 1986-87, vice chmn. 1984-85, chmn. elect 1985-86), Wash. State Bar Assn., Seattle Bar Assn., Phi Gamma Delta. Lodges: Rotary. Republican. Avocations: golf, skiing, fishing, hunting. Federal civil litigation, State civil litigation. Home: 8435 NE 21st Pl Bellevue WA 98004-2405 Office: Lane Powell Spears Lubersky 1420 5th Ave Ste 4100 Seattle WA 98101-2338

TOMLINSON, MARGARET LYNCH, lawyer; b. Cleve., June 21, 1929; d. John Joseph and Margaret (Stevenson) Lynch; m. Alexander C. Tomlinson. AB, Smith Coll., 1950; JD, N.Y. Law Sch., 1963. Bar: N.Y. 1963, D.C. 1971, U.S Ct. Appeals (D.C. cir.) 1971. Staff officer Dept. of State, 1950-55; U.S. Del. UN Gen. Assembly, N.Y.C., 1964-68; asst. legal adviser U.S. Mission to the UN, 1963-69; asst. to Sen. Claiborne Pell, Washington, 1969-71; sr. adviser U.S. Del. to the Law of the Sea Conf., 1972-78; ptnr. Dickey, Roadman & Dickey, Washington, 1978-82; cons. office gen. counsel CIA, Washington, 1987-93. Cons. Law of the Sea; bd. dirs. Coun. Ocean Law, Washington, 1984—, vice-chmn., 1994—; U.S. del. spl. session UN Gen. Assembly, 1994. Contbr. articles to profl. jours. Mem. ABA (internat. law sect., chmn. law of the sea com.), Am. Soc. Internat. Law, Internat. Law Assn., D.C. Bar Assn., Nat. Press Club, Sulgrave Club. Public international. Home: 3314 P St NW Washington DC 20007-2701

TOMLJANOVICH, ESTHER M. state supreme court justice; b. Galt, Iowa, Nov. 1, 1931; d. Chester William and Thelma L. (Brooks) Moellering; m. William S. Tomljanovich, Dec. 26, 1957; 1 child, William Brooks. AA, Itasca Jr. Coll., 1951; BSL, St. Paul Coll. Law, 1953, LLB, 1955. Bar: Minn. 1955, U.S. Dist. Ct. Minn. 1958. Asst. revisor of statutes State of Minn., St. Paul, 1957-66, revisor of statutes, 1974-77, dist. ct. judge Stillwater, 1977-90; assoc. justice Minn. Supreme Ct., St. Paul, 1990—98, ret., 1998. Mem. adv. bd. women offenders Minn. Dept. Corrections, 1999—; mem. leadership com. So. Minn. Legal Svcs. Corp., 1999—. Former mem. North St. Paul Bd. Edn., Maplewood Bd. Edn., Lake Elmo Planning Commn.; trustee William Mitchell Coll. Law, 1995—, Legal Rights Ctr., 1995—, pres., 1999; trustee So. Minn. Legal Svcs. Corp.; bd. dirs. Itasca C.C. Found., 1996—, Medica Health Ins. Co., 2001—. Recipient Centennial 2000 award William Mitchell Coll., also Disting. Alumna award; named one of One Hundred Who Made a Difference William Mitchell Coll. Law Mem. Minn. State Bar Assn., Bus. and Profl. Women's Assn. St. Paul (former pres.), Minn. Women Laywers (founding mem.). Office: 8533 Hidden Baytrail Lake Elmo MN 55042

TOMME, CURTIS RABON, lawyer; b. Brady, Tex., Feb. 18, 1956; s. William Rabon Tomme and Hannah Mae Curtis; m. Elizabeth Ann Watson, Nov. 1, 1997. BS in Indsl. Distribution, Tex. A&M U., 1978; JD, Tex. Tech U., 1988. Bar: Tex. 1989. Asst. dist. atty. Taylor County, Abilene, Tex. Bd. dirs. Salvation Army, Abilene, 1998—, sec., 1999—; staff Rdy Issard for Congress Camp, Abilene, 1995-96. Mem. Abilene Bar Assn., Abilene C. of C., Abilene A&M Club (pres. 2000). Office: Taylor County Criminal Dist Atty 400 Oak St Ste 110 Abilene TX 79602-1527

TOMPERT, JAMES EMIL, lawyer; b. Battle Creek, Mich., July 21, 1954; s. James Russell and Marjorie Mary (Storkan) T. BA, Duke U., 1976; JD, U. Mich., 1981. Bar: D.C. 1981, Md. 1985, Va. 1986. Legis. asst. to congressman U.S. Ho. of Rep., Washington, 1977—78; assoc. Baker & Hostetler, Washington, 1981—84, Cooter & Gell, Washington, 1984—86, ptnr., 1987—94, Cooter Mangold Tompert & Wayson L.L.P., Washington, 1995—. Mem. D.C. Bar Assn., Arts Club Washington, Univ. Club Washington. Federal civil litigation, General civil litigation, State civil litigation. Office: Cooter Mangold Tompert & Wayson LLP 5301 Wisconsin Ave NW Washington DC 20015-2015 E-mail: jtompert@cootermangold.com.

TOMPKINS, DWIGHT EDWARD, lawyer; b. Toledo, Ohio, June 29, 1952; s. Leonard Charles and Amanda Virginia (Bunce) T.; m. Marilyn Vergara, June 15, 1974; children: Jason, Kristin. BA in Anthropology, San Diego State U., 1974; MPA, Long Beach State U., 1981; JD, Loyola U., L.A., 1990. Bar: Calif. 1990, U.S. Dist. Ct. (ctrl. dist.) Calif. 1990, U.S. Dist. Ct. (so. dist.) Calif. 1991. Analyst City of Long Beach, 1985-89; law clk. Ching, Kurtz & Blix, Santa Ana, Calif., 1989-90; assoc. Ching & Assocs., Santa Ana, 1990-91; pvt. practice Downey, Calif., 1991—. Bd. dirs. Gladius, Inc., Las Vegas, Nev. Recipient Am. Jurisprudence Trial Advocacy award, 1990. Mem. Rotary (pres. 1997-98). Corporate, general, Estate planning. Office: 9530 Imperial Hwy Ste E Downey CA 90242-3041

TOMPKINS, JOSEPH BUFORD, JR., lawyer; b. Roanoke, Va., Apr. 4, 1950; s. Joseph Buford and Rebecca Louise (Johnston) T.; m. Nancy Powell Wilson, Feb. 6, 1993; children: Edward Graves, Claiborne Forbes; 1 stepchild, Clayton Tate Wilson. BA in Politics summa cum laude, Washington and Lee U., 1971; M Pub. Policy, JD, Harvard U., 1975. Bar: Va. 1975, U.S. Ct. Appeals (D.C. cir.), U.S. Ct. Appeals (5th cir.) 1977, U.S. Supreme Ct. 1977, U.S. Dist. Ct. D.C. 1982, U.S. Ct. Appeals (11th cir.) 1982, U.S. Ct. Appeals (3d cir.) 1983, U.S. Ct. Appeals (6th cir.) 1985, U.S. Ct. Appeals (7th cir.) 1991, U.S. Ct. Appeals (4th cir.) 1993, U.S. Ct. Internat. Trade 1996. Assoc. Sidley & Austin (now Sidley Austin Brown & Wood LLP), Washington, 1975-79, ptnr., 1982—; assoc. dir. Office Policy and Mgmt. Analysis criminal divsn. U.S. Dept. Justice, Washington, 1979-80, dep. chief fraud sect. criminal divsn., 1980-82. Contbr. articles to legal publs. Mem. Va. Bd. Health Professions, Richmond, 1984-92, vice chmn., 1984-86, chmn., 1986-88, 90-91. Mem. ABA (white collar crime com. criminal justice sect. 1980—, chmn. task force on computer crime 1982-92), Va. Bar Assn., D.C. Bar Assn., Phi Beta Kappa, Federal civil litigation, State civil litigation, Criminal. Home: 8146 Wellington Rd Alexandria VA 22308-1214 Office: Sidley Austin Brown & Wood LLP 1501 K St NW 8th Fl Washington DC 20005 Fax: 202-736-8711. E-mail: jtompkins@sidley.com.

TOMPKINS, RAYMOND EDGAR, lawyer; b. Oklahoma City, July 13, 1934; s. Charles Edgar and Eva Mae (Hodges) T.; m. Sue Anne Sharpe, June 10, 1963; children: Matthew Stephen, Christopher T., Katherine Anne. BS, Okla. State U., 1956; JD, U. Okla., 1963. Bar: Okla. 1963, U.S. Dist. Ct. (no. dist.) Okla. 1963, U.S. Dist. Ct. (we. dist.) Okla. 1964, U.S. Ct. Appeals (10th cir.) 1965, U.S. Supreme Ct. 1968, U.S. dist. Ct. (ea. dist.) Okla. 1969, U.S. Ct. Appeals (9th cir.) 1981, U.S. Ct. Appeals (4th cir.) 1986. Adminstrv. asst. U.S. Congress, 1966-68; ptnr. Linn & Helms, Oklahoma City, 1980-90, Daughery, Bradford, Haught & Tompkins, P.C., Oklahoma City, 1990-94; shareholder Conner & Winters, P.C., Oklahoma City, 1994—2003; sole practitioner Oklahoma City, 2003—. Past chmn. bd. trustees Okla. Ann. Methodist Conf., St. Luke's United Meth. Ch.; past chmn. adminstrv. bd.; mem. Okla. Bur. Investigation Commn., past chmn.; past gen. counsel Rep. State com., Interstate Oil Compact. Maj. USAR. Recipient award of Honor Oklahoma City Bi-Centennial Commn., 1976. Fellow Am. Coll. Civil Trial Mediators; master William S. Holliway Am. Inns of Ct. (emeritus, pres.), Robert J. Turner Am. Inn of Ct. (pres.); mem. ABA, Okla. County Bar Assn. (Pres.'s award 1988), Okla. Bar Assn. (chmn. bench and bar com. 1995-97, chmn. ADR sect., Law Day award), Nat. Arbitration Forum, Am. Arbitration Assn. (mediator/arbitrator), NASD (mediator, arbitrator), Am. Judicature Soc., Assn. Atty.-Mediators (past pres. Okla. chpt., nat. dir. and sec., Nat. President's award 2000), Blue Key, Lions (pres. Oklahoma City chpt.). General civil litigation. Home: 3148 Birch Bark Ln Oklahoma City OK 73120 Office: 1001 NW 63d St Ste 200 Oklahoma City OK 73116

TONER, STEPHEN, lawyer; b. Jan. 18, 1956; m. Pamela J.M. Toner; children: Carolyn L., Allison C. Student, St. Francis Coll., 1976; BS in Polit. Sci., U. Mass., 1978; postgrad., Kings Coll., London, 1980, U. Hong Kong, 1981; JD, New Eng. Sch. Law, 1983. Ptnr. Russo, Keane & Toner, N.Y.C., 1997—. Mem. Fairfield Harbor Mgmt. Commn., 1998—, elected vice commr., 2000; mem. Nat. Child Labor Com., 1986—98, elected exec. com., 1992. Mem.: ABA, Guild Cath. Lawyers, N.Y. Trial Lawyers Assn., Fairfield County Hunt Club (elected bd. govs. 2001). Avocations: sailing, skiing, horseback riding, tennis, golf. Insurance, Personal injury (including property damage), Professional liability. Office: Russo Keane Sokoloff & Toner 26 Broadway New York NY 10004-1703

TONG, PETER P. patent lawyer; PhD, Calif. Inst. Tech., 1985; MBA, Santa Clara U., 1992, JD, 1994. Bar: Calif. 1994. Engr. Hewlett Packard, Palo Alto, Calif., 1985-90, legal assoc., 1991-94, patent lawyer, 1994-95, McCutchen, Doyle, Palo Alto, 1995-97, Fliesler, Dubb, Meyer & Lovejoy, San Francisco, 1997-2000. CEO IP Learn, Mountain View, Calif., 1998—; CEO prof.Q San Jose, Calif., 2000-2002; pres. IpVenture, Cupertino, Calif., 2002-. Patentee in field. Mem. Caltech Alumni Assn. (pres. 1992-94), MBA Alumni Assn. Santa Clara Univ. (pres. 1996-97). Intellectual property. Office: ProfQ 690 Saratoga Ave Ste 201 San Jose CA 95129

TOOHEY, BRIAN FREDERICK, lawyer; b. Niagara Falls, N.Y., Dec. 14, 1944; s. Matthew and Marilyn (Hoag) T.; m. Mary Elizabeth Monihan; children: Maureen Elizabeth, Matthew Sheridan, Margaret Monihan, Mary Catherine, Elizabeth Warner. BS, Niagara U., 1966; JD, Cornell U., 1969. Bar: N.Y. 1969, N.Mex. 1978, Ohio 1980. Ptnr. Jones Day, Cleve., 1981—. Lt. JAG Corps, USNR, 1970-73. Mem. ABA, N.Y. State Bar Assn., State Bar N.Mex., Ohio State Bar Assn., Greater Cleve. Bar Assn. Roman Catholic. Federal civil litigation, Insurance. Home: 25 Pepper Creek Dr Cleveland OH 44124-5279 Office: Jones Day N Point 901 Lakeside Ave E Cleveland OH 44114-1190 E-mail: bftoohey@jonesday.com.

TOOLE, JOHN HARPER, lawyer; b. Johnson City, N.Y., Apr. 4, 1941; s. Edward Joseph and Anne (Junius) T.; m. Lamar Sparkman, May 30, 1969; children: John Carter, Lucy Bland. BS, U. Va., 1963; JD, Washington Coll. of Law, 1971. Bar: Va. 1971, D.C. 1972. From assoc. to ptnr. Lewis, Mitchell & Moore, Tysons Corner, Va., 1971-77; ptnr. Watt, Tieder, Killian, Toole & Hoffar, Tysons Corner, 1978-82; of counsel, ptnr. McGuire, Woods, Battle & Boothe, Tysons Corner, 1983-90, McLean, Va., 1990-99; ptnr. Cooley Godward LLP, Reston, Va., 2000—. 1st lt. U.S. Army, 1963—66. Mem. ABA, Va. State Bar, Va. Bar Assn., D.C. Bar Assn. Banking, Commercial, contracts (including sales of goods; commercial financing), Property, real (including real estate development, water). Office: Cooley Godward LLP 11951 Freedom Dr Reston VA 20190-5601 Fax: 703 456-8100. E-mail: jtoole@cooley.com.

TOOMAJIAN, WILLIAM MARTIN, lawyer; b. Troy, N.Y., Sept. 26, 1943; s. Leo R. and Elizabeth (Gundrum) T.; children: Andrew, Philip. AB, Hamilton Coll., 1965; JD, U. Mich., 1968; LLM, N.Y.U., 1975. Bar: N.Y. 1968, Ohio 1978. Mem. firm Cadwalader, Wickersham & Taft, N.Y.C., 1971-77, Baker & Hostetler, Cleve., 1977—. Served to lt. USCG, 1968-71. Mem. ABA, Ohio Bar Assn., Cleve. Bar Assn., Cleve. Tax Club. Commercial, contracts (including sales of goods; commercial financing), Corporate taxation, Personal income taxation. Home: 3582 Lytle Rd Cleveland OH 44122-4908 Office: Baker & Hostetler 3200 National City Ctr 1900 E 9th St Ste 3200 Cleveland OH 44114-3475

TOOTHMAN, JOHN WILLIAM, lawyer; b. Bryn Mawr, Pa., Dec. 6, 1954; m. Elizabeth McGee; 1 child, William. BS ChemE with honors, U. Va., 1977, MS ChemE, 1979; JD cum laude, Harvard U., 1981. Bar: D.C. 1981, Va. 1987, U.S. Dist. Ct. (ea. dist.) Va. 1987, U.S. Ct. Fed. Claims 1987, U.S. Ct. Appeals (4th and fed. cir.) 1987, U.S. Supreme Ct. 1987, Md. 1990, U.S. Bankruptcy Ct. (ea. dist.) Va. 1994, U.S. Dist. Ct. Colo. 1998. Assoc. Howrey & Simon, Washington, 1981-83, Akin, Gump, Strauss et al, Washington, 1983-84; trial atty. civil div. U.S. Dept. Justice, Washington, 1984-86; assoc. John Grad & Assocs., Alexandria, Va., 1986-88; ptnr. Grad, Toothman, Logan & Chabot, P.C., Alexandria, 1988-89, Shulman, Rogers, Gandal, Pordy & Ecker, P.A., Alexandria, 1989-93; founder The Devil's Advocate & The Toothman Law Firm, P.C., 1993—. Guest lectr. George Washington U. Law Sch., 1988; lectr. in field; founder LitWatch, 1999. Author: (with Douglas Danner) Danner & Toothman Trial Practice Checklists, 1989, 2d edit., 2001, (with William Ross) Toothman and Ross Legal Fees: Law and Management, 2003; contbr. articles to profl. jours. NSF fellow, 1977. Mem. ABA (Ross Essay award 1995), Sigma Xi, Tau Beta Pi. Address: 300 N Lee St Ste 450 Alexandria VA 22314-2640 E-mail: jtoothman@litwatch.com.

TOPELIUS, KATHLEEN ELLIS, lawyer; b. July 15, 1948; BA, U. Conn., 1970; postgrad., U. Md., 1971-74; JD, Cath. U. Am., 1978. Bar: D.C. 1978, U.S. Supreme Ct. 1988. Atty. office of gen. counsel Fed. Home Loan Bank Bd., 1978-80; ptnr. Morgan, Lewis & Bockius, Washington, 1985-93, Bryan Cave, Washington, 1993—. Recipient Alpha award Fed. Home Loan Bank Bds., 1979. Banking, Administrative and regulatory. Office: Bryan Cave 700 13th St NW Fl 7 Washington DC 20005-5921 Business E-Mail: ktopelius@bryancave.com.

TOPHAM, LEE EVANS, lawyer; MBA, Plymouth State Coll., 1988; JD, Franklin Pierce Law Ctr., Concord, N.H., 1991. Bar: N.H. 1991, U.S. Dist. Ct. N.H. 1991. Staff atty. N.H. Pub. Defender, Keene, 1991-93, Concord, 1993-95, mng. atty., 1995-2000; assoc. McSwiney, Semple, Bowers & Wise, P.C., New London, 2000—01; staff atty. N.H. Pub. Defender, 2001—. Town moderator Town of Wilmot, N.H., 1998—. Mem. N.H. Bar Assn., N.H. Assn. Criminal Def. Lawyers., Kearsarge Lodge No. 81 F.& A.M. Criminal. Office: 117 N State St Concord NH 03301

TOPOL, ROBIN APRIL LEVITT, lawyer; b. N.Y.C., Apr. 02; d. Anatole Roy and Phyllis Patricia (Redman) Levitt; m. Clifford Miles Topol, Oct. 23, 1982. Student, Stanford U., Eng., 1974; BA, Barnard Coll., 1976; JD, NYU, 1979; postgrad. exec. mgmt. program, Yale U., 1987. Bar: N.Y. 1980, Fla. 1981. Ptnr. real estate dept., comml. real estate and leasing Kurzman Eisenberg Corbin Lever & Goodwin LLP, White Plains, NY, 1996—. Trustee alumni bd. dirs. Yale U. Sch. Mgmt., 1987-88. Mem. ABA (vice chmn. real property com. 1986-90), N.Y. County Bar Assn. (real estate com. 1986-96), Women's Bar Assn. (chmn. real estate com. 1980-96). Avocations: tennis, golf, running. Property, real (including real estate development, water). Office: Kurzman Eisenberg Corbin Lever & Goodman LLP 1 N Broadway White Plains NY 10601-2310

TOPP, SUSAN HLYWA, lawyer; b. Detroit, Oct. 9, 1956; d. Michael Leo and Lucy Stella (Rusak) Hlywa; m. Robert Elwin Topp, July 25, 1985; children: Matthew, Sarah, Michael and Jamie (triplets). BS in Edn. cum laude, Ctrl. Mich. U., 1978; JD cum laude, Wayne State U., Detroit, 1991. Bar: Mich. 1992, U.S. Dist. Ct. (ea. dist.) Mich. 1992. Conservation officer Mich. Dept. Natural Resources, Pontiac, 1980-88, environ. conservation officer Livonia, 1988-93; pvt. practice Gaylord, Mich., 1993; ptnr. Rolinski & Topp, PLC, Gaylord, 1993; assoc. Plunkett & Cooney, PC, Gaylord, 1995—2001; pvt. practice Gaylord, 2001—. Adj. faculty Audubon Internat. Active Rocky Mountain Mineral Law Found., Urban Land Inst. Recipient Am. Jurisprudence award Wayne State U., 1987, Trial Advocacy award, 1988. Mem. ABA (nat. resources and environ. law com.), AAUW, Mich. State Bar Assn. (environ. law sect. coun. mem. 1999), Mich. C. of C. Roman Catholic. Avocations: backpacking, skiing, scuba diving, back-country camping, canoeing. Oil, gas, and mineral, Environmental, Property, real (including real estate development, water). Office: Susan Hlywa Topp Plc PO Box 1977 213 E Main Gaylord MI 49734 E-mail: susan@topplaw.com.

TORGERSON, LARRY KEITH, lawyer; b. Albert Lea, Minn., Aug. 25, 1935; s. Fritz G. and Lu (Hillman) T. BA, Drake U., 1958, MA, 1960, LLB, 1963, JD, 1968; MA, Iowa U., 1962; cert., The Hague Acad. Internat. Law, The Netherlands, 1965, 69; LLM, U. Minn., 1969, Columbia U., 1971, U. Mo., 1976; PMD, Harvard U., 1973; EdM, 1974. Bar: Minn. 1964, U.S. Dist. Ct. Minn. 1964, Wis. 1970, Iowa 1970, U.S. Dist. Ct. (no. dist.) Iowa 1971, U.S. Tax Ct. 1971, U.S. Supreme Ct. 1972, U.S. Dist. Ct. (ea. dist.) Wis. 1981, U.S. Ct. Appeals (8th cir.) 1981. Asst. corp. counsel 1st Bank Stock Corp. (88 Banks), Mpls., 1963-67, 1st Svc. Corp. (27 ins. agys., computer subs.), Mpls., 1965-67; v.p., trust officer Nat. City Bank, Mpls., 1967-69; sr. mem. Torgerson Law Firm, Northwood, Iowa, 1969-87; trustee, gen. counsel Torgerson Farms, Northwood, 19677—, Redbirch Farms, Kensett, Iowa, 1987—, Sunburst Farms, Grafton, Iowa, 1987—, Gold Dust Farms, Bolan, Iowa, 1988—, Torgerson Grain Storage, Bolan, 1988—, Indian Summer Farms, Bolan, 1991—, Sunset Farms, Bolan, 1992—, Sunrise Farms, Grafton, 1994—. CEO, gen. counsel Internat. Investments, Mpls., 1983-96, Transoceanic, Mpls., 1987-96, Torgerson Capital, Northwood, 1996—, Torgerson Investments, Northwood, 1984—, Torgerson Properties, Northwood, 1987—, Torgerson Ranches, Sundance, Wyo., 1998—, Hawaiian Investments Unltd., Maui, Hawaii, 1998—, Internat. Investments Unltd., San Pedro, Belize, 1999—. Recipient All-Am. Journalism award Thomas Arkle Clark Outstanding Achievement award, 1958, Dennis E. Brumfield Outstanding Achievement award, 1958, Johnny B. Guy Outstanding Leadership award, 1958; named to Outstanding Young Men of Am., U.S. Jaycees; Hagen scholar, Honor scholar. Mem. ABA, Am. Judicature Soc., Iowa Bar Assn., Minn. Bar Assn., Wis. Bar Assn., Hennepin County Bar Assn., Mensa, Drake Student-Faculty Coun., Drake Student Alumni Coun. (chmn.), Jaycees, Harvard Bus. Sch. Study (pres., exec. com., univ. editor in chief), Psi Chi, Circle K (pres. local chpt.), Phi Alpha Delta, Omicron Delta Kappa (pres. local chpt.), Pi Kappa Delta (pres. local chpt.), Alpha Tau Omega (pres. local chpt., Silver Bullet Outstanding Leadership award, 1965, 66), Pi Delta Epsilon (founder, chpt. pres.), Alpha Kappa Delta, Alpha Scholastic Hon. (U. editor-in-chief), Harvard Bus. Sch. Exec. Com. (U. editor-in-chief). Lutheran. Corporate, general, Property, real (including real estate development, water), Taxation, general.

TORKILDSON, RAYMOND MAYNARD, lawyer; b. Lake City, S.D., Nov. 19, 1917; s. Gustav Adolph and Agnes (Opitz) T.; m. Sharman Elizbeth Vaughn, Sept. 8, 1956; children: Stephen, Thomas. S.B., U. S.D., 1946; JD, Harvard U., 1948. Bar: Calif. 1949, Hawaii 1950. Assoc. James P. Blaisdell, Honolulu, 1949-52; ptnr. Moore, Torkildson & Rice and successors, Honolulu, 1955-64; exec. v.p. Hawaii Employers Council, Honolulu, 1964-67; ptnr. Torkildson, Katz, Fonseca, Jaffe, Moore & Hetherington and predecessors, Honolulu, 1967-72; sr. ptnr., 1972-92; of counsel, 1993—. Mem. mgmt. com. Armed Forces YMCA, Honolulu, 1971; treas. Hawaii Republican Com. 1977-83. Served with U.S. Army, 1941-46; lt. col. Res. ret. Mem. ABA, Hawaii Bar Assn. Clubs: Oahu Country, Pacific (Honolulu). Roman Catholic. Labor (including EEOC, Fair Labor Standards Act, labor-management relations, NLRB, OSHA).

TORNOW, THOMAS T. lawyer; b. Denver, July 29, 1954; s. Herbert H. and Mary A. (Flanagan) T.; m. Sue A. Brown, Mar. 2, 1992. BA magna cum laude, U. No. Colo., 1975; JD, U. Pa., 1979. Bar: Colo. 1979, Mont. 1991, U.S. Dist. Ct. Colo. 1979, U.S. Ct. Appeals (10th cir.) 1981, Soloman Islands 1988. Assoc. Calkind, Kramer, Denver, 1979-85; instr. U. Denver Coll. Law, 1984-87; legal advisor Solomon Islands Govt., Lata, Temotu, 1987-89; solo practitioner Whitefish, Mont., 1991—. Pres. Whitefish Planning Bd., 1991-96; advocate KC, Whitefish, 1992-97. Democrat. Buddhist. Avocation: racquetball. Commercial, contracts (including sales of goods; commercial financing), Land use and zoning (including planning), Property, real (including real estate development, water). Office: 100 2nd St E Whitefish MT 59937-2410

TORNSTROM, ROBERT ERNEST, lawyer, oil company executive; b. St. Paul, Jan. 17, 1946; s. Clifford H. and Janet (Hale) T.; m. Betty Jane Hermann, Aug. 5, 1978; children: Carter, Gunnar, Katherine. BA, U. Colo., 1968, JD, 1974; diploma grad. sch. mgmt. exec. program, UCLA, 1990. Bar: Colo. 1974, U.S. Dist. Ct. Colo. 1974, Calif. 1975, U.S. Dist. Ct. (cen. dist.) Calif. 1975. Atty. Union Oil Co. of Calif., L.A., 1974-76, counsel internat. div., 1977-78, regional counsel, 1976-77; sr. atty. Occidental Internat. Exploration and Prodn. Co., Bakersfield, Calif., 1978-81, mng. counsel, 1981-85, v.p., assoc. gen. counsel, 1985-88, v.p., regional ops. mgr., 1988-91; pres. Occidental Argentina, Buenos Aires, 1991-93, Occidental of Russia, Moscow, 1993-94; dir. comml. negotiations Occidental Internat., 1994-96; chmn. of bd. Sullivan Petroleum Co., 1997—. Bd. dirs., chmn. bd. Parmaneft Joint Venture, Vanyogannef JV, Moscow; bd. dirs. Calif. Land and Cattle Co., King City, 602 Operating Corp.; exec. bd. Cmty. House, Bakersfield; legal cons. Island Creek Coal Co., Lexington, Ky. Capt. U.S. Army, 1968-71, Vietnam. Decorated Bronze Star. Mem. Am. Soc. Internat. Law, Am. Corp. Counsel Assn., Soc. Mayflower Descendants, Moscow Country Club, Stockdale Country Club. Republican. Episcopalian. Avocations: skiing, tennis, golf, riding, collecting classic automobiles. Corporate, general, Oil, gas, and mineral, Private international. Home: 310 Mount Lowe Dr Bakersfield CA 93309-2468 Office: 1508 18th St Ste 222 Bakersfield CA 93301

TORPEY, SCOTT RAYMOND, lawyer; b. Detroit, July 4, 1955; s. Raymond George and Carmela Rose (Aquaro) T. BA in English, Wayne State U., 1978; JD, U. Detroit, 1982. Bar: Mich. 1984, D.C. 1985, N.Y. 1990, Ill. 1990, Calif. 1991, U.S. Dist. Ct. (ea. and we. dist.) Mich., U.S. Dist. Ct. (so., we., no. and ea. dists.) N.Y. 1990, U.S. Dist. Ct. (no., cen. and so. dists.) Ill. 1990, U.S. Dist. Ct. (D.C. dist.) 1989, U.S. Dist. Ct. (cen., so., no. and ea. dists.) Calif., 1991, U.S. Tax Ct., U.S. Ct. Appeals (D.C., fed., 2d, 6th, 7th and 9th cirs.), U.S. Supreme Ct. 1988. Litigation ptnr. Jaffe, Raitt, Heuer and Weiss, PC, Detroit, 2000—; assoc. Long & Levit, San Francisco, 1982-83, Keating, Canham & Wells, Detroit, 1983-85; ligitation ptnr. Kohl, Secrest, Wardle, Lynch, Clark & Hampton, Farmington Hills, Mich., 1985-2000. Editor Tax Law Jour., 1981, Corp., Fin. and Bus. Law Jour., 1982. Mem. ABA, Fed. Bar Assn., Lawyer-Pilots Bar Assn., Bar Assn. San Francisco, Mich. State Bar Assn. (chmn. aviation torts com. of aviation law sect. 1992—). Republican. Avocations: sports, music, sports cars. Aviation, General civil litigation, Product liability. Office: Jaffe Raitt Heuer & Weiss 1 Woodward Ave Ste 2400 Detroit MI 48226

TORRES, ERNEST C. federal judge; b. 1941; AB, Dartmouth Coll., 1963; JD, Duke U., 1968. Assoc. Hinckley, Allen, Salisbury & Parsons, 1968-74; ptnr. Saunders & Torres, 1974-80; assoc. justice R.I. Superior Ct., 1980-85; asst. v.p. Aetna Life and Casualty, 1985-86; ptnr. Tillinghast, Collins & Graham, 1986-87; chief judge U.S. Dist. Ct. R.I., Providence, 1988—. Pres. East Greenwich (R.I.) Town Coun., 1972-74; state rep. R.I. Ho. of Reps., 1975-80, dep. minority leader, 1977-80. Recipient Disting. Svc. award Jaycees, 1974; named Man of Yr., Prince Henry Soc. R.I., 1988, Prince Henry Soc. Mass., 1995; Alfred P. Sloan scholar Dartmouth Coll. Mem. ABA, ATLA, FBA, R.I. Bar Assn., Jaycees (Dist. Svc. award 1974), Prince Henry Soc. of R.I., Prince Henry Soc. of Mass. Office: US Dist Ct One Exchange Terrace Providence RI 02903

TORRES BLANQUEZ, MIGUEL, lawyer, law educator; b. Barcelona, Nov. 5, 1962; Degree in law, U. Barcelona, 1986. Assoc. Bufete Bertrán i Musitu, Barcelona, 1987—88, Bufete Mullerat & Rosell, 1989—92; ptnr. Bufete Mullerat & Roca, 1993—98, Mullerat, 1999—. Assoc. prof. law U. Barcelona, 1991—. Author: European Economic Interest Grouping. Mem.: Juristes Sans Frontières, Union Internationale des Avocats (vice-chmn.), Internat. Bar Assn. Corporate, general, Banking, Private international. Office: Mullerat Av Diagonal 640 Barcelona 08017 Spain Office Fax: 34.93.405.91.76. E-mail: m.torres@mullerat.com.

TORREY, CLAUDIA OLIVIA, lawyer; b. Nashville, June 10, 1958; d. Claude Adolphus and Rubye Mayette (Prigmore) T. BA in Econ., Syracuse U., 1980; JD, N.Y. Law Sch., 1985. Bar: N.Y. State 1988. Legal intern Costello, Cooney & Fearon, Syracuse, N.Y., 1979; legal clk. First Am. Corp., Nashville, 1981; legal asst. James I. Meyerson, N.Y.C., 1982-85; jud. law clk. N.Y. State Supreme Ct., N.Y.C., 1985; interim project supr., legal asst. CUNY Ctrl. Office, 1985-86; legal analyst Rosenman & Colin Law Firm, N.Y.C., 1986-87; asst. counsel N.Y. State Legis., Albany, 1988-90; atty., cons. pvt. practice, Nashville, Cookeville, Tenn., 1991—. Bd. dirs. Children's Corner Day Care Ctr., Albany, N.Y., 1989-90. Author column Health Law Jour. of N.Y. State Bar Assn., 1996—. Ch. rep. FOCUS exec. coun. Westminster Presbyn. Ch., Albany, 1990; mem. PDS/USN Alumni Bd., Nashville, 2001—; interim chair Synod of Living Waters COR Com., Presbyn. Ch. (U.S.A.), 2002. Mem. ABA (young lawyers divsn. liaison to ABA forum on health law 1994-96), Internat. Platform Assn., N.Y. State Bar Assn. (chmn. health law sect. study group on health info., privacy and confidentiality 1998-99), Alpha Kappa Alpha (treas., pres., corr. sec. IOTA Upsilon Chpt. Syracuse U.) Avocations: singing, reading, harp, travel, art. Education and schools, General practice, Health. Home and Office: PO Box 150234 Nashville TN 37215-0234 E-mail: jewel3@prodigy.net.

TOSCANO, OSCAR ERNESTO, lawyer; b. Ecuador, Jan. 24, 1951; s. Hugo and Maruja (Lopez) T.; children: Marina, Tracy, Oscar Emerson, Jacob, Nicole, David. BA, UCLA, 1975; JD, Loyola U., L.A., 1978. Bar: Calif. 1978, U.S. Dist. Ct. (9th dist.) Calif. 1978. Pvt. practice, Glendale, 1978—. Mem. Assn. Consumer Attys. of L.A., Consumer Attys. of Calif., Los Angeles County Bar, Mex.-Am. Bar Assn., State Bar Calif., Glendale Bar Assn., Hispanic Alumni Scholarship Found. Avocations: tennis, chess, trial work. Criminal, Family and matrimonial, Insurance. Office: 625 W Broadway Glendale CA 91204-1058

TOTENBERG, NINA, journalist; b. N.Y.C., Jan. 14, 1944; d. Roman and Melanie (Shroder) T.; m. Floyd Haskell, Feb. 3, 1979 (dec.); m. H. David Reines, 2000. Student, Boston U.; LLD (hon.), Haverford Coll., Chatham Coll., Gonzaga U., Northeastern U., St. Mary's, SUNY; LHD, Lebanon Valley Coll., Westfield State Coll., Pa. State U., Pine Manor Coll., De Paul U., Simmons Coll. Reporter Boston Record Am., 1965, Peabody Times, 1967, Nat. Observer, 1968-71, Newtimes, 1973, Nat. Pub. Radio, Washington, 1974—, Inside Washington, 1992—; reporter Nightline ABC, 1993-98. Contbr. articles to N.Y. Times Mag., Harvard Law Rev., Christian Sci. Monitor, N.Y. Mag., Parade. Recipient Sidney Hillman award, 1983, Alfred I. Dupont award Columbia U., 1988, 91, George Foster Peabody award, 1991, George Polk award, 1991, Joan Barone award, 1991, Silver Gavel award ABA, 1968-98, Woman of Courage award Women in Film, 1991, Athena award, 1994, Presdl. Commendation, Radcliffe Coll., 1998; named outstanding broadcast journalist of yr. Nat. Press Found., 1999. Mem. Sigma Delta Chi (award 1991). Office: NPR 635 Massachusetts Ave NW Washington DC 20001-3740

TOTTEN, RANDOLPH FOWLER, lawyer; b. Washington, June 20, 1943; s. Arthur Irving and Margaret Holland (Ross) Totten; m. Virginia Hunton, July 31, 1965; children: Louise, Fitz, Caroline. BA, Yale U., 1965; LLB, U. Va., 1968. Bar: Va. 1968. Law clk. to Hon. Gordon Va. Supreme Ct. Appeals, Richmond, 1968—69; from assoc. to ptnr. Hunton & Williams, Richmond, 1969—. Mem. editl. bd. Va. Law Rev. Chmn. Richmond Cmty. H.S., 1979—81; trustee Westminster-Canterbury Corp., 2003—, Ch. Schs. Episcopal Diocese Va., 1974—86; standing com. Diocese of Va., 1984—87; exec. bd. St. Andrew's Assn., 1981, pres., 1997—; exec. com. Christchurch Sch., 1982—86; exec. bd. Commonwealth Va. Bd. Mental Health, Mental Retardation and Substance Abuse Svcs., 1988—93. Mem.: ABA, Va. Bar Assn., Commonwealth Club, Country Club Va. Corporate, general. Office: Hunton & Williams Riverfront Plz PO Box 1535 Richmond VA 23218-1535

TOUBY, KATHLEEN ANITA, lawyer; b. Miami Beach, Feb. 20, 1943; d. Harry and Kathleen Rebecca (Hamper) T.; m. Joseph Thomas Woodward; children: Mark Andrew, Judson David Touby. BS in Nursing, U. Fla., 1965, MRC in Rehab. Counseling, 1967; JD with honors, Nova U., 1977. Bar: Fla. 1978, D.C. 1978. Counselor Jewish Vocat. Svc., Chgo., 1967-68; rehab. counselor Fla. Dept. Vocat. Rehab., Miami, 1968-70; spl. asst., asst. U.S. atty. U.S. Dept. Justice, Miami, 1978-80; assoc. Pyszka & Kessler, P.A., Miami, 1980-83; ptnr. Touby & Smith, P.A., Miami, 1983-89, Touby, Smith, DeMahy & Drake, P.A., Miami, 1989-94, Touby & Woodward, P.A., Miami, 1994—. Chmn. adv. exec. bd. Paralegal Edn. program Barry U., 1986-87; lectr. Food and Drug Law Inst., 1987-89, 91; lectr. environ. law Exec. Enterprises, 1987-88; lectr. trial techniques, Hispanic Nat. Bar Assn., St. Thomas Law Sch.; adj. prof. product liability Can. Govt., U.S. Trade and Mktg. Dept., 1989-95. Co-author: The Environmental Litigation Deskbook, 1989; contbr. chpts. to books, articles to profl. jours. Mem. ABA, Am. Inns of Ct. (pres. 1998-99, pres.-elect St. Thomas Law Sch. chpt. 1997-98, pres. 1998-99), Dade County Bar Assn. (legal aid, pub. svcs. com. 1988), Fed. Bar Assn. (bd. dirs. 1989—, v.p. 1991-92, pres.-elect So. Fla. chpt. 1992-93, pres. 1993-94), Phi Delta Phi (province pres. 1982-85, bd. dirs. 1985-87). Roman Catholic. General civil litigation, Insurance, Personal injury (including property damage). Home: 450 Sabal Palm Rd Miami FL 33137-3352 Office: Touby & Woodward PA 250 Bird Rd Ste 308 Miami FL 33146-1424

TOUCHY, DEBORAH K.P. lawyer, accountant; b. Pasadena, Tex., Dec. 9, 1957; d. Donald Carl and Bobbie Jo (Jackson) Putzka; m. Harry Roy Touchy, Jr., Feb. 23, 1980. BBA, Baylor U., 1979; JD, U. Houston, 1988. Bar: Tex. 1989; CPA, Tex.; cert. in estate planning and probate law Tex. Bd. Legal Specialization. Sr. mgr. tax KMPG Peat Marwick, Houston, 1980-86; assoc. Fizer Beck Webster & Bentley, Houston, 1989-90; pvt. practice law Houston, 1990—; chmn. spl. events Jr. League Houston, 1997-98. Editor Houston Law Rev., 1988-89. Chmn. ticket sales incentives Chi Omega, Houston, 1985; active ticket sales Mus. Fine Arts, Houston, 1984; facilities chmn. Woodland Trails West Civic Orgn., Houston, 1982-83; pres. Women Attys. in Tax & Probate, 1994-95, pres.-elect, 2003; bd. dirs. Episcopal Ch. Women at St. John the Divine; active St. John's Sch., 1999—, Lower Sch. Scrapbook Chmn. 2001-2002. Recipient Outstanding Alumni award, Beta Alpha Psi, 1997. Mem. ABA (estate-probate sect. 1989—, vice chmn. commn. property com. 1994—), AICPA (taxation sect., estate and gift tax com. 1992-95, 98-2000), Tex. Soc. CPAs (bd. dirs. 1995—, chmn. tax inst. com. 1996-97, estate planning com. 1990-94, 96—), Houston Chpt. CPAs (chmn. taxpayer edn. 1985-86, chmn. membership com. 1992-93, v.p. 1993-94, 96-97, chmn. tax forums 1994-95, long range planning com. 1995-96, chmn. leadership devel. 1997-98, treas. 1998-99, chmn. ann. charity event 1999-2000, bd. dirs. 1999-2000, 2002-03, pres. 2001-02), Houston Bar Assn. (estate-probate sect. 1989—), State Bar Tex. (estate-probate sect. 1989—, mem. elder law com. 1991-97), Houston Estate and Fin. Forum, Baylor U. Women's Assn. (treas. 1993-94, chmn. fin. com. 1994-95, parliamentarian 1995-96, sec. 1996-97, pres. 1997-98, chmn. audit com. 1999-2000), Chief Justice-Advocates, Tex. Bd. Legal Specializations (cert. estate planning, probate law 1994), Order of Coif, Omicron Delta Kappa, Phi Delta Phi, Beta Alpha Psi (Outstanding Alumni 1997). Estate planning, Probate (including wills, trusts), Taxation, general. Office: PO Box 130122 Houston TX 77219-0122

TOUMEY, DONALD JOSEPH, lawyer; BA, Williams Coll., 1978; JD, Yale U., 1981. Bar: N.Y. 1982, D.C. 1985, U.S. Supreme Ct. 1986. Law clk. to judge U.S. Ct Appeals (2d cir.), N.Y.C., 1981-82; spl. asst. to gen. counsel U.S. Dept. Treasury, Washington, 1982-85; assoc. Sullivan & Cromwell, N.Y.C., 1985-90; ptnr., 1990—. Republican. Banking, Mergers and acquisitions, Securities. Office: Sullivan & Cromwell LLP 125 Broad St New York NY 10004-2489

TOURKOW, JOSHUA ISAAC, lawyer; b. Fort Wayne, Ind., Mar. 5, 1947; s. Frederick Rhinehold and Leah Sarah (Schwartz) T.; m. Donna Susan Dubin, Aug. 30, 1970; children— Illana Joy, Lisa Michelle, Benjamin Ahron. Student Bar Ilan U., Israel, 1968; B.S. in Indsl. Mgmt., Purdue U., 1970; J.D., Ind. U.-Indpls., 1973. Bar: Ind. 1973, U.S. Dist. Cts. (no. and so. dists.) Ind. 1973, U.S. Ct. Appeals (7th cir.) 1973. Asst. dep. prosecutor Marion County, Indpls., 1972-73; ptnr. Tourkow, Crell, Rosenblatt & Johnston, Ft. Wayne, 1973— . Bd. dirs. Housing & Neighborhood Devel. Services, Inc., Ft. Wayne, 1980-84, Ft. Wayne Redevel. Com., 1983; atty. Ft. Wayne Housing Authority, 1983—87; advisor, atty. Parents Without Partners, Ft. Wayne, 1981-85, Fathers United for Equal Rights, Ft. Wayne, 1980— . Mem. ABA, Ind. Bar Assn. (chair of family law, 1992-994), Allen County Bar Assn (chair family law sect. 2000-02). Bankruptcy, Family and matrimonial, General practice. Home: 7022 Winchester Rd Fort Wayne IN 46819-1530 Office: Tourkow Crell Rosenblatt & Johnston 814 Anthony Wayne Building Fort Wayne IN 46802 Fax: 260-422-9991.

TOUSLEY, RUSSELL FREDERICK, lawyer; b. New Haven, Nov. 19, 1938; s. Russell F. and Della (Ermer) T.; m. Sarah Morford, July 23, 1963; children: Ellen Elizabeth, Kenneth Morford. BA cum laude, Yale Coll., 1960; JD, U. Wash., 1967. Bar: Wash. 1967. Assoc. Davis Wright, Seattle, 1967-69; v.p. Safecare Co., Inc., Seattle, 1969-78, Winmar Co., Inc., Seattle, 1977-78; ptnr. Tousley Brain Stephens PLLC, Seattle, 1978—. Trustee Seattle Opera Assn., 1980—, pres., chmn. bd., 1985-87; trustee Seattle Chamber Music Festival, 1990-93; moderator Plymouth Congl. Ch., Seattle, 1975-77, 83-85, trustee, 1969-93, adminstrn., property and fin. bd., 1999-2001. Lt. (j.g.) USN, 1960-64. Mem. ABA, Wash. State Bar Assn., Seattle-King County Bar Assn., Internat. Coun. Shopping Ctrs. (assoc.), Rainier Club, Seattle Tennis Club, Rotary. Avocations: opera, reading, collecting mint U.S. regular issue stamps. Finance, Private international, Property, real (including real estate development, water). Office: Tousley Brain Stephens PLLC Key Tower 56th Flr 700 5th Ave Ste 5600 Seattle WA 98104-5056 E-mail: rtousley@tousley.com.

TOWE, THOMAS EDWARD, lawyer; b. Cherokee, Iowa, June 25, 1937; s. Edward and Florence (Tow) T.; m. Ruth James, Aug. 21, 1960; children: James Thomas, Kristofer Edward. Student, U. Paris, 1956; BA, Earlham Coll., 1959; LLB, U. Mont., 1962; LLM, Georgetown U., 1965. Ptnr. Towe, Ball, Enright, Mackey & Sommerfeld, Billings, Mont., 1967—; legislator Mont. House of Rep., Billings, 1971-75, Mont. State Senate, Billings, 1975-87, 91-94. Served on various coms. Mont. Senate, 1975-87, 91-94. Contbr. articles to law revs. Mem. Alternatives, Inc., Halfway House, Billing, 1977-99, pres., 1985-86; mem. adv. com. Mont. Crime Control Bd., 1973-78, Youth Justice Coun., 1981-83; mem. State Dem. Exec. Com., 1969-73; Dem. candidate for Congress, 1976; bd. dirs. Mont. Consumer Affairs Coun., Regl. Cmty. Svcs. for the Devel. Disabled, 1975-77, Rimrock Guidance Found., 1975-80, Vols. of Am., Billings, 1984-89, Youth Dynamics Inc., 1989-96, Zoo Mont., 1985-2001, Inst. for Peace Studies, 1993—, Mont. State Parks Assn., 1993—. Capt. U.S. Army, 1962-65. Named as one of 100 Most Influential Montanans in 20th Century, Missoulian newspaper. Mem. Mont. Bar Assn., Yellowstone County Bar Assn., Am. Hereford Assn., Billings C. of C. Mem. Soc. Of Friends. Avocation: outdoor recreation. Federal civil litigation, Labor (including EEOC, Fair Labor Standards Act, labor-management relations, NLRB, OSHA), Probate (including wills, trusts). Home: 2739 S Gregory Dr Billings MT 59102-0509 Office: Towe Ball Enright Et Al 2525 6th Ave N Billings MT 59101-1358 E-mail: t.towe@attbi.com.

TOWERY, CURTIS KENT, lawyer; b. Hugoton, Kans., Jan. 29, 1954; s. Clyde D. and Jo June (Curtis) Towery. BA, Trinity U., 1976; JD, U. Okla., 1979; LLM in Taxation, Boston U., 1989. Mem. Curtis & Blanton, Pauls Valley, Okla., 1980-81; lawyer land and legal dept. Trigg Drilling Co., Oklahoma City, 1981-82; adminstrv. law judge Okla. Corp. Commn., Oklahoma City, 1982-85; counsel Curtis & Blanton, Pauls Valley, Okla., 1985-88; adminstrv. law judge Okla. Dept. Mines, Oklahoma City, 1985-88, assoc. gen. counsel, 1989-92; contracts and purchasing adminstr., atty. Okla. Turnpike Authority, Oklahoma City, 1992-93; asst. gen. counsel Okla. Corp. Commn., 1993-97; spl. judge City of Oklahoma City, 1997—2000; adminstrv. law judge Okla. Dept. of Labor, 1998, 2002—; v.p., trust officer Bank One Trust, Oklahoma City, 1998-2000; mgr. Cherokee Capital Holdings, 2000—. Assoc. bd. Okla. Mus. Art, 1985—88, Okla. Symphony Orch., 1987—92, Ballet Okla., 1987—92, sec., 1990—91, v.p., 1988—89. Mem.: ABA, Okla. Bar Assn., Tex. Bar Assn., Faculty Ho., Elks, Rotary, Sigma Nu, Phi Alpha Delta. Democrat. Presbyterian. Avocations: flying, golf, travel, investment analysis. Oil, gas, and mineral, Probate (including wills, trusts), Estate taxation. Office: PO Box 14891 Oklahoma City OK 73113-0891 Home: 11300 N Pennsylvania Ave Oklahoma City OK 73120

TOWNSEND, BRIAN DOUGLAS, paralegal; b. Tokyo, Sept. 22, 1961; s. Thomas and Juanita Evora (Sanford) T.; m. Gloria Ann Wigfall, Aug. 23, 1986; children: Brian D. Jr., Brianna A. BA in Criminology, U. Md., 1983. Legal aide Kirkland & Ellis, Washington, 1984-85; legal asst. to mng. clk. Cadwalader, Wickersham & Taft, Washington, 1985-87; paralegal specialist, Office of Chief Counsel U.S. Dept. Transp. Maritime Adminstrn., Washington, 1987-90, U.S. Dept. Treasury, IRS, Washington, 1990-92; litigation support specialist U.S. Dept. Justice, Tax Divsn., Washington, 1992-93; paralegal specialist Resolution Trust Corp., Washington, 1993-95, FDIC, Washington, 1996-98, U.S. Dept. Treasury, OIG, Washington, 1998-99; program specialist FOIA/PA U.S. Dept. Treasury, OFAC, Washington, 1999-2000; mgmt. analyst USDA, Washington, 2000—02; program analyst IRS/OPA, U.S. Dept. Treasury, Washington, 2002—. Avocations: bowling, fishing, swimming, chess, football. Office: US Dept Treasury IRS/OPA 1111 Constitution Ave NW Washington DC 20224-0002 E-mail: briandouglastownsend@yahoo.com., brian.d.townsend@irs.gov.

TOWNSEND, JOHN MICHAEL, lawyer; b. West Point, N.Y., Mar. 21, 1947; s. John D. and Vera (Nachman) T.; m. Frances M. Fragos, Oct. 8, 1994; children, James E., Patrick M. BA, Yale U., 1968, JD, 1971. Bar: N.Y. 1972, U.S. Dist. Ct. (so. and ea. dists.) N.Y. 1975, U.S. Ct. Appeals (2nd cir.) 1975, U.S. Supreme Ct. 1975, U.S. Ct. Appeals (8th cir.) 1982, U.S. Ct. Appeals (7th and 10th cirs.) 1986, D.C. 1990, U.S. Dist. Ct. D.C. 1990, U.S. Ct. Appeals (D.C. cir.) 1990, U.S. Ct. Appeals (4th cir.) 1991, U.S. Ct. Appeals (fed. cir.) 2000, U.S. Ct. Appeals (11th cir.) 2001, U.S. Ct. Fed. Claims, 2000, U.S. Ct. Appeals (1st cir.) 2003. Assoc. Hughes Hubbard & Reed, LLP, N.Y.C., 1971-73, 75-80, ptnr., 1980—; assoc. Hughes Hubbard & Reed, Paris, 1973-74. Bd. dirs., exec. com., chair law com. Am. Arbitration Assn.; trustee U.S. Coun. Internat. Bus. 1st lt. USAR, 1971-75. Mem. ABA, Am. Law Inst., Internat. Bar Assn., Assn. Bar City N.Y., Union Internat. des Avocats, Univ. Club, Yale Club (N.Y.C.). Democrat. Episcopalian. Antitrust, Alternative dispute resolution, Private international. Office: Hughes Hubbard & Reed LLP 1775 I St NW Washington DC 20006-2401 Fax: (202) 721-4646. E-mail: townsend@hugheshubbard.com.

TOWNSEND, ROBERT J. lawyer; b. Charlotte, Mich., Nov. 11, 1938; s. Robert Wright and Rhea Lucille (Jennings) T.; m. Thea E. Kolb, Aug. 1, 1964; children: Melissa, Bradley. BA, Mich. State U., 1960; LLB, Harvard U., 1963. Bar: Ohio 1964, U.S. Dist. Ct. (so. dist.) Ohio 1964, U.S. Ct. Appeals (6th cir.) 1971, U.S. Supreme Ct. 1992. Assoc. Taft, Stettinus & Hollister, Cin., 1963-72, ptnr., 1972—. Dir. Employers Resource Assn., Cin., 1989—. With U.S. Army, 1963-64, 68-69. Civil rights, General civil litigation, Labor (including EEOC, Fair Labor Standards Act, labor-management relations, NLRB, OSHA). Office: 1800 Firstar Tower 425 Walnut St Cincinnati OH 45202-3923 E-mail: townsend@taftlaw.com.

TOWNSEND, RODNEY ALLEN, lawyer; b. Port Arthur, Tex., Jan. 14, 1971; s. Rodney Allen and Debra Kay Townsend; m. Amy Michelle Judice, Jan. 4, 1997; 1 child, Alexandria Paige. BSc, Lamar U., 1994; JD, South Tex. Coll. Law, 2000. Bar: Tex. 2000, U.S. Dist. (so., ea.) Tex., cert.: mediator, Tex. 2000. Lawyer Provost and Umphrey, L.L.P., Beaumont, Tex., 2000—03, Barton, Price and McElroy, Orange, Tex., 2003. Sabine Chpt. Ducks Unltd. Orange, 2003—. Mem.: Orange County Bar Assn., Tex. Trial Lawyers Assn., Am. Trial Lawyers Assn. Personal injury (including property damage), Admiralty, Toxic tort. Office: Barton Price and McElroy 701 W Park Orange TX 77630 Business E-Mail: Barton@exp.net.

TOWNSEND, WILLIAM JACKSON, lawyer; b. June 4, 1932; s. Robert Glenn and Lois Juanita (Jackson) T. BS, Wake Forest U., 1954; student, U. Ky., 1957, U. Louisville, 1958; JD, U. N.C., 1960. Lawyer; b. Grayson, Ky., June 4, 1932; s. Robert Glenn and Lois Juanita (Jackson) T. BS, Wake Forest U., 1954; Student U. Ky., 1957, U. Louisville, 1958, U. N.C., 1960. Bar: N.C. 1965. Claims adjuster State Farm Ins. Co., 1963; sole practice, Fayetteville, N.C., 1965—; pub. adminstr. Robeson County, N.C., 1966; dir., treas. Colonial Foods, Inc., St. Paul, N.C., 1959—; tax atty. City of Lumberton, 1966-67 . Served as 1st lt. U.S. Army, 1954-56. Mem. N.C. Bar Assn., N.C. State Bar, Cumberland County Bar Assn., N.C. Bar Assn., Scabbard and Blade (pres.), Delta Theta Phi. Presbyterian. Club: Kiwanis (treas. Fayetteville 1973-82). Corporate, general, Family and matrimonial, Personal injury (including property damage). Office: PO Box 584 2109 Elvira St Apt 806 Fayetteville NC 28302

TOY, CHARLES DAVID, lawyer; b. N.Y.C., June 29, 1955; s. Frank H.F. and Louise S.K. (Louie) Toy; m. Sandra Lynn Youla, Mar. 10, 1984; 1 child, Alana May Youla. BA cum laude, Harvard U., 1977, JD, 1980. Bar: NY 1981, DC 2001. Assoc. Milbank, Tweed, Hadley & McCloy, N.Y.C., 1980-84, Kaye, Scholer, Fierman, Hays & Handler, Hong Kong, 1984-88, ptnr., 1989-91, 1991-93; v.p., gen. counsel Overseas Pvt. Investment Corp., Washington, 1993-2001, v.p. fin., 1995-96, v.p. investment funds, 1998-99; ptnr. Wilmer, Cutler & Pickering, Washington, 2001—02; bd. adv. GMI Capital Corp., Chevy Chase, Md., 2002—. Spkr. in field; profile subject Internat. Fin. Law Rev., 1996, Avenue Asia, 1996, 97, Assn. Bar City of N.Y., 2000, World Econ. Devel. Conf., 1996, Corp. Legal Times Roundtable, 1996, Com. of 100, 1996, Asian Am. Bar Assn., 1996, Asian Bus. Assn., 1996, Asian Pacific Am. Bar Assn., 1996, Forbes, 1997, Adam Smith Inst., 1998, Jerome Levy Econs. Inst. of Bard Coll., 1998, Asian Pacific Am. Inst. for Congl. Studies, 1998, Embassy of South Africa, 1998, Harvard Inst. for Internat. Devel., 1998, 99, Insight Info., 1998, 99, Nat. Asian Pacific Am. Bar Assn., 1998. U. Fla. Levin Coll. Law, 1999, CNA/Schinnerer Conf., 1999, Case We. Res. U. Sch. Law, 1999, Practising Law Inst., 1999, 2000, U. Iowa Tippie Sch. Mgmt., 2000, Met. Corp. Counsel Interview, 2000, Internat. Project Fin. Assn., 2000, Am. Corp. Counsel Assn., 2000, U.S. Inst. of Peace, 2001; interview Legal Times, 2001, Bloomberg, 2002. Contbg. editor Taxes and Investment in Asia and the Pacific, 1985, Tax News Svc., 1986—, Bull. for Internat. Fiscal Documentation, 1986—; bd. editors Strategic Alliance Alert, 1994-95. Bd. trustees Lower East Side Tenement Mus., 1994-98. Mem. ABA, N.Y. State Bar Assn., Assn. Bar City of N.Y., Nat. Asian Pacific Am. Bar Assn., Asian Pacific Am. Bar Assn., Harvard Law Sch. Assn., Am. Club (Hong Kong), Ladies Recreation Club (Hong Kong), Phi Beta Kappa Democrat. Roman Catholic. Commercial, contracts (including sales of goods; commercial financing), Corporate, general, Private international. Office: GMI Capital Corp 4701 Willard Ave Ste 413 Chevy Chase MD 20815-4610 E-mail: toy@globalmezzanine.com.

TRABUE, KENNETH ELLSWORTH, judge; b. Alton, Ill., Aug. 13, 1933; BS in Indsl. Econs., Purdue U., 1956; JD, Ind. U., 1961. Bar: Ind. 1961, Va. 1962. Multiple line adjuster St. Paul Fire and Marine Ins. Co., Indpls., 1956-61, claims mgr. Roanoke, Va., 1962-64; assoc. Hunter, Fox & Fox, Roanoke, 1965-66; ptnr. Hunter Fox & Trabue, Roanoke, 1967-77; judge 23d Jud. Cir. Ct. Va., 1977—95; mediator, arbitrator The McCammon Group, Richmond, Va., 1995—. Mem. faculty Va. Western Community Coll., Roanoke, 1972-75. Pres. Cave Spring Jaycees, 1964-66; group chmn. legal sect. United Fund Roanoke Valley, 1970, chmn. profl. div., 1971, chmn. svcs. div., 1972; pres. Hunting Hills Homeowners Assn., 1975-76; pres. Waters Edge Homeowner's Assn., 1999-2001. Fellow Va. Law Found.; mem. ABA, Va. Bar Assn., Roanoke Bar Assn. (dir. 1970-73), Va. Trial Lawyers Assn. (pres. 1976-77), Def. Rsch. Inst., Va. Assn. Def. Attys. (v.p. 6th dist. 1971). Home: 320 Island View Dr Penhook VA 24137 Office: McCammon Group Ltd 1111 E Main St Ste 1700 Richmond VA 23219

TRACHSEL, WILLIAM HENRY, corporate lawyer; b. El Paso, Tex., Apr. 20, 1943; BS in Aerospace Engring., U. Fla., 1965; JD, U. Conn., 1971. Bar: Conn. 1971. With United Tech. Corp., Hartford, Conn., 1965-93, v.p., sec. and dep. gen. counsel, 1993-98, sr. v.p., gen. counsel, sec., 1998—. Mem. ABA, Am. Corp. Counsel Assn. Office: United Tech Corp Bldg Hartford CT 06101 E-mail: trachswh@corphq.utc.com.*

TRACHTMAN, JERRY H. lawyer; b. Phila., Aug. 10, 1945; BSEE, Pa. State U., 1967; JD, U. Fla., 1976. Bar: Fla. 1976, U.S. Dist. Ct. (mid. dist.) Fla. 1978, U.S. Supreme Ct. 1980, U.S. Ct. Appeals (11th cir.) 1989; cert. aviation law. Elec. engr. N.Am. Aviation, Columbus, Ohio, 1967-68, Apollo spacecraft systems engr. Kennedy Space Ctr., Fla., 1968-71; Skylab project engr. Martin Marietta, Kennedy Space Ctr., 1971-74; pvt. practice Satellite Beach, Fla., 1976-80; atty., mng. ptnr. Trachtman, Henderson and Futchko, P.A., Melbourne, Fla., 1980—2002; pvt. practice Law Offices of Jerry H. Trachtman P.A., 2002—. Adj. prof. aviation law Fla. Inst. Tech., Melbourne, 1983-90; mem. adv. bd. Kaiser Coll., Melbourne, 1994—. Pres. Jewish Fedn. Brevard County, 2000—2001, bd. dirs. 1996—. Recipient Apollo achievement award NASA. Mem. ATLA, Fla. Bar Assn. (chmn. aviation law com. 1995-96, vice chmn. 1993-95, mem. aviation law cert. com. 2002-), Lawyer-Pilots Bar Assn., NTSB Bar Assn. (founder 1984—), Acad. Fla. Trial Lawyers. Aviation, Personal injury (including property damage), Product liability. Office: Ste #300 1735 W Hibiscus Blvd Melbourne FL 32901-2616 E-mail: jtrachtman@trachtman-law.com.

TRACT, MARC MITCHELL, lawyer; b. N.Y.C., Sept. 20, 1959; s. Harold Michael and Natalie Ann (Meyerowitz) T.; m. Sharon Beth Widrow; children: Melissa Hope, Harrison Michael, Sarah Michelle. BA in Biology, Ithaca Coll., 1981; JD, Pepperdine U., 1984. Bar: N.Y. 1985, N.J. 1985, D.C. 1986. Assoc. Kroll & Tract, N.Y.C., 1985—90, ptnr., 1990—94; ptnr. Rosenman & Colin LLP, N.Y.C., 1994—2002, Katten Muchin Zavis Rosenman, N.Y.C., 2002—. Bd. dirs. Rampart Ins. Co., Navigators Group Inc., N.Y.C., MAPFRE Reins. Corp., Florham Park, N.J., AXA Art Ins. Corp., N.Y.C., Rosemont, Ill. Bd. dirs. Italian Acad. Found. Decorated Order of Merit of Savoy. Mem. ABA, Assn. of Bar of City of N.Y., N.Y. State Bar Assn., N.J. State Bar Assn., N.Y. County Lawyers Assn., Am. Coun. Germany, Old Westbury Golf and Country Club, Met. Club, Econ. Club N.Y. Republican. Corporate, general, Insurance, Mergers and acquisitions. Office: KMZ Rosenman 575 Madison Ave Fl 11 New York NY 10022-2511

TRACTENBERG, CRAIG R. lawyer; b. Phila., Dec. 5, 1956; s. Jerome and Diane (Epstein) T. BA, La Salle Coll., Phila., 1979; JD, Temple U., 1981. Bar: Pa. 1981, N.J. 1983, U.S. Dist. Ct. (ea. dist.) Pa. 1981, U.S. Dist. Ct. N.J. 1983, U.S. Ct. Appeals (2d cir.) 1983, U.S. Ct. Appeals (3rd cir.) 1990, U.S. Supreme Ct. 1987. Assoc. Abraham, Pressman & Bauer, P.C., Phila., 1981-87, ptnr., 1987-97; shareholder Buchanan Ingersoll, Profl. Corp., Phila., 1998—2003; ptnr. Nixon Peabody LLP, 2003—. Bd. adv. Rita's Water Ice Franchising, Inc., ALS Assn. and Camp Ramah; judge pro tem Phila. Ct. Common Pleas. Contbg. editor Franchise Law Quar., Franchise Law Digest; articles editor ABA Franchise Law Jour.; contbr. articles to law jours. and profl. publs. Trustee Har Zion Temple, Penn Valley, Pa., 1988—2002. Mem. ABA, Pa. Bar Assn. (chmn. com. on franchising), Phila. Bar Assn., N.J. Bar Assn., Internat. Franchise Assn. Bankruptcy, Commercial, contracts (including sales of goods; commercial financing), Franchising. Home: 249 Ithan Creek Rd Villanova PA 19085-1339 Office: Nixon Peabody LLP 15th & JFK Blvd Ste 200 Two Penn Center Philadelphia PA 19102

TRACY, J. DAVID, lawyer, educator; b. Ft. Worth, Jan. 1, 1946; s. Dennis Ford and Virginia Eloise (Hall) T.; m. Jeral Ann Wilson, June 3, 1967; children: Bradley Wilson, Jennifer Diann. BA with honors, U. Tex., 1968, JD, 1970; LLM, So. Meth. U., 1971. Bar: Tex. 1971, U.S. Tax Ct. 1971, U.S. Ct. Appeals (5th cir.) 1976, U.S. Supreme Ct. 1978; cert. in estate planning, probate and tax law Tex. Bd. Legal Specialization. Ptnr. Cantey & Hanger, LLP, Ft. Worth. Bd. dirs. Ft. Worth Conv. and Vis. Bur., sec., 1987-89; adj. prof. advanced corp. taxation So. Meth. U., 1975-77; lectr. continuing legal edn.; council mem. real estate, probate and trust law sect. State Bar Tex., 1983-87; newsletter editor 1987-89, chmn., 1991-92; mem. Coll. State Bar Tex., tax law adv. commn. Tex. Bd. Legal Specialization, 1987-2000, chair, 1999-2000. Contbr. articles to law jours. Mem. adv. bd. dirs. Tarrant County Conv. Ctr., 1983-89, chmn., 1986-87. Named Outstanding Young Lawyer of Tarrant County, Tarrant County Young Lawyers Assn., 1982. Fellow Am. Coll. Trust and Estate Counsel, Am. Bar Found., Tex. Bar Found., Tarrant County Bar Found.; mem. ABA, Ft. Worth Club, Colonial Country Club, Phi Delta Phi. Presbyterian. Estate planning, Pension, profit-sharing, and employee benefits, Taxation, general. Office: 801 Cherry St Ste 2100 Fort Worth TX 76102-6881 E-mail: dtracy@canteyhanger.com.

TRACY, JAMES JARED, JR., accountant, financial executive, law firm administrator; b. Cleve., Jan. 17, 1929; s. James Jared and Florence (Comey) T.; m. Elizabeth Jane Bourne, June 30, 1953 (div. 1988); children: Jane Tracy Ahrens, Elizabeth Tracy Jenkins, James Jared IV, Margaret Tracy Rosen; m. Judith Anne Cooper, Feb. 18, 1989. AB, Harvard U., 1950, MBA, 1953. CPA, Ohio. Acct., sr. mgr. Price Waterhouse & Co., Cleve., 1953-65; treas., CFO Clevite Corp., Cleve., 1965-69; asst. treas. Republic Steel Corp., Cleve., 1969-70, treas., 1970-75; v.p., treas. Johns-Manville Corp., Denver, 1976-81; v.p., treas., CFO Internat. Techs. Corp., L.A., 1981-82; exec. dir. Hufstedler, Miller, Carlson & Beardsley, L.A., 1983-84, Shank, Irwin & Conant, Dallas, 1984-85, Pachter, Gold & Schaffer, L.A., 1985-86; v.p., sr. cons. Right Assocs., L.A., 1987-91; dir. adminstrn. Larson & Burnham, Oakland, Calif., 1991-95; adminstrv. dir. Law Offices of Thomas E. Miller, Newport Beach, Calif., 1996-97; human resources adminstr. Baker & McKenzie, San Francisco, 1997-98; dir. adminstrn. Wartnick, Chaber, Harowitz & Tigerman, San Francisco, 1998-2000, Kasdan, Simonds, & Epstein, Irvine, Calif., 2000—. Trustee, v.p. Miss Hall's Sch., Pittsfield, Mass., 1970-78; adv. bd. Arkwright-Boston Ins. Co., 1976-81. Trustee, v.p. Cleve. Soc. for Blind, 1965-76; trustee Western Res. Hist. Soc., Cleve., 1972-76; treas. St. Peters by the Sea Presbyn. Ch., Palos Verdes, Calif., 1981-91, Literacy Coun. Newport Beach (Calif.) Pub. Libr., 2002—; pres. Harvard Club, Cleve., 1958-59, Harvard Bus. Sch. Club, Cleve., 1959-60, Rocky Mountain Harvard Club, Denver, 1978-79; bd. dirs. Met. YMCA, Cleve., 1972-76, Fedn. for Cmty. Planning, Cleve., 1971-76, v.p. Recipient Alumni award Harvard U., Denver, 1981. Mem. AICPA, Ohio Soc. CPAs, Assn. Legal Adminstrs., Rotary (pres. Piedmont Montclair chpt. 1995-96), Harvard Radcliffe Club So. Calif. Avocations: sailing, golf, gardening. Home: 2204 Fortuna Newport Beach CA 92660 E-mail: jimjudytracy@adelphia.net.

TRACY, WILLIAM FRANCIS, II, lawyer; b. Decatur, Ill., Mar. 7, 1947; s. William Francis and Agnes Madonna (Ryan) Tracy; m. Elaine Baxter, Jan. 23, 1970; children: Katherine, Colleen, Ryan. AB, St. Louis U., 1969; JD, Northwestern U., 1972. Bar: Mo. 1972, Ill. 1977. Law clk. U.S. Dept. of Justice, Washington, 1971; jr. ptnr. Bryan, Cave, McPheeters & McRoberts, St. Louis, 1972—77; assoc. Doss, Simpson & Tracy, Monticello, Ill., 1977—78; ptnr. Miller, Tracy, Braun, Funk & Guenther, Monticello, 1978—. Spl. asst. atty. gen. State of Ill., Monticello, 1980—83; pub. adminstr., conservator, guardian Piatt County, Ill., 1978—90. Pres. Cmty. Coun., Bement, Ill., 1979. Mem.: ABA, Piatt County Bar Assn., Ill. Bar Assn., Mo. Bar Assn., Monticello Golf Club (treas., bd. dirs. 1982—84), Lions (pres. 1981), KC (adv. 1981—82), Rotary (treas. 1983—84). Estate planning, Probate (including wills, trusts), Estate taxation. Home: 807 N State St Monticello IL 61856-1145

TRAGER, DAVID G. federal judge; b. Mt. Vernon, N.Y., Dec. 23, 1937; s. Sol and Clara (Friedman) T.; m. Roberta E. Weisbrod, May 2, 1972; children: Mara Emet, Josiah Samuel, Naomi Gabrielle. BA, Columbia Coll., 1959; LL.B., Harvard U., 1962. Bar: N.Y. Assoc. Berman & Frost, 1963-65, Butler, Jablow & Geller, 1965-67; asst. corp. counsel Appeals Div. City of N.Y., 1967; law clk. Judge Kenneth B. Keating, N.Y. State Ct. Appeals, 1968-69; asst. U.S. atty. chief, appeals div., 1970-72; U.S. atty. Ea. Dist. N.Y., Bklyn., 1974-78; prof. Bklyn. Law Sch., 1972-94, dean, 1983-94; judge U.S. Dist. Ct. (ea. dist.) N.Y., Bklyn., 1994—; mem. adv. com. on criminal rules Jud. Conf. U.S., 2000—. Chmn. Mayor's Com. on Judiciary, 1982-89, N.Y. State Temp. Commn. on Investigation, 1983-90. Mem. N.Y.C. Charter Rev. Commn., 1986-89. With USAR, 1962-65, USNR, 1965-69. Mem.: Am. Law Inst., Fed. Bar Coun. (pres. 1986—88). Office: US Courthouse 225 Cadman Plz E Brooklyn NY 11201-1818

TRAGER, MICHAEL DAVID, lawyer; b. N.Y.C., Feb. 15, 1959; s. Philip and Ina (Shulkin) T.; m. Mariella Gonzalez, Sept. 12, 1987; children: Nicholas, Alexander. BA, Wesleyan U., Middletown, Conn., 1981; JD, Boston U., 1985. Bar: Mass. 1985, Conn. 1986, Fla. 1988, D.C. 1989. Staff atty. enforcement divsn. Securities & Exchange Com., Washington, 1985-87; assoc. Morgan, Lewis & Bockius, Miami, Fla., 1987-88; participating assoc. Fulbright & Jaworski, Washington, 1989-92; ptnr. Trager & Trager, Washington, 1992-93; of counsel Fulbright & Jaworski, Washington, 1993-94, ptnr., 1995—, co-head securities litigation and enforcement. Bd. dirs. Jewish Nat. Fund-Mid-Atlantic Region, 1993-97; officer Horace Mann PTA, 1997-99. Mem. ABA (bus. law sect. fed. regulation securities com. and civil litigation and SEC enforcement matters subcom., litigation sect. securities litigation com. and SEC enforcement subcom., class action and derivative litigation com. and securities litigation subcom., task force on SEC's insider trading and selective disclosure rules), Assn. SEC Alumni, Securities Industry Assn. (legal and compliance divsn.), D.C. Bar (corp., fin. and securities law sect. corp. counsel and planning group for broker-dealer programs 1992-94, broker-dealer regulation com., task force on SEC's proposed insider trading and selective disclosure rules), Mass. Bar, Fla. Bar., Conn. Bar., Bond Market Assn. (litigation adv. com.), Wesleyan Univ. Club of Washington (chair 2001--), Wesleyan U. Alumni Assn. (exec. com. 2001--). Administrative and regulatory, Federal civil litigation, Securities. Office: Fulbright & Jaworski 801 Pennsylvania Ave NW Fl 3-5 Washington DC 20004-2623

TRAHAIR, ANDREW JAMES, lawyer; b. Sydney, Australia, Sept. 7, 1963; s. Nicholas Snowden and Salley Marie Trahair; m. Nan Kathleen Dunham, Nov. 10, 1995; children: Esme, Linus. BCom./LLB, U. New South Wales, Australia, 1986. Bar: New South Wales 1987, Eng. and Wales 1991. Ptnr. Allen & Overy, London, 1994-97, Clayton Utz, Sydney, 1998-2000, Allen & Overy, Singapore, 2001—. Banking, Corporate, general, Finance. Office: Allen & Overy Singapore 24 Raffles Pl # 22-00 Clifford Ctr Singapore 048542 Singapore Fax: 656-6435 7474. E-mail: andrew.trahair@allenovery.com.

TRAMONTE, JAMES ALBERT, lawyer; b. New Orleans, Mar. 6, 1951; s. August Joseph and Genevieve Tramonte; m. Stephanie Thomas, Aug. 12, 1972; children: James Albert Jr., Karen Elizabeth, David August, Patrick Thomas, Mark Joseph. Student, U. Miss., 1968-70; BS in Acctg., La. State U., New Orleans, 1973; JD, Tulane U., 1976; LLM in Taxation, NYU, 1977. CPA La.; bar: La. 1976, U.S. Tax T. 1977, U.S. Ct. Claims 1978, U.S. Ct. Appeals (5th and 11th cirs.) 1981, Ga. 1989, cert.: La. (tax atty.). Ptnr. Hurt, Richardson, Garner, Todd & Cadenhead, Atlanta, 1988-92; gen. counsel Ctrl. Health Svcs., Inc., 1993-96, Simione Ctrl. Holdings, Inc., Atlanta, 1993-97; exec. v.p., chief legal officer LDC Direct, Ltd. Co., Atlanta, 1998-99; exec. v.p. R.S. Andrews Enterprises, Inc., Atlanta, 1999—2002; of counsel Gorby, Reeves and Peters, PC, Atlanta, 2002—03, Welch, Spell, Reemsnyder, Pless & Davis, P.C., Atlanta, 2003—. Author: (book) Estate Planning for Divorced and Remarried Persons, 1986; co-author: Loyola Law Rev. 5th Cir. Symposium, 1986. Mem.: AICPA, ABA (sect. on taxation), State Bar of Ga. (corp. coun. sect.), Ga. State Soc. CPAs (taxation com. 1989), La. State Bar Assn. (sec. on taxation, chmn. formularly com. 1981—82, chmn. liaison com. with dist. dir. IRS 1982—83). Roman Catholic. Corporate, general, Intellectual property, Mergers and acquisitions. Home: 5509 Mount Vernon Way Dunwoody GA 30338-2815 Office: Welch Spell Reemsnyder Pless & Davis PC Ste 1750 The Proscenium 1170 Peachtree St NE Atlanta GA 30309 Business E-Mail: james.tramonte@welchspell.com.

TRAMUTOLA, JOSEPH LOUIS, lawyer, educator; b. Union City, N.J., Mar. 6, 1931; s. Joseph Emil and Elda (Brioli) T.; m. Mary Ann Banull, Sept. 4, 1965; children Karen, Kim, Karla. BA, St. Peter's Coll., Jersey City, 1953; JD, Fordham U., 1959. Bar: N.J. 1961. Atty. Toolan, Haney, Romand, Perth Amboy, N.J.; prof. law Fairleigh Dickinson U., Madison, N.J., 1965—, creator, dir. ednl. program for older persons, 1972-2001, ret., 2001. Pre-legal advisor Silberman Coll. bus., Fairleigh Dickinson U.; cons. Am. Coun. on Edn., Washington, Am. Edn. Assn., Washington, Thomas Edison Coll., Trenton, N.J., Chartered Pub. Underwriters, East Orange, N.J., USDA; adj. faculty U. Mich., dir. Fairleigh Dickinson U. Patent Inst.. dir. ednl. seminars on student law; seminar dir. student law, Calif., Ill., Mass., N.Y., Ga. Author: Guide Book for Student Rights, Legal Perspective for Student Personal Administration, Legal Overview of the New Student; dir. CPA Law Rev. With U.S. Army, 1955-57. Named Outstanding Educator Outstanding Educators Inc., 1973, 1974, Commendation for Civic Contb. N.J. Legis., 1993. Roman Catholic. Avocations: bonsai, clock making, gardening, zymology, music. Education and schools. Home: 12 Browning Ct Mendham NJ 07945-3301 Fax: 973-543-6621. E-mail: jltram@earthlink.net.

TRANTER, TERENCE MICHAEL, lawyer; b. Cin., Nov. 26, 1944; s. John Lawrence and Florence Ellen (McGann) T.; m. Doris Ann Tepe, June 22, 1968; children— Amy, Terry, Michael, Christopher. A.B., Georgetown U., 1966; J.D., U. Cin., 1969. Bar: Ohio 1969, U.S. Dist. Ct. (so. dist.) Ohio 1969, U.S. Ct. Appeals (6th cir.) 1969. Asst. atty. gen. State of Ohio, Cin., 1970-71; sole practice law, Cin., 1969— ; mem. Ohio Ho. of Reps., Columbus, 1976-92; referee Domestic Relations Ct., Hamilton County, Ohio, 1975. Vice chmn. Hamilton County Democratic Exec. Com., Cin., 1984— ; mem. Ohio Dem. Cen. Com., Columbus, 1984-92; mem. city council Golf Manor, Ohio, 1971-76. Mem. ABA, Ohio Bar Assn., Cin. Bar Assn., Ohio Bd. Realtors, Cin. Bd. Realtors. Democrat. Roman Catholic. Lodges: K.C., Eagles. Avocation: fishing. General practice. Home: 7303 Fair Oaks Dr Cincinnati OH 45237-2923 Office: 606 American Bldg Cincinnati OH 45202

TRAPP, JAMES MCCREERY, lawyer; b. Macomb, Ill., Aug. 11, 1934; BA, Knox Coll., 1956; JD, U. Mich., 1961. Bar: Ill. 1961. Ptnr. McDermott, Will & Emery, Chgo., 1961-98, sr. counsel, 1998—. Chmn. Ill. Inst. Continuing Legal Edn., 1978-79, bd. dirs., 1980-86, pres., 1984-85. Fellow Am. Coll. Trust and Estate Counsel (Ill. chmn. 1980-83, nat. regent 1983—, treas. 1989-90, sec. 1990-91, v.p. 1991-92, pres.-elect 1992-93, pres. 1993-94, exec. com. 1986-94), Am. Bar Found., Ill. Bar Found.; mem. ABA, Ill. State Bar Assn., Chgo. Bar Assn. (chair trust law com. 1972-73, com. on coms. 1972-74), Internat. Acad. Estate and Trust Law, Am. Law Inst. (pres.), Chgo. Estate Planning Coun. Office: McDermott Will & Emery 227 W Monroe St Chicago IL 60606-5096

TRAPP, MARY JANE, lawyer; b. Columbus, Ohio, July 6, 1956; AB cum laude, Mount Holyoke Coll., 1978; JD, Case Western Reserve U., 1981. Bar: Ohio 1981, U.S. Supreme Ct. 1987. Ptnr. Apicella and Trapp, Cleve. Commr. Supreme Ct. Ohio Bd. Commrs. on Unauthorized Practice of Law, 1986—89; mem. Supreme Ct. Rules adv. com., 1997—2002. Fellow: Ohio State Bar Found., Am. Bar Found.; mem.: Cleve. Bar Assn. (trustee 1995—98), Cuyahoga County Bar Assn. (trustee 1986—93, 1999—), Ohio Acad. Trial Lawyers, Ohio State Bar Assn. (pres. 2001—02), ABA. Personal injury (including property damage), Family and matrimonial, Professional liability. Office: Apicella and Trapp 1200 Penton Media Bldg 1300 E 9th St Cleveland OH 44114-1503

TRAUB, RICHARD KENNETH, lawyer; b. Lakewood, N.J., Aug. 4, 1950; s. Harold W. and Muriel N. (Zurlin) T.; m. Barbara Lynn Wright, July 9, 1972; children: Russell S., Melissa L. BBA, U. Miami, Coral Gables, Fla., 1972, JD cum laude, 1975. Bar: Fla. 1975, N.Y. 1976, N.J. 1976, U.S. Dist. Ct. N.J. 1976, U.S. Supreme Ct. 1979, U.S. Dist. Ct. (ea. & so. dists.) N.Y. 1981. Ptnr. Wilson, Elser, Moskowitz, Edelman & Dicker, N.Y.C., 1975-95, Traub Eglin Lieberman Straus, Hawthorne, N.Y., 1996—. Ptnr. Time for Patty Stables, N.J., 1992—; officer, dir. X-Ray Duplications, Inc., N.J.; ptnr., founder Fractured Greetings, N.J.; mem., lectr. Fedn. Ins. and Corp. Counsel, 1993—, mem. admissions com., industry cooperation ins. coverage and alt. dispute resolution coms.; lectr. Inst. for Internat. Rsch., Washington, 1988, Engring. News Record Constrn. Claims Conf., 1991. Author: Legal and Professional Aspects of Construction Management, 1990, The Year 2000 and Potential Liabilities and Otherwise, 1999, Litigating Year 2000 Cases, Chapter 8, Insurance Coverage, 1999, Practical Environmental Forensics--Process and Case Histories, 2000; contbr. chpt.: Data Security and Privacy Law-Combatting Cyberthreats, The West Group, 2002; contbr. articles to profl. jours. Mem. ABA (forum com. on constrn. industry 1989, tort and ins. practice sect. 1985—, computer litigation sect.), N.Y. State Bar Assn., N.J. Bar Assn., Fla. Bar Assn., Fedn. Def. and Corp. Counsel (spkr. The Millenium Bug ins. coverage sect., vice chair ins. coverage and Y2K sects., chair tech. and e-commerce sect., chair tech. com., editor The Roster), Def. Rsch. Inst., Assn. Def. Trial Attys. Construction, Environmental, Insurance. Office: Traub Eglin Lieberman Straus Mid-Westchester Exec Park Three Skyline Dr Hawthorne NY 10532 also: 100 Metroplex Dr Ste 203 Edison NJ 08817- E-mail: rtraub@tels.com.

TRAUTH, JOSEPH LOUIS, JR., lawyer; b. Cin., Apr. 22, 1945; s. Joseph L. and Margaret (Walter) T.; m. Barbara Widmeyer, July 4, 1970; children: Jennifer, Joseph III, Jonathan, Braden, Maria. BS in Econs., Xavier U., 1967; JD, U. Cin., 1973. Bar: Ohio 1973, U.S. Dist. Ct. (so. dist.) Ohio 1973, U.S. Ct. Appeals (6th cir.) 1973, U.S. Supreme Ct. 1988, Ky. 2000. Ptnr. Keating, Muething & Klekamp, PLL, Cin., 1973-80, Keating, Muething & Klekamp, Cin., 1980—. Speaker real estate law, 1974—. Contbr. articles to real estate publs. Mem. Rep. Leadership Coun., Cin., 1987—, Parish Coun., Cin., 1990. Mem. Cin. Bar Assn. (grievance com., real estate com., negligence com.). Roman Catholic. Avocations: running, tennis, reading. General civil litigation, Land use and zoning (including planning), Property, real (including real estate development, water). Office: Keating Muething & Klekamp 1800 Provident Tower 1 E 4th St Ste 1400 Cincinnati OH 45202-3717 E-mail: jtrauth@kmklaw.com.

TRAUTMAN, HERMAN LOUIS, lawyer, educator; b. Columbus, Ind., Sept. 26, 1911; s. Theodore H. and Emma (Guckenberger) T.; m. Marian Lucille Green, Sept. 1, 1940; children: Stephen M., Pamela C.; LLB with distinction Ind. U., 1937, BA, 1946, JD with distinction, 1946; postgrad., NYU, 1953, Ford Found. faculty fellow, Harvard U., 1954-55. Bar: Ind. 1937, U.S. Tax Ct., U.S. Ct. Appeals (6th cir.) Tenn. Sole practice, Evansville, Ind., 1937-43; pres. Crescent Coal Co., Evansville, 1941-43; prof. law U. Ala. Tuscaloosa, 1946-49; prof. law Vanderbilt U., 1949—, prof. law emeritus, 1977; NYU vis. prof., 1955, U. Mich., Ann Arbor, 1963-64; ptnr. Trautman & Trautman, Nashville, 1976-85; sole practice, Nashville, 1986—. Served to lt. comdr. USN, 1943-46. Mem. ABA, Am. Law Inst., Tenn. Bar Assn., Nashville Bar Assn., Nat. Conf. Jud. Adminstrs., Estate Planning Coun., Order of Coif, Phi Gamma Delta, Belle Meade Club, Univ. Club, Kiwanis. Methodist. Probate (including wills, trusts), Estate taxation, Taxation, general. Address: PO Box 150862 Nashville TN 37215-0862

TRAUTMAN, WILLIAM ELLSWORTH, lawyer; b. San Francisco, Nov. 27, 1940; s. Gerald H. and Doris Joy (Tucker) T.; m. Dorothy (Williamson), June 17, 1962; children: Darcey, Torey. BA, U. Calif., Berkeley, 1962, LLB, 1965. Bar: Calif., 1965; U.S. Supreme Ct.; Calif. Dist. Ct.; U.S. Ct. Appeals (9th and Fed. Cir.). Assoc. Chickering and Gregory, San Francisco, 1965-71, ptnr., 1972-81, Brobeck, Phleger, and Harrison, San Francisco, 1981—2003, litig. dept. chair, 1984-91, San Francisco mng. ptnr., 1992-96; ptnr. Morgan, Lewis, and Bockius, San Francisco, 2003—. Pres. Oakland, Calif. Mus. Assn., 1981-83; mem. profl. ethics com. State Bar Calif., 1974-77. Fellow: Am. Coll. Trial Lawyers; mem.: Barrister's Club of San Francisco (v.p. 1973), Calif. Barristers (bd. dirs., v.p.), Bar Assn. San Francisco (bd. dirs. 1972—73), Legal Aid Soc. (bd. dirs. 1982—93, pres. 1985—88), U. Calif.-Berkeley Found. (trustee 1998—2000), Boalt Hall Alumni Assn. (bd. dirs. 1993—99, pres. 1997—98). Antitrust, General civil litigation, Insurance. Office: Morgan Lewis & Bockius 1 Market St San Francisco CA 94105-1420 E-mail: wtrautman@morganlewis.com.

TRAUTWEIN, BLAIR J. lawyer; b. Greeley, Feb. 16, 1952; s. Aronoel H. and Gertrude C. Trautwein; m. Suzanne E. Wolfstone, July 13, 1974; children: Mary R., John W. BS in Fin., U. Colo., 1974; JD with honors, U. Wyo., 1977. Bar: Wyo. 1977, U.S. Dist. Ct. Wyo. 1977, U.S. Dist. Ct. Nev. 1982, U.S. Ct. Appeals (9th cir.) 1985, U.S. Dist. Ct. Colo. 1988, Colo. 1995, U.S. Ct. Appeals (10th cir.) 1997. Atty. Hathaway, Speglit & Kunz, Cheyenne, Wyo., 1977—81; ptnr. Hathaway, Speglit, Kunz, Trautwein, Cheyenne, 1981—95; atty. Sommermieyer, Wick, Dow & Campbell, Ft. Collins, 1995; ptnr. Wick, Campbell, Bremer et. al., Ft. Collins, 1996—. Mem. Laramie County Bd. Health, Colo., 1997—, pres., 1999; various positions Laramie County Reps., 1977—84. Mem.: Ft. Collins Baseball Club, Sigma Phi Epsilon (bd. dirs. alumni bd. 1986—90). Avocations: bicycling, tennis, hiking, skiing, sports. Health, Personal injury (including property damage), General practice. Office: Wick Campbell Bremer et al 323 S College Ste 3 Fort Collins CO 80524 Office Fax: 970-482-8929. Business E-Mail: btrautwein@wicklaw.com.

TRAVIS, GRANT CARNER, lawyer; b. Cin., Sept. 24, 1969; BS in Polit. Sci., N.Y. Inst. Tech., Old Westbury, 1992; JD, Duquesne U., Pitts., 1995. Bar: Pa. 1995, U.S. Dist. Ct. (we. dist.) Pa. 1995, Erie County, Pa. Ct. of Pleas 1995. Law clk. Conner & Riley, Erie, Pa., 1993—95, atty., 1995—99; pvt. practice Law Offices of Grant C. Travis, Edinboro and Erie, 1999—. Bd. dirs. Erie County YMCA, Edinboro, 2000—, pres. bd. dirs., 2001—. Mem.: ATLA, Pa. Trial Lawyers Assn. (bd. govs. 2001—), Western Pa. Trial Lawyers Assn. (bd. govs. 1998—), Nat. Assn. Criminal Def. Lawyers, Pa. Assn. of Criminal Def. Lawyers, Erie County Bar Assn. (mem. Spkrs. Bur. 1999—), Pa. Bar Assn. Criminal, General civil litigation, Personal injury (including property damage). Office: Law Offices of Grant C Travis Travis Law Bldg 102 Lorna Ln Edinboro PA 16412

TRAXLER, WILLIAM BYRD, JR., federal judge; b. Greenville, S.C., May 1, 1948; s. William Byrd and Bettie (Wooten) Traxler; m. Patricia Alford, Aug. 21, 1972; children: William Byrd III, James McCall. BA, Davidson Coll., 1970; JD, U. S.C., 1973. Assoc. William Byrd Traxler, Greenville, 1973—75; asst. solicitor 13th Jud. Ct., Greenville, 1975—78, dep. solicitor, 1978—81, solicitor, 1981—85, resident cir. judge, 1985—92; U.S. Dist. judge Dist. of S.C., Greenville, 1992—98; judge U.S. Ct. of Appeals (4th cir.), Greenville, 1998—. Recipient Outstanding Svc. award, Solicitors Assn., S.C., 1987, Leadership award, Probation, Parole & Pardon Svcs., S.C., 1990. Office: PO Box 10127 Greenville SC 29603-0127

TRAYLOR, CHET D. state supreme court justice; b. Columbia, La., Oct. 12, 1945; s. John Hardy and Bernice (Bogan) T.; children: Mary Therese, Leigh Ann, Anna Marie. BA in Govt., N.E. La. State U., 1969; JD, Loyola U., 1974. Bar: La. Judge 5th Jud. Dist. Ct., Franklin, Richland and West Carroll Parishes, La., 1985-97; assoc. justice La. Supreme Ct., 1997—. Past legal advisor La. State Police; past investigator La. Dept. Justice; asst. dist. atty., Franklin Parish, 1975-76. Founding bd. mem. Winnsboro Econ. Devel. Found.; mem. Rocky Mountain Conservation Fund. With U.S. Army. Mem. ABA, La. Bar Assn., La. Dist. Judges Assn., NRA (life), Franklin Parish Mental Health Assn. (past bd. dirs.), Winnsboro Lions Club (past bd. dirs.), Greenwings (founder John Adams chpt.). Methodist. Office: Supreme Ct 301 Loyola Ave New Orleans LA 70112-1814

TRAYLOR, ROBERT ARTHUR, lawyer; b. Syracuse, N.Y., Jan. 15, 1949; s. Robert Arthur and Julia Elizabeth (McNulty) T.; m. Bonita Lynn Schmidt, Nov. 26, 1977. BS, LeMoyne Coll., 1970; JD cum laude, Syracuse U., 1975. Bar: N.Y., U.S. Dist. Ct. (no. dist.) N.Y., U.S. Tax Ct. Assoc. Love, Balducci & Scaccia, Syracuse, N.Y., 1976-77; estate tax atty. IRS, Syracuse, 1977-81; assoc. Scaccia Law Firm, Syracuse, 1981—. Contbr. articles to profl. jours. Of counsel St. Ann Sch., Syracuse, 1981—, mem. coordinating com. Vision 2000 1994—, mem. bd., 1998—. With U.S. Army, 1970-72. Mem. ABA, Onondaga County Bar Assn. (vol. lawyer program 1993—, Vol. Lawyer of Month 1994), World Wildlife Fedn. Republican. Roman Catholic. Avocations: motorsports, military history, catholic education. General civil litigation, Probate (including wills, trusts), Property, real (including real estate development, water). Home: 112 Knowland Dr Liverpool NY 13090-3130 Office: Scaccia Law Firm State Tower Bldg Ste 402 Syracuse NY 13202-1798

TRAYNOR, JOHN MICHAEL, lawyer; b. Oakland, Calif., Oct. 25, 1934; s. Roger J. and Madeleine (Lackmann) Traynor; m. Shirley Williams, Feb. 11, 1956; children: Kathleen Traynor Millard, Elizabeth Traynor Fowler, Thomas. BA, U. Calif., Berkeley, 1955; JD, Harvard U., 1960. Bar: Calif. 1961, U.S. Supreme Ct. 1966. Dep. atty. gen. State of Calif., San Francisco, 1961—63; spl. counsel Calif. Senate Com. on Local Govt., Sacramento, 1963; assoc. firm Cooley Godward, LLP, San Francisco, 1963—69, ptnr., 1969—. Adviser 3d Restatement of Unfair Competition, 1988—95, 3d Restatement of Torts, Products Liability, 1992—97, Apportionment, 1994—99, 2d Restatement of Conflict of Laws revs., 1988, 3d Restatement of Restitution and Unjust Enrichment, 1997—; lectr. Boalt Hall Sch. Law U. Calif., Berkeley, 1982—89, 1996—98; chmn. EarthJustice Legal Def. Fund (formerly Sierra Club Legal Def. Fund), 1989—91, pres., 1991—92, trustee, 1974—96. Mem. bd. overseers Inst. for Civil Justice The RAND Corp., 1991—97; bd. dirs. Environ. Law Inst., 1991—97, 2000—; Sierra Legal Def. Fund. Canada, 1990—96. 1st lt. USMC, 1955—57. Fellow: AAAS, Am. Bar Found. (life), Am. Acad. Arts and Scis.; mem.: Bar Assn. San Francisco (pres. 1973), Am. Law Inst. (coun. 1985—, pres. 2000—). Federal civil litigation, State civil litigation, Intellectual property. Home: 3131 Eton Ave Berkeley CA 94705-2713 Office: Cooley Godward LLP 1 Maritime Plz Ste 2000 San Francisco CA 94111-3580 E-mail: mtraynor@cooley.com.

TREACY, GERALD BERNARD, JR., lawyer; b. Newark, July 29, 1951; s. Gerald B. Sr. and Mabel L. (Nesbitt) T.; m. Joyce M. Biazzo, Apr. 6, 1974. BA summa cum laude, Rider Coll., 1973; JD, UCLA, 1981. Bar: Calif. 1981, Wash. 1982, D.C. 1995. Tchr. English Arthur L. Johnson Regional High Sch., Clark, N.J., 1973-77; assoc. Gibson, Dunn & Crutcher, L.A., 1981-82; ptnr. Perkins Coie, Bellevue, Wash., 1982-94, McGuire Woods Battle & Boothe, McLean, Va. and Bellevue, Va., 1994-96, Egger, Betts, Austin, Treacy, Bellevue, Wash., 1996-98; mem. Treacy Law Group, Bellevue, 1998—; of counsel Montgomery Purdue Blankinship and Austin, Seattle, 2000—. Chmn. bd. dirs. estate planning adv. bd. U. Wash., Seattle, 1990-92; presenter TV Seminar, Where There's a Will, PBS affiliate. Author: Washington Guardianship Law, Administration and Litigation, 1988, supplemented, 1991, 3d edit. supplemented, 2002, Supporting Organizations, 1996, 2d edit., 2002. Bd. dirs. Kitsap Opera, 2003—; mem. endowment fund com. Unitd Way, Seattle, 1987—89; mem. exec. com. Wash. Planned Giving Coun., 1993—94, 1996—98; bd. dirs., mem. adv. bd. ARC, Seattle, 1985—89, Arthritis Gift, 1987—89, Seattle Symphony, 1992, Seattle U., 1996. Mem. Eastside King County Estate Planning Coun., Order of Coif. Avocations: photography, hiking, ethnic and classical music, poetry, host/writer gilbert & sullivan radio show. Estate planning, Non-profit and tax-exempt organizations, Estate taxation. Office: PO Box 712 Keyport WA 98345 E-mail: gbtreacy@aol.com.

TREACY, VINCENT EDWARD, lawyer; b. Mass., Jan. 30, 1942; AB, Boston Coll., 1964; JD with honors, George Washington U., 1971. Bar: Va. 1972, D.C. 1973, Md. 1999; U.S. Supreme Ct. 1976. Atty. Fed. Labor Rels. Coun., Washington, 1971-73; legis. atty. Am. law divsn. Congrl. Rsch. Svc., Libr. Congress, Washington, 1973-98; sole practitioner Washington, 1998—. Legis. cons. Romanian Legal Analysis and Legis. Drafting Conf., Senate and Chamber Duputies Romania, Bucharest, 1996. Mem. law rev. staff George Washington Law Rev., 1970. Mem. Geroge Washington Law Alumni Assn. (pres. Capitol Hill chpt. 1986-87), Order of Coif. Entertainment, Labor (including EEOC, Fair Labor Standards Act, labor-management relations, NLRB, OSHA), Pension, profit-sharing, and employee benefits. E-mail: vtreacy@msn.com.

TREADWAY, JAMES CURRAN ERIK CORBETT, lawyer, investment company executive, former government official; b. Anderson, S.C., May 21, 1943; s. James C. and Maxine (Hall) T.; m. Susan Pepper Davis, Sept. 6, 1969; children: Elizabeth Pepper Hall, Caroline Worrell Harper Corbett. AB summa cum laude, Rollins Coll., 1964; JD summa cum laude, Washington and Lee U., 1967. Bar: Ga. 1967, Mass. 1968, D.C. 1970. Assoc. Candler, Cox, McClain & Andrews, Atlanta, 1967-68, Gadsby & Hannah, Boston and Washington, 1968-72; ptnr. Dickstein, Shapiro & Morin, Washington, 1972-82; commr. SEC, Washington, 1982-85; ptnr. Baker & Botts, Washington, 1985-87; exec. v.p., chmn. merchant banking dept., exec. com. Paine Webber Group Inc., N.Y.C., 1987—. Chmn. Nat. Commn. on Fraudulent Fin. Reporting, 1985—87; chmn. bds. dirs. Washington & Lee U. Sch. Law, 1992—94; dir. U. So. Calif., Sch. of Acctg. and Fin. Disclosure, 1985—93; mem. planning com. Garret Securities Law Inst., Northwestern U., 1985—92; spl. expert adviser, witness various U.S. congl. coms.; lectr. and author in field. Editor-in-chief Wash. & Lee U. Law review, 1966-67. Recipient Wildman Medal Am. Acctg. Assn., 1989. Mem. Mass. Bar Assn., Ga. Bar Assn., D.C. Bar Assn., Chevy Chase (Md.) Club, Bedford (N.Y.) Golf and Tennis Club, City Tavern Club, Met. Club, Univ. Club (Washington), Verbank Hunting and Fishing Club (Uniondale N.Y.; dir. 1995—), Order of Coif, Phi Beta Kappa, Omicron Delta Kappa. Home: Laurel Ledge Farm RD 4 Croton Lake Rd Bedford Corners NY 10549-4227 Office: PaineWebber Group Inc 1285 Ave of Americas New York NY 10019-6028

TREADWELL-RUBIN, PAMELA A. lawyer; b. Arlington, Tex., Dec. 15, 1960; BA in Polit. Sci., U. Ariz., 1982, JD, 1985. Bar: Ariz. 1985. Prosecutor, Tucson City, 1985—87; dep. atty. Pima County, 1987—93; atty. Moeller, Gage & Treadwell-Rubin, PC, Tucson. Mem. Ariz. Juvenile Justice Adv. Coun., 1993—96. Fellow: Ariz. Bar Found. (bd. dirs. 1991—94, chair victims' rights pro bono panel 1992—93); mem.: Pima County Bar Assn. (bd. dirs. 1989—90, pres. Young Lawyers divsn. 1989—90, bd. dirs. 1996—), Ariz. Women Lawyers Assn., State Bar Ariz. (bd. govs. 1994—95, pres. Young Lawyers divns. 1994—95, cert. specialist worker's compensation 1995—, bd. govs. 1996—, pres. 2003—, Outstanding Young Lawyer 1997). Workers' compensation, General civil litigation, Insurance. Office: Moeller Gage and Treadwell-Rubin 2606 E 10th St Tucson AZ 85716*

TREANOR, MARK C. lawyer, diversified financial services company executive; b. Proctor, Vt., Dec. 2, 1946; BS, U.S. Naval Acad., 1968; JD with honors, U. Md., 1976. Bar: Md. 1976, U.S. Dist. Ct. Md. 1977, U.S. Ct. Appeals (4th cir.) 1979, U.S. Tax Ct. 1980, U.S. Supreme Ct. 1980, Vt. 1997. Ptnr. Miles & Stockbridge, 1982—85, Treanor, Pope & Hughes, 1987—98; sr. exec. v.p., gen. counsel, sec. Wachovia Corp., Charlotte, NC, 1998—. Mem. Md. Law Rev., 1975—76. Bd. visitors U. Md. Sch. Law; bd. advisors U. N.C. Sch. Law Banking Inst., NC. Capt. USMC, 1968—73. Mem.: ABA, Order of Coif, Md. State Bar Assn., Phi Alpha Delta. Office: Wachovia Corp 1 Wachovia Ctr 301 S College St Charlotte NC 28288-0630 Office Fax: 704-374-3105.*

TREANOR, WILLIAM MICHAEL, law educator; b. Morristown, N.J., Nov. 16, 1957; s. William Joseph and Margaret Treanor; m. Allison Derivaux Ames, Oct. 15, 1994; children: William Paul Ames, Katherine Derivaux. BA, Yale U., 1979, JD, 1985; AM in History, Harvard U., 1982. Spl. asst. to dep. commr. U.S. Office Edn., Washington, 1979-80; speechwriter to sec. U.S. Dept. Edn., Washington, 1980; law clk. to Hon. James L. Oakes U.S. Ct. Appeals, 2d Cir., Brattleboro, Vt., 1985-86; spl. asst. to chmn. Com. on Govt. Integrity, N.Y.C., 1987; spl. asst. U.S. atty. U.S. Atty.'s Office, Washington, 1990; assoc. counsel Office of Ind. Counsel, Washington, 1987-90; assoc. prof. law Fordham U., N.Y.C., 1991-98, prof. law, 2001—, dean, 2002—; dep. asst. atty. gen. office of legal counsel U.S. Dept. Justice, N.Y.C., 1998-2001. Vis. prof. Univ. Paris I, Pantheon-Sorbonne, 1998, 2000. Contbr. articles to profl. jours. Democrat. Office: Fordham Law Sch Dean Office Rm110 140 W 62nd St New York NY 10023 E-mail: wtreanor@fordham.edu.*

TREBON, LAWRENCE ALAN, lawyer; b. Waterloo, Iowa, Mar. 28, 1949; s. Al C. and Ann (Ryan) T.; m. Lynn Kutsch, June 12, 1971; children: Scott, Luke. BA, Loras Coll., 1971; JD, Marquette U., 1974. Ptnr. Stepke & Trebon, Milw., 1974-76, Stepke, Kossow, Trebon & Stadtmueller, Milw., 1976-78, Stepke, Trebon & Schoenfeld, Milw., 1978-80, Trebon & Schoenfeld, Milw., 1980-85, Trebon & Polsky, Milw., 1985-94, Trebon & Mayhew, Milw., 1994—. Coach basketball and t-ball, Milw., 1981-90; chmn. fin. com. St. Monica Parish, Whitefish Bay, Wis., 1986-87, chmn. fin. resources com., 1990-94; pres. home and sch. com. St. Monica Sch., Whitefish Bay, 1987-88. Mem. Tripoli Country Club (bd. govs. 1991-94). Republican. Roman Catholic. Avocations: golf, tennis, downhill skiing. Corporate, general, Estate planning, Property, real (including real estate development, water). Office: Trebon & Mayhew 733 N Van Buren St Ste 770 Milwaukee WI 53202-4768

TRECKELO, RICHARD M. lawyer; b. Elkhart, Ind., Oct. 22, 1926; s. Frank J. and Mary T.; m. Anne Kosick, June 25, 1955; children: Marla Treckelo Buck, Mary Treckelo Lucchesi. AB, U. Mich., 1951, JD, 1953. Bar: Ind. 1953, U.S. Dist. Ct. (no. and so. dists.) Ind. Pvt. practice, Elkhart, 1953-70; ptnr. Barnes and Thornburg, Elkhart, South Bend, others, 1971-91, of counsel, 1992—. Sec. Skyline Corp., Elkhart, 1959-94, bd. dirs., 1961-91. Bd. dirs. Elkhart Gen. Hosp. Found., Elkhart Park Found.; co-chmn. Elkhart Constl. Bicentennial Commn. Served with USAF, 1945-46. Mem. ABA, Elkhart City Bar Assn. (pres. 1975), Ind. Bar Assn., Elkhart County Bar Assn., Pres.'s Club (U. Mich.), Christiana Country Club, Michiana Club (chmn., U. Mich. Elbel Scholarship award), Rotary. Republican. Office: Barnes & Thornburg 121 W Franklin St Ste 200 Elkhart IN 46516-3200

TREECE, JAMES LYLE, lawyer; b. Colorado Springs, Colo., Feb. 6, 1925; s. Lee Oren and Ruth Ida (Smith) T.; m. Ruth Julie Treece, Aug. 7, 1949 (div. 1984); children: James (dec.), Karen Pelletier, Teryl Wait, Jamilyn Smyser, Carol Crowder. Student, Colo. State U., 1943, Colo. U., 1943, U.S. Naval Acad., 1944-46; BS, Mesa Coll., 1946; JD, U. Colo., 1950; postgrad., U. N.C., 1976-77. Bar: Colo. 1952, U.S. Dist. Ct. Colo. 1952, U.S. Ct. Appeals (10th cir.) 1952, U.S. Supreme Ct. 1967. Assoc. Yegge, Hall, Treece & Evans and predecessors, 1951-59, ptnr., 1959-69; U.S. atty. Colo., 1969-77; pres. Treece & Bahr and predecessor firms, Littleton, Colo., 1977-91; mcpl. judge, 1967-68; mem. faculty Nat. Trial Advocacy Inst., 1973-76, Law-Sci. Acad., 1964. Chmn. Colo. Dept. Pub. Welfare, 1963-68; chmn. Colo. Dept. Social Svcs., 1968-69; mem. Littleton Bd. Edn., 1977-81. Served with USNR, 1944-46. Recipient awards Colo. Assn. Sch. Bds., 1981, IRS, 1977, FBI, 1977, DEA, 1977, Fed. Exec. Bd., 1977. Mem. Fed. Bar Assn. (pres. Colo. 1975, award 1975), Colo. Bar Assn. (bd. govs.), Denver Bar Assn. (v.p., trustee). Republican. Episcopalian. General civil litigation, Criminal, Insurance. Home: 12651 N Pebble Beach Dr Sun City AZ 85351-3327 E-mail: jltreece@juno.com.

TREIGER, IRWIN LOUIS, lawyer; b. Seattle, Sept. 10, 1934; s. Sam S. and Rose (Steinberg) T.; m. Betty Lou Friedlander, Aug. 18, 1957; children: Louis H., Karen I., Kenneth B. BA, U. Wash., 1955, JD, 1957; LLM in Taxation, NYU, 1958. Bar: Wash. 1958, D.C. 1982, U.S. Dist. Ct. (we. dist.) Wash., U.S. Ct. Appeals (9th cir.), U.S. Supreme Ct. Assoc. Bogle & Gates, Seattle, 1958-63, ptnr., 1964-99, chmn., 1986-94; ptnr. Dorsey & Whitney LLP, Seattle, 1999—. Pres. Jewish Fedn. Greater Seattle, 1993-95; chmn. Mayor's Symphony Panel, 1986, Corp. Coun. for the Arts, 1987-88; pres. Seattle Symphony Found., 1986—; trustee, co-chmn. Cornish Coll. of the Arts, 1990-96, chair elect 2003—; trustee The Seattle Found., 1992—, vice chair, 1999-2003, chair, 2003—; trustee., sec. Samis Found., 1989—; chmn. King County Baseball Pk. Commn., 1995. Fellow Am. Coll. Tax Counsel; mem. ABA (chmn. taxation sect. 1988-89, sect. del. 1990-96, bd. govs. 2000-03), Wash. State Bar Assn. (chmn. taxation sect. 1975, co-chmn. nat. conf. lawyers and accts. 1997-2000), Greater Seattle C. of C. (chmn. 1993-94), Seattle Rotary (trustee 1998-2000), Seattle Rotary Svc. Found. (v.p. 1995-96, pres. 1996-97). Jewish. Corporate, general, Estate planning, Taxation, general. Office: Dorsey & Whitney LLP Ste 3400 1420 5th Ave Seattle WA 98101-4010 E-mail: treiger.irwin@dorseylaw.com.

TREISTER, GEORGE MARVIN, lawyer; b. Oxnard, Calif., Sept. 5, 1923; s. Isadore Harry and Augusta Lee (Bloom) T.; m. Jane Goldberg, Jan. 24, 1946; children: Laura, Neil, Adam, Dana. BS, UCLA, 1943; LL.B., Yale U., 1949. Bar: Calif. 1950. Law clk. to chief justice Calif. Supreme Ct., 1949-50; law clk. to Assoc. Justice Hugo L. Black U. S. Supreme Ct., 1950-51; asst. U.S. atty. So. Dist. Calif., 1951-53; dep. atty. gen. Calif., 1953; practiced in, 1953—; mem. Stutman, Treister and Glatt, 1953—; instr. U. So. Calif. Law Sch., 1954-98, Stanford U. Law Sch., 1977-81. Mem., former vice chmn. Nat. Bankruptcy Conf.; former mem. adv. com. on bankruptcy rules Jud. Conf. U.S. Contbr. articles to profl. jours. Served with USNR, 1943-46. Mem. Am. Law Inst., Am. Judicature Soc. Home: 1201 Neil Creek Rd Ashland OR 97520-9778 Office: 3699 Wilshire Blvd Los Angeles CA 90010-2719

TREMAINE, H. STEWART, retired lawyer; b. St. Paul, Mar. 17, 1919; s. Hugh Milner and Sally (Fox) T.; m. Harriet Lupton, July 10, 1948; children: Sally, Victoria, Katherine. BA, U. Wash., 1940; LLB, Yale U., 1946. Bar: Oreg. 1947, Wash. 1947. Ptnr. Davis Wright Tremaine, Portland, Oreg., 1947—95; ret., 1995. Capt. USMC, 1942-45. Decorated Purple Heart (2). Mem. Arlington Club, Waverley Club, Multnomah Athletic Club (pres.). Republican. Presbyterian. Avocations: golf, hiking, climbing, fishing, bridge. Estate planning, Corporate taxation. Office: Davis Wright Tremaine 1300 SW 5th Ave Ste 2200 Portland OR 97201-5667

TREMBATH, JON R. lawyer; m. Shelle S. Scott. JD, Brigham Young U., 1991. Bar: Tex. 1991. Law clk. The Hon. Randall R. Rader, US Ct. Appeals (fed. cir.), Washington, 1991—92; assoc. Fish & Richardson, Houston, 1992—97; assoc./share holder Mcht. & Gould, Mpls., 1997—. Intellectual property, Federal civil litigation, Patent. Office: Merchant & Gould 3200 IDS 80 South 8th St Minneapolis MN 55402 E-mail: jtrembath@merchant-gould.com.

TRENEFF, CRAIG PAUL, lawyer; b. Columbus, Ohio, July 16, 1952; s. Christ and Marlene Sue (Bach) T.; m. Loraine Marsh Treneff, July 12, 1986. BA, Ohio State U., 1974; JD, Capital U., 1981. Bar: Ohio 1981, U.S. Dist. Ct. (so. dist.) Ohio 1982. Legis. asst. Ohio House Rep., Columbus, 1974-81; law clk. Ohio Supreme Ct., Columbus, 1981-83; assoc. Morrow, Gordon & Byrd, Newark, 1983-84; counsel atty. Teaford, Rich & Dorsey, Columbus, 1984-85; ptnr. Schottenstein, Treneff & Williams, Columbus, 1985-97, Treneff & Williams, Columbus, 1997-2001; prin. Craig P. Treneff Law Office, 2001—. Del. coord. Gore for Pres., Ohio, 1988; mgr. Franklin County Treas. campaign, 1988; rsch. coord. Brown for Ohio Sec. campaign, 1982, 90, Franklin County Pres. campaign, 1980' treas. Ohioans with Sherrod Brown; pres. bd. trustees Directions for Youth; mem. Zoning Bd. Appeals, Westerville, Ohio, 1990-95, 96; chmn. Planning Commn., Westerville, Ohio, 1996—. Fellow Am. Acad. Matrimonial Lawyers; mem. ABA, Columbus Bar Assn., Ohio Bar Assn. (bd. cert. family rels. law specialist). Democrat. Lutheran. Family and matrimonial. Home: 148 Executive Ct Westerville OH 43081-1474 Office: Craig P Treneff Law Offices 555 S Front St Ste 320 Columbus OH 43215-5668 E-mail: cptreneff@cs.com.

TREUSCH, PAUL ELLSWORTH, law educator, lawyer; b. Chgo. m. Phyllis Freedman, 1941; 1 child, Karen Treusch Lord. PhB, U. Chgo., 1932; JD cum laude, 1935. Bar: Ill. 1935, D.C. 1945, Mass. 1974, U.S. SUpreme Ct. 1939. Ovt. practice, Chgo., 1935-37; mem. law faculty La. State. U., Baton Rouge, 1937-38; atty. Office of Chief Counsel IRS, Washington, 1938-70; mem. excess profits tax coun., 1948-51; asst. chief counsel litigation, 1951-70; adj. prof. law Howard U., Washington, 1965-70; prof., 1970-73, 76-79; prof. emeritus, 1979—. Professorial lectr. law George Washington U., 1966-73; prof. law Boston U., 1973 -76, prof. emeritus, 1976—; head Washington office Winston Strawn, Washington, 1970-73; prof. Southwestern U., L.A., 1979—; lectr. Zhongshan U. Law Dept., 1991—, Hong Kong U. and City U. Law Schs., 1991—. Co-author: treatise: Tax Exempt Charitable Organizations, 1978, 83, 88; contbr. to numerous pubs. Bd. dirs., legal counsel Burgundy Farm Country Day Sch.; bd. dirs. Washington Inst. Mental Hygiene. Mem. Fed. Bar Assn. (nat. pres. 1969-70, nat. coun.), Fed. Bar Found (dir.), ABA (life; exempt orgn. and internat. law coms.), Am. Law Inst. (life). Clubs: Cosmos (Washington); Nat. Press (Washington), Nat. Lawyers; Los Angeles Athletic. Office: Southwestern U Sch Law 675 S Westmoreland Ave Los Angeles CA 90005-3905 Fax: 213-383-1688.

TREVENA, JOHN HARRY, lawyer; b. Dunedin, Fla., Dec. 28, 1961; s. Ernest Lewis and Lenora Geraldine (Adelson) T.; m. Susan Lee Corris, Nov. 23, 1988; 1 child, Samuel Alan. BA in criminal justice, Univ. S. Fla., 1982; Fla. Police standards, Pinellas Police Acad., 1982; JD, Stetson Univ., 1985. Bar: Fla., U.S. Dist. Ct. (mid. dist.) Fla. 1986; bd. cert. criminal trial lawyer, Fla. Pvt. practice, Largo, Fla. Editorial bd. Fla. Bar Jour., Fla. Bar News, 1990-93. Mem.: Tampa Bay Cath. Lawyers Guild, Inc., Am. Judicature Soc., Nat. Assn. Criminal Def. Lawyers, Pinellas County Criminal Def. Lawyers Assn., Pinellas County Trial Lawyers Assn., Fla. Bar Assn., Clearwater and Am. Bar Assn., Fla. Assn. Criminal Def. Lawyers (life). Roman Catholic. Democrat. Civil rights, Criminal. Home: 423 Buttonwood Ln Largo FL 33770-4060 Office: 801 W Bay Dr Ste 509 Largo FL 33770-3220 E-mail: trevenalaw@aol.com.

TREVES, ALBERT, advocate, educator; b. Marseille, France, Oct. 20, 1958; Grad. bus. law, Univ. Aix En Provace, Aix. Bar: Marseille. Lectr. in public law Air Force Acad., 1980—81, France. Mem.: Assn. Adovates Advisors Bus. Law (v.p. internat. divsn.). Office: Treves Internat Law Office 66 Rue St Jaacques 13006 Marseille France

TREVETT, THOMAS NEIL, lawyer; b. Rochester, N.Y., Mar. 14, 1942; S. Frank E. and Andrea (Kuhn) T.; m. Margaret H. Hepburn, July 29, 1967; children: Monica, Millicent, Thomas. BS, St. John Fisher Coll., 1964; JD, Albany Law Sch., 1967. Bar: N.Y. 1967, U.S. Dist. Ct. (we. dist.) N.Y. 1968. Assoc. Thomas J. Meagher, Rochester, 1967-68, Trevett, Lenweaver, Salzer, and predecessor Gough, Skipworth, Summers, Eves & Trevett, Rochester, 1968—; pres. Trevett, Lenweaver, Salzer, and predecessor Gough, Skipworth, 1985-89. N.Y. estate tax atty., 1974-92. State Dem. committeeman; bd. dirs. Genesee region March Dimes, Rochester Area Multiple Sclerosis Soc., chmn. bd., 1992-94; chmn. bd. trustees McQuaid Jesuit H.S., 1997-2003. Mem. ABA, N.Y. State Bar Assn., (ho. of dels. 1981, chmn. Ins. Negligence and Compensation Law sect. 1989-90, John E. Leach award, 1996), Monroe County Bar Assn. (trustee 1996—, pres. 1999—), Def. Rsch. Inst., Fedn. Ins. Corp. Counsel, Wayne County Bar. Assn. (pres. 1978-79). Roman Catholic. Estate planning, Personal injury (including property damage), Property, real (including real estate development, water). Office: 2 State St Ste 1000 Rochester NY 14614-1803 also: 2003 Ridge Rd Ontario NY 14519 E-mail: ttrevett@trevettetal.com.

TRICARICO, JOSEPH ARCHANGELO, lawyer; b. N.Y.C., May 6, 1940; s. Nicholas and Frances Tricarico; m. Mildred Grandi, Feb. 12, 1972; 1 child, Nicholas. BS, St. Johns U., 1963, JD, 1967. V.p. trust counsel U.S. Trust Co. N.Y., N.Y.C., 1973—. Author: Generation-Skipping Transfers: A Primer, 1984, Credit Card Rape: Learn How It Is Done; Learn How It Was Undone, 2002. Pro bono arbitrator small claims ct. Civil Ct. of City of N.Y., S.I., 1981—; trustee Eger Health Care Ctr., S.I., 1990—. Mem. ABA (com. bus. law 1990—, vice chair com. generation-skipping transfers 1993—, com. taxation 1984—), Am. Corp. Counsel Assn. (com. securities litigation 1991—, com. environ. law 1992—), N.Y. Bankers Assn. (spl. counsel trust legis. and regulatory com. 1991—), N.Y. Bar Assn., Assn. Bar City N.Y., New York County Lawyers Assn. (com. on legis. 1989—), Am. Judges Assn. (hon. judge 1985—), Am. Inn of Ct. Bankruptcy, Probate (including wills, trusts), Securities. Office: US Trust Co NY 114 W 47th St New York NY 10036-1510 E-mail: jtricarico@ustrust.com.

TRICE, WILLIAM HENRY, III, lawyer; b. Vicksburg, Miss., Nov. 19, 1946; s. William Henry and Ethel Preston Trice; m. Judy Martha Trice, July 26, 1976; 1 child, William Carl. BA, U. Ark., 1968, JD, 1971. Bar: Ark. 1974, U.S. Dist. Ct. (ea. and we. dists.) Ark., U.S. Ct. Appeals (5th cir.). Staff atty. Ark. Hwy. Dept., Little Rock, 1974—75; dep. pros. atty. 6th Jur. Dist. Ark., Little Rock, 1975—77; atty. Howell Trice Hope & Files, Little Rock, 1977—. Atty. Ark. State Bd. Dental Examiners, Little Rock, 1981—, Ark. State Med. Bd., Little Rock, 1989—, Ark. State Bd. Optometry, Little Rock, 2000—. Sr. warden vestry St. Margaret's Episcopal Ch., Little Rock, 1999—2001; lobbiest Dist. Judges Assn. Ark., 2000—. Lt. col. ret. Ark. Army Nat. Guard. Mem.: Ark. Criminal Def. Lawyers Assn. (pres.), Ark. Trial Lawyers Assn. (bd. govs.), Scottish Rite Freemasonry (venerable master 1995—2001). Democrat. Episcopalian. Personal injury (including property damage), Administrative and regulatory, Family and matrimonial. Office: Howell Trice Hope & Files PA 211 Spring Little Rock AR 72201

TRIMBLE, JAMES T., JR., federal judge; b. Bunkie, La., Sept. 13, 1932; s. James T. Sr. and Mabel (McNabb) T.; m. Murel Elise Biles, Aug. 18, 1956; children: Elise Rumsey, Mary Olive Beacham, Martha McNabb Elliott, Sarah Trimble Moritz. Student, U. La., Lafayette, 1950-52; BA in Law, La. State U., 1955, JD, 1956. Bar: La. 1956. With Gist, Murchison & Gist (now Gist, Methvin, Hughes & Munsterman), 1959-78, Trimble, Percy, Smith, Wilson, Foote, Walker & Honeycutt, 1979-86; U.S. magistrate U.S. Dist. Ct. (we. dist.) La., 1986-91, judge, 1991—. Lt. USAF, 1956-59. Mem. Southwest La. Bar Assn., La. Bar Assn., La. Bar Found. Office: 611 Broad St Ste 237 Lake Charles LA 70601-4380

TRIMBLE, WILLIAM CATTELL, JR., retired lawyer; b. Buenos Aires, Feb. 7, 1935; s. William Cattell and Nancy Gordon (Carroll) Trimble; m. Barbara Janney, June 19, 1960; children: William C, Margery M Kennelly. AB, Princeton U., 1958; LL.B., U. Md., 1964. Bar: Md 1965. With firm Ober, Grimes & Shriver, Balt., 1965-87, ptnr., 1970-87, mng. ptnr., 1973-77; counsel Semmes, Bowen & Semmes, Balt., 1987—2000; ret., 2000; mem. Gov.'s Commn. to Revise Annotated Code of Md., 1975-83. Hon consul, Netherlands, 1986—2003; pres bd trustees Valley Sch, 1968—73; trustee Garrison Forest Sch, 1975—95, Gilman Sch, 1980—84. Lt USNR, 1958—61. Mem.: ABA, Baltimore Bar Asn, Md Bar Asn, Soc Cincinnati, Greenspring Valley Hunt Club, Colonial Club (Princeton). Episcopalian. Education and schools, Estate planning, Probate (including wills, trusts). E-mail: wtrimble@msn.com.

TRIMMER, VICKY ANN, lawyer; b. Harrisburg, Pa., July 26, 1962; d. Ray E. and Saveria Sylvia Trimmer. BS, U. Pitts., 1984; JD, Dickinson U., 1987; AA, Harrisburg Area C.C., 1991. CPA Pa., 1995; bar: Pa. 1987. Sr. asst. counsel Pa. Dept. Revenue, Harrisburg, 1987—98; atty. Mette, Evans & Woodside, Harrisburg, 1999—. Dir. Leave A Legacy Harrisburg Area, Harrisburg, 2002—, Estate Planning Coun. of Ctrl. PA, Inc, Camp Hill, Pa., 2001—. Pres. Harrisburg 500 Club, Mechanicsburg, Pa., 2000—02; treas. Upper Allen Woman's Club Found., Mechanicsburg; pres.- elect/ 1st v.p. Upper Allen Woman's Club, Mechanicsburg, 2002—; mem. Gen. Fedn. of Woman's Clubs- Pa. Found. Com., Mechanicsburg, 2002—; bd. dirs. Harrisburg Area Woman's Bowling Assn., Mechanicsburg; mem. Pa. State Woman's 500 Club. Mem.: Pa. Inst. CPA's, Pa. Bar Assn., Dauphin County Bar Assn. (sect. chair probate sect. 2002, treas. probate sect., vice chair probate sect.). Roman Catholic. Avocations: bowling, reading, golf. Probate (including wills, trusts), Taxation, general, Estate planning. Home: 113 Cambridge Dr Mechanicsburg PA 17055 Office: Mette Evans & Woodside Box 5950 3401 N Front St Harrisburg PA 01711-0950 Office Fax: 717-236-1816. E-mail: vatrimmer@mette.com.

TRIMMIER, CHARLES STEPHEN, JR., lawyer; b. Chgo., June 25, 1943; s. Charles Stephen and Lucille E. (Anderson) T.; m. Rae Wade Trimmier, Aug. 19, 1966; children: Charles Stephen, Hallie Wade. BA, U. Ala., Tuscaloosa, 1965, JD, 1968. Bar: Ala. 1968. From assoc. to ptnr. Rives, Peterson, Pettus and Conway, Birmingham, Ala., 1968-77; pres. TrimmierLaw Firm, Birmingham and Mobile, Ala., Jacksonville, Fla., 1977—. Gen. counsel Nat. Assn. State Chartered Credit Union Suprs., 1983-2001, Ala. Credit Union League, Fla. Credit Union League, La. Credit Union League. Editor-in-chief: Ala. Law Rev., 1968. Mem. ABA (bus. and banking law sect., credit union com.), Ala. Bar Assn., Birmingham Bar Assn., Comml. Law League, Ala. Law Inst., Shades Valley Rotary, Shades Valley Jaycees (sec. 1973). Episcopalian. Commercial, contracts (including sales of goods; commercial financing), Corporate, general, Private international. Home: 3819 River View Cir Birmingham AL 35243-4801 Office: Trimmier Law Firm PO Box 1885 Birmingham AL 35201-1885 E-mail: steve@trimmier.com.

TRIMMIER, ROSCOE, JR., lawyer; b. Charlotte, N.C., July 22, 1944; s. Roscoe and Susie Elizabeth (Stitt) T.; divorced; 1 child, Leigh Snowden. AB, Harvard U., 1971, JD, 1974. Bar: Mass. 1974, U.S. Dist. Ct. Mass. 1975, U.S. Ct. Appeals (1st cir.) 1975, U.S. Supreme Ct. 1979, U.S. Claims Ct. 1983, U.S. Ct. Appeals (D.C. cir.) 2002. Assoc. Ropes & Gray, Boston, 1974-83, ptnr., 1983—. Mem. hearing com. Bd. Bar Overseers, 1983-89; bd. dirs., v.p. Family Counseling & Guidance Ctr., Inc., Boston, 1980-93; gov. Mus. of Sci., 1981-93; mem. exec. com. Jud. Nominating Commn., 1991-96; corp. mem. Mass. Gen. Hosp., 1992—; overseer N.E Med. Ctr. Hosps., 1992—; mem. Mass. Bd. Registration in Medicine, 2001--. 1st lt. U.S. Army, 1965-68. Fellow: Am. Coll. Trial Lawyers, Mass. Bar Found. (life), Am. Bar Found. (life); mem.: ABA (former chair standing com. on fed. judiciary), Am. Law Inst., Boston Bar Assn., Mass. Black Lawyers Assn. (life), Mass. Bar Assn. Federal civil litigation, State civil litigation, Environmental. Home: 1265 Beacon St Brookline MA 02446-5200 Office: Ropes & Gray 1 International Pl Boston MA 02110-2624

TRINDER, RACHEL BANDELE, lawyer; b. Ibadan, Nigeria, Feb. 21, 1955; came to U.S., 1977; d. Victor William John and Margaret (Almond) T. BA with honors, Oxford U., 1977, MA, 1994; LLM, U. Va., 1978. Bar: D.C. 1979, U.S. Dist. Ct. 1979, U.S. Ct. Appeals (D.C. cir.) 1980, U.S. Supreme Ct. 1986. Assoc. Zuckert, Scoutt & Rasenberger, LLP, Washington, 1978-85, ptnr., 1985—. V.p. aviation spl. interest chpt. Transp. Rsch. Forum, 1988-90, exec. v.p., 1990-91, gen. counsel, 1989-91; mem. bd. advisors 3d Ann. Symposium on Law and Outer Space, 1991, program dir., mem. bd. advisors, 4th Ann., 1991-92. Contbr. articles to legal jours. Bd. govs. Internat. Student House, 1986-93, mem. exec. com., asst. treas., 1987-88, mem. bd. advisors, 1993-97. Fellow English Speaking Union, 1977. Mem. ABA, FBA (chair space law com. 1990-94, chair internat. law sect. 1994-96), Fed. Bar Assn., Internat. Inst. Space Law (life), Internat. Aviation Women's Assn. (dir.-at-large 1996-98), Internat. Inst. Air and Space Law (bd. govs., exec. com. 1992-2002), Internat. Aviation Club (bd. govs. 1984-86, pres. 1986), Aero Club (bd. govs. 1993—, pres. 2000), Nat. Aeronautic Assn. (bd. govs. 2000-01). Aviation, Federal civil litigation, Corporate, general. Home: 1266 Dartmouth Ct Alexandria VA 22314-4784 Office: Zuckert Scoutt & Rasenberger LLP 888 17th St NW Washington DC 20006-3939 E-mail: rbtrinder@zsrlaw.com.

TRIPP, KAREN BRYANT, lawyer; b. Rocky Mount, NC, Sept. 2, 1955; d. Bryant and Katherine Rebecca (Watkins) Tripp; m. Robert Mark Burleson, June 25, 1977 (div. 1997); 1 child, Hamilton Chase Tripp Barnett. BA, U. NC, 1976; JD, U. Ala., 1981. Bar: Tex. 1981, US Dist. Ct. (so. dist.) Tex. 1982, US, Ct. Appeals (fed. cir.) 1983, US Dist. Ct. (ea. dist.) Tex. 1991, US Supreme Ct. 1994, US Dist. Ct. (no. dist.) Tex. 1998, US Ct. Appeals (5th and 9th cirs.) 2000, US Ct. Appeals (3d cir.) 2001. Law clk. Tucker, Gray & Espy, Tuscaloosa, Ala., 1978-81; law clk. to presiding justice Ala. Supreme Ct., Montgomery, Ala., summer 1980; atty. Exxon Prodn. Rsch. Co., Houston, 1981-86, coord. tech. transfer, 1986-87; assoc. Arnold, White and Durkee, Houston, 1988-93, shareholder, 1994-98; shareholder, head intellectual property sect. for Houston office Winstead, Sechrest & Minick, Attys. at Law, Houston, 1998; pres. Blake Barnett & Co., 1996—; pvt. practice, 1999—. Creator, program planner, master of ceremonies 1st and 2d intellectual property law confs. for women corp. counsels. Editor: Intellectual Property Law Rev., 1995—2003; contbr. articles to profl. jour. Chair U. Houston and Houston intellectual Property Law Assoc. Fall CLE Inst. on Intellectual Property, 2000. Mem. ABA (intellectual property law sect., ethics com. 1992-96), Houston Bar Assn. (interprofl. rels. com. 1988-90), Houston Intellectual Property Law Assn. (outstanding inventor com. 1982-84, chmn. 1994-95, sec. 1987-88, treas. 1991-92, bd. dir. 1992-94, 98-2000, nominations com. 1993, 96, chmn. fall CLE Inst. 2000), Tex. Bar Assn. (antitrust law com. 1984-85, chmn. internat. law com. intellectual property law sect. 1987-88, internat. transfer tech. com. 1983-84, planning com. continuing legal edn. conf. on intellectual property 2003), planning comm. for 2003 CLE Inst. on Intellectual property Law, Tex. Exec. Women, Women's Fin. Exch., Am. Intellectual Property Lawyers Assn. (patent law com. 1995), Intellectual Property Owners Assn. (copyright com.), Women in Tech. (founder), Lil Eli's Club (founder), Phi Alpha Delta. Republican. Episcopalian. Intellectual property, Patent, Trademark and copyright. Office: PO Box 1301 Houston TX 77251-1301 E-mail: ktripp@tripplaw.com.

TRIPP, THOMAS NEAL, lawyer, political consultant; b. June 19, 1942; s. Gerald Frederick and Kathryn Ann (Siebold) T.; m. Ellen Marie Larrimer, Apr. 16, 1966; children: David Larrimer, Bradford Douglas, Corinne Catherine. BA cum laude, Mich. State U., 1964; JD, George Washington U., 1967. Bar: Ohio 1967, U.S. Ct. Mil. Appeals 1968, U.S. Supreme Ct. 1968, Wyo. 1991. Pvt. practice, Columbus, Ohio, 1969—, Wilson, Wyo., 1991—. Real estate developer, Columbus, 1969—; chmn. bd. Black Sheep Enterprises, Columbus, 1969—; polit. cons. David A. Keene & Assocs., Washington, 1986-96; vice chmn. bd. Sun Valley-Elkhorn Assn., Idaho, 1983-85, chmn, 1986-91; vice chmn. Sawtooth Sports, Ketchum, Idaho, 1983-85; legal counsel Wallace F. Ackley Co., Columbus, 1973—; vice chmn. Triathlon LLC, 1996—; presiding judge Ohio Mock Trial Competition, 1986-94; chmn. bd. dirs. White House, 1996; mem. small bus. adv. coun. FCC, 1993-95; dep. spl. adviser to pres. N.Am. Free Trade Agreement, 1993; polit. columnist Trustee Americans for Responsible Govt., Washington, GOPAC; mem. Peace Corps Adv. Coun., 1981-85; mem. U.S. Commn. on Trade Policy and Negotiations, 1985-88; campaign mgr., fin. chmn. Charles Rockwell Saxbe, Ohio Ho. of Reps., 1974, 76, 78, 80; campaign mgr. George Bush for Pres., 1980, nat. dep. field dir., nat. dep. polit. dir., 1980; alumni admissions coun. Mich. State U., 1984—, George Washington U., 1988—; regional co-chmn. Reagan-Bush, 1984, nat. fin. com., 1984; mem. Victory '84 fin. com.; mem. Victory '88 fin. com. Bush-Quayle; co-chmn. Ohio Lawyers for Bush/Quayle, 1988; Rep. candidate 2d U.S. Congl. Dist., Idaho, 1988; candidate U.S. Senate, Wyo., 1996; transition dir. Ohio Sec. of State, 1990-91; bd. trustees Columbus Acad. Pvt. Co-ed Secondary Sch., 1991-94, Prescott (Ariz.) Coll., 1998-2000; chmn. bd. dirs. T.R.E.E. Coalition, 1991—; vice-chmn. Am. Conservative Union Found., 2002—. 1st lt. U.S. Army, 1967-69. Fellow Pi Sigma Alpha, Vietnam Vet. Am., Phi Delta Phi. Republican. Admiralty, General civil litigation, Non-profit and tax-exempt organizations. Home: 5420 Clark State Rd Columbus OH 43230-1956

TRITTER, DANIEL F. lawyer, writer; b. N.Y.C., Jan. 20, 1934; s. Maurice J. and Hermina (Ronay) T.; m. Rita Frances Shane, June 22, 1958; 1 child, Michael Shane. BA, Williams Coll., 1954; MA, Columbia U., 1957; cert., Inst. on East Cen. Europe, 1957; JD, Benjamin N. Cardozo Sch. Law, 1982. Bar: N.Y. 1984, U.S. Dist. Ct. (so. dist., ea. dist.) 1984, U.S. Supreme Ct. 1987. Writer, exec. Diener & Dorskind, Inc., N.Y.C., 1960-71, M.L. Grant, Inc., N.Y.C., 1971-79; pvt. practice, N.Y.C., 1984—. Adj. prof. Williams Coll., 1984, Touro Law Sch., 1989, Benjamin N. Cardozo Sch. Law, 1999. Contbr. essays to profl. jours. Bd. govs. N.Y. chpt. Arthritis Found., 1985-90. Spl. agt. CIC, U.S. Army, 1957-60. Mem. Assn. Trial Lawyers Am., Law and Humanities Inst. (pres. 1986-91, v.p. 1991—), Williams Club. Democrat. Avocations: classical music, writing, sports. General civil litigation, Entertainment. Office: 330 W 42nd St Fl 32 New York NY 10036-6902

TROCANO, RUSSELL PETER, lawyer; b. Hackensack, N.J., Sept. 7, 1963; s. Rosario Mario and Barbara Ann (Costa) T. BA, Seton Hall U., 1984; JD, Fordham U., 1987, LLM, 1992. Bar: N.J. 1987, N.Y. 1988. Law clk. to presiding justice County of Middlesex, New Brunswick, N.J., 1987-88; assoc. Sellar Richardson Law Firm, Newark and Roseland, N.J., 1988, Morgan Melhuish Monaghan Law Firm, Livingston, N.J., 1988-89; prin., owner Russell P. Trocano, Ridgewood, N.J., 1989—. Mem. San Guisseppe Societa de Santa Croce de Camerina, Paterson, N.J., 1989—. Fordham U. scholar, 1987. Mem. ABA, N.J. Bar Assn., N.Y. State Bar Assn., Bergen County Bar Assn., Passaic County Bar Assn., Brehon Law Soc., Arthur T. Vanderbilt Inn of Cts., Phi Alpha Theta. Roman Catholic. Avocations: mineral collecting, travel, reading. Bankruptcy, Commercial, consumer (including collections, credit), General practice. Home: 60 S Maple Ave Ridgewood NJ 07450-4542 Office: 7 E Ridgewood Ave Ridgewood NJ 07450-3807

TROFFKIN, HOWARD JULIAN, lawyer, diversified company executive; b. Port Chester, N.Y., Jan. 30, 1937; s. Irving and Frieda Troffkin; m. Rhea Dorothy, May 12, 1963; children: Stephen, Barbara. BS in Chemistry, St. Lawrence U., 1959; postgrad., Columbia U., 1959-60; JD, Georgetown U., 1970. Bar: Va. 1971, D.C. 1972. Rsch. chemist Am. Cyanamid Co., 1961-66, legal trainee, 1966-67, patent agt., 1967-71; assoc. Pennie, Edmonds, Morton, Taylor & Adams, Washington, 1971-77; patent atty. W.R. Grace & Co., Columbia, Md., 1977-86, sr. patent counsel, 1987-98; pvt. practice, 1998—; sec./counsel Concrete Corrosion Inhibitor Trade Assn. Patentee in chemistry field. Mem. Willerburn Civic Assn., 1971-75. Served with AUS, 1960-61. Mem. ABA, Va. Bar Assn., D.C. Bar Assn., Washington Patent Lawyers Assn., Md. Patent Law Assn. (pres. 1981-83), Am. Intellectual Property Law Assn., Am. Chem. Soc., Concrete Corrosion Inhibitors Assn. (sec./counsel). Jewish. Avocations: woodcrafting, travel. Intellectual property, Patent, Trademark and copyright. Home and Office: 7808 Ivymount Ter Potomac MD 20854-3218 E-mail: Troffkin@aol.com.

TROJACK, JOHN EDWARD, lawyer; b. St. Paul, Mar. 30, 1946; s. Albert G. and Eleanor (Mader) T.; m. Mary Jo LaNasa, Oct. 12, 1979; 4 children. BA, U. Minn., 1968; JD, William Mitchell Coll. Law, St. Paul, 1976. Bar: Minn. 1976, U.S. Dist. Ct. Minn. 1976, U.S. Ct. Appeals (8th cir.) 1980, U.S. Supreme Ct. 1980. Assoc. John E. Daubney, St. Paul, 1976-78; ptnr. Wagner, Rutchick & Trojack, P.A., St. Paul, 1978-83; sole practice St. Paul, 1983—. Conciliation Ct. referee Ramsey County Dist. Ct., St. Paul, 1979—; vol. atty. So. Minn. Regional Legal Svcs. Corp., St. Paul, 1982—; arbitrator Hennepin County Dist. Ct., 1986—, Am. Arbitration Assn., 1988—. Served with USN, 1968-72, capt. USNR. Mem.: Naval Res. Assn., Ramsey County Bar Assn., Minn. Bar Assn., Nat. Network of Estate Planning Attys., The Harvesters Club, Phi Alpha Delta. State civil litigation, General practice, Probate (including wills, trusts). Address: 1549 Livingston Ave Ste 101 Saint Paul MN 55118-3415 E-mail: jetlawoffice@aol.com.

TROLL, JOHN RICHARD, lawyer; b. Corning, N.Y., Oct. 30, 1947; s. John Richard Troll and Florence Estelle Keller; m. Suzanne Zimmerman, Aug. 25, 1990; 1 child, John Richard Troll III. BA, Antioch Coll., 1970; JD, SUNY, Buffalo. Bar: N.Y. 1981, Ohio 1984, Mich. 1997, Ind. 2002. Assoc. Graham, Campaign & McCurly, N.Y.C., 1980—81, Kane, Dalsimer, Kane Sullivan & Kurucz, N.Y.C., 1981—82; assoc. to ptnr. Porter & Keene, Porter & Bremer, Cleve., 1982—84; trademark counsel BP, Cleve., 1985—96; v.p., trademark counsel Harley-Davidson, Mich., Ann Arbor, 1996—2001; ptnr. Baker & Daniels, Indpls., 2002—. Mem.: AIPLA, ABA, Internat. Trademark Assn. (mem. designate), Brand Names Edn. Found. (chair bd. govs. 1999—2001), Indpls. Athletic Club. Avocations: cars, motorcycles, antiques, political theory, political history. Intellectual property, Trademark and copyright, Private international. Office: Baker & Daniels 300 N Meridian St Ste 2700 Indianapolis IN 46204-1782 E-mail: jrtroll@bakerd.com.

TROMBLEY, MICHAEL JEROME, lawyer; b. Bay City, Mich., Dec. 10, 1933; s. Clare F. and Sarah I. (Ingersol) T.; m. Anna K. Simons (div. 1963); children: Peter, Tad; m. Sandra V. Bybee (dec. 1980); children: Christine, Jacques; m. Sherry V. Cribbs, June 10, 1981. A.A., Menlo Coll., 1953; B.A., Stanford U., 1955; LL.B., U. Mo., 1960. Bar: Mo. 1960, Fla. 1974; bd. cert. elder law. Sole practice, Columbia, Mo., 1960-68; ptnr. Alexander, Wayland, Trombley, Butcher, Columbia, Mo., 1964-68; sole practice, 1969-79; ptnr. Trombley, Matheny & Schommer, Sebring, Fla., 1980-84, Trombley, Lobozzo, Schommer, Disler & Accorsi, Sebring, 1984— ; past chmn. Fla. Bar Cert. Com. Charter pres. Estate Planning Coun. of Highlands County, Fla., 1979-80. Served to 1st lt. USMCR, 1955-57. Mem. Am. Judicature Soc., Acad. Fla. Trial Lawyers, Nat. Acad. Elder Law Attys., Acad. Fla. Elder Law Attys. (pres.), Masons, Shriners, Elks. Republican. Episcopalian. Federal civil litigation, State civil litigation, Estate planning. Office: 329 S Commerce Ave Sebring FL 33870-3607

TROOBOFF, PETER DENNIS, lawyer; b. Balt., June 22, 1942; s. Benjamin M. and Rebecca (Cohen) Trooboff; m. Rhoda Morss, Aug. 10, 1969; children: Hannah, Abigail. BA cum laude, Columbia U., 1964; LLB cum laude, Harvard U., 1967; LLM, London Sch. Econs., 1968; diploma cum laude, Hague Acad. Internat. Law, Netherlands, 1968. Bar: N.Y. 1968, D.C. 1970. Rsch. assoc. Harvard U. Law Sch., Cambridge, Mass., 1968—69; asst. to exec. editor for The Advocates Sta. WGBH-TV, Boston, 1969; assoc. Covington & Burling, Washington, 1969—75, ptnr., 1975—. Lectr., dir. seminars The Hague Acad. Internat. Law, 1972, 82, lectr., 86, mem. curatorium, 1991—; lectr. The Hague Acad. External Program, Beijing, 1987, Harare, 93; lectr. internat. orgns. U. Va. Sch. Law, 1973; head U.S. del. 3d Inter-Am. Specialized Conf. Pvt. Internat. Law, La Paz, Bolivia, 1984; mem. U.S. del. Hague Conf. pvt. internat. law, 1993, 96, 1997—; arbitrator Internat. Ctr. Settlement of Investment Disputes. Contbr. chapters to books, articles to profl. publs.; editor: Law and Responsibility in Warfare-The Vietnam Experience, 1975. Frank Knox Meml. fellow. Mem.: Washington Inst. Fgn. Affairs, Internat. Law Assn., Am. Soc. Internat. Law (pres. 1990—92, bd. editors Am. Jour. Internat. Law 1980—92, 1994—), Am. Law Inst., Coun. Fgn. Rels., City Club (Washington), Cosmos Club. Corporate, general, Private international, Public international. Office: Covington & Burling PO Box 7566 1201 Pennsylvania Ave NW Washington DC 20044

TROPP, JONATHAN B. lawyer; b. Boston, July 7, 1967; s. Burton E. and Roslyn G. Tropp; m. Lauren M. Lublin, Aug. 20, 1989; children: Sarah, Rachel, Gabrielle. AB, Harvard U., 1988, JD, 1991. Bar: Conn. 1991, U.S. Dist. Ct. Conn. 1992, U.S. Dist. Ct. N.Y. (so. dist.) 1995, U.S. Dist. Ct. (no. dist.) 1997, U.S. Ct. Appeals (3d cir.) 1995, U.S. Ct. Appeals (2d cir.) 1999, U.S. PTO 2002, cert.: U.S. Ct. Appeals (fed. cir.) 2003. Law clk. Hon. Robert E. Keeton, 1991—92; atty. Day, Berry & Howard LLP, Hartford, Conn., 1992—95, Stamford, Conn., 1995—2001, ptnr., 2002—. Mem. regional bd. Anti-Defamation League, Conn., 2002—. Mem.: ABA, Fed. Bar Coun., Conn. Bar Assn. (exec. com. of fed. practice sect. 2001—). Federal civil litigation, Intellectual property, General civil litigation. Office: Day Berry & Howard LLP One Canterbury Green Stamford CT 06901

TROST, EILEEN BANNON, lawyer; b. Teaneck, N.J., Jan. 9, 1951; d. William Eugene and Marie Thelma (Finlayson) Bannon; m. Lawrence Peter Trost Jr., Aug. 27, 1977; children: Lawrence Peter III, William Patrick, Timothy Alexander. BA with great distinction, Shimer Coll., 1972; JD cum laude, U. Minn., 1976. Bar: Ill. 1976, U.S. Dist. Ct. (no. dist.) Ill. 1976, Minn. 1978, U.S. Tax Ct. 1978, U.S. Supreme Ct. 1981. Assoc. McDermott, Will & Emery, Chgo., 1976-82, ptnr., 1982-93; v.p. No. Trust Bank Ariz. N.A., Phoenix, 1993-95; ptnr. Sonnenschein Nath & Rosenthal, Chgo., 1995—. Mem. Am. Coll. Trust and Estate Coun., Minn. Bar Assn., Internat. Acad. Estate and Trust Law, Chgo. Estate Planning Coun. Roman Catholic. Estate planning, Probate (including wills, trusts), Estate taxation. Office: Sonnenschein Nath & Rosenthal 8000 Sears Tower Chicago IL 60606 E-mail: etrost@sonnenschein.com.

TROTT, DENNIS C(HARLES), lawyer; b. Ft. Wayne, Ind., Oct. 31, 1946; s. Charles and Eileen (Collins) T.; m. Nancy J. Servis, Aug. 4, 1973; children: Eileen Susanne, Duncan Eric. AB, Ind. U., 1968; JD, U. Mich., 1973. Bar: N.Y. 1974, U.S. Dist. Ct. (so. dist.) N.Y. 1974, U.S. Ct. Appeals (2d cir.) 1974, U.S. Dist. Ct. (ea. dist.) N.Y. 1978, U.S. Ct. Mil. Appeals 1985, U.S. Ct. Internat. Trade 1986, U.S. Tax Ct. 1986, U.S. Supreme Ct. 1986, U.S. Ct. Claims 1988, U.S. Ct. Appeals (fed. cir.) 1990, U.S. Ct. Appeals (3rd and 6th cirs.) 1991. Assoc. Haight, Gardner, N.Y.C., 1973-75, Breed, Abbott, N.Y.C., 1975-77; pres., chief exec. officer Luke Enterprises, Inc., N.Y.C., 1988—; ptnr. Trott & Appel, N.Y.C., 1989-91; pvt. practice N.Y.C., 1991—. Bd. dirs. Neighborhood Housing Services of N.Y.C., 1985-89. Served with U.S. Army, 1968-70. Mem. N.Y. County Lawyers Assn. Admiralty, Banking, Corporate, general. Home: 304 Sherman St Brooklyn NY 11218-1507 Office: 305 Broadway Ste 700 New York NY 10007-1109

TROTT, STEPHEN SPANGLER, federal judge, musician; b. Glen Ridge, N.J., Dec. 12, 1939; s. David Herman and Virginia (Spangler) Trott; m. Carol C. Trott; children: Christina, Shelley. BA, Wesleyan U., 1962; LLB, Harvard U., 1965; LLD (hon.), Santa Clara U., 1992; LLD (hon.), U. Idaho, 2001. Bar: Calif. 1966, U.S. Dist. Ct. (cen. dist.) Calif. 1966, U.S. Ct. Appeals (9th cir.) 1983, U.S. Supreme Ct. 1984. Guitarist, mem. The Highwaymen, 1958—; dep. dist. atty. L.A. County Dist. Atty.'s Office, L.A., 1966—75, chief dep. dist. atty., 1975—79; U.S. dist. atty. Central Dist. Calif., L.A., 1981—83; asst. atty. gen. criminal divsn. Dept. Justice, Washington, 1983—86; faculty Nat. Coll. Dist. Attys., Houston, 1973—; chmn. central dist. Calif. Law Enforcement Coord. Com., Houston, 1981—83; coord. L.A.-Nev. Drug Enforcement Task Force, 1982—83; assoc. atty. gen. Justice Dept., Washington, 1986—88; chmn. U.S. Interpol, 1986—88; judge U.S. Ct. of Appeals (9th cir.), Boise, Idaho, 1988—. Trustee Wesleyan U., 1984—87; adv. council Big Brothers, Big Sisters S.W. Idaho, 2001—; ofcl. photographer World Cup Wrestling Championship, 2003—; bd. dirs., pres. Children's Home Soc., Idaho, 1990—. Recipient Gold record as singer-guitarist for Michael Row the Boat Ashore, 1961, Disting. Faculty award, Nat. Coll. Dist. Attys., 1977. Mem.: Am. Coll. Trial Lawyers, Boise (Idaho) Philharm. Assn. (bd. dirs. 1995—, v.p. 1997—99, pres. 1999—2003, pre-concert lectr. 1997—), Idaho Classic Guitar Soc. (founder, pres. 1989—), Internat. Brotherhood Magicians, Idaho Racing Pigeon Assn., Magic Castle, Brentwood Racing Pigeon Club (pres. 1977—82), Wilderness Fly Fishers Club (pres. 1975—77). Republican. Office: US Ct Appeals 9th Cir 667 US Courthouse 550 W Fort St Boise ID 83724-0101

TROTTA, FRANK P., JR., lawyer; BA, JD, LLM, MBA. Bar: N.Y. U.S. Dist. Ct. (no. and we. dists.) N.Y., U.S. Ct. Mil. Appeals, U.S. Dist. Ct. (so. and ea. dists.) N.Y., U.S. Ct. Internat. Trade, U.S. Tax Ct., U.S. Supreme Ct., U.S. Ct. Appeals (D.C. cir.), U.S. Ct. Customs and Patent Appeals, D.C., Conn., Pa. Assoc. Weil, Gotshal & Manges, N.Y.C.; pvt. practice Washington, N.Y.C., New Rochelle, NY, Greenwich, Conn. Former mem. bd. govs ABA; mem. faculty Practicing Law Inst.; governing mem. Nat. Jud. Coll., Am. Bar Endowment, ABRA Pension Fund; chmn. bd. advisors Columbia U. Grad. Sch. Bus., Inst. for Non-for-Profit Mgmt. Bd. dirs. Boys Town of Italy; mem. Fund for Justice and Edn.; chmn. New Rochelle Rep. Party; mem. bd. edn. Greenwich Cath. Sch. Legislative.

TROTTER, RICHARD, law educator, arbitrator; b. East Orange, NJ, Feb. 9, 1943; s. Maurice S. and Leona S. Trotter. BS, Columbia U., 1965; MA, U. Pa., 1966, PhD, 1970; JD, Rutgers U., 1977. Bar: Pa. 1977, U.S. Dist. Ct. (ea. dist.) Pa. 1977, U.S. Ct. Appeals (3rd cir.) 1977, U.S. Supreme Ct. 1980. Asst. prof. Rutgers U., Camden, NJ, 1970—78; pvt. practice Phila., 1978—79; assoc. prof. U. Balt., 1979—. Labor arbitrator Fed. Mediation and Conciliation Svc., N.E. region, 1979—. Mem.: Indsl. Rels. Rsch. Assn. Avocations: scuba diving, bicycling, trekking. Office: Univ Balt 1420 N Charles St Baltimore MD 21201 Office Fax: 410-837-5675. Business E-Mail: rtrotter@ubmail.ubalt.edu.

TROUT, LINDA COPPLE, state supreme court chief justice; b. Tokyo, Sept. 1, 1951; BA, U. Idaho, 1973, JD, 1977; LLD (hon.), Albertson Coll. Idaho, 1999. Bar: Idaho 1977. Judge magistrate divsn. Idaho Dist. Ct. (2d jud. divsn.), 1983-90, dist. judge, 1991-92, acting trial ct. adminstr., 1987-91; justice Idaho Supreme Ct., 1992—, chief justice, 1997—. Instr. coll. law U. Idaho, 1983, 88. Mem. Idaho State Bar Assn., Clearwater Bar Assn. (pres. 1980-81).

TROUTMAN, E. MAC, federal judge; b. Greenwood Township, Pa., Jan. 7, 1915; s. Emmett Theodore and Kathryn (Holman) T.; m. Margaret Petrick, Nov. 23, 1944; children— Jane A., Jean K. AB, Dickinson Coll., 1934, LL.B., 1936. Bar: Pa. 1937. With Phila. and Reading Coal and Iron Co., 1937-58, gen. counsel, 1954-58; gen. atty. Phila. and Reading Corp., 1958-67; gen. counsel Reading Anthracite Co., 1958-61, Reserve Carbon Corp., 1961-66, So. Carbon Corp., 1966-67; solicitor Blue Mountain Sch. Dist., 1963-67, Blue Mountain Area Sch. Authority, 1963-67, Orwigsburg Municipal Authority, 1966-67, Am. Bank and Trust Co., Reading and Pottsville, Pa., 1957-67; exec. sec., gen. counsel Pa. Self-Insurers Assn., 1962-67; U.S. judge Eastern Dist. Pa., from 1967, sr. judge, 1982-98; retired, 1998. Bd. dirs. Greater Pottsville Indsl. Devel. Corp., 1963-67, Pa. C. of C., 1955-65, Greater Pottsville Area C. of C., 1961-64, Orwigsburg Community Meml. Assn., 1950-66, Schuylkill County Soc. Crippled Children, 1945-67; v.p., dir. Pottsville Hosp. and Warne Clinic, 1960-67. Served with AUS, World War II. Mem. ABA, Pa. Bar Assn., Schuylkill County Bar Assn. (vice chancellor 1955-57, chmn. jud. vacancies and unauthorized practice coms. 1960, chmn. medico-legal com. 1963-65) Lutheran (pres. coun. 1961—). Home: Kimmel's Rd Orwigsburg PA 17961

TROUTMAN, J. GREGORY, lawyer; b. Louisville, Dec. 7, 1966; BA in Polit. Sci. cum laude, U. Louisville, 1989, JD, 1992; LLM in Taxation, Boston U., 1993. Bar: Ky. 1992, U.S. Fed. Claims Ct. 1994, U.S. Dist. Ct. (we. dist.) Ky. 1995, U.S. Dist. Ct. (ea. dist.) Ky. 1998, U.S. Ct. Appeals (6th cir.) 1998, U.S. Ct. Appeals (7th cir.) 1999. Pvt. practice, Louisville, 1992-94; assoc. Morris, Garlove, Waterman & Johnson, Louisville, 1994—99, ptnr., 2000—. Mem. ABA, Ky. Bar Assn., Louisville Bar Assn. Office: Morris Garlove Waterman & Johnson 1000 One Riverfront Plaza Louisville KY 40202 Fax: 502-589-3219. E-mail: JGT@mgwj.com.

TROVER, ELLEN LLOYD, lawyer; b. Richmond, Va., Nov. 23, 1947; d. Robert Van Buren and Hazel (Urban) Lloyd; m. Denis William Trover, June 12, 1971; 1 dau., Florence Emma. AB, Vassar Coll., 1969; JD, Coll. William and Mary, 1972. Asst. editor Bancroft-Whitney, San Francisco, 1973-74; owner Ellen Lloyd Trover Atty.-at-Law, Thousand Oaks, Calif., 1974-82; ptnr. Trover & Fisher, Thousand Oaks, Calif., 1982-89; pvt. practice law Thousand Oaks, Calif., 1989-98; mng. ptnr. The Lloyd-Trover Partnership, Thousand Oaks, Calif., 1998—. Editor: Handbooks of State Chronologies, 1972. Trustee Conejo Future Found., Thousand Oaks, 1978—91, trustee emeritus, 1992—, vice chmn., 1982—84, chmn., 1984—88; pres. Zonta Club Conejo Valley Area, 1978—79; trustee Hydro Help for the Handicapped, 1980—85, Atlantis Found., 1994—; pres. Vista Santa Rosa Assn., 2001—. Mem. State Bar Calif., Va. State Bar, Phi Alpha Delta. Democrat. Presbyterian. Probate (including wills, trusts), Estate taxation. Home: PO Box 297 Coachella CA 92236 Office: 1107E E Thousand Oaks Blvd Thousand Oaks CA 91362-2816 E-mail: etrover@yahoo.com.

TROY, ANTHONY FRANCIS, lawyer; b. Hartford, Conn., Apr. 16, 1941; children: Anthony John, Francis Gerard II. BA in Govt., St. Michael's Coll., Vt., 1963; LLB, U. Richmond, Richmond, Va., 1966. Bar: Va. 1966, D.C. 1972, U.S. Dist. Ct. (ea. dist.) Va. 1966, U.S. Dist. Ct. (we. dist.) Va. 1967, U.S. Ct. Appeals (4th cir.) 1967, U.S. Supreme Ct. 1969. Asst. atty. gen. Commonwealth of Va., Richmond, 1966-72, atty. gen., 1977-78; assoc. Colson & Shapiro, Washington, 1972-74; ptnr. Troutman, Sanders LLP, Richmond, 1978—. Conard Mattox Disting. adj. prof. chair law U. Richmond Law Sch. Contbr. articles to profl. jours. Trustee Sci. Mus. Va. Fellow Am. Law Found., Va. Law Found. Antitrust, Criminal, Legislative. Home: 308 N Lombardy St Richmond VA 23220-3532 Office: Troutman Sanders LLP PO Box 1122 Richmond VA 23218-1122 E-mail: tony.troy@troutmansanders.com.

TROY, ROBERT SWEENEY, SR., lawyer; b. Quincy, Mass., Aug. 13, 1949; s. Robert F. and Winifred (Sweeney) T.; m. Sabina Greene, Oct. 12, 1985; children: Robert Sweeney Jr., Michael Francis, Matthew Thomas. AB, Georgetown U., 1971; JD, Boston Coll., 1974. Bar: Mass. 1974, Fla. 1976, U.S. Dist. Ct. Mass. 1976, U.S. Ct. Appeals 1977, U.S. Ct. Mil. Appeals 1982, U.S. Supreme Ct. 1990. Asst. dist. atty. Cape and Islands, Mass., 1974-76; counsel Town of Bourne, Mass., 1978—. Counsel Town of Duxbury, Mass., 1986—, Barnstable County, 1992—. Mem. Mass. Bar Assn. (bd. dels. 1977-80), Barnstable County Bar Assn., Plymouth County Bar Assn., Town Counsel Assn. Home: PO Box 125 West Barnstable MA 02668-0125 Office: 90 Route 6A Sandwich MA 02563-5301

TROYER, THOMAS ALFRED, lawyer; b. Omaha, Aug. 15, 1933; s. Robert Raymond and Dorothy (Darlow) T.; m. Sally Jean Brown, June 28, 1958; children: Kenneth D., Robert C., Virginia D., Thomas C. BA, Harvard U., 1955; JD, U. Mich., 1958. Bar: Colo. 1958, U.S. Ct. Appeals (D.C. cir.) 1967. Assoc. Holme, Roberts, More & Owen, Denver, 1958-61; USAF, Denver, 1961-62; trial atty. U.S. Dept. Justice, Washington, 1962-64; legal staff Asst. Sec. Treasury for Tax Policy, Washington, 1964-66; assoc. tax legis. counsel U.S. Dept. Treasury, Washington, 1966-67; mem. Caplin & Drysdale, Washington, 1967—. Pres. Stern Fund, N.Y.C., 1985—86; bd. dirs. Children's Def. Fund, Washington, Mineral Policy Ctr., Washington; trustee Natural Resources Def. Coun., N.Y.C., 1977—, Carnegie Corp., N.Y.C., 1983—91, Cmty. Found. Nat. Capital Region, 1992—2000; chairperson Charity Lobbying in Pub. Interest, Washington. Contbr. numerous articles to profl. jours. Bd. dirs. Common Cause, Washington, 1980-83; mem. Treasury Adv. Commn. on Pvt. Philanthropy and Pub. Needs, Washington, 1976-77; mem. adv. group to Commr. Internal Rev., Washington, 1978-80; mem. com. of visitors U. Mich. Law Sch., Ann Arbor, 1982—; mem. IRS Commr.'s Exempt Orgn. Adv. Group, Washington, 1987-90. Fellow Am. Bar Found., Am. Coll. Tax Counsel; mem. ABA (vice chmn. govt. rels. tax sect. 1989-91, commn. on homelessness and poverty 1992-94), Coun. for Excellence in Govt., Am. Law Inst. Democrat. Home: 5514 Cedar Pkwy Chevy Chase MD 20815-3444 Office: Caplin & Drysdale Chartered 1 Thomas Cir NW Ste 1100 Washington DC 20005-5894

TRUCANO, MICHAEL, lawyer; b. Washington, May 28, 1945; s. Peter Joseph and Fern Margaret (Bauer) T.; m. Doreen E. Struck, 1969; children: Michael, David. BA, Carleton Coll., 1967; JD, NYU, 1970. Assoc. Dorsey & Whitney, Mpls., 1970-75, ptnr., 1976—, head of office, 2000—. Corporate, general, Finance, Mergers and acquisitions. Office: Dorsey & Whitney LLP Ste 1500 50 S 6th St Minneapolis MN 55402-1498 E-mail: trucano.mike@dorseylaw.com.

TRUE, ROY JOE, lawyer; b. Shreveport, La., Feb. 20, 1938; s. Collins B. and Lula Mae (Cady) T.; m. Patsy Jean Hudsmith, Aug. 29, 1959; children: Andrea Alane, Alyssa Anne, Ashley Alisbeth. Student, Centenary Coll., 1957; BS, Tex. Christian U., 1961; LLB, So. Meth. U., 1963, postgrad., 1968-69. Bar: Tex. 1963. Pvt. practice, Dallas, 1963—; pres. Invesco Internat. Corp., 1969-70, True & Shackelford and predecessors, 1975—2002; of counsel Shackelford, Melton & McKinley, 2002. Bus. adviser, counselor Mickey Mantle, 1969-95; dir. The Mickey Mantle Found., 1995-98. Mem. editl. bd. Southwestern Law Jour, 1962-63. Served with AUS, 1956. Mem. ABA, Dallas Bar Assn., Tex. Assn. Bank Counsel, Phi Alpha Delta. Banking, Commercial, contracts (including sales of goods; commercial financing), Property, real (including real estate development, water). Home: 5601 Ursula Ln Dallas TX 75229-6429 Office: 10100 N Central Expy 6th Fl Dallas TX 75231

TRUETT, HAROLD JOSEPH, III, (TIM TRUETT), lawyer; b. Alameda, Calif., Feb. 13, 1946; s. Harold Joseph and Lois Lucille (Mellin) T.; 1 child, Harold Joseph IV; m. Anna V. Billante, Oct. 1, 1983 (dec. June 2000); 1 child, James S. Carstensen; m. Patricia Maynord, Mar. 5, 2002. BA, U. San Francisco, 1968, JD, 1975. Bar: Calif. 1975, Hawaii 1987, U.S. Dist. Ct. (ea., so., no., and cen. dists.) Calif. 1976, Hawaii 1987, U.S. Ct. Appeals (9th cir.) 1980, U.S. Supreme Ct. 1988, U.S. Ct. Fed. Claims, 1995. Assoc. Hoberg, Finger et al, San Francisco, 1975-78, Bledsoe, Smith et al, San Francisco, 1979-80, Abramson & Bianco, San Francisco, 1980-83; mem. Ingram & Truett, San Rafael, 1983-90; prin. Winchell & Truett, San Francisco, 1991—2002, Law Office of H.J. Tim Truett, San Francisco, 2003—. Lectr. trial practice Am. Coll. Legal Medicine, 1989-90, Calif. Continuing Edn. of the Bar. Bd. dirs. Shining Star Found. 1991—, pres., 2001—, Marin County, Calif.; mem. Marin Dem. Coun., San Rafael, 1983-90. Lt., aviator USN, 1967-74. Mem. ABA, Hawaii Bar Assn., Calif. Bar Assn. (com. for adminstrn. of justice, conf. of dels.), San Francisco Bar Assn., San Francisco Trial Lawyers Assn., Lawyers Pilots Assn. Roman Catholic. State civil litigation, Personal injury (including property damage), Product liability, Aviation, Professional liability. Home: 48 Valley Rd San Anselmo CA 94960 E-mail: hjtimtruett@attbi.com.

TRUHLAR, ROBERT T. lawyer; b. Chgo., Apr. 11, 1948; BA, St. Mary's Coll., 1970; JD, U. Denver, 1981. Bar: Colo. 1981, U.S. Dist. Ct. Colo. 1981, U.S. Ct. Appeals (10th cir.) 1981, U.S. Supreme Ct. 1981. Ptnr. Truhlar and Truhlar, LLP, Littleton, Colo. Part-time faculty master program in human resource mgmt. Chapman U., 1990—96; adj. prof. U. Denver Coll. Law, 1992—93. Bus. editor: Denver Law Jour., 1979—80; contbr. chapters to books. Mem.: Coll. Labor and Employment Lawyers, Arapahoe County Bar Assn. (bd. dirs. 1991—93, 1994—2001, officer 1996—2000, pres. 1999—2000), Colo. Bar Assn. (pres.-elect 2002—, v.p. 1997—98, bd. govs. 1997—2001, 2002—, mem. legal fee arbitration com. 1982—83, 1984—, labor law com. 1988—, co-chmn. 1989—92). Labor (including EEOC, Fair Labor Standards Act, labor-management relations, NLRB, OSHA). Office: Colo Bar Assn Ste 900 1900 Grant St Denver CO 80203 also: Truhlar and Truhlar LLP 1901 W Littleton Blvd Littleton CO 80120*

TRUITT, ROBERT RALPH, JR., lawyer; b. Lincoln-Chaves Counties, N.Mex., Jan. 21, 1948; s. Robert Ralph and Dorothy (Butler) T.; m. Susan Donovan, Nov. 28, 1981; children: Patrick Lynn, Maureen Elizabeth. BA, BBA, Southwestern U., 1970; JD, U. Tex., 1973. Bar: Tex. 1973, U.S. Ct. Appeals (5th cir.) 1976, U.S. Dist. Ct. (we. dist.) Tex. 1977, U.S. Dist. Ct. (no. dist.) Tex. 1981. Assoc. Turpin, Smith & Dyer, Midland, Tex., 1973-77; pvt. practice Midland, 1977—. Chmn. planning and zoning com., City of Midland, 1979-80; chmn., dir. and treas. Midland Downtown Lions Fire Prevention and Hist. Found., 1980—; dir. and sec.-treas. Midland Downtown Lions Youth Found., 1992-98, Midland Masonic Hist. Mus. and Libr. Found., 1996—; dir. Presdl. Mus., 1998-99; sec. El Paso Scottish Rite Libr. and Historical Mus. Found., 1999—. Mem. Tex. Bar Assn., Midland County Bar Assn. Banking, Bankruptcy, State civil litigation. Office: 901 W Texas Ave Midland TX 79701-6167

TRUJILLO, LORENZO A. lawyer, educator; b. Denver, Aug. 10, 1951; s. Filbert G. and Marie O. Trujillo; m. Ellen Alires; children: Javier Antonio, Lorenzo Feliciano, Kristina Alires. BA, U. Colo., 1972, MA, 1974, postgrad.; EdD, U. San Francisco, 1979; JD, U. Colo., 1993. Bar: Colo. 1994, U.S. Dist. Ct. Colo. 1994, U.S. Ct. Appeals (10th cir.) 1994, U.S. Supreme Ct. 1999; cert. edn. tchr., prin., supt., Colo. Exec. assoc. Inter-Am. Rsch. Assocs., Rosslyn, Va., 1980-82; exec. dir. humanities Jefferson County Pub. Schs., Golden, Colo., 1982-89; pvt. practice edn. cons. Lakewood, Colo., 1989-93; gen. corp. counsel Am. Achievement Schs., Inc., Lakewood, Colo., 1994-96; atty. Frie, Arndt & Trujillo Law Firm, Arvada, Colo., 1994-96, ptnr., 1995-97; dist. hearing officer, dir. of instrn. Adams County Sch. Dist. 14, 1996—97, dir. human resources, 1998-99, dist. attendance officer/legal counsel, prin. H.S., 1999—. Co-chair Mellon fellowships The Coll. Bd., N.Y.C., 1987-93; cons. U.S.I.A. Fulbright Tchr. Exch. Program, Washington, 1987-93; editl. advisor Harcourt, Brace, Jovanovich Pub., Orlando, Fla., 1988-93; mem. Colo. Supreme Ct. Multicultural Commn., 1996-98, 99—; mem. Colo. Supreme Ct. Families in the Cts. Commn., 2001-02; mem. 17th Jud. Dist. Nominating Com., 2002—; adj. prof. law U. Denver Sch. Law, 2002. Contbr. numerous articles to profl. jours. Mem. panel of arbitrators Am. Arbitration Assn., 1994-present; panelist, evaluator Nat. Endowment for the Arts, 1976—. Recipient Legal Aid Clinic Acad. award Colo. Bar Assn., 1993, Pro Bono award, 1993, Loyola U. Acad. award, 1993, Gov.'s award for excellence in the arts State of Colo., 1996, others. Mem. Am. Assn. Tchrs. of Spanish and Portuguese (pres. Colo. chpt. 1985-88), Colo. Hispanic Bar Assn. (bd. dirs. 2001-, pres.-elect 2003), Am. Immigration Lawyers Assn., Nat. Sch. Bds. Coun. Sch. Attys., Nat. Assn. Judiciary Interpreters and Translators, Colo. Bar Assn. (probate and trust sect., grievance policy com. 1995-97, ethics com. 1995-96), U. San Francisco Alumni Assn. (founder, pres. 1987-90), Phi Delta Kappa (chair internat. edn. com. 1988-89), Phi Alpha Delta. Avocation: violinist. Education and schools, Estate planning, General practice. Office: Adams County Sch Dist 14 6500 E 72d Ave Commerce City CO 80022-2380

TRUNZO, THOMAS HAROLD, JR., lawyer; b. McKeesport, Pa., Oct. 23, 1948; children: Melissa, Kirsten. BA, Tufts U., 1976; JD, Vt. Law Sch., 1980. Bar: N.H. 1980, Mass. 1981, Vt. 1988. Ptnr. Mullaly & Trunzo Law Offices, West Lebanon, N.H., 1980-87; pvt. practice Lebanon, N.H., 1987—. Active Sch. Bd. Orford (N.H.) Sch. Dist., 1980—87; mem. Orford Planning Bd., 1991—93; moderator Rivendale Sch. Dist., Orford, 1998—2002. Mem. Assn. Trial Lawyers Am., Nat. Lawyers Guild, N.H. Bar Assn. (Pro bono award 1987, 2003), Vt. Bar Assn., Grafton County Bar Assn. Democrat. Family and matrimonial, General practice, Property, real (including real estate development, water). Home: RR 1 Box 42 Orford NH 03777-9707 Office: Citizens Bank Bldg PO Box 825 20 W Park St Ste 415 Lebanon NH 03766-0825 E-mail: ttrunzo@innevi.com.

TRUSKOWSKI, JOHN BUDD, lawyer; b. Chgo., Dec. 3, 1945; s. Casimer T. and Jewell S. (Kirk) T.; m. Karen Lee Sloss, Mar. 21, 1970; children: Philip K., Jennifer B. BS, U. Ill., 1967; JD, U. Chgo., 1970. Bar: Ill. 1970, U.S. Dist. Ct. (no. dist.) Ill. 1970, U.S. Tax Ct. 1977. Assoc. Keck, Mahin & Cate, Chgo., 1970-71, 74-78, ptnr., 1978-97, Lord, Bissell & Brook, Chgo., 1997—. Author, editor Callaghan's Federal Tax Guide, 1987. Lt., USNR, 1971-74. Mem. ABA, Ill. State Bar Assn., Chgo. Bar Assn. Republican. Unitarian. Avocations: model railroading, stamp collecting. Corporate taxation, Taxation, general, Personal income taxation. Home: 251 Kimberly Ln Lake Forest IL 60045-3862 Office: Lord Bissell & Brook Harris Bank Bldg 115 S Lasalle St Chicago IL 60603-3801

TRYBAN, ESTHER ELIZABETH, lawyer; b. Chgo., Aug. 14, 1958; d. Chester Joseph and Lottie Elizabeth (Napora) T. AAS with honors, Elgin (Ill.) C.C., 1977, AS with honors, 1982; BS with honors, Roosevelt U., Chgo., 1986; JD, U. Chgo., 1989. Bar: Ill. 1989, U.S. Dist. Ct. (no. dist.) Ill. 1989, U.S. Ct. Appeals (7th cir.) 1990, U.S. Supreme Ct., 1996. Supr. adminstrv. svcs. law dept. Motorola, Inc., Schaumburg, Ill., 1977-86; staff law clk. U.S. Bankruptcy Ct., No. Dist. Ill., Chgo., 1989-90; asst. corp. counsel City of Chgo., 1990—. Mem. ABA, Nat. Lawyers Guild, Assn. Former Bankruptcy Law Clks, Ill. State Bar Assn., Chgo. Bar Assn. (chair govt. svc. com. 1996-97). Roman Catholic. Avocations: reading, football, traveling. Office: City Chgo Dept Law 30 N Lasalle St Ste 900 Chicago IL 60602-2503 E-mail: lw00026@ch.chi.il.us.

TRYGSTAD, LAWRENCE BENSON, lawyer; b. Holton, Mich., Mar. 22, 1937; BA, U. Mich., 1959; JD, U. So. Calif., 1967. Bar: Calif. 1968, U.S. Supreme Ct. 1974. Legal counsel Calif. Tchrs. Assn., United Tchrs. L.A., L.A., 1968-71; ptnr. Trygstad & Odell, L.A., 1971-80; pres. Trygstad Law Corp., L.A., 1980—. Instr., tchr. negotiation U. Calif.-Northridge; panelist TV shows Law and the Teacher. Bd. dirs. George Washington Carver Found., L.A. Mem. ABA, Calif. Bar Assn., L.A. County Bar Assn., Calif. Trial Lawyers Assn., L.A. Trial Lawyers Assn., Nat. Orgn. Lawyers for Edn. Assns., Am. Trial Lawyers Assn., Phi Alpha Delta. Civil rights, General civil litigation, Constitutional. Home: 4209 Aleman Dr Tarzana CA 91356-5405 Office: 1880 Century Park E Ste 404 Los Angeles CA 90067-1609

TSAI, RUEY-SEN, lawyer, law educator; b. Taipei, Taiwan, Jan. 17, 1965; s. Chen-Jen Tsai and Chiu-Chu Tsai-Li; m. Ya-Wen Yang, Mar. 11, 1997. LLB, Nat. Taiwan U., Taipei, 1987; LLM, Cornell U., 1991. Bar: (Taiwan) 1992. Counselor, sr. atty. Lee and Li, Attorneys-at-Law, Taipei, 1993—. Asst. prof. Nat. Chiao Tung U., Hsinchu, Taiwan, 2002—. Author, editor: Lee and Li Bull., 2000—; contbr. articles to profl. jours. 2nd lt. Republic of China Marine Corps, 1987—89. Mem.: Arbitration Assn. Republic of China, Taipei Bar Assn., Asia Patent Attys. Assn. Avocations: golf, swimming, hiking. Intellectual property. Office: Lee and Li Attorneys-at-Law 7F No 201 Tun-Hua N Rd Taipei 105 Taiwan E-mail: rueysentsai@leeandli.com.

TSATALIS, MARINA C. lawyer; b. Phila., Pa., Mar. 25, 1967; d. Peter and Anne Tsatalis. BA, Villanova U., 1989; JD, Harvard U., 1992. Bar: Pa. 1992, N.J. 1992, Calif. 1995. Mem.: ABA, Hellenic Lawyers Assn., San Francisco Bar Assn., Phi Beta Kappa. Labor (including EEOC, Fair Labor Standards Act, labor-management relations, NLRB, OSHA). Office: Wilson Sonsini Goodrich and Rosati 650 Page Mill Rd Palo Alto CA 94304

TSCHINKEL, ANDREW JOSEPH, JR., law librarian; b. Catskill, N.Y., Aug. 8, 1952; s. Andrew Joseph and Marie Frances (O'Connor) T.; m. Frances K. Quigley, Nov. 4, 1989. BA summa cum laude, St. John's Coll., Jamaica, N.Y., 1975, MLS, 1977; MBA, Fordham U., 1983. Grad. asst. div. libr. sci. St. John's U., Jamaica, 1975-77, asst. law libr., 1977-79, adj. law librarian, 1983-87; head librarian Christ the King High Sch., Middle Village, N.Y., 1979-80; sr. law librarian Bklyn. Supreme Ct., 1980-81; prin. law librarian N.Y. Supreme Ct., Jamaica, 1981—. Recipient Pub. Svc. award Queens Borough Pres. and N.Y. Tel. Co., 1986; named Alumnus of Yr. Grad. Sch. Arts & Scis. Divsn. Libr. & Info. Sci. St. John's U., 1993. Mem. Am. Assn. Law Librs., Law Libr. Assn. Greater N.Y. (bd. dirs. 2003—), Elks, Beta Phi Mu. Republican. Office: NY Supreme Ct Libr 88-11 Sutphin Blvd Jamaica NY 11435-3716

TSE, CHARLES YUNG CHANG, drug company executive; b. Shanghai, Mar. 22, 1926; s. Kung Chao and Say Ying (Chen) T.; m. Vivian Chang, Apr. 25, 1955; 1 dau., Roberta. BA in Econs, St. John's U., Shanghai, 1949; MS in Acctg, U. Ill., 1950; JD, N.Y. Law Sch., 1990. Asst. to controller Am. Internat. Group, N.Y.C., 1950-54, asst. mgr. Singapore-Malaysia, 1955-57; with Warner-Lambert Co., Morris Plains, N.J., 1957-86, area mgr. S.E. Asia, 1966-68, regional dir. S.E. Asia, 1968-69, v.p. Australasia, 1970-71, pres. Western Hemisphere Group, 1971-72, pres. Pan Am. Mgmt. Center, 1972-76, pres. European Mgmt. Center, 1976-78, pres. Internat. Group, 1979-86, sr. v.p. corp., 1980-83, exec. v.p. corp., 1984-85, vice chmn., 1985-86. Dir. Foster Wheeler Corp., Livingston, N.J., 1984-98, Superior Telecom., Inc., 1996—, Com. of 100; mem. faculty bus. adminstrn. dept. Fairleigh Dickinson U., 1961-64; pres. Cancer Rsch. Inst., Inc., N.Y.C., 1991-92. Bd. visitors CCNY, 1974-78; trustee Morristown Meml. Hosp.

(N.J.), 1982-86; bd. dirs. Bus. Council for Internat. Understanding, 1984-87. Mem. NAM (dir. 1984-86), Assn. of the Bar of the City of N.Y. (mem. Asian affairs com. 1991—). Office: 300 Park Ave Fl 17 New York NY 10022-7402

TU, HOANG HUY, lawyer; b. Saigon, Vietnam, May 22, 1963; arrived in U.S., 1975; s. Thanh Van Tu and Ky Tu Nguyen; m. Hang Thuy Chau Tran, Sept. 7, 1995; children: Huy Hoang, Dai Long. AA, El Camino Coll., 1984; BS, UCLA, 1992; JD, Western States Sch. Law, 1999. Bar: Calif., U.S. Dist. Ct. (ctrl. dist.) Calif., U.S. Dist. Ct. (so. dist.) Calif. Pres., CEO IBF Enterprise, L.A., 1990—96; pres. Escrow Divsn. Group, 1992—96; ptnr. Hoang Huy Tu Attys., Fountain Valley, 1999—. Mem.: Vietnamese Am. Bar Assn. (bd. dirs. 1999—), Consumer Atty. Calif., Orange County Bar Assn., Am. Immigration Lawyers Assn. Avocations: tennis, golf, Kung Fu, movies. Immigration, naturalization, and customs, Property, real (including real estate development, water), Family and matrimonial. Home: 56 Lakeside Dr Buena Park CA 90621 Office: 11770 E Warner Ave Fountain Valley CA 92708

TUBB, JAMES CLARENCE, lawyer; b. Corsicana, Tex. s. Cullen Louis and Sarah Elmore (Chapman) T.; m. Suzanne Alice Smith, Nov. 25, 1954; children: James Richard, Sara Elizabeth, Daniel Chapman. BA, So. Meth. U., 1951, JD, 1954. Bar: Tex. 1954, U.S. Dist. Ct. (no. dist.) Tex. 1955, U.S. Ct. Appeals (5th cir.) 1959, U.S. Supreme Ct. 1978; cert. comml. real estate specialist, 1983; lic. Tex. real estate broker; cert. mediator Dallas Bar Assn. With legal dept. Schlumberger Well Surveying Corp., Houston, 1954-55; claims atty. Franklin Am. Ins. Co., Dallas, 1957-58; ptnr. Vial, Hamilton, Koch, Tubb & Knox and predecessor firm Akin, Vial, Hamilton, Koch & Tubb, Dallas, 1958-84; dir., ptnr. Winstead, McGuire, Sechrest & Minick, Dallas, 1984-90; pvt. practice Dallas, 1990—. Guest lectr. on real estate broker liability Real Estate Ctr., Tex. A&M U., 1987. Mem. bd. deacons Highland Park Presbyn. Ch., Dallas, 1972—78, ruling elder, 1978—84, 1988—91; mem. permanent jud. commn. Grace Presbytery, 1984—90; bd. dirs. Christian Concern Found., 1965—71, Dallas County affiliate Am. Diabetes Assn., 1991—95. With Tex. Air N.G., 1949—51, 1st lt. JAGC, SAC USAF, 1955—57, 1st lt. USAF, ret. Recipient Outstanding Student award Student Bar Assn., 1954. Fellow Tex. Bar Found.; mem. ABA (chmn. comml. law com. gen. practice sect. 1982-84, real estate probate and trust law sect.), Tex. Bus. Law Found., Tex. Bar Assn., Am. Arbitration Assn. (sec. comml. arbitration panelist), Dallas Country Club, Dallas County Rep. Men's Club (sec. 1978-79). Estate planning, Probate (including wills, trusts), Property, real (including real estate development, water). Home and Office: 3407 Haynie Ave Dallas TX 75205-1842

TUBMAN, WILLIAM CHARLES, lawyer; b. N.Y.C., Mar. 16, 1932; s. William Thomas and Ellen Veronica (Griffin) T.; m. Dorothy Rita Krug, Aug. 15, 1964; children: William Charles Jr., Thomas Davison, Matthew Griffin. BS, Fordham U., 1953, JD, 1960; postdoctoral, NYU Sch. Law, 1960-61. Bar: N.Y. 1960, U.S. Ct. Appeals (2d cir.) 1966, U.S. Supreme Ct. 1967, U.S. Ct. Customs and Patent Appeals 1971. Auditor Peat, Marwick Mitchell & Co., N.Y.C., 1956-60; sr. counsel Kennecott Corp., N.Y.C., 1960-82, Phelps Dodge Corp., N.Y.C., 1982-85, sec., 1985-95, v.p., 1987-95; pres. Phelps Dodge Found., Phoenix, 1988-95. Author: Legal Status of Minerals Beyond the Continental Shelf, 1966. Mem. scholarship adv. coun. U. Ariz., 1990-92; active Big Bros., Inc., N.Y.C., 1963-73; trustee Phoenix Art Mus., 1989-94; bd. dirs. St. Joseph Hosp. Found., 1994—, chmn., 1994-95; bd. dirs. The Phoenix Symphony, 1994-95. Recipient Disting. Svc. cert. Big Brothers Inc., 1968. Mem.: ABA, N.Y. State Bar Assn. Democrat. Roman Catholic. Antitrust, Corporate, general, Securities. Home: 8008 N 66th St Paradise Valley AZ 85253-2612

TUCHMANN, ROBERT, lawyer; b. N.Y.C., July 7, 1946; s. Frederick C. and Hildegard (Jung) T.; m. Naomi R. Walfish, June 1, 1969; children; David, Paul. AB, Oberlin Coll., 1967; JD, Harvard U., 1971. Bar: Mass. 1971, U.S. Dist. Ct. Mass. 1971. Assoc. Hale and Dorr, Boston, 1971-76, jr. ptnr., 1976-80, sr. ptnr., 1980—. Lectr. Mass. Continuing Legal Edn., 1976—. Pres. Project Bread-The Walk for Hunger, Boston, 1990—98; mem. com. Oberlin Coll., 1990; chair Ctrl. Artery Environ. Oversight Com., 1992—; mem. New Fed. Courthouse Task Force, 1993—99; bd. overseers Rogerson Cmtys., 1995—; co-chair Mayor's Ctrl. Artery Completion Task Force, 2001—. Mem.: Island Alliance (trustee 1997—2000), Downtown Boston Transp. Mgmt. Assn. (chmn. 1996—), Mass. Conveyancers Assn. (com. chmn. 1984—89), Boston Bar Assn. (com. chmn. 1977—81), Abstract Club. Environmental, Property, real (including real estate development, water). Office: Hale and Dorr LLP 60 State St Boston MA 02109-1816 E-mail: robert.tuchmann@haledorr.com.

TUCK, AMY, lieutenant governor; b. Starkville, Miss., July 8, 1963; d. Grady William and Mary (Boykin) Tuck. BA in Polit. Sci., Miss. State U., Starkville, 1985; postgrad., Miss. State U., Miss. State U., Starkville, 1992—; JD, Miss. Coll., 1989. Legal asst. Ben. F. Hilburn Jr., Atty. at Law, Starkville, Miss., 1984-85; grad. asst. dept. polit. sci. Miss. State U., Starkville, 1986-87; law clk. Minor Buchanan, Jackson, Miss., 1987-88, Deposit Guaranty Nat. Bank, Jackson, 1988-89; state senator dist. 15 State of Miss., Jackson, 1990-99, lt. gov., 2000—. Adj. prof. Wood Jr. Coll., Mathiston, Miss., 1990—. Mem. Oktibbeha County Voter Re-Registration Com., Oktibbeha County Fedn. Dem. Women; bd. dirs. Oktibbeha County Am. Cancer Soc., 1991-92; mem. local rels. com. Children and Family Svcs.; assoc. mem. Nat. Mus. Women in the Arts, 1992-93. Mem. NAFE, Am. Legis. Exch. Com., Am. Soc. Pub. Adminstrs., Nat. Conf. State Legislature, Nat. Order Women Legislators, Miss. State U. Alumni Assn., Starkville Area Bus. and Profl. Women's Club, Oktibbeha County C. of C., Gamma Beta Phi, Pi Sigma Alpha, Omicron Delta Kappa, Phi Delta Phi (vice-magister 1988, historian 1988-89). Democrat. Methodist. Home: 3262 Highway 82 W Maben MS 39750-8674 Office: Miss Lt Governor PO Box 1018 Jackson MS 39215-1018*

TUCKER, BOWEN HAYWARD, lawyer; b. Providence, Apr. 13, 1938; s. Stuart Hayward and Ardelle Chase (Drabble) T.; m. Jan Louise Brown, Aug. 26, 1961; children: Stefan Kendric Slade, Catherine Kendra Gordon. AB in Math., Brown U., 1959; JD, U. Mich., 1962. Bar: R.I. 1963, Ill. 1967, U.S. Supreme Ct. 1970. Assoc. Hinckley & Allen, Providence, 1962-66; sr. atty. Caterpillar, Inc., Peoria, Ill., 1966-72; counsel FMC Corp., Chgo., 1972-82, sr. litigation counsel, 1982-95, assoc. gen. counsel, 1995-2000; v.p. eLaw Forum, Chgo., 2000—01; litig. mgmt. cons., 2000—. Chmn. legal process task force Chgo. Residential Sch. Study Com., 1973-74, mem. Commn. on Children, 1983-85, Ill. Com. on Rights of Minors, 1974-77, Com. on Youth and the Law, 1977-79; mem. White House Conf. on Children, ednl. svcs. subcom., 1979-80; chairperson Youth Employment Task Force, 1982-83; mem. citizens com. on Juvenile Ct. (Cook County), 1978-94, chmn. detention subcom., 1982-92; mem. econ. effects adv. com. Rand Inst. Civil Justice, 1990-92; bd. dirs. Voices Ill. Children, 1998—. 1st lt. U.S. Army, 1962-69. Mem. ABA, Am. Law Inst., Ill. State Bar Assn., R.I. Bar Assn., Chgo. (chmn. com. on juvenile law, 1976-77), Chgo. Lincoln Inn of Ct. (sec., treas. 1996-98), Constrn. Industry Mfrs. Assn. (exec. com. of Lawyers' Coun. 1972, 75-79, vice chmn. 1977, chmn. 1978-79), Mfrs. Alliance (products liability coun. 1974-95, vice chmn. 1981-83, chmn. 1983-85), Product Liability Adv. Coun. (bd. dirs. 1986-2000, exec. com. 1990-97, vice chmn. 1991-93, chmn. 1993-95), ACLU (bd. dirs. Ill. divsn. 1970-79, exec. com. 1973-79, sec. 1975-77), Am. Arbitration Assn. (mem. panel of arbitrators 1985-96), Phi Alpha Delta, Brown Univ. of Chgo. Club (nat. alumni schs. program 1973-85, v.p. 1980-81, pres. 1981-86), Lawyers Club of Chgo. General civil litigation, Juvenile, Product liability. Home: 107 W Noyes St Arlington Heights IL 60005-3747 E-mail: bhtu@att.net.

TUCKER, DAMIAN LADELL, lawyer; b. Rocky Mount, N.C., Feb. 7, 1973; s. Vernon Edward Tucker, Sr. and Ruby Lee Tucker. BA in Criminal Justice, U. N.C., Wilmington, 1995; JD, N.C. Ctrl. U., 1998. Bar: N.C. 1998, Ga. 2000. Asst. dist. atty. Edgecomb County Dist. Atty.'s Office, Tarboro, NC, 1998—2001; assoc. Hester & Moore, PLLC, Rocky Mount, 2001—. Mem.: N.C. Bar Assn., N.C. Acad. Trial Lawyers, Kappa Alpha Psi. Democrat. Baptist. Avocations: sports, travel. Criminal. Home: 104 St Annes Rd Nashville NC 27856 Office: Hester & Moore PLLC 3230 Zebulon Rd Rocky Mount NC 27804 Office Fax: 252-451-7774 . E-mail: dtucker@hesterlaw.com.

TUCKER, EDWIN WALLACE, law educator; b. N.Y.C., Feb. 25, 1927; s. Benjamin and May Tucker; m. Gladys Lipschutz, Sept. 14, 1952; children: Sherwin M., Pamela A. BA, NYU, 1948; LLB, Harvard U., 1951; LLM, N.Y. Law Sch., 1963, JSD, 1964; MA, Trinity Coll., Hartford, Conn., 1967. Bar: N.Y. 1955, U.S. Dist. Ct. (ea. and so. dists.) N.Y. 1958, U.S. Ct. Appeals (2d cir.) 1958, U.S. Supreme Ct. 1960. Pvt. practice, N.Y.C., 1955-63; Disting. Alumni prof. and prof. bus. law U. Conn., Storrs, 1963—, mem. bd. editors occasional paper and monograph series, 1966-70. Author: Adjudication of Social Issues, 1971, 2d edit., 1977, Legal Regulation of the Environment, 1972, Administrative Agencies, Regulation of Enterprise, and Individual Liberties, 1975, CPA Law Review, 1985; co-author: The Legal and Ethical Environment of Business, 1992; book rev. editor Am. Bus. Law Jour., 1964-65, adv. editor, 1974—; co-editor Am. Bus. Jour., 1965-73; mem. editl. bd. Am. Jour. Small Bus., 1979-86; adv. editor Jour. Legal Studies Edn., 1983-85, editor-in-chief, 1985-87, adv. editor, 1987—; mem. bd. editors North Atlantic Regional Bus. Law Rev., 1984—. With USAF, 1951-55. Recipient medal of excellence Am. Bus. Law Assn., 1979. Mem. Acad. Legal Studies in Bus., North Atlantic Regional Bus. Law Assn. Home: 11 Eastwood Rd Storrs Mansfield CT 06268-2401

TUCKER, MARCUS OTHELLO, judge; b. Santa Monica, Calif., Nov. 12, 1934; s. Marcus Othello Sr. and Essie Louvonia (McLendon) T.; m. Indira Hale, May 29, 1965; 1 child, Angelique. BA, U. So. Calif., 1956; JD, Howard U., 1960; MA in Criminal Justice, Chapman U., 1997; BS in Liberal Arts, Regents Coll., SUNY, 1999. Bar: Calif. 1962, U.S. Dist. Ct. (cen. dist.) Calif. 1962, U.S. Ct. Appeals (9th cir.) 1965, U.S. Ct. Internat. Trade 1970, U.S. Supreme Ct. 1971. Pvt. practice, Santa Monica, 1962-63, 67-74; dep. atty. City of Santa Monica, 1963-65; asst. atty. U.S. Dist. Ct. (Cen. Dist.) Calif., 1965-67; commr. L.A. Superior Ct., 1974-76; judge mcpl. ct. Long Beach (Calif.) Jud. Dist., 1976-85; judge superior ct. L.A. Jud. Dist., 1985—; supervising judge L.A. County Dependency Ct. L.A. Superior Ct., 1991-92, presiding judge Juvenile divsn., 1993-94. Asst. prof. law Pacific U., Long Beach, 1984, 86; justice pro tem Calif. State Ct. Appeals (2nd cir.), 1981; mem. exec. com. Superior Ct. of L.A. County, 1995-96. Mem. editl. staff Howard U. Law Sch. Jour., 1959-60. Pres. Community Rehab. Industries Found., Long Beach, 1983-86, Legal Aid Found., L.A., 1976-77; bd. dirs. Long Beach coun. Boy Scouts Am., 1978-92. With U.S. Army, 1960-66. Named Judge of Yr. Juvenile Cts. Bar Assn., 1986, Disting. Jurist Long Beach Trial Trauma Coun., 1987, Honoree in Law Handy Cmty. Ctr., L.A., 1987, Bernard S. Jefferson Jurist of Yr. John M. Langston Bar Assn. Black Lawyers, 1990, Judge of Yr. Long Beach Bar Assn., 1993, Judge of Yr., First Ann. Adoption Cong., 1997, Jurist of Yr., Juvenile Cts. Bar Assn., 1997, Daniel O'Connell award Irish-Am. Bar Assn., 1999, named to Nat. Bar Assn. Hall of Fame, 2002; recipient award for Law-Related Edn. Constl. Rights Found./L.A. County Bar Assn., 1992, commendation L.A. County Bd. Suprs., 1994. Fellow Internat. Acad. Trial Judges; mem. ABA, Calif. Judges Assn. (chmn. juvenile law com. 1986-87, Svc. award 2001), Langston Bar Assn. (pres. bd. dirs. 1972-73, named to hall of fame 2001), Calif. Assn. Black Lawyers, Santa Monica Bay Dist. Bar Assn. (treas. 1969-71), Am. Inns of Ct., Selden Soc. Avocations: comparative law, traveling. Office: 415 W Ocean Blvd Dept 245 Long Beach CA 90802-4512

TUCKER, WILLIAM P. lawyer, writer; b. Kingston, N.Y., Jan. 26, 1932; s. Philip and Mary (McGowan) T.; m. Dolores F. Beaudoin, June 10, 1961; children: Andrew M., Thomas B., Mary A. BA with honors, Hunter Coll., 1958; JD, St. John's U., 1962. Bar: N.Y. 1962, U.S. Dist. Ct. (ea. dist.) N.Y. 1963, Fla. 1980. Assoc. Mendes & Mount, N.Y.C., 1962-63; ptnr. Cullen and Dykman, Bklyn. and Garden City, N.Y., Washington and Newark, 1963-98, Golden, Wexler & Sarnese, Garden City/Purchase/S.I., 1998-2001; pvt. practice, 2001—. Former gen. counsel Broadway Nat. Bank, Wartburg Luth. Svcs., Luth. Ctr. for the Aging, Martin Luther Ter. Apts., Inc., Interfaith Med. Ctr., Roosevelt Savs. Bank, Olympian Bank, Green-Point Bank, Ridgewood Savs. Bank, Atlantic Liberty Savs., F.A., Bethpage Fed. Credit Union, Mcpl. Credit Union, Lincoln Savs. Bank, Bklyn. Savs. Bank, Met. Savs. Bank, Crossland Savs. Bank, Bushwick Savs. Bank, Anchor Savs. Bank; former spl. counsel OCI Mortgage Corp., Bklyn C. of C., Downtown Bklyn. Bus. Assn., Bank of N.Y., Chase Manhattan Bank, Fleet Bank, Kraft Credit Union, Apple Bank for Savs., Barclays Bank of N.Y.; chmn. bd. dirs. Broadway Nat. Bank. Author: DP-or Billy and Jerry in the Promised Land, 1996, Moving Home Plate, 1999, (novels) Excalibur, 2001, With Justice for All, 2003; contbr. articles to profl. jours. Past mem. Selective Svc. Bd.; past pres. St. Vincent Ferrer Home Sch. Assn.; del. Diocesan Union Holy Name Socs.; mem. coun. St. John's U.; mem. coun. of regents St. Francis Coll., Bklyn.; bd. dirs. Faith Home Found., St. Josephs Coll. Mem. Am. Coll. Real Estate Lawyers, N.Y. State Bar Assn., Fla. Bar Assn., Savs. Banks Lawyers Assn. Bklyn., N.Y. Land Title Assn., Suffolk County Bar Assn., Savs. Bank Assn. N.Y. State (law com.), Bklyn. Mcpl. Club (pres.), Knight of Malta. Avocations: co-owner Salem Keizer Volcanoes N.W. League baseball team, Norwich Navigators Ea. League baseball team; v.p. N.W. Profl. Baseball League; bd. dirs. Bklyn. Sportsplex Inc. Banking, General practice, Property, real (including real estate development, water). Home: 23 Bunker Hill Dr Huntington NY 11743-5705 Office: 145 East Main St Huntington NY 11743 E-mail: wptucker@optonline.net.

TUCKMAN, JOEL F. lawyer, researcher; b. Bristol, Pa., Aug. 28, 1970; s. Salus and Jean Linda Tuckman. BA, Temple U., 1992, JD, 1995. Bar: Pa. 1995, NJ 1995. Rsch. coord. Beasley Firm, Phila., 1999—. Mem.: Phila. Bar Assn., Phi Beta Kappa.

TUCK-RICHMOND, DOLETTA SUE, prosecutor; b. Hugo, Okla., June 18, 1966; d. Benny Doyle and Tommie Marie (Cousins) T.; m. Lyle Richmond, Sept. 30, 1995; children: Rachelle Jay Marie, Benjamin Lee. AS, Murray State Coll., Tishomingo, Okla., 1986; BS magna cum laude, S.E. Okla. State U., 1988; JD with highest honors, U. Okla., 1991. Bar: Okla. 1991, U.S. Dist. Ct. (we., ea., and no. dists.), U.S. Ct. Appeals (10th cir.). Summer assoc. Andrews Davis, Oklahoma City, 1989-90; instr. in legal rsch, writing and oral advocacy U. Okla., Norman, 1989-91; assoc. Crowe & Dunlevy, Oklahoma City, 1991-93, Tulsa, Okla., 1993-94; pvt. practice Antlers, Okla., 1994; exempt orgn. specialist IRS, Oklahoma City, Okla., 1994-95; asst. atty. gen. State of Okla., Oklahoma City, 1995—; asst. U.S. atty. U.S. Atty's. Office (we. dist.) Okla., Oklahoma City, 1999—. Author: Joint Defense Agreements Can It Help Your Client, 1998, King For a Day: An Overview of Federal and State Qui Jam Provisions, 1999, The Fifth Amendment Privilege Against Self-Incrimination: Walking the Tight-rope Between Civil and Criminal Law; contbg. author, editor: Oklahoma Environmental Law Practitioner's Handbook, 1992. Firm com. mem., participant Harvest Food Dr., Oklahoma City, 1991; chairperson Okla. Young Lawyers Rape Victims Assistance Com., 1992-94; bd. dirs. Okla. County Young Lawyers Divsn., 1993; participant, vol. Legal Aide of Western Okla., 1991. Named Miss Murray State Coll., Student Senate Pres., Tishomingo, Okla., 1986-86, Order of Coif U. Okla., Norman, Okla., 1991, Okla. Law Review U. Okla., Norman, 1991. Mem. FBA, Okla. Bar Assn. (bd. dirs., young lawyers divsn. 1993-95, mock trial com. 1994-95, liaison mental health com. 1994-95), Am. Agrl. Law Assn., Phi Delta Phi, Phi Kappa Phi (Spl. Act award for U.S. Atty. 1996, 97, 98). Democrat. Baptist. Avocations: tennis, reading, writing, knitting, sports events. Home: 1624 SW 128th Pl Oklahoma City OK 73170-5018 Office: US Atty's Office Western Dist of Okla 210 Park Ave Ste 400 Oklahoma City OK 73102-5628

TUDOR, JOHN MARTIN, lawyer, educator; b. Kenton, Ohio, 1937; s. Arthur Davis and Marjorie Maxie (Martin) T.; m. Anda Maija Vilums, Aug. 26, 1961; children: Mara Y. Tudor Ward, Andrew Roland. BA, Ohio State U., 1959; JD, Duke U., 1962. Bar: Ohio 1962, U.S. Dist. Ct. (no. dist.) Ohio 1963, U.S. Supreme Ct. 1973, U.S. Ct. Appeals (6th cir.) 1987, U.S. Dist. Ct. (ctrl. dist.) Ill. 1995. Assoc. Squire, Sanders & Dempsey, Cleve., 1962-65; ptnr. Mahon, Tudor & Van Dyne, Kenton, 1965-88, Tudor, Blue & Cloud, Columbus, Ohio, 1969-88, Tudor, Cloud & Cesner, Kenton, 1988-90; mng. mem. Tudor Law, LLC, Kenton, 1990—. Gen. counsel Am. BanCorp., Columbus, 1974-80; pres., dir. Village BancShares, Inc., Kenton, 1980-90, mng. mem. Latvian-Am. Trading Co., Ltd., 1997-2002. Author: We The People, 1987; contbr. articles to profl. jours. Founder Hardin County Hist. Soc., Kenton, 1966. Mem. ATLA, Am. Inns of Ct., Hardin County Bar Assn. (pres.), Eagle Scouts Assn. Republican. Presbyterian. Avocations: snow skiing, sail boating. General civil litigation, Corporate, general, Probate (including wills, trusts). Home: 411 Cecelia St Kenton OH 43326-1451 Office: 22 N Main St Kenton OH 43326-1552 Fax: 419-675-2145. E-mail: tudorlaw@kenton.com.

TUFTE, BRIAN NELSON, lawyer; b. Mpls., Dec. 9, 1961; s. Obert N. and Doris H. T.; m. Julie S. Tufte, July 22, 1993; children: Jessica, Brianna. BA in Physics/Math., St. Olaf Coll., 1984; JD magna cum laude, William Mitchell Coll. Law, 1994. Bar: Minn. 1994, U.S. Dist. Ct. Minn. 1994, U.S. Ct. Appeals (8th and fed. cirs.) 1994, U.S. Patent and Trademark Office. Sr. integrated cir. design engr. Honeywell Inc., Solid State Elecs. Ctr., Plymouth, Minn., 1985-93; assoc. atty. Nawrocki, Rooney & Siverston, P.A., Mpls., 1993-98; founding ptnr. Crompton, Seager & Tufte, LLC, Mpls., 1998—. Named a Super Lawyer, Minn. Law and Politics, Twin Cities Bus. Monthly and Mpls. St. Paul mags. Mem. Am. Intellectual Property Law Assn., Minn. Intellectual Property Law Assn., Minn. Bar Assn., Hennepin County Bar Assn. Intellectual property, Patent, Trademark and copyright. Office: Crompton Seager & Tufte LLC 331 2nd Ave S Ste 895 Minneapolis MN 55401-2260 E-mail: tufte@cstlaw.com.

TUKE, ROBERT DUDLEY, lawyer, educator; b. Rochester, N.Y., Dec. 5, 1947; s. Theodore Robert and Doris Jean (Smith) T.; m. Susan Devereux Cummins, June 21, 1969; children: Andrew, Sarah. BA with distinction, U. Va., 1969; JD, Vanderbilt U., 1976. Bar: Tenn. 1976, U.S. Dist. Ct. (mid. dist.) Tenn. 1976, U.S. Ct. Appeals (6th cir.) 1976, U.S. Ct. Appeals (4th cir.) 1978, U.S. Ct. Appeals (fed. cir.) 1993, U.S. Supreme Ct. 1986, U.S. Ct. Internat. Trade 1993. Assoc. Farris, Warfield & Kanaday, Nashville, 1976—79, ptnr., 1980—94, Tuke Yopp & Sweeney, Nashville, 1994—99, Trauger, Ney & Tuke, Nashville, 2000—. Adj. prof. law Vanderbilt U. Law Sch., Nashville; faculty PLI, 1995—; mem. AMA Drs.' Adv. Network. Author: (with others) Tennessee Practice, 1992—; editor-in-chief Vanderbilt Law Rev.; contbr. articles to profl. jours. Mem. Tenn. Adoption Law Study Commn., 1993-96, Metro CATV Com. Capt. USMC, 1969-73. Decorated Cross of Gallantry; Patrick Wilson Merit scholar. Mem. ABA, Am. Health Law Assn., Nat. Assn. Bond Lawyers, Am. Acad. Adoption Attys. (trustee), Tenn. Bar Assn., Nashville Bar Assn., Order of Coif. Democrat. Episcopalian. Avocations: rowing, running, cycling, hiking, travel. Corporate, general, Health, Securities. Office: 222 4th Ave N Nashville TN 37219-2115 E-mail: rtuke@tntlaw.net.

TUKEL, SUSAN, lawyer, mediator; b. Detroit, Apr. 5, 1955; d. Sherwin and Emily Tukel; m. Michael K. Balloch, May 24, 1988; 1 child, Adam Tukel-Finegood. BA with high honors and high distinction, U. Mich., 1976, JD cum laude, 1980. Bar: Mich. 1980, U.S. Dist. Ct. (ea. dist.) Mich. 1980, U.S. Ct. Appeals (6th cir.) 1981, U.S. Dist. Ct. Ariz. 1993, U.S. Ct. Appeals (9th cir.) 1994, U.S. Dist. Ct. (we. dist.) Mich. 1996. Assoc. atty. Denenberg, Tuffley, et. al., Southfield, Mich., 1981—86, Denenberg, Tuffley & Jamieson, P.C., Southfield, 1987—93; sr. atty. Morrison, Mahoney & Miller, Southfield, 1994—99; of counsel Feeney, Keellett, Wienner & Bush, Bloomfield Hills, Mich., 2000—01; ptnr. Williams, Mullen, Clark & Dobbins (formerly Wise & Marsac), Detroit, 2001—. Mediator Oakland County. Commercial, consumer (including collections, credit), Insurance, Corporate, general. Home: 3737 MacNichol Trail West Bloomfield MI 48323 Office: Williams Mullen Clark and Dobbins Buhl Bldg 11th Fl 535 Griswold St Detroit MI 48226-3604

TULACHOVA, ALENA, lawyer; b. Prague, Czech Republic, Nov. 8, 1969; d. Karel Marik and Alena Marikova; 1 child, Ema. ML, Charles U. of Prague, 1997. Bar: Czech Republic 2001. Legal clk. Ondrej Peterka, Prague, 1996—97, jr. atty. at law, 1997—2000, Peterka & Leuchterov v.o.s., 2000; assoc. Peterka & Leuchterova v.o.s., 2000—01; ptnr. Peterka, Leuchterova & Ptnrs. v.o.s., 2001—. Avocations: films, architecture, sports, travel, theater . Office: Peterka Leuchterova & Partners vos Na Prikope 15 Prague 110 00 Czech Republic

TULAFONO, TOGIOLA T.A. governor; b. Aunu'u Island, American Samoa, Feb. 28, 1947; s. Aitu and Silika (Vaatu'itu'i) T.; m. Maryann Taufaasau Mauga, Sept. 17, 1984; children: Puataunofo, Olita, Cherianne, Emema, Timoteo, Rosie. Grad., Honolulu Police Acad., 1967; BA, Chadron State Coll., 1970; JD, Washburn U., 1975. Bar: Kans., Am. Samoa. Police instr. Am. Samoa Police Dept., Pago Pago, 1967; adminstrv. asst. Sec. of Samoan Affairs, Pago Pago, 1970-71; legal asst. Atty. Gen., Pago Pago, 1971-72; assoc. Law Offices of George A. Wray, Pago Pago, 1975-77; v.p. South Pacific Island Airways, Pago Pago, 1977-79; judge Dist. Ct. of Am. Samoa, Pago Pago, 1979-80; chmn. bd. dirs. Am. Samoa Power Authority, Pago Pago, 1978-80; mem. Am. Samoa Senate, Pago Pago, 1981-85, 89—; pres. Nayram Samoa, Ltd., Pago Pago, 1985-88; lt. gov. Am. Samoa Pago Pago, 1997—2003; gov. Am. Samoa, 2003—. Chmn. Senate Investigation Com., 1993—. Chmn. Bd. Higher Edn., Am. Samoa, 1993—; bd. dirs. Am. Samoa Jr. Golfers' Assn.; deacon Sailele Congrl. Ch. Mem. ATLA, Am. Samoa Bar Assn., Kans. Bar Assn., Samoa Profl. Golfer's Assn. (pres. 1985-87), Am. Samoa Golf Assn. (pres.). Democrat. Congregationalist. Office: Office of the Gov Ter of American Samoa Pago Pago AS 96799*

TULLY, BERNARD MICHAEL, lawyer; b. Pitts., Aug. 28, 1952; s. Joseph J. and Mary Lorraine T.; m. Feb. 23, 1991; children: Elizabeth, Kevin, Michael, Jessica, Katie. BA, Duquesne, Pitts., 1974; JD, Ohio No. U., 1979. Asst. dist. atty., Pitts., 1979-85; assoc. Stokes, Lurie & Cole, Pitts., 1985-87; pvt. practice Pitts., 1987—. Solicitor Allegheny County Treas., Pitts., 1994-98. Criminal, Personal injury (including property damage). Office: Grant Bldg 310 Grant St Ste 716 Pittsburgh PA 15219-2200

TUNE, JAMES FULCHER, lawyer; b. Danville, Va., May 13, 1942; s. William Orrin and Susan Agnes (Fulcher) T.; m. Katherine Del Mickey, Aug. 2, 1969; children: Katherine Winslow, Jeffrey Bricker. BA, U. Va., 1964; MA, Stanford U., 1970, JD, 1974. Bar: Wash. 1974, U.S. Dist. Ct. (we. dist.) Wash. 1974. Assoc. Bogle & Gates, Seattle, 1974-79, ptnr., 1980-99, head comml./banking dept., 1985-93, mng. ptnr., 1986-93, chmn., 1994-99; ptnr. Dorsey & Whitney LLP, Seattle, 1999-2001, Stoel Rives LLP, Seattle, 2001—, Seattle mng. ptnr., 2002—. Bd. dirs. IBEC Internat. Inc., Vancouver, Wash., Keynetics Inc., Boise, Idaho, Nichirei U.S.A., Inc., Seattle, Tengu Co., Santa Fe Springs, Calif.; chmn. Seattle-King City Econ. Devel. Coun., 1992. Chmn. Seattle Repertory Theatre, 1995, Corp. Coun. for the Arts, 2001—02; chmn. elect United Way King County, 2003. Lt. USN, 1964—69, Vietnam. Woodrow Wilson fellow, 1964, Danforth Found. fellow, 1964. Mem. ABA, Wash. State Bar Assn. (lectr. CLE 1976, 78, 84, 99, 02), Seattle C. of C. (vice chmn. City Budget Task Force 1980-82),

Ranier Club, Seattle Tennis Club, Phi Beta Kappa. Presbyterian. Banking, Commercial, contracts (including sales of goods; commercial financing), Corporate, general. Office: Stoel Rives LLP 600 University St Ste 3600 Seattle WA 98101-3197 E-mail: jftune@stoel.com.

TUNG, KO-YUNG, lawyer; b. Peking, China, Feb. 20, 1947; came to U.S., 1964; s. Tien-chung and Hung-Fang (Wong) T.; m. Alison Heydt, Feb. 2, 1975; children: Vanessa, Adrian, Cameron, Gregory. BA, Harvard U., 1969; JD, U. Tokyo, 1971. Bar: N.Y., 1973. Assoc. Debevoise & Plimpton, N.Y.C., 1973-76; ptnr. Tung, Drabkin & Boynton, N.Y.C., 1976-84, O'Melveny & Myers, N.Y.C., 1985-99; v.p., gen. counsel The World Bank, Washington, 1999—; sec.-gen. Internat. Ctr. for Settlement of Investment Disputes, Washington, 2000—. Adj. assoc. prof. sch. law NYU, 1974-88. Mem. Coun. on Fgn. Rels., N.Y.C., 1986—, The Brookings Inst., 1990, Overseas Devel. Coun., Washington, 1990-99, The Japan Soc., 1990, Asia Soc., 1994—, Presl. Commn. U.S. Pacific Trade Investment Policy, 1996-97, Trilateral Commn., N.Y.C., 1990-97; chmn., bd. govs. East West Ctr., Honolulu, 1990-99; U.S. Nat. Commn. for Pacific Econ. Cooperation, 1991—; bd. dirs. Asian Am. Legal Def. and Edn. Fund, 1990—; vice chmn. adv. coun. Human Rights Watch/Asia, 1997-99, Am. Law Inst., 1997—. Law Faculty fellow Harvard U., 1993. Mem. Am. Law Inst., Am. Arbitration Assn., Internat. Panel Arbitrators, Phi Beta Kappa. Corporate, general, Private international, Mergers and acquisitions. Office: The World Bank 1818 H St NW Washington DC 20433-0001 E-mail: Ktung@worldbank.org.

TUNGATE, JAMES LESTER, lawyer; b. Sept. 27, 1947; s. Ernest O. Jr. and Diantha (Woltz) T.; m. Susan Sumner, Aug. 25, 1973; children: Edward Ernest, James Aaron. BS, Ill. Wesleyan U., 1969; MA, Northwestern U.-Ill., 1970, PhD, 1972; JD, U. Ill.-Urbana, 1979; hon. DHL, London Sch. (Eng.), 1972. Bar: Ill. 1979, U.S. Supreme Ct. 1985. Spl. instr. Northwestern U., Evanston, Ill., 1971; prof., chmn. Loyola U., New Orleans, 1971-76; state dir. News Election Svc., New Orleans, 1972-74; dir. Inst. Religious Communications, New Orleans, 1974-76; asst. to state's atty. Iroquois County, Watseka, Ill., 1978; ptnr. Tungate & Tungate, Watseka, Ill., 1979-98; pres. Tungate Law Offices, Ltd., Watseka, Ill., 1998—. Media cons. Inst. Politics, New Orleans, 1973-76; legal cons., lectr. Iroquois Mental Health Ctr., Watseka, 1980— ; lectr. law Kankakee Community Coll., Ill., 1982; instr. law, Purdue U., 2000; dir. Iroquois Mental Health Ctr., 1980— ; chmn. Iroquois County chpt. ARC, 1982-84, 85— ; dir. Iroquois Republican Council, 1983— . Author: Romantic Images in Popular Songs, 1972; Readings in Broadcast law, 1975. Recipient Internat. Radio and TV Found. award; Harnow scholar U. Ill., 1976. Mem. Ill. Bar Assn., Iroquois County Bar Assn. (Law Day chmn., pres. 1998—), Chgo. Bar Assn., AASR (mem. supreme coun., 2001, Internat. DeMolay Legion of Honor award 2002), Masons (master 1982-83), Scottish Rite (most wise master 1997-98, 33-degree 1999), Mohammed Shrine, Pi Alpha Delta. Republican. Methodist. Banking, General practice, Probate (including wills, trusts). Home: 146 W Hislop Dr Cissna Park IL 60924-8718 Office: Tungate Law Offices 744 E Walnut St PO Box 337 Watseka IL 60970-0337

TUOHEY, MARK HENRY, III, lawyer; b. Rochester, N.Y., Sept. 27, 1946; s. Mark Henry Tuohey; m. Martha Tuohey; children: Brendan, Sean, Devin. BA in History, St. Bonaventure U., 1968; JD, Fordham U., 1973. Bar: D.C. 1973, U.S. Supreme Ct. 1980, U.S. Ct. Appeals (D.C. cir.) 1974, U.S. Dist. Ct. D.C. 1974, N.Y. 1984. Asst. U.S. atty. U.S. Atty.'s Office, Washington, 1973-77; spl. trial counsel U.S. Dept. Justice, Washington, 1977-79; spl. counsel to U.S. Atty. Gen. Washington, 1979; co-adminstrv. ptnr. Washington office Vinson & Elkins, Washington; dep. ind. counsel Whitewater Investigation, 1994-95; spl. counsel D.C. City Coun. Investigation of Met. Police Dept., 1998. Served to 1st lt. U.S. Army, 1970—71. Master: Wm. Bryant Inn. of Ct.; fellow: Am. Bar Found. (bd. dirs. 1980—85), Am. Law Inst., Am. Coll. Trial Lawyers; mem.: ABA (chair standing com. on continuing edn. bar 1980—85, litig. sect. coun. 1980—90, mem. Am. Law Inst./ABA com. continuing profl. edn. 1983—), Bar Assn. D.C. (Lawyer of the Yr. 2001), Jud. Conf. U.S. Ct. Appeals (D.C. cir.), D.C. Bar Found. (chair 1998—), D.C. Bar (bd. govs. 1988—94, pres. 1993—94). Federal civil litigation, Criminal, Government contracts and claims. Home: 1655 Kalmia Rd NW Washington DC 20012-1125 Office: Vinson & Elkins The Willard Office Bldg 1455 Pennsylvania Ave NW Fl 7 Washington DC 20004-1013 E-mail: mtuohey@velaw.com.

TURANO, DAVID A. lawyer; b. Ashtabula, Ohio, Sept. 9, 1946; s. Egidio A. and Mary Agnes (Bartko) T.; m. Karen J. Emmel, Aug. 29, 1970; children: Aaron, Thad, Bethen, Kyle. BS, Kent State U., 1968; JD, Ohio State U., 1971. Bar: Ohio 1971. Staff atty. The Pub. Utilities Commn. Ohio, Columbus, 1971-72; assoc., then ptnr. George, Greek, King, McMahon and McConnaughey, Columbus, 1972-79; ptnr. Baker & Hostetler, Columbus, 1979-96, Harris, Carter, Mahota, Turano & Mazza, Columbus, 1996-97, Harris, Turano & Mazza, Columbus, 1997—2003; of counsel Shoemaker, Howarth & Taylor, LLP, Columbus, 2003—. Mem. ABA, Ohio State Bar Assn., Columbus Bar Assn., Transp. Lawyers Assn. Roman Catholic. Transportation. Office: Shoemaker Howarth & Tylor LLP 471 E Broad St Ste 2001 Columbus OH 43215

TURCOTTE, JOHN ARTHUR, JR., lawyer; b. Lowell, Mass., Mar. 27, 1950; s. John A. and Dorothy J. (Gillette) T.; m. Mary Catherine Willett, Nov. 12, 1976; 1 dau., Sarah Hamilton. B.S., Boston Coll., 1972; J.D., St. Louis U., 1976. Bar: Mo. 1977, U.S. Dist. Ct. (ea. dist.) Mo. 1979; U.S. Ct. Appeals (8th cir.) 1981. Law clk. to presiding justice Mo. Ct. Appeals (ea. dist.), St. Louis, 1976-78; assoc. Lashly, Caruthers, Baer & Hamel, St. Louis, 1978-81, ptnr., 1981-83; ptnr. Diekemper, Hammond, Shiners, Turcotte & Larrew, St. Louis, 1983—. Fellow Am. Acad. Matrimonial Lawyers; mem. ABA, Assn. Trial Lawyers Am., Mo. Assn. Trial Attys., Bar Assn. Met. St. Louis (chmn. com. on cts., Merit award 1983). Democrat. Roman Catholic. Family and matrimonial. Home: 139 Wildwood Ln Saint Louis MO 63122-5135 Office: Diekemper Hammond Shinners Turcotte & Larrew 7730 Carondelet Ave Ste 200 Saint Louis MO 63105-3326 Personal E-mail: jturx@aol.com. Business E-Mail: jturcotte@dhstl.com.

TUREK, DOUGLAS D. lawyer; b. Woodville, Tex., June 6, 1970; s. David E. and Linda M. Turek. BA in History, U. Tex., 1991; JD, U. Houston, 1994; attended, Nat. Inst. Trial Advocacy, 1999. Bar: Tex., 1995, Utah 2002, U.S. Dist. Ct. (so. dist.) Tex., 1996, U.S. Ct. Appeals (5th cir.), 1996, U.S. Dist. Ct. (we. dist.) Tex. 2000, U.S. Dist. Ct. Utah 2002. Assoc. atty. Glickman & Hughes LLP, Houston, 1995—2001; founding mem. The Turek Law Firm PLLC, Houston, 2001—. Mem. editl. adv. bd. Tex. Employment law, 1998; contbr. articles to profl. jours./seminars. Dir. Neartown Youth Baseball League, Houston, 1996-97, coach, 1997-98. Mem. ABA, State Bar Tex., Coll. of State Bar of Tex., Houston Bar Assn., Salt Lake County Bar Assn., Nat. Orgn. Social Security Reps., Houston Young Lawyers Assn., Phi Delta Phi. Avocations: golf, hunting, fishing, backpacking, camping. Appellate, General civil litigation, Labor (including EEOC, Fair Labor Standards Act, labor-management relations, NLRB, OSHA). Office: The Turek Law Firm PLLC 25231 Grogan's Mill Rd Ste 110 The Woodlands TX 77380 E-mail: dturek@tureklawfirm.com.

TURELLI, RICHARD DANIEL, judge; b. Denver, May 30, 1935; s. Niclo William and Mary Turelli; married, July 7, 1956; children: Paul William, Anne Marie. Bachelors, Regis Coll.; JD, Denver U. Law clk. Chief Justice Edward C. Day, Denver, 1961; asst. dist. atty. State of Colo., Commerce City, Colo., 1963—64; clk. Supreme Ct. Colo., Denver, 1965—76; judge Douglas County, Castle Rock, Colo., 1976—81; dist. judge 18th Jud. Dist., Colo., 1981—93. Office: 34 Oak Ridge Rd Castle Rock CO 80104 Fax: 303-663-2653.

TURETSKY, AARON, lawyer; b. Bklyn., Mar. 23, 1951; s. Victor and Edith (Levine) T.; m. Edna M. Real, July 21, 1990; children: Persephone Fatima, Aaron Jr. BA summa cum laude, Hunter Coll., N.Y.C., 1979; JD magna cum laude, N.Y. Law Sch., 1986. Bar: N.J. 1986, U.S. Dist. Ct. N.J. 1986, N.Y. 1987, U.S. Dist. Ct. (so. and ea. dist.) N.Y. 1987, U.S. Dist. Ct. (no. dist.) N.Y. 1988. Appellate law rsch. asst. appellate div. 2d dept. Supreme Ct. State of N.Y., 1986-87; atty. North Country Legal Svcs., Inc., Plattsburgh, N.Y., 1987-89; assoc. Holcombe & Bruno, Plattsburgh, 1989-90; pvt. practice, Keeseville, N.Y., 1990—. Law guardian Essex County Family Ct., 1990—; impartial hearing officer for children with disabilites, 1996—. Chmn. Essex County, N.Y. Conservative Com., 1990—; N.Y. St. Conservative Party N.E. regional vice. chmn., 1992—; eucharistic min. Cath. Community, Keeseville, N.Y. Mem. N.Y. State Bar Assn., Clinton County Bar Assn., Essex County Bar Assn., Elks, KC, Phi Beta Kappa. Roman Catholic. Education and schools, Family and matrimonial, General practice. Office: PO Box 367 Keeseville NY 12944-0367

TURK, ANDREW BORDERS, lawyer; b. San Diego, June 26, 1966; s. Rudy Henry and Wanda Lee (Borders) T.; m. Barbara Jay Kiffmeyer, Oct. 3, 1993. BA magna cum laude, Ariz. State U., 1988; JD, U. Wash., 1992. Bar: Ariz. 1993, Wash. 1993, U.S. Dist. Ct. Ariz. 1993, U.S. Ct. Appeals (9th cir.) 1993. Assoc. Muchmore & Wallwork, P.C., Phoenix, 1993-95; ptnr. Jennings, Strouss & Salmon, P.C., Phoenix, 1996—. Co-author: Arizona Environmental Law Manual, 1994, rev. edit., 1998; contbr. articles to profl. jours. Mem. bicycle adv. com. City of Tempe, Ariz., 1993-99, vice chair, 1996, mayoral appointee, chair subcom. on edn., 1996-98. Mem. Maricopa County Young Lawyers Divsn. (bd. dirs. 1997—, sec. 1998, pres.-elect 1999, pres. 2000-2001), Maricopa County Bar Assn. (bd. dirs. 2001-), Ariz. State Bar Assn. (civil practice and procedures com. 1998—), Phi Beta Kappa, Phi Alpha Delta. Avocations: cycling, golf, history, comic books, music. General civil litigation, Commercial, contracts (including sales of goods; commercial financing), Toxic tort. Office: Jennings Strouss & Salmon 2 N Central Ave Phoenix AZ 85004-2322 E-mail: abturk@jsslaw.com.

TURK, JAMES CLINTON, federal judge; b. Roanoke, Va., May 3, 1923; s. James Alexander and Geneva (Richardson) T.; m. Barbara Duncan, Aug. 21, 1954; children— Ramona Leah, James Clinton, Robert Malcolm Duncan, Mary Elizabeth, David Michael. AB, Roanoke Coll., 1949; L.L.B., Washington and Lee U., 1952. Bar: Va. bar 1952. Assoc. Dalton & Poff, Radford, Va., 1952-53; ptnr. Dalton, Poff & Turk, Radford, 1953-72; state senator from Va., 1959-72; judge U.S. Dist. Ct. (we. dist.) Va., Roanoke, 1972-73, chief judge, 1973—. Dir. 1st & Mchts. Nat. Bank of Radford Mem. Va. Senate, from 1959, minority leader.; Trustee Radford Community Hosp., 1959— . Served with AUS, 1943-46. Mem. Order of Coif, Phi Beta Kappa, Omicron Delta Kappa. Baptist (deacon). Home: 1002 Walker Dr Radford VA 24141-3018 Office: US Dist Ct 246 Franklin Rd SW # 220 Roanoke VA 24011-2214 Fax: (540) 857-5123.

TURLEY, J. WILLIAM, lawyer; b. Van Nuys, Calif., Jan. 11, 1948; s. Billy Brown and Kathryn Ann Turley; children: Timothy Jay, Damon Andrew, William Ross. BA, U. Mo., 1970, JD, 1974. Bar: Mo. 1974, U.S. Dist. Ct. (we. dist.) Mo. 1974. Stockholder Wesner, Turley & Kempton, Inc., Sedalia, Mo., 1975-84; ptnr. Carnahan, Carnahan & Turley, Rolla, Mo., 1984-87, ptnr. Williams, Robinson, Turley, Crump & White, 1987-96; sr. counsel Shelter Ins. Cos., 1996—. Author: Trial Handbook for Missouri Lawyers, 1984; contbr. articles to profl. jours. ; v.p. Mo. Lawyer's Trust Acct. Found., 1990. Mem. Mo. Bar Assn. (bd. govs. 1986-96, exec. com. 1989-90), Assn. Trial Lawyers Am. (bd. govs. 1985-89), Mo. Assn. Trial Attys. (pres. 1985). Federal civil litigation, Insurance, Personal injury (including property damage). Home: 2626 Huntleigh Pl Jefferson City MO 65109 Office: Shelter Ins Cos 1817 W Broadway Columbia MO 65218 Business E-Mail: bturley@shelterinsurance.com.

TURLEY, LINDA, lawyer; b. Altus, Okla., July 16, 1958; d. Windle and Shirley (Lacey) Turley; m. Thomas J. Stutz, Mar. 30, 1985; 1 child, Lacey. BS, Georgetown U., 1980; JD with honors, U. Tex., 1983. Bar: Tex. 1983; bd. cert. in personal injury trial law. Atty., head product liability dept. Law Offices of Windle Turley, P.C., Dallas, 1986-95; ptnr. Turley & Stutz, P.C., Dallas, 1997—2001; personal injury trial lawyer Law Offices of Windle Turley, P.C., 2001—. Mem. task force on Tex. rules of civil procedure Tex. Supreme Ct., 1992-93. Mem. ATLA (bd. govs. 1993-96, chair women trial lawyers' caucus 1989-90, chair product liability sect. 1996-97), Tex. Trial Lawyers Assn. (bd. dirs. 1989—). General civil litigation, Personal injury (including property damage), Product liability. Office: 1000 Turley Law Ctr 6440 N Central Expy Dallas TX 75206

TURLEY, ROBERT JOE, lawyer; b. Mt. Sterling, Ky., Dec. 6, 1926; s. R. Joe and Mavis Clare (Sternberg) T.; m. Mary Lynn Sanders, Dec. 17, 1948 (dv.); children: Leighton Turley Isaacs, Lynn Turley McComas, R. Joe, Mavis Lee Turley Scully. Student, Berea Coll., 1944-45, St. Mary's Coll., Calif., 1945-46; LLB, U. Ky., 1949. Bar: Ky. 1949, U.S. Dist. Ct. (ea. dist.) Ky. 1950, U.S. Supreme Ct. 1959. Ptnr. Mooney & Turley and successor firms, Lexington, Ky., 1949-84, Turley & Moore, Lexington, 1984-89, of counsel, 1989-93. Chmn. Fed. Jud. Selection Commn. Ky., 1985-89; gen counsel Shriners Hosps. for Children, 1976-77, trustee, 1981-90, emeritus trustee, 1990—; mem. exec. coun. and character first! edn. program team Character Coun. Ctrl. Ky., 2002—; mem. devel. team Lexington Leadership Found., 2001—. Author: The Choices Are Yours, 1997, The Bridge of Faith, 2000; contbr. articles to legal jours. Mem. devel. team Lexington Leadership Found., 2001-. With USNR, 1944-46. Diplomate Nat. Bd. Trial Advocacy, 1980. Fellow Am. Coll. Trial Lawyers, Ky. Bar Found. (life); mem. Ky. Bar Assn. (sr. counselor, Outstanding Lawyer award 2001, Ethics Hotline 1998—), St. Ives Jour. Club, Champions Trace Golf Club, Masons, Shriners. Home: 111 Woodland Ave Lexington KY 40502-6415

TURNAGE, FRED DOUGLAS, lawyer; b. Ayden, N.C., Sept. 24, 1920; s. Fred C. and Lou (Johnson) T.; m. Margaret Futrell, Aug. 21, 1943 (div. Nov. 1980); children: Betty Lou Griffith, Douglas C.; m. Elizabeth Louisa Turnage, Jan. 23, 1981. Grad. Naval Sch. on Far Eastern Civil Affairs, Princeton U., 1945; LLB, Wake Forest U., 1948, LLD, 1970. Bar: N.C. 1948, U.S. Supreme Ct. 1953, U.S. Dist. Ct. D.C. 1965, U.S. Ct. Appeals (D.C. cir.) 1967, U.S. Ct. Appeals (4th and 7th cirs.) 1979. Trial atty. antitrust div. U.S. Dept. Justice, Kansas City, Mo., 1948-51, sr. trial atty. antitrust div. Washington, 1951-65, spl. asst. to atty. gen., 1965; sr. ptnr. Cleary, Gottlieb, Steen & Hamilton, Washington, 1968—, counsel, 1990—. Lectr. continuing legal edn. courses, 1973-77. Contbr. articles to profl. jours. Bd. Visitors Wake Forest U. Sch. Law, Winston-Salem, N.C., 1980—. Served to 1st lt. AUS, 1942-46. Recipient Disting. Service in Law citation Wake Forest U., 1979. Mem. ABA (antitrust and litigation sects.), Fed. Bar Assn., Adv. Bd. Antitrust Bulletin, Wake Forest U. Alumni Assn. (pres. 1977), Nat. Lawyers Clubs. Methodist. Avocations: fishing, golf, writing. Antitrust, Federal civil litigation, Criminal. Home: 02 Fifth Ave Kitty Hawk NC 27949 Office: 2000 Pennsylvania Ave NW Washington DC 20006-1812

TURNAGE, JEAN ALLEN, retired state supreme court chief justice; b. St. Ignatius, Mont., Mar. 10, 1926; JD, Mont. State U., 1951; D Laws and Letters (non.), U. Mont., 1995. Bar: Mont. 1951, U.S. Supreme Ct. 1963. Formerly ptnr. Turnage, McNeil & Mercer, Polson, Mont.; formerly Mont. State senator from 13th Dist.; pres. Mont. State Senate, 1981—85; chief justice Supreme Ct. Mont., 1985-2001. Mem. Mont. State Bar Assn., Nat. Conf. Chief Justices (past pres.), Nat. Ctr. State Courts (past chair). Office: Turnage & Mercer PO Box 460 Polson MT 59860

TURNBULL, H. RUTHERFORD, III, law educator, lawyer; b. NYC, Sept. 22, 1937; s. Henry R. and Ruth (White) T.; m. Mary M. Slingluff, Apr. 4, 1964 (div. 1972); m. Ann Patterson, Mar. 23, 1974; children: Jay, Amy, Katherine. Grad., The Kent (Conn.) Sch., 1955; BA, Johns Hopkins U., 1959; LLB with hon., U. Md., 1964; LLM, Harvard U., 1969. Bar: Md., N.C. Law clerk to Hon. Emory H. Niles Supreme Bench Balt. City, 1959-60; law clerk to Hon. Roszel C. Thomsen U.S. Dist. Ct. Md., 1962-63; assoc. Piper & Marbury, Balt., 1964-67; prof. Inst. Govt. U. N.C., Chapel Hill, 1969-80, U. Kans., Lawrence, 1980—. Prof. spl. edn., courtesy prof. law U. Kans. Editor-in-chief Md. Law Review. Cons., author, lectr., co-dir. Beach Ctr. on Disability, U. Kans.; pres. Full Citizenship Inc., Lawrence, 1987-93; spl. staff-fellow U.S. Senate subcom. on disability policy, Washington, 1987-88; bd. dirs. Camphill Assn. N.Am., Inc., 1985-87; trustee Judge David L. Bazelon Ctr. Mental Health Law, 1993-2000, chmn., 1999—. With U.S. Army, 1960-65. Recipient Nat. Leadership award Nat. Assn. Pvt. Residential Resources, 1988, Internat. Coun. for Exceptional Children, 1996, Am. Assn. on Mental Retardation, 1997, Century award Nat. Trust for Hist. Preservation in Mental Retardation, 1999, Nat. Advocate award Am. Music Therapy Assn., 2002; named Nat. Educator of Yr., ARC, 1982; Public Policy fellow Joseph P. Kennedy, Jr. Found., 1987-88. Fellow Am. Assn. on Mental Retardation (pres. 1985-86, bd. dirs. 1980-86); mem. ABA (chmn. disability law commn. 1991-95), U.S.A. As sn. for Retarded Citizens (sec. and dir. 1981-83), Assn. for Persons with Severe Handicaps (treas. 1988, bd. dirs. 1987-90), Nat. Assn. Rehab. Rsch. and Tng. Ctrs. (chair govt. affairs com. 1990-93), Internat. Assn. Scientific Study of Mental Deficiency, Internat. League of Assns. for Persons with Mental Handicaps, Johns Hopkins U. Alumni Assn. (pres. N.C. chpt. 1977-79). Democrat. Episcopalian. Home: 1636 Alvamar Dr Lawrence KS 66047-1714 Office: U Kans 3111 Haworth Hall 1200 Sunnyside Ave Lawrence KS 66045-7534 E-mail: Rud@ku.edu.

TURNER, DAVID ELDRIDGE, lawyer; b. Washington, Jan. 16, 1947; s. Olan Eldridge and Bernice Adele (Bothwell) T.; m. Lauren Turner-Hudson; children: Matthew David, Elizabeth Kristine, Jacob Michael. BS, Pa. State U., 1969; JD cum laude, Temple U., 1974. Bar: Pa. 1974, U.S. Dist. Ct. (ea. and mid. dists.) Pa. 1974, U.S. Ct. Appeals (3d cir.) 1983, U.S. Supreme Ct. 1985. With Liberty Mut. Ins. Co., Allentown, Pa., 1969-71; ptnr. Rhoda, Stoudt & Bradley, Reading, Pa., 1974-80, Kozloff, Diener, Turner & Payne P.C., Wyomissing, Pa., 1980-84; pres. Bingaman, Hess, Coblentz & Bell, P.C., Reading, 1985—. Instr. Pa. State U., Berks County, 1974-80; jud. appointee Berks County Ct. of Common Pleas, Reading, 1982-83. Supr. Robeson Twp. Bd. Suprs., Berks County, Pa., 1980-82. Mem. ABA, Pa. Bar Assn., Berks County Bar Assn., Pa. Trial Lawyers Assn., Pa. Def. Inst., Endlich Law Club, Mensa. Avocations: sculpture, rock climbing. Federal civil litigation, State civil litigation, Insurance. Office: Bingaman Hess Coblentz & Bell Treeview Corp Ctr Ste 100 2 Meridian Dr Wyomissing PA 19610 E-mail: deturner@bhcb.com.

TURNER, DONALD ALLEN, lawyer; b. Cleve., Aug. 14, 1938; s. Louis O. and Harriet B. (Keizer) T.; m. Amy Glicksberg, Dec. 16, 1962 (div. Oct. 1980); children— Matthew, Kelli; m. Vikki Holley, Sept. 30, 1984 (div. 1989); m. Diane Fraunhoffer, 1992 (div. 1994); m. Renata Olgate, 1997. B. Metall. Engring., Ohio State U., 1963; J.D., Detroit Coll. Law, 1967. Bar: Mich. 1967, U.S. Dist. Ct. (ea. dist.) Mich. 1967. Ptnr., Turner & Schaden, Detroit, 1967-69, Nelson, Gracey, Turner, Detroit, 1969-72; pres. Turner & Turner, P.C., Southfield, Mich., 1972-91, ret. Served with USNR, 1956-58. Mem. Assn. Trial Lawyers Am., Mich. Trial Lawyers Assn., State Bar Mich., Southfield Bar Assn., Oakland County Bar Assn. Jewish. Civil rights, Federal civil litigation, Personal injury (including property damage). Home: 3923 Maple Hill St E West Bloomfield MI 48323-1742 Office: Turner & Turner PC 26000 W 12 Mile Rd Southfield MI 48034-1783

TURNER, DWAYNE CURTIS, lawyer; b. Atlanta, Sept. 13, 1960; s. George Aiken Turner and Mary Inez (Rowe) Holley. BA in Anthropology, Calif. State U., Long Beach, 1989; MA in Anthropology, UCLA, 1991, MPH, 1992, PhD in Anthropology, 1994; JD, Benjamin M. Cardozo Sch. Law, 1999. Bar: N.Y. First Dept. Assoc. dir. planning AIDS Project of L.A., 1992-94; adj. faculty anthropology Calif. State U., L.A., 1994-96; rsch. assoc. UCLA Sch. Medicine, Dept. Health Svcs., 1994-96; asst. prof. health scis. CUNY, 1996-99; asst. corp. coun. lead paint unit N.Y.C. Law Dept., 1999—2001; adj. prof. health law CUNY, 1999—2002; exec. dir. N.Y. State Task Force on Life and the Law, 2001—03; dir. Liberty County Health Dept., 2003—. Evaluation ocns. Teen Canteen/Travelers AID, L.A., 1993-94; adj. prof. health scis. CUNY, 1999—. Author: Risky Sex: Gay Men and HIV Prevention, 1997; contbr. articles to profl. jours. Bd. dirs. UCLA Ctr. for clin. AIDS Rsch. and Edn., 1994, AVANCE Humana Svcs., L.A., 1994, Liberty County Family Connections, 2003—, Liberty County United Way, 2003—, Liberty County YMCA, 2003; organizer Com. for Ann. Women and HIV Conf., L.A., 1992-94; vol. Being Alive, Long Beach. Calif., 1987-89; mem. AIDS Coalition to Unleash Power, L.A., 1990-92. Mem. APHA, Am. Anthropol. Assn., Soc. for Med. Anthropology, Soc. for Applied Anthropology (adv. bd. AIDS task force 1994), N.Y. State Bar Assn., City Bar Assn. of N.Y., N.Y. Acad. Scis. Avocation: music. Home: 204 Cherokee Tr Hinesville GA 31313 Office: PO Box 231 Hinesville GA 31310 E-mail: dcturner@gdph.state.ga.us.

TURNER, E. DEANE, lawyer; b. Auburn, N.Y., Aug. 4, 1928; s. Alfred Edward and Bertha (Deane) T. AB summa cum laude, Princeton U., 1950; LLB cum laude, Harvard U., 1953. Bar: N.Y. 1953. Assoc. Dewey Ballantine LLP and predecessor firms, N.Y.C., 1953-63, ptnr., 1963—, of counsel, 1991—. Treas. Harvard Law Sch. Assn., N.Y.C., 1964-83; elder, trustee Brick Presbyn. Ch., N.Y.C., 1976—, pres. bd. trustees, 1988-90; trustee Presbytery N.Y.C., 1993-98, pres. bd. trustees, 1995-98; com. to adminstr. James N. Jarvie Endowment, 1993-2000. Fellow Am. Coll. Investment Counsel (emeritus); mem. Union Club, John's Island Club, Phi Beta Kappa. Republican. Corporate, general, Finance. Home: 1120 5th Ave New York NY 10128-0144 also: 381 Llwyds Ln Johns Island Vero Beach FL 32963 Office: Dewey Ballantine LLP 1301 Avenue Of The Americas New York NY 10019-6022

TURNER, HARRY EDWARD, lawyer; b. Mt. Vernon, Ohio, Dec. 25, 1927; s. Paul Hamilton and Harriett (Krafft) T.; m. Shirley Marilyn Eggert, July 8, 1950; children: Harry Edward, Thomas Frederick (dec. Mar. 1995). BA, Baldwin Wallace Coll., 1951; JD, Ohio No. U., 1954. Bar: Ohio 1954, U.S. Supreme Ct. 1966. Practice in Mt. Vernon, 1954—; state rep. Ohio Gen. Assembly, 1973-85; solicitor Mt. Vernon, 1958-62. Prosecutor Mt. Vernon Municipal Ct., 1955-58 Mem. Mt. Vernon City Sch. Bd., 1964-70, pres., 1965-70; trustee Ohio Sch. Bd. Assn., 1968-70, Hannah Browning Home, 1987-2001, Sta. Break/Commn. on Planning Svcs., 1989-95; mem. Knox County Pub. Defender Commn., 1987-91. With USN, 1946-47. Mem. Ohio State Bar Assn., Knox County Bar Assn. (pres. 1970), Alpha Sigma Phi, Sigma Delta Kappa. Republican. Lutheran. Home: 1575 Yauger Rd Apt 15 Mount Vernon OH 43050-8299 Office: 118 E High St Mount Vernon OH 43050-3443

TURNER, HARRY WOODRUFF, lawyer; b. Blairsville, Pa., May 2, 1939; s. James McKinnie and Dorothy Elizabeth (Tittle) T.; m. Mary Elizabeth Phelan, Dec. 30, 1972; children: James William, David Woodruff. AB, U. Pitts., 1961; JD, Harvard U., 1964. Bar: Pa., 1965, U.S. Supreme Ct., 1979. Assoc. Kirkpatrick & Lockhart, LLP, Pitts., 1964-71; ptnr. Kirkpatrick & Lockhart, Pitts., 1971—. Mem. Fed. Jud. Selection Commn. Pa., 1995—, chair, 1997—. Trustee Hist. Soc. Western Pa. 1996—, vice-chmn., 1999—; trustee U. Pitts., 1995-2003, Wilson Coll., Chambersburg, Pa., 1978-89, Pitts. Cultural Trust, 2002—; trustee, pres. Pitts. Opera, 1993—, pres., 2001—; pres. U. Pitts. Nat. Alumni Assn., 2001—; alt. del. Rep. Nat. Conv., Miami, 1968, Houston, 1992, Phila., 2000, Rep. State Com., 1994—; trustee, v.p. Torrance (Pa.) State Hosp., 1969-73; trustee ann. giving fund U. Pitts. 1982-95; chair distbn. com. William L. Benz Found., 1985—; bd. dir. Pitts. divsn. Am. Heart Assn., 1993-2003; bd. vis. U. Pitts. Med. Sch., 1995-2000, U. Pitts. Coll. Arts & Sci., 1988-2003, chair bd. vis. Sch. Info. Sci., 1994-2002; trustee, Pittsbury Cultural Trust, 2002-. Mem. ABA, Pa. Bar Assn., Am. Law Inst., Internat. Acad. Trial Lawyers, Allegheny County Bar Assn., Allegheny County Acad. Trial Lawyers, SAR (pres. 1995-96), Fox Chapel Golf Club, Duquesne Club. Presbyterian. Antitrust, General civil litigation, Libel, Appellate. Office: Kirkpatrick & Lockhart 1500 Oliver Building Pittsburgh PA 15222-2312 E-mail: wturner@KL.com.

TURNER, HUGH JOSEPH, JR., lawyer; b. Paterson, N.J., Oct. 5, 1945; s. Hugh Joseph and Louise (Sullivan) T.; m. Charlene Chiappetta, Feb. 11, 1983. BS, Boston U., 1967; JD, U. Miami, Coral Gables, Fla., 1975. Bar: Fla. 1975, U.S. Dist. Ct. (so., no. and mid. dists.) Fla. 1975, U.S. Ct. Appeals (11th cir.) 1981, U.S. Supreme Ct. 1984. Tchr. Browne & Nichols, Cambridge, Mass., 1968-72; ptnr. Smathers & Thompson, Miami, Fla., 1981-87, Kelley Drye & Warren, Miami, 1987-93, English, McCaughan & O'Bryan, Ft. Lauderdale, 1993—2001, Redgrave & Turner LLP, Boca Raton, Fla., 2001—. Chmn. Fla. Bar internat. law sect., 1988-89. Contbg. author book on internat. dispute resolution Fla. Bar, 1989; contbr. articles to profl. jours. Bd. dirs. Japan Soc. South Fla., Miami, 1989-97; mem. Sea Ranch Lakes Village Coun., 1997-2000; mayor Sea Ranch Lakes, 2000-02. Mem. ABA, Def. Rsch. Inst. Avocation: running. General civil litigation, Product liability. Office: Redgrave & Turner LLP Ste 450 120 E Palmetto Park Rd Boca Raton FL 33432

TURNER, JAMES THOMAS, judge; b. Clifton Forge, Va., Mar. 12, 1938; s. James Thomas and Ruth (Greene) T.; m. Patricia Sue Renfrow, July 8, 1962; 1 child, James Thomas. BA, Wake Forest Coll., 1960; JD, U. Va., 1965. Bar: Va. 1965, U.S. Ct. Appeals (4th and fed. cirs.), U.S. Supreme Ct. Assoc. Williams, Worrell, Kelly & Greer, Norfolk, Va., 1965, ptrn., 1971-79; U.S. magistrate U.S. Dist. Ct. (ea. dist.) Va., Norfolk, 1979-87; judge U.S. Ct. Fed. Claims, 1987—. Mem. ABA, Fed. Bar Assn., Va. Bar Assn., Norfolk and Portsmouth Bar Assn. (sec. 1975-79). Office: 717 Madison Pl NW Washington DC 20439-0002

TURNER, LEE IRWIN, lawyer; b. Cleve., May 2, 1944; s. Louis and Harriet (Keizer) T.; married; children: Brooke, Brett, Brittany, Breanne, Brenna. B.S., Ohio State U., 1966, J.D. cum laude, 1969. Bar: Mich. 1969, Ohio, 1969, U.S. Dist. Ct. (no. dist.) Ohio 1971, U.S. Dist. (ea. dist.) Mich. 1971, U.S. Ct. Appeals (6th cir.) 1984. Assoc., Sommer, Schwartz, Silver, Schwartz, Detroit, 1969-73; ptnr. Turner & Turner, P.C., Southfield, Mich., 1973— . Mem. Assn. Trial Lawyers Am., Mich. Trial Lawyers, Detroit Bar Assn., Southfield Bar Assn., Oakland County Bar Assn. Democrat. Jewish. Federal civil litigation, State civil litigation, Personal injury (including property damage). Office: 26000 W 12 Mile Rd Southfield MI 48034-1783

TURNER, LESTER NATHAN, lawyer, international trade consultant; b. Colmar, Ky., July 11, 1933; s. Clifford G. and Minnie G. (Ensor) T.; m. Sandra B. Ward, July 3, 1976; children: Kimberly L., Michele M., Renee S., Mark L., Jeffrey S., Derek Kyle. BS, Lincoln Meml. U., 1955; JD, U. Mich., 1959. Bar: Mich. 1960, U.S. Dist. Ct. (ea. and we. dist.) Mich., U.S. Ct. Appeals (6th cir.), U.S. Supreme Ct. 1982. Law clk. to presiding justice, research atty. Mich. Supreme Ct., Lansing, 1960-62; ptnr. Sinas, Dramis, Brake & Turner, Lansing, 1960-78; sole law practice, bus. law, internat. cons. primarily in Mid. East Countries with emphasis on Palestine Nat. Authority, Lansing, Harbor Springs, Mich., 1978—; prin., CEO Palestinian Tourism Co. Ltd., Palestinian Co. Transp. Ltd., North Bay Ltd. Mem. std. jury instrn. com. Mich. Supreme Ct., Lansing, 1963-73; cons. higher commn. investment and fin. Palestinian Pres., 1997—. Mem. Mich. State Bar Assn., Mich. Trial Lawyers Assn. (bd. dirs. 1963-74, vice pres. 1974). Methodist. General civil litigation, General practice, Public international. Office: PO Box 499 Harbor Springs MI 49740-0499 E-mail: intlaw@chartermi.net.

TURNER, MARK MCDOUGALL, lawyer; b. Carlisle, Eng., Sept. 3, 1956; BA, Oxford U., 1979. Bar: solicitor, 1983. Ptnr. Denton Hall, London, 1988-95, Garrett & Co., London, 1995-97, Herbert Smith, London, 1998—. Author: Butterworth's Ency. of Competition Law, 1993, International Technology Transfers, 1995. Fellow Royal Soc. Arts; mem. United Oxford and Cambridge Univ. Club. Communications, Computer, E-business. Office: Herbert Smith Exchange House, Primrose St London EC2A 2HS England E-mail: mark.turner@herbertsmith.com.

TURNER, REGINALD MAURICE, JR., lawyer; b. Detroit, Feb. 25, 1960; s. Reginald and Anne Laura (Mims) T.; m. Marcia Holland, June 10, 1989. BS in Indsl. Psychology, Wayne State U., 1982; JD, U. Mich., 1987. Bar: Mich. With UPS, Livonia, Mich., 1977-83, Profl. Pers. Svc. div. B.P.A. Enterprises, Detroit, 1983-84; summer assoc. Office of the Gen. Counsel GM Corp., Detroit, 1985, 86; law clk. Sachs, Nunn, Kates, Kadushin, O'Hare, Helveston & Waldman, Detroit, 1987; jud. law clk. to Hon. Dennis W. Archer Mich. Supreme Ct., Detroit, 1987-89; ptnr. Sachs, Waldman, O'Hare, Helveston, Hodges & Barnes, P.C., Detroit, 1989—; atty. Clark Hill PLC, Detroit, 2000—. V.p. N.W. Detroiters for Better Govt.; chair MELL Team Against Substance Abuse. White House fellow, 1996-97; recipient Irving Stenn Jr. award U. Mich. Law Sch., 1987; named Barrister of the Yr., Outstanding Young Lawyer State Bar Mich., 1995. Mem. ABA, ACLU, NAACP, Fed. Bar Assn., Nat. Bar Assn., State Bar Mich. (commn., regional dir., pres. 2002-03), Wolverine Bar Assn. (past pres.), Detroit Assn. Black Orgns., Alpha Phi Alpha. Democrat. Episcopalian. Federal civil litigation, Labor (including EEOC, Fair Labor Standards Act, labor-management relations, NLRB, OSHA), Pension, profit-sharing, and employee benefits. Office: Clark Hill PLC 500 Woodward Ave Ste 3500 Detroit MI 48226-3435 Home: 19475 Cumberland Way Detroit MI 48203-1457 E-mail: rturner@clarkhill.com.*

TURNER, TOM, writer, editor; b. Oakland, Calif., 1942; m. Mary Jorgensen; children: Bret and Kathryn (twins). BA in Polit. Sci., U. Calif., 1965. Vol. Peace Corps, Turkey, 1965-67; grant analyst Head Start, 1968; editor, adminstrv. asst. Sierra Club, 1968-69; various positions including exec. dir. Friends of the Earth, 1969-86, also editor Not Man Apart; staff writer, dir. publs., sr. editor Earthjustice, 1986—. Author: Wild By Law: the Sierra Club Legal Defense Fund and the Places It Has Saved, 1990, Sierra Club: 100 Years of Protecting Nature, 1991, Justice on Earth, Earthjustice and the People It Has Served, 2002; contbr. to The Ency. of the Environment, 1994, also chpts. to books; contbr. articles to Sierra, Defenders, Wilderness, San Francisco Chronicle, San Francisco Examiner, L.A. Times, Oakland Tribune, Washington Post, Mother Earth News, Outside, others. Office: Earthjustice 426 17th St 6th Fl Oakland CA 94612 E-mail: tturner@earthjustice.org.

TURO, RON, lawyer; b. Fort Wayne, Ind., Apr. 2, 1955; s. John B. and Joan L. (Gluntz) T.; m. Claire Teresa Fetterman T., May 24, 1980; children: Andrew Jacob, Patricia Erin, Dominic Earl. BA in History with honors, Pa. State U., 1978; JD, Dickinson Sch. Law, 1981. Bar: Pa. 1981, U.S. Dist. (mid. dist.) Pa. 1982, U.S. Supreme Ct. 1987, U.S. Ct. Appeals (3d cir.) 1989. Ast. pub. defender Cumberland County, Carlisle, Pa., 1981-84; ptnr. Griffie & Turo, Carlisle, 1984-89; pvt. practice Carlisle, 1989—. Lectr. Dickinson Sch. Law, 1996—, Widener U. Sch. Law, 2000, adj. prof., 2001—, mem. trial advocacy program faculty, 2001—. Founder Cumberland County Police Recognition Dinner, Carlisle, Pa., 1985—; mem. Nat. Cath. Com. on Scouting, 1988—; chmn. Region III, Pa., N.J., 1993-95, parliamentarian and legal counsel, 1991-2002, advisor religious act, 1998-2000; bd. dirs. AHEDD, Inc., 1993-, vice chmn. 1994-95, chmn., 1995-2002; trustee David E. Baker Scholarship Trust, 1997—; bd. dirs. Pa. Assn. for the Blind, 1998—, exec. search com., 1999-2000. Recipient St. George Emblem Boy Scouts Am., 1983, Eagle Scout 1969, Golden AAD Emblem, 1989. Mem. Nat. Lawyers Assn., Nat. Assn. Criminal Def. Lawyers, Pa. Bar Assn., Pa. Assn. Criminal Def. Lawyers, Solicitor's Assn., Pa. Boroughs, Pa. Twp. Assns., Cumberland County Bar Assn. (social chmn. 1985-98, pub. rels. com. 1998—, bench-bar com. 1998—, membership chmn. 2000—), Nat. Assn. of Counsel for Children, St. Thomas More Soc. (v.p. 1996-98, treas. 1998—), Mensa (local sec. 1990-92, editor 1992-95, ombudsman 2000—), KC (pres. Capital area chpt. 1989, Knight of Yr. 1981, grand knight 1985-87, 93-95, fin. sec. 1996-2002, dist. dep. 1998-2002). Republican. Roman Catholic. Avocations: scuba diving, travel. General civil litigation, Criminal. Office: 28 S Pitt St Carlisle PA 17013-3211 E-mail: RonTuro@TuroLaw.com.

TUROW, SCOTT F. lawyer, writer; b. Chgo., Apr. 12, 1949; s. David D. and Rita (Pastron) Turow; m. Annette Weisberg, Apr. 4, 1971; 3 children. BA magna cum laude, Amherst Coll., 1970; MA, Stanford U., 1974; JD cum laude, Harvard U., 1978. Bar: Ill. 1978, U.S. Dist. Ct. (no. dist.) Ill. 1978, U.S. Ct. Appeals (7th cir.) 1979. Asst. U.S. atty. U.S. Ct. Appeals (7th dist.), Chgo., 1978—86; ptnr. Sonnenschein Nath & Rosenthal, Chgo., 1986—. E.H. Jones lectr. Stanford U., 1972—75. Author: One L.: An Inside Account of Life in the First Year at Harvard Law School, 1977, Presumed Innocent, 1987, The Burden of Proof, 1990, Pleading Guilty, 1993, The Laws of Our Fathers, 1996, Personal Injuries, 1999; contbr. articles to profl. jours. Mem.: Chgo. Coun. Lawyers, Chgo. Bar Assn. Office: Sonnenschein Nath Rosenthal 233 S Wacker Dr Ste 8000 Chicago IL 60606-6491

TURPENING, PATRICIA EILEEN KELLER, law librarian; b. Columbus, Ohio, Mar. 1, 1952; d. William Waite and Eileen Catherine (Miller) Keller; m. Richard Whitley Denham, Oct. 10, 1981 (div. Mar. 1986); 1 child, Michael Richard; m. Glen Thomas Turpening, Apr. 16, 1997. BS, Findlay Coll., 1974; MSLS, U. Ky., 1978. Cert. in preservation mgmt. Sch. Communication, Info. and Libr. Studies, Rutgers U., 1999. Acquisitions libr. Supreme Ct. Ohio Law Libr., Columbus, 1974-76, Robert S. Marx Law Libr., U. Cin., 1978-88, head preservation and archives, 1988—. Libr. Rendigs, Fry, Kiely & Dennis, Cin., 1979-85. Editor Tech. Svcs. Law Libr., 1990-94; contbr. articles to profl. jours. Mem. LWV, AAUW, NOW, AAUP, Am. Assn. Law Librs. (travel grantee 1984, preservation cons., coord. of library pgms.), Soc. Am. Archivists, Ohio Preservation Coun., Ohio Regional Assn. Law Librs. Episcopalian. Office: U Cin Robert S Marx Law Libr PO Box 210142 Cincinnati OH 45221-0142 E-mail: pat.turpening@law.uc.edu.

TURRENTINE, HOWARD BOYD, federal judge; b. Escondido, Calif., Jan. 22, 1914; s. Howard and Veda Lillian (Maxfield) T.; m. Virginia Jacobsen, May 13, 1965 (dec.); children: Howard Robert, Terry Beverly; m. Marlene Lipsey, Nov. 1, 1991. AB, San Diego State Coll., 1936; LLB, U. So. Calif., 1939. Bar: Calif. 1939. Practiced in, San Diego, 1939-68; judge Superior Ct. County of San Diego, 1968-70, U.S. Dist. Ct. (so. dist.) Calif., Calif., sr. judge, 1970—. Served with USNR, 1941-45. Mem. ABA, Fed. Bar Assn., Am. Judicature Soc. Office: US Dist Ct 940 Front St San Diego CA 92101-8994

TUSCHMAN, JAMES MARSHALL, lawyer; b. Nov. 28, 1941; s. Chester and Harriet (Harris) T.; m. Ina S. Cheloff, Sept. 2, 1967; children: Chad Michael, Jon Stephen, Sari Anne. BS in Bus., Miami U., Oxford, Ohio, 1963; JD, Ohio State U., 1966. Bar: Ohio 1966, U.S. Ct. Appeals (6th and 7th cirs.), U.S. Supreme Ct. Assoc. Shumaker, Loop & Kendrick, Toledo, 1966—84, ptnr., 1970—84; co-founder, chmn. ops. com. Jacobson Maynard Tuschman & Kalur, Toledo, 1985—97; COO Ohio Ferrous Group Omnisource Corp., Toledo, 1998—99, dir. bus. devel. No. Ohio group, 1999—2001; of counsel Barkan & Robon Ltd., Maumee, Ohio, 2002—. Chmn. bd., sec. Tuschman Steel Co., Toledo, 1969-76, Toledo Steel Supply Co., 1969-86; vice-chmn. bd. Kripke Tuschman Industries, Inc., 1977-85; ptnr. Starr Ave. Co., Toledo, 1969-86. Trustee, former chmn. bd. trustees U. Toledo; past trustee, chmn. fin. com., past treas. Maumee Valley Country Day Sch.; past trustee, v.p., treas. Temple B'nai Israel, 1984-88; mem. nat. alumni coun. Ohio State U. Coll. Law. Fellow Internat. Soc. Barristers; mem. Am. Bd. Trial Advocates, Ohio Bar Assn., Toledo Bar Assn., Ohio Trial Lawyers Assn., Million Dollar Advocates Forum, Toledo Club, Inverness Country Club, Zeta Beta Tau, Phi Delta Phi. State civil litigation, Product liability, Professional liability. Home: 2579 Olde Brookside Rd Toledo OH 43615-2233 Office: Barkan & Robon Ltd 1701 Woodlands Dr Maumee OH 43537-4092

TWARDY, STANLEY ALBERT, JR., lawyer; b. Trenton, N.J., Sept. 13, 1951; s. Stanley Albert Twardy and Dorothy M. Stonaker. BS with honors, Trinity Coll., 1973; JD, U. Va., 1976; LLM, Georgetown U., 1980. Bar: Conn. 1976, D.C. 1978, U.S. Supreme Ct. 1979, U.S. Ct. Appeals (2d cir.) 1984. Assoc. Whitman & Ransom, Greenwich, Conn., 1976-77; counsel com. on small bus. U.S. Senate, 1977-79, counsel to Senator Lowell Weicker Jr., 1979-80; ptnr. Silver, Golub & Sandak, Stamford, Conn., 1980-85; U.S. atty. Dist. of Conn., 1985-91; chief of staff Office of Gov. Lowell Weicker, Conn., 1991-93; ptnr. Day, Berry & Howard, Stamford, Conn., 1993—. Mem. nat. alumni exec. com. Trinity Coll., 1985—90, mem. athletic adv. com., 1992—, bd. dir.; chmn. City of Stamford Police Chief Selection Panel, 1993—94; mem. area adv. com. U. Conn. at Stamford, 1993—96; mem. strategic planning mgmt. com. U. Conn., 1993—95; bd. dirs. Drugs Don't Work!, 1989—93, 1994—2000, chmn. program com., 1989—91; bd. dirs. Rehab. Ctr., 1995—2002, Stamford Health Found., 1995—. Mem.: ABA, Conn. Trial Lawyers Assn., Assn. Trial Lawyers Am., Conn. Bar Assn., Phi Beta Kappa. Federal civil litigation, Constitutional, Criminal. E-mail: satwardy@dbh.com.

TWEEDIE, DAVID ALLISON OSBORNE, lawyer; b. Batu Gajah, Malaysia, Sept. 15, 1941; arrived in U.K., 1946; s. Dr. David Reid and Ruth Valentine Mary (Osborne) T.; m. Mary Elizabeth Maud Brewis, Oct. 24, 1970; children: Jeannie Anne Cecilia, Katherine Grace. MA in Modern History, New Coll. Oxford U., 1963; JD, Coll. of Law, London, 1967. Solicitor Supreme Ct. England, 1968. Ptnr. Gregory Rowcliffe & Milners, London, 1969-95; chmn. David Tweedie Assocs., 1995—. Cons. Gregory Rowcliffe & Milners, 1995-2000, Varies Ltd., Wroxeter; external rsch. assoc. Ctr. for Def. and Internat. Strategic Studies Lancaster U., 1995—. Contbr. articles to profl. jours. Councillor London Borough of Hammersmith and Fulham, 1982-86; active London Fire and Civil Def. Authority, 1985; trustee Burdett Coutts & Townshend Found. Sch., 1990—, Inst. for Study English Prints, 1996, Hoghton Tower Shakespeare Ctr., 1999; gov. Inst. Optimum Nutrition, 1998. Fellow Royal Soc. Arts, London, 1995. Mem. ABA, Internat. Bar Assn. Avocations: golf, tennis, modern history. Probate (including wills, trusts), Non-profit and tax-exempt organizations. Home and Office: Darnley House 31 Oxberry Av London SW6 5SP England E-mail: dtweedie41@aol.com.

TWIETMEYER, DON HENRY, lawyer; b. Rochester, N.Y., June 4, 1954; s. Frederick Herman and Norma Frances (Porter) T.; m. Victoria Lynne Engleman, July 1, 1989; children: Laura Elizabeth, Jill Ann Magoon, Anthony R. Cafarelli. BA in Polit. Sci., Econs. with honors, SUNY, Buffalo, 1976; JD, Union U., 1979; LLM in Taxation, U. Miami, 1980; MBA in Acctg., Rochester Inst. Tech., 1983. Bar: N.Y. 1980, Fla. 1980, U.S. Dist. Ct. (we. dist.) N.Y. 1980, U.S. Dist. Ct. (so. dist.) Fla. 1980, U.S. Tax Ct. 1980, U.S. Ct. Appeals (5th and 11th cirs.) 1981, U.S. Supreme Ct. 1994, U.S. Bankruptcy Ct. 1994; CPA, N.Y. Tax acct. Davie, Kaplan & Braverman, Rochester, 1980-82; assoc. DeHond-Stowe Law Office, Rochester, 1982-84, Lacy, Katzen, Ryen & Mittleman, Rochester, 1984-87; mng. atty. DeHond Law Office, Rochester, 1987-91, prin., 1991-92; assoc. Fix, Spindelman, Brovitz, Turk, Himelein & Shukoff, Rochester, 1992-98; of counsel Hiscock & Barclay, LLP, Rochester, 1998—. Lectr. estate and gift taxes Found. Acctg. Edn., 1987-96. Author: Review and Update for Experienced Practitioners: Fiduciary, Estate and Gift Taxation, 1987-96. V.p. coun. Hope Luth. Ch., 1989-91, active meml. fund com., 1990-91, chmn. bldg. use com., 1990-91; chmn. missions and social concerns com. Bethlehem Luth. Ch., 1992-2000, mem. ch. coun., 1993-95, pres. ch. coun., 1994-95, deacon, 1994-95; mem. orgn. com. Luth. Charities Rochester Region, 1993-95, pres., dir., 1995-2000, adv. bd. dirs., 2000—; dir. Prevention Ptnrs., Inc., 1997-03, pres., 2000-03, fin. com., 1997-03; mem. planned and deferred giving com. The Genesee Hosp. Found., 1998-2000; bd. dirs. Rochester Gen. Hosp. Found., 2003—, planned giving com., 2001—, com. chair, 2003—. Mem. ABA (tax sect., entertainment and sports industries forum) Fla. Bar Assn. (tax sect., out of state practitioners divsn., real property, probate and trust sect.), N.Y. State Bar Assn. (tax sect., entertainment and sports law sect, trusts and estates sect.), Monroe County Bar Assn. (tax sect. and trusts and estates sect., exec. coun. 1996-2003, sec. 2000-01, chair 2001-02, elder law com., intellectual property law com.), N.Y. State Soc. CPAs (relations with the legal cmty. com. 2003—), Am. Assn. Atty.-CPAs (mem. rels. with the legal cmty. com. 2003—), Estate Planning Coun. Rochester (exec. coun. 2000-03), Rotary (internat. svc. com. 1994-2002, Rotary Internat. Found. com. 1994-2002, chair com. 1996-2002, Rochester Rotary Golf Tournament com. 1995-2000, planned giving com. 1997—, com. co-chair 2003—, dist. conf. com. 2002-03), Phi Beta Kappa, Phi Alpha Delta, Omicron Delta Epsilon, Phi Eta Sima. Republican. Lutheran. Avocations: golf, tennis, skiing, philately. Entertainment, Estate planning, Taxation, general. Office: 2000 HSBC Plz Rochester NY 14604 Fax: 585-325-5458. E-mail: dtwietmeyer@hiscockbarclay.com.

TWILLEY, JOSHUA MARION, lawyer; b. Dover, Del., Mar. 23, 1928; s. Joshua Marion and Alice Hunn (Dunn) T.; m. Rebecca Jane Buchanan, Dec. 27, 1952; children: Stephanie, Jeffrey, Linda Edgar, Joshua; m. Rosemary Miller, Dec. 1, 1972. BA cum laude, Harvard U., 1950, JD, 1953. Bar: Del. 1953, U.S. Dist. Ct. Del. 1960, U.S. Supreme Ct. 1976. Pvt. practice, Dover, 1955-72; sr. ptnr. Twilley, Jones & Feliceangeli, Dover, 1972-88, Twilley, Street & Braverman, Dover, 1988-95, Twilley & Street, Dover, 1995—. Pres. Del. Indsl. Enterprises, Inc.; chmn. Incorporating Svcs. Ltd., Del. Incorporating Svcs. Ltd.; bd. dirs. 1st Nat. Bank Wyo.; sec. Sunshine Builders, Inc. mem. Del. Pub. Svc. Commn., 1975—, vice chmn. 1995—; pres. Kent County Levy Ct., 1970-75. Mem. exec. com. Del. Dem. Com., 1970-93; pres. Elizabeth Murphey Sch., 1957—. With U.S. Army, 1953-55. Mem ABA, Del. Bar Assn., Kent County Bar Assn. Democrat. Lutheran. Avocations: gardening, landscape architecture. Banking, Probate (including wills, trusts), Property, real (including real estate development, water). Home: 124 Meadow Glen Dr Dover DE 19901-5544 Office: 426 S State St Dover DE 19901-6724 E-mail: rtwilley@erols.com.

TWISS, ROBERT MANNING, prosecutor; b. Worcester, Mass., Aug. 2, 1948; s. Robert Sullivan Jr. and Marion (Manning) T.; m. Joan Marie Callahan, Aug. 4, 1979. BA, U. Mass., 1970; JD, U. San Francisco, 1975; MA in Criminal Justice, Wichita State U., 1979; LLM, Georgetown U., 1981. Bar: Mass. 1976, Calif., 1988, U.S. Ct. Appeals Armed Forces 1976, U.S. Dist. Ct. Mass. 1976, U.S. Ct. Appeals (1st cir.) 1976, U.S. Ct. Appeals (5th cir.) 1986, U.S. Ct. Appeals (9th cir.) 1988, U.S. Dist. Ct. (ea. and cen. dist.) Calif. 1989. Atty. office chief counsel IRS, Washington, 1980-86; trial atty. criminal div. U.S. Dept. Justice, Washington, 1986-87, asst. U.S. atty. Sacramento, 1987-93, 94—, chief organized crime and narcotics, 1991-92, 1st asst. U.S. atty., 1992-93, U.S. atty., 1993, exec. assst. U.S. atty., 1994, sr. litigation counsel, 2002—. Vis. prof. U. Calf. Law Sch., 2001—02; prof. The JAG Sch., 1998—. Contbr. articles to profl. jours. Capt. JAGC U.S. Army, 1980—85, mil. judge USAR, 1981—85, major JA USAR, 1998—. Named to McAuliffe Honor Soc. U. San Francisco, 1975; recipient Markham award Office Chief Counsel IRS, Washington, 1985. Avocation: athletics. Office: Office US Atty 501 I St 10th Fl Sacramento CA 95814-7306

TWITCHELL, E(RVIN) EUGENE, lawyer; b. Salt Lake City, Mar. 4, 1932; s. Irvin A. and E. Alberta (Davis) T.; m. Joyce A. Newey, Aug. 9, 1957 (div. May 1989); children: Robert R., Lauren E., David J., Michael S.; m. Linda Sue Wilson, 1991; children: Bonnie Wilson, Jimmy Wilson, Benjamin Wilson, Stefanie Wilson. Student, Brigham Young U., 1954-55; BA, Calif. State U., Long Beach, 1959; JD, UCLA, 1966. Bar: Mich. 1977, U.S. Dist. Ct. (ea. dist.) Mich., U.S. Supreme Ct. 1987. Contract adminstr. Rockwell No. Am. Aviation, Seal Beach, Calif., 1966-68; sr. contracts adminstr. McDonnell Douglas Corp., Long Beach, Calif., 1968-73; in-house counsel Albert C. Martin & Assocs., L.A., 1973-77; instr. bus. law Golden West Coll., Huntington Beach, 1973-74; corp. counsel, corp. sec. Barton Malow Co., Southfield, Mich., 1977-97, ret., 1997. Mem. Detroit EEO Forum, 1983-87; arbitrating and cons., 1997—. Editl. cartoonist Eufaula Tribune, 2001—; host (local TV show) Who's Who in Eufaula, 2002—. Pres. Corona (Calif.) Musical Theater, 1975-76; dist. chmn. Boy Scouts of Am.-North Trails, Oakland County, Mich., 1978-80; treas. Barton Malow PAC, Southfield, 1983-97. Sgt. USAF, 1950-52. Mem. ABA, Mich. Bar Assn., Am. Arbitration Assn. (arbitrator Detroit, Ala., Ga., and Fla. areas 1985-97, arbitrator Ala.-Ga. area 1997—), Am. Corp. Counsel Assn. (v.p., dir. 1983-97). Republican. Mem. Lds Ch. Avocations: cartooning, painting, Karate, music, theatre, writing. Alternative dispute resolution, Construction, Labor (including EEOC, Fair Labor Standards Act, labor-management relations, NLRB, OSHA). Home and Office: PO Box 747 Eufaula AL 36072-0747 Office Fax: 334-616-0014. E-mail: eetwitchell@earthlink.net.

TWOMEY, THOMAS A., JR., lawyer, educator; b. N.Y.C., Dec. 8, 1945; s. Thomas A. and Mary (Maloney) T.; m. Judith Hope Twomey, Dec. 15, 1979; stepchildren: Erling Hope, Nisse Hope. BA, Manhattan Coll., 1967; postgrad., U.Va., 1967-68; JD, Columbia U., 1970. Bar: N.Y. 1972, U.S. Tax Ct. 1974. Asst. town atty. Town of Southampton N.Y., 1973-74; spl. asst. dist. atty. Suffolk County, N.Y., 1973-74; pvt. practice law Riverhead, N.Y., 1974-75; ptnr. Hubbard & Twomey, Riverhead, 1976-79, Twomey, Latham, Shea & Kelley, Riverhead, 1980—. Chair N.Y. State East End Econ. and Environ. Task Force, 1993; mem. deans coun. Stonybrook Sch. Medicine, 1991—; adj. prof. environ. law Southampton Coll., 1977-78. Bd. dirs. East End Arts Coun., Riverhead, 1983, Guild Hall East Hampton, 1993—; bd. dirs. East Hampton Libr., 1994—, pres., 1998—; trustee L.I. Power Authority, 1989-94; town historian, Town of East Hampton, 1999, vice chair East Hampton Town 350th Anniversary com., 1998, editor East Hampton Histor. Collection; historian N.Y. State Dem. Com., 2000-01; chair East Hampton 350th lecture series, 1998. Recipient Environ. award, U.S. EPA, 1980, Citizen of Yr. award L.I. Farm Bur., 2002. Mem. ABA, Suffolk County Bar Assn., State Energy Coun., N.Y. State Fresh Water Wetlands Appeals Bd. Democrat. General practice, Estate planning, Land use and zoning (including planning). Home: #9 Two Holes of Water Rd East Hampton NY 11937

TYACK, THOMAS MICHAEL, lawyer; b. Columbus, Ohio, June 20, 1940; s. George E. and E. Naomi (Ballard) T.; m. Patricia J. Clark, Sept. 7, 1969; children: Jonathan, Jeffrey, James, Justin. BA cum laude, Ohio State U., Columbus, 1962, Jd, 1965. Bar: Ohio 1965, U.S. Ct. Appeals (6th cir.) 1970, U.S. Supreme Ct. 1970, U.S. Dist. Ct. (so. dist.) Ohio 1972. Ptnr. Tyack, Scott & Colley, Columbus, 1965-79, Tyack Scott & Wiseman, Columbus, 1979-81; prin. Thomas M. Tyack Assocs. Co., L.P.A., Columbus, 1981-90; ptnr. Tyack & Blackmore Co., L.P.A., Columbus, 1991-94; pres. Tyack, Blackmore & Liston Co. LPA, Columbus, 1994—. Bar examiner Ohio supreme Ct., 1975-80; lectr., legal asst. program Capitol U., Ohio, 1977-90. Fellow Am. Coll. Trial Lawyers; mem. ABA, Ohio Bar Assn., Columbus Bar Assn., Franklin Ct. and Trial Lawyers, Assn. Trial Lawyers Am., Ohio Acad. Trial Lawyers, Ohio Acad. Trial Lawyers, Ohio Acad. Criminal Def. Lawyers, NDCDL. Republican. Methodist. Criminal, Family and matrimonial, Personal injury (including property damage). Office: 536 S High St Columbus OH 43215-5605

TYDINGCO-GATEWOOD, FRANCES MARIE, judge; b. Oahu, Hawaii, Jan. 21, 1958; d. Daniel J. and Francesca S. Tydingco; m. Robert Gatewood; children: Daniel Gatewood, Michael Gatewood, Stephen Gatewood. BA in Polit. Sci., Marquette U., 1980; JD, U. Mo., Kansas City, 1983. Law clk. to Hon. Forest W. Hanna Jackson County Cir. Ct., Kansas City, 1983—84; asst. atty. gen. Govt. of Guam, 1984—88, chief prosecutor, 1990—94; asst. prosecutor Jackson County Prosecutor's Office, Mo., 1988—90; trial judge Superior Ct. Guam, 1994—2002; assoc. judge Supreme Ct. Guam, 2002—. Profl. Tech. scholar, Govt. of Guam. Office: Supreme Ct Guam Guam Jud Ctr Ste 300 120 W O'Brien Dr Hagatna GU 96910 Home: 222 Chalan Santo Papa Ste 222 Hagatna GU 96910 Office Fax: 671-475-3164. Business E-Mail: ftgate@guamsupremecourt.com.

TYGRETT, HOWARD VOLNEY, JR., judge, lawyer; b. Lake Charles, La., Jan. 12, 1940; s. Howard Volney and Hazel (Wheeler) T.; m. Linda Lee; children: Carroll Diane, Howard V. III. BA, Williams Coll., 1961; LLB, So. Methodist U., 1964. Bar: Tex. 1964. Gen. atty. SEC, 1964-65; law clk. to chief judge U.S. Dist. Ct. No. Dist. Tex., 1965-67; ptnr. Tygrett & Walker and predecessors, Dallas, 1968-98; state dist. judge, 86th dist. Kaufman County, Tex., 2003—. Bd. dirs. Routh St. Center, 1976-83, Theatre Three, 1974-75, Shakespeare Festival, 1978-81, Suicide and Crisis Ctr., 1983-8; chmn. Terrell Hist. Preservation Commn., 2000-2003. Mem. Tex. Bar Assn., Civitan (lt. gov. Tex. dist. 1976-77, gov. 1979-80), Terrell Heritage Soc. (v.p. 1999—), Delta Phi, Delta Theta Phi. Episcopalian. Home: 505 Pacific Ave Terrell TX 75160-2073 Office: Kaufman County Courthouse 100 W Mulberry Kaufman TX 75142

TYLER, BRIAN JOSEPH, lawyer; b. Hanover, Pa., Mar. 22, 1966; s. Joseph Glenn and Rose Marie (Neiderer) T. BA, Gettysburg U., 1991; JD, Widener U., 1996. Dep. clk. U.S. Bankruptcy Ct., Harrisburg, Pa., 1991-92; program adminstr. Chpt. 13 Trustee Office, Harrisburg, 1992-96; ptnr. Purcell, Krug & Haller, Harrisburg, 1996—. Lectr., faculty Pa. Bar Inst., Mechanicsburg, 1997-2001; mediator U.S. Bankruptcy Ct., Harrisburg, 1998. Bd. dirs. Harrisburg Cmty. Theatre, 1997-2001, chmn. bd., 2001-02. With USAF, 1984-88. Mem. Pa. Bankruptcy Bar Assn., Leadership Harrisburg Area. Bankruptcy, Commercial, consumer (including collections, credit), Private international. Office: Purcell Krug & Haller 1719 N Front St Harrisburg PA 17102-2392 E-mail: btyler@pkh.com.

TYLER, JOHN EDWARD, III, lawyer; b. Kansas City, Mo. BA, U. Notre Dame, 1986, JD, 1989. From assoc. to ptnr. Lathrop & Gage L.C., Kansas City, 1989-99; sr. v.p., gen. counsel, sec. Ewing Marion Kauffman Found., Kansas City, 1999—. Adj. prof. Rockhurst U., Kansas City, 2000—. Contbr. articles to profl. jours. Pres. Genesis Sch., Kansas City, 1995-96, 96-97; pres. Archbishop O'Hara H.S., Kansas City, 1994-95, 95-96, 96-97, bd. dirs.; pres. Sch. Bd. for Diocese of Kansas City-St. Joseph, 2003-; chair tax increment fin. commn. city of Raytown, Mo., 1997-99; bd. dirs. Ctr. for Mgmt. Assistance, Kansas City, pres., 1999-01. Named Man of Yr. Leukemia Soc., Kansas City, 1998, Bernie Hoffman award for cmty. svc. Cmty. Svc. Awards Found., 1997. Mem. ABA, Mo. Bar Assn. (Thomas D. Cochran award for cmty. svc. 1995), Kans. Bar Assn., Kansas City Metro. Bar Assn. (young lawyer of yr. 1998). Non-profit and tax-exempt organizations, Labor (including EEOC, Fair Labor Standards Act, labor-management relations, NLRB, OSHA), Trademark and copyright. Home: 2420 SW Wintercreek Ct Lees Summit MO 64081-4085 Office: Ewing Marion Kauffman Found 4801 Rockhill Rd Kansas City MO 64110-2046

TYLER, LLOYD JOHN, retired lawyer; b. Aurora, Ill., May 28, 1924; s. Lloyd J. and Dorothy M. (Curtis) T.; m. Inez Chappell Busener, Feb. 25, 1970; children by previous marriage: Barbara Tyler Miller, John R., Benjamin C., Robert B., Amy C. Tomas. BA, Beloit Coll., 1948; JD, U. Mich., 1951. Bar: Ill., Mich. bars 1951. Mem. firm Sears, Streit, Tyler and Dreyer and (predecessors), Aurora, Ill., 1951-62, Tyler and Hughes (P.A.), Aurora, 1962-99; ret. Lectr., speaker on profl. subjects, 1964— Contbr. chpts. to profl. books, articles to profl. jours. Democratic precinct committeeman, 1954-59; mem. Batavia (Ill.) Sch. Bd., 1959-62. Served with USAAF, 1943-46. Fellow Am. Bar Found.; mem. Am. Bar Assn. (Ho. of Dels. 1975-79), Ill. Bar Assn. (gov. 1970-78, pres. 1978-79, chmn. legislative com. 1980, task force on alternative forms of legal service 1981-82, long range planning com. 1982-88, fed. judiciary appointment com. 1984-90, spl. com. on merit selection 1987—), Ill. Bar Found. (pres. 1972-75), Ill. Inst. Continuing Legal Edn. (dir. 1971-75, 77-79), Ill. Lawyers Polit. Action Com. (trustee 1982— , chmn. 1987-88), Soc. Trial Lawyers Ill., Appellate Lawyers Assn., Phi Beta Kappa, Omicron Delta Kappa. Presbyterian. Home: 701 Fargo Blvd Geneva IL 60134-3227

TYMKOVICH, TIMOTHY, judge; b. Denver, Co., 1956; BA, Co. Coll., 1979; JD, Univ. of Co. Sch. of Law, 1982. Clk. Co. Supreme Ct., 1982—83; assoc. Davis, Graham, & Stubbs, 1983—89; of Counsel Bradley Campbel Carney & Madsen, 1990—91; solicitor gen. Office of the Co. Atty. Gen., 1991—96; ptnr. Hale Hackstaff Tymkovich & ErkenBrack, 1996—2003; US Supreme Ct. Judge 10th Circuit Ct. of Appeals, 2003—. Office: Byron White US Courthouse 1823 Stout St Denver CO 80257*

TYNEL, ANDRZEJ, lawyer; b. Warsaw, Nov. 18, 1937; s. Henryk and Maria (Kepinska) T.; married; two children. LLM, Jagiellonian U., 1962; LLD, Warsaw U., 1968. Legal advisor Polinex-Cekop, Warsaw, 1964-85, Agros, Warsaw, Poland, 1967-74, Polcoop, Warsaw, 1974-77; of counsel The Pres. of Polish Aippi Group, Warsaw, 1978-85; legal advisor Electrim, Warsaw, 1991-93. Arbitrator Internat. Arbitration Ct., Minsk, 1995, Moscow, 1996, Vilnins, 1997, Vienna, Austria, 1997, Prague, 1997; v.p. arbitration ct. Polish C. of C., Warsaw, 1978-85, 96-98; cons. in field. Mem. Internat. Law Assn., Polish Arbitration Assn. (pres. 1998). Democrat. Avocations: tennis, skiing, hunting. Home: Cypryjska 47 02-750 Warsaw Poland

TYNES, DOUGLAS LAMONT, lawyer; b. Poplarville, Miss., Dec. 14, 1943; s. Magnus Omar and Myrtle (Sones) T.; m. Mary Savan Wilby (div. July 1975); children: Christina Gustin, William Randall Tynes, Douglas L. Tynes, Jr.; m. Patricia Charlene Tynes; 1 child, Madison Claire; m. Kathleen Soyars (div. Apr. 1998). BS, U. So. Miss., 1966; JD, U. Miss., 1969. Bar: Miss. 1969, U.S. Dist. Ct. (no. dist.) Miss. 1969, U.S. Dist. Ct. (so. dist.) Miss. 1983, U.S. Ct. Appeals (5th cir.) 1983, U.S. Supreme Ct. 1972. Pvt. practice, Pascagoula, Miss., 1969—. Mem. Miss. Trial Lawyers Assn., Miss. Bar Assn., Miss. Bankruptcy Conf., Jackson County Bar Assn., Elks, Singing River Yacht Club, Delta Theta Pi. Episcopalian. Avocations: hunting, fishing, boating. Bankruptcy, Commercial, consumer (including collections, credit), General practice. Office: PO Box Drawer 966 525 Krebs Ave Pascagoula MS 39567-3123

UDALL, CALVIN HUNT, lawyer; b. St. Johns, Ariz., Oct. 23, 1923; s. Grover C. and Dora (Sherwood) U.; m. Doris Fuss, Dec. 11, 1943; children: Fredric, Margaret Udall Moses, Julie (Mrs. Blair M. Nash), Lucinda Udall Romney, Tina Udall Rodriguez. LL.B., U. Ariz., 1948. Bar: Ariz. 1948. Ptnr. Fennemore Craig, 1953—. Ariz. spl. counsel Arizona v. California, 1954-62; mem. Coun. on Legal Edn. Opportunity, 1983-93. Mem. cast, Phoenix Mus. Theatre, 1959-65. Fellow Am. Coll. Trial Lawyers, Am. Bar Found. (bd. dirs. 1986-89, fellows chmn. 1988-89), Ariz. Bar Found. (Disting. Svc. award 1993); mem. ABA (ho. dels. 1962-92, bd. govs. 1981-84, exec. com. 1983-84, chmn. task force on minorities 1984-86), Maricopa County Bar Assn. (pres. 1957, Disting. Pub. Svc. award 1986), State Bar Ariz. (bd. govs. 1960-65), Ariz. Law Coll. Assn. (bd. dirs. 1967-80, pres. 1978-79, U. Ariz. Disting. Citizen award 1984, bd. visitors 1991—). General civil litigation, General practice, Property, real (including real estate development, water). Office: Fennemore Craig 3003 N Central Ave Ste 2600 Phoenix AZ 85012-2913

UDALL, THOMAS (TOM UDALL), congressman; b. Tucson, May 18, 1948; s. Stewart and Lee Udall; m. Jill Z. Cooper; 1 child, Amanda Cooper. BA, Prescott Coll., 1970; LLB, Cambridge U., Eng., 1975; JD, U. N.Mex., 1977. Law clk. to Hon. Oliver Seth U.S. Ct. Appeals (10th cir.), Santa Fe, 1977-78; asst. U.S. atty. U.S. Atty.'s Office, 1978-81; pvt. practice Santa Fe, 1981-83; chief counsel N.Mex. Health & Environ. Dept., 1983-84; ptnr. Miller, Stratvert, Togerson & Schlenker, P.A., Albuquerque, 1985-90; atty. gen. State of N.Mex., 1991-98; mem. 106th Congress from NM 3rd dist., 1999—, mem. small bus. com., mem. resources com., mem. vets.' affairs com. Past pres. Rio Chama Preservation Trust; mem. N.Mex. Environ. Improvement Bd., 1986—87; bd. dirs. La Compania de Teatro de Albuquerque, Santa Fe Chamber Music Festival, Law Fund. Mem. Nat. Assn. Attys. Gen. (pres. 1996), Kiwanis. Democrat. Office: US Ho Reps 1414 Longworth HOB Washington DC 20515-0001

UDASHEN, ROBERT NATHAN, lawyer; b. Amarillo, Tex., June 10, 1953; s. Leo Joe and Esther K. (Klugsberg) U. BA with high honors, U. Tex., 1974, JD, 1977. Bar: Tex. 1977, U.S. Ct. Appeals (5th cir.) 1978, U.S. Dist. Ct. (no. and so. dists.) Tex. 1978, U.S. Ct. Appeals (11th cir.) 1981, U.S. Supreme Ct. 1981, U.S. Dist. Ct. (ea. dist.) Tex. 1989, U.S. Dist. Ct. (we. dist.) Tex. 1991, U.S. Dist. Ct. (ea. and we. dists.) Ark. 2000, U.S. Ct. Appeals (8th cir.) 2002. Staff atty. Staff Counsel for Inmates, Huntsville, Tex., 1977-79; assoc., ptnr. Crowder, Mattox & Udashen, Dallas, 1979-85; ptnr. Udashen & Goldstucker, Dallas, 1985-87; pvt. practice, 1987-94; ptnr. Milner, Lobel, Goranson, Sorrels, Udashen & Wells, Dallas, 1995-2000, Milner, Goranson, Sorrels, Udashen & Wells, Dallas, 2000—02, Sorrels & Udashen, Dallas, 2002—. Bd. dirs. Open, Inc., Dallas; instr. trial advocacy Sch. Law So. Meth. U., 1993-95; adj. prof. criminal procedure Sch. Law So. Meth. U., 1998-99, 2001-03. Contbr. articles to profl. jours. Adv. bd. Coalition for Safer Dallas, 1994. Mem. State Bar Tex. (penal code com. 1992-93), Nat. Assn. Criminal Def. Lawyers, Tex. Criminal Def. Lawyers Assn., Dallas Criminal Def. Lawyers Assn. Criminal. Office: Sorrels & Udashen 2301 Cedar Springs Rd Ste 400 Dallas TX 75201 E-mail: rnu@sorrelsudashen.com.

UFBERG, MURRAY, lawyer; b. Danville, Pa., July 30, 1943; s. Alfred Eugene and Leah (Abrams) U.; m. Margery Ann Fishman, June 29, 1969; children: Aaron, Joshua, Rachel. BA, Bucknell U., 1964; JD, Duquesne U., 1968. Bar: Pa. 1969, U.s. Dist. Ct. (mid. dist.) Pa. Assoc. Rosenn, Jenkins & Greenwald, Wilkes-Barre, Pa., 1969—74; ptnr. Rosenn, Jenkins & Greenwald, L.L.P., Wilkes-Barre, 1974—. Chair Greater Wilkes-Barre Partnership, Inc., 2000—02, bd. dirs., 2000—02, WVIA TV/FM/HDTV; mem. Commonwealth of Pa. Ind. Regulatory Rev. Commn., 2003—; mem. exec. com., Transition Team Gov.-elect Edward G. Rendell, 2002—03. Chmn. United Way Wyoming Valley Gen. Campaign, Wilkes-Barre, 1990, bd. dirs., 1992—99; mem. Luzerne County adv. com. Pa. Economy League; mem. pres. adv. coun. Keystone Coll.; mem. exec. com. transition team Gov.-elect Edward G. Rendell, 2002—03; past pres. Ohav Zedek Synagogue, Wilkes-Barre, 1986—88, Jewish Cmty. Ctr. Wyoming Valley, 1982—83, Seligman J. Strauss lodge B'nai B'rith, Wilkes-Barre, 1970—74; chmn. Jewish Cmty. Bd. of Wyoming Valley, 1997—; pres. Jewish Fedn. Greater Wilkes-Barre; trustee United Hebrew Inst.; bd. dirs., chmn. cmty. rels. coun. Jewish Cmty. Bd., 1993—97, 2000; trustee Coll. Misericordia. Recipient Disting. Svc. award Wilkes-Barre Jaycees, 1979, Cmty. Svc. award, Seligman J. Strauss Lodge No. 139 of B'nai B'rith, 2003. Mem. ABA, Pa. Bar Assn., Luzerne County Bar Assn. (chmn. cmty. rels. com. 1997—), Wilkes-Barre Law and Libr. Assn., Duquesne U. Law Alumni Assn. (bd. govs.). Jewish. Avocations: sports, recreational reading. Commercial, contracts (including sales of goods; commercial financing), Corporate, general, Property, real (including real estate development, water). Home: 644 Charles Ave Kingston PA 18704 Office: Rosenn Jenkins & Greenwald LLP 15 S Franklin St Wilkes Barre PA 18711-0075 also: 120 E Broad St Hazleton PA 18201 also: 120 Wyoming Ave Scranton PA 18503 E-mail: mufberg@rjglaw.com.

UFLAND, RICHARD MARK, lawyer; b. London, May 4, 1957; s. Bertram and Shirley Ufland; m. Jane Camilla Rapaport, Oct. 20, 1985; children: James Edward Alexander, William Rupert, Olivia Lily. BA and MA, Downing Coll., Cambridge, 1978. Solicitor Stephenson Harwood, London, 1981—86, ptnr., 1986—98, Lovells Downing, 1998—. Co-author: Venture Capital Law, 1991. Mem.: Law Soc. England & Wales. Avocations: opera, bridge, skiing, walking. Mergers and acquisitions, Corporate, general, Securities. Office: Lovells Atlantic House Holborn Viaduct London EC1A 2FG England Fax: 011 44 207 276 2001. E-mail: richard.ufland@lovells.com.

UGHETTA, WILLIAM CASPER, lawyer, manufacturing company executive; b. N.Y.C., Feb. 8, 1933; s. Casper and Frieda (Bohland) U.; m. Mary L. Lusk, Aug. 10, 1957; children: William C., Robert L., Edward F., Mark R. AB, Princeton U, 1954; LLB, Harvard U., 1959. Bar: N.Y. 1959. Assoc. Shearman & Sterling, N.Y.C., 1959-67; asst. sec. Corning Glass Works, N.Y., 1968-70, sec., counsel, 1971-72, v.p., gen. counsel, 1972-82, sr. v.p., gen. counsel, 1983-98. Bd. dirs. Chemung Canal Trust Co., Covance Inc. Bd. dirs. Steuben Area coun. Boy Scouts Am.; trustee Corning C.C. Lt. (j.g.) USN, 1954-56. Mem. Assn. of Bar of City of N.Y., ABA, N.Y. State Bar Assn., Am. Corp. Counsel Assn. (trustee 1982-85), Princeton Club (N.Y.C.), Univ. Club (N.Y.C.), Corning Country Club. Corporate, general. Home: 10519 North Rd Corning NY 14830-3235

UGRINOVA, ZDRAVKA MIRKOVA, lawyer, consultant; b. Plovdiv, Bulgaria, July 20, 1973; d. Rijrko Tsvetanov Ugrinov and Kina Anastassova Ugrinova. LLM, Sofia (Bulgaria) U., 1997. Bar: Sofia. Assoc. Djingov Gouginski Kyutchukov & Velichkov, Sofia, Bulgaria, 1995—98; law clk. Sofia (Bulgaria) City Ct., 1998—99; sr. assoc. Djingov Gouginski Kyutchukov & Velichkov, 1999—. Avocations: sports, music. Corporate, general, Commercial, contracts (including sales of goods; commercial financing), Mergers and acquisitions. Office: Djingov Gouginski Kyutchukov & Velichkov 10 Tsar Osvoboditel Blvd 1000 Sofia Bulgaria Fax: +3592 980 3586. E-mail: zdvavka.ugrinova@dgkv.com.

UHL, CHRISTOPHER MARTIN, lawyer; b. Balt., Feb. 21, 1958; s. Robert Henry and Marie Antoinette (Carosella) U.; m. Gael Anna Evangelista, Feb. 16, 1991; children: Christopher Martin Uhl, Grace Molinari Uhl. BS in Acctg., Northeastern U., 1989, MBA, 1991; JD, New Eng. Sch. Law, 1992. Bar: Mass. 1993, N.Y. 1993, U.S. Dist. Ct. Mass. 1993, D.C. 1994, Maine 1994, U.S. Dist. Ct. D.C. 1994, U.S. Dist. Maine 1994, Conn. 1995, U.S. Supreme Ct., 1998, U.S. Dist. Ct. (ea. and so. dists.) N.Y. 1999, U.S. Dist. Ct. Conn. 1999, U.S. Ct. Appeals (1st cir.) 2000. Fingerprint technician FBI, Washington, 1976-79; project mgr. various constrn. cos., Balt., 1979-87, Admiral Constrn. Co., Boston, 1987-91; asst. dist. atty. Worcester (Mass.) Dist. Atty.'s Office, 1992-96; prin. Christopher Uhl, Attorney at Law, Worcester, 1997—. Prof. Becker Coll., Worcester, 1993-97. Bd. dirs. Am. Cancer Soc., Boston, 1990-96; ward coord. Reelect Dist. Atty. Campaign, Worcester, 1994; elected mem. Southborough Rep. Town Com., Southborough Housing Authority, Northborough/Southborough Regional Sch. Com. Named Hon. Mem. Rep. State Com. Republican. Roman Catholic. Roman Catholic. Office: 5 State St Worcester MA 01609-2893 Fax: (508) 797-4210. E-mail: chris@uhllaw.com.

UILKEMA, JOHN K. lawyer; BSE in Mech. Engring., U. Mich., 1957; JD, George Washington U., 1961. Bar: Calif., D.C., U.S. Patent and Trademark Office, U.S. Dist. Ct. (all dists.) Calif., U.S. Ct. Appeals (Calif.), U.S. Dist. Ct. (all dists.) D.C., U.S. Ct. Appeals (D.C.), U.S. Ct. Appeals (fed. cir.). Ptnr. Thelen Reid & Priest LLP, San Francisco. Mem.: ABA (bd. govs. sect. intellectual property 2002—). Office: Thelen Reid & Priest LLP Ste 1800 101 Second St San Francisco CA 94105

UKROPINA, JAMES R. lawyer; b. Fresno, Calif., Sept. 10, 1937; s. Robert J. and Persida (Angelich) Ukropina. AB, Stanford U., 1959, MBA, 1961; LL.B., U. So. Calif., 1965. Bar: Calif. 1966. Assoc. firm O'Melveny & Myers, Los Angeles, 1965-72, ptnr., 1972—80, 1992—2000, of counsel, 2001—; exec. v.p., gen. counsel Santa Fe Internat. Corp., Alhambra, Calif., 1980-84, dir., 1981-86; exec. v.p., gen. counsel Pacific Enterprises, Los Angeles, 1984-86, pres. and dir., 1986-89, chmn. bd. and chief exec. officer, 1989-91. Bd. dirs. Lockheed Martin Corp., Pacific Life Ins. Co., Trust Co. of the West, Ctrl. Natural Resources., Indymac Bancorp, Keck Found. Editor in chief So. Calif. Law Rev, 1964-65. Trustee Stanford U., 1991-2000 Mem. ABA, Calif. Bar Assn., Los Angeles County Bar Assn., Annandale Golf Club, Calif. Club, Beta Theta Pi. Office: O'Melveny & Myers 400 S Hope St Los Angeles CA 90071-2899

ULRICH, PAUL GRAHAM, lawyer, writer, editor; b. Spokane, Wash., Nov. 29, 1938; s. Donald Gunn and Kathryn (Vandercook) U.; m. Kathleen Nelson Smith, July 30, 1982; children: Kathleen Elizabeth Pennington, Marilee Rae McCracken, Michael Graham Ulrich. BA with high honors, U. Mont., 1961; JD, Stanford U., 1964. Bar: Calif. 1965, Ariz. 1966, U.S. Supreme Ct. 1969, U.S. Ct. Appeals (9th cir.) 1965. Law clk. judge U.S. Ct. Appeals, 9th Circuit, San Francisco, 1964-65; assoc. Lewis and Roca, Phoenix, 1965-70, ptnr., 1970-85; pres. Paul G. Ulrich P.C., Phoenix, 1985-92, Ulrich, Thompson & Kessler, P.C., Phoenix, 1992-94, Ulrich & Kessler, P.C., Phoenix, 1994-95, Ulrich, Kessler & Anger, P.C., Phoenix, 1995-2000, Ulrich & Anger, P.C., Phoenix, 2000—03, Paul G. Ulrich PC, 2003—; owner Pathway Enterprises, 1985-91. Judge pro tem divsn. 1, Ariz. Ct. Appeals, Phoenix, 1986; instr. Thunderbird Grad. Sch. Internat. Mgmt., 1968-69, Ariz. State U. Coll. Law, 1970-73, 78, Scottsdale C.C., 1975-77, also continuing legal edn. seminars. Author and pub.: Applying Management and Motivation Concepts to Law Offices, 1985; editor: Arizona Appellate Handbook, 1978-2000, Working With Legal Assistants, 1980, 81, Future Directions for Law Office Management, 1982, People in the Law Office, 1985-86; co-author, pub.: Arizona Healthcare Professional Liability Handbook, 1992, supplement, 1994, Arizona Healthcare Professional Liability Defense Manual, 1995, Arizona Healthcare Professional Liability Update Newsletter, 1992-99; co-author, editor: Federal Appellate Practice: Ninth Circuit, 1994, 2d edit., 1999, supp. 2003; contbg. editor Law Office Econs. and Mgmt., 1984-97, Life, Law and the Pursuit of Balance, 1996, 2d edit., 1997. Mem. Ariz. Supreme Ct. Task Force on Ct. Orgn. and Adminstrn., 1988-89; mem. com. on appellate cts. Ariz. Supreme Ct., 1990-91; bd. visitors Stanford U. Law Sch., 1974-77; adv. com. legal assisting program Phoenix Coll., 1985-95; atty. rep. 9th Cir. Jud. Conf., 1997-2000. With U.S. Army, 1956. Recipient continuing legal edn. award State Bar Ariz., 1978, 86, 90, Harrison Tweed spl. merit award Am. Law Inst./ABA, 1987. Fellow Ariz. Bar Found. (founding 1985—); mem. ABA (chmn. selection and utilization of staff pers. com., econs. of law sect. 1979-81, mem. standing com. legal assts. 1982-86, co-chmn. joint project on appellate handbooks 1983-85, co-chmn. fed. appellate handbook project 1985-88, chmn. com. on liaison with non-lawyers orgns. Econs. of Law Practice sect. 1985-86), Am. Acad. Appellate Lawyers, Am. Law Inst. (life), Am. Judicature Soc. (Spl. Merit citation 1987), Ariz. Bar Assn. (chmn. econs. of law practice com. 1980-81, co-chmn. lower ct. improvement com. 1982-85, co-chmn. Ariz. appellate handbook project 1976-2000), Coll. Law Practice Mgmt., Maricopa County Bar Assn. (bd. dirs. 1994-96), Calif. Bar Assn., Phi Kappa Phi, Phi Alpha Delta, Sigma Phi Epsilon. Democrat. Appellate, Federal civil litigation, State civil litigation. Home and Office: 2223 E Shea Blvd Phoenix AZ 85028 E-mail: ulrichpc@aol.com.

ULRICH, THEODORE ALBERT, lawyer; b. Spokane, Wash., Jan. 1, 1943; s. Herbert Roy and Martha (Hoffman) Ulrich; m. Nancy Allison, May 30, 1966; children: Donald Wayne, Frederick Albert. BS cum laude, U.S. Mcht. Marine Acad., 1965; JD cum laude, Fordham U., 1970; LLM, NYU, 1974. Bar: N.Y. 1971, U.S. Ct. Appeals (2nd cir.) 1971, U.S. Supreme Ct. 1974, U.S. Ct. Claims 1977, U.S. Customs Ct. 1978, U.S. Ct. Internat. Trade 1981, U.S. Ct. Appeals (5th cir.) 1988, U.S. Ct. Appeals (D.C. cir.) 1992, Colo. 1993, U.S. Ct. Appeals (10 cir.) 1994. Mng. clk. U.S. Dept. Justice, N.Y.C., 1968-69, law clk. to federal dist. judge, 1969-70; assoc. Cadwalader, Wickersham & Taft, N.Y.C., 1970—94, ptnr., 1980-94, Popham, Haik, Schnobrich & Kaufman, Ltd., Denver, 1994-96; pvt. practice law Denver, 1996—. Author: Arbitration of Construction Contracts, V, 1991; co-author: Encyclopedia of International Commercial Litigation, 1991; contbg. author: Marine Engineering Economics and Cost Analysis, 1995; author, editor Fordham Law Rev., 1969. Leader Boy Scouts Am., Nassau County, N.Y., 1984-94, Denver, 1994—. Capt. USCGR, 1965-86. Mem. ABA, Colo. Bar, Denver Bar, Maritime Law Assn., Am. Soc. Internat. Law, Soc. Naval Architects and Marine Engrs., U.S. Naval Inst., Am. Arbitration Assn. Federal civil litigation, Commercial, contracts (including sales of goods; commercial financing), Private international. Home and Office: 4300 E 6th Ave Denver CO 80220-4940 E-mail: tnulrich@gte.net.

ULTIMO, PAUL JOSEPH, lawyer; b. Bklyn., Mar. 19, 1964; s. Frank Daniel and Kathryn Linda (Spingola) U.; 1 child, Anthony Joseph. BBA, Nat. U., 1992; JD, Western State U., 1995. Bar: U.S. Dist. Ct. (ctrl. dist.) Calif. 1996. Of counsel Curd, Galindo & Smith LLP, Long Beach, Calif. Donor Dem. Party, South Orange County, Calif., 1998. Recipient Am. Jurisprudence award in constnl. law Bancroft Whitney, 1995, Am. Jurisprudence award in comml. code Bancroft Whitney, 1995. Mem. ABA, Orange County Bar Assn. Roman Catholic. Avocations: water skiing, golfing, boating, sailing. Federal civil litigation, State civil litigation, Criminal. Office: The Ultimo Bldg 301 E Ocean Blvd Ste 460 Long Beach CA 90802-4880 also: Curd Galindo & Smith LLP Shoreline Sq Tower 301 E Ocean Blvd Ste 460 Long Beach CA 90802-4880

ULVEN, MARK EDWARD, lawyer; b. Sioux City, Iowa, Mar. 23, 1954; s. Marvin Edward and Bonnie Mae Ulven; m. Kathleen Lynn Lanini, Jan. 9, 1982 (div. June 1993); m. Debra Anne Cappellino, Sept. 3, 1993; children: Alexandra, Allison, Nicholas. BS, U. S.D., 1976; MA, U. Mo., 1982; JD, Georgetown U., 1994. Bar: Pa. 1994, DC 1994. Instr. U. Mo., Columbia, 1981-82; asst. editor Texarkana (Tex.) Gazette, 1982-83; legis. asst. U.S. Ho. of Reps., Washington, 1983-86, U.S. Senate, Washington, 1986-92; legis. analyst Dorsey & Whitney, Washington, 1992-94; assoc. Jones Day Reavis & Pogue, Washington, 1994-98, Klett Rooney Lieber & Schorling, Pitts., 1998-2001, Buchanan Ingersoll, Pitts., 2001—. Adj. instr. Dusquene U., 1999—2002. Contbr. articles to profl. jours. Recipient Am. Jurisprudence award, 1994, award for editl. cartooning/illustration Va. Press Assn., 1989. Mem.: Allegheny County Bar Assn. Republican. Episcopalian. Avocation: drawing and painting. Federal civil litigation, State civil litigation, Product liability. Home: 2006 White Oak Ct Moon Township PA 15108-9050 Office: Buchanan Ingersoll One Oxford Centre Pittsburgh PA 15219 E-mail: ulvenme@bipc.com.

UMBARGER, JASON T. lawyer; b. Wichita, Kans., Dec. 24, 1974; BS in Acctg., S.W. Mo. State U., 1996; MBA, JD, U. Mo., Kansas City, 2000. Bar: Mo. 01, U.S. Dist. Ct. (we. dist.) mo. 01. Assoc. Whiteaker & Wilson, P.C., Springfield, Mo., 2000—01; asst. pub. defender Mo. Pub. Defender's Office, Springfield, 2001—02; pvt. practice Law Office of Jason T. Umbarger, Springfield, 2002—. Bd. dirs. Citizens Adv. Com. on Cmty. Devel., Springfield, 2001—02. Mem.: Springfield Met. Bar Assn., Mo. Assn. Criminal Def. Lawyers. Criminal, Family and matrimonial, Personal injury (including property damage). Office: Law Office of Jason T Umbarger 333 Park Central E Ste 408 Springfield MO 65806 Fax: 417-865-4698. E-mail: jason.umbarger@sbcglobal.com.

UMEBAYASHI, CLYDE SATORU, lawyer; b. Honolulu, Sept. 2, 1947; s. Robert S. and Dorothy C. Umebayashi; m. Cheryl J. Much, June 27, 1975. BBA in Travel Industry Mgmt., U. Hawaii, 1969, JD, 1980. Spl. dept. atty.

gen. Labor and Indsl. Rels. Appeals Bd., Honolulu, 1980-81; atty., dir., shareholder Kessner, Duca, Umebayashi, Bain & Matsunaga, Honolulu, 1981—. Commr. Hawaii Criminal Justice Commn. Bd. dirs. Wesley Found., Honolulu, 1993-97. Mem. Hawaii State Bar Assn. Personal injury (including property damage), Property, real (including real estate development, water), Workers' compensation. Office: Kessner Duca Umebayashi Bain & Matsunaga 220 S King St Fl 19 Honolulu HI 96813-4526

UMMER, JAMES WALTER, lawyer; b. Pitts., July 16, 1945; s. Walter B. and Rose P. (Gerhardt) U.; m. Janet Sue Young, Dec. 21, 1968; children: James Bradley, Benjamin F. BA, Thiel Coll., 1967; JD, Duke U., 1972. Bar: Pa. 1972. Trust officer Pitts. Nat. Bank, 1972-75; tax atty., shareholder Buchanan Ingersoll P.C., Pitts., 1975-92; prin. Hirtle, Callaghan & Co., Pitts., 1992-93; shareholder Babst, Calland, Clements and Zomnir, Pitts., 1993-99; ptnr. Reed, Smith, Shaw & McClay, Pitts., 2000—. Golf course cons., Orlando, Fla. Trustee Thiel Coll., Greenville, Pa., 1984—, The Childrens' Inst., Pitts., 1984—; mem. bd. visitors Duke U. Div. Sch., 1999—. Fellow Am. Coll. Probate Counsel; mem. Estate Planning Coun. Western Pa. (pres. 1986-87), Tax Club (Pitts.), Duquesne Club, Rolling Rock Club, Oakmont Country Club. Republican. Presbyterian. Estate planning, Probate (including wills, trusts), Taxation, general. Home: 200 Woodland Farms Rd Pittsburgh PA 15238-2024 Office: Reed Smith LLP 435 6th Ave Ste 8 Pittsburgh PA 15219-1809

UNDERBERG, MARK ALAN, lawyer; b. Niagara Falls, N.Y., July 9, 1955; s. Alan Jack and Joyce Love (Wisbaum) U.; m. Diane Englander, Mar. 22, 1986; children: Andrew Englander, James Englander. BA, Cornell U., 1977, JD, 1981. Bar: N.Y. 1981. Law clk. to chief judge U.S. Ct. Appeals (3d cir.), Wilmington, Del., 1981-82; assoc. Debevoise & Plimpton, N.Y.C., 1982-87; mng. dir., dep. gen. counsel Henley Group, Inc., N.Y.C., 1987-90, mng. dir., gen. counsel, 1990-92; v.p., gen. counsel Abex Inc., Hampton, N.H., 1992-95. V.p., gen. counsel Fisher Sci. Internat. Inc., Hampton, N.H., 1991-97, cons. 1997-98; counsel Paul, Weiss, Rifkind, Wharton & Garrison, N.Y.C., 1998-99, ptnr., 2000—. Editor-in-chief Cornell Law Rev., 1980-81. Mem. ABA, Assn. of Bar of City of N.Y., Genesee Valley Club, University Club. Corporate, general, Securities. Office: Paul Weiss Rifkind Wharton & Garrison Rm 200 1285 Avenue Of The Americas New York NY 10019-6065

UNDERWOOD, MARK FOREST, lawyer; b. Ft. Campbell, Ky., Feb. 14, 1964; s. Harry Wayne and Alicia Elkins Underwood. BBA, Marshall U., 1986; JD, Pepperdine U., 1989; grad., Nat. Inst. Trial Advocacy, 1992, Am. Trial Lawyers Ultimate Advocacy Coll., 2002; diplomate, Gerry Spence Trial Lawyers Coll., 2002. Bar: Calif. 89, W.Va. 96, D.C. 97, U.S. Ct. Appeals (4th cir.) 99. Assoc. Hagenbaugh & Murphy, L.A., 1989—92, Crosby, Healey, Roach & May, L.A., 1992—94; ptnr. Fredeking & Fredeking, Huntington, W.Va., 1994—96; pvt. practice Underwood Law Offices, Huntington, 1997—. Mem. W.Va. Ho. of Dels., Charleston, 1997—98. Recipient Frasure Singleton Legis. fellowship, W.Va. Legislature, 1985. Mem.: ATLA, Nat. Coll. DUI Defense. Democrat. Presbyterian. Personal injury (including property damage), Criminal, Civil rights. Home: 910 Fourth Ave Ste 1111 Huntington WV 25701 Office: Underwood Law Offices 910 4th Ave Huntington WV 25701 Fax: 304-522-1763. E-mail: markunderwood@markunderwood.com.

UNGARETTI, RICHARD ANTHONY, lawyer; b. Chgo., May 25, 1942; s. Dino Carl and Antoinette (Calvetti) U.; children: Joy A., Paul R. BS, DePaul U., 1964, JD, 1970. Bar: Ill. 1970, U.S. Dist. Ct. (no. dist.) Ill. 1970, U.S. Supreme Ct. 1980. Assoc. Kirkland & Ellis, Chgo., 1970-74; ptnr. Ungaretti & Harris, Chgo., 1974—. Mem. adv. coun. DePaul Coll. Law, Chgo., 1988. Mem. ABA, Chgo. Bar Assn., Ill. State Bar Assn., Internat. Coun. Shopping Ctrs., Am. Coll. Real Estate Lawyers, Justinian Soc., Urban Land Inst. (assoc.), Lamda Alpha Avocations: golf, fishing, hunting. Land use and zoning (including planning), Landlord-tenant, Property, real (including real estate development, water). Office: Ungaretti & Harris 3500 Three First Nat Plz Chicago IL 60602 E-mail: raungaretti@uhlaw.com.

UNGARO-BENAGES, URSULA MANCUSI, federal judge; b. Miami Beach, Fla., Jan. 29, 1951; d. Ludivico Mancusi-Ungaro and Ursula Berliner; m. Michael A. Benages, Mar., 1988. Student, Smith Coll., 1968-70; BA in English Lit., U. Miami, 1973; JD, U. Fla., 1975. Bar: Fla. 1975. Assoc. Frates, Floyd, Pearson et al, Miami, 1976-78, Blackwell, Walker, Gray et al, Miami, 1978-80, Finley, Kumble, Heine et al, Miami, 1980-85, Sparber, Shevin, Shapo et al, Miami, 1985-87; cir. judge State of Fla., Miami, 1987-92; U.S. dist. judge U.S. Dist. Ct., Miami, 1992—. Mem. Fla. Supreme Ct. Race & Ethnic & Racial Bias Study Commn., Fla., 1989-92, St. Thomas U. Inns of Ct., Miami, 1991-92; mem. jud. resources com. Jud. Coun. U.S.; chmn. ct. svcs. com. So. Dist. Fla., chmn. magistrate judge com. Bd. dirs. United Family & Children's Svcs., Miami, 1981-82; mem. City of Miami Task Force, 1991-92. Mem. ABA, Fed. Judges Assn., Fla. Assn. Women Lawyers, Dade County Bar Assn., Eugene Spellman Inns of Ct. U. Miami. Office: US Dist Ct 301 N Miami Ave Fl 11 Miami FL 33128-7702

UNGER, GERE NATHAN, emergency physician, lawyer; b. Monticello, N.Y., May 15, 1949; s. Jessie Aaron and Shirley (Rosenstein) Unger; m. Alice J. McGowan, July 21, 1990; children: Elijah, Breena, Ari, Sasha, Arlen. JD, Bernadean U., 1979; MD, Inst. Polytecnico, Mexico City, 1986; D Phys. Medicine, Met. U., Mexico City, 1987; postgrad., Boston U., 1993, Harvard Law Sch., 1994-96; LLM in Med. Law, U. Glasgow, 2001. Diplomate Am. Bd. Forensic Examiners, Am. Bd. Med. Legal Analysis Medicine and Surgery, Am. Bd. Forensic Medicine, Am. Bd. Risk Mgmt., Am. Bd. Disability Analysts. Med. dir. Vietnam Vets. Post-Traumatic Stress Disorder Program, 1988-90; emergency rm. physician, cons. in medicaid fraud Bronx (N.Y.)-Lebanon Hosp., 1990—; clin. legal medicine Paladin Profl. Group, P.A., Palm Beach, Fla., 1992-98; pres. Albany Law Jour. Co., Inc., 1998—; jurisconsult Office of Gere Unger, M.D., J.D., 1999—. Mem. surg. critical care com. Am. Soc. Critical Care Medicine, 1992; mem. peer rev. com. Nat. Inst. Disability and Rehab. Rsch., Office Spl. Edn., U.S. Dept. Edn., 1993; mediator, arbitrator, negotiator World Intellectual Property Orgn., 1994; mem. clin. ethics com. Inst. Medecine Legale et de Medecine Sociale, Strasbourg, France, 1994; mediator, arbitrator World Bank, 2000—. Mem. editl. bd. Am. Bd. Forensic Examiners, 1993, Jour. Neurol. and Orthopaedic Medicine and Surgery, 1993. Comdt. Broward County Marine Corps League, 1995—. With USMC, 1968—72. Fellow: Exec. Practice Mgmt., Am. Coll. Forensic Examiners, Am. Acad. Neurol. and Orthopedic Surgeons, Am. Coll. Legal Medicine, Internat. Coll. Surgeons (mem. ethics com. 1994, mem. emergency response program eastern region 1994); mem.: FBA (mem. health com., rep. ABA 1994, chmn. med. malpractice/tort com., liaison to AMA), ATLA (N.Y. state capt. 1992), ABA, Internat. Criminal Law Network (The Hague), Internat. Assn. Prosecutors, Internat. Royal Soc. Medicine (London), Nat. Assn. Forensic Econs., Am. Soc. Laser Medicine and Surgery, Kennedy Inst. Ethics, Am. Coll. Physician Execs. (chair forum law and med. mgmt. 1995), Internat. Bar Assn., Nat. Coll. Advocacy. Avocations: flying, boating. Office: 1361 Elm St Manchester NH 03101 E-mail: jurismed@justicemail.com.

UNGER, HENRY MANNING, lawyer; b. Columbia, S.C., Mar. 10, 1972; BA, U. Va., 1994; MBA, JD, U. S.C., 1998. Bar: S.C. 1998, N.C. 1998. Lawyer Kennedy Covington Lobdell & Hickman, Charlotte, NC, 1998—2001, Moore & Van Allen, Charleston, SC, 2001—. Mem.: S.C. Econ. Developers Assn., N.C. Bar Assn., S.C. Bar. Corporate, general, Banking, Mergers and acquisitions. Office: Moore & Van Allen PLLC 40 Calhoun St Ste 300 Charleston SC 29401 Office Fax: 843-579-8072.

UNGER, PETER VAN BUREN, lawyer; b. Cin., Nov. 15, 1957; s. Sherman Edward and Polly Van Buren (Taylor) U.; m. Laura Meth Simone, June 29, 1991; children: Simone Taylor, Natalie Van Buren. BA in History, Polit. Sci., Miami U., Oxford, Ohio, 1980; JD, U. Cin., 1983; LLM in Securities, Georgetown U., 1987. Bar: Ohio 1984, D.C. 1985, U.S. Supreme Ct. 1991. Law clk. chief judge U.S. Dist. Ct. (so. dist.) Fla., Ft. Lauderdale, 1983-85; atty. enforcement divsn. SEC, N.Y.C., 1986-88; assoc. Fulbright & Jaworski, Washington, 1988-89, participating assoc., 1990-94, ptnr., 1995—. Mem. ABA (bus. law sect., com. fed. regulation of securities, sub-com. on civil litigation and SEC enforcement matters 1989—, litigation sect. com. on securities litigation sub-com. on SEC enforcement practice 1990—), Securities Industry Assn. (compliance and legal divsn.), D.C. Bar Assn. (corp., fin. and securities law sect. steering com.). Securities. Home: 3308 N St NW Washington DC 20007-2807 Office: Fulbright & Jaworski LLP 801 Pennsylvania Ave NW Washington DC 20004-2615 E-mail: punger@fulbright.com.

UNGERMAN, MAYNARD I. lawyer; b. Topeka, Dec. 5, 1929; s. Irvine E. and Hanna (Friedberg) U.; divorced; children: William Charles, Karla Beth, Rebecca Diane; m. Judith White, July 16, 1982; 1 child, Gregory. BA cum laude, Stanford U., 1951, JD, 1953. Owner Maynard I Ungerman Law Offices, Tulsa, 1956—. Spl. judge temp. div. 187, Okla. Ct. Appeals, 1982. Assoc. editor Comml. Law Jour., 1985—. Inaugural committeeman Pres. Johnson, 1965; chmn. Tulsa County Dems., 1967; pres. Community Service Council, Tulsa, 1986; past. pres., bd. dirs. Neighbor for Neighbor, Tulsa; bd. dirs. Oklahomans for Indian Opportunity, Norman, 1986; bd. dirs., chmn. community relations com. Tulsa Jewish Fedn., 1986. Named Citizen of the Yr. Okla. chpt. Nat. Assn. Social Workers, 1986. Mem. ABA, Comml. Law League, Okla. Bar Assn., Tulsa County Bar Assn. Democrat. Commercial, consumer (including collections, credit), Family and matrimonial, Labor (including EEOC, Fair Labor Standards Act, labor-management relations, NLRB, OSHA). Home: 6203 S Jamestown Ave Tulsa OK 74136-1424 Office: # 200 2512 E 21st St Tulsa OK 74114-1706

UNHOLZ, STEFAN PAUL, lawyer; b. London, June 13, 1953; s. Werner Albert and Lilly Emma (Denzler) U.; m. Brigitte Rutishauser, Nov. 22, 1990. Lic., Zurich U., 1979. Bar: Zurich, 1983. Legal probationer Dist. Ct. Bulach, Bulach-Zurich, Switzerland, 1979-80, clk. ct., 1981; lawyer Winterthur, Switzerland, 1983—. Contr. numerous articles and photographs on ry. transport to mags. and books in field. Mem. Swiss Bar Assn., Zurich Bar Assn., Zurich U. Soc., Cantonal High Sch. Soc. Winterthur, Tramway Mus. Zurich. Avocations: collecting records, photography. Office: Stadthausstrasse 39 CH-8402 Winterthur Switzerland

UNIS, RICHARD L. judge; b. Portland, Oreg., June 11, 1928; BS, JD, U. Oreg. Bar: Oreg. 1954, U.S. Dist. Ct. Oreg. 1957, U.S. Ct. Appeals (9th cir.) 1960, U.S. Supreme Ct. 1965. Judge Portland Mcpl. Ct., 1968-71, Multnomah County Dist. Ct., 1972-76, presiding judge, 1972-74; former judge Oreg. Cir. Ct. 4th Judicial Dist., 1977-90; former sr. dep. city atty. City of Portland; assoc. justice Oreg. Supreme Ct., Portland, 1990-96; spl. master U.S. Dist. Ct. House, Portland, 1996—. Adj. prof. of local govt. law and evidence Lewis & Clark Coll. Northwestern Sch. Law, 1969-76, 77-96; spl. master supr. La.-Pacific Inner-Seal Siding nationwide class action litig.; faculty mem. The Nat. Judicial Coll., 1971-2000; former faculty mem. Am. Acad. Judicial Edn. Author: Procedure and Instructions in Traffic Court Cases, 1970, 101 Questions and Answers on Preliminary Hearings, 1974. Bd. dirs. Oreg. Free from Drug Abuse; mem. Oreg. Adv. Com. on Evidence Law Revision, chmn. subcom., 1974-79. Maj. USAFR, JAGC, ret. Recipient Meritorius Svc. award U. Oregon sch. Law, 1988; named Legal Citizen of Yr. Oreg. Law Related Edn., 1987; inducted into The Nat. Judicial Coll. Hall of Honor, 1988. Mem. Am. Judicature Soc. (bd. dirs. 1975, Herbert Harley Nat. award 1999), Am. Judges Assn., Multnomah Bar Found., Oregon Judicial Conf. (chmn. Oreg. Judicial Coll. 1973-80, legis. com. 1976—, exec. com. of judicial edn. com., judicial conduct com.), N.Am. Judges Assn. (tenure, selection and compensation judges com.), Dist. Ct. Judges of Oreg. (v.p., chmn. edn. com.), Nat. Conf. Spl. Ct. Judges (exec. com.), Oreg. State Bar (judicial adminstrn. com., sec. local govt. com., com. on continuing certification, uniform jury instrn. com., exec. com. criminal law sect., trial practice sect. standards and certification com., past chmn., among others), Oreg. Trial Lawyers Assn. (named Judge of Yr. 1984). Office: US Dist Ct House 1000 SW 3rd Ave Portland OR 97204-2930

UNKELBACH, L. CARY, lawyer; b. NY, July 25, 1950; d. Kurt and Evelyn (Haskell) U.; m. David W. Olmstead, Sept. 11, 1993. BA, William Smith Coll., Geneva, N.Y., 1972; JD, U. Denver, 1979. Bar: Colo. 1979, U.S. Dist. Ct. Colo. 1979, U.S. Ct. Appeals (10th cir.) 1987, U.S. Supreme Ct. 2002. Dep. dist. atty. Jefferson County Dist. Attys. Office, Golden, Colo., 1979-84; asst. atty. gen. Atty. Gen.'s Office, Denver, 1984-86; assoc. John Faught PC, Englewood, Colo., 1986-90; asst. county atty. Arapahoe County, Littleton, Colo., 1990—. V.p., bd. mem. 2nd Appletree West Condo Assn., Denver, 1985-92. Mem.: Colo. County Attys. Assn. (bd. dirs. 1997—2000). Avocations: hiking, snowshoeing, travel, photography, animals. Home: PO Box 532 Franktown CO 80116-0532 Office: Arcpahoe County Atty Office 5334 S Prince St Littleton CO 80120-1136

UNPINGCO, JOHN WALTER SABLAN, federal judge; b. 1950; BA, St. Louis U., 1972; MBA, JD, NYU, 1976; LLM, Georgetown U., 1983. Bar: Guam 1977, D.C. 1983, Calif. 1992. Atty. Ferenz, Bramhall, Williams & Gruskin, Guam, 1976-77; atty. Office Staff Judge Advocate USAF, 1977-85, civilian atty., Office Staff Judge Advocate, 1985-87; counsel U.S. Naval Air Warfare Ctr., China Lake, Calif., 1987-92; fed. judge U.S. Dist. Ct. (Guam dist.), 1992—. Part-time instr. U. Md. Far East divsn., Yokota Air Base, Tokyo, 1983-87, European divsn., RAF Mildenhall, Suffolk, U.K., 1979-82, U. Guam, 1994-99. Pres. Guam Swim League, 2000; pres. parish coun. Our Lady of Hope Parish, 2000-. Mem. ABA, State Bar Calif., Guam Bar Assn., Internat. Legal Soc. Japan, D.C. Bar Assn., NWC Community Fed. Credit Union (bd. dirs. 1991-92). Office: US Dist Ct 4th Fl US Courthouse 520 W Soledad Ave Hagatna GU 96910

UPRIGHT, KIRBY GRANT, lawyer; b. South Canaan, Pa., Sept. 12, 1946; s. Lyle Lee and Ellen May (Kirby) U.; m. Joyce Ann Keyasko, Oct. 4, 1975; children: Chad, Scott. BS, Pa. State U., 1970; JD, U. Akron, 1973; LLM in Taxation, Temple U., 1977. Bar: Pa. 1973, U.S. Dist. Ct. (mid. dist.) Pa. 1978, U.S. Ct. Appeals (3d cir.) 1981, U.S. Tax Ct. 1979; CPA, Pa. Staff acct. Peat, Marwick, Mitchell, Phila., 1973-77; assoc. Henkleman, Kreder, O'Connell & Brooks, Scranton, Pa., 1977-82; ptnr. Young, Upright, Catina & Parker, Stroudsburg, Pa., 1982—. Paralegal instr., paralegal adv. bd. Pa. State U., Worthington Scranton Campus, Dunmore, Pa., 1978-82. With U.S. Army, 1964-67, Vietnam. Fellow Am. Coll. Trust and Estate Counsel; mem. Pa. Bar Assn. (chmn. probate and trust divsn.), Jaycees (bd. dirs. Scranton chpt. 1977-79), Pa. State U. Alumni Assn., Pocono Mountain Club (Stroudsburg, pres. 1982-85), Masons, Rotary (v.p.). Estate planning, Probate (including wills, trusts), Estate taxation. Home: 53 Wyndham Hills Cresco PA 18326-0053 Office: Young Upright Catina & Parker 300 Stroud Bldg Stroudsburg PA 18360-1602 E-mail: kupright@pennlawyers.com.

UPSON, THOMAS FISHER, judge, former state senator, lawyer; b. Waterbury, Conn., Sept. 30, 1941; s. J. Warren and Grace (Fisher) U.; m. Barbara Secor (div. Jan. 1979); children: Secor, Chauncey Julius; m. Katherine Wolff, June 1, 1996. BA in History, Washington and Jefferson Coll., 1963; LLB, U. Conn., 1968; postgrad., Trinity Coll., 1969-72, Georgetown U., 1971-72. Bar: Conn., 1969, U.S. Dist. Ct. (2d dist.), 1969, U.S. Supreme Ct. 1973. Lawyer Upson & Secor, Waterbury, 1969-70, 74-76; lawyer, spl. asst. U.S. Dept. Commerce, Washington, 1970-72; lawyer, spl. asst. to adminstr. GSA, Washington, 1973-74; dir. admissions St. Margaret's McTernan Sch., Waterbury, 1977-78; with div. spl. revenue State of Conn., Hartford, 1978-82; assoc. Moynahan & Ruskin, Waterbury, 1979-81; ptnr. Upson & Daly, Waterbury, 1981-2001; mem. Conn. Senate, Hartford, 1985-2001, chmn. gen. law com., vice-chmn. jud. com., majority whip, 1985-86, asst. minority leader, 1987-88, 89-90, minority leader protempore, 1991-92, dep. minority leader, 1993-94, dep. majority leader, chmn. jud. com., 1995-96, dep., then asst. minority leader, ranking mem. jud. com., 1997-2000; judge Superior Ct. State of Conn., Hartford, 2001—. Moderator 1st Congl. Ch., Waterbury, 1986-91; bd. dirs. Easter Seals-United Way, Waterbury, 1984-88; Rep. candidate for Congress, 6th Dist. Conn., 1976; mem. Conn. Rep. Ctrl. com., 1983-91; mem. Waterbury Rep. Town Com., 1980-85; dir. Mattatuck Mus., 1993—; former dir. Waterbury Symphony Orch.; former sec. and dir. First Ch. Housing, Inc.; pres. Naugatuck Valley Devel. Corp., 1975-76. Mem. ABA, Conn. Bar Assn., Waterbury Bar Assn., SAR, Soc. Colonial Wars, Soc. of the Founders of the Hartford, Phi Gamma Delta, Univ. Club (Waterbury). Lodges: Kiwanis (former pres., lt. gov. SW New Eng. dist.), Elks. Republican. Congregationalist. Avocations: hiking, music, history. Home: 210 Southwest Rd Waterbury CT 06708-3214 Office: Danbury Jud Dist 146 White St Danbury CT 06810

URAM, GERALD ROBERT, lawyer; b. Newark, July 11, 1941; s. Arthur George and Mildred (Stein) U.; m. Melissa Gordon, May 27, 1995; children: Michael, Alison, Carolyn Gordon Lewis. BA, Dartmouth Coll., 1963; LLB, Yale U., 1967. Bar: N.Y. 1967. Assoc. Paul, Weiss, Rifkind, Wharton & Garrison, N.Y.C., 1967-74; v.p., corp. counsel Prudential Bldg. Maintenance Corp., N.Y.C., 1974; ptnr. Davis & Gilbert, N.Y.C., 1974—. Lectr. N.Y. Law Sch. Contbr. to profl. publs. Bd. dirs. St. Francis Friends of Poor, Inc. Mem. ABA, N.Y. State Bar Assn., Assn. Bar City of N.Y. Landlord-tenant, Property, real (including real estate development, water). Office: 1740 Broadway Fl 3 New York NY 10019-4315

URANGA, JEAN R. lawyer; b. West Point, N.Y., Sept. 30, 1949; BA, Western Wash. U., 1971; JD, Willamette U., 1975. Bar: Idaho 1975, U.S. Dist. Ct. Idaho 1975, U.S. Ct. Appeals (9th cir.) 1980. Atty. Uranga & Uranga, Boise, Idaho. Mem.: Idaho State Bar (continuing legal edn. com. 1987—90, discipline hearing com. 1983—86, Supreme Ct. com. on child custody mediation 1989—, bankruptcy and family law sects., bar commr. 1990—93, pres. 1992). Administrative and regulatory, Family and matrimonial. Office: Uranga and Uranga PO Box 1678 714 N Fifth St Boise ID 83701-1678*

URBAN, DONALD WAYNE, lawyer; b. Belleville, Ill., Oct. 9, 1953; s. Andrew Anthony and Eileen Marie (Tibbitt) U.; m. Mary Beth Evans, June 9, 1979 (div. Oct. 1994); m. Georgianna Dowling, Feb. 2, 1995; 1 child, Andrew Jared. BA, So. Ill. U., 1976; JD, Washington U., 1979. Assoc. Sprague & Sprague, Belleville, 1979-96; ptnr. Sprague & Urban, Belleville, 1996—. Author, lectr. Ill. Inst. for CLE, Springfield. Author: Blasting & Subsidence Illinois Institute for Continuing Legal Education Handbook, 1983, vol. 2, 1986, vol. 3, 1989. Pres. Looking Glass Playhouse, Lebanon, Ill., 1988-90, 95-97, 99-01; spokesman St. Clair County Bicentennial, Belleville, 1989. Mem. Gamma Theta Upsilon. Democrat. Avocation: community theatre. Bankruptcy, Estate planning, Personal injury (including property damage). Home: 815 Belleville St Lebanon IL 62254-1312 Office: Sprague & Urban 26 E Washington St Belleville IL 62220-2101

URBANO, JAVIER, lawyer; b. Burgos, Spain, July 25, 1967; s. Honorio Urbano and Maria Teresa Jimenez; m. Marisa Martinez Escribano, July 9, 1994; children: Carolina, Ana, Javier. Degree in Law, Instituto Catolico de Administracion de Empresas (ICADE), Madrid, 1990; LLM, Harvard U., 1992. Bar: Madrid 1992. Assoc. Garrigues Law Firm, Madrid, 1992—2000, ptnr., 2001—. Founding ptnr. La Franco Argentine SA, Vervins, France, 1990—; prof. corp. law Assn. Parael Progreso de la Direccion, Madrid, 1993—96. Contbr. articles to profl. jours. Pres. European Assn., Harvard Law Sch., 1991. Mem.: Harvard Club Spain and European Assn. Avocations: opera, literature, history of art, skiing, golf. Mergers and acquisitions, Corporate, general. Office: Garrigues Abogados Jose Abascal 45 28003 Madrid Spain

URBANSKI, STEPHEN KARL, lawyer; b. Kingston, Pa., Jan. 29, 1964; s. Edward Kamil Urbanski and Bernadine Helen Mros; m. Christine Felia, May 26, 2002. children: Patricia, Kathleen, Robert. BA, Wilkes U., 1985; JD, Temple U., 1988. Bar: Pa. 1988, N.J. 1990. Asst. pub. defender Office of Luzerne County Public Defender, Wilkes-Barre, Pa., 1989; assoc. Anapol Schwartz Weiss & Schwartz, Phila., 1990, Leonard Zack and Assoc., Phila., 1991; pvt. practice Wilkes-Barre, 1992-95; sr. ptnr. Haggerty & Urbanski, Kingston, Pa., 1995—2002, Urbanski & Urbanski, Kingston, 2002—. Lectr. Coll. Misericordia, Dallas, Pa., 1992, Marywood U., Scranton, Pa., 1992, 93. Editor (periodical) Classless Action, 1987-88; author: One Vote Can't Make a Difference, 1998. Bd. dirs. Cultural Heritage Coun., Kingston, 1993—; mem. Kingston Republican Com., 1998—; councilman Municipality of Kingston, 1998—; mem. nat. alumni bd. Wilkes U., 2000—. With U.S. Army, 1983-85. Roman Catholic/Baptist Baptist. Criminal, Family and matrimonial. Home: 82 3d Ave Kingston PA 18704-5724 Office: Urbanski & Urbanski 575 Pierce St Ste 500 Kingston PA 18704 E-mail: steveurbanski@highpointing.com.

URBINA, RICARDO MANUEL, judge; b. 1946; BA, Georgetown U., 1967, JD, 1970. Trial atty. Pub. Defender Svc. for D.C., 1970-72; prin. Urbina & Libby, Washington, 1972-73, Law Office of Ricardo M. Urbina, Washington, 1973-74; prof. law, dir. criminal justice program Howard U., Washington, 1974-81; assoc. judge D.C. Superior Ct., 1981-94; judge U.S. Dist. Ct. D.C., 1994—. Adj. prof. Antioch Sch. Law, 1976, Georgetown U. Law Ctr., Washington, 1982, George Washington U. Nat. Law Ctr., Washington, 1993—; instr. Nat. Inst. Trial Advocacy, 1976, 78; vis. instr. trial advocacy Howard Law Sch., 1996—. Recipient VIDA award lifetime recognition comty. svc.; All-Am. track and field NCAA 880 Champion, 1966; named Georgetown U. Athletic Hall of Fame. Mem. ABA, D.C. Hispanic Bar Assn., Nat. Bar Assn., Hispanic Nat. Bar Assn., Washington Bar Assn., D.C. Bar Assn., Women's Bar Assn., Fahy Inns of Ct. (emeritus), Counsellors of Washington D.C., Coun. for Ct. Excellence, Nat. Coun. La Raza, Phi Delta Phi. Office: US Dist Ct DC US Courthouse Rm 4311 333 Constitution Ave NW Washington DC 20001-2802

URBISTONDO, IGNACIO, lawyer; b. Dec. 31, 1952; JD, U. Salamanca, Spain, 1975; LLM, Columbia U., 1978. Bar: Madrid 1978. Sr. ptnr. J&A Garrigues, Madrid, 1978—. Office: Garrigues Abogados Y Asesores Tributarios 45 Jose Abascal 28003 Madrid Spain

URBOM, WARREN KEITH, federal judge; b. Atlanta, Nebr., Dec. 17, 1925; s. Clarence Andrew and Anna Myrl (Irelan) U.; m. Joyce Marie Crawford, Aug. 19, 1951; children: Kim Marie, Randall Crawford, Allison Lee, Joy Renee. AB with highest distinction, Nebr. Wesleyan U., 1950, LLD (hon.), 1984; JD with distinction, U. Mich., 1953. Bar: Nebr. 1953. Mem. firm Baylor, Evnen, Baylor, Urbom, & Curtiss, Lincoln, Nebr., 1953-70; judge U.S. Dist. Ct. Nebr., 1970—; chief judge U.S. Dist. Ct. Dist. Nebr., 1972-86, sr. judge, 1991—. Mem. com. on practice and procedure Nebr. Supreme Ct., 1965-95; mem. subcom. on fed. jurisdiction Jud. Conf. U.S., 1975-83; adj. instr. trial advocacy U. Nebr. Coll. Law, 1979-90; bd. dirs. Fed. Jud. Ctr., 1982-86; chmn. com. on orientation newly apptd. dist. judges Fed. Jud. Ctr., 1986-89; mem. 8th Cir. Com. on Model Criminal and Civil Jury Instrns., 1983—; mem. adv. com. on alternative sentences U.S. Sentencing Com., 1989-91. Contbr. articles to profl. jours. Trustee St. Paul Sch. Theology, Kansas City, Mo., 1986-89; active United Methodist Ch. (bd. mgrs., bd. global ministries 1972-76, gen. com. on status and role of women, 1988-96, gen. conf. 1972, 76, 80, 88, 92, 96, 2000); pres. Lincoln YMCA, 1965-67; bd. govs. Nebr. Wesleyan U., chmn. 1975-80. With AUS, 1944-46. Recipient Medal of Honor, Nebr. Wesleyan U. Alumni Assn., 1983. Fellow Am. Coll. Trial Lawyers; mem. ABA, Nebr. Bar Assn. (ho. of dels. 1966-70, Outstanding Legal Educator award 1990), Lincoln Bar Assn. (Liberty Bell award 1993, pres. 1968-69), Kiwanis (Disting. Svc. award 1993), Masons (33 deg.), Am. Inns of Ct. (Lewis F. Powell Jr. award for Professionalism and Ethics 1995). Methodist. Home: 4421 Ridgeview Dr Lincoln NE 68516-1516 Office: US Dist Ct 586 Fed Bldg 100 Centennial Mall N Lincoln NE 68508-3859 E-mail: urboml@aol.com.

URIE, JOHN JAMES, lawyer, retired Canadian federal judge; b. Guelph, Ont., Can., Jan. 2, 1920; s. G. Norman and Jane A. U.; m. Dorothy Elizabeth James.; children: David, Janet, Alison. B.Commerce, Queen's U.; LL.B., Osgoode Hall Law Sch. Bar: Ont. 1948. Ptnr. firm Burke-Robertson, Urie, Weller & Chadwick, Ottawa, Ont., 1948-73; judge Fed. Ct. Can., Ottawa, 1973-90; counsel Scott and Aylen, Ottawa, 1991-2000, Borden, Ladner, Gervais, Ottawa, 2000—. Gen. counsel to Joint Com. of Senate and House of Commons on Consumer Credit; chmn. planning com. First Nat. Conf. on Law, Ottawa, 1972; judge Ct. Martial Appeal Ct., 1973-90. Past pres. County of Carleton Law Assn.; past v.p. Children's Aid Soc.; past pres. Eastern Profl. Hockey League. Served with Cameron Highlanders of Ottawa Can. Army, 1942-45. Mem. Royal Can. Mil. Inst., Phi Delta Phi. Mem. United Ch. of Canada. Clubs: Cameron Highlanders of Ottawa Assoc. (Ottawa), Ottawa Hunt and Golf (Ottawa), Rideau (Ottawa). Office: Borden Ladner Gervais 100 Queen St Ottawa ON Canada K1P1J9

UROWSKY, RICHARD J. lawyer; b. N.Y.C., June 28, 1946; s. Jacob and Anne (Granick) Urowsky. BA, Yale U., 1967, JD, 1972; BPhil, Oxford U., Eng., 1970. Bar: N.Y. 1973, U.S. Dist. Ct. (so. dist.) N.Y. 1973, U.S. Ct. Appeals (2d cir.) 1973, U.S. Supreme Ct. 1977. Law clk. to Justice Reed U.S. Supreme Ct., Washington, 1972-73; assoc. Sullivan & Cromwell, N.Y.C., 1973-80, ptnr., 1980—. Mem. ABA, Assn. of the Bar of the City of N.Y., Fed. Bar Coun., N.Y. County Lawyers Assn., Yale Club, Links, Lyford Cay Club. Antitrust, Securities, Appellate. Office: Sullivan & Cromwell 125 Broad St New York NY 10004-2498 E-mail: urowskyr@sullcrom.com.

UTRECHT, PAUL F. lawyer; b. The Hague, The Netherlands, Aug. 31, 1960; s. Robert Packard and Arnolda (Cohen) U. BA, Claremont McKenna Coll., 1980; student, Sorbonne, Paris, 1980; JD, U. Calif., Berkeley, 1983. Bar: Calif. 1985, U.S. Ct. Appeals (9th cir.) 1986, U.S. Supreme Ct. 1990. Law clk. to Judge M. Joseph Blumenfeld U.S. Dist. Ct., Hartford, Conn., 1983-84; assoc. Pillsbury Madison & Sutro, San Francisco, 1984-87, Law Offices of S.G. Archibald, Paris, 1987; pvt. practice San Francisco, 1987—. Contbr.: Rule 11 and Other Sanctions, 1986. Appellate, General civil litigation, Probate (including wills, trusts). Office: 235 Montgomery St Ste 1130 San Francisco CA 94104-2909

UTTAL, SUSAN, legal administrator; b. N.Y.C., Oct. 8, 1954; d. Sheldon and Jane Louise (Kaufmann) Uttal. BA, Clark U., 1976; cert. paralegal, Inst. Paralegal Tng., Phila., 1978. Legal asst. Winthrop, Stimson, Putnam & Roberts, N.Y.C., 1978-80; legal coord. Schroder Real Estate Corp., N.Y.C., 1980-83; legal asst. supr. real estate svcs. dept. Cravath, Swaine & Moore, N.Y.C., 1983-89; sr. legal asst. real estate dept. Rackemann, Sawyer & Brewster, Boston, 1989-90; sr. legal asst. leasing and real estate depts. Goulston & Storrs, Boston, 1990-97; contracts adminstr. Cabletron Systems, Inc., Rochester, N.H., 1997-99; v.p. ops. Nonpareil Software, New Durham, N.H., 1999—. Mem. Clark U. N.Y. Young Alumni Assn. (steering com.). Democrat. Jewish. Avocations: pottery, piano, photography, cycling, gourmet cooking. Office: Nonpareil Software Inc 39 N Shore Rd New Durham NH 03855-2113 E-mail: skosko@panaceapottery.com.

UTTER, ROBERT FRENCH, retired judge; b. Seattle, June 19, 1930; s. John and Besse (French) Utter; m. Elizabeth J. Stevenson, Dec. 28, 1953; children: Kimberly, Kirk, John. BS, U. Wash., 1952; LLB, 1954. Bar: Wash. 1954. Pros. atty., King County, Wash., 1955-57; individual practice law Seattle, 1957-59; ct. commr. King County Superior Ct., 1959-64, judge, 1964-69, Wash. State Ct. Appeals, 1969-71, Wash. State Supreme Ct., 1971-95, chief justice, 1979-81; ret., 1995; lectr. Ctrl. and Eastern European Legal Inst., Prague, Czech Republic, 2000, 01, 2002, dean faculty, 2001—. Lectr. in field; leader comparative law tour, China, 1986, China, 87, China, 88, China, 91, Russia, 89, South Africa, 97, Ukraine, 98, Hungary, 98, Czech Republic, 98; adj. prof. constl. law U. Puget Sound, 1987—94; cons. CEELI, 1991, 1993—, USIA, 1992; visitor to Kyrgystan Judiciary, Kazakhstan, 1993—96, Mongolia, 1997; lectr. Albanian Judiciary, 1994, 95, 2000, Georgian Judiciary, 1999, Serbian Judiciary, 2001—02. Editor: books on real property and appellate practice; author: books on state constl. law. Pres., founder Big Brother Assn., Seattle, 1955—67, Job Therapy Inc., 1963—71; mem. exec. com. Conf. Chief Justices, 1979—80, 1981—86; pres. Thurston County Big Bros./Big Sisters, 1984; lectr Soviet Acad. Moscow, 1991; USIA visitor to comment on jud. sys. Latvia, 1992, 1993—94; trustee Linfield Coll. Named Alumnus of the Yr., Linfield Coll., 1973, Judge of the Yr., Wash. State Trial Lawyers, 1989, Outstanding Judge, Wash. State Bar Assn., 1990, Seattle-King County Bar Assn., 1992, Conder-Faulkner lectr., U. Wash. Sch. Law, 1995, Disting. Alumnus, Sch. Law U. Wash., 1995; recipient Henry Jackson Disting. Pub. Svc. award, Nat. Wash. Sch. Law, 2000; scholar Disting. Jud., U. Ind., 1987. Fellow: Chartered Inst. Arbitrators; mem.: ABA (commentator on proposed constns. of Albania, Bulgaria, Romania, Russia, Lithuania, Azerbaijan, Uzbekistan, Byelarus, Kazakhstan, and Ukraine), Am. Judicature Soc. (sec. 1987—, chmn. bd. dirs., mem. exec. com., Herbert Harley award 1983, Justice award 1998), Order of Coif. Baptist.

UTUMI, ANA CLAUDIA AKIE, lawyer; b. São Paulo, São Paulo, Brazil, Nov. 13, 1970; d. Yoshio and Flavia (Echuya) Utumi; m. Rubens Teruyoshi Ozima, Nov. 6, 1999. Grad. in Bus. Adminstrn., Getulio Vargas Found., São Paulo, Brazil, 1992; Grad. in Law, U. São Paulo, Brazil, 1994; MBA - Fin. and Capital Mkts., Brazilian Instn. of Capital Mkts., São Paulo, SP, Brazil, 1996; MLL in Tax Law, Cath. U. of São Paulo, 2001. Bar: Brazilian Bar Assn. - São Paulo, Brazil 1996, CFP: 2003. Sr. cons. Coopers & Lybrand, São Paulo, Brazil, 1992—96; sr. assoc. lawyer - tax consulting Mattos Filho, Veiga Filho, Marrey Jr. e Quiroga Law Firm, São Paulo, 1996—2000; ptnr. in charge tax consulting dept. Tozzini, Freire, Teixeira e Silva Law Firm, São Paulo, 2000—02. Asst. prof. - post graduation - internat. tax Law Sch. - Cath. U. of São Paulo, São Paulo, São Paulo, Brazil, 2000—; commr. of cert. com. Brazilian Inst. of Cert. of Fin. Planners , São Paulo, São Paulo, Brazil, 2002; vis. prof. - post graduation - tax matters - mba in mgmt. and risk Sch. of Economy and Bus. Adminstrn.- U. of São Paulo, São Paulo, São Paulo, Brazil, 2002—. Corporate taxation, Taxation, general, State and local taxation. Office: TozziniFreireTeixeira e Silva Law Firm Rua Líbero Badaró 293 21st floor Sao Paulo São Paulo 01009-907 Brazil Office Fax: (55) (11) 3291.1111. E-mail: anautumi@tozzini.com.br.

UY, HAZEL J. lawyer; b. Manila; d. Thomas Y. and Rosita T. Uy. BS, U. of the Philippines, 1995; JD, Boston Coll., 2000. Bar: Minn. 2000, U.S. Dist. Ct. Minn. 2001, Calif. 2001, U.S. Ct. Appeals (8th cir.) 2003. Assoc. Best & Flanagan LLP, Mpls., 2000—. General civil litigation, Intellectual property, Labor (including EEOC, Fair Labor Standards Act, labor-management relations, NLRB, OSHA). Office: Best & Flanagan LLP Ste 4000 225 S 6th St Minneapolis MN 55402

UZEMACK, MARILYN V. lawyer; BS in Edn., No. Ill. U., 1971; JD, John Marshall Law Sch., 1977. Bar: Ill. 1977, U.S. Dist. Ct. (no. dist.) Ill. 1977. Pvt. practice, Park Ridge, Ill., 1977—. Office: 15 S Prospect Ave Park Ridge IL 60068-4120

VACCHELLI, ROBERT FRANCIS, lawyer; b. Hartford, Conn., Jan. 29, 1951; s. Frank P. and Helen (DeRobertis) V.; m. Cathy Kinnane; 1 child. AB, Coll. of the Holy Cross, Worcester, Mass., 1973; JD, Suffolk U., 1977. Bar: Conn. 1977, U.S. Dist. Ct. Conn. 1978, U.S. Ct. Appeals 1979, U.S. Supreme Ct. 1981, Calif. 1983. Assoc. Stoner, Gross & Chorches, Hartford, 1977-78; asst. atty. gen. Conn. Atty. Gen.'s Office, Hartford, 1978—. Tutor Sch. Law U. Conn., 1996—; contbr. seminar U.S. Bur. Alcohol, Tobacco & Firearms, 1984; spkr. various seminars, 1986—; argued before U.S. Supreme Ct., 1989; advisor Conn. Gen. Assembly Law Revision Commn., 1992; state coord. Internat. Extraditions, 1998—. Author: Liquor Licensing in Connecticut, 1987. Commr. Glastonbury, Conn. Pub. Bldg. commn., 1986, Glastonbury Wetlands Authority, 1987; mem. Dem. Town Com., Glastonbury, 1986-91; vice chmn. bd. dirs. Glastonbury ABC, 1989-94. Recipient Am. Jurisprudence Book prize Lawyer's Co-op. Publ. Co., 1976, proclamation Glastonbury Conservation Commn., 1988, Merit award State of Conn., 1986, 91, 92, 95, 97, 98. Mem. ABA, ATLA, Conn. Bar Assn. (chmn. adminstrv. law exec. com., specialization certification subcom. 1982-89, mcpl. law com. 1982-87), U.S. Supreme Ct. Hist. Soc., Conn. Bot. Soc., Wadsworth Atheneum. Avocation: astronomy. Office: Office of the Atty Gen Mackenzie Hall 110 Sherman St Hartford CT 06105-2267

VACHSS, ANDREW HENRY, lawyer, author, juvenile justice and child abuse consultant; b. N.Y.C., Oct. 19, 1942; s. Bernard and Geraldine (Mattus) V. BA, Case Western Res. U., 1965; JD magna cum laude, New Engl. Sch. Law, 1975. Bar: N.Y. 1976, U.S. Dist. Ct. (so. and ea. dists.) N.Y. 1976. Program rep. USPHS, Ohio, 1965-66; unit supr N.Y.C. Dept. Social Svcs., 1966-69; urban coord. Community Devel. Found., Norwalk, Conn., 1969-70; dir. Uptown Community Orgn., Chgo., 1970-71; dep. dir. Medfield (Mass.)-Norfolk Prison Project, 1971-72; dir. intensive treatment unit ANDROS II, Roslindale, Mass., 1972-73; project dir. Mass. Dept. Youth Svcs., Boston, 1972-73; dir. Juvenile Justice Planning Project, N.Y.C., 1975-85; pvt. practice N.Y.C., 1976—. Organizer, coord. Calumet (Ind.) Community Congress, 1970; bd. dirs. Libra Inc., Cambridge, Mass., Advocacy Assocs., N.Y. and N.J.; adj. prof. Coll. New Resources, N.Y.C., 1980-81; lectr. trainer, speaker to numerous orgns.; cons. on juvenile justice and child abuse to numerous orgns., 1971—. Author: The Life-Style Violent Juvenile: The Secure Treatment Approach, 1979, (novels) Flood, 1985, Strega, 1987, Blue Belle, 1988, Hard Candy, 1989, Blossom, 1990, Sacrifice, 1991, Shella, 1993, Another Chance to Get it Right, 1995, 2003, Down in the Zero, 1994, Footsteps of the Hawk, 1995, Batman: The Ultimate Evil, 1995, False Allegations, 1996, Safe House, 1998, Choice of Evil, 1999, Dead and Gone, 2000, Pain Management, 2001, Only Child, 2002, The Getaway Man, 2003, Down Here, 2004, (graphic novels) Predator: Race War, 1995, Hard Looks, 2002, (audiobook) Proving It, 2001, (short stories) Born Bad, 1994, Everybody Pays, 1999; editor-in-chief: New Eng. Law Rev., 1974—75; contbg. editor: Parade; contbr. articles. Bd. of counselors Childtrauma Acad., Baylor Coll. of Medicine; bd. adv. Protect PAC; mem. expert adv. panel on catastrophic child abuse N.Y. State Office of Mental Health. Recipient Grand Prix de Lit. Policiére, 1988, Falcon award Maltese Falcon Soc. Japan, 1988, Deutschen Krimi Preis, Die Jury des Bochumer Krimi Archivs, 1989, Raymond Chandler award Giuria a Noir Festival, 2000, 1st Annual Harvey R. Houck Award (Justice for Children) for Child Advocacy, 2003; Indsl. Area Found. Tng. Inst. fellow, 1970-71, John Hay Whitney Found. fellow, 1976-77. Mem. PEN, Writers Guild of Am. Juvenile. Office: Ste 2860 420 Lexington Ave New York NY 10170-2899

VADEN, FRANK SAMUEL, III, lawyer, engineer; b. San Antonio, Nov. 13, 1934; s. Frank Samuel Jr. and Helen Alyne (Roberts) V.; m. Caroline Chittenden Gerdes, Feb. 20, 1960; children: Christina Louise (Mrs. Eugene Linton), Olivia Anne (Mrs. Warren Augenstein), Cecilia Claire (Mrs. Scott Johnson). BSEE and BS in Indsl. Engring., Tex. A&M U., 1957; JD, So. Meth. U., 1963. Bar: Tex. 1963, U.S. Dist. Ct. (we. and so. dists.) Tex. 1963, U.S. Ct. Appeals (5th, 9th, 11th and Fed. cirs.) 1963, U.S. Supreme Ct. 1986; registered U.S. Patent and Trademark Office 1964. Assoc. Arnold & Roylance, Houston, 1963-66; ptnr. Arnold, White & Durkee, Houston, 1966-73, mng. ptnr., 1973-78; prin. Frank S. Vaden III, P.C., Houston, 1978-80; sr. ptnr. Vaden, Eickenroht & Thompson, L.L.P., Houston, 1980-98; ptnr. Felsman, Bradley, Vaden, Gunter & Dillon, L.L.P., Houston, 1999-2000; of counsel Bracewell & Patterson, L.L.P., 2001—02; cons in field. Lectr. in field. Author: Invention Protection for Practicing Engineers, 1971; contbr. numerous articles to profl. jours. Capt. S.C., U.S. Army, 1957-67. Fellow Tex. Bar Found. (sustaining), Houston Bar Found. (sustaining); mem. ABA (mem. standing com. on specialization 1993-96), Tex. Bar Assn. (chair intellectual property law sec. 1984-85), Houston Bar Assn., Am. Intellectual Property Law Assn., Houston Intellectual Property Law Assn. (pres. 1985-86), U.S. Trademark Assn., Licensing Exec. Soc. (chmn. Houston chpt. 1987-88). Republican. Episcopalian. Intellectual property, Patent, Trademark and copyright. Fax: 713-688-4177. E-mail: candfv@earthlink.net.

VAGTS, DETLEV FREDERICK, lawyer, educator; b. Washington, Feb. 13, 1929; s. Alfred and Miriam (Beard) V.; m. Dorothy Larkin, Dec. 11, 1954; children: Karen, Lydia. Grad., Taft Sch., 1945; AB, Harvard U., 1948, LLB, 1951. Bar: Mass. 1961. Assoc. Cahill, Gordon, Reindel & Ohl, N.Y.C., 1951-53, 56-59; asst. prof. law Harvard Law Sch., 1959-62, prof., 1962—, Eli Goldston prof., 1981-84, Bemis prof., 1984—, dir. internat. tax program, 1998-2000. Counselor internat. law Dept. State, 1976-77 Author: (with others) Transnational Legal Problems, 1968, 4th edit., 1994, Basic Corporation Law, 1973, 3d edit., 1989, Transnational Business Problems, 2d edit., 1998; editor: (with others) Secured Transactions Under the Uniform Commercial Code, 1963-64; assoc. reporter: (with others) Restatement of Foreign Relations Law; book rev. editor Am. Jour. Internat. Law, 1986-93, co-editor-in-chief, 1993-98. 1st lt. USAF, 1953-56. Recipient Max Planck Rsch. award, 1991. Mem. ABA, Am. Soc. Internat. Law, Coun. Fgn. Rels., Phi Beta Kappa. Home: 29 Follen St Cambridge MA 02138-3502 Office: Sch Law Harvard U Cambridge MA 02138 E-mail: vagts@law.harvard.edu.

VAIRA, PETER FRANCIS, lawyer; b. McKeesport, Pa., Mar. 5, 1937; s. Peter Francis and Mary Louise (Bedogne) V.; m. Mary Hohler, 1981. BA, Duquesne U., 1959, JD, 1962. Bar: Pa. 1963, D.C. 1968, Ill. 1984, U.S. Ct. Appeals (D.C. cir.) 1964, Ill. Supreme Ct. Ill. 1984, U.S. Dist. Ct. (no. dist.) Ill., U.S. Dist. Ct. (ea. dist.) Pa. Atty. Chgo. Strike Force, Justice Dept., 1968-72; atty. in charge Phila. Strike Force, 1972-73, Chgo. Strike Force on Organized Crime, 1973-78; U.S. atty. Ea. Dist. Pa., Phila., 1978—83; ptnr. Lord Bissel & Brook, Chgo., 1983-86, Fox, Rothschild, O'Brien & Frankel, Phila., 1986-90, Buchanan Ingersoll, Phila., 1990-92, Vaira & Assocs., Phila., 1992-93, Vaira & Riley, Phila., 1993—. Exec. dir. Pres.'s Commn. on Organized Crime, 1983; ind. hearing officer Laborers Internat. Union N.Am., 1995—; panelist, seminar, controlling internat. organized crime, Rome, Sorrento, Italy, June 1994; panelist, Internat. Conf. on Trial by Jury, Buenos Aires, Oct. 1996. Author: Corporate Responses to Grand Jury Investigations, 1984, Eastern District Practice Rules Annotated, 2002; contbr. articles to profl. jours. Mem. Mayor's Search Com. for Police Commr., Phila., 1992; corruption task force Phila. Police, 1997. Lt. USNR, 1963-68. Recipient Spl. Commendation award Justice Dept., 1976 Fellow Am. Coll. Trial Lawyers (chmn. criminal procedure com. 1995-98, mem. comms. com.); fellow Chartered Inst. Arbitrators; mem. ABA (mem. criminal justice coun. 1986), Am. Law Inst., Union League (Chgo.), Phila. Country Club. Alternative dispute resolution, Federal civil litigation, Criminal. Office: Vaira & Riley 1600 Market St Ste 2650 Philadelphia PA 19103-7226 E-mail: p.vaira@vairariley.com.

VAJTAY, STEPHEN MICHAEL, JR., lawyer; b. New Brunswick, N.J., Mar. 18, 1958; s. Stephen Michael and Veronica Gizella (Fehèr) V.; m. Gabriella Katherine Soltèsz, Aug. 5, 1989; children: Stephen, Andrew, Gregory, Daniel. BA, Rutgers U., 1980; JD, Georgetown U., 1983; LLM, NYU, 1989. Bar: N.J. 1984, U.S. Tax Ct. 1985. Assoc. McCarter and English LLP, Newark, N.J., 1983-91, ptnr., 1991—. Trustee Hungarian Scout Assn. in Exteris, Garfield, N.J., 1985—; trustee Partnership for a Drug-Free N.J., Inc., Montclair, 1993—; adj. prof. law Seton Hall U. Sch. Law, Newark, 1995—; spkr. at lectrs. and seminars, 1992—. Contbr. articles to profl. jours. Mem. Bd. of Adjustment, New Brunswick, N.J., 1993-98. Mem. ABA, N.J. Bar Assn. (chmn. tax sect. 2001-02), Essex County Bar Assn., Phi Beta Kappa. Roman Catholic. Mergers and acquisitions, Corporate taxation, Taxation, general. Office: McCarter and English LLP Four Gateway Ctr 100 Mulberry St Newark NJ 07102 E-mail: SVAJTAY@MCCARTER.com.

VAKERICS, THOMAS VINCENT, lawyer; b. Lorain, Ohio, Mar. 26, 1944; s. Paul Peter and Margaret Theresa (Dobos) V.; m. Kathryn Ida Rogers, Aug. 7,1965; children: Meredith Vakerics Ehler, Mitchell Thomas. BA, Bowling Green State U., 1965; JD with honors, George Washington U., 1968. Bar: U.S. Dist. Ct. D.C. 1968, U.S. Ct. Appeals (D.C. cir.) 1969, U.S. Supreme Ct. 1974, U.S. Ct. Internat. Trade 1982, U.S. Ct. Appeals (Fed. cir.) 1982. Antitrust trial atty. FTC, Washington, 1969-73; assoc. Gore, Cladouhos & Brashares, Washington, 1973-75; ptnr. O'Connor & Hannan, Washington, 1975-84, Bayh, Tabbert & Capehart, Washington, 1984-86, Morgan, Lewis & Bockius, Washington, 1986-88, Winthrop, Stimson, Putnam & Roberts, Washington, 1988-94, Perkins Coie, 1994—. Vis. prof. Nihon U., Tokyo, 1981-88. Author: Antitrust Basics, 1985, Antidumping, Countervailing Duty and Other Trade Actions, 1987; contbr. articles to profl. jours. Mem. ABA (vice chmn. internat. antitrust law com. sect. internat. law and practice 1992-95), Internat. Bar Assn., D.C. Bar Assn., Solar Energy Rsch. Inst. (editl. adv. bd. Solar Energy Law Reporter 1979-82), Order of Coif, Phi Delta Phi, Pi Sigma Alpha, Phi Alpha Delta, Sigma Chi. Democrat. Roman Catholic. Antitrust, Private international. Home: 12820 Tewksbury Dr Herndon VA 20171-2427 Office: Perkins Coie 607 14th St NW Ste 800 Washington DC 20005-2003 E-mail: vaket@perkinscoie.com.

VALADEZ, ROBERT ALLEN, lawyer; b. McAllen, Tex., May 27, 1960; s. Ventura S. and Maria G. (De los Santos) V.; 1 child, Ashley Marie. BBA, U. Tex., 1982, JD, 1985. Bar: Tex. 1985, U.S. Dist. Ct. (so., we., ea. & no. dists.) Tex. Briefing atty. Tex. Supreme Ct., Austin, 1985-86; assoc. Fulbright & Jaworski, San Antonio, 1986-89, participating assoc., 1989-92; assoc. Wright & Greenhill, San Antonio, 1992-93; shareholder Shelton & Valadez, San Antonio, 1993—. State civil litigation, Personal injury (including property damage), Product liability. Home: 15 Camden Oaks San Antonio TX 78248-1606 Office: Shelton & Valadez 600 Navarro Ste 500 San Antonio TX 78205 E-mail: rvaladez@shelton-valadez.com.

VALCHERA, VALERIA, lawyer; b. Fiuggi, Italy, May 21, 1973; d. Luigi Valchera and Adele Striani. Law Degree, Bologna (Italy) U., 1996. Bar: Italy 2000. Litigator Manca Graziadei, Rome, 1999, comml. law trade, 2000—. Roman Catholic. Avocations: travel, photography, sports. Office: Manca Graziadei Via Lombardia 00187 Rome Italy

VALDEZ, MELVA EVANGELISTA, lawyer; b. Binmaley, Philippines, Nov. 11, 1959; d. Melecio Baniqued and Lydia Manuel Evangelista; m. Enrico Gonzalez Valdez, Nov. 17; 1 child, Kathryn Brnadette. AB in Polit. Sci., U. The Philippines, 1979, LLB, 1985. Bar: The Philippines 1986. Sr. ptnr. Jimenez, Gonzales, Liwanag, Bello, Valdez, Caluya & Fernandez, Makati City, Philippines, 1998—. Pres. MCA Joint Venture Subic, Inc.; corp. sec. Asian Inst. Mgmt., Makati City, Tosoh Polyvin Corp., Balangas City, Capitol Med. Ctr., Inc., Quezon City, Worldmaster Corp., Makati City; others; presenter in field. Mem.: Inter-Pacific Bar Assn. (vice-chmn. immigration, nationality and employment com.), Philippine Bar Assn., UP Women Lawyers Cir., Integrated Bar of the Philippines, Philippine-New Zealand Bus. Coun., Australian-New Zealand C. of C., Canadian C. of C., Singapore Philippines Assn., Makati Bus. Club, Portia Sorority. Commercial, contracts (including sales of goods; commercial financing), Immigration, naturalization, and customs, Securities. Office: JGLaw SOL Bldg 6th Fl 112 Amoorsolo St Legaspi Village Philippines 1229 Fax: 632 8173 51. Business E-Mail: mevaldez@jglawph.com.

VALENCIA, MARC ANDREW, lawyer; BSc, U. Toronto, Can., 1990; LLB, U. Toronto, 1995. Bar: Ont., Can. 1997, Calif. 2001. Sr. Arthur Andersen & Co., Toronto, 1997—98; assoc. Osler, Hoskin & Harcourt, LLP, Toronto, 1998—2000, Shearman & Sterling, Menlo Park, Calif., 2000—. Mem.: ABA, Calif. Bar Assn., Law Soc. Upper Can. Mergers and acquisitions, Securities, Corporate, general. Office: Shearman and Sterling 1080 Marsh Rd Menlo Park CA 94025 Office Fax: 650-838-3699. Business E-Mail: mvalencia@shearman.com.

VALENTE, PETER CHARLES, lawyer; b. NYC, July 3, 1940; s. Francis Louis and Aurelia Emily (Cella) V.; m. Judith Kay Nemeroff, Feb. 19, 1966; children: Susan Lynn, David Marc. BA, Bowdoin Coll., 1962; LLB, Columbia U., 1966; LLM, NYU, 1971. Bar: N.Y. 1967. Assoc. Blank Rome LLP (formerly Tenzer Greenblatt LLP), N.Y.C., 1967-73, ptnr., 1973—, practice group leader pvt. client practice group, 2003—. Co-author column on wills, estates and surrogates's practice N.Y. Law Jour. Fellow Am. Coll. Trust and Estate Counsel; mem. ABA, N.Y. State Bar Assn. (lectr. on wills, trusts and estates), Assn. of Bar of City of N.Y., N.Y. County Lawyers' Assn. (former bd. dirs. and chmn. com. on surrogates' ct., lectr. on wills, trusts and estates), Phi Beta Kappa. Estate planning, Probate (including wills, trusts), Estate taxation. Office: Blank Rome 405 Lexington Ave New York NY 10174-0002 E-mail: pvalente@blankrome.com.

VALENTIN, JAMES, lawyer; b. Queens, NY, Feb. 24, 1949; m. Myrna Ilia Delfilar, Feb. 14, 1970. AAS, C.C. Air Force, 1977; BS, Embry-Riddle Aero. U., 1983; MS, Ctrl. Mich. U., 1987; JD, Temple U., 1997. Bar: Pa., NJ, U.S. Dist. Ct. NJ, U.S. Ct. Appeals (fed. cir.), U.S. Ct. Vet. Claims. Enlisted USAF, 1968, advanced to sgt., ret., 1993; self-employed pvt. detective Fairless Hills, Pa., 1994—96; assoc. Leventhal & Sutton, Longhorne, Pa., 1996—. Mem.: NRA. Roman Catholic. Labor (including EEOC, Fair Labor Standards Act, labor-management relations, NLRB, OSHA), Administrative and regulatory. Office: Leventhal & Sutton One Oxford Valley Ste 317 Langhorne PA 19047 E-mail: valentinlaw@aol.com.

VALENTINE, H. JEFFREY, legal association executive; b. Phila., Sept. 28, 1945; s. Joshua Morton and Olga W. (Wilson) V.; 1 child, Karyn. BS, St. Louis U., 1964, postgrad., 1966-68. Programmer, systems analyst Honeywell Electronic Data Processing, Wellesley Hills, Mass., 1964-66; account exec. Semiconductor div. Tex. Instruments, New Eng., 1966-68; New Eng. sales exec., Mid-Atlantic regional mgr. Electronic Instrumentation Co., 1968-70; pres. Nat. Free Lance Photographers Assn., Doylestown, Pa., 1970-89; pres., dir. Towne Print & Copy Ctrs. Inc.; v.p., exec. dir. Nat. Paralegal Assn., 1982—; pres. Paralegal Assocs., Inc., 1982—; chief operating officer Doylestown Parking Corp., 1977-88. Bd. dirs. Law Enforcement Supply Co., Solebury, Valtronics Supply Co., Towne Print & Copy Centers Inc., Solebury, Doylestown Stationery and Office Supply, Energy Mktg. Assocs., Inc., Solebury, Paralegal Placement Network; pres. Paralegal Pub. Corp., 1983-90; pub. Paralegal Jour.; pres. Valco Enterprises Inc., 1986—, Paralegal Employment Sys., Inc., 1988, Solebury Press, Inc., 1989—; ptnr. J&S Gen. Contractors, 1993—, J&S Landscaping Tree Svc., 1993—, J&S Estate and Property Mgmt., 2001--; owner Specialized Computer Consulting, 1992—. Author: Photographers Bookkeeping System, 1973, rev. edit., 1978, Photographers Pricing Guides, 1971, 72, 74, 75, Available Markets Director's - 4 Vols., 1973-77, National Model Sources Directory, Nat. Paralegal Salary and Employment Survey, 1985-86, 88, 90-92, 93-94; also articles, bulls. and pamphlets. Exec. sec. Doylestown Bus. Assn., 1972-78, pres., 1979, 83, v.p., 1981. Recipient Internat. Men of Achievement award, 1988; named Personalities of the Am., 1988. Mem. London Coll. Applied Scis., Nat. Fedn. Paralegal Assns., Photog. Industry Coun., Nat. Assn. Legal Assts., Am. Soc Assn. Execs., Soc. Assn. Mgrs.,

Nat. Fedn. Ind. Business (mem. action coun. com.), Nat. Parking Assn., Nat. Office Products Assn., Graphic Arts Assn. Delaware Valley, Nat. Assn. Federally Licensed Firearms Dealers, Nat. Compostition Assn., Internat. Platform Assn. Office: PO Box 406 Solebury PA 18963-0406

VALENZUELA, MANUEL ANTHONY, JR., lawyer; b. L.A., Dec. 4, 1955; s. Manuel and Artimesa B. (Ruiz) V.; m. Guadalupe Roa, Nov. 8, 1980; children: Manuel Anthony III, Nancy Christine. BA in Polit. Sci., UCLA, 1978; MPA, U. So. Calif., 1982; JD, Southwestern U., L.A., 1987. Bar: Calif. 1987, U.S. Dist. Ct. (cen. dist.) Calif. 1987, U.S. Ct. Appeals (9th cir.) 1988, U.S. Supreme Ct. 1991. Legis. analyst L.A. City Coun., 1981-88; legal extern ACLU, L.A., 1985; assoc. county counsel County of Los Angeles, 1988-89, sr. assoc county counsel, 1989-90, dep. county counsel, 1990-94, sr. dep. county counsel, 1994-98, prin. dep. county counsel, 1998—. Mem.: Constnl. Rights Found. (mock trial competition 1997—99, 2001), UCLA Latino Alumni Assn. (founder, bd. dirs. 1989—90, scholarship com. 1995—99), L.A. County Counsel Assn. (bd. dirs. 1989—99), Mexican Am. Bar Assn. (bd. dirs. 1990, 1991), L.A. County Bar Assn. (exec. com. govtl. law sect. 1990—91, sec. govtl. law sect. 1991—92, 2d vice chair govtl. law sect. 1992—93, 1st vice chair govtl. law sect. 1993—94, chair govtl. law sect. 1994—95, exec. com. govtl. law sect. 1995—96, bd. trustees 1995—96, exec. com. govtl. law sect. 1996—97). Democrat. Roman Catholic. Avocations: tennis, backpacking, photography, reading. Home: 9647 Val St Temple City CA 91780-1438 Office: Office of County Counsel 648 Hall of Adminstrn 500 W Temple St Los Angeles CA 90012-2713 E-mail: MValenzuela@counsel.co.la.ca.us.

VALERIO, MATTHEW F. lawyer; b. Lawrence, Mass., Sept. 28, 1963; s. Fred Ernest Jr. Valerio and Carole Elaine (Closson) Mimeault; m. Joanne F. Stockton, Aug. 6, 1988. BA, St. Michael's Coll., 1985; JD, Western New Eng. Coll., 1988. Bar: Mass. 1989, Vt. 1989, U.S. Dist. Ct. Mass. 1989, U.S. Dist. Ct. Vt. 1989, U.S. Ct. Appeals (2d cir.) 1998. Pvt. practice, Springfield, Mass., 1989; assoc. Abatiell & Wysolmerski, Rutland, Vt., 1989-94; ptnr. Abatiell & Valerio, Rutland, Vt., 1994—2001; defender gen. State of Vt., 2001—. Adj. prof. Coll. St. Joseph, Rutland, 1993-99. Fin. chmn. Rutland County Rep. Com., 1991-93. Mem. ABA (young lawyers divsn. dist. rep. Vt., Maine 1994-96, Vt. state membership chair 1995—), New Eng. Bar Assn. (bd. mem. 1997—, pres. 1999-2000), Vt. Trial Lawyers Assn., Vt. Bar Assn. (treas., exec. com. young lawyers sect. 1990-92, chmn.-elect exec. com. 1992, chmn. 1993-94, bd. bar mgr. 1992-2003, pres.-elect 2000-01, pres. 2001-02), Vt. Criminal Def. Lawyers Assn. (bd. dirs. 1993-96), Assn. Trial Lawyers Am., Kiwanis (bd. dirs. Rutland chpt. 1990-96, v.p. 1991-92, pres. 1993-94, pres. Rutland area mentor program 1994-96, disting. svc. award 1989-92, N.E. dis disting. pres. award 1993-94). Avocations: baseball, wrestling, blues. General civil litigation, Criminal, Personal injury (including property damage). Office: Office Defender Gen 120 State St Montpelier VT 05620-3301

VALLIANOS, CAROLE WAGNER, lawyer; b. Phila., Aug. 19, 1946; d. F. Leonard Wagner and Helen Rose Pikunas; m. Peter Denis Vallianos, June 22, 1963; children: Kelly, Denis, Jamie Vallianos-Healy. BA, Calif. State U., Fullerton, 1981; JD, Southwestern U., 1995. Bar: Calif. 1997. Nonprofit cons., Manhattan Beach, Calif., 1982—; atty. in pvt. practice, 1997—. Non-profit cons. USIA, Turkey, 1997, Cyprus, 1997, Bosnia, 1998, India, 1999. Pres. LWV Calif., 1989—91; mem. com. on pvt. judging Calif. Jud. Coun., 1989—91, mem. com. on race and ethic bias in the cts., 1991—96, mem. com. on access and fairness in the cts., 1994—97, 2002—, mem. task force on jury sys. improvements, 1998—2003; mem. Women Lawyers L.A. Jail Project; mem. adv. bd. U. Fla. Marion Brechner Citizen Access Project, 2000—02; bd. dirs. LWV U.S., 1992—98, LWV Edn. Fund U.S., 1992—98, Harbor-UCLA Rsch. and Edn. Inst., 2002—, treas., 2003—. Mem. LWV Beach Cities (former pres.), Am. Judicature Soc. (bd. dirs. 1996—, exec. com. 2001—, sec. 2003), First Amendment Coalition Calif. (bd. dirs. 1995—), Coalition for Justice (v.p. 1993—), Benjamin Aranda Inn of Ct. (exec. com. 2002—). Avocations: travel, political memorabilia, literature. Civil rights, Labor (including EEOC, Fair Labor Standards Act, labor-management relations, NLRB, OSHA), Non-profit and tax-exempt organizations.

VALLIANT, JAMES STEVENS, lawyer; b. Glendale, Calif., Sept. 29, 1963; s. William Warren and Carol Dee (Heath) V.; m. Holly Lynne White. BA, NYU, 1984; JD, U. San Diego, 1989. Bar: Calif. 1989. Law instr. U. San Diego, 1988-89; dep. dist. atty. Dist. Atty.'s Office, San Diego, 1989—. Host talk show WJM Prodns., Hollywood, Calif., 1996. Contbr. articles in objectivism and early Christianity. Recipient Citation of Appreciation, MADD, 1993. Office: Dist Attys Office 330 W Broadway San Diego CA 92101-3825

VALOIS, ROBERT ARTHUR, lawyer; b. N.Y.C., May 13, 1938; s. Frank Jacob and Harriet Frances (LaCroix) V.; m. Ruth Emilie Skacil, Dec. 23, 1961; children: Marguerite Jeannette, Robert Arthur Jr. BBA, U. Miami, 1962; JD, Wake Forest U., 1972. Bar: N.C. 1972, Fla. 1972, U.S. Ct. Appeals (4th cir.) 1973, U.S. Dist. Ct. (ea. and mid. dists.) 1974, U.S. Supreme Ct. 1975, U.S. Ct. Appeals (6th cir.) 1986. Field examiner NLRB, Winston-Salem, N.C., 1962-70; from assoc. to ptnr. Maupin, Taylor & Ellis, P.A., Raleigh, NC, 1972—, chmn. labor and employment sect., 1972-97, chmn. bd. dirs., pres., 1997—2002. Vice chmn. Legal Svcs. Corp., Washington, 1984-90, bd. dirs. Served with USN, 1956-59. Mem. Greater Raleigh C. of C. (chmn. fed. govt. com. 1991—). Democrat. Presbyterian. Labor (including EEOC, Fair Labor Standards Act, labor-management relations, NLRB, OSHA). E-mail: rvalois@maupintaylor.com.

VALVO, BARBARA-ANN, lawyer, surgeon; b. Elizabeth, N.J., June 7, 1949; d. Robert Richad and Vera (Kovach) V. BA in Biology, Hofsta U., 1971; MD, Pa. State U., 1975; JD, Loyola Sch. Law, 1993. Diplomate Am. Bd. Surgery; Bar: La. 1993. Surg. intern Nassau County Med. Ctr., East Meadow, N.Y., 1975-76; resident gen. surgery Allentown-Sacred Heart Med. Ctr., Allentown, Pa., 1976-80; asst. chief surgery USPHS, New Orleans, 1980-81; pvt. practice gen. surgery New Orleans, 1981-89; pvt. practice med. malpractice law, 1995—. Upjohn scholar, 1975. Fellow ACS; mem. ABA, FBA, La. Bar Assn., La. Trial Lawyers Assn. Republican. Avocations: computers, raising animals. Office: 4130 Loire Dr Ste A Kenner LA 70065 Fax: 504-467-8762. E-mail: bavalvo@att.net.

VAMOS, FLORENCE M. lawyer; b. N.Y.C., Apr. 09; d. Joseph Calabro and Louise Marie Horvath; m. Joseph S. Vamos. BA magna cum laude, U.Minn., 1974; JD, William Mitchell Coll. Law, St. Paul, 1978. Bar: Ind. 1978, Mich. 1982, U.S. Dist. Ct. (so. dist.) Ind. 1978, U.S. Dist. Ct. (no. dist.) Ind. 1979, U.S. Dist. Ct. (so. dist.) Mich. 1981, U.S. Dist. Ct (ea. dist.) Mich. 1982. Pvt. practice, South Bend, Ind., 1978-90, Mishawaka, Ind., 1990-2000, Edwardsburg, Mich., 2001—. Mem. Ind. State Bar Assn., Mich. State Bar Assn., Cass County (Mich.) Bar Assn., St. Joseph County (Ind.) Bar Assn., Nat. Inst. Trial Advocacy. Family and matrimonial, General practice, Trademark and copyright.

VAN ALLEN, WILLIAM KENT, lawyer; b. Albion, N.Y., July 30, 1914; s. Everett Kent and Georgia (Roberts) Van A.; m. Sally Schall, Nov. 11, 1944; children: William Kent, Jr., George Humphrey, Peter Cushing. AB, Hamilton Coll., 1935; LL.B., Harvard U., 1938. Bar: N.Y. 1938, D.C. 1939, N.C. 1951, U.S. Dist. Ct. (we. dist.) N.C. 1951, U.S. Dist. Ct. (mid. dist.) N.C. 1953, U.S. Ct. Appeals (4th cir.) 1951, U.S. Ct. Claims 1946, U.S. Tax Ct. 1940, FCC 1939, ICC 1940, U.S. Supreme Ct. 1946. With Hanson, Lovett & Dale, Washington, 1938-41, 46-50; ptnr. Lassiter, Moore and Van Allen and Moore and Van Allen, Charlotte, N.C., 1951-87; of counsel Moore & Van Allen, Charlotte, 1988—. Permanent mem. Jud. Conf. 4th Jud. Circuit. Vestryman Episc. Ch., 1957-60, 66-69; mem. Mecklenburg County Bd. Public Welfare, 1954-59, chmn. 1957-59; bd. dirs. N.C. Found. Commerce and Industry, 1965-73, Found. U. N.C. at Charlotte, 1979-89, Charlotte Symphony Orch., 1981-82, Mercy Health Svcs., 1983-88; chmn. Charlotte Area adv. coun. Am. Arbitration Assn., 1967-76; bd. dirs. United Community Svcs., 1972-77, v.p., 1972; bd. mgrs. Charlotte Country Day Sch., 1956-61, chmn., 1959-61, bd. visitors, 1978—, chmn., 1987-88; bd. advisers U. N.C.-Charlotte, 1983-84; trustee Spastics Hosp., 1951-60, Mint Mus. Art, 1976-79, Surtman Found., 1955-90, Mercy Hosp. Found., 1979-84; bd. visitors Johnson C. Smith U., 1978-89; pres. Charlotte Symphony League, 1980-81, Friends of U. N.C. at Charlotte, 1990-91. Served with USNR, 1941-45, commdg. officer destroyer escort ATO and PTO; released to inactive duty as lt. comdr. Mem. ABA, Charlotte C. of C. (bd. dirs. 1971-75, v.p. 1972-75). Mil. Order of Carabao, Holland Soc. N.Y., Charlotte Country Club, Charlotte City Club, Chevy Chase Club (Md.), Mullett Lake Country Club (Mich.), Mill Reef Club, Phi Beta Kappa, Chi Psi. Office: Moore & Van Allen Ste 4700 100 N Tryon St Charlotte NC 28202-4003

VAN ANTWERPEN, FRANKLIN STUART, federal judge; b. Passaic, NJ, Oct. 23, 1941; s. Franklin John and Dorothy (Hoedemaker) Van A.; m. Kathleen Veronica O'Brien, Sept. 12, 1970; children: Joy, Franklin W., Virginia. BS in Engring. Physics, U. Maine, 1964; JD, Temple U., 1967; postgrad., Nat. Jud. Coll., 1980. Bar: Pa. 1969, U.S. Dist. Ct. (ea. dist.) Pa. 1971, U.S. Ct. Appeals (3d cir.) 1971, U.S. Supreme Ct. 1972. Corp. counsel Hazeltine, Corp., N.Y.C., 1967-70; chief counsel Northampton County Legal Aid Soc., Easton, Pa., 1970-71; assoc. Hemstreet & Smith, Easton, 1971-73; ptnr. Hemstreet & VanAntwerpen, Easton, 1973-79; judge Ct. Common Pleas of Northampton County, Pa., 1979-87, U.S. Dist. Ct. (ea. dist.) Pa., Phila., 1987—. Apptd. to US Sentencing Commn. Jud. Working Group, 1992-93; apptd. to US Jud. Conf. Com. on Defender Svcs., 1997, chmn. subcom. on fed. defender funding, 2000-01; trial judge US vs. Scarfo, 1988-89; adj. prof. Northampton County Area CC, 1976-81; solicitor Palmer Twp., 1971-79; gen. counsel Fairview Savs. and Loan Assn., Easton, 1973-79; lectr. on law of evidence Pa. Bar Inst., 1985-92. Contbr. articles to Cardozo Law Rev. Recipient Booster award Bus. Indsl. and Profl. Assn., 1979, George Palmer award Palmer Twp., 1980, Citizen of Yr. award, 1981, Law Enforcement Commendation medal Nat. Soc. SAR, 1990, Disting. Alumni Achievement award Newark Acad., 2001; named an Alumnus Who Has Made a Difference in the World, U. Maine, 1991. Mem. ABA (com. on jud. edn.), Fed. Bar Assn. (hon.), Fed. Cir. Bar Assn., Pa. Bar Assn., Northampton County Bar Assn., Am. Judicature Soc., Fed. Judges Assn., Pomfret Club, Nat. Lawyers Club Washington, Union League Club, Pa. Soc. Club, Sigma Pi Sigma. Office: US Dist Ct Holmes Bldg 2nd and Ferry St Easton PA 18042

VANASKIE, THOMAS IGNATIUS, judge; b. Shamokin, Pa., Nov. 11, 1953; s. John Anthony and Delores (Wesoloski) V.; m. Dorothy Grace Williams, Aug. 12, 1978; children: Diane, Laura, Thomas. BA magna cum laude, Lycoming Coll., 1975; JD cum laude, Dickinson U., Carlisle, Pa., 1978. Bar: Pa. 1978, U.S. Dist. (mid. dist.) Pa. 1980, U.S. Ct. Appeals (3rd cir.) 1982, U.S. Supreme Ct. 1983. Law clk. to chief judge U.S. Dist. Ct. (mid. dist.) Pa., Scranton, 1978-80; assoc. Dilworth, Paxson, Kalish & Kauffman, Scranton, 1980-85, ptnr., 1986-92; prin. mem. Elliott, Vanaskie & Riley, 1992-94; dist. judge U.S. Dist. Ct. (mid. dist.) Pa., 1994—99, chief justice, 1999—. Counsel Gov. Robert P. Casey Com., Harrisburg, Pa., 1987-92; mem. Jud. Conf. Com. Info. Tech.; mem. Third Cir. Jud. Coun.; mem. automation and tech. com. U.S. Cir. Ct. 3d cir., 1998, co-chair 3d cir. task force on info. resources, 1998—; lectr. in field. Contbr. articles to profl. jours. Mem. Scranton Waste Mgmt. Com., 1989; trustee Scranton Prep. Sch., 1997—. Recipient James A. Finnegan award Finnegan Found. Mem. Judicature, Pa. Bar Assn., Fed. Judges Assn. (bd. dirs. 1998). Democrat. Avocations: golf, reading. Office: William J Nealon Fed Bldg & US Courthouse PO Box 913 235 N Washington Ave Scranton PA 18501

VAN ATTA, DAVID MURRAY, lawyer; b. Berkeley, Calif., Oct. 20, 1944; s. Chester Murray and Rosalind (Eisenstein) Van A.; m. Jo Ann Masaoka; 1 child, Lauren Rachel. BA, U. Calif., Berkeley, 1966; JD, U. Calif., Hastings, 1969. Bar: Calif. 1970. Asst. gen. counsel Boise Cascade Corp., Palo Alto, Calif., 1970-73; ptnr. Miller, Starr & Regalia, San Francisco, 1973-87, Graham & James, San Francisco, 1987-93, Hanna & Van Atta, Palo Alto, 1993—. Instr. Golden Gate U., San Francisco, 1984-85; U. Calif., Berkeley, 1976-84. Author: (with Hanna) California Common Interest Developments Law and Practice, 1999. Mem. ABA, Am. Coll. Real Estate Lawyers (bd. govs., sec.), Calif. Bar Assn. (vice chmn. exec. com. real property law sect. 1982-85, chmn. condominium and subdivsn. com. real property law sect. 1981-83), Cmty. Assn. Inst., Urban Land Inst., Anglo-Am. Real Property Inst., Rotary Club Palo Alto, Lambda Alpha Internat. Soc. Avocations: skiing, tennis, painting. Land use and zoning (including planning), Property, real (including real estate development, water), Personal income taxation. Office: Hanna & Van Atta 525 University Ave Ste 705 Palo Alto CA 94301-1921

VANBEBBER, GEORGE THOMAS, federal judge; b. Troy, Kans., Oct. 21, 1931; s. Roy Vest and Anne (Wenner) V.; m. Alleen Sara Castellani. AB, U. Kans., 1953, LLB, 1955. Bar: Kans. 1955, U.S. Dist. Ct. Kans. 1955, U.S. Ct. Appeals (10th cir.) 1961. Pvt. practice, Troy, 1955-58, 1961-82; asst. U.S. atty. Topeka, Kansas City, Kans., 1958-61; county atty. Doniphan County, Troy, 1963-69; mem. Kans. House of Reps., 1973-75; chmn. Kans. Corp. Commn., Topeka, 1975-79; U.S. magistrate Topeka, 1982-89; judge U.S. Dist. Ct., Kansas City, Kans., 1989-95, chief judge, 1995-2001. Mem. ABA, Kas. Bar Assn. Episcopalian. Office: US Dist Ct 529 US Courthouse 500 State Ave Kansas City KS 66101-2403

VAN BOKKELEN, JOSEPH SCOTT, prosecutor; b. Chgo., June 7, 1943; s. Robert W. and W. Louise (Reynolds) Van B.; m. Sally Wardall Huey, Aug. 14, 1971; children— Brian, Kate. B.A., U. Ind., 1966, J.D., 1969. Bar: Ind. 1969, U.S. Dist. Ct. (so. dist.) Ind. 1969, U.S. Dist. Ct. (no. dist.) Ind. 1973, U.S. Ct. Appeals (7th cir.) 1973, U.S. Supreme Ct. 1973. Dep. atty. gen. State of Ind., Indpls., 1969-71, asst. atty. gen., 1971-72; asst. U.S. atty. No. Dist. Ind., Hammond, 1972-75; ptnr. Goldsmith, Goodman, Ball & Van Bokkelen, Highland, Ind., 1975—2001 ; U.S. atty. Ind. No. Dist., 2001-. Recipient Outstanding Asst. U.S. Atty. award U.S. Dept. Justice, 1974. Mem. ABA, Fed. Bar Assn., Ind. Bar Assn., Criminal Def. Lawyers Assn. Home: 9013 Indianapolis Blvd Highland IN 46322-2502 Office: 1001 Main St Ste A Dyer IN 46311-1234*

VAN BUREN, LYNN MARIE, lawyer; b. Neillsville, Wis., Sept. 27, 1970; d. Gerald Francis and Sharon Mary Schug; m. Edward Morris Van Buren IV, July 8, 2000; 1 child, Thomas Edward. BA, St. Norbert Coll., 1992; JD, U. Wis., 1997. Bar: Wis. 1997, U.S. Dist. Ct. (we. dist.) Wis. 1997, Ct. Internat. Trade 1999, D.C. 2001. Counsel Ruder Wave and Michler, Wausau, Wis., 1997—99, Baker Botts, Washington, 1999—2000, Verner Liipfert, Bernhard McPherson and Hand, Washington, 2000—02, Piper Rudnick, Washington, 2002—. Bd. mem. Big Bros. Big Sisters, Wausau, 1997—99. Private international, Public international. Office: Piper Rudnick Washington DC 20005

VAN CAMP, BRIAN RALPH, judge; b. Halstead, Kans., Aug. 23, 1940; s. Ralph A. and Mary Margaret (Bragg) Van C.; m. Diane D. Miller, 1992; children: Megan M., Laurie E. AB, U. Calif., Berkeley, 1962, LLB, 1965. Bar: Calif. 1966. Dep. atty. gen., State Calif., 1965-67; agy. atty. Redevel. Agy., City of Sacramento, 1967-70; asst./acting sec. Bus. and Trans. Agy., State of Calif., 1970-71; commr. of corps. State of Calif., Sacramento, 1971-74; partner firm Diepenbrock, Wulff, Plant & Hannegan, Sacramento, 1975-77, Van Camp & Johnson, Sacramento, 1978-90; sr. ptnr. Downey, Brand, Seymour & Rohwer, 1990-97; judge Superior Ct., Sacramento County, 1997—. Lectr. Continuing Edn. Bar, Practicing Law Inst., Calif. CPA Soc. Contbr. articles to profl. jours. Mem. Rep. State Ctrl. Com. Calif., 1974-78; mem. electoral coll. Presdl. Elector for State of Calif., 1976; mem. Calif. Health Facilities Fin. Authority, 1985-89; mem. Capital Area Devel. Authority, 1989-97, chmn., 1990-97; mem. Calif. Jud. Coun. Task Force on Quality of Justice, 1998-99, Jud. Coun. Adv. Com. on Civil and Small Claims Law, 2000—; bd. dirs. Sacramento Symphony Assn., 1973-85, Sacramento Symphony Found., 1993—, Sacramento Area Commerce and Trade Orgn., pres. 1986-87, Sacramento Valley Venture Capital Forum, 1986-90, League to Save Lake Tahoe, 1988-95, Valley Vision, Inc., 1993-97; elder Fremont Presbyn. Ch., 1967—. Recipient Sumner-Mering Meml. award Sacramento U. of Calif. Alumni Assn., 1962, Thos. Jefferson award Am. Inst. Pub. Svc., 1994, Excellence in Achievement award Calif. Alumni Assn., 1997; named Outstanding Young Man of Yr., Sacramento Jaycees, 1970, Internat. Young Man of Yr., Active 20-30 Club Internat., 1973. Mem. Boalt Hall Alumni Assn. (bd. dirs. 1991-94), Lincoln Club Sacramento Valley (bd. dirs. 1975-90, pres. 1984-86), U. Calif Men's Club (pres. 1968), Sutter Club, Kanadhar Ski Club, Rotary Club Sacramento (pres. 1993-94, Paul Harris Fellow award 1995), Comstock Club (pres. 1976-77). Republican. Presbyterian. Office: 720 9th St Sacramento CA 95814-1302 E-mail: vancamp@saccourt.com.

VANCE, MICHAEL CHARLES, lawyer; b. Marshalltown, Iowa, May 31, 1951; s. Randall Scott and Irma Vance; m. Bonnie K. Becker, Jan. 1, 1995; children: Thomas Randall, Patrick Michael. BA in Polit. Sci. and Econs., U. Iowa, 1973, JD with distinction, 1976. Bar: Iowa 1976, U.S Dist. Ct. (so. dist.) Iowa 1976, U.S. Tax Ct. 1991. Sole practice, Mt. Pleasant, Iowa, 1976—. Atty. City of Wayland, Iowa, 1976—; instr. bus. law Iowa Wesleyan Coll., Mt. Pleasant, 1977-78; asst. county atty. Henry County, Mt. Pleasant, 1979-97, jud. magistrate, 1997—; mem. Iowa Supreme Ctr. Commn. on Unauthorized Practice of Law, 2002. Bd. dirs. Cmty. Mental Health of Henry, Louisa and Jefferson Counties, Mt. Pleasant, 1977-82; chairperson Henry County Dems., Mt. Pleasant, 1978-83; pres. Mt. Pleasant Sesquicentennial Assn., 1984-86; mem. St. Alphonsus Ch. Parish Coun. pres., 1983-85; trustee Mt. Pleasant, 1985—. Mem. ABA, Iowa Bar Assn. (bd. govs. 1996-2002, jud. adminstrn. com. 2002, scope and corralations 2003-), Henry County Bar Assn. (sec.-treas. 1977-78, v.p. 1978-79, pres. 1979-80, 88-91), Iowa Trial Lawyers Assn., Iowa Conf. Bar Assn. Presidents (bd. dirs. 1979-81), Iowa Assn. Jud. Magistrates (bd. dirs. 1998-2002), Mt. Pleasant C. of C. (bd. dirs. 1991-93, named Citizen of Yr. 1985), Mt. Pleasant Jaycees (bd. dirs. 1978-83), Rotary, KC, Omicron Delta Kappa, Omicron Delta Epsilon. Roman Catholic. General civil litigation, General practice, Probate (including wills, trusts). Home: 2005 Bittersweet Cir Mount Pleasant IA 52641-8301 Office: PO Box 469 101 N Jefferson St Mount Pleasant IA 52641-2039

VAN DE KAMP, JOHN KALAR, lawyer; b. Pasadena, Calif., Feb. 7, 1936; s. Harry and Georgie (Kalar) Van de K.; m. Andrea Fisher, Mar. 11, 1978; 1 child, Diana. BA, Dartmouth Coll., 1956; JD, Stanford U., 1959. Bar: Calif. 1960. Asst. U.S. atty., L.A., 1960-66; U.S. atty., 1966-67; dep. dir. Exec. Office for U.S. Attys., Washington, 1967-68, dir., 1968-69; spl. asst. Pres.'s Commn. on Campus Unrest, 1970; fed. pub. defender L.A., 1971-75; dist. atty. Los Angeles County, 1975-83; atty. gen. State of Calif., 1983-91; ptnr. Dewey Ballantine, L.A., 1991-96, of counsel, 1996—; pres. Thoroughbred Owners, Calif., 1996—. Bd. dirs. United Airlines. Mem. Calif. Dist. Attys. Assn. (pres. 1975-83), Nat. Dist. Attys. Assn. (v.p. 1975-83), Peace Officers Assn. L.A. County (past pres.), Nat. Assn. Attys. Gen. (exec. com. 1983-91), Conf. Western Attys. Gen. (pres. 1986), State Bar of Govs. Administrative and regulatory, General civil litigation, General practice. Office: Dewey Ballantine LLP 333 So Grand Ave Ste 2600 Los Angeles CA 90071-6511

VANDEMAN, GEORGE ALLEN, lawyer; b. Muncie, Ind., Jan. 16, 1940; s. George Edward and Nellie Florence (Johnson) V.; m. Judith Ellen Meyers, June 16, 1959 (div. 1976); m. Winifred Margaret Hayward, Jan. 15, 1977 (div. 2003); children: Shelli, Bradley, Craig. AB, U. So. Calif., 1963, JD, 1966. Bar: Calif. 1966. Atty., ptnr. Latham & Watkins, L.A., Calif., 1966-95; sr. v.p., gen. counsel, sec. Amgen Inc., 1995—2000. Mem. bd. councilors U. So. Calif. Sch. Law, 1988—. Mem. Calif. State Bar (com. on takeover and corp. govt. 1987—). Avocations: travel, water sports, skiing. Mergers and acquisitions. Home: 1652 Aldercreek Pl Westlake Village CA 91362-4270

VAN DEMARK, RUTH ELAINE, lawyer; b. Santa Fe, N.Mex., May 16, 1944; d. Robert Eugene and Bertha Marie (Thompson) Van D.; m. Leland Wilkinson, June 23, 1967; children: Anne Marie, Caroline Cook. AB, Vassar Coll., 1966; MTS, Harvard U., 1969; JD with honors, U. Conn., 1976; MDiv, Luth Sch. Theology, Chgo., 1999. Bar: Conn. 1976, Ill. 1977, U.S. Dist. Ct. Conn. 1976, U.S. Dist. Ct. (no. dist.) Ill., U.S. Ct. Appeals (7th cir.) 1984, U.S. Supreme Ct. 1983; ordained to ministry, Luth Ch., 1999. Instr. legal rsch. and writing Loyola U. Sch. Law, Chgo., 1976-79; assoc. Wildman, Harrold, Allen & Dixon, Chgo., 1977-84, ptnr., 1985-94; prin. Law Offices of Ruth E. Van Demark, Chgo., 1995—; pastor Wicker Park Luth. Ch., Chgo., 1999—. Mem. rules com. Ill. Supreme Ct., 1999—, chair appellate rules subcom., 1996—; mem. dist. ct. fund adv. com. U.S. Dist. Ct. (no. dist.) Ill., 1997—. Assoc. editor Conn. Law Rev., 1975-76. Bd. dirs. Lutheran Soc. Svcs. Ill., 1998—, sec., 2000—02, chmn., 2002-; mem. adv. bd. Horizon Hospice, Chgo., 1978—, YWCA Battered Women's Shelter, Evanston, Ill., 1982-86; del.-at-large White House Conf. on Families, L.A., 1980; mem. alumni coun. Harvard Divinity Sch., 1988-91; vol. atty. Pro Bono Advocates Chgo., 1982-92, bd. dirs., 1993-99, chair devel. com., 1993; bd. dirs. Friends of Pro Bono Advocates Orgn., 1987-89, New Voice Prodns., 1984-86, Byrne Piven Theater Workshop, 1987-90, Luth. Social Svcs. Ill. (sec., 2000—), 1998—; founder, bd. dirs. Friends of Battered Women and Their Children, 1986-87; chair 175th Reunion Fund Harvard U. Div. Sch., 1992. Mem. ABA, Ill. Bar Assn., Conn. Bar Assn., Chgo. Bar Assn., Appellate Lawyers Assn. Ill. (bd. dirs. 1985-87, treas. 1989-90, sec. 1990-91, v.p. 1991-92, pres. 1992-93), Women's Bar Assn. Ill., Jr. League Evanston (chair State Pub. Affairs Com. 1987-88, Vol. of Yr. 1983-84), Chgo. Vassar Club (pres. 1979-81), Cosmopolitan Club (N.Y.C.). Appellate, Federal civil litigation, State civil litigation. Home: 2046 W Pierce Ave Chicago IL 60622-1946 Office: 225 W Washington St Ste 2200 Chicago IL 60606-3408 E-mail: revlaw@msn.com.

VANDERBILT, ARTHUR T., II, lawyer; b. Summit, NJ, Feb. 20, 1950; s. William Runyon and Jean (White) V. BA, Wesleyan U., Middletown, Conn., 1972; JD, U. Va., 1975. Bar: N.J. 1975, U.S. Dist. Ct. N.J. 1975, U.S. Supreme Ct. 1978. Jud. clk. to presiding justice N.J. Superior Ct., 1975-76, dep. atty. gen., 1976-78, asst. counsel to gov., 1978-79; ptnr. Carella, Byrne, Bain & Gilfillan, Roseland, N.J., 1979—. Chmn. Supreme Ct. Ethics Com.; mem. Supreme Ct. Adv. Com. Profl. Ethics. Author: Changing Law 1976, Jersey Justice, 1978, Law School, 1981, Treasure Wreck, 1986, Fortune's Children, 1989 (Book of the Month Club, Readers Digest and fgn. edits.), New Jersey's Judicial Revolution, 1997, Golden Days, 1998 (fgn. edits.), Jersey Jurists, 1998, The Making of a Bestseller, 1999, Gardening in Eden, 2003. Trustee Elizabeth (NJ) Presbytery. Named to N.J. Literary Hall of Fame. Fellow: ABA Found.; mem.: ABA (Scribes award 1976), Nat. Writers Union, The Authors Guild, Inc., Nat. Assn. Bond Lawyers, Am. Judicature Soc., N.J. Bar Assn., Capitol Hill Club, Hyannis Yacht Club. Republican. Presbyterian. Avocation: writing. Administrative and regulatory, Municipal (including bonds), Utilities, public. Office: Carella Byrne Bain & Gilfillan 6 Becker Farm Rd Roseland NJ 07068-1735

VANDER LAAN, MARK ALAN, lawyer; b. Akron, Ohio, Sept. 14, 1948; s. Robert H. and Isabel R. (Bishop) Vander L.; m. Barbara Ann Ryzenga, Aug. 25, 1970; children: Aaron, Matthew. AB, Hope Coll., 1970; JD, U. Mich., 1972. Bar: Ohio 1973, U.S. Dist. Ct. (so. dist.) Ohio 1973, U.S. Ct. Appeals (6th cir.) 1978, U.S. Supreme Ct. 1981. Assoc. Dinsmore, Shohl,

Coates & Deupree, Cin., 1972-79; ptnr. Dinsmore & Shohl, Cin., 1979—. Chair litig. dept., 2001—, spl. counsel Ohio Atty. Gen.'s Office, 1983—; spl. prosecutor State of Ohio, 1985-94; city solicitor City of Blue Ash, Ohio, 1987—, City of Silverton, Ohio, 1999—; trustee Cin. So. Railway, 1994—, pres., 1999—; trustee, chair Grassroots Leadership Acad., 1997—. Mem. Cin. Human Rels. Commn., 1980-86; mem. Leadership Cin. Class XIII, 1989-90; trustee Legal Aid Soc. of Cin., 1981-94, pres., 1988-90; trustee Volunteer Lawyers for the Poor Found., pres., 2003—. Mem. ABA, Ohio Bar Assn., Cin. Bar Assn. (ethics com. 1983—), Sixth Cir. Jud. Conf. (life), Potter Stewart Inn of Ct. (master), Queen City Club. General civil litigation, Corporate, general. Office: Dinsmore & Shohl 1900 Chemed Ct 255 E 5th St Cincinnati OH 45202-4700

VANDER MOLEN, THOMAS DALE, lawyer; b. Ann Arbor, Mich., Oct. 30, 1950; s. John and Eleanor Ruth (Driesens) Vander M.; m. Judith P. Wrahlstad, June 16, 2001; children from previous marriage: Laura, David, Eric. BA, Calvin Coll., 1972; JD magna cum laude, Harvard U., 1975. Bar: Minn. 1976, U.S. Dist. Ct. Minn. 1981, U.S. Claims Ct. 1983, U.S. Tax Ct. 1977, U.S. Ct. Appeals 1988. Law clk. to judge U.S. Ct. Appeals-First Cir., Boston, 1975-76; assoc. Dorsey & Whitney, Mpls., 1976-81; ptnr. Dorsey & Whitney LLP, Mpls., 1982—, gen. counsel, 1993—2001. Mem. editorial bd. Harvard Law Rev., 1973-75. Presbyterian. Municipal (including bonds), Taxation, general, Non-profit and tax-exempt organizations. Office: Dorsey & Whitney LLP 50 South 6th St Minneapolis MN 55402-1498

VANDERSTAR, JOHN, lawyer; b. Jersey City, Sept. 17, 1933; s. John Vanderstar and Rosemarie (Torraco) Legette; m. Beth S. Vanderstar, Nov. 7, 1956 (div. Oct. 1984); children: Pippa, Alexandra, Thankful, Eliza; m. M. Elizabeth Culbreth, Mar. 16, 1985. BSE, Princeton U., 1954; LLB cum laude, Harvard U., 1961. Bar: D.C. 1961, U.S. Dist. Ct. (D.C. dist.) 1961, U.S. Dist. Ct. Md. 1985, U.S. Ct. Claims 1976, U.S. Ct. Appeals (8th cir.) 1966, U.S. Ct. Appeals (5th cir.) 1969, U.S. Ct. Appeals (1st cir.) 1971, U.S. Ct. Appeals (4th cir.) 1974, U.S. Ct. Appeals (3d cir.) 1979, U.S. Ct. Appeals 11th cir.) 1981, U.S. Ct. Appeals (Fed. cir.) 1983, U.S. Supreme Ct. 1966. Assoc. Covington & Burling, Washington, 1961-70, ptnr., 1970—2000. Pres. ACLU Nat. Capital Area, Washington, 1976-78, bd. dirs., 1971-78; bd. dirs. NOW Legal Def. and Edn. Fund, N.Y.C., 1979-94, Planned Parenthood Metro. Wash., 1998—. Lt. USNR, 1954-58. Recipient Alan Barth award, ACLU Nat. Capital Area, 1984. Mem. ABA, D.C. Bar (bd. govs. 1985-88). Episcopalian. Antitrust, Civil rights, Federal civil litigation. Office: Covington & Burling 1201 Pennsylvania Ave NW Washington DC 20004 Home: # 705 1300 Crystal Dr Arlington VA 22202-3234

VANDERVELDE, ERWIN, lawyer; b. Brussels, May 4, 1960; s. Louis Vandervelde and José Van Rillaer; m. Bieke Garcet, Oct. 5, 1985; children: Griet, Kaat, Lotte. Law Degree, Vrye U., Brussels, 1984. Bar: 1984. Legal cons., 1985; mgr. Deloitte & Touche, Brussels, 1992; ptnr., 1998, Laga & Philippe, Brussels, 2001. Labor (including EEOC, Fair Labor Standards Act, labor-management relations, NLRB, OSHA), Pension, profit-sharing, and employee benefits, Workers' compensation. Office: Laga & Philippe Berkenlaan 8A B-1831 Diegem Belgium

VANDEWALLE, GERALD WAYNE, state supreme court chief justice; b. Noonan, N.D., Aug. 15, 1933; s. Jules C. and Blanche Marie (Gits) VandeW. BSc, U. N.D., 1955, JD, 1958. Bar: N.D., U.S. Dist. Ct. N.D. 1959. Spl. asst. atty. gen. State of N.D., Bismarck, 1958-75, 1st asst. atty. gen., 1975-78; justice N.D. Supreme Ct., 1978-92, chief justice, 1993—. Mem. faculty Bismarck Jr. Coll., 1972-76; mem. Nat. Ctr. for State Cts. Rsch. adv. coun.; mem. fed.-state jurisdiction com. Jud. Conf. of the U.S. Editor-in-chief N.D. Law Rev, 1957-58. Active Bismarck Meals on Wheels Recipient Sioux award U. N.D., 1992, Ednl. Law award N.D. Coun. Sch. Attys., 1987, Love Without Fear award Abused Adult Resource Ctr., 1995, N. Dakota State Bar Assoc. Dist. Service Award, 1998. Mem. ABA (co-chmn. bar admissions com. 1991-99, mem. coun. sect. legal edn. and admissions, chmn. coun. sect. legal edn. and admissions), State Bar Assn. N.D., Burleigh County Bar Assn., Conf. of Chief Justices (past pres., bd. dirs. 1996-98, chmn. fed.-state tribal rels. com.), Am. Contract Bridge League, Order of Coif, N.D. Jud. Conf. (exec. com.), Elks, KC, Phi Eta Sigma, Beta Alpha Psi (Outstanding Alumnus award Zeta chpt. 1995), Beta Gamma Sigma, Phi Alpha Delta. Roman Catholic. Office: ND Supreme Ct State Capitol 600 E Boulevard Ave Bismarck ND 58505-0530 E-mail: gvandewalle@ndcourts.com.

VANDIVIER, BLAIR ROBERT, lawyer; b. Rapid City, S.D., Dec. 24, 1955; s. Robert Eugene and Barbara Jean (Kidd) V.; m. Elizabeth Louise Watson, July 26, 1980; children: Jessica Elizabeth, Jennifer Louise. BS magna cum laude, Butler U., 1978; JD cum laude, Ind. U., 1981. Bar: Ind. 1981, U.S. Dist. Ct. (so. dist.) Ind. 1981, U.S. Tax Ct. 1985. Assoc. Henderson, Daily, Withrow, Johnson & Gross, Indpls., 1981-83; assoc., ptnr. Johnson, Gross, Densborn & Wright, Indpls., 1983-85, of counsel, 1985-87; v.p., sec. Benchmark Products, Inc. (formerly Benchmark Chem. Corp.), Indpls., 1985-91, pres., 1991—, also bd. dirs.; ptnr. Gross & Vandivier, Indpls., 1987-89; of counsel Riley, Bennett & Egloff, Indpls., 1990—; mgmt. rep. Pro Com, L.L.C., 1991—. V.p. Seleco Inc., Indpls., 1988-93, pres., 1993—. Mem. com. Conner Prairie Settlement Fund Dr., Indpls., 1983-85, Riley Run, 1987—; mem. regulatory study com. City of Indpls., 1993-98. Mem. ABA, Ind. Bar Assn., Indpls. Bar Assn (bd. dirs. young lawyers divsn. 1982-85), Am. Electroplaters and Surface Finishers Soc. (chmn. nat. law com. 1986-97, pres. Indpls. br. 1989, bd. mgrs. 1997—, tech. conf. bd. 1991-97, chmn. surface finishers ann. tech. conf. and exhbn. 1994, chmn. surface finishers focus group 1994—, Tech. Conf. Bd. Recognition award 1996), Nat. Assn. Metal Finishers (bd. dirs. 1998—, exec. com. 1998—, sec./treas. 2000-2001, v.p. 2001-02, pres. 2002-03), Metal Finishing Suppliers Assn. (spl. projects svcs. com., 1988-93, chmn. 1993—, chmn. hazardous materials br. 1991-93, trustee 1992-95, v.p. 1995-97, pres. 1997-99, past pres. 1999—, Award of Merit 1997, August P. Munning Commemorative award of merit 2001), Crooked Stick Golf Club (house com. 2003), Highland Country Club (chmn. ins. com. 1989-94, golf. com. 1992-94, bd. dirs. 1995-97, chmn. fin. com. 1996-97), Surface Finishing Industry Coun. (bd. dirs., sec. 1997-98, pres. 1999), Econ. Club Indpls., Metal Finishing Found. (pres. 1999), Delta Tau Delta (chmn. 1987-97, bd. dirs. Beta Zeta Found. 1986, Outstanding Alumnus Beta Zeta chpt. 1986). Republican. Episcopalian. Avocations: reading, golf, aviation. Commercial, contracts (including sales of goods; commercial financing), Corporate, general, Property, real (including real estate development, water). Home: 8927 Woodacre Ln Indianapolis IN 46234-2848 Office: Benchmark Products Inc PO Box 68809 Indianapolis IN 46268-0809

VAN DYKE, JON MARKHAM MARKHAM, law educator; b. Washington, Apr. 29, 1943; s. Stuart Hope and Eleonora (Markham) Van D.; m. Sherry Phyllis Broder, Feb. 12, 1978; children: Jesse Bernard, Eric Gabriel, Michelle Tiare. BA, Yale U., 1964; JD, Harvard U., 1967. Bar: D.C. 1968, Calif. 1970, Hawaii 1976. Asst. prof. law Cath. U., Washington, 1967-69; law clk. Calif. Supreme Ct., San Francisco, 1969—70; vis. fellow Ctr. for Study of Democratic Instns., Santa Barbara, Calif., 1970-71; assoc. prof. law U. Calif., San Francisco, 1971—75, prof., 1975—76; prof. law U. Hawaii, Honolulu, 1976—, project dir. law of the sea Sea Grant Coll. Program, 1979-88, 90-92, assoc. dean, 1980-82. Rsch. assoc. East-West Ctr., Honolulu, 1982—84, adj. rsch. assoc., 1986—92, Honolulu, 2001—; exec. bd. Law of the Sea Inst., Honolulu, 1982—88; dir. U. Hawaii Inst. for Peace, 1988—90. Author: North Vietnam's Strategy for Survival, 1972, Jury Selection Procedures: Our Uncertain Commitment to Representative Panels, 1977; editor: Consensus and Confrontation: The United States and the Law of the Sea Convention, 1985, International Navigation: Rocks and Shoals Ahead?, 1988, Freedom for the Seas in the 21st Century, 1993, Sharing the Resources of the South China Sea, 1997, International Law and Litigation in the U.S., 2000, Checklists on Searches and Seizures in Public Schools, 2003. Mem. Reapportionment Commn., Honolulu, 1981-82, ACLU Litigation Com., Honolulu, 1986-87, Hawaii Bicentennial Commn. of U.S. Constitution, 1987. Recipient Presdl. Citation for Tchg. Excellence, 1987. Mem. Am. Soc. Internat. Law, Hawaii State Bar Assn., Internat. Coun. Environ. Law. Home: 4191 Round Top Dr Honolulu HI 96822-5039 Office: U Hawaii Law Sch 2515 Dole St Honolulu HI 96822-2328 E-mail: jvandyke@hawaii.edu.

VAN DYKE, PETER TYSON, lawyer; b. Glens Falls, N.Y., Mar. 3, 1942; s. Robert Tyson and Jonise Katherine (Rezzemini) Van D.; m. Prudence H., Dec. 10, 1942; children: Elizabeth, Katherine, Carolyn. BS, U. R.I., 1964; JD with honors, Albany Law Sch., 1968; LLM, George Washington U., 1973. Bar: N.Y. 1969, Okla. 1972, U.S. Supreme Ct., U.S. Ct. Appeals (5th and 10th cirs.), Okla., N.Y., U.S. Dist. Ct. (ea. dist.) N.Y., U.S. Dist. Ct. (we., ea. and no. dists.) Okla., U.S. Dist. Ct. (no. dist.) Tex. Atty. Lytle Soule & Curlee, Oklahoma City, 1972-97, McAfee & Taft, Oklahoma City, 1997—. Counsel Okla. chpt. Nat. Elec. Contractor's Assn., 1980—. Elder Trinity Bapt. Ch., Norman, 1988—. Capt. U.S. Army, 1969-73. Republican. Baptist. Labor (including EEOC, Fair Labor Standards Act, labor-management relations, NLRB, OSHA). Office: McAfee & Taft 2 Leadership Sq 10th Fl Oklahoma City OK 73102

VAN FLEET, GEORGE ALLAN, lawyer; b. Monterey, Calif., Jan. 20, 1953; s. George Lawson and Wilma Ruth (Williams) Van F.; m. Laurie Elise Koch, July 20, 1975; children: Katia Elaine, Alexander Lawson. BA summa cum laude, Rice U., 1976; JD summa cum laude, Columbia U., 1977. Bar: Tex. 1978, U.S. Dist. Ct. (so. dist.) Tex. 1978, U.S. Dist. Ct. (we. dist.) Tex. 1987, U.S. Dist. Ct. (no. dist.) Tex, 1988, U.S. Dist. Ct. (ea. dist.) Tex. 1991, U.S. Tax Ct., 1984, U.S. Ct. Appeals (5th cir.) 1978, U.S. Ct. Appeals (11th cir.) 1981, U.S. Ct. Appeals (D.C. cir.) 1982, U.S. Ct. Appeals (fed. cir.) 1993, U.S. Supreme Ct. 1981. Law clk. U.S. Ct. Appeals (2d cir.), N.Y.C., 1977; assoc. Vinson & Elkins, Houston, 1977-84, ptnr., 1984—. Co-chmn. Antitrust Practice Group. Editor: Annual Review of Antitrust Law Developments, 2000; co-author: Federal Civil Procedure Before Trial--Firth Circuit, 1997, supplement, 1999, The Competition Laws of NAFTA, Canada, Mexico and the United States, 1997, Business and Commercial Litigation in Federal Courts, 1998, American Legal Ethics Library, 2002, State Antitrust Practice and Statutes, 1999, Doing Business in Texas, 2003; contbr. articles to profl. jours. Mem. bd. visitors Columbia U., 1992—; mem. City of Houston Ethics Com., 1992—98, chmn., 1995—98; bd. dirs. Nat. Appleseed Found., 2002—, Tex. Appleseed Ctr., 1998—, vice chmn., 1999—2002, chmn., 2002—. Recipient Ordroneaux prize Columbia U., 1977, W. Frank Newton award for outstandign contbns. in provision of access to legal svcs. to the poor State Bar Tex., 2002; James Kent scholar Columbia U., 1974-77. Fellow Tex. Bar Found.; mem. ABA (com. chmn. 1987-95, mem. coun. 1996-99, com. chmn. 2000—, mem. ho. dels. 2002-, sect. officer 2002-, del. ho. dels. 2002-), State Bar Tex. (mem. coun. 2000-), Houston Bar Assn. (sect. chair 1991-93), Tex.-Mex. Bar Assn. (pres. 1998-2000), Phi Beta Kappa. Democrat. Jewish. Antitrust, General civil litigation, Professional liability. Home: 3430 S Parkwood Dr Houston TX 77021-1238 Office: Vinson & Elkins LLP 1001 Fannin St Ste 2300 Houston TX 77002-6760 E-mail: avanfleet@velaw.com.

VAN GESTEL, ALLAN, judge; b. Boston, Dec. 3, 1935; BA, Colby Coll., 1957; LLB, Boston U., 1961; MA (hon.), Colby Coll., 1999. Bar: Mass. 1961, U.S. Dist. Ct. Mass. 1963, U.S. Ct. Appeals (1st cir.) 1969, U.S. Supreme Ct. 1972, U.S. Ct. Claims 1979, U.S. Ct. Appeals (2d cir.) 1980, U.S. Dist. Ct. (no. dist.) N.Y. 1980, U.S. Dist. Ct. (we. dist.) N.Y. 1993, U.S. Ct. Appeals (3d cir.) 1993, U.S. Ct. Appeals (5th cir.) 1995. Assoc. firm Goodwin, Procter & Hoar, Boston, 1961-70, ptnr., 1970-96; assoc. justice Superior Ct. Mass., 1996—; presiding justice Suffolk County Bus. Litigation Session, 2000—. Spl. counsel Boston Fin. Commn., 1974; spl. counsel to Mass. Commn. on Jud. Conduct, 1986; mem. Scituate (Mass.) Bd. Zoning Appeals, 1970, Scituate Planning Bd., 1972; spl. counsel Gov. of N.Y. on Indian Land Claims, 1985-96; spl. counsel to Gov. and Atty. Gen. of Vt. on Indian Claims, 1987-90; chmn. standing adv. com. Mass. Rules Civil Procedure, 1986-93 ; overseer Colby Coll., 1990-99, trustee, 1999—. Contbr. numerous articles on Eastern Indian land claims, ct. administrn., capital punishment to profl. jours. Fellow Am. Coll. Trial Lawyers; mem. ABA, Mass. Bar Assn., Boston Bar Assn. (chmn., task force on drugs and the cts.), Supreme Jud. Ct. Hist. Soc. (chmn. bd. overseers 1993-96), Mass. Hist. Soc. General civil litigation, Environmental, Native American.

VAN GILDER, DEREK ROBERT, lawyer, engineer; b. San Antonio, Feb. 26, 1950; s. Robert Ellis and Genevieve Delphine (Hutter) Van G. Student, U.S. Mil. Acad., 1969-71; BS in Civil Engring., U. Tex., 1974, JD, 1981; MBA, U. Houston, 1976. Bar: Tex. 1981, U.S. Ct. Appeals (5th and 9th cirs.) 1982, Calif. 1982, U.S. Dist. Ct. (cen. dist.) Calif. 1982, U.S. Dist. Ct. (ea. and so. dists.) Tex. 1982, U.S. Dist. Ct. (we. dist.) Tex. 1983, U.S. Dist. Ct. (no. dist.) Tex. 1988, U.S. Supreme Ct. 1988, D.C. 1990, U.S. Patent/Trademark 1990. Engr. various engring cos., Houston, Longview and Austin, Tex., 1974-81; assoc. Thelen, Marrin, Johnson & Bridges, Los Angeles, 1981-82, Bean & Manning, Houston, 1982-85; pvt. practice Van Gilder & Assocs., Houston, 1985-94, Law Office of Derek R. Van Gilder, Bastrop, Tex., 1995—. Instr. Houston C.C., 1981-82; life mem., committeeman Houston Livestock Show & Rodeo, 1991-2000. Bd. dirs. Children's Advocacy Ctr. of Tex., Children's Advocacy Ctr. of Bastrop County, treas. 1996-2003; chmn. Friends of Science Park-MD Anderson Sci. Park., Smithville. Mem. Bastrop C. of C., Bastrop County Bar Assn., Rotary Club Bastrop County (v.p. 1996-97, pres.-elect 1997-98, pres. 1998-99, asst. dist. gov. 2000—). Republican. Roman Catholic. Avocations: golf, scuba diving, photography. General civil litigation, Construction, Patent. Office: 916 Main St Bastrop TX 78602-3810

VAN GORDER, JOHN FREDERIC, lawyer; b. Jacksonville, Fla., Mar. 22, 1943; s. Harold Burton and Charlotte Louise Van G.; m. Sandra Joan Hagen, June 4, 1977 (div. June 1995); children: Alyssa Jane, Kathryn Ann; m. Ann Michele Brancato, Oct. 7, 1995. Grad., Dover (Eng.) Coll., 1961; AB, Dartmouth Coll., 1965; postgrad., Air Force Inst. Tech., 1967-68; MS in Adminstrn., George Washington U., 1973; postgrad., U. Va., Coll. William and Mary, Cath. U. Am., Northeastern U., Babson Coll., U. South; JD, Fordham U., 1981. Bar: N.J. 1981, U.S. Dist. Ct. N.J. 1981, N.Y. 1983, U.S. Supreme Ct. 1989. Commd. 2d lt. USAF, 1965, advanced through grades to capt., 1968; weapons contr. Aerospace Def. Commd., Ft. Lee, Va., 1965-67; buyer electronics sys. divsn. Air Force Sys. Commd., Bedford, Mass., 1968-69; project mgr. rsch. and devel. Hdqrs. USAF, Washington, 1969-73, br. chief pers., 1973-74; presdl. social aide The White House, Washington, 1971-74; assoc. Louis C. Kramp & Assocs., Washington, 1975; program officer J.M. Found., N.Y.C., 1975-81; assoc. Winne, Banta & Rizzi Esqs., Hackensack, N.J., 1981-83; asst. sec., program adminstr. Glenmede Trust Co., Phila., 1983—86; exec. dir., asst. sec. Leon Lowenstein Found., 1986—. Atty. Rent Leveling Bd., Borough of Bergenfield, N.J., 1983; pres. Vanguard Corp., Massapequa, N.Y., 1996-2001; adj. prof. Grad. Sch. Edn., Fordham U., N.Y.C., 1997—. Chmn. N.Y.C. steering com. Nat. Congress on Volunteerism and Citizenship, 1976; mem. exec. com. Mayor's Vol. Action Coun., 1977-78; bd. govs. N.Y. Jaycees Found., 1978-79; bd. govs., 4th v.p. First Assembly Dist. Rep. Club, 1977-82; vestryman All Saints Episc. Ch., Bergenfield, 1982-83; mem. Tabernacle Twp. Planning Bd., 1985-88, Tabernacle Bd. Edn., 1988-91, Tabernacle Rep. Club, 1983-93; jr. warden, 1987-88, sr. warden, 1989-90, vestryman, lay reader St. Peter's Episc. Ch., Medford, N.J., 1985-93; program adv. com. Toshiba Am. Found., 1993-99; trustee, dir. Support Ctr. of N.Y., N.Y.C., 1995-97, Robert A. Taft Inst. Govt., N.Y.C., 1994-97; bd. dirs. N.Y. C. Pub./Pvt. Initiatives, Inc., 1996-2000, bd. dirs. NY Regional Assn. Grantmakers, 1998—; bd. trustees Calvin K. Kazanjian Econs. Found., 2002--. Col. USAFR, ret. Named Outstanding Young Man of VA., 1975, USAF Res. Officer of Yr., 1985. Mem. Internat. (senator; v.p. 1975; rep. to UN 1976), U.S. (nat. v.p. 1973-74), D.C. (pres. 1972-73), N.Y.C. (bd. govs. 1978-79) Jaycees, SAR, Soc. Mayflower Descs., ABA, N.Y. Bar Assn., Student Bar Assn. (class pres. 1978-81), Toastmasters (local pres. 1969-70, area gov. 1970-71), Lions (pres. Medford Twp. club 1985-86, co-chmn. Charity Ball 1987), Masons, Alpha Delta Phi. Republican. Episcopalian. General practice, Government contracts and claims. Address: 7 E Bayview St Massapequa NY 11758-7602

VAN GRAAFEILAND, ELLSWORTH ALFRED, federal judge; b. Rochester, N.Y., May 11, 1915; s. Ivan and (Gohr) Van Graafeiland; m. Rosemary Vaeth, May 26, 1945; children: Gary, Suzanne, Joan, John, Anne. AB, U. Rochester, 1937; LLB, Cornell U., 1940. Bar: N.Y. 1940. Practiced in, Rochester; judge U.S. Ct. Appeals (2nd cir), Rochester, NY, 1974—85; sr. judge U.S. Ct. Appeals (2d cir.), 1985—. Fellow: N.Y. Bar Found., Am. Bar Found.; mem.: ABA (ho. dels. 1973—75), Am. Coll. Trial Lawyers., Monroe County Bar Assn. (past pres.), N.Y. State Bar Assn. (v.p. 1972—73, pres. 1973—74, chmn. negligence compensation and ins. sect. 1968—69), Oak Hill Country Club, Kent Club, Masons. Home: 1 Tiffany Ct Pittsford NY 14534-1067 Office: Fed Bldg 100 State St Ste 423 Rochester NY 14614-1309

VAN GRACK, STEVEN, lawyer; b. Memphis, Oct. 6, 1948; s. Irving and Edna (Schwartz) Van Grack; m. Gail Beverly Lang, Nov. 18, 1972 (div.); children: Adam, Ryan, Brandon; m. Susan M Freeland, May 21, 1993. BA, U. Md., 1970, JD, 1974. Bar: 1974 (Md), DC 1976, US Dist Ct Md 1976, US Dist Ct DC 1976, US Ct Appeals (4th cir) 1977, US Supreme Ct 1978. Law clk. to presiding justice Montgomery County Cir. Ct., Rockville, Md., 1974-75; assoc. Joseph Roesser Law Offices, Silver Springs, Md., 1975-78; ptnr. Ebert & Bowytz, Washington, 1978-80; mng. ptnr. Van Grack, Axelson & Williamowsky, Rockville, 1980—. Instr, lectr Montgomery Col, Germantown, Md., 1983—85. Cubmaster packs 1343 and 1449 Boy Scouts Am; coach Rockville Baseball Asn; trustee Shady Grove Adventist Hosp Found; co-chmn Montgomery County March of Dimes WalkAmerica Comt, 1998—2000; campaign mgr Comt to Elect the Sitting Judges, Rockville, 1982; mayor City of Rockville, 1985—87; gen counsel Montgomery County Dem Cent Comt, Kensington, Md., 1978—82; Dem cand 8th Congl Dist Md, 1994; chmn Md Real Estate Comn, 2001—; bd dirs Washington Met Coun Govts. With USAR, 1970—71. Named one of Outstanding Young Men Am, Jaycees, 1978, 1981; recipient Fifth Ann Pro Bono Serv Award, Montgomery County Bar Found, 1998, Extraordinary Commitment to the Delivery of Legal Servs Award, 1999, Nancy Dworkin Award, Montgomery County Comn Children and Youth, 2001. Fellow: Md Bar Found (Profl. Legal Excellence award 2002); mem.: ATLA, ABA, Rockville CofC (bd dirs), Montgomery County Bar Asn (Outstanding Comt Chair of the Yr Award 2001), Md Trial Lawyers Asn, Md Bar Asn. Jewish. Avocations: running, swimming, exercising, coin collecting, political button collecting. Professional liability, Criminal, Personal injury (including property damage). Home: 808 Fordham St Rockville MD 20850-1018 Office: Van Grack Axelson & Williamowsky 110 N Washington St Fl 5 Rockville MD 20850-2223 E-mail: sug@vawlaw.com.

VAN GRUNSVEN, PAUL ROBERT, lawyer; b. Green Bay, Wis., Mar. 11, 1961; s. David Edward and Carol Ann (Janssen) Van G. BS, Marquette U., 1983, JD, 1986; LLM in Health Law, De Paul U., 1995. Bar: Wis. 1986, U.S. Dist. Ct. (ea. dist.) Wis. 1986. Mem. Techmeier & Van Grunsven, S.C., Milw., 1986-89, shareholder, 1989-2001; chair health law dept. Kasdorf, Lewis & Swietlik, S.C., 2001—. Adj. prof. Marquette U. Law Sch., Milw., 1995—. Recipient Am. Jurisprudence award Lawyer's Coop. Pub. Co., 1986. Mem. ATLA, Wis. Trial Lawyers for Public Justice, Wis. Acad. Trial Lawyers (bd. dirs., co-editor The Verdict), Wis. Bar Assn., Milw. Bar Assn. (co-chair health law sect.). Roman Catholic. Avocations: golf, football, baseball, basketball. General civil litigation, Health, Personal injury (including property damage). Office: Kasdorf Lewis & Swietlik SC 11270 W Park Pl Ste 500 Milwaukee WI 53224-

VAN GUNDY, GREGORY FRANK, lawyer; b. Columbus, Ohio, Oct. 24, 1945; s. Paul Arden and Edna Marie (Sanders) Van G.; m. Lisa Tamara Langer. BA, Ohio State U., Columbus, 1966, JD, 1969. Bar: N.Y. bar 1971. Asso. atty. firm Willkie Farr & Gallagher, N.Y.C., 1970-74; v.p. legal, sec. Marsh & McLennan Cos., Inc., N.Y.C., 1974-79, v.p., sec., gen. counsel, 1979-2000, sec., 2000—. Mem. ABA, Phi Beta Kappa. Clubs: University (N.Y.C.). Roman Catholic. Corporate, general. Home: 232 Fox Meadow Rd Scarsdale NY 10583-1640 Office: Marsh & McLennan Cos Inc 1166 Avenue Of The Americas New York NY 10036-2728

VAN HAREN, PETER, lawyer; b. 1945; BA, LLB, U. Ariz. Bar: Ariz. 1973. Asst. city atty. City of Phoenix, 1976—78, city atty., 2000—, City of Prescott, Ariz., 1978—84, City of Glendale, Ariz., 1984—2000. Town mgr. City of Paradise Valley, Ariz. Office: City Hall 200 W Washington St Ste 1300 Phoenix AZ 85003 Business E-Mail: peter.vanharen@phoenix.gov.*

VAN HAREN, W(ILLIAM) MICHAEL, lawyer; b. Grand Rapids, Mich., Feb. 15, 1948; s. Adrian William and Donna Bell (Burkett) Van H.; m. Kathryn Mary Desmet, Aug. 7, 1971; children: Ryan C., Amy K., Andrew M., Megan E. BS, U. Mich., 1970; JD magna cum laude, U. Detroit, 1975. Bar: Mich. 1975, U.S. Dist. Ct. (we. dist.) Mich. 1975. Assoc. Warner, Norcross & Judd, Grand Rapids, 1975-81, ptnr., 1981—. Adj. prof. taxation Seidman Sch. Bus., Grand Valley State U., Grand Rapids, 1983-85. Assoc. editor U. Detroit Sch. Law Jour. Urban Law, 1974-75; co-editor (handbook) Probate Practice in Decedents Estates, 1985. Co-chmn. profl. divsn. Kent County United Way, Grand Rapids, 1983, 84; pres. Garfield Pk. Nature Ctr., Grand Rapids, 1977, Garfield Pk. Neighborhhod Assn., Grand Rapids, 1979; bd. dirs. Western Mich. Estate Planning Coun., 1986-89, Cath. Social Svcs., 1997-2002, Goodwill Found., 2002—; mem. fin. com. St. Robert's Ch., Ada, Mich., 1997-2002. Fellow Am. Coll. Trust and Estate Coun.; mem. Mich. Bar Assn. (probate and estate planning coun. 1981-93, treas. 1987-88, sec. 1989-90, vice chmn. 1990-91, chair 1992-93, exec. officer 1993—), Mich. Bar Found., Univ. Club. Republican. Roman Catholic. Avocations: squash, golf, hunting. Corporate, general, Probate (including wills, trusts), Estate taxation. Home: 9007 Conservation St NE Ada MI 49301-9797 Office: Warner Norcross & Judd 900 Fifth Third Ctr 111 Lyon St NW Ste 900 Grand Rapids MI 49503-2487

VAN HOLLEN, J.B. lawyer; Grad., St. Olaf's Coll., U. Wis. Asst. U.S. atty. We. Dist. Wis., 1991—93; atty. Bayfield County, 1993—; U.S. atty. We. Dist. Wis., 2002—. Office: PO Box 1585 Madison WI 53701*

VAN HOOMISSEN, GEORGE ALBERT, state supreme court justice; b. Portland, Oreg., Mar. 7, 1930; s. Fred J. and Helen F. (Flanagan) Van H.; m. Ruth Madeleine Niedermeyer, June 4, 1960; children: Geroge T., Ruth Anne, Madeleine, Matthew. BBA, U. Portland, 1951; JD, Georgetown U., 1955, LLM in Labor Law, 1957; LLM in Jud. Adminstrn., U. Va., 1986. Bar: D.C. 1955, Oreg. 1956, Tex. 1971, U.S. Dist. Ct. Oreg. 1956, U.S. Ct. Mil. Appeals 1955, U.S. Ct. Customs and Patent Appeals 1955, U.S. Ct. Claims 1955, U.S. Ct. Appeals (9th cir.) 1956, U.S. Ct. Appeals (D.C. cir.) 1955, U.S. Supreme Ct. 1960. Law clk. for Chief Justice Harold J. Warner Oreg. Supreme Ct., 1955-56; Keigwin teaching fellow Georgetown Law Sch., 1956-57; dep. dist. atty. Multnomah County, Portland, 1957-59; pvt. practice Portland, 1959-62; dist. atty. Multnomah County, 1962-71; dean nat. coll. dist. attys., prof. law U. Houston, 1971-73; judge Cir. Ct., Portland, 1973-81, Oreg. Ct. Appeals, Salem, 1981-88; justice Oreg. Supreme Ct., Salem, 1988—2001. Adj. prof. Northwestern Sch. Law, Portland, Willamette U. Sch. Law, Portland State U.; mem. faculty Am. Acad. Judicial Edn., Nat. Judicial Coll.; Keigwin Teaching fellow Georgetown U. Law Sch. Mem. Oreg. Ho. of Reps., Salem, 1959-62, chmn. house jud. com. With USMC, 1951-53; col. USMCR (ret.). Recipient Disting. Alumnus award U. Portland, 1972. Master Owen M. Panner Am. Inn of Ct.; mem. ABA, Oreg. State Bar, Tex. Bar Assn., Oreg. Law Inst. (bd. dirs.), Arlington Club, Multnomah Athletic Club, Univ. Club. Roman Catholic. Office: Oreg Supreme Ct 2105 SW Elm St Portland OR 97201 E-mail: gavanhoomissen@qwest.net.

VAN HOY, PHILIP MARSHALL, lawyer; b. Washington, Nov. 8, 1947; s. Joe Milton and Helen Virginia (Spangler) V.; m. Sylvia Kathryn Smith, Dec. 30, 1972; children: Marshall, Travis. AB, Duke U., 1970; JD, U. N.C., 1973. Bar: N.C. 1973, U.S. Dist. Ct. (ea., we. and mid. dists.) N.C. 1974, U.S. Ct. Appeals (4th cir.) 1974, U.S. Supreme Ct. 1978. Labor counsel Duke Power Co., Charlotte, N.C., 1973-80; assoc. Siegel, O'Connor & Kaunen, Charlotte, N.C., 1980-83; ptnr. Mullins & Van Hoy, Charlotte, N.C., 1983-89, Van Hoy, Rentlinger & Dunn, Charlotte, 1989—. Mem. N.C. OSHA Rev. Bd., 1985-92, Mecklenburg County, N.C. Personnel Commn., 1985-92, N.C. Leadership Coun. Co-state chmn. Gardner for Lt. Gov., 1988, alt. del. Rep. Nat. Conv., Detroit, 1980; chmn. Mecklenburg County Young Rep. Com., 1979-93, vice chmn., 1980-83; Duke U. Athletics Coun., 1999-02. 1st lt. U.S. Army, 1973-81. Named top employment lawyer N.C., Bus. N.C. Magazine, 2002. Mem. N.C. Bar Assn. (councillor labor and employment law sect. 1985-88, chmn. EEOC com. 1983-92), N.C. State Bar, 4th Cir. Jud. Conf., Rotary, Charlotte Cotillion Club (pres. 1979-80), City Club, Myers Park Country Club (dir. 1994-96, 2000—). Republican. Methodist. Commercial, contracts (including sales of goods; commercial financing), Securities. Home: 2615 Hampton Ave Charlotte NC 28207-2521 Office: Van Hoy Reutlinger & Dunn 737 East Blvd Charlotte NC 28203-5113

VAN KAMPEN, AL, lawyer; b. Detroit; s. Al J. and Laureen Ann Van Kampen; m. Lisa Alice Gonnason, Sept. 1, 1990; children: Kyle, Grant. BA in Econs., U. Mich., 1979, JD, 1983. Bar: Wash. 1983. Ptnr. Bogle & Gates, Seattle, 1983-99. V.p. A.V. Kurt Constrn. Co., Ferndale, Mich., 1980-92. Editor, co-author: Contribution and Claims Reduction in Antitrust Litigation, 1986, Sample Jury Instructions in Civil Antitrust Cases, 1999. Mem. Mayor's Citizen Forecast Com., Seattle, 1987. Mem. ABA, Wash. State Bar Assn. (chair antitrust sect.). Avocations: sailing, skiing. Antitrust, Health, Intellectual property. Office: Rohde & Van Kampen 1000 2d Ave Ste 3110 Seattle WA 98104

VAN KERREBROOK, MARY ALICE, lawyer; b. Houston, Aug. 21, 1961; d. Richard Rene and Phyllis Law (Banks) Van K. BA in Econs., Northwestern U., 1983; JD, So. Meth. U., 1986. Bar: Tex. 1986, U.S. Dist. Ct. (so. dist.) Tex. 1987, U.S. Ct. Appeals (5th cir.) 1988, U.S. Dist. Ct. (ea. dist.) Tex. 1989, U.S. Supreme Ct. 2000. Assoc. Wilson, Cribbs, Goren & Flaum, P.C., Houston, 1986-94, shareholder, 1994—2003; ptnr. Edler, Van Kerrebrook & Corpening, LLP, Houston, 2003—. Trustee Tex. Com. on Natural Resources, Dallas, 1988—; mem. exec. com. Galveston Bay Found., Webster, Tex., 1991-93; pres. Katy Prairie Conservancy, Houston, 1995—. Construction, Property, real (including real estate development, water), State and local taxation. Office: Edler Van Kerrebrook & Corpening LLP 1300 Lyric Centre 440 Louisiana Houston TX 77002 E-mail: mary@evclawyers.com.

VAN KIRK, THOMAS L. lawyer; b. Pa., June 25, 1945; s. Theodore and Mary Jane (Young) Van K.; children: Thomas Jr., Christopher. BA, Bucknell U., 1967; JD cum laude, Dickinson U., 1970. Bar: Pa., U.S. Dist. Ct. (we. and ea. dists.) Pa. 1971, U.S. Ct. Appeals (3d cir.) 1972, U.S. Supreme Ct. 1976. Clk. Pa. Superior Ct., 1970-71; assoc. Buchanan Ingersoll, Pitts., 1971-77, ptnr., 1978—, chief oper. officer, 1985—. Bd. dirs. Buchanan Ingersoll P.C.; v.p. State Pa. Economy League; bd. dirs. Western Pa. Economy League, chair, 1998. Chmn. Allegheny County Heart Assn. Walk, 1992; chair Pitts. Downtown Partnership, 1995-97; bd. dirs. Capital divsn. Pa. Economy League, sec./treas., 1995; bd. dirs. Pitts. Cultural Trust, 1998, SPIRC bd., PEG bd., U. Pitts. Cancer Inst. bd. Mem.: ABA, Allegheny County Bar Assn., The Club at Nevillewood, Rivers Club, Duquesne Club. Democrat. Lutheran. Antitrust, Federal civil litigation, Public international. Home: 1010 Osage Rd Pittsburgh PA 15243-1014 Office: Buchanan Ingersoll PC 301 Grant St Fl 20 Pittsburgh PA 15219-1410

VAN LEUVEN, ROBERT JOSEPH, lawyer; b. Detroit, Apr. 17, 1931; s. Joseph Francis and Olive (Stowell) Van Leuven; m. Merri Lee Van Leuven; children: Joseph Michael, Douglas Robert, Julie Margaret. Attended, Albion Coll., 1949-51; BA, Wayne State U., 1953; JD, U. Mich., 1957. Bar: Mich. 1957. Practice in law, Muskegon, Mich.; ptnr. Hathaway, Latimer, Clink,and Robb, Mich., 1957-68, McCroskey, Libner, and Van Leuven, Mich., 1968-81, Libner and Van Leuven, Mich., 1982—99; ret. Mich., 1999. Mem. coun. negligence law sect. State Bar Mich. Bd. dir., Muskegon Children's Home, 1965—75. Served with Aus., 1953—55. Fellow: Am. Coll. Trial Lawyers, Mich. Bar Found.; mem.: Boca Royal Country Club, Delta Sigma Phi. Home: 410 Ruddi Man Dr # 4 Muskegon MI 49445-2795 Office: Libner-Van Leuven 4th Fl Comerica Bank Bldg 801 W Norton Ave Muskegon MI 49441

VAN METER, ABRAM DEBOIS, lawyer, retired banker; b. Springfield, Ill., May 16, 1922; s. A.D. and Edith (Graham) Van M.; m. Margaret Schlipf, Dec. 1, 1956; children: Andy, Alice, Ann. BS, Kings Point Coll., 1946; JD, Northwestern U., 1948. Bar: Ill. 1949. Ptnr. Van Meter, Oxtoby & Funk, Springfield, 1949—2001; adminstrv. asst. to treas. State of Ill., Springfield, 1963; v.p. Ill. Nat. Bank, Springfield, 1964-65, pres., 1965-88, chmn. bd. dirs., 1988-90, also bd. dirs.; chmn. bd. dirs. Nat. City, Springfield, 1990-93, dir. emeritus, 1993—. Chmn. bd. dirs. Ill. Housing Devel. Authority, 1977-2003; chmn. bd. trustees So. Ill. U., 1989-2001; bd. dirs., mem. exec. com. Meml. Med. Ctr. (emeritus). Mem. ABA, Ill. Bar Assn., Sangamon Bar Assn., Chgo. Club, Chgo. Athletic Club, Sangamo Club, Island Bay Yacht Club, Banking. Home: 6 Fair Oaks St Springfield IL 62704-3222 Office: Nat City 1 N Old State Capitol Plz Springfield IL 62701-1323

VANNATTA, SHANE ANTHONY, lawyer; b. Williston, N.D., May 5, 1968; s. Marlyn Laverne and Karen (Rossland) V. BA in Polit. Sci. with high honors, U. Mont., 1990, JD with honors, 1993. Bar: Mont. 1993, U.S. Dist. Ct. Mont. 1993. Clk./intern Worden Thane & Haines, P.C., Missoula, Mont., 1991-93, assoc., 1993-96, sr. assoc., 1996-2000, shareholder, 2001—. Contbr. articles to profl. jours. In-house campaign exec. United Way of Missoula, 1994—. Mem. Western Mont. Bar Assn. (pres. 2000-01), Mont. State Bar (new lawyers sect., pres. 1996-97, trustee 2002—), Missoula New Lawyers Assn. (pres. 1993-94), Missoula C. of C. (chair Leadership Missoula 1998-99). Roman Catholic. Avocations: Tae Kwon-Do (cert. 2d dan), bicycling. General civil litigation, Commercial, contracts (including sales of goods; commercial financing), Trademark and copyright. Office: Worden Thane PC 111 N Higgins Ave Ste 600 Missoula MT 59802-4494 E-mail: svanatta@wthlaw.net.

VAN NISPEN, CONSTANT J.J.C. lawyer, educator; b. Oudenbosch, Brabant, The Netherlands, Jan. 28, 1950; s. Constant. A.I.L. and Johanna A.M. (Dekkers) Van N.; m. Marianne L.E.E. Doon, Sept. 16, 1977; children: Louise, Constantijn. LLM, Leyden (The Netherlands) U., 1972, PhD, 1978. Assoc. De Brauw, The Hague, Netherlands, 1977-83, ptnr., 1984—; prof. Free U., Amsterdam, 1993—. Author: Injunctions, 1978, Remedies, 1988, 2d edit., 2003, Industrial Property, 1989, 2d edit. 2002; editor: Law on Civil Procedure, 1996, 2d edit., 2002. Chmn. Liberal Party, Leidschedam, 1980-83. With Intendance, 1975-76. Patent, Trademark and copyright. Home: koolmeeslaan 6 2261 EW Leidschendam Netherlands Office: De Brauw Zuid Hollandlaan 7 2596 AL The Hague Netherlands

VAN NOSTRAND, RICHARD CHARLES, lawyer; b. Johnstown, N.Y., Sept. 20, 1955; s. Charles F. and Delores M. (Trajlinek) Van N.; m. Deborah A. Genovese, Aug. 6, 1977; children: Emily Kate, Kelsey Lynn. BA in History, Binghamton U., Binghamton, 1977; JD, Duke U., 1980. Bar: Mass. 1980, U.S. Dist. Ct. Mass. 1981, U.S. Ct. Appeals (1st cir.) 1983, U.S. Ct. Claims 1983. Assoc. Bloom and Schwartz, Westborough, Mass., 1980-83, Bloom and Van Nostrand, Westborough, 1983-84; pvt. practice Westborough, 1984; assoc. Mirick, O'Connell, DeMallie and Lougee, Worcester, Mass., 1984-87, ptnr., 1988—. Atty. Vol. Lawyers Svc., Worcester, 1981—; legal counsel Mass. Jaycees, 1985-86; bd. dirs. Legal Assistance Corp. of Cen. Mass., treas., 1996—; chmn. Northborough Pers. Bd., 1994-97. Bd. dirs. United Way of Cen. Mass., 1991—, chmn. allocations divsn., 1991-93. Named one of Outstanding Young Men Am., 1985, Outstanding Young Leader of Worcester, 1995. Fellow Mass. Bar Found.; mem. ABA (nat. conf. bar pres. 1995-96), Mass. Bar Assn (bd. dels. 1995-96, budget and fin. com. 1997, pres.-elect, 2002-03, pres. 2003-), Worcester County Bar Assn. (pres. 1995-96, chmn. trial practice sect. 1988-90, exec. com. 1991-97, chmn. Superior Ct. com. 1990-91, Pres. award 1990, 95, 97), Worcester County Bar Found. (life, pres. 1996-97), Westborough Jaycees (pres. 1984-85), Mass. Continuing Legal Edn., Inc. (trustee 1997—). Democrat. Lutheran. General civil litigation, Commercial, contracts (including sales of goods; commercial financing), Labor (including EEOC, Fair Labor Standards Act, labor-management relations, NLRB, OSHA). Home: 109 Madison Rd Northborough MA 01532-2280 Office: Mirick OConnell 100 Front St Worcester MA 01608-1477 Office Fax: 508-791-8502. E-mail: rcvannostrand@MirickOConnell.com.*

VAN OEVEREN, EDWARD LANIER, lawyer, biologist, physician; b. Washington, Apr. 12, 1954; BA with high distinction, U. Va., 1976; MD, Med. Coll. Va., 1995; JD, U. Va., 1981; BS with distinction, George Mason U., 1983; MPH, Johns Hopkins U., 1998. Bar: Va. 1981, U.S. Dist. Ct. (ea. dist.) Va. 1988, U.S. Temporary Emergency Ct. Appeals 1989; lic. physician, Va.; bd. cert. pub. health & preventive medicine. Pvt. practice legal cons., Falls Church, Va., 1984-85; pvt. practice law, 1986-89; pvt. practice law and biology, 1989-95; intern Med. Coll. Va., 1996-97; resident in preventive medicine Johns Hopkins U., Balt., 1997-99; pvt. practice law, medicine and biology Falls Church, 1997—. Editor: Federal Special Court Litigation, 1982; contbr. articles to profl. jours. Election officer Fairfax County (Va.) Electoral Bd., 1989-90, 1994-2002. Capt. Va. Army NG, 1996-97; 1st lt. USAR, 1995-96, capt., 1997—. Mem.: George Mason U. Alumni Assn. (scholarship, awards, rules and policies coms. 1989—91), Va. State Bar Assn., Alpha Chi. Avocation: photography. Aviation, Federal civil litigation, Personal injury (including property damage). Home: 3304 Patrick Henry Dr Falls Church VA 22044-1514 E-mail: EVanOeveren@pol.net.

VAN REES, CORNELIUS S. lawyer; b. N.Y.C., May 29, 1929; s. Cornelius Richard and Beatrice Martin (Shreve) Van R.; m. Virginia Vandewater, Mar. 15, 1953 (div. 1984); children: Pamela Millet Van Rees Lundquist, Claire Katherine; m. Alix McIvor, Jan. 2, 1985. BA, Denison U., 1951; JD, Columbia U., 1954. Bar: N.Y. 1956, U.S. Dist. Ct. (so. dist.) N.Y. 1956, Conn. 1994. Assoc. Thacher Proffitt & Wood, N.Y.C., 1956-62, ptnr., 1963-93, of counsel, 1994—. Mem. exec. com., officer, bd. dirs. Graham Corp.; lectr. in field. Writer in field. Trustee, sec. Williston Northhampton Sch.; mem. senate, honors and prizes com. Columbia U. Harlem Fisk Stone scholar Columbia U., 1954. Mem. ABA (coms. on internat. fin. trans., maritime fin. and devel. in bus. fin.), Alumni Fedn. Columbia U., Inc. (Alumni medal 1984, pres. 1979-81). Avocation: sailing. Home and Office: 35 Cove Side Ln Stonington CT 06378-2902

VAN RYZIN, GARY JAMES, lawyer, accountant; b. Appleton, Wis., Apr. 26, 1953; s. Howard John and Roseanne Julie Van Ryzin; m. Pamela Jean Casey, Aug. 23, 1975; children: Kimberly, Andrew, Benjamin. MA, U. Ga., 1976; MBA in Acctg., Rosary Coll., 1979; MS in Bus., U. Wis., 1989, JD, 1994. CPA, Wis.; Bar: Wis., 1996, U.S. Dist. Ct. (we. dist.) Wis. 1996; cert. assn. exec., cert. mgmt. acct. Projects mgr. Nat. Roofing Contractors Assn., Chgo., 1977-80; v.p. fin. Credit Union Nat. Assn., Madison, Wis., 1980-88; CFO Bus. Graphics Group, Madison, 1989-94, Full Compass Sys., Ltd., Middleton, Wis., 1994-99; fin. mgr. Famous Footwear, Inc., 1999—2000; chief legal compliance officer Great Lakes Higher Edn. Corp., Madison, 2000—. Recipient Winners Circle award Am. Soc. Assn. Execs., 1987. Fellow Wis. Inst. CPAs, AICPA; mem. Inst. Cert. Mgmt. Accts., Inst. Mgmt. Accts., ABA (taxation divsn.), Wis. Bar Assn., Constrn. Industry Fin. Mgrs. Assn., Beta Gamma Sigma, Kappa Tau Alpha. Home: 50 Fuller Dr Madison WI 53704-5925 Office: Great Lakes Higher Edn Corp 2401 International Ln Madison WI 53704 E-mail: gvanryzin@glhec.org.

VAN SICKLE, BRUCE MARION, federal judge; b. Minot, N.D., Feb. 13, 1917; s. Guy Robin and Hilda Alice (Rosenquist) Van S.; m. Dorothy Alfreda Hermann, May 26, 1943; children: Susan Van Sickle Cooper, John Allan, Craig Bruce, David Max. BSL, JD, U. Minn., 1941. Bar: Minn. 1941, N.D. 1946. Pvt. practice law, Minot, 1947-71; judge U.S. Dist. Ct. N.D., 1971-85, sr. judge, 1985—. Mem. N.D. Ho. of Reps., 1957, 59. Served with USMCR, 1941-46. Mem. ABA, N.D. Bar Assn., N.W. Bar Assn., Ward County Bar Assn., Am. Trial Lawyers Assn., Am. Coll. Probate Counsel, Am. Judicature Soc., Bruce M. Van Sickle Inns of Ct., Masons, Shriners, Elks, Delta Theta Phi. Office: US Dist Ct US Courthouse Rm 428 PO Box 670 Bismarck ND 58502-0670

VAN STEENIS, JON ANTHONY, lawyer; b. Fremont, Calif., June 24, 1972; s. Dale Curtis and Gloria Dawn Van Steenis; m. Lou Starla White, Nov. 27, 1999. BA in History, U. Calif., Berkeley, 1996; JD, Regent U., 1999; LLM in Environ. and Energy Law, Tulane U., 2001. Bar: La. 00, U.S. Dist. Ct. (ea., we. and mid. dists.) La. 01, U.S. Ct. Appeals (5th cir.) 02. Assoc. Hemelt & Foshee, LLC, Covington, La., 2000—. Mem. fin. com. Habitat for Humanity, Covington, 2002. Mem.: Am. Health Lawyers Assn. Avocations: saltwater fishing, hunting, golf. Health, Insurance, Personal injury (including property damage). Office: Hemelt & Foshee LLC 717 W 175th Ave Covington LA 70433 Fax: 985-892-9605. E-mail: jsteenis@hemeltandfoshee.com.

VAN TATENHOVE, GREGORY F. prosecutor; JD, U. Ky. Aide to U.S. Senator Mitch McConnell, Ky.; law clerk 6th U.S. Cir. Ct. Appeals, Ky.; trial atty. Justice Dept., Ky.; chief of staff to 2nd dist. U.S. rep. Ron Lewis, Ky.; U.S. atty. ea. dist. U.S. Dept. of Justice, Ky., 2001—. Office: 110 W Vine St Ste 400 Lexington KY 40507-1671 Office Fax: 859-233-2666.*

VAN'T HOF, WILLIAM KEITH, lawyer; b. N.Y.C., Feb. 18, 1930; s. William and Nell (DeValois) Van't H.; m. Barbara Marie Rogers, Oct. 6, 1961; children: Sarah Lynn, David Edward. BA, Hope Coll., 1951; LLB, U. Mich., 1954. Bar: Mich. 1954, Conn. 1955, U.S. Dist. Ct. (we. dist.) Mich. 1956, U.S. Ct. Appeals (6th cir.) 1956. Assoc. Gumbart, Corbin, Tyler & Cooper, New Haven, 1954-56; ptnr. McCobb, Heaney & Van't Hof, Grand Rapids, Mich., 1959-72, Schmidt, Howlett, Van't Hof, Smell & Vana, Grand Rapids, 1972-82, Varnum, Riddering, Schmidt & Howlett, Grand Rapids, 1983-99. Mem. faculty Inst. Continuing Legal Edn., Ann Arbor, Mich., 1974-99. Chmn. Mich. Heart Assn., 1973-75; pres. United Way Kent County, 1979-80, hon. life mem., 1986—; chmn. Am. Heart Assn., Dallas, 1989-90. Mem. ABA, State Bar Mich. (grievance and arbitration panel 1970-91, 94-, chmn. com. on coops. and condos. 1982-86), Grand Rapids Bar Assn. (trustee 1965-67), West Mich. Hort. Soc. (pres. 1992-93), Cascade Hills Country Club, Univ. Club. Corporate, general, Land use and zoning (including planning), Property, real (including real estate development, water). Home: 3508 Windshire Dr SE Grand Rapids MI 49546-3698 Office: Varnum Riddering Schmidt & Howlett 333 Bridge St NW Ste 1700 Grand Rapids MI 49504-5356 E-mail: wkvanthof@varnumlaw.com.

VAN TINE, MATTHEW ERIC, lawyer; b. Tomahawk, Wis., June 21, 1958; s. Kenneth G. and Louise (Olson) Van T.; m. Rena Marie David, Apr. 30, 1988; 1 child, Kristen. AB cum laude, Harvard Coll., 1980; JD magna cum laude, Boston U., 1983. Bar: Ill. 1983, Mass. 1983, U.S. Dist. Ct. Mass. 1984, U.S. Dist. Ct. (no. dist.) Ill. 1986, Seventh Cir., 2001. Law clk. to Hon. Raymond J. Pettine U.S. Dist. Ct. R.I., Providence, 1983-84; assoc. Palmer & Dodge, Boston, 1984-85, Schiff, Hardin & Waite, Chgo., 1985-88; asst. corp. counsel City of Chgo., 1988-92; assoc. to ptnr. Saunders & Monroe, Chgo., 1993-99; of counsel Miller Faucher and Cafferty, Chgo., 2000—. Exec. editor: Boston University Law Rev., 1982-83. Mem. ABA, Chgo. Bar Assn., Inns of Ct. General civil litigation, Antitrust, Securities. Office: Miller Faucher and Cafferty 30 N Lasalle St Ste 3200 Chicago IL 60602-2506 E-mail: mvantine@millerfaucher.com.

VAN VALER, JOE NED, lawyer, land developer; b. Gas City, Ind., Mar. 13, 1935; s. Richard Carl and Wilma Amy (Kelly) Van V.; m. Constance Joy Richardson, June 25, 1960; children: Kimberly Joy, Kelli June, Lynn Louise, Joseph Jeffrey. AB, Franklin Coll., 1959; LLB, Ind. U., 1963. Bar: Ind. 1963, U.S. Dist. Ct. (so. dist.) Ind. 1963. Assoc. Van Valer Law Firm and predecessor firms, 1963-65, ptnr., 1965-75, sr. ptnr., 1975—. Pres. Home Owners Warranty Corp. of Central Ind., Indpls., 1984-91, chmn. bd. dirs. 1991-95; cons. bd. Nat. City Bank Greenwood; chmn. adv. group Home Owners Warranty Corp., Washington, 1988-90, 92-94 also bd. dirs.; pros. atty. 8th Jud. Dist., Franklin, Ind., 1967-74; chmn. Johnson County, Ind., Contractors' Listing Bd.; chmn. bd. Bldg. Industry Svc. Corp., 1995-2000. With AUS, 1957-58. Recipient Alumnus Citation award Franklin Coll., 1996. Mem. ABA, Indpls. Bar Assn., 8th Jud. Cir. Bar Assn., Nat. Assn. Home Builders (bd. dirs.), Ind. Home Builders Assn., Builders Assn. Greater Indpls. (dir.), Indpls. Soc. Republican. Methodist. State civil litigation, Land use and zoning (including planning), Property, real (including real estate development, water). Office: Van Valer Law Firm PO Box 7575 299 W Main St Greenwood IN 46142-3129 E-mail: Joe@vanvalerlaw.com.

VAN VALKENBURG, EDGAR WALTER, lawyer; b. Seattle, Jan. 8, 1953; s. Edgar Walter and Margaret Catherine (McKenna) Van V.; m. Turid L. Owren, Sept. 29, 1990; children: Ingrid Catherine, Andrew Owren. BA, U. Wash., 1975; JD summa cum laude, Willamette Coll. of Law, 1978; LLM, Columbia U., 1984. Bar: Oreg. 1978, U.S. Dist. Ct. Oreg. 1979, U.S. Ct. Appeals (9th cir.) 1980. Law clk. to assoc. justice Oreg. Supreme Ct., Salem, 1978-79; assoc. Stoel, Rives, Boley, Fraser & Wyse, Portland, Oreg., 1979-82, 84-86; ptnr. Stoel Rives LLP, Portland, Oreg., 1986—; instr. Columbia U., N.Y.C., 1982-84. Bd. dirs. Portland Oregon Sports Authority. Editor-in-chief: Williamette Law Jour. 1977-78. Bd. dirs., chmn. Multnomah County Legal Aid, 1997-98; bd. dirs. Oreg. Legal Aid, 1998—. Mem. ACLU (pres. Oreg. chpt. 1991-93), Oreg. State Bar (chmn. antitrust sect. 1989-90, mem. Ho. of Dels. 1996-98). Antitrust, Corporate, general, Intellectual property. Office: Stoel Rives LLP 900 SW 5th Ave Ste 2300 Portland OR 97204-1229 E-mail: wvanvalkenburg@stoel.com.

VAN WAGENEN, JEFFREY ANTHONY, prosecutor, consultant; b. Downey, Calif., June 27, 1972; s. Jeffrey Anthony and Cheryl Ann Van Wagenen; m. Dawn Nicole Osti, May 31, 1997; children: Tyler Anthony children: Brittany Nicole. JD, U. Calif., Hastings, 1997; BA, U. So. Calif., 1994. Sole propr. Law Offices of Jeffrey A. Van Wagenen, Riverside, Calif., 2000—; dep. dist. atty. Riverside County, Riverside, Calif., 1997—2000; apprentice investigator Mc Mackin Investigations, San Francisco, 1995—97; polit. cons. Eddie Mahe Co., Wahington, DC, 1992; congl. intern Congressman Robert K. Dornan, Garden Grove, Calif., 1991—92. Chmn. of criminal law sect. Riverside County Bar Assn., Riverside, 2002—, jud. liason bd. mem., Calif., 2002—; adv. bd. mem. Vols. in Parole, Riverside, Calif., 2000—. Recipient Employee of the Month, Riverside County Dist. Attorney's Office, 1998, 1999. Mem.: Calif. Attorneys Criminal Justice, Nat. Assn. Criminal Def. Lawyers, Leo Deegan Inn of Ct. (assoc. 2000). R-Consevative. Roman Catholic. Office: Law Offices of Jeffrey Van Wagenen Jr 4129 Main St Ste 207 Riverside CA 92501 Office Fax: 909-369-3777.

VAN WINKLE, DANNY L. lawyer; b. Houston, Feb. 20, 1947; BC, Rice U., 1969; JD, U. Tex., 1972. Bar: Tex. 1972. Mem. Vinson & Elkins, L.L.P., Houston. Mem. Phi Delta Phi. Office: Vinson & Elkins 2500 First City Tower 1001 Fannin St Ste 3300 Houston TX 77002-6706 Home: Rte 3 Box 263-B Mexia TX 76667

VAN ZANDT, DAVID E. dean; b. Princeton, N.J., Feb. 17, 1953; m. Lisa A. Huestis; children: Caroline, Nicholas. AB summa cum laude, Princeton U., 1975; JD, Yale U., 1981; PhD in Sociology, U. London, 1985. Bar: Ill. Clk. to Hon. Pierre N. Leval U.S. Dist. Ct. (so. dist.) N.Y., 1981-82; clk. to Hon. Harry A. Blackmun U.S. Supreme Ct., Washington, 1982-83; atty. Davis, Polk & Wardwell, 1984-85; mem. faculty Northwestern U. Law Sch., Chgo., 1985—, dean, 1995—. Mem. planning com. Northwestern U. Corporate Counsel Inst., Northwestern U. Corp. Counsel Ctr. Author: Living in the Children of God, 1991; mng. editor Yale Law Jour., 1980-81; contbr. articles to profl. jours. Office: Northwestern U Sch Law Office of Dean 357 E Chicago Ave Chicago IL 60611-3059*

VAN ZILE, PHILIP TAYLOR, III, lawyer, educator; b. Detroit, Feb. 17, 1945; s. Philip Taylor II and Ruth (Butzel) Van Z.; m. Susan Jones, Sept. 12, 1981; children: Caroline Sage, Philip Taylor IV. BA, Oberlin Coll., 1968; MDiv, Union Theol. Sem., 1971; JD, Mich. State U., 1975. Bar: Mich. 1976, D.C. 1976, U.S. Dist. Ct. (ea. dist.) Mich. 1976, U.S. Ct. Appeals (6th cir.) 1976, U.S. Supreme Ct. 1977, Pa. 1981. Law clk. Mich. Ct. Appeals, Detroit, 1976-78, Mich. Supreme Ct., Detroit and Lansing, Mich., 1978-80; asst. corp. counsel Office of Corp. Counsel, Washington, 1980-87; assoc. Killian & Gephart, Harrisburg, Pa., 1987-89; prin. Law Office of Philip T. Van Zile, Harrisburg, 1989-91; assoc. coun. Office Chief Coun. Pa. Dept. Conservation and Natural Resources, Harrisburg, 1991—; assoc. realtor M.C. Walker Realty, Mechanicsburg, Pa., 1997—. Teaching fellow Detroit Coll. Law, 1976-80; teaching asst. Detroit Gen. Hosp., 1978-80; teaching assoc. Acad. Med. Arts and Bus., Harrisburg, 1990-91. Contbr. articles to profl. jours. Ordained elder Mechanicsburg Presbyn. Ch., 1995—, chmn. vol. ministries, 1995, chmn. peacemaking, 1996, chmn. staff, 1997—. Mem. ABA, Kenwood Club (Chevy Chase, Md.). Administrative and regulatory, Environmental, Government contracts and claims. Office: Pa Dept Conservation/Natural Resources Office Chief Counsel 400 Market St Harrisburg PA 17101-2301

VARAT, JONATHAN D. dean, law educator; b. 1945; BA, U. Pa., Phila., 1967, JD, 1972. Law clk. to judge Walter Mansfield U.S. Ct. Appeals (2d cir.), N.Y.C., 1972-73; law clk. to justice Byron White U.S. Supreme Ct., Washington, 1973-74; assoc. O'Melveny & Myers, Los Angeles, 1974-76; acting prof. UCLA, 1976-81, prof., 1981—, assoc. dean, 1982-83, 91-92; dean UCLA Sch. Law, 1998—. Office: UCLA Sch Law PO Box 951476 Los Angeles CA 90095-1476

VARDAMAN, JOHN WESLEY, lawyer; b. Montgomery, Ala., Apr. 22, 1940; s. John Wesley and Elizabeth (Merrill) V.; m. Marianne Fay, June 14, 1969; children: Thomas, Shannon, John Wesley III, Davis. BA, Washington & Lee U., 1962; JD, Harvard U., 1965. Bar: D.C. 1966, U.S. Dist. Ct. (D.C.) 1967, U.S. Supreme Ct. 1970. Law clk. to justice Hugo Black U.S. Supreme Ct., 1965-66; assoc. Wilmer, Cutler & Pickering, Washington, 1966-70; ptnr. Williams & Connolly, Washington, 1970—; gen. counsel U.S. Golf Assn., 1999—2003, mem. exec. com., 2003—. Contbr. articles to profl. jours. Mem. exec. com. WGA; mem. ABA, Am. Coll. Trial Lawyers, U.S.

Golf Assn., Congl. Country Club (Bethesda, Md.). Baptist. Avocation: golf. Federal civil litigation, Criminal, Environmental. Office: Williams & Connolly 725 12th St NW Washington DC 20005-5901

VARELA, GERARDO, lawyer, educator; b. Santiago, Chile, June 15, 1963; s. Raul Varela and Esperanza Alfonso; m. Elna Barros; children: Gerardo, Elna, Sara, Lucas. LLB, U. Chile, Santiago, 1985. Lawyer legal dept. Nat. Bldg. and Constrn. Assn., Santiago, 1987—90; atty. So. Fishing Cos. Assn., Santiago, 1986—90, Cariola Diez Perez-Cotapos, Santiago, 1990—96, Knobbe, Martens, Olson & Bear, Newport, Calif., 1994; ptnr. Cariola Diez Perez-Cotapos, Santiago, 1996—. Prof. legal aspects of mktg. Pontificia U. Cath. Chile, Santiago, 1997—2001. Mem.: Chilean Bar Assn. Federal civil litigation, Antitrust, Mergers and acquisitions. Office: Cariola Diez Perez-Cotapos Ave Andres Bello 2711 19th Fl Santiago Chile

VARELLAS, SANDRA MOTTE, judge; b. Anderson, S.C., Oct. 17, 1946; d. James E. and Helen Lucille (Gilliam) Motte; m. James John Varellas, July 3, 1971; children: James John III, David Todd. BA, Winthrop U., 1968; MA, U. Ky., 1970, JD, 1975. Bar: Ky. 1975, Fla. 1976, U.S. Dist. Ct. (ea. dist.) Ky. 1975, U.S. Ct. Appeals (6th cir.) 1976, U.S. Supreme Ct. 1978. Instr. Midway Coll., Ky., 1970-72; adj. prof. U. Ky. Coll. Law, Lexington, 1976-78; instr. dept. bus. adminstrn. U. Ky., Lexington, 1976-78; ptnr. Varellas, Pratt & Cooley, Lexington, 1975-93, Varellas & Pratt, Lexington, 1993-97, Varellas & Varellas, Lexington, 1998—. Fayette County judge exec., Ky., 1980—; hearing officer Ky. Natural Resources and Environ. Protection Cabinet, Frankfort, 1984-88. Committeewoman Ky. Young Dems., Frankfort, 1977-80; pres. Fayette County Young Dems., Lexington, 1977; bd. dirs. Ky. Dem. Women's Club, Frankfort, 1980-84, bd. dirs., Bluegrass Estate Planning Coun., 1995-98; grad. Leadership Lexington, 1981; chairwoman Profl. Women's Forum, Lexington, Ky., 1985-86, bd. dirs., 1984-87, Aequum award com., 1989-92; mem. devel. coun. Midway Coll., 1990-92; co-chair Gift Club Com., 1992. Named Outstanding Young Dem. Woman, Ky. Young Dems., Frankfort, 1977, Outstanding Former Young Dem., Ky. Young Dems., 1983. Mem. Ky. Bar Assn. (treas. young lawyers divsn. 1978-79, long range planning com. 1988-89), Fla. Bar, Fayette County Bar Assn. (treas. 1977-78, bd. govs. 1978-80), LWV (nominating com. 1984-85), Greater Lexington C. of C. (legis. affairs com. 1994-95, bd.d irs. coun. smaller enterprises 1992-95). Club: The Lexington Forum (bd. dirs. 1996-99), Lexington Philharm. Guild (bd. dirs. 1979-81, 86—), Nat. Assn. Women Bus. Owners (chmn. cmty. liaison/govtl. affairs com. 1992-93), Lexington Network (bd. dirs. and sec. 1994-98). Office: Varellas & Varellas 167 W Main St Ste 1310 Lexington KY 40507-1398

VARET, MICHAEL A. lawyer; b. N.Y.C., Mar. 9, 1942; s. Guster V. and Frances B. (Goldberg) V.; m. Elizabeth R. Varet, June 3, 1973; 3 children. BS in Econs., U. Pa., 1962; LLB, Yale U., 1965. Bar: N.Y. 1966, U.S. Supreme Ct. 1975, U.S. Dist. Ct. (ea. and so. dists.) N.Y. 1975, U.S. Tax Ct. 1975, U.S. Claims Ct. 1975, U.S. Ct. Appeals (2d cir.) 1975. Mem., chmn. Varet & Fink P.C. (formerly Milgrim Thomajan & Lee P.C.), N.Y.C., 1982-95; mem. firm Piper Rudnick LLP, N.Y.C., 1995—. Bd dirs., exec. com., audit com. Salisbury Bank and Trust Co., Lakeville, Conn., Salisbury Bancorp, Inc., Lakeville. Trustee Montefiore Med. Ctr., Bronx, N.Y., 1980-92, mem. exec. com., 1985-92; bd. dirs. Sem. Libr. Corp. Jewish Theol. Sem., N.Y.C., 1983-87, United Jewish Appeal-Fedn. Jewish Philanthropies of Greater N.Y., Inc., 1979-86, mem. coun. of overseers, 1986-95; bd. dirs. Mosholu Preservation Corp., Bronx, 1982-88, Yale Law Sch. Fund, 2000—; bd. overseers Jewish Theol. Sem., 1982-90, Jewish Publ. Soc. of Am., 1986-96, exec. com., 1989-94, 95-96; mem. exec. com. Yale Law Sch. Assn., 1990-93; bd. dirs. B. de Rothschild Found. for Advancement Sci. in Israel, 1986—, Piatigorsky Found., 1990—; v.p., sec., bd. dirs. Am. Found. for Basic Rsch. in Israel, 1990—; dir. Plz. Jewish Cmty. Chapel, 2001—; bd. dirs. Am. and Internat. Friends of Victoria and Albert Mus., Inc., 1997-99, treas., 1997-99. Mem. ABA, N.Y. State Bar Assn., Assn. of Bar of City of N.Y. (bd. dirs., exec. com. 1971-75), Internat. Fiscal Assn., Internat. Tax Planning Assn., Yale Club of N.Y.C., Lotos Club. Democrat. Estate planning, Private international, Taxation, general. Office: Piper Rudnick LLP 1251 Ave of Americas New York NY 10020-1104 E-mail: mav@varet.com., michael.varet@piperrudnick.com.

VARN, WILFRED CLAUDE, lawyer; b. DeLand, Fla., Mar. 14, 1919; s. Claude Grady and Marjorie Amelia (Boor) Varn; m. Betty Jean Davenport, Nov. 12, 1949; children: Mary Patricia Varn Moore, Wilfred Claude Jr., George Seward. BSBA, U. Fla, 1947, LLB, (reconferred JD 1967), 1948. Bar: Fla. 1948, U.S. Dist. Ct. (no. dist.) Fla. 1948, U.S. Dist. Ct. (mid. dist. and trial bar so. dist.) Fla. 1956, U.S. Ct. Appeals (5th cir.) 1958, U.S. Supreme Ct. 1959, U.S. Ct. Appeals (5th and 11th cirs.), 1981. Ptnr. Spear and Varn, Panama City, Fla., 1948-54; asst. U.S. Atty. Dept. Justice No. Dist. Fla., 1954-58, U.S. Atty., 1958-61; ptnr. Ervin, Varn, Jacobs & Ervin, Tallahassee, 1961—92; of counsel Ervin, Boyd & Allaman, 1992—2001. Vice chancellor Episcopal Diocese of Fla., Jacksonville, 1994—; Rep. state com. mem. 1961-66. 2d lt. U.S. Army, 1942-46. PTO. Decorated Legion of Merit, U.S. Army, 1972. Fellow Am. Coll. of Trial Lawyers, Am. Bar Found.; mem. Fla. Bar Assn. (50 yr. Membership award 1998), Kiwanis Club (bd. dirs.). Avocations: painting, exercise, travel, hiking, swimming. General civil litigation, Condemnation (eminent domain), General practice. Home: 705 Kenilworth Rd Tallahassee FL 32312-3045

VASQUEZ, GERARD MANUEL, lawyer, international business consultant; b. Wallingford, Eng., Dec. 16, 1960; LLB with honors, Univ. Coll., London, 1983, LLM, 1984. Trainee solicitor Messrs. Knocker & Foskett, Sevenoaks, Kent, Eng., 1984-88; trainee Eduardo Amor Martinez & Asociados, Mojacar, Almeria, Spain, 1988-91; asst. solicitor Michael Soul & Assocs., London, 1991-93; cons. Malaga, Spain, 1993-95, Madrid, Spain, 1995-2000; gen. mgr., coord., cons. Lexfide, Madrid, 2000—. Co-author: International Personal Tax Planning Encyclopaedia, 2000; contbr. to Circulo de Dirigentes. Mem. Interat. Fiscal Assn. Avocations: internet, e-law. Computer, Corporate, general, Private international. Office: Lexfide C/Ortega y Gasset 34 1 oB Madrid 28006 Spain Fax: 34-91 4312793. E-mail: mail@spanishlegalnet.com.

VASSALLO, JOHN A. lawyer; b. N.Y.C., Aug. 19, 1937; s. John and Gilda (Di Desidero) Vassallo; married; children: John C., Edward F. AB, Columbia U., 1959, JD, 1962. Bar: N.Y. 1963, U.S. Dist. Ct. (so. and ea. dists.) N.Y. 1964, U.S. Ct. Appeals (2d cir.) 1965. Assoc. Saxe, Bacon & O'Shea, N.Y.C., 1962-68; ptnr. Barovick & Konecky, N.Y.C., 1968-70, Kurtz & Vassallo, N.Y.C., 1970-78, Franklin, Weinrib, Rudell & Vassallo, N.Y.C., 1978—. Fellow: Am. Coll. Family Trail Lawyers (diplomate), Am. Acad. Matrimonial Attys.; mem.: Friars Club. General civil litigation, Family and matrimonial. Home: 285 Central Park W New York NY 10024-3006 Office: Franklin Weinrib Rudell & Vassallo 488 Madison Ave New York NY 10022-5702

VASSIL, JOHN CHARLES, lawyer; b. Youngstown, Ohio, Mar. 3, 1930; s. Callias and Anastasia (Kyriakides) V.; m. Anita Devlin, Nov. 28, 1965; 1 son, Russell. BS in Chem. Engring., Carnegie Inst. Tech., 1952; JD, George Washington U., 1958. Bar: N.Y. 1960, U.S. Dist. Cts. (so. and ea. dists.) N.Y. 1961, U.S. Ct. Appeals (2d cir.) 1965, U.S. Ct. Appeals (fed. cir.) 1982, U.S. Supreme Ct. 1961. Patent examiner U.S. Patent Office, 1955-58; ptnr. Morgan & Finnegan, LLP, N.Y.C., 1961—. Lectr. in field. Served with C.E., U.S. Army, 1953-55. Mem. ABA, Assn. Bar City N.Y., N.Y. Patent Law Assn., Am. Patent Law Assn., Am. Arbitration Assn. Federal civil litigation, FERC practice, Intellectual property. Home: 420 E 54th St # 36H New York NY 10022-5179 Office: 345 Park Ave New York NY 10154-0004 E-mail: jcvassil@morganfinnegan.com.

VATER, CHARLES J. lawyer; b. Pitts., Feb. 8, 1950; s. Joseph A. and Helen M. (Genellie) V.; m. Diane E. Vater, June 10, 1972; children: Allison D., Elizabeth A. BA, U. Notre Dame, 1971; JD, U. Pitts., 1975. Bar: Pa. 1975, U.S. Dist. Ct. (we. dist.) Pa. 1975, U.S. Ct. Appeals (3d cir.) 1979. Assoc. Tucker Arensberg, P.C., Pitts., 1975-80, ptnr., shareholder, 1980—. Contbr. articles to profl. jours. Mem.: Estate Planning Coun. Pitts. (bd. dirs. 1988—90, 1995—97, past pres.), Allegheny County Bar Assn. (probate coun. 1988—98, 1999—2000, sec. 2003), Phi Beta Kappa, Order of Coif. Commercial, contracts (including sales of goods; commercial financing), Estate planning, Probate (including wills, trusts). Home: 1615 Trolist Dr Pittsburgh PA 15241-2650 Office: Tucker Arensberg 1 Ppg Pl Ste 1500 Pittsburgh PA 15222-5413 E-mail: cvater@tuckerlaw.com.

VAUGHAN, EDWARD GIBSON, lawyer; b. Dallas, Nov. 22, 1948; s. S.J. III and Martha (Gibson) V. BBA, U. Tex., 1971; cert., City of London Coll., 1970; JD, St. Mary's U., 1975. Bar: Tex. 1975. Assoc. Johnson & Jones, Austin, 1975-76; ptnr. Harris & Vaughan, Uvalde, Tex., 1976-79, Kessler, Kessler & Vaughan, Uvalde, 1979-94. Dir. First State Bank Uvalde, Security State Bank of Persall. Mem. ABA, Tex. and Southwestern Cattle Raisers (bd. dirs.), Uvalde C. of C. (bd. dirs. 1979-83), Tex. State C. of C. (bd. dirs. 1982-85), Tex. Lyceum Assn. (bd. dirs. 1980-85), Tex. Assn. Bank Counsel (bd. dirs. 1984-87), Southwestern Legal Found., State Bar Tex., Uvalde County Bar Assn. (pres. 1979-80), Kendall County Bar Assn., Tex. Water Found. (bd. dirs. 1998—). Banking, Oil, gas, and mineral, Property, real (including real estate development, water). Office: 1588 S Main St Ste 200 Boerne TX 78006-2300

VAUGHAN, HERBERT WILEY, retired lawyer; b. Brookline, Mass., June 1, 1920; s. David D. and Elzie G. (Wiley) Vaughan; m. Ann Graustein, June 28, 1941 (dec. June 2002). Student, U. Chgo., 1937-38; BS cum laude, Harvard U., 1941, LLB, 1948. Bar: Mass. 1948. Assoc. Hale and Dorr, Boston, 1948-54, jr. ptnr., 1954-56, sr. ptnr., 1956-89, co-mng. ptnr., 1976-80, of counsel, 1990—. Bd. dirs., fin. com. Boston and Maine R.R., 1961—64; vis. fellow New Coll., Oxford U., 1985. Mem. standing com. Trustees of Reservations, 1986—98, chmn., 1988—92, sec., 1992—98, asst. sec., mem. adv. coun., 1998—; mem. bd. trustees Am. Friends New Coll. (Oxford U.); mem. adv. coun. James Madison Program in Am. Ideals and Instns., Princeton U. Fellow: Mass. Hist. Soc., Am. Bar Found. (life); mem.: ABA, Am. Coun. Trustees and Alumni (mem. alumni leadership coun.), Am. Coll. Real Estate Lawyers, Am. Law Inst., Boston Bar Assn., Mass. Bar Assn., Longwood Cricket Club (Brookline), Boston Econ. Club, Union Club (Boston), Badminton and Tennis Club, Bay Club. Property, real (including real estate development, water). Office: Hale and Dorr LLP 60 State St Boston MA 02109-1816 E-mail: Herbert.Vaughan@haledorr.com.

VAUGHAN, JAMES JOSEPH MICHAEL, lawyer; b. Mar. 19, 1942; s. James M. and Elizabeth (McDonnell) Vaughan; m. Jeanette Rae Gerber, Aug. 5, 1967; children: Karen, Adrianne, Jennifer. BS, U. Scranton, 1963; JD, Cath. U., 1966. Bar: U.S. Dist. Ct. Md. 1979, U.S. Ct. Appeals (D.C. cir.) 1972, U.S. Ct. Claims 1973, U.S. Supreme Ct. 1977. Assoc. Dukes, Troese, et al, Chevy Chase, Md., 1969—72; atty. Assn. Am. Law Schs., Washington, 1972—76, 2001—; mem. firm Giordano, Villareale & Vaughan, Upper Marlboro, Md., 1976—2001; pvt. practice, 2001—. Mem.: Prince George's County Bar Assn., Md. Bar Assn., D.C. Bar Assn., Bar Assn. D.C., Assn. Trial Lawyers Am. Democrat. Roman Catholic. State civil litigation, Personal injury (including property damage), Workers' compensation. Office: 9658 Pennsylvania Ave Upper Marlboro MD 20773

VAUGHAN, PHILIP JOHN, lawyer; b. London, May 1, 1955; s. Richard John and Margaret Helm Vaughan; m. Jo Anna Shoubridge, July 6, 1991; children: Maria, Nicholas, Lydia, Cecilia. MA, Jesus Coll., 1976. Articled clk. Radcliffes & Co., London, 1977—79, solicitor, 1979—81, Simmons & Simmons, 1981—85, ptnr., 1985—98, head dispute resolution, 1998—. Fellow: Chartered Inst. Arbitrators; mem.: Internat. Bar Assn., Law Soc. England & Wales. Avocations: photography, music, marathon running. Alternative dispute resolution, Oil, gas, and mineral. Office: Simmons & Simmons 1 Ropemaker St London EC2Y 9SS England Fax: 0044 207 628 2070. E-mail: philip.vaughan@simmons-simmons.com.

VAUGHAN, STEPHEN MICHAEL, lawyer; b. Winchester, Ky., June 3, 1947; s. Harold Lee and Irene Marie (Wilson) V. BA, Yale U., 1969; JD, U. Tex., 1973. Bar: Tex., U.S. Dist. Ct. (no., so., ea. and we. dists.) Tex., U.S. Ct. Appeals (5th and 11th cirs.), U.S. Supreme Ct. Briefing atty. Ct. Criminal Appeals, Austin, Tex., 1973-74; assoc. Mandell & Wright, Houston, 1974-78, ptnr., 1978—. Cooperating atty. ACLU, Houston, 1975—. Mem. Tex. Bar. Assn., Houston Bar Assn., Am. Trial Lawyers Assn., Tex. Trial Lawyers Assn. (bd. dirs. 1984—), Houston Trial Lawyers Assn. (bd. dirs. 1984—), Tex. Consumer Assn. (pres. 1978). Democrat. Methodist. Avocations: running, scuba, sailplanes. Admiralty, Personal injury (including property damage), Workers' compensation. Home: 4706 Welford Dr Bellaire TX 77401-5332 Office: Mandell & Wright 712 Main St Ste 1600 Houston TX 77002-3297

VAUGHN, ROBERT CANDLER, II, lawyer; b. Winston Salem, North Carolina, Sept. 6, 1931; s. Robert Candler and Douglas Arthur V.; m. Carolyn (Hartford), May 2, 1959; children: Patricia Anne, Robert Candler III. BS in bus. adminstrn., U. N.C., 1953, JD, 1955. Bar: N.C., 1955, U.S. Dist. Ct. (mid. dist.), 1959, U.S. Tax Ct., 1981. Assoc. Petree, Stockton, Robinson, and predecessor firms, Winston Salem, NC, 1959-65, ptnr., 1965-2000. Bd. dirs., South Nat. Bank and predecessor bank, Winston Salem. Pres., United Way Forsyth County, Winston Salem, 1970-71; chmn., Winston Salem Coliseum and Conv. Ctr. Commn., 1974-78; bd. advs., U. N.C. Tax Inst., Chapel Hill; bd. dirs., Legal Svc. N.C., 1985-86,; Leadership, Winston Salem, chmn. Winston Salem Found., 2003; chmn. Forsyth Med. Ctr. Found., 1999-2001. Lt., USN, 1955-58. Fellow Am. Bar Found., Am. Coll. Trusts and Estates Counsel,(N.C.chmn.1990-1995); mem. N.C. Bar Assn. (pres. 1985-86, bd. dirs.), U. N.C. Law Alumni Assn. (pres. 1974-75), Am. Coll. Tax Counsel, Old Town Club, Piedmont Club, Rotary. Democrat. Methodist. Corporate, general, Probate (including wills, trusts), Estate taxation. Home: 2575 Club Park Rd. Winston Salem NC 27104-2009 Office: Vaughn Perkinson Ehlinger Moxley & Stogner PO Box 25715 Winston Salem NC 27114 E-mail: bob.vaughn@vpems.com.

VAZQUEZ, GILBERT FALCON, lawyer; b. Eagle Pass, Tex., Oct. 29, 1952; s. Catalina (Falcon) Vazquez. AB in Polit. Sci., Yale U., 1975; JD, Harvard U., 1978. Bar: Tex. 1978, U.S. Dist. Ct. (we. dist.) Tex. 1980, U.S. Ct. Appeals (5th and 11th cirs.) 1981. Ptnr. Matthews & Branscomb, San Antonio, Tex., 1978-85, Akin, Gump, Strauss, Hauer & Feld, L.L.P., San Antonio, 1985—. Co-chmn. issues com. H. Cisneros Mayoral Campaign, San Antonio, 1981; bd. dirs. Bexar County-San Antonio United Way, 1982-87, 91—, San Antonio World Affairs Coun., 1993-96, San Antonio Mus. Assn., 1993-95; mem. exec. com. Mayor's Target 90 Commn., San Antonio, 1985-89, vice chmn., 1987-89; chmn. City of San Antonio Charter Rev. Com., 1991-93, State of Tex. Pension Rev. Bd., 1991-96, vice-chmn., 1994, chair, 1995; bd. dirs. San Antonio Zool. Soc., 1988—, mem. exec. com.(1st v.p.), 2002-; bd. dirs. Harvard Law Sch. Alumni Assn., 2002—; mem. The Pro Bono Coll. of the State Bar of Tex., 2002—. Named Outstanding Young San Antonian, U.S. Jaycees, 1985, Outstanding Vol., J.C. Penny Co., 1984. Mem. ABA (internat. law sect., assoc. editor newsletter 1985-87), Nat. Assn. Bond Lawyers, Tex. Bar Assn. (governing coun. internat. law sect. 1985-88), San Antonio Bar Assn., San Antonio Young Lawyers Assn. (Outstanding Young Lawyer 1987), Hispanic Nat. Bar Assn. (regional pres. 1987-88, nat. sec. 1988-89, v.p. 1989-90), San Antonio World Trade Assn. (bd. dirs. 1987-90), Mexican C. of C. (bd. dirs. 1984-85), Greater San Antonio C. of C. (bd. dirs. 1992-95), Yale Club South Tex. (pres. 1982-85). Democrat. Roman Catholic. Avocations: community redevelopment, music, reading. Corporate, general, Private international, Municipal (including bonds). Office: Akin Gump Strauss Hauer & Feld LLP 300 Convent St Ste 1500 San Antonio TX 78205-3732

VAZQUEZ, MICHAEL ANTHONY, lawyer; b. Miami, Nov. 23, 1965; s. Luis Roman Vazquez and Caridad Proenza-Vazquez; m. Clarybel Arango Vazquez, Aug. 12, 1988; children: Michael Anthony Jr., Christopher Raymond. BA, U. Fla., 1990; JD, Nova Southeastern U., 1994. Bar: Fla. 1994. Atty. Nicklaus, Valle, Craig & Wicks, Miami, 1994—96, Proenza, Roberts & Hurst, 1996—97, Valle & Craig, 1997—. Mem. Bread for the World, Washington, 2000. Mem.: Dade County Bar Assn., Cuban-Am. Bar Assn., Fla. Bar Assn. Roman Catholic. Personal injury (including property damage). Office: Valle & Craig 9155 S Dadeland Blvd Ste 1000 Miami FL 33156 Fax: 305-373-2889. E-mail: vazquez@vallecraig.com.

VAZQUEZ, RAMON, lawyer; b. N.Y.C., Nov. 21, 1964; s. Ramon Vazquez and Maria Castro; m. Vivian L. Rivera; children: Alexander O., Christian G. BA magna cum laude, U. PR, Rio Predras, 1989, JD cum laude, 1994. Bar: PR 1995, U.S. Ct. Appeals (1st cir.) 1995, U.S. Supreme Ct. 1998, U.S. Dist. Ct. PR 1998, Fla. 2000, U.S. Ct. Appeals (11th cir.) 2000, U.S. Dist. Ct. (mid. dist.) Fla. 2001. Pvt. practice, Bayamon, PR, 1995—96; atty. Martinez-Alvarez, San Juan, PR, 1996—99, Drage, De Beaubien, et al, Orlando, Fla., 2000—02, Grower, Ketcham, et al, Orlando, 2002—. Moderator, chmn. Christian Ch. Disciples Christ, Casselberry, Fla., 2002. 2d lt. Air N.G., 1983—91. Mem.: ABA, Hispanic Bar Assn. Ctrl. Fla. General civil litigation, Insurance, Administrative and regulatory. Office: Grower Ketcham Rutherford et al 390 N Orange Ave Ste 1900 Orlando FL 32801 Office Fax: 407-425-7104. Business E-Mail: rvazquez@growerketcham.com.

VEACH, ROBERT RAYMOND, JR., lawyer; b. Charleston, S.C., Nov. 28, 1950; s. Robert Raymond and Evelyn Ardell (Vegter) V.; m. Lori Sue Erickson, May 27, 1989. Student, St. Olaf Coll., 1968-70; BS in Acctg., Ariz. State U., 1972; JD, So. Meth. U., 1975. Bar: Tex. 1975, Nebr. 1975, U.S. Dist. Ct. Nebr. 1975, U.S. Dist. Ct. (no. dist.) Tex. 1975, Temporary Emergency Ct. Appeals 1975. Acctg. instr. Sch. Bus. So. Meth. U., Dallas, 1973-74; law clk. to Hon. Joe E. Estes U.S. Dist. Ct. No. Dist. Tex.-Temp. Emergency Ct. Appeals, Dallas, 1975-76; assoc. Locke Purnell Boren Laney & Neely, Dallas, 1976-80; v.p. The Lomas & Nettleton Co., Dallas, 1980-83, Rauscher Pierce Refsnes, Inc., Dallas, 1983-87; pres. RPR Mortgage Fin. Corp., Dallas, 1985-87; sr. shareholder Locke Purnell Rain Harrell, Dallas, 1987-97; exec. v.p. Precision Imaging Solutions, Inc., Dallas, 1998—; pvt. practice Dallas, 1998—. Allied mem. N.Y. Stock Exch., 1985-87; lectr. securities and banking confs.; bd. dirs. pvt. corps.; trustee Correctional Properties Trust (NYSE-CPV), chmn. audit and finance com., 1998-2002, chmn. bd., 2002—. Author legal articles. Dir. North Tex. affiliate Am. Diabetes Assn., Dallas, 1978-81; mem. Gov.'s Task Force Wash. State Housing Commn., 1982-83. Mem. ABA, State Bar of Tex., Nebr. State Bar Assn., Fed. Bar Assn., Dallas Bar Assn. Republican. Methodist. Avocations: golf, antique American firearms. Corporate, general, Finance, Securities. Home: 4223 Brookview Dr Dallas TX 75220-3801 Office: 2911 Turtle Creek Blvd Ste 1240 Dallas TX 75219-6277

VEAL, REX R. lawyer; b. Lafayette, Ga., May 2, 1956; s. Boyd Herman and Barbara Ann (Sharp) V.; m. Vicky Elizabeth Wilkins, Dec. 13, 1980; children: Matthew Aaron and Richard Andrew (twins). BA, U. Tenn., 1978, JD, 1980. Bar: Tenn. 1981, U.S. Dist. Ct. (ea. dist.) Tenn. 1981, U.S. Ct. Appeals (10th cir.) 1981, U.S. Ct. Appeals (6th cir.) 1984, U.S. Ct. Appeals (4th cir.) 1987, Ga. 1991, U.S. Dist. Ct. (no. dist.) Ga. 1991, U.S. Ct. Appeals (11th cir.) 1991, D.C. 1993, U.S. Dist. Ct. D.C. 1993, U.S. Ct. Appeals (D.C. and fed. cir.) 1993. Assoc. Finkelstein, Kern, Steinberg & Cunningham, Knoxville, Tenn., 1980-83; atty. FDIC, Knoxville, 1983-84, sr. atty., 1984-88, counsel liquidation Washington, 1988-89, assoc. gen. counsel, 1989-90; spl. counsel Resolution Trust Corp., Washington, 1989-90; ptnr. Powell, Goldstein, Frazer & Murphy, Atlanta and Washington, 1990-99, Kilpatrick Stockton LLP, Atlanta, 1999—. Lectr. in field. Contbr. articles to profl. jours. Mem. ABA, Tenn. Bar Assn., Ga. Bar Assn., Atlanta Bar Assn. Avocations: hiking, golf, collecting books. Commercial, contracts (including sales of goods; commercial financing), Finance, Property, real (including real estate development, water). Home: 6201 Blackberry Hl Norcross GA 30092-1375 Office: Kilpatrick Stockton 1100 Peachtree St NE Ste 2800 Atlanta GA 30309-4501 E-mail: rveal@kilpatrickstockton.com.

VEASEY, EUGENE NORMAN, state supreme court chief justice; b. Wilmington, Del., Jan. 9, 1933; s. Eugene E. and Elizabeth B. (Norman) V.; m. Suzanne Johnson, Aug. 4, 1956; children: Andrew Scott, Dluglas Ross, E. Norman Jr., Marian Elizabeth. AB, Dartmouth Coll., 1954; LLB, U. Pa., 1957. Bar: Del. 158, U.S. Supreme Ct. 1963. Dep. atty. gen. State of Del., 1961-62; chief dep., 1962-63; ptnr. Richards, Layton & Finger, Wilmington, Del., 1963-92; chief justice Del. Supreme Ct., 1992—. Contbr. articles to profl. jours. Bd. advisors U. Pa. Inst. for Law and Econs. Capt. Del. Air N.G., 1957-63. Fellow Am. Bar Found., Am. Coll. Trial Lawyers, Am. Intellectual Property Law Assn.; mem. Del. Bd. Bar Examiners (chmn. 1973-80), Del. Bar Assn. (pres. 1982-83, chmn. corp. law com. 1969-74, chmn. rules com. Del. Supreme Ct. 1974-80), ABA (chair bus. law sect. 1994-95, chair spl. com. on ethics 2000 1997—), Am. Law Inst. (bd. dirs. conf. chief jusice 1994-96, chair professionalism com. 1994-98, 1st v.p. 1998, pres.-elect 1998-99, pres. 1999-00), Nat. Ctr. State Cts. (chair bd. dirs. 1999-00). Republican. Episcopalian. Office: Del Supreme Ct PO Box 1997 Wilmington DE 19899-1997 E-mail: e.norman.veasey@state.de.us.

VEEDER, PETER GREIG, lawyer; b. Pitts., Aug. 13, 1941; AB, Princeton U., 1963; JD, U. Pitts., 1966. Bar: Pa. 1966, D.C. 1976. Lawyer Thorp Reed & Armstrong, Pitts., 1970-99; of counsel Thorp, Reed & Armstrong LLP, Pitts., 1999—. Environmental. Office: Thorp Reed & Armstrong LLP 1 Oxford Ctr 301 Grant St Fl 14 Pittsburgh PA 15219-1425

VEGA, ALONSO, lawyer, consultant; b. Mexicali, Baja California, Mexico, Sept. 23, 1974; s. Octavio Alonso Vega and Celia Rosas. LLB, Escuela Libre de Derecho Sch. of Law, Mex. City Fed. Dist., 1998. Bar: Mexican Coll. Lawyers, Mex. City 2002. Assoc. Gonzalez Calvillo Y Forastieri, S.c., Mex. City, Mexico, 1995—97, Bufete Davalos and Assocs., Mex. City, 1998—2001; ptnr. Garcia Heres, S.C., Puebla, Mexico, 1998—2001; assoc. Bufete Ignacio Arturo Guajardo, S.C., Mexicali, Mexico, 2001—. General civil litigation, Criminal, Constitutional. Office: Bufete Ignacio Arturo Guajardo Sc Calle Mexi 100 Zona Ctrl Baja California Mexicali 21100 Mexico Home Fax: 011-52-686-554-44-04; Office Fax: 011-52-686-554-14-34. E-mail: avr@biag.com.mx.

VEGA, BENJAMIN URBIZO, retired judge, television producer; b. La Ceiba, Honduras, Jan. 18, 1916; m. Janie Lou Smith, Oct. 12, 1989; AB, U. So. Calif., 1938, postgrad., 1939-40; LLB, Pacific Coast U. Law, 1941, postgrad.Washington & Lee U., 1943. Bar: Calif. 1947, U.S. Dist. Ct. (so. dist.) Calif. 1947, U.S. Supreme Ct. 1958. Assoc. Anderson, McPharlin & Connors, L.A., 1947-48, Newman & Newman, L.A., 1948-51; dep. dist. atty. County of L.A., 1951-66; judge L.A., County Mcpl. Ct., East L.A. Jud. Dist., 1966-86, retired, 1986; leader faculty seminar Calif. Jud. Coll. at Earl Warren Legal Inst., U. Calif-Berkeley, 1978. Mem. Calif. Gov.'s Adv. Com. on Children and Youth, 1968; del. Commn. of the Califs., 1978; bd. dirs. Los Angeles-Mexico City Sister City Com.; pres. Argentine Cultural Found., 1983. Recipient award for outstanding services from Mayor of L.A., 1973, City of Commerce, City of Montebello, Calif. Assembly, Southwestern Sch. Law, Disting. Pub. Service award Dist. Atty. L.A. Mem. Conf. Calif. Judges, Mcpl. Ct. Judges' Assn. (award for Outstanding Services), Beverly Hills Bar Assn., Navy League, L.A. County, Am. Judicature Soc., World Affairs Council, Rotary (hon.), Pi Sigma Alpha. Home: 101 California Ave Apt 1207 Santa Monica CA 90403-3525

VELARDE, D. SEAN, lawyer, consultant; b. Denver, Oct. 9, 1967; BS in Bus. Adminstrn., Colo. State U., 1990; JD, U. Denver, 1994. Bar: Colo. 1994, U.S. Dist. Ct. Colo. 1996. Jud. law clk. to Hon. Daniel M. Taubman Colo. Ct. Appeals, Denver, 1994—95; assoc. Burns, Figa and Will, P.C., Englewood, Colo., 1995—99, shareholder, mem. exec. com., 2000—01, mng. dir., shareholder, 2002—. Mem. bd. dirs. Colo. Lawyers Com., Denver, 1996—98. Mem.: Colo. Bar Found. Republican. Corporate, general, Mergers and acquisitions, Commercial, contracts (including sales of goods; commercial financing). Office: Burns Figa & Will PC 6400 S Fiddlers Green Cir #1030 Englewood CO 80111 Office Fax: 303-796-2777.

VELAZQUEZ, AGUSTIN, lawyer; b. Mexico City, Dec. 19, 1968; Law Degree, U. Nuevo Mundo, Mexico City, 1992; postgrad. degree in intellectual property, U. Panamerican, Mexico City, 1996. Atty. clk. Guadarrama, Proal, Calva, Loyo, Mexico City, 1986—87, Basham, Ringe y Correa, S.C., Mexico City, 1987—93; assoc. Von Wobeser y Sierra, S.C., Mexico City, 1993—98, ptnr., 1999—. Contbr. articles to profl. jours. Mem.: Internat. C. of C. A.C. (sub-commr. for inventions intellectual property commn. Mexican chpt. 1996—), Illustre y Nacional Colegio de Abogados de Mexico, A.C., Am. Intellectual Property Law Assn., Mexican Inst. Mediation (alt. mem. bd. 2001—), Internat. Trademark Assn. (country reporter INTA Bull. com. 1996—97, customs procedure subcom. counterfeiting and enforcement com. 1997—98), Mexican Assn. for the Protection of Indsl. Property (various affairs commn. 1996, spl. ct. commn. 1996—98, copyright commn. 1997—98, trips commn. 1998, coord. litigation work group 1999—2002, pres. litigation work group 2002—), Mexican Bar Assn. (intellectual property law commn. 1993—, constnl. appeals law commn. 1995—, comml. law commn. 1995—). Trademark and copyright, Patent, Intellectual property. Office: Von Wobeser y Sierra SC G González Camarena 110 7th Col Santa Fe 01210 Mexico City Mexico

VELAZQUEZ DE LEON, CARLOS, lawyer; b. Garza Garcia, Mexico, Aug. 27, 1962; s. Ernesto Velazquez de leon and Elia Obregon; m. Jilda Ortego Contreras Velazquez de leon, June 29, 1990; children: Jimena, Juan Carlos. Law degree, Universidad Iberoamericana, Mexico City, 1987; LLM, Instituto de Empresa, Madrid, 1989. Assoc. atty. Basham, Ringe & Correa, S.C., Mexico City, ptnr. Bd. mem. Ctr. for Am. and Internat. Law, Dallas, 2000—03, Cancham, Monterey, 2000—03, Amcham, Monterey, 2000—03. Catholic. Avocations: tennis, skiing, soccer, reading, jogging. Home: Calleojon de las Privanzas 304-20 66269 Garza Garcia NL Mexico Office: Basham Ringe & Correa SC Batallon de San Patricio 109-P16 Garza Garcia NL Mexico Business E-Mail: carlosv@basham.com.mx.

VELTEMA, GREGORY N. lawyer; b. Lansing, Mich., Nov. 27, 1951; s. Corneal and Esther Ellen (Walenjus) V. BS, Grand Valley State U., 1974; JD, Cooley Law Sch., 1978. Bar: Mich. 1979, U.S. Dist. Ct. (we. dist.) Mich. 1981, U.S. Dist. Ct. (ea. dist.) Mich. 1987, U.S. Ct. Appeals (6th cir.) 1987. Assoc. Dood, Finn & Veltema, Lansing, 1981; pvt. practice Lansing, 1982—. Author: (with others) Michigan Sesquicentennial History of Delhi Township, 1987. Trustee Delhi Township, Holt, Mich., 1980-92. Mem. Ingham County Bar Assn., Eaton County Bar Assn. Republican. Episcopalian. Avocations: swimming, gardening. Family and matrimonial, Personal injury (including property damage), Property, real (including real estate development, water). Office: 2840 E Grand River Ste 1 East Lansing MI 48823

VENNING, ROBERT STANLEY, lawyer; b. Boise, Idaho, July 24, 1943; s. William Lucas and Corey Elizabeth (Brown) V.; m. Sandra Macdonald, May 9, 1966 (div. 1976); 1 child, Rachel Elizabeth; m. Laura Siegel, Mar. 24, 1979; 1 child, Daniel Rockhill Siegel. AB, Harvard U., 1965; MA, U. Chgo., 1966; LLB, Yale U., 1970. Bar: Calif., U.S. Dist. Ct. (no. dist.) Calif., 1971, U.S. Dist. Ct. (cen. dist.) Calif. 1973, U.S. Ct. Appeals (9th cir.) 1977, U.S. Supreme Ct. 1977, U.S. Ct. Appeals (fed. cir.) 1986, U.S. Ct. Appeals (D.C. cir.) 1987, U.S. Ct. of Fed. Claims 1996. Assoc. Heller Ehrman White & McAuliffe, San Francisco, 1970-73, 73-76, ptnr., 1977—, mem. exec. com., 1991-94. Vis. lectr. U. Wash., Seattle, 1973, Boalt Hall Sch. Law, U. Calif., Berkeley, 1982-85, 89, Sch. Bus., Stanford U., 1986-87. Editor Yale Law Jour., 1969-70. Early neutral evaluator U.S. Dist. Ct. (no. dist.) Calif., 1987—. Fellow Am. Bar Found. (life); mem. ABA, San Francisco Bar Assn. (past chair judiciary com.), CPR Inst. for Dispute Resolution, Olympic Club. Federal civil litigation, General civil litigation, State civil litigation. Office: Heller White & McAuliffe LLP 333 Bush St San Francisco CA 94104-2878

VENTO, M. THÉRÈSE, lawyer; b. N.Y.C., June 30, 1951; d. Anthony Joseph and Margaret (Stechert) V.; m. Peter Michael MacNamara, Dec. 23, 1977; children: David Miles, Elyse Anne. BS, U. Fla., 1974, JD, 1976. Bar: Fla. 1977, U.S. Dist. Ct. (so. and mid. dists.) Fla. 1982, U.S. Ct. Appeals (5th and 11th cirs.) 1981, U.S. Supreme Ct. 1985. Clk. to presiding justice U.S. Dist. Ct. (so. dist.) Fla., Miami, 1976-78; assoc. Mahoney, Hadlow & Adams, Miami, 1978-79, Shutts & Bowen, Miami, 1979-84, ptnr., 1985-95; founding ptnr. Gallwey Gillman Curtis & Vento, P.A., Miami, 1995—. Trustee Miami Art Mus., 1988—, v.p., 1999—; trustee The Beacon Coun., 1995-97, Law Sch. Alumni Coun., U. Fla., 1994—. Fellow Am. Bar Found.; mem. Dade County Bar Assn. (dir. young lawyers sect. 1978-83, editor newsletter 1981-83), Fla. Assn. for Women Lawyers, Fla. Bar Assn. (bd. govs., young lawyers div. 1983-85, civil procedure rules com. 1983-90, exec. coun. trial lawyers sect. 1996—), The Miami Forum (v.p. 1987-88, bd. dirs. 1989-91, co-pres. 2001-2002). Federal civil litigation, General civil litigation, Libel. Home: 3908 Main Hwy Miami FL 33133-6513 Office: Gallwey Gillman Curtis & Vento PA 200 SE 1st St Ste 1100 Miami FL 33131-1912 E-mail: TVento@GGCVH.com.

VENTRELLI, ANITA MARIE, lawyer; b. Berwyn, Ill., Apr. 20, 1964; d. Jose M. and Anita Marie (Loycano) Bolaños. AB, U. Mich., 1986; JD, DePaul U., 1989. Bar: Ill. 1990. Ptnr. Schiller DuCanto & Fleck, Chgo., 1997—. Fellow Am. Acad. Matrimonial Lawyers; mem. ABA, Ill. Bar Assn. Roman Catholic. Avocations: running, piano. Family and matrimonial. Office: Schiller DuCanto & Fleck 200 N La Salle St Ste 2700 Chicago IL 60601-1098 E-mail: aventrelli@sdflaw.com.

VENTRES, JUDITH MARTIN, lawyer; b. Ann Arbor, Mich., Feb. 10, 1943; d. D. Lawrence and Donna E. (Webb) Moran; children: Laura M. Buford, Paul M. Martin, A. Lindsay McGill; m. Daniel B. Ventres Jr., Dec. 27, 1984. BA, U. Mich., 1963; postgrad., U. Jean Moulin, Inst. du Droit, Lyon, France, 1981; JD, U. Minn., 1982. Bar: Minn. 1982, Fla. 1991, Colo. 1994, U.S. Tax Ct. 1989, U.S. Dist. Ct. Minn. 1989, U.S. Ct. Appeals (8th cir.) 1989. Tax supr., dir. fin. planning, asst. nat. dir. Coopers & Lybrand, Mpls., 1981-84; dir. fin. planning Investors Diversified Services subs. Am. Express, Mpls. and N.Y.C., 1984-85; sr. tax mgr., dir. fin. planning KPMG Peat Marwick Main & Co., Mpls., 1985-89; prin. Gray Plant Mooty Mooty & Bennett, P.A., Mpls., 2000—02; owner and mng. ptnr. Martin & Assoc., PA, Mpls., 1989—2000; mng. ptnr. Martin & Assocs., PA, Mpls., 2002—. Faculty Minn. CLE, 1994; adv. bd. Nicollet/Ebenezer, 1996. Mem. Mpls. C. of C. Campaign, Downtown Coun. Coms., Mpls., 1982-84, Metro Tax Planning Group, 1984-86, Mpls. Estate Planning Coun., 1985-99, Planned Giving Coun.; class chmn. fundraising campaign U. Minn. Law Sch., Mpls., 1985, 98; bd. dirs. Ensemble Capriccio, chmn. fundraising com., 1998-2002; usher Christ Presbyn. Ch., Edina, Minn., 1983—; mem. adv. coun. on planned giving ARC. Mem. ABA (task force on legal fin. planning), Minn. Bar Assn., Hennepin County Bar Assn., Fla. Bar Assn., Colo. Bar Assn., Minn. Soc. CPAs (instr. continuing legal edn. 1983-84, continuing profl. edn. 1982-86, individual, trust and estate provisions Tax Reform Act 1986, continuing legal edn. -estate planning 1994), Minn. Planned Giving Coun., Am. Assn. Ind. Investors (speaker), Am. Soc. CLUs, Minn. Soc. CLUs, Minn. Women Lawyers, Fla. Women Lawyers, Lex Alumnae, U. Mich. Alumni Assn. (coun. govs. 1989—, scholarship chmn.), U. Minn. Alumni Club (bd. dirs. 1996, coun. govs. 1988-96, pres., treas. mem. com.), Interlachen Club, Athletic Club, Lafayette Club, Montana Club, U. Minn. Alumni Assn. (mem. univ. issues com., nat. bd. dirs. 1996-99). Estate planning, Probate (including wills, trusts), Personal income taxation. Home: 1355 Vine Pl Mound MN 55364-9635 Office: Martin & Assoc PA 3800 W 80 St #270 Minneapolis MN 55431-

VERA, RONALD THOMAS, lawyer; b. Pomona, Calif., Oct. 16, 1946; s. Marcelino and Mary (Regaldo) V.; m. Christina Vega, June 10, 1972; children: Noah, Luis, Adam, Paul. BS, Mich. State U., 1970; JD, UCLA, 1973. Bar: Calif., 1974. Atty. Calif. Rural Legal Assistance, El Centro, Calif., 1973-77, dep. dir. San Francisco, 1977-79; staff atty. Mex.-Am. Legal Defense & Ednl. Fund, San Francisco, 1979-85; assoc. scholar Tomas Rivera Ctr. for Policy Studies, Claremont, Calif., 1985-86; ptnr. Barbosa & Vera, L.A., 1986-90; of counsel Best, Best & Krieger, Riverside, Calif., 1990-92; pvt. practice Claremont, 1994—; ptnr. Gutierrez & Vera, Claremont, 2003—. Vis. prof. law Loyola U. Law Sch., L.A., 1992-93, adj. prof. law, 1993-99. Contbr. articles to Ednl. Jours. Bd. dirs. Contra Costa Pers. Commn., Contra Costa County, Calif., 1984-86, Nat. Ctr. for Fair and Open Testing, Cambridge, Mass., 1986-94, Damien Prep. High Sch., La Verne, Calif., 1990-94, Pub. Counsel, 1989-92, Pomona Valley Med. Ctr., 1992—, Calif. Consortium of Edn. Found., 1995—. Recipient fellowship NEH, Harvard U. Law Sch., Cambridge, Mass., 1980, Tomas Rivera Ctr. for Policy Studies, Clarement, Calif., 1985-86. Mem.. ABA, Calif. State Bar Assn. (chair client security fund commn. 1993-97), L.A. County Bar Assn. Education and schools, Environmental, Municipal (including bonds). Office: 223 W Foothill Blvd Fl 2 Claremont CA 91711-2757

VERCAMMEN, KENNETH ALBERT, lawyer, prosecutor; b. Edison, N.J., Aug. 7, 1959; s. Albert Peter and Carol Ann (Rasche) V.; m. Cynthia Ann Bachenski, July 9, 1989. BS, U. Scranton, 1981; JD, Univ. Del. Law Sch., 1985. Bar: N.J., Pa. 1985, N.Y. 1986, D.C. 1987; cert. mediator N.J. Superior Ct., 1997-. Mng. atty., Cranbury, NJ, 1990—; prosecutor Township of Cranbury, Middlesex County, NJ, 1991—99; spl. acting prosecutor Delaware County, Pa. District Office, Middlesex County Probation Dept., Scranton Dist. Magistrate Office, Woodbridge, East Brunswick, Metuchen, South Brunswick, Clark, Berkeley; acting assoc. prosecutor Carteret Mcpl. Ct., Middlesex County, NJ, 2000. Adj. prof. Middlesex County Coll., Edison, 1990-91, 2001; instr. criminal law and procedure and bus. law; mem. com. mcpl. ct. edn. N.J. Supreme Ct., 1990-97; spkr. litig. engagements, wills, elder law and probate. Author 132 separate law rev. and legal periodicals articles to profl. jours. including N.J. Law Jour., ABA Barrister, N.J. Lawyer, ABA Law Practice Mgmt., Dictum; editor N.J. Municipal Ct. Law Review, 1993-; author, DWI & Drug Cases, 2002. Winner of the N.J. State Bar Gen. Practitioner of the Yr. award, 2002, N.J. Bar Assoc. Svc. to Bar award, N.J. State Bar Assn. YLD award, 1993. Mem.: N.J. State Bar Assn. (chair mcpl. ct. sect.), Middlesex Mcpl. Prosecutor's Assn. (co-chmn. mcpl. ct. practice com. 1997—, mem. bd. trustees 2000—). Avocations: cross-country running, soccer. Commercial, contracts (including sales of goods; commercial financing), Criminal, Personal injury (including property damage). Office: 2053 Woodbridge Ave Edison NJ 08817

VER DUGHT, ELGENE CLARK, lawyer/mediator; b. Des Moines, Oct. 8, 1951; s. Elvyn Eugene and Betty Louise (Clark) Ver D.; m. Juliann Esther Dieckmann, June 15, 1974; children: Janna, Jared. BA, U. Mo., 1973; JD cum laude, Hamline U., 1976. Bar: Mo. 1976, U.S. Dist. Ct. (we. dist.) Mo. 1976, U.S. Supreme Ct. 1979, U.S. Ct. Appeals (8th cir.) 1981. Ptnr. Ver Dught Law Offices, Higginsville, Mo., 1976—; city atty. Corder, Mo., 1977-85, Wellington, Mo., 1978-85, Napoleon, Mo., 1979-85; prosecuting atty. County of Lafayette, Lexington, Mo., 1979-80; city atty. Blackburn, Mo., 1982-87; city prosecutor Higginsville, Mo., 1986-88; counsel C-1 Sch. Dist., Higginsville, 1987-88, 90—; exec. dir., founder Mediation Svcs. Mo. Cons. Ver Dught Farms, Lexington and Higginsville, Mo., 1978—; founder Mediation Svcs. of Mo. V.p. Lafayette County Dems., Mo., 1977; bd. dirs., adv. coun. Foster Grandparent Assn. Mem. Nat. Acad. Family Mediators (sr.), Assn. Family and Conciliation Cts. Democrat. Reorganized Ch. Jesus Christ Latter Day Saints. Lodge: Rotary (pres. Higginsville club 1983-84, Paul Harris fellow, 1984). Alternative dispute resolution, State civil litigation, Family and matrimonial. Home: RR 2 Box 173 Higginsville MO 64037-9528 Office: 1814 N Main St # 174 Higginsville MO 64037-1525 also: 13910 Noland Ct Ste B-1 Independence MO 64055-3353 E-mail: elgene@aol.com.

VERGON, FREDERICK PORTER, JR., lawyer; b. Mesa, Ariz., June 12, 1944; s. Frederick Porter and Adalaide (Boyd) V.; children: Frederick Porter III, Heather Boyd, Sarah McCrea. BA, Denison U., 1966; JD, Case Western Res. U., 1969; postgrad., Cleve. Marshall Coll. Law, 1969-70. Bar: Ohio 1969, U.S. Dist. Ct. Ohio 1970, U.S. Supreme Ct. 1980. Assoc. McNeal & Schick, Cleve., 1969-79; ptnr. McNeal Schick, Archibald & Biro, Cleve., 1979-85; assoc. Cronquist Smith Marshall & Weaver, Cleve., 1985-86; ptnr. Smith Marshall Weaver & Vergon, Cleve., 1986—. Mem. ABA, Ohio State Bar Assn., Cleve. Bar Assn., Def. Rsch. Inst., Ohio Assn. Civil Trial Attys., Internat. Assn. Def. Counsel. Republican. Presbyterian. General civil litigation, Insurance, Product liability. Office: Smith Marshall Weaver & Vergon 500 National City-E 6 Bldg Cleveland OH 44114

VERHAAREN, HAROLD CARL, lawyer; b. Salt Lake City, Apr. 11, 1938; m. Cynthia Mary Hughes, Nov. 25, 1964; children: Scott Harold, Steven Robert, Jill, Brent Carl, Brian Hughes. JD, U. Utah, 1965. Bar: Utah 1965, U.S. Supreme Ct. 1978. Law clk. to chief justice Utah Supreme Ct., 1964-65; v.p., bd. dirs. Nielsen & Senior PC, Salt Lake City, 1992—. Judge pro tem Small Claims Ct. Salt Lake County, 1978-85. Chmn. Mt. Olympus Planning Dist., 1971-85; active Boy Scouts Am., 1967-97. Recipient Silver Beaver award Boy Scouts Am. Mem. Utah Bar Assn., Salt Lake County Bar Assn., Am. Arbitration Assn. (panel of arbitrators), Delta Theta Phi, Phi Kappa Phi, Phi Eta Sigma. Mem. Lds Ch. State civil litigation, Commercial, contracts (including sales of goods; commercial financing), Construction. Office: 60 E South Temple 11th Fl Salt Lake City UT 84111 E-mail: hcv@ns-law.com.

VERHOEVEN, CHARLES K. lawyer; BBA with distinction, U. Iowa, 1985, JD with high distinction, 1988. Assoc. Cravath, Swaine & Moore, N.Y.C., 1988—93; ptnr., head No. Calif. offices Quinn Emanuel et al, Redwood Shores, Calif., 1993—. Mem.: Iowa Law Rev., 1986—87, articles editor: , 1987—88. Named one of Top 20 Lawyers in Calif. Under 40 Yrs. Old, Calif. Law Bus. Mem.: ABA, Assn. Bar City of New York, State Bar N.Y., State Bar Calif. Intellectual property, Property, real (including real estate development, water), Antitrust. Office: Quinn Emauel et al 555 Twin Dolphin Dr Ste 560 Redwood City CA 94065 Office Fax: 650-620-4555. Business E-Mail: charlesverhoeven@quinnemanuel.com.*

VERNER, JAMES MELTON, lawyer; b. Selma, Ala., Sept. 19, 1915; s. Singleton Foster and Jennie (Harris) V.; m. Gretchen Gores, Aug. 12, 1939; children: Ann Verner Picardo, James Singleton, William Melton. Student, Biltmore Coll., 1932-34; AB, U. N.C., 1936, LL.B., 1938. Bar: N.C. 1938, Tenn. 1947, D.C. 1950, Va., 1986. Assoc. firm Gover & Covington, Charlotte, N.C., 1938; law clk. atty. gen. N.C., 1938-40; atty. CAB, Washington, 1940-43; asst. gen. counsel Chgo. & So. Airlines, Memphis, 1946-47; atty. Air Transport Assn. Am., Washington, 1947-49; hearing examiner CAB, 1949-50, exec. asst. to chmn., 1950, exec. dir., 1950-53; from atty. to ptnr. Turney & Turney, 1953—60; ptnr. firm Verner, Liipfert, Bernhard, McPherson & Hand, Chartered (and predecessor firms), 1960-88; hon. mem. bd. dirs., spl. coun. Piper Rudnick (formerly Verner, Liipfert, Bernhard, McPherson & Hand, Chartered, Washington, 1988—. Assoc. editor: N.C. Law Rev, 1937-38. Former mem., chmn. policy bd. Legal Counsel for Elderly, Washington. Served as lt. (j.g.) USNR, 1943-46; legal officer Naval Air Transport Svc., 1945-46. Mem. ABA, Order of Golden Fleece, Cosmos Club (Washington). Home: 900 N Taylor St # 2104-2106 Arlington VA 22203-1858 Office: Piper Rudnick 901 15th St NW Washington DC 20005-2327

VERNIERO, PETER G. state supreme court justice; married; 2 children. BA summa cum laude, Drew U., 1981; JD, Duke U., 1984. Law clk. to Justice Robert L. Clifford, 1984; with Pitney, Hardin, Kipp & Szuch, Morristown, NJ, 1985—87; dir. Herold & Haines P.A., Warren, NJ; chief counsel, chief of staff Gov. Christine Whitman, Trenton, NJ; atty. gen. State of N.J., Trenton, 1996—99; assoc. justice N.J. Supreme Ct., Trenton, 1999—. Adj. prof. bus. law County Coll. Morris, 1986. Exec. dir. Rep. State Com., 1989—90. Office: NJ Supreme Ct Hunterdon County Justice Ctr 65 Park Ave Flemington NJ 08822-0970

VERNON, DARRYL MITCHELL, lawyer; b. N.Y.C., May 4, 1956; s. Leonard and Joyce (Davidson) V.; m. Lauren Lynn Bernstein, Aug. 21, 1982. BA in Math., Tufts U., 1978; JD, Yeshiva U., 1981. Bar: N.Y. 1982, U.S. Dist. Ct. (so. and ea. dists.) N.Y. 1982, U.S. Ct. Appeals (2d cir.) 1987. Assoc. Hochberg & Greenberg, N.Y.C., 1981-82; ptnr. Greenberg & Vernon, N.Y.C., 1982-83, Law Offices of Darryl M. Vernon, N.Y.C., 1983—; pres., ptnr. Vernon & Ginsburg, LLP, N.Y.C., 1989—. Spkr. in field. Contbr. articles to profl. jours. Samuel Belkin scholar Yeshiva U., 1979. Mem. Assn. Bar City N.Y. (com. legal issues pertaining to animals). Landlord-tenant, Property, real (including real estate development, water), Animal welfare. Office: 261 Madison Ave New York NY 10016-2303

VERRELLI, ANTHONY LOUIS, lawyer; b. Bronx, Feb. 19, 1967; s. Sebastiano and Josephine V.; m. Sungho Pak, Feb. 16, 1997. BA cum laude, Iona Coll., 1989; MA summa cum laude, St. John's U., 1991; JD, Seton Hall U., 1994. Bar: N.J. 1994, N.Y. 1995, U.S. Dist. Ct. (so. and ea. dists.) N.Y. 1995. Atty. pvt. practice, Bronx, 1994—. St. John's U. Grad. Sch. scholar, Jamaica, N.Y., 1991. Mem. N.Y. State Trial Lawyers Assn., Bronx County Bar Assn. Avocations: soccer, hiking, golf. Pension, profit-sharing, and employee benefits, Personal injury (including property damage), Property, real (including real estate development, water). Office: 2701 Williamsbridge Rd Bronx NY 10469-4109 E-mail: atyalv@optonline.net.

VERRILL, CHARLES OWEN, JR., lawyer; b. Biddeford, Maine, Sept. 30, 1937; s. Charles Owen and Elizabeth (Handy) V.; m. Mary Ann Blanchard, Aug. 13, 1960 (dec.); children: Martha Anne, Edward Blanchard, Ethan Christopher, Elizabeth Handy, Matthew Lawton, Peter Goldthwait; m. Diana Baber, Dec. 11, 1993. AB, Tufts U., 1959; LLB, Duke U., 1962. Bar: D.C. 1962. Assoc. Weaver & Glassie, 1962-64, Barco, Cook, Patton & Blow, 1964-66, ptnr., 1967, Patton, Boggs & Blow, 1967-84, Wiley, Rein & Fielding, Washington, 1984—. Adj. prof. internat. trade law/internat. bus. transaction Georgetown U. Law Ctr., Washington, 1978—, Charles Fahy Disting. adj. prof., 1993; vis. sr. lectr. internat. trade law Duke U. Law Sch., 1998—; conf. chmn. The Future of Internat. Steel Industry, Bellagio, Italy, 1984, U.S. Agenda for Uruguay Round, Airlie House, Warrenton, Va., 1986, Polish Joint Venture Law, Cracow, Poland, 1987, Internat. Steel Industry II, Bellagio, 1987, Bulgaria and the GATT, Washington, 1977; chair, spkr. Protection of Intellectual Property from Theft and Piracy Abroad Southwestern Legal Found. Fgn. Investment Symposium, 1995, chair, panel on NAFTA 2 1/2 Years Later, 1996; nat. adv. bd. Natural Resources Coun. of Maine, 2002—; panel mem. CPR Washington, 2003—. Local dir. Tufts U. Ann. Fund, 1965-69; mem. Duke Law Alumni Coun., 1972-75; trustee Internat. Law Inst., 1981—, chmn. bd. trustees, 1983-87; apptd. to roster of dispute settlement panelists World Trade Orgn., 1995, 97; chmn. adv. bd. Inst. for Advancement of Svc., 1997—; adv. com. rules U.S. Ct. Internat. Trade, 1998—; chmn. D.C. Cable Television Adv. Com., 1999—; bd. visitors Duke U. Law Sch., 2000—. Mem. ABA, Internat. Bar Assn., D.C. Bar Assn., Order of Coif, Theta Delta Chi, Phi Delta Phi, Met. Club (Washington), Chevy Chase Club (Md.), Tarratine Club (Dark Harbor, Maine). Private international. Home: 3000 Q St NW Washington DC 20007-3080 Office: 1776 K St NW Washington DC 20006-2304 E-mail: cverrill@wrf.com.

VERRONE, PATRIC MILLER, lawyer, writer; b. Glendale, N.Y.C., Sept. 29, 1959; s. Pat and Edna (Miller) V.; m. Margaret Maiya Williams, 1989; children: Patric Carroll Williams, Marianne Emma Williams, Theodore Henry Williams. BA, Harvard U., 1981; JD, Boston Coll., 1984. Bar: Fla. 1984, Calif. 1988, U.S. Dist. Ct. (mid. dist.) Fla. 1984, U.S. Dist. Ct. (ctrl. dist.) Calif. 1995, U.S. Ct. Appeals (9th cir.) 1995. Assoc. Allen, Knudsen, Swartz, DeBoest, Rhoads & Edwards, Ft. Myers, Fla., 1984-86; writer The Tonight Show, Burbank, Calif., 1987-90. Adj. prof. Loyola Law Sch., LA, 1998—2000; lectr. U. Calif., LA, 2002—. Dir., producer, writer The Civil War-The Lost Episode, 1991; writer The Larry Sanders Show, 1992-94, The Critic, 1993-95; producer, writer The Simpsons, 1994-95, Muppets Tonight!, 1995-97 (Emmy award Best Children's Program 1998), Pinky and the Brain, 1998, Futurama, 1998-2002 (Environ. Media award 2000, Emmy nominee 1999, 2001, Emmy award for outstanding animated program 2002); editor Harvard Lampoon, 1978-84, Boston Coll. Law Rev., 1983-84, Fla. Bar Jour., 1987-88, L.A. Lawyer, 1994—; issue editor: Ann. Entertainment Law Issue, 1995-2003; contbr. articles to profl. jours. including Elysian Fields Quar., Baseball and the American Legal Mind, White's Guide to Collecting Figures, written by, Frank Sinatra: The Man, The Music, The Legend. Bd. dirs. Calif. Confedn. of Arts, 1994-98, Mus. Contemporary Art, 1994-95. Mem. ABA (vice-chair arts, entertainment and sports law com. 1995-96), Calif. Bar, Calif. Lawyers for Arts, L.A. County Bar Assn. (sec. barristers exec. com., chair artists and the law com., steering com. homeless shelter project, intellectual property and entertainment law sect., state appelate jud. evaluation com., legis. activity com.), Fla. Bar Assn., Writers Guild Am. West (exec. com. animation writers caucus, bd. dirs. 1999-2001, sec., treas., 2001-, membership fin. com. 1999—2001, chmn. 2001—02, contract negotiating com., chair organizing com. 2001-, animation writing award animation writers caucus, writers caucus animation writing award 2002), Harvard Club Lee County (v.p. 1985-86), Harvard Club So. Calif. Republican. Roman Catholic. Avocations: baseball, history. Home and Office: PO Box 1428 Pacific Palisades CA 90272-1428

VERSFELT, DAVID SCOTT, lawyer; b. Mineola, N.Y., Feb. 17, 1951; s. William H. and Ruth (Gerland) V.; m. Mary Deborah Garber, Aug. 31, 1974; children: Christopher L., William S., Kathryn H. AB, Princeton U., 1973; JD, Columbia U., 1976. Bar: N.Y. 1977, U.S. Dist. Ct. (so. and ea. dists.) N.Y. 1977, U.S. Ct. Appeals (D.C. cir.) 1979, U.S. Ct. Appeals (2d and 7th cirs.) 1980, U.S. Supreme Ct. 1980, U.S. Ct. Appeals (9th cir.) 1981, U.S. Ct. Appeals (3d cir.) 1982, Ct. Internat. Trade 1990, U.S. Ct. Appeals (fed. cir.) 1994, U.S. Ct. Appeals (6th cir.) 1996. Mem. Coun. of Community Law Office; vol. div. Legal Aid Soc., N.Y.C., 1985-88; dir. Partnership for a Drug-Free Am., 1989—. Mem. ABA, Fed. Bar Coun., Phi Beta Kappa. Federal civil litigation, Corporate, general, Securities. Office: Kirkpatrick & Lockhart LLP 599 Lexington Ave New York NY 10022-6030 E-mail: dversfelt@kl.com.

VERTEFEUILLE, CHRISTINE SIEGRIST, judge; b. New Britain, Conn., Dec. 10, 1950; BA in Polit. Sci., Trinity Coll., 1972; JD, U. Conn., 1975. Pvt. practice, 1975-89; judge Conn. Superior Ct., 1989—99; adminstrv. judge Waterbury Jud. Dist., 1994-99, complex litig. judge, 1999; judge Appellate Ct., 1999-2000; assoc. justice Conn. Supreme Ct., 2000—. Alternate mem. Waterbury and New Haven (Conn.) Grievance Panels, 1985-89; faculty Conn. Judges Inst., 1989-94. Recipient Jud. award Conn. Trial Lawyers Assn., 1995. Mem. Conn. Bar Assn. (mem. exec. com. real property 1988-89). Office: Supreme Ct Bldg 231 Capitol Ave Hartford CT 06106

VERTUN, ALAN STUART, lawyer; b. N.Y.C., Feb. 11, 1951; s. Simon and Dorothy (Weber) V.; m. Marion Vertun, May 20, 1983; children: Laura, Jeffrey, Amy. AB, UCLA, 1973; JD, Southwestern U., 1976. Bar: Calif. 1976. Atty. Potscrubber, Inc., L.A., 1978-81, NIS Corp., L.A., 1981-84; pvt. practice L.A., 1984—. Vol. Am. Cancer Soc., L.A., 1985-95, LIFE, L.A., 1984-87. Mem. Los Angeles County Bar Assn. General civil litigation, Corporate, general, Personal injury (including property damage). Office: 4250 Wilshire Blvd # 203 Los Angeles CA 90010-3508

VESSEL, ROBERT LESLIE, lawyer; b. Chgo., Mar. 21, 1942; s. Louis Frank and Margaret Ruth (Barber) V.; m. Diane White, Oct. 12, 1966; m. Lise Vessel, Dec. 19, 1992. BA, U. Ill., 1964; JD, Seton Hall U., 1973; LLM in Taxation, U. Miami, Coral Gables, Fla., 1980. Bar: N.J. 1973, Fla. 1981, U.S. Dist. Ct. (so. and mid. dists.) Fla. 1981, U.S. Ct. Appeals (11th cir.) 1981; bd. cert. civil trial, Fla. Assoc. Bennett & Bennett P.A., East Orange, N.J., 1973-76; ptnr. Kantor & Vessel, P.A., Wayne, N.J., 1976-81; assoc. Haddad Josephs & Jack, P.A., Coral Gables, Fla., 1981-85; ptnr. Mitchell Alley Rywant & Vessel, Tampa, 1985-89, Moffitt & Vessel, P.A., Tampa, 1989-94, Vessel & Morales, P.A., Tampa, 1994-99. With USNR, 1964-66. Mem. Assn. Trial Lawyers Am., Nat. Inst. Trial Advocacy, Acad. Fla. Trial Lawyers, Hillsboro County Bar Assn. Avocation: sailing. Estate planning, Personal injury (including property damage), Insurance. Office: Robert L Vessel PA 1100 W Kennedy Blvd Tampa FL 33606-1966 E-mail: veslaw@msn.com.

VESTAL, ALLAN W. dean, law educator; BA, Yale U., 1976, JD, 1979. Tchr. partnership and corp. law, comml. law, and real estate Washington and Lee U. Sch. Law , 1989—2000; dean U. Ky. Coll. Law, Lexington, 2000—. Practiced law for ten yrs., Wis., Iowa. Publ. (treatise with Prof. Hillman and Dean Weidner) The Revised Uniform Partnership Act ; contbr. chapters to books, articles to law revs. Mem.: Am. Law Inst. Office: Coll Law U Ky Lexington KY 40506-0048

VETTER, JAMES GEORGE, JR., lawyer; b. Omaha, Apr. 8, 1934; s. James George and Helen Louise (Adams) V.; m. Mary Ellen Froelich, June 25, 1960; 1 child, James G. III. BS, Georgetown U., 1954; JD, Creighton U., 1960. Bar: Nebr. 1960, Tex. 1967. Counsel IRS, Washington, 1960-64, Dallas, 1964-67; practiced in Dallas, 1967—; sr. ptnr. Vetter, Bates, Tibbals, Lee & DeBusk P.C., 1979-89; mem. Godwin & Gruber, P.C., 1989—, mng. dir., 1994-98. Lectr. taxation seminars; bd. dirs. Pilgrim's Pride Corp., AFV Energy, Inc., VLSIP Techs., Inc. Contbr. articles to profl. jours. Asst. sgt.-at-arms Tex. Dem. Conv., 1968; advisor selection com. Georgetown U., 1970-85; scoutmaster Boy Scouts Am., 1974-75; trustee St. Monica Sch. Endowment Trust, 1999—. With USAF, 1954-57; capt. USAFR, ret. Fellow Tex. Bar Found.; mem. Nebr. Bar Assn., State Bar Tex. (cert. tax law 1983—), Coll. State Bar Tex., Dallas Bar Assn. (chmn. fee disputes com. 1985, chmn. publs. com. 1988, chmn. pictoral directory com. 1993), Real Estate Fin. Execs. Assn. (pres. 1982-83), Cash Alliance (pres. 1987-88), Creighton U. Alumni Assn. (pres. Dallas-Ft. Worth 1969-70), Ctrl. Dallas Assn. (bd. dirs. 1994-95), Park Cities Club, Delta Theta Phi. Roman Catholic. Corporate taxation, Estate taxation, Personal income taxation. Home: 11023 Rosser Rd Dallas TX 75229-3915 Office: Godwin & Gruber PC 1201 Elm St Ste 1700 Dallas TX 75270 E-mail: jvetter@godwingruber.com.

VICK, JOSEPH JAMES, III, lawyer; b. Corpus Christi, Tex., June 4, 1954; s. James Andrew and Winnie Marie Vick; m. Patricia Burns, Aug. 11, 1979; children: Shelby C., Emmett J. A. BBA, U. Tex., 1976; JD, S. Tex. Coll. Law, 1979. Bar: Tex. 1980, Colo. 1981, U.S. Dist. Ct. Colo. 1981, U.S. Ct. Appeals (10th cir.) 1986, U.S. Supreme Ct. 1986. Pvt. practice, Ft. Collins, Colo., 1981—82, 1996—, Greeley, Colo., 1996—; assoc. Sleeper, Johnston & Helm, Waco, Tex., 1982; ptnr. Beatty & Vick, Ft. Collins, 1982—86; shareholder, ptnr. Wood, Herzog, Osborn & Bloom, PC, Ft. Collins, 1986—93; shareholder, mng. ptnr. Martinez, Perez & Vick, P.C., Ft. Collins, 1993—95. Part-time instr. Colo. State U., Ft. Collins, 1983—90; chmn. Larimer County Legal Aid Program, Ft. Collins, 1993. Coord., asst. com. pub. edn. Supreme Ct. Colo., Loveland, 1996. Lt. (j.g.) JAGC USNR, 1981—84. Mem.: ATLA, ABA, Larimer County Bar Assn. (pres. 1996—97), Colo. Trial Lawyers Assn. Republican. Roman Catholic. Avocations: reading, walking, travel. Personal injury (including property damage), Family and matrimonial, State civil litigation. Office: 315 W Oak St Ste 512 Fort Collins CO 80521

VICKERY, EDWARD DOWNTAIN, lawyer; b. Fort Worth, Tex., May 1, 1922; s. Charles Richard and Margaret May Vickery; children: Anne Vickery Stevenson, E.D. Jr. AS, North Tex. Agrl. Coll., 1941; BA, U. Tex., 1947, JD with honors, 1948. Bar: Tex. 1948, U.S. Dist. Ct. (so. dist.) Tex. 1948, U.S. Ct. Appeals (5th cir.) 1950, Bd. Immagration Appeals 1952, U.S. Supreme Ct. 1953. From assoc. to sr. ptnr. Royston, Rayzor, Vickery & Williams, Houston, 1948-55, sr. ptnr., 1955-98, of counsel, 1999—. Chmn. bd. dirs. First Nat. Bank Bellaire, Katy Bank, Tradition Bank, Houston. Deacon First Presbyn. Ch., Houston, 1958-64, elder 1965-94; mem. Brazos Presbyn. Ch., 1972-77, chmn. 1976-77; bd. trustees Austin (Tex.) Presbyn. Theol. Sem., 1976-85, 86-95, v. chmn. 1978-83, chmn. 1983-85, 89-95; bd. trustees Tex. Presbyn. Found. 1978-85. Fellow Am. Coll. Trial Lawyers, Internat. Acad. Trial Lawyers (Am. chpt.); mem. Internat. Assn. Ins. Counsel, Am. Judicature Soc., Maritime Law Assn. U.S. (exec. com. 1977-80), Hist. Soc. Supreme Ct. U.S., Tex. Assn. Def. Counsel (bd. dirs. 1965-67), Tex. Bar Found. (Houston chpt.), Tulane Admiralty Law Inst. (program, planning com., adv. bd., 1965-92), Propellor Club U.S. (nat. pres. 1965-66, 66-67, nat. first v.p. 1964-65, nat. exec. com. 1961-85, port of Houston pres. 1961-62), U. Tex. Littlefield Soc., Chancellor's Coun., T Assn., Longhorn Found., Law Sch. Found., Houston Club, Lakeside Country Club. Admiralty, Federal civil litigation, Insurance. Home: 610 Wellesley Dr Houston TX 77024-5507 Office: Royston Rayzor Vickery & Williams LLP 1001 McKinney Ste 1100 Houston TX 77002-6418 E-mail: ed.vickery@roystonlaw.com.

VICKERY, HAROLD KIRBY, JR., lawyer; b. Worcester, Mass., July 4, 1941; arrived in Thailand, 1968; s. Harold Kirby and Mary Letitia (Miller) V. BA, Trinity Coll., Hartford, Conn., 1963; JD, U. Pa., 1966. Bar: Mass., 1967, U.S. Supreme Ct., 1970. Asst. dir. Houston Hall Student Union, U. Pa., Phila., 1966-67; judge advocate USAF, Minot AFB, N.D., 1967-68, judge advocate, fgn. claims commr. U-Tapao Airfield, Thailand, 1968-70; mil. judge Headquarters, 7/13th Air Force, Bangkok, Thailand, 1970-72; assoc. Price, Sanond & Assocs., Ltd., Bangkok, 1972-74; ptnr. Vickery & Worachai Ltd., Bangkok, 1975—; ret.lt. col. USAFR, 1989. Bd. dirs., v.p. Community Svcs. of Bangkok, 1988-93; chmn. com. Reps. Abroad Thailand, 1990-92; vice chmn. Asia-Pacific Coun. Am. C. of C., 1992-94; mem. bd. fellows Trinity Coll., 1994-2000. Decorated Bronze Star. Mem. ABA, Mass. Bar Assn., Worcester County Bar Assn., Am. C. of C. in Thailand (gov. 1981-84, 86-87, 89-92, 94-97, 1999-2002, pres. 1984, Disting. Svc. award 1990), Am. Philatelic Soc., Army and Navy Club, Capitol Hill Club, Royal Bangkok Sports Club. Republican. Roman Catholic. Commercial, contracts (including sales of goods; commercial financing), Corporate, general, Taxation, general. Home: 31A Tower Pk, 52/144 Soi 3 (Nana Nua), Sukhumvit Rd Bangkok 10110 Thailand Office: 16th Fl Diethelm Tower A 93/1 Wireless Rd Bangkok 10330 Thailand E-mail: vwlaw@loxinfo.co.th.

VICTOR, A. PAUL, lawyer; b. N.Y.C., Nov. 6, 1938; s. Samuel L. and Sophie (Ostrow) V.; m. Ellen Grabois, Aug. 30, 1959; children: Stephanie, Rebecca, Diana. BBA, U. Mich., 1960, JD with distinction, 1963. Bar: N.Y. 1964, D.C. 1964. Atty. antitrust div. U.S. Dept. Justice, Washington, 1963-66; assoc. Kirkland, Ellis & Rowe, Washington, 1966-68, Weil, Gotshal & Manges, N.Y.C., 1968-72, ptnr., 1972—. Adj. prof. law Fordham U., N.Y.C., 1983—; mem. adv. bd. Ctr. for Am. and Internat. Law, Dallas, 1984—; bd. dirs. Toray Industries (Am.) Inc., N.Y.C., 1987—. Contbr. numerous articles to law revs., other legal publs. regarding U.S. internat. antitrust and trade law. Mem. visitors com. U. Mich. Law Sch., 1980—; trustee Mass. Sch. of Law, Andover, 1989—, chmn., 1998—; sec. Japan Soc., N.Y.C., 1999-2000. Mem. ABA (vice-chair 1994-95, coun. mem. sect. of antitrust law 1983-86, 91-94, chmn. internat. antitrust com. 1982-85, 87-90), Internat. Bar Assn., N.Y. State Bar Assn., Order of Coif. Jewish. Avocations: golf, travel, swimming. Office: Weil Gotshal & Manges LLP 767 5th Ave Fl Concl New York NY 10153-0119

VICTOR, MICHAEL GARY, lawyer, physician; b. Detroit, Sept. 20, 1945; s. Simon H. and Helen (Litsky) V.; children: Elise Nicole, Sara Lisabeth. Bar: Ill. 1980, U.S. Dist. Ct. (no. dist.) Ill. 1980, U.S. Ct. Appeals (7th cir.) 1981; diplomate Am. Bd. Legal Medicine. Pres. Advocate Adv. Assocs., Chgo., 1982-95; asst. prof. medicine Northwestern U. Med. Sch., Chgo., 1982—; pvt. practice law Barrington, Ill., 1982—; lectr. U. Ill., Chgo., 1999—. Dir. emergency medicine Loretto Hosp., Chgo., 1980-85, chief. sect. of emergency medicine St. Josephs Hosp., Chgo., 1985-87; v.p. Med. Emergency Svcs. Assocs., Buffalo Grove, Ill., 1989; v.p. MESA Mgmt. Corp.; of counsel Bollinger, Ruberry & Garvey, Chgo. Author: Informed Consent, 1980; Brain Death, 1980; (with others) Due Process for Physicians, 1984, A Physicians Guide to the Illinios Living Will Act, The Choice is Ours!, 1989. Recipient Service awards Am. Coll. Emergency Medicine, 1973-83. Fellow Am. Coll. Legal Medicine (bd. govs. 1996-97, alt. del. to AMA House of Dels. 1996-97), Chgo. Acad. Legal Medicine; mem. Am. Coll. Emergency Physicians (pres. Ill. chpt. 1980, med.-legal-ins. council 1980-81, 83-84), ABA, Ill. State Bar Assn., Am. Soc. Law and Medicine, Chgo. Bar Assn. (med.-legal council 1981-83), AMA, Ill. State Med. Soc. (med.-legal council 1980-86, 88), Chgo. Med. Soc. Jewish. State civil litigation, Health. Home and Office: 153 Aberdour Ln Palatine IL 60067-8001 E-mail: MGV@northwestern.edu.

VICTOR, RICHARD STEVEN, lawyer; b. Detroit, Mich., Aug. 3, 1949; s. Simon H. and Helen (Litsky) V.; m. Denise L. Berman, Nov. 26, 1978; children: Daniel, Ronald, Sandra. Bar: Mich. 1975, U.S. Dist. Ct. (ea. dist.) Mich. 1975. Assoc. Law Offices of Albert Best, Detroit, 1975; ptnr. Best & Victor, Oak Park, Mich., 1976-80; sole practice Oak Park, 1981-85; ptnr. Law Offices of Victor, Robbins and Bassett and predecessor firms, Birmingham, Mich., 1986-93, Victor and Robbins and predecessor firms, Birmingham, 1993-98, Bloomfield Hills, Mich., 1998-2000; pvt. practice Richard S. Victor, PLLC, Bloomfield Hills, Mich., 2000—. Instr. in family law Oakland U., Rochester, Mich., 1976—; bd. dirs. Agy. for Jewish Edn., 1990; legal advisor family law Sta. Ask the Lawyer WXYT radio. Author: (column) Legally Speaking, Stepfamily Bull., 1984—; author, genera editor: Michigan Practitioners Series: Family Law and Practice, 1997; tech. advisor Whose Mother Am I? Aaron Spelling Prodns./ABC Movies; bd. editors Mich. Lawyers Weekly newspaper, 2000-03. Recipient Award of Meritorious Svc. to the Chldren of Am., Nat. Coun. of Juvenile and Family Ct. Judges, 1993, Child Advocate of Yr. award Chld Abuse and Neglect Coun., 1994, Disting. Svc. award Oakland County Bar Assn., 1994, Lifetime Achievement award State Bar Mich., 1999, Disting. Alumni Award Nat. Alumni Assn. of Mich. State U.-Detroit Coll. of Law, 2000. Fellow Mich. State Bar Found., Am. Acad. Matrimonial Lawyers (bd. mgrs. Mich. chpt. 1999—, sec. 1999, treas. 2000, v.p. 2001, pres. 2003); mem. ABA (guest lectr. sem. 1988, exec. com. on custody 1989—), Mich. Bar Assn. (treas. family law sect. 1987-88, sec. 1988-89, chmn. continuing legal edn. com. family law sect., 1986-90, corr. sec. 1988-89, chmn. elect 1989-90, chmn. family law sect. 1990-91, Appreciation award from family law sect. 1987-89, Lifetime Achievement award family law sect. 1999, co-founder SMILE), Oakland County Bar Assn. (chmn. lawyer's admission com. 1981, unauthorized practice of law 1982, oldtimer's night 1984-85, speakers bur. 1985), Family Law Coun. (chmn. legis. com.), Grandparent Rights Orgn. (founder, exec. dir. 1984—, newsletter editor). Jewish. Avocation: playing piano. Family and matrimonial, Personal injury (including property damage). Office: Law Offices of Richard S Victor PLLC 100 W Long Lake Rd Ste 250 Bloomfield Hills MI 48304-2721 E-mail: rsvlaw@aol.com.

VICTORSON, MICHAEL BRUCE, lawyer; b. Fairmont, W.Va., July 13, 1954; s. Morton Jerome and Deborah (Jacobson) V.; m. Janet Harris, Mar. 8, 1981; children: David Solomon, Sara Lorraine. BA, W.Va. U., 1976, JD, 1979. Bar: W.Va. 1979, U.S. Dist. Ct. (so. and no. dists.) W.Va. 1979, U.S. Dist. Ct. (ea. dist.) Ky. 1986, U.S. Ct. Appeals (4th cir.) 1980, U.S. Supreme Ct., 1992. Assoc. Love, Wise, Robinson and Woodroe, Charleston, W.Va., 1979-83, Robinson & McElwee LLP, Charleston, 1983-84, ptnr., 1985-99; mem. Jackson Kelly PLLC, Charleston, 1999—. Spkr. in field. Contbr. articles to profl. jours. Chmn. appeal bd. U.S. Selective Svc. System, So. Dist. W.Va., Charleston, 1983—; lawyers' chmn. United Way Kanawha Valley, Charleston, 1988-92, chmn. profl. divsn., 1992-93, admissions com., 1990-92; treas., bd. dirs. Med. Eye Bank W.Va., Charleston, 1989—, treas., 2000—; bd. dirs. Sunrise Collectors Club, 2002—; trustee B'nai Jacob Synagogue, 1992-94, v.p. 1997-2001, pres. 2001-; trustee Federated Jewish Charities of Charleston, Inc., 1998—, vis. com. W.Va. U. Coll. Law, 1996-2000. Mem. ABA, Internat. Assn. Jewish Lawyers and Jurists, Am. Law Firm Assn. (products liability steering com., bd. dirs. 1998-99), W.Va. Bar Assn., W.Va. State Bar Assn., Kanawha County Bar Assn., Def. Rsch. Inst., Def. Trial Counsel W.Va. (charter, bd. govs. 1992-98), Order of Coif, Phi Beta Kappa, Phi Delta Phi, Phi Kappa Phi, Pi Sigma Alpha. General civil litigation, Environmental. Office: Jackson Kelly PLLC PO Box 553 Charleston WV 25322-0553 E-mail: mvictorson@jacksonkelly.com.

VICTORY, JEFFREY PAUL, state supreme court justice; b. Shreveport, La., Jan. 29, 1946; s. Thomas Edward and Esther (Horton) V.; m. Nancy Clark Victory, Jan. 20, 1973; children: Paul Bradford, William Peter, Christopher Thomas, Mary Katherine. BA in History and Govt., Centenary Coll., 1967; JD, Tulane U., 1971. Bar: La. 1971. Ptnr. Tucker, Jeter, Jackson & Victory, Shreveport, 1971-82; dist. ct. judge 1st Jud. Dist. Ct., Shreveport, 1982-90; appellate judge 2d Circuit Ct. of Appeal, Shreveport, 1991-95; assoc. justice Supreme Ct. La., 1995—. Bd. dirs. CODAC Drug Abuse, Shreveport; mem. La. Sentencing Commn. La. NG, 1969-75. Mem. ABA, Shreveport Bar Assn., La. Bar Assn. Republican. Baptist. Avocations: tennis, motorcycles, classic cars. Office: Supreme Ct 301 Loyola Ave New Orleans LA 70112-1814

VIDERMAN, LINDA JEAN, paralegal, corporate executive; b. Follansbee, W.Va., Dec. 4, 1957; d. Charles Richard and Louise Edith (LeBoeuf) Roberts; m. David Gerald Viderman Jr., Mar. 15, 1974; children: Jessica Renae, April Mae, Melinda Dawn. AS, W.Va. No. C.C., 1983; cert. income tax prep., H&R Block, Steubenville, Ohio, 1986. Cert. surg. tech., fin. counselor; lic. ins. agt. Food prep. pers. Bonanza Steak House, Weirton, W.Va., 1981—83; ward clk., food svcs. Weirton Med. Ctr., 1982—84; sec., treas. Mountaineer Security Systems, Inc., Wheeling, W.Va., 1983—86; owner, operator The Button Booth, Colliers, W.Va., 1985—; paralegal, adminstr. Atty. Dominic J. Potts, Steubenville, Ohio, 1987—92; gen. ptnr., executrix Panhandle Homes, Wellsburg, W.Va., 1988—96; sec.-treas., executrix Panhandle Homes, Inc., 1996—; ins. agt. Milico, Mass. Indemnity, 1991—92, L&L Ins. Svcs., 1992—94; paralegal Atty. Fred Risovich II, Weirton, 1991—93; sec. The Hon. Fred Risovich II, Wheeling, 1993; paralegal atty. Christopher J. Paull, Wellsburg, W.Va., 1993—; owner Wellsburg Office Supply, 1993—94; owner, operator Viderman Child Care Svcs. Co., Wellsburg, 1997—; owner, dir. Viderman & Assocs., Wellsburg, 1997—. Notary pub., 1991—. Contbr. articles to profl. jours.; author numerous poems. Chmn. safety com. Colliers (W.Va.) Primary PTA, 1985-87; founding mem. Brooke County Homeschoolers/Panhandle Homeschoolers Assn., 1999; editor Panhandle Homeschoolers Newsletter, 2000; mem., sec. LaLeche League, Steubenville, Ohio, 1978-80; vol. counselor W.Va. U. Counseling Svc., 1990—; IRS vol. Vol. Income Tax Assistance Program, 1991—. Mem. W.Va. Manufactured Housing Assn. (bd. dirs. 2001-), W.Va. Writers Assn., Legal Assts. of W.Va., Inc., Am. Affiliate of Nat. Assn. Legal Assts., W.Va. Trial Lawyers Assn., Wellsburg Art Assn., Brooke County Genealogical Soc., Phi Theta Kappa. Jehovah'S Witness. Avocations: christian ministry, home computing, camping, genealogy, home schooling. Home: RR2 Box 28 Wellsburg WV 26070-9500 Office: Panhandle Homes Inc RR 2 Box 27A Wellsburg WV 26070-9500 E-mail: lviderman@aol.com.

VIE, GEORGE WILLIAM, III, lawyer; b. Tampa, Fla., Mar. 21, 1961; s. George William Jr. and Cheri Ann (Bass) V. BS magna cum laude, U. Houston, Clear Lake, Tex., 1985; JD, U. Tex., 1988. Bar: Tex. 1989, Hawaii 2002, U.S. Dist. Ct. (so. dist.) Tex. 1990, U.S. Dist. Ct. Hawaii 2002, U.S. Ct. Appeals (5th cir.) 1990, U.S. Mil. Ct. Appeals 1995, U.S. Supreme Ct. 1995, U.S. Ct. Appeals (fed. cir.) 2002; bd. cert. civil appellate law Tex. Bd. Legal Specialization. Legal asst. Bankston, Wright & Greenhill, Austin, Tex., 1985-89, atty., 1989-90; ptnr. Mills Shirley, Galveston, Tex., 1990—. Spkr. in field. Contbr. articles to legal publs. Keeton fellow, Tex. Law Sch. Found. Fellow Tex. Bar Found.; mem. FBA, State Bar Tex., State Bar Hawaii, Phi Kappa Phi, Sigma Phi Epsilon. Appellate, Civil rights, Constitutional. Office: Mills Shirley 2228 Mechanic St Ste 400 Galveston TX 77550-1591 E-mail: gvie@millsshirley.com.

VIENER, JOHN D. lawyer; b. Richmond, Va., Oct. 18, 1939; s. Reuben and Thelma (Kurtz) V.; m. Karin Erika Bauer, Apr. 7, 1969; children: John D. Jr., Katherine Bauer Viener Riordan. BA, Yale U., 1961; JD, Harvard U., 1964. Bar: N.Y. State 1965, U.S. Supreme Ct. 1970, U.S. Dist. Ct. (so. dist.) N.Y. 1974, U.S. Tax Ct. 1975. Assoc. Satterlee, Warfield & Stephens, N.Y.C., 1964—69; sole practice N.Y.C., 1969—76; sr. ptnr. Christy & Viener, N.Y.C., 1976—98, Salans, Hertzfeld, Heilbronn, Christy & Viener, N.Y.C., 1999—2000; prin., dir. BFD Capital Beteiligungs GmbH, 2001—. Founder, bd. dirs., gen. counsel Foxfire Fund, Inc., 1968—88; gen. counsel, bd. dirs. Landmark Communities, 1970—99, Am. Continental Properties Group, 1978—, NF&M Internat., Inc., 1976—2003, Singer Fund, Inc., 1979—, Immunotherapy, Inc., 1997—99, Tupper Broadcasting Group Cos., 1996—, Viener Found., 1991—; gen. counsel Nat. Cancer Found. Cancer Care, 1982—85, Troster, Singer & Co., 1970—77; bd. dirs. Gen. Financiere Immob. et Commer. S.A., 1985—89; spl. counsel fin. instns., investment banking and securities concerns; real estate and tax advisor. Bd. dirs. York Theatre Co., 1999-2001, The N.Y. Pops, 1999-2002. Mem. Meeker Brook Sporting Assn., Fairfield County Hounds, Manursing Island Club, Washington Club, Palm Beach Polo. Property, real (including real estate development, water), Securities, Corporate taxation. Home: 650 Park Avenue New York NY 10021 Office: 620 5th Ave New York NY 10020-2402

VIETH, GIFFORD DUANE, lawyer; b. Omaha, Sept. 20, 1923; s. Walter E. and Irene E. (Horn) V.; m. Jane G. Richardson, Feb. 16, 1952; children: Peter D., Robert R., Jane G. BA, U. Iowa, 1947, JD, 1949. Bar: Iowa 1949, D.C. 1949, U.S. Dist. Ct. Iowa 1953, U.S. Dist. Ct. Md. 1955, U.S. Ct. Claims 1958, U.S. Ct. Appeals (3d cir.) 1960, U.S. Dist. Ct. (ea. dist.) Wis. 1965, U.S. Supreme Ct. 1966, U.S. Ct. Appeals (2d cir.) 1970, U.S. Ct. Appeals (7th cir.) 1971. Ptnr. Arnold & Porter, Washington, 1949—. Mem. D.C. Commn. on Budget and Financial Priorities, 1989-90. Trustee Iowa Law Sch. Found., Iowa City, 1971-88, Fed. City Council, Washington, 1972—. With USAAF, 1942-45, ETO. Mem. ABA, D.C. Bar Assn., Iowa State Bar Assn., Columbia Country Club, Burning Tree Club, Met. Club. Lutheran. Avocation: golf. General practice. Home: 4407 Chalfont Pl Bethesda MD 20816-1812 Office: Arnold & Porter 555 12th St NW Ste 1202 Washington DC 20004-1200

VIETOR, HAROLD DUANE, federal judge; b. Parkersburg, Iowa, Dec. 29, 1931; s. Harold Howard and Alma Johanna (Kreimeyer) V.; m. Dalia Artemisa Zamarripa Cadena, Mar. 24, 1973; children: Christine Elizabeth, John Richard, Greta Maria. BA, U. Iowa, 1955, JD, 1958. Bar: Iowa 1958. Law clk. U.S. Ct. Appeals 8th Circuit, 1958-59; ptnr. Bleakley Law Offices, Cedar Rapids, Iowa, 1959-65; judge Iowa Dist. Ct., Cedar Rapids, 1965-79, chief judge, 1970-79; U.S. dist. judge U.S. Dist. Ct. for So. Dist. Iowa, Des Moines, 1979-96, chief judge, 1985-92, sr. U.S. dist. judge, 1997—. Lectr. at law schs., legal seminars U.S. and Japan. Contbr. articles to profl. jours. in U.S. and Japan. Served with USN, 1952-54. Mem. Iowa Bar Assn. (pres. jr. sect. 1966-67), Iowa Judges Assn. (pres. 1975-76), 8th Cir. Dist. Judges Assn. (pres. 1986-88). Office: US Dist Ct 221 US Courthouse 123 E Walnut St Des Moines IA 50309-2035

VIG, VERNON EDWARD, lawyer; b. St. Cloud, Minn., June 19, 1937; s. Edward Enoch and Salley Johanna (Johnson) V.; m. Susan Jane Rosenow, June 10, 1961; 1 child, Elizabeth Karen. BA, Carleton Coll., 1959; LLB, NYU, 1962, LLM, 1963; postdoctoral studies, Univ. Paris, Fac. de Droit, 1964. Bar: N.Y. 1962; avocat, Paris, 1992. Assoc. Cleary, Gottlieb, Steen & Hamilton, Paris, 1964, Donovan, Leisure, Newton & Irvine, N.Y.C. and Paris, 1965-72, ptnr., 1972-86, LeBoeuf, Lamb, Greene & MacRae, LLP, N.Y.C., Brussels, 1986—2001, of counsel, 2002—. Editor: NYU Law Rev. Sr. warden Grace Ch., Bklyn., 1986-2001. George F. Baker scholar, Fulbright scholar, 1963-64, Ford Found. scholar, 1963-64. Mem. ABA (internat. and antitrust sects.), N.Y. State Bar Assn. (chmn. antitrust sect. 1987-88), Assn. of Bar of City of N.Y., Internat. Bar Assn., Union Internat. des Avocats, Heights Casino (bklyn.), Merriewold Club (Forestburgh, N.Y., bd. dirs. 1985-91), Phi Beta Kappa. Episcopalian. Antitrust, Corporate, general, Private international. Office: LeBoeuf Lamb Greene & MacRae LLP 125 W 55th St New York NY 10019-5369 E-mail: vvig@llgm.com.

VIGDOR, JUSTIN LEONARD, lawyer; b. N.Y.C., July 13, 1929; s. Irving Barton and Ida (Devins) V.; m. Louise Martin, Mar. 8, 1952; children: Robert, Jill Vigdor-Feldman, Lisa Vigdor-Peck, Wendy Vigdor-Hess. LLB magna cum laude, St. John's U., 1951; LLM, N.Y.U., 1952. Bar: N.Y. 1951, U.S. Supreme Ct 1951, Fla. 1975. Counsel Boylan, Brown, Code, Vigdor & Wilson LLP, Rochester, NY, 1958—. Bd. dirs.IEC Electronics Corp.; former mem. faculty Nazareth Coll.; mem. N.Y. Uniform Law Commn., Nat. Conf. Uniform Law Commrs. Contbr. articles to profl. jours. Bd. dirs. AAA Western/Central N.Y., Found. for Jewish Cmty., Ames Amzalak Meml. Trust; pres. AAA N.Y. State , Inc., Al Sigl Ptnrs. Foundn., also past pres.; chmn. N.Y. State IOLA Fund. Served with JAGC, AUS, 1952-54. Recipient Community Svc. award, 1960, award for Svc. to Community and Legal Profession, 1983, Disting. Svc. award N.Y. State Assn. County Clks., 1985. Fellow Am. Bar Found., N.Y. Bar Found. (Nathaniel award for cmty. svc. and profl. accomplishment); mem. Fla. Bar Assn., N.Y. State Bar Assn. (past pres. Ho. of Dels.), Monroe County Bar Assn. (past pres.), Estate Planning Coun., Am. Arbitration Assn. (nat. panel 1962—), N.Y. State C. of C. (Disting. Svc. award 1964), Irondequoit Country Club. Democrat. Jewish. Corporate, general, Alternative dispute resolution, Securities. Home: 16 Tobey Woods Pittsford NY 14534-1824 Office: Boylan Brown Code Vigdor & Wilson LLP 2400 Chase Sq Rochester NY 14604 E-mail: jvigdor@boylanbrown.com., jvigdor@aol.com.

VIGIL, DANIEL AGUSTIN, academic administrator; b. Denver, Feb. 13, 1947; s. Agustin and Rachel (Naranjo) V.; m. Claudia Cartier. BA in History, U. Colo., Denver, 1978, JD, 1982. Bar: Colo. 1982, U.S. Dist. Ct. Colo. 1983. Project mgr. Mathematics Policy Rsch., Denver, 1978; law clk. Denver Dist. Ct., 1982-83; ptnr. Vigil and Bley, Denver, 1983-85; asst. dean sch. law U. Colo., Boulder, 1983-89, assoc. dean sch. law, 1989—. Apptd. by chief justice of Colo. Supreme Ct. to serve on Colo. Supreme Ct. Ad Hoc Com. on miniority participation in legal profession, 1988-94; adj. prof. U. Colo. Sch. Law; mem. Gov. Colo. Lottery Commn., 1990-97; mem. Colo. Supreme Ct. Hearing Bd., 1998-2002; mem. atty. regulatory adv. com. Colo. Supreme Ct., 2002—. Editor (newsletter) Class Action, 1987-88; co-editor (ethics com. column) Colo. Lawyer, 1995-97. Bd. dirs. Legal Aid Soc. Met. Denver, 1986-99, chmn. bd. dirs., 1998-99; past v.p. Colo.

Minority Scholarhip Consortium, pres. 1990-91; bd. trustees Colo. Atty.'s Fund for Client Protection, 2001—; bd. trustees Boulder Bar Found., 2000-03; mem. Task Force on Community Race Rels., Boulder, 1989-94; past mem. jud. nomination rev. com. U.S. Senator Tim Wirth; chmn. bd. dirs. Colo. Legal Svcs., 2000-. Mem. Colo. Bar Assn. (mem. legal edn. and admissions com. 1989-94, chmn. 1989-91, bd. govs. 1991, 97—), Hispanic Nat. Bar Assn. (chmn. scholarship com. 1990-95), Colo Hispanic Bar Assn. (bd. dirs. 1985-89, pres. 1990), Denver Bar Assn. (joint com. on minorities in the legal profession 1993-95), Boulder County Bar Assn. (ex-officio mem., trustee), Inns of Ct. (Penfield Tate chpt.), Phi Delta Phi (faculty sponsor). Roman Catholic. Avocations: skiing, cosmology. Home: 2550 Winding River Dr 0-4 Broomfield CO 80020 Office: U Colo Sch Law PO Box 401 Boulder CO 80303 E-mail: daniel.vigil@colorado.edu.

VIGIL, DAVID CHARLES, lawyer; b. Bklyn., Jan. 29, 1944; s. Charles S. and Kathleen A. (Liebert) V. BA, U. Colo., 1966; JD, U. N.Mex., 1969. Bar: Colo. 1969, U.S. Dist. Ct. Colo. 1969, U.S. Ct. Appeals (10th cir.) 1969, U.S. Supreme Ct. 1974. Pvt. practice, Denver, 1969-80, 96—; ptnr. Vigil & Vigil, Denver, 1980-96; broker Perry & Butler Realty, Denver, 1996-97, Keller Williams Realty, Denver, 1997—. Bd. dirs. Archdiocesan Housing Commn. Inc., 1998—2003, Housing for All, 1999—2003. Grantee Nat. Inst. for Trial Advocacy, 1983. Mem.: NITA Advs. Assn., Cath. Lawyers Guild, Colo. Hispanic Bar Assn. (bd. dirs. 1986—89, treas. 1988), Assn. Trial Lawyers Colo., Am. Arbitration Assn. (comml. arbitrator 1993—95), Denver Bar Assn. (mem. jud. selection and benefits com. 1975—90, chmn. 1988—90), Colo. Bar Assn. (mem. ethics com. 1973—79, legal fee arbitration com. 1980—92), ATLA, ABA, Elks. Federal civil litigation, State civil litigation, Personal injury (including property damage). E-mail: davidcvigil@msn.com.

VIGNERI, JOSEPH WILLIAM, lawyer; b. Decatur, Ill., July 28, 1956; s. Joseph Paul and Thelma Lucille (Pettus) V.; m. Martha Suzanne Smith, May 19, 1984; children: Craig Ashley, Emily Carmela. BA in Polit. Sci., Millikin U., 1980; JD cum laude, St. Louis U., 1983. Bar: Ill. 1983, U.S. Dist. Ct. (ctrl. dist.) Ill. 1983, U.S. Supreme Ct. 1990. Assoc. Rosenberg, Rosenberg, Bickes, Johnson & Richardson, Decatur, 1983-86; ptnr. Brilley & Vigneri, Decatur, 1986-88; pvt. practice, Decatur, 1988-92; ptnr. Vigneri & Robinson, Decatur, Ill., 1993-95; pvt. practice Decatur, 1995—; asst. pub. defender Macon County, Ill., 1999—. Past mem. job. svc. employer com. Ill. Dept. Employment Security. Past mem. profl. adv. com. Vis. Nurses Assn.; past bd. dirs., treas. Macon County Mental Health Assn. Mem. ABA (sect. real property, probate and trust law, com. spl. needs and tech. com., vice chmn. gen. practice com. 1991-92, family law subcom., editor newsletter), Ill. Bar Assn. (sec. individual rights sect. 1986, mem. bus. advice and fin. planning sect. coun. 1995-97), Decatur Bar Assn. (continuing legal edn. com. 1994-95, tech. com. 1996-97). Republican. Roman Catholic. Avocations: reading, travel, computers. Criminal. Home: 65 Ridge Lane Dr Decatur IL 62521-5456 Office: 136 W Washington St Decatur IL 62522-3102 also: 212 W Vine St Taylorville IL 62568-1957 E-mail: jvigneri@earthlink.net.

VIGORITO, PHILIP MICHAEL, lawyer; b. Niles, Ohio, June 25, 1957; s. Philip Anthony and Annette Lucille (Pezzano) V.; m. Sharon Kay Patrick, July 14, 1995; children: Michael, Philip, Nicholas. BS in Applied Sci., Youngstown (Ohio) State U., 1984; JD cum laude, U. Akron, Ohio, 1989. Bar: Ohio 1989, U.S. Dist. Ct. (no. dist.) Ohio 1989.. Assoc. Baker, Meekison & Dublikar, Canton, Ohio, 1987-92, Law Offices of Marty White, Warren, Ohio, 1992-94; pvt. practice Warren, 1994—. Mem. Ohio State Bar Assn., Trumbull County Bar Assn. Roman Catholic. Avocations: hunting, fishing, camping, exercise. Commercial, consumer (including collections, credit), Criminal, Personal injury (including property damage). Office: PO Box 1150 Warren OH 44482-1150

VIKIÖ, JARI TAPANI, lawyer; b. Oulu, Finland, July 2, 1968; Degree in Common Law, U. Surrey, Eng., 1991; LLM, U. Turku, Finland, 1994. Bar: Finnish Assn. Lawyers 1998. Lawyer Attys. at Law Borenius & Kemppinen, Helsinki, Finland, 1994—2000, atty., 1998—, ptnr., 2001—. Vis. lawyer Clifford Chance, London, 1997. Antidumping and EU, 1995; contbr. articles to profl. jours. Avocation: sports. Mergers and acquisitions, Finance, Corporate, general. Office: Attys at Law Borenius & Kemppinen Yrjönkatu 13A 00120 Helsinki Finland

VILCHEZ, VICTORIA ANNE, lawyer; b. Tampa, Fla., Aug. 10, 1955; d. Angel and Mary Ida (Guarisco) V.; m. Louis J. Deutsch; children: Matthew Stephen Williams, Michael Paul Williams, Heather Margaret Williams. BA, Fla. State U., 1977; JD, Mercer U., 1980. Bar: Fla. 1980. Trial atty. Office Pub. Defender, Miami, Fla., 1980-83; pvt. practice, 1983—. Rep. Nat. Conf. on Women and Law, Atlanta, 1978; traffic magistrate Palm Beach County Ct., 1991-95. Vol. Cath. Home for Children, Miami, 1983-84; mem. Coun. Cath. Women; class 1994 Leadership Palm Beach County. Recipient cert. of achievement 8th Nat. Conf. Juvenile Justice, 1981, Livingstone Hall award Juvenile Justice ABA, 1998; grantee Mercer U., 1977. Mem. Fla. Bar, Fla. Assn. Women Lawyers (sec., newsletter editor Palm Beach County chpt. 1985-86, mentor chair 2003-03), Palm Beach County Bar Assn., Fla. State U. Alumni Assn., Palm Beach County Hispanic Bar Assn. (pres.-elect 1990-91, pres. 1991-92, bd. dirs. 1990—, treas. 1993-94, 94-97), Legal Aid Soc. Palm Beach (bd. dirs. 1992—, v.p. 1999-2001, pres. 2001-03), West Palm Beach Kiwanis Club, Leadership Palm Beach County (grad. 1994, bd. govs. 1999-2001). Roman Catholic. Criminal, Family and matrimonial, Juvenile. Office: 1803 S Australian Ave Ste F West Palm Beach FL 33409-6454

VILLA, JOHN KAZAR, lawyer; b. Ypsilanti, Mich., June 9, 1948; s. John Joseph and Susie (Hoogasian) V.; m. Ellen A. Edwards, June 3, 1990. AB, Duke U., 1970; JD, U. Mich., 1973. Bar: D.C. 1973. Trial atty. U.S. Dept. Justice, Washington, 1973-77; assoc. Williams & Connolly, Washington, 1977-81, ptnr., 1981—. Author: legal treatises. Federal civil litigation, Professional liability. Office: Williams & Connolly 725 12th St NW Washington DC 20005-5901

VILLAVASO, STEPHEN DONALD, lawyer, urban planner; b. New Orleans, July 12, 1949; s. Donald Philip and Jacklyn (Tully) V.; m. Regina Smith, Apr. 17, 1971; children: Christine Regina, Stephen Warner. BS in Econs., U. New Orleans, 1971, M in Urban and Regional Planning, 1976; JD, Loyola U., New Orleans, 1981. Bar: La. 1982; recognized ct. expert in land use, planning and zoning. Urban and regional planner Barnard & Thomas, New Orleans, 1976-78; dir. analysis and planning Office of Mayor, City of New Orleans, 1978-81; counsel for planning and devel. Office of City Atty., City of New Orleans, 1983-84; dir. planning and environ. affairs Tecon Realty, New Orleans, 1981-83; v.p. for planning and project mgmt. Morphy, Makofsky, Mumphrey & Masson, New Orleans, 1984-89; bus. devel. mgr. Waste Mgmt., Inc., New Orleans, 1989-96; pres. Villavaso & Assocs., LLC, New Orleans, 1996—, Brownfields Redevel. Profls. LLC, New Orleans, 2000—. Bd. dirs. Regional Loan Corp.; guest lectr., adj. prof. Coll. of Urban and Pub. Affairs, U. New Orleans, 1976—; spl. instr. grad. studies in urban planning So. U. New Orleans, 1987—. Bd. dirs. New Orleans Traffic and Transp. Bur., 1981-86, Riverfront Awareness, New Orleans, 1984-86; bd. dirs. Vols. Am. Greater New Orleans, 1987-96, vice chmn., 1990, chmn. bd., 1992-95. With USN, 1971-74. Named one of Outstanding Young Men of Am., 1980, 82. Mem. ABA, Am. Inst. of Cert. Planners, Am. Planning Assn. (pres. La. div. 1980-84, disting. svc. award 1985), Urban Land Inst., La. Bar Assn., U. New Orleans Alumni Assn. (bd. dirs. 1990—), Phi Kappa Phi, Delta Sigma Pi (pres. 1971), Omicron Delta Kappa. Democrat. Roman Catholic. Avocations: philately, camping, travel. E-mial. Environmental, Land use and zoning (including planning). Home: 6304 Beauregard Ave New Orleans LA 70124-4502 E-mail: villavaso.assoc.llc@worldnet.att.net.

VINAR, BENJAMIN, lawyer; b. Rock Island, Ill., Apr. 10, 1935; s. Isidore and Bessie (Sherman) Vinar; m. Rochelle Weinfeld, June 17, 1962; children: Jacqueline, Dov, Elana, Daniella. BA, U. Ill., 1957; LLB, NYU, 1960. Bar: N.Y. 1961, U.S. Dist. Ct. (so. dist.) N.Y. 1962, U.S. Ct. Appeals (2d cir.) 1964, U.S. Supreme Ct. 1966, U.S. Dist. Ct. (ea. dist.) N.Y. 1971. Assoc. Donovan, Leisure, Newton & Irvine, N.Y.C., 1961-71; pvt. practice N.Y.C., 1971-76, Garden City, N.Y. and N.Y.C., 1986—; ptnr. Siff & Newman, P.C., N.Y.C., 1976-86; assoc. Donovan, Leisure, Newton & Irvine, N.Y.C., 1961—71; pvt. practice N.Y.C., 1971—76, Garden City and N.Y.C., NY, 1986—; ptnr. Siff & Newman, P.C., N.Y.C., 1976—86. Contbr. articles to profl. jours. Mem. nat. law com. Anti-Defamation League, N.Y.C., 1975—2000; pres. Queens Jewish Cmty. Coun., N.Y.C., 1979—81, Young Israel of Queens Valley, N.Y.C., 1984—86; v.p. Nat. Coun. Young Israel, 1986—90, YM-YMHA of No. Queens, N.Y.C., 1989—91; bd. dirs. Met. Coun. on Jewish Poverty, N.Y.C., 1984—89. Mem.: ABA, NYU Law Rev. Alumni Assn. (pres. 1981—83), Nassau Bar Assn. (chair appellate practice com.), Phi Kappa Phi, Phi Beta Kappa, Order of Coif. Democrat. Appellate, State civil litigation, Insurance. E-mail: bvinar@compuserve.com.

VINCE, CLINTON ANDREW, lawyer; b. Bklyn., May 31, 1949; s. Tibor Andrew and Priscilla (Ward) V.; divorced; children: Matthew McHale, Jennifer Anne. AB, Trinity Coll., 1971; JD, Georgetown U., 1974. Bar: N.Y. 1975, U.S. Dist. Ct. (so. and ea. dists.) N.Y. 1975, U.S. Ct. Appeals (2nd cir.) 1975, D.C. 1976, U.S. Dist. Ct. D.C. 1976, U.S. Ct. Appeals (D.C. and 8th cirs.) 1976, U.S. Supreme Ct. 1979, U.S. Ct. Appeals (4th and 11th cirs.) 1984, U.S. Ct. Appeals (5th cir.) 1985, U.S. Ct. Appeals (10th cir.) 1988. Ptnr. Verner, Liipfert, Bernhard, McPherson & Hand, Washington, 1984—2001; ptnr., dir. energy group Sullivan & Worcester, LLP, 2001—. Chief energy cons. City of New Orleans, 1983—; gen. counsel Southeastern Power Resources Com., Tucker, Ga., 1986—. Contbr. articles to profl. jours. Bd. dirs. Fed. City Coun., bd. trustees Keystone Energy; treas. bd. dirs. The Writers Ctr., One Voice. Mem. ABA, ATLA, Fed. Energy Bar Assn. (chmn. bd. dirs., chmn. Fed. Energy Law Jour. Found.), DC Bar Assn., Econ. Club Washington, Cosmos Club. Avocations: sailing, skiing, tennis, literature, writing. Federal civil litigation, FERC practice, Private international. Office: Sullivan & Worcester LLP 1666 K St NW Ste 700 Washington DC 20006 E-mail: cvince@sandw.com.

VINCENT, JOHN K. prosecutor; U.S. atty. ea. dist., Calif., 2002; dir. criminal div. U.S. Atty. Office Ea. Dist., Calif., 2003—. Office Fax: 916-554-2900.*

VINCENTI, MICHAEL BAXTER, lawyer; b. Balt., Dec. 28, 1950; s. Rudolph and Betty (Jones) V.; m. Patricia Lynn Bishopp, Apr. 14, 1984; children: Sarah, Elizabeth. BA, Johns Hopkins U., 1972; JD, NYU Sch. Law, 1975. Bar: Ill. 1975, Ky. 1979; cert. comml. investor, Ky. Assoc. Sonnenschein, Nath & Rosenthal, Chgo., 1975-79; from assoc. to ptnr. Wyatt, Tarrant & Combs, Louisville, 1979—. Guest instr. Jefferson Cmty. Coll., Louisville, 1988-98. Sec., gen. counsel Louisville Sci. Ctr., 1993—; dir., counsel bd. trustees Chance Sch., Louisville, 1995-98. Mem. ABA, Internat. Coun. Shopping Ctrs., Ill. Bar Assn., Am. Land Title Assn. (lender's counsel group), Am. Coll. Real Estate Lawyers, Am. Coll. Mortgage Attys., Ky. Bar Assn., Louisville Bar Assn., Rotary, Louisville Boat Club, Lex Mundi. Episcopalian. Avocations: squash, racquetball, tennis, travel, reading. Commercial, contracts (including sales of goods; commercial financing), Landlord-tenant, Property, real (including real estate development, water). Office: Wyatt Tarrant & Combs 500 W Jefferson St Ste 2700 Louisville KY 40202-2898 Fax: 502-589-0309. E-mail: mvincenti@wyattfirm.com.

VINCENTI, SHELDON ARNOLD, law educator, lawyer; b. Ogden, Utah, Sept. 4, 1938; s. Arnold Joseph and Mae (Burch) V.; children: Matthew Lewis, Amanda Jo. AB, Harvard U., 1960, JD, 1963. Bar: Utah 1963. Sole practice law, Ogden, 1966-67; ptnr. Lowe and Vincenti, Ogden, 1968-70; legis. asst. to U.S. Rep. Gunn McKay, Washington, 1971-72, adminstrv. asst., 1973; prof., assoc. dean U. of Idaho Coll. of Law, Moscow, Idaho, 1973-83, dean, prof. law, 1983-95, prof. law, 1995—. Home: 2480 W Twin Rd Moscow ID 83843-9114 Office: U Idaho Coll Law 6th & Rayburn St Moscow ID 83843

VINEBERG, ROBERT SPENCER, lawyer; b. Montreal, Que., Can., June 23, 1943; s. Philip Fishel Vineberg and Miriam Sylvia Schachter; m. Rhoda Rosenoff Vineberg, Dec. 19, 1968; children: Justin, Deborah. BA, McGill U., Montreal, 1964, BCL, 1967. Bar: Que. 1968. Ptnr. Davies, Ward, Phillips & Vineberg, Montreal, 1968—. Bd. dirs. Am. Biltrite Ltd.; bd. dir. AOL Can., Inc., Coinmatic Can. Ltd., Reitmans Can. Ltd., Can. Jewish News. Pres. Jewish Cmty. Found. of Montreal, Montreal, Canada; v.p. Jewish Cmty. Found. Montreal, pres.; mem. McGill Fund Coun., Montreal. Mem.: ABA, Que. Bar Assn., Internat. Bar Assn., Can. Bar Assn., Montefiore Club, Univ. Club Montreal, Mt. Royal Club. Mergers and acquisitions, Property, real (including real estate development, water). Office: Davies Ward Phillips and Vineberg 1501 McGill College 26th Fl Montreal PQ Canada H3A 3N9 Office Fax: 514-841-6499. Business E-Mail: rvineberg@dwpv.com.

VINEGRAD, ALAN, prosecutor; Graduate Magna Cum Laude, U. Pa, 1980; JD, NYU, 1984. Staff acct. Price Waterhouse & Co.; clerk Honorable Leonard B. Sand, US Dist. Ct. for the Southern Dist., NY; private practice Meister Leventhal & Slade, 1985—90; chief of general crimes US Atty. Office, Brooklyn, NY, 1990—94, chief of civil rights, 1994—97, chief of the Criminal Div., 1999—; interim US Atty. US Atty. Office, Eastern Dist., New York, 2001. Adj. prof. New York Law Sch., 1996—; guest lectr. Brooklyn Law Sch., Cardozo Sch. Law, Fordham Law Sch., Hofstra Law Sch., New York U. Law Sch., Yale Law Sch., Dept. Justice's Office of Legal Edu. Recipient Atty. Gen. award for Distinguished Service, Stimson Medal for Outstanding Prosecutor, US Atty. Office for Eastern Dist. of NY. Office: US Attorney US Courthouse 147 Pierrepont St Brooklyn NY 11201 Fax: 718-254-6479.*

VINENT-CANTORAL, AIDA R. mediator; b. Havana, Cuba, Nov. 8, 1948; arrived in U.S., 1959; d. Roberto M. Vinent and Carmen; m. Ennio Cantoral, Dec. 26, 1979 (div. 1981); 1 child, Alfredo Cantoral. BA, Alverno Coll., 1969; MA, Marquette U., 1971, cert. dispute resolution, 1998; cert. negotiating labor agreements, Harvard U., 2000, U. Mich., 2002, Northwestern U. Family health asst. Milwaukee County Dept. Human Svcs. & Hosp., 1975—; human svcs. case coord. Milwaukee County Dept. Human Svcs. and Hosp., 1998—; mediator pvt. practice Milw., 1979—; mediator Milwaukee County Family Ct., 1998—, USPS, 1998—, Bus. to Bus., 1998—, CHIPS, 1997, Wis. Spl. Edn. Mediation Sys., 2001—; case mgr. Milw. Co. Disability Svs., 1996—. Cons. in field. Active ACR, 1998—, Wis. Assn. Homicide Investigators, 2000—. Named Human Svcs. Worker of Yr., Wis. Foster Parents, 1980. Republican. Address: PO Box 462 Greendale WI 53129-0462 E-mail: Avinent@aol.com.

VINES, JAMES, lawyer; b. Dec. 1959; BS, JD, Washington & Lee U. Law clk. to Judge Robert R. Merhige, U.S. Dist. Ct.; law clk. to Chief Justice William H. Rehnquist, U.S. Supreme Ct., 1989—90; assoc. King & Spalding, Atlanta, 1990—93; exec. dir., gen. counsel for environ. affairs Bridgestone/Firestone, Nashville, 1993—2000; ptnr. Baker, Donelson, Bearman & Caldwell, Nashville, 2000—02; U.S. atty. Mid. Dist. Tenn., 2002—. Office: 110 Ninth Ave S Ste A961 Nashville TN 37203*

VINSON, WILLIAM THEODORE, lawyer, diversified corporation executive; BS, USAF Acad., 1965; JD, UCLA, 1969. Bar: Calif. 1970. Judge advocate USAF, 1970-74; trial counsel Phillips Petroleum, San Mateo, Calif., 1974-75; atty. Lockheed Corp., Westlake Village, Calif., 1975-90, v.p. & sec., 1990-92, v.p., gen. couns., 92-95; v.p., chief counsel Lockheed Martin Corp., Westlake Village, 1995-98; cons. Lockheed Corp., Westlake Village, 1998; dir. Siemens Govt. Svcs., Inc., 2001—. Bd. dirs. Westminster Free Clinic, 2001—. Corporate, general, Government contracts and claims, Private international. Office: 5560 E Napoleon Ave Oak Park CA 91377-4746

VIOLANTE, JOSEPH ANTHONY, lawyer; b. Jersey City, June 15, 1950; s. Carmine Joseph and Rosa (Cardillo) V.; m. Linda Lee Munn, July 5, 1972; children: Joseph Anthony II, Christy Anne, Gina Lee. Student, St. Peter's Coll., Jersey City, 1972-74; BA, U. N.Mex., 1975; JD, U. La Verne (Calif.), 1980. Bar: Calif. 1981, D.C. 1990, U.S. Dist. Ct. (cen. dist.) Calif. 1982, (6th dist.) Ohio 1992, U.S. Ct. Appeals (fed. cir.) 1990, U.S. Ct. Appeals (D.C. cir.) 1991, U.S. Ct. Vets. Appeals 1990. Sole practice, Thousand Oaks, Calif., 1981-85; atty., cons. Bd. Vet. Appeals, Washington, 1985-90; staff counsel DAV, Washington, 1990-92, legis. counsel, 1992-96, dep. nat. legis. dir., 1996-97, nat. legis. dir., 1997—. Mem. adv. com. Bowie Cable TV, 1989-91, bd. dirs., 1992-94. Co-host cable TV show Vets. Forum, 1991-94. Asst. coach Am. Youth Soccer Orgn., Thousand Oaks, 1981-84, Little League, Thousand Oaks, 1981-84; del. John Glenn Calif. Dem. Presdl. Primary, Thousand Oaks, 1984; active campaign Combined Fed., Washington, 1985; mem. presdl. del. Prisoners of War/Missing in Action, Southeast Asia, 1996. With USMC, 1969-72. Mem.: FBA (vets. com. 1991—92, at-large bd. mem., contbg. writer Tommy), KC, ABA (vice chmn. vets. benefit com. 1991—98), DAV (life; comdr. 1990—91), Coun. of 2,000, Nat. Italian-Am. Found. (nat. mentors program), Italian-Am. Bar Assn., DC Bar Assn., Fed. Cir. Bar Assn. (chmn. vets appeal com. 1992—96, chmn. legis. com. 1996—2001, bd. govs. 2001—), Calif. Bar Assn., Nat. Found. Women Legislators (bd. dirs. 2001—), VFW (life; comdr. 1984—85), 2d Bn. 4th Marine Assn., Marine Corps League, Italian-Am. War Vets., Am. Legion, 3d Marine Divsn. Assn. (life). Democrat. Roman Catholic. Avocations: collecting coins, soccer, softball, reading. Administrative and regulatory, Government contracts and claims. Home: 2515 Ann Arbor Ln Bowie MD 20716-1562 Office: DAV Nat Svc & Legis Hdqrs 807 Maine Ave SW Washington DC 20024-2410

VIRELLI, LOUIS JAMES, JR., lawyer; b. Phila., Nov. 4, 1948; s. Louis James and Elsie Antoinette (Colombo) V.; m. Barbara Ann Rotella, Aug. 22, 1970; children: Louis J. III, Christopher F. BE in Mech. Engring., Villanova U., 1970; JD, U. Tenn., 1972. Bar: Pa. 1973, U.S. Patent and Trademark Office, 1973, U.S. Ct. Customs and Patent Appeals 1974, U.S. Dist. Ct. (we. dist.) Pa. 1976, U.S. Dist. Ct. (ea. dist.) Pa. 1977, U.S. Ct. Appeals (9th cir.) 1980, U.S. Ct. Appeals (D.C. cir.) 1982, U.S. Supreme Ct. 1982. Patent atty. Sperry New Holland Co., New Holland, Pa., 1973-74; assoc. counsel Westinghouse Co., Pitts., 1974-76; assoc. Paul & Paul, Phila., 1976-80, ptnr., 1980-84; patent counsel Nat. Starch and Chem. Co., Bridgewater, N.J., 1984-88, asst. gen. counsel, intellectual property, 1988-92, gen. counsel, intellectual property, 1992-95; asst. gen. counsel Patents Unilever U.S., Inc., Edgewater, NJ, 1988—95; v.p. gen. patent counsel Unilever N.V., P.L.C., Edgewater, NJ, 1995—96, sr. v.p., gen. patent counsel, 1997—, sr. v.p., gen. counsel intellectual property, 2003—. Arbitrator U.S. Dist. Ct. (ea. dist.) Pa., Phila., 1982-84. Mem.: ABA, Assn. Corp. Patent Counsel (treas., v.p., pres.), Phila. Patent Law Assn., NJ Patent Law Assn., Intellectual Property Owners Assn. (bd. dirs.). Corporate, general, Patent, Trademark and copyright. Office: Unilever US Inc 45 River Rd Edgewater NJ 07020-1017 also: Unilever PLC Unilever House Blackfriars London England E-mail: louis.virelli@unilever.com.

VITAL, PATRICIA BEST, lawyer; b. Pitts., Mar. 26; d. Clarence D. and Billie Lorraine (Wilson) B.; m. Leo Vital, Mar. 30. BA magna cum laude, U. Tenn., Chattanooga, 1989; JD with honors, U. Tenn., 1992. Bar: Ga. 1994, Tenn. 1993, U.S. Dist. Ct. (ea. dist.) Tenn. 1993, U.S. Dist. Ct. (no. dist.) Ga. 1995, U.S. Ct. Appeals (6th cir.) 1993, U.S. Ct. Appeals (11th cir.) 1995, U.S. Supreme Ct. 1996. Legal asst. Gleason & Assoc. Law Firm, Rossville, Ga., 1981-82; med. staff coord. Hutcheson Med. Ctr., Ft. Oglethorpe, Ga., 1982-86; rsch. asst. U. Tenn. Law Coll., Knoxville, 1991-92; from law clk. to assoc. atty. Lusk, Carter & McGhehey, Chattanooga, 1990-93; pvt. practice Chattanooga, 1993—; mediator, arbitrator Vital Dispute Resolution Svcs., Chattanooga, 1996—. Law clk. Hamilton County Attys. Office, Chattanooga, summer 1990; devel. coun. co-chair class 1992 U. Tenn. Coll. Law, alumni network mentoring program, 1995—, deans cir., 1992—; pres. adult scholars program U. Tenn., Chattanooga, 1988-89, adult scholars program adv. coun., scholarship com., 1994—; presenter in field; adj. prof. pre-trial litigation, legal asst. studies program U. Tenn., fall, 1997; instr. Law Sch. Admission Test preparation course KAPLAN, Inc., 1999-2000; commn. continuing legal edn. and specialization Tenn. Supreme Ct., 1996-2001; panel mediator, arbitrator (Ea. and Mid. dists.) Tenn. Fed. Mediation Programs, U.S. Dept. Justice, Key Bridge Found., Am. with Disabilities, Chattanooga Better Bus. Bur., Coun. Better Bus. Burs. AutoLine Arbitration, Hamilton County Tenn. Divorce Mediation, Am. Health Lawyers ADR Svc.; mem. panel, chair arbitration panel NASD, U.S. Dept. Labor/AEIDR; mem. adv. bd. ProLex, LLC, 2003—. Co-author: Tennessee Alternative Dispute Resolution Handbook, 1997; contbr. articles to profl. jours. Mentor Hamilton County Bd. Edn., 1995-96; cmty. resource person Ooltewah Middle and Chattanooga Phoenix Middle Schs., 1994-96; capt. attys. team presch. phon-a-thon Siskin Found., 1994-95; mem. Chattanooga Chamber Found. Leadership Chattanooga Class, 1997-98; nat. adv. bd. Ctr. for Enterprise Edn., Peabody Coll. Edn., Vanderbilt U., 1998-2000. Mem. ABA (ethics 2000 adv. coun. 1998, dispute resolution sect. Boston Conf. Planning Com. 1998-2000, co-chair dispute resolution sect. State and Local Bar Com. 1998-2000), AAUW, Fed. Bar Assn., Nat. Inst. Dispute Resolution, Nat. Assn. Mediators in Edn., Am. Health Lawyers Assn., Nat. Assn. Women Bus. Owners (local chpt. bd. dirs. 1994), Am. Soc. Law, Medicine and Ethics, Tenn. Bar Assn. (com. chair, sec. and spkr. ho. of dels. 1995—, com. chair law related edn. 1996-97, bd. dirs. law office tech. and mgmt. 1994-96, sec-treas., chair-elect, chair dispute resolution sect. 1995-98, Merit award 1995, mem. editl. bd. TBALink), Mediation Assn. Tenn. (chair continuing mediation edn., curriculum com. 1996-98), Tenn. Trial Lawyers Assn., Tenn. Assn. Med. Staff Svcs., Nat. and Tenn. Assn. Ptnrs. in Edn., Ga. State Bar Assn., Chattanooga Bar Assn. (bd. govs. 1996-97, chair bd. govs. task force on the future Tenn. judicial sys. 1995-96, centennial planning com. 1996-97, chair continuing legal edn. com. 1994-95, chair ethics rules rev. com. 1998-99, chair dispute resolution com. 1998—, First Beyond the Call of Duty award 1995), Chattanooga Trial Lawyers Assn. (dir., gov. bd. 1995-2000), Southeast Tenn. Lawyers Assn. Women (dir. at-large 1996-97), Better Bus. Bur., S.E. Tenn. Coun. on Children & Youth, Chattanooga Area C. of C., Phi Delta Phi. Avocations: whitewater rafting, mountain hiking, aerobics, reading. Alternative dispute resolution, General civil litigation, General practice. Office: Vital Law Offc & Dispute Resolution Svcs James Bldg Ste 801 735 Broad St Chattanooga TN 37402-1804 Fax: (423) 267-2376. E-mail: best-law@mindspring.com.

VITALE, LOUISE ANTOINETTE, lawyer; b. Cleve., Feb. 13, 1969; s. Louis and Margaret Vitale. BA, Cleve. State U., 1991, JD, 1995; LLM, George Washington U., 2001. Bar: Ohio. Assoc. Turoff & Turoff, Cleve., 1995—97; atty. Dept. of Navy, Washington, 1997—. Democrat.

VITKOWSKY, VINCENT JOSEPH, lawyer; b. Newark, Oct. 3, 1955; s. Boniface and Rosemary (Ofack) V.; m. Mary Gunzburg, May 16, 1981 (div. 1997); children: Vincent Jr., Victoria; m. Pandora Strasler, Sept. 18, 1999. BA, Northwestern U., 1977; JD, Cornell U., 1980. Bar: NY 1981. Assoc. Hart and Hume, N.Y.C., 1980-84, Kroll & Tract, N.Y.C., 1984-87; of counsel Nixon, Hargrave, Devans & Doyle, N.Y.C., 1988-89; ptnr. Buchalter, Nemer, Fields & Younger, N.Y.C., 1990-95, Edwards & Angell LLP, N.Y.C., 1996—. Mem. panel arbitration London Ct. Internat. Arbitration;

lectr. in field. Contbr. articles to profl. jours. Mem. ABA (com. chmn.), Am. Arbitration Assn. (inernat. panel arbitrators), Internat. Bar Assn. (com. officer), Internat. Law Assn., Assn. Bar City of N.Y., Cornell Club, Human Rights Watch, IBA Human Rights Inst. (officer, com. on interventions and trial observations), Lawyers Com. for Human Rights. Alternative dispute resolution, General civil litigation, Private international. Home: 422 E 72d St Apt 15E New York NY 10021 Office: Edwards & Angell LLP 750 Lexington Ave Fl 12 New York NY 10022-1253

VITOLA, JOHN RAYMOND, lawyer; b. N.Y.C., Dec. 10, 1957; s. Ralph M. and Lucille L. Vitola; m. Georgine Anne Hutton, June 2, 1984; children: Lindsay, Brandon, David, Jared, Elizabeth. AA, Broward C.C., Ft. Lauderdale, Fla., 1977; BA, U. Fla., 1979; JD, Nova Law Ctr., 1983. Bar: Fla. 83. Asst. state atty. State Atty.'s Office, Brooksville, Fla., 1983—85; assoc. Law Offices of James M. Brown, Brooksville, 1985—87; pvt. practice Law Offices of John R. Vitola, Brooksville, 1987—. Atty. Make A Wish Found., Brooksville, 1990. Coach, sponsor YMCA Baseball, Spring Hill, Fla., 1993—2000, FHYS Soccer, Spring Hill, 1993—, BUSA, Brooksville, 2000—01. Mem.: Fla. Bar Assn. (trial lawyers sect.), Hernando County Bar Assn. (pres. 1989), Fla. Assn. Criminal Def. Lawyers, Acad. Fla. Trial Lawyers. Republican. Mem. Assembly Of God. Personal injury (including property damage), Family and matrimonial, Criminal. Home: 7513 Oak Tree Ln Brooksville FL 34607 Office: Law Offices John R Vitola 218 S Broad St Brooksville FL 34601 Office Fax: 352-796-1097. E-mail: www.lojrv@yahoo.com.

VIVIANI, MONICA L. mediator, educator; b. Cleve., July 27, 1945; d. James Joseph and Isabelle Alberta Logan; m. James Leonard Viviani, June 24, 1972; children: Meghan, Bridget, James Logan. BA, St. John Coll., 1968; cert. in conflict resolution, Manchester Coll., 1993; cert. in divorce conflict mediation, Notre Dame Coll., 1997. Bar: Ohio 1997, Supreme Ct. Ohio. Tchr. Cleve. Cath. Diocese, Greater Cleve. area, 1968—96; presenter diversity workshop Nat. Coalition Bldg. Inst., Washington, 1995—; propr. Peaceful Response to Conflict, Chester Twp., Ohio, 1997—; presenter conflict skills Safe and Drug Free Schs., Ohio, 1999—, Ohio Dept. Edn., 2002—. Author: (book series) Peace Skills in Education Series, 2002. Vol. conciliator CALM, Cleve., 1992—95, trustee, 1993—96; sec. Joseph House, A Home for Refugees, Cleve., 1994—98, coord., 1997—2001, trustee, 1995—; trustee, v.p. bd. St. Francis Sch., Gates Mills, Ohio, 1983—89. Recipient Edn. award, CALM, 1995, Social Justice award, Cath. Diocese Cleve., 2001; grantee, Gund Found., Ohio, 1996, Safe and Drug Free Schs., Ohio, 1997—2002. Mem.: Assn. for Conflict Resolution. Roman Catholic. Office: Peaceful Response to Conflict 7931 Willowbrook Dr Chesterland OH 44026

VLADECK, JUDITH POMARLEN, lawyer; b. Norfolk, Va., Aug. 1, 1923; BA, Hunter Coll., 1945; JD, Columbia U., 1947. Bar: NY 1947, US Supreme Ct. 1962. Assoc. Conrad & Smith, N.Y.C., 1947-51; sole practice N.Y.C., 1951-57; mem. Vladeck, Elias, Vladeck & Engelhard P.C., N.Y.C., 1957—; sr. ptnr. Vladeck, Waldman, Elias & Englehard, P.C., N.Y.C. Bd. dir. Group Health Ins., Inc., Am. Arbitration Assn.; adj. prof. Fordham Law Sch.; mem. Civil Justice Reform Act Adv. Group of So. Dist. of NY; adv. coun. CPR Jud. Project. Mem. adv. bd. Inst. for Edn. and Rsch. on Women and Work, Cornell U.; bd. dirs. NY Civil Liberties Union, 1963-68; bd. dir., counsel Tamiment Inst., Inc.; bd. dirs. lawyers' coordinating com. AFL-CIO; bd. mem. Non-Traditional Employment for Women. Recipient Hunter Coll. Profl. Achievement award, 1992, Edith Spivack award, 1998, Women of Power and Influence award NY NOW, 1998, ORT Jurisprudence award, 1996; elected to Hunter Coll. Hall of Fame, 1988; non-traditional employment for women named building Judith P. Vladeck Ctr. for Women, 1989; Margaret Brent Award, ABA 2002; Columbia Law Sch. Assoc. Medal for Excellence, 2003; NEW 25th Anniv. Equity Leadership Award, 2003. Fellow Am. Bar Found., Coll. of Labor and Employment Lawyers; mem. ABA (co-chmn. labor law and equal employment coms., NY State Bar Assn. (labor law com.), Assn. of Bar of City of NY, NY County Lawyers Assn., Fed. Bar Assn., Women's Bar Assn., Am. Arbitration Assn. (panel of arbitrators), Columbia Law Sch. Alumni Assn. (bd. dir.), Harlem Inst. Fashion (counsel, bd. dir.). General civil litigation, Labor (including EEOC, Fair Labor Standards Act, labor-management relations, NLRB, OSHA). Home: 115 Central Park W New York NY 10023-4153 Office: Vladeck Waldman Elias & Engelhard 1501 Broadway Ste 800 New York NY 10036-5560 E-mail: jvladeck@vladeck.com.

VLEISIDES, GREGORY WILLIAM, lawyer; b. Kansas City, Mo., June 17, 1950; s. William Chris and Irene Helen (Karos) V. BA, U. Kans., 1972; JD, U. Mo., Kansas City, 1976. Bar: Mo. 1977, U.S. Dist. Ct. (Mo.) 1977, U.S. Ct. Appeals (8th cir.) 1977, U.S. Ct. Fed. Claims 1990. Law clk. presiding justice Circuit Ct. of Jackson County, Kansas City, 1976-78; assoc. Tierney & Ernst, Kansas City, 1978-86; of counsel Law Office of F. Lee Bailey, Boston, 1982-88; assoc. Turner & Boisseau, Kansas City, 1986-89; mng. ptnr. Vlesides, Donnelly & O'Leary, Kansas City, 1989—. Regional counsel Video Software Dealers Assn., Overland Park, Kans., 1986-89; v.p. legal affairs Nuvidia, LLC. Author: (with others) Challenges to Court Action in Child Abuse and Neglect Cases, 1976, Opening Statements by Julien, 1994, Stein on Closing Arguments, 1994. Mem. ABA, ATLA, Mo. Assn. Trial Lawyers, Kansas City Bar Assn. Republican. Greek Orthodox. Criminal, Personal injury (including property damage), Product liability. Home: 3008 W 84th Pl Leawood KS 66206-1309 Office: Vleisides Donnelly & O Leary LC 4006 Central PO Box 10084 Kansas City MO 64161-0084 E-mail: gvleisides@springmail.com.

VOGEL, CEDRIC WAKELEE, lawyer; b. Cin., June 4, 1946; s. Cedric and Patricia (Woodruff) V. BA, Yale U., 1968; JD, Harvard U., 1971. Bar: Ohio 1972, Fla. 1973, U.S. Tax Ct. 1972, U.S. Supreme Ct. 1975. Ptnr. Vogel, Heis, Wenstrup & Cameron, Cin., 1972-96; sole practice, 1997—. Bd. dirs. Pro Srs., 1994—. Chmn. mem.'s com. Cin. Art Mus., 1987-88; chmn. auction Cin. Hist. Soc., 1985; local pres. English Speaking Union, 1979-81, nat. bd. dirs., 1981; chmn. Keep Cin. Beautiful, Inc., 1994-96; active Bravo! Cin. Ballet, 1989; chmn. Act II Nutcracker Ball, 1987-88; bd. dirs. Merc Libr., 1991-98; bd. dirs. Cin. Preservation Assn., 1990-93, Cin. Opera Guild, 1997-99; vice chmn. Children's Heart Assn. Reds Rally, 1989; bd. dirs. Cin. Country Day Sch., 1983, pres. Alumni Coun. and Ann. Fund, 1983. Mem.: Fla. Bar Assn., Cin. Bar Assn., Yale Alumni Assn. (del. 1984—87), Harvard Law Sch. Assn. Cin. (pres. 1997—99, 2002—), Heimlich Inst. (trustee 1987—2001), Harvard Club of Cin. (bd. dirs. 1996—98, pres. 1999—2000), The Lawyers Club Cin. (pres. 1995), Cincinnatus, Cin. Yale Club (pres. 1980—81, 1996—97). Republican. Commercial, consumer (including collections, credit), General practice, Probate (including wills, trusts). Home: 2270 Madison Rd Cincinnati OH 45208-2659 Office: 817 Main St Ste 800 Cincinnati OH 45202-2183

VOGEL, DAVID SETH, lawyer; b. N.Y.C., July 11, 1955; s. Joshua Selig and Muriel Rita Vogel; m. Patrice Louise Jaxon; children: Claire, Jack. AB, Amherst Coll., 1973—77; JD magna cum laude, Boston U., 1979—82. Law clerk Hon. Frank M. Johnson, Jr., 11th Circuit Ct. of Appeals, Montgomery, Ala., 1982—83; assoc. Perkins Coie Law Firm, Seattle, 1983—84; dep. prosecutor King County Prosecutor's Office, Seattle, 1984—89; assoc. Levinson Friedman Law Firm, Seattle, 1989—92; prin. Law Offices of David S. Vogel, Seattle, 1992—. Editor: Boston U. Law Rev. Pres. Vashon-Maury Island Cmty. Coun., Vashon Island, Wash., 1986—93, bd. mem., 1985—2000, Vashon Household, Vashon Island, Wash., 1996—2002; chair Vashon Town Plan Com., Vashon Island, Wash., 1992—96. Recipient Cmty. Svc. award, Vashon-Maury Island Audubon Soc., 1994, Pilchuck Audubon Soc., 1997. Mem.: ABA, Wash. Assn. Criminal Defense Lawyers, Brain Injury Assn., Wash. State Trial Lawyers Assn., Assn. of Trial Lawyers of Am., Wash. State Bar Assn., Seattle-King County Bar Assn., WSTLA Eagles. Liberal. Jewish. Avocations: fishing, hiking, camping. Appellate, Personal injury (including property damage), Criminal. Office: Law Offices of David Vogel 2025 First Ave Penthouse Ste A Seattle WA 98121 Office Fax: 206-448-7950. Personal E-mail: dsvogel@earthlink.net.

VOGEL, HOWARD STANLEY, lawyer; b. N.Y.C., Jan. 21, 1934; s. Moe and Sylvia (Miller) V.; m. Judith Anne Gelb, June 30, 1962; 1 son, Michael S. BA, Bklyn. Coll., 1954; JD, Columbia U., 1957; LLM in Corp. Law, NYU, 1969. Bar: N.Y. 1957, U.S. Supreme Ct. 1964. Assoc. Whitman & Ransom, N.Y.C., 1961-66; with Texaco Inc., 1966-99, gen. atty., 1970-73, assoc. gen. counsel, 1973-81, gen. counsel Tex. Philanthropic Found. Inc., 1979-82; gen. counsel Jefferson Chem. Co. Texaco Chems. Can. Inc., 1973-82; assoc. gen. tax counsel, gen. mgr. adminstr. Texaco Inc., White Plains, N.Y., 1981-99; counsel Allegaert Berger & Vogel LLP, N.Y.C., 1999—. Gen. tax counsel Texaco Found. Inc., 1995-99; pres., dir. 169 E. 69th Corp., 1981— . Served to 1st lt. JAGC, U.S. Army, 1958-60. Mem. ABA, Aassn. Bar City N.Y., Fed. Bar Coun., Assn. Ex-Mems. of Squadron A., Princeton Club (N.Y.C.). Corporate, general, Securities, Corporate taxation. Home: 169 E 69th St Apt 9D New York NY 10021-5163 Office: 18th Fl 111 Broadway Fl 18 New York NY 10006-1901 E-mail: hvogel@abv.com.

VOGEL, JOHN WALTER, lawyer; b. Dansville, N.Y., Sept. 19, 1948; s. Walter Earl and Betty (Elston) V.; m. Pamela Hill; children: Michael John, Jennifer Alexandra. BA, SUNY, Albany, 1970; JD, Syracuse U., 1976. Bar: N.Y. 1976, U.S. Dist. Ct. (we. dist.) N.Y. 1979, U.S. Tax Ct. 1980, U.S. Supreme Ct., 1980, U.S. Dist. Ct. (no. dist.) N.Y. 1985, U.S. Ct. Appeals (2d cir.) 1985. Assoc. Edward J. Degnan Law Offices, Canisteo, NY, 1976-77; atty. N.Y. State Dept. Agrl. & Markets, Albany, 1977-78; sole practice law Dansville, 1978—. Legal counsel Dansville Econ. Devel. Corp., 1983—, Dansville Ctrl. Sch. Dist.; local counsel Danville Ctrl. Sch. Dist.; atty. Livingston County Habitat for Humanity, N.Y. State Festival of Balloons. Dir. Livingston County (N.Y.) Drug Abuse Prevention Coun., 1981-82. Served with U.S. Army, 1970—73. Mem. N.Y. State Bar Assn., Livingston County Bar Assn. (sec., treas. 1980-82, v.p. 1984-85, pres. 1985-86). Republican. Methodist. State civil litigation, General practice, Personal injury (including property damage). Home: 261 Main St Dansville NY 14437-1111 Office: 125 Main St Dansville NY 14437-1611

VOGEL, MART DANIEL, lawyer; b. Fargo, ND, Jan. 25, 1948; s. Mart R. and Louis F. (Fluetsch) V.; m. Belinda Wiman, May 23, 1996. Student, U. Calif., Berkeley; AB, Lawrence U., 1970; JD, U. Wis., 1974. Bar: N.D. 1974, Minn. 1981. Atty. Vogel, Weir, Hunke & McCormick Ltd., Fargo, ND. Recipient Fred Sievert award Defense Rsch. Inst., Chgo., 1993. General civil litigation, Insurance, Product liability. Office: Vogel Weir Hunke & McCormick Ltd 502 1st Ave N Fargo ND 58102-4804 E-mail: dvogel@vogellaw.com.

VOGEL, ROBERT, retired lawyer, educator; b. Coleharbor, N.D., Dec. 6, 1918; s. Frank A. and Louella (Larsen) V.; m. Elsa Mork, May 29, 1942; children: Mary Lou, Sarah May, Frank, Robert. BS, U. N.D., 1939; LL.B., Mpls. Coll. Law, 1942. Bar: N.D. 1943. Practiced in Garrison, 1943-54; state's atty., 1948-54; U.S. atty. Fargo, 1954-61; mem. Vogel, Bair & Brown, Mandan, N.D., 1961-73; justice N.D. Supreme Ct., 1973-78; prof. U. N.D. Law Sch., Grand Forks, 1978-95; ret., 1997. Democratic candidate for U.S. Ho. of Reps., 2d Dist. N.D., 1962; mem., sec. Nonpartisan League State Exec. Com., 1952; mem. N.D. Parole Bd., 1966-73. Home: 524 Harvard St Grand Forks ND 58203-2845 E-mail: rv5740@wiktel.com.

VOGELMAN, LAWRENCE ALLEN, law educator, lawyer; b. Bklyn., Feb. 24, 1949; s. Herman and Gertrude (Wohl) V.; m. Deborah Malka, Jan. 24, 1971 (div. Aug. 1980); m. Marcia Sikowitz, Mar. 3, 1985 (div. Nov. 1999). BA, Bklyn. Coll., 1970; JD, Bklyn. Law Sch., 1973. Bar: N.Y. 1974, U.S. Dist. Ct. (so. and ea. dists.) N.Y. 1975, U.S. Ct. Appeals (2d cir.) 1975, U.S. Ct. Appeals (3d cir.) 1983, U.S. Supreme Ct. 1983, N.H. 1994, U.S. Dist. Ct. N.H. 1994, U.S. Ct. Appeals (1st cir.) 2001. Trial atty. Legal Aid Soc., N.Y.C., 1973-77; assoc. appellate counsel Criminal Appeals Bur., N.Y.C., 1977-78; clin. prof. law Yeshiva U. Benjamin N. Cardozo Sch. Law, N.Y.C., 1979-93; dep. dir. N.H. Pub. Defender, Concord, NH, 1993-97; ptnr. Shuchman, Krause & Vogelman, 1997—. Adj. prof. law Franklin Pierce Law Ctr., 1994-98; faculty Inst. for Criminal Def. Advocacy, 1995—; program dir. Max Freund Litigation Ctr., 1984—; team leader Emory U. Trial Techniques Program, Atlanta, 1981-89, N.J. region, Nat. Inst. Trial Advocacy, 1997—; faculty N.E. region, Nat. Inst. Trial Advocacy, 1985—, Tom C. Clark Ctr. for Advocacy, Hofstra U. Sch. Law, 1985—, Legal Aid Socs. Trial Advocacy Program, 1986-89, Widener U. Law Sch. Intensive Trial Program, 1987-91, U. San Francisco Intensive Trial Advocacy Program, 1991—; mem. indigent's assigned counsel panel, appellate div. First Dept., N.Y.C., 1979-94; crminal justice act panel U.S. Dist. Ct. (so. and ea. dists.) N.Y., 1985-94, dist. N.H., 1997—; adminstrv. law judge N.Y.C. Environ. Control Bd., 1980-81. Author, editor: Cases and Materials on Clinical Legal Education, 1979; editor revisions to Eyewitness Identification. Pres. bd. trustees Woodward Park Sch., 1990—94; bd. dirs., legal coun. N.H. Civil Liberties Union. Fellow: Am. Bd. Criminal Lawyers; mem.: ATLA (exec. com. civil rights sect.), N.H. Trial Lawyers Assn., N.Y. State Defenders Assn., N.H. Bar Assn. (ethics com. 1995, dispute resolution com. 1999—, bd. law examiners 1999—, mem. adv.com. Fed. Ct. 2002—, fed. ct. adv. com. 2002—, sec. fed. practice sect. 2003—), N.H. Assn. Criminal Defense Lawyers, Nat. Assn. Criminal Defense Lawyers, Soc. Am. Law Tchrs., Assn. Legal Aid Attys. (chmn. bargaining com. 1974—79, exec. v.p. 1977—78, exec. com. 1984—86), Assn. of Bar of City of N.Y., Fortune Soc. (exec. com., bd. dirs.), Am. Inns of Ct. (master Daniel Webster Inn), Order of Barristers. Democrat. Jewish. Achievements include notable cases such as: People vs. Joel Steinberg, represented co-defendant, Hedda Nussbaum in homicide death Lisa Steinberg; U.S. vs. Falvey, in which Irish Rep. Army supporters were acquitted of gun running because of knowledge and approval of CIA; Bell vs. Coughlin, which involved highly publicized homicide of 2 N.Y. police officers; People vs. Roche, which established agy. def. to drug sale in State of N.Y.'s highest ct.; U.S. vs. Joseph, which appealed convictions in Brinks case. Home: 22 Cedar Point Rd Durham NH 03824 Office: Shuchman Krause & Vogelman PO Box 220 Exeter NH 03833-0220 E-mail: lav@sisna.com., larryvpd@aol.com.

VOGELZANG, JEANNE MARIE, professional association executive, lawyer; b. Hammond, Ind., Apr. 15, 1950; d. Richard and Laura Ann (Vanderaa) Jabaay; m. Nicholas John Vogelzang, May 17, 1971; children: Nick, Adam, Tim. BA, Trinity Christian Coll., Palos Heights, Ill., 1972; MBA, U. Minn., 1981; JD, U. Chgo., 1987. Bar: Ill. 1987; CPA, Ill.; CAE. Tchr. Timothy Christian H.S., Elmhurst, Ill., 1972-74; tchg. assoc. in fin. U. Minn., Mpls., 1980-81; fin. analyst Quaker Oats Co., Chgo., 1982-84; assoc. Baker & McKenzie, Chgo., 1987-89, Jenner & Block, Chgo., 1989-91; pres., owner J.M. Vogelzang & Assocs., Western Springs, Ill., 1991-99; exec. dir. Structural Engrs. Assn. Ill., Chgo., 1992—, Nat. Coun. Structural Engrs. Assns., Chgo., 1996—; pub., editor Structure mag., 1996—. Com. mem. Western Springs Planning Commn., 1991—95; village trustee Village of Western Springs, 1995—99, chmn. fin., chmn. gen. govt. com.; mem. adv. bd. Coll. DuPage Internat. Trade Ctr., Glen Ellyn, Ill., 1992—94; bd. dirs., mem. acad. affairs com., planning com., exec. com. sec. Trinity Christian Coll., 1992—98; mem. trustees' evaluation com. Christian Ref. Ch. N.Am., 1998—; treas. The Tower Party of Western Springs, 1999—2001; mem. jud. code com. Christian Reformed Ch. N.Am., Grand Rapids, Mich., 1991—97; bd. dirs. Austin Christian Law Ctr., Chgo., 1989—92, Barnabas Found., Palos Heights, Ill., 1989—95, Ctrl. Park Chapel, Holland, Mich., 2002—. Fellow Ill. Lincoln Excellence in Pub. Svc., 1999. Mem. ABA, Am. Soc. Assn. Execs., Ill. Bar Assn., Chgo. Bar Assn., Elim Work Svcs. Bus. Roundtable. Mem. Christian Reformed Ch. Office: 203 N Wabash Ave Ste 2010 Chicago IL 60601-2418

VOGRIN, JOSEPH EDWARD, III, lawyer; BA magna cum laude, Duquesne U., Pitts, 1969; JD, Duquesne U., 1972. Bar: Pa. 1972, U.S. Ct. Appeals (3rd cir.) 1972, US Supreme Ct. 1984. Dep. dist. atty. Dist. Atty's Office Allegheny County, Pitts., 1972—79; ptnr. Scott, Vogrin & Riester, Pitts., 1980—96, Vogrin & Riester, P.C., Pitts., 1996—2000, Meyer Darragh Buckler Bebenek & Eck, Pitts., 2000—. Program adv. com. Pa, Bar Inst. Mcpl. Solicitors, Pitts., 1999—; mem. curriculum rev. commn. Pa. Mcpl. Police Officer's Tng. Commn., Harrisburg, 2000—. Solicitor Ohio Twp. San. Authority, Pitts., 1983—, Twp. Shaler, Pitts., 1986—, Quaker Valley Coun. Govts., Pitts., 1987—, North Hills Coun. Govts., Pitts., 1989—, Borough's Assn. Allegheny County, Pitts., 1991—92, Borough Avalon, Pitts., 1992—, Ross Twp. CSC, Pitts., 1993—, Borough's Assn. Allegheny County, Pitts., 1994—95; co-counsel Allegheny County and Western Pa, Assn. Twp. Commissioners, Pitts., 1997—; solicitor Twp. Res., Pitts., 1998—. Mem.: Allegheny County Bar Assn. (chmn. assn. mcpl. and sch. solicitors Allegheny County 1998—99). Municipal (including bonds), Motor Vehicle Law. Office: Meyer Darragh Buckler Bebenek & Eck 2000 Frick Bldg Pittsburgh PA 15219 Home Fax: 412-471-2754; Office Fax: 412-471-2754. Personal E-mail: jvogrin@mdbbe.com.

VOIGHT, ELIZABETH ANNE, lawyer; b. Sapulpa, Okla., Aug. 6, 1944; d. Robert Guy and Garnetta Ruth (Bell) Voight; m. Bodo Barske, Feb. 22, 1985; children: Anne Katharine, Ruth Caroline. BA, U. Ark.-Fayetteville, 1967, MA, 1969; postgrad., U. Hamburg (W.Ger.), 1966-67; JD, Georgetown U., 1978. Bar: N.Y. 1979, Munich 1997. Lectr. German Oral Roberts U., Tulsa, 1968-69; tchr. German D.C. pub. schs., 1971-73; instr. German Georgetown U., Washington, 1973-74, adminstrv. asst. to dean Sch. Fgn. Svc., 1974-77; law clk. Cole Corette & Abrutyn (now Alston & Bird LLP), Washington, 1977-78; atty. Alston & Bird LLP (formerly Walter, Conston, Alexander & Green, P.C.), N.Y.C., 1978-88, Alston & Bird, LLP, Munich, 1990—. CMS Hasche Sigle, Munich, 1990—. Author (with Dr. Martin Peltzer): German Law Pertaining to Limited Liability Companies, German-English Text, 4th edit., 2000, German Securities Acquisition and Takover Act, 2002, German Commercial Code, German-English Text, 5th edit., 2002; trans. (articles for profl. jours.). Chmn. regional screening Am. Field Svc., N.Y.C., 1981-86; founding mem. Am. Berlin Opera Found. German Acad. Exchange Program fellow, 1966-67; adv. coun. Georgetown U. BMW Ctr. German and European Studies. Mem. Assn. Bar City N.Y., Munich Bar Assn., Internat. Fiscal Assn., Internat. Bar Assn., Am. C. of C. in Germany (Munich hospitality com.), Phi Beta Kappa, Kappa Kappa Gamma. Private international, Corporate, general, Mergers and acquisitions. E-mail: elizabeth.voight@cmslegal.de., voight@camelot.de.

VOIGT, BARTON R. state supreme court justice; BA and MA in Am. History, law degree, U. Wyo. Atty., Thermopolis, Wyo.; former Hot Springs County atty.; former county ct. judge; former dist. judge Douglas, Wyo.; justice Wyo. Supreme Ct., 2001—. Office: 2301 Capitol Ave Cheyenne WY 82001 Office Fax: 307-777-6129.*

VOIGT, STEVEN RUSSELL, lawyer; b. Geneva, Nebr., Dec. 29, 1952; s. James Leroy and Martha Anne (Erikson) V.; m. Barbara Jeane Molcyk, Apr. 23, 1983; children: Kelsey Marie, Katelyn Anne. BS, U. Nebr., 1975, JD, 1978. Bar: Nebr. 1978, U.S. Dist. Ct. Nebr. 1978, U.S. Tax Ct. 1980. Assoc. Nye, Hervert, Jorgensen & Watson, Kearney, Nebr., 1978-80; ptnr. Giese, Butler & Voigt, Kearney, 1980-82, Butler & Voigt, Kearney, 1982-85, Butler, Voigt & Brewster, Kearney, 1985-97, Butler, Voigt & Stewart P.C., Kearney, 1997—. Bd. dirs. Western Nebr. Legal Svcs., Scottsbluff, pres. bd. 1997—; pub. defender County of Kearney, Minden, Nebr., 1982—; pres. Nebr. Lawyers Trust Account Found., Lincoln, 1986-90. Mem. ABA (exec. coun. young lawyers div. 1985-86), Assn. Trial Lawyers Am., Nebr. State Bar Assn. (vice chair judiciary com.), Nebr. Criminal Defense Atty's. Assn., Sertoma (pres. Kearney chpt. 1983-84), Kearney Country Club (pres. of bd. dirs. 1995), Masons, Shriners. Avocations: golf, bicycling. Commercial, consumer (including collections, credit), Criminal, Family and matrimonial. Home: 5207 Avenue G Pl Kearney NE 68847-8598 Office: Butler Voigt & Stewart PC 2202 Central Ave Ste 200 Kearney NE 68847-5359

VOJCANIN, SAVA ALEXANDER, lawyer; b. Oak Lawn, Ill., Oct. 15, 1964; s. Jovan and Lili (Yovanovich) V.; m. Valerie S. Rupich, Oct. 12, 2002. Diploma, Culver Mil. Acad., 1981; BA with distinction, DePauw U., 1985; JD, Washington U., 1988. Bar: Ill. 1988, U.S. Dist. Ct. (no. dist.) Ill. 1989, U.S. Dist. Ct. (no. dist.) Tex. 1996. Assoc. Schaffenegger, Watson & Peterson Ltd., Chgo., 1988-91, Clausen Miller P.C., Chgo., 1991-98, ptnr., 1999—, shareholder, 2002—. Editor: Law, Culture and Values, 1989. Mem. Mayor's Adv. Coun. on Immigrant and Refugee Affairs, Chgo., 1992-97; trustee St. Basil Orthodox Ch. of Lake Forest, 1997—, sec. bd. trustees, 1999-2002, nominating com., 2002-. Mem.: Chgo. Bar Assn., Serbian Bar Assn. Am. (treas. 1999—2000, sec. 2000—01, v.p. 2001—02, pres. 2002—03, bd. dirs.). Orthodox. General civil litigation, Construction, Insurance. Office: Clausen Miller PC 10 S LaSalle St Chicago IL 60603-1098 E-mail: svojcanin@clausen.com.

VOLK, KENNETH HOHNE, lawyer; b. Hackensack, N.J., Nov. 8, 1922; s. Henry L. and Constance (Brady) V.; m. Joyce Geary, May 11, 1954; children: Christopher H., Cynthia. BS, U.S. Naval Acad., 1946; LLB, Yale U., 1953. Ptnr. Burlingham, Underwood, N.Y.C., 1955-92; of counsel McLane, Graf, Raulerson & Middleton, Portsmouth, N.H., 1992—. Speaker various symposia and confs. on maritime law. Assoc. editor Am. Maritime Cases; contbr. articles to profl. jours. Pres. Maritime Assocs., N.Y.C., 1967-68; chmn. bd. dirs. Seamen's House YMCA, N.Y.C., 1971-76; sec., bd. dirs. Seamen's Ch. Inst., N.Y.C., 1977-92; bd. dirs. Strawbery Banke Mus., Portsmouth, N.H.; mem. adv. bd. Tulane Admiralty Law Inst.. Fellow Am. Bar Found., Am. Coll. Trial Lawyers; mem. ABA, Assn. Bar of City of N.Y., Maritime Law Assn. U.S. (exec. com. 1977-80, pres. 1990-92), Comite Maritime Internat. (titulary mem.), Quaker Hill Country Club (pres. 1976-78). Republican. Espicopalian. Avocations: reading, hiking, fishing. Office: McLane Graf Raulerson & Middleton 10 Pleasant St Portsmouth NH 03801

VOLK, STEPHEN RICHARD, company executive, lawyer; b. Boston, Apr. 22, 1936; s. Ralph and Miriam (Rose) V.; m. Veronica J. Brown, June 19, 1959 (dec. Feb. 1989); children: Jeffrey A., Andrew M., Michael J.; m. Diane Kemelman, Apr. 22, 1990; 1 child, Anne. Student, Dartmouth Coll., 1957; JD, Harvard U., 1960. Bar: N.Y. 1961. Assoc. Sherman & Sterling, N.Y.C., 1960-68, ptnr., 1968—, dep. sr. ptnr., 1988-91, sr. ptnr., 1991—2001; vice chmn. Credit Suisse First Boston, N.Y.C., 2001—02, chmn., 2002—. Bd. dirs. ContiGroup Cos. Inc. Bd. dirs. Consol. Edison, Inc., 1996; trustee Consol Edison Co. N.Y.C., Inc., 1998, Harvard Law Sch. Assn., N.Y.C., 1999; mem. dean's adv. bd. Harvard Law Sch., 1997. Fellow Am. Bar Found.; mem. ABA (com. on securities regulation 1974), Assn. Bar City N.Y., Coun. on Fgn. Rels., Univ. Club, Phi Beta Kappa. Office: 11 Madison Ave 27th Fl New York NY 10010-3629

VOLLEN, ROBERT JAY, lawyer; b. Chgo., Jan. 23, 1940; s. Ben N. and Rose (Belonsky) V.; m. Judith Paula Spector, Aug. 12, 1961; children: Steven, Neil, Jennifer. AB, U. Mich., 1961; JD, U. Chgo., 1964. Bar: Ill. 1964, D.C. 1965, U.S. Supreme Ct. 1975. Atty. appellate sect. Civil Div., U.S. Dept. Justice, Washington, 1964-65; assoc. firm Schiff Hardin & Waite, Chgo., 1965-70, partner firm, 1971-72; gen. counsel BPI (Bus. and Profl. People for Pub. Interest), Chgo., 1972-83; ptnr. Schwartz & Freeman, Chgo., 1983-87. Mem. vis. com. U. Chgo. Law Sch., 1978-81. Mem. Chgo. Council Lawyers (gov. 1972-76, 79-81), ABA (ho. of dels. 1974-76) Home: 2 Kingswood Ct Deerfield IL 60015-1912 E-mail: rvollen@ameritech.net.

VOLZ, CHARLES HARVIE, JR., lawyer; b. Richmond, Va., Sept. 15, 1925; s. Charles Harvie and Mary V. (Mallory) V.; m. Constance A. Lewis, July 30, 1976; children: Charles Harvie III, Judith C. BS, U. Ala., 1950, JD, 1951. Bar: Ala. 1951, U.S. Dist. Ct. Ala., U.S. Ct. Appeals (5th cir.), U.S. Ct. Mil. Appeals, U.S. Ct. Appeals (11th cir.), U.S. Supreme Ct. 1962. Spl. agt. FBI, 1951; claim mgr. Allstate Ins. Co., 1952-54; claims atty. State Farm Ins. Co., 1954-57; ptnr. Roberts, Orme & Volz, 1957-59; sole practice Montgomery, 1961-63; asst. dir. Dept. Indsl. Rels., State of Ala., 1959-63; pntr. Volz, Capouano, Wampold & Prestwood, 1963-84, Volz & Volz, 1984-95, Volz, Prestwood & Hanan, 1995—2001; of counsel Prestwood and Assocs., 2001—. Note editor Ala. Law Rev., 1950-51. Campaign dir. March of Dimes, 1958, Am. Cancer Soc., 1967; exec. sec. Gov.'s Com. on Employment of Physically Handicapped, 1959-62; mem. Pres.'s Com. on Employment of Physically Handicapped, 1959-62; pres., bd. dirs. Montgomery chpt. Am. Cancer Soc. 2nd lt. USAAF, 1943-45. Recipient Outstanding Service award Am. Cancer Soc., 1967 Mem. ATLA (state committeeman 1973-75), Am. Arbitration Assn. (mem. nat. panel), ABA, Ala. Bar Assn., Ala. Trial Lawyers Assn., Farrah Law Soc., Montgomery Country Club, Masons, Kiwanis, Phi Alpha Delta. Methodist. Federal civil litigation, State civil litigation, Personal injury (including property damage). Home: 1638 Cobblestone Ct Montgomery AL 36117-1713 Office: 350 Adams Ave Montgomery AL 36104-4204

VON BERNUTH, CARL W. lawyer, diversified corporation executive; b. Feb. 2, 1944; BA, Yale U., 1966, LLB, 1969. Bar: N.Y. 1970, Pa. 1990. Corp. atty. White & Case, 1969-80; assoc. gen. counsel Union Pacific Corp., N.Y.C., 1980-83, dep. gen. counsel fin. and adminstrn., 1984-88, v.p., gen. counsel Bethlehem, Pa., 1988-91, sr. v.p., gen. counsel, 1991-97, sr. v.p., gen. counsel and sec. Omaha, 1997—. Mem. U. Pa. Inst. for Law and Econs. Mem. Am. Corp. Counsel Assn., Practicing Law Inst. Corporate, general, Securities. Office: Union Pacific Corp 1416 Dodge St Rm 1230 Omaha NE 68179-0001

VON BORRIES, CHRISTIAN RAMIRO, lawyer; b. Cochabamba, Bolivia, Apr. 18, 1967; s. Ramiro Von B. and Ana María Blanco; m. Daniela Hinojosa, Dec. 7, 1996; children: Matilda, Emilio, Vicente, Julian. LLB, U. Mayor San Andrés, La Paz, 1992; Atty., 1993. Assoc. Gutierrez Moscoso, La Paz, 1991-93; ptnr. Von Borries Blanco, La Paz, 1993—; counsel Banco Santander Central Hispano, 1996—. Cons. La Paz City Hall, 1996, Prudential Securities, La Paz, 1999; invited critic Analysis of Proposed Law, 1995. Author: Bases Juridico Institucionales Para Dar Mayor Competitividad al Sistema Búrsatil, 1992, Critics and Comments to Securities Code, 1997. Class pvt. Army (Branch XI-A), 1986-87. Mem. Internat. Bar Assn., La Paz Atty.'s Coll. Avocations: art collecting, tennis. Office: Von Borries Blanco Estudio Abogados Av Arc Esq Ros GutiEdi Mult Piso 16 1602 La Paz 6075 Bolivia Fax: 443381. E-mail: vborries@ceibo.entelnet.bo.

VON DEM KNESEBECK, DIRK WASMOD WERNER, lawyer; b. Munich, May 15, 1965; s. Werner Wasmod Paridam and Edda Von Dem Knesebeck; m. Ruth Hoeftmann, June 22, 1996; children: Sophie Knesebeck, Konstantin Knesebeck. Grad., U. Munich, 1992, grad., 1994, PhD, 1996. Lawyer Arcon Law Office, Munich, 1996—99, PWC Veltins Law Office, Munich, 1999—. Author: Comparison of German and U.S. Law, 1994—96. With German Mil., 1984—85. Avocations: windsurfing, surfing, Tae Kwon Do, skiing. Corporate, general. Office: PWC Veltins Rechtsanwalte Briennerstr 9 Amiraplatz 80538 Munich Germany

VON DER HEYDT, JAMES ARNOLD, federal judge; b. Miles City, Mont., July 15, 1919; s. Harry Karl and Alice S. (Arnold) von der H.; m. Verna E. Johnson, May 21, 1952. BA, Albion (Mich.) Coll., 1942; JD, Northwestern, 1951. Bar: Alaska 1951. Pvt. practice, Nome, 1953-59; judge superior ct. Juneau, Alaska, 1959-66; from judge to sr. judge U.S. Dist. Ct. Alaska, Alaska, 1966—; U.S. commr. Nome, Alaska, 1951—; U.S. atty. div. 2 Dist. Alaska, 1951-53; mem. Alaska Ho. of Reps., 1957-59. Author: Mother Sawtooth's Nome, 1990, Alaska, The Short and Long of It, 2000. Pres. Anchorage Fine Arts Mus. Assn. Recipient Disting. Alumni award Albion Coll., 1995. Mem. Alaska Bar Assn. (mem. bd. govs. 1955-59, pres. 1959-60), Am. Judicature Soc., Masons (32d degree), Shriners, Phi Delta Phi, Sigma Nu. Avocations: researching arctic bird life, creative writing. Office: US Dist Ct 222 W 7th Ave Box 40 Anchorage AK 99513-7564

VON KALINOWSKI, JULIAN ONESIME, lawyer; b. St. Louis, May 19, 1916; s. Walter E. and Maybelle (Michaud) von K.; m. Penelope Jayne Dyer, June 29, 1980; children by previous marriage: Julian Onesime, Wendy Jean von Kalinowski. BA, Miss. Coll., 1937; JD with honors, U. Va., 1940. Bar: Va. 1940, Calif. 1946. Assoc. Gibson, Dunn and Crutcher, L.A., 1946-52, ptnr., 1953-85, mem. exec. com., 1962-82, adv. ptnr., 1985—; CEO, chmn. Litigation Scis., Inc., Culver City, Calif., 1991-94, chmn. emeritus Torrance, Calif., 1994-96, Dispute Dyamics, Inc., Torrance, Calif., 1996-2000. Instr. Columbia Law Sch., Parker Sch. Fgn. and Comparative Law, 1981; instr. antitrust law So. Meth. Sch. of Law, 1982-84, bd. visitors, 1982-85; bd. dirs. W.M. Keck Found.; faculty Practising Law Inst., 1971, 76, 78-80; instr. in spl. course on antitrust litigation Columbia U. Law Sch., NYC, 1981; lawyers dels. com. to 9th Cir. Jud. Conf., 1953-67; UN expert Mission to People's Republic China, 1982. Contbr. articles to legal jours.; author: Antitrust Laws and Trade Regulation, 1969, desk edit., 1981; gen. editor: World Law of Competition, 1978, Antitrust Counseling and Litigation Techniques, 1984; gen. editor emeritus Antitrust Report. With USN, 1941-46, capt. Res. ret. Fellow Am. Bar Found., Am. Coll. Trial Lawyers (chmn. complex litigation com. 1984-87); mem. ABA (ho. of dels. 1970, chmn. antitrust law sect. 1972-73), State Bar Calif. (Anti-Trust Lawyer of Yr. award 2000), L.A. Bar Assn., U. Va. Law Sch. Alumni Assn. (mem. deans adv. coun.), Calif. Club, L.A. Country Club, La Jolla Beach and Tennis Club, Phi Kappa Psi, Phi Alpha Delta. Republican. Episcopalian. Antitrust, Federal civil litigation, General civil litigation. Home: 12320 Ridge Cir Los Angeles CA 90049-1151 Office: 12320 Ridge Cir Los Angeles CA 90049-1151 E-mail: j.ovnk@ason.com.

VON MANDEL, MICHAEL JACQUES, lawyer; b. Yokohama, Japan, Oct. 20, 1941; came to the U.S., 1946; s. Michael Maximillan and Suzanne (Jacques) V.M.; m. Mary Denise Bienvenue, Dec. 22, 1984; 1 child, Michelle Denise. AB in Econs., Georgetown U., 1964; JD, Cath. U., 1968; LLM in Taxation, NYU, 1970. Bar: Washington 1969, Conn. 1969, U.S. Supreme Ct. 1972, Ill. 1976, U.S. Dist. Ct. (no. dist.) Ill. 1976, U.S. Ct. Appeals (7th cir.) 1976, Fla. 1977. Trial atty. FTC, Washington, 1968-69; trial atty. tax divsn. U.S. Dept. Justice, Washington, 1970-76; pvt. practice Chgo., 1976-93; ptnr. Von Mandel & Von Mandel, Chgo., 1994—. Adj. prof. grad. tax program DePaul U., Chgo., 1980-83. Contbr. chapters to books. Mem. ABA (tax and litigation sects. 1976—), Chgo. Bar Assn. (fed. tax com. 1976—), Fed. Bar Assn. (bd. dirs. 1981-93), Seventh Cir Bar Assn., Union League Club. Roman Catholic. Taxation, general, Personal income taxation. Address: 79 W Monroe St Ste 1000 Chicago IL 60603-4901 Home: 1333 N Sandburg Terr Chicago IL 60610 E-mail: mvmtax@aol.com.

VON MEHREN, ARTHUR TAYLOR, lawyer, educator; b. Albert Lea, Minn., Aug. 10, 1922; s. Sigurd Anders and Eulalia Marion (Anderson) von M.; m. Joan Elizabeth Moore, Oct. 11, 1947; children— George Moore, Peter Anders, Philip Taylor S.B., Harvard U., 1942, LL.B., 1945, PhD, 1946; Faculty of Law, U. Zurich, 1946-47; Faculte de Droit, U. Paris, 1948-49; Doctor iuris (h.c.), Katholieke U., Leuven, 1985, U. Pantheon-Assas (Paris II), 2000. Bar: Mass. 1950, U.S. Dist. Ct. Mass. 1980. Law clk. U.S. Ct. Appeals (1st cir.), 1945-46; asst. prof. law Harvard U., 1946-53, prof., 1953-76, Story prof., 1976-93, prof. emeritus, 1993—, dir. East Asian legal studies program, 1981-83; acting chief legislation br., legal div. Occupation Mil. Govt. U.S.,Germany, 1947-48, cons. legal div., 1949. Tchr. Salzburg Seminar in Am. Studies, summers 1953, 54; Fulbright research prof. U. Tokyo, Japan, 1956-57, Rome, Italy, 1968-69; cons. legal studies Ford Found., New Delhi, 1962-63; vis. prof. U. Frankfurt, summer 1967, City Univ. Hong Kong, 1995; Ford vis. prof. Inst. Advanced Legal Studies, U. London, 1976; assoc. prof. U. Paris, 1977; Goodhart prof. legal sci. U. Cambridge, 1983-84, fellow Downing Coll., 1983-84, hon. fellow, 1984—; fellow Wissenschaftskolleg zu Berlin, 1990-91. Author: The Civil Law System: An Introduction to the Comparative Study of Law, 1957, 2d edit. (with J. Gordley), 1977, Law in the United States: A General and Comparative View, 1988, The Law of Multistate Problems: Cases and Materials in the Conflict of Laws, 1965, (with S. Symeonides and W. Perdue) Conflict of Laws: American, Comparative, International, 1998, International Commercial Arbitration, 1999, (with J. Varady, J. Barcelo) 2d edit., 2002; mem. editl. bd. Am. Jour. Comparative Law, 1952-86; contbr. articles to profl. jours.; editor: Law in Japan-The Legal Order in a Changing Soc., 1963; mem. editl. com. Internat. Ency. Comparative Law, 1969—. Mem. U.S. Del. Hague Conf. pvt. internat. law, 1966, 68, 76, 80, 85, 93, 96, 2001. Named to Order of the Rising Sun, golden rays Japanese Govt., 1989; Guggenheim fellow, 1968-69; inst. fellow Sackler Inst. Advanced Studies, 1986-87. Mem. ABA (Leonard J. Theberge Award for Pvt. Internat. Law 1997, Sect. of Internat. Law and Practice), Am. Acad. Arts and Scis., Internat. Acad. Comparative Law (Can. prize 2002), Institut de Droit Internat., Japanese Am. Soc. Legal Studies, Am. Soc. Comparative Law (bd. dirs., former pres.), Am. Soc. Polit. and Legal Philosophy, Institut Grand-Duchal (corr.), Phi Beta Kappa. Office: Harvard Law Sch/ AR-231 1545 Massachusetts Ave Cambridge MA 02138-2903 E-mail: vonmehre@law.harvard.edu.

VON MEHREN, ROBERT BRANDT, lawyer, retired; b. Albert Lea, Minn., Aug. 10, 1922; s. Sigurd Anders and Eulalia Marion (Anderson) von M.; m. Mary Katharine Kelly, June 26, 1948 (dec. Mar. 1985); children: Carl S., John M., Katharine, Jane, Margaret; m. Susan Heller Anderson, Apr. 2, 1988. BA summa cum laude with philosophical oration, Yale U., 1943; LLB magna cum laude, Harvard U., 1946. Bar: N.Y. 1946, U.S. Supreme Ct. 1954. Law clk. to Judge Learned Hand U.S. Ct. Appeals (2d cir.), 1946-47; law clk. to Assoc. Justice Stanley Reed U.S. Supreme Ct., 1947-48; assoc. Debevoise & Plimpton, N.Y.C., 1946, 48-57, ptnr., 1957-93, of counsel, 1994-95, ret., 1995. Arbitrator in internat. and other matters; sr. lectr. in law Wharton Sch. U. Pa., Phila., 1985-86; legal counsel Prep. Commn. for Internat. Atomic Energy Agy., N.Y.C., 1956-57; trustee Practising Law Inst., N.Y.C., 1972-96, emeritus, 1996, pres., 1979-86, chmn. bd., 1986-96. Bd. editors Harvard Law Rev., 1944-46, Am. Jour. Internat. Law, 1981-89, hon. editor, 1990-2000; contbr. articles to profl. jours. Trustee Axe Houghton Found., N.Y.C., 1965—; bd. dirs. Legal Aid Soc., N.Y.C., 1966-70; pres. Harvard Law Sch. Assn. N.Y., 1982-83. Mem. Assn. Bar City N.Y., Internat. Law Assn. (vice chmn. 1989—, pres. Am. br. 1978-86, chmn. exec. com. 1986-92), Coll. of Comml. Arbitrators, Coun. on Fgn. Rels., Univ. Club, Century Assn. N.Y.C., The Comml. Bar Assn. (hon. mem.). Corporate, general, Private international. Home: 925 Park Ave New York NY 10028-0210 Office: 919 3rd Ave 46th Fl New York NY 10022

VON RECHENBERG, WOLF G. lawyer; b. Bad Gandersheim, Germany, Mar. 20, 1954; m. Ute von Rechenberg, Sept. 29, 1984; 1 child, Ann-Cathrin. Law Degree, Albert-Ludwigs U., Freiburg, Germany, 1979, Doctorate in Law, 1984. Bar: Germany; cert. Berlin. Pvt. practice, Freiburg, 1982—88; assoc. SLS Sigle Loose, Stuttgart, Germany, 1988—89; fgn. assoc. Carter Ledyard Milburn, N.Y.C., 1989—90; ptnr. SLS Sigle Loose, Berlin, 1990—99; ptnr., head of tax CMS Hasche Sigle, Berlin, 1999—. Lectr. Freiburg Law Sch., 1984—90; mem. examination com. for tax advisors OFD, Berlin, 1996—; chmn. supervisory bd. OTG AG, St. Georgen, Germany, 2001—. Corporate, general, Taxation, general, Mergers and acquisitions. Office: CMS Hasche Sigle Markgrafenstrasse 36 10117 Berlin Germany

VON SAUERS, JOSEPH F. lawyer; b. N.Y.C. s. Joseph F. and Margaret von Sauers; m. June A. von Sauers. BEE, Manhattan Coll., 1980; MBA, Pepperdine U., 1987; JD, Southwestern U., 1991; LLM, Columbia U., 1995; DBA, North Central U., 2001. Bar: Calif. 1992, D.C. 1993, Minn. 1993, Tex. 1993, Colo. 1994, U.S. Patent and Trademark Office. Contracts negotiator Hughes Aircraft Co., El Segundo, Calif., 1985-92; atty. Jones, Day, Reavis & Pogue, Dallas, 1992-94, Loeb & Loeb, LLP, L.A., 1995-97, Gray, Cary, Ware & Freidenrich, Palo Alto, Calif., 1997-98; dep. gen. coun. Roland Corp. U.S., L.A., 1998—. Active Calif. Lawyers for Arts, L.A., 1996; guest spkr. Loyola U., L.A., 1996. Contbr. articles to profl. jours. Capt. USNR. Recipient Kuwait Liberation medal Saudi Arabian/Kuwaiti Govts., 1992, 96, Joint Svcs. Commendation medal, Navy Commendation medal (2), Navy Achievement medal; Wildman scholar Southwestern U., 1987-91. Mem. Naval Res. Assn., L.A. County Bar Assn. Avocations: sailing, golf, tennis. Commercial, contracts (including sales of goods; commercial financing), Entertainment, Intellectual property.

VON TEICHMAN, CHRISTOPH, lawyer; b. Magdeburg, Germany, Feb. 13, 1947; s. Horst and Marie-Luise von Teichman; m. Cornelia Wilcke, July 18, 1975; children: Caecilie, Cordelia. Law Grad. (1st State Exam.), Hamburg U., Germany, 1972; 2nd State Exam., Hamburg Ct. of Appeals, Germany, 1976. Bar: Hamburg Dist. Ct. 1976. Assoc. Nolte & Löwe, Hamburg, Germany, 1976—78; ptnr. Nolte & Löwe/Schön Nolte, Hamburg, Germany, 1979—2001, Latham & Watkins, Hamburg, Germany, 2001—. Lectr. bus. law course Hamburg U., Germany; vis. lectr. McGeorge Sch. of Law, European program, 1985—94. Contbr. legal textbook, chpt. to legal textbook. Mem.: German Bar Assn., Internat. Bar Assn. (sect. coun. mem. 1999—). Lutheran. Avocations: cooking, travel, films. Mergers and acquisitions, Finance, Banking. Office: Latham & Watkins Warburgstrasse 50 Hamburg 20354 Germany Office Fax: +49 40 41 40 31 30. E-mail: christoph.von.teichman@lw.com.

VON TEUFFEL, NIKOLAI, lawyer; b. Düsseldorf, Germany, May 25, 1954; s. Günther and Helga von Teuffel; m. Ursula Dietrich, Sept. 5, 1986; children: Antonia, Georgia. Degree in law, U. Munich, Germany, 1979, PhD in Law, 1983. Bar: Hamburg 1982. Pvt. practice, Hamburg, 1982—. Mem. German Bar Assn., German Maritime Assn., Hamburg Bar Assn. Admiralty, Commercial, contracts (including sales of goods; commercial financing), Corporate, general. Office: Kretschmar von Teuffel Leverkus Kleine Johannisstrasse 2-4 20457 Hamburg Germany

VON WALDOW, ARND N. lawyer; b. Moenchen-Gladbach, Germany, Mar. 15, 1957; came to U.S., 1966; s. Hans Eberhard and Brigitte H. (Schulze-Kadelbach) von W.; m. Esther R. Haguel, May 25, 1987; children: Rachel J., Danielle M. BA, Syracuse U., 1980; JD, U. Pitts., 1983. Bar: La. 1983, Pa. 1989. Assoc. Sessions & Fishman, New Orleans, 1983-90, Eckert, Seamans, Cherin & Mellott, Pitts., 1990-91; ptnr. Meyer, Darragh, Buckler, Bebenek & Eck, Pitts., 1991-99, Reed, Smith, Shaw & McClay, Pitts., 1999—. Mem. Product Liability Adv. Coun., Chgo., 1991—. Mem. ABA, Def. Rsch. Inst., Phi Beta Kappa. Commercial, contracts (including sales of goods; commercial financing), Insurance, Product liability. Home: 1738 Hempstead Ln Pittsburgh PA 15241-1376 Office: Reed Smith Shaw & McClay 435 6th Ave Ste 2 Pittsburgh PA 15219-1886

VON WITT, EDWARD ROBERT, lawyer; b. Bulaway, Zimbabwe, June 6, 1947; arrived in South Africa, 1947; s. Richard Philip and Florence Amy Von Witt; m. Jane Margaret Stevens, Jan. 18, 1975; children: Simon James, Caitlin Greta. BA, LLB, U. Stellenbosch, South Africa, 1971. Bar: 1974. Candidate atty. Findlay and Tait, Cape Town, South Africa, 1972—74, atty., 1974—77, dir., 1977—. Mem.: Arbitration and Mediation Svc. South Africa, Law Soc. Cape of Good Hope. Avocations: golf, hiking, bicycling. Labor (including EEOC, Fair Labor Standards Act, labor-management relations, NLRB, OSHA), Pension, profit-sharing, and employee benefits. Office: Findlay and Tait 60 St Georges Mall Cape Town 8001 South Africa

VOORHEES, JAMES DAYTON, JR., lawyer; b. Haverford, Pa., Nov. 14, 1917; s. James Dayton Voorhees and Elsa Denison Jameson; m. Mary Margaret Fuller, Sept. 5, 1942 (dec. Apr. 1991); children: J. Dayton III, Susan F. Voorhees-Maxfield, Jane Voorhees Kiss. BA, Yale U., 1940; JD, Harvard U., 1943. Bar: N.H. 1947, Colo. 1948, U.S. Dist. Ct. Colo. 1948, U.S. Ct. Appeals (10th cir.) 1949, U.S. Ct. Appeals (5th cir.) 1956, U.S. Supreme Ct. 1960. Assoc. Johnson & Robertson, Denver, 1947-50; atty. Conoco Inc., Denver, 1950-56; ptnr. Moran, Reidy & Voorhees, Denver, 1956-78, Kutak, Rock & Huie, Denver, 1978-80; ptnr., counsel Davis, Graham & Stubbs, Denver, 1980—. Mem. Denver Bd. Edn., 1965-71, pres. 1967-69. Lt. comdr. USNR, 1941-46, ATO, PTO. Mem.: ABA, Denver Bar Assn., Colo. Bar Assn., University Club, Denver Country Club. Republican. Avocation: golf.

VOORHEES, RICHARD LESLEY, federal judge; b. Syracuse, N.Y., June 5, 1941; s. Henry Austin and Catherine Adeline (Fait) V.; m. Barbara Holway Humphries, 1968; children: Martha Northrop, Steven Coerte. BA, Davidson Coll., 1963; JD, U. N.C., Chapel Hill, 1968. Bar: N.C. 1968, U.S. Dist. Ct. (we. dist.) N.C. 1969, U.S. Tax Ct. 1969, U.S. Ct. Appeals (4th cir.) 1978, U.S. Dist. Ct. (mid. dist.) N.C. 1981. Mem., ptnr. Garland, Alala, Bradley & Gray, Gastonia, N.C., 1968-80; pvt. practice Gastonia, N.C., 1980-88; judge U.S. Dist. Ct., Charlotte, N.C., 1988—, chief judge, 1991-98. Mem. N.C. State Rep. Exec. Com., Gaston County Rep. Com., chmn., 1979-83, U.S. Jud. Conf. Com., 1993—, case mgmt. and ct. adminstrn. com., 4th Cir. Ct. Appeals Jud. Coun., 1992-93; chmn. Gaston County Bd. Elections, Gastonia, 1985-86; alt. del. Rep. Nat. Conv., Kansas City, Kans., 1976. 1st lt. U.S. Army, 1963-65, U.S. Army Res., 1963-69. Mem. N.C. Bar Assn., Fed. Judges Assn., Dist. Judges Assn. Avocation: boating. Office: US Dist Ct WDNC 195 Fed Bldg 401 W Trade St Charlotte NC 28202-1619

VORE, COURTNEY CURRAN, lawyer; b. Winchester, Mass., June 10, 1975; d. Deborah Macbeth Curran; m. Jon Michael Brian Vore, Aug. 11, 2001. BA, Rutgers U., 1997; JD, Boston Coll., 2001. Bar: Mass. Law clk., assoc. McGrath and Kane, Boston, 1998—. Mem.: ABA, Mass. Bar Assn. Office: McGrath and Kane One Longfellow Pl Ste 3610 Boston MA 02114

VORT, ROBERT A. lawyer; b. Newark, N.J., Sept. 24, 1943; s. Saul S. and Ruth J. (Jacobson) Vort; m. Elizabeth Hornstein, June 25, 1968 (div. Nov. 1979); m. Marcelle Greenstein, Nov. 18, 1979 (div. Jan. 1991); children: Joel, Abigail, Rebecca; m. Tina Kruh, Feb. 4, 1996; 1 child, Hannah. BS in Econs., U. Pa., 1965; JD, Columbia U., 1968. Bar: N.J. 1968, N.Y. 1970, U.S. Ct. Appeals (2d and 3d cirs. 1975), U.S. Ct. Appeals (9th cir.) 1980, U.S. Ct. Appeals (5th cir.) 1981, U.S. Ct. Appeals (fed. cir.) 1984, U.S. Dist. Ct. N.J. 1968, U.S. Dist. Ct. (so. and ea. dists.) N.Y. 1984, U.S. Supreme Ct. 1977. Law clk. to Hon. Theodore I. Botter Superior Ct. of N.J., 1968-69; assoc. Davis & Cox, 1969-71, Israel B. Greene, 1971-73; sole practitioner, 1973-82; ptnr. Balk, Goldberger, Seligsohn, O'Connor & Rhatican, 1982-84, Kirsten, Friedman & Cherin, 1986; pvt. practice, 1984-85, 87-88; ptnr. Goldberg, Mufson & Spar, West Orange, N.J., 1988-91; counsel Donald Friedman, West Orange, 1991-92; pvt. practice Tenafly, N.J., 1997—; ptnr. Pearce, Vort & Fleisig LLC, Hackensack, N.J., 2001—. Mem. ABA (litigation sect., family law sect., legal econs. sect.), N.J. State Bar Assn. (appellate practice subcom.), Bergen County Bar Assn. Appellate, General civil litigation, Family and matrimonial. Office: Pearce Vort & Fleisig LLC Court Plaza North 25 Main St Hackensack NJ 07601 E-mail: rvort@pearcelawl.com.

VORYS, ARTHUR ISAIAH, lawyer; b. Columbus, Ohio, June 16, 1923; s. Webb Isaiah and Adeline (Werner) V.; m. Lucia Rogers, July 16, 1949 (div. 1980); children: Caroline S., Adeline Vorys Cranson, Lucy Vorys Noll, Webb I.; m. Ann Harris, Dec. 13, 1980. BA, Williams Coll., 1945; LLB, JD, Ohio State U., 1949. Bar: Ohio 1949. From assoc. to ptnr. Vorys, Sater, Seymour & Pease LLP, Columbus, 1949-82, sr. ptnr., 1982-93, of counsel, 1993—. Supt. ins. State of Ohio, 1957-59; bd. dirs Vorys Bros., Inc., others. Trustee, past pres. Children's Hosp., Greenlawn Cemetery Found.; trustee, former chmn. Ohio State U. Hosps.; regent Capital U.; del. Rep. Nat. Conv., 1968, 72. Lt. USMCR, World War II. Decorated Purple Heart. Fellow Ohio State Bar, Columbus Bar Assn.; mem. ABA, Am. Judicature Soc., Rocky Fork Headley Hunt Club, Rocky Fork Hunt and Country Club, Capital Club, Phi Delta Phi, Chi Psi. Home: 5826 Havens Corners Rd Columbus OH 43230-3142 Office: Vorys Sater Seymour & Pease LLP PO Box 1008 52 E Gay St Columbus OH 43216-1008

VOSBURG, BRUCE DAVID, lawyer; b. Omaha, June 17, 1943; s. Noble Perrin and Dena V. (Ferrari) V.; m. Susan Simpson, May 27, 1972; children: Margaret Amy, Wendy Christine, Bruce David. BA, U. Notre Dame, 1965; BSME, 1966; JD, Harvard U., 1969. Bar: Nebr. 1969, Ill. 1970, U.S. Supreme Ct. 1974. Law clk. U.S. Dist. Ct. Nebr., 1969-70; assoc. Kirkland & Ellis, Chgo., 1970-72; ptnr. Fitzgerald & Schorr, Omaha, 1972—. Author: Financing Small Businesses, 1981, Securities Law Practice, 1987, Securities Law-Going Public, 1989, Trade Secret Protection, 1994, Protecting Intellectual Property, 1998, Intellectual Property Law, 2000. Pres. Children's Crisis Ctr., 1984-85, bd. dirs., 1973-84, Childrens Savinds Inst. 1985-86, bd. dirs. 1984-90; pres. Nebr. Tennis Assn., 1976-77; mem. Leadership Omaha, 1979; chmn. bd. dirs. City of Omaha Parks and Recreation, 1985-92; founding dir. Friends of the Parks, 1988; bd. dirs. Omaha Pub. Libr. Found., 1997—, pres., 1999—; bd. dirs. Western Heritage Mus., 1998—. Named to, Nebr. Tennis Hall of Fame. Fellow Nebr. Bar Found.; mem. ABA, Nat. Assn. Bond Attys., Nebr. Bar Assn. (chmn. securities com.), Omaha Bar Assn. (exec. coun. 1983-86), Rotary (dir. 1993-98), USTA/Mo. Valley Tennis Assn. (chmn. grievance com. 1978—), Am. Intellectual Property Lawyers Assn., Tau Beta Pi. Republican. Roman Catholic. Corporate, general, Intellectual property, Securities. Office: Ste 400 13220 California St Omaha NE 68154-5228

VOSS, BARRY VAUGHAN, lawyer; b. St. Paul, July 25, 1952; s. James Lee and Stella Marie (Stewart) V.; m. Marilyn Williams, Jan. 25, 1980; children: Rori, Tiffini, Aaron. BA, U. Minn., 1975; JD, Hamline U., 1978. Bar: Minn. 1978, U.S. Dist. Ct. Minn. 1980, U.S. Ct. Appeals (8th cir.) 1982. Pres. Voss and Hickman, P.A., Mpls., 1978—. Spkr. in field. Author: A Taste of Cold Steel, 1999. Bd. dirs. Ramsey County Corrections Adv. Bd., St. Paul, 1977-79, RS Eden Program, 1998—. Recipient Most Well-Prepared award Minn. Lawyers Judges' Choice, 1991, Super Lawyer, Minn. Law and Politics Survey, 2000, 01, 02, 03, others. Mem. Am. Trial Lawyers Assn. (fire loss com.), Minn. Assn. Criminal Def. Attys. (bd. dirs. 1992-96), Minn. Trial Lawyers Assn., Minn. State Bar Assn. (civil litigation and criminal law sects.), Hennepin County Bar Assn. Democrat. Lutheran. Avocations: public speaking, sports, reading. General civil litigation, Criminal, Entertainment. Office: Voss and Hickman PA 527 Marquette Ave Ste 2355 Minneapolis MN 55402-1323 E-mail: b.v.voss@worldnet.att.net.

VOSS, KENNETH ERWIN, lawyer; b. Milw., Apr. 10, 1930; s. Andrew Hubert and Helen Lillian Voss; m. Charlotte Denise Gutierrez, Dec. 31, 1957; children: Christopher, Peter, Lisa, Michael, Timothy, Mark. BA, St. Francis Sem., Milw., 1952; JD, Marquette U., 1960. Bar: Wis. 1960, U.S. Dist. Ct. (ea. dist.) Wis. 1960, U.S. Supreme Ct. 1960. Gen. counsel Johnson Controls, Inc., Milw., 1960-84; pvt. practice Wickwire, Gavin & Gibbs, Vienna, Va and Madison, Wis., 1984-86, Fiorenza & Hayes, Milw., 1988-90, Suran & Suran, Milw., 1991-99, Hurtado S.C., Milw., 1999—. Author: (chpt.) Businessman's Guide to Construction, 1979, (chpt.) A Guide for the Foreign Investor, 1984, (chpts.) Wisconsin Construction Law, 1985. Sgt. U.S. Army, 1954-57; capt. JAGC U.S. Army, 1960-65. Mem.

Am. Arbitration Assn. (arbitrator 1968—), State Bar Wis. (mem. rels. com. pub. contract and constrn. law sect., 1995-2002). Roman Catholic. Alternative dispute resolution, Construction, Estate planning. Office: Hurtado SC 19395 W Capitol Dr Ste 200 Brookfield WI 53045-2736

VOXMAN, WILLIAM ALEXANDER, lawyer; b. Iowa City, Nov. 7, 1966; s. William Lloyd Voxman and Mary (Hazard) Foxman; m. Elizabeth Geib, May 22, 1993; children: William, Caroline, Thomas. BA, Amherst (Mass.) Coll., 1989; JD, U. Pa., 1993. Bar: Calif., Pa., D.C. Clk. Hon. Jerom Farris 9th Cir. Ct. Appeals, Seattle, 1993—94; assoc. Latham & Watkins, Washington and L.A., 1994—2000, ptnr. L.A., 2001—. Scholar Fulbright scholar, U. Bonn, Germany, 1990. Mem.: Town Hall, San Marino City Club. Mergers and acquisitions. Office: Latham & Watkins 633 W 5th St Ste 4000 Los Angeles CA 90071

VRABEL, JOSEPH P. lawyer; b. Adams, Mass., Feb. 8, 1948; BA, Lake Forest Coll., Ill., 1970; JD, Boston Coll., 1977; Mediator Cert., Harvard U., 1997. Bar: Mass., N.Y. Shareholder atty. Cope & Wilson, PC, 1979—84; sr. ptnr. Bowditch & Dewey, 1984—2001; v.p., gen. counsel Capital Risk Mgmt., Framingham, Mass., 2001—. Adj. prof. bus. law grad.-MBA program Babson Coll. Founder Crossroads Cmty. Found.; trustee Framingham State Coll.; treas., trustee Longfellow's Wayside Inn; former chmn. United Way MetroWest; trustee MCLE; dir. John J. Tobin Found., Maynard Food Pantry, Inc.; steering com. Equal Justice Coalition; former regional dir. Am. Cancer Soc.; mem. Maynard Town Counsel. Mem.: Worcester County Bar Assn., South Middlesex County Bar Assn., Boston Bar Assn., N.Y. Bar Assn., New Eng. Bar Assn. (bd. dirs.), Mass. Bar Assn. (chmn. bldg. and ops. com. 1988—, budget and fin. com. 1992—, exec. com. 1995—, governance task force 1996—98, pres., sec. 1998—99, dues restructuring task force 1999—2000, v.p. 1999—2000, treas. 2000—01, by-law com. 2001—02, pres.-elect 2001—02), ABA. Mergers and acquisitions, Commercial, consumer (including collections, credit). Office: Capital Risk Mgmt 1661 Worcester Rd Ste 303 Framingham MA 01701*

VRANICAR, MICHAEL GREGORY, lawyer; b. Hammond, Ind., Mar. 11, 1961; s. Melvin G. and Maryann R. (Szarek) V.; m. Marianna C. Livas, May 28, 1994. BSEE, U. Ill., 1983; JD, U. San Diego, 1987. Bar: Calif. 1987, Ill. 1988. Engr. Gen. Dynamics, San Diego, 1983-88; judge advocate USMC, Okinawa, Japan, 1988-91; assoc. Stellato & Schwartz, Chgo., 1992-94; ptnr. Plesha & Vranicar, Chgo., 1995—2001; atty. Fitch Even Tabin & Flannery, Chgo., 2001—. Arbitrator Cook County Arbitration Bd., Chgo., 1994—; judge regional competition Nat. Moot Ct., Chgo., 1992. Mem. Marine Corps Scholarship Found., Chgo. Ball Com. Lt. Col. USMC Res., 2001-. Mem. Chgo. Bar Assn., Okinawa Bench and Bar Assn., Am. Legion, Intellectual Property Lawyer's Assn., Chgo., Inst. Electrical and Electronics Engrs. Republican. Roman Catholic. Federal civil litigation, Intellectual property, Patent. Office: Fitch Even Tabin Flannery 120 S LaSalle Ste 1600 Chicago IL 60603

VRATIL, JOHN LOGAN, state legislator, lawyer; b. Great Bend, Kans., Oct. 28, 1945; s. Frank and Althea (Shoss) V.; m. Kathy Hoefer, June 21, 1971 (div. Dec. 1985); m. Anne Whitfill, Mar. 7, 1986 (div. Dec. 1992); m. Teresa Hobbs, Mar. 15, 1996; children: Alison, Andy, Ashley. BS in Edn., U. Kans., 1967; postgrad., U. Southampton, Eng., 1967-68; JD, U. Kans., 1971; postgrad., U. Exeter, Eng., 1972. Bar: Kans. 1971, U.S. Dist. Ct. Kans. 1971, U.S. Ct. Appeals (10th and 8th cirs.) 1975. From assoc. to ptnr. Bennett, Lytle, Wetzler & Winn, Prairie Village, Kans., 1972-83; with Lathrop & Gage, Overland Park, Kans., 1983—; v.p. Kans. Senate from 11th dist., 1998—. Contbr. articles to profl. jours. Mem. recreation commn. Prairie Village, 1982-83, mem. planning commn., 1983-84; v.p. Usher Mansion Hist. Found., Lawrence, Kans., 1990—. Fellow ABA Found.; mem. ABA, Kans. Bar Assn. (pres. 1995-96, gov. 1988-97), Kans. Bar Found. (trustee 1996-2002), Johnson County Bar Assn. (pres. 1979), Kans. Sch. Attys. Assn. (pres. 1985), Overland Park C. of C. (bd. dirs. 1985-94, pres. 1988). Republican. Avocations: sports, hunting, reading. Office: Lathrop & Gage 10851 Mastin Blvd Ste 1000 Overland Park KS 66210-2007 Address: Kansas Senate State Capitol Rm 255E Topeka KS 66612 E-mail: jvratil@lathropgage.com., vratil@senate.state.ks.us.

VRATIL, KATHRYN HOEFER, federal judge; b. Manhattan, Kans., Apr. 21, 1949; d. John J. and Kathryn Ruth (Fryer) Hoefer; children: Alison K., John A., Ashley A. BA, U. Kans., 1971, JD, 1975; postgrad., Exeter U., 1971-72. Bar: Kans. 1975, Mo. 1978, U.S. Dist. Ct. Kans. 1975, U.S. Dist. Ct. (we. dist.) Mo. 1978, U.S. Dist. Ct. (ea. dist.) Mo. 1985, U.S. Ct. Appeals (8th cir.) 1978, U.S. Ct. Appeals (10th cir.) 1980, U.S. Ct. Appeals (11th dist.) 1983, U.S. Supreme Ct., 1995. Law clk. U.S. Dist. Ct., Kansas City, Kans., 1975-78; assoc. Lathrop Koontz & Norquist, Kansas City, Mo., 1978-83; ptnr. Lathrop & Norquist, Kansas City, 1984-92; judge City of Prairie Village, Kans., 1990-92. Bd. dirs. Kans. Legal Bd. Svcs., 1991-92; mem. adminstrv. com. Judicial Conf. of the U.S., 2000—. Bd. editors Kans. Law Rev., 1974-75, Jour. Kans. Bar Assn., 1992—. Mem. Kansas City Tomorrow (XIV); bd. trustees, shepherd-deacon Village Presbyn. Ch.; nat. adv. bd. U. Kans. Ctr. for Environ. Edn. and Tng., 1993-95; bd. dirs. Kans. Legal Svcs., 1991-92. Fellow Kans. Bar Foun., Am. Bar Found.; mem. ABA (edtl. bd. Judges Jour. 1996—), Am. Judicature Soc., Nat. Assn. Judges, Fed. Judges Assn., Kans. Bar Assn. (mem. bench bar com., 2000—), Mo. Bar Assn., Kansas City Met. Area Bar Assn., Johnson County Bar Assn., Assn. Women Judges, Lawyers Assn. Kansas City, Supreme Ct. Hist. Soc., Kans. State Hist. Soc., U. Kans. Law Soc. (bd. govs. 1978-81), Kans. U. Alumni Assn. (mem. Kansas City chpt. alumni bd. 1990-92, nat. bd. dirs. 1991-96, bd. govs. Adams Alumni Ctr. 1992-95, mem. chancellor's club 1993—, mem. Williams ednl. fund 1993—, mem. Jayhawks for higher edn. 1993-95), Homestead Country Club Prairie Village (pres. 1985-86), Native Sons and Daus of Kans. (life), Jr. League Wyandotte and Johnson Counties, Order of Coif, Kans. Inn of Ct. (master 1993—, pres. 1999-2000), Phi Kappa Phi. Republican. Presbyterian. Avocations: cycling, sailing. Office: 511 US Courthouse 500 State Ave Kansas City KS 66101-2403

VREE, ROGER ALLEN, lawyer; b. Chgo., Oct. 2, 1943; s. Louis Gerard and Ruby June (Boersma) V.; m. Lauren Trumbull Gartside, Mar. 29, 1969; children: Jonathan Todd, Matthew David. BA, Wheaton Coll., 1965; MA, Stanford U., 1966, JD, 1969. Bar: Ill. 1969, U.S. Dist. Ct. (no. dist.) Ill. 1969. Assoc. Sidley & Austin, Chgo., 1969—75; ptnr. Sidley Austin Brown & Wood, Chgo., 1975—. Mem.: ABA, Univ. Club (Chgo.). Construction, Landlord-tenant, Property, real (including real estate development, water). Office: Sidley Austin Brown & Wood Bank One Plz 10 South Dearborn Chicago IL 60603-2000 E-mail: rvree@sidley.com.

VUKIĆ, ZORAN, lawyer, banking and corporate law consultant; b. Rijeka, Croatia, Apr. 3, 1962; s. Jure and Mila (Sjaus) V.; mem. Gina Kontić, Oct. 15, 1994; children: Luka, Iva, Ema. LLB, U. Rijeka, 1985. Assoc. Sprajc Law Office, Rijeka, 1985-88; ptnr. Sprajc and Vukić, Rijeka, 1989-95; sr. ptnr. Vukić, Jelušić & Šulina, Rijeka, 1996-2000, Vukić, Jelušić Šulina & Stanković, 2001—02; ptnr. Vukić, Jelušić Šulina, Stanković, Jurćan & Jabuka Law Firm, 2002—. Contbr. articles to profl. jours. Mem. Croatian Bar Assn., Internat. Bar Assn., Croatian C. of C. (arbitar permanent arbitration ct. 1997—), Yacht Club Galeb (Kostrena) (sec. 1987). Avocations: sailing, basketball, collecting art. Home: Tizianova 9 51000 Rijeka Croatia Office: Vukić Jelusić Sulina Stanković Jurcan& Jabuka N Tesle 9 51000 Rijeka Croatia E-mail: vukiclaw@ri.tel.hr.

VULEVICH, EDWARD, JR., prosecutor; b. Nov. 5, 1933; s. Edward J. and Minnie R. V.; m. Diane Misko; children: Erin, Jan, John. AB, U. Ala., 1955, JD, 1957. Bar: Ala., U.S. Supreme Ct., U.S. Ct. Appeals (11th cir.) Ala., U.S. Ct. Appeals (5th cir.) Ala. Atty. U.S. Dept. Justice, Mobile, Ala., 1969—, chief civil divsn. Office: US Attys Office 63 S Royal St Ste 1600 Mobile AL 36602-3245*

WAAGE, MERVIN BERNARD, lawyer; b. Spirit Lake, Iowa, May 12, 1944; s. Bernard and Pearl Peterson W.; children: Love Lee, Mark Warren. BA, Northwestern Coll., Roseville, Minn., 1966; MDiv, Southwestern Sem., 1969; JD, So. Methodist U., 1974. Bar: Tex. 1974, U.S. Dist Ct. (no. dist.) Tex. 1974, U.S. Dist. Ct. (ea. dist.) Tex. 1976, U.S. Supreme Ct. 1977, U.S. Tax Ct. 1978, U.S. Ct. Claims, 1978, U.S. Dist. Ct. (we. dist) Tex. 1988, U.S. Ct. Appeals (5th cir.) 1989. Asst. dist. atty. Denton County (Tex.) Atty.'s Office, 1974-76; pvt. practice law Denton, Tex., 1977—. Bankruptcy trustee, 1980-87. Mem. Tex. Bar Assn., Tex. State Bar (v.p. bankruptcy com., 2002-), Tex. Bd. Legal Specialization (cert. in consumer bankruptcy 1986, cert. in bus. bankruptcy 1988). Republican. Baptist. Avocation: singing. Bankruptcy. Office: Waage & Waage LLP 8350 S Stemmons St Denton TX 76210-2424

WAAGE, TORBEN PILEGAARD, lawyer; b. Copenhagen, Mar. 5, 1967; s. Georg Holger and Ruth (Pilegaard) W.; m. Lis Okkels Petersen; children:Georg Holger, Nikolaj, William. LLM, U. London, 1991; JD, U. Copenhagen, 1992. Asst. Danish Parliament, Copenhagen, 1987-90; lawyer Kromann Reumert, Copenhagen, 2000—. Tchr. U. Copenhagen, 1992-96, lectr., 1996—. Office: Kromann Reumert Sundkrogsgade 5 2100 OE Copenhagen Denmark

WACHENFELD, WILLIAM THOMAS, lawyer, foundation executive; b. Orange, N.J., Feb. 9, 1926; s. William A. and Ann (Weir) W.; children: William S., Robin A., John C. AB, Tufts U., 1947; LL.B., Duke U., 1950. Bar: N.J. 1949. Since practiced in Newark; mem. firm Lum, Biunno & Tompkins, 1957-58; pres. Charles Hayden Found., N.Y.C., 1968-97, chmn., 1997-99; prof. law Jersey City divsn. Jersey City divsn. Rutgers U., 1954-56; v.p., assoc. gen. counsel Prudential Ins. Co. Am., 1965-84; of counsel Tompkins, McGuire & Wachenfeld, Newark, 1984-00. Pres. Essex County Park Commn., 1960-65; chmn. bd. trustees Newark Acad., 1972-80; commr. pub. affairs, Orange, 1956-58; mem. N.J. Econ. Devel. Coun., 1980-88, 91-94, Mass. Audubon Coun., 2000—; bd. govs. N.J. Hist. Soc., 1981-83; mem. adv. bd. Wildlife Conservation Soc., 1983-93; trustee Liberty Sci. Ctr., 1988-93. Fellow Am. Bar Found.; mem. ABA, N.J. Bar Assn., Essex County Bar Assn., N.Y. Regional Assn. Grantmakers (bd. dirs. 1992-97), Eastward Ho Country Club, HC Yacht Club (commodore 1992-97). Home: 174 Sea Pine Rd North Chatham MA 02650-1077 Office: Tompkins McGuire & Wachenfeld 4 Gateway Ctr 100 Mulberry St Newark NJ 07102-4004

WACHSMUTH, ROBERT WILLIAM, lawyer; b. Crowell, Tex., Jan. 20, 1942; s. Frederick W. and Dorothy (McKown) W.; m. Karin Lynn Kusiak, Dec. 11, 1999; children: Wendi Leigh, Ashley Beth Bass, Matthew McKown, Daniel Kusiak. BA, U. Tex., 1965, JD, 1966, grad. bus. sch., 1976. Bar: Tex. 1966, U.S. Dist. Ct. (we. dist.) Tex. 1970, U.S. Ct. Appeals (5th cir., 11 cir.) 1975, U.S. Supreme Ct. 1979, U.S. Dist. Ct. (so. dist.) Tex. 1987. Assoc. Foster, Lewis, Langley, Gardner and Banack, San Antonio, 1969-73; of counsel H.B. Zachry Co., San Antonio, 1973-79; ptnr. Johnson, Johnston, Bowlin, Wachsmuth and Vives, San Antonio, 1973-79, Kelfer, Coatney & Wachsmuth, San Antonio, 1979-81, Kelfer, Coatney, Wachsmuth & Saunders, San Antonio, 1981-83, Brock & Kelfer, P.C., San Antonio, 1983-88, Coatney & Wachsmuth, P.C., San Antonio, 1989-92, Gendry, Sprague & Wachsmuth, P.C., San Antonio, 1992-94, The Kleberg Law Firm, P.C., San Antonio, 1994—. Panel arbitrators US Dist Ct. (we. dist.) Tex. Ct., 1985-88; instr. San Antonio Jr. Coll., 1972-74; bd. cert./civil trial law Tex. Bd. Legal Specialization, 1981—; faculty constrn. mgmt. and contrn. exec. program Tex. A&M U. Contbr. articles to profl. jours. Bd. dirs. Halfway House San Antonio, Jr. Achievement. Capt., mil. judge USMCR, 1966-69, Vietnam. Fellow Tex. Bar Found., Coll. of the State Bar; mem. ABA (vice chmn. comms. industry com. antitrust law sect. 1998-2001, steering com. divsn. 8 Forum on Constrn. Industry 1999—), State Bar of Tex. (bd. dirs., treas., sec., vice chmn. constrn. law sect. 1989-92, chmn. 1992-93), Am. Arbitration Assn. (panel of arbitrators, panel of mediators), San Antonio Bar Assn. (chmn. alternative dispute resolution com.), Fed. Bar Assn., Am. Subcontractors Assn. (gen. counsel San Antonio chpt. 1984-92), Assn. Gen. Contractors (gen. counsel San Antonio chpt. 1995—), Chartered Inst. Arbitrators, Plaza Club (social com.), Masons, Scottish Rite, Shriners, Optimists (pres. 1977-78). Republican. Episcopalian. Avocations: hunting, skiing, spectator sports, fishing, golf. Antitrust, General civil litigation, Construction. Office: The Kleberg Law Firm PC 112 E Pecan St Ste 1300 San Antonio TX 78205-1538 E-mail: rwachsmuth@kleberg.com.

WACHTEL, NORMAN JAY, lawyer; b. N.Y.C., June 1, 1941; s. A. Allen and Lillian (Rolnik) W.; m. C. Robin Fixler, June 12, 1969; children: Jonathan, Charles. AB, U. Pa., 1963, LLB, 1966; LLM, Boston U., 1967. Bar: N.Y. 1967. Assoc. Demov, Morris & Hammerling, N.Y.C., 1968-78, ptnr., 1978-87, Rogers & Wells, N.Y.C., 1987-96, of counsel, 1996—2003, Clifford Chance US LLP, N.Y.C., 2003—. Bd. advisors 1st Am. Title Ins. Co. N.Y., 1982—. Author: (chpt.) Real Estate Titles, 1984. Landlord-tenant, Property, real (including real estate development, water). Office: Clifford Chance US LLP 200 Park Ave Ste 5200 New York NY 10166-0005 E-mail: dex1125@aol.com., norman.wachtel@cliffordchance.com.

WADDEL, PATRICK OLYNN, lawyer; b. Tulsa, June 24, 1941; m. Robyn Watson Waddel, May 10, 1987; children: Laura D., Caroline D. Shaw, P. Clayton. BA, U. Tulsa, 1964; LLB, So. Meth. U., 1967. Law clk. U.S. Judiciary, Kansas City, Mo., 1967—69; atty. Haynes & Boone, Dallas, 1969—70, Sneed & Waddel, Tulsa, 1970—72, Waddel and Buzzard, 1972—87, Gable & Grotwals, 1987—97, Sneed Lang, 1998—. Chmn. Tulsa Devel. Authority, 1980—. Avocations: sports, hunting. Corporate, general, Securities, Administrative and regulatory. Office: Sneed Lang 2 W 2d St Tulsa OK 74103 E-mail: pwaddel@sneedlang.com.

WADDELL, PHILLIP DEAN, lawyer; b. Covington, Ky., Nov. 14, 1948; s. Ewell Edward and Sarah Isobel (Dean) W.; m. Jill Annette Tolson, Aug. 23, 1975; children: Nathan Ewell, James Seth. BA, Centre Coll. Ky., 1971; JD, No. Ky. U., 1982. Bar: Ky. 1982, Ohio 1983, Tenn. 1986. V.p., mgr. escrow Eagle Savings Assn., Cin., 1973-83; v.p. Union Planters Nat. Bank, Memphis, 1983-84; sr. v.p., liason First Nat. Bank & Trust Co., Oklahoma City, 1984-86; sr. v.p., sec., gen. counsel First Mortgage Strategies Group, Inc., Memphis, 1986-92; atty. pvt. practice, Memphis, 1992—. Mem. ABA, Am. Judicature Soc., Ky. Bar Assn., Tenn. Bar Assn. Lodges: Kiwanis. Republican. Presbyterian. Commercial, contracts (including sales of goods; commercial financing), Corporate, general, Property, real (including real estate development, water). Home: 9436 Summerlin Cove Memphis TN 38125 Office: 3169 Professional Plz Ste 2 Germantown TN 38138-7917

WADE, EDWIN LEE, author, lawyer; b. Yonkers, N.Y., Jan. 26, 1932; s. James and Helen Pierce (Kinne) W.; m. Nancy Lou Sells, Mar. 23, 1957; children: James Lee, Jeffrey K. BS, Columbia U., 1954; MA, U. Chgo., 1956; JD, Georgetown U., 1965. Bar: Ill. 1965. Fgn. svc. officer U.S. Dept. State, 1956-57; mktg. analyst Chrysler Internat., S.A., Switzerland, 1957-61; intelligence officer CIA, 1961-63; industry analyst U.S. Internat. Trade Commn., 1963-65; gen. atty. Universal Oil Products Co., Des Plaines, Ill., 1965-72; atty. Amsted Industries, Inc., Chgo., 1972-73; chief counsel dept. gen. svcs. State of Ill., Springfield, 1973-75; sr. atty. U.S. Gypsum Co., Chgo., 1975-84; gen. atty. USG Corp., 1985, corp. counsel, 1986, asst. gen. counsel, 1987, corp. sec., 1987-90, corp. sec., asst. gen. counsel, 1990-93; prin. Edwin L. Wade, 1993-95; instr. Roosevelt U., Chgo., 1995-96. Author: (books) Constitution 2000: A Federalist Proposal for the New Century, 2000, Talking Sense at Century's End: A Barbarous Time...Now What?, 2000; editor: Let's Talk Sense, A Pub. Affairs Newsletter, 1994-98. Fellow Chgo. Bar Assn. (life); mem. ABA, Ill. Bar Assn., Am. Philatelic Soc., Royal Philatelic Soc. Can. Constitutional, Corporate, general, Public international. Home: 434 Mary Ln Crystal Lake IL 60014-7257 Office: Let's Talk Sense Publishing Co PO Box 6716 Chicago IL 60680-6716 E-mail: edwade@mymailstation.com.

WADSWORTH, DYER SEYMOUR, retired lawyer; b. N.Y.C., June 16, 1936; s. Seymour and Phoebe Armistead (Helmer) W.; m. Beverley Allen Dunn Barringer, Feb. 2, 1963; children: Sophia, Jennifer. BA, Yale U., 1959; JD, Harvard U., 1962. Bar: N.Y. 1963, Pa. 1979. Assoc. Humes, Andrews & Botzow, N.Y.C., 1962-64; with Inco Ltd. and subs., N.Y.C., 1964-96; asst. gen. counsel Inco Ltd., N.Y.C., 1982-96; pres. Inco U.S., Inc., N.Y.C., 1993-96. Chmn., bd. dirs. Barringer Crater Co., Flagstaff, Ariz., 1996—; chmn., CEO, treas., dir. Cass County Iron Co., Linden, Tex., 1992— Gen. counsel Baseline Fin. Svcs., Inc., N.Y.C., 1997-2000, The Sailors Snug Harbor, Sea Level, N.C., 1987-2000; chmn., bd. dirs. Amsterdam Nursing Home Corp., N.Y.C., 1986-2000; trustee Isaac Tuttle Fund for the Aged, N.Y.C., 1968-96; bd. dirs. Frenchman Bay Conservancy, Hancock, Maine, 1997—. Named Trustee of Yr. N.Y. Assn. Homes and Svcs. for the Aging, 1995. Mem. Meteoritical Soc., Univ. Club, Ivy League Club, Union Club, (N.Y.C.), Pilgrims Soc. (N.Y.C.), Yale Club Suncoast (dir. 2001—, pres. 2002—). Home: 8466 Lockwood Ridge Rd PMB 304 Sarasota FL 34243-2951

WAGEMANS, MARC, lawyer; b. Brussels, May 17, 1947; m. Arielle Van Der Jeken, Sept. 18, 1980; children: Olivier, Marie-Ekristine, Fabienne, Caroline. Degree in law, U. Brussels, 1969; LLM, Harvard U., 1971. Bar: Belgium 1969. Ptnr. Stibbe, Brussels, 1969—. Maj. Belgium Air Force. Alternative dispute resolution, Commercial, contracts (including sales of goods; commercial financing), Corporate, general. Office: Stibbe Rue Henri Waffelaerts 47 1060 Brussels Belgium Fax: 2 5335378.

WAGGONER, JAMES CLYDE, lawyer; b. Nashville, May 7, 1946; s. Charles Franklin and Alpha (Noah) W.; m. Diane Dusenbery, Aug. 17, 1968; children: Benjamin, Elizabeth. BA, Reed Coll., 1968; JD, U. Oreg., 1974. Bar: Oreg. 1974, U.S. Dist. Ct. Oreg. 1975, U.S. Ct. Appeals (9th cir.) 1980, U.S. Tax Ct. 1979, U.S. Supreme Ct. 1979. Clerk to presiding justice Oreg. Supreme Ct., Salem, 1974-75; assoc. Martin, Bischoff & Templeton, Portland, Oreg., 1975-78, ptnr., 1978-82, Waggoner, Farleigh, Wada, Georgeff & Witt, Portland, 1982-89, Davis Wright Tremaine, Portland, 1990—. Contbr. articles to profl. jours. Fulbright scholar U. London, 1968-69. Mem. ABA, Oreg. Bar Assn., Multnomah Bar Assn., Reed Coll. Alumni Assn. (v.p. 1988, pres. 1989, bd. mgmt.) Alzheimers Assn. of Columbia-Willamette (v.p. 1992, pres. 1993), Order Coif, Phi Beta Kappa. Democrat. Avocations: wood turning, calligraphy. Bankruptcy, Commercial, consumer (including collections, credit), Property, real (including real estate development, water). Office: Davis Wright Tremaine 1300 SW 5th Ave Ste 2300 Portland OR 97201-5682

WAGGONER, LAWRENCE WILLIAM, law educator; b. Sidney, Ohio, July 2, 1937; s. William J. and Gladys L. Waggoner; m. Lynne S. Applebaum, Aug. 27, 1963; children: Ellen, Diane. BBA, U. Cin., 1960; JD, U. Mich., 1963; PhD, Oxford (Eng.) U., 1966. Assoc. Cravath, Swaine & Moore, N.Y.C., 1963; prof. law U. Ill., Champaign, 1968-72, U. Va., Charlottesville, 1972—74, U. Mich., Ann Arbor, 1974-84, Lewis M. Simes prof. law, 1987—. Dir. rsch., chief reporter joint editorial bd. for Uniform Trust and Estate Acts, 1986-94, dir. rsch., 1994—, joint editl. bd. uniform trust and estate acts; adviser restatement (2d) of property, 1987-90; reporter restatement (3d) of property, 1990—. Author: Estates in Land and Future Interests in a Nutshell, 1981, 2d edit., 1993, Federal Taxation of Gifts, Trusts, and Estates, 3d edit., 1997, Family Property Law: Wills, Trusts, and Future Interests, 1991, 3d edit., 2002. Served to capt., U.S. Army, 1966-68. Fulbright scholar Oxford U., 1963-65. Mem. Am. Law Inst., Am. Coll. Trust and Estates Counsel, Internat. Acad. Estate and Trust Law. Office: U Mich Law Sch 625 S State St Ann Arbor MI 48109-1215

WAGGONER, MICHAEL JAMES, law educator; b. Evanston, Ill., Sept. 21, 1942; s. Alva Madison and Martha W.; m. Cynthia Lynn Goff, Mar. 17, 1984; children: Julia Lauren, Thomas Charles. AB, Stanford U., 1964; LLB, Harvard U., 1967. Bar: D.C. 1968. Assoc. Wilmer, Cutler & Pickering, Washington, 1971-73; assoc. prof. law U. Colo., Boulder, 1973—, assoc. dean, 1998—. Served to capt. USAF, 1968-71. Home: 930 Crestmoor Dr Boulder CO 80303-3117 Office: U Colo Law Sch 401 UCB Boulder CO 80309-0401 E-mail: waggonem@spot.colorado.edu.

WAGNER, ANNICE MCBRYDE, judge; BA, law degree, Wayne State U. With Houston and Gardner; gen. counsel Nat. Capital Housing Authority; people's counsel D.C.; assoc. judge Superior Court D.C., 1977-90, D.C. Ct. Appeals, 1990—, now chief judge. Mem. teaching team, trial advocacy workshop Harvard U. Office: Dist of Columbia Court of Appeals 500 Indiana Ave NW Ste 6000 Washington DC 20001-2131

WAGNER, ARTHUR WARD, JR., lawyer; b. Birmingham, Ala., Aug. 13, 1930; s. Arthur Ward and Lucille (Lockheart) W.; m. Ruth Shingler, May 11, 1957; children: Celia Wagner Minter, Julia Wagner Dolce, Helen Wagner McAfee. BSBA, U. Fla., 1954, JD, 1957. Bar: Fla. 1957, U.S. Dist. Ct. (so. dist.) Fla. 1957, U.S. Dist. Ct. (mid. dist.) Fla. 1975. Ptnr. Wagner & McAfee, P.A., West Palm Beach, Fla., 1959-2000; ret., 2000—. Lectr. in field. Author: Art of Advocacy: Jury Selection, 1981; co-author: Anatomy of Personal Injury Lawsuit I & II, 1968 and 1981. Mem. 15th Jud. Nominating Com., Palm Beach City, 1979—82, 4th Dist. Nominating Commn., Palm Beach City, 1982—86; mem. pres.'s coun. U. Fla.; vestry Holy Trinity Parish, v.p., 2002—; bd. dirs., pres.-elect U. Fla. Found., 1996—. Fellow Internat. Acad. Trial Lawyers, Am. Coll. Trial Lawyers, Internat. Soc. Barristers, Am. Bd. Trial Advs.; mem. Assn. Trial Lawyers Am. (pres. 1975-76, hon. life trustee Roscoe Pound Found.), So. Trial Lawyers Assn. (pres. 1991), U. Fla. Law Coll. Alumni (mem. bd. govs.). Democrat. Episcopalian. Administrative and regulatory, General civil litigation, Personal injury (including property damage).

WAGNER, BURTON ALLAN, lawyer; b. Milw., June 13, 1941; s. Irwin and Jennie (Oxman) W.; m. Georgia Olchoff, Aug. 29, 1964; children: Andrew, Laura. BBA in Acctg, U. Wis., 1963, JD, 1966, MA in Health Services Adminstrn, 1976. Bar: Wis. 1966. Assoc. legal counsel U. Wis., 1968-74; asst. to vice chancellor, legal counsel U. Wis. Hosps., 1974-77; asst. sec. Wis. Dept. Health and Social Services, 1977-83, adminstr. div. community services, 1979-83; clin. assoc. prof. health adminstrn. U. Wis.; ptnr. Thomas Harnisch & Wagner, Madison, 1983-85, Whyte & Hirschboeck, Madison, 1985-90; ptnr. (of counsel) Katten Muchin and Zavis, Madison, 1990-93; ptnr. Reinhart Boerner Van Deuren Norris & Rieselbach, Madison, 1993—. Served with USAR, 1966-68, Vietnam. Decorated Bronze Star. Mem. Soc. Law and Medicine, Wis. Bar Assn., Dane County Bar Assn. Jewish. Office: PO Box 2018 Madison WI 53701-2018 E-mail: bwagner@reinhartlaw.com.

WAGNER, CHRISTOPH, lawyer; b. Feb. 4, 1962; m. Claudia Thamm; 1 child, Josephine Elsa. JD, U. Berlin, 1986, LLD, 1990. Bar: Berlin 1991. Assoc. Hogan & Hartson Raye, Berlin. Mem. German Media Ownership Control Commn. Mem.: Internat. Bar Assn. Avocation: sailing. Communications. Office: Hogan & Hartson Raye Potsdamer Platz 1 10785 Berlin Germany Office Fax: +49 30 726 115 102.

WAGNER, CURTIS LEE, JR., judge; b. Nov. 8, 1928; m. Jeanne E. Allen (dec.); children: Curtis L. III, Rex A. Student, Tenn. Poly. Inst., 1947-49; LLB, U. Tenn., 1951. Bar: Tenn. 1952. Assoc. Kramer, Dye, McNabb and Greenwood, Knoxville, Tenn., 1951-54; atty.-adv. gen. crimes and fraud sect. Criminal Divsn. Dept. Justice, Washington, 1954-56; trial atty. Dept. Justice, Washington, 1954-60; assigned to Ct. of Claims sect. Civil Divsn., Washington, 1956-60; spl. asst. comms., transp. and utilities JAG Dept. Army, Washington, 1960-64; chief Regulatory Law Divsn., Washington, 1964-74; adminstrv. law judge FERC, Washington, 1974-79, chief adminstrv. law judge, 1979—. Mem. civilian lawyer career com., 1960-74; chmn. JAG incentive awards com. 1960-74; mem. Army Staff Awards Bd., 1964-74, Army Environ. Policy Council, 1972-74. Dist. commr. Nat. Capital Area coun. Boy Scouts Am., 1967-69; mem. Bd. Govts. Watergate of Alexandria Condo, 1996—; commr. Alexandria Redevel. and Pub. Housing Commn., 1996-2000. Decorated Meritorious Civilian Svc. award, Exceptional Civilian Svc. award; recipient citation for outstanding performance Dept. Army, 1961-74, Scouter's Tng. award Boy Scouts Am., 1965, Scoutmaster's Key, 1966, Commr.'s Key, 1968, Commr.'s Arrowhead Honor, 1966, Silver Beaver award 1969. Mem. Order of Arrow, Annapolis Yacht (parliamentarian) Club. Methodist. Office: Fed Energy Regulatory Commn 888 1st St NE Washington DC 20426-0002 E-mail: curtis.wagner@ferc.gov.

WAGNER, DAVID JAMES, lawyer; b. Cleve., Feb. 7, 1946; m. Martha Wilson, June 22, 1979; 1 child, Diana Jane. BS, USAF Acad., 1969; JD, Georgetown U., 1973. Bar: Colo. 1973, U.S. Supreme Ct. 1975, U.S. Dist. Ct. of Colo. 1973, U.S. Tax Ct. 1974. Asst. assoc. gen. counsel Presdl. Clemency Bd., Washington, 1974-75; sec., gen. counsel Cablecomm-Gen. Inc., Denver, 1975-77; adj. prof. law Metro. State Coll., Denver, 1975-80; atty., mng. prin. Wagner & Waller, P.C., Denver, 1977-84; chmn. bd. GILA Comm., Inc., Denver, 1987; pvt. practice David Wagner & Assocs., P.C., Englewood, Colo., 1984—. Dir. Colo. Sch. of Mines Found., 1999, pres., 2002. Editor Am. Criminal Law Rev., Georgetown U. Law Sch., 1972-73. Trustee Kent Denver Sch., Cherry Hills Village, Colo., 1990-96, treas., 1992, pres., 1992-96; treas., dir. Denver Chamber Orch., 1979-81; dir. Leadership Denver Assn., 1978-80; trustee Colo. Sch. Mines, 1999. Capt. USAF, 1973-75. Republican. Episcopalian. Securities. Office: David Wagner & Assocs PC Penthouse 8400 E Prentice Ave Ph Englewood CO 80111-2927

WAGNER, FREDERICK WILLIAM (BILL WAGNER), lawyer; b. Daytona Beach, Fla., Apr. 13, 1933; s. Adam A. and Nella (Schroeder) W.; m. Ruth Whetstone; children: Alan Frederick, Darryl William, Thomas Adam. BA, U. Fla., 1955, LLB with honors, 1960. Bar: Fla. 1960, U.S. Supreme Ct. 1967, D.C. 1989; cert. civil trial lawyer, Fla. Bar; cert. aviation lawyer, Fla. Bar. Pvt. practice law, Miami, Fla., 1960-63, Orlando, Fla., 1963-65, Tampa, Fla., 1965—; ptnr. Nichols, Gaither, Beckham, Colson, Spence & Hicks, Tampa, Fla., 1965-67; ptnr. shareholder Wagner, Vaughan & McLaughlin (P.A. and predecessor names), 1967—. Mem. Gov.'s Judicial Nominations Commn., 1971-72, Constnl. Judicial Nominations Commn., 1972-75; mem. Fla. Bd. Bar Examiners, 1974-77, emeritus mem., 1995—; chmn. Civil Procedure Rules Com. Fla. Bar, 1977-78; bd. govs. Fla. Bar, 1978-83; trustee Roscoe Pound Inst., 1984-92; mem. civil jury instrn. com. Fla. Supreme Ct. Contbr. articles to profl. jours. 1st lt. USAF, 1955-57. Fellow Am. Bar Found., Am. Coll. Trial Lawyers, Internat. Acad. Trial Lawyers, Am. Bd. Trial Advs.; mem. Assn. Trial Lawyers Am. (bd. govs. 1973-80, 84-89, chmn. pub. affairs dept. 1984-89, treas. 1982-84, v.p. 1986-87, pres.-elect 1987-88, pres. 1988-89), Am. Inns of Ct. Found. (bd. trustees 1996-2000), Acad. Fla. Trial Lawyers (bd. dirs. 1965-84, pres. 1972-73), Bay Area Trial Lawyers Assn. (v.p. 1966-68), Am. Law Inst. (coun. 1993—), Lawyer-Pilots Bar Assn., Fla. Bar Found., U. Fla. Alumni Assn., Nat. Bd. Trial Advocacy (cert. civil), Assn. Personal Injury Lawyers, Australian Plaintiff Laywers Assn., Pan European Orgn. Personal Injury Lawyers, So. Trial Lawyers Assn., Nat. Transp. Safety Bd. Bar Assn., Tampa Bay Trail Lawyers Assn. Democrat. Methodist. Aviation, Personal injury (including property damage), Product liability. Home: 901 Mariner Way Tampa FL 33602-5759 Office: Wagner Vaughan & McLaughlin 601 Bayshore Blvd Ste 910 Tampa FL 33606-2786 E-mail: Bill@WagnerLaw.com.

WAGNER, GARY ALAN, lawyer; b. Queens, NY, June 20, 1952; s. Charles Wagner and Lillian Marie Paretys; m. Susan Wagner, May 30, 1981; 1 child, Jessica Nicole. BS, Manhattan Coll., 1974; JD, John Marshall Law Sch., 1978. Bar: NY 1979, Ill. 1978. Asst. state's atty. Cook County State's Atty. Office, Chgo., 1978; assoc. Furey & Mooney, Hempstead, NY, 1979—85; sr. ptnr. Farley, Holohan, Wagner & Doman, Mineola, NY, 1986—96, Wagner, Doman, & Leto, Mineola, NY, 1996—. Mem.: ATLA, ABA, Nassau-Suffolk Trial Lawyers, NY State Bar Assn. Avocations: music, sports, reading. Personal injury (including property damage), General civil litigation. Office: Wagner Doman & Leto 227 Mineola Blvd Mineola NY 11501 Office Fax: 516-742-1204.

WAGNER, JOHN LEO, lawyer, former magistrate judge; b. Ithaca, N.Y., Mar. 12, 1954; s. Paul Francis and Doris Elizabeth (Hoffschneider) W.; m. Marilyn Modin, June 18, 1987. Student, U. Nebr., 1973-74; BA, U. Okla., 1976, JD, 1979. Bar: Okla. 1980, Calif. 1999, U.S. Dist. Ct. (we. dist.) Okla. 1980, U.S. Dist. Ct. (no. and ea. dists.) Okla. 1981, U.S. Dist. Ct. (ctrl. dist.) Calif. 2000, U.S. Ct. Appeals (10th cir.) 1982. Assoc. Franklin, Harmon & Satterfield Inc., Oklahoma City, 1980-82; ptnr. Franklin, Harmon & Satterfield, Inc., Oklahoma City, 1982; assoc. Kornfeld, Franklin & Phillips, Oklahoma City, 1982-85, ptnr., 1985; magistrate judge U.S. Dist. Ct. No. Dist. Okla., Tulsa, 1985-97; dir. Irell & Manella LLP Alt. Dispute Resolution Ctr., Newport Beach, Calif., 1997—. Pres. U. Okla. Coll. Law Assn., 1991-92. Fellow Am. Coll. Civil Trial Mediators, Internat. Acad. Mediators, Fed. Magistrate Judge's Assn. (dir. 10th cir. 1987-89); mem. ABA, 10th Cir. Edn. Com., Okla. Bar Assn., Council Oak Am. Inn of Cts. (pres. 1992-93), Jud. Conf. U.S. (com. ct. adminstrn. and case mgmt. 1992-97), CPR-Georgetown Commn. Ethics and Standards in ADR. Republican. Office: Irell & Manella LLP Alt Dispute Resolution Ctr 840 Newport Ctr Dr Ste 450 Newport Beach CA 92660-6321 E-mail: jwagner@irell.com., usmag1@cox.net.

WAGNER, JOSEPH HAGEL, lawyer; b. Balt., June 4, 1947; s. Herman B. and Mary Louise (Hagel) W.; m. Hilary Reuss Becton, June 10, 1972; children: James Becton, Christopher Lowther. BA, Villanova U., 1969; JD, Syracuse U., 1972. Editor Bucks County Law Reporter, 1983-85, asst. editor, 85-86. Chmn. ch. com. ARC Bloodmobile, 1984-87; v.p. Bucks County Estate Planning Council, 1986-87, pres., 1987-88; former pres., v.p. New Britain Borough Civic Assn. Served to capt. USAR, 1972-81. Mem. Bucks County Bar Assn. (treas. 1983-85, bd. dirs. 1981-83). Republican. Roman Catholic. Estate planning, Probate (including wills, trusts), Property, real (including real estate development, water). Home: 25 Linda Ln Warrington PA 18976-1044 Office: 332 N Main St Doylestown PA 18901-3715

WAGNER, KENNETH LYNN, lawyer; b. McPherson, Kans., Oct. 13, 1956; s. Francis D. and Mary V. (Van Buren) W.; m. Lida Jane McNearney, Oct. 22, 1983; 1 child, Elizabeth Ann. BS in Journalism, U. Kans., 1979, JD, 1983; LLM, Georgetown U., 1987. Bar: Mo. 1983, Ill. 1984, D.C. 1985. Atty. div. corp. fin. SEC, Washington, 1984-86, spl. counsel, 1986-88; assoc. Schlafly, Griesedieck, Ferrell & Toft, St. Louis, 1983-84, Stinson, Mag & Fizzell, Kansas City, Mo., 1988-89, Arent, Fox, Kintner, Plotkin & Kahn, Washington, 1989-94; assoc. counsel Banc One Corp., 1994-98; sr. counsel Goodrich Corp., 1998—. Mem. ABA, Am. Soc. Corp. Secs., Mo. Bar Assn. Republican. Corporate, general, Finance, Securities. Office: Goodrich Corp 2730 W Tyvola Rd Charlotte NC 28217-4578 E-mail: kenneth.wagner@goodrich.com.

WAGNER, LESLIE, lawyer; b. Houston, July 18, 1953; d. Jacob and Geraldine (Harris) W. BA cum laude, U. Tex., 1975; JD, U. Houston, 1980. Bar: Tex. 1980, U.S. Dist. Ct. (so. dist.) Tex. 1981. Trial atty. civil rights EEOC, Houston, 1981-84; pvt. practice Houston, 1984-85, 87-88; dir. law placement U. Houston Law Ctr., 1985-87; employee rels. atty, sr. employee rels. analyst The Meth. Hosp. System, Houston, 1988—97; employee rels. cons. Prudential Fin., Houston, 1997—. Cons. EEOC, Houston, 1984—; v.p., treas. Houston Soc. Healthcare Human Resources Adminstrns., 1995-97; dir., gen. counsel Hematology/Oncology Assistance Resource Coalition, 1995-2002. Editor: U. Houston Law Rev., 1979, assoc. editor, 1980. Mem. health and edn. com. Jewish Cmty. Ctr., Houston, 1983-85; polit. cons., Houston, 1984-85. Named Honors Day Honoree U. Tex., 1971; Arts and Sciences scholar U. Tex., 1971-74. Mem. ABA (com. employee and labor rels. 1983-85, employment rights com. gen. practice sect. 1986), ATLA, Houston Bar Assn., Tex. Young Lawyers Assn. (job fair com.), Tex. Hosp. Assn., Tex. Hosp. Assn., Soc. of Human Resources Mgmt., Nat. Assn. Law Placement (careers com. 1986-87, minority placement com. 1987), Am. Studies Assn., Houston Festival Dancers (treas. 1976-77), Eta Phi Sigma. Democrat. Avocations: creative writing, dance, reading. General practice, Labor (including EEOC, Fair Labor Standards Act, labor-management relations, NLRB, OSHA). Home: 5407 Wigton Dr Houston TX 77096-4005 Office: Prudential Ins Co 435 B I FM 1092 #402 Stafford TX 77477-5494 E-mail: leslie.wagner@prudential.com.

WAGNER, MARK ALAN, lawyer; b. Papua New Guinea, Feb. 9, 1966; s. Merlyn Dean and Janet Bertha W. BS, U. Utah, 1988, JD, 1992. Bar: Utah. Jud. clk. U.S. Dist. Ct. Utah, Salt Lake City, 1993; from assoc. to shareholder Parr Waddoups Brown Gee & Loveless, Salt Lake City, 1994-2000; shareholder Van Cott, Bagley, Corwall & McCarthy, Salt Lake City, 2000—. Staff atty. Freedom of Info. Hotline Soc. Profl. Journalists, Salt Lake City, 1994-2000. Mng. editor Utah Law Rev., Salt Lake City, 1991-92. Com. Salt Lake City Mayor's Task Force on Access, 1997-00; vol. Am. Cancer Soc., 1987, 95—. Mem. ABA, ATLA, Fed. Bar Assn., Utah Trial Lawyers Assn., Fed. Bar Assn., AIA, Order of Coif. General civil litigation, Computer, Pension, profit-sharing, and employee benefits. Office: Van Cott Bagley Cornwall & McCarthy 50 S Main St Ste 1600 Salt Lake City UT 84144

WAGNER, SANDRA M. lawyer; b. Utica, N.Y., Feb. 9, 1952; BA, St. Lawrence U., Canton, N.Y., 1974; JD, U. San Diego, 1977. Bar: Calif. 1981, U.S. Dist. Ct. (no. dist.) Calif. 1981, U.S. Tax Ct. 1981. Assoc. Law Offices Timothy A. Tosta, San Francisco, 1981—83, Law Offices Jesse W. Jack, San Jose, Calif., 1983—87; pvt. practice Cupertino, Calif., 1987—89, San Diego, 1990—98; ptnr. Froman and Wagner LLP, San Diego, 1999—. Editor: (book) AILA's 12th Annual California Chapters Conference Handbook, 1999. Cub Scout leader Boy Scouts Am., San Diego, 1991—97, Boy Scout leader Solana Beach, Calif., 1994—. Recipient Scout Leader Recognition award, Del Mar Solana Beach Optimist Club, 1993, 1994, 1998, Dist. award Merit, Boy Scouts Am., 1996, Silver Beaver award, 2002. Mem.: Am. Immigration Lawyers Assn. (vice chair San Diego 2000—02, chair San Diego chapt. 2002—), Order of Arrow (mem. election com. 1999—), Rotary (mem. svc. com. 2000—), Sigma Delta Pi. Avocations: camping, backpacking, rock climbing, music. Immigration, naturalization, and customs, Corporate, general. Office: Froman and Wagner LLP 4370 La Jolla Village Dr Ste 400 San Diego CA 92122 Office Fax: 858-546-4706. Business E-Mail: smwsmw@attglobal.net.

WAGNER, THOMAS JOSEPH, lawyer, insurance company executive; b. Jackson, Mich., June 29, 1939; s. O. Walter and Dorothy Ann (Hollinger) Wagner; m. Judith Louise Bogardus, Jan. 15, 1961; children: Ann Louise, Mark Robert, Rachel Miriam. BA, Earlham Coll., 1957; JD, U. Chgo., 1965. Bar: Ill. 1968, U.S. Supreme Ct. 1975. Asst. to gov. State of Ill., Springfield, 1966—67, legal counsel, adminstrv. asst. to treas., 1967—70; adminstrv. asst. U.S. Senator Adlai E. Stevenson Washington, 1970—77; sr. v.p. govt. affairs divsn. Am. Ins. Assn., Washington, 1977—80; staff v.p. Ina Corp., Washington; v.p., chief counsel Property Casualty Group, CIGNA Corp., Phila., 1986—88, sr. v.p., corp. sec., 1988—91, exec. v.p., gen. counsel, 1992—2001; ret., 2001. Former trustee Eisenhower Exch. Fellowships, Inc.; past chmn. Phila. Crime Commn.; former bd. dirs. Inst. Law and Econs., U. Pa. Pub. Svc. fellow, Syracuse U., 1965—66. Mem.: ABA (bus. law com.), U.S.-Pacific Econ. Cooperation Coun., Am. Corp. Counsel Assn. Insurance, Legislative.

WAGONER, ANNA MILLS, prosecutor; BA, Agnes Scott Coll.; JD, Wake Forest U. Assoc. Woddson, Linn, Sayers, Lawther, Short and Wagoner, 1985—87, ptnr., 1987—90; judge Rowan County Dist. Ct., 1990—2001; U.S. atty. mid. dist. U.S. Dept. Justice, NC, 2001—. Office: PO Box 1858 Greensboro NC 27402*

WAGONER, DAVID EVERETT, lawyer; b. Pottstown, Pa., May 16, 1928; s. Claude Brower and Mary Kathryn (Groff) W.; children: Paul R., Colin H., Elon D., Peter B., Dana F.; m. Jean Morton Saunders; children: Constance A., Jennifer L., Melissa J. BA, Yale U., 1950; LLB, U. Pa., 1953. Bar: D.C. 1953, Pa. 1953, Wash. 1953. Law clk. U.S. Ct. Appeals (3d cir.), Pa., 1955-56; law clk. U.S. Supreme Ct., Washington, 1956-57; ptnr. Perkins & Coie, Seattle, 1957-96. Panel mem. of arbitration forum worldwide including People's Republic of China, B.C. Internat. Comml. Arbitration Ctr., Hong Kong Internat. Arbitration Centre, Asian/Pacific Ctr. for Resolution of Internat. Bus. Disputes and the Ctr. for Internat. Dispute Resolution for Asian/Pacific Region. Mem. sch. com. Mcpl. League Seattle and King County, 1958— , chmn., 1962-65; mem. Seattle schs. citizens coms. on equal ednl. opportunity and adult vocat. edn., 1963-64; mem. Nat. Com. Support Pub. Schs.; mem. adv. com. on community colls., to 1965, legislature interim com. on edn., 1964-65; mem. community coll. adv. com. to state supt. pub. instrn., 1965; chmn. edn. com. Forward Thrust, 1968; mem. Univ. Congl. Ch. Council Seattle, 1968-70; bd. dirs. Met. YMCA Seattle, 1968; bd. dirs. Seattle Pub. Schs., 1965-73, v.p., 1966-67, 72-73, pres., 1968, 73; trustee Evergreen State Coll. Found., chmn. 1986-87, capitol campaign planning chmn.; trustee Pacific NW Ballet, v.p. 1986. Served to 1st lt. M.C., AUS, 1953-55 Fellow Am. Coll. Trial Lawyers (mem. ethics com., legal ethics com.), Chartered Inst. Arbitrators, Singapore Inst. Arbitrators; mem. ABA (chmn. standing com. fed. jud. imprisonment, chmn. appellate advocacy com., mem. commn. on separation of powers and jud. independence), Wash. State Bar Assn., Seattle-King County Bar Assn., Acad. Experts, Swiss Arbitration Assn., Comml. Bar Assn. London, Nat. Sch. Bds. Assn. (bd. dirs., chmn. coun. Big City bds. edn. 1971-72), English-Speaking Union (v.p. Seattle chpt. 1961-62), Chi Phi. Alternative dispute resolution. Office: Internat Arbitration Chambers US BankCtr 1420 5th Ave Fl 22 Seattle WA 98101-4087 Home: 3916 E Pine St Seattle WA 98122-3517

WAGONER, WALTER DRAY, JR., lawyer; b. New Haven, Dec. 25, 1942; s. Walter D. and Mariana (Parcells) W.; m. Rosa Nilda Morales, Jan. 22, 1980; children— David, William Carlos, Brenda, Lisa. B.A., Yale U., 1965, LL.B., 1970. Bar: Conn. 1971, U.S. Dist. Ct. Conn. 1971. Staff atty. New Haven Legal Assistance Assn., 1970-74, mng. atty., 1974-76, dir. legal edn., 1976-78; sole practice, New Haven, 1978— . Chmn., New Haven City Commn. Cultural Affairs, 1977-79; trustee Conn. Public TV, 1977-83; trustee U.S. Bankruptcy Ct. for Dist. of Conn., 1983-87. Mem. Conn. Bar Assn. Democrat. Club: Loizenos (hon.). Bankruptcy. Office: 840 Elm St New Haven CT 06511-4010

WAHLEN, EDWIN ALFRED, lawyer; b. Gary, Ind., Mar. 12, 1919; s. Alfred and Ethel (Pearson) W.; m. Alice Elizabeth Condit, Apr. 24, 1943 (div. 1983); children: Edwin Alfred, Virginia Elizabeth, Martha Anne; m. Elizabeth L. Corey, Nov. 23, 1984. Student, U. Ala., 1936-38; AB, U. Chgo., 1942, JD, 1948. Bar: Ill. 1948. Practiced in, Chgo., 1948—; mem. firm Haight, Goldstein & Haight, 1948-55; ptnr. Goldstein & Wahlen, 1956-59, Arvey, Hodes, Costello & Burman (and predecessor), 1959-91, Wildman, Harrold, Allen & Dixon, 1992—. Author: Soldiers and Sailors Wills: A Proposal For Federal Legislation, 1948. Served to 2d lt. AUS, 1942-46. Decorated Silver Star medal, Bronze Star medal. Mem. ABA, Ill. Bar Assn., Chgo. Bar Assn., Order of Coif, Phi Beta Kappa, Phi Alpha Delta. Commercial, contracts (including sales of goods; commercial financing), Corporate, general, Property, real (including real estate development, water). Home: 1250 Breckenridge Ct Lake Forest IL 60045-3875 Office: 225 W Wacker Dr Chicago IL 60606-1224

WAHOSKE, MICHAEL JAMES, lawyer; b. Ripon, Wis., June 4, 1953; children: Jennifer, John. BA with highest honors, U. Notre Dame, 1975, JD summa cum laude, 1978. Bar: Minn. 1978, U.S. Dist. Ct. Minn. 1979, U.S. Ct. Appeals (7th cir.) 1979, U.S. Ct. Appeals (8th and 9th cirs.) 1980, U.S. Ct. Appeals (10th cir.) 1982, U.S. Supreme Ct. 1982, U.S. Ct. Appeals (6th cir.) 1988, U.S. Ct. Appeals (fed. cir.) 1989, U.S. Ct. Appeals (D.C. cir.) 1992, U.S. Ct. Appeals (4th cir.) 1994, U.S. Ct. Appeals (11th cir.) 1996, Supreme Ct. of Winnebago Tribe of Nebr., 1996. Law clk. to judge Luther M. Swygert U.S. Ct. Appeals (7th cir.), Chgo., 1978-79; law clk. to chief justice Warren E. Burger U.S. Supreme Ct., Washington, 1979-80; assoc. Dorsey & Whitney, Mpls., 1980-85, ptnr., 1986—. Adj. prof. law U. Minn., Mpls., 1981-83. Exec. editor U. Notre Dame Law Rev., 1977-78; co-editor: Freedom & Education: Pierce v. Society of Sisters Reconsidered, 1978. Recipient Vol. Recognition award Nat. Assn. Attys. Gen., 1993, Supreme Ct. Reception hons. State and Local Legal Ctr., 1991, 92, 93, 95. Fellow: Am. Acad. Appellate Lawyers; mem.: FBA, ABA (standing com. on Amicus Briefs 1997—2002), Hennepin County Bar Assn., Minn. Bar Assn., U.S. Ct. Appeals (8th cir.) Bar Assn., Phi Beta Kappa. Appellate. Office: Dorsey & Whitney LLP Ste 1500 50 S Sixth St Minneapolis MN 55402-1498

WAINWRIGHT, CARROLL LIVINGSTON, JR., lawyer; b. N.Y.C., Dec. 28, 1925; s. Carroll Livingston and Edith Katherine (Gould) W.; m. Nina Walker, July 2, 1948; children: Delos Walker, Mark Livingston. AB, Yale U., 1949; LL.B., Harvard U., 1952. Bar: N.Y. 1953. With Milbank, Tweed, Hadley & McCloy (and predecessor), N.Y.C., 1952-58, 60-62, ptnr., 1963—. Asst. counsel Gov. N.Y., 1959-60; mem. State Commn. Jud. Conduct, 1974-83; hon. dir. U.S. Trust Corp.; hon. trustee U.S. Trust Co. N.Y.; adj. prof. law Washington and Lee U. Sch. Law, 1991-97; mem. governing bd. N.Y. Community Trust, 1991—. Hon. trustee Am. Mus. Natural History; trustee Edward John Noble Found.; trustee Boys' Club N.Y., 1966—, pres., 1986-94, hon. trustee, 1999; vice-chmn. Cooper Union Advancement Sci. and Art, 1988-95, hon. trustee; trustee Ch. Pension Fund and Affiliates, 1974-91, treas. 1974-78; mem. univ. coun. Yale U., 1978-81; mem. vestry Trinity Ch., N.Y.C., 1983-90; dir. Greater Yellowstone Coalition, 1992-98, 99—. Served with USMCR, 1943-46. Mem. ABA, N.Y. State Bar Assn., Assn. Bar City N.Y. (treas. 1970-73, v.p. 1975-76), Union Club, Down Town Assn. (pres. 1985-92), Maidstone Club (pres. 1970-73). Probate (including wills, trusts), Charitable organizations. Home: 57 Dunemere Ln East Hampton NY 11937-2705 Office: Milbank Tweed Hadley & McCloy 1 Chase Manhattan Plz Fl 46 New York NY 10005-1401

WAINWRIGHT, DALE V. judge; b. Tenn. B, Howard U., 1983; JD, U. Chgo., 1988. With Andrews & Kurth, Houston, Haynes & Boone, Houston; dist. judge. Harris County, 1999—2002; justice Tex. Supreme Ct., 2002—. Fellow: Houston Bar Found., Tex. Bar Found.; mem.: ABA, Houston Bar Assn., State Bar Tex. Office: Tex State Supreme Ct PO Box 12248 Austin TX 78711 Office Fax: 512-463-1365.*

WAINWRIGHT, GEORGE, judge; b. Wilson County, N.C., Dec. 10, 1943; s. George Sr. and Susan Wainwright; m. Carol McChesney; children: Kennon, Ashton. Undergrad. degree, U. N.C., 1966; JD, Wake Forest U., 1984. Agribus. and real estate positions, Wilson, 1966-81; with Wheatly, Wheatly, Nobles & Weeks, Beaufort, N.C., 1986-90; apptd. judge Dist. Ct., 1991; resident Superior Ct. judge for N.C. Jud. Dist. 3B, 1994; justice Supreme Ct. N.C., 1999—. With USCGR, 1966-72 Morehead scholar, 1966. Mem. N.C. Bar Assn., Lookout Rotary Club. Presbyterian. Office: Supreme Ct NC Justice Bldg PO Box 1841 Raleigh NC 27602-1841

WAISANEN, CHRISTINE M. lawyer, writer; b. Hancock, Mich., May 27, 1949; d. Frederick B. and Helen M. (Hill) W.; m. Robert John Katzenstein, Apr. 21, 1979; children: Jeffrey Hunt, Erick Hill. BA with honors, U. Mich., 1971; JD, U. Denver, 1975. Bar: Colo. 1975, D.C. 1978. Labor rels. atty. U.S. C. of C., Washington, 1976-79; govt. rels. specialist ICI Americas, Inc., Wilmington, Del., 1979-87; dir. cultural affairs City of Wilmington, 1987; founder, chief writer Hill, Katzenstein & Waisanen, 1988—. Chmn. Delaware State Coastal Zone Indsl. Control Bd., 1993—. Mem. Fed. Bar Assn., Jr. League of Wilmington (v.p. 1985-86), Women's Rep. Club of Wilmington (bd. dirs. 1988-93), U. Mich. Club of Del. (pres. 1999—). Republican. Presbyterian. Administrative and regulatory, Environmental, Land use and zoning (including planning). Home: 1609 Mt Salem Ln Wilmington DE 19806-1134

WAITT, ROBERT KENNETH, lawyer; b. Seattle, Apr. 25, 1931; s. Charles Kenneth and Willa E. (Ryan) W.; m. Diane Dallam, Dec. 7, 1933; children: Mark Robert, Julie Lynn Reid. Student, Wash. State Coll., 1949-50, 52-53; LLB, Gonzaga U., 1957, JD, 1967. Bar: Wash. 1957, U.S. Supreme Ct., 1990. Assoc. Morrissey, Hedrick & Dunham, Seattle, 1957-59; ptnr. Benson & Waitt, Seattle, 1959-60; assoc. Walsh & Margolis, Seattle, 1960-62; ptnr. Murray, Dunham & Waitt, Seattle, 1962-81, Waitt, Johnson & Martens, Seattle, 1981-90, of counsel, 1990—99; retired, 1999. Judge King County Dist. Ct., Issaquah Dist., 1965-81, City of Issaquah Mcpl. Ct., 1961-81; chmn. City Issaquah Civil Service Commn., 1963-69; chmn. Gonzaga Law Council, Gonzaga U. Sch. Law, Spokane, Wash., 1983-85; regent Gonzaga U., 1982-88. With USMC, 1950-52. Mem. Wash. Bar Assn., Bermuda Dunes Country Club, Tradition Golf Club. State civil litigation, Insurance, Professional liability. Home: 3815 E Lake Sammamish Shorelane SE Sammamish WA 98075

WAKEFIELD, STEPHEN ALAN, lawyer; b. Olney, Ill., Oct. 18, 1940; s. George William and Blanche Lucille (Sheesley) W.; children from previous marriage: Melissa Hawley, Tracy Wakefield, Stephen Alan Jr.; m. Patricia Ann McGuire, Nov. 29, 1980; 1 child, Mark. LLB, U. Tex., Austin, 1965. Bar: Tex. 1965. Assoc. Baker & Botts, Houston, 1965-70, ptnr., 1974-84, sr. ptnr., chmn. energy dept., 1986-89; atty. Federal Power Commn., Washington, 1970-72; dep. asst. sec. energy programs Dept. Interior, Washington, 1972-73, asst. sec. energy and minerals, 1973-74; asst. adminstr. Fed. Energy Office, Washington, 1973-74; vice chmn., gen. counsel United Energy Resources, Inc., Houston, 1985-86; pres. United Gas Pipe Line Co., Houston, 1985-86; exec. v.p. MidCon Corp., 1985-86; gen. coun. Dept. Energy, Washington, 1989-91; ptnr. Akin, Gump, Strauss, Hauer & Feld, L.L.P., 1991-97; sr. v.p., gen. coun. Southern Co., 1997-2001; sr. counsel Southern Co. , 2001—. Bd. visitors M.D. Anderson Cancer Ctr.; bd. govs. Robert Packard Ctr. ALS Rsch. Johns Hopkins U. Mem. Tex. Bar Assn., Capital City Club (Atlanta). FERC practice, Private international, Utilities, public. Home: 201 Blackland Dr NW Atlanta GA 30342-4405 Office: Southern Company Ste 1400 270 Peachtree St NW Atlanta GA 30303-1263 E-mail: sawakefield@mindspring.com., sawakefi@southernco.com.

WALBAUM, ROBERT C. lawyer; b. Springfield, Ill., Nov. 13, 1933; s. George Crum and Mary Emma (Taylor) W.; m. Anita P. Walbaum, Aug. 6, 1960; children: John Taylor, Charles Robert. Student, Bradley U., Peoria, Ill., 1951-53; BS in Commerce, U. Ill., Urbana, 1955; JD, Washington, St. Louis, 1960. Bar: Ill. 1961, U.S. Dist. Ct. (so. dist.) Ill. 1964, U.S. Ct. Appeals (7th cir.) 1973, U.S. Supreme Ct. 1989. With Chgo. Title and Trust

Co., 1960-61; asst. states atty. County of Sangamon, Springfield, Ill., 1961-63; pvt. practice Springfield, 1963—. Atty. City Springfield, 1964-69, Village Pleasant Plains, Ill., 1970-93; tech. advisor Ill. Dept. Law Enforcement, 1969-73; counsel Springfield Park Dist., 1984—; dir. Pleasant Plains State Bank, 1982-95. Mem. Sangamon County Bd. Suprs., 1962-75, chmn., 1974; bd. dirs. Washington St. Mission, Springfield, 1966-90, pres. 1983-86. Served with U.S. Army, 1955-57. Mem. ABA, Ill. State Bar Assn., Sangamon County Bar Assn., Illini Country Club, Sangamo Club, Am. Bus. Club (Springfield). Republican. Epsicopalian. Banking, Corporate, general, Probate (including wills, trusts). Address: 1049 W Woodland Ave Springfield IL 62704-2863 E-mail: walbaumlaw@aol.com.

WALCH, SPENCER DAVID, lawyer; b. Burbank, Calif., Sept. 23, 1967; s. Victor Lloyd and Carole Foster Walch; m. Melissa Renae Heym, Oct. 21, 1995; children: Ethan Taylor, Carter Jameson. BS in Acctg., Brigham Young U., Provo, Utah, 1992; JD, Brigham Young U., 1995. Bar: Calif. 1996, U.S. Dist. Ct. (ctrl. dist.) Calif. 1996, U.S. Tax Ct. 1997, U.S. Supreme Ct. 2001. Lawk clk./assoc. Harney Law Offices, L.A., 1993—97; assoc. Law Offices of Victor L. Walch, Pasadena, 1997—2000; ptnr. Walch & Walch, LLP, Pasadena, 2000—. Bd. dirs. Kids' Cmty. Clinic of Burbank, Calif., 2001—, So. Calif. Conservatory of Music, La Canada, 2001—03. Mem.: Rotary Club of L.A. Probate (including wills, trusts), Taxation, general, Estate taxation. Office: Walch & Walch LLP 301 N Lake Ave 7th Fl Pasadena CA 91101-1807

WALCHER, ALAN ERNEST, lawyer; b. Chgo., Oct. 2, 1949; s. Chester R. and Dorothy E. (Kullgren) W.; children: Dustin Alan, Michael Alan, Christopher Ray. BS, U. Utah, 1971, cert. in internat. rels., 1971, JD, 1974. Bar: Utah 1974, U.S. Dist. Ct. Utah 1974, U.S. Ct. Appeals (10th cir.) 1977, Calif. 1979, U.S. Dist. Ct. (cen. dist.) Calif. 1979, U.S. Ct. Appeals (9th cir.) 1983, U.S. Dist. Ct. (ea., no., and so. dists.) Calif. 1994. Sole practice, Salt Lake City, 1974-79; ptnr. Costello & Walcher, L.A., 1979-85, Walcher & Scheuer, 1985-88, Ford & Harrison, 1988-91, Epstein Becker & Green, 1991—; judge pro tem Los Angeles Mcpl. Ct., 1986-91; dir. Citronia, Inc., Los Angeles, 1979-81. Trial counsel Utah chpt. Common Cause, Salt Lake City, 1978-79. Robert Mukai scholar U. Utah, 1971. Mem. Soc. Bar and Gavel (v.p. 1975-77), ABA, Fed. Bar Assn., Los Angeles County Bar Assn., Century City Bar Assn., Assn. Bus. Trial Lawyers, Phi Delta Phi, Owl and Key. Federal civil litigation, State civil litigation, Government contracts and claims. Home: 17933 Sunburst St Northridge CA 91325-2848 Office: Epstein Becker & Green Ste 1650 Two Embarcadero Ctr San Francisco CA 94111-5994 E-mail: awalcher@ebglaw.com., alan1002@earthlink.net.

WALD, BERNARD JOSEPH, lawyer; b. Bklyn., Sept. 14, 1932; s. Max and Ruth (Mencher) W.; m. Francine Joy Weintraub, Feb. 2, 1964; children— David Evan, Kevin Mitchell. B.B.A. magna cum laude, CCNY; J.D. cum laude, NYU, 1955. Bar: N.Y. 1955, U.S. Dist. Ct. (so. dist.) N.Y. 1960, U.S. Dist. Ct. (ea. dist.) N.Y. 1960, U.S. Ct. Appeals (2d cir.) 1960, U.S. Supreme Ct. 1971. Mem. Herzfeld & Rubin, P.C. and predecessor firms, N.Y.C., 1955— . Mem. ABA, N.Y. State Bar Assn., Assn. Bar City N.Y., N.Y. County Lawyers Assn. Commercial, contracts (including sales of goods; commercial financing), Corporate, general, Private international. Office: Herzfeld & Rubin PC 40 Wall St Ste 5400 New York NY 10005-2301 E-mail: bwald@herzfeld-rubin.com.

WALD, GERALD BARRY, lawyer; b. Feb. 9, 1944; s. Jack and Ruth (Fox) W.; m. ROberta Schneider, June 18, 1967; children: Lauren, Katherine. BA, Colgate U., 1966; JD, NYU, 1969. Bar: N.Y. 1970, U.S. Dist. Ct. (so. dist.) N.Y. 1971, U.S. Ct. Appeals 92nd cir.) 1972, U.S. Dist. Ct. (ea. dist.) N.Y. 1975, Fla. 1976, U.S. Dist. (so. dist.) Fla. 1976, U.S. Dist. (so. dist.) Fla. 1976, U.S. Cit. Appeals (5th cir.) 1976, U.S. Supreme Ct. 1976, U.S. Ct. Appeals (11th cir.) 1981. Law clk U.S. Dist. Ct. (so. dist.), N.Y., 1969-70; assoc. Hughes, Hubbard & Reed, N.Y.C., 1970-75; assoc., then ptnr. Paul, Landy, Beiley & Yacos, Miami, Fla., 1976-78, Murai, Wald, Biondo & Moreno, Miami, 1979—. Mem. panel arbitrators Am. Arbitration Assn. Mem. ABA, Fla. Bar, Dade County Bar Assn., Assn. Trial lawyers Am., Spellman-Hoeveler Inns of Ct. Federal civil litigation, State civil litigation. Home: 10745 SW 72nd Ave Miami FL 33156-3815 Office: 25 SE 2d Ave Suite 900 Miami FL 33131 E-mail: gwald@mwbm.com.

WALD, PATRICIA MCGOWAN, retired federal judge; b. Torrington, Conn., Sept. 16, 1928; d. Joseph F. and Margaret (O'Keefe) McGowan; m. Robert L. Wald, June 22, 1952; children: Sarah, Douglas, Johanna, Frederica, Thomas. BA, Conn. Coll., 1948; LLB, Yale U., 1951; HHD (hon.) , Mt. Vernon Jr. Coll., 1980; LLD (hon.) , George Washington Law Sch., 1983, CUNY, 1984; LLD (hon.) , Notre Dame U., John Jay Sch. Criminal Justice, Mt. Holyoke Coll., 1985, Georgetown U., 1987, Villanova U., Amherst Coll., N.Y. Law Sch., 1988, Colgate U., 1989, Hofstra U., 1991; LLD (hon.) , Hoffstra U., 1991; LLD (hon.) , New Eng. Coll., 1991, Vermont Law Sch., 1995, Yale U., 2001. Bar: D.C. 1952. Clk. to Hon. Jerome Frank U.S. Ct. Appeals, 1951—52; assoc. Arnold, Fortas & Porter, Washington, 1952—53; mem. D.C. Crime Commn., 1964—65; atty. Office of Criminal Justice, 1967—68, Neighborhood Legal Svc., Washington, 1968—70; co-dir. Ford Found. Project on Drug Abuse, 1970, Ctr. for Law and Social Policy, 1971—72, Mental Health Law Project, 1972—77; asst. atty. gen. for legis. affairs U.S. Dept. Justice, Washington, 1977—79; judge U.S. Ct. Appeals (D.C. cir.), 1979—99, chief judge, 1986—91; judge Internat. Criminal Tribunal for Former Yugoslavia, The Hague, Netherlands, 1999—2001. Author: Law and Poverty, 1965; co-author: Bail in the United States, 1964, Dealing with Drug Abuse, 1973; contbr. articles to profl. jours.; bd. editors: ABA Jour., 1978—86. Trustee Ford Found., 1972—77, Phillips Exeter Acad., 1975—77, Agnes Meyer Found., 1976—77, Conn. Coll., 1976—77; active Carnegie Council on Children, 1972—77. Mem.: ABA-Ctrl. and Ea. European Law Inst. (exec. bd. 1994—99), Inst. Justice Initiative, Am. Acad. Arts and Scis., Am. Law Inst. (coun. mem. 1979—, exec. com. 1985—99, 2d v.p. 1988—93, 1st v.p. 1993—98), Open Soc. Inst. (chair justice instrn. 2002—, chair), Phi Beta Kappa. Office: 2101 Connecticut Ave NW Washington DC 20008

WALDECK, JOHN WALTER, JR., lawyer; b. Cleve., May 3, 1949; s. John Walter Sr. and Marjorie Ruth (Palenschat) W.; m. Cheryl Gene Cutter, Sept. 10, 1977; children: John III, Matthew, Rebecca. BS, John Carroll U., 1973; JD, Cleve. State U., 1977. Bar: Ohio 1977. Product applications chemist Synthetic Products Co., Cleve., 1969-76; assoc. Arter & Hadden, Cleve., 1977-85, ptnr., 1986-88, Porter, Wright, Morris and Arthur, Cleve., 1988-90, ptnr. in charge, 1990-96; ptnr. Walter & Haverfield, Cleve., 1996—. Bd. advisors Litigation Mgmt., Inc., 2000—. Chmn. Bainbridge Twp. Bd. Zoning Appeals, Chagrin Falls, Ohio, 1984-94; trustee Greater Cleve. chpt. Lupus Found. Am., 1978-91, sec., 1979-86; trustee LeBlond Housing Corp., Cleve., 1990-96, sec., 1996, Univ. Circle, Inc., 1993-97, Fairmount Ctr. for Performing and Fine Arts, Novelty, Ohio, 1993-96, sect., 1994-95; bd. dirs. Geauga County Mental Health Alcohol and Drug Addiction Svc. Bd., Chardon, Ohio, 1988-97, treas., 1991-93, vice-chmn., 1993-95, chmn., 1995-97; mem. bd. advisors Palliative Care Svcs., Cleve. Clinic Cancer Ctr., 1989-91. Mem. Ohio State Bar Assn. (real property sect. bd. govs. 1992), Greater Cleve. Bar Assn. (real property, corp. banking sect, co-chair real estate law inst. 1990, 95, 96). Roman Catholic. Avocations: beekeeping, gardening, jogging. Corporate, general, Finance, Property, real (including real estate development, water). Home: 18814 Rivers Edge Dr W Chagrin Falls OH 44023-4968 Office: Walter & Haverfield 50 Public Square 1300 Terminal Tower Cleveland OH 44113 E-mail: jwaldeck@walterhav.com.

WALDMAN, DANIEL M. lawyer; b. 1945; BA, Franklin & Marshall Coll.; JD, Georgetown U., 1971. Bar: NJ. Ptnr. Waldman & Moriarty, Red Bank, NJ. Mem.: Assn. County Bar Pres., Monmouth Bar Assn. (former pres.), NJ Bar Assn. (pres. 2001—02). General civil litigation, Family and matrimonial, Criminal. Office: 212 Maple Ave Red Bank NJ 07701

WALDO, JAMES CHANDLER, lawyer; b. Seattle, Oct. 23, 1948; s. Burton Chandler and Margaret (Hoar) W.; m. Sharon B. Barber; children: Sara K., William K., John J. Grad., Whitman Coll., 1970; JD, Willamette U., 1974. Bar: Wash. 1974, U.S. Ct. Appeals (9th cir.) 1976. Exec. asst. Dept. of Labor, Washington, 1974-76; asst. U.S. atty. Justice Dept., Seattle, 1976-79; of counsel ESTEP & LI, Seattle, 1979-80; ptnr. Gordon, Thomas, Honeywell, Malanca, Peterson & Daheim LLP, Seattle, 1981—. Chmn. N.W. Renewable Resources Ctr., Seattle, 1984-97, Wash. State Energy Strategy Com., 1991-93; spl. counsel on Water for Gov., 2001—. Trustee Western Wash. U., 1981-93. Recipient Outstanding Alumnus of Yr. Whitman Coll., 1994, Dir.'s award Wash. Dept. Fisheries, 1986, Pres.'s award Assn. Wash. Bus., 1988, Outstanding Citizen award Western Assn. Fish & Wildlife Agys., 1987. Republican. FERC practice, Environmental, Government contracts and claims. Office: Gordon Thomas Honeywell Malanca Peterson & Daheim LLP PO Box 1157 Tacoma WA 98401-1157

WALDRON, JONATHAN KENT, lawyer; b. Washington, Feb. 11, 1949; s. Russell Lee and Ruth Magdalena Waldron; m. Janet Amy Roltsch, Dec. 8, 1973; children: Nathan Jay, Nicole Lee. BS in English, USCG Acad., 1971; JD, U. Miami, 1981. Bar: Fla. 1981, D.C. 1990. Comdr. USCG, 1971-91; sr. counsel Marine Spill Response Corp., Washington, 1991-95; ptnr. Blank Rome, Washington, 1996—. Recipient Schneider award Dept. Transp., 1990. Mem. Maritime Law Assn. Avocation: tennis. Administrative and regulatory, Environmental, Private international. Home: 3302 Lauren Oaks Ct Oak Hill VA 20171-1742 Office: Blank Rome Ste 1100 600 New Hampshire Ave NW Washington DC 20037-2485

WALDRON, KENNETH LYNN, lawyer; b. Cape Girardeau, Mo., Oct. 18, 1941; s. Leonard Vernal and Edna Marion (Baskerville) W.; children: Leonard, Matthew, Charles. Student, Westminster Coll., 1959-61; BS, U. Mo., 1963, JD, 1966. Bar: Mo. 1966, U.S. Dist. Ct. (ea. dist.) Mo. 1968, U.S. Ct. Appeals (8th cir.) 1971, U.S. Supreme Ct. 1975. Salesman Nat. Biscuit Co., various locations, 1963-66; assoc. Buerkle & Lowes, Jackson, Mo., 1966-71; ptnr. Waldron & Assocs., Jackson, 1971-91. Pres., CEO Eagle Environ. Products, Inc.; pres. Quail Springs Farm and Kennels, Inc., Stonewall Enterprises, Inc. Served to capt. U.S. Army, 1966-68. Decorated 2 Legions of Merit; named one of Outstanding Young Men in Am., 1972, 74, 76. Mem. Mo. Bar Assn., Assn. Trial Lawyers Am., Mo. Assn. Trial Attys., Am. Soc. Law and Medicine, Nat. Inst. Mcpl. Law Officers, Jackson Jaycees (Mo. legal counsel 1972-74, disting. service award 1968, 74), Am. Legion, Rotary. Republican. Baptist. Avocations: tennis, golf, hunting, bird dog field trials, music (vocal & guitar), songwriting. General civil litigation, Personal injury (including property damage). Home: PO Box 270 Jackson MO 63755-0270 Office: 417 N High St PO Box 270 Jackson MO 63755-0270 E-mail: kwaldron@eaglesystem.biz.

WALDROP, NORMAN ERSKINE, JR., lawyer; b. Gadsden, Ala., Feb. 27, 1946; s. Norman E. Sr. and Margaret Alice Waldrop; m. Margaret Ann Waldrop, Sept. 13, 1969; children: Margaret Carson, Norman Erskine III. BS, Auburn U., 1968; JD, U. Ala., 1971. Bar: Ala. 1971. Trial atty., ptnr. Armbrecht, Jackson LLP, Mobile, Ala., 1971—. Mem. Ala. Judicial Inquiry Commn., Montgomery, 1994-2003; chmn. so. dist. Ala. adv. bd., Mobile, 1992-96; mem. Ala. Permanent Code Commn. Capt. USAR Transp. Svc., 1971-77, Mobile. Mem. Ala. Bar Assn., Mobile County Bar Assn., Nat. Assn. R.R. Trial Counsel, Am. Bd. Trial Advocates, Maritime Law Assn., Fedn. Ins. and Corp. Counsel, Am. Inns of Ct., Order of Coif, Omicron Delta Kappa. Avocations: tennis, golf. Personal injury (including property damage), Professional liability. Office: Armbrecht Jackson LLP PO Box 290 Mobile AL 36601-0290

WALES, GWYNNE HUNTINGTON, retired lawyer; b. Evanston, Ill., Apr. 18, 1933; s. Robert Willett and Solace (Huntington) W.; m. Janet McCobb, Feb. 8, 1957; children— Thomas Gwynne, Catherine Anne, Louise Carrie. AB, Princeton U., 1954; JD, Harvard U., 1961. Bar: N.Y. 1962. Assoc. White & Case, N.Y.C., 1961-69, ptnr., 1969-2000, resident ptnr. Brussels, 1969-75, Ankara, Turkey, 1998-2000. Served with USN, 1954-58. Mem.: Am. Law Inst. (life), Round Hill (Greenwich, Conn.), Mountain Lake Colony House (Lake Wales, Fla.). Private international, Corporate taxation, Personal income taxation. Home: 25 Mountain Lake Lake Wales FL 33898

WALES, ROSS ELLIOT, lawyer; b. Youngstown, Ohio, Oct. 17, 1947; s. Craig C. and Beverly (Bromley) W.; m. Juliana Fraser, Sept. 16, 1972; children: Dod Elliot, James Craig. AB, Princeton U., 1969; JD, U. Va., 1974. Bar: Ohio 1974, U.S. Dist. Ct. (so. dist.) Ohio 1974, U.S. Ct. Appeals (5th cir.) 1979. Assoc. Taft, Stettinius & Hollister, Cin., 1974-81, ptnr., 1981—. Pres. U.S. Swimming, Inc., Colorado Springs, 1979-84, U.S. Aquatic Sports, Inc., Colorado Springs, 1984-88, 94-98; dir. Child Welfare League Am., 2003-. Pres. Cin. Active to Support Edn., 1987-88; chmn. sch. tax levy campaign, Cin., 1987; trustee The Childrens Home Cin., 1987—, v.p., 1995-98, pres., 1998-2002; bd. sec. Cin. State Tech. and C.C., 1995-98, vice-chmn., 1998-2000, chair 2000-02; pres. Cin. Arts Sch., Inc., 2000-01; sec. Greater Cin. Arts and Edn. Ctr., 1996—; mem. U.S. Anti-Doping Agy., Colo. Springs. Mem. ABA, Ohio Bar Assn., Cin. Bar Assn., Internat. Swimming Fedn. of Lausanne, Switzerland (sec. 1988-92, v.p. 1992-2000). Presbyterian. Corporate, general, Health, Private international. Office: 425 Walnut St Ste 1800 Cincinnati OH 45202-3923 E-mail: wales@taftlaw.com.

WALKE, GEARY LYNN, judge; b. Stephensville, Nfld., Can., Jan. 3, 1951; s. Emil Paul and Joyce Walke; m. Barbara Ann Cain, Mar. 18, 1972; children— Justin Paul, Collin Robert. B.A., U. Okla., 1973; J.D., Oklahoma City U., 1975. Bar: Okla. 1976, U.S. Dist. Ct. (we. dist.) Okla. 1976, U.S. Ct. Appeals (10th cir.) 1980, U.S. Supreme Ct. 1981. Editorial asst. Okla. Hist. Soc., Oklahoma City, 1974-75; legal intern Legal Aid Western Okla., Oklahoma City, 1975-76; ptnr. Coleman, Walke & Briggs, Del City, Okla., 1976—; spl. judge Dist. Ct. Oklahoma County, 2000—. Chmn. bd. dirs. Hope Community Mental Health Ctr., Oklahoma City, 1980-82; mem. accreditation com. Rose State Coll., Midwest City, Okla., 1984— ; chmn. Del City Bd. Adjustment, 1979— . Mem. ABA, Okla. Jaycees (state legal counsel 1980-81), Del City Area C. of C. (pres. 1984), Okla. Trial Lawyers Assn., Assn. Trial Lawyers Am., Okla. Bar Assn. Democrat. Presbyterian. Home: 32 N Bradbury Dr Edmond OK 73034 Office: Oklahoma County 321 Park Ave Rm123 Oklahoma City OK 73102

WALKER, ANDREW DOUGLAS, lawyer, solicitor; b. Liverpool, Eng., May 6, 1945; s. Malcolm Douglas and Jean Catherine Walker; m. Hilary Georgina Walker, Mar. 10, 1993. MA, Exeter Coll., Oxford, Eng., 1966. Trainee solicitor Wilkinson Kimbers & Staddon, London, 1968—70, solicitor, 1970—71, Lovell, White & King, London, 1971—78, ptnr., 1975—82, Hong Kong, 1982—87, mng. ptnr. London, 1987—88, Lovell White Durrant, London, 1988—93, ptnr., 1993—96; sr. ptnr. Lovell White Durrant (now Lovells), London, 1996—. Product liability. Office: Lovels Atlantic House Holdorn Viaduct London EC1A 2FG England

WALKER, BETTY STEVENS, lawyer; b. N.Y.C., Feb. 3, 1943; d. Randolph Blakney and Anne (Stevens) Wood; m. Paul Thomas Walker, Aug. 27, 1942; children: Camarf, Tarik, Kumi. BA in Polit. Sci. and History, Spelman Coll., 1964; JD, Harvard U., 1967. Bar: U.S. Dist. Ct. (DC) 1981, U.S. Ct. Appeals (DC cir.) 1977, U.S. Supreme Ct. 1996. Coord. southern schs. Legal Def. and Ednl. Fund, N.Y.C., 1964; asst. prof. polit. sci. Shaw U., Raleigh, N.C., 1968-69, faculty fellow, 1969-70; corp. atty. Southern Railway Co., Washington, 1974-77; exec. asst. to adminstr. Farmers Home Adminstrn. USDA, Washington, 1977-81; assoc. Walker & Walker Assoc., P.C., Washington, 1981—. Democrat. Mem. African Meth. Ch. Personal injury (including property damage). Office: Walker & Walker Assoc PC 2807 18th St NW Washington DC 20009-2205

WALKER, CLARENCE WESLEY, lawyer; b. Durham, N.C., July 19, 1931; s. Ernie Franklin and Mollie Elizabeth (Cole) W.; m. Ann-Heath Harris, June 5, 1954; children: Clare Ann, Wesley Gregg. AB, Duke U., 1953, LL.B., 1955. Bar: N.C. 1955. Assoc. Mudge Stern Baldwin & Todd, 1955-59; ptnr. Kennedy, Covington, Loddell & Hickman, Charlotte, N.C., 1961—. Bd. dirs. Lawyers Mut. Liability Ins. Co., Legal Services Corp. N.C., Oakwood Homes Corp. Glendale Group, Ltd.; lectr. N.C. Bar Found. Continuing Legal Edn. Insts., N.C. Jud. Planning Com., 1978-79; pres. Pvt. Adjudication Found. Chmn. bd. mgrs. Charlotte Meml. Hosp. and Med. Ctr., 1981-87; trustee N.C. Ctrl. U., 1979-83; vice-chmn. Charlotte-Mecklenburg Hosp. Authority, 1988-99; adv. bd. Ctrl. Piedmont Paralegal Sch.; trustee Carolinas Healthcare Found., Charlotte Country Day Sch., 1977-81; state chmn. Nat. Found. March of Dimes, 1968-70; chmn. Charlotte Park and Recreation Commn., 1970-73; bd. dirs. Charlotte Symphony, 1965-71, Bethlehem Ctr., 1975-77, N.C. Recreators Found., 1973-75; adv. bd. Charlotte Children's Theatre, 1972; bd. dirs. Charlotte C. of C., 1970-72; bd. visitors Duke U. Law Sch.; dir., gen. campaign chmn. United Way Ctrl. Carolinas, 1985. Fellow Am. Bar Found.; mem. N.C. Bar Assn. (pres. 1978-79, gov. 1971-75), ABA (state del. 1980-89, assembly del. 1989-97, bd. govs. 1997-2000, chair audit com. 2000—) 26th Jud. Dist. Bar Assn., Mecklenburg Bar Found. (trustee), Am. Law Inst., Order of Coif, Phi Eta Sigma, Phi Beta Kappa. Democrat. Methodist. Corporate, general, Utilities, public, Securities. Home: 1047 Ardsley Rd Charlotte NC 28207-1815 Office: Kennedy Covington Lobdell & Hickman Hearst Tower 47th Fl 214 N Tryon St Charlotte NC 28202

WALKER, CRAIG MICHAEL, lawyer; b. Vt., 1947; m. Patricia A. Magruder; two children. BA, Williams Coll., 1969; JD, Cornell U., 1972. Bar: N.Y. 1973, U.S. Dist. Ct. (so. dist.) N.Y. 1975, U.S. Ct. Appeals (2d cir) 1975, U.S. Supreme Ct 1976. Assoc. Alexander & Green, N.Y.C., 1972-80, ptnr., 1980-86, chmn. litigation dept., 1985-86; ptnr. Walter, Conston, Alexander & Green P.C., N.Y.C., 1987-89, Rogers & Wells LLP, N.Y.C., 1990-99, Clifford Chance Rogers & Wells LLP, NYC, 2000—02; spl. trial counsel Clifford Chance US LLP, NYC, 2002—03. Contbr. author: New York Forms of Jury Instruction, 1992; contbr. articles to profl. jours. Fellow Am. Bar Found.; mem. ABA, N.Y. State Bar Assn., Def. Rsch. Inst., Fed. Bar Coun. Democrat. Antitrust, Securities, Technology.

WALKER, FRANCIS JOSEPH, lawyer; b. Aug. 5, 1922; s. John McSweeney and Sarah Veronica (Meechan) W.; m. Julia Corinne O'Brien, Jan. 27, 1951; children: Vincent Paul, Monica Irene Hylton, Jill Marie Nudell, John Michael, Michael Joseph, Thomas More. BA, St. Martin's Coll., 1947; JD, U. Wash., 1950. Bar: Wash. Asst. atty. gen. State of Wash., 1950-51; pvt. practice Olympia, Wash., 1951—. Gen. counsel Wash. Cath. Conf., 1967-76. Lt. (j.g.) USNR, 1943-46; PTO. Commercial, consumer (including collections, credit), Probate (including wills, trusts), Estate taxation. Home and Office: 2723 Hillside Dr SE Olympia WA 98501-3460 E-mail: fjwalker1@msn.com.

WALKER, GEORGE KONTZ, law educator; b. Tuscaloosa, Ala., July 8, 1938; s. Joseph Henry and Catherine Louise (Indorf) W.; m. Phyllis Ann Sherman, July 30, 1966; children: Charles Edward, Mary Neel. BA, U. Ala., 1959; LLB, Vanderbilt U., 1966; AM, Duke U., 1968; LLM, U. Va., 1972; postgrad. (Sterling fellow), Law Sch. Yale U., 1975-76. Bar: Va. 1967, N.C. 1976. Law clk. U.S. Dist. Ct., Richmond, Va., 1966-67; assoc. Hunton, Williams, Gay, Powell & Gibson, Richmond, 1967-70; pvt. practice Charlottesville, Va., 1970-71; asst. prof. Law Sch. Wake Forest U., Winston-Salem, N.C., 1972-73, assoc. prof. Law Sch., 1974-77, prof. Law Sch., 1977—, mem. bd. advisors Divinity Sch., 1991-94; Charles H. Stockton prof. internat. law U.S. Naval War Coll., 1992-93. Vis. prof. Marshall-Wythe Sch. Law, Coll. William and Mary, Williamsburg, Va., 1979-80, U. Ala. Law Sch., 1985; cons. Naval War Coll., 1976—, Nat. Def. Exec. Res., 1991—, Naval War Coll., Internat. Law Dept. Adv. Bd., 1993—. Author: The Tanker War, 1980-88, 2000; contbr. articles to profl. jours. With USN, 1959-62, capt. USNR, ret. Woodrow Wilson fellow, 1962-63; decorated Order of the long Leaf Pine; recipient Joseph Branch Alumni Svc. award, Wake Forest, 1988, Meritorious Unit Commendation, 1992-93; named Hon. Atty. Gen. N.C., 1986. Mem.: ABA, Internat. Inst. Humanitarian Law, Maritime Law Assn., Am. Law Inst., Am. Judicature Soc., Internat. Law Assn. (exec. com. Am. br. 2001—), Am. Soc. Internat. Law (exec. coun. 1988—91), N.C. Bar Assn. (v.p. 1997—98), Va. Bar Assn., Order of Barristers (hon.), Piedmont Club, Phi Delta Phi, Sigma Alpha Epsilon, Phi Beta Kappa, Order of the Coif (hon.). Democrat. Episcopalian. Home: 3321 Pennington Ln Winston Salem NC 27106-5439 Office: Wake Forest U Sch Law PO Box 7206 Winston Salem NC 27109-7206

WALKER, GRAHAM RICHARD, international legal consultant; b. London, Jan. 21, 1959; s. Jack J. and Ruth F. H. Walker; m. Kristina Mary Thompson, July 18, 1958; children: Helena K. S., Thomas C. M. BA with 1st class honors, Manchester U., Eng., 1982; LLM, Cambridge U., Eng., 1984; JD, Inns of Ct. Sch. of Law, London, 1985. Barrister: Bar of Eng. & Wales 1985, Solicitor: Supreme Ct. of Eng. & Wales 1992, High Ct. of Hong Kong 1995, bar: Colo. (Bar) 2000. Barrister Inner Temple, Bar of Eng. & Wales, London, 1985—86; ptnr. Walker Enterprises LLLP, Boulder, Colo., 2000—; corp. fin. exec. Schroders, London, 1986—87; investment banker Samuel Montagu, London, 1987—89; sr. mgmt. group Brit. Telecom plc, London, 1989—90; barrister/assoc. solicitor Ince & Co, London, Great Britain and Northern Ireland, 1990—95; sr. assoc. solicitor Holman Fenwick & Willan, Hong Kong, 1995—96; cons. solicitor Jewkes Chan & Ptnrs., Hong Kong, 1996—2000; dir./ptnr. Asia Bus. Consulting LLC, Boulder, Colo., 2000—; vice pres./internat. legal cons. English & Continental (SW) Properties, Inc., Boulder, Colo., 2000—. Office: English & Continental Property Group 3100 Arapahoe Ave Ste 501 Boulder CO 80303 Office Fax: 303-402-1202. E-mail: grw@grw-kmw.com.

WALKER, IRVING EDWARD, lawyer; b. Balt., Jan. 31, 1952; s. Bertram and Mildred (Shapiro) W.; children: Brandon Harris, Aaron Seth, Emily Celeste. BA, Duke U., 1973; JD, U. Md., 1978. Bar: Md. 1978, U.S. Dist. Ct. Md. 1978, U.S. Ct. Appeals (4th cir.) 1980, U.S. Supreme Ct. 1995, U.S. Ct. Appeals (3d cir.) 2001. Assoc. Frank, Bernstein, Conaway & Goldman, Balt., 1978-85, ptnr., 1986-91; prin. Miles & Stockbridge, Balt., 1991-2001; ptnr. Saul Ewing LLP, Balt., 2001—. Chair Bankruptcy & Creditors Rights Group, 1991-2000. Contbg. author: Bankruptcy Deskbook, 1986. Bd. dirs. Jewish Cmty. Ctr. Greater Balt., 1986-88, Temple Emanuel of Balt., Inc., 1996-2002. Mem. ABA, Md. Bar Assn., Bar Assn. Balt. City (chmn. bankruptcy and bus. law com. 1989-90), Am. Bankruptcy Inst., Bankruptcy Assn. Dist. Md. (pres. 1992-93, chmn. Balt. chpt. 1989-91), Order of Coif. Avocations: soccer, weightlifting. Bankruptcy, Federal civil litigation. Office: Saul Ewing LLP 100 S Charles St 15th Fl Baltimore MD 21201 E-mail: iwalker@saul.com.

WALKER, JOHN LOCKWOOD, lawyer; b. Atlanta, Sept. 3, 1952; s. James William and Doris (Camp) W.; m. Caroline Asher Walker, Jan. 16, 1952; children: Ann Caroline, John Lockwood Jr., Elizabeth Davis, Lindsay Eleise. BA, Duke U., 1974, JD, 1977. Atty. legal div. bd. govs. FRS, Washington, 1977-79; assoc. Simpson Thacher & Bartlett, N.Y.C., 1979-84; ptnr. Simpson, Thacher & Bartlett, N.Y.C., 1984—. Mem. Fin. Svcs. Vol. Corps (dir., pres.), Coun. on Fgn. Rels., Met. Club of Washington, Univ. Club (N.Y.C.), Chevy Chase (Md.) Club, Bedford (N.Y.) Golf and Tennis

Club. Democrat. Episcopalian. Banking, Corporate, general, Securities. Office: Simpson Thacher & Bartlett 425 Lexington Ave Fl 11 New York NY 10017-3954 E-mail: JWalker@stblaw.com.

WALKER, JOHN MERCER, JR., federal judge; b. N.Y.C., Dec. 26, 1940; s. John Mercer and Louise (Mead) W.; m. Cristy West, June 20, 1980 (div. Apr. 1983); m. Katharine Kirkland, Feb. 14, 1987. BA, Yale U., 1962; JD, U. Mich., 1966. Bar: N.Y. 1969, U.S. Dist. Ct. (so. dist.) N.Y. 1971, U.S. Ct. Appeals (2d cir.) 1972, U.S. Supreme Ct. 1977, U.S. Ct. Appeals (D.C. cir.) 1982. Maxwell Sch. Pub. Adminstrn. fellow, state counsel Republic of Botswana, Africa, 1966-68; assoc. Davis, Polk and Warwell, N.Y.C., 1969-70; asst. U.S. atty. U.S. Dist. Ct. (so. dist.) N.Y., N.Y.C., 1971-75; assoc. to ptnr. Carter, Ledyard and Milburn, N.Y.C., 1975-81; asst. sec. enforcement ops. Dept. Treasury, Washington, 1981-85; judge U.S. Dist. Ct. (so. dist.) N.Y., 1985-89, U.S. Ct. Appeals (2nd cir.), 1989—, chief judge, 2000—. Adj. prof. NYU Law Sch., 1995—; gen. counsel Nat. Coun. on Crime and Deliquency, N.Y.C., 1977-81; chmn. Fed. Law Enforcement Tng. Ctr., Washington, 1981-85; spl. counsel Adminstrv. Conf. U.S., Washington, 1986-92; mem. budget com. jud. conf. Inst. Jud. Adminstrn., 1992—, dir., 1992—. Del. Rep. Nat. Conv., Detroit, 1980. With USMCR, 1963-67. Recipient Alexander Hamilton award Sec. of Treas., Washington, 1985, Secret Service Honor award, 1985. Mem. ABA, D.C. Bar Assn., Assn. Bar City of N.Y., Fed. Judges Assn. (pres. 1993-95). Republican. Episcopalian. Office: US Cir Ct 157 Church St New Haven CT 06510-2100

WALKER, JONATHAN LEE, lawyer; b. Kalamazoo, Mar. 8, 1948; s. Harvey E. and Olivia M. (Estrada) W. BA, U. Mich., 1969; JD, Wayne State U., 1977. Bar: Mich. 1977, U.S. Dist. Ct. (we. dist.) Mich. 1989, U.S. Dist. Ct. (no. dist.) Ill. 1991, U.S. Dist. Ct. (ea. dist.) Mich. 1983, Colo. 1996, U.S. Dist. Ct. Colo. 1996, U.S. Ct. Appeals (10th cir.) 1996. Assoc. Moore, Barr & Kerwin, Detroit, 1977-79; ptnr. firm Barr & Walker, Detroit, 1979-82; assoc. firm Richard M. Goodman, P.C., Detroit, 1983-87; hearing officer Mich. Civil Rights Commn., Detroit, 1983-86; pvt. practice Detroit, 1988-89, Birmingham, Mich., 1990—95; dep. pub. defender Office of State Pub. Defender, Colorado Springs, Colo., 1998—. Participant Detroit Bar Assn. Vol. Lawyer Program. Bd. dirs. Cmty. Treatment Ctr.-Project Rehab., Detroit, 1983-89; trustee ARC of Pikes Peak region; mem. scholarship com. Latino en Marcha Scholarship Fund, Detroit, 1984; treas. youth assistance program Citizens Adv. Coun., 1987; mem. State Domestic Violence Offenders' Mgmt. Bd., 2001—. Mem. State Bar Mich. Found., Wayne County Mediation Tribunal (mediator), Nat. Lawyers Guild (exec. bd. Detroit chpt. 1988-92, pres. Detroit chpt. 1988-90), Mich. Trial Lawyers Assn. (co-chair coalition com. 1988-90, exec. bd. 1988-96, co-chair pro bono com. 1991-96), State Bar Mich. (com. on underrepresented groups in law 1980-92, chmn. 1983-85, mem. com. jud. qualifications 1985-86, Latin Am. affairs coun. 1978-96), Colo. Criminal Def. Bar, Legal Aid and Def. Assn. (bd. dirs. 1990-95), Hispanic Bar Assn., Trial Lawyers for Pub. Justice (founder 1981, mem. amicus com. 1985-86, state capt. 1991-95), Ctr. for Auto Safety. Criminal. Office: 415 S Sahwatch Colorado Springs CO 80903 E-mail: jonathan.walker@state.co.us.

WALKER, MARK A. lawyer; b. N.Y.C., June 24, 1941; s. Joseph and Eleanor (Junger) W.; m. Tania Khodjamirian; children: Marie, Andrew. BA, Stanford U., 1963; LLB, Yale U., 1966. Bar: N.Y. 1967, U.S. Dist. Ct. (so. dist.) N.Y. 1977. Assoc. Cleary, Gottlieb, Steen & Hamilton, Paris, Brussels and N.Y., 1966-75, ptnr. N.Y.C., 1975—. Mem. Assn. Bar City N.Y. Finance, Private international, Public international. E-mail: mwalker@cgsh.com.

WALKER, RICHARD HENRY, lawyer; b. Wilmington, Del., Dec. 29, 1950; s. Henry H. and Mary L. (Meister) W. BA, Trinity Coll., 1972; JD, Temple U., 1975. Bar: Pa. 1976, U.S. Supreme Ct. 1977, N.Y. 1978, D.C. 1981. Law clk. to Hon. Collins J. Seitz U.S. Ct. Appeals (3rd cir.), Wilmington, Del., 1975-76; assoc., ptnr. Cadwalader, Wickersham & Taft, N.Y.C., 1976-91; regional dir. N.E. office U.S. SEC, N.Y.C., 1991-95, gen. counsel Washington, 1996-98, dir. enforcement, 1998—2001. Fellow Am. Bar Found.

WALKER, TIMOTHY BLAKE, lawyer, educator; b. Utica, N.Y., May 21, 1940; s. Harold Blake and Mary Alice (Corder) W.; m. Sandra Blake; children: Kimberlee Corder, Tyler Blake, Kelley Loren. AB magna cum laude, Princeton U., 1962; JD magna cum laude, U. Denver, 1967, MA in Sociology, 1969. Bar: Colo. 1968, Calif. 1969, Ind. 1971. Asst. prof. law U. Pacific, 1968-69; vis. assoc. prof. U. Toledo, 1969-70; assoc. prof. Indpls. Law Sch., Ind. U., 1970-71, U. Denver, 1971-75, prof., 1975-99; prof. emeritus, 1999—; dir. adminstrn. of justice program U. Denver, 1971-78; pvt. practice Denver, 1972-79; of counsel Robert T. Hinds, Jr. & Assocs. PC, Littleton, Colo., 1980-85; ptnr., of counsel Cox, Mustain-Wood, Walker & Schumacher, Littleton, 1985—. Cons., lectr. in field; rsch. on lay representation in adminstrv. agys., Colo., 1975-76. Contbr. articles to profl. jours.; editor: Denver Law Jour., 1966-67; editor-in-chief: Family Law Quar., 1983-92. Mem. Ind. Child Support Commn., 1970-71; pres. Shawnee (Colo.) Water Consumers Assn., 1975-84, 93-95; del. Colo. Rep. Conv., 1978. Colo. Bar Assn. grant, 1975-76. Fellow: Am. Bar Found., Internat. Acad. Matrimonial Lawyers, Am. Sociol. Assn., Am. Acad. Matrimonial Lawyers; mem.: ABA (vice chmn. child custody subcom., sec. Family Law sect. 1992—93, vice chmn., sec. 1993—94, chmn. elect family law sect. 1994—95, chmn. 1995—96, chmn. child custody task force 2000—, alimony, maintenance and support com. 2000—, family sect. del. ho. of dels. 2000—), Colo Trial Lawyers Assn., Ind. Bar Assn., Colo. Bar Assn., Calif. Bar Assn. Presbyterian. Home: 7329 Rochester Ct Castle Rock CO 80108-9281 Office: 1900 Olive St Denver CO 80220-1857 also: 6601 S University Blvd Littleton CO 80121-2913

WALKER, VAUGHN R. federal judge; b. Watseka, Ill., Feb. 27, 1944; s. Vaughn Rosenworth and Catharine (Miles) W. AB, U. Mich., 1966; JD, Stanford U., 1970. Intern economist SEC, Washington, 1966, 68; law clk. to the Hon. Robert J. Kelleher U.S. Dist. Ct. Calif., L.A., 1971-72; assoc. atty. Pillsbury Madison & Sutro, San Francisco, 1972-77, ptnr., 1978-90; judge U.S. Dist. Ct. (no. dist.) Calif., San Francisco, 1990—. Mem. Calif. Law Revision Commn., Palo Alto, 1986-89; bd. advisors Law and Econs. Ctr., George Mason U., 1999—. Dir. Jr. Achievement of Bay Area, San Francisco, 1979-83, St. Francis Found., San Francisco, 1991-97, 98—. Woodrow Wilson Found. fellow U. Calif., Berkeley, 1966-67. Fellow Am. Bar Found.; mem. ABA (jud. rep., antitrust sect. 1991-95), Lawyers' Club of San Francisco (pres. 1985-86), Assn. Bus. Trial Lawyers (dir. 1996-98), Am. Law Inst., Am. Saddlebred Horse Assn., San Francisco Mus. Modern Art, Bohemian Club, Olympic Club, Pacific-Union Club. Office: US Dist Ct 450 Golden Gate Ave San Francisco CA 94102-3482

WALKER, WALTER HERBERT, III, lawyer, writer; b. Quincy, Mass., Sept. 12, 1949; s. Walter H. Jr. and Irene M. (Horn) W.; m. Anne M. DiScuillo, June 17, 1972; children: Brett Daniel, Jeffrey St. John. BA, U. Pa., 1971; JD, U. Calif., San Francisco, 1974. Bar: Calif. 1974, Mass. 1981. Appellate atty. ICC, Washington, 1975-77; trial atty. Handler, Baker, Greene & Taylor, San Francisco, 1977-80; ptnr. Sterns and Walker and predecessor firm Sterns, Smith, Walker & Grell, San Francisco, 1981-88; ptnr. firm Walker & Durham, San Francisco, 1988—99, Walker & Hamilton, San Francisco, 2000—. Author: A Dime to Dance By, 1983 (Best 1st Novel by Calif. Author), The Two Dude Defense, 1985, Rules of The Knife Fight, 1986, The Immediate Prospect of Being Hanged, 1989, The Appearance of Impropriety, 1992. Mem. ATLA, Consumer Attys. of Calif., San Francisco Trial Lawyers Assn., Mystery Writers Am. Clubs: Hastings Rugby. Democrat. Insurance, Personal injury (including property damage), Product liability. Home: 604 Seminary Dr Mill Valley CA 94941-3169 Office: 50 Francisco St Ste 160 San Francisco CA 94133-2108

WALKER, WOODROW WILSON, retired lawyer, cattle and timber farmer, real estate investor; b. Greenville, Mich., Feb. 19, 1919; s. Craig Walker and Mildred Chase; m. Janet K. Keiter, Oct. 7, 1950; children: Jonathan Woodrow, William Craig, Elaine Virginia. BA, U. Mich., 1943; LLB, Cath. U., 1950. Bar: D.C. 1950, U.S. Supreme Ct. 1958, Va. 1959. Operator family farm, 1937-39; dir. Libr. of Congress Fed. Credit Union, 1957-60; atty. Am. law div. legis. reference Libr. Congress, Washington, 1951-60; pvt. practice, Arlington, Va., 1960-2000. Counsel, bd. dirs. Calvary Found., Arlington, 1970-85, first pres., 1972; judge moot ct. George Mason Law Sch., 1986; owner-operator Walker Farm Front Royal, Va., 1972—. Co-author rsch. publs. for U.S. Govt.; featured in Washington Post. V.p. Jefferson Civic Assn., Arlington, 1955-61; pres. Nellie Custis PTA, Arlington, 1960-61; sec. Arlington County Bd. Equalization Real Estate Assessment, 1962, chmn. 1963; com. chmn. Arlington Troop 108 Boy Scouts Am., 1964-69; mem. Arlington County Pub. Utilities Commn., 1964-66, vice chmn., 1965-66; pres. Betschler Class Adult Sunday Sch., Calvary United Meth. Ch., Arlington, 1965. Served with U.S. Army, 1943-45, PTO. Cited for notable deed in conduct of his legal duties Washington Post, 1996. Mem. ABA, Arlington County Bar Assn., Va. Farm Bur., Va. Cattleman's Assn. Methodist. Democrat. Commercial, consumer (including collections, credit), Commercial, contracts (including sales of goods; commercial financing), General practice. Home and Office: 2822 Ft Scott Dr Arlington VA 22202-2307

WALKOWIAK, VINCENT STEVEN, lawyer; b. Apr. 22, 1946; s. Vincent Albert and Elizabeth (Modla) W.; m. Linda Kae Schweigert, Aug., 1968; children: Jenifer, Steven. BA, U. Ill., 1968, JD, 1971. Bar: Ill. 1971, Tex. 1981, U.S. Ct. Appeals (8th cir.) 1971, (5th cir.) 1982, U.S. Dist. Ct. (ea., we., so., and no. dists.) Tex. 1982. Assoc. Dorsey, Marquart, Windhorst, West & Halladay, Mpls., 1971-74; ptnr. Fulbright & Jaworski LLP, Houston, 1982—. Prof. Fla. State U., Tallahassee, 1974-76, So. Meth. U., Dallas, 1976-84. Editor: Uniform Product Liability Act, 1980, Trial of a Product Liability Case, vol. 1, 1981, vol. 2, 1982, Preparation and Presentation of Product Liability, 1983, Attorney Client Privilege in Civil Litigation, 1997. Federal civil litigation, State civil litigation, Product liability. Office: Fulbright & Jaworski LLP 2200 Ross Ave Ste 2800 Dallas TX 75201-2784 E-mail: vwalkowiak@fulbright.com.

WALKUP, CHARLOTTE LLOYD, lawyer; b. N.Y.C., Apr. 28, 1910; d. Charles Henry and Helene Louise (Wheeler) Tuttle; m. David D. Lloyd, Oct. 19, 1940 (dec. Dec. 1962); children: Andrew M. Lloyd, Louisa Lloyd Hurley; m. Homer Allen Walkup, Feb. 4, 1967. AB, Vassar Coll., 1931; LLB, Columbia U., 1934. Bar: N.Y. 1935, U.S. Supreme Ct. 1939, U.S. Dist. Ct. D.C. 1953, Va. 1954. Asst. solicitor Dept. Interior, Washington, 1934-45; asst. gen. counsel UNRRA, Washington and London, 1945-48; assoc. and cons. firms Washington, 1953, 55, 60; atty., spl. asst. Office Treasury, Washington, 1961-65, asst. gen. counsel, 1965-73. Cons. Rogers & Wells, Washington, 1975-86. Editor Columbia Law Rev., 1933-34, Life Stories of a Celebrated Lawyer: Memoirs of Charles H. Tuttle, Esq., 2002. Pres. Alexandria Cmty. Welfare Coun., 1950-52; bd. dirs. Alexandria Coun. Human Rels., 1958-60, New Hope Found., 1977. Recipient Meritorious Svc. award Dept. Treasury, 1970, Exceptional Svc. award, 1973, Career Svc. award Nat. Civil Svc. League, 1973; named Hon. fellow Harry S. Truman Libr. Inst. Mem. Columbia U. Alumni Assn., Phi Beta Kappa. Democrat. Episcopalian. Home: 4800 Fillmore Ave Apt 1251 Alexandria VA 22311-5077 E-mail: walkup@comcast.net.

WALL, CHARLES R. lawyer; BA hist., Grinnell Coll., Iowa, 1967; JD, Univ. of Mo. Law Sch., Mo., 1970. V.p. and assoc. gen. coun. Philip Morris Co. Inc., New York, NY, 1990, sr. v.p., litig., 1994, Dep. gen. coun., 1995, gen. coun. and sr. v.p., 2000; assoc. and ptnr. Shook, Hardy & Bacon, Kans. City, Mo., 1970—90. Office: Philip Morris Altria Group 120 Park Ave New York NY 10017*

WALL, DONALD ARTHUR, lawyer; b. Lafayette, Ind., Mar. 17, 1946; s. Dwight Arthur and Myra Virginia (Peavey) W.; m. Cheryn Lynn Heinen, Aug. 29, 1970; children: Sarah Lynn, Michael Donald. BA, Butler U., 1968; JD, Northwestern U., 1971. Bar: Ohio 1971, U.S. Dist. Ct. (no. dist.) Ohio 1973, U.S. Supreme Ct. 1980, Ariz. 1982, U.S. Dist. Ct. (no. dist.) W.Va. 1982, U.S. Ct. Appeals (6th cir.) 1982, U.S. Dist. Ct. Ariz. 1983, U.S. Ct. Appeals (9th and 10th cirs.) 1984, U.S. Ct. Appeals (5th cir.) 1988. Assoc. Squire, Sanders & Dempsey, Cleve., 1971-80, ptnr., 1980-82, Phoenix, 1983—. Spkr. at profl. meetings; program moderator. Contbr. articles to profl. jours. Trustee Ch. of the Saviour Day Ctr., Cleveland Heights, 1979-82; mem. adminstrv. bd. Ch. of Saviour, Cleveland Heights, 1980-83; fin. com. Paradise Valley (Ariz.) United Meth. Ch., 1986-87; bd. dirs., divsn. commr. North Scottsdale (Ariz.) Little League, 1983-92; bd. dirs. Epilepsy Found. N.E. Ohio, 1976-82, pres., 1981-82; bd. dirs. N.E. Cmty. Basketball Assn., 1993-99; bd. visitors U. Ariz. Law Sch., 1996—; bd. mgrs. Scottsdale-Paradise Valley YMCA, 1999—. Mem. ABA (torts and ins. practice and litigation sect., past chmn. r.r. law com., litigation sect.), Def. Rsch. Inst., Ariz. Bar Assn. (labor and trial practice sects.), Maricopa County Bar Assn., Ariz. Assn. Def. Counsel. Methodist. Federal civil litigation, State civil litigation, Labor (including EEOC, Fair Labor Standards Act, labor-management relations, NLRB, OSHA). Office: Squire Sanders & Dempsey LLP 40 N Central Ave Ste 2700 Phoenix AZ 85004-4498 E-mail: dwall@ssd.com.

WALL, DUANE, lawyer; b. Amadarko, Okla., Jan. 10, 1940; BA, So. Nazarene U., 1962; JD, U. Okla., 1965; LLM, NYU, 1966. Bar: (N.Y.) 1969. Resident White & Case LLP, London, 1972—76, 1980—81, mng. ptnr. N.Y.C., 2000—. Mem.: ABA, Internat. Law Assn. (Am. br.), Assn. of Bar of City of N.Y., N.Y. State Bar Assn. Office: White & Case 1155 Ave of the Ams New York NY 10036

WALL, JOSEPH R. judge; b. Milw., Jan. 2, 1957; s. Paul B. and Nina A. Wall; 1 child, Justin M. BS in Acctg., Marquette U., 1979, JD magna cum laude, 1984. Bar: Wis., U.S. Dist. Ct. (ea. dist.) Wis., U.S. Ct. Appeals (7th cir.); CPA, Wis. Pub. acct. Touche Ross & Co., Milw., 1979-81; asst. dist. atty. Milw. County Dist. Atty.'s Office, 1984-86; asst. U.S. atty. U.S. Dept. Justice (ea. dist.) Wis., Milw., 1986—2001. Advisor St. Benedict The Moor Legal Clinic, Milw., 1983-90; mem. 7th Cir. Criminal Jury Instrn. Revision Com., Chgo., 1997-98. Contbr. articles to profl. jours. Site organizer Safe and Sound, Milw., 1998; reading tutor Milw. Pub. Schs., 1998. Avocation: long distance running. Office: 10201 W Watertown Plank Rd Wauwatosa WI 53226

WALL, KENNETH E., JR., lawyer; b. Beaumont, Tex., Apr. 6, 1944; s. Kenneth E. and W. Geraldine (Peoples) W.; m. Marjorie Lee Hughes, Dec. 21, 1968; children— Barbara, Elizabeth, Kenneth. Grad. Lamar U., 1966, U. Tex.-Austin, 1969. Bar: Tex. 1969, U.S. Supreme Ct. 1979. Asst. city atty., Beaumont, 1969-73, city atty., 1973-84; with firm Olson & Olson, Houston, 1984— ; dir. Tex. Mcpl. League Ins. Trust, 1979-84, vice chmn., 1983-84; counsel S.E. Tex. Regional Planning Commn., 1974, 76. Active Boy Scouts Am., Girl Scouts U.S.A. Mem. Nat. Inst. Mcpl. Law Officers (chmn. com. on local govt. pers. 1979-81, 82-84), State Bar Tex., Tex. City Attys. Assn. (pres. 1982-83), Jefferson County Bar Assn. (dir. 1975-77), Houston Bar Assn., Phi Delta Phi. Methodist. E-mail: kwall@olson.and-olson.com Land use and zoning (including planning), Municipal (including bonds), State and local taxation. Office: 333 Clay St Houston TX 77002-4000

WALL, ROBERT ANTHONY, JR., lawyer; b. Hartford, Conn., Mar. 3, 1945; s. Robert Anthony and Eileen (Fitzgerald) W.; children: Andrea, Melanie, Victoria, Robert, Natalie; m. Diana M. Wall. BA, Georgetown U., Washington, 1968; JD, Am. U., Washington, 1973. Bar: Conn. 1974, U.S. Ct. Appeals (D.C. cir.) 1974, U.S. Dist. Ct. Conn. 1974, U.S. Supreme Ct. 1977. Ptnr. Wall, Wall & Frauenhofer, Torrington, Conn., 1974-87; pvt. practice Torrington, 1987—. Mem. State of Conn. Rep. Ctrl. Com., 1976-79. Mem. Conn. Trial Lawyers Assn. (bd. govs. 1984-86), Ct. Washington #67 Foresters of Am. (trustee 1988—). Roman Catholic. Personal injury (including property damage). Home: 55 Quail Run Torrington CT 06790-2550 Office: 8 Church St Torrington CT 06790-5247 Fax: 860-496-0128. E-mail: wallgawrych@yahoo.com.

WALLACE, ANDERSON, JR., lawyer, educator; b. Cleve., Sept. 24, 1939; s. Anderson and Agatha Lee (Culpepper) Wallace; m. Kristine Lee Gough; children: Anderson III, Whitney. BA, George Washington U., 1962, JD, 1966. Bar: Tex. 68, U.S. Dist. Ct. (no. dist.) Tex. 68, U.S. Ct. Claims 68, U.S. Tax Ct. 68, U.S. Ct. Appeals (5th cir.) 68, U.S. Supreme Ct. 71, U.S. Ct. Appeals (11th cir.) 81. Program mgmt. asst. NASA, Washington, 1962—64; atty. U.S. Dept. Treasury, Washington, 1964—66; tax atty. Price Waterhouse & Co., Atlanta, 1966—67; tax ptnr. Jackson, Walker, Winstead, Cantwell & Miller, Dallas, 1967—84; dir. in charge tax dept. Baker, Mills & Glast, P.C., Dallas, 1984—93; pres. Anderson Wallace, Jr., P.C., Dallas, 1993—. Instr. Sch. Law So. Meth. U. Trustee S.W. Mus. Sci. and Tech., Dallas, 1974—, Girls Found. Dallas Inc.; chmn. Inst. on Employee Benefits, Southwestern Found., 1976. Mem.: ABA. Corporate taxation, Estate taxation, Personal income taxation. Office: 3328 Purdue Ave Ste 100 Dallas TX 75225-7635

WALLACE, DON, JR., law educator; b. Vienna, Apr. 23, 1932; s. Don and Julie (Baer) Wallace; m. Daphne Mary Wickham, 1963; children: Alexandra Creed, Sarah Anne, Benjamin James. BA with high honors, Yale U., 1953; LL.B. cum laude, Harvard U., 1957. Bar: N.Y. 1957, D.C. 1978. Assoc. Fleischmann, Jaeckle, Stokes and Hitchcock, N.Y.C., 1959-60, Paul, Weiss, Rifkind, Wharton and Garrison, N.Y.C., 1957-58, 60-62; rsch. asst. to faculty mem. Harvard Law Sch., Cambridge, Mass., 1958-59; regional legal adv. Middle East AID, Dept. State, 1963-65, dep. asst. gen. counsel, 1965-66; assoc. prof. law Georgetown U. Law Ctr., Washington, 1966-71, prof., 1971—2002; chmn. Internat. Law Inst., Washington, 1969—; adj./emeritus prof. Georgetown U. Law Ctr., Washington, 2002—. Cons. AID, 1966-70, UN Centre on Transnat. Corps., 1977-78; counsel Wald, Harkrader & Ross, Washington, 1978-86, Arnold & Porter, 1986-89, Shearman & Sterling, 1989-98, Morgan, Lewis & Bockius, 1998—; legal advisor State of Qatar, 1979-82; chmn. adv. com. on tech. and world trade Office of Tech. Assessment, U.S. Congress, 1976-79; mem. Sec. of State's Adv. Com. on Pvt. Internat. Law, 1979—; mem. U.S. del. UN Conf. on State Succession in Respect of Treaties, Vienna, 1978; mem. U.S. del. new internat. econ. order working group UN Commn. Internat. Trade Law, Vienna, 1981—; vis. com. Harvard Law Sch., 1996-97; mem. panel of judges World Trade Orgn., 1996-2000. Co-author: Internat. Business and Economics: Law and Policy; author: International Regulation of Multinational Corporations, 1976, Dear Mr. President: The Needed Turnaround in America's International Economic Affairs, 1984; editor: A Lawyer's Guide to International Business Transactions, 1977-87; contbr. numerous articles on internat. trade and law to profl. jours., books revs. on law and bus. to profl. jours. Coord. Anne Arundel County (Md.) Dem. Nat. Com., 1972-79; sec. Chesapeake Found., 1972-73; nat. chmn. Law Profs. for Bush and Quayle, 1988, 92, for Dole and Kemp, 1996; v.p., bd. govs. UNIDROIT Found., Rome, 1997—.$Dat. co-chmn. Law Profs. for Fulbright fellow, 1967, Eisenhower Exch. fellow, 1976. Mem. ABA (chmn. sect. internat. law 1978-79), Ho. of Dels. 1982-84), Am. Law Inst., Internat. Law Assn., Shaybani Soc. of Internat. Law (v.p.), Ctrl. and Ea. European Law Initiative (mem. adv. bd.), Cosmos Club, Met. Club, Coun. Postgraduate Sch. Internat. Bus. and European Law, European Ctr. Peace (pres.). Home: 2800 35th St NW Washington DC 20007-1411 Office: Georgetown U Law Ctr 600 New Jersey Ave NW Washington DC 20001-2022

WALLACE, ELAINE WENDY, lawyer; b. Worcester, Mass., Feb. 16, 1949; d. Louis S. and Ida (Zeiper) W. BA, Yeshiva U., 1971; JD, John F. Kennedy Sch. Law, 1976. Sole practice, Oakland, Calif. Civil rights, Government contracts and claims, Labor (including EEOC, Fair Labor Standards Act, labor-management relations, NLRB, OSHA). Home: 2430 Palmetto St # 1 Oakland CA 94602-2923 Office: 2430 Palmetto St # 2 Oakland CA 94602-2923

WALLACE, FRANKLIN SHERWOOD, lawyer, director; b. Bklyn., Nov. 24, 1927; s. Abraham Charles and Jennie (Etkin) Wolowitz; m. Eleanor Ruth Pope, Aug. 23, 1953; children: Julia Diane, Charles Andrew. Student, U. Wis., 1943-45; BS cum laude, U.S. Mcht. Marine Acad., 1950; LLB, JD, U. Mich., 1953. Bar: Ill. 1954. Practice law, Rock Island, Ill.; ptnr. Winstein, Kavensky & Wallace. Asst. state's atty. Rock Island County, 1967-68; local counsel UAW at John Deere-J.I. Case Plants. Former bd. dirs. Tri City Jewish Ctr.; former trustee United Jewish Charities of Quad Cities; former bd. dirs. Blackhawk Coll. Found. Mem. ABA, Ill. Bar Assn. (chmn. jud. adv. polls com. 1979-84), Rock Island County Bar Assn., Am. Trial Lawyers Assn., Ill. Trial Lawyers Assn., Nat. Assn. Criminal Def. Lawyers, Ill. Appellate Lawyers Assn., Am. Judicature Soc., Blackhawk Coll. Found. Democrat. Jewish. General civil litigation, Family and matrimonial, Labor (including EEOC, Fair Labor Standards Act, labor-management relations, NLRB, OSHA). Home: 3405 20th Street Ct Rock Island IL 61201-6201 Office: Rock Island Bank Bldg Rock Island IL 61201 Home: 36571 Tallowood Dr Palm Desert CA 92211 E-mail: fnewallace@aol.com.

WALLACE, HARRY LELAND, lawyer; b. San Francisco, June 26, 1927; s. Leon Harry and Anna Ruth (Haworth) W.; 1 child, Mary Ann Wallace Frantz. AB in Govt.; BS in Bus, Ind. U., 1949; JD, Harvard U., 1952. Bar: Wis. 1953. Law clk. U.S. Supreme Ct. Justice Sherman Minton, Washington, 1952-53; assoc. firm Foley & Lardner, Milw., 1953-61, partner, 1961-96, retired, 1996; officer and/or dir. various corps. Treas. Mequon-Thiensville Sch. Bds., 1966-67, 71-73, pres., 1965-66, 67-71, 73-75; bd. dirs. Milw. County Assn. for Mental Health, 1970-76, Milw. Mental Health Found., 1983-94; chmn. financing policies com. Gov.'s Commn. on Edn., 1969-70; mem. Gov.'s Task Force on Sch. Financing and Property Tax Reform, 1972-73; chmn. Gov.'s Commn. on State-Local Rels. and Fin. Policies, 1975-76; trustee Pub. Policy Forum, 1976-92, sec., 1984-86, pres., 1986-88. With USN, 1945-46. Mem. Wis. Bar Assn., Am. Law Inst., Phi Beta Kappa, Beta Gamma Sigma, Delta Tau Delta. Clubs: Milwaukee. Methodist. Corporate, general, Probate (including wills, trusts), Corporate taxation. Home: 1913 Somerset Ln Northbrook IL 60062-6067

WALLACE, HENRY JARED, JR., lawyer; b. Pitts., Oct. 26, 1943; s. Henry Jared and Jane (Bowman) Wallace. BA, Harvard U., 1965, JD, 1968. Bar: Pa. 1969, U.S. Supreme Ct. 1973. With Reed Smith Shaw & McClay, Pitts., 1968—94; pvt. practice Pitts., 1995—. Served with U.S. Army, 1968-70. Mem. Duquesne Club, Fox Chapel Golf Club, Harvard-Yale-Princeton Club (Pitts.). Federal civil litigation, State civil litigation, Labor (including EEOC, Fair Labor Standards Act, labor-management relations, NLRB, OSHA). Home and Office: 149 Ridgeview Dr New Kensington PA 15068-9389

WALLACE, HERBERT NORMAN, lawyer; b. Syracuse, N.Y., Oct. 19, 1937; s. Louis H. and Betty (Wagner) W.; m. Frances Adele Groobman, June 1, 1963 (div. Sept. 1976); children: Craig, Julie; m. Frances Mae Souza, Nov. 12, 1977; 1 child, John. BA, Davis & Elkins Coll., 1959; JD, Syracuse U., 1962. Bar: N.Y. 1962, U.S. Dist. Ct. (no. dist.) N.Y. 1962. Asst. atty. gen. State of N.Y., Albany, 1963-66, asst. atty. gen in charge of Poughkeepsie (N.Y.) office Poughkeepsie, 1966-79; counsel to banking com. N.Y. State Senate, Albany, 1979-84, counsel to Senator Rolison, asst. majority leader, 1984-88; sole practice Poughkeepsie, N.Y., 1979-86, 94—; ptnr. Wallace & Moore, Poughkeepsie, 1986-94, Wallace and Wallace,

2000—. Mem. Poughkeepsie Rep. Com., 1977-91. Recipient Ellis Island medal of hon. NECO, 1997. Mem. N.Y. State Bar Assn., Dutchess County Bar Assn. Jewish. Condemnation (eminent domain), General practice, Property, real (including real estate development, water). Home: 65 Cardinal Dr Poughkeepsie NY 12601-5703 Office: 299 Main St Poughkeepsie NY 12601-3144

WALLACE, J. CLIFFORD, federal judge; b. San Diego, Dec. 11, 1928; s. John Franklin and Lillie Isabel (Overing) Wallace; m. Virginia Lee Schlosser, 1957 (dec.); m. Elaine J. Barnes, Apr. 8, 1996 (dec.); m. Dixie Jenee Robison Zenger, Apr. 2, 2001. BA, San Diego State U., 1952; LLB, U. Calif., Berkeley, 1955. Bar: Calif. 1955. With Gray, Cary, Ames & Frye, San Diego, 1955—70; judge U.S. Dist. Ct. (so. dist.), Calif., 1970—72, U.S. Ct. Appeals (9th cir.), San Diego, 1972—96, chief judge, 1991—96, sr. judge, 1996—. Contbr. articles to profl. jours. Stake pres. San Diego East LDS Ch. , 1962—67, regional rep., 1967—74, 1977—79. With USN, 1946—49. Mem.: Inst. Jud. Adminstrn., Am. Bd. Trial Advocates. Mem. Lds Ch. Office: US Ct Appeals 9th Cir 940 Front St Ste 4192 San Diego CA 92101-8918

WALLACE, JAMES HAROLD, JR., lawyer; b. Atlanta, Feb. 8, 1941; s. James Harold Sr. and Ruth (Cocking) W. BSEE, U. S.C., 1963; JD, Georgetown U., 1966. Bar: D.C. 1967. Patent examiner U.S. Patent & Trademark Office, Washington, 1966-67; trial atty. antitrust div. U.S. Dept. Justice, Washington, 1967-70; from assoc. to ptnr. Kirkland & Ellis, Washington, 1970-83; ptnr. Wiley, Rein & Fielding, Washington, 1983—. Mem. adv. bd. BNA Patent, Trademark & Copyright Jour., Washington, 1971—. Contbr. articles to profl. jours. Mem. ABA. Antitrust, Federal civil litigation, Patent. Home: 3029 Cambridge Pl NW Washington DC 20007-2914 Office: Wiley Rein & Fielding 1776 K St NW Washington DC 20006-2304

WALLACE, KEITH M. lawyer; b. Evansville, Ind., Apr. 2, 1956; s. B. Joe and M. Joyce (Nicolaides) W.; 1 child, Elizabeth Anne. BA in Psychology, Ind. U., 1978; JD, Valparaiso U., 1983. Bar: Ky. 1984, Ind. 1983, U.S. Dist. Ct. (so. dist.) Ind. 1983, U.S. Ct. Appeals (7th cir.) 1985, U.S. Supreme Ct., 1997. Comml. credit analyst Old Nat. Bank, Evansville, 1978-79; assoc. Cubbage & Thomason, Henderson, Ky., 1983-84, Perdue & Stigger, Evansville, 1984-86; ptnr. Jones & Wallace, Evansville, 1987-90; fgn. expert Peking U. Law Dept., People's Republic China, 1990-91; ptnr. Wright, Evans & Daly, Evansville, 1991-95, Jones & Wallace, Evansville, 1996-2001; of counsel Bowers Harrison, 2001—. Asst. city atty., Evansville, 1984-90; hearing officer City of Evansville Dept. Code Enforcement, 1992-99. Steward Christian Fellowship Ch., Evansville, 1988-90; vol. Evansville Rescue Mission, 1987-92, Habitat for Humanity, 1992—; bd. dirs. Impact Ministries, 1992—; exec. dir. Families Thru Internat. Adoptions, Inc., 1995—. Recipient Sagamore of the Wabash award Gov. Frank O'Bannon, 1999, Disting. Hoosier award Gov. Evan Bayh, 1996. Mem. Am. Acad. Adoption Attys., Nat. Assn. of Counsel for Children, Ind. Bar Assn., Ky. Bar Assn., Evansville Bar Assn., Am. Immigration Lawyers Assn., Christian Legal Soc., Evansville Runners Club. Corporate, general, Environmental, Property, real (including real estate development, water). Office: PO Box 1287 Evansville IN 47706-1287 Fax: (812) 464-3676. E-mail: kwallace@ftia.org.

WALLACE, NORA ANN, lawyer; b. Phila., May 24, 1951; AB, Vassar Coll., 1973; JD cum laude, Harvard U., 1976. Bar: N.Y. 1977. Mem. Willkie Farr & Gallagher, N.Y.C. Trustee Vassar Coll., Bklyn. Acad. Music, Bklyn. Acad. Music Endowment Trust; pres. Harvard Law Sch. Assn. of N.Y.C.; bd. dirs. Joseph Collins Found. Securities, Corporate, general. Office: Willkie Farr & Gallagher 787 7th Ave New York NY 10019-6099

WALLACE, SEAN DANIEL, lawyer, judge; b. Walnut Creek, Calif., June 17, 1960; s. Daniel M. and Patricia Marie (Coyne) W.; m. Eileen Marie Lynch, May 29, 1999. BA, Hampden-Sydney Coll., 1982; JD, U. Md., 1985. Bar: Md. 1985, U.S. Dist. Ct. Md. 1986 (co-chmn. so. divsn. joint adv. com.), D.C. 1986, U.S. Dist. Ct. D.C. 1986, U.S. Ct. Appeals (4th, D.C. and Fed. cirs.) 1986. Spl. asst. to U.S. rep. Steny H. Hoyer, Washington, 1982; assoc. Knight, Manzi, Brennan & Ostrom, Upper Marlboro, Md., 1985-88; assoc. county atty. Prince George's County, Md., 1988-95, dep. county atty., chief litig., 1995-98, county atty., 1999—2002; cir. ct. judge 7th Jud. Cir., 2002—. Bd. dirs. moot ct. U. Md. Law Sch., Balt., 1983-85; adj. faculty Nat. Coll. Dist. Attys., 2002—. Mem. inquiry com. Md. Atty. Grievance Commn., 1986-02; bd. dirs. Associated Cath. Charities Archdiocese Washington, 1994-99, chmn. fin. com., 1996-98, bd. vice chair, 1999, fundraising gala chair, 2001; bd. dirs. SHARE, 2002—. Named one of Outstanding Young Men in Am. U.S. Jaycees, 1982, 84. Mem. ABA, Md. Assn. of Counties (co-chmn. govt. liability workgroup 1995-96), Prince George's County Bar Assn., Md. Bar Assn. (bd. dirs. 1997-99, sec. 1999-2000, treas. 2000-01, pres.-elect 2001-02, pres. 2002—), J. Dudley Digges Inn of Ct., Nat. Eagle Scout Assn. Roman Catholic. Federal civil litigation, State civil litigation. Office: Prince George's Co Cir Ct Courthouse Main St Upper Marlboro MD 20772

WALLACE, WALTER C. lawyer, government official; b. N.Y.C., Mar. 25, 1924; m. Frances Helm, Apr. 5, 1963; 1 dau., Laura. BA magna cum laude, St. John's U., Hillsdale, N.Y., 1948; LLB with distinction, Cornell U., 1951. Bar: N.Y. 1952, Calif. 1954, D.C. 1975, U.S. Dist. Ct. (no. dist.) Calif. 1954, U.S. Ct. Appeals (9th cir.) 1954, D.C. 1975, U.S. Dist. Ct. D.C. 1975, U.S. Ct. Appeals (D.C. cir.) 1975. Assoc. Cahill, Gordan & Reindel, N.Y.C., 1951-54; exec. asst. Sec. of Labor, Washington, 1955-60, asst. sec. of labor for manpower and employment, 1960-61; gen. counsel Presdl. R.R. Commn., Washington, 1961; v.p. labor rels. Hudson Pulp & Paper Corp., N.Y.C., 1963-73; pres. Bituminous Coal Operators Assoc., Washington, 1974-75; ptnr. Ables & Wallace, Washington, 1977-80; prin. Law Offices Walter C. Wallace, N.Y.C., 1981-82; mem. Nat. Mediation Bd., Washington, 1982—, chmn., 1983, 85, 88. U.S. del. Internat. Labor Orgn. Conf. on Labor Rels. in Timber Industry, Geneva, 1958; asst. to cabinet com. on oil imports chaired by John Foster Dulles, 1958. Mem. bd. editors Cornell Law Quar., 1950-51. Bd. dirs. Nat. Safety Coun., Washington, 1974-75; asst. to chmn. United Givers Fund, Washington, 1956, mem. admission and allocations com., 1957-58. Staff sgt. U.S. Army, 1943-45, ETO. Decorated Bronze Star; recipient Presdl. commendation Pres. Eisenhower, Washington, 1961, Disting. Svc. award United Givers Fund, 1956, Disting. Svc. award Nat. Mediation Bd., 1990. Mem. Calif. Bar Assn., N.Y. State Bar Assn., D.C. Bar Assn., Order of Coif. Republican. Roman Catholic. Home: 55 Central Park W New York NY 10023-6003

WALLACH, DAVID MICHAEL, lawyer; b. Ft. Worth, Nov. 13, 1954; s. David Edward and Zelma Jane (Gilbreath) W.; m. Susan Danell Hailey, Aug. 16, 1975; children: Landon James, Tyler Field, Carter Hailey. BA, Tex. Christian U., 1975; JD, U. Houston, 1979. Bar: Tex. 1979, U.S. Dist. Ct. (no. dist.) Tex. 1979, U.S. Ct. Appeals (5th and 11th cirs.) 1979, U.S. Dist. Ct. (so. dist.) Tex. 1986, U.S. Dist. Ct. (we. dist.) Tex. 1992. Assoc. Shannon, Gracey, Ratliff & Miller, Ft. Worth, 1979-83, ptnr., 1983-91; shareholder Wallach & Moore PC, Ft. Worth, 1991—. Contbr. articles to profl. jours. Named Boss of Yr. Fort Worth Legal Secs. Assn., 1991. Fellow Tex. Bar Found.; mem. Tex. Assn. Def. Counsel (v.p. programs 1993-96, bd. dirs. 1989-96, 97—, v.p. North Tex. region 1997-98, exec. v.p. 1999-2000, pres. 2001-02, pres.'s award 1992), Def. Rsch. Inst., Fedn. Def. and Corp. Counsel, Tarrant County Civil Trial Lawyers Assn. (pres. 1988-89, exec. v.p. 1987-88), State Bar Tex., Tarrant County Bar Assn., North Tex. Soc. for Health Care Risk Mgmt., Health Industry Coun. Dallas-Ft. Worth Region, Shriners, Masons. Republican. Methodist. Avocations: golf, snow skiing, racquetball. Personal injury (including property damage), Product liability, Professional liability. Office: Wallach Andrews Florsheim and Stouffer PC 1300 Summit Ave Ste 300 Fort Worth TX 76102-4417 E-mail: mwallach@wallach-law.com.

WALLACH, ERIC JEAN, lawyer; b. N.Y.C., June 11, 1947; s. Milton Harold and Jacqueline (Goldschmidt) W.; m. Miriam Grunberger, Mar. 21, 1976; children: Katherine, Emily, Peter. BA, Harvard U., 1968, JD, 1972. Bar: N.Y. 1973, U.S. Dist. Ct. (so. and ea. dists.) N.Y. 1973, U.S. Dist. Ct. (no. dist.) N.Y. 1989, U.S. Ct. Appeals (2nd cir.) 1973, (3d cir.) 1996, U.S. Tax Ct. 1976. Assoc. Webster & Sheffield, N.Y.C., 1972-77, Rosenman & Colin, N.Y.C., 1977-80, ptnr., 1981-96, mem. mgmt. com., 1993-96, chmn. employment practice group, 1985-96; ptnr., chmn. employment practice group Kasowitz, Benson, Torres & Friedman LLP, N.Y.C., 1996—. Presenter, chmn. CLE programs, Practising Law Inst., Cambridge Inst., others. Mem. editl. bd. You and the Law, 1992-96; contbr. articles to profl. jours. Sec.-treas. Art Dealers Assn. Am., Inc., N.Y.C., 1985-96; trustee C.G. Jung Found. for Analytical Psychology; trustee Am. Jewish World Svc., Inc., N.Y.C., 1989-97, chmn., 1995-97; dir. N.Y. Jr. Tennis League. Mem. Harvard Club N.Y.C. (admissions com. 1992-94), Sunningdale Country Club, Poughkeepsie Tennis Club. Democrat. Avocations: sports, travel, reading. General civil litigation, Labor (including EEOC, Fair Labor Standards Act, labor-management relations, NLRB, OSHA). Home: 940 Park Ave New York NY 10028 also: 16 Buttonwood Ln Rhinebeck NY 12572-3510 Office: Kasowitz Benson Torres & Friedman LLP 1633 Broadway New York NY 10019 E-mail: ewallach@kasowitz.com.

WALLACH, MARK IRWIN, lawyer; b. May 19, 1949; s. Ivan A. and Janice (Grossman) W.; m. Karla L. Wallach, 1996; children: Kerry Melissa, Philip Alexander; stepchildren: Daniel Kanter, Rachel Kanter, Adam Kanter. BA magna cum laude, Wesleyan U., 1971; JD cum laude, Harvard U., 1974. Bar: Ohio 1974, U.S. Dist. Ct. (no. dist.) Ohio, 1974, U.S. Ct. Appeals (6th cir.) 1985, U.S. Supreme Ct. 1985. Law clk. U.S. Dist. Ct., Cleve., 1974-75; assoc. Baker & Hostetler, Cleve., 1975-79; chief trial counsel City of Cleve., 1979-81; assoc. Calfee, Halter & Griswold, Cleve., 1981-82, ptnr., 1982—, exec. com., 1997-99. Mem. fed. ct. adv. com. U.S. Dist. Ct. (no. dist.) Ohio, 1991-95; chmn. bd. trustees Ohio Group Against Smoking Pollution, 1986-90; trustee Cleve. chpt. Am. Jewish Com., 1986—, sec. 1989-91, v.p., 1991-95, pres., 1995-97; bd. trustees Citizens League of Greater Cleve., 1978-79, 87-92. Author: Christopher Morley, 1976. Pres. Wesleyan Alumni Club, Cleve., 1983-87, 92—; trustee Lyric Opera, Cleve., 1995—, pres., 1996-98, Ratner Schs., 1994-96; pres. Performing Arts Together, 1997-2001; trustee The Sculpture Ctr.. 2001,pres., 2001—; trustee Bellefaire Jewish Children's Bur., 2001—. Mem. ABA, Ohio Bar Assn., Fed. Bar Assn., Cuyahoga County Law Dirs. Assn., The Cleve. Racquet Club, Greater Cleve. Bar Assn., The Club at Soc. Ctr. Avocations: reading, bicycling, space exploration, politics. Federal civil litigation, General civil litigation, State civil litigation. Home: 2758 Claythorne Rd Shaker Heights OH 44122-1938 Office: Calfee Halter & Griswold 1400 McDonald Investment Ctr 800 Superior Ave E Ste 1800 Cleveland OH 44114-2688 E-mail: mwallach@calfee.com.

WALLER, JOHN HENRY, JR., state supreme court justice; b. Mullins, S.C., Oct. 31, 1937; s. John Henry and Elnita (Rabon) Waller; m. Jane McLaurin Cooper, Nov. 16, 1963 (div.); children: John Henry III, Melissa McLaurin; m. Debra Ann Meares, May 9, 1981; children: Ryan Meares, Rand Ellis. AB in Psychology, Wofford Coll., 1959; LLB, JD, U. S.C., 1963. Mem. S.C. Ho. of Reps., 1967—77, S.C. Senate, 1977—80; judge S.C. Cir. Ct., 1980—94; assoc. justice S.C. Supreme Ct., 1994—. Capt. U.S. Army, 1959—60. Mem.: Millins Rotary Club (1st pres.), Shriners, Masons. Avocations: woodworking, golf, water sports, snow skiing. Office: SC Supreme Ct 103 Main St PO Box 1059 Marion SC 29571-1059 also: SC Supreme Ct Supreme Court PO Box 11330 Columbia SC 29211-1330

WALLER, PAUL PRESSLEY, JR., retired lawyer; b. East St. Louis, Ill., May 16, 1924; s. Paul Pressley and Rosamond Agnes (Mulqueeny) W.; m. Dolores A. Hartman; children: Mary Eleanor Waller Frascella, Paul P. III, Joseph H., J. Michael Waller, Kathleen A. Feist, Anne M. Meirink, Margaret M. Szendrey, Maureen R. Waller. JD, St. Louis U., 1948. Bar: Mo. 1949, Ill. 1950, U.S. Ct. Appeals (8th cir.) 1957, U.S. Supreme Ct. 1958. Assoc. Oemke & Dunham, East St. Louis, 1950-52; pvt. practice law East St. Louis, 1953-68, Belleville, Ill., 1969; ptnr. O'Connell & Waller, Belleville, 1969-82. Spl. asst. atty. gen. State of Ill., 1962-69, 83-86. Pres. St. Clair County Health and Welfare, St. Clair County Law Libr.; v.p. Legal Aid Soc. St. Clair County; bd. dirs. United Fund; chmn. St. Clair County chpt. ARC. With USN, 1943-46. Mem. St. Clair County Bar Assn., Ill. Bar Assn., Mo. Bar Assn., Bar Assn. Met. St. Louis, Serra (dist. gov.), K.C. (dist. dep.), Nat. Coun. Cath. Men (nat. chmn. com. on legislation), Miss. Atheltic Club. Democrat. General practice, Probate (including wills, trusts). Home: 121 Woods Edge Dr Belleville IL 62221-0453 Office: 211 S Jackson St Belleville IL 62220-2254

WALLER, WILLIAM LOWE, JR., state supreme court justice; b. Miss., Feb. 9, 1952; s. Bill Sr. and Carroll (Overton) W.; m. Charlotte Brawner, Aug. 4, 1979; children: William, Jeannie, Clayton. BA in Bus., Miss. State U., 1974; JD, U. Miss., 1977; grad., U.S. Army War Coll. Bar: Miss. 1977. Ptnr. Waller and Waller, 1977-97; judge City of Jackson, Miss., 1995-96; justice Miss. Supreme Ct., Jackson, 1998. Chmn. lawyer referral svc. Miss. State Bar, 1987-89; chmn. Miss. Pub. Defenders Task Force, 2000; mem. Study Commn. on the Miss. Jud. Sys.; panelist Miss. Pro Bon Svc. Tchr. Sunday sch. First Bapt. Ch., Jackson, Miss.; past gen. counsel Ctrl. Miss. chpt. Lupus Found. Am.; bd. dirs., chmn. Jackson Coun. Neighborhoods B.G., Miss. Nat. Guard. Mem. ABA, Miss. Bar Assn., Christian Legal Soc., Am. Legion, Miss. Nat. Guard Assn. (sec., chmn. legis. com., bd. dirs.). Office: PO Box 117 Jackson MS 39205-0117

WALLIN, JAMES PETER, lawyer; b. Huntington, N.Y., May 9, 1958; s. Jerome Peter and Margaret Mary (Gilvarry) W.; m. Julia Katherine Springen, Aug. 11, 1984; children: James Peter Jr., Thomas George, Katherine Grace, Sarah Elizabeth. BA in Econs., SUNY, Stony Brook, 1980; JD, N.Y. Law Sch., 1983. Bar: N.Y. 1984. Counsel Alliance Capital Mgmt., N.Y.C., 1982-86; assoc. Cole & Dietz (now Winston & Strawn), N.Y.C., 1986-87; counsel The Dreyfus Corp., N.Y.C., 1987-88; gen. counsel Yamaichi Capital Mgmt. Inc., N.Y.C., 1988-92, Yamaichi Internat. (Am.) Inc., N.Y.C., 1992-94, Evergreen Asset Mgmt. Corp., 1994-97; dir. Covenance Group Morgan Stanley Investment Mgmt., N.Y.C., 1997—. Faculty Practicing Law Inst., N.Y.C., 1992—. Author: (seminar materials) Broker Dealer Regulation, 1992. Avocations: aviation, skiing, sailing. Corporate, general, Private international, Securities.

WALLINGER, M(ELVIN) BRUCE, lawyer; b. Richmond, Va., Dec. 27, 1945; s. Melvin W. and Ellen Scott (Barnard) W.; m. Rosemary Moore Hynes, Aug. 8, 1970; children: Mary Moore, Ann Harrison, Carrie. BA, U. Va., 1968, JD, 1972. Bar: Va. 1972, U.S. Dist. Ct. (we. dist.) Va. 1972, U.S. Ct. Appeals (4th cir.) 1976, U.S. Supreme Ct. 1978, U.S. Dist. Ct. (ea. dist.) Va. 1986; mediator and arbitrator for Am. Arbitration Assn. (Comml., Employment and Large, Complex Case panels). Assoc. Wharton, Aldhizer & Weaver, Harrisonburg, Va., 1972-76, ptnr., 1976-98, mng. ptnr., 1998—2002. Bd. dirs. Shrine Mont, Inc., Orkney Springs, Va.; trustee Stuart Hall Sch., Staunton, Va., Shenandoah County Libr. Foun., Edinburg, Va. Fellow ABA, Am. Coll. Trial Lawyers, Va. Law Found.; mem. Va. Bar Assn. (exec. com. 1996-99), Harrisonburg Bar Assn. (pres. 1984), Va. State Bar (pres. young lawyers conf. 1981-82, chmn. 6th dist. disciplinary com. 1988-89), Va. Assn. Def. Attys. (pres. 1989-90). Avocations: cycling, scuba diving. Alternative dispute resolution, General civil litigation, Labor (including EEOC, Fair Labor Standards Act, labor-management relations, NLRB, OSHA). Office: Wharton Aldhizer & Weaver 100 S Mason St Harrisonburg VA 22801-4022

WALLIS, BEN ALTON, JR., lawyer; b. Llano County, Tex., Apr. 27, 1936; s. Ben A. and Jessie Ella (Longbotham) W.; children from previous marriage: Ben a. III, M. Jessica; m. Joan Mery, 1987. BBA, U. Tex., 1961, JD, 1971; postgrad., Law Sch. So. Meth. U. Bar: Tex. 1966, U.S. Dist. Ct. (no. dist.) Tex. 1971, U.S. Ct. Appeals D.C. 1974, U.S. Dist. Ct. D.C. 1975, U.S. Dist. Ct. (we. dist.) Tex. 1975, U.S. Dist. Ct. (no. dist.) Calif. 1983, U.S. Ct. Appeals (5th cir.) 1975, U.S. Ct. Appeals (8th cir.) 1980, U.S. Ct. Appeals (11th cir.) 1981, U.S. Dist. Ct. (ea. dist.) Wis. 1983, U.S. Supreme Ct. 1974. Pvt. practice, Llano, 1966-67, Dallas, 1971-73; investigator, prosecutor State Securities Bd. Tex., 1967-71; v.p. of devel. Club Corp. Am., Dallas, 1973; assoc. counsel impeachment task force U.S. Ho. of Reps. Com. on Judiciary, Washington, 1974; prin. Law Offices of Ben Wallis, P.C., San Antonio, 1974—. Chmn. Nat. Land Use Conf., 1979-81; mem. Gov.'s Areawide Planning Adv. Com., 1975-78; pres. Inst. Human Rights Rsch., 1979-2000. Mem. ATLA, FBA, Coll. of State Bar of Tex., State Bar Tex. (former chmn. agr. tax com.), D.C. Bar Assn., San Antonio Bar Assn., Delta Theta Phi, Delta Sigma Pi. Republican. Baptist. General civil litigation, Condemnation (eminent domain), General practice. Office: GPM South Tower 800 NW Loop 410 Ste 350 San Antonio TX 78216-5619 E-mail: wallis@stic.net.

WALLIS, OLNEY GRAY, lawyer; b. Llano, Tex., July 27, 1940; s. Ben Alton and Jessie Ella (Longbotham) W.; m. Linda Lee Johnson, June 29, 1963; children: Anne, Brett. BA, U. Tex., 1962, JD, 1965. Bar: Tex. 1965, U.S. Dist. Ct. (so. dist.) Tex. 1966, U.S. Ct. Mil. Appeals 1968, U.S. Surpeme Ct. 1970, U.S. dist. Ct. (we. dist.) Tex. 1976, U.S. Ct. Appeals (5th cir.) 1977, U.S. Tax Ct. 1980, U.S. Ct. Appeals (10th cir.) 1981, U.S. Ct. Appeals (11th cir.) 1983, U.S. Dist. Ct. (no. dist.) Tex. 1985, U.S. Dist. Ct. (ea. and we. dists.) Ark. 1985, U.S. Ct. Appeals (8th cir.) 1985. Assoc. Brown & Cecil, Houston, 1965-66; asst. U.S. atty. Dept. Justice, Houston, 1971-74; mem. Jefferson, Wallis & Sherman, Houston, 1975-81, Wallis & Pruitt, Houston, 1981-87, Wallis and Short, Houston, 1987—. Instr. U. Md., Keflauik, Iceland, 1968-69; mem. faculty continuing legal edn. U. Houston, 1981-84. Capt. USAF, 1969-70. Decorated Air Force Commendation medal. Mem. Assn. Trial Lawyers Am., Am. Judicature Soc., Tex. Trial Lawyers Assn., Houston Bar Found., Phi Delta Phi, Phi Kappa Tau. Federal civil litigation, State civil litigation, Criminal. Office: Wallis & Short 4300 Scotland St Houston TX 77007-7328 E-mail: ogwlawyer@earthlink.net.

WALLS, ROBERT HAMILTON, JR., lawyer; b. Austin, Tex., May 19, 1960; s. Robert Hamilton Sr. and Anita L. (Hoffman) W.; m. Nancy R. Ghormley, Aug. 11, 1984. BBA in Petroleum, U. Tex., 1983, JD, 1985. Bar: Tex. 1985. Assoc. Vinson & Elkins, Houston, 1985—; dep. gen. coun. Enron Corp., Houston, 1992—2002, exec. v.p. & gen. coun., 2002. Mem. ABA, Tex. Bar Assn., Houston Bar Assn. Corporate, general, Oil, gas, and mineral, Private international. Office: Office of Gen Coun Enron Corp 1400 Smith St PO Box 1188 Houston TX 77251-1188*

WALMER, EDWIN FITCH, lawyer; b. Chgo., Mar. 24, 1930; s. Hillard Wentz and Anna C. (Fitch) W.; m. Florence Poling, June 17, 1952; children: Linda Diane Walmer Dennis, Fred Fitch. BS with distinction, Ind. U., 1952, JD with high distinction, 1957. Bar: Wis. 1957, U.S. Dist. Ct. (ea. dist.) Wis. 1957. Assoc. Foley & Lardner, Milw., 1957-65, ptnr., 1965-90, ret., 1990. Served to 1st lt. U.S. Army, 1952-54. Recipient Cal. C. Chambers award Culver (Ind.) Mil. Acad., 1948. Fellow Am. Coll. Trust and Estate Counsel; mem. Order of Coif, Dairymen's Country Club (Boulder Junction, Wis.), Vineyards Country Club (Naples, Fla.), Phi Eta Sigma, Beta Gamma Sigma. Republican. Congregationalist. Avocations: golf, fishing. Probate (including wills, trusts), Estate taxation, Personal income taxation. Office: Foley & Lardner 777 E Wisconsin Ave Ste 3800 Milwaukee WI 53202-5367

WALMER, JAMES L. lawyer; b. Wabash, Ind., Oct. 18, 1948; s. Warren D. and Josephine (Clupper) W.; m. Carolyn Gwen Lackey, Apr. 23, 1977; children: Ryan, Christian, Jonathan, Geoffrey. BS, Ball State U., 1971; JD, U. Tulsa, 1973. Bar: Okla. 1974, Ind. 1974, U.S. Dist. Ct. (no. and ea. dists.) Okla. 1974, U.S. Dist. Ct. (so. dist.) Ind. 1974, U.S. Dist. Ct. (no. dist.) Ind. 1975. Sole practice, Warsaw, Ind., 1974—; dep. prosecutor Kosciusko County, Warsaw, 1976—96. Town atty. Winona Lake, Ind., 1976—, Pierceton, Ind., 1980—. Chmn. bd. dirs. Cardinal Ctr. Inc., Warsaw, 1978-84; mem. philanthropy com. Ball State U., Muncie, Ind., 1986—; pres. Lincoln PTO, 1989-90; co-pres. Harrison PTO, 1993-94; trustee First United Meth. Ch., 1992-94; dir. Ind. Prosecutors Child Support Alliance, 1994-96; bd. dirs. Warsaw Little League, 1994-98, coach, 1990-96, 98. Mem. ABA, Ind. Bar Assn. (chmn. surrogacy com. family law sect. 1987-88), Kosciusko County Bar Assn. (treas. 1979—), Okla. Bar Assn., Ind. Mcpl. Lawyers Assn. Lodges: Optimists (v.p. 1979-80), Shriners, Masons. Republican. Methodist. Family and matrimonial, General practice. Home: 1705 E Springhill Rd Warsaw IN 46580-1805 Office: PO Box 1056 Warsaw IN 46581-1056 Fax: 574-269-5593. E-mail: jwalmer@insightbb.com.

WALNER, ROBERT JOEL, lawyer; b. Chgo., Dec. 22, 1946; s. Wallace and Elsie W.; m. Charlene Walner; children: Marci, Lisa. BA, U. Ill., 1968; JD, De Paul U., 1972; MBA with distinction, Northwestern U., 1991. Bar: Ill. 1972, U.S. Dist. Ct. (no. dist.) Ill. 1972, U.S. Ct. Appeals (7th cir.) 1972, Fla. 1973. Atty. SEC, Chgo., 1972-73; pvt. practice Chgo., 1973—; adminstrv. law judge Ill. Commerce Commn., Chgo., 1973-76; atty. Allied Van Lines, Inc., Broadview, Ill., 1976-79; sr. v.p., gen. counsel, corp. sec. The Balcor Co., Skokie, Ill., 1979-92; prin. fin. ops. Balcor Securities divsn. The Balcor Co., Skokie, 1984-92, pres., 1989-92; of counsel Lawrence, Walner & Assocs., Ltd., Chgo., 1992-93; sr. v.p., gen. counsel, corp. sec. Grubb & Ellis Co., Northbrook, Ill., 1994—2001, exec. v.p., chief adminstrv. and legal officer, corp. sec., 2001—. Mem. securities adv. com. to Ill. Sec. of State, 1984-94; mem. editl. bd. Real Estate Securities Jour., Real Estate Securities and Capital Markets; program chmn. Regulators and You seminar. Contbr. chpts. to books, articles on real estate and securities law to profl. jours.; assoc. editor De Paul U. Law Rev. Mem. Kellogg Career Devel. Com., 1992-94, Kellogg Bus. Adv. Com., 1992-2001; mem. enterprise forum MIT, 1992—, mem. exec. com., 1993-94. With USAR, 1968-73. Mem. ABA, Ill. Bar Assn., Chgo. Bar Assn., Fla. Bar Assn., Am. Real Estate Com. (pres. com. 1985-90), Real Estate Syndication Com. (chmn. 1982-85), Ill. Inst. Continuing Legal Edn., N.Am. Securities Adminstrs. Assn. Inc. (industry adv. com. to real estate com., 1987-89), Real Estate Securities and Syndication Inst. of Nat. Assn. Realtors (chmn. regulatory and legis. com., 1984, 87, group v.p. 1987, exec. com. 1987-90, specialist, real estate investment), Nat. Real Estate Investment Forum (chmn. 1985, 88), Real Estate Investment Assn. (founder, exec. com. 1990-92), Kellogg Alumni Club (bd. dirs., event chmn. 1996-98, v.p., exec. com. 1998-99), Beta G amma Sigma. General civil litigation, Corporate, general, Securities.

WALPIN, GERALD, lawyer; b. N.Y.C., Sept. 1, 1931; s. Michael and Mary (Gordon) W.; m. Sheila Kainer, Apr. 13, 1957; children: Amanda Eve, Edward Andrew, Jennifer Hope BA, CCNY, 1952; LLB cum laude, Yale Law Sch., 1955. Bar: N.Y. 1955, U.S. Supreme Ct. 1965, U.S. Ct. Appeals (2d cir.) 1960, (6th cir.) 1969, (3d cir.) 1976, (8th cir.) 1982, (9th cir.) 1983, (llth cir.) 1983, (7th cir.) 1984, U.S. Ct. Claims 1984. Law clk. to Hon. E.J. Dimock U.S. Dist. Ct. (so. dist.) N.Y., N.Y.C.; law clk. to Hon. F.P. Bryan U.S. Dist. Judge (so. dist.) N.Y., N.Y.C., 1955-57; asst. U.S. atty., chief spl. prosecutions U.S. Atty. Office, N.Y.C., 1960-65; sr. ptnr. Katten Muchin Zavis Rosenman predecessor firms, N.Y.C., 1965—2002, chmn. litigation dept., 1985-96, counsel, 2002—. Adv. com. Fed. Ct. So. Dist. N.Y.,

1991-98; co-chmn. lawyers divsn. Anti-Defamation League, N.Y., 1994-97; bd. dirs. Ctr. for Individual Rights, 1997—, dir. 1989—; pres. Fed. Bar Coun., 2002—. Editor Yale Law Jour., 1953-54, mng. editor, 1954-55; contbr. articles to profl. jours. Pres. Parker Jewish Inst. for Health Care and Rehab., New Hyde Park, N.Y., 1987-90, trustee, 1979—; bd. dirs. Fund for Modern Cts., N.Y.C., 1985-91; mem. law com. Am. Jewish Com., 1980—; mem. Com. for Free World, N.Y.C., 1983-91; trustee, mem. exec. com. United Jewish Appeal-Fedn. Jewish Philanthropies, N.Y.C., 1984-96; mem. Nassau County Crime Commn., 1970; pres. Kensington Civic Orgn., Gt. Neck, N.Y., 1972-73. Recipient Quality of Life award United Jewish Appeal Fedn., 1978, Human Rels. award Am. Jewish Com., 1982, Gift of Life award Jewish Inst. Geriatric Care, 1987, Learned Hand award Am. Jewish Com., 1990, Human Rels. award Anti-Defamation League, 1998. Mem. ABA, Assn. Bar City N.Y., Fed. Bar Coun. (chmn. modern cts. com. 1989, v.p. 1991-95, chmn. bench and bar liaison com. 1994-95, vice chmn. 1995-97, chmn. bd. dirs. 1997-99, pres. 2002—), Federalist Soc. (chmn. litigation sect. 1996-99, mem. bd. visitors 1999—), Univ. Club. Republican. Jewish. General civil litigation, Criminal, Securities. Home: 875 Park Ave New York NY 10021-0341 Office: KMZ Rosenman 575 Madison Ave Fl 20 New York NY 10022-2511 E-mail: gerald.walpin@kmzr.com.

WALSER, DONALD H. lawyer; b. Mankato, Minn., May 5, 1943; s. Henry and Gladys Walser; m. Susan M. Johannsen, July 3, 1965; children: Jill, Amanda, Nicholas. BA, U. St. Thomas, St. Paul, MN, 1965; JD cum laude, U. Minn., Minneapolis, 1972. Civil Trial Specialist: Nat. Bd. Trial Advocacy 1988. Ptnr. Kraft, Walser, Hettig & Honsey, PLLP, Hutchinson, Minn., 1972—. Judge adv., legal adv. Minn. Am. Legion, St. Paul, 1995—. Commr. Hutchinson Cmty. Devel. Corp., 1994—2002, Hutchinson Utilities Commn., 2000—02. Sp5 U.S. Army, 1966—69, Germany. Mem.: ABA, Minn. State Bar Assn. Office: Kraft Walser Hettig & Honsey PLLP 131 S Main St Hutchinson MN 55350 Office Fax: 320-587-8152. E-mail: kwhh@hutchtel.net.

WALSH, DAVID GRAVES, lawyer; b. Madison, Wis., Jan. 7, 1943; s. John J. and Audrey B. Walsh; married; children: Michael, Katherine, Molly, John. BBA, U. Wis., 1965; JD, Harvard U., 1970. Bar: Wis. Law clk. Wis. Supreme Ct., Madison, 1970-71; ptnr. Walsh, Walsh, Sweeney & Whitney, Madison, 1971-86; ptnr.-in-charge Foley & Lardner, Madison, 1986—. Bd. regents U. Wis., 2003-; bd. dirs. Nat. Guardian Life, Madison, 1981—; lectr. U. Wis., Madison, 1974-75, 77-78, mem. bd. Regents U of Wis.. Chmn. State of Wis. Elections Bd., Madison, 1978. Lt. USN, 1965-67, Vietnam. Recipient Disting. Bus. Alumnus award U. Wis. Sch. Bus., 1997. Maple Bluff Country Club (Madison) (pres. 1987). Roman Catholic. Avocations: tennis, golf, fishing. Bankruptcy, Commercial, contracts (including sales of goods; commercial financing), Communications. Home: 41 Fuller Dr Madison WI 53704-5962 Office: Foley & Lardner PO Box 1497 Madison WI 53701-1497

WALSH, FRANCIS RICHARD, law educator, lawyer, arbitrator; b. Newark, Jan. 1, 1924; s. Francis R. Sr. and Loretta Anne (Norton) W.; m. Ethel Anne Walsh, Mar. 12, 1944; 1 child, Jeffrey R. BSBA, Seton Hall U., 1943; JD, Georgetown U., 1948. Prof. Law Sch. Georgetown U., Washington, 1949-51; law clk. to presiding justice U.S. Ct. Appeals (9th cir.), San Francisco, 1948-49; chief broadcast bur. FCC, Washington, 1970-71; pvt. practice San Francisco, 1954-70; prof. law U. San Francisco, 1951-54, 71-74, dean, prof. law, 1957-70; prof. law Hastings Coll. of Law, U. Calif., San Francisco, 1974—. Lt. USNR, 1943-46, PTO. Roman Catholic. Avocations: golf, travel. Home: 28 Spring Rd Kentfield CA 94904 Office: Hastings Coll Law 200 Mcallister St San Francisco CA 94102

WALSH, GERRY O'MALLEY, lawyer; b. Houston, Dec. 22, 1936; d. Frederick Harold and Blanche (O'Malley) W. BS, U. Houston, 1959; JD, South Tex. Coll. Law, 1966. Bar: Tex. 1966, U.S. Dist. Ct. (so. dist.) Tex. 1967, U.S. Dist. Ct. (we. dist.) Tex. 1976; cert. elem. tchr., Tex. Elem. tchr., Houston, 1959-65; instr. bus. law U. Houston, 1966-67; pvt. practice Houston, 1966—. Lectr. legal, jud. and civic orgns. Adviser, den mother Sam Houston coun. Boy Scouts Am.; mem. Mus. Fine Arts. Recipient den mother award Sam Houston coun. Boy Scouts Am. Mem. ABA, Houston Zool. Assn., Houston Archeol. Soc., Bus. and Profl. Women's Assn. (Woman of Yr. 1973), Am. Judicature Soc., Tex. Criminal Lawyers Assn., Harris County Criminal Lawyers Assn., Tex. Trial Lawyers Assn., State Bar Tex., Houston Bar Assn., U. Houston Alumni Assn., So. Tex. Coll. Law Alumni Assn., Nat. Criminal Def. Lawyers Assn., Zeta Tau Alpha (best mem. and rec. sec. 1958), Sigma Chi (award 1958). Criminal, Family and matrimonial, General practice.

WALSH, JAMES HAMILTON, lawyer; b. N.Y.C., N.Y., May 20, 1947; s. Edward James and Helen Smith (Hamilton) W.; m. Janice Ausherman, Aug. 3, 1967; children: Tracy, Courtney, Eric. BA in Psychology, Bridgewater Coll., 1968; JD, U. Va., 1975. Bar: Va. 1975, U.S. Dist. Ct. (ea. and we. dists.) Va. 1975, U.S. Ct. Appeals (4thc ir.) 1976, U.S. Supreme Ct. 1982. Assoc. McGuire, Woods LLPms), Richmond, Va., 1975-82; ptnr. McGuire, Woods, Battle & Boothe (and predecessor firms), Richmond, Va., 1982—. Instr. Nat. Inst. Trial Adv.; adj. prof. U. Richmond, 1992, 93; spl. prosecutor U.S. Dist. Ct. (ea. dist.) Va., 1979, 84. Contbr. articles to profl. jours. Mem. bd. trustees Bridgewater (Va.) Coll., mem. exec. com.; mem. staff Va. Law Rev. With U.S. Army, 1969-72. Mem. ABA (mem. antitrust sect. health care com., litigation sect.), Va. State Bar (bd. govs. antitrust sect. 1984-90, chmn. 1986), Va. Bar Assn. (chmn. criminal law sect. 1997, 98), Richmond Bar Assn., Best Lawyers in Am., 2003—, Va. Legal Elite, 2002, Willow Oaks, Order Coif, Phi Delta Phi. Episcopalian. Antitrust, Federal civil litigation, Product liability. Home: 113 Adingham Ct Richmond VA 23229-7761 Office: McGuire Woods LLP 1 James Ctr 910 E Cary St Richmond VA 23219-4004 E-mail: jwalsh@mcguirewoods.com.

WALSH, J(OHN) B(RONSON), lawyer; b. Buffalo, Feb. 20, 1927; s. John A. and Alice (Condon) W.; m. Barbara Ashford, May 20, 1966 (dec. Feb. 2001); 1 child, Martha. AB, Canisius Coll., 1950; JD, Georgetown U., 1952. Bar: N.Y. 1953, U.S. Supreme Ct. 1958, U.S. Ct. Internat. Trade 1969, U.S. Ct. Customs and Patent Appeals 1973. Trial atty. Garvey & Conway, N.Y.C., 1953-54; vol. atty. Nativity Mission, N.Y.C., 1953-54; ptnr. Jaeckle, Fleischmann, Kelly, Swart & Augspurger, Buffalo, 1955-60; pvt. practice Buffalo, 1961-75; ptnr. Jaeckle, Fleischmann & Mugel, Buffalo, 1976-80; with Walsh & Cleary, P.C., Buffalo, 1980-84; pvt. practice, 1984—; spl. counsel Ecology and Environment, Inc., Lancaster, N.Y., 1989—. Trial counsel antitrust div. Dept. Justice, Washington, 1960-61; spl. counsel on disciplinary procedures N.Y. Supreme Ct., 1960-76; appointee legal disciplinary coordinating com. State of N.Y., 1971; legis. counsel, spl. counsel to mayor Buffalo, 1995—; counsel to sheriff Erie County, 1969-72; legis counsel Niagara Frontier Transp. Authority; cons. Norfolk So. R.R., Ecology and Environment on Govtl. Affairs; guest lectr. univs. and profl. groups. Author: (TV series) The Law and You (Freedom Found. award, ABA award, Internat. Police Assn. award). Past pres. Ashford Hollow Found. Visual and Performing Arts; past trustee Dollar Bills, Inc.; past co-producer Grand Island Playhouse and Players. With U.S. Army, 1945-46. Recipient Gold Key Buffalo Jr. C. of C., 1962, award Freedom Found., 1966. Fellow Am. Bar Found.; mem. ABA (del. internat. conf. Brussels 1963, Mexico City 1964, Lausanne, Switzerland 1964, Award of Merit com. 1961-70, sec., vice chair, chmn. sect. bar activities 1965-69, mem. ho. of dels. 1969-70, mem. crime prevention and control com. 1968-70, vice chair sr. lawyers divsn., com. legislation and adminstrn. regulations 1992—, vice chair sr. lawyers divsn. membership com. 1993-94), N.Y. Trial Lawyers Assn., Am. Immigration Lawyers Assn., Am. Judicature Soc., N.Y. State Bar Assn. (past exec. sec.), Erie County Bar Assn., Buffalo Bar Assn., Nat. Pub. Employer Labor Relations Assn., Capital Hill Club of Buffalo, Am. Assn. Airport Execs., N.Y. State Bus. Coun. (environ. law subcom., chmn. subcom.), Buffalo Irish Club (bd. dirs.), Buffalo Athletic Club (past bd. dirs., past v.p.), Buffalo Canoe Club, Buffalo Club, Ft. Orange of Albany Club, KC, Knights of Equity, Leoknights, Phi Delta Phi, Delta Gamma. Roman Catholic. Environmental, Immigration, naturalization, and customs, Legislative. Office: 368 Pleasant View Dr Lancaster NY 14086-1316 also: 210 Ellicott Sq Bldg Buffalo NY 14203-2402 Home: Apt 302 1217 Delaware Ave Buffalo NY 14209-1432 E-mail: jbwalsh@ene.com.

WALSH, JOSEPH LEO, III, lawyer; b. St. Louis, Dec. 7, 1954; s. Joseph Leo and Joan Marie (Bocklage) W.; m. Eileen Rose Boland, June 11, 1982; children: Katie Rose, Joseph L. IV, Brian James, John Patrick, Mary Elizabeth. BS cum laude, Loras Coll., 1977; JD, St. Mary's U., 1984. Bar: Tex. 1984, U.S. Dist. Ct. (so. dist.) Tex. 1985, Mo. 1986, U.S. Dist. Ct. (ea. dist.) Mo. 1989, U.S. Ct. Appeals (8th cir.) 1989, U.S. Supreme Ct. 1991. Assoc. Chamberlain, Hrdlicka, White, Johnson & Williams, Houston, 1984-86; atty. Haley, Fredrickson & Walsh, St. Louis, 1986-88; assoc. Gray & Ritter, St. Louis, 1988-95; pvt. practice St. Louis, 1995—; mcpl. judge 21st Jud. Cir. Ct., Frontenac, 2000—01. Pro bono legal clinic St. Patrick Ctr., 1991—, Holy Guardian Angel Settlement, 1995—; jud. clk. U.S. Dist. Ct. (we. dist.) Tex., 1984. Co-author: Missouri Bar CLE Treatise on Torts, 2d edit., 1990; sr. assoc. editor St. Mary's U. Sch. Law Jour., 1983-84. Active Holly Hills Neighborhood Assn., 1991-93; v.p. Our Lady of Pillar Men's Club, 1998, pres., 1999-2000. Recipient Torts and Evidence award Lawyers' Co-op Pub. Co., 1982; named to Nat. Order Barristers, 1984. Mem. ATLA, Am. Bd. Trial Advocates, Mo. Assn. Trial Attys., Bar Assn. Met. St. Louis, Lawyers Assn. St. Louis, Phi Delta Phi (pres. 1984). Roman Catholic. General civil litigation, Personal injury (including property damage), Product liability. Home and Office: 10469 White Bridge Ln Saint Louis MO 63141-8415 Office: 720 Olive St Ste 750 Saint Louis MO 63101-2330

WALSH, JOSEPH RICHARD, lawyer; b. Atlanta, May 10, 1951; s. Joseph Radamaker and Meta Lucille (Cole) W.; m. Elisabeth Clare Kane, July 27, 1980; children: Lindsay Carolyn, Dana Elisabeth, Cameron Marisa. B in Indsl. Engring., Ga. Inst. Tech., 1973; JD, U. Ga., 1976; ML in Taxation, Georgetown Law Ctr., 1984. Bar: Ga. 1976, Va. 1978, D.C. 1979, Calif. 1984, U.S. Ct. Appeals (4th cir.) 1978, U.S. Ct. Appeals (5th cir.) 1976, U.S. Ct. Appeals (9th cir.) 1984, U.S. Ct. Appeals (11th cir.) 1982, U.S. Dist. Ct. (no. dist.) Ga. 1976, U.S. Dist. Ct. (no. dist.) Calif. 1984, U.S. Tax Ct. 1983, U.S. Claims Ct. 1983. Indsl. engr. So. Ry. System, Atlanta, 1973-74; atty. ICC, Washington, 1977-78, atty., asst. rail merger coordinator, 1979-84; assoc. Fulbright & Jaworski, Washington, 1978-79; counsel Bank of Am. Nat. Assn., San Francisco, 1984-85, sr. counsel, 1985-1998, asst. genl. counsel, 1998—; counselor Athens Legal Aid and Defender Soc., Ga., 1976; instr. comml. law San Francisco Law Sch., 1987-92. Contbg. author Federal Regulatory Process: Practice and Procedure, 1981. Campaign vol. Jimmy Carter Presdl. Campaign, New Hampshire, 1976. Recipient Spl. Achievement awards ICC, 1981, 82, 83, Chmn.'s Commendation award, ICC, 1982, Extraordinary award Bank Am., 1988; named Outstanding Young Men Am. U.S. Jaycees, 1982. Ga. Inst. Tech. nat. merit scholar 1969; NSF grantee 1972. Mem. D.C. Bar Assn., Ga. Bar Assn., ABA, Fed. Bar Assn., Va. Bar Assn., Calif. Bar Assn., San Francisco Bar Assn., San Francisco Leasing Lawyers Forum, Am. Inst. Indsl. Engrs., Sierra Club, Calif. Nature Conservancy, Phi Kappa Phi, Tau Beta Pi, Alpha Pi Mu. Presbyterian. Club: Lawyers (San Francisco), Commonwealth Calif. Banking, Commercial, contracts (including sales of goods; commercial financing), Corporate, general. Office: Bank of Am N A CA5-705-04-01 555 California St 4th Fl San Francisco CA 94137-0001 E-mail: joseph.r.walsh@bankofamerica.com.

WALSH, JOSEPH THOMAS, state supreme court justice; b. Wilmington, Del., May 18, 1930; s. Joseph Patrick and Mary Agnes (Bolton) W.; m. Madeline Maria Lamb, Oct. 6, 1955; children: Kevin, Lois, Patrick, Daniel, Thomas, Nancy. BA, LaSalle Coll., 1952; LLB, Georgetown U., 1955. Bar: D.C. 1955, Del. 1955. Atty. Ho. of Reps., Dover, Del., 1961-62; chief counsel Pub. Svc. Commn., Dover, 1964-72; judge Del. Superior Ct., Wilmington, 1972-84; vice chancellor Ct. of Chancery, Wilmington, 1984-85; justice Del. Supreme Ct., Wilmington, 1985—. Capt. U.S. Army, 1955-58. Democrat. Roman Catholic. Office: Del Supreme Ct Carvel State Bldg Wilmington DE 19801-3509

WALSH, LAWRENCE EDWARD, lawyer; b. Port Maitland, N.S., Can., Jan. 8, 1912; came to U.S., 1914, naturalized, 1922; s. Cornelius Edward and Lila May (Sanders) W.; m. Mary Alma Porter; children: Barbara Marie, Janet Maxine (Mrs. Alan Larson), Sara Porter, Dale Edward, Elizabeth Porter (Mrs. Joseph Wells). AB, Columbia, 1932, LL.B., 1935; LL.D., Union U., 1959, St. John's U., 1975, Suffolk U., 1975, Waynesburg Coll., 1976, Vt. Law Sch., 1976. Bar: N.Y. 1936, D.C. 1981, Okla. 1981, U.S. Supreme Ct. 1951. Spl. asst. atty. gen. Drukman Investigation, 1936-38; dep. asst. dist. atty. N.Y. County, 1938-41; assoc. Davis Polk Wardwell Sunderland & Kiendl, 1941-43; asst. counsel to gov. N.Y., 1943-49; counsel to gov., 1950-51; counsel Pub. Service Commn., 1951-53; gen. counsel, exec. dir. Waterfront Commn. of N.Y. Harbor, 1953-54; U.S. judge So. Dist. N.Y., 1954-57; U.S. dep. atty. gen., 1957-60; partner firm Davis, Polk & Wardwell, 1961-81; counsel firm Crowe & Dunlevy, Oklahoma City, 1981—. Ind. counsel Iran/Contra investigation, 1986-93; chmn. N.Y. State Moreland Commn. Alcoholic Beverage Control Law, 1963-64; pres. Columbia Alumni Fedn., 1968-69; dep. head with rank of amb. U.S. del. meetings on Vietnam, Paris, 1969; counsel to N.Y. State Ct. on Judiciary, 1971-72; 2d crct. mem. U.S. Crct. Judge Nominating Commn., 1978-80. Author: Firewall The Iran-Contra Conspiracy and Cover-Up, 1997, The Life of Insecurity, 2003. Trustee emeritus Columbia U., Mut. Life Ins. Co., N.Y. Recipient medal for excellence Columbia U., 1959, Law Sch., Columbia U., 1980, John Jay award Columbia Coll., 1989. Fellow Am. Bar Found., Am. Coll. Trial Lawyers; mem. Am. Law Inst., ABA (pres. 1975-76), N.Y. State Bar Assn. (pres. 1966-67), Oklahoma County Bar Assn., Okla. State Bar Assn., Internat. Bar Assn., Assn. of Bar of City of New York, N.Y. County Lawyers Assn., Fed. Bar Coun.; hon. mem. Law Soc. Eng. and Wales, Can. Bar Assn., Mexican Bar Assn., N.Y. Club, The Century Club, Oklahoma City Golf and Country Club, Petroleum Club (Oklahoma City), Beacon Club (Oklahoma City), Beta Theta Pi. Presbyterian. Home: 1902 Bedford Dr Oklahoma City OK 73116-5306 Office: 1800 Mid Am Towers Oklahoma City OK 73102

WALSH, MILTON O'NEAL, lawyer; b. Memphis, Tenn., June 17, 1941; BS, La. State U., 1964, JD, 1971. Bar: La. 1971. Salesman Met. Ins. Co., Baton Rouge, 1963-65; claims adjustor Safeco Ins. Co., Baton Rouge, 1965-68; law clk. Franklin, Moore, Beychok & Cooper, Baton Rouge, 1968-71, assoc., 1971-73; ptnr. Franklin, Moore, Cooper & Walsh, Baton Rouge, 1973-74, Franklin, Moore & Walsh, Baton Rouge, 1974-90; prin. O'Neal Walsh and Assocs., Baton Rouge, 1990—2002; atty. Walsh and Bailey, Baton Rouge, 2003—. Chmn. rules com. Baton Rouge City Ct., 1975-76, liaison com. 19th Jud. Dist. Ct., 1977; instr. in bus. law La. State U., 1974. Mem. ABA (mem. products liability com. 1978-79), Baton Rouge Bar Assn., La. Bar Assn., La. Assn. Def. Counsel (bd. dirs. 1982-84, 96-97), Internat. Assn. Def. Counsel (mem. casualty ins. com. 1980-81, mem. faculty 14th ann. counsel trial acad. 1986), Def. Rsch. Inst. (state chmn. 1980-82, regional v.p. 1983-86, bd. dirs. 1986-89, 96-98, mem. arbitration com., mem. nat. nominating com. 2000, Scroll of Merit award 1981, 82), Am. Bd. Trial Advocates (L.A. chpt., treas. 2000-01, v.p. 2001-02, pres. 2002, faculty mem. Masters in Trial 2000), Assn. Def. Trial Attys. (state chmn. 1984—, S.W. mem. chmn. 1985-95, v.p./pres.-elect 1995-96, pres. 1996-97, mem. exec. coun. 1990-93), Sherwood Forest Country Club (bd. dirs. 1977-79, pres. 1979), Phi Delta Phi. General civil litigation, Insurance. Office: O'Neal Walsh & Assocs 501 Louisiana Ave Baton Rouge LA 70802-5921 E-mail: onealwalsh@walshbailey.com.

WALSH, ROBERT ANTHONY, lawyer; b. Boston, Aug. 26, 1938; s. Frank and Emily Angelica (Bissitt) W.; m. Angela Rosalie Barile, Aug. 3, 1966; children: Maria, Robert II, Amy. SB, MIT, 1960; MS, Fla. Inst. Tech., 1967; JD, Suffolk U., 1971. Bar: Mass. 1971, U.S. Dist. Ct. Mass. 1972, U.S. Patent Office 1972, Can. Patent Office 1973, Ill. 1976, U.S. Supreme Ct. 1976, U.S. Ct. Appeals (Fed. cir.) 1982, U.S. Ct. Mil. Appeals 1983, Vt. 1996; registered profl. engr., Mass. Engr. Saturn Boeing, Michaud, La., 1964-65; program analyst RCA, Cape Canaveral, Fla., 1965-68; patent trainee, engr. Avco Research Lab., Everett, Mass., 1968-72; patent atty. GTE Labs., Waltham, Mass., 1972-73; group patent counsel Bell & Howell Co., Chgo., 1973-78; patent counsel ITT E. Coast Patents, Nutley, N.J., 1978-80, patent counsel internat., 1980-82, sr. patent counsel internat., 1982-86; dir. internat. patents ITT Corp., N.Y.C., 1986-87; gen. patent counsel ITT Def. Tech. Corp., Nutley, 1987-89; chief patent counsel, assoc. gen. counsel Allied-Signal Aerospace Co., Phoenix, 1989-94; atty. IBM Corp., Essex Junction, Vt., 1994—. Ednl. counselor admissions MIT, No. N.J., 1978-89, Ariz., 1989-94, Vt., 1998—; with Office of Judge Adv. Gen., Washington. Legal officer Civil Air Patrol Vt. Wing. Col. (ret.) USAF, 1960—92. Mem. ABA (co-chmn. subcom. PTC sect. 105), Tri-State USAFR Lawyers Assn. (Meritorious Achievement award 1980), KC (fin. sec. Scottsdale, Ariz. 1993-95), Internat. Patent Club (pres. 1988-89), Am. Intellectual Property Law Assn., Aerospace Industry Assn. (chmn. Intellectual Property com.), Chgo. Patent Law Assn., N.J. Patent Law Assn., Ariz. Patent Law Assn. (bd. dirs.), Sigma Xi. Roman Catholic. Patent, Trademark and copyright. Home: 171 Yacht Haven Dr Shelburne VT 05482-7776 Office: Intellectual Property Law Dept 915 1000 River St Essex Junction VT 05452-4201

WALSH, ROBERT K. dean; AB, Providence Coll., 1964; JD, Harvard U., 1967. Bar: Calif. 1967, Ark. 1979. Assoc. McCatchen, Black, Verleger & Shea, L.A., 1967-70; asst. prof. Villanova (Pa.) U., 1970-71, assoc. prof., 1971-73, prof., 1973-76; ptnr. Friday, Eldredge & Clark, Little Rock, 1981-89; dean, prof. Wake Forest Sch. Law, Winston-Salem, N.C., 1989—. Mem. ABA (chair accreditation com. 1984-86, chair standards rev. com. sect. legal edn. 1991—), N.C. Bar Assn. (chair bar bench and law schs. com. 1990-92, v.p., bd. govs. 1994-95). Office: Wake Forest Sch Law Dean's Office PO Box 7206 Winston Salem NC 27109-7206

WALSH, SEAN M. lawyer, audio-video computer forensics consultant; b. N.Y.C., Dec. 26, 1947; s. John W. and Catherine M. Walsh; m. Christine Ann Kull, June 10, 1978; children: Kathleen, Sean, Stephen. BS, Fordham U., 1970, JD, 1973. Bar: N.Y. 1974. Chief, asst. dist. atty. Dist. Atty.'s Office, N.Y.C., 1973-96; pres. Walsh Assocs. Forensic Cons., Douglaston, N.Y., 1997—. Officer/dir. Law Enforcement Video Assocs., Ft. Worth, 1989-95; counsel Office Inspector Gen., N.Y.C., 1996-. Author: Video and the Law, 1979; inventor non-linear video wire tapping rec. sys. Vice-chmn. N.Y.C. Cmty. Planning Bd., 1986-98; pres. Queens (N.Y.) Civic Congress, 1996—, past pres./dir. Douglaston Civic Assn. Recipient Outstanding Cmty. Bd. Work, N.Y.C., 1973, Outstanding Svc. to N.Y. State Police, 1992, Van Zandt Cmty. Svc. award, 1999; named Marshall to Little Neck Douglaston Meml. Day Parade, 1990. Mem. Assn. Bar City N.Y. (Comm. com. 1983-85, Computer com. 1997-2000), High Tech. Crime Investigation Assn. (pres. local chpt. 1994-96, internat. pres. 2000-2001). Avocations: sailing, skiing, scuba diving. Home: PO Box 238 Douglaston NY 11363-0238

WALSH, THOMAS CHARLES, lawyer; b. Mpls., July 6, 1940; s. William G. and Kathryne M. Walsh; m. Joyce Williams, Sept. 7, 1968; children: Brian Christopher, Timothy Daniel, Laura Elizabeth Smith. BS in Commerce magna cum laude, St. Louis U., 1962, LLB cum laude, 1964. Bar: Mo. 1964, U.S. Dist. Ct. (ea. dist.) Mo. 1964, U.S. Ct. Appeals (8th cir.) 1968, U.S. Supreme Ct. 1971, U.S. Ct. Appeals (6th cir.) 1972, U.S. Ct. Appeals (5th cir.) 1974, U.S. Ct. Appeals (D.C. cir.) 1980, U.S. Ct. Appeals (7th cir.) 1982, U.S. Ct. Appeals (9th cir.) 1987, U.S. Ct. Appeals (4th cir.) 1989, U.S. Ct. Appeals (11th and fed. cirs.) 1992, U.S. Ct. Appeals (2d and 10th cirs.) 1993. Jr. ptnr. Bryan, Cave, McPheeters & McRoberts, St. Louis, 1964-73; ptnr. Bryan Cave LLP, St. Louis, 1974—; mem. exec. com. Bryan Cave LLP, St. Louis, 1980-96. Mem. 8th Cir. Adv. Com., 1983-86. Bd. dirs. St. Louis Symphony Soc., 1983-95. With U.S. Army, 1965-66; lt. USNR, 1966-71. Fellow Am. Coll. Trial Lawyers, Am. Acad. Appellate Lawyers; mem. Mo. Bar Assn., St. Louis Bar Assn., Am. Law Inst., Mo. Athletic Club, Bellerive Country Club. Roman Catholic. Federal civil litigation, State civil litigation, Appellate. Office: Bryan Cave LLP 1 Metropolitan Sq 211 N Broadway Saint Louis MO 63102-2733 E-mail: tcwalsh@bryancave.com.

WALSH, THOMAS JOSEPH, lawyer; b. Kansas City, Mo., Oct. 3, 1932; s. Thomas E. and Clare E. (O'Leary) W.; m. Ellen B. Butler; children: Carolyn, David, Kathy. AB, U. Mo., 1953; JD, Georgetown U., 1958. Bar: D.C. 1958, Mo. 1958. Sole practice, Lee's Summit, Mo., 1958—. Mem. 4th Congl. Dist. Youth Coun., 1985-92; vice chmn. Mo. Coun. on Criminal Justice, 1977-80, chmn., 1977-80; atty. to Jackson County Sheriff's Dept., 1967-72; sec. Jackson County Bd. Election Commrs., 1993-96, chmn. 1997-2001. Served to 1st lt. U.S. Army, 1953-55. Mem. Mo. Bar Assn., Assn. Trial Lawyers Am., Met. Kansas City Bar Assn., Knights of Columbus. Lodges: Optimists (lt. gov. 1963-64, pres. 1960-61). Democrat. Roman Catholic. State civil litigation, Family and matrimonial, General practice. Home: 210 NW Hillcrest Ln Lees Summit MO 64063-2103 Office: 528 W 3rd St Lees Summit MO 64063-2248

WALSH, WILLIAM ARTHUR, JR., lawyer; b. Washington, Mar. 17, 1949; children: Jesse Creighton, Patrick McKay. BS in Econs. and Fin., U. Md., 1972; JD, U. Richmond, 1977. Bar: Va. Ptnr., head real estate, fin. and devel. team Hunton & Williams, Richmond, Va., 1977—. Mem. adv. bd. for law rev. U. Richmond. Trustee, bd. dirs. Va. Commonwealth U. Real Estate Found.; mem. Va. Commonwealth U. Real Estate Circle of Excellence. Mem. ABA, Va. Bar Assn., Richmond Bar Assn., Am. Coll. Real Estate Lawyers. Home: 4705 Leonard Pky Richmond VA 23226-1337 Office: Hunton & Williams Riverfront Plz East Tower 951 E Byrd St Richmond VA 23219-4074

WALTER, GLENN RICHARD, lawyer; b. Lancaster, Pa., May 16, 1962; s. Richard Kupp and Gayle Marie Walter; m. Nancy Donita Messer, Jan. 11, 1992; children: Jessica Morgan, Kyle Reed, Sydney Paige. BSBA, U. Pa., Bloomsburg, 1984; JD, U. Tenn., 1987. Bar: Tenn., U.S. Dist. Ct. (ea. dist.) Tenn., U.S. Ct. Appeals (6th cir.). Atty. Kramer Rayson Leake Rodgers & Morgan, Knoxville, 1987-96, Lewis King Krieg & Waldrop, Knoxville, 1996—. Mem. ABA (spl. projects coord. young lawyers divsn. 1997-98), Tenn. Bar Assn. (bd. govs. 1997-99, pres. young lawyers divsn. 1998-99), Knoxville Bar Assn. General civil litigation, Insurance, Labor (including EEOC, Fair Labor Standards Act, labor-management relations, NLRB, OSHA). Office: Lewis King Krieg & Waldrop 620 Market St Knoxville TN 37902-2231

WALTER, JEREMY CANNING, lawyer; b. Esher, U.K., Aug. 22, 1948; s. Richard and Beryl (Pugh) W.; m. Judith Jane Rowlands, Aug. 24, 1973 (div. 1983); children: Emma Canning, Alison Canning; m. Dawna Beth Rosenberg, Oct. 17, 1992. MA with double 1st class honors, Cambridge (Eng.) U., 1969, LLB with 1st class honors, 1970. Trainee solicitor Ellis Piers & Co., London, 1971-73; asst. solicitor Simmons & Simmons, London, 1973-77, ptnr., 1977—, dep. mng. ptnr. corp. dept., 1994-96, head corp. dept., 1996—, ptnr. in charge global energy utilities practice, 2001—. Mem. ICC Fin. Svcs. Commn., 1992—. Cons. editor Jour. Soc. Advanced Legal Studies, 1998—. Mem. East-West Forum of bus. law sect. IBA; co-chair IBA Arab Regional Forum Coun., 2000; com. mem. City of

London Law Soc., 1999—. Mem. ABA, Internat. Bar Assn., Securities Inst., Law Soc. (London ins. law com. 1991-99), Brit. Polish Legal Assn. (exec. com. 1992—). Office: Simmons & Simmons CityPoint 1 Ropemaker St London EC2Y 9SS England

WALTER, MICHAEL CHARLES, lawyer; b. Oklahoma City, Nov. 25, 1956; s. Donald Wayne and Viola Helen (Heffelfinger) W. BA in Polit. Sci., BJ Editl. Journalism, U. Wash., 1980; JD, Seattle U., 1983. Bar: Wash. 1985, U.S. Dist. Ct. (9th cir. 1985). Ptnr. Keating, Bucklin & McCormack, Seattle, 1985—. Instr. Bellevue (Wash.) C.C., 1983—. FAX: 206-223-9423. Mem. ABA, Wash. State Bar Assn., Seattle-King County Bar Assn., Wash. Def. Trial Laywers Assn., Seattle Claims Adjustors Assn., Wash. Assn. Mcpl. Attys., Def. Rsch. Inst., Am. Planning Assn. Avocations: running, swimming, hiking, coin collecting, photography. State civil litigation, Land use and zoning (including planning), Municipal (including bonds). Home: 11920 27th Pl SW Burien WA 98146-2438 Office: Keating Bucklin & McCormack Inc PS Bank of Am Plz 800 5th Ave Seattle WA 98104 Fax: 206- 223-9423. E-mail: mwalter@kbmlawyers.com.

WALTERS, BILL, former state senator, lawyer; b. Paris, Ark., Apr. 17, 1943; s. Peter Louis and Elizabeth Cecelia (Wilhelm) W.; m. Joyce Leslie Garrett Moore, Jan. 9, 1964 (div. 1970); children: Jamie, Sherry Ann; m. Shirley Ann Dixon, Aug. 20, 1971; 1 child, Sandra. BS, U. Ark., 1966, JD, 1971. Bar: Ark. 1971, U.S. Dist. Ct. Ark. 1971. Asst. prosecuting atty. 12th Jud. Dist. Ark., Ft. Smith, 1971-74; pvt. practice Greenwood, Ark., 1975—; mem. Ark. Senate, Little Rock, 1982-2000. Bd. dirs., sec.-treas. Mineral Owners Collective Assn. Inc., Greenwood; v.p., bd. dirs. Sebastian County Abstract & Title Ins. Co., Greenwood and Ft. Smith, Ark.; mem. Ark. Real Estate Commn., Ark. Abstract and Title Commn. Committeeman Rep. Ctrl. Com. Ark., Ft. Smith, 1980; search pilot CAP, Ft. Smith. Decorated Silver Medal of Valor; recipient Cert. of Honor Justice for Crime's Victims, 1983. Mem. Ark. Bar Assn., South Sebastian County Bar Assn. (pres. 1991-94), Profl. Landmen's Assn. Roman Catholic. Home: PO Box 280 Greenwood AR 72936-0280 Office: 1405 W Center Greenwood AR 72936-3200 E-mail: bwalters@waltlaw.net.

WALTERS, JESSE RAYMOND, JR., state supreme court justice; b. Rexburg, Idaho, Dec. 26, 1938; s. Jesse Raymond and Thelma Rachael (Hodgson) W.; m. Harriet Payne, May 11, 1959; children: Craig T., Robyn, J. Scott. Student, Ricks Coll., 1957-58; BA in Polit. Sci., U. Idaho, 1961, JD, 1963; postgrad., U. Washington, 1962; LLM, U. Va., 1990. Bar: Idaho 1963; U.S. Dist. Ct. Idaho 1964, U.S. Ct. Appeals (9th cir.) 1970. Law clk. to chief justice Idaho Supreme Ct., 1963-64; solo practice Boise, Idaho, 1964-77; atty. Idaho senate, Boise, 1965; dist. judge 4th Jud. Dist., Idaho, 1977-82, adminstrv. dist. judge, 1981-82; chief judge Idaho Ct. Appeals, Boise, 1982-97. Chmn. magistrate's commn. 4th jud. dist.; chmn. Supreme Ct. mem. services; chmn. Criminal Pattern Jury Instrn. Com.; mem. Civil Pattern Jury Instrn. Com. Republican committeeman Boise, 1975-77; mem. Ada County Rep. Ctrl. Com., 1975-77. Mem. Idaho Bar Assn. (bankruptcy com.), Idaho Adminstrv. Judges Assn., ABA, Am. Judicature Soc. (dir.), Assn. Trial Lawyers Am., Idaho Trial Layers Assn., Coun. Chief Judges Ct. Appeals (pres. 1994-95), Boise Estate Planning Coun., Jaycees (nat. dir. 1969-70, pres. Boise chpt. 1966-67), Lions, Elks, Eagles. Mem. Lds Ch. Office: Supreme Ct Idaho PO Box 83720 Boise ID 83720-3720

WALTHER, STEVEN T. lawyer; b. Reno, Nev., July 18, 1943; BA in Russian, U. Notre Dame, 1965; JD, U. Calif., Berkeley, 1968. Bar: Nev. 1968, (U.S. Dist. Ct. Nev.) 1969, Calif. 1986, (U.S. Ct. Appeals (9th cir.)) 1991, (U.S. Supreme Ct.). Guest lectr. Nat. Jud. Coll., chair exec. bd., 2001—; pres. legal adv. bd. Martindale-Hubbell LexisNexis, 2001—; panelist U.S. Magistrate Panelist, U.S. Magistrate Selection Panel, 1990; chair internat. bus. task force Coll. Bus. Adminstrn., U. Nev., Reno. Author: The Globalization of the Rule of Law and Human Rights; contbr. articles to profl. jours. Master: Am. Law Inst. (mem. consultative group transnat. civil procedure, mem. consultative group internat. jurisdiction and judgments); mem.: ATLA, ABA (bd. govs. 1995—97, fin. com. 1995—97, spl. adv. com. on internat. activities 1997—98, exec. adv. bd. 1998—2000, mem. UN coord. com. 1998—, subcom. on internat. jud. rels., mem. sect. on bus. and internat. law), Internat. Assn. Gaming Attys., Nev. Trial Lawyers Assn. Gaming Attys., Am. Inns of Ct. (Bruce R. Thompson chpt.), Nat. Conf. Bar Pres., Inc. (mem. sponsorship com. 1994—95), Washoe County Bar Assn., Calif. Bar Assn., Nev. Bar Assn. (gov., bd. govs. 1978—91, pres. 1990—91), Phi Delta Phi (trustee 2002—, bd. trustees 1990—94). Mailing: PO Box 30000 Reno NV 89520 Office: Walther Key Maupin Oats Cox & LeGoy Lakeside Profl Plz 3500 Lakeside Ct Reno NV 89509

WALTNER, ALAN CONRAD, lawyer; b. Glendale, Calif., Sept. 20, 1952; s. Peter Stephen and Aileen Elizabeth (Runck) W.; 1 child, Margaret Rose. AB, U. Calif., Berkeley, 1974, JD, 1978. Bar: Calif. 1978, U.S. Dist. Ct. (no. dist.) Calif. 1978, U.S. Ct. Appeals (9th cir.) 1979, U.S. Ct. Appeals (D.C. cir.) 1996, U.S. Supreme Ct., 1993. Assoc. Orrick, Herrington & Sutcliffe, San Francisco, 1978-83; supervisory atty. EPA, San Francisco, 1983-85; ptnr. Gorman & Waltner, Oakland, Calif., 1986-91; prin. Law Offices Alan Waltner, Oakland, Calif., 1991—98; u. counsel U. Calif., 1998—. Mem. ABA, Calif. Bar Assn., Phi Beta Kappa. Environmental. Office: 1111 Franklin St 8th fl Oakland CA 94607

WALTON, CHRISTOPHER JOHN, lawyer; BA with high honors, Coll. William and Mary, 1987; JD cum laude, Harvard Law Sch., 1990. Bar: NY 1991, registered: fgn. atty., N.Y. 2001. Assoc. Cleary, Gottlieb, Steen & Hamilton, N.Y.C., 1990—92, London, 1992—95, N.Y.C., 1995—98, spl. counsel, 1998—2001; ptnr. Clifford Chance LLP, London, 2001—. Mem.: The Law Soc. of Eng. and Wales. Securities, Mergers and acquisitions, Corporate, general. Office: Clifford Chance LLP 200 Aldersgate Street London EC1A 4JJ England Office Fax: 44-207-600-5555. E-mail: chris.walton@cliffordchance.com.

WALTON, DAN GIBSON, lawyer; b. Houston, Mar. 26, 1950; s. Dan Edward and Lucy Frances (Gibson) W.; m. Martha Sandlin, June 24, 1972; children: Cole Gibson, Emily Wyatt. BA with honors, U. Va., 1972; JD with honors, U. Tex., 1975. Bar: Tex. 1975, U.S. Dist. Ct. (so. dist.) Tex. 1977, U.S. Ct. Appeals (D.C. cir.) 1975, U.S. Ct. Appeals (5th cir.) 1981, U.S. Supreme Ct. 2001; bd. cert. in civil trial law. Law clk. to hon. Malcolm R. Wilkey D.C. Ct. Appeals (D.C. cir.), 1975-76; assoc. Vinson & Elkins, Houston, 1976-82, ptnr., 1982—. Bd. dirs. The Meth. Hosp., Houston. Bd. dirs. Tex. Equal Access to Justice Found., 2000—, State Bar of Tex., 1999-2002, South Tex. Coll. Law, Houston, 1994—, Briarwood Sch./Brookwood Cmty., Houston, 1991—; trustee St. John's Sch., Houston, 1997—, Good Samaritan Found., 1998—, Cullen Trust for Health Care, 2002-; co-chancellor Tex. Ann. Conf., United Meth. Ch., 1996—; admission commn. U.S. Dist. Cts. for So. Dist. Tex. Fellow Am. Bar Found., Tex. Bar Found., Houston Bar Found. (chair 1994), Houston Bar Assn. (pres. 1998-99), Garland Walker Am. Inn of Ct. (master), Am. Bd. Trial Advocates (assoc.), Internat. Soc. Barristers, Internat. Assn. Def. Counsel, Tex. Assn. Def. Counsel. Avocations: golf, skiing. General civil litigation, Construction, Professional liability. Office: Vinson & Elkins LLP 2300 First City Tower 1001 Fannin St Ste 3201 Houston TX 77002-6706

WALTON, LEWIS R. lawyer, writer; b. Santa Monica, Calif., Dec. 28, 1941; s. Lee Redford and Mabel B. (Nielsen) W.; m. Jo Ellen Walton, Dec. 19, 1971; 1 child, Richard. BA, La Sierra Coll., 1963; JD magna cum laude, U. San Diego, 1967, cert. tax law, 1989, LLM in Taxation, 1990. Bar: Calif. 1968, U.S. Supreme Ct. 1971, U.S. Tax Ct. 1973. Assoc. Clayton, Stark, Corona, Calif., 1970-71; pvt. practice Bakersfield, Calif., 1972—. Author: Omega, 1981, Omega II, 1995, Six Extra Years, 1981, Lucifer Diary, 1997. Bd. sec. SJCH Cmty. Hosp., Kern County, Calif., 1973-86; mem. presdl. task force Rep. Party, 1984-88; legal officer CAP, Calif., 1991-93; spl. advisor Congl. Adv. Bd., Washington, 1982-89. Lt. USCG, 1967-70, Vietnam. Recipient Burkan award ASCAP, 1966. Avocation: aviation. Personal income taxation. Office: 8825 Hwy 155 Glennville CA 93226

WALTON, MORGAN LAUCK, III, lawyer; b. Woodstock, Va., July 30, 1932; s. Morgan Lauck Jr. and Frances (Allen) W.; m. Jeannette Freeman Minor, Mar. 4, 1961; children: Morgan Lauck IV, Charles Lancelot Minor, Christopher Allen, Laura Cathlyn Hirschfeld. BA, Randolph-Macon Coll., 1953; LLB, U. Va., 1959. Bar: Va. 1959, N.Y. 1959, U.S. Ct. Appeals (2d cir.) 1959, U.S. Dist. Ct. (ea. and so. dists.) N.Y. 1960, U.S. Dist. Ct. (we. dist.) Va. 1988. Assoc. Donovan Leisure Newton & Irvine, N.Y.C., 1959-68, ptnr., 1968-84; counsel FDIC, Washington, 1989-90, asst. gen. counsel, 1990-97; mem. editl. adv. bd. Free Advice, San Francisco, 1997—. Contbr. articles to legal jours. Trustee Randolph-Macon Acad., Front Royal, Va., 1987-92, trustee emeritus, 2002—; trustee Unitarian Ch. Shenandoah Valley, Stephens City, Va., 1987—; mem. coun. Law Sch. U. Va., 1989-92; treas. Shenandoah Valley Music Festival, Woodstock, 1986-87; chmn. bd. All Souls Ch., N.Y.C., 1974-76; mem. Shenandoah County Dem. Com., 1999—. With U.S. Army, 1953-56. Mem. Univ. Club (N.Y.C.), Collectors Club, Order of Coif, Phi Beta Kappa. Democrat. Banking, Federal civil litigation, Professional liability. Home: 908 Kern Springs Rd Woodstock VA 22664-3216

WALTON, R. KEITH, academic administrator, lawyer; BA, Yale U., 1986; JD, Harvard U., 1990. Bar: Ga. Assoc. King & Spaulding, Atlanta, 1991-93; law clk. for Judge. U.W. Clemon U.S. Dist. Ct. (no. dist.) Ala., Birmingham, 1990-91; chief of staff Office Enforcement Dept. Treas., Washington, 1993-96; sec. of univ. Columbia U., N.Y.C., 1996—, polit. sci. lectr., 1997. Del. Young Leaders Conf., 1998. Del. Interpol, Rome, 1994, Beijing, 1995; treas. Yale Coll. Class of 1986, 1985-96; dep. dir. White House Security Rev., Washington, 1994-95; sr. advisor Good Ol' Boy Round Up Rev., Washington, 1995-96; U.S. Del., UN Crime Commn., Vienna, 1996; mem. adv. bd. Human Rights Watch, 1997—; bd. dirs. Sanctuary for Families, Apollo Theatre Found., Orch. St. Luke's. Mem. Am. Law Inst., Coun. for U.S. and Italy, Coun. Fgn. Rels. (adv. bd. 1997—), Enterprise Found. (N.Y. adv. bd. 1997—), Century Assn. Office: Columbia U Office of Sec 211 Low Meml Libr 535 W 116th St New York NY 10027-7030

WALTON, REGGIE BARNETT, judge; b. Feb. 8, 1949; m. Debra Walton; 1 child, Danon. BA, W.Va. State Coll., 1971; JD, Am. U., 1974. Staff atty. Defender Assn. Phila., 1974-76; asst. U.S. atty. Office of U.S. Atty., Washington, 1976-80, chief career criminal unit, 1979-80; assoc. judge Superior Ct. D.C., 1981—89, 1991—2001; exec. asst. U.S. atty. Office of U.S. Atty., Washington, 1980-81; dep. presiding judge criminal divsn. Superior Ct. D.C., 1986-89; assoc. dir. Office Nat. Drug Control Policy, Exec. Office of Pres., Washington, 1989-91; sr. White House advisor for crime, 1991; U.S. dist. judge U.S. Dist. Ct. for D.C., Wasington, 2001—. Mem. U.S. Dept. Justice and ABA Ctrl. and East European Law Initiative Reform Project, Irkutsk, Russia, 1996; instr. SEAK, Inc., 1993, 97, Criminal Practice Inst., Washington, 1996, 97, Ctrl. and East European Law Inst., ABA, 1996, Harvard U., 1994—; mem. faculty Nat. Jud. Coll., Reno, Nev., 1999—, George Washington U. Law Ctr., 1992—; instr. Nat. Inst. Trial Advocacy, Georgetown U. Law Sch., Washington, 1983—, U.S. Dept. Justice, 1993, ABA Traffic Ct. Sem., Washington, 1984, 87; disting. guest lectr. Lincoln U., Jefferson City, Mo., 1991, Albany (Ga.) State Coll., 1991; lectr. U.S. Atty.'s Office, Washington, 1979-81, D.C. Bar Assn., 1980, Graterford (Pa.) State Prison, 1974-76. Contbr. article to profl. jours. Active Big Brothers; mem. task force on interscholastic programs D.C. Pub. Schs., 1987; hon. mem. Capital Ballet Guild, Inc., 1989; mem. D.C. Cares, Inc., 1990; mem. Nat. Ctr. for Missing and Exploited Children, bd dirs., 1990-91; bd. dirs. Robert A. Shuker Scholarship Fund., Inc., 1993—, Hillcrest Children's Ctr., 1994-96; co-chmn. pub. safety com. D.C. Agenda Project, Fed. City Coun., 1995—. Recipient Dean's award Washington Coll. Law, 1989, Disting. Svc. award Young Lawyers sect. Bar Assn. D.C., 1989, H. Carl Moultrie award D.C. br. NAACP, 1989, Sec.'s award Dept. Vets. Affairs, 1990, James R. Waddy Meritorious Svc. award W.Va. State Coll. Nat. Alumni Assn., 1990, County Spotlight award Nat. Assn. Counties, 1990, William H. Hastie award Jud. coun. Nat. Bar Assn., 1993, Honorable Robert A. Shuker Meml. award Asst. U.S. Attys. Assn., 1997, Friendship award Best Friends Found., 1998, Disting. Alumni award Am. U., 1999, Angel award Bridging the Gap Tri-County Inc., Mt. Sinai Bapt. Ch., 2000, North Star award Washington Coll. of Law, Am. U., 2000, among others. Mem. ABA (lawyer competency com. 1984-87, del. nat. conf. state trial judges 1986), D.C. Bar Assn. (criminal instrns. com. 1984-86), Washington Bar Assn., Nat. Inst. Trial Advocacy Advocates Assn., Am. Inns of Ct. Republican. Office: US Dist Ct for DC 333 Constitution Ave NW Washington DC 20001-2131 E-mail: waltonrb@dcsc.gov.

WALTON, RODNEY EARL, lawyer; b. Corvallis, Oreg., Apr. 28, 1947; s. Ray Daniel Jr. and Carolyn Jane (Smith) W. BA, Coll. of Wooster, 1969; JD, Cornell U., 1976; MA in History, Fla. Internat. U., Miami, 2001. Bar: Fla. 1976, U.S. Dist. Ct. (so. dist.) Fla. 1976, U.S. Dist. Ct. (mid. dist.) Fla. 1977, U.S. Supreme Ct. 1980, U.S. Ct. Appeals (11th cir.) 1981. Assoc. to jr. ptnr. Smathers & Thompson, Miami, Fla., 1976-87; ptnr. Kelley, Drye and Warren, Miami, 1987-93; atty. Heinrich Gordon Hargrove Weihe & James, P.A., Ft. Lauderdale, 1994-97. Adj. instr. U.S. mil. history Fla. Internat. U., 2001. Sec. bd. dirs. Kings Creek Condominium Assn., Miami, 1984-89, treas., 1984, pres., 1990-91. 1st lt. U.S. Army, 1969-73, Vietnam. Decorated Bronze Star. Mem. ABA, Fla. Bar. Republican. Methodist. Avocations: travel, reading, tennis, history. Home: 7985 SW 86th St Apt 430 Miami FL 33143-7014 E-mail: RodneyEarlWalton@aol.com.

WALTON, STANLEY ANTHONY, III, lawyer; b. Chgo., Dec. 10, 1939; s. Stanley Anthony and Emily Ann (Pouzar) W.; m. Karen Kayser, Aug. 10, 1963; children: Katherine, Anne, Alex. BA, Washington and Lee U., 1962, LLB, 1965. Bar: Ill. 1965, U.S. Dist. Ct. (no. dist.) Ill. 1966, U.S. Ct. Appeals (7th cir.) 1966. Ptnr. Winston & Strawn, Chgo., 1965-89, Sayfarth Shaw Fairweather, Chgo., 1989-96. Trustee Village of Hinsdale (Ill.), 1985-89; bd. dirs. Washington and Lee Law Sch., Lexington, Va., 1975-78, bd. dirs. univ. alumni, 1983-87, pres., 1986-87; bd. dirs. UNICEF, Chgo., 1983; pres. Hinsdale Hist. Soc., 1979-81, 2001—, St. Isaac Jogues PTA, 1980; sec. Hinsdale Cmty. Svc., 2000—; bd. dirs. Hinsdale Ctrl. Found., 2000—. Mem. Ill. State Bar Assn., Phi Alpha Delta, Hinsdale Golf Club. Republican. Roman Catholic. Home and Office: 6679 Snug Harbor Dr Willowbrook IL 60527

WALTZ, JON RICHARD, lawyer, educator, author; b. Napoleon, Ohio, Oct. 11, 1929; s. Richard R. and Lenore (Tharp) W. BA with honors in Polit. Sci, Coll. Wooster, 1951; JD, Yale U., 1954. Bar: Ohio 1954, Ill. 1965. Assoc. Squire, Sanders & Dempsey, Cleve., 1954-64; chief prosecutor City of Willowick (Ohio), 1958-64; assoc. prof. law Northwestern U. Sch. Law, Chgo., 1964-65, prof. law, 1965-98, Edna B. and Ednyfed H. Williams prof. law emeritus; instr. med. jurisprudence Northwestern Med. Sch., 1969-74. Book critic Washington Post, Chgo. Tribune, others; Disting. vis. prof. law Ill. Inst. Tech.-Chgo.-Kent Coll. Law, 1974; lectr. Author: The Federal Rules of Evidence—An Analysis, 1973, Criminal Evidence, 1975, Chinese lang. edits., 1994, 2000, Evidence: A Summary Analysis, 1976, Introduction to Criminal Evidence, 1991, Chinese lang. edit., 1993; co-author: The Trial of Jack Ruby, 1965, Cases and Materials on Evidence, 1968, Principles of Evidence and Proof, 1968, Medical Jurisprudence, 1971, Cases and Materials on Law and Medicine, 1980, Evidence: Making the Record, 1981, Criminal Prosecution in the People's Republic of China and the United States of America: A Comparative Study, 1995; note and comment editor Yale Law Jour., 1953-54; mem. editorial adv. bd. Harcourt Brace Law Group,. 1978—; contbr. numerous articles to profl. jours. Mem. Ill. adv. com. U.S. Commn. on Civil Rights, 1971-74; mem. Ill. Criminal Justice System Policy and Planning Com., 1973-74, Ill. Jud. Inquiry Bd., 1980-88; mem. com. med. edn. AMA, 1982-83; mem. Gov.'s Task Force on Med. Malpractice, 1985; Capt. AUS, 1955-58. Decorated Commendation medal; recipient Disting. Svc. award Midland Authors, 1972, Disting. Alumni award Coll. Wooster, 1987. Mem. Assn. Am. Law Schs., Order of Coif, Phi Alpha Delta, Pi Sigma Alpha. Presbyterian. Home: 4005 Lakeridge Dr Holland MI 49424-2263

WALZ, GREGORY STEPHEN, lawyer; b. St. Cloud, Minn., Mar. 8, 1957; s. Wendelin George and Ilse Marie Walz; m. Sandra Jean Theis, Nov. 17, 1987; children: Nicole, Joseph, Jacob, Jessica, Alexandra. BA, St. Johns U., Collegeville, Minn., 1981; JD, William Mitchell Coll. Law, St. Paul, 1987. Bar: Minn. 1987, U.S. Dist. Ct. Minn. 1987. Atty. Walz Law Office, St. Cloud, 1990—. Criminal, Family and matrimonial, Personal injury (including property damage). Office: Walz Law Office PO Box 1794 Saint Cloud MN 56302-1794 E-mail: info@walzlaw.com.

WALZER, JAMES HARVEY, lawyer, author; b. Neptune, N.J., Jan. 24, 1949; s. Elwood John and Mary Elizabeth (Harvey) W.; m. Gloria Jean Demkowski, May 29, 1971; children: Sara, Emily, Amanda, Adam. BA, Bowdoin Coll., 1972; JD, Cleve. State U., 1975. Bar: N.J. 1975, U.S. Dist. Ct. N.J. 1975. Pvt. practice, Newark, 1975-78, Livingston, N.J., 1978-81, Boonton, N.J., 1981—. Legal forms editor All-State Legal, a div. of All-State Internat., Inc., Cranford, N.J., 1978—96. Author: Employment, Agency, Service Agreements, 1986, Motor Vehicle Law and Practice--Forms, 1988, 2 vols., 2000, Civil Practice Forms, 5 vols., 1990, 8 vols., 5th edit., 1998; editor, author: Legal Forms, 7 vols., 1995-96. Mem. Manville (N.J.) Bd. Adjustment, 1976; bd. dirs. Somerset-Sussex Legal Svcs. Mem. ABA, N.J. Bar Assn., Morris County Bar Assn. Democrat. Family and matrimonial, General practice, Property, real (including real estate development, water). Home: 18 Magda Ln Hillsborough NJ 08844-4217 Office: 103 William St PO Box 675 Boonton NJ 07005-0675 E-mail: jhwalzer@aol.com.

WAMPLER, ROBERT JOSEPH, lawyer; b. Greensboro, Ind., Mar. 3, 1936; s. Cruden V. and Mary L. (James) W.; m. Karen A. Wiggins, Feb. 19, 1977; children: Eric J., Kelly L., Michael J. AB, Yale U., 1959; JD, Ind. U., 1963. Bar: Ind. 1963, U.S. Dist. Ct. (so. dist.) Ind. 1963, U.S. Supreme Ct. 1966, U.S. Ct. Appeals (7th cir.) 1972. Assoc. Kightlinger & Gray, Indpls., 1963—, ptnr., 1968—, sr. ptnr., 1971—. Author handbook on product liability; co-author: Trial Advocacy in Indiana, 1989. Sec., bd. dirs. Ivy Ridge Civic Assn., Indpls., 1975—. Fellow Indpls. Bar Found.; mem. Indpls. Bar Assn. (chmn. litigation sect. 1987), Ind. Bar Assn., Def. Trial Counsel Ind., Masons, Order of Coif, Phi Delta Phi. Republican. Episcopalian. Alternative dispute resolution, General civil litigation, Professional liability. Home: 5939 Cape Cod Ct Indianapolis IN 46250-1845 Office: Kightlinger & Gray LLP 151 N Delaware St Ste 600 Indianapolis IN 46204-2574 E-mail: rwampler@k-glaw.com.

WAND, BARBARA FREEDMAN, lawyer; b. Worcester, Mass., Jan. 16, 1950; d. Abraham and Rose (Marcus) Freedman; m. Mitchell Wand, June 14, 1970; children: Rebecca, Jennifer, Joshua. BA, Brandeis U., 1972; JD, Ind. U., 1979. Bar: Ind. 1979, Mass. 1985. Assoc. Law Offices Andrew C. Mallor, Bloomington, Ind., 1979-81; asst. prof. sch. law Ind. U., Bloomington, 1981-83; vis. assoc. prof. sch. law Boston U., 1984-85; assoc. Hill & Barlow, Boston, 1985-89, ptnr., 1989—2002, Bingham McCutchen LLP, Boston, 2002—. Mem. ABA, Mass. Bar Assn., Boston Bar Assn. Estate planning, Probate (including wills, trusts), Estate taxation. Office: Bingham McCutchen LLP 150 Federal St Boston MA 02110-2607

WANDER, HERBERT STANTON, lawyer; b. Cin., Mar. 17, 1935; s. Louis Marvin and Pauline (Schuster) W.; m. Ruth Cele Fell, Aug. 7, 1960; children: Daniel Jerome, Susan Gail, Lois Marlene. AB, U. Mich., 1957; LLB, Yale U., 1960. Bar: Ohio 1960, Ill. 1960. Law clk. to judge U.S. Dist. Ct. (no. dist.) Ill., 1960—61; ptnr. Pope Ballard Shepard & Fowle, Chgo., 1961—78, Katten Muchin Zavis Rosenman, Chgo., 1978—. Trustee Michael Reese Found., 1991-; bd. dirs. Tel. & Data Systems, Chgo., 1968-, Advance Corp., 1991-96; mem. legal adv. com. to the bd. govs. N.Y. Stock Exch., 1989-92; mem. legal adv. bd. Nat. Assn. Securities Dealers, Inc., 1996-99. Editor: (jour.) Bus. Law Today, 1992-93; editor-in-chief: (jour.) The Bus. Lawyer, 1993-94; contbr. numerous articles to profl. jours. Bd. dirs. Jewish Fedn. Met. Chgo., 1972—, pres., 1981-83; bd. dirs. Jewish United Fund, 1972—, pres., 1981-83, chmn. pub. affairs com., 1984-87, gen. campaign chmn., 1993; former regional chmn. nat. young leadership cabinet United Jewish Appeal; vice-chmn. large city budgeting conf. Coun. Jewish Fedns., 1979-82, bd. dirs., 1980—, exec. com., 1983-84. Mem. ABA (sec. bus. law sect. 1992-93, vice-chair 1993-94, chair-elect 1994-95, chair 1995-96, apptd. to commn. on multidisciplinary practice 1998), Ill. State Bar Assn., Chgo. Bar Assn., Yale Law Sch. Assn. (exec. com. 1982-86), Std. Club, Econ. Club, Northmoor Country Club, Phi Beta Kappa. Corporate, general, Mergers and acquisitions, Securities. Home: 70 Prospect Ave Highland Park IL 60035-3329 Office: Katten Muchin Zavis Rosenman 525 W Monroe St Ste 1600 Chicago IL 60661-3693 E-mail: hwander@kmzr.com.

WANDERMAN, SUSAN MAE, lawyer; b. Mar. 12, 1947; d. Leo and Muriel D. Wanderman. AB, Wheaton Coll., Norton, Mass., 1967; JD, St. John's U., 1970; LLM, NYU, 1976. Bar: N.Y. 1971, U.S. Dist. Ct. (ea. and so. dists.) N.Y. 1972, U.S. Ct. Appeals (2d cir.) 1973, U.S. Supreme Ct. 1974. Asst. legal officer, legal dept. Chem. Bank, N.Y.C., 1972—75; 2d v.p. legal dept. Chase Manhattan Bank N.A., N.Y.C., 1975—82; asst. gen. counsel Citicorp Svcs., Inc., N.Y.C., 1982—84; v.p. Citibank, N.A., N.Y.C., 1984—. Instr. bus. law and law for the layman LaGuardia C.C., 1976—77; law day spkr. Queens County Supreme Ct., 1979—83; mem. Cmty. Bd. 6, Queens County, N.Y.C., 1987—. Contbr. articles to legal publs. Past vol. N.Y. State Bar Assn. Lawyers in the Classroom. Mem.: ABA, Queens County Bar Assn., N.Y. State Bar Assn. Banking, Computer, Pension, profit-sharing, and employee benefits. Office: Citibank NA One Court Sq Long Island City NY 11120

WANG, ALBERT HUAI-EN, lawyer; b. Tainan, Taiwan, Feb. 21, 1967; s. Tien-Yu Wang and Shiu-Yin Chen. BA magna cum laude, MA magna cum laude, UCLA, 1990; JD, Cornell U., 1994. Bar: N.Y. 1995. Tax specialist KPMG Peat Marwick, L.A., 1990-91; tchr. asst. Cornell Law Sch., 1993; assoc. Willkie Farr & Gallagher, N.Y.C., 1994-99, Schulte Roth & Zabel LLP, N.Y.C., 1999—2001. Legal counsel, adv. coun. Asian Am. Bus. Devel. ctr., N.Y.C., 1999—2002. U. Calif. regent scholar, 1986-90, Alumni scholar UCLA, 1986, Departmental scholar, 1989. Mem. ABA, N.Y. State Bar Assn., Chinese Fin. Soc. (dir., legal counsel 2000-2002), Taiwan Merchant Assn. N.Y., China Inst., Asia Soc., Chinese Am. Voters Assn. of Queens (dir. N.Y. chpt. 1999-2001), U.S.-China Lawyers Soc. (bd. dirs. 2002—), Phi Beta Kappa, Phi Delta Phi, Omicron Delta Epsilon. Democrat. Corporate, general, Private international, Securities. Home: 138-10 Franklin Ave Apt 5N Flushing NY 11355-3305 Office: Phillips Nizer LLP 666 Fifth Ave New York NY 10103-0084 Office Fax: 212-262-5152. Business E-Mail: awang@phillipsnizer.com.

WANG, ARTHUR CHING-LI, administrative law judge, law educator; b. Boston, Feb. 4, 1949; s. Kung Shou and Lucy (Chow) W.; m. Wendy F. Hamai, May 22, 1976 (div. 1981); m. Nancy J. Norton, Sept. 1, 1985; children: Alexander Xinglin, Sierra Xinan. BA, Franconia Coll., 1970; JD, U. Puget Sound, 1984. Bar: Wash. 1984. Printer Carmel Valley (Calif.) Outlook, 1970-73; project coord. Tacoma (Wash.) Cmty. House, 1973-76; rsch. analyst Wash. Ho. of Reps., Olympia, 1977-80, mem., 1981-94; of counsel Davies Pearson, P.C., Tacoma, 1984-94. Adj. prof. U. Puget Sound

Law Sch., Tacoma, 1987-93, Seattle U. Law Sch., Tacoma, 1995-98; chmn House Capital Budget Com., 1993-94, Revenue Com., 1989-92, Commerce and Labor Com., 1985-88; mem. Wash. Pers. Appeals Bd., Olympia, 1994-96; chief adminstrv. law judge Wash. Office Adminstrv. Hearings, 1997—; judge Wash. Ct. Appeals, 2000. Assoc. editor U. Puget Sound Law Review, 1983-84. Vista vol. Tacoma Urban League, 1973—74; del. Dem. Nat. Conv., 1976; bd. dirs. Pierce County AIDS Found., 1999—, pres., 2002; bd. dirs. Planned Parenthood of Western Wash., 2001—, vice chair, 2003—. Named Chinese Am. Man of Yr., Seattle Chinese Post, 1991, Legislator of Yr., Wash. Health Care Assn., 1992, Alumni of Yr., U. Puget Sound Law Sch. Alumni Assn., 1993; recipient Exemplary Leadership award, Wash. State Access to Justice Bd., 1999, Profl. Excellence award, Nat. Assn. Asian Am. Profls., Seattle, 2001, State Leadership award, Wash. State Combined Fund Dr., 2003. Democrat. Avocation: birding. Home: 3319 N Union Ave Tacoma WA 98407-6043 E-mail: awang@oah.wa.gov.

WANG, JUNFENG, lawyer; b. TongHua, JiLin, China, July 27, 1962; s. Yongxian Wang; m. Yue Fan; 1 child, Yu Chen. Bachelor Degree, Masters Degree, JSD, U. Calif., Berkeley. Lawyer China Coun. for the Promotion of Internat. Trade, Beijing, 1986—93, King & Wood PRC Lawyers, Beijing, 1993—. Office: King and Wood LLP 30 F North Tower Kerry Ctr Beijing 100020 China

WANKE, RONALD LEE, lawyer, educator; b. Chgo., June 22, 1941; s. William F. and Lucille (Kleinwachter) W.; m. Rose Klonowski, Oct. 23, 1987. BSEE, Northwestern U., 1964; JD, DePaul U., 1968. Bar: Ill. 1968. Assoc. Wood, Dalton, Phillips, Mason & Rowe, Chgo., 1968-71, ptnr., 1971-84, Jenner & Block, Chgo., 1984--. Lectr. John Marshall Law Sch., Chgo., 1985-94; mem. adv. com. intellectual property program, U. Fla. Coll. Law. Co-author: (book chpt.) International Intellectual Property Law, 1997; contbr. articles to Software Law Jour., 1987, Internat. Legal Strategy, 1995. Mem.: ABA, Intellectual Property Law Assn. Chgo. (chmn. inventor svcs. com. 1976, chmn. fed. rules com. 1981). Computer, Patent, Trademark and copyright. Home: 1806 N Sedgwick St Chicago IL 60614-5306 Office: Jenner & Block 1 E Ibm Plz Fl 4000 Chicago IL 60611-7603

WAPLER, VINCENT, legal auctioneer; b. Linares, Spain, Dec. 3, 1947; s. Jean Jacques and Helene (Huffmann de Cock) W. M. History of Art, Lille; M.Law and Bus., Paris. Self-employed legal auctioneer, Paris. Author: Jane Poupelet, Sculptor, 1969. Avocations: Karate, golf, stag hunting, alpinism, contemporary art collecting. Office: 16 Place Des Vosges 75004 Paris France E-mail: wapler@aol.com.

WARD, DENITTA DAWN, lawyer; b. Gardner, Kans., Apr. 29, 1963; d. Gerald Dee Ascue and Patricia Diane (Henderson) Ray; m. Kent Alan Ward, July 6, 1991; children: Alexander Patrick, Olivia Caitlyn. BA, U. Kans., 1985; JD magna cum laude, Georgetown U., 1989. Bar: Md. 1989, U.S. Ct. Appeals (fed. cir.) 1990, D.C. 1991, U.S. Ct. Internat. Trade 1991. Rsch. asst. Georgetown U., Washington, 1988-89; jud. clk. U.S. Ct. Appeals for Fed. Cir., Washington, 1989-90; assoc. Donovan Leisure Rogovin Huge & Schiller, Washington, 1990-94; atty. Fed. Election Commn., Washington, 1994-96, Marriott Internat., Inc., 1996-98; sr. v.p., gen. counsel Boulderbiz, Inc., 1999—. Mng. editor Law and Policy in Internat. Bus., 1988-89. Mem. ABA, Ct. of Appeals for Fed. Cir. Bar Assn., Ct. of Appeals for Fed. Cir. Former Jud. Clks. Assn., Order of Coif, Omicron Delta Kappa, Pi Sigma Alpha. Avocations: travel, gardening. Federal civil litigation, Commercial, contracts (including sales of goods; commercial financing), Labor (including EEOC, Fair Labor Standards Act, labor-management relations, NLRB, OSHA). Home: 6999 Firerock Ct Boulder CO 80301-3814

WARD, ERICA ANNE, lawyer, educator; b. Okiyama, Japan, Oct. 20, 1950; d. Robert Edward and Constance Regina (Barnett) W.; m. Ralph Joseph Gerson, May 20, 1979; children: Stephanie Claire, Madeleine Ward Gerson. BA, Stanford U., 1972; JD, U. Mich., 1975. Bar: Calif. 1975, D.C. 1976, U.S. Ct. Appeals (5th and D.C. cirs.) 1977, Temporary Emergency Ct. Appeals 1983, Mich. 1989. Assoc. Wilmer, Cutler & Pickering, Washington, 1975-77; staff counsel U.S. Senate Ethics Com., Washington, 1977-78; exec. asst. gen. counsel Dept. Energy, Washington, 1978-79, counsellor to dep. sec., 1980; assoc. dir. energy and natural resources, domestic policy staff White House, Washington, 1980-81; of counsel Skadden, Arps, Slate, Meagher & Flom, Washington, 1981-87, ptnr., 1987—; adj. prof. law U. Mich., Ann Arbor, 1984-85. Editor Mich. Law Rev., 1975. Commr. Mackinac Island (Mich.) State Park Commn., 1989-95; mem. adv. bd. Ctr. Edn. of Women U. Mich., Ann Arbor, 1989—; trustee Detroit Zool. Soc., 1997—, Cranbrook Ednl. Cmty., 1993—; mem. vis. com. U. Mich. Law Sch., 1989—. Recipient Outstanding Svc. medal Dept. Energy, 1981. Mem. ABA, Women's Bar Assn. D.C. Democrat. Jewish. Administrative and regulatory, FERC practice, Utilities, public. Office: Skadden Arps Slate Meagher Flom 1440 New York Ave NW Ste 600 Washington DC 20005-6000

WARD, GEORGE EDWARD, lawyer, law educator; b. Saginaw, Mich., Feb. 14, 1941; s. George E. and Mary Margaret (Hackett) W.; m. Margaret L. Barbour, June 13, 1968; children: Mary, William, Teresa, Anne, Thomas. AB, U. Detroit, 1963; JD, U. Mich., Ann Arbor, 1966. Bar: Mich. 1967. Rsch. atty. Mich. Supreme Ct., Lansing, 1966-67; assoc. Butzel, Long, Gust, Klein & VanZile, Detroit, 1967-71; exec. dir. Detroit Charter Commn., 1971-72; ptnr. Burgoyne, Kaufman, Roche & Ward, Detroit, 1972-82; pres. Wayne County Home Rule Charter Commn., 1981—82; of counsel Milmet, Vecchio, Ward & Carnago, Detroit, 1982-86; chief asst. pros. atty. Wayne County, 1986-2000; sole practice Detroit, 2000—. Adj. prof. U. Mich., MSU-DCL, WSU Law Sch., Dearborn, Mich. State U., Wayne State U. Law Sch.; cons. Pitts. Charter Commn., Pa., 1973, Pontiac Charter Commn., 1981; county pub. adminstr. State of Mich., Detroit, 1973—86; pres. Wayne Co. Charter Commn., 1981—82. Author: The Duties of Liberty, 1992, Cases and Materials on the Regulation of Business Franchises, 1997, Liberty and Law: Culture, Court, Consent of the Governed, 2001; contbr. articles to profl. jours. Mich. Law Revision Commn.; co-chmn. Gubernatorial Inaugural Com., 1983; bd. dirs. Wayne County Cath. Soc. Svcs., 1995—. Wayne County Neighborhood Legal Svcs., 1995—2002, Wayne Ctr. for Developmentally Disabled, 1995—2002, chmn. bd., 2001; mem. pres.'s cabinet U. Detroit, 1980—. Mem.: State Bar Mich. (Rep. Assembly 1979—82, bd. commrs. 1990—96), Inc. Soc. Irish-Am. Lawyers (pres. 2000), Scribes Club, U. Mich. Pres. Club, Alpha Sigma Nu. Alternative dispute resolution, Appellate, Condemnation (eminent domain), General civil litigation, Municipal (including bonds), Legislative, Probate (including wills, trusts). Address: 1100 Buhl Bldg Detroit MI 48226 E-mail: geoward41@hotmail.com.

WARD, HORACE TALIAFERRO, federal judge; b. LaGrange, Ga., July 29, 1927; m. Ruth LeFlore (dec.); 1 son (dec.). AB, Morehouse Coll., 1949; MA, Atlanta U., 1950; JD, Northwestern U., 1959. Bar: Ga. 1960. Instr. polit. sci. Ark. A.M. and N. Coll., 1950-51, Ala. State Coll., 1951-53, 55-56; claims authorizer U.S. Social Security Adminstrn., 1959-60; assoc. firm Hollowell Ward Moore & Alexander (and successors), Atlanta, 1960-69; individual practice law Atlanta, 1971-74; judge Civil Ct. of Fulton County, 1974-77, Fulton Superior Ct., 1977-79; U.S. Dist. Ct. judge No. Dist. Ga., Atlanta, 1979-93; sr. judge U.S. Dist. Ct. No. Dist. Ga., Atlanta, 1993—. Lectr. bus. and sch. law Atlanta U., 1965-70; dep. city atty., Atlanta, 1969-70, asst. county atty., Fulton County, 1971-74 Former Trustee Friendship Baptist Ch., Atlanta; mem. Ga. adv. com. U.S. Civil Rights Commn., 1963-65; assisting lawyer NAACP Legal Def. and Edn. Fund, Inc., 1960-70; mem. Jud. Selection Commn., Atlanta, 1972-74, Charter Commn., 1971-72; mem. Ga. Senate, 1964-74, jud. com., rules com., county and urban affairs com.; mem. State Democratic Exec. com., 1966-74; former bd. dirs. Atlanta Legal Aid Soc.; bd. dirs. Atlanta Urban League, Fed. Defender Program, No. Dist. Ga.; trustee Met. Atlanta Commn. on Crime and Delinquency, Atlanta U., Fledgling Found. Mem. Am. Bar Assn., Nat. Bar Assn. (chmn. jud. council 1978-79), State Bar Ga., Atlanta Bar Assn., Gate City Bar Assn. (pres. 1972-74), Atlanta Lawyers Club, Phi Beta Kappa, Alpha Phi Alpha, Phi Alpha Delta, Sigma Pi Phi. Office: US Dist Court 1252 US Courthouse 75 Spring St SW Atlanta GA 30303-3309

WARD, JOE HENRY, JR., retired lawyer; b. Childress, Tex., Apr. 18, 1930; s. Joe Henry and Helen Ida (Chastain) W.; m. Carlotta Agnes Abreu, Feb. 7, 1959; children: James, Robert, William, John. BS in Acctg., Tex. Christian U., 1952; JD, So. Meth. U., 1964. Bar: Tex. 1964, Va. 1972, D.C. 1974; CPA, Tex. Mgr. Alexander Grant & Co. CPA's, Dallas, 1956-64; atty. U.S. Treasury, 1965-68; tax counsel U.S. Senate Fin. Com., 1968-72; pvt. practice Washington, 1972-83; asst. gen. counsel, tax mgr. Epic Holdings, Ltd. and Crysopt Corp., 1983-87; pvt. practice Washington and Va., 1987-95; ret., 1995. Lt. USNR, 1952-56. Mem. ABA, AICPA, Am. Assn. Atty.-CPA's, Univ. Club. Home: 2639 Mann Ct Falls Church VA 22046-2721

WARD, ROBERT JOSEPH, federal judge; b. N.Y.C., Jan. 31, 1926; s. Joseph G. and Honor V. (Hess) W.; m. Florence C. Maisel, Apr. 15, 1951 (dec. Mar. 1994); children: Laura Alice, Carolyn; m. Renée J. Sokolow, May 28, 1995. SB, Harvard Coll., 1945, LLB, 1949. Bar: N.Y. 1949. Practiced in, N.Y.C., 1949-51, 61-72; asst. dist. atty. N.Y. County, 1951-55; asst. U.S. atty. So. Dist. N.Y., 1956-61; judge U.S. Dist. Ct. (so. dist.) N.Y., 1972-91, sr. judge, 1991—. With USNR, 1944-46. Mem. N.Y. State Bar Assn., Assn. of Bar of City of N.Y., Fed. Bar Coun. Office: US Dist Ct US Courthouse Foley Sq New York NY 10007-1501

WARD, RODMAN, JR., lawyer, director; b. Wilmington, Del., Apr. 8, 1934; s. Rodman and Dorcas (Andrews) W.; m. Susan Speakman Hill, Oct. 10, 1959; children: Margery Ward Garnett, Emily Ward Neilson, Rodman III, Jennifer Ward Oppenheimer. BA, Williams Coll., 1956; LLB, Harvard U., 1959. Bar: Del. 1959, D.C. 1959. Partner Prickett, Ward, Burt & Sanders, Wilmington, 1967-79, Skadden, Arps, Slate, Meagher & Flom, Wilmington, 1979—2001, counsel, 2002—. Bd. dirs. WMB Holdings, Inc. Author: (with Folk and Welch) Folk on the Delaware General Corporation Law, 1987; contbr. articles to profl. jours. Trustee Christiana Care Corp., Winterthur Mus. Gardens and Libr., chmn. acad. affairs com. Capt. USAF, 1960—63. Fellow: Am. Coll. Trial Lawyers; mem.: ABA, Am. Judicature Soc., Assn. of Bar of City of N.Y., D.C. Bar Assn., Am. Bar Found. (life), Del. State Bar Assn. (pres. 1989—90), Am. Law Inst., Vicmead Hunt Club, Wilmington Country Club, Wilmington Club. Home: 52 Selborne Dr Wilmington DE 19807-1216 Office: PO Box 636 Wilmington DE 19899-0636 E-mail: rward@skadden.com.

WARD, ROGER COURSEN, lawyer; b. Newark, June 19, 1922; s. Waldron Merry and Aline Toppin (Coursen) W.; m. Katharine More Stevens, Oct. 22, 1949; children: James Olney, Alexander More. Grad., Phillips Exeter Acad., 1940; AB, Princeton U., 1943; LL.B., Columbia U., 1949. Bar: N.J. 1949. Law clk. to justice N.J. Supreme Ct., 1951; since practiced in Newark, Morristown, Montclair, N.J.; ptnr. Pitney, Hardin, Kipp & Szuch, 1959-91, counsel, 1991-92, Schwartz, Tobia & Stanziale, 1993—. Bd. advisors Am. Inst. Law Tng. Within Office, Phila. 1986-88, Law Hiring and Tng. Report, Chgo., 1983-88. Bd. dirs. United Hosps. Newark, 1965-78, pres., 1973; trustee, v.p. Newark Mus. Assn., 1969-92; bd. dirs. Better Bus. Bur. Greater Newark, 1970-84; mem. Summit Zoning Bd. Adjustment, 1966-70; trustee Eye Inst. N.J., 1973, Pingry Sch., 1966-68, Summit YMCA, 1960-62, Newark Council Social Agys., 1956-60; vice chmn. Newark Mayor's Commn. on Youth, 1958-60. Served to lt. (j.g.) USNR, 1943-46, PTO, ETO. Harlan Fiske Stone scholar Columbia U., 1949. Mem. N.J. State Bar Assn., Essex County Bar Assn., Princeton Club N.Y., Short Hills (N.J.) Club, Phi Beta Kappa. Bankruptcy, Commercial, consumer (including collections, credit), Commercial, contracts (including sales of goods; commercial financing). Office: Schwartz Tobia Stanziale Rosensweig & Sedita 22 Crestmont Rd Montclair NJ 07042 E-mail: wardr@kipslaw.com.

WARD, SAMANTHA SNOW, lawyer; b. Clear Lake, Tex., Mar. 13, 1974; d. Emily Winchester Ryan. BA in Polit. Sci. and Spanish, Ctrl. Meth. Coll., Fayette, Mo., 1996; JD, U. of Missouri-Columbia, 1999. Bar: Mo. 2001, U.S. Dist. Ct. (we. dist.) Mo. 2002, Kans. Fed. 2002. Law clk. Mo. Pub. Defender, Farmington, 1999—2000; spl. asst. atty. gen. Mo. Dept. of Revenue, Jefferson City, 2001—. Spkr. Mo. Bar, Jefferson City, 2002—. Recipient Wall of Tolerance, Nat. Campaign of Tolerance. Mem.: Phi Alpha Delta, Omicron Delta Kappa, Sigma Pi Alpha (life). Office: Missouri Dept of Revenue PO Box 475 Jefferson City MO 65105

WARD, THOMAS JEROME, lawyer; b. New Kensington, Pa., May 6, 1936; s. Richard Thomas and Renatha Ann (Hruscienski) W.; m. Lindley Ann Bennett, Aug. 20, 1960; children: Christine Lester, Janice Nolte, Thomas, James, Jeffrey, Matthew. BS, Duquesne U., 1958; JD, Villanova U., 1961. Tax atty. Westinghouse Electric Corp., Pitts., 1961-65; successively atty., sr. atty., asst. gen. atty. Rockwell Mfg. Co., Pitts., 1965-71, mgr. corp. devel., 1971-73; v.p., gen. counsel, sec. Disston Inc., Pitts., 1973-78; ptnr. Meyer, Darragh, Buckler, Bebenek & Eck, Pitts., 1978-84; v.p. fin. and law, gen. counsel, sec. Dravo Corp., Pitts., 1984-87, sr. v.p. fin. and adminstrn., 1987-88, exec. v.p., 1988-90; sr. atty. Buchanan Ingersoll. PC, Pitts.; dir. Buchanan Ingersoll (Europa), Frankfurt, Germany, 1990-91; sr. v.p., gen. counsel Federated Svcs. Co., Pitts., 1991-99; spl. counsel Pietragallo, Bosick & Gordon, Pitts., 1999—. Editor Villanova Law Rev., 1960-61. Past bd. dirs., past pres. Cath. Charities of Pitts.; past bd. advisors Duquesne U. Sch. Bus. and Adminstrn., Pitts.; past bd. dirs., past pres. Bethel Park Cmty. Found. Mem. ABA, Pa. Bar Assn., Allegheny County Bar Assn., Century Club Disting. Alumni Duquesne U. Clubs: Duquesne. Democrat. Roman Catholic. Corporate, general, Finance, Mergers and acquisitions. Office: 38th Fl 1 Oxford Ct Fl 38 Pittsburgh PA 15219-1407 E-mail: tjw@pbandg.com.

WARDEN, JOHN L. lawyer; b. Evansville, Ind., Sept. 22, 1941; s. Walter Wilson and Juanita (Veatch) W.; m. Phillis Ann Rodgers, Oct. 27, 1960; children: Anne W. Clark, John L., W. Carson. AB, Harvard U., 1962; LLB, U. Va., 1965. Bar: N.Y. 1966, U.S. Ct. Appeals (2d cir.) 1966, U.S. Dist. Ct. (so. and ea. dists.) N.Y. 1967, U.S. Ct. Appeals (10th cir.) 1971, U.S. Supreme Ct. 1972, U.S. Ct. Appeals (D.C. cir.) 1980. Assoc. Sullivan & Cromwell, N.Y.C., 1965-73, ptnr., 1973—. Hon. trustee U. Va. Law Sch. Found.; trustee Am. Ballet Theatre. Editor-in-chief: Va. Law Rev., 1964-65. Fellow Am. Coll. Trial Lawyers; mem. ABA, Am. Law Inst., N.Y. State Bar Assn., Assn. Bar City N.Y., N.Y. County Lawyers Assn., Knickerbocker Club, Down Town Assn. Club, Doubles Club, Bedford Golf and Tennis Club, Lyford Cay Club. Republican. Episcopalian. Antitrust, General civil litigation, Mergers and acquisitions. Office: Sullivan & Cromwell 125 Broad St Fl 28 New York NY 10004-2489 E-mail: wardenj@sullcrom.com.

WARMAN, GUY LEE, lawyer; b. Lambert, Pa., July 11, 1929; s. Guy B. and Ida Grace (Lee) W.; m. Katherine V. Baldridge, Nov. 6, 1954; children: Katherine L., Cynthia V. BA, Pa. State U., 1953; JD, U. Pitts., 1956. Bar: Pa. 1957, U.S. Dist. Ct. (we. dist.) Pa. 1957, U.S. Ct. Appeals (3d cir.) 1976, U.S. Supreme Ct. 1971. Assoc. Metz, Cook, Hanna & Kelly, Pitts., 1957-63, ptnr. 1963-78; mem. Guy L. Warman and Assocs., P.C., Pitts., 1978-82; ptnr. Warman, Crone and Studeny, Pitts., 1982-98; spl. counsel Reed Smith LLP, 1998—. Republican county committeeman, 1970-80. Served with USAAF, 1946-49; 1st lt. USAFR 1953-56. Recipient Robert L. Vann award U. Pitts. Sch. Law, 1956. Mem. ABA, Pa. Bar Assn., Allegheny County Bar Assn. (chmn. membership com. 1968-69, chmn. ct. rules com. 1969-78, judiciary com. 1985). Republican. Presbyterian. Clubs: Longue Vue (Verona, Pa., pres. 1995-97), Duquesne Club (Pitts.), Masons, Shriners. Editor: The Allegheny County Common Pleas Court Manual, 1969-78. Contbr. articles to U. Pitts. Law Rev. General practice, Probate (including wills, trusts), Property, real (including real estate development, water). Home: 720 Shady Ave Pittsburgh PA 15232-2911 Office: 435 Sixth Ave Pittsburgh PA 15219-1886

WARMER, RICHARD CRAIG, lawyer; b. Los Angeles, Aug. 12, 1936; s. George A. and Marian L. (Paine) W.; children: Craig McEchron, Alexander Richard. AB, Occidental Coll., 1958; MA, Tufts U., 1959; LLB, NYU, 1962. Bar: Calif. 1963, D.C. 1976. Assoc. O'Melveny & Myers, LLP, Los Angeles, 1962-69, ptnr., 1970-75, mng. ptnr. Washington, 1976-92, mem. mgmt. com., 1986-92, with San Francisco, 1994—. Speaker in field. Contbr. articles to profl. jours. Trustee Law Ctr. Found. NYU, 1981-94; dir. Headland Ctr. for Arts, San Francisco Jazz Orgn. Mem. ABA, D.C. Bar, State Bar Calif., Order of Coif, Phi Beta Kappa, Cosmos Club. Administrative and regulatory, Antitrust, General civil litigation. Office: O'Melveny & Myers LLP Embarcadero Ctr W 275 Battery St San Francisco CA 94111-3305 E-mail: rwarmer@omm.com.

WARNCKE, JEFFREY SCOTT, lawyer; b. Bonne Terre, Mo., July 7, 1965; s. Frederick Charles Warncke Jr. and Connie J. Heefner; m. Janet Maria Hoffman, Nov. 12, 1992; children: Maxwell Scott, Adeline Elisabeth. BBA magna cum laude, Ga. State U., 1988; JD cum laude, U. Ga., 1991. Bar: Ga. 1991, U.S. Dist. Ct. 1995. Ptnr. Dietrick Evans Scholz & Williams, LLC, Atlanta, 1991—. Sec. Southeastern Masters Velo, Inc., Atlanta, 1999—; bd. dirs. Canterbury Sch., Atlanta, 2002—. Mem.: ATLA, Ga. Trial Laweyrs Assn., Patient Adv. Found. Democrat. Unitarian Universalist. Avocations: bicycle road racing, drums. Insurance, Personal injury (including property damage). Office: Dietrick Evans et al 3490 Piedmont Rd NE Ste 1500 Atlanta GA 30305 Office Fax: 404-869-0238. E-mail: jswarncke@desw.com.

WARNER, CHARLES COLLINS, lawyer; b. Cambridge, Mass., June 19, 1942; s. Hoyt Landon and Charlotte (Collins) W.; m. Elizabeth Denny, Aug. 24, 1964; children: Peter, Andrew, Elizabeth. BA, Yale U., 1964; JD cum laude, Ohio State U., 1970. Bar: Ohio 1970. Assoc. Porter, Wright, Morris & Arthur and predecessor, Columbus, 1970-76, ptnr., 1976—, also mgr. labor and employment law dept., 1988-92. Pres. Peace Corps Svc. Coun., Columbus, 1974—76, Old Worthington (Ohio) Assn., 1976—78, Worthington Ednl. Found., 1994—96, Opera Columbus, 1999—2001; chmn. lawyers sect. United Way, Columbus, 1983—84; mem. alumni adv. coun. Ohio State U.; pres. Alliance for Quality Edn., Worthington, 1987—89. Fellow Am. Bar Found., Ohio Bar Found., Columbus Bar Found., Coll. Labor and Employment Lawyers; mem. ABA (subcom. chmn. EEO com. 1986-89, co-chair 2000-02, exec. com. Met. Bar Caucus 1992-94, chmn. state & local bar ADR com. 1995-98), Ohio State Bar Assn. (coun. of dels. 1993—, chmn. fed. cts. com. 1992-94), Ohio Met. Bar Assn. (pres. 1991-92), Columbus Bar Assn. (pres. 1991-92, bd. govs. 1982-87, 88-93), FBA, Ohio Assn. Civil Trial Attys. (exec. bd. 1988-97), Ohio State U. Law Alumni Assn. (pres. 1996-97), Nat. Coun. Ohio State U. Coll. Law (pres. 2002—), Capital Club, Yale Club (pres. 1979-81). Avocations: clarinet, singing, tennis. Federal civil litigation, General civil litigation, Labor (including EEOC, Fair Labor Standards Act, labor-management relations, NLRB, OSHA). Home: 145 E South St Columbus OH 43085-4129 Office: Porter Wright Morris & Arthur 41 S High St Ste 2800 Columbus OH 43215-6194 E-mail: cwarner@porterwright.com.

WARNER, FRANK SHRAKE, lawyer; b. Ogden, Utah, Dec. 14, 1940; s. Frank D. and Emma (Sorensen) W.; 1 child, Sheri; m. Sherry Lynn Clary. JD, U. Utah, 1964. Bar: Utah 1964. Assoc. Young, Thatcher, Glasmann & Warner, and predecessor, Ogden, 1964-67, ptnr., 1967-72; chmn. Pub. Svc. Comn. Utah, Salt Lake City, 1972-76; ptnr. Warner & Wikstrom, Ogden, 1976-79, Warner, Marquardt & Hasenyager, Ogden, 1979-82; pvt. practice Ogden, 1982-89, Warner & Phillips, 1989-96, Warner Law Firm, 1996—. Mem. Utah Gov.'s Com. on Exec. Reorgn., 1978-80. Mem. Utah Bar Assn. (ethics and discipline com. 1981-90), Am. Inns of Ct, Am. Trial Lawyers Assn., Ogden Gun Club (past pres.). Administrative and regulatory, Personal injury (including property damage), Property, real (including real estate development, water). Office: Lincoln Pl 3544 Lincoln Ave # F Ogden UT 84401

WARNER, KARL K. prosecutor; BS, U.S. Mil. Acad.; JD, W.Va. U. Gen. counsel to 10th Mountain Div. U.S. Army, 1994—96; legal counsel to Multi-Nat. Force Joint Chiefs of Staff, Haiti, 1994—95, legal counsel to two chmn., joint chiefs staff, 1996—98; gen. counsel U.S. Spl. Ops. Command, 1998—2001; U.S. atty. so. dist. W.Va. U.S. Dept. Justice, 2001—. Office: PO Box 1713 Charleston WV 25326

WARNER, PAUL M. prosecutor; BA, Brigham Young U., 1973, JD, 1976, MPA, 1984. With Utah Atty. Gen.'s Office, 1991-98; asst. U.S. atty. U.S. Dept. Justice, Utah, 1998—2001, U.S. atty., 2001—. Office: 185 S State St Ste 400 Salt Lake City UT 84103-4139*

WARNER, TEDDY FLEMING, lawyer; b. Findlay, Ohio, Jan. 3, 1932; s. Freeman Dininger and Marjorie (Fleming) Warner; m. Carolyn Jean Warner, June 12, 1958; children: Wendy Ann, Randall Scott. AA, Phoenix Coll., 1955; BA with distinction, Ariz. State U., 1956; JD, U. Ariz., 1959. Bar: Ariz. 1959, U.S. Dist. Ct. Ariz. 1959, U.S. Supreme Ct. 1971. Prin. Warner Angle Roper Hallam Jackson & Formanek, Phoenix, 1962—82; sr. ptnr., pres. Warner Angle Roper & Hallam PC and predecessors, Phoenix, 1982—. Com. on fitness and character Ariz. Supreme Ct. , 1983—90, spl. com. legal aid and indigent defendants, ho. resolutions com., 1992—; bd. vis. Ariz. State U. Sch. Law, Ariz., 1979; lectr. in field. Bd. dirs. Phoenix and Valley of Sun YMCA, 1970—84, pres., 1977; bd. dirs. Sagauro-Grand Canyon chpt. March of Dimes, 1968—82, chmn., 1972—73, state chmn., 1974—82, nat. council chpt. vols., 1979—82; bd. dirs. Vol. Bur., 1975; active Fiesta Bowl Com., 1979—84; chmn. bd. trustees Ariz. Perinatal Trust, 1980—; active Ariz. Acad. With USAF, 1951—54. Fellow: Ariz. Bar Found. (Pro Bono Svc. award 1987), Am. Bar Found. (founding); mem.: ABA (ho. of dels. 1981—91, assembly del. 1992—), Law Coll. Assn. U. Ariz., Ariz. State Law Soc., State Bar Ariz. (chmn. com. on del. legal svcs. com.), Maricopa County Bar Found. (charter), Maricopa County Bar Assn. (pres., bd. dirs. 1981), Pinetop Country Club, Ariz. Country Club (sec., bd. dirs. 1971—73), Delta Sigma Phi, Phi Delta Phi. Republican. Corporate, general, Property, real (including real estate development, water). Office: Ste 1500 3550 N Central Ave Phoenix AZ 85012-2112

WARNER, THEODORE KUGLER, JR., lawyer; b. Phila., Sept. 13, 1909; s. Theodore Kugler and Anna (Allen) W.; m. Dorothy Wark Hoehler, Nov. 23, 1935 (dec. 1985); children: Betsy Ann, Peter Joyce; m. Lynn Howell, May 20, 1995. AB, U. Pa., 1931, LL.B. cum laude, 1934. Bar: Pa. 1934. With Pa. R.R., Phila., 1934-70, chief tax counsel, 1952-58, dir. taxation, 1958-68; v.p. taxes Penn Central, 1968, v.p. accounting and taxes, 1968-69, v.p. corp. adminstrn., 1969-70; pres. Can. So. Ry., 1968-70; v.p. Pitts. & Lake Erie R.R., 1968-70; officer, dir. other Penn Central cos., 1968-70; counsel Duane, Morris & Heckscher, Phila., 1970-71, Harper & Driver, 1975—. Lectr. on consol. returns various tax forums. Bd. suprs. Easttown Twp., Pa., 1962-70, chmn., 1966-70; bd. dirs. Independence Found., 1991—, sec. 1993, pres., 1993-95, sec.-treas., 1996— Mem. ABA, Nat. Tax Assn. (pres. 1965-66), Am. Law Inst. (life mem.), Pa. Bar Assn., Order of Coif, Union League, Masons (33 deg., com. on masonic homes 1970-84, chmn. 1975-77, 81-83, Franklin medal 1983, bd. dirs., treas. Masonic libr. and mus. 1991-99), Tau Kappa Epsilon. Republican. Presbyn. Home: 607 Benson House 930 W Montgomery Ave Bryn Mawr PA 19010 Office: 200 S Broad St Ste 1101 Philadelphia PA 19102

WARNOCK, WILLIAM REID, lawyer; b. Detroit, Mich., July 25, 1939; s. William G. and Margery E. (Ford) W.; m. Sandra L. Klarich, Dec. 27, 1961; children: Cheryl Lynn, Laura Ellen. BBA, U. Mich., 1961, JD with distinction, 1964. Bar: Ill. 1964, U.S. Dist. Ct. (no. dist.) Ill. 1965, U.S. Supreme Ct. 1972, Mich. 1995. With Ross & Hardies, Chgo., 1964-70; regional counsel U.S. Dept. HUD, Chgo., 1970-73; ptnr. Roan & Grossman, Chgo., 1973-82; sole practice Chgo., 1982-85; ptnr. Siegel & Warnock, Chgo., 1985-91; of counsel Donovan & Olsen, Chgo., 1991; pres. William R. Warnock P.C., LaGrange, Ill., 1992—2002, Three Rivers, Mich., 2002—. Cons. Ill. Dept. Bus. and Econ. Devel., Chgo., 1977-78, Ill. Housing Devel. Authority, Chgo., 1973-78, Council State Housing Financing Agys., Washington, 1975-78; past pres., chmn. Atty.'s Title Guaranty Fund, Inc., Chgo., 1986-88, also bd. dirs., 1976—. Author: (legal references) Land Use and Zoning, 1974-88, Ward on Title Examination, 1975, Illinois Real Property Service: Real Estate Exchanges, 1988, Environmental Law and the Real Estate Lawyer, 1989-90. Mem. Ill. State Bar Assn., Am. Coll. Real Estate Lawyers. Republican. Methodist. Avocations: boating, woodworking. Land use and zoning (including planning), Property, real (including real estate development, water). Home: 13556 Pleasant View Rd Three Rivers MI 49093-8406 Fax: 312-704-1105.

WARREN, ALVIN CLIFFORD, JR., lawyer, educator; b. Daytona Beach, Fla., May 14, 1944; s. Alvin Clifford and Barbara (Barnes) W.; m. Judith Blatt, Aug. 20, 1966; children— Allison, Matthew. B.A., Yale U., 1966; J.D., U. Chgo., 1969. Bar: Conn. 1970, Pa. 1975. Prof. law U. Conn.-West Hartford, 1969-73, Duke U., Durham, N.C., 1973-74, U. Pa., Phila., 1974-79, Harvard U. Law Sch., Cambridge, Mass., 1979— . Mem. ABA (tax sect.). Contbr. articles to law jours. Office: Law Sch Harvard U Cambridge MA 02138

WARREN, BRADFORD LLOYD, lawyer; b. Indpls., Oct. 2, 1948; s. Claude Marion and Nina Jean (Davidson) W. AB, Ind. U., Bloomington, 1970; JD, Ind. U., Indpls., 1973. Bar: Ind. 1973, U.S. Dist. Ct. (so. dist.) Ind. 1973, U.S. Supreme Ct. 1983. Tax staffman Arthur Andersen & Co., Indpls., 1972-74; ptnr. Warren, Snider & Warren, Indpls., 1974-77; sole practice Indpls., 1977—. Active Libertarian Party Ind. 1976—, candidate U.S. Ho. Reps., 1984, candidate U.S. Senate, 1986; guest lectr. dept. polit. sci. Ind. U., Bloomington, 1989—. Contbg. author: Party Politics in America, 10th edit. Mem. Ind. U. Alumni Assn., Delta Tau Delta (bd. dirs., sec., treas. Beta Alpha Shelter 1976-94). Lodges: Order of Demolay, Chevalier citation. Estate planning, Probate (including wills, trusts), Personal income taxation. Home: 5204 N Winthrop Ave Indianapolis IN 46220-3259 Office: 926 E 52nd St Indianapolis IN 46205-1124

WARREN, MARK EDWARD, lawyer; b. Rochester, Minn., Nov. 26, 1951; s. Edward Joseph and Eunice (Golberg) W.; m. Jasmine Margaret Syracuse, Feb. 18, 1984; children: Natalie, Stephanie. Cert., Instituto de Estudios Europeos, Madrid, 1972; BA, Gustavus Adolphus Coll., St. Peter, Minn., 1974; JD, U. Minn., 1977. Bar: Calif. 1977, U.S. Dist. Ct. (no. and cen. dists.) Calif. 1978, U.S. Ct. Appeals (9th cir.) 1985, U.S. Dist. Ct. (ea. dist.) Calif. 1986, U.S. Dist. Ct. (so. dist.) Calif. 1987, D.C. 1989, U.S. Supreme Ct. 1989, U.S. Ct. Appeals (D.C. cir.) 1989, U.S. Dist. Ct. (D.C. dist.) 1989, U.S. Dist. Ct. Md. 1991, Va. 1992. Assoc. Gibson, Dunn & Crutcher, L.A., 1977-78; spl. asst. to V.P. Walter Mondale Washington, 1979-80; assoc. Gibson, Dunn & Crutcher, L.A., 1980-84, ptnr. L.A. and Washington, 1985-93; sr. v.p., gen. counsel Princess Cruises, L.A., 1993-96; pres. The Gt. Am. Sta. Found., Washington, 1997-99. Mem. U. Minn. Law Alumni Assn. (bd. dirs. 1990-98).

WARREN, MARTIN HUGH, lawyer; b. Bideford, Devon, U.K., Feb. 12, 1961; LLB, Bristol, Avon, 1982. Solicitor, 1985. Trainee Osborne Clarke, 1983-85; solicitor Eversheds, 1986-88, assoc., 1988-89, ptnr., 1989—. Author: People Management. ABA, Am. Employment Law Coun., Reform Club. Labor (including EEOC, Fair Labor Standards Act, labor-management relations, NLRB, OSHA). Office: 1 Callaghan Sq Fitzalan R Cardiff CF10 5BT England Fax: 01633 882417; 029 2046 4347. E-mail: martinwarren@eversheds.com.

WARREN, WILLIAM BRADFORD, lawyer; b. Boston, July 25, 1934; s. Minton Machado and Sarah Ripley (Robbins) W.; children: John Coolidge, Sarah; m. Arete B. Swartz, Sept. 20, 1985. AB magna cum laude, Harvard U., 1956, LLB cum laude, 1959. Bar: N.Y. 1960. Assoc. Dewey Ballantine, N.Y.C., 1959-68; ptnr. Dewey Ballantine, LLP, 1968—. Lectr. Inst. Fed. Taxation, NYU, So. Fed. Tax Inst., Practicing Law Inst. Pres. Cintas Found., N.Y.C.; bd. dirs. St. John's Coll., Annapolis and Santa Fe; bd. dirs. emeritus John Carter Brown Libr., Providence, R.I.; adv. bd. dirs. Met. Opera Assn., N.Y.C.; mem. coun. fellows Morgan Libr., N.Y.C. Mem. Am. Law Inst., Am. Coll. Trust and Estate Counsel (former regent), Acad. Am. Poets (bd. dirs., treas.), Internat. Acad. Estate and Trust Law (former exec. com.), N.Y. State Bar Assn. (chmn. com. taxation of trust and estates sect. 1980-83), Assn. Bar City N.Y., Soc. Mayflower Descs., Harvard Club, Knickerbocker Club, Century Club, Grolier Club (past pres.). Home: 520 E 86th St New York NY 10028-7534 Office: Dewey Ballantine LLP 1301 Avenue Of The Americas New York NY 10019-6022

WARSHAVSKY, SUZANNE MAY, retired lawyer; b. N.Y.C., July 22, 1944; d. Charles Finke and Charlotte (Ceaser) Goldman; m. Mordechai Warshavsky, June 7, 1964; children: Oren Jay, Adam Stuart, Claire Faye. AB, Vassar Coll., 1965; JD cum laude, NYU, 1968. Bar: N.Y. 1968, U.S. Dist. Ct. (so. and ea. dists.) 1972, U.S. Ct. Appeals (2d cir.) 1972, U.S. Supreme Ct. 1973. Assoc. Dewey, Ballantine, Bushby, Palmer & Wood, N.Y.C., 1968—73, Milgrim Thomajan Jacobs & Lee PC, N.Y.C., 1973—76; ptnr. Warshavsky, Hoffman & Cohen PC, N.Y.C., 1976—91, Davis & Gilbert, N.Y.C., 1991—94; ret., 1994. Arbitrator Civil Ct. of N.Y.C., 1975—86. Mem.: ABA, Mag. Pubs. Assn. (legal affairs com. 1985—87), Am. Arbitration Assn. (panel comml. arbitrators 1976—77), N.Y. Women's Bar Assn. (com. bus. and tax laws 1985—92, chair com. profl. ethics and discipline 1986—87, chmn. judiciary com. 1988, trustee 1988—92), Assn. of Bar of City of N.Y. (profl. and judicial ethics com. 1976—79), N.Y. State Bar Assn. (pub. health com. 1972—77, com. on profl. discipline 1991—94). Computer, Libel, Trademark and copyright. Home: 158 Gates Ave Montclair NJ 07042-2009

WARSHAW, ALLEN CHARLES, lawyer; b. Harrisburg, Pa., Aug. 27, 1948; s. Julius and Miriam (Nepove) W.; m. Shirley Anne Nes, Aug. 23, 1970; children: Christopher James, Andrew Charles, William Robert. BA, U. Pa., 1970; JD, Villanova U., 1973. Bar: Pa. 1973, U.S. Dist. Ct. (ea. and mid. dists.) Pa. 1974, U.S. Ct. Appeals (3d cir.) 1975, U.S. Supreme Ct. 1977, Calif. 1978. Staff atty. Office Atty. Gen., State of Pa., Harrisburg, 1973-79, chief civil litigation, 1979-85, dir. civil law, 1985-86; ptnr. Duane, Morris & Heckscher, Harrisburg, 1986—2002; shareholder Klett, Rooney, Lieber & Schorling, Harrisburg, 2002—. Past pres. Mechanicsburg Soccer Assn.; Dem. committeeperson, area leader Cumberland County; mem. exec. com. Cumberland County Dem. Party; bd. dirs. Mechanicsburg Area Sch. Dist. Fellow Am. Bar Found.; mem. ABA, ABA Coun. Appelate Lawyers, Fed. Bar Assn., Am. Bankruptcy Inst., Pa. Bar Assn., Coun. Appellate Lawyers, Dauphin County Bar Assn., Turnabout Mgmt. Assn. Appellate, Bankruptcy, General civil litigation. Home: 1035 Mccormick Rd Mechanicsburg PA 17055-5970 Office: Klett Rooney Lieber & Schorling 240 N 3d St Harrisburg PA 17101 E-mail: acwarshaw@KlettRooney.com.

WARSHAW, ROBERTA SUE, lawyer, financial specialist; b. Chgo., July 10, 1934; d. Charles and Frieda (Feldman) Weiner; m. Lawrence Warshaw, July 5, 1959 (div. June 1978); children: Nan R., Adam; m. Paul A. Heise, Apr. 2, 1994. Student, U. Ill., 1952-55; BFA, U. So. Calif., 1956; JD, Northwestern U., 1980. Bar: Ill. 1980. Atty., fin. specialist Housing Svcs. Ctr., Chgo., 1980-84, Chgo. Rehab. Network, 1985-91, 92-95; dir. housing State Treas., State of Ill., Chgo., 1991; sole practitioner, 1995—. Legal worker Sch. of Law, Northwestern U. Legal Clinic, Chgo., 1977-80; real estate developer, mgr., marketer, Chgo., 1961-77; bd. dirs. Single Room Housing Assistance Corp., Lebanon County Mediation Svcs., mediator, sec., 2001; asst. dir. Lebanon Valley Coll. Program, Hania, Crete, 1998. Co-author: (manual) The Cook County Scavenger Sale Program and The City of Chicago Reactivation Program, 1991, (booklet) Fix the Worst First, 1989; co-editor: The Caring Contract, Voices of American Leaders, 1996. Alderman 9th ward City of Evanston, Ill., 1985-93, mem. planning and devel., rules com., unified budget com., chair flood and pollution control com.; pres. Sister Cities Found.; mem. cmty. and econ. devel. policy Nat. League Cities, 1990-93; mem. Dem. Nat. Com.; bd. dirs. Dem. Ctrl. Com. Evanston, 1973—; elected committeeman Evanston Twp. Dem. Com., 1994-98, dem. committeeman Mt. Gretna Borough, 2000—; del. Dem. Nat. Conv., 1996; Dem. committeeman Mt. Gretna Borough, 2000—; vol. tax preparer; tax counseling for elderly, 2000—; bd. dirs., mediator Lebanon County Mediation Svcs., 2000—, sec., 2001-03, pres., 2003—. Mem. ABA (affordable housing com.), Ill. State Bar Assn., Chgo. Bar Assn. (real estate coms.), Decalogue Soc. Lawyers, Chgo. Coun. Lawyers (housing com.), IRS Tax Counseling for the Elderly (vol. tax preparer). Avocations: politics, travel, hiking, camping, athletic activities. Home: 104 Brown Ave PO Box 537 Mount Gretna PA 17064-0537 E-mail: femdem1@narl.com.

WARTHEN, HARRY JUSTICE, III, lawyer; b. Richmond, Va., July 8, 1939; s. Harry Justice Jr. and Martha Winston (Alsop) W.; m. Sally Berkeley Trapnell, Sept. 7, 1968; children: Martha Alsop, William Trapnell. BA, U. Va., 1961, LLB, 1967. Bar: Va. 1967, U.S. Ct. Appeals (4th cir.) 1967, U.S. Dist. Ct. (ea. dist.) Va. 1969. Law clk. to judge U.S. Ct. Appeals (4th cir.), Richmond, Va., 1967-68; assoc. Hunton & Williams, Richmond, 1968—. Lectr. in field U. Va. Law Sch., Charlottesville, 1975—77. Trustee exec. com. Hist. Richmond Found., 1986-95, 96—, pres., 2000-02; trustee Woodrow Wilson Birthplace and Mus., 1997-2003; dir. exec. com. Preservation Alliance of Va., 1991-97, pres., 1994-96; Va. rep. bd. advisors The Nat. Trust for Historic Preservation, 2003—; elder, trustee endowment fund Grace Covenant Presbyn. Ch.; moderator Hanover Presbytery, Presbyn. Ch. (USA), 1988. Lt. U.S. Army, 1962-64. Fellow Am. Coll. Trust and Estate Counsel, Va. Law Found.; mem. ABA, Richmond Bar Assn., Va. Bar Assn. (chmn. sect. on wills, trusts and estates 1981-89), Antiquarian Soc. Richmond (pres. 1977-78, 98-99), Country Club Va., Deep Run Hunt Club. Republican. Probate (including wills, trusts), Estate taxation, Estate planning. Home: 1319 Shallow Well Rd Manakin Sabot VA 23103-2305 Office: Hunton & Williams Riverfront Plz E Tower 951 E Byrd St Richmond VA 23219 E-mail: hwarthen@hunton.com.

WARWICK, THOMAS JOSEPH, JR., lawyer; b. Hamilton Township, N.J., Nov. 17, 1946; 1 child, Thomas J. III; m. Cynthia Warwick. BSBA, Boston Coll., 1968; JD, U. San Diego, 1972. Bar: Calif. 1973. Ptnr. Grimes & Warwick, San Diego, 1974—; mem. Jud. Coun. Calif., 2001—. Recipient Outstanding Svc. award, San Diego Mcpl. Ct., 1999. Mem. State Bar Calif. (bd. govs. 1997-2000), San Diego County Bar Assn. (bd. dirs. 1986-88, 90-92, 2000-03), Consumer Attys. San Diego (bd. dirs. 1985—, pres. 1997—), San Diego County Bar, Appellate Defenders/Fed. Defenders (bd. dirs. 1986—, v.p. 1996-97, pres. 1997-98), San Diego Trial Lawyers Assn. (Trial Lawyer of Yr. award 1992, Outstanding Trial Lawyer award 1978, 93), Criminal Def. Lawyers Club (pres. 1991). Criminal. Office: Grimes and Warwick 2664 4th Ave San Diego CA 92103-6515

WASDEN, LAWRENCE, state attorney general; m. Tracey Wasden; children: Sean, Ashley, Cassidy, Blake. JD, U. Idaho. Bar: Idaho 1985. Dep. pros. atty. Canyon County, Idaho; dep. atty. gen. Idaho State Tax Commn.; dep. chief of staff State of Idaho, Boise, chief of staff to atty. gen., atty. gen., 2003—. Mem.: Idaho State Bar (founding mem., immediate past chmn. govt. and pub. lawyers sect.). Republican. Office: Office Atty Gen PO Box 83720 700 W Jefferson St Boise ID 83720*

WASDEN, MARK ROBERT, lawyer; b. Pomona, Calif., Apr. 5, 1961; s. James B. and Martha Wasden; m. Heidi Boettcher, Aug. 20, 1983; children: Chelsea Ann, Megan Lynn, Madison Rachel, Mark Tanner. BA, Brigham Young U., 1988; JD, U. Idaho, 1991. Bar: Idaho 94. Jud. clk. Judge Daniel Meehl, Twin Falls County, Idaho, 1991—92; jud. clk. Judge J. William Hart 5th Dist. Minidolca County, Rupert, Idaho, 1992—94; atty. Goicoechea Law Offices, Twin Falls, 1994—. Avocations: hunting, fishing, home remodeling. Personal injury (including property damage), Workers' compensation. Office: Goicoechea Law Offices 131 2d St W Twin Falls ID 83303 E-mail: hwasden@mindspring.com.

WASHBURN, DAVID THACHER, lawyer; b. Claremont, N.H., May 2, 1930; s. Walter Henry and Josephine Emmeline (Dana) W.; m. Joycemarie Springer, June 10, 1957 (div. Dec. 1975); children: Margaret Dana, David Thacher Jr., Robert Springer, John Putnam. BA, U. Vt., 1952; JD, NYU, 1955. Bar: N.Y. 1956, D.C. 1970, U.S. Supreme Ct. 1970. From assoc. to ptnr. Paul, Weiss, Rifkind, Wharton & Garrison, N.Y.C., 1955-95, of counsel, 1996—. Adj. prof. CUNY Law Sch., 1997-98. Trustee Rye Neck Bd. Edn., Mamaroneck, N.Y., 1971-73, Cambridge (Mass.) Coll., 1980-88, The Yard, N.Y.C., 1986-95, ARIA Found., Inc., Williston, Vt., 1991—; trustee, mem. exec. com. Rare Ctr. for Tropical Conservation, Phila., 1979-80; dir. Sanctuary for Families, Inc., N.Y.C., 1994—, mem. exec. com., treas. 1995-2000. Mem. ABA, N.Y. State Bar Assn., Assn. of Bar of City of N.Y., The Coffee House, Doubles, Westchester Country Club. Corporate, general, Mergers and acquisitions, Probate (including wills, trusts). Home: 10 W 66th St New York NY 10023-6206 Office: Paul Weiss Rifkind Wharton & Garrison Fl 2 1285 Avenue of the Americas New York NY 10019-6064 E-mail: dwashburn@paulweiss.com.

WASHINGTON, DONALD W. prosecutor; BS, U.S. Mil. Acad.; JD, S. Tex. Coll. Law. Capt. U.S. Army, 1977—82; with Conoco Inc., 1982—96, div. counsel, gen. litigation atty., 1991—96; ptnr. Jeansonne and Redmondet, Lafayette, La., 1996—2001; U.S. atty. we. dist. U.S. Dept. Justice, La., 2001—. Capt. USAR, 1982—90. Office: 300 Fannin St Ste 3201 Shreveport LA 71101*

WASHINGTON, ERIC T. state supreme court justice; Assoc. Fulbright and Jaworski, Houston and Washington; legis. dir., counsel Rep. Michael Andrews; spl. corp. counsel, prin. dep. corp. counsel; ptnr. Hogan & Hartson, Washington, 1990-95; apptd. Superior Ct., 1995; judge D.C. Ct. Appeals, 1999—. Office: DC Ct Appeals 6th Fl 500 Indiana Ave NW Fl 6 Washington DC 20001-2138

WASKO, STEVEN E. lawyer; b. Chgo., May 10, 1954; s. Theodore J. and Beverly W.; m. Elaine L. Enger, Oct. 3, 1981 (div. Aug. 1996); 1 child, Christine; m. Deborah Wasko; stepchildren: Tara, Raef, Brooke and Christopher. B in Spl. Studies cum laude, Cornell Coll., 1976; JD cum laude, Kent U., 1979. Bar: Ill. 1979, U.S. Dist. Ct. (no. dist.) Ill. 1979. Assoc. atty. Blanshan & Summerfield, Park Ridge, Ill., 1979-81; ptnr. Summerfield & Wasko, Park Ridge, 1981-86; sole practitioner Steven Wasko and Assocs., Park Ridge, 1986-90, mng. ptnr., 1992-95; ptnr. Wasko & Michaels, Park Ridge, 1990-91, Steponate & Wasko Ltd., Park Ridge and Chgo., 1995—. Dir. Kolan Corp., Park Ridge, 1988—. Great Books leader Field Sch. Dist., Park Ridge, 1997—. Avocations: weight training, watercolors, fine art. Family and matrimonial. Office: 1580 N Northwest Hwy Park Ridge IL 60068-1444

WASMAN, JANE G. lawyer; b. Miami Beach, Fla., May 9, 1956; BA magna cum laude, Princeton U., 1978; JD, Harvard U., 1981. Bar: Calif. 1981, D.C. 1983, N.Y. 1990. Assoc. Jones, Day Revis & Pogue, L.A., 1981-85; assoc. counsel U.S. Senate Com. on Vets. Affairs, Washington, 1987-89; assoc. Fried, Frank, Harris, Shriver & Jacobson, N.Y.C., 1989-95; dir. litigation Schering-Plough Corp., Kenilworth, NJ, 1995-98, staff v.p. European ops.-legal, chief counsel Europe, 1998-2000, staff v.p., assoc. gen. counsel, internat., 2001, staff v.p., assoc. gen. counsel, managed care/comml. licensing and regulatory, 2002—. Mem. Am. Corp. Counsel Assn., Phi Beta Kappa. General civil litigation, Health, Private international. Office: Schering-Plough Corp 2000 Galloping Hill Rd Kenilworth NJ 07033-1328 E-mail: jane.wasman@spcorp.com.

WASSERMAN, MARCIA WATSON, legal administration consultant; b. Bklyn., Dec. 17, 1949; d. Stanley and Seena (Klein) Watson; m. Charles Wasserman, Mar. 23, 2003. Student, UCLA, 1967-71, 80-81, UCLA Grad. Sch., 1987-88. Office mgr., paralegal Lewis, Marenstein & Kadar, L.A., 1977-81; office mgr. Rosenfeld, Meyer & Susman, Beverly Hills, Calif., 1981-83; adminstr. Rudin, Richman & Appel, Beverly Hills, 1983; dir. adminstrn. Kadison, Pfaelzer, L.A., 1983-87; exec. dir. Richards, Watson and Gershon, L.A., 1987-93; legal mgmt. cons. Wainess & Co., L.A., 1993-99; dir. law firm svcs. Dutch Franklin Bus. Svcs., Inc., 1999-2000; dir. client adv. svcs. Green Hasson & Janks LLP, L.A., 2000—. Adj. faculty U. West L.A. Sch. Paralegal Studies, 1997-98. Mem. ABA, L.A. County Bar Assn. (exec. com. law office mgmt. sect.), State Bar Calif. (exec. com. law practice mgmt. and tech. sect. 2002-), Assn. Legal Adminstrs. (mem. editl. adv. bd. 1998—, bd. dirs. 1990-92, asst. regional v.p. Calif. 1987-88, regional v.p. 1988-89, pres. Beverly Hills chpt. 1985-86, membership chair 1984-85, chair new adminstrn. sect. 1982-84, mktg. mgmt. sect. com. 1989-90, internat. conf. com.), Beverly Hills Bar Assn. (chair law practice mgmt. sect. 1998-2000, chair women in legal profession co. 2000-01). Avocations: historic preservation, antiques, interior design. Office: 10990 Wilshire Blvd Fl 16 Los Angeles CA 90024-3929 E-mail: mwwasserman@ghjadvisors.com.

WASSERMAN, RICHARD LEO, lawyer; b. Balt., Aug. 6, 1948; s. Jack B. and Claire (Gutman) W.; m. Manuele Delbourgo, May 13, 1973; children: Alexander E., Lauren E. AB, Princeton U., 1970; JD, Columbia U., 1973. Bar: N.Y. 1975, Md. 1978, U.S. Dist. Ct. (so. and ea. dists.) N.Y. 1975, U.S. Dist. Ct. Md. 1978, U.S. Ct. Appeals (2d cir.) 1975, U.S. Ct. Appeals (4th cir.) 1979, U.S. Supreme Ct. 1982. Law clk. to hon. Roszel C. Thomsen U.S. Dist. Ct. Md., Balt., 1973-74; assoc. Proskauer Rose Goetz & Mendelsohn, N.Y.C., 1974-78, Venable, Baetjer & Howard, Balt., 1978-81, ptnr., 1982—, also bd. dirs. Fellow Am. Coll. Bankruptcy, Md. Bar Found.; mem. ABA (bus. bankruptcy com.), Md. Bar Assn. (sec. coun. bus. law sect. 1989-92), Bar Assn. Balt. City (chmn. banking, bankruptcy and bus. law com. 1987-88), Bankruptcy Bar Assn. Dist. Md. (bd. dirs. 1988—, pres. 1990-91), Assn. Bar City N.Y., Am. Bankruptcy Inst., Princeton U. Alumni Assn. Md. (bd. dirs. 1980-98, pres. 1985-87), Suburban Club Baltimore County (bd. govs. 1982-89, 94-98, 2d v.p. 1986-87, sec. 1987-88, pres.-elect 1994-95, pres. 1995-97). Democrat. Jewish. Avocations: tennis, golf, bridge. Banking, Bankruptcy, Commercial, contracts (including sales of goods; commercial financing). Office: Venable Baetjer & Howard LLP 1800 Mercantile Bank Bldg Baltimore MD 21201 E-mail: rlwasserman@venable.com.

WASSERMAN, STEPHEN ALAN, lawyer; b. Cleve., Apr. 7, 1948; s. Myron Earl and Eve Ruth (Milstein) W.; m. Sandra Shulamith Moltz, Oct. 20, 1978. BA, U. Wis., 1970; JD, Northeastern U., Boston, 1978. Bar: Mass. 1978, U.S. Dist. Ct. Mass. 1978. Housing atty. Neighborhood Legal Svcs., Lynn, Mass., 1978-83; ptnr. Barmack, Boggs and Wasserman, Lynn, 1983-91; pvt. practice Salem, Mass., 1991-97, 98—, Boston, 1997-98. Bd. dirs. North Shore Cmty. Action Program, Peabody, Mass., 1995—. Avocations: reading, baseball, jogging. State civil litigation, Landlord-tenant, Personal injury (including property damage). Office: 32 Church St Salem MA 01970-3737 E-mail: S.A.Wasserman@verizon.net.

WATERHOUSE, RACHEL L. lawyer; b. Orlando, Fla., Oct. 17, 1962; d. Linton S. and Louise J. Waterhouse; m. James B. Selleh; 1 child, Sarah Louise. BA, U. S.C., 1984; JD cum laude, Stetson U., 1988. Bar: Fla. 1988, Tenn. 1989, U.S. Dist. Ct. (mid. dist.) Tenn. 1989, U.S. Dist. Ct. (we. dist.) Tenn. 1994, U.S. Ct. Appeals (6th cir.) 1994, U.S. Supreme Ct. 1994, U.S. Dist. Ct. (ea. dist.) Tenn. 1995. Jud. law clk. hon. Thomas A. Higgins U.S. Dist. Ct., Nashville, 1989-91; atty. King & Ballow, Nashville, 1991-94; asst. atty. gen. Tenn. Atty. Gens. Office, Nashville, 1994-95; asst. U.S. atty. U.S. Dept. Justice, Nashville, 1995—. Co-author: Americans With Disabilities Act, 1994; notes editor Stetson Law Rev., 1987. Stephen ministry Episcopal Ch., Nashville, 1989-91; bd. dirs. Focus, Nashville, 1991-94. Named to Outstanding Young Women of Am., 1988. Mem. ABA, Fla. Bar Assn., Nashville Bar Assn. (various coms.), Fed. Bar Assn. (pres.-elect Nashville chpt.), Lawyers Assn. for Women (various coms.). Avocations: running, reading, hiking. Office: US Attys Office Dept Justice 110 9th Ave S Ste A961 Nashville TN 37203-3870

WATERMAN, WILLIAM, JR., lawyer; b. Chgo., July 17, 1937; AB, Harvard U., 1959, LLB, 1962. Bar: Ill. 1962, N.Y. 1966, U.S. Ct. Dist. Ct. (so. and ea. dists.) 1968, U.S. Ct. Appeals (2nd cir.) 1975, U.S. Supreme Ct. 1976. Legal advisor Ministry Fin. No. Nigeria, Kaduna, 1963; asst. lectr. U. Lagos, Nigeria, 1963-64; assoc. Spear and Hill, N.Y.C., 1965-68; pvt. practice N.Y.C., 1969—. Co-author: Immigration Law and Defense, 1977, 4th rev. edit. 1986; contbr. articles to profl. jours. Mem. Am. Immigration Lawyers Assn., Nat. Lawyers Guild, N.Y. State Bar Assn., Assn. of Bar of City of N.Y. Corporate, general, Family and matrimonial, Immigration, naturalization, and customs. Address: 305 Broadway Fl 7 New York NY 10007-1109

WATERS, H. FRANKLIN, federal judge; b. Hackett, Ark., July 20, 1932; s. William A. and Wilma W.; m. Janie C. Waters, May 31, 1958; children—Carolyn Denise, Melanie Jane, Melissa Ann BS, U. Ark., 1955; LL.B., St. Louis U., 1964. Engr., atty. Ralston-Purina Co., St. Louis, 1958-66; ptnr. Crouch, Blair, Cypert & Waters, 1967-81; judge U.S. Dist. Ct. (we. dist.) Ark., from 1981, chief judge, sr. judge, 1997—. Former bd. dirs. Springdale Schs.; former bd. govs. Washington Regional Med. Ctr. Mem. ABA, Ark. Bar Assn., Springdale C. of C. (past bd. dirs.) Office: US Dist Ct PO Box 1908 Fayetteville AR 72702-1908

WATERSTON, TASS DEVER, lawyer; b. Dallas, Sept. 27, 1966; s. Tom Lee and Jean Ivy (Hollingsworth) W.; m. Laura Ann Lodewick, June 12, 1993. BA, U. Tex., 1988; MBA, Dallas Bapt. U., 1990; JD, So. Meth. U., 1997. Bar: Tex. 1997, U.S. Dist. Ct. (so., no., and ea. dists.) Tex. Adminstrv. intern Fed. Bur. Prisons, Seagoville, Tex., 1990-91; instr. Northwood U., Cedar Hill, Tex., 1991-96; intern 13th Dist. Ct. Appeals, Corpus Christi, Tex., 1996. Del. Tex. Dem. Conv., Houston, 1992, mem. state nominations com., Ft. Worth, 1994. Mem. ABA, FBA, Christian Legal Soc., Dallas County Bar Assn., Barristers, Delta Theta Phi. General civil litigation, Commercial, consumer (including collections, credit), General practice. Office: Francis & Orr LLP 2840 Lincoln Plz 500 N Alcord St Dallas TX 75201

WATHEN, DANIEL EVERETT, former state supreme court chief justice; b. Easton, Maine, Nov. 4, 1939; s. Joseph Jackson and Wilda Persis (Dow) W.; m. Judith Carol Foren, July 14, 1960; children: Julanne Carol, Daniel Arthur. AB, Ricker Coll., 1962; JD, U. Maine, 1965; LLM (hon.), U. Va. Law Sch., 1988. Bar: Maine 1965. Atty. Wathen & Wathen, Augusta, Maine, 1965-77; trial judge Superior Ct. Maine, Augusta, 1977-81; appellate judge Supreme Jud. Ct. Maine, Augusta, 1981-92, state chief justice, 1992—2001; of counsel Pierce Atwood, 2002—. Office: Pierce Atwood One Monument Sq Portland ME 04101*

WATSON, FORREST ALBERT, JR., lawyer, bank executive; b. Atlanta, May 7, 1951; s. Forrest Albert and Virginia Doris (Ritch) W.; m. Marlys Wise, Oct. 16, 1982; children: Annaliese Marie Elizabeth, Forrest Albert Watson III. AB, Emory U., 1973; JD, U. Ga., 1975; postgrad., Mercer U., 1979-80. Bar: Ga. 1975, U.S. Dist. Ct. (mid. dist.) Ga. 1976, U.S. Tax Ct. 1976, U.S. Ct. Appeals (5th cir.) 1977, U.S. Supreme Ct. 1980; cert. data processor; CFP. Assoc. Banks, Smith & Lambdin, Barnesville, Ga., 1976-78; ptnr. Watson & Lindsey, Barnesville, 1978-82; v.p., gen. counsel United Bank Corp., Barnesville, 1981-91, chief ops. officer, 1990-2000, exec. v.p., gen. counsel, 1991-2000, mem., bd. dirs., exec. v.p., 1991; pres. United Bank Mortgage; exec. v.p., sr. trust officer United Bank, Griffin, Ga., 1995-98, exec. v.p., bd. dir. Zebulon, Ga., 1998—, mem. audit com., 2002—. Pres. United Bank Mortgage, 1993-95; gen. counsel Lamar State Bank, Barnesville, 1976-84; judge Small Claims Ct., Lamar County, Ga., 1976, City Ct. of Milner, Ga., 1977; lectr. IBM, 1984-85; atty. City of Meansville, Ga., 1976, City of Milner, 1977; bd. dirs. United Bank Corp. Assoc. editor Ga. Jour. Internat. Law, 1975. Gen. counsel Lamar County Devel. Authority, 1977; mem. Zebulon Planning Commn., 2003—; vice-chmn. bd. trustees Wastwood Acad., Thomaston, Ga., 2001—; bd. dirs. Legaline Inc., Atlanta, 1983—85. Mem. ABA, Ga. Bar Assn., Cir. Ct. Bar Assn., Griffin Cir. Bar Assn., Ga. Rural Health Assn. (trustee 1981-82), S.E. Bank Card Assn. (operating com. 1986-91), Assn. Cert. Fin. Planners, Assn. Inst. Cert. Computer Profls., Internat. Assn. Fin. Planners. Methodist. Avocations: art, antiques, travel. Banking. Home: PO Box 347 Zebulon GA 30295-0347 Office: United Bank Corp PO Box 1337 110 Griffin St Zebulon GA 30295

WATSON, JACK CROZIER, retired state supreme court justice; b. Jonesville, La., Sept. 17, 1928; s. Jesse Crozier and Gladys Lucille (Talbot) W.; m. Henrietta Sue Carter, Dec. 26, 1958; children: Carter Crozier (dec.), Wells Talbot. BA, U. Southwestern La., 1949; JD, La. State U., 1956; completed with honor, Appellate Judges Seminar, N.Y. U., 1974, Sr. Appellate Judges Seminar, 1980. Bar: La. 1956. Atty. King, Anderson & Swift, Lake Charles, La., 1956-58; prosecutor City of Lake Charles, 1960; asst. dist. atty. Calcasieu Parish, La., 1961-64; ptnr. Watson & Watson, Lake Charles, 1961-64; judge 14th Jud. Dist., La., 1964-72; judge ad hoc Ct. Appeals, 1st Circuit, Baton Rouge, 1972-73; judge Ct. Appeals, 3rd Circuit, Lake Charles, 1973-79; assoc. justice La. Supreme Ct., New Orleans, 1979-96, ret., 1996. Faculty advisor Nat. Coll. State Judiciary, Reno, 1970, 73; adj. prof. law summer sch. program in Greece, Tulane U., 1988-2000; adj. prof. law So. U., Baton Rouge, 1998-99; del. NEH Seminar, 1976; La. del to Internat. Conf. Appellate Magistrates, The Philippines, 1977; mem. La. Jud. Coun., 1986-92. 1st lt. USAF, 1950-54. Mem. ABA, La. Bar Assn., S.W. La. Bar Assn. (pres. 1973), Law Inst. State of La., La. Coun. Juvenile Ct. Judges (pres. 1969-70), Am. Judicature Soc., S.W. La. Camellia Soc. (pres. 1973-74), Am. Legion (post comdr. 1963), Lake Charles Yacht Club (commodore 1974), Blue Key, Sigma Alpha Epsilon, Phi Delta Phi, Pi Kappa Delta. Democrat. Baptist.

WATSON, JOHN ALLEN, lawyer; b. Ft. Worth, Sept. 18, 1946; s. John and Mary (Barlow) W.; m. Patricia L. Clardy, Oct. 24, 1946; 1 child, Virginia E. BA, Rice U., 1968; JD, U. Tex., Austin, 1971. Bar: Tex. 1971. Assoc. Fulbright & Jaworski, Houston, 1971-78, ptnr., 1978—. Mem. ABA. Corporate, general, Finance, Securities. Office: Fulbright & Jaworski LLP 1301 McKinney St Ste 5100 Houston TX 77010-3031 E-mail: jwatson@fulbright.com.

WATSON, JOHN MICHAEL, lawyer; b. Karnes, Tex., May 9, 1956; s. Jarvis Schooley and Edwina Louise Watson; m. Margaret Marie Blackshear; children: Maggie, John. BA, Washington and Lee U., 1979; JD, U. Houston, 1982. Bar: Tex. 1982, U.S. Dist. Ct. (so., no., ea. and we. dists.) Tex. 1994. Counsel Union Bank Houston, 1982—85; asst. gen. counsel, v.p. Allied Bank Tex., Houston, 1985—88; asst. gen. counsel, sr. v.p. First Interstate Bank Tex., N.A., Houston, 1988—96; mng. counsel Wells Fargo Bank, Houston, 1996—. Dir. The Agnes Carter Helms Sch., Camden, Tex., 1986-89, Supreme Ct. Bd. Disciplinary Appeals, Houston, 1996—2002. Mem. Tex. Assn. Bank Counsel (dir. 1989-92). Republican. Methodist. Banking, State civil litigation, Commercial, contracts (including sales of goods; commercial financing). E-mail: watsonm1@wellsfargo.com.

WATSON, KIPP ELLIOTT, lawyer; b. L.A., Oct. 30, 1950; s. Benjamin And Irene Cohen; m. Emily Strauss; 1 child, Lisa Jo. BA, NYU, 1977; JD, Benjamin N. Cardozo Sch. Law, 1980. Bar: N.Y. Pvt. practice, N.Y.C., 1984—98; of counsel Mark B. Stumer & Assocs., N.Y.C., 1998—. Roothbert fellow, N.Y.C., 1979. Mem. N.Y. State Bar Assn. Civil Rights Com. (chair 1988-91), Nat. Employment Lawyers Assn. N.Y. (bd. dirs. 1992-99, newsletter editor 1994-97), 504 Dem. Club (pres. 1993). Avocations: computer programming, chess, wheelchair basketball-forward for L.I. Express. Office: Mark B Stumer & Assocs 101 5th Ave Rm 10E New York NY 10003-1008

WATSON, RICHARD ALLEN, lawyer; b. Oceanside, N.Y., Aug. 11, 1946; s. William Edgar and Grace (Brooks) W.; m. Mary Lee Brown, June 24, 1972; children: Rebecca, Sarah. BA, Hamilton Coll., 1967; JD, Columbia U., 1972. Bar: N.Y. 1973, U.S. Tax Ct. 1974, N.J. 1976. From assoc. to ptnr. Chamberlain, Willi, Ouchterloney & Watson, N.Y.C., 1972—. Mem. Morris Twp. Zoning Bd., N.J., 1981-88; mem. Morris Twp. Coun., 1988—; chmn. Morris Twp. Reps., 1985—; mayor of Morris Twp., 1991-92, 98-2000. Served with U.S. Army, 1969-71, Vietnam. Mem. ABA, N.J. Bar Assn. Republican. Presbyterian. Estate planning, General practice, Health. Home: 5 Quaker Ridge Rd Morristown NJ 07960-6502 Office: Chamberlain Willi Ouchterloney & Watson 15 Maiden Ln Ste 705 New York NY 10038-4029

WATSON, ROBERT FRANCIS, lawyer; b. Houston, Jan. 9, 1936; s. Louis Leon and Lora Elizabeth (Hodges) W.; m. Marietta Kiser, Nov. 24, 1961; children: Julia, Melissa, Rebecca. BA, Vanderbilt U., 1957; JD, U. Denver, 1959. Bar: Colo. 1959, U.S. Dist. Ct. (no. dist.) Tex. 1967, U.S. Supreme Ct. 1968, Tex. 1973, U.S. Ct. Appeals (5th cir.) 1973, U.S. Dist. Ct. (so. dist.) Tex. 1980, U.S. Ct. Appeals (11th cir.) 1981. Law clk. U.S. Dist. Ct. Colo., 1960-61; trial atty. SEC, Denver, 1961-67, asst. regional adminstr. Ft. Worth, 1967-72, regional adminstr., 1972-75; ptnr. Law, Snakard & Gambill, P.C., Ft. Worth, 1975-98, of counsel, 1998—; gen. counsel USPA&IRA (now First Command Fin. Svcs., Inc.), Ft. Worth, 1998—. Counsel City of Ft. Worth Police Investigation Commn., 1975; spl. counsel Office Atty. Gen. State Ariz., 1977-78. Contbr. articles to profl. jours. Mem. Ft. Worth Crime Commn., 1987-93. Honoree 27th Ann. Rocky Mountain State-Fed.-Provincial Securities Conf. Fellow: Coll. of State Bar Tex., U. Denver Law Sch. Alumni Coun., Tex. Bar Found. (life), Colo. Bar Assn. (life), Tarrant County Bar Assn., Ft. Worth Club; mem.: ABA, Tarrant County Bar Found., Tex. Bus. Law Found. (bd.dirs. 1988—93), State Bar Tex., Fed. Bar Assn., Shady Oaks Country Club (Ft. Worth), Phi Delta Phi. Republican. Presbyterian. Federal civil litigation, Corporate, general, Securities. Office: First Command 4100 S Hulen St Fort Worth TX 76109 also: Law Snakard & Gambill PC 1600 W 7th St Ste 500 Fort Worth TX 76102-3819 E-mail: rfwatson@firstcommand.com.

WATSON, ROBERTA CASPER, lawyer; b. Boise, Idaho, July 11, 1949; d. John Blaine and Joyce Lucile (Mercer) C.; m. Robert George Watson, July 22, 1972; 1 child, Rebecca Joyce. BA cum laude, U. Idaho, 1971; JD, Harvard U., 1974. Bar: Mass. 1974, U.S. Dist. Ct. Mass. 1975, U.S. Supreme Ct. 1979, U.S. Ct. Appeals (1st cir.) 1979, U.S. Tax Ct. 1979, Fla. 1985, U.S. Dist. Ct. (mid. dist.) Fla. 1985, U.S. Dist. Ct. (so. dist.) Fla. 1987. Assoc. Peabody & Brown, Boston, 1974-78, Mintz, Levin, Cohn, Ferris, Glovsky & Popeo, Boston, 1978-84; sr. dir. Wolper Ross & Co., Miami, 1983-85; assoc. Trenam, Kemker, Scharf, Barkin, Frye, O'Neill & Mullis, P.A., Tampa, Fla., 1985-87, ptnr., 1988—. Co-author: A Physician's Guide to Professional Corporations; co-editor-in-chief COBRA Adv. Newsletter, 1997-2000; contbr. articles to profl. jours. Pres. Performing Arts Ctr. Greater Framingham, Mass., 1983; bd. dirs., Northside Mental Health Ctr., 1987—, pres. 1999-2001; trustee Unitarian Universalist Found., Clearwater, Fla., 1986—; bd. dirs. Dist. 6 Cmty. Health Purchasing Alliance, pres. com. chair, 1998-2000. Named Bd. Mem. of Yr., Fla. Cmty. Mental Health, 1994. Mem.: ABA (chair employee benefit com sect. taxation 1995—96, chair employee benefits interest group health law sect. 1998—2001, chair joint com. on employee benefits 2002—03), Fla. West Coast Employee Benefits Coun. (bd. dirs., treas. 1997—98, v.p 1998—2001, pres. 2001—02), Am. Coll. Employee Benefits Counsel (charter mem.), Tampa Club, Harvard Club (bd. dirs. West Coast Fla. chpt.), Order Ea. Star. Democrat. Avocations: music, metaphysics, Lincoln historian, genealogy. Health, Pension, profit-sharing, and employee benefits. Home: 55 Martinique Ave Tampa FL 33606-4029 Office: Trenam Kemker et al 2700 Bank of Am Plz 101 E Kennedy Blvd Tampa FL 33602 E-mail: rcwatson@trenam.com.

WATSON, THOMAS C. lawyer; b. Poplar Bluff, Mo., Feb. 26, 1945; s. William C. and Dorothy E. (Whitson) W.; children: Thomas II, Nathan, Edward, Clay, Luke. BS, U. Memphis, 1967, MEd, 1968; JD, Washington U., St. Louis, 1972. Bar: Mo. 1972, D.C. 1973. Assoc. Morgan, Lewis & Bockius, Washington, 1973-78, ptnr., 1978-79, Crowell & Moring, Washington, 1979-95, Watson & Renner, 1996—. Avocations: hiking, biking, computers, hunting wild fowl. General civil litigation, Corporate, general, Toxic tort. Office: Watson & Renner 1919 M St NW Ste 400 Washington DC 20036

WATSON, THOMAS ROGER, lawyer; b. Concord, N.H., May 14, 1951; s. Roger Edward and Mary (Hannigan) W. BA in Polit. Sci. cum laude, U. N.H., 1973; JD, Franklin Pierce Law Ctr., 1978. Bar: N.H. 1978, U.S. Dist. Ct. N.H. 1978, U.S. Ct. Appeals (1st cir.) 1978, Maine 1982, U.S. Dist. Ct. Maine 1982, U.S. Supreme Ct. 1986. Ptnr. Tybursky & Watson, Portsmouth, N.H., 1979-86, Tybursky, Watson & Harman, Portsmouth, 1987-88, Taylor, Keane, Blanchard, Lyons & Watson, P.A., Portsmouth, 1988-94, Watson, Lyons, & Bosen, P.A., Portsmouth, 1994-99, Watson & Bosen, P.A., Portsmouth, 2000—01, Watson, Bosen, Harman, Venci & Lemire, P.A., Portsmouth, 2001—. Del. N.H. Constl. Conv., Concord, 1974. Mem. Maritime Heritage Commn., 1986-95, City of Portsmouth Hist. Dist. Commn., 1992, City of Portsmouth Planning Bd., 1992-94; bd. dirs. N.H. Small Bus. Devel. Ctr., 1993-95, N.H. Main St. Ctr., 1998-2002, sec., 2001-02; mem. adv. bd. Ballet New England, 1997—; bd. advisors N.H. Small Bus. Devel. Ctr., 1992-95; bd. trustees Strawberry Banke Mus., 2000—, sec., 2001-02, chmn., 2002—. Named Portsmouth Citizen of Yr., 1995. Mem. ABA, ATLA (state del. 1996—, chair-elect 1997-98, chair 1998-99, exec. com. 1998-99, co-chair coordinating com. on state rels. 1999-2000, mem. pub. affairs com. 1999-, Outstanding State Del. 1997, Wiedeman-Wysocki citation of excellence, 1999, 2000, 2002), N.H. Bar Assn. (bd. govs. 1985-90), N.H. Trial Lawyers Assn. (bd. govs. 1989—, sec. 1982-92, treas. 1993-94, pres. elect 1994-95, pres. 1995-96, chair legis. com. 1992-95, 96-2000, exec. com. 1992--, recipient Pres.'s award 1993, 97, Spl. Recognition award 2000), Rockingham County Bar Assn. (Profl. award 2001), Franklin Pierce Law Ctr. Alumni Assn. (pres. 1985-86), N.H. Bar Found. (bd. govs. 1987-90), Greater Portmouth C. of C. (bd. dirs. 1988-92, chmn. 1990-92), Portsmouth Hist. Soc. (trustee 1994—, pres. 1995-97), Portsmouth Atheneum (propr. 1991—). General civil litigation, Family and matrimonial, Personal injury (including property damage). Office: Watson Bosen Harman Venci & Lemire PA PO Box 469 Portsmouth NH 03802-0469

WATT, JOSEPH MICHAEL, state supreme court chief justice; b. Austin, Tex., Mar. 8, 1947; BA in History, Tex. Tech U., 1969; JD, U. Tex., 1972. Bar: Tex. 1972, Okla. 1974. Pvt. practice, Altus, Okla., 1972-85; judge Dist. Trial Ct., 1985-91; gen. counsel to gov. State of Okla., Oklahoma City, 1991-92; justice Okla. Supreme Ct., Okahoma City, 1992—2003, chief justice, 2003—. Office: Okla State Supreme Ct State Capitol Rm 245 Oklahoma City OK 73105 Fax: 405-521-6982.

WATTERS, EDWARD MCLAIN, III, lawyer; b. 1943; s. Edward McL. and Lucy F. (Disston) W.; m. Susan Secor, May 12, 1979; children: Jennifer Susan, Ann Elizabeth. BA cum laude, Yale U., 1965; JD cum laude, U. Pa., 1970. Bar: Pa. 1970. Ptnr. Pepper Hamilton LLP, Phila., 1977—. Lectr. programs on estate planning and will drafting Pa. Bar Inst. Bd. dirs. Children's Cruise and Playground Soc. Pa., Sanitarium Playgrounds of N.J., others. Lt. USNR, 1965-75; chair Decedents Estate Adv. Com. to Pa. Legislature's Joint State Govt. Commn. Fellow Am. Coll. Trust and Estate Counsel (com. state laws); mem. ABA, Phila. Bar Assn., Pa. Bar Assn. (past chmn. legis. com. probate sect.), Phila. Estate Planning Coun. (past pres.), Yale Club of Phila., Penn Club, Merion Golf Club. Probate (including wills, trusts), Estate taxation, Estate planning. Office: Pepper Hamilton LLP 400 Berwyn Park 899 Cassatt Rd Berwyn PA 19312-1183 E-mail: watterse@pepperlaw.com.

WATTERS, RICHARD DONALD, lawyer; b. Midland, Mich., May 3, 1951; s. Donald Wayne and Madalyn Bird (Tinetti) W.; m. Ann Elizabeth Hutchison, May 24, 1975; children: Kelly E., Nathan Paul. BS in Indsl. Engring., Bradley U., 1973; JD cum laude, St. Louis U., 1976. Bar: Mo. 1976, U.S. Dist. Ct. (we. and ea. dists.) Mo. 1976, Ill. 1977, U.S. Ct. Appeals (8th cir.) 1981; cert. healthcare mediator. Assoc. Lashly & Baer, P.C., St. Louis, 1976-81, ptnr., 1981—, dept. chmn., 1989—. Instr. St. Louis U. Sch. Law, 1977-79. Chmn., pres. United Cerebral Palsy Assn. St. Louis, 1985-88; bd. dirs. Canterbury Enterprises, sheltered workshop, St. Louis, 1988-94, participant Leadershp St. Louis, 1988-89; ethics com. DePaul Health Ctr., 1990—. Mem. Am. Health Lawyers Assn., Mo. Soc. Hosp. Attys. (bd. dirs. 1988-94, pres. 1990-91), Mo. Bar Assn. (vice chmn. health and hosp. com. 1988-90), Bar Assn. Metro. St. Louis (co-chmn. med.-legal com.). Republican. Avocation: sailing. Administrative and regulatory, Corporate, general, Health. Office: Lashly & Baer PC 714 Locust St Saint Louis MO 63101-1699 E-mail: rdwatters@lashlybaer.com.

WATTMAN, MALCOLM PETER, lawyer; b. N.Y.C., June 27, 1941; s. William and Irma (Turtletaub) W.; m. Donna Weber, Sept. 1, 1963. BS in Indsl. Engring., U. Buffalo, 1963; postgrad., Syracuse U., 1963-64; JD, Fordham U., 1968. Bar: N.Y. 1969. Engr. US Air Material Command, Rome, N.Y., 1963-64, Uniroyal, Passaic, N.J., 1964-66, M&M Candies, Hackettown, N.J., 1966-68; cons. Touche Ross Co., N.Y.C., 1968-69; assoc. Cadwalader Wickersham & Taft, N.Y.C., 1969-78, ptnr., 1978—. Mem. ABA, Assn. of Bar of City of N.Y. Corporate, general, Finance, Securities. Home: 1185 Park Ave Apt 8K New York NY 10128-1310 Office: Cadwalader Wickersham & Taft 100 Maiden Ln New York NY 10038-4818

WATTS, DAVID EIDE, lawyer; b. Fairfield, Iowa, June 13, 1921; BA, U. Iowa, 1941, JD, 1942; postgrad., Columbia Law Sch., 1946-47. Bar: Iowa 1942, Mass. 1950, N.Y. 1954. Instr. U. Iowa, Iowa City, 1947-48; asst. prof. U. Pa., 1948-49, Harvard Law Sch., 1949-52; ptnr. Dewey Ballantine, N.Y.C., 1958-90, of counsel, 1990—. Adj. assoc. prof. NYU, 1952-55; vis. lectr. Columbia U., 1954. Contbr. articles to legal jours. Mem. ABA, N.Y. State Bar Assn., Assn. Bar City N.Y., Am. Law Inst., Am. Coll. Tax Counsel, Am. Inst. Tax Policy. Corporate taxation, Taxation, general. Home: 33 W 74th St New York NY 10023-2402 Office: Dewey Ballantine LLP 1301 Ave Of The Americas New York NY 10019-6092

WATTS, STEVEN RICHARD, lawyer; b. Toledo, Oct. 5, 1955; s. James Hupp and Lona Jane Katherine (Miller) W.; m. Marcia Ann Jackson, Mar. 6, 1982; children: Lauren Brooke, Madison Ann. BA in History, Ohio State U., 1978; JD summa cum laude, U. Dayton, 1981. Bar: Ohio 1981, U.S. Dist. Ct. (so. dist.) Ohio 1981. Assoc. Smith & Schnacke, Dayton, Ohio, 1981-84, Porter, Wright, Morris & Arthur, Dayton, 1984-89, ptnr., 1990, Chernesky, Heyman & Kress P.L.L., Dayton, 1990—. Mem. ABA, Ohio State Bar Assn., Dayton Bar Assn. Presbyterian. Avocation: golf. Corporate, general, Securities. Home: 1101 Viewpoint Dr Dayton OH 45459-1442 Office: Chernesky Heyman & Kress PLL 1100 Courthouse Pla SW Dayton OH 45402

WAX, GEORGE LOUIS, lawyer; b. New Orleans, Dec. 6, 1928; s. John Edward and Theresa (Schaff) W.; LL.B., Loyola U. of South, 1952, B.C.S., 1960; m. Patricia Ann Delaney, Feb. 20, 1965; children: Louis Jude, Joann Olga, Therese Marie. Admitted to La. bar, 1952, practiced in New Orleans, 1954—. Served with USNR, 1952-54. Mem. La., New Orleans bar assns., Am. Legion. Roman Catholic. Kiwanian. Clubs: New Orleans Athletic, Suburban Gun and Rod, Southern Yacht. Estate planning, Probate (including wills, trusts), Property, real (including real estate development, water). Home: 6001 Charlotte Dr New Orleans LA 70122-2731 Office: 210 Baronne St Ste 1222 New Orleans LA 70112-1714

WAXMAN, BRUCE I. lawyer; b. N.Y.C., July 30, 1942; m. Sarah Jane Elpern, Mar. 17, 1974. BS, Cornell U., 1964; JD, Columbia U., 1967. Bar: D.C. 1970. Atty. Am. Fedn. of Govt. Employees, Washington, 1970—72; exec. dir. D.C. Pub. Employee Rels. Bd., 1972—80; dir. collective bargaining Assn. of Flight Attendants, Washington, 1980—82; atty. U.S. Dept. Commerce, Washington, 1983—2000, U.S. Dept. Justice, Washington, 2000—. Capt. U.S. Army, 1967—69. Office: US Dept Justice 5107 Leesburg Pike Ste 2600 Falls Church VA 22041

WAXMAN, SETH PAUL, lawyer; b. Hartford, Conn., Nov. 28, 1951; s. Felix H. and Frieda (Goodman) W.; m. Debra F. Goldberg, Mar. 20, 1977; children: Noah, Sarah, Ethan. AB summa cum laude, Harvard U., 1973; JD, Yale U., 1977. Bar: D.C. 1978, U.S. Dist. Ct. D.C., 1979, U.S. Ct. Appeals D.C Circuit, 1979, U.S. Supreme Ct. 1982, U.S. Ct. Appeals (1st cir.), 2000, (2d cir.), 1998, (3d cir.), 1983, (4th cir.), 1982, (5th cir.), 1997, (6th cir.), 1998, (7th cir.), 1998, (8th cir.), 1998, (9th cir.), 1989, (10th cir.), 1998, (11th cir.), 1989, U.S. Ct. Appeals Fed. Circuit, 1998. Law clk to Judge Gerhard A. Gesell, Washington, 1977-78; ptnr. Miller Cassidy Larroca & Lewin, Washington, 1978-94; assoc. dep. atty. gen. U.S. Dept. Justice, Washington, 1994-96, dep. solicitor gen., 1996-97, acting dep. atty. gen., 1997, solicitor gen. of the U.S., 1997-2001; partner Wilmer, Cutler & Pickering, 2001—. Disting. vis. from practice Georgetown U Law Ctr., 2001—; vis. prof. Georgetown U. Law Ctr., 2001; vis. fellow Harvard U. JFK Sch. Govt., 2001; fellow Am. Coll. Trial Lawyers, Am. Law Inst., Am. Acad. of Appellate Lawyers; dir. Supreme Ct. Inst., Georgetown U. Law Ctr.; lawyer Com. for Civil Rights Law. Prin. Coun. for Excellence in Govt.; trustee Supreme Ct. Hist. Soc.; director Nat. Found. for Jewish Culture; elected dir. Harvard Alumni Assn.; mem. com. to visit Harvard Coll. Harvard U.; trustee Bruce J. Ennis Found. Named hon. spl. agt., FBI, 2001; recipient Pro Bono Publico award, ABA, 1988, Edmund J. Randolph award, U.S. Dept. Justic, 2001, Benjamin L. Cardozo Cert. of Merit, Anti-Defamation League, 1987, Thomas Jefferson Found. medal in law, U. Va., 2002, Pursuit of Justice award, Internat. Assn. Jewish Lawyers and Jurists, 2001, Rex,Lee Advocacy Award, 2002; fellow Michael C. Rockefeller, Harvard U., 1973—74. Master: Edward Coke Appellate Inn Court; fellow: Am Acad. Appellate Attys., Am. Bar Found.; mem.: Am. Law Inst. Federal civil litigation, Constitutional, Criminal. E-mail: seth.waxman@wilmer.com.

WAXMAN, SHELDON ROBERT, lawyer; b. Chgo., Apr. 22, 1941; s. Henri and Ann (Sokolsky) W.; m. Katherine Slamski, Aug. 23, 1979; children: Josiah, Zoe. BA, U. Ill., 1963; JD, DePaul U., 1965. Bar: Ill. 1965, U.S. Supreme Ct. 1976, Mich. 1985. Staff atty. Argonne (Ill.) Nat. Lab., 1968-71; asst. U.S. Atty., Chgo., 1971-74; owner firm Waxman Tax & Legal Network, Chgo. and South Haven, Mich., 1976—. Owner Ind. Contractor Cons. Svcs. Author: In the Teeth of the Wind, 2002, All Anybody Needs to Know About Independent Contracting, 2003, (screenplay) The Raid, 2003; co-author: Piranhas on the Loose, 2003; editor-in-chief New Z Letter; contbr. articles to profl. jours. Founder Freedom Lawyers of Am., People for Simplified Tax Law, Nukes to the Sun. Civil rights, General civil litigation, Criminal. Office: PO Box 309 South Haven MI 49090-0309

WAXSE, DAVID JOHN, judge; b. Oswego, Kans., June 29, 1945; s. I. Joseph and Mary (Poole) W.; m. Linda Schilling (div.); children: Rachel, Ryan, Rebecca; m. Judy Pfannenstiel, May 29, 1982; 1 child, Elayna. BA, U. Kans., 1967; teaching cert., Columbia U., 1968, JD, 1971. Bar: Kans. 1971, U.S. Ct. Appeals (10th cir.) 1971, U.S. Supreme Ct. 1975, U.S. Ct. Appeals (8th Cir.) 1998. Dean of students Intermediate Sch. 88, N.Y.C., 1968-70; spl. edn. tchr. Peter Cooper Sch., N.Y.C., 1970-71; assoc. Payne & Jones, Olathe, Kans., 1971-74, ptnr., 1974-84; of counsel Shook, Hardy & Bacon, Overland Park, Kans., 1984-86, ptnr., 1986-95; shareholder Shook, Hardy & Bacon P.C., Overland Park, 1993-95; ptnr. Shook, Hardy & Bacon L.L.P., Overland Park, Kans., 1995-99; shareholder Shook, Hardy & Bacon P.C., Overland Park, 1993-95, v.p., asst. gen. counsel, 1995-99; U.S. magistrate judge Kansas City, 1999—. Mcpl. judge City of Shawnee, Kans., 1974-80; atty. City of DeSoto, Kans., 1972-79; adj. prof. U. Kans. Sch. Law, Lawrence, 1981-82; mem. juv. code adv. com. Kans. Jud. Coun., 1979-83, guardianship adv. com., 1982-83, atty. fees adv. com., 1986-87; mem. Civil Justice Reform Act Adv. Com., U.S. Dist. Ct. for Dist. Kans., 1991-95; mem. Kans. Commn. on Jud. Qualifications, 1992-99, vice-chmn. 1994-97, chair, 1997-99; v.p. Kans. Legal Svcs., Inc., 1980-82, pres., 1985-87; bd. advisors Kans. Coll. Advocacy, 1979-80; bd. trustees, lawyers' com. Civil Rights Under Law, 1997-99. Author: (with others) Kansas Employment Law, 1985, Litigating Employment Law Cases, 1987, Kansas Employment Law Handbook, 1991, supplements, 1992, 95, Kansas Annual Survey, 1990—; mem. bd. editors Profl. Lawyer, 2001—. Mem. Kan. Gov.'s Adv. Com. on Criminal Justice, 1974-77; mem. Kans. Justice Commn., 1997-99; gen. counsel Western Mo. Dist. ACLU, 1976-78, 86-97, v.p., 1983-86, nat. bd. dirs., 1979-86, 91-99, chmn. children's rights com., 1980-86; mem. AIDS Pol. Network, 1987-99, med. treatment issues com., 1991-96, constn. com., 1991-99; mem. med./tech. com. AIDS Coun. Greater Kans. City, 1986-98, ethics com. consortium Midwest Bioethics Ctr., 1990—; bd. dirs. Parents Anonymous Kans., 1978-83, pres., 1979; bd. dirs., mem. fin. com. Kans. Com. for Prevention Child Abuse, 1980-83. Fellow Am. Bar Found., Kans. Bar Found.; mem. ABA (chmn. children's rights com. and family law sects. 1985-86, mem. ho. of dels. 2000—, professionalism com. 2000—, bd. of editors The Profl. Lawyer, 2000—), Am. Judicature Soc. (bd. dirs. 1997—, adv. com. for ctr. for judicial conduct 1997—), Kans. Bar Assn. (chmn. legal aid com. 1978-83, bd. govs. 1988—, v.p. 1996-97, pres.-elect 1997-98, pres. 1998-99, mem. ABA ho. dels. 2000—, Pres.' Outstanding Svc. award 1982), Kans. City Met. Bar Assn., Johnson County Bar Assn. (chmn. legal aid com. 1975-82, 92-96), Earl E. O'Connor Am. Inn of Ct. (counselor, pres.-elect 2002, pres. 2003). Office: U S Courthouse 500 State Ave Rm 219 Kansas City KS 66101-2400 E-mail: judge_waxse@ksd.uscourts.gov.

WAYNE, ROBERT JONATHAN, lawyer, educator; b. Fresno, Calif., Apr. 4, 1951; s. William W. and Blanche Wayne; m. Dorothy A. Madden, Oct. 23, 1981; children: Daniel, Julia. BS, U. Oreg., 1971; JD, UCLA, 1974. Bar: Calif. 1974, Wash. 1975, U.S. Dist. Ct. (we. dist.) Wash. 1975, U.S. Ct. Appeals (9th and D.C. cirs.) 1975, U.S. Supreme Ct. 1979. Law clk. U.S. Ct. Appeals (D.C. cir.), 1974-75; assoc. Perkins, Coie, Stone, Olsen & Williams, Seattle, 1975-76; dep. prosecutor King County Prosecutor's Office, Seattle, 1976-78; pvt. practice, Seattle, 1978—. Instr. trial advocacy U. Wash., Seattle, 1977—; instr. trial advocacy Nat. Inst. Trial Advocacy, Seattle, 1979—, asst. team leader, 1990, team leader, 1991-2003, team leader nat. session, 1993, program dir. N.W. region, 1998—; lectr. implementing technology in trials. Mem. ATLA, NACDL (life, chmn. lawyers assistance strike force 1993-94), Wash. State Trial Lawyers Assn. (chmn.

tort sect. 1983-85), Wash. State Bar Assn. (chmn. criminal law sect. 1982-83, 86-87, exec. com. 1980-88), Seattle-King County Bar Assn. (jud. screening com. 1988-91), Wash. Assn. Criminal Def. Lawyers (founder, bd. govs. 1986-89, 99-2001, chmn. lawyers assistance strike force 1986-90, 91-93, chmn. ann. meeting 1989-90, 2001), Order of Coif, Order of Barristers. Avocations: skiing, flying. General civil litigation, Criminal, Professional liability. Office: 2110 N Pacific St Ste 100 Seattle WA 98103-9181 E-mail: bwayne@trialsnw.com.

WEADON, DONALD ALFORD, JR., lawyer; b. Brisbane, Australia, Sept. 15, 1945; arrived in U.S., 1946; s. Donald Alford and Ellen Martha (Salisbury) Weadon; m. Suzanne Hayden Cameron, Sept. 9, 1995. BA, Cornell U., 1967; JD, U. Calif., 1975; MBA, Harvard U., Iran Ctr. Mgmt. Studies, Tehran, 1976. Bar: Calif. 1976, D.C. 1988. Assoc. Hancock, Rothert & Bunshoft, San Francisco, 1977-80; ptnr. Bryan, Cave, McPheeters & McRoberts, Washington, 1980-83; ptnr., head internat. dept. Anderson Baker Kill & Olick, Washington, 1983-84; sr. ptnr. Weadon & Assocs., Washington, 1984—. Adj. prof. internat. law Golden Gate U., San Francisco, 1979—82, George Mason U., Arlington, Va., 1989—; spkr., cons. U.S. Dept. Commerce, 1980—83; cons. Internat. Mktg. Assn., 1980—, Sci. Apparatus Mfg. Assn., 1983—, Valve Mfrs. Assn., 1983—; internat. counsel Am. Electronics Assn., 1986—. Contbr. articles to profl. jours. Trustee coun. Cornell U., 2000—, Cornell Hold Soc., 2002—. Lt. comdr. USNR, 1968—72. Named Cornell U. Disting. Alumnus, 2000. Mem.: ABA (chmn. China trade law com. 1982—84, chmn. software and tech. data com. 1983—85), Press Club, Harvard Club, Savage Club, Metropolitan Club, Olympic Club, Sovereign Mil. Order Temple Jerusalem (Grand Cross, Order Merit), Delta Kappa Epsilon (alumni pres. 1997—, nat. bd. dirs. 1998—). Episcopalian. Intellectual property, Private international, Legislative. Office: Weadon & Assocs Internat House 3338 N St NW Washington DC 20007

WEATHERHEAD, LESLIE R. lawyer; b. Tacoma, Sept. 28, 1956; s. A. Kingsley and Ingrid A. (Lien) W.; m. Anali C. Torrado, June 24, 1985; children: Spencer, Madeleine, Audrey. BA, U. Oreg., 1977; JD, U. Wash., 1980. Bar: Wash. 1980, Oreg. 1996, U.S. Ct. Appeals (9th cir.) 1981, U.S. Dist. Ct. (ea. dist.) Wash. 1984, U.S. Ct. Internat. Trade 1984, Hawaii 1987, U.S. Dist. Ct. (we. dist.) Wash. 1989, Idaho 1989, U.S. Dist. Ct. Idaho 1989, U.S. Supreme Ct. 1994, Colville Tribal Ct. 1993, U.S. Ct. Appeals (10th cir.) 1995, U.S. Ct. Fed. Claims 1995, U.S. Ct. Appeals (fed. cir.) 1999. Asst. terr. prosecutor Territory of Guam, Agana, 1980-83; spl. asst. U.S. Atty. Dist. of Guam and No. Marianas, Agana, 1982-83; atty. Witherspoon, Kelley, Davenport & Toole, Spokane, 1984—. Lawyer-rep. 9th cir. jud. conf., 1989-95, lawyer-rep. chmn., 1995, 9th cir. adv. bd., 2001—; adj. faculty Gonzaga U. Sch. of Law, 1994-95. Contbr. articles on Indian law, administrv. investigations and fed. jurisprudence to profl. jours. Bd. dirs. Spokane Opera Co., 1989-96, pres., 1992-94. Fellow Am. Coll. Trial Lawyers; mem. ABA, Fed. Bar Assn. (pres. ea. dist. 1996-97), Hawaii Bar Assn., Idaho Bar Assn., Wash. State Bar Assn., Oreg. State Bar Assn. Avocations: sailing, scuba, skiing. Administrative and regulatory, Federal civil litigation, Criminal. Office: Witherspoon Kelley Davenport & Toole 428 W Riverside Ave Spokane WA 99201-0301

WEATHERUP, ROY GARFIELD, lawyer; b. Annapolis, Md., Apr. 20, 1947; s. Robert Alexander and Kathryn Crites (Hesser) W.; m. Wendy Gaines, Sept. 10, 1977; children: Jennifer, Christine. AB in Polit. Sci., Stanford U., 1968, JD, 1972. Bar: Calif. 1972, U.S. Dist. Ct. 1973, U.S. Ct. Appeals (9th cir.) 1975, U.S. Supreme Ct. 1980. Assoc. Haight, Brown & Bonesteel, L.A., Santa Ana, 1972—78, ptnr., 1979—. Judge Moot Ct. UCLA, Loyola U., Pepperdine U.; arbitrator Am. Arbitration Assn.; mem. com. Book Approved Jury Instrns. L.A. Superior Ct. Mem. ABA, Calif. Acad. Appellate Lawyers, Los Angeles County Bar Assn., Town Hall Calif. Republican. Methodist. Appellate, State civil litigation, Insurance. Home: 17260 Rayen St Northridge CA 91325-2919 Office: Haight Brown & Bonesteel Ste 800 6080 Center Dr Los Angeles CA 90045 E-mail: weatherup@hbblaw.com.

WEAVER, CLARK BRANSON, lawyer; b. Sterling, Ill., Apr. 28, 1934; s. Arthur Eugene and Lois (Clark) W.; m. Janet F. Holzman, Aug. 31, 1957; children— Kim, Tracey, Clark Jr. B.Sc., Ohio U., 1957; J.D., Salmon P. Chase Coll., 1965. Bar: Ohio 1966. Claims personnel mgr. Allstate Ins. Co., Ohio, 1959-69; ptnr. Lands Kroner & Weaver, Cleve., 1969-82, Weaver, Kolick, Georgeadis & Ernewein Co. L.P.A., Cleve., 1982—92; judge Common pLeas Ct. gen. divsn., 1992-93; judge eighth dist. ct. appeals, 1994-95; commr. Ohio Ct. Claims, 1996-; pvt. practice, 1995-. Mem. Strongsville Civil Service, Ohio, 1979-80, Strongsville Charter Commn., 1981; mem. Strongsville City Council, 1981—; trustee Southwest Gen. Hosp. Served with U.S. Army, 1957-59. Fellow Ohio Bar Assn. Fedn.; mem. Cleve. Bar Assn., Ohio Bar Assn., Parma Bar Assn. (trustee 1978-80). Republican. Presbyterian. Avocations: model trains; bridge; golf. Home: 11780 River Ridge Rd Cleveland OH 44136-3554 Office: Clark B Weaver Co LPA 1310 Illuminating Bldg 55 Public Sq Cleveland OH 44113

WEAVER, ELIZABETH A. state supreme court justice; b. New Orleans; d. Louis and Mary Weaver. BA, Newcomb Coll.; JD, Tulane U. Elem. tchr. Glen Lake Cmty. Sch., Maple City, Mich.; French tchr. Leelanau Sch., Glen Arbor, Mich.; pvt. practice Glen Arbor, Mich.; law clk. Civil Dist. Ct., New Orleans; atty. Coleman, Dutrey & Thomson, New Orleans; atty., title specialist Chevron Oil Co., New Orleans; probate and juvenile judge Leelanau County, Mich., 1975—86; judge Mich. Ct. of Appeals, 1987—94; justice Mich. Supreme Ct., Lansing, 1995—. Chief justice Mich. Supreme Ct., 1999—2000; instr. edn. dept. Ctr. Mich. U.; mem. Mich. Com. on Juvenile Justice, Nat. Conv. State Adv. Groups on Juvenile Justice for U.S.; chair Gov.'s Task Force on Children's Justice, Trial Ct. Assessment Commn., Office Juvenile Justice and Delinquency Prevention; jud. adv. bd. mem. Law and Orgnl. Econs. Ctr. U. Kans.; treas. Children's Charter of Cts. of Mich. Chairperson Western Mich. U. CLE Adv. Bd.; mem. steering com. Grand Traverse/Leelanau Commn. on Youth; mem. Glen Arbor Twp. Zoning Bd.; mem. charter arts north Leelanau County; mem. citizen's adv. coun. Arnell Engstrom Children's Ctr.; mem. cmty. adv. com. Pathfinder Sch. Treaty Law Demonstration Project; active Grand Traverse/Leelanau Mental Health Found. Named Jurist of Yr., Police Officers Assn. of Mich.; named one of five Outstanding Young Women in Mich., Mich. Jaycees; recipient Eastern award, Warren Easton Hall of Fame, Lifetime Dedication to Children award, Mich. Champions in Childhood Injury Prevention, 2000, Recognition award for outstanding svc. to Mich. children and families, Gov. Engler and Family Independence Agy., 2000, Profls. award, Mich. Assn. Drug Cts., 2002, Mary S. Coleman award, Ctr. for Civic Edn. Through Law, 2002. Fellow: Mich. State Bar Found.; mem.: ABA, Antrim County Bar Assn., Leelanau County Bar Assn., Grand Traverse County Bar Assn., La. Bar Assn., Nat. Coun. Juvenile and Family Judges, Mich. Bar Assn. (chair CLE adv. bd., chair crime prevention ctr., chair juvenile law com.), Delta Kappa Gamma (hon.). Office: Mich Supreme Ct 3300 Grandview Plz 10850 E Traverse Hwy Traverse City MI 49684-1364

WEAVER, JUDITH ANN, lawyer; b. South Bend, Ind., June 5, 1948; d. Raymond Joseph and Norma Jean DeVliegher; m. Edward Thomas Weaver, Sept. 3, 1983. BA, St. Mary's Coll., Notre Dame, Ind., 1970, JD, 1991; LLM, U. Mo., Kansas City, 1992. Bar: Mo. 1993, Kans. 1993, Colo. 2000. Social worker, dir. vol. svcs. S.C. Dept. Social Svcs., Charleston, 1970-73, adult day care licensure, 1973-75, title XX coord., 1975-78, asst. to commr., 1978-81, medicaid divsn. dir., 1981-83; mgmt. cons. Electronic Data Sys., Bethesda, Md., 1983-85; cons., adminstr. Booz Allen Hamilton, N.Y.C., 1985-89; pvt. practice Kansas City, Mo., 1992-93; assoc. Blackwood, Langworthy & Schmelzer, P.C., Kansas City, Mo., 1993-96; of counsel Lathrop & Gage, L.C., Kansas City, Mo., 1996—. Author: Health Law Handbook, 1995, 96; columnist Radiology Bus. Mgmt. Assocs. Jour., 1996-98. Bd. dirs. Samuel U. Rogers Cmty. Health Ctr., 1992-95, Mo. Family Health Coun., 1994-96, Katy's Place, 1996-99, Met. Orgn. to Combat Sexual Assault, 1998; trustee Swope Ridge Found., 1995-99; mem. Mo. Health Facilities Rev. Com., 1993-96, chair, 1995-96; Gubernatorial appointee Joint Legis. Com. to Study Health Planning Legislation, 1995; founder Fund for Gender Equity, Kansas City, 1998—; bd. dirs. Bristlecone Hosp., Summit, Colo., 1999—, chair, 2000— ; trustee Nat. Repertory Orch., Denver, 1999—. Gage fellow U. Mo., Kansas City, 1991-92. Mem. ABA, Am. Health Lawyers. Home and Office: PO Box 2146 Breckenridge CO 80424-2146 E-mail: ejweaver@earthlink.net.

WEAVER, MICHAEL JAMES, lawyer; b. Bakersfield, Calif., Feb. 11, 1946; s. Kenneth James and Elsa Hope (Rogers) W.; m. Valerie Scott, Sept. 2, 1966; children: Christopher James, Brett Michael, Karen Ashley. AB, Calif. State U., Long Beach, 1968; JD magna cum laude, U. San Diego, 1973. Bar: Calif., 1973, U.S. Dist. Ct. (so. dist.) Calif. 1973, U.S. Ct. Appeals (9th cir.) 1975, U.S. Supreme Ct. 1977. Law clk. to chief judge U.S. Dist. Ct. (so. dist.) Calif., San Diego, 1973-75; 1st v.p. Latham & Watkins, San Diego. Judge pro tem San Diego Superior Ct.; master of the Bench of the Inn, Am. Inns of Ct., Louis M. Welch chpt.; lectr. Inn of Ct., San Diego, 1981—, Continuing Edn. of Bar, Calif., 1983—, Workshop for Judges U.S. Ct. Appeals (9th cir.), 1990; mem. task force on establishment of bus. cts. sys. Jud. Coun. Calif., 1996-97. Editor-in-chief: San Diego Law Rev., 1973; contbr. articles to profl. jours. Bd. dirs., pres. San Diego Kidney Found., 1985-90; bd. dirs. San Diego Aerospace Mus., 1985-97; trustee La Jolla (Calif.) Playhouse, 1990-91. lt. USNR, 1968-74. Fellow Am. Coll. Trial Lawyers; mem. San Diego Assn. Bus. Trial Lawyers (founding mem., bd. govs.), San Diego Def. Lawyers Assn. (dir.), Am. Arbitration Assn., 9th Cir. Jud. Conf. (del. 1987-90), Calif. Supreme Ct. Hist. Assn. (bd. dirs. 1998—), Safari Club Internat. (San Diego chpt.), San Diego Sportsmen's Club, Coronado Yacht Club. Republican. Presbyterian. Avocations: reading, family activities, flying, skiing. Federal civil litigation, General civil litigation, State civil litigation. Office: Latham & Watkins 701 B St Ste 2100 San Diego CA 92101-8197 E-mail: mike.weaver@lw.com.

WEAVER, PAUL DAVID, lawyer; b. Chgo., Feb. 15, 1943; s. Paul Stanley and Margaret Elizabeth (Wurster) W.; m. Carol Lynne Homan, July 1, 1978; children: Paul Tyson, Samuel Lincoln. AB, Yale U., 1965; JD, U. Mich., 1971. Bar: Mass. 1971, Ohio 1972. Mgr. west coast Big 3 Industries, Houston, 1965-68; assoc. Goodwin, Procter & Hoar, Boston, 1971-78; sec., gen. counsel Houghton Mifflin Co., Boston, 1979-88, sr. v.p., gen. counsel, 1989—. Mem. Beverly (Mass.) Hosp. Corp., 1978—; town counsel Town of Wenham, Mass., 1976—, moderator, 1987—. Mem. ABA, Mass. Bar Assn., Boston Bar Assn., Assn. Am. Publs. (chmn. lawyers com. 1985-86), Am. Soc. Corp. Secs., Mass. City Solicitors/Town Counsels Assn., Mass. Moderators Assn., Myopia Hunt Club (Hamilton, Mass.), Yale Club (N.Y.C.), Phi Delta Phi. Avocations: antiques, skiing. Corporate, general, General practice, Trademark and copyright. Home: 30 Monument St Wenham MA 01984-1611 Office: Houghton Mifflin Co 222 Berkeley St Fl 5 Boston MA 02116-3748

WEAVER, ROBIN GEOFFREY, lawyer, educator; b. Columbus, Ohio, Aug. 19, 1948; s. Eugene Rudolph and Lois Ann (Banks) W.; m. Valerie Cheryl Waller, June 28, 1980; children: Allyson, Lauren, Meridith. BA, Ohio State U., 1970; JD, U. Mich., 1973. Bar: Ohio 1974, U.S. Dist. Ct. (no. dist.) Ohio 1974, U. S. Ct. Appeals (6th cir.) 1980. Assoc. Squire, Sanders & Dempsey, Cleve., 1973-83, ptnr., 1983—; mem. faculty Nat. Inst. for Trial Adv. Northwestern U., Chgo., 1983—. Mem. Ohio Supreme Ct. Bd. of Commrs. on Grievances and Discipline, chair, 1996, master commr., 2002-. With U.S. Army, 1974. Fellow Am. Coll. Trial Lawyers, Internat. Soc. Barristers; mem. Cleve. Bar Assoc. (pres. 2002-03); mem. ABA, Ohio Bar Assn., Cleve. Assn. Trial Attys. (life), 8th Appellate Jud. Conf., Am. Inns of Ct. (master bencher Cleve. chpt.). Episcopalian. General civil litigation, Personal injury (including property damage), Product liability. Office: Squire Sanders & Dempsey 4900 Key Tower Cleveland OH 44114

WEAVER, TIMOTHY ALLAN, lawyer; b. Elkhart, Ind., Nov. 30, 1948; s. Arthur and Joan Lucile (Yoder) W.; m. Catherine Anne Power, Nov. 23, 1974; children: Daniel Timothy, Christopher Matthew, David Colwell. AB, Brown U., 1971; JD, U. Ill., 1974. Bar: Ill. 1974, Wis. 1999, U.S. Dist. Ct. (no. dist.) Ill. 1975, U.S. Ct. Appeals (7th cir.) 1975, U.S. Dist. Ct. (no. dist. trial bar) Ill. 1982, U.S. Dist. Ct. (ea. dist.) Wis. 1999. Asst. pub. defender Cook County Pub. Defender, Chgo., 1974-75; trial atty. Chgo. Transit Authority, 1975-78; assoc. Philip E. Howard Ltd., Chgo., 1978, Pretzel & Stouffer, Chartered, Chgo., 1978-82, ptnr., 1982—. Editor: Medical Malpractice, 1989, 92, 96; contbr. chpts. to books. Mem. ABA, Ill. State Bar Assn., Ill. Assn. Def. Trial Counsel, State Bar of Wis., Civil Trial Counsel of Wis., The Lawyers Club of Chgo. General civil litigation, Personal injury (including property damage), Product liability. Office: Pretzel & Stouffer Chartered One S Wacker Dr #2500 Chicago IL 60606 E-mail: tweaver@pretzel-stouffer.com.

WEAVER, WILLIAM SCHILDECKER, retired electric power industry executive; b. Pitts., Jan. 15, 1944; s. Charles Henry and Louise (Schildecker) W.; m. Janet Kae Jones, Mar. 7, 1981. BA, Hamilton Coll., 1965; JD, U. Mich., 1968. Bar: Wash. 1968. Assoc. Perkins Coie, Seattle, 1968-74, ptnr., 1975-91; exec. v.p., CFO Puget Sound Power & Light Co., Bellevue, Wash., 1991-97; vice chmn., chmn. unregulated subsidiaries Puget Sound Energy, 1997—, pres., COO, 1997, pres., CEO, 1998—2002, also bd. dirs., ret. Bd. dirs. Kinetic Ventures, Chevy Chase, Md., 1998—2002. Bd. dirs., 1998-2002, Wash. Rsch. Coun., Seattle, 1991-97, chmn., 1995-97; trustee Seattle Repertory Theatre, 1992-95, 99-2000, chmn., 2000-02, Corp. Coun. Arts, 1995-02, Pacific Sci. Ctr., 1997-02. Mem. ABA, Wash. State Bar Assn., Seattle Yacht Club, Rainier Club, Flouder Bay Yacht Club.

WEBB, JOHN, retired state supreme court justice; b. Rocky Mount, N.C., Sept. 18, 1926; s. William Devin and Ella (Johnson) W.; m. Martha Carolyn Harris, Sept. 13, 1958; children: Caroline Webb Smart, William Devin. Student, U. N.C., 1946-49; LLB, Columbia U., 1952. Judge Superior Ct., Wilson, N.C., 1971-77, N.C. Ct. Appeals, Raleigh, 1977-86; justice Supreme Ct. N.C., Raleigh, 1986-99; ptnr. Webb & Webb, Raleigh, N.C., 1998—. Served with USN, 1944-46. Mem. N.C. Bar Assn. Democrat. Baptist. Home: 808 Trinity Dr W Wilson NC 27893-2131 Office: Webb & Webb 19 W Hargett St Raleigh NC 27601-1391

WEBB, JOHN GIBBON, III, lawyer; b. Flint, Mich., June 1, 1944; s. John Gibbon Jr. and Martha W.; m. Fain Murphey, July 6, 1968; children: Jennifer Horn, Philip, Andrew, John Matthew. AB, Davidson Coll., 1966; JD, Vanderbilt U., 1970. Bar: N.Y. 1971, N.J. 1981. Assoc. Curtis, Mallet-Prevost, Colt & Mosle, N.Y.C., 1970-80; gen. counsel, v.p & sec. J.M. Huber Corp., Edison, N.J., 1980-95; pvt. bus. law practice Mt. Olive, N.J., 1996—. Episcopalian. Commercial, contracts (including sales of goods; commercial financing), Corporate, general, Private international. Office: Ste 125 500 International Dr N Budd Lake NJ 07828 E-mail: webbgc@aol.com.

WEBB, KATHLEEN ROCHFORD, lawyer; b. Santa Ana, Calif., Apr. 30, 1956; d. Thomas Francis and Eileen (Travers) Rochford; m. William Alan Webb, May 27, 1978; children: Alan Travers, Shannon Kristin. BBA, Memphis State U., 1981, JD, 1987. Bar: Tenn. 1988. Real estate broker Rochford & Assocs., Cordova, Tenn., 1976-88; with Murphy, DeZonia & Webb, Memphis, 1987—2003. Instr. U. Memphis, 1985-98. Leader Girl Scouts USA, Memphis, 1993-2003. Mem. Memphis Bar Assn. (past chair real estate sect.), ABA, Tenn. Bar Assn., Real Estate Industry Trade Assn. (pres. 1996), Women's Coun. Realtors (local pres. 1983-84, Woman of Yr. 1984, state pres. 1988), Memphis Area Assn. Realtors (dir. 1986-87, trustee 1988-90, Affiliate of Yr. 1991). Republican. Roman Catholic. Avocations: fitness and exercise, outdoor activities, girl scouts. Property, real (including real estate development, water). Office: Murphy DeZonia & Webb 6389 N Quail Hollow Rd Ste 102 Memphis TN 38120-1422 E-mail: kwebb@mdwlaw.com.

WEBB, MICHAEL R. lawyer; b. Christchurch, New Zealand, Aug. 9, 1953; LLB, Victoria U. of Wellington, New Zealand, 1975. Barristr and solicitor High Ct. of New Zealand, 1976. Barrister, solicitor Brandons, Wellington, 1976-78, ptnr. Brookfield, Wellington, 1978-90, Simpson Grierson, Wellington, 1991-95; barrister Auckland/Wellington, New Zealand, 1995—. Chmn. Learning Media Ltd. (NZ), 1993-2000—; bd. dirs. Fulton Hogan Ltd., 1998-; mem. (acting chmn.), New Zealand Securities Commn., 1992—; dir. Tower Trust Ltd., 2001. Contbr. articles to legal jours. Mem. New Zealand Bar Assn., Arbitrators and Mediators Inst. New Zealand, New Zealand Law Soc. (legis. com. 2000), Internat. Law Assn. (mem. coun. New Zealand br.), Pacific Econ. Coop. Coun. (fin. markets devel. group). Administrative and regulatory, Banking, Corporate, general. Office: Level 3, The Annex, Axa Bldg, 41 Shortland St Auckland New Zealand E-mail: mw@michaelwebb.co.nz.

WEBB, THOMAS IRWIN, JR., lawyer, director; b. Toledo, Sept. 16, 1948; s. Thomas Irwin and Marcia Davis (Winters) W.; m. Polly S. DeWitt, Oct. 11, 1986; 1 child, Elisabeth Hurst. BA, Williams Coll., 1970; postgrad., Boston U., 1970-71; JD, Case Western Res. U., 1973. Bar: Ohio, Mich. Assoc. Shumaker, Loop & Kendrick, Toledo, 1973-79, ptnr., 1979—, chmn. corp. law dept., 1992-94, mgmt. com., 1994-99. Dir. Calphalon Corp., 1990-98, Yark Automotive Group, Inc. Mem. coun. Village of Ottawa Hills, Ohio, 1979-85, adviser Ohio divsn. Securities, 1979-85, commr. of taxation, Village of Ottawa Hills, Ohio, 1999—; bd. dirs. Kiwanis Youth Found. of Toledo, 1982-2002, Toledo Area Regional Transit Authority, 1989-91, Arts Commn. Greater Toledo, 1993-2003, exec. com., 1994-99, v.p., 1994-96, pres., 1996-97; bd. dirs. Jr. Achievement of Northwestern Ohio, Inc., 1992—, Lourdes Coll. Found., 1995-01, Toledo Orch. Assn., 1999—, Med. Coll. Ohio, 2001—, Lourdes Coll., 2001—. Mem. ABA, Ohio Bar Assn. (corp. law com. 1989—), Toledo Bar Assn., Mich. Bar Assn., Northwestern Ohio Alumni Assn. of Williams Coll. (pres. 1974-83), Toledo-Rowing Found. (trustee 1985-2001), Toledo Area C. of C. (trustee 1991-98, exec. com. 1993-98, fin. com. 1993—), Order of Coif, Crystal Downs Country Club, Toledo Country Club, The Toledo Club (trustee 1984-90, pres. 1987-90), Williams Club N.Y., Crystal Lake Yacht Club. Republican. Episcopalian. Corporate, general, Mergers and acquisitions, Securities. Office: Shumaker Loop & Kendrick 1000 Jackson St Toledo OH 43624-1573

WEBB, WILLIAM DUNCAN, lawyer, mediator; b. Dayton, Ohio, Feb. 14, 1930; s. Herbert Henry and Dorothy (Chamberlain) W.; m. Nancy Helen Regester, June 12, 1953; children: Joseph Chamberlain (dec.), Mary Helen, Nancy Katherine, Sarah Elizabeth, Lucy Ellen. AB, U. Mich., 1952, JD, 1956. Bar: Mo. 1956, Kans. 1958, U.S. Supreme Ct. 1969. Assoc. Stinson, Mag, Thomson, McEvers & Fizzell, Kansas City, Mo., 1956-58; sec. Kansas City (Mo.) Power & Light Co., 1960-78, asst. treas., 1969-78, asst. v.p. communications, 1978-79, asst. v.p. fed. affairs, 1979-84; v.p. investments Paine Webber, 1984-98. Legal counsel Fellowship of Christian Athletes. Mem. city coun. Roeland Park, Kans., 1960-62; chmn. Kansas City Myasthenia Gravis Found., 1965-67; bd. dirs. Boys Club of Kansas City, Mo., 1969-74, Greater Kansas City YMCA, Greater Kansas City chpt. ARC; chmn. bd. councilors Avila Coll., 1969-70; trustee, asst. sec., 1970-89; bd. dirs. Rural Water Dist. # 7, Johnson County, Kans., 1992-94. Mem. Internat. Maine-Anjou Assn. (dir., sec.-treas. 1969-76), Theta Delta Chi, Phi Alpha Delta. Presbyterian. Home and Office: 37000 W 155th St Gardner KS 66030-9617 E-mail: webb37ooo@aol.com.

WEBBER, BRIAN C. lawyer; b. Salt Lake City, July 26, 1969; s. William L. and Patricia G. Webber; m. Valerie Chase Webber, June 20, 1991; children: Madison, Parker, Spencer, Lauren. BA/BS in Fin., U. Utah, 1994, JD, 1997. Bar: Utah, U.S. Dist. Ct. Utah 1997. Assoc. McMurray, McMurray, Dale & Parkinson, Salt Lake City, 1997—99; law clk. Utah Ct. Appeals, Salt Lake City, 1999—2000; assoc. Richards, Brandt, Miller & Nelson, Salt Lake City, 2000—. Recipient Disting. Svc. award, Utah Ct. Appeals, 2000. Mem.: Def. Rsch. Inst. Avocations: golf, tennis, hiking. Product liability, General civil litigation, Health. Office: Richards Brandt Miller & Nelson 50 S Main #700 Salt Lake City UT 84110

WEBBER, RICHARD JOHN, lawyer; b. Mpls., July 27, 1948; s. Richard John and Mary Lee (Moore) W.; m. Susan Barbara Listerman, Jan. 8, 1972; children: Hillary, Joanna. BA, Princeton U., 1970; JD, U. Mich., 1973. Bar: D.C. Ct. Appeals 1974, U.S. Ct. Appeals (9th and D.C. cirs.) 1980, U.S. Dist. Ct. D.C. 1980, U.S. Claims Ct. 1974, U.S. Supreme Ct. 1980. Law clk. U.S. Ct. Claims, Washington, 1973-75; trial atty. U.S. Dept. Justice, Washington, 1975-80; assoc. Arent, Fox et al, Washington, 1980-85, ptnr., 1985—. Mem. ABA (chmn. fed. contract claims and remedies com. sect. pub. contract law 1986-91), Fed. Bar Assn. (chmn. ADP procurement com. govt. contracts sect. 1992-94, chmn. govt. contracts sect. 1994-96, chmn. ADR sect. 2002-03). Federal civil litigation, Construction, Government contracts and claims. Office: Arent Fox Washington Sq 1050 Connecticut Ave NW Ste 500 Washington DC 20036-5303 E-mail: webberr@arentfox.com.

WEBER, ALBAN, association executive, lawyer; b. Chgo., Jan. 29, 1915; s. Joseph A. and Anna (von Plachecki) W.; m. Margaret Kenny, Dec. 29, 1951; children: Alban III, Peggy Ann, Gloria, Brian. AB, Harvard U., 1935, JD, 1937; MA, Northwestern U., 1962; LLM, John Marshall Law sch., 1967. Bar: Ill. 1938, Mich. 1985, Fla. 1997, U.S. Supreme Ct. 1946. Ptnr. Weber & Weber, 1937-41; gen. counsel Fgn. Liquidation Commn., State Dept., 1946; trust officer Lake Shore Nat. Bank, Chgo., 1952-55; univ. counsel Northwestrn U., Evanston, Ill., 1955-70; pres. Fedn. Ind. Ill. Colls. and Univs., Evanston, 1970-85; of counsel Schuyler, Roche & Zwirner, Evanston, 1984-94; pres. Benjamin Franklin Fund, Inc., 1965-75, Northwestern U. Press, Inc., 1961-65; chmn. State Assn. Execs. Coun., 1981. Pres. N.E. Ill. coun. Boy Scouts Am., 1970-71, dist. chmn. Gulfstream coun., 1994-95; alderman City of Chgo., 1947-51. Comdr. USNR, 1941-45, rear adm., 1969-75. Recipient Silver Beaver award Boy Scouts Am., 1946, Meritorious Svc. award Loyola U., 1978, Edn. for Freedom award Roosevelt U., 1984. Mem. Nat. Assn. Coll. and Univ. Attys. (pres. 1962), Harvard Law Soc. Ill. (pres. 1984), Navy League (pres. Evanston coun. 1967-70), Univ. Risk Mgmt. Assn. (pres. 1965), Naval Order U.S. (nat. comdr. 1970-72), Harvard Club, Port St. Lucie Rotary Club, Chgo. Yacht Club, White Lake Yacht Club, Kiwanis (lt. gov., pres. Port St. Lucie club), St. Lucie River Power Squadron (comdr.), Anchor Line Yacht Club (commodore). Home: 1555 SE Sunshine Ave Port Saint Lucie FL 34952-6011 E-mail: StormyWeber2@aol.com.

WEBER, ARNOLD I. lawyer; b. Little Cedar, Iowa, Oct. 4, 1926; divorced; children: Katherine Weber Hickle, Thomas, Margaret Weber Robertson. PhB magna cum laude, Marquette U., 1949; MA, Harvard U., 1950; JD, George Washington U., 1954, LLM, 1956. Bar: D.C. 1954, Md. 1961, Calif. 1962, U.S. Dist Ct. D.C. 1954, (no. dist.) Calif. 1962, (cen. dist.) Calif. 1992, U.S. Ct. Claims 1960, U.S. Tax Ct. 1965, U.S. Ct. Appeals (D.C. cir.) 1954, (9th cir.) 1962, (fed. cir.) 1991, U.S. Supreme Ct. 1959. Lawyer Housing and Home Fin., Washington, 1954; pvt. practice Washington, 1954-55; lawyer Tariff Commn., Washington, 1954-55, FCC, Washington, 1955-56, IRS, Washington, 1956-61; assoc. Brobeck, Phleger & Harrison, San Francisco, 1961-64; sr. gen. atty. So. Pacific Transp., San Francisco, 1964-84; western tax counsel Santa Fe Pacific Corp., San Francisco, 1985-88; pvt. practice San Francisco, 1988—. With USNR,

1944-54, PTO. Mem. ABA, Olympic Club, Bar Assn. San Francisco, State Bar of Calif. Alternative dispute resolution, General civil litigation, Probate (including wills, trusts). Office: 57 Post St Ste 502 San Francisco CA 94104-5020

WEBER, FREDRIC ALAN, lawyer; b. Paterson, N.J., July 31, 1948; s. Frederick Edward and Alida (Hessels) W.; m. Mary Elizabeth Cook, June 18, 1983. BA in History, Rice U., 1970; JD, Yale U., 1976. Bar: Tex. 1976, U.S. Dist. Ct. (so. dist.) Tex. Assoc. Fulbright & Jaworski, Houston, 1976-80, participating assoc., 1980-83, ptnr., 1983—. Dir. Houston Symphony Soc., 1993—, v.p. devel., 2001—. Recipient Benjamin Scharps prize Yale Law Sch., 1976, Ambrose Gherini prize Yale Law Sch., 1976. Mem. ABA, Am. Coll. Bond Counsel, Nat. Assn. Bond Lawyers (bd. dirs. 1988-89, treas. 1989-90, pres.-elect 1991, pres. 1991-92), Houston Bar Assn. Finance, Municipal (including bonds), Securities. Office: Fulbright & Jaworski LLP 1301 Mckinney St Ste 5100 Houston TX 77010-3095 E-mail: fweber@fulbright.com.

WEBER, GERALD RICHARD, legal association administrator, educator; b. Middletown, Conn., June 2, 1964; s. Gerald Richard Sr. and Norma Jean W.; m. Stephanie Stuckey, May 27, 1996 (div. Dec. 1997). BS in Fin. and Law summa cum laude, Ill. State U., 1986; JD summa cum laude, U. Ga., 1989. Bar: Ga., 1990, U.S. Ct. Appeals (5th and 11th cirs.) U.S. Supreme Ct., 1990, U.S. Dist. Ct. (no. and mid. dists.) Ga., 1990. Jud. clk. to Hon. Thelma Wyatt Cummings Fulton Superior Ct., Atlanta, 1987; jud. clk. to Hon. Carolyn Dineen King U.S. Ct. Appeals (5th cir.), Houston, 1989-90; assoc. Dow, Lohnes & Albertson, Atlanta, 1990-91; legal dir. Am. Civil Liberties Union, Atlanta, 1991—. Adj. prof. Emory U. Sch. Law, Atlanta, 1997—, Ga. State U. Coll. Law, Atlanta, 1998—; chair legal com. Task Force for Homeless, 1992—; barrister Joseph Henry Lumpkin Inns of Ct., 1994-96; bd. dirs. Ga. First Amendment Found., 1994—, Ga. Ctr. Law in Pub. Interest, 1998-2000; mem. Atlanta steering com. Lawyers Com. Civil Rights Under Law, 1996—; co-chair access to justice com. State Bar Ga., 2002—; panelist in field; lectr. in field. Symposium editor Ga. Law Rev.; contbr. articles to mags. and profl. jours.; appearances in numerous local and nat. TV and radio shows. Trustee U. Ga. Libr., 1996-97; mem. Leadership Atlanta, 1997-98; pres. Cabbagetown Neighborhood Improvement Assn., 1998-2001, rep. neighborhood planning unit-N, 1998—; mem. adv. com. AID Atlanta, 1998-99; mem. adv. bd. Jeanette Rankin Found., 1997—; election monitor South African Elections, 1994; bd. dirs. Table of Elements. Recipient Cert. Appreciation, U.S. Dept. Justice, 1998; named one of 21 Young Lawyers Leading Us Into 21st Century, ABA, 1995, Forty Top Georgians Under 40, Ga. Trend Mag., 1997. Mem. FBA, State Bar Ga. (co-chair individual rights sect. 1998-2000, mem. various coms.), Lawyers Club Atlanta, Order of Coif. Democrat. Lutheran. Avocations: theremin musician, tennis, biking, fossil collecting. Office: Am Civil Liberties Union Ga 142 Mitchell St SW Ste 301 Atlanta GA 30303-3428 E-mail: gweber@acluga.org.

WEBER, HERMAN JACOB, federal judge; b. Lima, Ohio, May 20, 1927; s. Herman Jacob and Ada Minola (Esterly) W.; m. Barbara L. Rice, May 22, 1948; children: Clayton, Deborah. BA, Otterbein Coll., 1949; JD summa cum laude, Ohio State U., 1951. Bar: Ohio 1952, U.S. Dist. Ct. (so. dist.) Ohio 1954. Ptnr. Weber & Hogue, Fairborn, Ohio, 1952-61; judge Fairborn Mayor's Ct., 1956-58; acting judge Fairborn Mcpl. Ct., 1958-60; judge Greene County Common Pleas Ct., Xenia, Ohio, 1961-82, Ohio Ct. Appeals (2d dist.), Dayton, 1982-85, U.S. Dist. Ct. (so. dist.) Ohio, Cin., 1985—92, sr. judge, 1992—. Chmn. Sixth Cir. Dist. Judges Conf., 1988, Ohio Jud. Conf., Columbus, 1980-82; pres. Ohio Common Pleas Judges Assn., Columbus, 1975. Vice-mayor City of Fairborn, 1955-57, council mem., 1955-59. Served with USNR, 1945-46. Office: US Dist Ct 801 100 E 5th St Cincinnati OH 45202-3905

WEBER, JOHN WALTER, insurance company executive; b. Rochester, N.Y., Jan. 10, 1959; s. Donald J. and Patricia M. (Mangon) W. BS, U. Conn., 1984. Claims supr. Hartford Ins. Group, Southington, Conn., 1986-90; regional claims mgr. Housing Authority Risk Retention Group, Cheshire, Conn., 1990—. Mem. U. Conn. Alumni Assn. Avocations: running, reading, softball, cooking. E-mail: Jweber6@earthlink.net.

WEBER, MATTHEW BERNARD, lawyer; b. Visalia, Calif., Sept. 27, 1972; s. Robert Bernard and Margaret Frances Weber. BA in Psychology with honors, U. Calif., Santa Cruz, 1994; JD, U. Calif., San Francisco, 1999. Bar: Calif. 99, U.S. Dist. Ct. (no. and ea. dists.) Calif. 00, U.S. Ct. Appeals (9th cir.) 02. Case mgr. Harbor Hills Mental Health Clinic, Santa Cruz, 1994—95; bi-lingual sub. tchr. Santa Cruz/Hollister (Calif.) Sch. Dist., 1995—97; group supr. Juvenile Hall, Santa Cruz/Hollister, 1995—97; legal intern Gen. Assistance Advocacy Project, San Francisco, 1997—98; law clk. Gingras, Cates, Luebke, S.C., Madison, Wis., 1998—99; assoc. Schneider & Wallace, San Francisco, 1995—2000, Gildstein. Gellman, Melbostad Gibson & Harris, LLP, San Francisco, 2000—. Referral atty. AIDS Legal Referral Panel, San Francisco, 2001—; supervising atty. Legal Aid Employment Law Clinic, San Francisco, 2001—. Recipient Honors award, AIDS Legal Referral Panel, 2002. Mem.: Calif. Assn. Consumer Attys., Bar Assn. San Francisco, Phi Beta Kappa. Avocations: rollerblading, snowboarding, wakeboarding, drawing, biking. Civil rights, Landlord-tenant, Personal injury (including property damage). Office: Goldstein Gellman Melabostad Gibson & Harris 100 Van Ness Ave 21st Fl San Francisco CA 94102

WEBER, ROBERT CARL, lawyer; b. Chester, Pa., Dec. 18, 1950; s. Robert Francis and Lucille (Nobili) W.; m. Linda Brediger, June 30, 1972; children: Robert F., Mary Therese, David P., Joseph T. BA cum laude, Yale U., 1972; JD, Duke U., 1976. Bar: Ohio 1976, U.S. Dist. ct. (no. dist.) Ohio 1976, U.S. Ct. Claims 1980, U.S. Ct. Appeals (6th cir.) 1981, U.S. Ct. Appeals (5th cir.) 1995. Assoc. Jones, Day, Reavis & Pogue, Cleve., 1976-83, ptnr., 1983—. Bd. dirs. United Way Svcs. of Cleve., 1992-2002. Fellow Am. Coll. Trial Lawyers, Internat. Acad. Trial Lawyers; mem. Ohio Bar Assn., Am. Law Inst., Product Liability Adv. Coun., Cleve. Bar Assn. (chmn. jud. selection com. 1985-86, trustee 1990-93, pres.-elect 1994-95, pres. 1995-96), Jud. Conf. for 8th Jud. Dist. Ohio (life), Order of Coif. Roman Catholic. Federal civil litigation, General civil litigation, State civil litigation. Office: Jones Day Reavis & Pogue 901 Lakeside Ave E Cleveland OH 44114-1190 E-mail: rcweber@jonesday.com.

WEBER, WILLIAM RANDOLPH, lawyer; b. Columbia, Mo., Jan. 3, 1952; s. William Harry and Marie Antoinette (Fehlig) W.; m. Sondra Jean Gust, Aug. 12, 1972; children: Ashley Elizabeth, William Matthew, Stacey Pauline. BA cum laude, Vanderbilt U., 1974; JD, St. Louis U., 1977. Bar: Mo. 1977, Ill. 1978, U.S. Dist. Ct. (ea. dist.) Mo. 1978, U.S. Ct. Appeals (8th cir.) 1978. Ptnr. Thompson Coburn, St. Louis, 1977-99, Hazelwood & Weber LLC, St. Charles, Mo., 1999—. Chmn. adv. bd. U.S. Bank N.A.; mem. staff St. Louis U. Law Jour., 1975-76. Chmn. bd. advisors Salvation Army, St. Charles, 1980-83; chmn. St. Charles County Rep. Com., 1978-84; mem. Mo. State Rep. Com., Jefferson City, 1978-86; spl. counsel City of St. Peters, 1998—; counsellor St. Charles County, 1985-87, v.p. bd. govs., 1986-87; bd. govs. Truman State U., 1981-87; bd. dirs. St. Charles C. of C., 1984-98, pres., 1997; regional panel White House Fellowship Commn., 1988-92; chmn. bd. dirs. March of Dimes Birth Defects Found., St. Louis; vice-chmn. St. Charles County Transit Authority, 1992-2000; chmn. Boone Trails Dist., St. Louis Area coun. Boy Scouts Am., 2000-03. Recipient Disting. Cmty. Svc. award St. Charles Jaycees, 1984, Dist. award of merit and bronze pelican Boy Scouts Am., 2002 Mem. ABA (ho. of dels. 1987-89), Am. Soc. Hosp. Attys., Mo. Bar Assn. (rep. young lawyers sect. 1982-88), St. Charles County Bar Assn. (pres. 1984), Ill. Bar Assn., Eagle Scout Assn. Roman Catholic. Health, Property, real (including real estate development, water), Corporate, general. Office: Hazelwood & Weber LLC 200 N Third St Saint Charles MO 63301 E-mail: wweber@hazelwoodweber.com.

WEBSTER, C. EDWARD, II, lawyer, judge; b. Cody, Wyo., Mar. 27, 1944; s. Constant E. and Lucille (Moncur) W. BA in Bus. Adminstrn., U. Wyo., 1967, JD, 1969. Bar: Wyo. 1969. Legis asst. to U.S. Senator Clifford P. Hansen, U.S. Senate, Washington, 1969-72; ptnr. Housel and Webster, Cody, 1973-79; pvt. practice, Cody, 1979-99; prin. Webster & Thompson, LLC, Cody, 1999—. Judge mcpl. ct. Pres. Cody Stampede, 1980-84. Mem. ABA, Cody C. of C. (pres. 1974-75, 1975-2000), Eagles. Republican. Mem. Lds Ch. Property, real (including real estate development, water), Personal injury (including property damage), Probate (including wills, trusts). Office: 1226 11th St Cody WY 82414-3523 E-mail: weblaw@trib.com.

WEBSTER, DAVID MACPHERSON, lawyer; b. Chgo., June 22, 1950; s. Robert Fielden and Julia Orendorff (Macpherson) W.; m. Lucia Maxwell Blair, Oct. 3, 1987; 1 child, Jessie Maxwell. BA magna cum laude with hons. in History, Williams Coll., 1972; JD, U. Va., 1975; DD (hon.), Seabury-Western Theol. Sem., 2000. Bar: Ill. 1975. Assoc. Winston & Strawn, Chgo., 1975-81, ptnr., 1981-87; White House fellow Washington, 1987-88; spl. asst. to dir. FBI, Washington, 1988-89; asst. gen. counsel for multilateral negotiations U.S. Arms Control and Disarmament Agy., Washington, 1989—94; v.p., gen. counsel A.T. Kearney, Inc., Chgo., 1994—2002; of counsel Butler Rubin Saltarelli & Boyd, Chgo., 2002—. Mem. adv. com. on Ill. Bus. Corp. Act Ill. Sec. of State, Chgo., 1982-87. Bd. dirs. Ill. Soc. for Prevention of Blindness, Chgo., 1980—87, 1997—, pres., 1999—2001; bd. dirs. Better Govt. Assn., Chgo., 1997—99; trustee Episc. Charities and Profl. Svcs., Chgo., 1980—87; bd. dirs. WBEZ Alliance, Inc., Chgo., 1996—; chair bd. trustees Seabury-Western Theol. Sem., Evanston, Ill., 1993—96, trustee, 1988—96, 2002—, Village of Winnetka, Ill., 2003—. Mem. Am. Hist. Assn. (assoc.), Orgn. Am. Historians (assoc.), Ill. State Hist. Soc. (life), Chgo. Hist. Soc., Manuscript Soc., Abraham Lincoln Assn., White House Fellows Assn., Mid-Day Club (Chgo.), Univ. Club Chgo., Chgo. Coun. Fgn. Rels., Law Club City of Chgo., Phi Beta Kappa Assn. Chgo. (exec. com. 1996-98). Episcopalian. Avocations: history, writing. Home: 596 Arbor Vitae Rd Winnetka IL 60093-2302 Office: Butler Rubin Saltarelli & Boyd 70 W Madison St Ste 1800 Chicago IL 60602 Business E-Mail: dwebster@butlerrubin.com. E-mail: davidmwebster@attbi.com.

WEBSTER, PETER BRIDGMAN, lawyer; b. Boston, Jan. 11, 1941; s. John Archibald and Mildred (Bridgman) W.; m. Elaine Gerber, Dec. 20, 1964 (dec.); children: Amy Elizabeth, Peter Bridgman, Timothy James. AB, Bowdoin Coll., 1962; LLB, Cornell U., 1965. Bar: Maine 1965, U.S. Dist. Ct. Maine 1965. Assoc., then sr. ptnr. Verrill & Dana, LLP, Portland, Maine, 1965—. Mem. grievance commn. Maine Bd. Bar Overseers, Augusta, 1979-88, chmn., 1984-88, mem. 1986-94, chmn. 1990-92; adj. prof. law U. Maine, Portland, 1981; mem. Maine Commn. on Ethics and Govtl. Practices, 1991-2002, chair 1997-2002, chair Lawyers' Fund for Client Protection, 1997—. Recipient Alumni Svc. award Bowdoin Coll., 1999. Banking, Corporate, general, Education and schools. Home: 185 W Main St Yarmouth ME 04096-8400 E-mail: pwebster@verrilldana.com.

WEBSTER, PETER DAVID, judge; b. Framingham, Mass., Feb. 12, 1949; s. Waldo John and Helen Anne (Borovek) W.; m. Michele Page Hernandez, Jan. 13, 1989; 1 stepchild, Alana Perryman. BS, Georgetown U., 1971; JD, Duke U., 1974; LLM, U. Va., 1995. Bar: Fla. 1974, U.S. Dist. Ct. (mid. dist.) Fla. 1975, U.S. Ct. Appeals (5th cir.) 1975, U.S. Dist. Ct. (so. dist.) Fla. 1977, U.S. Dist. Ct. (no. dist.) Fla. 1978, U.S. Supreme Ct. 1978, U.S. Ct. Appeals (11th cir.) 1981. Law clk. U.S. Dist. Judge, Jacksonville, Fla., 1974-75; assoc. Bedell, Bedell, Dittmar, Smith & Zehmer, Jacksonville, 1975-78; ptnr. Bedell, Bedell, Dittmar & Zehmer, Jacksonville, 1978-85; cir. judge State Fla., Jacksonville, 1986-91; judge Dist. Ct. of Appeal, First Dist., State of Fla., Tallahassee, 1991—. Master of bench Chester Bedell Am. Inn of Ct., 1988-91, Tallahassee Am. Inn of Ct., 1992—; chmn. com. on standard jury instrns. in civil cases, chmn. court reporter cert. planning com.; mem. com. on trial ct. info. sys.; com. on confidentiality of records of jud. br. Fla. Supreme Ct. Contbg. author: Sanctions: Rule 11 and Other Powers, 1986, Florida Criminal Rules and Practice Manual, 1990. Bd. dirs. Jacksonville Area Legal Aid, Inc., 1978-82, River Region Human Svcs., Inc., Jacksonville, 1986-88; mem. adv. bd. P.A.C.E. Ctr. for Girls, Inc., Jacksonville, 1986-91; com. mem. Shawnee dist. North Fla. coun. Boy Scouts Am., 1974-78; mem. delinquency task force Mayor's Commn. on Children and Youth, City of Jacksonville, 1988-91; officer, mem. exec. bd. Suwanee River Area coun. Boy Scouts, 1991-96. Mem. Am. Judicature Soc. (bd. dirs. 2002—), Fla. Conf. Appellate Judges, Jacksonville Bar Assn., Tallahassee Bar Assn., Phi Beta Kappa, Phi Alpha Theta, Phi Eta Sigma. Office: 1st Dist Ct Appeal 301 Martin Luther King Blvd Tallahassee FL 32399-1850

WEBSTER, ROBERT BYRON, lawyer; b. Mar. 9, 1932; s. Don B. and Glennie E. (Cole) W.; children: Anne Elizabeth, Allison Dee, Peter Hey, James Byron. BA, U. Mich., 1955; JD, 1957. Bar: Mich. 1958, U.S. Dist. Ct. (ea. dist.) Mich., 1958, U.S. Dist. Ct. (we. dist.) Mich. 1972, U.S. Ct. Appeals (6th cir.) 1958, U.S. Supreme Ct. 1972. Law clk. U.S. Dist. Ct., 1957-59; assoc., ptnr. Hill, Lewis, Adams, Coodrich & Tait, 1959-73; judge Cir. Ct., Oakland County, 1973—82; chief judge, 1977; chmn. Hill Lewis PC, 1982—95, Clark Hill PLC, 1995—2002; shareholder Cox, Hodgman & Giarmarco, PC, Troy, Mich., 2003—. Chmn. Supreme Ct. Com. to Revise Ct Rules, 1975-78; mem. Mich. Ct. Rule Adv. Com., 1984; chair, State Bar Appellate Task Force, 1993; trustee, chmn. Horizon Health Systems, 1983-2002; co-chair Legis. Commn. on Cts. in 21st Century, 1990. Chmn. Oakland Rep. Com., 1970-71, commr. Nat. Commn. on Uniform State Laws, 1995—; chmn. State Officers Commn., 1998-2002; trustee Family and Children Svcs. Oakland County, 1976-84; mem. Oakland Cmty. Mental Health Bd. 1971-73; trustee Henry Ford Health Sys., 1995-2002; mem. jud. quality com. State Bar, 1990—. With USAF, 1951-53. Fellow Am. Bar Found. (life), State Bar Mich. Found. (life), Am. Coll. Trial Lawyers; mem. ABA (mem. ho. dels. 1990—), Am. Law Inst., Fed. Bar Assn., State Bar Mich. (commr. 1982-90, v.p. 1987-88, pres. elect 1988-89, pres. 1989-90), Oakland Bar Assn. Republican. Unitarian Universalist. Federal civil litigation, State civil litigation. Office: 101 W Big Beaver Rd 10th Fl Troy MI 48084-5280 Personal E-mail: rbwebster@hotmail.com. Business E-Mail: rwebster@chglaw.com.

WEBSTER, ROBERT KENLY, lawyer; b. N.Y.C., May 16, 1933; s. Francis Kenly and Mary Louise (Rathbone) W.; m. Sally Irene Stratton, Apr. 16, 1960; children: Timothy Kenly, Kimberly Anne. AB, Princeton U., 1955; LLB, U. Va., 1960. Assoc. Cadwalader, Wickersham & Taft, N.Y.C., 1960-65; asst. U.S. atty. Dept. of Justice, Washington, 1965-68; prin. dep. gen. counsel Dept. of Army, Washington, 1968-73; ptnr. Kennedy & Webster, Washington, 1973-81, Shaw, Pittman, Potts & Trowbridge, Washington, 1981-98; sole practice Washington, 1999—. Spl. investigator Iran FMS program Sec. of Def., Washington, 1977; advisor conflict of interest issues Watergate defendants Dept. Justice, Washington, 1977. Gen. counsel, bd. dirs. Princeton (N.J.) Project 55, Inc., 1989—. Lt. j.g. USN, 1955—57. Mem. ABA, Assn. Trial Lawyers Am., Fed. Bar Assn., Met. Club. Avocations: pottery, reading, travel, tennis. Fax: (202) 659-0084.

WEBSTER, WILLIAM HODGES, lawyer; b. N.Y.C., Oct. 26, 1946; s. Eugene Burnett and Verna May Webster; m. Joan Leslie Strawder, Dec. 30, 1967; 1 child, Sydney Kristen. BA cum laude, NYU, 1972; JD, U. Calif., Berkeley, 1975. Bar: Calif. 1976, U.S. Dist. Ct. (n.dist.) Calif. 1976, U.S. Tax Ct. 1984. Rsch. assoc. Nat. Econ. Devel. & Law Ctr., Berkeley, 1974-76, staff atty., 1976-81, mng. atty., 1981-83; ptnr. Hunter & Anderson, Oakland, Calif., 1983-86, mng. ptnr., 1986-93, Webster & Anderson, Oakland, Calif., 1993—. Contbr. articles to profl. jours. Mem. Mayor's Com. on Responsible Investments, City of Berkeley, 1990, Mayor's Housing Task Force, City of Berkeley, 1986; bd. dirs. Ctr. for Elders Independence, Inc., 2001—. Recipient Cert. of Merit, Nat. Congress for Cmty. Econ. Devel., 1983. Mem. Nat. Assn. Bond Lawyers, Calif. Bar Assn. (bus. law sect.), Charles Houston Bar Assn., Kappa Alpha Psi. Democrat. Avocations: yoga, bicycling, swimming, chess, reading. Corporate, general, Municipal (including bonds), Non-profit and tax-exempt organizations. Office: Webster and Anderson 469 9th St Ste 240 Oakland CA 94607-4068 E-mail: bwebster@websteranderson.com.

WECHSLER, MARY HEYRMAN, lawyer; b. Green Bay, Wis., Jan. 8, 1948; d. Donald Hubert and Helen (Polcyn) Heyrman; m. Roger Wechsler, Aug. 1971 (div. 1977); 1 child, Risa Heyrman; m. David Jay Sellinger, Aug. 15, 1981; 1 stepchild, Kirk Benjamin; 1 child, Michael Paul. Student, U. Chgo., 1966-67, 68-69; BA, U. Wash., 1971; JD cum laude, U. Puget Sound, 1979. Bar: Wash. 1979. Assoc. Law Offices Ann Johnson, Seattle, 1979-81; ptnr. Johnson, Wechsler, Thompson, Seattle, 1981-83; pvt. practice Seattle, 1984-87; ptnr. Mussehl, Rosenberg et al, Seattle, 1987-88, Wechsler, Becker, Erickson, Ross, Roubik & Edwards, Seattle, 1988—. Mem. Bd. of Ct. Edn., 1998—2003; bd. dirs. U. Wash. Law Sch. Child Advocacy Clinic, 1996—99; mem. Wash. State Commn. on Jud. Selection, 1995—96, Wash. State Commn. on Domestic Rels., 1996—97, 1999—2003; chair edn. com. Access to Justice Bd., 1996—99, mem. pub. trust and confidence com., 2000—; presenter in field. Author: Family Law in Washington, 1987, rev. edit., 1988, Marriage and Separation, Divorce and Your Rights, 1994; contbr. articles to legal publs. Mem. Wash. State Ethics Adv. Com., 1992-95; bd. dirs. Seattle LWV, 1991-92. Named one of Seattle's Top Lawyers, Seattle Mag., 2003. Fellow Am. Acad. Matrimonial Lawyers (Wash. state chpt., sec.-treas. 1996, v.p. 1997-98, pres. 1999-2000, nat. arbitration com. 1999-2000, nat. interdisciplinary com. 1999-2000, nat. admissions procedure com. 2000-02, nat. long range planning com. 2003); mem. ABA (chmn. membership Wash. state 1987-88), Wash. State Bar Assn. (exec. com. family law sect. 1985-91, chair 1988-89), profl. devel. com. 2002-03, media project com. 2001, ct. improvement com. 1998-2000, legs. com. 1991-96, Outstanding Atty. of Yr. family law sect. 1988, comms. com. 1997-98, disciplinary hearing officer 1998—), Wash. Women Lawyers, King County Bar Assn. (legis. com. 1985-2000, vice-chair 1990-91, chair family law sect. 1986-87, chair domestic violence com. 1986-87, trustee 1988-90, policy planning com. 1991-92, 2d v.p. 1992-93, 1st v.p. 1993-94, pres. 1994-95, long-range planning com. 1998-99, awards com. 1997-99, nominations com. 2003, Outstanding Atty. award 1999), Nat. Conf. of Bar Pres. (commn. com. 1994-95, long range planning com. 1998-99), King County Bar Found. (trustee 1997-2000), Am. Judicature Soc. (v.p. Washington chpt. 2000-03). State civil litigation, Family and matrimonial. Office: Wechsler Becker Erickson Ross Roubik & Edwards Ste 4550 701 5th Ave Seattle WA 98104-7097

WECKESSER, SUSAN ONEACRE, lawyer; b. Akron, Ohio, July 23, 1938; d. Leland E. and Maryethel (Parsons) Oneacre; m. John V. Rhinehart, Mar. 28, 1958 (div. 1971); children: Kirk Andrew Rhinehart, Kristin Rhinehart; m. John C. Weckesser, Aug. 19, 1972 (div. 1997). BEd, Ohio U., 1959; MA, CUNY, 1974; JD, U. N.Mex., 1983. Bar: N.Mex. 1983, U.S. Dist. Ct. (N.Mex.) 1984, U.S. Ct. Appeals (10th cir.) 1987. Dir. publs. N.Mex. Mcpl. League, Santa Fe, 1972-83; assoc. Patrick A. Casey, Santa Fe, 1983-86; pvt. practice Santa Fe, 1986-98; mem. legal bur. N. Mex. Risk Mgmt. Divsn., Santa Fe, 1998—2003; pvt. practice, 2003—. Bd. dirs. St. Elizabeth Shelter, Santa Fe, 1996—. Mem.: N.Mex. Trial Lawyers Assn. (bd. dirs. 1996—98). Democrat. Personal injury (including property damage), Probate (including wills, trusts), Workers' compensation. Office: PO Box 4819 Santa Fe NM 87502-4819

WEDDINGTON, SARAH RAGLE, lawyer, educator, speaker, writer; b. Abilene, Tex., Feb. 5, 1945; d. Herbert Doyle and Lena Catherine Ragle. BS magna cum laude, McMurry Coll., 1965, hon. doctorate, 1979; JD, U. Tex., 1967; hon. doctorate, Hamilton Coll., 1979, Southwestern U., 1989, Austin Coll., 1993, Nova Southeastern U., 1999. Bar: Tex. 1967, D.C. 1979, U.S. Dist. Ct. (we., no. and ea. dists.) Tex., U.S. Ct. Appeals (5th cir.), U.S. Supreme Ct. Pvt. practice law, Austin, 1967-77; gen. counsel Dept. Agr., Washington, 1977-78; spl. asst. to U.S. pres. Washington, 1978—79; asst. to U.S. pres., 1979—81; chmn. Interdepartmental Task Force on Women, 1978-81; mem. Pres.'s Commn. on Exec. Exchange, 1981; Carl Hatch prof. law and pub. adminstrn. U. N.Mex., Albuquerque, 1982-83; pvt. practice law Austin, Tex., 1985—; dir. Tex. Office State-Fed. Rels., Austin, Washington, 1983-85. Vis. prof. govt. Wheaton Coll., Norton, Mass., 1981-83; sr. lectr. Tex. Woman's U., Denton, 1981-90, 93, U. Tex., Austin, 1986-1989, adj. assoc. prof. 1989-2001, adj. prof., 2001-. Author: A Question of Choice, 1992; contbr. articles to various mags.; contbg. editor Glamour mag., 1981-83. Mem. Tex. Ho. of Reps., 1973-77; named hon. chair San Francisco Bar Assn. Breast Cancer Hotline/Network, 2001, named hon. chair ann. benefit for Breast Cancer Rsch. Ctr., Austin, 2002, named lecture showcase presenter Nat. Assn. Campus Activities, 2003. Recipient Woman of Yr. award Tex. Women's Polit. Caucus, 1973, Time Mag. Outstanding Young Am. Leaders, 1979, Leadership awards Ladies Home Jour., 1980, spl. recognition Esquire mag., 1984, Elizabeth (Betty) Boyer award Equity Action League, 1992, Woman Who Dares award Nat. Coun. Jewish Women, 1993, Woman of Distinction award Nat. Conf. for Coll. Women Student Leaders, 1993, Colby award for Pub. Svc. Sigma Kappa, 1996, Hummingbird award Leadership Am., 1998, Tallest Texan award Houston Chronicle, 2000, Speaking Out for Justice award AAUW Legal Advocacy Fund, 2001, Speaking Out for Justice award AAUW Ednl. Found., 2001, Ally award Possible Woman Leadership Conf., 2001; named Lectr. of Yr. Nat. Assn. for Coll. Activities, 1990, Tex. Women's C. of C. Tex. Woman of Century, 1999, San Antonio Express News Face of Century, 1999, 2000; named One of the Most Influential Lawyers of the 20th Century, Tex. Lawyer, 2000; hon. chair of Sarah Weddington Leadership Conf. named in her honor, Tex. Woman's U., 2001, hon. chair San Francisco Bar Assn Breast Cancer Hotline/Network, 2001, Annual Benefit for Breast Cancer Rsch., Austin, Tex., 2002, Lectr. Showcase Presenter Nat. Assn. Campus Activities, 2003. Mem. Tex. Bar Assn. Constitutional, Family and matrimonial, General practice. Office: The Weddington Ctr 709 W 14th St Austin TX 78701-1707 E-mail: sw@weddingtoncenter.com.

WEDGLE, RICHARD JAY, lawyer; b. Denver, Dec. 2, 1951; s. Joseph M. and Lillian E. (Brown) W.; m. Susan R. Mason, Oct. 17, 1987. BA, U. Calif., Berkeley, 1974; JD, U. Denver, 1978. Bar: Colo. 1978, U.S. Dist. Ct. Colo. 1978, U.S. Ct. Appeals (10th cir.) 1980. Ptnr. Cox, Wedgle & Padmore, P.C., Denver, 1978-85, Barnes, Wedgle & Shpall, P.C., Denver, 1986-87, Wedgle and Shpall, P.C., Denver, 1987-98, Wedgle and Friedman, P.C., Denver, 1998-2000, Wedgle and Kukrejs, P.C., 2000—. Vol. coord. Dick Lamm for Gov., 1974, citizen adv. office, 1975; bd. dirs. Cherry Creek Improvement Assn., 1985-88. Mem. ABA, Colo. Bar Assn., Denver Bar Assn., Jewish Cmty. Ctr. Avocations: running, biking, gardening. Federal civil litigation, State civil litigation, Family and matrimonial. Home: 365 Marion St Denver CO 80218-3927 Office: Wedgle & Kukrejs PC 730 17th St Ste 230 Denver CO 80202-3546

WEDGWOOD, RUTH, law educator, international affairs expert; b. N.Y.C. d. Morris P. and Anne (Williams) Glushien; m. Josiah Francis Wedgwood; May 29, 1982; 1 child, Josiah Ruskin Wedgwood. BA magna cum laude, Harvard U., 1972; fellow, London Sch. Econs., 1972-73; JD, Yale U., 1976. Bar: D.C., N.Y., U.S. Supreme Ct. Law clk. to judge Henry Friendly U.S. Ct. Appeals (2d cir.), N.Y.C., 1976-77; law clk. to justice Harry Blackmun U.S. Supreme Ct., Washington, 1977-78; spl. asst. to asst. atty. gen. U.S. Dept. Justice, Washington, 1978-80; asst. U.S. atty. U.S. Dist. Ct. (so. dist.) N.Y., N.Y.C., 1980-86; prof. law Yale U., New Haven,

1986—2002, fellow Inst. for Social and Policy Studies, 1989—; fellow Berkeley Coll., Yale U., 1989—; Edward B. Burling prof. internat. law and diplomacy Nitze Sch. Advanced Internat. Studies Johns Hopkins U., Washington, 2001—. Mem. Sec. of State's Adv. Com. Internat. Law, 1993—; dir., sr. fellow project internat orgns. and law Coun. Fgn. Rels., 1994—; Charles Stockton prof. internat. law U.S. Naval War Coll., Newport, RI, 1998—99; mem. Hart-Rudman Commn. on Nat. Security in the 21st Century, Def. Adv. Comm., 1999—2001; mem. acad. adv. com. to spl. rep. UN Sec.-Gen. for Children and Armed Conflict, 1999—; dir. studies Am. Soc. Internat. Law, 2000—; guest scholar U.S. Inst. Peace, 2001—02; dir. studies Hague Acad. Internat. Law, 2001—02; elected U.S. mem. UN Human Rights Com., Geneva, 2002—; mem. Hist. Rev. Panel advisory to dir. Ctrl. Intelligence, 2002; mem. def. policy adv. bd. U.S. Sec. Def., 2002—. Exec. editor Yale Law Jour., 1975-76; author: The Revolutionary Martyrdom of Jonathan Robbins, 1990, The Use of Force in International Affairs, 1992, American National Interest and the United Nations, 1996, Toward an International Criminal Court?, 1999, After Dayton: Lessons of the Bosnian Peace Process, 1999; mem. bd. editors Yale Jour. Law and Humanities, 1988-98, Am. Jour. Internat. Law, 1998—, World Policy Jour. (New Sch. Social Rsch.), 2001-; contbr. articles to profl jours. and popular publs. including N.Y. Times, Washington Post, Christian Sci. Monitor, Internat. Herald Tribune, Washington Times, Fin. Times, L.A. Times, Fgn. Affairs, Fgn. Policy, Nat. Interest, Time mag.; commentator for CNN, Fox. Nat. Pub. Radio, MSNBC, BBC. Prin. rapporteur U.S. Atty. Gen.'s Guidelines on FBI Undercover Ops., Informant Use and Racketeering and Gen. Crime Investigations, 1980; bd. dirs. Lawyers Com. for Human Rights, N.Y.C., 1988-94; mem. policy adv. com. UN Assn. U.S.A., 1998—; bd. dirs. Lawyers Alliance for World Security, 1999—, Freedom House, 2002—. Recipient Israel Peres prize, 1976, Disting. Contbn. to Internat. Law award N.Y. State Bar Assn., 2000; Ford Found. Rsch. grantee; Rockefeller Found. fellow. Mem. ABA (standing com. on law and national security 2002—), Am. Law Inst., Am. Soc. Internat. Law (exec. com. 1995-98), Internat. Law Assn. (v.p. 1994—, program chmn. Am. br. 1992), Assn. Am. Law Sch. (chmn. sect. internat. law 1995-96), Assn. of the Bar of the City of N.Y. (arms control and internat. security affairs com., chmn. 1989-92, chmn. internat. affairs coun. 1992-95, exec. com. 1995-99), Union Internationale des Avocats, U.S.A. (chpt. bd. govs. 1993-98), Coun. on Fgn. Rels., Elizabethan Club, Mory's Assn., Yale Club (N.Y.C.). also: Coun on Fgn Rels 58 E 68th St New York NY 10021-5953 Office: Johns Hopkins Sch Advanced Internat Studies 1619 Massachusetts Ave NW Washington DC 20036 E-mail: ruth.wedgwood@yale.edu., rwedgwood@jhu.edu.

WEDIG, REGINA SCOTTO, lawyer; b. Pensacola, Fla., July 30, 1955; d. Anthony P. and Janet (Treadway) Scotto; m. Eric M. Wedig. BA magna cum laude, Loyola U., 1977; MA, Tulane U., 1979; JD, La. State U., 1984. Bar: Tenn. 1984, U.S. Dist. Ct. (ea., mid. and we. dists.) Tenn. 1984, La. 1985, U.S. Dist. Ct. (ea., mid. and we. dists.) La. 1985, U.S. Ct. Appeals (5th cir.) 1985, U.S. Ct. Appeals (11th cir.) 1998. Assoc. Harkavy, Shainberg, Kosten, et al, Memphis, 1984-88, Bordelon, Hamlin & Theriot, New Orleans, 1988-94, ptnr., 1994—. Chmn. moot ct. bd. Paul M. Herbert Law Sch., La. State U., Baton Rouge, 1983-84. Editor: (newsletter) LSU-Coastal Law Newsletter, 1983-84; author: (law jour.) La. Bar Jour., 1996. Mem. La. Bar Assn., Tenn. Bar Assn., New Orleans Bar Assn. Commercial, contracts (including sales of goods; commercial financing), Probate (including wills, trusts), Property, real (including real estate development, water). Office: Bordelon Hamlin & Theriot 701 S Peters St New Orleans LA 70130-1588

WEEKS, ARTHUR ANDREW, lawyer, law educator; b. Hanceville, Ala., Dec. 2, 1914; s. A.A. and Anna S. (Seibert) W.; m. Carol P. Weeks; children: John David, Carol Christine, Nancy Anna. AB, Samford U., 1936; LL.B., JD, U. Ala., 1939; LL.M., Duke U., 1950; LL.D. (hon.), Widener U., 1980. Bar: Ala. 1939, Tenn. 1948. Sole practice, Birmingham, Ala., 1939-41, 1946-47, 1954-61; dean, prof. law Cumberland U. Sch. Law, 1947-54; dean, prof. Samford U., 1961-72, prof. law, 1972-74, Cumberland Sch. Law, Samford U., 1984—, Del. Sch. Law of Widener U., Wilmington, 1974-82, dean, 1974-80, interim dean, 1982-83, dean emeritus, prof., 1983—. Served to capt. AUS, 1941-46. Mem. ABA, Tenn. Bar Assn., Ala. Bar Assn., Birmingham Bar Assn., Del. Bar Assn. (assoc.), Phi Alpha Delta, Phi Kappa Phi, Delta Theta Phi Home: 1105 Water Edge Ct Birmingham AL 35244-1437

WEETH, GEORGE WRIGHT, lawyer; b. Houston, Apr. 1, 1954; s. Charles and Betty Weeth; m. Karen Weeth, Mar. 14, 1981. BA cum laude, U. Tex., 1976, JD, 1981. Bar: N.Mex. 1981, U.S. Dist. Ct. N.Mex. 1981, Tex. 1982, U.S. Dist. Ct. (we. dist.) Tex. 1986, U.S. Ct. Appeals (10th cir.) 1987. Assoc. Modrall, Sperling, Albuquerque, 1981-82, Butt, Thornton & Baehr, Albuquerque, 1982-88; pvt. practice Weeth Law Office, Albuquerque, 1988—. Mem. instnl. rev. bd. St. Joseph Healthcare, Albuquerque, 1993-97; pres. Acad. Hills Neighborhood, Albuquerque, 1989-91; v.p. Eastdale Little League, Albuquerque, 1997. Mem. State Bar of N.Mex. (sec. rep. young lawyers divsn. 1984-90, bd. dirs. trial practice sect. 1985-90, chair trial practice sect. 1990-91, bd. dirs. solo and small firm practitioners sect. 1999—, chair 2001-2002), N.Mex. Trial Lawyers Assn. (editor Worker's Compensation jour. 1994—). Avocations: basketball, skiing. Insurance, Personal injury (including property damage), Workers' compensation. Office: PO Box 91478 Albuquerque NM 87199-1478

WEGENER, MARK DOUGLAS, lawyer; b. Nov. 1, 1948; s. Virgil Albert and Jean Frances (Wilke) W.; m. Donna Chait, May 28, 1972; children: Tara, David, Marisa. BA cum laude, Cen. Coll., Pella, Iowa, 1970; JD, Rutgers U., 1973. Bar: D.C. 1974, U.S. Dist. Ct. D.C. 1974, U.S. Ct. Appeals (D.C. cir.) 1974. Assoc. Howrey & Simon, Washington, 1973-79; ptnr. Howrey Simon Arnold & White, Washington, 1979—. Mem.: ABA (antitrust sect., litig. sect.). Antitrust, Federal civil litigation, Private international. Office: Howrey Simon Arnold & White LLP 1299 Pennsylvania Ave NW Washington DC 20004-2400

WEGMANN, CYNTHIA ANNE, lawyer; b. New Orleans, July 12, 1949; d. Edward F. and Shirley (Caire) W.; m. James A. Babst, Nov. 17, 1973; children: Cynthia Morgan, James A. Jr. BFA, Sophie Newcomb Coll., 1971; LLB, Tulane U., 1973. Bar: La. 1973, U.S. Dist. Ct. (eas., mid. we. dists.) La. 1973, U.S. Dist. Ct. (so., no. dists.) Miss. 1995, U.S. Ct. Appeals (5th cir.) 1974, U.S. Supreme Ct. 1975. Assoc. Leach, Paysse & Baldwin, New Orleans, 1973-77, mem., 1977-84; ptnr. Wegmann & Wegmann, New Orleans, 1984-90; of counsel Terriberry, Carroll & Yancey, 1990—. Alumni editor Tulane Maritime Lawyer, New Orleans. Bd. dirs. Travelers Aid Soc. New Orleans, 1974-85, pres., 1983-85; bd. dirs. Vol. Info. Agy., Jr. League, United Way Greater New Orleans; mem. Jr. League New Orleans; chmn. Second Careers. Mem. ABA, Fed. Bar Assn., Maritime Law Assn. (proctor), Southeastern Admiralty Assn., Average Adjusters Assn. of U.S. Democrat. Roman Catholic. Admiralty, Estate planning, Probate (including wills, trusts). Office: Terriberry Carroll & Yancey 1100 Poydras St Ste 3100 New Orleans LA 70163-3101

WEGNER, JUDITH WELCH, law educator, former dean; b. Hartford, Conn., Feb. 14, 1950; d. John Raymond and Ruth (Thulen) Welch; m. Warren W. Wegner, Oct. 13, 1972. BA with honors, U. Wis., 1972; JD, UCLA, 1976. Bar: Calif. 1976, D.C. 1977, N.C. 1988, U.S. Supreme Ct. 1980, U.S. Ct. Appeals. Law clk. to Judge Warren Ferguson, U.S. Dist. Ct. for So. Dist. Calif., L.A., 1976-77; atty. Office Legal Counsel and Land & Natural Resources Divsn. U.S. Dept. Justice, Washington, 1977-79; spl. asst. to sec. U.S. Dept. Edn., Washington, 1979-80; vis. assoc. prof. U. Iowa Coll. Law, Iowa City, 1981; asst. prof. U. N.C. Sch. Law, Chapel Hill, 1981-84, assoc. prof., 1984-88, prof., 1988—, assoc. dean, 1986-88, dean, 1989-99; sr. scholar Carnegie Found. for Advancement of Tchg., 1999—. Spkr. in field. Chief comment editor UCLA Law Rev., 1975-76; contbr. articles to legal publs. Mem. ABA (chmn. planning com. African Law Sch. Initiative 1994, co-chmn. planning com. 1994 mid-yr. deans meeting sect. on legal edn. and admission to bar), N.C. Assn. Women Attys. (Gweneth Davis award 1989), N.C. State Bar Assn., Assn. Am. Law Schs. (mem. exec. com. sect. on law & edn. 1985-88, mem. exec. com. sect. on local govt. law 1989-92, mem. accreditation com. 1986-88, chmn. 1989-91, program chmn. 1992 ann. meeting, program chmn. 1994 ann. meeting, mem. exec. com. 1992-96, pres. 1995), Soc. Am. Law Tchrs., Nat. League Cities (coun.-mentor program 1989-91), Women's Internat. Forum, Order of Coif (nat. exec. com. 1989-91), Phi Beta Kappa. Democrat. Office: U NC Sch Law Van Hecke Wettach Hall Campus Box 3380 Chapel Hill NC 27599-3380 E-mail: judith_wegner@unc.edu.

WEHDE, ALBERT EDWARD, lawyer; b. Milw., Feb. 14, 1935; s. Albert Christian and Mary Hubbel (Dewey) W.; m. Joan M. Forney, Nov. 4, 1978; children: John C., Edward T. BS, Marquette U., 1956, JD, 1960. Bar: Wis. 1960, Calif. 1968. Atty. AEC, Albuquerque, 1963-66; counsel Lockheed Aircraft Co., Sunnyvale and Redlands, Calif., 1966-73; assoc. Schultz & Manfield, Palo Alto, Calif., 1973-74; sr. counsel FMC Corp., Santa Clara, Calif., 1974-95; atty. AEW Internat. Cons., Sunnyvale, 1995—. Bd. dirs. Tech. Credit Union, San Jose, Calif., 1982—, chmn., 1994-96. Pres. Mountain View (Calif.) Babe Ruth League, 1976; trustee Mid-Peninsula Family Services Assn., Palo Alto, 1973-74. Served to capt. U.S. Army, 1960-63. Mem. ABA (chmn. region VII pub. contracts sect. 1977-81), Santa Clara County Bar Assn. (co-chmn. corp. counsel sect. 1983-84, mem. exec. com.), Am. Corp. Counsel Assn. (chpt. sec., pres. 1988, bd. dirs. 1983-93), Wis. Bar Assn. (bd. dirs. non resident lawyers divsn. 2002—2003, pres.-elect 2003, bd. of govs. 2003-). Democrat. Roman Catholic. Avocations: gourmet cooking, music, sports. Government contracts and claims, Private international. Home: 1106 Lorne Way Sunnyvale CA 94087-5157

WEI, LI, lawyer; b. Shanghai, Aug. 19, 1957; s. Gregory Yang and Yongjing Wei; m. Li Li, Sept. 18, 1996; 1 child, William Liansi. BA, Fudan U., Shanghai, 1983; MA, Remin U. China, Beijing, 1986; JD, Willamette U., 1997. Lectr., dept. law Shanghai U., 1986—90; law clk. Oreg. Dept. Justice, Salem, 1996—97; assoc. Vander May Law Firm, Salem, 1997—99; solo practitioner Portland, Oreg., 1999—. Contbr. articles to law jours. Commercial, contracts (including sales of goods; commercial financing), Immigration, naturalization, and customs, Personal injury (including property damage). Office: 7059 SE Powell Blvd Portland OR 97206 Office Fax: 503-774-5338. E-mail: lilwei@hotmail.com.

WEIDEMEYER, CARLETON LLOYD, lawyer; b. Hebbville, Md., June 12, 1933; BA in Polit. Sci., U. Md., 1958; JD, Stetson U., 1961. Bar: Fla. 1961, D.C. 1971, U.S. Dist. Ct. (mid. dist.) Fla. 1963, U.S. Ct. Appeals (5th cir.) 1967, U.S. Ct. Appeals (D.C. cir.) 1976, U.S. Supreme Ct. 1966, U.S. Ct. Appeals (11th cir.) 1982. Rsch. asst. Fla. 2d Dist. Ct. Appeals, 1961-65; ptnr. Kalle and Weidemeyer, St. Petersburg, Fla., 1965-68; asst. pub. defender 6th Jud. Cir., Fla., 1966-69, 81-83; ptnr. Wightman, Weidemeyer, Jones, Turnbull and Cobb, Clearwater, Fla., 1968-82; pres. Carleton L. Weidemeyer, P.A. Law Office, 1982—; pres. So. Mcpl. Corp., 1997—. Guest lectr. Stetson U., 1978—80; lectr. estate planning seminars; bd. dirs. Watson Ctr. for the Blind, 1998—; trustee Tampa Bay Rsch. Inst., 2000—, Francis Prasse Scholarship Trust, 1984—; mem. bd. advisors to Fla. Sheriff's Youth Ranches, 1997—2001. Author: (handbook) Arbitration of Entertainment Claims, Baltimore County's Second District, The Emerging Thirties, 1990, Area History, Baltimore County, 1990, History of Musicians' Association of Clearwater, Local 729, AFM, 1999; editor Ad Lib mag., 1978-81; contbr. numerous articles to profl. jours. and general. pubs.; performer This Is Your Navy Radio Show, Memphis, 1951-52; leader Polka Dots, The Jazz Notes, 1976—; mem. St. Paul Ch. Orch., Fla. Hist. Soc., 1973—, Md. Hist. Soc., 1990—, Pinellas County Estate Planning Assn., 1997—; performer Clearwater Jazz Holiday, 1980, 81, co-chmn., 1981. Bd. advisors Musician Ins. Trust; trustee Francis G. Prasse Meml. Scholarship Trust, 1984—; mem. planned giving com. Upper Pinellas Assn. Retarded Citizens, 1996-2001; bd. trustees Tampa Bay Rsch. Inst., 2001—; adv. com. Fla. Sheriff Youth Ranches, 1997—; bd. dirs. Pinellas Ctr. for Visually Impaired, 1999-2000; bd. dirs. Watson Ctr. for the Blind, 2000—. Served with USN, 1951-54. Recipient Pres.'s award, Upper Pinellas Assn. Retarded Citizens, 1998. Mem. SAR, Musicians Assn. Clearwater (pres. 1976-81), Fla.-Ga. Conf. Musicians (sec., treas. 1974-76), NRA, ABA (sr. bar sect.), Fed. Bar Assn., Fla. State Hist. Soc., Md. Hist. Soc., Greater St. Petersburg Musicians Assn., Clearwater Bar Assn. (probate divsn.), Am. Fedn. Musicians (internat. law com. pres. so. conf. musicians 1979-80), Nat. Geneal. Soc., Clearwater Genealogy Soc., Md. Geneal. Soc., Augustan Soc., Lancaster (Pa.) Geneal. Soc., Pinellas (Fla.) Geneal. Soc. (lectr. 1995—), Carroll County (Md.) Geneal. Soc., Balt. County Geneal. Soc., Lancaster Mennonite Hist. Soc., Navy Hurricane Hunters, Sons Union Vets. Civil War, Md. Hist. Soc., Catonsville (Md.) Hist. Soc., Am. Legion, German Am. Geneal. Assn., DAV Fleet Res., Masons, Scottish Rite (Tampa), Egypt Temple Shrine, Moose, Sertoma (bd. dirs. Clearwater chpt. 1984-2002, v.p. 1989-92), Phi Delta Phi, Sigma Pi, Kappa Kappa Psi. Entertainment, Estate planning, General practice. Home: 2261 Belleair Rd Clearwater FL 33764-2761 Office: Legal Arts Bldg Ste 1 501 S Fort Harrison Ave Clearwater FL 33756-5317

WEIDENFELD, EDWARD LEE, lawyer; b. Akron, Ohio, July 15, 1943; s. Sam and Beatrice (Cooper) W.; m. Sheila Rabb, Aug. 11, 1968; children: Nicholas, Daniel. BS, U. Wis., 1965; JD, Columbia U., 1968. Bar: N.Y. 1968, U.S. Supreme Ct. 1972, D.C. 1973. Pvt. practice, N.Y.C., 1969-71, 73-82, Washington, 1982—. Spl. cons. N.Y.C. Dept. Bldgs., 1967; counsel, dir. energy staff Com. on Interior and Insular Affairs, U.S. Ho. of Reps., 1971—73; mem. faculty Am. Law Inst.-ABA CLE Programs; mem. Internat. Del. to Observe Philippine Election, 1986, Internat. Del. to Observe Republic Korea Election, 1987, Pakistan Election, 1988, Chilean Election, 1989, Albanian Election, 1997; mem. D.C. Bar Task Force on the Omnibus Trusts and Estates Amendment Act of 2000, 1999—2001; lectr. to profl. groups. Editor in chief Atomic Energy Law Jour., 1975-76; editor Conspectus Current Estate Planning Jour., 1998-2001; contbg. author: Generations: Planning Your Legacy, 1999. Mem. Pres.'s Commn. on White House Fellowships, 1977; nat. chmn. Lawyers for Reagan/Bush, 1980; chief dep. counsel Reagan/Bush Campaign, 1980; chmn. Reagan/Bush '84 Legal Adv. Bd., 1984; mem. D.C. Rep. Com., 1984-92, vice chmn., 1984-88; mem. Coun. Adminstrv. Conf. of U.S., 1981-92, sr. fellow, 1992-95; overseer dept. def. regional ctrs., sec.-treas. Salvation Army Adv. Bd.; trustee Danny Kaye and Sylvia Fine Kaye Found.; chmn. bd. visitors The Nat. Def. U. Recipient medal of Peter the Great, Russian Fedn., 2000. Mem. ABA, D.C. Bar Assn., Am. Law Inst. (life), Assn. Bar City N.Y., D.C. Estate Planning Coun. Clubs: Met. (Washington). Administrative and regulatory, Corporate, general, Private international. Office: 1828 L St NW Ste 500 Washington DC 20036-3806 E-mail: edward@weidenfeldlaw.com.

WEIDNER, LAUREN FINDER, lawyer; b. N.Y.C., Jan. 21, 1965; B in Commerce, McGill U., 1986; JD, U. Calif., Hastings, 1991. Bar: Calif. 1991, U.S. Dist. Ct. (no. and ctrl. dists.) Calif. 1991, U.S. Dist. Ct. (so. dist.) Calif. 1996. Assoc. Sedgwick, Detert, Moran & Arnold, San Francisco, 1991-95, Higgs Fletcher & Mack, San Diego, 1996-97, Gilbert, Kelly, Crowley & Jennett, San Diego, 1997—. Co-chair El Rancho del Ray Playground Renovation Com., Chula Vista, Calif., 1997-98; commr. City of Chula Vista Parks and Recreation, 1998— chair, 2000-02. Mem. San Diego Bar Assn. General civil litigation, Personal injury (including property damage), Professional liability. Office: Gilbert Kelly Crowley & Jennett 750 B St Ste 2600 San Diego CA 92101-8175

WEIGAND, WILLIAM LOREN, III, lawyer; b. Spokane, Wash., Sept. 8, 1965; s. William Loren Weigand Jr. and Mary Jean Weigand; m. Paula Stanley, June 5, 1999; children: William Loren IV, Cara Nicole. BA, U.Wash., Seattle, 1987; JD, U. Calif., San Francisco, 1990. Bar: Calif. 1991, Wash. 1991. Law clk. US Bankruptcy Ct. No. Dist. Wash., San Francisco, 1990—92; ptnr. Davis Wright Tremaine LLP, Seattle, 1992. Corporate, general. Office: Davis Wright Tremaine LLP 1501 4th Ave Ste 2600 Seattle WA 98101 Office Fax: 206-628-7699. E-mail: billweigand@dwt.com.

WEIGHT, MICHAEL ANTHONY, lawyer, former judge; b. Hilo, Hawaii, Jan. 5, 1940; s. Leslie A. and Grace B. (Brown) W.; m. Victoria Noel; children: Rachael R., Elizabeth G., Thomas P. BA in History, U. Rochester, 1961; LLB, Vanderbilt U., 1967. Bar: Hawaii 1967, U.S. Ct. Appeals (9th cir.) 1968, U.S. Supreme Ct. 1972. Pvt. practice, Honolulu, 1974-97; former judge Dist. Ct. (1st cir.) Hawaii; asst. fed. pub. defender Dists. of Hawaii and Guam, 1997—. Bd. dirs. Bishop Mus. Assn. 1st lt. USMC, 1961-63. Mem. Hawaii Bar Assn., Hawaii Assn. Criminal Def. Lawyers (pres. 1986). Criminal. Office: Fed Pub Defenders Office 300 Ala Moana Blvd Honolulu HI 96850-0001

WEIKSNER, SANDRA S. lawyer; b. D.C., Nov. 9, 1945; d. Donald B. and Dick (Cutter) Smiley; m. George B. Weiksner, Aug. 19, 1969; children: Michael, Nicholas. BA in Psychology, Stanford U., 1966, JD, 1969. Teaching fellow Stanford U., Calif., 1969-70; assoc. Cleary, Gottlieb, Steen & Hamilton, N.Y.C., 1970-77, ptnr., 1978—. Vis. lectr. Yale Law Sch., 1991-92. Bd. dirs. N.Y. Law Sch.; mem. Union Theol. Sem. Fellow Am. Bar Found., Am. Coll. Trusts and Estates Counsel, Internat. Acad. Estate and Trust Law; mem. ABA, N.Y. State Bar Assn., Assn. Bar of City of N.Y., Conn. Bar Assn. Democrat. Unitarian Universalist. Estate planning, Family and matrimonial, Probate (including wills, trusts). Home: 164 E 81st St New York NY 10028-1804 Office: Cleary Gottlieb Steen & Hamilton 1 Liberty Plz Fl 43 New York NY 10006-1404

WEIL, ANDREW LAWRENCE, lawyer; b. Highland Park, Ill., Dec. 19, 1960; s. Edward A. and Julie R. Weil. BA in Econs. with honors, Northwestern U., 1983, JD, 1986. Bar: Ill. 1986. Ptnr. Sonnenschein Nath & Rosenthal, Chgo., 1986—. Corp. sec. Donnelly Enterprise Solutions Inc., Chgo., 1997-98. Note and comment editor: Northwestern U. Jour. Internat. Law and Bus., 1984-86. Mem. Phi Beta Kappa. Commercial, contracts (including sales of goods; commercial financing), Corporate, general, Securities. Office: Sonnenschein Nath & Rosenthal 8000 Sears Tower Chicago IL 60606

WEIL, GARY RONALD, lawyer; b. N.Y.C., Oct. 1, 1953; s. Leopold and Margarete (Ofsijowitz) W. BS in Acctg., NYU, 1974; JD, NY Law Sch., 1978. Bar: N.Y. 1978, U.S. Dist. Ct. (so. dist.) N.Y. 1980. Asst. county atty. Westchester County Atty.'s Office, White Plains, N.Y., 1978-81; asst. dist. atty. Bronx (N.Y.) Dist. Atty.'s Office, 1981—, Spl. Narcotics Prosecutor's Office, N.Y.C., 1985-87. Mem. ABA, N.Y. State Bar Asn. Democrat. Jewish. Avocations: philately, photography. Office: Bronx Dist Attys Office 198 E 161st St Bronx NY 10451-3506 E-mail: geedubs@aol.com., weilg@bronxda.net.

WEIL, JEFFREY GEORGE, lawyer; b. Allentown, Pa., Apr. 28, 1951; s. Russel G.E. and Irene Marie (Kozlowski) W.; children: Michael, Stephen, Brooke. AB, Princeton U., 1973; JD, Harvard U., 1976. Bar: Pa. 1976, U.S. Dist. Ct. (ea. dist.) Pa. 1976, U.S. Ct. Appeals (3d cir.) 1976, U.S. Supreme Ct., 1988. Assoc. Dechert, Price & Rhoads, Phila., 1976-84, ptnr., 1984—, chmn. firm hiring com., 1987-89, mem. firm exec. com., 1990-94. Chmn. com. United Way Southeastern Pa., Phila., 1982-85, trustee, 1983-89, mem. funding policy com., 1987-90; participant Community Leadership Seminar Program, Phila., 1986; bd. dirs. Hawk Mountain Sanctuary, 1993-99, chmn. bd. dirs., 2000—; bd. dirs. Pa. Wildlife Fedn., 1996-99. Mem. ABA (vice chmn. admisntrn. law com. on pub. advs. and pub. representation 1985-88, mem. antitrust sect. pvt. litigation subcom. 1991—), Pa. Bar Assn., Phila. Bar Assn. (fed. cts. com. 1985—), Princeton U. Alumni Schs. Com., Princeton Club Phila. Avocations: fly-fishing, reading. Federal civil litigation, Securities, Health. Home: 195 Shelbourne Ln Phoenixville PA 19460-5710 Office: Dechert LLP 1717 Arch St Lbby 3 Philadelphia PA 19103-2713

WEIL, PETER HENRY, lawyer; b. N.Y.C., Nov. 20, 1933; s. Frank L. and Henrietta Amelia (Simons) W.; m. Helen Fay Kolodkin, Dec. 18, 1960; children: Karen W. Markus, Frank L. BA cum laude, Princeton U., 1954; LLB cum laude, Harvard U., 1957. Bar: N.Y. 1957, U.S. Dist. Cts. (so. and ea. dists.) N.Y. 1972. Assoc. Weil, Gotshal & Manges, N.Y.C., 1958-62; from assoc. to ptnr. Kaye Scholer, N.Y.C., 1962-95, ret., 1995. Lectr. SMU Inst. on Comml. Financing, 1985-94, Banking Law Inst., 1987-89. Author: Asset Based Lending: An Introductory Guide to Secured Financing, P.L.I., 1989, 3d edit., 1996. Fellow Am. Coll. of Commercial Fin. Lawyers; former chmn. N.Y. bd. overseers, former bd. govs. Hebrew Union Coll., Jewish Inst. Religion, Cin., N.Y.C., Los Angeles, Jerusalem. With U.S. Army 1957-58. Mem. Ringwood Golden Master Volleyball Team, U.S. Nat. Champions, 1983 Mem. ABA, Assn. of Bar of City of N.Y. (banking law com. 1975-78). Banking, Bankruptcy, Commercial, contracts (including sales of goods; commercial financing).

WEIL, ROBERT IRVING, lawyer, arbitrator, mediator, retired judge; b. N.Y.C., Apr. 6, 1922; s. Irving Julius and Esther (Aisenstein) W.; m. Carol Ethel Tannenbaum, Nov. 6, 1946 (div. 1953); children: David Irving, Timothy Robert; m. Dorothy Granet Kornhandler, Sept. 12, 1958. AB, UCLA, 1943; MS in Journalism, Columbia U., 1944; JD, U. So. Calif., L.A., 1951. Bar: Calif. 1951, U.S. Dist. Ct. (cen. dist.) Calif. 1951, U.S. Supreme Ct. 1961. Assoc. Pacht, Tannenbaum & Ross, L.A., 1951-54; ptnr. Tannenbaum, Steinberg & Shearer, Beverly Hills, Calif., 1954-58, Aaronson, Weil & Friedman, L.A., 1958-75; judge Calif. County Superior Ct., L.A., 1975-90; pvt. practice L.A., 1990—. V.p. L.A. Police Commn., 1973-75; chmn. Calif. Ctr. for Jud. Edn. and Rsch., Emoryville, 1989-90; lectr., seminar leader Calif. Jud. Coll., Berkeley, 1981—, The Rutter Group, L.A., 1981—. Co-author: California Practice Guide: Civil Procedure Before Trial, 1983; contbr. articles to profl. jours. Mem. ABA, Am. Judges Assn., Calif. Judges Assn. (pres. 1985-86, v.p. 1993-94), Pres.'s award 1987, v.p. 1993, Edn. award 1997), L.A. County Bar Assn., L.A. Copyright Soc., Beverly Hills Bar Assn. Avocations: writing, reading, travel, theatre. Alternative dispute resolution. Home and Office: 2686 Claray Dr Los Angeles CA 90077-2017 E-mail: robertweil@worldnet.att.net.

WEILAND, CHARLES HANKES, lawyer; b. Billings, Mont., Feb. 19, 1921; s. George Michael and Elizabeth (Hankes) W. AB cum laude, Johns Hopkins U., 1942; JD, Harvard U., 1948. Bar: Ill. 1949, U.S. Dist. Ct. (no. dist.) Ill. 1949, U.S. Ct. Appeals (7th cir.) 1949, U.S. Supreme Ct. 1968. Assoc. Lord, Bissell & Brook, Chgo., 1948-55, ptnr., 1956-83. Chmn. Cook County Inquiry Bd., Supreme Ct. Ill. Atty. Regis. and Disciplinary Commn., 1974-75 Served with AUS, 1942-46. Mem. Ill. Bar Assn., Chgo. Bar Assn. Clubs: The Lawyers Club of Chgo. Republican.

WEILER, JEFFRY LOUIS, lawyer; b. N.Y.C., Dec. 31, 1942; s. Kurt and Elaine (Kabb) W.; m. Susan Karen Goodman, June 8, 1964; children: Philip K., June M. BS, Miami U., Oxford, Ohio, 1964; JD, Cleve. State U., 1970. Bar: Ohio 1970, Fla. 1981; CPA, Ohio 1968. Acct. Meaden & Moore, CPAs, Cleve., 1964-65; IRS agt. U.S. Dept. Treasury, Cleve., 1965-70; assoc. Ulmer & Berne, Cleve., 1970-71; ptnr. Benesch, Friedlander, Coplan & Aronoff, LLP, Cleve., 1971—. Adj. assoc. prof. Cleve.-Marshall Coll. Law, Cleve. State U., 1980-87. Contbr. to profl. pubs. Fellow Am. Coll. Trust and Estate Counsel; mem. ABA (sect. taxation, estate and gift tax subcom.), Ohio State Bar Assn. (bd. govs. estate planning trust and probate law sect. 1999—), Cleve. Estate Planning Inst. (chmn. 1980), Cleve. Tax Inst. (chmn. 1983), Cleve. Bar Assn. (treas. 1993-96, trustee 1988-91), Tax Club of Cleve. (sec. 1996-97, v.p. 1997-99, pres. 1999-2000). Avocations: photography, sailboat racing, ice skating. Estate planning, Taxation, general, State and local taxation. Home: 24714 Maidstone Ln Beachwood OH 44122-1614 Office: Benesch Friedlander Coplan & Aronoff LLP 2300 BP Tower 200 Public Sq Cleveland OH 44114-2378 E-mail: jweiler@bfca.com.

WEILER, PAUL CRONIN, law educator; b. Port Arthur, Ont., Can., Jan. 28, 1939; s. G. Bernard and Marcella (Cronin) W.; m. Florrie Darwin, 1988; children: Virginia, John, Kathryn, Charles. BA with honors, U. Toronto, 1960, MA with honors, 1961; LLB, Osgoode Hall Law Sch., 1964; LLM, Harvard Law Sch., 1965; LLD, U. Victoria, 1981, U. Toronto, 2000. Bar: Ont. Prof. law Osgoode Hall Law Sch., 1965-72; chmn. Labour Rels. Bd. B.C., 1973-78; Mackenzie King prof. Can. studies Harvard Law Sch., 1978-80, prof. law, 1980—, Henry J. Friendly prof. law, 1993—. Chief counsel U.S. Commn. Future of Worker-Mgmt. Rels.; prin. legal investigator Harvard U. Med. Practice Study Group; impartial umpire AFL-CIO; chief reporter Am. Law Inst. Tort Reform Project; cons. to U.S. Commn. on Comprehensive Health Care (Pepper Commn.); spl. counsel Govt. of Ont. Rev. of Workers' Compensation, 1980-88; mem. pub. rev. bd. UAW, chief counsel Pres.' commn. Future Worker-Mgmt. Rels., 1993-94; panelist, U.S./Can. Free Trade Agreement Softwood Lumber Arbitration, 1992-93. Author: Labor Arbitration and Industrial Change, 1970, In the Last Resort: A Critical Study of the Supreme Court of Canada, 1974; (with others) Labor Relations Law in Canada, rev. edit., 1974; (with others) Studies in Sentencing in Canada, 1974, Reconcilable Differences: New Directions in Canadian Labour Law, 1980, Reforming Workers Compensation, 1980, MEGA Projects: The Collective Bargaining Dimensions, 1981, Protecting the Worker from Disability, 1983, Governing the Workplace: The Future of Labor and Employment Law, 1990, (with others) Patients, Doctors, and Lawyers: Medical Injury, Malpractice Litigation and Patient Compensation, 1990, Medical Malpractice on Trial, 1991, (with others) A Measure of Malpractice, 1992, Text, Cases, and Problems on Sports & the Law, 1993, 2d edit., 1998, Text, Cases, and Problems on Entertainment, Radio, and the Law, 1997, 2d edit., 2002, Leveling the Playing Field, 2000; contbr. articles to profl. jours. Mem. Nat. Acad. Arbitrators, Nat. Acad. Social Ins., Nat. Acad. Sci., Inst. Medicine. Clubs: Cambridge Tennis (Cambridge, Mass.). Roman Catholic. Office: Harvard U Law Sch 1525 Massachusetts Ave Cambridge MA 02138-2903 E-mail: pweiler@law.harvard.edu.

WEIMAR, ROBERT, law educator; b. Cologne, Fed. Republic Germany, May 13, 1932; s. Wilhelm and Agnes (Over) W.; m. Eva Zydek, June 18, 1974. JD, Licentiate, Basle U., Switzerland, 1965; PhD, Magister Artium Lib., Basle U., 1967, LLM, 2001; D in Pedagogics (hon.) , U. Moscow, 1992; LLM, U. Heidelberg, 2001. State examinations in law, Ministry of Justice, Dusseldorf, 1956, 60. Asst. U. Cologne, 1960-61; assoc. judge Cologne Dist. Ct., 1961-64; sci. staff Supreme Ct., Karlsruhe, 1964-67, Supreme Constl. Ct., Karlsruhe, 1970-72; appellate judge Dusseldorf Appell Ct., 1968-73; prof. law Siegen U., 1974—94; dir. Siegen Inst. Econ. Law & Legislation, 1974—; cons. European Faculty of Land Use and Devel., Strasbourg, France, 1981—; spokesman Inst. for German & European Econ. Law, Siegen U., 1989-90; lectr. law Heinrich-Heine U. Dusseldorf, 1989-90; dir. Siegen Inst. for Neurojurisprudence, 2000—. Vis. prof. U. Vienna, 1980—81, U. Luneburg, 2000—01, U. Heidelberg, 2001. Author: Studies in Product Liability, 1967, Psychological Structures of Judicial Decision-Making, 1996, Neuroscience Before the Gates of Jurisprudence, 2000, Evolution, Culture and Legal System, 2002; contbr. articles to profl. jours. Recipient Franz-Boehm medal, 1977. Mem. Internat. Assn. Philosophy of Law and Social Philosophy, Gesellschaft fur Rechtsvergleichung, German Assn. Univ. Profs., Goerres-Association. Avocation: painting. Home: Lagemannstrasse 30 D-57258 Siegen Germany

WEIMER, JOHN L. state supreme court justice; b. Thibodaux, Oct. 2, 1954; m. Penny Hymel; 3 children. BS (with honors), Nicholls State U., 1980; JD, La. State U., 1980. Pvt. practice law, 1980—95; judge 17th Judicial Dist. Ct., 1995—98, 1st Cir. Ct. of Appeal, Dist. 1, Divsn. B, 1998—2001; justice La. Supreme Ct., 2001—. Adj. prof. law Nicholls State U. , 1982—97, prof. law, 1982—97. Mem. Thibodaux Vol. Fire Dept. Recipient Crimefighter's Outstanding Jurist award . Mem.: Lafourche Parish Student Govt. Day Program (creator, coord.), Citizens' Summit Justice Reform (regional co-chmn. 1997), Assumption C. of C., Houma-Terrebonne C. of C., Thibodaux C. of C., Nicholls State U. (mem. alumni bd., former vol. legal counsel), Lafourche Parish Bar Assn., La. State Bar Assn. (del.), Rotary Club. Achievements include development of Lafourche Parish Drug Treatment Court. Mailing: 301 Loyola Ave New Orleans LA 70112

WEIMER, PETER DWIGHT, retired mediator, lawyer, corporate executive; b. Grand Rapids, Mich., Oct. 14, 1938; s. Glen E. and Clarabel (Kauffman) W.; children: Melanie, Kim; m. Judith Anne Minor. BA, Bridgewater Coll., 1962; JD, Howard U., 1969. Cert. mediator Supreme Ct. Va. Assoc. counsel Loporto & Weimer Ltd., Manassas, Va., 1970-75; chief counsel Weimer & Cheatle Ltd., Manassas, 1975-79, Peter D. Weimer, P.C., Manassas, 1979-83; pres., mediator Mediation Ltd., Manassas, 1981—2002, ret., 2002. Pres. Citation Properties, Inc., Manassas, 1971-93; pres. Preferred Rsch. of No. Va., Inc., 1985-89, Pro Rsch. Inc., 1989-93, Pro Mgmt., Inc., 1990-2002; cons. Continental Title & Escrow, Inc., 1992-96. Address: PO Box 7474 Sebring FL 33872

WEIN, BRUCE J. lawyer; b. N.Y.C., Jan. 15, 1944; s. Eber A. and Esther A. Wein; m. Penny Kirsch, June 24, 1967; children: Joseph, Howard, Michael, Rebecca. AB, Clark U., 1966; JD cum laude, Boston U., 1969. Bar: N.Y. 1970, U.S. Dist. Ct. (so. dist.) N.Y. 1970, U.S. Tax Ct. 1970. Assoc. Marshall, bratter, Greene, Allison, & Tucker, N.Y.C., 1969-75, ptnr., 1975-76, Gordon, Altman, Weitzen, Shalov & Wein, N.Y.C., 1976-2000; with Piper Rudnick LLP. Mem. ABA (taxation sect.), N.Y. State Bar Assn., Assn. of Bar of City of N.Y. (tax sect.). Corporate, general, Corporate taxation, Personal income taxation. Office: Piper Rudnick LLP 1251 Ave of the Americas New York NY 10020-1104 E-mail: Bruce.wein@piperrudnick.com.

WEIN, STEPHEN J. lawyer; married. BA Polit. Sci., Bklyn Coll., N.Y., 1972; JD, Stetson U., St. Petersburg, Fla., 1976. Bar: (Fla.) 1976, U.S. Dist. Ct., (Mid. Dist.) Fla. 1976, U.S. Ct. of Appeals (D.C. Cir.) 1979, U.S. Supreme Ct. 1980, U.S. Ct. of Appeals (5th and 11th cirs.) 1981, U.S. Tax Ct. 1985, U.S. Ct. of Appeals (Fed. Cir.) 2002. Assoc. Belcher & Fleece, St. Petersburg, Fla., 1976—78, Battaglia, Ross, Hastings & Dicus, P.A., St. Petersburg, Fla., 1979—81, shareholder, 1981—93, Battaglia, Ross, Dicus & Wein, P.A., St. Petersburg, Fla., 1993—. Bd. dirs. Pinellas County Jewish Day Sch., St. Petersburg, Fla., 1980—90, v.p., 1988, pres., 1989; bd. dirs. Jewish Fedn. of Pinellas County, Clearwater, Fla., 1989—2000, pres., 1991—93; bd. dirs./sec. Congregation Beth Chai, Seminole, Fla., 1978—84; trustee Menorah Manor Found., St. Petersburg, Fla., 1994—2002. Mem.: ABA, Cardozo Soc., St. Petersburg Bar Assn., The Fla. Bar, Nat. Assn. of Criminal Def. Lawyers. General civil litigation, Intellectual property, Criminal. Office: Battaglia Ross Dicus & Wein PA 980 Tyrone Blvd Saint Petersburg FL 33710 Office Fax: 727-343-4059. E-mail: swein@brdwlaw.com.

WEINBERG, HERSCHEL MAYER, lawyer; b. Bklyn., Oct. 13, 1927; s. Jacob and Gertrude (Wernick) W. BA, Bklyn. Coll., 1948; LL.B., Harvard U., 1952. Bar: N.Y. 1952. Atty. firm Payne & Steingarten, N.Y.C., 1952-57, Jacobs, Persinger & Parker, N.Y.C., 1957-61; partner firm Rubin, Rubin, Weinberg, & Di Paola, N.Y.C., 1961-78, Weinberg Tauber & Pressman, 1979-90; pvt. practice N.Y.C., 1990—. Served with AUS, 1946-47. Mem. Assn. of Bar of City of N.Y., N.Y. State Bar Assn. Clubs: Harvard (N.Y.C.). Home: 50 Sutton Pl S New York NY 10022-4167 Office: 110 E 59th St New York NY 10022-1304

WEINBERG, JEFFREY J. lawyer; b. N.Y.C., Aug. 27, 1948; s. Arnold Mitchell and Lucile (Barton) W.; m. Bonnie J. Sandhaus, Aug. 23, 1970; children: Seth, Andrew. BA, SUNY, Stony Brook, 1969; JD, Georgetown U., 1973. Bar: N.Y., U.S. Dist. Ct. (so. and ea. dists.). Assoc. Weil, Gotshal & Manges, N.Y.C., 1973-81, ptnr., 1981—. Acting judge Village of Roslyn Estates. Author: Sales of Troubled Business, 1991, 92, 93, 94. Former trustee Village of Roslyn Estate. Mem. Knickerbocker Y.C. (gov. 1990-91). Avocation: sailing. Office: Weil Gotshal & Manges 767 5th Ave Fl Concl New York NY 10153-0119

WEINBERG, LARRY, lawyer, labor union administrator; b. 1944; BA in Econs., U. Mich., JD, 1970. Bar: DC 1971. With FTC, Washington, Zwerdling, Washington, 1972—80; gen. counsel AFSCME, Washington, 1980—. Office: AFSCME 1101 17th St NW Washington DC 20036-4704*

WEINBERG, SARA CARYNA, lawyer; b. Houston, Jan. 10, 1973; d. Robert Stephen and Cathey Margaret Bienkowski; m. Justin Robert Weinberg, Aug. 14, 1997. BA, Binghamton U., 1994; JD, Boston U., 1997. Bar: Mass. 1998, D.C. 1999, N.Y. 2000, U.S. Ct. Fed. Claims 1999, U.S. Ct. Appeals (D.C. cir.) 1999. Assoc. Spiegel & McDiarmid, Washington, 1997—99, Swidler Berlin Sheriff Friedman, Washington, 1999—2001, Vinson & Elkins, Washington, 2001—. FERC practice, Utilities, public, Oil, gas, and mineral. Office: Vinson & Elkins Willard Office Bldg 1455 Pennsylvania Ave NW Washington DC 20004-1008

WEINBERG, STEVEN LEWIS, lawyer; b. NYC, Aug. 22, 1961; s. Harry and Florence Weinberg. BA in Polit. Sci., SUNY, Binghamton, 1982; JD, Albany Law Sch. Union Univ., 1985. Bar: N.Y. 1987, U.S. Ct. Appeals (2d cir.) 1987, U.S. Dist. Ct. (no., so., and ea. dists.) N.Y. 1987. Asst. dist. atty. Queens Dist. Atty., Kew Gardens, NY, 1985—87; mem. Gottesman Wolgel Secunda Malamy & Flynn, P.C., N.Y.C., 1987—. Dep. mayor Village of Thomaston, Great Neck, NY, 1997—. Appellate, General civil litigation. Office: Gottesman Wolgel Secunda Malamy & Flynn PC 11 Hanover Sq New York NY 10005

WEINBERGER, ALAN DAVID, lawyer, corporate executive; b. Washington, July 31, 1945; s. Theodore George and Shirley Sunshine (Gross) W.; m. Lauren Myra Kaminski, Dec. 2, 1979; children: Mark Henry, Benjamin Charles. BA, NYU, 1967, JD, 1970; LLM, Harvard U., 1973. Bar: N.Y. 1971, D.C. 1978, U.S. Supreme Ct. 1980. Assoc. White & Case, N.Y.C., 1970-72; founding law prof. Vt. Law Sch., South Royalton, 1973-75; atty. SEC and Fed. Home Loan Bank Bd., Washington, 1977-81; founder, chmn. bd. dirs., CEO The ASCII Group Inc., Washington, 1984—; founder, chmn. bd. dirs. Tech. Net, Inc., Bethesda, Md., 1995. Mem. adv. bd. Ashton Tate Inc., Torrance, Calif., 1986-87; sponsor, agt. All Union Fgn. Trade Acad., Acad. Nat. Economy of USSR in U.S.A., 1988-90; chmn. U.S. adv. bd. Moscow State U. of Commerce, 1992—; chmn. govt. affairs com. Computer Tech. Industry Assn., 1993-95; mem. U.S. adv. bd. U.S.-UK Fulbright Commn., 1999—. Author: White Paper to Reform Business Education in Russia, 1996; law rev. editor NYU Sch. Law, 1970. Named one of Top 25 Most Influential Execs. in Computer Industry, Computer Reseller News, 1988; recipient CEO of Yr. award Cyber Chanels, 1999; named eInnovator of Yr. Cyber Channels Assn., 2000. Mem. Nat. Orgn. on Disability (CEO coun.), D.C. Bar Assn., Order of Coif, Kenwood Country Club. Avocation: tennis. Computer, Corporate, general. Office: ASCII Group Inc 7101 Wisconsin Ave Bethesda MD 20814-4871

WEINBERGER, HAROLD PAUL, lawyer; b. N.Y.C., Mar. 12, 1947; s. Fred and Elaine (Schonfeld) W.; m. Toby Ann Strassman, Dec. 15, 1968; children: James David, Karen Ellen. BA, CCNY, 1967; JD, Columbia U., 1970. Bar: N.Y. 1971, U.S. Dist. Cts. (so., ea., and no. dists.) N.Y. 1972, U.s. Ct. Appeals (2d cir.) 1972. Law clk. to presiding justice U.S. Ct. Appeals (2d cir.), N.Y.C., 1970-71; assoc. Kramer Levin Naftalis Frankel LLP, N.Y.C., 1971-77, ptnr., 1978—. Recipient John Ordronaux prize Columbia U. Law Sch., 1970. Mem. ABA (intellectual property law sect. 1999—), Assn. Bar City N.Y. (com. fed. legislation 1975-78, com. on products liability 1983-86, mem. com. on trademarks and unfair competition 1995-97). Democrat. Jewish. Federal civil litigation, State civil litigation, Intellectual property. Home: 336 Central Park W New York NY 10025-7111 Office: Kramer Levin Naftalis & Frankel LLP 919 3rd Ave New York NY 10022-3902 E-mail: hweinberger@kramerlevin.com.

WEINBERGER, JOSEPH CHARLES, JR., lawyer; b. Bethlehem, Pa., Nov. 13, 1956; s. Joseph C. and Irene (Farkas) W.; m. Sallie Margaret Clayton, July 4, 1957; children: Joseph C. III, James Thomas, David C., William A. BA, Wake Forest U., Winston-Salem, N.C., 1978, JD, 1982. Bar: N.C. 1983, U.S. Dist. Ct. (mid. dist.) N.C. 1987. Assoc. Ramsey, Hubbard, Galloway & Cates, Roxboro, N.C., 1983-86; pvt. practice Roxboro, 1986—. City atty. City of Roxboro, 1994-96. Fellow N.C. Acad. Trial Lawyers, N.C. Bar Assn., Roxboro Area C. of C. (bd. dirs., pres. 2003), Kiwanis (pres. 1997-98, Kiwanian of Yr. 1994-95). Avocations: golf, racquetball. General civil litigation, Personal injury (including property damage), Property, real (including real estate development, water). Home: PO Box 1215 Roxboro NC 27573-1215 Office: 114 N Main St Roxboro NC 27573-5535

WEINBERGER, PETER HENRY, lawyer; b. Cleve., Nov. 15, 1950; s. Eric and Eva (Grant) W.; m. Laurie Ann Novak, Aug. 26, 1972; children: Kelly, Adam. AB in Psychology, Syracuse U., 1972; JD, Case Western Res. U., 1975. Bar: Ohio 1975, U.S. Ct. Appeals (6th cir.) 1975, U.S. Ct. Appeals (4th cir.) 1986, Pa. 1995, U.S. Supreme Ct. 1995. Ptnr. Kube & Weinberger, Cleve., 1975-88, Spangenberg, Shibley & Liber, Cleve., 1988—. Lectr. to bar assns., Case Western Res. U. Sch. Law. Contb. articles to legal jours. Chmn. Solon (Ohio) Cable TV Adv. Com., 1984-85; mem. Solon Civil Svc. Commn., 1985-87, vice chmn., 1986-87; bd. dirs. 1st Unitarian Ch. Cleve., pres., 1992-93. Fellow Am. Coll. Trial Lawyers; mem. ABA, Ohio Bar Assn., Cleve. Bar Assn. (chmn. young lawyers sect. 1980-81, charter mem. coun. litigation sect. 1987—), Cuyahoga Bar Assn. (pres. 1991-92, chmn. grievance com. 1984-86, trustee 1987—, cert. of appreciation 1985, 89, outstanding svc. award 1986), Assn. Trial Lawyers Am., Ohio Acad. Trial Lawyers (trustee 1999—), Cleve. Acad. Trial Attys. (pres. 1984-85, spl. merit award 1985), 8th Dist. Jud. Conf. (charter mem. commn. on pre-trials), Cuyahoga Bar Found. (pres. 1998—), Am. Bd. of Trial Advs. (adv.). Democrat. Unitarian Universalist. Personal injury (including property damage). Home: 34910 Forest Ln Cleveland OH 44139-1441 Office: Spangenberg Shibley & Liber 2400 National City Ctr Cleveland OH 44114 E-mail: phw@spanglaw.com.

WEINBERGER, STEVEN, lawyer, educator; b. Bklyn., Apr. 13, 1953; s. Robert Ira and Elaine (Lichtenthal) W.; m. Maureen Susan Horan, Oct. 15, 1978 (div. 1998); children: John William, Matthew Lawrence; m. Maria DiBenedetto, Sept. 26, 1998. BA, SUNY, Binghamton, 1974; JD, U. Miami, 1977; MS, Hartford Grad. Ctr., 1989. Bar: N.Y. 1978, Conn. 1987, U.S. Dist. Ct. (no. dist.) N.Y. 1981, U.S. Dist. Ct. Conn. 1990. Legis. atty. N.Y. City Council, 1977-78; asst. atty. Westchester County, White Plains, N.Y., 1978-79; sr. asst. atty. Broome County, Binghamton, N.Y., 1979-81, dep. personnel officer, 1981-82; from labor rels. specialist to chief employee svcs. bur. State of Conn., Hartford, 1982-95, dir. retirement and benefit svcs. divsn., 1995—. Adj. prof. Teikyo Post U., Waterbury, Conn., 1984—, Albertus Magnus Coll., New Haven, 2000—. Mem. N.Y. State Bar Assn. Democrat. Jewish. Office: State of Connecticut Retirement & Benefit Svcs 55 Elm St Hartford CT 06106-1746 E-mail: steve.weinberger@po.state.ct.us.

WEINCKE, THOMAS, lawyer; b. Denmark, Oct. 10, 1963; s. Mogens and Gudrun Weincke; children: Mille, Julie. LLM, Copenhagen U., 1990. Asst. atty. O. Bondo Svane Law Firm, Copenhagen, 1990—93, atty., 1994—98, ptnr., 1998—2000, Accura Law Firm, Hellerup, Denmark, 2000—.

WEINER, CHARLES R. federal judge; b. Phila., June 27, 1922; s. Max and Bessie (Chairney) W.; m. Edna Gerber, Aug. 24, 1947; children: William, Carole, Harvey. Grad., U. Pa., 1947, MA, 1967, PhD, 1972; LL.B., Temple U., 1950. Bar: Pa. bar 1951. Asst. dist. atty. Philadelphia County, 1952-53; mem. Pa. Senate from Phila. County, 1952-67, minority floor leader, 1959-60, 63-64, majority floor leader, 1961-62; U.S. dist. judge Eastern Dist. Pa., 1967—; now sr. judge. Mem. Phila. County Bd. Law Examiners, 1959—. Mem. Pres.'s Adv. Commn. Inter-Govtl. Rels., Phila., Pub. Policy Com., Phila. Crime Prevention Assn., Big Bros. Assn.; mem. Pa. Bd. Arts and Scis.; trustee, exec. com. Fedn. Jewish Philanthropies of Phila., Allied Jewish Appeal of Phila.; bd. dirs. Mental Health Assn. of Pa., Phila. Psychiat. Ctr., Phila. Tribune Charities, Phila. Wharton Ctr. Parkside YMCA, Jewish Publ. Soc. Am., The Athenaeum, and others. With USN, 1942—46. Recipient Phila. Fellowship award; Founder's Day award Temple U.; Alumni award U. Pa.; Founder's award Berean Inst.; others. Mem. ABA, Pa. Bar Assn., Phila. Bar Assn., Am. Law Inst. Office: US District Ct 6613 US Courthouse Ind Mall W 601 Market St Philadelphia PA 19106-1713

WEINER, DAVID P. lawyer; b. Portland, Oreg., Feb. 9, 1948; BA, Claremont McKenna Coll., 1969; JD magna cum laude, Willamette U., 1972. Law clk. U.S. Dist. Ct. Oreg., Portland, 1972-73; from assoc. to ptnr. Samuels, Yoelin, Weiner, Kanton & Seymour, Portland, 1973-96; of counsel Greene & Markley, P.C., Portland, 1996—. Mem. discipline rules and procedures com. Oreg. Supreme Ct., 1986—. Mem. ABA (real property sect. B-4 opinion letter com. 1994—), Oreg. State Bar (chair real property com. on opinion letters 1988—), Multnomah County Bar, Wash. State Bar Assn., Oreg. Golf Assn. (pres. 1998-2001). Commercial, contracts (including sales of goods; commercial financing), Property, real (including real estate development, water). Office: Greene and Markley PC 1515 SW 5th Ave Ste 600 Portland OR 97201-5449

WEINER, EARL DAVID, lawyer; b. Balt., Aug. 21, 1939; s. Jacob Joseph and Sophia Gertrude (Rachanow) W.; m. Gina Helen Priestley Ingoglia, Mar. 30, 1962; children: Melissa Danis Balmain, John Barlow. AB, Dickinson Coll., 1960; LL.B., Yale U., 1968. Bar: N.Y. 1969. Assoc. Sullivan & Cromwell, N.Y.C., 1968-76, ptnr., 1976—. Adj. prof. Rutgers U. Sch. Law, 1987-88; bd. dirs. Solvay Techs. Inc., Hedwin Corp., The Acting Co., vice chair, 1992—, v.p., 1991-92. Gov. Bklyn. Heights Assn., 1980-87, pres., 1985-87, adv. com., 1987—; gov. The Heights Casino, 1979-84, pres., 1981-84; trustee Bklyn. Bot. Garden, 1985—, chmn. 1998—; trustee Green-Wood Cemetery, 1986—, Bklyn. Hosp. Ctr., 1998—; bd. advisors Dickinson Coll., Carlisle, Pa., 1986-90, chmn., 1988-90, trustee, 1988-2002, vice chmn., 1998-2002; mem. adv. com. East Rock Inst., 1988—; bd. visitors U. Md. Ctr. for Environ. Sci., 2002—. Lt. USN, 1961-65. Fellow Fgn. Policy Assn. (sr.); mem. ABA, N.Y. State Bar Assn., Assn. Bar City N.Y. Corporate, general, Private international. Office: Sullivan & Cromwell 125 Broad St Fl 28 New York NY 10004-2489

WEINER, JODY CARL, lawyer, author, producer; b. Chgo., Oct. 19, 1948; s. Leo and Sarah Weiner; m. Nancy Calef, Mar. 4, 1993. BA, U. Wis., 1970; JD, DePaul U., 1974. Bar: Ill. 1974, U.S. Dist. Ct. (no. dist.) Ill. 1974, U.S. Ct. Appeals (6th and 7th cirs.) 1975, Calif. 1989, U.S. Dist. Ct. (no. dist.) Calif. 1989. Assoc. Law Offices Frazin & Frazin, Chgo., 1974-77; ptnr. Muslin & Weiner, Chgo., 1977-80; pvt. practice Chgo., 1980—85; sr. assoc. Law Offices James Duryea Jr., San Francisco, 1989-91; pvt. practice San Francisco, 1991—. Gen. mgr. The Island Hotel, Koh Samui, Thailand, 1994-96; corp. counsel Skyy Spirits, LLC, San Francisco, 1995-2000. Author: Raise Your Other Right Hand, 1987, Prisoners of Truth, 2002; assoc. prodr.: (feature film) Mama's Boy, 2000; (documentary) A Conversation with Koko, 1999. Cons., advisor Artist Guild San Francisco, 1996-99, Gorilla Found., Woodside, Calif., 1998-99, Eureka Theatre, San Francisco, 1998-2000; dir. Golda Found., Calif., 2001-. General practice, Entertainment, General civil litigation. Office: 846 Filbert St San Francisco CA 94133-2627 E-mail: jodycarlweiner@aol.com.

WEINER, KAREN COLBY (KAREN LYNN COLBY), psychologist, lawyer; b. Oak Park, Ill., Oct. 28, 1943; d. Leonard L. and Mildred Irene (Berman) Colby; m. J. Laevin Weiner, July 26, 1964; children: Joel Laevin, Doren Robin, Anthony Justin. BA, Mich. State U., East Lansing, 1964; JD, U. Detroit, 1977, MA, 1986, PhD, 1988. Bar: Mich. 1977, D.C. 1978. Speech therapist Oak Park Sch. Dist., 1965-68; law clk. justice G. Mennen Williams Mich. Supreme Ct., Lansing, 1977-79; assoc. Dickinson, Wright, Moon, Van Dusen & Freeman, Detroit, 1979-83; intern in psychology Detroit Psychiat. Inst., 1986-88; psychologist Northland Clinic, Southfield, Mich., 1987-88, Counseling Assocs., Southfield, 1988—; postdoctoral intern Wyandotte (Mich.) Hosp. and Health Ctr., 1988-90; dir. psychol. svcs., quality assurance coord. Counseling Assocs., Southfield, 1991-99. Hearing panelist Atty. Discipline Bd., Detroit, 1982-95; hearing referee Mich. Civil Rights Commn., Detroit, 1983-91; mem. Mich. Bd. Psychology, 1999—; adj. prof. U. Detroit Mercy, 2001—. Contbr. articles to profl. jours. Mem. adv. bd. Mich. chpt. Anti-Defamation League, 1981-90. Fellow Mich. Psychol. Assn. (mem. ethics com. 1992—, chmn. legis. com. 1993, chmn. ethics com. 1997-99); mem. APA, Mich. Soc. for Psychoanalytic Psychology (pres. 1995-97, sec. 1991-92, treas. 1992-94), Women Lawyers Assn. Mich. (pres. 1981-82, pres. Found. 1982-83), Mich. Bar Assn. (chmn. spl. com. for expansion under represented groups in law 1980-83). Jewish. Home: 2501 Long Lake Rd West Bloomfield MI 48323 Office: 29260 Franklin Rd Ste 115 Southfield MI 48034-1144 E-mail: drkcw@comcast.net.

WEINER, LAWRENCE, lawyer; b. Phila., Aug. 20, 1942; s. Robert A. and Goldie Weiner; m. Jane M. Coulthard, Feb. 28, 1976; 1 child, Kimberly. BS in Econs., U. Pa., 1964, JD, 1967. Bar: Pa. 1967, U.S. Dist. Ct. (ea. dist.) Pa. 1967, Fla. 1970, U.S. Dist. Ct. (so. dist.) Fla. 1976, U.S. Ct. Appeals (5th cir.) 1976, U.S. Tax Ct. 1984. Assoc., ptnr. Blank, Rome, Klaus & Comisky, Phila., 1967-71, 1975-77; ptnr. Weiner & Weisenfeld, P.A., Miami Beach, Fla., 1971-73, Pettigrew & Bailey, Miami, Fla., 1973-75; pres. Lawrence Weiner, P.A., Miami, 1977-83; ptnr. Spieler, Weiner & Spieler, P.A., Miami, 1983-89, Weiner & Cummings, P.A., Miami, 1989-94, Weiner, Cummings & Vittoria, Miami, 1994—. Lectr. Wharton Sch. U. Pa., Phila., 1968-70; instr. bus. law and acctg. Community Coll. Phila., 1967-70; lectr. estate planning various non-lawyer groups, Miami, 1972—. Mem. Fla. Bar (liaison non-lawyers groups 1980-87), Pa. Bar Assn., Phila. Bar Assn., Dade County Bar Assn. (chmn. ins. com. 1977-78, probate law com. 1992—). Democrat. Jewish. Corporate, general, Estate planning, Probate (including wills, trusts). Office: Weiner Cummings & Vittoria 1428 Brickell Ave Ste 400 Miami FL 33131-3436

WEINER, MARCIA MYRA, judge; b. Apr. 12, 1934; BA, St. Mary's U., San Antonio, 1965, JD, 1970. Bar: Tex. 1971. Atty-advisor HUD, San Antonio, 1971—84, chief counsel, 1984—97; elected justice of the peace Precinct 2 Pl., Bexar County, Tex., 2000—. Recipient Spl. Achievement awards, HUD, 1972, 1975, 1977, Hub Fed. Women's Program award, Leigh Curry award, Fed. Women's Program Coun. Mgmt. award, Outstanding Bus. Woman of Yr., 2000. Mem.: Coll. State Bar Tex., San Antonio Bar Assn., Bexar County Women's Bar Assn., Fed. Bar Assn., Tex. Bar Assn., Greyhound Pets of Am., Tex. Wanderers, Randolph Roadrunners, Alamo Unit #2 of Am. Legion Aux. Jewish. Office: Justice Ct Precinct 2 6715 Bandera Rd San Antonio TX 78238

WEINER, SANFORD ALAN, lawyer; b. Houston, Aug. 21, 1946; s. Abe I. and Zelda C. (Caplan) W.; m. Leslie Eve Grenadier, Aug. 16, 1970; children: Edward, David, Evan, Rebecca. BA, U. Tex., 1968; JD, Harvard U., 1971. Bar: Tex. 1971. Ptnr. Vinson & Elkins, Ltd. Liability Partnership, Houston, 1971—. Pres. Am. Coll. Real Estate Lawyers. Mem. Houston Bar Assn., Tex. Bar Assn., Houston Real Estate Lawyers Council, Anglo-Am. Real Property Inst. Jewish. Banking, Finance, Property, real (including real estate development, water). Office: Vinson & Elkins LLP 1001 Fannin St Ste 2300 Houston TX 07002-6760

WEINER, STEPHEN ARTHUR, lawyer; b. Bklyn., Nov. 20, 1933; s. Joseph Lee W. and Ruth Lessall (Weiner); m. Mina Rieur, Sept. 1, 1958; children: Karen, James. BA summa cum laude, Harvard U., 1954; JD cum laude, Yale U., 1957. Bar: N.Y. 1958, U.S. Supreme Ct. 1963. Assoc. Winthrop, Stimson, Putnam & Roberts, N.Y.C., 1958-65, ptnr., 1968—2000, vice chmn. mgmt. com., 1984-97; acting prof. law U. Calif., Berkeley, 1965-68; ptnr. Pillsbury Winthrop, LLP, N.Y.C., 2001, sr. counsel, 2002—. Arbitrator NASD Dispute Resolution, 2002—; mem. com. on character and fitness 1st dept. appellate divsn. N.Y. Supreme Ct., 1998—, spl. master, 1999—; mem. N.Y. State Jud. Inst. on Professionalism in the Law, 1999—. Contbr. articles to legal publs. Comment editor Yale Law Jour., 1956-57. Fellow Am. Coll. Trial Lawyers, Am. Bar Found.; mem. Assn. of Bar of City of N.Y. (chmn. recruitment of lawyers com., chmn. com. on Stimson medal), Fed. Bar Coun. (chmn. com. on 2d cir. cts., trustee), Order of Coif, Phi Beta Kappa. Federal civil litigation, State civil litigation. Home: 190 Harbor Rd Sands Point NY 11050-2636 Office: Pillsbury Winthrop LLP One Battery Park Plz New York NY 10004-1490 E-mail: sweiner@pillsburywinthrop.com.

WEINGARTEN, SAUL MYER, lawyer; b. Los Angeles, Dec. 19, 1921; s. Louis and Lillian Dorothy (Alter) W.; children: David, Steven, Lawrence, Bruce. AA, Antelope Valley Coll., 1940; AB, UCLA, 1942; cert., Cornell U., 1943; JD, U. Southern Calif., 1949. Bar: Calif. 1950, U.S. Supreme Ct., 1960, Calif. Supreme Ct., 1950, Fed. Dist. Ct., 1950, U.S. Ct. of Mil. Appeals, 1951, U.S. Supreme Ct., 1961. Prin. Saul M. Weingarten Assocs., Seaside, Calif., 1954—. Atty. City of Gonzales, Calif., 1954-74, City of Seaside, 1955-70; gen. counsel Redevel. Agy., Seaside, 1955-76, Security Nat. Bank, Monterey, Calif., 1968-74; bd. dirs., exec. com. Frontier Bank, Cheyenne, Wyo., 1984-99; pres. Quaestor, Inc., 1991-98. Author: Practice Compendium, 1950; contbr. articles to profl. jours. Del. Internat. Union of Local Authorities, Brussels, Belgium, 1963, 73; candidate state legislature Dem. Com., Monterey County, 1958; counsel Monterey Peninsula Mus. of Art, Inc., 1972-80; gen. counsel Monterey County Symphony Assn., Carmel, Calif., 1974-98, Mountain Plains Edn. Project, Glasgow, Mont., 1975-81; chmn. fund raising ARC, Monterey, 1964; chmn., bd. dirs. fund raising United Way, Monterey, 1962-63; pres., bd. dirs. Alliance on Aging, Monterey, 1968-82; bd. dirs. Family Svc. Agy., Monterey, 1958-66, Monterey County Cultural Coun., 1986-94, Clark Found., 1982—; dir., mem. exec. com. Monterey Bay Performing Arts Ctr., 1990. Served to commdr. USN, 1942-46, 50-54, Korea. Grad. fellow Coro Found., 1949-50. Mem. Calif. Bar Assn., Monterey County Bar Assn., Monterey County Trial Lawyers Assn., Rotary (pres. 1970-71, 82-83), Commonwealth Club, Meadowbrook Club. Jewish. Avocation: travel. Family and matrimonial, General practice, Property, real (including real estate development, water). Home: 4135 Crest Rd Pebble Beach CA 93953-3008 Office: Ste D 1123 Fremont Blvd Seaside CA 93955-5759 E-mail: lsm147@juno.com.

WEINIG, RICHARD ARTHUR, lawyer; b. Durango, Colo., Mar. 23, 1940; s. Arthur John and Edna (Novella) W.; m. Barbara A. Westerlund, June 16, 1964. BA in Polit. Sci., Stanford U., 1962, postgrad. in Soviet Studies, 1962-65; JD, U. Calif., San Francisco (Hastings), 1971. Bar: Alaska 1971, U.S. Dist. Ct. Alaska 1971, U.S. Ct. Appeals (9th cir.) 1978, U.S. Supreme Ct. 1979. Assoc. Burr, Pease & Kurtz, Anchorage, 1971-73, Greater Anchorage Area Borough, 1973-75, Municipality of Anchorage, 1975-82; ptnr. Pletcher & Slaybaugh, Anchorage, 1982-88, Pletcher, Weinig & Merriner, Anchorage, 1988-99, 1999—2001. Mem. editl. bd. Hastings Law Jour. Active Stanford U. Young Republicans, 1961-65, Sierra Club, Mountaineering Club, Knik Canoyers and Canoers of Alaska, Alaska Ctr. for Environ. Mem.: NRA (gunsite grad.), ABA, Anchorage Bar Assn., Alaska Bar Assn. Republican. Presbyterian. Condemnation (eminent domain), Insurance, Personal injury (including property damage). Office: Pletcher & Weinig 800 E Dimond Blvd Ste 3-615 Anchorage AK 99515-2045 Office Fax: 907-349-7758. E-mail: richard@akinsurancedefense.com.

WEINMAN, DARYL GAIL, lawyer; b. North Tarrytown, N.Y., Dec. 22, 1967; d. Lawrence S. Weinman and Serena Negrin Michelson; m. Donald Paul Morehart, July 19, 1997; children: Nathan Daniel Morehart, Benjamin Jake Morehart. BA, Colgate U., 1988; JD, N.Y. Law Sch., 1993. Bar: Tex. 1994, U.S. Dist. Ct. (we. dist.) Tex. 1994, U.S. Ct. Appeals (5th cir.) 1995, U.S. Supreme Ct. 1997, bd. cert. family law: 2000. Pvt. practice, Austin, Tex., 1994—2000; ptnr. Morehart and Weinman, Austin, 2000—. Vol. Sidelines, Austin, 1999—; mem. Jewish Cmty. Ctr., Austin, 1998—; local coord. Stepmothers Internat., Austin, 1999—. Mem.: Tex. Criminal Def. Lawyers Assn., Pro Bono Coll. State Bar, Estate Planning Coun. Cen. Tex., Coll. State Bar of Tex., State Bar Tex., Travis County Bar. Democrat. Jewish. Avocations: quilting, travel, children's activities. Family and matrimonial, Criminal, Probate (including wills, trusts). Office: Morehart and Weinman 821 W 11th St Austin TX 78701 Office Fax: 512-472-4086. E-mail: darylesq@aol.com.

WEINMAN, HOWARD MARK, lawyer; b. N.Y.C., May 6, 1947; s. Joseph and Kate (Dorn) Weinman; m. Pamela Eve Brodie, Jan. 6, 1980; children: David Lewis, Nathaniel Saul. BA magna cum laude, Columbia U., 1969; MPP, JD sum laude, Harvard U., 1973; LLM of Taxation highest honors, George Washington U., 1981. Assoc. Fried, Frank, Harris, Shriver & Kampelman, Washington and N.Y.C., 1973—78; legis. atty. Joint Com. on Taxation U.S. Congress, Washington, 1978—80; assoc. Sachs, Greenebaum & Tayler, Washington, 1980—82, Crowell & Moring LLP, Washington, 1982—84, ptnr., 1984—. Adj. prof. internat. tax Georgetown U. Law Ctr., Washington, 1988—89. Contbr. Mem.: ABA (taxation sect.), Kenwood Club, Phi Beta Kappa. Jewish. Corporate taxation. Home: 5404 Center St Bethesda MD 20815-7101 Office: Crowell & Moring LLP 1001 Pennsylvania Ave NW Fl 10 Washington DC 20004-2595

WEINMANN, RICHARD ADRIAN, lawyer, arbitrator; b. N.Y.C., Oct. 15, 1917; s. Randolph and Mae (Korber) W.; m. Bert Millicent Landes, Dec. 26, 1946; children: Harriet Joan, Elaine, Anita; m. Ginger Grace Rich, 1999. LLB, Bklyn. Law Sch., 1948; LLM, NYU, 1953. Bar: N.Y. 1958, U.S. Dist. Ct. (so. dist.) N.Y. 1960; U.S. Dist. Ct. (ea. dist.) N.Y. 1960, U.S. Ct. Appeals (2d cir.) 1965, U.S. Supreme Ct. 1964. Ptnr. Sipser, Weinstock & Weinmann, N.Y.C., 1953-71; sole practice N.Y.C., 1972—. Guest lectr. seminars; mem. staff Cornell U. Sch. Indsl. and Labor Relations; panel arbitrator Fed. Mediation and Conciliation Svc. Am. Arbitration Assn. Suffolk and Nassau Counties Pub. Employment Relations Bds. N.Y. State; N.Y. State Employment Rels. Bd. Committeeman Nassau County (N.Y.), 1965—; former mem. legal adv. bd. Union Lawyers Ednl. Conf. Served with AUS, 1943-46. Mem. ABA, ACLU, VFW, N.Y. State Bar Assn., Indsl. Rels. Rsch. Assn., B'nai B'rith. General practice, Labor (including EEOC, Fair Labor Standards Act, labor-management relations, NLRB, OSHA).

WEINSCHEL, ALAN JAY, lawyer; b. Bklyn., Feb. 9, 1946; m. Barbara Ellen Schure, Aug. 20, 1967; children: Lawrence, Adam, Naomi. BA, Bklyn. Coll., 1967; JD, NYU, 1969. Bar: N.Y. 1970, U.S. Dist. Ct. (so. and ea. dists.) N.Y. 1973, U.S. Ct. Appeals (2d cir.) 1979, U.S. Ct. Appeals (9th cir.) 1986, U.S. Ct. Appeals (3d cir.) 1993, U.S. Ct. Appeals (7th cir.) 1996. Assoc. Breed, Abbott & Morgan, N.Y.C., 1969-74, Weil, Gotshal & Manges, N.Y.C., 1974-78, ptnr., 1978—. Lectr. Practising Law Inst., Ohio Legal Ctr., Am. Mgmt. Assn., Law Jour. Seminars, Law and Bus. Seminars, Glasser Legalworks, Insight Seminars, Mfrs.' Alliance. Author: Antitrust Intellectual Property Handbook, 2000. Trustee N.Y. Inst. Tech., Old Westbury, N.Y., 1969-76, Temple Sinai, Roslyn, N.Y., 1981-87, 89-95. Capt. U.S. Army res., 1969-74. Mem. ABA (editl. bd. Antitrust Devels. 1981-87), N.Y. State Bar Assn. (chmn. antitrust sect. 1993-95), Assn. Bar of City of N.Y. Antitrust, General civil litigation, Intellectual property. Office: Weil Gotshal & Manges 767 5th Ave New York NY 10153-0119

WEINSCHELBAUM, EMILIO, lawyer; b. Rosario, Argentina, Oct. 25, 1935; s. Marcos Leib and Elka (Werbin) W.; m. Marina Lucila Scornik, Dec. 20, 1962; children: Fernando, Violeta. Student, Columbia U., 1952-53; Atty. at Law, Universidad Nacional, Buenos Aires, 1957, sociologist, 1975; postgrad., U. Sorbonne, Paris, 1978. Pvt. practice, Buenos Aires, 1957—. Personal del. from Pres. Alfonsin to Europe-Latin Am. Congress, Strasbourg, France, 1988; organizer Congreso Internacional sobre Reforma Constitucional, Buenos Aires, 1988. Editor, legal advisor Primera Plana newsmag., 1962-64; editor Plural newsmag., 1984—, El Ciudadano newsmag., 1988-89; editor: (TV program) Los Argentinos, 1987 (Martin Fierro award 1987). Pres. Fundacion Plural para la Participacion Democratica, Buenos Aires, 1984—; mem. Coun. for Consolidation of Democracy, Buenos Aires, 1985-89, Nat. Com. Politics and Strategies of Democracy, 1997—. Mem. Colegio Publico de Abogados de Buenos Aires, Fundacion Compromiso Ciudadano, Fundacion del Alvear (pres. 1999—), Club del Progreso (v.p. 1999—). Office: Av Santa Fe 900 piso 6 1059 Buenos Aires Argentina

WEINSTEIN, ALAN EDWARD, lawyer; b. Bklyn., Apr. 20, 1945; s. John and Matilda W.; m. Patti Kantor, Dec. 18, 1965; children: Steven R., David A. AA, U. Fla., 1964; BBA, U. Miami, Fla., 1965, JD cum laude, 1968. Bar: Fla. 1968, U.S. Dist. Ct. (so. dist.) Fla. 1968, U.S. Ct. Appeals (5th cir.) 1969, U.S. Supreme Ct. 1973, U.S. Ct. Appeals (4th & 11th cirs.) 1981. Assoc. Cohen & Hogan, Miami Beach, Fla., 1968-71; pvt. practice Miami Beach, 1972-81; sr. ptnr. Weinstein & Preira, Miami Beach, 1981-92; prin. Law Offices of Alan E. Weinstein, Miami, 1992—. Lectr. in field. Mem. ABA (criminal and family law sect. 1968—, white collar crime commn. 1986—), Nat. Assn. Criminal Def. Lawyers, 1st Family Law Am. Inn of Court, Fla. Bar Assn. (criminal and family law sect. 1968—, ethics com. 1987-88, bench/bar com. 1988-89, grievance com. 1999-2002, chmn. 2002, unlicensed practice of law com. 2002—), Fla. Criminal Def. Attys. Assn. (pres. 1978-79), Fla. Assn. Criminal Def. Lawyers (treas. 1989-90), Miami Beach Bar Assn., Soc. Wig and Robe, Phi Kappa Phi. Avocations: marlin fishing, reading, travel. Criminal, Family and matrimonial. Office: 1801 West Ave Miami FL 33139-1431 E-mail: defense1@bellsouth.net.

WEINSTEIN, ANDREW H. lawyer; b. Pitts., Oct. 5, 1943; s. Adolph J. and Meta I. (Schwarz) W.; m. Susan Balber, Aug. 11, 1968; children: Jodi L., Toby M., Jamie M. BSBA, Duquesne U., 1965; JD, U. Pitts., 1968; LLM in Tax Law, NYU, 1969. Bar: Pa. 1969, U.S. Tax Ct. 1969, Fla. 1970, U.S. Dist. Ct. (so. dist.) Fla., U.S. Ct. Fed. Claims. Trial atty. IRS, L.A., 1969-70, Miami, Fla., 1970-73; ptnr. Glass, Schultz, Weinstein & Moss, Coral Gables, Fla., 1973-80, Holland & Knight, Miami, 1980—. Contbr. articles to profl. jours. Bd. dirs. New World Symphony, Miami, Performing Arts Found., Zool. Soc. Fla. Fellow Am. Coll. Tax Counsel; mem. ABA (tax sect. com., chmn. subcom. 1981-87, chmn. CLE subcom., adminstrv. practice com., chmn. chief coun. liaison subcom.), The Fla. Bar Assn. Republican. Avocations: golf, swimming, travel. Corporate taxation, Estate taxation, Personal income taxation. Office: Holland & Knight 701 Brickell Ave Ste 3000 Miami FL 33131-2898

WEINSTEIN, ARTHUR GARY, lawyer; b. NYC, May 11, 1946; s. Jacob and Ada (Ambutter) W.; m. Judith Marilyn Rothstein, Dec. 24, 1969; children: Stephen, Marc. BA, Bklyn. Coll., 1967; JD, U. Pa., 1970. Bar: N.Y. 1971, N.J. 1977, U.S. Dist. Ct. (so. dist.) N.Y. 1973, U.S. Dist. Ct. N.J. 1977, U.S. Ct. Appeals (2d cir.) 1972, U.S. Supreme Ct. 1973. Asst. dist. atty. New York County, 1970-74, 85-86; asst. counsel Office of Ct. Adminstrn., N.Y., 1974-76; spl. asst. atty. gen. Dep. Atty. Gen.'s Office, N.Y.C., 1976—2001, counsel, 1981-85, spl. counsel, 1989-95; spl. asst. dist. atty. Monroe County, 2001—. Editor U. Pa. Law Sch. Yearbook Report, 1969-70. Business E-Mail: aweinstein@monroecounty.gov.

WEINSTEIN, DAVID AKERS, lawyer; b. Denver, Apr. 9, 1942; s. Sam and Rowena May (Akers) W.; m. Gayle Ann Sunshine. BA, U. Colo., 1963; JD, U. Denver, 1967. Bar: Colo. 1967, N.Y. 1970, Ohio 1972, Wis. 1993, U.S. Dist. Ct. Colo., U.S. Ct. Appeals (10th and fed. cirs.). Atty. U.S. Patent and Trademark Office, Washington, 1967-70, Gen. Foods Corp., White Plains, N.Y., 1970-71, Borden Inc., Columbus, Ohio, 1971-77; pvt. practice Denver, 1977-91; atty.-spl. counsel Reinhart, Boerner Van Deuren Norris & Rieselbach, Denver, 1991-94, Holme, Roberts & Owen, Denver, 1994-96; ptnr. Dorsey & Whitney, Denver, 1996-97. Legal cons. Republic of Bulgaria Patent Office, Sofia, 1996, Govt. of Egypt Trademark Office, Cairo, 1997-2002, Govt. of Jordan Ministry of Industry and Trade, 1999, Fed. Republic of Yugoslavia Intellectual Property Office, 2001—; mediator, mem. CPR/INTA Panel of Mediators. Author: How to Protect Your Creative Work, 1987, How to Protect Your Business, Professional & Brand Names, 1990. Past pres., bd. dirs. Colo. Lawyers for the Arts, Denver. Mem. Am. Intellectual Property Law Assn., Copyright Soc. U.S.A., Internat. Trademark Assn. Trademark and copyright. Office: Ste 2600 1600 Broadway Denver CO 80202-4989

WEINSTEIN, HARRIS, lawyer; b. Providence, May 10, 1935; s. Joseph and Gertrude (Rusitzky) W.; m. Rosa Grunberg, June 3, 1956; children: Teme Ring, Joshua, Jacob. BS in Math., MIT, 1956, MS in Math., 1958; LLB, Columbia U., 1961. Bar: D.C. 1962. Law clk. to Judge William H. Hastie U.S. Ct. Appeals (3d cir.), Phila., 1961-62; with Covington & Burling, Washington, 1962-67, 69-90, 1993—; chief counsel Office of Thrift Supervision U.S. Dept. of Treasury, Washington, 1990-92; asst. to solicitor gen. U.S. Dept. Justice, 1967-69. Pub. mem. Adminstrv. Conf. of U.S., 1982-90; lectr. U. Va. Law Sch., 1996; mgmt. com. Undiscovered Mgrs., LLC, 1998-2001. V.p. Jewish Social Svc. Agy., 1995-98; mem. MIT Corp., 1989-95. Mem. Nat. Press Club. Banking, General civil litigation. Home: 7717 Georgetown Pike Mc Lean VA 22102-1411 Office: Covington & Burling 1201 Pennsylvania Ave NW Washington DC 20004

WEINSTEIN, JACK BERTRAND, federal judge; b. Wichita, Kans., Aug. 10, 1921; s. Harry Louis and Bessie Helen (Brodach) W.; m. Evelyn Horowitz, Oct. 10, 1946; children: Seth George, Michael David, Howard Lewis. BA, Bklyn. Coll., 1943; LLB, Columbia, 1948; LLD (hon.), Bklyn. Law Sch., Yeshiva U., Albany Law Sch., Hofstra Law Sch., L.I. U., Yale U., NY Law Sch. Bar: N.Y. 1949. Assoc. Columbia Law Sch., 1948-49; law clk. N.Y. Ct. Appeals Judge Stanly H. Fuld, 1949-50; ptnr. William Rosenfeld, N.Y.C., 1950-52; mem. faculty Columbia Law Sch., 1952-67, prof. law, 1956-67, adj. prof., 1967-97; U.S. judge (Eastern Dist. N.Y.), 1967-93, chief judge, 1980-88; sr. judge Ea. Dist. N.Y., 1993—. Vis. prof. U. Tex., 1957, U. Colo., 1961, Harvard U., 1982, Georgetown U., 1991, Bklyn. Law Sch., 1988-97, others; counsel N.Y. Joint Legis. Com. Motor Vehicle Problems, 1952-54, State Sen. Seymour Halpern, 1952-54; reporter adv. com. practice and procedure N.Y. State Temp. Commn. Cts., 1955-58; adv. com. practice N.Y. Judicial Conf., 1963-66; adv. com. rules of evidence U.S. Jud. Conf., 1965-75, mem. com. jurisdiction, 1969-75, mem., 1983-86; mem. 2d Cir. Jud. Coun., 1982-88, U.S. Jud. Conf., 1983-86, others in past. Author: (with Morgan and Maquire) Cases and Materials on Evidence, 4th edit, 1965, (with Maguire, Chadbourne and Mansfield, 5th edit.), 1971, 6th edit., 1975, (with Mansfield, Abrams and Berger), 9th edit., 1997, (with Rosenberg) Cases and Materials on Civil Procedure, 1961, rev. edit, (with Smit), 1971, (with Smit, Rosenberg and Korn), 1976, (with Korn and Miller) New York Civil Procedure, 9 vols., rev. edit, 1966, Manual of New York Civil Procedure, 1967, Basic Problems of State and Federal Evidence, 1976, (with Berger) Weinstein's Evidence, 7 vols., 1967, rev. edit., 1993, Revising Rule Making Procedures, 1977, A New York Constitution Meeting Today's Needs and Tomorrow's Challenges, 1967, Disaster, A Legal Allegory, 1988, (with Greenawalt) Readings for Seminar on Equality and Law, 1979, (with Murphy) Readings for Seminar in Individual Rights in a Mass Society, 1990-91, (with Berger) Readings for Seminar in Science and Law, (with Feinberg) Mass Torts, 1992, 94, Individual Justice in Mass Litigation, 1995. Chmn. N.Y. Dem. adv. com. on Constl. Conv., 1955; bd. dirs. N.Y. Civil Liberties Union, 1956-62, Cardozo Sch. Law, Conf. on Jewish Social Studies, 1980-88; nat. adv. bd. Am. Jewish Congress, 1960-67, CARE, 1985-90, Fedn. Jewish Philanthropies, 1985-94; chmn. lay bd. Riverside Hosp. Adolescent Drug Users, 1954-55. Lt. USNR, 1943-46. Mem. ABA, N.Y. State Bar Assn., Assn. of Bar of City of N.Y., Nassau County Bar Assn., Am. Law Inst., Soc. Pub. Tchrs. Law (Eng.), Am. Acad. Arts and Scis. Jewish. Office: US Dist Ct US Courthouse 225 Cadman Plz E Brooklyn NY 11201-1818

WEINSTEIN, RUTH JOSEPH, lawyer; b. N.Y.C., Mar. 26, 1933; d. David Arthur and Toby (Landau) J.; m. Marvin Walter Weinstein, June 3, 1962; children: Rosalyn S., Steven M., Barbara E. AB magna cum laude, Radcliffe Coll., 1954; LLB, Harvard U., 1957. Bar: N.Y. 1957, D.C. 1966. Assoc. Hale Russell & Gray and predecessor firms, N.Y.C., 1957-66, ptnr., 1966-85, Winthrop Stimson Putnam & Roberts, N.Y.C., 1985-98, sr. counsel, 1999-2000, Pillsbury Winthrop, N.Y.C., 2000—. Chairperson Practising Law Inst. Forum, N.Y.C., 1978. Mem. sch. bd. Union Free Sch. Dist. 5, Rye Town, N.Y., 1976-79, pres., 1978-79; mem. The Friends of Crawford Park. Mem. ABA, Assn. of Bar of City of N.Y. (com. on Aeronautics Assn. 1987-90), Harvard-Radcliffe Club of Westchester. Avocations: boating, skiing. Home: 21 Meadowlark Rd Rye Brook NY 10573-1209 Office: Pillsbury Winthrop 1 Battery Park Plz New York NY 10004-1490

WEINSTEIN-BACAL, STUART ALLEN, lawyer, educator; b. Stuttgart, Germany, May 23, 1948; s. Marvin Stuart and Mae (Beal) W.; m. Holly Laurette Thompson, Aug. 7, 1982; children: Rachel Lee, Maximillian II, Sarah Nicole. BA, U. Va., 1970, MEd, 1973; JD cum laude, U. Miami, 1979. Bar: D.C. 1979, Va. 1981, V.I. 1985, P.R. 1988. Tchr., pvt. tutor various schs., Conn., Fla., Costa Rica, 1973-76; mem. prof. staff Merchant Marine and Fisheries Com. U.S. Ho. of Reps., Washington, 1978; assoc. Cameron, Hornbostel & Adelman, Washington, 1979-80, Burch, Kerns & Klimek, PC, Washington, 1980-81; staff atty. C.A.C.I., Washington, 1982-83; sr. assoc. Dudley, Dudley & Topper, St. Thomas, U.S. Virgin Islands, 1984-85; v.p. , gen. counsel Redondo Construction Corp., San Juan, PR, 1985-89; founder Indiano, Williams & Weinstein-Bacal, San Juan, PR, 1989-2000; owner Weinstein-Bacal & Assocs., P.S.C., Old San Juan, PR, 2000—. Contbr. articles to profl. jours. Capt. USAR, 1970-85. Mem. ABA, Am. Arbitration Assn. (pres., Caribbean region adv. coun. 1988—, arbitrator 1989—), Res. Officers Assn., Colegio de Abogados de P.R., U. Va. Alumni Assn., Nature Conservancy, Sovereign Order of the Oak (knight comdr.), Rotary Club of San Juan (bd. dirs. 1991-95), Middleburg Tennis Club, Bankers Club P.R., Phi Alpha Delta. Avocations: sailing, golf, tennis, riding, gourmet cooking, travel. Federal civil litigation, Commercial, contracts (including sales of goods; commercial financing), Construction. Home: Villas Del Mar E # 7D Carolina PR 00979 also: Mallory Chase Farm 35919 Turkey Roost Rd Middleburg VA 20117-3401 Office: Gonzalez Padin Bldg-Penthouse 154 Rafael Cordero St Plz Armas Old San Juan PR 00901 E-mail: sawbacal@aol.com.

WEINSTOCK, ALLISON SHIFF, lawyer; b. New Haven, Conn., Nov. 22, 1971; m. David Keith Weinstock. BA honors, U. Tex. Austin, 1993; JD, U. Ariz., 1996. Bar: Ariz. 1996, U.S. Dist. Ct. Ariz. 1999. Intern Hufford, Horstman, McCullough and Mongini, Flagstaff, Ariz., 1995, Atty. Gen. Office, Tucson, 1996; jud. clk. Ariz. Ct. Appeals, Phoenix, 1996—98; assoc. Mariscal, Weeks, McIntyre and Friedlander, Phoenix, 1998—. Kellogg Child Welfare fellow, U. Mich., 1995. Mem.: Maricopa County Bar Assn. (co-chair law week 1998—2000, Young Lawyers divsn. bd. dirs., family law sect.). Family and matrimonial. Office: Mariscal Weeks McIntyre and Friedlander 2901 N Central Ste 200 Phoenix AZ 85012

WEINSTOCK, HAROLD, lawyer; b. Stamford, Conn., Nov. 30, 1925; s. Elias and Sarah (Singer) W.; m. Barbara Lans, Aug. 27, 1950; children—Nathaniel, Michael, Philip. BS magna cum laude, N.Y. U., 1947; JD, Harvard, 1950. Bar: Conn. bar 1950, Ill. bar 1950, Calif. bar 1958. Atty. SEC, Washington, 1950-52, IRS, 1952-56; tax atty. Hunt Foods & Industries, Inc., Los Angeles, 1956-58; pvt. practice Beverly Hills, Calif., 1958-71, Los Angeles, 1971—; mem. Weinstock, Manion, Reisman, Shore & Neumann (and predecessor firms), 1958—. Lectr. extension div., estate planning courses U. Calif. at Los Angeles, 1959—86; estate planning and taxation courses Calif. Continuing Edn. of the Bar, 1960-87. Author: Planning An Estate, 4th edit., 2002; contbr. articles to profl. publs. Nat. trustee Union Am. Hebrew Congregations, 1976-79; trustee Jewish Cmty. Found., L.A., 1993-99; adv. bd. Estate Planning Inst. UCLA Law Sch., 1979-92, NYU Inst. on Fed. Taxation, 1986-95. Mem. ABA, Calif. Bar Assn., Beverly Hills Bar Assn. (chmn. probate and trusts com. 1967-68), Los Angeles Bar Assn., Beverly Hills Estate Planning Council (pres. 1968-69), Estate Counselors Forum of Los Angeles (pres. 1963-64) Jewish (pres. temple 1974-76). Estate planning, Probate (including wills, trusts), Estate taxation. Office: Weinstock Manion 1875 Century Park E Fl 15 Los Angeles CA 90067-2501

WEINSTOCK, LEONARD, lawyer; b. Bklyn., Aug. 18, 1935; s. Samuel Morris and Evelyn (Reiser) W.; m. Rita Lee Itkowitz, May 25, 1963; children: Gregg Douglas, Valerie Lisa, Tara Diane. BS, Bklyn. Coll., 1956; JD, St. John's U., Bklyn., 1959. Bar: N.Y. 1961, U.S. Supreme Ct. 1964, U.S. Ct. Appeals (2d cir.) 1963, U.S. Dist. Ct. (ea. and so. dists.) N.Y. 1963, U.S. Tax Ct. 1963. Assoc. Bernard Helfenstein law practice, Bklyn., 1962-63; supr. All State Ins. Co., Bklyn., 1963-64; atty. Hertz Corp., N.Y.C., 1964-65; ptnr. Nicholas & Weinstock, Flushing, N.Y., 1965-68; v.p., ptnr. Garbarini & Scher, P.C., N.Y.C., 1968—. Lectr. Practicing Law Inst., N.Y.C., 1975—; arbitrator Nassau County Dist. Ct., Mineola, N.Y., 1979—, U.S. Dist. Ct. (ea. dist.) N.Y. 1986—; mem. Med. Malpractice Mediation Panel, Mineola, 1978—. Legal counsel Massapequa Soccer Club, N.Y., 1981—; county committeeman Dem. Party, Massapequa Park, N.Y., 1979—. With U.S. Army, 1959-62. Mem. ABA, N.Y. State Bar Assn., Nassau County Bar Assn. (mem. med. jurisprudence ins. com. 1978), N.Y. Trial Lawyers Assn. Avocations: stamp collecting, softball, racquetball. Federal civil litigation, State civil litigation, Personal injury (including property damage). Home: 38 Barstow Rd Great Neck NY 11021-2218 Office: Garbarini and Scher PC 432 Park Ave S New York NY 10016-8013

WEINTRAUB, RUSSELL JAY, lawyer, educator; b. N.Y.C., Dec. 20, 1929; s. Harry and Alice (Lieberman) W.; m. Zelda Kresshover, Sept. 6, 1953; children— Sharon Hope, Harry David, Steven Ross. BA, NYU, 1950; JD, Harvard U., 1953. Bar: N.Y. 1955, Iowa 1961, Tex. 1980. Tchg. fellow Harvard U. Law Sch., 1955-57; asst. prof. law U. Iowa, 1957-61, prof., 1961-65, U. Tex., 1965—, Marrs McLean prof. law, 1970-80, Bryant Smith chmn., 1980-82, John B. Connally chmn., 1982-98, Powell chmn., 1998—. Vis. prof. law U. Mich., 1965, UCLA, 1967, U. Calif., Berkeley, 1973-74, Bklyn. Law Sch., 1990, 95, Inst. Internat. Comparative Law, Paris, 1975, Florence, Italy, 1997, Barcelona, 1999, 2002, London, 2000, U. Houston, 1979-80, Inst. Internat. and Comparative Law, Oxford, Eng., 1982-83, 86-87, 92, 2003, Dublin, Ireland, 1991, La. State U., Aix-en-Provence, France, 1993, Tulane U., Spetses, Greece, 1998, Australian Nat. U., 2001; Ronald Graveson Meml. lectr. King's Coll., London, 2000; lectr. Hague Acad. Internat. Law, 1984; cons. U.S. Dept. State, 1995—; cons. in field. Author: International Litigation and Arbitration, 1994, 3d revised edit., 2001, ann. supplement; (with Eugene Scoles) Cases and Materials on the Conflict of Laws, 1967, 2d rev. edit., 1972, supplement, 1978, Commentary on the Conflict of Laws, 1971, 4th rev. edit., 2000, ann. supplement; (with Hamilton and Rau) Cases and Materials on Contracts, 1984, 2d rev. edit., 1992; (with Hay and Borchers) Cases and Materials on the Conflict of Laws, 11th rev. edit., 2000, annual supplement; contbr. articles to profl. jours. Trustee U. Iowa Sch. Religion, 1960-65. With U.S. Army, 1953-55. Recipient Disting. Prof. award U. Tex. Sch. Law, 1977, Teaching Excellence award, 1979, cert. of meritorious service Am. Bar Assn., 1977, cert. of meritorious service Tex. Bar Assn., 1978, Best Tchr. award U. Houston, 1980, Carl Fulda award scholarship in internat. law, 1993. Mem. Am. Law Inst., Am. Bar Found. (life), Tex. Bar Found., Scribes. Jewish. Office: U Tex Sch Law 727 E Dean Keeton Austin TX 78705-3224 E-mail: rweintraub@mail.law.utexas.edu.

WEIR, PETER FRANK, lawyer; b. Mar. 26, 1933; s. Robert Henry and Ruth Sophie W.; m. Jean M., Sept. 27, 1958; children: Bradford F., Elizabeth A. BA, Williams Coll., 1955; LLB, Harvard U., 1958; MBA, N.Y.U., 1967. Bar: N.Y. 1959, Ga. 1957. Assoc. Winston & Strawn (formerly Cole and Deitz), N.Y.C., 1959-66; ptnr., 1966-92; ret. ptnr., 1992; pvt. practice, 1993—; chmn., CEO Northeast Internat. Soya, Inc., 1980—. Bd. dirs. Episc. Ch. Found., 1981-93, sec., 1989-93, also treas., chn. fin. com., 1982-89, chmn. audit com., 1982-88; mem. exec. com. N.Y. Regional Coun., 1975-81, chmn. 1979-81, mem. steering com., 1981-93; mem. adv. bd. First Am. Title Ins. Co. of N.Y., Inc., 1984-95. Bd. dirs., counsel Point O'Woods Assn., N.Y., 1976-91, v.p., 1982-91; alt. bd. dirs. Fire Island Assn., 1976-86, 92—; sec. and dir. Elderworks Found., 1982-92; dir. Episc. Preaching Found., 1995—; sec. and dir. The Point O'Woods Cmty. Trust, Inc., 1998—. Served with Air N.G., 1958-63. Mem. ABA, Internat. Bar Assn., N.Y. State Bar Assn., Assn. of Bar of City of N.Y., Church Club (trustee 1988-91), Downtown Assn. Club, Williams Club, Club at Point O'Woods (v.p., gov. 1970-79), Hillsboro Club. Republican. Probate (including wills, trusts), Property, real (including real estate development, water). Home: 49 E 86th St Apt 12C New York NY 10028-1060 Office: 49 E 86th St New York NY 10017

WEIR, ROBERT H. lawyer; b. Boston, Dec. 7, 1922; s. Abraham and Beatrice (Stern) W.; A.B., Harvard U., 1944, LL.B., 1948; m. Ruth Hirsch, July 2, 1954 (dec. Nov. 1965); children— Anthony, David, Michael H.; m. 2d, Sylvia T. Frias; children— Nicole F., Daniella F. Admitted to Mass. bar, 1948, Wash. bar, 1952, Calif. bar, 1957; spl. asst. to atty. gen. U.S. Dept. Justice, Seattle, 1948-53, Washington, 1953-56; practiced in San Jose, also Palo Alto, Calif., 1957— . Instr. taxation of real estate U. Calif. at San Jose and San Francisco, 1957— ; lectr. U. So. Calif. Tax Inst. Mem. prison com. Am. Friends Service Com. Bd. dirs. San Jose Light Opera Assn., Inc. Served with U.S. Army, 1942-45. CEO, Villa Tita Group, 1974-2001. Mem. Am., Santa Clara County bar assns., State Bar Calif., Am. Judicature Soc. Author: Advantages in Taxes, 1960. Tax columnist Rural Realtor, Chgo., 1959— . Speaker taxation annual meetings Nat. Assn. Real Estate Bds., 1958-60. Author: Taxes Working for You, 1966; How to Make the Most of Depreciation Write Off. Contbr. articles to profl. jours. E-mail: aveces@aol.com. Antitrust, Estate planning, Taxation, general. Address: 27743 Via Ventana Los Altos CA 94022-3241

WEIR, WILLIAM H. lawyer, judge, educator; b. East Orange, N.J., Mar. 16, 1947; s. William F. and Nela (Stinnett) W.; m. Marilyn Fowler, Dec. 6, 1969; 1 child, William Bradley. B.S., Eastern Ill. U., 1969; J.D., John Marshall Law Sch., 1977. Bar: Ill. 1977, U.S. Dist. Ct. (no. dist.) Ill. 1977. Field rep. Aetna Casualty, Chgo., 1972-76; assoc. Tomlinson & Thomas, Arlington Heights, Ill., 1976-77; ptnr. Brittain, Ketcham, Strass, Terlizzi, Flanagan, Weir & Johnson, P.C., Elgin, Ill., 1977—2003; prof. bus. law Elgin Community Coll., 1980—89; judge 16th Judicial Cir., 2003—. Author Tort Law Newsletter, 1981. Pres., Elgin YMCA, 1982-84. Served to capt. USMC, 1967-72. Mem. Assn. Trial Lawyers Am., Ill. Trial Lawyers Assn., ABA, Ill. State Bar Assn. (speaker, co-editor tort laws newsletter 1981-83), Kane County Bar Assn. (treas., civil practice com., speaker), Navy League, Am. Legion. Lodge: Kiwanis (Elgin). State civil litigation, Insurance, Personal injury (including property damage). Home: 41w058 Kingston Ct Saint Charles IL 60175-8432 Office: Kane County Judicial Ctr 37W777 Rte 38 Saint Charles IL 60175

WEIR, WILLIAM JOHN ARNOLD, lawyer; b. Phoenix, June 22, 1939; s. Arnold Miller and Jane (Kimmel) W.; m. Diana McGee, June 20, 1959; children— Derek Anthony, Brandon Kimmel, Donovan John Alan; m. 2d, Susan Armstrong Smith, Oct. 6, 1977; 1 dau., Robyn Smith. B.S., U. Calif.-Berkeley, 1965; J.D., U. Calif.-San Francisco, 1968. Bar: Calif. 1969, U.S. Dist. Ct. (no. dist.) Calif. 1969, U.S. Ct. Appeals (9th cir.) 1969, Dist. Ct. ct. (ea. dist.) Calif. 1971, U.S. Supreme Ct. 1980, U.S. Dist. Ct. (cen. dist.) Calif. 1982, U.S. Ct. Claims, 1975. Asst. gen. counsel Bank of Am., San Francisco, 1969-76; ptnr. Murphy, Weir & Butler, San Francisco, 1976-98; ptnr. Luce, Forward, Hamilton & Scripps, 1998—. Author: California Continuing Education of the Bar. Served in USMCR, 1957-65. Mem. ABA, Calif. Bar Assn., San Francisco Bar Assn. (chmn. comml. law and bankruptcy sect. 1980-82). Clubs: Commonwealth, St. Francis Yacht Club, Pacific-Union Club. Bankruptcy, Federal civil litigation, State civil litigation. Office: 121 Spear St Ste 200 San Francisco CA 94105

WEIS, JOSEPH FRANCIS, JR., federal judge; b. Pitts., Mar. 12, 1923; s. Joseph Francis and Mary (Flaherty) Weis; m. Margaret Horne Weis, Dec. 27, 1958; children: Maureen, Joseph Francis, Christine. BA, Duquesne U., 1941—47; JD, U. Pitts., 1950; LLD (hon.) , Dickinson Coll., 1989. Bar: Pa. 1950. Pvt. practice, Pitts., 1950—68; judge Ct. Common Pleas, Allegheny County, Pa., 1968—70, U.S. Dist. Ct. (we. dist.), Pa., 1970—73, U.S. Ct. Appeals (3d cir.), Pitts., 1973—88, sr. judge, 1988—. Lectr. trial procedures, 1965—; adj. prof. law U. Pitts., 1986—; chmn. Fed. Cts. Study Com., Jud. Conf. Com. on Experiment to Videotape Trial Proceedings within the 3rd Cir., Internat. Jud. Conf. the Joint Am.-Can. Appellate Judges Conf., Toronto, 1986, London, 85; futurist subcom. bicentennial com. Ct. Common Pleas, Allegheny County, Pa., 1988; participant programs legal medicine, Rome, London; mem. Am.-Can. Legal Exch., 1987; apptd. by Chief Justice Rehnquist U.S. Jud. Conf., Com. on Internat. Jud. Rels., 1998—2004; com. on adminstrn. bankruptcy sys., subcom. on jud. improvements Jud. Conf. U.S., 1983—87, chmn. civil rules com., 1986—87, chmn. standing com. rules of practice and procedure, 1988. Contbr. articles to profl. jours. Active Mental Health and Mental Retardation Bd., Allegheny County, 1970—73, Leukemia Soc., 1970—73, Disabled Am. Vets., Cath. War Vets, Mil. Order of the World Wars; trustee Forbes Hosp. Sys., Pitts., 1969—74; bd. adminstrn. Cath. Diocese Pitts., 1971—83. Capt. U.S. Army, 1943—48. Decorated Bronze Star, Purple Heart with oak leaf cluster; recipient St. Thomas More award, 1971, Phillip Amram award, 1991, Edward J. Devitt Disting. Svc. to Justice award, 1993, History Makers award, 1997. Fellow: Am. Bar Found., Internat. Acad. Trial Lawyers (hon.); mem.: ABA (chmn. appellate judges' conf. 1981—83), Inst. Jud. Adminstrn., Am. Judicature Soc., Acad. Trial Lawyers Allegheny County (past pres.), Allegheny Bar Assn. (past v.p.), Pa. Bar Assn., 4th Armored Divsn. Assn., Am. Legion, Knights of Malta, KC. Home: 225 Hillcrest Rd Pittsburgh PA 15238-2307 Office: US Ct Appeals US PO & Courthouse 7th & Grant St Rm 219 Pittsburgh PA 15219

WEISBERG, ADAM JON, lawyer; b. Cocoa Beach, Fla., June 5, 1963; s. Melvin H. Weisberg and Joan Julie (Carney) Vargo; m. Cheryl Lynn Scupp, June 25, 1994. BS in Bus. Econs., Rider Coll., 1985; JD, N.Y. Law Sch., 1988. Bar: N.Y. 1989, N.J. 1989, U.S. Dist. Ct. 1989, Fla. 1991. Law clk., asst. prosecutor Middlesex County Prosecutors Office, New Brunswick, N.J., 1988-90; workers' compensation atty. Levinson Axelrod Wheaton, Edison, N.J., 1990-91; trial atty. workers compensation Richard J. Simon, Esq., New Brunswick, 1991-92; pvt. practice lawyer New Brunswick, 1992—; pres. Asbury Music Co., Belmar, N.J. Mem. ABA, N.J. Bar Assn., Middlesex County Bar Assn., Monmouth County Bar Assn., Assn. Criminal Def. Lawyers. Avocations: fishing, surfing. Criminal, Personal injury (including property damage), Workers' compensation. Office: Monmouth Exec Plz II 1300 Highway 35 Ste 201 Ocean NJ 07712-3531 also: 200 Livingston Ave New Brunswick NJ 08901-2152

WEISBERG, DAVID CHARLES, lawyer; b. N.Y.C., June 25, 1938; s. Leonard Joseph and Rae M. (Kimberg) W.; m. Linda Gail Kerman, Aug. 27, 1975; children: Leonard Jay, Risa Beth. AB, U. Mich., 1958; LLB, Harvard U., 1961. Bar: N.Y. 1962, U.S. Dist. Ct. (so. and ea. dists.) N.Y. 1965, U.S. Supreme Ct. 1970. Assoc. Dreyer & Traub, Bklyn., 1962, Lee Franklin, Mineola, N.Y., 1962-65; pvt. practice, Patchogue, N.Y., 1965-67, 77-80; ptnr. Bass & Weisberg, Patchogue, 1967-77, Davidow, Davidow, Russo & Weisberg, Patchogue, 1981-82, Davidow, Davidow, Weisberg & Wismann, Patchogue, 1982-87, Davidow, Davidow & Wismann, Patchogue, 1988-92, Weisberg & Wismann, Patchogue, 1992-98; propr. The Lawyer's Equalizer, 2000—. Assoc. justice and justice Village of Patchogue, 1968-70, village atty., 1970-85; spl. asst. dist. atty. Suffolk County, Patchogue, 1970-85; assoc. estate tax atty., appraiser N.Y. State Dept. Taxation and Fin., Hauppauge, N.Y., 1975-85; lectr. estate tax Suffolk County Acad. Law, 1976-84, negligence law, 1994; cons. in field. Law chmn. Suffolk County Dem. Com., N.Y., 1975-85; bd. dirs. Temple Beth El of Patchogue. With USAR, 1961-62. Mem. ATLA, N.Y. State Bar Assn., Suffolk County Bar Assn., Nassau-Suffolk Trial Lawyers Sect., Lions (pres. Medford 1978-79, 2d v.p. 1984-85). Avocations: bicycling, skiing. Appellate, General civil litigation, Estate planning. E-mail: dcw@lawyersequalizer.com., dcw608@yahoo.com.

WEISBERGER, JOSEPH ROBERT, retired judge; b. Providence, Aug. 3, 1920; s. Samuel Joseph and Ann Elizabeth (Meighan) W.; m. Sylvia Blanche Pigeon, June 9, 1951; children: Joseph Robert, Paula Ann, Judith Marie. AB, Brown U., 1942; JD, Harvard U., 1949; LLD (hon.) , R.I. Coll., Suffolk U., Mt. St. Joseph Coll.; DCL (hon.) , Providence Coll.; DHL (hon.) , Bryant Coll.; LLD (hon.) , Roger Williams Coll., 1992; LLD (hon.) , Brown U., 1992, Constantine U., 1997; LLD, So. New England Sch. Law, 1998; DHL (hon.) , Salve Regina U., 2001. Bar: Mass. 1949, R.I. 1950. With Quinn & Quinn, Providence, 1951-56; solicitor Glocester, R.I., 1953-56; judge Superior Ct. R.I., Providence, 1956-72; presiding justice R.I. Superior Ct., Providence, 1972-78; justice R.I. Supreme Ct., Providence, 1978—, chief justice, 1993—2001; ret., 2001. Adj. prof. U. Nev., 1986—; mem. faculty Nat. Jud. Coll.; vis. lectr. Providence Coll., Suffolk Law Sch., Roger Williams Coll.; Chmn. New Eng. Regional Conf. Trial Judges, 1962, 63, 65; chmn. New Eng. Regional Commn. Disordered Offender, 1968-71, R.I. Com. Adoption on Rules Criminal Procedure, 1968-72, chmn. of R.I. Adv. Com. Corrections, 1973, Nat. Conf. State Trial Judges ABA, 1977-78; exec. com. Appelate Judges Conf. ABA, 1979—, vice chmn., 1983-85, chmn., 1985-86; bd. dirs. Nat. Ctr. for State Cts., 1975-81. Chmn. editorial bd. Judges Jour., 1973-75. Pres. R.I. Health Facilities Planning Coun., 1967-70; chmn. Gov. R.I. Coun. Mental Health, 1968-73; moderator Town of East Providence, 1954-56; mem. R.I. Senate, 1953-56, minority leader, 1955-56; vice chmn. bd. trustee R.I. Hosp., 1968-92, St. Joseph's Hosp., trustee, 1962—. Lt. comdr. USNR, 1941-46. Recipient Erwin Griswold award Nat. Jud. Coll., 1989; named to R.I. Hall of Fame; Paul Harris fellow Rotary Internat. Fellow Am. Bar Found.; mem. ABA (ho. of dels., task force on criminal justice stds. 1977-79, exec. com. appellate judges' conf. 1979-95), KC, R.I. Bar Assn., Am. Judges Assn. (gov.), Inst. Jud. Adminstrn., Am. Judicature Soc. (Herbert Harley award 1990), Am. Law Inst., Order of St. Gregory (knight comdr. with star 1989, Goodrich award for Svc. 1995), Phi Beta Kappa (past pres. Alpha chpt. Brown U.). Home: 60 Winthrop St Riverside RI 02915-2624 Office: RI Supreme Ct 250 Benefit St Ste 7 Providence RI 02903-2724 E-mail: jweisberger@courts.state.ri.us.

WEISCHADLE, DOUGLAS ERIC, lawyer, literary agent; b. Trenton, N.J., May 13, 1971; s. David E. and Mary Ann (Piscopo) W. BS, Trenton State Coll., 1992; JD, New England Sch. Law, 1995. Bar: Mass. 1995, N.J. 1995, D.C. 1996, U.S. Dist. Ct. Mass. 1996, U.S. Dist. Ct. N.J. 1996. Legis. aide N.J. Gen. Assembly, Trenton, 1991; law clk. N.J. Atty. Gen., Trenton, 1993, Mass. Atty. Gen., Boston, 1993; project asst., U.S. Senate Sen. Frank Lautenberg, Washington, 1994; ptnr. Weischadle & Weischadle, Quincy, Mass., 1995—; lit. agt., pres. The Gatsby Group, Inc., Boston, 1996—. Recipient Cum Laude award Am. Classic League, N.Y.C., 1985. Mem. ABA, Mass. Bar Assn., Mass. Acad. Trial Attys., Boston Bar Assn., D.C. Bar Assn., N.J. Bar Assn. Avocations: reading, writing, travel, science. Office: Weischadle and Weischadle 1212 Hancock St Ste 120 Quincy MA 02169-4300

WEISER, MARTIN JAY, lawyer; b. N.Y.C., Mar. 20, 1943; s. Jack J. and Esther (Attias) Weiser; m. Pamela D. Morgan, Sept. 4, 1966; children: Nicole, Jennifer. BA, Temple U., 1964; JD, Bklyn. Law Sch., 1967; LLM, NYU, 1975. Bar: N.Y. 1967, U.S. Dist. Ct. (ea. dist.) N.Y. 1975, U.S. Dist. Ct. (so. dist.) N.Y. 1990; cert. tchr. N.Y. Assoc. Newman & O'Malley, N.Y.C., 1967-69; ptnr., pres. Raiskin, Weiser & Donofrio, P.C., N.Y.C., 1970—99; pres. Weiser & Assocs., P.C., N.Y.C., 1999—. Counsel Metro N.Y. Oldsmobile Dealers Assn., 1988. Bd. dirs. East Hills, N.Y. Assn., 1986—87; v.p. Rio Assn., 1988, bd. dirs., pres., 1988—2002. Mem.: ATLA, Inst. Safety Analysis, Car and Truck Leasing Assn. Am., N.Y. State Trial Lawyers Assn., Nassau Bar Assn., N.Y. County Lawyers Assn., Nob Hill Club (v.p. 1985—86). General civil litigation, Insurance, Personal injury (including property damage). Office: Weiser & Assocs PC 215 Lexington Ave New York NY 10016-6023

WEISERT, KENT ALBERT FREDERICK, lawyer; b. Passaic, N.J., Sept. 9, 1949; s. Frederick William and Waleska Anna Sophia (Bischoff) W.; m. Deborah Jean Searing, Mar. 12, 1983; 1 child, Christianna Lillian. BA magna cum laude, Rutgers U., 1971, JD, 1974. Bar: N.J. 1974, U.S. Dist. Ct. N.J. 1974, U.S. Tax Ct. 1975, U.S. Ct. Appeals (3d cir.) 1978, U.S. Supreme Ct. 1987. Adminstrv. asst. trust dept. Howard Savs. Bank, Newark, 1973-74; ptnr. Schwartz, Tobia & Stanziale, Montclair, NJ, 1975—2001; pvt. practice law Bloomfield, NJ, 2001—. Arbitrator U.S. Dist. Ct., Newark, 1985—. Contbr. chpt. to book New Jersey Transaction Guide, 1987. Pres. ch. coun. Holy Trinity Luth. Ch., Nutley, N.J., 1982-83; session mem., elder Watchung Presbyn. Ch., Bloomfield, N.J.; mem. Greater N.J. Estate Planning Coun.; trustee, v.p. Oakeside Bloomfield Cultural Ctr. Mem. N.J. State Bar Assn., Essex County Bar Assn., Rutgers Law Sch. Alumni Assn., Nat. Trust Hist. Preservation, N.J. Hist. Soc., Phi Beta Kappa, Phi Alpha Theta, Pi Delta Epsilon. Republican. Presbyterian. Avocations: classical music, antiques, mil. and gen. history, hist. preservation, tennis. Estate planning, Labor (including EEOC, Fair Labor Standards Act, labor-management relations, NLRB, OSHA), Probate (including wills, trusts). Home and Office: Kent AF Weisert Esq 51 Fairway Bloomfield NJ 07003

WEISFELD, SHELDON, lawyer; b. McAllen, Tex., Feb. 20, 1946; s. Morris and Pauline (Horwitz) W.; m. Eve F. Weisfeld, Jan. 23, 1994; 1 child, Raquel Paolina. BBA, U. Tex., 1967; postgrad., Nat. U. Mex., Mexico City, 1969; JD, U. Houston, 1970. Bar: Tex. 1971, U.S. Dist. Ct. (so. dist.) Tex. 1978, U.S. Dist. Ct. (we. dist.) Tex. 1995, U.S. Dist. Ct. (ea. dist.) Tex. 2001, U.S. Ct. Appeals (5th cir.) 1978, U.S. Ct. Appeals (11th cir.) 1981, U.S. Supreme Ct. 1982. Pvt. practice, Austin, Tex., 1973-77; pvt. practice law Brownsville, Tex., 1980—. Asst. fed. pub. defender U.S. Dist. Ct. (so. dist.) Tex., Brownsville, 1977-80. Mem. Nat. Assn. Criminal Def. Lawyers (life), Tex. Criminal Def. Lawyers (dir.), ABA, Fed. Bar Assn., State Bar Tex., Cameron County (Tex.) Bar Assn., Hidalgo County (Tex.) Bar Assn., B'nai B'rith. Democrat. Federal civil litigation, Criminal. Office: 855 E Harrison St Brownsville TX 78520-7173 Fax: 956-544-7446. E-mail: isweisfeld@aol.com.

WEISGALL, JONATHAN MICHAEL, lawyer; b. Balt., Mar. 17, 1949; s. Hugo David and Nathalie (Shulman) W.; m. Ruth Macdonald, June 3, 1979; children: Alison, Andrew, Benjamin. BA, Columbia Coll., 1970; JD, Stanford U., 1973. Bar: D.C. 1974, N.Y. 1974, U.S. Supreme Ct. 1982, Marshall Islands 1983. Law clk. to judge U.S. Ct. Appeals (9th cir.), San Francisco, 1973-74; assoc. Covington & Burling, Washington, 1974-79; from assoc. to ptnr. Ginsburg, Feldman, Weil & Bress, Washington, 1980-83; pvt. practice Washington, 1983-99; v.p. Legis. and Regulatory Affairs MidAmerican Energy Holdings Co., 1995—. Adj. prof. Georgetown U. Law Ctr. Author: Operation Crossroads: The Atomic Tests at Bikini Atoll, 1994; exec. prodr. documentary film Radio Bikini. Chmn. bd. dirs. Ctr. for Energy Efficiency and Renewable Techs.; trustee Arena Stage, Washington; bd. dirs. Meet the Composer, Geothermal Resources Coun. Mem. Geothermal Energy Assn. (past v.p., bd. dirs., pres.), Geothermal Resources Coun. (bd. dirs.), Phi Beta Kappa. Jewish. Federal civil litigation, Public international, Legislative. Home: 5309 Edgemoor Ln Bethesda MD 20814-1323 Office: Ste 300 1200 New Hampshire Ave NW Washington DC 20036-6812 E-mail: jweisgall@aol.com.

WEISHAAR, AARON G. lawyer; b. St. Louis, Aug. 30, 1972; s. Lonnie George, Sr. and Colette Jean Weishaar; m. Cynthia Anne Halbert, Nov. 10, 2001. BA magna cum laude, St. Louis U., 1994, JD, 1999; postgrad., Kentick Sch. Theology, St. Louis, 1994—95. Bar: Mo. 2001, U.S. Dist. Ct. (ea. and we. dists.) Mo. 2001, Ill. 2002. Editor Fidelity & Surety News, St. Louis, 1997—98, editor-in-chief, 1998—99; assoc. atty. Reinert & Rourke, P.C., St. Louis, 1998—. Contbr. articles to profl. jours. Mem.: ATLA, ABA (mem. bus. law sect. 2002—, mem. ins. practice sect. 2002—), Bar Assn. Met. St. Louis, Chicago Bar Assn., St. Louis County Bar Assn., Mo. Athletic Club. Republican. Roman Catholic. Avocations: sports, camping, fishing. Construction, Corporate, general, Estate planning. Office: Reinert and Rourke PC 812 N Collins Saint Louis MO 63102 Office Fax: 314-621-8071. Business E-Mail: aweishaar@reinertrourke.com.

WEISMAN, MITCHELL ARTHUR, lawyer; b. Cleve., Sept. 20, 1958; s. Fred and Lois Jane (Kutler) W.; m. Mary Elizabeth Beathard, June 16, 1984; children: Matthew, Megan, Molly. BBA, Emory U., 1980; JD, Ohio State U., 1983. Bar: Ohio, 1983, N.Y., 1993. Ptnr. Weisman, Goldberg & Weisman, Cleve., 1983—. Speaker in field. Mem. ATLA, Ohio Bar Assn., Cleve. Bar Assn., Cuyahoga County Bar Assn. (bd. trustees 1990-93), Bar Assn. Greater Cleve. (young lawyers exec. com. 1987-90, chmn. civil litigation sect. 1987-88), Cleve. Acad. Trial Lawyers (bd. dirs. 1999—), Ohio State Bar Assn., Ohio Acad. Trial Lawyers, Cleve. Baseball Fedn. (bd. dirs. 1996—), Phi Sigma Tau, Masons, Cleve. Racquet Club. Avocations: softball, waterskiing, snow skiing, racquetball, squash. Home: 5917 Briardale Ln Solon OH 44139-2301 Office: Weisman Goldberg & Weisman 101 W Prospect Ave Cleveland OH 44115-1093

WEISMAN, PAUL HOWARD, lawyer; b. Los Angeles, Oct. 14, 1957; s. Albert L. and Rose J. (Zimman) W. BA cum laude, U. Calif., Davis, 1979; JD, Loyola U., Los Angeles, 1982. Bar: Calif. 1982. Tax atty. legis. and regulations div. office of chief counsel Dept. of Treasury IRS, Washington, 1982-83, tax atty. dist. counsel/office of chief counsel L.A., 1983-87; tax atty. Law Offices of Paul H. Weisman, L.A., 1987—. Registered players contract rep. Nat. Football League Players Assn. Co-author BNA Tax Mgmt. Portfolio 638 Federal Tax Collection Procedure, publs. in field. Participant vol. Income Tax Assistance, L.A., 1981-83; alt. mem. Los Angeles County Assessment Appeals Bd. Mem. San Fernando Valley Bar Assn., Beverly Hills Bar Assn. (co-chmn. tax ct. prose program). Republican. Avocations: sports, running, art, music, politics. Estate planning, Sports, Personal income taxation.

WEISS, ALLAN, lawyer; b. Louisville, Aug. 7, 1940; s. Morris M. and Evalyn (Brown) W.; m. Anne Pierce, Feb. 6, 1971; 1 child, John Allan. BS in Law, U. Louisville, 1962, JD, 1964. Bar: Ky. 1964, U.S. Dist. Ct. (we. dist.) Ky. 1965, U.S. Dist. Ct. (ea. dist.) Ky. 1973, U.S. Ct. Appeals (6th cir.) 1972; cert. arbitrator NASD Regulations Inc. 1998, NY Stock Exch., Am. Arbitration Assn.; cert. mediator/arbitrator Am. Health Lawyers Assn. Law clk. Ky. Supreme Ct., 1964-65; with Ferreri & Fogle, 1998—. Mem. panel Nat. Arbitration and Mediation, Nat. Arbitration Forum, 1999; bd. dirs. Mediation Assn. Ky. Adv. com. Learn More-Earn More Project Louisville Bd. Edn., 1965-68; chmn. citizens adv. com. 1967-68; bd. dirs. Louisville Sch. Autistic Children, 1973-83, pres., 1976-77; bd. dirs. Arts Forum, Inc., 1980-84, assoc. editor Beaux Arts Mag., 1980-81; bd. dirs. Bingham Child Guidance Clinic, 1979-90, treas., 1983, v.p., 1984; mem. Sunday Sch. com. The Temple, 1976-78; com. mem. Bur. Jewish Edn.-High Sch. Jewish Studies, 1980-82; pres. Ky. Legal Svcs. Inc., 1984, bd. dirs. 1981-85; bd. dirs. Cmty. Health Charities, 1990-99. Bingham fellow, 1997. Mem. Ky. State Bar Assn., Louisville Bar Assn. (chmn. pre-paid legal ins. com. 1982), Lawyers Alliance for World Security (bd. dirs.). Democrat. Alternative dispute resolution, Insurance, Workers' compensation. Home: 5910 Creighton Hill Rd Louisville KY 40207 Office: Ferreri & Fogle 203 Speed Bldg 333 Guthrie Grn Louisville KY 40202-1829 E-mail: aweiss@aol.com.

WEISS, CHARLES ANDREW, lawyer; b. Perryville, Mo., Jan. 24, 1942; s. Wallace Francis and Iola Francis Weiss; m. Marie Suzanne Desloge, June 10, 1972; children: Christopher, Robert, Julie, Anne. BJ with highest honors, U. Mo., 1964, AB in History, 1965; JD cum laude, Notre Dame U., 1968. Bar: Mo. 1968, U.S. Dist. Ct. (ea. dist.) Mo. 1968, U.S. Ct. Appeals (8th cir.) 1968, U.S. Supreme Ct. 1972, U.S. Ct. Appeals (9th cir.) 1974, U.S. Ct. Appeals (2d cir.) 1977, U.S. Ct. Appeals (1st cir.) 1987, U.S. Ct. Appeals (5th cir.) 1992, U.S. Ct. Appeals (fed. cir.) 2003, U.S. Ct. Appeals (7th cir.) 2003. Law clk. to chief judge U.S. Ct. Appeals (8th cir.), 1968; ptnr. Bryan Cave, St. Louis, 1969—. Lectr. St. Louis U. Law Sch., 1970-73. Supr. Red Cross Water Safety Program, Perry County, Mo., 1962-64; dir. Neighborhood Youth Corps., Perry County, 1965-66; pres. Perry County Young Democrats Club, 1965-67; committeeman Boy Scouts Am., 1982-86; mem. St. Louis Met. Sewer Dist. Civil Svc. Commn., 1999—; bd. dirs. United Way of Greater St. Louis, 1988-90. Fellow Am. Coll. Trial Lawyers; mem. ABA (ho. of dels. 1986-2002), Met. Bar Assn. St. Louis (pres. 1984-85), Mo. Bar Assn. (bd. govs. 1985, v.p. 1994-95, pres.-elect 1995-96, pres. 1996-97), St. Louis Bar Found. (pres. 1983), Mo. Lawyers Trust Account Found. (pres. 1992), Mo. Athletic Club (St. Louis), The Riverlands Assn., Inc. (pres. 1991-93), Jefferson Nat. Parks Assn. (chmn. 1993-2000), Notre Dame Club St. Louis (dir. 1983—), Notre Dame Law Assn. (dir., pres. 1997—). Roman Catholic. Federal civil litigation, Commercial, contracts (including sales of goods; commercial financing), Government contracts and claims. Office: Bryan Cave 211 N Broadway Saint Louis MO 63102-2733

WEISS, CHRISTOPHER JOHN, lawyer; b. Oswego, N.Y., Sept. 1, 1952; s. Robert Leo and Flora Elizabeth Weiss; m. Corinne Fratt, Mar. 28, 1973; children: Allison Ardis, Natalie Elizabeth, Christine Corinne, Kathryn Creigh. BS, Fla. State U., 1970, JD, 1977. Bar: Fla. 1977, U.S. Dist. Ct. (mid. and so. dists.) Fla. 1977, U.S. Supreme Ct. Ptnr. Holland and Knight (and predecessor firm), Orlando, Fla., 1977—. Lectr., author various constrn. litigation issues, 1977—. Mem. Orlando Rep. Com., 1975—. Mem. Fla. Bar, Orange County Bar Assn. (constrn. com. 1987—), Am. Arbitration Assn. (nat. panelist 1982—), Assoc. Gen. Contractors, Assoc. Builders and Contractors, Constrn. Fin. Mgrs. Assn. Avocations: camping, fishing, reading. State civil litigation, Construction. Office: Holland & Knight PO Box 1526 Orlando FL 32802-1526

WEISS, HARLAN LEE, lawyer; b. Washington, Dec. 6, 1941; s. Richard Stanley and Ethel (Shulman) Weiss; m. Elaine Sharon Schooler, Feb. 14, 1971; children: Rachel Shayna, Brian Adam. BA, U. Md.-College Park, 1963; JD with honors, U. Md.-Balt., 1966. Bar: Md. 1967, D.C. 1967, U.S. Dist. Ct. Md. 1967, U.S. Dist. Ct. D.C. 1967, U.S. Ct. Appeals (D.C. cir.)

1968, U.S. Ct. Appeals (4th cir.) 1977, U.S. Supreme Ct. 1970. Law clk. Ct. Appeals of Md., 1966-67; assoc. Surrey & Morse and predecessors, Washington, 1967-72, Sachs, Greenebaum, Tayler, Washington, 1972-76, ptnr., 1976-90; mem. Kivitz & Liptz, LLC, Chevy Chase, Md., 1990. Mem. Jud. Conf. D.C., 1978—79; mem. peer rev. com. Atty. Grievance Commn. Md., 2002—. Mem.: Jud. Conf. D.C. Federal civil litigation, State civil litigation, Insurance. Home: 12017 Cheyenne Rd Gaithersburg MD 20878-2011 Office: 650 Barlow Bldg 5454 Wisconsin Ave Chevy Chase MD 20815-6901

WEISS, LAWRENCE N. lawyer; b. N.Y.C., Aug. 9, 1942; s. Joseph and Martha (Guggenheimer) W.; m. Osnat Gad. BA, CCNY, 1963; LLB summa cum laude, Columbia U., 1966. Bar: N.Y. 1966, U.S. Ct. Appeals (2d cir.) 1967, U.S. Dist. Ct. (so. and ea. dists) N.Y. 1968, U.S. Supreme Ct. 1971, U.S. Ct. Appeals (3d cir.) 1968, U.S. Ct. Appeals (6th cir.) 1980, U.S. Tax Ct. 1977. Assoc. Kaye, Scholer, Fierman, Hayes & Handler, N.Y.C., 1966-67, 67-73; law clk. to judge N.Y. Ct. Appeals, Albany and N.Y.C., 1967; assoc. Botein, Hays, Sklar & Herzberg, N.Y.C., 1973-76, Weisman, Celler, Spett, Modlin & Wertheimer, N.Y.C., 1976, ptnr., 1977-79, counsel, 1979-81; prin. Lawrence N. Weiss, P.C., N.Y.C., 1981—, Pantaleoni & Weiss, N.Y.C., 1993—2001. Arbitrator Civil Ct., N.Y.C., 1985—; mediator U.S. Dist. Ct. (ea. dist.) N.Y. and N.Y. Supreme Ct. Mem. Assn. Bar of City of N.Y. (com. on legal edn. and admission to bar), N.Y. State Bar Assn. (chair com. CLE, com. on fed. judiciary, spl. com. on copyright, vice chair com. on UN, subcom. internat. cts., litig. sect., judiciary com.). Avocations: shakespearean studies, equestrian activities, scuba. General civil litigation, General practice, Trademark and copyright. Home: 107 E 37th St New York NY 10016-3065 E-mail: larry@lweiss.net.

WEISS, MARK ANSCHEL, lawyer; b. N.Y.C., NY, June 20, 1937; s. George and Ida (Galin) W.; m. Joan Roth, June 8, 1958; children: Rebecca, Sarabeth, Jonathan, Deborah. AB, Columbia U., 1958; LLB magna cum laude, Harvard U., 1961. Bar: N.Y. 1961, D.C. 1962, U.S. Supreme Ct. 1965. Assoc. Covington & Burling, Washington, 1961-66, 69-70, ptnr., 1970—; spl. asst. to Under Sec. Treasury Dept. Washington, 1966-68; spl. asst. to sec., 1968-69. Mem. editl. adv. bd. Electronic Banking Law and Commerce Report. Mem. ABA, D.C. Bar, Fed. Bar Assn. (chmn. banking law com.). Antitrust, Banking, Private international. Office: Covington & Burling 1201 Pennsylvania Ave NW Washington DC 20004-2401

WEISS, RHETT LOUIS, business executive, lawyer; b. Kyushu, Japan, May 22, 1961; came to U.S., 1961; s. Armand Berl and Judith (Bernstein) W.; m. Kristen Sue Krieger, Oct. 11, 1987; children: Aaron Bradford, Alexander Donald, Andrew Franklin, Alison Judith. BS in Mgmt. cum laude, Tulane U., 1983; JD, Coll. William and Mary, 1986; exec. internat. bus. cert., Georgetown U., 1996; postgrad., U. N.C., 2000. Bar: Va. 1986, D.C. 1993, N.Y. 1995, U.S. Ct. Appeals (4th cir.) 1986, U.S. Tax Ct. 1987, U.S. Dist. Ct. (we. dist.) Va. 1989, U.S. Bankruptcy Ct. (we. dist.) Va. 1989, U.S. Dist. Ct. (ea. dist.) Va. 1989, U.S. Bankruptcy Ct. (ea. dist.) Va. 1996. Chief ops. officer First Fed. Savs. Bank Shenandoah Valley, Front Royal, Va., 1990-92; sr. atty. Weil, Gotshal & Manges LLP, Washington, 1992-97; dir. strategic relocation/expansion svcs., mem. mgmt. com. Bus. Incentives Group, KPMG Peat Marwick LLP, McLean, Va., 1997-99; founder, CEO, chmn. DEALTEK, Ltd., Syracuse, NY, 1999—; former prin., dir. Adamson, Crump, Sharp & Weiss, P.C., Front Royal. Adj. prof. entrepreneurship and emerging enterprises Syracuse (NY) U. Sch. Mgmt., 2002—; bd. dirs. Pentathlon Corp., Winchester, Va., Assns. Internat. Inc., McLean, Va., Weiss Pub. Co., Inc., Richmond, Va.; asst. town atty., counsel to Front Royal Planning Commn., 1987-90. Author: Portfolio Transactions: The Anatomy of a Deal, 1994, The Basics of Successful Negotiating, 1994, The Negotiating Process: Optimizing Give and Take, 1995, 96, 97, Doing Global Business in a United States Foreign-Trade Zone, 1996, 97, Sales and Use Tax-Exempt Construction: An Innovative Economic Development Tool to Help Land the Deal, 1997, Facility Development, Expansion and Operations: The Major Tax and Related Cost Aspects, 1998, Doing a Deal in the U.S.: Incentives and the Project Negotiation Process, 1998, Business Expansion and Facility Development: Incentives and the Project Development Process, 1999, 2000, Working With Economic Developers, 2000; Web-Enabled Site Selection: Getting the Information You Need at Internet Speed, 2000, Economic Development in the Electronic Age, 2001, 02, Use Incentives to Make the Best Location Choice, 2001, Using the Internet to Move Technology Around the Globe Without Ever Leaving Home, 2002. Bd. dirs. Blue Ridge Arts Coun., Inc., 1987-92, v.p., 1989-90, pres., 1990-91; bd. dirs. Front Royal Little Theatre, Inc., 1988-89, Front Royal Warren County Unit Am. Heart Assn., 1991-92, Lord Fairfax C.C. Ednl. Found., 1991-94, Build-A-Future Found., 1994-98, v.p., 1997-98; Shenrapawa dist. chmn. Shenandoah area coun. Boy Scouts Am., 1988-89, coun. treas., 1991-92, coun. bd. dirs., 1987-94; adv. com. Small Bus. Assistance Ctr., Lord Fairfax C.C.; mem. Seaton Elem. Sch. devel. team D.C. Pub. Schs. Ptnrs. In Edn. Program, 1994-96; soccer coach Southwestern Youth Assn., 1998-2001. Recipient Nat. Quality Dist. award Boy Scouts Am., 1988, 89, Statuette award, 1992, Tech. Project of Yr. award, Tech. Alliance Ctrl. N.Y., 2003. Fellow John Marshall Soc. of Va. Bar Assn.; mem. Internat. Econ. Devel. Coun., D.C. Bar (vice chmn. comml. trans. com. 1994-96, vice chmn. real property trans. com. 1996-97, chmn. 1997-98, real estate, housing and land use sect.), Va. State Bar, N.Y. Bar Assn., Onondaga County Bar Assn., N.Y. State Bar Assn., Va., Econ. Developers Assn., S.C. Econ. Developers Assn., So. Econ. Devel. Coun., Greater Syracuse C. of C. (entrepreneurial coun., technology coun. 2002—), Ctrl. N.Y. Internat. Bus. Alliance (founding dir. 2002—), Tech. Alliance Ctr. N.Y. (bd. dir. 2003-), Valley Estate Planning Coun. (bd. govs. 1989-92, pres. 1992), Front Royal-Warren County C. of C. (bd. dirs. 1989-92, pres. 1990-91), Skaneateles Sunrise Rotary Club (bd. dirs. 2002—, pres.-elect 2003), Country Club Fairfax (Va.), Delta Tau Delta (sec. 1980-81), Beta Gamma Sigma, Beta Alpha Psi. Avocations: cars, outdoors, travel, music, sports. Corporate, general, Finance, Property, real (including real estate development, water). Office: 100 Madison St Ste 1200 Syracuse NY 13202 Home: 3767 Highland Ave Skaneateles NY 13152-9356 E-mail: rweiss@dealtek.com.

WEISS, RONALD PHILLIP, lawyer; b. Springfield, Mass., Apr. 28, 1947; s. Kermit Paul and Fay Roslyn (Robinovitz) W.; m. Janet Faye Landon, June 15, 1969; children: Emily, Katherine. BA, Dartmouth Coll., 1968; JD, U. Pa., 1972. Bar: Mass. 1972, U.S. Dist. Ct. Mass. 1975, U.S. Tax Ct. 1979, U.S. Ct. Appeals (1st cir.) 2000. Assoc. Bulkley, Richardson and Gelinas, Springfield, Mass., 1972-78; ptnr. Bulkley, Richardson and Gelinas, LLP, Springfield, 1978—. Pres. Estate Planning Coun. Hampden County, 1979-81; trustee Mass. Continuing Legal Edn. Inc., 1978-81. Author: (with others) Drafting Wills and Trusts in Massachusetts, 1990, 92, 94; editor: (with others) Massachusetts Corporate Tax Manual, 1986. Trustee Springfield Symphony Orch., 1986—, v.p., 1988—89, pres., 1989—91, chmn., 1991—94; mem. bd. advisors U. Mass. Family Bus. Ctr., 1992—; mem. adv. panel Hanson Initiative for Lang. and Literacy, MGH Inst. Health Professions, 2001—; counsel Cmty. Found. of Western Mass.; mem. appropriations com. Town of Longmeadow, Mass., 1990—96, chmn., 1991—92, 1995—96; trustee Jewish Fedn. Greater Springfield, 1986—90. Mem. ABA, Mass. Bar Assn. (chmn. taxation sect. 1978-81, bd. dels. 1979-81), Mass. Bar Found., Hampden County Bar Assn., Rotary. Corporate, general, Estate planning, Mergers and acquisitions. Office: Bulkley Richardson and Gelinas LLP 1500 Main St Ste 2700 Springfield MA 01115-0001

WEISS, SHERMAN DAVID, lawyer, consultant; b. Detroit, Dec. 26, 1929; s. Abraham and Eva (Lieberman) W.; m. Lorraine Gloria Moss, Apr. 5, 1952; children: Roger Kevin, Diane Leslie, Linda Beth. Student, U. Ill., 1947-48; BSC., Roosevelt U., 1951; JD, Chgo.-Kent Coll. Law, 1957. Bar: Ill. 1958, U.S. Dist. Ct. (no. dist.) Ill. 1958, U.S. Ct. Appeals (7th cir.) 1965. Mem. Deutsch & Kurlan, Chgo., 1959-60, Brody and Gore, Chgo., 1960-62, Arnstein, Gluck, Weitzenfeld and Minow, Chgo., 1963-65; asst. sec., asst. v.p. Walter E. Heller Internat. Corp., Chgo., 1965-75, Imperial Leather & Sportswear Ltd., L.A., 1975-76; exec. v.p. Roth Carpet Mills, Santa Monica, Calif., 1977-78; sr. research rep. Greenwich Assocs., 1985-87. Cons. fin. and bus. mgmt., L.A., 1979—; adj. prof. law John Marshall Sch. Law, Chgo., 1966-67. Case editor Chgo.-Kent Law Rev., 1956-57. Bd. dirs. Met. YMCA Chgo., 1961-64; gen. counsel Leukemia League Ill., 1960-70. Served with U.S. Army, 1952-54. Mem. Ill. Bar Assn., ABA. Jewish. Commercial, contracts (including sales of goods; commercial financing), Corporate, general, Private international. Home: 30 Parterre Foothill Ranch CA 92610-2341 E-mail: shrmwrm@hotmail.com.

WEISS, TERRI LYNN, lawyer; b. Oct. 9, 1957; AB, Georgetown U., 1978, JD, 1981. Bar: N.Y. 1982, U.S. Dist. Ct. (so. and ea. dists.) N.Y. 1982, U.S. Ct. Appeals (2nd cir.), 1982. Assoc. Morgan, Lewis & Bockius, N.Y.C., 1981-86, Rosenman & Colin, N.Y.C., 1986-90; ptnr. Marino & Weiss P.C., White Plains, N.Y., 1990—. Mem. editl. bd., Jour. Am. Acad. Matrimonial Lawyers; mem. editl. bd., Matrimonial Strategist; contbr. articles to profl. jours.; lectr. profl. orgns. Neutral evaluator Matrimonial Alt. Dispute Resolution Program, N.Y. County, N.Y.C., 1997—; arbitrator Domestic Rels. Fee Dispute Resolution Program, White Plains, N.Y., 1996—, Nat. Assn. Securities Dealers, N.Y.C., 1989—; bd. of profl. med. conduct N.Y. State Office Profl. Med. Conduct, N.Y. State Bd. Health, N.Y.C., 1988-98. Fellow Am. Acad. Matrimonial Lawyers (amicus com. N.Y. chpt. 1994—), Internat. Acad. Matrimonial Lawyers; mem. ABA (litigation and family law sects.), N.Y. State Bar Assn. (exec. com. family law sect. 1996—), Westchester County Bar Assn. (family law sect.), Westchester Women's Bar Assn. State civil litigation, Family and matrimonial. Office: Marino & Weiss PC 162 Grand St White Plains NY 10601-4803

WEISSENBERGER, HARRY GEORGE, lawyer; b. Berlin, Fed. Republic of Germany, Aug. 20, 1928; s. Georg Wilhelm and Gabriele Anna (Hochberg) W.; m. Margaret Looper, Dec. 23, 1950 (dec.); children: Carol Weissenberger Schlicht, Harry George Jr., Bruce Lee. Student, Swiss Inst. Tech., 1946-47; BEE, Ga. Tech. Inst., 1950; JD, Emory U., 1952; LLM, George Washington U., 1956. Bar: Ga. 1952, U.S. Dist. Ct. (no. dist.) Ga. 1952, U.S. Ct. Appeals (4th cir.) 1952, U.S. Supreme Ct. 1956, U.S. Ct. Customs and Patent Appeals 1956, Mo. 1957, U.S. Dist. Ct. (ea. dist.) Mo. 1957, U.S. Ct. Appeals (8th cir.) 1957, Mich. 1961, U.S. Dist. Ct. (we. dist.) Mich. 1961, U.S. Ct. Appeals (7th cir.) 1961, Calif. 1964, U.S. Dist. Ct. (no. and cen. dists.) Calif. 1964, U.S. Ct. Appeals (9th cir.) 1964, U.S. Dist. Ct. (ea. dist.) Calif. 1974, U.S. Dist. Ct. (we. dist.) Tex. 1976, U.S. Dist. ct. (so. dist.) Calif. 1982, U.S. Ct. Appeals (Fed. cir.) 1982. Examiner U.S. Patent Office, Washington, 1955-56; assoc. Bruninga & Sutherland, St. Louis, 1956-58, Sutherland, Polster & Taylor, St. Louis, 1958-59, Price & Heneveld, Grand Rapids, Mich., 1959-61, ptnr., 1961-63, Mellin, Hanscom & Hursh, San Francisco, 1963-67, Mellin, Hursh, Moore & Weissenberger, 1967-74, Phillips, Moore, Weissenberger, Lempio & Strabala, San Francisco, 1974-76, Phillips, Moore, Weissenberger, Lempio & Majestic, San Francisco, 1976-78, Newport Beach, Calif., 1978-81, Weissenberger & Peterson, Newport Beach, 1982-86, Laguna Hills, Calif., 1986-90, Weissenberger, Peterson, Uxa & Myers, Laguna Hills, 1990-93; pvt. practice atty. Laguna Hills, 1993-99; of counsel Stout, Uxa, Buyan & Mullins, Irvine, Calif., 1999—2001; pvt. practice cons., 2001—. Dir., gen. counsel Ctr. for Sutton Movement Writing, Inc., Newport Beach, Calif., 1983-93. Mem. Indsl. League Orange County, 1982-93; divsn. staff officer U.S. Coast Guard Aux., 2003—. Served to 1st lt. USAF, 1953-55. Recipient Honored Citizen award Orange County Bd. Suprs., 1992. Mem. Calif. Bar Assn., Am. Intellectual Property Law Assn., Orange County Patent Law Assn. (pres. 1985), Am. Arbitration Assn., Rotary (chpt. bd. dirs. 1988-94, 98, pres. 1991-92, Rotarian of the Yr. award 1989). Republican. Presbyterian. Patent, Trademark and copyright. Office: 2408-B S Grand Ave Ste 200 Carthage MO 64836 E-mail: weisspat@aol.com.

WEISSENBORN, SHERIDAN KENDALL, lawyer; b. Trenton, N.J., Oct. 3, 1948; d. Howard Weinstein and Shirleye Rose (Stanley) W.; m. Lee Edward, Mar. 19, 1977; stepchildren: Jim, Carol, Stephen. BA, U. Miami, 1970, JD, 1973. Bar: Fla. 1973, U.S. Dist. Ct. (so. dist.) Fla. 1974, U.S. Supreme Ct. 1980, U.S. Ct. Appeals (11th cir.) 1982, U.S. Dist. Ct. (mid. dist.) Fla. 1984. Ptnr. Papy Weissenborn, P.A., Coral Gables, Fla., 1974—. Mem. Fla. Bar Assn. Antitrust, Federal civil litigation, State civil litigation. Home: 14620 SW 82nd Ave Miami FL 33158-1902 Office: Vraspir & Puga PA 3001 Ponce De Leon Blvd # 214 Coral Gables FL 33134-6824

WEISSMAN, MATTHEW MARK, lawyer; b. Bklyn., Aug. 18, 1960; s. Abraham and Thelma Weissman; m. Susan C. Greenfield, June 28, 1987; children: Anna Sarah, Leonard Yale. ScB, AB, Brown U., 1983; MS, U. Pa., 1991; JD, Columbia U., 1991. Bar: N.Y. 1992, N.J. 1999, U.S. Dist. Ct. (so. dist.) N.Y. 1992, U.S. Dist. Ct. (ea. dist.) N.Y. 1993, U.S. Dist. Ct. N.J. 1999. Assoc. Fried, Frank, Haren, Shriver & Jacobsen, N.Y.C., 1991—97; ptnr. Wilentz Goldman & Spitzer, Woodbridge, NJ, 1998—. Contbr. articles to profl. publs. Mem.: Middlesex County Bar Assn., N.J. Bar Assn. (mem. pub. utility sect.). Utilities, public, Administrative and regulatory. Office: Wilentz Goldman & Spitzer 900 Woodbridge Ctr Dr Woodbridge NJ 07095

WEISSMAN, MICHAEL LEWIS, lawyer; b. Chgo., Sept. 11, 1934; s. Maurice and Sue (Goldberg) Weissman; m. Joanne Sherwin, Dec. 19, 1961; children: Mark Douglas, Greg Steven, Scott Adam, Brett Anthony. Student White scholar, U. Chgo., 1951-52; BS in Econs, Northwestern U., 1954; MBA in Acctg., U. Pa., 1956; JD, Harvard U., 1958; postgrad. Fulbright scholar, U. Sydney, Australia, 1958-59; postgrad., Hague Acad. Internat. Law, 1959. Bar: D.C. 1958, Ill. 1959. Asst. prof. bus. law Roosevelt U., Chgo., 1959-61; pvt. practice Chgo., 1959—; mem. firm Aaron, Aaron, Schimberg & Hess, 1969-78; sr. ptnr. Boorstein & Weissman, 1978-82, Weissman, Smolev & Solow, 1982-88, Foley & Lardner, 1988-92, McBride Baker & Coles, Chgo., 1992—2001; exec. v.p., gen. counsel Bridgeview Bank Group, Chgo.; of counsel Holland & Knight LLP, 2001—. Asst. prof. Roosevelt U., 1960—62; adj. prof. law John Marshall Law Sch., 2001—02; lectr. Lake Forest (Ill.) Coll., 1979—80; chmn. Banking Group, Union League Club Chgo.; panelist Robert Morris Assocs., Banking Law Inst., Midwest Fin. Conf., Greater O'Hare Assn., Mss. Law Inst., Bank Lending Inst., Chgo. Assn. Commerce and Industry, State of Art Seminars, Infocast Inc., SBA, Fed. Res. Bank Chgo., Lenders Ednl. Inst., Bank Adminstrn. Inst. Found., Lender's Forum, All Dist. Legal Edn. Author: (book) Lender Liability, 1988, Commercial Loan Documentation and Secured Lending, 1990, How to Avoid Career-Ending Mistakes in Commercial Lending, 1996, The Lender's Edge, 1997; mem. editl. bd.: Commercial Damages, 1985—; contbr. articles to profl. jours. Mem. adv. bd. Affective Disorders Clinic, U. Ill. Med. Sch., 1979—81. Scholar White, U. Chgo., 1951—52, Fulbright, U. Sydney, 1958—59. Mem.: ABA, Robert Morris Assn., Comml. Fin. Assn. Ednl. Found. (adv. bd.), Turnaround Mgmt. Assn. (steering com. Chgo. chpt.), Harvard Law Soc. Ill., Assn. Comml. Fin. Attys. (bd. dirs.), Ill. Inst. CLE (bd. dirs. 1989—2000, chmn. 2001—02), Ill. Bankers Assn. (mem. com. bank counsel 1987—88, vice chmn. 1988—89), Chgo. Bar Assn., Ill. Bar Assn., Beta Alpha Psi. Banking, Commercial, contracts (including sales of goods; commercial financing), Corporate, general. Home: 2067 Old Briar Rd Highland Park IL 60035-4245 Office: Holland & Knight LLP 131 S Dearborn St 30th Fl Chicago IL 60603-5506 also: Bridgeview Bank Group 1740 N Halsted St Chicago IL 60614 Business E-Mail: weissman@bridgeviewbank.com. E-mail: weissman@hklaw.com.

WEISSMAN, ROBERT ALLEN, lawyer, real estate broker; b. Los Angeles, May 26, 1950; s. Joseph Jonas and Shirley Rhoda (Solitare) W.; m. Susan Renee Bashner, Apr. 5, 1975; children: Evan Gregory, Russell Joseph, Dustin Raymond. Student, Chapman Coll., World Campus Afloat, 1970-71; BA, UCLA, 1972; JD, Southwestern U., 1975. Bar: Calif. 1975, U.S. Dist. Ct. Calif. 1976, D.C. 1980, U.S. Supreme Ct. 1982, U.S. Ct. Appeals (9th cir.) 1982. Ptnr., U.S. Dist. Ct. (no. dist.) Calif. 1985. Weissman & Weissman, L.A., 1975-81, prin., 1981—; speaker to profl. and trade groups. on creditor's rights, constrn. and mechanics' lien law. Co-author: How to Use the Mechanics' Lien Law, 1995, For Contractors Only, 1996, For Suppliers Only, 1996; contbg. author Calif. Real Property Jour., 1987; columnist on creditors rights and mechanics' lien law L.A. Daily Jour. contbr. articles to profl. jours. Pres.'s adv. coun. City of Hope, 1981-86. Named one of Outstanding Young Men of Am., U.S. Jaycees, 1980. Mem. ABA, State Bar Calif., L.A. County Bar Assn. (L.A. county founding mem., pre-judgement remedies sect., trustee, construc. Law subsection, 1994-95, constrn. law subsect.), San Fernando Valley Bar Assn. (co-chair bus. law sect. 1989-91, trustee 1991-92, treas. 1992-93, sec. 1993—, pres.- elect 1994, pres. 1995—, exec. com. 1996—), Calif. Lawyers for Arts, Acad. Magical Arts, Inc. Club. Democrat. Jewish. Commercial, consumer (including collections, credit), Construction, Property, real (including real estate development, water). Office: Weissman & Weissman 2660 Townsgate Rd Ste 350 Westlake Village CA 91361-5716

WEIST, WILLIAM BERNARD, lawyer; b. Lafayette, Ind., Dec. 23, 1938; s. Bernard Francis and Frances Loretta (Doyle) W.; m. Rosemary Elaine Anderson, Apr. 30, 1963; children: Sean M., Cynthia A. BBA, U. Notre Dame, 1961; JD, U. Louisville, 1970. Bar: Ky. 1971, Ind. 1971, U.S. Dist. Ct. (no. and so. dists.) Ind. 1971. Bank examiner Fed. Res. Bank, St. Louis, 1966-67; Trust officer Citizens Fidelity Bank, Louisville, 1967-71; pvt. practice Fowler, Ind., 1971—; sr. ptnr. Dumas, Weist and Mahnesmith. Bd. dirs. Benton Fin. Corp., Fowler, Fowler State Bank; pros. atty. 76th Jud. Cir., Benton County, Ind., 1975-98. Capt. USAF, 1961-65. Fellow Ind. Bar Found. (charter mem.); mem. Ind. State Bar Assn., Ind. Pros. Attys. Assn. (pres. 1979), Ind. Pros. Attys. Coun. (chmn. 1989), Nat. Dist. Attys. Assn. (bd. dirs.), Columbia Club (Indpls.), Elks, KC. Avocations: golf, reading. Estate planning, General practice, Probate (including wills, trusts). Home: 1000 E 5th St Fowler IN 47944-1520 Office: Weist Bldg Grant Ave Fowler IN 47944-0101

WEITZ, HARVEY, lawyer, educator; b. Bklyn., Aug. 16, 1933; AB, Bklyn. Coll.; JD, Bklyn. Law Sch. Bar: N.Y. 1954, U.S. Dist. Ct. (ea. and so. dists.) N.Y. 1956. Diplomate Am. Bd. Profl. Liability Attys. Ptnr. Schneider, Kleinick, Weitz, Damashek & Shoot, N.Y.C., 1966—; dean N.Y. State Trial Lawyers Inst.; adj. prof. Bklyn. Law Sch.; spl. master Supreme Ct., 1980-84. Author: A Compendium of the Art of Summation, Weitz on Automobile Litigation: The No-Fault Handbook, Vols. I & II; editor in chief Trial Lawyers Quar., 1972-80. Served with U.S. Army. Fellow Internat. Acad. Trial Lawyers, Internat. Soc. Barristers, Roscoe Pound Found.; mem. N.Y. State Trial Lawyers Assn. (bd. dirs.), Trial Lawyers for Pub. Justice (bd. dirs.), Am. Bd. Trial Advocates (nat. bd. mem.), ATLA (bd. govs. 1981-93, nat. sec. 1986-87), N.Y. State Trial Lawyers Assn. (pres. 1980-82), Bklyn. Law Sch. Alumni Assn. (bd. dirs.), Inner Circle of Advocates, Nat. Forensic Ctr. (mem. adv. panel), N.Y. State Bar (lectr.), Nat. Practice Inst. (lectr.), Assn. of the Bar, N.Y. County Lawyers Assn. (lectr.), N.Y.C. Trial Lawyers Assn. Personal injury (including property damage). Office: Schneider Kleinick Weitz & Damashek 233 Broadway Fl 5 New York NY 10279-0050 E-mail: hweitz@lawyer1.com.

WEITZEL, JOHN PATTERSON, lawyer; b. Pitts., Aug. 24, 1923; s. Albert Philip and Elizabeth (Patterson) W.; m. Elisabeth Swan, Mar. 20, 1965; children: Mary Middleton, Paul Patterson. Student, Deerfield (Mass.) Acad., 1937-40; AB, Yale U., 1946; LL.B., Harvard U., 1949. Bar: Mass. 1949, U.S. Supreme Ct. 1960. Asso. Herrick, Smith, Donald, Farley & Ketchum (now Herrick & Smith), Boston, 1949-53, ptnr., 1961-86, Palmer & Dodge, Boston, 1986-93; of counsel, 1993—; spl. asst. to asst. sec. treasury, 1953-55; asst. to under sec. treas, 1955-56; asst. gen. counsel Treasury Dept., 1956-59, dep. to sec. treasury, 1959-60, asst. sec. treasury, 1960-61; U.S. exec. dir. World Bank, 1960-61. Mem. planning bd. NSC, 1959-61; cons. to sec. def., 1973. Mem. Mass. Council Arts and Humanities, 1966-71; overseer, dir. sec. Boys and Girls Clubs, Boston; mem. corp. Mass. Gen. Hosp., Boston Mus. Sci.; trustee Roxbury Latin Sch. Served with USAAF, 1943-45. Mem. Am., Boston bar assns., Am. Law Inst. Clubs: Harvard (Boston), Union Boat (Boston). Home: 45 Devon Rd Chestnut Hill MA 02467-1851 Office: Palmer & Dodge LLP 111 Huntington Ave Boston MA 02199-7613

WEITZMAN, LINDA SUE, lawyer; b. Phila., July 27, 1959; d. Gerald and Elaine Weitzman. BA, Emory U., 1981; JD, U. Miami, 1984. Bar: Fla. 1984, Ga. 1989, U.S. Dist. Ct. (so. dist.) Fla. 1990. Assoc. Weiner, Shapiro & Rose, Miami; clk. Judge Mary Ann MacKenzie, Miami; in house counsel KRC Enterprises Inc., Ft. Lauderdale, Fla.; pvt. practice Coral Gables, Fla., 1989-99, Delray Beach, Fla., 1999-2001, West Palm Beach, Fla., 2001—. Mem. Am. Cancer Soc. Mem. ABA, ATLA, Dade County Bar Assn., Palm Beach County Bar Assn., Atty.'s Title Ins. Fund. General civil litigation, Commercial, contracts (including sales of goods; commercial financing), Property, real (including real estate development, water). Office: 4102 Washington Rd West Palm Beach FL 33405 Fax: 561-659-2996.

WEITZMAN, MARC HERSCHEL, lawyer; b. Milw., Feb. 1, 1950; s. J. Leonard and Esther (Charne) W.; m. Natalyn Ann Gipstein, Oct. 5, 1980; children: Benjamin, Marissa, Laura, Emily. BA, U. Calif., Santa Barbara, 1972; JD, Western State U., 1976. Bar: Calif. 1978, U.S. Dist. Ct. (cen. dist.) Calif. 1979, U.S. Ct. Appeals (9th cir.) 1981, U.S. Supreme Ct. 1987. Atty. State Compensation Ins. Fund, Long Beach, Calif., 1979-82, State Farm Ins. Co., Costa Mesa, Calif., 1982-85; assoc. Grancell, Grancell & Marshall, Santa Ana, Calif., 1985-88; ptnr. Hertz & Weitzman, Huntington Beach, Calif., 1988-89; pvt. practice Seal Beach, Calif., 1989—. Judge pro tem State of Calif. Divsn. Indsl. Rels.-Divsn. Indsl. Accidents, Norwalk, 1986—, Long Beach, 1984—, Santa Ana, 1995—; cert. workers' compensation specialist Calif. Bd. Legal Specialization-State Bar Calif., 1988—; arbitrator State of Calif. Divsns. Indsl. Rels. and Indsl. Accident, 1991. Mem. L.A. County Bar Assn., Orange County Bar Assn., Orange County Workers' Compensation Def. Assn., So. Calif. Rehab. Exch., Long Beach Bar Assn. Workers' compensation. Office: 3010 Old Ranch Pkwy Ste 200 Seal Beach CA 90740-2750

WELBORN, CARYL BARTELMAN, lawyer; b. Phila., Jan. 29, 1951; d. Raymond C. and Helen Ann (Roach) Bartelman; m. Lucien Ruby, Apr. 11, 1987. AB, Stanford U., 1972; JD, UCLA, 1976. Bar: Ill. 1976, Calif. 1978. Assoc. Isham Lincoln & Beale, Chgo., 1976—78; from assoc. to ptnr. Morrison & Foerster, San Francisco and L.A., 1978—95; prin. Law Office of Caryl Welborn, 1996—. Lectr. real property law. Mem. ABA (chmn. com. on partnerships, real property sect. 1989-93), Am. Coll. Real Estate Lawyers (bd. govs. 1994-2002, pres. 2001). Land use and zoning (including planning), Property, real (including real estate development, water). Office: Law Office of Caryl Welborn 601 Montgomery St Ste 700 San Francisco CA 94111

WELBORNE, JOHN HOWARD, railway company executive, lawyer; b. July 24, 1947; s. William Elmo and Pauline Cornwell (Schoder) W.; m. Mary Martha Lampkin, Oct. 8, 1994. AB, U. Calif.-Berkeley, 1969; MPA, UCLA, 1974; JD, U. Calif.-Davis, 1977. Bar: Calif. 1977, D.C. 1980. Congl. intern Congressman John V. Tunney, Washington, 1969; assoc. firm Adams, Duque & Hazeltine, L.A., 1979-84, of counsel, 1984-96; gen. counsel Magnum Software Corp., Chatsworth, Calif., 1989-98. Mgmt. cons., 1971—; dir. Pueblo Viejo Devel. Corp., 1979-88, Union Hardware & Metal Co., 1981—; pres. Angels Flight Railway Co., L.A., 1995—; COO Calif. Sesquicentennial Found., 1996-97; dir. Childrens Hosp. L.A. Centennial Celebration, 1998-2001. Contbr. articles to profl. jours. Mem. cen. bus. dist. project adv. com., downtown strategic plan adv. com., chmn. open space task force, mem. South Park task force City of L.A. Cmty. Redevel. Agy.; mem. L.A. Philharm. Men's Com., 1978-89; pres. L.A. County Host Com. for Olympic Games, 1984; mem. exec. com. Citizens's Task Force for Cen. Libr. Devel., L.A., 1981-83; bd. dirs. Children's Bur., L.A., 1982-88, El Pueblo Park Assn., 1983-89, L.A. Chpt. ARC, 1986-89, Angels Flight Rlwy. Found., 1995—, Friends of the USC Librs., 1999—, Inner City Law Ctr., 1992-95, Los Amigos del Pueblo, L.A. Libr. Assn., 1983-89, 1992-2002, Windsor Sq. Assn., 1980-87, 1999—, L.A. Beautiful, 1982-85, Pershing Sq. Restoration Campaign, 1986-87, Children's Bur. Found., 1997—; bd. dirs. In the Wings divsn. Music Ctr., Los Angeles County, 1982-86, pres. 1984-85; bd. dirs., officer L.A. 200 Com., 1978-91; bd. councilors U. So. Calif. Sch. Pub. Adminstrn., 1983-89; mem. adv. bd. The L.A. Conservancy, 1986—; trustee Windsor Sq-Hancock Park Hist. Soc., 1983-86, Nat. Trust Hist. Preservation, 1997—; fellow Amundsen Inst. U.S.-Mex. Studies, 1987. Capt. Adj. Gen.'s Corps., U.S. Army, 1970-71, USAR, 1972-79. Decorated Army Commendation medal with oak leaf cluster; Cross of Merit 1st class (Fed. Republic Germany). Mem. ABA, D.C. Bar Assn., State Bar Calif., Ordre des Coteaux de Champagne, Confrerie Saint-Etienne d'Alsace, Calif. Vintage Wine Soc. Episcopalian. Office: Angels Flight Railway PO Box 712345 Los Angeles CA 90071-7345

WELCH, DAVID WILLIAM, lawyer; b. St. Louis, Feb. 26, 1941; s. Claude LeRoy Welch and Mary Eleanor (Peggs) Penney; m. Candace Lee Capages, June 5, 1971; children: Joseph Peggs, Heather Elizabeth, Katherine Laura. BSBA, Washington U., St. Louis, 1963; JD, U. Tulsa, 1971. Bar: Okla. 1972, Mo. 1973, U.S. Dist. Ct. (we. dist.) Mo. 1973, U.S. Dist. Ct. (ea. dist.) Mo. 1974, U.S. Ct. Appeals (8th cir.) 1977, U.S. Ct. Appeals (7th cir.) 1991. Contract adminstr. McDonnell Aircraft Corp., St. Louis, 1965-66; bus. analyst Dun & Bradstreet Inc., Los Angeles, 1967-68; atty. U.S. Dept. Labor, Washington, 1972-73; ptnr. Moller Talent, Kuelthau & Welch, St. Louis, 1973-88, Lashly & Baer, St. Louis, 1988-96, Armstrong Teasdale LLP, St. Louis, 1996—. Author: (handbook) Missouri Employment Law, 1988; contbr. book chpts. Missouri Bar Employer-Employee Law, 1985, 87, 89, 92, 94, Missouri Discrimination Law, 1999; co-editor: Occupational Safety and Health Law, 1996. Mem. City of Creve Coeur Ethics Commn., 1987-88, Planning and Zoning Commn., 1988-96; bd. dirs. Camp Wyman, Eureka, Mo., 1982—, sec., 1987-88, 2nd v.p. 1988-89, 1st v.p. 1990-92, pres., 1992-94. Mem. ABA, Fed. Bar Assn., Mo. Bar Assn., Okla. Bar Assn., St. Louis Bar Assn., Kiwanis (bd. dirs. St. Louis 1979—, sec. 1982-83, 93-94, v.p. 1983-84, 88-90, 92-93, Man of Yr. award 1985). Democrat. Mem. Christian Ch. (Disciples Of Christ). Avocations: travel, music. Labor (including EEOC, Fair Labor Standards Act, labor-management relations, NLRB, OSHA). Home: 536 N Mosley Rd Saint Louis MO 63141-7633 Office: Armstrong Teasdale 1 Metropolitan Sq Ste 2600 Saint Louis MO 63102-2740

WELCH, JAMES DOUGLAS, lawyer, engineer; b. Omaha, Dec. 4, 1945; s. James J. and Lois V. (Hibbs) W.. BSEE, U. Nebr., 1969, JD, 1982, postgrad., 1993—; MS in Electronic Engring., U. Toronto, 1974. Registered profl. engr., Nebr.; bar: Nebr. 1982, U.S. Patent Bar 1984; lic. radio FCC. Technician Comm. Supply, Omaha, 1958-66; engr. Fed. Pacific Electric, Toronto, 1969-72; lab instr. Toronto U., 1972-74; lab technician Nebr. Med. Ctr., Omaha, 1975-76; engr. Omaha Pub. Power, 1977-78; pvt. practice lawyer and engr. Omaha, 1982—. Patentee in field. Grantee, U.S. Dept. Energy, 1993. Avocation: restoring 280z cars. Intellectual property. Home and Office: 10328 Pinehurst Ave Omaha NE 68124-1870

WELCH, JOSEPH DANIEL, lawyer; b. University City, Mo., Feb. 1, 1952; s. Robert Joseph and Mary Virginia (Church) W.; m. Sharon Susan Filipek, Mar. 16, 1973; children: Eric Ryan, Christopher Joseph, Colin Andrew, Maria Nicole, Theresa Katherine. BA cum laude, St. Louis U., 1974, JD, 1977. Bar: Mo. 1977, U.S. Dist. Ct. (ea. and we. dists.) Mo. 1977, U.S. Ct. Appeals (8th cir.) 1984, U.S. Supreme Ct. 1994. Assoc. Ely & Cary, Hannibal, Mo., 1977-79; ptnr. Ely, Cary & Welch, Hannibal, Mo., 1979-82, Ely, Cary, Welch & Hickman, Hannibal, Mo., 1982-99, Cary, Welch & Hickman, L.L.P., Hannibal, Mo., 1999—2001, Cary, Welch, Hickman, Walden & Porter, L.L.P., 2002—. Mem. Nat. Network of Estate Planning Attys, 2000-, Mississippi River Pky. Commn., St. Paul, 1988-95, head Mo. del., 1988; prof. bus. law Hannibal-LaGrange Coll., 1993-98; mem. Nat. Heritage Corridor Commn., Washington, 1990-96; speaker various orgns. Editor: Year in Review-Bankruptcy, 1991-94, co-author, 1988-90; speaker various profl. orgns.; contbr. articles to profl. jours. Bd. dirs. Hannibal Pks. and Recreation Dept., 2000-, Mark Twain Area Physician's Recruitment Assn., Hannibal, 1984-85, Hannibal Free Pub. Libr., 1980-82, Hannibal C. of C., 1978-80, pres. Hannibal Ctrl. Bus. Devel., Inc., 1982-85; mem. Mo. Right-to-Life, 1977—; community adv. bd. St. Elizabeth Hosp., 1985-86; Birthright of Hannibal, Inc., 1980—, Holy Family Sch. Bd., 1990-95. Acad. scholar St. Louis U., 1970-74; recognition for Significant Contribution to Bush Administrn., Dept. Interior, 1993. Mem. ATLA, Mo. Assn. Trial Lawyers., Mark Twain Astron. Soc. (co-founder), Nat. Network of Estate Planning Attys., Nat. Acad. Elder Law Attnys. Roman Catholic. Avocations: parenting, basketball, tennis, boating, creative writing. Banking, Bankruptcy, Estate planning. Home: 601 Country Club Dr Hannibal MO 63401-3033 Office: Cary Welch and Hickman LLP 1000 Center St Hannibal MO 63401-3449

WELCH, RICHARD LON See ABELL, RICHARD BENDER

WELCH, ROBERT MORROW, JR., lawyer; b. Wichita Falls, Tex., Dec. 17, 1927; s. Robert Morrow and Sue (Hays) W.; m. Victoria Swan; children: Catherine C., Robert Morrow III, Candice C. LLB, Baylor U., 1951. Bar: Tex. 1951, Colo. 1989. Briefing clk. Supreme Ct. Tex., Austin, 1951-52; from assoc. to ptnr. Fulbright & Jaworski, Houston, 1952-92, ret. sr. ptnr., 1992—. Sgt. USMC, 1946-48. Bankruptcy, Family and matrimonial. Home: PO Box 4628 Horseshoe Bay TX 78657

WELCH, THOMAS ANDREW, retired lawyer, arbitrator; b. Lincoln, Nebr., Dec. 22, 1936; s. Lawrence William and Edna Alberta (Tangeman) W.; m. Ann Reinecke, Sept. 12, 1959; children: Jonathan Thomas, Michael Andrew, Susan Jennifer. Student, Stanford U., 1955-56; BA, UCLA, 1959; JD, Harvard U., 1965. Bar: Calif. 1966, U.S. Dist. Ct. (no. dist.) 1966, U.S. Ct. Appeals (9th cir.) 1966, U.S. Supreme Ct. 1976. Assoc. Brobeck, Phleger & Harrison, San Francisco, 1965-71, ptnr., 1972-96; ret., 1996. Bd. dirs. Ctr. Internat. Dispute Resolution, Honolulu. Chmn. bd. dirs. Youth Law Ctr., San Francisco, 1990—. Lt. USNR, 1959-66. Mem. ABA, Calif. Bar Assn., Am. Law Inst., Am. Arbitration Assn. (large complex case panel of neutrals). Republican. Presbyterian. Alternative dispute resolution, State civil litigation. Home and Office: 449 S Clovercrest Lane San Ramon CA 94583-5505 E-mail: thomwelch@attbi.com.

WELD, JONATHAN MINOT, lawyer; b. Greenwich, Conn., Feb. 25, 1941; s. Alfred White and Sally (Duggan) W.; m. Jane Paige, June 19, 1965; children: Elizabeth, Eric. AB in History cum laude, Harvard U., 1963; JD, Cornell U., 1967. Bar: N.Y. 1967, U.S. Ct. Appeals (2d cir.) 1969, U.S. Dist. Ct. (ea. and so. dist.) N.Y. 1970. Assoc. Shearman & Sterling, N.Y.C., 1967-75, ptnr., 1976—, London, 1982-85. Bd. dirs. Bank of N.S. Internat.; chmn., bd. dirs. The Evergreens, Bklyn. Hosp., N.Y. Bd. dirs. N.Y. Presbyn. Healthcare Sys., St. Ann's Sch., Bklyn. Bot. Garden; former bd. dirs. Bklyn. Home for Children, Harvard Coll. Fund, Winant and Clayton Vols. Mem. ABA, N.Y. State Bar Assn. Banking, Corporate, general, Private international. Office: 599 Lexington Ave Fl C2 New York NY 10022-6030

WELDON, JEFFREY ALAN, lawyer; b. Billings, Mont., May 6, 1963; s. Richard Allen and Monica (Michaud) Weldon; m. Leslie Helen Boileau, July 7, 1990; 2 children. BA, U. Mont., 1986, MPA, 1994, JD, 1996. State senator, Mont., 1993-97; assoc. atty. Moulton Bellingham, Longo & Mather, P.C., Billings, Mont., 1997-2000; chief legal counsel Office of Pub. Instrn., State of Mont., Helena, 2000—. Education and schools, Estate planning, Property, real (including real estate development, water).

WELGE, JACK HERMAN , JR., lawyer; b. Austin, Tex., Sept. 12, 1951; s. Jack Herman and Regina Victoria (Hunger) W.; m. Frances Ava Roddy Avent, Dec. 23, 1977; children: Kirsten Frances Page Welge, Kathleen Ava Regina Welge. BA, U. Tex., 1974; JD, St. Mary's U., 1977. Bar: Tex. 1977, U.S. Dist. Ct. (ea. dist.) Tex. 1979, U.S. Dist. Ct. (no. dist.) Tex. 1982, U.S. Ct. Appeals (5th cir.) 1983, U.S. Supreme Ct., 1984; cert. family law Tex. Bd. Legal Specialization 1984. Asst. dist. atty. Gregg County Criminal Dist. Atty., Longview, Tex., 1978-79; assoc. Law Office of G. Brockett Irwin, Longview, 1979-81; judge Mcpl. Ct. of Record, Longview, 1979-81; ptnr. Adams & Sheppard, Longview, 1981-83; pvt. practice, 1983—. Of counsel East Tex. Assn. for Abused Families, Longview, 1985-90. Co-chair profl. divsn. Gregg County United Way, 1996—97; mem. vestry Trinity Episcopal Ch., Longview, 1993—96, 2001—; bd. directors Longview Cmty. Theater, 1979—82, East Tex. Coun. on Alcoholism and Drug Abuse, Longview, 1981—83, East Tex. Assn. for Abused Families, Longview, 1983—85, Longview Mus. and Arts Ctr., 1991—94; bd. directors adv. com. Salvation Army, 1994—, chmn., 1997; mem. sch. bd. Trinity Sch. of Tex., 2001—. Mem.: Tex. Acad. Family Law Specialists, Gregg County Bar Assn. (pres. 1983), N.E. Tex. Bar Assn., State Bar of Tex. (pro bono coll., contested custody case panel, protective case panel, Gregg County lawyers pro bono project, Outstanding Contbn. award 1990, Disting. Svc. award 1993, 1995, Outstanding Pro Bono Atty. 1994, 1997), East Tex. Knife and Fork Club (pres. 1983—84), Rotary (pres. Longview Club 1987—88, Paul Harris fellow 1982, 24 Yrs. Perfect Attendance 2002), Mason, Delta Upsilon (Tex. chpt. found. bd. 1974—78), Delta Theta Phi (dean 1977, Bickett Senate). General civil litigation, Family and matrimonial, Probate (including wills, trusts). Office: 413-415 S Green St PO Box 3624 Longview TX 75606-3624 E-mail: welgjhjr@hotmail.com.

WELLEN, ROBERT HOWARD, lawyer; b. Jersey City, Aug. 19, 1946; s. Abraham Louis and Helen Rose (Krieger) W.; m. Anita Fass, June 16, 1968; children: Elizabeth, Judith Maria. BA, Yale Coll., 1968; JD, Yale U., 1971; LLM in Taxation, Georgetown U., 1975. Bar: Conn. 1971, D.C. 1972, Colo. 1982. Assoc. Fulbright & Jaworski, Washington, 1975-76, participating assoc., 1976-79, ptnr., 1979-93, Ivins, Phillips & Barker, Washington, 1993—. Adj. prof. law Georgetown U. Law Ctr., 1982-85. Contbr. articles to legal publs. Served to lt. JAGC, USNR, 1971-75. Mem. ABA (past asst. sec., past chmn. com. on corp. tax, sect. taxation, past supr. editor sect. taxation newsletter, vice chair law devel. com. on corp. tax), Fed. Bar Assn. (coun. taxation), Phi Beta Kappa. Jewish. Corporate taxation, Taxation, general. Office: Ivins Phillips & Barker 1700 Pennsylvania Ave NW Washington DC 20006-4704 E-mail: rwellen@ipbtax.com.

WELLER, PHILIP DOUGLAS, lawyer; b. Richmond, Ind., May 5, 1948; s. Lawrence E. and Barbara Jean (Hughes) W.; m. Kathryn Jean Deucker, Apr. 3, 1971; 1 child, Leigh Rachel. Student, Ohio U., 1966-67; BS, Bowling Green State U., 1970; JD, Bates Coll. Law, 1975. Bar: Tex. 1975. Assoc. Vinson & Elkins, Houston, 1975-79, ptnr. Houston, Dallas, N.Y.C., 1980—, Baker, Brown, Sharman, Wise & Stephens, Houston, 1979-80. Speechwriter. Mem. ABA, ACMA, AARPI, ICSC, ULI, Am. Coll. Real Estate Lawyers, Tex. Bar Assn., Houston Bar Assn., Dallas Bar Assn., D.C. Bar Assn., Assn. Bar City N.Y. Property, real (including real estate development, water), Finance, Landlord-tenant. Office: 2300 First City Tower 1001 Fannin St Houston TX 77002-6760

WELLFORD, HILL B., JR., lawyer; b. Tulsa, Oklahoma, Apr. 30, 1942; BA, Davidson Coll., 1964; JD, U. N.C., 1967. Bar: Va., 1968. Ptnr.(group-head of firm's litig.,intellectual property and litig sections) Hunton and Williams, Richmond, Va. Lectr. in law. Mem. ABA; Va. Bar Assn. (chmn. com. labor rels. and employment law 1977-87); Assn. Trial Lawyers Am.; Phi Delta Phi. Office: Hunton & Williams Riverfront Plz East Tower 951 E Byrd St Richmond VA 23219-1535

WELLINGTON, HARRY HILLEL, lawyer, educator; b. New Haven, Aug. 13, 1926; s. Alex M. and Jean (Ripps) W.; m. Sheila Wacks, June 22, 1952; children: John, Thomas. AB, U. Pa., 1947; LLB, Harvard U., 1952; MA (hon.), Yale U., 1960. Bar: D.C. 1952. Law clk. to U.S. Judge Magruder, 1953-54, Supreme Ct. Justice Frankfurter, 1955-56; asst. prof. law Stanford U., 1954-56; mem. faculty Yale U., 1956—, prof. law, 1960—, Edward J. Phelps prof. law, 1967-83, dean Law Sch., 1975-85, Sterling prof. law, 1983-92, Sterling prof. emeritus law, 1992—, Harry H. Wellington prof. lectr., 1995—; pres., dean, prof. law N.Y. Law Sch., N.Y.C., 1992-2000, dean emeritus, prof., 2000—. Ford fellow London Sch. Econs., 1965; Guggenheim fellow; sr. fellow Brookings Instn., 1968-71; Rockefeller Found. fellow Bellagio Study and Conf. Ctr., 1984; faculty mem. Salzburg Seminar in Am. Studies, 1985; John M. Harlan disting. vis. prof. N.Y. Law Sch., 1985-86; review person ITT-SEC; moderator Asbestos-Wellington Group; cons. domestic and fgn. govtl. agys.; trustee N.Y. Law Sch.; bd. govs. Yale U. Press; mem. jud. panel, exec. com. Ctr. Public Resources Legal Program; Harry H. Wellington lectr., 1995—. Author: with Harold Shepherd) Contracts and Contract Remedies, 1957, Labor and the Legal Process, 1968, (with Clyde Summers) Labor Law, 1968, 2d edit., 1983, (with Ralph Winter) The Unions and the Cities, 1971, Interpreting the Constitution, 1990; contbr. articles to profl. jours. Mem. ABA, Bar Assn. Conn., Am. Law Inst., Am. Arbitration Assn., Am. Acad. Arts and Scis., Common Cause (nat governing bd.). Office: NY Law Sch 57 Worth St New York NY 10013-2959 also: Yale U Sch Law New Haven CT 06520

WELLIVER, WARREN DEE, lawyer, retired state supreme court justice; b. Butler, Mo., Feb. 24, 1920; s. Carl Winfield and Burdee Marie (Wolfe) W.; m. Ruth Rose Galey, Dec. 25, 1942; children: Gale Dee (Mrs. William B. Stone), Carla Camile (Mrs. Dayton Stone), Christy Marie. BA, U. Mo., 1945; JD, U. Mo., 1948. Bar: Mo. 1948. Asst. pros. atty. Boone County, Columbia, 1948-54; sr. ptnr. Welliver, Atkinson and Eng, Columbia, 1960-79; tchr. law Law Sch. U. Mo., 1948-49; mem. Mo. Senate, 1977-79; justice Supreme Ct. Mo., Jefferson City, 1979-89. Mem. Gov. Mo. Adv. Coun. Alcoholism and Drug Abuse, chmn. drug coun., 1970-72; chmn. Task Force Revision Mo. Drug Laws, 1970-71; liaison mem. coun. Nat. Inst. Alcoholism and Alcohol Abuse, 1973-76; mem. Cen. Regional Adv. Coun. Comprehensive Psychiat. Svcs., 1990-92. Bd. dirs. Nat. Assn. Mental Health, 1970-76, regional v.p., 1973-76; pres. Mo. Assn. Mental Health, 1968-69, Stephens Coll. Assocs., 1965-79; pres. Friends of Libr., U. Mo., 1976, bd. dirs., 1979-92; chmn. Dem. Com., 1954-64; hon. fellow Harry S. Truman Libr. Inst., 1979—; bd. dirs. Supreme Ct. Hist. Soc., 1982—; vice chair adv. bd. U. Mo. Multiple Sclerosis Inst., 1992—; bd. curators Stephen's Coll., 1980-92. With USNR, 1941-45. Recipient Disting. Alumni medal and award U. Mo., 1994. Fellow Am. Coll. Trial Lawyers, Am. Bar Found., Mo. Bar Found.; mem. ABA, Mo. Bar Assn. (pres. 1967-68), Boone County Bar Assn. (pres. 1970), Am. Judicature Soc., Am. Legion (past post comdr.), Multiple Sclerosis Soc. (Gateway chpt. bd. dirs. 1986-92), Order of Coif, Country Club of Mo., Columbia Country Club (past pres.). Home: 3430 Woodrail Ter Columbia MO 65203-0926

WELLNITZ, CRAIG OTTO, lawyer, English language educator; b. Elwood, Ind., Dec. 5, 1946; s. Frank Otto and Jeanne (Albright) W.; m. Karen Sue Thomas, Apr. 13, 1974 (div. Sept. 1987); children: Jennifer Suzanne, Anne Katherine; m. Carol L. Hinesley, Jan. 23, 1988. BA, Purdue U., 1969; MA, Ind. U., 1972; JD, Ind. U.-Indpls., 1978. Bar: Ind. 1978, U.S. Dist. Ct. (so. dist.) Ind. 1978, U.S. Supreme Ct. 1983, U.S. Ct. Appeals (7th and Fed. cirs.) 1984, U.S. Dist. Ct. (no. dist.) 1990; registered mediator, Ind. Instr. Danville Jr. Coll., Ill., 1972-74, S.W. Mo. State U., Springfield, Mo., 1974-75; ptnr. Coates, Hatfield, Calkins & Wellnitz, Indpls., 1978-98; pub. defender criminal divsn. Marion Superior Ct., Marion County, 1979-88, master commr. criminal divsn., 1988-96, registered mediator, 1998—; ptnr. Coates, Hatfield & Wellnitz, Indpls., 1999—2002; pvt. practice Indpls., 2002—. Instr. U. Indpls., 1981-82; mem. adj. faculty dept. English Butler U., Indpls., 1982—; instr. English Ind. U.-Purdue U., Indpls., 1987-90; pres. Ind. Account Mgmt., Inspls., 1985-94; v.p. Carol Craig Assocs., Indpls., 1987—; lectr. in field. Co-author: Successful Judgment Collection in Indiana, 1996, Emerging Trends in Indiana Commercial Collections, 2001; columnist A Jury of Your Peers, 1984-86. Vice committeeman Indpls. Rep. precinct, 1978; chmn. fin. com. St. Luke's United Meth. Ch., 1985-87; sponsor Christian Children's Fund, 1990—; active Am. Mus. Natural History, Indpls. Zoo, Children's Mus. Indpls., The Royal Oak Found. Postgrad. study grantee S.W. Mo. State U., Springfield, 1975. Mem.: MLA, AAUP, Broad Ripple Village Assn., Internat. Spkrs. Network., Spkrs. U.S.A., Libr. Congress Assocs., Smithsonian Assocs., Internat. Assn. Comml. Collectors, Creditors Internat., ACA Internat., Rivera Club Indpls., Columbia Club, Elks. State civil litigation, Commercial, consumer (including collections, credit), Personal injury (including property damage). Office: 2575 B East 55 Pl Indianapolis IN 46220 E-mail: Indplslaw@aol.com.

WELLON, ROBERT G. lawyer; b. Port Jervis, N.Y., Apr. 18, 1948; s. Frank Lewis and Alice (Stevens) W.; m. Jan Montgomery, Aug. 12, 1972; children: Robert F., Alice Wynn. AB, Emory U., 1970; JD, Stetson Coll. Law, 1974. Assoc. Turner, Turner & Turner, Atlanta, 1974-78; ptnr. Ridley, Wellon, Schwieger & Brazier, Atlanta, 1978-86; of counsel Wilson, Strickland & Benson, Atlanta, 1987—2000; pvt. practice Atlanta, 2000—. Adj. prof. Atlanta Law Sch., 1981-94; adj. prof. law Emory U. Sch. of Law, 1995—. Gov.'s task force chmn. Atlanta 2000, 1978; exec. com., treas., 2nd v.p. Atlanta Easter Seals Soc., 1983-88; rep. Neighborhood Planning Unit, 1981-83; adminstrv. bd. Northside United Meth. Ch., 1996-99, Stephen min. Served with USAR, 1970-76. Recipient Judge Joe Morris award Stetson Coll. Law, St. Petersburg, 1974. Master: Charles Longstreet Weltner Family Law Inn of Ct. (founding pres. 1997—2000); mem.: Atlanta Bar Found. (bd. dirs. 1996—), Am. Judicature Soc., Atlanta Bar Assn. (bd. dirs. 1978—88, pres. 1986—87, Atlanta continuing legal edn. bd. trustees 1994—97, del. to ho. of dels. 1999—, Charles E. Watkins Svc. award 1995), State Bar. of Ga. (professionalism com. 1994—), Fla. Bar, Atlanta Found. for Psychoanalysis, Inc. (bd. dirs. 1994—, exec. com. 1997—), Old War Horse Lawyers Club, Lawyers Club Atlanta. Methodist. State civil litigation, Family and matrimonial, Personal injury (including property damage). Office: Ste 1800 Promenade II 1230 Peachtree St NE Atlanta GA 30309 E-mail: rgwlaw@earthlink.net.

WELLS, BENJAMIN GLADNEY, lawyer; b. St. Louis, Nov. 13, 1943; s. Benjamin Harris and Katherine Emma (Gladney) W.; m. Nancy Kathryn Harpster, June 7, 1967; children: Barbara Gladney, Benjamin Harpster. BA magna cum laude, Amherst (Mass.) Coll., 1965; JD cum laude, Harvard U., 1968. Bar: Ill. 1968, Tex. 1973, U.S. Tax Ct. 1973, U.S. Ct. Claims 1975, U.S. Ct. Appeals (5th cir.) 1981, U.S. Dist. Ct. (so. dist.) Tex. 1985, U.S. Dist. Ct. (we. dist.) Tex. 1993. Assoc. Kirkland & Ellis, Chgo., 1968—69; assoc. to ptnr. Baker Botts, L.L.P. , Houston, 1973—, chmn. firmwide tax dept., 2002—. Contbr. articles to profl. jours. Mem. planned giving com. St. John's Sch., Houston (chmn. 1987-98); Harvard Legal Aid Bureau, 1966-68. Capt. U.S. Army, 1969-72. Fellow Am. Coll. Tax Counsel; mem. ABA (chair corp. tax com. sect. on taxation 2001-02), Houston Tax Roundtable (pres. 1994-95), The Forest Club, The Houston Club, Phi Beta Kappa. Presbyterian. Corporate taxation, Taxation, general. Office: Baker Botts LLP One Shell Plaza 910 Louisiana St Ste 3330 Houston TX 77002-4916 E-mail: benjamin.wells@bakerbotts.com.

WELLS, CHARLES TALLEY, state supreme court justice; b. Orlando, Fla., Mar. 4, 1939; Bar: Fla. 1965, U.S. Dist. Ct. (mid. dist.) Fla., U.S. Ct. Appeals (5th and 11th cirs.) 1966, U.S. Supreme Ct. 1969, U.S. Dist. Ct., U.S. Dist. Ct. (so. dist.) Fla. 1976, U.S. Ct. of Claims 1990. Trial atty. U.S. dept justice, Washington, 1969; pvt. practice Maguire, Voohris and Wells, PA, Orlando, Fla., 1965—68, 1970—75, Wells, Gattis, Hollowes & Carpenter, PA, Orlando, Fla., 1976—94; justice Fla. Supreme Ct., Tallahassee, 1994—. Methodist. Office: Fla Supreme Ct Supreme Ct Bldg 500 S Duval St Tallahassee FL 32399-1925

WELLS, DEWEY WALLACE, lawyer; b. Raleigh, N.C., Oct. 14, 1929; s. B.C. and Alma (Blanchard) W.; m. Ann D. Wells, Aug 25, 1951; children: Robert, Betty W., Daniel, Brady, Jeff. AA, Mars Hill Coll., 1950; BS, Wake Forest U., 1952, JD, 1954. Bar: N.C. 1954, U.S. Dist. Ct. (ea. dist.) N.C. 1960, U.S. Ct. Appeals (4th cir.) 1961, U.S. Dist. Ct. (mid. and we. dist.) N.C. 1985. Exec. sec. N.C. Jud. Council, Raleigh, 1954-55; ptnr. LeRoy, Wells, Shaw, Hornthal & Riley, Elizabeth City, N.C., 1958-85, Womble, Carlyle, Sandridge & Rice, PLLC, Winston Salem, N.C., 1985—. Judge Superior Ct., 1st Jud. Dist. N.C., 1974. Trustee N.C. Natural Heritage Trust, 1990-96, chmn. 1996-2003. 1st lt. USAR, 1954-58. Fellow Am. Coll. Trial Lawyers; mem. N.C. Bar Assn. (pres. 1980-81). Republican. Baptist. General civil litigation. Home: 1890 Pilot Ridge Rd Blowing Rock NC 28605-8917 Office: Womble Carlyle Sandridge & Rice 1 W 4th St Winston Salem NC 27102-0084

WELLS, ELIZABETH M. lawyer; b. Chgo., Apr. 9, 1954; d. Chester Bruno and Dorothy Mae Wells. BA in English magna cum laude, Hamline U., St. Paul, 1977; JD, IIT Chgo. Kent Sch. Law, 1995. Bar: Ill. 1996, U.S. Dist. Ct. (no. dist.) Ill. 1997. Mktg. and cons., computer software & svcs. Burroughs Corp., Control Data Corp., CompuServe Corp., 1977—86; prin. Employees Benefits Cons., Arlington Heights, Ill., 1986—92, student atty. asst., 1993—95, assoc. atty., 1996—97; prin. Law Offices of Elizabeth M. Wells, Chgo., 1997—. Lectr., author, cons., allocation of retirement plans in domestic rels. procs., 1997—; bd. mem. Loyola U. Chgo. Sch. Law Elder Law Clinic, 2002—. Recipient Vol. award, Chgo. Dept. on Aging, 2002. Mem.: Chgo. Bar Assn. (co-liaison matrimonial law legis. subcom. 2000—, chair legis. com. 2003—), Women's Bar Assn. of Ill. (co-chair task force on issues affecting women as they age 1999—), Ill. State Bar Assn., Phi Beta Kappa. Avocations: sailing, bridge, music, bicycling, hiking. Office: Law Offices of Elizabeth M Wells 980 N Michigan Ave Ste 1400 Chicago IL 60611

WELLS, LESLEY, judge; b. Muskegon, Mich., Oct. 6, 1937; d. James Franklin and Inez Simpson Wells; m. Charles F. Clarke, Nov. 13, 1998; children: Lauren Elizabeth, Caryn Alison, Anne Kristin, Thomas Eliot. BA, Chatham Coll., 1959; JD cum laude, Cleve. State U., 1974; cert., Nat. Jud. Coll., 1983, 85, 87, cert., 89. Bar: Ohio 1975, U.S. Dist. Ct. (no. dist.) Ohio 1975, U.S. Supreme Ct. 1989. Pvt. practice, Cleve., 1975; ptnr. Brooks & Moffet, Cleve., 1975-79; dir., atty. ABAR Litigation Ctr., Cleve., 1979-80; assoc. Schneider, Smeltz, Huston & Ranney, Cleve., 1980-83; judge Ct. of Common Pleas, Cleve., 1983-94, U.S. Dist. Ct. (no. dist.) Ohio 6th Cir., Cleve., 1994—. Adj. prof. law and urban policy Cleve. State U., 1980-83, 90-93. Editor, author: Litigation Manual, 1980. Past pres. Cleve. Legal Aid Soc.; legal chmn. Nat. Women's Polit. Caucus, 1981-82; chmn. Gov.'s Task Force on Family Violence, Ohio, 1983-87; mem. biomed. ethics com. Case Western Res. U. Med. Sch., 1985-94; mem. N.W. Ordinance U.S. Constn. Commn., Ohio, 1986-88; master Burton Inn of Ct., 1989—, counselor, 1993, pres., 1998-99; trustee Rosemary Ctr., 1986-92, Miami U., 1988-92, Urban League Cleve., 1989-90, Chatham Coll., 1989-94. Recipient Superior Jud. award Supreme Ct. Ohio, 1983, J. Irwin award Womenspace, Ohio, 1984, award Womens City Club, 1985, Disting. Alumna award Chatham Coll., 1988, Alumni Civic Achievement award Cleve. State U., 1992, Golden Gavel award Ohio Judges Assn., 1994, Outstanding Alumni award Cleve. Marshall Law Alumni Assn., 1994, Greater Cleve. Achievement award YWCA, 1995. Mem. ABA (coun. litigation sect. 1996-99), Am. Law

Inst., Ohio Bar Assn., Ohio Womens Bar Assn., Cleve. Bar Assn. (Merit Svc. award 1983), Cuyahoga County Bar Assn., Nat. Assn. Women Judges, Philos. Club Cleve. Office: 18-A US Court House 801 W Superior Ave Cleveland OH 44113-1836

WELLS, PETER NATHANIEL, judge, lawyer; b. Ogdensburg, N.Y., May 13, 1938; s. John Harris and Mary Theresa (Houlihan) W.; m. Diana Barry Wells, Apr. 8, 1967; childen: Mary, Sarah, Matthew. BS in Polit. Sci., Manhattan Coll., 1960; LLB, Boston Coll., 1963. Bar: N.Y. 1964, U.S. Dist. Ct. (no. dist.) N.Y. 1967, U.S. Dist. Ct. (we. dist.) N.Y. 1971, U.S. Ct. Appeals (d cir.) 1974, U.S. Ct. Appeals (3d cir.) 1978, U.S. Supreme Ct. 1974. Asst. atty. gen. State of N.Y., 1964-68; assoc. Costello, Cooney & Fearon, Syracuse, N.Y., 1968-70, ptnr., 1970-76, Williams, Micale & Wells, Syracuse, 1976-88, Mackenzie Smith Lewis, Michell & Hughes, Syracuse, 1988; surrogate ct. judge Onondaga County, 1989—. Mem. EPTL-SCPA Legis. adv. com. of N.Y. State. Editl. bd. Warren's Heaton on Surrogate Ct. Chmn. Dewitt Republican Com., 1976-87; town justice Dewitt, N.Y., 1987-88. Served with USAR, 1963-69. Mem. Onondaga County Bar Assn., Def. Rsch. Inst., Upstate Trial Lawyers Assn., N.Y. State Surrogates Assn. (pres. 1999-2001), Cavalry Club, Manlius Club (N.Y.). Roman Catholic. Home: 100 Downing Rd De Witt NY 13214-1503 Office: Surrogate Ct Chambers Onondaga County Courth Syracuse NY 13202

WELLS, ROGER W. lawyer, food products executive; b. Sioux Falls, S.D., May 7, 1957; BSBA summa cum laude, Creighton U., 1979, JD summa cum laude, 1981. Bar: Nebr. 1981, U.S. Dist. Ct. Nebr. 1981, U.S. Tax Ct. 1981. With McGrath, North, Mullin & Kratz, P.C., Omaha; gen. counsel ConAgra, Omaha, 2002—. Mem. editl. staff: Creighton U. Law Rev., 1980—81. Mem.: ABA (mem. corp., banking and bus. sect., mem. taxation sect., mem. internat. law sect.), Omaha Bar Assn., Nebr. Bar Assn., Beta Gamma Sigma. Office: ConAgra 1 Center Park Plz Ste 1400 222 S 15th St Omaha NE 68102 also: McGrath North Mullin and Kratz PC Ste 3700 1st Nat Tower 1601 Dodge St Omaha NE 68102 Office Fax: 402-341-0216., 402-341-0216. Business E-Mail: rwells@mnmk.com.*

WELLS, STEVEN WAYNE, lawyer; b. Ft. Walton Beach, Fla., Sept. 8, 1960; s. H. Wayne and Shirley A. W.; m. Lisa Stieler, May 20, 1983; Robert, James, Jessica. BA in Comm., Mich. State U., 1982; JD with distinction, Detroit Coll. of Law, 1985. Bar: Mich. Asst. prosecutor Oakland County, Pontiac, Mich., 1985-88; mng. ptnr. Schnelz, Bondy & Wells, PC, Troy, Mich., 1988-93; shareholder, mng. ptnr. Cross Wrock, PC, Detroit, 1993-99; prin. shareholder Schnelz, Wells, Monaghan, Wells & Parry PC, Birmingham, Mich., 1999—. Lectr., presenter in field. Contbr. articles to State Bar Jour. Pres. Bloomfield Village Bd. Fellow Mich. Bar Assn.; ABA, ATLA, Detroit Bar Assn., Mich. Trial Lawyers Assn., Nat. Dist. Attys. Assn. Avocations: golf, tennis, coaching youth baseball, soccer. Commercial, contracts (including sales of goods; commercial financing), Labor (including EEOC, Fair Labor Standards Act, labor-management relations, NLRB, OSHA), Land use and zoning (including planning). Address: 255 S Old Woodward Ave Ste 200 Birmingham MI 48009-6184

WELLS, WAYNE ALTON, lawyer; b. Abilene, Tex., Sept. 29, 1946; s. Thomas Edsel and Velma Pauline (Moseley) W.; married; children: Susannah, Emily. BA, U. Okla., 1969, JD, 1972. Bar: Supreme Ct. Okla. 1972, U.S. Dist Ct. (western dist.) Okla. 1973, U.S. Dist. Ct. (ea. dist.) Okla. 1985, U.S. Dist. Ct. (no. dist.) Okla. 1982, U.S. Ct. Appeals (10th cir.) 1976. Assoc. Lampkin, Wolfe, Burger, Abel, McCaffery & Norman, Oklahoma City, 1972-76; sole practice Edmond, Okla., 1976—. Athletic advisory bd. dirs. U.S. Olympic Com., Colorado Springs, 1973-76. Recipient Gold medal free style wrestling Internat. Olympics, Munich, 1972; named champion wrestler Nat. Colligate Athletic Assn., 1968, U.S. Wrestling Hall of Fame, 1982; named to Okla. Sports Hall of Fame, 2000. Mem. Okla. Bar Assn., Okla. Trial Lawyers Assn. (adv. bd. 1980), Okla. County Bar Assn., Citizens Savs. Athletic Found. Republican. Avocations: skiing, hunting, flying. Insurance, Personal injury (including property damage), Workers' compensation. E-mail: Wells_Law@msn.com.

WELMAKER, FORREST NOLAN, lawyer; b. McKinney, Tex., Aug. 13, 1925; s. Felix E. and Forrest Love (Baker) W.; div.; children: Forrest Nolan Jr., Mary Elizabeth Welmaker Young, Byron Skillin. BBA, U. Tex., 1950, LLD, 1953. Bar: Tex. 1953, U.S. Dist. Ct. (so. and we. dists.) Tex. 1956, U.S. Ct. Appeals (5th cir.) 1956, U.S. Tax Ct. 1959, U.S. Supreme Ct. 1956. Pvt. practice, San Antonio, 1953—. Past bd. dirs., officer United Fund San Antonio, San Antonio chpt. ARC, Children Welfare Bur. San Antonio, San Antonio YMCA. Capt. USNR, 1943-46, PTO, 1950-52, Korea. Fellow Tex. Bar Found., San Antonio Bar Found.; mem. San Antonio Bar Assn. (past bd. dirs., v.p., pres.), Tex. Assn. Def. Counsel, San Antonio Res. Officer Assn., Tex. Bar Assn. (past bd. dirs.), San Antonio Pla. Club, San Antonio German Club. Episcopalian. Avocations: handball, boating. General civil litigation, Personal injury (including property damage), Product liability. Home: 114 W Brandon Dr San Antonio TX 78209-6404

WELSH, SIR ALFRED JOHN, lawyer, consultant; b. Louisville, May 10, 1947; s. Elvin Alfred and Carol (Kleymeyer) W.; m. Lee Mitchell, Aug. 1, 1970; children: Charles Kleymeyer, Kathryn Thomas. BA, Centre Coll., 1969; JD, U. Ky., 1972; LLM in Internat. Law cum laude, U. Brussels, 1973. Bar: Ky. 1972, U.S. Dist. Ct. (we. and ea. dists.) Ky. 1972, U.S. Ct. Appeals (6th cir.) 1972. Asst. atty. Ky. Atty. Gen. Office, Frankfort, 1973-74; legis. counsel to congressman Ho. of Reps., Washington, 1974-77; mng. ptnr. Adams, Hayward and Welsh, Louisville, 1977—, Boone Welsh and Hayward Internat. Law. Hon. counsel of Belgium, 1983—; econ. devel. advisor Kingdom of Belgium; mem. Ky. Econ. Adv. Coun., 1991-94; pres. Transcontinental Trading Cons., Ltd.; del. North African Mideast Econ. Summit Conf., Morocco, 1994; bd. dirs. Intervention Resources Ctr., Inc. Bd. dirs. Greater Louisville Swim Found., 1983-94, exec. com., 1994—; bd. dirs. Louisville com. Coun. Fgn. Rels., 1993—, also pres.; bd. dirs. Jefferson County Alcohol and Drug Abuse Found., Louisville, 1986-98, Internat. Resolve, Louisville Internat. Cultural Ctr.; mem. econ. task force of Ky. Legis. Agts.; mem. Louisville Meml. Auditorium Commn., Louisville Meml. Commn. Decorated knight Order of the Crown (Belgium). Mem. ABA (internat. law sect., commn. on impairment), ATLA, Ky. Bar Assn. (bd. dirs. 1981-82, pres. young lawyers divsn. 1981-82), Ky. Acad. Trial Lawyers, Am. Judicature Soc., Louisville C. of C., Am. Ctr. Foreign Relations. Democrat. Presbyterian. Avocations: swimming, water polo, soccer. Corporate, general, Private international, Personal injury (including property damage). Office: Barristers Hall 1009 S 4th St Louisville KY 40203-3207

WELSH, H. RONALD, lawyer; b. Orange, N.J., Jan. 9, 1950; s. Harry A. and Faye L. (Neal) W.; 1 child, Austin. BS, Northwestern U., 1972; JD, U. Tex., 1975. Bar: Tex. 1975, U.S. Dist. Ct. (so. dist.) Tex. 1989, U.S. Ct. Appeals (5th and 11th cirs.) 1981; cert. in civil trial law and personal injury trial law Tex. Bd. Legal Specialization. Ptnr. Vinson and Elkins, Houston, 1982—. Fellow Am. Coll. Trial Lawyers, Am. Bd. Trial Advs., Tex. Bar Found., Houston Bar Found. General civil litigation, Product liability, Toxic tort. Office: Vinson & Elkins 3219 First City Tower 1001 Fannin St Ste 3300 Houston TX 77002-6706

WELSH, JOHN BERESFORD, JR., retired lawyer; b. Seattle, Feb. 16, 1940; s. John B. and Rowena Morgan (Custer) W. Student, U. Hawaii, 1960, Georgetown U., 1960; BA, U. Wash., 1962; LLB, 1965. Bar: Wash. 1965. Staff counsel Joint Com. on Govtl. Cooperation, 1965-66; asst. atty gen. Dept. Labor and Industries, 1966-67; atty. Legis Counsel; acting as counsel Pub. Health Com., Labor Com., Pub. Employees Collective Bargaining Com., Com. on State Instns. and Youth Devel., State of Wash., 1967-73; sr. counsel Wash. Ho. of Reps., Ho. Com. on Social and Health Svcs., Olympia, WA, 1973-86; atty., spkr. Ho. of Reps., 1973; counsel Ho. Com. Human Svcs., 1987-91, 93-95, Ho. Com. on Health Care, 1987—2003; ret., 2003. Counsel Ho. Com. on Trade and Econ. Devel., 1995-98, Joint Select Com. on Nurse Delegation, 1995-98, Joint Select Com. on Oral Health, 1996. legal cons. Gov's. Planning Commn. Vocat. Rehab., 1968, Gov.'s Commn. on Youth Involvement, 1969; envoy from Gov. Wash. to investiture of Prince of Wales, London, 1969, fac. Nat. Conf. State Legislatures, Denver, 1977, New Orleans, 1977; fac. Coun. Licensure, Enforcement and Regulation, San Francisco, 1984, Orlando, Fla., 1985, Denver, 1986, Kansas City, Mo., 1987, Washington, 1988, Indpls., 1989, Seattle, 1990, Ft. Lauderdale, Fla., 1991, Albuquerque, 1992, Boston, 1994, San Antonio, 1995, Norfolk, 1997; steering com., 1986-90, legis. issues com., 1986-88, Coun. of State Govts. com. on suggested state legis., 1988-95, subcom. scope and agenda, 1988-95. Vol. Hampton Rds. U.S. Naval Mus., mem. gov's. state medal merit com., 1986—. Recipient Gov.'s award for Excellence in State Health Care Policy, 2002. Mem. Wash. Bar Assn., Soc. des Amis du Musee de l'Armee, Paris, English Speaking Union, La Societe Napoleonienne (pres.), Medals Soc. Am., Sons of Union Veterans of the Civil War, Custer Battlefield Hist. & Mus. Assn., Northwest Hist. Assn. (pres., bd. dirs.), The Colonial Williamsburg Found., Napoleonic Alliance (bd. dirs.), World Affairs Coun., English Speaking Union, Friends of Old Ft. Stevens (bd. dirs.), Friends of Willie & Joe, Phi Delta Phi. Home: 1700 Evergreen Park Lane SW Olympia WA 98502

WELSH, PAUL PATRICK, retired lawyer; b. L.I., Dec. 13, 1941; s. Howard P. and Kathryn W.; m. Linda Franz, May 25, 1968; children: Sarah L., Carolyn A. AB, U. Pa., 1963, LLB, 1966. Bar: Pa. 1966, U.S. Dist. Ct. (ea. dist.) Pa. 1966, U.S. Dist. Ct. Del. 1970, U.S. Ct. Appeals (3d cir.) 1967, Del. 1968, U.S. Supreme Ct. 1972. Assoc. Morgan, Lewis & Bockius, Phila., 1966-67, Morris, Nichols, Arsht & Tunnell, Wilmington, Del., 1967-72, ptnr., 1972-99; Rep. candidate for Del. Senate, 2000. Mem. comty. adv. bd. Wilmington (Del.) News Jour., 1998—2000. Contbr. articles to profl jours. chpts to Lawyers Coop 3d cir. Practice Guide. Mem. N.J. and Newark Rep. Orgns. Mem.: ABA, Del. Bar Assn., Rodney Sq. Club, Whist Club, Univ. Club, Greenville Country Club. Unitarian Universalist. Bankruptcy, Federal civil litigation, State civil litigation. Home: 319 Cox Rd Newark DE 19711-3023 E-mail: paulwelsh@dca.net.

WELSH, SUE C. law librarian; b. Denver, Mar. 5, 1943; d. William Glenn and Viola West Calhoun; m. Neal W. Welsh, Oct. 5, 1968; children: Erick, Ethan. BA, Colo. State U., 1965; MS in Libr. Sci., Cath. U. Am., 1978. Info. specialist U.S. Fed. Jud. Ctr., Washington, 1972—81; deputy cir. libr. U.S. Ct. Appeals (9th cir.), San Francisco, 1981—90; head elec. info. U. Pacific, McGeorge Sch. Law, Sacramento, 1990—. Mem.: Western Pacific Chpt. Law Librs., No. Calif. Assn. Law Librs. (pres. 2001—02), Am. Assn. Law Librs., Kappa Delta. Office: U of Pacific McGeorge Sch Law Schaber Law Libr 3282 5th Ave Sacramento CA 95817 E-mail: swelsh@uop.edu.

WELT, PHILIP STANLEY, lawyer, consultant; b. Freeport, N.Y., July 5, 1959; s. Morris and Rose (Offenberg) W.; m. Karen Teresa Gault, May 22, 1994. BBA summa cum laude, Hofstra U., 1983; MBA, Columbia U., 1988; JD cum laude, NYU, 1995. Bar: N.J. 1995, N.Y. 1995; U.S. Dist. Ct. N.J. 1995, U.S. Dist. Ct. (so. and ea. dists.) N.Y. 1996, U.S. Ct. Appeals (2d cir.), 1997, U.S. Ct. Appeals Armed Forces, 2000, U.S. Supreme Ct. 1999; CPA, N.Y. Sr. mgr. Deloitte & Touche, N.Y.C., 1983-92; assoc. Reboul MacMurray Hewitt Maynard & Kristol, N.Y.C., 1993, Davis Polk & Wardwell, N.Y.C., 1994, 1996-2001; jud. clk. U.S. Dist. Ct. N.J., Newark, 1995-96; special asst. dist. atty. Kings Co., N.Y., 1999—; asst. gen. counsel Am. Internat. Group, Inc., 2001—. Bd. dirs., treas. Pub. Interest Law Found., N.Y.C., 1993-94; guest spkr. Boy Scouts Am., Nassau County, 1984-91, Nat. Assn. Accts., N.Y./N.J., 1988-92, others. Sr. editor Columbia Jour. World Bus., 1986-88; sr. exec. editor Ann. Survey Am. Law, 1993-95; contbr. articles to profl. jours. Vol. income tax asst. Dept. Treasury, IRS, N.Y.C., 1981-87; vol. Variety-The Children's Charity, N.Y.C., 1985-87; advisor Friends of Jon Kaiman, Nassau County, 1995. Provost's scholar Hofstra U., 1981-83, Deloitt & Touche fellow Columbia U., 1986-88; recipient Appreciation cert. Dept. Treasury, IRS, 1981-87, Variety, 1985-87, Bovenaan Outstanding Cmty. Svc. award Hofstra U., 1983, Orison S. Marden Moot Ct. Advocacy award NYU Sch. Law, 1993, Seymore A. Levy meml. award, 1995. Mem. ABA, AICPA, N.Y. State Bar Assn., N.Y. State Soc. CPAs, Beta Alpha Psi, Beta Gamma Sigma. Avocations: golf, rock climbing, photography, philately, amateur radio. Finance, Public international, Mergers and acquisitions. Home: 157 Mountain Wood Rd Stamford CT 06903-2107 Office: Am Internat Group Inc 70 Pine St New York NY 10270 E-mail: psw12@columbia.edu.

WENDEL, CHARLES ALLEN, lawyer; b. Lockport, N.Y., Aug. 13, 1942; s. Harold Henry and Doris Lillian (Gardner) W.; m. Helen W. Roberts, June 23, 1973; children: William Charles, Jonathan David. BChem Engrng., Rensselaer Poly Inst., 1964; JD, Am. U., 1968. Bar: N.Y. 1969, Va. 1971, D.C. 1980, U.S. Ct. Appeals (fed. and 4th cirs.), U.S. Dsit. Ct. (ea. and we. dists.) Va., U.S. Supreme Ct. Patent examiner U.S. Patent and Trademark Office, Washington, 1964-66; patent trainee Union Carbide Corp., Washington, 1966-68, patent atty. N.Y.C., 1968-70; assoc., then ptnr. Stevens, Davis, Miller & Mosher, Arlington, Va., 1970-83; ptnr. firm Wegner & Bretschneider, Washington, 1983-85; assoc. solicitor U.S. Patent and Trademark Office, 1985-88; assoc. Lyon & Lyon, Washington, 1988-90; founding ptnr. Parkhurst, Wendel & Rossi, Alexandria, Va., 1990-95. Contbr. articles to profl. jours. Mem. Va. State Bar (patent trademark copyright sect., chmn. 1977-78), Am. Intellectual Patent Law Assn., Patent Lawyers Club Washington (prs. 1982-83), Delta Theta Phi. Republican. Intellectual property. Office: Parkhurst & Wendel LLP 1421 Prince St Ste 210 Alexandria VA 22314-2805

WENGER, DANIEL ERIC, lawyer; b. Phila., Nov. 15, 1973; s. Alexander Azyk and Norma Lee Wenger. Bachelors, Washington U., 1995; JD, Hofstra U., 1999. Bar: NJ 2001, NY 2002. Legal asst. Shearman & Sterling, N.Y.C., 1995—96; intern Ct. TV, N.Y.C., 1997; jud. intern Hon. Cornelius Blackshear, N.Y.C., 1998; contract assoc. Wright, Pindulic & Hamelsky, Paramus, NJ, 2001—02; assoc. Costello, Shea & Gaffney, LLP, N.Y.C., 2002—. Mem.: ABA, NJ State Bar Assn., NY State Bar Assn. Democrat. Jewish. Avocations: tennis, weightlifting, water sports, travel. General civil litigation, Corporate, general. Home: 23 Bondsburry Ln Melville NY 11747 Office: Costello Shea & Gaffney LLP 44 Wall St New York NY 10005 E-mail: danwenger@lycos.com.

WENNER, CHARLES RODERICK, lawyer; b. New Haven, Jan. 10, 1947; s. Charles Bellew and Joan Rhoda (Morrison) W.; m. Jovita C. Vergara, June 11, 1999; children: Abigail Jessica, Charles Roderick Jr. BS, Coll. Charleston, 1969; JD, U. Conn., 1973. Bar: Conn. 1974, D.C. 1977. Law clk. Conn. Superior Ct., Hartford, 1973-74; staff atty. SEC, Washington, 1974-76, spl. counsel to chmn., 1976-77; assoc. Fulbright & Jaworski, Washington, 1977-81, ptnr., 1981—. Lectr. law Sch. Law U. Conn., 1973-74. Trustee Calvary United Meth. Ch., Arlington, Va., 1993-95, 97-98; counselor Gospel Mission of Washington, 1991—; bd. dirs. Operation Friendship Internat., Inc., Washington, 1993—. Recipient Am. Hist. award DAR, Charleston, 1969. Mem. ABA, D.C. Bar Assn. Methodist. Avocation: running. Securities. Home: 1808 South Lynn St Arlington VA 22202 Office: Fulbright & Jaworski 801 Pennsylvania Ave NW Fl 3-5 Washington DC 20004-2623

WENTWORTH, EARL JEFFREY, lawyer, realtor, state legislator; b. San Antonio, Nov. 20, 1940; s. Earl and Margaret Wentworth; m. Karla Whitsitt; children: Jason, Matthew. BA, Tex. A&M U., 1962; JD, Tex. Tech. U., 1972. Bar: Tex. 1971, DC. 1972. Staff mem. U.S. Congressman Bob Price; pvt. practice law San Antonio; mem. Tex. Ho. of Reps., 1988-92, Tex. Senate, 1993—. County commr. Bexar County, 1977-82; bd. regents Tex. State U. Sys. Spl. agt. U.S. Army Counterintelligence Corps, 1962—65. Republican. Office: PO Box 12068 Austin TX 78711-2068 also: 1250 NE Loop 410 Ste 720 San Antonio TX 78209-1525

WERDEGAR, KATHRYN MICKLE, state supreme court justice; b. San Francisco; d. Benjamin Christie and Kathryn Marie (Clark) Mickle; m. David Werdegar; children: Maurice Clark, Matthew Mickle. Student, Wellesley Coll., 1954—55; AB with honors, U. Calif., Berkeley, 1957; JD with highest distinction, George Washington U., 1962; JD, U. Calif., Berkeley, 1990. Bar: Calif. 1964, U.S. Dist. Ct. (no. dist.) Calif. 1964, U.S. Ct. Appeals (9th cir.) 1964, Calif. Supreme Ct. 1964. Legal asst. civil rights divsn. U.S. Dept. Justice, Washington, 1962—63; rsch. atty., author Calif. State Study Commn. on Mental Retardation, 1963—64; assoc. U. Calif. Ctr. for Study of Law and Soc., Berkeley, 1965—67; spl. cons. State Dept. Mental Health, 1967—68; cons., author Calif. Coll. Trial Judges, 1968—71; dir. criminal law divsn. Calif. Continuing Edn. of Bar, 1971—78; assoc. dean acad. and student affairs, assoc. prof. Sch. Law, U. San Francisco, 1978—81; sr. staff atty. Calif. 1st Dist. Ct. Appeal, 1981—85, Calif. Supreme Ct., 1985—91; assoc. justice Calif. 1st Dist. Ct. Appeal, 1991—94, Calif. Supreme Ct., San Francisco, 1994—. Regents' lectr. U. Calif., Berkeley, 2000. Author: Benchbook: Misdemeanor Procedure, 1971, Misdemeanor Procedure Benchbook rev., 1975, Misdemeanor Procedure Benchbook; supp., Misdemeanor Procedure Benchbook rev., 1983; contbr. California Continuing Education of the Bar books; editor: California Criminal Law Practice series, Discovery, 1975, California Uninsured Motorist Practice, 1973, I California Civil Procedure Before Trial, 1977. Recipient Charles Glover award, George Washington U., 1962, J. William Fulbright award for disting. pub. svc., George Washington U. Law Sch. Alumni Assn., 1996, excellence in achievement award, Calif. Alumni Assn., 1996, Roger J. Traynor Appellate Justice of Yr. award, 1996, Justice of Yr. award, Consumer Attys. of Calif., 1998, Citation award, Boalt Hall Sch. Law U. Calif., Berkeley, 2002, also 5 Am. Jurisprudence awards, 1960—62. Mem.: Am. Law Inst., Nev./Calif. Women Judges Assn., Calif. Judges Assn., Nat. Assn. Women Judges, Calif. Supreme Ct. Hist. Soc. (bd. dir.), Order of the Coif. Office: Calif Supreme Court 350 McAllister St San Francisco CA 94102-4797

WERDER, HORST HEINRICH, lawyer; b. Stettin, Germany, Aug. 13, 1924; arrived in U.S., 1937; BS, Columbia U., 1949, JD, 1951. Bar: N.Y. 1951, Ill. 1962. Ptnr. Haseltine & Lake, N.Y.C., 1952-61, Baker & McKenzie, Chgo., 1961-89. Mem. Columbia U. Club of S.W. Fla., Mich. Shores Club (Wilmette, Ill.). Intellectual property, Private international, Trademark and copyright. Office: 1001 Arbor Lake Dr Naples FL 34110-7080 Fax: 239-594-8498.

WERLEIN, EWING, JR., federal judge; b. Houston, Sept. 14, 1936; s. Ewing and Ruth (Storey) W.; m. Kay McGibbon Werlein, June 29, 1963; children: Ewing Kenneth, Emily Kay. BA, So. Meth. U., 1958; LLB, U. Tex., 1961. Bar: Tex. 1961, U.S. Dist. Ct. (so. dist.) Tex. 1965, U.S. Dist. Ct. (ea. dist.) Tex. 1990, U.S. Ct. Appeals (5th cir.) 1970, U.S. Ct. Appeals (10th cir.) 1980, U.S. Claims Ct. 1985, U.S. Tax Ct. 1985, U.S. Supreme Ct. 1983. Ptnr. Vinson & Elkins, Houston, 1964-92; dist. judge U.S. Dist. Ct. (so. dist.) Tex., 1992—. Trustee So. Meth. U., Dallas, 1976-92, Asbury Theol. Sem., Wilmore, Ky., 1989—; mem. gen. bd. pub. United Meth. Ch., Nashville, 1974-84, chmn., 1980-84, chancellor Tex. ann. conf., 1977—; mem. exec. com. World Meth. Counh., 1981-96, treas, 1991-93. Capt. USAF, 1961-64. Fellow Am. Coll. Trial Lawyers, 1984, Internat. Soc. Barristers, 1987; recipient Disting. Alumni award SMU Alumni Assn., 1994. Fellow Am. Bar Found., Tex. Bar Found., Houston Bar Found.; mem. State Bar Tex. (dir. 1990-93), Nat. Conf. Bar Pres., Houston Bar Assn. (pres. 1988-89), Houston C. of C. (life), SAR, Order of Coif, Petroleum Club, Houston Club, Phi Beta Kappa. Office: US Dist Ct Tex US Courthouse 515 Rusk St Ste 9136 Houston TX 77002-2605

WERNER, ROBERT J. lawyer; b. Wichita, Kans., Dec. 1, 1957; s. John Joseph and Lorreta Catherine Werner; m. Rebecca A. Winterscheidt, May 26, 1983; 1 child, Rachel C. BBA, Wichita State U., 1980; JD, U. Kans., 1983; LLM in Taxation, NYU, 1986. Atty. Jennings, Strouss & Salmon, PLC, Phoenix, 1983—99, Onsager, Werner & Oberg, PLC, Phoenix, 1999—. Taxation, general. Office: Onsager Werner and Oberg PLC 3200 N Central Ave Phoenix AZ 85012

WERNER, THOMAS M. lawyer; b. Des Moines, June 1, 1954; s. Charles T. and Olivia M. W.; m. Debra L. Miller, May 5, 1990. BA in journalism, Drake U., 1976, JD, 1979. Bar: Iowa 1980, U.S. Dist. Ct. (so. dist.) Iowa 1980, U.S. Ct. Appeals (8th cir.) 1980, U.S. Dist. Ct. (no. dist.) Iowa 1981. Asst. county atty. Polk County, Des Moines, 1980-82; with Anderson & Werner, Des Moines, 1982—. Mem. Iowa Trial Lawyers Assn., Des Moines Golf and Country Club. Avocations: travel, golf. Labor (including EEOC, Fair Labor Standards Act, labor-management relations, NLRB, OSHA), Personal injury (including property damage), Workers' compensation. Office: Anderson Werner & Romar 3030 Ingersoll Ave Des Moines IA 50312-3403

WERSHALS, PAUL LEONARD, lawyer; b. Bklyn., July 10, 1942; AA in Bus. Adminstrn., Midwest Inst. Bus. Adminstrn., 1963; BS in Bus. Adminstrn., Babson Coll., 1965; JD, Suffolk U., 1969; LLM, NYU, 1975. Bar: N.Y. 1974, U.S. Supreme Ct. 1974; cert. comml. mediator Nassau Co. Supreme Ct., 2002. Mem. Nassau County Assigned Counsel Defender Plan; mem. legal com., citizens adv. com. for cablevision Town of North Heampstead, N.Y., 1976-97. Mem. Sen. Michael J. Tully's legis. adv. com., 1982-97; dir. Great Neck (N.Y.) Sr. Citizens Ctr., Inc., Town of North Hempstead, 1985-89. Mem. Am. Judges Assn., N.Y. State Trial Lawyers Assn., Nassau County Bar Assn. (arbitrator 1981—, mem. arbitration tribunal panel 1984—), Great Neck (N.Y.) Lawyers Assn. (bd. dirs. 1973—, sec. 1981-84,pres. 1985, chmn. bd. dirs. 1986-87), Phi Alpha Delta (mem. moot ct.). General practice, Probate (including wills, trusts), Property, real (including real estate development, water). Office: 10 Cuttermill Rd Great Neck NY 11021-3201 Fax: 516 829-6219.

WERT, ROBERT CLIFTON, lawyer; b. Pleasantville, N.J., Jan. 8, 1944; s. Clifton Robert and Anna Louise (McLarren) W.; m. Grace Elizabeth Dunbar, Dec. 16, 1967; children: Andrew, Amy, Bethany, Laura. BS in Acctg., Temple U., 1965, JD, 1968; grad., JAG Sch., 1982, Command & Gen. Staff Coll., 1984, U.S. Army JFK Spl. Warfare Ctr, 1987. Bar: Pa. 1968, U.S. Dist. Ct. (ea. dist.) Pa. 1968, U.S. Ct. Mil. Appeals 1969, US. Supreme Ct. 1981. Commd. 2d lt. mil. police USAR, 1965, advanced through ranks to lt. col., 1984, ret., 1990; mil. judge U.S. Army, Okinawa, Japan, 1970-73, chief trial counsel, 1973, staff judge adv. Valley Forge Army Hosp., 1973-74, chief trial counsel, 1974—76, chief legal asst. and claims, 1976-77, ret., 1990; chief staff counsel Southeastern Penn Transp. Authority, Phila., 1977-78, acting chief counsel, 1978-80, gen. counsel, 1980-84, dept. gen. mgr., 1984-86; exec. dir. Blank Rome LLP, Phila., 1986—. Owner Insulco, King of Prussia, Pa., 1972-79; co-owner Master Page Inc., Malvern, Pa., 1985-93. Bd. dirs. Evang. Assn. for Promotion of Edn., St. David's, Pa., Ea. Coll., 1988—, Crime Prevention Assn. Charitable Giving, Phila., 1991—; bd. dirs. Caring People Alliance, Phila., 1988-2001, chair exec. com., 1992-94, 1998-2001, treas., 1994-96, v.p., 1997-98; pres. Charlestown Townwatch, 1980-2000; coord. Twp. Emergency, 1984-99; vice-chair bd. supr. Charlestown Twp., 1998-2000; mem. bd. trustees Great Valley Presbyn. Ch., 2001—; deacon, Sunday Sch. supt., mem. bldg. com., chmn. property com. Ch. of the Savior, Wayne, Pa.; bd. dirs., asst. treas. Adv. Meth. Ch., Phila. Decorated Meritorious Svc. medal, Army Achievement medal, Overseas Svc. medal, Nat. Def. Svc. medal, various Res. decorations; recipient Pa. Gov.'s award, 1989. Mem. Assn. of Legal Adminstrs., Phila. Bar Assn., Temple U. Law Alumni Assn. (exec. com. 1995-96), Masons. Avocation: woodworking. Corporate, general,

Military, Transportation. Office: Blank Rome LLP 1 Logan Sq Philadelphia PA 19103-6998 E-mail: wert@blankrome.com.

WESCH, ANGELIA DEAN, lawyer; b. Dallas, Feb. 18, 1964; d. Calvin W. and Judy D. Wesch; children: Austin, Travis. BA with honors, U. Tex., 1986; JD, Tex. Tech U., 1989. Bar: Tex. 1989, U.S. Dist. Ct. (so. dist.) Tex. 1991, U.S. Ct. Appeals (5th cir.) 1991, Wash. 1993, U.S. Dist. Ct. (we. dist.) Wash. 1993, Alaska 1996. Atty. Andrews & Kurth, Houston, 1989-93, Stanislaw Ashbaugh LLP, Seattle, 1993-97, Eisenhower & Carlson PLLC, Tacoma, 1997—. Pres., bd. dirs. Crew Network. Mem. Wash. State Bar Assn. (environ. and land use sect.), Master Builders Assn. Pierce County. Construction, Land use and zoning (including planning), Property, real (including real estate development, water). Office: Eisenhower & Carlson PLLC 1201 Pacific Ave Ste 1200 Tacoma WA 98402-4395 E-mail: awesch@eisenhowerlaw.com.

WESLEY, RICHARD C. judge; b. Canandaigua, N.Y., Aug. 1, 1949; s. Charles and Beatrice W.; m. Kathryn Rice; 2 children. BA summa cum laude, SUNY, Albany, 1971; JD, Cornell U., 1974. Assoc. Harris, Beach & Wilcox, 1974-76; assoc. atty. Welch, Streb & Porter, 1976-77; ptnr. Streb, Porter, Meyer & Wesley, 1977—87; asst. counsel to minority NY State Assembly, 1979—82; justice Supreme Ct. 7th Jud. Dist., 1987—94; supervising judge Criminal Cts. 7th Jud. Dist., 1991; judge appellate div. Supreme Ct. 4th Dept., 1994—96; assoc. judge N.Y. Ct. Appeals, Albany, 1997—2003; circuit judge U.S. Ct. Appeals, 2nd Cir., New York, NY, 2003—. Creator Felony Screening Program, 1993; lectr. in field; bd. trustees Ctr. Dispute Resolution, Pre-Trial Svcs. Corp. Editor: Cornell Law Rev. Asst. counsel to Assembly Rep. leader James L. Emery, 1979-1982; assemblyman N.Y. State 136th Assembly Dist., 1982-84, 84-86; chair Livingston County Alcohol and Drug Abuse Prevention Coun.; bd. trustees United Ch. Livonia, Chances and Changes, Charles Settlement House; bd. dirs. Myers' Found.; driver Livonia Vol. Ambulance. Named Legislator of Yr., Livingston-Wyoming Assn. Retarded Citizens, 1988; recipient Disting. SUNY Alumni award SUNY Alumni Assn., 1997. Fellow N.Y. State Bar Found.; mem. Livingston County Bar Assn. (sec.), Supreme Ct. Justices Assn. (pres. 7th jud. dist.). Office: 1702 US Courthouse 40 Centre St New York NY 10007-1561*

WESLEY, WILLIAM MATTHEW, lawyer; b. Green Bay, Wis., Dec. 19, 1943; BEE, Marquette U., 1966; JD cum laude, Loyola U., Chgo., 1971. Bar: Ill. 1971, U.S. Dist. Ct. (no. dist.) Ill. 1982, U.S. Ct. Appeals (7th cir. and fed. cir.) 1976, U.S. Supreme Ct. 1992. Engr. Tex. Instruments, Motorola; ptnr. McAndrews, Held & Malloy, Ltd., Chgo. Hearing officer Ill. Pollution Control Bd., 1972-85. Named one of Leading Experts in Patent Law, Euromoney Mag., 1997-99. Mem. ABA, Chgo. Bar Assn., Am. Intellectual Property Law Assn., Fed. Cir. Bar Assn., Intellectual Property Law Assn. Chgo., Internat. Trade Commn. Trial Lawyers Assn. (exec. com. 1991—), Licensing Execs. Soc., Tau Beta Pi, Eta Kappa Nu, Alpha Sigma Nu. Intellectual property, Public international, Patent. Office: McAndrews Held & Malloy Ltd 500 W Madison St Fl 34 Chicago IL 60661-2511 E-mail: bwesley@mhmlaw.com.

WESSEL, PETER, lawyer; b. N.Y.C., N.Y., Feb. 2, 1952; s. Harry Nathan Jr. and Charlene (Freimuth) W.; married Vicki Brodsky Scheck; children: Daniel, Elizabeth, Justin Scheck, Matthew Scheck. BS, Syracuse U., 1974, MPA, JD, 1980. Bar: N.Y. 1981, U.S. Dist. Ct. (no., so., ea. and we. dists.) N.Y. 1981, Fla. 1984, U.S. Ct. Mil. Appeals, 1988, U.S. Ct. Appeals (2d cir.) 1988, U.S. Supreme Ct. 1988. Confidential law clk. to Hon. David F. Lee Jr. N.Y. Supreme Ct., 1980-82; sr. atty. criminal def. div. The Legal Aid Soc., N.Y.C., 1982-87; pvt. practice N.Y.C., 1987—. Notes and comments editor Syracuse Law Rev., 1979-80; contbr. articles to profl. jours. Robert M. Anderson award for Writing and Legal Scholarship, 1980, Neal Brewster scholar, 1977-78, Syracuse U. Coll. Law scholar 1978-79, Louis Waters Meml. scholar, 1979-80, Hiscock, Cowie, Bruce & Lee scholar, 1979-80; Martindale-Hubbell a-v rated. Mem. ABA, N.Y. State Bar Assn., Assn. of Bar of City of N.Y., Fla. Bar Assn., Nat. Assn. Criminal Def. Lawyers, N.Y. State Assn. Criminal Def. Lawyers, N.Y. State Defender Assn., N.Y. State Trial Lawyers Assn., N.Y. County Lawyers Assn., N.Y. Criminal Bar Assn. General civil litigation, Criminal, Personal injury (including property damage).

WESSLING, ROBERT BRUCE, retired lawyer; b. Chgo., Oct. 8, 1937; s. Robert Euans and Marguerite (Rickert) W.; m. Judith Ann Hanson, Aug. 26, 1961; children: Katherine, Jennifer, Carolyn. BA, DePauw U., 1959; JD, U. Mich., 1962. Bar: U.S. Ct. Appeals (9th cir.) 1965. Assoc. Latham & Watkins, L.A., 1962-70, ptnr., 1970-94, of counsel, 1995—2002; ret., 2002. Bd. govs. Fin. Lawyers Conf., Los Angeles, 1974-2000. Mem. World Affairs Coun., L.A., Town Hall, L.A.; trustee DePauw U. Mem. ABA, Los Angeles Bar Assn., Phi Beta Kappa, Phi Delta Phi, Phi Eta Sigma, Order of Coif. Democrat. Methodist. Avocations: tennis, travel. Banking, Commercial, contracts (including sales of goods; commercial financing), Property, real (including real estate development, water). E-mail: bbwessling@aol.com.

WEST, CAROL CATHERINE, law educator; b. Phila., May 23, 1944; d. Scott G. and Helen (Young) West. BA, Miss. U. for Women, 1966; MLS, U. So. Miss., 1984; JD, U. Miss., 1970. Pub. svcs. law libr. U. Va., Charlottesville, 1966-67; catalog law libr. U. Miss., Oxford, 1967-70; legis. reference libr. Miss. Legislature, Jackson, 1970-75; law libr. Miss. Coll., Jackson, 1975-94, prof. law, 1975—. Del. White House Conf. Libr. and Info. Svcs., 1991; cons. to Parliament of Armenia, 1995, Parliament of Tanzania, 1997; mem. bd. commrs. Miss. Libr. Commn., 1993—98; mem., sec. Miss. Task Force on Gender Fairness in the Cts. Mem.: ABA, Miss. Women's Polit. Network (bd. dirs. 1998—2000), Miss. Libr. Assn., Miss. Women Lawyers Assn. (bd. dirs. 1991—93), Hinds County Bar, Miss. Bar Assn. (Susie Blue Buchanan award 2001). Methodist. Office: Miss Coll Law Sch 151 E Griffith St Jackson MS 39201-1302

WEST, JAMES C., JR., lawyer; b. White Sulphur Springs, W.Va., Mar. 15, 1932; LLB, W.Va. U., 1959. Bar: W.Va. 1959. Law clk. to Hon. Herbert S. Boreman, Judge of 4th Cir. Ct. Appeals, 1958—59; atty. Clifford, Jones & Williams, Clarksburg, W.Va., 1960—89, West & Jones (formerly Clifford, Jones & Williams), Clarksburg, W.Va., 1989—. Fellow: Am. Bd. Trial Advs., Am. Coll. Trial Lawyers; mem.: ABA, Assn. Trial Lawyers Am., W.Va. Trial Lawyers Assn. (pres. 1971), Harrison County Bar Assn., W.Va. State Bar (bd. govs. 1975 1978), Phi Delta Phi. Office: West and Jones PO Box 2348 360 Washington Ave Clarksburg WV 26301*

WEST, JAMES JOSEPH, lawyer; b. Tarentum, Pa., Nov. 26, 1945; s. Samuel Elwood and Rose (McIntyre) W.; m. Kathleen Geslak, Aug. 19, 1967; children: Joseph Allen, Yvonne Michelle, KaiLynn Ann. BS in Econs., St. Vincent Coll., 1967; JD, Duquesne U., 1970. Bar: Pa. 1971, U.S. Dist. Ct. (we. dist.) Pa. 1971, U.S. Ct. Appeals (3d cir.) 1971, U.S. Dist. Ct. (mid. dist.) Pa., 1980. Law clk. to presiding justice U.S. Dist. Ct., Pa., 1970-74; asst. U.S. atty. chief appellate sect. U.S. Atty.'s Office, Pitts., 1974-79; dep. dir. criminal law Pa. Atty. Gen.'s Office, Harrisburg, 1979-82; 1st asst. U.S. atty. U.S. Dist. Ct. (mid. dist.) Pa., Harrisburg, 1982-84, U.S. atty., 1984-93; assoc. Sprague & Sprague, Phila., 1993-95; pvt. practice Harrisburg, Pa., 1995—. Mem. Nat. Environ. Enforcement Council. Recipient Outstanding Performance award U.S. Dept. Justice, 1974-78, Commendation Gov. of Pa., 1981. Mem. Pa. Bar Assn., Allegheny County Bar Assn., Dauphin County Bar Assn. Republican. Roman Catholic. Home: 1222 Cardinal Way Rd Hummelstown PA 17036-8548 Office: James West 105 N Front St Harrisburg PA 17101-1483 E-mail: jwestlaw@aol.com.

WEST, JOHN CARL, lawyer, former ambassador, former governor; b. Camden, S.C., Aug. 27, 1922; s. Shelton J. and Mattie (Ratterree) W.; m. Lois Rhame, Aug. 29, 1942; children: John Carl Jr., Douglas Allen, Shelton West Bosley. BA, The Citadel, 1942; LB magna cum laude, U. S.C., 1948; D (hon.), The Citadel, U. S.C., Davidson Coll., Presbyn. Coll., Francis Marion Coll., Wofford Coll., Coll. Charleston. Bar: S.C. 1947. Ptnr. West, Holland, Furman & Cooper, Camden, S.C., 1947-70; state senator Kershaw County State of S.C., 1954-66; lt. gov. State of S.C., 1966-70, gov., 1971-75; ptnr. West, Cooper, Bowen, Beard & Smoot, Camden, S.C., 1975-77; amb. to Saudi Arabia, 1977-81; sr. ptnr. West & West, P.A., Hilton Head Island, 1981-88. Disting. prof. Middle East Studies U. S.C., 1981—; of counsel McNair Law Firm, Hilton Head Island, S.C., 1988-92, Bethea, Jordan & Griffin, P.A., Hilton Head Island, S.C., 1993—. Maj. AUS, 1942-46. Decorated Army commendation medal; comdr. Order of Merit (West Germany); recipient Freedom award S.C. C. of C. Mem. Phi Beta Kappa. Democrat. Presbyterian. Address: PO Box 13 Hilton Head Island SC 29938-0013

WEST, JOSEPH D. lawyer; b. Ashland, Pa., Apr. 18, 1949; BCE, Villanova U., 1971; JD, George Washington U., 1977. Bar: Va. 1977, D.C. 1977. Sr. ptnr. Arnold & Porter, Washington, 1993—. Mem. Order of Coif. Federal civil litigation, Construction, Government contracts and claims. Office: Arnold & Porter 555 12th St NW Washington DC 20004-1206 E-mail: Joseph_West@aporter.com.

WEST, LEE ROY, federal judge; b. Clayton, Okla., Nov. 26, 1929; s. Calvin and Nicie (Hill) W.; m. MaryAnn Ellis, Aug. 29, 1952; children: Kimberly Ellis, Jennifer Lee. BA, U. Okla., 1952, JD, 1956; LL.M. (Ford Found. fellow), Harvard U., 1963. Bar: Okla. 1956. Individual practice law, Ada, Okla., 1956-61, 63-65; faculty U. Okla. Coll. Law, 1961-62; Ford Found. fellow in law teaching Harvard U., Cambridge, Mass., 1962-63; judge 22d Jud. Dist. Okla., Ada, 1965-73; mem. CAB, Washington, 1973-78, acting chmn., 1977; practice law Tulsa, 1978-79; spl. justice Okla. Supreme Ct., 1965; judge U.S. Dist Ct. (we. dist.) Okla., 1979-94; sr. judge U.S. Dist. Ct. (we. dist.), Okla., 1994—. Editor: Okla. Law Rev. Served to capt. USMC, 1952-54. Recipient Humanitarian award Nat. Conf. Cmty. and Justice, 2000, Jud. Excellence award Okla. Bar Assn., 2000. Mem. U. Okla. Alumni Assn. (dir.), Phi Delta Phi (pres. 1956), Phi Eta Sigma, Order of Coif. Home: 6500 E Danforth Rd Edmond OK 73034-7601 Office: US Dist Ct 3001 US Courthouse 200 NW 4th St Oklahoma City OK 73102-3027

WEST, PEGGY A. lawyer; b. Memphis, Jan. 4, 1956; d. Eugene Conrad and Carol Hicks West; m. Jack Edwin Sinks, Sept. 17, 1983; 1 adopted child, Aimee Jade Sinks 1 child, Charles Andrew Sinks. BS in Com., Fla. State U., 1976, MS in Com., 1978, JD, 1984; ML in Taxation, Emory U. Coll. of Law, 1990. Bar: Ga. Assoc. atty. Arnall Golden & Gregory, Atlanta, 1984—88; fin. counsel, Legal Divsn. Securities and Acquisitions Group The Coca Cola Co., Atlanta, 1988—89, bus. devel. mgr., Corp. Bus. Devel., 1989—91, exec. asst. to sr. v.p. and gen. mgr., Coca Cola Fountain, 1991—93, bus. affairs counsel, 1993—94, sr. fin. counsel, Greater Europe Group, 1994—96, v.p., Bus. Affairs, 1996—. Rsch. asst. Fla. State Supreme Ct. Justice Raymond Ehrlich, 1983. Contbr. articles Fla. State U. Law Rev.; editor: Fla. State U. Law Rev., 1993. Mem.: ABA. Roman Catholic. Office: The Coca Cola Co P O Box 1734 Atlanta GA 30301 also: The Coca Cola Co 1 Coca Cola Plaza NW Atlanta GA 30313-2420

WEST, ROBERT GRADY, lawyer; b. Dallas, Aug. 13, 1947; s. Robert Sorrells and Thelma Grady W.; m. Marsha Lee Riegert, June 5, 1971; children: Kathryn Lee, Laura Elaine. BA, Midwestern State U., 1969; JD, U. Tex., 1972. Bar: Tex. 1972, U.S. Dist. Ct. (no. dist.) Tex. 1975, U.S. Dist. Ct. (ea. dist.) Tex. 1992, U.S. Ct. Appeals (5th cir.) 1976. Assoc. McGown, Godfrey, Decker, McMackin, Shipman & McClane, Ft. Worth, 1972-77, ptnr., 1977-88, Decker, McMackin & McClane, Ft. Worth, 1988-90, Decker, Jones, McMackin, McClane, Hall & Bates, Ft. Worth, 1990-93; assoc. Michener, Larimore, Swindle, Whitaker, et al, Ft. Worth, 1993-98, ptnr., 1999-2000, Whitaker, Chalk, Swindle & Sawyer, 2000—. Bd. regents Midwestern State U., Wichita Falls, Tex., 1992-98; dir. Grace Found., Dallas, 1990-92; mem. Tex. Ctr. Legal Ethics & Professionalism, 1994—, Leadership Ft. Worth, 1984. Mem. Am. Assn. Profl. Landmen, State Bar Tex., Tarrant County Bar Assn. Presbyterian. Avocations: travel, musical theatre, walking, volunteering. Non-profit and tax-exempt organizations, Probate (including wills, trusts), Property, real (including real estate development, water). Office: Whitaker Chalk Swindle & Sawyer 3500 City Ctr Tower II 301 Commerce St Fort Worth TX 76102-4186 E-mail: rwest@whitakerchalk.com.

WEST, SHAWNA, lawyer; b. Houston; m. Keith Rodario. BA, Yale U.; JD, Cornell U. Ptnr. O' Hair & Finch; pvt. practice; ptnr. Meriks, PC. Mem.: ABA, Am. Bar Found. (v.p., pres.-elect). Avocations: writing, basketball. Labor (including EEOC, Fair Labor Standards Act, labor-management relations, NLRB, OSHA), Appellate, Corporate, general. Office: Meriks PC 111 Mozart Ave W Mankato MN 56001

WEST, STEPHEN KINGSBURY, lawyer, director; b. Pittsfield, Mass., Sept. 28, 1928; s. William Bradford and Ruth (Osteyee) W.; m. Ann Wick, Apr. 30, 1955; children: Timothy Wick, Lucy West Engebretson, Todd Kingsbury, Daniel Wick. BA, Yale U., 1950; LL.B., Harvard U., 1953. Assoc. Sullivan & Cromwell, N.Y.C., 1957-64, ptnr., 1964-97, of counsel, 1997—. Bd. dirs. Pioneer Mut. Fund, Boston, AMVESCAP Plc, London, Swiss Helvetin Fund, Inc. Served to lst lt. inf. U.S. Army, 1953-56. Mem. ABA, N.Y. State Bar Assn., Assn. Bar City N.Y. Insurance, Securities, Mergers and acquisitions. Office: Sullivan & Cromwell 125 Broad St Fl 28 New York NY 10004-2489

WESTBROOK, JAMES EDWIN, lawyer, educator; b. Camden, Ark., Sept. 7, 1934; s. Loy Edwin and Helen Lucille (Bethea) W.; m. Elizabeth Kay Farris, Dec. 23, 1956; children: William Michael, Robert Bruce, Matthew David. BA with high honors, Hendrix Coll., 1956; JD with distinction, Duke U., 1959; LLM, Georgetown U., 1965. Bar: Ark. 1959, Okla. 1977, Mo. 1982. Assoc. Mehaffy, Smith & Williams, Little Rock, 1959-62; asst. counsel, subcom. of U.S. Senate Jud. Com., Washington, 1963; legis. asst. U.S. Senate, Washington, 1963-65; asst. prof. law U. Mo., Columbia, 1965-68, asst. dean, 1966-68, assoc. prof., 1968-70, prof., 1970-76, 80—, James S. Rollins prof. law, 1974-76, 80—, Earl F. Nelson prof. law, 1982-99, emeritus prof., 1999—, interim dean, 1981-82; dean U. Okla. Coll. Law, Norman, 1976-80. George Allen vis. prof. law, U. Richmond, 1987; vis. prof. law Duke U., 1988, Washington U., St. Louis, 1996, 2001; reporter Mid-Am. Assembly on Role of State in Urban Crisis, 1970; dir. Summer Internship Program in Local Govt., 1968; cons. various Mo. cities on drafting home-rule charters; mem. Gov.'s Adv. Coun. on Local Govt. Law, 1967-68, Fed. Practice Com. U.S. Dist. Ct. (we. dist.) Mo., 1986-90; chmn. Columbia Charter Revision Commn., 1973-74; mem. spl. com. labor relations Mo. Dept. Labor and Indsl. Rels., 1975; mem., chmn. subcom. on domestic violence Task Force on Gender and Justice, Mo. Jud. Conf., 1990-93; mem. com. to rev. govtl. structure of Boone County, Mo., 1991. Author: (with L. Riskin) Dispute Resolution and Lawyers, 1987, supplement, 1993, 2d edit., 1997, abridged edit. of 2d edit., 1998; contbr. articles to profl. jours. Chair search com. for chancellor U. Mo., Columbia, 1992, chair search com. for provost, 1998. Mem. ABA, Nat. Acad. Arbitrators, Assn. Am. Law Schs. (chmn. local govt. law round table coun. 1972), Ctrl. States Law Sch. Assn. (pres. 1982-83), Mo. Bar Assn. (vice chmn. labor law com. 1986-87, chmn. 1987-88, Spurgeon Smithton award 1995), Order of Coif, Blue Key, Alpha Chi. Roman Catholic. Home: 3609 S Woods Edge Rd Columbia MO 65203-6606 Office: U Mo Sch Law Columbia MO 65211-0001

WESTERBERG, SIV ÖMAN, lawyer, physician; b. Borås, Sweden, June 11, 1932; d. Bror and Magda (Karlsson) Öman; m. Per G.S. Westerberg, June 19, 1964; children: Eva, Carl, Gösta. Medicine Kandidat, U. Uppsala, Sweden, 1954, Medicine Licentiat, 1960; Juris Kandidat, U. Lund, Sweden, 1982. Bar: Sweden 1982, European Commn. Human Rights 1983, European Ct. Human Rights 1987. Physician Univ. Clinics, Gothenburg, Sweden, 1960-64; physician, rschr. Clin. Labs., Univ. Hosp. Sahlgrenska Sjukhuset, Gothenburg, 1961-63; pvt. practice gen. medicine, Gothenburg, 1964-79; pvt. practice law, 1982—. Author: Vaccination av utlandsresenärer, 1964, To Be a Physician, 1978, (with H.A. Hansen) A Handbook of Laboratory Work, 1962; contbr. articles on renal physiology to med. jours., articles on unnecessary taking of children into pub. care to Swedish and fgn. newspapers. Lutheran. Achievements include bringing to and winning number of cases in The European Court of Human Rights, Strasbourg, France. Civil rights, Family and matrimonial, Personal injury (including property damage). Home and Office: Skårsgatan 45 S-412 69 Göteborg Sweden

WESTERHAUS, DOUGLAS BERNARD, lawyer; b. Marion, Kans., Jan. 11, 1951; s. Edwin Gerard and Bernadine (Ullman) W.; m. Susan Elizabeth Scott, Aug. 20, 1973 (div. Jan. 1979); m. Karen Sue Giersch, Sept. 20, 1980 (div. Aug. 1997); children: John Joseph, Jamie Lynn, Jeffrey Michael; m. Victoria Lee Ruhga, March, 1998; 1 child: David Burton. BSBA, Kans. U., 1973, JD, 1976. Bar: Kans. 1976, U.S. Dist. Kans. 1976, U.S. Supreme Ct. 1980. Assoc. Harper & Hornbaker, Junction City, Kans., 1976-78, ptnr., 1978-80; prin. Westerhaus Law Office, Marion, Kans., 1980-86; pres. Hydrogen Energy Corp., 1986-91, also bd. dirs.; staff atty. THORN Ams., Inc., dba Rent-A-Ctr., Wichita, Kans., 1991-95, chief counsel human resources, 1995-96, assoc. gen. counsel, 1996-97; dir. Field Human Resources, 1997-98; exec. v.p. Mr. Goodcents Franchise Sys., Inc., 1999—2001, sr. v.p. and gen. counsel, 2002; pres. DVW Properties LLC, 2002—. Atty. City of Grandview Plaza, Kans. 1977-80, City of Lehigh, Kans. 1980-86, Marion County, 1981-85; gen. counsel The Hydrogen Energy Corp., Kansas City, Mo. 1984-86, Marion Die & Fixture, 1980-86. Bd. dirs. St. Luke's Hosp., Marion, 1985-86. Mem. ABA, Kans. Bar Assn. (chmn. Lawyer Referral Commn. 1979-84, Outstanding Service award 1984), Marion County Bar Assn. (pres. 1985), Sedgwick County Bar Assn. Republican. Lutheran. Corporate, general, Labor (including EEOC, Fair Labor Standards Act, labor-management relations, NLRB, OSHA). Home: 12813 King St Overland Park KS 66213-4416

WESTERVELT, CHARLES EPHRAIM, JR., lawyer; b. Columbus, Ohio, Mar. 10, 1922; s. Charles Ephraim and Winifred Reed (Wells) W.; m. Melba Louise Kuhlman, Mar. 3, 1946 (dec.); children: John Charles (dec.), Kirk Thomas, Todd William, Reed Matthew. BA, Ohio State U., 1943, LLB and JD, 1948. Ptnr. Graves & Westervelt, Columbus, 1948-53; chief right of way atty. Ohio Turnpike Commn., Columbus, 1953-55, asst. to exec. dir., 1956; pvt. practice C.E. Westervelt Jr., Westerville, Ohio, 1956—. Trustee Westerville Pub. Libr., 1958-75; twp. clk. Geona Twp., Ohio, 1960-72, mem. vol. fire dept., 1970-95; various offices Westerville Hist. Soc., 1948—. With USAAF, ETO, 1943-46. Decorated Air medal with 4 oak leaf clusters. Mem. Phi Beta Kappa. Republican. United Methodist. Avocations: reading, gardening, camping, fishing, genealogy. Estate planning, Probate (including wills, trusts), Estate taxation. Home: 7974 Africa Rd Westerville OH 43082-8818 Office: 18 W College Ave Westerville OH 43081-2176

WESTFALL, CONSTANCE COURTNEY, lawyer; b. Plainview, Tex., Nov. 29, 1960; d. M.H. and Carolyn Courtney; m. Monte Jay Westfall, Jan. 3, 1998; 1 child, William Henry Westfall. BS, U. Tex., 1982, JD, 1985. Bar: Tex., U.S. Dist. Ct. (we. and no. dists.) Tex., U.S. Dist. Ct. (we. and ea. dists.) Ark., U.S. Dist. Ct. (we. dist.) Okla., U.S. Ct. Appeals (5th and 8th cirs.) Tex. Com. clk. Natural Resources Com., Tex. Ho. of Rep., 1979; legis. staff to hon. Buck Florence Tex. Ho. of Rep., 1980-82; law clk. to hon. Jerre Williams U.S. Ct. Appeals (5th cir.), 1985-86; assoc. Thompson & Knight, Dallas, 1986-92, Brown McCarroll, Dallas, 1992-94; ptnr. Hutcheson & Grundy, Dallas, 1994-98, Strasburger & Price, Dallas, 1998—. Contbr. articles to profl. jours. Moderator So. Meth. U. Sch. Law Environ. Career Seminar, 1989-2000. Mem.: ABA, State Bar Coll., State Bar Tex. (mem. law sch. com. 1988—97, chair outreach com. environ. sect. 1989—92, chair law sch. com. 1997—, chair-elect environ. and natural resources sect. 2002—). Administrative and regulatory, Environmental. Office: Strasburger & Price 901 Main St Ste 4300 Dallas TX 75202-3724

WESTMAN, CARL EDWARD, lawyer; b. Youngstown, Ohio, Dec. 12, 1943; s. Carl H. and Mary Lillis (Powell) W.; m. Carolyn J., July 17, 1965; children: C. Forrest, Stephanie A. BBA, Sam Houston State U., 1966; JD, U. Miami, 1969, LLM in Taxation, 1972. Bar: Fla. 1969. Ptnr. Frost & Jacobs, 1983-93, Roetzel & Andress, 1993-98; mktg. and adminstrv. ptnr. Steel, Hector & Davis, Naples, Fla., 1999—. Active S.W. Fla. coun. Boy Scouts Am. Eagle Bd. of Rev., 1987—; chmn. planned giving com. Audobon of Fla. for Southwest Fla.; trustee David Lawrence Found. for Mental Health, Inc., 1976-86, chmn. 1985-86; trustee Pikeville Coll., 1993—; trustee, vice chmn., NCH Healthcare Sys. Inc., 1995—, chmn. profl. capabilities com. physician credentialing, 1998—; trustee, chmn. Naples Cmty. Hosp.; past pres. bd. trustees, elder Moorings Presbyn. Ch. Master lic. capt. USCG. Mem. ABA, Fla. Bar Assn. (exec. coun., cir. rep. real property, probate and trust law sect., probate law com., trust law com.), Collier County Bar Assn., Estate Planning Coun., Audubon Fla. (chair planned giving com.), Coral Reef Yacht Club, Useppa Island Club, Marco Island Yacht Club. Estate planning, General practice, Probate (including wills, trusts). Home: 1952 Crayton Rd Naples FL 34102-5070 Office: Collier Place I 3002 Tamiami Trail N Ste 300 Naples FL 34103-2718 E-mail: cwestman@steelhector.com.

WESTON, MICHAEL C. retired lawyer; b. Asheville, N.C., Aug. 13, 1938; m. Mary Ann Damme; two children. AB in English, Brown U., 1960; JD, U. Mich., 1963. Bar: Mich. 1964, Ill. 1973. Assoc. Clark Hill, Detroit, 1963-68; from sec. to pres. corp. and indsl. consortium Econ. Devel. Corp. of Greater Detroit, 1969-73; chief staff atty. Northwestern U., Evanston, Ill., 1973-81, v.p. legal affairs, 1981-89; v.p. and gen. counsel, 1990-2001. Lectr. minority bus. devel. Inst. Continuing Legal Edn., conflicts of interest Nat. Coun. Univ. Rsch. Adminstrs. Contbr. articles to profl. jours. Chmn. Univ. Gallery Com., 1982-85; bd. dirs. Northwestern U. Press. Mem. ABA (sec. taxation, com. on exempt orgns., ho. of dels., lectr. Inst. on Minority Bus. Devel.), Chgo. Coun. Lawyers, Nat. Assn. Coll. and Univ. Attys. (lectr. fed. tax matters, outside activities faculty mems. univ.-cmty. rels., med. risk mgmt., bd. dirs. 1985-88, 92-97, pres. 1995-96). E-mail: m-weston@northwestern.edu.

WESTPHAL, MARJORIE LORD, lawyer; b. Erie, Pa., July 24, 1940; d. Thomas and Dorothy (Hofft) Lord; m. David Melvin Zurn, Sept. 2, 1960 (div. Sept. 1970); children: Rena Zurn Fulweiler, Amelie Susan, Christopher F.; m. Lester Roy Westphal, May 26, 1971. Student, Brown U., 1958-60; BS, Gannon U., 1974; JD, Case Western Res. U., 1978. Bar: Ohio 1979. Assoc. Kohrman, Jackson, Weiss, Cleve., 1980-81; sole practice Cleve., 1981-92. Trustee Emma Willard Sch., Troy, N.Y., 1978-80; dir. Ohioans for Merit Selection of Judges, Cuyahoga County, 1979; mem. Vol. Lawyers for the Arts, Citizens League of Cleve., Women's Community Fund, 1990-92, Desert Foothills Music Fest; treas Women's City Club Found. Mem. ABA, Ohio Bar Assn., Cleve. Bar Assn., Cleve. Women's Bar Assn, Pi Gamma Mu. Clubs: Cleve. Skating, Desert Mountain. Avocations: reading, sailing, the arts. Non-profit and tax-exempt organizations, Estate planning, Personal income taxation. E-mail: joriel@earthlink.net.

WETHERELL, MICHAEL E. lawyer; b. Redding, Calif., Mar. 2, 1945; s. Robert Miles and Rose Clair (Hart) W.; m. Karen Lansdowne Mackenzie, Aug. 16, 1969; children: Kelly Mackenzie, Kristen Michelle, Katherine

Marie. BS in Edn., U. Idaho, 1967; JD, George Washington U., 1972. Bar: Idaho 1972, U.S. Dist. Ct. Idaho 1972, U.S. Ct. Appeals (9th cir.) 1984. Copywriter KBOI-AM-FM-TV, Boise, Idaho, 1965-67; legis. asst. Senator Frank Church, Washington, 1967-72, chief legal counsel, 1972-74, adminstrv. asst., 1975-76; sole practice Boise, 1977-78; assoc. Martin, Chapman & Hyde, Boise, 1978-82; ptnr. Hyde & Wetherell, Boise, 1982-85, Hyde, Wetherell, Bray & Haff, Boise, 1985-93, Hyde, Wetherell, Bray, Haff & French, A Profl. Co., Boise, 1993—98, Hyde Wetherell and Haff PLLC, 1998—2002; dist. judge Idahois 4th Jud. Dist., 2003—. Author: The Worker's Compensation Law of Idaho, 1989, 2d edit. 1991, 4th edit. 1996; contbr. articles to profl. jours. Dem. candidate for Idaho atty. gen., 1976; pres. Boise City Coun., 1988-92, 2002-03; mem. human welfare com. Mountain State Tumor Inst., Boise, 1985-2002, St. Lukes Regional Med. Ctr. (co-chmn. 1997-2002); bd. dirs. Epilepsy Found. am., 1980-87, United Way of Ada County, Boise, 1982-88, Idaho Epilepsy League, Boise, 1977—; chmn. Idaho State Dem. Party, 1991-93, exec. com. Nat. Dem. Party, 1993-97; candidate for Idaho Supreme Ct., 1998. Recipient Outstanding Personal Achievement award Epilepsy Found. Am., 1987. Mem. ABA, Idaho State Bar Assn. (Outstanding Service to Handicapped award 1981), Assn. Trial Lawyers Am., Idaho Trial Lawyers Assn. (editor Idaho Trial Lawyers Mag. 1978-85, bd. govs. 1979-85, Outstanding Svc. award 1990). Lodges: Kiwanis (Boise) (pres. 1985-86). Roman Catholic. Avocations: sailing, camping, photography, woodworking. State civil litigation, Personal injury (including property damage), Workers' compensation. Home: 1292 Candleridge Dr Boise ID 83712-6504 Office: 4th Jud Dist Ada County Courthouse 200 W Front St Boise ID 83702-7300

WETHERELL, T. KENT, II, judge; BS, Fla. State U., 1992, JD, 1995. Bar: Fla. 1995, Colo. 1997, U.S. Supreme Ct. 2001, U.S. Ct. Appeals (11th cir.) 2001. Atty. Hopping Green Sams & Smith, Talllahassee, 1995—99; dep. solicitor gen. Office of Atty. Gen., Tallahassee, 1999—2002; adminstrv. law judge Divsn. Adminstrv. Hearings, Tallahassee, 2002—. Office: Divsn Adminstrv Hearings 1230 Appalachee Pkwy Tallahassee FL 32399

WETHERILL, EIKINS, lawyer, stock exchange executive; b. Phila., Oct. 3, 1919; s. A. Hecksher and Edwina (Brunner) W. LL.B., U. Pa., 1948. Practiced in, Phila., 1948-55, Norristown, 1955-98; assoc. firm Evans, Bayard & Frick, 1948-50; ptnr. Reilly, Hepburn, Earle & Wetherill, 1950-55; firm Henderson, Wetherill, O'Hey & Horsey, 1955-98; pres. Phila. Stock Exchange, Inc., 1965-81. Bd. dirs. Germantown Savs. Bank; fin. commentator CBS-TV News, 1966-68; chmn. bd. Sta. WHYY-TV, 1970-76, dir., 1976-90; dir. 1st Pa. Corp., 1st Pa. Bank, solicitor to lt. gov. Pa., 1951-55, asst. U.S. atty. gen., 1953-55, treas., Montgomery County, 1956-59; pres. Montgomery County Bd. Commrs., 1960-63; chmn. Pa. Securities Commn., 1963-65; commr. Delaware Valley Regional Planning Commn., 1965—, chmn., 1968-69, 70-71, 78-79. Former bd. dirs. Greater Phila. Partnership; chmn. Phila. Drama Guild, 1975-80, dir., 1980-87; trustee Davis and Elkins Coll., 1973-91. Served to capt., cav. Signal Corps, OSS, AUS, 1941-45. Mem. Am., Phila. bar assns., Delta Psi. Clubs: Phila. (Phila.), Racquet (Phila.). Episcopalian.

WETMORE, KEITH CHIDESTER, lawyer; b. Valparaiso, Ind., Oct. 17, 1956; s. Leonard Leander and Dorisann (Chidester) W. BA, Northwestern U., 1977; JD magna cum laude, U. Mich., 1980. Bar: Calif. 1981, U.S. Dist. Ct. (no. dist.) Calif. 1981. Law clk. to presiding justice U.S. Ct. Appeals (2d cir.), 1980-81; assoc. Steinhart & Falconer, San Francisco, 1981-82, Morrison & Foerster, San Francisco, 1982-86, ptnr., 1986—. Articles editor U. Mich. Law Rev. 1980-81. Mem. ABA, Calif. Bar Assn., Bay Area Lawyers for Individual Freedom, San Francisco Bar Assn. Methodist. Bankruptcy, Commercial, contracts (including sales of goods; commercial financing), Corporate, general. Home: 17 Liberty St San Francisco CA 94110-2318 Office: Morrison & Foerster 345 California St San Francisco CA 94104-2606*

WETZEL, ROBERT CHARLES, lawyer; b. Hackensack, N.J., Sept. 27, 1952; s. George August and Gertrude Ruth (Dilba) W.; m. Nancy Archibald, July 24, 1976; children: Justin, Brian. BA, Wittenberg U., 1975; JD, Widener U., 1980. Bar: Va. 1981, Va. Supreme Ct. 1981, U.S. Ct. Appeals (4th cir.) 1981. Law editor Michies, Charlottesville, Va., 1980; claims adjustor Nationwide Insurance Co., Lynchburg, Va., 1980-81, trial atty., claim atty., 1981-87, sr. claims atty., 1987—; private practice Lynchburg, 1981—. Dir., legal counsel Campbell County Humane Soc., Rustburg, Va., 1982—, Federal Hills Hist. Dist., Lynchburg, 1990—. Insurance, Personal injury (including property damage). Home: 88 Mountain Dr Lynchburg VA 24504-9752 Office: Nationwide Ins Co 116 Nationwide Dr Lynchburg VA 24502-0669

WETZEL-WILLIAMS, KIMBERLY, lawyer; b. Ulysses, Kans., Jan. 27, 1958; d. Herbert O. and Manetta V. Wetzel; m. Robert E. Williams; 1 child, Matthew Williams. BS in Bus. Adminstrn., U. Kans., 1979, JD, 1982. Bar: Kans. 1982. Assoc. Mustaine & Newman, Kansas City, Kans., 1982—83; staff atty. Hyatt Legal Svcs., Kansas City, 1983—85; asst. dist. atty. Wyandotte County, Kansas City, 1985—2002; pvt. practice, 2002—. Adv. to youth officers Wyandotte County 4-H Coun., Kansas City, 2001—02; cmty. club leader Brauer Beavers 4-H Club, Kansas City, 2000—; chmn. Wyandotte County Ext. Coun., Kansas City, 2000—02; bd. dirs. Kans. State Ext. Adv. Coun., Manhattan, 2001—. Mem.: Kansas Bar Assn., Wyandotte County Bar Assn. Roman Catholic. Avocations: photography, gardening, gourmet cooking, working with youth. E-mail: kimwetzelwilliams@yahoo.com.

WEXELBAUM, MICHAEL, lawyer; b. Bklyn., Aug. 12, 1946; s. Joseph and Beatrice (Skurnick) W.; m. Cynthia Debra Schorr, Apr. 15, 1973 (dec. 1984); children: Joshua David, Stephanie Faye; m. Joan Brenda Math, Aug. 21, 1994; stepchildren: Jonathan David Kaye, Matthew Lawrence Kaye, Julie Dana Kaye. BA in Econs., Bucknell U., 1968; JD, NYU, 1971. Bar: N.Y. 1972, U.S. Dist. Ct. (so. and ea. dists.) N.Y. 1973, U.S. Dist. Ct. (ea. dist.) Wis. 1998. Assoc. Sherman, Citron & Karasik, P.C., N.Y.C., 1972-80, ptnr., head litigation dept., 1980-2001; ptnr. litigation dept. Snow Becker Krauss P.C., N.Y.C., 2001—. Arbitrator Nat. Arbitration Forum, 1999—. Arbitrator Am. Arbitration Assn. and Gen. Arbitration Coun. of Textile and Apparel Industries, N.Y.C., 1982—. Mem. Bankruptcy Lawyers Bar Assn., Lawyers Assn. Textile and Apparel Industries (bd. govs.), Am. Arbitration Assn. (arbitrator), Nat. Arbitration Forum (arbitrator), Assn. Comml. Fin. Attys. Democratic. Jewish. Avocations: tennis, skiing, biking, theatre. General civil litigation, Commercial, contracts (including sales of goods; commercial financing), General practice. Home: 85 Norrans Ridge Dr Ridgefield CT 06877-4237 Office: Snow Becker Krauss PC 605 Third Ave New York NY 10158-0125 Office Fax: 212-455-0455. E-mail: mwexelbaum@sbklaw.com.

WEXLER, RICHARD LEWIS, lawyer; b. Chgo., June 19, 1941; s. Stanley and Lottie (Pinkert) W.; m. Roberta Seigel, June 13, 1962; children: Deborah (Mrs. Jonathan Sokobin), Joshua, Jonathan. Student, U. Mich., 1959-1962; JD cum laude, John Marshall Law Sch., 1965. Bar: Ill. 1965, U.S. Dist. Ct. (no. dist.) Ill. 1967. Gen. counsel Metro. Planning Council, Chgo., 1965-67; ptnr. Wexler, Kane, Rosenzweig & Shaw, Chgo., 1967-71, Taussig, Wexler & Shaw, Chgo., 1971-78, Wexler, Siegel & Shaw, Ltd., Chgo., 1978-83, Sachnoff & Weaver, Ltd., Chgo., 1983-91, chair real estate dept., 1985-91, mng. ptnr., 1985-90; ptnr., chmn. real estate dept. Lord Bissell & Brook, Chgo., 1991-97, mem. compensation com., 1995. Legal cons. Zoning Laws Study Commn., Ill. Gen. Assembly, Springfield, 1969-71, Urban Counties Study Commn., Springfield, 1971-72; legal counsel Ill. Coastal Zone Mgmt. Program, Springfield, 1979-81, Northeastern Ill. Planning Commn., Chgo., 1969—. Contbr. numerous articles to profl. jours. Pres. Jewish Fedn. Met. Chgo., 1986-88, mem. numerous coms., also bd. dirs., 1978-90; pres. Jewish United Fund, 1986-88; bd. dirs. Coun. Jewish Fedns., 1980, mem. exec. com., 1985—, v.p., 1988—, chmn. planning steering com., 1990-95, chmn. fedn./agy. rels. com., 1988-90; co-chmn. Task Force on Poverty and Low Income, 1985-87; nat. vice-chmn. United Jewish Appeal, 1988, nat. chmn., 1996-98, regional allocations chmn., 1987-88, chmn. region II, 1988-90, budget com., 1989-92, allocations com., 1990-91, campaign exec., 1991-2000; chmn. Operation Exodus II, 1993-94, chmn. nat. mktg. com., 1994-95, chmn. 1997 campaign planning and budget com., nat. chmn., 1997-98, pres. bd. trustees, 1998-2000; co-chair United Jewish Appeal Fedns. N.Am., 1998-2000; bd. dirs. Jewish Edn. Soc. N.Am., 1982-85, Hebrew Immigrant Aid Soc., 1988—, Nat. Conf. on Soviet Jewry, 1989-95, vice chmn., 1989-92, nat. chmn., 1992-94; bd. dirs. Nat. Jewish Cmty. Rels. Adv. Coun., 1988-90, vice chmn., 1988-92; chmn. Jewish Com. Rels. Coun. Chgo., 1988-89. Fellow Eta Lambda; mem. ABA, Ill. State Bar Assn. (Lincoln award, Legal Writing, 1966). Avocations: tennis, reading, travel. Land use and zoning (including planning), Property, real (including real estate development, water). Office: Lord Bissell & Brook 115 S La Salle St Ste 3400 Chicago IL 60603-3801 E-mail: rwexler@lordbissell.com.

WEXLER, THOMAS CHARLES, lawyer; b. Princeton, N.J., Oct. 8, 1960; BA, Princeton U., 1983; LLB, Harvard U., 1988. Bar: Ill. 1988, England & Wales 1998. Assoc. Mayer Brown & Platt, Chgo., 1988—91, London, 1991—97, Ashukst Morris Crisp, 1997—99, ptnr., 1999—2002, Tokyo, 2002—. Avocations: athletics, languages, music. Banking, Private international, Oil, gas, and mineral. Office: Ashurst Morris Crisp Kioi-chō Bldg 8th Fl Kioi-chō 3-12 Chiyoda-ku Tokyo 102-0094 Japan Fax: 81-3-5276-5922. E-mail: thomaswexler@ashursts.com.

WHALE, ARTHUR RICHARD, retired lawyer; b. Detroit, Oct. 28, 1923; s. Arthur B. and Orpha Louella (Doak) W.; m. Roberta Lou Donaldson, Oct. 29, 1949; children: Richard Donaldson, Linda Jean. BSChemE, Northwestern U., 1945; LLB, George Washington U., 1956. Bar: D.C. 1957, Mich. 1957, Ind. 1977, U.S. Patent and Trademark Office 1957. Chem. engr. Ansul Chem. Co., Marinette, Wis., 1946-47, Parke, Davis & Co., Detroit, 1947-50, writer med. lit., 1950-52; chem. engr. Bur. Ships, U.S. Dept. Navy, Washington, 1952-55, dep. sect. head, indsl. gas sect., 1954-55; patent engr. Swift & Co., Washington, 1955-56; patent atty. Upjohn Co., Kalamazoo, 1956-65; asst. mgr. organic chems. sect. patent dept. Dow Chem. Co., Midland, Mich., 1965-66, mgr., 1967-73, mng. counsel, 1973-75; asst. sec., gen. patent counsel Eli Lilly & Co., Indpls., 1975-86; of counsel Miller, Morriss, & Pappas, Lansing, Mich., 1986-89, Baker & Daniels, Indpls., 1987—2003; ret., 2003. Lectr. Practicing Law Inst., John Marshall Law Sch. Contbr. articles to profl. jours. Pres. Nat. Inventors Hall of Fame Found., 1978-79; bd. dirs. Holcomb Rsch. Inst., INdpls, 1982-86. Served to lt. (j.g.) USNR, 1943-46. Mem. State Bar Mich. (chmn. patent trademark copyright sect. 1967-69), D.C. Bar Assn. (mem. patent trademark copyright div.), Midland County Bar Assn. (pres. 1974-75), Am. Bar Assn. (mem. patent trademark copyright sect.), Assn. Corp. Patent Counsel, Nat. Coun. Patent Law Assns. (chmn. 1979-80), Am. Intellectual Property Law Assn. (pres. 1974-75), Ashlar Lodge, Masons, Shriners. Republican. Presbyterian. Avocation: golf. Office: Baker & Daniels Ste 2700 300 N Meridian St Indianapolis IN 46204-1782

WHALE, MICHAEL JOHN, lawyer, consultant; b. Auckland, New Zealand, June 14, 1953; s. John Frederick and Sheila W.; m. Deborah Joan Alexander, Jan. 29, 1977; children: Andrew, Charlotte, Edward. BCom, Auckland U., 1974; LLB with honors, 1978. Ptnr. Phillips Fox Solicitors, New Zealand, 1981-98; cons., 1998-2000, Lowndes Assocs. Lawyers, New Zealand, 2000—. Bd. dirs. INSOL Internat., Eng. 2000-01; lectr. (part-time) U. Auckland, 1999-2000; co-convenor insolvency com. New Zealand Law Soc./Inst. Chartered Accts., 1993-2001. Bd. trustees Mt. Carmel Sch., Auckland, 1991-93; consul-gen. (hon.) for Thailand, Auckland, 1995—. Fellow Inst. Chartered Accts. (profl. conduct com.) New Zealand, Chartered Secretaries. New Zealand Inc.; mem. New Zealand Law Soc. Inst. of Dirs., Northern Club. Avocations: jogging, badminton, theatre, opera, reading. Bankruptcy, Commercial, contracts (including sales of goods; commercial financing), Franchising. Office: Lowndes Assocs Level 5 18 Shortland St Auckland New Zealand Fax: 373 3423. E-mail: mjwhale@xtra.co.nz., whale@lowndeslaw.com.

WHALEN, PAUL LEWELLIN, lawyer, educator, mediator; b. Lexington, Ky. s. Elza Boz and Barbara Jean (Lewellin) W.; m. Teena Gail Tanner, Jan. 26, 1985; children: Ashley, Lars, Lucy. BA, U. Ky.; JD, Northern Ky. U.; cert., Bonn U., Fed. Republic Germany, 1981; student, U.S. Army J.A.G. Sch., 1988; diploma, USAF Squadron Officers Sch., 1998. Bar: W.Va. 1984, U.S. Ct. Appeals (6th cir.) 1984, Ky. 1985, U.S. Ct. Appeals (4th cir.) 1985, Ohio 1993. Assoc. Geary Walker, Parkersburg, W.Va., 1984-85; prin. Paul L. Whalen, Ft. Thomas, Ky., 1985—; prof. Def. Acquisition U., WP AFB; prof. pub. contract law Air Force Inst. Tech., 1999-2000; atty. Dept. of Air Force, Office of Chief Trial Atty. Contract Law Ctr., Wright Patterson AFB, 1988—89; hearing officer, prosecutor Ky. Dept. Ednl. Profl. Stds. Bd., 1995—97; mem. arbitration panel No. Ky., 1997—, Montgomery County, Ohio, 1998—; hearing officer Ky. Dept. Edn. IDEA, 1999—2000; impartial due process hearing officer Ohio Dept. Edn., Ohio, 2002—. Mem. Leadership No. Ky., Ft. Thomas Bd. Edn., 1987—99, chmn., 1990—94; mem. Ky. Bd. Edn., 2000—, Ky. Commn. on Human Svcs.; pres. ch. coun. Highland United Meth. Ch., 2000; mem. Campbell County Foster Care Rev. Bd., Newport, Ky., 1986; bd. dirs. Ky. Coun. Child Abuse, Inc. Com. for Kids; dir. Ky. Sch. Bd. Assn., 1993—98; mem. Air Force Bicycle Team Ride Across Iowa, 1997—2000. Recipient Commendation No. Ky. Legal Aid, 1986-2002. Fellow Commonwealth Inst. Leadership; mem. Fed. Bar Assn., No. Ky. Bar Assn., So. Assn. Schs. (mem. com.), Optimist Club, Kiwanis Club, Phi Alpha Delta. Democrat. Methodist. Avocations: freelance writing, stamp collecting, politics, amateur radio, bicycling. Commercial, consumer (including collections, credit), Family and matrimonial, Government contracts and claims. Home: 113 Ridgeway Ave Fort Thomas KY 41075-1333 Office: PO Box 22 Fort Thomas KY 41075 E-mail: plewellinwhalen@aol.com.

WHALEN, THOMAS J. lawyer; b. Jersey City, July 29, 1938; s. Arthur and Mae (Cavannagh) W.; m. Anne Marie Donovan, Sept. 5, 1970; 1 child, Honore. B.A., St. Peter's Coll., Jersey City, 1960; J.D., Georgetown U., 1963. Bar: N.J. 1964, D.C. 1964, N.Y. 1968. Law sec. to judge U.S. Ct. Appeals (3d cir.), Newark, 1963-64; assoc. firm Condon & Forsyth, N.Y.C. and Washington, 1967-75, ptnr., 1975— ; author, spkr. on airline regulatory and liability law. Served to capt. JAGC, U.S. Army, 1964-67; Vietnam. Mem. ABA, Fed. Bar Assn., Univ. Club (Washington). Democrat. Roman Catholic. Commercial, contracts (including sales of goods; commercial financing), Aviation, Federal civil litigation. Address: Condon & Forsyth 1016 16th St NW Ste 700 Washington DC 20036-5724 E-mail: twhalen@condonlaw.com.

WHALEN, WAYNE W. lawyer; b. Savanna, Ill., Aug. 22, 1939; s. Leo R. and Esther M. (Yackley) W.; m. Paula Wolff, Apr. 22, 1970; children: Amanda, Clementine, Antonia, Nathaniel, Daniel. BS, U.S. Air Force Acad., 1961; JD, Northwestern U., 1967. Bar: Ill. 1967, U.S. Ct. Appeals (7th cir.) 1968, U.S. Supreme Ct. 1972. Commd. 1st lt. USAF, 1961, ret., 1964; assoc. Mayer, Brown & Platt, Chgo., 1967-74, ptnr., 1974, Skadden, Arps, Slate, Meagher & Flom (Ill.), Chgo., 1984—. Bd. dirs. Van Kampen Funds, Oak Brook, Ill. Author: Annotated Illinois Constitution, 1972. Del. 6th Ill. Constitutional Conv., 1969-70, chmn. style drafting and submission com. Named Outstanding Young Lawyer, Chgo. Bar Found., 1970. Mem. Chgo. Club. Corporate, general. Office: Skadden Arps Slate Meagher & Flom III 333 W Wacker Dr Ste 2100 Chicago IL 60606-1220

WHATLEY, JACQUELINE BELTRAM, lawyer; b. West Orange, N.J., Sept. 26, 1944; d. Quirino and Eliane (Gruet) Beltram; m. John W. Whatley, June 25, 1966 (dec. July 1998). BA, U. Tampa, 1966; JD, Stetson U., 1969. Bar: Fla. 1969, Alaska 1971; cert. real estate law splst. Assoc. Tucker, McEwen, Smith & Cofer, Tampa, Fla., 1969-71; pvt. practice Anchorage, Alaska, 1971-73; ptnr. Gibbons, Tucker, Miller, Whatley & Stein, P.A., Tampa, 1973—; pres., 1981—. Bd. dirs. Travelers Aid Soc., 1982-94; trustee Humana Women's Hosp., Tampa, 1987-93, Keystone United Meth. Ch., 1986-89, 99—. Mem. ABA, Fla. Bar Assn. (real estate cert. com. 1993-95), Alaska Bar Assn., Tenn. Walking Horse Breeders and Exhibitors Assn. (v.p. 1984-87, dir. Fla. 1981-87, 90-93, 97-99, adv. com. Tenn. Walking Horse Celebrateion 1994-97), Fla. Walking and Racking Horse Assn. (bd. dirs. 1988-89, pres. 1980-82), Athena Soc. (Tampa). Republican. Methodist. Commercial, contracts (including sales of goods; commercial financing), Property, real (including real estate development, water). Home: PO Box 17595 Tampa FL 33682-7595 Office: 101 E Kennedy Blvd Ste 1000 Tampa FL 33602-5146 E-mail: whatley@gte.net.

WHEATER, MURRAY RICHARD KENNETH, lawyer; b. Perth, Australia, Aug. 2, 1971; s. Richard Owen and Hilary Newton Wheater; m. Kylie Susanna Martens, Aug. 30, 1998. B of Commerce, B of Laws, Murdoch U., 1994. Bar: Western Australia 1996, England & Wales 2000. Assoc. Blake Dawson Waldron, Perth, Australia, 1995—98, Slaighter and May, London, 1998—2000, Shearman & Sterling, 2000—. Mergers and acquisitions, Corporate, general. Office: Shearman & Sterling 9 Appold St London EC2A 2AP England Fax: +44 207 655 5446.

WHEELAN, R(ICHELIEU) E(DWARD), lawyer; b. N.Y.C., July 10, 1945; s. Richard Fairfax and Margaret (Murray) W. BS, Springfield (Mass.) Coll., 1967; MS, Iona Coll., 1977; JD, Pace U., 1981. Bar: N.Y. 1982, Minn. 1983, Colo. 1989, Tex. 1990, U.S. Dist. Ct. (no dist.) Calif. 1982, (so. dist.) Tex. 1991, U.S. Internat. Trade 1982, U.S. Ct. Appeals (2d cir.) 1982, (9th cir.) 1983, (5th cir.) 1993, U.S. Supreme Ct. 1994, U.S. Tax Ct. 1998; bd. cert. criminal law, trial advocacy. Lt. of detectives White Plains (N.Y.) Police Dept., 1969-81; area counsel IBM, Armonk, N.Y., 1981-89; gen. counsel Kroll Assocs. (Asia), Hong Kong, 1989-91; pvt. practice, Houston, 1991—. Abogado consultor Mex. Consulate. Mem.: ABA (mem. sentencing guidelines com.), Tex. Assn. Criminal Def. Lawyers, Pro Bono Coll. State Bar Tex., New York County Lawyers Assn., N.Y. State Bar Assn., Coll. of State Bar Tex., Nat. Assn. Criminal Def. Lawyers (life; mem. death penalty com., Champion adv. bd.). Criminal, Personal income taxation. Office: 440 Louisiana St Houston TX 77002-1639

WHEELER, ALBERT LEE, III, lawyer, legal consultant; b. Oklahoma City, Sept. 28, 1954; s. Albert Lee Wheeler, Jr. and Mercedes Elizabeth Wheeler. BS in Mus. Edn., Central State U., Edmond, Okla., 1980; MBA in Fin., Oklahoma City U., 1983, JD with honors, 1990. Real estate appraiser Market Data Research Inc., Oklahoma City, 1977-79; real estate mgr. Kerr McGee Corp., Oklahoma City, 1979-80; prin. Al Wheeler Appraisal Co., Oklahoma City, 1980-99; pvt. practice law Oklahoma City, 1990—. Editor Oklahoma City U. Law Rev., 1989-90; contbr. articles to profl. jours. Mem. Oklahoma County Bar Assn. (chmn. workers compensation law sect. 1996-98), Am. Inst. Real Estate Appraisers, Merit Scholars Assn., Nat. Assn. Criminal Def. Lawyers, Phi Delta Phi. Democrat. Methodist. Avocations: music composition, blues guitar. Office: 9400 N Broadway Ste 515 Oklahoma City OK 73114 E-mail: al@alwheelerlaw.com.

WHEELER, EDD DUDLEY, lawyer; b. Macon, Ga., July 19, 1940; m. Frances Schnelker Rouhslange, Feb. 12, 1974; children: Diana Kaye, Catherine Anne, Emily Clare. BS, USAF Acad., 1962; MPA, U. Okla., 1968; PhD, Emory U., 1971; JD, Am. U., 1979. Bar: Ga. 1979, U.S. Dist. Ct. (no. dist.) Ga., U.S. Supreme Ct. 1991. Commd. 2d lt. USAF, Macon, 1962, advanced through grades to lt. col. Atlanta, 1976, ret. Tucker, Ga., 1978; pvt. practice Macon, 1979-83, Tucker, Ga., 1984-91; assoc. dir. Law & Econs. Ctr. Emory U., Atlanta, 1983-84. Spl. asst. atty. gen. Ga. Atty. Gen. Office, Atlanta, 1987-88; pres. Cronus, Inc., Atlanta, 1989-91; fed. adminstrv. law judge, 1991—. Author: From Games of God to Bubba's Field: A Century of the Modern Olympic Games, 1995, The Knot which Is Great within Us: Poems on Life, Law, and Other Imperfections, 1997. County commr. Bibb County Bd. of Commrs., Macon, 1980-82. Fellow Ga. Bar Found.; mem. Ga. Bar Assn., Com. on Lawyer Professionalism (reporter 1986-87). Episcopalian. Alternative dispute resolution, Constitutional, General practice. Office: 3598 Midvale Cv Tucker GA 30084-3208

WHEELER, JAMES JULIAN, lawyer; b. Independence, Mo., Mar. 20, 1921; s. Luther I. and Edith (Hesler) W.; m. Janet L. Esau, Apr. 28, 1951; children: Linnell Gretzinger, Robert W. LLB, U. Mo., 1948. Bar: Mo. 1948, U.S. Dist. Ct. (ea. dist.) Mo. 1956. Prosecuting atty. County of Chariton, Mo., 1950-54, probate judge, 1974-75; circuit judge 9th Judicial Circuit Court, Mo., 1976-82; sole practice Keytesville, Mo., 1948-74, 82—. Served as cpl. USMC, 1941-46, PTO. Mem. ABA, Mo. Bar Assn., Am. Judicature Soc., Assn. Trial Lawyers Am. Democrat. State civil litigation, Criminal, General practice. Home: 112 Kennedy Ave Keytesville MO 65261 Office: 304 Walnut St Keytesville MO 65261-1064

WHEELER, JOHN WATSON, lawyer; b. Murfreesboro, Tenn., Sept. 11, 1938; s. James William and Grace (Fann) W.; m. Dorothy Anita Pressgrove, Aug. 5, 1959; children: Jeffrey William, John Harold. BS in Journalism, U. Tenn., 1960, JD, 1968. Bar: Tenn. 1968, U.S. Dist. Ct. (ea. dist.) Tenn. 1968, U.S. Supreme Ct. 1974, U.S. Ct. Appeals (6th cir.) 1975. Editor The Covington (Tenn.) Leader, 1963-65; adminstrv. asst. to lab. dir. UT-AEC Rsch. Lab., Oak Ridge, Tenn., 1965-68; assoc. Hodges, Doughty & Carson, Knoxville, Tenn., 1968-72, ptnr., 1972—. Mem. commn. to study Apllellate Cts. in Tenn.; chair U.S. Magistrate Merit Selection Panel, Ea. Dist., Tenn., 1991, 2002, 03; mem. Bankruptcy Judge Merit Selection Panel, Ea. Dist. Tenn., 1992-94; chmn. Hist. Soc., U.S. Dist. Ct. (ea. dist.) Tenn. Mem. organizing com. Tenn. Supreme Ct. Hist. Soc. Lt. U.S. Army, 1961-63, capt. Res. Fellow Am. Bar Found. (life, Tenn. chair 1999—), Tenn. Bar Found. (life); mem. ABA (ho. of dels. 1986-2000), Tenn. Bar Assn. (pres. 1989-90, bd. govs. 1981-91), Nat. Conf. Bar Pres., Am. Inns. of Ct. (master of bench, emeritus), Internat. Assn. Def. Counsel, So. Conf. Bar Pres., 6th Cir. Jud. Conf. (life), Fox Den Country Club (bd. dirs. 2001—). Republican. Lutheran. Avocations: golf, travel. General civil litigation, Insurance, Workers' compensation. Home: 12009 N Fox Den Dr Knoxville TN 37922-2540 Office: Hodges Doughty & Carson PO Box 869 Knoxville TN 37901-0869 Business E-Mail: jwheeler@hdclaw.com.

WHEELER, MALCOLM EDWARD, lawyer, law educator; b. Berkeley, Calif., Nov. 29, 1944; s. Malcolm Ross and Frances Dolores (Kane) W.; m. Donna Marie Stambaugh, July 25, 1981; children: Jessica Ross, M. Connor. SB, MIT, 1966; JD, Stanford U., 1969. Bar: Calif. 1970, Colo. 1992, U.S. Dist. Ct (cen. dist.) Calif. 1970, U.S. Ct. Appeals (9th cir.) 1970, U.S. Ct. Appeals (10th cir.) 1973, U.S. Dist. Ct. (no., so., ea. and cen. dists.) Calif. 1975, U.S. Ct. Appeals (11th cir.) 1987, U.S. Ct. Appeals (D.C. cir.) 1987, U.S. Supreme Ct. 1976, U.S. Ct. Appeals (3d cir.) 1989, (4th cir.) 1992, (8th cir.) 1993, (5th cir.) 1995, (Fed. cir.) 1998. Assoc. Howard, Prim, Smith, Rice & Downs, San Francisco, 1969-71; assoc. prof. law U. Kans., Lawrence, 1971-74; assoc. Hughes Hubbard & Reed, Los Angeles, 1974-77, ptnr., 1977-81, 83-85, cons., 1981-83; ptnr. Skadden, Arps, Slate, Meagher & Flom, Los Angeles, 1985-91; dir. Parcel, Mauro, Hultin & Spaanstra P.C., Denver, 1991-98, Wheeler Trigg & Kennedy, P.C., Denver, 1998—. Vis. prof. U. Iowa, 1978, prof., 1979; prof. U. Kans., Lawrence, 1981-83; chief counsel U.S. Senate Select Com. to Study Law Enforcement Undercover Activities, Washington, 1982-83. Mem. editorial bd. Jour. Products Liability, 1984-90; bd. editors Fed. Litigation Guide Reporter, 1986-90; contbr. articles to profl. jours. Fellow Am. Coll. Trial Lawyers; mem. ABA, Calif. Bar Assn., Colo. Bar Assn., Am. Law Inst. Federal civil litigation, General civil litigation, Product liability. Home: 100 Humboldt St Denver CO 80218-3932

WHEELER, MARK ANDREW, SR., lawyer; b. Pitts., Feb. 14, 1963; s. Andrew Mate Wheeler and Anna Ruth (Whitfield) W.; m. Irina P. Wheeler, May 10, 1993; children: Mark Andrew Jr., Lauren Anna, Layne Allison, Livia Arden. BA in Philosophy, Hampden-Sydney Coll., 1985; JD, W.Va. U., 1991. Bar: Pa. 1992, U.S. Dist. Ct. (we. dist.) Pa. 1993; ordained to ministry Lighthouse Ch., 1997. Staff litigator W.Va. U. Coll. Law Legal Clinic, Morgantown, 1991-92; jud. clk. Mahoning County, Youngstown, Ohio, 1991-92; pvt. practice Reynoldsville, Pa., 1993—, Clarion, Pa., 1994—. Legal cons. S.T. & E., Inc., Punxsutawney, Pa., 1993—, Jefferson County Gun Owners Assn., Brookville, Pa., 1994—, Crimestoppers of Jefferson County, Brookville, 1993-94, Five Star Homes, Inc., 1995-97, Bembeng Cons., Inc., 1994—. Bd. dirs. Reynoldsville Area Indsl. Bd., 1993-96; mem. exec. dist. com. Boy Scouts Am., Dubois, Pa., 1993—; bd. dirs. Reynoldsville Pub. Libr. Assn., 1993-96; mem. Dubois Christian and Missionary Alliance Ch., mem. choir, 1995—. Mem. ABA, ATLA, Internat. Platform Assn., Pa. Bar Assn. (young lawyers divsn., chair zone 7), Am. Ctr. for Law and Justice, Pa. Trial Lawyers Assn., Pa. Assn. Notaries, Jefferson County Bar Assn., Western Pa. Trial Lawyers Assn., Clarion County Bar Assn., Nat. Eagle Scout Assn. Republican. Avocations: songwriting, public speaking, home renovation, car restoration. General civil litigation, Criminal, Family and matrimonial. Office: PO Box 176 512 Main St Reynoldsville PA 15851-1335 also: PO Box 770 Clarion PA 16214-0770

WHEELER, RAYMOND LOUIS, lawyer; b. Ft. Sill, Okla., Feb. 10, 1945; s. Raymond Louis and Dorothy Marie (Hutcherson) W.; m. Priscilla Wheeler, July 1, 1966 (div. 1982); children: Jennifer, Hilary; m. Cynthia Lee Jackson, July 14, 1984 (div. 1994); children: Matthew Raymond, Madeline Elizabeth; m. Freddie Kay Park, June 10, 1995. BA, U. Tex., 1967; JD, Harvard U., 1970. Bar: Calif. 1972, U.S. Dist. Ct. (no., cen., ea., so. dists.) Calif., U.S. Ct. Appeals (9th cir., 7th cir.), U.S. Ct. Appeals (7th cir.), U.S. Supreme Ct. Law clk. to hon. Irving L. Goldberg U.S. Ct. Appeals 5th cir., 1970-71; assoc. Morrison & Foerster, San Francisco, 1971-76, ptnr., 1976-90, Palo Alto, Calif., 1990—. Chmn. labor and employment law dept. Morrison & Foerster, San Francisco, 1984-88, 92—; lectr. labor and EEO law. Exec. editor Harvard Law Rev., 1969-70; editor in chief The Developing Labor Law; mem. nat. adv. bd. Berkeley Jour. Employment and Labor Law, 1980—; contbr. articles to law jours. Fellow Coll. Labor and Employment Lawyers; mem. ABA (chmn. com. on law devel. under labor rels. act 1990-93, coun. mem. sect. labor and employment 1994-02). Republican. Labor (including EEOC, Fair Labor Standards Act, labor-management relations, NLRB, OSHA). Office: Morrison & Foerster 755 Page Mill Rd Palo Alto CA 94304-1018 E-mail: rwheeler@mofo.com.

WHEELER, R(ICHARD) KENNETH, lawyer, educator; b. Washington, July 25, 1934; s. Nathaniel Dudley and Ruth Lee (Matthews) W.; m. Christine Kandris, Jan. 11, 1990; children by previous marriage: Jennifer L., Ruth E. BA, Emory and Henry Coll., U. Richmond, 1957; LLB, U. Richmond, 1964. Bar: Va. 1963, D.C. 1977, U.S. Tax Ct. 1978. Assoc., then ptnr. Hunton, Williams, Gay, Powell & Gibson and successor firms, Richmond, 1963-88; sr. ptnr. Kane, Wheeler, Fenderson & Jeffries, Richmond, 1988-90; counsel Durrette, Irvin, Lemons & Fenderson, P.C., Richmond, 1990-94; sr. ptnr. Wallace, Harris & Wheeler, Richmond, 1994-95. Adj. prof. law T.C. Williams Sch. Law, U. Richmond, 1966, 83, bd. dirs., 1977-79; adj. prof. law Va. Commonwealth U., 1970; lectr. trial practice U. Va., 1981-82, 85, 87; arbitrator Am. Arbitration Assn. Served to capt. USMCR, 1957-61. Williams scholar U. Richmond, 1961-63. Mem. Am. Law Inst., Va. State Bar (chmn. com. liaison with law schs. 1977-78, chmn. com. legal edn. and admission to bar 1978-80, spcl. com. on professionalism 1987-88), Web Soc., McNeill Law Soc., Marine Corps League (life), Rector's Club (U. Richmond, life), Pi Sigma Alpha, Phi Delta Phi, Omicron Delta Kappa (hon.). Federal civil litigation, State civil litigation, Personal injury (including property damage).

WHEELOCK, KENNETH STEVEN, chemist; b. Kansas City, Mo., Sept. 18, 1943; s. Kenneth Lewis and Clara Mae (Hanenkratt) W.; m. Mary Corinne Percy, June 30, 1972; children: Michael Steven, Celeste Marie. BSc, U. Mo., Kansas City, 1965; PhD, Tulane U., New Orleans, 1970; JD magna cum laude, Western New Eng. Coll., 1998. Bar: Mass.; registered patent atty. Chemist Exxon Rsch. & Devel. Labs., Baton Rouge, La., 1969-72, rsch. chemist, 1972-77, staff chemist, 1977-83, sr. staff chemist, 1983-86; assoc. prof. physics La. State U., Baton Rouge, 1987; sr. rsch. chemist Phillips Petroleum Co., Bartlesville, Okla., 1987-91; chmn. Prakti Katalysts, Bartlesville, Okla., 1992-93; patent agt. GE Plastics, Pittsfield, Mass., 1993-98, counsel intellectual property, 1998—. Cons. dept. chemistry Tulane U., New Orleans, 1970—75. Advisor Jr. Achievement, Baton Rouge, 1971; sec. Baton Rouge Orchid Soc., 1983, Bartlesville Gifted and Talented, 1989; vestry St. Stephen's, Pittsfield, 1999-2002. NDEA trainee, Tulane U., New Orleans, 1965-67, NASA fellow, 1967-69. Fellow Am. Inst. Chemists (profl. rels. com. 1991, 92, patents com. 1992); mem. ABA, Am. Chem. Soc. (program chmn. petroleum divsn. 1976-77, Snyder award Legal Ethics 1998), Am. Intellectual Property Law Assn., Mass. Bar Assn., N.Y. Acad. Sci., Sigma Xi. Episcopalian. Achievements include 20 patents; preparation and determination of crystal structure of (211) phase of 123 superconductors; invention of randomly cross-linked smectites, of high surface area supported perovskite catalysts and method for preparation; selective auto exhaust catalysts; theory of finely divided metals; bonding model for zerovalent acetylene and olefin complexes; fluidized catalytic cracking catalysts, sulfur tolerant catalytic reforming. Office: GE Plastics One Plastics Ave Pittsfield MA 01201

WHELAN, ROGER MICHAEL, lawyer, educator; b. Montclair, N.J., Nov. 12, 1936; s. John Leslie and Helen Louise (Callahan) W.; m. Rosemary Bogdan, Aug. 26, 1961; children: Helen, Theresa, John, James, Kathleen (dec.), Julie, Jennifer. AB cum laude, Georgetown U., 1959, JD, 1962. Bar: D.C. 1962, U.S. Dist. Ct. D.C. 1962, U.S. Ct. Appeals (D.C. cir.) 1962, U.S. Supreme Ct. 1968, U.S. Dist. Ct. Md. 1985. Assoc. Fried, Rogers & Ritz, Washington, 1961-66; ptnr. Doctor & Whelan, Washington, 1967-72; judge U.S. Bankruptcy Ct., Washington, 1972-83; sr. mem. Verner, Liipfert, Bernhard, McPherson & Hand, Chartered, Washington, 1984-89; ptnr., sr. counsel Shaw, Pittman, Potts & Trowbridge, Washington, 1989—2000; outside counsel to several Washington & Md. law firms, 2000—. Dir. Lincoln Ctr. for Legal Studies, Arlington, Va., 1974-84; disting. lectr. Columbus Sch. Law, Cath. U. Am., Washington, 1975—; bd. govs. Conf. on Consumer Fin. Law, 1995—. Sec. local campaign com., Alexandria, Va., 1964; trustee YMCAA, Silver Spring, Md., 1972-74. Recipient award D.C. Cir. Jud. Conf., 1984. Fellow: Am. Coll. Bankruptcy (bd. regents 1989—95, bd. dirs. 1995—2002); mem.: FBA (chmn. bankruptcy subcom. 1988, exec. com. 1993—96, pres. 1999—2000), Assn. Former Bankruptcy Judges (sec.-treas. 1996—), Am. Bankruptcy Inst. (bd. dirs. 1991—97, chmn. legis. com. 1991—99, exec. com. 1993—95), Walter Chandler Inn of Ct. (master emeritus 1990—). Republican. Roman Catholic. Avocations: fishing, hunting, boating. Home: 17908 Ednor View Ter Ashton MD 20861-9757

WHELESS, ALBERT EUGENE, lawyer; b. Timmonsville, S.C., Feb. 15, 1935; s. Albert B. and Marie (Martin) W.; m. Celeste Graham, Sept. 6, 1958; children— Al, Art, Ann Marie. BA, Wofford Coll., 1959; JD, U. S.C., 1969. Bar: S.C. 1969. Assoc. John W. Jenrette, North Myrtle Beach, S.C., 1969, ptnr. Jenrette & Wheless, North Myrtle Beach, 1970-75, Jenrette, Wheless, McInnis & Breeden, North Myrtle Beach, 1976-79, Wheless & McInnis, North Myrtle Beach, 1980— ; city recorder North Myrtle Beach, 1970-71, city atty., 1972-79. Mem. ABA, S.C. Bar Assn., Horry County Bar Assn. (pres. 1982-84), ATLA, S.C. Trial Lawyers Assn., S.C. Def. Attys. Assn. General practice, Personal injury (including property damage), Property, real (including real estate development, water). Office: 457 Main St North Myrtle Beach SC 29582-3023

WHELPLEY, DAVID B., JR., lawyer; b. Akron, Ohio, Apr. 21, 1964; s. David B. and JoAnn D. Whelpley; m. Teresa E. Dugger, Oct. 21, 1989; children: David III, Austin, Hannah. BS cum laude, Clemson U., 1986; JD, Emory U., 1989. Bar: N.C. 1989, Ga. 1989. Ptnr. Kilpatrick Stockton LLP, Charlotte, NC, 1989—. Advisor Legal Svcs. N.C., Raleigh, 1997—2003. Mem. exec. bd. Theatre Charlotte, 1995—2002; bd. dirs. Mecklenburg County Register Deeds Adv. Bd., 1995—2002, Charlotte Repertory Theatre, 2002—. Mem.: ABA (mem. com.), N.C. Bar Assn. (mem. com.). Avocations: travel, skiing, hiking. Commercial, contracts (including sales of goods; commercial financing), Finance, Mergers and acquisitions. Office: Kilpatrick Stockton LLP 3500 One Wachovia Ctr 301 S College St Charlotte NC 28202-6000

WHICHARD, WILLIS PADGETT, law educator, retired state supreme court justice; b. Durham, N.C., May 24, 1940; s. Willis Guilford and Beulah (Padgett) W.; m. Leona Irene Paschal, June 4, 1961; children: Jennifer Diane, Ida Gilbert. AB, U. N.C., 1962, JD, 1965; LLM, U. Va., 1984, SJD, 1994. Bar: N.C. 1965. Law clk. N.C. Supreme Ct., Raleigh, 1965-66; ptnr. Powe, Porter, Alphin & Whichard, Durham, 1966-80; assoc. judge N.C. Ct. Appeals, Raleigh, 1980-86; assoc. justice N.C. Supreme Ct., Raleigh, 1986-98; dean and prof. law Campbell U. Instr. grad. sch. bus. adminstrn. Duke U., 1978; vis. lectr. U. N.C. Sch. Law, 1986-98. Contbr. articles to profl. jours. Rep. N.C. Ho. of Reps., Raleigh, 1970-74; senator N.C. Senate, 1974-80, chair numerous coms. and commns.; N.C. legis. rsch. commn., 1971-73, 75-77, land policy coun., 1975-79; bd. dirs. Sr. Citizens Coordinating Coun., 1972-74; chair local crusade Am. Cancer Soc., 1977, state crusade chair, 1980, chair pub. issues com., 1980-84; pres., bd. chmn. Downtown Durham Devel. Corp., 1980-84; bd. dirs. Durham County chpt. ARC, 1971-79; Durham county campaign dir. March of Dimes, 1968, 69, chmn., 1969-74, bd. dirs. Triangle chpt., 1974-79; bd. advisors Duke Hosp., 1982-85, U. N.C. Sch. Pub. Health, 1985-96, U. N.C. Sch. Social Work, 1989—; bd. visitors N.C. Ctrl. U. Sch. Law, 1987—; mem. law sch. dean search com. U. N.C., 1978-79, 88-89, self-study com., 1985-86; pres. N.C. Inst. Justice, 1984-94; bd. dirs. N.C. Ctr. Crime and Punishment, 1984-94. Staff sgt. N.C. Army NG, 1966-72. Recipient Disting. Service award Durham Jaycees, 1971, Outstanding Legis. award N.C. Acad. Trial Lawyers, 1975, Outstanding Youth Service award N.C. Juvenile Correctional Assn., 1975, Citizen of Yr., Eno Valley Civitan Club, Durham, 1982, Faith Active in Pub. Life award N.C. Council of Churches, 1983, Outstanding Appellate Judge award N.C. Acad. Trial Lawyers, 1983, inducted Durham High Sch. Hall of Fame, 1987. Mem. ABA, N.C. Bar Assn. (v.p. 1983-84, 2001-02), Durham County Bar Assn., U. N.C. Law Alumni Assn. (pres. 1978-79, bd. dirs. 1979-82), Nat. Guard Assn. (judge advocate 1972-73, legis. com. 1974-76), Order of Golden Fleece, Order of Grail, Order of Old Well, Amphoterothen Soc., Order of Coif, Phi Alpha Theta, Phi Kappa Alpha. Clubs: Durham-Chapel Hill Torch (pres. 1984-85), Watauga (Raleigh, pres. 1994-95). Democrat. Baptist. Home: 84402 Winslow Chapel Hill NC 27517 Office: Wiggins Sch Law Campbell Univ PO Box 158 Buies Creek NC 27506-0158 E-mail: Whichard@webster.campbell.edu., whichoo1@earthlink.net.

WHINSTON, ARTHUR LEWIS, lawyer; b. N.Y.C., Feb. 5, 1925; s. Charles Nathaniel and Charlotte (Nalen) W.; m. Melicent Ames Kingsbury, Mar. 19, 1949; children: Ann Kingsbury, James Pierce, Melicent Ames, Louise Ellen, Patricia Kingsbury. B.C.E., Cornell U., 1945; MSE., Princeton U., 1947; JD, N.Y. U., 1957. Bar: N.Y. 1957, Oreg. 1964, U.S. Supreme Ct 1966, U.S. Patent Office 1958, U.S. Ct. Appeals (fed. cir.) 1959; registered profl. engr., N.Y., Oreg. Engr. Chas. N. & Selig Whinston, N.Y.C., 1947-50; lectr. Coll. City N.Y., 1950-51; structures engr. Republic Aviation Corp., Farmingdale, N.Y., 1951-57; patent lawyer Arthur, Dry & Kalish, 1957-64, Klarquist Sparkman, LLP, 1964—; chmn. Oreg. Bar com. on patent, trademark and copyright law, 1968-69, 77-78, mem. com. unauthorized practice law, 1970-73, chmn., 1972-73, com. on profl. responsibility, 1973-75. Served as ensign, C.E.C., USNR, 1945-46. Recipient Fuertes medal Cornell U. Sch. Civil Engring., 1945 Mem. ABA, Oreg. Bar Assn., N.Y. Bar Assn., Multnomah County Bar Assn., Am. Intellectual Property Law Assn., N.Y. Intellectual Property Law Assn., Oreg. Patent Law Assn. (pres. 1977-78), Profl. Engrs. Oreg. (past state legis. chmn.), Sigma Xi, Chi Epsilon, Phi Kappa Phi. Clubs: Multnomah Athletic. Republican. Unitarian Universalist. Home: 3824 SW 50th Ave Portland OR 97221-2112 Office: One World Trade Ctr Ste 1600 Portland OR 97204

WHINSTON, STEPHEN ALAN, lawyer; b. Stamford, Conn., Mar. 27, 1948; s. Alfred Leonard and Rose (Eisgrau) W.; m. Joan Lenett, June 4, 1978; children: Stephanie Portnoy, Brian Arasim, Joshua. BA, Colgate U., 1970; JD, Case Western Res. U., 1973. Bar: Pa. 1973, U.S. Dist. Ct. (ea. dist.) Pa. 1973, U.S. Ct. Appeals (3d cir.) 1973, U.S. Ct. Appeals (8th cir.) 1995, U.S. Ct. Appeals (2d cir.) 2000, U.S. Supreme Ct. 2001. Trial atty. U.S. Dept. Justice, Washington, 1974-79, sr. trial atty., 1979-83; atty. Berger & Montague, P.C., Phila., 1983-85, shareholder, 1986—. Bd. dirs. Disabilities Law Project, Phila., 1989—, Jewish Fedn. Housing, Inc., Cherry Hill, N.J., 1994-96. Mem. Pa. Prison Soc. (bd. dirs.). Avocation: music. Civil rights, General civil litigation, Securities. Office: Berger & Montague PC 1622 Locust St Philadelphia PA 19103-6305 E-mail: saw@bm.net.

WHIPPLE, DEAN, federal judge; b. 1938; BS, Drury Coll., 1961; postgrad., U. Tulsa, 1961-62; JD, postgrad., U. Mo., Kansas City, 1965. Pvt. practice, Lebanon, Mo., 1965-75; cir. judge div. II 26th Jud. Cir. Mo., 1975-87; judge U.S. Dist. Ct., Kansas City, Mo., 1987-2000, chief judge, 2000—. Prosecuting atty. Laclede County, Mo., 1967-71. Mem. Cen. United Meth. Ch., Kansas City. With Mo. N.G., 1956-61; USAR, 1961-66. Mem. Mo. Bar Assn. (mem. pub. info. com. 1971-72, mem. judiciary com. 1971-72, mem. bd. govs. 1975-87, mem. exec. com. 1983-84, 86-87, mem. planning com. for ann. meeting 1985, 87, chmn. 1986, mem. selection com. for Lon Hocker award 1986), Mo. Trial Judges Assn., 26th Jud. Bar Assn., Laclede County Bar Assn. (pres. 1968-69, 72-73), Kansas City Met. Bar Assn., Kansas City Inn of Ct. (instr. 1988-93), Mo. Hist. Soc., Phi Delta Phi. Office: US Courthouse 400 E 9th St Kansas City MO 64106-2607

WHITAKER, A(LBERT) DUNCAN, lawyer; b. Ft. Wayne, Ind., Jan. 3, 1932; s. Robert Lynn and Rhoda Irene (Duncan) W.; m. Adelaide B. Saccone, Aug. 13, 1955; children: Brent Robert, Alene G., Karen E. BA, Yale U., 1954; JD, U. Mich., 1957. Bar: Mich. 1957, U.S. Ct. Appeals D.C. 1959, U.S. Supreme Ct. 1961. Atty. antitrust div. U.S. Dept. Justice, 1957-59; assoc. Howrey & Simon, Washington, 1959-65, ptnr., 1965-97; pro bono atty., 1997—. Lectr. George Washington U., George Mason U. Law Sch. Contbr. articles to profl. jours. Mem. ABA, Fed. Bar Assn., D.C. Bar Assn., Order of Coif, Phi Beta Kappa Clubs: Metropolitan. Antitrust, Federal civil litigation, Corporate, general. Office: Howrey Simon Arnold and White 1299 Pennsylvania Ave NW Ste 1 Washington DC 20004-2420 E-mail: whitakerd@howrey.com., whitd1332@aol.com.

WHITAKER, ELIZABETH, lawyer; b. Washington, Feb. 20, 1953; BA magna cum laude, Wehaton Coll., 1975; JD with honors, So. Meth. U., 1980. Bar: Tex. 1980. Fellow: Dallas Bar Found., Tex. Bar Found.; mem.: Order of Coif, Coll. of State Bar Tex., State Bar Tex. (chair continuing legal edn. com. 1996—97, bd. dirs. 1996—99, chair bd. dirs. 1998—99). Office: Hankinson & Whitaker LLP 2305 Cedar Springs Ste 230 Dallas TX 75201*

WHITAKER, GLENN VIRGIL, lawyer; b. Cin., July 23, 1947; s. Glenn M. and Doris (Handlon) W.; m. Jennifer Lynn Angus, Oct. 22, 1990. BA, Denison U., 1969; JD, George Washington U., 1972. Bar: Md. 1972, D.C. 1973, Ohio 1980. Law clk. to judge U.S. Dist. Ct., Balt., 1972-73; assoc. O'Donoghue and O'Donoghue, Washington, 1973-76; trial atty. civil div. U.S. Dept. Justice, Washington, 1976-78, spl. litigation counsel, 1978-80; ptnr. Graydon, Head & Ritchey, Cin., 1980-92, Voyrs, Sater, Seymour & Pease, Cin., 1992—. Emeritus master of bench Potter Stewart Inn of Ct., Cin., 1985—; adj. prof. law Coll. Law U. Cin.; mem. Am. Bd. Trial Advocates. Fellow Am. Coll. Trial Lawyers; mem. ABA, Ohio Bar Assn., D.C. Bar Assn., Md. Bar Assn., Cin. Bar Assn. Avocations: hiking, exploring. General civil litigation, Criminal, Personal injury (including property damage). Office: Vorys Sater Seymour & Pease 221 E 4th St Ste 2100 Cincinnati OH 45202-5133

WHITAKER, LESLIE KENT, lawyer; b. Santa Monica, Calif., Aug. 10, 1938; s. Clarence Nelson and Dorothy (Stewart) W.; m. Elaine Croshier, Oct. 23, 1964 (div. Sept. 1975); children: Eric, Carol, Adrienne; m. Susan Snell, Aug. 14, 1997. AB, Stanford U., 1960; LLB, Yale U., 1965. Bar: Calif. 1966, U.S. Dist. Ct. (no., cen., ea. and so. dists.) Calif. 1966, U.S. Ct. Appeals (9th cir.) 1966, U.S. Supreme Ct. 1972. Assoc. Chickering & Gregory, San Francisco, 1966-73; counsel Kaiser Industries Corp., Oakland, Calif., 1973-77; v.p., sr. counsel, sec. Kaiser Steel Corp., Fontana, Calif., 1977-85; prin. Verdon & Whitaker, Newport Beach, Calif., 1986-88; atty. Calif. Ct. Appeals, Riverside, 1988—. Lt. USNR, 1960-62. Mem. Canyon Crest Country Club. Appellate, State civil litigation. Home: 1240 Country Club Dr Riverside CA 92506-3607 Office: Calif Ct Appeals 3389 12th St Riverside CA 92501-3851

WHITAKER, MARY FERNAN, lawyer; b. Kansas City, Mo., May 29, 1958; d. James Paul and Mildred Louise (Connor) Fernan; m. Mark Dwight Whitaker, May 28, 1983; children: Paul Connor, James Sullivan, Helen Foster. BSN, George Mason U., 1982, JD, 1987. Bar: Va. 1987, Pa. 1995; cert. swim coach, Md. cert. swim judge. Nurse George Washington Med. Ctr., Washington, 1980-82, Mt. Vernon Hosp., Alexandria, Va., 1982-84; atty. Legal Svcs. No. Va., Arlington, 1987, Office Rev. and Appeals, EEOC, Falls Church, Va., 1987-88; pvt. practice Annadale, Va., 1988-93, Pottsville, Pa., 1993-95, Coopersburg, Pa., 1995-96, Solomons, Md., 1996—2000; faculty St. Mary's Ryken High Sch., 1999—2000; lawyer pvt. law practice, 2001—. Adj. faculty paralegal program No. Va. C.C., 1992; counselor, mem. legal com. My Sister's Pl., Washington, 1987-93; mem. pro bono panel Legal Svcs. No. Va., Falls Church, 1997—. Vol. ARC, Alexandria, 1987; vol. atty. Women's Legal Def. Fund, Washington, 1989-91, Legal Svcs. No. Va., 1997—; mem. Shelter Outreach Program, 1990-93; v.p. Ravensworth Bristow Civic assn., 1990-93; head makeup design for cmty. theatre troupe Camelot Players, 1990-91; tchr. 3d grade religious edn. St. Michael's Ch. Choir, 1991-92, tchr. 8th grade religious edn., 1992-93, choir, 1992-93; tchr. 7th grade religious edn. St. Joseph Ch., 1995-96; swimmer U.S. Masters, 1997, 98; cert. stroke and turn judge Md. Swimming, 1998—2001. U.S. Master Swimmer, 1997-98. Mem. Va. State Bar Assn., Phi Delta Phi. Roman Catholic. Avocations: bicycling, swimming. Home and Office: 7104 Marlan Dr Alexandria VA 22307

WHITBECK, JILL KARLA, lawyer; b. Bangkok, Jan. 17, 1968; d. Joseph Kern Walter and Ruth Ann Tucker; m. Christopher Lee Whitbeck, July 20, 1991; children: Jasmine Claire, Donald Joseph, Jade Karin, Jennifer Morgan. BA, Calif. Luth. U., 1990; JD, Pepperdine U. Sch. Law, 1993. Bar: Nev. 1993, U.S. Dist. Ct. Nev. 1994. Atty. Laxalt & Nomura, Reno, 1993-94, Edward M. Bernstein & Assocs., Reno, 1994-97, Law Offices of White & Meany, Reno, 1997-2000; sole practitioner Reno, 2000—. Deaconess, sch. bd. New Beginnings Child Devel. Ctr., Washoe Valley, Nev., 1998—. Mem. ABA, ATLA, Nev. Trial Lawyers Assn., No. Nev. Women Lawyers Assn., Nev. State Bar Assn., Washoe County Bar Assn. Republican. Mem. Christian Ch. Personal injury (including property damage), Product liability, Family and matrimonial. Office: 955 S Virginia St Ste 220 Reno NV 89502 Fax: (775) 337-8873. E-mail: jkwhitbeck@aol.com.

WHITE, BARRY BENNETT, lawyer; b. Boston, Feb. 13, 1943; s. Harold and Rosalyn (Schneider) W.; m. Eleanor Greenberg; children: Joshua S., Adam J., Benjamin D. AB magna cum laude, Harvard U., 1964, JD magna cum laude, 1967. Bar: Mass. 1967, U.S. Dist. Ct. Mass. 1967, U.S. Ct. Appeals (1st cir.) 1967. Assoc. Foley Hoag & Eliot, Boston, 1969—74, ptnr., 1975—, chmn. exec. com., 1987—91, mng. ptnr., 1991—92, 1993—2001, sec., 1992—93. Chmn. Lex Mundi, 1994. Editor Harvard Law Rev., 1965-67. Sec., gen. counsel, exec. com. Greater Boston C. of C., Initiative for Competitive Inner City; bd. dirs., exec. com. Mass. Assn. Mental Health, 1985—, pres., 1993-95; bd. dirs. Boston Mcpl. Rsch. Bur., Vol. Lawyers Project, 1987-93, Support Ctr. of Mass., 1988-95; mem. Jewish Family and Children's Svcs., Boston, 1979-87; bd. visitors Boston U. Grad. Sch. Dentistry, 1981—; bd. trustees Jewish Cmty. Rels. Coun., 1988-92; chmn. com. for Clinton/Gore New Eng. Lawyers, 1992-96; chmn. Tsongas for Pres. Com., 1991-98. With USPHS, 1967-69. Mem. ABA, Mass. Bar Assn., Boston Bar Assn., Internat. Bar Assn., Am. Acad. Hosp. Attys., Am. Hosp. Assn. (adj. task force on health planning 1982-84, contbg. editor hosp. law manual 1981-84), Harvard Club Boston, Badminton and Tennis Club. Democrat. Corporate, general, Private international, Non-profit and tax-exempt organizations. Office: Foley Hoag LLP 155 Seaport Blvd Boston MA 02210 E-mail: bbwhite@foleyhoag.com.

WHITE, BENJAMIN VROOM, III, lawyer; b. Hartford, Conn., Nov. 25, 1941; s. Benjamin Vroom and Charlotte (Conover) W.; m. Elizabeth Dodge, Sept. 6, 1969; children: Constance Atwood, Charles Conover. AB, Harvard U., 1964; MAT, Harvard Grad. Sch. of Edn., 1970; JD, Boston U., 1974. Law clk. to Hon. Alfred H. Joslin R.I. Supreme Ct., Providence, 1974-75; assoc., ptnr. Hinckley, Allen, Salisburg & Parsons, Providence, 1975-81; ptnr. Vetter & White, Providence, 1981—. Mem. faculty MCLE and Nat. inst. Trial Advocacy, Boston, 1983—. Editor Note and Case, Boston U. Law Rev., 1993-94; contbr. articles to profl. jours. Bd. govs. Gordon Sch., East Providence, 1981-87, 1st v.p., 1984-87; bd. dirs. Lippit Hill Tutorial, Providence, 1978-82, Westport River Watershed Alliance, 1989-95, Westport Land Conservation Trust, 1997—; pres. Perishable Theatre, Providence, 1999—, bd. advisors, 1998—. Lt. USNR, 1964-68. Mem. ABA (litig. sect.), Am. Assn. Arbitration (comml. panel 1985—), Fed. Bar Assn. (chpt. pres. 1998-2001), R.I. Bar Assn. (fed. ct. bench and bar com. 1982—, chmn. 1993—), Boston Bar Assn., R.I. Fed. Ct. Bd. of Bar Examiners, New Bedford Yacht Club, Harvard (R.I. and N.Y.C.) Club, Hope (Providence) Club, Acoaxet (Westport, Mass.) Club. Republican. Episcopalian. Federal civil litigation, State civil litigation. Office: Vetter & White Inc 20 Washington Pl Ste 1 Providence RI 02903-1321

WHITE, BRANTLEY W. lawyer; b. Houston, Aug. 22, 1966; s. Michael J. and Gail G. White; m. Brandy White, July 11, 1998; 1 child, Abigail. BA in Govt., U. Tex., Austin, 1989; JD, Tex. Tech. Sch. Law, 1993. Bar: Tex., U.S. Dist. Ct. (no., so., ea., we. dists.) Tex., Tex. 1994. Assoc. Wilk Law Firm, Dallas, 1994—98; ptnr. Watts Law Firm, Corpus Christi, Tex., 1998—2002; prin. Sico, White & Braugh, Corpus Christi, Tex., 2002—. Mem.: ATLA, Attys. Info. Exch. Group, Tex. Trial Lawyers Assn. Personal injury (including property damage), Product liability. Office: Sico White & Braugh 900 Frost Bank Plaza 802 N Carancahua St Corpus Christi TX 78470 E-mail: bwhite@swbtrial.com.

WHITE, DANIEL BOWMAN, lawyer; b. Charlotte, N.C., Apr. 12, 1948; s. William Garner and Elizabeth (Bowman) W.; m. Sarah de Saussure Peterson, May 29, 1976; children: Bentley Parker, Sarah de Saussure. AB, Davidson Coll., 1970; JD, U. S.C., 1976. Bar: S.C. 1976, U.S. Dist. Ct. S.C. 1976, U.S. Ct. Appeals (4th cir.) 1978, U.S. Ct. Appeals (fed. cir.) 1990. Ptnr. Gallivan, White & Boyd P.A., Greenville, S.C., 1976—. Comments editor U. S.C. Law Rev., 1975-76. Commr. Greenville Zoning Commn., 1980-85; mem. Supreme Ct. Bd. Commrs. on Grievances and Discipline, 1988-91. 1st lt. U.S. Army, 1971-73. Decorated Bronze Star; Dana scholar Davidson Coll., N.C., 1966-70. Mem. S.C. Bar (ho. dels. 1986—, bd. govs. 1992-95, 2000—, chmn. ho. dels. 2000—, sec. 2002-03, treas. 2003-), Def. Rsch. Inst., Nat. Assn. R.R. Trial Counsel, Greenville Young Lawyers Club (pres. 1981), Fed. Cir. Jud. Conf., Internat. Assn. Def. Counsel, Assn. Def.

Trial Attys. Episcopalian. Federal civil litigation, State civil litigation, Environmental. Office: Gallivan White & Boyd PO Box 10589 Greenville SC 29603-2804 E-mail: dwhite@gwblawfirm.com.

WHITE, DOUGLAS JAMES, JR., lawyer; b. N.Y.C., Mar. 20, 1934; s. Douglas James and Margaret (Stillman) W.; m. Denise Beale, May 28, 1960; children: Brian Douglas, James Roderick. BA, U. Oreg., 1955; LLB, Willamette U., 1958. Bar: Oreg. 1958. Law clk. to assoc. justice Oreg. Supreme Ct., Salem, 1958-59; assoc. Schwabe, Williamson & Wyatt (formerly known as Mautz, Souther, Spaulding, Kinsey & Williamson), Portland, Oreg., 1959-69; shareholder, gen. ptnr. Schwabe, Williamson & Wyatt, P.C. (formerly known as Schwabe, Williamson, Wyatt, Moore & Roberts), Portland, Oreg., 1969-79, sr. ptnr., 1979-93; shareholder, 1994-98; of counsel, 1999—. Trustee Jesuit H.S., Beaverton, 1991-94; bd. dirs. St. Vincent de Paul Child Devel. Ctr., Portland, 1979-90, Portland Coun., Soc. St. Vincent de Paul, 1989-92, Portland House of Umoja, 1995—; bd. dirs., officer Maryville Nursing Home, Beaverton, 1993-99, St. Vincent de Paul Conf. of St. Thomas More, Portland, 1966—; active Saturday Acad. Beaverton, 1982—. Mem.: Oreg. State Bar Assn. (real estate and land use sect. exec. com. 1984—85), Flyfisher Club Oreg., Multnomah Athletic Club (Portland chpt.). Republican. Roman Catholic. Avocations: fly-fishing, cross-country skiing, bridge, hiking. Home: 6725 SW Preslynn Dr Portland OR 97225-2668 Office: Schwabe Williamson & Wyatt 1211 SW 5th Ave Ste 1600 Portland OR 97204-3713

WHITE, EDWARD GIBSON, II, lawyer; b. Lexington, Ky., Nov. 7, 1954; s. Russell Edwin White and Betty Lee White-Estabrook; m. Cynthia Ann Reisz, Mar. 10, 1979; children: Edward Gibson III, William Elliot, John Alexander, Albert Grahm. BA, U. Tenn., Chattanooga, 1980; JD, U. Tenn., Knoxville, 1983. Bar: Tenn. 1983, U.S. Dist. Ct. (ea. dist.) Tenn. 1984, U.S. Ct. Appeals (6th cir.) 1985. Assoc. Hodges, Doughty & Carson, Knoxville, 1983-87, ptnr., 1988—. Bd. dirs. Knoxville affiliate The Susan G. Komen Breast Cancer Found., Inc., Elizabeth R. Griffin Rsch. Found., West High Found., Inc. Fellow Knoxville Bar Found. (bd. dirs.); mem. ABA (litigation sect. 1985—), Tenn. Bar Assn. (interprofl. code com. 1989—, med./legal com. 1991—), Knoxville Bar Assn. (treas. 1995-96, continuing legal edn. com. 1985-86, 88-91, chmn. 1992-94, mem. naturalization com. 1985-87, bd. govs. 1993-94, pres. elect 1996, pres. 1997, Pres.'s award 1992), Tenn. Def. Lawyers Assn., Def. Rsch. Inst. (med./legal com. 1985—), Am. Bd. Trial Advocates, U. Tenn. Pres.'s Club, Univ. Club, Cherokee Country Club, Knoxville Racquet Club. Republican. Avocations: tennis, golf, boating, water sports, fishing. General civil litigation, Insurance, Personal injury (including property damage). Office: Hodges Doughty & Carson 617 Main St # 869 Knoxville TN 37902-2602

WHITE, EDWARD ALFRED, lawyer; b. Elizabeth, N.J., Nov. 23, 1934; BS in Indsl. Engring., U. Mich., 1957, JD, 1963. Bar: Fla. 1963, U.S. Ct. Appeals (5th cir.) 1971, U.S. Ct. Appeals (11th cir.) 1981, U.S. Supreme Ct. 1976. Assoc. Jennings, Watts, Clarke & Hamilton, Jacksonville, Fla., 1963-66, ptnr., 1966-69, Wayman & White, Jacksonville, Fla., 1969-72; pvt. practice Jacksonville, Fla., 1972—. Mem. aviation law com. Fla. Bar, 1972-94, chmn., 1979-81, bd. govs., 1984-88, admiralty com., 1984—, chmn., 1990-91, chmn. pub. relations com., 1986-88, exec. coun. trial lawyers sect., 1986-91, chmn. admiralty cert. com., 1995-97. Fellow Am. Bar Found.; mem. ABA (vice chmn. admiralty law com. 1995—), Fla. Bar Assn. (bd. cert. civil trial lawyer, bd. cert. admiralty lawyer), Jacksonville Bar Assn. (chmn. legal ethics com. 1975-76, bd. govs. 1976-78, pres. 1979-80), Assn. Trial Lawyers Am. (sustaining mem. 1984—), Acad. Fla. Trial Lawyers (diplomate), Fla. Coun. Bar Assn. Pres.'s, Lawyer-Pilots Bar Assn., Am. Judicature Soc., Maritime Law Assn. (proctor in admiralty), Southeastern Admiralty Law Inst. (bd. dirs. 1982-84, chmn., pres. 1994), Am. Bd. Trial Advocates. Admiralty, General civil litigation, Personal injury (including property damage). Home: 1959 Largo Rd Jacksonville FL 32207-3926 Office: 901 Blackstone Bldg 233 E Bay St Jacksonville FL 32202-3452 Fax: 904-356-6508. E-mail: cwitherwax@damato-lynch.com.

WHITE, EMMET, JR., retirement community administrator; b. Newark, Oct. 18, 1946; s. Emmet Sr. and June (Howlett) White; m. Betty Orr, June 7, 1970; children: Benjamin, Suzanne, George. BA, Lafayette Coll., 1968; JD, Coll. of William and Mary, 1971. Bar: Hawaii 1972; cert. nursing home adminstr., Hawaii. Law ptnr. Mau & White AAL, Honolulu, 1975-83, White & Tom AAL, Honolulu, 1983-95; pres., CEO Arcadia Retirement Residence, Honolulu, 1996—. Bd. trustees Ctrl. Union Ch., Honolulu, 1980-84, chmn. 1983-84, moderator, 1987. Col. USAR, 1968-94. Mem.: Hawaii Long Term Care Assn. (chmn. 2001—03), Hawaii Bar Assn. Avocations: family activities, physical activities. Office: Arcadia Retirement Residence 1434 Punahou St Honolulu HI 96822-4754 E-mail: ewhite@arcadia-hi.org.

WHITE, GEORGE EDWARD, law educator, lawyer; b. Northampton, Mass., Mar. 19, 1941; s. George LeRoy and Frances Dorothy (McCafferty) W.; m. Susan Valre Davis, Dec. 31, 1966; children: Alexandra V., Elisabeth McC. BA, Amherst Coll., 1963; MA, Yale U., 1964, PhD, 1967; JD, Harvard U., 1970. Bar: D.C. 1970, Va. 1975, U.S. Supreme Ct. 1973. Vis. scholar Am. Bar Found., 1970-71; law clk. to Chief Justice Warren U.S. Supreme Ct., 1971-72; asst. prof. law U. Va., 1972-74, assoc. prof., 1974-77, prof., 1977-86, John B. Minor prof. law and history, 1987—2003, disting. univ. prof., John B. Minor prof. law and history, 1992—2003, David and Mary Harrison disting. prof. law, 2003—. Vis. prof. Marshall-Wythe Law Sch. spring 1988, N.Y. Law Sch., fall 1988. Author books, including: The American Judicial Tradition, 1976, 2d edit., 1988, Tort Law in America: An Intellectual History (gavel award ABA 1981), 1980, ed edit., 2003, Earl Warren: A Public Life (gavel award ABA 1983), 1982, The Marshall Court and Cultural Change, 1988, 2d edit., 1991 (James Willard Hurst prize 1990), Justice Oliver Wendell Holmes: Law and the Inner Self, 1993 (gavel award ABA 1994, Scribes award, 1994, Littleton-Griswold prize 1994, Triennial Order of the Coif award 1996), Intervention and Detachment: Essays in Legal History and Jurisprudence, 1994; Creating the National Pastime: Baseball Transforms Itself, 1903-1953, 1996, The Constitution and The New Deal, 2000; editor Studies in Legal History, 1980-86, Delegate in Law, Oxford U. Press, 1986-97. Mem. AAAS, Am. Law Inst., Am. Soc. Legal History (bd. dirs. 1978-81), Soc. Am. Historians. Office: Law Sch U Va Charlottesville VA 22903-1789 E-mail: gew@virginia.edu.

WHITE, GREGORY A. lawyer; b. Nov. 1949; BA in Criminal Justice and Police Adminstrn., Kent State U., 1973; JD magna cum laude, Cleveland Marshall Coll., 1976. Atty. Wilcox and White Law Firm, 1977—84; law dir. City of Elyria, 1979; prosecutor Lorain County, Ohio, 1981—2002; U.S. atty. No. Dist. Ohio, 2003—. With USMC, Vietnam. Office: 1800 Bank One Ctr 600 Superior Ave E Cleveland OH 44114*

WHITE, HARRY EDWARD, JR., lawyer; b. Menominee, Mich., Apr. 26, 1939; s. Harry Edward and Verena Charlotte (Leisen) W.; m. Mary P.A. Sheaffer, June 7, 1980. BS in Fgn. Svc., Georgetown U., Washington, 1961; LLB, Columbia U., 1964. Bar: N.Y. 1965, U.S. Supreme Ct. 1970, U.S. Dist. Ct. (so. dist.) N.Y. 1979, U.S. Tax Ct. 1980. Assoc. Milbank, Tweed, Hadley & McCloy, N.Y.C., 1964-65, 67-73, ptnr., 1974—. Contbr. chpts. to books, articles to legal jours. Served with M.I., U.S. Army, 1965-66, Vietnam. Decorated Bronze Star. Mem. ABA, Internat. Bar Assn., N.Y. State Bar Assn. (chmn. taxation com. internat. law practice sect. 1987-90, co-chmn. exempt orgns. com. tax sect. 1987-88), Internat. Law Assn., ssn. Bar City N.Y., Internat. Fiscal Assn. Republican. Roman Catholic. Corporate taxation, Taxation, general, Personal income taxation. Home: 333 E 55th St New York NY 10022-8316 Office: Milbank Tweed Hadley & McCloy 1 Chase Manhattan Plz Fl 47 New York NY 10005-1413 E-mail: hwhite@milbank.com.

WHITE, JAMES ALFRED, lawyer; b. Bay City, Mich., Jan. 5, 1939; s. Gerald J. and Clara E. (Barnes) W.; m. Barbara J. White, Feb. 14, 1980. BA cum laude, Alma Coll., 1961; JD, U. Mich., 1964. Bar: Mich., 1964. Assoc. Foster, Swift, Collins & Coey, Lansing, Mich., 1964-69, ptnr., 1969-88, White, Schneider, Young & Chiodini, PC, Okemos, Mich., 1988—; . Csl. Mich. Edn. Assn., 1966— ; labor arbitrator labor panelAm. Arbitration Assn. Bd. dirs. Big Bros. and Big Sisters of Greater Lansing, Inc., 1972-80. Mem. ABA, Mich. Bar Assn., Ingham County Bar Assn. Club: Met. Flying (pres.). Labor (including EEOC, Fair Labor Standards Act, labor-management relations, NLRB, OSHA), Agricultural. Home: 2300 Jolly Oak Rd Okemos MI 48864 E-mail: jwhite@wsbyc.com.

WHITE, JAMES BARR, lawyer, real estate investor, consultant; b. Haverhill, Mass., June 13, 1941; s. Ned and Shirlee (Euster) W.; m. Carol Klein, June 23, 1963; children: Michael Andrew, Laurie Alison, Elizabeth Ellen. BS, Tufts U., 1962; LLB, Columbia U., 1965; MPA, Harvard U., 1988. Bar: Mass. 1965. Assoc. Goulston & Storrs, Boston, 1965—71, ptnr., 1971—74, Palmer & Dodge, Boston, 1974—89; pres. ELAW Corp., Concord, Mass., 1992—. Mem. adv. com. MIT Ctr. for Real Estate Devel., Cambridge, 1987-89; dir. Nat. Realty Com., Washington, 1987-89. Chmn., mem. Town of Wayland (Mass.) Planning Bd., 1974-78; mem. Route 128 Area Com., Lincoln, Mass., 1985-87; mem. Town of Lincoln Planning Bd., 1991-2001, Town of Lincoln Hist. Dist. Commn., 1992-2001; bd. overseers New Eng. Conservatory, 1995-98; chmn., bd. govs. Quansoo Beach Assn., Martha's Vineyard, Mass., 1998—; dir. Boston History Ctr. and Mus., Inc., 1999—, pres., 2000—. Mem. Handel and Haydn Soc. (gov. 1985-90, overseer 1990-94), Bostonian Soc. (bd. dirs. 1990-2002). Home: 38 Bedford Rd Lincoln MA 01773-2037 Office: ELAW Corp Office of Pres 175 Sudbury Rd Concord MA 01742-3419

WHITE, JAMES BOYD, law educator; b. Boston, July 28, 1938; s. Benjamin Vroom and Charlotte Green (Conover) W.; m. Mary Louise Fitch, Jan. 1, 1978; children: Emma Lillian, Henry Alfred; children by previous marriage: Catherine Conover, John Southworth. AB, Amherst Coll., 1960; AM, Harvard U., 1961, LLB, 1964. Assoc. Foley, Hoag & Eliot, Boston, 1964-67; asst. prof. law U. Colo., 1967-69, assoc. prof., 1969-73, prof., 1973-75; prof. law U. Chgo., 1975-83; Hart Wright prof. law and English U. Mich., Ann Arbor, 1983—. Vis. assoc. prof. Stanford U., 1972 Author: The Legal Imagination, 1973, (with Scarboro) Constitutional Criminal Procedure, 1976, When Words Lose Their Meaning, 1981, Heracles' Bow, 1985, Justice as Translation, 1990, "This Book of Starres", 1994, Acts of Hope, 1994, From Expectation to Experience, 1999, The Edge of Meaning, 2001. Sinclair Kennedy Traveling fellow, 1964-65; Nat. Endowment for Humanities fellow, 1979-80, 92; Guggenheim fellow, 1993; vis. scholar Phi Beta Kappa, 1997-98. Mem. AAAS, Am. Law Inst. Office: U Mich Law Sch 625 S State St Ann Arbor MI 48109-1215

WHITE, JAMES RICHARD, lawyer; b. McKinney, Tex., Jan. 22, 1948; s. James Ray and Maxine (Brown) W.; children: Nicole Olivia, Mandi Leigh, James Derek. BBA, So. Meth. U., 1969, MBA, 1970, JD, 1973, LLM, 1977. Bar: Tex. 1973, U.S. Tax Ct. 1975, U.S. Supreme Ct. 1989, U.S. Ct. Appeals (5th cir.) 1989); cert. Comml. Real Estate Law Tex. Bd. Legal Specialization. Assoc. Elliot, Meer, Vetter, Denton & Bates, Dallas, 1973-74, Atwell, Cain & Davenport, Dallas, 1974-75; atty. Sabine Corp., Dallas, 1975-77; assoc. Brice & Barron, Dallas, 1977-79; ptnr. Millard & Olson, Dallas, 1979-82, Johnson & Swanson, Dallas, 1982-83, Winstead, Sechrest & Minick P.C., Dallas, 1983—, hiring ptnr., 1987-2001, exec. com., 2000-01. Mem. staff Southwestern Law Jour., Dallas, 1971-73; mem. So. Meth. U. Moot Ct. Bd., Order Barristers, Dallas, 1972-73; prof. North Lake Coll., Dallas, 1985; bd. dirs. Tex. Assn. Young Lawyers, Austin, 1980-82; sec. bd. dirs. Dallas Assn. Young Lawyers, 1976-80. Contbr. articles to profl. jours. Chmn. bd. dirs. Tex. Lawyers Credit Union, Austin, 1980-82; pres. North Tex. Premier Soccer Assn., Dallas, 1979-81; v.p. Lake Highlands Soccer Assn., 1995-96, pres., 1996—; mem. regional mobility task force Real Estate Coun., City of Dallas, 1991-92, mem. downtown revitalization com., 1995-97; mem. Dallas Indsl. Devel. Bd., 1992-93, Dallas Higher Edn. Authority Bd., 1994-96; spkr.'s bur. and accreditation divsn. World Cup USA '94; mem. exec. coun. Recreational Interleague Assn. Dallas, 2002—. Mem. ABA (mem. title ins. and survey, mortgage loan origination and structure com., mortgage financing and opinion, non-traditional comml. real estate fin. coms.), Tex. Bar Assn. (cert. 1973, mem. mortgage loan opinion com.), Tex. Coll. Real Estate Attys., Coll. State Bar Tex. Methodist. Avocations: soccer, golf, skiing, racquetball. Banking, Finance, Property, real (including real estate development, water). Home: 8003 Hundley Ct Dallas TX 75231-4728 Office: Winstead Sechrest & Minick 5400 Renaissance Tower 1201 Elm St Ste 5400 Dallas TX 75270-2199 E-mail: jrwhite@winstead.com.

WHITE, JAMIE, lawyer; b. Dec. 18, 1968; BA in Politics, Lancaster U. Atty. DLA, 1993—2002; ptnr. Dinsents, 2002—. Avocations: golf, football, tennis. Bankruptcy. Office: Pinsents The Chancery 58 Spring Manchester M2 1EW England Fax: 0161 250 0142. E-mail: jamie.white@pinsents.com.

WHITE, JEFFERY HOWELL, lawyer; b. Tyler, Tex., Aug. 4, 1959; s. Bluford D. and Tempie R. (Tunnell) W.; m. Michael Anne Mackley, May 21, 1989; children: Kristin, Alex, Landry. BS in History, So. Ark. U., 1983; JD, Oklahoma City U., 1986. Bar: Tex. 1987. Assoc. Dean White, Canton, Tex., 1986-90; asst. dist. atty. Van Zandt Co., Canton, 1991-94; ptnr. Elliott Elliott & White, Canton, 1994-97; pvt. practice Canton, Tex., 1997—. Mem. Van Zandt County Bar Assn. (v.p. 1999-2000, pres. 2000-01), Tex. Criminal Def. Lawyers Assn. (sustaining), Tex. State Bar (dist. 1-A grievance com. 1996-2002). Democrat. United Methodist. Avocations: golf, tennis, spectator sports. Criminal, Juvenile. Home: Box 1200 Van TX 75790-1200 Office: 157 N Buffalo St Canton TX 75103-1353

WHITE, JERUSHA LYNN, lawyer; b. Kansas City, Mo., Nov. 30, 1950; d. Riley Vaughn and Edith Blynn (Ringen) W.; m. Larry D. Hancock, Jan. 5, 1969 (div. 1973); m. Stephen Perry Wasson, Nov. 30, 1978 (div. 1985); m. Charles Beam Westley, Feb. 14, 1994 (div.). AS, State Fair C.C., 1974; BS, Cen. Mo. State U., 1978; JD, U. Mo., Kansas City, 1981. Bar: Mo. 1981. With Montgomery Ward & Co., Sedalia, Mo., 1968-69, 73-74, Parkhurst Mfg. Co., Sedalia, Mo., 1969-71, United Farm Agy., Sedalia, Mo., 1972-73, Howard Truck & Equipment Co., Sedalia, Mo., 1974-75, McGraw-Edison Co., Sedalia, Mo., 1975-76, Rival Mfg. Co., Sedalia, Mo., 1977-78; buyer Hotel Equipment Co., Century City, Calif., 1978; law clk. Legal Aid Western Mo., Kansas City, 1979-80, Horowitz & Shurin PC, Kansas City, 1980-81; assoc. Steve Borel/Steve Streen, Kansas City, 1982-83; pvt. practice Sedalia, 1983-85; ptnr. Cope, Schuber & White, 1985-86; staff atty. Hyatt Legal Svcs., 1986-88; asst. dist. counsel U.S. Army Corps Engrs., Kansas City, 1988-2000; staff judge advocate contract atty. advisor Ft. Leavenworth, Kans., 2000—02; asst. dist. counsel U.S. Army Corps Engrs., Kansas City, 2002—. Mem.: Mo. Bar Assn. Democrat. Presbyterian. Government contracts and claims. Home: 6717 NW Chinquapin Ct Kansas City MO 64151-2326 Office: US Army Corps Engrs 601 E 12th St Rm 715 Kansas City MO 64106 E-mail: jerushawhite@aol.com., jerusha.l.white@usace.army.mil.

WHITE, JILL CAROLYN, lawyer; b. Santa Barbara, Calif., Mar. 20, 1934; d. Douglas Cameron and Gladys Louise (Ashley) W.; m. Walter Otto Weyrauch, Mar. 17, 1973. BA, Occidental Coll., L.A., 1955; JD, U. Calif., Berkeley, 1972. Bar: Fla. 1974, Calif. 1975, U.S. Dist. Ct. (no. and mid. dists.) Fla., U.S. Ct. Appeals (5th and 11th cirs.), U.S. Supreme Ct. Staff mem. U.S. Dept. State, Am. Embassy, Rio de Janeiro, 1956-58; with psychol. rsch. units Inst. Human Devel., Inst. Personality Assessment and Rsch., U. Calif., Berkeley, 1961-68; adj. prof. criminal justice program U. Fla., Gainesville, Fla., 1976-78; pvt. practice immigration and nationality law, Gainesville, 1976—2002. Contbr. articles to profl. jours. Mem.: Fla. Bar (immigration and nationality law cert. com. 1994—99, chmn. cert. com. 1997—98, cert. in immigration and nationality law 1995—), Bar Assn. 8th Jud. Cir. Fla., Am. Immigration Lawyers Assn. (bd. dirs. Ctrl. Fla. chpt. 1985—94, 1995—96, 1997—2000, chmn. Ctrl. Fla. chpt. 1988—89, co-chmn. so. regional liaison com. 1990—92, nat. bd. dirs. 1988—89), Altrusa. Democrat. Immigration, naturalization, and customs. Office: 2830 NW 41st St Ste C Gainesville FL 32606-6667 E-mail: jwhite49@earthlink.net.

WHITE, JOHN JOSEPH, III, lawyer; b. Darby, Pa., Nov. 23, 1948; s. John J. Jr. and Catherine (Lafferty) W.; m. Catherine M Staley, Dec. 9, 1983. BS, U. Scranton, 1970; MPA, Marywood U., 1977; JD, Loyola U., New Orleans, 1983. Bar: Pa. 1983, U.S. Dist. Ct. (ea. dist.) Pa. 1983, N.J. 1984, U.S. Ct. Appeals (3d cir.) 1983, U.S. Dist. Ct. N.J. 1984, U.S. Tax Ct. 1984, D.C. 1985, U.S. Supreme Ct. 1987. Exec. dir. Scranton (Pa.) Theatre Libre, Inc., 1973-77; pub. Libre Press Inc., Scranton, 1977-83; pvt. practice Phila., 1983—. Pres. eMercury, Inc., Lansdowne, Pa., 1987—; N.Am. agt. Palacky U. Med. Sch., Olomouc, Czech Republic, 1995—2001. Founder, pub. Metro Mag., 1977-83. Founder, Scranton Pub. Theatre, 1976; exec. dir. Scranton Theatre Libre, Inc., 1973. Capt. USAF, 1970-73; lt. col. Res., 1973-89, col. ANG, 1999-2000, ret. 2000. Mem.: ABA, N.G. Assn., Phila. Bar Assn., Nat. Acad. Elder Law Attys., Mil. Order of Fgn. Wars, Air Force Assn. (chpt. pres. 1975—), Phi Delta Phi Internat. Legal Frat. Democrat. Roman Catholic. Avocations: jogging, art collecting. General civil litigation, Private international, Personal injury (including property damage). E-mail: lawfirmusa@aol.com.

WHITE, KATHERINE PATRICIA, lawyer; b. N.Y.C., Feb. 1, 1948; d. Edward Christopher and Catherine Elizabeth (Walsh) W. BA in English, Molloy Coll., 1969; JD, St. John's U., 1971. Bar: N.Y. 1972, U.S. Dist. Ct. (ea. and so. dists.) N.Y., 1973, U.S. Supreme Ct. 1976. Atty. Western Electric Co., Inc., N.Y.C., 1971-79; sr. atty. AT&T Corp., N.Y.C., 1979-96, chief regulatory counsel-New Eng., 1996-97, law and govt. affairs v.p., gen. atty.-New Eng., 1997—2002. Adj. prof. law N.Y. Law Sch., N.Y.C., 1987-88, Fordham U. Sch. Law, 1988-91, 2002—; bd. dirs. First Security Benefit Life Ins. Co. N.Y. Vol. Sloan Kettering Inst., 1973, North Shore U. Hosp., 1975, various fed., state and local polit. campaigns; judge N.Y. State Bicentennial Writing Competition, N.Y.C., 1977-78; chmn. Com. to Elect Supreme Ct. Judge, N.Y.C., 1982; bd. dirs. The Flea Theatre Co., N.Y.C., 2000—. Mem. Am. Corp. Counsel Assn., N.Y. State Bar Assn. (bus. and banking law com. real estate law sect., corp. counsel sect.), Assn. Bar City N.Y. (adminstrv. law com. 1982-85, young lawyers com. 1976-79, judge nat. moot ct. competition 1979-91), Cath. Lawyers Guild for Diocese of Rockville Centre (pres. 1980-81), St. John's U. Sch. Law Alumni Assn. (pres. L.I. chpt. 1986-88), Women's Nat. Rep. Club (bd. govs. 1988-91), Met. Club. Avocations: racing sailboats, figure skating, golf, tennis. Administrative and regulatory, Commercial, contracts (including sales of goods; commercial financing), Utilities, public. Home: 1035 5th Ave Apt 14D New York NY 10028-0135 Office: AT&T 32 Avenue Of The Americas New York NY 10013-2473

WHITE, LINDA DIANE, lawyer; b. N.Y.C., Apr. 1, 1952; d. Bernard and Elaine (Simons) Schwartz; m. Thomas M. White, Aug. 16, 1975; 1 child, Alexandra Nicole. AB, U. Pa., 1973; JD, Northwestern U., 1976. Bar: Ill. 1976. Assoc. Walsh, Case, Coale & Brown, Chgo., 1976-77, Greenberger & Kaufmann (merged into Katten, Muchin), Chgo., 1977-82, ptnr., 1982-85, Sonnenschein Nath & Rosenthal, Chgo., 1985—. Mem. trustees coun. Penn Women; mem. Samuel Zell and Robert Lurie Real Estate Ctr., The Wharton Sch., U. Pa. Mem. ABA (real property fin. com., comml. leasing com., real property, probate and trust law sect. 1987—), Ill. Bar Assn., Chgo. Bar Assn., Practicing Law Inst. (chmn. program on negotiating comml. leases 1995-99, real estate law adv. com.). Commercial, contracts (including sales of goods; commercial financing), Landlord-tenant, Property, real (including real estate development, water). Office: Sonnenschein Nath & Rosenthal 8000 Sears Tower 233 S Wacker Dr Ste 8000 Chicago IL 60606-6491 E-mail: lwhite@sonnenschein.com.

WHITE, MARY JO, lawyer; b. Kans. City, Mo., Dec. 27, 1947; d. Carl and Ruth King Monk; m. John W. White, Jan. 24, 1970. BA, Coll. William & Mary, 1970; MA in Psychology, New Sch. for Soc. Rsch., 1971; JD, Columbia U., 1974. Bar: New York 1975. Law Clerk to Hon. Marvin E. Frankel, So. Dist. N.Y. , NY, 1975—76; assoc. Debevoise & Plimpton, 1976—78, litig. ptnr., 1983—90, ptnr., chair of litig., 2002—; asst. U.S. atty. So. Dist. N.Y., chief appellate atty. of criminal div. , 1978—81; instr. in Profl. Responsibility and Ethics Columbia Law Sch., 1982—; chief asst. U.S. atty. Ea. Dist. N.Y. , Bklyn., 1990—93; U.S. atty. So. Dist. N.Y., Manhattan, 1993—2002. Chairperson Atty. Gen. Janet Reno's advisory com. of U.S. Attys., 1993—94. Recipient Women of Power and Influence award, NOW, "Magnificent 7" award, Bus. & Profl. Women USA, Law Enforcement Person of the Year award, Soc. of Profl. Investigators, Human Relations Award, Anti-Defamation League Lawyer's Div., 1996, Edward Weinfeld award for disting. contbn. to Admin. of Justice, N.Y. County Lawyers' Assn., 1998, Nat. Law Jour. 2002 list of Top Women Litigators, John P. O'Neill Pillar of Justice award, Respect for Law Alliance, 2002, Sandra Day O'Connor award for Distinction in Public Svc., 2002, dir. of FBI's Jefferson Cup award for contbn. to Rule of Law in the fight against terrorism and crime, 2002, George H. W. Bush award for excellence in counter-terrorism and the Agency Seal Medallion, CIA, 2002; fellow Am. Coll. of Trial Lawyers. Mem.: ABA, N.Y. State Bar Assn., Assn. of the Bar of City of N.Y. (established tutorial prog. for minority canidates for admin. to bar). Achievements include First women to serve as U.S Atty. for So. Dist. of N.Y; first chairperson of Atty. Gen. Janet Reno's Advisory Com.of U.S. Attys. Office: Debevoise & Plimpton 919 Third Ave 47th Fl New York NY 10022

WHITE, NICHOLAS L. legal educator; b. 1925; AB, Ohio Wesleyan U., 1950; JD, U. Cin., 1956. Bar: Ohio 1956, Ind. 1971, Tenn. 1978. Assoc. Taft, Stettinius & Hollister, Cin., 1956-65, ptnr., 1965-70; asst. dean adminstrn. Ind. U., Bloomington, 1970-73, prof. law, 1970-77, assoc. dean, 1974-77; dean, prof. law Memphis State U., 1977-84; prof. law U. Memphis, 1985—. Vis. prof. McGeorge Sch. of Law, Sacramento, Calif., 1984-85; cons. EPA Water Planning Divsn., 1974-77, Nat. Commn. Water Quality, 1975. Served with USMC, 1943-46. Mem. Phi Beta Kappa, Order of Coif, Omicron Delta Kappa. Office: U Memphis School of Law Memphis TN 38152 E-mail: nlwhite@memphis.edu.

WHITE, PAMELA JANICE, lawyer; b. Elizabeth, NJ, July 13, 1952; d. Emmet Talmadge and June (Howlett) W. BA, Mary Washington Coll., 1974; JD, Washington and Lee U., 1977. Bar: Md. 1977, U.S. Dist. Ct. Md. 1978, D.C. 1979, U.S. Dist. Ct. D.C. 1979, U.S. Ct. Appeals (4th cir.) 1979, U.S. Ct. Appeals (D.C. cir.) 1981, U.S. Ct. Claims 1981, U.S. Ct. Appeals (2d cir.) 1983, N.Y. 1983, U.S. Dist. Ct. (so. dist.) N.Y. 1983, U.S. Ct. Appeals (9th cir.) 1988, U.S. Supreme Ct. 1981. Assoc. Ober, Grimes & Shriver, Balt., 1977-84; prin. Ober, Kaler, Grimes & Shriver, Balt., 1985—. Chair Employment Group, 1994—; mem. Md. Bd. Law Examiners, 1986-94, Md. Judiciary Pub. Trust and Confidence Com., 2001-03; select com. on Gender Equality, 1989-2000, chair, 1997-99, spl. com. on ethics 2002-03, spl. thesis com., 2002-03, pub. trust and confidence com., 2001-03; fed. dist. ct. adv. group Civil Justice Reform Act, 1990; exec. com. Md. Inst. for Continuing Profl. Edn. Lawyers, 2000-02; adv. bd. Md. Mediation and Conflict Resolution Ctr., 2001-02; equal justice coun. Legal Aid Bur., 2000—. Note and comment editor Washington and Lee Law Rev. 1976-77, Washington and Lee Law Council 1983-87, pres. 1991-92. Mem. Fed. Ct. Bicentennial Com., 1988-90; vol. Profl. Gov.'s Drug-Free Workplace Initiative, 1990-93; bd. trustees Washington and Lee U., 1995—. Named Disting. Alumna, Washington and Lee U., 1994, Hon. mem. Order of the Coif, 1994, Disting. Alumna, Mary Washington Coll., 2001. Fellow

Am. Bar Found., Md. Bar Found. (award for excellence 1996, bd. dirs. 2000-02); mem. ABA (chair-elect tort and ins. practice employer/employee rels. com. 1998-99, chair 1999-2000, del. 2000-2002), Am. Arbitration Assn. (arbitrator, mediator employment and comml. panels), Balt. Bar Found. (bd. dirs. 2003—), Fed. Bar Assn., N.Y. State Bar Assn., Md. Bar Assn. (coun. legal edn. sect. 1987-96, chmn. 1992-93, labor sect. coun. 1992-96, professionalism com. 1991—, chmn. 1994-97, bd. govs. 1993-95, 1998-2003, exec. com. 1994-95, 99-2001, pres.-elect 2000-2001, pres. 2001-02, past pres. 2002-2003, task force on professionalism chair 1996-97), D.C. Bar Assn., Balt. City Bar Assn. (exec. coun. 1995-96, 1997-98), Women's Bar Assn. Md. (treas. 1986-87, v.p. 1987-88, pres.-elect 1988-89, pres. 1989-90, bd. dirs. 1984-86, Rita C. Davidson award 2000), Md. Assn. Def. Counsel, Pro Bono Resource Ctr. (exec. com. 2000-02, bd. dirs. 2002—, Leaders of Equal Justice award 2002), Phi Beta Kappa (hon.). Presbyterian. Avocation: baseball. Federal civil litigation, Labor (including EEOC, Fair Labor Standards Act, labor-management relations, NLRB, OSHA), State civil litigation. Office: Ober Kaler Grimes & Shriver 120 E Baltimore St Ste 800 Baltimore MD 21202-1643

WHITE, PATRICIA DENISE, dean, law educator; b. Syracuse, N.Y., July 8, 1949; d. Theodore C. and Kathleen (Cowles) Denise; m. Nicholas P. White, Feb. 20, 1971 (div. 1997); children: Olivia Lawrence, Alexander Cowles. BA, U. Mich., 1971, MA, JD, 1974. Bar: D.C. 1975, Mich. 1988, Utah 1995. Assoc. Steptoe & Johnson, Washington, 1975-76; vis. asst. prof. Coll. of Law U. Toledo, 1976-77; assoc. Caplin & Drysdale, Washington, 1977-79; asst. prof. Law Ctr. Georgetown U., 1979-84, assoc. prof. Law Ctr., 1985-88; vis. prof. Law Sch. U. Mich., Ann Arbor, 1988-94; prof. U. Utah, Salt Lake City, 1994-98; counsel Parson, Behle and Latimer, Salt Lake City, 1995-98; dean, prof. Ariz. State U. Coll. Law, 1999—. Counsel Bodman, Longley and Dahling, Detroit, Ann Arbor, 1990-95. Contbr. articles to profl. jours. Office: Ariz State U Coll Law McAllister & Orange Sts PO Box 877906 Tempe AZ 85287-7906

WHITE, ROBERT ELLSWORTH, lawyer; b. Ottawa, Ill., Feb. 18, 1933; s. Lawrence James and Lura Mae (Ellsworth) White; m. Elinore Eileen Corrigan, Sept. 16, 1961; children: Leslie Marie, Michael Robert, Kathleen Marie, Brendan Michael. BS, U. Notre Dame, 1955, JD, 1961. Bar: Ill. 1961. Pvt. practice, Ottawa, Ill., 1961—65; ptnr. White & Marsh, Ottawa, Ill., 1965—. Served to capt. USAF, 1955—59. Mem.: LaSalle County Bar Assn., Ill. Bar Assn., KC, Elks. Roman Catholic. Banking, State civil litigation, Probate (including wills, trusts). Office: White Marsh Anderson Vickers and Doebler 511 Atna Rd Ottawa IL 61350

WHITE, ROBERT JOEL, lawyer; b. Chgo., Nov. 1, 1946; s. Melvin and Margaret (Hoffman) W.; m. Gail Janet Edenson, June 29, 1969 (div. Dec. 1982); m. Penelope K. Bloch, Dec. 22, 1985. BS in Accountancy, U. Ill., 1968; JD, U. Mich., 1972. Bar: Calif. 1972, N.Y. 1985, U.S. Dist. Ct. (cen., ea., so. dists.) Calif. 1972, U.S. Ct. Appeals (9th cir.) 1978, U.S. Ct. Appeals (5th cir.) 1983, U.S. Ct. Appeals (6th cir.) 1984, U.S. Supreme Ct. 1977. Staff auditor Haskin & Sells, Chgo., 1968-69; assoc. O'Melveny & Myers, L.A., 1972-79, ptnr., 1980-2001, chair reorgn. and restructuring dept., 1986—; CEO O'Melvey Cons. LLC, 2001—. Vis. lectr. U. Mich. Law Sch., Ann Arbor, 1986; lectr. Profl. Edn. Sys., Inc., Dallas, 1987, L.A., 1987, 89, Phoenix, 1990, Practicing Law Inst., San Francisco and N.Y.C., 1989-93, 2001-, Southwestern Legal Found., Dalalas, 1991, UCLA Bankruptcy Inst., 1993, UCLA, 1993; mem. L.A. Productivity Commn., 1993-96. Contbr. articles to profl. jours. Active Constl. Rights Found., 1980—; active Am. Cancer Soc., 1989—, mem. L.A. bd. dirs., 1995—; mem. Nat. Bankruptcy Conf., exec. com., 1999-2002. Fellow Am. Coll. Brankruptcy; mem. ABA (litigation sect., mem. comml. law and bankruptcy com. 1972—), L.A. County Bar Assn. (comml. law and bankruptcy sect., chmn. fed. cts. com. 1981-82, exec. com. 1982—), Assn. Bus. Trial Lawyers (bd. govs. 1983-85), Fin. Lawyers Conf. (bd. govs. 1986—, pres. 1990-91), Am. Bankruptcy Inst. Avocations: skiing, running, U.S. history. Bankruptcy, General civil litigation. Office: O'Melveny & Myers 1999 Ave of Stars Los Angeles CA 90067-6035

WHITE, RONNIE L. state supreme court justice; AA, St. Louis C.C., 1977; BA, St. Louis U., 1979; JD, U. Mo., Kansas City, 1983. Bar: Mo. Law intern Jackson County Prosecutors Office; legal asst. U.S. Def. Mapping Agy.; trial atty. Office of Pub. Defender; mem. Mo. Ho. of Reps., 1989-93; judge Mo. Ct. Appeals, 1994; spl. judge Mo. Supreme Ct., 1994-95, justice, 1994-95, assoc. justice, 1995—. Adj. faculty Washington U. Sch. Law, 1997—. Office: PO Box 150 Jefferson City MO 65102-0150

WHITE, THOMAS EDWARD, lawyer; b. N.Y.C., July 11, 1933; s. Thomas Aubrey and Gladys Mary (Piper) W.; m. Joan Carolyn Olsen, Dec. 2, 1967 (dec.); children: Charles Garret, Nancy Carolyn, Linda Marie, Penelope Lindsay, Elizabeth Ann. AB, Princeton U., 1955; LLB, Columbia U., 1960; BA summa cum laude, SUNY-Purchase Coll., 2002; student, NYU Inst. Fine Arts, 2002—. Bar: N.Y. 1961. Atty. Seward & Kissel, N.Y.C., 1960-69; gen. counsel Howmet Corp., N.Y.C., 1969-70; v.p., gen. counsel, sec. Howmedica, Inc., N.Y.C., 1970-74, sr. v.p., dir., 1974-83; pvt. practice N.Y.C., 1983-97. Ptnr. Westmed Venture Ptnrs. (formerly Integrated Med. Venture Ptnrs.), N.Y.C., 1987-99; chmn. Shoreside Cons. Ltd., Miami, Fla., 1987-98. Mem. Mamaroneck Town Coun., 1971-75; mem. vestry Episcopalian Ch., 1987-90; mem. diocesan coun. Episcopal Ch. N.Y., 2001--. Served to 1st lt. U.S. Army, 1955-57. Mem.: Larchmont (N.Y.) Yacht; Princeton (N.Y.C.). Republican. Home: 260 Barnard Rd Larchmont NY 10538-1941

WHITE, WALTER HIAWATHA, JR., lawyer; b. Milw., Aug. 21, 1954; s. Walter H. and Winifred (Parker) W.; m. Sonja Athene Rein, Dec. 30, 1977. Student, Leningrad Pedagogical Inst., USSR, 1976; BA, Amherst Coll., 1977; JD, U. Calif., Berkeley, 1980. Bar: Wis. 1980, U.S. Dist. Ct. (ea. dist.) Wis. 1980, U.S. Ct. Appeals (7th cir.) 1980, U.S. Supreme Ct. 1983. Assoc. Michael, Best & Friedrich, Milw., 1980-88; commr. securities State of Wis., 1988-91; ptnr. Quarles & Brady, Milw., 1991-94; mng. dir. Steptoe & Johnson Internat., Moscow, 1994-99; ptnr. Bryan Cave, London, 1999—2001, White Savelivea LLP, London, 2001—. Trustee Milw. Found., 1992-94; vice chmn. dist. com. Bd. Attys. Profl. Responsibility, Milw., 1984-87; bd. dirs. Wis. Trust Found., Madison, Church Mut. Ins. Co., Merrill, Wis., Ctrl. Asian Am. Enterprise Fund. Editor Black Law Jour., 1978-80; mem. editorial bd. Barrister Mag.; contbr. articles to profl. jours. Mem. Cardinal Stritch Coll. Bus. Adv. Bd., Milw., 1982-85, health law com. Wis. Civil Liberties Union, Milw., 1985-88, Gov.'s Adv. Bd. to Legal Services Corp., Madison, 1982-87; sec. Milw. Forum Inc., 1982-88; pres. Milw. Urban League, 1985; bd. dirs. WUWM Pub. Radio Sta., Milw., 1983-86, Family Service Milw., Inc., 1987-89, Neighborhood House of Milw., Inc., 1987-94. John Woodruff Simpson fellow, 1977; Named one of the 86 most interesting people in Milw., Milw. Mag., 1986. Mem. ABA (chair young lawyers div. 1989-90, commn. on opportunities for minorities in the profession, del. assn. Soviet lawyers, co-chair commonwealth of ind. states law com. of internat. law and practice sect. 1990-91, bd. govs. 2002—), Nat. Bar Assn., Assn. Internat. des Jeunes Avocats, Milw. Bar Assn., Wis. Black Lawyers Assn. (bd. dirs. 1982-83), Milw. Young Lawyers Assn. (pres. 1984-85, pres.'s award 1985), Bd. Bar Examiners, Milw. Found. Avocations: Russian lit., rowing, squash. Corporate, general, Health, Private international. Office: White Savelivea LLP 53 Davies St London W1K 5JH England

WHITE, WILLIAM NELSON, lawyer; b. Balt., Sept. 8, 1938; s. Nelson Cardwell and Ellen Atwell (Zoller) W.; m. Mary Kathleen Bitzel, Sept. 2, 1960 (div. 1971); children: Craig William, Jeffrey Alan, Colin Christopher; m. Christine Lewin Hanna, July 8, 1978. LLB, U. Md., 1968, JD, 1969. Bar: Md. 1972, U.S. Ct. Appeals (4th cir.) 1975, U.S. Dist. Ct. Md. 1976, U.S. Supreme Ct. 1976. Asst. state's atty., Balt., 1972; assoc. Brooks & Turnbull, Balt., 1973-76; pvt. practice Balt., 1977—. Counsel St. Andrews Soc. Balt., 1989—; counsel, bd. dirs. St. George's Soc. Former elder, pres. deacons, trustee Roland Park Presbyn. Ch.; former mem. worship, music and sacrament coun., former elder Second Presbyn. Ch. Mem. Md. Bar Assn., Baltimore County Bar Assn., U. Md. Alumni Assn. for Greater Balt. (pres. 1977), SAR (chancellor for Md. Soc.). Avocations: history, philosophy, classical music, tennis, sailing. General practice, Insurance, Personal injury (including property damage).

WHITEHEAD, JAMES FRED, III, lawyer; b. Atlanta, July 3, 1946; s. James Fred Jr. and Jessie Mae (Turner) W.; m. Joanne Christina Mayo, June 21, 1969 (div. Feb. 1992); children: Matthew Nicholas, Rebecca Catherine; m. Nancy Karean Hatley, May 28, 1992; stepchildren: Brandon, Madison. AB with distinction, Stanford U., 1968; JD, U. Mich., 1975. Bar: Wash. 1975, U.S. Dist. Ct. (we. dist.) Wash. 1975, U.S. Ct. Appeals (9th cir.) 1975, U.S. Supreme Ct. 1976, U.S. Dist. Ct. (ea. dist.) Wash. 1994, Alaska 1995, U.S. Dist. Ct. Alaska 1995. Assoc. LeGros, Buchanan, Paul & Madden, Seattle, 1975-79; dir., officer LeGros, Buchanan, Paul & Whitehead, Seattle, 1979-92; ptnr. McGee, Reno & Whitehead, Seattle, 1993; of counsel Holmes Weddle & Barcott, Seattle, 1993-97, shareholder, 1997—. Organizer, lectr. Pacific Northwest Admiralty Law Inst., Seattle, 1981—; chmn. Internat. Maritime Law Conf., Seattle, 1996. Assoc. editor Am. Maritime Cases, 1991—; contbr. articles to profl. jours. Mem. ABA, Maritime Law Assn. of U.S. (bd. dirs. 2000-2003). Avocations: tennis, golf, boating, birding. Admiralty, Construction, Personal injury (including property damage). Office: Holmes Weddle & Barcott Wells Fargo Center Ste 2600 Seattle WA 98104 E-mail: jwhitehe@sea.hwb-law.com.

WHITEHEAD, JOHN WAYNE, law educator, organization administrator, author; b. Pulaski, Tenn., July 14, 1946; s. John M. and Alatha (Wiser) W.; m. Virginia Carolyn Nichols, Aug. 26, 1967; children: Jayson Reau, Jonathan Mathew, Elisabeth Anne, Joel Christofer, Joshua Benjamen. BA, U. Ark., 1969, JD, 1974. Bar: Ark. 1974, U.S. Dist. Ct. (ea. and we. dists.) Ark. 1974, U.S. Supreme Ct. 1977, U.S. Ct. Appeals (9th cir.) 1980, Va. 1981, U.S. Ct. Appeals (7th cir.) 1981, U.S. Ct Appeals (4th and 5th cirs.). Spl. counsel Christian Legal Soc., Oak Park, Ill., 1977-78; assoc. Gibbs & Craze, Cleve., 1978-79; sole practice law Manassas, Va., 1979-82; pres. The Rutherford Inst., Charlottesville, Va., 1982—, also bd. dirs. Frequent lectr. colls., law schs.; past adj. prof. O.W. Coburn Sch. Law. Author: Schools on Fire, 1980, The New Tyranny, 1982, The Second American Revolution, 1982, The Stealing of America, 1983, The Freedom of Religious Expression in Public High Schools, 1983, The End of Man, 1986, An American Dream, 1987, The Rights of Religious Persons in Public Education, 1991, Home Education: Rights and Reasons, 1993, Religious Apartheid, 1994, Slaying Dragons, 1999, Grasping For the Wind, 2001, others; writer, dir.: (video series) Grasping for the Wind (Silver World medal N.Y. Film Festival), 1998-99; contbr. articles to profl. jours., chpts. to books. 1st lt. U.S. Army, 1969-71. Named Christian Leader of Yr. Christian World Affairs Conf., Washington, 1986; recipient Bus. and Profl. award Religious Heritage Am., 1990, Hungarian Freedom medal, Budapest, 1991. Mem. ABA, Ark. Bar Assn., Va. Bar Assn. Office: The Rutherford Inst PO Box 7482 Charlottesville VA 22906-7482

WHITEHEAD, PAUL, lawyer, labor union administrator; b. 1951; BA, U. Wis.; JD, Harvard U. Asst. gen. counsel United Steelworkers Am., Pitts., 2001—. Office: United Steelworkers Am 5 Gateway Center Pittsburgh PA 15222 Office Fax: 412-562-2484.*

WHITEHOUSE, SHELDON, lawyer, former state attorney general; b. N.Y.C., Oct. 20, 1955; s. Charles Sheldon and Mary (Rand) Whitehouse; m. Sandra Christine Thornton, Sept. 20, 1986; 2 children. BA, Yale U., 1978; JD, U. Va., 1982. Bar: W.Va. 1982, R.I. 1983, U.S. Dist. Ct. R.I. 1984, U.S. Supreme Ct. 1986, U.S. Ct. Appeals (1st cir.) 1984. Atty., Providence, 1983—84; spl. asst. atty. gen., 1985—90; chief regulatory unit, 1988—90; asst. atty. gen., 1989—90; exec. counsel Office of Gov., 1991, dir. gov. policy office, 1991—92; dir. Dept. Bus. Regulation, 1992—94; U.S. atty for dist. of R.I., 1994—98; atty. gen. State of R.I., 1999—2003. Democrat.

WHITEHURST, WILLIAM OSCAR, lawyer; b. Ardmore, Okla., Oct. 23, 1945; s. William Oscar and Freddie Elizabeth (Ormsby) W.; m. Stephanie Anne Evans, June 22, 1968; children: Emilee Dawn, Rebecca Danielle. BS in Pharmacy, U. Okla., 1968; JD, U. Tex., 1970. Bar: Tex. 1971, U.S. Dist. Ct. (we. dist.) Tex. 1971, U.S. Ct. Mil. Appeals 1971, U.S. Ct. Appeals (5th cir.) 1971, U.S. Supreme Ct. 1971. Assoc. Fulbright & Jaworski, Houston, 1971; counsel, staff dir. jud. affairs com. Tex. Ho. Reps., Austin, 1975; sr. shareholder Whitehurst, Harkness, Ozmun & Brees, P.C., Austin, 1975—. Mem. Senate-House Select Com. on the Judiciary, 1983-84, subcom. on Svc. Delivery, subcom. on Jurisdiction; faculty law U. Tex., 1979-86, 88, Tex. Coll. Trial Adv., 1984—. Served to capt. JAGC, USAF, 1971-75. Fellow Am. Bar Found., Tex. Bar Found. (chmn. bd. trustees 1992-93), Internat. Acad. Trial Lawyers (sec. internat. rels. 2002-03); mem. ABA, Nat. Conf. Bar Pres. (exec. coun. 1992-95), Tex. Bar Assn. (pres. 1986-87, exec. com. 1981-84, 85-88, bd. dirs. 1981-84, active various coms.), Travis County Bar Assn. (sec. 1980-81, bd. dirs. 1979-81), Am. Bd. Trial Advs., Tex. Young Lawyers Assn. (pres. 1982-83, bd. dirs. 1979-84), Austin Young Lawyers Assn. (pres. 1978-79), Tex. Trial Lawyers Assn. (pres. 1995), Am. Soc. Pharmacy Law, Am. Soc. Law and Medicine, Order of Barristers, Univ. Club, Austin Country Club. Democrat. Presbyterian. Avocations: flying, snow skiing, water skiing, travel. Personal injury (including property damage), Product liability, Professional liability. Home: 2703 Westlake Dr Austin TX 78746-1909 Office: Whitehurst Harkness et al 1122 Colorado St Austin TX 78701-2100

WHITEMAN, JOSEPH DAVID, retired lawyer, manufacturing company executive; b. Sioux Falls, S.D., Sept. 12, 1933; s. Samuel D. and Margaret (Wallace) W.; m. Mary Kelly, Dec. 29, 1962; children: Anne Margaret, Mary Ellen, Joseph David, Sarah Kelly, Jane. BA, U. Mich., 1955, JD, 1960. Bar: D.C. 1960, Ohio 1976. Assoc. Cox, Langford, Stoddard & Cutler, Washington, 1959-64; sec., gen. counsel Studebaker group Studebaker Worthington, Inc., N.Y.C., 1964-71; asst. gen. counsel. United Telecommunications, Inc., Kansas City, Mo., 1971-74; v.p., gen. counsel, sec. Weatherhead Co., Cleve., 1974-77, Parker Hannifin Corp., Cleve., 1977-98; ret., 1998. Immediate past chmn. bd. dirs. St. Lukes Med. Ctr. Served as lt. USNR, 1955-57. Mem. ABA, Beta Theta Pi, Phi Delta Phi. Republican. Roman Catholic. Home and Office: 2508 Robinson Springs Rd Stowe VT 05672

WHITESIDE, WILLIAM ANTHONY, JR., retired lawyer; b. Phila., Feb. 23, 1929; s. William Anthony and Ellen T. (Hensler) W.; m. Eileen Ann Ferrick, Feb. 27, 1954; children: William Anthony III, Michael P., Eileen A., Richard F., Christopher J., Mary P. BS, Notre Dame U., 1951; LLB, U. Pa., 1954. Bar: Pa. 1955. Assoc. Speiser, Satinsky, Gilliland & Packel, Phila., 1956-58, ptnr., 1958-61, Fox, Rothschild, O'Brien & Frankel, Phila., 1961—2001; ret., 2001. Chmn. Police Athletic League, Phila.; trustee Am. Coll. Mgmt. and Tech., Dubrovnik, Croatia; chmn. emeritus bd. trustees, emeritus trustee, Rochester Inst. of Tech.; trustee C.C. Phila. Found. trustee LaSalle Coll. HS, PA; trustee Cmty. Coll. of Phila. Found., pres. adv. coun. U. Notre Dame; emeritus trustee Germantown Acad., past pres. 1st lt. USAF, 1954-56. Named Man of Yr., Notre Dame Club Phila., 1967. Mem.: ABA, Pa. Soc., Phila. Bar Assn., Pa. Bar Assn., Wissahickon Skating Club, Union League Club Phila. Republican. Roman Catholic. Private international, Labor (including EEOC, Fair Labor Standards Act, labor-management relations, NLRB, OSHA), Pension, profit-sharing, and employee benefits. Home: 7808 Cobden Rd Glenside PA 19038-7256 also: 901 Gardens Plz Ocean City NJ 08226-4719 Office: Fox Rothschild O'Brien & Frankel 2000 Market St Ste 10 Philadelphia PA 19103-3231

WHITING, RICHARD ALBERT, lawyer; b. Cambridge, Mass., Dec. 2, 1922; s. Albert S. and Jessie (Coleman) W.; m. Marvelene Nash, Feb. 22, 1948 (div. 1984); children— Richard A. Jr., Stephen C., Jeffrey D., Gary S., Kimberly G.; m. Joanne Sherry, Oct. 14, 1984 AB, Dartmouth Coll., 1944; JD, Yale U., 1949. Bar: D.C. 1949. Assoc. Steptoe & Johnson, Washington, 1949-55, ptnr., 1956-86, of counsel, 1987—. Adj. prof. Vt. Law Sch., South Royalton, 1985-90; mem. exec. com. Yale Law Sch. Assn., New Haven, 1985-88; mem. adv. bd. The Antitrust Bull., N.Y.C., 1975-99. Contbr. articles to profl. jours. Trustee Colby-Sawyer Coll., 1987-97. 1st lt. U.S. Army, 1945-46. Mem. ABA (council mem. Antitrust Law sect. 1977-85, del. to Ho. Dels. 1982-83, chmn. 1984-85) Presbyterian. Home: PO Box 749 Grantham NH 03753-0749 Office: 1330 Connecticut Ave NW Washington DC 20036-1704 E-mail: whiting@srnet.com.

WHITING, STEPHEN CLYDE, lawyer; b. Arlington, Va., Mar. 20, 1952; s. Richard A. Whiting; m. Patrice Quinn, May 24, 1980; children: Kelsey, Daniel, Seth, Samuel. BA magna cum laude, Dartmouth Coll., 1974; JD, U. Va., 1978. Bar: Maine 1978, U.S. Dist. Ct. Maine 1978, U.S. Ct. Appeals (1st cir.) 1999. Ptnr. Douglas, Whiting, Denham & Rogers, Portland, Maine, 1978-98; founder The Whiting Law Firm, P.A., Portland, 1998—. Maine state dir. Am. Ctr. Law and Justice, 1998—. Co-author: Trying the Automobile Injury Case in Maine, 1993, Premises Liability: Preparation and Trial of a Difficult Case in Maine, 1994, Trying Soft Tissue Injury Cases in Maine, 1995, How to Litigate Your First Civil Trial in Maine, 2001. Mem. ATLA, Maine Bar Assn., Maine Trial Lawyers Assn., Phi Beta Kappa. General civil litigation, Insurance, Personal injury (including property damage). Office: The Whiting Law Firm PA 75 Pearl St Ste 207 Portland ME 04101 E-mail: mail@whitinglawfirm.com.

WHITLEY, JOE DALLY, lawyer; b. Atlanta, Nov. 12, 1950; s. Thomas Youngie and Mary Jo (Dally) W.; m. Kathleen Pinion, Sept. 27, 1975; children: Lauren Jacqueline, Thomas McMillan. BA, U. Ga., 1972, JD, 1975. Bar: Ga. 1975, U.S. Supreme Ct. 1989. Assoc. Kelly, Denney, Pease & Allison, Columbus, Ga., 1975-78; asst. dist. atty. Chattahoochee Jud. Cir., Columbus, 1978-79; assoc. Hirsch, Beil & Partin, P.C., Columbus, 1979-81; U.S. atty. Dept. Justice, Macon, Ga., 1981-87, dep. asst. atty. gen., Criminal Div. Washington, 1987-88, dep. assoc. atty. gen., 1988-89, acting assoc. atty. gen., 1989; ptnr. Smith, Gambrell & Russell, Atlanta, 1989-90; U.S. atty. Dept. of Justice, Atlanta, 1990-93; ptnr. Kilpatrick Stockton, Atlanta, 1993-97, Alston & Bird, Atlanta, 1997—. Mem. atty. gen.'s adv. com. Dept. Justice, Washington, 1982-85; chmn. organized crime and violent crime subcom. Atty. Gen.'s Adv. Com., 1990-93, mem. investigative subcom., chmn. white collar crime subcom., 1993-99. Treas. Muscogee County Young Reps., Columbus, 1979-80. Mem. Ga. Bar Assn., Macon Bar Assn., Young Lawyers Club (pres. Columbus chpt. 1980-81), Lawyers Club of Atlanta. Republican. Presbyterian. Criminal. Office: Alston & Bird 1201 W Peachtree St NW Atlanta GA 30309-3424 E-mail: jwhitley@alston.com.

WHITLOCK, JULIE MARIE, lawyer; b. Omaha, May 28, 1968; d. Larry F. and Barbara E. Schucht; m. Kevin M. Whitlock, June 25, 1994. BA in Fgn. Affairs, U. Va., 1990; JD, U. Richmond, 1994. Bar: Va. 1994, U.S. Dist. Ct. (ea. dist.) Va. 1994, U.S. Ct. Appeals (4th cir.) 1995. Ptnr. Thorsen Marchant & Scher LLP, Richmond, Va., 1996-98; assoc. Thompson & McMullan, PC, Richmond, 1998-2000; systems analyst, atty. Va. Dept. Motor Vehicles, Richmond, 2000—. Mem.: Richmond Bar Assn., Metro Richmond Women's Bar Assn. Computer, Government contracts and claims, Intellectual property. Office: Tech Procurement PO Box 27412 Richmond VA 23269 E-mail: dmvjxw@dmv.state.va.us.

WHITMAN, CHARLES S., III, lawyer; b. N.Y.C., Apr. 19, 1942; s. Charles S. Jr. and Janet (Russell) W; m. Christina L. Madden, Oct. 20, 1979; 1 child, Elizabeth R. AB, Harvard U., 1964, LLB, 1967; LLM, Cambridge U., 1989. BAr: N.Y. 1967, U.S. Supreme Ct. 1972. Asst. to chmn. U.S. SEC, Washington, 1971-74; gen. counsel Mitchell Hutchins Inc., N.Y.C., 1974; assoc. Davis Polk & Wardwell, N.Y.C., 1968-71, 74-76, ptnr., 1977—. Bd. dirs. British Schs. and Univs. Found., Inc., 2000—. Mem. Am. Law Inst. Republican. Presbyterian. Corporate, general, Securities. Office: Davis Polk & Wardwell 450 Lexington Ave Fl 18 New York NY 10017-3982

WHITMAN, MARA ARDEN, publishing executive; b. N.Y.C., Oct. 7, 1964; d. Robert and Edith Helen (Cybul) Whitman; m. Marc Stefan Edrich; children: Franklin Graham Whitman Edrich, Samantha Allison Whitman Edrich, Douglas Griffin Whitman Edrich, Mallory Sloan Whitman Edrich. BS in Bus., Skidmore Coll., 1986; MSLS, Simmons Coll., 1988; JD, U. Conn., 1992. Asst. librarian Warner & Stackpole, Boston, 1986—87; med. reference librarian Countway Library of Medicine Harvard U., 1987—88; law librarian New Eng. Sch. Law Library, 1987—88, Day, Berry & Howard, Hartford, Conn., 1988; asst. librarian U. Conn. Law Sch., 1988; law librarian Conn. Atty. Gen.'s Office, 1988—91; summer assoc. law clk. Lublin, Wolfe, Kantor & Silver, East Hartford, 1989; law libr. Tyler, Cooper & Alcorn, Hartford, 1992—97. Dir. The Grad. Group, 1987—. Sustainer Jr. League, Hartford. Grassroots grantee Jr. Mem. Roundtable Baker & Taylor, 1988: Starr fellow, 1989; Am. Assn. Law Librs. Mead Data Cen. scholar, 1989. Mem. ALA, Am. Assn. Law Librs., Spl. Libr. Assn., Student Bar Assn. (rep.), Jewish Law Students Assn. (pres.), Student Libr. Assn., New Eng. Libr. Assn., So. New Eng. Law Libr.'s Assn., Mass. Libr. Assn., Assn. Boston Law Librs., Hartford Assn. Law Librs., Skidmore Coll. Alumni Assn., Delta Delta Delta. Democrat. Avocations: travel, skiing, fishing, swimming, reading. Home: 86 Norwood Rd West Hartford CT 06117-2236

WHITMER, FREDERICK LEE, lawyer; b. Terre Haute, Ind., Nov. 5, 1947; s. Lee Arthur and Ella (Diekhoff) W.; m. Valeri Cade; children: Caitlin Margaret, Meghan Connors, Christian Frederick. BA, Wabash Coll., 1969; JD, Columbia U., 1973. Bar: N.Y. 1975, U.S. Dist. Ct. (so. dist.) N.Y. 1975, N.J. 1976, U.S. Dist. Ct. N.J. 1976, U.S. Ct. Appeals (3d cir.) 1977, U.S. Ct. Appeals (fed. cir.) 1983, U.S. Ct. Appeals (2d cir.) 1987, U.S. Supreme Ct. 1988, U.S. Ct. Appeals (7th cir.) 1994. Assoc. Kaye, Scholer, Fierman, Hays & Handler, N.Y.C., 1973-76, Pitney, Hardin & Kipp, Morristown, N.J., 1976-78; ptnr. Pitney, Hardin, Kipp & Szuch LLP, Morristown, 1979—. Mem. ABA, N.J. Bar Assn., Phi Beta Kappa. Republican. Episcopalian. Antitrust, Federal civil litigation, Trademark and copyright. Home: 190 Hurlbutt St Wilton CT 06897-2706 Office: Pitney Hardin Kipp & Szuch PO Box 1945 Morristown NJ 07962-1945 E-mail: fwhitmer@pitneyhardin.com.

WHITMER, JERRY F. lawyer; b. Fulton County, Ohio, Sept. 19, 1935; s. Frank Carlson and Bessie Merle (Saul) Whitmer; m. Kathleen Whitmer, Aug. 5, 1961. BA, Kent State U., 1957; JD, Case We. Res. U., 1960. Bar: Ohio 1960. Assoc. Johnston, Whitmer and Sayre, Akron, Ohio, 1960—68; ptnr. Roetzel, Hunsicker and Michaels, Akron, 1968—71; mng. ptnr. Brouse McDowell, Akron, 1971—. Airman USAF, 1957—59. Fellow: Akron Bar Assn. Found., Ohio State Bar Assn. Found.; mem.: ABA, Am. Inns of Ct., Akron Bar Assn. (bd. trustees 1994—97, pres. 1990—91, bd. trustees 1986—92, Sr. Lawyers award for Outstanding Svc. to Legal Profession and Cmty. 2000, Presdl. award of Spl. Merit 2000), Ohio State Bar Assn. (bd. govs. 1994—97, Coun. of Dels. 1994—97, alt. rep. to ABA Coun. of Dels. 1998—2000). Republican. Roman Catholic. Avocations: golf, woodworking, gardening, fishing. Bankruptcy, Criminal, Mergers and acquisitions. Home: 444 Burning Tree Dr Akron OH 44303 Office: Brouse McDowell 106 S Main St Akron OH 44308

WHITNEY, FRANK D. prosecutor; b. N.C., Nov. 22, 1959; s. A. Grant and Lillian (DeArmon) Whitney; m. Catherine Whitney; children: Anne Stone, Francis Hunter. BA, Wake Forest U., 1982; MBA, JD, U. N.C., 1987. Bar: N.C. 1987, D.C. 1988. Asst. U.S. atty. U.S. Dept. Justice, Ea. Dist. N.C., Raleigh, 1990—2001; counsel Kilpatrick Stockton LLP, Charlotte,

2001—02; assoc. McKenna Conner Cuneo, Washington, 1987—90; law clk. to Hon. David B. Sentelle U.S. Ct. Appeals (D.C. cir.), 1988—89. Presbyterian. Office: Ea Dist NC Fed Bldg 310 New Burn Ave Ste 800 Raleigh NC 27601-1461 Office Fax: 919-856-4487.

WHITNEY, RICHARD BUCKNER, lawyer; b. Corpus Christi, Tex., Mar. 1, 1948; s. Franklyn Loren and Betty Wolcott (Fish) Whitney; m. Chantal Marie Gindt, Aug. 18, 1972; children: Jennifer L, James R, Katherine E. BA in Polit. Sci., Union Coll., 1970; JD, Case Western Res. U., 1973. Bar: Ohio 1973, N.Y. 1998, US Ct Appeals (6th cir) 1974, US Ct Appeals (3d cir) 1987, US Dist Ct (so dist) NY 2000. From assoc. to ptnr. Jones Day, Reavis & Pogue, Cleve., 1973—. Trustee Hospice of the We. Res., Fairmount Music Edn. Found. Mem.: Am Inns Cts, Legal Aid Soc Cleveland (trustee), Cleveland Bar Asn, Order of Coif. General civil litigation, Product liability, Appellate. Home: 2750 Southington Rd Shaker Heights OH 44120-1603 Office: Jones Day 901 Lakeside Ave Cleveland OH 44114-1190 E-mail: rbwhitney@jonesday.com.

WHITSON, LISH, lawyer; b. Washington, Oct. 13, 1942; s. I. Lish and Clytie B. (Collier) W.; m. Barbara Lee Sullivan, Sept. 16, 1965; children: L. Richard, Kimberly S. BA in Philosophy, Pa. State U., 1965; JD, U. Wash., 1972. Bar: Wash. 1973, Oreg. 2002, U.S. Dist. Ct. (we. dist.) 1973, U.S. Dist. Ct. (ea. dist.) 1977, U.S. Supreme Ct. 1977. Assoc. Seattle-King County Pub. Defender Assn., 1972-76, Helsell, Fetterman, Martin, Todd & Hokanson, Seattle, 1976-81, ptnr., 1981-98; of counsel Badgley Mullins, Seattle, 1998-2000, Lish Whitson PLLC, Seattle, 2000—. Bd. dirs., past chmn. Downtown Emergency Svc. Ctr., Seattle, 1981-97; bd. dirs. Allied Arts, 1988-96, pres., 1994-96; mem. Allied Arts Found., 1997—; trustee Seattle Youth Symphony Orch., bd. dirs., 1986-95; mem. alumni bd. U. Wash. Law Sch., 1993-2001, treas., 1997-99, pres., 1999-2001; bd. dirs. Little Bit Therapeutic Riding Ctr., 2002—. Fellow Am. Bar Found., Am. Coll. Trial Lawyers; mem. ABA (young lawyers divsn. rep. to exec. coun. 1979, mem. standing com. on lawyer referral svc. 1990-96, chmn. 1992-96, commn. on women in the profn. 1998-2001), ATLA, Am. Bd. Trial Advocates (assoc., mem. nat. bd. 2003—), Wash. State Bar Assn. (gov. 1995-98, spl. hearing officer 1999—, jud. rev. com. 2000—, chmn. 2003), King County Bar Found. (mem. pres. coun.), King County Bar Assn. (pro bono com. chmn. 1981-84, bd. dirs. 1988-91, young lawyers sect. 1977-79, chmn. 1979, Pro Bono Svc. award 1993, Atty. of Yr. 2000), Fed. Bar Assn., Am. Judicature Soc. (bd. dirs. 1981-86, sec. Wash. chpt. 2002—), Seattle Pub. Def. Assn. (bd. dirs. 1982-86), Seattle C. of C., Wash. Athletic Club. Alternative dispute resolution, Personal injury (including property damage), Product liability. Office: Lish Whitson Pllc Ste 3800 999 3d Ave Seattle WA 98104 E-mail: lwhitson@whitsonlaw.com.

WHITTAKER, JUDITH ANN CAMERON, lawyer; b. N.Y.C., June 12, 1938; d. Thomas Macdonald and Mindel (Wallman) Cameron; m. Kent E. Whittaker, Jan. 30, 1960; children: Charles Evans II, Catherine Cameron. BA, Brown U., 1959; JD, U. Mo., 1963. Bar: Mo. 1963, U.S. Dist. Ct. (we. dist.) Mo. 1963, U.S. Ct. Appeals (8th cir.) 1965, U.S. Supreme Ct. 1980, D.C. 1987. Assoc. and ptnr. Sheffrey, Ryder & Skeer, Kansas City, Mo., 1963-72; asst. and assoc. gen. coun., exec. v.p. gen. coun. Hallmark Cards, Inc., Kansas City, 1972—; dir., v.p., gen. coun. Univision Holdings, Inc., Kansas City, 1988-92; dir. MCI Comm. Corp., 1985-98, Harmon Industries, 1993—2000. Dir. Am. Arbitration Assn., 1996—. Trustee Brown U. Providence, 1977-83, U. Mo. Law Found., Kansas City, 1977-90; dir. Kansas City (Mo.) Indsl. Devel. Authority, 1981-84, Legal Aid Kansas City, 1971-77, De La Salle Sch., 1993—. Episcopalian. Avocations: reading, skiing, hiking, piano, golf. General civil litigation, Corporate, general, Mergers and acquisitions. Office: Hallmark Cards Dept 339 PO Box 419126 Kansas City MO 64141-6126

WHITTEN, BEATRICE EHRENBERG, lawyer; b. Charleston, S.C., Oct. 19, 1959; d. David Owen and Susan Rush (Hills) W.; m. C. Patrick Leopold, Dec. 30, 1989; children: Jesse Lawrence, Susan Cameron. AS in Criminal Justice, Trident Tech. Coll., Charleston, 1980; BS in Criminal Justice, Charleston So. U., 1987; JD, U. S.C., 1990. Bar: S.C. 1990; cert. civil mediator. Assoc. Thomas W. Greene, Charleston, S.C., 1990-91; assoc./ptnr. Lucey & Whitten, PA, Charleston, 1991-93; pvt. practice Mt. Pleasant, S.C., 1993—. Adj. faculty Trident Tech. Coll., Charleston, 1994—; instr. legal writing U. S.C., Columbia, 1988-90. Named Pro Bono Atty. of Yr., 2000. Mem. S.C. Bar Assn. (bar pro bono program 1990—). Avocations: canoeing, camping. Administrative and regulatory, Family and matrimonial, Probate (including wills, trusts). Office: 745 A Johnnie Dodds Blvd Mount Pleasant SC 29464-3021

WHITTENBERG, IRA ORVILLE, lawyer; b. Ft. Worth; s. Ira Orville and Thyra Finch Whittenberg; m. Emma Jo Noland, Apr. 14, 1962; children: Ira Grant, Cheryl Lynn, Wendy Ann. BS in Indsl. Engring., So. Meth. U., 1957, LLB, 1961, LLM, 1977. Bar: Tex. 73. Contract mgr., corp. counsel Bell Helicopter Textron, Ft. Worth, 1961—89; dir. contracts, corp. counsel Murdock Engring., Irving, Tex., 1989—91; pvt. practice cons., mediator Colleyville, Tex., 1991—. Capt. USAF, 1955—57. Fellow: Nat. Contract Mgmt. Assn. (pres. 1962—); mem.: State Bar Tex. (award 2002), Toastmasters Internat. (chpt. pres. 1982—). Republican. Presbyterian. Avocations: sailing, bicycling. Alternative dispute resolution, Commercial, contracts (including sales of goods; commercial financing), Government contracts and claims. Home and Office: 3607 Cliffwood Dr Colleyville TX 76034

WHITTERS, JAMES PAYTON, III, lawyer, university administrator; b. Boston, Oct. 23, 1939; s. James P. Jr. and Norene (Jones) W.; m. Elizabeth Robertson, July 19, 1969; children: James P. IV, Catharine A. BA in History, Trinity Coll., Hartford, Conn., 1962; JD, Boston Coll., 1969; MA in Am. Studies, U. Mass., Boston, 2002. Bar: Mass. 1969, U.S. Dist. Ct. Mass. 1970, U.S. Ct. Appeals (1st cir.) 1972. Assoc. Ely, Bartlett, Brown & Proctor, Boston, 1969-74, Gaston Snow & Ely Bartlett, Boston, 1974-79, ptnr., 1979-88, Gaston & Snow, Boston, 1988-91; of counsel Peabody & Brown, Boston, 1991-95; dir. Office Career Devel., Suffolk U. Law Sch., Boston, 1995—, adj. prof. Am. legal history, 1997—. Bd. dirs., sec. Robertson Factories, Inc., Taunton, Mass., 1979—; v.p. Alkalol Co., Taunton, 1976-97, sr. v.p., 1997—; vis. tchr. Groton (Mass.) Sch., 1993-94; mem. Mass. Conflict Intervention Mediation Team, 1995—. Bd. dirs. New Eng. com. NAACP Legal Def. Fund, 1982—, Beacon Hill Nursery Sch., 1976-78, Mass. Appleseed Ctr. Law and Justice, 1997—; chmn. Mass. Outdoor Advt. Bd., Boston, 1975-81; vice chmn. Mass. Jud. Nominating Coun., Boston, 1983-87; trustee Trinity Coll., 1984-95; trustee, sec. Hurricane Island Outward Bound Sch., 1977-87; bd. dirs. Mass. affiliate Am. Heart Assn., 1979-98, chmn., 1989-91; bd. dirs. Greater Boston Legal Svcs., 1982-84, 93-99, Mass. Assn. Mediation Programs and Practitioners, 1993-98; founder Beacon Hill Seminars, 2000-2001, bd. dirs., 2001-02. Lt. (j.g.) USN, 1962-65. Recipient Alumni Excellence award Trinity Coll., 1987. Mem.: ABA, Boston Bar Assn. (standing com. on work-life balance, children's outreach task force, pub. svc. and criminal justice task force), Mass. Bar Assn., The Country Club (Brookline, Mass.). Democrat. Unitarian Universalist. Avocations: reading history, mountain climbing & jogging. Home: 44 Mount Vernon St Boston MA 02108-1302

WHITTIER, MONTE RAY, lawyer; b. Pocatello, Idaho, June 28, 1955; s. Raymond Max and Marjorie Lucille (Pea) W.; m. Denise Womack, May 29, 1982; children: Jason Dennis, Sarah Michelle, Sadie Mckenzie. BS in Acctg., U. Utah, 1976; JD, U. Idaho, 1978. Bar: U.S. Dist. Ct. Idaho, 1979, U.S. Supreme Ct. 1985, U.S. Tax Ct. 1989, U.S. Ct. Appeals (9th cir.) 1991, Idaho, 1979. Ptnr., shareholder Whittier & Souza, Pocatello, 1979—89; shareholder, mng. atty. Whittier, Souza & Naftz, Pocatello, 1989—97; asst. gen. counsel Melaleuca, Inc., Idaho Falls, 1997—2002; ptnr. Law Offices of Harmon & Whittier (divsn. of Northwest Ins. Co.), Boise, Idaho, 2002—. Vol. Internat. Spl. Olympics, South Bend, Ind., 1987, Mpls., 1991; mem. Magistrate Commn. 6th Jud. Dist., Pocatello, 1989-91; bd. dirs. Bannock Baseball, Inc., 1996-97; v.p. Idaho Falls Am. Legion Baseball, 2000-02. Mem. ATLA, Idaho Trial Lawyers Assn. (bd. dirs. 6th Jud. Dist. Pro Bono award 1994), Civitan (pres. Bannock chpt. 1983-84, bd. dirs. 1981-87, 92-93, lt. gov. Intermountain chpt. 1986-87, Outstanding Pres. award 1984, Outstanding Svc. award 1982-83, 86-88, 91). Avocations: bicycling, skiing, golfing, Spl. Olympics vol. activities. General civil litigation, Corporate, general, Personal injury (including property damage). Office: Harmon & Whittier Ste 100 390 E Parkcenter Blvd PO Box 6358 Boise ID 83716-6358 Business E-Mail: monte.whittier@llawoffice.com.

WHITTINGTON, THOMAS LEE, lawyer; b. Waukesha, Wis., July 14, 1943; s. Floyd Leon and Winifred Carol (McDonald) W.; m. Ashley J. Whittington; children: Erin Elizabeth, Hilary Ann. BA, Coll. of Wooster, 1965; JD, U. Mich., 1967. Bar: Trust Terr. of Pacific Islands 1967, Mich. 1969, Wash. 1974, U.S. Dist. Ct. (we. dist.) Wash. 1974. Vol. Peace Corps, Micronesia, 1967-69; staff asst. legis. office Dept. Interior, Washington, 1969-74; ptnr. Thomas, Whittington, Anderson, Bergan & Studebaker, Issaquah, Wash., 1974—2000, Scottsdale, Ariz., 2000—. Commercial, contracts (including sales of goods; commercial financing), Family and matrimonial, Property, real (including real estate development, water). Home: 27684 N 72d Way Scottsdale AZ 85262

WHITWORTH, J. BRYAN, JR., former oil company executive, lawyer; b. Baton Rouge, Aug. 14, 1938; s. Jennings Bryan Sr. and Virginia Ann (Calvert) W.; m. Sue Alice Walters, July 15, 1961 (Jan. 1982); children: Catherine Ann, Elizabeth, Suzanne Virginia; m. Donna Axum, Mar. 1, 1984. BS Pre-Law, U. Ala., 1961, LLM, 1964. Assoc. Cabaniss, Johnston, Gardner & Clark, Birmingham, Ala., 1964-66; gen. AT&T, Washington and N.Y.C., 1966-71; atty. Phillips Petroleum Co., Bartlesville, Okla., 1971-77, sr. counsel, 1977-79, assoc. gen. counsel, 1979-81, v.p. govt. relations, 1981-95, sr. v.p., gen. counsel and govt. relations, 1995—2003. Bd. dirs. Salk Inst. Biotechnology/Industry Assn. Inc., San Diego; mem. policy devel com. Am. Petroleum Inst., Washington, 1982—, Gov.'s Task Force on Higher Edn. in Okla. and the Council for Reorgn. of State Govt., Oklahoma City, 1985-87; bd. dirs. First Nat. Bank & First Bancshares Inc., Bartlesville. Former editor-in-chief Ala. Law Rev., U. Ala. Mem. Okla. Bar Assn., N.Y. Bar Assn., D.C. Bar Assn., Bartlesville Area C. of C. (v.p., bd. dirs. 1985-87, pres. 1987-88). Lodges: Rotary. *

WHORISKEY, ROBERT DONALD, lawyer; b. Cambridge, Mass., May 9, 1929; s. John Joseph and Katherine Euphemia (MacDonald) W.; m. Martha Beebe Poutas, Apr. 16, 1966; children: Alexandra, Jonathan, Eliza. AB, Harvard U., 1952; JD, Boston Coll., 1958; LLM, NYU, 1960. Bar: Mass. 1958, N.Y. 1963, U.S. Tax Ct. 1961, U.S. Claims Ct. 1969, U.S. Dist. Ct. (so. dist.) N.Y. 1969, U.S. Ct. Customs 1971, U.S. Ct. Appeals (2d cir.) 1972, U.S. Ct. Appeals (3d cir.) 1983, U.S. Ct. Appeals (D.C. cir.) 1991, U.S. Supreme Ct. 1974. Sr. trial atty. Office Chief Counsel, IRS, N.Y.C., 1960-67; assoc. Curtis, Mallet-Prevost, Colt & Mosle, N.Y.C., 1967-70, ptnr., 1970-2000, of counsel, 2001—, exec. com., 1978-82, chmn. tax dept., 1982-87. Bd. dirs. InterNat. Tax Inst., v.p., lectr., 1980-84, chmn. bd., pres., lectr., 1985-87; lectr. Practicing Law Inst., World Trade Inst., Tax Execs. Inst., Am. Mgmt. Assn., Coun. for Internat. Tax Edn.; bd. dirs. Life Ins. Co. of Boston and N.Y., Inc. Author: Foreign Trusts, 1977, Annual Institute on International Taxation, 1966, 80, 81, (with Sidney Pine, Ralph Seligman) Tax and Business Benefits of the Bahamas, 1986; contbg. author: International Boycotts, CCH Federal Tax Service, 1988, CCH Smart Tax CD-ROM: Third Party Information, John Wiley and Sons, Inc.'s Transfer Pricing, 1993, Transfer Pricing Under IRC & 482: Overview and Planning, Part I, 1996, Accuracy Related Penalty Regulations for Transfer Pricing, Part II, 1997, Third Party Information, Part III, 1997, U.S. Taxation of International Operations, Warren, Gorham Lamont, 1998; mem. editl. adv. bd. Corp. Bus. Taxation Monthly, 2000—. Trustee, treas. Montessori Sch. Westchester, 1974-77; mem. bd. ethics Village of Larchmont, N.Y., 1988—. With U.S. Army, 1952-54. Mem. ABA (com. on alternative tax sys. tax sect. 1994—, com. on ct. procedure tax sec. 1997—), N.Y. State Bar Assn. (com. on practice and procedure tax sect. 1990—), Harvard Club, Larchmont Yacht Club. Democrat. Roman Catholic. Corporate taxation, Estate taxation, Taxation, general. Office: Curtis Mallet-Prevost Colt & Mosle 101 Park Ave 35th Fl New York NY 10178-0061 E-mail: rwhoriskey@cm-p.com.

WHYLAND, CHRISTOPHER MARK, lawyer; b. Syracuse, N.Y., Apr. 16, 1965; s. John F. and Marie (Zirilli) W.; m. Melissa Anne Vincent, Oct. 19, 1991. BA, SUNY, Albany, 1987; MBA, JD, Syracuse U., 1990. Bar: N.Y. 1991, Mas. 1991, U.S. Dist. Ct. (no. dist.) N.Y. 1990. Assoc. atty. Charles M. Connelly & Assocs., Syracuse, 1990-93; ptnr. Whyland & Richmond, Syracuse, 1993-99; sole practitioner Manlius, N.Y., 1999—. Mem. ABA, N.Y. State Bar Assn., Onondaga County Bar Assn., Ctrl. N.Y. Workers' Compensation Bar Assn. Roman Catholic. Product liability, Workers' compensation. Office: 4500 Brickyard Falls Rd Manlius NY 13104 E-mail: whyland@twcny.rr.com.

WHYTE, RONALD M. judge; b. 1942; BA in Math., Wesleyan U., 1964; JD, U. So. Calif., 1967. Bar: Calif. 1967, U.S. Dist. Ct. (no. dist.) Calif. 1967, U.S. Dist. Ct. (cen. dist.) Calif. 1968, U.S. Ct. Appeals (9th cir.) 1986. Assoc. Hoge, Fenton Jones & Appel, Inc., San Jose, Calif., 1971-77, mem., 1977-89; judge Superior Ct. State of Calif., 1989-92, U.S. Dist. Ct. (no. dist.) Calif., San Jose, 1992—. Judge pro-tempore Superior Ct. Calif., 1977-89; lectr. Calif. Continuing Edn. of Bar, Rutter Group, Santa Clara Bar Assn., State Bar Calif.; legal counsel Santa CLara County Bar Assn., 1986-89; mem. county select com. Criminal Conflicts Program, 1988. Bd. trustees Santa Clara County Bar Assn., 1978-79, 84-85. Lt. Judge Advocate Gen.'s Corps, USNR, 1968-71. Recipient Judge of Yr. award Santa Clara County Trial Lawyers Assn., 1992, Am. Jurisprudence award. Mem. Calif. Judges Assn., Assn. Bus. Trial Lawyers (bd. govs. 1991-93), Santa Clara Inn of Ct. (exec. com. 1993—), San Francisco Bay area Intellectual Property Inn of Ct. (exec. com. 1994—). Office: US Courthouse 280 S 1st St Rm 2112 San Jose CA 95113-3002

WIANT, SARAH KIRSTEN, law library administrator, educator; b. Waverly, Iowa, Nov. 20, 1946; d. James Allen and Eva (Jorgensen) W.; m. Robert E. Akins. BA, Western State Coll., 1968; MLS, U. North Tex., 1970; JD, Washington & Lee U., 1978. Asst. law libr. Tex. Tech. U., 1970-72, 020, Washington & Lee U., Lexington, Va., 1972—, dir., 1978—, asst. prof. law, 1978-83, assoc. prof. law, 1984-92, prof. law, 1993—. Participant Conf. on Fair Use, NII, 1995-98. Co-author: Copyright Handbook, 1984, Libraries and Copyright: A Guide to Copyright Law in the 1990s, 1994, Legal Research in the District of Columbia, Maryland and Virginia, 1995, 2d edit., 2000; contbr. chapters to books; mem. adv. bd. Westlaw, 1988—93, 2003—. Mem.: ABA (com. on librs. 1987—93), U.S. Trademark Assn., Maritime Law Assn., Spl. Librs. Assn. (chair copyright com. 1990—96, John Cotton Dana award 1997), Am. Law Sch. (chmn. sec. on librs. 1990—92, accreditation com. 1991—94), Am. Assn. Law Librs. (mem. exec. bd. 1981—84, mem. copyright com. 1990—93, copyright office rep., chmn. 2003—, Pres.' award 2001, Spl. Dist. Svc. award Southeastern chpt. 1997). Office: Washington & Lee U Law Libr Lewis Hall Lexington VA 24450 E-mail: wiants@wlu.edu.

WICH, DONALD ANTHONY, JR., lawyer; b. Apr. 13, 1947; s. Donald Anthony and Margaret Louise (Blatz) W. BA with honors, Notre Dame U., Ind., 1969; JD, Notre Dame U., 1972. Bar: Fla. 1972, U.S. Dist. Ct. (so. dist.) Fla. 1972, U.S. Ct. Appeals (5th and 11th cirs.) 1982, U.S. Supreme Ct. 1976; cert. civil trial lawyer, 1983. Assoc. VISTA, Miami, Fla., 1972-74; atty. Legal Svcs., Miami, 1973-75; adj. prof. law U. Miami, 1974-75; ptnr. Wich, Wich & wich, P.A., Ft. Lauderdale, Fla., 1992—. Pres., dir. Legal Aid of Broward, Ft. Lauderdale, 1976-82; mem. 17th Cir. Jud. Nominating Commn., 1998-02; spl. prosecutor, grievance chmn. The Fla Bar, 1982-90; chmn. UPL Standing Com., 2001— Bd. dirs. St. Thomas More Sch. of So. Fla., 1989-2002. Mem. ATLA, Am. Arbitration Assn., North Broward Bar Assn. (pres. 1983-84), Acad. Fla. Trial Lawyers Assn. (sustaining mem.), Broward County Trial Lawyers Assn. (pres. 1988-89, sustaining mem.), Broward Bar Assn. (chmn. legis. com. 1984-85, exec. com. 1986-92, 94-98, chmn. bench-bar com. 1993-94, chmn. clk.-bar com. 1993-95, mem. 1998-99, pres. 1997-98), Tex. Trial Lawyers Assn., N.Y. Trial Lawyers Assn., Pompano Beach C. of C. (pres. 1989-90, dir. 1984-87, 92-95, govtl. affairs chmn. 1983-84, art show chmn. 1984-85, seafood festival chmn. 1986-90), Notre Dame Frederick Sorin Soc., Rotary (bd. dirs. 1987-91), Woodhouse (bd. dirs. 1990-91). General civil litigation, Personal injury (including property damage), Property, real (including real estate development, water). Office: Wich Wich & Wich PA 2400 E Commercial Blvd Fort Lauderdale FL 33308-4030 E-mail: wich3@msn.com.

WICHINSKY, GLENN ELLIS, lawyer; b. Monticello, N.Y., Dec. 22, 1952; s. Michael A. Wichinsky and Ann (Pesekow) Kaplan; m. Lillian Carol Rindom, June 6, 1976; children: Laura, David. BA in Polit. Sci., U. Miami, 1974; JD, U. Pacific, 1982. Bar: Fla. 1982, Nev. 1983, U.S. Dist. Ct. Nev. 1984. Legis. asst. Calif. Assembly, Sacramento, 1978-80; legal advisor Community Legal Svcs., Sacramento, 1980-81; jud. clk. Sacramento County Superior Ct., Sacramento, 1981-82; assoc. Rogers, Monsey, Woodbury, Las Vegas, Nev., 1983; pvt. practice Las Vegas and Boca Raton, Fla., 1983—2000. Mem. gaming law com. State Bar Nev., 1999; pres. Global Gaming and Tech., Inc., Boca Raton, 2000—02; of counsel Sheridan and Carroll, LLP, Sacramento, 2000—02. Chmn. transp. com. Palm Beach County (Fla.) Coop., 1987—89, Palm Beach County Task Force for Responsible Representation, 1989—91; mem. Palm Beach County Comprehensive Planning Adv. Com., 1988, Zoning Bd. Adjustment, 1991—2001, West Boca Action Com., Boca Raton, 1986—90; apptd. FAA Part 150 Noise Study Com. Boca Raton Mcpl. Airport, 1999—2000; mem., bd. dirs. Boca Raton Airport Action Group, 1999; pres. New Dems. Boca-Delray, Fla., 2003—. Music scholar U. Miami, 1970. Mem. ABA (com. on air and space law), Internat. Assn. Gaming Attorneys, Fla. Bar Assn. (aviation law com.), Palm Beach County Bar Assn., South Palm Beach County Bar Assn., Tau Epsilon Phi (pres. 1973-74). Democrat. Jewish. Avocations: skiing, travel, aviation, meteorology. Administrative and regulatory, Corporate, general, Probate (including wills, trusts). Office: 1200 N Fed Hwy Ste 200 Boca Raton FL 33432 E-mail: gwichinsky@aol.com.

WICK, HILTON ADDISON, lawyer; b. Mt. Pleasant, Pa., Feb. 11, 1920; m. Barbara G. Shaw; children: James H., William S., B. Jane, Ann W., Julia A. BA, Maryville Coll., 1942; JD, Harvard U., 1948. Bar: Vt. 1948. Practiced in Burlington; ptnr. Wick, Dinse & Allen, 1949-72; CEO Chittenden Bank, Chittenden Corp., 1969—85; bd. dirs. Sentinel Funds, 1970—76; of counsel Dinse, Allen & Erdmann, Burlington, 1972-80; bd. dirs. Nat. Life Ins. Co., 1976—92; of counsel Wick & Maddocks, Burlington, 1980—; state senator Vt., 1989-91; COO Gifford Med. Ctr., Inc., Randolph, 1993-95. Bd. dirs. Blue Cross/Blue Shield Vt., Beach Properties, Inc., Vt. Pub. Radio, chmn., 1990-96. Trustee Middlebury Coll., 1969-85, Champlain Coll., 1974-94, Maryville Coll., 1981-86, Shelburne Mus., 1985-94, Ethan Allen Homestead, 1989-96, Vt. Assn. for Blind and Visually Impaired, 1992-2001; pres. Coll. St. Congl. Ch., 1996-98; bd. dirs. Vt. divsn. Am. Cancer Soc., 1979-93, Intervale Found.; pres. bd. trustees Vt. Law Sch., 1975-95; chmn. bd. trustees Vt. Cmty. Found., 1985-91; chancellor Vt. State Colls., 1984-85; chmn. bd. dirs. Middlebury Coll., 1981-84. Mem. ABA, Vt. Bar Assn. (pres. 1967-68), Chittenden County Bar Assn. (pres. 1963-64), Internat. Soc. Barristers, Am. Bankers Assn. (bd. dirs. 1975-76), Vt. Bankers Assn. (pres. 1973-74), Ethan Allen Club, Harvard Club (Boston and N.Y.C.), Phi Kappa Delta. Home: Two Appletree Point Ln Burlington VT 05401 Office: 308 College St Burlington VT 05401-8319 E-mail: hiltbarb@aol.com.

WICK, LAWRENCE SCOTT, lawyer; b. San Diego, Oct. 1, 1945; children: Ryan Scott, Andrew Taylor, Hayley Lauren. BA, Northwestern U., Evanston, Ill., 1967; JD, Columbia U., 1970. Atty. Leydig Voit & Mayer Ltd., Chgo., 1978-84, shareholder, 1984-98; equity ptnr. Wildman, Harrold, Allen & Dixon, Chgo., 1998—2002; v.p., gen. counsel Lionheart Prodns., Ltd., Santa Ana, Calif., Lake Bluff, Ill., 1995—; pvt. practice Lake Bluff, Ill., 2002—. V.p., gen. counsel Purple Nurple Prodns. Ltd., Lake Bluff, Ill., 2001—; spkr. in field. Contbr. articles to profl. jours. Mem. ABA, Internat. Trademark Assn. (N.Y.), Internat. Trade Assn. (Chgo. chpt.), French-Am. C. of C., Brit.-Am. C. of C., Assn. Internat. pour la Protection de la Propriété Intellectuale (Zurich), Pharm. Trade Marks Group (London), Am. Film Inst. (L.A.), Chgo. Bar Assn. (mem. fin. com.). Avocations: international travel, film, swimming, snorkeling, free diving. Federal civil litigation, Intellectual property, Trademark and copyright. Home: 317 Rothbury Ct Lake Bluff IL 60044-1927 Office: P O Box 598 Lake Bluff IL 60044-0598 Office Fax: 847-615-7240. E-mail: wicklaw@aol.com.

WICKER, THOMAS CAREY, JR., judge; b. New Orleans, Aug. 1, 1923; s. Thomas Carey and Mary (Taylor) W.; children: Thomas Carey III, Catherine Anne; m. Jane Anne Trepanier, Dec. 29, 1995. BBA, Tulane U., 1944, LLB, 1949, JD, 1969. Bar: La. 1949. Law clk. La. Supreme Ct., New Orleans, 1949-50; asst. U.S. Atty., 1950-53; practiced in New Orleans, 1953-72; mem. firm Simon, Wicker & Wiedemann, 1953-67; partner firm Wicker, Wiedemann & Fransen, 1967-72; dist. judge Jefferson Parish (La.), 1972-85, judge, Court of Appeal 5th cir., 1985-98, mem. faculty Nat. Jud. Coll., 1979-93, Tulane U. Sch. Law, 1978-83. Past bd. visitors Tulane U.; bd. dirs. La. Jud. Coll.; past pres. Sugar Bowl. Author: (with others) Judicial Ethics, 1982, (with others) Modern Judicial Ethics, 1992; editor Tulane Law Review, 1949. Lt. (j.g.), USNR, 1944-46. Mem. ABA (jud. div. council), La. (chmn. jr. bar sect. 1958-59, gov. 1958, mem. ho. of dels. 1960-72), Jefferson Parish, bar assns., Tulane U. Alumni Assn. (past pres.), Am. Judicature Soc., La. Dist. Judges Assn. (past pres.), Order of Coif, Beta Gamma Sigma, Pi Kappa Alpha. Episcopalian. Clubs: Rotary (pres. 1971-72), Metairie (La.) Country. Avocations: golf, photography, military history.

WICKLUND, DAVID WAYNE, lawyer; b. St. Paul, Aug. 7, 1949; s. Wayne Glenwood and Elna Katherine (Buresh) W.; m. Susan Marie Bubenko, Nov. 17, 1973; children: David Jr., Kurt, Edward. BA cum laude, Williams Coll., 1971; JD cum laude, U. Toledo, 1974. Bar: Ohio 1974. Assoc. Shumaker, Loop & Kendrick, Toledo, 1974-80, ptnr., 1981—. Adj. instr. law, U. Toledo, 1988. Editor-in-chief U. Toledo Law Rev. 1973-74. Mem.: ABA, Toledo Bar Assn., Ohio State Bar Assn. (bd. govs. antitrust sect. 1994—2001), U. Toledo Coll. Law Alumni Assn. (pres. 1999—2000), Toledo Club, Inverness Club. Antitrust, Federal civil litigation, Patent. Office: Shumaker Loop & Kendrick N Courthouse Sq 1000 Jackson St Toledo OH 43624-1573 E-mail: dwicklund@slk-law.com.

WICKS, CHARLES CARTER, lawyer; b. Goshen, Ind., May 28, 1945; s. Charles Sterling and Christine (Carter) W.; m. Penny Rae Krull, Oct. 31, 1970; children: Jay, Kristin, Scott. BA, Tulane U., 1967; JD, Ind. U., 1970. Bar: Ind. 1970, U.S. Ct. Mil. Appeals 1971, U.S. Supreme Ct. 1991. Ptnr. Matthews Petsche-Wicks, South Bend, Ind., 1974-78, Virgil, Cawley, Platt & Wicks, Elkhart, Ind., 1978; pvt. practice Elkhart, 1979—; dep. pros. atty., 1978—; ptnr. Wicks & Rieff, Elkhart, 1988-89. Lectr. forensic medicine Goshen Coll. Sch. Nursing. Mem. vestry St. James Episcopal ch., 1977-79, 81-84, 86-88, sr. warden, 1989, diocesan coun. Episcopal Diocese No. Ind., 1988-89; mem. Rep. CTrl. Com., Goshen, 1978—, chmn., 2001--. Capt. USAF, 1970-74. Mem. ABA, ATLA, Ind. Bar Assn., Ind. Trial Lawyers Assn., Elkhart County Estate Planning Coun. (pres. 1982-83), Elkhart County Past Masters' Assn. (pres. 1984, 89), Elkhart C. of C., Goshen C. of

C., Goshen County Past Masters Assn., Am. Legion, Masons (master 1980, trustee 1981-83, 2001-2003, v.p. 33d deg. assn., comdr. in chief 1992-94, chmn. degree com. 1995-2000, Scottish Rite 1995-2001, dir. 24 degree 2001--, trustee 2001--), Shriners (pres. Goshen club 1983), Jesters, Red Cross of Constantine, Moose, Elkhart Kiwanis (bd. dirs. 1986-87, 97-99), Christiana Creek Country Club, Bent Oak Golf Club, Greater Elkhart Pachyderm Club (pres. 1989—), Nat. Pachyderm Club (bd. dirs. 1998-99), Masons. Rosicruiana. State civil litigation, Family and matrimonial, Personal injury (including property damage). Home: 26207 Hilly Ln Elkhart IN 46517-2243 Office: 514 S Main St PO Box 1884 Elkhart IN 46515-1884 E-mail: wix6316@aol.com.

WICKS, JEFFREY DONALD, lawyer; b. Springfield, Mo., Jan. 8, 1971; s. Jack and Janet Wicks. BA, U. Mo., Columbia, 1993; JD, Washburn U., 1996. Bar: Kans. 1996. Asst. pub. defender South Ctrl. Regional Pub. Defenders Office, Wichita, Kans., 1996—. Mem. Order of the Barristers, Kans. Assn. of Criminal Def. Lawyers. Criminal. Office: 604 N Main St Ste D Wichita KS 67203-3672 E-mail: jwicks@sbids.state.ks.us.

WIDDEL, JOHN EARL, JR., lawyer; b. Minot, N.D., Nov. 17, 1936; s. John Earl Sr. and Angela Victoria W.; m. Yvonne J. Haugen, Dec. 21, 1973; children: John P., James M., Susan N., Andrea K. B in Philosophy, BSBA, U. N.D., 1966, BSBA, 1971. Bar: N.D. 1971, U.S. Dist. Ct. N.D., 1971, U.S. Ct. Appeals (8th cir.) 1989. Ptnr. Thorsen & Widdel, Grand Forks, N.D., 1971-97; shareholder Law Offices ND, PC. Mcpl. judge City of Grand Forks, 1972—; ct. magistrate Grand Forks County, 1975. Mem. N.D. Foster Parent Program, 1974-87, Nat. Conf. of Bar Pres.; mem. bd. dirs. YMCA, Grand Forks, 1982; dist. chmn. Boy Scouts Am., 1987-88; corp. mem. ALTRU Hosp. With U.S. Army, 1960-62. Mem. State Bar Assn. N.D. (bd. govs. 1983-88, pres. 1986-87), Greater Grand Forks County Bar Assn. (pres. 1982), N.E. Cen. Jud. Dist. (pres. 1983), Grand Forks Cemetery Assn. (bd. dirs. 1984-96, pres. 1989-94), Grand Forks Hist. Soc. (pres. 1983), Grand Forks Jaycees, Antique Automobile Club Am. (nat. bd. dirs. 1984-2000, v.p. 1985-98, sec.-treas. 1989, pres. N.D . region 1977-78, 83-84), Sertoma (bd. dirs. 1994-99, pres. 1997-98, dist. gov. 2001-03), Elks (exalted ruler 1985-86), Masonic Bodies (Kem Temple Potentate 1995), Nat. Assn. Estate Planning Coun. (accredited estate planner, 1994), N.D. Mcpl. Judges Assn. (dir. 1993—). Roman Catholic. General practice, Probate (including wills, trusts), Property, real (including real estate development, water). Home: Box 5624 Grand Forks ND 58206-5624 Office: Law Offices North Dakota PC PO Box 5624 Grand Forks ND 58206-5624

WIDENER, HIRAM EMORY, JR., judge; b. Abingdon, Va., Apr. 30, 1923; s. Hiram Emory and Nita Douglas (Peck) Widener; children: Molly Berentd, Hiram Emory III. Student, Va. Poly. Inst., 1940—41; BS, U.S. Naval Acad., 1944; LLB, Washington and Lee U., 1953, LLD, 1977. Bar: Va. 1951. Pvt. practice, Bristol, Va., 1953—69; judge U.S. Dist. Ct. (we. dist.) Va., Abingdon, 1969—71, chief judge, 1971—72; judge U.S. Ct. of Appeals (4th cir.) , Abingdon, 1972—. U.S. commr. Western Dist. Va., 1963—66; mem. Va. Election Laws Study Commn., 1968—69. Chmn. Rep. 9th Dist. , Va., 1966—69; state exec. com. Va. Rep. State Ctrl. Com., 1966—69. Lt. (j.g.) USN, 1944—49, lt. USNR, 1951—52. Decorated Bronze Star with combat V. Mem.: Va. State Bar, Va. Bar Assn., Am. Law Inst., Phi Alpha Delta. Republican. Presbyterian. Office: US Courthouse 180 E Main St Rm 123 Abingdon VA 24210-2839

WIDMAN, DOUGLAS JACK, lawyer; b. Neptune, N.J., Feb. 28, 1949; s. Leonard and Phyllis (Rose) W.; m. Jill Rosenblad; children: Phyllis, Jared Leonard, Sarah. BA in Polit. Sci. cum laude, Syracuse U., 1971, JD, 1973. Bar: N.J. 1973, U.S. Dist. Ct. N.J. 1973, U.S. Supreme Ct. 1979, D.C. 1981, N.Y. 1990. Legal planner Syracuse-Onondaga (N.Y.) County Planning Agy., 1971-73; law sec. to presiding judges N.J. Dist. Ct. and N.J. Superior Ct., 1973-74; dep. atty gen. State Enforcement Bur. Div. Criminal Justice, Trenton, NJ, 1974; ptnr. Widman, Cooney & Wilson, Oakhurst, NJ, 1976—. Assoc. editor Syracuse Jour. Internat. Law & Commerce. Syracuse U. Coll. Law scholar, 1971-73; Syracuse U. Grad. Research fellow, 1972. Mem. N.J. Bar Assn., Phi Alpha Delta, Alpha Phi Omega, Pi Sigma Alpha. Alternative dispute resolution, Insurance, Personal injury (including property damage). Office: Widman Cooney & Wilson 1803 Hwy 35 Oakhurst NJ 07755-2911

WIDMARK, STEFAN, lawyer; b. Lund, Sweden, Aug. 16, 1963; LLM, U. Lund, 1989. Clk. Göteborg's (Sweden) Dist. Ct., 1989-92; assoc. Mannheimer Swartling, Stockholm, 1992-94, 96-98, Danowsky & Ptnrs., Stockholm, 1994-96, Vinge, Stockholm, 1998-2000; ptnr., 2001—. Entertainment, Intellectual property, Sports. Office: Vinge Smålandsgatan 20 111 87 Stockholm Sweden Fax: 46 8 6143190. E-mail: stefan.widmark@vinge.se.

WIEAND, JEFFREY SCOTT, lawyer; b. Harrisburg, Pa., Jan. 3, 1954; s. Richard Wilson and Annetta E. (Younker) W.; m. Janet G. Silver, Sept. 25, 1954; children: Douglas Leo, Roger Galvin. BA, Middlebury Coll., 1976; PhD, U. Chgo., 1981; JD, Harvard U., 1985. William Rainey Harper instr. U. Chgo., 1981-82; assoc. Hill & Barlow, Boston, 1985-87; mem. Hutchins, Wheeler & Dittmar, Boston, 1987-98; coun. Lane, Altman & Owens, Boston, 1998—99. Editor Boston Bar Jour., 1998-2001; contbr. articles to profl. jours. Mem. bd. of appeals Town of Concord, 1990-97, bd. dirs. Civic Symphony Orch., Boston, 1990-97; trustee Concord Open Land Found., 1998—, bd. of appeals Hist. Dists. Commn. Town of Concord, 1999-2003. Mem. ABA, Nat. Bus. Aviation Assn., Am. Philosophical Assn., Mass. Bar Assn., Boston Bar Assn. Aviation, Corporate, general, Mergers and acquisitions. Office: Boston Jetsearch Inc Civil Air Terminal Hanscom Field Bedford MA 01730

WIECHMANN, ERIC WATT, lawyer; b. Schenectady, N.Y., June 12, 1948; s. Richard Jerdone and Ann (Watt) W.; m. Merrill Metzger, May 22, 1971. BA, Hamilton Coll., 1970; JD, Cornell U., 1974. Bar: Conn. 1975, U.S. Dist. Ct. (so. and ea. dists.) N.Y. 1975, U.S. Dist. Ct. Conn. 1975, U.S. Dist. Ct. D.C. 1981, U.S. Ct. Appeals (2nd cir.) 1975, U.S. Ct. Appeals (9th cir.) 1980, U.S. Ct. Appeals D.C. 1982, U.S. Ct. Appeals (5th cir.) 1986, U.S. Ct. Appeals (10th cir.) 1989, U.S. Supreme Ct. 1978. Assoc. Cummings & Lockwood LLC, Stamford, Conn., 1974—82, ptnr., 1982—, mng. ptnr. Hartford office, bd. dirs., 1996—, bus. clients exec. com., 2003. Spl. pretrial master U.S. Dist. Ct. Conn. 1984—; state atty. trial referee, 1986—, mem. evidence code oversight com.; civil task force, civil jury instrn. com. Conn. Superior Ct., 1996-2000, docket control com., 2001—; comml. arbitrator Am. Arbitration Assn. Contbr. articles to profl. jours. Mem. Zoning Bd. Appeals, New Canaan, Conn., 1984-85; bd. dirs. Conn. Rivers coun. Boy Scouts Am., trustee, 2001—. Mem. ABA (vice-chmn. toxics and hazardous law com. TIPS sect.), Def. Rsch. Inst., Internat. Assn. Def. Counsel (mem. faculty Def. Trial Acad. 1996, chmn. toxic and hazardous substance com. 1998-99, chmn. CLE bd. 2000-02), Internat. Soc. Barristers, Conn. Bar Assn. (exec. com. antitrust sect. 1982—, ct. rules adv. com, chmn. 1991-93), Conn. Bar Found., Golf Club Avon. Republican. Episcopalian. Antitrust, General civil litigation, Product liability. Home: 10 Langley Park Farmington CT 06032-1541 E-mail: ewiech@yahoo.com., ewiech@cl-law.com.

WIEDER, BRUCE TERRILL, lawyer, electrical engineer; b. Cleve., Dec. 9, 1955; s. Ira J. and Judith M.W. BSEE, Cornell U., 1978; MBA, U. Tex., 1980, JD with honors, 1988. Bar: Tex. 1988, U.S. Dist. Ct. (we. dist.) Tex. 1989, U.S. Patent and Trademark Office 1989, U.S. Ct. Appeals (fed. cir.) 1990, D.C. 1991, U.S. Supreme Ct. 1992, U.S. Dist. Ct. (no. dist.) Tex. 1995, Va. 1997, U.S. Dist. Ct. (ea. dist.) Va. 1997. Engr. Motorola, Inc., Austin, Tex., 1979-85; assoc. Arnold, White & Durkee, Austin, 1988-90; law clk. U.S. Ct. Appeals (Fed. cir.), Washington, 1990-91; assoc. Burns, Doane, Swecker & Mathis, Alexandria, Va., 1991-97, ptnr., 1998—. Adj. prof. Georgetown U. Law Ctr., 1998—. Mem. IEEE, ABA, Am. Intellectual Property Law Assn., Alpha Phi Omega (life), Beta Gamma Sigma (life). Computer, Patent, Trademark and copyright. Office: Burns Doane Swecker & Mathis 1737 King St Ste 500 Alexandria VA 22314-2727

WIEDER, CATHERINE GRANT, prosecutor; d. Stoddard and Jane Catherine (Spencer) Baird; m. Terry A. Wieder, Aug. 16, 1996; children from previous marriage: Amanda Jane, Sybil Grace. BA, SUNY, New Paltz, 1974; JD, UCLA, 1977. Bar: Calif. 1982. Exec. sec. U.S.-China People's Friendship Assn., L.A., 1978-81; risk mgr. City of Fullerton (Calif.), 1981-84; atty. Community Legal Svcs., Compton, 1984-86, supervising atty. Norwalk, Calif., 1986-95; pvt. practice law Cerritos. Instr. bus. and law Coastline C.C., 1982-83, Cerritos Coll., 1989, Rio Hondo Coll., 1995-96. Mem. governing bd. ABC Unified Sch. Dist., Cerritos, 1985-93, pres., 1987-88, 92-93, clk., 1986-87; bd. mem. Su Casa Family Crisis and Support Ctr., 1989-97, sec., 1993-95, v.p., 1995-96; bd. mem. Cmty. Family Guidance Ctr., 1990-96, sec., 1992-93, v.p., 1993-94, pres. 1994-95. Recipient hon. service award Niemes Elem. Sch. PTA, 1987. Mem. Southeast Dist. Bar Assn. (named atty. of the yr. 1991), Los Angeles County Bar Assn., Am. Assn. of Univ. Women, LWV (treas. Downey, Calif., 1984-85). Democrat. Office: 13017 Artesia Blvd Ste D-120 Cerritos CA 90703-1364

WIENER, JACQUES LOEB, JR., judge; b. Shreveport, La., Oct. 2, 1934; s. Jacques L. and Betty (Eichenbaum) Wiener; m. Sandra Mills Feingerts; children: Patricia Wiener Shifke, Jacques L. III, Betty Ellen Wiener Spomer, Donald B. BA, Tulane U., 1956, JD, 1961. Bar: La. 1961, U.S. Dist. Ct. (we. dist.) La. 1961. Ptnr. Wiener, Weiss & Madison, Shreveport, 1961—90; judge U.S. Ct. Appeals (5th cir.), New Orleans, 1990—. Mem. coun. La. State Law Inst., 1963; master of the bench Am. Inn of Ct., 1990—98. Pres. United Way N.W. La., 1975, Shreveport Jewish Fedn., 1969—70. Fellow: La. Bar Found., Am. Bar Found., Am. Coll. Trust and Estates Counsel; mem.: ABA, Am. Law Inst., Shreveport Bar Assn. (pres. 1982), La. Bar Assn., Internat. Acad. Estate and Trust Law (academician). Avocations: fly fishing, upland game bird hunting, photography, travel. Office: Court of Appeals Building 600 Camp St Rm 244 New Orleans LA 70130-3425

WIENER, RONALD MARTIN, lawyer; b. Phila., June 1, 1939; s. William V. and Sylvia Wiener; children: Carol Jan, Alan Mark. AB, U. Pa., 1961; JD magna cum laude, Harvard U., 1964. Bar: D.C. 1965, Pa. 1966. Law clk. U.S. Tax Ct., 1964-66; assoc. Wolf, Block, Schorr and Solis-Cohen, Phila., 1966-72, ptnr., 1972—. Mem. commr.'s adv. group IRS, 1992-93. Fellow Am. Coll. Tax Counsel (regent 3d cir. 1996-2003); mem. ABA, Pa. Bar Assn., Phila. Bar Assn. (chair tax sect. 1989-90). Corporate taxation, , Taxation, general. Office: Wolf Block Schorr and Solis-Cohen LLP 1650 Arch St 22d fl Philadelphia PA 19103-2678 E-mail: rwiener@wolfblock.com.

WIER, RICHARD ROYAL, JR., lawyer; b. Wilmington, Del., May 19, 1941; s. Richard Royal and Anne (Kurtz) W.; m. Anne E. Edwards, Nov. 25, 1978; children— Melissa Royal, Emma Kurtz; children from previous marriage: Richard Royal, III, Mimi Poole. BA in English, Hamilton Coll., 1963; LLB, U. Pa., 1966; postgrad., Temple U., 1981-82. Bar: D.C. 1967, Del. 1967, Pa. 1980, U.S. Dist. Ct. Del., U.S. Ct. Appeals (3d cir.), U.S. Supreme Ct. Assoc. Connolly, Bove & Lodge, Wilmington, 1966-68; dep. atty. gen. State of Del., Wilmington, 1968-70; state prosecutor Del. Dept. Justice, Wilmington, 1970-74; atty. gen. State of Del., Wilmington, 1975-79; ptnr. Prickett, Jones, Elliott, Kristol & Schnee, Wilmington, 1979-92; pvt. practice Wilmington, 1993—. Lectr. criminal and labor law various instns. Active United Way campaign, 1976-77; supervisory bd. Gov.'s Commn. on Criminal Justice; bd. dirs. Del. Coun. Crime and Justice, 1982-89; adv. coun. Diabetes Control, 1990-92; dir. Project Assist, 1992-95, Commn. on Outreach, 1994—. Recipient Law Enforcement award Newark Police Dept., 1974; Law Enforcement Commendation medal Nat. Soc. SAR, 1976; Ideal Citizen award Am. Found. for Sci. Creative Intelligence, 1976; Commendation Del. Gen. Assembly Senate, 1976-77, 80; named one of Top Labor/Employment Attys. in Del., Del. Today, 1999—. Mem. ABA, Nat. Dist. Attys. Assn. (state dir.), Del. Bar Assn. (chmn. criminal law sect. 1987-91, co-chmn. on drug crisis 1993—, vice chmn. labor law sect. 1987-88, chmn. 1989-90), Pa. Bar Assn., D.C. Bar Assn., Nat. Assn. Attys. Gen. (hon. life, exec. com.), Soc. Attys. Gen. Execs. (emeritus), Am. Judicature Soc., Am. Del. Trial Lawyers Assn., Nat. Assn. Extradition Ofcls. (hon. life, regional v.p., exec. dir.), Italian Radio/TV Assn. (hon., Outstanding Achievement award), Internat. Platform Assn., Pi Delta Epsilon. Achievements include inventor in field. Criminal, Labor (including EEOC, Fair Labor Standards Act, labor-management relations, NLRB, OSHA), Personal injury (including property damage). Office: 1220 N Market St Ste 600 Wilmington DE 19801-2598 E-mail: rwier@wierlaw.com.

WIESE, KURT ROWLAND, lawyer; b. Fulton, Mo., Nov. 3, 1955; s. Donald Edgar Wiese and Bonnie Oliver Shaddock; m. Anne Carroll Gordon, July 8, 1978; children: Evelyn, Hollis. BS, Tulane U., 1978; JD, U. Ariz., 1984. Prin. atty. South Coast Air Quality Mgmt. Dist., Diamond Bar, Calif., 1989—. Adj. prof. Western State U. Coll. Law, Fullerton, 1993-98; instr. environ. compliance Calif. State U., Fullerton, 1998—. Mem. L.A. County Bar Assn. (environ. law sect., chair air quality com. 1996), Phi Beta Kappa, Order of Coif, Newport Harbor Yacht Club. Home: 666 Catalina Laguna Beach CA 92651-2545 E-mail: kwlese@agmd.gov.

WIEST, WILLIAM HARVEY, judge; b. Dalmatia, Pa., July 8, 1945; s. Nelson Earl and Elda Irene (Martz) Wiest; m. Karen Machtley Wiest, Dec. 27, 1969; children: Joel, Rachel, David(dec.) , Tobias(dec.) , Elisabeth, Chad, Patrick. BS/BA, Susquehanna U., 1967; JD, Cleveland-Marshall Coll., 1971. Tchr. music Carlisle Area Schs., Pa.; atty. Wiest, Wiest, Saylor & Muolo, Sunbury; judge Ct. Common Pleas, 1998—. Organist United Christ Ch. Mem.: Pa. Bar Assn., Pa. Juvenile Judges Assn., Pa. Trial Judges Assn., Lancaster Mennonite Hist. Soc., Johannes Schwalm Hist. Soc., Gratz Hist. Soc., Mahanoy & Mahantongo Hist. & Preservation Soc., Palatines to Am., Northumberland County Hist. Soc., Pa. German Soc. Republican. Mem. United Ch. Christ. Avocations: genealogy, history, antiques. Office: Northumberland County Cthse 201 Market St Sunbury PA 17801 Fax: 570-988-4497. E-mail: ncjudge2@ptdprolog.net.

WIGELL, RAYMOND GEORGE, lawyer; b. Chgo., Apr. 18, 1949; s. Raymond Carl and Amanda D. (Santiago) W.; m. Barbara E. Buettner, June 28, 1980; children: Katherine, Elizabeth, Charles. BA, U. Ill., Chgo., 1971; JD, John Marshall Law Sch., 1975; LLM in Taxation, DePaul U., 1991. Bar: Ill. 1975, U.S. Dist. Ct. (no. dist.) Ill. 1975, U.S. Dist. Ct. (no. dist.) Ind. 2002, U.S. Ct. Appeals (7th cir.) 1978, U.S. Supreme Ct. 1979, U.S. Tax Ct. 1987. Pvt. practice law Raymond G. Wigell, Chgo., 1975-77; trial atty. Cook County Pub. Defender, Chgo., 1977-78; pres., owner, atty. Wigell & Assocs., Matteson, Ill., 1978—. Instr. MacCormac Jr. Coll., Chgo., 1976-77; lectr. in bus. law Oakton C.C., Des Plaines, Ill., 1976-84; adj. prof. Govs. State U., University Park, Ill., 1984-92. Commn. chair inquiry bd. Atty. Registration Disciplinary Commn. Supreme Ct. Ill., Chgo., 1985-90, commn. chair hearing bd., 1990-95. With USN, 1971-77. Mem. Ill. State Bar Assn., South Suburban Bar Assn. (bd. dirs.), Nat. Assn. Criminal Def. Lawyers, U. Ill. Alumni Assn. (life). Roman Catholic. Entertainment, Corporate, general, Criminal. Office: Wigell & Assocs Atty at Law 4749 Lincoln Mall Dr Ste 505 Matteson IL 60443 E-mail: rwigell@waalaw.com.

WIGGER, JARREL L. lawyer; b. Wiesbaden, Germany, May 12, 1963; s. Philip Lee and Ervinetta (Maxey) W.; m. Rose Marie Riley, Aug. 1, 1987; children: Amy Elizabeth, Jordan Lee. BA in English, The Citadel, 1985; JD, Wake Forest U., 1988. Bar: S.C. 1988, U.S. Dist. Ct. S.C. 1993, U.S. Ct. Mil. Appeals 1991, U.S. Supreme Ct. 1998. Student prosecutor Forsyth County Dist. Atty. Office, Winston-Salem, N.C., 1988; assoc. Drose, Davidson & Bennett, Charleston, S.C., 1992-94, jr. ptnr., 1995-98; ptnr. Davidson, Bennett & Wigger, Charleston, 1999—. Real estate cons. Co-editor, author: U.S. Navy Mass Casualty Handbook, 1995. Lt. USN, 1986-92. Mem. ABA, ATLA, S.C. Trial Lawyers Assn., S.C. Bar Assn., Charleston County Bar Assn., Claimant Assn. for Workers Compensation (bd. govs.), Assn. Citadel Men (life), Citadel Brigadier Found., Charleston Area Citadel Club, Citadel Old Timers Wrestling Club (pres. 1996—), Sigma Tau Delta. Avocations: running, guitar, wrestling, coaching. General civil litigation, Personal injury (including property damage), Workers' compensation. Office: 8086 Rivers Ave North Charleston SC 29406

WIGGINS, CHARLES HENRY, JR., lawyer; b. Balt., July 15, 1939; s. Charles Henry and Kathryn Wilson (Walker) W.; m. Wendy Jane Horn, June 20, 1964 (div. 1996); children: Charles Hunter, Rebecca Rae, Melinda Marie; m. Karen Ann Kowal, Apr. 26, 1997 (div. 2002). BSEE, U. Ill., Urbana, 1962; JD with honors, U. Ill., 1965. Bar: Ill. 1965, U.S. Dist. (no. dist.) Ill. 1970, U.S. Tax Ct. 1974, U.S. Ct. Appeals (7th cir.) 1983. Assoc. Vedder, Price, Kaufman & Kammholz, Chgo., 1969-73, ptnr., 1974—. Mem. zoning bd. appeals Village of Indian Head Pk., Ill., 1984-91. Capt. U.S. Army, 1965-68. Mem. Chgo. Bar Assn., University Club (Chgo.), Edgewood Valley Country Club (LaGrange, Ill., bd. dirs. 1991-98), SAR. Avocations: golf, tennis, bridge. Estate planning, Probate (including wills, trusts), Estate taxation. Office: Vedder Price Kaufman & Kammholz 222 N La Salle St Fl 26 Chicago IL 60601-1003

WIGMORE, JOHN GRANT, lawyer; b. L.A., Mar. 14, 1928; s. George Theodore and Mary (Grant) W.; m. Dina Burnaby, July 27, 1968 (dec. 1994); children: Alexander Trueblood, Adam Trueblood, John G. Jr., Mary. BS in Geology, Stanford U., 1949; JD, UCLA, 1958. Geologist Western Geophys., Calif., Colo., Mo., 1953-55; assoc. Lawler, Felix & Hall, L.A., 1958-62, ptnr., 1963-86, Pillsbury, Madison & Sutro, L.A., 1986-90; ret. Lectr. in field. Contbr. articles to profl. jours. Trustee L.A. County Mus. Natural History, 1970—; participant various local & state election campaigns, 1965-80. Officer USN, 1950-53. Fellow Am. Coll. Trial Lawyers, Am. Bar Found.; mem. ABA (chair litigation com. antitrust sect. 1970-74), Calif. State Bar (L.A. County bar del. 1965-75), L.A. County Bar Assn. (exec. com. trial sect. 1965-68), L.A. County Bus. Trial Lawyers (exec. com. 1984-87), Barristers (exec. com. 1960-65). Antitrust, Federal civil litigation, Commercial, contracts (including sales of goods; commercial financing). Home: 870 Neptune Ave Encinitas CA 92024-2062

WILCHER, LARRY K. lawyer; b. Lebanon, Ky., July 19, 1950; s. Dwain LaRue and Juanita (Tungate) W.; m. Mary Jo Hayden, Aug. 21, 1971; children: Emily Jane, Joseph Keith. BS in Pharmacy, St. Louis Coll. Pharmacy, 1973; JD, No. Ky. U., 1984; program of instrn. for lawyers, Harvard U., 1987, 91, 94. Dir. real estate SuperX Drugs Corp., Cin., 1975-84; dir. real estate, real estate counsel Dollar Gen. Corp., Goodlettsville, Tenn., 1984-85, gen. counsel, 1985—2002; dir. U.S. Bank, 1995—; pres. Nations Title Co., Inc., 1999—2002; ptnr. Wyatt, Tarrant & Combs, 2002—. Presenter in field. Contbr. to book: Kentucky Business Organizations, 1989; presenter in field. Sec., dir. Scottsville-Allen County Leasing Corp., 1992—, Scottsville-Allen County Indsl. Devel. Authority, Inc., 1991—; dir. Leadership Ky., 1994—2000, mem. exec. com.., 1997—2000; dir. Bowling Green-Western Ky. U. Symphony Orch., 1998—2000; mem. Global Bus. Adv. Coun., Gordon Ford Coll.; chmn. Warren County Young Reps, Bowling Green, Ky., 1979, Scottsville-Allen County Planning Commn., 1997—. Named to Hon. Order Ky. Cols., 1968, One of Outstanding Young Men of Am., U.S. Jaycees, 1978; recipient Johnson & Johnson award St. Louis Coll. Pharmacy, 1973, Thurston B. Morton Leadership award Ky. Young Rep. Fedn., 1979. Mem. ABA, Nat. Assn. Corp. Dirs., Ky. Bar Assn. (recognition award 1987), Def. Rsch. Inst. Republican. Baptist. Office: Wyatt Tarrant & Combs 918 State St Bowling Green KY 42101

WILCOX, DONALD ALAN, lawyer; b. Grantsburg, Wis., July 18, 1951; s. John Charles and Lois Margaret (Finch) W.; m. Rachel Ann Johnson, Dec. 28, 1973; children: Benjamin Ray, Joseph Charles (dec.), Sara Johanna. BS, USAF Acad., 1973; JD, Georgetown U., 1979. Bar: Minn. 1979. Commd. 2d lt. USAF, 1973, advanced through grades to capt., resigned, 1979; assoc Holmquist & Holmquist, Benson, Minn., 1979-81; ptnr. Holmquist & Wilcox, 1981-90; shareholder Wilcox, Erhardt & Spates, P.A., Benson, 1990-91; pvt. practice Benson, 1991—2003; shareholder Wilcox & Ulmaniec, P.A., Benson, 2003—. Gen. counsel Swift County-Benson Hosp., 1981—, Farmers Mut. Coop., Bellingham, Minn., 1986—, Agralite Coop., Benson, 1986—, Kandiyohi Electric Coop., 1995—, Gardenville Coop. Tel. Assn., 2002—; atty. City of Benson, 1985—; examiner of titles Swift County, Benson, 1986—, Federated TE. Coop., Chokio, Minn., 1988—; bd. dirs. State Bank Danvers. Mem. Benson Planning Commn., 1979—; pres. Our Redeemer's Luth. Ch., Benson, 1985-86, 93-94; pres., bd. dirs. Swift County Homes, Inc., Benson, 1984-92. Recipient Lawyers Coop. Pub. award Lawyers Coop. Pub. Co., 1979. Mem. Minn. Bar Assn., Twelfth Dist. Bar Assn. (pres. 1995-96), Benson C. of C. (bd. dirs. 1981-84), Kiwanis (treas. Benson 1982-84, pres. 1999-00). Avocations: reading, golf, skiing. Commercial, contracts (including sales of goods; commercial financing), Probate (including wills, trusts), Property, real (including real estate development, water). Home: 604 13th St S Benson MN 56215-2017 Office: 1150 Wisconsin Ave Benson MN 56215-1841 E-mail: dwilcox@willmar.com.

WILCOX, JOHN CAVEN, lawyer, corporate consultant; b. N.Y.C., Nov. 12, 1942; s. Daniel A. and Jessie Alexandra (Caven) W.; m. Vanessa Guerrini-Maraldi, Sept. 30, 1983; children Daniel D.G., William G.M., Julia G.M. BA magna cum laude, Harvard U., 1964; MA, U. Calif., Berkeley, 1965; JD, Harvard U., 1968; LLM, NYU, 1981. Bar: N.Y. 1973. Account exec. Georgeson & Co. Inc., N.Y.C., 1973-79, mng. dir., 1979-90, chmn., 1990—99; vice chmn. Georgeson Shareholder Comm., Inc., 1999—. Dir. ACTV, Inc., GSC Proxitalia S.p.A.; bd. govs. Internat. Corp. Governance Network, chair ICGN com. on cross-border voting practices. Trustee Woodrow Wilson Nat. Fellowship Found., 1996, vice chmn., 1996—; trustee Bennington Coll., 1998—. With U.S. Army, 1968-70, Vietnam, trustee Family Dynamics, Inc., N.Y.C., 1979-1996. Woodrow Wilson fellow. Mem. ABA, NYSE (mem. shareholders comm. com. 1989-95), Am. Soc. Corp. Secs., Nat. Assn. Security Dealers (mem. issuer affairs com 1990—), The Brook, Downtown Assn., Harvard Club (N.Y.C.), Phi Beta Kappa. Democrat. Home: 580 West End Ave New York NY 10024-1723 E-mail: jwilcox@georgeson.com.

WILCOX, JON P. state supreme court justice; b. Berlin, Wis., Sept. 5, 1936; m. Jane Ann; children: Jeffrey, Jennifer. AB in Polit. Sci., Ripon Coll., 1958; JD, U. Wis., 1965. Pvt. practice Steele, Smyth, Klos and Flynn, LaCrosse, Wis., 1965-66, Hacker and Wilcox, Wautoma, Wis., 1966-69, Wilcox, Rudolph, Kubasta & Rathjen, Wautoma, 1969-79; mem. Wis. State Legislature, 1969—75; elected judge Waushara County Cir. Ct., 1979-92; apptd. justice Wis. Supreme Ct., 1992-97, elected justice 10-yr. term, 1997. Commr. Family Ct., Waushara County, 1977-79; Wis. state legislator, 1969-75; del. Wis. Conservation Congress, 1975-80; vice chmn., chmn. Wis. Sentencing Commn., 1984-92; chief judge 6th Jud. Dist., 1985-92; mem. State-Fed. Jud. Coun., 1992-99, Jud. Coun. Wis., 1993-98; mem. Prison Overcrowding Task Force, 1988-90; mem. numerous coms. Wis. Judiciary; mem. faculty Wis. Jud. Coll., 1986-97; chmn. Wis. Chief Judges Com., 1990-92; co-chair comm. on judiciary as co-equal br. of govt. Wis. State Bar, 1995-97; lectr. in field. Contbr. (with others): Wisconsin News Reporters Legal Handbook: Wisconsin Courts and Court Procedures, 1987. Bd. visitors U. Wis. Law Sch., 1970—76; del. Wis. Conservtion Congress,

1975—80. Lt. U.S. Army, 1959—61. Named Outstanding Jaycee Wautoma, 1974; recipient Disting. Alumni award Ripon Coll., 1993. Fellow Am. Bar Found.; mem. ABA (com. on continuing appellate edn.), Wis. Bar Assn. (bench bar com.), Wis. Law Found. (bd. dirs.), Tri-County Bar Assn., Dane County Bar Assn., Trout Unltd., Ducks Unltd., Rotary, Phi Alpha Delta. Office: Supreme Court State Capitol PO Box 1688 Madison WI 53701-1688

WILCOX, MARK DEAN, lawyer; b. May 25, 1952; s. Fabian Joseph and Zeryle Lucille (Tase) W.; m. Catherine J. Wertjes, Mar. 12, 1983; children: Glenna Lynn, Joanna Tessie, Andrew Fabian Joseph. BBA, U. Notre Dame, 1973; JD, Northwestern U., 1976; CLU, Am. Coll., 1979, ChFC, 1992. Bar: Ill. 1976, U.S. Dist. Ct. (no. dist.) Ill. 1976, Trial Bar 1982, U.S. Ct. Appeals (7th cir.) 1987, U.S. Supreme Ct. 1989. Staff asst. Nat. Dist. Attys. Assn., Chgo., 1974-75; trial asst. Cook County States Atty., Chgo., 1975; intern U.S. Atty. No. Dist. Ill., Chgo., 1975-76; assoc. Lord, Bissell & Brook, Chgo., 1976-85, ptnr., 1986—. Mem. YMCA Met. Chgo., Trinity United Meth. Ch., No Bats Baseball Club, Irving Park YMCA; venue ofcl. Internat. Spl. Olympics. Mem. ABA (tort and ins. practice sect.), Am. Soc. CLU and ChFC, Chgo. Bar Assn. (ins. law com.), Nat. Assn. Ins. and Fin. Advisors, Def. Rsch. Inst., Soc. Fin. Svc. Profls., Trial Lawyers Club Chgo., Notre Dame Nat. Monogram Club, Union League Club, Chgo. Lions Rugby Football Club, Beta Gamma Sigma. General civil litigation, Insurance, Professional liability. Office: Lord Bissell & Brook 115 S La Salle St Chicago IL 60603-3902

WILD, NELSON HOPKINS, lawyer; b. Milw., July 16, 1933; s. Henry Goetseels and Virginia Douglas (Weller) W.; m. Joan Ruth Miles, Apr. 12, 1969; children: Mark, Eric; m. Diana Morris, Sept. 7, 2002. AB, Princeton U., 1955; LL.B., U. Wis., 1961. Bar: Wis. 1962, Calif. 1967; cert. specialist in probate, estate planning and trust law State Bar of Calif. Research assoc. Wis. Legis. Council, Madison, 1955-56; assoc. Whyte, Hirschboeck, Minahan, Harding & Harland, Milw., 1961-67, Thelen, Marin, Johnson & Bridges, San Francisco, 1967-70; sole practice law San Francisco, 1970—. Mem. State Bar Calif. Client Trust Fund Commn., 1983, mem. exec. com. conf. dels., 1985-88. Contbr. articles to legal jours. Bd. dirs. Neighborhood Legal Assistance Found., San Francisco, 1974-85, chmn. bd., 1978-81. Served with USAF, 1956-58. Mem. ABA, Calif. Bar Assn., San Francisco Bar Assn., Am. Bar Found., Lawyers of San Francisco Club (gov. 1975, treas. 1981, v.p. 1982, pres.-elect 1983, pres. 1984), Calif. Tennis Club (bd. dirs. 1995-97, pres. 1997). Corporate, general, Estate planning, Probate (including wills, trusts). Office: 332 Pine St Ste 710 San Francisco CA 94104-3230

WILD, RICHARD P. lawyer; b. N.Y.C., Aug. 13, 1947; s. Alfred P. and Harriet C. (Hoffman) W.; m. Deirdre L. Felbin, June 15, 1969; children: Nicholas B., Daniel M. AB, Columbia U., 1968; JD, Yale U., 1971. Bar: Pa. 1971, U.S. Dist. Ct. (ea. dist.) Pa. 1971, U.S. Tax Ct. 1973, U.S. Claims Ct. 1977. Assoc. Dechert Price & Rhoads, Phila., 1971-78, ptnr., 1978—. Mem. Phila. Bar Assn. (tax sect.). Mergers and acquisitions, Corporate taxation, Taxation, general. Office: Dechert Price & Rhoads 4000 Bell Atlantic Tower 1717 Arch St Philadelphia PA 19103-2793

WILD, ROBERT WARREN, lawyer; b. Syracuse, N.Y., Mar. 25, 1942; s. Robert Sumner and Evelyn I. (Yorman) W.; m. Elizabeth Trowbridge, Sept. 5, 1965; children: Robert Mason, Alexander Lewis, Elizabeth Anne. BS, MIT, 1964; JD, Cornell U., 1970. Bar: N.Y. 1971, D.C. 1973. Engr. Smithsonian Astrophysical Obs., Cambridge, Mass., 1965-67; atty., advisor U.S. Dept. Justice, Washington, 1970-72; law clk. to Hon. Justice William H. Rehnquist U.S. Supreme Ct., Washington, 1972-73; ptnr. Nixon Peabody LLP, Rochester, N.Y., 1973—. Mem. Monroe County Bar Assn. (trustee 1990-91, 92-94, treas. 1992-94, counsel 1994—). Labor (including EEOC, Fair Labor Standards Act, labor-management relations, NLRB, OSHA), Pension, profit-sharing, and employee benefits, Taxation, general. Office: Nixon Peabody LLP Clinton Sq PO Box 31051 Rochester NY 14603-1051 E-mail: rwild@nixonpeabody.com.

WILDE, CARLTON D. lawyer, director; b. Houston, Apr. 11, 1935; s. Henry Dayton and Louise (Key) W.; m. Martha Cloyes, July 26, 1958; children: Carlton D. Jr., Jennifer. Student, Coll. of William and Mary, 1953-55; BA, U. Tex., 1957, JD, 1959. Assoc. Bracewell & Patterson, Houston, 1959-62, ptnr., 1962-67, 85—, mng. ptnr., 1967-85. Trustee Presbyn. Sch. Fellow Am. Bar Found., Tex. Bar Found., Houston Bar Found.; mem. ABA, State Bar Tex., River Oaks Country Club, Coronado Club (Houston), Biltmore Forest Country Club (Asheville, N.C.). Republican. Home: 3105 Reba Dr Houston TX 77019-6209 Office: Bracewell & Patterson 2900 S Tower Pennzoil Pl 711 Louisiana St Ste 2900 Houston TX 77002-2781 E-mail: cwilde@bracepatt.com.

WILDE, ROBERT, lawyer; b. Salt Lake City, Aug. 31, 1947; s. H. Gordon and Helen (Ross) W.; m. Deanne Henriksen, Feb. 13, 1973; 6 children. BS in Math., U. Utah, 1971; MA in Econs., U. N.H., 1977; JD, U. Utah, 1979. Bar: Utah 1979, U.S. Ct. Appeals (10th cir.). Pvt. practice, Salt Lake City. Mem. adv. com. on rules of evidence Utah Supreme Ct., 1991—; mem. admissions com. Utah State Bar, 2001—. Contbr. articles to profl. jours. Asst. dist. chmn. Boy Scouts Am., Salt Lake City, 1996-97, explorer scout leader, 1992-96, scoutmaster, 1989-92, 2001—. Col. USAFR, 1971-2001. Mem. ATLA, Utah Employment Lawyers Assn. (pres. 1994-96), Utah Trial Lawyers Assn. (pres. 1980-81, bd. govs. 1979-95), Nat. Employment Lawyers Assn. Labor (including EEOC, Fair Labor Standards Act, labor-management relations, NLRB, OSHA), Personal injury (including property damage). Office: PO Box 71922 Salt Lake City UT 84171-0922

WILDE, WILLIAM KEY, lawyer; b. Houston, May 3, 1933; s. Henry Dayton and Louise (Key) W.; m. Ann Jeannine Austin, Aug. 3, 1957; children— William Key, Austin, Adrienne, Michael AB, Coll. William and Mary, Williamsburg, Va., 1955; JD, U. Tex., Austin, 1958. Bar: Tex. 1958. Assoc. Bracewell & Patterson, Houston, 1958-61, ptnr., 1961—. Bd. dirs. Goodwill Industries Houston, 1972—; elder 1st Presbyn. Ch.; trustee Presbyn. Found. U.S.A., Ky., 1983-91; chmn. bd. trustees Schriener Coll., 1991-2000. Fellow ABA, Am. Bar Found., Am. Coll. Trial Lawyers; mem. Tex. Bar Assn. (bd. dirs. 1984-87), Houston Bar Assn. (pres. 1982-83), Houston Club (pres. 1981-82), Houston Country Club (bd. dirs., pres. 1989-90). Republican. Avocations: golf, skiing, scuba diving. Federal civil litigation, General civil litigation, State civil litigation. Home: 6206 Woods Bridge Way Houston TX 77007-7041 Office: Bracewell & Patterson 2900 S Tower Pennzoil Place Houston TX 77002

WILDE, WILLIAM RICHARD, lawyer; b. Markesan, Wis., Mar. 1, 1953; s. Leslie Maurice and Elaine Margaret (Schweder) W.; m. Carolyn Margaret Zieman, July 17, 1981 (div. 1987); 1 child, Leah Marie; m. Barbara Joan Rohlf, Jan. 6, 1990. BA, U. Wis., Milw., 1975; JD, Marquette U., 1980. Bar: Wis. 1980, U.S. Dist. Ct. (ea. and we. dists.) Wis. 1980. Dist. atty. Green Lake County, Green Lake, Wis., 1980—83, corp. counsel, 1981; ptnr. Curtis, Wilde and Neal, Oshkosh, Wis., 1983—97, Wilde Law Offices, LLC, Oshkosh, 1997—. Mem. ATLA, Wis. Bar Assn., Wis. Acad. Trial Lawyers (Amicus Curiae Brief com. 1987-92, bd. dirs., assoc. editor The Verdict, treas. 1993, sec. 1994, v.p. 1995, pres.-elect 1996, pres. 1997), Winnebago County Bar Assn., Green Lake County Bar Assn. Personal injury (including property damage), Alternative dispute resolution, Professional liability. Office: Wilde Law Offices LLC 600 S Main St 2d Fl PO Box 3422 Oshkosh WI 54903-3422 also: PO Box 282 Markesan WI 53946-0282 E-mail: wildelaw@expc.com.

WILDER, JAMES SAMPSON, III, lawyer, judge; b. Knoxville, Tenn., Mar. 15, 1949; s. James Sampson and Florence Louise (Summers) W. BS, Lambuth Coll., Jackson, Tenn., 1971; JD, Memphis State U., 1974. Bar: Tenn. 1974, U.S. Dist. Ct. (we. dist.) Tenn. 1975, U.S. Supreme Ct. 1981, U.S. Ct. Appeals (6th cir.) 1982. Assoc. Lt. Gov. John S. Wilder, Somerville, Tenn., 1974-75, ptnr., 1975-76, Wilder, Wilder & Johnson, Somerville, 1976-83; pvt. practice James S. Wilder III, Somerville, 1983-95; gen. sessions judge Fayette County, Somerville, 1985-90; assoc. Petkoff and Lancaster, Memphis, 1995—2000; pvt. practice Somerville, 2000—02; atty. Law Office of John M. Lannom, Dyersburg, Tenn., 2002—. Scoutmaster troop 95 Boy Scouts Am., Somerville, 1975-77, com. person, 1977—. Paul Harris fellow Rotary, Somerville, 1977. Mem. ABA, Assn. Trial Lawyers Am., Tenn. Bar Assn., Tenn. Trial Lawyers Assn. (dir. 1983-86), Fayette County C. of C. (dir. 1979—), Somerville Rotary (dir. 1976—, charter pres. 1976-78). Methodist. Avocations: hunting, fishing. Federal civil litigation, State civil litigation, Personal injury (including property damage). Home: PO Box 342 Dyersburg TN 38025 Office: 422 McGaughey St PO Box 1729 Dyersburg TN 38024

WILDER, MICHAEL STEPHEN, former insurance company executive; b. New Haven, Conn., Sept. 8, 1941; BA, Yale U., 1963; JD, Harvard U., 1966. Bar: Conn. 1966. Atty. Hartford (Conn.) Fire Ins. Co., 1967-69, asst. gen. counsel, 1969-71, assoc. gen. counsel, 1971-75, gen. coun., sec., 1975-87, sr. v.p., gen. counsel, sec., 1987-95; sr. v.p., gen. counsel The Hartford Fin. Svcs. Group, Inc., 1995—2001; ret., 2001. Mem. ABA, Conn. Bar Assn.*

WILDER, WILLIAM F. lawyer; b. Prescott, Ariz., Aug. 29, 1938; s. Carleton Stafford and Judith (Carlock) W.; m. Liisa Wilder, Oct. 18, 1975; children: Rebecca Files, Andrew. BS in Bus. Adminstrn., U. Ariz., 1962, LLB, 1964. Bar: Ariz. 1964. Atty., shareholder Ryley, Carlock & Applewhite, Phoenix, 1964—. Bd. dirs., chmn. Ariz. Heart Assn., 1977-83; trustee Desert Bot. Garden, Phoenix, 1996—; bd. dirs. Arizonans for Cultural Devel., 1994-2000, Phoenix Cmty. Alliance, 1993—. Served with USN, 1956-58. Mem. Nat. Assn. Bond Attys. Avocations: fishing, hiking, camping, tennis, skiing, travel. Corporate, general, Finance, Property, real (including real estate development, water).

WILDEROTTER, JAMES ARTHUR, lawyer; b. Newark, July 25, 1944; s. Arthur Walter and Dorothy Theresa (King) W.; m. Cheryl Lynn Clifford; children: James, Kristin, Kathryn. BA, Georgetown U., 1966; JD, U. Ill., 1969. Bar: D.C. 1969, U.S. Supreme Ct. 1974. Assoc. Covington & Burling, Washington, 1969-71; spl. asst. to Under Sec. Commerce, Washington, 1971-73; exec. asst. to Sec. HUD, Washington, 1973-74; assoc. dept. atty. gen. U.S. Washington, 1974-75; assoc. counsel to Pres. U.S., 1975-76; gen. counsel U.S. Energy Research and Devel. Adminstrn., Washington, 1976-77; of counsel Morgan, Lewis & Bockius, Washington, 1977-78; ptnr. Jones, Day, Reavis & Pogue, Washington, 1978-91, 95—; v.p., gen. counsel Internat. Paper Co., Purchase, N.Y., 1991-94. Editor in chief: U. Ill. Law Rev., 1968-69. Gen. counsel rules com. Rep. Nat. Conv., 1980; sec. James S. Brady Presdl. Found., 1982-88; gen. counsel Nat. Sudden Infant Death Syndrome Found., 1986-90, sec. Sudden Infant Death Syndrome Alliance, 1990-93. With USN, 1962-68. Mem. ABA Republican. Roman Catholic. Administrative and regulatory, Corporate, general. Home: 518 Duke St Alexandria VA 22314-3738 Office: Jones Day Reavis and Pogue 51 Louisiana Ave NW Washington DC 20001-2113

WILDMAN, MAX EDWARD, lawyer, director; b. Terre Haute, Ind., Dec. 4, 1919; s. Roscoe Ellsworth and Lena (Shaw) W.; m. Joyce Lenore Smith, Sept. 25, 1948; children: Leslie, William. BS, Butler U., 1941; JD, U. Mich., 1947; MBA, U. Chgo., 1952. Bar: Ill., Ind. Ptnr. Kirkland & Ellis, Chgo., 1947-67; mng. ptnr. Wildman, Harrold, Allen & Dixon, Chgo., 1967-89. Dir. Colt Industries, N.Y., Nat. Blvd. Bank, Ill. Contbr. articles to profl. jours. Trustee Butler U., Indpls., Lake Forest Hosp., Ill., Lake Bluff Library Bd., Ill.; chmn. Lake Bluff Zoning Bd. Served to lt. col. USAF, 1943-46; PTO Fellow Am. Coll. Trial Lawyers; mem. Soc. Trial Lawyers, Law Club, Legal Club, Trial Lawyers Club of Chgo. Clubs: Anglers (Chgo.), Pere Marquette Rod and Gun (Baldwin, Mich.), Shoreacres (Lake Bluff), Univ. of Chgo. Presbyterian. Antitrust, Federal civil litigation, State civil litigation. Office: Wildman Harrold Allen & Dixon 225 W Wacker Dr Chicago IL 60606-1224

WILEMAN, GEORGE ROBERT, lawyer; b. Ironton, Ohio, June 1, 1938; s. George Merchant and Marguerite (McCormick) W.; children: John Chandler, Julie Jo. AB, Duke U., 1960; JD, Georgetown U., 1963. Bar: Ohio 1968, Tex. 1977, U.S. Supreme Ct. 1993. Pvt. practice, Dallas, 1977—. Republican. Personal injury (including property damage), Professional liability. Home: 16143 Chalfont Cir Dallas TX 75248-3563 Address: # 445 15301 Spectrum Dr Addison TX 75001-4665

WILENSKY, SAUL, lawyer; b. Bklyn., Dec. 9, 1941; s. Morris and Pearl (Wagman) W.; m. Sandra J. Brunault, Nov. 11, 1979; 1 child, Margot. BA, Hunter Coll., 1963; LLB, St. John's U., Bklyn., 1966; LLM, NYU, 1976. Bar: N.Y. 1967, U.S. Dist. Ct. (ea. and so. dists.) N.Y. 1970, U.S. Supreme Ct. 1971, U.S. Ct. Appeals (2d cir.) 1973, U.S. Dist. Ct. (no. dist.) N.Y. 1974. Ptnr. Lester, Schwab, Katz & Dwyer, NYC, 1973—. Mem.: N.Y. State Bar Assn. (chair TICL 2000—01). State civil litigation, Personal injury (including property damage), Product liability. Office: Lester Schwab Katz & Dwyer 120 Broadway Fl 39 New York NY 10271-0002 E-mail: swilensky@lskdnylaw.com.

WILES, CHRISTOPHER, lawyer; b. Syracuse, N.Y., Mar. 18, 1943; s. Ben and Harriet Elizabeth (Brace) W.; m. Renée Arteaga Wiles, July 26, 1969; children: Allegra Cristina, Emilia Maxwell. BA cum laude, Princeton U., 1965; JD, Cornell U., 1971. Bar: N.Y. 1972, Minn. 1973, U.S. Dist. Ct. (no. dist.) N.Y. 1976. Peace corps volunteer, Montevideo, Uruguay, 1965-67; teaching fellow Latin Am. Teaching Fellowship, Caracas, Venezuela, 1971-73; gen. counsel Data 100 Corp., Mpls., 1974-75; pvt. practice Wiles & Wiles, Syracuse, N.Y., 1975-2001; asst. atty. gen. N.Y. State Atty. Gen., Syracuse, 2001—. Bd. dirs. Alzheimers Assn. Central N.Y., Syracuse, N.Y. 1988-93, Hiscock Legal Aid Soc., Syracuse, 1981-90; sch. bd. mem. Marcellus, N.Y. 1981-86, 90-96. Mem. Onondaga County Bar Assn., Onondaga County Bar Found., N.Y. State Bar Assn. Democrat. Avocations: tennis, canoeing, basketball. General civil litigation, General practice, Probate (including wills, trusts). Home: 305 Sedgwick Dr Syracuse NY 13203-1314 Office: Asst NY State Atty Gen Syracuse Regional Office 615 Erie Blvd W Ste 100 Syracuse NY 13204

WILEY, RICHARD ARTHUR, lawyer; b. Bklyn., July 18, 1928; s. Arthur Ross and Anna Thorsen (Holder) W.; m. Carole Jean Smith, Aug. 13, 1955; children: Kendra Elizabeth, Stewart Alan, Garett Smith. AB, Bowdoin Coll., Brunswick, Maine, 1948; BCL, Oxford (Eng.) U., 1951; LLM, Harvard U., 1959; LLD, Bowdoin Coll., 1994. Bar: Mass. 1954, U.S. Ct. Mil. Appeals 1954, U.S. Dist. Ct. Mass. 1962, U. S. Supreme Ct. 1985. Atty. John Hancock Mut. Life Ins. Co., Boston, 1956-58; from atty. to mng. ptnr. Bingham, Dana & Gould, Boston, 1959-76; gen. counsel, asst. sec. Dept. Def., 1976-77; v.p., counsel First Nat. Bank Boston, 1977-78, exec. v.p., 1978-85, Bank of Boston Corp., 1985; ptnr. Csaplar & Bok, Boston, 1986-90, mem. exec. com., 1987-90, chmn., 1989-90, of counsel, 1990, Gaston & Snow, Boston, 1990-91; dir. Powers and Hall P.C., Boston, 1991-94, of counsel, 1994-95, Hill & Barlow, Boston, 1995—2002, Foley & Hoag LLP , Boston, 2002—. Bd. dirs., chmn. Automated Assemblies Corp., Mass. Higher Edn. Assistance Corp.; bd. dirs. Edn. Rsch. Inst., Microwave Device Tech. Corp., Nomadic Structures, Inc., Nypro, Inc., Carlo Gavazzi Mupac, Inc.; lectr. Boston U. Law Sch., 1961-64; past vice chmn. New Eng. Conf. on Doing Bus. Abroad; trustee New Eng. Legal Found., chmn., 1980-83; adj. prof. govt. and legal studies Bowdoin Coll., 1995-2002; adj. prof. law Boston Coll. Law Sch., 1998—. Author: Cases and Materials on Law of International Trade and Investment, 1961; contbr. articles to profl. jours. Bd. overseers Bowdoin Coll., 1966-81, pres., 1977-80, trustee, 1981-93, trustee emeritus, 1993—; mem. Mass. Edn. Financing Authority, 1986-91, chmn., 1987-91; mem. Wellesley (Mass.) Town Meeting, 1971-75, mem. fin. adv. com., 1973-74; chmn. Mass. Bd. Regents of Higher Edn., 1991; bd. regents Task Force on Student Fin. Aid, 1987; mem. Mass. Higher Edn. Coord. Coun., 1991-95, vice chmn., 1991-93, chmn., 1993-95; chmn. lawyers divsn. United Way Mass. Bay, 1975; mem. devel. com., trustees of donations Episcopal Diocese Mass., 1971-75; trustee, exec. com. North Conway Inst., mem., 1980-92, chmn., 1988-92; bd. trustees Internat. Coun. Trust, Boston; trustee, mem. exec. com., chmn. Mass. Taxpayers Found., 1989-92; chmn. bd. trustees World Peace Found., Boston, 1983-95; corporator Schepens Eye Rsch. Inst., 1991-95; dep. chmn. planning Mass. rep. state com., 1971, vice chmn. fin. com., 1971-72. Officer USAF, 1953-56. Decorated Air Force Commendation medal; recipient Dep. Def. Disting. Pub. Svc. medal, 1977; Rhodes scholar, 1949. Mem. ABA (vice chmn. fgn. and internat. bus. law com. 1967-69), Boston Bar Assn. (exec. com., antitrust com. 1965-68), Council on Fgn. Relations, Boston Com. on Fgn. Relations (mem. exec. com., chmn. 1980-83), Phi Beta Kappa. Banking, Corporate, general, Finance.

WILEY, RICHARD EMERSON, lawyer; b. Peoria, Ill., July 20, 1934; s. Joseph Henry and Jean W. (Farrell) W.; m. Elizabeth J. Edwards, Aug. 6, 1960; children: Douglas S., Pamela L. BS with distinction, Northwestern U., 1955, JD, 1958; LLM, Georgetown U., 1962; LLD (hon.) , Cath. U. of Am., 1998. Bar: Ill. 1958, D.C. 1972. Pvt. practice, Chgo., 1962-70; gen. counsel FCC, Washington, 1970-72, mem., 1972-74, chmn., 1974-77, chmn. FCC's adv. com. on advanced TV svc., 1987-96; mng. ptnr. Wiley, Rein & Fielding, Washington, 1983—. Prof. law John Marshall Law Sch., U. Chgo., 1963-70. Chmn. bd. Media Inst., 1999—, Inst. for Tele-Info., Columbia U., 1997—. Capt. AUS, 1959-62. Recipient Emmy award Nat. Acad. Arts, 1997, Medal of Honor, Electronic Industries Am., 1996, Disting. Svc. award Nat. Assn. Broadcasters, 2002. Fellow: Am. Bar Found.; mem.: ABA (ho. of dels. 1969—71, 1977—84, chmn. young lawyers sect. 1977—84, chmn. Forum com. on comm. 1969, chmn. bd. editors ABA Jour. 1984—89, chmn. com. on scope and correlation of work 1989, chmn. adminstrv. law and regulatory practice 1993—94), Adminstrv. Conf. U.S. (coun., sr. fellow), Chgo. Bar Assn., Ill. Bar Assn., Fed. Comm. Bar Assn. (pres. 1987), Fed. Bar Assn. (pres. 1977), Phi Delta Kappa, Phi Delta Phi. Methodist. Communications. Home: 3818 N Woodrow St Arlington VA 22207-4345 Office: Wiley Rein & Fielding 1776 K St NW Ste 1100 Washington DC 20006-2332 E-mail: rwiley@wrf.com.

WILEY, ROBERT JOSEPH, lawyer; b. Lafayette, Ind., May 10, 1973; s. John Robert and Stephanie (Ferrante) Wiley. BS, Vanderbilt U., Nashville, 1996; JD, Tulane U., New Orleans, 1999. Bar: Tex. 1999, D.C. 2000, Calif. 2000. Law clk. Entergy Svcs., Inc., New Orleans, 1998—99; assoc. Bacher Assocs., Dallas, 2000; pres. Rob Wiley, P.C., Dallas, 2000—. Mem.: ATLA, Nat. Employment Lawyers Assn., Dallas Gay and Lesbian Bar Assn. (pres. 1999—2002), Stonewall Profl. Assn. (dir. 2001—02). Civil rights, Labor (including EEOC, Fair Labor Standards Act, labor-management relations, NLRB, OSHA). Office: Rob Wiley PC 3131 Turtle Creek Blvd #650 Dallas TX 75219

WILF, FREDERIC MARSHAL, lawyer; b. Phila., Mar. 3, 1959; s. Leonard R. and Phyllis Hope Wilf; m. Shirley Ann Segal; children: Chelsea Sarah, Robert Ethan. BA, Rutgers U., 1982; JD, Case Western Res. U., 1985. Bar: Pa. 1985, N.J. 1985, U.S. Dist. Ct. N.J. 1985, U.S. Dist. Ct. (ea. dist.) Pa. 1986, U.S. Dist. Ct. (middle dist.) Pa. 1992, U.S. Ct. Appeals (3d cir.) 1986, U.S. Ct. Appeals (Fed. cir.) 1989, U.S. Supreme Ct. 1989. Cons. atty. Bell Tel. Co. of Pa., Phila., 1985-86; assoc. Rapp, White, Janssen & German, Phila., 1986, Elman Assocs., Phila., 1986-88, Lipton, Famiglio & Elman, Media, Pa., 1988-89; ptnr. Elman Wilf & Fried, Media, 1990-95; spl. counsel Saul, Ewing, Remick & Saul LLP, Berwyn, Pa., 1995-99, Morgan, Lewis & Bockius LLP, Phila., 1999—. Mem. ABA, Internat. Trademark Assn., Copyright Soc. Am., Licensing Execs. Soc., Entrepreneurs Forum, Phila. Bar Assn., Computer Law Assn., Phila. Area New Media Assn., Phila. Intellectual Property Law Assn., Assn. for Computing Machinery, Electronic Frontier Found., Am. Civil Liberties Union. Democrat. Jewish. Avocation: photography. Commercial, contracts (including sales of goods; commercial financing), Computer, Intellectual property. Office: Morgan Lewis & Bockius LLP 1701 Market St Philadelphia PA 19103-2921 E-mail: fwilf@morganlewis.com.

WILFONG, HUGH C., II, lawyer; b. Waco, Tex., Feb. 6, 1942; BA, Baylor U., 1964; LLB, U. Tex., 1967. Bar: Tex. 1967. Lawyer Vinson & Elkins LLP, Houston. Mem. Chancellors, Order of Coif, Phi Delta Phi. Health, Joint ventures. Office: Vinson & Elkins 2500 First City Tower 1001 Fannin St Ste 3300 Houston TX 77002-6706 Home: 710 Saddlewood Ln Houston TX 77024

WILHELM, ROBERT OSCAR, lawyer, civil engineer, developer; b. Balt., July 7, 1918; s. Clarence Oscar and Agnes Virginia (Grimm) W.; m. Grace Sanborn Luckie, Apr. 4, 1959. BSCE, Ga. Tech. Inst., 1947, MSIM, 1948; JD, Stanford U., 1951. Bar: Calif. 1952, U.S. Supreme Ct. Mem. Wilhelm, Thompson, Redwood City, Calif., 1952—92; gen. counsel Bay Counties Gen. Contractors; pvt. practice civil engring., Redwood City, 1952. Pres. Bay Counties Builders Escrow, Inc., 1972-88. Author: The Manual of Procedures for the Construction Industry, 1971, Manual of Procedures and Form Book for Construction Industry, 9th edit., 1995, Construction Law for Contractors, Architects and Engineers; columnist Law and You in Daily Pacific Builder, 1955-2001. With C.E., AUS, 1942-46. Named to Wisdom Hall of Fame, 1999. Mem. Bay Counties Civil Engrs. (pres. 1957), Peninsula Builders Exch. (pres. 1958-71, dir.), Calif. State Builders Exch. (treas. 1971), Del Mesa Carmel Cmty. Assn. (bd. dirs. 1997-99), Masons, Odd Fellows, Eagles, Elks. Construction, Government contracts and claims. Home: 134 Del Mesa Carmel Carmel CA 93923-7950 Office: 600 Allerton St Ste 202 Redwood City CA 94083

WILKEN, CLAUDIA, judge; b. Mpls., Aug. 17, 1949; BA with honors, Stanford U., 1971; JD, U. Calif., Berkeley, 1975. Bar: Calif. 1975, U.S. Dist. Ct. (no. dist.) Calif. 1975, U.S. Ct. Appeals (9th cir.) 1976, U.S. Supreme Ct. 1981. Asst. fed. pub. defender U.S. Dist. Ct. (no. dist.) Calif., San Francisco, 1975-78, U.S. magistrate judge, 1983-93, dist. judge, 1993—; ptnr. Wilken & Leverett, Berkeley, Calif., 1978-84. Adj. prof. U. Calif., Berkeley, 1978-84; prof. New Coll. Sch. Law, 1980-85; mem. jud. br. com. Jud. Conf. U.S.; past mem. edn. com. Fed. Jud. Ctr.; chair 9th cir. Magistrates Conf., 1987-88. Mem. ABA (mem. jud. adminstrn. divsn.), Alameda County Bar Assn. (judge's membership), Nat. Assn. Women Judges, Order of Coif, Phi Beta Kappa. Office: US Dist Ct No Dist 1301 Clay St # 2 Oakland CA 94612-5217

WILKERSON, JAMES NEILL, retired lawyer; b. Tyler, Tex., Dec. 17, 1939; s. Hubert Cecil and Vida (Alexander) W.; m. Cal Cantrell; children: Cody, Ike; stepchildren: Janet, Joseph. AA, Tyler Jr. Coll., 1960; BBA, U. Tex., 1966, JD, 1968. Bar: Tex. 1968, U.S. Supreme Ct. 1973, U.S. Dist. Ct. (we. dist.) Tex. 1974. Pvt. practice, Georgetown and Mason, Tex., 1977-2001; ret., 2001. Instr. Cen. Tex. Coll., Copperas Cove, Tex., 1973-74; asst prof. law U.S. Mil. Acad., West Point, N.Y., 1971-73; pres. C&N Bus. Developers, 1992-95. Pres. Beautify Georgetown Assn., 1977-80, 81-82; pres. U. Tex. Young Reps., 1964-65; co-chmn. Bush for Pres., 1988, Reagan-Bush campaign, 1988; mem. Williamson County Rep. Com., 1977-81; chmn. Hist. Preservation Com., 1979-85; trustee 1st United Meth. Ch., 1994-95, chmn. bd. trustees, 1996-99; vol. Mason Lions Club, Steady Steps After Sch. Homework Helper; substitute tchr. Mason Schs.; vol. Sage Meml. Hosp., Navajo Health Found., Granada, Ariz., 2001-02. Col. USAR, 1968, trial judge JAGC, 1975-91, appellate judge Army Ct. Mil. Rev., 1991-93, ret. 1992. Decorated Legion of Merit, Bronze Star, Air medal.

Mem. Tex. State Bar Coll., Williamson County Bar Assn., Sertoma (v.p. 1981-83, 87, sec. 1988-89, pres. 1992-93), Lions (pres. 1982-83), Vietnam War Vets. Estate planning, Probate (including wills, trusts). Address: PO Box 1807 Mason TX 76856-1807

WILKINS, MICHAEL JON, state supreme court justice; b. Murray, Utah, May 13, 1948; s. Jack L. and Mary June (Phillips) W.; m. Diane W. Wilkins, Nov. 9, 1967; children: Jennifer, Stephanie, Bradley J. BS, U. Utah, 1975, JD, 1976; LLM, U. Va., 2001. Bar: Utah 1977, U.S. Dist. Ct. Utah 1977, U.S. Ct. Appeals (10th cir.) 1987, U.S. Supreme Ct. 1986. Mng. ptnr. Wilkins, Oritt & Headman, Salt Lake City, 1989-94; judge Utah Ct. Appeals, 1994—2000; justice Utah Supreme Ct, 2000—, mem. jud. coun., 2000—. Mem. Gov.'s Adv. Com. on Corp., Salt Lake City, 1989-94; mem. Utah Supreme Ct. Complex Steering Com., 1993-94; mem. Judiciary Standing Com. on Tech., 1995-2000, chmn., 1995-2000; mem. Legis. Compensation Commn., 1994-95. Trustee Utah Law Related Edn. Project, Inc., Salt Lake City, 1991-95, chmn., 1992-94. 1st lt. U.S. Army, 1968-72. Mem. Lds Ch. Office: Utah Supreme Ct 450 S State St PO Box 140210 Salt Lake City UT 84114-0210

WILKINS, WILLIAM WALTER, federal judge; b. Anderson, S.C., Mar. 29, 1942; s. W. Walter Wilkins and Evelyn Louise (Horton); m. Debra Ann Dill, Aug. 16, 1964; children: Lauren, Lyn, Walt. BA, Davidson Coll., 1964; JD, U. S.C., 1967. Bar: S.C. 1967, U.S. Dist. Ct. S.C. 1967, U.S. Ct. Appeals (4th cir.) 1969, U.S. Supreme Ct. 1970. Law clk. to Hon. Clement F. Haynsworth Jr. U.S. Ct. Appeals (4th cir.), 1969—70; legal asst. to U.S. Senator Strom Thurmond, 1970—71; ptnr. Wilkins & Wilkins, Greenville, SC, 1971—78; solicitor 13th Jud. Cir., 1974—81; judge U.S. Dist. Ct., Greenville, 1981—86, U.S. Ct. Appeals (4th cir.), 1986—, chief judge, 2003—. Lectr. Greenville Tech. Coll., 1973—97; chmn. U.S. Sentencing Commn., 1985—94; chmn. com. on criminal law Jud. Conf. U.S., 2000—03. Editor-in-chief : S.C. Law Rev., 1967; contbr. articles to profl. jours. With U.S. Army, 1967—69, with USAR, 1969—83, with S.C. Army Nat. Guard, 1983—94. Mem.: S.C. Bar Assn., Wig and Robe. Republican. Baptist. Office: US Cir Ct 4th Ct PO Box 10857 Greenville SC 29603-0857

WILKINSON, ALBERT MIMS, JR., lawyer; b. Nashville, June 29, 1925; s. Albert Mims and Mary Nelle (Derryberry) W.; m. Edythe Bush, Mar. 27, 1953 (div.); children: William Terry, Elizabeth Ann, David Bush; m. Dolores Jean Attard, Oct. 22, 1971 (div.); 1 child, Mary Dolores. Student, Emory U., 1942-43; JD, U. Ga., 1949. Bar: Ga. 1948. Pvt. practice law, Atlanta, 1950-85; gen. counsel GEC-Marconi Avionics Inc., Atlanta, 1985-98; hon. legal adviser to Brit. Consul Gen. at Atlanta. Author: The Winning of the Revolutionary War in the South, 1976, The Rights of Unsecured Creditors-The Law in Georgia, 1979. Mem. DeKalb County Bd. Elections, 1966-72; chmn. 4th Congl. Dist. Republican Exec. Com., 1968-70, Ga. State Rep. Exec. Com., 1968-74; 1st vice chmn. Ga. Rep. Party, 1972-74, asst. gen. counsel, 1974-75; vice chmn., trustee Atlanta Counseling Center, Inc., 1960-83. Served with USCGR, 1943-46. Decorated Order Brit. Empire. Fellow Comml. Law Found.; mem. BA, Ga. Bar Assn., Atlanta Bar Assn., Ga. Soc. (pres. 1962-63), SAR, Southeastern Mem.'s Assn. (pres. 1960-61), Comml. Law League Am., Ga. Soc. Colonial Wars, Old Guard of Gate City Guard (comdt. 1986), N.C. Soc. of Cincinnati, Sphinx Club, Gridiron Club, Commerce Club, Civitan, Masons, Blue Key, Omicron Delta Kappa. Baptist. Home and Office: 66 Demorest Ln # 333 Sky Valley GA 30537-2581 E-mail: amims@hemc.net.

WILKINSON, JAMES ALLAN, lawyer, healthcare executive; b. Cumberland, Md., Feb. 10, 1945; s. John Robinson and Dorothy Jane (Kelley) W.; m. Elizabeth Susanne Quinlan, Apr. 14, 1973; 1 child, Kathryn Barrett. BS in Fgn. Svc., Georgetown U., 1967; JD, Duquesne U., 1978; MA, U Pitts., 2001. Bar: Pa., U.S. Dist. Ct. (we. dist.) Pa. Legis. analyst Office of Mgmt. and Budget, Washington, 1972-73; dep. exec. sec. Cost of Living Coun., Washington, 1973-74; sr. fin. analyst U.S. Steel Corp., Pitts., 1974-82; ptnr. Buchanan Ingersoll, Pitts., 1982-88; exec. v.p., gen. counsel Meritcare, Pitts., 1988—; sr. v.p. Culwell Health Inc., 1991—2001. Adj. prof. U. Pitts. Sch. Law, 1988-91. Author: Financing and Refinancing Under Prospective Payment, 1985, Family Caregivers' Guide Planning and Decision Making for the Elderly, 1998; contbr. articles to profl. jours. Chmn. Oversight Com. on Organ Transplantation, Pitts., 1986–; sec.-treas. bd. dirs. Pitts. Symphony Soc., 1986-98, exec. com. bd. dirs., 1999-2002; bd. dirs. Western Pa. Com. of Prevention of Child Abuse, 1987-90, Comprehensive Safety Compliance, 1988-91, Buchanan Ingersoll Profl. corp., 1988-90, Parental Stress Ctr., 1990-94; sec. Ross Mountain Club, 1995-98, 99—, v.p., 1999-2001, pres., 2001—; exec. com. and bd. dirs. Carnegie Inst., 1997—, Carnegie Mus. Natural History, 1997—, Andy Warhol Mus., 1998—, Soc. for Contemporary Craft, 1999—, treas., 2000-01, v.p., 2001-02, pres., 2002—. Mem. Am. Health Lawyers Assn., Audubon Soc. Southwestern Pa. (treas. 1996-2000), Duquesne Club. Republican. Episcopalian. Corporate, general, Health, Mergers and acquisitions. Home: 1005 Elmhurst Rd Pittsburgh PA 15215-1819 Office: Meritcare Inc 2020 Ardmore Blvd Ste 335 Pittsburgh PA 15221 E-mail: wilkinso@bellatlantic.net.

WILKINSON, JAMES HARVIE, III, federal judge; b. N.Y.C., Sept. 29, 1944; s. James Harvie and Letitia (Nelson) W.; m. Lossie Grist Noell, June 30, 1973; children: James Nelson, Porter Noell. BA, Yale U., 1963-67; JD, U. Va., 1972, U. Richmond, 1997, U. S.C., 1998, Christopher Newport U., 2003. Bar: Va. 1972. Law clk. to U.S. Supreme Ct. Justice Lewis F. Powell, Jr., Washington, 1972-73; asst. prof. law U. Va., 1973-75, assoc. prof., 1975-78; editor Norfolk (Va.) Virginian-Pilot, 1978-81; prof. law U. Va., 1981-82, 83-84; dep. asst. atty. gen. Civil Rights div. Dept. Justice, 1982-83; judge U.S. Ct. Appeals (4th cir.), 1984—, chief judge, 1996—2003. Author: Harry Byrd and the Changing Face of Virginia Politics, 1968, Serving Justice: A Supreme Court Clerk's View, 1974, From Brown to Bakke: The Supreme Court and School Integration, 1979, One Nation Indivisible: How Ethnic Separatism Threatens America, 1997. Bd. Visitors U. Va., 1970-73; Republican candidate for Congress from 3d Dist. V a., 1970; bd. dirs. Fed. Jud. Ctr., 1992-96. Served with U.S. Army, 1968-69. Mem. Va. State Bar, Va. Bar Assn., Am. Law Inst. Episcopalian. Home: 1713 Yorktown Dr Charlottesville VA 22901-3035 Office: US Ct Appeals 255 W Main St Ste 230 Charlottesville VA 22902-5058

WILKINSON, JOHN HART, lawyer; b. Newton, Mass., Dec. 31, 1940; s. Roger Melvin and Margaret (Carter) Wilkinson; children: Heather, Carter. BA, Williams Coll., 1962; LLB, Fordham U., 1965. Bar: N.Y. 1965, U.S. Dist. Ct. (so. and ea. dists.) N.Y. 1968, U.S. Ct. Appeals (2d cir.) 1981, U.S. Ct. Appeals (11th cir.) 1982, U.S. Ct. Appeals (3d cir.) 1984, U.S. Ct. Appeals (5th cir.) 1987. Assoc. Donovan, Leisure, Newton & Irvine, N.Y.C., 1965, 67-73, ptnr., 1973-98, editor, contbg. author to firm's ADR Practice Book, 1990; law clk. to presiding justice U.S. Dist. Ct. (so. dist.) N.Y., 1967-68; of counsel Fulton, Rowe & Hart, N.Y.C., 1998—. Spkr. in field. Contbr. articles to profl. jours. Bd. dirs., pres. Childfind Am., Inc., 1993—94; vol. learning disabled children Chelsea Neighborhood, N.Y.C., 1965—67; v.p. bd. dirs. Pelham (N.Y.) Family Svc., 1982—85; bd. dirs. Catskill Ctr. Conservation and Devel., 1993—. Recipient Am. Jurisprudence award, Fordham U. Mem.: ABA (mem. alt. dispute resolution com. 1989—93), Assn. Bar City N.Y. (mem. profl. responsibility com. 1987—89, mem. pub. assistance com. 1991—94), N.Y. State Bar Assn. (mem. alt. dispute resolution com. 1989—93). Avocations: woodworking, fly fishing, bicycling, camping. Alternative dispute resolution, Federal civil litigation, State civil litigation. Office: Fulton Rowe & Hart One Rockefeller Plz New York NY 10020

WILKINSON, LESTER F., JR., lawyer; b. Mass., Nov. 12, 1956; BA, Bates Coll., 1978; JD, U. San Diego, 1981. Bar: Maine 1981, U.S. Dist. Ct. Maine 1981. Mng. shareholder Bernstein, Shur, Sawyer & Nelson, PA, Augusta, Maine. Instr. real estate law U. Maine, Augusta, 1988—89. Bd. dirs. Children's Ctr., 1990—93, pres., 1994; bd. dirs. Maine Gen. Health Assocs., 1997—2000. Mem.: Kennebec County Bar Assn., Maine State Bar Assn. (bd. govs., treas. 1994—2001, prest.-elect 2002, pres. 2003), Kennebec Valley C. of C. (dir. 1988—, pres. 2001). Commercial, consumer (including collections, credit), Mergers and acquisitions, Property, real (including real estate development, water). Office: Bernstein Shur Sawyer and Nelson 146 Capitol St Po Box 5057 Augusta ME 04330-5057*

WILKS, LARRY DEAN, lawyer; b. Columbia, S.C., Jan. 8, 1955; s. Ray Dean and Jean (Garrett) W.; m. Jan Elizabeth McIllwain, May 2,1981; children: John Ray, Adam Garrett. BS, U. Tenn., 1977, JD, 1980. Bar: Tenn. 1981, U.S. Dist. Ct. (mid. dist.) Tenn. 1981, U.S. Supreme Ct. 1986, U.S. Ct. Appeals (6th cir.) 1993, U.S. Dist. Ct. (we. dist.) Tenn. 1996. Assoc. Mayo & Norris, Nashville, 1981-82; sole practice Springfield, Tenn., 1982-84; ptnr. Walton, Jones & Wilks, 1984, Jones & Wilks, 1984-89; pvt. practice Springfield, Tenn., 1989—. Chmn. Dem. Orgn. Robertson County Tenn., 1986-93. Fellow Tenn. Bar Found.; mem. ABA, ATLA, Tenn. Bar Assn. (assoc. gen. counsel 1991-94, gen. counsel 1994-99, bd. profl. responsibility 1993-98, bd. govs. 1991—, young lawyers divsn. lifetime fellow, asst. treas. 1999-2000, treas. 2000—), Tenn. Assn. Criminal Def. Lawyers, Tenn. Trial Lawyers Assn. (bd. govs. 2002—), Robertson County Bar Assn. (pres. 1993-96), Nat. Assn. Criminal Def. Laywers, Tenn. Young Lawyers Conf. (bd. dirs. 1987, editor quar. newsletter 1987-88, Mid. Tenn. v.p. 1988-89, v.p. 1989-90, pres.-elect 1990-91, pres. 1991-92), Robertson County U. Tenn. Alumni Assn. (pres. 2003—). Methodist. Criminal, Personal injury (including property damage), Product liability. Office: 509 W Court Sq Springfield TN 37172-2413

WILL, ALFRED JOSEPH, lawyer, engineer; b. Jamaica, N.Y., Mar. 11, 1950; s. James George and Catherine Rose (Steinmuller) W.; m. Therese Catherine Buttner, Nov. 23, 1972; children— Peter Simon, Daniel Alfred, Meredith Marie, Eric James. B.S. in Engring., U.S. Merchant Marine Acad., 1972; J.D., St. John's Law Sch., 1975. Bar: N.Y. 1976, U.S. Dist. Cts. (so. and ea. dists.) N.Y. 1976, U.S. Ct. Appeals (2d cir.) 1982, U.S. Supreme Ct. 1982. Assoc. Tabak, Ezratty & Mellusi, N.Y.C., 1975-76; assoc., sr. Vincent, Berg, Russo, Marcigliano & Zawacki, N.Y.C., 1976-81; sr. ptnr. Badiak & Will, N.Y.C., 1981— ; past pres., founder Admiralty Law Sch. of St. John's Law Sch., N.Y.C., 1974-75. Served to lt. USNR, 1969-78. Recipient Gov.'s Scholastic award N.Y. State, 1967-68; named Athlete of Yr. (track) U.S. Merchant Marine Acad., 1972. Mem. Maritime Law Assn. of U.S., Average Adjusters Assn. of U.S., N.Y. County Bar Assn. Roman Catholic. E-mail: admiralaw@aol.com. Admiralty, Federal civil litigation, Insurance. Home: 23 Robbins DrE Williston Williston Park NY 11596-2009 Office: Badiak Will & Ruddy 120 Broadway Ste 1040 New York NY 10271-1040 Also: Badiak Will & Kallen 17071 W Dixie Hwy North Miami Beach FL 33160-3765

WILLARD, MATTHEW R. lawyer; b. Sept. 3, 1967; s. Ira and Pat Willard. AA, Tallahassee C.C., 1993; BA in Philosophy, Fla. State U., 1995, JD, 1998. Bar: Fla. 1998, U.S. Dist. Ct. (no. dist.) Fla. 2000. Atty. Jansen Law Firm, Tallahassee, 1998—. Mock trial team coach Fla. Coll. Law, Tallahassee, 1998; legal advisor, various fraternities and sororities Fla. State U., Tallahassee, 2000—. Mock trial team coach Leon H.S., Tallahassee, 1997. E-4 USN, 1987—91. Mem.: Tallahassee Bar Assn., Fla. Bar Assn. Avocation: tennis. Criminal. Office: Jansen Law Firm 1206 N Duval St Tallahassee FL 32303

WILLARD-JONES, DONNA C. lawyer; b. Calgary, Alberta, Can., Jan. 19, 1944; m. Douglas E. Jones. BA with honors, U. B.C., 1965, student, 1965-66; JD, U. Oreg., 1970. Bar: Ak. 1970, U.S. Dist. Ct. Ak. 1970, U.S. Ct. Appeals (9th cir.) 1971, U.S. Customs Ct. 1972, U.S. Tax Ct. 1975, U.S. Supreme Ct. 1981. Assoc. Boyko & Walton, 1970-71, Walton & Willard, 1971-73; ptnr. Gruenberg & Willard, 1974, Gruenberg, Willard & Smith, 1974-75, Richmond, Willoughby & Willard, 1976-81, Willoughby & Willard, 1981-89; pvt. practice Anchorage, 1990—. Chmn. fed. adv. group Implementation of Civil Justice Reform Act of 1990, 1991-92; lawyer rep. 9th Cir. Jud. Conf., 1979-80; mem. spl. com. on contempt Ak. Supreme Ct., 1991-92; chmn. Bankruptcy Judge Merit Screening com., 1979; mem. Am. Judicature Soc., 1973-92, Am. Trial Lawyers Assn., 1981-92; bd. dirs. Ak. Legal Svcs. Corp., 1979-80; spkr. in field. Mem. U. B.C. Law Rev.; assoc. editor Oreg. Law Rev.; copy editor Ak. Bar Rag, 1979-84, contbg. editor, 1979-92; annual reviser Probate Counsel, 1972-88. Mem. Anchorage Port Commn., 1987-93, chmn., 1990-93; chmn. Ak. State Officers Compensation Commn., 1986-92; mem. Anchorage Transp. Commn., 1983-87, chmn., 1986-87; vice-chmn. Ak. Code Revision Commn., 1976-78; bd. trustees Ak. Indian Arts, Inc., 1970-92; mem. Chilkat Dancer Ak., 1965—. Recipient Rikli Solo Lifetime Achievement. award, ABA Gen. Pract., 1998. Fellow Am. Bar Found. (life); mem. ABA (ho. dels. 1980-84, 86-96, bd. govs. 1992-96, sec. 1995-96), Nat. Conf. Bar Pres. (exec. coun. 1985-88), Nat. Conf. Bar Founds. (bd. trustees 1983-90), Am. Arbitration Assn., We. States Bar Conf. (pres. 1983-84), Ak. Bar Assn. (Bd. Govs. Disting. Svc. award 1991, bd. govs. 1977-80, pres. 1979-80, numerous coms.), Am. Law Inst. Presbyterian. Bankruptcy, Construction, Corporate, general. Office: 124 E 7th Ave Anchorage AK 99501-3608 also: Am Bar Assn 750 N Lake Shore Dr Chicago IL 60611-4403 Fax: 907-278-0449.*

WILLCOX, RODERICK HARRISON, lawyer; b. Columbus, Ohio, Jan. 10, 1934; s. Richard V. and Marcella A. (Rehl) W.; m. Rita Kay Click, July 2, 1955; children: Sharon Marie Willcox Hazlewood, Kathy Lynn, Patricia Ann Willcox Hanna, Roderick Harrison Jr. BA, Williams Coll., 1955; LLB, U. Mich., 1958. Ptnr. Chester, Willcox & Saxbe, Columbus, Ohio, 1971—. Corporate, general, Estate planning, Estate taxation. Office: Chester Willcox & Saxbe LLP 65 East State St Ste 1000 Columbus OH 43215-3442 E-mail: rwillcox@cwslaw.com.

WILLEE, PAUL ANDREW, lawyer; b. Brighton, Sussex, Eng., Nov. 20, 1941; s. Albert William and Kathleen Ann (Minter) W.;m. Barbara Alice Sadler, July 27, 1968; children: Justin Andrew, Benjamin Paul. LLB, U. Melbourne, Australia, 1965, LLM, 1980; postgrad. diploma E.D.P., Royal Melbourne Inst. Tech., 1986. Solicitor, 1966-67; barrister-at-law Victorian Bar, Melbourne, 1967-75, 86—; prosecutor for the Queen State Victoria, Melbourne, 1975-85; 1st gen. counsel Nat. Crime Auth., Melbourne, 1984-86; pvt. practice Queen's Counsel, 1991—. Cons. Leo Cussen Inst. Continuing Edn., 1983—99; convenor disciplinary appeal com. Merit Protection Rev. Agy., 1991—2001; dir. Time Base Pty. Ltd., Sydney, Australia, 1993—2000; mem. judge advs. panel Royal Australian Navy, 1985; apptd. Def. Force Magistrate, 1996; head Australian Mil. Bar , 2002—. Co-author: Preparation of Criminal Trials in Victoria, 1984. V.p. Univ. H.S. Alumni, Melbourne, 1986—96, Univ. H.S. Coun., 1983—86; leader the Mlanz del. com. Maritime Internat., China, 1981, The Mlaanz Del., China, 1984; mem. Australian del. OECD Conf., Berlin, Germany, 1984, Paris, France, 1984, 1985. Capt. Royal Australian Navy, 1961—. Recipient Res. Forces Decoration, with 2 clasps. Mem. Maritime Law Assn. Australia & New Zealand (v.p. 1981-86), the Naval & Mil. Club (pres. 1995-98), The Ran Ski CLub (v.p. 1989-96). Avocations: computers, squash, skiing, reading, swimming. Home: 32 Corby St Victoria 3104 Australia Office: PA Willee RFD QC 205 William St Melbourne 3000 Australia E-mail: willee@attglobal.net., pwillee@bigpond.net.au., willeeqc@vicbar.com.au.

WILLENBRINK, ROSE ANN, lawyer; b. Louisville, Ky., Apr. 20, 1950; d. J.L. Jr. and Mary Margaret (Williams) W.; m. William I. Cornett Jr. Student, U. Chgo., 1968-70; BA in Anthropology with highest honors, U. Louisville, 1973, JD, 1975. Bar: Ky. 1976, Ind. 1976, U.S. Dist. Ct. (we. dist.) Ky. 1976, Ohio 1999. Atty. Mapother & Mapother, Louisville, 1976-79; v.p., counsel Nat. City Bank, Louisville, 1980-99, v.p., sr. atty. Cleve., 1999—. Mem. ABA, Ohio Bar Assn., Ky. Bar Assn., Louisville Bar Assn., Conf. on Consumer Fin. Law, Corp. House Counsel Assn., Phi Kappa Phi. Banking, Commercial, consumer (including collections, credit), Finance. Home: 359 Glengarry Dr Aurora OH 44202-8584 Office: Nat City Bank 1900 E 9th St Cleveland OH 44114-3484 E-mail: Rose.Ann.Willenbrink@nationalcity.com.

WILLETT, THOMAS EDWARD, lawyer; b. N.Y.C., Nov. 8, 1947; s. Oscar Edward and Alice (Fleming) W.; m. Marilyn Kenney, Dec. 28, 1969; children: Thomas Justin, Christopher Joseph. BS, USAF Acad., Colo., 1969; JD with distinction, Cornell U., 1972. Bar: N.Y. 1973, U.S. Ct. Claims 1973, U.S. Supreme Ct. 1977. Judge advocate USAF, Syracuse, N.Y., 1973-75, Kincheloe AFB, Mich., 1975-77, USAF Hdqs., Washington, 1977-79; assoc. Harris Beach LLP, Rochester, NY, 1979-84, ptnr., 1985—. Pres. Monroe County Legal Assistance Corp., Rochester, 1983-89. Capt. USAF, 1969-79. Mem. ABA, N.Y. State Bar Assn., Monroe County Bar Assn., Order of Coif. Corporate, general, Securities. Office: Harris Beach LLP 99 Garnsey Rd Pittsford NY 14534 E-mail: twillett@harrisbeach.com.

WILLEY, CHARLES WAYNE, lawyer; b. Dillon, Mont., Oct. 7, 1932; s. Asa Charles and Elizabeth Ellen Willey; m. Helene D., July 21, 1962 (div.); children: Stephen Charles, Heather Helene, Brent David, Scott D.; m. Alexis W. Grant, Jan. 26, 1986. BS with honors, Mont. State U., 1954; JD with high honors, U. Mont., 1959. Bar: Mont. 1959, Calif. 1960, U.S. Ct. Claims 1975, U.S. Tax Ct. 1975, U.S. Ct. Appeals (9th cir.) 1959, U.S. Ct. Appeals (Fed. cir.) 1983, U.S. Supreme Ct. 1972. Law clk. to presiding judge U.S. Ct. Appeals (9th cir.), 1959-60; ptnr. Price, Postel & Parma, Santa Barbara, Calif., 1960-77; pvt. practice Santa Barbara, 1977-97; shareholder Hollister & Brace, Santa Barbara, 1998-2001. Prof. law corp.; instr. Santa Barbara City Coll., 1961-63, U. Calif., Santa Barbara, 1963-64; lectr. Mont. Tax Inst., 1990, 92, Am. Agr. Law Assn., 1993, 96. Chief editor Mont. Law Rev., 1958-59. Pres. Legal Aid Found. Santa Barbara, 1970; mem. Laguna Blanca Sch. Bd., pres. 1980-81; v.p. Phoenix of Santa Barbara. Served to capt. USAF, 1954-56. Mem. Santa Barbara County Bar Assn. (pres. 1972-73), State Bar of Calif., State Bar of Montana, Phi Kappa Phi, Phi Eta Sigma, Phi Delta Phi. Lodges: Kiwanis. Republican. Episcopalian. Avocations: reading, writing, traveling. State civil litigation, Estate planning, Property, real (including real estate development, water). Office: 806 Parkview Way Missoula MT 59803

WILLIAMS, BENJAMIN SUTTON, lawyer; b. Atlanta, Aug. 12, 1951; s. Kenneth Richmond and Maryanne (Sutton) Williams; 1 child, Abigail Sutton. BA cum laude, U. Ga., 1974, JD magna cum laude, 1976. Bar: Ga. 1977, U.S. Dist. Ct. (no. dist.) Ga., U.S. Ct. Appeals (5th cir.). Law clk. to Hon. James C. Hill U.S. Ct. Appeals (5th cir.), New Orleans, 1976—78; assoc. Long, Weinberg, Ansley & Wheeler, Atlanta, 1978—82, ptnr., 1982—86, Williams & Henry, LLP, Atlanta, 1986—99; owner, prin. Benjamin S. Williams & Assocs., LLC, Atlanta, 1999—. Mem.: TALA, ABA, Ga. Trial Lawyers Assn., Ga. Bar Assn. Avocations: antiques, historic house renovations, Civil War history. Office: Benjamin S Williams and Assocs Tower Pl 200 Ste 1050 3348 Peactree Rd NE Atlanta GA 30326

WILLIAMS, BETTY OUTHIER, lawyer; b. Woodward, Okla., Sept. 11, 1947; d. Robert E. and Ethel M. (Castiller) Outhier; children: Amanda J., Emily Rebecca. BA, Oklahoma City U., 1969; JD, Vanderbilt U., 1972. Bar: Okla. 1972, U.S. Dist. Ct. (no. dist.) Okla. 1972, U.S. Dist. Ct. (ea. dist.) Okla. 1973, (U.S. Ct. Appeals (10th cir.) 1973, U.S. Supreme Ct. 1980, U.S. Dist. Ct. (we. dist.) Okla. 1988. Atty. Regional Heber Smith Cmty. Lawyer Fellowship, Tulsa, 1972-73; asst. U.S. atty. Muskogee, Okla., 1973-81; U.S. atty., 1981-82; ptnr. Robinson, Locke, Gage, Fite & Williams, Muskogee, 1982-96, Robinson, Gage & Williams, Muskogee, 1996-97, Gage & Williams, Muskogee, 1997—2003; judge Jud. Appeals Tribunal, State of Okla., 2003—. Chair local rules com. U.S. Bankruptcy Ct. Ea. Dist., Okla., 1994, U.S. Dist. Ct. Ea. Dist. Okla., 1995; adj. settlement judge U.S. Dist. Ct. Ea. Dis. Okla., 1998—, Okla. Jud. Appeals Tribunal of Ct., 2003—; judge, judicial appeals. Mem. editl. bd. Okla. Law Enforcement Ops. Bull., 1993-94; editor Okla. Bar Jour., 1996-2002. Pres. Bus. and Profl. Women, Muskogee, 1975-77, 83; pres., bd. dirs. YWCA, Muskogee, 1975-82; bd. dirs. Green County Mental Health, Muskogee, 1986-88, WISH, 1990—; trustee Frontier Heritage Found., 1990-98; chmn. bd. commrs. Muskogee Housing Authority; adminstrv. bd. chmn., St. Paul United Meth. Ch., Muskogee, 1999-2001; state exec. com. Internat. Order the Rainbow for Girls. Named One of Outstanding Young Career Women, Bus. and Profl. Women, 1974. Fellow: Okla. Bar Found. (trustee 1989—, v.p. 1994, pres. 1996, gov. 2000—); mem.: Muskogee County Bar Assn. (pres. 1984—85), Okla. Bar Assn. (editl. bd. 1996—, bd. govs. 2000—), ABA, Soroptomists (pres. 1986—88), Order Eastern Star (Hope chpt.), Gamma Phi Beta (alumnae pres. 1993—). Republican. Methodist. Bankruptcy, Federal civil litigation, State civil litigation, Civil rights. Home: 4326 Oklahoma St Muskogee OK 74401-2351 Office: Gage & Williams PO Box 87 Muskogee OK 74402-0087 E-mail: bowlaw@swbglobal.net.

WILLIAMS, C. JAMES, III, (JIM WILLIAMS), lawyer; b. Verdun, Alsace, France, Dec. 8, 1960; s. Charles James Jr. and Monique Marielouise (Masure) W.; m. Elizabeth H. (Kessler) W.; 5 children. BS, George Mason U., 1983, JD, 1987. Bar: Va. 1987, U.S. Dist. Ct. Va. 1988, U.S. Ct. Appeals (4th cir.) 1988. Evaluator U.S. Gen. Acctg. Office, Washington, 1980-87; law clk. U.S. Dist. Ct. (we. dist.) Va., Big Stone Gap, 1987-88; assoc. Gentry, Locke, Rakes & Moore, Roanoke, Va., 1988—91, Morris & Morris, PC, 1991—93; house counsel mgr. Progressive Ins. Co., 1993—99; ptnr. Marks & Williams PC, Hopewell, Va., 1999—. Chmn. Roanoke City Rep. Com., 1990-91. Named Chevalier Order of Demolay, 1982. Mem. Masons. Republican. Roman Catholic. Avocations: private piloting, snow skiing. General civil litigation, Commercial, contracts (including sales of goods; commercial financing). Office: Marks & Williams PC PO Box 27 Hopewell VA 23850

WILLIAMS, CHARLES JUDSON, lawyer, writer; b. San Mateo, Calif., Nov. 23, 1930; s. John Augustus and Edith (Babcock) W.; children: Patrick, Victoria, Apphia. AB, U. Calif., Berkeley, 1952, LLB, 1955. Bar: Calif. 1955, U.S. Supreme Ct., 1970. Assoc. Kirkbride, Wilson, Harzfeld and Wallace, San Mateo County, Calif., 1956-59; sole practice Solano County, Calif., 1959-64, Martinez, Calif., 1964—, Benicia, Calif., 1981-88; city atty. Pleasant Hill, Calif., 1962-80, Yountville, Calif., 1965-68, Benicia, 1968-76, 80-82, Lafayette, Calif., 1968—, Moraga, Calif., 1974-92, Danville, Calif., 1982-88, Pittsburg, Calif., 1984-93, Orinda, Calif., 1985-97; of counsel Best Best and Krieger, Best, Best and Krieger, 2002—. Lectr. Calif. Continuing Edn. Bar 1964-65, U. Calif. Extension 1974-76, John F. Kennedy U. Sch. Law 1966-69; spl. counsel to various Calif. cities; legal advisor Alaska Legis. Council 1959-61; advisor Alaska sup. ct. 1960-61; advisor on revision Alaska statues 1960-62; atty. Pleasant Hill Redevel. Agy. 1978-82; sec., bd. dirs. Vintage Savs. & Loan Assn., Napa County, Calif., 1974-82; bd. dirs. 23d Agrl. Dist. Assn., Contra Costa County, 1968-70. Author: California Code Comments to West's Annotated California Codes, 3 vols., 1965, West' California Code Forms, Commercial, 2 vols., 1965, West's California Government Code Forms, 3 vols., 1971, Supplement to California Zoning Practice, 1978, 80, 82, 84, 85, 87, 89, 91, 94, 96, 98, 2000, 01; contbr. articles to legal jours. Mem. ABA, Calif. Bar Assn., Contra Costa County Bar Assn. Administrative and regulatory, State civil litigation. Office: 1330 Arnold Dr Ste 149 Martinez CA 94553-6538 E-mail: chaslaw@aol.com.

WILLIAMS, CLAY RULE, lawyer; b. Milw., Sept. 25, 1935; s. George Laverne and Marguerite Mae (Rule) W.; m. Jeanne Lee Huber, Jan. 18, 1986; children: Gwynne, Amy, Daniel, Sarah. BA, Lawrence U., 1957; LLB, U. Mich., 1960. Bar: Wis. 1960, U.S. Dist. Ct. (ea. and we. dists.) Wis. 1964, U.S. Ct. Appeals (7th cir.) 1965, U.S. Ct. Mil. Appeals 1963, U.S.

Supreme Ct. 1963. Assoc. Gibbs, Roper & Fifield, Milw., 1963-67; ptnr., shareholder Von Briesen & Roper, S.C., Milw., 1967-99, of counsel, 1999—. Mem. Gov.'s Task Force Creation Bus. Ct., 1994-99; instr. profl. seminars. Author: Berry, Davis, Deguire and Williams, Wisconsin Business Corporation Law, 1992; contbr. articles to profl. jours. Active Shorewood (Wis.) Sch. Bd., 1976-79. Capt. USAF, Judge Adv. Corps., 1960-63. Fellow Wis. Bar Found.; Fellow, ABA Found., mem. ABA (sect. antitrust law, corp. counseling com.), Wis. Bar Assn. (co-chmn. com. to revise corp. laws 1986-90, chmn. standing com. on bus. corp. law 1990-97, Pres.'s Award of Excellence 1990, 97), Milw. Bar Assn. (probate and real property sect., joint bench-bar com. Ct. Appeals, 1986-88, long-range planning com. 1987), Am. Law Inst., Milw. Club, Univ. Club. Republican. Episcopalian. Avocations: hunting, fishing, skiing, reading. General civil litigation, Corporate, general, Securities. Office: von Briesen & Roper SC 411 E Wisconsin Ave Milwaukee WI 53202 E-mail: cwilliam@vonbriesen.com.

WILLIAMS, DONALD CLYDE, lawyer; b. Oxnard, Calif., Oct. 12, 1939; s. Leslie Allen and Elizabeth Esther (Orton) W.; m. Miriam Arline, Oct. 5, 1966; children— Erin K., Nikki Dawn. BA in Gen. Bus, Fresno State Coll., 1963; JD, Willamette U., 1967. Bar: Oreg. 1967. Practice in, Grants Pass, 1967-70; ptnr. Myrick, Seagraves, Williams & Nealy, 1968-70, Carlsmith, Ball, Wichman, Murray & Ichiki, 1977—; asst. atty. gen. Am. Samoa, 1970-71, atty. gen., 1971-75; assoc. justice High Ct. Trust Ter. of Pacific Islands, 1975-77. Served with USCGR, 1958-59. Mem. ABA, Calif. Bar Assn., Oreg. Bar Assn., Am. Samoa Bar Assn., Guam Bar Assn., Hawaii Bar Assn., Commonwealth No. Mariana Islands Bar Assn., Fed. States of Micronesia Bar Assn., Guam C. of C. Office: Carlsmith Ball 444 S Flower St Fl 9 Los Angeles CA 90071-2901 E-mail: dwilliams@carlsmith.com.

WILLIAMS, EBB HARRY, III, lawyer; b. Danville, Va., Dec. 13, 1939; s. Ebb Harry Williams Jr. and Lillian (Shuping) Williams; m. Gayle Rae Gowdey, Dec. 31, 1960; children: Kevin T., Christa G. BA with honors, U. Richmond, 1961, JD with honors, 1964. Bar: Va. 1964, U.S. Dist. Ct. (we. dist.) Va. 1984, U.S. Ct. Appeals (4th cir.) 1988, U.S. Supreme Ct. Ptnr. Broaddus, Epperly, Broaddus and Williams, Martinsville, Va., 1964—73; pvt. practice Martinsville, 1973—. Assoc. prof. law Patrick Henry C.C., Martinsville, 1964—73; substitute judge Henry and Patrick Counties, 1969—81. Bd. trustees Averette U., Danville, Va., 1982—90, 1994—2002; bd. assocs. U. Richmond, 1994—. Mem.: ABA, Martinsville-Henry County Bar Assn. (pres. 1973—74), Va. State Bar (sec. 1968—69, Tradition of Excellence award 2000). Personal injury (including property damage), Criminal, Estate planning. Office: PO Box 1009 Martinsville VA 24114

WILLIAMS, FRANK J. judge, historian, writer; b. Providence, Aug. 24, 1940; s. Frank and Natalie L. (Corelli) W.; m. Virginia E. Miller, Aug. 24, 1966. BA, Boston U., 1962, JD, 1970; MS in Taxation, Bryant Coll., 1986; LHD, Lincoln Coll., 1987; LLD, So. New England Sch. Law, 2001; LHD, Johnson & Wales U., 2002; Lincoln Diploma of Honor (hon.) , Lincoln Meml. U., 2002. Bar: R.I. 1970, U.S. Dist. Ct. R.I. 1970, U.S. Supreme Ct. 1976. Assoc. Tillinghast, Collins & Graham, Providence, 1970-75, Leonard Decof Ltd., Providence, 1976-78; law clk. Graham, Reid, Ewing & Stapleton, Providence, 1969; law clk., adminstrv. asst. R.I. Atty. Gen., Providence, 1967-68; pres. Frank J. Williams Ltd., attys.-at-law, Providence, 1978-95; assoc. justice R.I. Superior Ct., 1995-2001; chief justice Supreme Ct. R.I., 2001—. Judge of probate Town of Hopkinton (R.I.), 1978-82, 84-90, solicitor, 1978-82, 84-87; judge of probate Town of West Greenwich, R.I., 1984-86, 92-95, solicitor, 1984-92, asst. solicitor, 1992—; dep. judge of probate, 1987-92; solicitor Town of Coventry, R.I., 1972-74, 76-78, Town of Barrington, R.I., 1993-95, Town of Bristol, R.I., 1995, Town of South Kingstown, R.I., 1995; past spl. counsel Towns of Westerly, Bristol, Hopkinton, South Kingstown, City of Providence; atty. Town of Smithfield Sewer Authority, 1974-90; legis. counsel R.I. Retail Fedn., 1975-93, Credit Info. Bur., R.I. Mortgage Bankers Assn., 1992-95; adj. prof. Roger Williams Sch. of Law, 1997—; lectr. bus. and legal practice R.I. Sch. Design, Providence, 1976-80; mem. panel of arbitrators Am. Arbitration Assn., panel of mediators R.I. Superior Ct., 1993-95; mem. R.I. Bd. Bar Examiners, 1987-95, chair, 1995; chair R.I. Housing and Mortgage Fin. Corp., 1995, The Lincoln Forum, 1996—. Pres. Lincoln Group of Boston, 1976—88, Abraham Lincoln Assn., Springfield, Ill., 1986—95, Ulysses S. Grant Assn., 1990—; elected del. R.I. Constnl. Conv., 1986; elected town moderator Richmond, RI, 1992—95; dist. moderator Chaniho Regional Sch. Dist., 1994; chmn. Lincoln adv. com. Brown U.; mem. Lincoln prize adv. com. Gettysburg Coll.; bd. dirs. John E. Fogarty Found. for Persons with Mental Retardation, 1975—, South County Hosp., 1995—, R.I. Com. for the Humanities, 2001—, Narraganset Coun. Boy Scouts Am., 1969—80, 1998—2001. Capt. U.S. Army, 1962—67, Germany and Vietnam. Decorated Bronze Star, Combat Infantryman's badge, Army Commendation medal, Air medal with 2 oak leaf clusters, Republic of Vietnam Gallantry Cross with silver star; recipient Disting. Svc. award, Mil. Order of Fgn. Wars, Commdg. Gen.'s Pub. Svc. award, Dept. of Army. Fellow: ATLA (jud.); mem.: RI Bar Assn. (ho. of dels. 1986—93, chmn. new lawyers adv. com. 1976—87, chmn. mcpl. law com. 1993), Conf. Chief Justices, Am. Law Inst., Nat. Assn. for Ct. Mgmt., Am. Judges Assn., Am. Antiquarian Soc., Phi Alpha Delta, Alpha Phi Sigma, Phi Sigma Alpha. Roman Catholic. Office: 250 Benefit St Providence RI 02903

WILLIAMS, GARY RANDALL, lawyer; b. Gainesville, Ga., Oct. 16, 1946; s. Ernest Eugene and Ruby Louise (Conner) W.; m. Linda (Meg) Eberhart, May 12, 1990. AA, SUNY, Albany, 1973; LLB, LaSalle U., 1969; JD, Woodrow Wilson Coll. Law, 1976. Bar: Ga. 1978, U.S. Tax Ct. 1978, U.S. Dist. Ct. (no. dist.) Ga. 1979, U.S. Ct. Claims 1980, U.S. Ct. Appeals (11th cir.) 1981, U.S. Supreme Ct., 1997. Atty. IRS, Washington, 1977-80; pvt. practice Marietta, Ga., 1980—86, Hiram, Ga., 1992—, Dallas, Ga., 1994—; lawyer ADP Pension Svcs., Inc., El Toro, Calif., 1981-82; tax specialist Ga. Dept. Revenue, Atlanta, 1986-92; judge protem Paulding County Probate Ct., 1997—; assoc. juvenile judge Tallapoosa Jud. Cir., 1999—. Affiliate atty. Am. Ctr. for Law and Justice. With U.S. Army, 1966-73. Mem. State Bar Ga., Paulding County Bar Assn. (sec., treas. 1994, pres. 1998-99), Christian Legal Soc. Avocations: computers, automobiles. Pension, profit-sharing, and employee benefits, Probate (including wills, trusts), Taxation, general. Office: 302 W I Pkwy Dallas GA 30132-5061

WILLIAMS, GERALD R. law educator; s. Ross Gerald and Luana Williams; m. Claudia Grace Clark, Dec. 17, 1965; children: Colette Williams Callister, Jennifer, Nicole Williams Bruderer, Michael Gerald, Daniel Clark. B.A., Brigham Young U., Provo, Utah, 1966; JD, U. Utah, Salt Lake City, 1969. Bar: Utah 1969, U.S. Dist. Ct. Utah 1969. Legal advisor to the prosecutor Navajo Tribe, Window Rock, Ariz., 1969—70; fellow Internat. Legal Ctr., Kabul, Afghanistan, 1970—72; prof. of law Brigham Young U. Law Sch., Provo, Utah, 1973—. Vis. prof. Ariz. State U. Coll. Law, Tempe, 1972—73, U. Cairo Faculty of Law, 1978—80; expert panel Internat. Devel. Law Inst., Rome, 1983—; pres., bd. of dirs Utah Legal Svcs., Inc., Salt Lake City, 1983—85; vis prof. Harvard Law Sch., Cambridge, Mass., 1986; editl. bd. Alternatives to the High Cost of Litig., N.Y.C., 1991—; editl. advisor Dispute Resolution Jour., Washington, 1992—; bd. dirs. Am. Arbitration Assn., Washington, 1992—96. Author: (book) Legal Negotiation and Settlement, article. Pres. Bd. of Edn., Provo, Utah, 1995—98. Grantee, NSF, 1973-76. Mem.: ABA (mem. standing com. on dispute resolutions 1989—92), Assn. for Conflict Resolution. Office: Brigham Young Univ 538 JRCB Provo UT 84602 Office Fax: 801-422-0391. E-mail: gerald.williams@byu.edu.

WILLIAMS, GLEN MORGAN, federal judge; b. Jonesville, Va., Feb. 17, 1920; s. Hughy May and Hattie Mae W.; m. Jane Slemp, Nov. 17, 1962; children: Susan, Judy, Rebecca, Melinda. AB magna cum laude, Milligan Coll., 1940; JD, U. Va., 1948. Bar: Va. 1947. Pvt. practice law, Jonesville, 1948-76; judge U.S. Dist. Ct. (we. dist.) Va., 1976-88, sr. judge, 1988—; commonwealth's atty. Lee County, Va., 1948-51; mem. Va. Senate, 1953-55. Mem. editorial bd.: Va. Law Rev, 1946-47. Mem. Lee County Sch. Bd., 1972-76; trustee, elder First Christian Ch., Pennington Gap, Va.; trustee Milligan Coll., 1990—, Appalachian Sch. of Law, 1995—. Lt. USN, 1942-46, MTO. Recipient Citation of Merit Va. Def. Lawyers Assn., Oustanding Alumnus award Milligan Coll., 1980, Svc. to Region award Emory & Henry Coll., 1996. Mem. ABA, Va. State Bar (citation of merit), Va. Bar Assn. (citation of merit), Fed. Bar Assn., Va. Trial Lawyers Assn. (Meritorious Svc. award 1986, Disting. Svc. award), Am. Legion, 40 and 8. Clubs: Lions, Masons, Shriners. Office: US Dist Ct Fed Bldg PO Box 339 Abingdon VA 24212-0339 E-mail: glenw@vawd.uscourts.gov.

WILLIAMS, HENRY NEWTON, retired lawyer; b. Dickson, Tenn., May 14, 1917; s. H. Newton and Cora Ethel (Wynns) W.; m. LaVerna Pearl Wharton, July 12, 1944 (dec.); children: John Wharton, George Wynns. BS, Mid. Tenn. State U., 1937; MA, U. Tenn., 1938; PhD, U. Chgo., 1951; JD, Vanderbilt U., 1952; LLM, Columbia U., 1954. Bar: Tenn. 1953, U.S. Ct. Appeals (3d cir.) 1954, U.S. Ct. Appeals (9th and 10th cirs.) 1955, U.S. Supreme Ct. 1956, U.S. Ct. Appeals (D.C. cir.) 1957, D.C. 1960. Asst. prof. polit. sci. Vanderbilt U., Nashville, 1946-53; assoc. prof. law Mercer U., Macon, Ga., 1954-56; atty. U.S. Dept. Justice, 1956-68, FTC, Washington, 1968-70; dep. gen. counsel Selective Svc. Sys., Washington, 1970-76, gen. counsel, 1976-99. Contbr. articles to law and polit. sci. jours. Col. U.S. Army, 1942-46. J.P. Chamberlain fellow Columbia U. Law Sch., 1953-54, Edward Hilman fellow U. Chgo., 1939-40, Univ. fellow, 1938-39. Mem. Am. Law Inst., ABA, Fed. Bar Assn., Tenn. Bar Assn., D.C. Bar Assn., Assn. of Bar of City of N.Y. Episcopalian. Home: 11811 Judson Rd Silver Spring MD 20902-2054

WILLIAMS, HENRY WARD, JR., lawyer, writer; b. Rochester, N.Y., Jan. 12, 1930; s. Henry Ward and Margaret Elizabeth (Simpson) W.; m. Christina M.; children: Edith Williams Linares, Margaret Williams Warren, Sarah Williams Farrand, Ann Williams Treacy, Elizabeth DeLancey, Victoria Maureen. AB, Dartmouth Coll., 1952; LLB, U.Va., 1958. Bar: N.Y. 1959, U.S. Dist. Ct. (we. dist.) N.Y. 1959, U.S. Dist. Ct. (so. dist.) Mich. 1982, U.S. Ct. Appeals (2d cir.) 1963, U.S. Tax Ct. 1960, U.S. Supreme Ct. 1968, D.C. 1978. Ptnr. Harris, Beach & Wilcox, Rochester, 1958-78, Robinson, Williams, Angeloff & Frank, Rochester, 1978-80, Weidman, Williams, Jordon, Angeloff & Frank, Rochester, 1980-82, The Williams Law Firm, Rochester, 1982—. Exec. editor Va. Law Rev., 1957-58. Chmn. Genesee Finger/Lakes Regional Planning Coun., 1973-89; majority leader Monroe County Legislature, 1967-73; councilman Town of Wheatland, N.Y., 2002–; mem. alumni coun. Dartmouth Coll., 1995-99; mem. no. 8020 Nat. Ski Patrol Sys. Lt. (j.g.) USN, 1952-55. Mem. ABA, N.Y. State Bar Assn., Monroe County Bar Assn. (trustee 1982-85), Rochester Yacht Club, Royal Can. Yacht Club, Lake Yacht Racing Assn. (pres. 1985-87, hon. pres. 1988-90), Royal Ocean Racing Club, Royal Nfld. Yacht Club, Raven Soc., Order of Coif, Omicron Delta Kappa. General practice. Office: The Williams Law Firm PO Box 8 Scottsville NY 14546-0008

WILLIAMS, HOWARD RUSSELL, lawyer, educator; b. Evansville, Ind., Sept. 26, 1915; s. Clyde Alfred and Grace (Preston) W.; m. Virginia Merle Thompson, Nov. 3, 1942 (dec. Dec. 2000); 1 son, Frederick S.T. AB, Washington U., St. Louis, 1937; LLB, Columbia U., 1940. Bar: N.Y. 1941. With firm Root, Clark, Buckner & Ballantine, N.Y.C., 1940-41; prof. law, asst. dean U. Tex. Law Sch., Austin, 1946-51; prof. law Columbia U. Law Sch., N.Y.C., 1951-63; Dwight prof. Columbia Law Sch., 1959-63; prof. law Stanford U., 1963-85, Stella W. and Ira S. Lillick prof., 1968-82, prof. emeritus, 1982, Robert E. Paradise prof. natural resources, 1983-85, prof. emeritus, 1985—. Oil and gas cons. President's Materials Policy Commn., 1951; mem. Calif. Law Revision Commn., 1971-79, vice chmn., 1976-77, chmn., 1978-79 Author or co-author: Cases on Property, 1954, Cases on Oil and Gas, 1956, 5th edit., 1987, Decedents' Estates and Trusts, 1968, Future Interests, 1970, Oil and Gas Law, 8 vols., 1959-64 (with ann. supplements/rev. 1964-95), abridged edit., 1973, Manual of Oil and Gas Terms, 1957, 11th edit., 2000. Bd. regents Berkeley Bapt. Divinity Sch., 1966-67; trustee Rocky Mountain Mineral Law Found., 1964-66, 68-85. With U.S. Army,(field arty.) 1941-46. Recipient Clyde O. Martz Tchg. award Rocky Mountain Mineral Law Found., 1994. Mem. Phi Beta Kappa. Democrat. Home: 360 Everett Ave Apt 4B Palo Alto CA 94301-1422 Office: Stanford U Sch Law Nathan Abbott Way Stanford CA 94305

WILLIAMS, J. BRYAN, lawyer; b. Detroit, July 23, 1947; s. Walter J. and Maureen June (Kay) Williams; m. Jane Elizabeth Eisele, Aug. 24, 1974; children: Kyle Joseph, Ryan Patrick. AB, U. Notre Dame, 1969; JD, U. Mich., 1972. Bar: Mich. 1972, U.S. Dist. Ct. (ea. dist.) Mich. 1972. Atty. Dickinson, Wright, PLLC (and predecessor firm), Detroit, 1972—, CEO Bloomfield Hills, Mich., 1991-2000. Pres. U.S. Law Firm Group, Inc., 2002. Mem.: ABA, Detroit Legal News Co. (bd. dirs.), Econ. Club Detroit (bd. dirs. 1996—2001), Detroit Bar Assn., Mich. Bar Assn., Detroit Regional C. of C. (bd. dirs., vice chmn. 1998—2002), Nat. Club Assn. (bd. dirs., sec. 1995—97, treas. 1997—98, v.p. 1998—2002, chmn. 2002—), Oakland Hills Country Club, Notre Dame Club Detroit (pres. 1984). Roman Catholic. Banking, Corporate, general. Home: 993 Suffield Ave Birmingham MI 48009-1242 Office: Dickinson Wright PLLC 38525 Woodward Ave Ste 2000 Bloomfield Hills MI 48304 E-mail: jwilliams@dickinson-wright.com.

WILLIAMS, J. VERNON, retired lawyer; b. Honolulu, Apr. 26, 1921; s. Urban and W. Amelia (Olson) W.; m. Malvina H. Hitchcock, Oct. 4, 1947 (dec. May 1970); children— Carl H., Karin, Frances E., Scott S.; m. Mary McLellan, Sept. 6, 1980. Student, Phillips Andover Acad., 1937-39; BA cum laude, Amherst Coll., 1943; LL.B., Yale, 1948. Bar: Wash. 1948. Assoc. Riddell, Riddell & Hemphill, 1948-50, ptnr., 1950-95; sr. prin. emeritus Riddell Williams, P.S., Seattle, 1996—. Sec., dir. Airborne Freight Corp., 1968-79, gen. counsel, 1968-96. Chmn. March of Dimes, Seattle, 1954-55; Mem. Mayor's City Charter Rev. Com., 1968-69; chmn. Seattle Bd. Park Commrs., 1966-68; co-chmn. parks and open space com. Forward Thrust, 1966-69; dir. bd. and commrs. br. Nat. Recreation and Parks Assn., 1968-69; chmn. Gov.'s adv. com. Social and Health Services, 1972-75; Bd. dirs. Seattle Met. YMCA, 1965— , pres., 1976-79; trustee Lakeside Sch., 1971-79; mem. alumni council Phillps Andover Acad., 1970-73, Yale Law Sch., 1969-77; chancellor St. Mark's Cathedral, Seattle, 1964-2000. Served with USAAF, 1943-45. Mem. Univ. Club, Seattle Tennis Club, Birnam Wood Golf Club. Home: 1100 38th Ave E Seattle WA 98112-4434 Office: 4500 1001 4th Ave Plz Seattle WA 98154-1065

WILLIAMS, J. WILLIAM, lawyer; b. Cleve., Apr. 29, 1972; s. William Francis and Reta E. Williams; m. Lauren Carson Williams, Aug. 9, 1997; 1 child, Grant Alexander. B in Acctg., U. Miss., 1994, M in Taxation, 1997, JD, 1998; LLM in Estate Planning, U. Miami, Coral Gables, Fla., 1999. Bar: Tenn. 1999, Miss. 1999, U.S. Dist. Ct. (no. and so. dist.) Miss. 1999, U.S. Ct. Appeals (5th cir.) 1999, U.S. Dist. Ct. (no. dist.) Ga. 2001, Ga. 2001, U.S. Tax Ct. 2001. Assoc. Hale Headrick, et. al., Memphis, 1999—2000, Alston & Bird, Atlanta, 2000—. Vol. Kids in Need of Dreams, Atlanta, 2000—; bd. dirs. Ga. Planned Giving Coun., Smyrna, 2002—; bd. dirs., pres.-elect Atlanta Interfaith AIDS Network, 2000—. Mem.: ABA (sect. taxation and real property, probate, trusts), Ga. Bar (fiduciary sect.), Nat. Planned Giving Coun. Avocations: golf, reading, gardening. Estate planning, Probate (including wills, trusts), Taxation, general. Office: Alston & Bird LLP 1201 W Peachtree St Atlanta GA 30309-3424 Office Fax: 404-881-7777. E-mail: jwwilliams@alston.com.

WILLIAMS, JACKIE N. law educator, former prosecutor; b. Roosevelt, Okla., Oct. 4, 1943; s. David Coleman and Grace Pearl (Southard) W.; children: Douglas Kennedy, Eric Neil. BBA, Wichita State U., 1967; JD, Washburn U. Law Sch., 1971. Bar: Kans. 1971. Asst. atty. gen. Kans. Atty. Gen.'s Office, Topeka, 1971-73; asst. dist. atty. Wichita, Kans., 1973-77; adminstrv. asst. U.S. Congressman Dan Glickman, Washington, D.C., 1977; asst. U.S. atty. Wichita, 1977-96; U.S. atty. Kans., 1996—2001; sr. fellow, criminal justice prog School of Community Affairs, Wichita State Univ , Kans., 2001—. Office: Wichita State Univ School of Community Affairs 302 Lindquist Hall, Box 135 Wichita KS 67260 E-mail: jackie.williams@wichita.edu.

WILLIAMS, JOEL CASH, lawyer; b. Dacula, Ga., Dec. 19, 1942; s. Joel Cash and Cora Belle W.; m. M'Liss Gurneym Dec. 11, 1976 (div.); children: Laurel M'Liss, Morgan Delannoy. BA, Shorter Coll., 1964; LLB, Mercer U., 1967. Bar: Ga., 1966, Ga. (no. dist.), 1967, Ga. (mid. dist.), 1967. Intern Atty. Gen. Ga., Atlanta, 1966, deputy asst. atty. gen., 1967-68, asst. atty. gen., 1968-69; legal counsel U.S. Senator Richard Russell, Washington, 1970-71, U.S. Senator David Gambrell, Washington, 1971; asst. to pres. Savannah (Ga.) Foods & Industry, 1971-78, v.p. corp. affairs, 1978-97; ptnr. Powell, Goldstein, Frazer & Murphy, Atlanta, 1998—. Chmn. adv. bd. 1st Liberty Bank, Savannah, 1993-97. Editor-in-chief Mercer LAw Rev., 1966-67. Chmn. bd. dirs. Savannah C. of C., United Way, Savannah, 1987-88. Mem. State Bar Ga. (corp. coun.), Ga. C. of C. (bd. dirs. 1994—). Corporate, general, Environmental, Public international. Office: Powell Goldstein Frazer & Murphy 191 Peachtree St NE Ste 1600 Atlanta GA 30303-1700

WILLIAMS, JOHN EDWARD, lawyer; b. Atlanta, May 21, 1946; s. Edward Carl and Mary E. (Griffin) W.; m. Kristin Forsberg, May 22, 1976; children: Alexandra, Courtney, Charles. BA, Yale U., 1968; JD, U. Va., 1974; LLM in Taxation, Georgetown U., 1977. Bar: Va. 1974, D.C. 1975, U.S. Dist. Ct. D.C. 1975, U.S. Tax Ct. 1975, U.S. Ct. Appeals (D.C. cir.) 1975, U.S. Supreme Ct. 1977. Law clk. to Judge Charles R. Richey U.S. Dist. Ct. (D.C. dist.), 1974-75; assoc. Patton, Boggs & Blow, Washington, 1975-78, Cadwalader, Wickersham & Taft, Washington, 1978-81; asst. to the commr. IRS, Washington, 1981-84; tax counsel Ropes & Gray, Washington, 1984-86; ptnr. David & Hagner, P.C., Washington, 1986-90, Winston & Strawn, Washington, 1990-2000. Mem. Jud. Conf. of D.C. Circuit, 1978, 82, 85, 87, 92. With U.S. Army, 1968-74. Mem. ABA (tax sect., chmn. tech. subcom., adminstrv. practice com. 1986-88), Met., Yale N.Y.C., Heritage Hunt Club. Corporate taxation, Estate taxation, Personal income taxation. Home: 4908A John Ticer Dr Alexandria VA 22304 Office: 3213 Duke St Ste 601 Alexandria VA 22314 E-mail: williamslawfirm@hotmail.com.

WILLIAMS, KAREN HASTIE, lawyer; b. Washington, Sept. 30, 1944; d. William Henry and Beryl (Lockhart) Hastie; m. Wesley S. Williams, Jr.; children: Amanda Pedersen, Wesley Hastie, Bailey Lockhart. Cert., U. Neuchatel, Switzerland, 1965; BA, Bates Coll., 1966; MA, Tufts U., 1967; JD, Cath. U. Am., 1973. Bar: D.C. 1973. Staff asst. internat. gov. relations dept. Mobil Oil Corp., N.Y.C., 1967-69; staff asst. com. Dist. Columbia U.S. Senate, 1970, chief counsel com. on the budget, 1977-80; law clk. to judge Spottswood Robinson III U.S. Ct. Appeals (D.C. Cir.), Washington, 1973-74; law clk. to assoc. justice Thurgood Marshall U.S. Supreme Ct., Washington, 1974-75; assoc. Fried, Frank, Harris, Shriver & Kampelman, Washington, 1975-77, 1975-77; adminstr. Office Mgmt. and Budget, Washington, 1980-81; of counsel Crowell & Moring, Washington, 1982, ptnr., 1982—. Bd. dirs. Chubb Corp., Gannett Co., Inc., Sun Trust Bank, Inc., Washington Gas Light Co., Continental Airlines. Trustee Greater Washington Research Ctr., chair. Mem. ABA (pub. contract law sect., past chair), Nat. Bar Assn., Washington Bar Assn., Nat. Contract Mgmt. Assn., NAACP (legal def. fund, bd. dirs.). Office: Crowell & Moring Ste 1200W 1001 Pennsylvania Ave NW Washington DC 20004-2595

WILLIAMS, MARCUS DOYLE, judge; b. Nashville, Oct. 24, 1952; s. John Freelander and Pansy (Doyle) W.; m. Carmen Myrie, May 21, 1983; children: Aaron Doyle, Adam Myrie. BA with honors, Fisk U., 1973; JD, Cath. U. of Am., 1977. Bar: Va. 1977, D.C. 1978. Asst. commonwealth's atty. County of Fairfax, Fairfax, Va., 1978-80, asst. county atty. Faifax, Va., 1980-87; dist. ct. judge 19th Jud. Dist., Va., 1987-90; judge 19th Jud. Cir., Va., 1990—. Lectr. bus. legal studies George Mason U., Fairfax, 1980-95; instr. pvt. investigators North Va. Community Coll., Fairfax, 1979; mem. Fairfax Criminal Justice Adv. Bd., 1980-86; faculty advisor Nat. Jud. Coll., 1991, faculty, 1992—; Am. participant lectr. for USIA, 1990; lectr. George Mason U. Law Sch., 1987. Book reviewer for ABA Jour., 1981-84; contbr. articles to legal jours. Bd. visitors Cath. U. Law Sch., 1998—. Recipient cert. of appreciation for outstanding svc. Burke-Fairfax Jack & Jill, Cert. of Appreciation, Nat. Forum for Black Pub. Adminstrs. and Black Women United for Action, 1995; Thomas J. Watson Found. fellow, 1977, Otis Smith award Black Law Students Assn. of Cath. U. Law Sch.; Outstanding Achievement and Svc. award Black Law Students Assn., 2001. Mem. ABA (chair subcom. Victims of Crimes 1996-2000), Fairfax Bar Assn. (CLE com., vice chmn. 1986-87), Am. Bus. Law Assn., Am. Judges Assn., Phi Alpha Delta, Beta Kappa Chi, Omega Psi Phi. Methodist. Office: Cir Ct 4110 Chain Bridge Rd Fairfax VA 22030-4009

WILLIAMS, MARY BETH, lawyer; b. Marshfield, Wis., Aug. 8, 1948; d. Delos A. and Leona E. (Kademan) Kobs; m. Ernest F. Wittwer, July 15, 1967 (div. Jan. 1989); children: Jake, Freddie; m. Paul L. Williams, July 22, 1989. BBA, U. Wis., 1983, JD, 1986. Bar: Wis. 1986, U.S. Dist. Ct. (we. dist.) Wis. 1986, U.S. Dist. Ct. (ea. dist.) Wis. 1988. Assoc. Wickhem & Gage, S.C., Janesville, Wis., 1986-88, Brennan, Steil, Basting & MacDougall, S.C., Janesville, 1988-91; pvt. practice law Janesville, 1991-2000; atty. Hill, Glowacki, Jaeger, Reiley, Zimmer & Hughes, LLP, 2000-01, Mary B. Williams Law Office, S.C., 2001—. Mem. legal secs. program adv. com. Blackhawk Tech. Coll., Janesville, 1992—; mem. alcohol license adv. com. City of Janesville, 1994-2000. Mem. ABA, State Bar Wis., Rock County Bar Assn. Avocations: reading, puzzle solving, piano playing, genealogy, historical restoration. Estate planning, Probate (including wills, trusts), Property, real (including real estate development, water). Office: PO Box 8066 20 S Main St Ste 23 Janesville WI 53545-3959 E-mail: pmwilli@inwave.com.

WILLIAMS, MAUREEN, lawyer, accountant; BSBA, Creighton U., 1985; JD, Hamline U., 1991. Bar: Minn. 1991, U.S. Dist. Ct. 1994, U.S. Ct. Appeals 1994; CPA 1988. CPA Ginoli & Co., Peoria, Ill., 1986, Woodward & Co., Kansas City, Mo., 1986-88; law clk. State Minn., 1990—93; pvt. practice Mpls., 1993—. Republican. Roman Catholic. Avocations: reading, biking. Appellate, Criminal. Office: PO Box 1895 Minneapolis MN 55337-0895

WILLIAMS, MICHAEL ANTHONY, lawyer; b. Mandan, N.D., Sept. 14, 1932; s. Melvin Douglas and Lucille Ann (Gavin) Williams; m. Marjorie Ann Harrer, Aug. 25, 1962 (div. 1989); children: Ann Margaret, Douglas Raymond, David Michael; m. Dorothy Ruth Hand, 1989. BA, Coll. of St. Thomas, 1954; LL.B., Harvard U., 1959. Bar: Colo. 1959, N.D. 1959, U.S. Dist. Ct. Colo. 1959, U.S. Ct. Appeals (10th cir.) 1959, U.S. Supreme Ct. 1967. Assoc. Sherman & Howard and predecessor Dawson, Nagel, Sherman & Howard, Denver, 1959—65, ptnr., 1965—91; pres. Williams, Youle & Koenigs, P.C., Denver, 1991—2002; prin. Michael A. Williams LLC, Denver, 2002—. Served as 1st lt. USAF, 1955—57. Mem.: ABA, Arapahoe County Bar Assn., Denver Bar Assn., Colo. Bar Assn., Am. Law Inst., Colo. Bar Found., Am. Bd. Trial Advs., Am. Coll. Trial Lawyers. Federal civil litigation, State civil litigation. Office: Michael A Williams LLC 950 17th St Ste 1700 Denver CO 80202-2811 E-mail: mwilliams@wyk.com.

WILLIAMS, MICHAEL EDWARD, lawyer; b. Ft. Worth, Aug. 10, 1955; s. Jerrol Evans and Helen Louise (Hoffner) W.; m. Jackie Ann Gordinier, Dec. 30, 1978; children: Margaret Eileen, James Andrew. BA, U. Calif.,

Riverside, 1977; JD, U. San Diego, 1980. Bar: Calif. 1980, U.S. Dist. Ct. (so. dist.) Calif. 1980, U.S. Tax Ct. 1981, U.S. Dist. Ct. (ea. and cen. dists.) Calif. 1982, U.S. Dist. Ct. (no. dist.) Calif. 1985. Assoc. Jamison & McFadden, Solana Beach, Calif., 1980-86, Dorazio, Barnhorst & Bonar, San Diego, 1986; sole practice Encinitas, Calif., 1987—. Pres. Casa de Amistad, Centro de Ensenaza, 2001—. Atty. pro bono Community Resource Ctr., Encinitas, Calif., 1984-96; vice moderator San Diego Presbytery, Presbyn. Ch. U.S.A., 1998, moderator, 1999; vice moderator SYNOD So. Calif. and Hawaii, Presbyn. Ch. U.S.A., 2003. Mem. Calif. State Bar Assn. (fee arbitrator 1992—), San Diego County Bar Assn. (client rels. com. 1990—, fee arbitration com. 1991—, ct. arbitrator). Democrat. Presbyterian. Bankruptcy, State civil litigation, Commercial, contracts (including sales of goods; commercial financing). Office: 4405 Manchester Ave Ste 206 Encinitas CA 92024-7902

WILLIAMS, NEIL, JR., lawyer; b. Charlotte, N.C., Mar. 22, 1936; s. Lyman Neil and Thelma (Peterson) W.; m. Sue Sigmon, Aug. 23, 1958; children: Fred R., Susan S. AB, Duke U., 1958, JD, 1961. Bar: Ga. 1962, U.S. Dist. Ct. (no. dist.) Ga. 1977, U.S. Ct. Appeals (11th cir.) 1977. Assoc. Alston & Bird (and predecessor firm), Atlanta, 1961—65, ptnr., 1966—99, mng. ptnr., 1984-96; gen. counsel, global ptnr. Amvescap PLC, Atlanta, 1999—2002; ret., 2002. Bd. dirs. NDC Health Corp., Atlanta, Printpack, Inc., Atlanta, Acuity Brands, Inc., Atlanta. Chmn. bd. trustees Duke U., 1983—88, trustee, 1980—93; chmn. bd. trustees Vasser Woolley Found., Atlanta, 1975—, Leadership Atlanta, 1976—80; trustee Brevard Music Ctr., 1977—86, 1991—2001, Presbyn. Ch. USA Found., Jeffersonville, Ind., 1983—90, Research Triangle Inst., 1983—88, The Duke Endowment, Charlotte, NC, 1997—; bd. dirs. Atlanta Symphony Orch., 1970—76, 1984—93, 1995—98, pres., 1988—90; bd. dirs. Woodruff Arts Ctr., 1987—98, 1999—, chmn., 2001—; bd. counsellors The Carter Ctr., Atlanta, 1987—96, Ctrl. Atlanta Progress, 1984—96; bd. dirs. Am. Symphony Orch. League, Washington, 1990—2000, chmn., 1995—99. Recipient Disting. Alumni award Duke U., 1991, Rhyne award, 1996. Mem. ABA, Am. Bar Found., State Bar Ga., Am. Law Inst., Atlanta C. of C. (bd. dirs. 1992-97, vice chmn. 1994-97), Piedmont Driving Club, Commerce Club (Atlanta), University Club (N.Y.C.), Phi Beta Kappa, Omicron Delta Kappa. Commercial, contracts (including sales of goods; commercial financing), Corporate, general, Securities. Home: 3 Nacoochee Pl NW Atlanta GA 30305-4164 Office: Amvescap PLC 1315 Peachtree St NE Atlanta GA 30309-3503 E-mail: neil_williams@amvescap.com.

WILLIAMS, PAUL STRATTON, lawyer; b. San Francisco, Calif., Oct. 9, 1959; s. Henry Stratton and Frances (Spurlock) W.; m. Laura Dawn Coleman, Sept. 15, 1984; children: Scott Coleman, Ryan Stratton. AB, Harvard Coll., 1981; JD, Yale U., 1984. Bar: Calif. 1984, Ohio 1987. Assoc. Gibson, Dunn & Crutcher, L.A., 1984-87, Vorys, Sater, Seymour & Pease, Columbus, Ohio, 1987-90; gen. counsel Info. Dimensions, Inc., Dublin, Ohio, 1994-95; v.p., asst. gen. counsel Cardinal Health, Inc., 1995—99, sr. v.p., dep. gen. counsel, 2000—01, exec. v.p., chief legal off. and sec., 2001—. Mem. ABA, Ohio Bar Assn., Columbus Bar Assn., Harvard Club Central Ohio, Yale Club Central Ohio. Democrat. Avocations: running, tennis. Corporate, general, Mergers and acquisitions, Securities. Home: 204 Springbrook Dr Gahanna OH 43230-6238 Office: Cardinal Health Inc 7000 Cardinal Pl Dublin OH 43017-1092*

WILLIAMS, QUINN PATRICK, lawyer; b. Evergreen Park, Ill., May 6, 1949; s. William Albert and Jeanne Marie (Quinlan) W.; m. Ingrid E. Haas; children: Michael Ryan, Mark Reed, Kelly Elizabeth. BBA, U. Wis., 1972; JD, U. Ariz., 1974. Bar: Ariz. 1975, N.Y. 1984, U.S. Dist. Ct. Ariz. 1976. V.p., sec., gen. counsel Combined Comm. Corp., Phoenix, 1975-80; sr. v.p. legal and adminstrn. Swensen's Inc., Phoenix, 1980-86; of counsel Winston & Strawn, Phoenix, 1985-87, ptnr., 1987-89, Snell & Wilmer, Phoenix, 1989—2002, Greenberg Traurig, 2002—; pres. Enterprise network, 2001. Bd. Ariz. Tech. Coun., 2001—, Ariz. Venture Capital Conf., 1993-2000; co-chmn. Gov.'s Small Bus. Advocate Exec. Coun., 1993—; chair, bd. dirs. Greater Phoenix Econ. Coun., 1996-2000, Scottsdale Area Chamber Partnership; vice-chair Gov. Regulatory Coun., 1995-97; sec. GSPED High Tech. Cluster, 1993—. With USAR, 1967-73. Mem. ABA, State Bar Ariz., Maricopa County Bar Assn., N.Y. Bar Assn., Internat. Franchise Assn., Scottsdale C. of C. (bd. dirs.), Paradise Valley Country Club, Scottsdale Charros. Republican. Roman Catholic. Corporate, general, Franchising, Securities. Home: 6201 E Horseshoe Rd Paradise Valley AZ 85253 Office: Greenberg Traurig 2375 E Camelback Rd Ste 700 Phoenix AZ 85016 E-mail: williamsq@gtlaw.com.

WILLIAMS, REBECCA LYNN, lawyer, nurse; b. LaGrange, Ill., Jan. 24, 1959; d. Richard Fowler and Anita (Albro) W. BSN magna cum laude, Duke U., 1981; JD, Loyola U., 1986. Bar: Ill. 1986, U.S. Dist. Ct. (no. dist.) Ill. 1986. Nurse Children's Meml. Hosp., Chgo., 1981-84, St. Jude's Hosp., Vieux Fort, St. Lucia, 1983; assoc. McDermott, Will & Emery, Chgo., 1986-88, Winston & Strawn, Chgo., 1988-93; ptnr. Sonnenschein Nath & Rosenthal, Chgo., 1993-98, Davis Wright Tremaine LLP, Seattle, 1998—. Contbr. articles to profl. jours. Patron various civic, environ., charitable and polit. groups. Mem.: ANA, ABA, Workgroup for Electronic Data Interchange (chair preemption subwork group), Am. Health Lawyers Assn. Avocations: scuba diving, reading, hiking, photography. Health. Office: Davis Wright Tremaine LLP 2600 Century Sq 1501 4th Ave Seattle WA 98101-1688 E-mail: beckywilliams@dwt.com.

WILLIAMS, RICHARD LEROY, federal judge; b. Morrisville, Va., Apr. 6, 1923; s. Wilcie Edward and Minnie Mae (Brinkley) W.; m. Eugenia Kellogg, Sept. 11, 1948; children: Nancy Williams Davies, R. Gregory, Walter L., Gwendolyn Mason. LLB, U. Va., 1951. Bar: Va. 1951. Ptnr. McGuire, Woods & Battle and predecessor firms, 1951-72; judge Cir. Ct. City of Richmond, 1972-76; ptnr. McGuire, Woods & Battle, 1976-80; dist. judge U.S. Dist. Ct., Richmond, Va., 1980—, sr. judge, 1992—. 2d lt. Air Corps., U.S. Army, 1940-45. Fellow Am. Coll. Trial Lawyers; mem. Va. State Bar, Va. Bar Assn., Richmond Bar Assn. Office: US Dist Ct/Lewis F Powell Ste 305 1000 E Main St Richmond VA 23219-3525 E-mail: barbarakreuter@uaed.uscourts.gov.

WILLIAMS, ROGER COURTLAND, lawyer; b. Atlanta, June 11, 1944; s. Ralph Roger and Beatrice (Hill) W.; m. Jo Ann Davenport, June 9, 1968; children: Melissa, Kimberly, Courtland. BS, U. Ala., 1966, JD, 1969. Bar: Ala. 1969, U.S. Dist. Ct. (no. and mid. dists.) Ala. 1969, U.S. Supreme Ct. 1972. V.p. Williams, Williams & Williams, P.C., Tuscaloosa, Ala., 1969-90, pres., 1990—. Adj. prof. U. Ala. Sch. Law, 1999—. Mem. bd. trustees Tuscaloosa Acad., 1987—, pres., 1990-94; bd. dirs. Children's Hands On Mus., Tuscaloosa, 1986-97. 1st lt. U.S. Army, 1969-71. Mem. ABA, Ala. State Bar Assn. (vice chmn. ADR com. 1997-98), Assn. Trial Lawyers Am., Nat. Acad. Arbitrators, Am. Arbitration Assn., Jaycees (nat. assoc. legal counsel 1979-80, state pres. 1978-79, pres. Ala. Found. 1980-81, Internat. Senator), Tuscaloosa Toastmasters (pres. 1975), Kiwanis of Tuscaloosa (bd. dirs. 1974, 90, v.p. 1995-98, pres. 1998-99), Kiwanis of Ala. (dist. lt. gov. 2001-2002), Indian Hills Country Club (bd. dirs. 1996—, v.p. 2003—). Methodist. Alternative dispute resolution, General civil litigation, General practice. Office: Williams Williams & Williams PC PO Box 2690 Tuscaloosa AL 35403-2690

WILLIAMS, RONALD DOHERTY, lawyer; b. New Haven, Conn., Apr. 6, 1927; s. Richard Hugh and Ethel W. (Nelson) w.; m. Laura Costarelli, Aug. 25, 1951; children: Craig F., Ronald D., Ellen A., Jane E. BA, U. Va., 1951; LLB, 1954. Bar: Conn. 1954. Assoc. Pullman, Comley, Bradley & Reeves, Bridgeport, Conn., 1954-60; ptnr., 1960-88, Williams, Cooney & Sheehy, 1989—. Mem. Fed. Jud. Com., 1988-91, com. unauthorized practice law, 1988-94, com. to study rules civil practice & procedure, 1984-86; atty. state trial referee, 1984-90. Selectman Town of Easton (Conn.), 1975-85, justice of the peace, 1977—, town atty., 1985-2000; mem. Bridgeport Area Found., 1971-90, adv. com. U. Bridgeport Law Sch., 1982-92; mem. statewide grievance com., 1985-91, chmn., 1989-91; mem. exec. bd. Sch. Law Quinnipiac Coll., 1994—. Served with U.S. Army, 1945-46. Fellow Am. Coll. Trial Lawyers; mem. ABA, Am. Bd. Trial Advs., Conn. Bar Assn. (bd. govs. 1975-78), Bridgeport Bar Assn. (pres. 1975), Conn. Def. Lawyers Assn. (pres. 1984-85), Trial Attys. Am. Republican. Roman Catholic. State civil litigation, Insurance, Personal injury (including property damage). Home: 14 Newman Dr Easton CT 06612-1915 Office: 799 Silver Ln Trumbull CT 06611-0753 E-mail: WilCooShee@aol.com.

WILLIAMS, SAMUEL ROBERT, lawyer; b. Chgo., Feb. 8, 1954; s. Samuel Wesley Williams Jr. and Lilla (Waring) Williams; m. Tracy S. Sherwood, June 8, 1991; children: Lauren Leigh, Haley Anne. BA, Lehigh U., 1976; JD, Syracuse U., 1979. Bar: N.Y. 1982, U.S. Dist. Ct. (no. dist.) N.Y. Assoc. Smiley, Schwartz and Captain, N.Y.C., 1982—84; asst. corp. counsel, sr. trial counsel Torts divsn. N.Y.C. Corp. Counsel, Bklyn., 1984—87; assoc. Sugarman, Wallace, Manheim and Schoenwald, Syracuse, NY, 1988—90; ptnr. Williams and Fleckenstein, Syracuse, 1990—94; pvt. practice Syracuse, 1994—. Mem.: ATLA, N.Y. State Trial Lawyers, Am. Bd. Trial Adv. Avocations: skiing, flying. Personal injury (including property damage). Office: 250 Harrison St Ste 302 Syracuse NY 13202

WILLIAMS, SPENCER MORTIMER, federal judge; b. Reading, Mass., Feb. 24, 1922; s. Theodore Ryder and Anabel (Hutchison) W.; m. Kathryn Bramlage, Aug. 20, 1943; children: Carol Marcia (Mrs. James B. Garvey), Peter, Spencer, Clark, Janice, Diane (Mrs. Sean Quinn). AB, UCLA, 1943; postgrad., Hastings Coll. Law, 1946; JD, U. Calif., Berkeley, 1948. Bar: Calif. 1949, U.S. Supreme Ct. 1952. Assoc. Beresford & Adams, San Jose, Calif., 1949, Rankin, O'Neal, Center, Luckhardt, Bonney, Marlais & Lund, San Jose, Evans, Jackson & Kennedy, Sacramento; county counsel Santa Clara County, 1955-67; adminstr. Calif. Health and Welfare Agy., Sacramento, 1967—70; judge U.S. Dist. Ct. (no. dist.) Calif., San Francisco, from 1971, now sr. judge. County exec. pro tem, Santa Clara County; adminstr. Calif. Youth and Adult Corrections Agy., Sacramento; sec. Calif. Human Relations Agy., Sacramento, 1967-70 Chmn. San Jose Christmas Seals Drive, 1953, San Jose Muscular Dystrophy Drive, 1953, 54; team capt. fund raising drive San Jose YMCA, 1960; co-chmn. indsl. sect. fund raising drive Alexian Bros. Hosp., San Jose, 1964; team capt. fund raising drive San Jose Hosp.; mem. com. on youth and govt. YMCA, 1967-68; Candidate for Calif. Assembly, 1954, Calif. Atty. Gen., 1966, 70; Bd. dirs. San Jose Better Bus. Bur., 1955-66, Boys City Boys' Club, San Jose, 1965-67; pres. trustees Santa Clara County Law Library, 1955-66. Served with USNR, 1943-46; to lt. comdr. JAG Corps USNR, 1950-52, PTO. Named San Jose Young Man of Year, 1954 Mem. ABA, Calif. Bar Assn. (vice chmn. com. on publicly employed attys. 1962-63), Santa Clara County Bar Assn., Sacramento Bar Assn., Internat. Assn. Trial Judges (pres. 1995-96), Calif. Dist. Attys. Assn. (pres. 1963-64), Nat. Assn. County Civil Attys. (pres. 1963-64), 9th Cir. Dist. Judges Assn. (pres. 1981-83), Fed. Judges Assn. (pres. 1982-87), Kiwanis, Theta Delta Chi.

WILLIAMS, STEPHEN FAIN, federal judge; b. N.Y.C., N.Y., Sept. 23, 1936; s. Charles Dickerman and Virginia (Fain) Williams; m. Faith Morrow, June 11, 1966; children: Susan, Geoffrey Fain, Sarah Margot Nu, Timothy Dwight, Nicholas Morrow. BA, Yale U., 1958; JD, Harvard U., 1961. Bar: N.Y. 1962, Colo. 1977. Assoc. Debevoise, Plimpton, Lyons & Gates, N.Y.C., 1962—66; asst. atty. U.S. Dist. Ct. (so. dist.), NY, 1966—69; asst. prof. law U. Colo., Boulder, 1969—77, prof., 1977—86; judge U.S. Ct. Appeals (D.C. cir.), Washington, 1986—. Vis. prof. UCLA, 1975—76; vis. prof., fellow in law and econs. U. Chgo., 1979—80; vis. William L. Hutchison prof. energy law So. Meth. U., 1983—84; cons. Adminstrv. Conf. U.S., 1974—76, FTC, 1983—85; mem. Boulder Area Growth Study Commn., 1972—73. Contbr. articles to profl. jours. and mags. With U.S. Army, 1961—62. Mem.: Am. Law Inst. Office: US Courthouse 3rd & Constitution Ave NW Washington DC 20001 E-mail: SFWilliams@cadc.uscourts.gov.

WILLIAMS, STEVEN MARK, lawyer; b. Guthrie, Okla., Mar. 25, 1954; s. Bob G. and Martha Jane Williams; m. Caron F. Henderson, Dec. 29, 1989 (div.); children: Casey, Blake, Steven Jr. BBA with hons., U. Tex., 1975; JD, Tex. Tech. U., 1979. Bar: Tex. Atty. El Paso Natural Gas Co., 1979-81, Transco Energy Co., Houston, 1981-83, Diamond Shamrock Corp., Dallas, 1983-85; assoc. Troy Douthitt, Wichita Falls, Tex., 1986-87; pvt. practice Wichita Falls, 1988—. Football coach, Boys Clubs Am., Wichita Falls, 1998. Voted Texhoma's Best Atty., Readers of Wichita Falls Times Record Newspaper, 98, 99, 2000, 02; Golden Gloves Boxer. Mem. ATLA, State Bar of Tex., Tex. Trial Lawyers Assn., Wichita County Bar Assn., Phi Delta Phi, Phi Beta Kappa. Bankruptcy, Criminal, Personal injury (including property damage). Office: 901 Lamar St Wichita Falls TX 76301-3414

WILLIAMS, THEODORE JOSEPH, JR., lawyer; b. Pitts., July 23, 1947; s. Theodore Joseph and Isabel (McAnulty) W.; m. Sherri Lynn Foust, July 4, 1970; children: Kelley Shields, Jonathan Stewart, Jordan Fuller. BA, Purdue U., 1969; JD, U. Tulsa, 1974. Bar: Ill. 1975, Colo. 1996, U.S. Ct. Appeals (7th cir.) 1975, U.S. Dist. Ct. (no., so. and cen. dists.) Ill. 1975, Mo. 1978, U.S. Ct. Appeals (8th cir.) 1978, U.S. Dist. Ct. (ea. and we. dists.) Mo. 1978, U.S. Supreme Ct. 1978, D.C. 1981, U.S. Ct. Appeals (D.C. cir.) 1988, U.S. Dist. Ct. D.C 1988, U.S. Ct. Mil. Appeals 1991, U.S. Ct. Appeals (10 cir.) 1996, U.S. Dist. Ct. (no. dist.) Ind. 2000. Asst. city prosecutor City of Tulsa, 1974; trial atty., law dept. Chgo. and North Western R.R., Chgo., 1975-78; assoc. Thompson and Mitchell, St. Louis, 1978-81, Shepherd, Sandberg & Phoenix, P.C., St. Louis, 1981-84, ptnr., 1984-88; ptnr., chmn. transp. law dept. Armstrong, Teasdale, Schlafly & Davis, St. Louis, 1988-2001, mem. mgmt. com., 1994—2000; ptnr. Williams, Venker & Sanders, LLC, St. Louis, 2001—. State Counsel for Mo. and Ill., Chgo. and North Western Transp. Co., 1981-95. Assoc. editor Law. Jour., U. Tulsa, 1974. Treas. sch. bd. Mary Queen of Peace Sch., Webster Groves, Mo., 1986, v.p., 1987. Lt. col. U.S. Army. Mem. ABA (vice chmn. rail and motor carrier law com., torts and ins. practice law sect. 1989-90, chair-elect 1990-91, chair 1991-92), Ill. Bar Assn., Mo. Bar Assn., Def. Rsch. Inst. (chair, railroad law com. 1996), Nat. Assn. R.R. Trial Coun. (exec. com. 2002--), We. Conf. Ry. Coun., Assn. ICC Practitioners, Maritime Law Assn., Internat. Assn. Def. Coun., Fedn. Def. and Ins. Counsel, Transp. Lawyers Assn., Assn. Transp. Practitioners, Fedn. Def. and Corp. Counsel, D.C. Bar Assn., Colo. Bar Assn. Republican. Roman Catholic. Personal injury (including property damage), Product liability, Transportation. Office: Williams Venker Sanders LLC Ste 1600 10 S Broadway St Saint Louis MO 63102 E-mail: Twilliams@wvslaw.com.

WILLIAMS, WALTER JOSEPH, lawyer; b. Detroit, Oct. 5, 1918; s. Joseph Louis and Emma Geraldine (Hewitt) W.; m. Maureen June Kay, Jan. 15, 1944; 1 child, John Bryan. Student, Bowling Green State U., 1935-36; BSBA, Ohio State U., 1940; JD, LL.B., U. Detroit, 1942. Bar: Mich. bar 1942. Title atty. Abstract & Title Guaranty Co., 1946-47; corp. atty. Ford Motor Co., 1947-51, Studebaker-Packard Corp., 1951-56; asst. sec., house counsel Am. Motors Corp., Am. Motors Sales Corp., Am. Motors Pan-Am. Corp., Evart Products Co., Ltd., 1956-65, corp. sec. house counsel, 1965-72; asst. corp. sec., dir. Am. Motors (Can.) Ltd.; dir. Evart Products Co., 1959-72; dir., corporate sec., house counsel Jeep Corp., Jeep Sales Corp., Jeep Internat. Corp., 1968-72; partner Gilman and Williams, Southfield, Mich., 1972-74; atty. Detroit Edison Co., 1974-75; asst. sec., sr. staff atty. Burroughs Corp. (and subsidiaries), 1975-84; pvt. practice, pres. Walter J. Williams P.C., Bloomfield Hills, Mich., 1984—. Charter commr., city of Dearborn Heights, Mich., 1960-63; dir. Detroit Met. Indsl. Devel. Corp., 1962-72, also asst. sec. Served to capt. U.S. Army, 1942-46. Mem. ABA, Detroit Bar Assn. (chmn. corp. gen. counsel com. 1965-68), Fed. Bar Assn., State Bar Mich., Ohio State U. Alumni Assn. (pres. Detroit 1961-63), U. Detroit Law Alumni, Delta Theta Phi. Clubs: Oakland Hills Country. Home and Office: 3644 Darcy Dr Bloomfield Hills MI 48301-2125

WILLIAMS, WAYNE LEROY, lawyer; b. Albany, Oreg., Feb. 21, 1945; s. Verne Delmer and Henrietta Jane (Zeller) W.; m. Kathleen Ann Sharar (div.); children: Brendan Wayne, Brooke Kathleen; m. Melanie Sue Stewart, Dec. 22, 1990; children: Sara Marie Stewart-Gerla, Blaire Starling Stewart-Gerla. BS in Journalism, U. Oreg., 1967, JD, 1970. Bar: Wash. 1970, U.S. Dist. Ct. (we. dist.) Wash. 1970, U.S. Dist. Ct. (ea. dist.) Wash. 1974, U.S. Ct. Appeals (9th cir.) 1972, U.S. Claims Ct. 1992, U.S. Supreme Ct. 1973. Asst. atty. gen. Wash. State Atty. Gen., Olympia, 1970-78; dir., counsel People's Orgn. for Washington Energy Resources, Olympia, 1978-80; pvt. practice Olympia, 1980-85; shareholder Rolland, O'Malley, Williams & Wyckoff, Olympia, 1986. Bar examiner Wash. State Bar, 1978. Coun. mem. City of Tumwater, Wash. Chmn. Parks and Recreation Bd., Tumwater, Wash., 1993-94. Mem.: Wash. State Trial Lawyers Assn. (chmn. workers compensation sect.). Avocations: flyfishing, golf. Administrative and regulatory, Personal injury (including property damage), Workers' compensation. Office: Rolland O'Malley et al 1405 Harrison Ave NW Olympia WA 98502-5360

WILLIAMS, WILLIAM JOHN, JR., lawyer; b. New Rochelle, N.Y., Feb. 6, 1937; s. William John and Jane (Gormley) W.; m. Barbara Reuter. BA, Holy Cross Coll., Worcester, Mass., 1958; LLB, NYU, 1961. Bar: N.Y. 1961. Practiced in, N.Y.C., 1962—; ptnr. firm Sullivan & Cromwell, 1969—. Trustee NYU Law Sch. Found., 1977—, Holy Cross Coll., 1988-96. Fellow Am. Bar Found.; mem. ABA, Am. Law Inst., N.Y. State Bar Assn., Assn. of Bar of City of N.Y., U.S. Golf Assn. (mem. exec. com. 1978-87, sec. 1980-81, v.p. 1982-85, pres. 1986-87). Democrat. Roman Catholic. Corporate, general, Private international, Securities. E-mail: williamsw@sullcrom.com.

WILLIAMSON, CHARLES READY, III, lawyer; b. Boston, Jan. 2, 1944; s. Charles Ready and Anne Margaret (Livingstone) W.; m. Julie Anne Williamson, Nov. 6, 1971; 1 dau., Anne Lucinda. B.A., Colgate U., 1965; LL.B., Suffolk U., 1968. Bar: Mass. 1968, Oreg. 1970, U.S. Supreme Ct. 1977. Law clk. to Judge Joseph B. Silverio, Mass. land ct., Boston 1968-69; VISTA atty., dep. dir. Multnomah County Legal Aid Service, Portland, 1970-74; assoc. Kell, Alterman & Runstein, Portland, 1974-78, 88—; pvt. practice, Portland, 1978-88; pres. Oreg. Legal Service Corp., 1976-77; mem. Oreg. Bd. Psychologist Examiners, 1973-74; chmn. Oreg. Grad. Sch. Profl. Psychology, Pacific U. Pres. Oreg. Consumer League, 1972-74; councilor Met. Service Dist. 1978-84; treas. Democratic Bus. Forum 1982-84. Mem. ABA, Oreg. Bar Assn. (pres.-elect 2002-03, pres. 2003-), Multnomah County Bar Assn. Club: Portland City. Contbr. in field. State civil litigation, General practice, Legislative. Home: 5304 SW 34th Pl Portland OR 97201-1125 Office: Kell Alterman & Runstein 520 SW Yamhill Ste 600 Portland OR 97204-1329*

WILLIAMSON, DOUGLAS FRANKLIN, JR., lawyer; b. Anniston, Ala., Mar. 23, 1930; s. Douglas Franklin and Elizabeth Louise (Connor) W.; m. Barbara Tuerk, Dec. 28, 1957; children: Mary Leyden, Douglas Franklin III, Bruce Reynolds. AB summa cum laude, Amherst Coll., 1952; LLB, Yale U., 1955. Bar: NY 1958, Fla. 1976. Assoc. Breed, Abbott & Morgan, N.Y.C., 1957-63, ptnr., 1963-72, Williamson & Hess and predecessor firm, N.Y.C., 1972-79; of counsel Winthrop, Stimson, Putnam & Roberts, N.Y.C., 1979-81, ptnr., 1982-95, sr. counsel, 1996-2000, Pillbury Winthrop LLP, N.Y.C., 2001—. Bd. dirs. World Wildlife Fund, Washington, 1979-88, treas., 1986-88, mem. nat. coun., 1988—; bd. dirs. Conservation Found., Washington, 1985-88, treas., 1986-88; bd. dirs. Lower Hudson chpt. Nature Conservancy, Katonah, N.Y., 1976-87, 93-97, sec., 1976-87, hon. dir., 1987—, chmn., 1993-94; bd. dirs. Oblong Land Conservancy, Pawling, N.Y., 1990-98, chmn. 1996-98; bd. dirs. Quaker Hill Civic Assn., Pawling, 1974-2000, past pres.; chmn. Pawling Assessment Rev. Bd., 1976-2001. With U.S. Army, 1955-57. Fellow N.Y. State Bar Found.; mem. Assn. Bar City N.Y. (life), English Spkg. Union, Old Guard Soc. Palm Beach Golfers, Everglades Club, Quaker Hill Country Club (pres. 1980-81), Phi Beta Kappa, Phi Beta Kappa Soc. (sec. 1975-77, v.p. 1977-79). Office: Pillsbury Winthrop LLP One Battery Park Plz New York NY 10004

WILLIAMSON, MELISSA, lawyer; b. Tallahassee, June 14, 1972; d. Dennis Arthur and Juanita Dolores Williamson. BA, U. Fla., 1994, JD, 1997. Bar: Fla. 1997. Asst. state atty. State Atty.'s Office, Jacksonville, 1997—. Mem.: Bedell Inns Ct. (barrister). Office: State Attys Office 330 E Bay St Jacksonville FL 32202 E-mail: melissaw@coj.net.

WILLIAMSON, PETER DAVID, lawyer; b. Houston, Oct. 13, 1944; s. Sam and Sophie Ann (Kaplan) W.; m. Patricia Golemon; children: Heather, Amber, Asia, Ginger. BA, U. Ill., 1966; JD, U. Tex., 1969. Bar: Tex. 1969, U.S. Supreme Ct. 1974, U.S. Ct. Appeals (4th, 5th, 6th, 8th, 9th, 10th, 11th and D.C. cirs.); lic. comml. pilot. Pvt. practice, Houston, 1971—. Founder IMMLAW, The Nat. Consortium of Immigration Law Firms. Mem. Am. Immigration Lawyers Assn. (pres. 1994-95). General civil litigation, Immigration, naturalization, and customs. Home: 2417 Branard St Houston TX 77098-2213 Office: 500 Jefferson Ste 2040 Houston TX 77002 E-mail: pwilliamson@pdwlaw.com.

WILLIAMSON, RONALD THOMAS, lawyer; b. Paterson, N.J., Nov. 12, 1948; s. Thomas Sim and Jessie Carnegie (Sandilands) W.; m. Nancy Anne Hough, June 13, 1982; children: Kate Elizabeth, Brad Francis Thomas. BA, Rutgers U., 1970; JD cum laude, Widener U., 1975. Bar: Pa. 1976, U.S. Dist. Ct. (ea. dist.) Pa. 1976, U.S. Supreme Ct. 1979, U.S. Ct. Appeals (3d cir.) 1980. Assoc. Modell, Pincus, Hahn and Reich, Phila., 1976-77; asst. dist. atty., chief of appeals County of Montgomery, Norristown, Pa., 1977-85; sr. dep. atty. gen. appeals and legal svcs. sect. Pa. Atty. Gen., Harrisburg, 1997—. 1997—. Instr. search and seizure Southeastern Tng. Ctr., Pa. State Police, Worcester, 1979-85; legal instr. Montgomery County C.C., Whitpain, Pa., 1984. Contbr. to profl. publs. Bd. dirs. Denbigh Group Foster Home, Bridgeport, Pa., 1979-83, pres., 1984; mem. Cen. Montgomery Optimist Club, Norristown, 1980-81. Mem. Pa. Bar Assn., Montgomery County Bar Assn. (chmn. appellate ct. practice com., bd. dirs.). Republican. Presbyterian. Avocations: tennis, squash, sailing, triathlon, reading. Office: Pa Office Atty Gen 2490 Blvd of the Generals Norristown PA 19403-5234 E-mail: rwilliamson@attorneygeneral.gov.

WILLIAMS-PEARSON, CYNTHIA L. lawyer, accountant; b. Biloxi, Miss., Dec. 30, 1955; d. Leroy and Hiltrud Williams; children: Jessica Christine Pearson, Kimberly Kristen Pearson. BA in Econs., U. Calif., Santa Barbara, 1979; MS in Bus. Taxation, Golden Gate U., 1986; JD, Tex. Wesleyan U., 2000. Bar: Tex. 2000, U.s. Dist. Ct. (no. dist.) Tex. 2000, U.S. Tax Ct. 2000. Tax mgr. KPMG PeatMarwick, Long Beach, Calif., 1986—88; pvt. practice CPA Manhattan Beach, Calif., 1988—91, Bedford, Tex., 1991—97; assoc. Whitaker, Chalk, Swindle & Sawyer, Ft. Worth, 1998—2003, Cynthia L. Williams-Pearson PLLC, 2003—. Co-chair tax and estate planning sect. Tarrant County Bar Assn., Ft. Worth, 2002—; dir. Tarrant County Probate Bar Assn., Ft. Worth, 2002—; adj. prof., area chair for law U. Phoenix, Dallas, Ft. Worth campus, 2001—; adj. prof. U. Tex. Arlington, 2003—. Mem.: ABA. Republican. Avocations: tennis, running, bicycling, Tae Kwon Do. Estate planning, Probate (including wills, trusts), Taxation, general. Home: PO Box 256 Bedford TX 76095 Office: 2324 Cheek Sparger RD Ste A Bedford TX 76021 Office Fax: 817-399-9785. E-mail: cwilliamspearson@aol.com.

WILLIAN, CLYDE FRANKLIN, lawyer; b. Indpls., Sept. 20, 1930; s. Clyde W. and Ruth L. (Robinson) W.; m. Patricia Strong, Aug. 16, 1953; children: James, Jeffrey, John, Mary, Michael. BS, Rose-Hulman Inst. Tech., 1952; postgrad. Ind. U., 1953-54; LLB, George Washington U., 1957; postgrad. Chgo. Kent Coll. Law, 1957. Bar: Ill. 1957, U.S. Supreme Ct. 1970, U.S. Dist. Ct. (no. dist.) Ill. 1957, U.S. Ct. Appeals (7th cir.) 1958. With Willian Brinks Hofer Gilson & Lione Ltd. and predecessors, Chgo., 1957—, pres., 1978—. Bd. dirs. Hadley Sch. for Blind, Rose-Hulman Inst. Tech. Mem. ABA, Chgo. Bar Assn., Ill. Bar Assn., Bar Assn. 7th Fed. Circuit, Am. Judicature Soc., Am. Patent Law Assn., Phi Alpha Delta. Republican. Episcopalian. Clubs: Union League (Chgo.); Skokie Country. Antitrust, Federal civil litigation, Patent. Office: Sidley Austin Brown and Wood Bank One Plz Chicago IL 60603-5503

WILLINGHAM, CLARK SUTTLES, lawyer; b. Houston, Nov. 29, 1944; s. Paul Suttles and Elsie Dell (Clark) W.; m. Jane Joyce Hitch, Aug. 16, 1969; children: Meredith Moores, James Barrett. BBA, Tex. Tech U., 1967; JD, So. Meth. U., 1971, LLM, 1984. Bar: Tex. 1971. Ptnr. Kasmir, Willingham & Krage, Dallas, 1972-86, Finley, Kumble et al, Dallas, 1986-87, Brice & Mankoff, Dallas, 1988-98, Moseley Martens, LLP, Dallas, 1999—. Contbr. articles to profl. jours. Exec. com. Dallas Summer Musicals, 1979-93, pres., 1994-95. Mem. ABA (chmn. agrl. com. tax sect. 1984-86), State Bar Tex. (chmn. agrl. tax com. 1985-87), Dallas Bar Assn., Am. Law Inst., Tex. Rangers Law Enforcement Assn.(bd. dirs. 2000—), Nat. Cattlemen's Beef Assn. (bd. dirs., pres. 1998), U.S. Meat Export Fedn. (exec. com. 1991-93), Beef Industry Coun. (exec. com. 1990-91, promotion chmn. 1992-94), Tex. Cattle Feeders Assn. (bd. dirs., pres. 1988), Tex. Bd. Vet. Med. Examiners (pres. 1994), Tex. Beef Coun. (bd. dirs., pres. 1989), Dallas Country Club. Republican. Episcopalian. Corporate taxation, Estate taxation, Personal income taxation. Home: 3824 Shenandoah St Dallas TX 75205-1702 Office: Moseley Martens LLP 3878 Oak Lawn Ave Fl 4 Dallas TX 75219-4460

WILLIS, BRUCE DONALD, judge; b. Mpls., Jan. 29, 1941; s. Donald Robert and Marie Evelyn (Edwards) W.; m. Elizabeth Ann Runsvold, July 17, 1971; children: Andrew John, Ellen Elizabeth. BA in English, Yale U., 1962; LLB, Harvard U., 1965. Bar: Minn., 1965, U.S. Dist. Ct. Minn. 1965, U.S. Ct. Fed. Claims 1989, U.S. Ct. Appeals (8th cir.) 1991, U.S. Supreme Ct. 1992. Assoc. Popham, Haik, Schnobrich & Kaufman, Ltd., Mpls., 1965-71, ptnr., 1971-95; judge Minn. Ct. Appeals, 1995—. Mem. jud. adv. bd. Law and Orgnl. Econs. Ctr., U. Kans., 1997—2001. Contbr. articles to profl. jours. Del. Rep. Nat. convs., 1976, 88; vice chmn. Ind.-Rep. Party Minn., 1979-81; mem. State Ethical Practices Bd., 1990-95, sec. 1990-91, vice chmn. 1991-92, chmn., 1992-93; mem. Minn. Commn. on Jud. Selection, 1991-94; mem. Minn. Bd. Jud. Stds., 1997—; mem. adv. com. on rules of civil appellate procedure Minn. Supreme Ct., 1997—. Named one of 1990's Lawyers of Yr., Minn. Jour. Law and Politics, 1991, one of Minn.'s Best Trial Lawyers, Minn. Lawyer, 1991. Mem.: ABA, Minn. Bar Assn. (professionalism com. 1998—). Mem. United Ch. of Christ. Home: 2940 Walnut Grove Ln N Plymouth MN 55447-1567 Office: Minn Jud Ctr 25 Rev Dr Martin Luther King Jr Blvd Saint Paul MN 55155-1500 E-mail: bruce.willis@courts.state.mn.us.

WILLIS, CALVIN C. lawyer; b. Shreveport, La., Dec. 15, 1958; s. A. C. and Bobbie Jane Willis. BA, La. Tech. U., 1980; JD, Boston Coll., 1986. Bar: Calif. Atty. pvt. practice. Pro bono legal svcs. African Am. Laywers Am. Mem.: ABA, C. of C. Avocations: tennis, basketball, weightlifting, bicycling. Probate (including wills, trusts). Home: 10806 Floralita Ave Sunland CA 91040 E-mail: calvincw@attbi.com.

WILLIS, DAWN LOUISE, legal assistant, small business owner; b. Johnstown, Pa., Sept. 11, 1959; d. Kenneth William and Dawn Louise (Joseph) Hagins; m. Marc Anthony Ross, Nov. 30, 1984 (div.); m. Jerry Wayne Willis, Dec. 16, 1989 (div.). Grad. high sch., Sacramento, Calif. Legal sec. Wilcoxen & Callahan, Sacramento, 1979-87, paralegal asst., 1987-88; legal adminstr. Law Office Jack Vetter, 1989-99; owner, mgr. Your Girl Friday Secretarial and Legal Support Svcs., 1991—; legal asst. Foley & Lardner, 1999-2001; case mgr. Larry Lockshin, Esq. Law Corp., 2001—02; legal asst. Hunter, Richey, Di Benedetto & Eisenbeis, 2002—03, Downey Brand LLP, 2003—. Vol ARC, 1985, Spec Olympics, 1997—. Mem.: Sacramento Legal Secys Asn. Democrat. Avocations: water sports, camping, reading, cooking. Office: Downey Brand LLP 555 Capitol Mall Sacramento CA 95814 E-mail: dwillis@downeybrand.com.

WILLIS, JOHN ALEXANDER, lawyer; b. Queens, N.Y., Feb. 3, 1966; s. John Joseph Willis and Dorothy Elizabeth (Savides) White. BA, SUNY, Stony Brook, 1989; JD, Nova Southeastern Law Ctr., 1994. Bar: Fla. 1994, U.S. Ct. Appeals (11th cir.) 1994, N.Y. 1995, U.S. Dist. Ct. (so. dist.) Fla. 1995, U.S. Supreme Ct., 1999. Acct. coord. Met. Life Ins. Co., Hauppauge, NY, 1989—91; cert. legal intern Palm Beach County State's Atty Office, West Palm Beach, Fla., 1994; assoc. David & French, P.A., Boca Raton, Fla., 1994—2000, Baker & Zimmerman, P.A., Boca Raton, 2000—01; ptnr. Law Offices of John A. Willis, P.A., Boca Raton, 2001—. Mem. ATLA, Acad. Fla. Trial Lawyers, South Palm Beach County Bar Assn. Avocations: golf, computers, softball. General civil litigation, Insurance, Personal injury (including property damage). Office: Law Offices of John A Willis 5355 Town Center Rd #801 Boca Raton FL 33486 E-mail: jawillis@aol.com.

WILLISCROFT-BARCUS, BEVERLY RUTH, lawyer; b. Conrad, Mont., Feb. 24, 1945; d. Paul A. and Gladys L. (Buck) W.; m. Kent J. Barcus, Oct. 1984. BA in Music, So. Calif. Coll., 1967; JD, John F. Kennedy U., 1977. Bar: Calif. 1977. Elem. tchr., Sunnyvale, Calif., 1968-72; legal sec., legal asst. various law firms, 1972-77; assoc. Neil D. Reid, Inc., San Francisco, 1977-79; sole practice Concord, Calif., 1979—. Exam. grader Calif. Bar, 1979—; real estate broker, 1980-88; tchr. real estate King Coll., Concord, 1979-80; judge pro-tem Mcpl. Ct., 1981-93; mem. Stage Right Drama Group, Concord, Calif., 1999—; lectr. in adoption law. Co-author: Adoption Law in California, Adoption Practice, Procedure and Pitfalls in California; lectr. in field. Bd. dirs. Contra Costa Musical Theatre, Inc., 1978-82, v.p. adminstrn., 1980-81, v.p. prodn., 1981-82; mem. community devel. adv. com. City of Concord, 1981-83, vice chmn., 1982-83, mem. status of women com., 1980-81, mem. redevel. adv. com., 1984-86, planning commnr. 1986-92, chmn., 1990; mem. exec. bd. Mt. Diablo coun. Boy Scouts Am., 1981-85; bd. dirs. Pregnancy Ctrs. Contra Costa County, 1991-2001, chmn., 1993-2000 Mem. Concord C. of C. (bd. dirs., chmn. govt. affairs com. 1981-83, v.p. 1985-87, pres. 1988-89, Bus. Person of Yr. 1986), Calif. State Bar (chmn. adoptions subcom. north, 1994), Contra Costa County Bar Assn., Christian Legal Soc., Todos Santos Bus. and Profl. Women (co-founder, pres. 1983-84, pub. rels. chmn. 1982-83, Woman of Achievement 1980, 81), Soroptimists (fin. sec. 1980-81). Office: PO Box 981 Pittsburg CA 94565-0098 E-mail: Barcus4@attbi.com.

WILLOUGHBY, KIMBERLY RAE, lawyer; b. Vermillion, S.D., July 3, 1968; d. H. William and Ardice Ann Willoughby. BA, U. Colo., 1991; JD, U. Va., 1994. Bar: Colo. 1994, U.S. Dist. Ct. Colo. 1994. Mgr. Willoughby Law Firm, Colo., 1996; clk. Colo. Ct. Appeals, 1996; Atty. Popham Heik, 1994—96. Contbr. articles to profl. jours. Bd. dirs. Equal Rights Colo., Denver, 2001—. Mem.: Thompson Marsh Inn of Ct. Avocations: history, Harley Davidson's, Scrabble. Office: Willoughby Law Firm 303 17th Ave Ste 840 Denver CO 80203 Fax: 303-839-1750. E-mail: kim@willoughbylaw.com.

WILLSON, PRENTISS, JR., lawyer; b. Durham, NC, Sept. 20, 1943; s. Prentiss and Lucille (Giles) W. AB, Occidental Coll., 1965; JD, Harvard U., 1968. Bar: Calif. 1969, U.S. Dist. Ct. (no. dist.) Calif. 1971, U.S. Ct. Appeals (9th cir.) 1971, U.S. Tax Ct. 1971, U.S. Supreme Ct. 1975. Instr. law Miles Coll., Birmingham, Ala., 1968-70; ptnr. Morrison & Foerster, San Francisco, 1970-98, Ernst & Young, Walnut Creek, Calif., 1998—. Prof. Golden Gate U., 1971-84; lectr. Stanford U. Sch. Law, 1985-88. Contbr. articles to profl. jours. Mem. ABA, Calif. Bar Assn. Democrat. Corporate taxation, Personal income taxation, State and local taxation. Office: Ernst & Young 1331 N California Blvd Walnut Creek CA 94596 E-mail: prentiss.willson@ey.com.

WILLY, THOMAS RALPH, lawyer; b. Phila., Sept. 30, 1943; s. Albert Ralph and Dorothy Rose (Driver) W.; m. Kay Harris, Jan. 12, 1968; children: Elyn Alexandria, Jon Charles. BA in History, U. Mo.-Kansas City, 1966, JD with distinction, 1974. Bar: Mo. 1974, U.S. Tax Ct. 1982. Assoc. Deacy & Deacy, Kansas City, 1974-75, Logan, Hentzen, Haitbrink & Moore, Kansas City, 1975; ptnr. Hentzen, Haitbrink & Moore, Kansas City, 1976-78, Hentzen, Moore & Willy, Kansas City, 1978-80, Moore & Willy Profl. Corp., Kansas City, 1980-87, pres., dir., 1987-94; shareholder, dir., v.p. Van Osdol, Magruder, Erickson & Redmond, P.C., Kansas City, 1994—. Cons. Ctr. for Mgmt. Assistance, Kansas City; presenter living will project, Midwest Bioethics Ctr. Pres. Kansas City Swiss Soc., 1989-91, bd. dirs. 1993-96; bd. dirs. Greater Kansas City People to People, 1995-98, 2000—; active Greater Kansas City Coun. Philanthropy, Mid-Am. Planned Giving Coun., Nat. Com. on Planned Giving, Friends of Art, Kansas City, Kansas City Consensus, Hist. Kansas City Found. Capt. USAF, 1966-70. Mem. ABA (sect. intellectual property law, sect. bus. law), Mo. Bar Assn., Lions (bd. dirs. Leawood 1986-88, 90-92, sec. 1988-90, v.p. 1996-97. Corporate, general, Estate planning, Intellectual property. Home: 10314 Lee Blvd Shawnee Mission KS 66206-2629 Office: 2400 Commerce Tower 911 Main St Kansas City MO 64105-2009 E-mail: twilly@vomer.com.

WILMER, CHARLES MARK, lawyer; b. Phoenix, Dec. 31, 1938; s. Mark Bernard and Genevieve (Tibshraeny) W.; m. Sandra Jean Provo; children: Charles M. Jr., Thomas C., Jeffrey A., Brian N. LLB, U. Ariz., 1964. Bar: Ariz. 1964, U.S. Dist. Ct. Ariz. 1964. Pvt. practice, Phoenix, 1964—. Judge pro tem Ariz. Ct. Appeals, 1985, 93. Contbr. numerous articles to law jours. Recipient Disting. Svcs. award Ariz. Ct. Appeals, 1985. Fellow Ariz. Bar Found. (founding); mem. Ariz. State Bar (bd. legal specialization 1979), Maricopa County Bar Assn. Avocation: all outdoor activities. Workers' compensation. Office: 2504 N 3d St Phoenix AZ 85004

WILMOTH, WILLIAM DAVID, lawyer; b. Elkins, W.Va., July 11, 1950; s. Stark Amasa and Goldie (Johnson) W.; m. Rebecca Weaver, Aug. 21, 1971; children: Charles, Anne, Samuel, Peter. BS in Fin. cum laude, W.Va. U., 1972, JD, 1975. Bar: W.Va. 1975, U.S. Dist. Ct. (so. dist.) W.Va. 1975, U.S. Dist. Ct. (no. dist.) W.Va. 1976, U.S. Ct. Appeals (4th cir.) 1977, U.S. Supreme Ct. 1981, Pa. 1986. Law clk. to presiding judge U.S. Dist. Ct. (no. dist.) W.Va., Elkins, 1975-76; assoc. Bachmann, Hess, Bachmann & Garden, Wheeling, W.Va., 1976-77; asst. U.S. atty. U.S. Dept. Justice, Wheeling, 1977-80; ptnr. Schrader, Byrd, Byrum & Companion, Wheeling, 1980-93; U.S. atty. U.S. Dist. Ct. (no. dist.) W.Va., Wheeling, W.Va., 1993-99; ptnr. Steptoe & Johnson, Wheeling, 1999—. Past pres., chmn. bd. dirs. nat. trail coun. Boy Scouts Am., Wheeling; chmn. bd. dirs. Wheeling Nat. Heritage Area Corp., Wheeling YMCA, State Coll. Sys. W.Va., past chmn. Named one of Best Lawyers in Am. Mem. Def. Research Inst., Def. Trial Counsel W.Va., Rotary Club Wheeling (past pres.). Democrat. Criminal, Health, Insurance. Home: 258 Arborland Rd Wheeling WV 26003-9314 Office: Steptoe & Johnson PO Box 751 Wheeling WV 26003-0751 E-mail: wilmotw@steptoe-johnson.com.

WILNER, ALAN M. judge; b. Balt., Jan. 26, 1937; AB, Johns Hopkins U., 1958, MLA, 1966; JD, U. Md., 1962. Assoc. Sherbow, Shea & Doyle, Balt., 1962-65; asst. atty. gen. State of Md., 1965-68; assoc. Venable, Baetjer & Howard, Balt., 1968-71; asst., then chief legis. officer, govs. staff, 1971-77; assoc. judge Ct. of Spl. Appeals, 1977-90, chief judge, 1990-96; judge Ct. of Appeals, Md., 1996—. Adj. faculty U. Md. Sch. of Law, U. Balt. Sch. of Law; with Judicial Inst. Md., 1997—, chmn. bd. dirs., 1999—; mem. Md. Alternative Dispute Resolution Commn., 1998—. Mem. ABA, Md. Bar. Found., Md. State Bar Assn., Balt. County Bar Assn. Office: Md Ct of Appeals County Courts Bldg 401 Bosley Ave Towson MD 21204

WILNER, THOMAS BERNARD, lawyer; b. Toronto, Ont., Can., July 7, 1944; came to U.S., 1944; s. Morton H. and Zelda (Dunkelman) W.; m. Jane Ten Broeck; children: Amanda, Adam, David. BA, Yale U., 1966; LLB, U. Pa., 1969. Clk. to Chief Judge William Hastie U.S. Ct. Appeals, Phila., 1969-70; assoc. Debevoise Plimpton, N.Y.C., 1970-72; counsel Amtrak, Washington, 1972-73; ptnr. Arnold & Porter, Washington, 1973-89, Shearman & Sterling, Washington and Tokyo, 1989—. General civil litigation, Private international, Legislative. Office: 801 Pennsylvania Ave NW Washington DC 20004-2615

WILSEY, STEVEN M. lawyer; b. St. Petersburg, Fla., Apr. 7, 1967; BS in Fin., Fla. State U., 1989; BS in Acctg., U. Fla., 1991, JD, 1992. Bar: Fla., 1992, U.S. Tax Ct., 1992. Ptnr. Fisher and Wilsey, P.A., St. Petersburg, Fla., 1992—. Mem. Suncoasters, St. Petersburg, 1998—; dir. Family Resources, Inc., St. Petersburg, 1995%. Mem. ABA, Fla. Bar Assn., Fla. Inst. CPAs, St. Petersburg Bar Assn. (past chair tax sect. 1992—), Exch. Club (past pres.). Probate (including wills, trusts), Property, real (including real estate development, water), Estate taxation. Office: Fisher and Wilsey PA 275 4th St N Saint Petersburg FL 33701-3290 E-mail: swilsey@fisher-wilsey-law.com.

WILSING, HANS ULRICH, lawyer; b. Bonn, Germany, Nov. 22, 1961; s. Karl Heinrich and Ursula Gela W.; m. Beate Elisabeth, Aug. 21, 1995; children: Caroline, Robert. Referendarexam, U. Bonn, 1992. Bar: Cologne 1992. Asst. U. Bonn, 1989-91; clk. Bauschert Law Office, Cologne, 1990-92, Bruckhaus Law Office, Düsseldorf, Germany, 1991. Co-author: Professional Partnerships, 1994; contbr. article to profl. jour. Obergefreiter S. Tank Divsn., 1980-82. Mem. German/U.S. Lawyers Assn., German Bar Assn. Corporate, general, Mergers and acquisitions, Securities. Home: Frankenstrasse 40 50858 Cologne NRW Germany Office: Linklater Oppenhoff & Raedler Hohenstaufenring 62 50674 Cologne NRW Germany Fax: 2091435. E-mail: hans-ulrich.wilsing@linklaters.com.

WILSKE, STEPHAN, lawyer; b. Ebingen, Germany, July 16, 1962; came to U.S., 1995; s. Manfred and Irmgard (Schwarz) W. Grad., U. Aix-Marseille III, Aix-en-Provence, France, 1987; JD, U. Tübingen (Germany), 1990, MA in Polit. Sci., 1991; LLM, U. Chgo., 1996; Dr.iur, U. Tübingen, 1998. Bar: N.Y. 1997, Germany 1997. Law clk. Higher Regional Ct., Stuttgart, Germany, 1990-93; rschr., tchg. fellow faculty of law U. Tübingen, 1990-96; assoc. Rogers & Wells, N.Y.C., 1996-97; ptnr. Gleiss Lutz, Stuttgart, Germany, 1997—. Mem. faculty law coun. U. Tübingen, 1994-95; internat. adv. Korean Inst. Technology & Law; lectr. Export Acad. Reutlingen, 1999-. Co-editor: The United Nations System, 2 vols., 1996; contbr. articles to profl. jours. Bd. dirs., gen. counsel, Culture Ctr. Kupferhammer, Tübingen, 1988—. Recipient Caspar Platt award U. Chgo. Law Sch., 1996. Mem. ABA, Am. Soc. Internat. Law, Internat. Bar Assn., N.Y. State Bar Assn. Avocations: music performances, coaching soccer team. Corporate, general, Private international, Public international. Home: Fritz Elsas Str 40 70174 Stuttgart Germany Office: Gleiss Lutz Maybach str 6 70469 Stuttgart Germany E-mail: stephan.wilske@gleisslutz.com.

WILSON, ALEXANDRA M. communications executive; B in Comm. summa cum laude, M in Comm., JD, U. Pa. Bar: D.C. 1984. Assoc. Crowell & Moring, Wiley, Rein & Fielding; chief cable svcs. bur. FCC, 1990—94; v.p. pub. policy Cox Enterprises, Atlanta, 1994—. Faculty mem. ann. conf. on cable TV law Practising Law Inst.; co-chair conf. on local cable and tel. competition Strategic Rsch. Inst.; spkr. in field. Mem.: Fed. Comm. Bar Assn. (pres.-elect 2002—03, sec., asst. sec., co-chair various coms., mem. exec. com.). Office: Cox Enterprises Inc 1400 Lake Hearn Dr Atlanta GA 30319*

WILSON, BRUCE BRIGHTON, retired transportation executive, lawyer; b. Boston, Feb. 6, 1936; s. Robert Lee and Jane (Schlotterer) W.; m. Elizabeth Ann MacFarland, Dec. 31, 1958; children: Mabeth, Mary, Bruce Robert, Caroline Daly. AB, Princeton U., 1958; LLB, U. Pa., 1961. Bar: Pa. 1962. Assoc. Montgomery, McCracken, Walker & Rhoads, Phila., 1962-69; atty. U.S. Dept. Justice, Washington, 1969-79, dep. asst. atty. gen. antitrust div., 1971-76; spl. counsel Consol. Rail Corp., Phila., 1979-81, gen. counsel litigation and antitrust, 1981-82, v.p., gen. counsel, 1982-84, v.p. law, 1984-87, sr. v.p. law, 1987-97, sr. v.p. merger, 1997. Bd. dirs. Phila. Indsl. Devel. Corp., Wayne Sr. Ctr., 2001—; mem. mgmt. com. Concord Resources Group, 1989-91. Chmn. Radnor Twp. Cable Commn. Coun., 1993—2000, mem., 2002—, Radnor Twp. Ethics Commn., 2000—01; bd. dirs. Wayne Sr. Ctr. Fellow Salzburg Seminar in Am. Studies (Austria), 1965; fellow Felz Inst. State and Local Govt., 1967 Mem. ABA, Phila. Bar Assn., Corinthian Yacht Club, Beach Club Cape May. Home: 224 Chamounix Rd Wayne PA 19087-3606 E-mail: bbwils24@erols.com.

WILSON, BRUCE DUXBURY, lawyer; b. Charleston, S.C., Feb. 12, 1948; BA, U. Vt., 1970; JD, Albany Law Sch., 1973. Bar: N.Y. 1974, U.S. Dist. Ct. (no. and we. dists.) N.Y. 1974, U.S. Supreme Ct. 1978. Clk. N.Y. State Atty. Gen., Albany, 1970; pvt. practice Ithaca, N.Y., 1974—; city prosecutor City of Ithaca, 1975-80; town atty. Town of Ulysses, Trumansburg, N.Y., 1993—; asst. county atty. Tompkins County, Ithaca, 1996—. Examining counsel Ticor Title Ins. Corp.; mem. faculty Tompkins-Cortland C.C., Ithaca, 1996. Bd. dirs. Greater Ithaca Activites Ctr., Inc., Alpha House, Inc. drug rehab. ctr., Ctr. for Arts at Ithaca, Inc., McGraw House, Hospicare; dir. Ithaca Theatre Guild; mem. Cmty. Arts Task Force; chmn. Lansing Village Bd. Zoning Appeals. Capt. U.S. Army. Mem. N.Y. State Bar Assn., Tompkins County Bar Assn. (v.p., pres.-elect, pres. 1996-97), U.S. Supreme Ct. Bar Assn., Sertoma (bd. dirs. local club). Estate planning, Family and matrimonial, Property, real (including real estate development, water). Office: 103 W Seneca St Ithaca NY 14850-4145 E-mail: brucedwilson@aol.com.

WILSON, CATINA L. lawyer; d. Ray L. and Helen Marie (Massey) Abrell; m. Jack W. Wilson, July 18, 1980; children: Johnny Ray, Jake Evertt. BA in Criminal Justice, Social Work, Psychology, Anderson Coll. (Now Anderson U.), Ind., 1974; BTh, The Way Coll., Emporia, Kans., 1980; AS, Okaloosa-Walton C.C., Niceville, Florida, 1990—91; JD, U.Fla. , Gainesville, 1994. Bar: Fla. 1995. Clk. ii Montgomery Police Dept., Ala., 1974—76; mountain guide Lead Outdoor Acad., Tinnie, N.Mex., 1977—82; staff The Way Internat., Inc., New Knoxville, Ohio, 1982—89; paralegal Fla. Dept. Health and Rehab. Svcs., Crestview, 1991; rsch. clk. So. Legal Counsel, Inc., Gainesville, Fla., 1993—95; lawyer Office of the Pub. Defender, Pensacola, Fla., 1995—96, Milton, Fla., 1996—98, Office of the State Atty., Milton, Fla., 1998—. Vol. Santa Rosa County Teen Ct., Milton, 1999—2002; charter mem. CEO Roundtable for the Prevention of Sch. Violence, Milton, Fla., 1999—; chmn. Santa Rosa County SHOCAP, Milton, Fla., 1999—; adj. prof. Troy State U., Milton - Whiting Naval Air Sta., 1999—2000; vol. Santa Rosa County Teen Ct., Milton, Fla., 1999—; co-chair Santa Rosa County Juvenile Justice Coun., Milton, Fla., 2002—. Big sister Big Bros. - Big Sisters, Milton, Fla. Avocations: golf, reading, exercising. Home: 4121 Barclay Dr Milton FL 32571 Office: Office of the State Atty 5185 Elmira St Milton FL 32570 Office Fax: 850-983-1024. E-mail: catina_wilson@co.escambia.fl.us.

WILSON, CHARLES FRANK, lawyer, law educator; b. Scranton, Pa., July 11, 1943; s. Victor Peter and Rose (Sposito) W.; m. Diane P. Cardoni, June 30, 1973 (dec. 1979); m. Kathleen Geary, Sept. 16, 1983; children: Nicole, Lisa. BS in Edn., Villanova U., 1965; JD, Dickinson U., 1969. Bar: U.S. Dist. Ct. (mid. dist.) Pa. 1969, U.S. Ct. Appeals (3d cir.) 1975. Assoc. Laster, Strohl, Kane, Mattes & McDonald, Scranton, Pa., 1969-71, Epstein, O'Neill & Utan, Scranton, 1971-83; asst. dist. atty. Dist. Attys. Office, Scranton, 1974-80; ptnr. Epstein, Utan, Wilson & Marsili, Scranton, 1983—. Instr. bus. law Pa. State U., 1971. Contbr. articles to profl. jours. Mem. ABA, Lackawanna County Bar Assn., Pa. Bar Assn., Pa. Trial Lawyers Assn., Scranton Lions Club. Republican. Roman Catholic. Avocations: fishing, boating, snorkeling. General practice, Personal injury (including property damage), Workers' compensation. Office: Epstein Utan Wilson & Marsili 800 Penn Security Bank Bldg 142 N Washington Ave Scranton PA 18503-2200

WILSON, CHARLES REGINALD, federal judge; b. Pensacola, FL, 1954; BS, U. Notre Dame, 1976, JD, 1979. Bar: Fla. 1979. Law clk. to Hon. Joseph W. Hatchett U.S. Ct. Appeal for 11th Cir., 1979—80; asst. county atty. Hillsborough county, Fla., 1980—81; county judge 13th Jud. Cir. of Fla., 1986—90; pvt. practice Fla., 1981—86; U.S. magistrate judge U.S. Dist. Ct. (mid. dist.) Fla., 1990—94, U.S. atty., 1994—99; U.S. cir. judge U.S. Ct. Appeals 11th Cir., Tampa, Fla., 1999—. Office: 11th Cir Ct Appeals 801 N Florida Ave Ste 14B Tampa FL 33602-3849

WILSON, CHRISTIAN BURHENN, lawyer; b. Balt., Feb. 24, 1946; s. Christian Columbus and Ruth Louise Frieda (Burhenn) W.; m. Kay Spencer Lewis, June 20, 1974. BA, Towson U., 1968; JD, U. Balt., 1975. Bar: Md. 1976, U.S. Dist. Ct. Md. 1976, U.S. Supreme Ct. 1980. Staff atty. Monumental Properties, Inc., Balt., 1977-79; counsel Mall Mgmt. Assocs., Balt., 1979-85; sole practice Bel Air, Md., 1986—. Sr. lectr. Towson (Md.) U., 1982-91. Served to 2d lt., Md. N.G., 1969-70. Mem. Md. State Bar Assn., Harford County Bar Assn., Sigma Delta Kappa. Republican. Lutheran. Commercial, consumer (including collections, credit), Landlord-tenant, Property, real (including real estate development, water). Home: 257 Victory Ln Bel Air MD 21014-5431 Office: 139 N Main St # 306 Bel Air MD 21014-8808

WILSON, CLARENCE SYLVESTER, JR., lawyer, educator; b. Bklyn., Oct. 22, 1945; s. Clarence Sylvester and Thelma Louise (Richards) W.; m. Helena Chapellin Iribarren, Jan. 26, 1972. BA, Williams Coll., 1967; JD, Northwestern U., 1974. Bar: Ill., 1975; U.S. Supreme Ct., 1985, U.S. Tax Ct. 1985, U.S. Ct. Appeals (7th cir.) 1985. Fgn. Svc. Res. officer U.S. Dept. of State, 1968-74; vice consul 3d sec. Am. Embassy, Caracas, Venezuela, 1969-71; adj. prof. law Kent Coll. of Law, Ill. Inst. Tech., Chgo., 1981-94; lecturer, Columbia Coll., Chgo., 1996—; mem. vis. com. music dept., visual arts, U. Chgo., 1991—; mem. bd. govs. Sch. of Art Inst. of Chgo., 1994-2002; vice chmn. Jazz Mus. of Chgo., 1994-97; adj. prof. The John Marshall Law Sch., 1999-2000. Trustee Chgo. Symphony Orch., 1987-96, Art Inst. Chgo., 1990—; mem. adv. bd. Chgo. Dept. Cultural Affairs, 1988-97; bd. dirs. Arts Midwest, Mpls., 1985-89, Harold Washington Found., Chgo., 1989-91; mem. MERIT Music Program, 1991-96, Ill. Arts Coun., 1984-89; project mgr. Dept. Justice Task Force. The Pres.'s Pvt. Sector Survey on Cost Control in the Fed. Govt. (Grace Commn.), 1982-84. Mem. com. to establish regional arts instns. Ill. Arts Coun., 1998—2003; mem. planned giving task force Diocese of Chgo. Mem. Lawyers for the Creative Arts (pres. 1987-88). Republican. Episcopalian. Avocations: music, art collecting. Corporate, general, Entertainment, Trademark and copyright. Office: 1130 S Michigan Ave #4303 Chicago IL 60605-2325 Fax: 312-583-0646. E-mail: hcwilson@ix.netcom.com.

WILSON, CLAUDE RAYMOND, JR., lawyer; b. Dallas, Feb. 22, 1933; s. Claude Raymond and Lottie (Watts) W.; m. Emilynn Wilson; children: Deidra Wilson Graves, Melissa Woodard Utley, Michele Woodard Dunn. BBA, So. Meth. U., 1954, JD, 1956. Bar: Tex. 1956; CPA, Calif., Tex. Assoc. firm Cervin & Melton, Dallas, 1956-58; atty. Tex. & Pacific R.R. Co., Dallas, 1958-60; atty. office regional counsel IRS, San Francisco, 1960-63, sr. trial atty. office chief counsel Washington, 1963-65; ptnr. Wilson & White, Dallas, 1965-98, Vial, Hamilton, Koch & Knox LLP, Dallas, 1998—. Chmn., Dallas dist. dir. IRS Adv. Commn., 1990-91. Chmn. Dallas Hist. Soc., 2000-01. Mem.: AICPA (coun. 1989—93, tax exec. com. 1998—2001), ABA, Tex. Soc. CPAs (pres. 1989—90, pres. Dallas chpt. 1983—84), Dallas Bar Assn. (pres. sect. taxation 1969—70), State Bar Tex., Greater Dallas C. of C. (chmn. appropriations and tax com. 1990—91), Dallas Petroleum Club, Montaigne Club, Masons, Delta Theta Phi., Delta Sigma Phi. Republican. Episcopalian. Taxation, general, Personal income taxation, State and local taxation. Office: Vial Hamilton Koch & Knox 1700 Pacific Ave Ste 2800 Dallas TX 75201-7388 E-mail: cwilson@vialaw.com.

WILSON, CRAIG P. lawyer; b. Southampton, N.Y., Sept. 7, 1965; BA, Dartmouth Coll., 1987; JD summa cum laude, M in environ. law summa cum laude, Vt. Law Sch., 1992. Bar: Pa. 1992, U.S. Supreme Ct. 2002, U.S. Ct. Appeals (3d and 4th cirs.), U.S. Dist. Ct. (ctrl. and ea. dists.) Pa. Assoc. Kirkpatrick & Lockhart LLP, Harrisburg, Pa., 1992—2000, ptnr., 2001—. Mem. adv. com. Vt. Law Sch. Environ. Law Ctr., South Royalton, 1995—; vestry St. Stephen's Episc. Cathedral, Harrisburg, 2002—. Mem.: ABA, Fed. Bar Assn., Pa. Bar Assn. Environmental, Administrative and regulatory, Land use and zoning (including planning). Office: Kirkpatrick & Lockhart LLP 240 N 3rd St Harrisburg PA 17101 Office Fax: 717-231-4501. E-mail: cwilson@kl.com.

WILSON, DAVID VANDIVER, II, lawyer; b. Houston, Jan. 9, 1968; s. David Vandiver and Emma Lee (Binion) W.; m. Susan Graham, Dec. 18, 1988; children: Katherine Elizabeth, Sarah Margaret. BS, Tex. A&M U., 1989; JD, South Tex. Coll. Law, Houston, 1993. Bar: Tex. 1993. Asst. dist. atty. Harris County, Houston, 1993-95; adj. prof. law South Tex. Coll. Law, 1994-95, 98—; asst. dist. atty. Angelina County, Lufkin, Tex., 1995-98; instr. Angelina Coll. Police Acad., Lufkin, 1995-98; shareholder Hays, McConn, Rice & Pickering, Houston, 1998—. Mem. editl. bd. Houston Lawyer, 2002—. Mem. exec. bd. Habitat for Humanity Angelina County, 1996-98; trustee First United Meth. Ch., Lufkin, 1996-98; mem. bd. stewards Meml. Dr. United Meth. Ch., 2001—. Named Child Advocate of Yr. Black Adoption Coun. S.E. Tex., Beaumont, 1997; awarded 1st prize Bruno Bitker Essay Contest, 1992. Mem. ABA (mem. ho. of dels. 1997-2000), Nat. Dist. Atty.'s Assn., Tex. Dist. and County Atty.'s Assn., Angelina County Bar Assn. (bd. dirs. 1996-98), Houston Bar Assn. Methodist. Avocations: hunting, fishing. General civil litigation, Insurance. Office: Hays McConn Rice & Pickering 1200 Smith St Ste 400 Houston TX 77002-4501 E-mail: dvw@haysmcconn.com.

WILSON, HUGH STEVEN, lawyer; b. Paducah, Ky., Nov. 27, 1947; s. Hugh Gipson and Rebekah (Dunn) W.; m. Clare Maloney, Apr. 28, 1973; children: Zachary Hunter, Samuel Gipson. BS, Ind. U., 1968; JD, U. Chgo., 1971; LLM, Harvard U., 1972. Bar: Calif. 1972, U.S. Dist. Ct. (cen. dist.) Calif. 1972, U.S. Dist. Ct. (so. dist.) Calif. 1973, U.S. Ct. Appeals (9th cir.) 1975, U.S. Dist. Ct. (no. dist.) Calif. 1977, U.S. Supreme Ct. 1978, U.S. Dist. Ct. (ea. dist.) 1980. Assoc. Latham & Watkins, L.A., 1972-78, ptnr., 1978—. Recipient Jerome N. Frank prize U. Chgo. Law Sch., 1971. Mem. Calif. Club., Coronado Yacht Club, Order of Coif. Republican. Avocations: lit., zoology. Federal civil litigation, Corporate, general, Mergers and acquisitions. E-mail: steve.wilson@lw.com.

WILSON, JAMES CHARLES, JR., lawyer; b. Birmingham, Ala., Sept. 13, 1947; s. James C. and Angelina (Serio) W.; m. Ann Bullock, Mar. 1, 1975; children: Brent Trammell, Lucy Bullock. BA, Tulane U., 1969, JD, 1972; MBA, Samford U., 1995. Ptnr. Bradley, Arant, Rose & White, Birmingham, 1972-90, Lange, Simpson, Robinson & Somerville, Birmingham, 1990-93, Sirote & Permutt, P.C., Birmingham, 1993-96; v.p. and gen. counsel Shop-A-Snak Food Mart, Inc., Birmingham, 1996; pres. Lucent Holdings, Inc., Golden, Miss., 1997-98; ptnr. Baker, Johnston & Wilson LLP, Birmingham, Ala., 1999—2002; shareholder Berkowitz, Lefkovits, Isom & Kushner, P.C., Birmingham, 2003—. Adj. prof. internat. bus. transactions and internat. law U. Ala., Tuscaloosa, 1983-85, 89-96; internat. bus. transactions Cumberland Sch. Law, 1990-95, adj. prof. corp. fin., 2001—, adj. prof. securities regulation, 2003—. Author: Alabama Business Corporation Law, 1980; co-author: Corporate Law for the Healthcare Provider: Organization, Operation, Merger and Bankruptcy, 1993, Alabama Business Corporation Law Guide, 1995. Adv. bd. Jr. League of Birmingham, 1984; bd. dirs. Ala. chpt. Am. Liver Found., 1993-97, sec., 1994-95; trustee The Altamont Sch., 1995-2001, v.p., 1996-98, pres., 1998-2000. With U.S. Army, 1972-76. Mem. ABA (sect. internat. law, tax and corp., banking and bus. law), Am. Law Inst., Ala. Bar Assn., Ala. Law Inst., Birmingham Bar Assn. (chmn. pub. rels. com. 1990, chmn. spl. projects com. 2002, chmn. membership benefits com. 2003), Birmingham Golf Assn. (pres., v.p., treas. 1982-84), Rotary (pres. Birmingham-Sunrise club 1986-87). Corporate, general, Private international, Securities. Office: 2501 20th Pl S Birmingham AL 35223

WILSON, JAMES HARGROVE, JR., lawyer; b. Oliver, Ga., Nov. 26, 1920; s. James Hargrove and Louise (Sealy) W.; m. Frances Audra Schaffer, Dec. 24, 1942 (dec. Nov. 1990); children: Susan Frances, James Hargrove. AB with honors, Emory U., 1940; LL.B. summa cum laude, Harvard U., 1947. Bar: Ga. 1947, D.C. 1951. Assoc. firm Sutherland, Tuttle & Brennan (now Sutherland, Asbill & Brennan LLP), Atlanta and Washington, 1947-53, ptnr., 1953—. Lectr. Emory U., 1959, chmn. bd. visitors, 1967-68; trustee The Northwestern Mut. Life Ins. Co., Milw., 1972-91; mem. advisory group Commr. of Internal Revenue, 1963-64 Pres.: Harvard Law Review, 1946-47. Chmn. bd. trustees Met. Atlanta Crime Commn., 1970-71; mem. Harvard U. Overseers Com. to Visit Law Sch., 1959-65; trustee Emory U., 1983-90, trustee emeritus, 1990—. Served to lt. comdr. USNR, 1942-46. Fellow Am. Bar Found., Am. Coll. Tax Counsel; mem. ABA, State Bar Ga., D.C. Bar, Atlanta Bar Assn., Am. Law Inst. (coun. 1974—), Lawyers Club Atlanta (pres. 1960-61), Am. Judicature Soc., Harvard Law Sch. Assn. (coun. 1981-85), Emory U. Alumni Assn. (pres. 1966-67), Capital City Club, Piedmont Driving Club, Peachtree Club, Phi Beta Kappa, Omicron Delta Kappa, Kappa Alpha. Methodist. Corporate, general, Mergers and acquisitions, Corporate taxation. Home: 3171 Marne Dr NW Atlanta GA 30305-1931 Office: Sutherland Asbill & Brennan LLP 999 Peachtree St NE Ste 2300 Atlanta GA 30309-3996

WILSON, JOHN PASLEY, law educator; b. Newark, Apr. 7, 1933; s. Richard Henry and Susan Agnes (Pasley) W.; m. Elizabeth Ann Reed, Sept. 10, 1955 (div.); children: David Cables, John Pasley, Cicely Reed. AB, Princeton U., 1955; LLB, Harvard U., 1962. Bar: N.J. 1962, Mass. 1963, U.S. Dist. Ct. N.J. 1962, U.S. Dist. Ct. Mass. 1963. Budget examiner Exec. Office of Pres., Bur. of the Budget, Washington, 1955-56; assoc. Riker, Danzig, Scherer & Brown, Newark, 1962-63; asst. dean Harvard U. Law Sch., Cambridge, Mass., 1963-67; assoc. dean Boston U. Law Sch., 1968-82; dean Golden Gate U. Sch. Law, San Francisco, 1982-88, prof., 1988—. Vis. prof. dept. health policy and mgmt. Harvard U., 1988; cons. Nat. Commn. for the Protection of Human Subjects of Biomed. and Behavioral Rsch.; mem. Mass. Gov.'s. Commn. on Civil and Legal Rights of Developmentally Disabled; former chmn. adv. com. Ctr for Cmty. Legal Edn., San Francisco. Author: The Rights of Adolescents in the Mental Health System; contbr. chpts. to books, articles to profl. jours. Bd. dirs. Greater Boston Legal Svcs., Chewonki Found.; mem. Health Facilities Appeals Bd., Commonwealth of Mass.; assoc. mem. Dem. Town Com., Concord; chmn. Bd. Assessors, Concord; bd. overseers Boston Hosp. for Women, past chmn. med. affairs com.; past mem. instl. rev. bd. Calif. Pacific Hosp., San Francisco. Served to lt. (j.g.) USNR, 1956-59. NIMH grantee, 1973. Mem. Nat. Assn. Securities Dealers (arbitrator). Office: Golden Gate U Sch Law 536 Mission St San Francisco CA 94105-2967 E-mail: jwilson@ggu.edu., jwlsn@earthlink.net.

WILSON, JOSEPH MORRIS, III, lawyer; b. Milw., July 26, 1945; s. Joseph Morris Jr. and Phyllis Elizabeth (Cresson) W.; children: Elizabeth J., Eric M.; m. Dixie Lee Brock, Mar. 23, 1984. BA, Calif. State U., Chico, 1967; MA, U. Washington, 1968; JD summa cum laude, Ohio State U., 1976. Bar: Alaska 1976, U.S. Dist. Ct. Alaska 1976, U.S. Ct. Appeals (9th cir.) 1986. Recruiter and vol. U.S. Peace Corps, Republic of Benin, 1969-73; legal intern U.S. Ho. of Reps., Washington, 1975; ptnr. Guess & Rudd P.C., Anchorage, 1976-88, chmn. comml. dept., 1981-82, ptnr. compensation com., 1982-84; mgr. Alaska taxes, sr. tax atty. BP Exploration Inc., Alaska, 1990-99. Bus. law instr. U. Alaska, Anchorage, 1977-78. Mem. Alaska Bar Assn., World Affairs Coun. Democrat. Avocations: music, sports, travel. Corporate, general, Corporate taxation, State and local taxation. Home and Office: 2556 Palmera Cir Las Vegas NV 89121-4016 E-mail: jsphwlsn@aol.com.

WILSON, JULIA ANN YOTHER, lawyer; b. Dallas, Sept. 6, 1958; d. Julian White and Mary Ann (Estes) Yother. BA, East Ctrl. U., Ada, Okla., 1980; JD, U. Okla., 1983. Bar: Okla. 1990, Calif. 1993, D.C. 1995; U.S. Ct. Appeals (9th cir.) Calif. 1993, U.S. Supreme Ct. 1993, U.S. Dist. Ct. (ctrl. dist.) Calif. 1993, U.S. Dist. Ct. (we. dist.) Okla., 1997. Assoc. Law Office of George Rodda Jr., Newport Beach, Calif., 1984-96; sole practice law Oklahoma City, 1996-97; assoc. Coldiron, Wilson & Assocs., Oklahoma City, 1997—. Served to 1st lt. USAR, 1980-86. Mem. ABA, D.C. Bar Assn., Calif. Bar Assn., Oklahoma County Bar Assn., Okla. Bar Assn. (litigation sect.), Orange County Bar Assn. General civil litigation, General practice, Probate (including wills, trusts). Office: Coldiron Wilson & Assocs 1800 E Memorial Rd Ste 106 Oklahoma City OK 73131-1827

WILSON, KAREN WILKERSON, paralegal; b. Reidsville, N.C., June 28, 1957; d. William Henry and Jean Gloria (Tiller) W.; married. Student, N.C. State U., 1975-77, Western Carolina U., Cullowhee, N.C., 1978-80; diploma, Profl. Ctr. Paralegal Studies, Columbia, S.C., 1988. Paralegal Ken H. Lester, Esquire, Columbia, 1989—, Lester & Jones, Columbia. Spkr. Alumni Profl. Ctr. Paralegal Studies, Columbia, 1988-95. Mem. ATLA, S.C. Trial Lawyers Assn. (paralegal rep. 1993-96). Democrat. Presbyterian. Office: Lester & Jones 1716 Main St Columbia SC 29201-2820

WILSON, MABLE JEAN, paralegal; b. Pine Bluff, Ark. d. James Arthur and Ruthia Mae (Dansby) Watson; children: Dana Eileen, Dana Kent, Carlos Alexander Fuller. BS, cert. in paralegal studies, U. So. Calif., 1982-86. Dep. sheriff L.A. County, 1971-80; ind. paralegal Wilson's Divorce Clinic, L.A., 1980—. Participant Dist. Atty. Victim Witness Program, L.A., 1991; active Brotherhood Crusade, L.A., 1992; mem. adv. bd. West L.A. Coll.-Paralegal Studies. Recipient Merit award L.A. County Bar Assn., 1993, Merit cert. City of L.A., County of L.A., Calif. Senate, U.S. Congress, Gov. State of Calif. Mem. Assn. Family and Conciliation Cts., Folk Power Inc. (bd. dirs. 1993—), Alpha Svc. Co. (v.p. 1993—, profl. women's adv. bd., Women's Inner Circle of Achievement), adv. bd on Paralegal Studies, W. L.A. Coll. Avocations: interior decorating, making stained glass windows, ceramics, painting, writing poetry. Office: 3860 Crenshaw Blvd Ste 201 Los Angeles CA 90008-1816

WILSON, MARGARET BUSH, lawyer; b. St. Louis, Jan. 30, 1919; married; 1 child, Robert Edmund. BA cum laude, Talladega Coll., 1940; LL.B., Lincoln U., 1943. Ptnr. Wilson & Wilson, St. Louis, 1947-65; now with firm Wilson & Assocs. Asst. dir. St. Louis Lawyers for Housing, 1969-72; asst. atty. gen. Mo., 1961-62; atty. Rural Electrification Adminstrn., Dept. Agr., St. Louis, 1943-45; instr. civil procedure St. Louis U. Sch. Law, 1971; chmn. St. Louis Land Reutilization Authority, 1975-76; mem. Mo. Coun. Criminal Justice, 1972—; chmn. Intergroup Corp., 1985-87; bd. dirs. Mut. of N.Y. Mem. gen. adv. com. ACDA, 1978-81; trustee emeritus Washington U., St. Louis; chmn. bd. trustees Talladega Coll., Ala., 1988-92; nat. bd. dirs. ARC, 1975-81, United Way, 1978-84, Police Found., 1976-93; treas. NAACP Nat. Housing Corp., 1971-84, chmn. nat. bd., 1975-84; dep. dir./acting dir. St. Louis Model City Agy., 1968-69; adminstr. Mo. Commn. Svc. and Continuing Edn., 1967-68. Recipient Bishop's award Episcopal Diocese Mo., 1962; Juliette Derricotte fellow, 1939-40, Disting. Lawyer award Bar Assn. Metro St. Louis, 1997. Mem. ABA (chmn. youth edn. for citizenship 1991-94, chmn. Nat. Law Day 1998-2000), Nat. Bar Assn., Mo. Bar Assn., Mound City Bar Assn., St. Louis Bar Assn., Alpha Kappa Alpha. Property, real (including real estate development, water), Probate (including wills, trusts), Condemnation (eminent domain). Office: Wilson & Assocs 4054 Lindell Blvd Saint Louis MO 63108-3202

WILSON, MICHAEL MOUREAU, lawyer, physician; b. Cheverly, Md., Dec. 30, 1952; s. Kenneth Moureau and Helen (Rice) Smith. BS, MIT, 1974; JD, Georgetown U., 1977, MD, 1986. Bar: D.C. 1977, N.Y. 1980, U.S. Dist. Ct. D.C. 1980, U.S. Dist. Ct. Md. 1992, U.S. Ct. Appeals (D.C. cir.) 1980, U.S. Supreme Ct. 1981. Law clk. Hon. John B. Hannum U.S. Dist. Ct., Phila., 1977-78; assoc. Cravath Swaine & Moore, N.Y.C., 1978-79; asst. to gen. counsel NSF, Washington, 1979-82; resident in psychiatry St. Elizabeth Hosp., Washington, 1986-89; pvt. practice med. malpractice litigation Washington, 1989—. Notes editor Am. Criminal Law Rev., 1976-77. Mem. ABA, Assn. Trial Lawyers Am., D.C. Trial Lawyers Assn., Phi Beta Kappa. Personal injury (including property damage). Office: 1120 19th St NW Ste LL-11 Washington DC 20036 Fax: 202-463-0590. E-mail: wilson@wilsonlaw.com.

WILSON, PAUL HOLLIDAY, JR., lawyer; b. Schenectady, N.Y., Sept. 4, 1942; s. Paul H. and Sarah Elizabeth (MacLean) W.; m. Elaine Hawley Griffin, May 30, 1964; children: Hollace, Paul, Kirsten, Katherine. AB, Brown U., 1964; LLB, MBA, Columbia U., 1967. Bar: N.Y. 1967, U.S. Dist. Ct. (so. dist.) 1968. Law clk. U.S. Dist. Ct. (so. dist.) N.Y., N.Y.C., 1967-68; assoc. Debevoise & Plimpton, N.Y.C., 1968-75, ptnr., 1976—, fin. ptnr., 1980-88, 91-93, 2001—, dep. presiding ptnr., 1993-98. Vice-chmn., trustee St. Michael's Montessori Sch., N.Y.C., 1977-79, chmn. bd. trustees, 1979-81. Mem. ABA, Assn. Bar City N.Y. (mem. commn. on securities regulations 1985-88). Clubs: Vineyard Haven Yacht (Mass.) (vice-commodore 1985, commodore 1986-87). Avocations: sailing, reading, music. Corporate, general, Mergers and acquisitions, Securities. Office: Debevoise & Plimpton 919 Third Ave 46th Fl New York NY 10022-6225 E-mail: phwilson@debevoise.com.

WILSON, PETER BOTTUM, retired lawyer; b. Bonners Ferry, Idaho, May 21, 1925; s. Oliver Chester and Margaret Amanda (Bottum) W.; m. Rhoda Marie Hill, Aug. 12,1950; children: Oliver C., Kevin P., Timothy B., Neal G. BA, U. Idaho, 1949, LLB, 1951. Bar: Idaho 1953, U.S. Dist. Ct. Idaho 1954, U.S. Supreme Ct. 1962. Atty. pvt. practice, Coeur d' Alene, Idaho, 1953-57, Bonners Ferry, Idaho, 1957-59, 66-67; ptnr. Prather & Wilson, Bonners Ferry, Idaho, 1959-66, Wilson & Walter, Bonners Ferry, Idaho, 1967-83; pvt. practice Bonners Ferry, Idaho, 1983-95; ret., 1995. Dir. KBFI Radio, Bonners Ferry; atty. Fry Hosp. Found., Bonners Ferry. Pres. Bonners Ferry C. of C., 1986; pres. NICC, North Idaho, 1986; city atty., Bonners Ferry, 1957-95, Moyie Springs, Idaho, 1986-95; atty. Boundary County Sch. Dist. # 101, 1980-95. Mem. Am. Legion (dept. comdr. 1959, nat. committeeman 1960-61), Lions Club. Republican. Episcopalian. Education and schools, General practice, Government contracts and claims. Office: PO Box 749 Bonners Ferry ID 83805-0749

WILSON, RHONDA HILL, lawyer; b. Phila., Aug. 20, 1955; d. Fleming and Emma (Woodson) Hill; m. Robert A. Wilson (div.); children: Mica, Christian. BA cum laude, C.W. Post Coll., 1976; JD, Am. U., 1979. Bar: Pa., Ohio, N.J. Asst. atty. gen. Office of Atty. Gen. Ohio, Columbus, 1979-81; pvt. practice law Phila., 1981-84; claims mgr. Allstate Ins., Horsham, Pa., 1984-86; atty. Am. Internat. Group, Phila., 1986-88, Crum & Forster Co., Phila., 1988-93; pvt. practice law Phila., 1993—. Host legal and current affairs WORD Radio, Phila., 1992—. Active Mt. Carmel Bapt. Ch., Phila.; past bd. dirs. Walden Sch., Swarthmore, Pa. Mem. Nat. Bar Assn. (pres. women lawyers divsn. Phila. 1993-94, presdl. award 1994), ATLA, Phila. Bar Assn., Barristers Assn. Phila. (bd. dirs. 1992-93), Pa. Trial Lawyers Assn., Phila. Trial Lawyers Assn., Phila. Assn. Def. Counsel (past bd. dirs.). Personal injury (including property damage). Office: Law Office Rhonda Hill Wilson PC 1500 John F Kennedy Blvd Ste 1050 Philadelphia PA 19102 Fax: 215-972-6756. E-mail: rhillwilso.@aol.com.

WILSON, RHYS THADDEUS, lawyer; b. Albany, Ga., May 9, 1955; s. Joseph Farr Jr. and Betty Ann (Wilkins) W.; m. Carolyn Reid Saffold, June 2, 1984. AB, Duke U., 1976; JD, U. Ga., 1979; LLM, Emory U., 1985. Bar: Ga. 1979. Pvt. practice law, Atlanta, 1979-89; sr. v.p., gen. counsel Monarch Capital Group, Inc., Atlanta, 1989-92, Jackson & Coker, Inc., Atlanta, 1992-93; pres. Jackson & Coker Locum Tenens, Inc., Atlanta, 1993-95; ptnr. Robins, Kaplan, Miller & Ciresi, Atlanta, 1995—. Spkr. continuing legal edn. seminars. Contbr. articles to profl. jours. Mem. ABA, Ga. Bar Assn. (chmn. internat. law sect. 1987-88, exec. com. corp. and banking law sect. 1987-89, editl. bd. Ga. State Bar Jour. 1986-89), Atlanta Bar Assn. (editor newsletter 1984-86, Outstanding Svc. award 1986), Assn. for Corp. Growth, Atlanta Network Alliance, Atlanta Tech. Angels, The Exec. Com. TEC, Atlanta Venture Forum, Capital City Club. Episcopalian. Corporate, general, Mergers and acquisitions, Securities.

WILSON, RICHARD RANDOLPH, lawyer; b. Pasadena, Calif., Apr. 14, 1950; s. Robert James and Phyllis Jean (Blackman) W.; m. Catherine Goodhugh Stevens, Oct. 11, 1980; children: Thomas Randolph, Charles Stevens. BA cum laude, Yale U., 1971; JD, U. Wash., 1976. Bar: Wash. 1976, U.S. Dist. Ct. (we. dist.) Wash. 1976, U.S. Ct. Appeals (9th cir.) 1977. Assoc. Hillis, Phillips, Cairncross, Clark & Martin, Seattle, 1976-81, ptnr., 1981-84, Hillis, Cairncross, Clark & Martin, Seattle, 1984-87, Hillis Clark Martin & Peterson, Seattle, 1987—, mem. mgmt. com., 1991—. Pres. Plymouth Housing Group, Seattle, 1998—2000, trustee, 1994—2001; bd. dirs. Plymouth Housing Properties, Seattle, 2001—, Quality Child Care Svcs., Inc., Seattle; lectr. various bar assns., 1980—. Contbr. articles to profl. jours. Chmn. class agts. Yale U. Alumni Fund, New Haven, 1985—87, class agt., 1971—2001, mem. class coun., 1991—96, mem. Western Wash. exec. com. Yale capital campaign, 1992—97, vice chmn. leadership gifts com. Yale 25th reunion, 1995—96, 30th reunion, 2000—01; mem., vice chmn. Medina (Wash.) Planning Commn., 1990—92; moderator, pres. ch. coun. Plymouth Congl. Ch., Seattle, 1998—2000; trustee, performer Gilbert & Sullivan Soc., 1984—91; chmn. capital campaign Plymouth Congl. Ch., 1995. Mem. ABA, Wash. State Bar Assn. (dir. environ. and land use law sect. 1985-88), Seattle-King County Bar Assn., Kingsley Trust Assn. (pres. 1996-98), Yale Assn. of Western Wash. Congregationalist. Avocations: acting, singing, rare book collecting. Environmental, Land use and zoning (including planning), Property, real (including real estate development, water). Home: 2305 86th Ave NE Bellevue WA 98004-2416 Office: Hillis Clark Martin & Peterson 1221 2nd Ave Ste 500 Seattle WA 98101-2925

WILSON, ROBERT FOSTER, lawyer; b. Windsor, Colo., Apr. 6, 1926; s. Foster W. and Anne Lucille (Svedman) W.; m. Mary Elizabeth Clark, Mar. 4, 1951 (div. Feb. 1972); children; Robert F., Katharine A.; m. Sally Anne Nemec, June 8, 1982. BA in Econs., U. Iowa, 1950, JD, 1951. Bar: Iowa 1951, U.S. Dist. Ct. (no. and so. dists.) Iowa 1956, U.S. Ct. Appeals (8th cir.) 1967. Atty. FTC, Chgo., 1951-55; pvt. practice, Cedar Rapids, Iowa, 1955—. Pres. Lawyer Forms, Inc.; dir. Lawyers Forms, Inc.; mem. Iowa Reapportionment Com., 1968; del. to U.S. and Japan Bilateral Session on Legal and Econ. Rels. Conf., Tokyo, 1988, Moscow Conf. on Law and Bilateral Rels., Moscow, 1990; U.S. del. to Moscow Conf. on Legal and Econ. Rels., 1990. Mem. Iowa Ho. of Reps., 1959-60; pres. Linn County Day Care, Cedar Rapids, 1968-70. Sgt. U.S. Army, 1944-46. Mem. ATLA, Am. Arbitration Assn. (panel arbitrators), Iowa Bar Assn., Iowa Trial Lawyers Assn., Linn County Bar Assn., Am. Legion (judge adv. 1970-75, 87-93), Cedar View Country Club, Elks, Eagles, Delta Theta Phi. Democrat. Personal injury (including property damage), Probate (including wills, trusts), Workers' compensation. Home: 2179 Blake Blvd SE Cedar Rapids IA 52403-1128 Office: 810 Dows Bldg Cedar Rapids IA 52403-7010 E-mail: RWilsonlaw@aol.com.

WILSON, ROGER GOODWIN, lawyer; b. Evanston, Ill., Sept. 3, 1950; s. G. Turner Jr. and Lois (Shay) W.; m. Giovinella Gonthier, Mar. 7, 1975. AB, Dartmouth Coll., 1972; JD, Harvard U., 1975. Bar: Ill. 1975, U.S. Dist. Ct. (no. dist.) Ill. 1976, U.S. Ct. Appeals (7th cir.) 1977, U.S. Dist. Ct. (no. dist.) Ind. 1985. Assoc. Kirkland & Ellis, Chgo., 1975-81, ptnr., 1981-86; sr. v.p., gen. counsel, corp. sec. Blue Cross/Blue Shield, 1986—. Speaker Nat. Healthcare Inst., U. Mich., 1987-93, Am. Law Inst.-ABA Conf. on Mng. and Resolving Domestic and Internat. Bus. Disputes, N.Y.C., 1988, Washington, 1990; cert. health cons. program Purdue U., 1993-94, Inst. for Bus. Strategy Devel., Northwestern U., 1993-94, The Health Care Antitrust Forum, Chgo., 1995, Am. Health Lawyers Assn Managed Care Law Inst., 1995, Am. Health Lawyers Assn. Conf. on Tax Issues in Healthcare Orgns., 1996. Contbg. editor Health Care Fraud and Abuse Newsletter, 1998—. Advisor Constl. Rights Found., Chgo., 1982-87; mem. So. Poverty Law Ctr., Montgomery, Ala., 1981—. Mem. ABA, Am. Health Lawyers Assn. (spkr. 1984, 96), Legal Assistance Found. of Chgo. (bd. dirs. 1998—), Chgo. Coun. Lawyers (bd. govs. 1988-92), Coun. Chief Legal Officers (conf. bd. 1995—), Coun. Corp. Governance (conf. bd. 1998-00), Dartmouth Lawyers Assn., Sinfonietta (bd. dirs. 1987—), Univ. Club, Mid-Am. Club, Phi Beta Kappa. Corporate, general, Health, Insurance. Home: 330 N Jefferson Ct Unit2004 Chicago IL 60661 Office: Blue Cross/Blue Shield 225 N Michigan Ave Ste 200 Chicago IL 60601-7601 E-mail: roger.wilson@bcbsa.com.

WILSON, STANLEY PATTERSON, retired lawyer; b. Hamlin, Tex., Sept. 1, 1922; s. Milton Young and Ethel M. (Patterson) W.; m. Claudie Park, Sept. 23, 1944; children: Stanley P., Russell Park, Marianne. BS, U. North Tex., Denton, 1943; LLB, U. Tex., Austin, 1948. Bar: Tex. 1948. Ptnr. McMahon, Smart, Wilson, Surovik & Suttle, Abilene, Tex., 1948-81; sr. v.p., gen. counsel Central and S.W. Corp., Dallas, 1981-86, exec. v.p., gen. counsel, 1986-88, ret., 1988. Lt. (j.g.) USN, 1943-46, PTO. Mem. ABA, State Bar Tex., Am. Coll. Trial Lawyers, Internat. Assn. Def. Counsel, Abilene Bar Assn., Abilene Country Club. Methodist. Home: 1921 Elmwood Dr Abilene TX 79605-4802 Office: Ste 800 First Nat Bank Bldg Abilene TX 79601 E-mail: swilson@mcmahonlawtx.com.

WILSON, THOMAS MATTHEW, III, lawyer; b. Ware, Mass., Feb. 22, 1936; s. Thomas Matthew Jr. and Ann Veronica (Shea) W.; m. Deborah Ord Lockhart, Feb. 10, 1962; children: Deborah Veronica, Leslie Lockhart, Thomas Matthew IV. BA, Brown U., 1958; JD, U. Md., 1971. Bar: Md. 1972, U.S. Ct. Appeals (4th cir.) 1976, U.S. Supreme Ct. 1977. Sales mgr. Mid-Ea. Box Mfg. Co., Balt., 1966-74; asst. atty. gen., chief antitrust divsn. State of Md., Balt., 1974-79; ptnr. Tydings & Rosenberg, LLP, Balt., 1979—. Author: Defending an Antitrust Action Brought by a State, 1987, The Spectre of Double Recovery in Antitrust Federalism, 1989; co-author: Reciprocity and the Private Plaintiff, 1972; mem. editl. adv. bd.: Bur. of Nat. Affairs Antitrust and Trade Regulation Report, 1979—. Mem. ABA (sect. on antitrust law 1974—, chmn. state antitrust enforcement com. 1986-89, antitrust sect. coun. 1990-93, coord. com. on legal edn. 1993—), Md. Bar

Assn. (antitrust subcom. 1975-78), Internat. Bar Assn. (sect. on bus. law, antitrust law and monopolies com. 1983—), Churchwarden's Chess Club, Annapolis Yacht Club. Republican. Achievements include patents for nail cartons. Antitrust, Appellate, Franchising. Home: Baobab Farm Hampstead MD 21074 Office: Tydings & Rosenberg LLP 100 E Pratt St Baltimore MD 21202-1009

WILSON, VIRGIL JAMES, III, lawyer; b. San Jose, Calif., July 25, 1953; s. Virgil James Wilson Jr. and Phyllis Emily (Mothorn) Brasser; children: Gabriel James Hekili, Alexander Robert Kaimoku, Hayley Noelani, Maia E. Kailani. BA with honors, U. Calif., Santa Cruz, 1975; JD cum laude, U. Santa Clara, 1981. Bar: Calif. 1981, U.S. Dist. Ct. (no. dist.) Calif. 1981, Hawaii 1982, U.S. Dist. Ct. Hawaii 1982, U.S. Ct. Appeals (9th cir.) 1987, U.S. Supreme Ct. 1987, Oreg. 1990, U.S. Dist. Ct. Oreg. 1998, U.S. Ct. Fed. Claims 1999; lic. pvt. investigator, Hawaii. Atty. James Krueger P.C., Wailuku, Maui, 1981-83; resident counsel Sterns & Ingram, Honolulu, 1983-89; pvt. practice Kailua, Hawaii, 1989—; assoc. Thorp, Purdy, Jewett, Urness & Wilkinson, P.C., Springfield, Oreg., 1998-99; of counsel Law Offices of Ian L. Mattoch, 1993-96, Gaydos, Churnside & Balthrop PC, Eugene, Oreg., 2001—. Owner Wilson Investigations, Santa Cruz, 1978-81, Honolulu, 1981—. Mem. Hawaii Bar Assn., Calif. State Bar Assn., Oreg. Bar Assn. Avocation: profl. magician. General civil litigation, Personal injury (including property damage), Product liability. Fax: 541-607-6565. E-mail: VJWILSONiii@msn.com.

WILSON, WALTER JOSEPH, lawyer; b. Oxnard, Calif., June 23, 1946; s. Walter Joseph and Eva Verling (Humphreys) W.; 1 child, Nicole Jacqueline. BA in Bus. Adminstrn., Calif. State U., Long Beach, 1972; JD, U. So. Calif., 1975. Bar: Calif. 1975, U.S. Dist. Ct. (ctrl. dist.) Calif. 1976. Assoc. Charles Gangloff & Assocs., Long Beach, 1977-80, Lichtman & Bruning, L.A. and Pasadena, Calif., 1984-86, Demler, Armstrong & Rowland, Long Beach, 1986-87; pvt. practice L.A., 1980-84, Long Beach, 1987—. Mem. Long Beach Bar Assn., Los Angeles County Bar Assn. Corporate, general, Personal injury (including property damage), Property, real (including real estate development, water). Office: 333 W Broadway Ste 200 Long Beach CA 90802-4439

WILSON, WILLIAM BERRY, lawyer; b. Cape Girardeau, Mo., June 17, 1947; s. Charles F. and Anita (Bartlum) Wilson; m. Suzanne T. Wilson; children: Matthew James, Sarah Talbot. BA summa cum laude, Westminster Coll., 1969; JD, U. Mich., 1972. Bar: Fla. 1972, U.S. Dist. Ct. (mid. dist.) Fla. 1972, U.S. Ct. Appeals (11th cir.) 1972, U.S. Supreme Ct. 1976, cert.: Civil Trial Lawyer Bd. 1983. Ptnr. Maguire, Voorhis & Wells P.A., Orlando, Fla., 1977-98, pres., 1984-97, chmn., 1997-98; ptnr. Holland & Knight LLP, Orlando, 1998—, dir., 1999—, exec. ptnr., 2003—. Mem. exec. com., trust com., bd. dirs. SunTrust Bank Ctrl. Fla., 1990—. Bd. overseers Crummer Sch. Bus., Rollins Coll., 1994—2002; chmn. Fla. Residential Property & Casualty Joint Underwriting Assn., 1995—2001; mem. Fla. Fed. Jud. Nominating Commn., 2001—; bd. dirs. Econ. Devel. Authority, Orlando, 1992—97, chmn., 1994—95, subcom. chmn. Project 2000 Orlando, 1985—87; bd. dirs. Fla. Symphony, Orlando1985; Fla. TaxWatch, Inc., 1992—98; bd. dirs. U. Ctrl. Fla. Found., 1996—, Jr. Achievement, 1998—; trustee Orlando Mus. Art, 1993—, pres., 1997—99. Mem.: Orlando Regional C. of C. (bd. dirs. 1997—, vice chmn. tech. 1999—, chair 2002—), Am. Bd. Trial Advocacy, Orange County Bar Assn. (chmn. fed. and state practice sect. 1982—84, mem. jud. rels. com. 1984—, chmn. 1987—98, chmn. professionalism com. 1997—99), Fla. Bar Assn. (code and rules of evidence com. 1982—88, chmn. 1986—88, mem. exec. coun. trial lawyers sect. 1987—98, chmn. 1996—97), ABA, Citrus Club (bd. dirs. 1994—2002, chmn. 1998—2002), Country Club of Orlando, Rotary. Republican. Presbyterian. Avocations: tennis, scuba diving. Federal civil litigation, State civil litigation, Construction. Office: Holland & Knight LLP PO Box 1526 200 S Orange Ave Ste 2600 Orlando FL 32801-3453 E-mail: bwilson@hklaw.com.

WILSON, WILLIAM R., JR., judge; b. 1939; Student, U. Ark., 1957-58; BA, Hendrix Coll., 1962; LLB, Vanderbilt U., 1965. Atty. Autrey & Goodson, Texarkana, Ark., 1965-66, Wright, Lindsey & Jennings, Little Rock, 1969-72, Wilson & Hodge, Little Rock, 1972-74; prin. William R. Wilson Jr., P.A., Little Rock, 1974-80, Wilson & Engstrom, Little Rock, 1980-83, Wilson, Engstrom & Vowell, Little Rock, 1984, Wilson, Engstrom, Corum & Dudley, Little Rock, 1984-93; judge U.S. Dist. Ct. (ea. dist.) Ark., Little Rock, 1993—. Chair Ark. Supreme Ct. Com. on Model Criminal Jury Instrns., 1978—; active Ark. Supreme Ct. Com. on Civil Practice, 1982—. Lt. USN, 1966-69. Named Disting. Alumnus, Hendrix Coll., 1993, Outstanding Lawyer, Pulaski County Bar Assn., 1993. Mem. ABA, ATLA, Am. Bd. Trial Advocates (Nat. Civil Justice award 1992), Am. Coll. Trial Lawyers, Internat. Acad. Trial Lawyers, Internat. Soc. Barristers, Ark. Bar Assn. (Outstanding Lawyer 1991), S.W. Ark. Bar Assn., Ark. Trial Lawyers Assn. (pres. 1982, Outstanding Trial Lawyer 1988-89), Pulaski County Bar Assn. (Outstanding Lawyer 1993). Office: US Dist Ct Ea Dist 600 W Capitol Ave Ste 423 Little Rock AR 72201-3320

WILTSE, PETER CHRISTIAN, lawyer; b. Buffalo, N.Y., Jan. 13, 1936; s. Harry Hersey and Sally K. (Lutzhoff) W. (div. 1988); m. Christine Wiltse, 1999; children: Lise Rene, Wende, Heather, Jessica. Student, Colgate U., 1953-56; JD, SUNY, Buffalo, 1960. Bar: N.Y., U.S. Dist. Ct. N.Y., U.S. Supreme Ct. Assoc. Saperston, Wiltse & Day, Buffalo, 1960-63; asst. trial atty. Erie County Dist. Atty., Buffalo, 1963; ptnr. Gross, Shuman & Wiltse, Buffalo, 1964-74; pvt. practice Hamburg, N.Y., 1974—. Avocations: marine aquaria, golf, boating. Estate planning, Family and matrimonial, Personal injury (including property damage). Office: 202 Main St Hamburg NY 14075-4917 E-mail: peteski@localnet.com.

WIMPFHEIMER, MICHAEL CLARK, lawyer; b. N.Y.C., July 9, 1944; s. Henry and Ruth (Rapp) Wimpfheimer; m. Susanne Rabner, June 11, 1968; children: Jan Steven, Barry Scott, Luba Rachel. BA, Columbia U., 1964; JD, Harvard U., 1967. Bar: N.Y. 1967, U.S. Dist. Ct. (ea. and so. dists.) N.Y. 1974, U.S. Ct. Appeals (2d cir.) 1974, U.S. Ct. Mil. Appeals 1979, U.S. Claims Ct. 1992. Ptnr. Wimpfheimer & Wimpfheimer, N.Y.C., 1970—. V.p. Union Orthodox Jewish Congregations Am., N.Y.C., 1978—2002, sr. v.p., 2002. Comdr. JAGC USNR. Mem.: ABA, Bronx County Bar Assn., N.Y. State Bar Assn. Jewish. Estate planning, General practice, Property, real (including real estate development, water). Home: 2756 Arlington Ave Riverdale Bronx NY 10463-4807 Office: Wimpfheimer & Wimpfheimer 330 W 58th St Ste 600 New York NY 10019-1818 Fax: 212-247-8196.

WIMPISSINGER, CHRISTIAN, lawyer; b. Vienna, Aug. 28, 1975; arrived in U.S., 2000; s. Thomas and Edith Wimpissinger. Student, London Sch. Econs.; magister juris, Vienna U., 1998; LLM in Internat. Taxation, NYU, 2002. Bar: N.Y. 2001. Assoc. KPMG Austria, Vienna, 1998—99; mem. dept. internat. and Austrian taxation Vienna U. Econ. & Bus. Admin., 1999—2000, instr., 2001—; assoc. Davis, Polk & Wardwell, N.Y.C., 2000—. Contbr. articles to profl. jours. Corporate taxation, Taxation, general. Office Fax: 212-450-3294. Business E-Mail: cwimpissinger@gmx.at.

WINARTA, FRANS HENDRA, advocate; b. Bandung, Indonesia, Sept. 17, 1943; s. Tan Tjin Giok and Gouw Pouw Nio; m. Miv Jatty Tanuwidjaja, Feb. 2, 1970; children: Patricia Ann, Randolph Jay. Bachelor Degree, Cath. U. Parahyangan, Bandung, 1970; M in Criminal Law, U. Indonesia, Jakarta, 1998. Mgr. Am. Home Products Singer Co., Procter & Gamble, Jakarata, 1970—80; founder, mng. ptnr. Frans Winarta & Ptnrs., Jakarata, 1981—. Trustee Legal Aid Found., Jakarta, 1989; mem. legal aid team Indonesian Bank Restructuring Agy., Jakarta, 2002—. Author: Indonesian Advocate, 1995, Legal Aid: A Human Right Not a Favor, 2000. Founder Indonesian Anti Discrimination Movement, Jakarta, 1998; chmn. Indonesian Inst. for the Independence of Judiciary, Jakarta, 1999; mem. Nat. Commn. Law, Jakarta, 2000. Mem.: Found. Law Practice Indonesia, Indonesian Bar Assn. (chmn. internat. rels. 1990—), Internat. Bar Assn. (coun. mem. human rights inst. 2000—). Avocations: reading, swimming, jogging. Home: Jl Tampak Siring Elok 2 North Jakarta 14240 Indonesia Office: Frans Winarta & Ptnrs Kompleks Bukit Grading Mediterania Blvd Bukit Gading Raya Blok A 16 17 North Jakarta 14240 Indonesia

WINCHELL, MICHAEL GEORGE, lawyer; b. Ardmore, Okla., Oct. 30, 1949; s. George Stockwell and Willis Marion (Woolery) W.; m. Donna Jean Winchell; children: Merridith Elaine, Candace Michelle. BBA, Cen. State U., 1974; JD, U. Okla., 1976. Bar: Okla. 1977. Assoc. Sokolsky & Becker, Oklahoma City, 1977; asst. regional counsel GSA, Ft. Worth, Tex., 1977-87; adminstrv. judge EEOC Commn., Dallas, 1987-88; counsel S.E. bases USMC, 1988-89; chief counsel John F. Kennedy Space Ctr., 1993-97, Johnson Space Ctr., 1997—. Pres. GSA employee's assn., 1982-84; chief KSC Inter-Tribal Coun., 1993-97. Named Meritorious Exec. of the Federal Sr. Exec. Svc., Pres. Clinton, 2000; recipient Meritorious Civilan Svc. medal, USN, 1993, Exceptional Svc. medal, NASA, 2001. Mem. Fed. Bus. Assn. (pres. 1984-85), FBA (pres. Ft. Worth chpt. 1981-82, bd. dirs. younger lawyers' div. 1981-85, 2d v.p. 5th cir. 1982-83, v.p. 1983-84, sec. cir. officers 1983-84, dep. chmn. cir. officers 1984-85, chmn. rules com. 1985-86), Southeastern Cherokee Confederacy (chief Eagle Clan 1992-93). Office: Code AL NASA Johnson Space Ctr Houston TX 77058

WINCHESTER, JAMES R. judge; m. Susan Winchester; 1 child, Davis. BA U. Okla, JD Oklahoma City U. Pvt. practice, Weatherford, Okla., Hinton, Okla.; assoc. dist. judge Caddo County, Okla., 1983; dist. judge 6th Judicial Dist. Okla., 1983—97; U.S. adminstrv. law judge, 1997—2000; justice Supreme Ct. Okla., 2000—. Mem.: Exec. Bd., Ok. Judicial Conf. (pres., 1995 1992—96). Office: Oklahoma Supreme Ct Admin Office 1915 N Stiles Ste 305 Oklahoma City OK 73104-2861*

WINCHESTER, RICHARD LEE, JR., lawyer; b. Memphis, May 21, 1924; s. Cassius Lee and Harriet Haywood (Bond) W.; m. Bette Anne Thompson, July 15, 1944; children— Robin Ann, Richard Lee Jr., John Thompson. LL.B., U. Tenn., 1949, J.D., 1965. Bar: Tenn. 1949. Sr. ptnr. Winchester Law Firm, Memphis, 1972— ; Shelby County atty., 1961-64; city atty., Arlington, Tenn., 1966— ; gen. counsel, bd. chmn. Community Bancshares, Inc.; sec. Beachfront Condos, Inc., N.Fla. Chmn. Germantown Planning Commn., 1958-61; mem. Gov.'s Commn. on Human Relations, 1962-68; vice chmn., treas. Memphis and Shelby County Democratic Exec. Com., 1958-72; state exec. com., pres. Tenn. Young Democrats, 1960-61; del. state and nat. Dem. Convs., 1964-68; nat. elector from Tenn., 1960-72; pres., bd. dirs. Mid-South Fair Assn., ARC.; trustee U. Tenn., 1975-84, Episcopal Girls Home, Bowld Hosp.; pres. Episcopal Planning Commn. Served to capt. inf. AUS, 1942-46, PTO. Fellow Tenn. Bar Found.; mem. ABA (past del.), Tenn. Bar Assn. (past pres. jr. sect.), Memphis Bar Assn. (past pres.), Shelby County Bar Assn. (past pres. jr. sect.), Am. Judicature Soc., Nat. Assn. Legal Aid and Pub. Defenders, Am. Legion (past post comdr., past state vice comdr.), 40 and 8, VFW (past post vice comdr.), U. Tenn. Alumni Assn. (past bd. govs., 9th dist. rep.), Sigma Alpha Epsilon, Phi Eta Sigma, Phi Kappa Phi, Omicron Delta Kappa. Episcopalian. Club: Tennessee. Lodges: Masons, Shriners, Jesters, Kiwanis. Banking, Probate (including wills, trusts). Office: Winchester Law Firm 6060 Poplar Ave Ste 38119 Memphis TN 38119

WINDER, RICHARD EARNEST, legal foundation administrator, writer, consultant; b. Vernal, Utah, Sept. 23, 1950; s. William Wallace and Winnifred (Jenkins) W.; m. Janice Fay Walker, Apr. 19, 1975; children: Scott Christian, Eric John, Brian Geoffrey, Laura Jeanne, Amy Elizabeth. BA magna cum laude, Brigham Young U., 1974, JD cum laude, 1978; MBA with honors, U. Michigan, Flint, 1988. Lic. life ins. agt. Mich.; bar: Utah 1978, U.S. Dist. Ct. Utah 1978, Mich. 1979, U.S. Dist. Ct. (ea. and we. dists.) Mich. 1979; lic. securities rep. series 6 and 63 NASD, Mich., first mortgage lic. Mich. Tchg. asst., grad. instr. Brigham Young U., Provo, Utah, 1976-78; law clk. Willingham & Coté, E. Lansing, Mich., 1978-79, atty., 1979-87; exec. v.p. Mgmt. Leasing, Inc., Battle Creek, Mich., 1987-88, Mgmt. Options, Inc., Lansing, Mich., 1988-91; fin. mgr. Mich. State Bar Found., Lansing, Mich., 1991-94, dep. dir., fin. mgr., 1994—. Panelist 9th Nat. Legis. Conf. Small Bus., San Antonio, 1987; adj. prof. Davenport Coll. Bus., Lansing, 1990-92, mgmt. adv. com., 1993-96; mem. founding steering com. Capital Quality Initiative, Lansing, 1992-96; liaison State Bar Mich. Long Range Planning Process, 1996-97; co-founder, rsch. prin. Quality Dynamics Rsch. Inst., Haslett, Mich., 1994-97; rsch. prin. Leadership Dynamics Rsch. Inst., Haslett, 1998—; sr. rep. Primerica Fin. Svcs., 2001—; co-founder, prin. Resilience, Inc. 2003-. Author: (with others) Value Sharing: Value Building, 1990, Corporate Orienteering, 1995; contbr., bd. editors: Summary of Utah Real Property Law, 1978. Vol. leader Boy Scouts Am., Chief Okemos Coun., Lansing, 1978—. Fellow Mich. State Bar Found.; mem. ABA, Am. Soc. Quality (chmn. Lansing-Jackson sect. 1994-95, spkr. and writer 1992-2000), Mich. Bar Assn., Utah Bar Assn., Lansing Regional C. of C. (small bus. coun., MBA task force Bus. and Edn. com. 1988-92, recipient Chmn.'s award 1992), Beta Gamma Sigma. Republican. Mem. Lds Ch. Avocations: writing, speaking, computer technology, research, teaching. Office: Mich State Bar Found 306 Townsend St Lansing MI 48933-2012

WINDHAM, JOHN FRANKLIN, lawyer, educator; b. Fayette, Ala., Jan. 21, 1948; s. Grover B. Windham Jr. and Nancy Katherine (McAdams) Haynie; 1 child, John Franklin Jr.; m. Denise Roche McNair, Apr. 6, 1999; 1 stepchild, Brittany Danielle McNair. BA, U. West Fla., 1970; JD, U. N.C., 1975. Bar: Fla. 1975, U.S. Dist. Ct. (no. dist.) Fla. 1976, U.S. Ct. Appeals (11th cir.) 1983, U.S. Supreme Ct. 1984. Acctg. supr. Monsanto Co., Research Triangle Park, N.C., 1970-72; law clk. to U.S. Atty Pensacola, Fla., 1974; assoc. Beggs & Lane, Pensacola, 1975-79, ptnr., 1979—. Adj. asst. prof. bus. law Troy State U., Pensacola, 1983-90. Mem. exec. com. Fla. divsn. Am. Cancer Soc., 1982-93, 95-2000, chmn. bd. 1998-99, chmn. elect bd. 1997-98; chmn. legis. and planned giving, 1986-88, chmn. inc. devel., 1989-91, chmn. ad hoc adv. com., 1991—, legal advisor, 1992—, bd. dirs., 1982—, mem. scholarship com., 1995-98, mem. Winn Dixie adv. com., 1996-99, chmn. dist. VII steering com., 1995-96. v.p, 1996-97, chmn. field ops. com., 1996-98, Nat. Assembly, 2002-, budget and fin. com. evaluation adv. com., nom. ad hoc com., bd. governance task force, bylaws com., 19990, chmn., 2002-; chmn. bd. Escambia Christian Sch., Pensacola, 1976-86; deacon Ch. of Christ, 1985-95, 1999-2002; adminstrv. team First City Ch., 2002-, mem. adv. bd.; mem. adv. bd. Interim Healthcare, 1993-96, Panhandle Rehab. Injury Mgmt. and Evaluation, 1993-96; mem. found. bd. East Hill Christian Sch., 1995-97; bd. govs. Pensacola chpt. Order Granaderos e Dames de Galvez, 1990-98, pres. 1995-98; mem. U. West Fla. Found., 1983-85. Mem. Fla. Bar (workers compensation rules com., 1995-2001, drafting subcom., 2000-01), Fla. Def. Lawyers Assn., Fla. Workers Compensation Inst., Southeastern Admiralty Law Inst. (bd. dirs. 1986-89), Northwest Fla. Blook Ctr. Found. (treas. 2002-), U. West Fla. Nat. Alumni Assn. (bd. dirs.), Kiwanis (pres. Pensacola 1978-79, 88-89). Republican. Avocation: church activities. Federal civil litigation, State civil litigation, Workers' compensation. Office: Beggs & Lane PO Box 12950 Pensacola FL 32591-2950

WINDHORST, JOHN WILLIAM, JR., lawyer; b. Mpls., July 6, 1940; s. John William and Ardus Ruth (Bottge) W.; divorced; 1 child, Diana Elizabeth. AB, Harvard U., 1962; LLB, U. Minn., 1965. Bar: Minn. 1965, U.S. Tax Ct., U.S. Ct. Appeals (8th cir.) 1965, U.S. Dist. Ct. Minn. 1967, U.S. Supreme Ct. 1975. Law clk. to Hon. H.A. Blackmun U.S. Cir. Ct., Rochester, Minn., 1965-66; assoc. Dorsey & Whitney, Mpls., 1966-70; with office of Revisor of Statutes State of Minn., 1967, 69; ptnr. Dorsey & Whitney, 1971-96, of counsel, 1997—. Bd. dirs. St. Paul Chamber Orch., 1980-86, Harry A. Blackmun Scholarship Found., 1996—, Minn. Taxpayers Assn., 1999—. Mem. ABA (com. on state and local taxes), Minn. Bar Assn., Hennepin County Bar Assn., Harvard Club of Minn. (pres. 1977-78). Home: 1235 Yale Pl Apt 1102 Minneapolis MN 55403-1946 Office: 50 S 6th St Ste 1500 Minneapolis MN 55402 E-mail: windhorst.john@dorseylaw.com.

WINDROW, RACHELLE L. lawyer; b. Murfreesboro, Tenn., Sept. 5, 1974; d. Eugene and Glenda Windrow. BS, Mid. Tenn. State U., 1996; JD, Miss. Coll., 1999. Assoc. Mitchell & Mitchell, Murfreesboro, Tenn., 2000—. Mem.: Am. Trial Lawyers Assn., Tenn. Bar Assn., Rutherford/Cannon County Bar Assn., Am. Inn of Ct. Family and matrimonial, Personal injury (including property damage). Office: Mitchell & Mitchell PO Box 1336 Murfreesboro TN 37130

WINDT, MARCEL, lawyer; b. Dinslaken, Germany, Mar. 7, 1965; s. J.A.M. Windt and D.C.M. Hogeland; m. Evelien Mentink, Aug. 19, 2000. M in law, Leiden (The Netherlands) U., 1989. Bar: Rotterdam 2001. From intern to assoc. Houthoff Buruma, Rotterdam, Netherlands, 1991—, ptnr., 2000—. Spkr. in field. Editor: Insolvency Guide. 2nd lt. Dutch Airforce, 1990—91. Mem.: INSOL Europe, INSOLAD. Office: Houthoff Buruma Weena 355 Weenatoren 3013 AL Rotterdam Netherlands

WINE, L. MARK, lawyer; b. Norfolk, Va., Apr. 16, 1945; s. Melvin Leon and Mildred Sylvia (Weiss) W.; m. Blanche Weintraub, June 8, 1969; children: Kim, Lara, Dana. BA with high honors, U. Va., 1967; JD, U. Chgo., 1970. Bar: D.C. 1970, U.S. Supreme Ct. 1977. Assoc. Kirkland & Ellis, Washington, 1970-72, ptnr., 1978—; trial atty. land and natural resources divsn. Dept. of Justice, Washington, 1972-78. Lawyer; b. Norfolk, Va., Apr. 16, 1945; s. Melvin Leon and Mildred Sylvia (Weiss) W.; m. Blanche Weintraub, June 8, 1969; children— Kim, Lara, Dana. B.A. with high honors, U. Va., 1967; J.D., U. Chgo., 1970. Bar: D.C. 1970, U.S. Supreme Ct. 1977. Assoc., Kirkland & Ellis, Washington, 1970-72; trial atty. land and natural resources div. Dept. of Justice, Washington, 1972-78; ptnr. Kirkland & Ellis, Washington, 1978— . Mem. ABA. Mem. ABA. Administrative and regulatory, Federal civil litigation, Environmental. Office: Kirkland & Ellis 655 15th St NW Ste 1200 Washington DC 20005-5793 E-mail: mark_wine@dc.kirkland.com.

WINE-BANKS, JILL SUSAN, lawyer; b. Chgo., May 5, 1943; d. Bert S. and Sylvia Dawn (Simon) Wine; m. Ian David Volner, Aug. 21, 1965; m. Michael A. Banks, Jan. 12, 1980. BS, U. Ill., Champaign, Urbana, 1964; JD, Columbia U., 1968; LLD (hon.), Hood Coll., 1975. Bar: N.Y. 1969, U.S. Ct. Appeals (2d, 4th, 5th, 6th, 7th and 9th cirs.), U.S. Supreme Ct. 1974, D.C. 1976, Ill. 1980. Asst. press and pub. rels. dir. Assembly of Captive European Nations, N.Y.C., 1965-66; trial atty. criminal divsn. organized crime & racketeering U.S. Dept. Justice, 1969-73; asst. spl. prosecutor Watergate Spl. Prosecutor's Office, 1973-75; lectr. law sem. in trial practice Columbia U. Sch. Law, N.Y.C., 1975-77; assoc. Fried, Frank, Harris, Shriver & Kampelman, Washington, 1975-77; gen. counsel Dept. Army, Pentagon, Washington, 1977-79; ptnr. Jenner & Block, Chgo., 1980-84; solicitor gen. State of Ill. Office of Atty. Gen., 1984-86, dep. atty. gen., 1986-87; exec. v.p., chief oper., officer ABA, Chgo., 1987-90; atty. pvt. practice, 1990-92; v.p., dir. transaction and govt. rels. Motorola Internat. Network Ventures, 1992-97; dir. strategic alliances Motorola Cellular Infrastructure Group, 1997—99; v.p. alliance mgmt. Maytag Corp., 1999-2001; CEO Winning Workplaces, Evanston, Ill., 2001—03; chief officer Chgo. Pub. Schs. Edn. to Careers, 2003—. Mem. EEC disting. vis. program European Parliament, 1987; chmn. bd. dirs. St. Petersburg Telecom., Russia, 1994-97, Omni Capital Ptnrs., Inc., 1994-97. Recipient Spl. Achievement award U.S. Dept. Justice, 1972, Meritorious award, 1973, Cert. Outstanding Svc., 1975; decorated Disting. Civilian Svc. Dept. Army, 1979; named Disting. Vis. to European Econ. Cmty. Mem.: The Chgo. Network, Internat. Women's Forum, Exec. Club (bd. dirs. 1999—2001), Econ. Club. Address: 1724 Asbury Ave Evanston IL 60201 E-mail: jwinebanks@winningworkplaces.org.

WINFIELD, RICHARD NEILL, lawyer; b. Chgo., Jan. 20, 1933; s. Richard Paul and Mary B. (Monaghan) W.; m. Deborah Mary Trainer, June 13, 1959; children: Richard Neill Jr., Pamela, Nicole. AB, Villanova U., 1955; LLB, Georgetown U., 1961. Bar: Va. 1961, N.Y. 1962, U.S. Dist. Ct. (so. dist.) N.Y. 1963. Assoc. Donovan, Leisure, Newton & Irvine, N.Y.C., 1961-65; asst. counsel to Gov. Nelson A. Rockefeller Gov.'s Office, Albany, N.Y., 1965-67; assoc. Royall, Koegel, Rogers & Wells, N.Y.C., 1967-69; ptnr. Clifford Chance US LLP (formerly known as Rogers & Wells), N.Y.C., 1969—. Bd. consultors Sch. Law Villanova U., Pa., 1980—; chmn. libel litigation confs. Practising Law Inst., N.Y.C., 1979-2000. faculty communications law confs, 1977-2001. prof. Columbia Law Sch., Fordham Law Sch., 2002— Editor: Libel Litigation, PLI, 1979, 81, 84, 86, 88, 90, 92, 94, 96, 98, 2000; contbr. articles to profl. jours. Chmn. bd. trustees Convent Sacred Heart Sch., N.Y.C., 1987-90; mem. bd. visitors Sch. Langs. and Linguistics, Georgetown U., Washington, 1987-93; bd. dirs. Fund for Peace, 2000—. Lt. USN, 1955-59. Recipient Loyalty award Villanova U., 1986, Alumni medallion Coll. Liberal Arts & Scis. Villanova U., 1984, First Amendment award Deadline Club 2002. Mem. ABA (chmn. media law reform working group 1996—), N.Y. State Bar Assn., Assn. of Bar of City of N.Y., Century Assn., Internat. Sr. Lawyers Project (treas., bd. dirs.). Republican. Roman Catholic. Avocations: travel, history. General civil litigation, Communications, Libel. Home: 40 5th Ave New York NY 10011-8843 Office: Clifford Chance US LLP 200 Park Ave Fl 54 New York NY 10166-0153

WING, ADRIEN KATHERINE, law educator; b. Aug. 7, 1956; d. John Ellison and Katherine (Pruitt) Wing; children: Che-Cabral, Nolan Felipe. AB magna cum laude, Princeton U., 1978; MA, UCLA, 1979; JD, Stanford, 1982. Bar: N.Y. 1983, U.S. Dist. Ct. (so. and ea. dists.) N.Y. 1983, U.S. Ct. Appeals (5th and 9th cirs.). Assoc. Curtis, Mallet-Prevost, Colt & Mosle, N.Y.C., 1982-86, Rabinowitz, Boudin, Standard, Krinsky & Lieberman, 1986-87; assoc. prof. law U. Iowa, Iowa City, 1987-93, prof., 1993—, disting. prof. law, 2001—. Mem. alumni council Princeton U., 1983-85, 96-2000, mem. exec. com., 2002—, trustee Class of '78 Alumni Found., 1984-87, 93—, v.p. Princeton Class of 1978 Alumni, 1993-98, trustee Princeton U. 1995; mem. bd. visitors Stanford Law Sch., 1993-96; vis. prof. U. Mich., 2002. Mem. bd. editors Am. J. Comp. Law, 1993—. Mem. Iowa Commn. on African Ams. in Prisons, 1999—. Mem.: ABA (exec. com. young lawyers sect. 1985—87, law sch. site inspector 2002—), U.S. Assn. Constl. Law (bd. dir.), Am. Assn. of Law Schs. (minority sect. bd. 1996—, chair 2002), Am. Friends Svc. Com. (bd. dirs. Mid. East 1998—), Am. Soc. Internat. Law (exec. coun. 1986—89, exec. com. 1988—99, nominating com. 1991, 1993, group chair S. Africa 1993—95, membership com. 1994—95, exec. coun. 1996—99), Internat. Assn. Dem. Lawyers (UN rep. 1984—87), Nat. Conf. Black Lawyers (chmn. internat. affairs sect. 1982—95, UN rep.), Internat. Third World Legal Studies Assn. (bd. dirs. 1996—, nominating trustee Princeton com. 1997—2000), Coun. on Fgn. Rels., Iowa Peace Inst. (bd. dirs. 1993—95), Iowa City Fgn. Rels. Coun. (bd. dirs. 1989—94), Transafrica Scholars Forum Coun. (bd. dirs. 1993—95), Black Alumni of Princeton U. (bd. dirs. 1982—87). Democrat. Avocations: photography, writing, poetry. Office: U Iowa Sch Law Boyd Law Bldg Iowa City IA 52242 E-mail: adrien-wing@uiowa.edu.

WING, JOHN RUSSELL, lawyer; b. Mt. Vernon, N.Y., Jan. 20, 1937; s. John R. and Elinore (Smith) W.; m. Mary Zeller, Aug. 24, 1963 (div. June 1975); children: Ethan Lincoln, Catherine Dorothy; m. Audrey Strauss, Aug. 12, 1979; children: Carlin Elinore, Matthew Lawrence. BA, Yale U., 1960; JD, U. Chgo., 1963. Bar: N.Y. 1964. Assoc. Sherman & Sterling,

N.Y.C., 1963-66; asst. U.S. atty. So. Dist. N.Y., N.Y.C., 1966-78; chief fraud unit U.S. Dist. Atty. So. Dist. N.Y., 1971-78; ptnr. Weil, Gotshal & Manges, N.Y.C., 1978—. Contbr. articles to profl. jours. Fellow Am. Coll. Trial Lawyers; mem. ABA (white collar crime com. criminal justice sect. 1978—, environ. task force com. 1983-85), Assn. Bar of City of N.Y. (criminal advocacy com. 1985-88), Fed. Bar Coun. (2d cir. cts. com. 1982-84), N.Y. Coun. Def. Lawyers (bd. dirs. 1986-90). Republican. Episcopalian. Avocation: sailing. Home: 52 Livingston St Brooklyn NY 11201-4813 Office: Weil Gotshal & Manges 767 5th Ave Fl Concl New York NY 10153-0119

WINGER, RALPH O. lawyer; b. Keokuk, Iowa, July 8, 1919; s. Ralph O. and Mary Ellen (Lee) W.; m. Irene L. Sutton, Apr. 5, 1941 (dec.); children: Ralph O. (dec.), Allen, Louise, Robert. BA, State U. Iowa, 1940; LLB, Harvard U., 1947. Bar: N.Y. 1948. Assoc. Cahill Gordon & Reindel and predecessor firms, N.Y.C., 1947-60, ptnr., 1960-91, sr. counsel, 1992—. Lt. USNR, 1942-46, PTO. Mem. ABA, N.Y. State Bar Assn. (chmn. tax sect. 1973-74, ho. of dels. 1974-75), Bay Terrace Country Club (N.Y.). Republican. Home: 20908 28th Rd Flushing NY 11360-2413 Office: Cahill Gordon & Reindel 80 Pine St Fl 17 New York NY 10005-1790

WINGET, WALTER WINFIELD, lawyer; b. Peoria, Ill., Sept. 12, 1936; s. Walter W. Winget and Arabella (Robinson) Richardson; m. Alice B. Winget, Sept. 23, 1993; children: Marie, Marshall. AB cum laude, Princeton U., 1958; JD, U. Mich., 1961. Bar: R.I. 1962, Ill. 1962, U.S. Supreme Ct. 1971; cert. civil trial advocate Nat. Bd. Trial Advocacy. Assoc. Edwards & Angell, Providence, 1961-64; ptnr. Winget & Winget, 1964—69; sole practice Peoria, 1969—77; ptnr. Winget & Kane, Peoria, 1977-2000, of counsel, 2000—. Asst. pub. defender Peoria, 1969-70; bd. dirs. various corps. Atty., bd. dirs. Better Bus. Bur. Cen. Ill., Inc. 1973-92, chmn., 1979-81. Served to sgt. U.S. Army, 1961-62. Mem. Ill. Bar Assn., Peoria County Bar Assn. (pres. 1991-92), Peoria Country Club, Princeton Club Chgo. (mem. schs. com. 1980—), Safari Club, Oakland Hall Club. Republican. Episcopalian. Avocations: competitive target shooting, big game and duck hunting, farm management. Federal civil litigation, State civil litigation, Corporate, general. Home: 6712 N Post Oak Rd Peoria IL 61615-2347 Office: Winget & Kane 416 Main St Ste 807 Peoria IL 61602-1177

WINKELMAN, JOHNNY MARTIN, lawyer, real estate development consultant and Indian gaming consultant; b. Bell, Calif., Nov. 17, 1946; s. Roy Hugh and Phyllis Lorrane (Jansen) W.; m. Brenda Jean Scott, July 4, 1979; children; Brian, Jennifer, Kristina, Diana. AA, Southwestern Coll., 1974; LLB, Western State U., 1976, JD, 1979. Bar: Calif. 1979, U.S. Dist. Ct. (so. dist.) Calif. 1979. Carpenter Local 1492, Los Angeles, 1969-70; constrn. mgr. Winkelman Constrn., Whittier, Calif., 1970-71; bldg. insp. City of Chula Vista, Calif., 1971-76; sr. bldg. insp. City of Nat. City, Calif., 1976-79; law practice San Diego, 1979—. Cons., instr. Southwestern Coll., 1979-85; corp. counsel Palm Homes, Inc., Chula Vista, 1979-88; tribal councilor Viejas Band Mission Indians, Alpine, Calif., 1985-91; advisor Bd. Appeals City of Chula Vista, 1981-88; CEO Viejas Casino & Turf, Club, 1991-99; bd. dirs. Multimedia Games, Inc., Austin, tex. Served with U.S. Army, 1966-68. Mem. Calif. State Bar, Kiwanis. Baptist. Avocations: skiing, travel, boating. E-mail: john@winkelman.ws.

WINKLER, ALLEN WARREN, lawyer, educator; b. Chgo., Dec. 11, 1954; s. Maurice A. and Florence (Klein) W.; m. Bett C. Gibson, Nov. 1, 1986. BS, No. Ill. U., 1977; JD, Tulane U., 1981. Bar: La. 1982, Ill. 1982, U.S. Dist. Ct. (ea. dist.) La. 1982, U.S. Dist. Ct. (mid. dist.) La. 1987. Atty. La. Legal Clinic, New Orleans, 1982-84; pvt. practice law New Orleans, 1984-85; staff atty. Oak Tree Savs. Bank, S.S.B., New Orleans, 1985-87, sr. atty., asst. v.p., 1987-90; atty. FDIC/Resolution Trust Corp., Baton Rouge, 1991-92, sr. atty. Atlanta, 1992-95; sr. corp. counsel Fleet Fin., Inc., Atlanta, 1996-97; pres. Legal Ease Inc., Atlanta, 1996—; corp. counsel Prudential Bank, Atlanta, 1997; gen. counsel, v.p. NCS Mortgage Svcs., Norcross, Ga., 1998-2000, gen. counsel, 1999-2000; exec. v.p., COO Companion Servicing Co., LLC, 1999-2000; corp. counsel Provident Bank, Atlanta, 2000-2001; sr. atty., v.p. SunTrust Bank, Atlanta, 2001—. Mem. faculty Franklin Coll. Ct. Reporting, Metairie, La., 1981-88; cons., guest lectr. paralegal studies Tulane U., New Orleans, 1982-90; guest lectr. U. New Orleans, 1988-90. Vol. Hawkins for Judge campaign, New Orleans. Mem. La. Bar Assn., Ill. Bar Assn. Commercial, consumer (including collections, credit), Commercial, contracts (including sales of goods; commercial financing), Property, real (including real estate development, water). Home: 4754 Forest Glen Court Marietta GA 30066 Office: SunTrust Bank 2950 SunTrust Plz 303 Peachtree St NE Atlanta GA 30308 E-mail: allen.winkler@suntrust.com.

WINKLER, CHARLES HOWARD, lawyer; b. NYC, Aug. 4, 1954; s. Joseph Conrad and Geraldine Miriam (Borok) W.; m. Joni S. Taylor, Aug. 28, 1993. BBA with highest distinction, Emory U., 1976; JD, Northwestern U., 1979. Bar: Ill. 1979, U.S. Dist Ct (no. dist.) Ill. 1979. Assoc. Levenfeld & Kanter, Chgo., 1979-80, Kanter & Eisenberg, Chgo., 1980-84, ptnr., 1985-86, Neal Gerber & Eisenberg, Chgo., 1986-96; sr. mng. dir., COO Citadel Investment Group, LLC, Chgo., 1996—2001; sr. mng. dir. Citadel Trading Group, Chgo., 1996—2000, Aragon Investments Ltd., Chgo., 1996—2000. Bd. dirs. Kensington Global Strategies Fund, Ltd., Antaeus Internat. Investments, Ltd., Jackson Investment Fund Ltd., Citadel Investment Group (Europe) Ltd., chief oper. officer, and sr. mng. dir. Amaranth Advisors, LLC, 2001—; hedge fund mgr. Author: (with others) Basic Tax Shelters, 1982, Limited Liability Companies: The Entity of Choice, 1995; mng. editor Northwestern Jour. Internat. Law and Bus., 1979. Mem. ABA (mem. sect. on taxation), Beta Gamma Sigma. Corporate, general, Securities, Taxation, general. Home: 10 Taconic Rd Greenwich CT 06830-3428 Office: Amaranth Advisors LLC One American Ln Greenwich CT 06831 E-mail: cwinkler@att.net.

WINKLER, DANA JOHN, lawyer; b. Wichita, Kans., Jan. 2, 1944; s. Donald Emil and Hazel Claire (Schmitter) W.; m. Mary Ann Seiwert, Oct. 14, 1967; 1 child, Jonathan. BA, Wichita State U., 1967; JD, Washburn Law Sch., 1971. Staff writer Wichita (Kans.) Eagle & Beacon, 1961-67; ptnr. Davis, Bruce, Davis & Winkler, Wichita, 1972-77; asst. city atty. City of Wichita, 1977-99; dir. Wichita Mcpl. Fed. Credit Union, 1980—, pres., 1982, 99-2000, sec.-treas., 1994-98, v.p., 1998-99. Dir. Deaf and Hard of Hearing Counseling Svc., 1979-80. Vol. Sedgwick County United Way, Wichita, 1973-74; vice-chmn. Wichita Pub. Schs. Spl. Edn. Adv. Coun., 1987-89. 1st lt. U.S. Army, 1967-69. Mem. Kans. Bar Assn., Wichita Bar Assn., Masons. Republican. Roman Catholic. Home and Office: 1621 Harlan St Wichita KS 67212-1842 E-mail: djwinkler@aol.com.

WINKLER, NICHOLAS GARY, lawyer; b. Sydney, Australia, June 24, 1948; BA, Sydney U., Australia, 1968, LLB, 1971, LLM, 1977. Law clk. Prudential Assurance Co., Sydney, Australia, 1969—71; solicitor State Bank of NSW, Sydney, Australia, 1971—82; chief solicitor Custom Credit Corp. Ltd., Sydney, Australia, 1982—87; prin. Nicholas Winkler & Turner, Sydney, Australia, 1984—94; sr. cons. Drake Mgmt. Cons., Sydney, Australia, 1994—96; dir. Nicholas Winkler Cons., Sydney, 1996—99; gen. counsel Tower Tech. Pty. Ltd., Lane Cove, Australia, 1999—2003; corp. counsel Caltex Australia Petroleum Pty Ltd., Sydney, 2003—. Contbr. articles to profl. jours. including Company Dir. and Law Soc. Jour. Patron, sponsor Pub. Info. Paper Series of Com. for Econ. Devel. of Australia, Sydney, 1993. Mem. Com. for Econ. Devel. of Australia (trustee 1990—, mem. internat. rels. com. 2000—), Law Soc. New South Wales, Australian Inst. of Co. Dir., Am. C. of C. in Australia, Am. Club Sydney, Cruising Yacht Club Australia. Commercial, contracts (including sales of goods; commercial financing), Computer, Oil, gas, and mineral. Home: 906-127 Kent St Sydney NSW 2000 Australia Office: Caltex Australia Petroleum Pty Ltd 19 Martin Pl Sydney NSWw 2000 Australia E-mail: nwinkler@caltex.com.au.

WINKLER, OSKAR WERNER, lawyer; b. Vienna, Apr. 3, 1959; s. Hugo and Ingrid (von Stockert) Winkler; m. Lisa Schreiner Winkler, June 29, 2002. M in Bus., U. Vienna, 1981, D in Law, 1984. Bar: Vienna 1996. Asst. judge Dist. Ct. Commerce, Vienna, 1984, Vienna Penal Ct., 1985, Vienna Ct. Commerce, 1985; sec.-gen. Wiener Allianz Versicherungs-AG, Vienna, 1985—90, Montana AG für Bergbau, Industrie und Handel, Vienna, 1990—91; assoc. Cerha Hempel Spiegelfeld, Vienna, 1992—96, ptnr., 1996—. Mem. supervisory bd. Worthington Cylinders GmbH, Kienberg, Austria, 1998—. Mem.: Gesellschaft der Musikfreunde Vienna, Vienna Bar Assn., Ski Club Arlberg, St. Johann's Club. Avocations: music, art, skiing. Corporate, general, Finance, Property, real (including real estate development, water). Home: Kopfgasse 8 A-1130 Vienna Austria Office: Cerha Hempel Spiegelfeld Partnerschaft von Rechtsanwalten Parkring 2 A-1010 Vienna Austria

WINN, JAMES JULIUS, JR., lawyer; b. Colon, Panama, Nov. 7, 1941; came to U.S., 1941; s. James Julius and Molly (Brown) W.; m. Elizabeth Kokernot Lacy, Aug. 15, 1970; children: Mary Ann W. Burns, Elizabeth Lacy, James Julius VI. AB, Princeton U., 1964; JD cum laude, Washington and Lee U., 1970. Bar: Md. 1970, U.S. Dist. Ct. Md. 1971, U.S. Dist. Ct. D.C. 1982. Assoc. Piper Marbury Rudnick & Wolfe, LLP, Balt., 1970-78; ptnr. Piper Rudnick LLP, Balt., 1978—. Assoc. editor, contbr. author Washington & Lee U. Law Rev., 1968-70. Counselor St. John's Ch., Western Run Parish, Glyndon, Md., 1974—; mem. com. on canons and other bus., investment com. Episc. Diocese Md., 1986—; dir. Ctr. for Ethics and Corp. Policy, 1988-95, chmn., 1991-95; dir. Ctr. Stage, 1986—; dir. Oldfields Sch., 1991-96; v.p., dir. Ruxton Country Sch., 1988-91; dir. The Jemicy Sch., 1999—. Mem. ABA (chmn. subcoms. on publs. and govt. acctg. standards of com. on law and acctg. of sect. of bus. law), Md. State Bar Assn. (com. on corp. law of sect. of bus. law). Banking, Corporate, general, Securities. Office: Piper Rudnick LLP 6225 Smith Ave Baltimore MD 21209-3600

WINNIG, JOEL BRUCE, lawyer; b. Wausau, Wis., Oct. 31, 1954; s. Sidney and Marion Rose (Marko) W.; m. Susan Rubnitz, July 20, 1980; children: Samuel David, Sarah Jo. BS, U. Wis., 1975, JD, 1977. Bar: Wis. 1978, U.S. Dist. Ct. (ea. and we. dists.) Wis. 1978. Pvt. practice, Madison, Wis., 1978—. Bd. dirs. Project Home Inc., Madison, 1985—. Mem. Wis. Acad. Trial Lawyers, Dane County Bar Assn., Dane County Criminal Def. Assn. Family and matrimonial, Personal injury (including property damage), Property, real (including real estate development, water). Office: Ste 200 455 County Road M Madison WI 53719-3823

WINNING, J(OHN) PATRICK, lawyer; b. Murphysboro, Ill., Oct. 29, 1952; s. William T. Jr. and Lillian (Albers) W.; m. Jessica Anne Yoder, June 17, 1978 (div. July 1999); children: Erika Anne, Brian Patrick, Derek Matthew. AB with distinction, Mo. Bapt. Coll., 1974; JD, St. Louis U., 1979. Bar: Mo. 1979, U.S. Dist. Ct. (ea. dist.) Mo. 1979, U.S. Ct. Appeals (8th cir.) 1979, U.S. Dist. Ct. (so. dist.) Tex. 1985, U.S. Ct. Appeals (5th cir.) 1987, U.S. Dist. Ct. (we. dist.) Tex. 1988, Tex. 1989. Assoc. Chused, Strauss, Chorlins, Goldfarb, Bini & Kohn, St. Louis, 1979-81; assoc. counsel Mfrs. Hanover Fin. Services, Phila., 1981-83; corp. counsel Cessna Fin. Corp., Wichita, Kans., 1983-85; atty. Southwestern Bell Publs., Inc., St. Louis, 1985-90; pvt. practice St. Louis, 1990-2000, 2001—; pres. Butler Hill Investments, Inc., St. Louis, 1990-91; prin. Success Mgmt. Group, 1991-96, DPPC Mgmt. Group, St. Louis, 1996-97; v.p., gen. counsel Winning Equipment Co., Herculaneum, Mo., 2000-01; assoc. Vogler Law Firm, P.C., Herculaneum, Mo., 2000—01; with Elco Chevrolet, Ballwin, Mo., 2002—. Sec., bd. dirs. Winning Equipment Co.; asst. prof. bus. adminstn. Mo. Bapt. Coll., 1986-91. Treas. Concerned Citizens of Chesterfield, 1989-91; deacon, mem. fin. com. 1st Bapt. Ch., Ellisville, Mo., 1992-93, vice chmn. fin. com., 1993-94, chmn. fin. com., 1994-95, vice chmn. deacons, 1993-95, chmn. deacons, 1997-98, dir. Sunday sch., 1993-94; trustee, chmn. athletic com., 1992-97, 98-2000, chmn. by-laws com. Mo. Bapt. Coll., 1992-96, sec. presdl. search com., 1994, mem., exec. com. bd. trustees, 1994-97, 98-2000; mgr. St. Louis Flames Youth Baseball, 1992-95; mgr. St. Louis Thunder Youth Baseball, 1995-97; coach St. Clare Bulls Basketball Team, 1994-97, St. Louis Wolfpack Youth Baseball, 1997-98; asst. scoutmaster troop 313, merit badge counselor Boy Scouts Am., 1997—; Camporee staff New Horizons dist. Boy Scouts Am., 1998-2000, adult leader tng. staff, 1998—, camping com., 1998-2000, dist. roundtable staff, 1999—, chmn. membership com. New Horizons dist., 1999—. Named one of Outstanding Young Men of Am., 1987, Outstanding Alumnus, Mo. Bapt. Coll., 1987-88; named to Athletic Hall of Fame, Mo. Bapt. Coll., 1989; recipient Wood Badge Adult Leadership Tng. award Boy Scouts Am., 1998. Mem. Nat. Lawyers Assn., Eagle Scouts Assn., Met. St. Louis Bar Assn., Christian Legal Soc., Acad. Family Mediators, Assn. Family and Conciliation Cts., Mo. Bapt. Coll. Alumni Assn. (pres. 1980-81, 88-90), St. Louis Assn., Christian Attys., West County C. of C., Chesterfield C. of C. Republican. Southern Baptist. Avocations: coaching baseball and basketball, reading, camping. Corporate, general, Family and matrimonial, Property, real (including real estate development, water). Home: 868 Gardenway Ballwin MO 63011 Office: 868 Gardenway Ballwin MO 63011

WINSLOW, F(RANCIS) DANA, state supreme court justice, former record company owner; b. N.Y.C., Feb. 20, 1939; s. Francis Dana and Flora Brady (Garvan) W.; m. Beverly June Bell, Aug. 25, 1984; children by previous marriage: Francis Dana III, Michael, Jennifer. BA, Am. U., 1966; JD, Cath. U. Am., 1969. Bar: N.Y. 1970, U.S. Ct. Appeals (2d cir.) 1972, U.S. Supreme Ct. 1975. Assoc. Beekman & Bogue (Now Gaston & Snow, N.Y.C., 1969-73; spl. counsel Sutter, Moffatt, Vannelli & Zevin, Mineola, N.Y., 1973-78; pvt. law practice Mineola, 1978-89; pres., owner Winslow Prodsn. Ltd., Mineola, 1983-96; ptnr. Schiavetti, Geiser, Corgan et al, various, N.Y., 1989-96; assoc. justice Village of Old Westbury, N.Y., 1991-96; village atty. Village of Centre Island, NY, 1988-96; justice N.Y. State Supreme Ct., 1996—. Chair adv. commn. N.Y. State Jud. Inst., 2000—; counsel World Tae Kwan Do championships, 1993; adj. prof. law sect. Grad. Bus. Law, St. John's U., 1998—2000. Judo instr. various univs. Washington met. area; instr. 2d Dan (Black Belt) Judo, 1963—, 5th Dan Tae Kwan Do, 1997; founding pres., chair Winslow Therapeutic Riding, Inc., 1974, bd. dirs., 1974—; founder, chmn. Helping Hand Horse Show, 1979-86; mem. N.Y. State Supreme Ct. Justice Task Force on N.Y. Ct. Reform, 1997—, chair, 2003; bd. dirs. N.Am. Riding for Handicapped Assn., 1983-87; chmn. publicity and pub. rels. Nat. Equestrian Sports Day; atty., legal counsel, advisor U.S. Tae Kwan Do Union, U.S. Olympic Com. for 1988 Olympics, 1984-89; co-organizer spl. song presentation for benefit Gift of Life program honoring Nancy Reagan, N.Y.C., 1984; appeared off-Broadway and cmty. prodns. musicals; pres. Glen Players, Glen Cove, N.Y., 1985-87, bd. dirs., 1986-90; trustee, police commr. Village of Old Wstbury, 1976-81, environ. commr., 19790-81. Spl. agt. M.I., U.S. Army, 1962-65, Korea. Recipient Outstanding Svc. award D.C. Bar Assn., 1968, citation of merit Uniformed Firefighters Assn., N.Y.C., 1983. Mem. Nassau County Bar Assn., Assn. N.Y. State Suprme Ct. Justices, Nassau County Magistrates Assn. (bd. dirs. 1995-96), The Creek Club (Locust Valley, N.Y.), Sigma Nu. Democrat. Corporate, general, Entertainment, General practice.

WINSLOW, JOHN FRANKLIN, lawyer; b. Houston, Nov. 15, 1933; s. Franklin Jarnigan and Jane (Shipley) W. BA, U. Tex., 1957, LLB, 1960. Bar: Tex. 1959, D.C. 1961. Atty., Hispanic law div. Library Congress, Washington, 1965-68; counsel, com. on the judiciary Ho. of Reps., Washington, 1968-71; atty., editor Matthew Bender & Co., Washington, 1973-79; atty. FERC, Washington, 1979-84; sole practice Washington, 1984—. Researcher Hispanic Law Research, Washington, 1979—. Author: Conglomerates Unlimited: The Failure of Regulation, 1974; editor: Fed. Power Service, 1974-79; contbr. articles to Washington Monthly, Nation, 1975—. Mem. Tex. Bar Assn., D.C. Bar Assn. Administrative and regulatory, Public international. E-mail: jfwinslow@aol.com.

WINSTEAD, GEORGE ALVIS, law librarian, biochemist, educator, consultant; b. Owensboro, Ky., Jan. 14, 1916; s. Robert Lee and Mary Oma (Dempsey) Winstead; m. Elisabeth Donelson Weaver, July 18, 1942. BS, We. Ky. U., 1938; MA, George Peabody Coll., 1940, MLS, 1957, MEd, 1958. Head chemistry and biology dept. Belmont Coll., Nashville, 1952-56; head chemistry dept. George Peabody Coll., Vanderbilt U., Nashville, 1956-58; assoc. law librarian Vanderbilt U., Nashville, 1958-76; dir. Tenn. State Supreme Ct. Law Libraries, Nashville, 1976—. Law cons. Tenn. Youth Legis., Nashville, 1976—; cons. civic clubs, local colls., 1976—, Tenn. State Govt. Depts. Archives, Nashville, 1976—. Author: Tenn. State Law Library Progress Reports, 1975, Supreme Court Library Personnel Guide, 1981, Designing Future Law Libraries' Growth and Expansion, 1982, Problem Identification and Solutions in Law Libraries, Tenn. Supreme Courts, 1985; mem. editl. bd. A Dictionary of Chemical Equations, 1952—. Mem. Col. Tenn. Gov.'s staff, Nashville, 1978. With USAAF, 1943-46. Named to Gov.'s Staff of Ky. Cols., Lexington, 1988. Fellow Am. Inst. Chemists, SAR. Baptist. Avocations: camping, hiking, traveling, crafts, antique cars. Home: 3819 Gallatin Pike Nashville TN 37216-2609 Office: Tenn Supreme Ct Libr Nashville TN 37219

WINSTEN, SAUL NATHAN, lawyer; b. Providence, Feb. 23, 1953; s. Harold H. and Anita E. Winsten; m. Patricia J. Miller, Aug. 7, 1977; children: David A., J. Benjamin, Jennifer M. BA, Beloit Coll., 1976; JD, Drake U., 1980. Shareholder Whyte Hirschboeck, Milw. Contbr. articles to profl. jours. Co-chmn. Wis. Gov.'s Adv. Coun. on Internat. Trade, 1996-2000, mem., 1996—, Wis. Gov.'s Internat. Edn. Task Force, 1997-98. Mem. ABA (chmn. com. young lawyers divsn. 1989-90, governing coun., antitrust, bus. and internat. law sects.), Wis. Bar Assn., Internat. Bar Assn., Japan-Am. Soc. Wis. (pres. 1993-94, co-founder 1990, sec. 1990-92), Nat. Assn. Japan-Am. Socs. (bd. dirs. 1991-97, exec. com. 1993-97), Order of Barristers, Hessen-Wisconsin, Inc. (bd. dirs.). Corporate, general, Private international, Non-profit and tax-exempt organizations. Office: Whyte Hirschboeck 111 E Wisconsin Ave Ste 2100 Milwaukee WI 53202-4108

WINSTON, HAROLD RONALD, lawyer; b. Atlantic, Iowa, Feb. 7, 1932; s. Louis D. and Leta B. (Carter) W.; m. Carol J. Sundeen, June 11, 1955; children: Leslie Winston Yannetti, Lisa Winston Shaw, Laura Winston Moritz. BA, U. Iowa, 1954, JD, 1958. Bar: Iowa 1958, U.S. Dist. Ct. (no. and so. dists.) Iowa 1962, U.S. Tax Ct. 1962, U.S. Ct. Appeals (8th cir.) 1970, U.S. Supreme Ct. 1969. Trust officer United Home Bank & Trust Co., Mason City, Iowa, 1958-59; mem. Breese & Cornwell, Mason City, 1960-62, Breese, Cornwell, Winston & Reuber, Mason City, 1963-73, Winston, Schroeder & Reuber, Mason City, 1974-79, Winston, Reuber, Swanson & Byrne, P.C., Mason City, 1980-92, Winston, Reuber & Byrne, Mason City, 1992-96, Winston & Byrne, P.C., Mason City, 1996—. Police judge, Mason City, 1961-73. Contbr. articles to profl. jours. Past pres. Family YMCA, Mason City, Cerro Gordo County Estate Planning Coun.; active local charitable orgns. Capt. USAF, 1955-57. Fellow Am. Coll. Trust and Estate Counsel, Am. Bar Found. (life), Iowa Bar Found. (life); mem. ABA, ATLA, Iowa Bar Assn. (gov., lectr. ann. meeting 1977-79), 2d Jud. Dist. Bar Assn. (lectr. meeting 1981-82), Cerro Gordo County Bar Assn. (past pres.), Am. Judicature Soc., Mason City Country Club, Kiwanis, Masons. Republican. Presbyterian. Corporate, general, General practice, Probate (including wills, trusts). Office: Winston & Byrne 119 2d St NW Mason City IA 50401-3105 E-mail: hwinston@netins.net.

WINSTON, JUDITH ANN, lawyer; b. Atlantic City, Nov. 23, 1943; d. Edward Carlton and Margaret Ann (Goodman) Marianno; m. Michael Russell Winston, Aug. 10, 1963; children: Lisa Marie, Cynthia Eileen. BA magna cum laude, Howard U., Washington, 1966; JD, Georgetown U., 1977. Bar: DC 1977, US Supreme Ct. Dir. EEO project Coun. Great City Schs., Washington, 1971-74; legal asst. Lawyers Com. for Civil Rights Under Law, Washington, 1975-77; spl. asst. to dir. Office for Civil Rights, HEW, Washington, 1977-79; exec. asst., legal counsel to chair U.S. EEO Commn., Washington, 1979-80; asst. gen. counsel U.S. Dept. Edn., 1980-86; dep. dir. Lawyers Com. for Civil Rights Under Law, 1986-88; dep. dir. pub. policy Women's Legal Def. Fund, Washington, 1988-90, chair employment discrimination com., 1979-88, ednl. cons., 1974-77; asst. prof. law Washington Coll. Law of Am. U., 1990-93, assoc. prof. law, 1993-95; gen. counsel U.S. Dept. Edn., Washington, 1993-2001; exec. dir. Pres.'s Initiative on Race, 1997-98; undersec. U.S. Dept. Edn., 2000-01; rsch. prof law Washington Coll. Law Am. U., Washington, 2001—02; prin. Winston Withers & Assocs., LLC, Washington, 2002—. Author: (book) Desegregating Schools in the Great Cities: Philadelphia, 1970, Chronicle of a Decade 1961-70, 1970, Desegregating Urban Schools: Educational Equality/Quality, 1970; contbr. articles to profl jours. Pres. bd. dirs. Higher Achievement Program; bd. dirs. Ptnrs. for Dem. Change, Nat. Pub. Radio, So. Edn. Found.; Nat. Law Ctr. on Poverty and Homelessness. Named Woman Lawyer of the Yr, Women's Bar Asn, 1997; recipient Margaret Brent, Am Bar Asn Comn Women in the Profession, 1998, Thurgood Marshall award, DC Bar, 1999. Fellow: ABA Found; mem.: ACLU, Lawyers Comt Civil Rights Under Law, Nat Bar Asn, Washington Bar Asn, Washington Coun Lawyers, DC Bar Asn, Fed Bar Asn, Links Inc, Phi Beta Kappa, Delta Theta Phi, Alpha Kappa Alpha. Democrat. Episcopalian. Home: 1371 Kalmia Rd NW Washington DC 20012-1444 Office: Winston Withers & Assocs Washington DC

WINTER, NELSON WARREN, lawyer; b. Williamsport, Pa., Nov. 4, 1950; s. John Calvin II and Margaret Jeanette (Stiber) W. BA with highest distinction, U. Va., 1972, JD, 1975. Bar: Pa. 1975, U.S. Dist. Ct. (we. dist.) Pa. 1975, U.S. Ct. of Appeals (3d cir.) 1976. Assoc. Reed Smith LLP, Pitts., 1975-84, ptnr., 1985—. Bd. dirs. Maglev, Inc.; bd. dirs. Inst. for German-Am. Rels., 1990—. Mem. Allegheny County Bar Assn., U.S. Tennis Assn. (treas. and dir. Middle States sect. 1993-2000, dir. Allegheny Mountain dist. 1993—), Oxford Athletic Club, Delta Tau Delta. Republican. Lutheran. Avocation: tennis. Banking, Corporate, general, Securities. Office: Reed Smith LLP 435 6th Ave Pittsburgh PA 15219-1886

WINTERER, PHILIP STEELE, lawyer; b. San Francisco, July 8, 1931; s. Steele Leland and Esther (Hardy) W.; m. Patricia Dowling, June 15, 1955; children: Edward J., Amey W. Marrella. BA, Amherst Coll., 1953; LLB, Harvard U., 1956. Bar: N.Y. 1957, Republic of Korea 1958. Assoc., then ptnr. Debevoise & Plimpton, N.Y.C., 1956-93, ret. ptnr., 1993, of counsel, 1994-96. Dir. Am. Savs. Bank, 1972-92. Contbr. articles to profl. publs. Past pres. Am. Italy Soc.; trustee Amherst Coll.; chmn. emeritus Sch. of Am. Ballet; chmn. exec. com. Phipps Houses; trustee emeritus N.Y. State Bd. Nature Conservancy; trustee, past chmn. Austen Riggs Ctr.; vice chmn. trustees Adelphi U.; bd. govs. Emily Dickinson Mus.; mem. Com. on the Folger Shakespeare Libr.; bd. dirs., v.p. Adirondack Trail Improvement Soc. Recipient Amherst Coll. medal for Eminent Svc., 1980. Mem.: Am. Coll. Tax Counsel, Tax Forum, N.Y. Acad. Scis., Citizens Housing and Planning Coun. N.Y., Am. Law Inst., Coun. on Fgn. Rels., Ausable Club (trustee, v.p.), Fellows of Phi Beta Kappa Soc. (bd. dirs.). Home: Gulf Brook Way Keene NY 12942 also: 1165 5th Ave New York NY 10029-6931 Office: Debevoise & Plimpton 919 3rd Ave New York NY 10022 E-mail: winterhil95@aol.com.

WINTERSHEIMER, DONALD CARL, state supreme court justice; b. Covington, Ky., Apr. 21, 1932; s. Carl E. and Marie A. (Kohl) W.; m. Alice T. Rabe, June 24, 1961; children: Mark D., Lisa Ann, Craig P., Amy T.,

Blaise Q. BA, Thomas More Coll., 1953; MA, Xavier U., 1956; JD, U. Cin., 1959; LHD (hon.), No. Ky. U., 1999. Bar: Ky. 1960, Ohio 1960. Pvt. practice, Covington, Ky., 1960-76; city solicitor City of Covington, 1962-76; judge Ky. Ct. Appeals, Frankfort, 1976-83; justice Ky. Supreme Ct., Frankfort, 1983—, chmn. criminal rules com., 1988-94, chmn. continuing jud. edn. com., 1983—, chmn. rules com., 1994—. Del. Foster Parent Rev. Bd., 1985-2002; mem. adv. bd. Sta. WNKU-FM, 1984-94, Am. Soc. Writers on Legal Subjects. Trustee Sta. WNKU-FM. Recipient Cmty. Svc. award Thomas More Coll., 1968; recipient Disting. Alumnus award Thomas More Coll., 1982, Disting. Alumni award Coll. Law/U.Cin., 1998; named Disting. Jurist Chase Coll. Law, 1983, Outstanding Jurist Phi Alpha Delta Law Frat., 1990. Mem. ABA, Am. Judicature Soc., Ky. Bar Assn., Ohio Bar Assn., Cin. Bar Assn., Inst. Jud. Adminstrn., Am. Inss of Ct. (founder Chase chpt.). Democrat. Roman Catholic. Home: 224 Adams Ave Covington KY 41014-1712 Office: Ky Supreme Ct Capitol Building Room 235 700 Capitol Ave Frankfort KY 40601-3410

WINTHROP, LAWRENCE FREDRICK, judge; b. Apr. 18, 1952; s. Murray and Vauneta (Cardwell) W. BA with honors, Whittier Coll., 1974; JD magna cum laude, Calif. Western Sch., 1977. Bar: Ariz. 1977, Calif. 1977, U.S. Dist. Ct. Ariz. 1977, U.S. Dist. Ct. (so. dist.) Calif. 1981, U.S. Ct. Appeals (9th cir.) 1981, U.S. Dist. Ct. (cen. dist.) Calif. 1983, U.S. Supreme Ct. 1983. Assoc. Snell and Wilmer, Phoenix, 1977—83, ptnr., 1984—93, Doyle, Winthrop, P.C., Phoenix, 1993—2002; judge divsn. one Ariz. Ct. Appeals, Phoenix, 2002—. Judge pro tem Maricopa County Superior Ct., 1987-97; lectr. Ariz. personal injury law and practice and state and local tax law Tax Exec. Inst., Nat. Bus. Inst., Profl. Edn. Systems, Inc., Ariz. Trial Lawyers Assn., Maricopa County Bar Assn.; bd. dirs. Valley of the Sun Sch., 1989-97, chmn., 1994-96; mem. Vol. Lawyers Program, Phoenix, 1980-2002. Editor-in-chief: Calif. Western Law Rev., 1976-77. Fellow Ariz. Bar Found., Maricopa Bar Found.; mem. ABA, Calif. Bar Assn., Ariz. Bar Assn. (mem. com. on exam. 1995-2002), Ariz. Tax Rsch. Assn. (bd. dirs. 1989-93), Maricopa County Bar Assn., Ariz. Assn. Def. Counsel (bd. dirs., pres. 1988-89, chmn. med. malpractice com. 1993-95), Am. Bd. Trial Advs., Aspen Valley Club, Forest Highlands Club. Republican. Methodist. Avocations: music, golf, tennis. Home: 6031 N 2nd St Phoenix AZ 85012-1210 Office: 1501 W Washington St Phoenix AZ 85007 E-mail: lwinthro@courts.sp.state.az.us.

WINTHROP, SHERMAN, lawyer; b. Duluth, Minn., Feb. 3, 1931; s. George E. and Mary (Tesler) W.; m. Barbara Cowan, Dec. 16, 1956; children: Susan Winthrop Crist, Bradley T., Douglas A. BBA, U. Minn., 1952; JD, Harvard U., 1955. Bar: Minn. 1955, U.S. Dist. Ct. Minn. 1955, U.S. Tax Ct. Law clk. to chief justice Minn. Supreme Ct., St. Paul, 1955-56; ptnr. Oppenheimer, Wolff & Donnelly, St. Paul, 1956-79; shareholder Winthrop & Weinstine P.A., St. Paul, 1979—. Bd. dirs. Bremer Fin. Corp., St. Paul, Minn., Capital City Partnership; bd. dirs., sec. St. Paul Progress Corp. Mem. ABA, Minn. Bar Assn. (chair exec. coun., bus. law sect. 1992-93), Ramsey County Bar Assn. Avocations: tennis, travel, family. Banking, Corporate, general, Property, real (including real estate development, water). Home: 1672 Pinehurst Ave Saint Paul MN 55116-2158 Office: Winthrop & Weinstine PA 3200 Minn World Trade Ctr 30 7th St E Saint Paul MN 55101-4914 E-mail: swinthrop@winthrop.com.

WINTRODE, RALPH CHARLES, lawyer; b. Hollywood, Calif., Dec. 21, 1942; s. Ralph Osborne and Maureen (Kavanagh) W.; m. Leslie Ann O'Rourke, July 2, 1966 (div. Feb. 1994); children: R. Christopher, Patrick L., Ryan B.; m. Denise A. Beetham, Aug. 24, 1999. BS in Acctg., U. So. Calif., 1966, JD, 1967. Bar: Calif. 1967, N.Y. 1984, Japan 1989, Washington 1990. From assoc. to ptnr. to of counsel Gibson, Dunn & Crutcher, Tokyo, L.A., Newport Beach and Irvine, Calif., 1967—. Sec. Music Ctr. Los Angeles County, 1986-88; bd. dirs. Coro Found., L.A. County, 1986-87. Mem. Newport Harbor Club, Am. Club Tokyo. Avocations: sailboat racing, car racing, flying. Corporate, general, Mergers and acquisitions, Property, real (including real estate development, water). Office: Gibson Dunn & Crutcher 4 Park Plz Ste 1400 Irvine CA 92614-8557 also: 333 S Grand Ave Ste 4400 Los Angeles CA 90071-1548

WINZENREID, JAMES ERNEST, lawyer, entrepreneur; b. Wheeling, W.Va., June 9, 1951; s. Ernest Christian and Dorothy Emma (Wolf) W.; m. Rebecca Lee Rice, Aug. 11, 1979; children: Diana Lee, Lauren Rice. AB, W. Liberty State Coll., 1973; MBA, W.Va. U., 1979; JD, Duquesne U., 1987; LLM, Wayne State U., 1989. Bar: Pa. 1987, U.S. Dist. Ct. (we. dist.) Pa. 1987. Staff asst. Wheeling Pitts. Steel Corp., Wheeling, 1974—78, supr. indsl. rels., 1978; mgr. profl. planning and devel. Copperweld Corp., Pitts., 1978—79, mgr. human resources Glassport, Pa., 1979—81, plant mgr., 1981—83, group mgr. human resources Pitts., 1984—85, market program mgr., 1986—87; with lab. and employment dept. Eckert, Seamans, Cherin & Mellott, Pitts., 1986—87; corp. staff rep. Tecumseh (Mich.) Products Co., 1987—89; v.p. human resources devel. Lafarge (Va.) Corp., 1989—94; v.p. human resources western region Lafarge Constrn. Materials, Calgary, Canada, 1994—96, Lafarge Can. Inc., Calgary, Canada, 1996—99; mgr. union rels. GE, Bloomington, Ind., 2000—01; dir. labor rels. and compliance Metaldyne Corp., Plymouth, Mich., 2002—. Mng. editor Juris mag., 1986. Bd. dirs. Wheeling Symphony Soc., 1977-86, Wheeling Jaycees, 1976-78; mem. adv. bd. Jr. Achievement Southwestern Pa., 1981-83. Named Outstanding Young Men Am. U.S. Jaycees, 1979. Mem. ABA, Pa. Bar Assn., Allegheny Bar Assn., Am. Soc. Human Resources Mgmt., Human Resource Planning Soc., Phi Alpha Delta. Republican. Lutheran. Avocations: golf, reading. Labor (including EEOC, Fair Labor Standards Act, labor-management relations, NLRB, OSHA). Home: 4647 Fox Moor Ln Greenwood IN 46143-9279 Office: Metaldyne Corp 47603 Halyard Dr Plymouth MI 48170-2429

WINZER, P.J. lawyer; b. Shreveport, La., June 7, 1947; d. C.W. Winzer and Pearlene Hall Winzer Tobin. BA in Polit. Sci., So. U., Baton Rouge, 1968; JD, UCLA, 1971. Bar: Bar: Calif. 1972, U.S. Supreme Ct. 1986. Staff atty. Office of Gen. Counsel, U.S. HEW, Washington, 1971-80; asst. spl. counsel U.S. Office of Spl. Counsel Merit Systems Protection Bd., Dallas, 1980-82; regional dir. U.S. Merit Systems Protection Bd., Alexandria, Va., 1982—. Mem. Calif. Bar Assn., Fed. Cir. Bar Assn., Delta Sigma Theta. Office: US Merit System Protection 1800 Diagnol Rd Ste 205 Alexandria VA 22314-2840

WIRKEN, CHARLES WILLIAM, lawyer; b. Moline, Ill., Aug. 29, 1951; s. Walter William and Elizabeth Claire (Mallory) W.; children: Nicole, Michelle. BS, U. Ariz., 1972, JD, 1975. Bar: Ariz. 1975, U.S. Dist. Ct. Ariz. 1976, U.S. Ct. Appeals (9th cir.) 1980, U.S. Ct. Appeals (Fed. cir.) 1985, U.S. Supreme Ct. 1980. Assoc. Killian, Legg & Nicholas, Mesa, Ariz., 1975-79; ptnr. Killian, Nicholas, Fischer, Wirken, Cook & Pew, Mesa, 1980-97, Gust Rosenfeld P.L.C., 1997—. Pres. Vol. Lawyers Project, Phoenix, 1981-83; judge pro tem Ariz. Ct. Appeals, 1985-99, Maricopa County Superior Ct., 1986—; mem. civil study com. Maricopa County Superior Ct., 1984—; bd. dirs. Cmty. Legal Svcs., Phoenix, 1979-82. Exec. v.p. East Valley Partnership, Mesa, 1984; pres. Tri-City Cath. Social Svc., Mesa, 1983, 84; bd. dirs. East Valley Cultural Alliance, Mesa, 1984. Mem. State Bar Ariz. (bd. govs. 1995—, pres.-elect 2003-), Maricopa County Bar Assn. (bd. dirs. 1983-91, pres. 1989-90), East Valley Bar Assn. (pres. 1979-80), Mesa C. of C. (dir. 1980-83), Am. Arbitration Assn. (arbitrator), Rotary (bd. dirs. 1980-89, pres. 1987-88). Democrat. Roman Catholic. Appellate, General civil litigation, Franchising. Home: 1708 E Knoll St Mesa AZ 85203-2171 Office: Gust Rosenfeld PLC 201 E Washington Ste 800 Phoenix AZ 85004-2327 E-mail: cwirken@gustlaw.com.

WIRKEN, JAMES CHARLES, lawyer; b. Lansing, Mich., July 3, 1944; s. Frank and Mary (Brosnahan) W.; m. Mary Morse, June 12, 1971; children: Christopher, Erika, Kurt, Gretchen, Jeffrey, Matthew. BA in English, Rockhurst Coll., 1967; JD, St. Louis U., 1970. Bar: Mo. 1970, U.S. Dist. Ct. (we. dist.) Mo. 1970. Asst. prosecuter Jackson County, Kans. City, Mo., 1970-72; assoc. Morris, Larson, King, Stamper & Bold, Kans. City, 1972-75; dir. Spradley, Wirken, Reismeyer & King, Kans. City, 1976-88, Wirken & King, Kans. City, 1988-93; CEO The Wirken Law Group, Kans. City, 1993—. Adj. prof. law U. Mo., Kansas City, 1984-89, 2001—. Author: Managing a Practice and Avoiding Malpractice, 1983; co-author Missouri Civil Procedure Form Book, 1984-; mem. editl. bd. Mo. Law Weekly, 1989-, Lender Liability News, 1990-, Emerging Trends and Theories of Lender Liability, 1991, Wirken Tips: Law Office Marketing Management and Economics, The Daily Record, 2003-; host. Wirken on the Law, KMBZ Radio, 1998-. Mem. ABA (exec. coun.), Nat. Conf. Bar Pres. (coun. 1992-96), Nat. Caucus of Met. Bar Leaders (exec. coun., pres. 1988-94), Am. Trial Lawyers Assn., L.P. Gas Group (founder, chair 1986-90, founder, chair lender liability group 1987-96), Mo. Bar Assn. (bd. govs. 1977-78, chmn. econs. and methods practice com. 1982-84, quality and methods of practice com. 1989-91, vice chmn. young lawyers sect. 1976-78), Mo. Assn. Trial Attys. (bd. govs. 1983-85), Kansas City Met. Bar Assn. (pres. young lawyers sect. 1975, chair legal assistance com. 1977-78, chair tort law com. 1982, pres. 1990). Federal civil litigation, State civil litigation, Personal injury (including property damage). Home: 47 W 53rd Kansas City MO 64112 Office: The Wirken Law Group PC 2600 Grand Blvd Ste 440 Kansas City MO 64108-4628

WIRTZ, GREGG LEE, lawyer; b. Pitts., Jan. 30, 1953; s. James Henry and Betty Lee (Pelissier) W.; m. Martha McMahon, Oct. 29, 1977. BA in Econs., Denison U., 1974; JD, Stetson U., 1977. Bar: Fla. 1977, U.S. Dist. Ct. (mid. dist.) Fla. 1977; cert. cir. civil mediator, civil trial specialist. Asst. staff judge adv. USAF, Shaw AFB, SC, 1978-80, area def. counsel, 1980-81, staff judge adv., 1981-82; ptnr. Boyd, Jenerette, Staas, Joos, Williams, Felton & Wirtz, Jacksonville, Fla., 1982—2002, Gregg L. Wintz, P.A., Jacksonville, 2002—. Speaker seminar on civil trial practice Fla. CLE, med. malpractice U. Hosp. Served to capt. (judge adv.) USAF, 1977-82. Mem. Fla. Bar Assn., Jacksonville Bar Assn., Am. Bd. Trial Advocates, Fla. Trial Lawyers Assn., Jacksonville Trial Lawyers Assn. (mediation rules and strategies com.), Omicron Delta Kappa, Omicron Delta Epsilon. Republican. Methodist. Avocation: sports. State civil litigation, Personal injury (including property damage), Professional liability. Office: 231 E Adams St Jacksonville FL 32202-3305

WIRTZ, WILLIAM WILLARD, lawyer; b. DeKalb, Ill., Mar. 14, 1912; s. William Wilbur and Alfa Belle (White) W.; m. Mary Jane Quisenberry, Sept. 8, 1936; children— Richard, Philip. Ed., No. Ill. State Teachers Coll., DeKalb, Ill., 1928-30, U. Calif. at Berkeley, 1930-31; AB, Beloit Coll., 1933; LL.B., Harvard, 1937. Instr. Kewanee (Ill.) High Sch., 1933-34; asst. prof. U. Iowa Sch. Law, 1937-39, Northwestern U. Sch. Law, 1939-42; asst. gen. counsel Bd. Econ. Warfare, 1942-43; with War Labor Bd., 1943-45, gen. counsel and pub. mem., 1945; chmn. Nat. Wage Stblzn. Bd., 1946; prof. law Northwestern U., 1946-54; engaged law practice, 1955-61; sec. of labor Dept. Labor, 1962-69. Prof. law U. San Diego, 0986-98. Mem. Ill. Liquor Control Commn., 1949-53. Mem. Am., D.C., Ill. bar assns., Phi Beta Kappa, Beta Theta Pi, Delta Sigma Rho.

WISBAUM, WAYNE DAVID, lawyer; b. Niagara Falls, N.Y., May 29, 1935; s. Franklin C. and Elizabeth (Boff) W.; m. Janet Katz, July 3, 1960; children— Karen, Wendy, Deborah. BA, Cornell U., 1956; LL.B., Harvard U., 1959. Bar: N.Y. 1960. Assoc. Kavinoky & Cook, Buffalo, 1960-66, sr. ptnr., 1966—. Mem. adv. com. Ticor Title Co.; pres., chmn. bd. dirs. Kleinhans Music Hall Mgmt. Inc., 1990-2000, life emeritus, 2003-. Pres. Buffalo Coun. on World Affairs, 1968-70; mem. Young Leadership Cabinet Nat. United Jewish Appeal, 1967-73; mem. com. on leadership devel. Nat. Coun. Jewish Fedn. and Welfare Funds, 1967— ; mem. Mayor's Com. on Youth Opportunity; bd. dirs. Anti-Defamation League; mem. Coun. Internat. Studies, SUNY, Buffalo; chmn. Buffalo chpt. Am. Jewish Com.; pres., chmn. bd. dirs. Buffalo Found. Jewish Philanthropies, 2001--; bd. govs. United Jewish Fedn., Buffalo; chmn. bd. dirs. Buffalo Philharm. Orch. Soc.; bd. dirs., mem. exec. com. Burchfield Art Ctr.; bd. dirs., pres. Jewish Family Service of Erie County; vice chmn., bd. dirs. Artpark, Irish Classical Theatre; trustee Buffalo and Erie County Park Libr. Served to capt. U.S. Army, 1964. Recipient United Jewish Fedn. Buffalo Leadership award, 1967, Community Relations award Am. Jewish Com., 1985, Abram Pugash award Jewish Family Service, 1985, Cmty. Leadership award Israel Bond, 2001; named Harvard Alumnus of Yr., 1990. Mem. ABA, N.Y. State Bar Assn. (chmn. com. lawyers title guaranty funds, Root/Stimson award 2003), Erie County Bar Assn., Am. Law Inst., Harvard Law Sch. Assn. Western N.Y. (sec.), Zool. Soc. Buffalo (dir., mem. exec. com.), Harvard Club (pres. Buffalo chpt., mem. N.Y.C. chpt.), Buffalo Club, Cornell Club (N.Y.C. chpt.), Zeta Beta Tau. Home: 180 Greenaway Rd Buffalo NY 14226-4166 Office: Kavinoky & Cook 120 Delaware Ave Rm 600 Buffalo NY 14202-2793

WISE, AARON NOAH, lawyer; b. Hartford, Conn., Feb. 14, 1940; s. Joseph J. and Ethel (Sklar) W.; m. Genevieve Ehrlich, Dec. 17. 1966; children: Haywood Martin, Paul Russell, Renee Alicia. AB, Boston U., 1962; JD, Boston Coll., 1965; LLM in Comparative/Internat. Law, NYU, 1971; certificat de Doctorat, d' Université en Droit, U. Paris Law Sch., 1970. Bar: N.Y., U.S. Dist. Ct. (so. dist.) N.Y. Internat. atty. Schering-Plough, Kenilworth, N.J., 1969-74; ptnr. Conboy Hewitt O'Brien & Boardman, N.Y.C., 1974-80, Wise Lerman & Katz P.C. (formerly Rosenbaum Wise Lerman & Katz), N.Y.C., 1981-95, Klepner & Cayea, N.Y.C., 1995-98, Brand, Cayea & Brand, LLC, 1998-2000, Siller Wilk LLP, N.Y.C., 2000—02, Gallet Dreyer & Berkey, LLP, N.Y.C., 2002—. Lectr. bus. and legal groups U.S., Europe, Latin Am. Author: International Sports Law and Business (Kluwer Law Internat., 1997, 3 vols.), Foreign Businessman's Guide to U.S. Law-Practice-Taxation; contbr. articles to pubs. in U.S. and Europe. Mem. ABA, N.Y. State Bar Assn. Avocations: multi-lingual including french, spanish, portuguese, italian, russian, japanese and german. Commercial, contracts (including sales of goods; commercial financing), Private international, Sports. Home: 38 Cummings Cir West Orange NJ 07052-2264 Office: Gallet Dreyer & Berkey LLP 845 Third Ave New York NY 10022-6601 E-mail: anw@gdblaw.com.

WISE, GEORGE EDWARD, lawyer; b. Chgo., Feb. 26, 1924; s. George E. and Helen L. (Gray) W.; m. Patricia E. Finn, Aug. 3, 1945; children: Erich, Peter, Abbe, Raoul, John. JD, U. Chgo. Bar: Calif. 1949, U.S. Dist. Ct. (no. dist.) Calif. 1948, U.S. Ct. Appeals (9th cir.) 1948, U.S. Dist. Ct. (cen. dist.) 1950, U.S. Supreme CT. 1955. Law clk. Calif. Supreme Ct., 1948-49; sr. ptnr. Wise, Wiezorek, Timmons & Wise, Long Beach, 1949—; of counsel Wise Pearce Yocis & Smith, Long Beach. With USNR, 1943-45. Fellow Am. Coll. Trial Lawyers; mem. ABA, Los Angeles County Bar Assn., Long Beach Bar Assn. (pres. 1970, Atty. of Yr. 1990), Calif. State Bar. General civil litigation, Corporate, general, Insurance. Home: 5401 E El Cedral St Long Beach CA 90815-4112 Office: Wise Pearce Yocis & Smith 249 E Ocean Blvd Ste 440 Long Beach CA 90802-4806

WISE, JOHN AUGUSTUS, lawyer, director; b. Detroit, Mar. 30, 1938; s. John Augustus and Mary Blanche (Parent) W.; m. Helga M. Bessin, Nov. 27, 1965; children: Monique Elizabeth, John Eric. Student, U. Vienna, 1957—58; AB honors cum laude, Coll. Holy Cross, 1959; JD, U. Mich., 1962; postgrad., U. Munich Law Faculty, 1962—63. Bar: Mich. 1963, D.C. 1966. Assoc. Dykema, Gossett, Detroit, 1962-64; asst. to pres. Internat. Econ. Policy Assn., Washington, 1964-66; assoc. Parsons, Tennent, Hammond, Hardig & Ziegelman, Detroit, 1967-70; pres. Wise & Marsac P.C., Detroit, 1970-2001; sr. ptnr. Williams, Mullen, Clark & Dobbins, PLLC. Dir. Peltzer & Ehlers Am. Corp., 1975-80, Colombian Am. Friends Inc., 1974-89. Bd. dirs. Hyde Park Coop., 1974-77; trustee Friends Sch., Detroit, 1977-81, Brighton Health Svcs. Corp., 1991-94, Providence Hosp., 2001—; chmn. bd. dirs. Brighton Hosp., 1995—; mem. Detroit Com. on Fgn. Rels. Ford Found. grantee U. Munich, 1962-63. Mem. ABA, Mich. Bar Assn., Detroit Bar Assn., Internat. Bar Assn., Detroit Athletic Club, Detroit Econ. Club. Roman Catholic. Corporate, general, Private international, Corporate taxation. Home: 1221 Yorkshire Rd Grosse Pointe Park MI 48230-1105 Office: Buhl Bldg 11th Fl 535 Griswold St Detroit MI 48226-3604 E-mail: jwise@williamsmullen.com.

WISE, ROBERT POWELL, lawyer; b. Jackson, Miss., Nov. 13, 1951; s. Sherwood Willing and Elizabeth (Powell) W. AB, Colgate U., 1973; MA, U. Va., 1975; JD, Washington & Lee U., 1979. Bar: Miss. 1979, U.S. Dist. Ct. Miss. 1979, U.S. Ct. Appeals (5th cir.) 1988. Ptnr. Wise, Carter, Child & Caraway, Jackson, 1979—. Lic. lay reader, chalice bearer St. Andrews Episc. Cathedral, Jackson, 1984—; pres. Caledonian Soc. Miss., Jackson, 1987, bd. dirs., 1985-90; bd. dirs. Belhaven Improvement Assn., 1991—, pres., 1994-97, v.p., 1999—, English Speaking Union of Miss., Jackson, 1985-92, Nat. Kidney Found. Miss., 1987—, v.p., 1988-92, pres. 1993-94; pres. Belhaven Security Assn., 1992-93. Mem. ABA (forums on constrn. and comm. law), Fed. Comm. Bar Assn., Miss. Bar Assn. Administrative and regulatory, Commercial, consumer (including collections, credit), Construction. Home: 1336 Olive St Jackson MS 39202-1809 Office: 600 Heritage Bldg PO Box 651 Jackson MS 39205-0651 E-mail: rpw@wisecarter.com.

WISE, RONNA F. lawyer; BA in Polit. Sci. cum laude, U. Mass., 1972; MSW, U. Conn., 1975; JD, Franklin Pierce Law Ctr., 1980. Mem. staff United Way of Southeastern Conn., Gales Ferry, 1975—77; assoc. McSwiney, Semple, Bowers & Wise, P.C., Concord, NH, 1980—84, ptnr., 1984—. Mem. NH Commn. on Status of Women, 2002—; bd. dirs. Havenwood-Heritage Heights, 2001—, Planned Parenthood of No. New Eng., 1996—2003, sec., 1998—; bd. dirs. Child and Family Svcs. NH, 1990—97, v.p., 1994—97; vol. mediator NH Superior Ct. Sys., 1994—; bd. dirs. Concord League NH Craftsmen, 1984—86, Friends Program, 1983—85; interfaith caregiver, 1998—2003. Mem.: ABA, Daniel Webster-Batchelder Am. Inns of Ct., Merrimack County Bar Assn., NH Bar Assn. Avocations: running, golf, reading. Mailing: 84 Woodwells Garrison Rd Contoocook NH 03229

WISE, STEVEN LANIER, lawyer, clergyman; b. Eufaula, Ala., Oct. 3, 1956; s. Edward Lanier and Cathryn (Ryals) W.; m. Eloise Massey, July 30, 1983. BA in English, U. Ala., 1978, MA in Counselling, 1979, JD, 1982; MDiv, New Orleans Bapt. Theol. Sem., 1993. Bar: Ala. 1982, U.S. Dist. Ct. (no. dist.) Ala. 1982. Staff atty. Ala. Ct. Civil Appeals, Montgomery, 1982-83; ptnr. Hardin & Wise, Tuscaloosa, Ala., 1983-88; pvt. practice Tuscaloosa, 1988-94; assoc. pastor 1st Bapt. Ch., Honea Path, S.C., 1994-98; assoc. N.Am. Mission Bd. SBC, 1998-2001; min. to singles 1st Bapt. Ch., Spartanburg, S.C., 2001—. Sec., bd. editors The Ala. Lawyer, Montgomery, 1983-88. Sponsor Ctrl. H.S. Key Club, Tuscaloosa, 1984-94, Belton-Honea Path H.S. Jr. Civitan Club, 1994-99; judge citizen lock-up March of Dimes, Tuscaloosa, 1986; mem. S.C. Youth and Recreation Min.'s Assn., 1995— (editor newsletter). Mem. ABA, Farrah Law Soc., Civitans, Kappa Delta Pi, Pi Tau Chi. Avocations: woodworking, golf, softball, music. Home: 400 Grayson Dr Moore SC 29369 Office: 250 E Main St Spartanburg SC 29306-5128 E-mail: notamagi@charter.net.

WISE, WILLIAM JERRARD, lawyer; b. Chgo., May 27, 1934; s. Gerald Paul and Harriet Muriel (Rosenblum) W.; m. Peggy Spero, Sept. 3, 1959; children: Deborah, Stephen, Betsy, Lynne. BBA, U. Mich., 1955, MBA, JD with distinction, U. Mich., 1958. Bar: Ill. 1959. Spl. atty. Office Regional Counsel, IRS, Milw., 1959-63; with firm McDermott, Will & Emery, Chgo., 1963-70, Coles & Wise, Ltd., Chgo., 1971-81, Wise & Stracks, Ltd., Chgo., 1982-2000, Querrey & Harrow Ltd., Chgo., 2000—. Lectr., contbr. Ill. Inst. Continuing Legal Edn.; arbitrator Cir. Ct. Cook County Ill., 1990—. Mem. Village of Winnetka (Ill.) Caucus, 1974-75; Bd. dirs. Blind Service Assn., Chgo., 1964-74; dir., treas. Suzuki Orff Sch. for Young Musicians, Chgo., 1981-91. Served with AUS, 1958-59. Mem. Chgo. Bar Assn. Pension, profit-sharing, and employee benefits, Corporate taxation, Personal income taxation. Home: 1401 Tower Rd Winnetka IL 60093-1628 Office: Querrey & Harrow Ltd 175 W Jackson Blvd Ste 1600 Chicago IL 60604-2827 E-mail: dididoe@yahoo.com.

WISEHEART, MALCOLM BOYD, JR., lawyer; b. Miami, Fla., Sept. 18, 1942; s. Malcolm B. and Dorothy E. (Allen) Wiseheart; m. Michele I. Romanens, Dec. 11, 1976. BA, Yale U., 1965; MA in English Jurisprudence, Cambridge U., 1973; JD with honors, U. Fla., 1970. Bar: Fla. 1970, Eng. 1970, Wales 1970, Jamaica 1970, Trinidad and Tobago 1971, DC 1980. Assoc. Helliwell, Melrose & DeWolf, Miami, 1970-72; pvt. practice Miami, 1973—86, 1987—; sr. ptnr. Wiseheart & Joyce, P.A., Miami, 1986—87. Sec., gen. counsel Wiseheart Found., pres., 1985—2003; spl. master Dade County Property Appraisal Adjustment Bd., 1977—90; pres. Fla. Law Inst., 1980—2003; dir. Yale Alumni Schs. Com. S. Fla., 2001—03; bd. dirs. Sta. WLRN Pub. Radio, 1982, Coun. Internat. Visitors. Trustee Ransom Everglades Sch., 1995—97; trustee, mem. exec. com. Players State Theater, 1982—84. Named Most Outstanding, U. Fla. Law Rev. Alumnus, 1981. Mem.: Gray's Inn of Ct., London (barrister), Order of Coif, Dade County Bar Assn. (dir. 1971—74, treas. 1974—75, sec. 1975—77, dir. 1986—89), Fla. Bar (chmn. grievance com. 1978—81), United Oxford and Cambridge Univs. Club (London), Yale Club (Miami pres. 1976—77). State civil litigation, Landlord-tenant, Property, real (including real estate development, water). Office: Wiseheart Bldg 2840 SW 3rd Ave Miami FL 33129-2317 E-mail: mbwjr@bellsouth.net.

WISEMAN, THOMAS ANDERTON, JR., federal judge; b. Tullahoma, Tenn., Nov. 3, 1930; s. Thomas Anderton and Vera Seleta (Poe) W.; m. Emily Barbara Matlack, Mar. 30, 1957; children: Thomas Anderton III, Mary Alice, Sarah Emily. BA, Vanderbilt U., 1952, LL.B., 1954; LLM, U. Va., 1990. Bar: Tenn. Pvt. practice, Tullahoma, 1956-63; ptnr. Haynes, Wiseman & Hull, Tullahoma and Winchester, Tenn., 1963-71; treas. State of Tenn., 1971-74; ptnr. Chambers & Wiseman, 1974-78; judge U.S. Dist. Ct. (mid. dist.) Tenn., Nashville, 1978—, chief judge, 1984-91, sr. judge, 1995—; 6th cir. rep. Jud. Conf. of the U.S., 1996—2001, chair dist. judges conf., 1998-99. Mem. Tenn. Ho. of Reps., 1964-68; adj. prof. law Vanderbilt U. Sch. Law; cons. to judiciary of Brcko, Bosnia, 2002. Asso. editor: Vanderbilt Law Rev, 1953-54. Democratic candidate for gov., Tenn., 1974; Chmn. Tenn. Heart Fund, 1973, Middle Tenn. Heart Fund, 1972. Served with U.S. Army, 1954-56. Fellow Tenn. Bar Found.; mem. Fed. Judges Assn. (bd. dirs. 1982-87, v.p. 1982-91, 87-91), Masons (33 deg.), Shriners, Amateur Chefs Soc. Presbyterian. Office: US Dist Ct 777 US Courthouse 801 Broadway Nashville TN 37203-3816

WISHEK, MICHAEL BRADLEY, lawyer; b. Pasadena, Calif., June 25, 1959; s. Homer Cedric and Donna Jean (Arnold) W.; m. Shari Patrice Rubin, June 7, 1981 (div. Feb. 1986); m. Dorothea Jean Palo, Feb. 12, 1988; children: Kirstin Alyce, Lauren Ashley. BS in Polit. Sci and Philosophy, Claremont Men's Coll., 1981; JD, U. Calif., Davis, 1985. Bar: Calif. 1986, U.S. Dist. Ct. (ea. dist.) Calif. 1986. Assoc. Michael S. Sands, Inc., Sacramento, 1986-91; ptnr. Rothschild & Wishek, Sacramento, 1991-96, Rothschild, Wishek & Sands, Sacramento, 1996—. Mem. Milton L. Schwartz Am. Inn of Ct., 2000—; adj. instr. trial practice U. Calif., Davis, Sch. Law, Davis. Mem. ABA, Calif. Bar Assn., Sacramento County Bar Assn. (co-chmn. criminal law sect. 1988-90), Calif. Attys. for Criminal Justice. Criminal. Office: 901 F St Ste 200 Sacramento CA 95814-0733

WISKING, STEPHEN, solicitor; b. Sale, Eng., Sept. 9, 1965; s. Derrick Lewis and Carmel Elizabeth Wisking; m. Louise Jane Turner, Mar. 11, 1994; 1 child, Allegra. LLB with honors, B in Econs., U. Adelaide,

Australia, 1987; LLM, U. Cambridge, Eng., 1991. Cert.: High Ct. Australia and South Australia (barrister and solicitor) 1988, Eng. and Wales (solicitor) 1998, Eng. and Wales (solicitor adv.) 1999. Assoc. Finlaysons, Adelaide, 1989—95, ptnr., 1995—97; asst. Herbert Smith, London, 1997—2000, ptnr., 2000—. Mem.: City London Law Soc., The Law Soc. Avocations: reading, travel. Antitrust. Home: 29 Tournay Rd London SW6 7UG England Office: Herbert Smith Primrose St London EC2A 2HS England

WISSBAUM, DONNA CACIC, lawyer; b. Portage, Wis., Dec. 3, 1956; d. Donald Richard and Rita Margaret (Polcyn) Cacic; m. David Michael Wissbaum, Dec. 29, 1984; children: Nicholas David, Heather Noelle. BA in Am. Instns., U. Wis., 1979; JD, Gonzaga U., 1982. Bar: Wis. 1982, U.S. Dist. Ct. (ea. and we. dists.) Wis. 1983. Assoc. Bennett & Bennett Law Offices, Montello, Wis., 1983-85, Gregory R. Wright Law Offices, Montello, 1985-89; prin. Donna Cacic Wissbaum, Atty. at Law, Montello, 1989—. Lt. col. USAR. Mem. ABA, Wis. Bar Assn., Tri-County Bar Assn. (sec.-treas. 1986-88, v.p. 1988-90, pres. 1990-92), Marquette County Crimestoppers, Inc. (vice chmn. 1994-96), Croatian Fraternal Union, Pardeeville Youth Wrestling Club (pres. 2001-2002). Roman Catholic. General practice. Home: W5436 County Road P Pardeeville WI 53954-9434 Office: 5 E Park St Montello WI 53949-9366

WITCOFF, SHELDON WILLIAM, lawyer; b. Washington, July 10, 1925; s. Joseph and Zina (Ceppos) W.; m. Margot Gail Hoffner, Sept. 6, 1953; children: Lauren Jill, David Lawrence, Lisa Ann, Julie Beth. BS in Elec. Engring, U. Md., 1949; JD, George Washington U., 1953. Bar: D.C. 1953, N.Y. 1955, Ill. 1956. Patent examiner Patent Office, Dept. Commerce, 1949-53; patent lawyer Bell Telephone Labs., Murray Hill, N.J., 1953-55; ptnr. Bair, Freeman & Molinare, Chgo., 1955-69, Allegretti, Newitt, Witcoff & McAndrews, Chgo., 1970-88, Allegretti & Witcoff, LTD, Chgo., 1988-95, Banner & Witcoff Ltd., Chgo., 1995—. V.p. Art Splty. Co., Chgo., 1967-84; v.p. Caspian Fur Trading Co., N.Y.C.; dir. Child Abuse Unit for Studies, Edn. and Svcs., Chgo. Fire and police commr., Skokie, Ill., 1960-63. Served with USNR, 1943-46. Mem. Am. Bar Assn., Intellectual Property Assn. of Chgo., Order of Coif, Tau Epsilon Phi, Phi Delta Phi., B'nai B'rith. Antitrust, Federal civil litigation, Patent. Home: 2180 Kipling Ln Highland Park IL 60035- Office: 10 S Wacker Dr Chicago IL 60606-7407 E-mail: witcoff@bannerwitcoff.com.

WITHERS, W. WAYNE, lawyer; b. Enid, Okla., Nov. 4, 1940; s. Walter O. and Ruby (Mackey) W.; m. Patricia Ann Peppers, Dec. 12, 1974; children: Jennifer Lynn, Whitney Lee. BA, U. Okla., 1962; JD, Northwestern U., 1965. Bar: Okla. 1965, Mo. 1970, U.S. Ct. Appeals (8th cir.), 1972, U.S. Supreme Ct. 1972, U.S. Ct. Appeals (fed. cir.) 1984, U.S. Ct. Appeals (D.C. cir.) 1985, U.S. Ct. Claims, 1984. Staff atty. FTC, Washington, 1965-68; co. atty. Monsanto Co., St. Louis, 1968-78, asst. gen. counsel, 1978—82; gen. counsel Monsanto Agrl. Co., St. Louis, 1978—89, v.p., gen. counsel; sr. v.p., sec., gen. counsel Emerson Electric Co., St. Louis, 1989—. V.p. Internat. Food Biotech. Coun., Washington, 1989-90; bd. dirs. Internat. Life Scis. Inst., Washington, 1988-89. Contbr. articles to profl. jours. Chmn. bd. Mo. Hist. Soc., 2002—; trustee MHS, 1995—; bd. dirs. World Agrl. Forum, 1999—. Mem. ABA (sect. bus. laaw, com. gen. counsel, antitrust, litigation), Am. Law Inst., Bar Assn. Met. St. Louis, Am. Corp. Counsel Assn., Am. Soc. Corp. Secs., Supreme Ct. Historic Soc., Warren E. Burger Soc., Nat. Ctr. for State Cts., Washington Legal Found., Indsl. Biotech. Assn. (chmn. law com.), Environ. Law Inst. (assoc.), Nat. Agrl. Chem. Assn. (chmn. law com. 1983-85), The Conf. Bd. Coun. for Gen. Counsel (vice chmn. 1992-98), MAPI Law Coun. Corporate, general, Product liability, Securities. Office: Emerson Electric Co 8100 W Florissant Ave Saint Louis MO 63136-1494

WITHERWAX, CHARLES HALSEY, lawyer, arbitrator, mediator; b. Schroon Lake, N.Y., July 24, 1934; s. Halsey Jerome and Elizabeth Daisy (Bingham) Witherwax; m. Marianne Jehander, June 24, 1980. BS in Marine Transp., N.Y. State Maritime Coll., 1956; LLB, Union U., 1959. Bar: N.Y. 1962, U.S. Dist. Ct. (so. dist.) N.Y. 1962, U.S. Supreme Ct. 1968, Hawaii 1971, U.S. Dist. Ct. Hawaii 1971, U.S. Ct. Appeals (9th cir.) 1984, U.S. Tax Ct. 1984, Nev. 1991, DC 1993, U.S. Ct. Appeals (2d cir.) 1995. Assoc. prof. N.Y. State Maritime Coll., Fort Schuyler, NY, 1963-64; asst. v.p., bond claims atty. Chubb Ins. Group, N.Y.C., 1961-70; v.p., gen. counsel Hawaiian Ins. Group, Honolulu, 1970-74; ptnr. Davis, Witherwax, Playdon & Gerson, Honolulu, 1974-78; prin. atty. Witherwax, Pottenger & Nishioka, Honolulu, 1978-91; of counsel D'Amato & Lynch, N.Y.C., 1992—. Author: (manual) Hawaii Construction Law, Mechanics Liens and Bond Claims, 1985; co-author, 1987. Bronx County chmn. N.Y. State Conservatives, 1962—67, state sec., 1967—70. Lt. comdr. USNR, 1959—79. Mem.: ABA (vice chair fidelity and surety com. 1978—83), Internat. Assn. Def. Counsel. Roman Catholic. Avocations: sailing, travel, golf. General civil litigation, Construction, Insurance. Office: D'Amato and Lynch 70 Pine St 37th Fl New York NY 10270-0002 E-mail: www.simpnas2@aol.com.

WITKIN, ERIC DOUGLAS, lawyer; b. Trenton, N.J., May 14, 1948; s. Nathan and Norma Shirley (Stein) W.; m. Regina Ann Bilotta, June 8, 1980; children: Daniel Robert, Sarah Ann. AB magna cum laude, Columbia U., 1969; JD, Harvard U., 1972. Bar: N.Y. 1973, D.C. 1989, U.S. Dist. Ct. (so. and ea. dists.) N.Y. 1974, U.S. Dist. Ct. (we. dist.) N.Y. 2001, U.S. Ct. Appeals (2d and D.C. cirs.) 1974, U.S. Supreme Ct. 1977, U.S. Dist. Ct. D.C. 1989. Assoc. Poletti, Freidin, Prashker & Gartner, N.Y.C., 1972-80, ptnr., 1980-85; sr. atty. labor Kaye, Scholer, Fierman, Hays & Handler, N.Y.C., 1985-88; of counsel Akin, Gump, Strauss, Hauer & Feld, Washington, 1988-90; counsel Benetar, Bernstein, Schair & Stein, N.Y.C., 1990-99; ptnr. Roberts & Finger, LLP, N.Y.C., 1999-2001, Greble & Finger, LLP, N.Y.C., 2001; counsel Brown, Raysman, Millstein, Felder, & Steiner LLP, N.Y.C., 2001—. Treas., founder Property Owners Against Unfair Taxation, N.Y.C., 1983-90; trustee Congregation Emanu-El of Westchester, 1996—, pres., 2002--. Lawrence Chamberlain scholar Columbia U., N.Y.C., 1968; recipient Alumni medal Alumni Fedn. Columbia U., 1982. Mem. ABA (labor and employment law sect.), N.Y. State Bar Assn. (labor and employment law sect., com. on equal employment opportunity law), Assn. of Bar of City of N.Y. (spl. com. on sex and law 1975-82, com. on labor and employment law 1982-85, 92-94), Westchester County Bar Assn., Columbia Coll. Alumni Assn. (pres. 1988-90, bd. dirs. 1974—, Robert Lincoln Carey prize, Alumni prize 1969, Lions award 1990), Alumni Fedn. Columbia U. (alumni trustee nominating com. 1990-97, pres. 1997-99), Am. Soc. Pers. Adminstrn. (contbr. monthly newsletter 1986-88), Soc. Human Resource Mgmt., Soc. Columbia Grads. (bd. dirs. 1994-97), Human Resources Assn. N.Y., Phi Beta Kappa. Clubs: Harvard (N.Y.C.). Avocations: piano, sailing. Federal civil litigation, State civil litigation, Labor (including EEOC, Fair Labor Standards Act, labor-management relations, NLRB, OSHA). Home: 103 Wendover Rd Rye NY 10580-1939 Office: Brown Raysman Millstein Felder & Steiner 900 3rd Ave Fl 23 New York NY 10022 E-mail: ewitkin@brownraysman.com., ericwitkin@aol.com.

WITMAN, LEONARD JOEL, lawyer; b. N.Y.C., Nov. 7, 1950; s. Seymour and Ruth W.; m. Mona Soled, Aug. 25, 1950; children: Rachel, Leah. BA, Rutgers Coll., 1972; JD, N.Y. Law Sch., 1975. Bar: N.J. 1975, U.S. Dist. Ct. N.J. 1975, U.S. Ct. Appeals (2d cir.) 1975, U.S. Dist. Ct. (so. and ea. dists.) N.Y., 1976, U.S. Tax Ct. 1976. Tax law specialist IRS, Newark, 1975-78; assoc. Lampf, Lipkind, West Orange, N.J, 1978-81; ptnr. Brach, Eichler, Rosenberg, Silver, Bernstein, Hammer & Gladstone, Roseland, N.J., 1981-89, Witman, Stadmauer & Michaels, P.A., Florham Park, N.J., 1990—. Adj. law prof. Seton Hall U., N.J., Rutgers U. Grad. Sch. Bus., 1996—. Author: Top Heavy Pension Plans, 1985; contbr. articles to profl. jours. Mem. ABA, N.J. Bar Assn., (chmn. employee benefit com. 1984-86, chmn. taxation sect. 1987-88), Essex County Bar Assn., Morris County Bar Assn. Jewish. Pension, profit-sharing, and employee benefits, Taxation, general. Home: 31 Conkling Rd Flanders NJ 07836-9106 Office: Witman Stadtmauer & Michaels 26 Columbia Tpke Florham Park NJ 07932-2213

WITMER, GEORGE ROBERT, JR., lawyer; b. Rochester, N.Y., Mar. 23, 1937; s. George Robert and Marian Pauline (Costello) W.; m. Nancy Rosetta Wenner, Dec. 28, 1968; children: Wendy Lynn, Heidi Dawn, George Robert, III, Frank David. AB, U. Rochester, 1959; LL.B., Harvard U., 1962. Bar: N.Y. 1962, U.S. Dist. Ct. (we. dist.) N.Y. 1963, U.S. Supreme Ct. 1967, U.S. Dist. Ct. (no. dist.) N.Y. 1977, U.S. Ct. Appeals (2d cir.) 1998. Assoc. Nixon, Hargrave, Devans & Doyle, Rochester, 1962-70, ptnr., 1970-99, Nixon Peabody, Rochester, 1999—. Instr. in bus. law U. Rochester, 1965-66; mem. com. to advise and cons. Jud. Conf. State N.Y. on Civil Practice Law and Rules, 1970-77; mem. N.Y. State Jud. Inst. on Professionalism in the Law, 1999—; mem. Adv. Group to N.Y. State and Fed. Jud. Coun., 1999—. Mem. N.Y. State Rep. Com., 1976-93; trustee Eastman Dental Ctr. Rochester, 1977-97, pres. bd. trustees, 1989-90; trustee U. Rochester, 1979—, chmn. exec. com., 1992-2003; trustee Eastman Dental Ctr. Found., 1997—. Fellow N.Y. Bar Found. (dir. 1991-96), ABA Found.; mem. ABA, Monroe County (N.Y.) Bar Assn., N.Y. State Bar Assn. (ho. of dels. 1978—, v.p. 1984-88, sec. 1989-90, pres.-elect 1993-94, pres. 1994-95, exec. com. environ. law sect. 1981-96, environ. law sect. Disting. Svc. award), Am. Law Inst., Rochester Rotary Club (dir. local club 1977-79, pres. local club 2001-02), Masons (master locla lodge 1971), Phi Beta Kappa. Republican. Lutheran. Environmental. Home: 892 Lake Rd Webster NY 14580-9008 Office: Nixon Peabody LLP PO Box 31051 Clinton Sq Rochester NY 14604-1729 E-mail: grwitmer@nixonpeabody.com.

WITMEYER, JOHN JACOB, III, lawyer; b. New Orleans, Dec. 18, 1946; s. John J. and Thais Audrey (Dolese) W. BS, Tulane U., 1968; JD with distinction, Duke U., 1971. Bar: N.Y. Assoc. Mudge Rose Guthrie & Alexander, N.Y.C., 1971-76; ptnr. Ford Marrin Esposito & Wittmeyer (now Ford, Marrin, Esposito, Witmeyer & Gleser LLP), N.Y.C., 1976—. Bd. trustees Gregorian U. Found., 1999—; adv. coun. Paul Tulane Coll., Tulane U., 1998—; bd. dirs. Tulane Assocs., Tulane U., 2001—. Col. U.S. Army. Mem.: Order of the Holy Sepulchre (knight). General civil litigation, Corporate, general. Office: Ford Marrin Esposito Witmeyer & Gleser LLP Wall St Plz New York NY 10005-1875

WITORT, JANET LEE, lawyer; b. Cedar Rapids, Iowa, Mar. 10, 1950; d. Charles Francis Svoboda and Phyllis Harriet (Wilber) Miller; m. Stephen Francis Witort, Oct. 27, 1979. Student, U. Colo., 1968-69, U. Iowa, 1971; BA, U. No. Colo., 1972; JD, Loyola U., 1979. Bar: Ill. 1979, U.S. Dist. Ct. (no. dist.) Ill. 1979, U.S. Dist. Ct. (no. dist.) Ill. 1979, U.S. Supreme Ct. 1987. Paralegal Fed. Nat. Mortgage Assn., Chgo., 1973-75, Sidley & Austin, Chgo., 1975-76; assoc. Frankel, McKay & Orlikoff, Chgo., 1979-81; atty. Mut. Trust Life Ins. Co., Oak Brook, Ill., 1981-86; assoc. counsel, asst. sec. N.Am. Co. for Life and Health Ins., Chgo., 1986-88; sr. atty. AMA, Chgo., 1988-89; gen. coun., sec. AMA Ins., Chgo., 1989-91, v.p. gen. counsel, sec., 1991-93; asst. gen. counsel Prudential Ins. and Fin. Svcs., Chgo., 1994—98; sr. counsel Allianz Life Ins. Co. of N.Am., 1998—99, v.p., dep. gen. counsel, 1999—. Author: (with others) The Legal Assistant-A Self Statement, 1974, (with others) Requirements and Limitations Imposed by Corporate Law, 1989, updated, 1992. Vol. Rep. Campaign, Chgo., 1974-76, 90-93, Children's Hosp. Guild, North Oaks, Minn., 1993—, v.p. 1994-95, pres. 1996; vol. Sci. Mus. Minn., St. Paul, 1994-2001; trustee Hindsdale Ill. Pub. Libr., 1987-93, v.p., 1991-93; bd. dirs. Suburban Libr. Sys., Burr Ridge, Ill., 1988-91, sec. 1990-91; bd. dirs. Children's Hosp. Assn., St. Paul, 1995-96; active Jr. League, St. Paul, 1997-2002, bd. dirs., 2000-01, sustainer, 2002—; active North Oaks (Minn.) Planning Commn., 2000—; del. Mo. State Rep. Conv., 2000. Mem. ABA, Am. Soc. Med. Assn. Coun., Ill. Bar Assn., Chgo. Assn. Paralegal Assts. (sec. 1973-74), Chgo. Bar Assn. (chair life & health ins. subcom. 1992-93), Womans Bar Assn. of Ill. (mem. ins. com. 1987-93), Ill. Paralegal Assn. (v.p. 1975-76), Nat. Fed. Paralegal Assns. (midwest reg. dir. 1975-76), Am. Corp. Counsel Assn. (membership com. 1988-90), Phi Alpha Delta, Student Bar Assn. (class rep. 1976-77). Republican. Avocations: golf, travel, skiing. Property, real (including real estate development, water), Securities, Insurance. Office: 1750 Hennepin Ave Minneapolis MN 55403-2115

WITTELS, BARNABY CAESAR, lawyer, writer; b. Phila., Mar. 28, 1948; s. David G. and Beatrice Tanya (Graitcr) W.; m. Heidi Jo Linsk, Sept. 8, 1974 (div. Aug. 1997); children: Kate Sophie, William David; m. Mary M. Labaree, Sept. 20, 1998. BA cum laude, Temple U., 1970; MA in Pol. Sci., Boston U., 1972, JD, 1975. Bar: Pa. 1975, U.S. Dist. Ct. (ea. dist.) Pa. 1985, U.S. Ct. Appeals (2d, 3d and 4th cir.) 1986. Asst. defender Defender Assn. of Phila., 1975-80; law clk. to Hon. Stanley Kubacki Ct. Common Pleas Phila. County, 1980-84; ptnr. Wittels, Newman & Bomstein, Phila., 1980-82; assoc. LaCheen & Alva, Phila., 1982-86; ptnr. LaCheen & Assoc., Phila., 1986—. Contbr. column to newspapers. Chair Northwest Victim Svcs., Phila., 1981-84, mem. counsel, 1984-90, mem. bd. dirs., 1983-90, chair, 1997— (outstanding svc. & leadership 1990), founding mem.; com. man 21st Divsn. Dem. Party, Phila., 1985-90, various polit. and jud. campaigns, 1980—; baseball coach Chestnut Hill Fathers Club, 1985-98, commr. 1991-93, 92-98; mem. exec. com. Northwest Interfaith Movement, 1985-86. Mem. NACDL, Pa. Assn. Criminal Def. Lawyers, Phila. Bar Assn. (fee dispute com. 1996—, mem. com. to elect good judges 1987-88, Pa. Bar Assn., Phila. Bar Found. (Apothaker award 1983). Democratic. Jewish. Avocations: writing, baseball, football, reading, woodworking. Appellate, Federal civil litigation, Criminal. Office: LaCheen & Assoc 3100 Lewis Tower Bldg Philadelphia PA 19102 Fax: 215 735-4649. E-mail: barnabyw@aol.com.

WITTENBRINK, JEFFREY SCOTT, lawyer; b. Cairo, Ill., May 24, 1960; s. Howard Samuel and Cherie Ellen (Martin) W.; m. Tamara Inez Parker, Aug. 5, 1989; children: Charlotte Jane, Jeffrey Scott Jr. BA, La. State U., 1984, JD, 1987. Bar: La. 1988, US Dist. Ct. (ea. and mid. dists.) La. 1988, US Dist. Ct. (we. dist.) La. 1989, US Ct. Appeals (5th cir.) 1989, US Supreme Ct. 1996. Law clk. to Judge William H. Brown, 19th Jud. Dist. Ct., Baton Rouge, 1987-88; assoc. Roy, Kiesel, Aaron & Tucker, Baton Rouge, 1988-91, Winston G. DeCuir & Assocs., Baton Rouge, 1991-93; pvt. practice Wittenbrink Law Firm, Baton Rouge, 1993—. Arbitrator Baton Rouge City Ct., 1993—; instr. CPCU's, Baton Rouge, 1991, Office Emergency Planning State of La., 1993; bd. dir. Capital Area Legal Svc., 2000—. Contbr. articles to Around the Bar legal newsletter, 1987—. Coach debate team Cath. HS, Baton Rouge, 1987-91, mock trial team Baton Rouge HS, 1989-93; treas. Ingleside United Meth. Ch., Baton Rouge, 1991-92, trustee, bd. dir., 1991-2001, chair pastor-parish com., 1992-2000, lay leader, 2001; mem., lectr. La. Vol. Lawyers for Arts, Baton Rouge, 1988-89; bd. dir. La. Crafts Coun., Baton Rouge, 1990. Mem. ABA, La. Bar Assn., Baton Rouge Bar Assn. (mem. newsletter com. 1987—, vol. indigent panel 1992, chair CLE 1992—, chmn. membership com. 1993, chair Law Expo com. 1998, chair family law sect. 2002, ex officio bd. dir. 2002, Pres.'s award 1993, Triple Century award 2001), Dean Henry George McMahon Am. Inn of Ct. (barrister, reporter 1993-95), Cortana Kiwanis (bd. dir. 1994-97, pres. 1998-99, Lt. Gov. 2001-2002, Kiwanis Internat., La.-Miss.-W.Tenn. Dist. Divn. 8-B). Avocations: photography, fencing, writing. General civil litigation, Family and matrimonial, Personal injury (including property damage). Office: 533 Europe St Baton Rouge LA 70802-6408 E-mail: jwbrink@aol.com.

WITTIG, DON, judge; b. San Antonio, Sept. 18, 1941; s. Don A. and Miriam (Moon) W.; children: Jeffrey A., Marie C., Sarah Elizabeth. Engring. student, U.S. Naval Acad., Annapolis, Md., 1960-61; BA in Govt., St. Mary's U., 1963, JD, 1965. Bar: Tex. 1965, U.S. Dist. Ct. (so. dist.) Tex. 1965, U.S. Ct. Claims 1965, U.S. Tax Ct. 1965, U.S. Ct. Customs and Patent Appeals 1965, U.S. Ct. Mil. Appeals 1965, U.S. Ct. Appeals (5th cir.) 1965. Ptnr. Lorance, Thompson & Wittig, Houston, 1972-80, Ellis, Wittig & Smith, Houston, 1984-85; pvt. practice Houston, 1985-88; judge 125th Dist. Ct., Houston, 1988—99, 14th Ct. Appeals, 1999—2001. Author: New Local Rules, 1988, A Practical Guide to Ct's. Charge, 1989, Streamlining Trial and Pretrial Practice, 1991. Mem. internat. com. Houston Livestock and Rodeo. Fellow Houston Bar Found.; mem. ABA (task force on fast track ligitation, cert. mediator), Am. Arbitration Assn., Nat. Arbitration Assn., State Bar Tex., Tex. Bar Found., Houston Bar Assn. Avocations: sailing, reading, golf.

WITTIG, RAYMOND SHAFFER, lawyer, technology management advisor; b. Allentown, Pa., Dec. 13, 1944; s. Raymond Battie and Alice (Shaffer) W.; m. Beth Glover, June 21, 1975; children: Meaghan G., Allison G. BA, Pa. State U., 1966, MEd, 1968; JD, Dickinson Sch. Law, 1974. Bar: Pa. 1974, U.S. Ct. Appeals (D.C. cir.) 1978. Rsch. psychologist Intext Corp., Scranton, Pa., 1968; minority counsel Small Bus. Com., U.S. Ho. Reps., Washington, 1975-84; pvt. practice Washington, 1984-92; tech. mgmt. group leader Geo-Ctrs., Inc., Newton Ctr., Mass., 1992—. Capt. U.S. Army, 1969-71. Mem. AAAS, ABA, Licensing Exec. Soc., Nat. Order Barristers, Fed. Lab. Consortium, Am. Intellectual Property Law Assn., Assoc. Univ. Tech. Mgrs. Administrative and regulatory, Government contracts and claims, Legislative. E-mail: wittigsall@aol.com.

WITWER, SAMUEL WEILER, JR., lawyer; b. Chgo., Aug. 5, 1941; s. Samuel Weiler and Ethyl Loraine (Wilkins) W.; m. Susan P. Stewart, Sept. 18, 1971; children: Samuel Stewart, Michael Douglas. AB with honors, Dickinson Coll., 1963; JD, U. Mich., 1966. Bar: Ill. 1967, U.S. Dist. Ct. (no. dist.) Ill. 1967, U.S. Ct. Appeals (7th cir.) 1972, U.S. Supreme Ct. 1973, U.S. Ct. Appeals (6th cir.) 1985, U.S. Dist. Ct. (ea. dist.) Mich., 1987. Assoc. Witwer, Moran, Burlage & Atkinson, Chgo., 1967-74; ptnr. Witwer, Poltrock & Giampietro, 1974-2003, mem. Witwer and Waldron, LLC, 2003-; mem. Fed. Trial Bar Admissions Com. No. Dist. Ill., 1982-97. Governing mem. Chgo. Zool. Soc., 1986-90; trustee United Meth. Homes and Services, Chgo., 1974—, Dickinson Coll., Carlisle, Pa., 1976-97; mem. Cook County Home Rule Commn., Chgo., 1974-75; chmn. Agy. Appeals Com. Chgo., 1975-78; atty. Glenview Park Dist., 1982—; spl. asst. atty. gen. Auditor Gen. Ill., 1984-92. Mem. ABA, Meth. Bar Assn. (pres. 1972-73), Chgo. Bar Assn., Ill. Bar Assn., Law Club of Chgo., Sigma Chi, Phi Delta Phi. Republican. Methodist. Club: Union League. Federal civil litigation, State civil litigation. Home: 1330 Overlook Dr Glenview IL 60025-5166 Office: Waldron LLC 1603 Orrington Ave Ste 2080 Evanston IL 60201 E-mail: witwer@wqglawyers.com.

WIZNIA, CAROLANN KAMENS, lawyer; b. Boston, Apr. 30, 1950; BA, Brandeis U., 1972; JD, Boston Coll., 1975. Bar: Conn. 1976. Pvt. practice, New Haven, 1976—. Mem. ABA, Conn. Bar Assn. Commercial, consumer (including collections, credit), General practice, Probate (including wills, trusts). Office: 850 Howard Ave New Haven CT 06519-1106

WOGLOM, ERIC COOKE, lawyer; b. Mar. 14, 1943; s. Joseph F. and Rita Mary (Cooke) W.; m. Joshan Robin Levitsky, May 11, 1968; children: Peter Douglas, Brian Stewart. BA, Yale U., 1964; LLB, U. Pa., 1967. Bar: N.Y. 1968, U.S. Patent and Trademark Office 1970, U.S. Ct. Appeals (9th cir.) 1972, U.S. Ct. Appeals (2d cir.) 1973, U.S. Dist. Ct. (so. and ea. dist.) N.Y. 1974, U.S. Supreme Ct. 1974, U.S. Ct. Appeals (7th cir.) 1980, U.S. Ct. Appeals (fed. cir.) 1982. With Fish & Neave, N.Y.C., 1967—, sr. ptnr., 1976—. Intellectual property adv. com. US Dist. Ct. Del., 1994—97. With U.S. Army, 1967. Mem.: ABA, N.Y. State Bar Assn., N.Y. Intellectual Property Law Assn. (past chair com. on econ. matters affecting the profession), N.Y. Law Inst., Assn. Bar City of N.Y. (past chair com. on patents), Am. Intellectual Property Law Assn., Shelter Island Yacht Club, Yale Club of N.Y.C. Republican. Roman Catholic. Federal civil litigation, Patent, Trademark and copyright. Home: 430 North St Harrison NY 10528-1118 Office: Fish & Neave Fl 50 1251 Avenue Of The Americas New York NY 10020-1105

WOHL, FRANK HAROLD, lawyer; b. Richmond, Va., June 5, 1942; AB, Dartmouth Coll., 1963; JD, U. of Chgo. Law, 1966. Bar: N.Y. 1967. Asst. U.S. atty. So. Dist. of N.Y., N.Y.C., 1971—79; ptnr. Rosenman & Colin, N.Y.C., 1979—84, Lankler Siffert & Wohl, LLP, N.Y.C., 1984—. Chair N.Y.C. Civilian Complaint Rev. Bd., 1999—2002. Fed. RICO adminstr. Fulton Fish Market, NY, 1988—92; dir. Broodwood Child Care, Bklyn., 1992—99. Lt. comdr. JAGC USNR, 1967—71. Fellow: Am. Coll. of Trial Lawyers (Access to Justice 2000); mem.: Fed. Bar Coun. (trustee 1999—2001), N.Y. Coun. of Def. Lawyers (bd. member 1998—), Fed. Bar Found. (dir. 1996—2002), Bar Assn. of the City of N.Y. Criminal. Office: Lankler Siffert & Wohl LLP 500 Fifth Ave New York NY 10110-3398

WOHLFORTH, ERIC EVANS, lawyer; b. N.Y.C., Apr. 17, 1932; s. Robert Martin and Mildred Campbell (Evans) W.; m. Caroline Penniman, Aug. 3, 1957; children: Eric Evans, Charles Penniman. AB, Princeton U., 1954; LLB, U. Va., 1957. Bar: N.Y. 1958, Alaska, 1967. Assoc. Hawkins, Delafield & Wood, N.Y.C., 1957-66; ptnr. McGrath & Wohlforth, Anchorage, 1966-70; commr. revenue State of Alaska, Anchorage, 1970-72; ptnr. McGrath, Wohlforth & Flint, Anchorage, 1972-74, Wohlforth & Flint, Anchorage, 1974-87, Wohlforth, Argetsinger, Johnson & Brecht, Anchorage, 1988-98, Wohlforth, Vassar, Johnson & Brecht, Anchorage, 1999—. Mem. Alaska Investment Adv. Com., 1973-80. Trustee Alaska Permanent Fund Corp., 1995—, vice-chair, 1995—97, 2001—02, chmn., 1997—99, 2002—; chancellor Episcopal Diocese of Alaska, 1972—. Mem. Alaska Bar Assn., Assn. of Bar of City of N.Y. Finance, Municipal (including bonds). Home: 7831 Ingram St Anchorage AK 99502-3965 Office: 900 W 5th Ave Ste 600 Anchorage AK 99501-2044

WOHLGENANT, RICHARD GLEN, lawyer, director; b. Porterville, Calif., Dec. 2, 1930; s. Carl Ferdinand and Sara Alice (Moore) W.; m. Teresa Joan Bristow, Dec. 27, 1959; children: Mark Thomas, Tracy Patrice, Timothy James. BA, U. Mont., Missoula, 1952; LL.B., Harvard U., Cambridge, Mass., 1957. Bar: Colo. 1957, U.S. Dist. Ct. Colo. 1957. Assoc. Holme Roberts & Owen LLP, Denver, 1957-62; ptnr./mem. Holme Roberts & Owen, Denver, 1962-99, of counsel, 2000—. Bd. dirs. Adopt-A-Sch., Denver, 1976-80, St. Joseph Found., Denver, 1990-93, Denver Com. Coun. Fgn. Rels., 1988-98, Japanese-Am. Soc. Colo., 1993-98, Rocky Mountain chpt. U.S. Mex. C. of C., 1993-00; bi-nat. bd. U.S./Mex. C. of C., 2000—; mem. Chamber of the Americas, 2001—; adv. bd. Human Med. Genetics Prgm., U. Colo. H.S.C., 2000—. Mem. ABA, Colo. Bar Assn., Denver Bar Assn., Am. Coll. Real Estate Lawyers, Univ. Club, Law Club, City Club, Cactus Club. Republican. Roman Catholic. Corporate, general, Finance, Property, real (including real estate development, water). Home: 300 Ivy St Denver CO 80220-5855 Office: Holme Roberts & Owen LLP 1700 Lincoln St Denver CO 80203-4500

WOLAVER, STEPHEN ARTHUR, lawyer; b. Springfield, Ill., Sept. 4, 1950; s. Lynn Ellsworth and Arah Dean Phyllis (Scheele) W.; m. Gayla Sue Howard, Feb. 28, 1987; children: Lindy Allison, Scott. BS, Miami U., Oxford, Ohio, 1972; JD, Valparaiso U., 1975. Bar: Ohio 1975, U.S. Dist. Ct. (so. dist.) Ohio 1976, U.S. Ct. Appeals (6th cir.) 1997, U.S. Tax Ct. 1990, U.S. Supreme Ct. 1979. Ptnr. Gill, Wolaver & Welch, Fairborn, Ohio, 1975-81; asst. pros. atty. Greene County (Ohio), Xenia, 1976—, chief trial counsel, 1989—; ptnr. Wolaver, Sheets & Lewis, Fairborn, 1981—2001, Wolaver, Mayer & Cusack, 2002—. Instr. Fairborn Bd. Edn., 1978—; adj. prof. Clark Tech. Coll., 1979-85; instr. Greene County Law Enforcement Police Acad., 1988—; faculty Nat. Advocacy Ctr. U. So. Carolina, 2001; lectr., 1982—, mem. law enforcement adv. com., 1983-86; advisor Fairborn (Ohio) H.S. Mock Trial Team, 1987-96; elected Common Pleas judge, Greene County, Ohio, 2003. Greene County campaign chmn. Gov. Rhodes re-election com., 1978, 86, Voinovich for U.S. Senate; mem. Greene County Rep. Ctrl. Com., 1978—; youth counselor Bethlehem Luth. Ch., Fairborn, 1980-96, head usher com. pres. Rona Village Homeowners Assn., 1981; pres. Greene County Rep. Club, 1999-2000. Named one of Outstanding Young Men Am., Jaycees, 1981, Greene County Legal Secs. Boss of Yr. award, 1985; named to Fairborn H.S. Hall of Honor, 2003; recipient Outstanding Asst. Prosecutor of Yr. award Ohio Pros. Attys. Assn., 1998, Outstanding Trial award Nat. Assn. Govt. Attys. in Capital Litigation, 2002, Meritorious Achievement award Ohio Pros. Attys. Assn., 2002. Mem. Greene County Bar Assn. (sec./treas. 1997, v.p. 1998, pres. 2000), Ohio Bar Assn., Assn. Trial Lawyers Am., Nat. Dist. Attys. Assn., Miami U. Alumni Assn., Sertoma (pres. 1982-83), Delta Tau Delta. Criminal, Probate (including wills, trusts), Estate taxation. Home: 3792 Westwind Dr Dayton OH 45440-3500 Office: Courthouse 45 N Detroit Ave Xenia OH 45385

WOLF, ALAN STEVEN, lawyer; b. Jersey City, Jan. 5, 1955; s. Lester Joel and Beatrice (Spiegel) W.; m. Donna Snow Wolf, Aug. 31, 1980; children: Lauren, Bradley. BA, Dartmouth Coll., 1977; JD, Southwestern U., L.A., 1980. Bar: Calif. 1980, U.S. Dist. Ct. (no., so., ea. and cen. dists.) Calif. 1980. With Alvarado, Rus & McClellen, Orange, Calif., 1981-84; ptnr. Cameron Dreyfuss & Wolf, Orange, 1984-89; pres. Gordon & Wolf, Newport Beach, Calif., 1989-91, Wolf & Pfeifer, Newport Beach, Calif., 1991-97, Wolf & Richards, Newport Beach, 1997—. Pres., founding dir. Laguna Beach (Calif.) Pop Warner Football, 1995-99, sec., 1996; chief Indian Princess Tribe, Laguna Beach, 1993; charter bd. dirs. Irvine Swim League, 1985. Mem. U.S. Foreclosure Network (bd. dirs. 1990-95, Com. Mem. of Yr. 1994), Calif. Mortgage Bankers Assn. (chmn. legal issues com. 1994-95), Dartmouth Club (pres. Orange County club 1991); fellow Am. Coll. Mortgage Attys. Avocations: computers, internet. Bankruptcy, Finance, Property, real (including real estate development, water). Office: The Wolf Firm 18 Corporate Plaza Dr Newport Beach CA 92660-7901

WOLF, BRUCE, lawyer; b. Phila., Dec. 16, 1955; s. Charles and Mary (Saionz) W. BA, Temple U., 1977; JD, Drake U., 1981. Bar: Pa. 1981, U.S. Dist. Ct. (ea dist.) Pa. 1981, U.S. Ct. Appeals (3d cir.) 1981. Assoc. LaCheen & Alva, Phila., 1981-88; pvt. practice Phila., 1989—. Mem. Fed. Criminal Justice Act Panel, Phila., 1998—. Committeeman Phila. Dem. Party 63rd ward, 1994-2000. Mem. Phila. Bar Assn., Pa. Assn. Criminal Def. Lawyers. Democrat. Jewish. Criminal, Family and matrimonial, General practice. Office: 612 S 6th St 1st Fl Philadelphia PA 19147-2108 Fax: (215) 922-2194. E-mail: bwolf.esq@erols.com.

WOLF, CHARLES BENNO, lawyer; b. Chgo., Apr. 16, 1950; s. Ludwig and Hilde (Mandelbaum) W.; m. Sarah Lloyd, Sept. 1, 1973; children: Walter Ludwig, Peter Barton. AB, Brown U., 1972; JD, U. Chgo., 1975. Bar: Ill. 1975, U.S. Dist. Ct. (no. dist.) Ill. 1975, U.S. Ct. Appeals (4th, 5th, 6th, 7th, 8th, 9th, 10th, and 11th cirs.) 1985, U.S. Supreme Ct. 1985. Ptnr. Vedder, Price, Kaufman & Kammholz, Chgo., 1975—, exec. com., 1999—. Co-author: ERISA Claims and Litigation, 10th edit., 1995; contbr. articles to profl. jours. Mem. ABA (co-chair labor sect. subcom. on collective bargaining and employee benefits, past co-chair subcom. on multi-employer plans), Internat. Found. Employee Benefit Plans. Labor (including EEOC, Fair Labor Standards Act, labor-management relations, NLRB, OSHA), Pension, profit-sharing, and employee benefits. Office: Vedder Price Kaufman & Kammholz 222 N La Salle St Ste 2600 Chicago IL 60601-1100 E-mail: cwolf@vedderprice.com.

WOLF, CYD BETH, lawyer, entrepreneur; b. N.Y.C., Oct. 6, 1957; d. Aaron Joseph and Sally (Marcus) Wolf; m. Germano Fabio Fabiani, Nov. 18, 1990; children: Alessandra Julia Fabiani, Francesca Isabella Fabiani. BA in Urban Studies with honors, U. Pa., 1977; JD, U. Balt., 1983. Bar: Md 1983, US Dist Ct Md 1983, US Ct Appeals (6th and 11th cir) 1986, US Ct Appeals (4th and 5th cir) 1989. Assoc. Weinberger, Weinstock, Sagner, Stevan & Harris, Balt., 1983-86, Semmes, Bowen & Semmes, Balt., 1986-90, Piper & Marbury, Balt., 1990-95; private practice Balt., 1995—2002; asst. atty. gen. Md. State Dept. Bus. and Econ. Devel., Balt., 2002—. Contbr. articles to profl jours. Mem leadership comt Univ Baltimore Educ Found, fundraiser, mentor. Mem.: ABA, Bar Asn Baltimore City (banking, bankruptcy and bus law sect), Bankruptcy Bar Asn (mem rules comt dist Md 1997—), Md State Bar Asn (banking and bus sect). Avocations: tennis, painting, drawing, fiction and non-fiction reading and writing. Bankruptcy, Commercial, consumer (including collections, credit). Home: 5 Hillchase Ct Baltimore MD 21208-6306 Office: Md State Dept Bus and Econ Devel Redwood Tower 11th Fl 217 E Redwood St Baltimore MD 21202

WOLF, G. VAN VELSOR, JR., lawyer; b. Balt., Feb. 19, 1944; s. G. Van Velsor and Alice Roberts (Kimberly) W.; m. Ann Holmes Kavanagh, May 19, 1984; children: George Van Velsor III, Timothy Kavanagh (dec.), Christopher Kavanagh, Elisabeth Huxley. BA, Yale U., 1966; JD, Vanderbilt U., 1973. Bar: N.Y. 1974, U.S. Dist. Ct. (so. dist.) N.Y. 1974, U.S. Ct. Appeals (2d cir.) 1974, Ariz. 1982, U.S. Dist. Ct. Ariz. 1982, U.S. Ct. Appeals (9th cir.) 1982. Agrl. advisor U.S. Peace Corps., Tanzania and Kenya, 1966-70; assoc. Milbank, Tweed, Hadley & McCloy, N.Y.C., 1973-75; vis. lectr. law Airlangga U., Surabaya, Indonesia, 1975-76; editor-in-chief Environ. Law Reporter, Washington, 1976-81; assoc. Lewis & Roca, Phoenix, 1981-84, ptnr., 1984-91, Snell & Wilmer, Phoenix, 1991—. Vis. lectr. law U. Ariz., 1990, Vanderbilt U., 1991, U. Md., 1994, Ariz. State U., 1995; cons. Nat. Trust Hist. Preservation, Washington, 1981. Editor: Toxic Substances Control, 1980; editor in chief Environ. Law Reporter 1976-81; contbr. articles to profl. jours. Bd. dirs. Ariz. divsn. Am. Cancer Soc., 1985—96, sec., 1990—92, vice-chmn., 1992—94, chmn., 1994—96, bd. dirs. S.W. divsn., 1996—, chmn., 1996—98, nat. bd. dirs., 1999—; bd. dirs. Herberger Theatre Ctr., 1998—, sec., 2001—; bd. dirs. Phoenix Little Theatre, 1983—90, chmn., 1986—88. Recipient St. George medal Am. Cancer Soc., 1998. Mem. ABA (vice-chmn. SONREEL commn. state and regional environ. coop. 1995-98, co-chmn. 1998-2000, vice-chmn. environ. audits task force 1998-99, vice-chmn. SONREEL ann. meeting planning com. 1998-99), Assn. of Bar of City of N.Y., Ariz. State Bar Assn. (coun. environ. & nat. res. law sect. 1988-93, chmn. 1991-92, CLE com. 1992-98, chmn. 1997-98), Maricopa County Bar Assn., Ariz. Acad., Union Club N.Y.C., Univ. Club Phoenix, Phoenix Country Club. Environmental, Legislative. Office: Snell & Wilmer 1 Arizona Ctr Phoenix AZ 85004-0001 E-mail: vwolf@swlaw.com.

WOLF, GARY WICKERT, lawyer; b. Slinger, Wis., Apr. 19, 1938; s. Leonard A. and Cleo C. (Wickert) W.; m. Jacqueline Weltzin, Dec. 17, 1960; children: Gary, Jonathan. BBA, U. Minn., 1960, JD cum laude, 1963. Bar: N.Y. 1964, U.S. Ct. Appeals (2d cir.) 1969, U.S. Dist. Ct. (so. dist.) N.Y. 1969, U.S. Supreme Ct. 1971. Assoc. Cahill, Gordon & Reindel, N.Y.C., 1963-70, ptnr., 1970—. Bd. dirs. N.J. Resources Corp. Mem. N.Y. State Bar Assn. (com. on securities regulation), Anglers Club (N.Y.C.), Downtown Assn. (N.Y.C.), Mashomack Fish and Game Club. Corporate, general, Finance, Mergers and acquisitions. Home: 35 Fieldstone Dr Basking Ridge NJ 07920-1605 Office: Cahill Gordon & Reindel 80 Pine St Fl 17 New York NY 10005-1790

WOLF, JEROME THOMAS, lawyer; b. Austin, Minn., June 13, 1937; s. William B. and Charlotte Elaine (Rosenstock) W.; m. Ellen L., Jan. 9, 1965; children: Margo Ann, Gregory Thomas. BA, Yale U., 1959; JD, Harvard U., 1962. Bar: Minn. 1962, Mo. 1966, Kans. 1984. Ptnr. Sonnerschein, Nath & Rosenthal, Kansas City, Mo., 1994—, mng. ptnr., mem. firm mgmt. com., 1994-2000, chmn. firm mktg. com., 1999—. Co-chair Justice for All campaign Legal Aid of Western Mo., 2000—; mem. coun. of fellows Nelson Atkins Mus., Kansas City, Mo., 2001—; chmn. Jewish Cmty. Rels. Bur. Kansas City, 1973—79, 2001—; mem. CPR commn. on future of arbitration Best Lawyers in Am. Capt. JAGC U.S. Army, 1962—66. Mem.: ABA, Mo. Bar, Kansas City Bar Found. (pres. 1979—80, founding), Kansas City Bar Assn. (pres. 1979), Phi Beta Kappa. Democrat. Federal civil litigation, State civil litigation. Home: 2411 W 70th Ter Shawnee Mission KS 66208-2741 Office: 4520 Main St Ste 1000 Kansas City MO 64111 E-mail: jw@sonnerschein.com.

WOLF, LAWRENCE, lawyer; b. L.A. BA cum laude, Calif. U., Northridge, 1972; JD cum laude, U. Calif., Santa Clara, 1975. Bar: Calif. 1975. Atty. City of Santa Monica, Calif., 1975-77, L.A. County Pub. Defender, 1977-79; pvt. practice law L.A., 1979—. Coord. law confs. Calif. Juvenile Cts., Inglewood, 1983. Mem. L.A. County Bar Assn., Juvenile Cts. Bar Assn. Administrative and regulatory, Criminal, Juvenile. Office: 10390 Santa Monica Blvd Ste 300 Los Angeles CA 90025-5091 Fax: (310) 277-1500. E-mail: info@youareinnocent.com.

WOLF, MARCUS ALAN, lawyer; b. Mansfield, Ohio, July 6, 1946; s. Carl Merle and Eunice Virginia (Beekman) W.; m. Terrie L. Wolf, May 18, 2001; children: Stephanie Ariah, Marcus André. BA, Northeast La. U., 1969; JD, Ohio No. U., 1980. Bar: Ohio 1980, U.S. Dist. Ct. (no. dist.) Ohio 1980. Tchr. Clearfork Valley Schs., Butler, Ohio, 1969-70, Shelby City Schools, Shelby, Ohio, 1972-77; prin. Marcus A. Wolf Co. L.P.A. (formerly Thompson & Wolf Co. L.P.A.), Mansfield, 1980—. Owner Marcus' Beauty Salon. Mem. exec. com. Richland County Dem. Com., 1986-93, 2000—, precinct committeeman, 1988, 90-93; chmn. adminstrv. bd. Main St. United Meth. Ch.; mem. dist. 7 Mansfield Power Squadron, 1985—. Mem. ABA, Ohio Bar Assn., Richland County Bar Assn. (chmn. cert. grievance com.), Masons, Elks. Methodist. Avocations: boating, fishing, skiing, hunting. Criminal, Family and matrimonial. Home: 457 Davis Rd Mansfield OH 44907-1121 Office: Marcus A Wolf Co LPA 13 Park Ave W Mansfield OH 44902-1714 also: Marcus' Salon 310 Lexington Ave Mansfield OH 44907

WOLF, MARK LAWRENCE, federal judge; b. Boston, Nov. 23, 1946; s. Jason Harold and Beatrice (Meltzer) W.; m. Lynne Lichterman, Apr. 4, 1971; children: Jonathan, Matthew. BA cum laude, Yale U., 1968; JD cum laude, Harvard U., 1971; hon. degree, Boston Latin Sch., 1990. Bar: Mass. 1971, D.C. 1972, U.S. Supreme Ct. 1976. Assoc. Surrey, Karasik & Morse, Washington, 1971-74; spl. asst. to dep. atty. gen. U.S. Dept. Justice, Washington, 1974-75, spl. asst. to atty. gen., 1975-76, dep. U.S. atty. Boston, 1981-85; from assoc. to ptnr. Sullivan & Worcester, Boston, 1977-81; judge U.S. Dist. Ct. Mass., Boston, 1985—. Lectr. Harvard U. Law Sch., Cambridge, Mass., 1990—; adj. prof. Boston Coll. Law Sch., 1992. Bd. dirs. Albert Schweitzer Fellowship, Boston, 1974—, pres., 1989-97, chmn., 1997—; chmn. John William Ward Fellowship, Boston, 1986—. Recipient cert. appreciation U.S. Pres., 1975, Disting. Service award U.S. Atty. Gen., 1985. Mem. Boston Bar Assn. (coun. 1982-85, Citation of Jud. Excellence 2002), Am. Law Inst. Office: US Dist Ct 1 Courthouse Way Boston MA 02210-3002

WOLF, MARTIN EUGENE, lawyer, educator; b. Balt., Sept. 9, 1958; s. Eugene Bernard and Mary Anna (O'Neil) W.; m. Nancy Ann Reinsfelder, May 9, 1980; children: Matthew Adam, Allison Maria, Emily Elizabeth. BA, Johns Hopkins U., 1980; JD, U. Md., 1991. Bar: Md. 1991, U.S. Dist. Ct. Md. 1992, U.S. Ct. Appeals (4th cir.) 1992, U.S. Ct. Appeals (2d cir.) 1993, U.S. Ct. Appeals (3d cir.) 1998, U.S. Ct. Appeals (11th cir.) 2000, U.S. Ct. Fed. Claims 2001. Mgmt. trainee Giant Foods, Inc., Landover, Md., 1980-82, dept. mgr., 1982-83, ops. analyst, 1983-86, fin. coord., 1986-89; law clk. Piper & Marbury, LLP, Balt., 1989-91, assoc., 1991-96; prin. Law Office of Martin E. Wolf, Abingdon, Md., 1996-99; ptnr. Quinn, Gordon & Wolf Chartered, Towson, Md., 2000—. Pres. bd. dirs. Chesapeake Search & Rescue Dog Assn., Inc., 2000—02. Mem. ABA, Md. State Bar Assn., Harford County Bar Assn., Harford County Bar Found. (Vol. Svc. award 1992, 94), Am. Trial Lawyers Assn. Democrat. Roman Catholic. Avocations: lacrosse, hockey. Appellate, General civil litigation, Condemnation (eminent domain). Home: 11 Mitchell Dr Abingdon MD 21009-1628 E-mail: mwolf@quinnlaw.com.

WOLF, RICHARD V. lawyer; b. Paris, 1962; DrIur, U. Vienna, 1985; LLM, Harvard U., 1986. 2d v.p. Chase Manhattan Bank, Austria, 1992-93; M&A mgr. Crédit Lyonnais, Austria, 1993-94; ptnr. Wolf Theiss & Ptnrs., Austria, 1994—. Served with Austrian Army, 1980-81. Fulbright scholar, 1985-86. Mem. Internat. Bar Assn. Banking, Mergers and acquisitions, Securities. Office: Wolf Theiss & Ptnrs Schubertring 6 A-1010 Vienna Austria

WOLF, ROBERT B. lawyer; b. Phila., Aug. 18, 1914; s. Morris and Pauline (Binswanger) W.; children— Edwin David, Virginia. BA, Haverford Coll., 1936; LL.B., Harvard U., 1939. Bar: Pa. 1939. Ptnr. Wolf, Block, Schorr & Solis-Cohen, 1940-43, 46-56, 57-85, of counsel, 1985—; gen. counsel FHA, Washington, 1956-57. Instr. humanities Haverford Coll., 1948-49, 71-72. Chmn. mayor's coordinated housing improvement program, Phila., 1951, Phila. Youth Svcs. Coordinating Com., 1978-84; past chmn. Pa. Com. Crime and Delinquency; mem. juvenile adv. com. Pa. Commn. on Crime and Delinquency, 1976-86; ct. master Phila. Youth Study Ctr., 1989-91; trustee Benjamin Franklin Found., Berlin, Germany, 1955-56 request Dept. State. Mem. Am., Pa., Phila. bar assns., Phi Beta Kappa. Home: 2101 Harts Ln Conshohocken PA 19428-2416 Office: Wolf Block Schorr & Solis-Cohen 1650 Arch St Fl 20 Philadelphia PA 19103-2029

WOLF, WILLIAM B., JR., lawyer; b. Washington, Sept. 11, 1927; s. William B. and Ruth (Pack) W.; m. Edna Russell Jacobs, Aug. 8, 1952 (div. Oct. 1976); children: Susan Marcia, William B. III, Victoria Katharine; m. Audrey Ann Riven, Nov. 29, 1980. AB, Princeton, 1948; postgrad., Oxford U., 1950; LLB, Yale U., 1951. Bar: D.C. 1951, U.S. Supreme Ct. 1954, Md. 1963. Ptnr. Wolf & Wolf, Washington, 1951-64, 82—; sole practice Washington, 1964-72, 75-81; ptnr. Wolf & Rosenblatt, Washington, 1972-75, Wolf, Amram & Hahn, P.C., Washington, 1981-82. Vice chmn. Security Nat. Bank, Washington, 1984-85. Author: Lawyers Are a Dime a Dozen, 1999. Pres. Nat. Capital USO, 1966—67, Jewish Hist. Soc. Greater WAshington, Brotherhood Washington Hebrew Congregation, 1967—68. With USN, 1945, sgt. U.S. Army, 1946—48. Mem.: ABA, Bar Assn. D.C., University (Washington), Nassau (Princeton, N.J.), Edgartown (Mass.) Yacht, Woodmont Country. Republican. Jewish. Banking, General practice, Property, real (including real estate development, water). Home: Watergate East Washington DC 20037 Office: Wolf & Wolf 2510 Virginia Ave NW Washington DC 20037

WOLFE, DEBORAH ANN, lawyer; b. Detroit, May 4, 1955; d. Adam and Mary A. (Smyth) Wolfe; m. Lester D. McDonald, May 23, 1987; children: Molly, Thomas. Student, Ariz. State U., Tempe, 1973-76; BA in Polit. Sci., Bus., Tex. Christian U., Ft. Worth, 1977; postgrad., So. Meth. U., 1977-78; JD, U. San Diego, 1980; grad., Gerry Spence's Trial Lawyers Coll., 1999. Bar: Calif. 1981, Ariz. 1982. Sole practice, San Diego, 1981-83; ptnr. Kremer & Wolfe, San Diego, 1983-86; assoc. D. Dwight Worden, Solana Beach, Calif., 1986-89; pvt. practice San Diego, 1989-91; owner Wolfe & McDonald, 1991-96; shareholder Nugent & Newnham, San Diego, 1996—. Instr. San Diego Inn of Ct. Evidence, 1988-95. Floutist San Diego City Guard Band, 1981-93, Grossmont Sinfonia, La Mesa, 1982-83, Classical/Chamber Music Quartet, San Diego, 1983-87, Foothills United Meth. Ch. band, 1997—; leader Girl Scouts. Named one of Lawyers of the Yr. Calif. Lawyer Mag., 1996, one of top ten plaintiff legal malpractice lawyers in Calif., 2001. Mem. ATLA, Consumer Attys. Calif., Consumer Attys. San Diego (pres. 1996, Outstanding Trial Lawyer award 1996, 2000, 02, Trial Lawyer of Yr. award 1996), Lawyers Club (San Diego), San Diego Trial Lawyers Assn. (Outstanding Trial Lawyers award 1987), Am. Inns of Ct. (master), Nat. Bd. Trial Advocates. Insurance, Personal injury (including property damage), Professional liability. Office: Nugent & Newnham 1010 2nd Ave Ste 2200 San Diego CA 92101-4911

WOLFE, HARRIET MUNRETT, lawyer; b. Mt. Vernon, N.Y., Aug. 18, 1953; d. Lester John Francis Jr. and Olga Harriet (Miller) Munrett; m. Charles Briant Wolfe, Sept. 10, 1983. BA, U. Conn., 1975; postgrad., Oxford (Eng.) U., 1976; JD, Pepperdine U., 1978. Bar: Conn. 1979. Assoc. legal counsel, asst. sec. Citytrust, Bridgeport, Conn., 1979-90; v.p., sr. counsel, asst. sec. legal dept. Shawmut Bank Conn., N.A., Hartford, 1990-96, pvt. practice, 1996-97; exec. v.p., gen. counsel, sec. Webster Fin. Corp., Waterbury, Conn., 1997—. Govt. rels. com. Electronic Funds Transfer Assn., Washington, 1983—. Mem. ABA, Conn. Bar Assn. (mem. legis. com. banking law sect.), Conn. Bankers Assn. (trust legis.com.), Guilford Flotilla Coast Guard Aux., U.S. Sailing Assn., Phi Alpha Delta Internat. (Frank E. Gray award 1978, Shepherd chpt. Outstanding Student award 1977-78). Banking, Corporate, general, Securities. Home: 621 Northwood Dr Guilford CT 06437-1124 Office: Webster Fin Corp Webster Plaza Waterbury CT 06702 E-mail: hwolfe@websterbank.com.

WOLFE, J. MATTHEW, lawyer; b. Pitts., Mar. 29, 1956; s. James Michael and Mary Evangeline (Andrews) Wolfe; children: James M. Jr., Ross M. BA, U. Pa., 1978; JD, Villanova U., 1981. Bar: Pa. 1981, U.S. Dist. Ct. (ea. dist.) Pa. 1985, U.S. Ct. Appeals (3rd cir.) 1985, U.S. Supreme Ct., 1992, U.S. Dist. Ct. (we. dist.) Pa. 1997. Atty. Cmty. Legal Svcs., Phila., 1981-82; pvt. practice Phila., 1981-82, 89-95, 97-99; asst. counsel Pa. Dept. of Transp., Phila, 1983-86; spl. prosecutor Pa., 1984-86; spl. asst. dist. atty. Berks County, Reading, Pa., 1984-86; dep. atty. gen. Commonwealth of Pa., Phila., 1986-89; spl. asst. dist. atty. Phila., 1991-92; chief counsel Pa. Dept. Law and Industry, 1995-97; atty. Law Offices of Alice Ballard, 1998—. Gen. counsel Univ. Bus. Machines, Inc., Upper Darby, Pa., 1989-95; instr. Pa. Bar Inst., Harrisburg, 1984; Pa. workers compensation rules com. Pa. Dept. Laor & Industry, 1995-97, Pa. Worker's Compensation Fraud task force, 1996-97. Assoc. editor The Docket newspaper, 1980-81; contbr. articles to The Univ. City Trumpet newspaper, 1981-95. Mem. Spruce Hill Cmty. Assn., Phila, 1980—, bd. dirs., 1982—96, 1999—; mem. sch. bd. task force on Scholastics and Sports Phila., 1986; mem. neighborhood adv. coun. 19th Police Dist., Phila., 1987—93; mem. Cedar Park Neighbors, 1986—; vice chmn. Woodland Dist. Phila.Coun. BSA, 1989—91; Ward leader 27th Ward Rep. Com., Phila., 1979—; chmn. Univ. City Rep.Com., 1990—96; eucharistic minister St. Francis de Sales Parish, 2000—; catechist Confraternity Christian Doctrine program, 1995—2002; lector St. Frances De Sales Parish, 1995—; bd. dirs. University City Town Watch, 1983—85. Mem. ABA, Pa. Bar Assn. (mem. com. legal ethics and profl. responsibility 1986-95), Phila. Bar Assn. (mem. com. labor and employment law, instr. 1995), West Phila. C. of C. (bd. dirs. 1989-95, gen. counsel 1993-95, 98—), Pi Sigma Alpha, Phi Delta Theta (editor Phi Oracle newsletter). Roman Catholic. Home: 4256 Regent Sq Philadelphia PA 19104-4439 Office: 1700 Lewis Tower 225 South 15th St Philadelphia PA 19102 E-mail: matthew@wolfe.org.

WOLFE, ROGER ALLEN, lawyer; b. Charleston, W.Va., Aug. 25, 1948; s. Jackson Clark and Imogene Ashley Wolfe; children: Matthew, Theresa, Katherine, Rebecca. BA in Psychology, W.Va. U., 1970, JD, 1973. Bar: W.Va. 1970, U.S. Ct. Appeals (4th cir.) 1975, U.S. Supreme Ct. 1979. Law clk. U.S. Dist. Ct., Charleston, 1973-74; mem. Jackson & Kelly, PLLC, Charleston, 1974—. Mem. W.Va. State Bar (chair employment law com. 1993-2001), Order of the Coif. Avocations: family activities, music, gardening, reading, outdoor activities. Labor (including EEOC, Fair Labor Standards Act, labor-management relations, NLRB, OSHA). Office: Jackson & Kelly PO Box 553 Charleston WV 25322-0553 E-mail: rwolfe@jacksonkelly.com.

WOLFEN, WERNER F. lawyer; b. Berlin, May 15, 1930; came to U.S., 1939; s. Martin and Ruth Eva (Hamburger) W.; m. Mary Glasier, July 1, 1956; children: Richard, James, Lawrence (dec.). BS, U. Calif., Berkeley, 1950, JD, 1953. Bar: Calif. 1953. Assoc. Irell & Manella, L.A., 1953-57, ptnr., 1957-98, sr. ptnr. emeritus, 1999—; pres. Capri Investment Co. LLC, 1999—. Bd. dirs. Broadcom Corp., Rokenbok Toy Co., Pre-Cash Corp.; mem. bd. visitors UCLA Sch. Arts and Arch., 1995—. Bd. govs. UCLA Found., 1992—, L.A. Goal, 1994-, pres., 1994-99. Mem. ABA. Democrat. Jewish. Office: Capri Investment Co LLC 1800 Avenue of the Stars Los Angeles CA 90067-4212 Business E-Mail: wwolfen@irell.com.

WOLFF, ALAN WILLIAM, lawyer; b. Malden, Mass., June 12, 1942; s. Louis K. and Etta (Bernstein) W.; m. Helene N. Novick, Mar. 3, 1965; children: Anna, Jeremy, Ewan. AB, Harvard U., 1963; LLB, Columbia U., 1966. Bar: Mass. 1967, N.Y. 1966, U.S. Supreme Ct. 1971, D.C. 1972, U.S. Ct. Appeals (fed. cir.) 1982, Ct. Internat. Trade 1993. Atty. Office Gen. Counsel, U.S. Treasury Dept., Washington, 1968—73; dep. gen. counsel Spl. Trade Rep. (now U.S. Trade Rep.), Washington, 1973-74, gen. counsel, 1974-76, dep. spl. trade rep. (with rank of ambassador), 1977-79; ptnr. Verner, Liipfert et al, Washington, 1979-85, Dewey, Ballantine, Bushby, Palmer & Wood (now Dewey Ballantine), Washington, 1985—, mng. ptnr., 1992—; mem. Nat. Rsch. Coun. Bd. on Sci., Tech. and Econ. Policy, 1997—. Mem. adv. com. for trade negotiations Office of the Pres., Washington, 1980—82; mem. policy adv. com. U.S. Trade Rep.'s Svcs., Washington, 1980—86; mem. adv. bd. Inst. Internat. Econs., Washington, 1981—, Ctr. Nat. Policy, Washington, 1988—, Econ. Strategy Inst., Washington, 1989—; mem. adv. com. on internat. econ. policy U.S. Dept. State, Washington, 1996—; chmn. adv. bd. Internat. Comml. Diplomacy Project, Washington, 1999—. Co-author: The Microelectronics Race, 1987, Steel and the State, 1988, Conflict Among Nations: Trade Policy for the 1990s, 1992; contbr. articles to profl. jours. Mem. Coun. Fgn. Rels., 1979—; bd. advisors Am. Edn. and Health Found., 2002—; trustee Monterey Inst. Internat. Studies, 1992—2001. Mem. ABA, Am. Soc. Internat. Law. Democrat. Unitarian Universalist. Private international, Public international, Legislative. Office: Dewey Ballantine LLP 1775 Pennsylvania Ave NW Washington DC 20006-4605 also: 1301 Avenue Of The Americas New York NY 10019-6022

WOLFF, CLIFFORD ALAN, lawyer; b. N.Y.C., Apr. 7, 1970; s. Malcolm and Judy Dale Wolff. BA, U. Fla., 1992, JD, 1995. Bar: Fla. 96, U.S. Dist. Ct. (so. and no. dists.) Fla. 96, U.S. Dist. Ct. (mid. dist.) Fla. 99, U.S. Ct. Appeals (11th cir.) 02. Assoc. Haddad Josephs Jack & Guete, P.A., Miami, Fla., 1996—98, Gunster Yoakley, P.A., Ft. Lauderdale, Fla., 1998—99, Heinrich Gordon Hargrove Weihe & James, P.A., Ft. Lauderdale, 2000—. Mem. Cystic Fibrosis Found., Ft. Lauderdale, 1996—, Ft. Lauderdale Riverwalk Trust, 1996—, Fla. Grand Opera, Ft. Lauderdale, 1997—. Named Champaion Advocate, ATLA, 1995. Mem.: Dade County Bar Assn., Broward County Bar Assn. Avocations: photography, travel, skiing, gourmet cooking. Product liability, Personal injury (including property damage). Office: Heinrich Gordon Hargrove Weihe & James PA 500 E Broward Blvd Ste 100 Fort Lauderdale FL 33394 Fax: 954-524-9481. E-mail: cwolff@heinrichgordon.com.

WOLFF, DEBORAH H(OROWITZ), lawyer; b. Phila., Apr. 6, 1940; d. Samuel and Anne (Manstein) Horowitz; m. Morris H. Wolff, May 15, 1966 (div.); children: Michelle Lynn, Lesley Anne; m. Walter Allan Levy, June 7, 1987. BS, U. Pa., 1962, MS, 1966; postgrad., Sophia U., Tokyo, 1968; JD, Villanova U., 1979, LLM, 1988. Tchr. Overbrook H.S., Phila., 1962-68; homebound tchr. Lower Merior Twp., Mongomery County, 1968-71; asst. dean U. Pa., Phila., 1975-76; law clk. Stassen, Kostos and Mason, Phila., 1977-78; assoc. Spencer, Sherr, Moses and Zuckerman, Norristown, Pa., 1980-81; ptnr. Wolff Assocs., Phila., 1981—. Lectr. law and estate planning, Phila., 1980—. Founder Take a Brother Program; bd. dirs. Germantown Jewish Ctr.; h.s. sponsor World Affairs Club, Phila., 1962-68; mem. exec.

com., sec. bd. Crime Prevention Assn., Phila., treas., bd. dirs., 1965—; v.p. bd. dirs. U. Pa. Alumnae Bd., Phila., 1965—, pres. bd. dirs., 1993—, v.p. organized classes, bd. crime prevention; chmn. urban conf. Boys Club Am., 1987, treas., 1999; active Hahnaman Brain Tumor Rsch. Bd.; v.p., bd. dirs. Crime Prevention; treas. Assn. of Alumnae Bd. Recipient 3d Ann. Cmty. Svc. award Phila. Mayor's Com. for Women, 1984; named Pa. Heroine of Month, Ladies Home Jour., 1984. Mem. Lions (pres. Germantown Club 1997—). Corporate, general, Probate (including wills, trusts), Taxation, general. Home and Office: 422 W Mermaid Ln Philadelphia PA 19118-4204 E-mail: debbyw@comcast.net.

WOLFF, FLORIAN, lawyer; b. Bochum, Germany, July 1, 1968; married. Law Degree, J.W. Goethe U., Frankfurt, Germany, 1993. Trainee German Law Firm, Moscow, 1995; assoc. Rossbach & Fischer, Frankfurt, Germany, 1996-98, ptnr., 1998—. Author: Tax and Bus. Law Guide, 2001—. Computer, Corporate, general, , Antitrust. Office: Rossbach & Fischer Schaumainkai 101-103 Frankfurt 60596 Germany Fax: (0049) 69 631571 99. E-mail: wolff@rolaw.de.

WOLFF, JESSE DAVID, lawyer; b. Mpls., Aug. 26, 1913; s. Maurice I. and Annalee (Weiskopf) W.; m. Elizabeth Hess, Nov. 22, 1939; children: Nancy Nicholas, Paula, Daniel Jesse. BA summa cum laude, Dartmouth Coll., 1935; JD, Harvard U., 1938. Bar: N.Y. 1938. Practiced in, N.Y.C., 1938—; assoc., then ptnr., to counsel Weil, Gotshal & Manges, 1938-88, 88—, sr. mng. ptnr., 1966-86. Past dir., dep. chmn. Sotheby Parke Bernet Group (Eng.); past mem. adv. bd. Sotheby's Inc. Hon. trustee Greatery N.Y. ARC; past mem. exec. com. Salvation Army, N.Y.C. Served with AUS, 1942-45. Mem. ABA, Judge Adv. Gen. Assn. General practice, Probate (including wills, trusts). Office: Weil Gotshal & Manges 767 5th Ave Fl Concl New York NY 10153-0119

WOLFF, JOEL HENRY, lawyer, human factors engineer; b. New Rochelle, N.Y., Oct. 29, 1966; s. Richard Eugene and Elise Leonora (Wolff) A.; m. Stacy J. Plotkin. BA, U. Nev. at Las Vegas, 1991; JD, Gonzaga U., 1995. Computer operator Sun Teleguide, Henderson, Nev., 1987-90; engring. aide Wojcik Engring., Las Vegas, 1989-90; computer cons. Ax Med. Interfaces, Las Vegas, 1990-91; programmer Biosoft, Las Vegas, 1991-92; computer cons., sys. analyst Wolff Legal Engines, 1995-99; mem. corp. legal dept. Graham and James LLP/Riddell-Williams P.S., Seattle, 1997-98; contractor for litigation dept. Preston, Gates and Ellis LLP, Seattle, 1998; staff atty. U.S. immigration and Visa law Law Offices of Dan P. Danilov, Seattle, 1999-2000; staff atty. immigration and Visa law Liebman-Mimbu, PLLC, Seattle, 2000; atty., owner immigration law Law Offices of Joel H. Wolff, Kirkland, Wash., 2000—01; shareholder Bergstedt, Clegg & Wolff, P.S., Lynnwood, Wash., 2001—. Contract reviewer, document coder Perkins Coie LLP, Seattle, 1999; legal database designer and cons., King County Prosecuting Atty.'s Office, civil divsn., employment law sect., Seattle, 1998-99. Named Eagle Scout Boy Scouts Am., 1984. Mem. ASCE (sec. student chpt. 1986-87), ABA (law student divsn. 1992-95), Internat. Law Soc. of Gonazaga Univ., Nat. Eagle Scout Assn., Fed. Bar Assn., Wash. State Bar Assn., Wash. State Trial Lawyers Assn., Phi Alpha Delta, Sigma Nu. Achievements include rsch. on systems engring. with emphasis of man/machine interface; stats. analysis of social power structures and how they interface with sci. and tech.; specialist in immigration and Visa law as it applies to high tech. corps. Immigration, naturalization, and customs, Private international, Public international. Office: Bergstedt Clegg & Wolff PS 3500 188th St SW # 550 Lynnwood WA 98037-4762 Office Fax: 425-673-2908. E-mail: joel@bcwlaw.info.

WOLFF, MICHAEL A. state supreme court judge; Grad., Dartmouth Coll., 1967; JD, U. Minn., 1970. Lawyer Legal Svcs.; mem. faculty St. Louis U. Sch. Law, 1975-98; judge Mo. Supreme Ct., 1998—. Chief counsel to gov., 1993-94, spl. counsel, 1994-98. Co-author: Federal Jury Practice and Instructions, 4th edit. Chief counsel to Gov. St. Louis, 1993-94, spl. counsel, 1994-98. Office: Supreme Ct MO PO Box 150 Jefferson City MO 65102-0150

WOLFF, PAUL MARTIN, lawyer; b. Kansas City, Mo., July 22, 1941; s. Joseph L. and Eleanor B. Wolff; m. Rhea S. Schwartz, Oct. 9, 1976. BA, U. Wis., 1963; LLB, Harvard U., 1966. Bar: D.C. 1968, U.S. Ct. Appeals (D.C. and 2d cir.) 1968, U.S. Supreme Ct. 1975, U.S. Ct. Appeals (10th and fed. cirs.) 1981, U.S. Ct. Appeals (8th cir.) 1982, U.S. Tax Ct. 1982, U.S. Ct. Claims 1984. Law clk. to Judge James R. Durfee U.S. Ct. Claims, Washington, 1966-67; assoc. Williams & Connolly, Washington, 1967-75, ptnr., 1976—. Adj. prof. Catholic U. Law Sch., 1970-73. Co-author: Forensic Sciences; contbr. articles to legal jours. Bd. dirs. Washington Coun. for Civil Rights Under Law, 1980-90, Renwick Alliance, Washington, 1987-93, Am. Jewish Com., Washington, 1988-92, Washington Legal Clinic for Homeless, 1988-99, Opportunities for Older Ams. Found., 1988-92, Emeritus Found., 1992-99; bd. dirs. Washington Performing Arts Soc., 1990-2002, hon. dir., 2002—; vice chmn. D.C. Pub. Charter Schs. Resource Ctr., 1999—; dir. D.C. Sports Commn., 1994-2000; dir. Com. Pub. Edn., 1994-99; trustee Fed. City Coun., bd. trustees, 1996—; dir. Am. U., Corcoran Mus. of Art, overseer, 1997—. Mem. Georgetown Club, Econ. Club Washington (dir.), Phi Beta Kappa. Democrat. Avocations: photography, gardening, fly fishing, sculpting. Banking, Federal civil litigation, General civil litigation. Home: 4770 Reservoir Rd NW Washington DC 20007-1905 also: Oak Ridge Warrenton VA 20186 Office: Williams & Connolly 725 12th St NW Washington DC 20005-5901 : 1250 Villager Sun Valley ID 83353 Fax: 202-434-5580. E-mail: pwolff@wc.com., dcpmw@aol.com.

WOLFSON, JEFFREY STEVEN, lawyer; b. Worcester, Mass., Jan. 9, 1954; s. Jack L. and Marcia (Paul) W.; m. Judy Rosen, Oct. 25, 1981. AB summa cum laude, Tufts U., 1976; JD, Yale U., 1979. Bar: Mass. 1979, U.S. Dist. Ct. Mass. 1980, U.S. Ct. Appeals (1st cir.) 1980. Assoc. Goulston & Storrs, P.C., Boston, 1979-86, ptnr., 1986—. Clk. Malden Mills Industries, Inc., Lawrence, Mass., 1981-90. Author: Practice Points for the Family Business Corporate Lawyer, 1996. Bd. dirs. Performers Ensemble, Inc., Boston, 1985-89; bd. advisors Northeastern U. Ctr. Family Bus., 1991—, chmn., 1995-99. Mem. ABA, Boston Bar Assn., Attys. for Family-Held Enterprises, Family Firm Inst., Phi Beta Kappa. Corporate, general, Commercial, contracts (including sales of goods; commercial financing), Mergers and acquisitions. Home: 140 Whitman Rd Needham MA 02492-1021 Office: Goulston & Storrs PC 400 Atlantic Ave Boston MA 02110-3333

WOLFSON, MICHAEL GEORGE, lawyer; b. Chgo., Sept. 1, 1938; s. A. Lincoln M. Weingarten and Brina (Nelson) W.; m. Rita Sue Parsont, Sept. 11, 1966; children: Bethany Lynne, Sara Wynne, Deborah Kay. Student, MIT, 1956-58; BA, U. Chgo., 1961, JD, 1964, postdoctoral, 1964-65. Bar: Ill. 1964, N.Y. 1969. Assoc. Cravath, Swaine & Moore, N.Y.C., 1965-71, Brown, Wood, Fuller, Caldwell & Ivey, N.Y.C., 1971-73; ptnr. Sidley Austin Brown & Wood LLP, N.Y.C., 1974—2002, sr. counsel, 2003—. Mediator, specializing in comml. and internat. disputes. Woodrow Wilson fellow, 1961; Ford Found. fellow in internat. trade and devel., 1965. Fellow Am. Bar Found. (life); mem. ABA. Avocations: reading, photography, fly fishing, bicycling. Corporate, general, Finance, Mergers and acquisitions. E-mail: mwolfson@sidley.com.

WOLFSON, SUSAN WARTUR, lawyer; b. Bklyn., May 2, 1938; d. Marcus Harry and Bertha (Stern) Wartur; m. Steven Wolfson, April 10, 1960; children: Ellen Paula, Roger Samuel. BA, Barnard Coll., 1959; JD, U. Conn., 1976. Bar: Conn. 1976, U.S. Dist. Ct. Conn. 1977. Assoc. Lieberman & Segaloff, New Haven, 1976-80; ptnr. Lieberman, Segaloff & Wolfson, New Haven, 1980-87, Susman, Duffy & Segaloff, P.C., New Haven, 1987—. Pres. Statewide Legal Svcs., 1996-98. Mem. editl. bd. Conn. Law Tribune, 1998—. Bd. dirs. Legal Assistance Assn. of New Haven, 1982-93. Fellow Conn. Bar Found. (bd. dirs. 1992—); mem. ABA (ho. of dels. 1989-93, chair alimony com. family law sect.), Conn. Bar Assn. (ho. of dels. 1983-87, counsel of pres. 1983-84, bd. govs. 1983-87, sec. 1987-89, v.p. 1989-90, pres. 1991-92), New Haven County Bar Assn. (exec. bd. 1978-88, pres. 1983-84). Family and matrimonial, Personal injury (including property damage), Property, real (including real estate development, water), Alternative dispute resolution. Home: 571 Muirfield Ln New Haven CT 06516-7904 Office: Susman Duffy & Segaloff PC 55 Whitney Ave New Haven CT 06510-1300

WOLK, BRUCE ALAN, law educator; b. Bklyn., Mar. 2, 1946; s. Morton and Gertrude W.; m. Lois Gloria Krepliak, June 22, 1968; children: Adam, Daniel. BS, Antioch Coll., 1968; MS, Stanford U., 1972; JD, Harvard U., 1975. Bar: D.C. 1975. Assoc. Hogan & Hartson, Washington, 1975-78; prof. U. Calif. Sch. Law, Davis, 1978—, acting dean, 1990-91, dean, 1993-98. Danforth Found. fellow, 1970-74, NSF fellow, 1970-72, Fulbright sr. research fellow, 1985-86. Mem. ABA, Am. Law Inst. Office: Univ Cal Davis Sch Law King Hall 400 Mrak Hall Dr Davis CA 95616-5201

WOLKOFF, EUGENE ARNOLD, lawyer; b. N.Y.C., June 9, 1932; s. Oscar and Jean (Zablow) W.; m. Judith Gail Edwards, Oct. 15, 1967; children— Mandy, Elana, Alexa, Justine. AB, Bklyn. Coll., 1953; LLB, St. John's U., 1961. Bar: N.Y. 1962, N.Mex. 1994. Practiced in, N.Y.C and Santa Fe; mem. Callahan & Wolkoff, N.Y.C., 1965—; gen. counsel BGK Group of Cos. Bd. dirs. Babylon Enterprises, Inc., Hist. Newspaper Archives, Inc., Beacon Concessions, Inc.; mem. nat. panel arbitrators Am. Arbitration Assn. Served to lt. col. USAFR, 1953-75. Mem. N.Y. State Bar Assn., N.Mex. Bar Assn., Pi Beta Gamma. Office: 2124 Broadway New York NY 10023-1722 also: 330 Garfield St Santa Fe NM 87501-2640 E-mail: gene@bgkgroup.com.

WOLLAN, EUGENE, lawyer; b. N.Y.C., Nov. 2, 1928; s. Isidor and Mollie (Elterman) W.; m. Jean B. Sack, June 6, 1954 (div. 1974); children— Eric G., Jennifer J.; m. Marjorie Cama, Nov. 25, 1977; stepchildren— Valerie M. Rosenwasser, Jon J. Rosenwasser. B.A. cum laude, Harvard U., 1948, J.D., 1950. Bar: N.Y., 1950, U.S. Dist. Ct. (so. and ea. dists.) N.Y. 1953. U.S. Ct. Appeals (2d cir.) 1955, U.S. Ct. Mil. Appeals 1951, U.S. Supreme Ct. 1960; cert. arbitrator and umpire. Assoc. Rein Mound & Cotton, N.Y.C., 1953-62, ptnr., 1963-87, Mound, Cotton, Wollan & Greengrass, 1987—. Served to col. USAR, 1951-81. Mem. Internat. Assn. Ins. Counsel, Def. Rsch. Inst., Internat. Soc. Barristers, Assn. Internationale De Droit Des Assurances, N.Y.C. Bar Assn., N.Y. County Lawyers, Judge Advocates Assn., Aida Reins. and Ins. Arbitration Soc., Harvard Club (N.Y.C.), Met. Opera Guild (N.Y.C.). Federal civil litigation, State civil litigation, Insurance. Home: 430 E 57th St New York NY 10022-3061 Office: Mound Cotton Wollan & Greengrass One Battery Park Plz New York NY 10004 E-mail: ewollan@moundcotton.com.

WOLLE, CHARLES ROBERT, federal judge; b. Sioux City, Iowa, Oct. 16, 1935; s. William Carl and Vivian (Down) W.; m. Kerstin Birgitta Wennerstrom, June 26, 1961; children: Karl Johan Knut, Erik Vernon, Thomas Dag, Aaron Charles. AB, Harvard U., 1959; JD, Iowa Law Sch., 1961. Bar: Iowa 1961. Assoc. Shull, Marshall & Marks, Sioux City, 1961-67, ptnr., 1968-80; judge Dist. Ct. Iowa, Sioux City, 1981-83; justice Iowa Supreme Ct., Sioux City and Des Moines, 1983-87; judge U.S. Dist. Ct. (so. dist.) Iowa, Des Moines, 1987-92, chief judge, 1992-99, sr. U.S. dist. judge, 2001—. Faculty Nat. Jud. Coll., Reno, 1983—. Editor Iowa Law Rev., 1960-61 Vice pres. bd. dirs. Sioux City Symphony, 1972-77; bd. dirs. Morningside Coll., Sioux City, 1977-81 Fellow Am. Coll. Trial Lawyers; mem. ABA, Sioux City C. of C. (bd. dirs. 1977-78) Avocations: sports, art, music, literature. Office e-mail: charles r. Office: Sr US Dist Judge US Dist Ct SD IA 110 E Ct St Des Moines IA 50309 E-mail: wolle@iasd.uscourts.gov.

WOLLER, JAMES ALAN, lawyer; b. Adrian, Mich., Dec. 27, 1946; s. Robert Arthur and Florence Emma (Jacob) W.; m. Jill Ann Samis, Aug. 18, 1968 (div. Aug. 1978); 1 child, Emily Erin; m. Elizabeth Julia Frey, May 22, 1982 (div. Apr. 1999); m. Carol Pierini, Oct. 29, 1999. BA, U. Mich., 1969; JD, Columbia U., 1974. Bar: N.J. 1974, U.S. Dist. Ct. N.J. 1974, U.S. Tax Ct. 1976, U.S. Supreme Ct. 1995. Assoc. McCarter & English, Newark, 1974-79; v.p. Pfaltz & Woller, PA, Summit, N.J., 1979-86, pres., 1987—. Editor Columbia U. Human Rights Law Rev., 1973-74. Mem.: ABA, Summit Bar Assn. (pres. 1987—88), Union County Bar Assn., NJ Bar Assn., Columbia Law Sch. Assn. NJ (trustee 1992—97, v.p. 1997—2001, pres. 2001—), Raritan Yacht Club (Perth Amboy, NJ) (fin. sec. 1988—89, treas. 1989—92, vice commodore 1993—94, commodore 1994—95), Downtown Club (trustee 1997—99, treas. 1999, v.p. 2000, pres. 2001). Republican. Methodist. Avocation: sailing. Banking, Corporate, general, Property, real (including real estate development, water). Home: The Gatehouse 249 Hanover St Annapolis MD 21401 Office: Pfaltz & Woller PA 382 Springfield Ave Ste 217 Summit NJ 07901-2780 E-mail: jimwoller@aol.com.

WOLLINS, DAVID HART, lawyer; b. N.Y.C., Nov. 1, 1952; s. Donald John Wollins and Constance Joy Graham; m. Leslie Bjerg Lilly, Apr. 1, 1989; children: Alexandra Bjerg Lilly W., David Hart Jr. BS in Fin. and Mktg., U. Pa., 1974; JD, New Eng. Sch. Law, 1978. Bar: N.Y. 1979, U.S. Dist. Ct. (ea. and so. dists.) N.Y. 1979, U.S. Dist. Ct. Colo. 1986, U.S. Dist. Ct. (ea. dist.) Calif. 1999 U.S. Ct. Appeals (10th cir.) 1986, U.S. Ct. Appeals (fed., D.C. and 2d cirs.) 1990, U.S. Ct. Appeals (9th cir.), 1992, U.S. Ct. Claims 1983, U.S. Supreme Ct. 1994. Pres. Nature's Way Recycling Co., Boston, 1974-75; summer assoc. Phillips, Nizer, Benjamin, Krim & Ballon, N.Y.C., 1976-78, assoc., 1978-86; of counsel Cortez and Friedman, P.C., Englewood, Colo., 1986-87; mem. firm, co-head litigation dept. Brenman, Raskin, Friedlob & Tenenbaum, P.C., Denver, 1987-91; shareholder, head litigation dept. McGeady Sisneros & Wollins, P.C., Denver, 1991-95; spl. counsel Jonathan J. Hellman & Assoc., P.C., Englewood, Colo., 1995-96; mng. ptnr. Wollins, Hellman & Green, Denver, 1996—2001, Wollins & Hellman, P.C., Denver, 2001—. Pro bono atty., City N.Y., 1978-86. Author short stories and numerous poems. Mem.: Denver Bar Assn., Colo. Trial Lawyers Assn., Colo. Bar Assn., NY Bar Assn. Federal civil litigation, General civil litigation, Securities. Home: 120 Fairfax St Denver CO 80220 Office: Wollins & Hellman PC 720 S Colorado Blvd Ste 620S Denver CO 80246-1943 Fax: 303-758-8111. E-mail: dhwollins@cs.com.

WOLLMAN, ERIC, lawyer; b. Bklyn., May 26, 1951; s. Harry and Lillian (Levine) W. AA, Kingsborough Community Coll., 1970; BA, Bklyn. Coll., 1973; JD, Bklyn. Law Sch., 1993. Bar: N.J. 1994, N.Y. 1996. Exec. asst. to treas. Dept. Fin., N.Y.C., 1973-76; supervising investment analyst Office of Comptroller, N.Y.C., 1976-85, project mgr., 1985-90, adminstrv. mgr.proxy unit, 1990-92, dir. corp. governance, 1993-94, adminstrv. mgr., 1994-96, assoc. gen. counsel, 1996—2001, dep. dir. contracting, 2001—. Exec. prodr., host Second to None TV program, 1995-2001. Vice pres. Com. to Preserve Brighton Beach, Bklyn., 1989; aux. capt. N.Y.C. Police Dept., 1973—; mem. Pub. Works Forum, 1991-96, commr. of deeds. Recipient award of valor N.Y.C. Police Dept., award of merit United Fund of Greater N.Y. Mem. ABA, NRA, N.Y. County Lawyers Assn., Am. Assn. Jewish Lawyers and Jurists, Bklyn. Coll. Alumni Assn., Bklyn. Law Sch. Alumni Assn., Aux. Police Benevolent Assn., Phi Delta Phi. Democrat. Jewish. Government contracts and claims. Home: 2209 E 28th St Brooklyn NY 11229-5057 Office: NYC Office of Comptroller 1 Centre St Rm 736 New York NY 10007-1602 E-mail: stnonradio@yahoo.com.

WOLLMAN, ROGER LELAND, federal judge; b. Frankfort, S.D., May 29, 1934; s. Edwin and Katherine Wollman; m. Diane Marie Schroeder, June 21, 1959; children: Steven James, John Mark, Thomas Roger. BA, Tabor Coll., Hillsboro, Kans., 1957; JD magna cum laude, U. S.D., 1962; LLM, Harvard U., 1964. Bar: S.D. 1964. Sole practice, Aberdeen, 1964—71; justice S.D. Supreme Ct., 1971—85, chief justice, 1978—82; judge U.S. Ct. Appeals (8th cir.), 1985—, chief judge, 1999—2002; states atty. Brown County, Aberdeen, 1967—71. Served with U.S. Army, 1957—59. Office: US Ct Appeals US Courthouse & Fed Bldg 400 S Phillips Ave Rm 315 Sioux Falls SD 57104-6851

WOLNITZEK, STEPHEN DALE, lawyer; b. Covington, Ky., Mar. 13, 1949; s. Frederick William Jr. and Mary Ruth (Meiners) W.; m. Katherine Anita Bishop, Dec. 15, 1972; children: Marcus Stephen, Justin Bishop. BA cum laude, U. Notre Dame, 1970; JD, U. Cin., 1974. Bar: Ky. 1975, U.S. Dist. Ct. (ea. dist.) Ky. 1976, U.S. Supreme Ct. 1978, U.S. Dist. ct. (we. dist.) Ky. 1981, U.S. Ct. Appeals (6th cir.) 1991. Dep. sheriff Kenton County, Covington, 1971—74; assoc. Taliaferro & Smith, Covington, 1975-80; ptnr. Taliaferro, Smith, Mann, Wolnitzek & Schachter, Covington, 1980-86; officer Smith, Wolnitzek, Schachter & Rowekamp P.S.C., Covington, 1986-96; pres. Wolnitzek, Rowekamp, Bender & Bonar, P.S.C., Covington, 1996-98, Wolnitzek, Rowekamp & Bonar, P.S.C., Covington, 1998—2002, Wolnitzek & Rowekamp PSC, Covington, 2002—. Bd. dirs. Ky. Legal Svcs. Plan Inc., 1984-96; adj. prof. Samuel Chase Coll. Law, No. Ky. U., 1995-98; mem. Ky. Jud. Retirement and Removal Commn. (now Ky. Jud. Conduct Commn.), 1995—, chair, 1996— Mem. exec. com. Kenton County Boys-Girls Club, 1981-2003, sec., 1995, v.p., 1996, pres., 1997; mem. exec. com. Ky. Law Enforcement Coun., Frankfort, 1984-93, vice chmn., 1991-93, chair cert. com., 1986-93; mem. City Coun., Ft. Wright, Ky., 1984-85, mem. Bd. Adjustment, 1986-97, vice chair, 1995-97; pres. No. Ky. Comty. Ctr., Covington, 1985-86; mem. bd. visitors Chase Coll. Law, no. Ky. U., 1995-97; bd. dirs. Kenton Housing Inc., 1986—, sec., 1991-93, v.p., 1993-95, pres., 1995-97; trustee No. Ky. Youth Leadership Found., 1992-2003, exec. com. bd. dirs., 1992-2003, pres., 1996-2001; gen. chair diocesean annual appeal Diocese of Covington, Ky., 2001. Recipient Roy Taylor award No. Ky. Legal Aid Soc., 1985, Disting. Lawyer award No. Ky. Bar Assn., 1998; named Vol. of Yr., Community Chest United Appeal, Cin., 1986. Fellow: No. Ky. Bar Found. (charter life), Ky. Bar Found. (bd. dirs. 1989—94, 1995—2000, charter life), Am. Bar Found.; mem.: So.Conf. Bar Presidents, Nat. Conf. Bar Presidents, Fraternal Order Police (Ky. gen. counsel 1975—), U. Cin. Alumni Assn. (trustee, bd. dirs. 1999—, treas. 2002—), Def. Rsch. Inst., Ky. Def. Counsel. (bd. dirs. 1982—86), Nat. Coun. Sch. Bd. Attys., Ky. Coun. Sch. Bd. Attys. (bd. dirs. 1981—87), Assn. Def. Trial Attys., Ky. Bar Assn. (bd. govs. 1984—96, chmn. ann. conv. 1986, chmn. ho. of dels. 1986, v.p. 1992—93, pres. 1994—95), Notre Dame Club Cin. Democrat. Roman Catholic. Avocations: sports, reading. State civil litigation, Education and schools, Insurance. Home: 1836 Beacon Hl Covington KY 41011-3684 Office: PO Box 352 502 Greenup St Covington KY 41011-2522 E-mail: wolnitfam@fuse.net.

WOLPER, BEATRICE EMENS, lawyer; b. New Haven, Nov. 28, 1945; BA, U. Cin., 1974; JD cum laude, No. Ky. U., 1978. Bar: Ohio 1979. Assoc., then ptnr. Emens, Kegler, Brown, Hill & Ritter, Columbus, Ohio, 1979-97; ptnr. Chester, Willcox & Saxbe, LLP, Columbus, 1997—. Pres., founder Women's Bus. Bd., Columbus, 1984—; bd. mem., exec. com. Ctr. Sci. and Industry, Columbus, 1994—. Author: Family Business Basics, 2000. Participant NAFTA, Washington, 1993; del. White House Conf. on Small Bus., Washington, 1995. Named Entrepreneur of the Yr., YWCA, Columbus, 1993, Women of Achievement, Ernst & Young/Inc. Mag., Columbus, 1993. Mem. Internat. Women's Forum (pres. Ohio chpt. 1994—), Columbus Bar Assn. (chair securities commn. 1987-89), Capital Club (chair 1994-96), Columbus C. of C. (bd. mem. 1994—). Avocations: fly fishing, geology, hiking, reading. Corporate, general, Estate planning. Home: 9592 Lake Of The Woods Dr Galena OH 43021-9622 Office: Chester Willcox & Saxbe LLP 65 East State St Ste 1000 Columbus OH 43215

WOLSON, CRAIG ALAN, lawyer; b. Toledo, Feb. 20, 1949; s. Max A. and Elaine B. (Cohn) W.; m. Ellen Carol Schulgasser, Oct. 26, 1986; children: Lindsey, Michael and Geoffrey (triplets). BA, U. Mich., 1971, JD, 1974. Bar: N.Y. 1975, U.S. Dist. Ct. (so. and ea. dists.) N.Y. 1975, U.S. Ct. Appeals (2d cir.) 1975, U.S. Supreme Ct. 1978. Assoc. Shearman & Sterling, N.Y.C., 1974—81; v.p., asst. gen. counsel Thomson McKinnon Securities Inc., N.Y.C., 1981—85; v.p., sec., gen. counsel J.D. Mattus Co., Inc., Greenwich, Conn., 1985—88; also bd. dirs. J.D. Mattus Co., Inc. and affiliated cos., Greenwich, Conn.; v.p., asst. gen. counsel Chem. Bank, N.Y.C., 1988—95; of counsel Williams & Harris, N.Y.C., 1995-96; ptnr. Williams & Harris LLP, N.Y.C., 1996-97; counsel Brown & Wood L.L.P., N.Y.C., 1997-98, Mayer, Brown & Platt, N.Y.C., 1999-2001; spl. counsel Schulte Roth & Zabel LLP, N.Y.C., 2001—03; ptnr. Duane Morris, LLP, N.Y.C., 2003—. Dep. clk. Lucas County Courthouse, Toledo, 1968-69, 71-72. Articles and administrv. editor U. Mich. Law Rev., 1973-74. Mem. ABA, N.Y. State Bar Assn., Assn. of Bar of City of N.Y. (securities regulation com. 1994-97, corp. law com. 1997-2000, project fin. com. 2000—), Corp. Bar. Assn. of Westchester and Fairfield, Phi Beta Kappa, Phi Eta Sigma, Pi Sigma Alpha. Avocations: reading, playing piano, fine dining, theater. Corporate, general, Securities, Banking. Home: 29 Punch Bowl Dr Westport CT 06880-2130 Office: Duane Morris LLP 380 Lexington Ave New York NY 10168

WONG, ALFRED MUN KONG, lawyer; b. Honolulu, Sept. 12, 1930; s. Inn and Mew Kung (Choy) Wong; m. Laureen Hong, Nov. 20, 1965; children: Peter Marn On, Julie Li Sharn. Student, U. Hawaii, 1948—50; BS, Marquette U., Milw., 1953; JD, U. Calif., 1964. Bar: Hawaii 1964. With Thomas Lee, CPA, 1961—62; mem. firm Scott and Balacco, San Francisco, 1962—64; contract atty. Honolulu Redevel. Agy., 1968—71; mng. dir. Takushi, Funaki Wong & Stone, Attys.-at-Law, Honolulu, 1964—2002; of counsel Takushi Wong Lee & Yee, Honolulu, 2002—. Adj. prof. U. Hawaii Law Sch., 1980—82; mem. bd. bar examiners State of Hawaii, 1968—79; mem. Hawaii Jud. Selection Commn., 1979—85, chmn., 1983—85. Bd. dirs. Pacific coun. Girls Scouts U.S., 1973—78; pres. Niu Valley Cmty. Assn., 1975, bd. dirs., 1974, 1976—77; dir. Maryknoll Schs., 1995—, v.p., 1999—2002, chmn., 2002—; mem. exec. com. Friends Hawaii Charities; mem. spl. rev. com. William S. Richardson Law Sch., U. Hawaii, 1995. Capt. C.E. U.S. Army, 1953—61. Recipient medal, Chgo. Tribune, 1952, 1953, award, Soc. Am. Mil. Engrs., 1952, 1953, Outstanding Svc. award, Pacific coun. Girl Scouts U.S., 1978, Cmty. Benefactor award, 1992. Mem.: ABA, Hawaii Bar Assn. (dir., chmn. unauthorized practice of law com., nominating com., real property and fin. svcs. sect.), Am. Law Inst., Friends of U. Hawaii Law Sch. (bd. dirs. 1987—93, pres. 1991—93), Hastings Coll. Law Alumni Assn. (bd. govs. 1978—, mem. bd. trustees 1066 Found. 1992—, nat. chair Hastings ann. fund 1993—94, v.p. 1995, Disting. Svc. award 1987, Alumnus of the Yr. award 1997), Honolulu Club (founding dir.), Waialae Country Club (bd. dirs. 1991—93, pres. 1993). Banking, Landlord-tenant, Property, real (including real estate development, water). Office: Takushi Wong Lee & Yee 841 Bishop St Honolulu HI 96813

WONG, CHRISTOPHER WAI C. lawyer; b. Kuala Lumpur, Federal Territory, Malaysia, Feb. 3, 1967; s. Kon Min Wong and Sow Yoong Chan. LLB with honors, U. Sheffield (Eng.), 1990. Bar: solicitor Supreme Ct. Eng. and Wales 1993; adv., solicitor Supreme Ct. Singapore 1995; legal practitioner High Ct. New South Wales, Australia 2000. Qualified arbitrator Denton Hall, London, 1991—93; pupil Khattar Wong & Ptnrs., Singapore, 1993-94; adv., solicitor Wong Partnership, Singapore, 1995-97, Kelvin Chia Partnership, Singapore, 1997-98, Harry Elias Partnership, Singapore, 1998-99; solicitor Baker & McKenzie, Sydney, 1999-2000, Minter Ellison, Sydney, 2000—, liaison officer Asian Focus Group, 2001—. Coach mock trial U. Sydney, 2000; presenter in field. Contbr. articles to profl. jours. Vol. multicultural affairs U. Sydney, 2000; mem. bd. legal edn. Student CTTE, Singapore, 1994. Mem. Law Soc. Eng. and Wales, Law Soc. Singapore, Law Soc. New South Wales, Malaysian & Singaporean Students Soc. (pres. 1987). Avocations: reading, travel, gym, swimming, music. Bankruptcy, Commercial, consumer (including collections, credit), Construction. Office: Minter Ellison Aurora Pl 88 Phillip St Sydney NSW 2000 Australia Fax: 612 9921-8123. E-mail: chris.wong@minterellison.com.

WONG, REUBEN SUN FAI, lawyer; b. Honolulu, Mar. 12, 1936; s. Lin and Ella Mew Quon (Ching) W.; m. Vera Hui, Dec. 4, 1966; children: Delwyn, Irwyn. BSCE, U. Hawaii, 1958; JD, U. Ill., 1964. Bar: Hawaii 1964, U.S. Dist. Ct. Hawaii 1964, U.S. Ct. Appeals (9th cir.) 1967, U.S. Supreme Ct. 1974. Law clk. Supreme Ct. of Hawaii, Honolulu, 1964-65; dep. corp. counsel City and County of Honolulu, 1965-67; adminstrv. asst. Hawaii Ho. of Reps., Honolulu, 1967; atty. pvt. practice, Honolulu, 1976—. Lectr. U. Hawaii, 1967-70. Vice chairperson Legislature's Adv. Study Commn. on Water Resources, Honolulu, 1982-85. Served to capt. USAF, 1959-62. Mem. ABA, Am. Judicature Soc., Assn. Trial Lawyers Am., Hawaii C. of C. (bd. dirs. 1976-80, v.p. 1977-78), Chinese C. of C. Hawaii (pres. 2002), Phi Alpha Delta. Lodges: Aloha Temple. Banking, General civil litigation, Property, real (including real estate development, water). Home: 15 Homelani Pl Honolulu HI 96817-1113 Office: 220 S King St Ste 2288 Honolulu HI 96813-4538

WONG-DIAZ, FRANCISCO RAIMUNDO, lawyer, educator; b. Havana, Cuba, Oct. 29, 1944; came to U.S., 1961; s. Juan and Teresa (Diaz de Villegas) Wong; 1 child, Richard Alan. BA with honors, No. Mich. U., 1965; MA with highest honors, U. Detroit, 1967; PhD, MA, U. Mich., 1974; JD, U. Calif., Berkeley, 1976. Bar: Calif. 1980, U.S. Dist. Ct. (no. dist.) Calif. 1990, Fla. 1987. Prof. City Coll. San Francisco, 1975—, dept. chmn., 1978-85; rsch. atty. Marin Superior Ct., 1980-81; ct. arbitrator Marin Mcpl. Ct., 1985; atty. pvt. practice, Kentfield, Calif., 1980—. Adj. asst. prof. San Francisco State U., 1977; assoc. dean Miami-Dade Coll., 1986; dir. Cutcliffe Cons., Inc., Hawthorne, LaFamila Ctr., Inc., San Rafael, Calif., 1980-85, Small Bus. Inst., Kentfield, 1982-86; cons. ICC Internat., San Francisco, 1980-82; polit. commentator Univision KDTV, 1980—. Author: American Politics in a Changing World, 1999; bd. editors Indsl. Rels. Law Jour., 1975-76; mem. editl. bd. Calif. Lawyer, 1991-93. Lector St. Sebastian's Ch., 1984—, parish coun., 1995; bd. dirs. Am. Cancer Soc., 1999—; mem. devel. rsch. program, fellowship com. U. Calif.-San Francisco, 2002-. Vis. scholar U. Calif., Berkeley Sch. Bus., 1983-84, U.S. Dept. State scholar, Washington, 1976; Horace C. Rackham fellow U. Mich., 1970, summer fellow U. Calif. Berkeley, 1995, Nat. Security Law Ctr. U. Va., 1996; named Best New Vol. of Yr., Am. Cancer Soc., 2000, One of One Hundred Most Influential Hispanics in the Nation, Hispanic Bus. Mag., Oct. 2000. Mem. ABA, Am. Polit. Sci. assn., Latino Ednl. Assn. (treas. 1985), Cuban Am. Nat. Coun., World Affairs Coun. (sem. leader San Francisco 1980), U. Calif. San Francisco PC Advocates, Commonwealth Club. Roman Catholic. General civil litigation, General practice, Other.

WONNELL, THOMAS BURKE, lawyer; b. Jan. 29, 1970; BA, U. Calif., San Diego, 1993; JD, Washington and Lee U., 1996. Bar: Alaska 1996, U.S. Dist. Ct. Alaska 1996, U.S. Ct. Appeals (9th cir.) 1998. Asst. mcpl. prosecutor Municipality of Anchorage, 1996-98; pvt. practice, Anchorage, 1998—. General civil litigation, Criminal, Family and matrimonial. Office: 2600 Denali St Ste 460 Anchorage AK 99503-2754

WOO, CHANG ROK, lawyer; b. Gyeongju, South Korea, Feb. 14, 1953; m. Ho Goun Chung Woo; children: Hye Won, Jae Hyong, Jae Ha. LLB, Seoul Nat. U., Korea, 1974; LLM, U. Wash. Law Sch., U.S.A, 1983. Judge advocate Navy, Seoul, Republic of Korea, 1976-79; assoc. Kim & Chang, Seoul, Republic of Korea, 1979-84, ptnr., 1984-92, Woo & Ptnrs., Seoul, Republic of Korea, 1992-97; mng. ptnr. Woo Yun Kang Jeong & Han, Seoul, Republic of Korea, 1997—. Lectr. Jud. Tng. and Rsch. Insts., The Supreme Ct. of Korea, 1995—99, vis. lawyer, 1976, Coudert Bros., N.Y.C., 1984; vis. scholar U. Calif., Boalt Hall, 1983. Author: A Brief Survey of Korean Corporate Liquidation and Bankruptcy Law, 1980, Residency as the Base for Tax Jurisdiction, 1996, Deductibility of Illegal Expenses, 1997, Tax Issues Related to Merger and Acquisition, 1997. Trustee EWHA Women's U., Republic of Korea, 1997—. Mem.: Inter-Pacific Bar Assn., Internat. Fiscal Assn., Internat. Bar Assn., Korean Bar Assn. Corporate, general, Government contracts and claims, Estate taxation. Office: Textile Ctr 11-13 Fl 944-31 Daechi-dong 135-713 Gangnam-gu Seoul Republic of Korea Fax: 82 2-528-5228. E-mail: crwoo@wooyun.co.kr.

WOO, VERNON YING-TSAI, lawyer, real estate developer, judge; b. Honolulu, Aug. 7, 1942; s. William Shu-Bin and Hilda Woo; children: Christopher Shu-Bin, Lia Gay. BA, U. Hawaii, 1964, MA, 1966; JD, Harvard U., 1969. Pres. Woo Kessner Duca & Maki, Honolulu, 1972-87; pvt. practice law Honolulu, 1987—. Judge per diem Honolulu Dist. Family Ct., 1978-84, 1995-2002. Bd. dirs. Boys and Girls Club of Honolulu,. 1985-95, pres., 1990-92. Mem.: ABA, Honolulu Bd. Realtors, Hawaii Bar Assn. Property, real (including real estate development, water). Home: 3936 Waokanaka St Honolulu HI 96813 Office: Harbor Ct 55 Merchant St Ste 1900 Honolulu HI 96813

WOOD, ALLISON LORRAINE, lawyer; b. N.Y.C., May 30, 1962; d. Walter C. and Joan T. Wood. BA, Pace U., 1984; JD, DePaul U., 1987; postgrad., Northwestern U. Bar: Ill. 1987, U.S. Dist. Ct. (no. dist.) Ill. 1989, Fed. Trial Bar 1990. Judicial extern U.S. Bankruptcy Ct., Chgo., 1987; pub. defender, Office of Pub. Defender Cook County, Ill., 1987-89; counsel Peoples Energy Corp., Chgo., 1989-93; ptnr. Albert, Whitehead, P.C., Chgo., 1993—. Adj. prof. DePaul U. Coll. Law, 1992—; hearing bd. chair Atty. Registration Disciplinary Commn. Chmn. bd. dirs. Ctrs. for New Horizons, 2001—; mem. Target Hope-Mentor; spkr. We Care Role Model. Mem. ABA (products sect., columnist trial sect. newsletter), Chgo. Bar Assn. (mem. editl. bd., columnist trial practice), Cook County Bar Assn. (bd. dirs., treas. 1993-98). Bankruptcy, General civil litigation, Commercial, consumer (including collections, credit). Office: Albert Whitehead PC Ten N Dearborn Ste 600 Chicago IL 60602

WOOD, DIANE PAMELA, judge; b. Plainfield, N.J., July 4, 1950; d. Kenneth Reed and Lucille (Padmore) Wood; m. Dennis James Hutchinson, Sept. 2, 1978 (div. May 1998); children: Kathryn Hutchinson, David Hutchinson, Jane Hutchinson. BA, U. Tex., 1971, JD, 1975. Bar: Tex. 1975, D.C. 1978, Ill. 1993. Law clk. U.S. Ct. Appeals (5th cir.), 1975—76, U.S. Supreme Ct., 1976—77; atty.-advisor U.S. Dept. State, Washington, 1977—78; assoc. Covington & Burling, Washington, 1978—80; asst. prof. law Georgetown U. Law Ctr., Washington, 1980—81, U. Chgo., 1981—88, prof. law, 1988—95, assoc. dean, 1989—92, Harold J. and Marion F. Green prof. internat. legal studies, 1990—95, sr. lectr. law, 1995—; spl. cons. antitrust divsn. internat. guide U.S. Dept. Justice, 1986—87, dep. asst. atty. gen. antitrust divsn., 1993—95; judge U.S. Ct. Appeals (7th cir.), 1995—. Contbr. articles to profl. jours. Bd. dirs. Hyde Park-Kenwood Cmty. Health Ctr., 1983—85. Mem.: Internat. Acad. Comparative Law, Am. Law Inst., Am. Soc. Internat. Law, Phi Alpha Delta. Democrat.

WOOD, DONALD F. lawyer; b. Bonne Terre, Mo., July 25, 1944; BSBA, Washington U., 1966; JD, Harvard U., 1969. Bar: Tex. 1970. Mng. ptnr. Vinson & Elkins, L.L.P., Austin. Fellow Houston Bar Found. (chmn. 1991); mem. Beta Gamma Sigma, Omicron Delta Kappa. Taxation, general. Office: Vinson & Elkins LLP 2801 Via Fortuna Ste 100 Austin TX 78746 E-mail: dwood@velaw.com.

WOOD, FRANK MAXWELL, lawyer; b. Forest Park, Ga. m. Suzanne Brunson; children: Frank, Sydney, James. BA, LaGrange Coll., 1981; JD, U. Ga., 1985. Law clk. Floyd County Superior Ct., 1985—87; staff atty. Pros. Attys.' Coun. Ga., 1992—94; asst. dist. atty. Ocmulgee Dist. Atty.'s Office, 1994—97; pvt. practice Macon, Ga.; U.S. atty. Mid. Dist. Ga., 2001—. Mem. Martha Bowman Meml. United Meth. Ch. With USAF, lt. col. Ga. Air Nat. Guard. Office: Mid Dist Ga Thomas Jefferson Bldg 433 Cherry St Macon GA 31201*

WOOD, HARLINGTON, JR., federal judge; b. Springfield, Ill., Apr. 17, 1920; s. Harlington and Marie (Green) W. AB, U. Ill., 1942, JD, 1948. Bar: Ill. 1948. Practiced in, Springfield, 1948-69; mem. firm Wood & Wood, 1948—58, 1961—69; U.S. atty. So. Dist. Ill., 1958-61; assoc. dep. atty. gen. for U.S. attys. Justice Dept., Washington, 1969-70, assoc. dep. atty. gen., 1970-72, asst. atty. gen. civil div., 1972-73; U.S. dist. judge So. Dist. Ill., Springfield, 1973-76; circuit judge U.S. Ct. Appeals (7th cir.), Springfield, 1976—92, sr. judge, 1992—. Adj. prof. Sch. Law, U. Ill., Champaign, 1993; disting. vis. prof. St. Louis U. Law Sch., 1996—. Chmn. Adminstrv. Office Oversight Com., 1988-90; mem. Long Range Planning Com., 1991-96. U.S. Army, 1942—46. Recipient Profl. Lifetime Achievement award, Inns of Ct., 2002. Office: US Ct Appeals PO Box 299 600 E Monroe St Springfield IL 62701-1626*

WOOD, JAMES ALLEN, retired lawyer; b. McMinnville, Tenn., Jan. 14, 1906; s. Ira and Emma (Calhoun) W.; m. Eva Beth Sellers, Dec. 28, 1941; 1 son, Eben Calhoun. AB, U. Tenn., 1929; LL.B., U. Tex., 1934. Bar: Tex. 1934. Tchr. Bolton H.S., Alexandria, La., 1929-32; since practiced in Corpus Christi, 1971-97; ret., 1998. State dist. judge, Corpus Christi, 1941-43; mem. rules adv. com. Supreme Ct. Tex., 1949-86. Author 7 vols. poetry; contbr. articles to profl. jours.; author: Life on a Warren County Farm (Tenn.) 1906-1923, 1996, Early Bench and Bar of Corpus Christi, 1996, Items: Serious of Not, 1997, Moody Shadows, 1962, Muted Echoes, 1970, For Exiles, 1973, Last Sunset, 1974, Blunt Arrows, 1979, Bottom Lines, 1987, Wandering Lines, 1993. Bd. dirs. Nueces River Authority, 1972-89, pres., 1981-84, life time hon. dir., 1989—. Lt. USNR, 1943-45. Fellow Am. Coll. Trial Lawyers; mem. ABA, Tex. Bar Assn., Nueces County Bar Assn. (pres. 1941) General practice. Home and Office: 458 Dolphin Pl Corpus Christi TX 78411-1514

WOOD, JAMES JERRY, lawyer; b. Rockford, Ala., Aug. 13, 1940; s. James Ronald and Ada Love Wood; m. Earline Luckie, Aug. 9, 1959; children: James Jerry, William Gregory, Diana Lynn. AB, Samford U., 1964, JD, 1969. Bar: Ala. 1969, U.S. Supreme Ct. 1976. Dir. legal affairs Med. Assn. State of Ala., Montgomery, 1969-70; asst. atty. gen. State of Ala., Montgomery, 1970-72; asst. U.S. atty. Middle Dist. Ala., Montgomery, 1972-76; pvt. practice, 1977-78; pres. Wood & Parnell, P.A., Montgomery, Ala., 1979-89; pvt. practice Montgomery, 1990—. Gen. counsel Ala. Builders Self-Insurers Fund, Home Builders Assn. of Ala.; chmn. character and fitness com. Ala. State Bar, 1981-84, 86-89, chair task force on quality of life, 1990-92, chair task force on mem. svcs., 1994-96. Capt. USAR, 1974-79. Fellow Am. Bar Found. (Ala. state chair), Ala. Law Found.; mem. ABA (ho. of dels. 1990-98), FBA (pres. Montgomery chpt. 1974-75), Am. Nat. Inns of Ct., Am. Soc. Assn. Execs., Ala. Assn. Workers Compensation Group Self-Insured Funds (chmn.), Ala. Bar Assn., Montgomery Bar Assn., Ala. Def. Lawyers Assn., Ala. Law Inst., Ala. Coun. Assn. Execs. (pres. 2001), Def. Rsch. Inst., Rotary (pres. Montgomery Capital chpt. 1986-87, 96-97). Republican. Baptist. Construction, Corporate, general, Workers' compensation. Office: PO Box 241206 Montgomery AL 36124-1206 E-mail: jjwood@mindspring.com.

WOOD, JENNIFER LYNN, lawyer; b. Redwood Falls, Minn., Mar. 14, 1964; d. David George and Jacqueline (Palmer) W. BA cum laude, Gustavus Adolphus Coll., 1986; JD cum laude, U. Minn., 1995. Bar: Minn. 1995, Fla. 2000. Law clk. Dist. Ct. Minn., Mpls., 1995-97; assoc. Zalk & Eayrs, Mpls., 1997-98; shareholder Zalk & Wood, Mpls., 1999-2000; staff atty. U.S. Dist. Ct. (no. dist.) Fla., Pensacola, 2000—. Humphrey fellow Humphrey Inst. Policy Forum, Mpls., 1995-96. Mem. Fla. Bar, Escambia-Santa Rosa Bar Assn. Family and matrimonial. Office: US Dist Ct 1 N Palafax St Pensacola FL 32501

WOOD, JOHN MARTIN, lawyer; b. Detroit, Mar. 29, 1944; s. John Francis and Margaret Kathleen (Lynch) Wood; m. Judith Anne Messer; children: Timothy Peter, Meagan Anne. BA, Boston Coll., 1966; JD, Cath. U. Am., 1969. Bar: D.C. 1970, Va. 2001, U.S. Dist. Ct. D.C. 1970, U.S. Dist. Ct. Va. 2001, U.S. Ct. Appeals (D.C. cir.) 1973, U.S. Ct. Appeals (3d cir.) 1973, U.S. Ct. Appeals (4th cir.) 1973, U.S. Supreme Ct. 1973. Trial atty, tax divsn. Dept. Justice, Washington, 1969-73; assoc. Reed Smith LLP, Washington, 1973-80, ptnr., 1980—, mng. ptnr., 1989-95, dir. legal pers., 1995-98. Dir. adv. bd. Salvation Army, Va. and Met. Washington, Leadership Washington, 1993—. Mem.: Fairfax Bar Assn., D.C. Bar Assn., The Currituck Club N.C., River Bend Golf and Country Club, Barristers Club Washington, Delta Sigma Pi, Phi Alpha Delta. Administrative and regulatory, General civil litigation, Federal civil litigation. Home: 9490 Oak Falls Ct Great Falls VA 22066-4143 Office: Reed Smith LLP 3110 Fairview Park Dr Ste 1400 Falls Church VA 22042 E-mail: jwood@reedsmith.com.

WOOD, JUDSON ROBERT, lawyer; b. Sherman, Tex., July 21, 1928; s. James Ralph and Kathleen (Cook) W.; m. Nancy Matthews, June 22, 1957; children: Judson Jr., Wright Matthews, John Charles. BBA, U. Tex., Austin, 1949, LLB, 1951. Bar: Tex. 1951, U.S. Dist. Ct. (no. dist.) Tex. 1957, U.S. Dist. Ct. (ea. dist.) Tex. 1962, U.S. Dist. Ct. (so. dist.) Tex. 1964, U.S. Ct. Appeals (5th cir.) 1964, U.S. Ct. Appeals (11th cir.) 1981. Assoc. Scurry, Scurry & Pace, Dallas, 1951-57; ptnr. Vinson & Elkins, Houston, 1957—. 1st lt. U.S. Army, 1952-54. Fellow Tex. Bar Found. (life); mem. Am. Bd. Trial Advocates, Tex. Assn. Def. Counsel, Houston Racquet Club, Houston Ctr. Club. Avocations: golf, photography. Insurance, Personal injury (including property damage). Home: 3229 Ella Lee Ln Houston TX 77019-5923 Office: Vinson & Elkins 3300 First City Tower 1001 Fannin St Ste 3300 Houston TX 77002-6706

WOOD, LEONARD JAMES, lawyer; b. Camden, N.J., Dec. 21, 1949; s. Leonard and Virginia (Ferraro) W.; m. Catherine Mary Dugan, June 29, 1979; children: Leonard James III, Tara Kathleen. BA, Manhattan Coll., 1972; JD, Rutgers U., 1976. Bar: N.J. 1976, U.S. Ct. Appeals (3d cir.) 1977, U.S. Supreme Ct. 1980. Law clk. to presiding judge Chancery div. Superior Ct. of N.J., Camden, 1976-77; ptnr. Console, Marmero, Li Volsi, Wood, Curcio, Berlin, NJ, 1977-89, Ferreri and Wood, Voorhees, NJ, 1989-95, Morelli & Rinaldi, 1995-97; sole practice, 1997-99; ptnr. Wade & Wood LLC, 2000—02; mng. ptnr. Wade, Long, Wood & Kennedy, LLC, 2003—. Mem. ABA (family law sect.), N.J. State Bar Assn. (family law sect.), Camden County Bar Assn. Family and matrimonial, Personal injury (including property damage), Property, real (including real estate development, water). Office: 1250 Chews Landing Rd Laurel Springs NJ 08021-2816

WOOD, PAULA DAVIDSON, lawyer; b. Oklahoma City, Dec. 20, 1952; d. Paul James and Anna Mae (Ferrero) Davidson; m. Andrew E. Wood; children: Michael Paul, John Roland. BS, Okla. State U., 1976; JD, Oklahoma City U., 1982. Bar: Okla. 1983, U.S. Dist. Ct. (we. dist.) Okla. 1983, U.S. Supreme Ct. 1995; cert. pub. mgr. Pvt. practice, Oklahoma City, 1984-85; ptnr. Davidson & Wood, Oklahoma City, 1985-87; child support enforcement counsel Okla. Dept. Human Svcs., Oklahoma City, 1987-92, child support adminstr. (IV-D dir.), 1992-96; pvt. practice Oklahoma City, Okla., 1997—. Adj. instr. Tech. Inst. Okla. State U., Oklahoma City, 1985. Articles editor Oklahoma City U. Law Rev., 1982. Bd. dirs. Okla. Youth Symphony, 2000-01. Mem. Okla. Bar Assn. (sec. family law sect. 1987, Golden Gavel award 1987, Artist of the Yr. 1999), Nat. Child Support Enforcement Assn. (bd. dirs. 1995, sec. 1997), Okla. Child Support Enforcement Assn. (pres. 1992), S.W. Regional Child Assn. (pres. 1996), Western Interstate Child Support Enforcement Coun. (sec. 1995). Republican. Roman Catholic. Home: 3020 Shadybrook Dr Midwest City OK 73110-4133 Office: 3904 E Reno Oklahoma City OK 73117 Office Fax: 405-619-9338. E-mail: pwoodatty@aol.com.

WOOD, ROBERT ALEXANDER, lawyer; b. Cleve., Sept. 4, 1939; m. Dorita M. Wood, June 18, 1966; children: Melissa, Robert Gregory; m. Zoe Breen, Apr. 25, 1992; children: Liana, Ashley, Cara. BA, U. Mich., 1961; JD, Cleve. Marshall Sch. Law, 1969. Bar: Conn. 1972, Ohio 1969, U.S. Ct. Mil. Appeals 1973. Pvt. practice, Avon, Conn., 1972-89; claims counsel Lawyers Title Ins. Co., Richmond, Va., 1989-91; dist. counsel Stewart Title, Norfolk, Va., 1991-93; asst. gen. counsel Midland Title Security, Inc., Cleve., 1993—. Lectr. in field. Jr. warden Trinity Cathedral, Cleve., 1996—. Comdr. JAGC USNR, 1961-83. Mem. Ohio Bar Assn., Cleve. Bar Assn. (real estate sect.), Naval Res. Lawyers Assn., Ohio Land Title Assn. Insurance. Office: Midland Title Security Inc 1360 E 9th St Ste 500 Cleveland OH 44114-1705 E-mail: rawood@firstam.com.

WOOD, ROBERT CHARLES, lawyer, real estate developer; b. Chgo., Apr. 8, 1956; s. Roy Edward and Mildred Lucille (Jones) W.; m. Jennifer Jo Briggs, Oct. 1984; children: Jacqueline Jones, Reagan Keith. BA in History, BBA in Real Estate, So. Meth. U., 1979, JD, 1982. Bar: Tex. 1983. Appraiser McClellan-Massey, Dallas, 1977-79; researcher, acquisitions officer Amstar Fin. Corp., Dallas, 1979-80; prin. Robert Wood Cons., Dallas, 1981-98; ptnr. Welch & Wood Attys. and Y2K Cons., Dallas, 1998-2000; pvt. practice, Dallas, 1995—; real estate investor and developer, 1998—. Cons. Plan Mktg. Cos., 1983-84; pvt. practice law, Dallas, 1983-84; gen. counsel Diversified Benefits, Inc., Dallas, 1984-86; nat. accts. mgr. Lomas & Nettleton Real Estate Group, Dallas, 1987-88; sr. pension cons., prin. Eppler, Guerin &Turner, 1988-93; chmn. adv. coun. on devel. Medisend, 1991; nat. consulting coord. fin. advisors coun., v.p. Callan Assocs., San Francisco, 1994-95; atty. at law, 1995—; exec. v.p., gen. counsel, Rushmore Investment Advisors, Plano, Tex., 2002-. Author: Electionomics: How the Money Managers View the Election, 1992, After the Congress Vote: How the Managers See Things Now, 1993, Y2K--The Year 2000 Issue: How Y2K Affects the Markets, 1998; mem. So. Meth. U. Law Rev., 1981-82; contbr. articles to profl. publs. Bd. dirs. Dallas unit Am. Cancer Soc., 1982-87, mem. spl. events com., 1986-87, mem. crusade com., 1987-88, mem. medisend adv. com., 1988-94, chmn. corp. devel. bd., 1989-95. Mem. Tex. Bar Assn., Phila. Bar Assn., Phi Gamma Delta. Avocations: skiing, tennis, bicycling. Finance, Corporate, general, Securities. E-mail: rccwood@aol.com.

WOOD, ROBERT WARREN, lawyer; b. Des Moines, July 5, 1955; s. Merle Warren and Cecily Ann (Sherk) W.; m. Beatrice Wood, Aug. 4, 1979; 1 child, Bryce Mercedes. Student, U. Sheffield, Eng., 1975-76; AB, Humboldt State U., 1976; JD, U. Chgo., 1979. Bar: Ariz. 1979, Calif. 1980, Wyo. 2000, N.Y. 1989, D.C. 1993, Mont. 1998, U.S Tax Ct. 1980, Wyo.; Roll of Solicitors of Eng. and Wales, 1998. Assoc. Jennings, Strouss, Phoenix, 1979-80, McCutchen, Doyle, San Francisco, 1980-82, Broad, Khourie, San Francisco, 1982-85, Steefel, Levitt & Weiss, San Francisco, 1985-87, ptnr., 1987-91, Bancroft & McAlister, San Francisco, 1991-93; prin. Robert W. Wood, P.C., San Francisco, 1993—. Instr. in law U. Calif. San Francisco, 1981-82. Author: Taxation of Corporate Liquidations: A Complete Planning Guide, 1987, 2nd edit., 1994, The Executive's Complete Guide to Business Taxes, 1989, Corporate Taxation: Complete Planning and Practice Guide, 1989, S Corporations, 1990, The Ultimate Tax Planning Guide for Growing Companies, 1991, Taxation of Damage Awards and Settlement Payments, 1991, 2nd edit., 1998, Tax Strategies in Hiring, Retaining and Terminating Employees, 1991, The Home Office Tax Guide, 1991; co-author: (with others) California Closely Held Corporations: Tax Planning and Practice Guide, 1987, Legal Guide to Independent Contractor Status, 3d edit., 2000; editor: California Small Busines Guide, 4 vols., 1998, Home Office Money & Tax Guide, 1992, Tax Aspects of Settlements and Judgements, 1993, 2d edit., 1998, cumulative supplement, 2000; editor-in-chief The M & A Tax Report; editor: Limited Liability Companies: Formation, Operation and Conversion, 1994, 2d edit., 2001, Limited Liability Partnerships: Formation, Operation and Taxation, 1996; mem. editl. bd. Real Estate Tax Digest, The Practical Accountant, Jour. Real Estate Taxation. Fellow Am. Coll. Tax Counsel; mem. Calif. Bd. Legal Specialization (cert. specialist taxation), Can. Bar Assn., Bohemian Club, Law Coun. Australia. Republican. Mergers and acquisitions, Corporate taxation, Personal income taxation. Office: 639 Front St #200 San Francisco CA 94111

WOOD, TRACEY ANN, lawyer; b. Milw., June 21, 1967; d. Kenneth J. and Susan J. (Hayden) Wood; 1 child, Alexander Case Roller. BA, Marquette U., 1988; JD, U. Wis., 1992. Bar: Wis. 1993, U.S. Dist. Ct. (we. and ea. dists.) Wis. 1993, U.S. Ct. Appeals (7th cir.) 1993. Atty. Kalal & Assocs., Madison, 1993-96, Thomas, Kelly, Habermehl & Wood, S.C., Madison, 1996-98; ptnr. Van Wagner & Wood, S.C., Madison, 1998—. Mem. Nat. Assn. Criminal Def. Lawyers (bd. dirs.), Wis. Assn. Criminal Def. Lawyers, Dane County Criminal Def. Lawyers Assn. (pres. 1998), DUI Coll. (state del.). Avocations: bicycling, hiking, yoga. Criminal, Juvenile. Office: Van Wagner & Wood SC 10 E Doty St Ste 701 Madison WI 53703 E-mail: traceyawood@yahoo.com.

WOOD, WILLIAM MCBRAYER, lawyer; b. Greenville, S.C., Jan. 27, 1942; s. Oliver Gillan and Grace (McBrayer) W.; m. Nancy Cooper, 1973 (dec. 1993); children: Walter, Lewis; m. Jeanette Dobson Haney, June 25, 1994. BS in Acctg., U. S.C., 1964, JD cum laude, 1972; LLM in Estate Planning (scholar), U. Miami, 1980. Bar: S.C. 1972, Fla. 1979, D.C. 1973, U.S. Tax Ct. 1972, U.S. Ct. Claims 1972, U.S. Supreme Ct. 1977. Intern ct. of claims sect., tax divsn. U.S. Dept. Justice, 1971; law clk. to chief judge U.S. Ct. Claims, Washington, 1972-74; ptnr. firm Edwards Wood, Duggan & Reese, Greer and Greenville, 1974-78; asst. prof. law Cumberland Law Sch., Samford U., Birmingham, Ala., 1978-79; faculty Nat. Inst. Trial Advocacy: N.E. Regional Inst., 1979, 83-90, 95-97, Fla. Regional Inst., 1989; teaching team 5th intensive trial techniques course Hofstra U., 1983; assoc. then capital ptnr. firm Shutts & Bowen, Miami, 1980-85; sole practice Miami, 1985—; also Rock Hill, S.C., 1994—; of counsel Griffin, Smith, Caldwell, Helder & Lee, Monroe, N.C., 2001—. Contbg. editor: The Lawyers PC; Fla. editor: Drafting Wills and Trust Agreements; substantive com. editor ABA: The Tax Lawyer, 1983—. Pres. Piedmont Heritage Found., Inc. 1975-78; del. State Rep. Conv., 1985, 87, 90; exec. committeeman Miami-Dade County Republicans, 1988-94, co-gen. counsel, 1990-91; apptd. Miami-Dade County Indsl. Devel. Authority, 1990-94; mem. vestry Episc. Ch., 1993-94. With USAF, 1965-69, Vietnam. Decorated Air Force Commendation medal; recipient Am. Jurisprudence award in real property and tax I, 1971; winner Grand prize So. Living Mag. travel photo contest, 1969. Mem. ABA (taxation sect., teaching law com., 1994—), Greer C. of C. (pres. 1977, Outstanding leadership award 1976), Greater Greenville C. of C. (dir. 1977), Order Wig and Robe, Estate Planning Council South Fla., Omicron Delta Kappa. Club: Bankers (bd. govs. 1989-94). Lodge: Masons, Scottish Rite, Rotary. Estate planning, Probate (including wills, trusts), Estate taxation. Office: 5345 Wilgrove Mint Hill Rd Charlotte NC 28227-3467

WOODALL, PAUL OLIVER, JR., lawyer; b. Birmingham, Ala., June 4, 1968; m. Susan Kerns Woodall, Sept. 13, 1997. BA, U. of the South, 1991; JD magna cum laude, U. Ala., Tuscaloosa, 1995. Bar: Ala., U.S. Dist. Ct. (no. and mid. dists.) Ala. Atty. Gordon, Silberman, Birmingham, Ala., 1995—99, Ogletree, Deakins, Birmingham, 1999—2000, Walston, Wells, Anderson & Bains, Birmingham, 2000—. Mem.: ABA, Ala. Bar Assn.,

Birmingham Bar Assn., Order of Coif. Avocations: travel, music. Corporate, general, Mergers and acquisitions, Commercial, contracts (including sales of goods; commercial financing). Office: Walston Wells Anderson & Bains LLP Ste 500 505 20th St Birmingham AL 35203- Office Fax: 205-251-9600.

WOODALL, SAMUEL ROY, JR., lawyer; b. July 8, 1936; s. Samuel Roy Woodall; m. Jane Marvin Brock, Aug. 5, 1958; children: Samuel Roy III, Lawrence B., Claiborne A., George G. BA, U. Ky., 1958, LLB, 1962; postgrad., Yale U., 1959. Bar: Ky. 1962. Atty. Ky. Dept. Ins., 1962-64, gen. counsel, 1965-66; commr. ins. Commonwealth Ky., 1966-68; assoc. firm Wyatt, Grafton and Sloss, Louisville, 1968-69, ptnr., 1969-72; pres. Western Pioneer Life Ins. Co. (and predecessors), Louisville, 1972-76; asst. to pres. Am. Life & Accident Ins. Co., Louisville, 1976-80; pres. Nat. Assn. Life Cos., Washington, 1980-93; v.p. and chief counsel state rels. Am. Coun. Life Ins., Washington, 1993-98; with Morris, Manning & Martin (Atlanta-based firm), Washington, 1998—2001; ins. cons. Congl. Rsch. Svc., Libr. of Congres, Washington, 2001—; sr. ins. policy analyst U.S. Treasury Dept., 2002—. Guest instr. ins. law U. Louisville, 1968—69. Note editor: U. Ky. Law Rev., 1961—62. Pres. Citizen's Met. Planning coun., Louisville, 1970—71; chmn. City of Louisville Riverfront Commn., 1970—75, Ky. Heritage Commn., 1964—77; bd. dirs. Bingham Child Guidance Clinic, Louisville, 1969—76, Youth Performing Arts Coun., 1979—80. Named one of Ky.'s 3 Outstanding Young Men, Ky. Jr. C. of C., 1968; recipient Sullivan medallion, U. Ky., 1958; fellow Woodrow Wilson, Yale U., 1959. Mem.: ABA, Fedn. Ins. Counsel, D.C. Bar Assn., Ky. Bar Assn., Phi Beta Kappa, Phi Alpha Delta (pres. chpt. 1961—62). Home: 2851 29th St NW Washington DC 20008-4111 Office: US Dept Treasury 15th and Pennsylvania Ave NW Washington DC 20220

WOODALL, THOMAS A. state supreme court justice; b. Meridian, Miss., July 14, 1950; m. Debbie Bogan, 1972; children: Scott, Matthew, Claire. BA in History, Millsaps Coll., 1972; JD, U. Va., 1975. With Rives and Peterson, Birmingham, Ala., 1975—91; ptnr. Woodall and Maddox, Birmingham, 1991—96; circuit judge Jefferson County, 1996—2001; assoc. justice Ala. Supreme Ct., 2001—. Mem. Ala. Pattern Jury Instrn.-Civil Com., 1985—2001, vice chmn., 1992—2001. Republican. Methodist. Office: 300 Dexter Ave Montgomery AL 36104-3741

WOODARD, JOSEPH LAMAR, law librarian, law educator; b. Auburndale, Fla., Dec. 28, 1937; s. Wilbur Allen and Florence Virginia (Ladd) W.; m. Eleanor Eugenia Cummings, Aug. 7, 1964; children: Robert Edward, James Frederick. BA, U. Fla., 1959, J.D., 1962; MS in Libr. Sci., Columbia U., 1964. Bar: Fla. 1962, U.S. Dist. Ct. (mid. dist.) Fla. 1970. Asst. reference libr. Columbia U., NYC, 1962-64; asst. libr.Cahill, Gordon, Reindel and Ohl, NYC, 1964-65; law libr. Tulane U., 1965-69; ptnr. Schuh, Schuh and Woodard, St. Petersburg, Fla., 1969-71; law librarian Stetson U., 1971-2001, prof. law, 1979-2001; Law libr. and prof. emeritus, 2001-. Pres. Tampa Bay Library Consortium, 1981, 88-89. Served with USAR, 1957-63. Mem. Fla. Bar, Am. Assn. Law Librs. (sec.-treas. S.E. chpt. 1975-78), Pinellas Pub. Lib. Coop. (sec.-treas. 1993-94, pres. 1994-95). Republican. Presbyterian. Office: 1401 61st St S Saint Petersburg FL 33707-3246 E-mail: jwoodar2@tampabay.rr.com.

WOODBURN, RALPH ROBERT, JR., lawyer; b. Haverhill, Mass., Nov. 3, 1946; s. Ralph Robert and Josephine Marie (McClure) W.; m. Janet M. Smith, Sept. 15, 1985. BA, Mich. State U., 1967; JD, Harvard U., 1972; LLM, Boston U., 1981. Bar: Mass. 1972, U.S. Tax Ct. 1987. Assoc. Bowers, Fortier & Lakin, Boston, 1972-76; from assoc. to ptnr. Hausserman, Davison & Shattuck, Boston, 1976-83; ptnr. Palmer & Dodge, Boston, 1983—. Tchr. Harvard Ctr. for Lifelong Learning, Cambridge, Mass., 1986-89; chmn. Wellesley Cable Access Bd., 1993-95. Contbr. articles to Boston Bar Jour. and Estate Planning. Treas. Exeter Assn. of New Eng., Boston, 1985-89, v.p., 1989-91, pres., 1991-93. Fellow Am. Coll. Trust and Estate Counsel; mem. ABA, Boston Bar Assn. (chmn. probate legislation 1983-93), Brae Burn Country Club (Newton, Mass.), Harvard Club of Boston, Boston Probate and Estate Planning Forum (program chair 1996-97, moderator 1997-98), Harvard Travellers Club. Estate planning, Probate (including wills, trusts), Estate taxation. Home: 25 Cypress Rd Wellesley MA 02481-2918 Office: Palmer & Dodge LLP 111 Huntington Ave Boston MA 02199-7613 E-mail: rwoodburn@palmerdodge.com.

WOODHOUSE, GAY VANDERPOEL, former state attorney general, lawyer; b. Torrington, Wyo., Jan. 8, 1950; d. Wayne Gaylord and Sally (Rouse) Vanderpoel; m. Randy Woodhouse, Nov. 26, 1953; children: Dustin, Houston. BA with honors, U. Wyo., 1972, JD, 1977. Bar: Wyo. 1978, U.S. Dist. Ct. Wyo., U.S. Supreme Ct. Dir. student Legal Svcs., Laramie, Wyo., 1976—77; assoc. Donald Jones Law Offices, Torrington, 1977—78; asst. atty. gen. State of Wyo., Cheyenne, 1978—84, sr. asst. atty. gen., 1984—89, spl. U.S. atty., 1987—89, asst. U.S. atty., 1990—95, chief dept. atty. gen., 1995—98, atty. gen., 1998—2000. Chmn. Wyo. Tel. Consumer Panel, Casper, 1982—86; advisor Cheyenne Halfway House, 1984—93; chmn. Wyo. Silent Witness Initiative Zero Domestic Violence by 2010, 1997, Wyo. Domestic Violence Elimination Coun., 1999—2001; spl. projects cons. N.Am. Securities Adminstrs. Assn., 1987—89; Chmn. bd. Pathfinder, 1987; S.E. Wyo. Mental Health. Mem.: Prevent Child Abuse Wyo. Rotary, Laramie County Bar Assn. Republican. Avocations: inline speed skating, stained glass. Address: 211 W 19th St Ste 308 Cheyenne WY 82001 Office: 123 Capitol Bldg Cheyenne WY 82002-0001 Fax: 307-638-1975. E-mail: gwoodh@state.wy.us.

WOODHOUSE, THOMAS EDWIN, lawyer; b. Cedar Rapids, IA, Apr. 30, 1940; s. Keith Wallace and Elinor Julia (Cherny) W.; m. Kiyoko Fujiie, May 29, 1965; children: Miya, Keith, Leighton. AB cum laude, Amherst Coll., 1962; JD, Harvard U., 1965. Bar: N.Y. 1966, U.S. Supreme Ct. 1969, Calif. 1975. Assoc. Chadbourne, Parke, Whiteside & Wolff, N.Y.C., 1965-68; atty./adviser AID, Washington, 1968-69; counsel Pvt. Investment Co. for Asia S.A., Tokyo, 1969-72; ptnr. Woodhouse Lee & Davis, Singapore, 1972-74; assoc. Graham & James, San Francisco, 1974-75; asst. gen. counsel Natomas Co., San Francisco, 1975-81; mem. Lasky, Haas, Cohler & Munter, San Francisco, 1982-90; trust adminstr. Ronald Family Trust A, 1989—. Gordon P. Getty Family Trust, 1994—; sole practice Berkeley, 1990—2001. Of counsel Wilson, Sonsini, Goodrich & Rosati, Palo Alto, Calif., 1992-95; instr. law faculty U. Singapore, 1972-74; CEO, Vallejo Investments, 1997—. chmn. Police Rev. Com. of Berkeley (Calif.), 1980-84; mem. Berkeley Police Res., 1986—; bd. dirs. Friends Assn. of Svcs. for Elderly, 1979-84; clk. fin. com. Am. Friends Svc. Com. of No. Calif., 1979-83; pres. Zyzzyva Inc., lit. quar., 1985-87. Trustee Freedom from Hunger, 1989-99, Coun. of Friends Bancroft Libr., 1997-2002, chmn. 2002-2003, Mark Twain Luncheon Club, 2002—, Dominican Sch. of Philosophy and Theology, 1998-2003. With U.S. Army, 1958. Fellow Am. Bar Found. (life); mem. Calif. Bar Assn., Assn. Internat. de Bibliophilie, Harvard Club, Univ. Club, Book Club Calif., Roxburghe Club, Travellers Club, Grolier Club, Faculty Club U. Calif.-Berkeley, Mira Vista Golf and Country Club. Republican. Roman Catholic. Corporate, general, Private international, Patent. Home and Office: 1800 San Antonio Ave Berkeley CA 94707-1618 E-mail: tewoodhouse@earthlink.net.

WOODKE, ROBERT ALLEN, lawyer; b. Schaller, Iowa, Dec. 23, 1950; s. Everett Albert and Helen Marie (Breihan) W.; m. Jan Melanie Lawrence, Aug. 15, 1987 (div. 1997). BS, Iowa State U., 1973; JD, Creighton U., 1977. Bar: Iowa 1977, Minn. 1978, U.S. Dist. Ct. (no. dist.) Iowa 1977, U.S. Dist. Ct.Minn. 1980. Law clk. Minn. 5th Dist. Ct., Marshall, 1977-78; assoc. Powell Law Office, Bemidji, Minn., 1978-82; pvt. practice Bemidji, 1982—. Cons. Mgmt. Tng. Inst., Bemidji, 1987-88. Contbg. author: Flying Solo: A Survival Guide for Solo Lawyers, 1984, 2d edit., 1994, Going to Trial, 1989, 2d edit. 1999, Personal Injury Handbook, 1991. Bd. dirs. Bemidji chpt. Am. Red. Cross, 2001—. Recipient Ann. Legal Svc. award N.W. Minn. Legal Svcs., Moorehead, 1987. Mem. ABA (coun. mem. sect. gen. practice 1994-98; co-editor-in-chief Legal Tech. and Practice Guide 1996-98, mem. editl. bd. 1996-2002), Minn. Trial Lawyers Assn., Minn. Bar Assn. (chair sect. of gen. practice 1990-92, chair GP solo and small firm sect. 2000-02), Beltrami County Bar Assn. (pres. 1988-89), 15th Dist. Bar Assn. (treas. 1986-87, pres. 1997-98), Downtown Bus. and Profl. Assn., Bemidji C. of C., Jaycees (v.p. 1986-87), Lions Club (2d v.p. Bemidji chpt. 1987-88, 1st v.p. 1988—, pres. 1989—). Republican. Lutheran. General civil litigation, General practice, Personal injury (including property damage). Office: Brouse Woodke & Meyer PLLP 312 America Ave NW Bemidji MN 56601-3121 E-mail: rawoodke@paulbunyan.net.

WOODLAND, IRWIN FRANCIS, lawyer; b. New York, Sept. 2, 1922; s. John James and Mary (Hynes) W.; m. Sally Duffy, Sept. 23, 1954; children: Connie, J. Patrick, Stephen, Joseph, William, David, Duffy. BA, Columbia U., 1948; JD, Ohio State U., 1959. Bar: Calif. 1960, Wash., 1991, U.S. Dist. Ct. (cen. dist.) Calif. 1960, U.S. Dist. Ct. (no. dist.) Calif. 1962, U.S. Dist. Ct. (so. dist.) Calif. From assoc. to ptnr. Gibson, Dunn & Crutcher, L.A., 1959-88. Bd. dirs. Sunlaw Energy Corp., Vernon, Calif. With USAF, 1942-45, ETO. Mem. ABA, Calif. Bar Assn., L.A. Bar Assn., Wash. State Bar Assn., Phi Delta Phi, Jonathan Club. Roman Catholic. Antitrust, General civil litigation, FERC practice. Address: Gibson Dunn & Crutcher 333 S Grand Ave Ste 4400 Los Angeles CA 90071-1548

WOODLOCK, DOUGLAS PRESTON, judge; b. Hartford, Conn., Feb. 27, 1947; s. Preston and Kathryn (Ropp) W.; m. Patricia Mathilde Powers, Aug. 30, 1969; children: Pamela, Benjamin. BA, Yale U., 1969; JD, Georgetown U., 1975. Bar: Mass. 1975. Reporter Chgo. Sun-Times, 1969-73; staff mem. SEC, Washington, 1973-75; law clk. to Judge F.J. Murray U.S. Dist. Ct. Mass., Boston, 1975-76; assoc. Goodwin, Procter & Hoar, Boston, 1976-79, 83-84, ptnr., 1984-86; asst. U.S. atty. Boston, 1979-83; judge U.S. Dist. Ct., Boston, 1986—. Instr. Harvard U. Law Sch., 1981, 82; mem. U.S. Jud. Conf. Com. on Security Space and Facilities, 1987-95; chmn. New Boston Fed. Courthouse Bldg. Com., 1987-98. Articles editor Georgetown Law Jour., 1973-75; contbr. articles to profl. jours. Chmn. Commonwealth of Mass. Com. for Pub. Counsel Svcs., 1984-86, Town of Hamilton Bd. Appeals, 1978-79. Recipient Dir.'s award U.S. Dept. Justice, 1983, Thomas Jefferson award for Pub. Architecture, AIA, 1996. Mem. ABA, Mass. Bar Assn., Boston Bar Assn., Am. Law Inst., Am. Judicature Soc., Am. Bar Found., Fed. Judges Assn. (bd. dirs. 1996-01), Mass. Hist. Soc. Office: US Courthouse 1 Courthouse Way Ste 4110 Boston MA 02210-3006

WOODMAN, WALTER JAMES, lawyer; b. Talara, Peru, Jan. 21, 1941; s. Walter James and Nora Carmen (Wensjoe) W.; m. Ruth Meyer, Dec. 19, 1970; children: Justin Meyer, Jessica Hilary. BA, U. Miami, 1964; JD, So. Meth. U., 1967. Bar: Tex. 1967, La. 1980, U.S. Dist. Ct. (no. dist.) Tex. 1967, U.S. Ct. Appeals (5th cir.) 1981, U.S. Supreme Ct. 1971, U.S. Dist. Ct. (we. dist.) La. 1980, U.S. Dist. Ct. (ea. dist.) Tex. 1983, U.S. Dist. Ct. (mid. dist.) La. 1988, U.S. Dist. Ct. (ea. dist.) La. 1989. Pvt. practice, Dallas, 1967-72, Waxahachie, Tex., 1972-79, Shreveport, La., 1979—. Bd. dirs. N.W. La. Legal Svcs., Shreveport, 1993-96. Contbr. articles to profl. jours. Candidate Tex. Ho. of Reps., 1972; bd. dirs. Gov.'s Pan Am. Commn., Baton Rouge, 1993-96. General civil litigation, Private international. Home: Nonesuch Farm 12250 Ellerbe Rd Shreveport LA 71115 Office: 9045 Ellerbe Rd Ste 103 Shreveport LA 71106-6799

WOODROW, RANDALL MARK, lawyer; b. Anniston, Ala., June 17, 1956; s. Herbert Milisam and Rose (Marshall) W.; m. Carolyn Ann Jackson, Jan. 7, 1977; children: Amanda Lauren, Emily Claire, Taylor Jackson, Douglas Cockrell. BA in Polit. Sci., Jacksonville (Ala.) State U., 1978; JD, Samford U., 1981. Bar: Ala. 1981. Law clk. to judge U.S. Dist. Ct. (no. dist.) Ala., 1981-82; ptnr. Doster & Woodrow, Anniston, Ala., 1990—. Asst. dist. atty. 7th Jud. Cir., Anniston, 1983; adj. prof. Jacksonville State U., 1985-86; gen. counsel Jacksonville Univs., 1985—. Chmn. crusade Calhoun County Cancer Soc., Anniston, 1983; mem. adminstrv. bd. dirs. 1st United Meth. Ch., Jacksonville, 1994—; pres. Boys Clubs of Anniston, Inc., 1985; mem. Calhoun County Econ. Devel. Coun., 1995—; mem. Jacksonville (Ala.) Planning Commn., 1995—; mem. City of Jacksonville Bd. Edn., 1996—. Mem. ABA, Ala. Bar Assn., Calhoun County Bar Assn., Calhoun County C. of C. Federal civil litigation, State civil litigation, Corporate, general. Home: 509 6th St NE Jacksonville AL 36265-1617 Office: Doster & Woodrow PO Box 2286 Anniston AL 36202-2286

WOODRUFF, BRUCE EMERY, lawyer; b. Mason City, Iowa, June 23, 1930; s. Frederick Bruce and Grace (Emery) W.; m. Carolyn Clark, Aug. 18, 1956; children: David. C., Douglas B., Lynn M., Daniel R. BS in Bus., U. Ill., 1952; JD, Washington U., St. Louis, 1959. Bar: Mo. 1959, D.C. Dist. Ct. (ea. dist.) Mo. 1959, U.S. Ct. Appeals (8th cir.) 1960, U.S. Supreme Ct. 1979. Assoc. Armstrong, Teasdale, Schlafly, Davis & Dicus, St. Louis, 1959-65; ptnr. Armstrong Teasdale, Schlafly & Davis (and predecessor firms), St. Louis, 1966-95; sr. counsel Armstrong Teasdale LLP, St. Louis, 1996—. Prin. counsel St. Louis C.C., 1962-89; bd. dirs. Cass Bank & Trust Co., Cass Info. Sys., Inc., Red Lion Beef Corp., Manor Grove Corp., Rainbow Village, Inc.; city atty., Kirkwood, Mo., 1986. Named Kirkwood Citizen of Yr., 1983. Mem. ABA (banking law com.), Mo. Bar Assn., Bar Assn. Met. St. Louis, Health Lawyers Assn. Clubs: Algonquin (Glendale, Mo.); Noonday (St. Louis (bd. dirs. 1988-91). Republican. Presbyterian. Avocations: golf, swimming, sailing, photography. Banking, Corporate, general, Mergers and acquisitions. Home: 9 Taylor Est Kirkwood MO 63122-2914 Office: Armstrong Teasdale LLP 1 Metropolitan Sq Ste 2600 Saint Louis MO 63102-2740

WOODRUFF, RANDALL LEE, lawyer; b. Anderson, Ind., July 31, 1954; s. Billy Max and Phyllis Joan (Helmick) W.; m. Lucetta Farnham, Aug. 15, 1976. BA, Ind. U., 1976, JD, 1985. Bar: Ind. 1985, U.S. Dist. Ct. (no. and so. dists.) Ind. 1985, U.S. Supreme Ct. 1989. Exec. dir Cmty. Justice Ctr., Anderson, 1979-85; assoc. Shearer, Schrock & Woodruff, Anderson, 1985-87; pvt. practice Anderson, 1987-97, Woodruff Law Offices, P.C., Anderson, 1997—. Bd. dirs. East Ctrl. Legal Svcs. Program, Anderson, 1986—89; trustee Chpt. 7 Bankruptcy Panel, So. Dist. Ind., 1991—. Bd. dirs. Offender Aid & Restoration of the U.S., 1988-93; chmn. Bd. Zoning Appeals, Town of Edgewood, Ind., 1998—. Mem. Ind. Assn. Criminal Def. Lawyers, Ct. Appointed Spl. Advocates (bd. dirs. 1988), Madison County Bar Assn. (sec./treas. 1990, v.p. 1991, pres. 1992). Mem. Christian Ch. (Disciples Of Christ). Criminal, General practice, Personal injury (including property damage). Office: 115-A E 9th St Anderson IN 46016 E-mail: rlwtrustee@insightbb.com., rlwoodruff@insightbb.com.

WOODS, DANIEL JAMES, lawyer; b. Bklyn., Nov. 12, 1952; s. James J. and Elinor (Masten) W.; m. Kathryn Anne Morris, Dec. 27, 1974; children: Meghan M., Alexandra K., Shauna E. AB cum laude, U. So. Calif., 1974, JD, 1977. Bar: Calif. 1977, U.S. Dist. Ct. (cen., ea., so., and no. dists.) Calif., U.S. ct Appeals (9th cir.) 1978, U.S. Supreme Ct. 1981. Law clk. to judge U.S. Dist. Ct. (ctrl. dist.), Calif., 1977-78; assoc. Brobeck, Phleger & Harrison, L.A., 1978-84, ptnr., 1984-96, White & Case LLP, 1996—. Vol. pro tem L.A. Mcpl. Ct., 1985—, L.A. Superior Ct., 1989—. Roman Catholic. Avocations: tennis, bicycling, travel. Appellate, Federal civil litigation, State civil litigation. Office: White & Case LLP 633 W 5th St Los Angeles CA 90071-2627 E-mail: dwoods@whitecase.com.

WOODS, GEORGE EDWARD, judge; b. 1923; m. Janice Smith. Student, Ohio No. U., 1941-43, 46, Tex. A&M Coll., 1943, Ill. Inst. Tech., 1943; JD, Detroit Coll. Law, 1949. Sole practice, Pontiac, Mich., 1949-51; asst. pros. atty. Oakland County, Mich., 1951-52; chief asst. U.S. atty. Ea. Dist. Mich., 1953-60, U.S. atty., 1960-61; assoc. Honigman, Miller, Schwartz and Cohn, Detroit, 1961-62; sole practice Detroit, 1962-81; judge U.S. Bankruptcy Ct., 1981-83, U.S. Dist. Ct. (ea. dist.) Mich., Detroit, 1983-93, sr. judge, 1993—. Served with AUS, 1943-46. Fellow Internat. Acad. Trial Lawyers, Am. Coll. Trial Lawyers; mem. Fed. Bar Assn., State Bar Mich. Office: US Dist Ct 277 US Courthouse 231 W Lafayette Blvd Detroit MI 48226-2700

WOODS, GERALD WAYNE, lawyer; b. Durham, N.C., Sept. 15, 1946; m. Deborah Jordan Bates, Apr. 30, 1983; children: Paul Ellis, Katherine Jordan. BS, U. N.C., 1968; JD, Emory U., 1973. Bar: Ga. 1973, U.S. Dist. Ct. (no. dist.) Ga. 1974, U.S. Supreme Ct. 1980, U.S. Dist. Ct. (so. dist.) Ga. 1987. With retail mgmt. Sears, Roebuck & Co., Atlanta, 1968-70; asst. to exec. sec. bd. regents U. Ga. System, Atlanta, 1973-76, asst. exec. sec., 1976-78; legal advisor to pres. Med. Coll. of Ga., Augusta, 1978-2000, v.p. for bus. ops., legal advisor to the pres., asst. prof. med. jurisprudence, 1990-2000; of counsel Kilpatrick Stockton LLP, 2001—. Mem. faculty Sr. Acctg. Officers Workshop Nat. Assn. of Coll. and Univ. Bus. Officers, Myrtle Beach, S.C., 1981; lectr. law seminars and med. confs., nationwide. Contbr. articles to profl. jours. Councilman City of Augusta, 1984-95; pres. YMCA of Augusta, Inc., 1987-88; bd. dirs. Leadership Augusta, 1982-85, 94-96, others; bd. dirs. Augusta Symphony, 1988-90, pres., 1990-91; trustee Augusta-Richmond County Pub. Libr., 1984-85; mem. Richmond County Dem. Exec. Com., 1983-86, Richmond County Bd. of Health, 1986-95, Augusta Symphony League, 1986—; bd. dirs. Augusta Youth Ctr., 1988-93, Southea. Nat. Scis. Acad., 1998—, Southeastern Natural Scis. Acad. Land Trust, Inc., 2001—02; chmn. cultural action plan steering com. Greater Augusta Arts Coun., 1992, active, 1994-2001, pres., 1999; mem. air svc. task force Augusta C. of C., 1990-93; mem. Cmtys. in Sch. Inc. Bd., 1996-98, Southeastern Tech. Ctr. Bd., 1996-2000; trustee Historic Augusta, Inc., 1998—, treas., 2002—; active Ga.-Carolina coun. Boy Scouts Am., 1999—2002; co-chair exec. forum Leadership Augusta, 1994-96, 2002; asst. scoutmaster Boy Scouts Am., 1998--. Mem. State Bar Ga. (medico-legal liaison and mental health coms. 1979, vice chmn. coll. and univ. com., sch. and coll. law sect. 1986-88), Augusta Bar Assn., Ga. Soc. Hosp. Attys., Nat. Assn. Coll. and Univ. Attys. (exec. bd. 1983-86, co-vice chair fin. com. 2002—), Nat. Health Lawyers Assn., Kiwanis (treas. Ansley club 1977, bd. dirs. 1977-78), Nat. Assn. Coll. and Univ. Bus. Officers, Forrest Hills Assn. (pres. 1982-85, bd. dirs. 1985-94), Met. Augusta C. of C. (co-chair govt. affairs com.), U. N.C. Alumni Assn. (v.p. Augusta chpt. 1984-90), Pinnacle Club, Augusta Country Club, Rotary (bd. dirs. Augusta 2002—). Avocation: photography. Office: Kilpatrick & Stockton LLP 1400 Wachovia Bldg Augusta GA 30903

WOODS, HARRY ARTHUR, JR., lawyer; b. Hartford, Ark., Feb. 15, 1941; s. Harry Arthur and Viada (Young) W.; m. Carol Ann Meschter, Jan. 21, 1967; children: Harry Arthur III, Elizabeth Ann. BA in Econs., Okla. State U., 1963; JD, NYU, 1966. Bar: N.Y. 1966, Okla. 1970. Assoc. White & Case, NYC, 1966—67, Crowe & Dunlevy, Okla. City, 1971—75, ptnr., 1976—. Councilman City of Edmond, 1975-79, mayor pro tem, 1977-79. Capt. JAGC U.S. Army, 1967-71. Mem. ABA, Am. Law Inst., Internat. Assn. Def. Counsel, Okla. Bar Assn., pres. elect, 2003,(bd. govs. 2001-02, pres.-elect 2003, profl. responsibility tribunal 1999-2004, Outstanding Svc. award 1982, Golden Gavel award 1998, Neil Bogan Professionalism award 1998), Ruth Bader Ginsburg Inn of Ct. (pres. 1998-2000), Okla. County Bar Assn. (bd. dirs. 2001-2003). Democrat. Methodist. Avocations: rock climbing, flying, jogging, photography. Federal civil litigation, State civil litigation, Product liability. Office: Crowe & Dunlevy 1800 Mid-America Tower 20 N Broadway Ave Ste 1800 Oklahoma City OK 73102-8273

WOODS, JAMES ROBERT, lawyer; b. San Francisco, Aug. 3, 1947; AB with honors, U. Calif., Berkeley, 1969; JD, U. Calif., Davis, 1972. Bar: Calif. 1972, N.Y. 1973, U.S. Dist. Ct. (so. & ea. dists.) N.Y. 1975, U.S. Ct. Appeals (2d cir.) 1975, U.S. Dist. Ct. (no. dist.) Calif. 1984. Ptnr. LeBoeuf, Lamb, Greene & MacRae L.L.P., San Francisco, 1983—. Co-author: California Insurance Law and Practice; contbr. articles to profl. jours. Corporate, general, Insurance. Office: LeBoeuf Lamb Greene & MacRae LLP 1 Embarcadero Ctr Ste 400 San Francisco CA 94111-3619

WOODS, JOHN WILLIAM, retired lawyer; b. Ft. Worth, Dec. 10, 1912; s. John George and Eugenia (Smith) W.; m. Gertie Leona Parker, Apr. 15, 1954. BS, North Tex. State U., 1951, M.Ed., 1952; JD, St. Mary's U., San Antonio, 1967; postgrad., Fresno State Coll., 1952, West Tex. State U., 1959. Bar: Tex. bar 1966. Tchr., Corcoran, Calif., 1952-53, Pampa (Tex.) Ind. Sch. Dist., 1953-63, Harlandale Sch. Dist., San Antonio, 1963-67; practicing atty. Amarillo, Tex., 1967-68; county atty. Sherman County, Tex., 1969-72; county judge, 1988; ret., 1988; justice of peace, 1975-88; pvt. practice, 1968-95; ret., 1995. Served to ensign USN, 1930-47, ETO. Mem. Tex. Bar Assn., Amarillo Bar Assn., Am. Legion, Masons, Shriners, Scottish Rite, York Rite. Democrat. Mem. Christian Ch. (Disciples Of Christ). Home: # 911 1300 S Jackson St Amarillo TX 79101-4146

WOODS, LARRY DAVID, lawyer, educator; b. Martinsburg, WV, Sept. 10, 1944; s. Allen Noel and Loyce L. (Dillingham) W.; children— Rachel, Allen, Sarah. B.A., Emory U., 1966; J.D., Northwestern U., 1969. Bar: Tenn. 1969, Ga. 1970. Dir. litigation Atlanta Legal Aid Soc., Inc., 1969-71; assoc. dir. Atlanta Mcpl. Defender Project, 1970; ptnr. Woods & Woods, Nashville, 1971—; assoc. prof. Tenn. State U., 1972-84, prof., 1984— ; bd. dirs. Citizen's Bank; lectr. Taft Ins., 1974-79, Am. Criminology Soc., 1984; chmn. bd. Southeastern Inst. Paralegal Tng. Nat. bd. editors' Matthew Benders, 1984—; Del., Tenn. Democratic Conv., 1972, 76, 80. debate coach for V.P. Al Gore, 1992, 1996; sr. strategist, Bredesen for Governor campaign, 2002; chmn. TennCare Transition com. for Gov. Bredesen, 2003; coord. Dept. Transp. Transisiton Com., 2003; keynote spkr. Nat. Debate Tournament, 2003. mem. Tenn. Bar Assn. (ho. of dels. 1979-85), Ga. Bar Assn., ABA, Fed. Bar Assn., Tenn. Assn. Criminal Def. Lawyers (dir. 1975-78). Methodist. Author: (with Fowler) Crime and Investigation, 1967; Compulsory Service and the Alternatives, 1968; The Strategy of Intervention, 1969; Pollution: Problems and Proposals, 1970; Co-editor: Tools for the Ultimate Trial: Tennessee Death Penalty Practice and Procedure, 1985; mem. editl. bd. James Pub. Co., 1993-95, The Fed. Lawyer, 1994-95. Federal civil litigation, Corporate, general, General practice. Office: 631 2nd Ave S Ste 1-R Nashville TN 37210-2025

WOODS, ROBERT EDWARD, lawyer; b. Albert Lea, Minn., Mar. 27, 1952; s. William Fabian and Maxine Elizabeth (Schmit) W.; m. Cynthia Anne Pratt, Dec. 26, 1975; children: Laura Marie Woods, Amy Elizabeth Woods. BA, U. Minn., 1974, JD, 1977; MBA, U. Pa., 1983. Bar: Minn. 1977, U.S. Dist. Ct. Minn. 1980, U.S. Ct. Appeals (8th cir.) 1980, Calif. 2000. Assoc. Moriarty & Janzen, Mpls., 1977-81, Berger & Montague, Phila., 1982-83, Briggs and Morgan, St. Paul and Mpls., 1983-84, ptnr., 1984-99; exec. v.p., gen. counsel InsWeb Corp., Redwood City, Calif., 1999-2000; gen. counsel BORN Info. Svcs., Inc., Mpls., 2000—. Adj. prof. William Mitchell Coll. Law, St. Paul, 1985; exec. com., bd. dirs. LEX MUNDI, Ltd., Houston, 1989-93, chmn. bd. 1991-92; bd. dirs. Midwest Asia Ctr., 1993-95, chmn. bd., 1994-95. Author (with others) Business Torts, 1989; sr. contbg. editor: Evidence in America: The Federal Rules in the States, 1987. Mem. ABA, Minn. State Bar Assn., State Bar of Calif., Hennepin County Bar Assn., Ramsey County Bar Assn. (chmn. corp., banking and bus. law sect. 1985-87), Assn. Trial Lawyers Am., Wharton Club of Minn., Phi Beta Kappa. Federal civil litigation, General civil litigation, Securities. Home: 28 N Deep Lake Rd North Oaks MN 55127-6506

WOODSIDE, FRANK C., III, lawyer, educator, physician; b. Glen Ridge, N.J., Apr. 18, 1944; s. Frank C. and Dorothea (Poulin) W.; m. Julia K. Moses, Nov. 15, 1974; children: Patrick Michael, Christopher Ryan. BS, Ohio State U., 1966, JD, 1969; MD, U. Cin., 1973. Diplomate Am. Bd.

Legal Medicine, Am. Bd. Forensic Medicine, Am. Bd. Profl. Liability Attys. Mem. Dinsmore & Shohl, Cin.; clin. prof. pediats.emeritus U. Cin., 1992—. Adj. prof. law U. Cin., 1973—. Editor: Drug Product Liability, 1985—. Fellow Am. Coll. Legal Medicine, Am. Coll. Forensic Examiners, Am. Soc. Hosp. Attys., Soc. Ohio Hosp. Attys.; mem. ABA, FBA, Ohio Bar Assn., Internat. Assn. Def. Counsel, Def. Rsch. Inst. (chmn. drug and med. svc. com. 1988-91), Cin. Bar Assn. Personal injury (including property damage), Product liability, Professional liability. Office: Dinsmore & Shohl 1900 Chemed Ctr 255 E 5th St Cincinnati OH 45202-4700 E-mail: frank.woodside@dinslaw.com.

WOODWARD, DAVID LUTHER, lawyer, consultant; b. Alexandria, La., Mar. 18, 1942; s. Luther Washburn and Ruby Ellen (Robertson) W.; m. Adeline Myree Peterson, July 12, 1965 (div. 1971); m. Louisette Marie Forget, Nov. 12, 1973. BA, Fla. State U., 1965, JD, 1969; LLM, U. London, 1982. Bar: Fla. 1969, Okla. 1982, Tex. 1987, U.S. Dist. Ct. (mid. and so. dists.) Fla. 1971, U.S. Dist. Ct. (no. and we. dists.) Okla. 1983, U.S. Dist. Ct. (no. and ea. dists.) Tex. 1985, U.S. Dist. Ct. (ea. dist.) Wis. 1992, U.S. Dist. Ct. (no. dist.) Fla. 1997, U.S. Ct. of Claims 1970, U.S. Ct. Appeals (fed. and D.C. cirs.) 1970, (5th and 11th cirs.) 1981, (10th cir.) 1982, (9th cir.) 1985, U.S. Tax Ct. 1970, U.S. Ct. Mil. Appeals 1970, U.S. Supreme Ct. 1973. Trial atty. USDA, Washington, 1970; asst. atty. gen. State of Fla., Tampa, 1971-73; ptnr. Rose & Woodward, Tampa, 1973-76; pvt. practice The Law Offices of David Luther Woodward, Tampa, 1976-80; appellate pub. defender State of Okla., 1980-81; instr. U. Okla. Coll. Law, Norman, 1980-81; assoc. Jones, Gungoll, Jackson, Collins & Dodd, Enid, Okla., 1982-84, Brice & Barron, Dallas, 1985-86; pvt. practice Dallas, 1986-97; of counsel Kenneth R. Guest & Assocs., Dallas, 1990-91, Sapp & Madden, Dallas and Austin, 1991, Bennett & Kurtzman, Dallas, 1991-93; supervising atty. Bond & Botes PC, Pensacola, Fla., 1997-98; of counsel Reeves & Davis, Pensacola, 1998—2001; sole practitioner Pensacola, 2001—. Contbr. articles to profl. jours. Vis. scholar Hattie M. Strong Found. fellow. Episcopalian. Bankruptcy, General civil litigation, Private international. Office: Law Offices of David Luther Woodward 111 Bayshore Dr PO Box 4475 Pensacola FL 32507-0475

WOODWARD, LESTER RAY, lawyer; b. Lincoln, Nebr., May 24, 1932; s. Wendell Smith and Mary Elizabeth (Theobald) W.; m. Marianne Martinson, Dec. 27, 1958; children: Victoria L. Woodward Eisele, Richard T., David M., Andrew E. BSBA, U. Nebr., 1953; LLB, Harvard U., 1957; LLD (hon.), Bethany Coll., 1974. Bar: Colo., 1957. Assoc. Davis, Graham & Stubbs, Denver, 1957-59, 60-62, ptnr., 1962—. Teaching fellow Sch. Law Harvard U., 1959-60. Bd. dirs. Bethany Coll., Lindsborg, Kans., 1966-74, 87-95, chmn., 1989-92; bd. dirs. Pub. Edn. Coalition, Denver, 1985-92, chmn., 1988-89; mem. Colo. Commn. Higher Edn., Denver, 1977-86, chmn., 1979-81; mem. bd. edn. Denver Pub. Schs., 1999—. Mem. ABA, Colo. Bar Assn., Am. Law Inst. Republican. Lutheran. Home: 680 Bellaire St Denver CO 80220-4935 Office: Davis Graham & Stubbs 1150 17th St Ste 500 Denver CO 80202-5682

WOODWORTH, RAMSEY LLOYD, lawyer; b. Syracuse, N.Y., Dec. 26, 1941; s. Woodrow Lloyd and Helen (Ramsey) W.; m. Diane Elizabeth McMillion, June 12, 1971; children: Scott, Ashley, Jeffrey. AB, Brown U., 1964; LLM cum laude, Syracuse (N.Y.) U., 1967. Bar: N.Y. 1967, D.C. 1968, U.S. Ct. Appeals (D.C. cir.) 1968. Atty., advisor FCC, Washington, 1967-68; from assoc. to ptnr. Hedrick & Lane, Washington, 1968-82; prin. Wilkes, Artis, Hedrick & Lane, Chartered, Washington, 1982-99; of counsel Shook, Hardy & Bacon LLP, Washington, 1999—. Convenor Peace Luth. Ch., Alexandria, 1985-86; pres. Broadcast Pioneers Ednl. Fund, Inc., 1997—. Mem. Fed. Comm. Bar Assn. (exec. com. 1986-89, chair profl. responsibility com. 1984-86, treas. 1989-90, chmn. Fed. Commn. Bar Assn. Found. 1991-93, trustee 1991-94, Univ. Club Washington, Order of Coif. Avocation: swimming. Administrative and regulatory, Communications, Intellectual property. Office: Shook Hardy & Bacon LLP 600 14th St NW Ste 800 Washington DC 20005-2099 E-mail: rwoodworth@shb.com.

WOOLARD, WILLIAM LEON, lawyer, electrical distributing company executive; b. Bath, N.C., Aug. 26, 1931; s. Archie Leon and Pearl Irene (Boyd) W.; m. Virginia Harris Stratton, June 17, 1961; children: William Leon Jr., Margaret Anne. AB, Duke U., 1953, LLB, JD, 1955. Bar: N.C. 1955, U.S. Dist. Ct. (we. and mid. dists.) N.C. 1960. Claims analyst Md. Casualty Co., Charlotte, N.C., 1955-56; dist. mgr. Chrysler Corp., Charlotte, 1956-60; ptnr. Jones, Hewson & Woolard, Charlotte, 1960-86, of counsel, 1986—; pres. Armature Winding Co., Inc., Charlotte, 1970—, also bd. dirs.; v.p. Power Products Mfg. Co., Charlotte, 1970—, also bd. dirs. Mem. adminstrv. bd. 1st United Meth. Ch., Charlotte, 1961-78, trustee, 1984-87; trustee Lawyers Ednl. Found., Charlotte, 1970-78, N.C. Sch. Sci. and Math., 1997—; bd. dirs. Christian Rehab. Ctr., Charlotte, 1972-73, N.C. Eye and Human Tissue Bank, Winston-Salem, 1978-79. Recipient Order of Civil Merit Moran award Republic of Korea, 1990, Disting. Svc. medal Republic of China, 1990, Medal of Friendship Pope John Paul II, 1990, Humanitarian Citizen of Merit medal Republic of China, 1990, Humanitarian medal France, 1990, Outstanding Svc. medal Mayor of Paris, 1990, Order of Long Leaf Pine, Gov. of N.C., 1990, numerous others; Angier B. Duke scholar Duke U., 1949-53; Carnegie Found. fellow Duke U., 1951-52, Melvin Jones fellow Lions Found., 1978. Mem. ABA, N.C. Bar Assn., N.C. State Bar Assn., 26th Jud. Dist. Bar Assn., Am. Judicature Soc., Lions (pres. Charlotte Ctrl. club 1972-73, pres., trustee ednl. found. 1973-87, dist. gov., chmn. coun. govs. internat. orgn. 1978-79, internat. bd. dirs. 1981-85, Ambassador of Goodwill award 1983, internat. 3rd v.p. 1986-87, 2nd v.p. 1987-88, 1st v.p. 1988-89, internat. pres. 1989-90, immediate past pres. 1990-91, chmn. bd. trustees 1990-91), Masons, Shriners, Phi Kappa Sigma, Delta Theta Phi. Avocations: collecting antique and rare books, opera, boating, fishing. Home: 638 Hempstead Pl Charlotte NC 28207-2320 Office: PO Box 32277 Charlotte NC 28232-2277

WOOLDRIDGE, WILLIAM CHARLES, lawyer; b. Miami, Fla., Feb. 24, 1943; s. Clarence Edward and Easter Marguerite (Souders) W.; m. Joyce L. Norton, June 15, 1968; children: William Charles, John Michael. BA, Harvard U., 1965; LLB, U. Va., 1969. Bar: Va. 1969. Atty. Norfolk and Western Ry. Co., 1973-82; with Norfolk So. Corp., 1982-2000, v.p. dept. law, 1996-2000. Pres. John Marshall Found., Richmond, Va., 1992-94; pres. Norfolk Hist. Soc., 1995-96; chair Friends of Chrysler Mus. Hist. Houses, 1997-99; bd. dirs. Sta. WHRO (FM and TV), 1997-2000, WHRO Found., Libr. of Va. Found. Capt. JAGC, U.S. Army, 1969-73. Mem. Va. Bar Assn. Republican. Administrative and regulatory, Antitrust, Corporate, general.

WOOLSEY, JOHN MUNRO, JR., retired lawyer; b. NYC, Apr. 22, 1916; s. John M. and Alice B. (Bacon) W.; m. Ledlie Laughlin, Dec. 27, 1948; children: John, Alice, Henry, Mary. BA, Yale U., 1938, LL.B., 1941. Bar: N.Y. 1941, Mass. 1947. Assoc. Debevoise, Stevenson, Plimpton & Page, N.Y.C., 1941-42; with Bd. Econ. Warfare, Washington, 1942, Herrick & Smith and predecessor firms, Boston, 1946—86; of counsel Palmer & Dodge, Boston, 1986—2001; ret., 2001. With Office of U.S. Chief of Counsel, Nürnberg Trials, Germany, 1945-46 Former pres. Trustees of Reservations, Shady Hill Sch. Served to lt. USNR, 1942-46. Decorated Order of White Lion (Czechoslovakia) Mem. Am. Antiquarian Soc., Am. Law Inst., Century Assn., Tavern Club.

WOOLSON, CHARLES E., JR., lawyer; b. Woodbury, N.J., June 6, 1953; s. Charles E. and Alice Woolson; 1 child, Jennifer E. BA, Temple U., 1975; JD, Widener U., 1977. Bar: N.J., Va., U.S. Dist. Ct. N.J., U.S. Ct. Appeals (3d cir.), U.S. Supreme Ct; cert. N.J. Supreme Ct. Asst. claims atty. Fidelity & Deposit, Richmond, Va., 1978-81; atty. Davidow & Davidow, Millville, NJ, 1981, Montano Summers Mullen Manuel & Owens, Cherry Hill, NJ, 1982—86, Law Offices of Roger Steedle, Absecon, NJ, 1986—2002; prin. Law Firm of Charles E. Woolson, Jr., L.L.C., Hammonton, NJ, 2002—. Mem. Atlantic County Rep. Com., 1996—. Mem. Trial Attys. of N.J. (trustee 1996—), N.J. Bar Assn. (spl. com. mcpl. ct. practice). General civil litigation, Insurance, Municipal (including bonds). Office: 104 Bellevue Ave PO Box 851 Hammonton NJ 08037 E-mail: woollaw@eticomm.net.

WOOSNAM, RICHARD EDWARD, venture capitalist, lawyer; b. Anderson, Ind., June 27, 1942; s. Richard Wendell and Ruth (Cleveland) W.; m. Diane Dalto; children: Cynthia S., Elizabeth C. BS, Ind. U., 1964, JD, 1967, MBA, 1968. Bar: Ind. 1967, U.S. Dist. Ct. (so. dist.) Ind. 1967. Instr. bus. law Ind. U., Bloomington, 1966-68; assoc. Ferguson, Ferguson & Lloyd, Bloomington, 1967-68; dep. pros. Monroe County, Bloomington, 1967-68; tax acct. Price Waterhouse, Phila., 1968-69; v.p., treas. Innovest Group, Inc., Phila., 1969-82, chmn., pres., 1983—. Guest lectr. Wharton Sch. Bus., U. Pa., Kelley Sch. Bus., Ind. U., Bloomington, 1975—; bd. dirs. Capital Mgmt. Corp., N.Y. Achievement, L.L.C., Innovest Talent Svcs., Inc., Command Equity Group, LLC, Bridges Learning Sys., Inc., Ind. U. Found., World Affairs Coun. of Phila., Fairmount Park Conservancy, Phila. Hospitality, Inc., Ctr. for Entrepreneurship and Innovation, Pa. Acad. Fine Arts. Mem. Walnut St. Theatre. Mem. ABA, Ind. Bar Assn., Union League of Phila., Sunday Breakfast Club, The Pa Soc. Home: 1810 Spruce St Philadelphia PA 19103-6677 Office: 1528 Walnut St Ste 1701 Philadelphia PA 19102

WOOSTER, KELLY C. lawyer; b. San Francisco, Dec. 18, 1942; AB cum laude, Stanford U., 1964; JD, U. Calif., Berkeley, 1967. Bar: Calif. 1967. Ptnr. Brobeck, Phleger & Harrison, San Francisco, 1978—2002. Note and comment editor: Calif. Law Rev., 1966-67. Mailing: PO Box 62 Copperopolis CA 95228

WORD, TERRY MULLINS, lawyer; b. Corpus Christi, Tex., Dec. 30, 1943; s. Terrence Stuart and Leila Elba (Mullins) W.; m. ALice G. Hector, Jan. 27, 1971 (div. 1977); children: Morgan Anna, Zachary Hector; m. Mary Ann L. Rios Garcia, May 28, 1983; children: Jettie Laure, Terrence Rios; 1 stepson, John Jarrett Garcia. BA in Econs., Math., U. Tex., 1966, JD, 1973. Bar: Tex. 1973, N.Mex. 1973, U.S. Dist. Ct. N.Mex. 1973. Ptnr. Stribling, Anderson, Read & Word, Albuquerque, 1973-74; atty. N.Mex. Pub. Defender, Albuquerque, 1974-76; pvt. practice Albuquerque, 1976-77; assoc. Richard E. Ransom, P.A., Albuquerque, 1977-83; pres. pvt. practice, Albuquerque, 1983—. Mem. rules of civil procedures com N.Mex. Supreme Ct., 1989—92. Workmen's compensation editor The N.Mex. Trial Lawyer, Albuquerque, 1982-84. Bd. dirs. Big Bros./Big Sisters Albuquerque, 1983-86. Lt. USN, 1966-70, Vietnam. Fellow Am. Coll. Trial Lawyers; mem. ATLA (sustaining mem., bd. govs. 1991-94), N.Mex. Trial Lawyers Assn. (chmn. continuing legal edn. com. 1984-85, treas. 1984-85, bd. dirs. 1984—, pres. elect 1985-86, pres. 1986-87), Am. Bd. Trial Advocates (pres. N.Mex. chpt. 1996-97). Democrat. Episcopalian. Civil rights, Personal injury (including property damage), Workers' compensation. Home: 6401 Caballero Pkwy NW Albuquerque NM 87107-5635 Office: 500 Tijeras Ave NW Albuquerque NM 87102-3133 E-mail: twordpc@swcp.com.

WORK, CHARLES ROBERT, lawyer; b. Glendale, Calif., June 21, 1940; s. Raymond P. and Minna M. (Fricke) W.; m. Linda S. Smith, Oct. 4, 1965 (div.); children: Matthew Keehn, Mary Lucila Landis, Benjamin Reed; m. Veronica A. Haggart, Apr., 1985, 1 child, Andrew Haggart. BA, Wesleyan U., 1962; JD, U. Chgo., 1965; LLM, Georgetown U., 1966. Bar: D.C. 1965, Utah 1965. Asst. U.S. atty. D.C., 1966-73; dep. adminstr. law enforcement assistance adminstrn., U.S. Dept. Justice, 1973-75; ptnr. Peabody, Lambert & Meyers, Washington, 1975-82, McDermott, Will & Emery, Washington, 1982—. Recipient Rockefeller Pub. Service award 1978. Mem. D.C. Bar (pres. 1976-77). Federal civil litigation, State civil litigation, Private international. Office: McDermott Will & Emery 600 13th St NW Fl 12-8 Washington DC 20005-3005 E-mail: cwork@mwe.com.

WORK, MICHAEL JAY, lawyer; b. Maysville, Ky., Oct. 7, 1946; s. Clarence Lee and Marjorie (Lemon) W.; m. Christine Marion Dignan, Aug. 2, 1969; children: Thomas M., Meghan E., Kristen C. BA, Ohio State U., 1968, JD, 1971. Bar: N.H. 1972, U.S. Dist. Ct. N.H. 1972. Atty., examiner Pub. Utilities Commn. Ohio, Columbus, 1971; criminal justice planner N.H. Gov.'s Commn. on Crime and Delinquency, Concord, 1972-73; assoc. Law Offices of John C. Fairbanks, Newport, N.H., 1973-75; sole practice Newport, N.H., 1975—. Mem. adv. bd. Lake Sunapee Bank, Newport, 1980—; mem. N.H. Supreme Ct. Profl. Conduct Commn., Concord, 1981-90. Dir. YMCA Camp Coniston, Inc., Croydon, N.H., 1981—. Named Outstanding Young Man Am., 1978. Mem. ABA, N.H. Bar Assn. (gov. 1982-84), Sullivan County Bar Assn. (pres. 1982), New London Bar Assn. (pres. 1983), Newport C. of C. (pres. 1980), Rotary (pres. Newport chpt. 1984-85). Democrat. Avocations: sports, coin collecting. Probate (including wills, trusts), Property, real (including real estate development, water). Home: 126 Squires Ln PO Box 552 New London NH 03257-0552 Office: 7a Main St PO Box 627 Newport NH 03773-0627 E-mail: mjwork@earthlink.net.

WORLEY, JANE LUDWIG, lawyer; b. Reading, Pa., Sept. 4, 1917; d. Walter Schearer and Marion Grace (Johns) L.; m. Floyd Edwin Worley, Oct. 30, 1946 (dec. Jan. 1982); children: Laetitia Anne, Thomas Allen, Christopher Ludwig. AB, Bryn Mawr Coll., 1938; JD, Temple U., 1942. Bar: Pa. 1943, U.S. Dist. Ct. (ea. dist.) Pa. 1980, U.S. Supreme Ct. 1968. Assoc. Richardson Moss & Richardson, Reading, 1943-48; pvt. practice Wernersville, Pa., 1948—. V.p., bd. dirs. Worley Lumber Co. Inc., Wernersville, 1955—. Sec. Friends of Reading Mus., 1986-91; sec. Berks County chpt. ARC, 1986-87, v.p., 1987-91. Mem. ABA, Pa. Bar Assn., Berks County Bar Assn., DAR, Jr. League Reading. Republican. Mem. United Ch. of Christ. Avocations: antique and art collecting, travel. Family and matrimonial, General practice, Property, real (including real estate development, water). Office: 404 Sheridan Rd Womelsdorf PA 19567

WORLEY, ROBERT WILLIAM, JR., retired lawyer; b. Anderson, Ind., June 13, 1935; s. Robert William and Dorothy Mayhew (Hayler) W.; m. Diana Lynn Matthews, Aug. 22, 1959; children: Nathanael, Hope Hillegas. BS in Chem. Engring., Lehigh U., 1956; LLB, Harvard U., 1960. Bar: Conn. 1960, U.S. Supreme Ct. 1966, Fla. 1977. Assoc. then ptnr. Cummings & Lockwood, Stamford, Conn., 1960-91; gen. counsel Consol. Asset Recover Corp. sub. Chase Manhattan Corp., Bridgeport, Conn., 1991-94; v.p., asst. gen. counsel The Chase Manhattan Bank, N.Y.C., 1994-2001; ret., 2001. Mem. trustees com. on bequests and trusts Lehigh U., 1979—; mem. Conn. Legis. Task Force on Probate Court Sys., 1991-93; chmn. Greenwich Arts Coun., 1981-82; v.p., bd. dirs. Greenwich Choral Soc., 1962-77, 80, mem., 1960-95; bd. dirs. Greenwich Ctr. for Chamber Music, 1981-85, Greenwich Symphony, 1986-89; commr. Greenwich Housing Authority, 1972-77; past mem. Rep. Town Com. Greenwich; mem. bldg. com. for sr. ctr. Greenwich Bd. Selectman, 1980-81. Capt. JAGC, AUS, 1965. Mem. Conn. Bar Assn. (exec. com. probate sect. 1980), Harvard Club Boston. Christian Scientist. Banking, Estate planning, Probate (including wills, trusts). Home: PO Box 1055 Marion MA 02738-0019

WORTHINGTON, BRUCE R. lawyer; b. 1949; BA Econ.(hon.) , Claremont KcKenna Coll.; JD, King Hall, Univ. of Calif. at Davis, Calif. Bar: State Bar of Calif. 1974. Sr. v.p. and gen. counsel PG&E Corp, San Francisco, 1995—; sr. v.p. and gen. coun. Pacific Gas and Electric Co., 1974; v.p. and gen. coun. PG&E Corp., San Francisco, 1994. Mem.: Section of Pub. Utility, Comm. and Transportation Law of the Am. Bar Assoc., Calif. Bar Assoc., San Francisco Bar Assoc. Worthington has more than 20 years in the energy industry legal sector and is responsible for the corp. legal, internal auditing, business ethics, and compliance functions. He provides oversight of these functions for the Company's bus. including PG&E Nat. Energy Group, Pacific Gas and Electric Co. and Pacific Venture Captial, LLC. Office: PG&E Corp Ste 2400 One Market Spear Tower San Francisco CA 94105*

WORTHINGTON, DANIEL GLEN, lawyer, educator; b. Rexbury, Idaho, Aug. 15, 1957; BA magna cum laude, Brigham Young U., 1982, MEd, 1986, EdD, JD cum laude, Brigham Young U., 1989; LLM in Taxation, U. Fla., 2002. Bar: Utah 1990. Asst. to assoc. dean students Brigham Young U., 1986—88, cons., 1987—89, mgr. planned giving, tech. cons., 1989—90, adj. prof. law and edn., 1989—; asst. dean students Coll. Eastern Utah, 1985—86; assoc. dean, exec. dir. devel. Porterville Coll. Found., 1990—91; prin. Worthington & Assocs., Provo, Utah, 1991—93; mng. atty., ptnr. Walstad & Babcock, Provo; assoc. dean U. S.D. Sch. Law, 1994—95, exec. v.p. found., 1995—2001. Assoc. v.p. gen. counsel U. Ctrl. Fla. Found., Orlando, adj. faculty Masters of Tax Program; sr. cons. Fla. Hosp. and the U. S.D. Bus. Sch., 1997—2001; cons. Citigroup Trust Svcs., 1997—2001; sr. cons. Fla. Hosp., 1997—99, v.p. gen. counsel, 1999—2003. Editor-in-chief jour. Edn. & Law Perspectives, 1986-88, co-chair, exec. adv. bd., dir., 1988-91; contbr. articles to profl. jours. Exec. v.p. S.D. Planned Giving Coun., 1994-2001, nat. task force valuation, 2002—; nat. assembly del. Nat. Com. on Planned, 1994—; pres. Greater Orlando Planned Giving Round Table, 1999—; v.p., gen. counsel Fla. Hosp. Found., 1999-2003; v.p. Wealth Mgmt. Group; bd. dirs. S.D. Turst Co., 2002—; pres. Family Bank Design Ctr., 2002—. With USAFR, 1982-88. Mem. Supreme Ct. Hist. Soc., Federalist Soc., Nat. Soc. Fund Raising Execs., Phi Kappa Phi. Alternative dispute resolution, Corporate, general, Probate (including wills, trusts). Home and Office: 3229 King George Dr Orlando FL 32835 E-mail: dan.worthington@flhosp.org.

WORTHINGTON, SANDRA BOULTON, lawyer; b. Phila., July 12, 1956; BA with high distinction, U. Va., 1978; JD, Temple U., 1983. Bar: Pa. 1983, U.S. Dist. Ct. (ea. dist.) Pa. 1984. Summer clk. Ct. of Common Pleas Montgomery County, Pa., summer 1981; legal intern Peruto, Ryan & Vitullo, Phila., 1982-83; assoc. Michael D. Fioretti Law Office, Phila., 1983-84; founding ptnr. Stocker & Worthington Law Office, Jenkintown, Pa., 1984—. Legal counsel Phila. Women's Squash Racquets Assn., 1985—. Mem. Pa. Trial Lawyers Assn., Phila. Trial Lawyers Assn., Pa. Bar Assn., Montgomery County Bar Assn. Avocations: small business consulting, squash, tennis. Commercial, consumer (including collections, credit), Family and matrimonial, Personal injury (including property damage). Office: Stocker & Worthington Law Offices The Rectory Ste 2 436 Old York Rd Jenkintown PA 19046-2840

WORTHINGTON, WILLIAM ALBERT, III, lawyer; b. June 26, 1950; s. William Albert Jr. and Patricia Lou (Reynolds) W.; m. Melanie Ann McDonald, Oct. 30, 1993; children: Elizabeth Clark, Emily Robin, Katherine Anne, William Jackson. BS, U. Utah, 1972; JD, Washington and Lee U., 1976. Bar: Tex. 1976, U.S. Dist. Ct. (so. dist.) Tex. 1977, U.S. Ct. Appeals (5th cir.) 1977, U.S. Ct. Appeals (11th cir.) 1981, U.S. Supreme Ct. 1981, U.S. Dist. Ct. (we. dist.) Tex. 1982, U.S. Dist. Ct. (ea. dist.) Tex. 1986, U.S. Dist. Ct. (no. dist.) Tex. 1993. Assoc. Sewell & Riggs, Houston, 1976-82, ptnr., 1982-89, shareholder, 1990-94; ptnr. Strasburger & Price, LLP, Houston, 1994—. Exec. editor Washington and Lee Law Rev., 1976; contbr. articles to law jours. Active Houston YMCA, Amnesty Internat. U.S.A., ARC; del. state bar of Tex. to Rep. Cuba, 2001. Mem. Am. Law Inst., Tex. Assn. Def. Counsel, Def. Rsch. Inst., Product Liability Adv. Coun., Houston Bar Found., Tex. Bd. Legal Specialization (cert. civil trial lawyer, personal injury trial lawyer), U.S. Cycling Fedn., Sierra Club. General civil litigation, Insurance, Product liability. Office: Strasburger & Price LLP 1401 Mckinney Ste 2200 Houston TX 77010-3033 E-mail: bill.worthington@strasburger.com.

WOUNG-CHAPMAN, MARGUERITE NATALIE, lawyer; b. Kingston, Jamaica, Aug. 11, 1965; came to U.S., 1978; d. Maurice Lascelles and Lois (Ogle) W.; m. Kevin Troy Bingham May 27, 1990 (div. Apr. 1998); 1 child, Jordan Nile Bingham; m. Stanley G. Chapman III, May 28, 1999. BSLI, Georgetown U., 1986, JD, 1989. Bar: D.C., 1989, U.S. Dist. Ct. D.C., 1991. Assoc. Arter & Hadden, Washington, 1989-91; sr. atty. Tenneco Energy, Houston, 1991-95, counsel, 1995-97; atty. ARCO Pipeline Co., Houston, 1995; sr. counsel El Paso Corp., Houston, 1997-99, assoc. gen. counsel, v.p., 2000—; gen. counsel Tenn. Gas Pipeline Co., 2000—, ANR Pipeline Co., 2000—. Contbg. author: Banks and Thrifts - Government Enforcement and Receivership, 1991. Mem.: D.C. Bar Assn., Energy Bar Assn. FERC practice. Office: El Paso Corp 9 E Greenway Plz Ste 734 Houston TX 77046-0908 E-mail: Marguerite.Woung-Chapman@ElPaso.com.

WOVSANIKER, ALAN, lawyer, educator; b. Newark, Mar. 19, 1953; s. Harold and Sally (Gooen) W.; m. Susan Orme, Aug. 23, 1987. AB, Brown U., 1974; JD, Harvard U., 1977. Bar: N.J. 1977. Law clk. to presiding judge U.S. Dist. Ct. N.J., Camden, 1977-78; ptnr. Lowenstein Sandler PC, Roseland, N.J., 1978—. Adj. prof. Seton Hall Law Sch., 1988-91, Rutgers U. Law Sch., 1989-95; chmn. dist. ethics com. Supreme Ct. Contbr. articles to profl. jours. Mem. exec. com. N.J. chpt. Anti-Defamation League. Mem. Essex County Bar Assn. (trustee 1996-99, chmn. banking law com. 1994-97, chmn. corp. law com. 1999—). Banking, Mergers and acquisitions, Securities. Office: Lowenstein Sandler PC 65 Livingston Ave Roseland NJ 07068-1791 E-mail: awovsaniker@lowenstein.com.

WRAGE, JEFFREY S. lawyer; b. Rockford, Ill., Dec. 6, 1968; s. Keith L. Wrage and Jeanne W. Hart; m. Christine M. Hollis, Sept. 24, 1994; 1 child, Kendall M. BS in Bus. Econ. and Pub. Policy, Ind. U., 1991; JD, Valparaiso U., 1994. Bar: Ind. 1994, Ill. 1994. Assoc. atty. Christopher A. McQuillin & Assoc., Valparaiso, Ind., 1995—96, Dowd & Dowd, Chgo., 1996—97, Stellato & Schwartz, Chgo., 1997—98, Kopka, Landau & Pinkus, Crown Point, Ind., 1998—2000, Blachly, Tabor, Bozik & Hartman, Valparaiso, Ind., 2000—. Contbr. articles to profl. jours. Parish pastoral coun. St. Elizabeth Ann Seton Ch., Valparaiso, 2002. Mem.: ATLA (assoc.), Ind. Trial Lawyers Assn. (assoc.). Personal injury (including property damage), Transportation, General civil litigation. Office: Blachly Tabor Bozik & Hartman 56 S Washington St Ste 401 Valparaiso IN 46383 Office Fax: 219-464-0927. Business E-Mail: jswrage@btbhlaw.com.

WRAY, CECIL, JR., lawyer; b. Memphis, Nov. 19, 1934; s. Thomas Cecil and Margaret (Malone) W.; m. Gilda Gates, Sept. 11, 1964; children: Christopher A., Kathleen Wray Baughman. Student, U. Va., 1952-53; BA magna cum laude, Vanderbilt U., 1956; LLB, Yale U., 1959. Bar: Tenn. 1959, N.Y. 1961, U.S. Supreme Ct. 1964. Registered counseil juridique, France, 1978-82. Law clk. to justice Tom C. Clark U.S. Supreme Ct., Washington, 1959-60; assoc. Debevoise & Plimpton, N.Y.C., 1960-67, ptnr., 1968-96, of counsel, 1997-99, resident ptnr. Paris, 1976-79. Adj. prof. N.Y. Law Sch., 1997-2001. Co-author: Innovative Corporate Financing Techniques, 1986. Pres. Search & Care, Inc., N.Y.C., 1981-87, Episcopal Charities, N.Y.; vestryman St. James' Ch., N.Y.C., 1982-87, warden, 1988-94; trustee Fondation des Etats-Unis, Paris, 1976-79, Ch. Pension Fund; bd. dirs. East Side Comty. Ctr., Inc.; bd. fgn. parishes Episcopal Ch., 1995—; bd. dirs. Hudson Highlands Land Trust; commr. Adirondack Park Agy.; bd. dirs. Ch. Life Ins. Co. Fellow Am. Coll. Investment Counsel (trustee 1981-86, pres. 1983-84); mem. Am. Law Inst., Assn. Bar City N.Y., Coun. Fgn. Rels., Ausable Club (St. Huberts, N.Y.), Union Club, Century Club, Order of Coif, Phi Beta Kappa. Episcopalian. Corporate, general. Home: 47 E 88th St New York NY 10128-1152 Office: Debevoise & Plimpton 919 3rd Ave New York NY 10022-3902

WRAY, ROBERT, lawyer; s. George and Ann (Moriarty) W.; m. Lila Keogh (dec.); children: Jennifer, Edward, Hillary. BS, Loyola U., 1957; JD, U. Mich., 1960. Bar: DC, Ill. 1960. Assoc. Hopkins & Sutter, Chgo., 1964-69; gen. counsel Agy. for Internat. Devel., 1969-71; sr. counsel TRW, Inc., 1972-73, Export-Import Bank of the U.S., 1974-79; prin. Robert Wray Assocs., 1979-86; internat. ptnr. Pierson, Ball & Dowd, 1986-87; prin. Robert Wray Assocs., 1988—; spec. counsel Graham & James, 1988-97; ptnr. Holland & Knight, Washington, 1997—2003; mng. mem. Robert Wray PLLC, Washington, 2003—. Recipient medal of superior honor Dept. of State. Mem.: ABA, Internat. Bar Assn., Am. Soc. Internat. Law, Fed. Bar Assn., Chevy Chase Club, Annapolis Yacht Club, Talbot Country Club, Met. Club, Bretton Woods Com. Aviation, Private international. Office: 1150 Connecticut Ave NW Ste 350 Washington DC 20036

WRAY, THOMAS JEFFERSON, lawyer; b. Nashville, July 17, 1949; s. William Esker and Imogene (Cushman) W.; m. Susan Elizabeth Wells, Aug. 19, 1972; children: William Clark, Caroline Kell. BA, Emory U., 1971; JD, U. Va., 1974. Bar: Tex. 1974, U.S. Dist. Ct. (so., no. and ea. dists.) Tex. 1976, U.S. Ct. Appeals (5th and 11th cirs.) 1976, U.S. Supreme Ct. 1987. Assoc. Fulbright & Jaworski, L.L.P., Houston, 1974-82; ptnr. Fulbright & Jaworski, Houston, 1982—. Mem. ABA, Coll. Labor and Employment Lawyers, Houston Bar Assn., Houston Mgmt. Lawyers Forum (chmn. 1981-82), Briar Club, Phi Beta Kappa. Republican. Episcopalian. Civil rights, Federal civil litigation, Labor (including EEOC, Fair Labor Standards Act, labor-management relations, NLRB, OSHA). Home: 3662 Ella Lee Ln Houston TX 77027-4105 Office: Fulbright & Jaworski 1301 Mckinney St Ste 5100 Houston TX 77010-3095 E-mail: tjwray@fulbright.com.

WRIGHT, DANIEL A. lawyer; b. Washington, Sept. 30, 1946; s. William L. and Mary J. Wright; m. Deborah J. Wright, Sept. 5, 1981. BA, U. Calif., Davis, 1968; JD, Golden Gate U., 1978; Cert. in Pub. Adminstrn., U. Ala., 1969. Bar: Wash., U.S. Dist. Ct. (we. dist.) Wash. Claims officer Dept. Social and Health Svcs., Olympia, Wash., 1979—85; staff atty. Dept. of Licensing, Olympia, 1985—95; sole practitioner Tumwater, Wash., 1986—96; atty. William B. Pope & Assocs., Olympia, 1996—2001, McConnell, Meyer & Assocs., LLP, Olympia, 2001—. Adjudicator VA, San Francisco, 1979; law examiner Wash. State Bar Assn., Seattle, 1998. Asst. scoutmaster Boy Scouts Am., 1990—2001. Capt. U.S. Army, 1969-71, Vietnam. Regional Tng. Program in Pub. Adminstrn. fellow, 1968-69. Mem.: Wash. State Bar Assn. (fee dispute arbitration com. 1988—90, com. on professionalism 1998—2000, law office mgmt. assistance program com.), Clan Gregor (elections com., fundraising chmn. Pacific N.W. chpt. 1995—, fundraising chmn. 2000—). Avocations: woodworking, auto racing, astronomy, photography. Administrative and regulatory, Family and matrimonial, Probate (including wills, trusts). Office: McConnell, Meyer & Assocs 2112 Black Lake Blvd SE Olympia WA 98512 E-mail: dwright@lewiscountylaw.com.

WRIGHT, EUGENE ALLEN, federal judge; b. Seattle, Feb. 23, 1913; s. Elias Allen and Mary (Bailey) W.; m. Esther Ruth Ladley, Mar. 19, 1938; children: Gerald Allen, Meredith Ann Wright Morton. AB, U. Wash., 1935, JD, 1937; LLD, U. Puget Sound, 1984. Bar: Wash. 1937. Assoc. Wright & Wright, Seattle, 1937-54; judge Superior Ct. King County, Wash., 1954-66; v.p., sr. trust officer Pacific Nat. Bank Seattle, 1966-69; judge U.S. Ct. Appeals (9th cir.), Seattle, from 1969. Acting municipal judge, Seattle, 1948-52; mem. faculty Nat. Jud. Coll., 1964-72; lectr. Sch. Communications, U. Wash., 1965-66, U. Wash. Law Sch., 1952-74; lectr. appellate judges' seminars, 1973-76, Nat. Law Clks. Inst., La. State U., 1973; chmn. Wash. State Com. on Law and Justice, 1968-69; mem. com. on appellate rules Jud. Conf., 1978-85, mem. com. on courtroom photography, 1983-85, com. jud. ethics, 1984-92, com. Bicentennial of Constn., 1985-87. Author: (with others) The State Trial Judges Book, 1966; also articles; editor: Trial Judges Jour., 1963-66; contbr. articles to profl. jours. Chmn. bd. visitors U. Puget Sound Sch. Law, 1979-84; mem. bd. visitors U. Wash. Sch. Law, 1996; bd. dirs. Met. YMCA, Seattle, 1955-72; lay reader Episc Ch. Served to lt. col. USAR, 1941-46, col. Res., ret. Decorated Bronze Star, Combat Inf. badge; recipient Army Commendation medal, Disting. Service award U.S. Jr. C. of C., 1948, Disting. Service medal Am. Legion. Fellow Am. Bar Found.; mem. ABA (coun. div. jud. adminstrn. 1971-76), FBA (Disting. Jud. Svc. award 1984), Wash. Bar Assn. (award of merit 1983), Seattle-King County Bar Assn. (Spl. Disting. Svc. award 1984. William L. Dwyer Outstanding Jurist award 2001), Order of Coif, Wash. Athletic Club, Rainier Club, Masons (33 degree), Shriners, Delta Upsilon (Disting. Alumni Achievement award 1989), Phi Delta Phi. Home: Seattle, Wash. Died Sept. 3, 2002.

WRIGHT, FRANCES JOHNSON, mediator, arbitrator; b. Ind., Sept. 18, 1950; d. James and Frances Johnson; 1 child, Leila. BA, Duke U., 1972; JD, U. Fla., 1975; postgrad., Oxford (Eng.) U., 1974. Trial counsel Fla. Power Corp., St. Petersburg, Fla., 1975—78. Bd. dirs. So. Meth. U., Dallas, 1992—2002, Dallas Crime Commn., Dallas, 1992—97. Mem.: Dallas Bar Assn., Fla. Bar Assn., Tex. Bar Assn. Republican. Methodist. Office: Frances Johnson Wright PC 6223 Park Ln Dallas TX 75225

WRIGHT, FREDERICK LEWIS, II, lawyer; b. Roanoke, Va., Sept. 17, 1951; s. Frederick Lewis and Dorothy Marie (Trent) W.; m. Margaret Suzanne Rey, Oct. 16, 1982; children: Lauren Elizabeth, Emily Trent. BA, Ga. State U., 1978; JD, U. Ga., 1981. Bar: Ga. 1982, U.S. Dist. Ct. (no. dist.) Ga. 1984, U.S. Ct. Appeals (11th, 8th and 4th cirs.) 1984, U.S. Supreme Ct. 1990. Law clk. to presiding justice U.S. Ct. Appeals, Atlanta, 1981-82; ptnr. Smith, Currie and Hancock, Atlanta, 1982-96, Vaughn, Wright and Stearns, Atlanta, 1997—. Articles editor Ga. Law Rev., 1980—81. Mem.: ABA (forum com. constrn. industry), Ga. Def. Lawyers Assn. (chmn. constrn. law com.), Fed. Bar Assn., Def. Rsch. Inst., Order of Coif. Methodist. General civil litigation, Construction, Environmental. Office: One Paces West Ste 1740 2727 Paces Ferry Rd Atlanta GA 30339 E-mail: fwright@vws-attys.com.

WRIGHT, J(AMES) LAWRENCE, lawyer; b. Portland, Oreg., Apr. 12, 1943; s. William A. and Esther M. (Nelson) W.; m. Mary Aileene Roche, June 29, 1968; children: Rachel, Jonathan, Christopher. BBA, Gonzaga U., 1966, JD, 1972; LLM, NYU, 1977. Bar: Wash. 1972, U.S. Ct. Mil. Appeals 1974, U.S. Tax Ct. 1976, U.S. Supreme Ct. 1976. Prin. Halverson & Applegate, P.S., Yakima, Wash., 1972-74, 77—, pres., 1998—. Mem. St. Elizabeth Hosp. Found., Yakima, 1986-89, Yakima Meml. Hosp. Found., 1990—; pres. fin. bd. St. Paul's Cathedral, Yakima, 1979—; mem. fin. coun. Diocese of Yakima, 1994—; v.p. Apple Tree Racing Assn., 1986-87; bd. dirs. Capital Theatre, Yakima, 1985-95. Capt. U.S. Army, 1966-68, 74-76. Mem. ABA, Wash. Bar Assn., Yakima County Bar Assn., Rotary. Roman Catholic. Avocations: tennis, golf. Corporate, general, Estate planning, Taxation, general. Office: Halverson & Applegate PS PO Box 22730 311 N 4th St Yakima WA 98901-2467

WRIGHT, JOHN F. judge; BS, U. Nebr., 1967, JD, 1970. Atty. Wright & Simmons, 1970-84, Wright, Sorensen & Brower, 1984-91; mem., coord. Commn. on Post Secondary Edn., 1991-92; judge Nebr. Ct. Appeals, 1992-94; assoc. justice Nebr. Supreme Ct., 1994—. Chmn. bd. dirs. Panhandle Legal Svcs., 1970. Mem. Scottsbluff Bd. Edn., 1980-87, pres., 1984, 86. Served with U.S. Army, 1970, Nebr. N.G., 1970-76. Recipient Friend of Edn. award Scottsbluff Edn. Assn., 1992. Office: Nebr Supreme Ct 2207 State Capitol PO Box 98910 Lincoln NE 68509-8910

WRIGHT, JUDITH MARGARET, law librarian, educator, dean; b. Jackson, Tenn., Aug. 16, 1944; d. Joseph Clarence and Mary Catherine (Key) Wright; m. Mark A. Johnson, Apr. 17, 1976; children— Paul, Michael BS, U. Memphis, 1966; MA, U. Chgo., 1971; JD, DePaul U., 1980. Bar: Ill. 1980. Librarian Oceanway Sch., Jacksonville, Fla., 1966-67; program dir. ARC, South Vietnam, 1967-68; documents and reference librarian D'Angelo Law Library, U. Chgo., 1970-74, reference librarian, 1974-77, dir., lectr. in law, 1980-99, assoc. dean for libr. and info. svcs., lectr. in law, 1999—. Mem. adv. bd. Legal Reference Svcs. Quar., 1981—. Mem. ABA, Am. Assn. Law Libraries, Chgo. Assn. Law Libraries. Democrat. Methodist. Office: U Chgo Law Sch D'Angelo Law Libr 1121 E 60th St Chicago IL 60637-2745 Fax: 773-702-2889. E-mail: jm-wright@uchicago.edu.

WRIGHT, KENNETH BROOKS, lawyer; b. Whittier, Calif., June 5, 1934; s. Albert Harold and Marian (Schwey) W.; m. Sandra Beryl Smith, June 20, 1959; children: Margo Teresa, Daniel Brooks, John Waugh. BA cum laude, Pomona Coll., 1956; JD, Stanford U., 1960. Bar: Calif. 1961, U.S. Supreme Ct. 1979. Assoc., then ptnr. Lawler, Felix & Hall, 1961-77; ptnr. Morgan, Lewis & Bockius, LA, 1978—99, counsel, 1999—2003. Teaching team leader Nat. Inst. Trial Advocacy, 1978-80; mem. governing com. Calif. Continuing Edn. of Bar, 1973-77, chmn., 1975-76; nat. panel arbitrators Am. Arbitration Assn., 1970—; lectr. ABA Sect. Litigation Nat. Inst., 1979-86; bd. dirs. L.A. Internat. Comml. Arbitration Ctr. Chmn. bd. editors: Am. Bar Jour, 1977-81. Pres. Pomona Coll. Alumni Assn., 1970-71; pres. parent tchr. coun. Campbell Hall Sch., 1973-74, bd. dirs., 1976—, vice chmn., 1994—; counsel Vol. League San Fernando Valley, 1979-81; chmn. sect. adminstrn. of justice Town Hall of Calif., 1970-71; sr. warden Episcopal Ch., 1973-74. Served with U.S. Army, 1956-57. Mem. ABA (dir. programs litigation sect. 1977-81, mem. coun. 1982-88, mem. standing com on comm. 1978-88, chmn. 1987-88, chmn. sect. book pub. com. 1986-89, pres. fellows young lawyers 1985-86, bd. dirs. 1980-89), Internat. Bar Assn., Assn. Bus. Trial Lawyers (chair com. alt. dispute resolution 1991-93, bd. dirs. 1993-96), Am. Law Inst., Am. Bar Found., State Bar Calif. (mem. gov. com. continuing edn. of the bar 1972-77, chmn. 1975-76), Conf. Barristers (exec. com. 1966-69, 1st v.p. 1969), L.A. County Bar Assn. (com. on judiciary 1981-83, chmn. continuing legal edn. adv. com. 1989-91, vice-chmn. continuing legal edn. com. 1991-93, bd. dirs. L.A. Lawyers 1989-94), L.A. County Bar Found. (bd. dirs., trustee 1993-99, mem. exec. com. internat. sect. 1996-99), Jonathan Club, Chancery Club, Phi Beta Kappa. Republican. Avocations: skiing, tennis. Federal civil litigation, State civil litigation, Environmental. Home: 3610 Longridge Ave Sherman Oaks CA 91423-4918 Office: Morgan Lewis & Bockius 300 S Grand Ave Los Angeles CA 90071-3109

WRIGHT, MINTURN TATUM, III, lawyer; b. Phila., Aug. 7, 1925; s. Minturn T. and Anna (Moss) W.; m. Nonya R. Stevens, May 11, 1957; children: Minturn T., Richard S., Robert M., Marianne F. BA, Yale U., 1949; LLB, U. Pa., 1952. Bar: Pa. 1953, U.S. Ct. Appeals (3d cir.) 1953, U.S. Supreme Ct. 1962. Law clk. U.S. Ct. Appeals (3d cir.), 1952-53; assoc. Dechert, Price & Rhoads, Phila., 1953-61, ptnr., 1961-95, chmn., 1982-84. Bd. dirs. Cotiga Devel. Co.; vis. prof. U. Pa. Law Sch., 1965—69, 1993—97. Contbr. articles to profl. jours. Trustee Acad. Natural Scis. Phila., 1958—, chmn., 1976-81; trustee Hawk Mountain Sanctuary Assn., chmn. bd. dirs., 1992-97; trustee Rare Ctr., Pa. chpt. The Nature Conservancy, Exec. Svc. Corps.; trustee Marshall-Reynolds Found. Served with U.S. Army, 1943-46. Mem. ABA, Pa. Bar Assn., Phila. Bar Assn., Nat. Coal Lawyers Assn., Eastern Mineral Law Assn. (trustee), Phila. Club, Milldam Club. Episcopalian. Commercial, contracts (including sales of goods; commercial financing), Probate (including wills, trusts). Office: Dechert Price & Rhoads 4000 Bell Atlantic Tower 1717 Arch St Ste 4000 Philadelphia PA 19103-2793

WRIGHT, PAUL WILLIAM, lawyer, oil company executive; b. Jamestown, N.Y., July 7, 1944; s. Julian M. and Ruth (Blake) W.; m. Elizabeth O'Rourke Wright, Nov. 22, 1975; children: Jeffrey, Stephen. BS in Bus. Adminstrn., Georgetown U., 1966, JD, 1969. Bar: Va. 1969, D.C. 1972, Tex. 1973, La. 1985, U.S. Supreme Ct. 1972. Staff atty. Fed Power Commn., 1969-70; assoc. Wolf & Case, Washington, 1970-72; atty. Exxon Corp., Houston, 1973—, chief atty., 1986-92; sr. staff counsel Exxon Co. Internat. Bd. dirs. La. Pro Bono-Project, 1986-90. Mem. ABA, Tex. Bar Assn., La. Bar Assn., Va. Bar Assn., D.C. Bar Assn., La. Bar Found. (bd. dirs., sec., treas. 1986-87, v.p. 1987-89, pres. 1989-91). Alternative dispute resolution, General civil litigation, Private international. Office: Exxon Mobil Corp PO Box 2180 Houston TX 77252-1347 E-mail: paul.w.wright@exxonmobil.com., pwwright66@yahoo.com.

WRIGHT, PETER MELDRIM, lawyer; b. Charlottesville, Va., Apr. 10, 1946; s. David McCord and Caroline Wallace (Jones) W.; m. Astrid Gabriella Mercedes Sandberg, June 4, 1972; children: David Habersham, Christian Langdon. AB, U. Ga., 1967, JD, 1972. Bar: Ga. 1972, U.S. Dist. Ct. (no. dist.) Ga. 1972. Assoc. Jones, Bird & Howell, Atlanta, 1972-77, ptnr., 1977-82, Alston & Bird, Atlanta, 1982-2001; gen. counsel Resource Healthcare of Am., Inc., 2001—; pres., chmn. bd. dirs. Skidaway Health & Living Svcs., Inc., 2003—. Author: A Survey of State Blue Sky Laws Applicable to Tax Exempt Bonds, 1987, Long Term Care Facilities, Chapter 7 of Health Care Corporate Law—Facilities and Transactions, 1996. Sec. Atlanta coun. Soc. Colonial Wars in Ga., 1975-88, dep. gov., 1989-91, mem. coun., 2003—; mem. Soc. Cin. Ga., Savannah, historian, 1996—, v.p., 1998—. Mem. Ga. Bar Assn., Nat. Assn. Bond Lawyers (chmn. blue sky laws and legal investment law coms. 1982-85, bd. dirs. 1985-86), Ga. Hist. Soc. (bd. curators 1993-2000, sec. 1994-98; v.p. Atlanta chpt. 1998-2000), Skidway Health and Living Svs., Inc (pres., dir. 2003-), Oglethorpe Club (Savannah, Ga.), St. Andrew's Soc. Savannah. Corporate, general, Finance, Health. Home: 3502 Woodhaven Rd NW Atlanta GA 30305-1011 Office: Resource Healthcare Am One Buckhead Plaza Ste 900 3060 Peachtree Rd NW Atlanta GA 30305

WRIGHT, ROBERT JOSEPH, lawyer; b. Rome, Ga., Dec. 13, 1949; s. Arthur Arley and Maude T. (Lacey) W.; m. Donna Ruth Bishop, Feb. 18, 1972; children: Cynthia Ashley, Laura Christine. BA cum laude, Ga. State U., 1979; JD cum laude, U. Ga., 1983. Bar: GA 1983, U.S. Dist. Ct. (no. dist.) Ga. 1983, U.S. Dist. Ct. (mid. dist.) Ga. 1985. Assoc. Craig & Gainer, Covington, Ga., 1983-84, Heard, Leverett & Adams, Elberton, Ga., 1984-86; gen. counsel Group Underwriters, Inc., Elberton, Ga., 1987—2002. Mem. editl. staff Ga. Jour. Internat. and Comparative Law, 1981-82. Mem. State Bar Ga. (sec. legal econs. sect. 1987-88, chmn. legal econs. sect. 1988-90), Order of the Coif, Masons, Phi Alpha Delta. Baptist. Insurance, Land use and zoning (including planning), Personal injury (including property damage). Home: 1030 E Canyon Creek Ct Watkinsville GA 30677-1500

WRIGHT, ROBERT PAYTON, lawyer; b. Beaumont, Tex., Feb. 15, 1951; s. Vernon Gerald and Huberta Read (Nunn) W.; m. Sallie Chesnutt Smith, July 16, 1977; children: Payton Cullen, Elizabeth Risher. AB, Princeton U., 1972; JD, Columbia U., 1975. Bar: Tex. 1975. Ptnr. Baker Botts L.L.P., Houston, 1975—. Author: The Texas Homebuyer's Manual, 1986. Mem. Am. Coll. Real Estate Lawyers (bd. govs. 2002—), State Bar Tex. (chmn. coun. real estate, probate, trust law sect. 1994-95), Houston Bar Assn. (chmn. real estate sect. 1989-90), Tex. Coll. Real Estate Lawyers, Houston Real Estate Lawyers Coun., Houston Club. Episcopalian. Environmental, Finance, Property, real (including real estate development, water).

WRIGHT, ROBERT ROSS, III, law educator; b. Ft. Worth, Nov. 20, 1931; m. Susan Webber; children: Robert Ross IV, John, David, Robin. BA cum laude, U. Ark., 1953, JD, 1956; MA (grad. fellow), Duke U., 1954; SJD (law fellow), U. Wis., 1967. Bar: Ark. 1956, U.S. Supreme Ct. 1968, Okla. 1970. Instr. polit. sci. U. Ark., 1955-56; mem. firm Forrest City, Ark., 1956-58; ptnr. Norton, Norton & Wright, Forrest City, 1959; asst. gen. counsel, asst. sec. Crossett Co., Ark.; atty. Crossett div. Ga.-Pacific Corp., 1960-63; asst. sec. Pub. Utilities Co., Crossett, Triangle Bag Co., Covington, Ky., 1960-62; faculty U. Ark. Law Sch., 1963-70; asst. prof., dir. continuing legal edn. and research, then asst. dean U. Ark., Little Rock, 1965-66, prof. law, 1967-70; prof. U. Okla., 1970-77; dean U. Okla. Coll. Law; dir. U. Okla. Law Center, 1970-76; vis. prof. U. Ark., Little Rock, 1976-77; Donaghey Disting. prof. U. Ark, 1977-99, Donaghey disting. prof. emeritus, 1999—. Vis. disting. prof. U. Cin., 1983; vis. prof. law U. Iowa, 1969-70; vis. prof. U. Ark., Little Rock, 1976-77; Ark. commr. Nat. Conf. Commrs. Uniform State Laws, 1967-70; past chmn. Com. Uniform Eminent Domain Code; past mem. Com. Uniform Probate Code, Ark. Gov.'s Ins. Study Commn.; chmn. Gov. Commn. on Uniform Probate Code; chmn. task force joint devel. Hwy. Research Bd.; vice chmn. Okla. Jud. Council, 1970-72, chmn., 1972-75; chmn. Okla. Center Criminal Justice, 1971-76 Author: Arkansas Eminent Domain Digest, 1964, Arkansas Probate Practice System, 1965, The Law of Airspace, 1968, Emerging Concepts in the Law of Airspace, 1969, Cases and Materials on Land Use, 3d edit., 1982, supplement, 1987, 5th edit., 1997, Uniform Probate Code Practice Manual, 1972, Model Airspace Code, 1973, Land Use in a Nutshell, 1978, 4th edit., 2000, The Arkansas Form Book, 1979, 2d edit., 1988, Zoning Law in Arkansas: A Comparative Analysis, 1980, Old Seeds in the New Land: A History and Reminiscences of the Bar of Arkansas, 2001; contbr. articles to profl. jours. Mem. Little Rock Planning Commn., 1978-82, chmn., 1982. Named Ark. Man of Year Kappa Sigma, 1958. Fellow: Am. Coll. Trust and Estate Counsel (acad.), Am. Law Inst.; mem.: ABA (past chmn., exec. coun. gen. practice, solo and small firm sect., former chmn. new pubs. editl. bd., sect. officers conf., ho. of dels. 1994—2000, standing com. fed. jud. improvements 1998—), Pulaski County Bar Assn., Ark. Bar Assn. (life; exec. coun. 1985—88, ho. of dels., chmn. eminent domain code com., past mem. com. new bar ctr., past chmn. preceptorship com., exec. com. young laywers sect.), Okla. Bar Assn. (past vice-chmn. legal internship com., former vice-chmn. gen. practice sect.), U. Ark. Alumni Assn., U. Wis. Alumni Assn., Duke U. Alumni Assn., Omicron Delta Kappa, Phi Alpha Delta, Phi Beta Kappa, Order of Coif. Episcopalian. Home: 249 Pleasant Valley Dr Little Rock AR 72212-3170

WRIGHT, ROBERT THOMAS, JR., lawyer; b. Detroit, Oct. 4, 1946; s. Robert Thomas and Jane Ellen (Blandin) W.; m. Diana Feltman, June 8, 1994; children: Sarah Allison, Jonathan Brian. BA in History and Polit. Sci., U. N.C., 1968; JD, Columbia U., 1974. Bar: Fla. 1974. Assoc. Paul & Thomson, Miami, Fla., 1974-77, Mershon, Sawyer, Johnston, Dunwoody & Cole, Miami, 1977-81, ptnr., 1981-95, Shutts & Bowen, Miami, 1995-98; shareholder, dir. Verner, Liipfert, Bernhard, McPherson & Hand, Miami, 1998—2001; founding ptnr. Coffey & Wright, L.L.P., Miami, 2002—. 1st lt. U.S. Army, 1968-71. Mem. ABA, Fla. Bar, Dade County Bar Assn. Avocations: golf, rugby, African cichlids. Federal civil litigation, State civil litigation, Insurance. Home: 11095 SW 84th Ct Miami FL 33156-4311 Office: Coffey & Wright LLP Penthouse 2-B 2665 S Bayshore Dr Miami FL 33133 E-mail: RTWJr1@aol.com., RWright@Coffeywright.com.

WRIGHT, SCOTT OLIN, federal judge; b. Haigler, Nebr., Jan. 15, 1923; s. Jesse H. and Martha I. Wright; m. Shirley Frances Young, Aug. 25, 1972. Student, Central Coll., Fayette, Mo., 1940-42; LLB, U. Mo., Columbia, 1950. Bar: Mo. 1950. City atty., Columbia, 1951-53; pros. atty. Boone County, Mo., 1954-58; practice of law Columbia, 1958-79; U.S. dist. judge Western Dist. Mo., Kansas City, from 1979. Pres. Young Democrats Boone County, 1950, United Fund Columbia, 1965. Served with USN, 1942-43; as aviator USMC, 1943-46. Decorated Air medal. Mem. ABA, Am. Trial Lawyers Assn., Mo. Bar Assn., Mo. Trial Lawyers Assn., Boone County Bar Assn. Clubs: Rockhill Tennis, Woodside Racquet. Lodges: Rotary (pres. Columbia 1965). Unitarian Universalist. Office: Charles E Whitaker Courthouse 400 E 9th St Ste 8662 Kansas City MO 64106-2684

WRIGHT, SUSAN WEBBER, judge; b. Texarkana, Ark., Aug. 22, 1948; d. Thomas Edward and Betty Jane (Gary) Webber; m. Robert Ross Wright, III, May 21, 1983; 1 child, Robin Elizabeth. BA, Randolph-Macon Woman's Coll., 1970; MPA, U. Ark., 1972, JD with high honors, 1975. Bar: Ark. 1975. Law clk. U.S. Ct. Appeals (8th Cir.), 1975-76; from asst. prof. to assoc. prof. law U. Ark., Little Rock, 1976—83, prof., 1983-90, asst. dean, 1976-78; dist. judge U.S. Dist. Ct. (ea. dist.) Ark., Little Rock, 1990—, chief judge, 1998—. Vis. assoc. prof. Ohio State U., Columbus, 1981, La. State U., Baton Rouge, 1982—83; mem. adv. com. U.S. Ct. Appeals (8th cir.), St. Louis, 1983—88. Author (with R. Wright): (book) Land Use in a Nutshell, 1978, Land Use in a Nutshell, 2d edit., 1985; editor-in-chief: Ark. Law Rev., 1975; contbr. articles to profl. jours. Mem.: Ark. Assn. Women Lawyers (v.p. 1977—78), Am. Law Inst., Pulaski County Bar Assn., Ark. Bar Assn., Am. Judicature Soc., Ark. Women's Forum. Episcopalian. Office: US District Court 600 W Capitol Ave Ste 520 Little Rock AR 72201-3329

WRIGHT, WILLIAM EVERARD, JR., lawyer; b. New Orleans, Dec. 4, 1949; s. William E. and Claire (Carter) W.; m. Alice Marquez, May 26, 1972; children: Matthew, Caroline. BA, Tulane U., 1971, JD, 1974. Bar: La. 1974. Assoc. Little, Schwartz & Dussom, New Orleans, 1974-76; ptnr. Baldwin & Haspel, New Orleans, 1976-91, Deutsch, Kerrigan & Stiles, New Orleans, 1991—. Mem. La. Bd. Examiners, 1981-84. Mem. ABA (chmn. profl., officers' and dirs. liability law com. 1997-98, constrn. forum), Associated Builders and Contractors (bd. dirs.), La. Bar Assn. (bd. dels. 1985-90), New Orleans Bar Assn. (exec. com. 1980-86, officer 1983-86), New Orleans C. of C. General civil litigation, Construction, Professional liability. Home: 700 Eleonore St New Orleans LA 70115-3249 Office: Deutsch Kerrigan & Stiles 755 Magazine St Ste 100 New Orleans LA 70130-3672 E-mail: wwright@dkslaw.com.

WRIGLEY, DREW H. lawyer; b. Fargo, N.D., Oct. 1965; BA, U. N.D., 1988; JD, Am. U., 1991. Pros. atty. City of Fargo, 1992—93; asst. dist. atty. Phila. Dist. Atty.'s Office, 1993—98; gen. counsel for pub. policy N.D. Workers Compensation Bur., 1998—99; exec. dir., legal counsel ND Rep. Party, 1999—2000; dep. chief of staff Office of Gov. of N.D., 2000—01; U.S. atty. N.D., 2001—. Office: 655 First Ave N Ste 250 Fargo ND 58102

WROBLE, ARTHUR GERARD, judge; b. Taylor, Pa., Jan. 21, 1948; s. Arthur S. and Sophia P. Wroble; m. Mary Ellen Sheehan, Nov. 19, 1977; children: Sophia Ann, Sarah Jean, Stacey Margaret. BSBA with honors, U. fla., 1970, MBA, 1971, JD, 1973. Bar: Fla. 1973, U.S. Ct. Appeals (5th cir.) 1974, U.S. Ct. Appeals (11th cir.) 1981, U.S. Dist. Ct. (so. dist.) Fla. 1974, U.S. Dist. Ct. (mid. dist.) 1982, U.S. Dist. Ct. (no. dist.) Fla. 1986, U.S. Army Ct. Mil. Rev. 1989, U.S. Ct. Mil. Appeals 1990, U.S. Supreme Ct. 1976. Ptnr. Burns, Middleton, Farrell & Faust (now Steel, Hector, Davis, West), Palm Beach, Fla., 1973-82, Wolf, Block, Schorr & Solis-Cohen, Phila. & West Palm Beach, 1982-87, Scott, Royce, Harris & Bryan, P.A., Palm Beach, 1987-89, Grantham and Wroble, P.A., Lake Worth, 1989-92; prin. Arthur G. Wroble, P.A., West Palm Beach, 1992-2000; cir. judge 15th Jud. Ct. Fla., Palm Beach, 2001—. Mem. 15th Jud. Cir. Ct. Nominating Commn., 1979-83; mem. U. Fla. Law Ctr. Council, 1981-84, 99—, U.S. Magistrate Merit Selection Panel, so. dist. Fla., 1987; mem. adv. bd. alternative sentencing program Palm Beach County Pub. Defender's Office; adj. instr. bus. law Coll. of Boca Raton (now Lynn U.), 1988; mem. U.S. Military Acad. Screening com., 16th Dist., Fla., 2001-. Contbr. to profl. jours. Bd. dirs. Palm Glades Girl Scout Coun., 1996—. Served to lt. col. JAG, USAR. Named Eagle Scout, Boy Scouts Am., 1962. Mem. ABA, Fla. Bar (bd. govs. young lawyers sect. 1979-83, bd. govs. 1985-89), Palm Beach County Bar Assn. (pres. young lawyers sect. 1978-79, bd. dirs. 1979-81, sec.-treas. 1981-83, pres. 1984-85), Fla. Bar Found. (bd. dirs. 1990-93), Fla. Assn. Women Lawyers, Fla. Coun. Bar Assn. Pres. (bd. dirs. 1986-92), Hispanic Bar Assn. of Palm Beach County, F.M. Cunningham Bar Assn., Guild Cath. Lawyers Diocese Palm Beach, Inc. (pres. 1980-81, bd. dirs. 1981-2001, Monsignor Jeremiah P. O'Mahoney Outstanding

Lawyer award 1993), Legal Aid Soc. Palm Beach County, Inc. (bd. dirs. 1981-2000), Univ. Fla. Alumni Assn., Palm Beach County Club (pres. 1983-84), Kiwanis (pres. 1980-81, pres. West Palm Beach found. 1989-2000, dir. 1991—, Citizen of Yr. 1994, George F. Hixon fellowship 1999), KC (grand knight 1978-79), Am. Inns of Ct LIV (West Palm Beach chpt. pres. 1999-2000, bd. dirs. 1995-2000). Roman Catholic. Office: Palm Beach County Cthse 205 N Dixie Hwy West Palm Beach FL 33401-4522

WROBLESKI, JEANNE PAULINE, lawyer; b. Phila., Feb. 14, 1942; d. Edward Joseph and Pauline (Popelak) Wrobleski; m. Robert J. Klein, Dec. 3, 1979. BA, Immaculata Coll., 1964; MA, U. Pa., 1966; JD, Temple U., 1975. Bar: Pa. 1975. Pvt. practice law, Phila., 1975—; pres., shareholder Jeanne Wrobleski & Assocs., LLC, Phila., 1999—. Lectr. Bus. Law Wharton Sch., Phila.; mem. Commn. on Women and the Legal Profession, 1986—89; v.p. Center City Residents' Assn.; Eisenhower Citizen Amb. del. Soviet Union; judge Pro Tem Phila. Ct. Common Pleas; bd. dirs. Charlotte Cushman Found. Bd. dirs., mem. exec. com. Temple Law Alumni; del. Moscow Conf. on Law and Econ. Coop., 1990; del. to jud. conf. 3d Cir. U.S. Ct. Appeals, 1991; mediator U.S. Dist. Ct. (ea. dist.) Pa., 1996; bd. trustees Phila. Prisons; Bd. dirs. South St. Dance Co., Women in Transition; bd. dirs., vice chair The Wilma Theater. Rhea Liebman scholar, 1974. Mem.: ABA, AAUW, Jagiellonian Law Soc. (exec. com.), Am. Judicature Soc., Phila. Bar Assn. (chmn. women's rights com. 1986, com. on jud. selection and retention 1986—87, chmn. appellate cts. com. 1992, bus. cts. task force, com. on bus. litigation), Pa. Bar Assn., Phila. Art Alliance, Nat. Mus. Women in the Arts, Pa. Acad. Fine Arts, Penn Club, Lawyers Club, Founders Club, The Cosmopolitan Club, Lambda Iota Tau, Alpha Psi Omega. Democrat. Federal civil litigation, General civil litigation. Office: Jeanne Wrobleski & Assocs LLC 1845 Walnut St Fl 24 Philadelphia PA 19103-4708 E-mail: jwrobleski@wwdlaw.com.

WRUBLE, BERNHARDT KARP, lawyer; b. Wilkes-Barre, Pa., Mar. 21, 1942; s. Maurice and Ruth Yvonne (Karp) W.; m. Judith Marilyn Eyges, Nov. 16, 1968 (div. 1987); children: Justine, Vanessa, Alexis; m. Jill Diamond, Nov. 24, 1990; children: Mattia, Austin. BA in Polit. Sci., Williams Coll., Williamstown, Mass., 1963; LLB, U. Pa., 1966; postgrad., NYU, 1972-74, Harvard U., 1978. Bar: U.S. Dist. Ct. (so. dist.) N.Y. 1969, U.S. Dist. Ct. (ea. dist.) N.Y. 1972, U.S. Ct. Appeals (2d cir.) 1972, U.S. Supreme Ct. 1972, U.S. Ct. Appeals (7th cir.) 1974, U.S. Ct. Appeals (D.C. and 4th cirs.) 1984, U.S. Ct. Appeals (5th cir.) 1985, U.S. Ct. Appeals (11th cir.) 1986. Law clk. to presiding judge U.S. Ct. Appeals (3d cir.), 1966-67; assoc. Simpson, Thacher & Bartlet, N.Y.C., 1968-73; ptnr. Simpson, Thatcher & Bartlet, N.Y.C., 1974-77; prin. dep. gen. counsel U.S. Dept. Army, Washington, 1977-79; dir. Office Govt. Ethics, Washington, 1979; exec. asst. to sec. and dep. sec. U.S. Dept. Energy, Washington, 1979-81; dir. Pres.'s Interagy. Coal Export Task Force, Washington, 1980-81; ptnr. Verner, Liipfert, Bernhard, McPherson and Hand, Washington, 1981-99; sr. v.p. legal affairs Northwest Airlines, St. Paul, 1999—2001. Bd. dirs. Epilepsy Found. Am., 1983, chmn., 1991. Mem. ABA, D.C. Bar Assn., N.Y. State Bar Assn., Williams Coll. Alumni Assn. (pres. Washington chpt. 1986-91), Williams Coll. Soc. Alumni Assn. (exec. com. 1988-91). Democrat. Antitrust, Federal civil litigation, Corporate, general. E-mail: bkwruble@yahoo.com.

WU, ROBIN CHI CHING, lawyer; b. Guangxi, People's Republic of China, Jan. 6, 1941; came to U.S., 1955; s. Paul S.C. and Janny S.F. (Wong) W. BA, Fordham U., 1964; MA, Columbia U., 1967; LLD, N.Y. Law Sch., 1983. Bar: N.Y. 1983, N.J. 1984. Asst. libr. Fed. Res. Bank N.Y., N.Y.C., 1967-68; asst. dir. rsch. Nat. Rev. mag., N.Y.C., 1968-72, dir. rsch., 1972-79; dir. rsch. TV program Firing Line, N.Y.C., 1972-79; pvt. practice N.Y.C., 1983—. Editor Bridge, 1972, Asian-Am. jour. Mem. N.Y. State Bar Assn., N.Y. County Lawyers Assn., N.J. State Bar Assn. Avocations: reading, writing, movies. Commercial, contracts (including sales of goods; commercial financing), General practice, Property, real (including real estate development, water). Office: 8 Chatham Sq New York NY 10038-1000

WU, SUI-YU, lawyer; LLB, Nat. Taiwan U., 1980; LLM, U. Mich., 1987, JD, 1995. Bar: Taiwan 1983, N.Y. 1990. Assoc. Lee & Li, 1981—82, sr. atty., 1983—86, 1989—94; assoc. prof. Soochow U. Law Sch., 1996—; of counsel Perkins Cole, Taipei, Taiwan, 1996—97, mng. ptnr., 1997—2000; assoc. prof. Inst. Law Sci. and Tech., Tsing Huw U. Law Sch., 2002—. Vis. atty. Van Bael & Bellis, Brussels, 1988, Nishimura & Assocs., Tokyo, 1989; vis. rschr. European Law Rsch. Ctr., Harvard Law Sch., 1993. Contbr. articles to profl. jours. Mem.: ABA, Assn. Comml. Arbitration (arbitrator 1990), State Bar N.Y., Internat. Bar Assn., Taipei Bar Assn. (vice chair com. internat. affairs 1993—96, dir. 1993—96), Inter-Pacific Bar Assn. (chair internat. trade com. 1999—2001, vice chair internat. trade com. 1995—99, coun. mem. 1991—94). Office: Lec Tsai and Ptnrs 5A 218 Tun Hwa S Rd Sect 2 Taipei 106 Taiwan

WUERMELING, ULRICH URBAN, lawyer; b. Muenster, Germany, Dec. 24, 1964; s. Georg and Ursula Wuermeling. LLB, U. Bayreuth, Germany, 1992. Atty. Wessing, Frankfurt, Germany, 1996; editor Verlagsgruppe Handelsblatt, Dusseldorf, Germany, 1991; head multimedia law group Wessing, Frankfurt, Germany, 1999—2001; mem. IT Group Latham & Watkins Schön Nolte, Frankfurt, 2001—. Communications, Computer, Mergers and acquisitions. Office: Latham & Watkins Schön Nolte Platz Der Einheit 2 D-60327 Frankfurt Main Germany E-mail: ulrich.wuermeling@lw.com.

WUERZNER, ANDREA, lawyer; b. Yverdon, Switzerland, Sept. 7, 1969; d. Peter and Dorothee W. Degree in law, U. Lausanne, Switzerland, 1993, U. N.C., 1998. Bar: Geneva 1995, Zürich 1998. Lawyer Pestalozzi Lachenal Patry, Zürich, 1998—. Commercial, contracts (including sales of goods; commercial financing), Corporate, general. Office: Pestalozzi Lachenal Patry Löwenstr 1 8001 Zürich Switzerland Fax: 41.1.217.92.17.

WUNDER, DAVID HART, lawyer; b. Argo, Ill., Dec. 6, 1925; s. Mylton Bowerman and Marian Antoinette (Richcreek) W.; m. Shirley May Dahlin, June 10, 1950 (dec. Oct. 1974); children: Rebecca Anne, David Hart II; m. Mary Ann Koestner, May 9, 1980. BA, Wabash Coll., Crawfordsville, Ind., 1950; JD, ITT-Chgo. Kent Coll. Law, 1962. Bar: Ind., U.S. Dist. Ct. (no. and so. dists.) 1985, U.S. Supreme Ct. 1974. Enforcement atty., officer, mgr. Ill. Sec. of State, Chgo., 1963-72, securities commr. Springfield, 1972-84; ptnr. Wunder and Wunder, Indpls., 1985—. Sgt. U.S. Army, 1944-46, PTO. Mem. Am. Legion (dist. comdr. 1972), SAR, Soc. Mayflower Descs. Avocations: reading, exercise sports. Bankruptcy, Commercial, consumer (including collections, credit), Family and matrimonial. Home: 40 W Thompson Rd Indianapolis IN 46217-3558 Office: Wunder and Wunder 7551 S Shelby St Ste #303 Indianapolis IN 46227

WUNNICKE, BROOKE, lawyer; b. Dallas, May 9, 1918; d. Rudolph von Falkenstein and Lulu Lenore Brooke; m. James M. Wunnicke, Apr. 11, 1940; (dec. 1977); 1 child, Diane B. BA, Stanford U., 1939; JD, U. Colo., 1945. Bar: Wyo. 1946, Colo. 1969, U.S. Dist. Ct. Wyo. 1947, U.S. Dist. Ct. Colo. 1970, U.S. Supreme Ct. 1958, U.S. Ct. Appeals (10th cir.) 1958. Pvt. practice law, 1946-56; ptnr. Williams & Wunnicke, Cheyenne, Wyo., 1956-69; of counsel Calkins, Kramer, Grimshaw & Harring, Denver, 1969-73; chief appellate dep. atty. Dist. Atty's Office, Denver, 1973-86; of counsel Hall & Evans L.L.C., Denver, 1986—. Adj. prof. law U. Denver Coll. of Law, 1978-97; lectr. Internat. Practicum Inst. Denver, 1978—. Author: Ethics Compliance for Business Lawyers, 1987; co-author: Standby Letters of Credit, 1989, Corporate Financial Risk Management, 1992, Legal Opinion Letters Formbook, 2d edit., 2002, UCP 500 and Standby Letters of Credit-Special Report, 1994, Standby and Commercial Letters of Credit, 1996, 3d edit., 2000, Supplement, 2003; contbr. articles to profl. jours. Pres. Laramie County Bar Assn., Cheyenne, Wy., 1967-68; Dir. Cheyenne C. of C., Cheyenne, Wy., 1965-68. Recipient awards for Outstanding Svc., Colo. Dist. Attys. Coun., 1979, 82, 86, Disting. Alumni award U. Colo. Sch. of Law, 1986, 93, Lathrop Trailblazer award Colo. Women's Bar Assn., 1992, William Lee Knous award U. Colo., 1997, Eleanor P. Williams award disting. svc. to legal profession, 1997, Potter Lifetime Profl. Svc. award, 1999, Def. Rsch. Inst. Ann. Nat. award, 1999; named first Frank H. Ricketson Jr. Adj. Prof., U. Denver Coll. Law, 1997. Fellow Colo. Bar Found. (hon.); mem. ABA, Wyo. State Bar, Denver Bar Assn. (hon. life; trustee 1977-80), Colo. Bar Assn. (hon., life, Award of Merit 1999), Am. Arbitration Assn. (nat. panel, regional panel), William E. Doyle Inn of Ct. (hon.), Order of Coif, Phi Beta Kappa. Republican. Avocations: reading, writing, teaching, lecturing. Office: Hall & Evans L L C 1125 17th St Ste 600 Denver CO 80202 also: 1125 17th St Ste 600 Denver CO 80202

WUNSCH, KATHRYN SUTHERLAND, retired lawyer; b. Tipton, Mo., Jan. 30, 1935; d. Lewis Benjamin and Norene Marie (Wolf) Sutherland; m. Charles Martin Wunsch, Dec. 22, 1956 (div. May 1988); children: Debra Kay Wolff, Laura Ellen Stubberud. AB, Ind. U., 1958, JD summa cum laude, 1977; postgrad., Stanford (Calif.) U., 1977. Founder Wunsch and George, San Francisco, 1989-93, Kathryn Wunsch and Assoc. Counsel, San Francisco, 1993-99; ret., 1999. Articles editor Ind. U. Law Rev., 1975-76. Trustee Minuteman Found., 2002—; sec. Opera Las Vegas Guild, 2002—. Mem. Sun City Anthem Garden Club (founder, pres. 2001—), Phi Beta Kappa (v.p. no. calif. 1995-97). Republican. Avocations: collecting fine art and antiques, theater, opera, gardening, hiking.

WUORI, MATTI OSSIAN, lawyer, environmental affairs consultant; b. Helsinki, July 15, 1945; s. Ossi Valdemar and Toini (Tjaga) W. LLM, Helsinki U., 1979. Lic. advocate, Finland. Jr. lawyer Asianajotoimisto Erhard Galle, Kerava, Finland, 1967-68; sr. ptnr. Asianajotoimisto Matti Wuori Ky, Helsinki, 1970—. Ombudsman, arbitrator Helsinki Journalists Assn., Helsinki, 1970-83; chmn. Greenpeace Internat., 1991-93; mem. various state coms. in Finland. Contbr. articles to various publs. Spl. advisor Truth and Reconciliation Commn., South Africa, 1996—98; mem., human rights rapporteur European Parliament, 1999—; founder, v.p. Suomen Varusmiesliitto, Helsinki, 1970—73; v.p. Am. Field Svc. - Finland, 1966—67. Mem. Finnish Bar Assn., Internat. Bar Assn., Internat. Commn. Jurists (pres. Helsinki chpt. 1988—), Union Internat. Avocats Human Rights Commn. Avocation: history. Office: Arkadiankatu 12 B 48 SF-00100 Helsinki Finland E-mail: mwuori@europarl.eu.int., matti.wuori@mattiwuori.fi.

WYATT, DEBORAH CHASEN, lawyer; b. Atlanta, Apr. 19, 1949; d. S.H. and Catherine Jane (Hudlow) Chasen; m. Richard Haste Wyatt, Jr., Feb. 19, 1972; children: Thomas Clayton, William Tyler. Student, Sweet Briar Col., 1968-70; BA, Tufts U., 1971; JD, U. Va., 1978. Bar: Va. 1978, U.S. Dist. Ct. (we. and ea. dists.) Va. 1978, U.S. Ct. Appeals (4th cir.) 1980, U.S. Ct. Appeals (D.C. cir.) 1984, U.S. Supreme Ct. 1983. Assoc. Lowe & Gordon, Charlottesville, Va., 1978-80; ptnr. Wyatt & Rosenfield, Charlottesville, Va., 1980-83, Gordon & Wyatt, Charlottesville, Va., 1984-92, Wyatt & Carter, Charlottesville, Va., 1993-2000, Wyatt & Assocs., PLC, Charlottesville, Va., 2000—02, Wyatt & Armstrong PLC, Charlottesville, 2002—. Mem. ATLA, Va. Coll. Criminal Def. Attys. (bd. dirs. 1997—), Charlottesville-Albemarle Criminal Bar Assn., Charlottesville Bar Assn. Avocations: writing, painting. Civil rights, Criminal, Personal injury (including property damage). Office: Wyatt & Armstrong PLC 300 Court Sq Charlottesville VA 22902-5160

WYATT, JOHN BRUNDIGE, III, lawyer, educator; b. Marion, Ohio, Aug. 27, 1953; s. John Brundige Jr. and Mary Elizabeth (Lodwig) W.; children: John Brundige IV, Jacqueline Eva-Marie. Student, U. Madrid, 1974; BA, Findlay Coll., 1975; JD, U. Dayton, Ohio, 1978. Bar: Ohio 1978, U.S. Dist. Ct. (so. dist.) Ohio 1978, U.S. Supreme Ct. 1984, U.S. Ct. Claims 1985, U.S. Ct. Appeals (Fed. cir.) 1988. Staff atty. Dayton Power & Light Co., 1978-82; sr. staff atty. Mead Data Cen. Co., Dayton, 1982-84; pvt. practice Dayton, 1984-90; prof. fin., real estate and law Calif. State Poly. U., Pomona, 1990—. Prof. govt. contract law and contract mgmt. Sch. Systems and Logistics, Air Force Inst. Tech., Wright-Patterson AFB, Ohio, 1985-90; adj. prof. govt. contract law Ind. U.-Purdue U., Indpls., 1987-98; adj. asst. prof. bus. law Wright State U., Dayton, 1988-90. Co-author: Government Contract Law, 1986; assoc. editor Govt. Contract Law, 1987, 88. Fellow Nat. Contract Mgmt. Assn. (Nat. Edn. award 2001); Outstanding Fellow Natl. Contract Mgmt. Assn., 1994, Natl. Vice Pres., 1998-99, Natl. Contract Mgmt. Assn., mem. ABA, Fed. Bar Assn. (mem. govt. contracts com. 1985-90), Nat. Contract Mgmt. Assn., Nat. Property Mgmt. Assn., Am. Bus. Law Assn., Nat. Property Mgmt. Assn., Am. Bus. Law Assn. (peer reviewer Am. Bus. Law Jour.). Administrative and regulatory, Commercial, contracts (including sales of goods; commercial financing), Government contracts and claims. Office: Calif State Poly U Dept FRL 3801 W Temple Ave Dept FRL Pomona CA 91768-2557 E-mail: jwyatt3@aol.com., jbwyatt@csupomona.edu.

WYATT, JOSEPH LUCIAN, JR., lawyer, writer; b. Chgo., Feb. 21, 1924; s. Joseph Lucian and Cecile Gertrude (Zadico) W.; m. Marjorie Kathryn Simmons, Apr. 9, 1954; children: Daniel, Linn, Jonathan. AB in English Lit. with honors, Northwestern U., 1947; LLB, Harvard U., 1949. Bar: Calif. 1950, U.S. Dist. Ct. (cen. dist.) Calif. 1950, U.S. Ct. Appeals (9th cir.) 1950, U.S. Tax Ct., U.S. Supreme Ct. 1965. Assoc. firm Brady, Nossaman & Walker, Los Angeles, 1950-58, ptnr. L.A., 1958-61; pvt. practice L.A., 1961-71; sr. mem. Cooper, Wyatt, Tepper & Plant, P.C., L.A., 1971-79; of counsel Beardsley, Hufstedler & Kemble, L.A., 1979-81; ptnr. Hufstedler & Kaus, L.A., 1981-95; sr. of counsel Morrison & Foerster, L.A., 1995—. Mem. faculty Pacific Coast Banking Sch., Seattle, 1963-92, Southwestern Grad. Sch. Banking, 1988-89; adviser Am. Law Inst., 1988—, Restatement, Trusts 3d, 1988—. Author: Trust Administration and Taxation, 4 vols., 1964—; editor: Trusts and Estates, 1962-74. Lectr. continuing legal edn. programs, Calif. and Tex.; trustee Pacific Oaks Coll. and Children's Sch., 1969-97; counsel, parliamentarian Calif. Democratic party and presdl. conv. dels., 1971—; mem. Calif. State Personnel Bd., 1961-71, v.p., 1963-65, pres., 1965-67; bd trustees Calif. Pub. Employees Retirement System, 1963-71. Served with USAAF, 1943-45. Fellow Am. Coll. of Trust and Estate Counsel; mem. ABA, Internat. Acad. Estate and Trust Law (treas. 1990-96), Am. Law Inst., Calif. State Bar Assn. (del. state conf. 1956, 62-67), L.A. Bar Assn. (trustee 1956). Democrat. Christian Scientist. Avocations: poetry, fishing. Home: 1119 Armada Dr Pasadena CA 91103-2805 E-mail: jwyatt@mofo.com., jwyatt3@earthlink.net.

WYATT, ROBERT LEE, IV, lawyer; s. Robert Lee III and Louise Carole (Bard) W.; m. Vicki Harris Wyatt. BS, Southeastern Okla. State U., 1986; JD, U. Okla., 1989. Bar: Okla. 1989, U.S. Dist. Ct. (we. dist.) Okla. 1990, U.S. Ct. Appeals (10th cir.) 1990, U.S. Dist. Ct. (no. dist.) Okla. 1991, U.S. Ct. Appeals (8th cir.) 1991, U.S. Supreme Ct. 1993. Intern Okla. State Bur. Investigation, Oklahoma City, 1988-89, guest lectr., 1989; dep. spl. counsel Gov. of Okla., 1995; atty. Jones & Wyatt, Enid, Okla., 1989-2000. Criminal justice panel atty. We. Dist. Okla. Contbr. Counsel to Fire Civil Svc. Commn. City of Enid, 1998-2000. Mem. ABA (mem. criminal and litigation sects.), Okla. Bar Assn. (mem. ins., mem. criminal law com.), Oklahoma County Bar Assn., Okla. Criminal Def. Lawyers Assn., Nat. Inst. for Trial Advocacy, Nat. Assn. Criminal Defense Lawyers, Luther Bohanon Am. Inn of Ct. (barrister), Phi Delta Phi, Alpha Chi. Democrat. Baptist. General civil litigation, Criminal, Insurance. E-mail: bobwyatt@wyattlaw.com.

WYATT, THOMAS CSABA, lawyer; b. Toronto, Ont., Can., Mar. 19, 1952; came to U.S., 1979; s. Charles Wojatsek and Marietta Marcinkova; m. Helen A. Johnson, Dec. 24, 1979; children: J.P. Max, Stephen M. BA, Bishop's U., 1975; BCL, McGill U., 1974; JD, U. San Francisco, 1981; LLM, U. Montréal, 1980. Bar: Que. 1975, Calif. 1982, U.S. Dist. Ct. (no. dist.) Calif. 1982, U.S. Ct. Appeals (9th cir.) 1982. Assoc. counsel Can. Gen. Electric, Montreal, 1975—77; solicitor Du Pont Can., Inc., Montreal, 1977—79; internat. counsel Computerland Corp., Oakland, Calif., 1982—85; sr. counsel Bank of Am., San Francisco, 1985—87, Intel Corp., Santa Clara, Calif., 1987—90; gen. counsel Philips Semiconductors, Sunnyvale, Calif., 1990—2001; founder, dir. Actineon, Inc., Sunnyvale, Calif., 2001—. Arbitrator Am. Arbitration Assn., San Francisco, 1985—. Bd. dirs. Silicon Valley Law Found., 2000—02. Mem. Silicon Valley Assn. of Gen. Counsel (chmn. 1998-2000), Santa Clara County Bar Assn. (bd. trustees 2001-2002), Knightly Order of Vitez, Knights of Malta. Roman Catholic. Commercial, contracts (including sales of goods; commercial financing), Computer, Intellectual property. Office: Actineon Inc 1230 Oakmead Pkwy # 306 Sunnyvale CA 94085 E-mail: twyatt@actineon.com.

WYCHE, CYRIL THOMAS, lawyer; b. Greenville, S.C., Jan. 28, 1926; C. Granville and Mary (Wheeler) W.; m. Harriet Smith, June 19, 1948; children: Sara McCall, Bradford Wheeler, Mary Frances. BE, Yale U., 1946; LLB, U. Va., 1949; LLD (hon.), Clemson U., 1997, Furman U., 1997; HLD (hon.), Wafford Coll. Bar: S.C. 1948, U.S. Dist. Ct. S.C. 1950, U.S. Ct. Appeals (4th cir.) 1952, U.S. Ct. Claims 1964, U.S. Supreme Ct. 1970. Ptnr. Wyche, Burgess, Freeman & Parham, P.A., Greenville, S.C., 1948—. Pres., bd. dirs. YMCA, Greenville, 1960; pres. Greenville Little Theatre, 1965, Arts Festival Assn., Greenville, 1970, Greenville Community Corp., 1976—; bd. dirs. Greater Greenville C. of C., 1980. Served with USN, 1943-46. Named Environmentalist of Yr., State of S.C., 1979; recipient Conservation award Gulf Oil Corp., 1983, Alexander Calder award, 1996, Garden Clubs Am., 1999, Oak Leaf award The Nature Conservancy, 1996, Order of the Palmetto award S.C. Gov., 1996. Mem. ABA, S.C. Bar Assn., Greenville County Bar Assn., Am. Judicature Soc. Presbyterian. Avocations: skiing, scuba diving, piano, tennis, white water canoeing. Corporate, general, Probate (including wills, trusts), Corporate taxation. Office: Wyche Burgess Freeman & Parham 44 E Camperdown Way PO Box 728 Greenville SC 29602-0728 E-mail: twyche@wyche.com.

WYCHE, MADISON BAKER, III, lawyer; b. Albany, Ga., Aug. 11, 1947; s. Madison Baker Jr. and Merle (McKemie) W.; m. Marguerite Jernigan Ramage, Aug. 7, 1971; children: Madison Baker IV, James Ramage. BA, Vanderbilt U., 1969, JD, 1972. Bar: Ga. 1972, U.S. Dist. Ct. (mid. dist.) Ga. 1972, U.S. Ct. Appeals (5th cir.) 1973, S.C. 1976, U.S. Dist. Ct. S.C. 1977, U.S. Ct. Appeals (4th cir.) 1977, U.S. Supreme Ct. 1980, U.S. Ct. Appeals (11th cir.) 1981, U.S. Dist. Ct. (no. dist.) Ga. 1995. Assoc. Perry, Walters, Lippitt & Custer, Albany, 1972-76, Thompson, Ogletree & Deakins, Greenville, S.C., 1976-77, Ogletree, Deakins, Smoak & Stewart, Greenville, 1977-80; ptnr. Ogletree, Deakins, Nash, Smoak & Stewart P.C., Greenville, 1980—. Bd. dirs. Happy Ho., Inc., Albany. Co-editor Labor and Employment Law for South Carolina Lawyers, 1999. Co-incorporator, sec. State of Tenn. Intercollegiate State Legislature, Nashville, 1967-69; mem. employer and employee rels. com. N.C. Citizens for Bus. and Industry, Raleigh, 1984—; mem. Greenville C. of C., gen. counsel, 2003; mem. 300 for Greenville; mem. United Way Greenville; bd. dirs., 1992—; mem. Christ Episcopal Ch., Greenville, vestry, 1981-85; mem. bd. visitors Clemson U., 1998-2001, mem. continuing/distance edn. advancement bd., 2003; bd. dirs. Blue Ridge Coun., Boy Scouts Am., 1999-2000. Capt. U.S. Army, 1969-77. Recipient Eagle Scouts award Boy Scouts Am., 1961. Mem. ABA, Coll. of Labor and Employment Lawyers, S.C. Bar Assn. (unauthorized practice of law com. 1977-95, chmn. 1982-92, ho. of dels. 1991-98, nominating com. 1992-95, CLE divsn., chmn., 1997-98, exec. com. 1995-99, chmn. seminars subcom. 1995-97), Ga. Bar Assn., Atlanta Bar Assn., S.C. Def. Trial Lawyers Assn., St. Andrews Soc. Upper S.C. (bd. dirs. 1979-81, v.p. 1986-87, pres. 1988-90, scholarship chmn. 1998—), Vanderbilt U. Alumni Assn. (pres. S.C. chpt. 1990-95, bd. dirs. 1994—), The Poinsett Club (v.p., bd. dirs.) (Greenville, S.C.), Rotary (bd. dirs. 1982-84, Paul Harris fellow 1986), Commerce Club of Greenville (bd. dirs. 1990—), Phi Delta Phi. General civil litigation, Environmental, Labor (including EEOC, Fair Labor Standards Act, labor-management relations, NLRB, OSHA). Office: Ogletree Deakins Nash Smoak & Stewart PO Box 2757 Greenville SC 29602-2757

WYCKOFF, E. LISK, JR., lawyer; b. Middletown, N.J., Jan. 29, 1934; m. Elizabeth Ann Kuphal; children: Jenny Adele, Edward Lisk III, Elizabeth Hannah Longstreet. BA, Duke U., 1955; JD, U. Mich., 1960. Bar: N.Y. 1961, U.S. Dist. Ct. (so. and ea. dists.) N.Y. 1962, U.S. Ct. Appeals (2d cir. 1963), U.S. Tax Ct. 1974. Ptnr. Trubin Sillcocks, 1975—79, Kelley Drye & Warren, 1979—93, Kramer, Levin, N.Y.C., NY, 1993—2001. Lectr. Practising Law Inst., 1970—, various profl. and bus. orgns. in U.S. and abroad; spl. counsel N.Y. Bankers Assn., 1974-98; counsel N.Y. State Senate Com. Housing and Urban Renewal, 1969-71, N.Y. State Senate Com. Judiciary, 1963-64, Com. Affairs of the City of N.Y., 1962; mem. N.Y.C. Mayor's Taxi Study Commn., 1967 Directing editor, author West's McKinney's Forms on Estates and Trusts, 1974—; commentator McKinney's Not-For-Profit Corp. law, 1995—; contbr. articles to profl. jours. Trustee Inner-City Scholarship Fund., Inc., 1993—; chmn., bd. dirs. 1652 Wyckoff House and Assn., Inc., 1982—; trustee Goodspeed Opera Co., 1996—, Florence Griswold Mus., 1997—, Wildlife Conservation Soc., 1993—; elector Wadsworth Atheneum; trustee, pres. Homeland Found., 1988—; mem. Concilium Socalium to Vatican Mus., 1991—; dir., treas. NY Geneal. and Biographic Soc., 2002—. Named papal hon. Knight Commdr., Order of St. Gregory the Great, 1998; recipient Star, 2002. Fellow: Am. Bar Found., Am. Coll. Trust and Estate Counsel; mem.: ABA, St. Nicholas Soc., Holland Soc., Assn. of Bar of City of N.Y., N.Y. State Bar Assn., Internat. Bar Assn., Internat. Fiscal Assn., N.Y. Yacht Club, Essex Yacht Club (Conn.), Mashomack Fish and Game Preserve Club (Pine Plains, N.Y.), Racquet and Tennis Club (N.Y.C.), Knickerbocker Club. Avocations: tennis, sailing. General practice, Non-profit and tax-exempt organizations, Estate taxation. Office: 20th Fl 505 Park Ave New York NY 10022 E-mail: eliskwyckoff@aol.com.

WYGONIK, RICHARD, lawyer; b. Dearborn, Mich., June 2, 1944; s. Albin and Genevieve Wygonik; m. Adrenne Margarete Sindel, Apr. 19, 1968. BS, We. Mich. U., 1966; JD, Wayne State U., 1972. Bar: U.S. Dist. Ct. (ea. dist.) Mich. 1972, U.S. Ct. Appeals (6th cir.) 1983, U.S. Supreme Ct. 1988, U.S. Dist. Ct. V.I. 1992. Tchr. Detroit Pub. Schs., 1967—70; assoc., ptnr. Hurwitz, Karp and Wygonik, Dearborn Heights, Mich., 1972—81; ptnr. Wygonik and Walsh, Dearborn, 1981—2001; pvt. practice Dearborn, 2001—. Hearing panelist State of Mich. Atty. Discipline Bd., Detroit, 1991—; mediator, case evaluator Wayne County Mediation Bd., Detroit, 1991—; participant Mich. Protection and Adv., Dearborn, 1992—2002. Mem.: Mich. Trial Lawyers Assn. (exec. bd. 1991—, co-chair Cmty. Action com. 2000—02), KC (3d degree 1990). Democrat. Roman Catholic. Avocations: reading, travel, politics, weight training. Office: 24240 Michigan Ave Dearborn MI 48124

WYLE, FREDERICK S. lawyer; b. Berlin, May 9, 1928; came to U.S., 1939, naturalized, 1944; s. Norbert and Malwina (Mauer) W.; m. Katinka Franz, June 29, 1969; children: Susan Kim, Christopher Anthony, Katherine Anne. BA magna cum laude, Harvard U., 1951, LL.B., 1954. Bar: Mass. 1954, Calif. 1955, N.Y. 1958. Teaching fellow Harvard Law Sch., 1954-55; law clk. U.S. Dist. Ct., No. Dist. Calif., 1955-57; assoc. firm Paul, Weiss, Rifkind, Wharton & Garrison, NYC, 1957-58; pvt. practice San Francisco, 1958-62; spl. asst. def. rep. U.S. del. to NATO, Paris, 1962-63; mem. Policy Planning Council, Dept. State, Washington, 1963-65; dep. asst. sec. def. for European and NATO affairs Dept. Def., Washington, 1966-69; v.p. devel., gen. counsel Schroders, Inc., NYC, 1969-71, atty., cons., 1971-72; chief exec. officer Saturday Rev. Industries, Inc., San Francisco, 1972-76; individual practice law San Francisco, 1976—82. Internat. counsel to Fed.

States Micronesia, 1974-82; cons. Rand Corp., Dept. Def., Nuclear Regulatory Commn. Contbr. to: Ency. Brit, 1972, also articles in profl. publs., newspapers. Trustee US Interest Bicycle Club Casino, 1996-99; trustee in bankruptcy Garden City, Inc., 2000-; liquidating trustee Synthetic Industries, 2000—, Biosurg. Industries, 2000—; Negotiator for gov., Calif., Indian Tribes organizing, with AUS, 1946-47. Mem. Internat. Inst. Strategic Studies, Phi Beta Kappa. Office: 3 Embarcadero Ctr Fl 7 San Francisco CA 94111-4065

WYNN, STANFORD ALAN, lawyer; b. Milw., May 9, 1950; s. Sherburn and Marjory (Tarrant) W. BBA, U. Wis., Milw., 1972; JD, Case Western Res. U., 1975; LLM in Taxation, U. Miami, 1976. Bar: Wis. 1975, Fla. 1976. Assoc. Walsh and Simon, Milw., 1976-78; atty., asst. dir. advanced mktg. Northwestern Mut. Life Ins. Co., Milw., 1978—. Author: The Insurance Counselor-Split Dollar Life Insurance, 1991; cons. editor: The Insurance Counselor-The Irrevocable Life Insurance Trust, 1995. Bd. dirs. Waukesha Estate Planning Coun., 1985-86. Estate planning, Insurance, Estate taxation. Office: Northwestern Mut Life Ins Co 720 E Wisconsin Ave Milwaukee WI 53202-4703

WYRSCH, JAMES ROBERT, lawyer, educator, author; b. Springfield, Mo., Feb. 23, 1942; s. Louis Joseph and Jane Elizabeth (Welsh) W.; m. B. Darlene Wyrsch, Oct. 18, 1975; children: Scott, Keith, Mark, Brian, Marcia. BA, U. Notre Dame, 1963; JD, Georgetown U., 1966; LLM, U. Mo., Kansas City, 1972. Bar: Mo. 1966, U.S. Ct. Appeals (8th cir.) 1971, U.S. Ct. Appeals (10th cir.) 1974, U.S. Ct. Appeals (5th cir.) 1974, U.S. Ct. Appeals (6th cir.) 1982, U.S. Ct. Appeals (11th cir.) 1984, U.S. Ct. Appeals (7th cir.) 1986, U.S. Ct. Appeals (4th cir.) 1990, U.S. Ct. Appeals (9th cir.) 1998, U.S. Ct. Mil. Appeals 1978, U.S. Tax Ct. 1983, U.S. Supreme Ct. 1972. Assoc. Wyrsch, Hobbs & Mirakian P.C., Kansas City, 1970-71, of counsel, 1972-77, ptnr., 1978—, pres., shareholder, 1988—; adj. prof. U. Mo., 1981—. Mem. Mo. Supreme Ct., 1983—, procedures com., 2003—; mem. adv. coun. legal assts. program U. Mo. at Kansas City , 1985-88; mem. cir. ct. adv. com. Jackson County, Mo., 1998—; mem. jud. selection com. U.S. Magistrate we. dist., Mo., 1985; mem. fed. practice subcom. we. dist. U.S. Dist. Ct., Mo., 1985-88; mem. subcom. to draft model criminal instrns.for dist. cts. of 8th cir., 1986—; bd. dirs. Kansas City Bar Found.; Mo. membership co-chmn. U.S. Supreme Ct. Hist. Soc., 2002-03. Co-author: Missouri Criminal Trial Practice, 1994; contbr. articles to profl. jours. Capt. U.S. Army, 1966—69. Recipient Joint Svcs. Commendation medal U.S. Army, 1969, U. Mo. Kansas City Svc. award Law Found., 1991-92, Lawyer of Yr. award Mo. Lawyers Weekly, 2001, Dean of Trial Bar award Kansas City Met. Bar Assn., 2002, Practitioner of the Yr. award U. Mo. Kans. City Law Sch. Alumni Assn., 2002; named Best of the Bar, Kansas City Bus. Jour., 2002. Fellow: Mo. Bar Found. (vice chmn. criminal law com. 1978—79), Am. Coll. Trial Lawyers (access to justice com., Mo. State com. 2002—03), Am. Bar Found. (life); mem.: ATLA, ABA, Coll. Master Advs. and Barristers (sr. counsel), Mo. Assn. Criminal Def. Attys. (dir. 1978, sec. 1982, dir. 1983, justice com., Mo. state com. 2002—03), Nat. Assn. Criminal Def. Attys., Am. Bd. Trial Advs. (adv.), Kansas City Bar Assn. (chmn. anti-trust com. 1981, chmn. bus. tort, anti-trust, franchise com. 1998), Mo. Bar Assn., Am. Arbitration Assn. (panel arbitrators 1976—2000), U.S. Supreme Ct. Hist. Soc. (co-chmn. Mo. membership 2002—03), Country Club of Blue Springs, Kansas City Club, Phi Delta Phi. Democrat. Roman Catholic. Antitrust, Criminal. Home: 1501 NE Sunny Creek Ln Blue Springs MO 64014-2044 Office: Wyrsch Hobbs & Mirakian PC 1101 Walnut St Fl 13 Kansas City MO 64106-2134

WYSE, WILLIAM WALKER, lawyer, real estate executive; b. Spokane, Wash., July 20, 1919; s. James and Hattie (Walker) W.; m. Janet E. Oswalt, Jan. 30, 1944; children: Wendy L., Scott C., Duncan E. AB, U. Wash., 1941; JD, Harvard U., 1948. Bar: Oreg. 1948. Pvt. practice, Portland; ptnr. Stoel, Rives, Boley, Jones & Gray, 1953-88; pres. Wyse Investment Svcs., 1988—. Past dir. Treasureland Savs. and Loan Assn.; past trustee, sec. Pacific Realty Trust; past trustee Holladay Park Plaza; dir. Costa Pacific Co., 1999-2000. Chmn. ctrl. budget com. United Fund, 1958—60; 1st v.p. United Good Neighbors; chmn. bd. dirs. Portland Sch. Bd., 1959—66; pres. Tri-County Cmty. Coun., 1970—71; bd. dirs., sec. Oreg. Parks Found.; bd. dirs. Cmty. Child Guidance Clinic, 1950—57, pres., 1956—57; bd. dirs. Oreg. Symphony Soc., 1965—74, 1993—99, pres., 1968; bd. dirs. Loaves and Fishes Ctrs., Inc., 1997—. Mem. ABA, Oreg. Bar Assn., Multnomah County Bar Assn., Am. Coll. Real Estate Lawyers, Univ. Club, Arlington Club, Portland City Club (past gov.), Wauna Lake Club, Delta Upsilon. Republican. Presbyterian. Home: 3332 SW Fairmount Ln Portland OR 97201-1446 Office: 111 SW Fifth Ave Ste 1100 Portland OR 97204-5753

WYSS, JOHN BENEDICT, lawyer; b. Evanston, Ill., Nov. 23, 1947; s. Walther Erwin and Caroline Nettie (Benedict) W.; m. Joanne P. Comstock, Oct. 22, 1994; children: John Christian, Kirsten Dunlop. BS in Physics summa cum laude, Stanford U., 1969; JD, Yale U., 1972. Bar: Calif. 1972, D.C. 1974, U.S. Supreme Ct. 1976. Trial atty. antitrust div. U.S. Dept. Justice, Washington, 1972-74; assoc. Kirkland & Ellis, Washington, 1974-78, ptnr., 1978-83, Wiley, Rein & Fielding, Washington, 1983—. Mem. ABA, Phi Beta Kappa. Antitrust, Patent, General civil litigation. Office: Wiley Rein & Fielding 1776 K St NW Washington DC 20006-2304 E-mail: jwyss@wrf.com.

WYSS, LUKAS F. lawyer; b. Bern, Switzerland, June 4, 1965; s. Ernst Wyss and Elisabeth Wyss-Ritter; m. Brigitte U. Emch-Wyss, July 19, 1995; children: Stephanie, Michelle, Raphael. Degree in law, U. Bern, 1992; M in Internat. Legal Studies, Georgetown U., 2002. Asst. tax dept. Arthur Andersen, Zurich, Switzerland, 1992—93; sr. legal advisor Swiss Mobilias Ins. Corp., Bern, 1993—97; sr. assoc. Bratschi Emch & Ptnrs., Bern and Zurich, 1998—. Contbr. articles to profl. jours.; jazz musician, 1984—97. Capt. Swiss mil., 1996. Mem.: Swiss Bar Assn., Bernese Bar Assn., Swiss-Chinese C. of C., Inst. European Law. Avocations: sports, music, Asian and European culture. Commercial, contracts (including sales of goods; commercial financing), Private international, Product liability. Home: Hangweg 104 3095 Spiegel b Berne Switzerland Office: Bratschi Emch & Ptnrs Bollwerk 15 3001 Bern Switzerland Office Fax: (++41) 31 310 19 20. E-mail: l.wyss@bep.ch.

XAVIER, HELENA DE ARAUJO LOPES, lawyer, consultant; b. Lisbon, Portugal, Dec. 5, 1952; arrived in Brazil, 1991; d. Jose and Hortense Araújo Lopes. LLB, Lisbon U., 1975. Bar: Lisbon 1975, Munich 1989, Rio de Janeiro 1992, Sao Paulo 1995, Santa Catarina 2000, Brasilia 2002. Lectr. adminstrv. law Lisbon U. Law Sch., 1977—86; ptnr. R. Tavares, H. Araújo Lopes, A. Lopes, Lisbon, 1977—91; mem. com. adminstrv. code Portuguese Govt., Lisbon, 1981—83; lectr. adminstrv. law Free Lusiada U., Lisbon, 1982—86; sr. assoc. Castro, Barros, Sobral E. Xavier, Rio de Janeiro, 1992—95; sr. ptnr. Xavier, Bernardes, Braganca, Rio de Janeiro, 1995—. Guest rschr. Inst. for Politics and Pub. Law, Munich, 1986—91; dir. Pagenet do Brasil SA, Sao Paulo, 1996—2000; officer Brazilian Assn. for Informatics and Telecomms. Law, Sao Paulo, 1999—, SR Telecom Do Brasil Ltda., Rio de Janeiro, 2000—. Contbr. articles to profl. jours. Named Recommended Practitioner, European Coun., 2000—02, Recommended Individual, Global Counsel 3000, 2001—02, Highly Recommended Individual, 2002—03. Mem.: Associacao Portuguesa para Desenvolvimento das Comunicacoes, United Telecom Coun., Computer Law Assn. Avocations: literature, opera, winter sports. Administrative and regulatory, Communications, General practice. Office: Xavier Bernardes Braganca Sociedade de Advogados Av Rio Branco 1-14 20090-003 Rio de Janeiro Brazil Fax: 5521 2283 0023. E-mail: helenaxavier@xbb.com.br.

XIE, JEFF ZHENGQUAN, lawyer; b. Hubei, China, Mar. 18, 1963; m. Bin Wu; 1 child, Maylene. JD, Ga. State U., 1999. Bar: Ga. 2000, U.S. Dist. Ct. (no. dist.) Ga. 2000, U.S. Ct. Internat. Trade 2001. Asst. counsel Ga. Dept. Corrections, Atlanta, 1999—2000; mng. mem. Xie Law Offices, LLC, Norcross, Ga., 2000—. Mem.: ABA, Am. Immigration Lawyers Assn. Immigration, naturalization, and customs, Private international. Office: Xie Law Offices LLC 5430 Jimmy Carter Blvd Ste 230 Norcross GA 30093 Office Fax: 678-421-0668. E-mail: jeffxie@uslawnet.com.

YABE, KOZO, lawyer; b. Tokyo, Jan. 22, 1962; s. Tetsuo and Tomoko (Hirayama) Y. LLB, Chuo U., Tokyo, 1985; cert. Am. law program, U. Calif., Davis, 1993; LLM, U. Ill., 1994. Atty. Yuasa & Hara, Tokyo, 1991—, ptnr., 2000—; vis. fgn. lawyer Keck, Mahin & Cate, Chgo., 1994-95, Graham & James, L.A., 1995-96. Mem. Internat. Conf. Assigned Numbers Names Intellectual Property Constituence, 2000—; adj. prof. U. Ill. Coll. Law, 2000—. Mem. ABA (assoc.), Japan Patent Atty. Assn., Daiichi Tokyo Bar Assn., Am. Soc. of Internat. Law, Am. Intellectual Property Law Assn., Japan Trademark Assn. (vice chmn. legal sys. com. 1998—, bd. dirs.), Law and Computer Assn. (Japan), Copyright Law Assn. (Japan). Avocations: study of history, classical music. Office: Yuasa & Hara Sec 206 New Ohtemachi Bldg 2-2-1 Ohtemachi Chiyoda-ku Tokyo 100-0004 Japan

YAGER, THOMAS C. retired judge; b. L.A., Feb. 16, 1918; s. Thomas C. and May M. (McGowan) Yager; m. Antonia M. Gussenhoven, Nov. 2, 2000. AB in pol. sci., UCLA, 1939, gen. secondary lifetime tchg. credential, 1940; JD, USC, 1948; LLD, Western State U., Calif., 1972. Reader UCLA Philosophy Dept., 1940; atty. L.A., 1949-57; legal advisor Gov. Calif., 1957, 58; superior ct. sr. judge, 1959-78; founder Cmty. Betterment Svc., L.A. Author: numerous legal and religious books; contbr. articles to profl. jours. Founder Judge Thomas C. Yager Found., L.A., Cmty. Betterment Svc., L.A. Maj. U.S. Army, 1942—46. Office: The Cmty Betterment Svc 108 N Gower St Los Angeles CA 90004-3828 E-mail: pvtsecty@aol.com.

YAKOWICZ, VINCENT X, lawyer, consultant; b. New Castle, Pa., July 29, 1932; s. Vincent William and Anna (Kahocka) Y.; m. Marlene Brown, Apr. 2, 1977; children: Meredythe, Megan, Michelle. BA in Polit. Sci., Pa. State U., 1953; JD, U. Pa., 1956; postgrad., U. Va., 1968-69. Bar: Pa. 1957, U.S. Dist. Ct. (mid. dist.) Pa. 1962, U.S. Supreme Ct. 1970, U.S. Ct. Appeals (3d cir.) 1983. Asst. atty. gen. Pa. Dept. Revenue, Harrisburg, 1958-59, bur. dir., 1959-62; dep. atty. gen. State of Pa., Harrisburg, 1962-71, dep. sec. of revenue, 1971-74, sec. of revenue, 1974-75, solicitor gen., 1975-78; chief dep. counsel, chief of litigation Pa. Dept. Treasury, Harrisburg, 1979-87; pvt. practice law Harrisburg, 1987—. Chief of litigation, Pa. Dept. Ins., 1979; chief tax litigation, Pa. Dept. Justice, 1979; adv. com. Decedent Estate Laws of Joint State Govt. Com.; legal counselor to Pa. Constl. Conv. on Revisions; bd.d irs. Pa. Employees Retrement Fund, Pa. Sch. Employees Retirement Fund; author, lectr. tax seminars, U. Pa., Pa. Bar Inst. Bd. dirs. Pa. State Employee's Retirement Sys., 1973—78, Pa. Pub. Sch. Employee's Retirement Sys., 1979—81. Mem. ABA, Pa. Bar Assn., Lawrence County Bar Assn., Nat. Tax Assn., Nat. Assn. Tax Adminstrs., Fed. Bench-Bar Exec. Com., Nat. Assn. Atty. Gens. (antitrust subcom.), Gov.'s Tax Reform Com., Multi-state Taxation Commn. (chmn. subcom.). General civil litigation, State civil litigation, Constitutional. Home and Office: 227 Oak Knoll Rd New Cumberland PA 17070-2836

YALE-LOEHR, STEPHEN WILLIAM, lawyer, editor; b. Newport News, Va., June 10, 1954; s. Raymond Charles and Joan Mary (Briggs) Loehr; m. Amy Janet Yale, July 16, 1977; children: Elizabeth, Jonathan, Alexander. BA, Cornell U., 1977, JD cum laude, 1981. Bar: D.C. 1981, U.S. Dist. Ct. D.C. 1982, U.S. Ct. Appeals (D.C. cir.) 1983, U.S. Supreme Ct. 1990, N.Y. 1993. Co-founder, editor Imagework mag., 1977; law clk. to chief judge U.S. Dist. Ct. (no. dist.) N.Y., Syracuse, 1981-82; assoc. Sutherland, Asbill & Brennan, Washington, 1982-86; co-editor Interpreter Releases, Washington, 1986-94; exec. editor Immigration Briefings, Washington, 1988-94; of counsel True, Walsh & Miller, Ithaca, N.Y., 1990—. Adj. prof. Georgetown U. Law Sch., 1988-90, Cornell Law Sch., 1991—; cons. Ford Found., 1997-99. Author: (with others) Understanding the 1986 Immigration Law, 1987, Understanding the Immigration Act of 1990, 1991, Immigration Law and Procedure, 1994— (20 vols.), Carnegie Endowment for Internat. Peace, 1994-96, Balancing Interests: Rethinking U.S. Selection of Skilled Immigrants, 1996; immigration law columnist N.Y. Law Jour., 1997—; contbr. articles to profl. jours. Mem.: ABA (immigration coord. com. 1998—2001), Am. Immigration Lawyers Assn. (chmn. investors com., bus. immigration com., Elmer Fried award for excellence in tchg. 2001), D.C. Bar Assn., N.Y. Bar Assn., Amnesty Internat., Phi Beta Kappa. Democrat. Avocations: photography, hockey. Home: 301 Highgate Rd Ithaca NY 14850-1437 Office: True Walsh & Miller 202 E State St Ithaca NY 14850-5551 E-mail: syl@twmlaw.com.

YALOWITZ, KENNETH GREGG, lawyer; b. Moline, Ill., Apr. 9, 1954; s. Jerome M. and Esther F. (Falkoff) Y.; m. Jan A. Albright, Jan. 4, 1976; children: Kevan, James T. BS, Ill. State U., 1976; JD, So. Ill. U., 1979. Bar: Ill. 1979, Mo. 1980, Wash. 1982, U.S. Dist. Ct. (ea. and we. dists.) Wash. 1982, U.S. Ct. Appeals (9th cir.) 1985. Assoc. Peper, Martin, Jensen, Maichel & Hetlage, St. Louis, 1979-82, Nourse & Assocs., Seattle, 1982-86, Hight Green & Yalowitz, Seattle, 1986—2001, Green & Yalowitz PLLC, 2001—. Instr. Bellevue Community Coll., Wash., 1985; bd. dirs. construction law sect. WSBA, chmn. 2000-01. Commr. Issaquah (Wash.) Planning Commn., 1986-94; dir. Luana Water Assn., 1994-97; mem. exec. bd. Issaquah Little League, 1996-99. Mem. ABA, Wash. State Bar Assn., King County Bar Assn., Associated Gen. Contractors (v. chair legal affairs com. 2001-02, chair 2003). Avocations: hiking, skiing, running. Federal civil litigation, Commercial, contracts (including sales of goods; commercial financing), Construction. Office: Ste 1310 1000 2nd Ave Seattle WA 98104-1082 Home: 19119 SE 62nd Pl Issaquah WA 98027

YAMASAKI, YUKUZO, lawyer; b. Yamaguchi, Japan, Oct. 12, 1924; s. Bunsaburo and Yasuko (Ueda) Y. m. Keiko Furubayashi, Aug. 15, 1961; children: Takao, Chiyo. BA, Tokyo U., 1952; M of Comparative Law, So. Meth. U., 1965. Assoc. Shozawa & Nagashima, Tokyo, 1961-72; trainee Kaye, Scholer, Fierman, Hayes & Handler, N.Y.C., 1965-66; sr. ptnr. Yamasaki Law & Patent Office, Tokyo, 1972—. Author: Digest of Japanese Patent Infringement Cases 1966-68, 1970; contbr. articles to Jour. of Assn. Internat. pour Protection Propriété Indsl. Mem. Indsl. Property Coun. of the Patent Office, Tokyo, 1991-96. Recipient commendation Ministry Internat. Trade and Industry. Mem. First Tokyo Bar Assn., Japanese Bar Assn. (chmn. intellectual property com. 1989-90), Patent Attys. Assn. of Japan, Inter-Pacific Bar Assn. (chmn. intellectual property com. 1991-93), Japanese Br. Assn. Internat. Protection Propriété Indsl. (councillor, commendation 1986). Home: 2-20-21 Higashi Kunitachi Tokyo 186-0002 Japan Office: Yamasaki Law & Patent Office 1-11-28 Nagatacho Chiyoda-ku Tokyo 100-0014 Japan E-mail: yukuzo@nn.iij4u.or.jp., moveon@yamasaki-law.com.

YAMBRUSIC, EDWARD SLAVKO, lawyer, consultant; b. Conway, Pa., Mar. 9, 1933; s. Michael Misko and Slavica Sylvia (Yambrusic) Y.; m. Natalie Visniak, 1990. BA, Duquesne U., 1957; postgrad., Georgetown U. Law Ctr., 1959-61; JD, U. Balt., 1966; cert., The Hague (Netherlands) Acad. Internat. Law, 1967, 69; diploma, Ctr. Study and Rsch. Internat. Law and Internat. Rels., 1970; PhD in Pub. Internat. Law, Cath. U. Am., 1984. Bar: Md. 1969, U.S. Ct. Customs and Patent Appeals 1972, U.S. Supreme Ct. 1972, U.S. Ct. Internat. Trade 1988. Copyright examiner U.S. Copyright Office, Libr. of Congress, Washington, 1960-69; atty. adviser Office Register of Copyrights, 1969-98; pvt. practice internat. and immigration law, 1969—. Legal counsel Nat. Ethnic Studies Assembly, 1976—, Soc. Fed. Linguists, 1980; pres. AMCRO Internat. Consulting, Inc., 1995—. Author: Treat Interpretation: Theory and Reality, 1987, The Trade-Based Approaches to the Protection of Intellectual Property, 1990; contbr. articles to ofcl. newsletter Nat. Confedn. Am. Ethnic Groups, also legal jours. Pres. Nat. Confedn. Am. Ethnic Groups, Washington; nat. chmn. Croatian-Am. Bicentennial Com. nat. chmn. Nat. Pilgrimage of Croatian-Ams. to Nat. Shrine of Immaculate Conception, Washington; v.p. Croatian Acad. Am. Served to capt. U.S. Army, 1957-59. Duquesne U. Tamburitzans scholar, 1953-57; Hague Acad. Internat. Law fellow, 1970. Mem. ABA, Md. Bar Assn., Internat. Law Assn., Internat. Fiscal Assn., Am. Soc. Internat. Law, Croatian Cath. Union Am., Croatian Frat. Union Am. Republican. Roman Catholic. Certificate issued by the Librarian of Congress in recognition of 40 years of distinguished service to the people of the United States of America, 1957-98. Home and Office: 4720 Massachusetts Ave NW Washington DC 20016-2346

YAMIN, DIANNE ELIZABETH, judge; b. Danbury, Conn., June 4, 1961; d. Raymond Joseph and Linda May (Bucko) Goetz; m. Robert Joseph Yamin, Sept. 3, 1988; children: Samantha Blythe, Rebecca Anne. AB, Lehigh U., 1983; JD, Mercer U., 1986. Bar: Conn. 1986, U.S. Dist. Ct. Conn. 1989. Atty. Gerald Hecht & Assocs., Danbury, 1986-92; judge State Conn., Danbury, 1991—. Atty. Yamin & Yamin, Danbury, 1992—; chmn. ethics com. Conn. Probate Assembly, 1994—; mem. Conn. Coun. on Adoptions, 1992—; mem. Conn. Probate Assembly, 1991—, 2d v.p., 2003—. Bd. dirs. Big Bros./Big Sisters, Danbury, 1987-94, Conn Brass Soc., Inc., 1991—, Friends of Tarrywile Park, Inc., Danbury, 1993-99, Danbury Music Ctr., 1996—, Hispanic Ctr. Greater Danbury, 1999—; pres. coun. women Lehigh U, 2000—. Recipient outstanding young citizen award Conn. Jaycees, 1994, pro bono award Conn. Legal Svcs., 1993; named as one of 21 Young Lawyers Leading Us into the 21st Century, ABA Mag., 1995. Mem. ABA, Conn. Bar Assn., Conn. Health Lawyers Assn., Danbury Bar Assn., Greater Danbury C. of C. (bd. dirs. 2003—), Omicron Delta Kappa. Republican. Roman Catholic. Avocations: ballet, volunteerism, travel, outdoor activities. Home: 66 Barnum Rd Danbury CT 06811-2938 Office: 155 Deer Hill Ave Danbury CT 06810-7726

YAMIN, MICHAEL GEOFFREY, lawyer; b. N.Y.C., Nov. 10, 1931; s. Michael and Ethel Yamin; m. Martina Schaap, Apr. 16, 1961; children: Michael Jeremy, Katrina. AB magna cum laude, Harvard U., 1953, LLB, 1958. Bar: N.Y. 1959, U.S. Dist. Ct. (so. and ea. dists.) N.Y., U.S. Ct. Appeals (2d cir.) 1966, U.S. Supreme Ct. 1967. Assoc. Weil, Gotshal & Manges, N.Y.C., 1958-65; sr. ptnr. Colton, Hartnick, Yamin & Sheresky, N.Y.C., 1966-93, Kaufmann, Feiner, Yamin, Gildin & Robbins, LLP, N.Y.C., 1993—. Trustee Gov.'s Com. Scholastic Achievement, 1976—; mem. Manhattan Cmty. Bd. 6, 1974—88, chmn., 1986—88; mem. Manhattan Borough Bd., 1986—88. Mem. ABA, N.Y. State Bar Assn., Assn. Bar City N.Y., Fed. Bar Coun., Am Fgn. Law Assn. (Am. br.), Internat. Law Assn., Societe de Legislation Comparee, Internat. Bar Assn., Harvard Faculty Club (Cambridge, Mass.), Harvard Club of N.Y.C. (trustee N.Y. Found. 1981—, pres. 1999—, sub-chmn. schs. and scholarships com. 1972-93, bd. mgrs. 1985-88, 93-98, chair house com. 1992-95, v.p. 1995-98, chair comms. com. 1997-99, chair membership svcs. com. 1999-2000), Harvard Alumni Assn. (bd. dirs. 1995-98). Corporate, general, Mergers and acquisitions, Commercial, contracts (including sales of goods; commercial financing). Office: 777 3rd Ave New York NY 10017-1401

YANAS, JOHN JOSEPH, lawyer; b. Albany, N.Y., July 18, 1929; m. Mary Faith Casey; children: John J., Joseph J., Kathleen Ann, Mary Patricia. Student Russell Sage Coll., 1947-50; LLB, Albany Law Sch., 1953, LLD, 1989. Bar: N.Y. 1954, U.S. Ct. Appeals (2d cir.) 1962. Assoc. Casey, Honikel and Wisely, Albany, 1954-60; ptnr. Dugan, Casey, Burke & Lyons, Albany, 1960-69; ptnr. Casey, Yanas, Mitchell & Amerling, Albany, 1969-84, Casey, Yanas, Clyne, Mitchell & Amerling, Albany, 1984-88; ptnr. Degraff, Foy, & Devine, 1989—; counsel Albany County Pub. Welfare Dist., 1959-60; mem. Albany City CSC, 1970-73, Albany County CSC, 1970-73; justice Albany City Ct., 1973-77; Bank. Trustee Christian Bros. Acad., Albany, 1972-2002, chair, 1992, Albany Law Sch., 1975-2001, chair, 1993. Fellow Am. Bar Found., N.Y. Bar Found., ABA; mem. Am. Coll. Real Estate Lawyers, N.Y. State Bar Assn. (chmn. real property law sect. 1974-75, (chmn. com. to confer with N.Y. State Realty Bd. 1975-77, chmn. com. continuing legal edn. 1977-80, treas. 1980-86, chmn. fin. com. 1987, pres.-elect 1988, pres. 1989), Albany County Bar Assn. (pres. 1978). Banking, Probate (including wills, trusts), Property, real (including real estate development, water). Office: 90 State St Albany NY 12207

YANDLE, STEPHEN THOMAS, dean; b. Oakland, Calif., Mar. 7, 1947; s. Clyde Thomas and Jane Walker (Hess) Y.; m. Martha Anne Welch, June 26, 1971. BA, U. Va., 1969, JD, 1972. Bar: Va. 1972. Asst. dir. admissions U. Va. Law Sch., Charlottesville, 1972-76; from asst. to assoc. dean Northwestern U. Sch. Law, Chgo., 1976-85; assoc. dean Yale U. Law Sch., New Haven, 1985—2002; exec. dir. Housing Authority of New Haven, 2002—. Bd. dirs. The Access Group; lectr. in law Yale Law Sch., 2002—. Commr. New Haven Housing Authority, 1998-2002; trustee Nat. Assoc. for Law Placement Found. for Rsch. and Edn., 2000—. Capt. U.S. Army, 1972. Mem. Law Sch. Admission Coun. (programs, edn. and prelaw com. 1978-84), Assn. Am. Law Schs. (chmn. legal edn. and admissions sect. 1979, nominations com. 1987, chmn. adminstrn. of law schs. sect. 1991), Nat. Assn. for Law Placement (pres. 1984-85, co-chmn. Joint Nat. Assn. com. on placement 1986-88), New Haven Legal Assistance Assn. (bd. dirs., treas. 1992-98). Office: Yale Law Sch PO Box 208215 New Haven CT 06520-8215 E-mail: stephen.yandle@yale.edu.

YANG, DEBRA W. lawyer; b. L.A. Grad., Boston Coll. Lawyer; judge L.A. Mcpl. and Superior Cts.; fed. prosecutor; U.S. atty., 2002—. Adj. prof. U. So. Calif. Law Sch. Office: Ctrl Dist Calif US Courthouse Rm 1200 312 N Spring St Los Angeles CA 90012*

YANG, JOHN, lawyer; AB, Washington U.; JD with honors, George Washington U. Bar: D.C., Ill. Ptnr. Wiley Rein & Fielding, Washington. Assoc. professorial lectr. law George Washington U. Law Sch., 1994—2000. Mem. editl. adv. bd.: Environ. Claims Jour., book rev. and articles editor: The George Washington Law Rev.; contbr. articles to profl. jours. Mem. citizens adv. coun. D.C. Met. Police Dept. Mem.: Nat. Asian Pacific Am. Legal Consortium (mem. nat. adv. coun. 1998—2000, bd. dirs. 2001—, treas. 2002—), Orgn. Chinese Am. (gen. counsel 2000—), Asian Pacific Am. Bar Assn. Greater Washington (bd. dirs. 1995—2001, pres. 1997—98), D.C. Bar (sec. 1998—99, gen. counsel 2000—02), Nat. Asian Pacific Am. Bar Assn. (S.E. regional gov. 1999—2001, pres.-elect). Office: Wiley Rein & Fielding 1776 K St NW Washington DC 20006*

YANNUCCI, THOMAS DAVID, lawyer; b. Springfield, Ohio, Mar. 30, 1950; s. David Marion and Patricia (Wilson) Y.; m. Lisa Marie Copeland, June 30, 1972; children: Teresa, Andrea, Thomas D. Jr. AB, U. Notre Dame, 1972, JD, 1976. Bar: Ohio 1977, U.S. Ct. Appeals (D.C., 1st, 2d, 3d, 4th, 5th, 6th, 7th, 8th, 11th and 10th cirs.) 1980, U.S. Supreme Ct. 1980, D.C. 1981. Law clk. to presiding justice U.S. Ct. Appeals (D.C. cir.), Washington, 1976-77; trial atty. U.S. Dept. Justice, Washington, 1977-80; ptnr. Kirkland & Ellis, Washington, 1980—. Editor-in-chief U. Notre Dame Law Rev., 1975-76. Roman Catholic. Antitrust, Federal civil litigation, State civil litigation. Office: Kirkland & Ellis 655 15th St NW Ste 1200 Washington DC 20005-5793 E-mail: thomas_yannucci@dc.kirkland.com.

YARBRO, ALAN DAVID, lawyer; b. Huntington, W.Va., Sept. 16, 1941; s. John David and Bernice (Bulette) Y.; m. Lee Merryman Myers, July 1961; children: Wendy, Jennifer, Caroline. AB magna cum laude, Harvard U., 1962, LLB cum laude, 1966. Bar: Md. 1966, U.S. Ct. Appeals (4th cir.) 1966, U.S. Dist. Ct. Md. 1966. Assoc. Venable Baetjer & Howard, Balt., 1966-72, ptnr., 1973-96, of counsel, 2002—; gen. counsel Mercantile Bankshares Corp., 1996—2002, corp. sec., 2002. Pres. W.S. Baer Corp., 1990-99. Trustee Children's Hosp., Balt., 1986-99, Children's Hosp. at Sinai Found., 1999—, Sinai Hosp. of Balt., 1999—; bd. dirs. The Park

Heights St. Acad., Balt., 1986-89. Fellow Am. Bar Found., Md. Bar Found.; mem. ABA, Md. Bar Assn., Bar Assn. of Balt. (chmn. ethics com. 1988-89). Corporate, general, Mergers and acquisitions, Securities.

YARMEY, RICHARD ANDREW, investment manager; b. Kingston, Pa., Aug. 23, 1948; s. Stanley Richard and Rose Mary (Rees) Y.; m. Jeanne Marie Cappelli, Aug. 5, 1972; children: Lynn Rees, Jessica Brett, Kristen Alexandra. BS, U. Scranton, 1970; JD, Cath. U., 1975. Bar: Pa. 1975, D.C. 1976, U.S. Ct. Appeals (5th cir.) 1976, U.S. Tax Ct. 1978, U.S. Ct. Appeals (D.C. cir.) 1980. Contract adjudicator GAO, Washington, 1970-73; program asst. EPA, Washington, 1973; assoc. Sharon, Pierson, et al, Washington, 1975-82; of counsel Pierson, Semmes et al, Washington, 1982-93; prin. Yarmey Capital Mgmt., 1989-95; sr. portfolio mgr. PNC Advisors, 1995—; mng. dir. Instl. Investment Group, 2000—02; portfolio mgr. profl. investment advisory program Merrill Lynch, 2002—. Fin. cons. various pension plans, individuals and bus. concerns, 1976—; TV panelist, speaker, writer on portfolio mgmt.; instr. fin. mgmt. and investments continuing edn. Wilkes U., Wilkes-Barre. Mem. Pa. Bar Assn., Aircraft Owners and Pilots Assn., Alpha Sigma Nu. Democrat. Avocation: cabinetmaking. Office: 600 Balt Dr Wilkes Barre PA 18702 also: One PNC Plz Fifth Ave & Wood St Pittsburgh PA 15265-0001 E-mail: ryarmey@pclient.ml.com.

YASHIRO, JUNJIRO, pharmaceutical executive, patent lawyer; b. Niigata, Japan, Sept. 5, 1940; m. Ikuko. Degree in pharmacy, Tohoku Pharm. U., Sendai, Japan, 1963; degree in patent law, Patent Acad., Tokyo, 1969. Mgr. licensing Eisai Co., Ltd., Tokyo, 1975-88, dir. licensing, 1988-93, dir. intellectual Property, 1993-2000; auditor Genox Rsch., Inc., Kawasaki-shi, Kanagawa, Japan, 2000—. Mem. Licensing Exec. Soc. Internat. (vice chair biotechnology com. 1999-2000), Japan Pharm. Mfrs. Assn. (chair intellectual property com. 1999-2000), Licensing Exec. Soc. Japan (healthcare com. 1995-97, trustee 1995-98, v.p. 1999—). Home: 10-17 Negishidai-7 Asaka 351 0005 Japan Office: Genox Rsch Inc 907 Nogawa, Miyamae-ku Kawasaki Kanagawa Japan

YATES, ALFRED GLENN, JR., lawyer; b. Sarver, Pa., June 17, 1946; s. Alfred Glenn and Mary Etta (Best) Y.; m. Barbara Jean Lang, June 12, 1982; children: Jennifer Christine, Elizabeth Ann. BA in Philosophy, Coll. William and Mary, 1968; JD, U. Pitts., 1973. Bar: Pa. 1973, U.S. Dist. Ct. (we. dist.) Pa. 1973, U.S. Ct. Appeals (3d cir.) 1984, W.Va. 1987, U.S. Dist. Ct. (so. dist.) W.Va. 1987. Asst. v.p. trust dept. Pitts. Nat. Bank, 1973-79; assoc. Wayman, Irvin & McAuley, Pitts., 1979-80; sole practice, Pitts., 1981—; instr. taxation Robert Morris Coll., Pitts., 1982; founder, dir. Inst. for Corp. Litigation Reform, 1988. Developer (book) Pocket Tax Calculators, 1976—. Legal counsel, founding mem. West Pa. chpt. Lupus Found. Am., Pitts., 1982-91. Served with U.S. Army, 1968-70. Decorated Joint Service Commendation medal. Mem. Pa. Bar Assn., Assn. Trial Lawyers Am. General civil litigation, Estate planning, Probate (including wills, trusts). Office: 519 Allegheny Bldg 429 Forbes Ave Pittsburgh PA 15219-1622

YATES, GRACE KATHARINE, lawyer; b. Ponca City, Okla., Sept. 22, 1974; d. John Michael and Mary Grace Yates. BA, Okla. State U., 1996; JD, U. Okla., 1999. Bar: Okla., U.S. Dist. Ct. (we. and no. dists.) Okla. Assoc. Mee, Mee & Hoge, Oklahoma City, 1999—2000; ptnr. Holmes and Yates, Ponca City, 2000—. Bd. dirs. Ponca City Humane Soc., 2001—. Mem.: ABA, Cleveland County Bar Assn., Kay County Bar Assn., Okla. Bar Assn. Office: Holmes and Yates 914 E Overbrook Ave Ponca City OK 74601-3418

YATES, LEIGHTON DELEVAN, JR., lawyer; b. Atlanta, Sept. 4, 1946; s. Leighton Delevan and Stella Louise (Hill) Y.; m. Phyllis Jeanne Hummer, Dec. 22, 1968; children: Leighton Delevan III, Lauren Jeanne. BA, Hampden-Sydney Coll., Va., 1968; JD with high honors, U. Fla., 1973. Bar: Fla. 1974, U.S. Dist. Ct. (middle dist.) Fla. 1975. Assoc. Maguire, Voorhis & Wells, P.A., Orlando, Fla., 1974-77, shareholder, 1978-98, dept. chmn., 1985-90; ptnr. Holland & Knight LLP, Orlando, Fla., 1998—. Bd. dirs. Hubbard Constrn. Co., Winter Park , Fla., 1985—, Blythe Constrn., Inc., Charlotte, NC, 1999—; adminstrv, dir. SunTrust Bank, Orlando, Fla., 1990—. Exec. editor U. Fla. Law Rev., 1973. Mem. Fla. Bd. Bar Examiners, 1992-97, 2002—, vice chmn., 1995-96, chmn. 1996-97, 2002—; chmn. Fla.'s Blood Ctrs., 1995—, vice chmn., 1980-95; chmn. Orlando Opera Co., 1994, pres., 1993. Fellow Am. Bar Found.; mem. ABA, Fla. Bar Assn., Orange County Bar Assn., Univ. Club of Orlando, Country Club of Orlando, Order of the Coif, Omicron Delta Kappa, Phi Kappa Phi. Republican. Presbyterian. Avocations: scuba diving, cycling, music, reading. Banking, Corporate, general, Mergers and acquisitions. Home: 3218 S Osceola Ave Orlando FL 32806-6251 Office: Holland & Knight LLP 200 S Orange Ave Ste 2600 Orlando FL 32801-3453 Personal E-mail: lyates@cfl.rr.com. Business E-Mail: lyates@hklaw.com.

YATES, LINDA SNOW, financial services marketing executive, real estate; b. St. Louis, July 20, 1938; d. Robert Anthony Jerrue and June Alberta (Crowder) Armstrong; m. Charles Russell Snow, Nov. 26, 1958 (div. 1979); children: Cathryn Louise, Christopher Armstrong, Heather Highstone, Sean Webster; m. Alan Porter Yates, July 22, 1983. BBA, Auburn U., 1973, MEd, 1975, EdD, 1998. Cert. profl. sec. Div. head placement div. Solutions Group, Atlanta, 1981-83; employment coord. Fulton Fed. Savs., Atlanta, 1983-84; owner, recruiter Data One, Inc., Atlanta, 1984-85; ops. mgr. Talent Tree Temporaries, Atlanta, 1985-87; legal asst., sec. Rice & Keene, Atlanta, 1987-90; legal word processing asst. Kilpatrick & Cody, Atlanta, 1990-94; pres., owner Power Comm., Cashiers, N.C., 1994-98; regional coord. S.E. region, regional mktg. rep. WorldConnect Comms., Tulsa; dir. mktg. electronic collection divsn. Am. Fin. and Credit Svcs., Inc.; area v.p., loan agent Enterprise Lenders, LLC; bd. dirs., corp. sec. The Hilltop Assocs. Inc., 1999—; real estate sales Apex Realty, Inc. Adj. instr. DeKalb Coll., Atlanta, 1980-84, Mercer U., Atlanta, 1981-82; instr. bus. So. Union State Jr. Coll., Valley, Ala., 1974-75; legal sec. Swift, Currie, McGhee & Hiers, Atlanta, 1979-80, Samford, Torbert, Denson & Horsley, Opelika, Ala., 1969-71; dir. acad. planning, chmn. edn. divsn., mem. part-time faculty in ednl. adminstrn. CEU Grad. Coll., Nuevo Leon, Mex. Columnist Neon News Flash, 1995. Mem. Paralegal Assn. Beaufort County (charter mem., sec. 1993-94), Women Bus. Owners, Nat. Assn. Pers. Cons., Internat. Soc. Poets (Disting. mem., Internat. Poet of Merit 1996, Internat. Poetry Hall of Fame 1996), Cashiers Writers Group, Phi Delta Kappa, Alpha Xi Delta. Republican. Episcopalian. Avocations: golf, writing, international travel. Office: 1 Wade Hampton Dr Ladys Island SC 29907

YATES-CARTER, LYNNE, lawyer; b. Oakland, Calif., June 1, 1950; d. Charles and Bernice (Rose) Yates; m. William Matthew Carter, July 9, 1972; 1 child, Alexander. BA in English, U. Santa Clara, 1972, JD, 1976. Bar: Calif. 1976, U.S. Dist. Ct. (no. dist.) Calif. Pvt. practice, San Jose, 1976—. Judge pro tempore family law dept. Santa Clara County Superior Ct., 1979—, spl. master, 1988—, arbitrator in family matters, 1988—; adj. prof. family law Santa Clara U., 1989-90, 92; lectr. in field. Contbr. articles to profl. jours.; cons./contbr.: California Family Law Service, 1986. Active various polit. and civic orgns. Recipient Resolution of Commendation Santa Clara County Bd. Suprs., 1986. Mem. ABA, Santa Clara County Bar Assn. (conf. of dels. 1984—, sec. 1986, program com. chmn. 1991, Justice Bryl R. Salsman award for community svc. 1986, Cert. of Appreciation 1983, 86, family law exec. com.), Am. Acad. Matrimonial Lawyers (past pres. No. Calif. chpt.), Calif. State Bar Assn. (former chair family law sect.), Calif. Women Lawyers. Democrat. Avocations: cooking, reading, gardening. Family and matrimonial. Office: 111 W Saint John St Ste 300 San Jose CA 95113-1104

YAZIJI, NEJD, lawyer; b. Syria, Aug. 10, 1965; arrived in U.S., 1987; d. Isber Gabriel Yaziji and Taghrid Merhej; m. Darrow Gary Zeidenstein, Oct. 23, 1992; 1 child, Julian Zeidenstein. PhD in Comparative Lit., U. Tex., 1994, JD, 2000. Bar: Tex. 2001, U.S. Dist. Ct. (so. dist.) Tex. Assoc. Williams Bailey Law Firm, Houston, 2000—02. Adj. prof. NYU, N.Y.C., 1995—97. Report writer Lawyers Com. Human Rights, N.Y.C., 1994. Univ. Continuing fellow, U. Tex., 1992. Mem.: ATLA, Tex. Trial Lawyers Assn. Personal injury (including property damage), Toxic tort. Home: 3031 Covebrook Dr Pearland TX 77584

YEAGER, DENNIS RANDALL, lawyer; b. Dallas, Jan. 10, 1941; s. William C. and Katherine (Payne) Y.; m. Jere Jones, Aug. 31, 1963; children: Stephanie Ann O'Donnell, Karen Elizabeth Kimball, Brenda Marie. BSS, Loyola U. of South, 1964; LLB, Columbia U., 1967. Bar: N.Y. 1967, D.C. 1979, U.S. Supreme Ct., 1971, U.S. Ct. Appeals (2d cir.) 1972. Assoc. Willkie Farr & Gallagher, N.Y.C., 1967-69; dir., chief exec. officer Nat. Employment Law Project, N.Y.C., 1969-75; from assoc. to ptnr. Tufo, Johnston & Allegaert, N.Y.C., 1975-80; ptnr. Yeager & Barrett, N.Y.C., 1980-93; pvt. practice N.Y.C., 1993—. Chmn. program on bus. errors and omissions ins. Practicing Law Inst., 1983, program on role of outside counsel in bus. investigation, 1985; panelist program on dirs. and officers liabilities, 1988. Mem. Am. Coun. on Germany, N.Y.C., 1995—. Mem. N.Y. State Bar Assn., Assn. of Bar of City of N.Y., Blue Key, Alpha Sigma Nu. Roman Catholic. Federal civil litigation, State civil litigation, Insurance. Home and Office: 70 W 95th St New York NY 10025-6721 Office Fax: 212-245-9778. E-mail: dryeagerlaw@cs.com.

YEAGER, JOSEPH HEIZER, JR., lawyer; b. Indpls., Jan. 8, 1957; s. Joseph Heizer and Marilyn Virginia (Hillyard) Y.; m. Candance A. Grass, June 2, 1984; children: Samuel, Henry. AB cum laude, Harvard U., 1979; JD cum laude, Ind. U., 1983. Bar: Ind. 1983, U.S. Dist. Ct., (so. and no. dist.) Ind. 1983, U.S. Ct. Appeals (7th cir.) 1986, U.S. Supreme Ct. 1996. Dir. ops. Penn and Schoen Assocs., N.Y.C., 1979-80; assoc. Baker & Daniels, Indpls., 1983-89, ptnr., 1990—. Bd. dirs. Indpls. Legal Aid Soc., 1990-99, pres. 1992-94; chmn. Indpls. Com. for UNICEF, 1986-91; mem. Indpls. Com. for Fgn. Affairs, 1986-91. Mem. Ind. Bar Assn., Indpls. Bar Assn. (litigation sect. exec. com. 1985-86, 1996-2000, chair 1999, mem. jud. evaluation com.), Cen. Ind. Regional Citizens League (bd. dirs. 1997-99, mgmt. com. 2001—). Democrat. Avocation: private pilot. Aviation, Federal civil litigation, State civil litigation. Office: Baker & Daniels 300 N Meridian St Ste 2700 Indianapolis IN 46204-1782

YEAGER, RUTH, lawyer; Asst. U.S. Atty., Dept. Justice, Tyler, Tex., chief civil divsn., 1988—2002; U.S. Atty., Ea. Dist. Tex., 1993—94. Office: US Attys Office 110 N College Ave Ste 700 Tyler TX 75702-0204 E-mail: ruth.yeager@usdoj.gov.

YEAZEL, KEITH ARTHUR, lawyer; b. Fayetteville, N.C., Feb. 14, 1956; s. Russell E. and Barbara E. (Weaver) Y.; m. Deborah M. MacDonald, Aug. 30, 1986. BA, Ohio State U., 1983; JD, Capital U., 1989. Bar: Ohio 1989, U.S. Dist. Ct. (so. dist.) Ohio 1989, U.S. Ct. Appeals (6th cir.) 1990, U.S. Supreme Ct. 1992. Law clk. to judge George C. Smith U.S. Dist. Ct., Columbus, Ohio, 1988-89; prin. Keith A. Yeazel, Atty. at Law, Columbus, 1989—. Mem. Ohio Bar Assn., Columbus Bar Assn., Nat. Assn. Criminal Def. Lawyers, Ohio Assn. Criminal Def. Lawyers, Order of Curia. Republican. Lutheran. Federal civil litigation, Criminal, Personal injury (including property damage). Office: 65 S 5th St Columbus OH 43215-4307

YELENICK, MARY THERESE, lawyer; b. Denver, May 17, 1954; d. John Andrew and Maesel Joyce (Reed) Y. B.A. magna cum laude, Colo. Coll., 1976; J.D. cum laude, Georgetown U., 1979. Bar: D.C. 1979, U.S. Dist. Ct. D.C. 1980, U.S. Ct. Appeals (D.C. cir.) 1981, N.Y. 1982, U.S. Dist. Ct. (so. and ea. dists.) N.Y. 1982, U.S. Supreme Ct. 1992, U.S. Ct. Appeals (5th cir.) 1995. Law clk. to presiding justices Superior Ct. D.C., 1979-81; ptnr. Chadbourne & Parke, LLP, N.Y.C., 1981—. Editor Jour. of Law and Policy Internat. Bus., 1978-79. Mem. Phi Beta Kappa. Democrat. Roman Catholic. Product liability, Toxic tort. Home: 310 E 46th St New York NY 10017-3002 Office: Chadbourne & Parke LLP 30 Rockefeller Plz Fl 31 New York NY 10112-0129

YERIGAN, DEBRA E. lawyer; BA, St. Cloud State U., 1982; JD, Hamline U. Sch. of Law, 1985. Atty. Robert Latz, P.A., Mpls., 1985—87, pvt. practice, Brooklyn Park, 1987—2000. Mem.: ABA. Family and matrimonial. Office: Rider Bennett LLP 333 South Seventh St Ste 2000 Minneapolis MN 55402 Office Fax: 612-340-7900. E-mail: deyerigan@riderlaw.com.

YERMAN, FREDRIC WARREN, lawyer; b. N.Y.C., Jan. 8, 1943; s. Nat W. and Tina (Barotz) Y.; m. Ann R. Rochlin, May 31, 1965; children: Emily, Deborah. BA, CUNY, 1963; LLB, Columbia U., 1966. Bar: N.Y. 1967. Assoc. Kaye, Scholer, Fierman, Hays & Handler, N.Y.C., 1966-74, ptnr., 1974—, chmn. exec. com., 1990-92. Bd. dirs. United Way Tri-State, Jewish Bd. Family and Children Svcs., N.Y.C. Fellow Am. Coll. Trial Lawyers. Home: 31 Sheridan Rd Scarsdale NY 10583-1523 Office: Kaye Scholer LLP 425 Park Ave New York NY 10022-3506

YERRID, C. STEVEN, lawyer; b. Charleston, W.Va., Sept. 30, 1949; s. Charles George and Audrey Faye Yerrid; m. Sharon Wainman, Feb. 13, 2000. BA in History and Polit. Sci., La. State U., 1971; JD, Georgetown U., 1975. Bar: Fla. 1975, Va. 1975, U.S. Supreme Ct. 1979, D.C. 1984; cert. civil trial advocate Nat. Bd. Trial Advocacy. Aide U.S. Senator Ellender, Washington, 1971-73; ptnr. Holland & Knight, Tampa, Fla., 1975-86; pres. Stagg, Hardy & Yerrid, Tampa, 1986-89, Yerrid, Knopik & Krieger PA, Tampa, 1990-2000, The Yerrid Law Firm, Tampa, 2000—. Mediator and Cir. Ct. arbitrator Fla. and Fed. Cts. Mem. ABA, Va. Bar Assn., D.C. Bar Assn., Fla. Bar Assn. (chmn. admiralty law com. 1984-85, bd. cert. com. 1988-91, vice chmn. 1990-91, chmn. 1994-95, bd. cert. civil trial lawyer), Southeastern Admiralty Law Inst., Am. Judicature Soc., Assn. Trial Lawyers Am. (sustaining), Am. Bd. Trial Advocates (advocate), Maritime Law Assn. (proctor), Tex. Trial Lawyers Assn., Acad. Fla. Trial Lawyer (designated continuing legal edn. speaker 1982—, bd. dirs. 1989-97 2000-2001), Inner Cir. Advocates, Internat. Soc. Barristers, Am. Inns. of Ct. (supporting fellow), Cousteau Soc., Centre Club, Tampa Club, Univ. Club, Grand Havana Club, Old Memorial Golf Club. Democrat. Avocations: fishing, tennis, boxing. General civil litigation. Office: The Yerrid Law Firm 101 E Kennedy Blvd Ste 3910 Tampa FL 33602-5187

YETTER, R. PAUL, lawyer; b. Milw., Aug. 5, 1958; s. Richard and Lobelia (Gutierrez) Y.; m. Patricia D. Yetter, May 6, 1983; children: Chris, Mark, Michael, Joseph, Thomas, Andrew, Daniel. BA, U. Tex., El Paso, 1980; JD, Columbia U., 1983. Bar: Tex. 1983, U.S. Dist. Ct. (so., ea., no. and we. dists.) Tex., U.S. Ct. Appeals (5th cir.); bd. cert. in civil trial law and personal injury trial law Tex. Bd. Legal Specialization. Law clk. to Hon. John R. Brown U.S. Ct. Appeals (5th cir.), Houston, 1983-84; assoc. Baker & Botts, L.L.P., Houston, 1984-89, ptnr., 1990-97; name ptnr. Yetter & Warden, L.L.P., Houston, 1997—. Chair state judiciary rels. com. State Bar, 1995-96; mem. Funding Parity Task Force, 1995-97; mem. ex officio Jud. Selection Task Force, 1995-97; chair Alliance for Jud. Funding, Inc., 1996—; mem. ex officio contbns. com. Tex. Ctr. for the Judiciary, mem. com. on admissions, So. Dist., Tex., 2000—. Contbr. articles to profl. jours. Recipient Presdl. citation State Bar Tex., 1996; Southwestern Legal Found. rsch. fellow. Fellow Tex. Bar Foun., Houston Bar Found. Federal civil litigation, State civil litigation. Office: Yetter & Warden LLP 909 Fannin Ste 3600 Houston TX 77010-

YETTER, RICHARD, lawyer; b. Phila., Mar. 14, 1929; s. Frederick Jacob and Marie (Kircher) Y.; m. Lobelia Gutierrez, Feb. 4, 1955; children: Bruce, Tina Marie, Richard Paul, Erich David. BS, Pa. State U., 1951; JD, Marquette U., 1960. Bar: Wis. 1960, U.S. Dist. Ct. (ea. dist.) Wis. 1960, Tex. 1961, U.S. Dist. Ct. (we. dist.) Tex. 1971, U.S. Ct. Appeals (5th cir.) 1972. Adjuster Md. Casualty Co., El Paso, Tex., 1960-62; pres. Richard Yetter & Assocs. Inc., El Paso, 1970-90; sole practitioner, El Paso, 1962-70, 90—. Assoc. judge Mcpl. Ct., El Paso, 1967-71; adj. prof. law Webster U., St. Louis. Pres. Pleasantview Home for Sr. Citizens, Inc., 1968-76; state committeeman Tex. Rep. Com., El Paso, 1968-70; chmn. adv. bd. SBA, Lubbock, Tex., Salvation Army, El Paso; active El Paso County Civil Svc. Commn., 1992-96. With USAF, 1951-60. Recipient William Booth award Salvation Army, 1997. Mem. Wis. State Bar, Tex. State Bar, El Paso Bar Assn., Coll. of the State Bar of Tex., El Paso Trial Lawyers Assn. (past bd. dirs.), El Paso Probate Bar Assn. (past bd. dirs.), Optimist (life, pres. El Paso), Mil. Order World Wars (life), Phi Delta Phi. Methodist. Avocation: walking. Probate (including wills, trusts), Estate planning. Office: 6070 Gateway Blvd E Ste 501 El Paso TX 79905-2031

YEUNG, ADRIENNE, lawyer; d. Sandford and Jet Yeung. JD, Calif. Western Sch. Law, 1996; LLM in Taxation, U. San Diego, 1998. Bar: Calif. 1997, Nev. 1997, U.S. Patent Trademark Office 1996. Assoc. Skinner Watson & Pounds, Reno, 1999—2000, THelen Reid & Priest, San Jose, Calif., 2000—. Mem. faculty U. Phoenix, San Jose, 2002—. Contbr. articles to profl. jours. Avocations: triathlete, bird breeding. Intellectual property, Trademark and copyright. E-mail: ayyeung@juno.com.

YIM, EDWARD CHANG, lawyer; b. L.A., Aug. 27, 1971; s. Hyang Keun and Jean Chin Yim; m. Johnna Marian Shia, Sept. 2, 2000. BA in English, UCLA, 1993; JD, U. Dayton, Ohio, 1996. Bar: Ohio 1996, Calif. 2002, U.S. Dist. Ct. (so. dist.) Ohio 2001. Asst. pros. atty. Montgomery County Prosecutor, Dayton, 1996—2001; atty. Dyer, Garofalo Mann & Schultz, Dayton, 2001—. Scholar Dean's scholar, U. Dayton Sch. Law, 1993—96, Alumni scholar, UCLA, 1989—93. Mem.: ATLA, Dayton Bar Assn., Ohio Bar Assn. Avocations: golf, guitar. Personal injury (including property damage). Office: Dyer Garofalo Mann &Schultz 131 N Ludlow St Dayton OH 45402

YIN, DOMINIC DAVID, police officer, educator, lawyer; b. Tokyo, Jan. 3, 1966; came to U.S., 1972; s. Winsor and Helen Yin; m. Kimberly Hyon Kim, Feb. 14, 1996. BA, U. Calif., Berkeley, 1989; JD, UCLA, 1993; MS, San Francisco State U., 1996; postgrad., U. So. Calif., 1998—. Bar: Calif. Atty. JAGC USN, Alexandria, Va., 1991-95; police officer San Francisco Police Dept., 1995—. Lectr. Calif. State U., Hayward, 1996—, City Coll. San Francisco, 1999—; instr. San Francisco Police Acad., 1997—; instr. Calif. Specialized Tng., San Luis Obisbo, 1997—. Vol. Chinatown Youth Ctr., San Francisco, 1998. Lt. (j.g.) USNR, 1991-95; 1st lt. Calif. N.G., 1995—. Mem. San Francisco Police Officers Assn. Avocations: reading, travelling, fitness. Home: 576 41st Ave San Francisco CA 94121-2527 Office: 372 7th Ave San Francisco CA 94118-2322

YIRA, MARKUS CLARENCE, lawyer; b. St. Croix Falls, Wis., Feb. 6, 1971; s. Robert Gordon and Ruth Elizabeth Yira; m. Dawn Susanne Nelson, June 19, 1993; children: Jordan M., Kaitlin E., Alison M., Brandon M. BA magna cum laude, Hamline U., 1993; JD, William Mitchell Coll. Law, St. Paul, 1996. Bar: Minn. 1996, Wis. 2002, U.S. Dist. Ct. Minn. 1996, U.S. Ct. Appeals (8th cir.) 1997, U.S. Supreme Ct. 1999. Rsch. asst. William Mitchell Coll. Law, 1993-95; assoc. Eckman, Strandness & Egan, P.A., Wayzata, Minn., 1996-99, Lommen, Nelson, Cole & Stageberg, P.A., Mpls., 1999—2003, Bradford Yira, Hutchinson, Minn., 2003—. Mem.: ATLA, Hennepin County Bar Assn., Wis. Acad. Trial Lawyers, Minn. Trial Lawyers Assn., Minn. Bar Assn., Phi Beta Kappa. General civil litigation, Personal injury (including property damage), Product liability. Office: Bradford Yira PO Box 130 75 Hassan St S Hutchinson MN 55350 Office Fax: 320-587-5007. E-mail: mcy@hutchtel.net.

YODOWITZ, EDWARD JAY, lawyer; b. N.Y.C., 1943; BS, Long Island U., 1965; JD, U. Balt., 1969. Bar: N.Y. 1972. With Skadden, Arps, Slate, Meagher & Flom, L.L.P., N.Y.C., 1969—, now sr. ptnr. Chmn. securities litigation seminar Practicing Law Inst., 1984-95; bd. trustees L.I. U., 1990-99. Mem.: ABA. Federal civil litigation, Securities. Home: 105 Ocean Ave Lawrence NY 11559-2006 Office: Skadden Arps Slate Meagher & Flom LLP Four Times Sq New York NY 10036-6522 Business E-Mail: eyodowit@skadden.com.

YOHALEM, HARRY MORTON, lawyer; b. Phila., Jan. 21, 1943; s. Morton Eugene and Florence (Mishnun) Y.; m. Martha Caroline Remy, June 9, 1967; children: Seth, Mark. BA with honors, U. Wis., 1965; JD cum laude, M in Internat. Affairs., Columbia U., 1969. Bar: N.Y. 1969, D.C. 1981, Calif. 1992, U.S. Supreme Ct. 1985. Assoc. Shearman & Sterling, N.Y.C., 1969-71; asst. counsel to gov. State of N.Y., Albany, 1971-73, counsel office planning svcs., 1973-75; asst. gen. counsel FEA, Washington, 1975-77; mem. staff White House Energy Policy and Planning Office, Washington, 1977; dep. gen. counsel for legal svcs. Dept. Energy, Washington, 1978-80, dep. under sec., 1980-81; ptnr. Rogers & Wells, Washington, 1981-91; gen. counsel Calif. Inst. Tech., Pasadena, 1991—. Editor comments Columbia Jour. Transnat. Law, 1967-68, rsch. editor, 1968-69. Prin. Coun. for Excellence in Govt., Washington, 1990—; pres. Opera Bel Canto, Washington, 1984-87; mem. Lawyers Com. for Arts, Washington, 1981-88; bd. visitors dept. English U. Wis., 1999—. Harlan Fiske Stone scholar Columbia U., 1967, 69. Mem. ABA, Calif. Bar Assn., D.C. Bar Assn. Athenaeum, Phi Kappa Phi, Columbia Club N.Y. Corporate, general, Education and schools, General practice. Home: 702 E California Blvd Pasadena CA 91106 Office: Calif Inst Tech Mail Code 109-31 1200 E California Blvd Pasadena CA 91125 E-mail: harry.yohalem@caltech.edu.

YOHN, WILLIAM H(ENDRICKS), JR., federal judge; b. Pottstown, Pa., Nov. 20, 1935; s. William H. and Dorothy C. (Cornelius) Y.; m. Jean Louise Kochel, Mar. 16, 1963; children: William H. III, Bradley G., Elizabeth Y. Lerman. AB, Princeton U., 1957; JD, Yale U., 1960. Bar: Pa. 1961, U.S. Dist. Ct. D.C. 1961. Ptnr. Wells Campbell Reynier & Yohn, Pottstown, 1961-71; mem., chmn. coms. Pa. House of Reps., Harrisburg, 1968-80; ptnr. Binder Yohn & Kalis, Pottstown, 1971-81; judge Montgomery County Ct. of Common Pleas, Norristown, Pa., 1981-91, U.S. Dist. Ct., ea. dist., Pa., 1991—. Asst. D.A., Montgomery County D.A. Office, 1962-65; instr. Am. Inst. of Banking, 1963-66; bd. dirs. Fed. Jud. Ctr., 1999-2003. Bd. dirs. Greater Pottstown Drug Abuse Prevention Program, 1970-76, Pottstown Meml. Med. Ctr., 1974-95, chmn., 1984-95; mem. exec. com. Yale LAw Sch. Alumni Assn., 1998—. Cpl. USMCR, 1960-66. Mem. Pa. Bar Assn., Montgomery Bar Assn. (bd. dirs. 1967-70). Republican. Office: US Dist Ct 14613 US Courthouse 601 Market St Philadelphia PA 19106-1713

YOHO, BILLY LEE, lawyer; b. Huntington, W.Va., Oct. 24, 1925; s. Wilbert Wiley Yoho Sr. and Nellie Pansy (Bryan) Hawkins; m. Martha Sue Carroll; children: Kevin Richard, Karen Lee; m. Shirley Ann Stone Morris. BA, U. Md., 1950; LLD, U. Md., Balt., 1953. Bar: Md. 1953. Ptnr. Hoyert & Yoho Chartered, Lanham, Md., 1953—; gen. counsel City of College Park, Md., 1959-62; town atty. Town of Colmar Manor, Md., 1956-72; gen. counsel Prince George's Gen. Hosp., Cheverly, Md., 1955-74, MD22 Lions Rsch. Found., Balt., 1988—; ptnr. Hoyert & Yoho Chartered, Lanham, Md., 1987—. Mem. College Park airport program in saving the oldest airport in the world, 1968. With USN, 1943-47. Mem. ABA, Prince George's County Bar Assn. (pres. 1976-77), Md. Assn. Trial Attys., Lions Clubs Internat. (dist. gov. 1989-90, life mem.), NRA, U. Md. Alumni Assn. Democrat.

Presbyterian. Avocations: computing, genealogy, christian study. Corporate, general, Family and matrimonial, Personal injury (including property damage). Home: 5950 Westchester Park Dr College Park MD 20740-2802

YOO, GRACE, legal association administrator; Exec. dir. Nat. Asian Pacific Am. Bar Assn., Washington. Office: Nat Asian Pacific Am Bar Assn Ste 315 733 15th St NW Washington DC 20005*

YORK, ALEXANDRA, lawyer; b. Jersey City, Feb. 9, 1939; d. Daniel Simpson and Regina (Norwich) S. BA, Tulane U., 1960; JD, Fordham U., 1976. Bar: N.Y. 1978, N.J., 1984; U.S. Dist. Ct. (so. and ea. dists.) N.Y. 1978, U.S. Dist. Ct. N.J. 1984, U.S. Ct. Appeals (2d cir.) 1987. Vol. Peace Corps, Philippines, 1961-63; legis. adviser Speaker of the Philippine House of Reps., Manila, 1964; speechwriter Mems. U.S. Congress, Washington, 1965; compliance officer U.S. Equal Employment Opportunity Commn., Washington, 1966-68; cons. N.Y.C. Dept. Consumer Affairs, 1969; cons., speechwriter N.Y.C. Dept. Air Resources, 1970-72; assoc. Shea and Gould, N.Y.C., 1977-79, Leopold Kaplan P.C., N.Y.C., 1980-86; asst. atty. gen. N.Y. State Dept. of Law, N.Y.C., 1987-93; spl. counsel external affairs Congress of Federated States of Micronesia, Pohnpei, 1993-95. Del. Federated States of Micronesia Internat. Climate Change Neg., Geneva, 1994; sr. policy adv. Philippine Sen. Com. Environment, 1996; U.N. devel. prog. cons. Philippine Dept. Environment and Natural Resources, 1996-97; mem., adv. com. environ. law, Practicing Law Inst., N.Y.C., 1991-93; prof. environ. policy, Ateneo de Manila U., Philippines, 1996-97; ofcl. del. UN Conf. on Environ. and Devel., Rio de Janiero, 1992; spkr. in field. Contbr. articles on environ. mgmt., internat. environ. law and climate change to profl. jours. Mem. ABA (natural resources sect., energy and environ. sect., internat. law and practice sect. 1990-93, program chair ann. meeting 1991, 92, chair subcom. on Human Rights and Environ., goal IX officer, 1992-93), Assn. of Bar of City of N.Y. (mem. internat. law com. 1990-93, mem., originator spl. com. internat. environ. law 1991, environ. com. 1987-90), Am. Soc. Internat. Law (environ. sect. 1991-92). E-mail: silva@fpfc.com.ph.

YORK, DAVID P. lawyer; b. 1963; BA, Birmingham So. Coll.; JD, Samford U. Asst. dist. atty. Douglas Jud. Cir., 1990—91; assoc. atty. Johnston, Wilkins, Druhan & Holz, 1991—92; asst. dist. atty. 13th Jud. Cir., 1992—97; atty. Pierce, Ledyard, Latta, Wasden & Bowron, Mobile; U.S. atty. So. Dist. Ala. Office: River View Plz 63 S Royal St Mobile AL 36602*

YOSKOWITZ, IRVING BENJAMIN, lawyer, merchant banker; b. Bklyn., Dec. 2, 1945; s. Rubin and Jennie Y.; m. Carol L. Magil, Feb. 11, 1973; children: Stephen M., Robert J. BA, CCNY, 1966; JD, Harvard U., 1969; postgrad., London Sch. Econs., 1971-72. Bar: N.Y. 1970, D.C. 1970, Conn. 1982. Programmer IBM, East Fishkill, N.Y., 1966; systems analyst Office Sec. Def., Washington, 1969-71; assoc. Arnold & Porter, Washington, 1972-73; atty. IBM, 1973-79, regional counsel, to 1979; dep. gen. counsel United Technologies Corp., Hartford, Conn., 1979-81, v.p. and gen. counsel, 1981-86, sr. v.p., gen. counsel, 1986-90, exec. v.p., gen. counsel, 1990-98; sr. ptnr. Global Tech. Ptnrs., L.L.C., Washington, 1998—; sr. counsel Crowell & Moring, Washington, 2001—. Bd. dirs. BBA Group, PLC, Equant, N.V. Mem. editorial bd. Harvard Law Rev., 1968-69. With U.S. Army, 1969-71. Knox fellow, 1971-72 Mem. ABA, Am. Corp. Counsel Assn. (bd. dirs. 1982-85), Assn. Gen. Counsel. Antitrust, Commercial, contracts (including sales of goods; commercial financing), Corporate, general.*

YOSKOWITZ, MARLENE, lawyer, educator; b. Russia, Mar. 27, 1943; BA, Rutgers U., 1964; MA, Kean U., 1968; JD cum laude, Seton Hall U., 1975. Bar: N.J. 1975, N.Y. 1983, U.S. Dist. Ct. 1975, U.S. Supreme Ct. 1983. With firm Timins & Lesniak, Elizabeth, N.J., 1987-88, Norman A. Cohen, Perth Amboy, N.J., 1977-92; sole practitioner Union, N.J., 1992—. Adj. instr. Kean U. N.J., Union, 1995—. General civil litigation, Family and matrimonial, General practice. Office: PO Box 484 Union NJ 07083-6132

YOST, GERALD B. lawyer; b. Harvey, Ill., Dec. 21, 1954; s. Richard Dennis and Marilyn Patricia (Moore) Y.; m. Kay Lynn Benton, Apr. 16, 1977; children: Matthew Brian, Benjamin Gerald, Andrew Richard. BA in Journalism, Drake U., 1976; student, Purdue U., 1975; JD, Hamline U., 1980. Bar: Minn. 1980, U.S. Dist. Ct. Minn. 1980, Wis. 1987. Assoc. Bergman, Street & Ulmen, Mpls., 1980—84; ptnr. Wasserman and Baill, Mpls., 1984—90, Yost, Stephenson & Sanford, Mpls., 1990—95, Yost & Baill LLP, Mpls., 1996—. Editor: Student Osteo. Med. Assn. Publ. mag., 1976; mem. Law Review Hamline U., 1978-80. Active YMCA, St. Paul. Recipient Am. Jurisprudence award, Lawyers Coop. Pub. Co., St. Paul, 1979. Mem. ABA, Minn. State Bar Assn., Wis. Bar Assn., Phi Alpha Delta, Sigma Delta Chi. Avocations: tennis, racquetball, boating and water skiing, jogging. Corporate, general, Mergers and acquisitions, Property, real (including real estate development, water). Home: 422 Mt Curve Blvd Saint Paul MN 55105 Office: Yost & Baill LLP 2350 One Fin Plz 120 S 6th St Minneapolis MN 55402-1803 E-mail: gyost@yostbaill.com.

YOUNEY, JOHN WILLIAM, lawyer; b. Manchester, N.H., May 10, 1954; s. William John and Christine (Zoulias) Y.; m. Karol A. Kish. BS in Resource Devel., Mich. State U., 1975; JD, Western New Eng. Coll., 1980; LLM in Taxation, Boston U., 1981. Bar: Maine 1980, Mass. 1980. Sole practice, Boston and Skowhegan, Maine, 1980-81; sr. tax specialist Laventhol & Horwath, Tucson, 1981-83; mgr. Tax Computer Systems, Inc., Tucson, 1984; adminstrv. law judge Office of Appeals State of Ariz., Tucson, 1984-89; atty. Law Offices of Ron Cullenberg, Farmington, Maine, 1989-90; ptnr., prin. Merrill, Hyde, Fortier & Youney, P.A., Skowhegan, Maine, 1991—. Bus. and tax cons. 1980—. Rep. campaign coordinator, Augusta, Maine, 1976; campaign mgr. Laos for Congress Com., Tucson, 1982; Rep. Com. mem. Skowhegan, 1972-80, 89—; state committeeman Maine Rep. State Commn., 1992-98; chmn. assembly St. Demetrios Greek Orthodox Ch., 1986, Tucson, Ariz., parish coun. St. George Greek Orthodox Ch., Bangor, Maine, 1991-95. Recipient Eagle Scout award Boy Scouts Am., 1969. Mem. Maine Bar Assn., Mich. State U. Alumni Club (advisor Tucson chpt., bd. govs.), Am. Hellenic Ednl. Progressive Assn. (warden 1985-86, bd. govs. 1986-88), Masons, Lions (past pres., Dist. Cabinet 1994—, vice dist. gov. 1998-99, dist. gov. 1999-2000, MD Parlimentarian 2001—, USA/Can. Lions leadership, forum presenter, moderator and discussion leader.). General civil litigation, General practice, Probate (including wills, trusts). Home: 161 Madison Ave Skowhegan ME 04976-1345 Office: Merrill Hyde Fortier & Youney PA PO Box 3100 Skowhegan ME 04976-3100

YOUNG, ALICE, lawyer; b. Washington, Apr. 7, 1950; d. John and Elizabeth (Jen) Y.; m. Thomas L. Shortall, Sept. 22, 1984; children: Amanda, Stephen. AB magna cum laude, Yale U., 1971; JD, Harvard U., 1974. Bar: N.Y. 1975. Assoc. Coudert Bros., N.Y.C., 1974-81; mng. ptnr. Graham & James, N.Y.C., 1981-87; ptnr. Milbank, Tweed, Hadley & McCloy, N.Y.C., 1987-93; ptnr., chair Asia Pacific Practice (U.S.) Kaye, Scholer LLP, N.Y.C., 1994—. Bd. dirs. Mizuho Trust & Banking Co. Contbr. articles to profl. jours. Bus. com. Nat. Com. on U.S.-China Rels., 1993—, U.S.-China Bus. Coun., 1993—, Com. of 100, 1993—, vice-chmn., 1999—; bd. overseers visitation com. to Law Sch. Harvard U., 1994—99, chair subcom. on grad. program, 1996; trustee Lingnan Found., N.Y.C., 1984—91, Pan-Asian Repertory Theatre, N.Y.C., 1987—90, Aspen (Colo.) Inst., 1988—, Am. Assembly, 2000—; bus. com. Met. Mus. Art, N.Y.C., 1989—94; active Coun. on Fgn. Rels., 1977—, Chmn.'s Forum, 2000—; trustee Asia Found., 2002—. Named one of Top 100 Minority Leaders, 1998, one of 40 Under 40 Crain's Bus., N.Y.C., 1989; Bates fellow Yale U., 1970, NDFL fellow Harvard U., 1967-68; recipient Star award N.Y. Women's Agenda, 1992. Mem. ABA, N.Y. State Bar Assn. (fgn. investment com.), Assn. Bar City N.Y. (spl. com. on rels. with Japanese bar, Union Internat. des Avocats), Nat. Asian Pacific Am. Bar Assn., Asian Am. Bar Assn. N.Y., Coun. on Fgn. Rels., Chmn.'s Forum, Harvard Law Sch. Assn. N.Y.C. (trustee 1990-94), Japan Soc. (sec. 1989-97), Asia Soc. (pres.'s coun. 1984—). Corporate, general, Private international, Mergers and acquisitions. Office: Kaye Scholer LLP 425 Park Ave New York NY 10022-3506 E-mail: ayoung@kayescholer.com.

YOUNG, BARNEY THORNTON, lawyer; b. Chillicothe, Tex., Aug. 10, 1934; s. Bayne and Helen Irene (Thornton) Y.; m. Sarah Elizabeth Taylor, Aug. 31, 1957; children: Jay Thornton, Sarah Elizabeth, Serena Taylor. BA, Yale U., 1955; LLB, U. Tex., 1958. Bar: Tex. 1958. Assoc. Thompson, Knight, Wright & Simmons, Dallas, 1958-65; ptnr. Rain, Harrell, Emery, Young & Doke, Dallas, 1965-87; mem. firm Locke Purnell Rain Harrell (A Profl. Corp.), 1987-98; of counsel Locke, Liddell & Sapp LLP, 1999—. Mem. adv. coun. Dallas Cmty. Chest Trust Fund, Inc., 1964-66; bd. dirs. Mental Health Assn. Dallas County, Inc., 1969-72, Trammell Crow Family Found., 1984-87; trustee Hockaday Sch., Dallas, 1971-77, 90—, chmn., 1994-96, Dallas Zool. Soc., 1986-92, Lamplighter Sch., Dallas, 1976-99, chmn., 1983-86, St. Mark's Sch., Dallas, 1970—, pres., 1976-78, The Found. for Callier Ctr. and Comm. Disorders, 1988-99, Friends of Ctr. for Human Nutrition, 1988—, Shelter Ministries of Dallas Found., 1993—, Dallas Hist. Soc., 1993-2001; bd. dirs. Susan G. Komen Breast Cancer Found., 2000—, Nat. Assn. Ind. Schs., 2000—; mem. Yale Devel. Bd., 1984-91, 1998—. Fellow Tex. Bar Found., Dallas Bar Found.; mem. ABA, Tex. Bar Assn., Dallas Bar Assn., Am. Judicature Soc., Order of Coif, Phi Beta Kappa, Pi Sigma Alpha, Phi Gamma Delta, Phi Delta Phi, Dallas Country Club., Petroleum Club (Dallas), Yale Club (Dallas, N.Y.C.). Corporate, general, Mergers and acquisitions, Securities. Home: 6901 Turtle Creek Blvd Dallas TX 75205-1251 Office: Locke Liddell & Sapp LLP 2200 Ross Ave Ste 2200 Dallas TX 75201-6776

YOUNG, BRYANT LLEWELLYN, lawyer, business executive; b. Rockford, Ill., Mar. 9, 1948; s. Llewellyn Anker and Florence Ruth Y. AB, Cornell U., 1970; JD, Stanford U., 1974. Bar: Calif. 1974, Nev. 1975, D.C. 1979. Law clk. U.S. Dist. Ct. (no. dist.) Calif., San Francisco, 1974-75; assoc. Dinkelspiel, Pelavin, Steefel & Levitt, San Francisco, 1975-77; White House fellow, spl. asst. to sec. HUD, Washington, 1977-78, spl. asst. to sec., 1978-79, acting dep. exec. asst. for ops. Office of Sec., 1979; from dep. gen. mgr. to acting gen. mgr. New Cmty. Devel. Corp., 1979-80; mgmt. cons. AVCO Corp., 1980; spl. asst. to chmn. bd., CEO U.S. Synthetic Fuels Corp., Washington, 1980-81, project dir., 1981; pres. Trident Mgmt. Corp., San Francisco, 1981-87; of counsel Pelavin, Norberg, Harlick & Beck, San Francisco, 1981-82, ptnr., 1982-87; mng. ptnr. bus. section Carroll, Burdick & McDonough, San Francisco, 1987-90; founding ptnr. Young, Vogl & Harlick, San Francisco, 1990-93, Young, Vogl, Harlick, Wilson & Simpson, LLP, San Francisco, 1993-99; pres. Young Enterprises, Inc., 1995—; mgr. SRY Industries LLC, 1997—, KML Hospitality Industries LLC, 1997—; ptnr. Young Vogl LLP, 1999—2001; prin. Law Offices of Bryant L. Young, 2002—. Dir. The Whitman Inst. Pub. affairs com. San Francisco Aid Retarded Citizens, Inc., 1977; U.S. co-chmn. New Towns Working Group, U.S.-USSR Agreement on Cooperation in Field of Housing and Other Constrn., 1979-80; treas., bd. dirs. White House Fellows Found., 1980-84; prin. Coun. Excellence in Govt., Washington, 1986-94; adv. com. Nat. Multi-Housing Coun., 1987-92; mem. Ross Sch. Found., 1994-97, sec., 1995-97; bd. dirs. Marin AIDS Project, 1996-97, sec., 1997; trustee Ross Sch., 1997-2002, pres. 2002—. Mem. ABA (real property, trust and probate law sects. 1975-96), White House Fellows Assn. (chmn. ann. meeting 1979, del. China 1980), Marin County Sch. Bds. Assn., Am. Field Svc. Returnees Assn., Can.-Am. C. of C. No. Calif. (v.p., bd. dirs. 1992), Chile-Calif. Found. (exec. com., bd. dirs. 1993-96). Corporate, general, Private international, Property, real (including real estate development, water). Office: 44 Montgomery St ste 4020 San Francisco CA 94104-4602 E-mail: bly@ebzlaw.net.

YOUNG, DEBORAH SCHWIND, lawyer; b. Buffalo, Feb. 28, 1955; d. Richard G. and Rhoda R. Schwind; m. Thomas Paul Young, May 23, 1981. BA, Dartmouth Coll., 1976; JD, SUNY, Buffalo, 1979. Bar: N.Y. 1980, U.S. Dist. Ct. (we. dist.) N.Y. 1980. Assoc. Harter, Secrest and Emery, Rochester, N.Y., 1979-83; asst. v.p., asst. counsel Chase Lincoln First Bank, Rochester, 1983-85, v.p., sr. counsel, 1985-92; v.p., sr. assoc. counsel The Chase Manhattan Bank, Rochester, 1993-96, v.p., asst. gen. counsel, 1997—2000, J.P. Morgan Chase & Co., Rochester, 2001—. Mem. pension com. Rochester Philharm. Orch., 1983-91; mem. Rochester-Monroe County Youth Bd., 1987-88. Mem. N.Y. Bar Assn. Banking. Office: JP Morgan Chase & Co 1 Chase Sq Rochester NY 14643-0002

YOUNG, DOUGLAS HOWARD, lawyer; b. Bronxville, N.Y., Oct. 16, 1948; s. Joseph Paul and Frances (Lally) Y.; m. Betsy Baker, Apr. 24, 1971; children: Jeffrey D., Kevin C. BA, Gettysburg Coll., 1970; JD magna cum laude, Syracuse U., 1978. Bar: N.Y. 1979, U.S. Dist. Ct. (no. dist.) N.Y. 1979, U.S. Claims Ct. 1992. Ptnr. Melvin & Melvin, Syracuse, N.Y., 1978—. Bd. dirs. Onondaga County Legal Svcs. Corp., Syracuse, pres., 1995-96; village atty. Village of Jordan, N.Y., 1980—. Editor Syracuse Law Rev., 1977-78; contbr. articles to profl. jours. Cub scout leader Boy Scouts Am., Syracuse, 1980-81; umpire Liverpool (N.Y.) Little League, Babe Ruth League, 1981-90, Optimists Basketball, Liverpool, 1985-87; coach Babe Ruth Baseball, Liverpool, 1989-90. Capt. USAF, 1971-76. Named Eagle Scout Boy Scouts Am., 1965. Mem. N.Y. State Bar Assn., N.Y.S. Trial Lawyers Assn., Onondaga County Bar Assn. Episcopalian. Avocations: gardening, golf, outdoor hiking. General civil litigation, Condemnation (eminent domain). Home: 4058 Pawnee Dr Liverpool NY 13090-2853 Office: Melvin & Melvin 217 S Salina St Syracuse NY 13202-1390 E-mail: DYoung@melvinlaw.com.

YOUNG, DOUGLAS REA, lawyer; b. L.A., July 21, 1948; s. James Douglas and Dorothy Belle (Rea) Y.; m. Terry Forrest, Jan. 19, 1974; 1 child, Megann Forrest. BA cum laude, Yale U., 1971; JD, U. Calif., Berkeley, 1976. Bar: Calif., 1976, U.S. Dist. Ct. (no. dist.) Calif. 1976, U.S. Ct. Appeals (6th and 9th cirs.) 1977, U.S. Dist. Ct. (ctrl. dist.) Calif. 1979, U.S. Dist. Ct. Hawaii, U.S. Dist. Ct. (so. dist.) Calif., U.S. Supreme Ct. 1982; cert. specialist in appellate law. Law clk. U.S. Dist. Ct. (no. dist.) Calif., San Francisco, 1976-77; assoc. Farella, Braun & Martel LLP, San Francisco, 1977-82, ptnr., 1983—. Spl. master U.S. Dist. Ct. (no. dist.) Calif., 1977-78, 88, 96, 2000; mem. Criminal Justice Act Def. Panel no. dist. Calif.; mem. faculty Calif. Continuing Edn. of Bar, Berkeley, 1982—, Nat. Inst. Trial Advocacy, Berkeley, 1984—, Practicing Law Inst., 1988—; adj. prof. Hastings Coll. Advocacy, 1985—; vis. lectr. law Boalt Hall/U. Calif., Berkeley, 1986; judge pro tem San Francisco Mcpl. Ct., 1984—, San Francisco Superior Ct., 1990—. Author: (with Purver and Davis) California Trial Handbook, ed edit., (with Hon. Richard Byrne, Purver and Davis), 3d edit., (with Purver, Davis and Kerper) The Trial Lawyers Book, (with Hon. Eugene Lynch, Taylor, Purver and Davis) California Negotiation and Settlement Handbook; contbr. articles to profl. jours. Bd. dirs. Berkeley Law Found., 1977-78, chmn., 1978-79; bd. dirs. San Francisco Legal Aid Soc., pres., 1993—; bd. dirs. Pub. Interest Clearinghouse, San Francisco, chmn., 1987—, treas., 1988—; chmn. Attys. Task Force for Children, Legal Svcs. for Children, 1987—; mem. State Bar Appellate Law Adv. Commn., 1994—. Recipient award of appreciation Berkeley Law Found., 1983, Criminal Justice Achievement award Criminal Trial Lawyers Assn. of No. Calif., 2002. Fellow Am. Coll. Trial Lawyers, Am. Acad. Appellate Lawyers; mem. ABA (Pro Bono Pub. award 1992), San Francisco Bar Assn. (founding chmn. litigation sect. 1988-89, award of appreciation 1989, bd. dirs. 1990-91, pres. 2001), Calif. Acad. Appellate Lawyers, McFetridge Am. Inn of Ct. (master), Lawyers Club San Francisco. Democrat. Federal civil litigation, State civil litigation, Criminal. Office: Farella Braun & Martel 235 Montgomery St Ste 3000 San Francisco CA 94104-2902

YOUNG, GEORGE CRESSLER, federal judge; b. Cin., Aug. 4, 1916; s. George Philip and Gladys (Cressler) Y.; m. Iris June Hart, Oct. 6, 1951; children: George Cressler, Barbara Ann. AB, U. Fla., 1938, LLB, 1940; postgrad., Harvard Law Sch., 1947. Bar: Fla. 1940. Practice in, Winter Haven, 1940-41; asso. firm Smathers, Thompson, Maxwell & Dyer, Miami, 1947; adminstrv., legislative asst. to Senator Smathers of Fla., 1948-52; asst. U.S. atty. Jacksonville, 1952; partner firm Knight, Kincaid, Young & Harris, Jacksonville, 1953-61; U.S. dist. judge No., Middle and So. dists. Fla., 1961-73; chief judge Middle Dist., 1973-81, sr. judge, 1981—. Mem. com. on adminstrn. fed. magistrates system Jud. Conf. U.S., 1973-80 Bd. dirs. Jacksonville United Cerebral Palsy Assn., 1953-60. Served to lt. (s.g.) USNR, 1942-46. Mem. Rollins Coll. Alumni Assn. (pres. 1968-69), ABA (spl. com. for adminstrn. criminal justice), Fla. Bar Assn. (gov. 1960-61), Jacksonville Bar Assn. (past pres.), Order of Coif, Fla. Blue Key, Phi Beta Kappa, Phi Kappa Phi, Phi Delta Phi, Sigma Alpha Epsilon. Home: 2424 Shrewsbury Rd Orlando FL 32803-1334 Office: US Dist Ct 635 US Courthouse 80 N Hughey Ave Orlando FL 32801-2278

YOUNG, HUBERT HOWELL, JR., lawyer, real estate investor and developer; b. Franklin, Va., May 30, 1945; s. Hubert Howell and Elizabeth Ann (Davidson) Y.; m. Christine P. Brooks, Dec. 31, 1964; 1 son, Hubert Howell, III. BA, Washington Lee U., 1967, LLB, magna cum laude, 1969. Bar: Va. 1969, U.S. Supreme Ct. 1972, Tex. 1974, U.S. Dist. Ct. Tex. 1974, U.S. Dist. Ct. (ea. dist.) Va. 1980. Assoc., Johnson, Bromberg, Leeds and Riggs, Dallas, 1973-75; gen. counsel Trammel Crow Co., Dallas, 1975-79; sole practice, Suffolk, Va., 1979— ; gen. counsel Young Properties, Suffolk, 1979— ; dir. Young Properties Devel. Corp., Trammel Crow Investment Corp., Suffolk Broadcasting Corp. Pres. Suffolk (Va.) Found. Trust, 1982-83; vice chmn. Suffolk Coalition for Sr. Citizen Housing, Inc., 1982-83; mem. Suffolk Substance and Abuse and Youth Council, 1982-84; chmn. Suffolk Rep. Party, 1982-85; commr. Med. Coll. Hampton Roads, 1990-96; dir. Va. Symphony, 1991-94. Served as lt. JAG, USN, 1969-73. Designated col. Confederate Army The Lee-Jackson Meml. Inc., 1981. Mem. ABA, Suffolk Bar Assn. (pres. 1994), Property Owners and Mgrs. Assn. (pres. 1995-96). Club: Town Point, Sports, Ducks Unlimited (Suffolk). Fax: 757-539-5130. E-mail: yprop@msn.com. Corporate, general, General practice, Property, real (including real estate development, water). Office: Young Properties 444 N Main St Suffolk VA 23434-4425

YOUNG, JAMES EDWARD, lawyer; b. Painesville, Ohio, Apr. 20, 1946; s. James M. and Isabel P. (Rogers) Y. BBA, Ohio U., 1968; JD, Ohio State U., 1972. Bar: Ohio 1972. Law clk. to chief judge U.S. Ct. Appeals, Nashville, 1972-73; chief counsel City of Cleve., 1980-81, law dir., 1981-82; assoc. Jones, Day, Reavis & Pogue, Cleve., 1973-79, ptnr., 1983—. Product liability, Environmental, Toxic tort. Office: Jones Day Reavis & Pogue 901 Lakeside Ave E Cleveland OH 44114-1190 E-mail: jameseyoung@jonesday.com.

YOUNG, JAMES MARION, lawyer; b. Winston-Salem, N.C., Nov. 15, 1930; s. William Rector and Celia Marie (Pasley) Y.; m. Barbara Marie Pultz, Feb. 2, 1957; children: Deborah Marie, Rebecca Anne, Catherine Arline, Cynthia Louise. BA, U. Va., 1953, LLB, 1957. Bar: Va. Assoc. M.S. McChung, Salem, Va., 1957-58, A. Tracy Loyd, Roanoke, 1958-64, Dodson, Pence & Coulter, Roanoke, 1964-66; ptnr. Dodson Pence Viar Young and Woodrum, Roanoke and Salem, Va., 1966—. Pres. Roanoke County Council PTA, 1970; mem. exec. bd. Blue Ridge Mountains council Boy Scouts Am., 1960—, pres., 1975-77; chmn. City of Salem Electoral Bd., 1968-83. Recipient Disting. Service award Salem Jaycees, 1964; Silver Beaver award Boy Scouts Am., 1976. Mem. ABA, Va. Bar Assn., Roanoke County Bar Assn. (pres. 1970), Salem-Roanoke County C. of C. (pres. 1972). Democrat. Presbyterian. Club: Salem Kiwanis (pres. 1981-82). Probate (including wills, trusts). Home: 412 N Shank St Salem VA 24153-2655 Office: James M Young PC Atty at Law 25 Library Sq Salem VA 24153-3846

YOUNG, JEFFREY, lawyer; b. Cleve., Jan. 5, 1953; s. Sheldon Michael and Margery Polster Young; m. Elizabeth Ann Mahoney, Sept. 14, 1986; children: Brendan, Celeste, Amara. BA, Brown U., 1976; JD, Case Western Res. U., 1982. Bar: D.C. 1982, U.S. Dist. Ct. D.C. 1982, Md. 1983, U.S. Ct. Appeals (D.C. cir.) 1983, Maine 1988, U.S. Dist. C. Md. 1988, U.S. Ct. Appeals (1st cir.) 1993, U.S. Ct. Appeals (4th cir.) 1984, U.S. Ct. Appeals (2d cir.) 1994. Atty. Lechner & Butsavage, Washington, 1982—86, Baptiste & Wilder, 1986—88, McTeague Higbee Case Cohen Whitney & Baker, Topsham, Maine, 1988—92, ptnr., shareholder, 1992—. Mem.: Maine Civil Liberties Union, Maine Employment Lawyers Assn., Nat. Employment Lawyers Assn. Civil rights, Labor (including EEOC, Fair Labor Standards Act, labor-management relations, NLRB, OSHA), Workers' compensation. Office: 4 Union Park Box 5000 Topsham ME 04086-5000 Fax: 207-725-1090. E-mail: jyoung@me-law.com.

YOUNG, JOHN EDWARD, lawyer; b. Tulsa, July 11, 1935; s. Russell Edward and Frances Lucille (Wetmore) Y.; m. Mary Moore Nason, Dec. 27, 1966; children: Cynthia Nason, Abigail Brackett. BS with honors, Calif. Inst. Tech., 1956; LLB magna cum laude, Harvard U., 1959. Bar: N.Y. 1961, U.S. Dist. Ct. (so. dist.) N.Y. 1973. Assoc. Cravath, Swaine & Moore LLP, N.Y.C., 1960-67, ptnr., 1968-95, resident ptnr. Paris, 1971-73, London, 1990-95, sr. counsel, 1996—. Editor Harvard Law Rev., 1958-59. Trustee Internat. Sculpture Ctr., 1997—, vice chmn., 2000—; trustee Royal Oak Found., 1997-2002, chmn., 1999-2002; gov. Am. Crafts Mus., 1997—. Sheldon Traveling fellow Harvard U., 1959-60. Mem. Assn. of Bar of City of N.Y., Century Assn., Harvard Club of N.Y.C., N.Y. Yacht Club, City Univ. Club London. Democrat. Episcopal. Corporate, general, Finance, Securities. Home: 1088 Park Ave New York NY 10128-1132 Office: Cravath Swaine and Moore LLP 825 Eighth Ave New York NY 10019 E-mail: jeyoung@attglobal.net.

YOUNG, JOHN HARDIN, lawyer, corporate executive; b. Washington, Apr. 25, 1948; s. John D. and Laura Virginia (Gwathmey) Y.; m. Mary Frances (Farley) Crosby. JD, U. Va., 1973; BCL, Oxford U., Eng., 1976. Bar: Va. 1973, D.C. 1974, U.S. Dist. Ct. (Va.) 1974, U.S. Dist. Ct. D.C. 1974, Internat. Trade Ct. 1974, U.S. Ct. Fed. Claims 1974, (U.S. Ct. Appeals (4th, 5th, Fed.and D.C. cirs.)), Pa. 1976, U.S. Supreme Ct. 1977, U. S. Dist. Ct. (Md.) 1989, cert.: Va. Supreme Ct. (mediator 1998-2001). Pvt. practice, 1973—75, 1978—81, 1983—; ptnr. Porter Wright Morris & Arthur, Washington, 1988-92, of counsel, 1992-99; gen. counsel, adminstr. Exec. Office of Pres., Washington, 2000; of counsel Sandler, Reiff & Young, PC, 2001—. Mem. adv. bd. Antitrust Bull.; mem. U.S. Sec. State's adv. com. Pvt. internat. Law, 1987-95; chmn. Va. Retirement Sys. Rev. Bd., 1990-94; asst. atty. gen. Commonwealth of Va., 1976-78; moderator Alexandria Forum, 1993-98, Fedn. Forum/TV Channel 10, 1989-91; gen. counsel, adminstr. Exec. Office of Pres., Washington, 2000; sr. v.p., gen. counsel various profit and not-for-profit tech. cos. Author: Federal Rules of Evidence, Mastering Written Discovery, Federal Rules of Evidence; contbr. articles to profl. jours. on litigation, evidence and technology contracting. Spl. counsel Dem. Nat. Com., 1998—99, chair nat. lawyers coun., 1998—; lead recount counsel for V.P. Gore Fla., 2000. Mem.: ABA (chmn. trade regulation and competition com. 1983—86, chmn. dispute resolution com. 1984—96, chmn. adminstrv. law and regulatory practice sect. 1999—2000, standing com. on continuing edn. of the bar 2002—, fellow adminstrv. law 2001—), Temple Bar Found. (founding mem., bd. dirs.), Comml. Bar Assn. U.K. (overseas mem.), George Mason Am. Inn of Ct. (master 1990—, pres. 2002—03, Spl. Projects award 2003), Am. Law Inst., Phi Alpha Theta (history honors), Hon. Soc. Mid Temple U.K. Episcopalian. Administrative and regulatory, Federal civil litigation, Computer. E-mail: young@sandlerreiff.com.

YOUNG, MARVIN OSCAR, lawyer; b. Union, Mo., Apr. 4, 1929; s. Otto Christopher and Irene Adelheide (Barlage) Y.; m. Sue Carol Mathews, Aug. 23, 1952; children: Victoria Leigh, Kendall Marvin. AB, Westminster Coll., 1951; JD, U. Mich., 1954; LLD, Westminster Coll., 1989. Bar: Mo. 1954. Practice law firm Thompson, Mitchell, Thompson Douglas, St. Louis, 1954-55, 57-58; atty. Mo. Farmers Assn., Columbia, 1958-67; exec. v.p. First Mo. Corp., Columbia, 1965-68; v.p. ops. MFA-Central Coop., Columbia, 1967-68; v.p., gen. counsel, sec. Peabody Coal Co., St. Louis, 1968-82; gen. counsel Peabody Holding Co., Inc., St. Louis, 1983-85; also dir., sec. subs. and affiliates Peabody Coal Co.; ptnr. Gallop, Johnson & Neuman, St. Louis, 1986—, chmn. corp. dept., 1988-90, chmn. energy dept., 1990—. City atty. Warson Woods, Mo., 1990—; spkr. in field. Assoc. editor Mich. Law Rev., 1953-54; contbr. articles to profl. jours. Pres. Warson Woods PTA, 1974-75; trustee Met. Sewer Dist. St. Louis, 1974-80, chmn. 1978-80; active Mo. Energy Coun., 1973-77, Mo. Environ. Improvement and Energy Resources Athority, 1983-87, vice-chmn. 1986-87; trustee Eastern Mineral Law Found., 1983-98; pres. Alumni Assn. Westminster Coll., Fulton, Mo., 1978-80, trustee coll., 1977—, exec. com., 1978-2003, chmn. 1986-90, chmn. investment com., 1998-2002; chmn. Churchill Meml. and Libr., Fulton, 1992-2000; mem. chancellor's coun. adv. bd. U. Mo., St. Louis, 1992—; trustee Stages--St. Louis, 2001—; lawyers adv. coun. Gt. Plains Legal Found., Kansas City, Mo., 1976-84; mem. Rep. Com. Boone County, Mo., 1962-68, chmn. legis. dist. com., 1962-64, 66-68; alt. del. Rep. Nat. Conv., 1968; pres. Clayton Twp. Rep. Club, 1973-77; sr. warden Episcopal Ch., 1988-89. Capt. USAF, 1955-57. Recipient alumni award of merit, 1972; named Coal Lawyer of Yr., Nat. Coal Assn., 1994; Churchill fellow, 1990. Mem. ABA, Mo. Bar Assn., Bar Assn. Met. St. Louis, Barristers Soc., Round Table Club St. Louis, John Marshall Rep. Lawyers Club (pres. 1977), Mo. Athletic Club, Shamrock Club St. Louis County, Rotary (bd. dirs. St. Louis club 1993-95), Masons, Order of Coif, Shriners. Alternative dispute resolution, Corporate, general, Natural resources. Home: 555 Flanders Dr Saint Louis MO 63122-1617 Office: Gallop Johnson & Neuman LC 101 S Hanley Rd Ste 1600 Saint Louis MO 63105-3489 E-mail: moyoung@gjn.com.

YOUNG, MICHAEL ANTHONY, lawyer; b. Lima, Ohio, Sept. 3, 1960; s. William John and Bettye Jean (Day) Y. BS magna cum laude, U. Cen. Fla., 1981; JD with honors, Fla. State U., 1984. Bar: Ga. 1984, Fla. 1985. Assoc. Kilpatrick & Cody, Atlanta, 1984-86, Stokes, Lazarus & Carmichael, Atlanta, 1986-89; pvt. practice, Atlanta, 1989—. Jud. intern U.S. Dist. Ct. (no. dist.) Fla., 1984; weekend atty. Atlanta Legal Aid Soc., 1985-86. Rsch. editor Fla. State U. Law Rev., 1982-84; contbr. articles to legal jours. Dir., pres. ChildKind Found. Mem. ABA, Assn. Trial Lawyers of Am., Fla. Bar Assn., Ga. Bar Assn., Atlanta Bar Assn. Avocations: scuba diving, golf, weightlifting. General civil litigation, Labor (including EEOC, Fair Labor Standards Act, labor-management relations, NLRB, OSHA), Personal injury (including property damage). Home: 5275 S Trimble Rd NE Atlanta GA 30342-2174 Office: 1050 Crown Pointe Pkwy Ste 330 Ste 440 Atlanta GA 30338

YOUNG, MICHAEL KENT, dean, lawyer, educator; b. Sacramento, Nov. 4, 1949; s. Vance Lynn and Ethelyn M. (Sowards) Young; m. Suzan Kay Stewart, June 1, 1972; children: Stewart, Kathryn, Andrew. BA summa cum laude, Brigham Young U., 1973; JD magna cum laude, Harvard U., 1976. Bar: Calif. 1976, N.Y. 1985. Law clk. to Justice Benjamin Kaplan, Supreme Jud. Ct. Mass., Boston, 1976-77; assoc. prof., prof., Fuyo prof. Japanese law Columbia U., N.Y.C., 1978-98; dir. Ctr. Japanese Legal Studies Ctr. for Korean Legal Studies, N.Y.C., 1985-98; dir. Program Internat. Human Rights and Religious Liberties Columbia U., N.Y.C., 1995-98; dep. legal advisor U.S. Dept. State, Washington, 1989-91, dep. under sec. for econ. affairs, 1991-93, amb. for trade and environ. affairs, 1992-93; law clk. to Justice William H. Rehnquist U.S. Supreme Ct., Washington, 1977-78; dean, Lobingier prof. comparative law and jurisprudence George Washington U. Sch. of Law, Washington, 1998—. Chair U.S. Commn. on Internat. Religious Freedom, 2001—02, vice chair, 2002—03; vis. scholar law faculty U. Tokyo, 1978—80, 1983; vis. prof. Waseda U., 1989; chmn. bd. advisors Japan Soc., 1996—98; counsel select subcom. on arms transfers to Bosnia U.S. Ho. of Reps., 1996; mem. steering com. Law Profs. for Dole, 1996; mem. com. on internat. jud. rels. U.S. Jud. Conf., 1999—; mem. Brown v. Bd. Edn. 50th Anniversary Commemoration Com.; chair NAFTA labor agreement adv. com. Dept. of Labor, 2002—; mem. trade and environ. policy adv. com. U.S. Trade Rep. Office, 2003—. Author: Fundamentals of U.S. Trade Law, 2001, Japanese Law in Context, 2001. Bd. visitors USAF Acad., 2000—02. Fellow, POSCO Rsch. Inst., 1995—98, Japan Found., 1979—80, Fulbright, 1983—84. Fellow: Am. Bar Found.; mem.: Coun. Fgn. Rels. Mem. Lds Ch. Avocation: Avocations: skiing, scuba diving, photography. Fax: 202-994-5157. E-mail: myoung@law.gwu.edu.

YOUNG, MICHAEL RICHARD, lawyer; b. Wiesbaden, Federal Republic Germany, May 12, 1956; parents Am. Citizens; s. Richard Barton and Janet (Crawford) Y.; m. Leslie Anne Carroll, Aug. 11, 1984. BA, Allegheny Coll., 1978; JD, Duke U., 1981. Bar: N.Y. 1982, U.S. Dist. Ct. (so. and ea. dists.) N.Y. 1982, U.S. Ct. Appeals (9th cir.) 1990, (2d. cir.) 1996, U.S. Supreme Ct. 1994. Assoc. Willkie Farr & Gallagher, N.Y.C., 1981-90, ptnr., 1990—. Rsch. and mng. editor Duke Law Jour., 1980-81; editor: Accounting Irregularities and Financial Fraud, 2000, 2d edit., 2002. Mem. ABA (com. on law and acctg.), Assn. of Bar of City of N.Y. (com. on legal edn. and admission to bar 1983-87), Phi Beta Kappa. Republican. Avocations: sailing, riding. General civil litigation. Home: 645 W End Ave Apt 1A New York NY 10025-7347 Office: Willkie Farr & Gallagher 787 Seventh Ave New York NY 10019-6099

YOUNG, RANDY WILLIAM, lawyer; b. Ft. Wayne, Ind., Oct. 19, 1949; s. Robert Arnold and Genevieve Mary (Obert) Y.; m. Julie Maree Brunson, June 16, 1984; children: Maree Elizabeth, Ann Elaine. BBA, U. Notre Dame, 1972; JD, Ind. U., 1975. Bar: Ind. 1975, U.S. Dist. Ct. (no. dist.) Ind. 1976. Law clk. to judge Ind. Ct. Appeals, Indpls., 1975-76; ptnr. Christoff, Cornelius & Young, Ft. Wayne, 1976-80; sole practice Ft. Wayne, 1980—. Recipient Silver Beaver award Boy Scouts Am., 1981, dist. award of Merit, 1985, Sagamore of Wabash, Gov. of Ind., 1990. Mem. Allen County Bar Assn. (treas. 1983-85), Allen County Law Library Assn. (treas. 1980-98). Clubs: St. Vincent Men's (Ft. Wayne), Notre Dame of Ft. Wayne (award of the Yr. 1985). Avocations: scouting, skiing, camping, backpacking. Family and matrimonial, Personal injury (including property damage), Probate (including wills, trusts). Home: 2115 Carroll Rd Fort Wayne IN 46818-8908 Office: 202 W Berry St Ste 710 Fort Wayne IN 46802-2273 E-mail: ry@randyyoung.com.

YOUNG, ROBERT P., JR., state supreme court justice; Bachelor's degree cum laude, Harvard Coll., 1974; JD, Harvard U., 1977. With Dickinson, Wright, Moon, Van Dusen & Freeman, 1977-1992; v.p., corp. sec., gen. counsel AAA Mich., 1992; appt. Mich. Ct. Appeals 1st Dist., 1995; appt. justice Mich. Supreme Ct., 1998, elected justice, 2000. Mem. Mich. Civil Svc. Commn.; bd. trustees Cen. Mich. U. Office: PO Box 30052 Lansing MI 48909-7552

YOUNG, ROLAND FREDERIC, III, lawyer; b. Norway, Maine, Apr. 8, 1954; s. Roland Frederic Jr. and Marylyn May (Bartlett) Y.; m. Dona Davis Gagliano, Aug. 18, 1979; children: Meghan, Wesley, Taylor. AB, Cornell U., 1976; JD, U. Conn., 1979. Bar: Conn. 1979, U.S. Dist. Ct. Conn., U.S. Tax Ct., U.S. Ct. Appeals (2d cir.). Ptnr. Howard, Kohn, Sprague & FitzGerald, Hartford, Conn., 1984-91, O'Brien, Tanski & Young, Hartford, Conn., 1991—. Lectr. Hartford Grad. Ctr., 1991-98. Author (seminar booklet) Confidentiality of Med. Records, 1989, Limiting Damages, 1990; co-author (seminar booklet) Med. Malpractice in Conn., 1992; editor Conn. Risk Mgmt. Assn., 1986-98. Trustee Mooreland Mill Sch.; vice chmn. Conn. Nat. Kideny Found. Mem. Conn. Hosp. Assn., Hartford County Bar Assn. (chmn. medico-legal liaison com.). Avocation: golf. Federal civil litigation, Health, Personal injury (including property damage). Office: O'Brien Tanski & Young City Place II 16th Fl Hartford CT 06103 E-mail: rfy@otylaw.com.

YOUNG, SHERILYN BURNETT, lawyer; b. Providence, Nov. 7, 1953; d. Archie C. III and Hope (Westcott) Burnett; m. Gary Richard Young, Oct. 9, 1977; children: Garrett, Alanna, Valerie. BA, Cornell U., 1975; JD, Franklin Pierce Law Ctr., 1982. Bar: N.H. 1982, U.S. Dist. Ct. N.H. 1982, U.S. Tax Ct. 1983. Assoc. Orr & Reno, P.A., Concord, N.H., 1982-87; ptnr. Rath, Young and Pignatelli, P.A., Concord, 1987—. Trustee Univ. Systems N.H., Concord Hosp., 1991-98, N.H. Hist. Soc., 2001-; legis. counsel to Gov. Gregg, Concord, 1989-90; mem. adv. coun. to ins. commr., 1989-93; spkr. in field. Legal counsel Rudman for U.S. Senate campaign, Concord, 1984-93; bd. dirs. Concord chpt. ARC, 1988-91; mem. N.H. adv. bd. New Eng. Legal Found., 1991-97; pres. Concord Hosp. Assn., 1991-97, bd. dirs. Mem. ABA, N.H. Bar Assn., New Eng. Coun., Concord C. of C. (bd. dirs. 1988-91), Bus. and Industry Assn., Cornell Club N.H. Republican. Avocations: skiing, tennis. Corporate, general, Environmental, Probate (including wills, trusts). Office: One Capital Pla PO Box 1500 Concord NH 03302-1500

YOUNG, SIDNEY DAVID, lawyer; b. N.Y.C., Jan. 10, 1916; s. Benjamin and Pauline (Simmons) Y.; married, Dec. 10, 1939; children: Alan H., Estelle, Robert, Wendy. BS, Bklyn. Coll., 1937, LLB, 1939. Bar: N.Y. 1939, U.S. Dist. Ct. (ea. and so. dists.) N.Y. 1966. Ptnr. Dreyer and Traub, Bklyn., 1937-49; sr. ptnr. Lindenbaum and Young, Bklyn., 1949—. Pres. U.S. Com. Sports for Israel, N.Y.C., 1972-76. Mem. Bklyn. Bar Assn. (bd. dirs. real estate tax 1980-82), Rev. Bar Assn. Lodges: B'nai Brith. Landlord-tenant, Property, real (including real estate development, water), State and local taxation. Office: 16 Court St Brooklyn NY 11241-0102

YOUNG, THOMAS PAUL, lawyer; b. Jamestown, N.Y., Dec. 11, 1955; s. Burdette R. and Ruth Ann Y.; m. Deborah Ann Schwind, May 23, 1981; 1 child, Amanda Marie. BA, SUNY, Geneseo, 1977; JD, Georgetown U., 1980. Bar: N.Y. 1981, U.S. Dist. Ct. (we. dist.) N.Y. 1981. Assoc. Hodgson & Russ LLP, Buffalo, 1980—81; asst. counsel Gannett Co., Inc., Rochester, N.Y., 1982-84; assoc. Underberg & Kessler, Rochester, 1984-91, sr. atty., 1991-98; of counsel Harter, Secrest & Emery LLP, Rochester, 1998-2000; gen. counsel, sec. Xelus, Inc., Fairport, N.Y., 2000—. Mem. Perinton (N.Y.) Rep. Com., 1989—; mem. coun. Bethlehem Luth. Ch., Fairport, N.Y., 1984-90; bd. dirs. Geneseo Found., Inc., 1982—; bd. dirs., sec. Martin Luther Found., Rochester, 1986-89; mem. allocations com. United Way Greater Rochester, 1990-95; mem. zoning bd. appeals, Town of Perinton, N.Y., 1997—. Mem. ABA, N.Y. State Bar Assn. Corporate, general, Computer, Securities. Office: Xelus Inc 290 Woodcliff Dr Fairport NY 14450-4212 E-mail: tom_young@xelus.com.

YOUNG, VERNON LEWIS, lawyer; b. Seaman, Ohio, Oct. 13, 1919; s. Ezra S. and Anna (Bloom) Y.; m. Eileen Humble, Sept. 20, 1941; children: Robert, Loretta, Bettie Jo, Jon W., Denise L. Student, Alfred Holbrook Coll., 1938-39; JD, Ohio No. U., 1942. Bar: Ohio 1942. Employee War Dept., 1942; sole practice West Union, Ohio, 1942-50, 78-81; ptnr. Young & Young, West Union, 1959-78, Young & Caldwell, 1978-81, 95—, Young-Caldwell & BUBP, West Union, 1981-95. Spl. counsel Office of Atty. Gen., State of Ohio, West Union, solicitor Cities of Jamestown, Seaman, Winchester, Manchester, Ohio; pros. atty. Adams County, Ohio, 1952-56, acting county judge, 1968-79. Mayor City of Seaman, 1944-46; mem. Adams County Health Bd., West Union, 1968-75; chmn. membership com. Eastern Shore Inst. Lifelong Learning, Fairhope, Ala., 1983-84; mem. Rep. Presdl. Task Force, 1980-94. Mem. Ohio State Bar Assn., Adams County Bar Assn. (former pre.), Masons (32 degree), Lions (pres. 1950-51, dist. gov. 1951-52), Sigma Delta Kappa (chancellor 1940). Avocations: fishing, hunting, gardening. Banking, State civil litigation, Finance. Home and Office: 10 Hickory Dr Seaman OH 45679-9762

YOUNG, VICTORIA E. occupational health and pediatrics nurse practitioner, lawyer; b. Concord, Mich., Apr. 20, 1933; d. Arthur Raymond and Edith Louise (Hands) Y. Diploma, Mercy Sch. Nursing, Jackson, Mich., 1954; JD, U. West Los Angeles, Culver City, Calif., 1973; BSN, UCLA, 1960, MPH in Adminstrn., 1966. Bar: Calif., U.S. Dist. Ct., Calif.; RN, Calif.; cert. pub. health nurse, pediatric nurse practitioner. Pub. health nurse L.A. City and Los Angeles County Health Dept.; exec. dir. Santa Monica (Calif.) Vis. Nurse Assn.; sch. nurse practitioner L.A. Unified Schs.; relief nurse L.A. Times. Vol. Moorpark City Hall, Moorpark Sr. Ctr; mem. Disaster Assistance Response Team, Moorpark. Ret. capt. USNR, Desert Storm. Mem. Nat. Assn. Pediatric Nurse Assocs. and Practitioners, Calif. Bar Assn., Fleet Res. Assn., Moorpark Woman's Fortnightly Club (treas. 1998-99). Home: 4359 Brookdale Ln Moorpark CA 93021-2302

YOUNG, WILLIAM GLOVER, federal judge; b. Huntington, N.Y., Sept. 23, 1940; s. Woodhull Benjamin and Margaret Jean (Wilkes) Y.; m. Beverly June Bigelow, Aug. 5, 1967; children: Mark Edward, Jeffrey Woodhull, Todd Russell. AB, Harvard U., 1962, LLB, 1967; LLD, New Eng. Sch. Law, 2001. Bar: Mass. 1967, U.S. Supreme Ct. 1970. Law clk. to chief justice Supreme Jud. Ct., Mass., 1967-68; spl. asst. atty. gen. Mass., 1969-72; chief legal counsel to gov., 1972-74; asso. firm Bingham, Dana and Gould, Boston, 1968-72, ptnr., 1975-78; assoc. justice Superior Ct., Commonwealth of Mass., Boston, 1978-85; judge U.S. Dist. Ct. Mass., Boston, 1985-99, chief judge, 1999—. Mem. budget com., 1987-2001, chmn. economy subcom., 1991-2001; lectr. part time Boston Coll. Law Sch., 1968-90, Boston U. Law Sch., 1979—, Harvard Law Sch., 1979—1990. Served to capt. U.S. Army, 1962-64. Mem. Am. Law Inst., Mass. Bar Assn., Boston Bar Assn., Harvard Alumni (pres. 1976-77) Office: US Courthouse Rm 5710 Boston MA 02210 E-mail: william_young@mad.uscourts.gov., bjbg2y3@earthlink.net.

YOUNGBLOOD, DEBORAH SUE, lawyer, speech pathology/audiology services professional; b. Fairview, Okla., July 29, 1954; d. G. Dean and Beatrice J. (Hiebert) White. BS with honors, Okla. State U., 1976, MA with honors, 1979; JD cum laude, Boston Coll. Law Sch., 1991; MPH in Health Care Mgmt., Harvard U., 1992. Bar: Colo., U.S. Ct. Appeals (10th cir.). Jud. law clk. Colo. Supreme Ct., 1992-94; assoc. atty. Patton Boggs, L.L.P., Denver, 1994—97; sr. assoc. atty. Vaglica & Meinhold, L.L.C., Colorado Springs, 1997-99; speech-lang. pathologist North Conway, NH, 1999—2001; atty. in pvt. practice, speech-lang. pathologist Sun Valley, Idaho, 1999—. Recipient Lexis Legal Rsch. and Writing award. Mem.: ABA, Minoru Yasui Am. Inns of Ct. (exec. coun. 1995—97), Colo. Bar Assn., Sun Valley Edn. Found. (bd. dirs.), Phi Kappa Phi. Administrative and regulatory, General civil litigation, Constitutional. Office: 201 Bullion St Hailey ID 83333 E-mail: youngblood@peoplepc.com.

YOUNGDAHL, JAY THOMAS, lawyer; b. St. Louis, May 29, 1952; s. James Edward and Patricia Ruth (Lucy) Y.; m. Mary Ellen Vogler, Dec. 12, 1981; children: Benjamin Douglass, Colleen Alexandra. BS, U. Houston, 1978; JD, U. Tex., 1980. Bar: Ark. 1981, Tex., 1992, D.C. 1993, U.S. Dist. Ct. (ea. and we. dists.) Ark. 1981, U.S. Ct. Appeals (8th, 10th and 11th cirs.) 1981, U.S. Claims Ct. 1992, U.S. Tax Ct. 1981, Tex. 1994. Ptnr. Provost, Umphrey, LLP, Youngdahl, Sadin P.C., Little Rock, 2001—03; mng. ptnr. Youngdahl, Sadin P.C., Friendswood, Tex., 1993—; ptnr. Youngdahl, Youtz & Youngdahl PC; gen. counsel Vox.com. Adj. instr. Webster Coll., Little Rock, 1983-95; adj. prof. U. Ark., Little Rock Sch. of Law, 1988-90; mem. Ark. Employment Security Div. Adv. Coun., Little Rock, 1980-97, Gov.'s Workers Compensation Study Com., Little Rock, 1985-86. With U.S. Army, 1972-74. Mem. ABA, Ark. Bar Assn. (chmn. labor law sect. 1983-84), ATLA, Ark. Trial Lawyers Assn., AFL-CIO Lawyers Coordinating Com. (adv. bd.), Acad. Rail Labor Attys., Tex. Trial Lawyers Assn., State Bar Tex. (Pro Bono Coll. 1996). Avocations: running, reading, culinary arts. Federal civil litigation, Labor (including EEOC, Fair Labor Standards Act, labor-management relations, NLRB, OSHA), Personal injury (including property damage). Office: Youngdahl Youtz & Youngdahl 1414 S Friendswood Friendswood TX 77546 E-mail: jyoungdahl@youngdahl.com.

YOUNGER, STEPHEN P. lawyer; b. N.Y.C., May 9, 1956; s. George D. and Doris Anne (Hill) Y.; m. Prudence Madden, Aug. 7, 1982; children: Millicent, Willard, Coleman, Emery. BA, Harvard Coll., 1977; JD magna cum laude, Albany Law Sch., 1982. Bar: N.Y. 1983, U.S. Dist. Ct. (so. and ea. dists.) N.Y. 1986, U.S. Ct. Appeals (2d cir.) 1986, U.S. Tax Ct. 1989. Law clk. to assoc. judge N.Y. State Ct. Appeals, Albany, 1982-84; assoc. Patterson Belknap Webb & Tyler, N.Y.C., 1985-91, ptnr., 1991—. Asst. counsel N.Y. State Commn. on Jud. Nomination, 1994—; spl. asst. N.Y. Corp. Counsel's Office, N.Y.C., 1990; staff counsel Gov.'s Commn. on Liability Ins., N.Y.C., 1986-87. Editor-in-chief Albany Law Rev., 1981-82. Active Glen Ridge Congl. Ch.; trustee Albany Law Sch., 1994—; trustee Sorrento V.I.A., 1996—, NY Theol. Sem., 2002—. Mem. Bar Assn. City N.Y. (com. on arbitration 1995—), N.Y. State Bar Assn. (chair securities litigation com., vice chmn., comml. and fed. litigation sect.), Harvard Club of the City of N.Y., Albany Law Sch. Nat. Alumni Coun. (pres. 1992-93), Sorrento Yacht Club (commodore 1996-99), Stuyvesant Alumni Assn. (bd. dirs. 1997-2000), Hist. Soc. NY State Cts. (treas. 2002—). Congregationalist. Avocations: sailing, golf. Alternative dispute resolution, Property, real (including real estate development, water), General civil litigation. Home: 26 Hillcrest Rd Glen Ridge NJ 07028 Office: Patterson Belknap & Tyler LLP 1133 Ave of Ams New York NY 10036

YOUNGLOVE, MICHAEL ROBERT, lawyer; b. Chgo., Dec. 7, 1955; s. Robert Frederick and Mary Louise Younglove; m. Wendy Sue Koenen; children: Samantha Elizabeth, Benjamin Michael. BS, Mt. Senario Coll., Ladysmith, Wis., 1987; JD, John Marshall Law Sch., Chgo., 2001. Bar: Wis. 2002, US Dist. Ct. (ea. and we. dists.) Wis. 2002. Chief of police City of Oak Creek, Wis., 1990—97; atty. at law Law Offices of Michael R. Younglove, Racine, Wis., 2002—; criminal investigator Kenosha County Dist. Atty.'s Office, Kenosha, Wis., 1985—89. General practice, Civil rights, Criminal. Office: Law Offices of Michael R Younglove 209 Eighth St Racine WI 53403-1508 Office Fax: 262-632-3888. E-mail: myounglove@ameritech.net.

YOUNGWOOD, ALFRED DONALD, lawyer; b. N.Y.C., Apr. 27, 1938; s. Milton and Lillian (Ginsburg) Y.; m. Judith Goldfarb, June 24, 1963; children: Jonathan David, Stephen Michael. BA magna cum laude, Yale U., 1959; LLB magna cum laude, Harvard U., 1962. Bar: N.Y. 1962, D.C. 1970, U.S. Tax Ct. 1964, U.S. Ct. Appeals (2d cir.) 1969. Law clk. to judge U.S. Dist. Ct. N.Y., 1962-63; assoc. Paul, Weiss, Rifkind, Wharton & Garrison, N.Y.C., 1964-70, ptnr., 1970—, chair, 1999—. Fulbright scholar, London, 1963-64. Fellow Am. Coll. Tax Counsel; mem. ABA, N.Y. State Bar Assn. (chmn. tax sect. 1978-79, exec. com. 1971—, ho. of dels. 1979-80), Assn. of Bar of City of N.Y., Coun. on Fgn. Rels. Corporate taxation, Taxation, general, Personal income taxation. Home: 1125 Park Ave New York NY 10128-1243 Office: Paul Weiss Rifkind Wharton 1285 Avenue Of The Americas New York NY 10019-6064 E-mail: ayoungwood@paulweiss.com.

YUDOF, MARK GEORGE, law educator, university system chancellor; b. Phila., Oct. 30, 1944; s. Jack and Eleanor (Parris) Y.; m. Judith Lynn Gomel, July 11, 1965; children: Seth Adam, Samara Lisa BA, U. Pa., 1965, LLB, 1968. Bar: Pa. 1970, U.S. Supreme Ct. 1974, U.S. Dist. Ct. (we. dist.) Tex. 1975, U.S. Ct. Appeals (5th cir.) 1976, Tex. 1980. Law clk. to judge U.S. Ct. Appeals (5th cir.), 1968-69; assoc. gen. counsel to ABA study FTC, 1969; rsch. assoc. Harvard Ctr. Law and Edn., 1969-70, sr. staff atty., 1970-71; lectr. Harvard Grad. Sch. Edn., 1970-71; asst. prof. law U. Tex., Austin, 1971-74, prof., 1974—97, assoc. dean, 1979-84, James A. Elkins Cent. chair in law, 1983-97, dean, 1984-94, exec. v.p., provost, 1994-97, John Jeffers rsch. chair in law, 1991-94; pres. U. Minn., 1997—2002; chancellor U. Tex. Sys., 2002—, Jamail regents chair higher edn. leadership, 2002—, Wright chair fed. courts, 2002—. Of counsel Pennzoil vs. Texaco, 1987. Author: When Government Speaks, 1983 (Scribes Book award 1983, cert. merit ABA 1983), (with others) Educational Policy and the Law, 1992, (with others) Gender Justice, 1986. Mem. Tex. Gov.'s Task Force on Sch. Fin., 1989-90, Tex. Gov.'s Select Com. on Edn., 1988; bd. dirs. Freedom to Read Found., 1989-91; mem. Austin Cable Commn., 1981-84, chmn., 1982; mem. nat. panel on sch. desegregation rsch. Ford Found., 1977-80; mem. state exec. com. Univ. Interscholastic League, 1983-86; bd. dirs. Jewish Children's Regional Svc., 1980-86; mem. Gov.'s Select Task Force on Pub. Edn., 1995; mem. Telecomms. Infrastructure Fund Bd., State of Tex., 1995-97; adv. bd. Nat. Inst. for Literacy, 2002-. Recipient Teaching Excellence award, 1975, Most Meritorious Book award Scribes, 1983, Humanitarian award Austin region NCCJ, 1988, Antidefamation League Jurisprudence award, 1991; hon. fellow Queen Mary and Westfield Coll., U. London. Fellow: Am. Acad. Arts & Sci., Am. Bar Found., Tex. Bar Found.; mem.: Edn. Testing Svc. (mem. bd. dirs. 2000—02), Am. Coun. Edn. (mem. com. on leadership and instl. effectiveness 2000), Assn. Am. Law Schs. (chmn. law and edn. sect. 1983—84, exec. com. 1988—90), Tex. Bar Found., Am. Law Inst. Avocation: collecting antique maps. Office: U Texas System 601 Colorado St Austin TX 78701-2904

YUHNKE, ROBERT E. lawyer, educator, consultant; b. Buffalo, Dec. 13, 1943; s. Edward L. and Marjorie T. Y.; m. Stephanie Mines; 1 stepdaughter, Rachel Erdman. BS, Canisius Coll., 1965; student, Columbia U., 1968-69; JD, Yale U., 1972. Bar: Pa 1972, U.S. Supreme Ct. 1977, Ill. 1980, Colo. 1981, U.S. Ct. Appeals (D.C. cir.) 1979, (7th cir.) 1983, (9th cir.) 1986, (10th cir.) 1985, (11th cir.) 2000, (5th cir.) 2001. Spl. asst. atty. gen. Pa. Dept. Environ. Resources, Harrisburg, 1972-78; asst. regional solicitor U.S. Dept. Interior, Denver, 1978-79; pvt. practice Chgo., 1979-80; sr. atty. Environ. Def. Fund, Boulder, 1980-92; prin. Robert E Yuhnke & Assocs., 1992—. Founder, treas. DOM Project, Eldorado Springs, Colo., 1993—; adj. prof. environ. law U. Colo. Sch. Law, Boulder, 1998—. Contbr. articles to profl. jours. Tenor Rocky Mountain Chorale, Boulder, 1994—. 1st lt. U.S. Army Res., 1965-68. Avocations: flute, paddling, yoga. trout fishing. Environmental. Office: 2910-B County Road 67 Boulder CO 80303-9639

YURASKO, FRANK NOEL, judge; b. Rahway, N.J., Dec. 22, 1938; s. Frank H. and Estelle (Yurasko) mm. Mary Byrd, July 23, 1966 (dec. 1991); children: Elizabeth Anne, Suzanne, Frank; m. Rosalee Yurasko, May 1997. BA, Brown U., 1960; cert., London Sch. Econs., 1961; student, Gray's Inn., London, 1960-61; JD, Yale U., 1964. Bar: N.J. 1964, Fla. 1979, U.S. Dist. Ct. N.J. 1965, U.S. Ct. Appeals (3d cir.) 1980, U.S. Supreme Ct. 1969; cert. civil trial atty., N.J. Judge's law clk. N.J. Dept. Judiciary, Trenton, 1964-66; ptnr. Graham, Yurasko, Golden, Lintner & Rothchild, Somerville, N.J., 1966-80; pvt. practice Somerville, 1980—. Judge Montgomery Twp. (N.J.) Mcpl. Ct., 1973-84; twp. atty. Hillsborough Twp. (N.J.), 1973-2000; atty. Green Brook (N.J.) Bd. Adjustment, 1973-2001. Trustee Gill/St. Bernard Sch., Bernardsville, N.J.; mem. alumni bd. trustees Peddie Sch., Hightstown, N.J. Mem. ABA, Am. Jud. Soc., N.J. Bar Assn., Fla. Bar Assn., Somerset County Bar Assn., Mercer County Bar Assn., Assn. Trial Lawyers Am., Trial Attys. N.J., N.J. Fedn. Planning Ofcls., Fed. Bar Assn. Office: PO Box 1041 139 W End Ave Somerville NJ 08876-1809

YURCHUCK, ROGER ALEXANDER, retired lawyer; b. Amityville, N.Y., June 9, 1938; s. Alexander and Ella Marie (Munley) Y.; m. Sally Ward, Apr. 14, 1961 (div. 1972); children: Scott, Lauren; m. Susan Holland, June 1, 1985. AB cum laude, Northwestern U., 1959; LLB, Harvard U., 1962. Bar: Ohio 1962. Assoc. Vorys, Sater Seymour and Pease, Columbus,

Ohio, 1962-68, ptnr., 1969—71, 1973—2002, ptnr. Cin. office, 1984—2002; v.p., gen. counsel Fed. Home Loan Mortgage Corp., Washington, 1971-73. Vice chmn., bd. dirs. Securities Investors Protection Corp., Washington, 1982-88. Del. Rep. Nat. Conv., 1980, 84. Mem. ABA, Ohio Bar Assn., Phi Beta Kappa. Clubs: Queen City (Cin.). Republican. Episcopalian. Office: Vorys Sater Seymour and Pease 221 E 4th St Ste 2100 Cincinnati OH 45202-5133

YUSPEH, ALAN RALPH, lawyer, healthcare company executive; b. New Orleans, June 13, 1949; s. Michel and Rose Fay (Rabenovitz) Y.; m. Janet Horn, June 8, 1975. BA, Yale U., 1971; MBA, Harvard U., 1973; JD, Georgetown U., 1978. Bar: D.C. 1978. Mgmt. cons. McKinsey & Co., Washington, 1973-74; adminstrv. asst., legis. asst. Office of U.S. Senator J. Bennett Johnston, Washington, 1974-78; atty. Shaw, Pittman, Potts & Trowbridge, Washington, 1978-79, Ginsburg, Feldman, Weil and Bress, Washington, 1979-82; gen. counsel Com. on Armed Services-U.S. Senate, Washington, 1982-85; ptnr. Preston, Thorgrimson, Ellis & Holman, Washington, 1985-88, Miller & Chevalier, Washington, 1988-91, Howrey & Simon, Washington, 1991-97; sr. v.p. ethics, compliance and corp. responsibility HCA, Nashville, 1997—. Coord. Def. Industry Initiative on Bus., Ethics and Conduct, 1987-97; v.p. Health Care Compliance Assn., 2002. Editor Law and Policy in Internat. Business jour., 1978-79, Nat. Contract Mgmt. Jour., 1988-92; assoc. editor Pub. Contract Law jour., 1987-91. Chmn. bd. ethics, City of Balt., 1988-96, planning commn. City Balt., 1996-97; pres., bd. dirs. Health Care Compliance Assn.,; bd. dirs. Ethics Officer Assn.; chmn. bd. dirs. Tenn. Repertory Theater; bd. dirs. YMCA Mid. Tenn. Camp, 2002—, Balt. Housing Authority, 1996-97. 1st lt. USAR, 1971-77. Health. Office: HCA One Park Plaza Nashville TN 37203 Home: 126 Third Ave N Franklin TN 37064 E-mail: alan.yuspeh@hcahealthcare.com.

ZABANAL, EDUARDO OLEGARIO, lawyer; b. Legazpi City, Albay, The Philippines, Aug. 8, 1952; came to U.S., 1986; s. Jose Agas and Maria Soledad (Olegario) Z.; m. Leorosie Rebodos Nabor, June 18, 1983; children: Shalimar Rosary, Angelica Almira, Regina Tatiana, Lorelei Blossom, Eduardo Olegario, Jr. BA, Aquinas U., The Philippines, 1972; BL, U. The Philippines, 1978. Bar: Hawaii 1990, The Philippines 1979, U.S. Dist. Ct. Hawaii 1990, U.S. Ct. Appeals (9th cir.) 2002. Assoc. Pacis & Reyes, Manila, 1979-86; pvt. practice Honolulu, 1990—. Contbr. articles to profl. jours. Bd. dirs. Kahaluu Neighborhood Bd., Honolulu, 1991-93; active Filipino Coalition for Solidarity, Honolulu, 1991—. Recipient recognition among Disting. Filipinos in Oahu, FIL-AM Courier, 1995. Mem. ABA, ATLA, Hawaii State Bar Assn., Am. Civil Lawyers Assn., Hawaii Filipino Lawyers Assn., Integrated Bar The Philippines, Philippine Bar Assn., Filipino C. of C. Hawaii. Roman Catholic. Avocations: jogging, travel, reading. Estate planning, Immigration, naturalization, and customs, Personal injury (including property damage). Home: 91-1146 Lanakoi St Kapolei HI 96707-2907 E-mail: e.zabanal@worldnet.att.net.

ZABEL, SHELDON ALTER, lawyer, law educator; b. Omaha, Apr. 25, 1941; s. Louis Julius and Anne (Rothenberg) Z.; m. Roberta Jean Butz, May 10, 1975; children: Andrew Louis, Douglas Patrick, Robert Stewart Warren. AB cum laude, Princeton U., 1963; JD cum laude, Northwestern U., 1966. Bar: Ill. 1966, U.S. Supreme Ct. 1976. Law clk. to presiding justice Ill. Supreme Ct., 1966-67; assoc. Schiff, Hardin & Waite, Chgo., 1967-73, ptnr., 1973—. Instr. environ. law Loyola U., Chgo. Mem. governing bd. Chgo. Zool. Soc. Mem. ABA, Chgo. Bar Assn., Chgo. Coun. Lawyers, Order of Coif, Union League Club, Met. Club (Chgo.) Jewish. Avocations: skiing, squash. Environmental, Utilities, public. Office: Schiff Hardin & Waite Sears Tower 233 S Wacker Dr Ste 6600 Chicago IL 60606-6473 E-mail: szabel@schiffhardin.com.

ZABKA, SVEN PAUL, lawyer; b. Heide, Germany, May 11, 1971; s. Clifton Thomas and Lieselotte A.M. Zabka. BA cum laude with dept. honors in econs., Union Coll., Schenectady, N.Y., 1993; JD, Emory U., 1996. Bar: Ga. 1996, D.C. 1997. Assoc. Smith, Gambrell & Russell, LLP, Atlanta, 1997—. Mem. Emory Law Rev., 1994. Mem.: Econ. Honor Soc. Avocations: water polo, skiing. Computer, Corporate, general, Mergers and acquisitions. Office: Smith Gambrell & Russell 1230 Peachtree St NE Ste 3100 Atlanta GA 30309-3592 E-mail: szabka@sgrlaw.com.

ZACHARSKI, DENNIS EDWARD, lawyer; b. Detroit, Feb. 25, 1951; s. Edward J. and Margaret R. (Cendrowski) Z.; m. Susan G. Foster, Aug. 8, 1975; children: Jeffrey Alan, Lauren Michelle. BBA, U. Mich., 1973; JD, Mich. State U., 1977. Bar: Mich. 1977, U.S. Dist. Ct. (ea. dist.) Mich. 1977, U.S. Dist. Ct. (we. dist.) Mich. 1982, U.S. Supreme Ct. 1988, U.S. Ct. Appeals (6th cir.) 1990, Ohio, 1993. Atty. Lacey & Jones, Birmingham, Mich., 1977—. Case evaluator Mediation Tribunal Assn., Detroit; arbitrator Am. Arbitration Assn., Southfield, Mich. Mem. Oakland County Bar Assn., Assn. Trial Def. Counsel, Mich. Trial Def. Counsel. Avocations: golf, skiing, soccer, tennis, cycling. General civil litigation, Insurance, Personal injury (including property damage). Office: Lacey & Jones 600 S Adams Rd Ste 300 Birmingham MI 48009-6827 E-mail: dzacharski@laceyjones.com.

ZACHOS, KIMON STEPHEN, lawyer; b. Concord, N.H., Nov. 20, 1930; s. Stephen and Sophia (Bacogiannis) Z.; m. Anne Colby, July 5, 1959; children: Ellen, Elizabeth, Sarah. BA, Wesleyan U., 1952; JD, NYU, 1955; LLM, Boston U., 1968; LLD (hon.), N.H. Coll., 1992, St. Anselm Coll., 1994. Bar: N.H. 1955, U.S. Dist. Ct. N.H. 1957, U.S. Supreme Ct. 1963. Ptnr. Sheehan, Phinney, Bass & Green, Manchester, N.H., 1957—. White House fellow, spl. asst. to atty. gen. Nicholas deB. Katzenbach, Washington, 1965-66; bd. dirs. New Eng. Tel., Bank of Ireland 1st Holdings Inc., Citizens Bank N.H., Hitchiner Mfg. Co., Inc., also others. Dep. speaker N.H. Ho. Reps., 1969-74; active various charitable and ednl. orgns. Named Man of Yr., Manchester C. of C., 1985, Disting. Citizen, Boy Scouts Am., 1987, Bus. Leader of Yr., New Hampshire Assn. C of C., 1994; recipient Brotherhood award NCCJ, 1966, Disting. Alumnus award, Wesleyan U., 1997, Lifetime Achievement award N.H. Bus. and Industry Assn., 2000. Mem. ABA, N.H. Bar Assn. Republican. Greek Orthodox. Avocation: stamp collecting. Banking, Corporate, general, Probate (including wills, trusts). Home: 2093 Elm St Manchester NH 03104-2316 Office: Sheehan Phinney Bass & Green 1000 Elm St Ste 1801 Manchester NH 03101-1792 E-mail: kzachos@sheehan.com.

ZACK, ARNOLD MARSHALL, lawyer, mediator, arbitrator; b. Lynn, Mass., Oct. 7, 1931; s. Samuel George and Bess Ethel (Freedman) Z.; m. Norma Eta Wilner, Aug. 10, 1969; children: Jonathan Samuel, Rachel Ann. AB, Tufts Coll., 1953; LLB, Yale U., 1956; MPA, Harvard U., 1961. Asst. to Saul Wallen (arbitrator), 1956-63; cons. govt. South Africa UN Mission to Congo, 1960; cons. U.S. Peace Corps, 1961-63, Labor Dept., 1962-79, Pres.'s Study Commn. on Nat. Service Corps, 1962-63, U.S. AID, 1963—, Friedrich Ebert Stiftung, 1963-64, Nat. Center for Dispute Settlement, 1968-76. Cons. IMF, 2000—02, Govt. Italy, 2002—, Internat. Labor Orgn., 1961—; mem. steering com. Permanent Ct. Arbitration, 2002—; vis. Fulbright lectr. Haile Selassie U., Addis Ababa, Ethiopia, 1963—64; referee Nat. R.R. Adjustment Bd., 1964—; mem. faculty labor and worklife program Harvard Law Sch., 1985—; full time mediator/arbitrator, Boston, 1968—; bd. dirs. Ctr. for Socio-Legal Studies faculty of law U. Natal, South Africa, 1986—92; mem. Fgn. Svc. Labor Rels. Bd., 1982—84, Presdl. Emergency Bds. 221 and 222; chair Presdl. Emergency Bd. 232, 234; chmn. Essential Industries Dispute Settlement Bd. Bermuda, 1993—2000; chair Essential Svcs. Dispute Settlement Bd. Bermuda, 1996—2000; vis. lectr. Yale Law Sch., 1995—96; permanent arbitrator Am. Airlines & APA, IRS & NTEU, Commonwealth Mass., Capital ABC and NABET, Overseas Fedn. Tchrs., Def. Dept. Author: Labor Training in Developing Countries, 1964, Ethiopia's High Level Manpower-Analysis and Projections, 1964, Handbook on Grievance Arbitration in the Public Sector, 1974, Handbook on Fact Finding and Arbitration in the Public Sector, 1974, Grievance Arbitration, A Practical Guide, 1977; (with R. Bloch) Arbitration of Discipline and Discharge Cases, 1979, (with R. Bloch) The Agreement in Negotiation and Arbitration, 1983, 2d edition, 1995, Arbitration in Practice, 1984, Mediation in the Public Sector, 1985, Grievance Arbitration: Cases on the Merits in Discipline Discharge and Contract Interpretation, 1989, Handbook on Grievance Arbitration: Issues on Procedure and Ethics, 1992, (with J. Dunlop) Mediation and Arbitration of Employment Disputes, 1997, Arbitration Discipline and Discharge Cases, 2000; contbr. articles to profl. jours. Bd. visitors Harvard U. Recipient Whitney North Seymour medal for oustanding contbn. to arbitration, 1980, Cushing Gavin award, 1986, Mildred Spaulding award, 1987, Disting. Svc. award for arbitration of labor-mgmt. disputes, 1989; Wertheim fellow Harvard U., 1996-97. Fellow: African Studies Assn.; mem.: ABA (pub. mem. coun. labor and employment law sect. 2000—), Coll. Labor and Employment Lawyers, Internat. Soc. for Labor Law and Social Security (bd. dirs.), Indsl. Rels. Rsch. Assn. (bd. dirs.), Am. Arbitration Assn. (dir. Labor-Mgmt. Inst. 1966—68), Nat. Acad. Arbitrators (treas. 1972—75, bd. govs. 1977—79, v.p. 1980—82, pres. Rsch. and Edn. Found. 1989—91, pres. 1994—95), Yale Law Sch. Assn., Yale Club (N.Y.C.), Harvard Club. Private international, Labor (including EEOC, Fair Labor Standards Act, labor-management relations, NLRB, OSHA). Address: 170 W Canton St Boston MA 02118-1216

ZACKS, DAVID N. lawyer; b. Detroit, July 23, 1956; s. Joel Norman Zacks and Bernice Davidson; m. Elizabeth Anne Zacks, Sept. 1, 1981 (div. June 1982); children: Steven Michael, Jeremy Adam. BS, Eastern Mich. U., 1978; JD, Thomas Cooley Law Sch., 1982. Bar: Mich. 1982, Fla. 1982, U.S. Dist. Ct. (so. dist.) Mich. 1983, U.S. Ct. Appeals (6th cir.) 1983, U.S. Surpeme Ct. 1985. Atty. Gropman, Kaplan, Sims & Gibons, Southfield, Mich., 1982—84; ptnr. Harrison & Zacks, Bloomfield Hills, 1985—94; ptnr., litigation chmn. Lewis, White & Clay, Detroit, 1994—. Staff asst. U.S Sen. Donald Riegle, Livonia, Mich., 1978. Fellow: Assn. Cert. Fraud Examiners; mem.: Assn.. Trial Lawyers Am., Nat. Assn. Criminal Def. Attys. Federal civil litigation, General civil litigation, Criminal. Office: Lewis & Munday 1300 1st Nat Bldg Detroit MI 48226 Fax: 313-961-1270. E-mail: david.zacks@lewismunday.com.

ZAGER, STEVEN MARK, lawyer; b. Memphis, Nov. 16, 1958; s. Jack and Sylvia (Bloomfield) Z.; m. Debra D'Angelo; children: Samantha, Amanda, Kathryn, Jackson. BA, Vanderbilt U., 1979, JD, 1983. Bar: Tex. 1984, U.S. Dist. Ct. (all dists.) Tex. 1984, U.S. Dist. Ct. Ariz. 1992, U.S. Dist. Ct. (D.C.) 1998, U.S. Ct. Appeals (5th, 6th, and 11th cirs.) 1983, U.S. Ct. Appeals (D.C. cir.) 1991, U.S. Ct. Appeals (Fed. cir.) 1997, U.S. Supreme Ct. 1991. Assoc. Fulbright & Jaworski, Houston, 1983-86, Weil, Gotshal & Manges, Houston, 1986-90, ptnr., 1990-98, head Houston office litigation sect., 1994-96; head natl. litigation grp., 2001—03; mng. ptnr. Tex. offices Brobeck, Phleger & Harrison, 1999—2001, firm ops. com., 1999—2003, Akin, Gump, Strauss, Hauer & Feld, LLP, Austin, 2003—. Adj. prof. U. Houston Sch. Law, 1990—95; nat. adv. bd. NALP, 1996—99. Contbr. articles to Tex. Bar Jour., Texas Lawyer, Houston Lawyer. Bd. dirs., exec. com. Alley Theatre, Houston, 1988-96, Tex. Accts. and Lawyers for the Arts, Houston, 1984-88; adv. bd. Montgomery Bell Acad., 1996—; bd. dirs. Vol. Legal Svcs. Ctrl. Tex., 2000-01, TV Sta. KLRU, 2001-03. Named Outstanding Young Man in Am., U.S. Jaycees, 1983, Best Civil Def. Trial Lawyer in Tex., Tex. Lawyer, 2003; named one of 45 Best Lawyers Under 45 in Am.; recipient Frank J. Scurlock award, State Bar Tex., 1991, Outstanding Pro Bono Svc., Professionalism award, Tex. Ctr. for Legal Ethics, 2002. Mem. ABA (litigation sect.), State Bar Tex. (dir. 1997-98, Frank J. Scurlock award 1991), Houston Bar Assn. (sec. 1996-97, v.p. 1997-98, bd. dirs. 1993-96, chair law and arts com. 1994, chair adminstrn. of justice com. 1995, rodeo com. 1997, bd. dirs. 1998, Outstanding Young Lawyer in Houston 1991, Pres.'s award 1996-98), Houston Vol. Lawyers Program (bd. dirs. 1997-98, chair 1998), Travis County Bar Assn. (bd. dirs. 2001-03, chair bench bar program 2000, chair, 2003, mem. jud. affairs com. 1999-2000), Fed. Bar Assn. Federal civil litigation, State civil litigation, Computer. Office: Akin Gump Strauss Hauer & Feld 1900 Pennzoil Pl Houston TX 77002

ZAGORIN, JANET SUSAN, legal firm administrator, marketing professional; b. Lakewood, NJ; d. Irving C. and Dorothy (Tarshish) Z. BA, Douglass Coll., 1975; MLS, Rutgers U., 1977. Asst. law libr. N.J. Atty. Gen., Trenton, 1977-78; head of reference sect. Cardozo U. Law Sch., N.Y.C., 1978-79; law and legis. svcs. libr. FTC, Washington, 1979-81; dir. of reference Paul Weiss Rifkind, N.Y.C., 1981-82; libr. dir. Riker Danzig Scherer & Hyland, Morristown, N.J., 1982; libr., profl. devel. dir. Baker & McKenzie, N.Y.C., 1982-96; dir. practice devel. and info. svcs. Stroock & Stroock & Lavan LLP, N.Y.C., 1996-98; dir. practice devel. Cadwalader, Wickersham & Taft, N.Y.C., 1998-99, Gibson, Dunn & Crutcher, N.Y.C., 1999—2001; dir. mktg. Sidley Austin Brown & Wood, N.Y.C., 2001—. Bd. dirs. N.Y. Cares, 1998—. Mem. ABA (vice chmn. standing com. Law Libr. Congress 1995-96, chmn. 1996—, mem. law 2000 steering com. Libr. Congress), Fin. Women's Assn. (mem. bd. dirs. 1993-95, 99—), Bus. Women's Network, Am. Assn. Law Librs. (chair fgn. comparative internat. law com. 1990-91, vice chair pvt. law librs. 1990-91, chair 1991—, chair com. on recruitment 1991), Spl. Librs. Assn., Hadassah. E-mail: jzagorin@sidley.com.

ZAHAROFF, HOWARD GEORGE, lawyer; b. Bronx, N.Y., Apr. 30, 1951; s. Arthur Charles and Dorothy (Einhorn) Z.; m. Deborah J. Whitehill, Dec. 28, 1975; children: Joshua, Marta, Leah. BA in Philosophy, Lafayette Coll., 1973; MA, Johns Hopkins U., 1975, PhD in Philosophy, 1979; JD, Harvard U., 1980. Bar: Mass. 1980, U.S. Ct. Appeals (1st cir.) 1981, U.S. Dist. Ct. Mass. 1981. Assoc., ptnr., shareholder Brown Rudnick Freed & Gesmer, Boston, 1980-98; shareholder Morse, Barnes-Brown & Pendleton, Waltham, Mass., 1998—. Trustee Vol. Lawyers for the Arts, Inc., Boston, 1997-99. Contbr. numerous articles to profl. jours. Mem. ABA, Internat. Bar Assn., Boston Bar Assn. (co-chair arts and entertainment law com. 1996-98, co-chair computer and internet law com. 1997-99, co-chair intellectual property sect. 1999-2001), Computer Law Assn., Copyright Soc. USA, Licensng Execs. Soc., Mass. Software Coun., Nat. Writers Union. Avocations: creative writing, reading history. Computer, Entertainment, Intellectual property. E-mail: hgz@mbbp.com.

ZAHN, RICHARD WILLIAM, JR., lawyer; b. Richmond, Va., Oct. 1, 1964; s. Richard William and Frances Ellen Z.; m. Kerry Ellen Mahaney, Aug. 7, 1988; children: Ryan William, Allison McKenzie. BA, Washington Lee U., 1986; JD, New Eng. Sch. Law, Boston, 1993. Bar: Va. 1993, U.S. Dist. Ct. (ea. dist.) Va. 1993, U.S. Ct. Appeals (4th cir.) 1994, U.S. Supreme Ct. 2000. Law clk. to Hon. John A. MacKenzie U.S. Dist. Ct., Norfolk, Va., 1993-94; assoc. Taylor & Walker, P.C., Norfolk, 1994—. Bd. dirs., 2d v.p. Big Bros./Big Sisters of South Hampton Roads, Norfolk, 1996-2000. Mem. Va. Assn. Def. Attys. (bd. dirs. 2000—), Def. Rsch. Inst., Norfolk/Portsmouth Bar Assn. Federal civil litigation, State civil litigation, Insurance. Office: Taylor & Walker PC 555 E Main St Ste 1300 Norfolk VA 23510-2235 E-mail: rzahn@taywal.com.

ZAHND, RICHARD H. professional sports executive, lawyer; b. N.Y.C., July 22, 1946; s. Hugo and Rose (Genovese) Z.; m. Phyllis Beth Workman, Aug. 13, 1978; children: Andrew Richard, Melissa Dawn. AB, NYU, 1968, JD, 1971. Bar: N.Y. 1972. Assoc. Paul, Weiss, Rifkind, Wharton & Garrison, N.Y.C., 1971-74; staff atty. Madison Square Garden Corp., N.Y.C., 1974-75; v.p. legal affairs Madison Square Garden Center, Inc., N.Y.C., 1975-79; v.p., gen. counsel Madison Square Garden Corp., N.Y.C., 1979-86; v.p. N.Y. Knickerbockers Basketball Club, N.Y.C., 1979-86, N.Y. Rangers Hockey Club, N.Y.C., 1979-86; ptnr. Morrison & Foerster, N.Y.C., 1986-91; exec. v.p., gen. counsel NHL Enterprises, L.P., N.Y.C., 1992—. Served to capt. U.S. Army, 1972. John Norton Pomeroy scholar NYU Law Sch., 1969; Mortimer Bishop scholar NYU Law Sch., 1969; Judge Jacob Markowitz scholar NYU Law Sch., 1970; recipient Am. Jurisprudence prize NYU Law Sch., 1969 Episcopalian. Office: NHL Enterprises LP Fl 46 1251 Ave of the Americas New York NY 10020-1104 E-mail: rzahnd@nhl.com.

ZAITZEFF, ROGER MICHAEL, lawyer; b. Detroit, June 25, 1940; s. Peter and Mary (Fedchenia) Z.; children: Zachary, Natasha, Zoe, Peter. BA with high honors and high distinction, U. Mich., 1962; MA with distinction, U. Calif., Berkeley, 1963, JD, 1969. Bar: N.Y. 1970, U.S. Dist. Ct. (so. dist.) N.Y. 1975, U.S. Ct. Appeals (2nd cir.) 1975, D.C. 1985. Assoc. Seward & Kissel, N.Y.C., 1969-77, ptnr., 1977-94, Latham & Wakins, N.Y.C., 1994-2000, LeBoeuf Lamb Greene & MacRae, N.Y.C., 2000—02, Swidler Berlin Shereff Friedman, N.Y.C., 2002—. Contbr. articles to profl. jours. Mem. Tribar Opinion Com., 1990-93. Heller grantee U. Mich., 1962; recipient William Jennings Bryan Prize. Mem.: ABA, N.Y. County Lawyers Assn. (spl. com. legal opinions in comml. transactions), N.Y. State Bar Found., Phi Beta Kappa. Banking, Finance, Securities. Office: Swidler Berlin Shereff Friedman 405 Lexington Ave 11th Fl New York NY 10174

ZAK, ROBERT JOSEPH, lawyer; b. Steubenville, Ohio, July 29, 1946; s. Joseph and Pearl (Munyas) Zak; m. Kristy Hubbard Winkler, Sept. 13, 1980; children: Elizabeth Adele, Robert Joseph Jr, Barbara Ann. BS, W.Va. U., 1968, JD, 1975. Bar: WVa 1975, US Dist Ct (so dist) WVa 1975, US Dist Ct (no dist) WVa 1989, US Ct Appeals (4th cir) 1990. Staff atty. Pub. Svc. Commn. of W.Va., Charleston, 1975-76; assoc. Preiser & Wilson L.C., Charleston, 1976-81, ptnr., 1981-85; sr. ptnr. Zak & Assocs., Charleston, 1985—. Hearing examiner W.Va. Bd. Regents, Charleston, 1987—90; spl. asst. atty. gen. State of W.Va., 1987—90, mem. workers compensation appeals , 1991—97, 2001—. With U.S. Army, 1969—71, Vietnam. Fellow: Am Acad Matrimonial Lawyers; mem.: Order Barristers. Republican. Presbyterian. General civil litigation, Family and matrimonial, Personal injury (including property damage). Office: Zak & Assocs 607 Ohio Ave Charleston WV 25302-2228

ZALESNE, DEBORAH, law educator; b. Phila., Mar. 27, 1966; d. Saul and Rachelle (Brody) Zalesne. BA, Williams Coll., 1988; JD, U. Denver, 1992; LLM, Temple U., 1997. Bar: Colo. 1992. Assoc. Pendleton & Sabian, P.C., Denver, 1992-94; jud. clk. Colo. Supreme Ct., Denver, 1994-95; Hon. Abraham L. Freedman tchg. fellow Temple Law Sch., Phila., 1995-97; assoc. prof. law CUNY Sch. Law, Flushing, 1997—. Advisor Russian Commn. on Securities and Exchs., Moscow, 1994. Contbr. articles to profl. jours. Vol., Cmty. Outreach Law Program, N.Y.C., 1999, Jews for Racial and Econ. Justice, N.Y.C., 1999. Securities Law fellow Denver Law Sch., 1991-92. Mem. ABA. Democrat. Office: CUNY Law Sch 65-21 Main St Flushing NY 11367

ZALK, ROBERT H. lawyer; b. Albert Lea, Minn., Dec. 1, 1944; s. Donald B. and Juliette J. (Erickson) Z.; m. Ann Lee Anderson, June 21, 1969; children: Amy, Jenna. BA, Carleton Coll., 1966; JD, U. Minn., 1969. Bar: Minn. 1969, U.S. Dist. Ct. Minn. 1969. Assoc. Popham, Haik, Schnobrich, Kaufman & Doty, Mpls., 1969-72; atty. No. States Power Co., Mpls., 1972-73, Wright, West & Diessner, Mpls., 1973-84, Fredrikson & Byron P.A., Mpls., 1984-94, Zalk & Assocs., Mpls., 1994-95; ptnr. Zalk & Eayrs, Mpls., 1995-98, Zalk & Wood, Mpls., 1999, Zalk & Bryant, Mpls., 2000—. Fellow Am. Acad. Matrimonial Lawyers (pres. Minn. chpt. 2000-01), Minn. Bar Assn. (co-chmn. maintenance guideline com. 1991-94), Hennepin County Bar Assn. (co-chmn. family law sect. 1990-91). General civil litigation, Family and matrimonial. Office: Zalk & Bryant Sunset Ridge Bus Park 5861 Cedar Lake Rd Minneapolis MN 55416-1481 E-mail: rzalk@zalkbryant.com.

ZALUTSKY, MORTON HERMAN, lawyer; b. Schenectady, Mar. 8, 1935; s. Albert and Gertrude (Daffner) Z.; m. Audrey Englebardt, June 16, 1957; children: Jane, Diane, Samuel BA, Yale U., 1957; JD, U. Chgo., 1960. Bar: Oreg. 1961. Law clk. to presiding judge Oreg. Supreme Ct., 1960-61; assoc. Hart, Davidson, Veazie & Hanlon, 1961-63, Veatch & Lovett, 1963-64, Morrison, Bailey, Dunn, Cohen & Miller, 1964-69; prin. Morton H. Zalutsky, P.C., 1970-76; ptnr. Dahl, Zalutsky, Nichols & Hinson, 1977-79, Zalutsky & Klarquist, P.C., Portland, Oreg., 1980-85, Zalutsky, Klarquist & Johnson, Inc., Portland, 1985-94; Zalutsky & Klarquist, P.C., Portland, 1994—. Instr. Portland State U., 1961-64, Northwestern Sch. of Law, 1969-70; assoc. prof. U. Miami Law Sch.; lectr. Practising Law Inst., 1971—, Oreg. State Bar Continuing Legal Edn. Program, 1970, Am. Law Inst.-ABA Continuing Legal Edn. Program, 1973—, 34th, 37th NYU ann. insts. fed. taxation, So. Fed. Tax Inst., U. Miami Inst. Estate Planning, Southwestern Legal Found., Internat. Foun. Employee Benefit Plans, numerous other profl. orgns.; dir. A-E-F-C Pension Plan, 1994-99, chmn., 1989-99. Author: (with others) The Professional Corporation in Oregon, 1970, 82; contbg. author: The Dentist and the Law, 3d edit.; editor-in-chief (retirement plans) Matthew Bender's Federal Tax Service, 1987-90; contbr. to numerous publs. in field. Mem. vis. com. U. Chgo. Law Sch., 1986-88. Mem. ABA (vice chair profl. svcs. 1987-89, mem. coun. tax sect. 1985-87, spl. coord. 1980-85), Am. Law Inst., Am. Bar Retirement Assn. (trustee, bd. dirs., vice chair 1990-91, chair 1991-92), Am. Coll. Employee Benefits Coun. (charter mem.), Am. Coll. Tax Coun. (charter mem.), Multnomah County Bar Assn., Am. Tax Lawyers (charter mem.), Oreg. Estate Planning Coun. Jewish. Pension, profit-sharing, and employee benefits, Corporate taxation, Estate taxation. Home: 3118 SW Fairmount Blvd Portland OR 97201-1466 Office: 215 SW Washington St Fl 3 Portland OR 97204-2636 E-mail: mort@erisalaw.com.

ZAMBOLDI, RICHARD HENRY, lawyer; b. Kittanning, Pa., Nov. 22, 1941; s. Henry F. and Florence E. (Colligan) Z.; m. Maria Therese Reiser, Aug. 12, 1967; children: Elizabeth M., Richard H. Jr., Margaret B. BBA, St. Bonaventure U., 1963; JD, Villanova U., 1966. Bar: U.S. Dist. Ct. (we. dist.) Pa. 1966, Pa. 1968, U.S. Ct. Appeals (3d cir.) 1970, U.S. Supreme Ct. 1981. Law clk. U.S. Dist. Ct. (we. dist.) Pa., Pitts., 1966-67; atty. Nat. Labor Rels. Bd., Pitts., 1967-68; assoc. Kanehann & McDonald, Allentown, Pa., 1968-69; ptnr. Elderkin Martin Kelly Messina & Zamboldi, Erie, Pa., 1969-90, Knox McLaughlin Gornall & Sennett, Erie, 1990—, pres., 1997—. Author (student articles) Villanova Law Rev., 1964-65, editor, 1965-66. Mem. Pa. Bar Assn., Erie County Bar Assn. Republican. Roman Catholic. Labor (including EEOC, Fair Labor Standards Act, labor-management relations, NLRB, OSHA). Home: 6206 Lake Shore Dr Erie PA 16505-1013 Office: Knox McLaughlin Gornall & Sennett 120 W 10th St Erie PA 16501-1410

ZAMBORSKY, DONALD A. lawyer; b. Allentown, Pa., Dec. 21, 1947; s. Edward J. and Helen A. (Gresko) Z.; m. Joan E. Gallo, July 19, 1969; children: Sonia, Eric, Laura, David. BA, U. Pa., 1969; JD, Villanova U., 1972. Law clk. to Hon. Martin Coyne County Ct., Allentown, Pa., 1972-73; ptnr. Zamborsky & Zamborsky, Allentown, 1973-92; pvt. practice Allentown, 1992-97; ptnr. Tallman, Hudders & Sorrentino, P.C., Allentown, 1998—. Mental health rev. officer Lehigh County Ct., Allentown, 1977—; adj. prof. Cedar Crest Coll., Allentown, 1978-93, Pa. State U., Fogelsville, 1978-92. Mem. Lehigh Valley Estate Planning Coun., pres., 1982-83. Mem. Lehigh Country Club (bd. dirs. 1993-97, sec. 1999-2001). Roman Catholic. Avocations: golf, paddle tennis. Estate planning, Probate (including wills, trusts), Estate taxation. Office: 1611 Pond Rd Ste 300 Allentown PA 18104-2258 E-mail: dzamborsky@thslaw.com.

ZAMMIT, JOSEPH PAUL, lawyer; b. N.Y.C., May 19, 1948; s. John and Farla (Rudolph) Z.; m. Dorothy Therese O'Neill, June 6, 1970; children: Michael, Paul, Brian. AB, Fordham U., 1968; JD, Harvard U., 1971; LLM, NYU, 1974. Bar: N.Y. 1972, U.S. Dist. Ct. (so. and ea. dists.) N.Y. 1973, U.S. Dist. Ct. (no. dist.) Ala. 1989, U.S. Dist. Ct. (we. dist.) N.Y., 1991, U.S.

Ct. Appeals (2d cir.) 1973, U.S. Supreme Ct. 1978, U.S. Dist. Ct. (no. dist.) N.Y. 1983, U.S. Ct. Appeals (11th cir.) 1987, U.S. Ct. Appeals (fed. cir.) 1995. Assoc. Reavis & McGrath, N.Y.C., 1971-74; asst. prof. law St. John's U., Jamaica, N.Y., 1974-76, assoc. prof., 1976-78; assoc. Reavis & McGrath, N.Y.C., 1978-79, ptnr., 1979-88, Fulbright & Jaworski L.L.P. (formerly Fulbright Jaworski & Reavis McGrath), N.Y.C., 1989—. Adj. assoc. prof. St. John's U., Jamaica, 1979-83, adj. prof., 1984—; mem. panel comml. arbitrators tech. panel Am. Arbitration Assn., N.Y.C., 1977—. Bd. editors E-commerce Law and Strategy, 1987—; contbr. articles to profl. jours. Mem. ABA, N.Y. State Bar Assn., Assn. of Bar of City of N.Y. (chmn. com. on computer law 1995-98, chmn. comml. liability subcom. 1981-87, fed. cts. com. 1998-2001), Computer Law Assn., Phi Beta Kappa. General civil litigation, Commercial, contracts (including sales of goods; commercial financing), Computer. Office: Fulbright & Jaworski LLP 666 5th Ave Fl 31 New York NY 10103-0001 E-mail: jzammit@fulbright.com.

ZAMORA, RODRIGO, lawyer; JD, Escuela Libre De Derecho, Mexico, 1996; LLM, NYU, 1999. Bar: Mexican Bar Assn. Fgn. vis. atty. Kelley Drye & Warren, N.Y.C., 1999—2000. Mem.: Mexican Bar Assn. (chair comml. arbitration com.). Alternative dispute resolution, Private international, General civil litigation, Arbitration. Office: Bufete Zamora Pierce Porfirio Diaz 102-4 03720 Mexico City Mexico Office Fax: (52) (55) 55985933. E-mail: zapj3707@prodigy.net.mx.

ZANOT, CRAIG ALLEN, lawyer; b. Wyandotte, Mich., Nov. 15, 1955; s. Thomas and Faye Blanch (Sperry) Zanot. AB with distinction, U. Mich., 1977; JD cum laude, Ind. U., 1980. Bar: Ind. 1980, Mich. 1981, U.S. Dist. Ct. (so. dist.) Ind. 1980, U.S. Dist. Ct. (no. dist.) Ind. 1981, U.S. Ct. Appeals (6th cir.) 1985, U.S. Dist. Ct. (ea. dist.) Mich. 1987, U.S. Dist. Ct. (we. dist.) Mich. 1990. Law clk. to presiding justice Allen County Superior Ct, Ft. Wayne, 1980-81; ptnr. Davidson, Breen & Doud P.C., Saginaw, Mich., 1981—. Mem. ABA, Mich. Bar Assn., Saginaw County Bar Assn., Bay County Bar Assn., Genesee County Bar Assn. Roman Catholic. Insurance, Personal injury (including property damage), Workers' compensation. Home: 547 S Linwood Beach Rd Linwood MI 48634-9432 Office: Davidson Breen & Doud PC 1121 N Michigan Ave Saginaw MI 48602-4762

ZAPHIRIOU, GEORGE ARISTOTLE, lawyer, educator; b. July 10, 1919; came to U.S., 1973, naturalized, 1977; s. Aristotle George and Callie Constantine (Economou) Z.; m. Peaches J. Griffin, June 1, 1973; children: Ari, Marie. JD, U. Athens, 1940; LLM, U. London, 1950. Bar: Supreme Ct. Greece 1946, Eng. 1956, Ill. 1975, Va. 1983. Gen. counsel Counties Ship Mgmt. and R & K Ltd., London, 1951-61; practicing barrister, lectr. City of London Poly., 1961-73; vis. prof. Ill. Inst. Tech.-Chgo. Kent Coll. Law, 1973-76; pvt. practice Northbrook, Ill., 1976-78; prof. law George Mason U. Sch. Law, 1978-94, prof. law emeritus, adj. prof., 1994—. Prof. internat. transactions George Mason U. Internat. Inst., 1992-94; mem. Odin, Feldman & Pittelman P.C., Fairfax, Va., 1994-96; mem. study group on internat. elec. commerce conv. and other pvt. internat. law convs. U.S. Dept. of State. Author: Transfer of Chattels in Private International Law, 1956, U.S. edit., 1981, European Business Law, 1970; co-author: Declining Jurisdiction in Private International Law, 1995; joint editor: Jour. Bus. Law, London, 1962-73; bd. dirs. and bd. editors Am. Jour. Comp. Law of Am. Soc. Comparative Law, 1980-94; contbr. articles to profl. jours. Mem.: ABA (sect. internat. law and practice and dispute resolution), George Mason Am. Inn of Ct. (founder, master, emeritus), Am. Arbitration Assn. (panel comml. arbitrators), Chgo. Bar Assn., Ill. Bar Assn. Alternative dispute resolution, Commercial, contracts (including sales of goods; commercial financing), Private international. Home: 400 Green Pasture Dr Rockville MD 20852-4233 Fax: 301-984-1164. E-mail: gzaphiri@gmu.edu.

ZARELLA, PETER T. state supreme court justice; BS, Northeastern U., 1972; JD, Suffolk U., 1975. Bar: Mass. 1975, Conn. 1977, U.S. Dist. Ct. Mass. 1976, U.S. Dist. Ct. Conn. 1977, U.S. Supreme Ct. 1985, U.S. Ct. Appeals (2d cir.) 1985, U.S. Dist. Ct., So. Dist. N.Y. 1990. Pvt. practice, 1977—96; ptnr. Brown, Paindiris & Zarella, Hartford, Conn., 1978—96; judge Superior Ct., 1996—99, Appellate Ct., 1999—2001; assoc. justice Conn. Supreme Ct., 2001—. Chmn. Criminal Justice Commn., 2001—; chmn. rules com. Superior Ct., 2001—. Mem.Ethics Commn., Town of West Hartford, Conn., 1992—95, mem. Charter Revision Commn., 1995—96. Mem.: Conn. Bar Assn. (mem. exec. com. coml. law and bankruptcy sect. 1985—90, mem. banking law com. 1990—94). Office: Conn Supreme Ct 231 Capitol Ave Hartford CT 06106

ZAREMSKI, MILES JAY, lawyer; b. Chgo., Aug. 16, 1948; s. Samuel and Ann (Levine) Z.; m. Elena Cinthia Resnik, July 19, 1970; children: Jason Lane, Lauren Devra. BS, U. Ill., 1970; JD, Case Western Res. U., 1973. Bar: Ill. 1973, Pa. 2000, Ind. 2000, U.S. Dist. Ct. (no. dist.) Ill. 1973, U.S. Dist. Ct. Nebr. 1996, U.S. Dist. Ct. (ea. dist.) Tenn. 1997, U.S. Dist. Ct. (no. dist.) Ind. 2001, U.S. Ct. Appeals (7th cir.) 1973, U.S. Ct. Appeals (8th cir.) 1988, U.S. Ct. Appeals (6th cir.) 1998, U.S. Ct. Appeals (9th cir.) 2002, U.S. Supreme Ct. 1977. Spl. asst. state's atty. Lake County, Ill., 1980-82; ptnr. Kamensky & Rubinstein, Lincolnwood, Chgo., Ill., 2000—. Arbitrator, mandatory arbitration programs Cook and Lake Counties, Ill., 1990—; asst. prof. med. jurisprudence Finch U. Health Scis./Chgo. Med. Sch., 1991—; adj. faculty U. Chgo. Law Sch., 1999—2001; adj. asst. prof. Case Western Res. Law Sch., 2001—; advisor to congressman and staffs on patient rights, 1999—. Editor: Medical and Hospital Negligence, 4 vols., 1988, supplement, 1993, 95-99; contbr. chpts. in books and articles to profl. jours.; author: Reengineering Healthcare Liability Litigation, 1997, supplement, 1999; patentee in field. Oversight com. law sch. Case Western Res. U., Cleve., 1985-99, alumni bd. dirs., 1996-99; mem. exec. com. law sch. ctr for health care Loyola U., Chgo., 1987-89; mem. lakefront commn. City of Highland Park, Ill., 1982-84; bd. dirs., officer Regional Organ Bank Ill., Chgo., 1986-91; bd. dirs. The Lambs, Libertyville, Ill., 1982-84, Jocelyn Ctr. for Mental Health, 1994-96; field play marshall U.S. Olympics Baseball, Atlanta, 1996. Named one of Outstanding Young Men in Am., U.S. Jaycees, 1979. Fellow: Am. Bar Found., Am. Coll. Legal Medicine (assoc. in law 1973—91, editl. bd. Jour. Legal Medicine 1981—, chair legal com. 1996—98, chair Amicus com. 1997—2000, bd. govs., sec. 1999—2000, treas. 2000—01, pres.-elect 2001—02, pres. 2002—03); mem.: ABA (editor-in-chief Forum 1979—81, vice chmn. 1979—90, chmn. med. and law com. 1984—85, editl. bd. Forum on Health Law 1989—91, spl. com. on med. profl. liability 1991—95, 1998—, chmn. spl. com. on med. profl. liability 2000—03, chmn. 2000—, various coms. tort, trial and ins. practice sect.), Ill. Assn. Healthcare Attys., Quality Mgmt. Health Care (editl. bd.), Am. Soc. Writers on Legal Subjects (scribes), Am. Health Law Assn. (vice chair hosp. liability com. 1999—2001), Am. Soc. Law and Medicine (editor-in-chief 1981—83, bd. editors 1983—86), Lake County Bar Assn., Ill. Bar Assn. (1st and 3d prizes 1978—79). Jewish. Avocations: baseball, soccer, coaching athletic teams. State civil litigation, Personal injury (including property damage), Product liability. Office: Kamensky & Rubinstein 7250 N Cicero Ave Ste 200 Lincolnwood IL 60712

ZARRILLO, TERI DAWN, lawyer; b. Bklyn., Jan. 18, 1969; d. Barnet Irwin and Patricia Alpert; m. Michael Thomas Zarrillo, Mar. 4, 2000. BA, Emory U., 1990, JD, 1993. Bar: Ga. 1993, Fla. 1993. Atty. Mullman & Alpert, Atlanta, 1993—97, Hicks, Casey & Barber, Marietta, Ga., 1998—2000, Gorby, Reeves, Peters & Burns, Atlanta, 2000—; pvt. practice Atlanta, 1997—98. Mem.: ABA, Lawyers Club, Atlanta Trial Lawyers Assn., State Bar Ga. Workers' compensation, Personal injury (including property damage), Insurance. Office: Gorby Reeves and Peters 945 E Paces Ferry Rd # 250 Atlanta GA 30326 Office Fax: 404-239-1179. Business E-Mail: tzarrillo@gorbyreeves.com.

ZARZUR, CRISTIANNE SACCAB, lawyer; b. São Paulo, Brazil, Aug. 13, 1971; d. Camilo and Ivany Saccab Zarzur. Law Degree, Mackenzie U., São Paulo, 1995; Grad in Economy/Bus. Adminstrn., Getutio Vargas U., 2002. Bar: Brazil 1995. Trainee Arruda Alyim Advogados, São Paulo, 1992, Pinheiro Neto Advogados, São Paulo, 1992—95, jr. assoc., 1996—99, full assoc., 1999—2003, sr. assoc., 2000—01; fgn. legal cons. Howrey Simon Arnold & White LLP, Washington, 2002—, leading atty. antitrust law, 2003—. Author: Chambers Global, 2002. Mem.: Brazilian Bar Assn. Antitrust, Administrative and regulatory, Mergers and acquisitions. Office: Pinheiro Neto Advogados Rua Boavista 254 9o and 01014-907 São Paulo Brazil Home: Rua Honduras 256 São Paulo 01428-000 Brazil

ZASLOWSKY, DAVID PAUL, lawyer; b. N.Y.C., Dec. 30, 1960; s. Daniel N. and Rhoda Z.; m. Lisa Ann Freudenberger, Aug. 26, 1982; children: Amanda Lauren, Michael Joel, Steven Ira. BS in Computer/Info. Sci. summa cum laude, Bklyn. Coll., 1981; JD, Yale U., 1984. Bar: N.Y. 1984, N.J. 1984, U.S. Dist. Ct. (so. and ea. dist.) N.Y. 1985, U.S. Dist. Ct. N.J. 1985, U.S. Cir. Ct. (2d cir.) 1992. Assoc. Baker & McKenzie, N.Y.C., 1984-94, ptnr., 1994—. Author: (with others) Federal Civil Practice, 1989, Transnational Litigation in U.S. Federal Courts, 1991, Litigating International Commercial Disputes, 1996; editor: International Litigation and Arbitration Alert, 2001-. Mem. ABA (litigation sect.), N.Y. State Bar Assn. (comml. and fed. litigation sect.), Assn. Bar City N.Y. General civil litigation, Commercial, contracts (including sales of goods; commercial financing). Office: Baker & McKenzie 805 3rd Ave Fl 29 New York NY 10022-7513 E-mail: david.zaslowsky@bakernet.com.

ZAUN, ANNE MARIE, lawyer; b. N.Y.C., Aug. 1, 1949; d. George F. and Clara J. (Varriale) Z.; m. Stephen A. Lokos, Oct. 17, 1987; children: Debra M., Anthony G. BS, Fordham U., 1970; JD cum laude, Seton Hall U., 1979. Assoc. mgr. Prudential Property and Casualty Ins. Co., Woodbridge, N.J., 1972-76; dep. atty. gen. State of N.J., Trenton, 1980-84; staff atty. Knapp & Blejwas, Edison, N.J., 1984-87; dir. legal writing program Law Sch. Seton Hall. U., Newark, 1987-89; prin. Anne M. Zaun, East Brunswick, N.J., 1989—. Adj. prof. paralegal program Middlesex County Coll., 1992—. Mem. N.J. Bar Assn. (elder law sect.), Middlesex County Bar Assn. (elder law sect.). Democrat. Avocations: reading, music, tennis, swimming. Estate planning, Family and matrimonial, Probate (including wills, trusts). Office: G 12A Brier Hill Ct East Brunswick NJ 08816-3000 E-mail: azaun@compuserve.com.

ZAUSNER, BARBARA T. arbitrator, mediator; married; 1 child, Erica Cotto. MA, Rutgers U., 1976. Tchr. N.Y.C. Sch., 1967—69; vocat. rehab. counselor State of N.J., Trenton, 1970—74; coord. employee rels. Rutgers U., New Brunswick, 1976—76, rsch. assoc., 1975—77, lectr., adj. prof., 1980—85; adj. prof. Phila. Coll. Textile & Sci., 1982; pvt. practice Mt. Tremper, NY, 1976—. Mem.: Nat. Acad. Arbitrators (v.p. 2000—01). Home and Office: PO Box 300 Mount Tremper NY 12457 Home Fax: 845-688-2411. Personal E-mail: bzausner@hvc.rr.com.

ZAVACKY, SUSAN KLINE, law librarian; b. Doylestown, Pa., May 5, 1953; d. Percy H. and Helen C. K.; m. Stephen C. Zavacky, Sept. 12, 1981. BS in Libr. Edn., Millersville (Pa.) U., 1971-75. Asst. libr. Legis. Reference Bureau, Harrisburg, Pa., 1975-79, libr., 1979—. Vice chair. legis. rsch. librs. staff sect. Nat. Conf. of State Legis., Denver, 1987-88, chair, 1988-89; mem. Dauphin County Libr. Sys. Mem. Greater Phila. Law Libr. Assn., Easter Seal Soc., Chesapeake Bay Found. Office: Legis Reference Bur Main Capitol Building Rm 641 Harrisburg PA 17120-0033

ZAVATSKY, MICHAEL JOSEPH, lawyer; b. Wheeling, W.Va., Dec. 15, 1948; s. Mike and Mary (Mirich) Z.; m. Kathleen Hanson, May 28, 1983; children: David, Emily. BA in Internat. Studies, Ohio State U., 1970; MA in Polit. Sci., U. Hawaii, 1972; JD, U. Cin., 1980. Bar: Ohio 1980, U.S. Dist. Ct. (so. dist.) Ohio 1981, U.S. Ct. Appeals (6th cir.) 1985, U.S. Supreme Ct. 1989. Ptnr. Taft, Stettinius & Hollister, Cin., 1980—. Adj. prof. in trial practice and immigration law U. Cin., 1986— Trustee Internat. Visitors Ctr., Cin., 1984-86; bd. dirs. Cin. Charter Com., 1988-91; bd. dirs., mem. steering com. Leadership Cin., 1994-96. Capt. USAF, 1973-77. William Graham fellow U. Cin., 1979, East West Ctr. fellow U. Hawaii, 1970. Mem ABA, Ohio Bar Assn., Cin. Bar Assn., Am. Immigration Lawyers Assn. (chmn. Ohio chpt. 1987-88, 90-93), Potter Stewart Inn of Ct., Order of Coif. Federal civil litigation, State civil litigation, Immigration, naturalization, and customs. Home: 3820 Eileen Dr Cincinnati OH 45209-2013 Office: 1800 US Bank Tower Cincinnati OH 45202

ZAX, LEONARD A. lawyer; b. Paterson, N.J., July 16, 1950; s. Harry and Shirley Jeanne (Hollander) Z.; m. Helen Kemp, May 25, 1980; children: David Hollander, Laura Alexandra. BA, U. Chgo., 1971; M of City Planning, JD, Harvard U., 1975. Bar: N.J. 1978, D.C. 1978. Spl. asst. to gen. counsel HUD, 1975-76, spl. asst. to sec., 1976-77; lectr., mem. faculty Harvard U., Cambridge, Mass., 1977-78; assoc. Fried, Frank, Harris, Shriver & Kampelman, Washington, 1977-82, ptnr., 1982-95, Latham & Watkins, Washington, 1995—, also chmn. real estate group. Co-chmn. Mayor's Downtown Housing Commn., Washington, 1986-89, D.C. Enterprise Zones Study Commn., 1986-89; D.C. Downtown Interactive Retail Task Force, 1996-98; co-chmn. Washington adv. com. Asian Real Estate Assn., Washington, 1991-92. Contbg. author Nat. Law Jour., N.Y. Times, L.A. Times, Harvard Law Bull., Real Estate Fin. Jour., Urban Land, Washington Business Jour., Washington Post; editor: Real Estate and the RTC: A Guide to Asset Purchases and Contracting, Urban Land Inst., 1990. Trustee Nat. Bldg. Mus., D.C. Preservation League, 1988-95; mem. Fannie Mae Nat. Adv. Coun., 1994-95; mem. vis. com. Harvard Design Sch., 2000—. Mem. ABA (chmn. com. on housing and urban devel. law 1986-89, steering com. representation of the Homeless Project 1988-91, governing bd. forum com. affordable housing and community devel. 1991-94), D.C. Bar Assn., Urban Land Inst., Nat. Multi Housing Coun. Property, real (including real estate development, water). Home: 4511 28th St NW Washington DC 20008-1035 Office: Latham & Watkins 555 11thSt NW Ste 1000 Washington DC 20004-1304

ZAZZALI, JAMES R. state supreme court associate justice; b. Newark, N.J., June 17, 1937; m. Eileen Fitzsimmons; children: Mara, James Jr., Robert, Courtney, Kevin. BA, JD, Georgetown U. Bar: NJ, NY, DC. Law clk. U.S. Dist. Ct. Judge Lawrence A. Whipple, 1964—65; from asst. prosecutor to chief appellate sect. Essex County Prosecutor's Office, 1965—68; ptnr. Zazzali, Fagella, & Nowak, Newark; atty. gen. State of NJ, 1981—82; gen. counsel NJ Sports and Exposition Authority; assoc. justice NJ Supreme Ct., 2000—. Adj. prof. Seton Hall Law Sch., 1984—; commr. NJ State Commn. of Investigation, 1984—94, chmn., 1990—94; vice-chair Disciplinary Rev Bd., 1984—2000. Democrat. Office: NJ Supreme Court Hughes Justice Complex PO BOX 23 Trenton NJ 08625-0023

ZEALEY, SHARON JANINE, lawyer; b. St. Paul, Aug. 30, 1959; d. Marion Edward and Freddie Zealey. BS, Xavier U. of La., 1981; JD, U. Cin., 1984. Bar: Ohio 1984; U.S. Dist. Ct. (so. dist.) Ohio 1985; U.S. Ct. Appeals (6th cir.) 1990; U.S. Supreme Ct. 1990. Law clk. U.S. Atty. for S. Dist. of Ohio, Cin., 1982; trust adminstr. Firstar Bank, Cin., 1984-86; atty. UAW Legal Svcs., Cin., 1986-88; assoc. Manley, Burke, Lipton & Fischer, Cin., 1988-91; mng. atty. and dep. atty. gen. Ohio Atty. Gen. Office, Cin., 1991-95; asst. U.S. atty. criminal div. for So. Dist. Ohio U.S. Attys. Office, Cin., 1995-97; United States atty. So. Dist. Ohio, Cin., 1997—2001; ptnr. Blank Rome Comisky & McCauley, 2001—. Adj. instr. lawU. Cin., 1997—; mem. U.S. Atty. Gen.'s Adv. Com., 1999—2001, chair civil rights subcom., 2001; mem. merit selection com. Sixth Cir. Ct. of Appeals Bankruptcy Ct., 1992—96. Mem. commn. Cin. Cmty. Action Now, 2001—; commr. Tall Stacks Commn., City of Cin., 1990—94, Mayor's Commn. on Children, City of Cin., 1992—94; mem. equal employment adv. rev. panel City of Cin., 1989—91; trustee, bd. visitors U. Cin. Coll. Law, 1992—; trustee Legal Aid Soc. Cin., 1987—92. Named Career Woman of Achievement, Cin. YWCA, 1988; recipient Disting. Alumni award, Friends of Women's Studies, U. Cin., 2001, Theodore M. Berry award for outstanding achievement in politics and in svc. to cmty., Cin. chpt. NACCP, 1998, Nicholas Longworth III Alumni Achievement award for disting. pub. svc., U. Cin. Coll. Law, 1997. Mem. Black Lawyers Assn. of Cin. (pres. 1989-91, round table 1988-), Legal Aid Soc. (sec. 1991-92), ABA, Fed. Bar Assn., Ohio Bar Assn., Nat. Bar Assn. (bd. govs. 1988-1990, Mem. of Yr. region VI 1990), Cin. Bar Assn. (trustee 1989-94), Cin. CAN Commn. Democrat. Episcopalian. Office: 1700 PNC Ctr 201 E 5th St Cincinnati OH 45202 Fax: 513-362-8787. E-mail: zealey@blankRome.com.*

ZEARFOSS, HERBERT KEYSER, lawyer; b. Montandon, Pa., Oct. 13, 1929; s. Dean Wilson and Susan Lesher (Keyser) Z.; m. Thelma Mary McCarthy, Dec. 19, 1953 (dec. 1984); children: Timothy McCarthy, Jonathan Andrew, Sarah Creighton; m. Suzanne VanderVeer, Nov. 14, 1992. AB, Bucknell U., 1951; postgrad., Yale U., 1951-53; JD, Am. U., 1958. Bar: Pa. 1959, U.S. Dist. Ct. (mid. dist.) Pa. 1959, U.S. Dist. Ct. (ea. dist.) Pa. 1975, U.S. Supreme Ct. 1975. Ptnr. Fetter & Zearfoss, Lewisburg, Pa., 1959-60; asst. counsel Fidelity Mut. Life Ins. Co., Phila., 1960-67, sr. v.p., gen. counsel, 1978-82; sec., mgr. Ins. Fedn. of Pa. Inc., 1967-68; ptnr. Zearfoss & Campbell, 1968-78; sr. v.p., sec., gen. counsel Provident Indemnity Life Ins. Co. and parent co. Provident Am. Corp., Norristown, Pa., 1982-87; sole practice Radnor, Pa., 1987-91; adj. faculty Cabrini Coll., 1988-90; asst. gen. counsel, asst. sec. Teleflex Inc., Limerick, Pa., 1991-2001. Author: The Life Insurance Law of Pennsylvania, 1983; book rev. editor Am. U. Law Rev., 1956-58. Rep. Pa. Gen. Assembly from 167th dist., 1968-78; justice of the Peace, Radnor Twp., Delaware County, Pa., 1966-67; v.p. Valley Forge coun. Boy Scouts Am., 1982-86 (silver beaver award 1989); treas. Netherlands-Am. Amity Trust, Inc., 1981-86. Lt. comdr. USNR, 1954-58. Decorated officer Order of Orange-Nassau (Netherlands), 1992. Mem. ABA, Pa. Bar Assn., Assn. Life Ins. Counsel, Netherlands Soc. Phila. (pres. 1979-83), SAR (pres. Phila. Continental chpt. 1986-87), Colonial Soc. Pa. (gov. 1988-91), Del. Soc. Cin. (pres. 1996-99), Pa. Geneal. Soc. (counsel 1987-91, pres. 1995—), Soc. War 1812 (pres. gen. 1996-99), Mil. Order Loyal Legion U.S. (comdr., Pa. comdr. 1999-2001, judge adv.-in-chief 2001—), Sovereign Mil. Order Temple Jerusalem (grand officer), Priory of Phila. (prior 1994-98), Yale Club of Phila., Phila. Club, Penn Club, Merion Cricket Club, Omicron Delta Kappa, Phi Alpha Delta, Phi Alpha Theta, Tau Kappa Alpha, Pi Sigma Alpha. Republican. Presbyterian. Corporate, general, Product liability, Securities. Home: 532 Candace Ln Villanova PA 19085-1702 E-mail: hzearfoss@aol.com.

ZEIGLER, ANN DEPENDER, lawyer; b. Spokane, Wash., June 7, 1947; d. F. Norman and Dorothy (Wolter) dePender; m. Paul Stewart Zeigler, June 20, 1970; 1 child, Kate Elizabeth. BA magna cum laude, Ft. Wright Coll. Holy Names, Spokane, 1969; MFA in Creative Writing, U. Mont., 1975; JD, U. Houston, 1984. Bar: Tex. 1984. Course adminstr. legal communications U. Houston, 1982-84; assoc. Dula, Shields & Egbert, 1984-87; ind. project atty., 1987; assoc. Dow, Cogburn & Friedman, 1987-90; assoc. bankruptcy sect./avoidance litigation Hughes, Watters & Askanase, Houston, 1990—. Co-editor: Insurance Guide-Arts Nonprofits, 1993, Basic Issues in Estate Planning-Representing the Artist, 1994, Leading the Arts Nonprofit: Duties of Officers and Directors, 1999; editl. bd. Houston Lawyer, 1999—, guest editor spl. hist. issue 2000, 01; assoc. editor Keeping Up With, 2002-03; contbr. articles to profl. jours. Mem. publs. com., writer Tex. Accts. and Lawyers for Arts, Houston, 1988—; mem. Supreme Ct. of Tex. Unauthorized Practice of Law Com., Houston; vol. Houston Lawyers for Hunger Relief, 1988-90. Mem. ABA, State Bar Tex., Houston Bar Assn. (chair law and the arts com. 1996-97, co-chair ann. fiction contest), Can. Bar Assn., Phi Alpha Delta. Democrat. Bankruptcy, General civil litigation, Property, real (including real estate development, water). Home: 4038 Cheena Dr Houston TX 77025-4702 Office: Hughes Watters & Askanase 1415 Louisiana St Fl 37 Houston TX 77002-7360 E-mail: azeigler@hwallp.com.

ZEISEL, LAURA, lawyer, educator, environ. counsel; b. Bklyn., June 9, 1948; d. Melvin and Shirley Martha (Weinstein) Z.; m. David Seymour Strong, Nov. 20, 1970; children— Sara Zeisel, Elizabeth Pearl. Student Smith Coll., 1966-68; B.A., Washington Sq. Coll., NYU, 1970, postgrad., 1970-72; J.D., SUNY-Buffalo, 1975. Bar: N.Y. 1976, U.S. Dist. Ct. (so. dist.) N.Y. 1976, U.S. Ct. Appeals (2d cir.) 1977, U.S. Dist. Ct. (no. dist.) N.Y. 1979. Atty. Mid-Hudson Legal Services, Poughkeepsie, N.Y., 1975-80; ptnr. Lazar & Zeisel, Poughkeepsie, 1980-82; regional atty. N.Y. State Dept. Environ. Conservation, New Paltz, 1982-85; resident counsel Mid-Hudson br. office Sive, Paget & Riesel, P.C., 1985-88; adj. prof. Marist Coll., Poughkeepsie, 1976—93 ; mem. Gov.'s Commn. Domestic Violence, Albany, N.Y., 1983-88. Recipient Bennett award Faculty Law and Jurisprudence SUNY, Buffalo, 1975. Mem. N.Y. State Bar Assn., Ulster County Bar Assn., Mid-Hudson Women's Bar Assn. (pres. 1983-84). Democrat. Jewish. Office: Drake Sommers Loeb et al 1 Corwin Ct Newburgh NY 12550 Office Fax: 845-565-1999. E-mail: lzeisel@dsltc.com.

ZEITLAN, MARILYN LABB, lawyer; b. N.Y.C., Sept. 17, 1938; d. Charles and Florence (Geller) Labb; m. Barrett M. Zeitlan, Apr. 14, 1957; children: Adam Scott, Daniel Craig. BA, Queens Coll., 1958, MS, 1970; JD, Hofstra U., 1978. Bar: N.Y. 1979. Tchr. N.Y.C., 1958-61; pvt. practice matrimonial law, Roslyn, N.Y., 1980—. Assoc. editor: Law Rev., Hofstra U., 1977-78; contbr. articles to profl. jours. Commr. East Hills Environ. Commn., 1971-75; co-founder Roslyn Environ. Assn., 1970; v.p. Roslyn LWV, 1974-75. Hofstra Law Sch. fellow, 1976. Mem. Nassau County Bar Assn., N.Y. State Bar Assn., Phi Beta Kappa. Avocation: horseback riding. Family and matrimonial. Office: 1025 Northern Blvd Ste 201 Roslyn NY 11576-1506

ZELDES, ILYA M. forensic scientist, lawyer; b. Baku, Azerbaidjan, Mar. 15, 1933; came to U.S., 1976; s. Michael B. and Pauline L. (Ainbinder) Z.; m. Emma S. Kryss, Nov. 5, 1957; 1 child, Irina Zeldes Rieser. JD, U. Azerbaidjan, Baku, 1955; PhD in Forensic Scis., U. Moscow, 1969. Expert-criminalist Med. Examiner's Bur., Baku, 1954-57; rsch. assoc. Criminalistics Lab., Moscow, 1958-62; sr. rsch. assoc. All-Union Sci. Rsch. Inst. Forensic Expertise, Moscow, 1962-75; chief forensic scientist S.D. Forensic Lab., Pierre, 1977-93. Owner Forensic Scientist's Svcs., Pierre, 1977-93. Author: Physical-Technical Examination, 1968, Complex Examination, 1971, The Problems of Crime, 1981; contbr. numerous articles to profl. publs. in Australia, Austria, Bulgaria, Can., Eng., Germany, Holland, India, Ireland, Israel, Rep. of China, Russia, U.S. and USSR. Mem. Internat. Assn. Identification (rep. S.D. chpt. 1979-93, chmn. forensic lab. analysis subcom. 1991-98, firearm and toolmark identification subcom. 2001—), Am. Soc. Crime Lab. Dirs., Am. Assn. Firearm and Toolmark Examiners (emeritus). Avocation: travel. Home: 5735 Foxlake Dr Apt 1 Fort Myers FL 33917-5661 E-mail: ilyaz@earthlink.net.

ZELDES, JACOB DEAN, lawyer; b. Galesburg, Ill., Dec. 10, 1929; s. Louis Herman and Sophia Ruth (Koren) Z.; m. Nancy S. Zeldes, Aug. 23, 1953; children: Stephen, Kathryn, Amy. BS, U. Wis., 1951; LLB, Yale U., 1957. Bar: Conn. 1957, U.S. Dist. Ct. Conn. 1958, U.S. Ct. Appeals (2nd cir.) 1959, U.S. Supreme Ct. 1960, U.S. Tax Ct. 1966. Ptnr. Zeldes Needle & Cooper PC, Bridgeport, Conn. Lt. (j.g.) USNR, 1951-53, Korea. Fellow Am. Bar Found., Am. Coll. Trial Lawyers; mem. ABA Assn. Profl. Responsibility Lawyers, Conn. Bar Assn. (lawyer to lawyer dispute resolution com., spl. counsel Conn. Ho. of Reps., select com. to investigate impeachment of probate judge 1985), Conn. Trial Lawyers Assn., Assn. Trial Lawyers of Am., Nat. Assn. Criminal Def. Lawyers, Conn. Criminal

Def. Lawyers Assn., Bridgeport Bar Assn. Democrat. Jewish. Avocations: swimming, hiking, travel. General civil litigation, Criminal. Office: Zeldes Needle & Cooper PC 1000 Lafayette Blvd Fl 5 Bridgeport CT 06604-4725 E-mail: jzeldes@znclaw.com.

ZELECHIWSKY, BOHDAN JOHN, lawyer; b. Pottsville, Pa., July 6, 1951; s. Bohdan Stephen and Nadia Z.; m. Chrystyna Hawrylak, Sept. 15, 1978 (div. Jan. 1989); children: Sophia, Adrian; m. Anita Louise Walters, Dec. 5, 1993; children: Roman, Zenia. BA, Moravian Coll., 1973; JD, Vt. Law Sch., 1976. Bar: Pa. 1977. Pvt. practice, Bethlehem, Pa., 1978—. Coun. mem. Ukranian Orthodox Ch., N.J., 1993. With USMC, 1971-72. Avocations: skiing, biking. General civil litigation, Criminal, General practice. Fax: (610) 866-4626. E-mail: BJZLaw@fast.net.com.

ZELENAK, EDWARD MICHAEL, lawyer, musician; b. Dearborn, Mich., Aug. 28, 1953; s. Edward Patrick and Irene Elaine (Maruska) Z.; m. Angeline Rose Cianfarani, May 24, 1986; children: Amelia Mary Rose and Edward Patrick (twins), Elliott William. BA, Wayne State U., 1975, JD, 1977. Bar: Mich. 1977, U.S. Dist. Ct. (ea. dist.) Mich. 1977, 6th Cir. Ct. of Appeals 1987. Leader Ed Zelenak Orch., Lincoln Park, Mich., 1971—; dir. pub. affairs Sta. WDRQ, Southfield, Mich., 1977-83, host talk show, 1978-83; instr. Wayne State Univ., Detroit, 1977-84; pvt. practice, Lincoln Park, 1977—; atty. Cities of Lincoln Park and Southgate (Mich.), 1978—. Hon. consul Slovak Republic, 2001—; corr. RKO Network, 1980-83; host talk show United Cable TV Mich., Woodhaven, 1980—, Sta. WXYT, 1988-94; gen. counsel Pat Paulsen for Pres., 1996; hon. consul Slovakia, 2001. Composer, performer (album) C. B. Polka, 1977. Alt. del. Dem. Nat. Conv., Miami, Fla., 1972, mem. staff Dem. Nat. Conv., N.Y.C., 1976; exec. bd. 16th Dist. Dems., Dearborn, 1975-87; gen. counsel First Cath. Slovak Union U.S. and Can., 1988-99, Pat Paulsen for Pres. Campaign, 1996; spl. counsel City of Ecorse, Mich., 1989—; bd. dirs. People's Cmty. Svcs. of Detroit, 1992-98; dir. Downriver Coun. for the Arts, 1997—; mem. Congress on New Urbanism, Seaside Inst. Recipient Commendation Mich. State Senate, 1982; named One of Five Outstanding Young Michiganders, Mich. Jaycees, 1990. Mem. Am. Fedn. Musicians, State Bar Mich., Wayne State U. Law Sch. Alumni Assn. (dir. 1998—, sec., v.p. 2001, pres. 2002), Downriver Bar Assn., Slovak League Am. (nat. dir. 1985—, del. meeting with Vaclav Havel and Alexander Dubcek conf. in Czecho-Slovakia 1990), Wayne State U. Law Alumni Assn. (mem. exec. com., v.p. 2001, pres. 2002), Slovak Cath. Sokol Club, First Cath. Slovak Union, KC (fin. com. Robert Jones chpt. 1987-96), Kiwanis (pres. local chpt. 1981-82), Rotary Internat. Home: 711 Saint Johns Blvd Lincoln Park MI 48146-4925 Office: 2933 Fort St Lincoln Park MI 48146-2425

ZELENKA, DONALD JOHN, lawyer; b. Akron, Ohio, Feb. 16, 1952; s. Donald Banser and Jane (Cunningham) Z.; m. Leslie Rock, May 24, 1975. BA in Arts and Scis., Ohio State U., 1974; JD, U. S.C., 1977. Bar: S.C. 1977, U.S. Ct. Appeals (4th cir.) 1978, Va. 1980, U.S. Dist. Ct. S.C. 1981, U.S. Supreme Ct. 1983, U.S. Ct. Appeals (11th cir.) 1985. Law clk., research asst. U.S. Ct. Appeals (4th cir.), Richmond, Va., 1977-79; from asst. to chief dep. atty. gen. S.C. Atty. Gen., Columbia, 1979-94; asst. dep. atty. gen. supr. Capital Litigation/Fed. Habeas Corpus unit S.C. Atty. Gen., 1995—. Tchr., instr. clin. programs U. S.C. Law Sch., Columbia, 1983-84. Mem. Sentencing Guidelines Commn., Columbia, 1983-89, S.C. Victim-Witness Task Force. Recipient Silver Scales of Justice award S.C. Victim Assistance Network, 1991. Mem. ABA (pub. sector lawyers divsn.), Richland County Bar Assn., Assn. Govt. Attys. in Capital Litigation (exec. bd. dirs. 1985—, pres. 1992-93, Excellence award 1995), S.C. Bar Assn. (sec. criminal law sect.), Nat. Dist. Attys. Assn. Methodist. Home: 320 Hunters Blind Dr Columbia SC 29212-1610 Office: SC Atty Gen PO Box 11549 Columbia SC 29211-1549

ZELENOCK, KATHERYNE L. lawyer; b. Detroit, Aug. 7, 1966; d. Gerald B. and Mary K. Z. BA in Polit. Sci., U. Mich., 1987; JD, U. Notre Dame, 1991. Bar: Mich. 1991, U.S. Dist. Ct. (ea. and we. dists.) Mich. 1991. Atty. Simpson & Berry, Birmingham, Mich., 1991-95; ptnr. Simpson, Zelenock, Birmingham, Mich., 1995—2001; of counsel Dykema Gossett, 2001—. Vol. counselor Women's Survival Ctr., Pontiac, Mich., 1996—; vol. coach Birmingham Groves High Sch. Mock Trial Team, 1995-2000. Mem. Notre Dame Club Detroit (dir. 1995—), Mortgage Banker's Assn., Conn. Mortgage Securitization Assn., Mortgage Group, Comml. Mortgage Industry Std. Maintainance Orgn., U. Mich. Alumnae Club Oakland County. Avocations: golf, tennis. Commercial, contracts (including sales of goods; commercial financing), Corporate, general, Property, real (including real estate development, water). Office: Simpson Zelenock 260 E Brown St Ste 300 Birmingham MI 48009-6232

ZELL, GLENN, lawyer; b. N.Y.C., Nov. 2, 1934; s. Joseph and Rose (Hyman) Z.; m. Gloria Wynne, Apr. 16, 1961; children: Jeffrey, Rodney, Barbara. BS, N.Y.U., 1954; LLB, Emory U., 1965. Bar: Ga. 1965. Pvt. practice Zell & Zell, Atlanta, 1965—. Mem. Ga. Bar Assn., Ga. Assn. Criminal Def. Lawyers. Jewish. Constitutional, Criminal. Office: Zell & Zell 729 Piedmont Ave NE Atlanta GA 30308

ZELLER, MICHAEL EUGENE, lawyer; b. Queens, N.Y., June 19, 1967; s. Hans Ludwig and Geri Ann (Schottenstein) Z. BA, Union Coll., 1989; JD, Temple Law Sch., 1992; LLM magna cum laude, U. Hamburg, Germany, 1994. Bar: N.Y. 1992, U.S. Dist. Ct. (so. and ea. dists.) N.Y. 1995, N.C. 1996. Fgn. intern Bryan Gonzalez Vargas y Gonzalez Baz, Mexico City, 1990; student law clk. Hon. Jane Cutler Greenspan, Phila., 1990-91; fgn. clk. DROSTE, Hamburg, 1991, fgn. assoc., translator, 1992-94; freelance translator Charlotte, N.C., 1995—; mem. Internat. and Corp. Law Group of Moore & Van Allen PLLC, Charlotte, 1995—; owner, restaurateur Salad Garden, LLC. and Salad Garden Café, LLC, 1998—2001; owner Nighttime Entertainment LLC, 1999—2001, BGZ Properties, LLC. Active Charlotte World Affairs Coun., Charlotte Mayor's Internat. Cabinet; bd. dirs. Alemannia Soc., 1996-2000, Young Affiliates of Mint Mus., 1999-2000; bd. dirs., pres. Southgate Commons Homeowners Assn., 1998-2002; vol. atty. Children's Law Ctr., 1995- (bd. dirs., 2003-). Named Vol. Lawyer of Yr., Children's Law Ctr., 1998, 2003; scholar, Fedn. German/Am. Clubs, 1987. Mem. ABA, N.Y. State Bar Assn., N.C. Bar Assn., Mecklenburg County Bar Assn., ESOP Assn., Nat. Ctr. for Employee Ownership, Esop Assn., Nat. Ctr. Employee Ownership, Gewerblicher Rechtsschutz und Urheberrecht e.V., European Am. Bus. Forum. Avocations: singing, theater, golf, fictional writing. Corporate, general, Private international, Mergers and acquisitions. Office: 100 N Tryon St Fl 47 Charlotte NC 28202-4003

ZELLER, RONALD JOHN, lawyer; b. Phila., Jan. 28, 1940; m. Lucille Bell; children: John, Kevin, Suzanne. BSBA, LaSalle Coll., 1964; JD, Ohio State U., 1967. Bar: Mich. 1968, Fla. 1971. Ptnr. Zeller & Kanner, Miami, Fla., 1973-80, of counsel, 1980-89; pres., chief exec. officer Norwegian Cruise Lines, 1980-86; pres. Twenty First Century Mgmt. Group, Inc., Coconut Grove, Fla., 1986-90, Miami Voice Corp., 1990-92; gen. counsel Splty. Mgmt. Co., Delray Beach, Fla., 1992-93, pres., 1994-96; ptnr. Zeller & Assocs., LLC, Palm Beach, Fla., 1996—. Dep. chmn. Cruise Lines Internat. Assoc., N.Y.C., 1981-85, chmn., 1986. Trustee United Way Dade County, 1981-86; pres. Cath. Charities, Archdiocese of Miami 1976-78, Broward County, 1975-76, Excalibur Devel. Ctrs., Inc., 1973-75; mem. citizens bd. U. Miami, 1980-92; mem. exec. bd. New World Sch. Arts, 1986-87; mem. centennial campaign com. Ohio State U. Coll. Law, 1982-92, also mem. nat. coun.; mem. coun. Pres.'s Assocs., LaSalle U., 1982-87; mem. Fla. Postsecondary Edn. Planning Commn., 1986-87; mem. Cmty. Assns. Inst., 1995-2000; chmn. exec. com. Maritime Inst., 1997-99; mem. utility rev. bd. Village of Wellington, 1997-98; mem. gen. counsel Palm Beach Maritime Mus.; mem. Fla. com. Affirm Thy Friendship Campaign, Ohio State U., 1997-2000; mem. cruise line incentive com. Port of Palm Beach, 1997-2000; mem. ecumenical rev. bd. Diocese Palm Beach, 2002—. Mem. ABA (sect. taxation, closely held businesses. com.), Fla. Bar Assn. (lawyers and CPA's com., long range planning com. 2001--), Maritime Law Assn. (proctor in admiralty), Pres.' Club Ohio State U. General civil litigation, Corporate, general, Taxation, general. Office: Zeller & Assocs LLC Esperante Bldg 222 Lakeview Ave Ste 260 West Palm Beach FL 33401 Fax: 561 802-4387. E-mail: zellerlawfirm@cs.com.

ZELMAN, ANDREW E. lawyer; b. N.Y.C., Dec. 3, 1941; s. Benjamin M. and Beatrice (Feldman) Z.; m. Marjorie Ann Sussman, June 21, 1964; children: Lorraine Amy, Elissa Karen. BA, Colgate U., 1963; LLB, Columbia U., 1966. Bar: D.C. 1967, U.S. Ct. Appeals (D.C. cir.) 1967, U.S. Dist. Ct. (so. and ea. dists.) N.Y. 1970, U.S. Ct. Appeals (2d cir.) 1970, U.S. Supreme Ct. 1976. Assoc. Collier, Shannon, Rill, Edwards & Scott, Washington, 1966-67; asst. to chmn. NLRB, 1967-69; assoc. Polletti, Freidin, Prashker, Feldman & Gartner, N.Y.C., 1969-71, Surrey & Morse, N.Y.C., 1971-73, ptnr., 1974-79, Klein, Zelman, Rothermel & Dicter, N.Y.C., 1979—. Lectr. Cornell Sch. Indsl. and Labor Rels.; adj. prof. Bklyn. Law Sch., 1996—. Columnist N.Y.C. Bus. Mag. Mem. ABA (labor law sect. com. NLRB practice and procedure), Phi Beta Kappa. Labor (including EEOC, Fair Labor Standards Act, labor-management relations, NLRB, OSHA). Office: Klein Zelman Rothermel & Dicter 15th Floor 485 Madison Ave Fl 15 New York NY 10022-5803

ZELON, LAURIE DEE, lawyer; b. Durham, N.C., Nov. 15, 1952; d. Irving and Doris Miriam (Baker) Z.; m. David L. George, Dec. 30, 1979; children: Jeremy, Daniel. BA in English with distinction, Cornell U., 1974; JD, Harvard U., 1977. Bar: Calif. 1977, U.S. Ct. Appeals (9th cir.) 1978, U.S. Supreme Ct. 1989. Assoc. Beardsley, Hufstedler & Kemble, L.A., 1977-81, Hufstedler, Miller, Carlson & Beardsley, L.A., 1981-82, ptnr., 1983-88, Hufstedler, Miller, Kaus & Beardsley, L.A., 1988-90, Hufstedler, Kaus & Ettinger, L.A., 1990-91, Morrison & Foerster, L.A., 1991-2000; judge L.A. Superior Ct., 2000—. Contbg. author: West's California Litigation Forms: Civil Procedure Before Trial, 1996; editor-in-chief Harvard Civil Rights and Civil Liberties Law Rev., 1976-77 Bd. dirs. N.Y. Civil Liberties Union, 1973-74. Mem. ABA (chmn. young lawyers divsn. pro bono project 1981-83, delivery and pro bono projects com. 1983-85, subgrant competition-subgrant monitoring project 1985-86, chair standing com. on lawyers pub. svc. responsibility 1987-90, chair law firm pro bono project 1989-91, standing com. legal aid and indigent defendants 1991-97, chmn. 1993-97, mem. ho. dels. 1993—, state del. 1998—, commn. on ethics 2000 1997-2003), Calif. Bar Assn. (bd. dirs. appellate project 1995-2000, chair commn. on access to justice 1997-99), L.A. County Bar Assn. (trustee 1989-91, v.p. 1992-93, sr. v.p. 1993-94, pres.-elect 1994-95, pres. 1995-96, fed. cts. and practices com. 1984-93, vice chmn. 1987-88, chmn. 1988-89, chmn. judiciary com. 1991-92, chmn. real estate litigation subsect. 1991-92), Women Lawyers Assn. L.A., Calif. Women Lawyers Assn. Democrat. Federal civil litigation, State civil litigation. Office: Los Angeles Superior Ct 111 N Hill St Los Angeles CA 90012-3117

ZERGER, KIRSTEN LOUISE, mediator, lawyer; b. Newton, Kans., Oct. 15, 1950; d. Homer Joshua and Karolyn Louise (Kaufman) Z.; m. Edward Peters Dick, Mar. 28, 1969 (div. 1978); 1 child, Daagya Shanti; m. Sanford Norman Nathan, June 14, 1980; children: Jesse Zerger, Jonathan Kaufman, Joshua Zev. BA with highest distinction, Bethel Coll., 1973; JD, U. Calif.-Berkeley, 1977. Bar: Calif. 1977, U.S. Dist. Ct. (no. dist.) Calif. 1977, U.S. Ct. Appeals (9th cir.) 1987, U.S. Supreme Ct. 1985. Staff atty. United Farm Workers, AFL-CIO, Salinas, Calif., 1977-79; staff atty. Calif. Tchrs. Assn., Burlingame, 1979-85, chief counsel, 1985-88; pvt. practice, Berkeley, Calif., 1988-93; mediator, facilitator, and trainer, Kansas Inst. for Peace and Conflict Resolution, North Newton, Kansas, 1994-; coll. instr. Bethel Coll., North Newton, Kansas, 1996-; approved mediator, trainer Kans. Supreme Ct., 1998-; speaker ednl., profl. confs. Writer on mediation, facilitation and tng. as well as on public sector labor law issues; co-editor book California Public Sector Labor Law, 1989; contbr. articles to profl. jours. Mem. Heartland Mediators Assn., Calif. Bar Assn.(labor and employment law sect., chmn. pub. sector com. 1983-85, membership com. 1982-83, exec. com., 1985-89, treas. 1986-87, vice-chair 1987-88, advisor 1988-89). E-mail: snkz@mtelco.net.

ZERR, RICHARD KEVIN, lawyer; b. St. Charles, Mo., Apr. 10, 1949; s. Elmer George and Lillian Grace (Gross) Z.; m. Martha Jo Zerr, Mar. 19, 1969 (div. June 1976); m. Judy Ann Yeager, Aug. 8, 1978; 1 child, Richard Kevin Jr. AB in Polit. Sci., U. Mo., 1971; JD, U. Ark., 1974. Bar: Mo. 1974, U.S. Dist. Ct. (we. dist.) Mo. 1974, U.S. Dist. Ct. (ea. dist.) Mo. 1983, U.S. Ct. Appeals (8th cir.) 1985, U.S. Supreme Ct. 1985. Asst. to pros. atty. County of St. Charles, 1974; magistrate judge City of St. Charles, 1975-78; assoc. judge Cir. Ct., St. Charles, 1979-82; ptnr. Beck, Tiemeyer, Zerr, Frailily and Wulff, P.C., St. Charles, 1983—. Bd. dirs. St. Charles County Police Acad., 1978-88, Legal Svcs. Ea. Mo., 1978—. Bd. dir. St. Charles City-County Libr. Dist., 1991—. Mem. ABA (state chmn. small claims ct. com. 1978-82), Mo. Bar Assn. (bd. govs. 1999—), St. Charles County Bar Assn., Metro. St. Louis Bar Assn., U. Mo. Columbia Alumni Assn. (nat. bd. dirs. 1994—). Lodges: Kiwanis. Democrat. Roman Catholic. Avocation: high sch. and coll. football official. Criminal, Family and matrimonial, Personal injury (including property damage). Home: 176 Huntington Downs Saint Charles MO 63301-8700 Office: Beck Tiemeyer & Zerr 2777 W Clay St Saint Charles MO 63301-2539 E-mail: rzerr@btzlaw.com.

ZERUNYAN, FRANK VRAM, lawyer; b. Istanbul, Turkey, Sept. 17, 1959; came to U.S., 1978; s. Jack Hagop and Ayda (Yagupyan) Z.; m. Jody Lynn Forman, May 18, 1986; children: Daniel, Nicole. French Baccalaureat, Coll. Samuel Moorat, Paris, 1978; BA, Calif. State U., Long Beach, 1982; JD, Western State U., Fullerton, Calif., 1985; postgrad., U. Southern Calif., 1988. Bar: Calif. 1989, D.C. 1995, U.S. Dist. Ct. (ctrl. dist.) Calif. 1989, U.S. Dist. Ct. (no. dist.) Calif. 2001, U.S. Ct. Internat. Trade 1994, U. S. Supreme Ct. 2000. V.p. law Internat. Mktg. Alliance, Torrance, Calif., 1985-89; pvt. practice L.A., 1989-92; mng. mem. Yacoubian & Zerunyan, P.C., L.A., 1992-95; shareholder Sulmeyer, Kupetz, Baumann & Rothman, L.A., 1995—. Instr. law Alex Pilibos Sch., L.A., 1993-99; judge pro tem, L.A. Superior Ct.; mem. adv. com. Bus. Tech. Ctr. of L.A., Calif., 2003—. Editor SKB&R Newsletter, 1995—. Chmn. scholarship com. Orgn. Istanbul Armenians, Van Nuys, Calif., 1992—94; legal counsel and policy adv. com. Armenian Nat. Com. of Am., Armenian Nat. Com. of Am., Washington, 1993—; planning commr., past chmn. City of Rolling Hills Estates, 2000; mem. police svc. task force Little Company of Mary Hosp., 2003—; bd. dirs. Am. Youth Soccer Orgn., Palos Verdes, Calif., 1995—, referee adminstr., 1995—; bd. dirs., vice-chmn., chmn. Daniel Freeman Hosps. Found., 1998—2003, chmn., 1998—2002. Mem.: Financial Lawyers Conf., Armenian Bar Assn. (bd. govs. 2003—). Avocations: golf, soccer. Bankruptcy, Commercial, contracts (including sales of goods; commercial financing), Property, real (including real estate development, water). Office: Sulmeyer Kupetz 333 S Hope St 35th Fl Los Angeles CA 90071 E-mail: fzerunyan@sulmeyerlaw.com.

ZEVNIK-SAWATZKY, DONNA DEE, retired litigation coordinator, art gallery owner; b. Tulsa, Dec. 15, 1946; d. Robert Joseph Z. and Dorothy Dee (Robertson) Zink; m. Kenneth Sawatzky, May 30, 1965; children: K. Brian, Kaira D. Student, U. Ctrl. Okla., 1977, Okla. State U., 1984. Cert. AIDS educator, State of Okla., 1995-97. Sec. Farmers Ins. Co., Oklahoma City, 1974-80; office mgr. S.A.F.E., Inc., Oklahoma City, 1980-83; jr. acct. Southeast Exploration Corp., Oklahoma City, 1983-84; acct. Young Bros., Inc., Oklahoma City, 1984-88, The Denman Co., Inc., Oklahoma City, 1988-89; litigation coord. ACLU Okla., Oklahoma City, 1994—2003; ret., 2003; founder, owner Otherwhere Arts, 1999—2001. Bd. dirs. ACLU Okla., 1995—; founder, CEO Otherwhere Arts. Author and illustrator: That Place--Otherwhere, 1994, Something for Otherwhere, 1995; author: At Our House, 1979-83; columnist Putnam City-N.W. News, Warr Acres, Okla., 1979-83; designer stage sets Miss Warr Acres Pageant, 1971-88. Bd. dirs. Miss Warr Acres (Okla.) Pageant, 1984-88, Warr Acres C. of C., 1981-85; treas. ACLU of Okla., 1995—, bd. dirs., 1994—; child welfare advocate Okla. State Dept. Human Svcs., Oklahoma City, 1987-89; coord. AIDS clinic Triangle Assn., Oklahoma City, 1994-97; founder Circle of Friends with Arachnoiditis World Wide Web Chronic Pain Support Group, 1997. Named Honorary Mayor of Warr Acres, 1971, Super Citizen, 1973, Outstanding Vol. Okla. State Dept. Human Svcs., 1988; recipient Svc. award Warr Acres C. of C., 1979, Legis. Commendation State of Okla., 1988, numerous Okla. Newspaper Column of Month awards Okla. Press Assn., Oklahoma City, 1981-82. Mem. NAFE, ACLU (Exec. Dir. Vol. Svc. award 1996), Nat. Notary Assn., Am. Inst. Profl. Bookkeepers, Amnesty Internat., The Interfaith Alliance, Pflag, Human Rights Campaign, Okla. Coalition to Abolish the Death Penalty. Democrat. Methodist. Avocations: painting, writing, photography, family. Office: 3000 Paseo Dr Oklahoma City OK 73103

ZHANG, CHUANPING **See JONG, JAMES C.**

ZHAO, JIWEI, lawyer; b. Macheng City, Hubei, May 21, 1966; arrived in U.S., 1996; s. Bin Fu Zhao and Yuan Hua Jiang; m. Xuefei Feng Zhao, Sept. 18, 1993; 1 child, Virginia F. BS, Northeastern U., Shenyang China, 1988; MS, Northeastern U., Shenyang, 1991; JD, Rutgers U., Camden, N.J., 2001. Bar: N.J. 2001, N.Y. 2002. V.p. Qinhuanadao Empire Trading Co., China, 1993—96; CEO Mighty Dragon Inc., Edison, NJ, 1996—2001; pvt. practice Law Office of Jiwei Zhao, Esq., Edison, 2001—02; of counsel Kline & Gast, P.A., Edison, 2002—. Chmn. bd. dirs. Mighty Dragon, Inc., Edison, 0199—2002; adv. bd. Huaxia Chinese Sch. USA, Edison, 2002—; bd. dirs. The Am. Chinese Times, Edison, 2001—. Author: A Review of China Coastal City Development, 1994; editor: Handbook for Chinese Economists, 1991. Legal counsel Chinese Culture Day of N.J., Jersey City, 2002—; gen. counsel N.J. Chinese Dancing Assn., Livingston, NJ. Fellow: Rutgers Alumni Assn.; mem.: Am. Immigration Lawyers Assnj., N.Y. State Bar Assn., N.J. State Bar Assn. Avocations: reading, soccer. Corporate, general, Immigration, naturalization, and customs, Property, real (including real estate development, water). Office: Law Offices of Jiwei Zhao Esq 1967 Lincoln Hwy Ste 22 Edison NJ 08817

ZHAO, QIAN, lawyer; b. Dalian, Liaoning, China, Aug. 24, 1968; LLB, UIBE, Beijing, 1990; JD, NYU, 1998. Bar: N.Y. 1999, People's Rep. China 1992. Ptnr. Haiwen & Ptnr., Beijing, 1990-94; assoc. Sullivan & Cromwell, N.Y.C., 1998-2000, Skadden Arps, Beijing, 2000—. Private international, Mergers and acquisitions, Securities. Office: Skadden Arps Slate Meagher & Flom East Wing Office China World Trade Ctr 100004 Beijing China E-mail: Qzhao@skadden.com.

ZHU-CLARK, INGRID WENYING, lawyer; b. Beijing, July 31, 1958; d. Baozhen Zhu and Yiping Feng; m. Nigel Bruce Clark, July 12, 2000. BA in English, Beijing Tchrs. Coll., 1977; LLM in Internat. Law, CASS, Beijing, 1985; LLM in Asian Law, U. Wash., 1993, JD, 1996. Bar: China, Wash. Atty. China Legal Affairs Ctr., Beijing, 1985—87; vis. prof. Duke U. Sch. Law, Durham, NC, 1990—91; atty., con. Hillis Clark Martin & Peterson, Seattle, 1992—97; atty. Lovells, Hong Kong, 1997—98, mng. atty. Beijing, 1998—2001; mng. ptnr. LeBoeuf, Lamb, Greene & MacRae, Beijing, 2001—. V.p. China Profls. Assn., Seattle, 1992—96; lectr. Aspen Inst., 1993. Contbr. articles to profl. jours. Ford Found. scholar, 1988—91. Avocations: swimming, climbing, singing, hiking. Insurance, Finance, Corporate, general. Office: LeBoeuf Lamb Greene & MacRae 1 Jian Gao Men Wai Ave Ste 1908 Beijing 100004 China

ZIEGLER, DONALD EMIL, federal judge; b. Pitts., Oct. 1, 1936; s. Emil Nicholas and Elizabeth Ziegler; m. Claudia J. Chermak, May 1, 1965; 1 son, Scott Emil. BA, Duquesne U., 1958; LL.B., Georgetown U., 1961. Bar: Pa. 1962, U.S. Supreme Ct. 1967. Practice law, Pitts., 1962-74; judge Ct. of Common Pleas of Allegheny County, Pa., 1974-78, U.S. Dist. Ct. (we. dist.) Pa., Pitts., 1978—, chief judge, 1994-2001. Mem. Jud. Conf. U.S., 1997-2000. Treas. Big Bros. of Allegheny County, 1969-74. Mem. ABA, Pa. Bar Assn., Allegheny County Bar Assn., Am. Judicature Soc., St. Thomas More Soc. Clubs: Oakmont Country. Democrat. Roman Catholic. Office: 649 U S Post Office & Courthouse Bldg 7th and Grant St Pittsburgh PA 15219

ZIEGLER, HAL JEFFREY, lawyer; b. Syracuse, N.Y., Nov. 27, 1954; m. Sheila E. Levine, June 3, 1984; 1 child, Matthew Eric. BS, Syracuse U., 1972; MHS, Johns Hopkins U., 1978; JD, U. Balt., 1993. Bar: Md. 1994, D.C. 1994, U.S. Ct. Appeals (4th cir.) 1996. Health planner Md. Health Planning Agy., Balt., 1977-79; dir. govt. rels. Md. Med. Soc., Balt., 1979-84; pres. Ziegler & Assocs., Balt., 1984-88; dir. provider rels. Md. Mobile Ultrasound, Lutherville, 1988-90; media rels. specialist Milner-Fenwick, Inc., Timonium, Md., 1990—2000; pvt. practive law Balt., 1993—99; assoc. Weinstock, Friedman & Friedman, P.A., 2000—. Avocations: model trains, swimming. Health, Insurance, Legislative. Address: 7104 Plymouth Rd Baltimore MD 21208-6033 E-mail: jz@weinstocklegal.com.

ZIEGLER, JOHN AUGUSTUS, JR., lawyer; b. Grosse Pointe, Mich., Feb. 9, 1934; s. John Augustus and Monnabell M. Ziegler; m. G. Kay Brubeck; children: John Augustus III, Laura, Lisa, Adeline. AB, U. Mich., JD, 1957. Bar: Mich. 1957. Since practiced in, Detroit; assoc. Dickinson, Wright, McKean & Cudlip, 1957-65, ptnr., 1965-68, Parsons, Tennent, Hammond, Hardig & Ziegelman, 1969-70, Ziegler, Dykhouse & Wise, 1970-77; pres., CEO Nat. Hockey League, 1977-92, chmn. bd. govs., 1976-78; of counsel Dickinson, Wright, PLLC, Bloomfield Hills, 1992—99. Office: 375 Park Ave Ste 2004 New York NY 10152-2099

ZIEGLER, R. W., JR., lawyer, consultant; b. Pitts. children: Caroline, Gretchen, Jeremy, Benjamin, Phoebe, Polly. Student, Carnegie Tech., U. Pitts.; JD, Duquesne U., 1972. Bar: Pa. 1972, Calif. 1981, U.S. Ct. Appeals (3d cir.) 1977, U.S. Dist. Ct. (we. dist.) Pa. 1972, U.S. Supreme Ct. 1977, U.S. Tax Ct. 1978, Calif. 1982, U.S. Dist. Ct. (no. dist.) Calif. 1982, U.S. Ct. Appeals (9th cir.) 1982. Ptnr. Ziegler & Ombres, Pitts., 1973-79; pres. Ziegler Ross Inc., San Francisco, 1979—. Lectr. for Bar Assns. Author: Law Practice Management; editor: Law Office Guide in Computing. Mem. ABA, Am. Mgmt. Assn., Pa. State Bar Assn., Calif. State Bar Assn., Assn. of Legal Admin., Young Presidents' Org., Am. Assn. of Law Librarians., San Francisco Bar Assn. Office: 580 Market St Ste 500 San Francisco CA 94104-5413

ZIEGLER, WILLIAM ALEXANDER, lawyer; b. N.Y.C., July 15, 1924; s. William Alexander and Sally (Cootes) Z.; m. Glenn Crawley, Feb. 10, 1950; children: Richard S., Daryl A. Henning, Susan G. Barrows, W. Thomas. AB, Harvard U., 1944, JD, 1949. Bar: N.Y. 1949, U.S. Tax Ct. 1950, U.S. Dist. Ct. (so. dist.) N.Y. 1949, U.S. Dist. Ct. (ea. dist.) N.Y. 1957, U.S. Dist. Ct. (no. dist.) Ohio 1973, U.S. Dist. Ct. (ea. dist.) Mich. 1983, U.S. Ct. Apppeals (1st cir.) 1963, U.S. Ct. Appeals (2d cir.) 1957, U.S. Ct. Appeals (3d cir.) 1986, U.S. Ct. Appeals (4th cir.) 1979, U.S. Ct. Appeals (5th cir.) 1987, U.S. Ct. Appeals (6th cir.) 1984, U.S. Ct. Appeals (7th cir.) 1992, U.S. Ct. Appeals (8th cir.) 1981, U.S. Ct. Appeals (9th cir.) 1973, U.S. Ct. Appeals (10th and 11th cirs.) 1983, U.S. Ct. Appeals (D.C. cir.) 1972, U.S. Supreme Ct. 1972. Assoc. Sullivan & Cromwell, N.Y.C., 1949-56, ptnr., 1957-89. Bd. dirs. Std. Comml. Corp. Bd. dirs. Wilton (Conn.) Land Conservation Trust. Mem. Assn. Bar City N.Y., Riverside Country Club (Mont.), Harvard Club of N.Y.C., Harvard Club of Fairfield Country (bd. dirs.), Harvard Club Mont. Federal civil litigation, Corporate, general, Labor (including EEOC, Fair Labor Standards Act, labor-management relations, NLRB, OSHA).

ZIERDT, ALYSON KATHLEEN, lawyer; b. Milw., Feb. 10, 1947; d. Edward Paul and Alyce Ann (Burt) Dietzmann; m. William Henry Zierdt III, July 12, 1991. Student, St. Norbert Coll., West DePere, Wis., 1964-66; BA, U. Wis., Milw., 1969; JD, Marquette U., 1981. Bar: Wis. 1981, U.S. Dist. Ct. (we. and ea. dist.) Wis. 1981, U.S. Ct. Appeals (7th cir.) 1986. Asst. buyer/sales mgr. Boston Store divsn. Federated Dept. Stores, Milw., 1969-71, buyer, dept. mgr., 1971-78; law clk. Warshafsky, Rotter, Tarnoff, Gesler, Reinhardt & Bloch, S.C., Milw., 1979-81, assoc., 1981-86, Mulcahy & Wherry, S.C., Milw., 1986-89, atty./shareholder, 1989-91, Davis & Kuelthau, S.C., Milw., 1991-94, Reff Baivier Bermingham Zierdt & Lim, S.C., Oshkosh, Wis., 1994-2000, Davis & Kuelthau S.C., Oshkosh, Wis., 2000—. Mem. dist. III com. Office of Lawyer Regulation, Oshkosh, Fox Valley, 1997—, com. chmn., 2003-. Co-author: Wisconsin Trial Practice, 1999, The Law of Damages in Wisconsin, 1988, 2d edit., 1996. Vol. mediator Winnebago Conflict Resolution Ctr., Oshkosh, 1995—; vols. Irish Fest, Milw., 1990—; bd. dirs., trustee Paine Art Ctr. and Gardens, Oshkosh, 1996—, pres. 2001-02; pres. TEMPO, Milw., 1987-88, bd. dirs. TEMPO Fox Valley, 1995-98, pres. 1995-97; pres. Women's Fund of Oshkosh Area Cmty. Found., 1998-2000, bd. dirs. 1998—. Thomas More scholar Marquette U., 1980. Mem. State Bar Wis. (editl. bd. Wis. Lawyer 1988-95, 96-02, bd. dirs. alternative dispute resolution sect., 1996-98), Assn. for Women Lawyers (bd. dirs. 1984-89, pres. 1987-88), Wisc. Assn. Mediators, Wisc. Sch. Attys. Assn., Milw. Bar Assn. (bd. dirs. 1987-88, sec. 1988-91), Oshkosh C. of C. (bd. dirs. 1997—, pres. 1999-2000), Fond du Lac Yacht Club. Alternative dispute resolution, General civil litigation, Labor (including EEOC, Fair Labor Standards Act, labor-management relations, NLRB, OSHA). Office: Davis & Kuelthau PO Box 1278 219 Washington Ave Oshkosh WI 54903-1278 E-mail: azierdt@dkattorneys.com.

ZIERING, WILLIAM MARK, lawyer; b. New Britain, Conn., Feb. 4, 1931; s. Jacob Max and Esther (Freedman) Z.; m. Harriet Koskoff, Aug. 20, 1958 (div. Sept. 1993); 1 son, Benjamin. BA, Yale U., 1952; JD, Harvard U., 1955. Bar: Conn. 1955, Calif. 1962. Assoc. Koskoff & McMahon, Plainville, Conn., 1959-60; sr. trial atty. SEC, San Francisco, 1960-65; pvt. practice law San Francisco, 1965—; ptnr. Bremer & Ziering, 1972-77. Instr. Golden Gate U. Law Sch., San Francisco, 1968-75 Vice pres., bd. dirs. Calif. League Handicapped, 1972— . Served to comdr. USNR, 1955-58. Mem. ABA, Calif. Bar Assn., San Francisco Bar Assn. (past chmn. securities, corps. and banking), Navy League (dir.) Clubs: Commonwealth. Corporate, general, Securities. Home: 440 Davis Ct Apt 620 San Francisco CA 94111-2418

ZIESER, JOHN S. lawyer, publishing executive; m. Adele Zieser; children: John, Philip, Allison. BBA, MBA, U. Iowa; JD, Cornell U. With Sullivan & Cromwell; assoc. gen. counsel First Data Corp., 1993—99; group pres. First Data Mcht. Svcs. subs. First Data Corp.; v.p. corp. and employee svcs. group, gen. counsel Meredith Corp., Des Moines, 1999—, also sec. bd. dirs. Office: Meredith Corp 1716 Locust St Des Moines IA 50309-3023*

ZIFCHAK, WILLIAM C. lawyer; b. 1948; BA, Harvard U., 1970; JD, Columbia U., 1973. Bar: N.Y. 1974, U.S. Ct. Appeals (2d cir.) 1975, U.S. Ct. Appeals (3d cir., D.C. cir.) 1983, U.S. Dist. Ct. (so. dist.) N.Y. 1984. Ptnr., co-chair labor and employment law dept. Kaye, Scholer, Fierman, Hays & Handler, N.Y.C. Planning com. NYU Ann. Nat. Conf. Labor, 1991-97. Contbr. articles to profl. jours. Mem. ABA (sect. labor and employment law 1975—, subcom. antitrust, RICO and labor rels. law), Assn. Bar City of N.Y. (sec. com. labor and employment law 1984-87), N.Y. State Bar (comml.-fed. litig. sect. co-chair labor and employment law com. 1995-97). Alternative dispute resolution, General civil litigation, Labor (including EEOC, Fair Labor Standards Act, labor-management relations, NLRB, OSHA). Office: Kaye Scholer LLP 425 Park Ave New York NY 10022-3506

ZIKA, PATRICK JOHN, judge; b. Ottumwa, Iowa, Dec. 14, 1948; AB, U. Notre Dame, 1970; JD, Ind. U., 1973. Judge Alameda County Superior Ct., Oakland, Calif. Office: Alameda County Superior Ct 661 Washington St Oakland CA 94607-3922

ZILLY, THOMAS SAMUEL, federal judge; b. Detroit, Jan. 1, 1935; s. George Samuel and Bernice M. (McWhinney) Z.; divorced; children: John, Peter, Paul, Luke; m. Jane Greller Noland, Oct. 8, 1988; stepchildren: Allison Noland, Jennifer Noland. BA, U. Mich., 1956; LLD, Cornell U., 1962. Bar: Wash. 1962, U.S. Ct. Appeals (9th cir.) 1962, U.S. Supreme Ct. 1976. Ptnr. Lane, Powell, Moss & Miller, Seattle, 1962-88; dist. judge U.S. Dist. Ct. (we. dist.) Wash., Seattle, 1988—. Judge pro tem Seattle Mcpl. Ct., 1972-80; mem. adv. com. bankruptcy rules U.S. Judicial Conf. Contbr. articles to profl. jours. Mem. Cen. Area Sch. Council, Seattle, 1969-70; scoutmaster Thunderbird Dist. council Boy Scouts Am. Seattle, 1976-84; bd. dirs. East Madison YMCA. Served to lt. (j.g.) USN, 1956-59. Recipient Tuahku Dist. Service to Youth award Boy Scouts Am., 1983. Mem. ABA, Wash. State Bar Assn., Seattle-King County Bar Assn. (treas. 1979-80, trustee 1980-83, sec. 1983-84, 2d v.p. 1984-85, 1st v.p. 1985-86, pres. 1986-87). Office: US Dist Ct 410 US Courthouse 1010 5th Ave Seattle WA 98104-1189

ZIMAND, HARVEY FOLKS, lawyer; b. N.Y.C., Aug. 28, 1928; s. Savel and Gertrude (Folks) Z.; m. Ingeborg Rockosch, 1963 (div. 1980); children— Patricia Folks Carpenter, Stephanie Folks; m. Noel French, Apr. 30, 1983 BA, Colgate U., 1950; postgrad., Oxford U., Eng., 1950; MA, U. Chgo., 1951; postgrad., Columbia U., 1952-53; LL.B., Yale U., 1957. Bar: N.Y. 1957. Rapporteur Council for Fgn. Relations, N.Y.C., 1952-53; atty. Dept. Navy, Washington, 1956-70; ptnr. Kelley Drye & Warren, N.Y.C., 1970—. Dir. Toronto-Dominion Trust Co., N.Y.C., 1975-83. Bd. editors The Chase Jour. Bd. dirs. Virginia Day Nursery, N.Y.C., 1980-84. Served to cpl. U.S. Army, 1951-53 Fellow N.Y. Bar Found., Am. Coll. Trust and Estate Counsel; mem. ABA, N.Y. State Bar Assn., Assn. Bar City of N.Y., Estate Planning Coun., Univ. Club. Clubs: Yale (N.Y.C.); Randolph Mountain (N.H.). Republican. Episcopalian. Home: 120 E 81st St New York NY 10028-1428 Office: Kelley Drye & Warren LLP 101 Park Ave New York NY 10178-0002

ZIMMER, RICHARD ALAN, lawyer, former congressman; b. Newark, N.J., Aug. 16, 1944; s. William and Evelyn (Schlank Rader) Zimmer; m. Marfy Goodspeed Zimmer, Dec. 27, 1965; children: Carl William, Benjamin Goodspeed. BA, Yale U., 1966, LLB, 1969. Bar: N.Y. 1971, U.S. Dist. Cts. (so. and ea. dists.) N.Y. 1974, N.J. 1975, U.S. Dist. Ct. N.J. 1975, U.S. Supreme Ct. 1980. Assoc. Cravath, Swaine and Moore, N.Y.C., 1969—75; gen. atty. Johnson & Johnson, New Brunswick, NJ, 1976—91; mem. N.J. Gen. Assembly, 1982—87, chmn. state govt. com., 1986—87; mem. N.J. Senate, 1987—91, 102nd-104th Congresses from 12th N.J. dist., Washington, 1991—96; with Dechert Price & Rhoads, Princeton, NJ, 1997—2001, Gibson, Dunn & Crutcher, Washington, 2001—. Lectr. pub. and internat. affairs Woodrow Wilson Sch., Princeton U., 1997—2000. Chmn. Citizens for a Better N.J., 1997—2000, Study Commn. on the Implementation of the Death Penalty, 1997—98; trustee Freedom House Found., 1997—. Mem.: ABA. Republican. Home: Locktown-Flemington Rd Flemington NJ 08822-9541 Office: Gibson Dunn & Crutcher 1050 Connecticut Ave NW Washington DC 20036 E-mail: rzimmer@gibsondunn.com.*

ZIMMERMAN, AARON MARK, lawyer; b. Syracuse, N.Y., Jan. 28, 1953; s. Julius and Sara (Lavine) Z. B.S., Syracuse U., 1974, J.D., 1976. Bar: N.Y. 1977, Pa. 1977, D.C. 1978, S.C. 1978, Fla. 1978, U.S. Dist. Ct. S.C. 1978, U.S. Dist. Ct. (no. dist.) N.Y. Corp. atty., asst. sec. Daniel Internat. Corp., Greenville, S.C., 1977-79; ptnr. Abend, Driscoll & Zimmerman, 1979-81; Zimmerman Law Office, Syracuse, 1981— . Bd. dirs. Syracuse Friends Ametuer Boxing, 1982-92. Mem. Am. Arbitration Assn. (arbitrator), Workers Compensation Com. N.Y. State Bar (exec. com. 1984—), Workers Compensation Assn. of Cen. N.Y. (charter mem., dir., treas. 1980-95), N.Y. State Bar, S.C. State Bar, D.C. State Bar, Fla. State Bar, ABA. Lodge: Masons. State civil litigation, Personal injury (including property damage), Workers' compensation. Home: 602 Standish Dr Syracuse NY 13224-2018 Office: 117 S State St Syracuse NY 13202-1103

ZIMMERMAN, ALVIN LOUIS, lawyer; b. Houston, June 28, 1943; s. Sam J. and Dorothy (Sakowitz) Z.; m. Ellen Sue Davis, Aug. 22, 1965; children: Brian Weil, Gary Jay. BS, U. Houston, 1964, JD, 1967. Bar: Tex. 1967, U.S. Ct. Appeals (5th cir.) 1968, U.S. Supreme Ct. 1968; cert. in family law Tex. Bd. Legal Specialization. Asst. atty. gen., Austin, Tex., 1967-68; gen. counsel, v.p. Sterling Electronics Corp., Houston, 1969-80; judge State of Tex., Houston, 1980-84; chmn., dir. Zimmerman, Axelrad, Meyer & Wise, Houston, 1984—. Pres. Houston Law Rev. Found., 1990—. Pres. YMCA, 1985—86. Recipient Deans award U. Houston Law Ctr., 1988. Fellow Am. Acad. Matrimonial Lawyers, Internat. Acad. Mediators, Tex. Bar Found., Houston Bar Found. (vice-chmn. 1991-92); mem. ABA (faculty family law advocacy), Houston Bar Assn. (pres. family law sect. 1992). Alternative dispute resolution, State civil litigation, Family and matrimonial. Office: Zimmerman Axelrad Meyer & Wise PC 3040 Post Oak Blvd Ste 1300 Houston TX 77056-6584 E-mail: azimmerman@zommerlaw.com.

ZIMMERMAN, D(ONALD) PATRICK, lawyer; b. Albany, N.Y., Mar. 20, 1942; s. Bernard M. and Helen M. (Eshelman) Z. Student, Lawrenceville Sch., 1960, McDonogh Sch.; BA , Rollins Coll., 1964; JD, Dickinson Sch. Law, 1967. Bar: Pa. 1968, U.S. Supreme Ct. 1971. Atty. Legal Aid, 1968-69; pub. defender Lancaster County, Pa., 1969-72; pvt. practice Lancaster, 1974—. Instr. Ct. Common Pleas for Constables, 1976—; solicitor Lancaster County Dep. Sheriff Assn., 1977—, Lancaster County Constable Assn., 1975—; instr. sheriff's dept. Lancaster County for Dep. Sheriffs, 1978-85; of counsel to Dep. Sheriff Assn. Pa., 1979-81; spl. counsel Pa. State Constables Assn., 1981; chmn. Bd. Arbitrators Lancaster County, 1975-81; spl. counsel Legislative Com. to Constable Assn. Pa., 1982. Author: The Pennsylvania Landlord and Tenant Handbook, 1982, revised edit., 1993; editor (with J. Hatfield and A. Taylor) Pennsylvania Constable Handbook, 1998; contbr. articles to profl. jours. Mem. pastoral coun. St. Anthony's Cath. Ch., 1995-98. Recipient Ofcl. Commendation of Merit, Lancaster County Sheriff's Dept., 1979, Ofcl. Commendation of Merit, F.O.P. State Police Lodge 66, 1985, Disting. Svc. award, 1987, Cert. of Appreciation, Lancaster Crime Commn., 2003; named Extraordinary Min., 2002. Mem. ABA, ATLA, Pa. Bar Assn., Acad. Family Mediators, Lancaster County Bar Assn., W. Hensel Brown Inn of Ct., Lancaster County Constables Assn. (Outstanding Leadership award 1988, Disting. Svc. award as solicitor 1998, 25 Yrs. Dedicated Svc. award 2000). Family and matrimonial, Landlord-tenant, Personal injury (including property damage). Office: 214 E King St Lancaster PA 17602-2977

ZIMMERMAN, EDWIN MORTON, lawyer; b. N.Y.C., June 11, 1924; s. Benjamin and Tobie (Fuchs) Z.; m. Caroline Abbot, July 3, 1956; children: Sarah Abbot, Lyle Benjamin, Miriam Appleton. AB, Columbia U., 1944, LLB, 1949. Bar: N.Y. 1949, D.C. 1969, U.S. Supreme Ct 1969. With Hoover Commn. Reorgn. Exec. Br., 1948; law clk. to Hon. Stanley F. Reed U.S. Supreme Ct., 1950-51; law clk. to Judge Simon H. Rifkind U.S. Dist. Ct., 1949-50; pvt. practice law N.Y.C., 1951-59; prof. law Stanford U., 1959-69; with Justice Dept., 1965-69, asst. atty. gen. charge antitrust div., 1968-69; mem. Covington & Burling, Washington, 1969-94, sr. counsel, 1994—. Mem. coun. Adminstrv. Conf. U.S., 1975—78; mem. mfg. studies bd. Nat. Acad. Sci., 1983—87; adj. prof. George Washington Sch. Law, 1996—2001. Trustee Textile Mus., 1983—, pres. bd. trustees, 1987-96; mem. Folger Poetry Bd., 1990—; mem. adv. bd. Partisan Rev., 1996—. 1st lt. AUS, 1944-46. Mem. ABA, Assn. of Bar of City of N.Y., Am. Law Inst., Coun. Fgn. Rels., Phi Beta Kappa. Administrative and regulatory, Antitrust, Mergers and acquisitions. Home: 1820 Kalorama Sq NW Washington DC 20008-4022 Office: Covington & Burling PO Box 7566 1201 Pennsylvania Ave NW Washington DC 20004-2401 E-mail: ezimmerman@cov.com.

ZIMMERMAN, ELLIOT MICHAEL, lawyer; b. Bklyn., July 11, 1953; s. Leo and Regina (Zelman) Z.; m. Cynthia Sue Odeneal, June 23, 1985; children: Jacob Alan, Maxwell Isaac. BBA cum laude, Bernard M. Baruch Coll., 1976; JD, Cardozo Sch. Law, 1979. Bar: Fla. 1981, U.S. Dist. Ct. (so. dist.) Fla. 1981. Pvt. practice, Ft. Lauderdale, Fla., 1981—. Lectr. Continuing Legal Edn., 1986-2000. Author, editor: Mardindale-Hubbell Jour., 1991-92. Mem. Fla. Bar Assn. (chmn. spl. com. on entertainment law 1982-85, chmn. cert. com. EASL, 1994-1995, chmn. multimedia & internet com., 1998-1999, mem. exec. coun. entertainment, arts and sports law, 1998-2002, webmaster for entertainment, arts and sports law sec. 1998-2001, designee-qualified in entertainment arts and sports law designation plan 1985-88, 91-96). Avocations: musician, record producer, songwriter, computer programming. Federal civil litigation, State civil litigation, Entertainment. Home: 8900 S Lake Dasha Dr Plantation FL 33324-3014 Office: 5353 N Fed Hwy PH 405 Fort Lauderdale FL 33308

ZIMMERMAN, HERBERT ALAN, mediator; b. Detroit, July 23, 1934; s. Israel Jacob and Flora Zimmerman; m. Barbara Jean Greenbaum, Nov. 26, 1995; m. Jacqueline Audrey Waronoff, July 24, 1976 (dec. Mar. 4, 1994); children: Rodney, Stanley, Leslie. BA, U. Mich., 1956; cert., Oakland Mediation Ctr., 1997. Pres. Levine Waste Paper Co., Detroit, 1957—59, Mich. Paper Stock Co., Detroit, 1965—90; v.p. Paper Mills Trucking Co., Kalamazoo, 1985—94, Internat. Paper Recycling Co., Detroit, 1997—2003; mediator Oakland Mediation Ctr., Bloomfield Hills, Mich., 2002, 48th Dist. Ct., Bloomfield Hills, 2001—, Nat. Ctr. for Dispute Settlement, Southfield, Mich., 2001—, 6th Cir. Ct., Pontiac, Mich., 2001—, Washtenaw County Trial Ct., Ann Arbor, Mich., 2001—. Mem.: Assn. Conflict Resolution. Home and Office: 22522 Ivanhoe Ln Southfield MI 48034

ZIMMERMAN, JEAN, lawyer; b. Berkeley, Calif., Dec. 3, 1947; d. Donald Scheel Zimmerman and Phebe Jean (Reed) Doan; m. Gilson Berryman Gray III, Nov. 25, 1982; children: Charles Donald Buffum and Catherine Elisabeth Phebe (twins); stepchildren: Alison Travis, Laura Rebecca, Gilson Berryman. BSBA, U. Md., 1970; JD, Emory U., 1975. Bar: Ga. 1975, D.C. 1976, N.Y. 1980. Asst. mgr. investments FNMA, Washington, 1970-73; assoc. counsel Fuqua Industries Inc., Atlanta, 1976-79; assoc. Sage Gray Todd & Sims, N.Y.C., 1979-84; from assoc. counsel to sr. v.p., gen. counsel, sec. IBJ Whitehall Bank & Trust Co., N.Y.C., 1994-99; sr. v.p., gen. counsel, sec., bd. dirs. IBJ Schroder Bus. Credit Corp., N.Y.C., 1996-98, Innovest Capital Mgmt., Inc., N.Y.C., 1997-99; sr. v.p., gen. counsel, sec. Innovest Corp., N.Y.C., 1997-99; from gen. counsel, sec. to exec. v.p. ops. and legal ArrowSight, Inc. (formerly ParentWatch.com), N.Y.C., 2001—. From asst. sec. to sr. v.p., gen. counsel, sec., bd. dirs. IBJ Whitehall Bus. Credit Corp., IBJ Whitehall Capital Corp., IBJ Whitehall Securities, Inc., Delphi Asset Mgmt., Inc., Innovest Asset Mgmt., Inc., N.Y.C., 1997-99; from asst. sec. to v.p., gen. counsel, sec. IBJ Schroder Internat. Bank, Miami, Fla., 1989-98; sr. v.p., gen. counsel, sec. Execution Svcs., N.Y.C., 1991-93. Founder, officer ERA Ga., Atlanta, 1977-79; bd. dirs. Ct. Apptd. Spl. Advs., 1988-94. Named one of Outstanding Atlantans, 1978-79; recipient Disting. Alumni award Emory U. Sch. Law, 1999. Mem.: LWV, Am. Soc. Corp. Secs., Inc., Ga. Assn. Women Lawyers (bd. dirs. 1977—79), Assn. of Bar of City of N.Y., ABA, Assn. Emory Alumni (pres. 1999—, bd. govs. 2001—), DAR. Computer, Corporate, general.

ZIMMERMAN, MICHAEL DAVID, lawyer; b. Chgo., Oct. 21, 1943; s. Elizabeth Porter; m. Lynne Mariani (dec. 1994); children: Evangeline Albright, Alessandra Mariani, Morgan Elisabeth; m. Diane Hamilton, 1998. BS, U. Utah, 1966, JD, 1969, PhD (hon.) , 2001. Bar: Calif. 1971, Utah 1978. Law clk. to Chief Justice Warren Earl Burger U.S. Supreme Ct., Washington, 1969-70; assoc. O'Melveny & Myers, L.A., 1970-76; assoc. prof. law U. Utah, 1976-78, adj. prof. law, 1978-84, 89-93; of counsel Kruse, Landa, Zimmerman & Maycock, Salt Lake City, 1978-80; spl. counsel Gov. of Utah, Salt Lake City, 1978-80; ptnr. Watkiss & Campbell, Salt Lake City, 1980-84; assoc. justice Supreme Ct. Utah, Salt Lake City, 1984-93, 98-00, chief justice, 1994-98; atty., mediator, arbitrator, of counsel Snell & Wilmer, Salt Lake City, 2000—. Co-moderator Justice Soc. Program of Snowbird Inst. for Arts and Humanities, 1991, 92, 93, 94, 95, 97, 98; moderator, Tanner lecture panel dept. philosophy U. Utah, 1994; faculty Judging Sci. Program Duke U., 1992, 93; bd. dirs. Conf. of Chief Justices, 1995-98. Note editor: Utah Law Rev., 1968-69; contbr. numerous articles to legal publs. Mem. Project 2000, Coalition for Utah's Future, 1985—96; trustee Hubert and Eliza B. Michael Found., 1994—98; bd. dirs. Rowland-Hall St. Mark's Sch., 1997—; bd. assoc. Utah Mus. Natural History Found., 1995—; bd. dirs. Summit Inst. for Arts and Humanities, 1998—, chair, 1999—; bd. dirs. Hansen Planetarium , 1997—, Snowbird Inst. for Arts and Humanities, 1989—98, Deer valley Inst. for Arts and Humanities, 1996—98, Kanzeon Zen Ctr., 1999—, chair, 2000—; bd. dirs. Utah Coun. on Conflict Resoultion, 1999—, chair, 1999—; bd. dirs. Pvt. Adjudication Ctr.; mem. Duke U., 2000—; co-dir. Registry of Ind. Sci. and Tech. Advisors, Duke U., 2000—; chair Utah Jud. Coun. Task Force on Racial and Ethnic Fairness in the Jud. Sys., 1996. Named Utah State Bar Appellate Ct. Judge of Yr., 1998; recipient Excellence in Ethics Award, Ctr. for Study of Ethics, 1994, Disting. Svc. Award Utah State Bar, 1998, Individual Achievement Award Downtown Alliance, 1997, The Peter W. Billings, Sr. American Arbitration Assoc. Outstanding Dispute Resolution Svc. Award, 1997, participant Justice and Soc. Program of Aspen Inst. for Humanistic Studies, 1998, co-moderator, 1989. Fellow: Am. Bar Found.; mem.: Gov. Radiation Exposure Study Mgmt. Com., Ririe-Woodbury Dance Co. (exec. bd. 1982—84), U.S. Dept. of Energy Dose Assessment Adv. Group of the Off-Site Radiation Exposure Reconstruction Project (Utah citizen rep. 1980—84), Utah Legal Svc. Corp. (Bd. of Trustees 1985—87), U. Utah Master of Pub. Adminstrn. Program Practitioners' Adv. Com. (mem 1985—89), U.S. Vet. Adminstrn. Adv. Com. on Environ. Hazzards (e.g., agent orange, nuclear radiation 1985—89), Nat. Endowment for the Humanities Scholar in Residence at Utah Valley Cmty. Coll. (Orem, Utah 1990), Order of Coif, Am. Judicature Soc. (bd. dirs. 1995—2001), Am. Inns of Ct. VII, Utah Jud. Coun. (supreme ct. rep. 1986—91, chair 1994—98), Jud. Conf. U.S. (adv. com. civil rules 1985—91), Salt Lake County Bar Assn., Utah Bar Assn., Am. Law Inst., ABA (faculty mem. appellate judges' seminar 1993), Phi Kappa Phi. Office: Snell & Wilmer 15 West South Temple Ste 1200 Salt Lake City UT 84101*

ZIMMETT, MARK PAUL, lawyer, educator; b. Waukegan, Ill., July 4, 1950; s. Nelson H. Zimmett and Roslyn (Yastrow) Zimmett Grodzin; m. Joan Robin Urken, June 11, 1972; children: Nora Helene, Lili Eleanor. BA, Johns Hopkins U., 1972; JD, NYU, 1975. Bar: N.Y. 1976, U.S. Dist. Ct. (so. and ea. dists.) N.Y. 1976, U.S. Dist. Ct. (no. dist.) Calif. 1980, U.S. Ct. Appeals (2d cir.) 1980, U.S. Supreme Ct. 1981, U.S. Ct. Appeals (5th cir.) 1986, U.S. Ct. Appeals (9th cir.) 1988. Assoc. Shearman & Sterling, N.Y.C., 1975-83, ptnr., 1984-90; adj. assoc. prof. internat. law NYU, 1986-88; lectr. internat. comml. litig. and arbitration Practicing Law Inst., 2000—02. Author: Letters of Credit, New York Practice Guide Business and Commerical Law, 1990; contbr. articles to profl. jours. Mem. ABA (subcom. on letters of credit, com. on uniform comml. code sect. bus. law), N.Y. State Bar Assn., Assn. of the Bar of the City of N.Y., N.Y. County Lawyers Assn. (com. on bus. bankruptcy law), Citizens Union. Democrat. Jewish. Federal civil litigation, State civil litigation, Private international. Office: 126 E 56th St New York NY 10022-3613

ZIMRING, FRANKLIN E. law educator, lawyer; b. 1942; BA, Wayne State U., 1963; JD, U. Chgo., 1967. Bar: Calif. 1968. Asst. prof. U. Chgo., 1967-69, assoc. prof., 1969-72, prof., 1972-85; co-dir. Ctr. for Studies in Criminal Justice, 1973-75, dir., 1975-86; prof. law dir. Earl Warren Legal Inst., Univ. Calif., Berkeley, 1985—2002. Author: (with Newton) Firearms and Violence in American Life, 1969; The Changing Legal World of Adolescence, 1982; (with Hawkins): Deterrence, 1973, Capital Punishment and the American Agenda, 1986, The Scale of Imprisonment, 1991, The Search for Rational Drug Control, 1992, Incapacitation: Penal Confinement and the Restraint of Crime, 1995, Crime is Not the Problem, 1997, American Youth Violence, 1998, Punishment and Democracy, 2001, The Contradictions of American Capital Punishment, 2003. Mem. Am. Acad. Arts and Scis. Office: U Calif Earl Warren Legal Inst Boalt Hall Berkeley CA 94720 E-mail: zimring@law.berkeley.edu.

ZIMRING, STUART DAVID, lawyer; b. L.A., Dec. 12, 1946; s. Martin and Sylvia (Robinson) Z.; m. Eve Axelrad, Aug. 24, 1969 (div. 1981); m. Carol Grenert, May 24, 1981; children: Wendy Lynn Martin, Joseph Noah, Matthew Kevin Grenert, Dov Shimon. BA in U.S. History, UCLA, 1968, JD, 1971. Bar: Calif. 1972, U.S. Dist. Ct. (cen. dist.) Calif. 1972, U.S. Dist. Ct. (no. dist.) Calif. 1984; U.S. Supreme Ct., 1994; cert. specialist in estate planning, probate and trust law. Assoc. Law Offices Leonard Smith, Beverly Hills, Calif., 1971-73; ptnr. Law Offices Smith & Zimring, Beverly Hills, Calif., 1973-76; assoc. Levin & Ballin, North Hollywood, Calif., 1976-77; prin. Levin, Ballin, Plotkin, Zimring & Goffin, A.P.C., North Hollywood, 1978-91, Law Offices Stuart D. Zimring, North Hollywood, 1991—. Lectr. Los Angeles Valley Coll., Van Nuys, Calif., 1974-82. Author: Inter Vivos Trust Trustees Operating Manual, 1994, Durable Powers of Attorney for Health Care--A Practical Approach to an Intimate Document, 1995, Reverse Mortgages--An Update, 1996, Cultural and Religious Concerns in Drafting Advance Directives, 1996, Drafting for Multi-Cultural Diversity in Advance Directives, 2000; co-author: California Guide to Tax, Estate and Financial Planning for the Elderly, 2001. Bd. dirs. Bet Tzedek, Jewish Legal Svcs., L.A., 1975-88, chmn. legal svcs. com., 1978-82; bd. dirs. Brandeis-Bardin Inst., Simi Valley, Calif., 1976-80; bd. dirs. Bur. Jewish Edn., L.A., 1973-88, chmn. com. on parent and family edn., 1985-87; trustee Adat Ari El Synagogue, L.A., 1982-2000; bd. dirs. Orgn. for the Needs of the Elderly, 1994, 1st v.p. 1995-97, pres., 1997-2001. Recipient Circle award Juvenile Justice Connection Project, L.A., 1989, Wiley W. Manuel award for pro bono legal svcs., 1994, 95, 96, 97, 98; named Vol. Atty. of Yr., Bet Tzedek Legal Svcs., 2002. Fellow: Am. Coll. Trusts and Estates Counsel, Nat. Acad. Elder Law Attys. (pres. So. Calif. chpt. 1997, nat. bd. dirs. 1997—2001, sec. 2001—, chair nat. tech. com., pres.); mem.: San Fernando Bar Assn. (trustee 1979—86), State Bar Calif. Democrat. Avocations: music, collecting wine, travel, photography. Commercial, contracts (including sales of goods; commercial financing), Estate planning, Probate (including wills, trusts). Office: 12650 Riverside Dr North Hollywood CA 91607-3421 E-mail: zimzim@elderlawca.com.

ZINK, CHARLES TALBOTT, lawyer; b. Long Beach, Calif., Oct. 27, 1937; s. William Talbott and Nellie Grace (Hoskins) Z.; m. Deborah Sidney Burks, Nov. 26, 1983. AB, Princeton U., 1959; LLB, U. Va., 1965. Bar: Va. 1965, Ga. 1965. Mng. ptnr. Hansell & Post, Atlanta, 1965-89; ptnr. Jones, Day, Reavis & Poque, Atlanta, 1989-93, Long, Aldridge & Norman, Atlanta, 1993—2002, McKenna Long & Aldridge LLP, 2002—. Lectr. N.W. Ctr. for Profl. Edn., Washington, Atlanta and Tampa, Fla., 1983—; mem. faculty Atlanta Coll. Trial Advocacy, 1985, mem. exec. com., 1984—, pres., 1985, 86. Bd. dirs. Atlanta Humane Soc., 1983—. Lt. (j.g.) USN, 1959-62. Mem. Lawyers Club Atlanta, Atlanta Tax Forum, Capital City Club. Republican. Episcopalian. Office: 1 Peachtree Center Ave NE # 5300 Atlanta GA 30303-3002

ZINTER, STEVEN L. state supreme court justice; m. Sandra Zinter; 2 children. Doctorate, Univ. So. Dakota, 1975, BS, 1972. Judge Supreme Court, 2002—; pvt. practice, 1978—86; practice as asst. atty. gen. State So. Dakota; cir. judge State of So. Dakota, 1987—97; presiding judge Sixth Judicial Cir., 1997—2002. Mem. Harry S. Found.; trustee So. Dakota Retirement Sys.; elect. pres. So. Dakota Corrections Commn. Mem.: Am. Bar Assn. Office: Supreme Court S Dakota State Capital Bldg E Capitol Ave Pierre SD 57501-5070*

ZIPF, ROBERT EUGENE, JR., legal medicine consultant, pathologist; b. Sept. 18, 1940; s. Robert Eugene and Meriam (Murr) Z.; m. Nancy J. Gaskell, Sept. 11, 1965; children: Karin Lorene, Marjorie Kristine. BA, DePauw U., 1962; MD, Ohio State U., 1966. Diplomate Am. Bd. Pathology. Intern Miami Valley Hosp., Dayton, Ohio, 1966-67; dir. forensic pathology Duke U. Med. Ctr., Durham, N.C., 1967-72; dir. radioisotope pathology Riverside Meth. Hosp., Columbus, 1974-78; dep. coroner, forensic pathologist Franklin County, Columbus, 1974-78; regional forensic pathologist State of N.C., Rocky Mount, 1978—. Clin. asst. prof. East Caroline U. Med. Sch., Greenville, N.C., 1979—; adj. prof. Atlantic Christian Coll., Wilson, N.C., 1980-89, dir. Sch. Med. Tech., 1983-89; cons. in field. Contbr. articles to profl. jours. Trustee United Fund, 1979-84; mem. Mayor's Com. on Drug and Substance Abuse, 1987—. Maj. USAF, 1972-74. Fellow Am. Soc. Clin. Pathologist, Am. Acad. Forensic Scientists; mem. SMS (clin. adv. bd. 1988-91, lab. advisors bd. 1989-91), Assn. Clin. Scientists, Am. Coll. Nuclear Medicine, N.C. Med. Soc., N.Y. Acad. Scis. (pres. Lab. Users Group 1988-90, 92), Nash County Med. Soc. (pres. 1995). Home: 120 Newby Ct Rocky Mount NC 27804-3322 Office: Nash Gen Hosp Pathology Lab Rocky Mount NC 27804 E-mail: rezpath@email.com.

ZIPFINGER, FRANK PETER, lawyer; b. Sydney, Australia, Feb. 27, 1953; s. Franz Johann and Annie Thea (Van Kooij) Z.; m. Susan Elizabeth Gulliver, Jan. 5, 1979; children: Sarah Elizabeth, Jonathan Francis, Nicholas James. BA in Econs., Macquarie U., Sydney, 1974; LLB, Sydney U., 1977, LLM, 1986. Bar: Australia 1977, High Ct. Australia 1977, N.Y. 1981. Assoc. Stephen Jaques and Stephen, Sydney, 1977-80, Winthrop, Stimson, Putnam & Roberts, N.Y.C., 1980-81, Stephen Jaques Stone James, Sydney, 1982-83; ptnr. Mallesons Stephen Jaques, Sydney, 1983—. Author: Australian Stamp Duties Law, 1982, Stamp Duty Aspects of Trusts Settlements and Gifts in Australia, 1984, The Stamp Duty Book - NSW, 1994. Mem. ABA, Law Soc. New South Wales, Killara Golf Club, Australian Club. Avocations: philately, tennis, golf. Property, real (including real estate development, water), Securities, State and local taxation. Home: 1 Arthur St Killara Australia 2071 E-mail: frank.zipfinger@msj.com.au.

ZIPKIN, SHELDON LEE, lawyer, educator; b. Washington, June 10, 1951; s. Sol and Selma (Rumerman) Z.; m. Ellen Linda Reitman, July 1, 1973; children: Saul Moshe, Shana Chaya, Joel Mordechai, Abigail Deborah. Student, Hebrew U., Jerusalem, 1970-71; BA, U. Fla., 1973, MA, Cert. in Urban Studies, 1977; JD, Emory U., 1980. Bar: Ga. 1980, Fla. 1980, U.S. Dist. Ct. (so. dist.) Fla. 1983. Assoc. Gladstone Assocs., Miami, Fla., 1973-75; ptnr. Emory Assocs., Atlanta, 1979-80; dep. consumer adv. Metro Dade County, Miami, 1980-81; asst. pub. defender 11th Jud. Cir., Miami, 1981-83; ptnr. Roth & Zipkin, Miami, 1984-86; pvt. practice, Miami, 1986-87, 88-91; chief consumer litigation sect. Fla. Dept. Legal Affairs, Miami and Tallahassee, 1987-88; ptnr. Roth, Zipkin, Cove & Roth, Miami, 1991-95; pvt. practice law, 1995—. Adj. prof. law U. Miami, St. Thomas U., 1998—; pres., chmn. bd. Analytic Prognostication, Inc., Miami, 1988—. Pres., chmn. bd. dirs. Sta. WDNA-FM Pub. Radio, Miami, 1981-82; mem. consumer adv. coun. Fla. Hosp. Cost Containment Bd., Tallahassee, 1988-89. Fellow Soc. for Applied Anthropology; mem. ABA, ATLA, North Dade Bar Assn. (dir. 1997—), Dade County Bar Assn. (dir. 2000), Fla. Bar Assn. (consumer protection com. 1988—), Omicron Delta Kappa. Democrat. Jewish. Avocations: chess, sailing. General civil litigation, Criminal, General practice. Office: 2020 NE 163rd St North Miami Beach FL 33162-4927 E-mail: zipkin@aol.com.

ZIPP, JOEL FREDERICK, lawyer; b. Shaker Heights, Ohio, Feb. 12, 1948; s. Jack David and Eleanor Adele Zipp; m. Elizabeth Ann Frieden, Dec. 4, 1976; 1 child, Carlyn Leigh. BS, U. Wis., 1970, MS, 1972; JD, Case Western Res. U., 1975. Bar: Ohio 1975, D.C. 1976, U.S. Claims Ct., U.S. Ct. Appeals (D.C. cir.) 1976, U.S. Ct. Appeals (5th cir.) 1979, U.S. Ct. Appeals (11th cir.) 1983, U.S. Supreme Ct. 1983. Trial atty. Fed. Energy Regulation Com., Washington, 1975-79, asst. dir. office of enforcement, 1979; assoc. Morley & Caskin, Washington, 1979-80; ptnr. Morley, Caskin & Generelly, Washington, 1981-98; mng. ptnr. Cameron McKenna LLP, Washington, 1998—; gen. counsel, sec. Portland Natural Gas Transmission Sys., 1993-99. Notes editor: Energy Law Jour., 1990—98; contbr. articles to profl. jours. Bd. dirs. Westmoreland Children's Ctr., Washington, 1987—88, Found. Energy Law Jour., 1999—2001. Fellow Smithsonian, 1969. Mem.: ABA, Energy Bar Assn. (v.p. 1989—99, past com. chair ann. meeting 1992, 1993, bd. dirs. 1993—96, pres. 2000—01, bd. dirs. 2001—02, mem. nominations com. 2002—). Jewish. Avocations: skiing, running, bicycling. Administrative and regulatory, FERC practice, Utilities, public. Home: 9216 Burning Tree Rd Bethesda MD 20817-2251 Office: Cameron McKenna LLP 2175 K St NW Washington DC 20037-1831 E-mail: jzipp@cmcklaw.com.

ZIPP, RONALD DUANE, judge, priest, real estate broker; b. New Braunfels, Tex., Dec. 7, 1946; s. Nolan William and Irene Alyce (Stiba) Z.; children: Robert Andrew, Kristi Nicole; m. Saundra Zipp, Mar. 5, 1989. BBA, Tex. A&M U., 1968; JD, St. Mary U., San Antonio, 1971; MA, Oxford (Eng.) U., 1997. Bar: Tex., U.S. Dist. Ct. (so. dist.) Tex., U.S. Ct. Appeals (5th cir.) 1973, U.S. Supreme Ct. 1974; ordained to ministry Anglican Ch., 1998. Assoc. Kelley, Looney, Alexander & Hiester, Edinburg, Tex., 1971-73; ptnr. Pena, McDonald, Prestia & Zipp, Edinburg, Tex., 1973-81; pvt. practice New Braunfels, Tex., 1981-82, 89—; real estate broker. Judge Comal County (Tex.) Ct.-at-Law, New Braunfels, 1983—; adj. prof. San Antonio Coll.; real estate broker. Author local newspaper column; contbr. articles to profl. jours. Bd. dirs. New Braunfels Cmty. Svcs., 1992—, prse., 1981-83, 97-98, sec., 1994; bd. dirs. Child Welfare, vice chmn., 1981-82, chmn., 1982-83; dir. Drover-Comal County Fair Assn.; vol. H.O.S.T.S.; vice chmn. Folkfest, 1994, chmn., 1995—; pres. Cmty. Svc. Ctr., 1997; bd. dirs., trustee Sr. Citizens Ctr. and Found.; dir. Comal County Fair Assn.; mentor New Braunfels Ind. Sch. Dist.; clergyman, chancellor Anglican Diocese of S.W. Fellow Coll. of State Bar; mem. ABA, Greater New Braunfels C. of C. (legis. com., resources com., heritage com.), Tex. State Jr. Bar (criminal law com. 1975-76), Tex. Criminal Def. Lawyers' Assn. (bd. dirs. 1976-77, various coms.), Tex. Aggie Bar Assn. (charter), Comal County Bar Assn. (past pres.), Comal County A&M Club (pres., treas.), Hidalgo County Bar Assn. (treas. 1972-75), Opa and Kleine Opa of Wurstfest Assn. (chmn. Folkfest), Hidalgo County A&M Club (pres.), Elks, Kiwanis, Lions (sec. 1996, pres. 1997), Phi Delta Phi. Lutheran/Anglican. Office: 384 Landa St New Braunfels TX 78130-5401 Fax: (830) 629-5754. E-mail: rzipp@nbtx.com.

ZIRINSKY, BRUCE R. lawyer; b. N.Y.C., Sept. 6, 1947; BS, Cornell U., 1969; JD, NYU, 1972. Bar: N.Y. 1973, U.S. Dist. Ct. (so. and ea. dists.) N.Y. 1973, U.S. Ct. Appeals (2d cir.) 1974, U.S. Ct. Appeals (1st cir.) 1980, U.S. Ct. Appeals (11th cir.) 1981, U.S. Ct. Appeals (5th cir.) 1986, U.S. Supreme Ct. 1991, U.S. Ct. Appeals (6th cir.), 1995. Mem. Weil, Gotshal & Manges, N.Y.C., 1999; ptnr. Cadwalader, Wickersham & Taft, N.Y.C. Mem. ABA (sect. corp., banking and bus. law), N.Y. State Bar Assn. (mem. com. bankruptcy laws banking and bus. law sects. 1979—). Office: Cadwalader Wickersham & Taft 100 Maiden Ln New York NY 10038-4818 E-mail: bruce.zirinsky@cwt.com.

ZISMAN, BARRY STUART, lawyer; b. N.Y.C., Sept. 18, 1937; s. Harry and Florence Rita (Tucker) Z.; m. Maureen Frances Brumond, Dec. 30, 1979; children: Michael Glenn, Marlene Ann. AB, Columbia U., 1958, JD, 1961. Bar: D.C. 1962, N.Y. 1965, Tex. 1986, U.S. Dist. Ct. (ea. and so. dists.) N.Y. 1967, U.S. Ct. Appeals (D.C. cir.) 1967, U.S. Dist. Ct. (no. and so. dists.) Tex. 1986, U.S. Ct. Appeals (5th cir.) 1988, U.S. Supreme Ct. 1967. With U.S. Govt., 1962-66; pvt. practice Syosset, N.Y., 1966-71; sr. counsel CBS Inc., N.Y.C., 1972-75; asst. gen. counsel, asst. sec. M. Lowenstein & Sons, N.Y.C., 1975-79; gen. counsel Grumman Allied Indsl. Inc., Bethpage, N.Y., 1979-83; asst. gen. counsel Grumman Corp., Bethpage, 1982-83; sr. atty. FDIC, Dallas, 1984-87; of counsel Arter & Hadden, Dallas, 1987-88, ptnr., 1988, Winstead, McGuire, Sechrest & Minick, Dallas, 1988-90, Arter & Hadden, Dallas and Washington, 1990-91, Rubinstein & Perry, Dallas, 1991-93, The Zisman Law Firm, P.C., Dallas, 1993—. Advisor in field; vice-chmn. Assn. of Bank and Thrift Receivership Coun. Editor and author: Banks and Thrifts: Government Enforcement and Receivership Law, 1991. With U.S. Army, 1961-62. Banking, General civil litigation, Corporate, general. Home: 905 Murl Dr Irving TX 75062-4441 Office: 1412 Main St Fl 23 Dallas TX 75202 E-mail: zislaw@aol.com.

ZISSU, MICHAEL JEROME, lawyer; b. N.Y.C., June 3, 1934; s. Leonard and Ruth Edith (Katz) Z.; m. Maria Theresia Duffner, June 27, 1960 (div. Feb. 1971); children: Audrey Lynn Zissu Hensley, Erik March; m. Patricia Joan Murphy, Feb. 20, 1971 (div. 1977); 1 child, Jacob Royal. AB, Dartmouth Coll., 1956; postgrad., U. Chgo., 1956-58; LLB, New Eng. Law Sch., 1962. Bar: Mass. Supreme Jud. Ct. 1963, N.Y. (app. divsn. 1st. dept.) 1964. Assoc. Zissu, Marcus & Stein, N.Y.C., 1962-68, Regan Goldfarb Powell & Quinn, N.Y.C., 1968-71; ptnr. Zissu & Harris, N.Y.C., 1972-82, Murphy & Zissu, N.Y.C., 1985-96. With U.S. Army, 1958-60. Mem. Assn. of the Bar of the City of N.Y., Copyright Soc. USA. Jewish. General civil litigation, Entertainment, Trademark and copyright. Home: 12800 Vonn Rd Apt 7603 Largo FL 33774-2590 Office: 375 Riverside Dr Apt 9E New York NY 10025-2120

ZITANI, GREGORY ANTHONY, lawyer; b. Aversa, Italy, July 1, 1957; d. Genius Ares and Rosemarie Catherine (Spina) Z.; m. Brenda Louise Oliver, June 12, 1990; 1 child, Michael. BS, U. Calif., Berkeley, 1979; JD magna cum laude, California Western U., 1983. Bar: Calif. 1984, Fla. 1999, U.S. Dist. Ct. (so. dist.) Calif. 1984, U.S. Dist. Ct. (no. dist.) Calif. 1991, U.S. Dist. Ct. (mid. dist.) Fla. 2000, U.S. Ct. Appeals for the Armed Forces 1991. Pvt. practice, Imperial Beach, Calif., 1987-90, San Diego, 1993—95; litigation atty. Quintrall & Assocs., San Diego, 1990-92, Haas & Hout, San Diego, 1992-93, Agnes, Lewis & Zitani, Chartered, Sarasota, Fla., 1996—2001. Lt. USN, 1983-87. Mem. ABA, Sarasota County Bar Assn. Avocations: athletics, coins. Health, Insurance, Probate (including wills, trusts). Office: Agnes Lewis Zitani Chartered 4046 Sawyer Rd Ste D Sarasota FL 34233

ZLAKET, THOMAS ANDREW, attorney, former state supreme court chief justice; b. May 30, 1941; AB in Polit. Sci., U. Notre Dame, 1962; LLB, U. Ariz., 1965; LLM, U. Va., 2001. Bar: Ariz. 1965, U.S. Dist. Ct. Ariz. 1967, U.S. Ct. Appeals (9th cir.) 1969, Calif. 1976. Atty. Lesher Scruggs Rucker Kimble & Lindamood, Tucson, 1965-68, Maud & Zlaket, 1968-70, Estes Browning Maud and Zlaket, 1970-73, Slutes Estes Zlaket Sakrison & Wasley, 1973-82, Zlaket & Zlaket, 1982-92; judge pro tempore Pima County (Ariz.) Superior Ct., 1983—; justice Ariz. Supreme Ct., 1992—2002, vice chief justice, 1996—97, chief justice, 1997—2002. Fellow Am. Coll. Trial Lawyers, Am. Bar Found., Ariz. Bar Found.; mem. ABA, Pima County Bar Assn., Am. Bd. Trial Advocates, Ariz. Coll. Trial Advocacy, U. Ariz. Law Coll. Assn., Ariz. Law Rev. Assn. Office: 310 S Williams Blvd Ste 170 Tucson AZ 85711 E-mail: tazlaket@qwest.net.

ZLOCH, WILLIAM J. federal judge; b. 1944; Judge U.S. Dist. Ct. (so. dist.) Fla., Ft. Lauderdale, 1985—. Office: US Dist Ct 299 E Broward Blvd Fort Lauderdale FL 33301-1944

ZLOTNICK, NORMAN LEE, lawyer; b. Bklyn., Nov. 2, 1947; s. Harry S. and Frances Zlotnick; m. JoAnn L. Zlotnick, Nov. 26, 1976; m. Sharon Harris, Mar. 12, 1990. BA in History, CCNY, 1969; JD, Rutgers U., 1972. Bar: N.J. 1972, U.S. Dist. Ct. N.J. 1972, U.S. Ct. Appeals (3d cir.) 1974, U.S. Supreme Ct. 1976, N.Y. 1990. Assoc. Perskie & Callinan, 1972-77; ptnr. Perskie, Bloom & Zlotnick, P.A., 1977-79, Bloom & Zlotnick, 1979-82, Marione, Biel, Zlotnick & Feinberg, P.A., Atlantic City, 1982—. Contbr. Rutgers-Camden Law Jour. Mem. ABA, ATLA, N.J. Bar Assn., N.Y. Bar Assn., Cape May County Bar Assn., Atlantic County Bar Assn. (N.J. Supreme Ct. spl. ethics master, Atlantic County civil case arbitrator, cert. civil trial atty.). General civil litigation, Commercial, contracts (including sales of goods; commercial financing), Property, real (including real estate development, water). Office: 3201 Atlantic Ave Atlantic City NJ 08401-6216 Address: 20 Devon Dr Egg Harbor Township NJ 08234-7569 E-mail: normanzlotnick@mbzflaw.com.

ZOBEL, RYA WEICKERT, federal judge; b. Germany, Dec. 18, 1931; AB, Radcliffe Coll., 1953; LLB, Harvard U., 1956. Bar: Mass. 1956, U.S. Dist. Ct. Mass., 1956, U.S. Ct. Appeals (1st cir.) 1967. Assoc. Hill & Barlow, Boston, 1967-73, Goodwin, Procter & Hoar, Boston, 1973-76, ptnr., 1976-79; judge U.S. Dist. Ct. Mass., Boston, 1979—; dir. Fed. Jud. Ctr., Washington, 1995-99. Mem. ABA, Boston Bar Assn., Am. Bar Found., Mass. Bar Assn., Am. Law Inst. Office: US District Ct 1 Courthouse Way Boston MA 02210-3002

ZOELLER, DONALD J. lawyer; b. Queens Village, N.Y., Mar. 18, 1930; s. Henry Adolph and Marion Elizabeth (Brodie) Z.; m. Susan Josephine Campisi, Sept. 3, 1955; children— Paul Joseph, Jean Marie, Diane Marie AB, Fordham Coll., 1951; LL.B., Fordham Sch. Law, N.Y.C., 1958. Bar: N.Y. 1959, D.C. 1967. Law clk. to judge U.S. Dist. Ct. (so. dist.) N.Y., N.Y.C., 1958-59; assoc. Mudge Rose Guthrie Alexander & Ferdon, N.Y.C., 1959-68, ptnr., 1968-95, exec. ptnr., 1991-95, chmn. exec. com., 1995; counsel Carter, Ledyard & Milburn, N.Y.C., 1995-96, ptnr., 1997-98, of counsel, 1999—. Adj. prof. law Fordham U. Law Sch., 1989—; lectr. in field. Contbr. articles to legal publs. 1st lt. U.S. Army, 1951-53, Korea. Mem. ABA, N.Y. State Bar Assn., Bar Assn. City of N.Y., Inst. Jud. Adminstrn., Am. Judicature Soc., Fed. Bar Coun. Republican. Roman Catholic. Avocations: skiing, swimming, tennis, reading. Antitrust, Federal civil litigation, Construction. Office: Carter Ledyard & Milburn 2 Wall St Fl 13 New York NY 10005-2072 Business E-Mail: dzoeller@optonline.net.

ZOHN, MARTIN STEVEN, lawyer; b. Denver, Oct. 22, 1947; s. William and Alice Zohn; m. Carol Falender, June 6, 1980; children: David Joseph, Daniel Robert. BA, Ind. U., 1969; JD, Harvard U., 1972. Bar: Calif. 1972, Ind. 1973, U.S. Ct. Claims 1980, U.S. Supreme Ct. 1980, U.S. Ct. Appeals (9th cir.) 1981. Assoc. Cadick, Burns, Duck & Neighbors, Indpls., 1972-77, ptnr., 1977-80, Pacht, Ross, Warne, Bernhard & Sears, Inc., L.A., 1980-86, Shea & Gould, L.A., 1986-89, Proskauer Rose LLP, L.A., 1989—. Pres. Indpls. Settlements, Inc., 1977-79. Bd. dirs. Pub. Counsel, 2001—. Mem. Fin. Lawyers Conf., L.A. County Bar Assn. (exec. com. prejudgment remedies sect. 1985-92, exec. com. bankruptcy sect. 2001-02), Beverly Hills Bar Assn. (exec. com. bus. law sect. 1985-92, exec. com. bankruptcy sect. 2003—), Phi Beta Kappa. Bankruptcy, General civil litigation, Corporate, general. E-mail: mzohn@proskauer.com.

ZOLA, MICHAEL S. lawyer; b. Madison, Wis., Dec. 15, 1942; s. Emanuel and Harriet (Sher) Zola; 1 child, Emanuel David. BS cum laude, U. Wis., 1964; LLB, Columbia U., 1967. Bar: D.C. 1968, Wis. 1968, U.S. Dist. Ct. (we. dist.) Wis. 1968, Calif. 1969, U.S. Dist. Ct. (no. dist.) Calif. 1969, U. S. Ct. Appeals (9th cir.) 1969, Hawaii 1981, U.S. Dist. Ct. Hawaii 1981. Law clk. to judge U.S. Dist. Ct. (we. dist.) Wis., 1967—68; mng. atty. San Francisco Neighborhood Legal Assistance Found., 1968—70; sole practice Calistoga, Calif., 1970—73; directing atty. Mendocino Legal Svcs., Ukiah, Calif., 1973—76; state chief of legal svcs. State of Calif., Sacramento, 1976—78, dep. state pub. defender, 1978—79; sole practice Kailua-Kona, Hawaii, 1981—. Mem. adv. bd. Kona Salvation Army, 1983—93; chmn. Mendocino County Dem. Ctrl. Com., Ukiah, 1975—76; pres. Kona Beth Shalom Congregation, 1991—94. Reginald Heber Smith Poverty Law fellow, 1968—70. Mem.: Legal Aid Soc. Hawaii (bd. dirs. 1985—86), Nat. Assn. Criminal Def. Lawyers, Hawaii Assn. Criminal Def. Lawyers (bd. dirs. 1989—), Rotary Club Kona (pres. 1998—99). Criminal, Family and matrimonial, Personal injury (including property damage). Office: 75-5744 Alii Dr Ste 223 Kailua Kona HI 96740-1740 E-mail: zolalaw@aol.com.

ZONANA, VICTOR, lawyer, educator; b. Zagazig, Eqypt, Aug. 28, 1940; s. Isaac A. and Fortunee (Cohen Beyda) Z.; m. Mary Linda Haynie, Aug. 22, 1964; children: David A., Nancy B. Zonana Dickinson. BS in Econs., Hofstra U., 1961; LLB, NYU, 1964, LLM, 1966. Bar: N.Y. 1965. Assoc. Kaye, Scholer, Fierman, Hays & Handler, N.Y.C., 1966-69; asst. prof. NYU, 1969-80, adj. prof., 1981—, Charles S. Lyon vis. prof., 1994; dep. tax legis. counsel U.S. Dept. Treasury, 1975-76; cons. to asst. commr. IRS, 1975, office of chief counsel, 1994; counsel, ptnr. Kaye, Scholer, Fierman, Hays & Handler, N.Y.C., 1980-87, Arnold & Porter, N.Y.C., 1988—2001; prof. Bklyn. Law Sch., 1996—2002; prin. KPMG LLP, London, 2002—. Mem., chmn. adv. bd. NYU Tax Inst. Fellow Am. Coll. Tax Counsel; mem. ABA, N.Y. State Bar Assn. (co-chmn. com. on fgn. activities of U.S. taxpayers, chmn. com. on depreciation and investment credit, co-chmn. com. tax acctg. matters, com. tax policy). Private international, Corporate taxation. Office: KPMG LLP 8 Salisbury Sq London EC4Y 8BB England

ZOOGMAN, NICHOLAS JAY, lawyer; b. N.Y.C., Apr. 2, 1947; s. Morris William and Hannah (Stern) Z.; m. Carla Ganz, June 7, 1970; children: Sarah Elizabeth, Peter William. BA, NYU, l967; MA, Harvard U., l969, JD, l973. Bar: N.Y. 1974, U.S. Dist. Ct. (so. and ea. dists.) N.Y. 1974, U.S. Ct. Appeals (2d cir.) 1975, U.S. Supreme Ct. 1979, U.S. Dist. Ct. (ea. dist.) Mich. 1988, U.S. Ct. Appeals (D.C. cir.) 1990, U.S. Ct. Appeals (6th cir.) 1993, U.S. Ct. Appeals (5th cir.) 1997. Assoc. Donovan Leisure Newton & Irvine, N.Y.C., 1973-75; ptnr. Anderson Kill & Olick, N.Y.C., 1976-2000; counsel Dickstein Shapiro Morin & Oshinsky, N.Y.C., 2000—. Mem. ABA, N.Y. State Bar Assn., Assn. Bar City N.Y., Phi Beta Kappa, Pi Sigma Alpha. General civil litigation, Insurance. Office: Dickstein Shapiro Morin & Oshinsky 1177 Avenue of Americas New York NY 10036-2714 E-mail: zoogmann@dsmo.com.

ZORIE, STEPHANIE MARIE, lawyer; b. Walla Walla, Wash., Mar. 18, 1951; d. Albert Robert and L. Ruth (Land) Z.; m. Francis Benedict Buda, Apr. 18, 1981 (div. 1985). BA, U. Fla., 1974, JD, 1978. Bar: N.Mex. 1991, Fla. 1978, U.S. Dist. Ct. (so. and mid. dists.) Fla. 1979, U.S. Ct. Appeals (5th cir.) 1979, U.S. Tax Ct. 1980, U.S. Ct. Customs and Patent Appeals 1980, U.S. Customs Ct. 1980, U.S. Ct. Mil. Appeals 1980, U.S. Ct. Claims 1981, U.S. Ct. Internat. Trade 1981, U.S. Ct. Appeals (11th cir.) 1981, U.S. Ct. Appeals (fed. cir.) 1982, U.S. Supreme Ct. 1988; cert. civil ct. mediator Fla. Supreme Ct.; cert. family mediator, N.Mex. Assoc. Richard Hardwich, Coral Gables, Fla., 1978-79, Brown, Terrell & Hogan P.A., Jacksonville, Fla., 1979-80, Dorsey, Arnold & Nichols, Jacksonville, Fla., 1980-81; sole practice Jacksonville, Fla., 1981-84; ptnr. Blakeley & Zorie P.A., Orlando, Fla., 1985-86; sole practice Orlando, Fla., 1986—, Santa Fe. Owner Coyote Cody Co., 1991. Recipient Rep. Claude Pepper award, 1978. Mem. John Marshall Bar Assn., Spanish-Am. Law Students Assn., Phi Alpha Delta (local sec.-treas. 1978-79). Avocations: water sports, needlework, cooking. State civil litigation, Family and matrimonial, Personal injury (including property damage). Office: PO Box 2898 Santa Fe NM 87504-2898 also: PO Box 372118 Melbourne FL 32937-0118

ZORNOW, DAVID M. lawyer; b. N.Y.C., Mar. 31, 1955; s. Jack and Marion (Gilden) Z.; m. Martha Malkin, July 21, 1985; children: Samuel Morris, Hannah Jane, Ethan Lewis. AB summa cum laude, Harvard U., 1976; JD, Yale U., 1980. Bar: N.Y. 1981, D.C. 1988, U.S. Ct. Appeals (3d cir.) 1982, U.S. Dist. Ct. (so. dist.) N.Y. 1983, U.S. Ct. Appeals (2d cir.) 1984, U.S. Dist. Ct. D.C. 1989, U.S. Ct. Appeals (D.C. cir.) 1989, U.S. Dist. Ct. Ariz. 1990, U.S. Dist. Ct. (ea. dist.) N.Y. 1993. Law clerk to Judge Herbert J. Stern U.S. Dist. Ct. N.J., Newark, 1980-82; assoc. Kramer Levin Kamin Nessen & Frankel, N.Y.C., 1982-83; asst. U.S. atty. so. dist. N.Y. U.S. Atty.'s Office, N.Y.C., 1983-87; assoc. counsel Office Ind. Counsel-Iran/Contra Investigation, Washington, 1987-89; ptnr. Skadden Arps Slate Meagher & Flom LLP, N.Y.C., 1989—. Chmn. N.Y.C. Civilian Complaint Rev. Bd., 1994-96; vis. faculty Trial Advocacy Workshop Harvard Law Sch., Cambridge, Mass., 1988. Mem. ABA (com. on white collar crime), Fed. Bar Coun., Assn. of Bar of City of N.Y., N.Y. Coun. Def. Lawyers. Criminal. Office: Skadden Arps Slate Meagher & Flom LLP 4 Times Sq Fl 39 New York NY 10036-6595 E-mail: dzornow@skadden.com.

ZOUB, BURTON IRVING, lawyer; b. Chgo., Feb. 1, 1926; s. Morris B. and Taubie M. (Gertz) Z.; m. Barbara H. Zoub, Nov. 14, 1954 (div. 1971); children: Jeffrey R., Debra J., Andrew S.; m. Eleanor Weiss, Apr. 19, 1986. BS, U. Ill., 1948; JD, Northwestern U., 1952. Bar: Ill. 1952. Lawyer Ruttenberg & Ruttenberg, Chgo., 1952-54; pvt. practice Chgo., 1954—. Pres. Acad. of Family Mediators, Lexington, Ma., 1987-88; founding pres. Meditation Coun. of Ill., 1982. Author: Mediating Child Custody Disputes, 1992. With U.S. Army, 1944-46. Mem. Chgo. Bar Assn. (chmn. matrimonial law com. 1974-75). Avocations: tennis, swimming, gardening, travelogues. Alternative dispute resolution, Family and matrimonial. Office: 155 N Michigan Ave Chicago IL 60601-7511

ZSCHAU, JULIUS JAMES, lawyer; b. Peoria, Ill., Apr. 1, 1940; s. Raymond Johann Ernst and Rosamond Lillian (Malicoat) Z.; m. Leila Joan Krueger, Aug. 7, 1971; children: Kristen Elisabeth, Kimberly Erna, Kira Jamie, Karla Johanna. BS, U. Ill., Champaign, 1964, JD, 1966; LLM, John Marshall Law Sch., 1978. Bar: Ill. 1966, Fla. 1975. Atty. Ill. Central Gulf R.R. Co., Chgo., 1966-68; assoc. Coin & Sheerin, Chgo., 1968-70, Snyder, Clarke et al, Waukegan, Ill., 1970-72; counsel Ill. Ctr. Corp., Chgo., 1972-74; v.p., gen. counsel, sec. Am. Agronomics Corp., Tampa, Fla., 1974-76; pres. Sorota & Zschau, Clearwater, Fla., 1976-90; shareholder Baynard, Harrell, Ostow & Ulrich PA, 1990-94, Johnson, Blakely, Pope, Bokor, Ruppel and Burns, Clearwater, 1994—2002, Pennington Moore Wilkinson Bell & Dunbar PA, 2002—. Bd. dirs. Attys. Title Ins. Fund, Inc. (chmn. bd. dirs. 1994-95); chmn. com. on land trusts, dir. real property divsn. Real Property, Probate and Trust Law sect., vice chair grievance com., 1985-87, Fla. Bar, chair leadership conf., 1987; chmn. Jud. Nominating Commn. of 6th Jud. Dist., 1991-94. Bd. dirs. Nat. Attys. Title Assurance Fund, Attys. Title Ins. Fund, Attys. Title Guaranty Fund of Colo., treas.; mem. Pinellas County Exec. Com., Tampa Regional Planning Coun., 1988-92. Served to capt. USNR, 1962-92. Fellow Am. Bar Found. (life); mem. ABA (chmn. land trust com., chmn. standing com. lawyers title guaranty funds 1991-94), Am. Coll. Real Estate Lawyers (chmn. condominium com.), Ill. Bar Assn., Chgo. Bar Assn., Clearwater Bar Assn. (past pres.), Fla. Coun. Bar Assn. (past pres., past chmn. vol. bar liaison com.), Fla. Bar Found. (legal aid to poor com., chmn. jud. nominations procedures com. 1992-93), Clearwater C. of C. (bd. govs., exec. com., past v.p.). Clubs: Countryside Country (Clearwater, Fla.); Masons, Scottish Rite, Shriners. Republican. Corporate, general, Probate (including wills, trusts), Property, real (including real estate development, water). Home: 1910 Saddlehill Rd N Dunedin FL 34698-2437 Office: Pennington Moore et al 133 N Fort Harrison Clearwater FL 33607 E-mail: jayz@penningtonlawfirm.com.

ZUCKER, DAVID G. lawyer; b. Bronx, N.Y., Apr. 6, 1949; BA, CUNY, 1971; JD, St. John's U., N.Y.C., 1974. Bar: N.Y., U.S. Supreme Ct., U.S. Dist. Ct. (ea. and so. dists.) N.Y. Asst. dist. atty. Queens (N.Y.) Dist. Atty., 1974—77; ptnr. Schwed & Zucker, Queens, 1977—. Hearing officer Taxi & Limosine Commn., N.Y.C., 1977—80; adminstrv. law judge EPA, N.Y.C., 1980—84. Pres. Merrick (N.Y.) Little League, 1999—2000. Appellate, Criminal, Family and matrimonial. Office: 12510 Queens Blvd Ste 6 Kew Gardens NY 11415-1522 Office Fax: 718-263-2911.

ZUCKER, HOWARD, lawyer; b. N.Y.C., June 21, 1952; s. Morris Milton and Sarah Shirley (Spector) Z.; m. Lynn Carol Bierschenk; children: Lauren Heather, Erica Rachael, Monica Juliet. Student, London Sch. Econs., 1973; BS in Econs. summa cum laude, U. Pa., 1973, JD, 1977. Bar: N.Y. 1978. Ptnr. Hawkins, Delafield & Wood, N.Y.C., 1977—. Author: ABCs of Housing Bonds, 5th edit., 1993. Mem. ABA (chmn. pub. fin. com. of state and local govt. law sect. 1996-98), N.Y. State Bar Assn., Nat. Assn. Bond Lawyers (bd. dirs. 1994-2001, pres.-elect 1998-99, pres. 1999-2000), Omicron Delta Epsilon. Municipal (including bonds), Taxation, general. Office: Hawkins Delafield & Wood 67 Wall St Fl 11 New York NY 10005-3155

ZUCKERMAN, HERBERT LAWRENCE, lawyer; b. Newark, June 11, 1928; s. David and Adele Zuckerman; m. Janet Albert, Sept. 10, 1950; children: Julia, Elizabeth, William. BSBA, Lehigh U., 1949; JD, Rutgers U., 1953. Acct. Zuckerman & Black, Newark, 1949-56; pvt. practice law Newark, 1956-71; ptnr. Zuckerman, Aronson & Horn, Newark, 1971-81; ptnr., v.p. Sills Cummis, Newark, 1981-98, sr.counsel, 1998—. Bd. dirs. Am. Jewish Com., 1990—; vol. The Hospice, Glen Ridge, N.J., 1985-93. Fellow Coll. of Tax Counsel; mem. ABA, N.J. Bar Assn., Fed. Bar Assn., Essex County Bar Assn., Mental Health Assn. (bd. dirs. 1997-99), Mensa. Avocations: tennis, music, theater, opera, reading. Estate taxation, Taxation, general, State and local taxation. Office: Sills Cummis 1 Riverfront Plz 13th Fl Newark NJ 07102-5400 E-mail: hzuckerman@sillscummis.com.

ZUCKERMAN, JOSEPH, lawyer; b. Bridgeport, Conn., Aug. 15, 1938; s. Max and Pearl (Glantz) Z.; m. Theda Lehrer, July 6, 1968; children: Brian, Lawrence, Beth. BA, U. Conn., 1960; LLB, Columbia U., 1962. Bar: N.Y. 1963. Counsel Katten Muchen Zavis Rosenman, N.Y.C., 1963—. Mem. ABA. Democrat. Jewish. Federal civil litigation, Environmental, Professional liability. Office: Katten Muchen Zavis Rosenman 575 Madison Ave Fl 26 New York NY 10022-2585

ZUCKERMAN, PAUL HERBERT, lawyer; b. Bklyn., Mar. 7, 1935; s. Max B. and Minnie (Mendelson) Z.; m. Sara Shiffman, Aug. 25, 1963; children: David Isaac, Daniel Mark. BS in Econs., Wharton Sch., U. Pa., 1957; MBA in Corp. Fin., NYU, 1964; JD, Bklyn. Law Sch., 1967. Bar: N.Y. 1968, U.S. Dist. Ct. (so. and ea. dists.) N.Y. 1975, U.S. Tax Ct. 1977, U.S. Ct. Appeals (2d cir.) 1972, U.S. Supreme Ct. 1973. Security analyst U.S. Trust Co., N.Y.C., 1962-66; sr. security analyst CNA Mgmt. Rsch. Corp., N.Y.C., 1966-71, mgr. dept. investment rsch., 1971-73; sole practice N.Y.C., 1973—. Speaker and writer in field; radio, TV appearances. Trustee Sutton Place Synagogue. Served to lt. (j.g.) USN, 1957-60. Mem. Assn. Bar City N.Y., Wharton Bus. Sch. (N.Y.C.). Corporate, general, Estate planning, Probate (including wills, trusts). Office: 8th Fl 226 W 26th St New York NY 10001-6785

ZUETEL, KENNETH ROY, JR., lawyer; b. L.A., Apr. 5, 1954; s. Kenneth Roy Sr. and Adelle Francis Z.; m. Cheryl Kay Morse, May 29, 1976; children: Bryan, Jarid, Christopher, Lauren. BA, San Diego State U., 1974; JD, U. San Diego, 1978. Bar: Calif. 1978 U.S. Ct. Appeals (9th cir.) 1979, U.S. Dist. Ct. (ctrl. dist.) Calif. 1979, U.S. Dist. Ct. (so. and no. dists.) Calif. 1980, U.S. Dist. Ct. (ea. dist.) 1981. Clk. to fed. Judge Martin Pence U.S. Dist. Ct. Hawaii, Honolulu, 1978-79; assoc. litigation Buchalter, Nemer, L.A., 1979-83, Thelen, Marrin, L.A., 1983-88; ptnr. Zuetel & Torigian, Pasadena, Calif., 1988—. Superior ct. arbitrator L.A. Superior Ct., 1982-90, superior ct. settlement officer, 1988-93; judge pro temp L.A. Mcpl. Ct., 1983-94, L.A. Superior Ct., 1989-94; guest lectr. Loyola U. Sch. Law, 1986-95; CEB lectr. Author: Civil Procedure Before Trial, 1992; cons. editor: Cal. Civ. Proc., 1992; contbr. articles to profl. jours. Recipient Recognition award L.A. (Calif.) Bd. Suprs., 1988. Mem. State Bar Calif. (mem. adv. com. continuing edn. 1985-88, trial practice subcom. 1985-88, disciplinary examiner 1986), Los Angeles County Bar Assn. (chair trial atty. project 1982-83, mem. L.A. del. conf. of dels. 1986-96, chair L.A. de. conf. of dels. 1995, exec. com. barristers 1984-88, superior ct. com. 1985-88, civil practice com. 1992-94, exec. com. litigation sect. 1989-90), Pasadena Bar Assn., Inns of Ct. (barrister L.A. chpt. 1991-92), Phi Beta Kappa, Phi Kappa Phi, Phi Alpha Theta, Pi Sigma Alpha. Republican. Presbyterian. General civil litigation, Health. Office: Zuetel & Torigian 215 N Marengo Ave 3d Fl Pasadena CA 91101 E-mail: krzuetel@ztlaw.net.

ZUKERMAN, MICHAEL, lawyer; b. Bklyn., Oct. 3, 1940; s. Charles Morris and Gertrude Ethel Zukerman; m. Claire J. Goldsmith, June 25, 1961 (div. 1986); children: Steven, Amy; m. Elaine DeMasi, Nov. 21, 1986 (div. 1999); children: Jaclyn, Laura; m. Janey Alexander, Feb. 2, 2001. BS, U. Fla., 1961; LLB, St. John's U., 1964; LLM, NYU, 1966. Bar: N.Y. 1965, Pa. 1983, U.S. Tax Ct. 1984. Credit analyst, loan officer Franklin Nat. Bank, 1964-66; assoc. Jaffin, Schneider, Kimmel & Galpeer, N.Y.C., 1966-67; ptnr. Zukerman, Licht & Friedman and predecessors, N.Y.C., 1967-79, Baskin & Sears, P.C., N.Y.C., 1979-85, Graubard, Moskowitz, Dannett, Horowitz & Mollen, N.Y.C., 1985-86, Gersten, Savage, Kaplowitz & Zukerman, N.Y.C., 1986-89; of counsel Olsham, Grundman, Frome & Rosenzweig, N.Y.C., 1990-95, Graham & James, N.Y.C., 1995-2000, Bryan Cave LLP, 2000—; exec. v.p. Brookhill Group, 1986-89. Pres. First Ptnrs. Credit Corp., N.Y.C., 1988—93; bd. dirs. Interjurist Ltd., Whitestone Realty Capital, Inc.; mng. dir. Life Sci. Found., 1993—, trustee, 2001—; lectr. in field. Contbr. articles to profl. jours. Trustee Temple Beth Torah, Melville, N.Y., 1972-80, YMHA Suffolk County, Hauppague, N.Y., 1980-85; bd. dirs. Dayton Mgmt. Corp., 1974-2001, Suffolk Jewish Cmty. Planning Bd., Hauppague, 1982-85, Congregation Bnai Elohim, 1994, 2nd v.p., 1995; co-chmn. bus. adv. coun. Town of Greenburgh, 1992. Mem. ABA. Home: 915 Cherry Ln Valley Stream NY 11581-2722 Office: Bryan Cave LLP 31st Flr 1290 Ave of the Americas New York NY 10104 E-mail: mmzukerman@BryanCave.com.

ZUMBACH, STEVEN ELMER, lawyer; b. Jan. 12, 1950; s. Elmer J. and Mary C. (Frese) Zumbach; m. Kathy J. Case, June 5, 1971; children: Stephanie L., Mathew J. BS, Iowa State U., 1973, PhD, 1980; JD, U. Iowa, 1975. CPA; bar: Iowa 1975. Assoc. Belin Lamson McCormick Zumbach Flynn, P.C., Des Moines, 1977—, ptnr., 1980—. Lectr. law Drake U., Des Moines, 1980—84; mem. Iowa Bd. Regents, 1973—77; trustee, bd. dir. Iowa State U. Found., Ames, Iowa, 1986—. Fellow: Am. coll. Trust and Estate Counsel; mem.: Polk County Bar Assn., Iowa Soc. CPAs, Greater Des Moines Partnership Chair (chair C. of C. Fedn. 1993), Iowa State U. Alumni Assn. (pres. 1986—87), Gamma Sigma Delta, Omocron Delta Kappa, Phi Kappa Phi, Order of Coif. Republican. Probate (including wills, trusts), Corporate taxation, Estate taxation. Home: 708 38th St West Des Moines IA 50265-3176 Office: Belin Lamson McCormick Zumbach Flynn PC 666 Walnut St Ste 2000 Des Moines IA 50309-3989

ZUMBRUN, ALVIN JOHN THOMAS, law and criminology educator; b. Balt., Aug. 9, 1926; s. Orrell Sylvester Tilton and Mary Kathryn (Sprinkle) Z.; m. Marianne Jane Nolan, Aug. 26, 1950; children: Mary Susan, Alvin J.T. Jr., Steven M., Diane, MaryAnn, Mary Kathleen. BA, U. Md., 1952, MA, 1956; MEd in Spl. Edn., Coppin State U., 1972, MEd in Adminstrn., 1974; JD, U. Balt., 1970. Probation officer Supreme Bench of Balt., 1950-52; budget and program dir. Cmty. Chest, Balt., 1953-55; mng. dir. Criminal Justice Commn., Balt., 1956-59; exec. dir., criminologist Md. Crime Investigating Com., Balt., 1960-96; dept. chmn., prof. criminal justice Catonsville (Md.) C.C., 1968-94; dept. chmn., dir. grad. program, prof. criminal justice U. Balt., 1974-76. Adj. prof. criminal justice U. Md., Hood Coll., Coppin State U., Md. State Police Acad., Balt. County Police Acad., 1969—; mem. adv. bd. U. Balt. Criminal Justice Program, 1976-94; cons. Am. Edn. Assn., Washington, 1980—; mem. senate Catonsville C.C., 1970-83; mem. Nat. Disaster Med. System, 1993—; mem. acad. stds. senate com. U. Md., College Park, 1997-99. Author: Maryland Crime Report, 5 vols., 1959-94, Directory of Criminal Justice Agencies, 22 vols., 1962-94, Civil Disturbance Riots of 1968, 69, also rsch. in field. Mem. scholarship com. Md. Troopers Assn., Pikesville, 1990-93; mem. adv. bd. articulation com. U. Md., College Park, 1977-94; lay pres., mem. coun. Salem Luth. Ch., Catonsville, 1956-59, 65-68; pres. Maplewoods Home Owners Assn., 1996-97. Lt. (j.g.) USN, 1943-50. Recipient Superior Pub. Svc. award Afro Am. Newspaper, 1962, Excellence in Teaching award Md. State Bd. C.C.s, 1987, Superior Ednl. Svcs. award Balt. County Police Chief, 1994, Gov.'s citation for ednl. achievements Gov. of Md., 1994, Hon. Trooper 25 Yrs. Acad. Teaching Md. State Police, 1995. Mem. VFW (life), Am. Legion (life), Md. Acad. Criminal Justice Profs. (pres. 1971-94), Internat. Soc. Criminology, Nat. Dist. Attys. Assn., Internat. Assn. Chiefs of Police, Maplewoods Homeowners Assn. (pres. 1995-96). Avocations: walking, biking, family activities, world travel. Home and Office: 438 Maple Forest Rd Catonsville MD 21228-1783 E-mail: ajtz@juno.com.

ZWEIACHER, BRIAN DEAN, lawyer; b. Red Bank, N.J., Nov. 11, 1963; s. Norman Lee and June Carol Zweiacher; m. Terry Collett Zweiacher, July 12, 1987; children: Holly, Kristy. BA, Montclair State U., 1986; JD, Widener U., 1993. Bar: Pa. 1994, U.S. Dist. Ct. (mid. dist.) Pa. 1999, U.S. Ct. Appeals (3d cir.) 2000. Asst. Office of Gen. Counsel Commonwealth of Pa., Harrisburg, 1993—. Mem.: Pa. Bar Assn. Avocation: coaching soccer. Office: Commonwealth Pa Office of Budget Bell Tower 7th Fl 303 Walnut St Harrisburg PA 17101-1808

ZYCHICK, JOEL DAVID, lawyer; b. Cleve., June 23, 1954; s. Eugene K. and Myra (Rotblatt) Z. BBA, George Washington U., 1976; JD, Case Western Res. U., 1979; LLM in Taxation, NYU, 1979. Bar: Ohio 1979, N.Y. 1985, D.C. 1985, U.S. Tax Ct. 1980, U.S. Ct. Claims 1980, U.S. Ct. Appeals (fed. cir.) 1982. Assoc. Jones, Day, Reavis & Pogue, Cleve., 1980-83, Milbank, Tweed, Hadley & McCloy, N.Y.C., 1983-85; ptnr. Hertzog, Calamari & Gleason, N.Y.C., 1986-98; pres. Zcounsel LLC; pres., CEO, GETKO Group, Inc., Westbury, NY, 1998—2001. Former gen. counsel, dir. The Egg Factory, LLC, Va; contbr. articles to profl. jours. Dir., treas. Northside Ctr. for Child Devel., N.Y.C. Mem. ABA (past sec., dir. coun. tax sect., nominating com., former chmn. sales and fin. trans. com., past vice chmn. regulations com. govt. submissions), N.Y. State Bar Assn. Avocations: hiking, music, traveling. Corporate, general, Corporate taxation, Personal income taxation. Home: PO Box 1097 Amagansett NY 11930-1097 E-mail: JZ@Zcounsel.com.

Fields of Practice Index

Cambridge
Jenkins, Robert Rowe

Greenbelt
Brugger, George Albert

North Potomac
Lehman, Leonard

Potomac
Meyer, Lawrence George

Rockville
Berryman, Richard Byron
Cheston, Sheila Carol
Rachanow, Gerald Marvin

Westminster
Dulany, William Bevard

MASSACHUSETTS

Ashfield
Pepyne, Edward Walter

Boston
DiCara, Lawrence S.

Holyoke
Ferriter, Maurice Joseph

Springfield
Burke, Michael Henry
Gelinas, Robert Albert

MICHIGAN

Ann Arbor
Anderson, Austin Gothard

Detroit
Babcock, Charles Witten, Jr.,
Calkins, Stephen
Gottschalk, Thomas A.
Mamat, Frank Trustick

Lansing
Fink, Joseph Allen
Marvin, David Edward Shreve

Warren
Bridenstine, Louis Henry, Jr.,

MINNESOTA

Edina
Burk, Robert S.

Minneapolis
Comstock, Rebecca Ann
French, John Dwyer
Keppel, William James
Marshall, Siri Swenson

Saint Paul
Galvin, Michael John, Jr.,

MISSISSIPPI

Hattiesburg
Davis-Morris, Angela Elizabeth

Jackson
Chinn, Mark Allan
Hemleben, Scott P.
Martinez, Eduardo Vidal
Peden, James Alton, Jr.,
Wise, Robert Powell

MISSOURI

Columbia
Harter, Philip J.

Jefferson City
Angstead, Robert Kenneth
Martin, Cathleen A.
Tettlebaum, Harvey M.

Kansas City
Cross, William Dennis
King, Richard Allen
Sader, Neil Steven
Satterlee, Terry Jean

Saint Louis
Gilhousen, Brent James
Sullivan, Edward Lawrence
Watters, Richard Donald

MONTANA

Billings
Sites, James Philip

Missoula
Loring, Emilie

NEBRASKA

Omaha
Krutter, Forrest Nathan
Lee, Dennis Patrick
Stenberg, Donald B.

NEVADA

Carson City
Crowell, Robert Lamson

Las Vegas
Brown, Joseph Wentling
Curran, William P.
Hilbrecht, Norman Ty
Jost, Richard Frederic, III,

Reno
Hill, Earl McColl

NEW HAMPSHIRE

Concord
Rath, Thomas David

NEW JERSEY

Bridgewater
Conroy, Robert John

Hackensack
Navatta, Anna Paula

Hillsborough
Ames, Marc L.

Morristown
Pellecchia, John Michael

New Providence
Bernstein, Nadia J.

Newark
Cummis, Clive Sanford
Miller, Richard Allan

Princeton
Picco, Steven Joseph

Roseland
Carella, Charles Carmine
Eichler, Burton Lawrence
Vanderbilt, Arthur T., II,

Somerville
Laskey, James Howard

Summit
Pearlmutter, Fredi L.

Vauxhall
Ross, Mark Samuel

Woodbridge
Weissman, Matthew Mark

NEW MEXICO

Santa Fe
Green, Barry

NEW YORK

Albany
Barsamian, J(ohn) Albert
Fernandez, Hermes A., III,
Hanna, John, Jr.,

Ardsley On Hudson
Stein, Milton Michael

Brooklyn
Jacobson, Barry Stephen

Huntington
Augello, William Joseph

Larchmont
Berridge, George Bradford

New York
Abrams, Robert
Allen, Leon Arthur, Jr.,
Clapman, Peter Carlyle
Davidson, Sheila Kearney
Douchkess, George
Fleischman, Edward Hirsh
Gottlieb, Paul Mitchel
Gotts, Ilene Knable
Greilsheimer, James Gans
Helfer, Michael Stevens
Jacobson, Jerold Dennis
Juceam, Robert E.
Klapper, Molly
Kreitzman, Ralph J.
Lifland, William Thomas
Lord, Barbara Joanni
Lowenfels, Lewis David
Lupkin, Stanley Neil
Marshall, Sheila Hermes
Most, Jack Lawrence
Rossen, Jordan
Schumacher, Harry Richard
Semaya, Francine Levitt
Shoss, Cynthia Renée
White, Katherine Patricia

Pittsford
George, Richard Neill

Purchase
Andrews, David Ralph

Smithtown
Dowis, Lenore

White Plains
Taft, Nathaniel Belmont

NORTH CAROLINA

Durham
Markham, Charles Buchanan

Fairview
Rhynedance, Harold Dexter, Jr.,

Greensboro
Koonce, Neil Wright

Raleigh
Carmichael, Carson, III,
Currin, Samuel Thomas
Dixon, Wright Tracy, Jr.,
Dunn, Hubert Glenn Tolson
Kapp, Michael Keith
Maupin, Armistead Jones
Mitchell, Henry Allen, Jr.,
Thomas, Jason Selig

NORTH DAKOTA

Bismarck
Klemin, Lawrence R.

OHIO

Cincinnati
Kelley, John Joseph, Jr.,
O'Reilly, James Thomas

Cleveland
Gippin, Robert Malcolm
Hardy, Michael Lynn
Kola, Arthur Anthony
Millstone, David Jeffrey

Columbus
Booker, James Douglas
Cox, Paul L.
Deal, John Charles
Graff, Douglas Eric
Maynard, Robert Howell
McKenna, Alvin James
Morgan, Dennis Richard
Schneider, Karl Herbert
Taft, Sheldon Ashley
Taylor, Joel Sanford

Dayton
Kinlin, Donald James

Howard
Lee, William Johnson

Lancaster
Libert, Donald Joseph

Mayfield Heights
Rosenfeld, Robert Thomas

Portsmouth
Gerlach, Franklin Theodore

OKLAHOMA

Edmond
Loving, Susan Brimer

Oklahoma City
Decker, Michael Lynn

Tulsa
Waddel, Patrick Olynn

OREGON

Portland
Brenneman, Delbert Jay
Dotten, Michael Chester
Harrell, Gary Paul
Matarazzo, Harris Starr
Sullivan, Edward Joseph

PENNSYLVANIA

Blue Bell
Teklits, Joseph Anthony

Harrisburg
Burcat, Joel Robin
Kelly, Robert Edward, Jr.,
Kury, Franklin Leo
Van Zile, Philip Taylor, III,
Wilson, Craig P.

Langhorne
Valentin, James

Media
Durham, James W.

Philadelphia
Collings, Robert L.
Dabrowski, Doris Jane
Fineman, S. David
McKeever, John Eugene
Reiss, John Barlow
Stevens, Mark Alan

Pittsburgh
Bleier, Michael E.
DeForest, Walter Pattison, III,
Kobell, Gerald
Leibowitz, Marvin

RHODE ISLAND

North Providence
Lombardi, Valentino Dennis

SOUTH CAROLINA

Beaufort
Harvey, William Brantley, Jr.,

Charleston
Cannon, Hugh
Freer, Robert Elliott, Jr.,

Columbia
Carpenter, Charles Elford, Jr.,
Harvey, Jonathan Matthew
Scott, Ronald Charles

Mount Pleasant
Whitten, Beatrice Ehrenberg

SOUTH DAKOTA

Rapid City
Goodsell, G. Verne

TENNESSEE

Hendersonville
McCaleb, Joe Wallace

Johnson City
Epps, James Haws, III,

Nashville
Jacobs, Sharon O.

TEXAS

Austin
Black, William Earl
Brim, Jefferson Kearney, III, (Jay)
Cortez, Hernan Glenn
Cunningham, Judy Marie
Davis, Creswell Dean
Demond, Walter Eugene
Donley, Dennis W.
Golemon, Ronald Kinnan
Hale, Louis Dewitt
Heath, Claude Robert
Moss, Bill Ralph
Nevola, Roger
Patman, Philip Franklin
Roan, Forrest Calvin, Jr.,
Strauser, Robert Wayne
Temple, Larry Eugene

Dallas
Douglass, Frank Russell
Dutton, Diana Cheryl
Westfall, Constance Courtney

Fort Worth
Chalk, John Allen, Sr.,

Houston
Eiland, Gary Wayne
Epstein, Jon David
Kelly, Hugh Rice
Kennedy, John Edward
Ney, Judy Larson
Rozzell, Scott Ellis
Salch, Steven Charles

Mc Kinney
Dowdy, William Clarence, Jr.,

Mcallen
Jarvis, Robert Glenn

San Antonio
Lutter, Charles William, Jr.,

UTAH

Ogden
Warner, Frank Shrake

Provo
Abbott, Charles Favour

Salt Lake City
Heaton, Jon C.
Jensen, Dallin W.

VERMONT

Montpelier
Cheney, Kimberly Bunce

Springfield
Boxer, Andrew Carey

VIRGINIA

Abingdon
Shortridge, Judy Beth

Arlington
Cohen, Sheldon Irwin
Morris, Roy Leslie

Charlottesville
Merrill, Richard Austin

Fairfax
Abrams, Sheri

Falls Church
Kirk, Dennis Dean
Meserve, Richard Andrew
Wood, John Martin

Glen Allen
Page, Eric Michael

Mc Lean
Byrnes, William Joseph
Herge, J. Curtis
Ingersoll, William Boley
Olson, William Jeffrey

Montross
Monaco, Grace Powers

Nellysford
Sims, John Rogers, Jr.,

Reston
Platt, Leslie A.
Rau, Lee Arthur
Scharff, Joseph Laurent

Richmond
Brasfield, Evans Booker
Flippen, Edward L.
Freeman, George Clemon, Jr.,

Roanoke
Glover, Harry Allen, Jr.,

Spotsylvania
Manthei, Richard Dale

Vienna
Hagberg, Chris Eric

WASHINGTON

Olympia
Williams, Wayne Leroy
Wright, Daniel A.

Seattle
Blom, Daniel Charles
Freeman, Antoinette Rosefeldt
Redman, Eric
Rosen, Jon Howard
Sausser, Gail Dianne

Spokane
Weatherhead, Leslie R.

WEST VIRGINIA

Bluefield
Kantor, Isaac Norris

Wheeling
Bailey, John P.

WISCONSIN

Appleton
Thenell, Heather Jo

Colby
Nikolay, Frank Lawrence

Madison
Fleischli, George Robert

Milwaukee
Fitzgerald, Kevin Gerard
Hase, David John
Scrivner, Thomas William

TERRITORIES OF THE UNITED STATES

PUERTO RICO

San Juan
Pierluisi, Pedro R.

AUSTRALIA

Brisbane
Perrett, Ross Graham

BRAZIL

Rio de Janeiro
Basilio, Ana Tereza Palhares
Xavier, Helena de Araujo Lopes

São Paulo
Inglez de Souza, Ricardo Norouha
Padovan, Lira Renardini
Zarzur, Cristianne Saccab

COSTA RICA

San José
Retana, Vanessa

ADMIRALTY

ALTERNATIVE DISPUTE RESOLUTION

Naples
Berning, Randall Karl
Buckley, Frederick Jean

Orlando
Adler, Marshall Stuart
Nadeau, Robert Bertrand, Jr.,
Worthington, Daniel Glen

Pembroke Pines
Granata, Linda M.

Sarasota
Phillips, Elvin Willis
Salomone, William Gerald

Starke
Green, Robert Alexis, Jr.,

Tampa
MacDonald, Thomas Cook, Jr.,
Stagg, Clyde Lawrence
Thomas, Wayne Lee

West Palm Beach
Beasley, James W., Jr.,

Winter Springs
Fernandez, William Warren, Sr.,

GEORGIA

Atlanta
Bloodworth, A(lbert) W(illiam) Franklin
Croft, Terrence Lee
Hinchey, John William
Linder, Harvey Ronald
Myers, Lawrence Joseph
Oakley, Mary Ann Bryant
Smith, George Anthony
Smith, Sidney Oslin, Jr.,

Augusta
Cooney, William J.

Metter
Doremus, Ogden

Tucker
Wheeler, Edd Dudley

HAWAII

Honolulu
Crumpton, Charles Whitmarsh
Deaver, Phillip Lester

IDAHO

Boise
Clark, Merlyn Wesley

ILLINOIS

Chicago
Boies, Wilber H.
Cass, Robert Michael
Hofer, Roy Ellis
Karon, Sheldon
McMahon, Thomas Michael
Muller, Kurt Alexander
Niro, Cheryl
Nugent, Lori S.
Partridge, Mark Van Buren
Schoonhoven, Ray James
Zoub, Burton Irving

Park Ridge
LaRue, Paul Hubert

INDIANA

Indianapolis
Shula, Robert Joseph
Wampler, Robert Joseph

La Porte
Kaminski, Leon R.

Merrillville
Gioia, Daniel August

Vincennes
Emison, Ewing Rabb, Jr.,

IOWA

Des Moines
Bennett, Edward James

KENTUCKY

Louisville
Ballantine, John Tilden
Tannon, Jay Middleton
Weiss, Allan

LOUISIANA

New Orleans
Molony, Michael Janssens, Jr.,

Shreveport
Clark, James E.

MAINE

Portland
McHold, Sharon Lawrence

MARYLAND

Baltimore
McWilliams, John Michael

Bethesda
Pipkin, James Harold, Jr.,

Brookeville
Johns, Warren LeRoi

Rockville
Zaphiriou, George Aristotle

MASSACHUSETTS

Boston
Aresty, Jeffrey M.
Hoffman, David Alan
O'Neill, Philip Daniel, Jr.,
Ristuben, Karen R.

Cambridge
Esher, Jacob Aaron

Northampton
Thomas, Margot Eva

Stow
Golder, Leonard Howard

Weymouth
Fitzsimmons, B. Joseph, Jr.,

Winchester
Bigelow, Robert P.

MICHIGAN

Bingham Farms
Larky, Sheldon Glen

Bloomfield
Kanter, Alan Michael

Bloomfield Hills
Morganroth, Fred

Detroit
Schochet, P(aula) Rivka
Ward, George Edward

Grand Rapids
Bransdorfer, Stephen Christie

Schoolcraft
Foley, John Francis

Traverse City
Hornberger, Lee

MINNESOTA

Burnsville
Dewalt, Deborah N.

Edina
Landrum, Michael Arthur

Minneapolis
Biglow, Robert Roy
Lazar, Raymond Michael

Saint Cloud
Carpenter, Kevin Starr

Saint Louis Park
Nightingale, Tracy Irene

Saint Paul
Carruthers, Philip Charles
Noonan, James C.

MISSISSIPPI

Biloxi
Dornan, Donald C., Jr.,

Hernando
Brown, William A.

Jackson
Purdy, William Richard

MISSOURI

Columbia
Harter, Philip J.

Higginsville
Ver Dught, ElGene Clark

Saint Louis
Switzer, Frederick Michael, III,
Young, Marvin Oscar

Springfield
FitzGerald, Kevin Michael

MONTANA

Kalispell
Kaufman, Leonard Lee

NEBRASKA

Omaha
Brownrigg, John Clinton

NEW JERSEY

Bedminster
Spierer, Howard

Hackensack
Spiegel, Linda F.

Morristown
Pollock, Stewart Glasson

Mountainside
Helander, Robert Charles

Newark
Michels, Herman D.

Oakhurst
Widman, Douglas Jack

Somerville
Dreier, William Alan

NEW YORK

Buffalo
Pearson, Paul David

Dobbs Ferry
Juettner, Diana D'Amico

Flushing
Deerson, Adele Shapiro

Mamaroneck
Du Boff, Michael H(arold)

Mineola
Klein, Arnold Spencer

New York
Bach, Thomas Handford
Bassen, Ned Henry
Beitel, Bernard
Canoni, John David
Creel, Thomas Leonard
Davidson, Robert Bruce
DeCarlo, Donald Thomas
Drucker, Jacquelin F.
Freyer, Dana Hartman
Friedman, Victor Stanley
Gans, Walter Gideon
Hochman, Stephen Allen
Holtzmann, Howard Marshall
Hulbert, Richard Woodward
Itzkoff, Norman Jay
Jacobowitz, Harold Saul
Kandel, William Lloyd
Klapper, Molly
Levine, Richard L.
Lynn, Theodore Stanley
Milmed, Paul Kussy
Ringer, James Milton
Rovine, Arthur William
Savitt, Susan Schenkel
Schiffer, Larry Philip
Smoak, Evan L.
Vitkowsky, Vincent Joseph
Wilkinson, John Hart
Younger, Stephen P.
Zifchak, William C.

Port Washington
Herz, Arnold D.

Rochester
Vigdor, Justin Leonard

Uniondale
Eilen, Howard Scott

Valley Stream
Levine, Marilyn Markovich

NORTH CAROLINA

Asheville
Hiller, Aleece

Charlotte
Mack, Susan Elizabeth
Sterrett, Tate Kincaid

Fayetteville
Ruppe, Arthur Maxwell

Hickory
Farthing, Edwin Glenn

Leland
Barnhardt, Zeb Elonzo, Jr.,

Raleigh
Hunter, Richard Samford, Jr.,

Sanford
Raisig, Paul Jones, Jr.,

OHIO

Cincinnati
Hardy, William Robinson
Lawrence, James Kaufman Lebensburger

Cleveland
Skulina, Thomas Raymond
Sogg, Wilton Sherman

Columbus
Hutson, Jeffrey Woodward

Mayfield Heights
Rosenfeld, Robert Thomas

OKLAHOMA

Mcalester
Pendell, Terry Ashley

Tulsa
Ballard, Elizabeth Ann
Kroblin, Lucy S.

OREGON

Portland
Meyer, Paul Richard

Salem
Gangle, Sandra Smith

PENNSYLVANIA

Ardmore
Narin, Stephen B.

Harrisburg
Miller, Leslie Anne

Media
Durham, James W.

Philadelphia
Berger, Harold
Blumstein, Edward
Dubin, Leonard
Lotman, Arline Jolles
Milbourne, Walter Robertson
Mullinix, Edward Wingate
Rosenstein, James Alfred
Sonnenfeld, Marc Jay
Vaira, Peter Francis

Pittsburgh
Cusick, Daniel Francis

Plymouth
Musto, Joseph John

RHODE ISLAND

Providence
Bulman, John

TENNESSEE

Chattanooga
Vital, Patricia Best

Knoxville
Campbell, Robert Roe
Lloyd, Francis Leon, Jr.,

Nashville
Gannon, John Sexton

TEXAS

Arlington
Dowdy, John Vernard, Jr.,

Austin
Davis, Robert Larry
Gambrell, James Bruton, III,
Saltmarsh, Sara Elizabeth

Colleyville
Whittenberg, Ira Orville

Corpus Christi
Coover, Ann E.

Dallas
DelHomme, Beverly Ann
Goodstein, Barnett Maurice
Greiner, Mary Louise
McGowan, Patrick Francis
Mighell, Kenneth John
Prather, Robert Charles, Sr.,

El Paso
Morton, Fred J.

Fort Worth
Broiles, David
Shannon, Joe, Jr.,
Swift, Thomas Grover, Jr.,

Houston
Ali, Arif Hyder
Kaighen, Sondra
Moroney, Linda L.S. (Muffie)
Pannill, William Presley
Prestridge, Pamela Adair
Salch, Steven Charles
Shurn, Peter Joseph, III,
Susman, Morton Lee
Wright, Paul William
Zimmerman, Alvin Louis

Mc Kinney
Roessler, P. Dee

San Antonio
Javore, Gary William
Pfeiffer, Philip J.

UTAH

Salt Lake City
Lee, James B.

VERMONT

Burlington
Frank, Joseph Elihu

Concord
Norsworthy, Elizabeth Krassovsky

VIRGINIA

Falls Church
Birch, Terrell Colhoun

Harrisonburg
Wallinger, M(elvin) Bruce

Richmond
Merhige, Robert Reynold, Jr.,

Roanoke
Effel, Laura

Vienna
Titus, Bruce Earl

WASHINGTON

Bellevue
Sebris, Robert, Jr.,

Bellingham
Garrett, Deborra Elizabeth

Enumclaw
Hart, Trip

Everett
Dewell, Julian C.

Pullman
Savage, David William

Seattle
Blair, M. Wayne
Cutler, Philip Edgerton
Loftus, Thomas Daniel
O'Connor, Bruce Edward
Tarshes, David C.
Tausend, Fredric Cutner
Wagoner, David Everett
Whitson, Lish

Spokane
Harbaugh, Daniel Paul

WEST VIRGINIA

Huntington
Bagley, Charles Frank, III,

WISCONSIN

Brookfield
Voss, Kenneth Erwin

Milwaukee
Michelstetter, Stanley Hubert
Nelson, Roy Hugh, Jr.,

Oshkosh
Lampe, Ronald L.
Wilde, William Richard
Zierdt, Alyson Kathleen

Stevens Point
Hamlar, Portia Yvonne Trenholm

Sun Prairie
Eustice, Francis Joseph

Waukesha
Moran, Kevin Paul

MEXICO

Mexico City
Monterrubio Alcántara, Luis Manuel
Zamora, Rodrigo

AUSTRALIA

Brisbane
Perrett, Ross Graham

Sydney
Eggleton, Glenn David
L'Estrange, Timothy I.

BELGIUM

Brussels
Barnum, John Wallace
Wagemans, Marc

BRAZIL

Rio de Janeiro
Basilio, Ana Tereza Palhares
Lopes, Beatriz

CZECH REPUBLIC

Prague
Cerny, Jiri

DENMARK

Copenhagen
Kjaeldgaard, Joergen

ENGLAND

London
Bishop, John Maurice
Dickey, John W.
Galloway, Diane
Mackie, David Lindsay
Vaughan, Philip John

FINLAND

Helsinki
Isotupa, Sirpa Hannele

FRANCE

Bayon
Cochran, John M., III,

Paris
Dupuis, Delphine Marie
Salans, Carl Fredric

HONG KONG

Hong Kong
Tang, Cynthia Yuen-shun

INDONESIA

Jakarta
Mills, Karen

JAPAN

Tokyo
Stoupe, Louise

NEW ZEALAND

Auckland
Laxon, William Allan

Wellington
Pol, Ronald Franciscus

NIGERIA

Lagos
Braithwaite, Kunbi

ROMANIA

Bucharest
Predoiu, Cătălin Marian

SPAIN

Madrid
Fernandez Aguado, Juan Ignacio
Mantilla-Serrano, Fernando

SWEDEN

Stockholm
Edlund, Lars Harald
Nilsson, Bo Gustaf Herman

SWITZERLAND

Zürich
Stieger, Werner

UKRAINE

Kiev
Golub, Andrey Vladimirovich

VENEZUELA

Caracas
Mezgravis, Andrés A.

ADDRESS UNPUBLISHED

Atchison, Rodney Raymond
Bakkensen, John Reser
Bandy, Jack D.
Bowman, Reid C.
Dickstein, Michael Ethan
Dubuc, Carroll Edward
Fryburger, Lawrence Bruce
Glanzer, Mona N.
Gorske, Robert H.
Harp, Chadwick Allen
Harris, Janine Diane
Hershatter, Richard Lawrence
Humphreys, Robert Russell
Jaynes, Gordon Leslie
Kahn, Laurence Michael
Painton, Russell Elliott
Peccarelli, Anthony Marando
Reath, George, Jr.,
Siegel, Sarah Ann
Siemon, Joyce Marilyn
Silver, Carol Ruth
Swacker, Frank Warren
Tierney, Kevin Joseph

ANTITRUST

UNITED STATES

ALABAMA

Birmingham
Avant, Grady, Jr.,
Givhan, Robert Marcus
Hinton, James Forrest, Jr.,
Long, Thad Gladden
Stabler, Lewis Vastine, Jr.,

ARIZONA

Paradise Valley
Tubman, William Charles

Phoenix
Allen, Robert Eugene Barton
Bouma, John Jacob
Galbut, Martin Richard
Klausner, Jack Daniel
Price, Charles Steven
Sanders, Barry R.

Scottsdale
Titus, Jon Alan

Tucson
Maltz, Gerald Stuart
Staubitz, Arthur Frederick

ARKANSAS

Little Rock
Anderson, Philip Sidney
Jennings, Alston

CALIFORNIA

Beverly Hills
Sherwood, Arthur Lawrence

Chino Hills
Pearson, April Virginia

Encinitas
Wigmore, John Grant

La Jolla
Kirchheimer, Arthur E(dward)

Los Altos
Weir, Robert H.

Los Angeles
Bernhard, Herbert Ashley
Cohen, Cynthia Marylyn
Fredman, Howard S.
Hanson, John J.
Hayutin, David Lionel
Hufstedler, Seth Martin
Medearis, Miller
Pruetz, Adrian M.
von Kalinowski, Julian Onesime
Woodland, Irwin Francis

Mill Valley
Salomon, Darrell Joseph

Modesto
Mussman, William Edward, III,

Palo Alto
Steer, Reginald David
Tiffany, Joseph Raymond, II,

Redwood City
Verhoeven, Charles K.

San Francisco
Alexis, Geraldine M.
Anderson, Edward Virgil
Byrne, Robert William
Campbell, Scott Robert
Dell, Robert Michael
Fergus, Gary Scott
Gelhaus, Robert Joseph
Gowdy, Franklin Brockway
Miller, William Napier Cripps
Odgers, Richard William
Popofsky, Melvin Laurence
Rosch, John Thomas
Taylor, William James (Zak Taylor)
Trautman, William Ellsworth
Warmer, Richard Craig

San Rafael
Duke, George F.

Walnut Creek
Pagter, Carl Richard

COLORADO

Boulder
Dickinson, Nancy

Denver
Harris, Dale Ray
Miller, Gale Timothy
Thomasch, Roger Paul
Timmins, Edward Patrick

Durango
Burnham, Bryson Paine

Fort Collins
Hjelmfelt, David Charles

CONNECTICUT

Darien
Prince, Kenneth Stephen

Fairfield
Huth, William Edward

Farmington
Wiechmann, Eric Watt

Hartford
Dennis, Anthony James

New Haven
Belt, David Levin

DELAWARE

Wilmington
Magee, Thomas Hugh

DISTRICT OF COLUMBIA

Washington
Adler, Howard, Jr.,
Attridge, Daniel F.
Atwood, James R.
Barnes, Donald Michael
Bennett, Alexander Elliot
Berner, Frederic George, Jr.,
Bleakley, Peter Kimberley
Blumenfeld, Jeffrey
Bray, John Martin
Burchfield, Bobby Roy
Campbell, James Sargent
Cutler, Lloyd Norton
Davidow, Joel
deKieffer, Donald Eulette
Denger, Michael Louis
Dubrow, Jon B.
Ewing, Ky Pepper, Jr.,
Funkhouser, Robert Bruce
Gellhorn, Ernest Albert Eugene
Gold, Peter Frederick
Goodman, Alfred Nelson
Gorinson, Stanley M.
Gribbon, Daniel McNamara
Heckman, Jerome Harold
Henke, Michael John
Hewitt, Paul Buck
Hills, Carla Anderson
Hobbs, Caswell O., III,
Hoffman, Joel Elihu
Jacobsen, Raymond Alfred, Jr.,
Johnson, Shirley Z.
Jordan, Robert Elijah, III,
Klarfeld, Peter James
Lackey, Michael E., Jr.,
Lavelle, Joseph P.
Marks, Herbert Edward
McDavid, Janet Louise
McDiarmid, Robert Campbell
Melamed, Arthur Douglas
Mierzewski, Michael Brian
Miller, Andrew Pickens
Moates, G. Paul
Murphy, James Paul
Murry, Harold David, Jr.,
Owen, Roberts Bishop
Pfeiffer, Margaret Kolodny
Prettyman, Elijah Barrett, Jr.,
Rein, Bert Walter
Rockefeller, Edwin Shaffer
Roll, David Lee
Ryan, Stephen Michael
Schmidt, Edward Craig
Smith, Brian William
Stock, Stuart Chase
Stromberg, Clifford Douglas
Taurman, John David
Temko, Stanley Leonard
Townsend, John Michael
Turnage, Fred Douglas
Vakerics, Thomas Vincent
Vanderstar, John
Wallace, James Harold, Jr.,
Wegener, Mark Douglas
Weiss, Mark Anschel
Whitaker, A(lbert) Duncan
Wyss, John Benedict
Yannucci, Thomas David
Zimmerman, Edwin Morton

FLORIDA

Alachua
Gaines, Weaver Henderson

Boca Raton
Kassner, Herbert Seymore

Coral Gables
Kearns, John W.
Weissenborn, Sheridan Kendall

Lecanto
Corsi, Philip Donald

Miami
Houlihan, Gerald John
Nachwalter, Michael
Nagin, Stephen Elias

Naples
Ericson, Roger Delwin
Steinhouse, Carl Lewis

Orlando
Subin, Eli Harold

Tampa
Blau, Richard M.
Smith, William Reece, Jr.,

GEORGIA

Atlanta
Alexander, Miles Jordan
Bratton, James Henry, Jr.,
Doyle, Michael Anthony
Genberg, Ira
Grady, Kevin E.
Izard, John
Killorin, Robert Ware
Lotito, Nicholas Anthony
Reynolds, Bradley Kenneth
Rhodes, Thomas Willard

HAWAII

Honolulu
Char, Vernon Fook Leong

ILLINOIS

Barrington
Lee, William Marshall

Chicago
Abrams, Lee Norman
Allen, Henry Sermones, Jr.,
Barrett, Roger Watson
Bunge, Jonathan Gunn
Crane, Mark
Cusack, John Thomas
Dechene, James Charles
Dixon, Stewart Strawn
Donner, Ted A.
Downing, Robert Allan
Eimer, Nathan Philip
Esrick, Jerald Paul
Finke, Robert Forge
Franch, Richard Thomas
Gibbons, William John
Gordon, James S.
Gustman, David Charles
Hardgrove, James Alan
Harrold, Bernard
Hoskins, Richard Jerold
Howell, R(obert) Thomas, Jr.,
Hunter, James Galbraith, Jr.,
Hyman, Michael Bruce
Johnson, Lael Frederic
Joseph, Robert Thomas
Kamin, Chester Thomas
King, Michael Howard
Michaels, Richard Edward
Montgomery, William Adam
Nord, Robert Eamor
Pascal, Roger
Pollock, Earl Edward
Sanchez, Christopher Benjamin
Saunders, George Lawton, Jr.,
Sfikas, Peter Michael
Silberman, Alan Harvey
Simon, Seymour
Streff, William Albert, Jr.,
Van Tine, Matthew Eric
Wildman, Max Edward
Willian, Clyde Franklin
Witcoff, Sheldon William

Hinsdale
Hetke, Richard Louis

Park Ridge
LaRue, Paul Hubert

Prospect Heights
Leopold, Mark F.

Warrenville
Johnson, Douglas Wells

INDIANA

Indianapolis
Knebel, Donald Earl
Lipshaw, Jeffrey Marc
McTurnan, Lee Bowes

IOWA

Des Moines
Bennett, Edward James

KENTUCKY

Louisville
Reed, John Squires, II,

Newport
Siverd, Robert Joseph

LOUISIANA

Metairie
Kutcher, Robert A.

New Orleans
Lee, Wayne J.
Marcus, Bernard
Masinter, Paul James

MAINE

Brunswick
Owen, H. Martyn

MARYLAND

Baltimore
Cole, Emried Dargan, Jr.,
Liebmann, George W(illiam)
Wilson, Thomas Matthew, III,

Bethesda
Dickstein, Sidney
Ross, William Warfield

Potomac
Meyer, Lawrence George

Rockville
Cheston, Sheila Carol

MASSACHUSETTS

Boston
Buchanan, Robert McLeod

Framingham
Gould, Rodney Elliott

Newton
Messing, Arnold Philip

Springfield
Dibble, Francis Daniel, Jr.,

MICHIGAN

Ann Arbor
Britton, Clarold Lawrence

Detroit
Calkins, Stephen
Driker, Eugene
Gottschalk, Thomas A.
Krsul, John Aloysius, Jr.,

Lansing
Baker, Frederick Milton, Jr.,

Monroe
Lipford, Rocque Edward

Troy
Alterman, Irwin Michael

MINNESOTA

Crystal
Reske, Steven David

Minneapolis
Bress, Michael E.
Clary, Bradley G.
Cullen, Terrance Michael
Duncan, Richard Alan
French, John Dwyer
Long, James Jay
Safley, James Robert
Silver, Alan Irving
Sippel, William Leroy

Minnetonka
Carpenter, Norman Roblee

Saint Paul
Maclin, Alan Hall

MISSISSIPPI

Jackson
Henegan, John C(lark)

MISSOURI

Clayton
Schwartz, Theodore Frank

Kansas City
Cross, William Dennis
Egan, Charles Joseph, Jr.,
Wyrsch, James Robert

Saint Louis
Berendt, Robert Tryon
Clear, John Michael
Joerling, Dale Raymond
Luberda, George Joseph

NEW JERSEY

Florham Park
Laulicht, Murray Jack

Iselin
Dornbusch, Arthur A., II,
Goodman, Barry S.

Kenilworth
Hoffman, John Fletcher

Morristown
Whitmer, Frederick Lee

Parsippany
Stein, Julie Lynne

Roseland
Eakeley, Douglas Scott

Somerville
Laskey, James Howard

NEW MEXICO

Albuquerque
Bardacke, Paul Gregory

NEW YORK

Buffalo
Halpern, Ralph Lawrence
Mucci, Gary Louis

Corning
Hauselt, Denise Ann

Larchmont
Gaffney, Mark William

New York
Altieri, Peter Louis
Arenson, Gregory K.
Arquit, Kevin James
Axinn, Stephen Mark
Barron, Francis Patrick
Barthold, Walter
Benjamin, Jeff
Bialo, Kenneth Marc
Blumkin, Linda Ruth
Broder, Douglas Fisher
Cirillo, Richard Allan
Clark, Merrell Edward, Jr.,
Clary, Richard Wayland
Collins, John F.
Collins, Wayne Dale
Cooper, Michael Anthony
Critchlow, Charles Howard
Dallas, William Moffit, Jr.,
DiBlasi, Gandolfo Vincent
Donovan, Richard Edward
Elwin, James William, Jr.,
Epstein, Michael Alan
Evans, Martin Frederic
Foster, David Lee
Friedman, Victor Stanley
Gold, Stuart Walter
Golden, Arthur F.
Goott, Alan F(ranklin)
Gotts, Ilene Knable
Harbison, James Wesley, Jr.,
Hartzell, Andrew Cornelius, Jr.,
Heller, Robert Martin
Holley, Steven Lyon
Holman, Bud George
Hruska, Alan J.
Hurlock, James Bickford
Jackson, Thomas Gene
Joffe, Robert David
John, Ian Grant
Joseph, Leonard
Kalish, Myron
Karmali, Rashida Alimahomed
Kaye, Stephen Rackow
Keany, Sutton
Kempf, Donald G., Jr.,
Kessler, Jeffrey L.
Kezsbom, Allen
King, Henry Lawrence
Kirby, John Joseph, Jr.,
Kleinberg, Norman Charles
Kobak, James Benedict, Jr.,
Koob, Charles Edward
Kurzweil, Harvey
Lifland, William Thomas
Logan, Kenneth Richard
London, Martin
Luria, Mary Mercer
Maulsby, Allen Farish
Mc Inerney, Denis
McMahon, James Charles
Millstein, Ira M.
Norfolk, William Ray
Primps, William Guthrie
Quinlan, Guy Christian
Quinn, Yvonne Susan
Reinthaler, Richard Walter
Reynolds, Michael Timothy
Rifkind, Robert S(inger)
Ringel, Dean
Rolfe, Ronald Stuart
Saunders, Paul Christopher
Serota, James Ian
Sesser, Gary Douglas
Silverman, Moses
Sobel, Gerald
Steuer, Richard Marc
Stoll, Neal Richard
Struve, Guy Miller
Taylor, Job, III,
Thackeray, Jonathan E.
Urowsky, Richard J.
Vig, Vernon Edward
Warden, John L.
Weinschel, Alan Jay
Zoeller, Donald J.

Pittsford
Braunsdorf, Paul Raymond

Rochester
Payment, Kenneth Arnold
Sheller, Patrick Michael
Smith, John Stuart

Schenectady
Cusick, Ernest George

Syracuse
Bullock, Stephen C.

NORTH CAROLINA

Fairview
Rhynedance, Harold Dexter, Jr.,

Wilmington
Jones, Lucian Cox

OHIO

Cincinnati
Hill, Thomas Clark

Cleveland
Bates, Walter Alan
Collin, Thomas James
Jacobs, Leslie William
Rains, M. Neal

Dayton
Faruki, Charles Joseph
Saul, Irving Isaac
Taronji, Jaime, Jr.,

Lancaster
Libert, Donald Joseph

Toledo
Wicklund, David Wayne

OREGON

Portland
Hanlon, Michael Gregory
Van Valkenburg, Edgar Walter

PENNSYLVANIA

Blue Bell
Elliott, John Michael

Kennett Square
Partnoy, Ronald Allen

Lancaster
Nast, Dianne Martha

Malvern
Quay, Thomas Emery

Philadelphia
Asher, Steven Alan
Berger, David
Bissell, Rolin Plumb
Calvert, Jay H., Jr.,
Grady, Thomas Michael
Haviland, Bancroft Dawley
Kessler, Alan Craig
Mannino, Edward Francis
Poul, Franklin
Schneider, Richard Graham
Tiger, Ira Paul

Pittsburgh
Drake, Edwin P.
Hershey, Dale
O'Connor, Edward Gearing
Turner, Harry Woodruff
Van Kirk, Thomas L.

RHODE ISLAND

Barrington
Soutter, Thomas Douglas

Providence
Medeiros, Matthew Francis

Wakefield
Hart, Kenneth Nelson

SOUTH CAROLINA

Charleston
Freer, Robert Elliott, Jr.,

Columbia
Dibble, Robert Wightman, Jr.,

Greenville
Phillips, Joseph Brantley, Jr.,
Todd, John Dickerson, Jr.,

TENNESSEE

Nashville
Mathies, Jordon Dean

TEXAS

Austin
Judson, Philip Livingston

Baytown
Chavez, John Anthony

Dallas
Frisbie, Curtis Lynn, Jr.,
Harrison, Orrin Lea, III,
Hinshaw, Chester John
Huffman, Gregory Scott Combest
Kearney, Douglas Charles
Lippe, Emil, Jr.,
McAtee, David Ray
McNamara, Anne H.
Price, John Aley

Fort Worth
Mack, Theodore

Houston
Barnett, Edward William
Carter, John Loyd
Devlin, Francis James
Harvin, David Tarleton
Kruse, Layne E.
McClure, Daniel M.
Owens, Betty Ruth
Reasoner, Harry Max
Smith, Alison Leigh
Van Fleet, George Allan

San Antonio
Wachsmuth, Robert William

UTAH

Salt Lake City
Berman, Daniel Lewis

VIRGINIA

Arlington
Kelly, John James

Reston
Rau, Lee Arthur

Richmond
Clinard, Robert Noel
Patterson, Robert Hobson, Jr.,
Slater, Thomas Glascock, Jr.,
Troy, Anthony Francis
Walsh, James Hamilton

WASHINGTON

Seattle
Boeder, Thomas L.
Clinton, Richard M.
Gray, Marvin Lee, Jr.,
Sandler, Michael David
Van Kampen, Al

WEST VIRGINIA

Morgantown
Fusco, Andrew G.

WISCONSIN

Madison
Barnhill, Charles Joseph, Jr.,

Milwaukee
Babler, Wayne E., Jr.,
Holz, Harry George
Levit, William Harold, Jr.,
Martin, Quinn William

MEXICO

Bosques de las Lomas
Duarte Coppel, Luis A.

Mexico City
Fuentes-Ostos, Francisco
Garcia Santos Coy, Luis Gerardo
Monterrubio Alcántara, Luis Manuel

AUSTRALIA

Sydney
L'Estrange, Timothy I.

BELGIUM

Brussels
Barnum, John Wallace

BRAZIL

São Paulo
Alves, Rodney Almeida
Inglez de Souza, Ricardo Norouha
Padovan, Lira Renardini
Zarzur, Cristianne Saccab

BULGARIA

Sofia
Gouginski, Nikolai Todorov

CHILE

Santiago
Letelier, Jose Luis
Varela, Gerardo

CZECH REPUBLIC

Prague
Cerny, Jiri

DENMARK

Copenhagen
Lokdam, Lars

Kolding
Ohrt, Hans-Christian

ENGLAND

London
Haubold, Samuel Allen
Wisking, Stephen

FINLAND

Helsinki
Kauppi, Matti Risto Sakari
Mentula, Arttu

FRANCE

Lyon
Girerd, Carole

Paris
Caritoux, Valérie Francoise Cecile
Condomines, Aurélien

GERMANY

Frankfurt
Ewen, Michael
Schulte, Josef L.
Wolff, Florian

Hamburg
Núñez Müller, Marco A.

Stuttgart
Mailaender, Karl Peter

IRELAND

Dublin
Calvani, Terry

NEW ZEALAND

Wellington
Pol, Ronald Franciscus

PERU

Lima
Rebaza, Alberto

REPUBLIC OF KOREA

Seoul
Hong, Dong Oh

SOUTH AFRICA

Sandown
Meijer, Jean Yvonne

SPAIN

Barcelona
Baches, Sergio
Girbau, Ramon

Madrid
Gutierrez, Alfonso

SWEDEN

Stockholm
Bergqvist, Trine Osen
Bökwall, Carl

ADDRESS UNPUBLISHED

Belleville, Philip Frederick
Berrey, Robert Forrest
Beukema, John Frederick
Blumenthal, William
Braun, Jerome Irwin
Colman, Richard Thomas
Dillon, Clifford Brien
Epstein, Judith Ann
Gass, Raymond William
Gladden, Joseph Reah, II,
Harris, Richard Eugene Vassau
Joelson, Mark René
Lea, Lorenzo Bates
McCobb, John Bradford, Jr.,
Mitchell, William Graham Champion
Newman, Carol L.
Pratt, Robert Windsor
Quillen, Cecil Dyer, Jr.,
Roberts, William H.
Skolnik, Barnet David
Springer, Paul David
Swacker, Frank Warren
Tapley, James Leroy
Tasker, Joseph
Tingle, James O'Malley
Walker, Craig Michael
Wooldridge, William Charles
Wruble, Bernhardt Karp
Yoskowitz, Irving Benjamin

APPELLATE

UNITED STATES

ALABAMA

Birmingham
Mills, William Hayes

Mobile
Cleveland, Lila Virginia

ALASKA

Anchorage
Gruenberg, Max F., Jr.,
Lerman, Averil

ARIZONA

Phoenix
Corson, Kimball Jay
Ulrich, Paul Graham
Wirken, Charles William

Tucson
Errico, Melissa
Lesher, Stephen Harrison

ARKANSAS

Fayetteville
Kester, Charles Melvin

CALIFORNIA

Belvedere Tiburon
Allan, Walter Robert

Berkeley
Pyle, Walter K.

Beverly Hills
Amado, Honey Kessler

Fresno
Little, Kevin Gerard

Irvine
Hensley, William Michael

Los Angeles
Adler, Erwin Ellery
Barth, Karen Ann
Cleary, William Joseph, Jr.,
Cole, Curtis Allen
Heinke, Rex S.
Hufstedler, Shirley Mount (Mrs. Seth M. Hufstedler)
Imre, Christina Joanne
Kanner, Gideon
Scoular, Robert Frank
Weatherup, Roy Garfield
Woods, Daniel James

Kittrell, Pamela R.
Logan, James Kenneth
Mugridge, David Raymond
Newman, Carol L.
Ostergaard, Joni Hammersla
Pagano, Eugene Salvatore Rooney
Peccarelli, Anthony Marando
Phillips, Dorothy Kay
Roberts, William H.
Sanders-Cochran, Rachel Deanna
Siemon, Joyce Marilyn
Vinar, Benjamin
Weisberg, David Charles

AVIATION

UNITED STATES

ALABAMA

Mobile
Roedder, William Chapman, Jr.,

ARIZONA

Phoenix
Tennen, Leslie Irwin

Tucson
Heaphy, John Merrill

ARKANSAS

Little Rock
Bohannon, Charles Tad

CALIFORNIA

Los Angeles
Foley, Martin James
Greaves, John Allen
Guilford, Robert E.
Hedlund, Paul James
Johnson, Philip Leslie
Margo, Rod David
Pascotto, Alvaro

Redwood City
Coddington, Clinton Hays

San Anselmo
Truett, Harold Joseph, III, (Tim Truett)

San Francisco
Dworkin, Michael Leonard

Santa Monica
Bower, Allan Maxwell
Boyle, Kevin Richard
Hofer, Stephen Robert

COLORADO

Denver
Byrne, Thomas J.

CONNECTICUT

Stamford
Burton, David K.

DISTRICT OF COLUMBIA

Washington
Carneal, George Upshur
Davison, Calvin
Keiner, R(obert) Bruce, Jr.,
Littell, Richard Gregory
Pogue, L(loyd) Welch
Schafrick, Frederick Craig
Trinder, Rachel Bandele
Whalen, Thomas J.
Wray, Robert

FLORIDA

Coral Gables
Hoffman, Carl H.

Melbourne
Trachtman, Jerry H.

Miami
Aronovitz, Tod
Becerra, Robert John
O'Connor, Kathleen Mary
Podhurst, Aaron Samuel

Tampa
Wagner, Frederick William (Bill Wagner)

GEORGIA

Atlanta
Harkey, Robert Shelton
Strauss, Robert David

Tucker
Armstrong, Edwin Alan

HAWAII

Honolulu
Char, Vernon Fook Leong
Fried, L. Richard, Jr.,

ILLINOIS

Chicago
Bogaard, Jonathan Harvey
Goldschmidt, Lynn Harvey
Rapoport, David E.
Salzetta, Paul Louis

INDIANA

Indianapolis
Yeager, Joseph Heizer, Jr.,

KANSAS

Wichita
Hodge, Ray

KENTUCKY

Louisville
Helm, T. Kennedy, III,

LOUISIANA

New Orleans
King, Rebecca J.

MARYLAND

Baltimore
Orman, Leonard Arnold

Columbia
Jacobs, William Michael

Rockville
Cheston, Sheila Carol

MASSACHUSETTS

Bedford
Wieand, Jeffrey Scott

MICHIGAN

Detroit
Torpey, Scott Raymond

East Lansing
Joseph, Raymond

MISSOURI

Kansas City
Robb, Gary Charles

NEBRASKA

Omaha
O'Connor, Robert Edward, Jr.,

NEVADA

Reno
Hibbs, Loyal Robert

NEW JERSEY

Woodcliff Lake
Clemen, John Douglas

NEW YORK

New York
Barry, Desmond Thomas, Jr.,
Mentz, Lawrence
Romans, John Niebrugge

Williamsville
Ross, Christopher T.W.

OHIO

Cincinnati
Lloyd, David Livingstone, Jr.,

Cleveland
Rosenbaum, Jacob I.

Columbus
Eichenberger, Jerry Alan

PENNSYLVANIA

Chadds Ford
Lamonaca, Joseph Michael

Philadelphia
Goldberg, Marvin Allen

SOUTH CAROLINA

Columbia
Ratchford, David Maurice

Greenville
Phillips, Joseph Brantley, Jr.,

TENNESSEE

Memphis
Lee, Samuel S.

TEXAS

Austin
Davis, Don Lawrence
Spivey, Broadus Autry

Lindale
Anderson, Lawrence Worthington

San Antonio
Guess, James David

VIRGINIA

Falls Church
Van Oeveren, Edward Lanier

Lynchburg
Healy, Joseph Francis, Jr.,

WASHINGTON

Hoquiam
Kessler, Keith Leon

Tacoma
Riggio, Michael V.

BRAZIL

São Paulo
Lynch, Maria Regina Mangabeira Albernaz

FRANCE

Paris
Honig, Gérard

GREECE

Athens
Papantonopoulu, Katia

JAPAN

Tokyo
Grondine, Robert Francis

PERU

Lima
Lozano-Merino, Raul Santiago

PHILIPPINES

Makati City
Gonzales, Ponciano Jr. Concepcion

SWITZERLAND

Zollikon Zurich
Neupert, Walter Dieter

Zürich
Kammerer, Adrian W.

UKRAINE

Kiev
Kolesnyk, Oleg Ivanovich

ADDRESS UNPUBLISHED

Alberger, William Relph
Dubuc, Carroll Edward
Johnson, Richard Tenney

BANKING *See also* Commercial

UNITED STATES

ALABAMA

Birmingham
Brooke, William Wade
Carmody, Richard Patrick
Childs, Larry Brittain
Hagefstration, John E., Jr.,

Dadeville
Adair, Charles Robert, Jr.,

Mobile
Oldweiler, Thomas Patrick

Montgomery
Leslie, Henry Arthur

ALASKA

Anchorage
Ostrovsky, Lawrence Zelig

ARIZONA

Phoenix
Rudolph, Gilbert Lawrence

ARKANSAS

Pine Bluff
Strode, Joseph Arlin

CALIFORNIA

Costa Mesa
Marshall, Ellen Ruth

Encino
Levine, Thomas Jeffrey Pello

Los Angeles
Clark, R(ufus) Bradbury
Dunham, Scott H.
Farrar, Stanley F.
Hudson, Jeffrey Reid
MacLaughlin, Francis Joseph
Marcus, Stephen Howard
Millard, Neal Steven
Morgenthaler-Lever, Alisa
Thoren-Peden, Deborah Suzanne

Pacific Palisades
Share, Richard Hudson

Pasadena
Logan, Francis Dummer

San Diego
Shippey, Sandra Lee

San Francisco
Abbott, Barry Alexander
Coombe, George William, Jr.,
Halloran, Michael James
Howard, Carl
Smith, Robert Michael
Stroup, Stanley Stephenson
Walsh, Joseph Richard

San Rafael
Duke, George F.

Santa Barbara
Cappello, A. Barry

Santa Monica
Preble, Laurence George

COLORADO

Colorado Springs
Buell, Bruce Temple

Denver
Bain, Donald Knight
Hawley, Robert Cross
Moye, John Edward
Otten, Arthur Edward, Jr.,
Stockmar, Ted P.

Fort Collins
Gast, Richard Shaeffer
Rogers, Garth Winfield

CONNECTICUT

Litchfield
Fiederowicz, Walter Michael

Stamford
Rose, Richard Loomis

Washington
Fishman, Mitchell Steven

Waterbury
Wolfe, Harriet Munrett

Westport
Lindskog, David Richard

DELAWARE

Dover
Steele, Myron Thomas
Twilley, Joshua Marion

Wilmington
Salinger, Frank Max

DISTRICT OF COLUMBIA

Washington
Alexander, Clifford Joseph
Bachman, Kenneth Leroy, Jr.,
Buckley, Jeremiah Stephen
Clark, Paul Thomas
Comstock, Robert Francis
Glancz, Ronald Robert
Haines, Terry L.
Horn, Charles M.
Hyde, Howard Laurence
Kaufman, Thomas Frederick
Leibold, Arthur William, Jr.,
Levenson, Alan Bradley
Lybecker, Martin Earl
Mierzewski, Michael Brian
Miles, David Michael
Oppenheimer, Franz Martin
Pape, Stuart M.
Policy, Vincent Mark
Smith, Brian William
Stock, Stuart Chase
Topelius, Kathleen Ellis
Weinstein, Harris
Weiss, Mark Anschel
Wolf, William B., Jr.,
Wolff, Paul Martin

FLORIDA

Boca Raton
McNair, Russell Arthur, Jr.,

Coconut Grove
Arboleya, Carlos Joaquin

Coral Gables
Sacasas, Rene

Deerfield Beach
Buck, Thomas Randolph

Jacksonville
Christian, Gary Irvin
Hodge, James Edward
Kent, John Bradford

Jasper
McCormick, John Hoyle

Miami
Berley, David Richard
Garrett, Richard G.
Hajek, Robert J., Sr.,
Miller, James M.
Murai, Rene Vicente

Naples
Petersen, David L.

Orlando
Christiansen, Patrick T.
Jontz, Jeffry Robert
Neff, A. Guy
Yates, Leighton Delevan, Jr.,

Palm Coast
Patz, Edward Frank

Sarasota
Abel, Harvey Joseph
Raimi, Burton Louis

Tallahassee
Elliott, Timothy B.

Tampa
Gardner, J. Stephen
Roberson, Bruce Heerdt

Vero Beach
Gordon, William Stout

West Palm Beach
Koffler, Warren William

Winter Park
Hadley, Ralph Vincent, III,

GEORGIA

Atlanta
Carson, Christopher Leonard

Collins, Steven M.
Driver, Walter W., Jr.,
Jordan, Hilary Peter
Kessler, Richard Paul, Jr.,
Moeling, Walter Goos, IV,
Sibley, James Malcolm
Smith, Alexander Wyly, Jr.,
Stallings, Ronald Denis

Brunswick
McLemore, Gilbert Carmichael, Jr.,

Savannah
Searcy, William Nelson

Zebulon
Watson, Forrest Albert, Jr.,

HAWAII

Honolulu
Nakata, Gary Kenji
Okinaga, Lawrence Shoji
Wong, Alfred Mun Kong
Wong, Reuben Sun Fai

ILLINOIS

Barrington
Cloney, Terence J.

Burr Ridge
Brennan, James Joseph

Chicago
Burke, Richard William
Cohen, Melanie Rovner
Duncan, John Patrick Cavanaugh
Field, Robert Edward
Franklin, Christine Carroll
Golden, Bruce Paul
Jacobson, Ronald H.
Kallick, David A.
Kaufman, Andrew Michael
Kohn, William Irwin
Kravitt, Jason Harris Paperno
Malkin, Cary Jay
McCrohon, Craig
McDermott, John H(enry)
McMenamin, John Robert
Prochnow, Herbert Victor, Jr.,
Schwartz, Donald Lee
Tarun, Robert Walter
Weissman, Michael Lewis

Gurnee
Southern, Robert Allen

Highland Park
Tabin, Seymour

Lincolnshire
Bartlett, Robert William

Marengo
Franks, Herbert Hoover

Ottawa
White, Robert Ellsworth

Springfield
Van Meter, Abram DeBois
Walbaum, Robert C.

Watseka
Tungate, James Lester

Wheaton
Stein, Lawrence A.

Winnetka
Fawcett, Dwight Winter
Greenblatt, Ray Harris

INDIANA

Brazil
Deal, James Edward

Indianapolis
Kleiman, Mary Margaret
Neff, Robert Matthew
Talesnick, Stanley

Richmond
Bever, Robert Lynn

South Bend
Ford, George Burt

Vincennes
Smith, Bruce Arthur

IOWA

Des Moines
Flynn, Thomas Lee

Iowa City
Downer, Robert Nelson

KANSAS

Overland Park
Ayers, Jeffrey David

KENTUCKY

Bowling Green
Catron, Stephen Barnard

Flemingsburg
McCartney, Frank Howard, III,

Glasgow
Gardner, Woodford Lloyd, Jr.,

Hazard
Barker, Stephen Gerald

Lexington
Byrne, Walter Robbins, Jr.,

Louisville
Conner, Stewart Edmund
Fenton, Thomas Conner
Helm, T. Kennedy, III,
Maggiolo, Allison Joseph

LOUISIANA

Monroe
Sartor, Daniel Ryan, Jr.,

New Orleans
Bieck, Robert Barton, Jr.,
Getten, Thomas Frank
Maloney, Marilyn C.
McMillan, Lee Richards, II,

Shreveport
Cox, John Thomas, Jr.,
Goodman, Robert Uhle

MAINE

Portland
Hirshon, Robert Edward

Yarmouth
Webster, Peter Bridgman

MARYLAND

Annapolis
Lucas, Steven Mitchell
Michaelson, Benjamin, Jr.,

Baltimore
Haines, Thomas W. W.
Wasserman, Richard Leo
Winn, James Julius, Jr.,

New Market
Gabriel, Eberhard John

MASSACHUSETTS

Arlington
Keshian, Richard

Boston
Fischer, Eric Robert
Loria, Martin A.
Perkins, John Allen
Ragalevsky, Stanley Victor
Read, Nicholas Cary
Smith, Edwin Eric

Greenfield
Blanker, Alan Harlow

Lincoln
Gnichtel, William Van Orden

Marion
Worley, Robert William, Jr.,

MICHIGAN

Battle Creek
Steffel, Vern John, Jr.,

Bloomfield Hills
Ledwidge, Patrick Joseph
Williams, J. Bryan

Detroit
Howbert, Edgar Charles
Lawrence, John Kidder
Rohr, Richard David
Targan, Holli Hart

Grosse Pointe Farms
Brucker, Wilber Marion

Kalamazoo
Gordon, Edgar George

Muskegon
Fauri, Eric Joseph

MINNESOTA

Duluth
Nys, John Nikki

Eden Prairie
Nilles, John Michael

Fridley
Savelkoul, Donald Charles

Golden Valley
Schlichting, William Henry

Minneapolis
Kantor, David
Palmer, Brian Eugene

Saint Paul
Winthrop, Sherman

MISSISSIPPI

Gulfport
Harral, John Menteith

Jackson
Hammond, Frank Jefferson, III,

MISSOURI

Hannibal
Welch, Joseph Daniel

Kansas City
Deacy, Thomas Edward, Jr.,
Frisbie, Charles
Graham, Harold Steven
Parres, Cynthia Dillard

Saint Louis
Graham, Robert Clare, III,
Inkley, John James, Jr.,
Poscover, Maury B.
Rubenstein, Jerome Max
Woodruff, Bruce Emery

NEBRASKA

Lincoln
Guthery, John M.

Omaha
Hamann, Deryl Frederick

Valentine
O'Kief, W. Gerald

NEW HAMPSHIRE

Manchester
Stebbins, Henry Blanchard
Zachos, Kimon Stephen

NEW JERSEY

Bridgewater
Linett, David

Florham Park
Freis, James Henry

Garwood
Maher, Gary Laurence

Morris Plains
Mellinger, Louis Philip

Morristown
O'Grady, Dennis Joseph

Newark
Radin, Steven S.

Oakhurst
Rescinio, Albert John

Roseland
Carella, Charles Carmine
McMahon, Edward Richard
Wovsaniker, Alan

Short Hills
Siegfried, David Charles

Somerville
Hutcheon, Peter David

Summit
Pfaltz, Hugo Menzel, Jr.,
Woller, James Alan

Trenton
Frost, Barry Warren

Union
Greenstein, Richard Henry

Woodbridge
Hoberman, Stuart A.

NEW MEXICO

Albuquerque
Fish, Paul Mathew

Clovis
Skarda, Lynell Griffith

Ruidoso
Dutton, Dominic Edward

Santa Fe
Justice, Jack Burton

NEW YORK

Albany
Yanas, John Joseph

Hauppauge
Cummings, Anthony William

Hudson
Howard, Andrew Baker

Huntington
Tucker, William P.

Lake George
Hayes, Norman Robert, Jr.,

Larchmont
Berridge, George Bradford
Kullen, Richard Charles, Jr.,

Long Island City
Wanderman, Susan Mae

Melville
Lane, Arthur Alan

New York
Adair, Wendell Hinton, Jr.,
Bergan, Philip James
Bernstein, Donald Scott
Brundige, Robert William, Jr.,
Caytas, Ivo George
Chen, Wesley
Christenfeld, Alan M.
Christopherson, David Victor
Cohen, Henry Rodgin
Corbin, Sol Neil
Daitz, Ronald Frederick
Das, Kalyan
Davis, Richard Ralph
Douglas, James McCrystal
Doyle, Joseph Anthony
Dropkin, Charles Edward
Dwyer, Cornelius J., Jr.,
Feintuch, Richard David
Fernandez, Jose Walfredo
Fewell, Charles Kenneth, Jr.,
Franklin, Blake Timothy
Freedman, Gerald M.
Genova, Diane Melisano
Greene, Ira S.
Grew, Robert Ralph
Harper, Emery Walter
Hauser, Rita Eleanore Abrams
Helfer, Michael Stevens
Henze, William F., II,
Hill, Joseph C.
Huck, L. Francis
Isaacson, Allen Ira
Jock, Paul F., II,
Jong, James C. (Chuanping Zhang)
Knight, Townsend Jones
Kraemer, Lillian Elizabeth
Lee, In-Young
Leichtling, Michael Alfred
Levine, Robert Jay
Lindsay, George Peter
Lynch, Luke Daniel, Jr.,
MacRae, Cameron Farquhar, III,
Marcus, Eric Peter
McBryde, Thomas Henry
McDavid, William Henry
McLaughlin, Joseph Thomas
Minsky, Bruce William
O'Hara, Robert Sydney, Jr.,
Oshima, Michael W.
Pidot, Whitney Dean
Puleo, Frank Charles
Quale, Andrew Christopher, Jr.,
Radon, Jenik Richard
Rocklen, Kathy Hellenbrand
Rosenblum, William F., Jr.,
Ross, Michael Aaron
Russo, Thomas Anthony
Schwab, Terrance W.
Serchuk, Ivan
Sheehan, Robert C.
Skigen, Patricia Sue
Smith, Bradley Youle
Taylor, Richard Trelore
Tehan, John Bashir
Thaler, Craig H.
Thomas, Jeremiah Lindsay, III,
Toumey, Donald Joseph
Trott, Dennis C(harles)
Walker, John Lockwood
Weld, Jonathan Minot
Wolson, Craig Alan
Zaitzeff, Roger Michael

Rochester
Galbraith, Robert Lyell, Jr.,
Young, Deborah Schwind

Scarsdale
Kanter, Carl Irwin

Syracuse
Ackerman, Kenneth Edward
Barclay, H(ugh) Douglas
Hubbard, Peter Lawrence

NORTH CAROLINA

Charlotte
Loughridge, John Halsted, Jr.,
Monge, Jay Parry
Taylor, David Brooke

Greensboro
Davis, Herbert Owen

Murphy
Bata, Rudolph Andrew, Jr.,

Raleigh
Carlton, Alfred Pershing, Jr.,
Jernigan, John Lee

Wilmington
Jones, Lucian Cox
McCauley, Cleyburn Lycurgus

Winston Salem
Adams, Alfred Gray

Herring, Jerone Carson
Sandridge, William Pendleton, Jr.,

OHIO

Ashland
Leper, Paul

Celina
Luth, Thomas Edward

Cincinnati
Ashdown, Philomena Saldanha
Coffey, Thomas William

Cleveland
Coquillette, William Hollis
Goins, Frances Floriano
Hollington, Richard Rings, Jr.,
Lawniczak, James Michael
Stevens, Thomas Charles
Willenbrink, Rose Ann

Columbus
Deal, John Charles
Frasier, Ralph Kennedy

Seaman
Young, Vernon Lewis

Toledo
Hilbert, John Warren, II,

Upper Sandusky
Fox, Mary Ellen

Warren
McGeough, Robert Saunders

OKLAHOMA

Jones
Dean, Bill Verlin, Jr.,

Muskogee
Robinson, Adelbert Carl

Norman
Hastie, John Douglas

Oklahoma City
Beech, Johnny Gale
Elder, James Carl

OREGON

Lake Oswego
Byczynski, Edward Frank
Rasmussen, Richard Robert

Portland
Arthur, Michael Elbert

PENNSYLVANIA

Allison Park
Ries, William Campbell

Exton
Teti, Louis N.

Hermitage
McKay, Donald Ross

Mc Murray
Brzustowicz, John Cinq-Mars

Philadelphia
Berger, Lawrence Howard
Dilks, Park Bankert, Jr.,
Genkin, Barry Howard
Haley, Vincent Peter
Hunter, James Austen, Jr.,
Loveless, George Group
Maxey, David Walker
Spolan, Harmon Samuel

Pittsburgh
Bleier, Michael E.
Restivo, James John, Jr.,
Singer, Paul Meyer
Winter, Nelson Warren

Reading
Kline, Sidney DeLong, Jr.,

Warren
Ristau, Mark Moody

Washington
Posner, David S.

Williamsport
Knecht, William L.

RHODE ISLAND

Providence
Furness, Peter John

SOUTH CAROLINA

Charleston
Unger, Henry Manning

Columbia
Johnson, Lawrence Wilbur, Jr.,
Price, Robert Grant

Greenville
Riley, Richard Wilson

SOUTH DAKOTA

Sioux Falls
Prendergast, Terry Neill

TENNESSEE

Memphis
Winchester, Richard Lee, Jr.,

Nashville
Bass, James Orin
Camp, Randy Coleman
Eisen, Steven Jeffrey

TEXAS

Addison
Kneipper, Richard Keith

Amarillo
Cox, Roger Stephen

Austin
Laves, Alan Leonard
Temple, Larry Eugene

Boerne
Vaughan, Edward Gibson

Brownsville
Fleming, Tommy Wayne

Dallas
Baggett, W. Mike
Beuttenmuller, Rudolf William
Brady, Jack Edgar
Hicks, Marion Lawrence, Jr., (Larry Hicks)
Jones, Lindy Don
Kearney, Douglas Charles
Peterson, Edward Adrian
Riddle, Michael Lee
True, Roy Joe
White, James Richard
Zisman, Barry Stuart

Houston
Bistline, F. Walter, Jr.,
Block, Nelson R(ichard)
Bridges, David Manning
Moehlman, Michael Scott
Weiner, Sanford Alan

Midland
Meyers, Alan Hoge
Truitt, Robert Ralph, Jr.,

Missouri City
Hodges, Jot Holiver, Jr.,

Plainview
Lafont, William Harold

Rockport
Porter, Charles Raleigh, Jr.,

San Marcos
Kyle, Henry Carper, III,

Sherman
Freels, Jesse Saunders, Jr.,

The Woodlands
Hagerman, John David

Tyler
Lake, David Alan

Victoria
McKay, Robert Connally

Weslaco
Pomerantz, Jerald Michael

Yorktown
Barry, Thomas Joseph

UTAH

Saint George
Gallian, Russell Joseph

Salt Lake City
Callister, Louis Henry, Jr.,

VIRGINIA

Abingdon
Copeland, Robert Tayloe

Charlottesville
Hodous, Robert Power

Falls Church
Christman, Bruce Lee
Jennings, Thomas Parks

Reston
Toole, John Harper

Richmond
Buford, Robert Pegram
Pinckney, Charles Cotesworth

Roanoke
Densmore, Douglas Warren

Springfield
Englert, Roy Theodore

Sterling
McBarnette, Bruce Olvin

Woodstock
Walton, Morgan Lauck, III,

WASHINGTON

Seattle
Kuhrau, Edward W.
Ritter, Daniel Benjamin
Tune, James Fulcher

WEST VIRGINIA

Charleston
O'Connor, Otis Leslie

WISCONSIN

La Crosse
Klos, Jerome John

Milwaukee
Adashek, James Lewis
Flynn, William Frederick
Friedman, James Dennis

Sun Prairie
Eustice, Francis Joseph

WYOMING

Casper
Lowe, Robert Stanley

Cheyenne
Dyekman, Gregory Chris

TERRITORIES OF THE UNITED STATES

VIRGIN ISLANDS

Christiansted
Grey, Samuel T.

AUSTRALIA

Melbourne
Paterson, Robert

Sydney
Seidler, Robert Leslie

AUSTRIA

Vienna
Wolf, Richard V.

BELGIUM

Antwerp
De Roeck, Martine M.

Brussels
Delsaut, Philippe Patrick
Lohest, Thierry

BRAZIL

Rio de Janeiro
Pinheiro-Guimarães, Plinio

São Paulo
Padovan, Lira Renardini

BULGARIA

Sofia
Poshtakova, Dora Hristova

CHILE

Santiago
Laval, Juan Esteban

CZECH REPUBLIC

Prague
Krejci, Kvetoslav

DENMARK

Copenhagen
Sogaard, Klaus

ENGLAND

London
Barratt, Jeffrey Vernon
Brownwood, David Owen
Cole, Richard A.
Quillen, Cecil Dyer, III,

FRANCE

Paris
Boiron, Jean-Eric
Plankensteiner, Marco

GERMANY

Düsseldorf
Gillessen, Frederick

Hamburg
von Teichman, Christoph

Nuremberg
Schwartz, Harald Josef

Stuttgart
Mailaender, Karl Peter

GREECE

Athens
Georgacopulos, Dimitris Haralambos

Piraeus
Bowen-Morris, Nigel Vaughan

INDONESIA

Jakarta
Djemat, Humphrey Rithan

ITALY

Milan
Codurri, Maurizio

JAPAN

Tokyo
Impastato, David John, III,
Sedlak, Eric William
Wexler, Thomas Charles

LUXEMBOURG

Luxembourg
Kremer, Christian

NEW ZEALAND

Auckland
Webb, Michael R.

Wellington
Craig, David J.

PANAMA

Panama
Martínez Saenz, Ivette Elisa

PORTUGAL

Lisbon
Ferreira, Anabela Gonçalves
Lowndes Marques, Filipe

ROMANIA

Bucharest
Angelo, Florentina Daniela
Predoiu, Cătălin Marian

SINGAPORE

Singapore
Trahair, Andrew James

SOUTH AFRICA

Sandton
Cron, Kevin Richard

SPAIN

Barcelona
Torres Blanquez, Miguel

SWEDEN

Stockholm
Romander, Clas Gustav Johannes

SWITZERLAND

Geneva
De Pfyffer, Andre
Equey, Robert

Zürich
Feller, Urs P.
Maurenbrecher, Benedikt

THAILAND

Bangkok
Periera, Santhapat

ADDRESS UNPUBLISHED

Allen, Wayne Alan
Babb, Frank Edward
Beattie, Charles Robert, III,
Bennett, Steven Alan
Berti-Azar, Joseph
Brown, Charles Dodgson
Crook, Donald Martin
Cumberland, William Edwin
Derman, Emre
Field, Arthur Norman
Ginsberg, Ernest
Goebel, Hans P.
Gregory, George G.
Gross, Richard Benjamin
Hackett, Robert John
Harman, Wallace Patrick
Johnson, Leonard Hjalma
June, Roy Ethiel
Kaufman, James Jay
Kelly, Anastasia Donovan
Marker, Marc Linthacum
Ober, Richard Francis, Jr.,
Padilla, James Earl
Reiter, Glenn Mitchell
Ring, Renee Etheline
Shambaugh, Stephen Ward
Watson, John Michael
Weil, Peter Henry
Wessling, Robert Bruce
Wiley, Richard Arthur

BANKRUPTCY *See also* Commercial

UNITED STATES

ALABAMA

Birmingham
Carmody, Richard Patrick
Irons, William Lee
Johnson, Eric Heath

Enterprise
Price, Robert Allan

Tuscaloosa
Crownover, Walter Parker

ALASKA

Anchorage
Bundy, David Hollister
Ostrovsky, Lawrence Zelig
Willard-Jones, Donna C.

ARIZONA

Flagstaff
Cowser, Danny Lee

Phoenix
Lee, Richard H(arlo)
Meyers, Howard Craig
Rathwell, Peter John

Prescott
Chamberlain, David Alanson

Tempe
Palmer, Janice Maude

ARKANSAS

Fort Smith
Foster, M. Shannon

CALIFORNIA

Bakersfield
Gong, Gloria Margaret

Beverly Hills
Brickwood, Susan Callaghan

Burbank
McNally, Gerald, Jr.,

Downey
Schauf, Carolyn Jane

East Palo Alto
Bates, William, III,

El Cajon
Graf, Sheryl Susan

Encinitas
Williams, Michael Edward

Escondido
Godone-Maresca, Lillian

Huntington Beach
Armstrong, Alan Leigh

Los Angeles
Cohen, Cynthia Marylyn
Davidson, Jeffrey H.
Freier, Elliot G.
Gilhuly, Peter Martin
Havel, Richard W.
Huben, Brian David
Neely, Sally Schultz
O'Leary, Prentice L.
Ohlgren, Joel R.
Sands, Velma Ahda
White, Robert Joel
Zerunyan, Frank Vram

Newport Beach
Wolf, Alan Steven

Oakland
Allen, Jeffrey Michael
Buckley, Mike Clifford

Pacific Palisades
Kelley, Thomas Joseph

Pleasanton
Opperwall, Stephen Gabriel

Point Richmond
Edginton, John Arthur

Sacramento
Felderstein, Steven Howard

San Diego
Shapiro, Philip Alan

San Francisco
Holden, Frederick Douglass, Jr.,
Kelly, J. Michael
Lapping, Richard A.
Stinnett, Terrance Lloyd
Weir, William John Arnold
Wetmore, Keith Chidester

San Jose
Katzman, Irwin

Stanford
Sofaer, Abraham David

Ventura
Kump, Kary Ronald

Walnut Creek
Rathjen, Jon Laurence

COLORADO

Colorado Springs
Gefreh, Paul Thomas
Slivka, Michael Andrew

Denver
Anstine, Glen Roscoe
Babiniec, Dennis Henry
Cohen, Jeffrey
Dowdle, Patrick Dennis
Long, Martin Edward
Smiley, John Clinton

Littleton
Perlman, B. Arthur

CONNECTICUT

Farmington
Grafstein, Joel M.

Hartford
Sosensky, Steven Charles

New Haven
Skalka, Douglas Scott
Wagoner, Walter Dray, Jr.,

Roxbury
Friedman, John Maxwell, Jr.,

DELAWARE

Newark
Welsh, Paul Patrick

Wilmington
Flame, Andrew Jay
Melnik, Selinda A.

DISTRICT OF COLUMBIA

Washington
Black, Stephen Franklin
Cohen, Nelson Craig
Mackiewicz, Edward Robert

Pearlstein, Paul Davis
Samuelson, Kenneth Lee

FLORIDA

Brandon
England, Lynne Lipton

Coconut Creek
Sheehy, Frances Diane

Hudson
Hay, Cedric Peter

Jacksonville
McBurney, Charles Walker, Jr.,

Miami
Baena, Scott Louis
Miller, Raymond Vincent, Jr.,
Pastoriza, Julio
Scheer, Mark Jeffrey
Stein, Allan Mark

New Port Richey
Focht, Theodore Harold

Orlando
Jontz, Jeffry Robert

Palm Coast
Patz, Edward Frank

Palm Harbor
Summers-Powell, Alan

Pensacola
Woodward, David Luther

Saint Petersburg
Kersker, Peter Wheeler

Sarasota
Fetterman, James Charles

Tampa
Arcuri, Shirley Copeland
Lau, Mary Applegate
Olson, John Karl

West Palm Beach
Dunkum, Betty Lee
Mrachek, Lorin Louis

GEORGIA

Atlanta
Campbell, Charles Edward
Carson, Christopher Leonard
Cohen, Ezra Harry
Frenzel, James Charles
Kessler, Richard Paul, Jr.,
McCloud, Robert Olmsted, Jr.,

Columbus
Johnson, Walter Frank, Jr.,

Roswell
Mimms, Thomas Bowman, Jr.,

Statesboro
Stone, Ralph Kenny

HAWAII

Honolulu
Bocken, R. Charles
Gelber, Don Jeffrey

Wailuku
Barbin, Ryther Lynn

IDAHO

Blackfoot
Sorensen, Murray Jim

Boise
Noack, Harold Quincy, Jr.,

Coeur D Alene
Garbrecht, Louis

Twin Falls
Sudweeks, Jay Dean

ILLINOIS

Alton
Struif, L. James

Aurora
Mateas, Kenneth Edward

Belleville
Urban, Donald Wayne

Chicago
Berkoff, Mark Andrew
Cohen, Melanie Rovner
Collen, John
Cunningham, Thomas Justin
Feinstein, Fred Ira
French, Timothy A.
Gordon, James S.
Hoseman, Daniel
Kohn, Shalom L.
Kohn, William Irwin
Murray, Daniel Richard
Peterson, Ronald Roger
Rosenbloom, Lewis Stanley
Schwartz, Donald Lee
Wood, Allison Lorraine

La Grange
Kerr, Alexander Duncan, Jr.,

Normal
Bender, Paul Edward

Paris
Bell, Allen Andrew, Jr.,

Springfield
Duggan, Timothy E.

INDIANA

Fort Wayne
Tourkow, Joshua Isaac

Indianapolis
Abels, Jonathan Berle
Bruns, Beverly A.
Capehart, Craig Earl
Carlberg, James Edwin
Knauer, James A.
Silver, Gregory K.
Talesnick, Stanley
Wunder, David Hart

Lafayette
Hoffman, John Frederick

Vincennes
Smith, Bruce Arthur

IOWA

Des Moines
Flynn, Thomas Lee
Neiman, Donald Flint

Sioux City
Giles, William Jefferson, III,

KANSAS

Leawood
Bohm, Jack Nelson

Neodesha
Depew, Harry Luther

Topeka
Barnes, Tom R., II,

KENTUCKY

Lexington
Masterton, Lucinda Cronin

Louisville
Bubalo, Gregory Joe
Shaikun, Michael Gary

Monticello
Tobbe, Leonard Lee

LOUISIANA

Baton Rouge
Anderson, Lawrence Robert, Jr.,

New Orleans
Brouphy, Greta Manning
Johnson, Patrick, Jr.,
Jones, Philip Kirkpatrick, Jr.,
Title, Peter Stephen

MAINE

Bass Harbor
Ervin, Spencer

MARYLAND

Baltimore
Berlage, Jan Ingham
Coppel, Lawrence David
Katz, Lawrence Edward
Liebmann, George W(illiam)
Walker, Irving Edward
Wasserman, Richard Leo
Wolf, Cyd Beth

Bethesda
Bason, George F., Jr.,

Frederick
Borison, Scott Craig

Lutherville
Fascetta, Christopher Michael

Rockville
Barkley, Brian Evan
Stolker, Richard Samuel

Silver Spring
Davis, Richmond T.P.

MASSACHUSETTS

Boston
Berman, Mark Niles
Bodoff, Joseph Samuel Uberman
Daley, Paul Patrick
Glosband, Daniel Martin
Lamb, Kevin Thomas
Macauley, William Francis
Rodman, John Slater
Smith, Edwin Eric

Cambridge
Esher, Jacob Aaron

Stoughton
Gabovitch, Steven Alan

MICHIGAN

Ann Arbor
Ellmann, Douglas Stanley

Birmingham
Smith, Patti

Bloomfield Hills
Cunningham, Gary H.

Detroit
Fellrath, Richard Frederic
Howbert, Edgar Charles
Pirtle, H(arold) Edward
Toll, Sheldon Samuel

Grand Rapids
Curtin, Timothy John
Mears, Patrick Edward

Kalamazoo
Borsos, Robert Bruce
Bus, Roger Jay

Midland
Battle, Leonard Carroll

MINNESOTA

Duluth
Nys, John Nikki

Edina
Gurstel, Norman Keith

Minneapolis
Baillie, James Leonard

Owatonna
Rask, Kelly Scott

MISSISSIPPI

Hattiesburg
Davis-Morris, Angela Elizabeth

Jackson
King, Robert Wilson
Mitchell, Meade Westmoreland
O'Mara, James Wright
Scanlon, Pat H.

Pascagoula
Tynes, Douglas Lamont

MISSOURI

Hannibal
Welch, Joseph Daniel

Kansas City
Carter, J. Denise
Foster, Mark Stephen
Parres, Cynthia Dillard
Redmond, Christopher John

Maryland Heights
Cooper, Richard Alan

Saint Louis
Komen, Leonard
Palans, Lloyd Alex

Springfield
Carlson, Thomas Joseph

MONTANA

Great Falls
Smartt, Michael Stewart

NEBRASKA

Lincoln
Rowe, David Winfield

Omaha
Frank, Julie Ann

NEVADA

Las Vegas
Hill, Judith Deegan
Miller, Rebecca Anne

Reno
Fletcher, Douglas Charles
Picker, Marc

NEW HAMPSHIRE

Gorham
Cote, Thomas Jacques

Newport
Shklar, Michael Charles

NEW JERSEY

Bayonne
Olsen, Mary Ann

Bloomfield
Caccavale, Stephen Joseph

Montclair
Ward, Roger Coursen

Morristown
O'Grady, Dennis Joseph

New Providence
Chobot, John Charles

Newark
Fiore, William Joseph
Radin, Steven S.

Parsippany
Gallagher, Jerome Francis, Jr.,

Pitman
Cloues, Edward Blanchard, II,

Red Bank
Anderson, James Francis

Ridgewood
Trocano, Russell Peter

Roseland
Schenkler, Bernard

Trenton
Frost, Barry Warren

Union
Suplee, Katherine Ann

West Orange
Cuozzi, William Francis, Jr.,

NEW MEXICO

Albuquerque
Fish, Paul Mathew
Mann, Nathan Huguenor

Carlsbad
Byers, Matthew T(odd)

Santa Fe
Justice, Jack Burton

NEW YORK

Auburn
Gunger, Richard William

Buffalo
Brown, Lawrence Charles
Fisher, Cheryl Smith

Garden City
Fischoff, Gary Charles

Geneseo
Macko, John

Hamburg
Gaughan, Dennis Charles

New York
Aloe, Paul Hubschman
Antonucci, Peter A.
Beitel, Bernard
Beltzer, Howard Stewart
Bernstein, Donald Scott
Berzow, Harold Steven
Blackman, Kenneth Robert
Blair, James Newell
Booth, Edgar Hirsch
Broude, Richard Frederick
Bursky, Herman Aaron
Cannell, John Redferne
Chaitman, Helen Davis
Christenfeld, Alan M.
Cook, Michael Lewis
Davis, Michael Steven
De Natale, Andrew Peter
Drebsky, Dennis Jay
Dresner, Byron
Emrich, Edmund Michael
Epling, Richard Louis
Feintuch, Richard David
Freedman, Gerald M.
Freedman, Theodore Levy
Gadsden, James
Greene, Ira S.
Handelsman, Lawrence Marc
Hazan, Scott L.
Hershcopf, Gerald Thea
Hirshfield, Stuart
Hirshon, Sheldon Ira
Hughes, Kevin Peter
Jacob, Marvin Eugene
Jerome, John James
Kinzler, Thomas Benjamin
Klein, Martin I.
Kornberg, Alan William
Kraemer, Lillian Elizabeth
Krasnow, Richard P.
Lacy, Robinson Burrell
Langer, Bruce Alden
Leinwand, Harris Donald
Levine, Robert Jay
Linker, Arthur S.
Lipton, Robert Steven
Luskin, Michael
Mayerson, Sandra Elaine
Miller, Richard Steven
Minkel, Herbert Philip, Jr.,
Moloney, Thomas Joseph
Nelson, Lester
Novikoff, Harold Stephen
O'Dea, Dennis Michael
Posner, Louis Joseph
Reilly, Conor Desmond
Scheler, Brad Eric
Silverberg, Jay Lloyd
Strickon, Harvey Alan
Tricarico, Joseph Archangelo

Olean
Heyer, John Henry, II,

Rochester
Lustig, Douglas James

Syracuse
Ackerman, Kenneth Edward
Goldberg, Harold Philip
Hubbard, Peter Lawrence

Troy
Marinstein, Elliott Fred

NORTH CAROLINA

Beaufort
Tilghman, Carl Lewis

Durham
Carpenter, Charles Francis

Gastonia
Cooper, Langdon McIlroy

Winston Salem
Schollander, Wendell Leslie, Jr.,

OHIO

Akron
Lammert, Thomas Edward
Whitmer, Jerry F.

Ashland
Leper, Paul

Celina
Luth, Thomas Edward

Cincinnati
Ashdown, Philomena Saldanha
Bissinger, Mark Christian
Candito, Joseph
Coffey, Thomas William

Cleveland
Eisen, Saul
Felty, Kriss Delbert
Lawniczak, James Michael
Meyer, G. Christopher
Sicherman, Marvin Allen

Columbus
Schaeffer, Matthew Thomas
Sidman, Robert John
Swetnam, Daniel Richard

Kent
Nome, William Andreas

Massillon
Breyfogle, Edwin Howard

Westerville
Lancione, Bernard Gabe

OKLAHOMA

Muskogee
Williams, Betty Outhier

Oklahoma City
Gibson, Keith Russell
Kline, David Adam
Kline, Timothy Deal
Schwabe, George Blaine, III,

Tulsa
Abrahamson, A. Craig
Clark, Gary Carl
Eliot, Theodore Quentin
Haynie, Tony Wayne
Moffett, J. Denny

OREGON

Eugene
Palmer, Russell Scott

Portland
Anderson, Herbert Hatfield
Waggoner, James Clyde

PENNSYLVANIA

Abington
Budman, Alan David

Blue Bell
Siedzikowski, Henry Francis

Brookville
Smith, Sharon Louise

Center Valley
Smillie, Douglas James

Harrisburg
Tyler, Brian Joseph
Warshaw, Allen Charles

Philadelphia
Aaron, Kenneth Ellyot
Berger, David
Bressler, Barry E.
Bressler, Gary David
Gough, John Francis
Grunfeld, David I.
Huntington, Stephen N.
Loveless, George Group
McMichael, Lawrence Grover
Reed, Michael Haywood
Schorling, William Harrison
Temin, Michael Lehman
Tractenberg, Craig R.

Pittsburgh
Aderson, Sanford M.
Helmrich, Joel Marc
Hollinshead, Earl Darnell, Jr.,
Leibowitz, Marvin
Miller, David A.
Murdoch, David Armor
Singer, Paul Meyer

Warren
Ristau, Mark Moody

Williamsport
Knecht, William L.

York
Ream, Jack Frantz

RHODE ISLAND

Providence
Furness, Peter John

Westerly
Panciera, Richard Conner

SOUTH CAROLINA

Aiken
Marine, Andrew Craig

Columbia
Johnson, Lawrence Wilbur, Jr.,

Myrtle Beach
Breen, David Hart

SOUTH DAKOTA

Sioux Falls
Hayes, Robert E.

TENNESSEE

Chattanooga
Ragan, Charles Oliver, Jr.,

Cleveland
Miller, Rodney Craig

Knoxville
Lucas, John Allen

Memphis
Matthews, Paul Aaron

Nashville
Mendes, Robert Joseph

TEXAS

Abilene
Boone, Celia Trimble

Amarillo
Cox, Roger Stephen

Dallas
Brister, Bill H.
Creel, Luther Edward, III,
Johnson, James Joseph Scofield
Nolan, John Michael
Phelan, Robin Eric
Portman, Glenn Arthur

Denton
Waage, Mervin Bernard

Fort Worth
Mack, Theodore
Tillman, Karen Sue

Galveston
Caldwell, Garnett Ernest

Horseshoe Bay
Welch, Robert Morrow, Jr.,

Houston
Banks, John Robert, Jr.,
Kay, Joel Phillip
Kemp, Roland Connor
McDaniel, Jarrel Dave
Miller, Gary C.
Prestridge, Pamela Adair
Ray, Hugh Massey, Jr.,
Sheinfeld, Myron M.
Sing, William Bender
Zeigler, Ann dePender

Lubbock
Crowson, James Lawrence

Midland
Truitt, Robert Ralph, Jr.,

Richardson
Olson, Dennis Oliver

San Antonio
Biery, Evelyn Hudson
Spears, Sally

Sherman
Freels, Jesse Saunders, Jr.,

Tyler
Patterson, Donald Ross

Wichita Falls
Williams, Steven Mark

UTAH

Provo
Hill, Richard Lee

Salt Lake City
Lochhead, Robert Bruce
Mabey, Ralph R.
Manning, Brent V.
Swinton, Jeffrey Cheever

VERMONT

Burlington
Lang, Richard Arnold, Jr.,

VIRGINIA

Abingdon
Copeland, Robert Tayloe

Charlottesville
Musselman, Robert Metcalfe

Danville
Abreu, Luis Alberto
Goodman, Lewis Elton, Jr.,

Hopewell
Clark, Bruce Arlington, Jr.,

Mc Lean
Morse, Duane D(ale)

Newport News
Nachman, Erwin B(ehr)

Norfolk
Gibson, Beverly Cullen

Richmond
Pinckney, Charles Cotesworth

Roanoke
Butler, Manley Caldwell

Virginia Beach
Harrell, Charles Lydon, Jr.,
Spitzli, Donald Hawkes, Jr.,

WASHINGTON

Kennewick
Hames, William Lester

Seattle
Bergstedt, Anders Spencer
Kriegman, Bruce Peter
MacLean, Merrilee Ann
Sandman, Irvin W(illis)

Spokane
Esposito, Joseph Anthony

WEST VIRGINIA

Charleston
Chaney, Michael Thomas

WISCONSIN

La Crosse
Russell, David Brent

Madison
Doran, Kenneth John
Prange, Roy Leonard, Jr.,
Temkin, Harvey L.
Walsh, David Graves

Milwaukee
Adashek, James Lewis
Blain, Peter Charles
Casper, Richard Henry
Medved, Paul Stanley
Sturm, William Charles

Sheboygan
Gass, David

WYOMING

Riverton
Girard, Nettabell
Scott, Beverly J.

TERRITORIES OF THE UNITED STATES

GUAM

Hagatna
Butler, George Morton

MEXICO

Mexico City
Garcia Giorgana, Ricardo

AUSTRALIA

Sydney
L'Estrange, Timothy I.
Wong, Christopher Wai C.

BELGIUM

Brussels
Bosly, Thierry H.
Delsaut, Philippe Patrick

BRAZIL

Rio de Janeiro
Basilio, Ana Tereza Palhares

BULGARIA

Sofia
Poshtakova, Dora Hristova

CHINA

Hong Kong
Rapinet, Crispin William

CZECH REPUBLIC

Prague
Peroutka, Hynek

ENGLAND

Manchester
White, Jamie

FRANCE

Paris
Boiron, Jean-Eric

GERMANY

Nuremberg
Schwartz, Harald Josef

NETHERLANDS

Amsterdam
Schaink, Paul Reinier Willem

NEW ZEALAND

Auckland
Whale, Michael John

PERU

Lima
Castle, Percy

SCOTLAND

Glasgow
Burrow, Alistair Stewart

Midlothian
Barnes, Joy Chappell

SPAIN

Madrid
Fernandez Aguado, Juan Ignacio

SWITZERLAND

Zürich
Kammerer, Adrian W.

ADDRESS UNPUBLISHED

Carpenter, Victoria J.
Carroll, Diane C.
Crown, Nancy Elizabeth
Drabkin, Murray
Field, Arthur Norman
Fisher, Joseph Freiler
Gray, Lillia Ann
Kippur, Merrie Margolin
Lichtenstein, Sarah Carol
Padilla, James Earl
Perlstein, William James
Putney, Wainscott Walker
Seifert, Stephen Wayne
Weil, Peter Henry
Zohn, Martin Steven

CIVIL LITIGATION, FEDERAL

UNITED STATES

ALABAMA

Andalusia
Fuller, William Sidney

Anniston
Woodrow, Randall Mark

Birmingham
Childs, Larry Brittain
Newton, Alexander Worthy
Rountree, Asa
Selfe, Edward Milton
Stabler, Lewis Vastine, Jr.,

Dothan
Huskey, Dow Thobern

Huntsville
Huckaby, Gary Carlton

Mobile
Holmes, Broox Garrett
Pierce, Donald Fay

Montgomery
Byram, James Asberry, Jr.,
Lawson, Thomas Seay, Jr.,
Volz, Charles Harvie, Jr.,

ARIZONA

Phoenix
Bain, C. Randall
Bakker, Thomas Gordon
Beggs, Harry Mark
Bivens, Donald Wayne
Bouma, John Jacob
Coghill, William Thomas, Jr.,
Condo, James Robert
Corson, Kimball Jay
Gomez, David Frederick
Grant, Merwin Darwin
Knoller, Guy David
Leonard, Jeffrey S.
Lyons, George Harris
Petitti, Michael Joseph, Jr.,
Rathwell, Peter John
Ulrich, Paul Graham
Wall, Donald Arthur

Tucson
Hyams, Harold
Kimble, William Earl
Kitchen, Charles William
Maltz, Gerald Stuart
Mc Donald, John Richard
Meehan, Michael Joseph

ARKANSAS

Fort Smith
Foster, M. Shannon

Little Rock
Anderson, Philip Sidney
Drummond, Winslow
Griffin, William Mell, III,
Jennings, Alston

CALIFORNIA

Burlingame
Cotchett, Joseph Winters

Costa Mesa
Guilford, Andrew John

Danville
Candland, D. Stuart

Encinitas
Wigmore, John Grant

Huntington Beach
Nikas, Richard John

Irvine
Friedland, Michael Keith
Martens, Don Walter

Laguna Hills
Reinglass, Michelle Annette

Long Beach
Haile, Lawrence Barclay
Stolpman, Thomas Gerard
Ultimo, Paul Joseph

Los Angeles
Angel, Arthur Ronald
Bakaly, Charles George, Jr.,
Barrett, Jane Hayes
Bender, Charles William
Bernhard, Herbert Ashley
Bodkin, Henry Grattan, Jr.,
Bortman, David
Bressan, Paul Louis
Bridges, B. Ried
Chiate, Kenneth Reed
Daniels, John Peter
Fairbank, Robert Harold
Fisher, Barry Alan
Franceschi, Ernest Joseph, Jr.,
Galton, Stephen Harold
Handzlik, Jan Lawrence
Heller, Philip
Hight, B. Boyd
Kirwan, R. DeWitt
Krupka, Robert George
Lauchengco, Jose Yujuico, Jr.,
Litvack, Sanford Martin
Long, Gregory Alan
Metzger, Robert Streicher
Miller, Milton Allen
Neufeld, Timothy Lee
Newman, Michael Rodney
Oliver, Dale Hugh
Stoner, William Edward
Strong, George Gordon, Jr.,
von Kalinowski, Julian Onesime
Woods, Daniel James
Wright, Kenneth Brooks
Zelon, Laurie Dee

Menlo Park
Dyer, Charles Arnold
Edwards, John Wesley, II,

Mill Valley
Cole, Richard Charles

Mountain View
Pasahow, Lynn H(arold)

Napa
Snow, Tower Charles, Jr.,

Newport Beach
Millar, Richard William, Jr.,
Rudolph, George Cooper

Oakland
Bjork, Robert David, Jr.,

Oxnard
Gerber, David A.

Pacific Palisades
Dickson, Robert Lee

Palo Alto
Baron, Frederick David
O'Rourke, C. Larry
Steer, Reginald David
Tiffany, Joseph Raymond, II,

Pasadena
Tanner, Dee Boshard

Redwood City
Coddington, Clinton Hays

Sacramento
Goode, Barry Paul

San Diego
Clark, David Robert
Klinedinst, John David
Longstreth, Robert Christy
McDermott, Thomas John, Jr.,
Weaver, Michael James

San Francisco
Alexis, Geraldine M.
Barbagelata, Robert Dominic
Borowsky, Philip
Brown, Donald Wesley
Bushnell, Roderick Paul
Dell, Robert Michael
Finberg, James Michael
Friese, Robert Charles
Gelhaus, Robert Joseph
Gowdy, Franklin Brockway
Heilbron, David M(ichael)
Ladar, Jerrold Morton
Martel, John Sheldon
Meadows, John Frederick
Miller, William Napier Cripps
Phillips, Richard Myron
Popofsky, Melvin Laurence
Ragan, Charles Ransom
Renfrew, Charles Byron
Richards, Norman Blanchard
Robertson, J. Martin
Rosch, John Thomas
Rubin, Michael
Traynor, John Michael
Venning, Robert Stanley
Walcher, Alan Ernest
Weir, William John Arnold
Young, Douglas Rea

Lake Forest
Emerson, William Harry
Galatz, Henry Francis

Libertyville
DeSanto, James John

Lombard
O'Shea, Patrick Joseph

Northbrook
Dilling, Kirkpatrick Wallwick
Irons, Spencer Ernest

Park Ridge
LaRue, Paul Hubert

Peoria
Winget, Walter Winfield

Rockford
Mateer, Don M.

Rosemont
Nichols, Robert Hastings

Shorewood
Copeland, Charlene Carole

Wheaton
Mirabile, Thomas Keith

INDIANA

Beech Grove
Brown, Richard Lawrence

Evansville
Berger, Charles Lee
Bodkin, Robert Thomas

Hammond
Ruman, Saul I.

Indianapolis
Albright, Terrill D.
Bennett, Bryce Hugh, Jr.,
Conour, William Frederick
Elberger, Ronald Edward
Fisher, James R.
Kashani, Hamid Reza
Knauer, James A.
Knebel, Donald Earl
McTurnan, Lee Bowes
Reuben, Lawrence Mark
Ryder, Henry C(lay)
Stayton, Thomas George
Steger, Evan Evans, III,
Taylor, Brent Douglas
Yeager, Joseph Heizer, Jr.,

Lafayette
Bodle, John Frederick
Layden, Charles Max

Seymour
Pardieck, Roger Lee

Terre Haute
Coleson, Richard Eugene
Frey, Eric Alan

IOWA

Des Moines
Frederici, C. Carleton
Koehn, William James
Peddicord, Roland Dale
Phipps, David Lee
Rickert, Brian Patrick

Marshalltown
Brooks, Patrick William

Sioux City
Mayne, Wiley Edward

KANSAS

Overland Park
Abele, Robert Christopher
Keplinger, Bruce (Donald Keplinger)
Klamann, John Michael
Sampson, William Roth

Prairie Village
Stanton, Roger D.

Shawnee Mission
Badgerow, John Nicholas
Helder, Jan Pleasant, Jr.,
Sparks, Billy Schley

Topeka
Hamilton, John Richard
Schroer, Gene Eldon

Wichita
Hund, Edward Joseph
Kennedy, Joseph Winston
Sevart, Daniel Joseph

KENTUCKY

Bowling Green
Rudloff, William Joseph

Hazard
Roark, Jimmy Lee

Lexington
Fryman, Virgil Thomas, Jr.,

Louisville
Chauvin, Leonard Stanley, Jr.,
Cohen, Edwin Louis
Dolt, Frederick Corrance
Stavros, Peter James

Newport
Siverd, Robert Joseph

LOUISIANA

Baton Rouge
Dugas, David Roy
Jones, Johnnie Anderson
Rubin, Michael Harry

Lafayette
Bengtson, Karl W.
Davidson, James Joseph, III,

Lake Charles
Parkerson, Hardy Martell

Metairie
Bains, David Paul
Dean, Bruce Campbell
Harris, Thorne D., III,
Kutcher, Robert A.

New Orleans
Allen, Frank Clinton, Jr.,
Bieck, Robert Barton, Jr.,
Combe, John Clifford, Jr.,
Gertler, Meyer H.
Herman, Russ Michel
Johnson, Patrick, Jr.,
Jones, Philip Kirkpatrick, Jr.,
Kupperman, Stephen Henry
McGlone, Michael Anthony
Ostendorf, Lance Stephen

Slidell
Shamis, Edward Anthony, Jr.,

MAINE

Camden
Sanford, John Joseph

Portland
Culley, Peter William
Harvey, Charles Albert, Jr.,
Lancaster, Ralph Ivan, Jr.,
Marjerison, Thomas Sydney

MARYLAND

Baltimore
Ayres, Jeffrey Peabody
Baker, William Parr
Carbine, James Edmond
Crowe, Thomas Leonard
Dubé, Lawrence Edward, Jr.,
Fax, Charles Samuel
Golomb, George Edwin
Hansen, Christopher Agnew
Himeles, Martin Stanley, Jr.,
Johnson, Harry Sterling
Kramer, Paul R.
Pappas, George Frank
Radding, Andrew
Schochor, Jonathan
Sfekas, Stephen James
Walker, Irving Edward
White, Pamela Janice

Bethesda
Baird, Bruce Allen

Chevy Chase
Mackall, Laidler Bowie
Weiss, Harlan Lee

Parkville
Hill, Milton King, Jr.,

Patuxent River
Fitzhugh, David Michael

Potomac
Meyer, Lawrence George
Mullenbach, Linda Herman

Rockville
Dugan, John R.

Salisbury
Clarke, Wm. A. Lee, III,

Silver Spring
Gagliardo, Thomas James

Upper Marlboro
Wallace, Sean Daniel

MASSACHUSETTS

Boston
Carpenter, Robert Brent
Curley, Robert Ambrose, Jr.,
Dillon, James Joseph
Felter, John Kenneth
Fox, Francis Haney
Gelb, Richard Mark
Gilmore, John Allen Dehn
Hieken, Charles
Keating, Michael Burns
Macauley, William Francis
Mone, Michael Edward
Moriarty, George Marshall
Sullivan, Edward Michael
Trimmier, Roscoe, Jr.,

Concord
Glovsky, Susan G. L.

Newton
Messing, Arnold Philip

Sudbury
Dignan, Thomas Gregory, Jr.,

Truro
Friedman, Edward David

MICHIGAN

Ann Arbor
Britton, Clarold Lawrence

Bloomfield Hills
Googasian, George Ara
Pappas, Edward Harvey
Rader, Ralph Terrance

Detroit
Andreoff, Christopher Andon
Brady, Edmund Matthew, Jr.,
Cothorn, John Arthur
Jacobs, John Patrick
Longhofer, Ronald Stephen
Monsanto, Raphael Angel
Saxton, William Marvin
Smith, James Albert
Toll, Sheldon Samuel
Turner, Reginald Maurice, Jr.,
Zacks, David N.

East Lansing
Joseph, Raymond

Flint
Hart, Clifford Harvey

Holland
Bidol, James Alexander

Kalamazoo
Geary, James H.
Lubben, Craig Henry

Lansing
Coey, David Conrad
Rasmusson, Thomas Elmo

Midland
Battle, Leonard Carroll

New Buffalo
Stevens, William J.

Northville
Leavitt, Martin Jack

Southfield
Fieger, Geoffrey Nels
Forrest, Robert Edwin
Israel, Stuart Michael
Morganroth, Mayer
Ponitz, John Allan
Turner, Donald Allen
Turner, Lee Irwin

Traverse City
Quick, Albert Thomas

Troy
Alber, Phillip George
Alterman, Irwin Michael
Webster, Robert Byron

MINNESOTA

Crystal
Reske, Steven David

Duluth
Thibodeau, Thomas Raymond

Golden Valley
Hagglund, Clarance Edward

Mankato
Gage, Fred Kelton

Minneapolis
Ciresi, Michael Vincent
Eckland, Jeff Howard
Finzen, Bruce Arthur
French, John Dwyer
Gagnon, Craig William
Gordon, John Bennett
Hanson, Bruce Eugene
Hanson, Kent Bryan
Hart, Buster Clarence
Jarpe, Geoffrey Pellas
Keppel, William James
Klaas, Paul Barry
Lonergan, Lauren Elizabeth
Magnuson, Roger James
Rockwell, Winthrop Adams
Saeks, Allen Irving
Safley, James Robert
Silver, Alan Irving
Sippel, William Leroy
Tanick, Marshall Howard
Trembath, Jon R.

Minnetonka
Carpenter, Norman Roblee

North Oaks
Woods, Robert Edward

Saint Paul
Allison, John Robert
Maclin, Alan Hall

MISSISSIPPI

Clarksdale
Cocke, John Hartwell

Jackson
Clark, David Wright
Currie, Edward Jones, Jr.,
Hafter, Jerome Charles
Hemleben, Scott P.
Henegan, John C(lark)
Hewes, George Poindexter, III,
Howell, Joel Walter, III,

Kosciusko
Pickle, L. Scott

New Albany
Sumners, Lester Furr

MISSOURI

Clayton
Schwartz, Theodore Frank

Columbia
Turley, J. William

Jefferson City
Barrett, David F.

Kansas City
Beck, William G.
Beckett, Theodore Charles
Cowden, John William
Cross, William Dennis
Johnson, Mark Eugene
Kilroy, John Muir
Levings, Theresa Lawrence
Lolli, Don R(ay)
Palmer, Dennis Dale
Price, James Tucker
Redmond, Christopher John
Spalty, Edward Robert
Stoup, Arthur Harry
Wirken, James Charles
Wolf, Jerome Thomas

Maryland Heights
Cooper, Richard Alan

Saint Louis
Brown, Paul Sherman
Clear, John Michael
Collins, James Slade, II,
Conran, Joseph Palmer
DeWoskin, Alan Ellis
Douaihy, Toni Patricia
Feder, Gary Harold
Gianoulakis, John Louis
Gilhousen, Brent James
Guerri, William Grant
Hullverson, James Everett, Jr.,
Lucchesi, Lionel Louis
Marks, Murry Aaron
Noel, Edwin Lawrence
Palans, Lloyd Alex
Rice, Canice Timothy, Jr.,
Sestric, Anthony James
Smith, Arthur Lee
Sneeringer, Stephen Geddes
Sugg, Reed Waller
Tierney, Betty Thorne
Walsh, Thomas Charles
Weiss, Charles Andrew

Springfield
McDonald, William Henry
Myers, Ronald Lynn

MONTANA

Billings
Malee, Thomas Michael
Towe, Thomas Edward

Great Falls
Blewett, Alexander, III,

Missoula
Sullivan, Robert John

NEBRASKA

Lincoln
Colleran, Kevin

North Platte
Kay, Stephen William

Omaha
Dolan, James Vincent
Jensen, Sam
Lamson, William Maxwell, Jr.,

NEVADA

Las Vegas
Reilly, Patrick John

Reno
Kent, Stephen Smiley

NEW HAMPSHIRE

Concord
Hodes, Paul William
Johnson, Robert Veiling, II,

Exeter
Engel, David Chapin

Hanover
Lundquist, Weyman Ivan

Portsmouth
Shaines, Robert Arthur

NEW JERSEY

Asbury Park
Darnell, Alan Mark

Bloomfield
Caccavale, Stephen Joseph

Bridgewater
Dahling, Gerald Vernon

Chatham
Jacobs, Andrew Robert

Cherry Hill
Garrigle, William Aloysius
Kole, Janet Stephanie
Korin, Joel Benjamin

Cranford
De Luca, Thomas George

Fairfield
Connell, William Terrence

Haddonfield
Fuoco, Philip Stephen

Iselin
Rowe, Paul Andrew

Jersey City
Frisch, Harry David

Kenilworth
Hoffman, John Fletcher

Lawrenceville
Blumstein, Jeffrey Phillip

Little Silver
Robertson, Lewis Harold

Morristown
Bartkus, Robert Edward
Humick, Thomas Charles Campbell
Whitmer, Frederick Lee

Newark
Cahn, Jeffrey Barton
Cummis, Clive Sanford
Eittreim, Richard MacNutt
Haring, Eugene Miller
Maderer, William F.
McGuire, William B(enedict)
Miller, Richard Allan
Rak, Lorraine Karen
Reilly, William Thomas
Robertson, William Withers

Parsippany
Kallmann, Stanley Walter

Roseland
Eakeley, Douglas Scott
McMahon, Edward Richard

Saddle Brook
Knopf, Barry Abraham
Pearlman, Peter Steven

Ship Bottom
Shackleton, Richard James

Short Hills
Marshall, John Patrick

Somerville
Sponzilli, Edward George

Summit
Katz, Michael Albert

Trenton
Campbell, Bernard Alexander, Jr.,

West Orange
Gordon, Michael

NEW MEXICO

Albuquerque
Bardacke, Paul Gregory
Bohnhoff, Henry M.
Messersmith, Lanny Dee
Roehl, Jerrald J.
Slade, Lynn

Santa Fe
Burton, John Paul (Jack Burton)
Huffaker, Gregory Dorian, Jr.,
Schwarz, Michael

NEW YORK

Albany
Linnan, James Daniel

Binghamton
Chivers, James Leeds
Gouldin, David Millen

Buffalo
Brown, Jerrold Stanley
Fisher, Cheryl Smith
Glanville, Robert Edward
Halpern, Ralph Lawrence
Herdzik, Arthur Alan
Manning, Kenneth Alan
Mattar, Lawrence Joseph

Canaan
Pennell, William Brooke

East Meadow
Hyman, Montague Allan

Garden City
Kroll, Martin N.

Glen Cove
Mills, Charles Gardner

Great Neck
Kimm, Michael S.

Huntington
German, June Resnick

Jericho
Rehbock, Richard Alexander

Larchmont
Davis, Wendell, Jr.,
Gaffney, Mark William

Melville
Agoglia, Emmet John
Cahn, Richard Caleb

Mineola
Klein, Arnold Spencer
Lippe, Richard Allen
Monaghan, Peter Gerard

Mount Kisco
Curran, Maurice Francis

New York
Alcott, Mark Howard
Amsterdam, Mark Lemle
Arenson, Gregory K.
Avery, Patricia I.
Axinn, Stephen Mark
Baechtold, Robert Louis
Barasch, Clarence Sylvan
Barenholtz, Celia Goldwag
Bazerman, Steven Howard
Behrendt, John Thomas
Benedict, James Nelson
Berman, Tony
Bezanson, Thomas Edward
Bialo, Kenneth Marc
Blumkin, Linda Ruth
Bodovitz, James Philip
Booth, Edgar Hirsch
Bosses, Stevan J.
Braid, Frederick Donald
Brown, Paul M.
Brown, Peter Megargee
Buchwald, Don David
Burns, John MacDougal, III,
Burrows, Michael Donald
Carter, James Hal, Jr.,
Cashman, Gideon
Castel, P. Kevin
Chan, Lai Lee
Cirillo, Richard Allan
Clark, Merrell Edward, Jr.,
Cohen, Robert Stephan
Cole, Charles Dewey, Jr.,
Coleman, Jerome P.
Coll, John Peter, Jr.,
Cook, Michael Lewis
Cooper, Michael Anthony
Critchlow, Charles Howard
Dallas, William Moffit, Jr.,
Davidson, Robert Bruce
Diskant, Gregory L.
Donovan, Craig Thomas
Dopf, Glenn William
Doyle, Paul Francis
Edelson, Gilbert Seymour
Evans, Martin Frederic
Fagen, Leslie Gordon
Fasman, Zachary Dean
Fiske, Robert Bishop, Jr.,
Fitzpatrick, Joseph Mark
Flamm, Leonard N(athan)
Fletcher, Anthony L.
Forstadt, Joseph Lawrence
Foster, David Lee
Fox, Donald Thomas
Freeman, David John
Friedman, Victor Stanley
Gitter, Max
Glekel, Jeffrey Ives
Gold, Stuart Walter
Golden, Arthur F.
Goldstein, Howard Warren
Golomb, David Bela
Goltz, Susan Ackerman
Greenawalt, William Sloan
Greenspon, Robert Alan
Habian, Bruce George
Haig, Robert Leighton
Hall, John Herbert
Halperin, Kyle Mallary
Handelsman, Lawrence Marc
Handler, Arthur M.
Harbison, James Wesley, Jr.,
Harris, Joel B(ruce)
Hartmann, Carl Joseph
Hartzell, Andrew Cornelius, Jr.,
Helfer, Michael Stevens
Heller, Robert Martin
Hirsch, Jerome S.
Hoffman, Mathew
Hollyer, A(rthur) Rene
Hritz, George F.
Hruska, Alan J.
Huffman, Richard Lee
Hughes, Kevin Peter
Hyde, David Rowley
Hynes, Patricia Mary
Iannuzzi, John Nicholas
Isquith, Fred Taylor
Jackson, Thomas Gene
Jacob, Edwin J.
Jacob, Marvin Eugene
Jacobs, Randall Scott David
Jacobson, Jeffrey E.
Joffe, Robert David
Joseph, Gregory Paul
Joseph, Leonard
Kandel, William Lloyd
Karmali, Rashida Alimahomed
Katz, Jerome Charles
Kaufman, Stephen Edward
Kaye, Stephen Rackow
Kende, Christopher Burgess
Keneally, Kathryn Marie
Kenney, John Joseph
Kessler, Jeffrey L.
Kidd, John Edward
King, Henry Lawrence
Kinnally, William Lee, Jr.,
Kinzler, Thomas Benjamin
Kirby, John Joseph, Jr.,
Klein, Martin I.
Klingsberg, David
Kobak, James Benedict, Jr.,
Koegel, William Fisher
Koob, Charles Edward
Kramer, Daniel Jonathan
Krane, Steven Charles
Krasner, Daniel Walter
Kuh, Richard Henry
Kurland, Paul Carl
Lack, Robert Joel
Lacy, Robinson Burrell
Langer, Bruce Alden
Lans, Deborah Eisner
Lauer, Eliot
Lee, Jerome G.
Lesch, Michael Oscar
Levine, Alan
Lifland, William Thomas
Linsenmeyer, John Michael
Lupert, Leslie Allan
Mandelker, Lawrence Arthur
Marion, Roger K.
Martone, Patricia Ann
McCormack, Howard Michael
McLaughlin, Joseph Thomas
Mentz, Lawrence
Millstein, Ira M.
Moerdler, Charles Gerard
Moloney, Thomas Joseph
Moy, Mary Anastasia
Muccia, Joseph William
Mullaney, Thomas Joseph
Munzer, Stephen Ira
Muskin, Victor Philip
Nearing, Vivienne W.
Newman, Lawrence Walker
O'Donnell, John Logan
O'Sullivan, Thomas J.
Phillips, Anthony Francis
Primps, William Guthrie
Quinn, Yvonne Susan
Rand, Harry Israel
Raylesberg, Alan Ira
Reich, Larry Sam
Reinthaler, Richard Walter
Reiss, Steven Alan
Rifkind, Robert S(inger)
Ringer, James Milton
Robertson, Edwin David
Rogers, Laurence Steven
Rosenberg, Gerald Alan
Rosenfeld, Steven B.
Rosensaft, Menachem Zwi
Rosenzweig, Charles Leonard
Rothman, Dennis Michael
Rovine, Arthur William
Salomon, Philippe M.
Saunders, Paul Christopher
Savitt, Susan Schenkel
Schmidt, Charles Edward
Schumacher, Harry Richard
Schwab, Harold Lee
Schwartz, Barry Fredric
Schwartz, Herbert Frederick
Seidel, Selvyn
Serota, James Ian
Sesser, Gary Douglas
Shentov, Ognjan V.
Silverberg, Michael Joel
Silverman, Leon
Silverman, Moses
Sladkus, Harvey Ira
Smiley, Guy Ian
Smith, Robert Everett
Smith, Robert Sherlock
Smoak, Evan L.
Snow, Charles
Soyster, Margaret Blair
Spivak, Leonard A.
Sternman, Joel W.
Stever, Donald Winfred
Stoll, Neal Richard
Strum, Jay Gerson
Swire, James Bennett
Taylor, Job, III,
Terry, James Joseph, Jr.,
Thackeray, Jonathan E.
Tilewick, Robert
Vassil, John Charles
Versfelt, David Scott
Weinberger, Harold Paul
Weiner, Stephen Arthur
Weinstock, Leonard
Wilkinson, John Hart
Will, Alfred Joseph
Witkin, Eric Douglas
Woglom, Eric Cooke
Wollan, Eugene
Yeager, Dennis Randall
Yodowitz, Edward Jay
Zimmett, Mark Paul
Zoeller, Donald J.
Zuckerman, Joseph

Pittsford
Braunsdorf, Paul Raymond
Hartman, James Matthew

Rochester
Geiger, Alexander
Law, Michael R.
Payment, Kenneth Arnold
Smith, John Stuart
Smith, Jules Louis

Sands Point
Hoynes, Louis LeNoir, Jr.,

Southampton
Lopez, David

Staten Island
Howard, Davis Jonathan

Syracuse
DiLorenzo, Louis Patrick

Troy
Jones, E. Stewart, Jr.,

Waterford
Novotny, F. Douglas

White Plains
Doyle, Dennis T.
Halpern, Philip Morgan

NORTH CAROLINA

Asheville
Davis, Roy Walton, Jr.,

Charlotte
Bell, Paul Buckner
Raper, William Cranford

Fairview
Rhynedance, Harold Dexter, Jr.,

New Bern
McCotter, Charles Kennedy, Jr.,

Raleigh
Currin, Samuel Thomas
Dorsett, James K., III,
Maupin, Armistead Jones

Tabor City
Jorgensen, Ralph Gubler

Wilmington
Baldwin, Charles Selden, IV,

Winston Salem
Barnhill, Henry Grady, Jr.,
Dahl, Tyrus Vance, Jr.,
Gitter, Allan Reinhold
Stockton, Ralph Madison, Jr.,

OHIO

Akron
Ruport, Scott Hendricks
Tipping, Harry A.

Cincinnati
Cioffi, Michael Lawrence
Cissell, James Charles
DeLong, Deborah
Dornette, W(illiam) Stuart
Frantz, Robert Wesley
Holschuh, John David, Jr.,
Manley, Robert Edward
Shea, Joseph William, III,
Zavatsky, Michael Joseph

Cleveland
Adamo, Kenneth R.
Ashmus, Keith Allen
Berger, Sanford Jason
Collin, Thomas James
Crist, Paul Grant
Dunlap, Jeffrey Scott
Fay, Regan Joseph
Fisher, Thomas Edward
Gold, Gerald Seymour
Goldfarb, Bernard Sanford
Hardy, Michael Lynn
Kahrl, Robert Conley
Karp, Marvin Louis
Kelly, Dennis Michael
Kilbane, Thomas Stanton
Kola, Arthur Anthony
Kramer, Edward George
Krembs, Peter Joseph
Lowe, James Allison
Mc Cartan, Patrick Francis
Moore, Kenneth Cameron
Pollock, R. Jeffrey
Schiller, James Joseph
Sicherman, Marvin Allen
Skulina, Thomas Raymond
Stewart, Lawrence Edward
Toohey, Brian Frederick
Wallach, Mark Irwin
Weber, Robert Carl

Columbus
Ferguson, Gerald Paul
Hollenbaugh, H(enry) Ritchey
Johnson, Mark Alan
Long, Thomas Leslie
McKenna, Alvin James
Reasoner, Willis Irl, III,
Sidman, Robert John
Todd, William Michael
Warner, Charles Collins
Yeazel, Keith Arthur

Dayton
Faruki, Charles Joseph
Saul, Irving Isaac

Dublin
Coco, Mark Steven

Portsmouth
Crowder, Marjorie Briggs

Toledo
Baker, Richard Southworth
Dane, Stephen Mark
Jackson, Reginald Sherman, Jr.,
Wicklund, David Wayne

OKLAHOMA

Antlers
Stamper, Joe Allen

Muskogee
Williams, Betty Outhier

Oklahoma City
Fenton, Elliott Clayton
Kenney, John Arthur
Paul, William George
Woods, Harry Arthur, Jr.,

Tulsa
Biolchini, Robert Fredrick
Eldridge, Richard Mark
Eliot, Theodore Quentin
Haynie, Tony Wayne
Herrold, David Henry
Howard, Gene Claude
Imel, John Michael
Luthey, Graydon Dean, Jr.,
Matthies, Mary Constance T.
Strecker, David Eugene

OREGON

Eugene
Lowry, Robert Dudley

Medford
Deatherage, William Vernon
O'Connor, Karl William (Goodyear Johnson)
Thierolf, Richard Burton, Jr.,

Portland
Bailey, Ronald E.
Eakin, Margaretta Morgan
Hanlon, Michael Gregory
Houser, Douglas Guy
Rosenbaum, Lois Omenn
Shorr, Scott Alden

Salem
Haselton, Rick Thomas
Spooner, Ralph Charles

PENNSYLVANIA

Allentown
McGinley, Paul Anthony, Jr.,

Blue Bell
Siedzikowski, Henry Francis
Teklits, Joseph Anthony

Clarks Summit
Beemer, John Barry

Doylestown
Renz, William Tomlinson

Erie
McNair, Timothy Dean

Harrisburg
Kelly, Robert Edward, Jr.,

Lancaster
Lewis, Alvin Bower, Jr.,
Nast, Dianne Martha

New Kensington
Wallace, Henry Jared, Jr.,

Newtown
Godwin, Robert Anthony

Norristown
Cowperthwait, Lindley Murray

Philadelphia
Asher, Steven Alan
Barrett, John J(ames), Jr.,
Berger, David
Berger, Harold
Binder, David Franklin
Bissell, Rolin Plumb
Bressler, Gary David
Brown, William Hill, III,
Calvert, Jay H., Jr.,
Collins, Todd Stowe
Cox, Roger Frazier
Cramer, Harold
D'Angelo, George A.
Donohue, John Patrick
Durant, Marc
Epstein, Alan Bruce
Fiebach, H. Robert
Grant, M. Duncan
Hangley, William Thomas
Haviland, Bancroft Dawley
Kessler, Alan Craig
Klein, Howard Bruce
Ledwith, John Francis
Levin, Murray Simon
Lillie, Charisse Ranielle
Lowery, William Herbert
Madva, Stephen Alan
Mathes, Stephen Jon
McGurk, Eugene David, Jr.,
McKeever, John Eugene
McMichael, Lawrence Grover
Milbourne, Walter Robertson
Milone, Francis Michael
Mullinix, Edward Wingate
Phelan, John M.
Pokotilow, Manny David
Poul, Franklin
Rainville, Christina
Resnick, Stephanie
Roberts, Carl Geoffrey
Sheils, Denis Francis
Shestack, Jerome Joseph
Sigmond, Richard Brian
Smith, John Francis, III,
Sonnenfeld, Marc Jay
Tiger, Ira Paul
Vaira, Peter Francis
Weil, Jeffrey George
Wittels, Barnaby Caesar
Wrobleski, Jeanne Pauline

Pipersville
Carr, Stephen Kerry

Pittsburgh
Acheson, Amy J.
Baldauf, Kent Edward
Basinski, Anthony Joseph
Blenko, Walter John, Jr.,
Brown, James Benton
Candris, Laura A.
Connors, Eugene Kenneth
Fischer, Nora Barry
Fort, James Tomlinson
Hershey, Dale
Hull, John Daniel, IV,
Hurnyak, Christina Kaiser
Jones, Craig Ward
Kenrick, Charles William
Klett, Edwin L.
Leech, Jeffrey James
Litman, Roslyn Margolis
McGinley, John Regis, Jr.,
O'Connor, Edward Gearing
Plowman, Jack Wesley
Sokol, Stephen M.
Ulven, Mark Edward
Van Kirk, Thomas L.

Scranton
Howley, James McAndrew

Stroudsburg
Catina, Janet K.

Wyomissing
Turner, David Eldridge

RHODE ISLAND

Providence
Labinger, Lynette J.
Medeiros, Matthew Francis
White, Benjamin Vroom, III,

Wakefield
Hart, Kenneth Nelson

SOUTH CAROLINA

Aiken
Amabile, John Louis

Charleston
Kahn, Ellis Irvin

Columbia
Babcock, Keith Moss
Dibble, Robert Wightman, Jr.,
Ratchford, David Maurice
Sheftman, Howard Stephen
Tate, Harold Simmons, Jr.,

Florence
Lee, Robert E.

Greenville
Cowan, John Joseph
Shoemaker, James Marshall, Jr.,
White, Daniel Bowman

Hilton Head Island
McKay, John Judson, Jr.,

SOUTH DAKOTA

Sioux Falls
Prendergast, Terry Neill

TENNESSEE

Chattanooga
Bahner, Thomas Maxfield

Campbell, Paul, III,
Cooper, Gary Allan
Gearhiser, Charles Josef
Moore, Hugh Jacob, Jr.,

Collierville
Scroggs, Larry Kenneth

Cookeville
Acuff, John Edgar

Dyersburg
Wilder, James Sampson, III,

Hendersonville
McCaleb, Joe Wallace

Kingsport
Shine, David Bruce

Knoxville
Hagood, Lewis Russell
Lucas, John Allen

Memphis
Carr, Oscar Clark, III,
Clark, Ross Bert, II,
Garts, James Rufus, Jr.,
Hancock, Jonathan Cromwell
McQuiston, John Ward, II,
Newman, Charles Forrest
Noel, Randall Deane
Sossaman, William Lynwood

Nashville
DeLanis, James Alfred
Hardin, Hal D.
Sims, Wilson
Woods, Larry David

Soddy Daisy
Leitner, Paul Revere

TEXAS

Abilene
Suttle, Stephen Hungate

Arlington
Jensen, John Robert

Austin
Donaldson, David Howard, Jr.,
Gambrell, James Bruton, III,
Harrison, Richard Wayne
Judson, Philip Livingston
Lochridge, Lloyd Pampell, Jr.,
Schuurman, Willem Gerhard

Baytown
Chavez, John Anthony

Beaumont
Black, Robert Allen

Brownsville
Weisfeld, Sheldon

Dallas
Atwood, Roy Tress
Baggett, Steven Ray
Bickel, John W., II,
Biermacher, Kenneth Wayne
Brin, Royal Henry, Jr.,
Case, Thomas Louis
Coleman, Robert Winston
Evans, Roger
Fanning, Barry Hedges
Figari, Ernest Emil, Jr.,
Flegle, Jim L.
Freytag, Sharon Nelson
Harrison, Orrin Lea, III,
Haworth, Charles Ray
Hinshaw, Chester John
Huffman, Gregory Scott Combest
Hytken, Franklin Harris
Jayson, Melinda Gayle
Jones, James Alton
Kearney, Douglas Charles
Keithley, Bradford Gene
Lippe, Emil, Jr.,
Lowenberg, Michael
Maris, Stephen S.
Mc Elhaney, John Hess
McAtee, David Ray
Mow, Robert Henry, Jr.,
Price, John Aley
Ringle, Brett Adelbert
Selinger, Jerry Robin
Sides, Jack Davis, Jr.,
Smith, Russell Bryan
Walkowiak, Vincent Steven

Flower Mound
Hunt, David Ford

Fort Worth
Brunig, Robert Arthur
Chappell, David Franklin
Elliott, Frank Wallace
Larimore, Tom L.
Mack, Theodore
Rutherford, Jay K.
Streck, Frederick Louis, III,
Watson, Robert Francis

Friendswood
Youngdahl, Jay Thomas

Houston
Adair, William B. (Ben Adair)
Addison, Linda Leuchter
Amdur, Arthur R.
Atlas, Scott Jerome
Ballanfant, Richard Burton
Bayko, Emil Thomas
Beirne, Martin Douglas
Brinson, Gay Creswell, Jr.,
Burch, Voris Reagan
Caldwell, Rodney Kent
Carr, Edward A.
Craig, Robert Mark, III,
Crinion, Gregory Paul
Cunningham, Tom Alan
Durham, William Andrew
Epstein, Jon David
Essmyer, Michael Martin
Gayle, Gibson, Jr.,
Gonynor, Francis James
Harvin, David Tarleton
Hilder, Philip H.
Holstead, John Burnham
Hudspeth, Chalmers Mac
Jordan, Charles Milton
Kaplan, Lee Landa
Ketchand, Robert Lee
Kinnan, David Emery
Krieger, Paul Edward
Lopez, David Tiburcio
McDade, Thomas Rambaut
McFall, Donald Beury
Miller, Gary C.
Nunnally, Knox Dillon
Pettiette, Alison Yvonne
Pugsley, Frank Burruss
Ray, Hugh Massey, Jr.,
Reasoner, Harry Max
Redden, Joe Winston, Jr.,
Rowland, Robert Alexander, III,
Schwartz, Charles Walter
Smith, Alison Leigh
Susman, Morton Lee
Susman, Stephen Daily
Tartt, Blake
Toedt, D(ell) C(harles), III,
Vickery, Edward Downtain
Wallis, Olney Gray
Wilde, William Key
Wray, Thomas Jefferson
Yetter, R. Paul
Zager, Steven Mark

Midland
Estes, Andrew Harper

San Antonio
Biery, Evelyn Hudson
Moynihan, John Bignell

Sugar Land
Greer, Raymond White

UTAH

Salt Lake City
Christensen, Patricia Anne Watkins
Christensen, Ray Richards
Colessides, Nick John
Lochhead, Robert Bruce
Scofield, David Willson
Slaughter, David Wayne

VERMONT

Burlington
Cory, Barbara Ellen

VIRGINIA

Abingdon
Copeland, Robert Tayloe
McElroy, Howard Chowning

Alexandria
Carter, Richard Dennis
DiMuro, Bernard Joseph
Georges, Peter John

Arlington
Green, Richard Alan
Kelly, John James

Fairfax
Folk, Thomas Robert

Falls Church
Van Oeveren, Edward Lanier
Wood, John Martin

Fredericksburg
Billingsley, Robert Thaine

Nellysford
Sims, John Rogers, Jr.,

Newport News
Thro, William Eugene

Norfolk
Albert, Alan Dale
Baird, Edward Rouzie, Jr.,
Clark, Morton Hutchinson
Zahn, Richard William, Jr.,

Richmond
Bing, Richard McPhail
Clinard, Robert Noel
Hall, Stephen Charles
Patterson, Robert Hobson, Jr.,
Slater, Thomas Glascock, Jr.,
Walsh, James Hamilton

Roanoke
Harris, Bayard Easter

Springfield
Chappell, Milton Leroy

Vienna
Bredehoft, John Michael

Virginia Beach
Clark, Donald H.
Dumville, S(amuel) Lawrence
Hajek, Francis Paul

Warrenton
Howard, Blair Duncan

Woodstock
Walton, Morgan Lauck, III,

WASHINGTON

Seattle
Andrews, J. David
Bagshaw, Bradley Holmes
Bateman, Heidi S.
Bringman, Joseph Edward
Freedman, Bart Joseph
Gray, Marvin Lee, Jr.,
Hendricks, Katherine
McKay, Michael Dennis
McKinstry, Ronald E.
Mines, Michael
Robinson-Dorn, Michael Jay
Schwartz, Irwin H.
Squires, William Randolph, III,
Tausend, Fredric Cutner
Taylor, David F.
Tomlinson, John Randolph
Yalowitz, Kenneth Gregg

Spokane
Weatherhead, Leslie R.

Tacoma
Mungia, Salvador Alejo

WEST VIRGINIA

Charleston
Bell, Harry Fullerton, Jr.,
Neely, Richard

Wheeling
Hill, Barry Morton

WISCONSIN

Cross Plains
Atterbury, Lee Richard

Kenosha
Clarke, Alan William

La Crosse
Ablan, Michael Charles

Madison
Bruchs, Amy O'Brien
Hildebrand, Daniel Walter
Skilton, John Singleton

Milwaukee
Babler, Wayne E., Jr.,
Busch, John Arthur
Frauen, Kurt Herman
Grzezinski, Dennis Michael
Habush, Robert Lee
Levit, William Harold, Jr.,
Melin, Robert Arthur
Pollen, Raymond James
Terschan, Frank Robert
Titley, Robert L.

Pepin
Seymour, Mary Frances

Racine
Gasiorkiewicz, Eugene Anthony

WYOMING

Casper
Combs, W(illiam) Henry, III,

Cheyenne
Dyekman, Gregory Chris

Cody
Stradley, Richard Lee

Jackson
Schuster, Robert Parks
Shockey, Gary Lee

Wheatland
Hunkins, Raymond Breedlove

TERRITORIES OF THE UNITED STATES

PUERTO RICO

Old San Juan
Weinstein-Bacal, Stuart Allen

CHILE

Santiago
Varela, Gerardo

ENGLAND

London
Haubold, Samuel Allen

NETHERLANDS

The Hague
Brower, Charles Nelson

SWITZERLAND

Zürich
Stieger, Werner

ADDRESS UNPUBLISHED

Alexander, Richard Elmont
Belleville, Philip Frederick
Blevins, Jeffrey Alexander
Bloom, Charles Joseph
Braun, Jerome Irwin
Brumbaugh, John Moore
Campbell, Frank Andrew Scott
Campion, Thomas Francis
Colman, Richard Thomas
Comisky, Ian Michael
Dolan, John F.
Dolan, Peter Brown
Dubuc, Carroll Edward
Eaton, Larry Ralph
Erlebacher, Arlene Cernik
Flanary, Donald Herbert, Jr.,
Frank, James Stuart
Gladden, Joseph Reah, II,
Glosser, Jeffrey Mark
Goddard, Claude Philip, Jr.,
Goldberg, Michael Bradley
Golder, Frederick Thomas
Greenebaum, Leonard Charles
Grier, Phillip Michael
Grutman, Jewel Humphrey
Hall, John Hopkins
Harnack, Don Steger
Harris, Janine Diane
Heins, Samuel David
Heise, John Irvin, Jr.,
Howard, John Wayne
Humphreys, Robert Russell
Joelson, Mark René
Johnson, Edward Michael
Madsen, H(enry) Stephen
Manos, Christopher Lawrence
Mc Donough, John Richard
McCoy, John Joseph
McDuffy, Aditya
Merritt, Bruce Gordon
Muri, Anthony Frederick
Pereyra-Suarez, Charles Albert
Reiss, Jerome
Roethe, James Norton
Sanders-Cochran, Rachel Deanna
Siemer, Deanne Clemence
Smith, James A.
Smouse, H(ervey) Russell
Speight, John B.
Stream, Arnold Crager
Sulton, Anne Thomas
Sussman, Howard S(ivin)
Szuch, Clyde Andrew
Tasker, Joseph
Terrell, G. Irvin
Twardy, Stanley Albert, Jr.,
Vigil, David Charles
Waxman, Seth Paul
Wheeler, R(ichard) Kenneth
Wilson, Hugh Steven
Wruble, Bernhardt Karp
Young, John Hardin
Ziegler, William Alexander

CIVIL LITIGATION, GENERAL

UNITED STATES

ALABAMA

Anniston
Klinefelter, James Louis

Birmingham
Albritton, William Harold, IV,
Blan, Ollie Lionel, Jr.,
Boardman, Mark Seymour
Childs, Larry Brittain
Clark, William Northington
Donahue, Timothy Patrick
Gale, Fournier Joseph, III,
Givhan, Robert Marcus
Henry, James Fred
Hinton, James Forrest, Jr.,
Long, Thad Gladden
McWhorter, Hobart Amory, Jr.,
Mills, William Hayes
Nettles, Bert Sheffield
Norris, John E.
Rowe, Stephen Ashford
Scherf, John George, IV,

Dadeville
Oliver, John Percy, II,

Dothan
Derrick, Raymond Todd

Gadsden
Cornett, Bradley Williams

Guntersville
McLaughlin, Jeffrey Rex

Huntsville
Richardson, Patrick William

Mobile
Baxley, Phillip Kent
Braswell, Louis Erskine
Harris, Benjamin Harte, Jr.,
Helmsing, Frederick George
Holmes, Broox Garrett
McCoy, Douglas Leon
Roedder, William Chapman, Jr.,

Montgomery
Harris, George Bryan
Laurie, Robin Garrett
Lawson, Thomas Seay, Jr.,
McFadden, Frank Hampton
Morrow, Dorsey W., Jr.,

Moulton
Dutton, Mark Anthony

Tuscaloosa
Williams, Roger Courtland

ALASKA

Anchorage
Dickson, Robert Jay
Evans, Charles Graham
Flynn, Charles P.
Wonnell, Thomas Burke

Kodiak
Jamin, Matthew Daniel
Ott, Andrew Eduard

ARIZONA

Phoenix
Allen, Robert Eugene Barton
Beggs, Harry Mark
Bouma, John Jacob
Calderon, Ernest
Galbut, Martin Richard
Goldstein, Stuart Wolf
Halpern, Barry David
Harris, Ray Kendall
Harrison, Mark Isaac
Himelrick, Richard G.
Johnston, Logan Truax, III,
Klausner, Jack Daniel
Litteral, Daniel Pace
McRae, Hamilton Eugene, III,
Platt, Warren E.
Postal, David Ralph
Preston, Bruce Marshall
Rivera, Jose de Jesus
Rose, David L.
Sanders, Barry R.
Sherk, Kenneth John
Turk, Andrew Borders
Udall, Calvin Hunt
Wirken, Charles William

Rio Rico
Ryan, John Duncan

Sun City
Treece, James Lyle

Tempe
Fanning, Francis Gerard

Tucson
D'Antonio, James Joseph
Heaphy, John Merrill
Jacobs, William Russell, II,
Lesher, Stephen Harrison
Treadwell-Rubin, Pamela A.

ARKANSAS

Bryant
Jackson, James Ralph (Jim Jackson)

Crossett
Hubbell, Billy James

Hot Springs National Park
Schnipper, Don Martin

Jonesboro
Deacon, John C.

Little Rock
May, Ronald Alan

CALIFORNIA

Alameda
Dósa, Andrew Alexander

Alamo
Madden, Palmer Brown

Bakersfield
Karcher, Steven Michael

Belvedere Tiburon
Bremer, William Richard

Berkeley
Pyle, Walter K.
Sparks, John Edward

Beverly Hills
Amado, Honey Kessler
Burns, Marvin Gerald
Dent, John Robert
Isaacman, Alan L.
Kadisha, Sheila
Sherwood, Arthur Lawrence

Calabasas
Grimwade, Richard Llewellyn

Cambria
Stotter, James, II,

Claremont
Ferguson, Cleve Robert

Del Mar
Seitman, John Michael

East Palo Alto
Bates, William, III,

Encino
Magidsohn, Herman Edward
Sperber, David Sol

Fallbrook
Leehey, Paul Wade

Fresno
Jamison, Daniel Oliver

Fullerton
Moerbeek, Stanley Leonard

Glendale
MacDonald, Kirk Stewart

Indio
De Salva, Christopher Joseph

Irvine
Hensley, William Michael
Ingram, James Michael
Petrasich, John Moris

Long Beach
Dawson, Norma Ann
Wise, George Edward

Los Angeles
Adamek, Charles Andrew
Barrett, Jane Hayes
Bosl, Phillip L.
Brodka, Mark A.
Byrd, Christine Waterman Swent
Cathcart, David Arthur
Cathcart, Robert James
Chu, Morgan
Cohen, Cynthia Marylyn
Cole, Curtis Allen
Dunham, Scott H.
Fredman, Howard S.
Gest, Howard David
Heller, Philip
Hight, B. Boyd
Holtzman, Robert Arthur
Huben, Brian David
Hufstedler, Seth Martin
Hutt, Laurence Jeffrey
Kirwan, R. DeWitt
Kolber, Richard A.
Litvack, Sanford Martin
MacLaughlin, Francis Joseph
Marcus, Stephen Howard
Miller, Milton Allen
Mitchell, Briane Nelson
Morgenthaler-Lever, Alisa
Neufeld, Timothy Lee
Ogbogu, Cecilia Ify
Olivas, Daniel Anthony
Pasich, Kirk Alan
Peterson, Linda S.
Reed, Leland
Renwick, Edward S.
Rutter, Marshall Anthony
Schulman, Robert S.
Scoular, Robert Frank
Shacter, David Mervyn
Shapiro, Robert
Sheller, John Willard
Tarr, Ralph William
Trygstad, Lawrence Benson
Van de Kamp, John Kalar
Vertun, Alan Stuart
von Kalinowski, Julian Onesime
White, Robert Joel
Woodland, Irwin Francis

Mill Valley
Nemir, Donald Philip

Modesto
Mussman, William Edward, III,

Napa
Kuntz, Charles Powers
Meyers, David W.

Newport Beach
Carman, Ernest Day
Johnson, Thomas Webber, Jr.,
Schiff, Laurie

Oakland
Allen, Jeffrey Michael
Berry, Phillip Samuel
Bryant, Arthur H.
Condie, Robert Stevens
Johnson, Kenneth F.
Quinby, William Albert

Oxnard
Gerber, David A.

Pacific Palisades
Dickson, Robert Lee
Kelley, Thomas Joseph

Palm Springs
FitzGerald, John Edward, III,

Palo Alto
Johnston, Alan Cope

Pasadena
Zuetel, Kenneth Roy, Jr.,

Pleasanton
Opperwall, Stephen Gabriel
Scott, G. Judson, Jr.,

Point Richmond
Edginton, John Arthur

Riverside
Marlatt, Michael James

Sacramento
Brazier, John Richard
Brookman, Anthony Raymond
Daniel, Lance
Houpt, James Edward

San Diego
Clark, David Robert
Estep, Arthur Lee
Guinn, Stanley Willis
Herring, Charles David
Iredale, Eugene Gerald
Margolis, Anita Joy
McDermott, Thomas John, Jr.,
Schwartz, Jeffrey Scott
Shelton, Dorothy Diehl Rees
Sullivan, William Francis
Weaver, Michael James
Weidner, Lauren Finder

San Francisco
Bleich, Jeffrey Laurence
Bostwick, James Stephen
Boutin, Peter Rucker
Briscoe, John
Callison, Russell James
Diekmann, Gilmore Frederick, Jr.,
Donovan, Charles Stephen
Getto, Ernest John
Knebel, Jack Gillen
Koeppel, John A.
Kornblum, Guy Orville
Lapping, Richard A.
Miller, William Napier Cripps
Penskar, Mark Howard
Popofsky, Melvin Laurence
Reese, John Robert
Richardson, Daniel Ralph
Seabolt, Richard L.
Smith, Robert Michael
Taylor, William James (Zak Taylor)
Trautman, William Ellsworth
Utrecht, Paul F.
Venning, Robert Stanley
Warmer, Richard Craig
Weber, Arnold I.
Weiner, Jody Carl

San Jose
Bennion, David Jacobsen
Bohn, Robert Herbert
Cummins, Charles Fitch, Jr.,
Denver, Thomas H. R.
Hernández, Fernando Vargas
McManis, James
Narayan, Beverly Elaine
Stein, John C.

San Mateo
Slabach, Stephen Hall

San Rafael
Bloomfield, Neil Jon
Fairbairn, Sydney Elise
Roth, Hadden Wing

Santa Ana
Mosich, Nicholas Joseph
Patt, Herbert Jacob

Santa Barbara
Ah-Tye, Kirk Thomas
Cappello, A. Barry
Metzinger, Timothy Edward
Pyle, Kurt H.

Santa Cruz
Seligmann, William Robert

Santa Monica
Bower, Allan Maxwell
Fagen, Peter Kirk
Pizzulli, Francis Cosmo Joseph

Stockton
Malm, Scott

Sunnyvale
Thornton, D. Whitney, II,

Torrance
Johnson, Einar William

Tracy
Hay, Dennis Lee

Tustin
Gaughan, John Stephen

Van Nuys
Mikesell, Richard Lyon

Ventura
Leach, Donald Lee

Walnut Creek
Cameron, Mark Alan
Rathjen, Jon Laurence
Schreiber, John T.

Weaverville
Correll, Joanna Rae

Westlake Village
Mittenthal, Peter A.

Woodland Hills
Johnson-Champ, Debra Sue

Yuba City
Doughty, Mark Anthony

COLORADO

Arvada
Carney, T.J
Peck, Kenneth E.

Basalt
Shipp, Dan Shackelford

Boulder
Cope, Joseph Adams
Ranniger, Leslie Jean

Broomfield
Jonsen, Eric Richard

Canon City
McDermott, John Arthur

Colorado Springs
Kennedy, Richard Joseph
McCready, Guy Michael
Purvis, Randall W. B.
Sheffield, Alden Daniel, Jr.,
Slivka, Michael Andrew

Denver
Bain, Donald Knight
Ceriani, Gary James
Dowdle, Patrick Dennis
Dunn, Randy Edwin
Fowler, Daniel McKay
Green, Jersey Michael-Lee
Hamel, Fred Meade
Harris, Dale Ray
Hawley, Robert Cross
Holme, Richard Phillips
Horowitz, Robert M.
Kahn, Benjamin Alexander
Kaplan, Marc J.
Kintzele, John Alfred
Long, Martin Edward
Malatesta, Mary Anne
McIntosh, Carolyn Leigh
Merritts, Jack Michael
Mitchem, James E.
Munteanu, Victor John
Murane, William Edward
Pack, Stuart Harris
Pineau, John Kenneth
Rench, Stephen Charles
Shore, Heather Field
Solano, Henry L.
Timmins, Edward Patrick
Wheeler, Malcolm Edward
Wollins, David Hart

Durango
Burnham, Bryson Paine

Englewood
Orsini, Rosemary

Fort Collins
Downey, Arthur Harold, Jr.,

Frisco
McElyea, Monica Sergent

Golden
Eiberger, Carl Frederick
Snead, Kathleen Marie

Grand Junction
Griff, Harry

Greeley
Frey, Henry Charles

Greenwood Village
Gallegos, Larry Duayne

Highlands Ranch
Hagen, Glenn W.

Littleton
Robinson, Warren A. (Rip Robinson)

CONNECTICUT

Bridgeport
Katz, Stuart Michael
Zeldes, Jacob Dean

Fairfield
Denniston, Brackett Badger, III,

Farmington
Wiechmann, Eric Watt

Glastonbury
Rintoul, David Skinner

Greenwich
Forrow, Brian Derek

Hamden
Bershtein, Herman Sammy

Hartford
Bonee, John Leon, III,
Donnell, Brian James
Orth, Paul William
Packard, Stephen Michael
Rosengren, David E.
Sosensky, Steven Charles
Space, Theodore Maxwell
Stravalle-Schmidt, Ann Roberta

Meriden
Lowry, Houston Putnam
Luby, Thomas Stewart

New Haven
Babbin, Jeffrey R.
Belt, David Levin
Carty, Paul Vernon

New London
Reardon, Robert Ignatius, Jr.,

Southport
Sanetti, Stephen Louis

Stamford
Tropp, Jonathan B.

Torrington
Leard, David Carl

West Hartford
Swerdloff, Mark Harris

Westport
Arons, Mark David

DELAWARE

Dover
Sherlock, Mary Eva

Wilmington
Curtin, Christopher James
Finkelstein, Jesse Adam
Flame, Andrew Jay
Goldman, Michael David
Julian, J. R.
Katzenstein, Robert John
Semple, James William
Smith, Craig Bennett

DISTRICT OF COLUMBIA

Washington
Attridge, Daniel F.
Barnett, Robert Bruce
Baum, Lynne Miriam
Bernabei, Lynne Ann
Black, Stephen Franklin
Bleakley, Peter Kimberley
Boss, Lenard Barrett
Buckley, John Joseph, Jr.,
Buscemi, Peter
Canfield, Edward Francis
Carome, Patrick Joseph
Carter, William Joseph
Casey, Bernard J.
Chang, Deanna J.
Collins, Daniel Francis
Cooper, Clement Theodore
Denison, Mary Boney
Deso, Robert Edward, Jr.,
Dolin, Mitchell F.
Eastment, Thomas James
Ellis, Courtenay
Fedders, John Michael
Funkhouser, Robert Bruce
Gelb, Joseph Donald
Goldfarb, Ronald Lawrence
Greenfeld, Alexander
Hassett, Joseph Mark
Huddleson, Edwin Emmett, III,
Jones, George Washington, Jr.,
Kent, M. Elizabeth
Klarfeld, Peter James
Lackey, Michael E., Jr.,
Latham, Peter Samuel
Lazarus, Kenneth Anthony
McConnell, Nicholas Stillwell
McDaniels, William E.
Miller, Andrew Pickens
Montedonico, Joseph
Moses, Alfred Henry
O'Donnell, Terrence
Profaizer, Joseph Rudolph
Reid, Inez Smith
Rezneck, Daniel Albert
Salsbury, Michael H.
Sherman, Lawrence Jay
Singleton, Harry Michael
Splitt, David Alan
Tompert, James Emil
Watson, Thomas C.
Weinstein, Harris
Wilner, Thomas Bernard
Wolff, Paul Martin
Wyss, John Benedict

FLORIDA

Bay Harbor Islands
Ryce, Donald Theodore

Boca Raton
Barwell, Cindy Ann
Beber, Robert H.
Comiter, Lloyd Alan
Silver, Barry Morris
Turner, Hugh Joseph, Jr.,
Willis, John Alexander

Clearwater
Swope, Scott Paul

Coral Gables
Buell, Rodd Russell
Gonzalez, Ervin Amado
Hoffman, Carl H.
McGrane, Miles A., III,

Fort Lauderdale
Fanizza, Joanne
Hoines, David Alan
James, Gordon, III,
Wich, Donald Anthony, Jr.,

Gainesville
Kurrus, Thomas William

Gulf Breeze
Burr, Timothy Fuller

Gulfport
Allen, John Thomas, Jr.,

Jacksonville
Ansbacher, Barry Barnett
Boyer, Tyrie Alvis
Bradford, Dana Gibson, II,
Bullock, Bruce Stanley
Coker, Howard Coleman
Korn, Michael Jeffrey
Liles, Rutledge Richardson
McBurney, Charles Walker, Jr.,
Posgay, Matthew Nichols
Rinaman, James Curtis, Jr.,
Schulz, George E., Jr.,
White, Edward Alfred

Key West
Brihammar, B. Niklas

Lake Worth
Kreidler, Frank Allan

Lakeland
Knowlton, Kevin Charles

Leesburg
Austin, Robert Eugene, Jr.,

Maitland
Bailey, Michael Keith

Melbourne
Cacciatore, S. Sammy

Miami
Aronovitz, Tod
Bartelstone, Ted Henry
Berger, Steven R.
Bronis, Stephen Jay
Burr, Scott Allen
Castillo, Angel, Jr.,
Critchlow, Richard H.
Curtis, Karen Haynes
Hartz, Steven Edward Marshall
Hauser, Helen Ann
Jimenez, Marcos Daniel
Johnson, Alise M.
Klock, Joseph Peter, Jr.,
Korchin, Judith Miriam
Levine, Robert Jeffrey
Long, Maxine Master
Maher, Stephen Trivett
Miller, James M.
Osman, Edith Gabriella
Russell, Patrick
Santoro, Thomas Mead
Schnapp, Mark Paul
Stansell, Leland Edwin, Jr.,
Touby, Kathleen Anita
Vento, M. Thérèse

Naples
Buckley, Frederick Jean

North Miami Beach
Zipkin, Sheldon Lee

Orlando
Blackwell, Bruce Beuford
Handley, Leon Hunter
Hartley, Carl William, Jr.,
Hurt, Jennings Laverne, III,
Jontz, Jeffry Robert
Kelaher, James Peirce
Metz, Larry Edward
Motes, Carl Dalton
Murrell, Robert George
Nadeau, Robert Bertrand, Jr.,
Neal, Thomas Frederick
Paul, David Aaron
Pierce, John Gerald (Jerry Pierce)
Spoonhour, James Michael
Subin, Eli Harold
Vazquez, Ramon

Palm Beach
Devins, Robert Sylvester

Palm Beach Gardens
Pumphrey, Gerald Robert

Panama City
Fensom, James B.

Pensacola
Bozeman, Frank Carmack
Jones, Julie Laura
McKenzie, James Franklin
Soloway, Daniel Mark
Woodward, David Luther

Pompano Beach
Shulmister, M(orris) Ross

Saint Petersburg
Henniger, David Thomas
Mann, Sam Henry, Jr.,
Ross, Howard Philip
Wein, Stephen J.

Sarasota
Christopher, William Garth
Garland, Richard Roger
Lamia, Christine Edwards

Tallahassee
Davis, William Howard
Kitchen, E.C. Deeno
Sheffield, Frank Elwyn
Varn, Wilfred Claude

Tampa
Anton, David
Berkowitz, Herbert Mattis
Blau, Richard M.
Boos, Robert Walter, II,
Campbell, Richard Bruce
Cook, William John
Davis, Kirk Stuart
Jordan-Holmes, Clark
MacDonald, Thomas Cook, Jr.,
Nutter, Robert Heinrich
Olson, John Karl
Robinson, John William, IV,
Stagg, Clyde Lawrence
Taub, Theodore Calvin
Yerrid, C. Steven

Vero Beach
Stewart, John Mitchell

West Palm Beach
Beasley, James W., Jr.,
Damsel, Charles H., Jr.,
Dunkum, Betty Lee
Lane, Matthew Jay
Mrachek, Lorin Louis
Norton, William Alan
Scarola, John
Spillias, Kenneth George
Weitzman, Linda Sue
Zeller, Ronald John

Winter Park
Johnson, Kraig Nelson

GEORGIA

Atlanta
Beckham, Walter Hull, III,
Blackstock, Jerry B.
Bonds, John Wilfred, Jr.,
Bramlett, Jeffrey Owen
Brown, John Robert
Calvert, Matthew James
Campbell, Charles Edward
Chilivis, Nickolas Peter
Collins, Steven M.
Croft, Terrence Lee
Fellows, Henry David, Jr.,
Gambrell, David Henry
Hughes, David Andrew
Janney, Donald Wayne
Jenkins, Albert Felton, Jr.,
Jones, Frank Cater
Killorin, Robert Ware
Kitchens, Joyce Ellen
Koplan, Andrew Bennet
Lackland, Theodore Howard
Leach, James Glover
Manley, David Bott, III,
Marshall, Thomas Oliver, Jr.,
McAlpin, Kirk Martin
Paquin, Jeffrey Dean
Persons, W. Ray
Rhodes, Thomas Willard
Savell, Edward Lupo
Tanner, W(alter) Rhett
Wright, Frederick Lewis, II,
Young, Michael Anthony

Augusta
Cooney, William J.

Cartersville
Ford, Vickie Louise Arp

College Park
Stokes, Arch

Columbus
Harp, John Anderson

Decatur
Apolinsky, Stephen Douglas

Metter
Doremus, Ogden

Nashville
Ellis, Robert Bryan, Jr.,

Norcross
Hahn, Stanley Robert, Jr.,

Roswell
England, John Melvin

Savannah
Gannam, Michael Joseph

Statesboro
Brogdon, W.M. "Rowe"
Classens, Michael John

HAWAII

Honolulu
Ching, Gale Lin Fong
Ching, Wesley H. H.
Edmunds, John Sanford
Fong, Peter C. K.
Godbey, Robert Carson
Grande, Thomas Robert
Heller, Ronald Ian
Kawachika, James Akio
Lau, Eugene Wing Iu
Lau, Jeffrey Daniel
Okinaga, Carrie Kiyono
Reinke, Stefan Michael
Sato, Glenn Kenji
Sumida, Kevin P.H.
Wong, Reuben Sun Fai

IDAHO

Boise
Dryden, William George
Greener, Richard H.
Hoagland, Samuel Albert
Lombardi, David Richard
Noack, Harold Quincy, Jr.,
Scanlan, Kevin J.
Schild, Raymond Douglas
Shurtliff, Marvin Karl
Whittier, Monte Ray

Hailey
Hogue, Terry Glynn
Youngblood, Deborah Sue

Pocatello
Nye, W. Marcus W.

ILLINOIS

Arlington Heights
Giampietro, Wayne Bruce
Tucker, Bowen Hayward

Belleville
Bauman, John Duane
Boyle, Richard Edward

Bloomington
Bragg, Michael Ellis

Carrollton
Strickland, Hugh Alfred

Champaign
Harden, Richard Russell

Chicago
Adelman, Stanley Joseph
Alberts, Barry S.
Allen, Thomas Draper
Anderson, Kimball Richard
Angst, Gerald L.
Banta, Don Arthur
Barron, Howard Robert
Belz, Edwin J.
Bernick, David M.
Blatt, Richard Lee
Brice, Roger Thomas
Burke, William Joseph
Burns, Terrence Michael
Connelly, Mary Jo
Cusack, John Thomas
Daniels, John Draper
Davis, Scott Jonathan
Donner, Ted A.
Downing, Robert Allan
Drumke, Michael William
Eggert, Russell Raymond
Eimer, Nathan Philip
Elden, Gary Michael
Esrick, Jerald Paul
Feagley, Michael Rowe
Finke, Robert Forge
Formeller, Daniel Richard
Franklin, Christine Carroll
Frazen, Mitchell Hale
French, Timothy A.
Fuller, Perry Lucian
Geraldson, Raymond I., Jr.,
Gerske, Janet Fay
Gilford, Steven Ross
Golden, Bruce Paul
Gustman, David Charles
Halloran, Michael John
Harper, Steven James
Harrold, Bernard
Henry, Brian Thomas
Herald, J. Patrick
Herman, Stephen Charles
Hickey, John Thomas, Jr.,
Hoffa, Thomas Edward
Horwich, Allan
Howe, Jonathan Thomas
Hyman, Michael Bruce
Jacobson, Richard Joseph
Johnson, Richard Fred
Kaminsky, Richard Alan
Kasson, Constantine D.
Kikoler, Stephen Philip
Kim, Michael Charles
Kunkle, William Joseph
Lynch, John James
McFadden, Monica Elizabeth
McLaren, Richard Wellington, Jr.,
McVisk, William Kilburn
Molo, Steven Francis
Montgomery, William Adam
Niro, Cheryl
Nora, Gerald Ernest
Panich, Danuta Bembenista
Pelton, Russell Meredith, Jr.,
Pope, Michael Arthur
Price, Paul L.
Roberson, G. Gale, Jr.,
Rutkoff, Alan Stuart
Sanchez, Christopher Benjamin
Saunders, Terry Rose
Shank, William O.
Simon, John Bern
Simon, Seymour
Stavins, Richard Lee
Stick, Michael Alan
Stiegel, Michael A.
Suskin, Howard Steven
Tenenbaum, J. Samuel
Thomson, George Ronald
Tinaglia, Michael Lee
Van Tine, Matthew Eric
Vojcanin, Sava Alexander
Weaver, Timothy Allan
Wilcox, Mark Dean
Wood, Allison Lorraine

Columbia
Gutknecht, Timothy Arthur

Edwardsville
Hunsaker, Richard Kendall

Elgin
Roeser, Ronald O.

Elmhurst
Blain, Robert Krieger

Evanston
Creamer, Robert Allan

Homewood
Olofsson, Daniel Joel

Jacksonville
Kuster, Larry Donald

La Grange
Kerr, Alexander Duncan, Jr.,

Mattoon
Corn, Stephen Leslie

Mundelein
Ackley, Robert O.

Naperville
Levy, Steven B.

Northfield
Giza, David Alan

Oak Brook
Oldfield, E. Lawrence

Oakbrook Terrace
Tibble, Douglas Clair

Oswego
May, Frank Brendan, Jr.,

Peoria
Bertschy, Timothy L.
Prusak, Maximilian Michael

Rock Island
Wallace, Franklin Sherwood

Urbana
Thies, David Charles

Wauconda
Malik, Thomas Warren

Westchester
Castellano, Christine Marie

Wheaton
Butt, Edward Thomas, Jr.,

Wilmette
Griffith, James D.
McNeill, Thomas B.

INDIANA

Danville
Baldwin, Jeffrey Kenton

Evansville
Hayes, Philip Harold

Fort Wayne
Colvin, Sherrill William
Pope, Mark Andrew

Gary
Hall, John Henry

Indianapolis
Albright, Terrill D.
Barrett, David Olan
Blythe, James David, II,
Carr, David J.
Choplin, John M., II,
Conour, William Frederick
Johnstone, Robert Philip
Kautzman, John Fredrick
Leitch, Ryan L.
McTurnan, Lee Bowes
Moffatt, Michael Alan
Petersen, James L.
Scaletta, Phillip Ralph, III,
Stayton, Thomas George
Wampler, Robert Joseph

Lafayette
Hart, Russell Holiday
Hoffman, John Frederick

Merrillville
Miller, Richard Allen

New Albany
Bourne, James E.

South Bend
Phillipoff, Mark James
Reinke, William John

Terre Haute
Bopp, James, Jr.,
Kesler, John A.

Valparaiso
Wrage, Jeffrey S.

Vincennes
Emison, Ewing Rabb, Jr.,

IOWA

Cedar Rapids
Collins, Kevin Heath

Des Moines
Conlin, Roxanne Barton
Norris, Glenn L.
Phipps, David Lee
Rickert, Brian Patrick
Soulati, Behnaz

Dubuque
Hammer, David Lindley

Iowa City
Hayek, John William

Le Mars
Murphy, Patrick Neil

Mount Pleasant
Vance, Michael Charles

KANSAS

Hays
Boone, Thomas Caleb

Kansas City
Brown, Norman Jack
O'Neill, Thomas Tyrone

Lawrence
Huff, Barbara Kay

Manhattan
Miller, Anne Burke

Olathe
Scott, Robert Gene

Overland Park
Griswold, Thomas L.
Smith, Daniel Lynn
Smith, Jill Galbreath

Prairie Village
Sharp, Rex Arthur

Shawnee Mission
Badgerow, John Nicholas
Helder, Jan Pleasant, Jr.,
Smith, Edwin Dudley

KENTUCKY

Bowling Green
Sparks, David Thomas

Covington
Stepner, Donald Leon

Crestwood
Ray, Ronald Dudley

Flemingsburg
McCartney, Frank Howard, III,

Glasgow
Gardner, Woodford Lloyd, Jr.,

Lexington
Bagby, Glen Stovall
Beshear, Steven Lynn
Deener, Larry Colby
Kessinger, B.L., Jr.,
Matl, Lois Tudor

London
Keller, John Warren

Louisville
Ballantine, John Tilden
Bubalo, Gregory Joe
Carroll, Wayne Jackson
Cowan, Frederic Joseph
Ethridge, Larry Clayton
Manly, Samuel
Reed, John Squires, II,
Schecter, Benjamin Seth
Swyers, Walter John, Jr.,
Talbott, Ben Johnson, Jr.,

Paintsville
Massengale, Roger Lee

Shepherdsville
Givhan, Thomas Bartram

LOUISIANA

Alexandria
Gist, Howard Battle, Jr.,

Baton Rouge
Johnson, Joseph Clayton, Jr.,
Walsh, Milton O'Neal
Wittenbrink, Jeffrey Scott

Chalmette
Mumphrey, J. Wayne

Hammond
Ross, Kenneth L.

Jefferson
Conino, Joseph Aloysius

Lafayette
Morgan, Glenn L.
Pate, James Lavert

Lake Charles
Judice, Gregory Van
Sanchez, Walter Marshall

Leesville
Smith, Simeon Christie, IV,

Metairie
Album, Jerald Lewis
Gauthier, Celeste Anne

New Orleans
Abaunza, Donald Richard
Barnett, William Michael
David, Robert Jefferson
Dittman, Stevan Craig
Eustis, Richmond Minor
Fierke, Thomas Garner
Gagnard, Candyce C.
Guidry, Susan Gail
Hearin, Robert Matlock, Jr.,
Herman, Fred L.
Hoffman, Donald Alfred
Levin, Richard Barry
Molony, Michael Janssens, Jr.,
Pearce, John Y.
Pugh, William Whitmell Hill, III,
Redmann, John William
Rodriguez, Antonio Jose
Sinor, Howard Earl, Jr.,
Stag, Michael Gregory
Steinberg, Sylvan Julian
Wright, William Everard, Jr.,

Shreveport
Clark, James E.
Woodman, Walter James

MAINE

Bass Harbor
Ervin, Spencer

Kennebunk
Clifford, Peter

Portland
Culley, Peter William
Dinan, Christopher Charles
Harvey, Charles Albert, Jr.,
Hirshon, Robert Edward
Martin, Michael Keith
Whiting, Stephen Clyde

Skowhegan
Youney, John William

MARYLAND

Abingdon
Wolf, Martin Eugene

Annapolis
Ferris, William Michael

Baltimore
Archibald, James Kenway
Bartlett, James Wilson, III,
Berlage, Jan Ingham
Burch, Francis Boucher, Jr.,
Ellin, Marvin
Fax, Charles Samuel
Friedman, Barry Howard
Hafets, Richard Jay
Himeles, Martin Stanley, Jr.,
Kandel, Nelson Robert
Lynch, Timothy Cronin
Messina, Bonnie Lynn
Plummer, Risque Wilson
Powell, Roger Norman
Schreiber, Martin Harold, II,
Stiller, Shale David
Sykes, Melvin Julius

Bel Air
Miller, Max Dunham, Jr.,

Bethesda
Bauersfeld, Carl Frederick
Eisen, Eric Anshel
Frosh, Brian Esten
Moss, Stephen Edward

Bowie
McCarthy, Kevin John

Cockeysville
Barnes, Peter

College Park
Neal, Edward Garrison

Greenbelt
Greenwald, Andrew Eric

Leonardtown
Lacer, Alfred Antonio

Rockville
Barkley, Brian Evan
Friedman, Greg Stuart
Stolker, Richard Samuel
Titus, Roger Warren
Tomar, Richard Thomas

Showell
Grech, Christopher Alan

Silver Spring
Ahmed, Atiq Rahman

Towson
Borgerding, Francis Xavier, Jr.,

MASSACHUSETTS

Amherst
Howland, Richard Moulton

Boston
Adler, Sidney W.
Berry, Janis Marie
Brody, Richard Eric
Buchanan, Robert McLeod
Carpenter, Robert Brent
Daley, Paul Patrick
Dillon, James Joseph
Gilmore, John Allen Dehn
Goldman, Eric Scot
Gossels, Claus Peter Rolf
Graham, John Joseph
Hess-Mahan, Theodore Michael
Hoffman, David Alan
Johnston, Richard Alan
Kaler, Robert Joseph
Keating, Michael Burns
Koutoujian, Peter John
Lanckton, Arthur Van Cleve
Licata, Arthur Frank
Lyons, Nance
McKittrick, Neil Vincent
Meserve, William George
Moriarty, George Marshall
Muldoon, Robert Joseph, Jr.,
Redlich, Marc
Richmond, Alice Elenor
Ritvo, Elizabeth Ann
Schlichtmann, Jan R.
Spelfogel, Scott David
Stern, Donald Kenneth
Sullivan, Edward Michael

Chelmsford
Grossman, Debra A.
Lerer, Neal M.

Florence
Park, Beverly Goodman

Newton
Peterson, Osler Leopold

Orleans
Chaplin, Ansel Burt

Quincy
Motejunas, Gerald William

Salem
Frattaroli, Carmen Aniello

Somerville
Dash, Adam S.

Springfield
Burke, Michael Henry
Dibble, Francis Daniel, Jr.,
Low, Terrence Allen

Wakefield
Lucas, Robert Frank

Wellesley
Giroux, Eugene Xavier

Worcester
Donnelly, James Corcoran, Jr.,
Feener, Donald Edward
Fox, Douglas Lee
Van Nostrand, Richard Charles

MICHIGAN

Ann Arbor
Ellmann, Douglas Stanley
Joscelyn, Kent B(uckley)
Niehoff, Leonard Marvin

Bingham Farms
Lebow, Michael Jeffrey

Birmingham
Zacharski, Dennis Edward

Bloomfield Hills
Baumkel, Mark S.
Clippert, Charles Frederick
Cranmer, Thomas William
Cunningham, Gary H.
Hertz, Howard
Snyder, George Edward

Dearborn
Demorest, Mark Stuart

Detroit
Brady, Edmund Matthew, Jr.,
Driker, Eugene
Gottschalk, Thomas A.
Mamat, Frank Trustick
Torpey, Scott Raymond
Ward, George Edward
Zacks, David N.

Farmington Hills
Fershtman, Julie Ilene
Foley, Thomas John
Taravella, Christopher Anthony

Flint
Hart, Clifford Harvey
Henneke, Edward George

Grand Rapids
Blackwell, Thomas Francis
Bransdorfer, Stephen Christie
Buquicchio, Steven T.
Drew, Stephen Richard
Marshall, J. Stephen
Neckers, Bruce Warren

Grosse Pointe
Goss, James William

Grosse Pointe Park
McIntyre, Anita Grace Jordan

Harbor Springs
Turner, Lester Nathan

Kalamazoo
Bauhof, James Francis
Hatch, Hazen van den Berg

Lansing
Clarke, Hugh B., Jr.,
Fink, Joseph Allen

Mount Pleasant
Plachta, Thomas J.

South Haven
Waxman, Sheldon Robert

Southfield
Israel, Stuart Michael
Morganroth, Mayer
Sullivan, Robert Emmet, Jr.,

West Bloomfield
Gullen, Christopher Roy

MINNESOTA

Bemidji
Woodke, Robert Allen

Edina
Ashley, James Patrick

Hallock
Malm, Roger Charles

Hawley
Baer, Zenas

Hopkins
Hunter, Donald Forrest

Hutchinson
Yira, Markus Clarence

Minneapolis
Ayling, Corey John
Baillie, James Leonard
Barnard, Allen Donald
Bland, J(ohn) Richard
Bodas, Margie Ruth
Borger, John Philip
Bruner, Philip Lane
Christensen, Robert Paul
Clary, Bradley G.
Cole, Phillip Allen
Eck, George Gregory
Gagnon, Craig William
Gill, Richard Lawrence
Heffelfinger, Thomas Backer
Jarpe, Geoffrey Pellas
Johannsen, Marc Alan
Klaas, Paul Barry
Long, James Jay
Manning, William Henry
McNamara, Michael John
Palmer, Brian Eugene
Reinhart, Robert Rountree, Jr.,
Roe, Roger Rolland, Jr.,
Rothenberg, Elliot Calvin
Schermer, Judith Kahn
Silver, Alan Irving
Smith, Curtis David
Sortland, Paul Allan
Uy, Hazel J.
Voss, Barry Vaughan
Zalk, Robert H.

Minnetonka
Kunert, Paul Charles
Schechtman, Steven Lawrence

North Oaks
Woods, Robert Edward

Saint Cloud
Hughes, Kevin John

Saint Paul
Bell, Robert Charles
Cassidy, Edward Q.

South Saint Paul
O'Reilly, Ann Catherine

Wayzata
Reutiman, Robert William, Jr.,

MISSISSIPPI

Batesville
Baglan, Charles E., Jr.,

Drew
Holladay, Robert Lawson, Sr.,

Gulfport
Allen, Harry Roger
Harral, John Menteith

Jackson
Corlew, John Gordon
Harkins, Patrick Nicholas, III,
Langford, James Jerry
O'Mara, James Wright
Scanlon, Pat H.

Mccomb
Starrett, Keith

Ridgeland
Boackle, K F.

Tupelo
Clayton, Claude F., Jr.,

University
Howorth, David Bishop

MISSOURI

Clayton
Fluhr, Steven Solomon
Klein, Jerry A.

Hannibal
Terrell, James Daniel

Independence
Smith, R(onald) Scott

Jackson
Waldron, Kenneth Lynn

Jefferson City
Angstead, Robert Kenneth
Doerhoff, Dale Charles
Martin, Cathleen A.
Riner, James William

Kansas City
Bellmann, Thomas Richard
Brake, Timothy L.
Cowden, John William
Deacy, Thomas Edward, Jr.,
Eldridge, Truman Kermit, Jr.,
Foster, Mark Stephen
Hubbell, Ernest
Johnston, John Steven
Joyce, Michael Patrick
Lotven, Howard Lee
McManus, James William
Modin, Richard F.
Newsom, James Thomas
Palmer, Dennis Dale
Sands, Darry Gene
Siro, Rik Neal
Small, Stephen Bradley
Smithson, Lowell Lee
Stoup, Arthur Harry
Whittaker, Judith Ann Cameron

Saint Charles
Dorsey, Mary Elizabeth

Saint Louis
Bailey, R(obert) Greg
Barken, Bernard Allen
Berendt, Robert Tryon
Blanke, Richard Brian
Boggs, Beth Clemens
Burke, Thomas Michael
Carr, Gary Thomas
Corrigan, Ann Phillips
Corrigan, William M.
Downey, Michael Patrick
Elbert, Charles Steiner
Gullborg, Peter William
Hartweger, Gordon Gravius
Joerling, Dale Raymond
Klobasa, John Anthony
Komen, Leonard
Luberda, George Joseph
Massey, Raymond Lee
McDaniel, James Edwin
Michenfelder, Albert A.
Newman, Charles A.
Riggio, Nicholas Jospeh, Sr.,
Ringkamp, Stephen H.
Schramm, Paul Howard
Shalowitz, Howard A.
Switzer, Frederick Michael, III,
Tierney, Betty Thorne
Walsh, Joseph Leo, III,

Springfield
Lowther, Gerald Halbert
Roberts, Patrick Kent
Sherwood, Devon Fredrick

MONTANA

Billings
Beiswanger, Gary Lee
Cromley, Brent Reed
Malee, Thomas Michael
Murphy, Gregory Gerard

Bozeman
Conover, Richard Corrill
Nelson, Steven Dwayne

Livingston
Jovick, Robert L.

Missoula
Sullivan, Robert John
Vannatta, Shane Anthony

NEBRASKA

Lincoln
Blake, William George
Guthery, John M.
Rowe, David Winfield
Sapp, Susan Kubert

Omaha
Achelpohl, Steven Edward
Brownrigg, John Clinton
Fitzgerald, James Patrick
Grant, John P.
Lamson, William Maxwell, Jr.,

NEVADA

Las Vegas
Kirsch, Lynn
Lovell, Carl Erwin, Jr.,
Mansfield, Lorraine J.

Reno
Hibbs, Loyal Robert
Hornbeck, David Arthur
Shaffer, Wayne Alan

NEW HAMPSHIRE

Concord
Chapman, William Lansing
Rath, Thomas David

Dover
Catalfo, Alfred, Jr., (Alfio Catalfo)

Manchester
Hanna, Katherine Merritt
Harvell, Michael Cleland
Middleton, Jack Baer
Rubin, Jeffrey Mark

Nashua
Jette, Ernest Arthur
Raudonis, Valerie Christine

Portsmouth
Doleac, Charles Bartholomew
Watson, Thomas Roger

NEW JERSEY

Atlantic City
Zlotnick, Norman Lee

Bedminster
Spierer, Howard

Bridgewater
Conroy, Robert John
Linett, David

Cherry Hill
Tomar, William

Clark
Barr, Jon-Henry

East Hanover
Kayser, Kenneth Wayne

Edison
O'Brien, John Graham

Flemington
Michels, Kevin Howard

Florham Park
Chase, Eric Lewis
Laulicht, Murray Jack
Reid, Charles Adams, III,

Freehold
Brown, Sanford Donald

Garwood
Maher, Gary Laurence

Glen Rock
Markey, Brian Michael

Hackensack
Spiegel, Linda F.
Vort, Robert A.

Haddonfield
Heuisler, Charles William
Mitnick, Craig Robert

Hammonton
Woolson, Charles E., Jr.,

Hoboken
Sommers, George R.

Holmdel
Suhr, J. Nicholas

Iselin
Goodman, Barry S.

Kearny
Brady, Lawrence Peter

Kenilworth
Wasman, Jane G.

Livingston
Milstein, Rachelle H. (Shelly Milstein)
Nagel, Bruce H.

Millburn
Diamond, Richard S.

Morris Plains
Pluciennik, Thomas Casimir

Morristown
Clark, Grant Lawrence
Clemente, Mark Andrew
Geppert, John Gustave, Jr.,
Kreindler, Peter Michael
O'Grady, Dennis Joseph
Pellecchia, John Michael
Pollock, Stewart Glasson
Rose, Robert Gordon
Sperling, Joy Harmon

Mount Holly
Mintz, Jeffry Alan

Newark
Brenner, John Finn
Cahn, Jeffrey Barton
Creenan, Katherine Heras
Garde, John Charles
Kraus, Alan Edward
Maderer, William F.
Michels, Herman D.
Reilly, William Thomas
Salyer, John Clark, IV,
Siegal, Joel Davis
Slavitt, Ben J.

North Haledon
Harrington, Kevin Paul

Parsippany
Markus, Allan Lewis

Pine Brook
Henschel, John James

Pleasantville
Sinderbrand, David I.

Princeton
Benesch, Katherine
Greene, Steven Kevin
Karpoff, Michael Steven
Shaver, Philip Alcott
Sutphin, William Taylor

Red Bank
Waldman, Daniel M.

Roseland
Drasco, Dennis J.
Eakeley, Douglas Scott
Hayden, Joseph A., Jr.,
Kenny, George James
LaVecchia, John B.
Rubin, Alix R.
Schenkler, Bernard
Tarino, Gary Edward

Saddle Brook
Cohn, Albert Linn

Scotch Plains
Klock, John Henry

Short Hills
Kaye, Marc Mendell
Leviss, Stewart Michael

Somers Point
Baylinson, Christopher Michael

Somerville
Dreier, William Alan
Sozansky, Michael William, Jr.,

Springfield
Mytelka, Arnold Krieger

Stone Harbor
Taylor, Robert Lee

Trenton
Bigham, William J.
Glassen, James Warren

Union
Mark, Michael David
Yoskowitz, Marlene

Vineland
O'Neill, Joseph Dean

Westwood
McGuirl, Robert Joseph

Woodbridge
Golden, Daniel Lewis

Woodcliff Lake
Clemen, John Douglas

NEW MEXICO

Albuquerque
Beach, Arthur O'Neal
Bova, Vincent Arthur, Jr.,
Caruso, Mark John
Farmer, Terry D(wayne)
Lopez, Floyd William
Lopez, Martin, III,
Mann, Nathan Huguenor

Shane, Richard J.

Deming
Sherman, Frederick Hood

Farmington
Moeller, Floyd Douglas

Hobbs
Stout, Lowell

Las Cruces
Murphy, Michael Terrence

Los Alamos
Herr, Bruce

Roswell
Kraft, Richard Lee

Santa Fe
Bienvenu, John Charles
Brannen, Jeffrey Richard
Casey, Patrick Anthony
Pound, John Bennett

NEW YORK

Albany
Alessi, Robert Joseph
Fanciullo, William Patrick
Laird, Edward DeHart, Jr.,
Lauricella, Peter Alan
Pozner, Louis-Jack

Amherst
Jones, E. Thomas

Bethpage
Burian, Lawrence J.

Binghamton
Chivers, James Leeds
Gates, Gregory Ansel
Kramer, Philip Joseph

Bronxville
Fuller, David Otis, Jr.,

Buffalo
Brown, Lawrence Charles
Feuerstein, Alan Ricky
Fisher, Cheryl Smith
Goldberg, Neil A.
Hayes, J. Michael
Herdzik, Arthur Alan
Jasen, Matthew Joseph
Lazroe, Jeffrey Alan
Magavern, James L.
Manning, Kenneth Alan
Murray, Glenn Edward

Central Islip
Bronstein, Richard M.

Garden City
Balkan, Kenneth J.
DaSilva, Willard H.
Fischoff, Gary Charles
Kroll, Martin N.
Sawyer, James

Glens Falls
Bartlett, Richard James

Great Neck
Breitenbach, Roy W.
Lowenbraun, Solomon Mortimer

Hicksville
Giuffré, John Joseph

Hudson
Davis, Deborah Lynn
Howard, Andrew Baker

Latham
Couch, Mark Woodworth

Long Beach
Solomon, Robert H.

Manlius
Mathewson, George Atterbury

Medina
Mark, Lance Joseph

Melville
Adler, Kenneth

Mineola
Bartlett, Clifford Adams, Jr.,
Bartol, Ernest Thomas
Wagner, Gary Alan

New City
Fenster, Robert David

New Hyde Park
Lee, Brian Edward

New York
Alcott, Mark Howard
Aloe, Paul Hubschman
Altieri, Peter Louis
Appel, Albert M.
Arkin, Stanley S.
Bainton, J(ohn) Joseph
Barasch, Clarence Sylvan
Barist, Jeffrey
Barron, Francis Patrick
Barthold, Walter
Beitel, Bernard
Berman, Tony
Blair, James Newell
Bluestone, Andrew Lavoott
Boddie, Reginald Alonzo
Bodovitz, James Philip
Braun, Jeffrey Louis
Broadwater, Douglas Dwight
Broder, Douglas Fisher
Brodsky, David Michael
Brown, Peter Megargee
Brundige, Robert William, Jr.,
Burrows, Michael Donald
Butterman, Jay Ronald
Calvaruso, Joseph Anthony
Cantor, Melvyn Leon
Carley, John Halliday
Carling, Francis
Castel, P. Kevin
Colfin, Bruce Elliott
Coll, John Peter, Jr.,
Collins, John F.
Conboy, Kenneth
Connuck, Eric S.
Constantine, Heidi Christine
Cuneo, Donald Lane
Dankner, Jay Warren
Davidson, George Allan
Davis, Michael Steven
Derzaw, Richard Lawrence
DiBlasi, Gandolfo Vincent
Donovan, Richard Edward
Dorkey, Charles E., III,
Doyle, Paul Francis
Drebsky, Dennis Jay
Dropkin, Charles Edward
Elsen, Sheldon Howard
Fallek, Andrew Michael
Finkelstein, Ira Allen
Fishbein, Peter Melvin
Fleischman, Keith Martin
Frankel, Sandor
Freyer, Dana Hartman
Gadsden, James
Ganz, Howard Laurence
Garland, Sylvia Dillof
Genel, Noah D.
Getnick, Neil Victor
Goott, Alan F(ranklin)
Gordon, Evan L.
Graham, Philip L., Jr.,
Grassi, Joseph F.
Greenberg, Philip Alan
Greenman, Frederick F., Jr.,
Greilsheimer, James Gans
Gruen, Michael Stephan
Gulino, Frank
Haig, Robert Leighton
Handler, Arthur M.
Harrison, Tomasita L.
Herman, Kenneth Beaumont
Hirshowitz, Melvin Stephen
Holman, Bud George
Hulbert, Richard Woodward
Hynes, Patricia Mary
Jaffe, Mark M.
Juceam, Robert E.
Katsh, Salem Michael
Katz, Jerome Charles
Keany, Sutton
Kempf, Donald G., Jr.,
Kilsch, Gunther H.
Kirschbaum, Myron
Kleinberg, Norman Charles
Kostelanetz, Boris
Kurzweil, Harvey
Laufer, Jacob
LeBlang, Skip Alan
Lesser, Seth Richard
Levander, Andrew Joshua
Levine, Richard L.
Levine, Ronald Jay
Levinson, Paul Howard
Lindenauer, Susan B(adian)
Linker, Arthur S.
Linsenmeyer, John Michael
Lipton, Robert Steven
Logan, Kenneth Richard
London, Martin
Lunding, Christopher Hanna
Lupkin, Stanley Neil
Luskin, Michael
Lyddane, John Lawrence Ashton
Lynton, Harold Stephen
Maulsby, Allen Farish
Mc Inerney, Denis
McGrath, Christopher Thomas
Meister, Robert Allen
Milmed, Paul Kussy
Moore, Thomas A.
Moore, Thomas Ronald (Lord Bridestowe)
Munzer, Stephen Ira
Naftalis, Gary Philip
Nonna, John Michael
Norfolk, William Ray
O'Connell, Margaret Sullivan
Oberman, Michael Stewart
Oechler, Henry John, Jr.,
Orden, Stewart L.
Owen, Robert Dewit
Panken, Peter Michael
Pinczower, Kenneth Ephraim
Puccio, Thomas P.
Raab, Sheldon
Rand, William
Reynolds, Michael Timothy
Rivera, Walter
Rogers, Theodore Otto, Jr.,
Rogoff, Jeffrey Scott
Rolfe, Ronald Stuart
Rosner, Jonathan Levi
Rubin, Herbert
Sahid, Joseph Robert
Salomon, Philippe M.
Schiffer, Larry Philip
Schlain, Barbara Ellen
Seiff, Eric A.
Seligman, Delice
Silverberg, Michael Joel
Silverman, Arthur Charles
Simmons, Peter Lawrence
Sobel, Gerald
Steuer, Richard Marc
Struve, Guy Miller
Suh, Sung-Hee
Tilewick, Robert
Tritter, Daniel F.
Vassallo, John A.
Vitkowsky, Vincent Joseph
Vladeck, Judith Pomarlen
Wallach, Eric Jean
Walpin, Gerald
Warden, John L.
Weinberg, Steven Lewis
Weinschel, Alan Jay
Weiser, Martin Jay
Weiss, Lawrence N.
Wenger, Daniel Eric
Wexelbaum, Michael
Winfield, Richard Neill
Witherwax, Charles Halsey
Witmeyer, John Jacob, III,
Young, Michael Richard
Younger, Stephen P.
Zammit, Joseph Paul
Zaslowsky, David Paul
Zifchak, William C.
Zissu, Michael Jerome
Zoogman, Nicholas Jay

Newburgh
Liberth, Richard Francis

Niagara Falls
Anton, Ronald David
Berrigan, Patrick Joseph

Nyack
Seidler, B(ernard) Alan

Patchogue
Esteve, Edward V.

Perry
Kelly, Michael Joseph

Riverhead
Maggipinto, V. Anthony

Rochester
Gross, Bryon William
Smith, Jules Louis

Rockville Centre
Buchman, Lawrence Jay

Salamanca
Brady, Thomas Carl

Scarsdale
Perko, Kenneth Albert, Jr.,
Sabadie, Francisca Alejandra
Sweeney, John J(oseph)

Smithtown
Spellman, Thomas Joseph, Jr.,

Somers
Keeffe, John Arthur

Staten Island
Howard, Davis Jonathan
Landron, Michel John
Parnese, John S.

Syracuse
Murphy, Timothy Paul
Pinsky, Roy David
Traylor, Robert Arthur
Wiles, Christopher
Young, Douglas Howard

Troy
Finkel, Sanford Norman

Uniondale
Cassidy, David Michael
Eilen, Howard Scott
Good, Douglas Jay

Watertown
Gebo, Stephen Wallace

West Harrison
Johnson, Craig Edward

West Point
Stock, Margaret Deborah

Westbury
Dwyer, Diane Marie

White Plains
Doyle, Dennis T.
Greenspan, Leon Joseph
Greenspan, Michael Evan
Halpern, Philip Morgan
Keane, Thomas J.
Null, William Seth
Ryan, Robert Davis

NORTH CAROLINA

Asheville
Leake, Larry Bruce

Chapel Hill
Crohn, Max Henry, Jr.,

Charlotte
Chesson, Calvin White
McLoughlin, James Patrick, Jr.,
Newitt, John Garwood, Jr.,
Ogburn, Thomas Lynn, III,
Stephens, Robert C.

Durham
Carpenter, Charles Francis

Gastonia
Cooper, Langdon McIlroy

Greensboro
Clark, David McKenzie
Floyd, Jack William
Harris, Terrill Johnson

High Point
Baker, Walter Wray, Jr.,

Mooresville
Homesley, Clifton W.

New Bern
Durr, William Scott

Raleigh
Dixon, Wright Tracy, Jr.,
Ellis, Lester Neal, Jr.,
Glass, Fred Stephen
Hunter, Richard Samford, Jr.,
Kapp, Michael Keith
Kurtz, Howard Arthur
Millberg, John C.
Thomas, Jason Selig

Roxboro
Weinberger, Joseph Charles, Jr.,

Smithfield
Schulz, Bradley Nicholas

Wilmington
Seagle, J. Harold

Winston Salem
Kelly, James Howard, Jr.,
Wells, Dewey Wallace

NORTH DAKOTA

Bismarck
Edin, Charles Thomas
Klemin, Lawrence R.

Dickinson
Greenwood, Dann E.

Fargo
Crothers, Daniel J.
Vogel, Mart Daniel

Grand Forks
Cilz, Douglas Arthur

Mandan
Bair, Bruce B.

OHIO

Akron
Cahoon, Peter Thomas
Lammert, Thomas Edward
Lombardi, Frederick McKean

Cincinnati
Bissinger, Mark Christian
Burke, Timothy Michael
Chesley, Stanley Morris
Cioffi, Michael Lawrence
Cohen, Edward
Faller, Susan Grogan
Frantz, Robert Wesley
Hardy, William Robinson
Holschuh, John David, Jr.,
Lutz, James Gurney
Parker, R. Joseph
Rose, Donald McGregor
Scacchetti, David J.
Shea, Joseph William, III,
Townsend, Robert J.
Trauth, Joseph Louis, Jr.,
Vander Laan, Mark Alan
Whitaker, Glenn Virgil

Cleveland
Bacon, Brett Kermit
Bates, Walter Alan
Boukis, Kenneth
Cohn, Mark Barry
Crist, Paul Grant
Duncan, Ed Eugene
Eklund, Claudia Rieth
Ernst, Christopher Mark
Gardner, Steven Leslie
Gippin, Robert Malcolm
Goins, Frances Floriano
Grossman, Theodore Martin
Havens, Hunter Scott
Hollington, Richard Rings, Jr.,
Jacobs, Leslie William
Kelly, Dennis Michael
McLaughlin, Patrick Michael
Newman, John M., Jr.,
Osborne, Frank R.
Pollock, R. Jeffrey
Rains, M. Neal
Schiller, James Joseph
Solomon, Randall Lee
Stuhan, Richard George
Summers, William Lawrence
Szaller, James Francis
Vergon, Frederick Porter, Jr.,
Wallach, Mark Irwin
Weaver, Robin Geoffrey
Weber, Robert Carl
Whitney, Richard Buckner

Columbus
Adams, John Marshall
Ayers, James Cordon
Binning, J. Boyd
Blackburn, Thomas Irven
Chappelear, Stephen Eric
Chester, John Jonas
Draper, Gerald Linden
Eblin, Robert L.
Gall, John R.
Hardymon, David Wayne
Hockstad, Karen Sue
McDermott, Kevin R.
Mirman, Joel Harvey
Neuman, Todd Howard
Phillips, James Edgar
Plymale, Ronald Elton
Ray, Frank Allen
Robol, Richard Thomas
Ryan, Joseph W., Jr.,
Schaeffer, Matthew Thomas
Swetnam, Daniel Richard
Taylor, Joel Sanford
Tripp, Thomas Neal
Warner, Charles Collins

Dayton
Faruki, Charles Joseph
Krebs, Leo Francis

Delaware
Martin, Stephen David

Dublin
Tenuta, Luigia

Fairborn
Miles, David R.

Findlay
Kentris, George Lawrence

Ironton
Collier, James Bruce

Jackson
Lewis, Richard M.

Kenton
Tudor, John Martin

Lima
Jacobs, Ann Elizabeth

North Olmsted
Dorchak, Thomas J.

Portsmouth
Crowder, Marjorie Briggs

Saint Marys
Huber, William Evan

Sandusky
Bailey, K. Ronald

Toledo
Baker, Richard Southworth
Dalrymple, Thomas Lawrence
Pletz, Thomas Gregory
Thacker, Joseph Phillip

Twinsburg
Doyle, Duane Lynn

Wooster
Kennedy, Charles Allen

Youngstown
Blair, Richard Bryson

Zanesville
Micheli, Frank James

OKLAHOMA

Chandler
Swanson, Robert Lee

Cherokee
Stein, Sam L.

Edmond
Lester, Andrew William

Enid
Jones, Stephen

Norman
Talley, Richard Bates

Oklahoma City
Bailey, Burck
Christiansen, Mark D.
Coats, Andrew Montgomery
Cunningham, Stanley Lloyd
Gibson, Keith Russell
Gordon, Kevin Dell
Kline, David Adam
Lindsey, Lori Dawn
Necco, Alexander David
Nesbitt, Charles Rudolph
Schuster, E. Elaine
Tompkins, Raymond Edgar
Wilson, Julia Ann Yother

Tulsa
Arrington, John Leslie, Jr.,
Clark, Joseph Francis, Jr.,
Dexter, Deirdre O'Neil Elizabeth
Eliot, Theodore Quentin
Haynie, Tony Wayne
Herrold, David Henry
Imel, John Michael
Medina, J. Michael
Miller, James Anthony
Moffett, J. Denny
Scott, Roger Roy

Norfolk
Davis, Terry Hunter, Jr.,
McCaa, James Cureton, III,
Pearson, John Yeardley, Jr.,
Rashkind, Alan Brody
Ryan, John M.

Norton
Jessee, Roy Mark

Portsmouth
Moody, Willard James, Sr.,

Reston
Anderson, Charles Anthony
Bredehoft, Elaine Charlson

Richmond
Bing, Richard McPhail
Booker, Lewis Thomas
Ellis, Andrew Jackson, Jr.,
Hall, Stephen Charles
King, William H., Jr.,
Levit, Jay J(oseph)
Merhige, Robert Reynold, Jr.,
Rucker, Douglas Pendleton, Jr.,
Spahn, Gary Joseph
Thomas, John Charles

Roanoke
Barnhill, David Stan
Densmore, Douglas Warren
Effel, Laura
Hylton, Myles Talbert
McGarry, Richard Lawrence
Mundy, Gardner Marshall

Schley
McVey, Henry Hanna, III,

Spotsylvania
Pugh, Randall Scott

Vienna
Cochran, Stephen Grey

Virginia Beach
Clark, Donald H.
Dumville, S(amuel) Lawrence
Harrell, Charles Lydon, Jr.,
Swope, Richard McAllister

Warrenton
Howard, Blair Duncan

Winchester
Adams, Nate Lavinder, III,

Wise
Rogers, Leonard David

Woodbridge
Roberts, Charles Bren

WASHINGTON

Bainbridge Island
Otorowski, Christopher Lee

Bellevue
Medved, Robert Allen

Bellingham
Raas, Daniel Alan

Centralia
Tiller, Laurel Lee

Everett
Davies, Gregory Lane

Gig Harbor
Thompson, Ronald Edward

Seattle
Boeder, Thomas L.
Boman, Marc Allen
Bucklin, Mark Richard
Budigan, William Clay
Clinton, Richard M.
Ferrer, Rafael Douglas Paul
Freedman, Bart Joseph
Johnson, Bruce Edward Humble
Lemly, Thomas Adger
Longfelder, Lawrence Lee
Losey, Beverley Brown
Lundgren, Gail M.
Manning, J. Richard
Massong, Judy Irene
McCune, Philip Spear
McKay, John
McKinstry, Ronald E.
Paul, Thomas Frank
Radtke, Derek Paul
Robinson-Dorn, Trilby C. E.
Rummage, Stephen Michael
Sandler, Michael David
Smith, Scott A.
Taylor, David F.
Wayne, Robert Jonathan

Spokane
Antonietti, Joan L(ynn)
Eymann, Richard Charles
Leipham, Jay Edward
Stone, Donald Gene

Tacoma
Bergsten, William P.
Hostnik, Charles Rivoire
Krueger, James A.

Yakima
Tenney, Robert Carl

WEST VIRGINIA

Bluefield
Evans, Wayne Lewis
Henderson, Susan Ellen Fortune

Charleston
Berthold, Robert Vernon, Jr.,
Crislip, Stephen Ray
Neely, Richard
Robinson, E. Glenn
Teare, John Richard, Jr.,
Victorson, Michael Bruce
Zak, Robert Joseph

Huntington
Offutt, Denver Clyde, Jr.,

Morgantown
Fusco, Andrew G.

Summersville
Davis, Stephen Allen

Wheeling
Bailey, John P.

WISCONSIN

Deerfield
Pappas, David Christopher

Evansville
Decker, John Robert

Germantown
Ehlinger, Ralph Jerome

Green Bay
Burnett, Ralph George

Madison
Anderson, Michael Steven
Blanchard, Brian Wheatley
Doran, Kenneth John
Peterson, H. Dale
Prange, Roy Leonard, Jr.,
Ragatz, Thomas George
Schmid, John Henry, Jr.,
Schooler, Steven James
Shumaker, Robert E.
Skilton, John Singleton

Milwaukee
Ballman, Patricia Kling
Clark, James Richard
Daily, Frank J(erome)
Donovan, Michael Joseph
Frauen, Kurt Herman
Hase, David John
Nelson, Roy Hugh, Jr.,
Shriner, Thomas L., Jr.,
Terschan, Frank Robert
Van Grunsven, Paul Robert
Williams, Clay Rule

Oshkosh
Kelly, John Martin
Zierdt, Alyson Kathleen

Osseo
Feltes, Charles Victor

Pepin
Seymour, Mary Frances

Racine
Rudebusch, Alice Ann

Rhinelander
Saari, John William, Jr.,

Waukesha
Bohren, Michael Oscar

Wausau
Connell, James Bernard

WYOMING

Cheyenne
Mackey, Terrence Wayne

Riverton
Hursh, John R.

Rock Springs
Honaker, Richard Henderson

Sheridan
Cannon, Kim Decker
Riggs, Dan Britt

TERRITORIES OF THE UNITED STATES

GUAM

Tamuning
Aguigui, Ignacio Cruz

PUERTO RICO

San Juan
Pierluisi, Pedro R.

CANADA

ONTARIO

Toronto
Heintzman, Thomas G.

MEXICO

Coahuila
Hernandez, Juan Ignacio

Mexicali
Vega, Alonso

Mexico City
Zamora, Rodrigo

Monterrey
Rios-Farjat, Margarita

Sonora
Medrano, Roberto M.

AUSTRALIA

Brisbane
Perrett, Ross Graham

BRAZIL

São Paulo
Azevedo, Renato Olimpio Sette de
Chiavassa, Tercio
Oliveira-Ramos, Luiz Gustavo

CHINA

Hong Kong
Rapinet, Crispin William

CZECH REPUBLIC

Prague
Cerny, Jiri
Peterka, Ondrej

ENGLAND

London
Carrow, Robert Duane
Dickey, John W.
Duesenberg, Mark Hugo
Galloway, Diane
Mendelowitz, Michael Sydney

FRANCE

Paris
Dupuis, Delphine Marie
Norris, Pascale Danielle
Powell-Smith, Marc Edgar Raoul

GERMANY

Berlin
Schoene, Friedrich Tobias

Frankfurt
Baeumer, Ulrich J.P.

IRELAND

Dublin
Preston, Caroline Mary

ISRAEL

Ramat-Gan
Aron, Roberto

ITALY

Padova
Grossi, Francis Xavier, Jr.,

JAPAN

Tokyo
Stoupe, Louise

NEW ZEALAND

Wellington
Pol, Ronald Franciscus

NORWAY

Oslo
Keiserud, Erik
Klingenberg, Olav E.

PERU

Lima
Lee, Henry

PORTUGAL

Lisbon
Mónica, António De Carvalho Godinho
Talhão, Luis

SPAIN

Madrid
Fernandez Aguado, Juan Ignacio

SWEDEN

Orebro
Dicksen, Dennis Johansson

VENEZUELA

Caracas
Mezgravis, Andrés A.

ADDRESS UNPUBLISHED

Beldock, Myron
Berger, Marc Joseph
Beukema, John Frederick
Bibik, Jacqueline Avis
Boone, Richard Winston, Sr.,
Braun, Jerome Irwin
Brumbaugh, John Moore
Carmack, Mildred Jean
Collins, Theodore John
Connell, William D.
Coviello, Frank Joseph
Diamond, Paul Steven
Dickstein, Michael Ethan
Dolan, John F.
Dolan, Peter Brown
Dondanville, John Wallace
Eldridge, David P.
Farley, Barbara Suzanne
Fischer, David Jon
Fleischman, Herman Israel
Giovanniello, Joseph, Jr.,
Goddard, Claude Philip, Jr.,
Goldberg, Michael Bradley
Hagelien, Per
Haley, George Brock, Jr.,
Hall, John Hopkins
Hansen, John Alton
Harman, Wallace Patrick
Harvey, Marc S(ean)
Heinrich, Steven Allan
Herman, Richard Bruce
Hess, Chad Brandon
Holmes, Michael Gene
Kapnick, Richard Bradshaw
Killeen, Michael John
Klein, Linda Ann
Lichtenstein, Sarah Carol
Lilly, Thomas Gerald
Lipsman, Richard Marc
Martin, Thomas MacDonald
McCormick, Homer L., Jr.,
McNeil Staudenmaier, Heidi Loretta
Metz, Eric Bennett
Missan, Richard Sherman
Moehle, Carm Robert
Mudd, John O.
Newman, Carol L.
Norman, Albert George, Jr.,
O'Leary, Sean Edward
Pagano, Eugene Salvatore Rooney
Paul, Richard Wright
Quillen, Cecil Dyer, Jr.,
Roethe, James Norton
Schroeder, Edward James
Schultz, Dennis Bernard
Seifert, Stephen Wayne
Shapiro, Edwin Stanley
Siporin, Sheldon
Skinner, Gwynne Lynette
Skolnik, Barnet David
Smith, James A.
Smith, Ronald Ehlbert
Stream, Arnold Crager
Swann, Barbara
Szuch, Clyde Andrew
Terp, Thomas Thomsen
Terrell, G. Irvin
Thornton, J. Pat
van Gestel, Allan
Wagner, Arthur Ward, Jr.,
Walner, Robert Joel
Weisberg, David Charles
Wessel, Peter
White, John Joseph, III,
Wilson, Virgil James, III,
Wong-Diaz, Francisco Raimundo
Wyatt, Robert Lee, IV,
Zelechiwsky, Bohdan John
Zohn, Martin Steven

CIVIL LITIGATION, STATE

UNITED STATES

ALABAMA

Andalusia
Fuller, William Sidney

Anniston
Woodrow, Randall Mark

Birmingham
Kracke, Robert Russell
Newton, Alexander Worthy
Rountree, Asa
Stabler, Lewis Vastine, Jr.,

Demopolis
Dinning, Woodford Wyndham, Jr.,

Florala
Duplechin, D. James

Huntsville
Huckaby, Gary Carlton

Mobile
Holmes, Broox Garrett

Montgomery
Byram, James Asberry, Jr.,
Volz, Charles Harvie, Jr.,

Moulton
Dutton, Mark Anthony

Sheffield
Hamby, Gene Malcolm, Jr.,

ALASKA

Sitka
Graham, David Antony

ARIZONA

Phoenix
Bain, C. Randall
Bakker, Thomas Gordon
Beggs, Harry Mark
Bouma, John Jacob
Coghill, William Thomas, Jr.,
Condo, James Robert
Gomez, David Frederick
Grant, Merwin Darwin
Knoller, Guy David
Leonard, Jeffrey S.
Petitti, Michael Joseph, Jr.,
Ulrich, Paul Graham
Wall, Donald Arthur

Prescott
Goodman, Mark N.

Scottsdale
Smith, David Burnell

Tempe
Palmer, Janice Maude

Tucson
Cope, Thom K.
Kimble, William Earl
Kitchen, Charles William
Maltz, Gerald Stuart
Mc Donald, John Richard

Yuma
Hossler, David Joseph

ARKANSAS

Little Rock
Drummond, Winslow
Griffin, William Mell, III,
Jennings, Alston

CALIFORNIA

Auburn
Lyon, Bruce Arnold

Bakersfield
Kind, Kenneth Wayne

Berkeley
Sparks, John Edward

Beverly Hills
Jaffe, F. Filmore
Juno, Cynthia

Burbank
Ajalat, Sol Peter

Burlingame
Cotchett, Joseph Winters

Campbell
Castello, Raymond Vincent

Costa Mesa
Frieden, Clifford E.
Guilford, Andrew John

Emeryville
Howe, Drayton Ford, Jr.,

Encinitas
Williams, Michael Edward

Fresno
Nunes, Frank M.

Glendale
Kazanjian, Phillip Carl
Martinetti, Ronald Anthony

Granada Hills
Sindon, Geoffrey Stuart

Huntington Beach
Garrels, Sherry Ann

Irvine
Specter, Richard Bruce

Laguna Hills
Reinglass, Michelle Annette

Laguna Niguel
McEvers, Duff Steven

Long Beach
Haile, Lawrence Barclay
Ultimo, Paul Joseph

Los Angeles
Bakaly, Charles George, Jr.,
Baumann, Richard Gordon
Bender, Charles William
Bernhard, Herbert Ashley
Bodkin, Henry Grattan, Jr.,
Bressan, Paul Louis
Bridges, B. Ried
Chiate, Kenneth Reed
Daniels, John Peter
Fairbank, Robert Harold
Galton, Stephen Harold
Grush, Julius Sidney
Handzlik, Jan Lawrence
Heller, Philip
Hight, B. Boyd
Imre, Christina Joanne
Kanner, Gideon
Kirwan, R. DeWitt
Long, Gregory Alan
Lurvey, Ira Harold
Lysle, Richard Scott
Neufeld, Timothy Lee
Newman, Michael Rodney
Nia, Firoozeh
Robison, William Robert
Snyder, Arthur Kress
Stoner, William Edward
Strong, George Gordon, Jr.,
Weatherup, Roy Garfield
Woods, Daniel James
Wright, Kenneth Brooks
Zelon, Laurie Dee

Martinez
Williams, Charles Judson

Menlo Park
Dyer, Charles Arnold
Edwards, John Wesley, II,

Napa
Snow, Tower Charles, Jr.,

Newport Beach
Cordova, Ron
Millar, Richard William, Jr.,
Rudolph, George Cooper

Oakland
Bjork, Robert David, Jr.,

Pacific Palisades
Dickson, Robert Lee

Palo Alto
Baron, Frederick David
Steer, Reginald David
Tiffany, Joseph Raymond, II,

Pasadena
Brenner, Anita Susan
Calvert, Melanie A.
Myers, R(alph) Chandler
Telleria, Anthony F.

Redwood City
Coddington, Clinton Hays

Riverside
Whitaker, Leslie Kent

Sacramento
Brookman, Anthony Raymond
Goode, Barry Paul
McGrath, William Arthur

Salinas
Bolles, Donald Scott

San Anselmo
Truett, Harold Joseph, III, (Tim Truett)

San Diego
Christensen, Charles Brophy
Klinedinst, John David
McDermott, Thomas John, Jr.,
Roseman, Charles Sanford
Sceper, Duane Harold
Weaver, Michael James

San Francisco
Barbagelata, Robert Dominic
Borowsky, Philip
Brown, Donald Wesley
Bushnell, Roderick Paul
Coombe, George William, Jr.,
Dell, Robert Michael
Friese, Robert Charles
Gowdy, Franklin Brockway
Heilbron, David M(ichael)
Ladar, Jerrold Morton
Martel, John Sheldon
Matthews, Philip Richard
Richards, Norman Blanchard
Rosch, John Thomas
Rosen, Sanford Jay
Traynor, John Michael
Venning, Robert Stanley
Walcher, Alan Ernest
Weir, William John Arnold
Young, Douglas Rea

San Jose
Hannon, Timothy Patrick
Morgan, Robert Hall
Stutzman, Thomas Chase, Sr.,

San Rafael
Chilvers, Robert Merritt

San Ramon
Welch, Thomas Andrew

Santa Ana
Ingalsbe, William James

Santa Barbara
Bauer, Marvin Agather
Herman, James Edward

Sherman Oaks
Joyce, Stephen Michael

Stockton
Parish, William Henry

Tustin
Madory, Richard Eugene

Universal City
Golper, John Bruce

Ventura
Gartner, Harold Henry, III,
Kump, Kary Ronald

Visalia
Crowe, Daniel Walston

Walnut Creek
Medak, Walter Hans
Pinkerton, Albert Duane, II,
Skaggs, Sanford Merle

West Covina
Ebiner, Robert Maurice

Westlake Village
Hoefflin, Richard Michael
Sullivan, Mark Francis

COLORADO

Boulder
Purvis, John Anderson

Denver
Babiniec, Dennis Henry
Bain, James William
Campbell, Leonard M.
Ceriani, Gary James
Cohen, Jeffrey
Conover, Frederic King
Cox, William Vaughan
Daily, Richard W.
Donnelly, Frederick James
Green, Philip Burton
Hoffman, Daniel Steven
Kahn, Edwin Sam
Miller, Gale Timothy
Quiat, Marshall
Roth, Robert Charles
Samuels, Donald L.
Starrs, Elizabeth Anne
Thomasch, Roger Paul
Wedgle, Richard Jay
Williams, Michael Anthony

Fort Collins
Vick, Joseph James, III,

Frisco
Helmer, David Alan

Golden
Carney, Deborah Leah Turner

Grand Junction
Erkenbrack, Stephen Kenneth

CONNECTICUT

Bristol
Hayes, Margaret Mary

Fairfield
Osis, Daiga Guntra

Hartford
Pepe, Louis Robert
Sussman, Mark Richard

Madison
Clendenen, William Herbert, Jr.,

Middletown
Adams, Richard Glen

Milford
Sagarin, J. Daniel

New Haven
Geisler, Thomas Milton, Jr.,

Norwich
Masters, Barbara J.

Roxbury
Friedman, John Maxwell, Jr.,

Stamford
Cacace, Michael Joseph
Livolsi, Frank William, Jr.,
Shanman, James Alan

Trumbull
Brennan, Daniel Edward, Jr.,
Williams, Ronald Doherty

West Hartford
Elliot, Ralph Gregory

Westport
Johnson, Allan Richard

Willimantic
Schiller, Howard Barry

DELAWARE

Dover
Steele, Myron Thomas

Newark
Welsh, Paul Patrick

Wilmington
Carpenter, Edmund Nelson, II,
Crompton, Charles Sentman, Jr.,
Johnston, William David
Kirkpatrick, Andrew Booth, Jr.,
Rothschild, Steven James

DISTRICT OF COLUMBIA

Washington
Bellinger, Edgar Thomson
Bucklin, Donald Thomas
Cooter, Dale A.
Fox, Hamilton Phillips, III,
Hassett, Joseph Mark
Kuder, Armin Ulrich
Medaglia, Mary-Elizabeth
Murphy, James Paul
Nace, Barry John
Policy, Vincent Mark
Sandman, James Joseph
Tompert, James Emil
Tompkins, Joseph Buford, Jr.,
Work, Charles Robert
Yannucci, Thomas David

FLORIDA

Altamonte Springs
Heindl, Phares Matthews
Hoogland, Robert Frederics

Boca Raton
David, Ronald Albert
Golis, Paul Robert

Coconut Grove
McAmis, Edwin Earl

Coral Gables
Kearns, John W.
Weissenborn, Sheridan Kendall

Fort Lauderdale
Bayon, Antonio
Bunnell, George Eli
Bustamante, Nestor
Hirsch, Jeffrey Allan
Zimmerman, Elliot Michael

Fort Pierce
Sneed, Richard Durwood, Jr.,

Hollywood
Phillips, Gary Stephen

Jacksonville
Bradford, Dana Gibson, II,
Cowles, Robert Lawrence
Gabel, George DeSaussure, Jr.,
O'Neal, Michael Scott, Sr.,
Pillans, Charles Palmer, III,
Wirtz, Gregg Lee

Lake Worth
Rose, Norman

Lakeland
Martin, Michael David

Longwood
Cordes, Alexander Charles

Miami
Berman, Bruce Judson
Burnett, Henry
Critchlow, Richard H.
Eaton, Joel Douglas
Evans, Thomas William
Ferrell, Milton Morgan, Jr.,
Glickman, Fred Elliott
Glinn, Franklyn Barry
Greer, Alan Graham
Hall, Miles Lewis, Jr.,
Miller, Raymond Vincent, Jr.,
Nachwalter, Michael
Rogers, Harvey Delano
Scott, Thomas Emerson, Jr.,
Starr, Ivar Miles
Wald, Gerald Barry
Wiseheart, Malcolm Boyd, Jr.,
Wright, Robert Thomas, Jr.,

Naples
Cimino, Richard Dennis

Orlando
deBeaubien, Hugo H.
Dempsey, Bernard Hayden, Jr.,
Eagan, William Leon
Losey, Ralph Colby
Motes, Carl Dalton
Reinhart, Richard Paul
Weiss, Christopher John
Wilson, William Berry

Pensacola
Gaines, Robert Pendleton
Windham, John Franklin

Plantation
Sperry, Martin Jay

Saint Petersburg
Glass, Roy Leonard

Sarasota
Rossi, William Matthew

Sebring
Trombley, Michael Jerome

South Miami
Keedy, Christian David

Tallahassee
Anderson, Bruce Paige
Aurell, John Karl
Ervin, Robert Marvin
Gary, Thomas
Gievers, Karen A.
Simpson, Larry Dean

Tampa
Barkin, Marvin E.
Boos, Robert Walter, II,
Butler, Paul Bascomb, Jr.,
DeVaney, Donna Brookes
Gonzalez, Joe Manuel
Murphy, James Burton, Jr.,
Smith, William Reece, Jr.,
Somers, Clifford Louis
Thomas, Wayne Lee

Vero Beach
Stewart, John Mitchell

West Palm Beach
Chopin, Susan Gardiner
Djokic, Walter Henry
Farina, John
Lane, Matthew Jay
Montgomery, Robert Morel, Jr.,
Norton, William Alan
Orlovsky, Donald Albert

Winter Park
Ackert, T(errence) W(illiam)
Godbold, Gene Hamilton
Helms, Roger D.

GEORGIA

Alpharetta
Boynton, Frederick George

Atlanta
Blank, A(ndrew) Russell
Doyle, Michael Anthony
Duffey, William Simon, Jr.,
Farnham, Clayton Henson
Fleming, Julian Denver, Jr.,
Frankel, Craig M.
Jones, Frank Cater
Marshall, John Treutlen
Paquin, Jeffrey Dean
Smith, Grant Butler
Wellon, Robert G.

Augusta
Miller, Alfred Montague

Decatur
Skinner, William French Cochran, Jr.,

Macon
Elliott, James Sewell

Marietta
Dalziel, Charles Meredith, Jr.,
Ingram, George Conley

Newnan
Franklin, Bruce Walter

Savannah
Ladson, M. Brice

Snellville
Giallanza, Charles Philip

Statesboro
Franklin, James Burke
Stone, Ralph Kenny

HAWAII

Honolulu
Crosier, Douglas A.
Devens, Paul
Freed, Michael Leonard
Iwai, Wilfred Kiyoshi
Kemper, Edward Crawford
Kobayashi, Bert Takaaki, Jr.,
Louie, David Mark
Morse, Jack Craig
Potts, Dennis Walker
Taylor, Carroll Stribling

IDAHO

Boise
Clark, Merlyn Wesley
Risch, James E.
Wetherell, Michael E.

Lewiston
Tait, John Reid

ILLINOIS

Aurora
Dreyer, John Edward

Champaign
Rawles, Edward Hugh

Chicago
Adelman, Stanley Joseph
Allen, Thomas Draper
Anderson, Craig Edgar
Baugher, Peter V.
Bellah, Kenneth David
Biebel, Paul Philip, Jr.,
Boies, Wilber H.
Bresnahan, Arthur Stephen
Bridgman, Thomas Francis
Brown, Donald James, Jr.,
Burke, John Michael
Burke, Thomas Joseph, Jr.,
Chemers, Robert Marc
Cherney, James Alan
Cicero, Frank, Jr.,
Coughlin, Terrance J.
De Jong, David John
Deitrick, William Edgar
Ditkowsky, Kenneth K.
Donlevy, John Dearden
Eaton, J(ames) Timothy
Feagley, Michael Rowe
Fina, Paul Joseph
Franch, Richard Thomas
Futterman, Ronald L.
Gibbons, William John
Halloran, Michael John
Hammesfahr, Robert Winter
Hardgrove, James Alan
Harper, Steven James
Harrington, James Timothy
Harris, Donald Ray
Herald, J. Patrick
Hoover, Russell James
Hunter, James Galbraith, Jr.,
Johnson, Garrett Bruce
Joseph, Robert Thomas
Kamin, Chester Thomas
Katz, Harold Ambrose
Kroll, Barry Lewis
Kroot, Jason M.
Leyhane, Francis John, III,
Lichtenstein, Nathan H.
Marick, Michael Miron
Meyer, John Albert
Montgomery, Julie-April
Nash, Gordon Bernard, Jr.,
Nowacki, James Nelson
Nussbaum, Bernard J.
Palmer, Robert Towne
Parson, Jason A.
Prior, Gary L.
Prochnow, Douglas Lee
Redmond, Richard Anthony
Richter, Tobin Marais
Rundio, Louis Michael, Jr.,
Schoumacher, Bruce Herbert
Sfikas, Peter Michael
Stavins, Richard Lee
Theis, William Harold
Van Demark, Ruth Elaine
Wildman, Max Edward

Elgin
Carbary, Jonathan Leigh

Elmhurst
Blain, Robert Krieger

Elmwood Park
Spina, Anthony Ferdinand

Evanston
Schulte, Bruce John
Witwer, Samuel Weiler, Jr.,

Galesburg
Mustain, Douglas Dee

Lake Forest
Emerson, William Harry

Libertyville
DeSanto, James John

Lincolnwood
Ghezzi, Sheryl Rae
Zaremski, Miles Jay

Mattoon
Horsley, Jack Everett

Mount Vernon
Harvey, Morris Lane

Ottawa
White, Robert Ellsworth

Palatine
Victor, Michael Gary

Peoria
Winget, Walter Winfield

Rockford
Mateer, Don M.

Saint Charles
Weir, William H.

Schaumburg
Shapiro, Edwin Henry

Shorewood
Copeland, Charlene Carole

Skokie
Plotnick, Paul William

Vernon Hills
Richards, Alan Edward

Wheaton
Cunningham, William Francis
Didzerekis, Paul Patrick

Winnetka
Krucks, William Norman

INDIANA

Beech Grove
Brown, Richard Lawrence

Columbus
Harrison, Patrick Woods

Elkhart
Wicks, Charles Carter

Evansville
Berger, Charles Lee
Bodkin, Robert Thomas
Clouse, John Daniel

Greenwood
Van Valer, Joe Ned

Hammond
Ruman, Saul I.

Indianapolis
Bennett, Bryce Hugh, Jr.,
Elberger, Ronald Edward
Fisher, James R.
Koch, Edna Mae
Lisher, John Leonard
Schreckengast, William Owen
Steger, Evan Evans, III,
Taylor, Brent Douglas
Wellnitz, Craig Otto
Yeager, Joseph Heizer, Jr.,

Kokomo
Russell, Richard Lloyd

Lafayette
Bodle, John Frederick
Layden, Charles Max

Lebanon
Donaldson, John Weber

Seymour
Pardieck, Roger Lee

Shelbyville
McNeely, James Lee

Terre Haute
Frey, Eric Alan

IOWA

Cedar Rapids
Read, Thomas Buchanan

Des Moines
Doyle, Richard Henry, IV,
Duckworth, Marvin E.
Foxhoven, Jerry Ray
Frederici, C. Carleton
Koehn, William James

Iowa City
Spies, Leon Fred

Keokuk
Hoffman, James Paul

Sioux City
Mayne, Wiley Edward

KANSAS

Emporia
Helbert, Michael Clinton

Garden City
Pierce, Ricklin Ray

Overland Park
Keplinger, Bruce (Donald Keplinger)
Klamann, John Michael

Pittsburg
Short, Timothy Allen

Shawnee Mission
Helder, Jan Pleasant, Jr.,
Sparks, Billy Schley

Topeka
Hamilton, John Richard
Schroer, Gene Eldon

Wichita
Hund, Edward Joseph

KENTUCKY

Bowling Green
Rudloff, William Joseph

Covington
Wolnitzek, Stephen Dale

Hazard
Roark, Jimmy Lee

Lexington
Fryman, Virgil Thomas, Jr.,

Louisville
Chauvin, Leonard Stanley, Jr.,
Dolt, Frederick Corrance
Karageorge, Thomas George

LOUISIANA

Baton Rouge
Dugas, David Roy

Covington
Miltenberger, Henry James, Jr.,

Franklin
McClelland, James Ray

Kenner
Todaro, Laura Jean

Lafayette
Davidson, James Joseph, III,

Lake Charles
Parkerson, Hardy Martell

Metairie
Dean, Bruce Campbell

New Orleans
Gertler, Meyer H.
Herman, Russ Michel
Johnson, Patrick, Jr.,
Kupperman, Stephen Henry
Lowe, Robert Charles

Slidell
Shamis, Edward Anthony, Jr.,

MAINE

Camden
Sanford, John Joseph

Lewiston
Burke, Edmund James, III,

Portland
Lancaster, Ralph Ivan, Jr.,
Marjerison, Thomas Sydney
Rundlett, Ellsworth Turner, III,

MARYLAND

Annapolis
Perkins, Roger Allan

Baltimore
Ayres, Jeffrey Peabody
Carbine, James Edmond
Crowe, Thomas Leonard
Gilbert, Blaine Louis
Golomb, George Edwin
Grady, Joseph Harold
Gray, Oscar Shalom
Hansen, Christopher Agnew
Johnson, Harry Sterling
Kramer, Paul R.
Kuryk, David Neal
Pappas, George Frank
Radding, Andrew
Schochor, Jonathan
Summers, Thomas Carey
White, Pamela Janice

Chevy Chase
Weiss, Harlan Lee

Easton
Foster, Philip Carey

Parkville
Hill, Milton King, Jr.,

Rockville
Dugan, John R.
Thompson, James Lee

Salisbury
Clarke, Wm. A. Lee, III,

Upper Marlboro
Vaughan, James Joseph Michael
Wallace, Sean Daniel

MASSACHUSETTS

Ashfield
Pepyne, Edward Walter

Boston
Arrowood, Lisa Gayle
Carpenter, Robert Brent
Curley, Robert Ambrose, Jr.,
Dillon, James Joseph
Felter, John Kenneth
Fox, Francis Haney
Gelb, Richard Mark
Howard, Gregory Charles
Lee, David Harold
Macauley, William Francis
Mone, Michael Edward
Moriarty, George Marshall
Packenham, Richard Daniel
Trimmier, Roscoe, Jr.,

Cambridge
Crawford, Linda Sibery

New Bedford
Murray, Robert Fox

Newton
Messing, Arnold Philip
Monahan, Marie Terry

Northampton
Miles, Harry Lehman

Salem
Wasserman, Stephen Alan

Wellesley
Goglia, Charles A., Jr.,

MICHIGAN

Ann Arbor
Britton, Clarold Lawrence
O'Brien, Darlene Anne

Bay City
Greve, Guy Robert

Bloomfield Hills
Googasian, George Ara
Pappas, Edward Harvey

Detroit
Andreoff, Christopher Andon
Brady, Edmund Matthew, Jr.,
Cothorn, John Arthur
Jacobs, John Patrick
Leuchtman, Stephen Nathan
Longhofer, Ronald Stephen
Mengel, Christopher Emile
Saxton, William Marvin

Flint
Hart, Clifford Harvey

Holland
Bidol, James Alexander

Kalamazoo
Geary, James H.
Lubben, Craig Henry

Lansing
Coey, David Conrad
Rasmusson, Thomas Elmo
Stackable, Frederick Lawrence

Midland
Battle, Leonard Carroll

New Buffalo
Stevens, William J.

Pontiac
Pierson, William George

Rapid City
Ring, Ronald Herman

Romeo
Clark, Mark Lee

Southfield
Fieger, Geoffrey Nels
Thurswell, Gerald Elliott
Turner, Lee Irwin

Troy
Alber, Phillip George
Kruse, John Alphonse
May, Alan Alfred
Webster, Robert Byron

MINNESOTA

Duluth
Thibodeau, Thomas Raymond

Golden Valley
Hagglund, Clarance Edward

Mankato
Gage, Fred Kelton

Minneapolis
Ciresi, Michael Vincent
Finzen, Bruce Arthur
Gordon, John Bennett
Hanson, Bruce Eugene
Hanson, Kent Bryan
Hart, Buster Clarence
Jarpe, Geoffrey Pellas
Jepsen, William E.
Rockwell, Winthrop Adams
Safley, James Robert
Tanick, Marshall Howard

Saint Cloud
Provinzino, John C.

Saint Paul
Allison, John Robert
Degnan, John Michael
Gehan, Mark William
Trojack, John Edward

MISSISSIPPI

Jackson
Clark, David Wright
Currie, Edward Jones, Jr.,
Hewes, George Poindexter, III,
Howell, Joel Walter, III,
King, Robert Wilson
Mitchell, Meade Westmoreland

New Albany
Sumners, Lester Furr

MISSOURI

Clayton
Schwartz, Theodore Frank

Columbia
Schwabe, John Bennett, II,

Higginsville
Ver Dught, ElGene Clark

Independence
Minton, Kent W.

Kansas City
Beckett, Theodore Charles
Clarke, Milton Charles
Cowden, John William
Johnson, Mark Eugene
Kilroy, John Muir
Lolli, Don R(ay)
Price, James Tucker
Redfearn, Paul L., III,
Spalty, Edward Robert
Wirken, James Charles
Wolf, Jerome Thomas

Keytesville
Wheeler, James Julian

Lees Summit
Walsh, Thomas Joseph

Saint Ann
Johnson, Harold Gene

Saint Charles
Fleddermann, Stephen Roy

Saint Louis
Brown, Paul Sherman
Collins, James Slade, II,
Conran, Joseph Palmer
DeWoskin, Alan Ellis
Douaihy, Toni Patricia
Guerri, William Grant
Gunn, Michael Peter
Hullverson, James Everett, Jr.,
Noel, Edwin Lawrence
Rice, Canice Timothy, Jr.,
Sestric, Anthony James
Sneeringer, Stephen Geddes
Sugg, Reed Waller
Tierney, Betty Thorne
Walsh, Thomas Charles

Springfield
McDonald, William Henry

MONTANA

Kalispell
Lerner, Alan Jay

Lolo
Hansell, Ronald Stephen

Missoula
Sullivan, Robert John
Willey, Charles Wayne

NEBRASKA

Lincoln
Colleran, Kevin

Omaha
Lee, Dennis Patrick
O'Connor, Robert Edward, Jr.,

NEVADA

Henderson
Eskin, Jeffrey Laurence

Las Vegas
Reilly, Patrick John

Reno
Pagni, Albert Frank

NEW HAMPSHIRE

Concord
Johnson, Robert Veiling, II,

Exeter
Engel, David Chapin

Hanover
Lundquist, Weyman Ivan

Portsmouth
Shaines, Robert Arthur
Tober, Stephen Lloyd

NEW JERSEY

Asbury Park
Darnell, Alan Mark

Cape May Court House
Fineberg, Robert Alan

Chatham
Jacobs, Andrew Robert

Cherry Hill
Garrigle, William Aloysius
Kole, Janet Stephanie
Korin, Joel Benjamin

Clark
Farina, Mario G.

Clifton
Goldberger, Alan Steven
Palma, Nicholas James

Cranford
De Luca, Thomas George
Gurrieri, Mario Charles
McCreedy, Edwin James

Englewood Cliffs
Masi, John Roger

Hackensack
Greenberg, Steven Morey
Sosland, Karl Z.

Hackettstown
Mulligan, Elinor Patterson

Haddonfield
Andres, Kenneth G., Jr.,

Hoboken
Greco, Joseph Dominic, Jr.,

Iselin
Rowe, Paul Andrew

Jersey City
D'Alessandro, Daniel Anthony

Kearny
Brady, Lawrence Peter

Kendall Park
Fisch, Joseph

Kenilworth
Hoffman, John Fletcher

Lawrenceville
Blumstein, Jeffrey Phillip

Little Silver
Robertson, Lewis Harold

Millburn
Madden, Edward George, Jr.,

Morristown
Bartkus, Robert Edward
Humick, Thomas Charles Campbell
Rosenthal, Meyer L(ouis)

Newark
Cummis, Clive Sanford
Haring, Eugene Miller
McGuire, William B(enedict)
Rak, Lorraine Karen
Robertson, William Withers

Newton
Morgenstern, Robert Terence

Parsippany
Gallagher, Jerome Francis, Jr.,
Kallmann, Stanley Walter

Princeton
Karpoff, Michael Steven

Randolph
Scheneck, Carol Ann

Red Bank
Klatsky, Fred M.

Roseland
McMahon, Edward Richard
Smith, Dennis Jay

Saddle Brook
Knopf, Barry Abraham
Pearlman, Peter Steven

Ship Bottom
Shackleton, Richard James

Short Hills
Marshall, John Patrick

Somerville
Sponzilli, Edward George

Trenton
Campbell, Bernard Alexander, Jr.,
Doherty, Robert Christopher

Warren
Kraus, Steven Gary

West Orange
Gordon, Michael

Woodbridge
Estis, Dennis Arnold

Woodbury
Adler, Lewis Gerard

Woodcliff Lake
Phillips, John C.

NEW MEXICO

Alamogordo
Bloom, Norman Douglas, Jr.,

Albuquerque
Bardacke, Paul Gregory

Ruidoso
Mitchell, Gary Colas

Santa Fe
Schwarz, Michael
Zorie, Stephanie Marie

NEW YORK

Albany
Linnan, James Daniel

Binghamton
Chivers, James Leeds
Gouldin, David Millen

Buffalo
Brown, Jerrold Stanley
De Marie, Anthony Joseph
Elibol, David Hakan
Glanville, Robert Edward
Herdzik, Arthur Alan
Mattar, Lawrence Joseph
Stachowski, Michael Joseph

Canaan
Pennell, William Brooke

Carmel
Grossman, Victor G.

Central Valley
Levinson, David Lawrence

Chestnut Ridge
Burns, Richard Owen

Commack
Steindler, Walter G.

Dansville
Vogel, John Walter

Glens Falls
Meyer, Martin Arthur

Gouverneur
Leader, Robert John

Great Neck
Salzman, Stanley P.

Hauppauge
Clayton, David William

Ithaca
Patte, George David, Jr.,

Jericho
Corso, Frank Mitchell

Larchmont
Davis, Wendell, Jr.,
Gaffney, Mark William

Long Island City
Forchelli, Charles Nicholas

Melville
Cahn, Richard Caleb

Mineola
Fowler, David Thomas
Klein, Arnold Spencer
Monaghan, Peter Gerard
Raab, Ira Jerry
Sandback, William Arthur

Mohegan Lake
Stokes, Ron

Mount Kisco
Curran, Maurice Francis

New York
Amsterdam, Mark Lemle
Avery, Patricia I.
Barenholtz, Celia Goldwag
Benedict, James Nelson
Bezanson, Thomas Edward
Braid, Frederick Donald
Brown, Paul M.
Brown, Peter Megargee
Buchwald, Don David
Burns, John MacDougal, III,
Burrows, Michael Donald
Cantor, Melvyn Leon
Cashman, Gideon
Castel, P. Kevin
Cohen, Robert Stephan
Cole, Charles Dewey, Jr.,
Coll, John Peter, Jr.,
Dallas, William Moffit, Jr.,
Damashek, Philip Michael
Dopf, Glenn William
Doyle, Paul Francis
Easton, Reed W.
Edelson, Gilbert Seymour
Eiseman, Neal Martin
Fagen, Leslie Gordon
Feder, Saul E.
Fiske, Robert Bishop, Jr.,
Fletcher, Anthony L.
Forstadt, Joseph Lawrence
Frankel, Sandor
Gitter, Max
Goldstein, Kenneth B.
Golomb, David Bela
Greenawalt, William Sloan
Greene, Bernard Harold
Gurfein, Richard Alan
Habian, Bruce George
Haig, Robert Leighton
Hall, John Herbert
Halperin, Kyle Mallary
Handler, Arthur M.
Harbison, James Wesley, Jr.,
Harris, Joel B(ruce)
Hartzell, Andrew Cornelius, Jr.,
Heisler, Stanley Dean
Hirsch, Jerome S.
Hirshowitz, Melvin Stephen
Hoffman, Mathew
Hollyer, A(rthur) Rene
Hritz, George F.
Hughes, Kevin Peter
Hyde, David Rowley
Iannuzzi, John Nicholas
Isquith, Fred Taylor
Jacob, Edwin J.
Jacobs, Randall Scott David
Joseph, Gregory Paul
Katz, Jerome Charles
Kaufman, Stephen Edward
Kaye, Stephen Rackow
Kelmachter, Leslie Debra
Kinnally, William Lee, Jr.,
Kinzler, Thomas Benjamin
Klingsberg, David
Koegel, William Fisher
Kuh, Richard Henry
Kurland, Paul Carl
Kushel, Glenn Elliot
Lack, Robert Joel
Langer, Bruce Alden
Lans, Deborah Eisner
Leaf, Martin Norman
Lesch, Michael Oscar
Lesman, Michael Steven
Levine, Melvin Charles
Lipton, Robert Steven
Loscalzo, Anthony Joseph
Lupert, Leslie Allan
Mandelker, Lawrence Arthur
Mantel, Allan David
Marion, Roger K.
McGrath, Christopher Thomas
Moloney, Thomas Joseph
Muccia, Joseph William
Mullaney, Thomas Joseph
Muskin, Victor Philip
Neff, Michael Alan
O'Dea, Dennis Michael
O'Donnell, John Logan
O'Sullivan, Thomas J.
Oliveri, Paul Francis
Phillips, Anthony Francis
Quinn, Yvonne Susan
Rabin, Jack
Rand, Harry Israel
Raylesberg, Alan Ira
Reich, Larry Sam
Rifkind, Robert S(inger)
Rikon, Michael
Rivera, Walter
Rosenberg, Gerald Alan
Rosenfeld, Steven B.
Rosner, Jonathan Levi
Rothman, Bernard
Rothman, Dennis Michael
Salomon, Philippe M.
Saunders, Paul Christopher
Schwab, Harold Lee
Silverberg, Michael Joel
Silverman, Leon
Silverman, Moses
Sladkus, Harvey Ira
Smiley, Guy Ian
Smith, Robert Everett
Smith, Robert Sherlock
Smoak, Evan L.
Soyster, Margaret Blair
Spivak, Leonard A.
Sternman, Joel W.
Terry, James Joseph, Jr.,
Weinberger, Harold Paul
Weiner, Stephen Arthur
Weinstock, Leonard
Wilensky, Saul
Wilkinson, John Hart
Witkin, Eric Douglas
Wollan, Eugene
Yeager, Dennis Randall
Zimmett, Mark Paul

Newburgh
Milligram, Steven Irwin

Pittsford
Braunsdorf, Paul Raymond
Hartman, James Matthew

Poughkeepsie
Ostertag, Robert Louis
Shatz, Phillip
Sproat, Christine A.

Rochester
Geiger, Alexander
Law, Michael R.
Payment, Kenneth Arnold
Servis, William George

Saratoga Springs
Harper, David Alexander

Syracuse
Goldberg, Harold Philip
Zimmerman, Aaron Mark

Warsaw
Cook, Charlotte Smallwood

Waterford
Novotny, F. Douglas

White Plains
Bender, Joel Charles
Doyle, Dennis T.
Halpern, Philip Morgan
Jacobson, Sandra W.
Kalish, Daniel A.
Nesci, Vincent Peter
Weiss, Terri Lynn

Yonkers
Connors, James Patrick

NORTH CAROLINA

Asheville
Davis, Roy Walton, Jr.,
Frue, William Calhoun
Sharpe, Keith Yount

Beaufort
Tilghman, Carl Lewis

Cary
Cromer, Charles Lemuel
Montgomery, Charles Harvey

Charlotte
Bragg, Ellis Meredith, Jr.,
Cannon, Thomas Roberts
Eve, Robert Michael, Jr.,
Raper, William Cranford

Dunn
Pope, Patrick Harris

Greenville
Romary, Peter John Michael

Newton
Cutchin, John Franks

Raleigh
Dorsett, James K., III,
Maupin, Armistead Jones
Parker, John Hill

Tabor City
Jorgensen, Ralph Gubler

Winston Salem
Barnhill, Henry Grady, Jr.,
Gitter, Allan Reinhold
Stockton, Ralph Madison, Jr.,

OHIO

Akron
Ruport, Scott Hendricks
Tipping, Harry A.

Cincinnati
Davis, Robert Lawrence
DeLong, Deborah
Dornette, W(illiam) Stuart
Manley, Robert Edward
Shea, Joseph William, III,
Zavatsky, Michael Joseph

Cleveland
Ashmus, Keith Allen
Birne, Kenneth Andrew
Brown, Seymour R.
Crist, Paul Grant
Dunlap, Jeffrey Scott
Gold, Gerald Seymour
Karp, Marvin Louis
Kelly, Dennis Michael
Kilbane, Thomas Stanton
Krembs, Peter Joseph
LaFond, Thomas Joseph
Mc Cartan, Patrick Francis
Moore, Kenneth Cameron
Pollock, R. Jeffrey
Spero, Keith Erwin
Stewart, Lawrence Edward
Wallach, Mark Irwin
Weber, Robert Carl

Columbus
Belton, John Thomas
Campbell, Joel Roderick
Cline, Richard Allen
Drexel, Ray Phillips
Ferguson, Gerald Paul
Hollenbaugh, H(enry) Ritchey
Johnson, Mark Alan
Long, Thomas Leslie
O'Shaughnessy, Christopher T.
Schneider, Karl Herbert
Selcer, David Mark
Tait, Robert E.
Todd, William Michael

Dayton
Jenks, Thomas Edward
Roberts, Brian Michael
Rogers, Richard Hunter
Saul, Irving Isaac
Schneble, Alfred William, III,

Dublin
Coco, Mark Steven

Fairfield
Grove, Jack Frederick

Findlay
Kostyo, John Francis

Franklin
Ruppert, Rupert Earl

Ironton
Allen, Craig Adams

Logan
Kernen, Will

Maumee
Tuschman, James Marshall

Painesville
Dean, J. Thomas

Ravenna
Giulitto, Paula Christine

Seaman
Young, Vernon Lewis

Toledo
Baker, Richard Southworth
Jackson, Reginald Sherman, Jr.,

Twinsburg
Doyle, Duane Lynn

Warren
Kafantaris, George Nicholas

Wooster
Kennedy, Charles Allen

OKLAHOMA

Antlers
Stamper, Joe Allen

Broken Arrow
Frieze, H(arold) Delbert

Claremore
Gordon, Jack Elliott, Jr.,

Muskogee
Williams, Betty Outhier

Oklahoma City
Beech, Johnny Gale
Epperson, Kraettli Quynton
Fenton, Elliott Clayton
Kenney, John Arthur
Paul, William George
Woods, Harry Arthur, Jr.,

Tulsa
Eldridge, Richard Mark
Imel, John Michael
Luthey, Graydon Dean, Jr.,

OREGON

Brookings
Hinton, Floyd

Eugene
Palmer, Russell Scott
Sahlstrom, E(lmer) Bernard

Medford
Deatherage, William Vernon

Portland
Eakin, Margaretta Morgan
Houser, Douglas Guy
Johnston, Ronald Allen
Marandas, John Steve
Williamson, Charles Ready, III,

Salem
Feibleman, Gilbert Bruce
Haselton, Rick Thomas
Mannix, Kevin Leese
Spooner, Ralph Charles

PENNSYLVANIA

Allentown
Brown, Robert Wayne

Beaver
Petrush, John Joseph

Blue Bell
Elliott, John Michael

Bryn Mawr
Hankin, Mitchell Robert

Clarks Summit
Beemer, John Barry

Doylestown
Renz, William Tomlinson

Feasterville Trevose
Osterhout, Richard Cadwallader

Glenside
Mermelstein, Jules Joshua

Harrisburg
Kelly, Robert Edward, Jr.,

Hazleton
Schiavo, Pasco Louis

Hermitage
McKay, Donald Ross

Indiana
Barbor, John Howard

Lancaster
Lewis, Alvin Bower, Jr.,

Meadville
Barrett, Bruce Alan

Media
Cramp, John Franklin

Natrona Heights
Maleski, Cynthia Maria

New Cumberland
Yakowicz, Vincent X

New Kensington
Wallace, Henry Jared, Jr.,

Newtown
Godwin, Robert Anthony

Norristown
Cowperthwait, Lindley Murray

Philadelphia
Auerbach, Sheryl Lynn
Barrett, John J(ames), Jr.,
Binder, David Franklin
Brown, William Hill, III,
Cox, Roger Frazier
Fiebach, H. Robert
Grant, M. Duncan
Kormes, John Winston
Ledwith, John Francis
Lillie, Charisse Ranielle
Mathes, Stephen Jon
McGurk, Eugene David, Jr.,
Milbourne, Walter Robertson
Milone, Francis Michael
Phelan, John M.
Savett, Stuart Hubert
Schoener, George Francis, Jr.,
Sheils, Denis Francis
Sonnenfeld, Marc Jay
Tiger, Ira Paul

Pittsburgh
Acheson, Amy J.
Basinski, Anthony Joseph
Connors, Eugene Kenneth
Fischer, Nora Barry
Hurnyak, Christina Kaiser
Jones, Craig Ward
Kenrick, Charles William
Klett, Edwin L.
Litman, Roslyn Margolis
McGinley, John Regis, Jr.,
O'Connor, Edward Gearing
Pfaff, Robert James
Plowman, Jack Wesley
Ulven, Mark Edward

Reading
Eshelman, David Richard

Scranton
Howley, James McAndrew

Stroudsburg
Catina, Janet K.

White Oak
Pribanic, Victor Hunter

Wyomissing
Turner, David Eldridge

RHODE ISLAND

Providence
White, Benjamin Vroom, III,

SOUTH CAROLINA

Aiken
Amabile, John Louis

Charleston
Kahn, Ellis Irvin
Spitz, Hugo Max

Columbia
Babcock, Keith Moss
Sheftman, Howard Stephen
Tate, Harold Simmons, Jr.,

Greenville
Cowan, John Joseph
Kappel, Matthew Jay
Massey, Raymond David
Shoemaker, James Marshall, Jr.,
Todd, John Dickerson, Jr.,
White, Daniel Bowman

Hilton Head Island
McKay, John Judson, Jr.,

Sumter
Seth, J. Cabot

SOUTH DAKOTA

Pierre
Thompson, Charles Murray

TENNESSEE

Bolivar
Cary, Charles Muse

Chattanooga
Akers, Samuel Lee
Bahner, Thomas Maxfield
Campbell, Paul, III,
Cooper, Gary Allan

Church Hill
Faulk, Michael Anthony

Collierville
Scroggs, Larry Kenneth

Cookeville
Acuff, John Edgar

Dyersburg
Wilder, James Sampson, III,

Knoxville
Hagood, Lewis Russell

Memphis
Carr, Oscar Clark, III,
Garts, James Rufus, Jr.,
Newman, Charles Forrest
Noel, Randall Deane

Nashville
Cooney, Charles Hayes
DeLanis, James Alfred
Hardin, Hal D.
Sims, Wilson

Soddy Daisy
Leitner, Paul Revere

TEXAS

Abilene
Suttle, Stephen Hungate

Arlington
Jensen, John Robert
Rosenberry, William Kenneth

Austin
Donaldson, David Howard, Jr.,
Harrison, Richard Wayne
Hernandez, Mack Ray
Judson, Philip Livingston
Kilgore, Gary Lynn
Smith, Peyton Noble

Brownwood
Bell, William Woodward

Corpus Christi
Alberts, Harold

Dallas
Abney, Frederick Sherwood
Atwood, Roy Tress
Baggett, Steven Ray
Bickel, John W., II,
Biermacher, Kenneth Wayne
Blount, Charles William, III,
Brin, Royal Henry, Jr.,
Coleman, Robert Winston
Evans, Roger
Fanning, Barry Hedges
Figari, Ernest Emil, Jr.,
Flegle, Jim L.
Freytag, Sharon Nelson
Harrison, Orrin Lea, III,
Hartnett, Will Ford
Haworth, Charles Ray
Huffman, Gregory Scott Combest
Hytken, Franklin Harris
Jayson, Melinda Gayle
Jones, Lindy Don
Lippe, Emil, Jr.,
Lowenberg, Michael
May, April Michelle
McAtee, David Ray
Mow, Robert Henry, Jr.,
Mueller, Mark Christopher
Ringle, Brett Adelbert
Selinger, Jerry Robin
Sides, Jack Davis, Jr.,
Smith, Russell Bryan
Walkowiak, Vincent Steven

El Paso
Dinsmoor, Robert Davidson

Farmersville
Seward, Richard Bevin

Flower Mound
Hunt, David Ford

Fort Worth
Brunig, Robert Arthur
Chappell, David Franklin
Crumley, John Walter
Elliott, Frank Wallace
Larimore, Tom L.
Myers, Thomas Everett
Rutherford, Jay K.

Garland
Irby, Holt

Hallettsville
Baber, Wilbur H., Jr.,

Harlingen
Johnson, Orrin Wendell

Houston
Addison, Linda Leuchter
Atlas, Scott Jerome
Ballanfant, Richard Burton
Bayko, Emil Thomas
Beirne, Martin Douglas
Brinson, Gay Creswell, Jr.,
Burch, Voris Reagan
Carr, Edward A.
Craig, Robert Mark, III,
Crinion, Gregory Paul
Cunningham, Tom Alan
Gayle, Gibson, Jr.,
Gilbert, Keith Thomas
Harvin, David Tarleton
Holstead, John Burnham
Horrigan, Joseph Stewart
Jordan, Charles Milton
Kaplan, Lee Landa
Ketchand, Robert Lee
Lovelace, Byron Keith
McFall, Donald Beury
McQuarrie, Claude Monroe, III,
Nunnally, Knox Dillon
Ray, Hugh Massey, Jr.,
Reasoner, Harry Max
Redden, Joe Winston, Jr.,
Rowland, Robert Alexander, III,
Smith, Alison Leigh
Susman, Morton Lee
Susman, Stephen Daily
Tartt, Blake
Wallis, Olney Gray
Wilde, William Key
Yetter, R. Paul
Zager, Steven Mark
Zimmerman, Alvin Louis

Killeen
Roberts, Burk Austin

Midland
Estes, Andrew Harper
Truitt, Robert Ralph, Jr.,

Richardson
Austin, Ann Sheree

Rockport
Porter, Charles Raleigh, Jr.,

San Antonio
Hohman, A. J., Jr.,
Labay, Eugene Benedict
Maloney, Marynell
Valadez, Robert Allen

Sugar Land
Aldrich, Lovell W(eld)
Greer, Raymond White

The Woodlands
Hagerman, John David

UTAH

Ogden
Sullivan, Kevin Patrick

Salt Lake City
Christensen, Patricia Anne Watkins
Christensen, Ray Richards
Colessides, Nick John
Verhaaren, Harold Carl

VERMONT

Essex Junction
Gannon, Michael John

Montpelier
Cheney, Kimberly Bunce

VIRGINIA

Abingdon
McElroy, Howard Chowning

Alexandria
Burch, John Thomas, Jr.,
Carter, Richard Dennis

Arlington
Green, Richard Alan

Fairfax
Arnold, William McCauley

Fredericksburg
Billingsley, Robert Thaine

Great Falls
Preston, Charles George

Mc Lean
Church, Randolph Warner, Jr.,

Mechanicsville
Martin, Ronald Allen

Norfolk
Fletcher, John Richard
Zahn, Richard William, Jr.,

Petersburg
Shell, Louis Calvin
Spero, Morton Bertram

Radford
Davis, Richard Waters

Richmond
Hall, Stephen Charles
Patterson, Robert Hobson, Jr.,

Vienna
Razzano, Frank Charles

Virginia Beach
Clark, Donald H.
Hajek, Francis Paul

WASHINGTON

Centralia
Buzzard, Steven Ray

Renton
Swanson, Arthur Dean

Sammamish
Waitt, Robert Kenneth

Seattle
Andrews, J. David
Bagshaw, Bradley Holmes
Bateman, Heidi S.
Bringman, Joseph Edward
Cornell, Kenneth Lee
Hendricks, Katherine
McKay, Michael Dennis
Mines, Michael
Petrie, Gregory Steven
Sayre, Matt Melvin Mathias
Tomlinson, John Randolph
Walter, Michael Charles
Wechsler, Mary Heyrman

Tacoma
Mungia, Salvador Alejo

WEST VIRGINIA

Charleston
Bell, Harry Fullerton, Jr.,
Kiblinger, Cindy Jo
Neely, Richard

Fairmont
Sawyer, Sean Jeffrey

Lewisburg
Ford, Richard Edmond

Romney
Saville, Royce Blair

Weirton
Fahey, William Thomas, II,

Wheeling
Hill, Barry Morton

WISCONSIN

Amery
Gust, Gerald Norman

Cross Plains
Atterbury, Lee Richard

Green Bay
Schober, Thomas Leonard

Kenosha
Clarke, Alan William
Higgins, John Patrick

La Crosse
Sleik, Thomas Scott

Madison
Field, Henry Augustus, Jr.,
Hildebrand, Daniel Walter

Milwaukee
Busch, John Arthur
Grzezinski, Dennis Michael
Habush, Robert Lee
Levit, William Harold, Jr.,
Melin, Robert Arthur
Pollen, Raymond James

Oshkosh
Curtis, George Warren

Pepin
Seymour, Mary Frances

Wausau
Grischke, Alan Edward

WYOMING

Casper
Combs, W(illiam) Henry, III,

Cheyenne
Dyekman, Gregory Chris

Jackson
Clauss, C. David
Schuster, Robert Parks
Shockey, Gary Lee

CZECH REPUBLIC

Prague
Honsa, Frantisek

ADDRESS UNPUBLISHED

Adams, Thomas Lawrence
Alexander, Richard Elmont
Bakkensen, John Reser
Belleville, Philip Frederick
Blevins, Jeffrey Alexander
Brumbaugh, John Moore
Campion, Thomas Francis
Carlson, Alan Douglas
Cohen, Anita Marilyn
Corlett, Edward Stanley, III,
Dolan, John F.
Dolan, Peter Brown
Ehrlich, Stephen Richard
Erlebacher, Arlene Cernik
Flanary, Donald Herbert, Jr.,
Gilbert, Ronald Rhea
Goldberg, Michael Bradley
Guehl, Robert Lee
Hall, John Hopkins
Harper, Harlan, Jr.,
Heins, Samuel David
Hoffman, Alan Craig
Horn, Andrew Warren
Howard, John Wayne
Hughes, Roy Fredericks
Johnson, Richard Wesley
Kellerman, Edwin
MacLaren, Robert Ian, II,
Madsen, H(enry) Stephen
Manos, Christopher Lawrence
Martin, Robert James
Mc Donough, John Richard
McCoy, John Joseph
Merritt, Bruce Gordon
Muri, Anthony Frederick
Orlebeke, William Ronald
Peccarelli, Anthony Marando
Pereyra-Suarez, Charles Albert
Phillips, Dorothy Kay
Richeson, Hugh Anthony, Jr.,
Ricks, Cecil Earl, Jr.,
Saliterman, Richard Arlen
Siemer, Deanne Clemence
Smith, James A.
Smouse, H(ervey) Russell
Speight, John B.
Strick, Gerald Jay
Szuch, Clyde Andrew
Terrell, G. Irvin
Vigil, David Charles
Vinar, Benjamin
Watson, John Michael
Wheeler, R(ichard) Kenneth

CIVIL RIGHTS

UNITED STATES

ALABAMA

Tuskegee
Gray, Fred David

ALASKA

Fairbanks
Schendel, William Burnett

ARIZONA

Phoenix
McKee, Roger A.
Nelson, Douglas Clarence

Tucson
Bainton, Denise Marlene
Cope, Thom K.
Esposito, Joseph Louis
Mc Donald, John Richard

ARKANSAS

Fayetteville
Kester, Charles Melvin

Little Rock
Jones, Stephen Witsell

CALIFORNIA

Beverly Hills
Juno, Cynthia

Clovis
Ninnis, William Raymond, Jr.,

Fresno
Little, Kevin Gerard

Fullerton
Talmo, Ronald Victor

Los Angeles
Feigen, Brenda S.
Franco, Maria-Lorinda D.
Lavin, Laurence Michael
Trygstad, Lawrence Benson

Newport Beach
Carman, Ernest Day

Oakland
Lomhoff, Peter George
Wallace, Elaine Wendy

Pasadena
Poole, Heather L.

San Francisco
Rosen, Sanford Jay
Rubin, Michael
Weber, Matthew Bernard

Sanger
Chynoweth, W. Edward

Venice
Schanes, Christine

Woodland Hills
Kaufman, Albert I.

COLORADO

Boulder
Echohawk, John Ernest

Denver
Breeskin, Michael Wayne
Corry, Robert J., Jr.,
Nathan, J(ay) Andrew
Nier, Harry Kaufman
Roesler, John Bruce

CONNECTICUT

Hartford
Dempsey, Edward Joseph

Stamford
Margolis, Emanuel

DISTRICT OF COLUMBIA

Washington
Berenson, Aimee Robin
Bernabei, Lynne Ann
Deutsch, David
Keeney, John Christopher, Jr.,
Nolan, John Edward
Payton, John
Sheehy, Barbara
Sherman, Lawrence Jay
Vanderstar, John

FLORIDA

Boca Raton
Silver, Barry Morris

Coral Gables
McGrane, Miles A., III,

Largo
Trevena, John Harry

Miami
Campos-Orrego, Nora Patricia
Connor, Terence Gregory
Kurzban, Ira Jay
Maher, Stephen Trivett

Miami Lakes
Cohen, Ronald J.

Palm Bay
Tietig, Edward Chester

Pensacola
Soloway, Daniel Mark

Saint Petersburg
Escarraz, Enrique, III,

Tampa
Munoz, Shane Thomas

West Palm Beach
Hoch, Rand

GEORGIA

Atlanta
Barwick, William D.
Bramlett, Jeffrey Owen
Gepp, Randy C.
González, Carlos A.
Harness, William Walter
Patrick, Deval Laurdine

HAWAII

Honolulu
Gierlach, David J.
Schweigert, Jack

COLLECTIONS. *See* Commercial, consumer.

COMMERCIAL FINANCING. *See* Commercial, contracts.

COMMERCIAL, CONSUMER

ARIZONA

Phoenix
Clarke, David Alan
Rudolph, Gilbert Lawrence

Prescott
Chamberlain, David Alanson
Goodman, Mark N.

ARKANSAS

Fayetteville
Pettus, E. Lamar

Fort Smith
Daily, Thomas A.

North Little Rock
Patty, Claibourne Watkins, Jr.,

CALIFORNIA

Bakersfield
Karcher, Steven Michael

Costa Mesa
Frieden, Clifford E.

Del Mar
Seitman, John Michael

Downey
Duzey, Robert Lindsey

Encino
Levine, Thomas Jeffrey Pello

Los Angeles
Barth, Karen Ann
Baumann, Richard Gordon
Gilhuly, Peter Martin
Marcus, Stephen Howard
O'Leary, Prentice L.
Ohlgren, Joel R.
Porter, Verna Louise

Pacific Palisades
Share, Richard Hudson

Pleasanton
Opperwall, Stephen Gabriel

San Diego
Guinn, Stanley Willis

San Francisco
Kelly, J. Michael

San Jose
Hannon, Timothy Patrick

Santa Barbara
Cappello, A. Barry

Tracy
Hay, Dennis Lee

Tustin
Gaughan, John Stephen

Westlake Village
Weissman, Robert Allen

COLORADO

Arvada
Kreis, Elizabeth Susan

Colorado Springs
Gefreh, Paul Thomas

Pueblo
Kogovsek, Daniel Charles

CONNECTICUT

Hartford
Stravalle-Schmidt, Ann Roberta

Madison
Clendenen, William Herbert, Jr.,

New Haven
Skalka, Douglas Scott
Wiznia, Carolann Kamens

West Hartford
Swerdloff, Ileen Pollock

DELAWARE

Wilmington
Curtin, Christopher James
Flame, Andrew Jay
Salinger, Frank Max

DISTRICT OF COLUMBIA

Washington
Cohen, Nelson Craig
Kass, Benny Lee

FLORIDA

Altamonte Springs
Hoogland, Robert Frederics

Boca Raton
Comiter, Lloyd Alan

Brandon
England, Lynne Lipton

Coral Gables
Rothstein, David Alan

Edgewater
Dunagan, Walter Benton

Fort Lauderdale
Hirsch, Jeffrey Allan

Jacksonville
Coker, Howard Coleman
Siegel, Edward

Miami
Hartz, Steven Edward Marshall
Podhurst, Aaron Samuel
Russell, Patrick
Stein, Allan Mark

Ocala
Hatch, John D.

Orlando
Christiansen, Patrick T.

Palm Harbor
Summers-Powell, Alan

Tampa
Anton, David
Cook, William John
Jordan-Holmes, Clark
Roberson, Bruce Heerdt

GEORGIA

Atlanta
Jordan, Hilary Peter
Kessler, Richard Paul, Jr.,
Tanner, W(alter) Rhett
Winkler, Allen Warren

HAWAII

Honolulu
Dang, Marvin S. C.
Lau, Jeffrey Daniel
Lee, Dale W.
Sato, Glenn Kenji

Wailuku
Kinaka, William Tatsuo

IDAHO

Boise
Fawcett, Charles Winton

Idaho Falls
Hart, Stephen Strong

ILLINOIS

Belleville
Gossage, Roza

Bloomington
Deneen, Daniel Guy

Chicago
Berkoff, Mark Andrew
Hoseman, Daniel
Hyman, Michael Bruce
Kawitt, Alan
Neumeier, Matthew Michael
Wood, Allison Lorraine

Moline
Cleaver, William Lehn

Paris
Bell, Allen Andrew, Jr.,

Prospect Heights
Leopold, Mark F.

INDIANA

Crawfordsville
Donaldson, Steven Bryan

Fort Wayne
Gehring, Ronald Kent

Indianapolis
Abels, Jonathan Berle
Wellnitz, Craig Otto
Wunder, David Hart

New Albany
Bourne, James E.

IOWA

Davenport
Phelps, Robert J.

Mason City
Duffy, John Leonard

KANSAS

Arkansas City
Templar, Ted Mac

Lawrence
Karlin, Calvin Joseph

KENTUCKY

Fort Thomas
Whalen, Paul Lewellin

New Castle
Brammell, William Hartman

LOUISIANA

New Orleans
Barnett, William Michael
Lee, Wayne J.
Levin, Richard Barry

Shreveport
Feldman, Larry, Jr.,

MAINE

Augusta
Wilkinson, Lester F., Jr.,

MARYLAND

Baltimore
Erwin, H. Robert
Goldman, Brian Arthur
Wolf, Cyd Beth

Bel Air
Wilson, Christian Burhenn

Lutherville
Fascetta, Christopher Michael

New Market
Gabriel, Eberhard John

MASSACHUSETTS

Amesbury
Swartz, Mark Lee

Boston
Bodoff, Joseph Samuel Uberman
Lowney, Timothy Jay
Read, Nicholas Cary

Florence
Park, Beverly Goodman

Framingham
Vrabel, Joseph P.

MICHIGAN

Birmingham
Harms, Steven Alan

Detroit
Tukel, Susan

Grand Rapids
Brinkmeyer, Scott S.
Buquicchio, Steven T.
Mears, Patrick Edward

Grosse Pointe Farms
Brucker, Wilber Marion

Grosse Pointe Woods
Pytell, Robert Henry

Marquette
Osstyn, Randolph Beier

MINNESOTA

Minneapolis
Kantor, David

Minnetonka
Schechtman, Steven Lawrence

Wayzata
Reutiman, Robert William, Jr.,

MISSISSIPPI

Bay Springs
Shoemaker, Bobby Lynn

Jackson
Eicher, Donald E., III,
Wise, Robert Powell

Pascagoula
Tynes, Douglas Lamont

MISSOURI

Kansas City
Joyce, Michael Patrick
Small, Stephen Bradley

Lexington
Giorza, John C.

Saint Louis
Bloom, Allen Jerry
Kramer, Donald Burton
Riggio, Nicholas Jospeh, Sr.,

MONTANA

Lolo
Hansell, Ronald Stephen

NEBRASKA

Kearney
Voigt, Steven Russell

Omaha
Lee, Dennis Patrick

NEVADA

Las Vegas
Goodwin, John Robert

NEW HAMPSHIRE

Concord
Hilliard, Russell F.

NEW JERSEY

Cranbury
Gupta, Rajat Kumar

Montclair
Ward, Roger Coursen

Morris Plains
Mellinger, Louis Philip

Morristown
Sperling, Joy Harmon

Newark
Corbin Walker, Karol
Rak, Lorraine Karen

Oakhurst
Rescinio, Albert John

Parsippany
Gallagher, Jerome Francis, Jr.,

Red Bank
Anderson, James Francis

Ridgewood
Trocano, Russell Peter

NEW MEXICO

Albuquerque
Bova, Vincent Arthur, Jr.,

Farmington
Morgan, Jack M.

Santa Fe
Green, Barry

NEW YORK

Albany
Lauricella, Peter Alan

Baldwin
Naranjo, Carolyn R.

East Northport
Ryesky, Kenneth H.

Great Neck
Salzman, Stanley P.

Huntington
Houslanger, Todd Eric

Mineola
Lung, Henry

New York
Anker, Kent Kari
Epling, Richard Louis
Jacobs, Randall Scott David

Rochester
Lustig, Douglas James

Scarsdale
Sabadie, Francisca Alejandra

Syracuse
Goldberg, Harold Philip

Troy
Marinstein, Elliott Fred

NORTH CAROLINA

Charlotte
Buckley, Charles Robinson, III,
Ogburn, Thomas Lynn, III,

Durham
Carpenter, Charles Francis

Greensboro
Galloway, Hunter Henderson, III,
Glover, Durant Murrell

OHIO

Beavercreek
Stadnicar, Joseph William

Cincinnati
Vogel, Cedric Wakelee

Cleveland
Eisen, Saul
Felty, Kriss Delbert
Willenbrink, Rose Ann

Columbus
Drexel, Ray Phillips
Robinson, Randal D.

Massillon
Breyfogle, Edwin Howard

Shaker Heights
Cherchiglia, Dean Kenneth

Warren
Vigorito, Philip Michael

OKLAHOMA

Cherokee
Stein, Sam L.

Oklahoma City
Gibson, Keith Russell
Schwabe, George Blaine, III,

Tulsa
Abrahamson, A. Craig
Herrold, David Henry
Ungerman, Maynard I.

OREGON

Brookings
Hinton, Floyd

Lincoln City
Elliott, Scott

Oregon City
McFarland, Carol Anne

Portland
Johnston, Ronald Allen
Waggoner, James Clyde

PENNSYLVANIA

Abington
Budman, Alan David

Doylestown
Goldman, William Lewis

Harrisburg
Lighty, Fredrick W.
Tyler, Brian Joseph

Jenkintown
Worthington, Sandra Boulton

Lemoyne
Stewart, Richard Williams

Philadelphia
Grunfeld, David I.

Pittsburgh
Helmrich, Joel Marc
Krebs, Robert Alan

Reading
Thornton, William P., Jr.,

Wellsboro
Duff, Brian S.

York
Ream, Jack Frantz

RHODE ISLAND

Cranston
Coletti, John Anthony

SOUTH CAROLINA

Charleston
Hood, Robert Holmes

Columbia
Johnson, Lawrence Wilbur, Jr.,

West Columbia
Applegate, William Russell

SOUTH DAKOTA

Sioux Falls
Hayes, Robert E.
Johnson, Richard Arlo

COMMERCIAL, CONTRACTS

UNITED STATES

Lakeland
Harris, Christy Franklin

Melbourne
Dixon, Richard Dean
Hedman, George William

Miami
Baena, Scott Louis
Hoffman, Larry J.
Jeffrey, Douglas Jason
Kanov, Jonathan E.
Long, Maxine Master
Milian, David Philip
Murai, Rene Vicente
Osman, Edith Gabriella
Reive, Kevin Christopher
Schuette, Charles A.
Stein, Allan Mark

Orlando
Fildes, Richard James
Hartley, Carl William, Jr.,
Pierce, John Gerald (Jerry Pierce)

Pembroke Pines
Granata, Linda M.

Saint Petersburg
Ross, Howard Philip

Sarasota
Christopher, William Garth
Miller, Harold O.

Tampa
Barkin, Marvin E.
Hadlow, Richard B.
Olson, John Karl
Schwenke, Roger Dean
Teblum, Gary Ira
Whatley, Jacqueline Beltram

Vero Beach
Case, Douglas Manning

West Palm Beach
Weitzman, Linda Sue

Winter Park
Ackert, T(errence) W(illiam)
Hadley, Ralph Vincent, III,

GEORGIA

Atlanta
Antonino, Lauren Slepin
Bratton, James Henry, Jr.,
Byrne, Granville Bland, III,
Calhoun, Scott Douglas
Cargill, Robert Mason
Driver, Walter W., Jr.,
Hinchey, John William
Jones, Glower Whitehead
Koplan, Andrew Bennet
Lackland, Theodore Howard
Linder, Harvey Ronald
Liss, Matthew M.
Reynolds, Bradley Kenneth
Strauss, Robert David
Thompson, Philip C.
Veal, Rex R.
Williams, Neil, Jr.,
Winkler, Allen Warren

Marietta
Ahlstrom, Michael Joseph

Perry
Geiger, James Norman

Roswell
Mimms, Thomas Bowman, Jr.,

Saint Simons Island
Thau, William Albert, Jr.,

Swainsboro
Cadle, Jerry Neal

HAWAII

Honolulu
Asai-Sato, Carol Yuki
Ching, Gale Lin Fong
Deaver, Phillip Lester
Gay, E(mil) Laurence
Sato, Glenn Kenji

Paia
Richman, Joel Eser

ILLINOIS

Bloomington
Deneen, Daniel Guy

Buffalo Grove
Robins, Martin B.

Chicago
Anderson, J. Trent
Baer, John Richard Frederick
Berger, Robert Michael
Cohen, Melanie Rovner
Cunningham, Thomas Justin
Fazio, Peter Victor, Jr.,
Feldman, Scott Milton
Field, Robert Edward
French, Timothy A.
Golan, Stephen Leonard
Grant, Robert Nathan
Heist, Robert Connor
Henry, Robert John
Hoseman, Daniel
Jacobson, Ronald H.
Kaplan, Howard Gordon
Kasson, Constantine D.
Kohn, William Irwin
Kravitt, Jason Harris Paperno
Laidlaw, Andrew R.
Lapin, Andrew William
Looman, James R.
Mandel, Reid Alan
Martin, Arthur Mead
Mehlman, Mark Franklin
Miller, Paul J.
Murray, Daniel Richard
Peterson, Ronald Roger
Rohrman, Douglass Frederick
Rosenbloom, Lewis Stanley
Shank, Suzanne Adams
Sullivan, Marcia Waite
Thompson, Michael
Wahlen, Edwin Alfred
Weil, Andrew Lawrence
Weissman, Michael Lewis
White, Linda Diane

Elgin
Roeser, Ronald O.

Lafox
Seils, William George

Lake Forest
Francois, William Armand

Long Grove
Obert, Paul Richard

Moline
Cleaver, William Lehn

Naperville
Fenech, Joseph Charles

Northfield
Giza, David Alan

Oakbrook Terrace
Tibble, Douglas Clair

Urbana
Thies, David Charles

Vernon Hills
Richards, Alan Edward

Warrenville
Johnson, Douglas Wells

Westchester
Castellano, Christine Marie

Wilmette
McNeill, Thomas B.

Winnetka
Fawcett, Dwight Winter
Greenblatt, Ray Harris

INDIANA

Evansville
Harrison, Joseph Heavrin

Fort Wayne
Murphy, Patrick Guyon
Pope, Mark Andrew

Highland
Fine, William Irwin

Indianapolis
Carlberg, James Edwin
Kahlenbeck, Howard, Jr.,
Kleiman, Mary Margaret
Knauer, James A.
Miller, David Anthony
Talesnick, Stanley
Vandivier, Blair Robert

Merrillville
Bowman, Carol Ann

Peru
Grund, James Arthur

Plainfield
Carpenter, Craig M.

Richmond
Bever, Robert Lynn

South Bend
Reinke, William John

Terre Haute
Britton, Louis Franklin

Vincennes
Smith, Bruce Arthur

IOWA

Des Moines
Jensen, Dick Leroy
Neiman, Donald Flint

Iowa City
Holland, Charles Joseph

Sioux City
Madsen, George Frank

KANSAS

Hutchinson
Chalfant, William Young

Lincoln
Crangle, Robert D.

Manhattan
Miller, Anne Burke

Topeka
Elwood, H. Philip

KENTUCKY

Lexington
Lester, Roy David

Louisville
Fenton, Thomas Conner
Shaikun, Michael Gary
Vincenti, Michael Baxter

LOUISIANA

Baton Rouge
Anderson, Lawrence Robert, Jr.,
Richards, Marta Alison

Metairie
Hardy, Ashton Richard
Kutcher, Robert A.

New Orleans
Brouphy, Greta Manning
Getten, Thomas Frank
Pugh, William Whitmell Hill, III,
Steeg, Moise S., Jr.,
Steinberg, Sylvan Julian
Wedig, Regina Scotto

Shreveport
Bryant, J(ames) Bruce

MAINE

Portland
Martin, Michael Keith
Stauffer, Eric P.

MARYLAND

Baltimore
Baker, William Parr
Blakeslee, Wesley Daniel
Kandel, Nelson Robert
Kuryk, David Neal
Mogol, Alan Jay
Wasserman, Richard Leo

Bethesda
Ballman, B. George
Frosh, Brian Esten
Goodwin, Robert Cronin
Himelfarb, Stephen Roy
Rosenberg, Mark Louis
Tanenbaum, Richard Hugh

Chevy Chase
Toy, Charles David

Easton
Maffitt, James Strawbridge

Leonardtown
Lacer, Alfred Antonio

Rockville
Axelson, Jeffrey Mark
Zaphiriou, George Aristotle

West Bethesda
Scully, Roger Tehan, II,

MASSACHUSETTS

Boston
Berman, Mark Niles
Bodoff, Joseph Samuel Uberman
Daley, Paul Patrick
Hester, Patrick Joseph
Huang, Thomas Weishing
Lamb, Kevin Thomas
Read, Nicholas Cary
Rudolph, James Leonard
Shapiro, Sandra
Smith, Edwin Eric
Wolfson, Jeffrey Steven

Cambridge
Esher, Jacob Aaron

Framingham
Meltzer, Jay H.

Medford
Berman, David

Wellesley
Marx, Peter A.

Worcester
Van Nostrand, Richard Charles

MICHIGAN

Alpena
Hunter, Mark John

Ann Arbor
Ellmann, Douglas Stanley
Hahn, Gary Lynn

Battle Creek
Steffel, Vern John, Jr.,

Bingham Farms
Berman, Leonard Keith

Birmingham
Harms, Steven Alan
McCarthy, Daniel J.
Schaefer, John Frederick
Wells, Steven Wayne
Zelenock, Katheryne L.

Bloomfield
Kanter, Alan Michael

Bloomfield Hills
Clippert, Charles Frederick
Dawson, Stephen Everette

Clinton Township
Theut, C. Peter

Detroit
Collier, James Warren
Dunn, William Bradley
Fromm, Frederick Andrew, Jr.,
Targan, Holli Hart
Thorpe, Norman Ralph
Toll, Sheldon Samuel

Flint
Powers, Edward Herbert

Grand Rapids
Curtin, Timothy John
Dewey, Charles Nichols, Jr.,
Mears, Patrick Edward

Kalamazoo
Lubben, Craig Henry

Muskegon
Fauri, Eric Joseph

Plymouth
Koroi, Mark Michael

Southfield
Jacobs, John E.

Troy
Robinson, Logan Gilmore

MINNESOTA

Andover
Lodge, Steven John

Austin
Schneider, Mahlon C.

Benson
Wilcox, Donald Alan

Edina
Gurstel, Norman Keith

Hopkins
Hunter, Donald Forrest

Minneapolis
Anderson, Eric Scott
Baillie, James Leonard
Nelson, Steven Craig
Opdahl, Clark Donald
Peterson, Mark Bradley

Rochester
Lantz, William Charles

Saint Cloud
Hughes, Kevin John

Saint Paul
Rebane, John T.

MISSISSIPPI

Jackson
Grant, Russell Porter, Jr.,
Hafter, Jerome Charles
O'Mara, James Wright

MISSOURI

Chesterfield
Pollihan, Thomas Henry

Kansas City
Bartunek, Robert R(ichard), Jr.,
Doan, Kirk Hugh
Frisbie, Charles
Herman, Robert Stephen
Parres, Cynthia Dillard
Parrette, Leslie Jackson

Maryland Heights
Cooper, Richard Alan

Saint Louis
Carr, Gary Thomas
Duesenberg, Richard William
Godiner, Donald Leonard
Goldenhersh, Robert Stanley
Green, Dennis Joseph
Hetlage, Robert Owen
Komen, Leonard
Leontsinis, George John
Lowther, Thomas Edward
Olson, Robert Grant
Palans, Lloyd Alex
Poscover, Maury B.
Sullivan, Edward Lawrence
Weiss, Charles Andrew

Springfield
Carlson, Thomas Joseph

MONTANA

Missoula
Vannatta, Shane Anthony

Whitefish
Tornow, Thomas T.

NEBRASKA

Omaha
Fitzgerald, James Patrick

NEVADA

Henderson
Eskin, Jeffrey Laurence

Las Vegas
Buckley, Michael Edward
Singer, Michael Howard

NEW HAMPSHIRE

Concord
Potter, Fred Leon

Portsmouth
Doleac, Charles Bartholomew

NEW JERSEY

Atlantic City
Zlotnick, Norman Lee

Bloomfield
Caccavale, Stephen Joseph

Bridgewater
Dahling, Gerald Vernon

Budd Lake
Webb, John Gibbon, III,

Cliffside Park
Diktas, Christos James

Cranbury
Amzel, Viviana

East Brunswick
Applebaum, Charles

Edison
Vercammen, Kenneth Albert

Florham Park
Freis, James Henry
Hardin, William Downer

Hackensack
Greenberg, Steven Morey
Miller, Harvey Allan
Sosland, Karl Z.

Kenilworth
LaRosa, Joseph J.

Montclair
Ward, Roger Coursen

Morristown
Aspero, Benedict Vincent
Campbell, William F., III,
Clark, Grant Lawrence
Rosenthal, Meyer L(ouis)

New Providence
Chobot, John Charles

Newark
Day, Edward Francis, Jr.,

Parsippany
Borger, John Emory
Stein, Julie Lynne

Piscataway
Smith, Bob

Princeton
Miller, Richard Mark

Roseland
Rosen, Charles Arthur
Smith, Dennis Jay

Short Hills
Fast, Kenneth H.
Siegfried, David Charles

Somerset
Green, Jeffrey C.

Teaneck
Kaplan, Howard M(ark)

Trenton
Frost, Barry Warren

Union
Suplee, Katherine Ann

Warren
Rana, Harminderpal Singh

Woodbridge
Felton, William Raymond

NEW MEXICO

Albuquerque
Farmer, Terry D(wayne)
Fish, Paul Mathew
Lopez, Martin, III,
Moughan, Peter Richard, Jr.,

Santa Fe
Burton, John Paul (Jack Burton)
Green, Barry
Justice, Jack Burton

NEW YORK

Brooklyn
Johnson, Donald Raymond

Buffalo
Brown, Lawrence Charles
Oppenheimer, Randolph Carl

Cedarhurst
Taubenfeld, Harry Samuel

Corning
Hauselt, Denise Ann

Croton On Hudson
Hoffman, Paul Shafer

Flushing
Deerson, Adele Shapiro

Geneseo
Macko, John

Great Neck
Rockowitz, Noah Ezra

Hillsdale
Lunde, Asbjorn Rudolph

Jericho
Rehbock, Richard Alexander

Lake George
Hayes, Norman Robert, Jr.,

Larchmont
Kullen, Richard Charles, Jr.,

Long Beach
Solomon, Robert H.

Malverne
Benigno, Thomas Daniel

Mamaroneck
Du Boff, Michael H(arold)

Mineola
Tannenbaum, Bernard

New York
Adair, Wendell Hinton, Jr.,
Bernstein, Daniel Lewis
Bernstein, Donald Scott
Berzow, Harold Steven
Bianco, S. Anthony
Bidwell, James Truman, Jr.,
Bluestone, Andrew Lavoott
Booth, Edgar Hirsch
Broude, Richard Frederick
Browne, Jeffrey Francis
Bursky, Herman Aaron
Carpenter, Randle Burt
Chaitman, Helen Davis
Chen, Wesley
Chin, Sylvia Fung
Cho, Tai Yong
Christenfeld, Alan M.
Chromow, Sheri P.
Clapman, Peter Carlyle
Cook, Michael Lewis
Cowan, Wallace Edgar
Das, Kalyan
De Natale, Andrew Peter
DeOrchis, Vincent Moore
Derzaw, Richard Lawrence
Devine, Michael Buxton
Drucker, Jacquelin F.
Dwyer, Cornelius J., Jr.,
Epling, Richard Louis
Feder, Saul E.
Feintuch, Richard David
Fernandez, Jose Walfredo
Fier, Elihu
Filler, Ronald Howard
Freedman, Theodore Levy
Gadsden, James
Ganz, David L,
Gelfman, Peter Trustman
Goebel, William Horn
Granoff, Gary Charles
Greene, Ira S.
Greenspon, Robert Alan
Grover, Douglas E.
Hackett, Kevin R.
Herbst, Todd L.
Herz, Andrew Lee
Hirshfield, Stuart
Huhs, John I.
Jerome, John James
Kawano, Arnold Hubert
Kinney, Stephen Hoyt, Jr.,
Koblenz, Michael Robert
Kornberg, Alan William
Kornreich, Edward Scott
Lee, In-Young
Lefkowitz, Howard N.
Levy, Herbert Monte
Lieberman, Nancy Ann
Lighter, Lawrence
Lindsay, George Peter
Lunding, Christopher Hanna
Luskin, Michael
Lutringer, Richard Emil
Maney, Michael Mason
Mansour, Jana Williamson
Mantle, Raymond Allan
Marcus, Eric Peter
Modlin, Howard S.
Newman, Lawrence Walker
O'Dea, Dennis Michael
Otero, Brian V.
Owen, Robert Dewit
Pollan, Stephen Michael
Puleo, Frank Charles
Resnicow, Norman Jakob
Savell, Polly Carolyn
Schaab, Arnold J.
Scheler, Brad Eric
Schwab, Terrance W.
Seltzer, Richard C.
Sharpe, Robert Francis, Jr.,
Sheikh, Kemal A.
Sher, Michael Lee
Silverberg, Jay Lloyd
Smith, Bradley Youle
Strickon, Harvey Alan
Stringer, Ronald E.
Teiman, Richard B.
Wald, Bernard Joseph
Wexelbaum, Michael
White, Katherine Patricia
Wise, Aaron Noah
Wu, Robin Chi Ching
Yamin, Michael Geoffrey
Zammit, Joseph Paul
Zaslowsky, David Paul

Nyack
Cember, M. Nathan

Pittsford
Hampson, Thomas Meredith

Port Washington
Satovsky, Stacey Yael

Rochester
Galbraith, Robert Lyell, Jr.,
Sheller, Patrick Michael

Sherrill
Campanie, Samuel John

Syracuse
Ackerman, Kenneth Edward
Bogart, William Harry
Hubbard, Peter Lawrence

Uniondale
Good, Douglas Jay

Walden
Gubits, David Barry

Westbury
Nogee, Jeffrey Laurence

White Plains
Rosenberg, Michael

NORTH CAROLINA

Cary
Taylor, Marvin Edward, Jr.,

Chapel Hill
Hultquist, Steven John

Charlotte
Chesson, Calvin White
Eve, Robert Michael, Jr.,
Goodwin, Walter Henry
Van Hoy, Philip Marshall
Whelpley, David B., Jr.,

Raleigh
Harazin, William Dennis
Jernigan, John Lee
Robinson, David Spencer

Wilmington
Jones, Lucian Cox

Winston Salem
Sandridge, William Pendleton, Jr.,

OHIO

Akron
Lammert, Thomas Edward
Lombardi, Frederick McKean

Cincinnati
Ashdown, Philomena Saldanha
Coffey, Thomas William
Corwin, Melanie S.
Meyers, Pamela Sue
Strauss, William Victor
Tobias, Charles Harrison, Jr.,

Cleveland
Bacon, Brett Kermit
Boukis, Kenneth
Brown, Seymour R.
Gardner, Steven Leslie
Groetzinger, Jon, Jr.,
Kahn, Scott Harris
Lawniczak, James Michael
Meyer, G. Christopher
Osborne, Frank R.
Sicherman, Marvin Allen
Striefsky, Linda A(nn)
Toomajian, William Martin

Columbus
Buchenroth, Stephen Richard
Deal, John Charles
Johnson, Mark Alan
Robinson, Randal D.
Schaeffer, Matthew Thomas
Sidman, Robert John
Sully, Ira Bennett

Dayton
Kinlin, Donald James
Krygowski, Walter John

Findlay
Kostyo, John Francis

Lakewood
Baxter, Howard H.

Shaker Heights
Cherchiglia, Dean Kenneth

Toledo
Gouttiere, John P.

Warren
McGeough, Robert Saunders

Wickliffe
Kidder, Fred Dockstater

Wooster
Haught, Sharon Kay

OKLAHOMA

Bartlesville
Roff, Alan Lee

Broken Arrow
Frieze, H(arold) Delbert

Norman
Hastie, John Douglas
Talley, Richard Bates

Oklahoma City
Elder, James Carl
Schwabe, George Blaine, III,

Tulsa
Butler, Robert Carlyle, III,
Chandler, Ronald Jay

OREGON

Cannon Beach
Hillestad, Charles Andrew

Eugene
Palmer, Russell Scott

Medford
Shaw, Barry N.

Portland
Eakin, Margaretta Morgan
Stewart, Milton Roy
Wei, Li
Weiner, David P.

PENNSYLVANIA

Allentown
Brown, Robert Wayne

Bryn Mawr
Hankin, Mitchell Robert

Center Valley
Smillie, Douglas James

Harrisburg
Sullivan, John Cornelius, Jr.,

Kennett Square
Partnoy, Ronald Allen

Mc Murray
Brzustowicz, John Cinq-Mars

Philadelphia
Aaron, Kenneth Ellyot
Bochetto, George Alexander
Cross, Milton H.
Denmark, William Adam
Finkelstein, Joseph Simon
Foxman, Stephen Mark
Haley, Vincent Peter
Huntington, Stephen N.
Ominsky, Andrew Michael
Rainone, Michael Carmine
Schorling, William Harrison
Temin, Michael Lehman
Tractenberg, Craig R.
Wilf, Frederic Marshal
Wright, Minturn Tatum, III,

Pittsburgh
Brown, David Ronald
Hartman, Ronald G.
Kalil, David Thomas
Murdoch, David Armor
Vater, Charles J.
von Waldow, Arnd N.

Warren
Ristau, Mark Moody

Wayne
Spiess, F. Harry, Jr.,

West Chester
Osborn, John Edward

Wilkes Barre
Roth, Eugene
Ufberg, Murray

York
Perry, Ronald
Ream, Jack Frantz

RHODE ISLAND

Providence
Furness, Peter John
Salvadore, Guido Richard

Westerly
Nardone, William Andrew

SOUTH CAROLINA

Columbia
Gray, Elizabeth Van Doren
Pansegrau, Phaedra Renée

Hilton Head Island
Bethea, William Lamar, Jr.,

Kingstree
Jenkinson, William Eldridge, III,

North Charleston
Laddaga, Lawrence Alexander

TENNESSEE

Brentwood
Provine, John Calhoun

Cookeville
Day, David Owen

Germantown
Waddell, Phillip Dean

Hermitage
Burkett, Gerald Arthur

Memphis
Clunan, Amy Marie
Crone, Alan Grady
Matthews, Paul Aaron

Nashville
Mendes, Robert Joseph

Sweetwater
Ridenour, Charles Edward

TEXAS

Abilene
Sartain, James Edward

Addison
Hranitzky, Rachel Robyn

Amarillo
Cox, Roger Stephen

Austin
Borden, Diana Kimball
Hernandez, Mack Ray

Brownsville
Fleming, Tommy Wayne

Colleyville
Whittenberg, Ira Orville

Dallas
Bromberg, John E.
Clark, Robert Murel, Jr.,
Gores, Christopher Merrel
Helfand, Marcy Caren Caren
Hunter, Robert Frederick
Jones, Lindy Don
Lowenberg, Michael
Portman, Glenn Arthur
Prather, Robert Charles, Sr.,
Rodgers, John Hunter
True, Roy Joe

El Paso
Skipworth, Robert Allison

Garland
Irby, Holt

Henderson
Adkison, Ron

Houston
Barton, Sarah Muriel
Bistline, F. Walter, Jr.,
Block, Nelson R(ichard)
Bradie, Peter Richard
Bridges, David Manning
Carmody, James Albert
Cline, Vivian Melinda
Crocker, Samuel Sackett
Ewen, Pamela Binnings
Farnsworth, T. Brooke
Harris, Warren Wayne
Heinrich, Timothy John
Hollyfield, John Scoggins
Hoyt, Mont Powell
Kay, Joel Phillip
Morgan, Richard Greer
O'Donnell, Lawrence, III,
Taheri, Marshall M.

Kerrville
Parmley, Robert James

Killeen
Kleff, Pierre Augustine, Jr.,

New Braunfels
Nolte, Melvin, Jr.,

Richardson
Martin, Richard Kelley

Rockwall
Holt, Charles William, Jr.,

San Antonio
Becker, Douglas Wesley
Shearn, Michael Joseph

Stephenville
Batson, David Warren

Sugar Land
Koh, Chye Hock

The Woodlands
Hagerman, John David

UTAH

Logan
Honaker, Jimmie Joe

Salt Lake City
Beckstead, John Alexander
Castleton, David J.
Jones, Michael Frank
Lochhead, Robert Bruce
Ockey, Ronald J.
Reeder, F. Robert
Verhaaren, Harold Carl

VERMONT

Burlington
Lang, Richard Arnold, Jr.,
McMahon, Dennis C.

Woodstock
Dagger, William Carson

VIRGINIA

Alexandria
Goolrick, Robert Mason

Arlington
Walker, Woodrow Wilson

Charlottesville
McKay, John Douglas
Robinette, Christopher John

Danville
Abreu, Luis Alberto

Fairfax
Downey, Richard Lawrence

Falls Church
Jennings, Thomas Parks
Nunes, Morris A.

Haymarket
Frank, Jacob

Hopewell
Williams, C. James, III, (Jim Williams)

Leesburg
Price, Stephen Conwell

Mc Lean
Morse, Duane D(ale)

Norfolk
Parker, Richard Wilson
Pearson, John Yeardley, Jr.,
Russell, C. Edward, Jr.,
Smith, Richard Muldrow

Portsmouth
Brennan, John William

Reston
Toole, John Harper

Richmond
Bing, Richard McPhail
Carter, Joseph Carlyle, Jr.,
Pinckney, Charles Cotesworth

WASHINGTON

Issaquah
Benoliel, Joel

Olympia
Scuderi, Joseph

Port Angeles
Gay, Carl Lloyd

Seattle
Cutler, Philip Edgerton
Ferrer, Rafael Douglas Paul
Franke, Patrick Joseph
Graham, Stephen Michael
Kriegman, Bruce Peter
MacLean, Merrilee Ann
McLean, Dennis Edgar
Olsen, Harold Fremont
Ritter, Daniel Benjamin
Sandman, Irvin W(illis)
Tune, James Fulcher
Yalowitz, Kenneth Gregg

Spokane
Esposito, Joseph Anthony

Yakima
Larson, Paul Martin

WEST VIRGINIA

Charleston
Chaney, Michael Thomas

Martinsburg
Martin, Clarence Eugene, III,

Summersville
Davis, Stephen Allen

WISCONSIN

Chippewa Falls
Hunt, Heather M.

Kohler
Sheedy, Kathleen Ann

Madison
Boucher, Joseph W(illiam)
Croake, Paul Allen
Peterson, H. Dale
Walsh, David Graves

Milwaukee
Adashek, James Lewis
Casper, Richard Henry
Martin, Quinn William
Maynard, John Ralph
Medved, Paul Stanley
Rintelman, Donald Brian
Ryan, Patrick Michael

Sheboygan
Rice, Shawn G.

Sun Prairie
Eustice, Francis Joseph

WYOMING

Gillette
Lubnau, Thomas Edwin, II,

Riverton
Girard, Nettabell

TERRITORIES OF THE UNITED STATES

PUERTO RICO

Old San Juan
Weinstein-Bacal, Stuart Allen

San Juan
Rodriguez-Diaz, Juan E.

MEXICO

Mexico City
Grau, Vicente
Perez Elizundia, Rodrigo

AUSTRALIA

Melbourne
Paterson, Robert

Sydney
Machin, Peter William
Seidler, Robert Leslie
Winkler, Nicholas Gary

BELGIUM

Antwerp
De Roeck, Martine M.

Brussels
Wagemans, Marc

BRAZIL

Rio de Janeiro
Basilio, Ana Tereza Palhares
Lopes, Beatriz

São Paulo
Coelho da Rocha, Paulo Frank
Flesch, Marcos Rafael
Inglez de Souza, Ricardo Norouha
Lynch, Maria Regina Mangabeira Albernaz
Meira, Fernando Alves
Rodrigues, Fabiana Utrabo
Suchodolski, Beno

BULGARIA

Sofia
Georgiev, Georgi Vladimirov
Gouginski, Nikolai Todorov
Poshtakova, Dora Hristova
Ugrinova, Zdravka Mirkova

CHILE

Santiago
Letelier, Jose Luis

CHINA

Beijing
Fiske, Harold Parker

COLOMBIA

Bogotá
Cajiao, Ximena T.

CZECH REPUBLIC

Prague
Cermak, Karel
Hajkova, Gabriela
Peroutka, Hynek
Peterka, Ondrej

DENMARK

Copenhagen
Horten, Eric Korre
Overgaard, Finn

Kolding
Ohrt, Hans-Christian

ENGLAND

London
McGeachie, Jeffrey Stuart
Rashidmanesh, Hamid Reza

FINLAND

Helsinki
Isotupa, Sirpa Hannele
Kauppi, Matti Risto Sakari

FRANCE

Lyon
Girerd, Carole

Paris
Baum, Axel Helmuth
de Castellan, Elisabetta Ferruta
Norris, Pascale Danielle
Powell-Smith, Marc Edgar Raoul

GERMANY

Bonn
Goeckeler, Stephan

Cologne
Siepelt-Babilon, Stefan

Dortmund
Nockelmann, Wolfgang

Frankfurt
Jung, Harald H.
Peter, Anne-Marie

Hamburg
von Teuffel, Nikolai

Munich
Hallweger, Matthias
Preisenberger, Simon Andreas

GREECE

Athens
Cocalis, Dimitri N.
Papantonopoulu, Katia

HONG KONG

Hong Kong
Randt, Clark Thorp, Jr.,

ISRAEL

Ramat-Gan
Aron, Roberto

Tel Aviv
Raved, Yoram

ITALY

Milan
Codurri, Maurizio
Graffer, Jacopo

Padua
Polettini, Alessandro

Rome
Apuzzo, Ernesto
Lo Faso, Giovanni

Tuscany
Monaci Naldini, Jacopo

Udine
Braggion, Antonio

JAPAN

Osaka
Kanai, Michiko

Tokyo
Grondine, Robert Francis
Gustafson, Albert Katsuaki
Sekine, Osamu

LUXEMBOURG

Luxembourg
Kremer, Christian

NEW ZEALAND

Auckland
Whale, Michael John

Wellington
Craig, David J.

NORWAY

Oslo
Erno, Torkel
Keiserud, Erik

Stavanger
Koppang, Baard Ivar

PANAMA

Panama
Arias, Ramon Ricardo

PERU

Lima
Chabaneix, Jean Paul
Gotuzzo, Gianina
Lee, Henry
Lozano-Merino, Raul Santiago

PHILIPPINES

Legaspi Village
Valdez, Melva Evangelista

Makati City
Mamuric, Jose Roberto Lota

Manila
Siguion-Reyna, Leonardo

PORTUGAL

Lisbon
Ferreira, Anabela Gonçalves
Martins, Belarmino Gonçalves

Porto
Pessanha, Tomas Vasconcelos

REPUBLIC OF KOREA

Seoul
Jin, Hong Ki

ROMANIA

Bucharest
Angelo, Florentina Daniela
Predoiu, Cătălin Marian

SAUDI ARABIA

Riyadh
Taylor, Frederick William, Jr., (Fritz Taylor)

SCOTLAND

Edinburgh
Hook, Christian Robert Malnachtan

SINGAPORE

Singapore
Ackermann, Reudiger Friederich

SLOVAKIA

Bratislva
Marek, Premysl

SOUTH AFRICA

Johannesburg
Lomax, Ross Donald
Mackenzie, Janet Lynne

Sandton
Cron, Kevin Richard
Pinnock, David Bruce

SPAIN

Barcelona
Marin, Daniel
Pallares, Ignacio

Bilbao
Armesto, Ana

Madrid
Benavides, Alfonso
Blanco, Raquel
de la Calle, José Antonio
Hunter, George S.

SWEDEN

Orebro
Dicksen, Dennis Johansson

Stockholm
Bergqvist, Trine Osen
Blomberg, Erik Bïson

SWITZERLAND

Bern
Wyss, Lukas F.

Geneva
De Pfyffer, Andre
Equey, Robert

Lausanne
Reeves, Simon

Zürich
Kanzig, David Frederic
Ladner, Thomas F.
Lutz, Martin J.
Wuerzner, Andrea

THAILAND

Bangkok
Periera, Santhapat
Smuthranond, Archava
Vickery, Harold Kirby, Jr.,

UKRAINE

Kiev
Kolesnyk, Oleg Ivanovich

VENEZUELA

Caracas
Eljuri, Elisabeth

ADDRESS UNPUBLISHED

Atchison, Rodney Raymond
Beattie, Charles Robert, III,
Berry, Robert Worth
Bloom, Charles Joseph
Bloomer, Harold Franklin, Jr.,
Brodhead, David Crawmer
Brown, Charles Dodgson
Clabaugh, Elmer Eugene, Jr.,
Cornish, Jeannette Carter
Friedlander, James Stuart
Giusti, William Roger
Gold, Martin Elliott
Gora, Daniel Martin
Hagelien, Per
Hagerman, Michael Charles
Harshman, Raymond Brent
Hernandez, David N(icholas)
Idzik, Daniel Ronald
Kahn, Laurence Michael
Kallgren, Edward Eugene
Kaufman, James Jay
Klaus, Charles
Kunkel, David Nelson
Lalla, Thomas Rocco, Jr.,
Landy, Lisa Anne
Lilly, Thomas Gerald
Locke, William Henry
Marker, Marc Linthacum
O'Dell, Joan Elizabeth
Oz, Yilmaz
Padilla, James Earl
Pallot, Joseph Wedeles
Phillips, Leo Harold, Jr.,
Pratt, Robert Windsor
Reath, George, Jr.,
Rodenburg, Clifton Glenn
Samuels, Janet Lee
Schultz, Dennis Bernard
Schwartz, Arthur Jay
Seifert, Stephen Wayne
Simmons, Raymond Hedelius
Smagula, John William
Stone, Andrew Grover
Swinnen, Benoit M.J.
von Sauers, Joseph F.
Watson, John Michael
Weil, Peter Henry
Wessling, Robert Bruce
Yoskowitz, Irving Benjamin

COMMUNICATIONS

UNITED STATES

ARIZONA

Phoenix
Silverman, Alan Henry

Tucson
Meehan, Michael Joseph

CALIFORNIA

El Cajon
Lee, Ernest J., Sr.,

Los Angeles
Lederman, Bruce Randolph

San Diego
Eger, John Mitchell

San Francisco
Tobin, James Michael

COLORADO

Denver
Hubbard, Melissa
Quiat, Marshall

CONNECTICUT

Darien
Beach, Stephen Holbrook

Hartford
Knickerbocker, Robert Platt, Jr.,

DISTRICT OF COLUMBIA

Washington
Bell, Stephen Robert
Besozzi, Paul Charles
Blake, Jonathan Dewey
Blumenfeld, Jeffrey
Brinkmann, Robert Joseph
Brown, Richard L.
Carome, Patrick Joseph
Casserly, James Lund
Cohen, Edward Barth
Cox, Kenneth Allen
Davidson, Tom William
Disenhaus, Helen Elizabeth
Fisher, Benjamin Chatburn
Hammerman, Edward Scott
Harris, Scott Blake
Heckman, Jerome Harold
Lane, John Dennis
Lowe, Randall Brian
Malone, William Robert
Marks, Herbert Edward
Marks, Richard Daniel
McAvoy, John Joseph
McReynolds, Mary Armilda
Michaels, Gary David
Price, Richard Edward
Quale, John Carter
Rhyne, Sidney White
Russo, Roy R.
Salsbury, Michael H.
Sanford, Bruce William
Shepard, Julian Leigh
Spector, Phillip Louis
Tannenwald, Peter
Wiley, Richard Emerson
Woodworth, Ramsey Lloyd

Larchmont
Davis, Wendell, Jr.,

Long Island City
Wanderman, Susan Mae

New York
Black, Louis Engleman
Einhorn, David Allen
Epstein, Michael Alan
Fricklas, Michael David
Glazer, Steven Donald
Jaglom, Andre Richard
Kinney, Stephen Hoyt, Jr.,
Lefkowitz, Howard N.
Prochnow, Thomas Herbert
Spiegel, Jerrold Bruce
Taylor, Job, III,
Zammit, Joseph Paul

Poughkeepsie
Taphorn, Joseph Bernard

NORTH CAROLINA

Charlotte
Linker, Raymond Otho, Jr.,

OHIO

Cleveland
Ernst, Christopher Mark
Kahrl, Robert Conley
Stovsky, Michael David

Columbus
Rector, Susan Darnell

PENNSYLVANIA

Conshohocken
Bramson, Robert Sherman

New Buffalo
Cramer, John McNaight

Philadelphia
Damsgaard, Kell Marsh
Simkanich, John Joseph
Wilf, Frederic Marshal

Pittsburgh
Salpietro, Frank Gugliotta
Silverman, Arnold Barry

TEXAS

Austin
Borden, Diana Kimball

Houston
Anani, Tarig
Toedt, D(ell) C(harles), III,
Zager, Steven Mark

Humble
Gaffney, Richard Cook

UTAH

Salt Lake City
Ockey, Ronald J.
Wagner, Mark Alan

VIRGINIA

Alexandria
Greigg, Ronald Edwin
Wieder, Bruce Terrill

Arlington
Doyle, Gerard Francis

Haymarket
Frank, Jacob

Richmond
Whitlock, Julie Marie

WASHINGTON

Seattle
Prentke, Richard Ottesen

WISCONSIN

Milwaukee
O'Shaughnessy, James Patrick

AUSTRALIA

Sydney
Winkler, Nicholas Gary

AUSTRIA

Vienna
Frank, Alix

DENMARK

Copenhagen
Lokdam, Lars

ENGLAND

London
Rawkins, Jason W.D.
Turner, Mark McDougall

GERMANY

Frankfurt
Baeumer, Ulrich J.P.
Wolff, Florian
Wuermeling, Ulrich Urban

Hamburg
Dieselhorst, Jochen

GREECE

Athens
Moutzouridou, Victoria G.

JAPAN

Osaka
Iijima, Ayumu

SPAIN

Barcelona
Agustinoy Guilayn, Albert
Darna, Pablo
Fernandez, Rodolfo

Madrid
Vasquez, Gerard Manuel

SWITZERLAND

Lausanne
Reeves, Simon

Zürich
Auf der Maur, Rolf

ADDRESS UNPUBLISHED

Dupree, David H.
Fischer, David Jon
Gora, Daniel Martin
Hagerman, Michael Charles
Keys, Jerry Malcom
Kunkel, David Nelson
McCobb, John Bradford, Jr.,
Miller, John Eddie
Pear, Charles E., Jr.,
Stone, Andrew Grover
Young, John Hardin
Zaharoff, Howard George
Zimmerman, Jean

CONDEMNATION

UNITED STATES

ALASKA

Anchorage
Weinig, Richard Arthur

CALIFORNIA

El Segundo
Schimmenti, John Joseph

Los Angeles
Kanner, Gideon
Salvaty, Benjamin Benedict

Oakland
Hausrath, Les A.

Walnut Creek
Skaggs, Sanford Merle

COLORADO

Colorado Springs
Sheffield, Alden Daniel, Jr.,

FLORIDA

Boca Raton
Golis, Paul Robert

Jacksonville
Boyer, Tyrie Alvis

Orlando
Harris, Gordon H.
Spoonhour, James Michael

Tallahassee
Varn, Wilfred Claude

Tampa
Buell, Mark Paul
DeVaney, Donna Brookes

GEORGIA

Atlanta
Janney, Donald Wayne

Smyrna
Seigler, Michael Edward

HAWAII

Honolulu
Bunn, Robert Burgess

ILLINOIS

Chicago
Redmond, Richard Anthony

INDIANA

Merrillville
Miller, Richard Allen

Vincennes
Emison, Ewing Rabb, Jr.,

KANSAS

Topeka
Hamilton, John Richard

KENTUCKY

Louisville
Cohen, Edwin Louis
Schecter, Benjamin Seth

LOUISIANA

Lafayette
Davidson, James Joseph, III,

MARYLAND

Abingdon
Wolf, Martin Eugene

Greenbelt
Brugger, George Albert

MICHIGAN

Detroit
Ward, George Edward

Muskegon
Briggs, John Mancel, III,

MINNESOTA

Minneapolis
Barnard, Allen Donald

Saint Paul
Spencer, David James

MISSOURI

Kansas City
Smithson, Lowell Lee

Saint Louis
Riggio, Nicholas Jospeh, Sr.,
Wilson, Margaret Bush

NEBRASKA

Lincoln
Blake, William George

NEW JERSEY

Allendale
Rosenblum, Edward G.

Roseland
Drasco, Dennis J.

NEW MEXICO

Albuquerque
Salazar, John Paul

NEW YORK

New York
Rikon, Michael

Poughkeepsie
Wallace, Herbert Norman

Syracuse
Young, Douglas Howard

NORTH CAROLINA

Greensboro
Cahoon, Robert Strange

Raleigh
Davis, Thomas Hill, Jr.,

OREGON

Portland
Maloney, Robert E., Jr.,

PENNSYLVANIA

Pittsburgh
Hess, Emerson Garfield
Richards, John Thomas, Jr.,

West Chester
Ewing, Joseph Neff, Jr.,

SOUTH CAROLINA

Columbia
Babcock, Keith Moss

TENNESSEE

Knoxville
Hartsoe, Mark Charles

TEXAS

Houston
Bellatti, Lawrence Lee
Kendall, Frank Russell, Sr.,
Montague, H. Dixon

San Antonio
Wallis, Ben Alton, Jr.,

VERMONT

Burlington
Frank, Joseph Elihu

VIRGINIA

Leesburg
Price, Stephen Conwell

Richmond
Ellis, Andrew Jackson, Jr.,
Pearsall, John Wesley

Springfield
Costello, Daniel Brian

WASHINGTON

Seattle
Daudt, Michael D.

ADDRESS UNPUBLISHED

Barry, David F.
Hall, Ralph Carr
Martin, Gary Duncan
McCormick, Homer L., Jr.,

CONSTITUTIONAL

UNITED STATES

ALABAMA

Birmingham
Hopkins, Harry L.

ALASKA

Anchorage
Lerman, Averil

ARIZONA

Tucson
Esposito, Joseph Louis

CALIFORNIA

Berkeley
Ogg, Wilson Reid

Los Angeles
Arkoz, David X.
Cleary, William Joseph, Jr.,
Fisher, Barry Alan
Trygstad, Lawrence Benson

Oakland
Bryant, Arthur H.

San Francisco
Hilton, Stanley Goumas
Rossmann, Antonio

Santa Monica
Pizzulli, Francis Cosmo Joseph

COLORADO

Colorado Springs
McCready, Guy Michael

Denver
Corry, Robert J., Jr.,
Nier, Harry Kaufman

DELAWARE

Wilmington
Mekler, Arlen B.

DISTRICT OF COLUMBIA

Washington
Ayer, Donald Belton
Bernabei, Lynne Ann
Brame, Joseph Robert, III,
Burchfield, Bobby Roy
Poe, Luke Harvey, Jr.,
Reid, Inez Smith

FLORIDA

Boca Raton
Kassner, Herbert Seymore

Miami
Horn, Mark
Jimenez, Marcos Daniel
Rashkind, Paul Michael

Palm Bay
Tietig, Edward Chester

Tampa
Blau, Jeffrey Alan
Thomas, Gregg Darrow

GEORGIA

Atlanta
Bramlett, Jeffrey Owen
Schroeder, Eric Peter
Shapiro, George Howard
Zell, Glenn

Tucker
Tewes, R. Scott
Wheeler, Edd Dudley

IDAHO

Hailey
Youngblood, Deborah Sue

ILLINOIS

Arlington Heights
Giampietro, Wayne Bruce

Chicago
Wade, Edwin Lee

Joliet
Lenard, George Dean

INDIANA

Indianapolis
Korin, Offer

Terre Haute
Bopp, James, Jr.,
Coleson, Richard Eugene

KANSAS

Hutchinson
Chalfant, William Young

KENTUCKY

Louisville
Lilly, Nolte Scott Ament

LOUISIANA

Baton Rouge
Anderson, Lawrence Robert, Jr.,

Riddick, Winston Wade, Sr.,

MAINE

Lewiston
Burke, Edmund James, III,

MASSACHUSETTS

Florence
Park, Beverly Goodman

MICHIGAN

Ann Arbor
Niehoff, Leonard Marvin

Detroit
Schochet, P(aula) Rivka

Southfield
Sullivan, Robert Emmet, Jr.,

MINNESOTA

Crystal
Reske, Steven David

Minneapolis
Rothenberg, Elliot Calvin

MISSOURI

Kansas City
Owens, Dennis James Campbell
Sader, Neil Steven

NEBRASKA

Omaha
Runge, Patrick Richard

NEW JERSEY

Greenwich
Lane, Mark

Montclair
Gutman, Richard Martin

Newark
Salyer, John Clark, IV,

NEW MEXICO

Ruidoso
Mitchell, Gary Colas

NEW YORK

Glen Cove
Lewis, Felice Flanery

New York
Bamberger, Michael Albert
Buckley, Susan
Collins, Wayne Dale
Conboy, Kenneth
Davidson, George Allan
Glekel, Jeffrey Ives
Greilsheimer, James Gans
Gruen, Michael Stephan
Levitan, David M(aurice)

NORTH CAROLINA

Raleigh
Kurtz, Howard Arthur

OHIO

Cleveland
Berger, Sanford Jason

Columbus
McDermott, Kevin R.

OKLAHOMA

Edmond
Lester, Andrew William

Oklahoma City
Cantrell, Charles L.

OREGON

Portland
Byrne, Gregory William
Hinkle, Charles Frederick

PENNSYLVANIA

Blue Bell
Elliott, John Michael

Glenside
Mermelstein, Jules Joshua

New Cumberland
Yakowicz, Vincent X

Philadelphia
Feirson, Steven B.

Pittsburgh
Pushinsky, Jon

SOUTH CAROLINA

Aiken
Pearce, Richard Lee

TENNESSEE

Clarksville
Love, Michael Joseph

Fayetteville
Dickey, John Harwell

TEXAS

Austin
Bray, Austin Coleman, Jr.,
Hamilton, Dagmar Strandberg
Weddington, Sarah Ragle

Dallas
Gibson, John Wheat

Eldorado
Kosub, James Albert

Fort Worth
Sharpe, James Shelby

Galveston
Vie, George William, III,

VERMONT

Montpelier
Putter, David Seth

VIRGINIA

Alexandria
Hirschkop, Philip Jay

Mc Lean
Olson, William Jeffrey

Newport News
Thro, William Eugene

Richmond
Freeman, George Clemon, Jr.,
Ryland, Walter H.

WASHINGTON

Seattle
Johnson, Bruce Edward Humble
Muenster, John Rolfing

WISCONSIN

Milwaukee
Shriner, Thomas L., Jr.,

MEXICO

Mexicali
Vega, Alonso

PERU

Lima
Quiroga-Leon, Anibal

ADDRESS UNPUBLISHED

Albin, Barry G.
Boyd, Thomas Marshall
Diamond, Paul Steven
Gersch, Charles Frant
Grutman, Jewel Humphrey
Harp, Chadwick Allen
Howard, John Wayne
Siporin, Sheldon
Swann, Barbara
Twardy, Stanley Albert, Jr.,
Waxman, Seth Paul

CONSTRUCTION

UNITED STATES

ALABAMA

Eufaula
Twitchell, E(rvin) Eugene

Montgomery
McFadden, Frank Hampton
Wood, James Jerry

ALASKA

Anchorage
Dickson, Robert Jay
Evans, Charles Graham
Willard-Jones, Donna C.

ARIZONA

Phoenix
Calderon, Ernest
Lyons, George Harris

CALIFORNIA

El Segundo
Muhlbach, Robert Arthur

Glendale
MacDonald, Kirk Stewart

Los Angeles
Cathcart, Robert James
Lund, James Louis
Moloney, Stephen Michael
Pieper, Darold D.
Robison, William Robert

Marina Del Rey
Smolker, Gary Steven

Oakland
Johnson, Kenneth F.
Leslie, Robert Lorne

Pasadena
Hunt, Gordon

Redwood City
Wilhelm, Robert Oscar

San Diego
Bleiler, Charles Arthur

San Francisco
Berning, Paul Wilson
Heilbron, David M(ichael)
Koeppel, John A.

San Pedro
Russell, Thomas Arthur

Santa Ana
Ingalsbe, William James

Sunnyvale
Thornton, D. Whitney, II,

Walnut Creek
Cameron, Mark Alan

Westlake Village
Weissman, Robert Allen

COLORADO

Aurora
Staelin, Earl Hudson

Colorado Springs
Gefreh, Paul Thomas

Denver
Bain, James William
Donnelly, Frederick James
Jablonski, James Arthur

Highlands Ranch
Hagen, Glenn W.

CONNECTICUT

Hartford
Donnell, Brian James
Pepe, Louis Robert
Rosengren, David E.

West Hartford
Dowling, Vincent John

Westport
Lindskog, David Richard

DISTRICT OF COLUMBIA

Washington
Alexander, Allison L(eslie)
Kent, Alan Heywood
Lifschitz, Judah
Mitchell, Roy Shaw
Ness, Andrew David
Perlman, Matthew Saul
Schor, Laurence
Webber, Richard John
West, Joseph D.

FLORIDA

Altamonte Springs
Gunewardene, Roshani Mala

Fort Lauderdale
Bustamante, Nestor

Miami
DeMaria, Joseph Angelo
Greenleaf, Walter Franklin
Hajek, Robert J., Sr.,
Hogg, Jesse Stephen
Jeffrey, Douglas Jason

Orlando
Harris, Gordon H.
Nadeau, Robert Bertrand, Jr.,
Neal, Thomas Frederick
Weiss, Christopher John
Wilson, William Berry

Palm Beach Gardens
Seidman, Jennifer L.

Pompano Beach
Shulmister, M(orris) Ross

Sarasota
Christopher, William Garth
Lamia, Christine Edwards
Phillips, Elvin Willis

Tallahassee
Anderson, Bruce Paige

Tampa
Campbell, Richard Bruce

GEORGIA

Atlanta
Abernathy, Thomas Edwards, IV,
Croft, Terrence Lee
Genberg, Ira
Hinchey, John William
Jones, Glower Whitehead
Sibley, Horace Holden
Smith, George Anthony
Sweeney, Neal James
Wright, Frederick Lewis, II,

Madison
DuBose, Charles Wilson

Saint Simons Island
Thau, William Albert, Jr.,

HAWAII

Honolulu
Deaver, Phillip Lester
Freed, Michael Leonard
Iwai, Wilfred Kiyoshi
Kobayashi, Bert Takaaki, Jr.,
Kupchak, Kenneth Roy

Paia
Richman, Joel Eser

ILLINOIS

Chicago
Angst, Gerald L.
Bormes, James X.
Doyle, John Robert
Hummel, Gregory William
Jacobson, Richard Joseph
Jahns, Jeffrey
Kikoler, Stephen Philip
Kim, Michael Charles
Nowacki, James Nelson
Schoumacher, Bruce Herbert
Vojcanin, Sava Alexander
Vree, Roger Allen

Crystal Lake
Franz, William Mansur

Oakbrook Terrace
Tibble, Douglas Clair

Schaumburg
Frano, Andrew Joseph

INDIANA

Indianapolis
Albright, Terrill D.
Lowe, Louis Robert, Jr.,

South Bend
Reinke, William John

IOWA

Des Moines
Koehn, William James
Rickert, Brian Patrick

Sioux City
Fredregill, Alan

KENTUCKY

Louisville
Cohen, Edwin Louis
Ethridge, Larry Clayton
Schecter, Benjamin Seth
Swyers, Walter John, Jr.,

LOUISIANA

New Orleans
Katz, Morton Howard
Sinor, Howard Earl, Jr.,
Wright, William Everard, Jr.,

MARYLAND

Cockeysville
Barnes, Peter

Columbia
Jacobs, William Michael

Frederick
Beam, Bethamy N.

MASSACHUSETTS

Boston
DiNicola, John W., II,
Edwards, Richard Lansing
James, Paul M.
Meserve, William George

Norwell
Moriarty, Paul J.

Worcester
Moschos, Michael Christos

MICHIGAN

Birmingham
McCarthy, Daniel J.

Burton
Breczinski, Michael Joseph

Detroit
Candler, James Nall, Jr.,

Southfield
Antone, Nahil Peter

Troy
Alber, Phillip George

MINNESOTA

Edina
Landrum, Michael Arthur

Minneapolis
Bruner, Philip Lane
Eck, George Gregory
Forneris, Jeanne M.
Hart, Buster Clarence

Saint Paul
Hassett, Timothy John

MISSISSIPPI

Jackson
Purdy, William Richard
Scanlon, Pat H.
Wise, Robert Powell

MISSOURI

Saint Louis
Colagiovanni, Joseph Alfred, Jr.,
Hetlage, Robert Owen
Kelly, Maura Patricia
Weishaar, Aaron G.

NEBRASKA

Omaha
Lash, Douglas Steven

NEVADA

Las Vegas
Kirsch, Lynn

NEW HAMPSHIRE

Manchester
Hanna, Katherine Merritt
Stebbins, Henry Blanchard

NEW JERSEY

Cherry Hill
Shapiro, Richard Allen

Cranford
De Luca, Thomas George

Fair Lawn
Delloff, Stefan T.

Florham Park
Calabrese, Arnold J.

Morristown
Rose, Robert Gordon

Mountain Lakes
Daniel, Royal Thomas, III,

Roseland
Drasco, Dennis J.
Smith, Wendy Hope

Scotch Plains
Klock, John Henry

Woodbridge
Estis, Dennis Arnold

NEW MEXICO

Albuquerque
Bohnhoff, Henry M.

NEW YORK

Gouverneur
Leader, Robert John

Greenvale
Halper, Emanuel B(arry)

Hawthorne
Traub, Richard Kenneth

Ithaca
Patte, George David, Jr.,

Latham
Couch, Mark Woodworth

Malverne
Benigno, Thomas Daniel

New Rochelle
Stevens, Roger Ross

New York
Berman, Tony
Brown, Paul M.
Eiseman, Neal Martin
Grassi, Joseph F.
Herbst, Todd L.
Sigmond, Carol Ann
Silverman, Arthur Charles
Terry, James Joseph, Jr.,
Witherwax, Charles Halsey
Zoeller, Donald J.

White Plains
Colistra, Brian William

NORTH CAROLINA

Charlotte
Sink, Robert C.
Stephens, Robert C.

Raleigh
Davis, Thomas Hill, Jr.,

Winston Salem
Humphrey, Dudley

OHIO

Akron
Lombardi, Frederick McKean
Ruport, Scott Hendricks

Cincinnati
Bissinger, Mark Christian
Parker, R. Joseph

Cleveland
Kahn, Scott Harris
Kilbane, Thomas Stanton
McAndrews, James Patrick
Sogg, Wilton Sherman
Solomon, Randall Lee

Columbus
Eichenberger, Jerry Alan
Hutson, Jeffrey Woodward
O'Shaughnessy, Christopher T.

Dayton
Hadley, Robert James
Hayslip, Michael Warren
Rogers, Richard Hunter

OKLAHOMA

Broken Arrow
Jones, Ronald Lee

Muskogee
Frix, Paige Lane

PENNSYLVANIA

Philadelphia
Auerbach, Sheryl Lynn
Donner, Henry Jay
Jurewicz, Richard Michael
Miller, Henry Franklin
Roberts, Carl Geoffrey
Segal, Robert Martin

Pittsburgh
Doty, Robert Walter
Douglass, Kevin K.
Farley, Andrew Newell
Mall, James Richard
Picadio, Anthony Peter
Stroyd, Arthur Heister

RHODE ISLAND

Providence
Bulman, John

SOUTH CAROLINA

Charleston
Leath, William Jefferson, Jr.,

Florence
Lee, Robert E.

Hilton Head Island
Laughlin, Drew Alan

TENNESSEE

Collierville
Scroggs, Larry Kenneth

Memphis
Carter, Richard Murrell
Harvey, Albert C.
Hunt, Sean Antone
Soefker, Curt Reid

TEXAS

Austin
Davis, Robert Larry
Greig, Brian Strother
Hile, Richard C.

Bastrop
Van Gilder, Derek Robert

Dallas
Doke, Marshall J., Jr.,

Flower Mound
Hunt, David Ford

Fort Worth
Crumley, John Walter

Houston
Bellatti, Lawrence Lee
Bridges, David Manning
Diaz-Arrastia, George Ravelo
Van Kerrebrook, Mary Alice
Walton, Dan Gibson

Richardson
Austin, Ann Sheree

San Antonio
Goff, Colleen Mullen
Javore, Gary William
Wachsmuth, Robert William

UTAH

Salt Lake City
Anderson, Robert Monte
Slaughter, David Wayne
Verhaaren, Harold Carl

VIRGINIA

Charlottesville
Jones, Christopher Andrew

Chester
Connelly, Colin Charles
Gray, Charles Robert

Fairfax
Arnold, William McCauley

Mc Lean
Molineaux, Charles Borromeo
Stump, John Sutton

Roanoke
Barnhill, David Stan

Vienna
Stearns, Frank Warren
Titus, Bruce Earl

WASHINGTON

Issaquah
Oles, Stuart Gregory

Olympia
Scuderi, Joseph

Seattle
Boman, Marc Allen
Daudt, Michael D.
Murray, Michael Kent
Petrie, Gregory Steven
Prentke, Richard Ottesen
Squires, William Randolph, III,
Whitehead, James Fred, III,
Yalowitz, Kenneth Gregg

Spokane
Sullivan, Patrick Arthur

Tacoma
Wesch, Angelia DeAn

WISCONSIN

Brookfield
Voss, Kenneth Erwin

Evansville
Decker, John Robert

Janesville
Steil, George Kenneth, Sr.,

Milwaukee
Clark, James Richard
Rieselbach, Allen Newman

WYOMING

Wheatland
Hunkins, Raymond Breedlove

TERRITORIES OF THE UNITED STATES

PUERTO RICO

Old San Juan
Weinstein-Bacal, Stuart Allen

CANADA

ONTARIO

Toronto
Heintzman, Thomas G.

AUSTRALIA

Melbourne
Delkousis, Jim

Sydney
Wong, Christopher Wai C.

DENMARK

Copenhagen
Tarnoe, Rune

Valby
Hansen, Johannus Egholm

ENGLAND

London
Bishop, John Maurice

Reigate
Sheridan, Peter Louis

GERMANY

Düsseldorf
Mütze, Michael W.

GREECE

Athens
Georgacopulos, Dimitris Haralambos

PORTUGAL

Lisbon
Melo, Pedro

SPAIN

Madrid
Blanco, Raquel
Mantilla-Serrano, Fernando

TAIWAN

Taipei
Hsiao, Joanne Y.

ADDRESS UNPUBLISHED

Bakkensen, John Reser
Dondanville, John Wallace
Hall-Barron, Deborah
Hartley, Karen Jeanette
Jaynes, Gordon Leslie
Klein, Linda Ann
Kunkel, David Nelson
Reiss, Jerome
Schultz, Dennis Bernard
Stinchfield, John Edward

CONSUMER CREDIT. *See* **Commercial, consumer.**

CONTRACTS. *See* **Commercial, contracts.**

CORPORATE, GENERAL

UNITED STATES

ALABAMA

Anniston
Woodrow, Randall Mark

Birmingham
Avant, Grady, Jr.,
Baker, David Remember
Barber, Peter Earl
Brooke, William Wade
Gamble, Joseph Graham, Jr.,
Garner, Robert Edward Lee
Hagefstration, John E., Jr.,
Lacy, Alexander Shelton
Martin, Arthur Lee, Jr.,
Rotch, James E.
Stewart, Joseph Grier
Theibert, Richard Wilder
Trimmier, Charles Stephen, Jr.,
Wilson, James Charles, Jr.,
Woodall, Paul Oliver, Jr.,

Dadeville
Adair, Charles Robert, Jr.,

Dothan
Huskey, Dow Thobern

Guntersville
McLaughlin, Jeffrey Rex

Mobile
Murchison, David Roderick
Oldweiler, Thomas Patrick

Montgomery
Gregory, William Stanley
Wood, James Jerry

Northport
Allen, Randy Lee

Opelika
Samford, Yetta Glenn, Jr.,

ALASKA

Anchorage
Ebell, C(ecil) Walter
Rosston, Richard Mark
Willard-Jones, Donna C.

ARIZONA

Kingman
Basinger, Richard Lee

Mesa
Smith, Kenneth M.

Paradise Valley
Tubman, William Charles

Phoenix
Bixby, David Michael
Case, David Leon
Clarke, David Alan
Coppersmith, Sam
Curzon, Thomas Henry
Dunipace, Ian Douglas
Hay, John Leonard
Hienton, James Robert
Mangum, John K.
Martori, Joseph Peter
McRae, Hamilton Eugene, III,
McRae, Stephanie A.
Olson, Kevin Lory
Perry, Lee Rowan
Pidgeon, Steven D.
Pietzsch, Michael Edward
Thompson, Terence William
Tomback, Jay Loren
Warner, Teddy Fleming
Williams, Quinn Patrick

Prescott
Madden, Paul Robert

Scottsdale
Lindgren, D(erbin) Kenneth, Jr.,

Tempe
Moya, Patrick Robert

Tucson
Pace, Thomas M.
Staubitz, Arthur Frederick
Tindall, Robert Emmett

ARKANSAS

Fayetteville
Pettus, E. Lamar

Little Rock
Anderson, Philip Sidney
Campbell, George Emerson
Marshall, William Taylor
Nelson, Edward Sheffield

Newport
Thaxton, Marvin Dell

Pine Bluff
Ramsay, Louis Lafayette, Jr.,

Warren
Claycomb, Hugh Murray

CALIFORNIA

Alamo
Fleisher, Steven M.

Auburn
Moglen, Leland Louis

Bakersfield
Tornstrom, Robert Ernest

Berkeley
Woodhouse, Thomas Edwin

Beverly Hills
Bordy, Michael Jeffrey
Schiff, Gunther Hans

Burbank
McNally, Gerald, Jr.,

Burlingame
Denten, Christopher Peter

Chino Hills
Pearson, April Virginia

Claremont
Ferguson, Cleve Robert

Costa Mesa
Daniels, James Walter
Marshall, Ellen Ruth
Schaaf, Douglas Allan
Tarwater, Jeremy Ryan

Cypress
Olschwang, Alan Paul

Downey
Tompkins, Dwight Edward

El Segundo
Hunter, Larry Dean
Pearce, Harry Jonathan

Escondido
Mayer, James Hock

Foothill Ranch
Weiss, Sherman David

Foster City
Lonnquist, George Eric

Fremont
Kitta, John Noah

Fresno
Ewell, A. Ben, Jr.,

Irvine
Bastiaanse, Gerard C.
Beard, Ronald Stratton
Black, William Rea
Doan, Gerald Xuyen Van
Wintrode, Ralph Charles

La Jolla
Kirchheimer, Arthur E(dward)

Laguna Niguel
Apke, Thomas Michael

Long Beach
Cockriel, Stephen Eugene
Wilson, Walter Joseph
Wise, George Edward

Los Angeles
Adams, Thomas Merritt
Allred, Gloria Rachel
Barnes, Willie R.
Barton, David Joseph
Basile, Paul Louis, Jr.,
Baumgarten, Ronald Neal
Bernacchi, Richard Lloyd
Blencowe, Paul Sherwood
Boehmer, Richard A.
Boxer, Lester
Camp, James Carroll
Carrey, Neil
Carter, Bret Robert
Castro, Leonard Edward
Clark, R(ufus) Bradbury
Costales, Marco Daniel
De Brier, Donald Paul
de Castro, Hugo Daniel
Dienes, Louis Robert
Fein, Ronald Lawrence
Forster, Jonathan Shawn
Gilhuly, Peter Martin
Grush, Julius Sidney
Haakh, Gilbert Edward
Hahn, Elliott Julius
Heyler, Grover Ross
Hyman, Milton Bernard
Katz, Jason Lawrence
Kupietzky, Moshe J.
Lederman, Bruce Randolph
Lesser, Joan L.
May, Lawrence Edward
McKinzie, Carl Wayne
McLane, Frederick Berg
Miyoshi, David Masao
Morgan, R. Gregory
Niemeth, Charles Frederick
Parsky, Gerald Lawrence
Pircher, Leo Joseph

Byrne, Granville Bland, III,
Calhoun, Scott Douglas
Cargill, Robert Mason
Chisholm, Tommy
Cohen, George Leon
Davis, Frank Tradewell, Jr.,
Drucker, Michael Stuart
Durrett, James Frazer, Jr.,
Forbes, Theodore McCoy, Jr.,
Gambrell, David Henry
Ganz, Charles David
Grant, Walter Matthews
Greer, Bernard Lewis, Jr.,
Harkey, Robert Shelton
Harrold, Thomas J., Jr.,
Hawks, Barrett Kingsbury
Hoffman, Michael William
Hopkins, John David
Isaf, Fred Thomas
Izard, John
Kaufman, Mark David
Kelley, James Francis
Lackland, Theodore Howard
Leach, James Glover
Linder, Harvey Ronald
Manley, David Bott, III,
McCloud, Robert Olmsted, Jr.,
McMahon, Teri Lynn
Moderow, Joseph Robert
Moeling, Walter Goos, IV,
Morgan, Charles Russell
Ortiz, Jay Richard Gentry
Pike, Larry Samuel
Pless, Laurance Davidson
Pryor, Shepherd Green, III,
Rayis, James Y.
Sibley, Horace Holden
Sibley, James Malcolm
Silverstein, Leonard A.
Stallings, Ronald Denis
Tanenbaum, Allan Jay
Taylor, George Kimbrough, Jr.,
Tramonte, James Albert
Williams, Joel Cash
Williams, Neil, Jr.,
Wilson, James Hargrove, Jr.,
Wright, Peter Meldrim
Zabka, Sven Paul

Augusta
Lee, Lansing Burrows, Jr.,

Duluth
Sloan, Donnie Robert, Jr.,

Dunwoody
Callison, James W.

Fayetteville
Johnson, Donald Wayne

Macon
Elliott, James Sewell

Madison
DuBose, Charles Wilson

Marietta
Ahlstrom, Michael Joseph

Savannah
Searcy, William Nelson

Stone Mountain
Minter, Kendall Arthur

Tifton
Reinhardt, George Robert

HAWAII

Honolulu
Akinaka, Asa Masayoshi
Asai-Sato, Carol Yuki
Bocken, R. Charles
Case, James Hebard
Char, Vernon Fook Leong
Gay, E(mil) Laurence
Ingersoll, Richard King
Katayama, Robert Nobuichi
Keppeler, H(erbert) K(arl) Bruss
Marks, Michael J.
Miller, Clifford Joel
Nakata, Gary Kenji
Okinaga, Lawrence Shoji
Suzuki, Norman Hitoshi
Taira, Darryl M.

IDAHO

Boise
Fawcett, Charles Winton
Risch, James E.
Schild, Raymond Douglas
Whittier, Monte Ray

ILLINOIS

Alton
Hoagland, Karl King, Jr.,

Belleville
Mathis, Patrick Bischof

Buffalo Grove
Robins, Martin B.

Chicago
Anderson, Craig Edgar
Anderson, J. Trent
Barack, Peter Joseph
Barron, Harold Sheldon
Berens, Mark Harry
Berner, Robert Lee, Jr.,
Bitner, John Howard
Bogaard, Jonathan Harvey
Brizzolara, Charles Anthony
Bunge, Jonathan Gunn
Burgdoerfer, Jerry
Clemens, Richard Glenn
Clinton, Edward Xavier
Craven, George W.
Custer, Charles Francis
Davis, Scott Jonathan
Delp, Wilbur Charles, Jr.,
Docksey, John Ross
Domanskis, Alexander Rimas
Donohoe, Jerome Francis
Dunn, Edwin Rydell
Durchslag, Stephen P.
Dykstra, Paul Hopkins
Edelman, Alvin
Esrick, Jerald Paul
Felsenthal, Steven Altus
Finke, Robert Forge
Gerlits, Francis Joseph
Gerstein, Mark Douglas
Golan, Stephen Leonard
Grant, Robert Nathan
Gregg, Jon Mann
Hannah, Wayne Robertson, Jr.,
Head, Patrick James
Heatwole, Mark M.
Heist, Robert Connor
Helman, Robert Alan
Henning, Joel Frank
Henry, Robert John
Hess, Sidney J., Jr.,
Hodes, Scott
Holleb, Marshall Maynard
Holsinger, John Paul
Hormeku, Lebene Abena
Howell, R(obert) Thomas, Jr.,
Hubbard, Elizabeth Louise
Jacobson, Marian Slutz
Jenkins, James R.
Johnson, Elmer William
Johnson, Gary Thomas
Johnson, Lael Frederic
Junewicz, James J.
Kallick, David A.
Kaufman, Andrew Michael
Kelly, Charles Arthur
Kenney, Frank Deming
Kirkpatrick, John Everett
Ladd, Jeffrey Raymond
Lang, Gordon, Jr.,
Levin, Jack S.
Levin, Michael David
Lichtenstein, Nathan H.
Looman, James R.
Lubin, Donald G.
Malkin, Cary Jay
Manzoni, Charles R., Jr.,
Martin, Arthur Mead
McCann, Bradley
McCrohon, Craig
McDermott, John H(enry)
McDermott, Robert B.
McLaren, Richard Wellington, Jr.,
McMahon, Thomas Michael
McMenamin, John Robert
Metzger, Paul Thomas
Michaels, Richard Edward
Michod, Charles Louis, Jr.,
Miller, John Leed
Miller, Paul J.
Miller, Stanton Bernett
Neis, James Michael
Newman, Dennis Nathan
Niehoff, Philip John
Peter, Bernard George
Pirok, Edward Warren
Redman, Clarence Owen
Reich, Allan J.
Reicin, Ronald Ian
Rhind, James Thomas
Roberson, G. Gale, Jr.,
Robson, Douglas Spears
Rudnick, Paul David
Ruiz, Michele Ilene
Sanders, Richard Henry
Sawdey, Richard Marshall
Schilt, Margaret Anne
Schreck, Robert A., Jr.,
Schulz, Keith Donald
Shank, Suzanne Adams
Shank, William O.
Shapiro, Harold David
Shindler, Donald A.
Siegel, Howard Jerome
Silets, Harvey Marvin
Simon, John Bern
Smedinghoff, Thomas J.
Smith, Gordon Howell
Sprowl, Charles Riggs
Stassen, John Henry
Swibel, Steven Warren
Thomas, Frederick Bradley
Thomas, Stephen Paul
Wade, Edwin Lee
Wahlen, Edwin Alfred
Wander, Herbert Stanton
Weil, Andrew Lawrence
Weissman, Michael Lewis
Whalen, Wayne W.
Wilson, Clarence Sylvester, Jr.,
Wilson, Roger Goodwin

Deerfield
Oettinger, Julian Alan

Glenview
Knox, James Edwin

Gurnee
Southern, Robert Allen

Highland Park
Nelson, Richard David
Tabin, Seymour

Hinsdale
Hetke, Richard Louis

La Grange
Kerr, Alexander Duncan, Jr.,

Lafox
Seils, William George

Lake Forest
Francois, William Armand

Lake Zurich
Scott, John Joseph

Lincolnshire
Para, Gerard Albert

Long Grove
Obert, Paul Richard

Matteson
Wigell, Raymond George

Morris
Rooks, John Newton

Naperville
Fenech, Joseph Charles

North Chicago
de Lasa, José M.

Northbrook
Bohlender, Hugh Darrow
Irons, Spencer Ernest
Lapin, Harvey I.
Sernett, Richard Patrick
Wallace, Harry Leland

Northfield
Giza, David Alan

Oak Brook
Foltz, Michael Craig
O'Brien, Walter Joseph, II,
Oldfield, E. Lawrence

Oswego
May, Frank Brendan, Jr.,

Palatine
Pinderski, Jerome Wilbert, Jr.,

Park Ridge
Hegarty, Mary Frances

Peoria
Winget, Walter Winfield

Quincy
Rapp, James Anthony

Rockford
Johnson, Thomas Stuart

Rolling Meadows
Sullivan, Michael D.

Schiller Park
Congalton, Christopher William

Skokie
Gopman, Howard Z.

Springfield
Rowe, Max L.
Walbaum, Robert C.

Taylorville
Austin, Daniel William

Westchester
Castellano, Christine Marie

Wilmette
Frick, Robert Hathaway

Winnetka
Greenblatt, Ray Harris
Ryan, Robert Jeffers

INDIANA

Evansville
Harrison, Joseph Heavrin
Wallace, Keith M.

Fort Wayne
Cain, Tim J.
Dean, Laura Hansen
Lawson, Jack Wayne
Shoaff, Thomas Mitchell
Smith, Maxwell Paul

Indianapolis
Abels, Jonathan Berle
Barrett, David Olan
Blythe, James David, II,
Carlberg, James Edwin
Dorocke, Lawrence Francis
Dutton, Stephen James
Gilliland, John Campbell, II,
Hackman, Marvin Lawrence
Kahlenbeck, Howard, Jr.,
Kalsi, Swadesh Singh
Kappes, Philip Spangler
Klimek, James
Koeller, Robert Marion
Lipshaw, Jeffrey Marc
Maine, Michael Roland
Merrill, William H., Jr.,
Neff, Robert Matthew
Reynolds, Robert Hugh
Roberts, Patricia Susan
Russell, David Williams
Schneider, Michael J.
Sommer, James Koch
Strain, James Arthur
Vandivier, Blair Robert

Lafayette
Bodle, John Frederick

Merrillville
Bowman, Carol Ann

Plainfield
Carpenter, Craig M.

South Bend
Carey, John Leo
Ford, George Burt
Mintz, Richard L.
Seall, Stephen Albert

Zionsville
Bradley, Charles Harvey

IOWA

Burlington
Hoth, Steven Sergey

Davenport
Shaw, Elizabeth Orr

Des Moines
Bennett, Edward James
Brown, Paul Edmondson
Carroll, Frank James
Grefe, Rolland Eugene
Hansell, Edgar Frank
Harris, Charles Elmer
Jensen, Dick Leroy
Neumann, Gordon Richard, Jr.,
Simpson, Lyle Lee
Tipton, Sheila Kay

Iowa City
Downer, Robert Nelson

Mason City
Winston, Harold Ronald

Muscatine
Coulter, Charles Roy

Sioux City
Dykstra, Daniel D.
Madsen, George Frank

KANSAS

Bucyrus
Hoffman, John Raymond

Garden City
Pierce, Ricklin Ray

Hutchinson
Swearer, William Brooks

Leawood
Bohm, Jack Nelson

Lincoln
Crangle, Robert D.

Olathe
Taylor, L(ynn) Franklin

Overland Park
Devlin, James Richard
Sherlock, E. Todd
Steinkamp, Robert Theodore
Westerhaus, Douglas Bernard

Shawnee Mission
Snyder, Willard Breidenthal

Topeka
Conroy, Christopher S.
Elwood, H. Philip
Snyder, Brock Robert

Wichita
Arvin, Lester Cave
Depew, Spencer Long
Steele, Thomas Lee
Stephenson, Richard Ismert

KENTUCKY

Bowling Green
Catron, Stephen Barnard

Lexington
Byrne, Walter Robbins, Jr.,
Jefferson, Wade Hampton, IV,
Lester, Roy David
Terry, Joseph H.

Louisville
Buckaway, William Allen, Jr.,
Conner, Stewart Edmund
Daniel, William LaRue, II,
Fassler, Charles
Helm, T. Kennedy, III,
Mellen, Francis Joseph, Jr.,
Northern, Richard
Reed, D. Gary
Renau, Donald Irwin
Talbott, Ben Johnson, Jr.,
Tannon, Jay Middleton
Welsh, Sir Alfred John

Newport
Hartmann, Markus Uwe
Siverd, Robert Joseph

Owensboro
Miller, James Monroe

LOUISIANA

Baton Rouge
Richards, Marta Alison

Hammond
Ross, Kenneth L.

Lafayette
Breaux, Paul Joseph
Myers, Stephen Hawley
Skinner, Michael David

Lake Charles
Judice, Gregory Van

Metairie
Derbes, Albert Joseph, III,

Monroe
Curry, Robert Lee, III,
Sartor, Daniel Ryan, Jr.,

New Orleans
Abbott, Hirschel Theron, Jr.,
Allen, Frank Clinton, Jr.,
Beahm, Franklin D.
Coleman, James Julian, Jr.,
Curtis, Charles Thach, Jr.,
Fierke, Thomas Garner
Katz, Morton Howard
Marcus, Bernard
Mintz, Albert
Simon, H(uey) Paul
Snyder, Charles Aubrey
Title, Peter Stephen

Shreveport
Cox, John Thomas, Jr.,
Goodman, Robert Uhle
Hardtner, Quintin Theodore, III,

MAINE

Brunswick
Owen, H. Martyn

Portland
Ingalls, Everett Palmer, III,

Yarmouth
Webster, Peter Bridgman

MARYLAND

Baltimore
Bruner, William Gwathmey, III,
Chernow, Jeffrey Scott
Chriss, Timothy D.A.
Cook, Bryson Leitch
Curran, Robert Bruce
Dopkin, Mark Dregant
Goldman, Brian Arthur
Haines, Thomas W. W.
Hubbard, Herbert Hendrix
Johnston, Edward Allan
Mogol, Alan Jay
Moser, M(artin) Peter
Robinson, Zelig
Scriggins, Larry Palmer
Winn, James Julius, Jr.,

Bel Air
Miller, Max Dunham, Jr.,

Bethesda
Bauersfeld, Carl Frederick
Dickstein, Sidney
Hagberg, Viola Wilgus
Hendricks, John Charles
Himelfarb, Stephen Roy
Menaker, Frank H., Jr.,
Stentz, Jon William
Tanenbaum, Richard Hugh
Weinberger, Alan David

Brookeville
Johns, Warren LeRoi

Burtonsville
Covington, Marlow Stanley

Chevy Chase
Toy, Charles David

Cockeysville
Bowen, Lowell Reed

College Park
Yoho, Billy Lee

Columbia
Cooney, Teresa M.
Maseritz, Guy B.

Easton
Ikenberry, Henry Cephas, Jr.,
Maffitt, James Strawbridge

Fort Washington
Bowman, Denise Marie

Greenbelt
Jackley, Michael Dano

Leonardtown
Lacer, Alfred Antonio

Lutherville
Fascetta, Christopher Michael
Freeland, Charles

New Market
Gabriel, Eberhard John

Rockville
Axelson, Jeffrey Mark
Berryman, Richard Byron
Katz, Steven Martin
Patrick, Philip Howard
Roberts, Christopher Chalmers
Stolker, Richard Samuel

Towson
Miller, Herbert H.

Westminster
Staples, Lyle Newton

MASSACHUSETTS

Bedford
Wieand, Jeffrey Scott

Belmont
Greer, Gordon Bruce

Boston
Benjamin, William Chase
Berman, Mark Niles
Bernhard, Alexander Alfred
Bines, Harvey Ernest
Bloch, Donald Martin
Bohnen, Michael J.
Bornheimer, Allen Millard
Brountas, Paul Peter
Burr, Francis Hardon
Caccese, Michael Stephen
Engel, David Lewis
Fischer, Eric Robert
Goldman, Richard Harris
Haddad, Ernest Mudarri
Hester, Patrick Joseph
Jordan, Alexander Joseph, Jr.,
Keller, Stanley
King, William Bruce
Kreisler, David P.
Milder, Forrest David
Mooney, Michael Edward
O'Neill, Philip Daniel, Jr.,
Patterson, John de la Roche, Jr.,
Redlich, Marc
Rosenbloom, Thomas Adam
Rowe, Larry Jordan
Rudolph, James Leonard
Saltiel, David Michael
Sargeant, Ernest James
Soden, Richard Allan
Soehle, Tracy Morse
Spelfogel, Scott David
Thibeault, George Walter
Weaver, Paul David
White, Barry Bennett
Wolfson, Jeffrey Steven

Brookline
Goldenberg, Stephen Bernard

Cambridge
Connors, Frank Joseph

Framingham
Meltzer, Jay H.
Munro, Meredith Vance

Greenfield
Blanker, Alan Harlow

Holden
Price, Robert DeMille

Holyoke
Ferriter, Maurice Joseph

Lincoln
Schwartz, Edward Arthur

Longmeadow
Quinn, Andrew Peter, Jr.,

Lowell
Curtis, James Theodore

Natick
Grassia, Thomas Charles

New Bedford
Hurwitz, Barrett Alan

Newton
Frankenheim, Samuel
Glazer, Donald Wayne

Northampton
Fierst, Frederick Udell

Norwell
Mullare, T(homas) Kenwood, Jr.,

Somerville
Dash, Adam S.

Springfield
Weiss, Ronald Phillip

Tyngsboro
Farkas, Stephen Gerard

Waltham
Barnes-Brown, Peter Newton
Dickie, Robert Benjamin

Wellesley
Goglia, Charles A., Jr.,
Marx, Peter A.

Weston
Bateman, Thomas Robert

Worcester
Donnelly, James Corcoran, Jr.,
Lougee, David Louis
Silver, Marvin S.

MICHIGAN

Ada
Mc Callum, Charles Edward

Ann Arbor
Dew, Thomas Edward
Hahn, Gary Lynn
Keppelman, Nancy

Birmingham
Zelenock, Katheryne L.

Bloomfield Hills
Berlow, Robert Alan
Callow, Thomas Edward
Cunningham, Gary H.
Deron, Edward Michael
Gold, Edward David
Kasischke, Louis Walter
Klein, Coleman Eugene
Ledwidge, Patrick Joseph
LoPrete, James Hugh
Meyer, George Herbert
Williams, J. Bryan

Dearborn
Demorest, Mark Stuart

Detroit
Babcock, Charles Witten, Jr.,
Brustad, Orin Daniel
Calkins, Stephen
Collier, James Warren
Darlow, Julia Donovan
Deason, Herold McClure
Driker, Eugene
Hampton, Verne Churchill, II,
Hoops, Frederick Kurre
Howbert, Edgar Charles
Johnson, Cynthia L(e) M(ae)
Krsul, John Aloysius, Jr.,
Kuehn, George E.
Lewand, F. Thomas
McKim, Samuel John, III,
Myers, Rodman Nathaniel
Rohr, Richard David
Semple, Lloyd Ashby
Shaevsky, Mark
Sparrow, Herbert George, III,
Thoms, David Moore
Tukel, Susan
Wise, John Augustus

Dexter
Millman, Jode Susan

East Lansing
Story, Monte Robert

Farmington
Harms, Donald C.

Grand Rapids
Hogan, Thomas Patrick
Titley, Larry J.
Van Haren, W(illiam) Michael
Van't Hof, William Keith

Grosse Pointe
Cobau, John Reed

Grosse Pointe Woods
Pytell, Robert Henry

Ishpeming
Steward, James Brian

Kalamazoo
Borsos, Robert Bruce
Gordon, Edgar George

Lansing
Gallagher, Byron Patrick, Jr.,

Livonia
Hoffman, Barry Paul

Midland
Gootee, Jane Marie

Monroe
Lipford, Rocque Edward

Northville
Leavitt, Martin Jack

Plymouth
Morgan, Donald Crane

Southfield
Dawson, Dennis Ray
Jacobs, John E.
Kaplow, Robert David
Ponitz, John Allan
Silber, Albert J.

Troy
Chapman, Conrad Daniel
Dillon, Joseph Francis
Haron, David Lawrence
Robinson, Logan Gilmore

Walled Lake
Seglund, Bruce Richard

Warren
Bridenstine, Louis Henry, Jr.,

MINNESOTA

Andover
Lodge, Steven John

Bayport
Bernick, Alan E.

Bloomington
Broeker, John Milton

Duluth
Nys, John Nikki

Eden Prairie
Nilles, John Michael

Fridley
Savelkoul, Donald Charles

Hopkins
Hunter, Donald Forrest

Mankato
Gage, Fred Kelton
West, Shawna

Minneapolis
Al, Marc Andre
Anderson, Eric Scott
Bergerson, David Raymond
Chosy, James Louis
Crosby, Thomas Manville, Jr.,
Cullen, Terrance Michael
Devgun, Dharminder Singh
Erhart, John Joseph
Flom, Gerald Trossen
Forneris, Jeanne M.
Freeman, Todd Ira
Garton, Thomas William
Gottschalk, Stephen Elmer
Greener, Ralph Bertram
Hayward, Edward Joseph
Kaplan, Sheldon
Marshall, Siri Swenson
McNamara, Michael John
McNeil, Mark Sanford
Mellum, Gale Robert
Minish, Robert Arthur
Nelson, Steven Craig
Opdahl, Clark Donald
Peterson, Mark Bradley
Sanner, Royce Norman
Stageberg, Roger V.
Trucano, Michael
Yost, Gerald B.

Minnetonka
Kunert, Paul Charles
Lubben, David J.

Rochester
Orwoll, Gregg S. K.

Saint Paul
Dietz, Charlton Henry
Hassett, Timothy John
Karasov, Phyllis
Rebane, John T.
Sheahan, Michael John
Winthrop, Sherman

MISSISSIPPI

Bay Saint Louis
Bernstein, Joseph

Diamondhead
Reddien, Charles Henry, II,

Jackson
Clark, David Wright
Corlew, John Gordon
Hafter, Jerome Charles
Houston, Jamie Giles, III,
Martinez, Eduardo Vidal
Shinn, Clinton Wesley

Laurel
McKenzie, Franklin Cooper, Jr.,

Tupelo
Bush, Fred Marshall, Jr.,

MISSOURI

Ballwin
Winning, J(ohn) Patrick

Chesterfield
Fagerberg, Roger Richard
Hier, Marshall David
Pollihan, Thomas Henry

Cuba
Lange, C. William

Hillsboro
Howald, John William

Joplin
Scott, Robert Haywood, Jr.,

Kansas City
Anderson, Christopher James
Bartunek, Robert R(ichard), Jr.,
Bates, William Hubert
Becker, Thomas Bain
Brous, Thomas Richard
Crawford, Howard Allen
Egan, Charles Joseph, Jr.,
Graham, Harold Steven
Howes, Brian Thomas
Kitchin, John Joseph
Lombardi, Cornelius Ennis, Jr.,
Murguia, Ramon
Parrette, Leslie Jackson
Pemberton, Bradley Powell
Selzer, James Otto
Shughart, Donald Louis
Sparks, Stephen Stone
Spencer, Richard Henry
Stremming, Troy Alan
Whittaker, Judith Ann Cameron
Willy, Thomas Ralph

Lamar
Geddie, Rowland Hill, III,

Saint Charles
Dorsey, Mary Elizabeth
Weber, William Randolph

Saint Louis
Appleton, R. O., Jr.,
Arnold, Fred English
Barken, Bernard Allen
Berger, John Torrey, Jr.,
Boggs, Beth Clemens
Brickler, John Weise
Bryan, Henry C(lark), Jr.,
Cullen, James D.
Donaho, Timothy Lawrence, Jr.,
Dorwart, Donald Bruce
Duesenberg, Richard William
Elbert, Charles Steiner
Fogle, James Lee
Godiner, Donald Leonard
Graham, Robert Clare, III,
Guerri, William Grant
Gullborg, Peter William
Harris, Harvey Alan
Hartweger, Gordon Gravius
Inkley, John James, Jr.,
Kelly, Maura Patricia
Lattinville, Robert Henry
Lause, Michael Francis
Leontsinis, George John
Lowther, Thomas Edward
Luberda, George Joseph
Mandelstamm, Jerome Robert
McCarter, Charles Chase
Metcalfe, Walter Lee, Jr.,
Neville, James Morton
Poscover, Maury B.
Rose, Albert Schoenburg
Rubenstein, Jerome Max
Schoene, Kathleen Snyder
Schramm, Paul Howard
Tierney, Michael Edward
Watters, Richard Donald
Weishaar, Aaron G.
Withers, W. Wayne
Woodruff, Bruce Emery
Young, Marvin Oscar

MONTANA

Great Falls
Berry, Anders Taylor

Missoula
George, Alexander Andrew

NEBRASKA

Omaha
Burke, Thomas Raymond
Dolan, James Vincent
Hamann, Deryl Frederick
Krutter, Forrest Nathan
Lash, Douglas Steven
Moylan, James Harold
Stenberg, Donald B.
von Bernuth, Carl W.
Vosburg, Bruce David

NEVADA

Carson City
Crowell, Robert Lamson

Las Vegas
Brown, Joseph Wentling
Singer, Michael Howard
Wilson, Joseph Morris, III,

Reno
Fletcher, Douglas Charles

NEW HAMPSHIRE

Concord
Chamberlain, Douglas Reginald
Potter, Fred Leon
Young, Sherilyn Burnett

Laconia
Martin, Willard Gordon, Jr.,

Manchester
Harvell, Michael Cleland
Monson, John Rudolph
Rubin, Jeffrey Mark
Zachos, Kimon Stephen

Portsmouth
Shaines, Robert Arthur

NEW JERSEY

Bridgewater
Chandonnet, Sheila Wohl

Budd Lake
Webb, John Gibbon, III,

Camden
Furey, John J.
Lario, Frank M., Jr.,

Cherry Hill
Shapiro, Richard Allen

Cranbury
Iatesta, John Michael

Edgewater
Virelli, Louis James, Jr.,

Edison
Zhao, Jiwei

Englewood Cliffs
Masi, John Roger

Far Hills
Corash, Richard

Flemington
Michels, Kevin Howard

Florham Park
Hardin, William Downer
Kandravy, John

Fort Lee
Cox, Melvin Monroe

Garfield
Herpst, Robert Dix

Hackensack
Greenberg, Steven Morey
Steinbach, Harold I.

Iselin
Dornbusch, Arthur A., II,

Jersey City
Longo, Mellissa Layla

Morristown
Aspero, Benedict Vincent
Campbell, William F., III,
Gillen, James Robert
Humick, Thomas Charles Campbell
Kreindler, Peter Michael
Sherman, Sandra Brown

Mountain Lakes
Daniel, Royal Thomas, III,

New Brunswick
Scott, David Rodick

New Providence
Bernstein, Nadia J.
Chobot, John Charles

Newark
Creenan, Katherine Heras
Liftin, John Matthew

Parsippany
Borger, John Emory
Markus, Allan Lewis

Pine Brook
Henschel, John James

Pitman
Cloues, Edward Blanchard, II,

Princeton
Alford, Duncan Earl
Katzenbach, Nicholas deBelleville
Kenny, Robert
Miller, Richard Mark
Mulchinock, David Steward

Ramsey
Jalil, James Paul

Ridgewood
Harris, Micalyn Shafer

Roseland
Carella, Charles Carmine
Danzis, Colin Michael
Rosen, Charles Arthur

Saddle Brook
Pearlman, Peter Steven

Secaucus
Fitzpatrick, Harold Francis

Somerset
Green, Jeffrey C.

Somerville
Hutcheon, Peter David
Sozansky, Michael William, Jr.,

Springfield
Kraemer, Waldron

Summit
Macioce, Frank Michael
Woller, James Alan

Union
Bottitta, Joseph Anthony
Greenstein, Richard Henry
Suplee, Katherine Ann

Westfield
Gutterman, Alan J.

Woodbridge
Felton, William Raymond
Harris, Brett Rosenberg
Hoberman, Stuart A.
Schaff, Michael Frederick

Woodbury
Carter, James M.

Woodcliff Lake
Nachtigal, Patricia

NEW MEXICO

Albuquerque
Haltom, B(illy) Reid
Mann, Nathan Huguenor
Moore, Charles Loyd
Mueller, Diane Mayne
Roehl, Jerrald J.
Schuler, Alison Kay

Farmington
Morgan, Jack M.

Santa Fe
Pound, John Bennett

NEW YORK

Albany
Provorny, Frederick Alan

Amagansett
Zychick, Joel David

Amherst
Harvey, Timothy Robert

Batavia
Saleh, David John

Bedford
Atkins, Ronald Raymond

Bethpage
Burian, Lawrence J.
Lemle, Robert Spencer

Binghamton
Gerhart, Eugene Clifton

Bronx
Balka, Sigmund Ronell

Brooklyn
Johnson, Donald Raymond

Buffalo
Bailey, Thomas Charles
Day, Donald Sheldon
Fine, Robert Paul
Gardner, Arnold Burton
Greene, Robert Michael
Halpern, Ralph Lawrence
Heilman, Pamela Davis
Jasen, Matthew Joseph
Mattar, Lawrence Joseph
Mucci, Gary Louis
Oppenheimer, Randolph Carl
Rachlin, Lauren David

Cedarhurst
Klein, Irwin Grant

Corning
Hauselt, Denise Ann
Ughetta, William Casper

Dobbs Ferry
Scudder, Charles Seelye Kellgren

Fairport
Young, Thomas Paul

Farmingville
Pruzansky, Joshua Murdock

Forest Hills
Grant, Susan Irene

Glen Cove
Shields, Craig M.

Glens Falls
McMillen, Robert Stewart

Great Neck
Rockowitz, Noah Ezra

Hamburg
Glose, Herbert James
Hargesheimer, Elbert, III,

Harrison
Strone, Michael Jonathan

Hauppauge
Cummings, Anthony William

Hillsdale
Lunde, Asbjorn Rudolph

Jamestown
Beckstrom, Charles G.

Jericho
Corso, Frank Mitchell
Shulman, Madelyn R. Spatt

Lake George
Hayes, Norman Robert, Jr.,

Larchmont
Kullen, Richard Charles, Jr.,

Manhasset
Gastwirth, Stuart Lawrence

Melville
Lane, Arthur Alan

Middletown
Kossar, Ronald Steven

Mineola
Bee, Peter Aloysius
Lippe, Richard Allen
Schaffer, David Irving

Montauk
Kahn, Richard Dreyfus

New City
Fenster, Robert David

New Rochelle
Kreppel, Milton Mark
Stevens, Roger Ross

New York
Adams, George Bell
Andrus, Roger Douglas
Atkins, Peter Allan
Backman, Gerald Stephen
Bamberger, Michael Albert
Bancroft, Margaret Armstrong
Barth, Mark Harold
Bartlett, Joseph Warren
Baumgardner, John Ellwood, Jr.,
Beattie, Richard Irwin
Beck, Andrew James
Begley, Louis
Behrendt, John Thomas
Beller, Gary A.
Bender, John Charles
Benjamin, Jeff
Bennett, Scott Lawrence
Bernstein, Daniel Lewis
Berzow, Harold Steven
Beshar, Robert Peter
Bialkin, Kenneth Jules
Bick, John Alan
Bickford, Nathaniel Judson
Bicks, David Peter
Bidwell, James Truman, Jr.,
Black, Louis Engleman
Blackman, Kenneth Robert
Boehner, Leonard Bruce
Borisoff, Richard Stuart
Brauner, David A.
Bring, Murray H.
Brome, Thomas Reed
Brown, Meredith M.
Browne, Jeffrey Francis
Brumm, James Earl
Bryan, Barry Richard
Buckman, James Edward
Burak, H(oward) Paul
Burns, Arnold Irwin
Burns, John MacDougal, III,
Bushnell, George Edward, III,
Butler, Samuel Coles
Cannell, John Redferne
Carpenter, Randle Burt
Cashman, Gideon
Chappell, John Charles
Chasey, Jacqueline
Chazen, Hartley James
Chilstrom, Robert Meade
Chin, Sylvia Fung
Cho, Tai Yong
Christopherson, David Victor
Clark, Celia Rue
Cohen, Edward Herschel
Cohen, Henry Rodgin
Cohen, Howard Marvin
Cole, Lewis George
Cooper, Stephen Herbert
Corbin, Sol Neil
Cowan, Wallace Edgar
Cranney, Marilyn Kanrek
Daitz, Ronald Frederick
Davidson, Sheila Kearney
Davis, Richard Ralph
Derzaw, Richard Lawrence
Detjen, David Wheeler
Devine, Michael Buxton
Diamant, Aviva F.
Dlugoff, Marc Alan
Dorado, Marianne Gaertner
Doyle, Joseph Anthony
Drebsky, Dennis Jay
Dresner, Byron
Dubin, James Michael
Dundas, Philip Blair, Jr.,
Dunham, Wolcott Balestier, Jr.,
Dwyer, Cornelius J., Jr.,
Eagan, David Eugene
Easton, Reed W.
Eiseman, Neal Martin
Eisert, Edward Gaver
Elwin, James William, Jr.,
Epstein, Melvin
Fass, Peter Michael
Feit, Glenn M.
Feldman, Franklin
Fewell, Charles Kenneth, Jr.,
Finkelstein, Allen Lewis
Fischer, Mark David
Fisher, Robert I.
Fortenbaugh, Samuel Byrod, III,
Fox, Donald Thomas
Frank, Lloyd
Franklin, Blake Timothy
Fredericks, Wesley Charles, Jr.,
Freedman, Theodore Levy
French, John, III,
Fried, Donald David
Friedman, Bart
Friedman, Samuel Selig
Galant, Herbert Lewis
Gambro, Michael S.
Gans, Walter Gideon
Garvey, Richard Anthony
Gelfman, Peter Trustman
Getnick, Neil Victor
Gettner, Alan Frederick
Gibbons, Robert John
Gill, E. Ann
Gold, Simeon
Goldstein, Howard Sheldon
Golino, Antonio
Goltz, Susan Ackerman
Goodale, James Campbell
Gottesman, A(rthur) Edward
Grader, Scott Paul
Grant, Stephen Allen
Greenberg, Philip Alan
Greilsheimer, William Henry
Grew, Robert Ralph
Gruen, Michael Stephan
Haje, Peter Robert
Hamel, Rodolphe
Hart, Robert M.
Hartmann, Carl Joseph
Hayden, James Francis
Healy, Harold Harris, Jr.,
Heftler, Thomas E.
Henderson, Donald Bernard, Jr.,
Henderson, Kenneth Lee
Hendry, Andrew Delaney
Henze, William F., II,
Herold, Karl Guenter
Herzeca, Lois Friedman
Hiden, Robert Battaile, Jr.,
Hirsch, Barry
Hirsch, Daniel
Hirshon, Sheldon Ira
Hochman, Stephen Allen
Hodes, Robert Bernard
Hoffmann, Brian
Hooker, Wade Stuart, Jr.,
Hurlock, James Bickford
Iseman, Joseph Seeman
Jacobs, Paul
Jacobs, Reuven
Jaffe, Mark M.
Jenner, Eva C.
Jerome, John James
Jock, Paul F., II,
Jones, Douglas Wiley
Kalish, Myron
Kane, Alice Theresa
Kaplan, Carl Eliot
Kaplan, Mark Norman
Katz, Stuart Z.
Kaufman, Robert Max
Kawano, Arnold Hubert
Keene, Lonnie Stuart
Kelly, John Fleming
Kern, George Calvin, Jr.,
Kessel, Mark
Klemann, Gilbert Lacy, II,
Klink, Fredric J.
Koblenz, Michael Robert
Kobrin, Lawrence Alan
Komaroff, Stanley
Kornberg, Alan William
Krinsly, Stuart Z.
Larose, Lawrence Alfred
Leaf, Martin Norman
Lederman, Lawrence
Lefkowitz, Howard N.
Leichtling, Michael Alfred
Leonard, Edwin Deane
Levin, Ezra Gurion
Levine, Robert Jay
Lieberman, Nancy Ann
Lindenauer, Susan B(adian)
Littenberg, Michael Richard
Lovejoy, Paul Robert
Lowenfels, Lewis David
Lutringer, Richard Emil
Lutzker, Elliot Howard
Lynch, Luke Daniel, Jr.,
Lynton, Harold Stephen
Lyon, Carl Francis, Jr.,
Maney, Michael Mason
Mansour, Jana Williamson
Mantle, Raymond Allan
Marcusa, Fred Haye
Mark, Jonathan I.
Marks, Theodore Lee
Martin, George J., Jr.,
Masters, Jon Joseph
Matteson, William Bleecker
Mayerson, Sandra Elaine
Mc Inerney, Denis
McBryde, Thomas Henry
McCarthy, Robert Emmett
McDavid, William Henry
McSloy, Steven Paul
Meltzer, Roger
Merrill, George Vanderneth
Mestres, Ricardo Angelo, Jr.,
Milgrim, Roger Michael
Miller, Paul S(amuel)
Minsky, Bruce William
Modlin, Howard S.
Morgan, Frank Edward, II,
Moskin, Morton
Most, Jack Lawrence
Mullman, Michael S.
Nance, Allan Taylor
Neidell, Martin H.
Nelson, Lester
Norwitz, Trevor S.
O'Hara, Robert Sydney, Jr.,
Orce, Kenneth W.
Papernik, Joel Ira
Parent, Louise Marie
Parish, J. Michael
Passer-Muslin, Juliette Mayabelle
Pavia, George M.
Pelz, Robert Leon
Perell, Edward Andrew
Perkins, Roswell Burchard
Perlmuth, William Alan
Pettibone, Peter John
Pidot, Whitney Dean
Pierce, Morton Allen
Pisano, Vincent James
Posen, Susan Orzack
Poster, Michael Sollod
Profusek, Robert Alan
Puleo, Frank Charles
Quinn, Linda Catherine
Rabb, Bruce
Rabin, Jack
Radon, Jenik Richard
Rankin, Clyde Evan, III,
Ray, Jeanne Cullinan
Reid, Edward Snover, III,
Reilly, Conor Desmond
Robinson, Irwin Jay
Rocklen, Kathy Hellenbrand
Rodman, Leroy Eli
Romney, Richard Bruce
Rosen, Richard Lewis
Rosenblum, William F., Jr.,
Rosenzweig, Charles Leonard
Rothman, Henry Isaac
Rubin, Herbert
Rubin, Richard Allan
Rubinstein, Frederic Armand
Ruegger, Philip T., III,
Rusmisel, Stephen R.
Russo, Thomas Anthony
Ryan, J. Richard
Saunders, Mark A.
Schaab, Arnold J.
Schmidt, Joseph W.
Schneider, Howard
Schneiderman, Irwin
Seifert, Thomas Lloyd
Semaya, Francine Levitt
Senzel, Martin Lee
Serchuk, Ivan
Seward, George Chester
Seymour, Everett Hedden, Jr.,
Shapiro, Aleena Rieger
Sharpe, Robert Francis, Jr.,
Sheehan, Robert C.
Shenker, Joseph C.
Sher, Michael Lee
Siegel, Jeffrey Norton
Silkenat, James Robert
Siller, Stephen I.
Silverberg, Jay Lloyd
Skigen, Patricia Sue
Smith, Robert Everett
Smith, Thomas A.
Snow, Charles
Solomon, Stephen L.
Spanbock, Maurice Samuel
Spatt, Robert Edward
Spiegel, Jerrold Bruce
Spivak, Leonard A.
Squire, Walter Charles
Steinberg, Howard Eli
Stephenson, Alan Clements
Stringer, Ronald E.
Strom, Milton Gary
Stuart, Alice Melissa
Taub, Cathy Ellen
Taylor, Richard Trelore
Tehan, John Bashir
Teiman, Richard B.
Thaler, Craig H.
Thomas, Jeremiah Lindsay, III,
Tom, Roslyn
Tract, Marc Mitchell
Trott, Dennis C(harles)
Turner, E. Deane
Underberg, Mark Alan
Van Gundy, Gregory Frank
Versfelt, David Scott
Vig, Vernon Edward
Vogel, Howard Stanley
von Mehren, Robert Brandt
Wald, Bernard Joseph
Walker, John Lockwood
Wallace, Nora Ann
Wang, Albert Huai-En
Washburn, David Thacher
Waterman, William, Jr.,
Wattman, Malcolm Peter
Wein, Bruce J.
Weiner, Earl David
Weld, Jonathan Minot
Wenger, Daniel Eric
Whitman, Charles S., III,
Wilson, Paul Holliday, Jr.,
Witmeyer, John Jacob, III,
Wolf, Gary Wickert
Wolson, Craig Alan
Wray, Cecil, Jr.,
Yamin, Michael Geoffrey
Young, Alice
Young, John Edward
Zuckerman, Paul Herbert

Niagara Falls
Berrigan, Patrick Joseph

Oswego
Greene, Stephen Craig

Pittsford
Hampson, Thomas Meredith
Willett, Thomas Edward

Pleasantville
Ahrensfeld, Thomas Frederick

Port Washington
Satovsky, Stacey Yael

Poughkeepsie
Shatz, Phillip

Purchase
Kelly, Edmund Joseph

Riverhead
Maggipinto, V. Anthony

Rochester
Doyle, Justin P.
Goldman, Arnold Joseph
Vigdor, Justin Leonard

Rye
Dixon, Paul Edward
Roberts, Thomas Alba

Sands Point
Hoynes, Louis LeNoir, Jr.,

Scarsdale
Kanter, Carl Irwin
Perko, Kenneth Albert, Jr.,

Sherrill
Campanie, Samuel John

Somers
Keeffe, John Arthur

Southampton
Lopez, David

Syracuse
Barclay, H(ugh) Douglas
Bullock, Stephen C.
Evans, Thomas Steven
Rivette, Francis Robert
Weiss, Rhett Louis

Uniondale
Bennett, James Davison
Kestenbaum, Harold Lee

White Plains
Bender, Joel Charles
Berlin, Alan Daniel
Carlucci, Joseph P.
Feder, Robert
Silverberg, Steven Mark

NORTH CAROLINA

Asheville
Bissette, Winston Louis, Jr.,
Dillard, John Robert
Hamilton, Jackson Douglas

Burlington
Slayton, John Howard

Cary
Reinhard, Steven Ira
Taylor, Marvin Edward, Jr.,

Chapel Hill
Lilley, Albert Frederick

Charlotte
Belthoff, Richard Charles, Jr.,
Bernstein, Mark R.
Chesson, Calvin White
Culbreth, James Harold, Jr.,
Loughridge, John Halsted, Jr.,
McBryde, Neill Gregory
Monge, Jay Parry
Newitt, John Garwood, Jr.,
Preston, James Young
Pruden, James Norfleet, III,
Robinson, Russell Marable, II,
Smart, Roy Louis, III,
Smith, Laura Chalk
Taylor, David Brooke
Wagner, Kenneth Lynn
Walker, Clarence Wesley
Zeller, Michael Eugene

Cherryville
Huffstetler, Palmer Eugene

Concord
Holland, Michael Wade

Durham
Du Sartel, Alexandre
Gudaitis, Christy Myers

Elizabeth City
Riley, John Frederick

Fayetteville
Townsend, William Jackson

Greensboro
Davis, Herbert Owen
Koonce, Neil Wright

Greenville
Dixon, Phillip Ray, Sr.,

Leland
Barnhardt, Zeb Elonzo, Jr.,

Mooresville
Homesley, Clifton W.

Morganton
Simpson, Daniel Reid

Raleigh
Hale, Grayson S.
Harazin, William Dennis
Hargrove, Wade Hampton
Jernigan, John Lee
Joyner, Walton Kitchin
Mallard, Heather K.
Mitchell, Henry Allen, Jr.,

Taylor, Ritchie W.

Wilkesboro
Hellrung, Stephen Andrew

Wilmington
McCauley, Cleyburn Lycurgus

Winston Salem
Early, James H., Jr.,
Greason, Murray Crossley, Jr.,
Herring, Jerone Carson
Schollander, Wendell Leslie, Jr.,
Stockton, Ralph Madison, Jr.,
Vaughn, Robert Candler, II,

OHIO

Akron
Allan, Ronald Curtis
Harvie, Crawford Thomas
Rooney, George Willard

Athens
Gall, Robert Jay

Canfield
Hill, Thomas Allen

Cincinnati
Anthony, Thomas Dale
Buechner, Robert William
Carr, George Francis, Jr.,
Flanagan, John Anthony
Goodman, Stanley
Heldman, Paul W.
Kelley, John Joseph, Jr.,
Lindberg, Charles David
Meranus, Leonard Stanley
Meyers, Karen Diane
Meyers, Pamela Sue
Neumark, Michael Harry
Olson, Robert Wyrick
Petrie, Bruce Inglis
Porter, Robert Carl, Jr.,
Ruby, Stanley L.
Schwab, Nelson, Jr.,
Tobias, Charles Harrison, Jr.,
Vander Laan, Mark Alan
Wales, Ross Elliot

Cleveland
Braverman, Herbert Leslie
Coquillette, William Hollis
Dampeer, John Lyell
Ebert, Gary Andrew
Ernst, Christopher Mark
Falsgraf, William Wendell
Friedman, Harold Edward
Groetzinger, Jon, Jr.,
Horvitz, Michael John
Koblenz, N(orman) Herschel
Krembs, Peter Joseph
Markey, Robert Guy
Mc Cartan, Patrick Francis
Meyer, G. Christopher
Ollinger, W. James
Pearlman, Samuel Segel
Presti, Geralyn Marie
Sawyer, Raymond Terry
Schiller, James Joseph
Stevens, Thomas Charles
Stovsky, Michael David
Taft, Seth Chase
Waldeck, John Walter, Jr.,

Columbus
Anderson, Jon Mac
Archer, Michael Dale
Bailey, Daniel Allen
Balthaser, James Harvey
Barrett, Phillip Heston
Brinkman, Dale Thomas
Carnahan, John Anderson
Casey, John Frederick
Chappano, Perry Michael
Cross, Jeffrey D.
Druen, William Sidney
Dunlay, Catherine Telles
Emens, J. Richard
Frasier, Ralph Kennedy
Gibson, Rick J.
Hockstad, Karen Sue
Mone, Robert Paul
Rector, Susan Darnell
Robins, Ronald Albert, Jr.,
Selcer, David Mark
Shayne, Stanley H.
Tarpy, Thomas Michael
Willcox, Roderick Harrison
Wolper, Beatrice Emens

Dayton
Lamme, Kathryn Anne
Schneble, Alfred William, III,
Taronji, Jaime, Jr.,
Watts, Steven Richard

Dublin
Inzetta, Mark Stephen
Williams, Paul Stratton

Findlay
Kline, James Edward

Grove City
Dodd, Jerry Lee

Ironton
Allen, Craig Adams

Jefferson
Lemire, Jerome Albert

Kenton
Tudor, John Martin

Lakewood
Baxter, Howard H.

Lancaster
Libert, Donald Joseph

Massillon
Netzly, Dwight H.

Mount Vernon
Rose, Kim Matthew

North Canton
Dettinger, Warren Walter

Painesville
Dean, J. Thomas

Shaker Heights
Band, Jordan Clifford
Cherchiglia, Dean Kenneth
Messinger, Donald Hathaway

Toledo
Doner, Gary William
Hilbert, John Warren, II,
O'Connell, Maurice Daniel
Webb, Thomas Irwin, Jr.,

Wadsworth
McIlvaine, James Ross

Warren
Letson, William Normand
McGeough, Robert Saunders

Westerville
Flaherty, James Grant

Wickliffe
Kidder, Fred Dockstater

Youngstown
Giannini, Matthew Carlo
Lenga, Robert Allen
Petrony, John Francis
Roth, Daniel Benjamin

OKLAHOMA

Alva
Mitchell, Allan Edwin

Bartlesville
Koch, Robert Charles
Roff, Alan Lee

Broken Arrow
Jones, Ronald Lee

Chandler
Swanson, Robert Lee

Muskogee
Frix, Paige Lane

Norman
Talley, Richard Bates

Oklahoma City
Derrick, Gary Wayne
Paliotta, Armand
Paul, William George
Rockett, D. Joe
Stanley, Brian Jordan
Steinhorn, Irwin Harry

Tulsa
Arrington, John Leslie, Jr.,
Biolchini, Robert Fredrick
Chandler, Ronald Jay
Gaberino, John Anthony, Jr.,
Howard, Gene Claude
Kihle, Donald Arthur
Sneed, James Lynde
Waddel, Patrick Olynn

OREGON

Lake Oswego
Kuntz, Joel Dubois
Rasmussen, Richard Robert

Medford
Shaw, Barry N.

Portland
Abravanel, Allan Ray
Arthur, Michael Elbert
Cable, John Franklin
DuBoff, Leonard David
Epstein, Edward Louis
Grossmann, Ronald Stanyer
Hanna, Harry Mitchell
Harrell, Gary Paul
Krahmer, Donald Leroy, Jr.,
Pratt, Scott Owen
Simpson, Robert Glenn
Stewart, Milton Roy
Van Valkenburg, Edgar Walter

Salem
Mannix, Kevin Leese

PENNSYLVANIA

Allentown
McGinley, Paul Anthony, Jr.,

Ardmore
Narin, Stephen B.

Bala Cynwyd
Garrity, Vincent Francis, Jr.,

Beaver
Petrush, John Joseph

Berwyn
Damstra, Daniel Louis

Bradford
Hauser, Christopher George

Elkins Park
Schneider, Carl William

Grove City
McBride, Milford Lawrence, Jr.,

Jenkintown
Robbins, Jack Winton

Kennett Square
Partnoy, Ronald Allen

Lancaster
Lewis, Alvin Bower, Jr.,

Malvern
Cameron, John Clifford
Quay, Thomas Emery

Media
Cramp, John Franklin
Rainer, G. Bradley

Merion Station
Henry, Ragan Augustus

Mount Pleasant
Johnson, Michael A.

Newtown Square
Bower, Ward Alan

Norristown
Aman, George Matthias, III,
Milner, Kenneth Paul

Philadelphia
Berenato, Mark Anthony
Berger, Lawrence Howard
Blum, Howard Alan
Bogutz, Jerome Edwin
Chimples, George
Clark, William H., Jr.,
Cross, Milton H.
DeBunda, Salvatore Michael
Del Raso, Joseph Vincent
Doran, William Michael
Drake, William Frank, Jr.,
Dubin, Stephen Victor
Frank, Harvey
Goldman, Gary Craig
Goldman, Jerry Stephen
Gough, John Francis
Grady, Thomas Michael
Hunter, James Austen, Jr.,
Koplin, Bernice Judith
Krzyzanowski, Richard L.
Leonard, Thomas
Lipman, Frederick D.
Loveless, George Group
Luongo, Stephen Earle
O'Brien, William Jerome, II,
Pauciulo, John William
Promislo, Daniel
Reed, Michael Haywood
Reiss, John Barlow
Sartorius, Peter S.
Scullin, Michael E.
Spolan, Harmon Samuel
Staffieri, Nicholas J.
Subak, John Thomas
Wert, Robert Clifton
Wolff, Deborah H(orowitz)

Pittsburgh
Aderson, Sanford M.
Barrett, Karen Moore
Boswell, William Paret
Cowan, Barton Zalman
Demmler, John Henry
Drake, Edwin P.
Farley, Andrew Newell
Fox, Michael David
Hardie, James Hiller
Helmrich, Joel Marc
Hess, Emerson Garfield
Kalil, David Thomas
Letwin, Jeffrey William
McCague, John Joseph, III,
Murdoch, David Armor
Reed, W. Franklin
Singer, Paul Meyer
Stepanian, Steven Arvid, II,
Sweeney, Clayton Anthony
Thompson, Thomas Martin
Ward, Thomas Jerome
Wilkinson, James Allan
Winter, Nelson Warren

Valley Forge
Bovaird, Brendan Peter

Villanova
Zearfoss, Herbert Keyser

Washington
Lerner, William C.

West Chester
Osborn, John Edward

Wilkes Barre
Roth, Eugene
Ufberg, Murray

Williamsport
Ertel, Allen Edward

Wormleysburg
Cherewka, Michael

RHODE ISLAND

Barrington
Soutter, Thomas Douglas

Newport
McConnell, David Kelso

Pawtucket
Kranseler, Lawrence Michael

Providence
Carlotti, Stephen Jon
Decarvalho, Kas R.
Gasbarro, Pasco, Jr.,
Olsen, Hans Peter
Salvadore, Guido Richard

Warwick
Battle, Leslie Anne Elizabeth
St. Pierre, Michael A.

SOUTH CAROLINA

Aiken
Alan, Matthew W. A.

Beaufort
Harvey, William Brantley, Jr.,

Charleston
Cannon, Hugh
Freer, Robert Elliott, Jr.,
Unger, Henry Manning

Columbia
Nexsen, Julian Jacobs
Pansegrau, Phaedra Renée
Price, Robert Grant
Tate, Harold Simmons, Jr.,

Conway
Martin, Gregory Keith

Greenville
Dobson, Robert Albertus, III,
Edwards, Harry LaFoy
Phillips, Joseph Brantley, Jr.,
Reese, Kevin Wayne
Riley, Richard Wilson
Shoemaker, James Marshall, Jr.,
Wyche, Cyril Thomas

Greenwood
Nexsen, Julian Jacobs, Jr.,

Hilton Head Island
Hagoort, Thomas Henry
Rose, William Shepard, Jr.,
Scarminach, Charles Anthony

Kiawah Island
Coyle, Martin Adolphus, Jr.,

Salem
Everett, C(harles) Curtis

SOUTH DAKOTA

Rapid City
Foye, Thomas Harold

TENNESSEE

Brentwood
Provine, John Calhoun
Schreiber, Kurt Gilbert

Chattanooga
Bahner, Thomas Maxfield
Durham, J(oseph) Porter, Jr.,

Germantown
Sisson, Jerry Allan
Waddell, Phillip Dean

Greeneville
Bell, William Hall

Knoxville
Campbell, Robert Roe
Howard, Lewis Spilman
McCall, Jack Humphreys, Jr.,

Memphis
Broadhurst, Jerome Anthony
Clunan, Amy Marie
Gentry, Gavin Miller
Lee, Samuel S.
Masterson, Kenneth Rhodes
Matthews, Paul Aaron
McQuiston, John Ward, II,
Rawlins, Donald R.
Rutledge, Roger Keith

Murfreesboro
Heffington, Jack Grisham

Nashville
Bass, James Orin
Carr, Davis Haden
Cheek, James Howe, III,
Eisen, Steven Jeffrey
Habermann, Ted Richard
Lamar, Howard Henry, III,
Lowell, Roland M.
Mayden, Barbara Mendel
Sawyer, Christy Carlson
Sims, Wilson
Spining, W. Carl
Tuke, Robert Dudley
Woods, Larry David

Signal Mountain
Anderson, Charles Hill

TEXAS

Abilene
Sartain, James Edward

Amarillo
Hill, Edward Haynes

Arlington
Dowdy, John Vernard, Jr.,
Pierson, Grey

Austin
Borden, Diana Kimball
Donley, Dennis W.
Gangstad, John Erik
Godfrey, Cullen Michael

Brownsville
Ray, Mary Louise Ryan

Cypress
Callegari, William A., Jr.,

Dallas
Beuttenmuller, Rudolf William
Blount, Charles William, III,
Brady, Jack Edgar
Crowley, James Worthington
Estep, Robert Lloyd
Feld, Alan David
Fishman, Edward Marc
Glancy, Walter John
Glendenning, Don Mark
Gores, Christopher Merrel
Hennessy, Daniel Kraft
Hunter, Robert Frederick
Joplin, Julian Mike
Kennedy, Marc J.
Malorzo, Thomas Vincent
McNamara, Anne H.
Morrison, David Eugene
Peterson, Edward Adrian
Pleasant, James Scott
Rodgers, John Hunter
Schrauff, Christopher Wesley
Smith, Russell Bryan
Spears, Robert Fields
Steinberg, Lawrence Edward
Storey, Charles Porter
Veach, Robert Raymond, Jr.,
Young, Barney Thornton
Zisman, Barry Stuart

El Paso
Smith, Tad Randolph

Ennis
Swanson, Wallace Martin

Farmersville
Seward, Richard Bevin

Fort Worth
Brown, C. Harold
Chalk, John Allen, Sr.,
Larimore, Tom L.
Mercer, Edwin Wayne
Watson, Robert Francis

Galveston
O'Toole, Austin Martin

Garland
Tankersley, Rebecca Elizabeth Guldi

Georgetown
Bryce, William Delf

Houston
Allender, John Roland
Anani, Tarig
Anderson, Eric Severin
Barton, Sarah Muriel
Bech, Douglas York
Beirne, Martin Douglas
Bland, John Lloyd
Campbell, Bert Louis
Cline, Vivian Melinda
Conlon, Michael William
Craig, Robert Mark, III,
Curry, Alton Frank
Dilg, Joseph Carl
Ewen, Pamela Binnings
Finch, Michael Paul
Forbes, Arthur Lee, III,
Gates, Stephen Frye
Goldman, Nathan Carliner
Hartrick, Janice Kay
Hoyt, Mont Powell
Kelly, Hugh Rice
Kinnan, David Emery
Marlow, Orval Lee, II,
Massad, Stephen Albert
Moehlman, Michael Scott
Murphy, Ewell Edward, Jr.,
Nacol, Mae
Nolen, Roy Lemuel
O'Donnell, Lawrence, III,
Oldham, Darius Dudley
Parker, Dallas Robert
Plaeger, Frederick Joseph, II,
Rogers, Arthur Hamilton, III,
Sapp, Walter William
Saunders, Charles Albert

Shouse, August Edward
Simmons, Stephen Judson
Smith, Walter John
Strock, William Matthew
Szalkowski, Charles Conrad
Thomas, John A.
Walls, Robert Hamilton, Jr.,
Watson, John Allen

Irving
Falgour, Tilman Joseph, III,
Reed, Anthony W.

Lubbock
Crowson, James Lawrence

Mc Kinney
Dowdy, William Clarence, Jr.,

Plano
Blachly, Jack Lee

San Antonio
Becker, Douglas Wesley
Biery, Evelyn Hudson
Bramble, Ronald Lee
Case, Jeff Dean
Harkins, Thad
Lutter, Charles William, Jr.,
Pipkin, Marvin Grady
Shearn, Michael Joseph
Vazquez, Gilbert Falcon

Sherman
Munson, Peter Kerr

Temple
Cuba, Benjamin James
Pickle, Jerry Richard

Waco
Page, Jack Randall
Smith, Cullen

UTAH

Ogden
Mecham, Glenn Jefferson

Provo
Hill, Richard Lee

Saint George
Slemboski, James E.

Salt Lake City
Atkin, Gary Eugene
Baucom, Sidney George
Callister, Louis Henry, Jr.,
Heaton, Jon C.
Jones, Michael Frank
Lee, James B.
Mabey, Ralph R.
Ockey, Ronald J.
Ricks, Lyndon Lee
Sine, Wesley Franklin

Spanish Fork
Ashworth, Brent Ferrin

VERMONT

Rutland
Taylor, A. Jeffry

VIRGINIA

Alexandria
Beach, Barbara Purse
Goolrick, Robert Mason
Higgins, Mary Celeste
Klewans, Samuel N.
Lauderdale, Katherine Sue
Maloof, Farahe Paul

Arlington
Kelly, John James

Charlottesville
Hodous, Robert Power
Stroud, Robert Edward

Danville
Regan, Michael Patrick
Talbott, Frank, III,

Fairfax
Downey, Richard Lawrence
Sanderson, Douglas Jay
Schwartz, Philip

Falls Church
Jennings, Thomas Parks
Kirk, Dennis Dean
Nunes, Morris A.

Glen Allen
Pace, Nicholas Joseph

Great Falls
Neidich, George Arthur
Preston, Charles George
Rath, Francis Steven

Hampton
McNider, James Small, III,

Heathsville
McKerns, Charles Joseph

Leesburg
Kushner, Gordon Peter

Lynchburg
Healy, Joseph Francis, Jr.,

Mc Lean
Armstrong, Arthur John
Baker, Keith Leon
Brown, Thomas Cartmel, Jr.,
Church, Randolph Warner, Jr.,
Halagao, Avelino Garabiles
Hammons, Terrence Gordon, Jr.,
McCorkindale, Douglas Hamilton
Morris, James Malachy
Morse, Duane D(ale)
Stephens, William Theodore

Nellysford
Sims, John Rogers, Jr.,

Newport News
Kamp, Arthur Joseph, Jr.,
Segall, James Arnold

Norfolk
Baird, Edward Rouzie, Jr.,
Hamar, Michael Bruce
Handford, Lee A.
Poston, Anita Owings
Russell, C. Edward, Jr.,

Oakton
Duesenberg, Robert H.
Randolph, Christopher Craven

Reston
Rau, Lee Arthur
Scharff, Joseph Laurent

Richmond
Baer, Tommy Percy
Belcher, Dennis Irl
Buford, Robert Pegram
Carter, Joseph Carlyle, Jr.,
Cutchins, Clifford Armstrong, IV,
Denny, Collins, III,
Elmore, Edward Whitehead
Goodpasture, Philip Henry
Mezzullo, Louis Albert
Minardi, Richard A., Jr.,
Musick, Robert Lawrence, Jr.,
Pearsall, John Wesley
Redmond, David Dudley
Starke, Harold E., Jr.,
Strickland, William Jesse
Totten, Randolph Fowler

Roanoke
Butler, Manley Caldwell
Dellinger, Mark Wayne
Densmore, Douglas Warren
Glenn, Robert Eastwood
Glover, Harry Allen, Jr.,

Spotsylvania
Manthei, Richard Dale

Suffolk
Young, Hubert Howell, Jr.,

Vienna
Maiwurm, James John

Virginia Beach
Frantz, Thomas Richard

Williamsburg
Church, Dale Walker

WASHINGTON

Centralia
Bates, Charles Walter

Hoquiam
Rutledge, John Paul

Issaquah
Benoliel, Joel
Moch, Robert Gaston

Montesano
Stewart, James Malcolm

Seattle
Blair, M. Wayne
Blom, Daniel Charles
Cook, Charles Ryan
Creim, Jerry Alan
Ferrer, Rafael Douglas Paul
Franke, Patrick Joseph
Giles, Robert Edward, Jr.,
Graham, Stephen Michael
Hilpert, Edward Theodore, Jr.,
Hoffman, Mark Frederick
Judson, C(harles) James (Jim Judson)
Kilbane, Thomas M.
Lamb, Mark Christopher
Malone, Thomas William
Manning, J. Richard
Palmer, Douglas S., Jr.,
Propst, Andrew J.
Schneidler, Jon Gordon
Treiger, Irwin Louis
Tune, James Fulcher
Weigand, William Loren, III,

Tacoma
Krueger, James A.

Walla Walla
Hayner, Herman Henry

Yakima
Wright, J(ames) Lawrence

WEST VIRGINIA

Charleston
Berthold, Robert Vernon, Jr.,
Chaney, Michael Thomas
Chaney, Vincent Verlando
Davis, James Hornor, III,

Martinsburg
Martin, Clarence Eugene, III,

Morgantown
Fusco, Andrew G.

WISCONSIN

Elkhorn
Sweet, Lowell Elwin

Germantown
Ehlinger, Ralph Jerome

Janesville
Steil, George Kenneth, Sr.,

Kohler
Sheedy, Kathleen Ann

La Crosse
Ablan, Michael Charles
Klos, Jerome John

Madison
Anderson, Michael Steven
Boucher, Joseph W(illiam)
Brewster, Francis Anthony
Hanson, David James
Heymann, S. Richard
Peterson, H. Dale
Ragatz, Thomas George
Sweet, Howard A.
Temkin, Harvey L.

Manitowoc
Muchin, Arden Archie

Menasha
Franzoi, Joseph Frank, IV,

Milwaukee
Abraham, William John, Jr.,
Barnes, Paul McClung
Bliss, Richard Jon
Bratt, Herbert Sidney
Bremer, John M.
Calise, William Joseph, Jr.,
Connolly, Gerald Edward
Donahue, John Edward
Duback, Steven Rahr
Friedman, James Dennis
Galanis, John William
Goodkind, Conrad George
Holz, Harry George
Iding, Allan Earl
Kubale, Bernard Stephen
Kurtz, Harvey A.
Martin, Quinn William
Maynard, John Ralph
McGaffey, Jere D.
Medved, Paul Stanley
Rintelman, Donald Brian
Ryan, Patrick Michael
Skipper, Walter John
Trebon, Lawrence Alan
Williams, Clay Rule
Winsten, Saul Nathan

New Berlin
Bembenek, Alan R.
Schober, Thomas Gregory

Oak Creek
Giblin, Louis

Racine
Coates, Glenn Richard
Du Rocher, James Howard
Smith, Stephen James

Sheboygan
Rice, Shawn G.

WYOMING

Casper
Gray, Jan Charles
Lowe, Robert Stanley

Sheridan
Riggs, Dan Britt

TERRITORIES OF THE UNITED STATES

GUAM

Tamuning
Aguigui, Ignacio Cruz

PUERTO RICO

San Juan
Pierluisi, Pedro R.
Rodriguez-Diaz, Juan E.

MEXICO

Coahuila
Hernandez, Juan Ignacio

Huixquilucan
Garcia-Ruiz, Fernando

Mexico City
Ayala-Aguirre, Jose Ramon
Carpio, Miguel Angel
Fonseca, Gerardo
Garcia Giorgana, Ricardo
Garcia Santos Coy, Luis Gerardo
González Luna, Rodrigo
Grau, Vicente
Luna-Arena, Alejandro
Perez Elizundia, Rodrigo

Sonora
Medrano, Roberto M.

ARGENTINA

Buenos Aires
Parisier, Carlos

AUSTRALIA

Melbourne
Paterson, Robert

Sydney
Bateman, Gregory Anthony
Seidler, Robert Leslie

AUSTRIA

Vienna
Winkler, Oskar Werner

BELGIUM

Antwerp
De Roeck, Martine M.

Brussels
Bustin, George Leo
Delsaut, Philippe Patrick
Lohest, Thierry
Wagemans, Marc

Liège
Bernard, Vincent Jacques Nicolas

BRAZIL

Rio de Janeiro
Lopes, Beatriz
Muniz, Joaquim Tavares de Paiva
Muniz, Renata Maria (Renata Novotny)
Pinheiro-Guimarães, Plinio

São Paulo
Alves, Rodney Almeida
Azevedo, Renato Olimpio Sette de Carmo, Lie Uema do
Coelho da Rocha, Paulo Frank
Flesch, Marcos Rafael
Gutiérrez Chamlati, Jorge
Hong, Byung Soo
Lynch, Maria Regina Mangabeira Albernaz
Meira, Fernando Alves
Müller Filho, Luiz Eugênio Araújo
Padovan, Lira Renardini
Rodrigues, Fabiana Utrabo
Rossi, Carlos Alberto de Souza

BULGARIA

Sofia
Djingov, Assen Alexandrov
Georgiev, Georgi Vladimirov
Komitova, Emilia Eneva
Kunze, Violetta Detkova
Ugrinova, Zdravka Mirkova

CHILE

Santiago
Letelier, Jose Luis

CHINA

Beijing
Fiske, Harold Parker
Liu, Ge
Zhu-Clark, Ingrid Wenying

COLOMBIA

Bogotá
Cajiao, Ximena T.

COSTA RICA

San José
Peralta, Federico
Retana, Vanessa

CROATIA

Zagreb
Cirkveni, Neven

CZECH REPUBLIC

Prague
Hajkova, Gabriela
Leuchterova, Darina

DENMARK

Copenhagen
Horten, Eric Korre
Mogelmose, Henrik
Overgaard, Finn
Philip, Marianne

ENGLAND

Birmingham
Hull, David Julian

London
Bafi, Alex
Barnes, Oliver William Abbott
Booker, Russell Stuart
Brownwood, David Owen
Childs, David Robert
Cole, Richard A.
Duesenberg, Mark Hugo
Exley, Paul Marcus
Glazer, Barry David
Goldenberg, Philip
Katkin, Elizabeth Lynn
Kelly, Christopher Richard
Liston, Stephanie W.
McGeachie, Jeffrey Stuart
McLeod, Simon Nicholas
Page, Timothy A.C.
Rashidmanesh, Hamid Reza
Rosenberg, Daniel P.
Sheach, Andrew Jonathan
Smith, Jerry Leon
Spindler, Kester Lars
Thomas, Allen Lloyd
Ufland, Richard Mark
Walton, Christopher John
Wheater, Murray Richard Kenneth
White, Walter Hiawatha, Jr.,

Oxford
Loake, Jonathan David

FINLAND

Helsinki
Savela, Ari Juhani
Vikiö, Jari Tapani

FRANCE

Paris
Bedos, Jean-Luc
de Castellan, Elisabetta Ferruta
Dehe, Richard
Fischer, Cédric Henri
Lee, Eun Hwa
Letréguilly, Hervé
Mitrovic, Laurence
Pavec, Arnaud
Poli, Frédéric Charles
Tézé, Bernard André

GERMANY

Berlin
Kautzsch, Christof
Rodewald, Joerg
Schoene, Friedrich Tobias
von Rechenberg, Wolf G.

Bonn
Goeckeler, Stephan

Cologne
Luer, Hans-Jochem
Rizor, Stefan
Siepelt-Babilon, Stefan
Wilsing, Hans Ulrich

Düsseldorf
Gillessen, Frederick
Pathe, Ilmo
Schiessl, Maximilian

Frankfurt
Andres, Ingrid
Dienst, Armin
Gross, Wolfgang
Hartmann, Uwe
Ihrig, Hans-Christoph
Jung, Harald H.
Klerx, Oliver
Peter, Anne-Marie
Schroeder, Oliver Marcus
Wolff, Florian

CREDITOR. *See* **Commercial, consumer.**

CRIMINAL

Burlingame
Lowenstein, Anthony

El Cajon
Graf, Sheryl Susan

Fresno
Little, Kevin Gerard

Fullerton
Talmo, Ronald Victor

Glendale
Toscano, Oscar Ernesto

Huntington Beach
Garrels, Sherry Ann

Indio
De Salva, Christopher Joseph

Laguna Beach
Simons, Barry Thomas

Long Beach
Ultimo, Paul Joseph

Los Angeles
Bortman, David
Handzlik, Jan Lawrence
Holliday, Thomas Edgar
Lauchengco, Jose Yujuico, Jr.,
Medearis, Miller
Reed, Leland
Rozanski, Stanley Howard
Shapiro, Robert
Wolf, Lawrence

Manhattan Beach
Hallett, James M.

Newport Beach
Cordova, Ron

Oakland
Koch, Richard Phillips (Terry Koch)

Palm Desert
La Rocca, Phillip R.

Paramount
Hall, Howard Harry

Pasadena
Brenner, Anita Susan

Sacramento
Daniel, Lance
Wishek, Michael Bradley

San Diego
Goldberg, Charles L.
Iredale, Eugene Gerald
King, Nicholas Spencer
Shapiro, Philip Alan
Shelton, Dorothy Diehl Rees
Warwick, Thomas Joseph, Jr.,

San Francisco
Bondoc, Rommel
Bruen, James A.
Cohn, Nathan
Ladar, Jerrold Morton
Philipsborn, John Timothy
Russoniello, Joseph Pascal
Young, Douglas Rea

San Jose
McManis, James

Sanger
Chynoweth, W. Edward

Santa Ana
Harley, Robison Dooling, Jr.,

Santa Barbara
Herman, James Edward

Santa Monica
Genego, William Joseph
Hirsch, Richard Gary

Sebastopol
Hillberg, Marylou Elin

Sherman Oaks
Ardalan, Pezhman Christopher

Ventura
Bray, Laurack Doyle

Walnut Creek
Larkin, David Joseph

Weaverville
Correll, Joanna Rae

Windsor
Greiner, Robert Philip

Woodland
Melton, Barry

COLORADO

Boulder
Mulligan, Casey John

Centennial
Carlton, Diane Michele

Colorado Springs
Fisher, Robert Scott
Walker, Jonathan Lee

Denver
Anstine, Glen Roscoe
Brega, Charles Franklin
Bronstein, Robert
Corry, Robert J., Jr.,
Furtado, David Jeffrey
Malatesta, Mary Anne
Palmer, David Gilbert
Pineau, John Kenneth
Rench, Stephen Charles
Springer, Jeffrey Alan

Englewood
Coffee, Melvin Arnold

Fort Collins
Johnson, Donald Edward, Jr.,

Frisco
McElyea, Monica Sergent

Grand Junction
Erkenbrack, Stephen Kenneth
Gurley, Richard T.

Littleton
Perlman, B. Arthur

CONNECTICUT

Bridgeport
Harrell, Kyle Alexander
Katz, Stuart Michael
Zeldes, Jacob Dean

Danbury
Arconti, Richard David

Fairfield
Denniston, Brackett Badger, III,

Guilford
Noonan, Patrick Matthew

Hartford
Bennett, Jessie F.

New Haven
Carty, Paul Vernon

Norwich
Francoline, Stacey

Ridgefield
Foster, Julie Irene

Stamford
Margolis, Emanuel

Torrington
Conti, William Achille

Wallingford
Farrell, Lynne S.

Waterbury
Marano, Richard Michael

DELAWARE

Wilmington
Malik, John Stephen
Mekler, Arlen B.
Wier, Richard Royal, Jr.,

DISTRICT OF COLUMBIA

Washington
Best, Judah
Boss, Lenard Barrett
Bray, John Martin
Buckley, John Joseph, Jr.,
Bucklin, Donald Thomas
Buscemi, Peter
Durney, Michael Cavalier
Feffer, Gerald Alan
Fox, Hamilton Phillips, III,
Geniesse, Robert John
Goldfarb, Ronald Lawrence
Greenfeld, Alexander
Kent, M. Elizabeth
Luskin, Robert David
McDaniels, William E.
O'Neil, Thomas Francis, III,
Peters, Frederick Whitten
Pierson, Stuart F.
Povich, David
Rezneck, Daniel Albert
Ryan, Stephen Michael
Salsbury, Michael H.
Spaeder, Roger Campbell
Starr, Judson Wilmarth
Stuart, Pamela Bruce
Tompkins, Joseph Buford, Jr.,
Tuohey, Mark Henry, III,
Turnage, Fred Douglas
Vardaman, John Wesley

FLORIDA

Altamonte Springs
Gunewardene, Roshani Mala

Arcadia
Cherry, Paul Stephen

Brooksville
Hallman, William H., III,
Vitola, John Raymond

Clearwater
Rose, Donna

Coconut Grove
Denaro, Gregory

Coral Gables
Cano, Mario Stephen

Daytona Beach
Neitzke, Eric Karl

Fort Lauderdale
Behr, Ralph Steven
Benjamin, James Scott
Bogenschutz, J. David
Dutko, Michael Edward
Harris, Jeffrey Mark
Sale, David Todd
Schreiber, Alan Hickman

Gainesville
DeThomasis, Craig Constantine
Kurrus, Thomas William

Jacksonville
Link, Robert James
Pillans, Charles Palmer, III,

Lake Worth
Kreidler, Frank Allan

Largo
Trevena, John Harry

Longwood
Hernandez, H(ermes) Manuel

Miami
Becerra, Robert John
Berger, Steven R.
Bronis, Stephen Jay
Cohn, Don Stephen
DeMaria, Joseph Angelo
Ferrell, Milton Morgan, Jr.,
Hartz, Steven Edward Marshall
Hirsch, Milton
Horn, Mark
Houlihan, Gerald John
Katz, Lawrence Sheldon
Kritzer, Glenn Bruce
Lebowitz, Walter Bernard
Poston, Rebekah Jane
Quirantes, Albert M.
Rashkind, Paul Michael
Rogers, Harvey Delano
Rosen, Michael James
Rothman, David Bill
Scott, Thomas Emerson, Jr.,
Seiden, Mark
Weinstein, Alan Edward

Naples
Steinhouse, Carl Lewis

North Miami Beach
Zipkin, Sheldon Lee

Orlando
deBeaubien, Hugo H.
Dempsey, Bernard Hayden, Jr.,
Kehoe, Terrence Edward
Lubet, Marc Leslie
Murrell, Robert George
Russ, James Matthias

Palm Beach
Devins, Robert Sylvester

Palm Beach Gardens
Auerbach, Paul Ira

Panama City
Sutton, Pamela Dru

Punta Gorda
Goldman, Jason Brian

Saint Petersburg
Wein, Stephen J.

Sarasota
Byrd, L(awrence) Derek

St Petersburg Beach
Milham, Julee Lynn

Tallahassee
Davis, William Howard
Kitchen, E.C. Deeno
Morphonios, Dean B.
Sheffield, Frank Elwyn
Simpson, Larry Dean
Willard, Matthew R.

Tampa
Blau, Jeffrey Alan
Clendinen, Craig P.
Garrett, Howard Leon
Givens, Stann William
Loewenthal, Steven Richard
Nutter, Robert Heinrich

West Palm Beach
Prather, David C.
Strolla, Cory Carsan
Vilchez, Victoria Anne

GEORGIA

Acworth
Pope, Robert Daniel

Albany
Collum, Rick Daniel

Atlanta
Billington, Barry E.
Bogart, Jeffrey B.
Chilivis, Nickolas Peter
Duffey, William Simon, Jr.,
Lotito, Nicholas Anthony
Mull, Gale W.
Patrick, Deval Laurdine
Pilcher, James Brownie
Whitley, Joe Dally
Zell, Glenn

Douglas
Sims, Rebecca Littleton

Gainesville
Hester, Francis Bartow, III, (Frank Hester)

Jasper
Marger, Edwin

Lawrenceville
Clark, David Edward

Moultrie
Forehand, Jon Vincent

Nashville
Ellis, Robert Bryan, Jr.,

Roswell
England, John Melvin

Statesboro
Classens, Michael John

Sugar Hill
Hamby, Lee Ellen

Valdosta
Dodd, Roger J.
Edwards, Edith Martha
Terry, Guyton Otis, III,

HAWAII

Honolulu
Edmunds, John Sanford
Harrison, William A.
Schweigert, Jack
Weight, Michael Anthony

Kailua Kona
Zola, Michael S.

Kilauea
Polli, Robert Paul

IDAHO

Boise
Marsters, LaDawn Marie
Shurtliff, Marvin Karl

Idaho Falls
Hart, Stephen Strong

ILLINOIS

Aurora
Camic, David Edward
Mateas, Kenneth Edward

Chicago
Bailey, Robert Short
Barnett, William A.
Coulson, William Roy
Crane, Mark
Donlevy, John Dearden
Farber, Bernard John
Flessner, Mark Alan
Harris, Donald Ray
Hoffa, Thomas Edward
Hoover, Russell James
King, Michael Howard
Kunkle, William Joseph
Meyer, John Albert
Molo, Steven Francis
Murray, Daniel Charles
Nash, Gordon Bernard, Jr.,
Nora, Gerald Ernest
Pugh, Todd Selby
Roustan, Yvon Dominique
Silets, Harvey Marvin
Smith, Ronald Charles
Tarun, Robert Walter
Theis, William Harold
Tobin, Craig Daniel

Chicago Heights
Cifelli, John Louis

Decatur
Vigneri, Joseph William

Homewood
Olofsson, Daniel Joel

Joliet
Lenard, George Dean

Lombard
O'Shea, Patrick Joseph

Matteson
Wigell, Raymond George

Murphysboro
McCann, Maurice Joseph

Palos Heights
Taylor, Joseph Henry

Skokie
Plotnick, Paul William

INDIANA

Anderson
Woodruff, Randall Lee

Evansville
Clouse, John Daniel

Fort Wayne
Murphy, Patrick Guyon

Gary
Lewis, Robert Lee

Greenfield
Dobbins, Caryl Dean

Indianapolis
Kautzman, John Fredrick

Lebanon
Donaldson, John Weber

Peru
Grund, James Arthur

Shelbyville
Lisher, James Richard

Terre Haute
Kesler, John A.

IOWA

Davenport
Phelps, Robert J.

Des Moines
Branstad, Christine Ellen
Foxhoven, Jerry Ray

Iowa City
Spies, Leon Fred

KANSAS

Cottonwood Falls
North, William T.

Garden City
Pierce, Ricklin Ray

Lawrence
Huff, Barbara Kay

Overland Park
Spaeth, Nicholas John

Topeka
Schultz, Richard Allen

Wichita
Wicks, Jeffrey Donald

KENTUCKY

Frankfort
Chadwick, Robert

Lexington
Fryman, Virgil Thomas, Jr.,

Louisville
Cooper, Richard Earl
Manly, Samuel

Shelbyville
Igleheart, Ted Lewis

LOUISIANA

Baton Rouge
Boren, James Edgar

Covington
Paddison, David Robert

Franklin
McClelland, James Ray

Lafayette
Morgan, Glenn L.
Skinner, Michael David

Lake Charles
Sanchez, Walter Marshall

Leesville
Smith, Simeon Christie, IV,

New Orleans
Hantel, Philip Edward
Reed, John Wilson

MAINE

Kennebunk
Clifford, Peter

Portland
Marjerison, Thomas Sydney

Waterville
Sandy, Robert Edward, Jr.,

MARYLAND

Baltimore
Arnick, John Stephen
Crowe, Thomas Leonard
Himeles, Martin Stanley, Jr.,
Kramer, Paul R.
Radding, Andrew
Schreiber, Martin Harold, II,
Silverman, Steven Donald
Snyder, Mark Allen

Bethesda
Baird, Bruce Allen

College Park
Neal, Edward Garrison

Easton
Foster, Philip Carey

Glen Burnie
Lilly, John Richard, II,

Potomac
Mullenbach, Linda Herman

Rockville
Van Grack, Steven

Salisbury
Clarke, Wm. A. Lee, III,

Showell
Grech, Christopher Alan

Silver Spring
Ahmed, Atiq Rahman
Davis, Richmond T.P.

Towson
Gunning, Timothy Michael

Westminster
Preston, Charles Michael

MASSACHUSETTS

Barnstable
Mycock, Frederick Charles

Boston
Berry, Janis Marie
Goldman, Eric Scot
Hrones, Stephen Baylis
Keating, Michael Burns
Levine, Julius Byron
Lowney, Timothy Jay
McKittrick, Neil Vincent
Rabinovitz, Daniel M.
Savage, Joseph Francis
Stern, Donald Kenneth
Sultan, James Lehman

Cambridge
Ta, Tai Van

Hopkinton
Titlebaum, Earl Stanley

Lenox
Coffin, Mary McCarthy

Newton
Lowinger, Lazar

Northampton
Kunkel, Leah R.

Springfield
Maidman, Stephen Paul

Wellesley
Giroux, Eugene Xavier

MICHIGAN

Ann Arbor
O'Brien, Darlene Anne

Bloomfield Hills
Cranmer, Thomas William

Burton
Breczinski, Michael Joseph

Clinton Township
Lucido, Peter J.

Detroit
Andreoff, Christopher Andon
Pirtle, H(arold) Edward
Zacks, David N.

Farmington Hills
Bagley, Dennis Joseph

Greenville
Mullendore, James Myers

Holt
Legere Jr, Henry J.

Inkster
Bullock, Steven Carl

Irons
Getty, Gerald Winkler

Jackson
Jacobs, Wendell Early, Jr.,

Kalamazoo
Bauhof, James Francis

Lansing
Clarke, Hugh B., Jr.,
Kronzek, Charles Michael
Rasmusson, Thomas Elmo

Midland
Beale, Michael John

Mount Pleasant
Plachta, Thomas J.

New Buffalo
Stevens, William J.

South Haven
Waxman, Sheldon Robert

Southfield
Forrest, Robert Edwin
Morganroth, Mayer

Troy
Morgan, Michael Vincent

MINNESOTA

Bemidji
Kief, Paul Allan

Hawley
Baer, Zenas

Mankato
Manahan, James Hinchon

Minneapolis
Ayling, Corey John
Heffelfinger, Thomas Backer
Magnuson, Roger James
McNamara, Michael John
Nemo, Anthony James
Palmer, Brian Eugene
Resnick, Phillip Stanley
Voss, Barry Vaughan
Williams, Maureen

Saint Cloud
Provinzino, John C.
Walz, Gregory Stephen

Saint Paul
Carruthers, Philip Charles
Duckstad, Jon Robert

South Saint Paul
O'Reilly, Ann Catherine

MISSISSIPPI

Bay Springs
Shoemaker, Bobby Lynn

Drew
Holladay, Robert Lawson, Sr.,

Gloster
Davis, Cynthia D'Ascenzo

Hattiesburg
Adelman, Michael Schwartz
Davis-Morris, Angela Elizabeth

Jackson
Hutchison, Mark Stevenson

Ocean Springs
Denham, Earl Lamar

Oxford
Lewis, Ronald Wayne

MISSOURI

Cape Girardeau
Lowes, Albert Charles

Columbia
Moore, Mitchell Jay

Kansas City
Carter, J. Denise
Handley, Gerald Matthew
Joyce, Michael Patrick
Keller, Marilyn B.
Lotven, Howard Lee
Rogers, Charles Myers
Sader, Neil Steven
Vleisides, Gregory William
Wyrsch, James Robert

Keytesville
Wheeler, James Julian

Marshall
Peterson, William Allen

Saint Charles
Zerr, Richard Kevin

Saint Louis
Marks, Murry Aaron
Shalowitz, Howard A.

Springfield
Groce, Steven Fred
Royce, James Richard
Sherwood, Devon Fredrick
Umbarger, Jason T.

MONTANA

Bozeman
Nelson, Steven Dwayne

Great Falls
Smartt, Michael Stewart

Kalispell
Nardi, Stephen J.

NEBRASKA

Kearney
Voigt, Steven Russell

Omaha
Achelpohl, Steven Edward
Fellman, Richard Mayer
Frank, Julie Ann
Runge, Patrick Richard

NEVADA

Las Vegas
Hill, Judith Deegan

Reno
Cornell, Richard Farnham
Dunn, Larry K.
Picker, Marc

NEW HAMPSHIRE

Concord
Hodes, Paul William
Topham, Lee Evans

Dover
Catalfo, Alfred, Jr., (Alfio Catalfo)

Exeter
Lytton, William Bryan

NEW JERSEY

Chatham
Jacobs, Andrew Robert
Kean, Sharon Bittner

Cherry Hill
D'Alfonso, Mario Joseph
Korin, Joel Benjamin

Clark
Barr, Jon-Henry
Farina, Mario G.

Clifton
Feinstein, Miles Roger
Palma, Nicholas James
Randazzo, Anthony J.

East Hanover
Kayser, Kenneth Wayne

Edison
Garasia, Anjana
Vercammen, Kenneth Albert

Flemington
Miller, Louis H.

Hackensack
Mullin, Patrick Allen

Haddonfield
Fuoco, Philip Stephen
Mitnick, Craig Robert

Hainesport
Gallagher, R. Louis, II,

Hazlet
Brown, Christopher Robert

Linden
Littman, David Bernard

Morris Plains
Pluciennik, Thomas Casimir

Newark
Maderer, William F.
Robertson, William Withers

Ocean
Weisberg, Adam Jon

Old Bridge
Downs, Thomas Edward, IV,

Princeton
Greene, Steven Kevin

Randolph
Bilinkas, Edward J.

Red Bank
Moore, Francis Xavier
Waldman, Daniel M.

Ridgewood
Seigel, Jan Kearney

Roseland
Hayden, Joseph A., Jr.,
Tarino, Gary Edward

South Orange
Feinberg, Paul H.

Trenton
Glassen, James Warren

Vineland
O'Neill, Joseph Dean

Wall
Nucciarone, A. Patrick

Westfield
Hrycak, Michael Paul
Stahl, Robert George

NEW MEXICO

Albuquerque
Leavell, Julita Ann
Lopez, Floyd William
Lopez, Martin, III,

Farmington
Titus, Victor Allen

Las Cruces
Kirschner, William Steven

Raton
Montoya, Sarah Marie

Ruidoso
Mitchell, Gary Colas

Santa Fe
Farber, Steven Glenn

NEW YORK

Albany
Barsamian, J(ohn) Albert
Devine, Eugene Peter
Dulin, Thomas N.
Fanciullo, William Patrick

Binghamton
Gates, Gregory Ansel

Briarcliff Manor
Rosen, Paul Maynard

Brooklyn
Jacobson, Barry Stephen
Kamins, Barry Michael

Buffalo
Ewing, Charles Patrick
Murray, Glenn Edward

Carle Place
Mulhern, Edwin Joseph

Carmel
Grossman, Victor G.
Levy, Adam B.

Cedarhurst
Klein, Irwin Grant

Central Islip
Bronstein, Richard M.

Central Valley
Levinson, David Lawrence

East Northport
Juliano, John Louis

Hamburg
Gaughan, Dennis Charles

Hauppauge
Clayton, David William

Herkimer
Kirk, Patrick Laine

Highland
Schonberg, Bruce A.

Huntington
Houslanger, Todd Eric

Islandia
Buckley, Terrence Patrick

Jericho
Rehbock, Richard Alexander

Kew Gardens
Nizin, Leslie Stephen
Schechter, Donald Robert
Sparrow, Robert E.
Zucker, David G.

Mineola
Daniels, John Hill
Lung, Henry
Rubine, Robert Samuel
Sandback, William Arthur

Mohegan Lake
Stokes, Ron

New York
Amsterdam, Mark Lemle
Arkin, Stanley S.
Baker, Mark M.
Barenholtz, Celia Goldwag
Brodsky, David Michael
Buchwald, Don David
Checkman, Neil Bruce
Elsen, Sheldon Howard
Fiske, Robert Bishop, Jr.,
Frankel, Sandor
Genel, Noah D.
Getnick, Neil Victor
Glekel, Jeffrey Ives
Goldstein, Howard Warren
Grimaldi, Neil Vincent
Grover, Douglas E.
Keneally, Kathryn Marie
Kennedy, Michael John
Kenney, John Joseph
Kostelanetz, Boris
Kuh, Richard Henry
Lauer, Eliot
Laufer, Jacob
Lerner, Max Kasner
Levander, Andrew Joshua
Levine, Alan
Levinson, Paul Howard
Lindenauer, Susan B(adian)
London, Martin
Lupert, Leslie Allan
Lupkin, Stanley Neil
Marion, Roger K.
Orden, Stewart L.
Passonneau, Polly Nicole
Puccio, Thomas P.
Reiss, Steven Alan
Rosner, Jonathan Levi
Salvan, Sherwood Allen
Schwartz, Jeffrey Todd
Seiff, Eric A.
Seligman, Delice
Seligman, Frederick
Smith, Morton Alan
Suh, Sung-Hee
Walpin, Gerald
Wohl, Frank Harold
Zornow, David M.

Nyack
Seidler, B(ernard) Alan

Patchogue
Esteve, Edward V.

Rochester
Spoto, David Dennis

Saratoga Springs
Harper, David Alexander

Scarsdale
Roseman, Arnold David

Smithtown
Brooks, Sondra

South Richmond Hill
Scheich, John F.

Syracuse
Duffy, Shirley Kathleen
Hildebrandt, George Frederick
Rosenthal, Alan

Troy
Frost, Jerome Kenneth
Jones, E. Stewart, Jr.,

Valley Stream
Isaacs, Leonard Bernard

Westbury
Dwyer, Diane Marie

White Plains
Greenspan, Leon Joseph
Greenspan, Michael Evan

Williamsville
Ross, Christopher T.W.

NORTH CAROLINA

Asheboro
Bunch, W(alter) Edward

Asheville
Sharpe, Keith Yount

Beaufort
Tilghman, Carl Lewis

Candler
Sutton, John Richard, Sr.,

Cary
Cromer, Charles Lemuel

Charlotte
Brackett, Martin Luther, Jr.,
McLoughlin, James Patrick, Jr.,

Elkin
Gillespie, James Davis

Greensboro
Cahoon, Robert Strange
O'Neal, Lee C.
Oakley, Joel Neese

Greenville
Romary, Peter John Michael

Newton
Cutchin, John Franks

Raleigh
Currin, Samuel Thomas
Hall, John Thomas
Kurtz, Howard Arthur
Suhr, Paul Augustine

Rocky Mount
Tucker, Damian Ladell

Southern Pines
Foyles, Kirsten Ellefson

Warsaw
Thompson, Eugene Cebron, III,

Winston Salem
Klinkosum, Maitri (Mike Klinkosum)

NORTH DAKOTA

Grand Forks
Arnason, Joel Frederick
Seaworth, Mary Ellen

OHIO

Akron
Cahoon, Peter Thomas
Cody, Daniel Schaffner
Glinsek, Gerald John
Whitmer, Jerry F.

Barnesville
Jefferis, Paul Bruce

Beavercreek
Stadnicar, Joseph William

Cincinnati
Cissell, James Charles
Hust, Bruce Kevin
Scacchetti, David J.
Whitaker, Glenn Virgil

Cleveland
Coyne, John Coughlin
Gold, Gerald Seymour
Smaili, Jihad M.
Summers, William Lawrence

Columbus
Belton, John Thomas
Binning, J. Boyd
Cline, Richard Allen
Hollenbaugh, H(enry) Ritchey
Ketcham, Richard Scott
Lippe, Jerry Leonard
Phillips, James Edgar
Tyack, Thomas Michael
Yeazel, Keith Arthur

Dayton
Holz, Michael Harold

Fairborn
Miles, David R.

Findlay
Kentris, George Lawrence

Girard
Denney, James Allen

Mansfield
Wolf, Marcus Alan

Marion
Slagle, James William

Marysville
Hamilton, Robert Otte

Salem
Slack, Mark Robert

Sandusky
Bailey, K. Ronald

Toledo
Pooley, Christopher J.
St. Clair, Donald David

Twinsburg
Doyle, Duane Lynn

Warren
Vigorito, Philip Michael

Xenia
Chappars, Timothy Stephen
Wolaver, Stephen Arthur

OKLAHOMA

Alva
Mitchell, Allan Edwin

Claremore
Gordon, Jack Elliott, Jr.,

Enid
Gill, Amber McLaughlin
Jones, Stephen

Oklahoma City
Cantrell, Charles L.
Ferguson, Steven Edward
Kline, David Adam

Ponca City
Raley, John W., Jr.,

Sayre
Brooks, David Eugene

Tulsa
Brewster, Clark Otto
Cowdery, Allen Craig
Dunn, Frederick Louis, III,
Nigh, Robert Russell, Jr.,

Vinita
Johnston, Oscar Black, III,

Walters
Flanagan, Kathleen

Yukon
Hixson, Wendell Mark

OREGON

Hillsboro
Cross, Daniel Albert

Medford
O'Connor, Karl William (Goodyear Johnson)

Newport
Greco, Guy Benjamin

Oregon City
McFarland, Carol Anne

Portland
Bender, Laurie
Rieke, Forrest Neill

The Dalles
Hashizume, Kevin

PENNSYLVANIA

Allentown
Moyer, Michael Edward

Carlisle
Turo, Ron

Clarks Summit
Beemer, John Barry

Du Bois
Blakley, Benjamin Spencer, III,

Edinboro
Travis, Grant Carner

Elkins Park
Shmukler, Stanford

Frackville
Domalakes, Paul George

Harrisburg
Lappas, Spero Thomas

Johnstown
Kaharick, Jerome John

Kingston
Urbanski, Stephen Karl

Lancaster
Pyfer, John Frederick, Jr.,

Lock Haven
Smith, Stephen Chadwick

Meadville
Barrett, Bruce Alan

Media
Rubin, Arnold E.

Mercer
Kochems, Robert Gregory

Newtown
Kardos, Mel D.

Norristown
Gregg, John Pennypacker

Philadelphia
Caravasos, NiaLena
Durant, Marc
Gianfrancesco, Paul Richard
Hoffman, Alan Jay
Ivey, Stephen David
Klein, Howard Bruce
Rainville, Christina
Siegel, Bernard Louis
Vaira, Peter Francis
Wittels, Barnaby Caesar
Wolf, Bruce

Pittsburgh
Corbett, Thomas Wingett, Jr.,
McGough, Walter Thomas, Jr.,
Sokol, Stephen M.
Tully, Bernard Michael

Reading
Eshelman, David Richard

Reynoldsville
Wheeler, Mark Andrew, Sr.,

Somerset
Carroll, William Richard

State College
Nollau, Lee Gordon

Stroudsburg
Catina, Janet K.

Trevose
McEvilly, James Patrick, Jr.,

Uniontown
Davis, James Thomas

White Oak
Pribanic, Victor Hunter

RHODE ISLAND

West Warwick
Pollock, Bruce Gerald

SOUTH CAROLINA

Columbia
Harvey, Jonathan Matthew
Strom, J. Preston, Jr.,

Greenville
Cowan, John Joseph
Kappel, Matthew Jay
Steele, C. Carlyle

Hilton Head Island
Esposito, John Vincent

Kingstree
Jenkinson, William Eldridge, III,

Seneca
Sires, Norman Gruber, Jr.,

Summerville
Hardee-Thomas, Marva A.

SOUTH DAKOTA

Gregory
Johnson, Charles Rick

Rapid City
Murphy, John Richard

Sioux Falls
Johnson, Richard Arlo

TENNESSEE

Chattanooga
Moore, Hugh Jacob, Jr.,

Clarksville
Love, Michael Joseph

Fayetteville
Dickey, John Harwell

Knoxville
Dillard, W. Thomas
Giordano, Lawrence Francis
Oberman, Steven
Routh, John William

Memphis
Garts, James Rufus, Jr.,
Klein, Henry Leonard
McAfee, Chesney Falk

Nashville
Gross, Edward Jordan
Hardin, Hal D.

Springfield
Wilks, Larry Dean

TEXAS

Austin
Dudley, Todd Steven
Feazell, Vic
Shapiro, David L.
Weinman, Daryl Gail

Beaumont
Lawrence, Edward Jack, III,

Brownsville
Weisfeld, Sheldon

Canton
White, Jeffery Howell

Cleburne
MacLean, John Ronald

Corpus Christi
Miller, Carroll Gerard, Jr., (Gerry Miller)

Dallas
Coggins, Paul Edward, Jr.,
Miller, Deborah Slye
Rucker, R.D.
Udashen, Robert Nathan

El Paso
Dinsmoor, Robert Davidson
Leachman, Russell DeWitt

Fort Worth
Brunig, Robert Arthur
Dickson, Victor Paul
Myers, Thomas Everett

Graham
Richie, Boyd Lynn

Houston
Berg, David Howard
Disher, David Alan
Essmyer, Michael Martin
Hilder, Philip H.
Lamson, Michael Alan
McDade, Thomas Rambaut
McWherter, Louis Alfred
Rustay, Jennifer B.
Shefman, Daucie Elana
Wallis, Olney Gray
Wheelan, R(ichelieu) E(dward)

Lubbock
Brock, Ralph Haney

Mason
Johnson, Rufus Winfield

Mc Kinney
Pikl, James Alan

Mcallen
Connors, Joseph Aloysius, III,

Odessa
Cliff, John William, Jr.,

Plainview
Lafont, William Harold

San Angelo
Sutton, John Ewing

San Antonio
Raign, Michael Stephen

Spring
Beauchamp, Gary Fay

Temple
Mischtian, John Michael

Wichita Falls
Williams, Steven Mark

UTAH

Ogden
Kaufman, Steven Michael
Sullivan, Kevin Patrick

Salt Lake City
Mooney, Jerome Henri
Rasmussen, Thomas Val, Jr.,

VERMONT

Montpelier
Valerio, Matthew F.

VIRGINIA

Abingdon
Conway, Berry Leslie, II,

Amherst
Martin, Stephen Clarke

Arlington
Green, Richard Alan

Charlottesville
Armstrong, Richard Charles
Wyatt, Deborah Chasen

Fairfax
Sriskandarajah, Atchuthan

Hot Springs
Deeds, Robert Creigh

Lebanon
Compton, Carnis Eugene

Leesburg
Tichenor, Patricia E.M.

Lynchburg
Angel, James Joseph
Packert, G(ayla) Beth

Martinsville
Williams, Ebb Harry, III,

Newport News
Saunders, Bryan Leslie

Norfolk
Fletcher, John Richard
Gibson, Beverly Cullen

Petersburg
Spero, Morton Bertram

Powhatan
Carrico, Lucretia A.

Richmond
Troy, Anthony Francis

Roanoke
Hylton, Myles Talbert
Thomson, Paul Rice, Jr.,

Salem
Griffith, H(oward) Morgan

Vienna
Razzano, Frank Charles

Virginia Beach
Holmes, William James
Schafer, Gerard Thomas Roger

Warrenton
Howard, Blair Duncan
Morrison, Paul A.

Wytheville
Baird, Thomas Bryan, Jr.,
Crewe, Trenton Guy, Jr.,

WASHINGTON

Everett
Mestel, Mark David

Mount Vernon
Moser, C. Thomas

Seattle
Gonick, Peter B.
McKay, Michael Dennis
Muenster, John Rolfing
Novotny, Patricia Susan
Schwartz, Irwin H.
Taylor, David F.
Vogel, David Seth
Wayne, Robert Jonathan

Spokane
Weatherhead, Leslie R.

WEST VIRGINIA

Bluefield
Henderson, Susan Ellen Fortune

Charleston
Cline, Michael Robert

Huntington
Underwood, Mark Forest

Romney
Saville, Royce Blair

Wheeling
Bailey, John P.
Wilmoth, William David

WISCONSIN

Casco
Richards, Steven George

Colby
Nikolay, Frank Lawrence

Kenosha
Clarke, Alan William

Madison
Blanchard, Brian Wheatley
Kelly, T. Christopher
Mowris, Gerald William
Wood, Tracey Ann

Menomonie
Steans, Phillip Michael

Racine
Younglove, Michael Robert

Waukesha
Bohren, Michael Oscar

Wausau
Connell, James Bernard
Drengler, William Allan John

Wauwatosa
Bonneson, Paul Garland

WYOMING

Cheyenne
Mackey, Terrence Wayne
Scorsine, John Magnus

Evanston
Combs, William L.

Jackson
Spence, Gerald Leonard

Rock Springs
Honaker, Richard Henderson

Worland
Richins, Kent Alan
Sweeny, Wendy Press

TERRITORIES OF THE UNITED STATES

VIRGIN ISLANDS

St Thomas
Caffee, Lorren Dale

MEXICO

Guadalajara
Godoy, Cesar Eduardo

Mexicali
Vega, Alonso

CZECH REPUBLIC

Prague
Honsa, Frantisek

GEORGIA

Atlanta
Wakefield, Stephen Alan

IDAHO

Boise
Meyer, Christopher Hawkins

ILLINOIS

Chicago
Fazio, Peter Victor, Jr.,
Holsinger, John Paul

Lake Forest
Emerson, William Harry

MARYLAND

Bethesda
Eisen, Eric Anshel
Rivkin, Steven Robert

MASSACHUSETTS

Boston
Hester, Patrick Joseph

MISSOURI

Kansas City
Bates, William Hubert

NEW YORK

New York
Adair, Wendell Hinton, Jr.,
Allen, Leon Arthur, Jr.,
Kelly, John Fleming
Martin, George J., Jr.,
Vassil, John Charles

Pittsford
George, Richard Neill

OREGON

Portland
Dotten, Michael Chester

TEXAS

Dallas
Armour, James Lott
Keithley, Bradford Gene

Houston
Hartrick, Janice Kay
Kelly, Hugh Rice
Kennedy, John Edward
Martin, Jay Griffith
Ryan, Thomas William
Woung-Chapman, Marguerite Natalie

VIRGINIA

Alexandria
Sczudlo, Walter Joseph

Norfolk
Smith, Richard Muldrow

WASHINGTON

Tacoma
Waldo, James Chandler

GERMANY

Frankfurt
Just, Christoph Oliver Thomas

ITALY

Milan
Parola, Lorenzo

ADDRESS UNPUBLISHED

Choukas-Bradley, James Richard
Harshman, Raymond Brent
Tanenbaum, Jay Harvey

ENERGY, NUCLEAR POWER

UNITED STATES

ALABAMA

Birmingham
Robin, Theodore Tydings, Jr.,

CALIFORNIA

San Francisco
Morrissey, John Carroll, Sr.,

CONNECTICUT

Hartford
Knickerbocker, Robert Platt, Jr.,

DISTRICT OF COLUMBIA

Washington
McBride, Michael Flynn
McMahon, Joseph Einar
Ruddy, Frank

FLORIDA

Naples
Doub, William Offutt

ILLINOIS

Chicago
Rooney, Matthew A.

MARYLAND

Saint Michaels
Brown, Omer Forrest, II,

MASSACHUSETTS

Sudbury
Dignan, Thomas Gregory, Jr.,

NEW YORK

New York
Hayes, Gerald Joseph

NORTH CAROLINA

Raleigh
Glass, Fred Stephen

PENNSYLVANIA

Media
Durham, James W.

Pittsburgh
Cowan, Barton Zalman

TEXAS

Houston
Morgan, Richard Greer
Tartt, Blake

Sugar Land
Koh, Chye Hock

AUSTRALIA

Sydney
Machin, Peter William

ENGLAND

London
Haubold, Samuel Allen

ITALY

Milan
Tedeschi, Edoardo

PORTUGAL

Lisbon
Melo, Pedro

TAIWAN

Taipei
Hsiao, Joanne Y.

ADDRESS UNPUBLISHED

Eaken, Bruce Webb, Jr.,
Fetzer, Mark Stephen

ENTERTAINMENT

UNITED STATES

ARIZONA

Phoenix
Lubin, Stanley
Silverman, Alan Henry

CALIFORNIA

Beverly Hills
Brown, Hermione Kopp
Isaacman, Alan L.
Schiff, Gunther Hans

Encinitas
Nemeth, Valerie Ann

Irvine
Specter, Richard Bruce

Los Angeles
Bennett, Bianca Cherie
Boxer, Lester
Demoff, Marvin Alan
Diamond, Stanley Jay
Donaldson, Michael Cleaves
Feigen, Brenda S.
Lurvey, Ira Harold
MacIntosh, Jay W.
Meisinger, Louis M.
Menes, Paul Ira
Pascotto, Alvaro
Pasich, Kirk Alan
Robertson, Hugh Duff
Rosenthal, Sol

Newport Beach
Schiff, Laurie

Redwood City
Mandel, Martin Louis

San Francisco
Getto, Ernest John
Weiner, Jody Carl

Santa Monica
Cooper, Jay Leslie
Pizzulli, Francis Cosmo Joseph
Roberts, Virgil Patrick

Sausalito
Gordon, Robert Eugene

Sherman Oaks
Joyce, Stephen Michael

Universal City
Husband, Bertram Paul

Westlake Village
Hoefflin, Richard Michael

COLORADO

Centennial
Barnthouse, William Joseph

Denver
McCabe, John L.

CONNECTICUT

New Haven
Gastwirth, Donald Edward

DISTRICT OF COLUMBIA

Washington
Babby, Lon S.
Barnett, Robert Bruce
May, Randolph Joseph
Mc Pherson, Harry Cummings, Jr.,
O'Connor, Charles P.

FLORIDA

Boca Raton
Jacobs, Joseph James

Clearwater
Weidemeyer, Carleton Lloyd

Fort Lauderdale
Benjamin, James Scott
Zimmerman, Elliot Michael

West Palm Beach
Finley, Chandler R.

GEORGIA

Atlanta
Koplan, Andrew Bennet
Smith, Jeffrey Michael

Stone Mountain
Minter, Kendall Arthur

HAWAII

Honolulu
Bourgoin, David L.

ILLINOIS

Chicago
Crull, Jan, Jr.,
Durchslag, Stephen P.
Hoffman, Valerie Jane
Rubin, E(rwin) Leonard
Sennet, Charles Joseph
Wilson, Clarence Sylvester, Jr.,

Matteson
Wigell, Raymond George

Oak Brook
Mlsna, Kathryn Kimura

INDIANA

Indianapolis
Carr, David J.
Elberger, Ronald Edward

LOUISIANA

Shreveport
Bryant, J(ames) Bruce

MARYLAND

Baltimore
Gilbert, Blaine Louis
Katz, Lawrence Edward

MASSACHUSETTS

Boston
Fischer, Mark Alan
Geismer, Alan Stearn, Jr.,
Koutoujian, Peter John
Larson, Olive Elizabeth
Litwin, Paul Jeffrey

Northampton
Fierst, Frederick Udell
Kunkel, Leah R.

MICHIGAN

Bloomfield Hills
Hertz, Howard

Dexter
Millman, Jode Susan

MINNESOTA

Minneapolis
Street, Erica Catherine
Voss, Barry Vaughan

MISSOURI

Kansas City
Kitchin, John Joseph
Stremming, Troy Alan

Saint Louis
Cullen, James D.

Springfield
Evans, William Ellis

NEVADA

Las Vegas
Goodwin, John Robert

NEW HAMPSHIRE

Concord
Hodes, Paul William

NEW JERSEY

Montclair
Brown, Ronald Wellington

NEW YORK

Bethpage
Lemle, Robert Spencer

Chappaqua
Castrataro, Barbara Ann

Kew Gardens
Schechter, Donald Robert

New York
Breglio, John F.
Butterman, Jay Ronald
Colfin, Bruce Elliott
Collyer, Michael
Cramer, Edward Morton
Curtis, Frank R.
Dretzin, David
Goldberg, David
Greenbaum, Jeffrey Alan
Greenberg, Hayley
Grossberg, David
Indursky, Arthur
Jacobson, Jeffrey E.
Laufer, Jacob
Levinson, Paul Howard
Lighter, Lawrence
McCarthy, Robert Emmett
Nearing, Vivienne W.
Oppenheimer, Martin J.
Papernik, Joel Ira
Plotkin, Loren H.
Poster, Michael Sollod
Ryan, J. Richard
Spanbock, Maurice Samuel
Tritter, Daniel F.
Zissu, Michael Jerome

Pound Ridge
Golenbock, Susan A.

Rochester
Twietmeyer, Don Henry

Scarsdale
Angel, Dennis

Westbury
Nogee, Jeffrey Laurence

OKLAHOMA

Norman
Fairbanks, Robert Alvin

PENNSYLVANIA

Philadelphia
Berger, Harold
DeBunda, Salvatore Michael

Pittsburgh
Stepanian, Steven Arvid, II,

RHODE ISLAND

Providence
Decarvalho, Kas R.

TENNESSEE

Memphis
Moore, Dwight Terry

Nashville
Bramlett, Paul Kent
Lyon, Philip K(irkland)

TEXAS

Austin
Black, William Earl

Dallas
Coggins, Paul Edward, Jr.,
DelHomme, Beverly Ann
McGarry, Charles William

Houston
Bargfrede, James Allen

Lubbock
Saied, Robert Mack

UTAH

Salt Lake City
Mooney, Jerome Henri

VIRGINIA

Alexandria
Lauderdale, Katherine Sue

Richmond
Goodpasture, Philip Henry

WASHINGTON

Seattle
Bergstedt, Anders Spencer
Sussman, Neil A.

WISCONSIN

Milwaukee
Misey, Robert J., Jr.,

CHINA

Beijing
Liu, Ge

ENGLAND

Birmingham
Hull, David Julian

Oxford
Loake, Jonathan David

GERMANY

Nuremberg
Schwartz, Harald Josef

ITALY

Milan
Peron, Sabrina

JAPAN

Osaka
Iijima, Ayumu

NORWAY

Oslo
Strømme, Vidar

SWEDEN

Stockholm
Danowsky, Peter
Widmark, Stefan

SWITZERLAND

Zürich
Auf der Maur, Rolf

ADDRESS UNPUBLISHED

Davis, Donald Glenn
Fantino, Lisa Maria
Harvey, Marc S(ean)
Lightstone, Ronald
Meyerson, Stanley Phillip
Muller, Peter
Noddings, Sarah Ellen
O'Connor, Edward Vincent, Jr.,
Satorius, Daniel Mark
Siporin, Sheldon
Spira, Immanuel Isaac
Springer, Paul David
Treacy, Vincent Edward
von Sauers, Joseph F.
Winslow, F(rancis) Dana
Zaharoff, Howard George

ENVIRONMENTAL

UNITED STATES

ALABAMA

Birmingham
Alford, Margie Searcy
Brown, T. Michael
Gale, Fournier Joseph, III,
Palmer, Robert Leslie
Pritchett, Rebecca Wright
Robin, Theodore Tydings, Jr.,

Mobile
Johnston, Neil Chunn
Pierce, Donald Fay

ALASKA

Anchorage
Flynn, Charles P.
Linxwiler, James David
Owens, Robert Patrick

Kodiak
Ott, Andrew Eduard

ARIZONA

Flagstaff
Gliege, John Gerhardt
Lacey, Henry Bernard

Phoenix
Curry, J. Stanton
Henze, Tom
Storey, Lee A.
Wolf, G. Van Velsor, Jr.,

Scottsdale
Jorden, Douglas Allen

Tempe
Shimpock, Kathy Elizabeth

ARKANSAS

Little Rock
Julian, Jim Lee

CALIFORNIA

Beverly Hills
Bordy, Michael Jeffrey

Campbell
Bass, Lewis

Chino Hills
Pearson, April Virginia

Claremont
Vera, Ronald Thomas

Fremont
Cummings, John Patrick

La Jolla
Peterson, Paul Ames

Los Angeles
Fisher, Barry Alan
Gest, Howard David
Hieronymus, Edward Whittlesey
Moskowitz, Joel Steven
Olivas, Daniel Anthony
Renwick, Edward S.
Rutter, Marshall Anthony
Tarr, Ralph William
Wright, Kenneth Brooks

Moraga
Kilbourne, George William

Oakland
Waltner, Alan Conrad

Sacramento
Brewer, Roy Edward
Eickmeyer, Evan
Goode, Barry Paul
Robbins, Stephen J. M.
Thorme, Melissa Anne

San Diego
Dawe, James Robert
Longstreth, Robert Christy

San Francisco
Bruen, James A.
Byrne, Robert William
Gibson, Virginia Lee
Matthews, Philip Richard
Penskar, Mark Howard
Robertson, J. Martin
Rossmann, Antonio
Seneker, Carl James, II, (Kim Seneker)

Santa Barbara
Metzinger, Timothy Edward

COLORADO

Boulder
Gray, William R.
Yuhnke, Robert E.

Denver
Benton, Auburn Edgar
Goldberg, Gregory Eban
Grant, Patrick Alexander
Holme, Howard Kelley
McIntosh, Carolyn Leigh
Merritts, Jack Michael
Ray, Bruce David
Rockwood, Linda Lee
Sayre, John Marshall
Shepherd, John Frederic

Golden
Hughes, Marcia Marie
Snead, Kathleen Marie

Littleton
Cypser, Darlene Ann

Thornton
Sherk, George William

CONNECTICUT

Greenwich
Pascarella, Henry William

Hartford
Buck, Gurdon Hall
Davis, Andrew Neil
Merriam, Dwight Haines
Sussman, Mark Richard

DELAWARE

Wilmington
Waisanen, Christine M.

DISTRICT OF COLUMBIA

Washington
Abeles, Charles Calvert
Adams, John Jillson
Bardin, David J.
Bernstein, Mitchell Harris
Bleicher, Samuel Abram
Bruce, E(stel) Edward
Carr, Lawrence Edward, Jr.,
Chang, Deanna J.
Durnil, Gordon Kay
Ewing, Ky Pepper, Jr.,
Faron, Robert Steven
Frost, Edmund Bowen
Garrett, Theodore Louis
Haynes, William J(ames), II,
Hollis, Sheila Slocum
Huddleson, Edwin Emmett, III,
Hutt, Peter Barton
Joseph, Daniel Mordecai
Keiner, Suellen Terrill
Kirsch, Laurence Stephen
Kovacs, William Lawrence
Legro, Stanley Wayne
Lettow, Charles Frederick
Lewis, William Henry, Jr.,
Littell, Richard Gregory
Macleod, John Amend
McElveen, Junius Carlisle, Jr.,
McMahon, Joseph Einar
Mills, Kevin Paul
Raul, Alan Charles
Rose, Jonathan Chapman
Ruddy, Frank
Smith, Turner Taliaferro, Jr.,
Starr, Judson Wilmarth
Stoll, Richard G(iles)
Vardaman, John Wesley
Waldron, Jonathan Kent
Wine, L. Mark

FLORIDA

Apopka
Seward, Jeffrey James

Gainesville
Boyes, Patrice Flinchbaugh

Key Largo
Mattson, James Stewart

Lake Buena Vista
Schmudde, Lee Gene

Lakeland
Martin, Michael David

Miami
Fleming, Joseph Z.
Halsey, Douglas Martin
Thornton, John William, Sr.,

Miami Lakes
Sharett, Alan Richard

Orlando
Sims, Roger W.

Palm Bay
Tietig, Edward Chester

Pensacola
Smith, G. Thomas

Sarasota
Salomone, William Gerald

Tallahassee
Alderman, Silvia Morell
Curtin, Lawrence N.
DeFoor, J. Allison, II,
Dix, Martin Robert
Downie, Robert Collins, II,

Tampa
Brown, Enola T.
Schwenke, Roger Dean

GEORGIA

Atlanta
Killorin, Robert Ware
Ortiz, Jay Richard Gentry
Smith, Walton Napier
Stokes, James Sewell
Williams, Joel Cash
Wright, Frederick Lewis, II,

Macon
Ennis, Edgar William, Jr.,

Metter
Doremus, Ogden

HAWAII

Honolulu
Lombardi, Dennis M.
Okinaga, Carrie Kiyono

IDAHO

Boise
Meyer, Christopher Hawkins

ILLINOIS

Chicago
Eggert, Russell Raymond
Feinstein, Fred Ira
Greenspan, Jeffrey Dov
Hammesfahr, Robert Winter
Harrington, James Timothy
Harrold, Bernard
Lockwood, Gary Lee
McMahon, Thomas Michael
Murray, Daniel Charles
Olian, Robert Martin
Pirok, Edward Warren
Pope, Michael Arthur
Rohrman, Douglass Frederick
Rundio, Louis Michael, Jr.,
Schink, James Harvey
Schoenfield, Rick Merrill
Shindler, Donald A.
Stick, Michael Alan
Thomson, George Ronald
Zabel, Sheldon Alter

Glen Ellyn
O'Connell, Daniel James

Shorewood
Copeland, Charlene Carole

Springfield
Immke, Keith Henry
Rominger, M. Kyle

Western Springs
Hanson, Heidi Elizabeth

INDIANA

Evansville
Wallace, Keith M.

Indianapolis
Beckwith, Lewis Daniel
Korin, Offer
Scaletta, Phillip Ralph, III,
Silver, Gregory K.

Lafayette
Benton, Anthony Stuart
Hart, Russell Holiday

IOWA

Davenport
Shaw, Elizabeth Orr

KANSAS

Overland Park
Sherlock, E. Todd

Wichita
Badger, Ronald Kay

KENTUCKY

Frankfort
Chadwick, Robert

LOUISIANA

Metairie
O'Donnell, Barbara Bourdonnay

New Orleans
Coleman, James Julian, Jr.,
Grant, Arthur Gordon, Jr.,
Pearce, John Y.
Rodriguez, Antonio Jose
Sinor, Howard Earl, Jr.,
St. John, James Berry, Jr.,
Stag, Michael Gregory
Villavaso, Stephen Donald

MARYLAND

Baltimore
Fisher, Morton Poe, Jr.,
Sack, Sylvan Hanan

Bethesda
Hagberg, Viola Wilgus
Pipkin, James Harold, Jr.,
Rivkin, Steven Robert

Gaithersburg
Sherer, Samuel Ayers

Glen Burnie
Lilly, John Richard, II,

Hagerstown
Berkson, Jacob Benjamin

Saint Michaels
Brown, Omer Forrest, II,

MASSACHUSETTS

Boston
Arrowood, Lisa Gayle
Cohn, Andrew Howard
Hackney, H(iram) Hamilton, III,
Hugo, Michael R.
Johnston, Richard Alan
Last, Michael P.
McKenna, Karen L.
Stevenson, Philip Davis
Trimmier, Roscoe, Jr.,
Tuchmann, Robert

New Bedford
Murray, Robert Fox

Orleans
Chaplin, Ansel Burt

Sudbury
Dignan, Thomas Gregory, Jr.,

MICHIGAN

Bloomfield Hills
Charla, Leonard Francis
Gotthelf, Beth

Detroit
Collier, James Warren
Fromm, Frederick Andrew, Jr.,
Sparrow, Herbert George, III,

Gaylord
Topp, Susan Hlywa

Grand Rapids
Birkbeck, A.J. Koerts
Brinkmeyer, Scott S.

Lansing
Baker, Frederick Milton, Jr.,

Southfield
Cassar, George V., Jr.,

Traverse City
Quandt, Joseph Edward

MINNESOTA

Minneapolis
Comstock, Rebecca Ann
Duncan, Richard Alan
Goodman, Elizabeth Ann
Gordon, John Bennett
Keppel, William James

Plymouth
Saville, Derric James

MISSISSIPPI

Jackson
Hemleben, Scott P.
Shinn, Clinton Wesley

MISSOURI

Kansas City
Beck, William G.
Eldridge, Truman Kermit, Jr.,
Gardner, Brian E.
Price, James Tucker
Satterlee, Terry Jean
Smithson, Lowell Lee

Maryville
McLaughlin, James Patrick

Saint Louis
Berendt, Robert Tryon
Gilhousen, Brent James
Hiles, Bradley Stephen
Joerling, Dale Raymond
Massey, Raymond Lee
Noel, Edwin Lawrence

MONTANA

Billings
Murphy, Gregory Gerard

Butte
Carlson, Robert M.

NEBRASKA

Lincoln
Colleran, Kevin

NEVADA

Reno
Hornbeck, David Arthur

NEW HAMPSHIRE

Concord
Young, Sherilyn Burnett

Exeter
Donahue, Michael Joseph

Hanover
Lundquist, Weyman Ivan

Warner
Coolidge, Daniel Scott

NEW JERSEY

Cherry Hill
Kole, Janet Stephanie
Tomar, William

Florham Park
Pantel, Glenn Steven

Freehold
Lijoi, Peter Bruno

Hackensack
Duus, Gordon Cochran

Lyndhurst
McNamara, Patrick James

Montville
Buzak, Edward Joseph

Morristown
Bromberg, Myron James
Rose, Robert Gordon

Newark
Corbin Walker, Karol

Princeton
Picco, Steven Joseph

Roseland
Hayden, Joseph A., Jr.,
LaVecchia, John B.

Scotch Plains
Klock, John Henry

Secaucus
Fitzpatrick, Harold Francis

Summit
English, Jerry Fitzgerald
Pearlmutter, Fredi L.

Trenton
Bigham, William J.
Glassen, James Warren

Wall
Nucciarone, A. Patrick

West Orange
Gordon, Michael

Woodbury
Adler, Lewis Gerard

NEW MEXICO

Albuquerque
Ausherman, Larry Price

Santa Fe
Huffaker, Gregory Dorian, Jr.,

NEW YORK

Albany
Alessi, Robert Joseph
Hanna, John, Jr.,

Binghamton
Kramer, Philip Joseph

Buffalo
Brown, Jerrold Stanley
Slater, Craig Allyn

Hawthorne
Traub, Richard Kenneth

Lancaster
Walsh, J(ohn) B(ronson)

New York
Beattie, Richard Irwin
Benjamin, Jeff
Burgweger, Francis Joseph Dewes, Jr.,
Freeman, David John
French, John, III,
Huffman, Richard Lee
Kafin, Robert Joseph
Kezsbom, Allen
Levine, Ronald Jay
Miller, Paul S(amuel)
Milmed, Paul Kussy
Quinlan, Guy Christian
Riley, Scott C.
Seymour, Everett Hedden, Jr.,
Shea, Edward Emmett
Stever, Donald Winfred
Zuckerman, Joseph

Orangeburg
Rivet, Diana Wittmer

Purchase
Andrews, David Ralph

Rochester
Witmer, George Robert, Jr.,

Syracuse
Baldwin, Robert Frederick, Jr.,
Duffy, Shirley Kathleen
Regan, Paul Michael

West Harrison
Johnson, Craig Edward

White Plains
Feder, Robert
Silverberg, Steven Mark

NORTH CAROLINA

Asheville
Lawrence, Betty Tenn

Charlotte
Belthoff, Richard Charles, Jr.,

Raleigh
Carmichael, Carson, III,
Dunn, Hubert Glenn Tolson
Ellis, Lester Neal, Jr.,
Thomas, Jason Selig

Wilmington
Seagle, J. Harold

OHIO

Cincinnati
Cioffi, Michael Lawrence
Frantz, Robert Wesley
Hill, Thomas Clark
O'Reilly, James Thomas
Parker, R. Joseph

Cleveland
Falsgraf, William Wendell
Gippin, Robert Malcolm
Hardy, Michael Lynn
Janke, Ronald Robert
Moore, Kenneth Cameron
Young, James Edward

Columbus
Hardymon, David Wayne
Maynard, Robert Howell
Taylor, Joel Sanford

Jefferson
Lemire, Jerome Albert

Medina
Arnold, Alanna S. Welling

Wooster
Haught, Sharon Kay

OKLAHOMA

Oklahoma City
Steinhorn, Irwin Harry

OREGON

Portland
Dailey, Dianne K.
Sokol, Larry Nides

PENNSYLVANIA

Bala Cynwyd
Manko, Joseph Martin, Sr.,

Harrisburg
Burcat, Joel Robin
Burcat, Joel Robin
Downey, Brian Patrick
Kury, Franklin Leo
Van Zile, Philip Taylor, III,
Wilson, Craig P.

New Buffalo
Cramer, John McNaight

Philadelphia
Auerbach, Sheryl Lynn
Collings, Robert L.
Cox, Roger Frazier
Leonard, Thomas
Maxey, David Walker
Rosenstein, James Alfred
Stevens, Mark Alan

Pittsburgh
Hull, John Daniel, IV,
Picadio, Anthony Peter
Veeder, Peter Greig

Williamsport
Ertel, Allen Edward

RHODE ISLAND

Providence
McConnell, John James, Jr.,
Murphy, James Truden

Warwick
Reilly, John B.

SOUTH CAROLINA

Charleston
Robinson, Neil Cibley, Jr.,

Columbia
Dibble, Robert Wightman, Jr.,

Greenville
Smoak, Lewis Tyson
White, Daniel Bowman
Wyche, Madison Baker, III,

TENNESSEE

Hendersonville
McCaleb, Joe Wallace

Memphis
Broadhurst, Jerome Anthony
Carr, Oscar Clark, III,
McLean, Robert Alexander

Nashville
Jacobs, Sharon O.

TEXAS

Austin
Golemon, Ronald Kinnan
Nevola, Roger
Patman, Philip Franklin
Rider, Brian Clayton

Corpus Christi
Coover, Ann E.

Dallas
Dutton, Diana Cheryl
Flowers, Bruce Marvin
Johnson, James Joseph Scofield
Westfall, Constance Courtney

Henderson
Adkison, Ron

Houston
Ballanfant, Richard Burton
Bayko, Emil Thomas
Crinion, Gregory Paul
Dinkins, Carol Eggert
Edwards, Blaine Douglass
Forbes, Arthur Lee, III,
Gonynor, Francis James
Martin, Jay Griffith

Mcallen
Jarvis, Robert Glenn

San Antonio
Labay, Eugene Benedict

UTAH

Logan
Honaker, Jimmie Joe

Salt Lake City
Adams, John A.
Becker, Ralph Elihu, Jr.,
Beless, Rosemary June
Dragoo, Denise Ann
Manning, Brent V.

VERMONT

Burlington
Rendall, Donald James, Jr.,
Schroeder, William Wayne

VIRGINIA

Charlottesville
Merrill, Richard Austin

Falls Church
Meserve, Richard Andrew
Middleton, J. Howard, Jr.,

Norfolk
Baird, Edward Rouzie, Jr.,
Parker, Richard Wilson

Richmond
Freeman, George Clemon, Jr.,
Landin, David Craig
Pomeroy, Christopher Donald

Roanoke
Thomson, Paul Rice, Jr.,

Williamsburg
Graham, David Browning

WASHINGTON

Bellevue
Medved, Robert Allen

Olympia
Miller, Allen Terry, Jr.,

Richland
Norris, Kenneth Michael

Seattle
Blumenfeld, Charles Raban
Freedman, Bart Joseph
Kilbane, Thomas M.
Leed, Roger Melvin
McCann, Richard Eugene
McCune, Philip Spear
McKinstry, Ronald E.
Redman, Eric
Robinson-Dorn, Michael Jay
Robinson-Dorn, Trilby C. E.
Wilson, Richard Randolph

Tacoma
Goodstein, Robert I.
Mack, Robert E.
Waldo, James Chandler

Vancouver
Karpinski, John Stanley

WEST VIRGINIA

Charleston
Victorson, Michael Bruce

Fairview
Bunner, William Keck

WISCONSIN

Madison
Heymann, S. Richard
Rankin, Gene Raymond

Milwaukee
Grzezinski, Dennis Michael

WYOMING

Sheridan
Cannon, Kim Decker

COSTA RICA

San José
Retana, Vanessa

GERMANY

Frankfurt
Just, Christoph Oliver Thomas

INDIA

New Delhi
Kachwaha, Sumeet

ISRAEL

Jerusalem
Stern, Doron Daniel

NEW ZEALAND

Auckland
Laxon, William Allan

ADDRESS UNPUBLISHED

Adams, Thomas Lynch, Jr.,
Ayers, Kristen Ness
Connell, William D.
Eaton, Larry Ralph
Fetzer, Mark Stephen
Francis, Jerome Leslie
Garner, Mary Martin
Gold, Martin Elliott
Klaus, Charles
Lippes, Richard James
Meraz, Salvador Adrian
Minahan, Daniel Francis
Moyer, Craig Alan
Muri, Anthony Frederick
Myers, Bill
Orloff, Neil
Rosen, Martin Jack
Terp, Thomas Thomsen
van Gestel, Allan
Wright, Robert Payton

ESTATE PLANNING *See also* Probate; Taxation, estate

UNITED STATES

ALABAMA

Birmingham
Foster, Arthur Key, Jr.,

Mobile
Armbrecht, William Henry, III,
Brock, Glen Porter, Jr.,
Holland, Lyman Faith, Jr.,

Montgomery
Leslie, Henry Arthur
Smith, Jerome David

ALASKA

Anchorage
Brautigam, Peter Bryan

ARIZONA

Mesa
Gunderson, Brent Merrill
Smith, Kenneth M.

Phoenix
Case, David Leon
Ehmann, Anthony Valentine
Litteral, Daniel Pace
Olsen, Alfred Jon
Swartz, Melvin Jay
Tomback, Jay Loren

Scottsdale
Lindgren, D(erbin) Kenneth, Jr.,
Lowry, Edward Francis, Jr.,
Roberts, Jean Reed

Yuma
Hunt, Gerald Wallace

ARKANSAS

Fayetteville
Lushbaugh, Brad

Fort Smith
Daily, Thomas A.

Harrison
Pinson, Jerry D.

Little Rock
Haught, William Dixon
Stockburger, Jean Dawson

Warren
Claycomb, Hugh Murray

CALIFORNIA

Alameda
Dósa, Andrew Alexander
Stonehouse, James Adam

Camarillo
Dunlevy, William Sargent
Pugh, Francis Leo

Cerritos
Sarno, Maria Erlinda

Downey
Tompkins, Dwight Edward

Emeryville
Howe, Drayton Ford, Jr.,

Fullerton
Roberts, Mark Scott

Grass Valley
Hawkins, Richard Michael

Greenbrae
Bonapart, Alan David

Huntington Beach
Armstrong, Alan Leigh

Long Beach
Tikosh, Mark Axente

Los Altos
Weir, Robert H.

Los Angeles
Antin, Michael
Basile, Paul Louis, Jr.,
Campbell, Jennifer Louise
Carter, Bret Robert
Forster, Jonathan Shawn
Gorman, Joseph Gregory, Jr.,
Grobe, Charles Stephen
May, Lawrence Edward
Rae, Matthew Sanderson, Jr.,
Ruskey, John A.
Shacter, David Mervyn
Stephens, George Edward, Jr.,
Tobisman, Stuart Paul
Weinstock, Harold

Mill Valley
Dyer, Gregory Clark

Morgan Hill
Foster, John Robert

Newport Beach
Allen, Russell G.
Mortensen, Arvid LeGrande

North Hollywood
Kreger, Melvin Joseph
Zimring, Stuart David

Oakland
McDonnell, John L., Jr.,

Palm Desert
Reinhardt, Benjamin Max

Palos Verdes Estates
Toftness, Cecil Gillman

Pasadena
Calleton, Theodore Edward

D'Angelo, Robert William
Davis, Edmond Ray

Petaluma
Eller, Leslie Robert

Rancho Mirage
Leydorf, Frederick Leroy

Sacramento
Craven, Thomas Arthur
Mueller, Virginia Schwartz

Saint Helena
Marvin, Monica Louise Wolf

Salinas
Etienne, Myron E., Jr.,

San Diego
Hofflund, Paul
Payne, Margaret Anne
Sceper, Duane Harold

San Francisco
Friedman, K. Bruce
Greene, Richard Lawrence
Guggenhime, Richard Johnson
Manning, Jerome Alan
Sugarman, Myron George
Wild, Nelson Hopkins

San Jose
Cummins, Charles Fitch, Jr.,

San Luis Obispo
Dorsi, Stephen Nathan
Krout, Michael Seth

San Mateo
Bhatnagar, Mary Elizabeth
Slabach, Stephen Hall

San Rafael
Drexler, Kenneth

Santa Barbara
Egenolf, Robert F.
McEwen, Willard Winfield, Jr.,

Santa Monica
Axe, Norman Gold

Stockton
Blewett, Robert Noall

Torrance
Moore, Christopher M.

Victorville
Kennedy, Jeanne Elizabeth

Walnut Creek
Baker, Roy Gordon, Jr.,

Yuba City
Doughty, Mark Anthony

COLORADO

Arvada
Johnson, Christian Kent

Colorado Springs
Buell, Bruce Temple
Keene, Kenneth Paul
Kendall, Phillip Alan
Palermo, Norman Anthony

Commerce City
Trujillo, Lorenzo A.

Crested Butte
Renfrow, Jay Royce

Denver
Atlass, Theodore Bruce
Cain, Douglas Mylchreest
Crow, Nancy Rebecca
McMichael, Donald Earl
Mitchem, Allen P.
Olsen, M. Kent
Phelps, Robert Frederick, Jr.,
Schmidt, L(ail) William, Jr.,

Durango
Sherman, Lester Ivan

Lakewood
Brant, John Getty
Thome, Dennis Wesley

Littleton
Carleno, Harry Eugene

Parker
Greenberg, Morton Paul

Pueblo
O'Callaghan, R.J. Patrick

Rocky Ford
Mendenhall, Harry Barton

CONNECTICUT

Colchester
Broder, Joseph Arnold

Greenwich
Bentley, Peter
Brandrup, Douglas Warren
Selby, Leland Clay

Hartford
Appel, Robert Eugene
Richter, Donald Paul

New Britain
Hogan, John W., Jr.,

New London
Johnstone, Philip MacLaren

Stamford
Bobrow, Henry Bernard
Sarner, Richard Alan

Waterbury
Dost, Mark W.

West Hartford
Lynch, Karen Renzulli
Storm, Robert Warren

Westport
Carr, Cynthia
Dimes, Edwin Kinsley
Kosakow, James Matthew

DELAWARE

Wilmington
Grossman, Jerome Kent
Jewell, George Benson
Jolles, Janet K. Pilling
Reiver, Joanna
Tigani, Bruce William

DISTRICT OF COLUMBIA

Washington
Bergner, Jane Cohen
Blazek-White, Doris
Colson, Earl Morton
Damico, Nicholas Peter
Determan, Sara-Ann
Faley, R(ichard) Scott
Mayfield, Richard Heverin
McCoy, Jerry Jack
Ostrov, Jerome
Pearlstein, Paul Davis
Plaine, Lloyd Leva
Silver, Sidney J.

FLORIDA

Boca Raton
Reinstein, Joel
Tescher, Donald R.

Boynton Beach
Solkoff, Scott M.

Bradenton
Lopacki, Edward Joseph, Jr.,
St. Paul, Alexandra De La Vergne

Clearwater
Weidemeyer, Carleton Lloyd

Coral Springs
Polin, Alan Jay

Fort Lauderdale
Dressler, Robert A.
Gore, George Henry
Hess, George Franklin, II,
Katz, Thomas Owen
Nyce, John Daniel

Jacksonville
Steffey, Fred H.

Jupiter
Click, David Forrest

Lakeland
Harris, Christy Franklin
Martin, Michael David

Miami
Chabrow, Penn Benjamin
Ersek, Gregory Joseph Mark
Glickman, Fred Elliott
Hall, Miles Lewis, Jr.,
Lancaster, Kenneth G.
Morgan, Charles Oxford, Jr.,
Ruffner, Charles Louis
Scheer, Mark Jeffrey
Weiner, Lawrence

Naples
Anderson, John Thomas
Cimino, Richard Dennis
Rigor, Bradley Glenn
Stevens, William Kenneth
Strauss, Jerome Manfred
Westman, Carl Edward

North Miami Beach
Slewett, Robert David

Orlando
Boyles, William Archer
Lefkowitz, Ivan Martin

Ormond Beach
Logan, Sharon Brooks

Palm Beach Gardens
Flemiing, Joshua Michael

Plant City
Sparkman, Steven Leonard

Port Charlotte
Levin, Allen Jay

Sarasota
Conetta, Tami Foley

Sebring
Trombley, Michael Jerome

Tallahassee
Dariotis, Terrence Theodore
France, Belinda Takach

Tampa
Ellwanger, Thomas John
Gonzalez, Joe Manuel
O'Neill, Albert Clarence, Jr.,
Vessel, Robert Leslie

Venice
Britton, Andrew James

West Palm Beach
Henry, Thornton Montagu
Lampert, Michael Allen

GEORGIA

Atlanta
Bird, Wendell Raleigh
Calhoun, Scott Douglas
Durrett, James Frazer, Jr.,
Hoffman, Michael William
Kitchens, Joyce Ellen
Lamon, Harry Vincent, Jr.,
Linkous, William Joseph, Jr.,
Manigault, Edward Middleton
Salo, Ann Sexton Distler
Smith, Alexander Wyly, Jr.,
Thrower, Randolph William
Williams, J. William

Augusta
Lee, Lansing Burrows, Jr.,

Doraville
Gerstein, Joe Willie

Savannah
Dickey, David Herschel
Searcy, William Nelson

Tifton
Reinhardt, George Robert

HAWAII

Honolulu
Adams, Jo-Ann Marie
Bunn, Robert Burgess
Gerson, Mervyn Stuart
Keppeler, H(erbert) K(arl) Bruss
Taylor, Carroll Stribling

Kapolei
Zabanal, Eduardo Olegario

Kihei
Burns, Richard Gordon

Wailuku
Bodden, Thomas Andrew

IDAHO

Boise
Erickson, Robert Stanley

Caldwell
Kerrick, David Ellsworth

Moscow
Bielenberg, Leonard Herman

Saint Maries
Park, Jerrold Elliott

ILLINOIS

Alton
Struif, L. James

Arlington Heights
Biestek, John Paul

Belleville
Mathis, Patrick Bischof
Urban, Donald Wayne

Bourbonnais
Engels, Patricia Louise

Carrollton
Strickland, Hugh Alfred

Champaign
Miller, Harold Arthur

Chicago
Acker, Frederick George
Bixby, Frank Lyman
Brown, Alan Crawford
Carr, Walter Stanley
Chandler, Kent, Jr.,
Chiles, Stephen Michael
Corwin, Sherman Phillip
Ellwood, Scott
English, John Dwight
Felsenthal, Steven Altus
Gertz, Theodore Gerson
Hannah, Wayne Robertson, Jr.,
Harrington, Carol A.
Heisler, Quentin George, Jr.,
Herpe, David A.
Hess, Sidney J., Jr.,
Holleb, Marshall Maynard
Kirkpatrick, John Everett
Lutter, Paul Allen
Marshall, John David
McCann, Bradley
Nitikman, Franklin W.
Robson, Douglas Spears
Sawdey, Richard Marshall
Schar, Stephen L.
Shank, William O.
Stanhaus, James Steven
Trost, Eileen Bannon
Wiggins, Charles Henry, Jr.,

Crystal Lake
Thoms, Jeannine Aumond

Elmwood Park
Spina, Anthony Ferdinand

Genoa
Cromley, Jon Lowell

Glenview
Baetz, W. Timothy

Highland Park
Schindel, Donald Marvin

Long Grove
Fisher, Joy Deborah

Monticello
Tracy, William Francis, II,

Naperville
Klein, Richard Dennis

Oak Brook
Foltz, Michael Craig

Peoria
Coletta, Ralph John
Tomlin, James Milton

Rockford
Johnson, Thomas Stuart

Skokie
Kahn, Bert L.

South Holland
Bell, Jason Cameron

Tinley Park
Kenny, Mary Alice

Western Springs
Rhoads, Paul Kelly

Wilmette
Griffith, James D.

INDIANA

Bloomington
Tackitt, Sylvan Wright

Columbus
Crump, Francis Jefferson, III,

Fort Wayne
Dean, Laura Hansen
Fink, Thomas Michael
Springer, James Elten

Fowler
Weist, William Bernard

Indianapolis
Ewbank, Thomas Peters
Korin, Offer
Leitch, Ryan L.
Padgett, Gregory Lee
Rothbaum, Sandra Lazarus
Schneider, Michael J.
Warren, Bradford Lloyd

IOWA

Davenport
Dettmann, David Allen

Des Moines
Campbell, Bruce Irving
Simpson, Lyle Lee

Garner
Hovda, Theodore James

Muscatine
Nepple, James Anthony

KANSAS

Cottonwood Falls
North, William T.

Iola
Toland, Clyde William

Lawrence
Karlin, Calvin Joseph
Springer, Byron Eugene

Olathe
Haskin, J. Michael

Wichita
Depew, Spencer Long

KENTUCKY

Louisville
Duffy, Martin Patrick
Hallenberg, Robert Lewis

LOUISIANA

Baton Rouge
Blitzer, Sidney Milton, Jr.,

Jefferson
Conino, Joseph Aloysius

Monroe
Curry, Robert Lee, III,

New Orleans
Abbott, Hirschel Theron, Jr.,
Benjamin, Edward Bernard, Jr.,
Lemann, Thomas Berthelot
McDaniel, Donald Hamilton
Neff, Carole Cukell
Simon, H(uey) Paul
Snyder, Charles Aubrey
Wax, George Louis
Wegmann, Cynthia Anne

Shreveport
Hardtner, Quintin Theodore, III,

MAINE

Augusta
Johnson, Phillip Edward

Portland
Hunt, David Evans
Ingalls, Everett Palmer, III,
LeBlanc, Richard Philip

MARYLAND

Baltimore
Ferro, Elizabeth Krams
Mitchell, Hugh Allen, Jr.,
Moser, M(artin) Peter

Bethesda
Burton, Charles Henning
Eastman, Hope Beth
Hendricks, John Charles
Nelson, William Eugene

Phoenix
Anderson, Mary Ellen

Potomac
Redding, Robert Ellsworth

Rockville
Katz, Steven Martin

Ruxton
Lewis, Alexander Ingersoll, III,

Takoma Park
Dunn, John Benjamin

Westminster
Staples, Lyle Newton

MASSACHUSETTS

Boston
Clymer, John Howard
de Rham, Casimir, Jr.,
Kidder, George Howell
Li, Winifred I.
Milstein, Richard Sherman
Perkins, John Allen
Roche, John Jefferson
Smith, Perry Marshall
Wand, Barbara Freedman
Woodburn, Ralph Robert, Jr.,

Brookline
Alban, Ludwig

Framingham
Munro, Meredith Vance

Greenfield
Blanker, Alan Harlow

Holden
Price, Robert DeMille

Hyannis
Haddleton, Russell Edgecomb

Lexington
Hines, Edward Francis, Jr.,

Marblehead
Kirsch, Florence Weitz

Marion
Worley, Robert William, Jr.,

Needham
Cox, Gilbert W., Jr.,

Sharon
Brown, Barbara A.

South Hamilton
Campbell, Diana Butt

Springfield
Weiss, Ronald Phillip

Wellesley
Riley, Michael Hylan

West Chatham
Rowley, Glenn Harry

Weston
Thomas, Roger Meriwether

Worcester
Silver, Marvin S.

Yarmouth Port
Paquin, Thomas Christopher

MICHIGAN

Ann Arbor
Joscelyn, Kent B(uckley)

Bloomfield Hills
Deron, Edward Michael
Kirk, John MacGregor
Klein, Coleman Eugene
Solomon, Mark Raymond
Sommerfeld, David William

Center Line
Litch, John Michael

Detroit
Miller, George DeWitt, Jr.,
Rasmussen, Douglas John
Thoms, David Moore

East Lansing
Story, Monte Robert

Farmington
Harms, Donald C.

Flint
Cooley, Richard Eugene

Grand Rapids
Davis, Henry Barnard, Jr.,
Hogan, Thomas Patrick

Grosse Pointe
Goss, James William

Kalamazoo
Borsos, Robert Bruce
Hatch, Hazen van den Berg

Menominee
Rolfs, Craig Alan

Monroe
Lipford, Rocque Edward

Muskegon
Briggs, John Mancel, III,

Niles
Stone, Donald P.

Saint Clair Shores
Joslyn, Robert Bruce

Southfield
DeLong, Donald Alan
Kaplow, Robert David

Troy
Chapman, Conrad Daniel
Gregory, George William

West Bloomfield
Glazier, Sandra Deborah

MINNESOTA

Duluth
Burns, Richard Ramsey

Kenyon
Peterson, Franklin Delano

Minneapolis
Berens, William Joseph
Freeman, Todd Ira
Johnson, Gary M.
Struyk, Robert John
Ventres, Judith Martin

Minnetonka
Heckt, Melvin Dean

Saint Louis Park
Nightingale, Tracy Irene

Saint Paul
Noonan, James C.

MISSISSIPPI

Jackson
Houston, Jamie Giles, III,

MISSOURI

Florissant
Boyle, Patrick Otto

Hannibal
Welch, Joseph Daniel

Hillsboro
Howald, John William

Independence
Minton, Kent W.

Kansas City
Anderson, Christopher James
Bernard, James Harvey, Jr.,
Davis, John Charles
Dicus, Stephen Howard
Herman, Robert Stephen
Hubbard, William L.
Langworthy, Robert Burton
Lombardi, Cornelius Ennis, Jr.,
Setzler, Edward Allan
Shughart, Donald Louis
Toll, Perry Mark
Willy, Thomas Ralph

Rock Port
Mulvania, Walter Lowell

Rolla
Hickle, William Earl

Saint Louis
Baldwin, Edwin Steedman
Cornfeld, Dave Louis
Cullen, James D.
Fogle, James Lee
Greenley, Beverly Jane
Gunn, Michael Peter
Harris, Harvey Alan
McCarter, Charles Chase
Redd, Charles Appleton
Rose, Albert Schoenburg
Sestric, Anthony James
Sherby, Kathleen Reilly
Weishaar, Aaron G.

Salem
Hall, Glenn Allen

Springfield
Pruitt, Rebecca Lee

MONTANA

Billings
Thompson, James William

Havre
Moog, Mary Ann Pimley

Missoula
Willey, Charles Wayne

NEBRASKA

Gretna
Bergren, Colleen Doyle

Lincoln
Rembolt, James Earl

Omaha
Burke, Thomas Raymond
Hamann, Deryl Frederick
Lieben, Thomas Geoffrey
Niemann, Nicholas Kent

Valentine
O'Kief, W. Gerald

NEVADA

Las Vegas
Greene, Addison Kent
Gubler, John Gray
Lovell, Carl Erwin, Jr.,

NEW HAMPSHIRE

Concord
McDonald, Joseph F., III,

Hooksett
Rogers, David John

Manchester
Monson, John Rudolph

Plymouth
Deachman, Ross Varick

NEW JERSEY

Bloomfield
Weisert, Kent Albert Frederick

East Brunswick
Zaun, Anne Marie

Far Hills
Corash, Richard

Florham Park
LeVine, Walter Daniel

Lyndhurst
Donegan, Joseph Michael

Mc Afee
Fogel, Richard

Morristown
Sherman, Sandra Brown
Sweeney, John Lawrence

Newark
Schlesinger, Norman E.

Pennington
Gorrin, Eugene

Point Pleasant Beach
Herr, Philip Michael

Princeton
Kenny, Robert
Shaver, Philip Alcott

Red Bank
Neff, Robert Carey

Summit
Kenyon, Edward Tipton

Teaneck
Kaplan, Howard M(ark)

Verona
Hock, Frederick Wyeth

West Orange
Cuozzi, William Francis, Jr.,
Laves, Benjamin Samuel
Richmond, Harold Nicholas

Woodbridge
Lepelstat, Martin L.

NEW MEXICO

Albuquerque
Keleher, Michael Lawrence

Santa Fe
Hickey, John Miller
Schliemann, Walter Charles

NEW YORK

Baldwin
Naranjo, Carolyn R.

Binghamton
Gerhart, Eugene Clifton
Price, Paul Marnell

Buffalo
Fine, Robert Paul
Newman, Stephen Michael
Rachlin, Lauren David

Cedarhurst
Klein, Irwin Grant

Corning
Becraft, Charles D., Jr.,

Cortlandt Manor
DeLaMothe, Cassandra Macon

East Hampton
Twomey, Thomas A., Jr.,

Garden City
Haskel, Jules J.

Hamburg
Wiltse, Peter Christian

Huntington
Hochberg, Ronald Mark

Ithaca
Wilson, Bruce Duxbury

Jericho
Hecht, Donald Stuart

Kew Gardens
Adler, David Neil

Mineola
Bartol, Ernest Thomas
Smolev, Terence Elliot

Mount Vernon
Ross, Richard C.

New York
Alessandroni, Venan Joseph
Angus, Patricia Marie
Barasch, Mal Livingston
Bell, Jonathan Robert
Black, James Isaac, III,
Blumberg, Gerald
Bockstein, Herbert
Boehner, Leonard Bruce
Brauner, David A.
Clark, Celia Rue
Crary, Miner Dunham, Jr.,
Engel, Ralph Manuel
Evans, Douglas Hayward
Finkelstein, Bernard
Forger, Alexander Darrow
Gelb, Judith Anne
Gifford, William C.
Heineman, Andrew David
Herbst, Abbe Ilene
Hess, P. Gregory
Jasper, Seymour
Josephson, Mark A.
Kamin, Sherwin
Karan, Paul Richard
Kartiganer, Joseph
Kavoukjian, Michael Edward
Kitay, Harvey Robert
Lesk, Ann Berger
Lipsky, Burton G.
Malkin, Peter Laurence
Martin, Malcolm Elliot
Materna, Joseph Anthony
McGrath, Thomas J.
Merrill, George Vanderneth
Moore, Thomas Ronald (Lord Bridestowe)
Nathan, Frederic Solis
Newman, Lawrence
O'Grady, John Joseph, III,
Paul, Herbert Morton
Pershan, Richard Henry
Pollan, Stephen Michael
Posner, Louis Joseph
Ralli, Constantine Pandia
Robinson, Barbara Paul
Saufer, Isaac Aaron
Savrin, Louis
Schlesinger, Sanford Joel
Shapiro, Aleena Rieger
Spanbock, Maurice Samuel
Valente, Peter Charles
Varet, Michael A.
Watson, Richard Allen
Weiksner, Sandra S.
Wimpfheimer, Michael Clark
Zuckerman, Paul Herbert

Oyster Bay
Bernstein, Jacob

Pearl River
Riley, James Kevin

Poughkeepsie
Ostertag, Robert Louis

Rochester
Buckley, Michael Francis
Clifford, Eugene Thomas
Colby, William Michael
Gross, Bryon William
Palermo, Anthony Robert
Schumacher, Jon Lee
Trevett, Thomas Neil
Twietmeyer, Don Henry

Somers
Keeffe, John Arthur

Uniondale
Bennett, James Davison

White Plains
Danziger, Joel Bernard
Rosenberg, Michael

NORTH CAROLINA

Asheville
Lavelle, Brian Francis David

Chapel Hill
Herman-Giddens, Gregory

Charlotte
McBryde, Neill Gregory
Pleicones, Laura
Preston, James Young
Wood, William McBrayer

Durham
Buchanan, Phillip Hoge

Goldsboro
Hine, John Charles

Greenville
Dixon, Phillip Ray, Sr.,

Jamestown
Schmitt, William Allen

Raleigh
Taylor, Ritchie W.

Warsaw
Thompson, Eugene Cebron, III,

Winston Salem
Humphrey, Dudley

NORTH DAKOTA

Grand Forks
Cilz, Douglas Arthur

Mandan
Bair, Bruce B.

OHIO

Akron
Kaufmann, Philip Seil

Athens
Gall, Robert Jay

Beavercreek
Stier, Charles Herman, Jr.,

Cincinnati
Bahlman, William Thorne, Jr.,
Buechner, Robert William
Goodman, Stanley
Hoffheimer, Daniel Joseph
Neltner, Michael Martin
Petrie, Bruce Inglis
Phillips, T. Stephen
Ruby, Stanley L.
Schwab, Nelson, Jr.,
Strauss, William Victor

Cleveland
Braverman, Herbert Leslie
Brucken, Robert Matthew
Cairns, James Donald
Ebert, Gary Andrew
Fabens, Andrew Lawrie, III,
Hochman, Kenneth George
Horvitz, Michael John
Lease, Robert K.
Shapiro, Fred David
Weiler, Jeffry Louis

Columbus
Anderson, Jon Mac
Balthaser, James Harvey
Casey, John Frederick
Emens, J. Richard
Oman, Richard Heer
Willcox, Roderick Harrison
Wolper, Beatrice Emens

Dayton
Conway, Mark Allyn
Johnson, C. Terry
Roberts, Brian Michael

Findlay
Jetton, Girard Reuel, Jr.,

Mentor
Driggs, Charles Mulford

Oak Harbor
Robertson, Jerry D.

Salem
Bowman, Scott McMahan

Springfield
Husted, Stanley Neal, II,

Toledo
Calcamuggio, Larry Glenn
Jackson, Louise Anne
Stupsker, Charles A.

Warren
Kearney, Patricia Ann
Letson, William Normand

Westerville
Flaherty, James Grant
Westervelt, Charles Ephraim, Jr.,

Worthington
Juhola, Michael Duane

Youngstown
Lenga, Robert Allen
Roth, Daniel Benjamin

OKLAHOMA

Broken Arrow
Stewart, Murray Baker

Muskogee
Robinson, Adelbert Carl

Oklahoma City
Cook, Gayle Freeman
Ross, William Jarboe

Tulsa
Bowles, Margo La Joy
Butler, Robert Carlyle, III,
Clark, Gary Carl
Draughon, Scott Wilson
Hatfield, Jack Kenton
Nemec, Michael Lee
Sneed, James Lynde

Vinita
Curnutte, Mark William

OREGON

Florence
Clark, David Lewis

Grants Pass
Sloan, William Marshall

La Grande
Joseph, Steven Jay

Pendleton
Rew, Lawrence Boyd

Portland
Froebe, Gerald Allen
Klarquist, Kenneth Stevens, Jr.,
Pratt, Scott Owen
Strader, Timothy Richards
Tremaine, H. Stewart

PENNSYLVANIA

Allentown
Zamborsky, Donald A.

Berwyn
Watters, Edward McLain, III,

Bryn Mawr
Frick, Benjamin Charles

Doylestown
Wagner, Joseph Hagel

FAMILY AND MATRIMONIAL

UNITED STATES

Woodland Hills
Kaufman, Albert I.

COLORADO

Arvada
Kreis, Elizabeth Susan

Aurora
Staelin, Earl Hudson

Centennial
Carlton, Diane Michele

Colorado Springs
Adams, Deborah Rowland
Evans, Paul Vernon
Fisher, Robert Scott

Denver
Babiniec, Dennis Henry
Brega, Charles Franklin
Bronstein, Robert
Kaplan, Marc J.
McDowell, Karen Ann
McGuane, Frank L., Jr.,
Quiat, Marshall
Wedgle, Richard Jay

Englewood
Ambrose, Arlen S.

Fort Collins
Johnson, Donald Edward, Jr.,
Vick, Joseph James, III,

Golden
Hughes, Marcia Marie

Grand Junction
Griff, Harry

Lakewood
Freed, Diane Susan

Littleton
Robinson, Warren A. (Rip Robinson)

CONNECTICUT

Bristol
Hayes, Margaret Mary

Fairfield
Osis, Daiga Guntra

Greenwich
Schoonmaker, Samuel Vail, III,

New Haven
Greenfield, James Robert
Reiner, Leona Hudak
Wolfson, Susan Wartur

Norwich
Masters, Barbara J.

Ridgefield
Foster, Julie Irene
Fricke, Richard John

South Windsor
Gerlt, Wayne Christopher

West Hartford
Nereberg, Eliot Joel
Swerdloff, Ileen Pollock
Swerdloff, Mark Harris

Westport
Johnson, Allan Richard

Willimantic
Sinder, Joan B.

DELAWARE

Wilmington
Bounds, Curtis Preston
Kelleher, Daniel Francis
Mekler, Arlen B.
Tenenbaum, Joel David

DISTRICT OF COLUMBIA

Washington
Ain, Sanford King
Feldman, Clarice Rochelle
Karpinski, Irena Izabella
Kuder, Armin Ulrich
Lewis, Glenn C.
Maginnis, John C., III,
Medalie, Susan Diane
Richards, Suzanne V.

FLORIDA

Bascom
Brooten, Kenneth Edward, Jr.,

Bradenton
St. Paul, Alexandra De La Vergne

Brooksville
Vitola, John Raymond

Clearwater
Borja, Mary Ellen Murphy
Free, E. LeBron
Rose, Donna

Coral Gables
Cano, Mario Stephen
Fletcher, Paul Gerald
Mitchell, David Benjamin

Daytona Beach
Neitzke, Eric Karl

Fort Lauderdale
Brawer, Marc Harris
Brydger, Gordon Charles
Glantz, Wendy Newman
Nyce, John Daniel
Sanders, Dale R.

Fort Myers
Delizia, Carolyn
Finman, Sheldon Eliot
Rubinstein, Alan Jay

Jacksonville
Siegel, Edward

Jupiter
Brophy, Gilbert Thomas

Key West
Brihammar, B. Niklas

Lauderdale Lakes
Russell, Antonette Patrice

Miami
Katz, Lawrence Sheldon
Lebowitz, Walter Bernard
Osman, Edith Gabriella
Pastoriza, Julio
Pruna, Laura Maria
Samole, Myron Michael
Weinstein, Alan Edward

Naples
Rocuant, Paul A.

Orlando
Blackwell, Bruce Beuford
deBeaubien, Hugo H.
Lubet, Marc Leslie

Palatka
Baldwin, Allen Adail

Palm Beach
Devins, Robert Sylvester

Palm Beach Gardens
Auerbach, Paul Ira
Kahn, David Miller

Panama City
Sutton, Pamela Dru

Pensacola
Wood, Jennifer Lynn

Sarasota
Byrd, L(awrence) Derek

St Petersburg Beach
Milham, Julee Lynn

Tallahassee
Gary, Thomas
Morphonios, Dean B.

Tampa
Anton, David
Caveda, David Martin
Givens, Stann William
Gonzalez, Joe Manuel
Loewenthal, Steven Richard

West Palm Beach
Chopin, Susan Gardiner
Vilchez, Victoria Anne

GEORGIA

Atlanta
Billington, Barry E.
Bogart, Jeffrey B.
Mull, Gale W.
Wellon, Robert G.

Cartersville
Ford, Vickie Louise Arp

Decatur
Skinner, William French Cochran, Jr.,

Douglas
Sims, Rebecca Littleton

Jasper
Marger, Edwin

Nashville
Ellis, Robert Bryan, Jr.,

Norcross
Hahn, Stanley Robert, Jr.,

Snellville
Giallanza, Charles Philip

Statesboro
Classens, Michael John

Valdosta
Dodd, Roger J.
Edwards, Edith Martha

HAWAII

Honolulu
Crosier, Douglas A.
Kimura, Kevin

Kailua Kona
Zola, Michael S.

Wailuku
Kinaka, William Tatsuo

IDAHO

Boise
Uranga, Jean R.

Hailey
Hogue, Terry Glynn

Idaho Falls
Hart, Stephen Strong

ILLINOIS

Aurora
Mateas, Kenneth Edward

Belleville
Gossage, Roza

Bourbonnais
Engels, Patricia Louise

Chicago
Auerbach, Marshall Jay
Caner, Emin David
Davis, Muller
DuCanto, Joseph Nunzio
Feinstein, Paul Louis
Glieberman, Herbert Allen
Grant, Burton Fred
Hubbard, Elizabeth Louise
Jaconetty, Thomas Anthony
Muller, Kurt Alexander
Pritikin, James B.
Schilt, Margaret Anne
Schupp, Anastasia Luka
Sproger, Charles Edmund
Ventrelli, Anita Marie
Zoub, Burton Irving

Homewood
Olofsson, Daniel Joel

Joliet
Drell, Lea Armstrong

Lincolnwood
Ghezzi, Sheryl Rae

Mount Vernon
Harvey, Morris Lane

Mundelein
Ackley, Robert O.

Naperville
Klein, Richard Dennis

Niles
Sassan, Dennis Donald

Park Ridge
Wasko, Steven E.

Rock Island
Wallace, Franklin Sherwood

Springfield
Reed, Robert Phillip

Wheaton
DaRosa, Ronald Anthony
Didzerekis, Paul Patrick

Wheeling
Kulinsky, Lois

Woodstock
Gray, Paulette Michelle

INDIANA

Crawfordsville
Donaldson, Steven Bryan

Elkhart
Wicks, Charles Carter

Evansville
Clouse, John Daniel

Fort Wayne
Springer, James Elten
Tourkow, Joshua Isaac
Young, Randy William

Gary
Lewis, Robert Lee

Indianapolis
Avery, Melissa J.
Blythe, James David, II,
Bruns, Beverly A.
Pennamped, Bruce Michael
Silver, Gregory K.
Wunder, David Hart

Kokomo
Russell, Richard Lloyd

Lebanon
Donaldson, John Weber

Merrillville
Gioia, Daniel August

South Bend
Phillipoff, Mark James

Warsaw
Walmer, James L.

IOWA

Boone
Danilson, David Ray

Indianola
Ouderkirk, Mason James

Sioux City
Giles, William Jefferson, III,

KANSAS

Manhattan
Miller, Anne Burke

Overland Park
Griswold, Thomas L.
Short, Joel Bradley

Shawnee Mission
Gastl, Eugene Francis

Topeka
Hejtmanek, Danton Charles

KENTUCKY

Fort Thomas
Whalen, Paul Lewellin

Lexington
Bagby, Glen Stovall
Davidson, Michael
Goldman, Elisabeth Paris
Matl, Lois Tudor

Louisville
Brown, Bonnie Maryetta
Cooper, Richard Earl
Gowin, Richard Bryan
Karageorge, Thomas George
Morgan-White, Stephanie Lynn
Spalding, Catherine

LOUISIANA

Baton Rouge
Taylor, John McKowen
Wittenbrink, Jeffrey Scott

Covington
Paddison, David Robert

Kenner
Todaro, Laura Jean

Lafayette
Theall, Susan Lorna

Lake Charles
Sanchez, Walter Marshall

New Orleans
King, Rebecca J.
Levin, Richard Barry
Lowe, Robert Charles

Shreveport
Politz, Nyle Anthony

MAINE

Brewer
Ebitz, Elizabeth Kelly

Portland
Altshuler, Kenneth Paul

Waterville
Sandy, Robert Edward, Jr.,

MARYLAND

Annapolis
Ferris, William Michael
Perkins, Roger Allan

Baltimore
Cohen, Hyman K.
Meiselman, Alyson

Bethesda
Moss, Stephen Edward

Chestertown
Mowell, George Mitchell

College Park
Yoho, Billy Lee

Owings Mills
Silverman, Steven D.

Rockville
Avery, Bruce Edward
Barkley, Brian Evan
Tomar, Richard Thomas

Takoma Park
Dunn, John Benjamin

Towson
Campion, Renée
Putzel, Constance Kellner

MASSACHUSETTS

Amherst
Howland, Richard Moulton

Boston
Geismer, Alan Stearn, Jr.,
Gossels, Claus Peter Rolf
Hoffman, David Alan
Katz, Donald H.
Larson, Olive Elizabeth
Lee, David Harold
Packenham, Richard Daniel
Perera, Lawrence Thacher

Chelmsford
Grossman, Debra A.

Haverhill
Cox, William Donald, Jr.,

Hopkinton
Titlebaum, Earl Stanley

Lenox
Coffin, Mary McCarthy

Lowell
Maille, Brenda Patricia

Natick
Marr, David E.

Newton
Monahan, Marie Terry

North Andover
Fernandez, Patricia S.

Salem
Marks, Scott Charles

Sharon
Brown, Barbara A.

South Hamilton
Campbell, Diana Butt

Springfield
Dibble, Francis Daniel, Jr.,

Walpole
Ryan, Marilynne R.

Worcester
Moschos, Michael Christos

MICHIGAN

Bay City
Greve, Guy Robert

Bingham Farms
Larky, Sheldon Glen

Birmingham
Schaefer, John Frederick
Smith, Patti

Bloomfield Hills
Gold, Edward David
Hertz, Howard
Morganroth, Fred
Snyder, George Edward
Victor, Richard Steven

Clinton Township
Lucido, Peter J.

Detroit
Pirtle, H(arold) Edward

Dexter
Millman, Jode Susan

East Lansing
Veltema, Gregory N.

Farmington Hills
Bagley, Dennis Joseph

Flint
Cooley, Richard Eugene

Greenville
Mullendore, James Myers

Grosse Pointe
Barnhart, Katherine Louise

Grosse Pointe Park
McIntyre, Anita Grace Jordan

Grosse Pointe Woods
Prather, Kenneth Earl

Holland
Murphy, Max Ray

Inkster
Bullock, Steven Carl

Jackson
Jacobs, Wendell Early, Jr.,

Salem
Slack, Mark Robert

Toledo
Stupsker, Charles A.

Upper Sandusky
Fox, Mary Ellen

Wadsworth
McIlvaine, James Ross

Westerville
Lancione, Bernard Gabe

Worthington
Juhola, Michael Duane

Youngstown
Briach, George Gary
Giannini, Matthew Carlo
Roth, Daniel Benjamin

OKLAHOMA

Enid
Gill, Amber McLaughlin

Norman
Petersen, Catherine Holland

Oklahoma City
Ferguson, Steven Edward
Necco, Alexander David

Sayre
Brooks, David Eugene

Tulsa
Abrahamson, A. Craig
Butler, Robert Carlyle, III,
Cowdery, Allen Craig
Kroblin, Lucy S.
Steltzlen, Janelle Hicks
Ungerman, Maynard I.

Vinita
Johnston, Oscar Black, III,

Walters
Flanagan, Kathleen

Yukon
Hixson, Wendell Mark

OREGON

Brookings
Hinton, Floyd

Eugene
Sahlstrom, E(lmer) Bernard

Florence
Clark, David Lewis

Oregon City
McFarland, Carol Anne

Portland
Bender, Laurie
Carr, Kathleen M.
Cooper, Nancy M.
Gottlieb, Ira Leonard
Johnson, Mark Andrew
Johnston, Ronald Allen

Salem
Feibleman, Gilbert Bruce

The Dalles
Hashizume, Kevin

PENNSYLVANIA

Abington
Blessing, Maribeth

Bethlehem
Spry, Donald Francis, II,

Chadds Ford
Lamonaca, Joseph Michael

Doylestown
Bolla, William Joseph
Goldman, William Lewis

Du Bois
Blakley, Benjamin Spencer, III,

Exton
Ashton, Mark Randolph

Feasterville Trevose
Osterhout, Richard Cadwallader

Girard
Steadman, James Robert

Hatboro
John, Robert McClintock

Jenkintown
Worthington, Sandra Boulton

Kingston
Meyer, Martin Jay
Urbanski, Stephen Karl

Lancaster
Pyfer, John Frederick, Jr.,
Zimmerman, D(onald) Patrick

Langhorne
Hillje, Barbara Brown

Media
DiOrio, Robert Michael
Rubin, Arnold E.
Tomlinson, Herbert Weston

Mercer
Kochems, Robert Gregory

Monroeville
Cohen, Laura

Newport
Scaringi, Melanie Walz

Norristown
DeMatteo, Christina M.
Gold-Bikin, Lynne Z.
Gregg, John Pennypacker
Rounick, Jack A.

Perkasie
Roeger, William Coley, Jr.,

Philadelphia
Blumstein, Edward
Cramer, Harold
Dubin, Leonard
Grunfeld, David I.
Haviland, Bancroft Dawley
Kormes, John Winston
Wolf, Bruce

Pittsburgh
Chase, Norma
Fall, Robert J.
Goldberg, Mark Joel
Isabella, Mary Margaret
Mahood, James Edward
Miller, David A.
Pollock, David Samuel

Reading
Eshelman, David Richard

Reynoldsville
Wheeler, Mark Andrew, Sr.,

Somerset
Carroll, William Richard

West Chester
Litvin, William Joseph

Womelsdorf
Worley, Jane Ludwig

RHODE ISLAND

Middletown
Barrow, Barbara A.

Providence
DiMonte, Vincent A.

SOUTH CAROLINA

Columbia
Burnette, Mary Malissa
Sheftman, Howard Stephen

Greenville
Kappel, Matthew Jay
Steele, C. Carlyle

Laurens
Burney, Rhett D.

Mount Pleasant
Whitten, Beatrice Ehrenberg

Myrtle Beach
Breen, David Hart

Newberry
Partridge, William Franklin, Jr.,

Seneca
Sires, Norman Gruber, Jr.,

Summerville
Hardee-Thomas, Marva A.

West Columbia
Applegate, William Russell
Dickerson, Michelle Moody

SOUTH DAKOTA

Sioux Falls
Hattervig, Karen Ann
Johnson, Richard Arlo

TENNESSEE

Cleveland
Miller, Rodney Craig

Knoxville
Cremins, William Carroll

Memphis
Gipson, Harvey Lofton
McGinnis, Mary Margaret
Rice, George Lawrence, III, (Larry Rice)

Morristown
Murphy, Michael Cary

Murfreesboro
Windrow, Rachelle L.

Nashville
Gross, Edward Jordan
Levy, Jeffrey Lawrence

Rogersville
Skelton, Mark Albert

TEXAS

Abilene
Boone, Celia Trimble

Arlington
Rosenberry, William Kenneth

Austin
Saltmarsh, Sara Elizabeth
Shapiro, David L.
Weddington, Sarah Ragle
Weinman, Daryl Gail

Beaumont
Bias, Dana G.
Lawrence, Edward Jack, III,

Bellaire
Soffar, William Douglas

Cleveland
Campbell, Selaura Joy

Dallas
Greenwald, Thomas Albert
May, April Michelle
McCurley, Carl Michael
McCurley, Mary Johanna
Miller, Deborah Slye
Nelson, Keith Milton

El Paso
Dinsmoor, Robert Davidson

Fort Worth
Shannon, Joe, Jr.,

Graham
Richie, Boyd Lynn

Horseshoe Bay
Welch, Robert Morrow, Jr.,

Houston
Adair, William B. (Ben Adair)
Burg, Brent Lawrence
Covington, Vonda Russell
Disher, David Alan
Fason, Rita Miller
Handlin, Danita L.
Kaighen, Sondra
Kemp, Roland Connor
Pesikoff, Bette Schein
Prater, Wendy Lea
Short, J. Lindsey, Jr.,
Zimmerman, Alvin Louis

Killeen
Roberts, Burk Austin

Longview
Harrison, Guy Newell
Johnson, Darryl Todd
Welge, Jack Herman , Jr.,

Lubbock
Purdom, Thomas James

Odessa
Cliff, John William, Jr.,

San Angelo
Sutton, John Ewing

San Antonio
Spears, Sally
Tharp, Christine M.

Sherman
Munson, Peter Kerr

Sugar Land
Greer, Raymond White

Temple
Mischtian, John Michael

Waco
Hall, Donald Orell

Wharton
Roades, John Leslie

UTAH

Ogden
Kaufman, Steven Michael

Saint George
Slemboski, James E.

Salt Lake City
Sine, Wesley Franklin

VERMONT

Montpelier
Cheney, Kimberly Bunce
Diamond, M. Jerome

VIRGINIA

Alexandria
Cassell, Richard Emmett
Cottrell, James Ray
Gannon, Martin C.

Arlington
Korman, James William
Malone, William Grady

Bristol
Alan, Sondra Kirschner

Charlottesville
Raynor, Steven Leigh

Chesapeake
Leftwich, James Asbury, Jr.,

Danville
Abreu, Luis Alberto

Fairfax
Byrd Mische, Richard J.
Sanderson, Douglas Jay
Schwartz, Philip
Spratt, David Howard
Sriskandarajah, Atchuthan

Lebanon
Compton, Carnis Eugene

Leesburg
Saunders, Richard R.
Tichenor, Patricia E.M.

Lynchburg
Packert, G(ayla) Beth

Newport News
Nachman, Erwin B(ehr)
Segall, James Arnold

Norfolk
Gibson, Beverly Cullen

Petersburg
Baskervill, Charles Thornton
Spero, Morton Bertram

Powhatan
Carrico, Lucretia A.

Reston
Anderson, Charles Anthony

Roanoke
Mundy, Gardner Marshall

Suffolk
McLemore, James Latinus, III,

Vienna
Cochran, Stephen Grey
Condo, Joseph A.

Virginia Beach
Holmes, William James

Warrenton
Morrison, Paul A.

Woodbridge
Roberts, Charles Bren

WASHINGTON

Bellevue
Hand, Bruce George

Enumclaw
Hart, Trip

Everett
Davies, Gregory Lane

Gig Harbor
Morales, Debra A.

Moses Lake
Black, Barbara Jean

Olympia
Wright, Daniel A.

Seattle
Boxx, Karen Elizabeth
Clark, Cornelia
Koehler, Reginald Stafford, III,
Lawless, Janine A.
Novotny, Patricia Susan
Pritchard, Llewelyn G.
Wechsler, Mary Heyrman

Spokane
Lineberger, Peter Saalfield
Scanlon, Robert Charles

WEST VIRGINIA

Bluefield
Kantor, Isaac Norris

Charleston
Zak, Robert Joseph

Gassaway
Jones, Jeniver James

Huntington
Ransbottom, Jennifer Dickens

Morgantown
Ringer, Darrell Wayne (Dan Ringer)

WISCONSIN

Cross Plains
Moretti, Jay Donald

Deerfield
Pappas, David Christopher

Delafield
Hausman, C. Michael

Elkhorn
Eberhardt, Daniel Hugo

Elm Grove
Kaestner, Richard Darwin

La Crosse
Sleik, Thomas Scott

Madison
Mowris, Gerald William
Roberson, Linda
Winnig, Joel Bruce

Milwaukee
Ballman, Patricia Kling
Karp, David Barry
Meldman, Clifford Kay
Peckerman, Bruce Martin

Wausau
Drengler, William Allan John
Molinaro, Thomas J.

Wauwatosa
Baird, Kathleen Mary
Bonneson, Paul Garland

WYOMING

Evanston
Combs, William L.

Jackson
Clauss, C. David

Riverton
Scott, Beverly J.

Worland
Sweeny, Wendy Press

AUSTRALIA

Mount Gambier
Rymill, Thomas Mark

GERMANY

Berlin
Scharioth, Ulrike

ITALY

Palermo
Palmigiano, Alessandro

NORWAY

Oslo
Aars-Rynning, Jacob

PORTUGAL

Lisbon
Talhão, Luis

SCOTLAND

Midlothian
Barnes, Joy Chappell

SWEDEN

Göteborg
Westerberg, Siv Öman

ADDRESS UNPUBLISHED

Beitling, S. Richard
Carroll, Diane C.
Carter, Jeanne Wilmot
Chernett, Robert Irwin
Cohen, Anita Marilyn
Cohen, Jason Jay
DiMento, Carol A.G.
Gourvitz, Elliot Howard
Habeck, James Roy
Heinrich, Steven Allan
Hickey, Timothy Andrew
Kell, Scott K.
Kiefer, Karen LaVerne
Leaf, Frederick Peter
Lynch, Robert Berger
Markham, Rosemary
Marshall, Kathryn Sue

FINANCE

UNITED STATES

Falls Church
Christman, Bruce Lee

Mc Lean
Hammons, Terrence Gordon, Jr.,
Stump, John Sutton

Newport News
Kamp, Arthur Joseph, Jr.,

Norfolk
Hamar, Michael Bruce

Richmond
Strickland, William Jesse

WASHINGTON

Seattle
Hoffman, Mark Frederick
Kuhrau, Edward W.
Lamb, Mark Christopher
Propst, Andrew J.
Tousley, Russell Frederick

WISCONSIN

Milwaukee
Galanis, John William

Oak Creek
Giblin, Louis

TERRITORIES OF THE UNITED STATES

VIRGIN ISLANDS

Charlotte Amalie
Bolt, Thomas Alvin Waldrep

MEXICO

Mexico City
Castro Díaz, Alfonso
Fuentes-Ostos, Francisco

AUSTRIA

Vienna
Winkler, Oskar Werner

BRAZIL

Rio de Janeiro
Pinheiro-Guimarães, Plinio

BULGARIA

Sofia
Djingov, Assen Alexandrov

CHILE

Santiago
Laval, Juan Esteban

CHINA

Beijing
Zhu-Clark, Ingrid Wenying

CROATIA

Zagreb
Cirkveni, Neven

CZECH REPUBLIC

Prague
Krejci, Kvetoslav

DENMARK

Copenhagen
Kjaeldgaard, Joergen
Mogelmose, Henrik

Rungsted Kyst
Berning, Jesper

ENGLAND

London
Astleford, Peter David
Lakhdhir, David Karim
Newburg, Andre
Nugee, Edward George
Thomas, Allen Lloyd

FINLAND

Helsinki
Vikiö, Jari Tapani

FRANCE

Paris
Bedos, Jean-Luc
Dehe, Richard

GERMANY

Frankfurt
Hartmann, Uwe
Klerx, Oliver

Hamburg
von Teichman, Christoph

GREECE

Athens
Georgacopulos, Dimitris Haralambos

Piraeus
Bowen-Morris, Nigel Vaughan
Sofianopoulos, Dimitrios

HUNGARY

Budapest
Dederick, David
Grmela, Zoltan

INDONESIA

Jakarta
Madian, Ferry Pauliansyah
Mills, Karen

ISRAEL

Jerusalem
Stern, Doron Daniel

Tel Aviv
Shaham, Shiri

ITALY

Milan
Tedeschi, Edoardo

JAPAN

Tokyo
Hashidate, Kenji

NETHERLANDS

Amsterdam
Liem, Edwin T.H.

NEW ZEALAND

Auckland
Owles, Peter Gary

NORWAY

Oslo
Erno, Torkel

PANAMA

Panama
Martínez Saenz, Ivette Elisa

PERU

Lima
Chabaneix, Jean Paul

POLAND

Warsaw
Gessel Kalinowska vel Kalisz, Beata

PORTUGAL

Lisbon
Lowndes Marques, Filipe

SINGAPORE

Singapore
Trahair, Andrew James

SOUTH AFRICA

Johannesburg
Baillie, Brigette Ann

SPAIN

Barcelona
Darna, Pablo

Bilbao
Armesto, Ana

Valencia
Navarro-González, Antonio J.

SWEDEN

Stockholm
Alhanko, Peter

SWITZERLAND

Basel
Eulau, Peter H.

Geneva
Equey, Robert

Zürich
Gericke, Dieter Andreas

ADDRESS UNPUBLISHED

Ayers, Kristen Ness
Bloomer, Harold Franklin, Jr.,
Brodhead, David Crawmer
Campbell, Frederick Hollister
Colton, Sterling Don
Cumberland, William Edwin
Diehl, Deborah Hilda
Elliott, Edward Sporl
Giusti, William Roger
Gutman, Richard Edward
Howell, Donald Lee
Locke, William Henry
O'Brien, Charles H.
Pear, Charles E., Jr.,
Pratt, Robert Windsor
Pusateri, Lawrence Xavier
Ruhm, Thomas Francis
Shaffer, Richard James
Walker, Mark A.
Wilder, William F.
Wiley, Richard Arthur
Wolfson, Michael George
Wood, Robert Charles
Wright, Robert Payton

FRANCHISING

UNITED STATES

ARIZONA

Phoenix
Hay, John Leonard
Williams, Quinn Patrick
Wirken, Charles William

CALIFORNIA

Los Angeles
Barnes, Willie R.
Barton, David Joseph

San Ramon
Freed, Kenneth Alan

DISTRICT OF COLUMBIA

Washington
Klarfeld, Peter James
McDavid, Janet Louise

FLORIDA

Orlando
Blaher, Neal Jonathan
Chong, Stephen Chu Ling

West Palm Beach
Brams, Jeffrey Brent

GEORGIA

Atlanta
Barkoff, Rupert Mitchell

Duluth
Sloan, Donnie Robert, Jr.,

ILLINOIS

Chicago
Abrams, Lee Norman
Baer, John Richard Frederick
Joseph, Robert Thomas
Lapin, Andrew William

Lincolnshire
Para, Gerard Albert

Warrenville
Johnson, Douglas Wells

INDIANA

Indianapolis
Klimek, James
Petersen, James L.

KANSAS

Wichita
Stephenson, Richard Ismert

LOUISIANA

New Orleans
Curtis, Charles Thach, Jr.,

MARYLAND

Baltimore
Chernow, Jeffrey Scott
Wilson, Thomas Matthew, III,

Bethesda
Stentz, Jon William

MINNESOTA

Minneapolis
Long, James Jay

MISSISSIPPI

Olive Branch
Carnall, George Hursey, II,

MISSOURI

Kansas City
Palmer, Dennis Dale
Spalty, Edward Robert

Saint Louis
Hartweger, Gordon Gravius

NEW JERSEY

Florham Park
Chase, Eric Lewis

Hackensack
Miller, Harvey Allan

NEW YORK

Buffalo
Bailey, Thomas Charles

Mineola
Schaffer, David Irving

New York
Rosen, Richard Lewis

Uniondale
Kestenbaum, Harold Lee

NORTH CAROLINA

Charlotte
Smart, Roy Louis, III,

Morganton
Simpson, Daniel Reid

Raleigh
Kapp, Michael Keith
Taylor, Ritchie W.

Winston Salem
Schollander, Wendell Leslie, Jr.,

OHIO

Cincinnati
Lutz, James Gurney

Columbus
Buchenroth, Stephen Richard

OKLAHOMA

Tulsa
Slicker, Frederick Kent

OREGON

Lake Oswego
Byczynski, Edward Frank

PENNSYLVANIA

Blue Bell
Siedzikowski, Henry Francis

Norristown
Milner, Kenneth Paul

Philadelphia
Tractenberg, Craig R.

TENNESSEE

Nashville
Habermann, Ted Richard

TEXAS

Houston
Devlin, Francis James
Hinton, Paula Weems
Simmons, Stephen Judson

UTAH

Salt Lake City
Swinton, Jeffrey Cheever

VIRGINIA

Richmond
Clinard, Robert Noel

WISCONSIN

Milwaukee
Casper, Richard Henry

AUSTRIA

Innsbruck
Schurr, Francesco Armando

FRANCE

Lyon
Girerd, Carole

Paris
Baum, Axel Helmuth

JAPAN

Tokyo
Sekine, Osamu

NEW ZEALAND

Auckland
Whale, Michael John

NORWAY

Osteras
Drevvatne, Dag

ADDRESS UNPUBLISHED

Horwitz, Donald Paul

GENERAL PRACTICE

UNITED STATES

ALABAMA

Birmingham
Cicio, Anthony Lee
Friend, Edward Malcolm, III,
Thompson, Charles Amos

Brewton
Garrett, Broox Gray, Jr.,

Clanton
Jackson, John Hollis, Jr.,

Florence
Schuessler, Cindy Sandlin

Mobile
Armbrecht, William Henry, III,
Baxley, Phillip Kent

Montgomery
Byars, Walter Ryland, Jr.,
Byram, James Asberry, Jr.,

Opelika
Samford, Yetta Glenn, Jr.,

Tuscaloosa
Williams, Roger Courtland

Crawfordsville
Donaldson, Steven Bryan

Danville
Baldwin, Jeffrey Kenton

Fort Wayne
Lebamoff, Ivan Argire
Springer, James Elten
Tourkow, Joshua Isaac

Fowler
Weist, William Bernard

Gary
Hall, John Henry

Indianapolis
Kautzman, John Fredrick
Rothbaum, Sandra Lazarus

Lagrange
Glick, Cynthia Susan

Merrillville
Irak, Joseph S.

Muncie
Reed, Samuel Lee

Shelbyville
Harrold, Dennis Edward
Lisher, James Richard

Terre Haute
Bitzegaio, Harold James
Britton, Louis Franklin
Frey, Eric Alan
Kesler, John A.

Warsaw
Walmer, James L.

IOWA

Boone
Danilson, David Ray

Burlington
Hoth, Steven Sergey

Cedar Rapids
Nazette, Richard Follett

Davenport
Phelps, Robert J.

Des Moines
Jensen, Dick Leroy

Grundy Center
Kliebenstein, Don

Humboldt
Sandblom, Steven Kirk

Iowa City
Hayek, John William

La Porte City
Lubben, Rick Ronald

Mason City
Winston, Harold Ronald

Mount Pleasant
Vance, Michael Charles

Wapello
Hicklin, Edwin Anderson

KANSAS

Arkansas City
Templar, Ted Mac

Cottonwood Falls
North, William T.

Hutchinson
Chalfant, William Young

Iola
Toland, John Robert

Kansas City
O'Neill, Thomas Tyrone

Lawrence
Nordling, Bernard Erick
Smith, Glee Sidney, Jr.,

Lincoln
Marshall, Susan

Neodesha
Depew, Harry Luther

Olathe
Scott, Robert Gene

Prairie Village
Sharp, Rex Arthur

Shawnee Mission
Sparks, Billy Schley

Topeka
Schultz, Richard Allen
Snyder, Brock Robert

Ulysses
Hathaway, Gary Ray

Wichita
Arvin, Lester Cave
Sevart, Daniel Joseph

KENTUCKY

Florence
Frohlich, Anthony William

Frankfort
Chadwick, Robert

Glasgow
Gardner, Woodford Lloyd, Jr.,

Hazard
Barker, Stephen Gerald

Lebanon
Higdon, Frederick Alonzo

Lexington
Hickey, John King

Louisville
Osborn, John Simcoe, Jr.,
Pettyjohn, Shirley Ellis

New Castle
Brammell, William Hartman

Owensboro
Miller, James Monroe

Shelbyville
Igleheart, Ted Lewis

Shepherdsville
Givhan, Thomas Bartram

Somerset
Prather, John Gideon
Prather, John Gideon, Jr.,

LOUISIANA

Metairie
Harris, Thorne D., III,

New Orleans
Barham, Mack Elwin
Herman, Fred L.
King, Rebecca J.
Lowe, Robert Charles

Slidell
Singletary, Alvin D.

MAINE

Bass Harbor
Ervin, Spencer

Camden
Sanford, John Joseph

Farmington
Holman, Joseph Frederick

Portland
Berry, Henry Newhall, III,
Rundlett, Ellsworth Turner, III,

Skowhegan
Youney, John William

Waterville
Sandy, Robert Edward, Jr.,

MARYLAND

Baltimore
Arnick, John Stephen
Baker, William Parr
Cohen, Hyman K.
Ferro, Elizabeth Krams
Grady, Joseph Harold
Kandel, Nelson Robert
Powell, Roger Norman
Thompson, Craig A.

Bethesda
Eastman, Hope Beth
Moss, Stephen Edward

Brookeville
Johns, Warren LeRoi

Chestertown
Mowell, George Mitchell

Columbia
Cooney, Teresa M.

Easton
Foster, Philip Carey

Frederick
Beam, Bethamy N.
Sica, John

Hagerstown
Berkson, Jacob Benjamin

Owings Mills
Silverman, Steven D.

Phoenix
Anderson, Mary Ellen

Rockville
Thompson, James Lee

Showell
Grech, Christopher Alan

Towson
Borgerding, Francis Xavier, Jr.,

Westminster
Dulany, William Bevard

Wheaton
Kirchman, Eric Hans

MASSACHUSETTS

Amherst
Howland, Richard Moulton

Barnstable
Mycock, Frederick Charles

Boston
Graham, John Joseph
Katz, Donald H.
Kidder, George Howell
Lyons, Nance
McAuliffe, Rosemary
Milstein, Richard Sherman
Perera, Lawrence Thacher
Politi, Stephen Michael
Redlich, Marc
Weaver, Paul David

Brookline
Lipson, Roger Russell

Cambridge
Ta, Tai Van

East Boston
Mason, Thomas Owen

Framingham
Heng, Gerald C. W.

Haverhill
Cox, William Donald, Jr.,

Hopkinton
Titlebaum, Earl Stanley

Lowell
Curtis, James Theodore

New Bedford
Hurwitz, Barrett Alan

Newton
Lowinger, Lazar
Stern, Edward Mayer

Orleans
Chaplin, Ansel Burt

Quincy
Motejunas, Gerald William

Salem
Marks, Scott Charles

Springfield
Maidman, Stephen Paul

Watertown
Kaloosdian, Robert Aram

Wellesley
Giroux, Eugene Xavier

West Springfield
Ely, John P.

MICHIGAN

Albion
Moore, David Gregory

Bingham Farms
Berman, Leonard Keith
Larky, Sheldon Glen

Bloomfield Hills
Ledwidge, Patrick Joseph

Brighton
Gardella, Robert Christopher

Burton
Breczinski, Michael Joseph

Decatur
Kinney, Gregory Hoppes

Detroit
Johnson, Cynthia L(e) M(ae)
Mengel, Christopher Emile

Farmington Hills
Blizman, Paul John

Fenton
Hildner, Phillips Brooks, II,

Flint
Powers, Edward Herbert

Greenville
Palmer, Richard Douglas

Harbor Springs
Turner, Lester Nathan

Holland
Murphy, Max Ray

Jackson
Jacobs, Wendell Early, Jr.,

Midland
Beale, Michael John

Niles
Stone, Donald P.

Plymouth
Koroi, Mark Michael
Morgan, Donald Crane

Rapid City
Ring, Ronald Herman

Rochester Hills
Diehl, Richard Paul

Romeo
Clark, Mark Lee

Shelby
Burrows, Jay Edward

Ypsilanti
Barr, John Monte
McLain, Dennis O.

MINNESOTA

Bemidji
Kief, Paul Allan
Woodke, Robert Allen

Brainerd
O'Hara, William Desmond, Jr.,

Chanhassen
Peterson, Steven A.

Chatfield
Opat, Matthew John

Hallock
Malm, Roger Charles

Kenyon
Peterson, Franklin Delano

Saint Paul
Galvin, Michael John, Jr.,
Jacobs, Stephen Louis
Trojack, John Edward

MISSISSIPPI

Bay Saint Louis
Bernstein, Joseph

Bay Springs
Shoemaker, Bobby Lynn

Gloster
Davis, Cynthia D'Ascenzo

Jackson
King, Robert Wilson

Kosciusko
Pickle, L. Scott

Laurel
McKenzie, Franklin Cooper, Jr.,

Mccomb
Starrett, Keith

New Albany
Sumners, Lester Furr

Pascagoula
Tynes, Douglas Lamont

Raymond
Moss, Jack Gibson

MISSOURI

Ballwin
Banton, Stephen Chandler

Cape Girardeau
McManaman, Kenneth Charles

Cuba
Lange, C. William

Florissant
Boyle, Patrick Otto

Kansas City
Carter, J. Denise

Keytesville
Wheeler, James Julian

Lees Summit
Walsh, Thomas Joseph

Lexington
Giorza, John C.

Maryville
McLaughlin, James Patrick

Saint Ann
Johnson, Harold Gene

Saint Joseph
Kranitz, Theodore Mitchell

Saint Louis
Barken, Bernard Allen
Bloom, Allen Jerry
Carp, Larry
DeWoskin, Alan Ellis
Duesenberg, Richard William
Neill, Joseph Vincent
Shalowitz, Howard A.

Salem
Hall, Glenn Allen

Sedalia
Rice, James Briggs, Jr.,

MONTANA

Billings
Cromley, Brent Reed

Bozeman
Nelson, Steven Dwayne

Superior
Austin, Douglas Robert

NEBRASKA

Gretna
Bergren, Colleen Doyle

Lincoln
McClain, Richard Douglas

Valentine
O'Kief, W. Gerald

NEVADA

Las Vegas
Brown, Joseph Wentling
Goldberg, Aubrey

NEW HAMPSHIRE

Concord
Johnson, Robert Veiling, II,

Hooksett
Rogers, David John

Lebanon
Trunzo, Thomas Harold, Jr.,

Manchester
Borofsky, Stephen Eric
Craig, James William

Nashua
Hanson, Arnold Philip
Jette, Ernest Arthur

Newport
Shklar, Michael Charles

Portsmouth
Tober, Stephen Lloyd

Salem
Jones, Michael Earl

Seabrook
Ganz, Mary Keohan

NEW JERSEY

Bloomfield
Lordi, Katherine Mary

Boonton
Walzer, James Harvey

Brick
Tivenan, Charles Patrick

Caldwell
Castano, Gregory Joseph

Camden
Lario, Frank M., Jr.,

Cherry Hill
D'Alfonso, Mario Joseph
Shapiro, Richard Allen

Clark
Barr, Jon-Henry

Cliffside Park
Diktas, Christos James

Clifton
Pincus, Sheldon H.

Edison
Fink, Edward Murray
Garasia, Anjana

Elmwood Park
Mangano, Louis

Glen Ridge
Connolly, Joseph Thomas

Glen Rock
Markey, Brian Michael

Hackensack
Curtis, Robert Kern

Hammonton
Howell, Brian Graham

Hillsdale
Hodinar, Michael

Jersey City
D'Alessandro, Daniel Anthony
Signorile, Vincent Anthony

Kearny
Dunne, Frederick R., Jr.,

Kendall Park
Fisch, Joseph

Liberty Corner
Apruzzese, Vincent John

Linden
Littman, David Bernard

Montclair
Bate, David Soule

Princeton
Keephart, Lydia Fabbro

Ridgewood
Trocano, Russell Peter

Roseland
Smith, Dennis Jay

Salem
Petrin, Helen Fite

Sewell
Crouse, Farrell R.
Fichera, Lewis Carmen

Somers Point
Beakley, Robert Paul

Somerset
Green, Jeffrey C.

South Plainfield
Santoro, Frank Anthony

Spring Lake
Pandolfe, John Thomas, Jr.,

Stone Harbor
Taylor, Robert Lee

Trenton
Doherty, Robert Christopher
Levin, Susan Bass

Union
Rosenberg, A. Irving
Yoskowitz, Marlene

Vauxhall
Ross, Mark Samuel

Warren
Gargano, Francine Ann
Rana, Harminderpal Singh

West Orange
Cuozzi, William Francis, Jr.,

Westfield
Stahl, Robert George

Willingboro
Tarver, Margaret Leggett

Wyckoff
Spizziri, John Anthony

NEW MEXICO

Alamogordo
Bloom, Norman Douglas, Jr.,

Albuquerque
Lopez, Floyd William

Carlsbad
Byers, Matthew T(odd)

Clovis
Skarda, Lynell Griffith

Farmington
Moeller, Floyd Douglas

Las Cruces
Kirschner, William Steven

Raton
Montoya, Sarah Marie

Roswell
Bassett, John Walden, Jr.,

Santa Fe
George, W. Peyton
Schliemann, Walter Charles

NEW YORK

Albany
Devine, Eugene Peter
Pozner, Louis-Jack

Amherst
Jones, E. Thomas
Murray, William Michael

Auburn
Gunger, Richard William

Binghamton
Beck, Stephanie G.

Bronxville
Fuller, David Otis, Jr.,

Brooklyn
Schussler, Theodore

Buffalo
McElvein, Thomas Irving, Jr.,

Commack
Somer, Stanley Jerome

Corning
Becraft, Charles D., Jr.,

Dansville
Vogel, John Walter

Delmar
Cavanaugh, John Joseph, Jr.,

Douglaston
Salvo, Joseph Aldo

East Hampton
Twomey, Thomas A., Jr.,

Elma
Markello, Jeffrey Philip

Flushing
Deerson, Adele Shapiro

Garden City
DiMascio, John Philip
Jones, Lawrence Tunnicliffe

Glen Cove
Lewis, Felice Flanery

Glens Falls
Bartlett, Richard James

Gouverneur
Leader, Robert John

Great Neck
Lowenbraun, Solomon Mortimer
Wershals, Paul Leonard

Groton
Henry, James Richard

Hamburg
Hargesheimer, Elbert, III,

Houghton
Brautigam, David Clyde

Huntington
German, June Resnick
Levitan, Katherine D.
Munson, Nancy Kay
Tucker, William P.

Keeseville
Turetsky, Aaron

Kew Gardens
Reichel, Aaron Israel
Schechter, Donald Robert
Sparrow, Robert E.

Lockport
Brodsky, Felice Adrienne

Mahopac
Sequeira, Manuel Alexandre, Jr.,

Manlius
Mathewson, George Atterbury

Massapequa
Van Gorder, John Frederic

Melville
Lane, Arthur Alan

Middletown
Kossar, Ronald Steven

Mineola
Bee, Peter Aloysius
Clark, Paul Jay
Levin, A. Thomas
Monaghan, Peter Gerard
Raab, Ira Jerry

New Hartford
McKennan, John T.

New Rochelle
Kreppel, Milton Mark

New York
Aloe, Paul Hubschman
Annenberg, Norman
Beshar, Robert Peter
Bianco, S. Anthony
Boddie, Reginald Alonzo
Burns, Arnold Irwin
Donovan, Craig Thomas
Feder, Saul E.
Felder, Raoul Lionel
Friedman, Elaine Florence
Goldstein, Howard Sheldon
Greenberg, Hayley
Grossberg, David
Hodes, Robert Bernard
Hollyer, A(rthur) Rene
Huffman, Richard Lee
Josephson, Mark A.
Klein, Martin I.
Klemann, Gilbert Lacy, II,
Kobrin, Lawrence Alan
Lande, David Steven
Levy, Herbert Monte
Marks, Theodore Lee
Masters, Jon Joseph
Minsky, Bruce William
Morganstern, Gerald H.
Neff, Michael Alan
Plotkin, Loren H.
Rice, Donald Sands
Salvan, Sherwood Allen
Seligman, Delice
Seligman, Frederick
Siegel, Edward M.
Smit, Robert H.
Thompson, Katherine Genevieve
Watson, Richard Allen
Weiss, Lawrence N.
Wexelbaum, Michael
Wimpfheimer, Michael Clark
Wolff, Jesse David
Wu, Robin Chi Ching
Wyckoff, E. Lisk, Jr.,

Orchard Park
Sullivan, Mortimer Allen, Jr.,

Ossining
Daly, William Joseph

Perry
Kelly, Michael Joseph

Port Jefferson
Hindin, Seymour

Port Washington
Herz, Arnold D.

Poughkeepsie
Dietz, Robert Barron
Wallace, Herbert Norman

Rochester
Goldman, Arnold Joseph
Palermo, Anthony Robert
Rosner, Leonard Allen

Rome
Griffith, Emlyn Irving

Scarsdale
Roseman, Arnold David

Schoharie
Duncombe, Raynor Bailey

Scottsville
Williams, Henry Ward, Jr.,

Sea Cliff
McGill, Gilbert William

Sherrill
Campanie, Samuel John

Smithtown
Dowis, Lenore

South Richmond Hill
Goldsmith, Michael Lawrence

Staten Island
Ferranti, Thomas, Jr.,
Landron, Michel John
Miller, Claire Cody

Suffern
Reda, Robert L.

Syracuse
Butler, John Edward
Kram, Richard Corey
Rivette, Francis Robert
Wiles, Christopher

Tupper Lake
Johnson, David Wesley

Utica
Brennan, John Joseph

Walden
Gubits, David Barry

Waterford
Glavin, A. Rita Chandellier (Mrs. James Henry Glavin III)

White Plains
Cohn, Julius W.
Levine, Steven Jon

NORTH CAROLINA

Asheboro
Bunch, W(alter) Edward

Asheville
Hyde, Herbert Lee

Candler
Sutton, John Richard, Sr.,

Charlotte
Bragg, Ellis Meredith, Jr.,
Buckley, Charles Robinson, III,

Dunn
Pope, Patrick Harris

Greensboro
Cahoon, Robert Strange

Hickory
Adams, Valeree R.
Farthing, Edwin Glenn

Mooresville
Homesley, Clifton W.

Southern Pines
Foyles, Kirsten Ellefson

NORTH DAKOTA

Grand Forks
Arnason, Joel Frederick
Widdel, John Earl, Jr.,

OHIO

Barnesville
Jefferis, Paul Bruce

Brecksville
McBride, Judith Bliss

Celina
Luth, Thomas Edward

Cincinnati
Hoffheimer, Daniel Joseph
Hust, Bruce Kevin
Schwab, Nelson, Jr.,
Tranter, Terence Michael
Vogel, Cedric Wakelee

Cleveland
Boukis, Kenneth
Boyko, Christopher Allan
Goldfarb, Bernard Sanford
Hollington, Richard Rings, Jr.,
LaFond, Thomas Joseph
Sanislo, Paul Steve
Sogg, Wilton Sherman

Columbus
Carnahan, John Anderson
Casey, John Frederick
Chester, John Jonas
Cline, Richard Allen
Cox, Paul L.
Drexel, Ray Phillips
Phillips, James Edgar

Dayton
Holz, Michael Harold
Schmidt, Matthew Martin

Dublin
Tenuta, Luigia

Findlay
Kostyo, John Francis

Girard
Denney, James Allen

Howard
Lee, William Johnson

Kent
Nome, William Andreas

Lima
Jacobs, Ann Elizabeth
Robenalt, John Alton

Logan
Kernen, Will

London
Rolfes, James Walter, Sr.,

Marysville
Hamilton, Robert Otte

Maumee
Marsh, Benjamin Franklin

Mount Vernon
Rose, Kim Matthew

North Olmsted
Dorchak, Thomas J.

Ravenna
Nolfi, Edward Anthony

Saint Marys
Huber, William Evan
Kemp, Barrett George

Salem
Slack, Mark Robert

Springfield
Browne, William Bitner
Husted, Stanley Neal, II,

Tiffin
Huth, Lester Charles

Toledo
St. Clair, Donald David

Twinsburg
Doyle, Duane Lynn

Upper Sandusky
Fox, Mary Ellen

Westerville
Lancione, Bernard Gabe

Wilmington
Schutt, Walter Eugene

Youngstown
Ausnehmer, John Edward
Briach, George Gary

OKLAHOMA

Alva
Mitchell, Allan Edwin

Antlers
Stamper, Joe Allen

Chandler
Swanson, Robert Lee

Claremore
Gordon, Jack Elliott, Jr.,

Edmond
Loving, Susan Brimer

Guthrie
Davis, Frank Wayne

Kingfisher
Baker, Thomas Edward

Mcalester
Cornish, Richard Pool

Oklahoma City
Cunnyngham, Maxine Brown
Lindsey, Lori Dawn
Nesbitt, Charles Rudolph
Ross, William Jarboe
Wilson, Julia Ann Yother

Ponca City
Raley, John W., Jr.,

Sayre
Brooks, David Eugene

Tulsa
Bryant, Hubert Hale
Cowdery, Allen Craig
Dunn, Frederick Louis, III,
Scott, Roger Roy

Yukon
Hixson, Wendell Mark

OREGON

Eugene
DuPriest, Douglas Millhollen
Mumford, William Porter, II,

Grants Pass
Baker, Lindi L.

Medford
Thierolf, Richard Burton, Jr.,

Pendleton
Rew, Lawrence Boyd

Portland
Marandas, John Steve
Matarazzo, Harris Starr
Williamson, Charles Ready, III,

PENNSYLVANIA

Abington
Budman, Alan David

Ardmore
Narin, Stephen B.

Doylestown
Elliott, Richard Howard
Goldman, William Lewis

Du Bois
Blakley, Benjamin Spencer, III,

Feasterville Trevose
Osterhout, Richard Cadwallader

Frackville
Domalakes, Paul George

Hatboro
John, Robert McClintock
Nicholson, Bruce Allen

Hazleton
Schiavo, Pasco Louis

Honey Brook
DePaul, Anthony Kenneth

Jenkintown
Friedman, Ralph David
Robbins, Jack Winton

Kingston
Meyer, Martin Jay

Lancaster
Pyfer, John Frederick, Jr.,

Mc Keesport
Kessler, Steven Fisher

Meadville
Barrett, Bruce Alan

Natrona Heights
Maleski, Cynthia Maria

New Castle
Manolis, James William

Newport
Scaringi, Melanie Walz

Newtown
Godwin, Robert Anthony

Philadelphia
Hoffman, Alan Jay
O'Brien, William Jerome, II,
Savett, Stuart Hubert
Wolf, Bruce

Pittsburgh
Fall, Robert J.
Litman, Roslyn Margolis
McLaughlin, John Sherman
Pushinsky, Jon
Warman, Guy Lee

Pottsville
Jones, Joseph Hayward

Scranton
Wilson, Charles Frank

Trevose
McEvilly, James Patrick, Jr.

Warminster
Hetherington, John Joseph

Wayne
Spiess, F. Harry, Jr.,

West Chester
Litvin, William Joseph

Womelsdorf
Worley, Jane Ludwig

York
Hoffmeyer, William Frederick

RHODE ISLAND

Cranston
Coletti, John Anthony
Tammelleo, A. David

Middletown
Barrow, Barbara A.

Newport
McConnell, David Kelso

Pawtucket
Kranseler, Lawrence Michael

Providence
Demopulos, Harold William
Gasbarro, Pasco, Jr.,
Long, Nicholas Trott
McElroy, Michael Robert

West Warwick
Pollock, Bruce Gerald

SOUTH CAROLINA

Aiken
Marine, Andrew Craig

Beaufort
Harvey, William Brantley, Jr.,

Greenville
Horton, James Wright

Hilton Head Island
Esposito, John Vincent
Scarminach, Charles Anthony

North Myrtle Beach
Wheless, Albert Eugene

Seneca
Sires, Norman Gruber, Jr.,

Spartanburg
Smith, William Douglas

Sumter
Seth, J. Cabot

SOUTH DAKOTA

Pierre
Thompson, Charles Murray

Rapid City
Graslie, Thomas Eric

Spearfish
Hood, Earl James

TENNESSEE

Bolivar
Cary, Charles Muse

Chattanooga
Vital, Patricia Best

Church Hill
Faulk, Michael Anthony

Etowah
Parker, Eugene LeRoy, III,

Hermitage
Burkett, Gerald Arthur

Jackson
Pietrowski, R. Scott

Johnson City
Epps, James Haws, III,

Knoxville
Giordano, Lawrence Francis
Routh, John William

Memphis
Allen, Newton Perkins
Jackson, Thomas Francis, III,
Moore, Dwight Terry
Newman, Charles Forrest
Rutledge, Roger Keith

Nashville
Camp, Randy Coleman
Torrey, Claudia Olivia
Woods, Larry David

Newport
Bell, John Alton
Myers, John William

Rogersville
Skelton, Mark Albert

South Pittsburg
Ables, Charles Robert

Sweetwater
Ridenour, Charles Edward

TEXAS

Austin
Hale, Louis Dewitt
Weddington, Sarah Ragle

Bellaire
Soffar, William Douglas

Borger
Pace, Rosa White

Brenham
Tate, Milton York, Jr.,

Brownsville
Fleming, Tommy Wayne

Brownwood
Bell, William Woodward

Cleveland
Campbell, Selaura Joy

Corpus Christi
Alberts, Harold
Wood, James Allen

Cypress
Callegari, William A., Jr.,

Dallas
Anderson, E. Karl
Levin, Hervey Phillip
Mueller, Mark Christopher
Nichols, Henry Louis
Ringle, Brett Adelbert
Sloman, Marvin Sherk
Waterston, Tass Dever

El Paso
Morton, Fred J.

Farmersville
Seward, Richard Bevin

Fort Worth
Brown, C. Harold
Phillips, Robert James, Jr.,

Garland
Irby, Holt

Georgetown
Bryce, William Delf

Houston
Adair, William B. (Ben Adair)
Bradie, Peter Richard
Burton, Joseph Randolph
Covington, Vonda Russell
Forbes, Arthur Lee, III,
Gayle, Gibson, Jr.,
Gutheinz, Joseph Richard, Jr.,
Ney, Judy Larson
Pesikoff, Bette Schein
Plaeger, Frederick Joseph, II,
Prater, Wendy Lea
Simoneaux, Jerry W.

Kerrville
Parmley, Robert James

Killeen
Kleff, Pierre Augustine, Jr.,

Lockhart
Scudday, Roy George

Longview
Harrison, Guy Newell
Johnson, Darryl Todd

Lubbock
Brock, Ralph Haney

Odessa
Cliff, John William, Jr.,

Richardson
Olson, Dennis Oliver

San Angelo
Moeller, Galen Ashley

San Antonio
Case, Jeff Dean
Wallis, Ben Alton, Jr.,

San Saba
Senterfitt, Reuben

Spring
Beauchamp, Gary Fay

Stafford
Wagner, Leslie

Waco
Hall, Donald Orell
Smith, Cullen

Wharton
Roades, John Leslie

UTAH

Brigham City
Bunderson, Jon J.

Park City
Schiesswohl, Cynthia Rae Schlegel

Salt Lake City
McConkie, Oscar Walter
Scofield, David Willson

VIRGINIA

Alexandria
Beach, Barbara Purse
Burch, John Thomas, Jr.,
Straub, Peter Thornton

Amherst
Martin, Stephen Clarke

Arlington
Walker, Woodrow Wilson

Bristol
Alan, Sondra Kirschner

Chester
Gray, Charles Robert

Danville
Conway, French Hoge

Falls Church
Kirk, Dennis Dean

Hopewell
Clark, Bruce Arlington, Jr.,

Hot Springs
Deeds, Robert Creigh

Lynchburg
Angel, James Joseph

Manassas
Scriven, Wayne Marcus

Martinsville
Smith, James Randolph, Jr.,

Mc Lean
Morris, James Malachy
Redmond, Robert

Mechanicsville
d'Evegnee, Charles Paul

Newport News
Cuthrell, Carl Edward
Saunders, Bryan Leslie

Powhatan
Carrico, Lucretia A.

Providence Forge
Richardson, William Winfree, III,

Reston
Anderson, Charles Anthony

Richmond
Pearsall, John Wesley
Thomas, John Charles

Salem
Griffith, H(oward) Morgan

Springfield
Chappell, Milton Leroy
Costello, Daniel Brian

Suffolk
Young, Hubert Howell, Jr.,

Virginia Beach
Spitzli, Donald Hawkes, Jr.,

Winchester
Adams, Nate Lavinder, III,

WASHINGTON

Bellevue
McCutcheon, James Edward, III,

Centralia
Buzzard, Steven Ray

Issaquah
Moch, Robert Gaston
Oles, Stuart Gregory

Montesano
Stewart, James Malcolm

Seattle
Budigan, William Clay
Cavin, Clark
Davis, Noah
Pritchard, Llewelyn G.
Sayre, Matt Melvin Mathias

Selah
Ring, Lucile Wiley

Spokane
Scanlon, Robert Charles

WEST VIRGINIA

Bluefield
Henderson, Susan Ellen Fortune

Fairview
Bunner, William Keck

Gassaway
Jones, Jeniver James

Romney
Saville, Royce Blair

WISCONSIN

Colby
Nikolay, Frank Lawrence

Deerfield
Pappas, David Christopher

La Crosse
Russell, David Brent

Milwaukee
Donahue, John Edward
Michelstetter, Stanley Hubert

Monroe
Kittelsen, Rodney Olin

Montello
Wissbaum, Donna Cacic

Oshkosh
Kelly, John Martin

Osseo
Feltes, Charles Victor

Port Washington
Meyer, Raymond George, II,

Racine
Younglove, Michael Robert

Salem
Edenhofer, Carl R.

Sheboygan
Gass, David

Wausau
Connell, James Bernard
Deffner, Roger L.
Drengler, William Allan John

WYOMING

Cheyenne
Scorsine, John Magnus

Laramie
Kinney, Lisa Frances

Riverton
Girard, Nettabell

Worland
Richins, Kent Alan
Sweeny, Wendy Press

ARGENTINA

Buenos Aires
Parisier, Carlos

AUSTRALIA

Mount Gambier
Rymill, Thomas Mark

BRAZIL

Rio de Janeiro
Xavier, Helena de Araujo Lopes

São Paulo
Azevedo, Renato Olimpio Sette de

CHILE

Santiago
López Escarcena, R. Sebastián

FRANCE

Paris
Dupuis, Delphine Marie

NIGERIA

Lagos
Braithwaite, Kunbi

NORWAY

Oslo
Keiserud, Erik

Osteras
Drevvatne, Dag

PHILIPPINES

Makati City
Gonzales, Ponciano Jr. Concepcion

PORTUGAL

Lisbon
Mónica, António De Carvalho Godinho

SCOTLAND

Midlothian
Barnes, Joy Chappell

THAILAND

Pathumwan
Sutham, Apisith John

VENEZUELA

Caracas
Eljuri, Elisabeth

ADDRESS UNPUBLISHED

Amughan, Kennedy Abba Keday
Barry, David F.
Bibik, Jacqueline Avis
Boensch, Arthur Cranwell
Boner, Eleanor Katz
Burgess, Hayden Fern
Campbell, Frank Andrew Scott
Carroll, Diane C.
Easterling, Charles Armo
Feldkamp, John Calvin
Fleischman, Herman Israel
Greenebaum, Leonard Charles
Guehl, Robert Lee
Gutis, Mark Philip
Hartley, Karen Jeanette
Heinrich, Steven Allan
Herman, Richard Bruce
Hubbard, Michael James
Kiefer, Karen LaVerne
Leb, Arthur Stern
Licke, Wallace John
Lynch, Robert Berger
Mangler, Robert James
Margolis, Benjamin Robert
Martin, Thomas MacDonald
Maynard, Peter David
McAlhany, Toni Anne
McDonald, Bradley G.
Natcher, Stephen Darlington
O'Dell, Joan Elizabeth
Orlebeke, William Ronald
Perry, George Williamson
Purtle, John Ingram
Rawls, Frank Macklin
Regenstreif, Herbert
Rogovin, Lawrence H.
Rosenn, Harold
Rosner, Seth
Saliterman, Richard Arlen
Saporito, Steven
Schmoll, Harry F., Jr.,
Schroeder, Edward James
Sheble, Walter Franklin
Sussman, Howard S(ivin)
Vamos, Florence M.
Walsh, Gerry O'Malley
Weinmann, Richard Adrian
White, William Nelson
Winslow, F(rancis) Dana
Wong-Diaz, Francisco Raimundo

Zelechiwsky, Bohdan John

GOVERNMENT CONTRACTS AND CLAIMS

UNITED STATES

ALABAMA

Birmingham
Pritchett, Rebecca Wright

CALIFORNIA

California City
Friedl, Rick

Los Angeles
Metzger, Robert Streicher
Oliver, Dale Hugh
Pieper, Darold D.

Oak Park
Vinson, William Theodore

Oakland
Leslie, Robert Lorne
Wallace, Elaine Wendy

Pomona
Wyatt, John Brundige, III,

Redwood City
Wilhelm, Robert Oscar

San Francisco
Russoniello, Joseph Pascal
Walcher, Alan Ernest

San Juan Capistrano
Graves, Patrick Lee

San Pedro
Russell, Thomas Arthur

Sunnyvale
Thornton, D. Whitney, II,
Wehde, Albert Edward

DISTRICT OF COLUMBIA

Washington
Churchill, David A.
Crowell, Eldon Hubbard
Dembling, Paul Gerald
Feldman, Roger David
Hatcher, Michael Robert
Haynes, William J(ames), II,
Johnson, David Raymond
Kent, Alan Heywood
Kessler, Judd Lewis
Latham, Peter Samuel
Latham, Weldon Hurd
Ledeman, Gordon Nathaniel
Lifschitz, Judah
Mann, Donegan
Mitchell, Roy Shaw
Nemeroff, Michael Alan
Ness, Andrew David
O'Sullivan, Lynda Troutman
Perlman, Matthew Saul
Ryan, Stephen Michael
Schmidt, William Arthur, Jr.,
Schor, Laurence
Silver, Harry R.
Splitt, David Alan
Tuohey, Mark Henry, III,
Violante, Joseph Anthony
Webber, Richard John
West, Joseph D.

FLORIDA

Fort Pierce
Conklin, Howard Lawrence

Jasper
McCormick, John Hoyle

Key Biscayne
Pearson, John Edward

Miami
Mehta, Eileen Rose

Pensacola
George, Katie

Sarasota
Phillips, Elvin Willis

Tampa
Campbell, Richard Bruce
Jordan-Holmes, Clark

GEORGIA

Atlanta
Abernathy, Thomas Edwards, IV,
Dattolo, Alphonse Robert
Sweeney, Neal James

HAWAII

Honolulu
Katayama, Robert Nobuichi

IDAHO

Boise
Leroy, David Henry

Bonners Ferry
Wilson, Peter Bottum

KENTUCKY

Fort Thomas
Whalen, Paul Lewellin

Lexington
Beshear, Steven Lynn

Louisville
Ethridge, Larry Clayton

LOUISIANA

New Orleans
Fierke, Thomas Garner

MARYLAND

Bethesda
Hagberg, Viola Wilgus
Menaker, Frank H., Jr.,
Stentz, Jon William

Patuxent River
Fitzhugh, David Michael

MASSACHUSETTS

Carlisle
Hensleigh, Howard Edgar

MICHIGAN

Bloomfield Hills
Birnkrant, Sherwin Maurice

Detroit
Fellrath, Richard Frederic
Lewand, F. Thomas
Thorpe, Norman Ralph

Rochester Hills
Diehl, Richard Paul

MINNESOTA

Minneapolis
Bruner, Philip Lane
Eckland, Jeff Howard
Forneris, Jeanne M.
Smith, Curtis David

MISSISSIPPI

Jackson
Purdy, William Richard

MISSOURI

Kansas City
White, Jerusha Lynn

Saint Louis
Arnold, John Fox
Carr, Gary Thomas
Weiss, Charles Andrew

NEVADA

Las Vegas
Kirsch, Lynn

NEW JERSEY

Morristown
Clark, Grant Lawrence

NEW YORK

Albany
Fernandez, Hermes A., III,

Massapequa
Van Gorder, John Frederic

New Rochelle
Stevens, Roger Ross

New York
Grassi, Joseph F.
Sigmond, Carol Ann
Wollman, Eric

NORTH CAROLINA

Charlotte
Sink, Robert C.

NORTH DAKOTA

Grand Forks
Hand, James Stanley

OHIO

Columbus
Haught, Jack Gregg

Grove City
Dodd, Jerry Lee

Marion
Slagle, James William

OREGON

Coquille
Lounsbury, Steven Richard

PENNSYLVANIA

Harrisburg
Van Zile, Philip Taylor, III,

SOUTH CAROLINA

Aiken
Alan, Matthew W. A.
Pearce, Richard Lee

SOUTH DAKOTA

Sioux Falls
Hattervig, Karen Ann

TENNESSEE

Knoxville
Dillard, W. Thomas

Nashville
Cobb, Stephen A.

TEXAS

Colleyville
Whittenberg, Ira Orville

Dallas
Crowley, James Worthington
Doke, Marshall J., Jr.,

Houston
Eiland, Gary Wayne

Mc Kinney
Roessler, P. Dee

San Antonio
Goff, Colleen Mullen

VIRGINIA

Alexandria
Burch, John Thomas, Jr.,

Arlington
Doyle, Gerard Francis

Fairfax
Folk, Thomas Robert

Mc Lean
Baker, Keith Leon

Oakton
Duesenberg, Robert H.
Randolph, Christopher Craven

Petersburg
Rosenstock, Louis Anthony, III,

Richmond
Ryland, Walter H.
Whitlock, Julie Marie

Vienna
Hagberg, Chris Eric
Settle, Eric Lawrence

WASHINGTON

Issaquah
Oles, Stuart Gregory

Seattle
Boman, Marc Allen
Bucklin, Mark Richard
Freeman, Antoinette Rosefeldt
Olsen, Harold Fremont

Tacoma
Mack, Robert E.
Waldo, James Chandler

WEST VIRGINIA

Charleston
Lane, Charlotte

ENGLAND

London
McLeod, Simon Nicholas

REPUBLIC OF KOREA

Seoul
Woo, Chang Rok

TAIWAN

Taipei
Hsiao, Joanne Y.

UKRAINE

Kiev
Golub, Andrey Vladimirovich

ADDRESS UNPUBLISHED

Casselman, William E., II,
Collins, Theodore John
Dowben, Carla Lurie
Goddard, Claude Philip, Jr.,
Hoffman, Ira Eliot
Johnson, Richard Tenney
Levy, Kenneth St. Clair
Martin, Gary Duncan
McCabe, Thomas Edward
McDuffy, Aditya
Reiss, Jerome
Stone, Andrew Grover
Wittig, Raymond Shaffer

HEALTH

UNITED STATES

ALABAMA

Birmingham
Friend, Edward Malcolm, III,
Givhan, Robert Marcus
Henry, James Fred
Levy, Jack B.
Rowe, Stephen Ashford

Mobile
Pierce, Donald Fay

Montgomery
Porter, Cheairs Mayes

ALASKA

Anchorage
Dickson, Robert Jay

ARIZONA

Phoenix
Barclay, Steven Calder
Bixby, David Michael
Halpern, Barry David
Johnston, Logan Truax, III,
Pietzsch, Michael Edward
Thompson, Terence William

Tucson
Kaucher, James William

ARKANSAS

Little Rock
Marshall, William Taylor

Rogers
Myers, Dane Jacob

CALIFORNIA

Alamo
Fleisher, Steven M.

Fresno
Jamison, Daniel Oliver

Los Angeles
Carrey, Neil
Kessler, Robert Mark
Kollar, Linda Randlett
Lavin, Laurence Michael
Mancino, Douglas Michael
Memel, Sherwin Leonard
Stromberg, Ross Ernest

Oakland
Koch, Richard Phillips (Terry Koch)

Pasadena
Zuetel, Kenneth Roy, Jr.,

San Francisco
DeMuro, Paul Robert
Taylor, William James (Zak Taylor)

San Rafael
Duke, George F.

Santa Barbara
Ah-Tye, Kirk Thomas

COLORADO

Denver
McManus, Richard Griswold, Jr.,

Fort Collins
Trautwein, Blair J.

Pueblo
Farley, Thomas T.

CONNECTICUT

Hartford
Del Negro, John Thomas
Dennis, Anthony James
Lloyd, Alex
Space, Theodore Maxwell
Young, Roland Frederic, III,

Manchester
Horwitz, Melvin

New Haven
Birnbaum, Irwin Morton
Knag, Paul Everett

Stamford
Lalli, Michael Anthony

DELAWARE

Wilmington
Rodgers, Stephen John

DISTRICT OF COLUMBIA

Washington
Berenson, Aimee Robin
Boggs, Judith Susan
Cook, Michael Harry
Flannery, Ellen Joanne
Hastings, Douglas Alfred
Hoffman, Joel Elihu
Hutt, Peter Barton
Kingham, Richard Frank
Kuder, Armin Ulrich
McAnaney, Kevin George
McConnell, Nicholas Stillwell
McHugh, James Lenahan, Jr.,
Miller, Charles A.
Montedonico, Joseph
Navarro, Bruce Charles
O'Neil, Thomas Francis, III,
Rabecs, Robert Nicholas
Silver, Harry R.
Stromberg, Clifford Douglas
Temko, Stanley Leonard

FLORIDA

Boca Raton
Kornberg, Joel Barry

Fort Walton Beach
Lester, Arthur H.

Jacksonville
Korn, Michael Jeffrey
Prom, Stephen George

Lakeland
Knowlton, Kevin Charles

Miami
Ersek, Gregory Joseph Mark
Fishman, Lewis Warren
Pons, Elizabeth S.
Quirantes, Albert M.

Miami Lakes
Sharett, Alan Richard

Naples
Berning, Randall Karl

Orlando
Henry, William Oscar Eugene

Pensacola
Bozeman, Frank Carmack

Ponte Vedra Beach
Horty, John Francis

Sarasota
Garland, Richard Roger
Zitani, Gregory Anthony

Tallahassee
Dix, Martin Robert
Miller, Morris Henry

Tampa
Davis, Kirk Stuart
Pellett, Jon Michael
Rosenkranz, Stanley William
Watson, Roberta Casper

West Palm Beach
Terry, Karen Elizabeth

GEORGIA

Atlanta
Brown, John Robert
Grady, Kevin E.
Ide, Roy William, III,
Schroder, Jack Spalding , Jr.,
Wright, Peter Meldrim

HAWAII

Honolulu
Grande, Thomas Robert

IDAHO

Boise
Lombardi, David Richard

ILLINOIS

Chicago
Allen, Henry Sermones, Jr.,
Cherney, James Alan
Cusack, John Thomas
Dechene, James Charles
Egan, Kevin James
Gilbert, Howard N(orman)
Ladd, Jeffrey Raymond
McVisk, William Kilburn
Parson, Jason A.
Pelton, Russell Meredith, Jr.,
Reed, Keith Allen
Sanders, Richard Henry
Shields, Thomas Charles
Wilson, Roger Goodwin

Mattoon
Horsley, Jack Everett

North Chicago
de Lasa, José M.

Northbrook
Dilling, Kirkpatrick Wallwick
Staab, Michael Joseph

Palatine
Victor, Michael Gary

Roselle
Bassitt, Janet Louise

Springfield
Morse, Saul Julian

Waukegan
Henrick, Michael Francis

Western Springs
Shannon, Peter Michael, Jr.,

INDIANA

Hammond
Diamond, Eugene Christopher

Indianapolis
Gilliland, John Campbell, II,
Horn, Brenda Sue
Kemper, James Dee
Shula, Robert Joseph

South Bend
Phillipoff, Mark James

KANSAS

Prairie Village
Stanton, Roger D.

KENTUCKY

Flemingsburg
McCartney, Frank Howard, III,

Louisville
Ament, Mark Steven
Reed, D. Gary

LOUISIANA

Baton Rouge
Riddick, Winston Wade, Sr.,

Covington
Miltenberger, Henry James, Jr.,
Van Steenis, Jon Anthony

Lafayette
Breaux, Paul Joseph

Metairie
Ford, Robert David

New Orleans
Beahm, Franklin D.
David, Robert Jefferson
Steinberg, Sylvan Julian

MAINE

Manchester
MacLean, Andrew Bishop

MARYLAND

Baltimore
Friedman, Barry Howard
Moser, M(artin) Peter
Sfekas, Stephen James
Ziegler, Hal Jeffrey

Phoenix
Anderson, Mary Ellen

MASSACHUSETTS

Boston
Adler, Sidney W.
Haddad, Ernest Mudarri
Johnston, Richard Alan
Lanckton, Arthur Van Cleve
Ristuben, Karen R.

Cambridge
Crawford, Linda Sibery

Newton
Isselbacher, Rhoda Solin

Springfield
Fein, Sherman Edward

Worcester
Donnelly, James Corcoran, Jr.,

MICHIGAN

Ann Arbor
Muraski, Anthony Augustus

Bloomfield
Kanter, Alan Michael

Detroit
Johnson, Cynthia L(e) M(ae)

Grand Rapids
Kolenic, Anthony James, Jr.,

MINNESOTA

Bloomington
Broeker, John Milton

Hallock
Malm, Roger Charles

Minneapolis
Bress, Michael E.
Hanson, Bruce Eugene
Struthers, Margo S.

Saint Paul
Duckstad, Jon Robert

MISSOURI

Independence
Cady, Elwyn Loomis, Jr.,

Jefferson City
Tettlebaum, Harvey M.

Kansas City
Brous, Thomas Richard
Chase, Curt J.
Doan, Kirk Hugh
Toll, Perry Mark

Saint Charles
Weber, William Randolph

Saint Louis
Schoene, Kathleen Snyder
Watters, Richard Donald

MONTANA

Billings
Murphy, Gregory Gerard

NEW HAMPSHIRE

Concord
Chamberlain, Douglas Reginald

Manchester
Hanna, Katherine Merritt

NEW JERSEY

Berlin
Goldstein, Benjamin

Bridgewater
Conroy, Robert John
Feingold, Mark Howard

Kenilworth
Wasman, Jane G.

New Providence
Bernstein, Nadia J.

Princeton
Benesch, Katherine

Roseland
Eichler, Burton Lawrence

Woodbridge
Schaff, Michael Frederick

NEW MEXICO

Santa Fe
Pound, John Bennett

NEW YORK

Albany
Fernandez, Hermes A., III,
Sciocchetti, Nancy

Brooklyn
Schussler, Theodore

Buffalo
Fine, Robert Paul
Greene, Robert Michael
Magavern, James L.

Great Neck
Breitenbach, Roy W.

Medina
Mark, Lance Joseph

New York
Appel, Albert M.
Beattie, Richard Irwin
Chazen, Hartley James
Donovan, Richard Edward
Garson, Andrew S.
Hanover, Richard
Jacobson, Jerold Dennis
Kaplan, Susan
Kaufman, Robert Max
Kornreich, Edward Scott
Moore, Thomas A.
Naftalis, Gary Philip
Watson, Richard Allen

Niskayuna
Sokolow, Lloyd Bruce

Rochester
Stewart, Sue S.

Syracuse
Pinsky, Roy David

NORTH CAROLINA

Asheville
Bissette, Winston Louis, Jr.,

Durham
Du Sartel, Alexandre
Gudaitis, Christy Myers

Greensboro
Harris, Terrill Johnson

Raleigh
Glass, Fred Stephen
Simpson, Steven Drexell

OHIO

Athens
Hedges, Richard Houston

Cincinnati
Anthony, Thomas Dale
Markesbery, Maria Saba
Wales, Ross Elliot

Cleveland
Brown, Harry M.
Koblenz, N(orman) Herschel

Columbus
Ballard, Catherine Anne Martine
Dunlay, Catherine Telles
Frasier, Ralph Kennedy
Graff, Douglas Eric
Todd, William Michael

Dayton
Hadley, Robert James

Dublin
Maloon, Jerry L.

Howard
Lee, William Johnson

OKLAHOMA

Oklahoma City
Gordon, Kevin Dell

Stillwater
Fischer, Richard Samuel

Tulsa
Draughon, Scott Wilson
Gaberino, John Anthony, Jr.,

OREGON

Eugene
Lowry, Robert Dudley

Portland
Anderson, Herbert Hatfield
Epstein, Edward Louis
Harrell, Gary Paul
Hart, John Edward
Simpson, Robert Glenn

PENNSYLVANIA

Malvern
Cameron, John Clifford

Natrona Heights
Maleski, Cynthia Maria

Philadelphia
Brier, Bonnie Susan
Cramer, Harold
Flanagan, Joseph Patrick, Jr.,
Haley, Vincent Peter
Lowery, William Herbert
Luongo, Stephen Earle
Reed, Michael Haywood
Reiss, John Barlow
Weil, Jeffrey George

Pittsburgh
Farley, Andrew Newell
Kabala, Edward John
Lyncheski, John E.
Springer, Eric Winston
Sweeney, Clayton Anthony
Thurman, Andrew Edward
Wilkinson, James Allan

Plymouth
Musto, Joseph John

West Chester
Ewing, Joseph Neff, Jr.,

RHODE ISLAND

Cranston
Tammelleo, A. David

Providence
Olsen, Hans Peter

SOUTH CAROLINA

Columbia
Scott, Ronald Charles

North Charleston
Laddaga, Lawrence Alexander

SOUTH DAKOTA

Pierre
Gerdes, David Alan

TENNESSEE

Johnson City
King, Robert Lewis

Knoxville
Lloyd, Francis Leon, Jr.,

Memphis
Gentry, Gavin Miller

Nashville
Gillmor, John Edward
Sawyer, Christy Carlson
Torrey, Claudia Olivia
Tuke, Robert Dudley
Yuspeh, Alan Ralph

TEXAS

Abilene
Robinson, Vianei Lopez

Austin
Davis, Creswell Dean

Dallas
Gerberding Cowart, Greta Elaine
Green, Jesse Joseph
Greiner, Mary Louise
Humble, Monty Garfield
Stinnett, Mark Allan

Fort Worth
Hayes, Larry B.

Harlingen
Pope, William L.

Houston
Blackshear, A. T., Jr.,
Campbell, Bert Louis
Crocker, Samuel Sackett
Eiland, Gary Wayne
Epstein, Jon David
McQuarrie, Claude Monroe, III,
Rogers, Arthur Hamilton, III,
Sumers, Jean Petersen
Wilfong, Hugh C., II,

Temple
Pickle, Jerry Richard

Tyler
Lake, David Alan

UTAH

Salt Lake City
Owen, Langdon Talbot, Jr.,
Webber, Brian C.

VIRGINIA

Alexandria
Carter, Richard Dennis
Franklin, Jeanne F.
Klewans, Samuel N.

Arlington
Mossinghoff, Gerald Joseph

Charlottesville
Merrill, Richard Austin

Chesapeake
Leftwich, James Asbury, Jr.,

Great Falls
Neidich, George Arthur

Mc Lean
Brown, Thomas Cartmel, Jr.,

Montross
Monaco, Grace Powers

Norfolk
Poston, Anita Owings

Reston
Platt, Leslie A.

Roanoke
Lemon, William Jacob

Spotsylvania
Manthei, Richard Dale

WASHINGTON

Everett
Ferguson, Gordon Douglas

Seattle
Hutcheson, Mark Andrew
Lamb, Mark Christopher
Losey, Beverley Brown
Sausser, Gail Dianne
Van Kampen, Al
Williams, Rebecca Lynn

Spokane
Connolly, K. Thomas

WEST VIRGINIA

Bluefield
Evans, Wayne Lewis

Wheeling
Wilmoth, William David

WISCONSIN

Germantown
Ehlinger, Ralph Jerome

Madison
Baldwin, Janice Murphy
Hanson, David James

Milwaukee
Berkoff, Marshall Richard
Biehl, Michael Melvin
Busch, John Arthur
Friedman, James Dennis
Shapiro, Robyn Sue
Van Grunsven, Paul Robert

MEXICO

Mexico City
Ayala-Aguirre, Jose Ramon

AUSTRALIA

Sydney
Bateman, Gregory Anthony

ENGLAND

London
White, Walter Hiawatha, Jr.,

GERMANY

Villingen
Koenig, Hans-Joachim

ADDRESS UNPUBLISHED

Bales, John Foster, III,
Bennett, Steven Alan
Boone, Richard Winston, Sr.,
Burgess, Hayden Fern
Cazalas, Mary Rebecca Williams
Clarke, Edward Owen, Jr.,
Dikeou, George Demetrios
Dowben, Carla Lurie
Hough, Thomas Henry Michael
Kaufman, James Jay
Kellerman, Edwin

IMMIGRATION, NATURALIZATION, AND CUSTOMS

UNITED STATES

MEXICO

BELARUS

ENGLAND

FRANCE

NORWAY

PHILIPPINES

PORTUGAL

SWITZERLAND

ADDRESS UNPUBLISHED

INSURANCE *See also* Personal injury

UNITED STATES

Long Beach
Haile, Lawrence Barclay
Wise, George Edward

Los Angeles
Adamek, Charles Andrew
Adler, Erwin Ellery
Bodkin, Henry Grattan, Jr.,
Bradley, Lawrence D., Jr.,
Daniels, William Anthony
Galton, Stephen Harold
Garretson, Robert H.
Hufstedler, Seth Martin
Imhoff, Earl J.
Imre, Christina Joanne
Jacobs, Randall Brian
Johnson, Philip Leslie
Katz, Jason Lawrence
MacLaughlin, Francis Joseph
Margo, Rod David
Miller, Milton Allen
Newman, Michael Rodney
Pasich, Kirk Alan
Rozanski, Stanley Howard
Schulman, Robert S.
Weatherup, Roy Garfield

Mill Valley
Cole, Richard Charles

Napa
Kuntz, Charles Powers

Newport Beach
Johnson, Thomas Webber, Jr.,

Paramount
Hall, Howard Harry

Pleasanton
Scott, G. Judson, Jr.,

Sacramento
Campos, Dennis M.

San Clemente
Fisher, Myron R.

San Diego
Christensen, Charles Brophy
Gomez, John Hamilton
Herring, Charles David
Longstreth, Robert Christy
McIntyre, Monty Alan
Roseman, Charles Sanford
Sceper, Duane Harold
Wolfe, Deborah Ann

San Francisco
Callison, Russell James
Dworkin, Michael Leonard
Hofmann, John Richard, Jr.,
Kasanin, Mark Owen
Kornblum, Guy Orville
Matthews, Philip Richard
Meadows, John Frederick
Staring, Graydon Shaw
Trautman, William Ellsworth
Walker, Walter Herbert, III,
Woods, James Robert

San Jose
Narayan, Beverly Elaine

Santa Barbara
Bauer, Marvin Agather

Santa Monica
Morgan, Kermit Johnson

Tahoe City
Hirshon, Jack Thomas

Tustin
Madory, Richard Eugene

Ukiah
Sager, Madeline Dean

Ventura
Gartner, Harold Henry, III,

Walnut Creek
Medak, Walter Hans
Pinkerton, Albert Duane, II,

COLORADO

Denver
Burke, Gay Ann Wolesensky
Byrne, Thomas J.
Fowler, Daniel McKay
Furtado, David Jeffrey
Nathan, J(ay) Andrew
Pack, Stuart Harris
Reilly, Daniel M.

Englewood
Orsini, Rosemary

Fort Collins
Downey, Arthur Harold, Jr.,

Greenwood Village
Karr, David Dean

CONNECTICUT

Danielson
Jungeberg, Thomas Donald

Farmington
McCann, John Joseph

Hartford
Fain, Joel Maurice
Packard, Stephen Michael
Taylor, Allan Bert

New Britain
Hogan, John W., Jr.,

New Haven
Gildea, Brian Michael

Stamford
Hubschman, Henry A.
Shanman, James Alan

Trumbull
Williams, Ronald Doherty

Weatogue
Greenlaw, Dawn Sharon

DELAWARE

Dover
Sherlock, Mary Eva
Steele, Myron Thomas

Wilmington
Julian, J. R.
Katzenstein, Robert John
Semple, James William

DISTRICT OF COLUMBIA

Washington
Bellinger, Edgar Thomson
Boehm, Steven Bruce
Carpenter, Russell H., Jr.,
Carr, Lawrence Edward, Jr.,
Carter, William Joseph
Cummings, Frank
Dolin, Mitchell F.
Faron, Robert Steven
Funkhouser, Robert Bruce
Handleman, Aaron L.
Havens, Charles W., III,
Lanam, Linda Lee
Marks, Andrew H.
Medaglia, Mary-Elizabeth
Schwartz, Victor Elliot
Skinner, William Polk
Solomons, Mark Elliott

FLORIDA

Alachua
Gaines, Weaver Henderson

Boca Raton
David, Ronald Albert
Willis, John Alexander

Boynton Beach
Hermann, Philip J.

Bradenton
Groseclose, Lynn Hunter

Clearwater
Fine, A(rthur) Kenneth

Coral Gables
Gonzalez, Ervin Amado
McGrane, Miles A., III,

Fort Lauderdale
Bunnell, George Eli
Flynn, RoseAnn
Pomeroy, Gregg Joseph

Hollywood
Korthals, Candace Durbin

Jacksonville
Posgay, Matthew Nichols
Reed, Ronald Ernst

Lake Worth
Rose, Norman

Maitland
Bailey, Michael Keith

Miami
Fishman, Lewis Warren
Greenleaf, Walter Franklin
Hauser, Helen Ann
Jeffrey, Douglas Jason
Johnson, Alise M.
Kritzer, Glenn Bruce
Levine, Robert Jeffrey
Long, Maxine Master
Mazer, Jason S.
O'Connor, Kathleen Mary
Russell, Patrick
Silverman, Bradley Allan
Skolnick, S. Harold
Stansell, Leland Edwin, Jr.,
Thornton, John William, Sr.,
Touby, Kathleen Anita
Wright, Robert Thomas, Jr.,

Ocala
Hatch, John D.

Orlando
Hurt, Jennings Laverne, III,
Motes, Carl Dalton
Shapiro, Peter A.
Vazquez, Ramon

Panama City
Fensom, James B.

Pembroke Pines
Murray, Claude Robert, Jr.,

Pensacola
Bozeman, Frank Carmack
Jones, Julie Laura
McKenzie, James Franklin

Plantation
Ogden, Anne D.
Sperry, Martin Jay

Pompano Beach
Hasenauer, Judith Anne

Saint Petersburg
Glass, Roy Leonard
Hungate, Mark Edward

Sarasota
Zitani, Gregory Anthony

Tallahassee
Elliott, Timothy B.
Levine, A. Kenneth
Mang, Douglas Arthur

Tampa
Berkowitz, Herbert Mattis
Butler, Paul Bascomb, Jr.,
Cook, William John
Murphy, James Burton, Jr.,
Somers, Clifford Louis
Vessel, Robert Leslie

Tavares
Johnson, Terri Sue

Vero Beach
Stewart, John Mitchell

West Palm Beach
McAfee, William James

GEORGIA

Atlanta
Altman, Robert
Barwick, William D.
Bonds, John Wilfred, Jr.,
Eckl, William Wray
Farnham, Clayton Henson
Glaser, Arthur Henry
Kneisel, Edmund M.
Leach, James Glover
Persons, W. Ray
Savell, Edward Lupo
Smith, Alexander Wyly, Jr.,
Smith, Walton Napier
Warncke, Jeffrey Scott
Zarrillo, Teri Dawn

Augusta
Smith, Larry Ira

Decatur
Apolinsky, Stephen Douglas

Douglas
Hayes, Dewey

Roswell
Roland, Raymond William

Savannah
Bowman, Catherine McKenzie
Forbes, Morton Gerald

Smyrna
Seigler, Michael Edward

Watkinsville
Wright, Robert Joseph

HAWAII

Honolulu
Ching, Gale Lin Fong
Ching, Wesley H. H.
Crumpton, Charles Whitmarsh
Fong, Peter C. K.
Kawachika, James Akio
Lau, Jeffrey Daniel
Louie, David Mark
Reinke, Stefan Michael
Sumida, Kevin P.H.

ILLINOIS

Bloomington
Bragg, Michael Ellis

Chicago
Angst, Gerald L.
Bellah, Kenneth David
Berens, Mark Harry
Blatt, Richard Lee
Bresnahan, Arthur Stephen
Cass, Robert Michael
Chemers, Robert Marc
Daniels, John Draper
Donner, Ted A.
Downing, Robert Allan
Doyle, John Robert
Elden, Gary Michael
Franklin, Christine Carroll
Frazen, Mitchell Hale
Friedman, Lawrence Milton
Gilford, Steven Ross
Hammesfahr, Robert Winter
Jacobson, Richard Joseph
Johnson, Richard Fred
Kawitt, Alan
Kroll, Barry Lewis
Leyhane, Francis John, III,
Lockwood, Gary Lee
Lynch, John James
Marick, Michael Miron
McVisk, William Kilburn
Nugent, Lori S.
Palmer, Robert Towne
Pope, Michael Arthur
Prochnow, Douglas Lee
Shank, Suzanne Adams
Simon, John Bern
Spector, David M.
Thomson, George Ronald
Vojcanin, Sava Alexander
Wilcox, Mark Dean
Wilson, Roger Goodwin

DeKalb
Davidson, Kenneth Lawrence

Des Plaines
Kotelman, Laura Mary

Edwardsville
Gorman, James Edward
Hunsaker, Richard Kendall

Evanston
Creamer, Robert Allan

Glen Ellyn
O'Connell, Daniel James

Northbrook
Ihm, Stephen Lawrence
Rotchford, Patricia Kathleen

Peoria
Prusak, Maximilian Michael

Saint Charles
Weir, William H.

Springfield
Abbott, Randall (Lee Abbott)
Morse, Saul Julian

Wheaton
Butt, Edward Thomas, Jr.,
Cunningham, William Francis

INDIANA

Bloomington
O'Connor, Joseph Daniel

Indianapolis
Bennett, Bryce Hugh, Jr.,
Choplin, John M., II,
Helm, John R.
Johnstone, Robert Philip
Koch, Edna Mae
Lisher, John Leonard
McKeon, Thomas Joseph
Roberts, Patricia Susan
Schreckengast, William Owen

Lafayette
Hart, Russell Holiday

New Albany
Bourne, James E.

Richmond
Bever, Robert Lynn

Shelbyville
Harrold, Dennis Edward
McNeely, James Lee

South Bend
Norton, Sally Pauline

IOWA

Des Moines
Brown, Paul Edmondson
Duckworth, Marvin E.
Hill, Luther Lyons, Jr.,
Peddicord, Roland Dale
Phipps, David Lee

Dubuque
Hammer, David Lindley

Le Mars
Murphy, Patrick Neil

Marshalltown
Brooks, Patrick William

Sioux City
Fredregill, Alan
Mayne, Wiley Edward

KANSAS

Hutchinson
Hayes, John Francis

Kansas City
Brown, Norman Jack

Overland Park
Abele, Robert Christopher

Topeka
Conroy, Christopher S.

Wichita
Hodge, Ray

KENTUCKY

Bowling Green
Rudloff, William Joseph
Sparks, David Thomas

Covington
Stepner, Donald Leon
Wolnitzek, Stephen Dale

Hazard
Roark, Jimmy Lee

Lexington
Kessinger, B.L., Jr.,

London
Keller, John Warren

Louisville
Bubalo, Gregory Joe
Carroll, Wayne Jackson
Osborn, John Simcoe, Jr.,
Reed, D. Gary
Weiss, Allan

Paintsville
Massengale, Roger Lee

LOUISIANA

Alexandria
Gist, Howard Battle, Jr.,

Baton Rouge
Dugas, David Roy
Riddick, Winston Wade, Sr.,
Walsh, Milton O'Neal

Covington
Miltenberger, Henry James, Jr.,
Rice, Winston Edward
Thornton-Ermes, Lucie Elizabeth
Van Steenis, Jon Anthony

Lafayette
Judice, Marc Wayne

Lake Charles
Judice, Gregory Van

Metairie
Ford, Robert David
McMahon, Robert Albert, Jr.,
O'Donnell, Barbara Bourdonnay
St. Pe, Philippi Pierre

New Orleans
Abaunza, Donald Richard
Combe, John Clifford, Jr.,
Eustis, Richmond Minor
Gisleson, Soren Erik
Guidry, Susan Gail
Lee, Wayne J.
Sinnott, John William
Sutterfield, James Ray

Shreveport
Politz, Nyle Anthony

MAINE

Portland
Dinan, Christopher Charles
Hirshon, Robert Edward
Lancaster, Ralph Ivan, Jr.,
Whiting, Stephen Clyde

MARYLAND

Baltimore
Gray, Oscar Shalom
Hansen, Christopher Agnew
Hubbard, Herbert Hendrix
Messina, Bonnie Lynn
Ziegler, Hal Jeffrey

Burtonsville
Covington, Marlow Stanley

Chevy Chase
Mackall, Laidler Bowie
Weiss, Harlan Lee

Columbia
Jacobs, William Michael

Parkville
Hill, Milton King, Jr.,

Rockville
Dugan, John R.

MASSACHUSETTS

Boston
Goldman, Eric Scot
Lanckton, Arthur Van Cleve
Neumeier, Richard L.
Richmond, Alice Elenor

Canton
Masiello, Thomas Philip, Jr.,

Chelmsford
Lerer, Neal M.

Longmeadow
Quinn, Andrew Peter, Jr.,

Quincy
Motejunas, Gerald William

Worcester
Balko, George Anthony, III,
Feener, Donald Edward

MICHIGAN

Birmingham
Zacharski, Dennis Edward

Detroit
Beyer, Daniel G.
Cothorn, John Arthur
Smith, James Albert
Tukel, Susan

East Lansing
Joseph, Raymond

Farmington Hills
Fershtman, Julie Ilene

Flint
Henneke, Edward George

Grand Rapids
Spies, Frank Stadler

Lansing
Fink, Joseph Allen
Nicolucci, John Peter

Pontiac
Pierson, William George

Royal Oak
Monnich, John Robert

Saginaw
Zanot, Craig Allen

Southfield
Gordon, Louis

Troy
Kruse, John Alphonse

MINNESOTA

Duluth
Balmer, James Walter

Edina
Ashley, James Patrick

Golden Valley
Hagglund, Clarance Edward

Minneapolis
Al, Marc Andre
Barrett, Michael D.
Greener, Ralph Bertram
Hektner, Candice Elaine
Lonergan, Lauren Elizabeth
Sanner, Royce Norman
Witort, Janet Lee

Minnetonka
Carpenter, Norman Roblee
Kunert, Paul Charles

Saint Paul
Bell, Robert Charles
Degnan, John Michael
Maclin, Alan Hall

MISSISSIPPI

Biloxi
Dornan, Donald C., Jr.,

Columbus
Hicks, Dewitt T., Jr.,

Gulfport
Allen, Harry Roger
Harral, John Menteith

Jackson
Currie, Edward Jones, Jr.,
Langford, James Jerry
Mitchell, Meade Westmoreland
Quin, William Monroe, II,

Pascagoula
Hunter, John Leslie

Tupelo
Bush, Fred Marshall, Jr.,
Deaton, Chris Harold

MISSOURI

Cape Girardeau
Lowes, Albert Charles

Columbia
Turley, J. William

Hannibal
Terrell, James Daniel

Jefferson City
Angstead, Robert Kenneth

Kansas City
Bryant, Richard Todd
Levings, Theresa Lawrence
Milton, Chad Earl
Modin, Richard F.
Todd, Stephen Max

Saint Louis
Boggs, Beth Clemens
Brown, Paul Sherman
Johnson, Weldon Neal
McDaniel, James Edwin
Reeg, Kurtis Bradford

Springfield
FitzGerald, Kevin Michael
Myers, Ronald Lynn
Roberts, Patrick Kent

MONTANA

Butte
Carlson, Robert M.

Great Falls
Blewett, Alexander, III,

Kalispell
Lerner, Alan Jay

NEBRASKA

North Platte
Kay, Stephen William

Omaha
Gleason, James Mullaney
Krutter, Forrest Nathan

NEVADA

Las Vegas
Sturman, Glorida J.

Reno
Kent, Stephen Smiley
Pagni, Albert Frank

NEW HAMPSHIRE

Concord
Hilliard, Russell F.

Manchester
Hutchins, Peter Edward
Rubin, Jeffrey Mark

NEW JERSEY

Asbury Park
Cernigliaro, Michael Joseph

Cherry Hill
Garrigle, William Aloysius

Edison
O'Brien, John Graham

Fairfield
Connell, William Terrence

Florham Park
Reid, Charles Adams, III,

Hammonton
Woolson, Charles E., Jr.,

Keyport
Colmant, Andrew Robert

Millburn
Madden, Edward George, Jr.,

Morris Plains
Pluciennik, Thomas Casimir

Morristown
Clemente, Mark Andrew
Gillen, James Robert

Mountainside
Helander, Robert Charles

Newark
Eittreim, Richard MacNutt
Garde, John Charles
Haring, Eugene Miller
Radin, Steven S.

North Haledon
Harrington, Kevin Paul

Oakhurst
Widman, Douglas Jack

Parsippany
Kallmann, Stanley Walter

Princeton
Stern, Bruce H.
Theroux, William Gerard

Roseland
LaVecchia, John B.
Smith, Wendy Hope

Short Hills
Kaye, Marc Mendell

Summit
Pearlmutter, Fredi L.

Warren
Kraus, Steven Gary

Westfield
Smith, Francis M.

Woodcliff Lake
Clemen, John Douglas

NEW MEXICO

Albuquerque
Beach, Arthur O'Neal
O'Brien, Daniel J.
Roehl, Jerrald J.
Shane, Richard J.
Thiel, Albert Nicholas, Jr.,
Weeth, George Wright

Roswell
Haines, Thomas David, Jr.,

NEW YORK

Albany
Laird, Edward DeHart, Jr.,

Binghamton
Gerhart, Eugene Clifton

Buffalo
De Marie, Anthony Joseph
Goldberg, Neil A.

Garden City
Balkan, Kenneth J.

Hawthorne
Traub, Richard Kenneth

Melville
Adler, Kenneth
Agoglia, Emmet John
Schoenfeld, Michael P.

Mineola
Fowler, David Thomas
Kelly, Shawn Paul
Stock, Thomas John

New Hyde Park
Jaffe, Richard S.

New York
Barry, Desmond Thomas, Jr.,
Birnbaum, Sheila L.
Connuck, Eric S.
Cunha, Mark Geoffrey
Davis, Michael Steven
DeCarlo, Donald Thomas
DeOrchis, Vincent Moore
Dopf, Glenn William
Dunham, Wolcott Balestier, Jr.,
Evans, Martin Frederic
Foster, David Lee
Gabay, Donald David
Halperin, Kyle Mallary
Hayden, Raymond Paul
Hayes, Gerald Joseph
Henderson, Donald Bernard, Jr.,
Hirsch, Daniel
Jacobowitz, Harold Saul
Juceam, Robert E.
Kende, Christopher Burgess
Kirschbaum, Myron
Klapper, Molly
Kleinberg, Norman Charles
Kramer, Alan Sharfsin
Kroll, Sol
Kushel, Glenn Elliot
LeBlang, Skip Alan
Lesman, Michael Steven
Lynch, Luke Daniel, Jr.,
Marshall, Sheila Hermes
McBryde, Thomas Henry
McCormack, Howard Michael
McCormick, Hugh Thomas
Mentz, Lawrence
Nonna, John Michael
O'Connell, Margaret Sullivan
Oliveri, Paul Francis
Paul, James William
Primps, William Guthrie
Quinlan, Guy Christian
Reilly, Conor Desmond
Riley, Scott C.
Rogoff, Jeffrey Scott
Schiffer, Larry Philip
Schmidt, Charles Edward
Semaya, Francine Levitt
Shoss, Cynthia Renée
Squire, Walter Charles
Toner, Stephen
Tract, Marc Mitchell
Weiser, Martin Jay
West, Stephen Kingsbury
Will, Alfred Joseph
Witherwax, Charles Halsey
Wollan, Eugene
Yeager, Dennis Randall
Zoogman, Nicholas Jay

Newburgh
Milligram, Steven Irwin

Rochester
Heyman, Sidney
Spoto, David Dennis

Scarsdale
Perko, Kenneth Albert, Jr.,

Smithtown
Spellman, Thomas Joseph, Jr.,

Staten Island
Howard, Davis Jonathan

Uniondale
Cassidy, David Michael

Watertown
Gebo, Stephen Wallace

White Plains
Keane, Thomas J.
Klein, Paul E.
Taft, Nathaniel Belmont

Yonkers
Connors, James Patrick

NORTH CAROLINA

Asheville
Chidnese, Patrick N.
Davis, Roy Walton, Jr.,
Leake, Larry Bruce

Chapel Hill
Crohn, Max Henry, Jr.,

Charlotte
Mack, Susan Elizabeth

Greensboro
Agapion, Bill

Marion
Burgin, Charles Edward

Raleigh
Dixon, Wright Tracy, Jr.,
Millberg, John C.
Mitchell, Henry Allen, Jr.,

Smithfield
Schulz, Bradley Nicholas

Winston Salem
Dahl, Tyrus Vance, Jr.,
Gitter, Allan Reinhold
Kelly, James Howard, Jr.,
Osborn, Malcolm Everett

NORTH DAKOTA

Bismarck
Edin, Charles Thomas

Fargo
Vogel, Mart Daniel

OHIO

Cincinnati
Hill, Thomas Clark
Meyers, Karen Diane
Neltner, Michael Martin

Cleveland
Duncan, Ed Eugene
Karp, Marvin Louis
Maher, Edward Joseph
Toohey, Brian Frederick
Vergon, Frederick Porter, Jr.,
Wood, Robert Alexander

Columbus
Adams, John Marshall
Blackburn, Thomas Irven
Draper, Gerald Linden
Druen, William Sidney
Eblin, Robert L.
Hutson, Jeffrey Woodward
Ryan, Joseph W., Jr.,

Dayton
Jenks, Thomas Edward
Schmidt, Matthew Martin

Portsmouth
Crowder, Marjorie Briggs

Toledo
Thacker, Joseph Phillip

Youngstown
Blair, Richard Bryson

OKLAHOMA

Broken Arrow
Stewart, Murray Baker

Jones
Dean, Bill Verlin, Jr.,

Mcalester
Neal, Charles D., Jr.,

Oklahoma City
Gordon, Kevin Dell

Tulsa
Atkinson, Michael Pearce
Ballard, Elizabeth Ann
Clark, Joseph Francis, Jr.,

OREGON

Eugene
Lowry, Robert Dudley

Medford
Deatherage, William Vernon

Portland
Brenneman, Delbert Jay
Dailey, Dianne K.
Kennedy, Jack Leland
Kester, Randall Blair

Salem
Mannix, Kevin Leese
Spooner, Ralph Charles

PENNSYLVANIA

Bala Cynwyd
Aris, John Lynnwood

Gladwyne
Booth, Harold Waverly

Harrisburg
Gale, Randall Glenn
Hafer, Joseph Page
Nauman, Spencer Gilbert, Jr.,

Hermitage
McKay, Donald Ross

Horsham
Best, Franklin Luther, Jr.,

Lancaster
Eagan, Michele
Roda, Joseph Francis

Media
Cramp, John Franklin

Monroeville
Baum, Alan Stuart

Paoli
Griffith, Edward

Perkasie
Roeger, William Coley, Jr.,

Philadelphia
Aaron, Kenneth Ellyot
Berenato, Mark Anthony
Bogutz, Jerome Edwin
Fineman, S. David
Goldberg, Marvin Allen
Hanselmann, Fredrick Charles
Huntington, Stephen N.
Ledwith, John Francis
Lowery, William Herbert
Park, Elena
Resnick, Stephanie
Shestack, Jerome Joseph

Pittsburgh
Beck, Christopher Alan
Bochicchio, Vito Salvatore
Mulvihill, Keithley D.
Pfaff, Robert James
Restivo, James John, Jr.,
Salpietro, Frank Gugliotta
von Waldow, Arnd N.

Wyomissing
Turner, David Eldridge

RHODE ISLAND

Warwick
Battle, Leslie Anne Elizabeth
Reilly, John B.

SOUTH CAROLINA

Charleston
Groves, Stephen Peterson, Sr.,

Columbia
Brown, Robert Charles
Carpenter, Charles Elford, Jr.,
Jones, Hartwell Kelley, Jr.,

SOUTH DAKOTA

Pierre
Gerdes, David Alan
Thompson, Charles Murray

TENNESSEE

Chattanooga
Campbell, Paul, III,
Cooper, Gary Allan
Hays, Melissa Padgett

Cookeville
Acuff, John Edgar

Jonesborough
Jenkins, Ronald Wayne

Knoxville
Walter, Glenn Richard
Wheeler, John Watson
White, Edward Gibson, II,

Memphis
Russell, James Franklin

Signal Mountain
Anderson, Charles Hill

TEXAS

Austin
Barnes, Natasha Lynn
Roan, Forrest Calvin, Jr.,

Beaumont
Dowell, James Dale
Orwig, Matthew Dane
Scofield, Louis M., Jr.,

Corpus Christi
Fancher, Rick

Dallas
Bradley, Jean Marie
Brin, Royal Henry, Jr.,
Dyess, Bobby Dale
Ellis, Alfred Wright (Al Ellis)
Fanning, Barry Hedges
Kent, David Charles
Pruessner, David Morgan
Schrauff, Christopher Wesley
Ticer, Mark Allen

Fort Worth
Cottongame, W. Brice
Dent, Edward Dwain
Shannon, Joe, Jr.,

Houston
Bluestein, Edwin A., Jr.,
Carver, Teresa Ann
Durham, William Andrew
Dykes, Osborne Jefferson, III,
Hawash, Michael Andrew
Silva, Eugene Joseph
Smith, Langdon
Sorrels, Randall Owen
Vickery, Edward Downtain
Wilson, David Vandiver, II,
Wood, Judson Robert
Worthington, William Albert, III,

Lindale
Anderson, Lawrence Worthington

Lubbock
Purdom, Thomas James

Midland
MacDonald, Leland Lloyd

Odessa
Hendrick, Benard Calvin, VII,

San Antonio
Henry, Peter York
Patrick, Dane Herman

Temple
Pickle, Jerry Richard

The Woodlands
Schlacks, Stephen Mark

Waco
Tekell, David Glenn

Wichita Falls
Altman, William Kean

UTAH

Salt Lake City
Adams, John A.
Humpherys, LeGrande Rich

South Jordan
Larson, Bryan A.

VERMONT

Burlington
Cain, Robert Gaynor
Rendall, Donald James, Jr.,

Rutland
Faignant, John Paul

Springfield
Boxer, Andrew Carey

VIRGINIA

Abingdon
McElroy, Howard Chowning
Shortridge, Judy Beth

Alexandria
Summers, Alicia Lehnes

Lynchburg
Wetzel, Robert Charles

Mc Lean
Alexander, Fred Calvin, Jr.,
Corson, J. Jay, IV,

Montross
Monaco, Grace Powers

Norfolk
Davis, Terry Hunter, Jr.,
McCaa, James Cureton, III,
Rashkind, Alan Brody
Zahn, Richard William, Jr.,

Radford
Davis, Richard Waters

Richmond
Ellis, Andrew Jackson, Jr.,
Spahn, Gary Joseph

Schley
McVey, Henry Hanna, III,

Virginia Beach
Dumville, S(amuel) Lawrence
Swope, Richard McAllister

Wytheville
Baird, Thomas Bryan, Jr.,

WASHINGTON

Renton
Swanson, Arthur Dean

Sammamish
Waitt, Robert Kenneth

Seattle
Blom, Daniel Charles
Bucklin, Mark Richard
Corning, Nicholas F.
Loftus, Thomas Daniel
Mines, Michael
Radtke, Derek Paul

Spokane
Pontarolo, Michael Joseph

WEST VIRGINIA

Charleston
Bell, Harry Fullerton, Jr.,
Brenneman Harrah, Sandra
Rowe, Larry Linwell
Salango, C. Benjamin

Fairmont
Sawyer, Sean Jeffrey

Huntington
Bagley, Charles Frank, III,
Offutt, Denver Clyde, Jr.,

Wheeling
Wilmoth, William David

WISCONSIN

Appleton
Lonergan, Kevin
Thenell, Heather Jo

Elm Grove
Miracle, Dale Neil

Green Bay
Schober, Thomas Leonard

Kenosha
Higgins, John Patrick

Madison
Croake, Paul Allen
Field, Henry Augustus, Jr.,
Schmid, John Henry, Jr.,

Milwaukee
Bremer, John M.
Fitzgerald, Kevin Gerard
Gaines, Irving David
Galanis, John William
Wynn, Stanford Alan

Monona
Boller, Matthew Hubly

Rhinelander
Saari, John William, Jr.,

WYOMING

Sheridan
Riggs, Dan Britt

CHINA

Beijing
Zhu-Clark, Ingrid Wenying

ENGLAND

London
Arthur, David Anthony Dering
Mendelowitz, Michael Sydney
Page, Timothy A.C.

FRANCE

Paris
Tézé, Bernard André

GERMANY

Cologne
Luer, Hans-Jochem

Duedenbuettel
Pfennigstorf, Werner

GREECE

Athens
Murray, Virginia

SOUTH AFRICA

Johannesburg
Lomax, Ross Donald

ADDRESS UNPUBLISHED

Bandy, Jack D.
Berman, Richard Bruce
Blazzard, Norse Novar
Campion, Thomas Francis
Corlett, Edward Stanley, III,
Dikeou, George Demetrios
Dimitry, Theodore George
Dondanville, John Wallace
Eaton, Larry Ralph
Erwin, Gregory Scott
Flanary, Donald Herbert, Jr.,
Gilbert, Ronald Rhea
Grady, Maureen Frances
Griffith, Steven Franklin, Sr.,
Harper, Harlan, Jr.,
Hoglund, John Andrew
Howell, Ally Windsor
Hughes, Roy Fredericks
Johnson, Edward Michael
King, Jack A.
Klein, Judah Baer
Lederer, Peter David
Levy, David
Radogno, Joseph Anthony
Tierney, Kevin Joseph
Vinar, Benjamin
Wagner, Thomas Joseph
Wells, Wayne Alton
White, William Nelson
Wyatt, Robert Lee, IV,

INTELLECTUAL PROPERTY

UNITED STATES

ALABAMA

Birmingham
Barber, Peter Earl
Hinton, James Forrest, Jr.,
Long, Thad Gladden

ARIZONA

Flagstaff
Lacey, Henry Bernard

Phoenix
Allen, Robert Eugene Barton
Bain, C. Randall
Corson, Kimball Jay
Harris, Ray Kendall
Henze, Tom
Meschkow, Jordan M.
Price, Charles Steven
Sanders, Barry R.
Sutton, Samuel J.

Tempe
Shimpock, Kathy Elizabeth

ARKANSAS

Pine Bluff
Strode, Joseph Arlin

CALIFORNIA

Cerritos
Sarno, Maria Erlinda

Claremont
Ansell, Edward Orin

Cupertino
Simon, Nancy Ruth

Davis
Chander, Anupam

East Palo Alto
Bates, William, III,

Encinitas
Nemeth, Valerie Ann

Irvine
Friedland, Michael Keith
Ingram, James Michael
Knobbe, Louis Joseph
Stone, Samuel Beckner

Los Angeles
Adler, Erwin Ellery
Arkoz, David X.
Barrett, Jane Hayes
Barsky, Wayne Mitchell
Chan, Thomas Tak-Wah
Dienes, Louis Robert
Donaldson, Michael Cleaves
Foley, Martin James
Fredman, Howard S.
MacIntosh, Jay W.
Meisinger, Louis M.
Menes, Paul Ira
Pruetz, Adrian M.
Scoular, Robert Frank

Mill Valley
Salomon, Darrell Joseph

Mountain View
Radlo, Edward John

Newport Beach
Rudolph, George Cooper

Pacific Palisades
Flattery, Thomas Long

Palo Alto
Johnston, Alan Cope
Sano, Jeannine Yoo
Sato, Greg Y.
Simon, James Lowell

Redlands
Nassar, William Michael

Redwood City
Verhoeven, Charles K.

San Diego
Chatroo, Arthur Jay
Preston, David Raymond
Sullivan, William Francis

San Francisco
Anderson, Edward Virgil
Bleich, Jeffrey Laurence
Chambers, Guy Wayne
Traynor, John Michael

San Jose
Denver, Thomas H. R.
Hernández, Fernando Vargas
Jorgensen, Norman Eric
McManis, James
Tong, Peter P.

Sunnyvale
Wyatt, Thomas Csaba

COLORADO

Broomfield
Jonsen, Eric Richard

Denver
Dorr, Robert Charles
Hendrix, Lynn Parker

CONNECTICUT

New Haven
De Lio, Anthony Peter
Gastwirth, Donald Edward

Stamford
Tropp, Jonathan B.

DELAWARE

Wilmington
Blumenfeld, Jack Barry
Devine, Donn
Magee, Thomas Hugh

DISTRICT OF COLUMBIA

Washington
Aisenberg, Irwin Morton
Attridge, Daniel F.
Browne, Richard Cullen
Cantor, Herbert I.
Dinan, Donald Robert
Greenberger, I. Michael
Hammerman, Edward Scott
McDaniels, William E.
Pfeiffer, Margaret Kolodny
Potenza, Joseph Michael
Price, Griffith Baley, Jr.,
Weadon, Donald Alford, Jr.,
Woodworth, Ramsey Lloyd

FLORIDA

Melbourne
Dixon, Richard Dean

Miami
Kanov, Jonathan E.
Milian, David Philip
Nagin, Stephen Elias
Perwin, Jean Shapiro

Miami Lakes
Dominik, Jack Edward

Naples
Werder, Horst Heinrich

Saint Petersburg
Wein, Stephen J.

Tampa
Thomas, Gregg Darrow

GEORGIA

Atlanta
Blackstock, Jerry B.
Fleming, Julian Denver, Jr.,
Rayis, James Y.
Tramonte, James Albert

HAWAII

Honolulu
Godbey, Robert Carson

IDAHO

Boise
Scanlan, Kevin J.

ILLINOIS

Chicago
Altman, Louis
Amend, James Michael
Delaney, Timothy Quinn
Geraldson, Raymond I., Jr.,
Gills, Jeanne M.
Hilliard, David Craig
Hodes, Scott
Karon, Sheldon
Lane, Bradley Glenn
Maher, David Willard
Neumeier, Matthew Michael
Partridge, Mark Van Buren
Roper, Harry Joseph
Shurtz, Steven Park
Smedinghoff, Thomas J.
Streff, William Albert, Jr.,
Sweeney, James Raymond
Thompson, Michael
Vranicar, Michael Gregory
Wesley, William Matthew

Kenilworth
Feng, Paul Yen-Hsiung

Lake Bluff
Wick, Lawrence Scott

Oak Brook
Mlsna, Kathryn Kimura

Roselle
Bassitt, Janet Louise

Tinley Park
Chin, Davis

INDIANA

Indianapolis
Cole, Roland Jay
Knebel, Donald Earl
Troll, John Richard

IOWA

Des Moines
Fisher, Thomas George

KANSAS

Overland Park
Sampson, William Roth

KENTUCKY

Louisville
Stavros, Peter James

LOUISIANA

Jennings
Miller, Ruth Loyd

New Orleans
Curtis, Charles Thach, Jr.,

MARYLAND

Baltimore
Berlage, Jan Ingham
Blakeslee, Wesley Daniel
Haines, Thomas W. W.
Pappas, George Frank

Potomac
Troffkin, Howard Julian

MASSACHUSETTS

Boston
Deutsch, Stephen B.
Litwin, Paul Jeffrey
Patterson, John de la Roche, Jr.,
Savage, Joseph Francis

Lexington
Dulchinos, Peter

Newton
Appleman, Lawrence Joel

INTERNATIONAL, PRIVATE

Eger, John Mitchell
LeBeau, Charles Paul
Pugh, Richard Crawford
Snaid, Leon Jeffrey

San Francisco
Baker, Cameron
Berning, Paul Wilson
Donovan, Charles Stephen
Finck, Kevin William
Freud, Nicholas S.
Gresham, Zane Oliver
Hinman, Harvey DeForest
McKenzie, John F.
Offer, Stuart Jay
Ragan, Charles Ransom
Seavey, William Arthur
Sullivan, Robert Edward
Young, Bryant Llewellyn

San Jose
Kraw, George Martin

San Marino
Cranston, Howard Stephen

Santa Monica
Schlei, Norbert Anthony
Scott, Michael Dennis

Sunnyvale
Wehde, Albert Edward

Visalia
Atkins, Thomas Jay

COLORADO

Boulder
Manka, Ronald Eugene

Castle Rock
Procopio, Joseph Guydon

Centennial
Barnthouse, William Joseph

Denver
Campbell, William J.
Jones, Richard Michael
Nier, Harry Kaufman
Rich, Robert Stephen
Ulrich, Theodore Albert

Englewood
Choi, Jay Junekun

CONNECTICUT

Bloomfield
Messemer, Glenn Matthew

Fairfield
Huth, William Edward

Farmington
Herzog, Brigitte

Greenwich
Cantwell, Robert
Nimetz, Matthew

Meriden
Lowry, Houston Putnam

New Canaan
Bennett, James H.

Simsbury
Soler, Leslie T.

West Hartford
Storm, Robert Warren

Westport
Daw, Harold John
Lindskog, David Richard

DELAWARE

Wilmington
Melnik, Selinda A.

DISTRICT OF COLUMBIA

Washington
Atwood, James R.
Ball, Markham (Robert Ball)
Batla, Raymond John, Jr.,
Bierman, James Norman
Blake, Jonathan Dewey
Bodansky, Robert Lee
Bogard, Lawrence Joseph
Bregman, Arthur Randolph
Brown, David Nelson
Burt, Jeffrey Amsterdam
Busby, David
Butler, Michael Francis
Cameron, Duncan Hume
Carey, Sarah Collins
Carpenter, Russell H., Jr.,
Carroll, J. Speed
Cassidy, Robert Charles, Jr.,
Chanin, Michael Henry
Christaldi, Brian
Clagett, Brice McAdoo
Cole, Robert Theodore
Cutler, Lloyd Norton
Cymrot, Mark Alan
Danas, Andrew Michael
Davidow, Joel
deKieffer, Donald Eulette
Denison, Mary Boney
Dinan, Donald Robert
Ehrenhaft, Peter David
Ellicott, John LeMoyne
Ellis, Courtenay
Epstein, Gary Marvin
Faron, Robert Steven
Fate, Aaron Alan
Feldhaus, Stephen Martin
Fishburne, Benjamin P., III,
Fisher, Benjamin Chatburn
Flowe, Benjamin Hugh, Jr.,
Geniesse, Robert John
Gold, Peter Frederick
Graham, Thomas Richard
Green, Donald Hugh
Gulland, Eugene D.
Harris, Scott Blake
Harrison, Donald
Harrison, Earl David
Harrison, Marion Edwyn
Heron, Julian Briscoe, Jr.,
Hirschhorn, Eric Leonard
Horlick, Gary Norman
Houlihan, David Paul
Hunnicutt, Charles Alvin
Ives, Stephen Bradshaw, Jr.,
Johnson, Oliver Thomas, Jr.,
Kaplan, Gilbert B.
Karpinski, Irena Izabella
Keiner, R(obert) Bruce, Jr.,
Kessler, Judd Lewis
Kramer, William David
Kriesberg, Simeon M.
Kronstein, Werner J.
La Force, Pierre Joseph
Lambert, Jeremiah Daniel
Lamm, Carolyn Beth
Landfield, Richard
Lavine, Henry Wolfe
Lazarus, Kenneth Anthony
Ledeman, Gordon Nathaniel
Leonard, Will Ernest, Jr.,
Lowe, Randall Brian
Mashruwala, Anish Subhash
Mazo, Mark Elliott
Mc Phee, Henry Roemer
Mendelsohn, Martin
Mitchell, Roy Shaw
Moyer, Homer Edward, Jr.,
Owen, Roberts Bishop
Palmeter, N. David
Poe, Luke Harvey, Jr.,
Price, Daniel Martin
Price, Joseph Hubbard
Profaizer, Joseph Rudolph
Raul, Alan Charles
Reade, Claire Elizabeth
Rein, Bert Walter
Rivers, Richard Robinson
Robinson, Davis Rowland
Rocque, Vincent Joseph
Rosenblatt, Peter Ronald
Ross, Stanford G.
Ruddy, Frank
Samuelson, Kenneth Lee
Santos, Leonard Ernest
Spector, Phillip Louis
Stayin, Randolph John
Stern, Samuel Alan
Stuart, Pamela Bruce
Theroux, Eugene
Townsend, John Michael
Trooboff, Peter Dennis
Tung, Ko-Yung
Vakerics, Thomas Vincent
Van Buren, Lynn Marie
Verrill, Charles Owen, Jr.,
Vince, Clinton Andrew
Waldron, Jonathan Kent
Weadon, Donald Alford, Jr.,
Wegener, Mark Douglas
Weidenfeld, Edward Lee
Weiss, Mark Anschel
Wilner, Thomas Bernard
Wolff, Alan William
Work, Charles Robert
Wray, Robert

FLORIDA

Boca Grande
Brock, Mitchell

Coral Gables
Sacasas, Rene

Fort Lauderdale
Barnard, George Smith
Clubb, Bruce Edwin

Lake Placid
Roberts, William B.

Lake Wales
Wales, Gwynne Huntington

Miami
Alvarez-Farré, Emilio José
Berley, David Richard
Berman, Bruce Judson
Burr, Scott Allen
Castillo, Angel, Jr.,
Hudson, Robert Franklin, Jr.,
Klock, Joseph Peter, Jr.,
Landy, Burton Aaron
Murphy, Timothy James
Poston, Rebekah Jane
Pruna, Laura Maria

Miami Lakes
Dominik, Jack Edward

Naples
Werder, Horst Heinrich

Orlando
Hendry, Robert Ryon
Neff, A. Guy

Pensacola
Woodward, David Luther

Tampa
Grammig, Robert James

Vero Beach
Case, Douglas Manning

West Palm Beach
Brams, Jeffrey Brent
Finley, Chandler R.
Koffler, Warren William
Moore, George Crawford Jackson

Winter Park
Johnson, Kraig Nelson

GEORGIA

Atlanta
Barker, Clayton Robert, III,
Cargill, Robert Mason
Greer, Bernard Lewis, Jr.,
Harrold, Thomas J., Jr.,
Kelley, James Francis
McNeill, Thomas Ray
Miller, Douglas L.
Rayis, James Y.
Reynolds, Bradley Kenneth
Schock, Robert Christopher
Taylor, George Kimbrough, Jr.,
Thompson, Philip C.
Wakefield, Stephen Alan

Norcross
Xie, Jeff Zhengquan

HAWAII

Honolulu
Boas, Frank
Bourgoin, David L.
Ingersoll, Richard King
Katayama, Robert Nobuichi
Miller, Clifford Joel

ILLINOIS

Barrington
Cloney, Terence J.

Chicago
Archer, James G.
Barack, Peter Joseph
Baugher, Peter V.
Beem, Jack Darrel
Berner, Robert Lee, Jr.,
Burgdoerfer, Jerry
Cass, Robert Michael
Cicero, Frank, Jr.,
Crull, Jan, Jr.,
Cunningham, Robert James
Docksey, John Ross
Henry, Frederick Edward
McLees, John Alan
Meltzer, Robert Craig
Michaels, Richard Edward
Morrow, John E.
Prochnow, Herbert Victor, Jr.,
Rizowy, Carlos Guillermo
Schink, James Harvey
Shapiro, Harold David
Stevenson, Adlai Ewing, III,
Thomas, Stephen Paul
Thompson, Michael

Highland Park
Nelson, Richard David

Hinsdale
Hetke, Richard Louis

Naperville
Fenech, Joseph Charles
Larson, Mark Edward, Jr.,

North Chicago
de Lasa, José M.

Northbrook
Ihm, Stephen Lawrence

INDIANA

Fort Wayne
Cain, Tim J.

Indianapolis
Kalsi, Swadesh Singh
Reynolds, Robert Hugh
Russell, David Williams
Troll, John Richard

IOWA

Burlington
Hoth, Steven Sergey

KENTUCKY

Louisville
Northern, Richard
Welsh, Sir Alfred John

LOUISIANA

Covington
Rice, Winston Edward

Lafayette
Myers, Stephen Hawley

New Orleans
Jones, Philip Kirkpatrick, Jr.,

Shreveport
Woodman, Walter James

MARYLAND

Annapolis
Lucas, Steven Mitchell

Baltimore
Robinson, Zelig

Bethesda
Daniels, Michael Paul
English, William deShay
Goodwin, Robert Cronin

Chevy Chase
Toy, Charles David

North Potomac
Lehman, Leonard

Rockville
Berryman, Richard Byron
Zaphiriou, George Aristotle

West Bethesda
Scully, Roger Tehan, II,

MASSACHUSETTS

Amherst
Mednicoff, David Michael

Belmont
Greer, Gordon Bruce

Boston
Aresty, Jeffrey M.
Benjamin, William Chase
Bernhard, Alexander Alfred
Bines, Harvey Ernest
Chow, Stephen Y(ee)
Gonson, S. Donald
Graham, John Joseph
Huang, Thomas Weishing
Kaler, Robert Joseph
Kopelman, Leonard
Licata, Arthur Frank
Menoyo, Eric Felix
O'Neill, Philip Daniel, Jr.,
Thibeault, George Walter
White, Barry Bennett
Zack, Arnold Marshall

Brookline
Burnstein, Daniel

Cambridge
Ta, Tai Van

Carlisle
Hensleigh, Howard Edgar

Lincoln
Gnichtel, William Van Orden

Newton
Singer, Paula Noyes

Waltham
Barnes-Brown, Peter Newton

MICHIGAN

Ada
Mc Callum, Charles Edward

Ann Arbor
Muraski, Anthony Augustus

Battle Creek
Markey, James Kevin

Birmingham
Elsman, James Leonard, Jr.,

Clinton Township
Theut, C. Peter

Detroit
Darlow, Julia Donovan
Lawrence, John Kidder
Thorpe, Norman Ralph
Wise, John Augustus

Grand Rapids
Mitchell, James Albee

Troy
Dillon, Joseph Francis
Robinson, Logan Gilmore

MINNESOTA

Minneapolis
Devgun, Dharminder Singh
Hayward, Edward Joseph
McNeil, Mark Sanford
Nelson, Steven Craig
Sippel, William Leroy

Saint Paul
Dordell, Timothy Paul

MISSOURI

Chesterfield
Hier, Marshall David

Kansas City
Parrette, Leslie Jackson
Redmond, Christopher John

Saint Louis
Bailey, R(obert) Greg
Leontsinis, George John

NEW JERSEY

Budd Lake
Webb, John Gibbon, III,

Fort Lee
Cox, Melvin Monroe

Garfield
Herpst, Robert Dix

Kenilworth
Wasman, Jane G.

Keyport
Colmant, Andrew Robert

Montclair
Brown, Ronald Wellington

Mountainside
Helander, Robert Charles

Ramsey
Jalil, James Paul

Short Hills
Marshall, John Patrick
Siegfried, David Charles

Summit
English, Jerry Fitzgerald

Woodbridge
Golden, Daniel Lewis

NEW MEXICO

Albuquerque
Messersmith, Lanny Dee
Schuler, Alison Kay

Placitas
Schoen, Stevan Jay

Santa Fe
McClaugherty, Joe L.

NEW YORK

Albany
Hanna, John, Jr.,

Brooklyn
Johnson, Donald Raymond

Buffalo
Heilman, Pamela Davis
Rachlin, Lauren David

Canaan
Pennell, William Brooke

Dobbs Ferry
Scudder, Charles Seelye Kellgren

Hillsdale
Lunde, Asbjorn Rudolph

Larchmont
Berridge, George Bradford

New Rochelle
Ferencz, Benjamin Berell

New York
Adams, George Bell
Allen, Leon Arthur, Jr.,
Andersen, Richard Esten
Angus, Patricia Marie
Barist, Jeffrey
Barth, Mark Harold
Bason, George R., Jr.,
Begley, Louis
Behrendt, John Thomas
Bickford, Nathaniel Judson
Bidwell, James Truman, Jr.,
Brumm, James Earl
Brundige, Robert William, Jr.,
Bryan, Barry Richard
Burak, H(oward) Paul
Carpenter, Randle Burt
Carter, James Hal, Jr.,
Chilstrom, Robert Meade
Cho, Tai Yong
Clapman, Peter Carlyle
Cohen, Edmund Stephen
Cohen, Howard Marvin
Cooper, Stephen Herbert
Crane, Benjamin Field
Critchlow, Charles Howard
Cuneo, Donald Lane
Davidson, Robert Bruce
Detjen, David Wheeler

THAILAND

Pathumwan
Sutham, Apisith John

ADDRESS UNPUBLISHED

Agraz, Francisco Javier, Sr.,
Alberger, William Relph
Baker, Donald
Bateman, David Alfred
Berry, Robert Worth
Bloomer, Harold Franklin, Jr.,
Boner, Eleanor Katz
Boulanger, Carol Seabrook
Branagan, James Joseph
Casselman, William E., II,
Castro, Raul Hector
Catuzzi, J(erome) P(rimo), Jr.,
Chamberlin, Michael Meade
Clark, Donald Otis
D'Avignon, Roy Joseph
Dimitry, Theodore George
Edwards, James Malone
Estes, Carl Lewis, II,
Foster, Judith Christine
Friedlander, James Stuart
Garner, Mary Martin
Gianotti, Ernest F.
Guttentag, Joseph Harris
Hoffman, Ira Eliot
Hyde, Alan Litchfield
Idzik, Daniel Ronald
Jaynes, Gordon Leslie
Joelson, Mark René
Klapper, Gail Heitler
Landy, Lisa Anne
Lederer, Peter David
Lilly, Thomas Gerald
Lipsman, Richard Marc
McCobb, John Bradford, Jr.,
Michel, Clifford Lloyd
Miller, John Eddie
Mitchell, Carol Ann
Oz, Yilmaz
Peshkin, Samuel David
Phillips, Leo Harold, Jr.,
Potter, Tanya Jean
Prem, F. Herbert, Jr.,
Quigley, Leonard Vincent
Silberman, Curt C.
Squires, Katherine Landey
Tasker, Joseph
Voight, Elizabeth Anne
Walker, Mark A.
Wallin, James Peter
White, John Joseph, III,
Williams, William John, Jr.,

INTERNATIONAL, PUBLIC

UNITED STATES

ARIZONA

Phoenix
Koester, Berthold Karl

Prescott
Chamberlain, David Alanson

CALIFORNIA

San Diego
Eger, John Mitchell
Pugh, Richard Crawford

San Francisco
Philipsborn, John Timothy

San Mateo
Monaco, Daniel Joseph

Stanford
Sofaer, Abraham David

Venice
Schanes, Christine

CONNECTICUT

Stamford
Rose, Richard Loomis

DISTRICT OF COLUMBIA

Washington
Bachman, Kenneth Leroy, Jr.,
Ball, Markham (Robert Ball)
Batla, Raymond John, Jr.,
Bennett, Alexander Elliot
Bregman, Arthur Randolph
Cameron, Duncan Hume
Carneal, George Upshur
Christaldi, Brian
Clagett, Brice McAdoo
Cymrot, Mark Alan
deKieffer, Donald Eulette
Dembling, Paul Gerald
Fate, Aaron Alan
Glick, Leslie Alan
Graham, Thomas Richard
Horlick, Gary Norman
Ives, Stephen Bradshaw, Jr.,
Johnson, Oliver Thomas, Jr.,
Kaplan, Gilbert B.
Kessler, Judd Lewis
Kriesberg, Simeon M.
Leonard, Will Ernest, Jr.,
Marks, Herbert Edward
Mendelsohn, Martin
Miller, Gay Davis
Moyer, Homer Edward, Jr.,
Palmeter, N. David
Perry, Rotraud Mezger
Price, Daniel Martin
Reade, Claire Elizabeth
Rivers, Richard Robinson
Robinson, Davis Rowland
Rosenblatt, Peter Ronald
Tomlinson, Margaret Lynch
Trooboff, Peter Dennis
Van Buren, Lynn Marie
Weisgall, Jonathan Michael
Wolff, Alan William

FLORIDA

Bascom
Brooten, Kenneth Edward, Jr.,

Fort Lauderdale
Behr, Ralph Steven
Clubb, Bruce Edwin

Lake Placid
Roberts, William B.

Miami
Katz, Lawrence Sheldon
Kurzban, Ira Jay
Schuette, Charles A.

Miami Beach
Bratter, Joshua Peppercorn

GEORGIA

Atlanta
Jones, Glower Whitehead
Schock, Robert Christopher
Williams, Joel Cash

HAWAII

Honolulu
Boas, Frank

ILLINOIS

Chicago
Block, Neal Jay
Rizowy, Carlos Guillermo
Rudo, Saul E.
Smith, Ronald Charles
Wade, Edwin Lee
Wesley, William Matthew

KANSAS

Shawnee Mission
Snyder, Willard Breidenthal

KENTUCKY

Lexington
Hickey, John King

MARYLAND

Crownsville
Irish, Leon Eugene

Gaithersburg
Sherer, Samuel Ayers

Saint Michaels
Brown, Omer Forrest, II,

MASSACHUSETTS

Amherst
Mednicoff, David Michael

Boston
Kopelman, Leonard

Carlisle
Hensleigh, Howard Edgar

Quincy
Hayes, Mary Dianne Wixted

Tyngsboro
Farkas, Stephen Gerard

Weston
Bateman, Thomas Robert

MICHIGAN

Harbor Springs
Turner, Lester Nathan

Southfield
Antone, Nahil Peter

MINNESOTA

Minneapolis
Brink, David Ryrie

MISSOURI

Saint Louis
Green, Dennis Joseph

NEW HAMPSHIRE

Hollis
Merritt, Thomas Butler

NEW JERSEY

Morristown
Fishman, Richard Glenn

NEW YORK

New Rochelle
Ferencz, Benjamin Berell

New York
Burns, Arnold Irwin
Frank, Lloyd
Hauser, Rita Eleanore Abrams
Holtzmann, Howard Marshall
Huhs, John I.
Kailas, Leo George
Rosner, Jonathan Levi
Sassoon, Andre Gabriel
Welt, Philip Stanley

OKLAHOMA

Oklahoma City
Cantrell, Charles L.

PENNSYLVANIA

Philadelphia
Krzyzanowski, Richard L.

Pittsburgh
Van Kirk, Thomas L.

TENNESSEE

Greeneville
Bell, William Hall

TEXAS

Austin
Dyer, Cromwell Adair, Jr.,

Fort Worth
Mercer, Edwin Wayne

Houston
Ali, Arif Hyder

VIRGINIA

Alexandria
Buechner, Jack W(illiam)
Higgins, Mary Celeste

Arlington
Landry, Walter Joseph

Great Falls
Rath, Francis Steven

WASHINGTON

Lynnwood
Wolff, Joel Henry

MEXICO

Mexico City
Leycegui, Gardoqul Beatriz

BELARUS

Minsk
Todorovic, Ilija Ika

CHILE

Santiago
López Escarcena, R. Sebastián

ENGLAND

London
Mackie, David Lindsay
Newburg, Andre

FRANCE

Paris
Meyer-Fabre, Nathalie
Plankensteiner, Marco
Salans, Carl Fredric

GERMANY

Stuttgart
Wilske, Stephan

ITALY

Rome
Dalla Vedova, Riccardo

NETHERLANDS

The Hague
Brower, Charles Nelson

THAILAND

Pathumwan
Sutham, Apisith John

ADDRESS UNPUBLISHED

Boner, Eleanor Katz
Burgess, Hayden Fern
Castro, Raul Hector
Clark, Donald Otis
Davis, Donald Glenn
DiFronzo, Michael A.
English, Richard D.
Hoffman, Ira Eliot
Lichtenstein, Natalie G.
Muller, Peter
Rosseel-Jones, Mary Louise
Sheble, Walter Franklin
Walker, Mark A.
Winslow, John Franklin

JUVENILE

UNITED STATES

ALABAMA

Montgomery
Petersen, Michael John

ALASKA

Palmer
Bales, Candice Marie

ARIZONA

Lake Havasu City
Cookson, Kirk S.

Phoenix
Feder, Bruce
Klahr, Gary Peter

Tucson
Blackman, Jeffrey William

ARKANSAS

Little Rock
Smith, Anne Orsi

CALIFORNIA

Laguna Beach
Simons, Barry Thomas

Los Angeles
Wolf, Lawrence

Manhattan Beach
Hallett, James M.

Oakland
Koch, Richard Phillips (Terry Koch)

Sebastopol
Hillberg, Marylou Elin

Woodland
Melton, Barry

COLORADO

Boulder
Mulligan, Casey John

Denver
Green, Philip Burton

Littleton
Perlman, B. Arthur

CONNECTICUT

Ridgefield
Sherman, Harold

Wallingford
Farrell, Lynne S.

West Hartford
Saegaert, Ellen C.

FLORIDA

Lauderdale Lakes
Russell, Antonette Patrice

West Palm Beach
Strolla, Cory Carsan
Vilchez, Victoria Anne

ILLINOIS

Arlington Heights
Tucker, Bowen Hayward

Chicago
Muller, Kurt Alexander

Joliet
Drell, Lea Armstrong

Mundelein
Ackley, Robert O.

KENTUCKY

Lexington
Davidson, Michael

Louisville
Spalding, Catherine

LOUISIANA

La Place
Cicet, Donald James

New Orleans
Hantel, Philip Edward

MARYLAND

Towson
Campion, Renée

MASSACHUSETTS

Newton
Stern, Edward Mayer

MICHIGAN

Holt
Legere Jr, Henry J.

MINNESOTA

Minneapolis
Niemi, Andrea Kay

NEBRASKA

Omaha
Boyle, Lynnette Zellner
Frank, Julie Ann

NEW HAMPSHIRE

Newport
Shklar, Michael Charles

NEW JERSEY

Chatham
Kean, Sharon Bittner

Clark
Farina, Mario G.

Hazlet
Brown, Christopher Robert

South Orange
Feinberg, Paul H.

NEW MEXICO

Alamogordo
Bloom, Norman Douglas, Jr.,

Albuquerque
Leavell, Julita Ann

NEW YORK

Buffalo
Ewing, Charles Patrick

New York
Reiniger, Douglas Haigh
Rothberg, Glenda Fay Morris
Vachss, Andrew Henry

NORTH CAROLINA

Charlotte
Rockey, Arlaine

NORTH DAKOTA

Grand Forks
Anderson, Damon Ernest

OHIO

Toledo
Pooley, Christopher J.

OKLAHOMA

Enid
Gill, Amber McLaughlin

OREGON

Hillsboro
Cross, Daniel Albert

Portland
Bender, Laurie

The Dalles
Hashizume, Kevin

PENNSYLVANIA

Honey Brook
DePaul, Anthony Kenneth

Mercer
Kochems, Robert Gregory

Monroeville
Cohen, Laura

Philadelphia
Gianfrancesco, Paul Richard

TENNESSEE

Fayetteville
Dickey, John Harwell

Nashville
Levy, Jeffrey Lawrence

South Pittsburg
Ables, Charles Robert

TEXAS

Austin
Dudley, Todd Steven

Canton
White, Jeffery Howell

Houston
Burton, Joseph Randolph
Forlano, Frederick Peter

UTAH

Salt Lake City
Rasmussen, Thomas Val, Jr.,

VERMONT

Concord
Norsworthy, Elizabeth Krassovsky

VIRGINIA

Martinsville
Smith, James Randolph, Jr.,

Newport News
Saunders, Bryan Leslie

WEST VIRGINIA

Huntington
Ransbottom, Jennifer Dickens

WISCONSIN

Madison
Wood, Tracey Ann

ADDRESS UNPUBLISHED

Hickey, Timothy Andrew
Schmidt, Kathleen Marie
Shattuck, Cathie Ann

LABOR *See also* Workers' compensation; Pension

UNITED STATES

ALABAMA

Birmingham
Hopkins, Harry L.
Norris, John E.

Eufaula
Twitchell, E(rvin) Eugene

ALASKA

Anchorage
Flynn, Charles P.

Fairbanks
Schendel, William Burnett

ARIZONA

Eloy
O'Leary, Thomas Michael

Phoenix
Gomez, David Frederick
Knoller, Guy David
Lubin, Stanley
Lundeen, Bradley Curtis
McKee, Roger A.
Petitti, Michael Joseph, Jr.,
Wall, Donald Arthur

Tempe
Fanning, Francis Gerard
Shimpock, Kathy Elizabeth

Tucson
Bainton, Denise Marlene
Cope, Thom K.
Corey, Barry Martin
Esposito, Joseph Louis
Kaucher, James William
Rabb, Lloyd Leath

ARKANSAS

Little Rock
Gunter, Russell Allen
Jones, Stephen Witsell
Ross, Robert Dwain

CALIFORNIA

Glendale
Martinetti, Ronald Anthony

Irvine
Black, William Rea
Ristau, Kenneth Eugene, Jr.,

Laguna Hills
Reinglass, Michelle Annette

Los Angeles
Adell, Hirsch
Allred, Gloria Rachel
Bakaly, Charles George, Jr.,
Bressan, Paul Louis
Carr, Willard Zeller, Jr.,
Cathcart, David Arthur
Dunham, Scott H.
Emanuel, William Joseph
Feigen, Brenda S.
Foley, Martin James
Franco, Maria-Lorinda D.
Gross, Allen Jeffrey
Hahn, Elliott Julius
Lipsig, Ethan
MacIntosh, Jay W.
Moloney, Stephen Michael
Silbergeld, Arthur F.
Thoren-Peden, Deborah Suzanne

Menlo Park
Kennelly, Dennis L.

Oakland
Wallace, Elaine Wendy

Orinda
Sohnen, Harvey

Palm Springs
FitzGerald, John Edward, III,

Palo Alto
Tsatalis, Marina C.
Wheeler, Raymond Louis

Pasadena
Calvert, Melanie A.

San Diego
Bleiler, Charles Arthur

San Francisco
Boutin, Peter Rucker
Bushnell, Roderick Paul
Diekmann, Gilmore Frederick, Jr.,
Gelhaus, Robert Joseph
Hilton, Stanley Goumas
Libbin, Anne Edna
Rubin, Michael

Santa Barbara
Pyle, Kurt H.

Santa Monica
Fagen, Peter Kirk

Stockton
Malm, Scott

Torrance
Johnson, Einar William

Universal City
Golper, John Bruce

Walnut Creek
Burnison, Boyd Edward

Westlake Village
Sullivan, Mark Francis

COLORADO

Boulder
Ward, Denitta Dawn

Denver
Breeskin, Michael Wayne
Holme, Richard Phillips
Jablonski, James Arthur
McManus, Richard Griswold, Jr.,
Solano, Henry L.
Timmins, Edward Patrick
Truhlar, Robert T.

Englewood
Orsini, Rosemary

Golden
Eiberger, Carl Frederick
Snead, Kathleen Marie

Placerville
Reagan, Harry Edwin, III,

Sedalia
Ewing, Mary

CONNECTICUT

Bloomfield
Messemer, Glenn Matthew

Bridgeport
Katz, Stuart Michael

Danielson
Jungeberg, Thomas Donald

Glastonbury
Rintoul, David Skinner

Greenwich
Bentley, Peter

Hartford
Dempsey, Edward Joseph
O'Donnell, Edward Francis, Jr.,
Orth, Paul William

Trumbull
Brennan, Daniel Edward, Jr.,
Czajkowski, Frank Henry

DELAWARE

Wilmington
Bounds, Curtis Preston
Wier, Richard Royal, Jr.,

DISTRICT OF COLUMBIA

Washington
Berman, Marshall Fox
Brame, Joseph Robert, III,
Casey, Bernard J.
Deso, Robert Edward, Jr.,
Donegan, Charles Edward
Elcano, Mary S.
Esslinger, John Thomas
Flowe, Carol Connor
Foster, C(harles) Allen
Gibson, Calvin Roe
Goldsmith, Willis Jay
Guerrieri, Joseph, Jr.,
Heenan, Michael Terence
Horne, Michael Stewart
Lapidus, Lawrence Searle
Lopatin, Alan G.
Mackiewicz, Edward Robert
McElveen, Junius Carlisle, Jr.,
Miller, Gay Davis
Natalie, Ronald Bruce
O'Connor, Charles P.
Rabekoff, Elise Jane
Railton, William Scott
Rissetto, Harry A.
Sacher, Steven Jay
Sheehy, Barbara
Skinner, William Polk
Stern, Elizabeth Espin
Tallent, Stephen Edison

FLORIDA

Bay Harbor Islands
Ryce, Donald Theodore

Clearwater
McCormack, John Robert

Coral Springs
Saltman, Stuart Ivan

Hollywood
Laura, Elaine S.

Jacksonville
Cramer, Jeffrey Allen
Thomas, Archibald Johns, III,

Miami
Bartelstone, Ted Henry
Burr, Scott Allen
Campos-Orrego, Nora Patricia
Connor, Terence Gregory
Fleming, Joseph Z.
Hogg, Jesse Stephen
Korchin, Judith Miriam
Mazer, Jason S.
Reynardus, Jorge Edgardo
Santoro, Thomas Mead

Miami Lakes
Cohen, Ronald J.
Sharett, Alan Richard

Pensacola
George, Katie

Pineland
Donlon, William James

Sarasota
Rossi, William Matthew

Tampa
Alley, John-Edward
Lau, Mary Applegate
McAdams, John Pope
Munoz, Shane Thomas
Robinson, John William, IV,

West Palm Beach
Dunkum, Betty Lee
Hoch, Rand

GEORGIA

Albany
Collum, Rick Daniel

Athens
Davis, Claude-Leonard

Atlanta
Gepp, Randy C.
Harkey, Robert Shelton
Harness, William Walter
Hughes, David Andrew
Hunter, Forrest Walker
Kitchens, Joyce Ellen
Kneisel, Edmund M.
Oakley, Mary Ann Bryant
Remar, Robert Boyle
Stine, J(ames) Larry
Young, Michael Anthony

College Park
Stokes, Arch
Stokes, Arch

Macon
Ennis, Edgar William, Jr.,

Savannah
Bowman, Catherine McKenzie

HAWAII

Honolulu
Chun-Hoon, Lowell Koon Ying
Freed, Michael Leonard
Moore, Ernest Carroll, III,
Okinaga, Carrie Kiyono
Reinke, Stefan Michael

IDAHO

Boise
Seiniger, William Breck, Jr.,

ILLINOIS

Arlington Heights
Giampietro, Wayne Bruce

Aurora
Dreyer, John Edward

Chicago
Adelman, Steven Herbert
Antognoli, Anthony E.
Badel, Julie
Bailey, Robert Short
Banta, Don Arthur
Barron, Howard Robert
Bashwiner, Steven Lacelle
Brice, Roger Thomas
Connelly, P. Kevin
Fellows, Jerry Kenneth
Gladden, James Walter, Jr.,
Greenfield, Michael C.
Hoffman, Valerie Jane
Jenkins, James R.
Kaminsky, Richard Alan
Katz, Harold Ambrose
Kipperman, Lawrence I.
Laner, Richard Warren
Panich, Danuta Bembenista
Pelton, Russell Meredith, Jr.,
Peter, Bernard George
Redman, Clarence Owen
Reed, Keith Allen
Schoonhoven, Ray James
Serwer, Alan Michael
Smith, Arthur B., Jr.,
Stiegel, Michael A.
Tinaglia, Michael Lee
Wolf, Charles Benno

DeKalb
Davidson, Kenneth Lawrence

Edwardsville
Carlson, Jon Gordon

Kenilworth
McKittrick, William Wood

Lake Forest
Galatz, Henry Francis
Palmer, Ann Therese Darin

Prospect Heights
Leopold, Mark F.

Rock Island
Wallace, Franklin Sherwood

Rosemont
Nichols, Robert Hastings

Springfield
Kerr, Gary Enrico

Winnetka
Krucks, William Norman

INDIANA

Bloomington
Bingham, Lisa Blomgren

Fort Wayne
Cain, Tim J.

Indianapolis
Beckwith, Lewis Daniel
Boldt, Michael Herbert
Born, Samuel Roydon , II,
Carr, David J.
Gilliland, John Campbell, II,
Klaper, Martin Jay
Maine, Michael Roland
Moffatt, Michael Alan
Reuben, Lawrence Mark
Ryder, Henry C(lay)
Scism, Daniel Reed

Lafayette
Benton, Anthony Stuart

Shelbyville
McNeely, James Lee

IOWA

Cedar Rapids
O'Brien, David A.

Des Moines
Werner, Thomas M.

KANSAS

Overland Park
Smith, Jill Galbreath
Westerhaus, Douglas Bernard

KENTUCKY

Louisville
Effinger, Cynthia Lynn
Fenton, Thomas Conner
Hopson, Edwin Sharp

Newport
Hartmann, Markus Uwe

LOUISIANA

Baton Rouge
Jones, Johnnie Anderson

New Orleans
Marcus, Bernard
Molony, Michael Janssens, Jr.,

Shreveport
Cox, John Thomas, Jr.,

MAINE

Topsham
Young, Jeffrey

MARYLAND

Baltimore
Ayres, Jeffrey Peabody
Bruner, William Gwathmey, III,

Carey, Jana Howard
Dubé, Lawrence Edward, Jr.,
Hafets, Richard Jay
Pokempner, Joseph Kres
Rosenthal, William J.
White, Pamela Janice

Bethesda
Eastman, Hope Beth
Eisen, Eric Anshel

Crownsville
Irish, Leon Eugene

Potomac
Mullenbach, Linda Herman

Silver Spring
Gagliardo, Thomas James

MASSACHUSETTS

Boston
Deutsch, Stephen B.
Lyons, Nance
Lyons, Paul Vincent
Zack, Arnold Marshall

Quincy
Hayes, Mary Dianne Wixted

Truro
Friedman, Edward David

Woburn
Kuelthau, Paul Stauffer

Worcester
Felper, David Michael
Moschos, Demitrios Mina
Van Nostrand, Richard Charles

MICHIGAN

Ann Arbor
Muraski, Anthony Augustus

Bingham Farms
Berman, Leonard Keith

Birmingham
Kienbaum, Thomas Gerd
Wells, Steven Wayne

Bloomfield Hills
Cranmer, Thomas William
McDonald, Patrick Allen

Dearborn
Demorest, Mark Stuart

Detroit
Beyer, Daniel G.
Cohen, Norton Jacob
Glotta, Ronald Delon
Hanson, Victor G.
Mamat, Frank Trustick
Nemeth, Patricia Marie
Saxton, William Marvin
Turner, Reginald Maurice, Jr.,

Farmington Hills
Fershtman, Julie Ilene

Grand Rapids
Barnes, Thomas John
Khorey, David Eugene

Jenison
Kruse, Pamela Jean

Kalamazoo
Geary, James H.
Morris, Christopher David

Northville
Leavitt, Martin Jack

Okemos
Schneider, Karen Bush
White, James Alfred

Plymouth
Winzenreid, James Ernest

Saint Clair Shores
Danielson, Gary R.

Southfield
Israel, Stuart Michael
McClow, Roger James

Traverse City
Hornberger, Lee

Walled Lake
Seglund, Bruce Richard

Warren
Bridenstine, Louis Henry, Jr.,

MINNESOTA

Bloomington
Broeker, John Milton

Edina
Burk, Robert S.
Landrum, Michael Arthur

Mankato
West, Shawna

Minneapolis
Corwin, Gregg Marlowe
Kraus, Leslie Jay
Lonergan, Lauren Elizabeth
Miller, Michael Thomas
Nelson, Richard Arthur
Reinhart, Robert Rountree, Jr.,
Schermer, Judith Kahn
Uy, Hazel J.

Saint Cloud
Hughes, Kevin John

Saint Paul
Cassidy, Edward Q.
Galvin, Michael John, Jr.,
Karasov, Phyllis

MISSISSIPPI

Gulfport
Desmond, Susan Fahey

Jackson
Roberts, Richard C., III,

Oxford
Lewis, Ronald Wayne

MISSOURI

Jefferson City
Barrett, David F.
Martin, Cathleen A.
Riner, James William

Kansas City
Foster, Mark Stephen
Sands, Darry Gene
Siro, Rik Neal
Tyler, John Edward, III,

Saint Louis
Douaihy, Toni Patricia
Elbert, Charles Steiner
Gianoulakis, John Louis
Hiles, Bradley Stephen
Jaudes, Richard Edward
Johnson, Weldon Neal
Kelly, Maura Patricia
McDaniel, James Edwin
Switzer, Frederick Michael, III,
Welch, David William

MONTANA

Billings
Towe, Thomas Edward

Missoula
Loring, Emilie

NEBRASKA

Lincoln
Sapp, Susan Kubert

Omaha
Boyle, Lynnette Zellner
Jensen, Sam
Lieben, Thomas Geoffrey

NEW JERSEY

Bloomfield
Weisert, Kent Albert Frederick

Clifton
Pincus, Sheldon H.

Hillsborough
Ames, Marc L.

Liberty Corner
Apruzzese, Vincent John

Morristown
Stanton, Patrick Michael

New Providence
Hurley, Lawrence Joseph

Princeton
Innamorato, Don Anthony

Roseland
Goodman, Stanley Lewis
Ploscowe, Stephen Allen
Rubin, Alix R.

Somerville
Sponzilli, Edward George

Summit
Katz, Michael Albert

Toms River
Berman, Michael Barry

Trenton
Bigham, William J.

Voorhees
Suflas, Steven William

Warren
Bernstein, Eric Martin

Woodbury
Carter, James M.

NEW MEXICO

Albuquerque
Thiel, Albert Nicholas, Jr.,

Las Cruces
Neumann, Rita Nunez

Los Alamos
Herr, Bruce

NEW YORK

Albany
Barsamian, J(ohn) Albert
Devine, Eugene Peter

Amherst
Harvey, Timothy Robert

Buffalo
Brydges, Thomas Eugene
Doren, Robert Alan
Odza, Randall M.
Oppenheimer, Randolph Carl
Salisbury, Eugene W.

Chestnut Ridge
Burns, Richard Owen

Garden City
Lilly, Thomas Joseph

Huntington Station
Binder, Harry J.

Jamestown
Beckstrom, Charles G.
Idzik, Martin Francis

Latham
Couch, Mark Woodworth

Mineola
Bee, Peter Aloysius
Millman, Bruce Russell
Paterson, Basil Alexander
Pogrebin, Bertrand B.
Sandback, William Arthur

New York
Altieri, Peter Louis
Auclair, Suzanne C.
Bassen, Ned Henry
Bianco, S. Anthony
Braid, Frederick Donald
Budd, Thomas Witbeck
Canoni, John David
Carling, Francis
Chan, Lai Lee
Coleman, Jerome P.
Dretzin, David
Drucker, Jacquelin F.
Duff, William Brandon
Estock, Howard Gordon
Fallek, Andrew Michael
Fasman, Zachary Dean
Flamm, Leonard N(athan)
Friedman, Eugene Stuart
Ganz, Howard Laurence
Glanstein, Joel Charles
Hartmann, Carl Joseph
Jacobson, Jerold Dennis
Kandel, William Lloyd
Kiok, Joan Stern
Krupman, William Allan
McMahon, James Charles
Moerdler, Charles Gerard
Moss, Franklin Kass
Oechler, Henry John, Jr.,
Oppenheimer, Martin J.
Panken, Peter Michael
Rogers, Theodore Otto, Jr.,
Rossen, Jordan
Savitt, Susan Schenkel
Schwartz, Arthur Zachary
Shaw, Melvin Robert
Shen, Michael
Soyster, Margaret Blair
Vladeck, Judith Pomarlen
Wallach, Eric Jean
Witkin, Eric Douglas
Zelman, Andrew E.
Zifchak, William C.

Niagara Falls
Berrigan, Patrick Joseph

Rochester
Gootnick, Margery Fischbein
Paley, Gerald Larry
Rosenhouse, Michael Allan
Smith, Jules Louis
Wild, Robert Warren

Sands Point
Hoynes, Louis LeNoir, Jr.,

Syracuse
DiLorenzo, Louis Patrick
Gaal, John
King, Bernard T.

Valley Stream
Levine, Marilyn Markovich

West Point
Stock, Margaret Deborah

White Plains
Longo, Ronald Anthony

NORTH CAROLINA

Charlotte
Belthoff, Richard Charles, Jr.,
Goodwin, Walter Henry

Cherryville
Huffstetler, Palmer Eugene

Durham
Fisher, Stewart Wayne

High Point
Sheahan, Robert Emmett

Raleigh
Davis, Thomas Hill, Jr.,
Duncan, Allyson K.

Winston Salem
Early, James H., Jr.,

OHIO

Akron
Flannery, Harry Audley
Rooney, George Willard
Tipping, Harry A.

Athens
Hedges, Richard Houston

Cincinnati
Adams, Deborah Susan
Corwin, Melanie S.
DeLong, Deborah
Hermanies, John Hans
Lawrence, James Kaufman Lebensburger
Mann, David Scott
Smith, Sheila Marie
Swigert, James Mack
Tobias, Paul Henry
Townsend, Robert J.

Cleveland
Ashmus, Keith Allen
Dunlap, Jeffrey Scott
Duvin, Robert Phillip
Goldfarb, Bernard Sanford
Kola, Arthur Anthony
Kramer, Edward George
Lewis, John Francis
Millstone, David Jeffrey
Pace, Stanley Dan
Ross, Harold Anthony
Strimbu, Victor, Jr.,

Columbus
Bridgman, G(eorge) Ross
Cox, Paul L.
Eblin, Robert L.
Haught, Jack Gregg
McKenna, Alvin James
Minor, Robert Allen
Morgan, Dennis Richard
Pressley, Fred G., Jr.,
Reasoner, Willis Irl, III,
Selcer, David Mark
Tarpy, Thomas Michael
Warner, Charles Collins

Dayton
Lamme, Kathryn Anne

Dublin
Coco, Mark Steven

Ironton
Allen, Craig Adams

Mayfield Heights
Rosenfeld, Robert Thomas

Medina
Arnold, Alanna S. Welling

Toledo
Dane, Stephen Mark
O'Connell, Maurice Daniel

Warren
Kafantaris, George Nicholas

OKLAHOMA

Mcalester
Pendell, Terry Ashley

Oklahoma City
Court, Leonard
Van Dyke, Peter Tyson

Tulsa
Dexter, Deirdre O'Neil Elizabeth
Draughon, Scott Wilson
Matthies, Mary Constance T.
Strecker, David Eugene
Ungerman, Maynard I.

OREGON

Medford
O'Connor, Karl William (Goodyear Johnson)

Portland
Bovarnick, Paul Simon
Cooper, Nancy M.
Harnden, Edwin A.
Jolles, Bernard
Smith, Lester V., Jr.,

PENNSYLVANIA

Berwyn
Markle, John, Jr.,

Blue Bell
Teklits, Joseph Anthony

Erie
Cullen, James Donald
Zamboldi, Richard Henry

Lancaster
Eagan, Michele

Langhorne
Valentin, James

Lansdale
Sultanik, Jeffrey Ted

New Castle
Babb, Alfred Ward

New Kensington
Wallace, Henry Jared, Jr.,

Norristown
Rees, Thomas Dynevor

Philadelphia
Bernard, John Marley
Bildersee, Robert Alan
Brown, William Hill, III,
Dabrowski, Doris Jane
Dichter, Mark S.
Epstein, Alan Bruce
Feirson, Steven B.
Fine, Lawrence B.
Gilberg, Kenneth Roy
Goldman, Gary Craig
Hagan, Mary Ann
Lillie, Charisse Ranielle
Lotman, Arline Jolles
McCausland, Margaret A.
Milone, Francis Michael
O'Reilly, Timothy Patrick
Pasek, Jeffrey Ivan
Reisman, Jason Eric
Satinsky, Barnett
Sigmond, Richard Brian
Smith, John Francis, III,
Whiteside, William Anthony, Jr.,

Pittsburgh
Artz, John Curtis
Bellisario, Domenic Anthony
Brown, James Benton
Candris, Laura A.
Chaban, Lawrence Richard
Connors, Eugene Kenneth
Cowan, Barton Zalman
DeForest, Walter Pattison, III,
Denys, Sylvia
Harty, James Quinn
Kobell, Gerald
Lyncheski, John E.
Olson, Stephen M(ichael)
Orsatti, Ernest Benjamin
Post, Peter David
Scheinholtz, Leonard Louis

RHODE ISLAND

Providence
Labinger, Lynette J.
Long, Nicholas Trott
McAndrew, Thomas Joseph

SOUTH CAROLINA

Columbia
Burnette, Mary Malissa

Greenville
Hutson, Melvin Robert
Smoak, Lewis Tyson
Wyche, Madison Baker, III,

TENNESSEE

Chattanooga
Phillips, John Bomar

Collierville
Thomas, Keith Richard

Kingsport
Shine, David Bruce

Knoxville
Hagood, Lewis Russell
Walter, Glenn Richard

Memphis
Clark, Ross Bert, II,
Crone, Alan Grady
Hancock, Jonathan Cromwell
Sossaman, William Lynwood

Morristown
Murphy, Michael Cary

Nashville
Barrett, George Edward
Gannon, John Sexton
Lyon, Philip K(irkland)
Mathies, Jordon Dean
Sharp, Kevin Hunter

Signal Mountain
Anderson, Charles Hill

LAND USE AND ZONING

MISSOURI

Kansas City
Bryant, Richard Todd
Gardner, Brian E.
Moore, Stephen James

Saint Louis
Biesterfeld, Craig Stewart
Michenfelder, Albert A.

MONTANA

Whitefish
Tornow, Thomas T.

NEVADA

Las Vegas
Curran, William P.

NEW HAMPSHIRE

Exeter
Donahue, Michael Joseph

NEW JERSEY

East Brunswick
Applebaum, Charles

Freehold
Brown, Sanford Donald

Hackensack
Duus, Gordon Cochran
Navatta, Anna Paula

Lyndhurst
McNamara, Patrick James

Montville
Buzak, Edward Joseph

Newton
Cox, William Martin

Piscataway
Smith, Bob

Princeton
Karpoff, Michael Steven
Sutphin, William Taylor

Roseland
Rosen, Charles Arthur

Somers Point
Baylinson, Christopher Michael

Springfield
Grayson Kurzweil, Bette Rita
Mytelka, Arnold Krieger

Union
Greenstein, Richard Henry

Woodcliff Lake
Phillips, John C.

Wyckoff
Spizziri, John Anthony

NEW MEXICO

Albuquerque
Salazar, John Paul

NEW YORK

Amherst
Murray, William Michael

East Hampton
Twomey, Thomas A., Jr.,

Glen Cove
Rathkopf, Daren Anthony

Mineola
Levin, A. Thomas

New York
Braun, Jeffrey Louis
Kafin, Robert Joseph

White Plains
Null, William Seth

NORTH CAROLINA

Asheville
Lawrence, Betty Tenn

Cary
Montgomery, Charles Harvey

OHIO

Akron
Schrader, Alfred Eugene

Cincinnati
Burke, Timothy Michael
Mara, Timothy Gerald
Trauth, Joseph Louis, Jr.,

Columbus
Neuman, Todd Howard

Fairfield
Grove, Jack Frederick

Findlay
Hackenberg, David Alan

OKLAHOMA

Oklahoma City
Epperson, Kraettli Quynton

OREGON

Coquille
Lounsbury, Steven Richard

Eugene
Brotherton, Kathryn Piele
DuPriest, Douglas Millhollen

Portland
Firestone, Gary
Hribernick, Paul R.
Sullivan, Edward Joseph

Salem
Lien, Wallace Wayne

PENNSYLVANIA

Bala Cynwyd
Manko, Joseph Martin, Sr.,

Doylestown
Bolla, William Joseph

Harrisburg
Wilson, Craig P.

Lancaster
Shirk, Kenelm Lawrence, Jr.,

Norristown
Rees, Thomas Dynevor

Philadelphia
Kupperman, Louis Brandeis

Pittsburgh
Mall, James Richard

RHODE ISLAND

Jamestown
Parks, Albert Lauriston

Providence
Decarvalho, Kas R.
Smith, Robert Ellis

Westerly
Nardone, William Andrew

SOUTH CAROLINA

Charleston
Robinson, Neil Cibley, Jr.,

Greenwood
Nexsen, Julian Jacobs, Jr.,

TEXAS

Dallas
Nichols, Henry Louis

Houston
Wall, Kenneth E., Jr.,

UTAH

Salt Lake City
Becker, Ralph Elihu, Jr.,
Hunter, M(ilton) Reed, Jr.,

VERMONT

Rutland
Facey, John Abbott, III,

VIRGINIA

Alexandria
Beach, Barbara Purse

Richmond
Cohn, David Stephen
Redmond, David Dudley

Vienna
Stearns, Frank Warren

WASHINGTON

Mount Vernon
Moser, C. Thomas

Olympia
Miller, Allen Terry, Jr.,

Seattle
Aramburu, John Richard
Blumenfeld, Charles Raban
Brower, Joshua Christopher Allen
Leed, Roger Melvin
McCann, Richard Eugene
McCune, Philip Spear
Murray, Michael Kent
Walter, Michael Charles
Wilson, Richard Randolph

Tacoma
Wesch, Angelia DeAn

Vancouver
Karpinski, John Stanley

WISCONSIN

Madison
Rankin, Gene Raymond

Milwaukee
Jost, Lawrence John
Rieselbach, Allen Newman

Waukesha
Macy, John Patrick

GERMANY

Düsseldorf
Mütze, Michael W.

ADDRESS UNPUBLISHED

Bateman, David Alfred
Dickerman, John Melvin
Martin, Gary Duncan

LANDLORD-TENANT *See also* Commercial

UNITED STATES

ALABAMA

Birmingham
Theibert, Richard Wilder

ARIZONA

Phoenix
Lee, Richard H(arlo)

CALIFORNIA

Costa Mesa
Daniels, James Walter

Irvine
Farrell, Teresa Joanning

Los Angeles
Porter, Verna Louise

Placentia
Evans, Winthrop Shattuck

Sacramento
Giguiere, Michele Louise

San Francisco
Weber, Matthew Bernard

Torrance
Johnson, Einar William

COLORADO

Aspen
Peirce, Frederick Fairbanks

DELAWARE

Wilmington
Kristol, Daniel Marvin

DISTRICT OF COLUMBIA

Washington
Majev, Howard Rudolph

FLORIDA

Boca Raton
Barwell, Cindy Ann
Comiter, Lloyd Alan

Miami
Feinsmith, Paul Lowell
Wiseheart, Malcolm Boyd, Jr.,

West Palm Beach
Layman, David Michael

HAWAII

Honolulu
Wong, Alfred Mun Kong

Wailuku
Kinaka, William Tatsuo

ILLINOIS

Chicago
Bernstein, Charles Bernard
Copeland, Edward Jerome
Kawitt, Alan
Rudnick, Paul David
Ungaretti, Richard Anthony
Vree, Roger Allen
White, Linda Diane

INDIANA

Gary
Hall, John Henry

Indianapolis
Dorocke, Lawrence Francis

KENTUCKY

Louisville
Vincenti, Michael Baxter

MARYLAND

Baltimore
Chriss, Timothy D.A.

Bel Air
Wilson, Christian Burhenn

Silver Spring
Hannan, Myles

MASSACHUSETTS

Boston
Bloch, Donald Martin
Hawkey, G. Michael
Katz, Donald H.
Saltiel, David Michael
Surkin, Elliot Mark

Brookline
Lerman, Herbert S.
Lipson, Roger Russell

Salem
Wasserman, Stephen Alan

MICHIGAN

Bloomfield Hills
Berlow, Robert Alan
Dawson, Stephen Everette

Detroit
Candler, James Nall, Jr.,

Farmington Hills
Blizman, Paul John

MINNESOTA

Minneapolis
Heiberg, Robert Alan
Jensch, Charles Campbell

Owatonna
Rask, Kelly Scott

Rochester
Lantz, William Charles

Saint Paul
Spencer, David James

NEW HAMPSHIRE

Manchester
Craig, James William

NEW JERSEY

Hackensack
Navatta, Anna Paula

Short Hills
Fast, Kenneth H.

NEW YORK

Brooklyn
Young, Sidney David

Chittenango
Baum, Peter Alan

Commack
Somer, Stanley Jerome

Hudson
Davis, Deborah Lynn

Long Island City
Forchelli, Charles Nicholas

Mineola
Lung, Henry

New York
Goldstein, Kenneth B.
Hackett, Kevin R.
Intriligator, Marc Steven
Levine, Melvin Charles
Lynn, Theodore Stanley
Powell, James Henry
Sanseverino, Raymond Anthony
Uram, Gerald Robert
Vernon, Darryl Mitchell
Wachtel, Norman Jay

Port Washington
Forman, James Douglas

Rochester
Rosner, Leonard Allen

NORTH CAROLINA

Greensboro
Agapion, Bill

OHIO

Cleveland
McAndrews, James Patrick

OKLAHOMA

Oklahoma City
Johnson, Robert Max

OREGON

Cannon Beach
Hillestad, Charles Andrew

Portland
Matarazzo, Harris Starr

PENNSYLVANIA

Lancaster
Zimmerman, D(onald) Patrick

Philadelphia
Bressler, Barry E.
Glazer, Ronald Barry
Goldman, Gary Craig
Ominsky, Harris
Panzer, Mitchell Emanuel
Segal, Robert Martin

Pittsburgh
Hartman, Ronald G.

RHODE ISLAND

West Warwick
Pollock, Bruce Gerald

TENNESSEE

Knoxville
Ritchie, Albert

TEXAS

Dallas
Fishman, Edward Marc

Houston
Hollyfield, John Scoggins
Shouse, August Edward
Weller, Philip Douglas

VIRGINIA

Portsmouth
Brennan, John William

Richmond
Cohn, David Stephen

WASHINGTON

Seattle
McLean, Dennis Edgar

WISCONSIN

Milwaukee
Hoffman, Nathaniel A.
Jost, Lawrence John

BRAZIL

Rio de Janeiro
Pinheiro, Guilherme Martins

Kennedy, Michael John
Kurnit, Richard Alan
Otero, Brian V.
Ringel, Dean
Robertson, Edwin David
Schlain, Barbara Ellen
Schwartz, Renee Gerstler
Winfield, Richard Neill

NORTH CAROLINA

Marion
Burgin, Charles Edward

OHIO

Cincinnati
Faller, Susan Grogan

Toledo
Pletz, Thomas Gregory

OREGON

Portland
Hinkle, Charles Frederick

PENNSYLVANIA

Harrisburg
Sullivan, John Cornelius, Jr.,

Philadelphia
Harvey, Gregory Merrill
McHugh, James Joseph
Solano, Carl Anthony

Pittsburgh
Doty, Robert Walter
McGough, Walter Thomas, Jr.,
Turner, Harry Woodruff

RHODE ISLAND

Providence
Smith, Robert Ellis

SOUTH CAROLINA

Charleston
Kahn, Ellis Irvin

TENNESSEE

Chattanooga
Phillips, John Bomar

TEXAS

Austin
Donaldson, David Howard, Jr.,

Beaumont
Black, Robert Allen

Dallas
Mc Elhaney, John Hess

Fort Worth
Sharpe, James Shelby

VIRGINIA

Hampton
Smith, Stephen Mark

WASHINGTON

Seattle
Johnson, Bruce Edward Humble

CANADA

ONTARIO

Toronto
Chester, Robert Simon George

ITALY

Milan
Peron, Sabrina

NORWAY

Oslo
Strømme, Vidar

ADDRESS UNPUBLISHED

Bloom, Charles Joseph
Epstein, Judith Ann
Grutman, Jewel Humphrey
Kapnick, Richard Bradshaw
Swann, Barbara

MALPRACTICE. *See* Personal injury.

MERGERS AND ACQUISITIONS

UNITED STATES

ALABAMA

Birmingham
Baker, David Remember
Barber, Peter Earl
Rotch, James E.
Stewart, Joseph Grier
Woodall, Paul Oliver, Jr.,

Mobile
Oldweiler, Thomas Patrick

ARIZONA

Phoenix
Cohen, Jon Stephan
Curzon, Thomas Henry
Dunipace, Ian Douglas
Hienton, James Robert
McRae, Stephanie A.

Tempe
Moya, Patrick Robert

ARKANSAS

Fayetteville
Lushbaugh, Brad

CALIFORNIA

Burlingame
Denten, Christopher Peter

Cypress
Olschwang, Alan Paul

Irvine
Black, William Rea
Wintrode, Ralph Charles

Los Angeles
Barton, Alan Joel
Blencowe, Paul Sherwood
Boehmer, Richard A.
Costales, Marco Daniel
de Castro, Hugo Daniel
Farrar, Stanley F.
Fein, Ronald Lawrence
Haakh, Gilbert Edward
Havel, Richard W.
Heyler, Grover Ross
McKinzie, Carl Wayne
McLane, Frederick Berg
Morgan, R. Gregory
Power, John Bruce
Shilling, Monica Jill
Voxman, William Alexander

Menlo Park
Kaufman, Christopher Lee
Kelly, Daniel Grady, Jr.,
Valencia, Marc Andrew

Mill Valley
Cole, Richard Charles

Newport Beach
Cano, Kristin Maria

Palo Alto
Benton, Lee F.
Chacon, Gerald Gilbert
Gaither, James C.
Lesser, Henry
Nopar, Alan Scott
Phair, Joseph Baschon

Redwood City
Millard, Richard Steven
Mo, Curtis Luke

San Diego
Brooks, John White
Copeland, Robert Glenn
Eigner, William Whitling
Kuntz, William Richard, Jr.,

San Francisco
Baker, Cameron
DeMuro, Paul Robert
Evers, William Dohrmann
Holden, Frederick Douglass, Jr.,
Larson, John William
Loeb, Ronald Marvin
Mann, Bruce Alan
Wood, Robert Warren

San Ramon
Freed, Kenneth Alan

Walnut Creek
Rainey, William Joel

Westlake Village
Vandeman, George Allen

COLORADO

Boulder
Deaktor, Darryl Barnett
Manka, Ronald Eugene

Denver
Grissom, Garth Clyde
Newcom, Jennings Jay
Ruppert, John Lawrence

Englewood
Lidstone, Herrick Kenley, Jr.,
Velarde, D. Sean

Littleton
Ross, William Robert

Westminster
Gaither, John Francis, Jr.,

CONNECTICUT

Darien
Prince, Kenneth Stephen

Farmington
McCann, John Joseph

Hartford
Davis, Andrew Neil

Simsbury
Soler, Leslie T.

DELAWARE

Wilmington
Finkelstein, Jesse Adam
Goldman, Michael David

DISTRICT OF COLUMBIA

Washington
Adler, Howard Bruce
Alexander, Allison L(eslie)
Bierman, James Norman
Brown, David Nelson
Carroll, J. Speed
Czarra, Edgar F., Jr.,
Dubrow, Jon B.
Fishburne, Benjamin P., III,
Goldstein, Michael B.
Hebert, Jay Howell
Jacobson, Raymond Alfred, Jr.,
Lambert, David
Mashruwala, Anish Subhash
Mazo, Mark Elliott
Pusey, William Anderson
Rafferty, James Gerard
Repper, George Robert
Stock, Stuart Chase
Strong, Carter
Tung, Ko-Yung
Zimmerman, Edwin Morton

FLORIDA

Boca Raton
Klein, Peter William

Miami
Alvarez-Farré, Emilio José
Friedman, Richard Nathan
Grossman, Robert Louis
Jacobson, Bernard
Nuernberg, William R(ichard)

Naples
Berning, Randall Karl

Orlando
Blackford, Robert Newton
Capouano, Albert D.
Conti, Louis Thomas Moore
Yates, Leighton Delevan, Jr.,

Tampa
Doliner, Nathaniel Lee
Janney, Oliver James
Patrick, Victor Phillip
Rasmussen, Robert Carl

Wellington
Beck, Jan Scott

West Palm Beach
Gildan, Phillip Clarke

Winter Park
Heinle, Richard Alan

GEORGIA

Atlanta
Barker, Clayton Robert, III,
Chait, Gregory Marshall
Cohen, George Leon
Grant, Walter Matthews
Hopkins, John David
Kaufman, Mark David
Kelley, James Francis
McMahon, Teri Lynn
McNeill, Thomas Ray
Morgan, Charles Russell
O'Callaghan, William Lawrence, Jr.,
Pless, Laurance Davidson
Schulte, Jeffrey Lewis
Sibley, Horace Holden
Silverstein, Leonard A.
Thompson, Philip C.
Tramonte, James Albert
Wilson, James Hargrove, Jr.,
Zabka, Sven Paul

ILLINOIS

Chicago
Ackerman, David Paul
Anderson, J. Trent
Archer, James G.
Barron, Harold Sheldon
Bitner, John Howard
Brown, Gregory K.
Burke, Richard William
Clemens, Richard Glenn
Cole, Thomas Amor
Crawford, Dewey Byers
Crull, Jan, Jr.,
Davis, Scott Jonathan
Docksey, John Ross
Duncan, John Patrick Cavanaugh
Dunn, Edwin Rydell
Emerson, Carter Whitney
Friedman, Lawrence Milton
Gerlits, Francis Joseph
Gerstein, Mark Douglas
Gregg, Jon Mann
Heatwole, Mark M.
Howell, R(obert) Thomas, Jr.,
Kaplan, Jared
Levin, Jack S.
Martin, Arthur Mead
McLees, John Alan
Metzger, Paul Thomas
Morrow, John E.
Perl, Sanford Eric
Reum, James Michael
Rizowy, Carlos Guillermo
Rosenbloom, Lewis Stanley
Rudo, Saul E.
Schreck, Robert A., Jr.,
Schulz, Keith Donald
Scogland, William Lee
Thomas, Frederick Bradley
Wander, Herbert Stanton

Northbrook
Sernett, Richard Patrick

INDIANA

Indianapolis
Kahlenbeck, Howard, Jr.,
Lipshaw, Jeffrey Marc
Reynolds, Robert Hugh
Schneider, Michael J.
Strain, James Arthur

Plainfield
Carpenter, Craig M.

IOWA

Des Moines
Neumann, Gordon Richard, Jr.,

KENTUCKY

Lexington
Jefferson, Wade Hampton, IV,
Terry, Joseph H.

Louisville
Ament, Mark Steven
Mellen, Francis Joseph, Jr.,
Tannon, Jay Middleton

LOUISIANA

New Orleans
Correro, Anthony James, III,
Eckstein, Michael Lehman
McMillan, Lee Richards, II,

MAINE

Augusta
Wilkinson, Lester F., Jr.,

Portland
Stauffer, Eric P.

MARYLAND

Baltimore
Hubbard, Herbert Hendrix
Robinson, Zelig
Stiller, Shale David

Bethesda
Menaker, Frank H., Jr.,

Rockville
Roberts, Christopher Chalmers

MASSACHUSETTS

Bedford
Wieand, Jeffrey Scott

Boston
Bohnen, Michael J.
Brountas, Paul Peter
Gonson, S. Donald
Greer, Allen Curtis, II,
Kreisler, David P.
Patterson, John de la Roche, Jr.,
Rosenbloom, Thomas Adam
Sargeant, Ernest James
Wolfson, Jeffrey Steven

Framingham
Vrabel, Joseph P.

Norwell
Mullare, T(homas) Kenwood, Jr.,

Springfield
Weiss, Ronald Phillip

Worcester
Lougee, David Louis

MICHIGAN

Ada
Mc Callum, Charles Edward

Detroit
Deason, Herold McClure
Kuehn, George E.
Lawrence, John Kidder
Semple, Lloyd Ashby

Midland
Gootee, Jane Marie

MINNESOTA

Minneapolis
Bergerson, David Raymond
Devgun, Dharminder Singh
Erhart, John Joseph
Flom, Gerald Trossen
Garton, Thomas William
Kaplan, Sheldon
Martin, Phillip Hammond
Mellum, Gale Robert
Minish, Robert Arthur
Opdahl, Clark Donald
Stageberg, Roger V.
Trucano, Michael
Yost, Gerald B.

Saint Paul
Dordell, Timothy Paul
Rebane, John T.

MISSOURI

Chesterfield
Denneen, John Paul

Kansas City
Pemberton, Bradley Powell
Spencer, Richard Henry
Whittaker, Judith Ann Cameron

Saint Louis
Berger, John Torrey, Jr.,
Dorwart, Donald Bruce
Tierney, Michael Edward
Woodruff, Bruce Emery

NEBRASKA

Lincoln
Rembolt, James Earl

NEW HAMPSHIRE

Concord
Potter, Fred Leon

NEW JERSEY

Bridgewater
Chandonnet, Sheila Wohl

Florham Park
Kandravy, John

Fort Lee
Cox, Melvin Monroe

Garfield
Herpst, Robert Dix

Newark
Vajtay, Stephen Michael, Jr.,

Pitman
Cloues, Edward Blanchard, II,

Princeton
Miller, Richard Mark

Roseland
Wovsaniker, Alan

NEW YORK

Buffalo
Day, Donald Sheldon

New York
Alpert, Laurent

Pavec, Arnaud
Poli, Frédéric Charles
Poncelet, Aline
Raffin, Marie-Hélène J.
Schultze, Pascal
Tézé, Bernard André

GERMANY

Berlin
Kautzsch, Christof
von Rechenberg, Wolf G.

Bonn
Goeckeler, Stephan

Cologne
Luer, Hans-Jochem
Rizor, Stefan
Siepelt-Babilon, Stefan
Wilsing, Hans Ulrich

Dortmund
Nockelmann, Wolfgang

Düsseldorf
Gillessen, Frederick
Pathe, Ilmo
Schiessl, Maximilian

Frankfurt
Andres, Ingrid
Dienst, Armin
Gross, Wolfgang
Hartmann, Uwe
Jung, Harald H.
Klerx, Oliver
Peter, Anne-Marie
Roch, Michael Peter
Schroeder, Oliver Marcus
Strelow, Markus
Wolff, Florian
Wuermeling, Ulrich Urban

Hamburg
Núñez Müller, Marco A.
von Teichman, Christoph

Munich
Friedl, Birgit E.
Preisenberger, Simon Andreas
Schleifenbaum, Eckhart Johannes

Stuttgart
Mailaender, Karl Peter

Villingen
Koenig, Hans-Joachim
Piazolo, Kathrin Barbara

GREECE

Athens
Cocalis, Dimitri N.
Georgacopulos, Dimitris Haralambos

GRENADA

Saint George's
Helgerson, John Walter

HONG KONG

Hong Kong
Chow, Stanley
Graham, David

HUNGARY

Budapest
Dederick, David
Grmela, Zoltan

INDONESIA

Jakarta
Madian, Ferry Pauliansyah

IRELAND

Dublin
Brady, George Eoghan

ISRAEL

Jerusalem
Stern, Doron Daniel

ITALY

Milan
Parola, Lorenzo
Tedeschi, Edoardo

Padua
Polettini, Alessandro

Rome
Apuzzo, Ernesto
Fahey Sandell, Jacquelyn Marie
Giarda, Raffaele
Lo Faso, Giovanni

JAPAN

Osaka
Solberg, Norman Robert

Tokyo
Fujieda, Atsushi
Hashidate, Kenji
Sedlak, Eric William

LUXEMBOURG

Luxembourg
Garban, Blaise Jean-Francois
Kremer, Christian

MALAYSIA

Kuala Lumpur
Lim, Michael Hee Kiang

NETHERLANDS

Amsterdam
Liem, Edwin T.H.

Rotterdam
Booysen, Willem Hendrik

NEW ZEALAND

Auckland
Owles, Peter Gary

NORWAY

Oslo
Dahl, Torleif Peder
Fitzpatrick, Whitfield Westfeldt
Moljord, Kare I.
Sven, Robert
Thogersen, Kai
Thyness, Erik

Stavanger
Koppang, Baard Ivar

PANAMA

Panama
Arias, Ramon Ricardo

PERU

Lima
Gotuzzo, Gianina
Rebaza, Alberto

PHILIPPINES

Makati City
Mamuric, Jose Roberto Lota
Tan, Eusebio Valdez

POLAND

Lomianki
Deeg-Dabrowska, Agnieszka

Warsaw
Chajec, Andrzej Bogdan
Gessel Kalinowska vel Kalisz, Beata

PORTUGAL

Lisbon
Gomes, Joao Jose Veiga
Martins, Belarmino Gonçalves

Porto
Pessanha, Tomas Vasconcelos

REPUBLIC OF KOREA

Seoul
Jin, Hong Ki

SCOTLAND

Edinburgh
Hook, Christian Robert Malnachtan

Glasgow
Burrow, Alistair Stewart

SLOVAKIA

Bratislva
Marek, Premysl

SOUTH AFRICA

Benmore
Ewing, Christopher Haig

Sandton
Pinnock, David Bruce
Schlosberg, Jonathan Harry

SPAIN

Barcelona
Baches, Sergio
Casanueva, Fernando
Girbau, Ramon
Marin, Daniel
Pallares, Ignacio

Madrid
Blanco, Raquel
Diez, Maite
Hunter, George S.
Lincke, Karl Heinrich
Rueda, Pedro Antonio
Urbano, Javier

Valencia
Navarro-González, Antonio J.

SWEDEN

Gothenburg
Edh, Staffan

Helsingborg
Swanstein, Jerker

Stockholm
Alhanko, Peter
Blomberg, Erik Bïson
Bökwall, Carl

SWITZERLAND

Basel
Eulau, Peter H.

Zürich
Gericke, Dieter Andreas
Kanzig, David Frederic
Ladner, Thomas F.

THAILAND

Bangkok
John, Phillip L.M.
Periera, Santhapat
Pichedvanichok, Arkrapol
Smuthranond, Archava

TURKEY

Istanbul
Limnili, Duygu
Selcuk, Galip Murat

ADDRESS UNPUBLISHED

Ball, James Herington
Blumenthal, William
Catuzzi, J(erome) P(rimo), Jr.,
Crook, Donald Martin
D'Avignon, Roy Joseph
Delafield, Joseph Livingston, III,
Derman, Emre
Diehl, Deborah Hilda
Edwards, James Malone
Firestone, Bruce Michael
Fischer, David Charles
Fraidin, Stephen
Goebel, Hans P.
James, Michael Andrew
Kapnick, Richard Bradshaw
Lefkowitz, Alan Zoel
Madden, John J.
Meyer, Max Earl
Millimet, Erwin
Mitchell, William Graham Champion
Painton, Russell Elliott
Voight, Elizabeth Anne
Wilson, Hugh Steven
Wilson, Rhys Thaddeus
Wolfson, Michael George
Yarbro, Alan David

MILITARY

UNITED STATES

ALABAMA

Birmingham
Norris, Robert Wheeler

ARIZONA

Eloy
O'Leary, Thomas Michael

CALIFORNIA

Santa Ana
Harley, Robison Dooling, Jr.,

KENTUCKY

Crestwood
Ray, Ronald Dudley

Fort Campbell
Ruth, Bryce Clinton, Jr.,

Lexington
Davidson, Michael
Hickey, John King

MARYLAND

Annapolis
Ferris, William Michael

Glen Burnie
Lilly, John Richard, II,

MISSOURI

Springfield
Royce, James Richard

NEW YORK

New York
Einhorn, David Allen
Shaw, Melvin Robert

NORTH CAROLINA

Raleigh
Huggard, John Parker

OHIO

Dayton
Kinlin, Donald James

PENNSYLVANIA

Elkins Park
Shmukler, Stanford

Philadelphia
Wert, Robert Clifton

Pittsburgh
Orsatti, Ernest Benjamin

Souderton
Marden, Jack Mortimer

TENNESSEE

Newport
Bell, John Alton

TEXAS

Mason
Johnson, Rufus Winfield

VIRGINIA

Arlington
Cohen, Sheldon Irwin

Sterling
McBarnette, Bruce Olvin

Virginia Beach
Buzard, David Andrew
Holmes, William James

WEST VIRGINIA

Morgantown
Cohen, Richard Paul

SCOTLAND

Balintore
Cook, Glen André

ADDRESS UNPUBLISHED

Marshall, Kathryn Sue

MUNICIPAL (include BONDS)

UNITED STATES

ALABAMA

Birmingham
Foster, Arthur Key, Jr.,
Haskell, Wyatt Rushton

Montgomery
Gregory, William Stanley

ALASKA

Anchorage
Wohlforth, Eric Evans

ARIZONA

Flagstaff
Gliege, John Gerhardt

ARKANSAS

Little Rock
Bohannon, Charles Tad

CALIFORNIA

Claremont
Vera, Ronald Thomas

Los Angeles
Carroll, Raoul Lord

Napa
Meyers, David W.

Oakland
Webster, William Hodges

COLORADO

Denver
Grimshaw, Thomas Tollin

CONNECTICUT

Hartford
Anthony, J(ulian) Danford, Jr.,
See, Edmund M.

Westport
Saxl, Richard Hildreth

DELAWARE

Wilmington
McDowell, Charles S.

DISTRICT OF COLUMBIA

Washington
Journey, Drexel Dahlke

FLORIDA

Miami
Johnson, Alise M.

Plant City
Buchman, Kenneth William

West Palm Beach
Spillias, Kenneth George

GEORGIA

Atlanta
Ide, Roy William, III,
Mobley, John Homer, II,

IDAHO

Boise
Fawcett, Charles Winton

NATIVE AMERICAN

UNITED STATES

NATURAL RESOURCES

UNITED STATES

PENNSYLVANIA

Pittsburgh
Kalil, David Thomas

TENNESSEE

Knoxville
Howard, Lewis Spilman

TEXAS

Houston
Hurd, John R.

UTAH

Salt Lake City
Becker, Ralph Elihu, Jr.,
Dragoo, Denise Ann
Jensen, Dallin W.
Lee, James B.

VIRGINIA

Mc Lean
Armstrong, Arthur John

Richmond
Denny, Collins, III,

Roanoke
Thomson, Paul Rice, Jr.,

WASHINGTON

Seattle
Aramburu, John Richard
Robinson-Dorn, Michael Jay

NON-PROFIT AND TAX-EXEMPT ORGANIZATIONS

UNITED STATES

ARIZONA

Phoenix
Dunipace, Ian Douglas

CALIFORNIA

Alamo
Fleisher, Steven M.

Los Angeles
Clark, R(ufus) Bradbury
Costales, Marco Daniel

Oakland
Webster, William Hodges

San Diego
Dostart, Paul Joseph

San Francisco
Sugarman, Myron George

Toluca Lake
Runquist, Lisa A.

COLORADO

Lakewood
Thome, Dennis Wesley

Littleton
Cypser, Darlene Ann

CONNECTICUT

Hartford
Anthony, J(ulian) Danford, Jr.,

DISTRICT OF COLUMBIA

Washington
Beckwith, Edward Jay
Boskey, Bennett
Browne, Richard Cullen
Dye, Alan Page
Frost, Edmund Bowen
McCoy, Jerry Jack
McHugh, James Lenahan, Jr.,
Nelson, Robert Louis
Schmidt, William Arthur, Jr.,

FLORIDA

Cocoa Beach
Church, Glenn J.

GEORGIA

Atlanta
Bird, Wendell Raleigh
Rhodes, Thomas Willard

Moultrie
Forehand, Jon Vincent

HAWAII

Honolulu
Tanna, Wayne Mitsuo

Kihei
Burns, Richard Gordon

ILLINOIS

Chicago
Hahn, Frederic Louis
Howe, Jonathan Thomas
Paprocki, Thomas John
Sanders, Richard Henry

Park Forest
Goodrich, John Bernard

INDIANA

Terre Haute
Bopp, James, Jr.,

KANSAS

Lincoln
Crangle, Robert D.

Shawnee Mission
Snyder, Willard Breidenthal

KENTUCKY

Louisville
Buckaway, William Allen, Jr.,

MARYLAND

Crownsville
Irish, Leon Eugene

MASSACHUSETTS

Boston
Caccese, Michael Stephen
Clymer, John Howard
Haddad, Ernest Mudarri
Rowe, Larry Jordan
White, Barry Bennett

MICHIGAN

Detroit
Darlow, Julia Donovan

Grand Rapids
Kolenic, Anthony James, Jr.,

MINNESOTA

Minneapolis
Greener, Ralph Bertram
Vander Molen, Thomas Dale

MISSOURI

Columbia
Parrigin, Elizabeth Ellington

Kansas City
Langworthy, Robert Burton
Tyler, John Edward, III,

Saint Louis
Baum, Gordon Lee

NEW JERSEY

Clifton
Goldberger, Alan Steven

NEW YORK

Buffalo
Heilman, Pamela Davis

Hamburg
Glose, Herbert James

Montauk
Kahn, Richard Dreyfus

New York
Davidson, George Allan
Finch, Edward Ridley, Jr.,
Haims, Bruce David
Josephson, William Howard
Kaufman, Robert Max
Knight, Townsend Jones
Kornreich, Edward Scott
Morganstern, Gerald H.
Neuwirth, Gloria S.
Reilly, Edward Arthur
Reynolds, Michael Timothy
Schwartz, Arthur Zachary
Solomon, Stephen L.
Wyckoff, E. Lisk, Jr.,

Rochester
Stewart, Sue S.

Syracuse
Evans, Thomas Steven

NORTH CAROLINA

Durham
Buchanan, Phillip Hoge

Raleigh
Simpson, Steven Drexell

OHIO

Akron
Allan, Ronald Curtis

Cleveland
Dampeer, John Lyell
Leavitt, Jeffrey Stuart
Taft, Seth Chase

Columbus
Oman, Richard Heer
Tripp, Thomas Neal

Marion
Frericks, Timothy Matthew

Wilmington
Schutt, Walter Eugene

PENNSYLVANIA

King Of Prussia
Gadsden, Christopher Henry

Philadelphia
Berger, Lawrence Howard
Scullin, Michael E.

Pittsburgh
Johnson, Robert Alan

SOUTH DAKOTA

Rapid City
Thatcher, Anna Marie

TEXAS

Austin
Osborne, Duncan Elliott

Dallas
Bumpas, Stuart Maryman
Green, Jesse Joseph
Humble, Monty Garfield

Fort Worth
West, Robert Grady

Houston
Grossberg, Marc Elias

VIRGINIA

Charlottesville
Middleditch, Leigh Benjamin, Jr.,

Mc Lean
Herge, J. Curtis
LeSourd, Nancy Susan Oliver
Olson, William Jeffrey

WASHINGTON

Everett
Dewell, Julian C.

Keyport
Treacy, Gerald Bernard, Jr.,

WISCONSIN

Madison
Brewster, Francis Anthony
Sweet, Howard A.

Milwaukee
Melin, Robert Arthur
Winsten, Saul Nathan

AUSTRIA

Innsbruck
Schurr, Francesco Armando

ENGLAND

London
Tweedie, David Allison Osborne

ADDRESS UNPUBLISHED

Paul, Eve W.
Vallianos, Carole Wagner
Westphal, Marjorie Lord

OIL, GAS, AND MINERAL

UNITED STATES

ALABAMA

Mobile
Armbrecht, William Henry, III,
Harris, Benjamin Harte, Jr.,

Northport
Allen, Randy Lee

ALASKA

Anchorage
Linxwiler, James David

CALIFORNIA

Bakersfield
Tornstrom, Robert Ernest

Pasadena
Armour, George Porter

San Francisco
Hinman, Harvey DeForest

COLORADO

Centennial
Barnthouse, William Joseph

Colorado Springs
MacDougall, Malcolm Edward

Denver
Hawley, Robert Cross
Hendrix, Lynn Parker
Irwin, R. Robert
Jones, Richard Michael
Kirchhoff, Bruce C.
Merritts, Jack Michael
Roth, Robert Charles
Shepherd, John Frederic

DISTRICT OF COLUMBIA

Washington
Allan, Richmond Frederick
Avil, Richard Daniel, Jr.,
Bardin, David J.
Eastment, Thomas James
Ellis, Courtenay
Jordan, Robert Elijah, III,
Manning, Michael J.
Weinberg, Sara Caryna

ILLINOIS

Mount Carmel
Rhine, John E.

Pinckneyville
Johnson, Don Edwin

Wilmette
Frick, Robert Hathaway

KANSAS

Lawrence
Nordling, Bernard Erick

Ulysses
Hathaway, Gary Ray

Wichita
Depew, Spencer Long

LOUISIANA

Baton Rouge
Johnson, Joseph Clayton, Jr.,
Taylor, John McKowen

Jennings
Miller, Ruth Loyd

Lafayette
Durio, William Henry
Mansfield, James Norman, III,

Monroe
Sartor, Daniel Ryan, Jr.,

New Orleans
Pearce, John Y.

MICHIGAN

Gaylord
Topp, Susan Hlywa

MISSISSIPPI

Jackson
Eicher, Donald E., III,
Grant, Russell Porter, Jr.,
Hughes, Byron William

NEVADA

Reno
Hill, Earl McColl

NEW MEXICO

Albuquerque
Haltom, B(illy) Reid
Moise, Steven Kahn

Roswell
Nibert, Gregory James

NEW YORK

Babylon
Hennelly, Edmund Paul

Buffalo
Day, Donald Sheldon

New York
Harley, Colin Emile
Owen, Robert Dewit
Stein, Stephen William

Olean
Heyer, John Henry, II,

White Plains
Berlin, Alan Daniel

OHIO

Canfield
Hill, Thomas Allen

Jefferson
Lemire, Jerome Albert

OKLAHOMA

Broken Arrow
Jones, Ronald Lee

Kingfisher
Baker, Thomas Edward

Oklahoma City
Christiansen, Mark D.
Cook, Gayle Freeman
Cunningham, Stanley Lloyd
Decker, Michael Lynn
Kallstrom, James David
Nesbitt, Charles Rudolph
Stanley, Brian Jordan
Towery, Curtis Kent

Seminole
Elsener, G. Dale

Tulsa
Kihle, Donald Arthur
Medina, J. Michael
Sneed, James Lynde

PENNSYLVANIA

Pittsburgh
Boswell, William Paret

SOUTH CAROLINA

Newberry
Partridge, William Franklin, Jr.,

SOUTH DAKOTA

Rapid City
Graslie, Thomas Eric

TEXAS

Amarillo
Hill, Edward Haynes

Austin
Black, William Earl
Clark, Pat English
Godfrey, Cullen Michael
Lochridge, Lloyd Pampell, Jr.,
Patman, Philip Franklin

Boerne
Vaughan, Edward Gibson

Borger
Edmonds, Thomas Leon

Dallas
Armour, James Lott
Douglass, Frank Russell
Keithley, Bradford Gene

Edinburg
Looney, Cullen Rogers

Hallettsville
Baber, Wilbur H., Jr.,

Houston
Anderson, Doris Ehlinger
Burch, Voris Reagan
Dykes, Osborne Jefferson, III,
Farnsworth, T. Brooke
Gibson, Rex Hilton
Kinnan, David Emery
Martin, Jay Griffith
McClure, Daniel M.
Morgan, Richard Greer
Plaeger, Frederick Joseph, II,
Poitevent, Edward Butts, II,
Ryan, Thomas William
Sheppard, Ben H., Jr.,
Walls, Robert Hamilton, Jr.,

Humble
Hinton, Quincy Thomas, Jr.,

Kilgore
Rorschach, Richard Gordon

Lockhart
Scudday, Roy George

Lubbock
Saied, Robert Mack

Plano
Blachly, Jack Lee

Rockport
Porter, Charles Raleigh, Jr.,

San Antonio
Labay, Eugene Benedict

Tyler
Hadden, Arthur Roby

Victoria
McKay, Robert Connally

Yorktown
Barry, Thomas Joseph

UTAH

Salt Lake City
Beless, Rosemary June

WEST VIRGINIA

Charleston
Chaney, Vincent Verlando

WYOMING

Casper
Durham, Harry Blaine, III,
Lowe, Robert Stanley

Gillette
Lubnau, Thomas Edwin, II,

AUSTRALIA

Sydney
Machin, Peter William
Winkler, Nicholas Gary

BRAZIL

Rio de Janeiro
Muniz, Joaquim Tavares de Paiva

São Paulo
Padovan, Lira Renardini

ENGLAND

London
Barratt, Jeffrey Vernon
Exley, Paul Marcus
Kelly, Christopher Richard
Vaughan, Philip John

INDONESIA

Jakarta
Mills, Karen

ITALY

Milan
DePalma, Giuseppe
Parola, Lorenzo

Tuscany
Monaci Naldini, Jacopo

JAPAN

Tokyo
Wexler, Thomas Charles

NORWAY

Oslo
Fitzpatrick, Whitfield Westfeldt

VENEZUELA

Caracas
Eljuri, Elisabeth

ADDRESS UNPUBLISHED

Choukas-Bradley, James Richard
Giusti, William Roger
Lynch, Thomas Wimp
Moyer, Craig Alan
Oz, Yilmaz
Quigley, Leonard Vincent
Shambaugh, Stephen Ward

PATENT

UNITED STATES

ALABAMA

Birmingham
Robin, Theodore Tydings, Jr.,

ARIZONA

Phoenix
Flickinger, Don Jacob
Meschkow, Jordan M.
Phillips, James Harold
Sutton, Samuel J.

Sun City
Hauer, James Albert

CALIFORNIA

Berkeley
Woodhouse, Thomas Edwin

Cerritos
Sarno, Maria Erlinda

Claremont
Ansell, Edward Orin

Cupertino
Simon, Nancy Ruth

Irvine
Knobbe, Louis Joseph
Martens, Don Walter
Stone, Samuel Beckner
Tachner, Leonard

Los Angeles
Barsky, Wayne Mitchell
Chu, Morgan
Green, William Porter
Krupka, Robert George

Mountain View
Pasahow, Lynn H(arold)
Radlo, Edward John

Palo Alto
O'Rourke, C. Larry
Simon, James Lowell

San Diego
Preston, David Raymond

San Francisco
Anderson, Edward Virgil
Chambers, Guy Wayne
Richardson, Daniel Ralph
Smegal, Thomas Frank, Jr.,

San Jose
Jorgensen, Norman Eric

Van Nuys
Mikesell, Richard Lyon

COLORADO

Breckenridge
Fromm, Jeffery Bernard

Denver
Dorr, Robert Charles

Golden
Phillipson, Donald E.

CONNECTICUT

Enfield
Smith, Spencer Thomas

Monroe
Oliver, Milton McKinnon

New Haven
De Lio, Anthony Peter

Westport
Razzano, Pasquale Angelo

DELAWARE

Wilmington
Blumenfeld, Jack Barry
Magee, Thomas Hugh

DISTRICT OF COLUMBIA

Washington
Aisenberg, Irwin Morton
Cantor, Herbert I.
Goodman, Alfred Nelson
Hefter, Laurence Roy
Henderson, Douglas Boyd
Laughlin, James Harold, Jr.,
Lavelle, Joseph P.
McCann, Clifton Everett
Railton, William Scott
Repper, George Robert
Sears, Mary Helen
Wallace, James Harold, Jr.,
Wyss, John Benedict

FLORIDA

Melbourne
Dixon, Richard Dean

Miami
Fleit, Martin

GEORGIA

Norcross
Anderson, Albert Sydney, III,

Tucker
Tewes, R. Scott

Valdosta
Sinnott, John Patrick

HAWAII

Honolulu
Hsia, Martin Edgar

ILLINOIS

Barrington
Lee, William Marshall

Chicago
Altman, Louis
Amend, James Michael
Berenzweig, Jack Charles
Berghoff, Paul Henry
Boehnen, Daniel A.
Geren, Gerald S.
Gerstman, George Henry
Hofer, Roy Ellis
Hoffman, Richard Bruce
Hoskins, Richard Jerold
Kozak, John W.
Lane, Bradley Glenn
Lyerla, Bradford Peter
Maher, David Willard
Nicolaides, Mary
Parkhurst, Todd Sheldon
Roper, Harry Joseph
Schneider, Robert Jerome
Sheppard, Berton Scott
Sweeney, James Raymond
Vranicar, Michael Gregory
Wanke, Ronald Lee
Wesley, William Matthew
Willian, Clyde Franklin
Witcoff, Sheldon William

Lansing
Hill, Philip

Urbana
Fitz-Gerald, Roger Miller

IOWA

Cedar Rapids
Harms, Allan L.

KENTUCKY

Louisville
Reed, John Squires, II,
Stavros, Peter James

MARYLAND

Potomac
Hall, William Darlington
Troffkin, Howard Julian

MASSACHUSETTS

Boston
Chow, Stephen Y(ee)
Deutsch, Stephen B.
Hieken, Charles

Concord
Glovsky, Susan G. L.

Framingham
Kriegsman, Edward Michael

MICHIGAN

Bloomfield Hills
Rader, Ralph Terrance

Detroit
Monsanto, Raphael Angel

Farmington Hills
Taravella, Christopher Anthony

Grand Rapids
Mitchell, James Albee

Troy
Cantor, Bernard Jack

MINNESOTA

Minneapolis
Gill, Richard Lawrence
Sawicki, Zbigniew Peter
Trembath, Jon R.
Tufte, Brian Nelson

MISSOURI

Carthage
Weissenberger, Harry George

Saint Louis
Evans, Lawrence E.
Lucchesi, Lionel Louis

MONTANA

Bozeman
Conover, Richard Corrill

Lolo
Hansell, Ronald Stephen

NEVADA

Reno
Ryan, Robert Collins

NEW HAMPSHIRE

New London
Plant, David William

NEW JERSEY

Bridgewater
Dahling, Gerald Vernon

Edgewater
Virelli, Louis James, Jr.,

Edison
Fink, Edward Murray

Iselin
Dornbusch, Arthur A., II,

Morristown
Huettner, Richard Alfred

NEW YORK

Brooklyn
Rubenstein, Allen Ira

Huntington
Robinson, Kenneth Patrick

New York
Baechtold, Robert Louis
Bazerman, Steven Howard
Bosses, Stevan J.
Brooks, Lorimer Page
Calvaruso, Joseph Anthony
Coggio, Brian D.
Creel, Thomas Leonard
Dunham, Christopher Cooper
Faber, Robert Charles
Fitzpatrick, Joseph Mark
Frommer, William S.
Glazer, Steven Donald
Hamburg, Charles Bruce
Herman, Kenneth Beaumont
Katsh, Salem Michael
Kidd, John Edward
Lee, Jerome G.
Martone, Patricia Ann
Pegram, John Braxton
Rogers, Laurence Steven
Schwartz, Herbert Frederick
Seltzer, Richard C.
Shentov, Ognjan V.
Smith, Robert Blakeman
Sobel, Gerald
Stathis, Nicholas John
Woglom, Eric Cooke

Poughkeepsie
Taphorn, Joseph Bernard

NORTH CAROLINA

Chapel Hill
Hultquist, Steven John

Charlotte
Bell, Paul Buckner
Linker, Raymond Otho, Jr.,

Durham
Priest, Peter H.

Greensboro
Floyd, Jack William

OHIO

Akron
Kreek, Louis Francis, Jr.,

Cleveland
Burge, David Alan
Crehore, Charles Aaron
Fay, Regan Joseph
Fisher, Thomas Edward

Cuyahoga Falls
Jones, John Frank

Toledo
Wicklund, David Wayne

OREGON

Lincoln City
Arant, Eugene Wesley

Portland
Noonan, William Donald

PENNSYLVANIA

Bala Cynwyd
Chovanes, Eugene

Conshohocken
Bramson, Robert Sherman

Philadelphia
Frank, George Andrew
Pokotilow, Manny David
Seidel, Arthur Harris
Simkanich, John Joseph

Pittsburgh
Baldauf, Kent Edward
Blenko, Walter John, Jr.,
Colen, Frederick Haas
Silverman, Arnold Barry

SOUTH CAROLINA

Greenville
Bagarazzi, James Michael
Csontos, Alan Arthur

TEXAS

Austin
Schuurman, Willem Gerhard

Bastrop
Van Gilder, Derek Robert

Dallas
McGowan, Patrick Francis
Mills, Jerry Woodrow
Mondul, Donald David

Houston
Bargfrede, James Allen
Bliss, Ronald Glenn
Caldwell, Rodney Kent
Fladung, Richard Denis
Kaplan, Lee Landa
Kirk, John Robert, Jr.,
Krieger, Paul Edward
Larkin, Lee Roy
Pravel, Bernarr Roe
Pugsley, Frank Burruss
Rosenthal, Alan D.
Shurn, Peter Joseph, III,
Toedt, D(ell) C(harles), III,
Tripp, Karen Bryant

Humble
Gaffney, Richard Cook

Plano
Levine, Harold

Sugar Land
Hitchcock, Bion Earl

Tyler
Alworth, Charles Wesley

UTAH

Provo
Brown, Joseph William

Salt Lake City
Cornaby, Kay Sterling

VERMONT

Essex Junction
Walsh, Robert Anthony

VIRGINIA

Alexandria
Georges, Peter John
Greigg, Ronald Edwin
Mar, Eugene
Swift, Stephen Christopher
Wieder, Bruce Terrill

Arlington
Landry, Walter Joseph
Litman, Richard Curtis
Mossinghoff, Gerald Joseph
Scafetta, Joseph, Jr.,

Falls Church
Birch, Terrell Colhoun
Brady, Rupert Joseph

Hampton
Hammerle, Kurt Georg

Mc Lean
Kondracki, Edward John
Shapiro, Nelson Hirsh

WISCONSIN

Madison
Bremer, Howard Walter

Milwaukee
O'Shaughnessy, James Patrick

Waukesha
Moran, Kevin Paul

MEXICO

Mexico City
Cardenas, Alejandro
Carpio, Miguel Angel
Velázquez, Agustin

BRAZIL

São Paulo
Giacchetta, Andre Zonaro

CZECH REPUBLIC

Prague
Kroft, Michal

ENGLAND

London
Gilbert, Penny Xenia

ITALY

Milan
Graffer, Jacopo

NETHERLANDS

The Hague
Van Nispen, Constant J.J.C.

SWITZERLAND

Zürich
Auf der Maur, Rolf

WALES

Cardiff
Lindsey, Michael

ADDRESS UNPUBLISHED

Adams, Thomas Lawrence
Antolin, Stanislav
Beck, Stuart Edwin
Campagna, Mark V.
Carten, Francis Noel
Corle, James Thomas
Fiorito, Edward Gerald
Gray, John Leonard
McCullough, Edward Eugene
Peters, R. Jonathan
Phelan, Charles Scott
Sprung, Arnold
Vaden, Frank Samuel, III,

PENSION, PROFIT-SHARING, AND EMPLOYEE BENEFITS

UNITED STATES

ALABAMA

Bessemer
Fawwal, Audeh Edward

Birmingham
Levy, Jack B.

ARIZONA

Phoenix
Ehmann, Anthony Valentine
Hoecker, Thomas Ralph
Lundeen, Bradley Curtis
Pietzsch, Michael Edward

CALIFORNIA

Costa Mesa
Marshall, Ellen Ruth

Fallbrook
Leehey, Paul Wade

Irvine
Maldonado, Kirk Francis

Los Angeles
Carrey, Neil
Cathcart, David Arthur
Lipsig, Ethan

Oakland
Reese, Charles Woodrow, Jr.,

San Francisco
Foster, David Scott
Gibson, Virginia Lee
Homer, Barry Wayne

San Jose
Kraw, George Martin

Walnut Creek
Rainey, William Joel

COLORADO

Denver
Crow, Nancy Rebecca
Solano, Henry L.

Golden
Boumann, Robert Lyle

Placerville
Reagan, Harry Edwin, III,

CONNECTICUT

New London
Johnstone, Philip MacLaren

Stamford
Lalli, Michael Anthony

Trumbull
Czajkowski, Frank Henry

DISTRICT OF COLUMBIA

Washington
Alexander, Donald Crichton
Bostick, George Hale
Cummings, Frank
Damico, Nicholas Peter
Faley, R(ichard) Scott
Flowe, Carol Connor
Goldsmith, Willis Jay
Horahan, Edward Bernard, III,
Kautter, David John
Lopatin, Alan G.
Mackiewicz, Edward Robert
Miller, Evan
Oliphant, Charles Frederick, III,
Quintiere, Gary Gandolfo
Sacher, Steven Jay
Stauffer, Ronald Eugene

FLORIDA

Bradenton
Lopacki, Edward Joseph, Jr.,

Fort Lauderdale
Ruback, Alan Steven

Miami Lakes
Cohen, Ronald J.

Orlando
Lefkowitz, Ivan Martin

Pembroke Pines
Murray, Claude Robert, Jr.,

Saint Petersburg
Escarraz, Enrique, III,

Tampa
Robinson, John William, IV,
Watson, Roberta Casper

Venice
Brott, Irving Deerin, Jr.,

GEORGIA

Atlanta
Forbes, Theodore McCoy, Jr.,
Lamon, Harry Vincent, Jr.,
Tanenbaum, Allan Jay

Dallas
Williams, Gary Randall

Sugar Hill
Hamby, Lee Ellen

ILLINOIS

Chicago
Ackerman, David Paul
Brown, Gregory K.
Daley, Susan Jean
Fellows, Jerry Kenneth
Ferencz, Robert Arnold
Gerske, Janet Fay
Greenfield, Michael C.
Kaplan, Jared
Kelly, Peter McClorey, II,
Krueger, Herbert William
Margolin, Stephen M.
Michalak, Edward Francis
Miller, Stephen Ralph
Peter, Bernard George
Rizzo, Ronald Stephen
Scogland, William Lee
Serwer, Alan Michael
Siske, Roger Charles
Tinaglia, Michael Lee
Wise, William Jerrard
Wolf, Charles Benno

Kenilworth
McKittrick, William Wood

Oak Brook
Barnes, Karen Kay

Riverside
Kubiczky, Stephen Ralph

INDIANA

Indianapolis
Boldt, Michael Herbert
Kemper, James Dee
Ritz, Stephen Mark
Roberts, Patricia Susan

IOWA

Davenport
Dettmann, David Allen

Muscatine
Nepple, James Anthony

KENTUCKY

Louisville
Gilman, Sheldon Glenn
Hallenberg, Robert Lewis

LOUISIANA

Baton Rouge
Bayard, Alton Ernest, III,

MAINE

Brewer
Ebitz, Elizabeth Kelly

MARYLAND

Baltimore
Bruner, William Gwathmey, III,
Curran, Robert Bruce
Dubé, Lawrence Edward, Jr.,

Cambridge
Jenkins, Robert Rowe

MASSACHUSETTS

West Falmouth
Carlson, David Bret

Worcester
Felper, David Michael

MICHIGAN

Ann Arbor
Keppelman, Nancy
Stevenson, Robert Bruce

Bloomfield Hills
Callow, Thomas Edward

Detroit
Brustad, Orin Daniel
Turner, Reginald Maurice, Jr.,

Grand Rapids
Kolenic, Anthony James, Jr.,
Titley, Larry J.

Muskegon
McKendry, John H., Jr.,

Southfield
McClow, Roger James

Troy
Brody, Jay Howard

MINNESOTA

Duluth
Burns, Richard Ramsey

Minneapolis
Cullen, Terrance Michael
Freeman, Todd Ira
Gottschalk, Stephen Elmer
Nelson, Richard Arthur
Shnider, Bruce Jay

Rochester
Jacobsen, Van Paul

Saint Cloud
Provinzino, John C.

MISSOURI

Columbia
Crepeau, Dewey Lee

Kansas City
Brous, Thomas Richard
Toll, Perry Mark

Saint Louis
Crowe, Robert Alan
Farnam, Thomas Campbell
Fogle, James Lee
Kandel, Alan Harold

NEVADA

Las Vegas
Greene, Addison Kent

NEW HAMPSHIRE

Concord
Chamberlain, Douglas Reginald

Portsmouth
Mason, J. William L.

NEW JERSEY

Camden
Furey, John J.

Florham Park
Reid, Charles Adams, III,
Witman, Leonard Joel

Mc Afee
Fogel, Richard

Morristown
Doyle, David Perrie

Newark
Fiore, William Joseph

Point Pleasant Beach
Herr, Philip Michael

Sewell
Fichera, Lewis Carmen

South Orange
Delo, Ellen Sanderson

NEW MEXICO

Albuquerque
Lieuwen, John N.
Ramo, Roberta Cooper

Deming
Sherman, Frederick Hood

NEW YORK

Bronx
Verrelli, Anthony Louis

Buffalo
Newman, Stephen Michael

Flushing
Schwartz, Estar Alma

Garden City
Lilly, Thomas Joseph

Harrison
Strone, Michael Jonathan

Hartsdale
Kroll, Arthur Herbert

Huntington
Hochberg, Ronald Mark

Huntington Station
Binder, Harry J.

Jamestown
Beckstrom, Charles G.

Kingston
Ellison, Patricia Lee

Lockport
Brodsky, Felice Adrienne

Long Island City
Wanderman, Susan Mae

Mineola
Pogrebin, Bertrand B.

New Rochelle
Lurie, Alvin David

New York
Barry, David Earl
Budd, Thomas Witbeck
Canoni, John David
Carling, Francis
Cornell, John Robert
Duff, William Brandon
Estock, Howard Gordon
Friedman, Eugene Stuart
Glanstein, Joel Charles
Macris, Michael
Moore, Donald Francis
Moss, Franklin Kass
Nassau, Michael Jay
Oppenheimer, Martin J.
Panken, Peter Michael
Ray, Jeanne Cullinan
Reifler, Stewart
Rover, Edward Frank
Serota, Susan Perlstadt
Simone, Joseph R.
Thompson, Loran Tyson

Rochester
Colby, William Michael
Wild, Robert Warren

Syracuse
King, Bernard T.

White Plains
Alin, Robert David
Danziger, Joel Bernard
Klein, Paul E.
Taft, Nathaniel Belmont

Yonkers
Steinberg, Avery

NORTH CAROLINA

Asheville
Gantt, Charles David

Charlotte
Culbreth, James Harold, Jr.,
Daniel, James Edward

Tarboro
O'Malley, Susan Marie

Winston Salem
Gunter, Michael Donwell

NORTH DAKOTA

Fargo
Ficek, Gary A.

OHIO

Cincinnati
Fink, Jerold Albert
Levin, Debbe Ann

Cleveland
Leavitt, Jeffrey Stuart
Ollinger, W. James
Shaw, Russell Clyde

Columbus
Tarpy, Thomas Michael

Warren
Letson, William Normand

OKLAHOMA

Stillwater
Fischer, Richard Samuel

OREGON

Portland
Froebe, Gerald Allen
Grossmann, Ronald Stanyer
Klarquist, Kenneth Stevens, Jr.,
Zalutsky, Morton Herman

PENNSYLVANIA

Allison Park
Ries, William Campbell

Philadelphia
Abramowitz, Robert Leslie
Bernard, John Marley
Bildersee, Robert Alan
Cannon, John, III,
Dabrowski, Doris Jane
Donner, Henry Jay
Drake, William Frank, Jr.,
Fox, Gregory John
Gilberg, Kenneth Roy
Lichtenstein, Robert Jay
Magargee, W(illiam) Scott, III,
O'Reilly, Timothy Patrick
Sigmond, Richard Brian
Thomas, Lowell Shumway, Jr.,
Whiteside, William Anthony, Jr.,

Pittsburgh
Candris, Laura A.
Chaban, Lawrence Richard
Johnson, Robert Alan
Kabala, Edward John
Kearns, John J., III,
Leech, Jeffrey James

Reading
Linton, Jack Arthur

TENNESSEE

Kingsport
Shine, David Bruce

Nashville
Gannon, John Sexton

TEXAS

Austin
Fink, Vella Mary

Dallas
Bumpas, Stuart Maryman
Cowart, T(homas) David
Crowley, James Worthington
Finston, Felicia A.
Gerberding Cowart, Greta Elaine
Gully, Russell George
Pingree, Bruce Douglas

Fort Worth
Tracy, J. David

Houston
Amaon, Gary P.
Croom, Sam Gaston, Jr.,
Dworsky, Clara Weiner
Harper, Alfred John, II,
Jansen, Donald Orville
Segal, Steven E.
Seymour, Barbara Laverne

Mansfield
Bright, Thomas Lynn

Richardson
Conkel, Robert Dale

San Antonio
Goff, Colleen Mullen

UTAH

Salt Lake City
Wagner, Mark Alan

VIRGINIA

Amherst
Martin, Stephen Clarke

Charlottesville
Hodous, Robert Power

Danville
Regan, Michael Patrick

Fairfax
Abrams, Sheri

Richmond
Musick, Robert Lawrence, Jr.,

Wise
Rogers, Leonard David

WASHINGTON

Centralia
Bates, Charles Walter

Seattle
Birmingham, Richard Joseph
Parks, Patricia Jean

Spokane
Connolly, K. Thomas

WEST VIRGINIA

Morgantown
Cohen, Richard Paul

WISCONSIN

Milwaukee
Donahue, John Edward
Kurtz, Harvey A.
Levy, Alan M.

Wausau
Gray, Robert Joseph

BELGIUM

Diegem
Vandervelde, Erwin

ENGLAND

London
Nugee, Edward George

PORTUGAL

Lisbon
Leitao, Maria Da Gloria

SOUTH AFRICA

Cape Town
Von Witt, Edward Robert

SPAIN

Madrid
García-Perrote, Ignacio

ADDRESS UNPUBLISHED

Coleman, Richard William
Erlenborn, John Neal
Freedman, Barbara Widman
Glanzer, Mona N.
Hammond, Glenn Barry, Sr.,
Harris, Morton Allen
Piga, Stephen Mulry
Portnoy, Sara S.
Pustilnik, David Daniel
Stinchfield, John Edward
Treacy, Vincent Edward

PERSONAL INJURY *See also* Insurance

UNITED STATES

ALABAMA

Andalusia
Fuller, William Sidney

Birmingham
Alford, Margie Searcy
Blan, Ollie Lionel, Jr.,
Boardman, Mark Seymour
Cicio, Anthony Lee
Donahue, Timothy Patrick
McWhorter, Hobart Amory, Jr.,
Newton, Alexander Worthy
Norris, Robert Wheeler
Palmer, Robert Leslie
Scherf, John George, IV,

Enterprise
Hollingsworth, John R.
Price, Robert Allan

Florala
Duplechin, D. James

Jasper
Thomas, Steven Allen

Mobile
Baxley, Phillip Kent
Waldrop, Norman Erskine, Jr.,

Montgomery
Volz, Charles Harvie, Jr.,

Sheffield
Hamby, Gene Malcolm, Jr.,

Tuscaloosa
Crownover, Walter Parker

ALASKA

Anchorage
Pradell, Steven
Ross, Wayne Anthony
Weinig, Richard Arthur

Sitka
Graham, David Antony

ARIZONA

Flagstaff
Stoops, Daniel J.

Phoenix
Adelman, Daniel J.
Bakker, Thomas Gordon
Begam, Robert George
Brewer, Charles Moulton
Feder, Bruce
Goldstein, Stuart Wolf
Horan, Adnan
Klahr, Gary Peter
Leshner, Stephen I.
Marks, Lawrence J.
O'Steen, Van
Plattner, Richard Serber
Preston, Bruce Marshall
Rivera, Jose de Jesus
Sherk, Kenneth John

Rio Rico
Ryan, John Duncan

Scottsdale
Crawford, Robert F.
Smith, David Burnell

Tucson
Clark, Douglas H., Jr.,
Corey, Barry Martin
D'Antonio, James Joseph
Errico, Melissa
Feldman, Stanley George
Gonzales, Richard Joseph
Heaphy, John Merrill
Hyams, Harold
Jacobs, William Russell, II,
Kaucher, James William
Osborne, John Edwards
Rabb, Lloyd Leath
Samet, Dee-Dee
Stompoly, John George

Yuma
Hossler, David Joseph

ARKANSAS

Bryant
Jackson, James Ralph (Jim Jackson)

Crossett
Hubbell, Billy James

Fayetteville
Pearson, Charles Thomas, Jr.,

Fort Smith
Karr, Charles

Harrison
Pinson, Jerry D.

Jonesboro
McNeill, Paul Deane

Little Rock
Drummond, Winslow
Trice, William Henry, III,

Marion
Fogleman, John Nelson

Mena
Thrailkill, Daniel B.

Searcy
Hughes, Thomas Morgan, III,

CALIFORNIA

Alameda
Dósa, Andrew Alexander

Auburn
Moglen, Leland Louis

Bakersfield
Gong, Gloria Margaret

Belvedere Tiburon
Bremer, William Richard

Berkeley
Ross, Julia

Beverly Hills
Bear, Jeffrey Lewis

Brentwood
Biren, Matthew Bennett

Cambria
Stotter, James, II,

Campbell
Bass, Lewis
Castello, Raymond Vincent

Cathedral City
Paul, Vivian

Chico
Lenzi, Albert James, Jr.,

Clovis
Ninnis, William Raymond, Jr.,

Cupertino
Svalya, Phillip Gordon

El Cajon
Lee, Ernest J., Sr.,

Escondido
Godone-Maresca, Lillian

Fremont
Kitta, John Noah

Fresno
Jamison, Daniel Oliver
Nunes, Frank M.

Fullerton
Moerbeek, Stanley Leonard

Glendale
Kazanjian, Phillip Carl
Martinetti, Ronald Anthony

Laguna Hills
Mathews, Stanton Terry

Long Beach
Dawson, Norma Ann
Stolpman, Thomas Gerard
Wilson, Walter Joseph

Los Angeles
Angel, Arthur Ronald
Arkoz, David X.
Bridges, B. Ried
Chiate, Kenneth Reed
Daniels, William Anthony
Franceschi, Ernest Joseph, Jr.,
Greaves, John Allen
Guilford, Robert E.
Hedlund, Paul James
Jacobs, Randall Brian
Lauchengco, Jose Yujuico, Jr.,
Lysle, Richard Scott
Medearis, Miller
Moloney, Stephen Michael
Ogbogu, Cecilia Ify
Polakov, Anthony Scott
Rozanski, Stanley Howard
Sands, Velma Ahda
Shacter, David Mervyn
Vertun, Alan Stuart

Moraga
Kilbourne, George William

Napa
Kuntz, Charles Powers

Newport Beach
Johnson, Jennifer Rose
LeSage, Tracy Rochelle

Oakland
Berry, Phillip Samuel
Bjork, Robert David, Jr.,
Lomhoff, Peter George
Mendelson, Steven Earle

Orinda
Sohnen, Harvey

Paramount
Hall, Howard Harry

Pasadena
Telleria, Anthony F.

Placentia
Evans, Winthrop Shattuck

Pleasanton
Scott, G. Judson, Jr.,

Riverside
Darling, Scott Edward
Marlatt, Michael James

Sacramento
Brookman, Anthony Raymond
Burton, Randall James
Daniel, Lance
Friedman, Morton Lee
Owen, Allan Jacobs

San Anselmo
Truett, Harold Joseph, III, (Tim Truett)

San Clemente
Fisher, Myron R.

San Diego
Bleiler, Charles Arthur
Gomez, John Hamilton
King, Nicholas Spencer
Margolis, Anita Joy
McClellan, Craig Rene
McIntyre, Monty Alan
Roseman, Charles Sanford
Shapiro, Philip Alan
Sussman, Nancy
Weidner, Lauren Finder
Wolfe, Deborah Ann

San Francisco
Barbagelata, Robert Dominic
Bostwick, James Stephen
Cohn, Nathan
Dryden, Robert Eugene
Kornblum, Guy Orville
Walker, Walter Herbert, III,
Weber, Matthew Bernard

San Jose
Bennion, David Jacobsen
Bohn, Robert Herbert
Hernández, Fernando Vargas
Katzman, Irwin
Narayan, Beverly Elaine
Stein, John C.

San Juan Capistrano
Graves, Patrick Lee

San Marino
Tomich, Lillian

San Mateo
Monaco, Daniel Joseph
O'Reilly, Terence John

San Rafael
Fairbairn, Sydney Elise

Santa Ana
Patt, Herbert Jacob

Santa Barbara
Bauer, Marvin Agather
Pyle, Kurt H.

Santa Monica
Boyle, Kevin Richard
Morgan, Kermit Johnson

Santa Rosa
Clark, Kim Rogers

Sherman Oaks
Ardalan, Pezhman Christopher

Tahoe City
Hirshon, Jack Thomas

Tustin
Madory, Richard Eugene

Ventura
Gartner, Harold Henry, III,
Kump, Kary Ronald

Visalia
Hart, Timothy Ray

Walnut Creek
Larkin, David Joseph
Medak, Walter Hans

West Covina
Ebiner, Robert Maurice

Westlake Village
Mittenthal, Peter A.

Woodland Hills
Johnson-Champ, Debra Sue
Kaufman, Albert I.

Yuba City
Doughty, Mark Anthony

COLORADO

Arvada
Peck, Kenneth E.

Aurora
Staelin, Earl Hudson

Basalt
Shipp, Dan Shackelford

Boulder
Gray, William R.
Purvis, John Anderson

Canon City
McDermott, John Arthur
Slater, Daniel B.

Centennial
Carlton, Diane Michele

Colorado Springs
Evans, Paul Vernon
Fisher, Robert Scott
Kennedy, Richard Joseph
McCready, Guy Michael
Slivka, Michael Andrew

Denver
Brega, Charles Franklin
Cooper, Paul Douglas
Fowler, Daniel McKay
Furtado, David Jeffrey
Hoffman, Daniel Steven
Kaplan, Marc J.
Kintzele, John Alfred
McConnell, Michael Theodore
Nathan, J(ay) Andrew
Pack, Stuart Harris
Reilly, Daniel M.
Shapiro, Steven Andy
Springer, Jeffrey Alan

Fort Collins
Downey, Arthur Harold, Jr.,
Trautwein, Blair J.
Vick, Joseph James, III,

Frisco
McElyea, Monica Sergent

Golden
Carney, Deborah Leah Turner

Grand Junction
Griff, Harry
Gurley, Richard T.

Greeley
Conway, Rebecca Ann Koppes
Frey, Henry Charles

Greenwood Village
Karr, David Dean

Nixon, Scott Sherman

Littleton
Robinson, Warren A. (Rip Robinson)

Sedalia
Ewing, Mary

CONNECTICUT

Bridgeport
Harrell, Kyle Alexander

Bristol
Hayes, Margaret Mary

Colchester
Broder, Joseph Arnold

Danbury
Arconti, Richard David

Fairfield
Osis, Daiga Guntra

Guilford
Noonan, Patrick Matthew

Hamden
Bershtein, Herman Sammy

Hartford
Fain, Joel Maurice
Foden, Maria Luisa de Castro
Gale, John Quentin
Young, Roland Frederic, III,

Manchester
Horwitz, Melvin

Meriden
Luby, Thomas Stewart

Milford
Benedosso, Anthony Nechols

New Haven
Carty, Paul Vernon
Katz, Jonathan
Wolfson, Susan Wartur

New London
Reardon, Robert Ignatius, Jr.,

Norwich
Francoline, Stacey

Stratford
O'Rourke, James Louis

Torrington
Conti, William Achille
Leard, David Carl
Wall, Robert Anthony, Jr.,

Trumbull
Williams, Ronald Doherty

Waterbury
Marano, Richard Michael

West Hartford
Swerdloff, Mark Harris

Westport
Arons, Mark David
Cramer, Allan P.
Johnson, Allan Richard

Willimantic
Schiller, Howard Barry

Windsor
Morelli, Carmen

DELAWARE

Dover
Sherlock, Mary Eva

Wilmington
Curtin, Christopher James
Kelleher, Daniel Francis
Wier, Richard Royal, Jr.,

DISTRICT OF COLUMBIA

Washington
Gelb, Joseph Donald
Green, James Francis
Lapidus, Lawrence Searle
Maginnis, John C., III,
Mann, Lawrence Moses
McConnell, Nicholas Stillwell
Montedonico, Joseph
Nace, Barry John
Olender, Jack Harvey
Povich, David
Schmidt, Edward Craig
Schwartz, Victor Elliot
Singleton, Harry Michael
Walker, Betty Stevens
Wilson, Michael Moureau

FLORIDA

Altamonte Springs
Heindl, Phares Matthews

Boca Raton
David, Ronald Albert
Kitzes, William Fredric
Silver, Barry Morris
Willis, John Alexander

Boynton Beach
Hermann, Philip J.

Bradenton
Groseclose, Lynn Hunter

Brooksville
Vitola, John Raymond

Bushnell
Hagin, T. Richard

Clearwater
Free, E. LeBron

Cocoa Beach
Church, Glenn J.

Coral Gables
Anthony, Andrew John
Buell, Rodd Russell
Friedman, Marvin Ross
Gonzalez, Ervin Amado
Hoffman, Carl H.

Daytona Beach
Neitzke, Eric Karl

Fort Lauderdale
Bunnell, George Eli
Flynn, RoseAnn
James, Gordon, III,
Pomeroy, Gregg Joseph
Romanello, Nicholas Williams
Roselli, Richard Joseph
Sale, David Todd
Wich, Donald Anthony, Jr.,
Wolff, Clifford Alan

Fort Myers
Spivey, Randall L.

Fort Walton Beach
Lester, Arthur H.

Gainesville
Kurrus, Thomas William

Gulf Breeze
Burr, Timothy Fuller

Hobe Sound
Buetens, Eric D.

Hollywood
Korthals, Candace Durbin
Laura, Elaine S.
Phillips, Gary Stephen

Jacksonville
Bullock, Bruce Stanley
Coker, Howard Coleman
Cramer, Jeffrey Allen
Liles, Rutledge Richardson
Link, Robert James
O'Neal, Michael Scott, Sr.,
Reed, Ronald Ernst
White, Edward Alfred
Wirtz, Gregg Lee

Key West
Brihammar, B. Niklas

Lake Worth
Rose, Norman

Leesburg
Austin, Robert Eugene, Jr.,

Maitland
Bailey, Michael Keith
Edwards, James Alfred

Melbourne
Cacciatore, S. Sammy
Trachtman, Jerry H.

Miami
Arbuz, Joseph Robert
Aronovitz, Tod
Blumberg, Edward Robert
Burnett, Henry
Glinn, Franklyn Barry
Hickey, John Heyward (Jack Hickey)
Kritzer, Glenn Bruce
Lebowitz, Walter Bernard
Lipcon, Charles Roy
Podhurst, Aaron Samuel
Rosenn, Jonathan Rudge
Silverman, Bradley Allan
Stansell, Leland Edwin, Jr.,
Thornton, John William, Sr.,
Touby, Kathleen Anita
Vazquez, Michael Anthony

Miami Beach
Hertz, Stephen G.

Naples
Crehan, Joseph Edward
Rocuant, Paul A.

Orlando
Blackwell, Bruce Beuford
Handley, Leon Hunter
Hurt, Jennings Laverne, III,
Kelaher, James Peirce
Metz, Larry Edward
Mooney, Thomas Robert
Morgan, Mary Ann
Murrell, Robert George
Paul, David Aaron
Shapiro, Peter A.

Palm Beach Gardens
Telepas, George Peter

Panama City
Fensom, James B.
Sutton, Pamela Dru

Pensacola
McKenzie, James Franklin
Soloway, Daniel Mark

Plantation
Ogden, Anne D.
Sperry, Martin Jay

Punta Gorda
Goldman, Jason Brian

Saint Petersburg
Glass, Roy Leonard
Mann, Sam Henry, Jr.,
McKeown, H. Mary
Scott, Kathryn Fenderson

Sarasota
Byrd, L(awrence) Derek
Duggan, Kevin

Tallahassee
Davis, William Howard
Fonvielle, Charles David
Gievers, Karen A.
Kitchen, E.C. Deeno
Sheffield, Frank Elwyn

Tampa
Berkowitz, Herbert Mattis
Buell, Mark Paul
Clendinen, Craig P.
Epperson, Joel Rodman
Garrett, Howard Leon
Givens, Stann William
Loewenthal, Steven Richard
Martinez, Neri L.
Nutter, Robert Heinrich
Oehler, Richard Dale
Rardon, Larry L.
Somers, Clifford Louis
Vessel, Robert Leslie
Wagner, Frederick William (Bill Wagner)

Tavares
Johnson, Terri Sue

West Palm Beach
Djokic, Walter Henry
McAfee, William James
Montgomery, Robert Morel, Jr.,
Patterson, John B.
Prather, David C.
Scarola, John
Terry, Karen Elizabeth

Winter Park
Helms, Roger D.

GEORGIA

Acworth
Pope, Robert Daniel

Albany
Collum, Rick Daniel

Atlanta
Altman, Robert
Beckham, Walter Hull, III,
Billington, Barry E.
Blank, A(ndrew) Russell
Davis, E(dward) Marcus
Eckl, William Wray
Glaser, Arthur Henry
McAlpin, Kirk Martin
Pilcher, James Brownie
Smith, Walton Napier
Warncke, Jeffrey Scott
Wellon, Robert G.
Young, Michael Anthony
Zarrillo, Teri Dawn

Augusta
Miller, Alfred Montague
Smith, Larry Ira

Columbus
Brinkley, Jack Thomas
Harp, John Anderson
McGlamry, Max Reginald

Decatur
Apolinsky, Stephen Douglas

Douglas
Hayes, Dewey

Fayetteville
Johnson, Donald Wayne

Jasper
Marger, Edwin

Moultrie
Forehand, Jon Vincent

Newnan
Franklin, Bruce Walter

Norcross
Hahn, Stanley Robert, Jr.,

Roswell
England, John Melvin
Roland, Raymond William

Savannah
Kraeuter, R. Scot
Ladson, M. Brice
Lowry, Stephen Glenn
McCracken, Eugene Luke

Snellville
Giallanza, Charles Philip

Statesboro
Brogdon, W.M. "Rowe"
Franklin, James Burke

Tucker
Armstrong, Edwin Alan

Valdosta
Dodd, Roger J.
Terry, Guyton Otis, III,

Watkinsville
Wright, Robert Joseph

HAWAII

Honolulu
Ching, Wesley H. H.
Crumpton, Charles Whitmarsh
Edmunds, John Sanford
Fried, L. Richard, Jr.,
Fritz, Collin Martin
Gierlach, David J.
Harrison, William A.
Kawachika, James Akio
Kemper, Edward Crawford
Lawson, William Homer
Lee, Dale W.
Louie, David Mark
Morse, Jack Craig
Pavey, Judith Ann
Potts, Dennis Walker
Sumida, Kevin P.H.
Tam, Raymond J.
Umebayashi, Clyde Satoru

Kailua Kona
Zola, Michael S.

Kapolei
Zabanal, Eduardo Olegario

IDAHO

Blackfoot
Sorensen, Murray Jim

Boise
Dryden, William George
Lombardi, David Richard
Marsters, LaDawn Marie
Seiniger, William Breck, Jr.,
Wetherell, Michael E.
Whittier, Monte Ray

Caldwell
Kerrick, David Ellsworth

Idaho Falls
Ohman, John Michael

Twin Falls
Berry, L. Clyel
Sudweeks, Jay Dean
Wasden, Mark Robert

ILLINOIS

Alton
Talbert, Hugh Mathis

Belleville
Bauman, John Duane
Boyle, Richard Edward
Gossage, Roza
Heiligenstein, Christian E.
Ripplinger, George Raymond, Jr.,
Urban, Donald Wayne

Bloomington
Bragg, Michael Ellis
Kelly, Timothy William

Bourbonnais
McClure, Thomas Edward

Champaign
Harden, Richard Russell
Rawles, Edward Hugh

Chicago
Brown, Donald James, Jr.,
Burke, John Michael
Burke, William Joseph
Burns, Terrence Michael
Caner, Emin David
Connelly, Mary Jo
Costello, James Paul
Coughlin, Terrance J.
Daniels, John Draper
De Jong, David John
Doyle, John Robert
Fina, Paul Joseph
Frazen, Mitchell Hale
Henry, Brian Thomas
Karnezis, John T.
Knox, James Marshall
Kroot, Jason M.
Kunkle, William Joseph
Lavin, Terrence J.
Lowery, Timothy J.
McFadden, Monica Elizabeth
Menaker, Pamela Sakowicz
Motherway, Nicholas J.
Napleton, Robert Joseph
Nemeroff, David Brian
Pavalon, Eugene Irving
Pirok, Edward Warren
Rapoport, David E.
Roustan, Yvon Dominique
Salzetta, Paul Louis
Schoenfield, Rick Merrill
Tobin, Craig Daniel
Weaver, Timothy Allan

Chicago Heights
Cifelli, John Louis

Edwardsville
Carlson, Jon Gordon
Gorman, James Edward
Hopkins, John J.

Elgin
Carbary, Jonathan Leigh

Hoopeston
Manion, Paul Thomas

Jacksonville
Kuster, Larry Donald

La Grange
Coplan, Gregory Forrest

Libertyville
DeSanto, James John
Rallo, Douglas

Lincolnwood
Zaremski, Miles Jay

Lombard
O'Shea, Patrick Joseph

Mattoon
Corn, Stephen Leslie
Horsley, Jack Everett

Mount Vernon
Harvey, Morris Lane

Naperville
Levy, Steven B.

Peoria
O'Brien, Daniel Robert
Prusak, Maximilian Michael
Strodel, Robert Carl

Rockford
Mateer, Don M.

Saint Charles
Weir, William H.

Springfield
Duggan, Timothy E.

Waukegan
Henrick, Michael Francis

Wheaton
Cunningham, William Francis
Pollock, Bradley Neil

INDIANA

Anderson
Woodruff, Randall Lee

Bloomington
O'Connor, Joseph Daniel

Columbus
Harrison, Patrick Woods

Elkhart
Wicks, Charles Carter

Evansville
Berger, Charles Lee
Bodkin, Robert Thomas

Fort Wayne
Colvin, Sherrill William
Lebamoff, Ivan Argire
Murphy, Patrick Guyon
Young, Randy William

Gary
Lewis, Robert Lee

Greenfield
Dobbins, Caryl Dean

Hammond
Ruman, Saul I.

Indianapolis
Bruns, Beverly A.
Choplin, John M., II,
Cline, Lance Douglas
Conour, William Frederick
Eckert, Stephen Paul
Fisher, James R.
Helm, John R.
Hovde, Frederick Boyd
Hovde, Frederick Russell
Koch, Edna Mae
Lisher, John Leonard
Schreckengast, William Owen
Wellnitz, Craig Otto

Kokomo
Russell, Richard Lloyd

Lafayette
Layden, Charles Max

McManus, James William
Murguia, Ramon
Redfearn, Paul L., III,
Rooney, Robert Gerard
Siro, Rik Neal
Small, Stephen Bradley
Stoup, Arthur Harry
Vleisides, Gregory William
Wirken, James Charles

Lake Saint Louis
Callahan, Robert John, Jr.,

Lees Summit
Cownie, Willian Garry

Marshall
Peterson, William Allen

Maryville
McLaughlin, James Patrick

Rolla
Hickle, William Earl

Saint Ann
Johnson, Harold Gene

Saint Charles
Fleddermann, Stephen Roy
Ritter, Robert Thornton
Zerr, Richard Kevin

Saint Joseph
Kranitz, Theodore Mitchell

Saint Louis
Baum, Gordon Lee
Blanke, Richard Brian
Burke, Thomas Michael
Collins, James Slade, II,
Corrigan, William M.
Donaho, Timothy Lawrence, Jr.,
Farris, Spencer Edward
Floyd, Walter Leo
Hagerty, Patrick John
Hullverson, James Everett, Jr.,
Johnson, Weldon Neal
Marks, Murry Aaron
Neill, Joseph Vincent
Rabbitt, Daniel Thomas, Jr.,
Rice, Canice Timothy, Jr.,
Ringkamp, Stephen H.
Sugg, Reed Waller
Walsh, Joseph Leo, III,
Williams, Theodore Joseph, Jr.,

Sedalia
Rice, James Briggs, Jr.,

Springfield
Groce, Steven Fred
Lowther, Gerald Halbert
McDonald, William Henry
Myers, Ronald Lynn
Roberts, Patrick Kent
Umbarger, Jason T.

MONTANA

Billings
Dalthorp, George Carrol
Malee, Thomas Michael

Dillon
Suenram, Andy

Great Falls
Blewett, Alexander, III,

Helena
Doubek, John C.

Kalispell
Lerner, Alan Jay
Nardi, Stephen J.

Livingston
Jovick, Robert L.

Missoula
Morales, Julio K.

NEBRASKA

Lincoln
Guthery, John M.

North Platte
Kay, Stephen William

Omaha
Fellman, Richard Mayer
Gleason, James Mullaney
Grant, John P.

NEVADA

Carson City
Nelson, Bryan Maynard

Las Vegas
Galatz, Neil Gilbert
Goldberg, Aubrey
Gostin, Irwin
Lucas, Craig John
Sturman, Glorida J.

Reno
Kent, Stephen Smiley
Pagni, Albert Frank
Picker, Marc
Shaffer, Wayne Alan

Whitbeck, Jill Karla

NEW HAMPSHIRE

Contoocook
Mekeel, Robert K.

Exeter
Engel, David Chapin

Gorham
Cote, Thomas Jacques

Keene
Gardner, Eric Raymond

Manchester
Borofsky, Stephen Eric
Craig, James William
Dugan, Kevin F.
Hutchins, Peter Edward
Middleton, Jack Baer

Nashua
Hanson, Arnold Philip
Jette, Ernest Arthur

Portsmouth
Mason, J. William L.
Tober, Stephen Lloyd
Watson, Thomas Roger

NEW JERSEY

Asbury Park
Cernigliaro, Michael Joseph
Darnell, Alan Mark

Berlin
Goldstein, Benjamin

Brick
Tivenan, Charles Patrick

Cape May Court House
Fineberg, Robert Alan

Cherry Hill
D'Alfonso, Mario Joseph
Spielberg, Joshua Morris
Tomar, William

Clifton
Palma, Nicholas James
Randazzo, Anthony J.

Cranford
Gurrieri, Mario Charles
McCreedy, Edwin James

Edison
O'Brien, John Graham
Vercammen, Kenneth Albert

Englewood Cliffs
Masi, John Roger

Flemington
Miller, Louis H.

Florham Park
Calabrese, Arnold J.

Haddonfield
Andres, Kenneth G., Jr.,

Hammonton
Howell, Brian Graham

Hazlet
Brown, Christopher Robert

Hillsdale
Hodinar, Michael

Hoboken
Sommers, George R.

Jersey City
Nwele, Kenneth F.

Kearny
Brady, Lawrence Peter

Laurel Springs
Wood, Leonard James

Livingston
Nagel, Bruce H.
Rinsky, Joel Charles
Sukoneck, Ira David

Morris Plains
Mellinger, Louis Philip

Morristown
Clemente, Mark Andrew

Mount Holly
Mintz, Jeffry Alan

Newton
Morgenstern, Robert Terence

North Haledon
Harrington, Kevin Paul

Oakhurst
Rescinio, Albert John
Widman, Douglas Jack

Ocean
Weisberg, Adam Jon

Pleasantville
Sinderbrand, David I.

Princeton
Benesch, Katherine
Greene, Steven Kevin
Stern, Bruce H.
Theroux, William Gerard

Randolph
Scheneck, Carol Ann

Ridgewood
Seigel, Jan Kearney

Roseland
Smith, Wendy Hope

Saddle Brook
Knopf, Barry Abraham

Sewell
Crouse, Farrell R.

Short Hills
Kaye, Marc Mendell
Leviss, Stewart Michael

Somerville
Lieberman, Marvin Samuel

South Orange
Feinberg, Paul H.

Teaneck
Kaplan, Howard M(ark)

Trenton
Campbell, Bernard Alexander, Jr.,
Doherty, Robert Christopher

Warren
Kraus, Steven Gary

Wayne
Fiedler, Laurie W.

Westfield
Smith, Francis M.

Westwood
McGuirl, Robert Joseph

Woodcliff Lake
Phillips, John C.

NEW MEXICO

Albuquerque
Beach, Arthur O'Neal
Cargo, David Francis
Caruso, Mark John
Moughan, Peter Richard, Jr.,
Rawley, James Albert
Thiel, Albert Nicholas, Jr.,
Weeth, George Wright
Word, Terry Mullins

Deming
Sherman, Frederick Hood

Farmington
Moeller, Floyd Douglas
Titus, Victor Allen

Hobbs
Stout, Lowell

Roswell
Haines, Thomas David, Jr.,
Kraft, Richard Lee

Ruidoso
Dutton, Dominic Edward

Santa Fe
Brannen, Jeffrey Richard
Casey, Patrick Anthony
Farber, Steven Glenn
McClaugherty, Joe L.
Weckesser, Susan Oneacre
Zorie, Stephanie Marie

NEW YORK

Albany
Dulin, Thomas N.
Fanciullo, William Patrick
Laird, Edward DeHart, Jr.,
Linnan, James Daniel

Binghamton
Gates, Gregory Ansel
Gouldin, David Millen
Kramer, Philip Joseph
Price, Paul Marnell

Bronx
Verrelli, Anthony Louis

Brooklyn
Rayo, Mark James
Schussler, Theodore

Buffalo
De Marie, Anthony Joseph
Dietrich, Joseph Edward, III,
Elibol, David Hakan
Feuerstein, Alan Ricky
Gentile, Carmen James
Hayes, J. Michael
Jasen, Matthew Joseph
Lazroe, Jeffrey Alan
Pajak, David Joseph

Stachowski, Michael Joseph
Szanyi, Kevin Andrew

Camillus
Endieveri, Anthony Frank

Carle Place
Mulhern, Edwin Joseph
Seiden, Steven Jay

Carmel
Collins, John Peter

Chestnut Ridge
Burns, Richard Owen

Dansville
Vogel, John Walter

Delmar
Cavanaugh, John Joseph, Jr.,

East Northport
Juliano, John Louis

Elma
Markello, Jeffrey Philip

Farmingdale
O'Brien, Joan Susan

Flushing
Schwartz, Estar Alma
Suh, Edward H.

Garden City
Sawyer, James

Glens Falls
Meyer, Martin Arthur

Great Neck
Kors, Murray Daniel
Lowenbraun, Solomon Mortimer

Hamburg
Wiltse, Peter Christian

Hauppauge
Scheine, Edward Robert

Hicksville
Giuffré, John Joseph

Highland
Schonberg, Bruce A.

Hornell
Pulos, William Whitaker

Hudson
Howard, Andrew Baker

Islandia
Buckley, Terrence Patrick

Jericho
Corso, Frank Mitchell

Kew Gardens
Reichel, Aaron Israel
Sparrow, Robert E.

Latham
Brearton, James Joseph

Long Island City
Forchelli, Charles Nicholas

Mahopac
Sequeira, Manuel Alexandre, Jr.,

Melville
Agoglia, Emmet John
Schoenfeld, Michael P.

Mineola
Bartlett, Clifford Adams, Jr.,
Fowler, David Thomas
Kelly, Shawn Paul
Raab, Ira Jerry
Rubine, Robert Samuel
Stock, Thomas John
Wagner, Gary Alan

New Hartford
McKennan, John T.

New Hyde Park
Jaffe, Richard S.
Lee, Brian Edward

New Rochelle
Kreppel, Milton Mark

New York
Bluestone, Andrew Lavoott
Colbert, Douglas Marc
Damashek, Philip Michael
Dankner, Jay Warren
Edelman, Paul Sterling
Gair, Anthony Henry
Garfield, Martin Richard
Garson, Andrew S.
Golomb, David Bela
Greenberg, Hayley
Gulino, Frank
Gurfein, Richard Alan
Habian, Bruce George
Hanover, Richard
Issler, Harry
Jacobowitz, Harold Saul
Kelmachter, Leslie Debra
Kilsch, Gunther H.
Koob, Charles Edward
Kushel, Glenn Elliot
LeBlang, Skip Alan

Lesman, Michael Steven
Liss, Norman
Loscalzo, Anthony Joseph
McGrath, Christopher Thomas
Moore, Thomas A.
O'Connell, Margaret Sullivan
Oliveri, Paul Francis
Pecoraro, Steven John
Pinczower, Kenneth Ephraim
Ritter, Ann L.
Rivera, Walter
Salvan, Sherwood Allen
Shandell, Richard Elliot
Smiley, Guy Ian
Strober, Eric Saul
Toner, Stephen
Weinstock, Leonard
Weiser, Martin Jay
Weitz, Harvey
Wilensky, Saul

Newburgh
Liberth, Richard Francis
Milligram, Steven Irwin

Ossining
Daly, William Joseph

Poughkeepsie
Kranis, Michael David
Sproat, Christine A.

Rhinebeck
Melley, Steven Michael

Rochester
Geiger, Alexander
Heyman, Sidney
Law, Michael R.
Palermo, Anthony Robert
Spoto, David Dennis
Trevett, Thomas Neil

Rockville Centre
Buchman, Lawrence Jay

Salamanca
Brady, Thomas Carl

Schenectady
Taub, Eli Irwin

Smithtown
Brooks, Sondra
Spellman, Thomas Joseph, Jr.,

South Richmond Hill
Goldsmith, Michael Lawrence
Scheich, John F.

Staten Island
Parnese, John S.

Syracuse
Bogart, William Harry
Butler, John Edward
Hildebrandt, George Frederick
King, Bernard T.
Murphy, Timothy Paul
Piraino, Andrew Norman
Rivette, Francis Robert
Rosenthal, Alan
Williams, Samuel Robert
Zimmerman, Aaron Mark

Troy
Finkel, Sanford Norman
Frost, Jerome Kenneth
Jones, E. Stewart, Jr.,

Valley Stream
Isaacs, Leonard Bernard

Warsaw
Cook, Charlotte Smallwood

Watertown
Gebo, Stephen Wallace

White Plains
Cohn, Julius W.
D'Aloise, Lawrence T., Jr.,
Greenspan, Michael Evan
Kalish, Daniel A.
Keane, Thomas J.
Nesci, Vincent Peter
Ryan, Robert Davis
Silverman, Donald N.

Williamsville
Ross, Christopher T.W.

Yonkers
Connors, James Patrick

NORTH CAROLINA

Asheboro
Bunch, W(alter) Edward

Asheville
Chidnese, Patrick N.
Leake, Larry Bruce
Sharpe, Keith Yount

Charlotte
Brackett, Martin Luther, Jr.,
Campbell, Clair Gilliland
Eve, Robert Michael, Jr.,
Goodwin, Walter Henry
Raper, William Cranford

Dunn
Pope, Patrick Harris

Durham
Fisher, Stewart Wayne
Markham, Charles Buchanan

Elkin
Gillespie, James Davis

Fayetteville
Townsend, William Jackson

Greensboro
Clark, David McKenzie
Koonce, Neil Wright

Greenville
Batten, Stephen John
Melvin, R. Bailey
Romary, Peter John Michael

Hickory
Adams, Valeree R.

High Point
Baker, Walter Wray, Jr.,

Jamestown
Schmitt, William Allen

Marion
Burgin, Charles Edward

Raleigh
Hunter, Richard Samford, Jr.,
Millberg, John C.
Suhr, Paul Augustine

Roxboro
Weinberger, Joseph Charles, Jr.,

Selma
Bryant, Robert W., Jr.,

Smithfield
Schulz, Bradley Nicholas

Tarboro
O'Malley, Susan Marie

Warsaw
Thompson, Eugene Cebron, III,

Winston Salem
Early, James H., Jr.,
Kelly, James Howard, Jr.,

NORTH DAKOTA

Dickinson
Greenwood, Dann E.

Fargo
Ficek, Gary A.

Grand Forks
Arnason, Joel Frederick
Seaworth, Mary Ellen

OHIO

Akron
Cody, Daniel Schaffner
Glinsek, Gerald John
Schrader, Alfred Eugene

Avon Lake
Long, David Carter

Beavercreek
Stadnicar, Joseph William

Canton
Huryn, Christopher Michael

Cincinnati
Chesley, Stanley Morris
Cohen, Edward
Davis, Robert Lawrence
Gehrig, Michael Ford
Harris, Jerald David
Holschuh, John David, Jr.,
Lutz, James Gurney
Mann, David Scott
Mara, Timothy Gerald
Neltner, Michael Martin
Scacchetti, David J.
Whitaker, Glenn Virgil
Woodside, Frank C., III,

Cleveland
Alcox, Patrick Joseph
Bacon, Brett Kermit
Birne, Kenneth Andrew
Cohn, Mark Barry
Coyne, John Coughlin
Domiano, Joseph Charles
Duncan, Ed Eugene
Eklund, Claudia Rieth
Gardner, Steven Leslie
Havens, Hunter Scott
Lowe, James Allison
Maher, Edward Joseph
Sanislo, Paul Steve
Shapiro, Fred David
Spero, Keith Erwin
Stewart, Lawrence Edward
Summers, William Lawrence
Szaller, James Francis
Trapp, Mary Jane
Weaver, Robin Geoffrey
Weinberger, Peter Henry

Columbus
Adams, John Marshall
Ayers, James Cordon
Belton, John Thomas
Binning, J. Boyd
Burchfield, James Ralph
Campbell, Joel Roderick
Chappelear, Stephen Eric
Lippe, Jerry Leonard
Plymale, Ronald Elton
Radnor, Alan T.
Ray, Frank Allen
Robol, Richard Thomas
Tait, Robert E.
Tyack, Thomas Michael
Yeazel, Keith Arthur

Dayton
Jenks, Thomas Edward
Krebs, Leo Francis
Schneble, Alfred William, III,
Yim, Edward Chang

Dublin
Maloon, Jerry L.

Findlay
Kentris, George Lawrence

Franklin
Ruppert, Rupert Earl

Hamilton
Holcomb, Jeffrey G.

Jackson
Lewis, Richard M.

Lima
Jacobs, Ann Elizabeth

Portsmouth
Gerlach, Franklin Theodore

Ravenna
Giulitto, Paula Christine

Sandusky
Bailey, K. Ronald

Toledo
St. Clair, Donald David

Twinsburg
Doyle, Duane Lynn

Wadsworth
McIlvaine, James Ross

Warren
Kafantaris, George Nicholas
Vigorito, Philip Michael

Wooster
Kennedy, Charles Allen

Xenia
Chappars, Timothy Stephen

Youngstown
Ausnehmer, John Edward
Blair, Richard Bryson
Carlin, Clair Myron
Giannini, Matthew Carlo

Zanesville
Micheli, Frank James

OKLAHOMA

Cherokee
Stein, Sam L.

Norman
Fairbanks, Robert Alvin

Oklahoma City
Fenton, Elliott Clayton
Ferguson, Steven Edward
Phelps, Anthony David

Ponca City
Raley, John W., Jr.,

Tulsa
Atkinson, Michael Pearce
Brewster, Clark Otto
Bryant, Hubert Hale
Dunn, Frederick Louis, III,
Howard, Gene Claude
Miller, James Anthony

OREGON

Eugene
Mumford, William Porter, II,
Sahlstrom, E(lmer) Bernard

Newport
Greco, Guy Benjamin

Portland
Bovarnick, Paul Simon
Carr, Kathleen M.
Clark, Jennie L.
Foote, Jeffrey Paul
Hart, John Edward
Jolles, Bernard
Kennedy, Jack Leland
Rieke, Forrest Neill
Robinowitz, Charles
Savage, John William
Schuster, Philip Frederick , II,
Shinn, Michael Robert
Sokol, Larry Nides
Swanson, Leslie Martin, Jr.,
Wei, Li

Salem
Feibleman, Gilbert Bruce
Roy, Matthew Lansing

PENNSYLVANIA

Allentown
Altemose, Mark Kenneth

Altoona
Serbin, Richard Martin

Bala Cynwyd
Aris, John Lynnwood
Olley, Michael Joseph

Beaver
Petrush, John Joseph

Easton
Brown, Robert Carroll

Edinboro
Travis, Grant Carner

Erie
Bernard, Bruce William
McNair, Timothy Dean

Harrisburg
Angino, Richard Carmen
Cooper, Jeffrey
Gale, Randall Glenn
Hafer, Joseph Page
Lighty, Fredrick W.
Miller, Leslie Anne
Stefanon, Anthony

Hazleton
Schiavo, Pasco Louis

Indiana
Bell, Paul Anthony, II,

Jenkintown
Friedman, Ralph David
Worthington, Sandra Boulton

Johnstown
Glosser, William Louis

Kingston
Meyer, Martin Jay

Lancaster
Hall, Thomas Wayne
Roda, Joseph Francis
Zimmerman, D(onald) Patrick

Mc Keesport
Kessler, Steven Fisher

Media
D'Amico, Andrew J.
DiOrio, Robert Michael
Farber, Howard
Firkser, Robert Michael
Smith, John Churchman
Tomlinson, Herbert Weston

New Castle
Babb, Alfred Ward
Manolis, James William

Newtown
Kardos, Mel D.

Norristown
Devine, James I.

Paoli
Griffith, Edward

Perkasie
Roeger, William Coley, Jr.,

Philadelphia
Bartolomeo, Paul Joseph, Jr.,
Binder, David Franklin
Blumstein, Edward
Buccino, Ernest John, Jr.,
Coleman, Robert J.
Collings, Robert L.
D'Angelo, George A.
Dragon, Albert
Goldberg, Joseph
Goldberg, Marvin Allen
Hanselmann, Fredrick Charles
Kanter, Seymour
Kline, Thomas Richard
Koral, Mark A.
Kormes, John Winston
McHugh, James Joseph
Patton, Peter Mark
Rhoads, Nancy Glenn
Rosenberg, Howell K.
Schoener, George Francis, Jr.,
Wilson, Rhonda Hill

Pipersville
Carr, Stephen Kerry

Pittsburgh
Bellisario, Domenic Anthony
Bochicchio, Vito Salvatore
Breault, Theodore Edward
Cusick, Daniel Francis
Fishman, Craig L.
Hurnyak, Christina Kaiser
Krebs, Robert Alan
Meyers, Jerry Ivan
Miller, David A.
Perry, Jon Robert
Sokol, Stephen M.
Strader, James David
Tarasi, Louis Michael, Jr.,
Tully, Bernard Michael

Pottsville
Tamulonis, Frank Louis, Jr.,

Scranton
Wilson, Charles Frank

State College
Nollau, Lee Gordon

Trevose
McEvilly, James Patrick, Jr.,

Uniontown
Davis, James Thomas

Washington
Richman, Stephen I.

White Oak
Pribanic, Victor Hunter

Wilkes Barre
O'Donnell, Catherine Rose

Williamsport
Ertel, Allen Edward

RHODE ISLAND

Cranston
Tammelleo, A. David

Providence
Demopulos, Harold William
Jones, Lauren Evans
McConnell, John James, Jr.,
Murphy, James Truden

Warwick
St. Pierre, Michael A.

Woonsocket
Koutsogiane, Phillip Charles

SOUTH CAROLINA

Charleston
Hood, Robert Holmes
Kahn, Ellis Irvin
Spitz, Hugo Max

Columbia
Blanton, Hoover Clarence
Brown, Robert Charles
Harvey, Jonathan Matthew
Jones, Hartwell Kelley, Jr.,
Sheftman, Howard Stephen

Greenville
Christian, Warren Harold, Jr.,
Christophillis, Constantine S.
Steele, C. Carlyle

Hilton Head Island
McKay, John Judson, Jr.,

Langley
Bell, Robert Morrall

Laurens
Burney, Rhett D.

Mount Pleasant
Hahn, H. Blair

Myrtle Beach
Breen, David Hart

North Charleston
Wigger, Jarrel L.

North Myrtle Beach
Wheless, Albert Eugene

Pawleys Island
Daniel, J. Reese

Spartanburg
Anthony, Kenneth C., Jr.,
Smith, William Douglas

Summerville
Hardee-Thomas, Marva A.

Sumter
Seth, J. Cabot

West Columbia
Applegate, William Russell

SOUTH DAKOTA

Belle Fourche
Day, Michael W.

TENNESSEE

Chattanooga
Gearhiser, Charles Josef

Cleveland
Miller, Rodney Craig

Cookeville
Day, David Owen

Dyersburg
Wilder, James Sampson, III,

Etowah
Parker, Eugene LeRoy, III,

Jackson
Pietrowski, R. Scott

Johnson City
King, Robert Lewis

Knoxville
Cremins, William Carroll
Hartsoe, Mark Charles
Oberman, Steven
Ownby, Jere Franklin, III,
Routh, John William
White, Edward Gibson, II,

Memphis
Gipson, Harvey Lofton
Green, Sheldon Neal
Harvey, Albert C.
Hunt, Sean Antone
Ledbetter, Paul Mark
Taylor, Jerry F(rancis)

Morristown
Murphy, Michael Cary

Murfreesboro
Windrow, Rachelle L.

Nashville
Barrow, Clisby Hall
Bramlett, Paul Kent
Cooney, Charles Hayes
Day, John Arthur
Gross, Edward Jordan

Newport
Bell, John Alton

Paris
Rose, Todd Alan

Rogersville
Skelton, Mark Albert

Soddy Daisy
Leitner, Paul Revere

Springfield
Wilks, Larry Dean

TEXAS

Arlington
Jensen, John Robert

Austin
Allison, James Purney
Barnes, Natasha Lynn
Bishop, Daniel W.
Cortez, Hernan Glenn
Davis, Don Lawrence
Feazell, Vic
Hile, Richard C.
Kilgore, Gary Lynn
McConnico, Stephen E.
Pena, Richard
Probus, Michael Maurice, Jr.,
Smith, Peyton Noble
Spivey, Broadus Autry
Tighe, Austin
Whitehurst, William Oscar

Azle
Henvey, John William

Beaumont
Black, Robert Allen
Dowell, James Dale
Orwig, Matthew Dane
Scofield, Louis M., Jr.,

Bellaire
Soffar, William Douglas

Cleburne
MacLean, John Ronald

Corpus Christi
Fancher, Rick
Miller, Carroll Gerard, Jr., (Gerry Miller)
White, Brantley W.

Dallas
Anderson, E. Karl
Biermacher, Kenneth Wayne
DelHomme, Beverly Ann
Ellis, Alfred Wright (Al Ellis)
Girards, James Edward
Holmes, James Hill, III,
Kent, David Charles
Malouf, Stephen Ferris
Mighell, Kenneth John
Miller, Deborah Slye
Murray, Jay J.
Smith, Larry Francis
Stinnett, Mark Allan
Ticer, Mark Allen
Turley, Linda
Wileman, George Robert

Edinburg
Julia, Katherine Driscoll

El Paso
Marshall, Richard Treeger
McDonald, Charles Edward

Fort Worth
Berenson, William Keith
Broiles, David
Chappell, David Franklin

Cottongame, W. Brice
Dean, Beale
Dent, Edward Dwain
Hayes, Larry B.
Jensen, Keith Michael
Soward, Joe Weldon, II,
Streck, Frederick Louis, III,
Swift, Thomas Grover, Jr.,
Wallach, David Michael

Friendswood
Youngdahl, Jay Thomas

Galveston
Neves, Kerry Lane

Houston
Agosto, Benny, Jr.,
Berg, David Howard
Brinson, Gay Creswell, Jr.,
Carver, Teresa Ann
Coghlan, Kelly Jack
Eckhardt, William Rudolf, III,
Elias, Raymon Todd
Essmyer, Michael Martin
Fudge, Edward William
Harris, Warren Wayne
Hawash, Michael Andrew
Hooper, Scott Alan
Kline, Allen Haber, Jr.,
Lamson, Michael Alan
Lilly, Joyce Stamp
Mallia, Michael Patrick
McFall, Donald Beury
McQuarrie, Claude Monroe, III,
McWherter, Louis Alfred
Nacol, Mae
Nations, Howard Lynn
Nunnally, Knox Dillon
Pettiette, Alison Yvonne
Pitts, Gary Benjamin
Raley, John Wesley, III,
Redden, Joe Winston, Jr.,
Schechter, Arthur Louis
Smith, Langdon
Sorrels, Randall Owen
Taheri, Marshall M.
Vaughan, Stephen Michael
Wood, Judson Robert

Lamesa
Saleh, John

Longview
Harrison, Guy Newell

Lubbock
Harrell, Walter Hugh
Purdom, Thomas James
Saied, Robert Mack

Mc Kinney
Dowdy, William Clarence, Jr.,

Mcallen
Carrera, Victor Manuel

Midland
MacDonald, Leland Lloyd

Odessa
Hendrick, Benard Calvin, VII,

Orange
Townsend, Rodney Allen

Pearland
Yaziji, Nejd

Rockwall
Holt, Charles William, Jr.,

San Angelo
Moeller, Galen Ashley

San Antonio
Branton, James LaVoy
Crosley, Thomas Andrew
Henry, Peter York
Hohman, A. J., Jr.,
Maloney, Marynell
Maloney, Pat, Sr.,
Patrick, Dane Herman
Putman, Michael (Michael James Putman)
Valadez, Robert Allen
Welmaker, Forrest Nolan

Spring
Beauchamp, Gary Fay

Sugar Land
Aldrich, Lovell W(eld)

Tyler
Ellis, Donald Lee
Green, Jay Nelson

Uvalde
Kerby, Yale Leland

Waco
Hall, Donald Orell
Tekell, David Glenn

Wharton
Roades, John Leslie

Wichita Falls
Altman, William Kean
Williams, Steven Mark

UTAH

Logan
Jenkins, James C.

Ogden
Kaufman, Steven Michael
Sullivan, Kevin Patrick
Warner, Frank Shrake

Provo
Abbott, Charles Favour

Salt Lake City
Atkin, Gary Eugene
Humpherys, LeGrande Rich
Lambert, Dale John
Sine, Wesley Franklin
Wilde, Robert

South Jordan
Larson, Bryan A.

VERMONT

Burlington
Cory, Barbara Ellen
McMahon, Dennis C.
Shoup, Tina Louise

Montpelier
Diamond, M. Jerome
Valerio, Matthew F.

Rutland
Faignant, John Paul

Shelburne
Molloy, Maureen Katherine

VIRGINIA

Abingdon
Conway, Berry Leslie, II,
Shortridge, Judy Beth

Alexandria
Cassell, Richard Emmett
DiMuro, Bernard Joseph
Hirschkop, Philip Jay
Levine, Steven Mark
Summers, Alicia Lehnes

Arlington
Korman, James William
Malone, William Grady

Charlottesville
Armstrong, Richard Charles
Chandler, Lawrence Bradford, Jr.,
Jones, Christopher Andrew
Slaughter, Edward Ratliff, Jr.,
Wyatt, Deborah Chasen

Chester
Gray, Charles Robert

Danville
Conway, French Hoge

Fairfax
Keith, John A.C.

Falls Church
Van Oeveren, Edward Lanier

Fredericksburg
Allen, Edward Lefebvre

Galax
Kapp, John Paul

Hampton
Smith, Stephen Mark

Hot Springs
Deeds, Robert Creigh

Lynchburg
Angel, James Joseph
Wetzel, Robert Charles

Manassas
Scriven, Wayne Marcus

Martinsville
Frith, Douglas Kyle
Williams, Ebb Harry, III,

Mc Lean
Corson, J. Jay, IV,
Halagao, Avelino Garabiles
Redmond, Robert

Mechanicsville
Martin, Ronald Allen

Newport News
Segall, James Arnold

Norfolk
Davis, Terry Hunter, Jr.,
Drescher, John Webb
Fletcher, John Richard
McCaa, James Cureton, III,
Rashkind, Alan Brody

Norton
Jessee, Roy Mark

Petersburg
Shell, Louis Calvin

Portsmouth
Moody, Willard James, Sr.,

Radford
Davis, Richard Waters

Reston
Bredehoft, Elaine Charlson

Richmond
Baer, Tommy Percy
Cantor, Irvin Victor
Levit, Jay J(oseph)
Spahn, Gary Joseph

Roanoke
Hylton, Myles Talbert
McGarry, Richard Lawrence
Mundy, Gardner Marshall

Salem
Griffith, H(oward) Morgan

Vienna
Cochran, Stephen Grey

Virginia Beach
Blachman, Michael Joel
Buzard, David Andrew
Hajek, Francis Paul
Schafer, Gerard Thomas Roger

Warrenton
Morrison, Paul A.

Woodbridge
Roberts, Charles Bren

Wytheville
Crewe, Trenton Guy, Jr.,

WASHINGTON

Bainbridge Island
Otorowski, Christopher Lee

Centralia
Buzzard, Steven Ray

Everett
Mestel, Mark David

Gig Harbor
Thompson, Ronald Edward

Hoquiam
Kahler, Ray William
Kessler, Keith Leon

Kennewick
Hames, William Lester

Mount Vernon
Moser, C. Thomas

Olympia
Chambers, Thomas Jefferson
Williams, Wayne Leroy

Pullman
Savage, David William

Renton
Barber, Mark Edward
Swanson, Arthur Dean

Seattle
Bailey, William Scherer
Budigan, William Clay
Cornell, Kenneth Lee
Corning, Nicholas F.
Davis, Susan Rae
Kraft, Robert Morris
Leed, Roger Melvin
Loftus, Thomas Daniel
Longfelder, Lawrence Lee
Losey, Beverley Brown
Lundgren, Gail M.
Mussehl, Robert Clarence
Peterson, Jan Eric
Radtke, Derek Paul
Scott, Brian David
Stevens, David Bruce
Vogel, David Seth
Whitehead, James Fred, III,
Whitson, Lish

Spokane
Eymann, Richard Charles
Harbaugh, Daniel Paul
Leipham, Jay Edward
Pontarolo, Michael Joseph
Stone, Donald Gene

Tacoma
Condon, David Bruce
Hostnik, Charles Rivoire
Morgan, Cynthia Makie
Riggio, Michael V.

Vancouver
Karpinski, John Stanley

Yakima
Tenney, Robert Carl

WEST VIRGINIA

Bluefield
Evans, Wayne Lewis
Kantor, Isaac Norris

Charleston
Berthold, Robert Vernon, Jr.,
Brenneman Harrah, Sandra
Cline, Michael Robert
Crislip, Stephen Ray
Kiblinger, Cindy Jo
Rowe, Larry Linwell
Salango, C. Benjamin
Zak, Robert Joseph

Fairmont
Sawyer, Sean Jeffrey
Stanton, George Patrick, Jr.,

Huntington
Offutt, Denver Clyde, Jr.,
Underwood, Mark Forest

Martinsburg
Martin, Clarence Eugene, III,

Morgantown
Ringer, Darrell Wayne (Dan Ringer)

Parkersburg
Merriman, William Otto, Jr.,

Weirton
Fahey, William Thomas, II,

Weston
Oldaker, Bradley Russell

WISCONSIN

Amery
Gust, Gerald Norman

Appleton
Lonergan, Kevin
Lorge, Robert Gerald Augustine

Cross Plains
Atterbury, Lee Richard

Delafield
Hausman, C. Michael

Elm Grove
Miracle, Dale Neil

Franklin
Konstantakis, Georgia L.

Green Bay
Burnett, Ralph George

La Crosse
Skemp, William

Madison
Kelly, T. Christopher
Mowris, Gerald William
Schooler, Steven James
Steingass, Susan R.
Winnig, Joel Bruce

Menomonie
Steans, Phillip Michael

Milwaukee
Daily, Frank J(erome)
Donovan, Michael Joseph
Gaines, Irving David
Habush, Robert Lee
Hoefle, Paul Ryan
Karp, David Barry
Kmiec, Steven Gerard
Levine, Herbert
Slavik, Donald Harlan
Terschan, Frank Robert
Van Grunsven, Paul Robert

Monona
Boller, Matthew Hubly

Oshkosh
Curtis, George Warren
Kelly, John Martin
Lampe, Ronald L.
Wilde, William Richard

Osseo
Feltes, Charles Victor

Racine
Gasiorkiewicz, Eugene Anthony
Rudebusch, Alice Ann

Rhinelander
Saari, John William, Jr.,

Wausau
Gray, Robert Joseph
Grischke, Alan Edward
Molinaro, Thomas J.

Wauwatosa
Bonneson, Paul Garland

WYOMING

Casper
Combs, W(illiam) Henry, III,

Cheyenne
Mackey, Terrence Wayne

Cody
Webster, C. Edward, II,

Gillette
Bailey, Daniel B.

Jackson
Clauss, C. David
Shockey, Gary Lee
Spence, Gerald Leonard

Rock Springs
Honaker, Richard Henderson

Wheatland
Hunkins, Raymond Breedlove

TERRITORIES OF THE UNITED STATES

PUERTO RICO

Ponce
Leon-Sotomayor, Jose Rafael

MEXICO

Guadalajara
Godoy, Cesar Eduardo

AUSTRIA

Vienna
Frank, Alix

CZECH REPUBLIC

Prague
Honsa, Frantisek

GERMANY

Duedenbuettel
Pfennigstorf, Werner

PHILIPPINES

Makati City
Gonzales, Ponciano Jr. Concepcion

SCOTLAND

Balintore
Cook, Glen André

SWEDEN

Göteborg
Westerberg, Siv Öman

ADDRESS UNPUBLISHED

Ashkin, Roberta Ellen
Bandy, Jack D.
Bell, Pamela Cole
Berman, Richard Bruce
Boone, Richard Winston, Sr.,
Buford, Floyd Moye, Jr.,
Carlson, Alan Douglas
Carmack, Mildred Jean
Clark, Richard Edward
Corlett, Edward Stanley, III,
Coviello, Frank Joseph
Dupree, David H.
Ehrlich, Stephen Richard
Embry, Stephen Creston
Erwin, Gregory Scott
Fleischman, Herman Israel
Gilbert, Ronald Rhea
Grady, Maureen Frances
Griffith, Steven Franklin, Sr.,
Guehl, Robert Lee
Hall-Barron, Deborah
Harper, Harlan, Jr.,
Hess, Chad Brandon
Hoffman, Alan Craig
Hoglund, John Andrew
Horn, Andrew Warren
Howell, Ally Windsor
Hughes, Roy Fredericks
Johnson, Richard Wesley
Kell, Scott K.
Kellerman, Edwin
Klein, Linda Ann
Leaf, Frederick Peter
Lippes, Richard James
Mallas, Kostantinos
McAlhany, Toni Anne
Moehle, Carm Robert
Moore, Lloyd Evans
Mugridge, David Raymond
Pennington, Alyce Loraine
Purtle, John Ingram
Rawls, Frank Macklin
Rawls, John D.
Richeson, Hugh Anthony, Jr.,
Ricks, Cecil Earl, Jr.,
Saporito, Steven
Schmoll, Harry F., Jr.,
Speight, John B.
Strick, Gerald Jay
Subin, Florence
Swinnen, Benoit M.J.
Tanenbaum, Jay Harvey
Thornton, J. Pat
Vigil, David Charles
Wagner, Arthur Ward, Jr.,
Wells, Wayne Alton
Wessel, Peter
Wheeler, R(ichard) Kenneth
White, John Joseph, III,
White, William Nelson

Wilson, Virgil James, III,

PROBATE *See also* Estate planning; Taxation, estate

UNITED STATES

ALABAMA

Birmingham
Cicio, Anthony Lee
Foster, Arthur Key, Jr.,
Gamble, Joseph Graham, Jr.,
Irons, William Lee
Thompson, Charles Amos

Florence
Schuessler, Cindy Sandlin

Guntersville
McLaughlin, Jeffrey Rex

Huntsville
Richardson, Patrick William

Jasper
Thomas, Steven Allen

Mobile
Brock, Glen Porter, Jr.,
Holland, Lyman Faith, Jr.,

Montgomery
Leslie, Henry Arthur
Smith, Jerome David

Opelika
Samford, Yetta Glenn, Jr.,

ALASKA

Anchorage
Bundy, David Hollister

Kodiak
Jamin, Matthew Daniel

Salcha
Rice, Julian Casavant

ARIZONA

Kingman
Basinger, Richard Lee

Lake Havasu City
Cookson, Kirk S.

Mesa
Gunderson, Brent Merrill

Phoenix
Haga, David L.
Olsen, Alfred Jon
Swartz, Melvin Jay

Rio Rico
Ryan, John Duncan

Scottsdale
Crawford, Robert F.
Lowry, Edward Francis, Jr.,
Roberts, Jean Reed

Yuma
Hunt, Gerald Wallace

ARKANSAS

Fayetteville
Epley, Lewis Everett, Jr.,
Lushbaugh, Brad

Hot Springs National Park
Schnipper, Don Martin

Little Rock
Haught, William Dixon
Stockburger, Jean Dawson

Monticello
Ball, William Kenneth

Morrilton
Denniston, Jeannie L.

North Little Rock
Patty, Claibourne Watkins, Jr.,

Pine Bluff
Ramsay, Louis Lafayette, Jr.,

Searcy
Hughes, Thomas Morgan, III,

Warren
Claycomb, Hugh Murray

CALIFORNIA

Alameda
Stonehouse, James Adam

Antioch
Richards, Gerald Thomas

Berkeley
Ogg, Wilson Reid
Ross, Julia

Beverly Hills
Brown, Hermione Kopp

Campbell
Castello, Raymond Vincent

Downey
Schauf, Carolyn Jane

Fullerton
Roberts, Mark Scott

Granada Hills
Sindon, Geoffrey Stuart

Grass Valley
Hawkins, Richard Michael

Greenbrae
Bonapart, Alan David

Hayward
Smith, John Kerwin

Huntington Beach
Armstrong, Alan Leigh

La Jolla
Shannahan, William Paul

Long Beach
Cockriel, Stephen Eugene
Tikosh, Mark Axente

Los Angeles
Antin, Michael
Campbell, Jennifer Louise
Gorman, Joseph Gregory, Jr.,
Rae, Matthew Sanderson, Jr.,
Rogers, John Torrey, Jr.,
Ruskey, John A.
Stephens, George Edward, Jr.,
Tobisman, Stuart Paul
Weinstock, Harold

Mill Valley
Dyer, Gregory Clark

Morgan Hill
Foster, John Robert

Newport Beach
Allen, Russell G.
Mallory, Frank Linus

North Hollywood
Kreger, Melvin Joseph
Zimring, Stuart David

Palm Desert
Reinhardt, Benjamin Max

Palo Alto
Miller, Michael Patiky

Palos Verdes Estates
Toftness, Cecil Gillman

Pasadena
Ashley-Farrand, Margalo
Calleton, Theodore Edward
D'Angelo, Robert William
Davis, Edmond Ray
Myers, R(alph) Chandler
Walch, Spencer David

Paso Robles
Knecht, James Herbert

Placentia
Evans, Winthrop Shattuck

Rancho Mirage
Leydorf, Frederick Leroy

Sacramento
Burton, Randall James
Craven, Thomas Arthur
Mueller, Virginia Schwartz

San Clemente
Fisher, Myron R.

San Diego
Hansotte, Louis Bernard
Hofflund, Paul
Payne, Margaret Anne

San Francisco
Friedman, K. Bruce
Guggenhime, Richard Johnson
Manning, Jerome Alan
Seavey, William Arthur
Silk, Thomas
Thomas, William Scott
Utrecht, Paul F.
Weber, Arnold I.
Wild, Nelson Hopkins

San Jose
Morgan, Robert Hall

San Marino
Tomich, Lillian

Santa Ana
Patt, Herbert Jacob

Santa Monica
Axe, Norman Gold
Jung, Karen Eunkyung

Sonoma
Obninsky, Victor Peter

Stockton
Blewett, Robert Noall

Sunland
Willis, Calvin C.

Thousand Oaks
Trover, Ellen Lloyd

Torrance
Moore, Christopher M.

Tustin
Gaughan, John Stephen

Ukiah
Sager, Madeline Dean

Ventura
Leach, Donald Lee

Victorville
Kennedy, Jeanne Elizabeth

Visalia
Crowe, Daniel Walston

Walnut Creek
Baker, Roy Gordon, Jr.,

West Covina
Ebiner, Robert Maurice

COLORADO

Arvada
Johnson, Christian Kent

Colorado Springs
Gaddis, Larry Roy
Keene, Kenneth Paul
Kendall, Phillip Alan
Kennedy, Richard Joseph
Purvis, Randall W. B.

Denver
Atlass, Theodore Bruce
McMichael, Donald Earl
Mitchem, Allen P.
Olsen, M. Kent
Phelps, Robert Frederick, Jr.,
Schmidt, L(ail) William, Jr.,

Lakewood
Brant, John Getty
Thome, Dennis Wesley

Longmont
Hopp, Walter James

Pueblo
O'Callaghan, R.J. Patrick

Rocky Ford
Mendenhall, Harry Barton

Steamboat Springs
Holloway, John P.

CONNECTICUT

Bethel
Medvecky, Thomas Edward

Canaan
Capecelatro, Mark John

Enfield
Berger, Robert Bertram

Greenwich
Brandrup, Douglas Warren
Pascarella, Henry William
Selby, Leland Clay

Hartford
Berall, Frank Stewart
Bonee, John Leon, III,
Gale, John Quentin
Milliken, Charles Buckland

Lakeville
Rout, Robert Howard

Milford
Broughel, Andrew Joseph

Mystic
Palmer, Richard Crist

New Haven
Auerbach, Hillel Joshua
Wiznia, Carolann Kamens

Ridgefield
Foster, Julie Irene
Sherman, Harold

Stamford
Bobrow, Henry Bernard
Sarner, Richard Alan
Teitell, Conrad Laurence

Wallingford
Galligan, Matthew G.

Waterbury
Dost, Mark W.

West Hartford
Lynch, Karen Renzulli

Saegaert, Ellen C.

Westport
Kosakow, James Matthew
Saxl, Richard Hildreth

Willimantic
Sinder, Joan B.

Wilton
Adams, Thomas Tilley
Slater, Ralph Evan

Windsor
Morelli, Carmen

DELAWARE

Dover
Twilley, Joshua Marion

Newark
McCann, Richard Stephen

Wilmington
Jewell, George Benson
Jolles, Janet K. Pilling
Reiver, Joanna

DISTRICT OF COLUMBIA

Washington
Beckwith, Edward Jay
Bellinger, Edgar Thomson
Blazek-White, Doris
Boskey, Bennett
Close, David Palmer
Coerper, Milo George
Comstock, Robert Francis
Damico, Nicholas Peter
Determan, Sara-Ann
Freedman, Jay Weil
Ginsburg, Charles David
Isbell, David Bradford
Lessenco, Gilbert Barry
Maginnis, John C., III,
Mayfield, Richard Heverin
Ostrov, Jerome
Perry, Rotraud Mezger
Plaine, Lloyd Leva
Rhyne, Sidney White
Richards, Suzanne V.

FLORIDA

Apopka
Seward, Jeffrey James

Boca Raton
Harris, Michael Robert
Wichinsky, Glenn Ellis

Boynton Beach
Solkoff, Scott M.

Bradenton
Lopacki, Edward Joseph, Jr.,

Brooksville
Hallman, William H., III,

Clearwater
Free, E. LeBron
Rose, Donna
Swope, Scott Paul
Zschau, Julius James

Coral Gables
Fletcher, Paul Gerald

Fort Lauderdale
Dressler, Robert A.
Fanizza, Joanne
Gardner, Russell Menese
Golden, E(dward) Scott
Gore, George Henry
Hess, George Franklin, II,
Hoines, David Alan
Katz, Thomas Owen
Meeks, William Herman, III,

Fort Pierce
Sneed, Richard Durwood, Jr.,

Hobe Sound
Buetens, Eric D.

Jacksonville
Ansbacher, Lewis
Steffey, Fred H.

Jasper
McCormick, John Hoyle

Jupiter
Brophy, Gilbert Thomas
Click, David Forrest

Lutz
Hayes, Timothy George

Melbourne
Hedman, George William

Miami
Amber, Laurie Kaufman
Greenleaf, Walter Franklin
Lancaster, Kenneth G.
Morgan, Charles Oxford, Jr.,
Skolnick, S. Harold
Weiner, Lawrence

Miami Beach
Brodie, Ronald
Hertz, Stephen G.

Naples
Buckley, Frederick Jean
Budd, David Glenn
Stevens, William Kenneth
Strauss, Jerome Manfred
Westman, Carl Edward

North Miami Beach
Slewett, Robert David

North Palm Beach
Daniels, Bruce Joel

Orlando
Worthington, Daniel Glen

Ormond Beach
Logan, Sharon Brooks

Palatka
Baldwin, Allen Adail

Palm Beach Gardens
Auerbach, Paul Ira
Flemiing, Joshua Michael
Kahn, David Miller

Palm Harbor
Summers-Powell, Alan

Pompano Beach
Shulmister, M(orris) Ross

Port Charlotte
Levin, Allen Jay

Saint Petersburg
Mann, Sam Henry, Jr.,
Wilsey, Steven M.

Saint Petersburg Beach
Gagan, James Ephriam

Sarasota
Conetta, Tami Foley
Miller, Harold O.
Zitani, Gregory Anthony

Tallahassee
Boyd, Joseph Arthur, Jr.,
Dariotis, Terrence Theodore
France, Belinda Takach

Tampa
Ellwanger, Thomas John
Gardner, J. Stephen
Garrett, Howard Leon
Oehler, Richard Dale

Venice
Britton, Andrew James

Vero Beach
Gordon, William Stout

West Palm Beach
Farina, John
Henry, Thornton Montagu

Winter Springs
Fernandez, William Warren, Sr.,

GEORGIA

Alpharetta
Bettis, Barry Phillip

Atlanta
Linkous, William Joseph, Jr.,
Pike, Larry Samuel
Salo, Ann Sexton Distler
Sibley, James Malcolm
Williams, J. William

Augusta
Cooney, William J.
Lee, Lansing Burrows, Jr.,

Brunswick
McLemore, Gilbert Carmichael, Jr.,

Columbus
Brinkley, Jack Thomas
Johnson, Walter Frank, Jr.,

Dallas
Williams, Gary Randall

Doraville
Gerstein, Joe Willie

Douglas
Sims, Rebecca Littleton

Fayetteville
Johnson, Donald Wayne

Hamilton
Byrd, Gary Ellis

Savannah
Dickey, David Herschel
Gannam, Michael Joseph
McCracken, Eugene Luke

Swainsboro
Cadle, Jerry Neal

Valdosta
Cork, Robert Lander

HAWAII

Honolulu
Dang, Marvin S. C.
Gerson, Mervyn Stuart
Suzuki, Norman Hitoshi
Taylor, Carroll Stribling

Wailuku
Bodden, Thomas Andrew

IDAHO

Boise
Erickson, Robert Stanley
Schild, Raymond Douglas

Moscow
Bielenberg, Leonard Herman

Saint Maries
Park, Jerrold Elliott

ILLINOIS

Alton
Struif, L. James

Arlington Heights
Biestek, John Paul

Aurora
Lowe, Ralph Edward

Belleville
Waller, Paul Pressley, Jr.,

Champaign
Mamer, Stuart Mies

Chicago
Acker, Frederick George
Bernstein, Charles Bernard
Bixby, Frank Lyman
Brown, Alan Crawford
Carr, Walter Stanley
Chandler, Kent, Jr.,
Corwin, Sherman Phillip
Coughlin, Terrance J.
Dixon, Stewart Strawn
Edelman, Alvin
English, John Dwight
Harrington, Carol A.
Heisler, Quentin George, Jr.,
Herpe, David A.
Kaplan, Howard Gordon
Kelly, Charles Arthur
Kirkpatrick, John Everett
Lutter, Paul Allen
Marshall, John David
Miller, Stanton Bernett
Nicolaides, Mary
Nitikman, Franklin W.
Schar, Stephen L.
Schupp, Anastasia Luka
Shields, Thomas Charles
Sprowl, Charles Riggs
Stanhaus, James Steven
Trost, Eileen Bannon
Wiggins, Charles Henry, Jr.,

Crystal Lake
Thoms, Jeannine Aumond

Downers Grove
Siedlecki, Nancy Therese

Genoa
Cromley, Jon Lowell

Glenview
Baetz, W. Timothy
Marmet, Gottlieb John

Highland Park
Schindel, Donald Marvin

Long Grove
Fisher, Joy Deborah

Monticello
Tracy, William Francis, II,

Morris
Rooks, John Newton

Murphysboro
McCann, Maurice Joseph

Niles
Sassan, Dennis Donald

Northbrook
Wallace, Harry Leland

Oak Brook
O'Brien, Walter Joseph, II,

Ottawa
White, Robert Ellsworth

Park Ridge
Hegarty, Mary Frances

Peoria
Coletta, Ralph John
Tomlin, James Milton

Pinckneyville
Johnson, Don Edwin

Rock Island
Ciaccio, Karin McLaughlin

Skokie
Kahn, Bert L.

Springfield
Reed, Robert Phillip
Walbaum, Robert C.

Taylorville
Austin, Daniel William

Watseka
Tungate, James Lester

Wauconda
Malik, Thomas Warren

Waukegan
Bairstow, Richard Raymond

West Frankfort
Riva, David Michael

Western Springs
Rhoads, Paul Kelly

Wheaton
Didzerekis, Paul Patrick
Stein, Lawrence A.

Wheeling
Kulinsky, Lois

Winnetka
Ryan, Robert Jeffers

INDIANA

Bloomington
Tackitt, Sylvan Wright

Columbus
Crump, Francis Jefferson, III,

Fort Wayne
Fink, Thomas Michael
Gehring, Ronald Kent
Smith, Maxwell Paul
Young, Randy William

Fowler
Weist, William Bernard

Greenfield
Dobbins, Caryl Dean

Highland
Fine, William Irwin

Indianapolis
Ewbank, Thomas Peters
Koeller, Robert Marion
Leitch, Ryan L.
Lofton, Thomas Milton
Lowe, Louis Robert, Jr.,
Padgett, Gregory Lee
Rothbaum, Sandra Lazarus
Warren, Bradford Lloyd

Knox
Gudeman, Leroy Dennis

Lawrenceburg
Ewan, William Kenneth

Muncie
Reed, Samuel Lee

Peru
Grund, James Arthur

South Bend
Ford, George Burt

IOWA

Cedar Rapids
Nazette, Richard Follett
Wilson, Robert Foster

Des Moines
Grefe, Rolland Eugene
Harris, Charles Elmer
Hill, Luther Lyons, Jr.,
Zumbach, Steven Elmer

Garner
Hovda, Theodore James

Humboldt
Sandblom, Steven Kirk

Indianola
Ouderkirk, Mason James

Iowa City
Downer, Robert Nelson

La Porte City
Lubben, Rick Ronald

Mason City
Duffy, John Leonard
Heiny, James Ray
Winston, Harold Ronald

Mount Pleasant
Vance, Michael Charles

Muscatine
Coulter, Charles Roy

Parkersburg
Lawler, Thomas Albert

Sioux City
Dykstra, Daniel D.

KANSAS

Arkansas City
Templar, Ted Mac

Hutchinson
Hayes, John Francis
Swearer, William Brooks

Iola
Toland, Clyde William
Toland, John Robert

Lawrence
Karlin, Calvin Joseph
Nordling, Bernard Erick
Smith, Glee Sidney, Jr.,
Springer, Byron Eugene

Leawood
Bohm, Jack Nelson

Lincoln
Marshall, Susan

Neodesha
Depew, Harry Luther

Olathe
Haskin, J. Michael
Taylor, L(ynn) Franklin

Shawnee Mission
Gastl, Eugene Francis

Topeka
Barnes, Tom R., II,
Hejtmanek, Danton Charles

Ulysses
Hathaway, Gary Ray

Wichita
Badger, Ronald Kay

KENTUCKY

Lebanon
Higdon, Frederick Alonzo

Lexington
Bagby, Glen Stovall

Louisville
Buckaway, William Allen, Jr.,
Chauvin, Leonard Stanley, Jr.,
Duffy, Martin Patrick
Gilman, Sheldon Glenn
Hallenberg, Robert Lewis
Manly, Samuel
Pettyjohn, Shirley Ellis
Renau, Donald Irwin

Shelbyville
Igleheart, Ted Lewis

Somerset
Prather, John Gideon
Prather, John Gideon, Jr.,

LOUISIANA

Alexandria
Gist, Howard Battle, Jr.,

Baton Rouge
Bayard, Alton Ernest, III,
Blitzer, Sidney Milton, Jr.,

Hammond
Ross, Kenneth L.

Lafayette
Durio, William Henry
Mansfield, James Norman, III,

Metairie
Derbes, Albert Joseph, III,

New Orleans
Barnett, William Michael
Lemann, Thomas Berthelot
Neff, Carole Cukell
Steeg, Moise S., Jr.,
Wax, George Louis
Wedig, Regina Scotto
Wegmann, Cynthia Anne

Shreveport
Goodman, Robert Uhle
Hardtner, Quintin Theodore, III,

Slidell
Singletary, Alvin D.

MAINE

Farmington
Holman, Joseph Frederick

Portland
Cowan, Caspar Frank
Hunt, David Evans
LeBlanc, Richard Philip

Skowhegan
Youney, John William

MARYLAND

Annapolis
Michaelson, Benjamin, Jr.,

Baltimore
Johnston, Edward Allan
Mitchell, Hugh Allen, Jr.,
Plant, Albin MacDonough
Plummer, Risque Wilson
Sykes, Melvin Julius

Bethesda
Burton, Charles Henning
Nelson, William Eugene

Columbia
Cooney, Teresa M.

Rockville
Katz, Steven Martin
Rachanow, Gerald Marvin

Ruxton
Lewis, Alexander Ingersoll, III,

Takoma Park
Dunn, John Benjamin

Towson
Miller, Herbert H.

Westminster
Dulany, William Bevard

MASSACHUSETTS

Amesbury
Swartz, Mark Lee

Arlington
Keshian, Richard

Boston
Clymer, John Howard
de Rham, Casimir, Jr.,
Goldman, Richard Harris
Kidder, George Howell
Lee, David Harold
Levine, Julius Byron
Li, Winifred I.
Menoyo, Eric Felix
Milstein, Richard Sherman
Perera, Lawrence Thacher
Perkins, John Allen
Roche, John Jefferson
Smith, Perry Marshall
Sullivan, Edward Michael
Wand, Barbara Freedman
Woodburn, Ralph Robert, Jr.,

Brookline
Alban, Ludwig
Goldenberg, Stephen Bernard
Lerman, Herbert S.

Haverhill
Cox, William Donald, Jr.,

Hyannis
Haddleton, Russell Edgecomb

Lexington
Dulchinos, Peter

Lincoln
Lufkin, Martha B.G.

Lowell
Maille, Brenda Patricia

Marblehead
Kirsch, Florence Weitz

Marion
Worley, Robert William, Jr.,

Needham
Cox, Gilbert W., Jr.,

New Bedford
Hurwitz, Barrett Alan

Newton
Isselbacher, Rhoda Solin
Monahan, Marie Terry

North Andover
Bialla, Rowley

Northampton
Thomas, Margot Eva

South Hamilton
Campbell, Diana Butt

Wakefield
Lucas, Robert Frank

Walpole
Ryan, Marilynne R.

Watertown
Kaloosdian, Robert Aram

Wellesley
Riley, Michael Hylan

West Chatham
Rowley, Glenn Harry

West Springfield
Ely, John P.

Weston
Thomas, Roger Meriwether

Yarmouth Port
Paquin, Thomas Christopher

MICHIGAN

Alpena
Hunter, Mark John

Ann Arbor
Dew, Thomas Edward

Birmingham
Smith, Patti
Sweeney, Thomas Frederick

Bloomfield Hills
Kirk, John MacGregor
LoPrete, James Hugh

Bridgeport
Haines, John Alden

Center Line
Litch, John Michael

Decatur
Kinney, Gregory Hoppes

Detroit
Miller, George DeWitt, Jr.,
Rasmussen, Douglas John
Ward, George Edward

East Lansing
Story, Monte Robert

Farmington Hills
Bagley, Dennis Joseph
Blizman, Paul John

Fenton
Hildner, Phillips Brooks, II,

Flint
Henneke, Edward George

Grand Rapids
Davis, Henry Barnard, Jr.,
Marshall, J. Stephen
Van Haren, W(illiam) Michael

Grosse Pointe
Cobau, John Reed

Grosse Pointe Farms
Brucker, Wilber Marion

Grosse Pointe Woods
Pytell, Robert Henry

Harbor Springs
Smith, Wayne Richard

Ishpeming
Steward, James Brian

Kalamazoo
Gordon, Edgar George

Lansing
Gallagher, Byron Patrick, Jr.,
Stackable, Frederick Lawrence

Menominee
Rolfs, Craig Alan

Niles
Stone, Donald P.

Shelby
Burrows, Jay Edward

Southfield
Cassar, George V., Jr.,
Silber, Albert J.

Troy
Brody, Jay Howard
May, Alan Alfred

Waterford
Hall, Terrence Lyon

West Bloomfield
Glazier, Sandra Deborah

MINNESOTA

Benson
Wilcox, Donald Alan

Chanhassen
Peterson, Steven A.

Chatfield
Opat, Matthew John

Crosby
Barnum, Charles Earl, III,

Kenyon
Peterson, Franklin Delano

Minneapolis
Berens, William Joseph
Biglow, Robert Roy
Brink, David Ryrie
Johnson, Gary M.
Rachie, Cyrus
Saeks, Allen Irving
Struyk, Robert John

Mara, Timothy Gerald
Phillips, T. Stephen
Porter, Robert Carl, Jr.,
Tobias, Charles Harrison, Jr.,
Vogel, Cedric Wakelee

Cleveland
Alcox, Patrick Joseph
Boyko, Christopher Allan
Braverman, Herbert Leslie
Brucken, Robert Matthew
Cairns, James Donald
Fabens, Andrew Lawrie, III,
Falsgraf, William Wendell
Hochman, Kenneth George
Katcher, Richard
Kundtz, John Andrew
Lease, Robert K.
Maher, Edward Joseph
Shapiro, Fred David
Steiger, Sheldon Gerald

Columbus
Burchfield, James Ralph
Carnahan, John Anderson
Fisher, Lloyd Edison, Jr.,
Sowald, Beatrice Kronick
Sully, Ira Bennett

Dayton
Conway, Mark Allyn
Johnson, C. Terry
Krebs, Leo Francis
Roberts, Brian Michael
Taylor, Edward McKinley, Jr.,

Findlay
Jetton, Girard Reuel, Jr.,

Franklin
Ruppert, Rupert Earl

Garfield Heights
Demer, Margaret Elizabeth

Ironton
Collier, James Bruce

Kent
Nome, William Andreas

Kenton
Tudor, John Martin

Lima
Robenalt, John Alton

Marion
Frericks, Timothy Matthew

Marysville
Hamilton, Robert Otte

Massillon
Netzly, Dwight H.

Maumee
Marsh, Benjamin Franklin

Mentor
Driggs, Charles Mulford

Mount Vernon
Rose, Kim Matthew

Newark
Hite, David L.
Mantonya, John Butcher

Oak Harbor
Robertson, Jerry D.

Painesville
Dean, J. Thomas

Salem
Bowman, Scott McMahan

Springfield
Browne, William Bitner
Husted, Stanley Neal, II,

Toledo
Calcamuggio, Larry Glenn
Gouttiere, John P.
Jackson, Louise Anne
Stupsker, Charles A.

Warren
Kearney, Patricia Ann

Westerville
Flaherty, James Grant
Westervelt, Charles Ephraim, Jr.,

Wilmington
Schutt, Walter Eugene

Worthington
Albert, Robert Hamilton
Juhola, Michael Duane

Xenia
Wolaver, Stephen Arthur

Youngstown
Briach, George Gary
Lenga, Robert Allen

OKLAHOMA

Guthrie
Davis, Frank Wayne

Kingfisher
Baker, Thomas Edward

Mcalester
Cornish, Richard Pool
Pendell, Terry Ashley

Oklahoma City
Cook, Gayle Freeman
Cunnyngham, Maxine Brown
Lindsey, Lori Dawn
Necco, Alexander David
Ross, William Jarboe
Schuster, E. Elaine
Towery, Curtis Kent
Wilson, Julia Ann Yother

Seminole
Elsener, G. Dale

Tulsa
Bowles, Margo La Joy
Clark, Gary Carl
Eagleton, Edward John
Hatfield, Jack Kenton
Nemec, Michael Lee
Scott, Roger Roy
Steltzlen, Janelle Hicks
Taylor, Varley H.

Vinita
Curnutte, Mark William

Walters
Flanagan, Kathleen

OREGON

Eugene
Horn, John Harold
Mumford, William Porter, II,

Florence
Clark, David Lewis

Grants Pass
Sloan, William Marshall

Medford
Shaw, Barry N.

Pendleton
Rew, Lawrence Boyd

Portland
Klarquist, Kenneth Stevens, Jr.,
Schuster, Philip Frederick , II,
Strader, Timothy Richards

PENNSYLVANIA

Allentown
Zamborsky, Donald A.

Berwyn
Watters, Edward McLain, III,

Brookville
Smith, Sharon Louise

Bryn Mawr
Frick, Benjamin Charles

Doylestown
Elliott, Richard Howard
Wagner, Joseph Hagel

Easton
Brown, Robert Carroll

Erie
Cullen, James Donald

Exton
Buckwalter, Wayne Clark

Girard
Steadman, James Robert

Greensburg
Gounley, Dennis Joseph

Grove City
McBride, Milford Lawrence, Jr.,

Harrisburg
Nauman, Spencer Gilbert, Jr.,
Trimmer, Vicky Ann

Hatboro
John, Robert McClintock
Nicholson, Bruce Allen

Horsham
Best, Franklin Luther, Jr.,

Indiana
Barbor, John Howard
Bell, Paul Anthony, II,

Johnstown
Glosser, William Louis

King Of Prussia
Gadsden, Christopher Henry
Schneider, Pam Horvitz

Lancaster
Minney, Michael Jay

Langhorne
Hillje, Barbara Brown

Lemoyne
Stewart, Richard Williams

Lock Haven
Smith, Stephen Chadwick
Snowiss, Alvin L.

Mc Keesport
Kessler, Steven Fisher

Media
Farber, Howard
Firkser, Robert Michael
Rubin, Arnold E.
Tomlinson, Herbert Weston

Monroeville
Cohen, Laura

New Castle
Babb, Alfred Ward

Philadelphia
Bartolomeo, Paul Joseph, Jr.,
Browne, Stanhope Stryker
D'Angelo, George A.
Freedman, Robert Louis
Hagan, Mary Ann
Kaier, Edward John
Koplin, Bernice Judith
Lombard, John James, Jr.,
Magargee, W(illiam) Scott, III,
Mirabello, Francis Joseph
Putney, Paul William
Rabinowitz, Samuel Nathan
Wolff, Deborah H(orowitz)
Wright, Minturn Tatum, III,

Pittsburgh
Brown, David Ronald
Daniel, Robert Michael
Fall, Robert J.
Hollinshead, Earl Darnell, Jr.,
McLaughlin, John Sherman
Richards, John Thomas, Jr.,
Ummer, James Walter
Vater, Charles J.
Warman, Guy Lee
Yates, Alfred Glenn, Jr.,

Pottsville
Jones, Joseph Hayward

Reading
Kline, Sidney DeLong, Jr.,

Stroudsburg
Upright, Kirby Grant

Uniontown
Coldren, Ira Burdette, Jr.,
Davis, James Thomas

Washington
Posner, David S.

Wilkes Barre
O'Donnell, Catherine Rose

York
Hoffmeyer, William Frederick

RHODE ISLAND

North Providence
Lombardi, Valentino Dennis

Providence
Demopulos, Harold William
Field, Noel Macdonald, Jr.,
Hastings, Edwin H(amilton)
Mulhearn, Christopher Michael
Salter, Lester Herbert
Silver, Paul Allen

Westerly
Panciera, Richard Conner

Woonsocket
Koutsogiane, Phillip Charles
Roszkowski, Joseph John

SOUTH CAROLINA

Charleston
Branham, C. Michael

Columbia
Cotty, William Frank (Bill Cotty)
Gibbes, William Holman
Nexsen, Julian Jacobs

Conway
Martin, Gregory Keith

Greenville
Massey, Raymond David
Wyche, Cyril Thomas

Mount Pleasant
Whitten, Beatrice Ehrenberg

Pawleys Island
Daniel, J. Reese

West Columbia
Dickerson, Michelle Moody

SOUTH DAKOTA

Rapid City
Graslie, Thomas Eric

Spearfish
Hood, Earl James

TENNESSEE

Chattanooga
Akers, Samuel Lee

Columbia
Moore, Tom White, Jr.,

Germantown
Sisson, Jerry Allan

Hermitage
Burkett, Gerald Arthur

Knoxville
Roach, Jon Gilbert

Memphis
Allen, Newton Perkins
Bland, James Theodore, Jr.,
Jackson, Thomas Francis, III,
Patton, Charles Henry
Taylor, Jerry F(rancis)
Winchester, Richard Lee, Jr.,

Nashville
Jordan, James D(ee)
Spining, W. Carl
Trautman, Herman Louis

Sweetwater
Ridenour, Charles Edward

TEXAS

Amarillo
Burnette, Susan Lynn

Arlington
Dowdy, John Vernard, Jr.,

Austin
Fink, Vella Mary
Helman, Stephen Jody
Hernandez, Mack Ray
Ikard, Frank Neville, Jr.,
Osborn, Joe Allen
Weinman, Daryl Gail

Bedford
Williams-Pearson, Cynthia L.

Bellaire
Jacobus, Charles Joseph
Rhodes, George Frederick, Jr.,

Borger
Pace, Rosa White

Brenham
Fisher, Edwin H.

Brownsville
Ray, Mary Louise Ryan
Ray, Mary Louise Ryan

Corpus Christi
Alberts, Harold

Dallas
Abney, Frederick Sherwood
Adams, Carl David
Anderson, Barbara McComas
Anderson, E. Karl
Brady, Jack Edgar
Copley, Edward Alvin
Emery, Herschell Gene
Goodstein, Barnett Maurice
Hartnett, Will Ford
Jones, Grier Patterson
Reid, Rust Endicott
Stalcup, Joe Alan
Storey, Charles Porter
Tubb, James Clarence

East Bernard
Boettcher, Armin Schlick

Edinburg
Looney, Cullen Rogers

El Paso
Cox, Sanford Curtis, Jr.,
Feuille, Richard Harlan
Marshall, Richard Treeger
Yetter, Richard

Fort Worth
Brown, C. Harold
Crumley, John Walter
West, Robert Grady

Galveston
Caldwell, Garnett Ernest

Georgetown
Bryce, William Delf

Hallettsville
Baber, Wilbur H., Jr.,

Harlingen
Johnson, Orrin Wendell

Houston
Amann, Leslie Kiefer
Andrews, Sally S.
Cox, James Talley
Eubank, J. Thomas
Fason, Rita Miller
Forlano, Frederick Peter
Gissel, L. Henry, Jr.,
Horrigan, Joseph Stewart
Jansen, Donald Orville
Jeske, Charles Matthew
Kemp, Roland Connor
Kline, Allen Haber, Jr.,
Linden, William M.
Martin, Paul Edward
McWherter, Louis Alfred
Moncure, John Lewis
Saunders, Charles Albert
Schwartzel, Charles Boone
Seale, Robert Arthur, Jr.,
Sumers, Jean Petersen
Touchy, Deborah K.P.

Hurst
Leach, Terry Ray

Lamesa
Saleh, John

Longview
Welge, Jack Herman , Jr.,

Lubbock
Barnhill, Robert Edwin, III,
Harrell, Walter Hugh

Mason
Wilkerson, James Neill

Midland
Meyers, Alan Hoge

New Braunfels
Nolte, Melvin, Jr.,

San Angelo
Joynton, Stanley Forrest
Moeller, Galen Ashley

San Antonio
Bayern, Arthur Herbert
Ross, James Ulric
Spears, Sally

San Marcos
Kyle, Henry Carper, III,

San Saba
Senterfitt, Reuben

Temple
Mischtian, John Michael

Tyler
Hadden, Arthur Roby

Uvalde
Kerby, Yale Leland

UTAH

Salt Lake City
Owen, Langdon Talbot, Jr.,

VIRGINIA

Arlington
Malone, William Grady

Bristol
Alan, Sondra Kirschner

Charlottesville
Middleditch, Leigh Benjamin, Jr.,
Musselman, Robert Metcalfe

Danville
Conway, French Hoge
Goodman, Lewis Elton, Jr.,

Eastville
Tankard, Baxley Trower

Fairfax
Arntson, Peter Andrew
Callahan, Timothy J.

Lexington
Anderson, Richard Gardiner

Madison
Coates, Frederick Ross

Mc Lean
Herge, J. Curtis
Morris, James Malachy
Tansill, Frederick Joseph

Newport News
Nachman, Erwin B(ehr)

Petersburg
Baskervill, Charles Thornton

Providence Forge
Richardson, William Winfree, III,

Richmond
Addison, David Dunham
Aghdami, Farhad
Belcher, Dennis Irl
Millhiser, Thomas McNally
Stevens, Charles Daniel
Warthen, Harry Justice, III,

Roanoke
Dellinger, Mark Wayne
Lemon, William Jacob

Salem
Young, James Marion

Suffolk
McLemore, James Latinus, III,

PRODUCT LIABILITY

KENTUCKY

Covington
Pierce, Delana S.

Lexington
O'Brien, Stephen Mazyck, III,

LOUISIANA

Lafayette
Bass, William Morris

Metairie
Ford, Robert David
Gauthier, Celeste Anne
McMahon, Robert Albert, Jr.,

New Orleans
Ates, J. Robert
Combe, John Clifford, Jr.,
Gertler, Meyer H.
Grant, Arthur Gordon, Jr.,
Hoffman, Donald Alfred
Masinter, Paul James
Sinnott, John William

MAINE

Portland
Culley, Peter William

MARYLAND

Baltimore
Archibald, James Kenway
Bartlett, James Wilson, III,
Burch, Francis Boucher, Jr.,
Cardea, James Donald
DeVries, Donald Lawson, Jr.,
Erwin, H. Robert
Sly, John T.

Bowie
McCarthy, Kevin John

Greenbelt
Greenwald, Andrew Eric

Rockville
Michael, Robert Roy

MASSACHUSETTS

Boston
Edwards, Richard Lansing
Hugo, Michael R.
Kenney, Raymond Joseph , Jr.,
Muldoon, Robert Joseph, Jr.,

Worcester
Balko, George Anthony, III,
Fox, Douglas Lee

MICHIGAN

Ann Arbor
Joscelyn, Kent B(uckley)

Bingham Farms
Goren, Steven Eliot

Birmingham
Elsman, James Leonard, Jr.,

Bloomfield Hills
Baumkel, Mark S.

Detroit
Babcock, Charles Witten, Jr.,
Torpey, Scott Raymond

Farmington Hills
Foley, Thomas John

Grand Rapids
Blackwell, Thomas Francis
Brinkmeyer, Scott S.
Neckers, Bruce Warren
Spies, Frank Stadler

Midland
Gootee, Jane Marie

Southfield
Gordon, Louis

Troy
Hintzen, Erich Heinz

MINNESOTA

Austin
Schneider, Mahlon C.

Edina
Ashley, James Patrick

Hutchinson
Yira, Markus Clarence

Minneapolis
Bailey, Timothy Gordon
Christensen, Robert Paul
Finzen, Bruce Arthur
Flom, Katherine S.
Gill, Richard Lawrence
Hanson, Kent Bryan
Manning, William Henry
Nemo, Anthony James
Roe, Roger Rolland, Jr.,

Saint Cloud
Carpenter, Kevin Starr

Saint Paul
Allison, John Robert

Winona
Borman, John

MISSISSIPPI

Clarksdale
Chapman, Ralph E.

Columbus
Hicks, Dewitt T., Jr.,

Jackson
Corlew, John Gordon
Harkins, Patrick Nicholas, III,
Hewes, George Poindexter, III,
Langford, James Jerry

Ocean Springs
Luckey, Alwyn Hall

Tupelo
Clayton, Claude F., Jr.,

MISSOURI

Independence
Smith, R(onald) Scott

Kansas City
Eldridge, Truman Kermit, Jr.,
Hubbell, Ernest
Johnston, John Steven
Kaplan, Harvey L.
Levings, Theresa Lawrence
Modin, Richard F.
Newsom, James Thomas
Redfearn, Paul L., III,
Robb, Gary Charles
Rooney, Robert Gerard
Vleisides, Gregory William

Rolla
Hickle, William Earl

Saint Louis
Donaho, Timothy Lawrence, Jr.,
Downey, Michael Patrick
Farris, Spencer Edward
Green, Dennis Joseph
Gullborg, Peter William
Hagerty, Patrick John
Rabbitt, Daniel Thomas, Jr.,
Reeg, Kurtis Bradford
Ringkamp, Stephen H.
Walsh, Joseph Leo, III,
Williams, Theodore Joseph, Jr.,
Withers, W. Wayne

Springfield
FitzGerald, Kevin Michael

MONTANA

Billings
Dalthorp, George Carrol

Butte
Carlson, Robert M.

Helena
Doubek, John C.

NEVADA

Las Vegas
Galatz, Neil Gilbert

Reno
Shaffer, Wayne Alan
Whitbeck, Jill Karla

NEW HAMPSHIRE

Contoocook
Mekeel, Robert K.

Keene
Gardner, Eric Raymond

Manchester
Hutchins, Peter Edward

NEW JERSEY

Haddonfield
Andres, Kenneth G., Jr.,

Holmdel
Suhr, J. Nicholas

Livingston
Nagel, Bruce H.

Morristown
Bromberg, Myron James

Newark
Brenner, John Finn
Garde, John Charles
Kraus, Alan Edward

Pine Brook
Henschel, John James

Pleasantville
Sinderbrand, David I.

Ship Bottom
Shackleton, Richard James

Somerville
Dreier, William Alan
Lieberman, Marvin Samuel

Westwood
McGuirl, Robert Joseph

NEW MEXICO

Albuquerque
Caruso, Mark John

Santa Fe
Brannen, Jeffrey Richard
Casey, Patrick Anthony
McClaugherty, Joe L.

NEW YORK

Buffalo
Goldberg, Neil A.
Hayes, J. Michael
Pajak, David Joseph
Szanyi, Kevin Andrew

Camillus
Endieveri, Anthony Frank

Farmingdale
O'Brien, Joan Susan

Flushing
Schwartz, Estar Alma

Manlius
Whyland, Christopher Mark

Melville
Schoenfeld, Michael P.

Mineola
Bartlett, Clifford Adams, Jr.,
Kelly, Shawn Paul

New Hyde Park
Lee, Brian Edward

New York
Antonucci, Peter A.
Bainton, J(ohn) Joseph
Bezanson, Thomas Edward
Birnbaum, Sheila L.
Cunha, Mark Geoffrey
Dankner, Jay Warren
Dorkey, Charles E., III,
Fallek, Andrew Michael
Gair, Anthony Henry
Garfield, Martin Richard
Goott, Alan F(ranklin)
Gurfein, Richard Alan
Harrison, Tomasita L.
Holman, Bud George
Jacob, Edwin J.
Kalish, Myron
Kroll, Sol
Levine, Ronald Jay
Lyddane, John Lawrence Ashton
Marshall, Sheila Hermes
Otero, Brian V.
Romans, John Niebrugge
Schwab, Harold Lee
Shandell, Richard Elliot
Strober, Eric Saul
Wilensky, Saul
Yelenick, Mary Therese

Newburgh
Liberth, Richard Francis

Salamanca
Brady, Thomas Carl

Scarsdale
Sweeney, John J(oseph)

Syracuse
Murphy, Timothy Paul

White Plains
Colistra, Brian William
D'Aloise, Lawrence T., Jr.,
Ryan, Robert Davis
Silverman, Donald N.

NORTH CAROLINA

Chapel Hill
Crohn, Max Henry, Jr.,

Raleigh
Dorsett, James K., III,

Winston Salem
Barnhill, Henry Grady, Jr.,
Maready, William Frank

NORTH DAKOTA

Fargo
Vogel, Mart Daniel

OHIO

Avon Lake
Long, David Carter

Cincinnati
Chesley, Stanley Morris
Woodside, Frank C., III,

Cleveland
Bates, Walter Alan
Baughman, R(obert) Patrick
Havens, Hunter Scott
Lowe, James Allison
McLaughlin, Patrick Michael
Stuhan, Richard George
Vergon, Frederick Porter, Jr.,
Weaver, Robin Geoffrey
Whitney, Richard Buckner
Young, James Edward

Columbus
Blackburn, Thomas Irven
Eichenberger, Jerry Alan
Hardymon, David Wayne
Radnor, Alan T.
Ray, Frank Allen

Maumee
Tuschman, James Marshall

Youngstown
Carlin, Clair Myron

Zanesville
Micheli, Frank James

OKLAHOMA

Oklahoma City
Coats, Andrew Montgomery
Phelps, Anthony David
Woods, Harry Arthur, Jr.,

Tulsa
Atkinson, Michael Pearce
Ballard, Elizabeth Ann
Eldridge, Richard Mark

OREGON

Portland
Bailey, Ronald E.
Duden, Paul Russell
Foote, Jeffrey Paul
Maloney, Robert E., Jr.,
Swanson, Leslie Martin, Jr.,

Salem
Roy, Matthew Lansing

PENNSYLVANIA

Allentown
Altemose, Mark Kenneth

Bala Cynwyd
Olley, Michael Joseph

Easton
Brown, Robert Carroll

Harrisburg
Angino, Richard Carmen
Downey, Brian Patrick
Stefanon, Anthony

Lancaster
Hall, Thomas Wayne
Nast, Dianne Martha

Norristown
Devine, James I.

Philadelphia
Barrett, John J(ames), Jr.,
Coleman, Robert J.
Damsgaard, Kell Marsh
Dragon, Albert
Fickler, Arlene
Jurewicz, Richard Michael
Kanter, Seymour
Koral, Mark A.
Levin, Murray Simon
Madva, Stephen Alan
Patton, Peter Mark
Phelan, John M.
Rosenberg, Howell K.
Schoener, George Francis, Jr.,

Pittsburgh
Beck, Christopher Alan
Douglass, Kevin K.
Mulvihill, Keithley D.
Perry, Jon Robert
Stroyd, Arthur Heister
Ulven, Mark Edward
von Waldow, Arnd N.

Villanova
Zearfoss, Herbert Keyser

SOUTH CAROLINA

Mount Pleasant
Hahn, H. Blair

Spartanburg
Anthony, Kenneth C., Jr.,

SOUTH DAKOTA

Rapid City
Goodsell, G. Verne

TENNESSEE

Knoxville
Ownby, Jere Franklin, III,

Memphis
Harvey, Albert C.
Ledbetter, Paul Mark
Taylor, Jerry F(rancis)

Nashville
Barrow, Clisby Hall
Bramlett, Paul Kent
Tarpley, John R.

Paris
Rose, Todd Alan

Springfield
Wilks, Larry Dean

TEXAS

Austin
Davis, Don Lawrence
Hile, Richard C.
Probus, Michael Maurice, Jr.,
Whitehurst, William Oscar

Azle
Henvey, John William

Corpus Christi
Fancher, Rick
White, Brantley W.

Dallas
Holmes, James Hill, III,
Moore, Edward Warren
Smith, Larry Francis
Turley, Linda
Walkowiak, Vincent Steven

Edinburg
Julia, Katherine Driscoll

El Paso
McDonald, Charles Edward
Skipworth, Robert Allison

Fort Worth
Hayes, Larry B.
Jensen, Keith Michael
Soward, Joe Weldon, II,
Swift, Thomas Grover, Jr.,
Wallach, David Michael

Galveston
Neves, Kerry Lane

Houston
Elias, Raymon Todd
Mallia, Michael Patrick
Nations, Howard Lynn
Pettiette, Alison Yvonne
Sorrels, Randall Owen
Welsh, H. Ronald
Worthington, William Albert, III,

Mc Kinney
Pikl, James Alan

Richardson
Austin, Ann Sheree

San Antonio
Branton, James LaVoy
Crosley, Thomas Andrew
Guess, James David
Maloney, Pat, Sr.,
Putman, Michael (Michael James Putman)
Valadez, Robert Allen
Welmaker, Forrest Nolan

Wichita Falls
Altman, William Kean

UTAH

Salt Lake City
Atkin, Gary Eugene
Christensen, Ray Richards
Webber, Brian C.

VERMONT

Burlington
Shoup, Tina Louise

Shelburne
Molloy, Maureen Katherine

VIRGINIA

Hampton
Smith, Stephen Mark

Norfolk
Bishop, Bruce Taylor
Drescher, John Webb

Norton
Jessee, Roy Mark

Richmond
Cantor, Irvin Victor
King, William H., Jr.,
Landin, David Craig
Walsh, James Hamilton

Roanoke
McGarry, Richard Lawrence

WASHINGTON

Hoquiam
Kahler, Ray William

Pullman
Savage, David William

Renton
Barber, Mark Edward

Seattle
Corning, Nicholas F.
Davis, Susan Rae
Kraft, Robert Morris
Lundgren, Gail M.
Paul, Thomas Frank
Peterson, Jan Eric
Scott, Brian David
Smith, Scott A.
Whitson, Lish

Yakima
Tenney, Robert Carl

WEST VIRGINIA

Charleston
Brenneman Harrah, Sandra
Kiblinger, Cindy Jo
McCuskey, John F.

Parkersburg
Merriman, William Otto, Jr.,

Wheeling
Hill, Barry Morton

WISCONSIN

Appleton
Lonergan, Kevin

Green Bay
Burnett, Ralph George

Madison
Anderson, Michael Steven
Field, Henry Augustus, Jr.,
Skilton, John Singleton

Menomonie
Steans, Phillip Michael

Milwaukee
Clark, James Richard
Daily, Frank J(erome)
Donovan, Michael Joseph
Frauen, Kurt Herman
Hoefle, Paul Ryan
Kmiec, Steven Gerard
Slavik, Donald Harlan

Oshkosh
Curtis, George Warren

Salem
Edenhofer, Carl R.

Wausau
Grischke, Alan Edward

WYOMING

Jackson
Spence, Gerald Leonard

Sheridan
Cannon, Kim Decker

TERRITORIES OF THE UNITED STATES

PUERTO RICO

Ponce
Leon-Sotomayor, Jose Rafael

AUSTRALIA

Melbourne
Morrison, Andrew

Sydney
Eggleton, Glenn David

BELGIUM

Brussels
Bustin, George Leo

ENGLAND

London
Walker, Andrew Douglas

FRANCE

Paris
Honig, Gérard

GREECE

Athens
Moutzouridou, Victoria G.

IRELAND

Dublin
Preston, Caroline Mary

JAPAN

Tokyo
Arai, Yuki

SOUTH AFRICA

Johannesburg
Lomax, Ross Donald

SWITZERLAND

Bern
Wyss, Lukas F.

ADDRESS UNPUBLISHED

Ashkin, Roberta Ellen
Carmack, Mildred Jean
Connell, William D.
Coviello, Frank Joseph
Embry, Stephen Creston
Erlebacher, Arlene Cernik
Grady, Maureen Frances
Hansen, John Alton
Mitchell, William Graham Champion
Paul, Richard Wright
Rosseel-Jones, Mary Louise
Wilson, Virgil James, III,

PROFESSIONAL LIABILITY

UNITED STATES

ALABAMA

Birmingham
Nettles, Bert Sheffield

Mobile
Waldrop, Norman Erskine, Jr.,

ARIZONA

Phoenix
Adelman, Daniel J.
Bouma, John Jacob
Harrison, Mark Isaac

ARKANSAS

Fort Smith
Karr, Charles

CALIFORNIA

Calabasas
Grimwade, Richard Llewellyn

Danville
Candland, D. Stuart

Los Angeles
Garretson, Robert H.
Kollar, Linda Randlett

Riverside
Marlatt, Michael James

San Anselmo
Truett, Harold Joseph, III, (Tim Truett)

San Diego
McIntyre, Monty Alan
Sussman, Nancy
Weidner, Lauren Finder
Wolfe, Deborah Ann

San Francisco
Bostwick, James Stephen
Callison, Russell James

Santa Monica
Hinerfeld, Robert Elliot

Sherman Oaks
Feldman, Phillip

COLORADO

Denver
Cooper, Paul Douglas
McConnell, Michael Theodore
Starrs, Elizabeth Anne

Greenwood Village
Nixon, Scott Sherman

CONNECTICUT

Hartford
Fain, Joel Maurice

Meriden
Luby, Thomas Stewart

DISTRICT OF COLUMBIA

Washington
Handleman, Aaron L.
Marks, Andrew H.
McAvoy, John Joseph
Olender, Jack Harvey
Sundermeyer, Michael S.
Villa, John Kazar

FLORIDA

Bradenton
Groseclose, Lynn Hunter

Hollywood
Korthals, Candace Durbin

Jacksonville
Cowles, Robert Lawrence
Wirtz, Gregg Lee

Miami
Blumberg, Edward Robert
Greer, Alan Graham
Milian, David Philip

Orlando
Motes, Carl Dalton
Shapiro, Peter A.

Tallahassee
Fonvielle, Charles David

West Palm Beach
Patterson, John B.

GEORGIA

Atlanta
Smith, Jeffrey Michael

Marietta
Dalziel, Charles Meredith, Jr.,

Savannah
Kraeuter, R. Scot

HAWAII

Honolulu
Fritz, Collin Martin
Gierlach, David J.
Harrison, William A.
Lawson, William Homer

IDAHO

Boise
Scanlan, Kevin J.

ILLINOIS

Belleville
Ripplinger, George Raymond, Jr.,

Chicago
Alberts, Barry S.
Costello, James Paul
Fuller, Perry Lucian
George, John Martin, Jr.,
Heist, Robert Connor
Henry, Brian Thomas
Kroot, Jason M.
Lynch, John James
Motherway, Nicholas J.
Napleton, Robert Joseph
Pavalon, Eugene Irving
Price, Paul L.
Rieger, Mitchell Sheridan
Rutkoff, Alan Stuart
Salzetta, Paul Louis
Wilcox, Mark Dean

Naperville
Levy, Steven B.

Peoria
Strodel, Robert Carl

Wheaton
Pollock, Bradley Neil

INDIANA

Fort Wayne
Roby, Daniel Arthur

Indianapolis
Hovde, Frederick Boyd
Shula, Robert Joseph
Wampler, Robert Joseph

KANSAS

Fort Scott
Hudson, Leigh Carleton

Shawnee Mission
Smith, Edwin Dudley

Wichita
Hodge, Ray

KENTUCKY

Louisville
Ballantine, John Tilden

LOUISIANA

Lafayette
Bass, William Morris
Judice, Marc Wayne

New Orleans
Beahm, Franklin D.
Masinter, Paul James
Wright, William Everard, Jr.,

MAINE

Augusta
Johnson, Phillip Edward

MARYLAND

Baltimore
DeVries, Donald Lawson, Jr.,
Orman, Leonard Arnold
Summers, Thomas Carey

Rockville
Michael, Robert Roy
Van Grack, Steven

Towson
Gunning, Timothy Michael

MASSACHUSETTS

Boston
Adler, Sidney W.
Hinchey, Edward Thomas
Kenney, Raymond Joseph , Jr.,

Springfield
Burke, Michael Henry

MICHIGAN

Bingham Farms
Larky, Sheldon Glen
Lebow, Michael Jeffrey

MINNESOTA

Minneapolis
Ayling, Corey John
Bland, J(ohn) Richard
Cole, Phillip Allen
Gagnon, Craig William
Saeks, Allen Irving

Winona
Borman, John

MISSISSIPPI

Clarksdale
Cocke, John Hartwell

Jackson
Quin, William Monroe, II,

MISSOURI

Kansas City
Koelling, Thomas Winsor

Saint Louis
Downey, Michael Patrick
Floyd, Walter Leo

NEW HAMPSHIRE

Keene
Gardner, Eric Raymond

NEW JERSEY

Berlin
Goldstein, Benjamin

Cranford
McCreedy, Edwin James

Flemington
Michels, Kevin Howard

Haddonfield
Heuisler, Charles William

Iselin
Goodman, Barry S.

Morristown
Bromberg, Myron James

Newark
McGuire, William B(enedict)
Reilly, William Thomas

Princeton
Theroux, William Gerard

Short Hills
Leviss, Stewart Michael

NEW MEXICO

Albuquerque
Bohnhoff, Henry M.

NEW YORK

Buffalo
Pajak, David Joseph

Camillus
Endieveri, Anthony Frank

Garden City
Balkan, Kenneth J.

Islandia
Buckley, Terrence Patrick

New York
Connuck, Eric S.
Garson, Andrew S.
Kaplan, Susan
Kilsch, Gunther H.
Kramer, Daniel Jonathan
Kroll, Sol
Lyddane, John Lawrence Ashton
Paul, James William
Toner, Stephen
Zuckerman, Joseph

NORTH CAROLINA

Greenville
Batten, Stephen John

Winston Salem
Maready, William Frank

OHIO

Cincinnati
Woodside, Frank C., III,

Cleveland
Domiano, Joseph Charles
McLaughlin, Patrick Michael
Swartzbaugh, Marc L.
Trapp, Mary Jane

Columbus
Bailey, Daniel Allen
Draper, Gerald Linden
O'Shaughnessy, Christopher T.
Plymale, Ronald Elton

Dublin
Maloon, Jerry L.

Maumee
Tuschman, James Marshall

Youngstown
Carlin, Clair Myron

OREGON

Portland
Savage, John William

PENNSYLVANIA

Allentown
Altemose, Mark Kenneth

Altoona
Serbin, Richard Martin

Easton
Noel, Nicholas, III,

Greensburg
Belden, H. Reginald, Jr.,

Harrisburg
Angino, Richard Carmen
Hafer, Joseph Page

Lancaster
Hall, Thomas Wayne

Media
Smith, John Churchman

Monroeville
Baum, Alan Stuart

Norristown
Devine, James I.

Philadelphia
Bochetto, George Alexander
Bogutz, Jerome Edwin
Kanter, Seymour
Mannino, Edward Francis
McCarron, Jeffrey Baldwin
Mullinix, Edward Wingate

Pittsburgh
Fishman, Craig L.

SOUTH DAKOTA

Rapid City
Goodsell, G. Verne

TENNESSEE

Jonesborough
Jenkins, Ronald Wayne

Nashville
Cooney, Charles Hayes

TEXAS

Austin
Moss, Bill Ralph
Probus, Michael Maurice, Jr.,
Whitehurst, William Oscar

Dallas
Adams, Carl David
Coleman, Robert Winston
Maris, Stephen S.
Mow, Robert Henry, Jr.,
Smith, Larry Francis
Ticer, Mark Allen
Wileman, George Robert

El Paso
Skipworth, Robert Allison

Fort Worth
Wallach, David Michael

Harlingen
Pope, William L.

Houston
Smith, Langdon
Van Fleet, George Allan
Walton, Dan Gibson

San Antonio
Branton, James LaVoy

Tyler
Green, Jay Nelson

VERMONT

Burlington
Shoup, Tina Louise

Rutland
Taylor, A. Jeffry

Shelburne
Molloy, Maureen Katherine

VIRGINIA

Charlottesville
Chandler, Lawrence Bradford, Jr.,

Mc Lean
Alexander, Fred Calvin, Jr.,

Norfolk
Pearson, John Yeardley, Jr.,

Richmond
Rucker, Douglas Pendleton, Jr.,

Vienna
Titus, Bruce Earl

Virginia Beach
Buzard, David Andrew

Woodstock
Walton, Morgan Lauck, III,

WASHINGTON

Renton
Barber, Mark Edward

Sammamish
Waitt, Robert Kenneth

Seattle
Bringman, Joseph Edward
Longfelder, Lawrence Lee
Peterson, Jan Eric
Wayne, Robert Jonathan

WEST VIRGINIA

Charleston
Crislip, Stephen Ray

Parkersburg
Merriman, William Otto, Jr.,

WISCONSIN

Milwaukee
Hoefle, Paul Ryan

Oshkosh
Wilde, William Richard

ENGLAND

London
Arthur, David Anthony Dering

FRANCE

Paris
Honig, Gérard

IRELAND

Dublin
Preston, Caroline Mary

SWEDEN

Stockholm
Edlund, Lars Harald

ADDRESS UNPUBLISHED

Harris, Richard Eugene Vassau
Paul, Richard Wright
Roberts, William H.
Rosner, Seth

PROPERTY DAMAGE. *See* Personal injury.

PROPERTY, REAL

UNITED STATES

ALABAMA

Birmingham
Friend, Edward Malcolm, III,
Hagefstration, John E., Jr.,
Irons, William Lee
Martin, Arthur Lee, Jr.,
Pritchett, Rebecca Wright
Theibert, Richard Wilder

Brewton
Garrett, Broox Gray, Jr.,

Dadeville
Adair, Charles Robert, Jr.,
Oliver, John Percy, II,

Dothan
Huskey, Dow Thobern

Huntsville
Richardson, Patrick William

Mobile
Braswell, Louis Erskine
Holland, Lyman Faith, Jr.,
Johnston, Neil Chunn
Quina, Marion Albert, Jr.,

Sheffield
Hamby, Gene Malcolm, Jr.,

ALASKA

Anchorage
Nosek, Francis John
Rosston, Richard Mark

ARIZONA

Kingman
Basinger, Richard Lee

Mesa
Smith, Kenneth M.

Phoenix
Baker, William Dunlap
Cole, George Thomas
Coppersmith, Sam
Klausner, Jack Daniel
Koester, Berthold Karl
Lee, Richard H(arlo)
Mangum, John K.
Martori, Joseph Peter
Perry, Lee Rowan
Postal, David Ralph
Storey, Lee A.
Udall, Calvin Hunt
Warner, Teddy Fleming

Prescott
Goodman, Mark N.

Scottsdale
Jorden, Douglas Allen
Lowry, Edward Francis, Jr.,
Titus, Jon Alan
Whittington, Thomas Lee

Sun City
Hauer, James Albert

Tucson
D'Antonio, James Joseph
Pace, Thomas M.

ARKANSAS

Fayetteville
Epley, Lewis Everett, Jr.,
Pearson, Charles Thomas, Jr.,
Pettus, E. Lamar

Little Rock
Campbell, George Emerson
Haley, John Harvey

Mena
Thrailkill, Daniel B.

Newport
Thaxton, Marvin Dell

CALIFORNIA

Arcadia
Gelber, Louise C(arp)

Auburn
Lyon, Bruce Arnold
Moglen, Leland Louis

Bakersfield
Karcher, Steven Michael
Kind, Kenneth Wayne

Berkeley
Ross, Julia

Beverly Hills
Bordy, Michael Jeffrey
Burns, Marvin Gerald
Schiff, Gunther Hans

California City
Friedl, Rick

Camarillo
Dunlevy, William Sargent

Costa Mesa
Daniels, James Walter
Frieden, Clifford E.
Simon, John Roger

Encinitas
Forrester, Kevin Kreg

Foster City
Lonnquist, George Eric

Fountain Valley
Tu, Hoang Huy

Fremont
Kitta, John Noah

Fresno
Ewell, A. Ben, Jr.,
Nunes, Frank M.

Fullerton
Moerbeek, Stanley Leonard

Glendale
Scott, A. Timothy

Hayward
Smith, John Kerwin

Huntington Beach
Garrels, Sherry Ann

Hydesville
Shulman, Adley M.

Irvine
Clark, Karen Heath
Farrell, Teresa Joanning
Hurst, Charles Wilson
Ingram, James Michael
Petrasich, John Moris
Wintrode, Ralph Charles

La Jolla
Peterson, Paul Ames

Laguna Niguel
Apke, Thomas Michael
McEvers, Duff Steven

Long Beach
Wilson, Walter Joseph

Los Angeles
April, Rand Scott
Baker, Donald P.
Baumgarten, Ronald Neal
Boxer, Lester
Camp, James Carroll
Carter, Bret Robert
Cathcart, Robert James
de Castro, Hugo Daniel
Grush, Julius Sidney
Hieronymus, Edward Whittlesey
Hutt, Laurence Jeffrey
Lesser, Joan L.
Lund, James Louis
May, Lawrence Edward
Millard, Neal Steven
Miyoshi, David Masao
Nicholas, Frederick M.
Pircher, Leo Joseph
Porter, Verna Louise
Robertson, Hugh Duff
Robison, William Robert
Shapiro, Marvin Seymour
Slavitt, Earl Benton
Snyder, Arthur Kress
Strickstein, Herbert Jerry
Tan, William Lew
Tarr, Ralph William
Zerunyan, Frank Vram

Marina Del Rey
Smolker, Gary Steven

Mill Valley
Nemir, Donald Philip

Napa
Meyers, David W.

Newport Beach
Wolf, Alan Steven

Oakland
Allen, Jeffrey Michael
Hausrath, Les A.
Ong, George E.
Reese, Charles Woodrow, Jr.,

Pacific Palisades
Lagle, John Franklin

Palo Alto
Nopar, Alan Scott
Van Atta, David Murray

Petaluma
Eller, Leslie Robert

Pleasanton
Staley, John Fredric

Redwood City
Verhoeven, Charles K.

Riverside
Darling, Scott Edward

Sacramento
Brewer, Roy Edward
Giguiere, Michele Louise
McGrath, William Arthur
Robbins, Stephen J. M.

Salinas
Etienne, Myron E., Jr.,

San Diego
Clark, David Robert
Dorne, David J.
Hansotte, Louis Bernard
Heidrich, Robert Wesley
Herring, Charles David
Schwartz, Steven Norman

San Francisco
Briscoe, John
Burden, James Ewers
Edwards, Robin Morse
Hunter, William Dennis
La Vine, Robert L.
Seneker, Carl James, II, (Kim Seneker)
Welborn, Caryl Bartelman
Young, Bryant Llewellyn

San Jose
Gonzales, Daniel S.
Mitchell, David Walker
Rossi, Dean Christopher
Stutzman, Thomas Chase, Sr.,

San Juan Capistrano
Graves, Patrick Lee

San Luis Obispo
Dorsi, Stephen Nathan
Krout, Michael Seth

San Mateo
Kenney, William Fitzgerald

San Rafael
Bloomfield, Neil Jon
Fairbairn, Sydney Elise

Santa Barbara
Egenolf, Robert F.
McEwen, Willard Winfield, Jr.,

Santa Cruz
Seligmann, William Robert

Santa Monica
Hofer, Stephen Robert
Jung, Karen Eunkyung
Kinney, James Howard
Preble, Laurence George

Seaside
Weingarten, Saul Myer

Torrance
Matsunaga, Geoffrey Dean

Ukiah
Sager, Madeline Dean

Van Nuys
Mikesell, Richard Lyon

Ventura
Leach, Donald Lee

Visalia
Crowe, Daniel Walston

Walnut Creek
Cameron, Mark Alan
Curtin, Daniel Joseph, Jr.,

Westlake Village
Hoefflin, Richard Michael
Weissman, Robert Allen

Windsor
Greiner, Robert Philip

COLORADO

Arvada
Carney, T.J
Peck, Kenneth E.

Aspen
Peirce, Frederick Fairbanks

Aurora
Katz, Michael Jeffery

Boulder
Ranniger, Leslie Jean

Canon City
Slater, Daniel B.

Colorado Springs
Everson, Steven Lee
Gaddis, Larry Roy
MacDougall, Malcolm Edward
Palermo, Norman Anthony
Purvis, Randall W. B.
Sheffield, Alden Daniel, Jr.,

Crested Butte
Renfrow, Jay Royce

Denver
Blitz, Stephen M.
Braverman, Janis Ann Breggin
Dowdle, Patrick Dennis
Fanganello, Joseph Michael
Grant, Patrick Alexander
Grimshaw, Thomas Tollin
Hamel, Fred Meade
Hopfenbeck, George Martin, Jr.,
Horowitz, Robert M.
Irwin, R. Robert
Long, Martin Edward
Mitchem, James E.
Munteanu, Victor John
Sayre, John Marshall
Wohlgenant, Richard Glen

Durango
Sherman, Lester Ivan

Englewood
Ambrose, Arlen S.

Fort Collins
Gast, Richard Shaeffer
Rogers, Garth Winfield

Frisco
Helmer, David Alan

Lakewood
Freed, Diane Susan

Longmont
Hopp, Walter James

Pueblo
O'Callaghan, R.J. Patrick

Rocky Ford
Mendenhall, Harry Barton

Steamboat Springs
Holloway, John P.

Thornton
Sherk, George William

Westcliffe
Snyder, Paul

CONNECTICUT

Avon
Godbout, Arthur Richard, Jr.,

Bethel
Medvecky, Thomas Edward

Canaan
Capecelatro, Mark John

Enfield
Berger, Robert Bertram

Farmington
Mandell, Joel

Greenwich
Pascarella, Henry William

Hartford
Buck, Gurdon Hall
Merriam, Dwight Haines

Union
Mark, Michael David
Rosenberg, A. Irving

Wayne
Fiedler, Laurie W.

Westfield
Gutterman, Alan J.

NEW MEXICO

Albuquerque
Farmer, Terry D(wayne)
Gorman, Robert Dennis
Keleher, Michael Lawrence
Moise, Steven Kahn
Ramo, Roberta Cooper
Salazar, John Paul

Placitas
Schoen, Stevan Jay

Roswell
Bassett, John Walden, Jr.,
Nibert, Gregory James

Ruidoso
Dutton, Dominic Edward

Santa Fe
Burton, John Paul (Jack Burton)
Cohen, Saul
Schliemann, Walter Charles

Seneca
Monroe, Kendyl Kurth

NEW YORK

Albany
Yanas, John Joseph

Ballston Spa
Brown, Ifigenia Theodore

Binghamton
Price, Paul Marnell

Briarcliff Manor
Rosen, Paul Maynard

Bronx
Verrelli, Anthony Louis

Brooklyn
Young, Sidney David

Buffalo
Bailey, Thomas Charles
Mucci, Gary Louis

Carle Place
Moroney, Francis Xavier

Cedarhurst
Taubenfeld, Harry Samuel

Chittenango
Baum, Peter Alan

Commack
Somer, Stanley Jerome

Corning
Becraft, Charles D., Jr.,

Cortland
Taylor, Leland Baridon

Cortlandt Manor
Galella, Joseph Peter

Dobbs Ferry
Juettner, Diana D'Amico
Maiocchi, Christine

Douglaston
Salvo, Joseph Aldo

East Meadow
Adler, Ira Jay
Hyman, Montague Allan

Farmingville
Pruzansky, Joshua Murdock

Floral Park
Goldman, Alan Barry

Garden City
DaSilva, Willard H.
Fischoff, Gary Charles
Jones, Lawrence Tunnicliffe

Geneseo
Macko, John

Geneva
Brind, David Hutchison

Glens Falls
McMillen, Robert Stewart

Great Neck
Wershals, Paul Leonard

Greenvale
Halper, Emanuel B(arry)

Groton
Henry, James Richard

Harrison
Strone, Michael Jonathan

Hornell
Pulos, William Whitaker

Houghton
Brautigam, David Clyde

Hudson
Davis, Deborah Lynn

Huntington
Houslanger, Todd Eric
Munson, Nancy Kay
Tucker, William P.

Ithaca
Wilson, Bruce Duxbury

Jamesport
Cardinale, Philip John

Mahopac
Sequeira, Manuel Alexandre, Jr.,

Malverne
Benigno, Thomas Daniel

Manhasset
Gastwirth, Stuart Lawrence

Manlius
Mathewson, George Atterbury

Melville
D'Angelo-Mayer, Ida

Middletown
Kossar, Ronald Steven

Mineola
Daniels, John Hill
Tannenbaum, Bernard

Mount Vernon
Ross, Richard C.

New City
Fenster, Robert David

New Rochelle
Herzberg, Sydelle Shulman

New York
Abelman, Arthur F.
Alden, Steven Michael
Altschuler, Fredric Lawrence
Barasch, Clarence Sylvan
Barry, David Earl
Bennett, Scott Lawrence
Black, James Isaac, III,
Boxer, Leonard
Brauner, David A.
Browdy, Joseph Eugene
Burgweger, Francis Joseph Dewes, Jr.,
Chen, Wesley
Chromow, Sheri P.
Colbert, Douglas Marc
Cuiffo, Frank Wayne
Diamond, Bernard Robin
Dresner, Byron
DuLaux, Russell Frederick
Fier, Elihu
Finkelstein, Allen Lewis
Goebel, William Horn
Goldstein, Charles Arthur
Granoff, Gary Charles
Grew, Robert Ralph
Gruenberger, Peter
Hackett, Kevin R.
Handlin, Joseph Jason
Herbst, Todd L.
Hershcopf, Gerald Thea
Herz, Andrew Lee
Ingram, Samuel William, Jr.,
Intriligator, Marc Steven
Jacobs, Reuven
Kalikow, Richard R.
Kawano, Arnold Hubert
Kobrin, Lawrence Alan
Kreitzman, Ralph J.
Kuklin, Anthony Bennett
Kuntz, Lee Allan
Kuntz, Lee Allan
Lambert, Judith A. Ungar
Lascher, Alan Alfred
Levine, Melvin Charles
Liss, Norman
Lynn, Theodore Stanley
Lynton, Harold Stephen
Malkin, Peter Laurence
Marks, Theodore Lee
Miller, Richard Steven
Mills, Barry
Moerdler, Charles Gerard
Montgomerie, Bruce Mitchell
Morganstern, Gerald H.
Mullman, Michael S.
Munzer, Stephen Ira
Nance, Allan Taylor
Neveloff, Jay A.
Paul, Robert Carey
Pinover, Eugene Alfred
Plotkin, Loren H.
Pollan, Stephen Michael
Powell, James Henry
Rabin, Jack
Richards, David Alan
Rikon, Michael
Rosen, Richard Lewis
Rosenberg, Gerald Alan
Saft, Stuart Mark
Sanseverino, Raymond Anthony
Savrin, Louis
Seifert, Thomas Lloyd
Seltzer, Richard C.
Shenker, Joseph C.
Shipper, David W.
Siegel, Edward M.
Silverman, Arthur Charles
Siskind, Donald Henry
Solomon, Stephen L.
Strauss, Gary Joseph
Uram, Gerald Robert
Vernon, Darryl Mitchell
Viener, John D.
Wachtel, Norman Jay
Weir, Peter Frank
Wimpfheimer, Michael Clark
Wu, Robin Chi Ching
Younger, Stephen P.

Niagara Falls
Levine, David Ethan

Niskayuna
Sokolow, Lloyd Bruce

Nyack
Cember, M. Nathan

Olean
Heyer, John Henry, II,

Orangeburg
Rivet, Diana Wittmer

Oswego
Greene, Stephen Craig

Oyster Bay
Bernstein, Jacob

Patchogue
Esteve, Edward V.

Port Jefferson
Hindin, Seymour

Port Washington
Forman, James Douglas

Poughkeepsie
Dietz, Robert Barron
Kranis, Michael David
Wallace, Herbert Norman

Purchase
Gioffre, Bruno Joseph

Queensbury
Sleight, Virginia Mae

Rochester
Blyth, John E.
Clifford, Eugene Thomas
Galbraith, Robert Lyell, Jr.,
Goldman, Arnold Joseph
Lustig, Douglas James
Rosner, Leonard Allen
Servis, William George
Trevett, Thomas Neil

Rockville Centre
Buchman, Lawrence Jay

Rome
Griffith, Emlyn Irving

Saratoga Springs
Harper, David Alexander

Scarsdale
Sabadie, Francisca Alejandra

Staten Island
Ferranti, Thomas, Jr.,
Miller, Claire Cody

Suffern
Reda, Robert L.

Syracuse
Cirando, John Anthony
Fitzpatrick, James David
Regan, Paul Michael
Traylor, Robert Arthur
Weiss, Rhett Louis

Uniondale
Kestenbaum, Harold Lee

Walden
Gubits, David Barry

West Hempstead
Mendola, Joseph Vincent

White Plains
Carlucci, Joseph P.
Feder, Robert
Gjertsen, O. Gerard
Null, William Seth
Rosenberg, Michael
Silverberg, Steven Mark
Topol, Robin April Levitt

NORTH CAROLINA

Asheville
Dillard, John Robert
Frue, William Calhoun

Cary
Reinhard, Steven Ira

Charlotte
Beddow, John Warren
Sink, Robert C.

Elizabeth City
Riley, John Frederick

Greensboro
Agapion, Bill
Galloway, Hunter Henderson, III,
Glover, Durant Murrell

Murphy
Bata, Rudolph Andrew, Jr.,

Roxboro
Weinberger, Joseph Charles, Jr.,

Southern Pines
Foyles, Kirsten Ellefson

Winston Salem
Adams, Alfred Gray

NORTH DAKOTA

Bismarck
Edin, Charles Thomas
Klemin, Lawrence R.

Casselton
Burgum, Bradley Joseph

Grand Forks
Widdel, John Earl, Jr.,

OHIO

Athens
Lavelle, William Ambrose

Beavercreek
Stier, Charles Herman, Jr.,

Canfield
Hill, Thomas Allen

Cincinnati
Goodman, Stanley
Heldman, James Gardner
Manley, Robert Edward
Meranus, Leonard Stanley
Naylor, Paul Donald
Petrie, Bruce Inglis
Strauss, William Victor
Trauth, Joseph Louis, Jr.,

Cleveland
Brown, Seymour R.
Felty, Kriss Delbert
Friedman, Harold Edward
Kahn, Scott Harris
Mason, Thomas Albert
McAndrews, James Patrick
Pearlman, Samuel Segel
Presti, Geralyn Marie
Rosenbaum, Jacob I.
Striefsky, Linda A(nn)
Waldeck, John Walter, Jr.,

Columbus
Barrett, Phillip Heston
Buchenroth, Stephen Richard
Burchfield, James Ralph
Chester, John Jonas
Graff, Douglas Eric
Schneider, Karl Herbert
Sully, Ira Bennett

Dayton
Hadley, Robert James
Holz, Michael Harold
Taylor, Edward McKinley, Jr.,

Dublin
Inzetta, Mark Stephen

Fairfield
Grove, Jack Frederick

Findlay
Hackenberg, David Alan

Garfield Heights
Demer, Margaret Elizabeth

Lima
Robenalt, John Alton

Logan
Kernen, Will

Newark
Mantonya, John Butcher

Salem
Bowman, Scott McMahan

Shaker Heights
Band, Jordan Clifford

Toledo
Gouttiere, John P.
Hilbert, John Warren, II,

Warren
Kearney, Patricia Ann

Wooster
Haught, Sharon Kay

Worthington
Albert, Robert Hamilton

Youngstown
Petrony, John Francis

OKLAHOMA

Broken Arrow
Frieze, H(arold) Delbert

Guthrie
Davis, Frank Wayne

Jones
Dean, Bill Verlin, Jr.,

Muskogee
Robinson, Adelbert Carl

Norman
Hastie, John Douglas

Oklahoma City
Cunnyngham, Maxine Brown
Elder, James Carl
Epperson, Kraettli Quynton
Johnson, Robert Max
Kallstrom, James David
Schuster, E. Elaine
Stanley, Brian Jordan

Seminole
Elsener, G. Dale

Tulsa
Chandler, Ronald Jay
Steltzlen, Janelle Hicks

OREGON

Cannon Beach
Hillestad, Charles Andrew

Eugene
DuPriest, Douglas Millhollen
Horn, John Harold

Grants Pass
Baker, Lindi L.
Sloan, William Marshall

La Grande
Joseph, Steven Jay

Lake Oswego
Byczynski, Edward Frank

Portland
Anderson, Herbert Hatfield
Arthur, Michael Elbert
Byrne, Gregory William
Feuerstein, Howard M.
Hanna, Harry Mitchell
Pratt, Scott Owen
Waggoner, James Clyde
Weiner, David P.

Salem
Lien, Wallace Wayne

PENNSYLVANIA

Allentown
Brown, Robert Wayne
McGinley, Paul Anthony, Jr.,

Bradford
Hauser, Christopher George

Brookville
Smith, Sharon Louise

Bryn Mawr
Hankin, Mitchell Robert

Doylestown
Bolla, William Joseph
Wagner, Joseph Hagel

Du Bois
Blakley, Benjamin Spencer, III,

Erie
Bernard, Bruce William

Exton
Teti, Louis N.

Girard
Steadman, James Robert

Greensburg
Gounley, Dennis Joseph

Grove City
McBride, Milford Lawrence, Jr.,

Harrisburg
Kury, Franklin Leo

Hatboro
Nicholson, Bruce Allen

Honey Brook
DePaul, Anthony Kenneth

Indiana
Barbor, John Howard
Bell, Paul Anthony, II,

Jenkintown
Friedman, Ralph David

Lancaster
Minney, Michael Jay
Shirk, Kenelm Lawrence, Jr.,

Lock Haven
Smith, Stephen Chadwick
Snowiss, Alvin L.

Media
D'Amico, Andrew J.

Mount Pleasant
Johnson, Michael A.

Norristown
Milner, Kenneth Paul

Philadelphia
Cherken, Harry Sarkis, Jr.,
Cross, Milton H.
Denmark, William Adam
Dubin, Stephen Victor
Finkelstein, Joseph Simon
Foxman, Stephen Mark
Glazer, Ronald Barry
Goldberg, Richard Robert
Hunter, James Austen, Jr.,
Keene, John Clark
Kupperman, Louis Brandeis
Maxey, David Walker
Miller, Henry Franklin
O'Brien, William Jerome, II,
Ominsky, Harris
Panzer, Mitchell Emanuel
Pauciulo, John William
Pollack, Michael
Rosenstein, James Alfred
Schwartz, Robert M.
Segal, Robert Martin
Stevens, Mark Alan

Pittsburgh
Brown, David Ronald
Ehrenwerth, David Harry
Hartman, Ronald G.
Hollinshead, Earl Darnell, Jr.,
Letwin, Jeffrey William
Reed, W. Franklin
Richards, John Thomas, Jr.,
Stepanian, Steven Arvid, II,
Warman, Guy Lee

Reading
Kline, Sidney DeLong, Jr.,

Somerset
Carroll, William Richard

Washington
Posner, David S.

Wilkes Barre
Ufberg, Murray

Williamsport
Knecht, William L.

Womelsdorf
Worley, Jane Ludwig

York
Hoffmeyer, William Frederick
Perry, Ronald

RHODE ISLAND

Cranston
Coletti, John Anthony

North Providence
Lombardi, Valentino Dennis

Providence
Carlotti, Stephen Jon

Westerly
Nardone, William Andrew
Panciera, Richard Conner

Woonsocket
Roszkowski, Joseph John

SOUTH CAROLINA

Aiken
Marine, Andrew Craig

Charleston
Robinson, Neil Cibley, Jr.,

Columbia
Cotty, William Frank (Bill Cotty)
Price, Robert Grant
Scott, Ronald Charles

Conway
Martin, Gregory Keith

Greenville
Edwards, Harry LaFoy
Reese, Kevin Wayne

Greenwood
Nexsen, Julian Jacobs, Jr.,

Hilton Head Island
Bethea, William Lamar, Jr.,
Laughlin, Drew Alan
Scarminach, Charles Anthony

Laurens
Burney, Rhett D.

North Myrtle Beach
Wheless, Albert Eugene

SOUTH DAKOTA

Sioux Falls
Hayes, Robert E.
Prendergast, Terry Neill

TENNESSEE

Bolivar
Cary, Charles Muse

Germantown
Sisson, Jerry Allan
Waddell, Phillip Dean

Knoxville
Ritchie, Albert

Memphis
deWitt, Charles Benjamin, III,
Doggrell, Henry Patton
Webb, Kathleen Rochford

Nashville
Camp, Randy Coleman
Jordan, James D(ee)

TEXAS

Arlington
Pierson, Grey
Rosenberry, William Kenneth

Austin
Clark, Pat English
Davis, Robert Larry
Nevola, Roger
Osborn, Joe Allen
Rider, Brian Clayton

Bellaire
Jacobus, Charles Joseph

Boerne
Vaughan, Edward Gibson

Brenham
Fisher, Edwin H.

Brownsville
Ray, Mary Louise Ryan

Dallas
Baggett, W. Mike
Beuttenmuller, Rudolf William
Bromberg, John E.
Fishman, Edward Marc
Goodstein, Barnett Maurice
Helfand, Marcy Caren Caren
Hennessy, Daniel Kraft
Hicks, Marion Lawrence, Jr., (Larry Hicks)
Levin, Hervey Phillip
Massman, Richard Allan
McWilliams, Mike C.
Mueller, Mark Christopher
Nolan, John Michael
Peterson, Edward Adrian
Pleasant, James Scott
Portman, Glenn Arthur
Prather, Robert Charles, Sr.,
Riddle, Michael Lee
Schrauff, Christopher Wesley
Stalcup, Joe Alan
True, Roy Joe
Tubb, James Clarence
White, James Richard

El Paso
Cox, Sanford Curtis, Jr.,
Morton, Fred J.

Ennis
Swanson, Wallace Martin

Fort Worth
Phillips, Robert James, Jr.,
West, Robert Grady

Galveston
Caldwell, Garnett Ernest

Houston
Anderson, Doris Ehlinger
Heinrich, Timothy John
Hollyfield, John Scoggins
Hudspeth, Chalmers Mac
Marlow, Orval Lee, II,
Moncure, John Lewis
Shouse, August Edward
Simmons, Stephen Judson
Sing, William Bender
Van Kerrebrook, Mary Alice
Weiner, Sanford Alan
Weller, Philip Douglas
Zeigler, Ann dePender

Kerrville
Parmley, Robert James

Killeen
Kleff, Pierre Augustine, Jr.,

Lockhart
Scudday, Roy George

Mcallen
Jarvis, Robert Glenn

Midland
Meyers, Alan Hoge

Missouri City
Hodges, Jot Holiver, Jr.,

New Braunfels
Nolte, Melvin, Jr.,

Richardson
Martin, Richard Kelley

Rockwall
Holt, Charles William, Jr.,

San Antonio
Barton, James Cary
Pipkin, Marvin Grady

San Marcos
Kyle, Henry Carper, III,

Sherman
Munson, Peter Kerr

Spring
Hendricks, Randal Arlan

Temple
Cuba, Benjamin James

Tyler
Hadden, Arthur Roby
Lake, David Alan

Uvalde
Kerby, Yale Leland

Victoria
McKay, Robert Connally

Weslaco
Pomerantz, Jerald Michael

UTAH

Logan
Honaker, Jimmie Joe
Jenkins, James C.

Ogden
Mecham, Glenn Jefferson
Warner, Frank Shrake

Saint George
Gallian, Russell Joseph

Salt Lake City
Anderson, Robert Monte
Beless, Rosemary June
Castleton, David J.
Colessides, Nick John
Cornaby, Kay Sterling
Dragoo, Denise Ann
Heaton, Jon C.
Jensen, Dallin W.
Jones, Michael Frank

VERMONT

Burlington
Schroeder, William Wayne

Rutland
Facey, John Abbott, III,

Woodstock
Dagger, William Carson

VIRGINIA

Alexandria
Maloof, Farahe Paul
McClure, Roger John

Charlottesville
Kudravetz, David Waller

Chester
Connelly, Colin Charles

Danville
Goodman, Lewis Elton, Jr.,

Eastville
Tankard, Baxley Trower

Fairfax
Byrd Mische, Richard J.
Keith, John A.C.
Sanderson, Douglas Jay

Falls Church
Christman, Bruce Lee
Goldrosen, Donald Norman
Middleton, J. Howard, Jr.,
Nunes, Morris A.

Great Falls
Preston, Charles George

Lexington
Anderson, Richard Gardiner

Madison
Coates, Frederick Ross

Martinsville
Frith, Douglas Kyle

Mc Lean
Ingersoll, William Boley

Mechanicsville
Martin, Ronald Allen

Newport News
Kamp, Arthur Joseph, Jr.,

Norfolk
Parker, Richard Wilson
Russell, C. Edward, Jr.,

Portsmouth
Brennan, John William

Providence Forge
Richardson, William Winfree, III,

Reston
Toole, John Harper

Richmond
Bagley, Philip Joseph, III,
Cohn, David Stephen
Redmond, David Dudley
Rucker, Douglas Pendleton, Jr.,

Roanoke
Glenn, Robert Eastwood
Lemon, William Jacob

Springfield
Costello, Daniel Brian

Suffolk
McLemore, James Latinus, III,
Young, Hubert Howell, Jr.,

Vienna
Stearns, Frank Warren

Virginia Beach
Harrell, Charles Lydon, Jr.,
Spitzli, Donald Hawkes, Jr.,

Wise
Rogers, Leonard David

Wytheville
Baird, Thomas Bryan, Jr.,
Crewe, Trenton Guy, Jr.,

WASHINGTON

Bellevue
Medved, Robert Allen

Bremerton
Cunningham, Gary Allen

Centralia
Tiller, Laurel Lee

Everett
Dewell, Julian C.

Gig Harbor
Thompson, Ronald Edward

Hoquiam
Rutledge, John Paul

Issaquah
Benoliel, Joel

Olympia
Miller, Allen Terry, Jr.,

Port Angeles
Gay, Carl Lloyd

Seattle
Aramburu, John Richard
Bateman, Heidi S.
Blair, M. Wayne
Brower, Joshua Christopher Allen
Cornell, Kenneth Lee
Creim, Jerry Alan
Daudt, Michael D.
Kilbane, Thomas M.
Kriegman, Bruce Peter
Kuhrau, Edward W.
McCann, Richard Eugene
McLean, Dennis Edgar
Murray, Michael Kent
Palmer, Douglas S., Jr.,
Panchot, Dudley Bradford
Schneidler, Jon Gordon
Smith, Scott A.
Tousley, Russell Frederick
Wilson, Richard Randolph

Spokane
Esposito, Joseph Anthony
Michaelsen, Howard Kenneth

Tacoma
Goodstein, Robert I.
Wesch, Angelia DeAn

Yakima
Larson, Paul Martin

WEST VIRGINIA

Charleston
O'Connor, Otis Leslie

Fairmont
Stanton, George Patrick, Jr.,

Fairview
Bunner, William Keck

Gassaway
Jones, Jeniver James

Lewisburg
Ford, Richard Edmond

Romney
Saville, Royce Blair

Summersville
Davis, Stephen Allen

WISCONSIN

Chippewa Falls
Hunt, Heather M.

Cross Plains
Moretti, Jay Donald

Elkhorn
Eberhardt, Daniel Hugo
Sweet, Lowell Elwin

Evansville
Decker, John Robert

Franklin
Konstantakis, Georgia L.

Janesville
Williams, Mary Beth

Kohler
Sheedy, Kathleen Ann

Lodi
Smith, Michael W.

Madison
Kuehling, Robert Warren
Rankin, Gene Raymond
Temkin, Harvey L.
Winnig, Joel Bruce

Milwaukee
Abraham, William John, Jr.,
Biehl, Michael Melvin
Bratt, Herbert Sidney
Bremer, John M.
Connolly, Gerald Edward
Gaines, Irving David
Hoffman, Nathaniel A.
Jost, Lawrence John
Levine, Herbert
Rieselbach, Allen Newman
Trebon, Lawrence Alan

New Berlin
Schober, Thomas Gregory

Port Washington
Check, Melvin Anthony

Racine
Du Rocher, James Howard

Wausau
Deffner, Roger L.

WYOMING

Cody
Webster, C. Edward, II,

Gillette
Bailey, Daniel B.

Worland
Richins, Kent Alan

TERRITORIES OF THE UNITED STATES

PUERTO RICO

Ponce
Leon-Sotomayor, Jose Rafael

VIRGIN ISLANDS

Charlotte Amalie
Bolt, Thomas Alvin Waldrep

Saint Thomas
Nichols, David E.

CANADA

Montreal
Vineberg, Robert Spencer

MEXICO

Mexico City
González Luna, Rodrigo

AUSTRALIA

Killara
Zipfinger, Frank Peter

Mount Gambier
Rymill, Thomas Mark

AUSTRIA

Vienna
Winkler, Oskar Werner

BRAZIL

Rio de Janeiro
Basilio, Ana Tereza Palhares

Pinheiro, Guilherme Martins

BULGARIA

Sofia
Petkov, Petko Angelov

COSTA RICA

San José
Peralta, Federico

DENMARK

Valby
Hansen, Johannus Egholm

ENGLAND

London
Nugee, Edward George

FRANCE

Paris
Meyer, Michel
Schultze, Pascal

GERMANY

Cologne
Rizor, Stefan

Düsseldorf
Mütze, Michael W.

GRENADA

Saint George's
Helgerson, John Walter

ISRAEL

Haifa
Permut, Scott Richard

Tel Aviv
Raved, Yoram

ITALY

Padua
Polettini, Alessandro

PHILIPPINES

Makati City
Tan, Eusebio Valdez

REPUBLIC OF KOREA

Seoul
Jin, Hong Ki

SLOVAKIA

Bratislva
Marek, Premysl

SPAIN

Madrid
Benavides, Alfonso

SWITZERLAND

Lausanne
Reeves, Simon

THAILAND

Bangkok
Smuthranond, Archava

ADDRESS UNPUBLISHED

Allen, Wayne Alan
Amughan, Kennedy Abba Keday
Atchison, Rodney Raymond
Ball, James Herington
Bateman, David Alfred
Branagan, James Joseph
Brehl, James William
Carpenter, Victoria J.
Cazalas, Mary Rebecca Williams
Chasnoff, Jules
Chernett, Robert Irwin
Clabaugh, Elmer Eugene, Jr.,
Colton, Sterling Don
Cook, David Lee
Crown, Nancy Elizabeth
Cumberland, William Edwin
Dickerman, John Melvin
Eaken, Bruce Webb, Jr.,
Edwards, Daniel Paul
Engelhardt, John Hugo
Fetzer, Mark Stephen
Francis, Jerome Leslie
Garner, Mary Martin
Gold, Martin Elliott
Gordon, David Zevi
Gregory, George G.
Griffith, Steven Franklin, Sr.,
Hackett, Wesley Phelps, Jr.,
Hall, Ralph Carr
Hall-Barron, Deborah
Harman, Wallace Patrick
Hemingway, Whitley Maynard
Hernandez, David N(icholas)
Hess, Chad Brandon
Holden, William Hoyt, Jr.,
Holtzschue, Karl Bressem
Hybl, William Joseph
Johnson, Leonard Hjalma
Klein, Judah Baer
Leaf, Frederick Peter
Locke, William Henry
MacLaren, Robert Ian, II,
Markham, Rosemary
Martin, Connie Ruth
Martin, James William
McCormick, Homer L., Jr.,
McCurley, Robert Lee, Jr.,
McGinty, Brian Donald
Meli, Salvatore Andrew
Missan, Richard Sherman
Moehle, Carm Robert
Naughton, John Alexander
Oates, Carl Everette
Pallot, Joseph Wedeles
Pear, Charles E., Jr.,
Peterson, Howard Cooper
Poliakoff, Gary A.
Regenstreif, Herbert
Rivera, Oscar R.
Rogovin, Lawrence H.
Rosen, Martin Jack
Rosenberg, Sheli Zysman
Shaffer, Richard James
Siebert, William Alan
Siegel, Sarah Ann
Silver, Carol Ruth
Silverberg, Mark Victor
Simmons, Raymond Hedelius
Smith, Walter Ernest
Speaker, Susan Jane
Stinchfield, John Edward
Thiele, Howard Nellis, Jr.,
Torgerson, Larry Keith
Weldon, Jeffrey Alan
Wessling, Robert Bruce
Wilder, William F.
Wright, Robert Payton

REAL ESTATE DEVELOPMENT. *See* Property, real.

SALES OF GOODS. *See* Commercial, contracts.

SECURITIES

UNITED STATES

ALABAMA

Birmingham
Avant, Grady, Jr.,
Baker, David Remember
Garner, Robert Edward Lee
McWhorter, Hobart Amory, Jr.,
Rotch, James E.
Selfe, Edward Milton
Wilson, James Charles, Jr.,

Mobile
McCoy, Douglas Leon

ARIZONA

Paradise Valley
Tubman, William Charles

Phoenix
Bivens, Donald Wayne
Bouma, John Jacob
Cohen, Jon Stephan
Curzon, Thomas Henry
Galbut, Martin Richard
Himelrick, Richard G.
McRae, Stephanie A.
Olson, Kevin Lory
Pidgeon, Steven D.
Price, Charles Steven
Thompson, Terence William
Williams, Quinn Patrick

Prescott
Madden, Paul Robert

Scottsdale
Titus, Jon Alan

Tempe
Moya, Patrick Robert

Tucson
Meehan, Michael Joseph
Pace, Thomas M.

CALIFORNIA

Beverly Hills
Sherwood, Arthur Lawrence

El Segundo
Hunter, Larry Dean

Irvine
Creatura, Mark Anthony
Hensley, William Michael

La Jolla
Kirchheimer, Arthur E(dward)

Los Angeles
Adams, Thomas Merritt
Barnes, Willie R.
Barton, Alan Joel
Blencowe, Paul Sherwood
Boehmer, Richard A.
Bortman, David
Bosl, Phillip L.
Castro, Leonard Edward
Fairbank, Robert Harold
Farrar, Stanley F.
Fein, Ronald Lawrence
Haakh, Gilbert Edward
Heyler, Grover Ross
McKinzie, Carl Wayne
McLane, Frederick Berg
Mitchell, Briane Nelson
Morgan, R. Gregory
Presant, Sanford Calvin
Sheehan, Lawrence James
Stoner, William Edward

Menlo Park
Gunderson, Robert Vernon, Jr.,
Kaufman, Christopher Lee
Kelly, Daniel Grady, Jr.,
Valencia, Marc Andrew

Monte Sereno
Allan, Lionel Manning

Napa
Snow, Tower Charles, Jr.,

Newport Beach
Cano, Kristin Maria
Jeffers, Michael Bogue
Jones, Sheldon Atwell

Pacific Palisades
Lagle, John Franklin

Palo Alto
Benton, Lee F.
Gaither, James C.
Lesser, Henry
Morando, Marta Lucile Hope
Phair, Joseph Baschon
Tanner, Douglas Alan

Redwood City
Millard, Richard Steven
Mo, Curtis Luke

San Diego
Brooks, John White
Kuntz, William Richard, Jr.,
Sullivan, William Francis

San Francisco
Boutin, Peter Rucker
Campbell, Scott Robert
Edwards, Robin Morse
Evers, William Dohrmann
Finberg, James Michael
Friese, Robert Charles
Halloran, Michael James
Hofmann, John Richard, Jr.,
Larson, John William
Loeb, Ronald Marvin
Mann, Bruce Alan
Olson, Walter Gilbert
Palmer, Venrice Romito
Phillips, Richard Myron
Sullivan, Robert Edward
Ziering, William Mark

Santa Barbara
Howell, Weldon U., Jr.,

Toluca Lake
Runquist, Lisa A.

Torrance
Petillon, Lee Ritchey

Walnut Creek
Rainey, William Joel

COLORADO

Boulder
Deaktor, Darryl Barnett

Denver
Campbell, William J.
Grissom, Garth Clyde
Hanna, Juliet Marie
Hubbard, Melissa
Matsukage, Fay Mariko
Mauro, Richard Frank
Newcom, Jennings Jay
Wollins, David Hart

Englewood
Choi, Jay Junekun
Lidstone, Herrick Kenley, Jr.,
Wagner, David James

Westminster
Gaither, John Francis, Jr.,

CONNECTICUT

Fairfield
Denniston, Brackett Badger, III,

Greenwich
Cantwell, Robert
Lowenstein, Peter David
Nimetz, Matthew
Winkler, Charles Howard

Milford
Sagarin, J. Daniel

New Britain
Hogan, John W., Jr.,

Stamford
Hubschman, Henry A.

Washington
Fishman, Mitchell Steven

Waterbury
Wolfe, Harriet Munrett

Westport
Daw, Harold John

Wilton
Auchincloss, John Winthrop

Windsor
Lerman, Kenneth B.

DELAWARE

Wilmington
Smith, Craig Bennett

DISTRICT OF COLUMBIA

Washington
Abeles, Charles Calvert
Adler, Howard Bruce
Alexander, Clifford Joseph
Berl, Joseph M.
Black, Stephen Franklin
Boehm, Steven Bruce
Brown, David Nelson
Clark, Paul Thomas
Cobb, Calvin Hayes, Jr.,
Cohen, Louis Richard
Craft, Robert Homan, Jr.,
Fedders, John Michael
Finkelstein, Jay Gary
Freedman, Jay Weil
Goelzer, Daniel Lee
Goldstein, Frank Robert
Greenberger, I. Michael
Haines, Terry L.
Halpern, James Bladen
Hebert, Jay Howell
Horahan, Edward Bernard, III,
Horn, Charles M.
Hyde, Howard Laurence
Johnson, Philip McBride
Kronstein, Werner J
Lambert, David
Laporte, Gerald Joseph Sylvestre
Levenson, Alan Bradley
Lybecker, Martin Earl
Mashruwala, Anish Subhash
Miles, David Michael
Mixter, Christian John
Mostoff, Allan Samuel
Muir, J. Dapray
Pusey, William Anderson
Schropp, James Howard
Stevens, Herbert Francis
Stromberg, Jean Wilbur Gleason
Strong, Carter
Trager, Michael David
Unger, Peter Van Buren
Wenner, Charles Roderick

FLORIDA

Boca Raton
Buckstein, Mark Aaron

Coral Gables
Rothstein, David Alan

Fort Lauderdale
Schneider, Laz Levkoff

Jacksonville
Kelso, Linda Yayoi
Liles, Rutledge Richardson

Lecanto
Corsi, Philip Donald

Miami
Critchlow, Richard H.
Ersek, Gregory Joseph Mark
Friedman, Richard Nathan
Garrett, Richard G.
Grossman, Robert Louis
Hoffman, Larry J.
Jacobson, Bernard
Miller, James M.
Nuernberg, William R(ichard)
Sacher, Barton Stuart

Naples
Anderson, John Thomas

New Port Richey
Focht, Theodore Harold

Orlando
Blackford, Robert Newton
Blaher, Neal Jonathan
Pierce, John Gerald (Jerry Pierce)

Pompano Beach
Hasenauer, Judith Anne

Saint Petersburg
Kiefner, John Robert, Jr.,

Sarasota
Raimi, Burton Louis

Tampa
Grammig, Robert James
Hadlow, Richard B.
Janney, Oliver James
Rasmussen, Robert Carl
Teblum, Gary Ira

Vero Beach
Goff, Michael Harper

Winter Park
Heinle, Richard Alan

GEORGIA

Atlanta
Antonino, Lauren Slepin
Beckham, Walter Hull, III,
Byrne, Granville Bland, III,
Chait, Gregory Marshall
Cohen, George Leon
Collins, Steven M.
Ganz, Charles David
Greer, Bernard Lewis, Jr.,
Isaf, Fred Thomas
Kaufman, Mark David
Morgan, Charles Russell
Prince, David Cannon
Savell, Edward Lupo
Schulte, Jeffrey Lewis
Silverstein, Leonard A.
Williams, Neil, Jr.,

HAWAII

Honolulu
Case, James Hebard
Gay, E(mil) Laurence

ILLINOIS

Barrington
Cloney, Terence J.

Chicago
Barack, Peter Joseph
Barron, Harold Sheldon
Bashwiner, Steven Lacelle
Bitner, John Howard
Bramnik, Robert Paul
Burgdoerfer, Jerry
Clemens, Richard Glenn
Clinton, Edward Xavier
Cole, Thomas Amor
Crawford, Dewey Byers
Custer, Charles Francis
Delp, Wilbur Charles, Jr.,
Donohoe, Jerome Francis
Dunn, Edwin Rydell
Dykstra, Paul Hopkins
Emerson, Carter Whitney
Feldman, Scott Milton
George, John Martin, Jr.,
Gerlits, Francis Joseph
Gerstein, Mark Douglas
Golden, Bruce Paul
Gregg, Jon Mann
Helman, Robert Alan
Henry, Robert John
Hodes, Scott
Johnson, Gary Thomas
Johnson, Lael Frederic
Junewicz, James J.
Kravitt, Jason Harris Paperno
Lang, Gordon, Jr.,
Levin, Michael David
Manzoni, Charles R., Jr.,
McDermott, John H(enry)
Miller, Paul J.
Newman, Dennis Nathan
Niehoff, Philip John
Pascal, Roger
Prior, Gary L.
Reich, Allan J.
Reum, James Michael
Rhind, James Thomas
Roberson, G. Gale, Jr.,
Ruiz, Michele Ilene
Sanchez, Christopher Benjamin
Schreck, Robert A., Jr.,
Suskin, Howard Steven
Thomas, Stephen Paul
Van Tine, Matthew Eric
Wander, Herbert Stanton
Weil, Andrew Lawrence

Deerfield
Oettinger, Julian Alan

Gurnee
Southern, Robert Allen

Lafox
Seils, William George

Lake Zurich
Scott, John Joseph

Naperville
Larson, Mark Edward, Jr.,

Schiller Park
Congalton, Christopher William

Skokie
Gopman, Howard Z.

Wheaton
Mirabile, Thomas Keith

INDIANA

Indianapolis
Dutton, Stephen James
Kleiman, Mary Margaret
Klimek, James
Koeller, Robert Marion
Lowe, Louis Robert, Jr.,
Neff, Robert Matthew
Padgett, Gregory Lee
Strain, James Arthur

IOWA

Des Moines
Neumann, Gordon Richard, Jr.,

KANSAS

Overland Park
Ayers, Jeffrey David

Prairie Village
Stanton, Roger D.

Shawnee Mission
Gaar, Norman Edward

Wichita
Steele, Thomas Lee

KENTUCKY

Louisville
Conner, Stewart Edmund

LOUISIANA

New Orleans
Bieck, Robert Barton, Jr.,
Correro, Anthony James, III,
Kupperman, Stephen Henry
McMillan, Lee Richards, II,

MARYLAND

Annapolis
Lucas, Steven Mitchell

Baltimore
Burch, Francis Boucher, Jr.,
Chernow, Jeffrey Scott
Lynch, Timothy Cronin
Scriggins, Larry Palmer
Winn, James Julius, Jr.,

Bethesda
Baird, Bruce Allen
Dickstein, Sidney
Rivkin, Steven Robert

Columbia
Maseritz, Guy B.

Easton
Ikenberry, Henry Cephas, Jr.,

Rockville
Roberts, Christopher Chalmers

MASSACHUSETTS

Boston
Bines, Harvey Ernest
Bohnen, Michael J.
Brountas, Paul Peter
Caccese, Michael Stephen
Engel, David Lewis
Fischer, Eric Robert
Greer, Allen Curtis, II,
Hess-Mahan, Theodore Michael
Jordan, Alexander Joseph, Jr.,
Keller, Stanley
King, William Bruce
Kreisler, David P.
Rosenbloom, Thomas Adam
Rowe, Larry Jordan
Soden, Richard Allan
Soehle, Tracy Morse
Thibeault, George Walter

Framingham
Meltzer, Jay H.

Newton
Glazer, Donald Wayne

Waltham
Dickie, Robert Benjamin

Weston
Bateman, Thomas Robert

Worcester
Lougee, David Louis

MICHIGAN

Battle Creek
Markey, James Kevin

Detroit
Hampton, Verne Churchill, II,
Hoops, Frederick Kurre
Semple, Lloyd Ashby
Shaevsky, Mark

MINNESOTA

Golden Valley
Schlichting, William Henry

Minneapolis
Bergerson, David Raymond
Chosy, James Louis
Cole, Phillip Allen
Flom, Gerald Trossen
Mellum, Gale Robert
Minish, Robert Arthur
Peterson, Mark Bradley
Potuznik, Charles Laddy
Sanner, Royce Norman
Stageberg, Roger V.
Witort, Janet Lee

Minnetonka
Lubben, David J.

North Oaks
Woods, Robert Edward

MISSOURI

Chesterfield
Denneen, John Paul
Hier, Marshall David

Kansas City
Selzer, James Otto

Lamar
Geddie, Rowland Hill, III,

Saint Louis
Arnold, John Fox
Brickler, John Weise
Clear, John Michael
Conran, Joseph Palmer
Schoene, Kathleen Snyder
Smith, Arthur Lee
Sneeringer, Stephen Geddes
Tierney, Michael Edward
Withers, W. Wayne

MONTANA

Great Falls
Berry, Anders Taylor

NEBRASKA

Omaha
Ellsworth, John David
von Bernuth, Carl W.
Vosburg, Bruce David

NEW HAMPSHIRE

Grantham
Goss, Richard Henry

NEW JERSEY

Bridgewater
Chandonnet, Sheila Wohl

Camden
Furey, John J.

Florham Park
Hardin, William Downer

Jersey City
Frisch, Harry David

Kenilworth
LaRosa, Joseph J.

Morristown
Campbell, William F., III,

Newark
Kraus, Alan Edward
Liftin, John Matthew
Miller, Richard Allan

Ramsey
Jalil, James Paul

Roseland
Wovsaniker, Alan

Somerville
Hutcheon, Peter David

Summit
Macioce, Frank Michael

Woodbridge
Felton, William Raymond

NEW MEXICO

Albuquerque
Moore, Charles Loyd
Schuler, Alison Kay

Seneca
Monroe, Kendyl Kurth

NEW YORK

Ardsley On Hudson
Stein, Milton Michael

Dobbs Ferry
Scudder, Charles Seelye Kellgren

Fairport
Young, Thomas Paul

Forest Hills
Grant, Susan Irene

Glen Cove
Shields, Craig M.

Great Neck
Rockowitz, Noah Ezra

Jericho
Shulman, Madelyn R. Spatt

Mamaroneck
Du Boff, Michael H(arold)

Mineola
Schaffer, David Irving

Montauk
Kahn, Richard Dreyfus

New York
Andrus, Roger Douglas
Arenson, Gregory K.
Arkin, Stanley S.
Atkins, Peter Allan
Avery, Patricia I.
Bach, Thomas Handford
Backman, Gerald Stephen
Bancroft, Margaret Armstrong
Barnett, Gary
Barth, Mark Harold
Bartlett, Joseph Warren
Beck, Andrew James
Benedict, James Nelson
Bennett, Scott Lawrence
Bergan, Philip James
Besen, Stephen M.
Bialkin, Kenneth Jules
Bicks, David Peter
Blackman, Kenneth Robert
Bodovitz, James Philip
Boehner, Leonard Bruce
Borisoff, Richard Stuart
Broder, Douglas Fisher
Brodsky, David Michael
Brome, Thomas Reed
Brown, Meredith M.
Browne, Jeffrey Francis
Bryan, Barry Richard
Buckman, James Edward
Butler, Samuel Coles
Caytas, Ivo George
Chappell, John Charles
Chazen, Hartley James
Cirillo, Richard Allan
Clary, Richard Wayland
Cohen, Edward Herschel
Cole, Lewis George
Collins, John F.
Conboy, Kenneth
Cooper, Michael Anthony
Cooper, Stephen Herbert
Corbin, Sol Neil
Cowan, Wallace Edgar
Crane, Benjamin Field
Cranney, Marilyn Kanrek
Cunha, Mark Geoffrey
Daitz, Ronald Frederick
Davidson, Sheila Kearney
De Sear, Edward Marshall
Diamant, Aviva F.
DiBlasi, Gandolfo Vincent
Dorado, Marianne Gaertner
Dropkin, Charles Edward
Dubin, James Michael
Dunham, Wolcott Balestier, Jr.,
Dunn, M(orris) Douglas
Eisert, Edward Gaver
Elsen, Sheldon Howard
Epstein, Melvin
Fass, Peter Michael
Feit, Glenn M.
Filler, Ronald Howard
Finch, Edward Ridley, Jr.,
Fischer, Mark David
Fisher, Robert I.
Fleischman, Edward Hirsh
Fleischman, Keith Martin
Fortenbaugh, Samuel Byrod, III,
Frank, Lloyd
French, John, III,
Fricklas, Michael David
Fried, Donald David
Friedman, Bart
Friedman, Samuel Selig
Galant, Herbert Lewis
Gambro, Michael S.
Garvey, Richard Anthony
Gibbons, Robert John
Gold, Simeon
Golino, Antonio
Gottlieb, Paul Mitchel
Grader, Scott Paul
Grant, Stephen Allen
Greilsheimer, William Henry
Haje, Peter Robert
Hart, Robert M.
Healy, Harold Harris, Jr.,
Heftler, Thomas E.
Henderson, Kenneth Lee
Hendry, Andrew Delaney
Herzeca, Lois Friedman
Hiden, Robert Battaile, Jr.,
Hirsch, Barry
Hirsch, Jerome S.
Hoffman, Mathew
Hoffmann, Brian
Holley, Steven Lyon
Hruska, Alan J.
Hynes, Patricia Mary
Isquith, Fred Taylor
Jacob, Marvin Eugene
Jenner, Eva C.
Jock, Paul F., II,
Jones, Douglas Wiley
Kaplan, Carl Eliot
Kaplan, Mark Norman
Katz, Stuart Z.
Kenney, John Joseph
Kern, George Calvin, Jr.,
Kessel, Mark
Kinney, Stephen Hoyt, Jr.,
Kirschbaum, Myron
Klink, Fredric J.
Koblenz, Michael Robert
Kramer, Alan Sharfsin
Kramer, Daniel Jonathan
Krasner, Daniel Walter
Lack, Robert Joel
Leonard, Edwin Deane
Levander, Andrew Joshua
Levin, Ezra Gurion
Levine, Richard L.
Littenberg, Michael Richard
Lowenfels, Lewis David
Lowy, George Theodore
Lutzker, Elliot Howard
MacRae, Cameron Farquhar, III,
Marcusa, Fred Haye
Mark, Jonathan I.
Masters, Jon Joseph
Meister, Robert Allen
Meltzer, Roger
Mestres, Ricardo Angelo, Jr.,
Miller, Arthur Madden
Modlin, Howard S.
Morgan, Frank Edward, II,
Morphy, James Calvin
Morris, Edward William, Jr.,
Moskin, Morton
Muccia, Joseph William
Mullaney, Thomas Joseph
Neidell, Martin H.
Norwitz, Trevor S.
O'Donnell, John Logan
Orce, Kenneth W.
Oshima, Michael W.
Papernik, Joel Ira
Parent, Louise Marie
Parish, J. Michael
Pedreira, Jorge
Perell, Edward Andrew
Perlmuth, William Alan
Pettibone, Peter John
Pierce, Morton Allen
Pisano, Vincent James
Posen, Susan Orzack
Profusek, Robert Alan
Purtell, Lawrence Robert
Quinn, Linda Catherine
Raab, Sheldon
Ray, Jeanne Cullinan
Raylesberg, Alan Ira
Reid, Edward Snover, III,
Reinthaler, Richard Walter
Ringer, James Milton
Robertson, Edwin David
Robinson, Irwin Jay
Rocklen, Kathy Hellenbrand
Rolfe, Ronald Stuart
Romney, Richard Bruce
Rosenblum, William F., Jr.,
Rosensaft, Menachem Zwi
Rothman, Henry Isaac
Rubin, Richard Allan
Rubinstein, Frederic Armand
Rusmisel, Stephen R.
Russo, Thomas Anthony
Saunders, Mark A.
Schneider, Howard
Schneiderman, Irwin
Schorr, Brian Lewis
Schueller, Thomas George
Schwartz, Barry Fredric
Senzel, Martin Lee
Sharpe, Robert Francis, Jr.,
Shenker, Joseph C.
Shepard, Robert M.
Siegel, Jeffrey Norton
Siller, Stephen I.
Smith, Thomas A.
Snow, Charles
Spatt, Robert Edward
Steinberg, Howard Eli
Stephenson, Alan Clements
Stone, David Philip
Strom, Milton Gary
Strum, Jay Gerson
Stuart, Alice Melissa
Tehan, John Bashir
Thalacker, Arbie Robert
Thomas, Jeremiah Lindsay, III,
Tom, Roslyn
Toumey, Donald Joseph
Tricarico, Joseph Archangelo
Underberg, Mark Alan
Urowsky, Richard J.
Versfelt, David Scott
Viener, John D.
Vogel, Howard Stanley
Walker, John Lockwood
Wallace, Nora Ann
Walpin, Gerald
Wang, Albert Huai-En
Wattman, Malcolm Peter
West, Stephen Kingsbury
Whitman, Charles S., III,
Wilson, Paul Holliday, Jr.,
Wolson, Craig Alan
Yodowitz, Edward Jay
Young, John Edward
Zaitzeff, Roger Michael

Pittsford
Willett, Thomas Edward

Rochester
Doyle, Justin P.
Vigdor, Justin Leonard

Rye
Roberts, Thomas Alba

Southampton
Lopez, David

Uniondale
Eilen, Howard Scott

NORTH CAROLINA

Burlington
Slayton, John Howard

Chapel Hill
Lilley, Albert Frederick

Charlotte
Nadelman, Cary
Pruden, James Norfleet, III,
Robinson, Russell Marable, II,
Smith, Laura Chalk
Van Hoy, Philip Marshall
Wagner, Kenneth Lynn
Walker, Clarence Wesley

Greensboro
Clark, David McKenzie

Leland
Barnhardt, Zeb Elonzo, Jr.,

Raleigh
Carlton, Alfred Pershing, Jr.,
Hale, Grayson S.
Mallard, Heather K.

OHIO

Aurora
Berry, Dean Lester

Cincinnati
Heldman, James Gardner
Heldman, Paul W.
Olson, Robert Wyrick

Cleveland
Dampeer, John Lyell
Goins, Frances Floriano
Markey, Robert Guy
Stevens, Thomas Charles
Stovsky, Michael David

Columbus
Bailey, Daniel Allen
Brinkman, Dale Thomas
Dunlay, Catherine Telles
McDermott, Kevin R.
Neuman, Todd Howard
Robins, Ronald Albert, Jr.,
Tannous, Robert Joseph

Dayton
Watts, Steven Richard

Dublin
Williams, Paul Stratton

Findlay
Kline, James Edward

Shaker Heights
Messinger, Donald Hathaway

Toledo
Webb, Thomas Irwin, Jr.,

OKLAHOMA

Bartlesville
Koch, Robert Charles

Oklahoma City
Derrick, Gary Wayne
Rockett, D. Joe
Steinhorn, Irwin Harry

Tulsa
Biolchini, Robert Fredrick
Kihle, Donald Arthur
Luthey, Graydon Dean, Jr.,
Slicker, Frederick Kent
Waddel, Patrick Olynn

SOCIAL SECURITY. *See* Pension.

SPORTS

WASHINGTON

Seattle
Mussehl, Robert Clarence

BRAZIL

Rio de Janeiro
Pinheiro, Guilherme Martins

ITALY

Tuscany
Monaci Naldini, Jacopo

SWEDEN

Helsingborg
Swanstein, Jerker

Stockholm
Widmark, Stefan

SWITZERLAND

Zürich
Gasser, Christoph Johannes

ADDRESS UNPUBLISHED

Bronner, James Russell
Mihov, Julian
Weisman, Paul Howard

TAXATION, CORPORATE

UNITED STATES

ALABAMA

Birmingham
Levy, Jack B.
Selfe, Edward Milton

Montgomery
Proctor, David Ray

ARIZONA

Phoenix
Ehmann, Anthony Valentine
Everett, James Joseph
Hienton, James Robert
Martori, Joseph Peter
Olsen, Alfred Jon

Scottsdale
Lindgren, D(erbin) Kenneth, Jr.,

ARKANSAS

Little Rock
Haley, John Harvey
Marshall, William Taylor

CALIFORNIA

Beverly Hills
Karlin, Michael Jonathan Abraham

Burlingame
Denten, Christopher Peter

Costa Mesa
Schaaf, Douglas Allan

Emeryville
Howe, Drayton Ford, Jr.,

Laguna Niguel
Apke, Thomas Michael

Larkspur
Greenberg, Myron Silver

Los Angeles
Freier, Elliot G.
Goldstein, Michael Gerald
Hyman, Milton Bernard
Maeder, Gary William
Mancino, Douglas Michael
Pircher, Leo Joseph
Presant, Sanford Calvin
Stone, Lawrence Maurice

Palo Alto
Bradley, Donald Edward
Sprague, Gary David

Paso Robles
Knecht, James Herbert

Rancho Santa Margarita
Curtis, John Joseph

Redlands
Shimoff, Paul Martin

Sacramento
Arkin, Michael Barry

San Diego
Pugh, Richard Crawford
Shaw, Richard Allan

San Francisco
Greene, Richard Lawrence
Homer, Barry Wayne
Klott, David Lee
Livsey, Robert Callister
Martin, Stephen James
Offer, Stuart Jay
Silk, Thomas
Spiegel, Hart Hunter
Wood, Robert Warren

Santa Cruz
Schalk, Robert Partridge

Walnut Creek
Willson, Prentiss, Jr.,

COLORADO

Aurora
Stauffer, Scott William

Denver
Cain, Douglas Mylchreest
Callison, James William
Rich, Robert Stephen
Ruppert, John Lawrence

Parker
Greenberg, Morton Paul

CONNECTICUT

Darien
Dale, Erwin Randolph

Hartford
Coyle, Michael Lee
Lloyd, Alex
Lyon, James Burroughs

Monroe
Cleland, Edward Gordon

Westport
Sheiman, Ronald Lee

DELAWARE

Wilmington
Baumann, Julian Henry, Jr.,
Grossman, Jerome Kent

DISTRICT OF COLUMBIA

Washington
Alexander, Donald Crichton
Bostick, George Hale
Brady, Richard Alan
Caplin, Mortimer Maxwell
Cohen, Sheldon Stanley
Cole, Robert Theodore
Colson, Earl Morton
Davidson, Daniel Morton
Fries, Joseph Michael
Halvorson, Newman Thorbus, Jr.,
Harris, Don Victor, Jr.,
Heffernan, James Vincent
Jacobson, David Edward
Lane, Bruce Stuart
Laughlin, Felix B.
Magee, John Benjamin
Nauheim, Stephen Alan
Paul, William McCann
Rafferty, James Gerard
Richmond, David Walker
Rubin, Blake Douglas
Shay-Byrne, Olivia
Silver, Sidney J.
Stauffer, Ronald Eugene
Weinman, Howard Mark
Wellen, Robert Howard

FLORIDA

Boca Raton
Klein, Peter William
Reinstein, Joel

Coral Gables
Gonzalez, Renee E.

Fort Lauderdale
Stankee, Glen Allen

Lake Wales
Wales, Gwynne Huntington

Miami
Border, James Robert
Friedman, Richard Nathan
Gragg, Karl Lawrence
Hudson, Robert Franklin, Jr.,
Scheer, Mark Jeffrey
Simmons, Sherwin Palmer
Weinstein, Andrew H.

Miami Beach
Brodie, Ronald

Orlando
Boyles, William Archer
Conti, Louis Thomas Moore
Henry, William Oscar Eugene
Lefkowitz, Ivan Martin

Tampa
Barton, Bernard Alan, Jr.,
Rosenkranz, Stanley William
Teblum, Gary Ira

Wellington
Beck, Jan Scott

GEORGIA

Atlanta
Abrams, Harold Eugene
Chait, Gregory Marshall
Ganz, Charles David
Taylor, George Kimbrough, Jr.,
Wilson, James Hargrove, Jr.,

HAWAII

Honolulu
Ingersoll, Richard King

IDAHO

Boise
Erickson, Robert Stanley

ILLINOIS

Chicago
Ackerman, David Paul
Banoff, Sheldon Irwin
Berens, Mark Harry
Block, Neal Jay
Bogaard, Jonathan Harvey
Boocock, Stephen William
Bowen, Stephen Stewart
Craven, George W.
Cunningham, Robert James
Ellwood, Scott
Ferencz, Robert Arnold
Freeman, Louis S.
Friedman, Lawrence Milton
Hahn, Frederic Louis
Henry, Frederick Edward
Kaplan, Howard Gordon
Kaplan, Jared
Levin, Jack S.
Lipton, Richard M.
Litwin, Burton Howard
Margolin, Stephen M.
McDermott, Robert B.
McKenzie, Robert Ernest
McLees, John Alan
Metzger, Paul Thomas
Michalak, Edward Francis
Myers, Lonn William
Palmer, John Bernard, III,
Rizzo, Ronald Stephen
Siske, Roger Charles
Swibel, Steven Warren
Truskowski, John Budd
Wise, William Jerrard

Downers Grove
Kirvelaitis, Vytenis P.

Glenview
Marmet, Gottlieb John

Hoffman Estates
Simmons, Myriam Michele Sido

Kenilworth
McKittrick, William Wood

Lake Forest
Palmer, Ann Therese Darin

Naperville
Larson, Mark Edward, Jr.,

Northbrook
Lapin, Harvey I.
Wallace, Harry Leland

INDIANA

Indianapolis
Kemper, James Dee
Lofton, Thomas Milton

South Bend
Carey, John Leo

IOWA

Des Moines
Carroll, Frank James
Harris, Charles Elmer
Zumbach, Steven Elmer

KANSAS

Topeka
Elwood, H. Philip

Wichita
Sorensen, Harvey R.

KENTUCKY

Louisville
Fassler, Charles
Gilman, Sheldon Glenn

LOUISIANA

Baton Rouge
Blackman, John Calhoun, IV,

Metairie
Nuzum, Robert Weston

New Orleans
Benjamin, Edward Bernard, Jr.,
Eckstein, Michael Lehman
Simon, H(uey) Paul

MAINE

Portland
Sellers, Elizabeth Martin
Smith, William Charles

Tenants Harbor
Bates, John Cecil, Jr.,

Trenton
Sang, Peter Bennett

MARYLAND

Baltimore
Cook, Bryson Leitch
Curran, Robert Bruce
Shapiro, Harry Dean

Bethesda
Burton, Charles Henning

Greenbelt
Jackley, Michael Dano

Lutherville
Freeland, Charles

Rockville
De Jong, David Samuel

MASSACHUSETTS

Boston
Benjamin, William Chase
Bernhard, Alexander Alfred
Jacobs, Michael A.
Milder, Forrest David
Mooney, Michael Edward
Ritt, Roger Merrill

Newton
Metzer, Patricia Ann

Springfield
Gelinas, Robert Albert

West Falmouth
Carlson, David Bret

MICHIGAN

Bloomfield Hills
Kasischke, Louis Walter
Solomon, Mark Raymond

Detroit
Thoms, David Moore
Wise, John Augustus

East Lansing
Essa, Daniel F.

Grand Rapids
Oetting, Roger H.

Troy
Chapman, Conrad Daniel

West Bloomfield
Tobin, Bruce Howard

MINNESOTA

Bayport
Bernick, Alan E.

Golden Valley
Schlichting, William Henry

Minneapolis
Garton, Thomas William
Kaplan, Sheldon
Shnider, Bruce Jay

Saint Paul
Geis, Jerome Arthur

MISSOURI

Saint Louis
Farnam, Thomas Campbell
Gorham, Charles
Keller, Juan Dane
Mandelstamm, Jerome Robert
Rose, Albert Schoenburg

Springfield
Evans, William Ellis

MONTANA

Missoula
George, Alexander Andrew

NEBRASKA

Omaha
Ellsworth, John David
Niemann, Nicholas Kent

NEVADA

Las Vegas
Wilson, Joseph Morris, III,

NEW JERSEY

Boonton
Massler, Howard Arnold

Cherry Hill
Liebman, Emmanuel

Englewood Cliffs
Cohen, Philip Gary

Kenilworth
LaRosa, Joseph J.

Livingston
Rosenberg, Paul I.

Morristown
Fishman, Richard Glenn

Newark
O'Connor Quinn, Deirdre
Vajtay, Stephen Michael, Jr.,

Pennington
Gorrin, Eugene

Roseland
Danzis, Colin Michael

West Orange
Richmond, Harold Nicholas

Woodbridge
Lepelstat, Martin L.

NEW MEXICO

Albuquerque
Lieuwen, John N.

Seneca
Monroe, Kendyl Kurth

NEW YORK

Albany
Koff, Howard Michael

Amagansett
Zychick, Joel David

Eastchester
Katz, Kenneth Arthur

Hartsdale
Kroll, Arthur Herbert

Mineola
Smolev, Terence Elliot

New Rochelle
Lurie, Alvin David

New York
Agranoff, Gerald Neal
Aidinoff, M(erton) Bernard
Amdur, Martin Bennett
Andersen, Richard Esten
Baity, John Cooley
Beerbower, Cynthia Gibson
Cohen, Edmund Stephen
Cohen, Richard Gerard
Connors, Peter J.
Cornell, John Robert
Cubitto, Robert J.
Dixon, William
Einstein, Steven Henry
Faber, Peter Lewis
Feder, Arthur A.
Feeney, David Wesley
Ferguson, Milton Carr Carr, Jr.,
Finkelstein, Stuart M.
Flanagan, Deborah Mary
Forry, John Ingram
Gamboni, Ciro Anthony
Garfunkel, Alan J.
Gifford, William C.
Goldman, Richard Lurie
Gordon, Stephen Louis
Gottesman, A(rthur) Edward
Haims, Bruce David
Harley, Colin Emile
Hayden, James Francis
Heitner, Kenneth Howard
Henderson, Donald Bernard, Jr.,
Hirschfeld, Michael
Hodes, Robert Bernard
Jacobs, Robert Alan
Jassy, Everett Lewis
Kalish, Arthur
Koch, Edward Richard
Levitan, James A.
Macan, William Alexander, IV,

MacLean, Babcock
McCormick, Hugh Thomas
McFadyen, Douglas Robert Andrew
Montgomerie, Bruce Mitchell
Nicholls, Richard H.
Odell, Stuart
Osborn, Donald Robert
Paul, Herbert Morton
Phillips, Barnet, IV,
Rappaport, Charles Owen
Rice, Donald Sands
Roberts, Sidney I.
Rooney, Paul C., Jr.,
Rosow, Stuart L.
Rover, Edward Frank
Sachs, David
Samuels, Leslie B.
Schneider, Willys Hope
Shepard, Robert M.
Shoss, Cynthia Renée
Staffaroni, Robert J.
Strock, Marcus
Thomas, Roger Warren
Thompson, Loran Tyson
Tillinghast, David Rollhaus
Viener, John D.
Vogel, Howard Stanley
Watts, David Eide
Wein, Bruce J.
White, Harry Edward, Jr.,
Whoriskey, Robert Donald
Youngwood, Alfred Donald

Purchase
McKenna, Matthew Morgan

Rochester
Kraus, Sherry Stokes
Stewart, Sue S.

White Plains
Danziger, Joel Bernard
Klein, Paul E.

NORTH CAROLINA

Asheville
Hamilton, Jackson Douglas

Burlington
Slayton, John Howard

Goldsboro
Hine, John Charles

Wilmington
McCauley, Cleyburn Lycurgus

Winston Salem
Gunter, Michael Donwell
Osborn, Malcolm Everett

OHIO

Cincinnati
Fink, Jerold Albert
Flanagan, John Anthony
Levin, Debbe Ann

Cleveland
Currivan, John Daniel
Doris, Alan S(anford)
Glaser, Robert Edward
Katcher, Richard
Toomajian, William Martin

Dayton
Hitter, Joseph Ira

Findlay
Kline, James Edward

Grove City
Dodd, Jerry Lee

Toledo
Doner, Gary William

Youngstown
Matune, Frank Joseph

OKLAHOMA

Oklahoma City
Burget, Mark Edward
Kornfeld, Julian Potash
Paliotta, Armand

Tulsa
Eagleton, Edward John
Taylor, Varley H.

OREGON

Lake Oswego
Kuntz, Joel Dubois

Portland
Epstein, Edward Louis
Strader, Timothy Richards
Tremaine, H. Stewart
Zalutsky, Morton Herman

PENNSYLVANIA

Bala Cynwyd
Odell, Herbert

Harrisburg
Nauman, Spencer Gilbert, Jr.,

Philadelphia
Bernard, John Marley
Bildersee, Robert Alan
Davis, C. VanLeer, III,
Frank, Barry H.
Lichtenstein, Robert Jay
McQuiston, Robert Earl
Rachofsky, David J.
Strasbaugh, Wayne Ralph
Thomas, Lowell Shumway, Jr.,
Wiener, Ronald Martin
Wild, Richard P.

Pittsburgh
Hitt, Leo N.
Kearns, John J., III,
Ketter, David Lee
Lauterbach, Paul D.
Phillips, Larry Edward

Spring House
Rosoff, William A.

RHODE ISLAND

Providence
Reilly, Charles James

SOUTH CAROLINA

Greenville
Wyche, Cyril Thomas

TENNESSEE

Memphis
Cook, August Joseph

TEXAS

Dallas
Bumpas, Stuart Maryman
Crichton, Thomas, IV,
Emery, Herschell Gene
Glancy, Walter John
Hughes, Vester Thomas, Jr.,
Kerridge, Ronald David
Lan, Donald Paul, Jr.,
Massman, Richard Allan
Pingree, Bruce Douglas
Vetter, James George, Jr.,
Wallace, Anderson, Jr.,
Willingham, Clark Suttles

Houston
Allender, John Roland
Blackshear, A. T., Jr.,
Gibson, Rex Hilton
Grossberg, Marc Elias
Jewell, George Hiram
Lowy, Peter Andrew
Osterberg, Edward Charles, Jr.,
Salch, Steven Charles
Seymour, Barbara Laverne
Wells, Benjamin Gladney

San Antonio
Ross, James Ulric

UTAH

Salt Lake City
Barusch, Lawrence Roos

VERMONT

Burlington
Schroeder, William Wayne

VIRGINIA

Alexandria
Klewans, Samuel N.
Sczudlo, Walter Joseph
Williams, John Edward

Charlottesville
Stroud, Robert Edward

Glen Allen
Pace, Nicholas Joseph

Hampton
McNider, James Small, III,

Mc Lean
Susko, Carol Lynne

Richmond
Canup, James W.C.
Graves, H. Brice
Howell, George Cook, III,
Kelly, John Francis
Mezzullo, Louis Albert
Minardi, Richard A., Jr.,

Williamsburg
Merritt, James Edward

WASHINGTON

Seattle
Giles, Robert Edward, Jr.,

Spokane
Connolly, K. Thomas

WISCONSIN

Hales Corners
Case, Karen Ann

Madison
Boucher, Joseph W(illiam)
Pitzner, Richard William
Ragatz, Thomas George

Menasha
Franzoi, Joseph Frank, IV,

Milwaukee
Kurtz, Harvey A.
McGaffey, Jere D.
Meldman, Robert Edward
Misey, Robert J., Jr.,
Schnur, Robert Arnold

BELGIUM

Liège
Bernard, Vincent Jacques Nicolas

BRAZIL

São Paulo
Rossi, Carlos Alberto de Souza
Utumi, Ana Cláudia Akie

DENMARK

Rungsted Kyst
Berning, Jesper

ENGLAND

London
Aleksander, Nicholas P.
Gething, Heather
Lubar, Charles Gordon
Zonana, Victor

FRANCE

Neuilly-sur-Seine
Leherissel, Herve

Paris
Poirier, Roland Albert
Raffin, Marie-Hélène J.
Renoux, Vincent Andre
Schultze, Pascal

ITALY

Rome
Lupo, Antonello

JAPAN

Tokyo
Arai, Yuki

NORWAY

Oslo
Klingenberg, Olav E.
Moljord, Kare I.
Thyness, Erik

Stavanger
Koppang, Baard Ivar

PORTUGAL

Lisbon
Nuncio, Paulo

SPAIN

Barcelona
Casanueva, Fernando

SWITZERLAND

Zürich
O'Donnell, Thomas Alexander

UKRAINE

Kiev
Kolesnyk, Oleg Ivanovich

ADDRESS UNPUBLISHED

Baker, Donald
Berti-Azar, Joseph
Blazzard, Norse Novar
Bost, Thomas Glen
Buttrey, Donald Wayne
DiFronzo, Michael A.
Doyle, Austin Joseph
Estes, Carl Lewis, II,
Freedman, Barbara Widman
Guttentag, Joseph Harris
Handler, Harold Robert
Harnack, Don Steger
Harris, Morton Allen
Heath, Charles Dickinson
Kusma, Kyllikki
Levy, David
Marinis, Thomas Paul, Jr.,
Mossawir, Harve H., Jr.,
Peshkin, Samuel David
Petrie, Richard Allen
Pustilnik, David Daniel
Rubenfeld, Stanley Irwin
Serumgard, John R.
Wimpissinger, Christian

TAXATION, ESTATE *See also* Estate planning; Probate

UNITED STATES

ALASKA

Anchorage
Brautigam, Peter Bryan

ARIZONA

Phoenix
Everett, James Joseph
Swartz, Melvin Jay

ARKANSAS

Little Rock
Haley, John Harvey
Haught, William Dixon

North Little Rock
Patty, Claibourne Watkins, Jr.,

CALIFORNIA

Alameda
Stonehouse, James Adam

Grass Valley
Hawkins, Richard Michael

Greenbrae
Bonapart, Alan David

Indio
De Salva, Christopher Joseph

Larkspur
Greenberg, Myron Silver

Long Beach
Cockriel, Stephen Eugene

Los Angeles
Campbell, Jennifer Louise
Goldstein, Michael Gerald
Gorman, Joseph Gregory, Jr.,
Grobe, Charles Stephen
Rae, Matthew Sanderson, Jr.,
Rogers, John Torrey, Jr.,
Stephens, George Edward, Jr.,
Tobisman, Stuart Paul
Weinstock, Harold

Newport Beach
Allen, Russell G.

Palo Alto
Miller, Michael Patiky

Palos Verdes Estates
Toftness, Cecil Gillman

Pasadena
Calleton, Theodore Edward
Davis, Edmond Ray
Walch, Spencer David

Paso Robles
Knecht, James Herbert

Rancho Mirage
Leydorf, Frederick Leroy

Redlands
Shimoff, Paul Martin

Riverside
Darling, Scott Edward

Sacramento
Arkin, Michael Barry
Craven, Thomas Arthur

San Diego
Payne, Margaret Anne
Shaw, Richard Allan

San Francisco
Friedman, K. Bruce
Guggenhime, Richard Johnson
Manning, Jerome Alan

San Jose
Mitchell, David Walker

San Mateo
Kenney, William Fitzgerald

Thousand Oaks
Trover, Ellen Lloyd

COLORADO

Arvada
Johnson, Christian Kent

Colorado Springs
Keene, Kenneth Paul
Kendall, Phillip Alan

Denver
Atlass, Theodore Bruce
Olsen, M. Kent
Phelps, Robert Frederick, Jr.,
Schmidt, L(ail) William, Jr.,

Lakewood
Brant, John Getty

Westcliffe
Snyder, Paul

CONNECTICUT

Greenwich
Selby, Leland Clay

Hartford
Appel, Robert Eugene
Berall, Frank Stewart

New London
Johnstone, Philip MacLaren

Stamford
Sarner, Richard Alan

Waterbury
Dost, Mark W.

Westport
Kosakow, James Matthew
Sheiman, Ronald Lee

Wilton
Slater, Ralph Evan

DELAWARE

Wilmington
Jewell, George Benson
Jolles, Janet K. Pilling
Reiver, Joanna

DISTRICT OF COLUMBIA

Washington
Blazek-White, Doris
Cohen, Sheldon Stanley
Determan, Sara-Ann
Durst, Michael C.
Geske, Alvin Jay
Harris, Don Victor, Jr.,
Heffernan, James Vincent
Mayfield, Richard Heverin
McCoy, Jerry Jack
Plaine, Lloyd Leva

FLORIDA

Boca Raton
Harris, Michael Robert

Fort Lauderdale
Barnard, George Smith
Dressler, Robert A.
Gardner, Russell Menese

Jacksonville
Braddock, Donald Layton

Miami
Simmons, Sherwin Palmer
Weinstein, Andrew H.

Naples
Stevens, William Kenneth
Strauss, Jerome Manfred

Palm Beach Gardens
Flemiing, Joshua Michael

Saint Petersburg
Wilsey, Steven M.

Sarasota
Conetta, Tami Foley

Tampa
Ellwanger, Thomas John

West Palm Beach
Chopin, L. Frank
Henry, Thornton Montagu

GEORGIA

Atlanta
Abrams, Harold Eugene
Linkous, William Joseph, Jr.,
Liss, Matthew M.

Thrower, Randolph William

HAWAII

Honolulu
Gerson, Mervyn Stuart

IDAHO

Moscow
Bielenberg, Leonard Herman

ILLINOIS

Arlington Heights
Biestek, John Paul

Champaign
Mamer, Stuart Mies

Chicago
Acker, Frederick George
Bixby, Frank Lyman
Brown, Alan Crawford
Carr, Walter Stanley
Chiles, Stephen Michael
English, John Dwight
Harrington, Carol A.
Heisler, Quentin George, Jr.,
Herpe, David A.
Hess, Sidney J., Jr.,
Marshall, John David
Nitikman, Franklin W.
Schar, Stephen L.
Siske, Roger Charles
Sprowl, Charles Riggs
Trost, Eileen Bannon
Wiggins, Charles Henry, Jr.,

Highland Park
Schindel, Donald Marvin

Monticello
Tracy, William Francis, II,

Western Springs
Rhoads, Paul Kelly

INDIANA

Fort Wayne
Fink, Thomas Michael

Indianapolis
Ewbank, Thomas Peters
Lofton, Thomas Milton

IOWA

Des Moines
Campbell, Bruce Irving
Zumbach, Steven Elmer

KANSAS

Iola
Toland, Clyde William

Lawrence
Smith, Glee Sidney, Jr.,
Springer, Byron Eugene

Wichita
Sorensen, Harvey R.

KENTUCKY

Louisville
Duffy, Martin Patrick

Somerset
Prather, John Gideon

LOUISIANA

Baton Rouge
Bayard, Alton Ernest, III,
Blackman, John Calhoun, IV,
Blitzer, Sidney Milton, Jr.,

New Orleans
Benjamin, Edward Bernard, Jr.,
Eckstein, Michael Lehman
Lemann, Thomas Berthelot
McDaniel, Donald Hamilton
Mintz, Albert

MAINE

Portland
LeBlanc, Richard Philip
Sellers, Elizabeth Martin
Smith, William Charles

Trenton
Sang, Peter Bennett

MARYLAND

Baltimore
Cook, Bryson Leitch
Mitchell, Hugh Allen, Jr.,
Plant, Albin MacDonough

Bethesda
Ballman, B. George

Rockville
De Jong, David Samuel

Ruxton
Lewis, Alexander Ingersoll, III,

MASSACHUSETTS

Boston
de Rham, Casimir, Jr.,
Li, Winifred I.
McKenna, Karen L.
Menoyo, Eric Felix
Roche, John Jefferson
Smith, Perry Marshall
Wand, Barbara Freedman
Woodburn, Ralph Robert, Jr.,

Holden
Price, Robert DeMille

Hyannis
Haddleton, Russell Edgecomb

Lincoln
Lufkin, Martha B.G.

Newton
Metzer, Patricia Ann
Singer, Paula Noyes

North Andover
Bialla, Rowley

Wellesley
Riley, Michael Hylan

West Chatham
Rowley, Glenn Harry

Weston
Thomas, Roger Meriwether

Worcester
Silver, Marvin S.

Yarmouth Port
Paquin, Thomas Christopher

MICHIGAN

Ann Arbor
Dew, Thomas Edward

Birmingham
Sweeney, Thomas Frederick

Bloomfield Hills
Kirk, John MacGregor
LoPrete, James Hugh
Sommerfeld, David William

Detroit
Hoops, Frederick Kurre
Miller, George DeWitt, Jr.,

Grand Rapids
Van Haren, W(illiam) Michael

Saint Clair Shores
Joslyn, Robert Bruce

Southfield
Cassar, George V., Jr.,

Troy
Gregory, George William

West Bloomfield
Tobin, Bruce Howard

MINNESOTA

Minneapolis
Berens, William Joseph
Martin, Phillip Hammond
Struyk, Robert John

MISSISSIPPI

Jackson
Houston, Jamie Giles, III,

MISSOURI

Kansas City
Bartunek, Robert R(ichard), Jr.,
Crawford, Howard Allen
Davis, John Charles
Setzler, Edward Allan

Saint Louis
Baldwin, Edwin Steedman
Gorham, Charles
Mulligan, Michael Dennis
Redd, Charles Appleton
Sherby, Kathleen Reilly

MONTANA

Billings
Thompson, James William

Havre
Moog, Mary Ann Pimley

NEW HAMPSHIRE

Concord
McDonald, Joseph F., III,

NEW JERSEY

Boonton
Massler, Howard Arnold

Hoboken
Greco, Joseph Dominic, Jr.,

Livingston
Rosenberg, Paul I.

Lyndhurst
Donegan, Joseph Michael

Newark
Zuckerman, Herbert Lawrence

Red Bank
Neff, Robert Carey

Summit
Kenyon, Edward Tipton
Pfaltz, Hugo Menzel, Jr.,

West Orange
Laves, Benjamin Samuel

Woodbridge
Lepelstat, Martin L.

NEW MEXICO

Albuquerque
Lieuwen, John N.

NEW YORK

Babylon
Garvey, Jane Roberts

Bedford
Atkins, Ronald Raymond

Cortland
Taylor, Leland Baridon

Eastchester
Katz, Kenneth Arthur

Garden City
Haskel, Jules J.

Huntington
Hochberg, Ronald Mark

Kew Gardens
Adler, David Neil

Lawrence
Goldstein, Irwin Melvin

New Hyde Park
Rose, Elihu Isaac

New York
Angus, Patricia Marie
Barasch, Mal Livingston
Bell, Jonathan Robert
Blumberg, Gerald
Bockstein, Herbert
Christensen, Henry, III,
Cohen, Richard Gerard
Connors, Peter J.
Crary, Miner Dunham, Jr.,
DuLaux, Russell Frederick
Einstein, Steven Henry
Engel, Ralph Manuel
Evans, Douglas Hayward
Feder, Arthur A.
Finch, Edward Ridley, Jr.,
Gelb, Judith Anne
Greene, Bernard Harold
Herbst, Abbe Ilene
Hershcopf, Gerald Thea
Hess, P. Gregory
Karan, Paul Richard
Kartiganer, Joseph
Kavoukjian, Michael Edward
Klipstein, Robert Alan
Levitan, David M(aurice)
Levitan, James A.
Martin, Malcolm Elliot
Materna, Joseph Anthony
McGrath, Thomas J.
Neuwirth, Gloria S.
O'Grady, John Joseph, III,
Pershan, Richard Henry
Ralli, Constantine Pandia
Reilly, Edward Arthur
Robinson, Barbara Paul
Rodman, Leroy Eli
Rover, Edward Frank
Saufer, Isaac Aaron
Schlesinger, Sanford Joel
Valente, Peter Charles
Whoriskey, Robert Donald
Wyckoff, E. Lisk, Jr.,

Old Chatham
Severs, Charles A., III,

Pearl River
Meyer, Irwin Stephan

Port Jefferson
Hindin, Seymour

Rochester
Buckley, Michael Francis
Schumacher, Jon Lee

Syracuse
Baldwin, Robert Frederick, Jr.,

White Plains
Gjertsen, O. Gerard
Kurzman, Robert Graham

NORTH CAROLINA

Chapel Hill
Herman-Giddens, Gregory

Charlotte
Pleicones, Laura
Wood, William McBrayer

Winston Salem
Vaughn, Robert Candler, II,

OHIO

Akron
Kaufmann, Philip Seil

Cincinnati
Bahlman, William Thorne, Jr.,
Levin, Debbe Ann
Phillips, T. Stephen

Cleveland
Brucken, Robert Matthew
Fabens, Andrew Lawrie, III,
Hochman, Kenneth George
Katcher, Richard
Lease, Robert K.
Strauss, David J.

Columbus
Anderson, Jon Mac
Fisher, Lloyd Edison, Jr.,
Oman, Richard Heer
Willcox, Roderick Harrison

Dayton
Conway, Mark Allyn
Johnson, C. Terry

Mentor
Driggs, Charles Mulford

Oak Harbor
Robertson, Jerry D.

Toledo
Calcamuggio, Larry Glenn

Westerville
Westervelt, Charles Ephraim, Jr.,

Xenia
Wolaver, Stephen Arthur

OKLAHOMA

Oklahoma City
Kornfeld, Julian Potash
Towery, Curtis Kent

Tulsa
Nemec, Michael Lee
Taylor, Varley H.

OREGON

Portland
Zalutsky, Morton Herman

PENNSYLVANIA

Allentown
Zamborsky, Donald A.

Berwyn
Watters, Edward McLain, III,

Bryn Mawr
Frick, Benjamin Charles

Exton
Buckwalter, Wayne Clark

King Of Prussia
Schneider, Pam Horvitz

Philadelphia
Frank, Barry H.
Freedman, Robert Louis
Kaier, Edward John
Lombard, John James, Jr.,
Rabinowitz, Samuel Nathan
Richards, Bonnie E.

Pittsburgh
Daniel, Robert Michael
Ketter, David Lee
Phillips, Larry Edward

Reading
Linton, Jack Arthur

Stroudsburg
Upright, Kirby Grant

Uniontown
Coldren, Ira Burdette, Jr.,

SOUTH CAROLINA

Charleston
Branham, C. Michael

Greenville
Massey, Raymond David

TENNESSEE

Columbia
Moore, Tom White, Jr.,

Memphis
Patton, Charles Henry

Nashville
Jordan, James D(ee)
Trautman, Herman Louis

TEXAS

Austin
Helman, Stephen Jody
Ikard, Frank Neville, Jr.,
Osborne, Duncan Elliott

Corpus Christi
Stukenberg, Michael Wesley

Dallas
Anderson, Barbara McComas
Copley, Edward Alvin
Emery, Herschell Gene
Hughes, Vester Thomas, Jr.,
Owens, Rodney Joe
Vetter, James George, Jr.,
Wallace, Anderson, Jr.,
Willingham, Clark Suttles

El Paso
Feuille, Richard Harlan

Houston
Andrews, Sally S.
Eubank, J. Thomas
Gissel, L. Henry, Jr.,
Jeske, Charles Matthew
Kepke, Carlos Erwin
Martin, Paul Edward
Moncure, John Lewis
Osterberg, Edward Charles, Jr.,
Schwartzel, Charles Boone
Seale, Robert Arthur, Jr.,

Hurst
Leach, Terry Ray

Lubbock
Barnhill, Robert Edwin, III,

San Angelo
Joynton, Stanley Forrest

San Antonio
Bayern, Arthur Herbert

VIRGINIA

Alexandria
McClure, Roger John
Straub, Peter Thornton
Williams, John Edward

Eastville
Tankard, Baxley Trower

Fairfax
Arntson, Peter Andrew
Callahan, Timothy J.

Mc Lean
Aucutt, Ronald David

Richmond
Aghdami, Farhad
Belcher, Dennis Irl
Kelly, John Francis
Rowe, William L. S.
Stevens, Charles Daniel
Warthen, Harry Justice, III,

WASHINGTON

Keyport
Treacy, Gerald Bernard, Jr.,

Olympia
Walker, Francis Joseph

Spokane
Antonietti, Joan L(ynn)

WISCONSIN

Madison
Pitzner, Richard William

Menasha
Franzoi, Joseph Frank, IV,

Milwaukee
Christiansen, Keith Allan
Gallagher, Richard Sidney
Harrington, John Timothy
McGaffey, Jere D.
Walmer, Edwin Fitch
Wynn, Stanford Alan

Racine
Smith, Stephen James

Wauwatosa
Alexander, Robert Gardner

WYOMING

Cody
Stradley, Richard Lee

ENGLAND

London
Lubar, Charles Gordon
Simon, M. Daniel

FRANCE

Neuilly-sur-Seine
Leherissel, Herve

Paris
Renoux, Vincent Andre

PORTUGAL

Lisbon
Nuncio, Paulo

REPUBLIC OF KOREA

Seoul
Woo, Chang Rok

SWITZERLAND

Zürich
O'Donnell, Thomas Alexander

ADDRESS UNPUBLISHED

Buechel, William Benjamin
Engelhardt, John Hugo
Gamble, E. James
Green, Harland Norton
Hansen, Scott William
Hauver, Constance Longshore
Kerner, Michael Philip
Merrill, Abel Jay
Milsten, Robert B.
Reber, Joseph E.
Reiche, Frank Perley
Sliger, Herbert Jacquemin, Jr.,
Stickney, John Moore
Stuart, Michael George
Surratt, John Richard
Sweeney, Deidre Ann

TAXATION, GENERAL

UNITED STATES

ALABAMA

Mobile
Brock, Glen Porter, Jr.,

ARIZONA

Phoenix
Case, David Leon
Haga, David L.
McRae, Hamilton Eugene, III,
Tomback, Jay Loren
Werner, Robert J.

Yuma
Hunt, Gerald Wallace

ARKANSAS

Little Rock
Bohannon, Charles Tad

CALIFORNIA

Burbank
McNally, Gerald, Jr.,

Camarillo
Pugh, Francis Leo

Glendale
Scott, A. Timothy

La Jolla
Shannahan, William Paul

Los Altos
Weir, Robert H.

Los Angeles
Antin, Michael
Basile, Paul Louis, Jr.,
Freier, Elliot G.
Grobe, Charles Stephen
Shapiro, Marvin Seymour
Stone, Lawrence Maurice

North Hollywood
Kreger, Melvin Joseph

Palo Alto
Chacon, Gerald Gilbert

Pasadena
D'Angelo, Robert William
Walch, Spencer David

San Diego
Dorne, David J.
Dostart, Paul Joseph
Guinn, Stanley Willis
LeBeau, Charles Paul
Shaw, Richard Allan

San Francisco
Foster, David Scott
Freud, Nicholas S.
La Vine, Robert L.
Sugarman, Myron George

San Jose
Mitchell, David Walker

San Rafael
Bloomfield, Neil Jon

Santa Barbara
Egenolf, Robert F.

Santa Cruz
Schalk, Robert Partridge

Universal City
Husband, Bertram Paul

COLORADO

Colorado Springs
Everson, Steven Lee

Denver
Burke, Gay Ann Wolesensky
Cain, Douglas Mylchreest
Callison, James William
Crow, Nancy Rebecca
Rich, Robert Stephen

Englewood
Coffee, Melvin Arnold

Golden
Boumann, Robert Lyle

CONNECTICUT

Bridgeport
Harrell, Kyle Alexander

Greenwich
Winkler, Charles Howard

Hartford
Anthony, J(ulian) Danford, Jr.,
Del Negro, John Thomas
Milliken, Charles Buckland

Westport
Carr, Cynthia

DELAWARE

Wilmington
Baumann, Julian Henry, Jr.,
Grossman, Jerome Kent
Tigani, Bruce William

DISTRICT OF COLUMBIA

Washington
Alexander, Donald Crichton
Bergner, Jane Cohen
Campos, Alfred
Caplin, Mortimer Maxwell
Davidson, Daniel Morton
Dolan, Michael William
Durney, Michael Cavalier
Dye, Alan Page
Faley, R(ichard) Scott
Feldhaus, Stephen Martin
Geske, Alvin Jay
Kafka, Gerald Andrew
Kies, Kenneth J.
Kyhos, Thomas Flynn
Lazarus, Kenneth Anthony
Oliphant, Charles Frederick, III,
Ostrov, Jerome
Ross, Stanford G.
Rubin, Blake Douglas
Shay-Byrne, Olivia
Stevens, Herbert Francis
Wellen, Robert Howard

FLORIDA

Boca Raton
Tescher, Donald R.

Coconut Creek
Sheehy, Frances Diane

Fort Lauderdale
Hoines, David Alan
Katz, Thomas Owen

Jacksonville
Steffey, Fred H.

Miami
Border, James Robert
Chabrow, Penn Benjamin
Gragg, Karl Lawrence
Hudson, Robert Franklin, Jr.,
Ruffner, Charles Louis
Simmons, Sherwin Palmer

Orlando
Boyles, William Archer
Capouano, Albert D.

Tallahassee
France, Belinda Takach

Tampa
Barton, Bernard Alan, Jr.,
Doliner, Nathaniel Lee
O'Neill, Albert Clarence, Jr.,

West Palm Beach
Chopin, L. Frank
Lampert, Michael Allen
Zeller, Ronald John

GEORGIA

Atlanta
Abrams, Harold Eugene
Dattolo, Alphonse Robert
Durrett, James Frazer, Jr.,
Forbes, Theodore McCoy, Jr.,
Hoffman, Michael William
Lamon, Harry Vincent, Jr.,
Manigault, Edward Middleton
O'Callaghan, William Lawrence, Jr.,
Pike, Larry Samuel
Thrower, Randolph William
Williams, J. William

Dallas
Williams, Gary Randall

Doraville
Gerstein, Joe Willie

Savannah
Dickey, David Herschel

Smyrna
Seigler, Michael Edward

HAWAII

Honolulu
Heller, Ronald Ian
Taira, Darryl M.
Tanna, Wayne Mitsuo

ILLINOIS

Belleville
Mathis, Patrick Bischof

Chicago
Banoff, Sheldon Irwin
Barnett, William A.
Boocock, Stephen William
Craven, George W.
Cunningham, Robert James
Felsenthal, Steven Altus
Freeman, Louis S.
Litwin, Burton Howard
Mandel, Reid Alan
McCann, Bradley
Neis, James Michael
Rudo, Saul E.
Ryder, David R.
Silets, Harvey Marvin
Truskowski, John Budd
Von Mandel, Michael Jacques

Highland Park
Nelson, Richard David

Kenilworth
Feng, Paul Yen-Hsiung

Lake Forest
Palmer, Ann Therese Darin

Rolling Meadows
Sullivan, Michael D.

South Holland
Bell, Jason Cameron

Tinley Park
Chin, Davis

INDIANA

Fort Wayne
Dean, Laura Hansen

Indianapolis
Kappes, Philip Spangler
Ritz, Stephen Mark

South Bend
Seall, Stephen Albert

IOWA

Des Moines
Campbell, Bruce Irving
Grefe, Rolland Eugene

Muscatine
Nepple, James Anthony

Parkersburg
Lawler, Thomas Albert

KANSAS

Lincoln
Marshall, Susan

Overland Park
Steinkamp, Robert Theodore

Wichita
Melgren, Eric Franklin
Sorensen, Harvey R.

KENTUCKY

Lebanon
Higdon, Frederick Alonzo

Louisville
Fassler, Charles

LOUISIANA

Metairie
Derbes, Albert Joseph, III,
Nuzum, Robert Weston

Monroe
Curry, Robert Lee, III,

New Orleans
Abbott, Hirschel Theron, Jr.,
McDaniel, Donald Hamilton

MAINE

Portland
Hunt, David Evans
Sellers, Elizabeth Martin

MARYLAND

Baltimore
Hirsh, Theodore William
Johnston, Edward Allan
Shapiro, Harry Dean
Stiller, Shale David

Bethesda
Bauersfeld, Carl Frederick
Rosenberg, Mark Louis

Greenbelt
Jackley, Michael Dano

Rockville
Friedman, Greg Stuart
Katz, Steven Martin

Westminster
Staples, Lyle Newton

MASSACHUSETTS

Boston
Jacobs, Michael A.
Larson, Olive Elizabeth
Ritt, Roger Merrill
Solet, Maxwell David

Cambridge
Connors, Frank Joseph

Framingham
Heng, Gerald C. W.

Lexington
Hines, Edward Francis, Jr.,

Newton
Metzer, Patricia Ann

Stoughton
Gabovitch, Steven Alan

MICHIGAN

Ann Arbor
Keppelman, Nancy

Birmingham
Sweeney, Thomas Frederick

Bloomfield Hills
Callow, Thomas Edward
Deron, Edward Michael
Kasischke, Louis Walter
Klein, Coleman Eugene
Solomon, Mark Raymond

Detroit
Rasmussen, Douglas John

Grand Rapids
Oetting, Roger H.

Grosse Pointe
Goss, James William

Southfield
DeLong, Donald Alan
Forrest, Robert Edwin

Troy
Brody, Jay Howard
Dillon, Joseph Francis
Gregory, George William

MINNESOTA

Minneapolis
Erhart, John Joseph
Martin, Phillip Hammond
Shnider, Bruce Jay
Vander Molen, Thomas Dale

MISSISSIPPI

Jackson
Hammond, Frank Jefferson, III,

MISSOURI

Chesterfield
Fagerberg, Roger Richard

Kansas City
Egan, Charles Joseph, Jr.,
Pemberton, Bradley Powell

Saint Louis
Cornfeld, Dave Louis
Goldenhersh, Robert Stanley
Gorham, Charles
Greenley, Beverly Jane
Keller, Juan Dane

MONTANA

Kalispell
Kaufman, Leonard Lee

NEW JERSEY

Cherry Hill
Liebman, Emmanuel

Florham Park
LeVine, Walter Daniel
Witman, Leonard Joel

Hackensack
Mullin, Patrick Allen

Jersey City
Guarini, Frank Joseph

Morristown
Doyle, David Perrie
Fishman, Richard Glenn
Sherman, Sandra Brown
Sweeney, John Lawrence

Newark
Costenbader, Charles Michael
O'Connor Quinn, Deirdre
Vajtay, Stephen Michael, Jr.,
Zuckerman, Herbert Lawrence

Point Pleasant Beach
Herr, Philip Michael

Princeton
Kenny, Robert
Mulchinock, David Steward

Roseland
Danzis, Colin Michael

South Orange
Delo, Ellen Sanderson

West Orange
Richmond, Harold Nicholas

NEW MEXICO

Albuquerque
Gorman, Robert Dennis

Santa Fe
Hickey, John Miller

NEW YORK

East Northport
Ryesky, Kenneth H.

Floral Park
Goldman, Alan Barry

Jericho
Shulman, Madelyn R. Spatt

New Rochelle
Herzberg, Sydelle Shulman

New York
Aidinoff, M(erton) Bernard
Black, Louis Engleman
Clark, Celia Rue
Cohen, Edmund Stephen
Cubitto, Robert J.

Darrow, Jill E(llen)
Dixon, William
Dlugoff, Marc Alan
Easton, Reed W.
Fass, Peter Michael
Feder, Arthur A.
Ferguson, Milton Carr Carr, Jr.,
Finkelstein, Stuart M.
Gifford, William C.
Gordon, Stephen Louis
Haims, Bruce David
Hirschfeld, Michael
Josephson, Mark A.
Kamin, Sherwin
Keneally, Kathryn Marie
Kitay, Harvey Robert
Kolbe, Karl William, Jr.,
Kurtz, Jerome
Lipsky, Burton G.
Loengard, Richard Otto, Jr.,
MacLean, Babcock
Meyers, Donal Alexander
Moore, Thomas Ronald (Lord Bridestowe)
Odell, Stuart
Phillips, Barnet, IV,
Posner, Louis Joseph
Reifler, Stewart
Rooney, Paul C., Jr.,
Rosenberg, Alan Stewart
Sachs, David
Samuels, Leslie B.
Schneider, Willys Hope
Serota, Susan Perlstadt
Shapiro, Aleena Rieger
Shipper, David W.
Smith, Morton Alan
Staffaroni, Robert J.
Strock, Marcus
Thompson, Loran Tyson
Varet, Michael A.
Watts, David Eide
White, Harry Edward, Jr.,
Whoriskey, Robert Donald
Youngwood, Alfred Donald
Zucker, Howard

Pearl River
Meyer, Irwin Stephan

Rochester
Colby, William Michael
Kraus, Sherry Stokes
Twietmeyer, Don Henry
Wild, Robert Warren

White Plains
Berlin, Alan Daniel
Greenspan, Leon Joseph

NORTH CAROLINA

Asheville
Hamilton, Jackson Douglas
Lavelle, Brian Francis David

Charlotte
Preston, James Young

Durham
Buchanan, Phillip Hoge

Raleigh
Simpson, Steven Drexell

Tabor City
Jorgensen, Ralph Gubler

NORTH DAKOTA

Grand Forks
Cilz, Douglas Arthur

OHIO

Cincinnati
Flanagan, John Anthony
Neumark, Michael Harry
Porter, Robert Carl, Jr.,
Ruby, Stanley L.

Cleveland
Cohn, Mark Barry
Conner, William Herbert
Currivan, John Daniel
Doris, Alan S(anford)
Friedman, Harold Edward
Horvitz, Michael John
Koblenz, N(orman) Herschel
Ollinger, W. James
Weiler, Jeffry Louis

Columbus
Balthaser, James Harvey
Hockstad, Karen Sue
Shayne, Stanley H.

Dayton
Hitter, Joseph Ira

Findlay
Jetton, Girard Reuel, Jr.,

Massillon
Netzly, Dwight H.

Toledo
Doner, Gary William
Jackson, Louise Anne

Worthington
Albert, Robert Hamilton

Youngstown
Matune, Frank Joseph

OKLAHOMA

Enid
Jones, Stephen

Muskogee
Frix, Paige Lane

Oklahoma City
Kornfeld, Julian Potash

Tulsa
Eagleton, Edward John
Moffett, J. Denny

OREGON

Portland
Froebe, Gerald Allen
Hanna, Harry Mitchell

PENNSYLVANIA

Bala Cynwyd
Odell, Herbert

Exton
Teti, Louis N.

Harrisburg
Cooper, Jeffrey
Trimmer, Vicky Ann

Philadelphia
Brier, Bonnie Susan
Chimples, George
Frank, Barry H.
Goldman, Jerry Stephen
Koplin, Bernice Judith
Lichtenstein, Robert Jay
McQuiston, Robert Earl
Richards, Bonnie E.
Strasbaugh, Wayne Ralph
Wiener, Ronald Martin
Wild, Richard P.
Wolff, Deborah H(orowitz)

Pittsburgh
Hitt, Leo N.
Montgomery, Richard C.
Ummer, James Walter

Pottsville
Jones, Joseph Hayward

Wellsboro
Duff, Brian S.

Wormleysburg
Cherewka, Michael

York
Perry, Ronald

RHODE ISLAND

Providence
Olsen, Hans Peter
Salter, Lester Herbert

SOUTH CAROLINA

Greenville
Dobson, Robert Albertus, III,

Hilton Head Island
Rose, William Shepard, Jr.,

SOUTH DAKOTA

Rapid City
Foye, Thomas Harold

TENNESSEE

Knoxville
Gentry, Mack A.

Memphis
Bland, James Theodore, Jr.,

Nashville
Trautman, Herman Louis

TEXAS

Austin
Wood, Donald F.

Bedford
Williams-Pearson, Cynthia L.

Brenham
Fisher, Edwin H.

Corpus Christi
Stukenberg, Michael Wesley

Dallas
Brewer, David Madison
Chapman, Robert T.
Crichton, Thomas, IV,
Gerberding Cowart, Greta Elaine
Glancy, Walter John
Kerridge, Ronald David
Lan, Donald Paul, Jr.,
Mankoff, Ronald Morton
Nolan, John Michael
Owens, Rodney Joe
Wilson, Claude Raymond, Jr.,

Fort Worth
Tracy, J. David

Houston
Allender, John Roland
Caudill, William Howard
Cox, James Talley
Grossberg, Marc Elias
Linden, William M.
Osterberg, Edward Charles, Jr.,
Segal, Steven E.
Sheinfeld, Myron M.
Touchy, Deborah K.P.
Wells, Benjamin Gladney

Waco
Page, Jack Randall

VIRGINIA

Mc Lean
Aucutt, Ronald David
Susko, Carol Lynne
Tansill, Frederick Joseph

Norfolk
Old, William Abner

Orange
Thomas, Franklin A., III,

Richmond
Addison, David Dunham
Canup, James W.C.
Denny, Collins, III,
Starke, Harold E., Jr.,

Williamsburg
Merritt, James Edward

WASHINGTON

Seattle
Boxx, Karen Elizabeth
Judson, C(harles) James (Jim Judson)
Malone, Thomas William
Parks, Patricia Jean
Sussman, Neil A.
Treiger, Irwin Louis

Yakima
Wright, J(ames) Lawrence

WISCONSIN

Madison
Baldwin, Janice Murphy
Croake, Paul Allen

Milwaukee
Duback, Steven Rahr
Frautschi, Timothy Clark
Gallagher, Richard Sidney
Peltin, Sherwin Carl
Schnur, Robert Arnold

New Berlin
Bembenek, Alan R.

TERRITORIES OF THE UNITED STATES

PUERTO RICO

San Juan
Rodriguez-Diaz, Juan E.

BRAZIL

Recife
Caldas de Sá, Rodrigo Cesar

Rio de Janeiro
Muniz, Renata Maria (Renata Novotny)

São Paulo
Chiavassa, Tercio
Utumi, Ana Cláudia Akie

ENGLAND

London
Aleksander, Nicholas P.
Lubar, Charles Gordon

FRANCE

Neuilly-sur-Seine
Leherissel, Herve

Paris
Plankensteiner, Marco
Poirier, Roland Albert
Raffin, Marie-Hélène J.
Renoux, Vincent Andre

GERMANY

Berlin
Rodewald, Joerg
von Rechenberg, Wolf G.

Düsseldorf
Pathe, Ilmo

INDONESIA

Jakarta
Hsi, Edward Yang

ITALY

Rome
Lupo, Antonello

JAPAN

Tokyo
Fujieda, Atsushi

PERU

Lima
Castle, Percy

PORTUGAL

Lisbon
Nuncio, Paulo

SPAIN

Madrid
Mullerat, Ramon, Jr.,

SWITZERLAND

Zürich
O'Donnell, Thomas Alexander
Oberle, Andreas

THAILAND

Bangkok
Vickery, Harold Kirby, Jr.,

ADDRESS UNPUBLISHED

Alfred, Stephen Jay
Boulanger, Carol Seabrook
Clark, Donald Otis
Comisky, Ian Michael
DiFronzo, Michael A.
Freedman, Barbara Widman
Freund, Samuel J.
Harmon, Gail McGreevy
Holden, William Hoyt, Jr.,
Houle, Jeffrey Robert
Kerner, Michael Philip
Kusma, Kyllikki
Levy, David
Lipsman, Richard Marc
Lubick, Donald Cyril
Marks, Bernard Bailin
Meyer, Max Earl
Milsten, Robert B.
Peterson, Howard Cooper
Petrie, Richard Allen
Putney, Wainscott Walker
Rodriguez, Vivian N.
Sabino, William
Sliger, Herbert Jacquemin, Jr.,
Stuart, Michael George
Torgerson, Larry Keith
Wimpissinger, Christian

TAXATION, PERSONAL INCOME

UNITED STATES

ALABAMA

Montgomery
Proctor, David Ray

ARIZONA

Phoenix
Everett, James Joseph

CALIFORNIA

Costa Mesa
Schaaf, Douglas Allan

Glendale
Scott, A. Timothy

Glennville
Walton, Lewis R.

Larkspur
Greenberg, Myron Silver

Los Angeles
Hyman, Milton Bernard
Maeder, Gary William
Presant, Sanford Calvin
Stone, Lawrence Maurice

Palo Alto
Miller, Michael Patiky
Van Atta, David Murray

Redlands
Shimoff, Paul Martin

Sacramento
Arkin, Michael Barry

San Francisco
Greene, Richard Lawrence
Livsey, Robert Callister
Martin, Stephen James
Thomas, William Scott
Wood, Robert Warren

Santa Barbara
Howell, Weldon U., Jr.,

Santa Cruz
Schalk, Robert Partridge

Santa Monica
Axe, Norman Gold

Walnut Creek
Willson, Prentiss, Jr.,

COLORADO

Aurora
Stauffer, Scott William

Colorado Springs
Everson, Steven Lee

Denver
Ruppert, John Lawrence

Parker
Greenberg, Morton Paul

CONNECTICUT

Darien
Dale, Erwin Randolph

Hartford
Appel, Robert Eugene
Lyon, James Burroughs

Monroe
Cleland, Edward Gordon

New Haven
Auerbach, Hillel Joshua

Stamford
Burton, David K.
Teitell, Conrad Laurence

Westport
Sheiman, Ronald Lee

Wilton
Slater, Ralph Evan

DELAWARE

Wilmington
Baumann, Julian Henry, Jr.,

DISTRICT OF COLUMBIA

Washington
Campos, Alfred
Cohen, Sheldon Stanley
Davidson, Daniel Morton
Harris, Don Victor, Jr.,
Heffernan, James Vincent
Jacobson, David Edward
Kafka, Gerald Andrew
Kautter, David John
Paul, William McCann
Rubin, Blake Douglas

FLORIDA

Boca Raton
Harris, Michael Robert

Fort Lauderdale
Barnard, George Smith
Gore, George Henry

Lake Wales
Wales, Gwynne Huntington

Miami
Weinstein, Andrew H.

Miami Beach
Brodie, Ronald

TAXATION, STATE AND LOCAL

MONTANA

Billings
Sites, James Philip

NEVADA

Las Vegas
Wilson, Joseph Morris, III,

NEW JERSEY

Allendale
Rosenblum, Edward G.

Hamilton
Haushalter, Harry

Newark
Costenbader, Charles Michael
Zuckerman, Herbert Lawrence

Somerville
Sozansky, Michael William, Jr.,

NEW YORK

Albany
Koff, Howard Michael

Brooklyn
Young, Sidney David

East Meadow
Hyman, Montague Allan

New York
Agranoff, Gerald Neal
Faber, Peter Lewis
Flanagan, Deborah Mary
Garfunkel, Alan J.
Koch, Edward Richard
Rosenberg, Alan Stewart
Rosenberg, Jerome Roy
Sachs, David
Shea, James William

OHIO

Cleveland
Conner, William Herbert
Kramer, Eugene Leo
Rosenbaum, Jacob I.
Weiler, Jeffry Louis

Columbus
Fisher, Lloyd Edison, Jr.,

Dayton
Hitter, Joseph Ira

Youngstown
Matune, Frank Joseph

OREGON

Coquille
Lounsbury, Steven Richard

PENNSYLVANIA

Philadelphia
Ominsky, Harris

RHODE ISLAND

Providence
Reilly, Charles James
Salter, Lester Herbert

TEXAS

Austin
Cunningham, Judy Marie
Harrison, Richard Wayne

Dallas
Bonesio, Woodrow Michael
Mankoff, Ronald Morton
Wilson, Claude Raymond, Jr.,

Houston
Seymour, Barbara Laverne
Van Kerrebrook, Mary Alice
Wall, Kenneth E., Jr.,

VIRGINIA

Hampton
McNider, James Small, III,

Mc Lean
Susko, Carol Lynne

Richmond
Kelly, John Francis
Millhiser, Thomas McNally
Rowe, William L. S.

WASHINGTON

Seattle
Hilpert, Edward Theodore, Jr.,
Judson, C(harles) James (Jim Judson)

WISCONSIN

Milwaukee
Frautschi, Timothy Clark
Schnur, Robert Arnold

New Berlin
Bembenek, Alan R.

Waukesha
Macy, John Patrick

AUSTRALIA

Killara
Zipfinger, Frank Peter

BRAZIL

Rio de Janeiro
Muniz, Renata Maria (Renata Novotny)

São Paulo
Utumi, Ana Cláudia Akie

ADDRESS UNPUBLISHED

Bost, Thomas Glen
Drabkin, Murray
Freund, Samuel J.
Haley, George Brock, Jr.,
Harnack, Don Steger
Harris, Richard Eugene Vassau

TOXIC TORT

UNITED STATES

ALABAMA

Birmingham
Brown, T. Michael
Palmer, Robert Leslie

ARIZONA

Phoenix
Turk, Andrew Borders

CALIFORNIA

Fresno
Runyon, Brett L.

Moraga
Kilbourne, George William

Oakland
Mendelson, Steven Earle

Sacramento
Eickmeyer, Evan

San Francisco
Fergus, Gary Scott
Getto, Ernest John

DISTRICT OF COLUMBIA

Washington
Adamson, Terrence Burdett
Watson, Thomas C.

GEORGIA

Atlanta
Myers, Lawrence Joseph

ILLINOIS

Chicago
Drumke, Michael William
Menaker, Pamela Sakowicz
Schoenfield, Rick Merrill

Edwardsville
Hopkins, John J.

KENTUCKY

Lexington
Masterton, Lucinda Cronin

LOUISIANA

Chalmette
Mumphrey, J. Wayne

Lake Charles
Parkerson, Hardy Martell

Metairie
O'Donnell, Barbara Bourdonnay

New Orleans
Hoffman, Donald Alfred

MARYLAND

Baltimore
Sack, Sylvan Hanan

MASSACHUSETTS

Boston
Schlichtmann, Jan R.

MICHIGAN

Grand Rapids
Birkbeck, A.J. Koerts

MISSISSIPPI

Tupelo
Deaton, Chris Harold

MISSOURI

Kansas City
Beck, William G.
Koelling, Thomas Winsor
Rooney, Robert Gerard

Saint Louis
Rabbitt, Daniel Thomas, Jr.,
Reeg, Kurtis Bradford

NEW JERSEY

Cherry Hill
Spielberg, Joshua Morris

Newark
Corbin Walker, Karol

NEW YORK

Buffalo
Szanyi, Kevin Andrew

New Hyde Park
Jaffe, Richard S.

New York
Antonucci, Peter A.
Birnbaum, Sheila L.
Harrison, Tomasita L.
Kelmachter, Leslie Debra
Riley, Scott C.
Strober, Eric Saul
Yelenick, Mary Therese

White Plains
Colistra, Brian William

NORTH CAROLINA

Winston Salem
Maready, William Frank

OHIO

Cleveland
Solomon, Randall Lee
Young, James Edward

Medina
Arnold, Alanna S. Welling

OKLAHOMA

Oklahoma City
Phelps, Anthony David

OREGON

Portland
Bailey, Ronald E.
Duden, Paul Russell

PENNSYLVANIA

Philadelphia
Fickler, Arlene
Hoyle, Lawrence Truman, Jr.,
Madva, Stephen Alan

Pittsburgh
Tarasi, Louis Michael, Jr.,

TEXAS

Houston
Edwards, Blaine Douglass
Oldham, Darius Dudley
Welsh, H. Ronald

Orange
Townsend, Rodney Allen

Pearland
Yaziji, Nejd

VIRGINIA

Norfolk
Bishop, Bruce Taylor

Richmond
King, William H., Jr.,
Landin, David Craig

WASHINGTON

Hoquiam
Kahler, Ray William

WEST VIRGINIA

Huntington
Bagley, Charles Frank, III,

Weston
Oldaker, Bradley Russell

AUSTRALIA

Melbourne
Morrison, Andrew

Sydney
Eggleton, Glenn David

ENGLAND

London
Mendelowitz, Michael Sydney

ADDRESS UNPUBLISHED

Ashkin, Roberta Ellen

TRADEMARK AND COPYRIGHT

UNITED STATES

ARIZONA

Phoenix
Meschkow, Jordan M.
Phillips, James Harold
Sutton, Samuel J.

CALIFORNIA

Beverly Hills
Brown, Hermione Kopp

Claremont
Ansell, Edward Orin

Encinitas
Nemeth, Valerie Ann

Irvine
Knobbe, Louis Joseph
Martens, Don Walter
Stone, Samuel Beckner
Tachner, Leonard

Los Angeles
Chu, Morgan
Green, William Porter
Heinke, Rex S.
Krupka, Robert George
Menes, Paul Ira

Mountain View
Pasahow, Lynn H(arold)

Oxnard
Gerber, David A.

Palo Alto
Nycum, Susan Hubbell
Patten, Valerie Lynn
Simon, James Lowell

Sacramento
Houpt, James Edward

San Francisco
Chambers, Guy Wayne
Smegal, Thomas Frank, Jr.,

San Luis Obispo
Dorsi, Stephen Nathan

Santa Monica
Scott, Michael Dennis

Sausalito
Gordon, Robert Eugene

COLORADO

Breckenridge
Fromm, Jeffery Bernard

Denver
Dorr, Robert Charles
Samuels, Donald L.
Weinstein, David Akers

CONNECTICUT

Enfield
Smith, Spencer Thomas

Monroe
Oliver, Milton McKinnon

New Haven
De Lio, Anthony Peter

Westport
Razzano, Pasquale Angelo

DISTRICT OF COLUMBIA

Washington
Aisenberg, Irwin Morton
Cantor, Herbert I.
Coerper, Milo George
Cooper, Alan Samuel
Davidson, Tom William
Denison, Mary Boney
Glick, Leslie Alan
Goodman, Alfred Nelson
Hefter, Laurence Roy
Henderson, Douglas Boyd
Hobbs, J. Timothy, Sr.,
Malone, William Robert
Marks, Richard Daniel
McCann, Clifton Everett
Potenza, Joseph Michael
Price, Griffith Baley, Jr.,
Repper, George Robert
Sears, Mary Helen

FLORIDA

Jacksonville
Hill, Debra S.

Miami
Bartelstone, Ted Henry
Castillo, Angel, Jr.,
Fleit, Martin

Naples
Werder, Horst Heinrich

Orlando
Blaher, Neal Jonathan

GEORGIA

Atlanta
Alexander, Miles Jordan
Drucker, Michael Stuart
Schroeder, Eric Peter

Norcross
Anderson, Albert Sydney, III,

Valdosta
Sinnott, John Patrick

HAWAII

Honolulu
Hsia, Martin Edgar

ILLINOIS

Barrington
Lee, William Marshall

Chicago
Altman, Louis
Amend, James Michael
Berenzweig, Jack Charles
Berghoff, Paul Henry
Boehnen, Daniel A.
Geraldson, Raymond I., Jr.,
Geren, Gerald S.
Gerstman, George Henry
Hilliard, David Craig
Hofer, Roy Ellis
Hoffman, Richard Bruce
Kozak, John W.
Parkhurst, Todd Sheldon
Partridge, Mark Van Buren
Rubin, E(rwin) Leonard
Schneider, Robert Jerome
Sheppard, Berton Scott
Sweeney, James Raymond
Wanke, Ronald Lee
Wilson, Clarence Sylvester, Jr.,

Lake Bluff
Wick, Lawrence Scott

Northbrook
Bohlender, Hugh Darrow
Sernett, Richard Patrick

Urbana
Fitz-Gerald, Roger Miller

INDIANA

Indianapolis
Cole, Roland Jay
Troll, John Richard

TRANSPORTATION

LOUISIANA

Metairie
McMahon, Robert Albert, Jr.,

New Orleans
Ostendorf, Lance Stephen

MARYLAND

Bethesda
Pankopf, Arthur, Jr.,

Potomac
Redding, Robert Ellsworth

MICHIGAN

Brighton
Gardella, Robert Christopher

MISSOURI

Saint Louis
Newman, Charles A.
Williams, Theodore Joseph, Jr.,

NEVADA

Las Vegas
Hilbrecht, Norman Ty

NEW JERSEY

Millburn
Madden, Edward George, Jr.,

NEW YORK

Brooklyn
Jacobson, Barry Stephen

Huntington
Augello, William Joseph

Melville
Adler, Kenneth

New York
McMahon, James Charles
Oechler, Henry John, Jr.,

Syracuse
Pinsky, Roy David

White Plains
Nesci, Vincent Peter

NORTH CAROLINA

Cherryville
Huffstetler, Palmer Eugene

OHIO

Cleveland
Kundtz, John Andrew
Skulina, Thomas Raymond

Columbus
Turano, David A.

OREGON

Portland
Kester, Randall Blair
Simpson, Robert Glenn

PENNSYLVANIA

Philadelphia
Staffieri, Nicholas J.
Wert, Robert Clifton

TENNESSEE

Memphis
Russell, James Franklin
Soefker, Curt Reid

Nashville
Lowell, Roland M.

TEXAS

Fort Worth
Soward, Joe Weldon, II,

VIRGINIA

Charlottesville
Chandler, Lawrence Bradford, Jr.,

Mc Lean
Olsen, Robert Eric

Norfolk
Bishop, Bruce Taylor

WISCONSIN

Green Bay
Schober, Thomas Leonard

MEXICO

Mexico City
Garcia Giorgana, Ricardo

BELGIUM

Brussels
Barnum, John Wallace

ENGLAND

London
Arthur, David Anthony Dering

GREECE

Piraeus
Sofianopoulos, Dimitrios

ADDRESS UNPUBLISHED

Beitling, S. Richard
Tavrow, Richard Lawrence

TRIAL. *See* **Civil Litigation; Criminal.**

TRUSTS. *See* **Probate.**

UTILITIES, PUBLIC

UNITED STATES

ALABAMA

Montgomery
Harris, George Bryan
Laurie, Robin Garrett

ARIZONA

Phoenix
Baker, William Dunlap
Lyons, George Harris
Nelson, Douglas Clarence

CALIFORNIA

Fresno
Ewell, A. Ben, Jr.,

Oakland
Skaff, Andrew Joseph

San Francisco
Morrissey, John Carroll, Sr.,
Odgers, Richard William

COLORADO

Denver
Campbell, Leonard M.

Fort Collins
Hjelmfelt, David Charles

CONNECTICUT

Hartford
Taylor, Allan Bert

DISTRICT OF COLUMBIA

Washington
Avil, Richard Daniel, Jr.,
Batla, Raymond John, Jr.,
Beresford, Douglas Lincoln
Besozzi, Paul Charles
Betts, Kirk Howard
Downs, Clark Evans
Emery, Nancy Beth
Feldman, Roger David
Jacobson, David Edward
Littell, Richard Gregory
MacDougall, Gordon Pier
Mallory, Charles King, III,
Mann, Donegan
May, Randolph Joseph
Moring, John Frederick
O'Neill, Brian Dennis
Oliver, Joseph McDonald, Jr.,
Simons, Barbara M.
Ward, Erica Anne
Weinberg, Sara Caryna
Zipp, Joel Frederick

FLORIDA

Naples
Doub, William Offutt

Pensacola
Jones, Julie Laura

West Palm Beach
Gildan, Phillip Clarke

GEORGIA

Atlanta
Hawks, Barrett Kingsbury
Miller, Douglas L.
Wakefield, Stephen Alan

HAWAII

Honolulu
Case, James Hebard

ILLINOIS

Chicago
Delp, Wilbur Charles, Jr.,
Fazio, Peter Victor, Jr.,
Helman, Robert Alan
Horwich, Allan
Zabel, Sheldon Alter

INDIANA

Indianapolis
Allen, David James
Schlegel, Fred Eugene

Lawrenceburg
Ewan, William Kenneth

IOWA

Des Moines
Fisher, Thomas George, Jr.,
Graziano, Craig Frank
Tipton, Sheila Kay

KANSAS

Bucyrus
Hoffman, John Raymond

KENTUCKY

Owensboro
Miller, James Monroe

MARYLAND

Baltimore
Cole, Emried Dargan, Jr.,

Bethesda
Gottlieb, Jonathan W.
Ross, William Warfield

MICHIGAN

Detroit
Smith, James Albert

Lansing
Marvin, David Edward Shreve

MINNESOTA

Saint Paul
LeVander, Harold Powrie, Jr.,

MISSISSIPPI

Bay Saint Louis
Bernstein, Joseph

MISSOURI

Saint Louis
Godiner, Donald Leonard
Smith, Arthur Lee

NEBRASKA

Omaha
Dolan, James Vincent

NEVADA

Las Vegas
Hilbrecht, Norman Ty

Reno
Marshall, Robert William

NEW JERSEY

Roseland
Vanderbilt, Arthur T., II,

Somerville
Laskey, James Howard

Woodbridge
Weissman, Matthew Mark

NEW MEXICO

Albuquerque
Moore, Charles Loyd

Santa Fe
Carpenter, Richard Norris

NEW YORK

Albany
Alessi, Robert Joseph

Buffalo
Glanville, Robert Edward

New York
Dunn, M(orris) Douglas
Joseph, Leonard
Lyon, Carl Francis, Jr.,
Parish, J. Michael
Schwartz, Renee Gerstler
White, Katherine Patricia

Pittsford
George, Richard Neill

NORTH CAROLINA

Charlotte
Walker, Clarence Wesley

Raleigh
Carmichael, Carson, III,
Hargrove, Wade Hampton

OHIO

Akron
Flannery, Harry Audley

Columbus
Cross, Jeffrey D.
Mone, Robert Paul
Ryan, Joseph W., Jr.,
Taft, Sheldon Ashley

Newark
Hite, David L.

OKLAHOMA

Tulsa
Arrington, John Leslie, Jr.,
Gaberino, John Anthony, Jr.,

OREGON

Portland
Dotten, Michael Chester

PENNSYLVANIA

Philadelphia
Satinsky, Barnett

Pittsburgh
Boswell, William Paret
Demmler, John Henry
Reed, W. Franklin

RHODE ISLAND

Providence
Gasbarro, Pasco, Jr.,
McElroy, Michael Robert

SOUTH CAROLINA

Charleston
Groves, Stephen Peterson, Sr.,

SOUTH DAKOTA

Pierre
Gerdes, David Alan

TENNESSEE

Nashville
Bass, James Orin

TEXAS

Austin
Demond, Walter Eugene

Houston
Gover, Alan Shore
Hartrick, Janice Kay
Rozzell, Scott Ellis

UTAH

Salt Lake City
Baucom, Sidney George
Reeder, F. Robert

VERMONT

Rutland
Taylor, A. Jeffry

VIRGINIA

Glen Allen
Page, Eric Michael

Norfolk
Smith, Richard Muldrow

Richmond
Brasfield, Evans Booker
Flippen, Edward L.

WASHINGTON

Seattle
Redman, Eric

Spokane
Stone, Donald Gene

Tacoma
Mack, Robert E.

WEST VIRGINIA

Charleston
Chaney, Vincent Verlando
Lane, Charlotte

WISCONSIN

Madison
Hanson, David James

Milwaukee
Barnes, Paul McClung

ENGLAND

London
Phillips, Robert John

SOUTH AFRICA

Johannesburg
Baillie, Brigette Ann

ADDRESS UNPUBLISHED

Baker, William Thompson, Jr.,
Branstetter, Cecil Dewey, Sr.,
Eaken, Bruce Webb, Jr.,
Eichhorn, Frederick Foltz, Jr.,
Gorske, Robert H.
Haley, George Brock, Jr.,
Harshman, Raymond Brent
Heath, Charles Dickinson
Howell, Donald Lee
Mayer, James Joseph
Norman, Albert George, Jr.,
Ostergaard, Joni Hammersla
Polsky, Howard David
Powers, Elizabeth Whitmel
Roethe, James Norton

WATER. *See* **Property, real.**

WILLS. *See* **Probate.**

WORKERS' COMPENSATION *See also* Labor; Personal injury

UNITED STATES

ALABAMA

Bessemer
Fawwal, Audeh Edward

Birmingham
Albritton, William Harold, IV,
Donahue, Timothy Patrick

Dadeville
Oliver, John Percy, II,

North Charleston
Wigger, Jarrel L.

Spartanburg
Smith, William Douglas

TENNESSEE

Etowah
Parker, Eugene LeRoy, III,

Knoxville
Ownby, Jere Franklin, III,
Wheeler, John Watson

Memphis
Gipson, Harvey Lofton
Russell, James Franklin

TEXAS

Austin
Kilgore, Gary Lynn
Pena, Richard

Cleburne
MacLean, John Ronald

Dallas
Finston, Felicia A.
Levin, Hervey Phillip

Fort Worth
Streck, Frederick Louis, III,

Houston
Ney, Judy Larson
Pitts, Gary Benjamin
Vaughan, Stephen Michael

San Antonio
Henry, Peter York

VERMONT

Burlington
Cain, Robert Gaynor

VIRGINIA

Alexandria
Cassell, Richard Emmett

Mechanicsville
d'Evegnee, Charles Paul

WASHINGTON

Olympia
Williams, Wayne Leroy

Seattle
Scott, Brian David

Spokane
Harbaugh, Daniel Paul
Pontarolo, Michael Joseph

Tacoma
Condon, David Bruce

WEST VIRGINIA

Charleston
Rowe, Larry Linwell

WISCONSIN

Amery
Gust, Gerald Norman

Delafield
Hausman, C. Michael

La Crosse
Skemp, William

Madison
Bruchs, Amy O'Brien
Schmid, John Henry, Jr.,

Milwaukee
Kmiec, Steven Gerard

Racine
Rudebusch, Alice Ann

Wausau
Gray, Robert Joseph
Molinaro, Thomas J.

BELGIUM

Diegem
Vandervelde, Erwin

PORTUGAL

Lisbon
Leitao, Maria Da Gloria

SPAIN

Madrid
García-Perrote, Ignacio

ADDRESS UNPUBLISHED

Berman, Richard Bruce
Branstetter, Cecil Dewey, Sr.,
Carlson, Alan Douglas
Embry, Stephen Creston
Erwin, Gregory Scott
Hoffman, Alan Craig
Kell, Scott K.
Seagull, Keith Allen
Wells, Wayne Alton

OTHER

UNITED STATES

ALABAMA

Birmingham
Norris, Robert Wheeler *Ethics*

Montgomery
Smith, Jerome David *Elder law*

ARIZONA

Phoenix
McRae, Stephanie A. *Licensing*
Platt, Warren E. *Accountant*

Scottsdale
Roberts, Jean Reed *Elder*

CALIFORNIA

Beverly Hills
Dent, John Robert *Hotel Development & Operations*

Newport Beach
Jones, Sheldon Atwell *Investment*

Oakland
Bryant, Arthur H. *Public interest*
Lomhoff, Peter George *Elder*

Palo Alto
Patten, Valerie Lynn *Art Law*
Patterson, Robert Edward *High technology*

Pasadena
Poole, Heather L. *domestic violence*
Tanner, Dee Boshard *Corporate Fraud*

San Francisco
Baker, James P. *ERISA*

Sanger
Chynoweth, W. Edward

Santa Ana
Mosich, Nicholas Joseph

Universal City
Husband, Bertram Paul *Equine law*

COLORADO

Denver
Austin, H(arry) Gregory *Partnership*

DELAWARE

Wilmington
Tenenbaum, Joel David *Adoption*

DISTRICT OF COLUMBIA

Washington
Beers, Donald Osborne *Food and drug*
Johnson, Philip McBride *Commodities*
Keeney, John Christopher, Jr., *Political campaigns*
Matisik, Edward Newton
Pierson, Stuart F. *Media law*
Rosenblatt, Peter Ronald *Government*
Schneider, Matthew Roger *Government Relations*

FLORIDA

Fort Pierce
Conklin, Howard Lawrence *Trade*

Miami
Perdomo, Michelle *consular law*

Pensacola
Jones, Julie Laura *Risk Management*

Tallahassee
DeFoor, J. Allison, II, *Technology*

West Palm Beach
Moore, George Crawford Jackson *British law*

GEORGIA

Sugar Hill
Hamby, Lee Ellen *Elder*

ILLINOIS

Chicago
Bogaard, Jonathan Harvey *Equipment Finance*
Bormes, James X. *Commercial litigation*
Emerson, Carter Whitney *Venture capital*
Nicolaides, Mary *Elder*

INDIANA

Indianapolis
Capehart, Craig Earl *Contract Law*
Capehart, Craig Earl *Business Law*
McKeon, Thomas Joseph *Arson, fraud*

KENTUCKY

Florence
Frohlich, Anthony William

LOUISIANA

New Orleans
Correro, Anthony James, III,

MARYLAND

Baltimore
Meiselman, Alyson *Gender & Sexuality*

Fort Washington
Bowman, Denise Marie *Government ethics compliance*
Bowman, Denise Marie *Campaign finance compliance*

Frederick
Sica, John *Agriculture*

MASSACHUSETTS

Boston
Buchanan, Robert McLeod *Legal Ethics*
Hess-Mahan, Theodore Michael *Class Actions*
Soehle, Tracy Morse *Financial Services*

Framingham
Gould, Rodney Elliott *Travel*

Lincoln
Lufkin, Martha B.G. *Art*

Northampton
Fierst, Frederick Udell *Licensing*

Winchester
Bigelow, Robert P.

MICHIGAN

Bingham Farms
Larky, Sheldon Glen *Legal malpactice*

Bloomfield Hills
Charla, Leonard Francis *Art*

Detroit
Hanson, Victor G. *Maritime*
Peters, John Douglas *Drug and Medical Device Litigation*
Peters, John Douglas *Complex Litigation*

Grand Rapids
Buquicchio, Steven T. *receiverships*

Okemos
White, James Alfred *Agricultural*

MISSOURI

Kansas City
Hubbard, William L. *Elder*
Robb, Gary Charles *Medical Negligence*

Saint Louis
Brickler, John Weise *Municipal Finance*

NEW JERSEY

Bridgewater
Feingold, Mark Howard *Transactions*

Montclair
Gutman, Richard Martin *Freedom of Information*

Parsippany
Stein, Julie Lynne *Advertising*

Pompton Plains
Ludemann, Cathie Jane *Elder*

NEW YORK

Huntington
Robinson, Kenneth Patrick *Technology*

Jamaica
Angione, Howard Francis *Elder Law*

Jericho
Hecht, Donald Stuart *Elder*

New York
Darrow, Jill E(llen) *Partnership taxation*
Diskant, Gregory L. *Pharmaceuticals*
Edelson, Gilbert Seymour *Art*
Feldman, Franklin *Art Law*
Filler, Ronald Howard *Commodities*
Gold, Simeon *Restructuring*
Harley, Colin Emile *Equipment leasing*
Heftler, Thomas E. *Commodities*
Jaglom, Andre Richard *Distribution and Marketing Law*
Kailas, Leo George *Commodities*
Leichtling, Michael Alfred *Equipment leasing*
Littenberg, Michael Richard *Venture*
Reifler, Stewart *executive compensation*
Rosenberg, Alan Stewart *International taxation*
Smit, Robert H. *International Arbitration*
Vernon, Darryl Mitchell *Animal welfare*
Wainwright, Carroll Livingston, Jr., *Charitable organizations*

NORTH CAROLINA

Raleigh
Hargrove, Wade Hampton *Media*

OHIO

Delaware
Martin, Stephen David *Business*

Shaker Heights
Messinger, Donald Hathaway *Public*

OREGON

Portland
DuBoff, Leonard David *Art*

PENNSYLVANIA

Greensburg
Belden, H. Reginald, Jr., *Business litigation*

Lancaster
Eagan, Michele *class actions and complex litigation*

Langhorne
Hillje, Barbara Brown *Elder*

Media
Rainer, G. Bradley *Ethics*

Philadelphia
McKeever, John Eugene *Postal*
Palmer, Richard Ware *Marine Insurance*
Palmer, Richard Ware *International Law*
Rachofsky, David J. *International taxation*

Pittsburgh
Vogrin, Joseph Edward, III, *Motor Vehicle Law*

Warminster
Hetherington, John Joseph *Elder*

TEXAS

Austin
Bray, Austin Coleman, Jr., *Election*
Moss, Bill Ralph *Ethics*
Tighe, Austin *Consumer Class Action*

Baytown
Chavez, John Anthony *Trade*

Houston
Gilbert, Keith Thomas *Election*
Lowy, Peter Andrew *Tax Litigation*
Wilfong, Hugh C., II, *Joint ventures*

VIRGINIA

Arlington
Cragin, Charles Langmaid *Veteran*

WASHINGTON

Seattle
Boeder, Thomas L. *Trade*

Tacoma
Bergsten, William P. *Arbitration and mediation*

MEXICO

Mexico City
Fonseca, Gerardo *Telecommunications, Foreign Investment*
Garcia Giorgana, Ricardo *Mexican*
Zamora, Rodrigo *Arbitration*

BELARUS

Minsk
Todorovic, Ilija Ika *Refugee law*

BRAZIL

Rio de Janeiro
Basilio, Ana Tereza Palhares *Insolvency & Reorganization*

CZECH REPUBLIC

Prague
Kroft, Michal *Information Technology*

ENGLAND

London
Galloway, Diane *Shipping/Commodities*

Reigate
Sheridan, Peter Louis *Arbitration*

FRANCE

Paris
Caritoux, Valérie Francoise Cecile *Advertising, Internet, Distbn.*
Doumenge, Arnaud *Labor Litigation*
Meyer-Fabre, Nathalie *Arbitration*
Poncelet, Aline *Capital Market*

GERMANY

Frankfurt
Strelow, Markus *Private equity*
Strelow, Markus *Joint ventures*

ISRAEL

Tel Aviv
Raved, Yoram *Hi-tech and venture*

JAPAN

Tokyo
Fujieda, Atsushi *Transfer pricing*

NORWAY

Oslo
Aars-Rynning, Jacob *political asylum*
Thogersen, Kai *IT and Telecomms*

PERU

Lima
Quiroga-Leon, Anibal *Human Rights*

PHILIPPINES

Makati City
Gonzales, Ponciano Jr. Concepcion *Aerospace*

SPAIN

Madrid
Benavides, Alfonso *hotels*

SWITZERLAND

Zürich
Auf der Maur, Rolf *IT and telecommunication*

UKRAINE

Kiev
Golub, Andrey Vladimirovich *International trade law*

ADDRESS UNPUBLISHED

Professional Index

Saltzburg, Stephen Allan *law educator, consultant*
Starrs, James Edward *law and forensics educator, consultant*
Wallace, Don, Jr., *law educator*
Wedgwood, Ruth *law educator, international affairs expert*

FLORIDA

Coral Gables
Swan, Alan Charles *law educator*

Fort Lauderdale
Cane, Marilyn Blumberg *lawyer, educator*
Jarvis, Robert Mark *law educator*
Joseph, Paul R *law educator*
Mintz, Joel Alan *law educator*

Fort Myers
Zeldes, Ilya M. *forensic scientist, lawyer*

Gainesville
Mills, Jon *dean, law educator*

Jacksonville
Schupp, Robert Warren *law educator*

Jupiter
del Russo, Alessandra Luini *retired law educator*

Miami
Butterworth, Robert A. *dean, former state attorney general*
Matthews, Douglas Eugene *lawyer, educator, consultant*

Opa Locka
Light, Alfred Robert *lawyer, political scientist, educator*

Orlando
Glynn, Gerard Francis *law educator*

Saint Petersburg
Carrere, Charles Scott *law educator, judge*
Jacob, Bruce Robert *law educator*

Tallahassee
D'Alemberte, Talbot (Sandy D'Alemberte) *academic administrator, lawyer*
Schroeder, Edwin Maher *law educator*

GEORGIA

Athens
Beaird, James Ralph *law educator, dean*
Carlson, Ronald Lee *lawyer, educator*
Cooper, James Russell *retired law educator*
Kurtz, Paul Michael *law educator*
Shipley, David Elliott *dean, lawyer*

Atlanta
Arthur, Thomas Carlton *law educator*
Hay, Peter Heinrich *law educator*
Hunter, Howard Owen *academic administrator, law educator*
Knowles, Marjorie Fine *lawyer, educator, dean*
Landau, Michael B. *law educator, musician, writer*
Marvin, Charles Arthur *law educator*
Podgor, Ellen Sue *law educator*

HAWAII

Honolulu
Bloede, Victor Carl *lawyer, academic executive*
Callies, David Lee *lawyer, educator*
Iijima, Chris K. *law educator*
Miller, Richard Sherwin *law educator*
Van Dyke, Jon Markham Markham *law educator*

IDAHO

Moscow
Vincenti, Sheldon Arnold *law educator, lawyer*

ILLINOIS

Champaign
Etienne, Margareth *law educator*
Hurd, Heidi M. *law educator, dean*
Kindt, John Warren *lawyer, educator, consultant*
Mc Cord, John Harrison *lawyer, educator*
Nowak, John E. *law educator*
Stone, Victor J. *law educator*

Chicago
Alschuler, Albert W. *law educator*
Appel, Nina Schick *law educator, dean*
Baird, Douglas Gordon *law educator, dean*
Bennett, Robert William *law educator*
Garth, Bryant Geoffrey *law educator, foundation executive*
Helmholz, R(ichard) H(enry) *law educator*
Hutchinson, Dennis James *law educator*
Landes, William M. *law educator*
Levmore, Saul *law educator, dean*
McGovern, Peter John *law educator*
Meltzer, Bernard David *law educator*
Peterson, Randall Theodore *law educator*
Simoni, Christopher *dean, law educator*
Stone, Geoffrey Richard *law educator, lawyer*
Van Zandt, David E. *dean*

Highland Park
Ruder, David Sturtevant *lawyer, educator, government official*

Saint Charles
Alfini, James Joseph *dean, educator, lawyer*

INDIANA

Bloomington
Aman, Alfred Charles, Jr., *law educator*
Dilts, Jon Paul *law educator*
Palmer, Judith Grace *university administrator*
Robel, Lauren *law educator*
Shreve, Gene Russell *law educator*

Fort Wayne
Spielman, Kim Morgan *lawyer, educator*

Indianapolis
Funk, David Albert *retired law educator*

Notre Dame
Gunn, Alan *law educator*
O'Hara, Patricia A. *dean, law educator*
Smithburn, John Eric *law educator, judge*

West Lafayette
Scaletta, Phillip Jasper *lawyer, educator*

IOWA

Des Moines
Begleiter, Martin David *law educator, consultant*
Edwards, John Duncan *law educator, librarian*

Grinnell
Osgood, Russell King *academic administrator*

Iowa City
Hines, N. William *dean, law educator, administrator*
Wing, Adrien Katherine *law educator*

KANSAS

Lawrence
Turnbull, H. Rutherford, III, *law educator, lawyer*

Topeka
Concannon, James M. *law educator, university dean*
Elrod, Linda Diane Henry *lawyer, educator*

Wichita
Williams, Jackie N. *law educator, former prosecutor*

KENTUCKY

Lexington
Michael, Douglas Charles *law educator*
Vestal, Allan W. *dean, law educator*

LOUISIANA

Baton Rouge
Schroeder, Leila Obier *retired law educator*

New Orleans
Childress, Steven Alan *law educator*
Ciolino, Dane Stephen *law educator*
Friedman, Joel William *law educator*
Osakwe, Christopher *lawyer, educator*
Palmer, Vernon Valentine *law educator*
Ponoroff, Lawrence *law educator, legal consultant*
Sherman, Edward Francis *dean, law educator*

MAINE

Lewiston
Kessler, Mark *political scientist, educator*
Kessler, Mark Allen *political scientist, educator*

MARYLAND

Baltimore
McLain, Lynn *law educator*
Rothenberg, Karen H. *dean, law educator*
Trotter, Richard *law educator, arbitrator*

Catonsville
Zumbrun, Alvin John Thomas *law and criminology educator*

MASSACHUSETTS

Boston
Abrams, Roger Ian *law educator, arbitrator*
Bae, Frank S. H. *law educator, law library administrator*
Carter, T(homas) Barton *law educator*
Cass, Ronald Andrew *dean*
Daynard, Richard Alan *law educator*
Freehling, Daniel Joseph *law educator, law library director*
Hall, David *law educator, dean, law educator, department chairman*
Kindregan, Charles Peter *law educator*
Park, William Wynnewood *law educator*
Samuelson, Susan Stobaugh *law educator*
Whitters, James Payton, III, *lawyer, university administrator*

Cambridge
Andrews, William Dorey *law educator, lawyer*
Dershowitz, Alan Morton *lawyer, educator*
Fisher, Roger Dummer *lawyer, educator, negotiation expert*
Frug, Gerald E. *law educator*
Glendon, Mary Ann *law educator*
Kagan, Elena *law educator*
Kaplow, Louis *law educator*
Kaufman, Andrew Lee *law educator*
Martin, Harry S., III, *law educator, law librarian*
Patton, Bruce M. *law educator, management consultant*
Ray, Stephen Alan *academic administrator, lawyer*
Schauer, Frederick Franklin *law educator*
Steiner, Henry Jacob *law and human rights educator*
Vagts, Detlev Frederick *lawyer, educator*
von Mehren, Arthur Taylor *lawyer, educator*
Warren, Alvin Clifford, Jr., *lawyer*
Weiler, Paul Cronin *law educator*

Medford
Salacuse, Jeswald William *lawyer, educator*

Newton
Coquillette, Daniel Robert *lawyer, educator*
Huber, Richard Gregory *lawyer, educator*

Newton Center
Garvey, John Hugh *dean, law educator*
Soifer, Aviam *law educator, dean*

North Easton
Cregan, Mark Thomas *academic administrator, lawyer, priest*

MICHIGAN

Ann Arbor
Allen, Layman Edward *law educator, research scientist*
Dobranski, Bernard *law educator*
Duquette, Donald Norman *law educator*
Kamisar, Yale *lawyer, educator*
Reed, John Wesley *lawyer, educator*
St. Antoine, Theodore Joseph *retired law educator, arbitrator*
Waggoner, Lawrence William *law educator*
White, James Boyd *law educator*

Detroit
Lamborn, LeRoy Leslie *law educator*
Sedler, Robert Allen *law educator*

East Lansing
Bitensky, Susan Helen *law educator*
Blackburn, Terence Lee *dean*
Ten Brink, Charles J. *law educator*

Grosse Pointe Park
Centner, Charles William *lawyer, educator*

Lansing
Rooney, John Philip *law educator*
Stockmeyer, Norman Otto *law educator, consultant*

MINNESOTA

Minneapolis
Kilbourn, William Douglas, Jr., *law educator*
Kirtley, Jane Elizabeth *law educator*
Mengler, Thomas M. *dean*
Sullivan, E. Thomas *law educator*

Saint Paul
Daly, Joseph Leo *law educator*
Jones, C. Paul *lawyer, educator*

MISSISSIPPI

Jackson
West, Carol Catherine *law educator*

MISSOURI

Columbia
Peth, Howard Allen *lawyer, educator*
Westbrook, James Edwin *lawyer, educator*

Saint Louis
Seligman, Joel *dean*

Springfield
Sanders, Bryan Howard *law educator, department chair, consultant*

MONTANA

Missoula
Kende, Mark Steven *law educator*

Whitehall
Bernard, Donald Ray *law educator, international business counselor*

NEBRASKA

Lincoln
Ogle, Robbin Sue *criminal justice educator*

NEW HAMPSHIRE

Exeter
DeMitchell, Terri Ann *law educator*
Vogelman, Lawrence Allen *law educator, lawyer*

Hanover
Prager, Susan Westerberg *law educator, provost*

NEW JERSEY

Lyndhurst
Bunda, Stephen Myron *political advisor, counselor, lawyer, classical philosopher*

Newark
Defeis, Elizabeth Frances *law educator, lawyer*

Oakhurst
Konvitz, Milton Ridbaz *law educator*

NEW YORK

Flushing
Zalesne, Deborah *law educator*

Fresh Meadows
Greenberg, Robert Jay *law educator*

Hempstead
Liebmann, Theodor S. *law educator*

Hudson
Agata, Burton C. *law educator, lawyer*

Huntington
Glickstein, Howard Alan *law educator*

Ithaca
Alexander, Gregory Stewart *law educator, educator*
Barcelo, John James, III, *law educator*
Clermont, Kevin Michael *law educator*
Cramton, Roger Conant *law educator, lawyer*
Eisenberg, Theodore *law educator*
Hillman, Robert Andrew *law educator, former academic dean*
Lehman, Jeffrey Sean *academic administrator, educator*
Roberts, E. F. *lawyer, educator*
Rossi, Faust F. *lawyer, educator*
Simson, Gary Joseph *law educator*
Teitelbaum, Lee E. *dean, law educator*

Neponsit
Re, Edward Domenic *law educator, retired federal judge*

New York
Amsterdam, Anthony Guy *law educator*
Arlen, Jennifer Hall *law educator*
Bell, Derrick Albert *law educator, author, lecturer*
Black, Barbara Aronstein *legal history educator*
Carden, Constance *law educator, lawyer*
Chase, Oscar G(ottfried) *law educator, consultant, author*
Dorsen, Norman *lawyer, educator*
Dworkin, Ronald Myles *legal educator*
Estreicher, Samuel *lawyer, educator*
Eustice, James Samuel *legal educator, lawyer*
Farnsworth, E(dward) Allan *lawyer, educator*
Feerick, John David *law educator*
Fine, Toni Michele *law educator*
Grad, Frank Paul *law educator, lawyer*
Greenawalt, Robert Kent *lawyer, law educator*
Greenberg, Jack *lawyer, law educator*
Greenberger, Howard Leroy *lawyer, educator*
Guggenheim, Martin Franklin *law educator, lawyer*
Halberstam, Malvina *law educator, lawyer*
Henkin, Louis *lawyer, law educator*
Hill, Alfred *lawyer, educator*
Kaden, Lewis B. *law educator, lawyer*
Kernochan, John Marshall *lawyer, educator*
Leebron, David Wayne *dean, law educator*
Liebman, Lance Malcolm *law educator, lawyer*
Lowenstein, Louis *legal educator*
Marcus, Maria Lenhoff *lawyer, law educator*
Maxfield, Guy Budd *lawyer, educator*
Merrill, Thomas Wendell *lawyer, law educator*
Mundheim, Robert Harry *law educator*
Murphy, Arthur William *lawyer, educator*
Parsons, Inga L. *law educator*
Redlich, Norman *lawyer, educator*
Revesz, Richard Luis *law educator*
Rubino, Victor Joseph *academic administrator, lawyer*
Sandler, Ross *law educator*
Schwartz, William *lawyer, educator*
Sexton, John Edward *academic administrator, law educator*
Siegel, Stanley *lawyer, educator*
Stewart, Richard Burleson *law educator*
Strauss, Peter L(ester) *law educator*
Tancredi, Laurence Richard *law and psychiatry educator, physician*
Treanor, William Michael *law educator*
Walton, R. Keith *academic administrator, lawyer*
Wellington, Harry Hillel *lawyer, educator*

Uniondale
Pratt, George Cheney *law educator, retired federal judge*

White Plains
Ottinger, Richard Lawrence *dean emeritus*
Sloan, F(rank) Blaine *law educator*

NORTH CAROLINA

Buies Creek
Davis, Ferd Leary, Jr., *law educator, lawyer, consultant*
Whichard, Willis Padgett *law educator, retired state supreme court justice*

Chapel Hill
Nichol, Gene Ray, Jr., *dean, department chairman*
Wegner, Judith Welch *law educator, former dean*

TURKEY

Istanbul
Nomer, Ergin Nami *law educator, academic administrator, principal*

ADDRESS UNPUBLISHED

Anderson, John Bayard *lawyer, educator, former congressman*
Areen, Judith Carol *law educator, university dean*
Bakken, Gordon Morris *law educator*
Bernstein, Merton Clay *law educator, lawyer, arbitrator*
Bork, Robert Heron *lawyer, author, educator, former federal judge*
Brewer, Edward Cage, III, *law educator*
Chin, Kelvin Henry *university ombudsperson*
Clark, Robert Charles *dean, law educator*
Davis, Frederick Benjamin *law educator*
Dutile, Fernand Neville *law educator*
Fiss, Owen M. *law educator, educator*
Freedman, Monroe Henry *lawyer, educator, columnist*
Fried, Charles *law educator*
Green, Carol H. *lawyer, educator, journalist*
Hazard, Geoffrey Cornell, Jr., *law educator*
Hermann, Donald Harold James *lawyer, educator*
Heymann, Philip Benjamin *law educator, academic director*
Jones, William Rex *law educator*
Kerstetter, Wayne Arthur *law educator, lawyer*
Loser, Joseph Carlton, Jr., *dean, retired judge*
Manne, Henry Girard *lawyer, educator*
Matheson, Scott Milne, Jr., *dean, law educator*
Merrifield, Leroy Sorenson *law educator*
Michaelis, Karen Lauree *law educator*
Olson, Dennis Alan *law educator*
Post, Ruth-Ellen *lawyer, educator*
Reidenberg, Joel R. *law educator*
Roe, Mark J. *law educator*
Schiffman, Howard Scott *law educator*
Schlueter, Linda Lee *law educator*
Schrag, Philip Gordon *law educator*
Siegan, Bernard Herbert *lawyer, educator*
Termini, Roseann Bridget *lawyer, educator*
Young, Michael Kent *dean, lawyer, educator*

FINANCE AND REAL ESTATE

UNITED STATES

CALIFORNIA

Encino
Luna, Barbara Carole *financial analyst, accountant, appraiser*

Los Angeles
Chan, David Ronald *tax specialist, lawyer*

Newport Beach
Harley, Halvor Larson *banker, lawyer*
Tracy, James Jared, Jr., *accountant, financial executive, law firm administrator*

Santa Monica
Malayil, Thomas Connolly *real estate developer*

COLORADO

Denver
Lincoln, Alexander, III, *financier, lawyer, private investor*

Monument
Boggs, Steven Eugene *real estate broker, lawyer*

DISTRICT OF COLUMBIA

Washington
Ansary, Cyrus A. *investment company executive, lawyer*

FLORIDA

Celebration
Crabtree, Valleri Jayne *real estate executive, lawyer*

HAWAII

Honolulu
Ng, Wing Chiu *accountant, educator, application developer, lawyer, educator, advocate*

ILLINOIS

Bloomington
Brunner, Kim M. *insurance company executive*

Chicago
DeMoss, Jon W. *insurance company executive, lawyer*

Deerfield
Lifschultz, Phillip *financial and tax consultant, accountant, lawyer*

Northbrook
McCabe, Michael J. *insurance executive*

Oak Park
Kinzie, Raymond Wyant *banker, lawyer*

KANSAS

Leawood
Gregory, Lewis Dean *trust company executive*

MARYLAND

Baltimore
Dubin, Charles Thomas *accountant, consultant*
Morris, David Michael *insurance executive, lawyer*

Columbia
Kurlander, Neale *accounting and law educator, lawyer*

MASSACHUSETTS

Boston
Mansfield, Christopher Charles *insurance company legal executive*

Gloucester
Means, Elizabeth Rose Thayer *financial consultant, writer, lawyer*

MINNESOTA

Minneapolis
Boelter, Philip Floyd *real estate company officer, mortgage company executive*

NEBRASKA

Lincoln
Lundstrom, Gilbert Gene *banker, lawyer*

NEVADA

Las Vegas
Di Palma, Joseph Alphonse *investment company executive, lawyer*

NEW JERSEY

Cherry Hill
Copsetta, Norman George *real estate executive*

NEW YORK

Hempstead
Aaron, Merik Roy *financial executive, educator, lawyer*

New York
Barbeosch, William Peter *bank executive, lawyer*
Dallen, Russell Morris, Jr., *investment company executive, lawyer, publishing company executive*
Felner, Richard M. *real estate consultant, lawyer*
Friedman, Robert Laurence *investment professional*
Kaplan, Keith Eugene *insurance company executive, lawyer*
Seltzer, Jeffrey Lloyd *diversified financial services company executive*
Volk, Stephen Richard *company executive, lawyer*

White Plains
Gillingham, Stephen Thomas *financial planner*

Whitestone
Brill, Steven Charles *financial advisor, lawyer*

NORTH CAROLINA

Asheville
Cragnolin, Karen Zambella *real estate developer, lawyer*

OHIO

Mentor
Krone, Norman Bernard *commercial real estate developer, lawyer*

Toledo
Batt, Nick *property and investment executive*

PENNSYLVANIA

Philadelphia
Gowa, Andrew *real estate investor, lawyer*
Woosnam, Richard Edward *venture capitalist, lawyer*

Wilkes Barre
Yarmey, Richard Andrew *investment manager*

TEXAS

Austin
Lemens, William Vernon, Jr., *banker, finance company executive, lawyer*

Tyler
Guin, Don Lester *insurance company executive*

WASHINGTON

Seattle
Campbell, Robert Hedgcock *investment banker, lawyer*

WISCONSIN

Milwaukee
Fitzpatrick, Dennis John *insurance company executive, lawyer*
Franklin, Scott Bradley *accountant, lawyer*

BRAZIL

Curitiba
Pereira dos Santos, Sandro Wilson *tax specialist*

ADDRESS UNPUBLISHED

Barr, Michael Charles *financial journalist*
Kass, David Norman *accountant, lawyer*
McLaughlin, Michael John *retired insurance company executive*
Moore, Andrew Given Tobias, II, *investment banker, law educator*
Nelson, Walter Gerald *retired insurance company executive*
Powell, Kathleen Lynch *lawyer, real estate executive*
Rondepierre, Edmond Francois *insurance executive*
Scipione, Richard Stephen *insurance company executive, lawyer, retired*
Weber, John Walter *insurance company executive*
Wilder, Michael Stephen *former insurance company executive*

FOUNDATIONS AND ASSOCIATIONS

UNITED STATES

ALABAMA

Montgomery
Hamner, Reginald Turner *lawyer*

ARKANSAS

Little Rock
Malone, David Roy *educational association administrator*

CALIFORNIA

Corona
Everett Nollkamper, Pamela Irene *legal management company executive, educator*

Long Beach
Heggeness, Julie Fay *foundation administrator, lawyer*

Los Angeles
Lindley, F(rancis) Haynes, Jr., *foundation executive, lawyer*
Wasserman, Marcia Watson *legal administration consultant*

Pasadena
Hunter, Harold J., Jr., *legal association administrator*

COLORADO

Denver
Fevurly, Keith Robert *educational administrator*

CONNECTICUT

Riverside
Coulson, Robert *retired association executive, arbitrator, author*

DISTRICT OF COLUMBIA

Washington
Bronstein, Alvin J. *lawyer*
Evans, Robert David *legal association executive*
Henderson, Thomas Henry, Jr., *lawyer, legal association executive*
Kim, Charles Changyoung *trade association executive, lawyer*
Kreig, Andrew Thomas *trade association executive*
Lichtenstein, Elissa Charlene *legal association executive*
Murphy, Laura *legal association administrator*
Rasmus, John Charles *trade association executive, lawyer*
Yoo, Grace *legal association administrator*

FLORIDA

Port Saint Lucie
Weber, Alban *association executive, lawyer*

GEORGIA

Atlanta
Weber, Gerald Richard *legal association administrator, educator*

HAWAII

Honolulu
Matayoshi, Coralie Chun *lawyer, bar association executive*
White, Emmet, Jr., *retirement community administrator*

ILLINOIS

Argonne
Tanzman, Edward Alan *lawyer*

Chicago
Hayes, David John Arthur, Jr., *legal association executive*
Stein, Robert Allen *legal association executive, law educator*
Vogelzang, Jeanne Marie *professional association executive, lawyer*

Vernon Hills
Michalik, John James *legal educational association executive*

INDIANA

Bloomington
Franklin, Frederick Russell *retired legal association executive*

MAINE

Falmouth
Burns, Jennifer D. *advocate, lawyer*

MARYLAND

Baltimore
Carlin, Paul Victor *legal association executive*
Eveleth, Janet Stidman *law association administrator*

Lanham Seabrook
Littlefield, Roy Everett, III, *association executive, legal educator*

MASSACHUSETTS

Waltham
Roosevelt, James, Jr., *health plan executive, lawyer*

MICHIGAN

Detroit
Holiday, Gregory *administrative law judge*

Lansing
Lobenherz, William Ernest *container company/association executive, lawyer*
Winder, Richard Earnest *legal foundation administrator, writer, consultant*

MISSOURI

Jefferson City
Baker, Wade Franklin *retired state bar executive*

NEW YORK

Albany
Bellizzi, John J. *law enforcement association administrator, educator, pharmacist*

Clinton
McKee, Francis John *medical association consultant, lawyer*

New York
Baird, Zoë *foundation president, lawyer*
Giuffra, Robert Joseph, Jr., *lawyer*
Helton, Arthur Cleveland *advocate, lawyer, scholar, writer*
McKay, Donna *legal association administrator*
Romero, Anthony D. *legal association administrator*

NORTH CAROLINA

Waynesville
Cole, James Yeager *foundation executive*

OHIO

Columbus
Ramey, Denny L. *bar association executive director*

PENNSYLVANIA

Philadelphia
Carroll, Mark Thomas *lawyer*

Stern, Gerald Mann *lawyer*
Stevens, Paul Schott *lawyer*
Stewart, David Pentland *lawyer, educator*
Stucky, Jean Seibert *lawyer*
Stucky, Scott Wallace *lawyer*
Targ, Nicholas William *lawyer*
Teal, Arabella W. *state attorney general*
Tetzlaff, Charles Robert *lawyer*
Timmer, Barbara *United States Senate official, lawyer*
Udall, Thomas (Tom Udall) *congressman*
Winston, Judith Ann *lawyer*
Yambrusic, Edward Slavko *lawyer, consultant*

FLORIDA

Bartow
Cury, Bruce Paul *lawyer, magistrate, law educator*

Clearwater
Dougall-Sides, Leslie K. *lawyer*
Falkner, William Carroll *lawyer*

Fort Lauderdale
Roberts, Derrick Stacy *federal official*
Silvershein, Joel Michael *lawyer*

Gulfport
Jackson, Nicholas Miller *lawyer, researcher*

Jacksonville
Carlson, Raymond Howard *retired naval officer, prosecutor*
Williamson, Melissa *lawyer*

Live Oak
Peters, Lee Ira, Jr., *public defender*

Miami
Darmody, Stephen Jerome *lawyer*
Elliot, Cameron Robert *lawyer*
Miller Udell, Bronwyn *lawyer*
Ronzetti, Thomas A. Tucker *lawyer, law educator*

Milton
Wilson, Catina L. *lawyer*

North Miami
Dellagloria, John Castle *city attorney, educator*

Orlando
Citro, Vincent A. *prosecutor, educator*
Gold, I. Randall *lawyer*

Panama City
Roberson, Kelly McIntosh *lawyer*

Pensacola
Negron, Francisco Maria, Jr., *lawyer*

Tallahassee
Crist, Charles (Charlie Crist) *state attorney general*
Herskovitz, S(am) Marc *lawyer*
Kerns, David Vincent *lawyer*
Kirwin, Thomas F. *prosecutor*
Marshall, Marilyn Josephine *lawyer*
Miller, Gregory R. *lawyer*
Rodriguez, Raquel *lawyer*
Thiele, Herbert William Albert *lawyer*

Tampa
Perez, Paul Ignatius *lawyer*

Tequesta
Kay, Richard Broughton *lawyer*

West Palm Beach
Damico, Paul Anthony *lawyer, educator*

GEORGIA

Atlanta
Baker, Thurbert E. *state attorney general*
Murphy, Richard Patrick *lawyer*
Parker, Wilmer, III, *lawyer, educator*
Raby, Kenneth Alan *lawyer, retired army officer*

Augusta
Booth, Edmund A., Jr., *prosecutor*

Douglas
Hayes, Dewey Norman, Jr., *lawyer*

Fort Stewart
Hansen, Michelle Ann *lawyer*

Hinesville
Turner, Dwayne Curtis *lawyer*

Loganville
Murphy, Deborah Jane *lawyer*

Macon
Scarbary, Otis Lee *lawyer*
Wood, Frank Maxwell *lawyer*

Savannah
Dixon, Harry D., Jr., (Donnie Dixon) *former prosecutor*
Thompson, Richard S. *lawyer*

HAWAII

Honolulu
Bennett, Mark J. *state attorney general*
Cowan, Stuart Marshall *lawyer*
Moroney, Michael John *lawyer*

IDAHO

Boise
Moss, Thomas E. *prosecutor*
Wasden, Lawrence *state attorney general*

Eagle
Richardson, Betty H. *lawyer, former prosecutor*

ILLINOIS

Chicago
Abt, Ralph Edwin *lawyer*
Bodenstein, Ira *lawyer*
DeVine, Richard A. (Dick DeVine) *lawyer*
Fitzgerald, Patrick J. *prosecutor*
Kerycznskyj, Leo Ihor *county official, educator, lawyer*
Krakowski, Richard John *lawyer, public relations executive*
Kuczwara, Thomas Paul *postal inspector, lawyer*
Landsberg, Jill Warren *lawyer, educator, arbitrator*
Lassar, Scott R. *lawyer*
Madigan, Lisa *state attorney general*
Mansfield, Karen Lee *lawyer*
Mikva, Abner Joseph *lawyer, retired federal judge*
Morgan, William Adams *lawyer*
Olk, Frederick James *county official, paralegal*
Richmond, James Glidden *lawyer*
Taren, Jeffrey Lynn *lawyer*
Tryban, Esther Elizabeth *lawyer*

Effingham
Bower, Glen Landis *lawyer*

Elgin
Moltz, Martin Paul *lawyer*

Fairview Heights
Miquelon, Miriam F. *lawyer*

Glen Ellyn
Hudson, Dennis Lee *lawyer, retired government official, arbitrator, educator*

Normal
Spears, Larry Jonell *lawyer*

Springfield
Miller, Jan Paul *lawyer*

Waterloo
Coffee, Richard Jerome, II, *lawyer*

INDIANA

Dyer
Van Bokkelen, Joseph Scott *prosecutor*

Evansville
Miller, Daniel Raymond *prosecutor*

Franklin
Hamner, Lance Dalton *prosecutor*

Indianapolis
Brizzi, Carl *prosecutor*
Brooks, Susan W. *prosecutor*
Carter, Steve *state attorney general*
Lamkin, Martha Dampf *lawyer*
McCarthy, Kevin Bart *lawyer*

Lafayette
Gerde, Carlyle Noyes (Cy Gerde) *lawyer*

Munster
Amber, Douglas George *lawyer*

IOWA

Cedar Rapids
Larson, Charles W. *prosecutor*
Reppert, Nancy Lue *former county official, legal consultant*

Des Moines
Burns, Bernard John, III, *public defender*
Kelly, Edwin Frost *prosecutor*
Miller, Thomas J. *state attorney general*

Dubuque
Ernst, Daniel Pearson *lawyer*

Le Mars
Raymond, Darin James *lawyer*

West Des Moines
Johnson, John Paul *lawyer, administrative law judge*

KANSAS

Hutchinson
O'Neal, Michael Ralph *state legislator, lawyer*

Kansas City
Coleman, Thomas *federal lawyer*

Overland Park
Vratil, John Logan *state legislator, lawyer*

Topeka
Kline, Phillip D. *state attorney general*
Moler, Donald Lewis, Jr., *lawyer*

Wichita
Randels, Ed L. *lawyer*
Winkler, Dana John *lawyer*

KENTUCKY

Bowling Green
Chism, Timothy Kirkpatrick, Jr., *lawyer*

Frankfort
Chandler, Albert Benjamin, III, *state attorney general*
Gilley, Stephen D. *prosecutor*
Gillig, John Stephenson *lawyer*
Sonego, Ian G. *assistant attorney general*
Taylor, Kembra Sexton *lawyer, state agency administrator*

Lexington
Van Tatenhove, Gregory F. *prosecutor*

Louisville
Barr, James Houston, III, *lawyer*
Smith, R(obert) Michael *lawyer*

Munfordville
Craddock, John Durrett, III, *lawyer*

Whitesburg
Banks, Edison G., II, *lawyer*

LOUISIANA

Baton Rouge
Ieyoub, Richard Phillip *state attorney general*
Parks, James William, II, *public facilities executive, lawyer*

Lafayette
Mickel, Joseph Thomas *lawyer*

Marksville
Riddle, Charles Addison, III, *district attorney, former state legislator*

New Orleans
Jordan, Eddie J. *lawyer, former prosecutor*
Letten, James *prosecutor*
Ortique, Revius Oliver, Jr., *city official, retired state supreme court justice*

Shreveport
Johnson, Tommy J. *prosecutor, legal association administrator*
Washington, Donald W. *prosecutor*

MAINE

Augusta
Ketterer, Andrew *state commissioner, former state attorney general*
Rowe, G. Steven *state attorney general*

Portland
Silsby, Paula *prosecutor*

MARYLAND

Baltimore
Curran, J. Joseph, Jr., *state attorney general*
DiBiagio, Thomas M. *prosecutor*

Bel Air
Comeau, Michael Gerard *lawyer*

Bethesda
Keplinger, Michael Scott *lawyer*
Morrison, Bruce Andrew *government executive, public affairs consultant*
Schoem, Alan Howard *lawyer*

Chevy Chase
Ragland, Robert Allen *lawyer*

Columbia
Closson, Walter Franklin *child support prosecutor*

Gaithersburg
McCann, Joseph Leo *lawyer, former government official*

Hyattsville
Rummel, Edgar Ferrand *retired lawyer*

Kensington
Dauster, William Gary *lawyer, economist*

Potomac
Broder, Gail Steinmetz *lawyer*

Rockville
Boetticher, Helene *lawyer*
Frye, Roland Mushat, Jr., *lawyer*

Silver Spring
Lederer, Max Donald, Jr., *lawyer*
Williams, Henry Newton *retired lawyer*

MASSACHUSETTS

Boston
Casper, Denise Jefferson *lawyer*
Conley, Daniel F. *prosecutor*
Del Bono, Irene Lillian (Irene Stone Guild Del Bono) *lawyer*
Donahue, Charlotte Mary *lawyer*
McCourt, Joyce Elise *lawyer*
Nemon, Nancy Susan Schectman *lawyer*
Reilly, Thomas F. *state attorney general*
Shapiro, Benjamin Louis *lawyer, law association administrator*
Sullivan, Michael J. *prosecutor*

Brighton
Schatkin, Sidney Bernhard *lawyer*

Hanscom AFB
Harms, John Kevin *lawyer*

Pittsfield
Green, Nathaniel Kimball *lawyer*

Salem
Hayes, John Charles *lawyer*

Sandwich
Troy, Robert Sweeney, Sr., *lawyer*

Springfield
Goodhines, James Richard *prosecutor, law educator*
Susse, Sandra Slone *lawyer*

MICHIGAN

Detroit
Brown, Zenell Bridgette *lawyer, mediator*
Collins, Jeffrey G. *lawyer*
Duggan, Michael E. *prosecutor*
Gershel, Alan M. *prosecutor*
Humphries, James Nathan *lawyer*
Quinn, John Peter *lawyer, software designer*

Grand Rapids
Chiara, Margaret Mary *United States attorney*

Kalamazoo
Cinabro, Robert Henry *lawyer*

Lansing
Cox, Mike *state attorney general*
Granholm, Jennifer Mulhern *governor*

Livonia
Fisher, Michael Ernest *lawyer*

Mount Clemens
Brumbaugh, George Edwin, Jr., *lawyer*

Warren
Dalenberg, David Lyle *lawyer*

MINNESOTA

Anoka
Goodell, Robert D. *lawyer, educator*

Hallock
Hane, Jeffrey W. *lawyer*

Minneapolis
Genia, James Michael *lawyer*
Johnson, Thomas Edward *lawyer*

Rochester
Canan, Thomas Michael *lawyer*

Saint Paul
Black, Bert *state administrator, lawyer*
Hatch, Mike *state attorney general*

MISSISSIPPI

Grenada
Hill, Clyde Vernon, Jr., *prosecutor*

Gulfport
Faneca, Cy T. *lawyer*

Jackson
Hill, Tina *prosecutor*
Lampton, Dunn O. *prosecutor*
Moore, Mike *state attorney general*
Tuck, Amy *lieutenant governor*

Oxford
Greenlee, Jim Ming *prosecutor*

Tylertown
Mord, Irving Conrad, II, *lawyer*

MISSOURI

Farmington
Pratte, Geoffrey Lynn *lawyer, arbitrator*

Independence
Lashley, Curtis Dale *lawyer*

Jefferson City
Lanning, Linda Lee *lawyer*
Maxwell, Joe Edwin *lieutenant governor*
Nixon, Jeremiah W. (Jay Nixon) *state attorney general*
Pritchett, Michael Eugene Cook *lawyer*
Ward, Samantha Snow *lawyer*

Kansas City
Graves, Todd Peterson *prosecutor*

Licking
Katz, Aya *jurist, linguist, writer*

Saint Louis
Banks, Eric Kendall *lawyer*
Gruender, Raymond W. *prosecutor*
Johnson, William Ashton *retired lawyer*
O'Malley, Kevin Francis *lawyer, writer, educator*

MONTANA

Billings
Aldrich, Richard Kingsley *lawyer*

Hu, Daniel David *lawyer*
Keller, Brenda Ann Schrader *lawyer*
Newton, Brent Evan *defender*
Rosenthal, Charles A., Jr., *prosecutor*
Serres, Gregory A. *prosecutor*
Shelby, Michael T. *lawyer*
Winchell, Michael George *lawyer*

Huntsville
Peck, Leonard Warren, Jr., *lawyer*

Irving
Cunningham, Cathy Meyer *lawyer*

Lubbock
Davis, Jimmy Frank *assistant attorney general*

Mineola
Bruce, Robert Denton *lawyer*

San Antonio
Cavazos-Garza, Belinda *lawyer*
Durbin, Richard Louis, Jr., *lawyer*
Frigerio, Charles Straith *lawyer*
Fuller, Debra Lynn *lawyer, consultant*
Mathy, Pamela Ann *lawyer*
McCray, Hubert Todd *lawyer*
Reed, Susan D. *prosecutor*
Sutton, Johnny K. *lawyer*
Weiner, Marcia Myra *judge*

Tyler
Yeager, Ruth *lawyer*

UTAH

Provo
Gregerson, Gary LeRoy *lawyer*

Salt Lake City
Moore, Debra *lawyer*
Shurtleff, Mark L. *state attorney general*
Warner, Paul M. *prosecutor*

Vernal
Judd, Dennis L. *lawyer*

VERMONT

Burlington
Hall, Peter W. *prosecutor*
Shattuck, Gary G. *lawyer*

Montpelier
Sorrell, William H. *state attorney general*

VIRGINIA

Abingdon
Brownlee, John L. *prosecutor*

Alexandria
Abell, Richard Bender (Richard Lon Welch) *lawyer, federal judicial official*
Burgess, David *lawyer*
Bussewitz, Roy Jon *lawyer, pharmacist*
Guevara, Rogelio E. *federal agency administrator*
Kalder, Frank M. *federal agency administrator*
Kaplan, Richard Alan *government official*
Kotlarchuk, Ihor O. E. *lawyer*
Mastromarco, Dan Ralph *lawyer, consultant*
McNulty, Paul J. *prosecutor*
Retson, Nicholas Philip *lawyer, military officer*
Simpkins, William B. *federal agency administrator*
Whitaker, Mary Fernan *lawyer*
Winzer, P.J. *lawyer*

Arlington
Barry, Lance Leonard *judge*
Gilmore, Marjorie Havens *civic worker, lawyer*
Monroe, Carl Dean, III, *lawyer*
Rynearson, Arthur John *lawyer*

Blackstone
Allen, Jeffrey Rodgers *lawyer*

Centreville
Etters, Ronald Milton *lawyer, former government official*

Dulles
Flannery, John Philip *lawyer*

Fairfax
Hopson, Everett George *retired lawyer*

Fairfax Station
Bishop, Alfred Chilton, Jr., *lawyer*
Carver, George Allen, Jr., *retired lawyer*

Falls Church
Waxman, Bruce I. *lawyer*

Fort Belvoir
Brittigan, Robert Lee *lawyer*

Leesburg
Hoffman, Bonnie Hope *lawyer*

Mc Lean
Mater, Maud *lawyer*
Rawls, Charles Richardson *lawyer, government official*

Pulaski
McCarthy, Thomas James, Jr., *lawyer*

Richmond
Crouch, Robert P., Jr., *state agency administrator, former prosecutor*
Kaine, Timothy M. *lieutenant governor*
Kilgore, Jerry *state attorney general*
McFarlane, Walter Alexander *lawyer, educator*
Pollard, Overton Price *state agency executive, lawyer*

Spotsylvania
Neely, William F. *lawyer*

Springfield
Basham, W. Ralph *federal agency administrator*

Vienna
Anderson, Earl E. *retired military officer, legal association administrator*

Virginia Beach
McCrimmon, Teresa Norvell *lawyer*
Schon, Alan Wallace *lawyer, actor*

Williamsburg
Burdette, Robert Bruce *retired lawyer*

WASHINGTON

Bellevue
Andrews, Richard Lee *lawyer*

Bremerton
Rieke, Davin Eric *lawyer, military officer*

Forks
Fleck, William Rodney *lawyer*

Olympia
Gregoire, Christine O. *state attorney general*
Roe, Charles Barnett *lawyer*
Welsh, John Beresford, Jr., *retired lawyer*

Seattle
Frost, Barbara Sherry *lawyer*

Spokane
Jude, Carlin M. *prosecutor*
Lister, Stephanie Joyce *lawyer*
McDevitt, James A. *lawyer*

Tacoma
Diaz, Joseph Michael *lawyer*
George, Nicholas *lawyer, entrepreneur*

Tumwater
Edmondson, Frank Kelley, Jr., *lawyer, legal administrator*

Vancouver
Dodds, Michael Bruce *lawyer*

Walla Walla
Leonhard, Matthew Brent *prosecutor*

WEST VIRGINIA

Charleston
Betts, Rebecca A. *lawyer*
Mc Graw, Darrell Vivian, Jr., *state attorney general*
Warner, Karl K. *prosecutor*

Wheeling
Johnston, Thomas E. *prosecutor*

WISCONSIN

Eau Claire
Frank, John LeRoy *lawyer, government executive, educator*

Madison
Doyle, James E(dward) *governor*
Lautenschlager, Peggy A. *state attorney general*
Strebe, Galen George *lawyer, educator*
Van Hollen, J.B. *lawyer*

Milwaukee
Biskupic, Steven M. *lawyer*
Santelle, James Lewis *prosecutor*
Stephens, Marla Jean *lawyer*

WYOMING

Cheyenne
Crank, Pat *state attorney general*
Mead, Matthew Hansen *prosecutor*
Woodhouse, Gay Vanderpoel *former state attorney general, lawyer*

TERRITORIES OF THE UNITED STATES

AMERICAN SAMOA

Pago Pago
Sunia, Fiti *American Samoa attorney general*
Tulafono, Togiola T.A. *governor*

GUAM

Hagatna
Black, Frederick A.
Moylan, Douglas *state attorney general*

NORTHERN MARIANA ISLANDS

Saipan
Manglona, Ramona V. *state attorney general*
Soll, Herbert D. *lawyer*

PUERTO RICO

San Juan
Garcia, Humberto Sigifredo *lawyer*
Gil, Guillermo *prosecutor*
Rodriguez, Annabelle *state attorney general*

VIRGIN ISLANDS

Charlotte Amalie
Stridiron, Iver Allison *attorney general*

Saint Thomas
Nissman, David M. *lawyer*

MILITARY ADDRESSES OF THE UNITED STATES

EUROPE

Apo
Kammerer, Kelly Christian *lawyer*

CANADA

ONTARIO

Harrow
Kurtz, James P. *administrative law judge*

Ottawa
Buchanan, John MacLennan *Canadian provincial official*

Whale Cove
Rodnunsky, Sidney *lawyer, educator*

AUSTRIA

Vienna
Halphen-Perez, Jorge Enrique *ambassador, lawyer*

BRAZIL

Rio De Janeiro
Catanante, Alessandra *lawyer*

DENMARK

Copenhagen
Erichsen, Kield-Gustav *lawyer*

ENGLAND

Beverley
Edles, Gary Joel *lawyer*

FRANCE

Villamblard
Barnes, James Neil *lawyer*

JAPAN

Hagatna
Rapadas, Leonardo M. *lawyer*

NETHERLANDS

The Hague
Brunetti, Maurizio *international lawyer*

SWITZERLAND

Geneva
Kwakwa, Edward Kwaku *lawyer*

TANZANIA

Arusha
Rapp, Stephen John *international prosecutor*

ADDRESS UNPUBLISHED

Adams, Frances Grant, II, *lawyer*
Anzai, Earl I. *former state attorney general*
Avallone, Anthony Francis *lawyer*
Barnett, Mark William *former state attorney general*
Block, Richard Raphael *lawyer, arbitrator*
Bloomfield, David Charles *lawyer, educator, not-for-profit executive*
Booher, Alice Ann *lawyer*
Botelho, Bruce Manuel *former state attorney general, mayor*
Bradley, Amelia Jane *lawyer*
Brieger, George *lawyer*
Buchbinder, Darrell Bruce *lawyer*
Calhoun-Senghor, Keith *lawyer*
Cambrice, Robert Louis *lawyer*
Campbell, John William *prosecutor*
Carpenter, Susan Karen *defender*
Cauley, Michael A. *prosecutor*
Cologne, Gordon Bennett *lawyer*
Condon, Charles Molony *former state attorney general*
Condra, Allen Lee *lawyer, state official*
Del Papa, Frankie Sue *former state attorney general*
Dietel, James Edwin *lawyer, consultant*
Dokurno, Anthony David *lawyer*
DuMontier, Clarissa Williams *lawyer*
Famularo, Joseph L. *former prosecutor*
Fellers, Rhonda Gay *lawyer*
Finelsen, Libbi June *lawyer*
Grab, Frederick Charles *lawyer*
Grace, Walter Charles *retired prosecutor*
Hulin, Frances C. *retired prosecutor*
Jallins, Richard David *lawyer*
Jochner, Michele Melina *lawyer*
Johnson, Christopher George *lawyer*
Kanrek, Victoria Jane *lawyer*
Kubo, Edward Hachiro, Jr., *prosecutor*
Lance, Alan George *former state attorney general*
Landers, Sharon L. *transportation management and policy consultant*
Lazarus, Linda Iris *lawyer*
Levinson, Peter Joseph *retired lawyer*
MacMillan, Hoke *former state attorney general*
Maple, Johanna Philhower *lawyer*
Martin, Alice Howze *prosecutor*
McCormick, David Arthur *lawyer*
McDougall, Roderick Gregory *lawyer*
Metzger, Jeffrey Paul *lawyer*
Miller, Charles T. *lawyer*
Modisett, Jeffrey A. *lawyer, state attorney general, business executive*
Olivier, William K. *lawyer*
Pence, Stephen Beville *prosecutor*
Poppler, Doris Swords *lawyer*
Roark, Candice Renau *lawyer*
Ruschky, Eric William *prosecutor*
Ryan, James E. *former state attorney general*
Ryan, Kelly *lawyer*
Samuel, Raphael *lawyer*
Shaffert, Kurt *retired lawyer, chemical engineer*
Sherling, Fred W. *lawyer*
Smith, Deirdre O'Meara *lawyer*
Soble, Mark Richard *lawyer*
Steinberg, Mark Robert *lawyer*
Stillman, Elinor Hadley *retired lawyer*
Stovall, Carla Jo *former state attorney general*
Tobin, Richard Willis, II, *state government executive*
Vincent, John K. *prosecutor*
Vitale, Louise Antoinette *lawyer*
Weinstein, Arthur Gary *lawyer*
Whitehouse, Sheldon *lawyer, former state attorney general*
York, Alexandra *lawyer*

INDUSTRY

UNITED STATES

CALIFORNIA

Oakland
Meyer, Carl Beat *chemical consultant, mediator, arbitrator, lawyer*

Pleasanton
Gordon, Robert A. *food products executive*

DELAWARE

Wilmington
Mobley, Stacey J. *consumer products company executive*

DISTRICT OF COLUMBIA

Washington
Moore, Robert Madison *food industry executive, lawyer*
Thompson, Richard Leon *pharmaceutical company executive, lawyer*

IDAHO

Boise
Sims, John R. *food products executive*

INDIANA

Indianapolis
Greer, Charles Eugene *company executive, lawyer*

MARYLAND

Baltimore
Rheinstein, Peter Howard *healthcare company executive, consultant, physician, lawyer*

MASSACHUSETTS

Pittsfield
Wheelock, Kenneth Steven *chemist*

Quincy
McClung, J(ames) David *corporate executive, lawyer, academic administrator*

MICHIGAN

Benton Harbor
Hopp, Daniel Frederick *manufacturing company executive, lawyer*

Dearborn
Rintamaki, John M. *automotive executive*
Ross, Dennis E. *automotive executive*

Midland
Manetta, Richard *chemicals executive*

MINNESOTA

Eden Prairie
Cohen, Robert *medical device manufacturing and marketing executive*

Saint Paul
Boehnen, David Leo *lawyer*

NEW JERSEY

New Brunswick
Fine, Roger Seth *pharmaceutical executive, lawyer*

Whitehouse Station
Frazier, Kenneth C. *pharmaceutical executive*

NEW YORK

New York
Kelson, Richard B. *metal products executive*
Tse, Charles Yung Chang *drug company executive*

OHIO

Miamisburg
Thompson, Holley Marker *lawyer, marketing professional*

OREGON

Dundee
Sadler, Richard Lawrence *food company executive, lawyer*

PENNSYLVANIA

Bethlehem
Barnette, Curtis Handley *steel company executive, lawyer*

TENNESSEE

Bristol
Macione, Kyle Pritchett *pharmaceutical company executive, lawyer*

Nashville
Hofstead, James Warner *laundry machinery company executive, lawyer*

TEXAS

San Antonio
McCoy, Reagan Scott *oil company executive, lawyer*

JAPAN

Kawasaki
Yashiro, Junjiro *pharmaceutical executive, patent lawyer*

ADDRESS UNPUBLISHED

Brown, Rhonda Rochelle *chemist, health facility administrator, lawyer*
Chaykin, Robert Leroy *manufacturing and marketing executive*
Crawford, William Walsh *retired consumer products company executive*
Nichols, Michael C. *food company executive, lawyer*
Ormasa, John *retired utility executive, lawyer*
Sissel, George Allen *manufacturing executive, lawyer*
Weaver, William Schildecker *retired electric power industry executive*

JUDICIAL ADMINISTRATION

UNITED STATES

ALABAMA

Ashland
Ingram, Kenneth Frank *retired state supreme court justice*

Birmingham
Acker, William Marsh, Jr., *federal judge*
Blackburn, Sharon Lovelace *federal judge*
Ferguson, Ralph Alton, Jr., (Sonny Ferguson) *circuit court judge*
Goldstein, Debra Holly *judge*
Guin, Junius Foy, Jr., *federal judge*
Pointer, Sam Clyde, Jr., *retired federal judge, lawyer*
Privett, Caryl Penney *judge*

Cullman
Chaney, Kim J. *judge*

Enterprise
McAliley, Gary Lex *judge, prosecutor, educator*

Gadsden
Sledge, James Scott *judge*

Mobile
Butler, Charles Randolph, Jr., *federal judge*
Cox, Emmett Ripley *judge*
Pittman, Virgil *federal judge*

Montgomery
Brown, Jean Williams *state supreme court justice*
De Ment, Ira *judge*
Dubina, Joel Fredrick *federal judge*
Godbold, John Cooper *judge*
Harwood, Robert Bernard, Jr., *state supreme court justice*
Hobbs, Truman McGill *federal judge*
Houston, James Gorman, Jr., *state supreme court justice*
Johnstone, Douglas Inge *state supreme court justice*
Lyons, Champ, Jr., *state supreme court justice*
Maddox, Alva Hugh *retired state supreme court justice*
Moore, Roy S. *state supreme court chief justice*
See, Harold Frend *judge, law educator*
Steele, Rodney Redfearn *judge*
Stuart, Lyn (Jacquelyn L. Stuart) *judge*
Woodall, Thomas A. *state supreme court justice*

ALASKA

Anchorage
Branson, Albert Harold (Harry Branson) *judge, educator*
Bryner, Alexander O. *state supreme court justice*
Eastaugh, Robert L. *state supreme court justice*
Fabe, Dana Anderson *state supreme court chief justice*
Singleton, James Keith *federal judge*
von der Heydt, James Arnold *federal judge*

Fairbanks
Kleinfeld, Andrew J. *federal judge*

Juneau
Carpeneti, Walter L. *judge*

ARIZONA

Bisbee
Holland, Robert Dale *retired judge*

Florence
O'Neil, William Joseph *judge*

Green Valley
McDonough, Russell Charles *retired state supreme court justice*

Mesa
Hicks, Bethany Gribben *judge, commissioner, lawyer*

Phoenix
Berch, Rebecca White *state supreme court justice, lawyer*
Broomfield, Robert Cameron *federal judge*
Canby, William Cameron, Jr., *judge*
Carroll, Earl Hamblin *federal judge*
Hurwitz, Andrew D. *judge*
Jones, Charles E. *chief justice supreme court*
Martone, Frederick J. *judge*
McNamee, Stephen M. *federal judge*
Rosenblatt, Paul Gerhardt *judge*
Ryan, Michael D. *state supreme court justice*
Schroeder, Mary Murphy *federal judge*
Silverman, Barry G. *federal judge*
Strand, Roger Gordon *federal judge*
Winthrop, Lawrence Fredrick *judge*

Springerville
Geisler, Sherry Lynn *magistrate*

Tucson
Browning, William Docker *federal judge*
Druke, William Erwin *lawyer, judge*
Marquez, Alfredo C. *federal judge*
Roll, John McCarthy *judge*
Zlaket, Thomas Andrew *attorney, former state supreme court chief justice*

ARKANSAS

Batesville
Harkey, John Norman *judge*

El Dorado
Barnes, Harry Francis *federal judge*

Fayetteville
Hendren, Jimm Larry *federal judge*
Waters, H. Franklin *federal judge*

Little Rock
Arnold, Morris Sheppard *judge*
Arnold, Richard Sheppard *federal judge*
Arnold, W. H. (Dub Arnold) *state supreme court chief justice*
Corbin, Donald L. *state supreme court justice*
Glaze, Thomas A. *state supreme court justice*
Hannah, Jim *judge*
Imber, Annabelle Clinton *state supreme court justice*
Reasoner, Stephen M. *federal judge*
Thornton, Ray *state supreme court justice, former congressman*
Wilson, William R., Jr., *judge*
Wright, Susan Webber *judge*

CALIFORNIA

Chatsworth
Schwab, Howard Joel *judge*

Fort Bragg
Lehan, Jonathan Michael *judge*

Fresno
Coyle, Robert Everett *federal judge*

Glendale
Early, Alexander Rieman, III, *judge*

Gualala
Kalustian, Richard Peter *judge*

Long Beach
Tucker, Marcus Othello *judge*

Los Angeles
Bufford, Samuel Lawrence *federal judge*
Collins, Audrey B. *judge*
Curry, Daniel Arthur *judge*
Fischer, Dale Susan *judge*
Hupp, Harry L. *federal judge*
Johnson, Earl, Jr., *judge, author*
Kelleher, Robert Joseph *judge*
Marrs, Bruce F. *judge*
Marshall, Consuelo Bland *federal judge*
Mohr, Anthony James *judge*
Mosk, Richard Mitchell *judge*
Rafeedie, Edward *senior federal judge*
Takasugi, Robert Mitsuhiro *federal judge*
Tevrizian, Dickran M., Jr.,
Yager, Thomas C. *retired judge*

Mendocino
Masterson, William A. *retired judge*

Modesto
Siefkin, Susan Deeble *judge*

Oakland
Jensen, D. Lowell *federal judge, lawyer, government official*
Newsome, Randall Jackson *judge*
Wilken, Claudia *judge*
Zika, Patrick John *judge*

Oroville
Howell, Steven John *judge*

Panorama City
Chen, Edward M. *judge*

Pasadena
Boochever, Robert *judge*
Fernandez, Ferdinand Francis *federal judge*
Fisher, Raymond Corley *judge*
Goodwin, Alfred Theodore *federal judge*
Hall, Cynthia Holcomb *federal judge*
Johnson, Barbara Jean *retired judge, lawyer*
Nelson, Dorothy Wright (Mrs. James F. Nelson) *federal judge*
Rymer, Pamela Ann *federal judge*

Ramona
Jordan, David Francis, Jr., *retired judge*

Riverside
Holmes, Dallas Scott *judge, educator*
Timlin, Robert J. *judge*

Sacramento
Gilmour, Richard H. *judge*
Karlton, Lawrence K. *federal judge*
Kolkey, Daniel Miles *judge*
Levi, David F. *federal judge*
Moulds, John F. *federal judge*
Schwartz, Milton Lewis *federal judge*
Van Camp, Brian Ralph *judge*

San Diego
Bowie, Peter Wentworth *judge, educator*
Brewster, Rudi Milton *judge*
Harutunian, Albert T(heodore), III, *judge*
Jones, Napoleon A., Jr., *judge*
Lewis, Gerald Jorgensen *judge*
McKeown, Mary Margaret *federal judge*
Rhoades, John Skylstead, Sr., *federal judge*
Thompson, Gordon, Jr., *federal judge*
Turrentine, Howard Boyd *federal judge*
Wallace, J. Clifford *federal judge*

San Francisco
Baxter, Marvin Ray *state supreme court justice*
Berzon, Marsha S. *federal judge*
Brown, Janice Rogers *state supreme court justice*
Browning, James Robert *federal judge*
Bybee, Jay Scott *judge, federal agency administrator*
Callahan, Consuelo Maria *judge*
Chin, Ming *state supreme court justice*
Conti, Samuel *federal judge*
George, Ronald M. *state supreme court chief justice*
Kennard, Joyce L. *judge*
Moreno, Carlos R. *state supreme court justice*
Noonan, John T., Jr., *judge, law educator*
Schwarzer, William W *federal judge*
Walker, Vaughn R. *federal judge*
Werdegar, Kathryn Mickle *state supreme court justice*

San Jose
Whyte, Ronald M. *judge*

San Marino
Mortimer, Wendell Reed, Jr., *judge*

Santa Ana
Barr, James Norman *federal judge*
Colaw, Thierry Patrick *judge*
Ferguson, Warren John *judge*
Stotler, Alicemarie Huber *judge*

Santa Barbara
Aldisert, Ruggero John *judge*

Santa Monica
Vega, Benjamin Urbizo *retired judge, television producer*

Van Nuys
Kolostian, Richard George, Sr., *judge*

Woodland Hills
Mund, Geraldine *judge*

COLORADO

Castle Rock
Turelli, Richard Daniel *judge*

Denver
Bender, Michael Lee *judge*
Coats, Nathan B. *state supreme court justice*
Ebel, David M. *federal judge*
Felter, Edwin Lester, Jr., *judge*
Hobbs, Gregory James, Jr., *state supreme court justice*
Kane, John Lawrence, Jr., *judge*
Keithley, Roger Lee *judge*
Kirshbaum, Howard M. *retired judge, arbiter*
Kourlis, Rebecca Love *state supreme court justice*
Martinez, Alex J. *state supreme court justice*
Mc Connell, Michael W. *judge, law educator*
McWilliams, Robert Hugh *federal judge*
Mullarkey, Mary J. *state supreme court chief justice*
Nottingham, Edward Willis, Jr., *federal judge*
Porfilio, John Carbone *federal judge*
Rice, Nancy E. *judge*
Rovira, Luis Dario *state supreme court justice*
Satter, Raymond Nathan *judge*
Tymkovich, Timothy *judge*

Englewood
Coffman, Penelope Dalton *judge*
Erickson, William Hurt *retired state supreme court justice*

Fort Collins
Gandy, H. Conway *retired judge, state official*

Golden
Rodgers, Frederic Barker *judge*

Hotchkiss
Ela, William MacHarg *judge, mediator, arbitrator*

CONNECTICUT

Bridgeport
Eginton, Warren William *federal judge*

Danbury
Upson, Thomas Fisher *judge, former state senator, lawyer*
Yamin, Dianne Elizabeth *judge*

Deep River
Spallone, Jeanne Field *retired state judge*

Hartford
Bieluch, William Charles *judge*
Borden, David M. *state supreme court justice*
Chatigny, Robert Neil *judge*
Droney, Christopher F. *judge*
Dupont, Antoinette Loiacono *judge*
Katz, Joette *state supreme court justice*
Killian, Robert Kenneth, Jr., *judge, lawyer*
Newman, Jon O. *federal judge*
Norcott, Flemming L., Jr., *state supreme court justice*
Palmer, Richard N. *state supreme court justice*
Peters, Ellen Ash *judge, trial referee, retired state supreme court justice*
Schaller, Barry R. *judge*

Shea, David Michael *state supreme court justice*
Sullivan, William J. *state supreme court justice*
Thompson, Alvin W. *judge*
Vertefeuille, Christine Siegrist *judge*
Zarella, Peter T. *state supreme court justice*

New Britain
Meskill, Thomas J. *federal judge*

New Haven
Arterton, Janet Bond *judge*
Berdon, Robert Irwin *judge trial referee, retired state supreme court justice*
Burns, Ellen Bree *federal judge*
Cabranes, José Alberto *judge*
Calabresi, Guido *judge, law educator*
Dorsey, Peter Collins *federal judge*
Walker, John Mercer, Jr., *federal judge*

Stamford
Callahan, Robert Jeremiah *retired judge, mediator*
Karazin, Edward Robert, Jr., *judge*

Vernon Rockville
Purnell, Oliver James, III, *judge*

Waterbury
Goettel, Gerard Louis *federal judge*

DELAWARE

Georgetown
Holland, Randy James *state supreme court justice*

Wilmington
Ambro, Thomas L. *federal judge*
Balick, Helen Shaffer *retired judge*
Berger, Carolyn *state supreme court justice*
Jacobs, Jack Bernard *judge*
Latchum, James Levin *federal judge*
Roth, Jane Richards *federal judge*
Stapleton, Walter King *federal judge*
Veasey, Eugene Norman *state supreme court chief justice*
Walsh, Joseph Thomas *state supreme court justice*

DISTRICT OF COLUMBIA

Washington
Bartnoff, Judith *judge*
Bayly, John Henry, Jr., *judge*
Beghe, Renato *federal judge*
Belson, James Anthony *judge*
Breyer, Stephen Gerald *United States supreme court justice*
Burnett, Arthur Louis, Sr., *judge*
Chabot, Herbert L. *judge*
Chiechi, Carolyn Phyllis *federal judge*
Clevenger, Raymond Charles, III, *federal judge*
Cohen, Mary Ann *judge*
Couvillion, David Irvin *federal judge*
Cowen, Wilson *judge*
Crawford, Susan Jean *federal judge*
Edwards, Harry T. *judge*
Farley, John Joseph, III, *federal judge*
Farrell, Michael W. *state supreme court justice*
Ferren, John Maxwell *judge*
Flannery, Thomas Aquinas *federal judge*
Friedman, Daniel Mortimer *federal judge*
Gajarsa, Arthur J. *circuit court judge*
Gallagher, George R. *retired judge*
Garland, Merrick Brian *federal judge*
Gerber, Joel *federal judge*
Gibson, Reginald Walker *federal judge*
Glickman, Stephen *state supreme court justice*
Goldberg, Stanley Joshua *federal judge*
Green, Joyce Hens *federal judge*
Holdaway, Ronald M. *retired federal judge*
Ivers, Donald Louis *judge*
Jackson, Thomas Penfield *federal judge*
Jacobs, Julian I. *federal judge*
Johnson, Norma Holloway *federal judge*
Kennedy, Anthony McLeod *United States supreme court justice*
Kern, John Worth, III, *judge*
Kline, Norman Douglas *federal judge*
Kramer, Kenneth Bentley *federal judge, former congressman*
Laro, David *judge*
Leon, Richard J. *federal judge*
Liberty, Arthur Andrew *judge*
Lourie, Alan David *federal judge*
Mack, Julia Cooper *retired judge*
Margolis, Lawrence Stanley *federal judge*
Marvel, L. Paige *federal judge*
Mayer, Haldane Robert *federal chief judge*
Michel, Paul Redmond *federal judge*
Miller, Christine Odell Cook *judge*
Newman, Pauline *judge*
Oberdorfer, Louis F. *federal judge*
Plager, S. Jay *judge*
Prost, Sharon *federal judge*
Randolph, A(rthur) Raymond *federal judge*
Ruiz, Vanessa *judge*
Scalia, Antonin *judge*
Schall, Alvin Anthony *federal judge*
Schwelb, Frank Ernest *appellate judge*
Sentelle, David Bryan *federal judge*
Smith, Loren Allan *federal judge*
Smith, Roy Philip *judge*
Steadman, John Montague *appellate court judge*
Steinberg, Jonathan Robert *judge*
Stevens, John Paul *judge*
Sullivan, Eugene Raymond *federal judge*
Swift, Stephen Jensen *federal judge*
Sypolt, Diane Gilbert *federal judge*
Terry, John Alfred *state supreme court judge*
Thomas, Clarence *United States supreme court justice*
Turner, James Thomas *judge*
Urbina, Ricardo Manuel *judge*
Wagner, Annice McBryde *judge*
Wagner, Curtis Lee, Jr., *judge*
Wald, Patricia McGowan *retired federal judge*
Walton, Reggie Barnett *judge*
Washington, Eric T. *state supreme court justice*
Williams, Stephen Fain *federal judge*

FLORIDA

Boca Raton
Bernstein, Edwin S. *judge*

Clearwater
Peters, Robert Timothy *judge*

Daytona Beach
Palmer, William D. *judge*

Deland
Rouse, Robert Kelly, Jr., *judge*
Sanders, Edwin Perry Bartley *judge*

Destin
Robinson, Wilkes Coleman *retired federal judge*

Fort Lauderdale
Gonzalez, Jose Alejandro, Jr., *federal judge*
Zloch, William J. *federal judge*

Jacksonville
Gooding, David Michael *judge*
Melton, Howell Webster, Sr., *federal judge*
Schlesinger, Harvey Erwin *judge*

Miami
Barkett, Rosemary *circuit judge*
Brown, Stephen Thomas *judge*
Cristol, A. Jay *federal judge*
Davis, Edward Bertrand *retired federal judge, lawyer*
Freeman, Gill Sherryl *judge*
Graham, Donald Lynn *federal judge*
Highsmith, Shelby *federal judge*
King, James Lawrence *federal judge*
Rosinek, Jeffrey *judge*
Seitz, Patricia Ann *judge*
Ungaro-Benages, Ursula Mancusi *federal judge*

Orlando
Arnold, C. Jeffery *judge, educator*
Fawsett, Patricia Combs *federal judge*
Young, George Cressler *federal judge*

Saint Petersburg
Andrews, Horace A. *retired judge*
Chipman, Marion Walter *retired judge*
Grube, Karl Bertram *judge*
Roney, Paul H(itch) *federal judge*

Tallahassee
Anstead, Harry Lee *state supreme court justice*
Bell, Kenneth B. *judge*
Cantero, Raoul G., III, *judge*
Grimes, Stephen Henry *retired state supreme court justice*
Lewis, R. Fred *judge*
McCord, Guyte Pierce, Jr., *retired judge*
Pariente, Barbara J. *state supreme court justice*
Quince, Peggy A. *state supreme court justice*
Shaw, Leander Jerry, Jr., *state supreme court justice*
Webster, Peter David *judge*
Wells, Charles Talley *state supreme court justice*
Wetherell, T. Kent, II, *judge*

Tampa
Corcoran, Clement Timothy, III, *judge*
Dail, Joseph Garner, Jr., *judge*
Kovachevich, Elizabeth Anne *judge*
Wilson, Charles Reginald *federal judge*

West Palm Beach
Wroble, Arthur Gerard *judge*

GEORGIA

Atlanta
Benham, Robert *state supreme court justice*
Camp, Jack Tarpley, Jr., *judge*
Carley, George H. *judge*
Carnes, Julie Elizabeth *judge*
Deane, Richard Hunter, Jr., *lawyer, former federal judge*
Fletcher, Norman S. *state supreme court justice*
Forrester, J. Owen *federal judge*
Hines, Preston Harris *state supreme court justice*
Hull, Frank Mays *federal judge*
Hunstein, Carol *state supreme court justice*
Kravitch, Phyllis A. *federal judge*
Moore, Thelma Wyatt *judge*
O'Kelley, William Clark *federal judge*
Sears, Leah J. *state supreme court justice*
Thompson, Hugh P. *state supreme court justice*
Ward, Horace Taliaferro *federal judge*

Augusta
Bowen, Dudley Hollingsworth, Jr., *federal judge*

Brunswick
Alaimo, Anthony A. *federal judge*

Cleveland
Barrett, David Eugene *judge*

Columbus
Laney, John Thomas, III, *federal judge*

Jeffersonville
Fitzpatrick, Duross *federal judge*

Lawrenceville
Iannazzone, Joseph Charles *judge*
Reeves, Gene *judge*

Macon
Anderson, Robert Lanier, III, *judge*
Hershner, Robert Franklin, Jr., *judge*
Owens, Wilbur Dawson, Jr., *federal judge*

Rome
Murphy, Harold Loyd *federal judge*

Savannah
Edenfield, Berry Avant *federal judge*

HAWAII

Honolulu
Acoba, Simeon Rivera, Jr., *state supreme court justice, educator*
Choy, Herbert Young Cho *federal judge*
Clifton, Richard Randall *judge*
Levinson, Steven Henry *state supreme court justice*
Moon, Ronald T. Y. *state supreme court chief justice*
Nakayama, Paula Aiko *state supreme court justice*
Ramil, Mario R. *judge*

IDAHO

Boise
Kidwell, Wayne L. *state supreme court justice*
McDevitt, Charles Francis *retired state supreme court justice, lawyer*
Silak, Cathy R. *former state supreme court justice*
Trott, Stephen Spangler *federal judge, musician*
Walters, Jesse Raymond, Jr., *state supreme court justice*

Idaho Falls
Shindurling, Jon J. *judge*

Pocatello
Murray, Bryan Kenneth *judge*

Soda Springs
Harding, Don L. *judge*

Twin Falls
Hohnhorst, John Charles *judge*

ILLINOIS

Belleville
Ferguson, John Marshall *retired federal judge*

Benton
Foreman, James Louis *retired judge*
Gilbert, J. Phil *federal judge*

Bridgeview
Berry, J. Martin *judge*

Chicago
Alesia, James H(enry) *judge*
Aspen, Marvin Edward *federal judge*
Bauer, William Joseph *federal judge*
Conlon, Suzanne B. *federal judge*
Cousins, William, Jr., *retired judge*
Cudahy, Richard D. *judge*
Fairchild, Thomas E. *federal judge*
Fitzgerald, Thomas Robert *judge*
Flaum, Joel Martin *judge*
Funderburk, Raymond *judge*
Grady, John F. *federal judge*
Hart, William Thomas *federal judge*
Leighton, George Neves *retired federal judge*
Leinenweber, Harry D. *federal judge*
McMorrow, Mary Ann G. *state supreme court chief justice*
Moran, James Byron *federal judge*
Morrissey, George Michael *judge*
Nordberg, John Albert *federal judge*
Norgle, Charles Ronald, Sr., *federal judge*
O'Malley, Denise Margaret *judge*
Pallmeyer, Rebecca Ruth *judge*
Posner, Richard Allen *federal judge*
Roti, Thomas David *judge*
Rovner, Ilana Kara Diamond *federal judge*
Shadur, Milton Irving *judge*
Sonderby, Susan Pierson *federal judge*
Squires, John Henry *judge*

Danville
Garman, Rita B. *judge*

East Saint Louis
Stiehl, William D. *federal judge*

Edwardsville
Crowder, Barbara Lynn *judge*

Hennepin
Bumgarner, James McNabb *judge*

Joliet
Bertani-Tomczak, Amy Marie *circuit judge*

Maple Park
Nickels, John L. *retired state supreme court justice*

Northbrook
Leikin, Mitchell *retired judge*

Peoria
Mihm, Michael Martin *federal judge*

Pontiac
Glennon, Charles Edward *retired judge, lawyer*

Rockford
Reinhard, Philip G. *federal judge*

Springfield
Gramlich, Charles J. *judge*
Miller, Benjamin K. *retired state supreme court justice*
Mills, Richard Henry *federal judge*
Rarick, Philip Joseph *judge*
Wood, Harlington, Jr., *federal judge*

Taylorville
Spears, Ronald Dean *judge*

Waukegan
Brady, Terrence Joseph *judge*

Wheaton
Thomas, Robert R. *state supreme court justice*

Wilmette
Bowman, George Arthur, Jr.,

INDIANA

Boonville
Campbell, Edward Adolph *judge, electrical engineer*

Crown Point
Dywan, Jeffery Joseph *judge*

Evansville
Capshaw, Tommie Dean *judge*

Fort Wayne
Lee, William Charles *judge*
Reyes Robbins, Ann Marie *magistrate, judge*

Frankfort
Smith, Kathy Rae *judge*

Greenwood
Gregory, Lewis J. *judge, lawyer*

Hammond
Rodovich, Andrew Paul *magistrate*

Indianapolis
Boehm, Theodore Reed *judge*
Dickson, Brent E(llis) *state supreme court justice*
Givan, Richard Martin *retired state supreme court justice*
Hamilton, David F. *judge*
McKinney, Larry J. *federal judge*
Rucker, Robert D. *judge*
Shepard, Randall Terry *state supreme court chief justice*
Staton, Robert Howard *retired judge*
Sullivan, Frank, Jr., *state supreme court justice*

Lagrange
Brown, George E. *judge, educator*

South Bend
Brueseke, Harold Edward *magistrate*
Ripple, Kenneth Francis *federal judge*
Sharp, Allen *federal judge*

IOWA

Algona
Andreasen, James Hallis *retired state supreme court judge*

Cedar Rapids
Hansen, David Rasmussen *federal judge*
Mc Manus, Edward Joseph *federal judge*

Chariton
Stuart, William Corwin *judge*

Council Bluffs
Peterson, Richard William *retired judge, lawyer*

Des Moines
Cady, Mark S. *judge*
Carter, James H. *judge*
Fagg, George Gardner *federal judge*
Harris, K. David *senior state supreme court justice*
Larson, Jerry Leroy *state supreme court justice*
Lavorato, Louis A. *state supreme court chief justice*
Streit, Michael J. *state supreme court justice*
Ternus, Marsha K. *state supreme court justice*
Vietor, Harold Duane *federal judge*
Wolle, Charles Robert *federal judge*

Ida Grove
Snell, Bruce M., Jr., *retired judge*

Sioux City
O'Brien, Donald Eugene *federal judge*

KANSAS

Kansas City
Lungstrum, John W. *federal judge*
VanBebber, George Thomas *federal judge*
Vratil, Kathryn Hoefer *federal judge*
Waxse, David John *judge*

Lawrence
Six, Fred N. *retired state supreme court justice*

Topeka
Abbott, Bob *state supreme court justice*
Allegrucci, Donald Lee *state supreme court justice*
Crow, Sam Alfred *judge*
Davis, Robert Edward *state supreme court justice*
Gernon, Robert L. *judge*
Larson, Edward *state supreme court justice*

Wright, John F. *judge*

Omaha
Riley, William Jay *federal judge*
Shanahan, Thomas M. *judge*
Strom, Lyle Elmer *judge*

NEVADA

Carson City
Agosti, Deborah Ann *state supreme court chief justice*
Gibbons, Mark *judge*
Leavitt, Myron E. *judge*
Maupin, A. William *state supreme court justice*
Rose, Robert E(dgar) *state supreme court justice*
Springer, Charles Edward *retired judge*

Las Vegas
Becker, Nancy Anne *state supreme court justice*
Bell, Stewart Lynn *judge*
Hardcastle, Gerald Wayne *judge*
Mahan, James Cameron *judge*
Pro, Philip Martin *judge*
Rawlinson, Johnnie Blakeney *federal judge*
Steffen, Thomas Lee *retired judge, lawyer*

Reno
Brunetti, Melvin T. *federal judge*
Hagen, David Warner *judge*
Hug, Procter Ralph, Jr., *federal judge*
McKibben, Howard D. *federal judge*
Reed, Edward Cornelius, Jr., *federal judge*

NEW HAMPSHIRE

Concord
Barbadoro, Paul James *federal judge*
Brock, David Allen *state supreme court chief justice*
Broderick, John T., Jr., *state supreme court justice*
Dalianis, Linda Stewart
DiClerico, Joseph Anthony, Jr., *federal judge*
Duggan, James E., Jr., *state supreme court justice*
Howard, Jeffrey R. *judge, lawyer, former state attorney general*
McAuliffe, Steven James *federal judge*
Nadeau, Joseph P. *state supreme court justice*

Rochester
Jones, Franklin Charles *judge*

NEW JERSEY

Camden
Brotman, Stanley Seymour *federal judge*
Irenas, Joseph Eron *judge, director*
Simandle, Jerome B. *federal judge*

Egg Harbor Township
Lashman, Shelley Bortin *retired judge*

Flemington
Verniero, Peter G. *state supreme court justice*

Freehold
Newman, James Michael *judge, lawyer*

Hackensack
Cipollone, Anthony Dominic *judge, educator*
Stein, Gary S. *retired judge, lawyer*

Morristown
Hansbury, Stephan Charles *judge*
LaVecchia, Jaynee *state supreme court justice*
Muir, Robert, Jr., *retired judge, lawyer*

Newark
Ackerman, Harold A. *federal judge*
Alito, Samuel Anthony, Jr., *federal judge*
Barry, Maryanne Trump *federal judge*
Bissell, John W. *federal judge*
Debevoise, Dickinson Richards *federal judge*
Garth, Leonard I. *judge*
Hochberg, Faith S. *U.S. district court judge*
Lechner, Alfred James, Jr., *judge*

Red Bank
O'Hern, Daniel Joseph *retired state supreme court justice*

Somerville
Yurasko, Frank Noel *judge*

Trenton
Albin, Barry Todd *judge*
Cooper, Mary Little *federal judge, former banking commissioner*
Gindin, William Howard *judge*
Greenberg, Morton Ira *federal judge*
Long, Virginia *state supreme court justice*
Poritz, Deborah T. *state supreme court chief justice, former attorney general*
Zazzali, James R. *state supreme court associate justice*

Warren
Coleman, James H., Jr., *former state supreme court justice*

NEW MEXICO

Albuquerque
Conway, John E. *federal judge*
Dal Santo, Diane *writer, retired judge*
Hansen, Curtis LeRoy *federal judge*
Hartz, Harris L. *federal judge*
Parker, James Aubrey *federal judge*

Roswell
Baldock, Bobby Ray *judge*

Santa Fe
Baca, Joseph Francis *state supreme court justice*
Bosson, Richard Campbell *judge*
Chavez, Edward L. *judge*
Kelly, Paul Joseph, Jr., *judge*
Maes, Petra Jimenez *state supreme court justice*
Minzner, Pamela Burgy *state supreme court justice*
Serna, Patricio *state supreme court justice*

NEW YORK

Albany
Graffeo, Victoria A. *state supreme court judge*
Kaye, Judith Smith *judge*
Meader, John Daniel *judge*
Miner, Roger Jeffrey *judge*
Read, Susan *judge*

Amsterdam
Aison, Howard M. *judge*

Binghamton
Regenbogen, Adam *judge*

Bronx
Bamberger, Phylis Skloot *judge*
Crispino, Jerry L. *judge*
Engoron, Arthur Fredericks *judge*
Salman, Barry *judge*

Brooklyn
Amon, Carol Bagley *federal judge*
Glasser, Israel Leo *federal judge*
Korman, Edward R. *federal judge*
Levy, Robert Morris *judge*
Reichbach, Gustin Lewis *state supreme court justice*
Ryan, Leonard Eames *judge*
Sifton, Charles Proctor *federal judge*
Tomei, Albert *county supreme court justice*
Trager, David G. *federal judge*
Weinstein, Jack Bertrand *federal judge*

Buffalo
Elfvin, John Thomas *federal judge*
Foschio, Leslie George *judge*
Ne Moyer, Edgar Carroll *judge*
Skretny, William Marion *federal judge*

Carmel
Hickman, S. Barrett *judge*

Central Islip
Platt, Thomas Collier, Jr., *federal judge*
Seybert, Joanna *federal judge*
Spatt, Arthur Donald *federal judge*

Hempstead
Sher, Denise Linda *judge*

Jamaica
Grayshaw, James Raymond *judge*

Mamaroneck
Sirlin, Roger H. *judge*

Mount Vernon
Dowery-Rodriquez, Brenda *judge*

New York
Aquilino, Thomas Joseph, Jr., *federal judge, law educator*
Blinder, Albert Allan *judge*
Buchwald, Naomi Reice *judge*
Cedarbaum, Miriam Goldman *federal judge*
Ciparick, Carmen Beauchamp *judge*
Feinberg, Wilfred *judge*
Francis, James Clark, IV, *judge*
Freedman, Helen E. *justice*
Gerber, Robert Evan *judge*
Griesa, Thomas Poole *federal judge*
Gropper, Allan Louis *bankruptcy judge*
Haight, Charles Sherman, Jr., *federal judge*
Jurow, George *judge*
Katzmann, Robert Allen *judge*
Kearse, Amalya Lyle *federal judge*
Keenan, John Fontaine *judge*
Knapp, Whitman *federal judge*
Koeltl, John George *judge*
Leisure, Peter Keeton *federal judge*
Maas, Frank *judge*
Martin, John Sherwood, Jr., *federal judge*
McLaughlin, Joseph Michael *federal judge, law educator*
Motley, Constance Baker (Mrs. Joel Wilson Motley) *federal judge, former city official*
Mukasey, Michael B. *federal judge*
Musgrave, R. Kenton *federal judge*
Nelson, Barbara Anne *judge*
Owen, Richard *federal judge*
Patterson, Robert Porter, Jr., *federal judge*
Pollack, Milton *federal judge*
Preska, Loretta A. *federal judge*
Raggi, Reena *circuit judge*
Sack, Robert David *judge, educator*
Sand, Leonard B. *federal judge*
Smith, George Bundy *state supreme court justice*
Sotomayor, Sonia *judge*
Sprizzo, John Emilio *judge*
Straub, Chester John *judge*
Titone, Vito Joseph *state supreme court justice*
Ward, Robert Joseph *federal judge*
Wesley, Richard C. *judge*

Niagara Falls
Boniello, Ralph Anthony, III, *judge*

Penn Yan
Falvey, W(illiam) Patrick *judge*

Poughkeepsie
Rosenblatt, Albert Martin *state appeals court judge*

Rochester
Telesca, Michael Anthony *federal judge*
Van Graafeiland, Ellsworth Alfred *federal judge*

Rome
Simons, Richard Duncan *lawyer, retired judge*

Sag Harbor
Pierce, Lawrence Warren *retired federal judge*

Schenectady
Levine, Howard Arnold *state supreme court justice*

Syracuse
McCurn, Neal Peters *federal judge*
Munson, Howard G. *federal judge*
Scullin, Frederick James, Jr., *federal judge*
Wells, Peter Nathaniel *judge, lawyer*

Utica
Cardamone, Richard J. *judge*

White Plains
Brieant, Charles La Monte *federal judge*
Conner, William Curtis *judge*
Hardin, Adlai Stevenson, Jr., *judge*
Parker, Barrington D., Jr., *federal judge, lawyer*

NORTH CAROLINA

Asheville
Thornburg, Lacy Herman *federal judge*

Charlotte
Campbell, Hugh Brown, Jr., *judge*
Mullen, Graham C. *federal judge*
Voorhees, Richard Lesley *federal judge*

Graham
Allen, Bradley Reid, Sr., *judge*

Greensboro
Bullock, Frank William, Jr., *federal judge*
Frye, Henry E. *retired state supreme court chief justice*
Osteen, William L. *federal judge*
Tilley, Norwood Carlton, Jr., *federal judge*

Hendersonville
Franks, Stephen F. *retired judge*

Raleigh
Brady, Edward Thomas *judge*
Britt, W. Earl *federal judge*
Brown, James Joseph *judge*
Butterfield, G. K., Jr., *state supreme court justice*
Eagles, Sidney Smith, Jr., *judge*
Edmunds, Robert H., Jr., *state supreme court justice*
Lake, I. Beverly, Jr., *judge*
Martin, John Charles *judge*
Martin, Mark D. *state supreme court justice*
Orr, Robert F. *judge*
Parker, Sarah Elizabeth *state supreme court justice*
Small, Alden Thomas *judge*
Wainwright, George *judge*
Webb, John *retired state supreme court justice*

Randleman
Jordan, Lillian B. *judge*

Wilmington
Fox, James Carroll *federal judge*

Winston Salem
Eliason, Russell Allen *judge*

NORTH DAKOTA

Bismarck
Conmy, Patrick A. *federal judge*
Kapsner, Carol Ronning *state supreme court justice*
Maring, Mary Muehlen *state supreme court justice*
Neumann, William Allen *state supreme court justice*
Sandstrom, Dale Vernon *judge*
VandeWalle, Gerald Wayne *state supreme court chief justice*
Van Sickle, Bruce Marion *federal judge*

Fargo
Bright, Myron H. *federal judge*
Bye, Kermit Edward *federal judge, lawyer*
Magill, Frank John *federal judge*

Minot
Kerian, Jon Robert *retired judge*

OHIO

Akron
Bell, Samuel H. *federal judge, educator*

Chillicothe
Street, John Benson *judge*

Cincinnati
Beckwith, Sandra Shank *judge*
Black, Robert L., Jr., *retired judge*
Cook, Deborah L. *judge, former state supreme court justice*
Jones, Nathaniel Raphael *retired federal judge*
Karam, Ernest *chief magistrate*
Kennedy, Cornelia Groefsema *federal judge*
Nelson, David Aldrich *judge*
Painter, Mark Philip *judge*
Panioto, Ronald Angelo *judge*
Perlman, Burton *judge*
Rogers, John Marshall *judge, law educator*
Spiegel, S. Arthur *federal judge*
Sutton, Jeffrey S. *judge*
Weber, Herman Jacob *federal judge*

Cleveland
Coyne, William Joseph *judge*
Kilbane, Anne L. *judge*
Krupansky, Robert Bazil *federal judge*
Manos, John M. *federal judge*
Matia, Paul Ramon *federal judge*
Moore, Karen Nelson *judge*
Oliver, Solomon, Jr., *judge*
Wells, Lesley *judge*

Columbus
Calhoun, Donald Eugene, Jr., *federal judge*
Cole, Ransey Guy, Jr., *federal judge*
Douglas, Andrew *retired state supreme court justice*
Graham, James Lowell *federal judge*
Holschuh, John David *federal judge*
Miller, Nodine *judge*
Moyer, Thomas J. *state supreme court chief justice*
Norris, Alan Eugene *federal judge*
O'Connor, Maureen *judge*
Pfeifer, Paul E. *state supreme court justice*
Resnick, Alice Robie *judge*
Sargus, Edmund A., Jr., *judge*
Sellers, Barbara Jackson *federal judge*
Smith, George Curtis *judge*
Stratton, Evelyn Lundberg *judge*
Sweeney, Asher William *state supreme court justice*
Sweeney, Francis E. *state supreme court justice*

Dayton
Knapp, James Ian Keith *judge*
Merz, Michael *federal judge*
Petzold, John Paul *judge*

Delaware
Louden, Thomas Edward *judge*

Ironton
McCown, Frank J. *judge*

Lisbon
Dailey, Coleen Hall *magistrate, lawyer*

Lucasville
Reno, Ottie Wayne *former judge*

Marion
Rogers, Richard Michael *judge*

Medina
Batchelder, Alice M. *federal judge*

New Lexington
Cooperrider, Luann *judge*

Portsmouth
Harcha, Howard H., III, *judge*

Sandusky
Stacey, James Allen *retired judge*

Toledo
Carr, James Gray *judge*
Potter, John William *federal judge*
Resnick, Melvin L. *judge*

OKLAHOMA

Atoka
Gabbard, Douglas, II, (James Gabbard) *judge*

Boise City
Kincannon, Ronald Lynn *judge*

Guthrie
Brooks, Larry Roger *judge*

Oklahoma City
Alley, Wayne Edward *federal judge, retired army officer*
Bohanon, Luther L. *federal judge*
Cauthron, Robin J. *federal judge*
Hargrave, Rudolph *state supreme court chief justice*
Henry, Robert Harlan *federal judge, former attorney general*
Hodges, Ralph B. *state supreme court justice*
Holloway, William Judson, Jr., *federal judge*
Lavender, Robert Eugene *state supreme court justice*
Leonard, Timothy Dwight *judge*
Lumpkin, Gary leonard *judge*
Opala, Marian P(eter) *state supreme court justice*
Russell, David L. *federal judge*
Summers, Hardy *state supreme court justice*
Thompson, Ralph Gordon *federal judge*
Walke, Geary Lynn *judge*
Watt, Joseph Michael *state supreme court chief justice*
West, Lee Roy *federal judge*
Winchester, James R. *judge*

Pryor
McBride, Terry H. *judge*

Seminole
Snow, Gary Paul *judge, lawyer*

Tulsa
Brett, Thomas Rutherford *federal judge*
Eagan, Claire Veronica *judge*
Frizzell, Gregory Kent K. *judge*
Kern, Terry C. *judge*
Seymour, Stephanie Kulp *federal judge*
Taylor, Joe Clinton *judge*

OREGON

Eugene
Hogan, Michael R(obert) *judge*

Oregon City
Herndon, Robert D. *judge*

Portland
Fisher, Ann Lewis *judge*
Frye, Helen Jackson *federal judge*
Jones, Robert Edward *federal judge*
King, Garr Michael *federal judge*
Leavy, Edward *federal judge*
Marsh, Malcolm F. *federal judge*
O'Scannlain, Diarmuid Fionntain *federal judge*
Panner, Owen M. *federal judge*
Redden, James Anthony *federal judge*
Rosenblum, Ellen F. *judge*
Roth, Phillip Joseph *retired judge*
Skopil, Otto Richard, Jr., *federal judge*
Todd, Steven A. *judge*
Unis, Richard L. *judge*
Van Hoomissen, George Albert *state supreme court justice*

Salem
Armstrong, Rex *judge*
Balmer, Thomas Ancil *state supreme court justice*
Carson, Wallace Preston, Jr., *judge*
De Muniz, Paul J. *state supreme court justice*
Durham, Robert Donald, Jr., *state supreme court justice*
Leeson, Susan M. *state supreme court judge*
Peterson, Edwin J. *retired judge, mediator, law educator*
Riggs, R. William *judge*

PENNSYLVANIA

Allentown
Platt, William Henry *judge*

Devon
Lamb, William H. *judge*

Doylestown
Rubenstein, Alan Morris *county judge*

East Lansdowne
Tolliver, Elkin, Jr., *judge*

Easton
Van Antwerpen, Franklin Stuart *federal judge*

Erie
Mencer, Glenn Everell *federal judge*

Harrisburg
Rambo, Sylvia H. *federal judge*
Saylor, Thomas G. *state supreme court justice*

Johnstown
Getty, Charles A. *judge*
Smith, D. Brooks *federal judge*

Mechanicsburg
Eakin, J. Michael *judge*

Newtown Square
Scholl, David Allen *former federal judge, lawyer*

Orwigsburg
Troutman, E. Mac *federal judge*

Philadelphia
Angell, M(ary) Faith *federal magistrate judge*
Bartle, Harvey, III, *federal judge*
Baylson, Michael Morris *judge*
Bechtle, Louis Charles *lawyer, retired federal judge*
Becker, Edward Roy *judge*
Buckwalter, Ronald Lawrence *federal judge*
Castille, Ronald D. *judge*
Chertoff, Michael *judge*
Dalzell, Stewart *federal judge*
Joyner, J(ames) Curtis *judge*
Kelly, Robert F. *federal judge*
Ludwig, Edmund Vincent *federal judge*
Newcomer, Clarence Charles *federal judge*
Nigro, Russell M. *state supreme court justice*
O'Neill, Thomas Newman, Jr., *federal judge*
Pollak, Louis Heilprin *judge, educator*
Reed, Lowell A., Jr., *federal judge*
Robreno, Eduardo C. *federal judge*
Rufe, Cynthia Marie *judge*
Scirica, Anthony Joseph *federal judge*
Sloviter, Dolores Korman *federal judge*
Weiner, Charles R. *federal judge*
Yohn, William H(endricks), Jr., *federal judge*

Pittsburgh
Bloch, Alan Neil *federal judge*
Cappy, Ralph Joseph *judge*
Cohill, Maurice Blanchard, Jr., *federal judge*
Colville, Robert E. *judge*
Conti, Joy Flowers *judge*
Diamond, Gustave *federal judge*
Fitzgerald, Judith Klaswick *federal judge*
Flaherty, John Paul, Jr., *state supreme court chief justice emeritus*
Lally-Green, Maureen Ellen *superior court judge, law educator*
Lee, Donald John *federal judge*
Sensenich, Ila Jeanne *judge*
Skwaryk, Robert Francis *judge*
Standish, William Lloyd *judge*
Weis, Joseph Francis, Jr., *federal judge*
Ziegler, Donald Emil *federal judge*

Scranton
Conaboy, Richard Paul *federal judge*
Nealon, William Joseph, Jr., *federal judge*
O'Malley, Carlon Martin *judge*
Vanaskie, Thomas Ignatius *judge*

Sunbury
Wiest, William Harvey *judge*

Towanda
Mott, John C. *judge*

Uniontown
Franks, William J. *judge*

Washington
Gilmore, David L. *judge*
Mc Cune, Barron Patterson *retired federal judge*

West Conshohocken
Newman, Sandra Schultz *state supreme court justice*

Wilkes Barre
Schwartz, Roger Alan *judge*

Williamsport
McClure, James Focht, Jr., *federal judge*
Muir, Malcolm *federal judge*

RHODE ISLAND

Providence
Flaherty, Francis Xavier *judge*
Flanders, Robert G., Jr., *state supreme court justice*
Goldberg, Maureen McKenna *state supreme court justice*
Hagopian, Jacob *federal judge*
Lagueux, Ronald Rene *federal judge*
Lisi, Mary M. *federal judge*
Torres, Ernest C. *federal judge*
Weisberger, Joseph Robert *retired judge*
Williams, Frank J. *judge, historian, writer*

SOUTH CAROLINA

Camden
Chapman, Robert Foster *judge*
Jacobs, Rolly Warren *judge*

Charleston
Hawkins, Falcon Black, Jr., *federal judge*

Columbia
Bristow, Walter James, Jr., *retired judge*
Burnett, E. C., III, *state supreme court justice*
Hamilton, Clyde Henry *judge*
Pleicones, Costa M. *state supreme court justice*
Shedd, Dennis W. *federal judge*
Toal, Jean Hoefer *state supreme court chief justice*

Greenville
Herlong, Henry Michael, Jr., *federal judge*
Traxler, William Byrd, Jr., *federal judge*
Wilkins, William Walter *federal judge*

Greenwood
Moore, James E. *state supreme court justice*

Marion
Waller, John Henry, Jr., *state supreme court justice*

Myrtle Beach
Harwell, David Walker *retired state supreme court chief justice*

Orangeburg
Finney, Ernest Adolphus, Jr., *retired state supreme court chief justice*

SOUTH DAKOTA

Deadwood
Johns, Timothy Robert *judge*

Pierre
Gilbertson, David *state supreme court justice*
Konenkamp, John K. *state supreme court justice*
Sabers, Richard Wayne *state supreme court justice*
Zinter, Steven L. *state supreme court justice*

Sioux Falls
Meierhenry, Judith Knittel *judge, lawyer*
Piersol, Lawrence L. *federal judge*
Wollman, Roger Leland *federal judge*

TENNESSEE

Chattanooga
Barker, William M. *state supreme court justice*
Edgar, R(obert) Allan *federal judge*
Franks, Herschel Pickens *judge*

Greeneville
Hull, Thomas Gray *federal judge*

Jackson
Todd, James Dale *federal judge*

Johnson City
Kiener, John Leslie *judge*

Kingsport
Beck, Ronald Jerry *judge*

Knoxville
Anderson, Edward Riley *state supreme court justice*
Garrett, Carey Edward *judge*
Jarvis, James Howard, II, *judge*
Jordan, Robert Leon *judge*
Murrian, Robert Phillip *retired state judge, educator*

Memphis
Gibbons, Julia Smith *federal judge*
Gilman, Ronald Lee *judge*
Holder, Janice Marie *state supreme court justice*
McRae, Robert Malcolm, Jr., *federal judge*
Robilio, Kay Spalding *judge*

Nashville
Birch, Adolpho A., Jr., *state supreme court justice*
Brown, Joe Blackburn *judge*
Daughtrey, Martha Craig *federal judge*
Drowota, Frank F., III, *state supreme court chief justice*
Echols, Robert L. *federal judge*
Nixon, John Trice *judge*
Wiseman, Thomas Anderton, Jr., *federal judge*

Newport
Porter, James Kenneth *retired judge*

Signal Mountain
Cooper, Robert Elbert *state supreme court justice*

TEXAS

Amarillo
Johnson, Philip Wayne *judge*
Robinson, Mary Lou *federal judge*

Angleton
Germany, Garvin Holt, Jr., *retired judge, lawyer*

Austin
Benavides, Fortunato Pedro (Pete Benavides) *federal judge*
Coronado, Santiago Sybert (Jim Coronado) *judge*
Garwood, William Lockhart *judge*
Gonzalez, Raul A. *retired state supreme court justice, lawyer*
Hecht, Nathan Lincoln *state supreme court justice*
Hudspeth, Harry Lee *federal judge*
Jefferson, Wallace B. *state supreme court justice*
Johnson, Cheryl Ann *judge*
Jones, Robert D. *judge*
Keller, Sharon Faye *judge*
Miller, Charles E. (Chuck Miller) *judge*
Nowlin, James Robertson *federal judge*
O'Neill, Harriet *state supreme court justice*
Owen, Priscilla Richman *state supreme court justice*
Phillips, Thomas Royal *judge*
Pitman, Robert L. *judge*
Pope, Andrew Jackson, Jr., (Jack Pope) *retired judge*
Reavley, Thomas Morrow *federal judge*
Schneider, Michael H. *judge*
Smith, Steven W. *judge*
Sparks, Sam *federal judge*
Wainwright, Dale V. *judge*

Beaumont
Cobb, Howell *federal judge*

Bellaire
Martin, John Randolph *judge*

Brownsville
Garza, Reynaldo G. *federal judge*

Bryan
Smith, Steven Lee *judge*

Corpus Christi
Jack, Janis Graham *judge*

Dallas
Higginbotham, Patrick Errol *federal judge*
Sanders, Harold Barefoot, Jr., *judge*

Del Rio
Thurmond, George Murat *judge*

Edinburg
Hinojosa, Federico Gustavo, Jr., *judge*

El Paso
Briones, David *judge*

Fort Worth
McBryde, John Henry *federal judge*
Tillman, Massie Monroe *mediator, arbitrator, art gallery owner, retired federal judge*

Houston
Blackmon, Willie Edward Boney *judge, military officer*
DeMoss, Harold Raymond, Jr., *federal judge*
Hanks, George Carol, Jr., *state judge*
Hittner, David *federal judge*
Hoyt, Kenneth M. *federal judge*
Hughes, Lynn Nettleton *federal judge*
King, Carolyn Dineen *federal judge*
Lake, Sim *federal judge*
Rosenthal, Lee H. *federal judge*
Sondock, Ruby Kless *retired judge*
Werlein, Ewing, Jr., *federal judge*

Kaufman
Tygrett, Howard Volney, Jr., *judge, lawyer*

Laredo
Kazen, George Philip *federal judge*

Lockhart
McCormick, Michael Jerry *retired judge*

Mcallen
Hinojosa, Ricardo H. *federal judge*

Midland
Furgeson, William Royal *federal judge*

New Braunfels
Hathcock, J. Andrew *judge*
Zipp, Ronald Duane *judge, priest, real estate broker*

Richmond
Elliott, Brady Gifford *judge*

San Antonio
King, Ronald Baker *federal judge*

Sherman
Brown, Paul Neeley *federal judge*

Temple
Skelton, Byron George *federal judge*

Texarkana
Ross, Donald Rae *judge*

Tyler
Guthrie, Judith K. *federal judge*
Rogers, Randall Lee *judge*
Steger, William Merritt *federal judge*

Victoria
Rainey, John David *federal judge*

UTAH

Provo
Harding, Ray Murray, Jr., *judge*
Schofield, Anthony Wayne *judge*

Salt Lake City
Anderson, Stephen Hale *federal judge*
Clark, Glen Edward *judge*
Durham, Christine Meaders *state supreme court chief justice*
Durrant, Matthew B. *state supreme court justice*
Greene, John Thomas *judge*
Howe, Richard Cuddy *state supreme court justice*
Jenkins, Bruce Sterling *federal judge*
McKay, Monroe Gunn *federal judge*
Murphy, Michael R. *federal judge*
Russon, Leonard H. *state supreme court justice*
Sam, David *federal judge*
Wilkins, Michael Jon *state supreme court justice*

VERMONT

Brattleboro
Oakes, James L. *federal judge*

Montpelier
Dooley, John Augustine, III, *state supreme court justice*
Gibson, Ernest Willard, III, *retired state supreme court justice*
Johnson, Denise Reinka *state supreme court justice*
Skoglund, Marilyn *state supreme court justice*

Waterbury Center
Amestoy, Jeffrey Lee *state supreme court chief justice*

Woodstock
Billings, Franklin Swift, Jr., *federal judge*

VIRGINIA

Abingdon
Widener, Hiram Emory, Jr., *judge*
Williams, Glen Morgan *federal judge*

Alexandria
Kloch, John E. *judge, educator*

Annandale
Hollis, Daryl Joseph *judge*

Charlottesville
Crigler, B. Waugh *US magistrate judge*
Michael, James Harry, Jr., *federal judge*
Wilkinson, James Harvie, III, *federal judge*

Chesterfield
Davis, Bonnie Christell *judge*

Covington
Stephenson, Roscoe Bolar, Jr., *state supreme court justice*

Danville
Kiser, Jackson L. *federal judge*
Milam, Joseph Walton, Jr., *judge*

Fairfax
Williams, Marcus Doyle *judge*

Falls Church
Barton, Robert Leroy, Jr., *judge, educator*

Fredericksburg
Brown, Harold Eugene *retired magistrate*

King George
Revercomb, Horace Austin, III, *judge*

Lynchburg
Burnette, Ralph Edwin, Jr., *judge*

Mc Lean
Anthony, Joan Caton *administrative judge*

Norfolk
Adams, David Huntington *judge*
Bonney, Hal James, Jr., *federal judge*

Clarke, J. Calvitt, Jr., *federal judge*
Jackson, Raymond A. *federal judge*
Morgan, Henry Coke, Jr., *judge*
Prince, William Taliaferro *retired federal judge*
Thomas, Norman Allan *judge*

Pennington Gap
Sergent, Birg Eugene *judge*

Richmond
Agee, G. Steven *judge*
Butzner, John Decker, Jr., *retired federal judge*
Carrico, Harry Lee *retired judge*
Compton, Asbury Christian *state supreme court justice*
Hassell, Leroy Rountree, Sr., *state supreme court chief justice*
Kinser, Cynthia D. *state supreme court justice*
Lacy, Elizabeth Bermingham *state supreme court justice*
Lemons, Donald W. *state supreme court justice*
Poff, Richard Harding *retired state supreme court justice*
Russell, Charles Stevens *judge, educator*
Tice, Douglas Oscar, Jr., *federal bankruptcy judge*
Trabue, Kenneth Ellsworth *judge*
Williams, Richard Leroy *federal judge*

Roanoke
Turk, James Clinton *federal judge*

Salem
Koontz, Lawrence L., Jr., *state supreme court justice*
Pearson, Henry Clyde *judge*

Stuart
Clark, Martin F(illmore), Jr., *judge*

Virginia Beach
Keenan, Barbara Milano *judge*

WASHINGTON

Bellevue
Andersen, James A. *retired state supreme court justice*

Ephrata
Fitterer, Richard Clarence *judge*

Everett
Bowden, George Newton *judge*

Kent
McDermott, Richard Francis *judge*

Mercer Island
Noe, James Alva *retired judge*

Olympia
Alexander, Gerry L. *state supreme court chief justice*
Bridge, Bobbe J. *state supreme court justice*
Fairhurst, Mary E. *judge*
Ireland, Faith *state supreme court justice*
Johnson, Charles William *state supreme court justice*
Madsen, Barbara A *state supreme court justice*
Owens, Susan *state supreme court justice*
Sanders, Richard Browning *judge*
Smith, Charles Z. *retired state supreme court justice*

Seattle
Beezer, Robert Renaut *federal judge*
Bladen, Edwin Mark *lawyer, judge*
Dimmick, Carolyn Reaber *federal judge*
Farris, Jerome *federal judge*
Fletcher, Betty Binns *judge*
Mc Govern, Walter T. *federal judge*
Roberts, Mary Ellen *judge*
Rothstein, Barbara Jacobs *federal judge*
Tallman, Richard C. *federal judge, lawyer*
Wright, Eugene Allen *federal judge*
Zilly, Thomas Samuel *federal judge*

Spokane
Quackenbush, Justin Lowe *federal judge*

Tacoma
Bryan, Robert J. *federal judge*

Tukwila
Talmadge, Philip Albert *former state supreme court justice, former state senator*

Vancouver
Harris, Robert L(ee) *judge*

Yakima
McDonald, Alan Angus *federal judge*
Suko, Lonny Ray *judge*

WEST VIRGINIA

Beckley
Faber, David Alan *federal judge*

Charleston
Albright, Joseph P. *state supreme court justice*
Brewer, Lewis Gordon *judge, lawyer, educator*
Copenhaver, John Thomas, Jr., *federal judge*
Goodwin, Joseph R. *judge*
Haden, Charles Harold, II, *federal judge*
Hallanan, Elizabeth Virginia *federal judge*
King, Robert Bruce *federal judge*
Marland, Melissa Kaye *judge*
Maynard, Elliott *state supreme court justice*
McGraw, Warren Randolph *state supreme court justice*
Michael, M. Blane *federal judge*
Starcher, Larry Victor *state supreme court chief justice*

Elkins
Maxwell, Robert Earl *federal judge*

Sutton
Facemire, Richard Allen *judge*

Wayne
Pratt, Darrell *judge*

WISCONSIN

Madison
Abrahamson, Shirley Schlanger *state supreme court chief justice*
Bablitch, William A. *state supreme court justice*
Bradley, Ann Walsh *state supreme court justice*
Crabb, Barbara Brandriff *federal judge*
Crooks, N(eil) Patrick *state supreme court justice*
Heffernan, Nathan Stewart *retired state supreme court chief justice*
Martin, Robert David *judge, educator*
Prosser, David Thomas, Jr., *state supreme court justice, retired state legislator*
Shabaz, John C. *judge*
Sykes, Diane S. *state supreme court justice*
Wilcox, Jon P. *state supreme court justice*

Milwaukee
Shapiro, James Edward *judge*
Siefert, John *judge*
Stadtmueller, Joseph Peter *federal judge*

Superior
Lucci, Michael T. *judge*

Wauwatosa
Wall, Joseph R. *judge*

WYOMING

Casper
Downes, William F. *judge*

Cheyenne
Brimmer, Clarence Addison *federal judge*
Golden, T. Michael *state supreme court justice*
Hill, William U. *state supreme court chief justice*
Kite, Marilyn S. *state supreme court justice, lawyer*
Lehman, Larry L. *state supreme court justice*
O'Brien, Terrence Leo *federal judge*
Voigt, Barton R. *state supreme court justice*

Cody
Patrick, H. Hunter *judge*

TERRITORIES OF THE UNITED STATES

AMERICAN SAMOA

Pago Pago
Kruse, F. Michael *judge*
Richmond, Lyle L. *judge*

GUAM

Hagatna
Carbullido, F. Philip *judge*
Siguenza, Peter Charles, Jr., *territory supreme court justice*
Tydingco-Gatewood, Frances Marie *judge*
Unpingco, John Walter Sablan *federal judge*

NORTHERN MARIANA ISLANDS

Saipan
Castro, Alexandro C. *judge*
Demapan, Miguel S. *judge*
Manglona, John A. *judge*
Munson, Alex Robert *judge*

PUERTO RICO

San Juan
Acosta, Raymond Luis *federal judge*
Andreu-Garcia, Jose Antonio *territory supreme court chief justice*
Casellas, Salvador E. *judge*
Corrada del Rio, Baltasar *supreme court justice*
Fusté, José Antonio *federal judge*
Fuster, Jaime B. *supreme court justice*
Gierbolini-Ortiz, Gilberto *federal judge*
Hernandez-Denton, Federico *supreme court justice*
Merly, Miriam Naveira *state supreme court justice*
Negron-Garcia, Antonio S. *former territory supreme court justice*
Rebollo-Lopez, Francisco *judge*
Rivera Perez, Efrain E. *state supreme court justice*

VIRGIN ISLANDS

Charlotte Amalie
Barnard, Geoffrey W. *judge*

Christiansted
Finch, Raymond Lawrence *chief judge*
Resnick, Jeffrey Lance *federal magistrate judge*

St Thomas
Moore, Thomas Kail *district court judge*

CANADA

ONTARIO

Ottawa
Bastarache, Michel *judge*
Binnie, William Ian Cornell *judge*
Deschamps, Marie *judge*
LeBel, Louis *judge*

MEXICO

Mexico City
Aquirre Anguiano, Sergio Salvador *judge*
Azuela Guitron, Mariano *judge*
Castro y Castro, Juventino Victor *judge*
de Garcia Villegas, Olga Sanchez Cordero *judge*
Gudino Pelayo, Jose de Jesus *judge*
Ortiz Mayagoitia, Guillermo Iberion *judge*
Roman Palacios, Humberto *judge*
Romero, Juan Diaz *judge*
Silva Meza, Juan N. *judge*

GERMANY

Munich
Davies, Gillian *judge, writer, educator*

GREECE

Athens
Rigos, George *retired judge*

NETHERLANDS

The Hague
Allison, Richard Clark *judge*

SWEDEN

Stockholm
Sterzel, Fredrik Albert Christian *judge, researcher*

ADDRESS UNPUBLISHED

Albritton, William Harold, III, *federal judge*
Askey, William Hartman *US magistrate judge, lawyer*
Austin, John DeLong *judge*
Barliant, Ronald *federal judge*
Barrett, James Emmett *judge*
Bertelsman, William Odis *federal judge*
Boudreau, Daniel J. *state supreme court justice*
Brackett, Colquitt Prater, Jr., *judge, lawyer*
Brown, Robert Laidlaw *state supreme court justice*
Callow, William Grant *retired judge*
Campbell, Vincent Bernard *judge, lawyer*
Castagna, William John *federal judge*
Ceci, Louis J. *former state supreme court justice*
Cochran, George Moffett *retired judge*
Coffey, John Louis *judge*
Cohn, Avern Levin *district judge*
Compton, Allen T. *retired state supreme court justice*
Cook, Julian Abele, Jr., *federal judge*
Cyr, Conrad Keefe *federal judge*
Daugherty, Frederick Alvin *federal judge*
Davis, Marguerite Herr *judge*
Day, Roland Bernard *retired chief justice state supreme court*
Dela Cruz, Jose Santos *retired state supreme court justice*
Eaton, Joe Oscar *federal judge*
Edwards, Ninian Murry *judge*
Engel, Albert Joseph *retired federal judge*
Enoch, Craig Trively *state supreme court justice*
Fadeley, Edward Norman *retired state supreme court justice*
Fahrnbruch, Dale E. *retired state supreme court justice*
Flynn, Peter Anthony *judge*
Freeman, Charles E. *state supreme court justice*
Gardner, Anne Lancaster *judge*
Garibaldi, Marie Louise *former state supreme court justice*
Gillette, W. Michael *state supreme court justice*
Goetz, Clarence Edward *retired judge, retired chief magistrate judge*
Golden, Elliott *judge*
Goldstein, Samuel S. *judge*
Grant, Isabella Horton *retired judge*
Griffin, Robert Paul *former United States senator, state supreme court justice*
Hamblen, Lapsley Walker, Jr., *judge*
Harding, Major Best *former state supreme court chief justice*
Hawkins, Michael Daly *federal judge*
Hayek, Carolyn Jean *retired judge*
Heard, Wyatt H. *retired judge*
Hightower, Jack English *former state supreme court justice, congressman*
Howard, Alex T., Jr., *federal judge*
Howard, George, Jr., *federal judge*
Joiner, Charles Wycliffe *judge*
Kauger, Yvonne *state supreme court justice*
Kenney, James Albert, III, *judge*
Kenworthy, William Eugene *judge*
Kilbride, Thomas L. *judge*
Lancaster, Joan Ericksen *state supreme court justice*
Lee, Dan M. *retired state supreme court chief justice*
Lively, Pierce *federal judge*
Magnuson, Paul Arthur *federal judge*
Mahon, Eldon Brooks *former federal judge*
Mai, Harold Leverne *retired judge*
Matthews, Warren Wayne *state supreme court justice*
McClure, Ann Crawford *judge, lawyer*
McKee, Roger Curtis *retired federal judge*
Metzner, Charles Miller *federal judge*
Muecke, Charles Andrew (Carl Muecke) *former federal judge*
Murray, Florence Kerins *retired state supreme court justice*
Nangle, John Francis *federal judge*
Nesbit, Phyllis Schneider *judge*
Neuman, Linda Kinney *state supreme court justice*
Newbern, William David *retired state supreme court justice*
Newman, Theodore Roosevelt, Jr., *judge*
Porter, James Morris *retired judge*
Potter, Robert Daniel *federal judge*
Prather, Lenore Loving *former state supreme court chief justice*
Pusateri, James Anthony *judge*
Ramsey, Edward Lawrence *judge*
Reinhardt, Stephen Roy *federal judge*
Rice, Walter Herbert *federal judge*
Ross, Donald Roe *federal judge*
Roszkowski, Stanley Julian *retired federal judge*
Schroeder, Gerald Frank *state supreme court vice chief justice*
Schultz, Louis William *retired judge*
Shearing, Miriam *state supreme court justice*
Shubb, William Barnet *judge*
Silberman, Laurence Hirsch *federal judge*
Souter, David Hackett *United States supreme court justice*
Stahl, Madonna *retired judge*
Staker, Robert Jackson *judge*
Stanton, Louis Lee *federal judge*
Sweet, Robert Workman *federal judge*
Tacha, Deanell Reece *federal judge*
Trout, Linda Copple *state supreme court chief justice*
Utter, Robert French *retired judge*
Watson, Jack Crozier *retired state supreme court justice*
Wicker, Thomas Carey, Jr., *retired judge*
Williams, Spencer Mortimer *federal judge*
Wittig, Don *judge*
Wood, Diane Pamela *judge*

LIBRARY

UNITED STATES

ALABAMA

Birmingham
Feenker, Cherie Diane *law librarian*

Montgomery
Sinclair, Julie Moores Williams *lawyer, law library consultant*

ARIZONA

Phoenix
Schneider, Elizabeth Kelley *law librarian*

Tucson
Chiorazzi, Michael Gerard *law librarian, educator*

ARKANSAS

Little Rock
Fitzhugh, Kathryn Corrothers *law librarian*
Ligon, Stark *lawyer*

CALIFORNIA

Hacienda Heights
Pearson, David Brooksbank *lawyer, educator*

Los Angeles
Arouoff, Vera *law librarian*
Dryden, Mary Elizabeth *law librarian, writer, actress*
Gray, Randall Joshua *law librarian*
Iamele, Richard Thomas *law librarian*
Murray, Jennifer Sue *law librarian*
Raffalow, Janet Terry *law librarian*

Oakland
Stromme, Gary L. *law librarian*

Ontario
Dunn, Donald Jack *law librarian, law educator, dean, lawyer*

Sacramento
Welsh, Sue C. *law librarian*

San Diego
Dyer, Charles Richard *law librarian, law educator*

San Francisco
Futch, Dorothy Helen *librarian, paralegal*
Jones, Frances Mary *law librarian*

MEDIA

UNITED STATES

Rogers, Thomas Sydney *communications executive*

SOUTH CAROLINA

Ladys Island
Yates, Linda Snow *financial services marketing executive, real estate*

TEXAS

Jacksonville
Thrall, Gordon Fish *publishing executive*

San Antonio
Ellis, James D. *communications executive, corporate lawyer*

VIRGINIA

Charlottesville
Parrish, David Walker, Jr., *legal publishing company executive*

WISCONSIN

Madison
Drechsel, Robert Edward *journalism educator*

Milwaukee
Kritzer, Paul Eric *media executive, communications lawyer*

ADDRESS UNPUBLISHED

Quade, Vicki *editor, writer, playwright, producer*
Roberts, Delmar Lee *editor*

OTHER

UNITED STATES

ALABAMA

Auburn
Samford, Thomas Drake, III, *lawyer*

Birmingham
Farley, Joseph McConnell *lawyer*
Goodrich, Thomas Michael *engineering and construction executive, lawyer*
Johnson, Joseph H., Jr., *lawyer*
Mc Millan, George Duncan Hastie, Jr., *lawyer, former state official*

Lillian
Ray, Betty Jean G. *retired lawyer*

ALASKA

Anchorage
Hayes, George Nicholas *lawyer*

ARIZONA

Paradise Valley
Lisa, Isabelle O'Neill *law firm administrator, mergers and acquisitions executive*

Peoria
Engelhardt, Thomas Francis *lawyer, consultant*

Phoenix
Breecher-Breen, Sheila Rae *lawyer*
Griller, Gordon Moore *court administrator*
Hurtt, Harold L. *protective services official*

Tempe
Bender, Paul *lawyer, educator*

Tucson
Gantz, David Alfred *lawyer, university official*
Ruth, Henry Swartley *retired lawyer*

ARKANSAS

Apo
Gordon, Carey Nathaniel *lawyer, federal agency administrator*

Little Rock
Fogleman, John Albert *lawyer, retired judge*

CALIFORNIA

Atherton
Davidson, Duncan Mowbray *lawyer, management consultant, entrepreneur*

Berkeley
Harris, Michael Gene *optometrist, educator, lawyer*

Beverly Hills
Holmes, Henry W. *lawyer*

Costa Mesa
Caldwell, Courtney Lynn *lawyer, real estate consultant*
Jones, H(arold) Gilbert, Jr., *lawyer*

Fallbrook
Sorbello, Joseph Charles *retired lawyer*

Fresno
Howe, Ronald Evans *lawyer, minister, small business owner*

Fullerton
Goldstein, Edward David *lawyer, former glass company executive*
Steinmeyer, Robert Jay *lawyer*

Huntington Beach
Jensen, Dennis Lowell *lawyer*

Irvine
Hancock, S. Lee *business executive*
Hilker, Walter Robert, Jr., *lawyer*

Lafayette
Davies, Paul Lewis, Jr., *retired lawyer*

Los Angeles
Christol, Carl Q(uimby) *lawyer, political science educator*
Collier, Charles Arthur, Jr., *lawyer*
Irwin, Philip Donnan *lawyer*
Kundinger, Mathew Hermann *lawyer, engineer, author, entrepreneur*
Lappen, Timothy *lawyer, investor*
Levine, Meldon Edises *lawyer, former congressman*
Lindholm, Dwight Henry *lawyer*
Neumeyer, Richard Albert *lawyer*
O'Connell, Kevin *lawyer*
Peck, Austin H., Jr., *lawyer*
Pollock, John Phleger *lawyer*
Ray, Gilbert T. *lawyer*
Stamm, Alan *lawyer*
Welborne, John Howard *railway company executive, lawyer*

Marina Del Rey
Annotico, Richard Anthony *legal administrator, real estate investor*

Mission Viejo
Ruben, Robert Joseph *lawyer*

Modesto
Murphy, John Thomas *lawyer*

Newport Beach
Lawless, William Burns *lawyer, retired judge, academic administrator*
Wagner, John Leo *lawyer, former magistrate judge*

North Fork
Flanagan, James Henry, Jr., *lawyer, writer, business educator*

Pacific Palisades
Verrone, Patric Miller *lawyer, writer*

Palm Springs
Kimberling, John Farrell *retired lawyer*

Palo Alto
Casillas, Mark *lawyer*

Pasadena
Wyatt, Joseph Lucian, Jr., *lawyer, writer*

Pebble Beach
Robinson, William Adams *lawyer*

Rancho Mirage
Reuben, Don Harold *lawyer*

Riverside
Sklar, Wilford Nathaniel *retired lawyer, real estate broker*

Sacramento
Root, Gerald Edward *legal administrator*

San Bernardino
Eskin, Barry Sanford *court investigator*

San Diego
Bejarano, David *protective services official*

San Francisco
Bertram, Manya M. *retired lawyer*
Coleman, Thomas Young *lawyer*
Sutton, John Paul *lawyer*
Yin, Dominic David *police officer, educator, lawyer*
Ziegler, R. W., Jr., *lawyer, consultant*

San Jose
Chandler, Mark *telecommunications industry executive*
Terry, Michael Joseph *legal process supervisor, court trainer*

Santa Ana
Dillard, John Martin *lawyer, pilot*

Sausalito
Berkman, William Roger *lawyer, army reserve officer*

Sherman Oaks
Crump, Gerald Franklin *retired lawyer*

Stanford
Grossman, Claudio M. *lawyer*

Tustin
Kraft, Henry Robert *lawyer*

West Covina
McHale, Edward Robertson *retired lawyer*

Westlake Village
Pardau, Stuart Lloyd *market research company executive, lawyer, educator*

COLORADO

Boulder
Moses, Raphael Jacob *lawyer*
Walker, Graham Richard *international legal consultant*

Breckenridge
Weaver, Judith Ann *lawyer*

Canon City
Fredrickson, Bryan Timothy *lawyer*

Denver
Burford, Anne McGill *lawyer*
Burkhardt, Donald Malcolm *lawyer*
Faxon, Thomas Baker *retired lawyer*
Keatinge, Robert Reed *lawyer*
Martz, Clyde Ollen *lawyer, educator*
Seawell, Donald Ray *lawyer, publisher, arts center executive, producer*
Wunnicke, Brooke *lawyer*

Englewood
Grant, Paul *chemical engineer, manufacturer's representative, real estate broker*

Littleton
Meyer, Milton Edward, Jr., *lawyer, artist*

Lone Tree
Spelts, Richard John *lawyer*

CONNECTICUT

Greenwich
Cantor, Samuel C. *lawyer, company executive*
McDonald, Paul Kimball *lawyer, investment executive*

Hamden
Greenblatt, Morton Harold *retired assistant attorney general*

Hartford
Cain, George Harvey *lawyer, business executive*
Cullina, William Michael *lawyer*
Pinney, Sidney Dillingham, Jr., *lawyer*

Lakeville
Jones, Ronald David *lawyer*

New Canaan
Coughlin, Francis Raymond, Jr., *surgeon, educator, lawyer*

New Haven
Gewirtz, Paul D. *lawyer, legal educator*

Norfolk
Jessup, Philip Caryl, Jr.,

Redding
Gooch, Anthony Cushing *lawyer*

Stamford
Bowen, Patrick Harvey *lawyer, consultant*
Della Rocco, Kenneth Anthony *lawyer*
Perle, Eugene Gabriel *lawyer*

Stonington
Van Rees, Cornelius S. *lawyer*

Weston
Aibel, Howard J. *lawyer, arbitrator, mediator*

DELAWARE

Wilmington
Mullen, Regina Marie *lawyer*

DISTRICT OF COLUMBIA

Washington
Augustyn, Noel James *lawyer*
Bauleke, Howard Paul *lawyer*
Blair, William McCormick, Jr., *lawyer*
Branfman, Eric Jay *lawyer*
Brown, Charles Freeman, II, *lawyer*
Cobbs, Louise Bertram *lawyer*
Cohrssen, John Joseph *lawyer, consultant*
Condrell, William Kenneth *lawyer*
Eghbal, Morad *geologist, lawyer*
Flood, John Joseph *lawyer*
Fowler, Paul Raymond *physician, lawyer*
Frank, Richard Asher *lawyer, health products executive*
Ginsburg, Martin David *lawyer, educator*
Glitzenstein, Eric Robert *lawyer*
Greif, Joseph *lawyer*
Husband, Phillip Lyle *lawyer*
Jackson, John Howard *lawyer, educator*
Kahn, Edwin Leonard *lawyer*
Kimmitt, Robert Michael *executive, banker, diplomat, lawyer*
Lehr, Dennis James *lawyer*
Loevinger, Lee *lawyer, science writer*
Maechling, Charles, Jr., *lawyer, diplomat, educator, writer*
Marinaccio, Charles Lindbergh *lawyer, consultant*
Martin, Guy *lawyer*
McLean, Christopher Anthony *lawyer, former government official*
Medalie, Richard James *lawyer*
Mishkin, Barbara Friedman *lawyer*
Monk, Carl Colburn *lawyer, academic administrator*
Pedersen, William Francis *lawyer*
Pickering, John Harold *lawyer*
Poneman, Daniel Bruce *lawyer*
Potts, Ramsay Douglas *lawyer, aviator*
Schmidt, Richard Marten, Jr., *lawyer*
Sterrett, Samuel Black *lawyer, former judge*
Strauss, Stanley Robert *lawyer*
Verner, James Melton *lawyer*
Whiting, Richard Albert *lawyer*
Zimmer, Richard Alan *lawyer, former congressman*

FLORIDA

Boca Raton
Garlick, Michael *lawyer*

Boynton Beach
Babler, Wayne E. *lawyer, retired telephone company executive*

Bradenton
Thomas, Ella Cooper *lawyer*

Cocoa Beach
Burch, William Mark, II, *retired lawyer*

Coral Gables
Ely, John Hart *lawyer, university dean*
Moss, Ambler Holmes, Jr., *lawyer, former ambassador*
O'Donnell, Anthony Joseph, Jr., *lawyer, educator*
Simpson, Russell Gordon *lawyer, former mayor, not-for-profit developer, consultant*

Deerfield Beach
Caso, Dawn Marie *lawyer, consultant, law educator*

Delray Beach
Armstrong, Jack Gilliland *lawyer*
Larry, R. Heath *lawyer, director*

Fort Lauderdale
Di Giulian, Bruno L. *lawyer*

Fort Myers
Consilio, Barbara Ann *legal administrator, management consultant*
Morse, John Harleigh *lawyer, director*

Gainesville
Kaimowitz, Gabe Hillel *lawyer*

Jacksonville
Crawford, John Richard *lawyer*
Criser, Marshall M. *lawyer, retired university president*

Key West
Eden, Nathan E. *lawyer*

Lecanto
Fischer, Theodore David *retired lawyer*

Leesburg
Fechtel, Vincent John *legal administrator*

Longboat Key
Freeman, Richard Merrell *lawyer, corporate director*

Naples
Norton, Elizabeth Wychgel *lawyer*
Putzell, Edwin Joseph, Jr., *lawyer, mayor*

Palm Beach
Rauch, George Washington *lawyer, director*

Panama City Beach
Patterson, Christopher Nida *lawyer*

Pensacola
Jespersen, Robert Randolph *legal consultant*

Pompano Beach
Szilassy, Sandor *retired lawyer, library director, educator*

Saint Petersburg
Harrell, Roy G., Jr., *lawyer*

Sarasota
Heitler, George *lawyer*
Hull, J(ames) Richard *retired lawyer, business executive*
Kimbrough, Robert Averyt *lawyer*
Wadsworth, Dyer Seymour *retired lawyer*

Sun City Center
Fuller, Samuel Ashby *lawyer, mining company executive*

Tallahassee
Holcomb, Lyle Donald, Jr., *retired lawyer*

Tampa
Carlucci, Paul Pasquale *lawyer*
Kelly, Thomas Paine, Jr., *lawyer*
Scaglione, Cynthia M. *lawyer, consultant*

Vero Beach
Parlin, Charles C., Jr., *retired lawyer*

GEORGIA

Athens
Chaffin, Verner Franklin *lawyer, educator*

Yale-Loehr, Stephen William *lawyer, editor*

Jamaica
Hall, Michael *disability processing specialist*

Jamesville
DeCrow, Karen *lawyer, author, lecturer*

Long Beach
Levine, Samuel Milton *lawyer, retired judge, mediator, arbitrator*

Melville
Fine, Barry Kenneth *lawyer*

Mineola
Taub, Stephen Richard *lawyer*

New Rochelle
Gunning, Francis Patrick *lawyer, insurance association executive*

New York
Ames, John Lewis *lawyer*
Anthoine, Robert *lawyer, educator*
Arther, Richard Oberlin *polygraphist, educator*
Berkowsky, Peter Arthur *lawyer, retired military officer*
Boros, Jerome S. *lawyer*
Borsody, Robert Peter *lawyer*
Brown, Ralph Sawyer, Jr., *retired lawyer, business executive*
Conston, Henry Siegismund *lawyer*
Costikyan, Edward N. *lawyer*
Crowell, Kenneth E. *lawyer, chemical engineer*
Cucin, Robert Louis *plastic surgeon, lawyer*
Darrell, Norris, Jr., *lawyer*
Dunham, Corydon Bushell *lawyer, broadcasting executive*
Eakins, William Shannon *lawyer*
Esposito, Joseph J. *protective services official*
Farber, Donald Clifford *lawyer, educator*
Fishman, Fred Norman *lawyer*
Flint, George Squire *lawyer*
Freund, Fred A. *retired lawyer*
Goetz, Maurice Harold *lawyer*
Goodfriend, Herbert Jay *lawyer*
Grant, Paula DiMeo *lawyer, nursing educator, mediator*
Greenbaum, Maurice Coleman *lawyer*
Hoblin, Philip J., Jr., *securities lawyer*
Holtzman, Elizabeth *lawyer*
Hull, Philip Glasgow *lawyer*
Hyman, Jerome Elliot *lawyer*
Kaplan, Madeline *legal administrator*
Katsoris, Constantine Nicholas *lawyer, consultant*
Kilbourn, Joseph A. *lawyer*
Kleckner, Robert George, Jr., *lawyer*
Lahoud, Nina Joseph *lawyer, international organization assistant*
Lazerus, Gilbert *lawyer*
Leitner, Anthony Joseph *lawyer*
Lindenbaum, Samuel Harvey *lawyer*
Mahon, Arthur J. *lawyer*
Maneker, Morton M. *lawyer*
Mathers, William Harris *lawyer*
McHenry, Barnabas *lawyer*
McNally, John Joseph *retired lawyer*
Merow, John *lawyer*
Montellaro, Randell *lawyer*
Morris, Eugene Jerome *retired lawyer*
Mosenson, Steven Harris *lawyer*
Nimkin, Bernard William *retired lawyer*
Peterson, Charles Gordon *retired lawyer*
Richman, Martin Franklin *lawyer*
Roberts, Burton Bennett *lawyer, retired judge*
Ross, Matthew *lawyer*
Schmertz, Eric Joseph *lawyer, educator*
Schwartz, Marvin *lawyer*
Shientag, Florence Perlow *lawyer*
Sidamon-Eristoff, Constantine *lawyer*
Sinsheimer, Warren Jack *lawyer*
Stevenson, Douglas Bruce *lawyer*
Stratton, Walter Love *lawyer*
Taylor, John Chestnut, III, *lawyer*
Terry, Frederick Arthur, Jr., *lawyer*
Wallace, Walter C. *lawyer, government official*
Watson, Kipp Elliott *lawyer*
Wilcox, John Caven *lawyer, corporate consultant*
Williamson, Douglas Franklin, Jr., *lawyer*
Winger, Ralph O. *lawyer*
Winterer, Philip Steele *lawyer*
Zukerman, Michael *lawyer*

Rochester
McCrory, John Brooks *retired lawyer*
Swett, Albert Hersey *retired lawyer, business executive, consultant*

Sands Point
Busner, Philip H. *retired lawyer*

Scarsdale
Callaghan, Georgann Mary *lawyer*
Macchia, Vincent Michael *lawyer*
O'Brien, Edward Ignatius *private investor, corporation director*

Schenectady
Levine, Sanford Harold *lawyer*

Smithtown
Goodman, Richard Shalem *lawyer, orthopedic surgeon*

Syracuse
Day, Christian C. *lawyer, educator*
Hayes, David Michael *lawyer*

Valley Stream
Blakeman, Royal Edwin *lawyer*

Walden
Starkman, Mark T. *lawyer, health care consultant*

Woodmere
Jeffries, Seymour Barnard *lawyer*

NORTH CAROLINA

Chapel Hill
Broun, Kenneth Stanley *lawyer, educator*
Brower, David John *lawyer, urban planner, educator*
Gressman, Eugene *lawyer*

Charlotte
Chambers, Julius LeVonne *lawyer*
Dagenhart, Larry Jones *lawyer*
Van Allen, William Kent *lawyer*
Woolard, William Leon *lawyer, electrical distributing company executive*

Davidson
Carroll, W. Donald, Jr., *lawyer, consultant*

Durham
Horowitz, Donald Leonard *lawyer, educator, researcher, political scientist, arbitrator*

Raleigh
Davis, Egbert Lawrence, III, *lawyer*
Graham, William Edgar, Jr., *lawyer, retired utility company executive*
Kurz, Mary Elizabeth *lawyer*
Roach, Wesley Linville *lawyer, insurance executive*

Rocky Mount
Zipf, Robert Eugene, Jr., *legal medicine consultant, pathologist*

NORTH DAKOTA

Bismarck
Nelson, Keithe Eugene *state court administrator, lawyer*

Grand Forks
Vogel, Robert *retired lawyer, educator*

OHIO

Ada
Streib, Victor Lee *dean*

Beachwood
Lewis, Cherie Sue *lawyer, English language and journalism educator*

Cincinnati
Bruvold, Kathleen Parker *lawyer*
Kordons, Uldis *lawyer*
McClain, William Andrew *lawyer*

Cleveland
Austin, Arthur Donald, II, *lawyer, educator*
Schatz, William Bonsall *lawyer*

Cleveland Heights
Gutfeld, Norman E. *lawyer*

Columbus
Federle, Katherine Hunt *lawyer*
Greek, Darold I. *lawyer*
Hill, Kathleen Blickenstaff *lawyer, mental health nurse, nursing educator*
Jackson, James G. *protective services official*
Kilgore, Terry Lee *lawyer*
McConnaughey, George Carlton, Jr., *retired lawyer*
McCutchan, Gordon Eugene *retired lawyer, insurance company executive*
Vorys, Arthur Isaiah *lawyer*

Cuyahoga Falls
Kreiner, Margaret Helen *sales/marketing executive*

Dayton
Rapp, Gerald Duane *lawyer, manufacturing company executive*

Gambier
Leech, Charles Russell, Jr., *lawyer*

Maumee
McBride, Beverly Jean *lawyer*

Mechanicsburg
Saxbe, William Bart *lawyer, former government official*

Miamisburg
Andreozzi, Louis Joseph *lawyer*

Shaker Heights
Donnem, Roland William *retired lawyer, real estate owner, developer*

Toledo
Boggs, Ralph Stuart *retired lawyer*

Troy
Bazler, Frank Ellis *retired lawyer*

OKLAHOMA

Oklahoma City
Allen, Robert Dee *lawyer*
Busey, Phil Gordon *lawyer*
Davenport, Gerald Bruce *lawyer*
Hemry, Jerome Eldon *lawyer*
Walsh, Lawrence Edward *lawyer*
Wheeler, Albert Lee, III, *lawyer, legal consultant*
Zevnik-Sawatzky, Donna Dee *retired litigation coordinator, art gallery owner*

Tulsa
Bereolos, Demetrius Theodore *lawyer*

OREGON

Astoria
Haskell, Donald McMillan *lawyer*

Eugene
Etter, Orval

Portland
Backlar, Byron *lawyer*
Lavigne, Peter Marshall *environmentalist, lawyer, educator*
Lezak, Sidney Irving *lawyer, mediator*

PENNSYLVANIA

Bethlehem
Styer, Jane M. *computer consultant*

Carlisle
Strong, Sara Dougherty *psychologist, marriage and family therapist, mediator*

Cecil
Keddie, Roland Thomas *physician, hospital administrator, lawyer*

Lake Harmony
Polansky, Larry Paul *court administrator, consultant*

Philadelphia
Cappella, Elena A. *lawyer, legal association administrator*
Coyne, Charles Cole *lawyer*
Johnson, Sylvester *protective services official*
Kemler, R(obert) Michael *lawyer*
Moss, Arthur Henshey *lawyer*
Nocella, Richard J. *lawyer*
Nofer, George Hancock *lawyer*
Reiter, Joseph Henry *lawyer, retired judge*
Rhodes, Alice Graham *lawyer*
Spaeth, Edmund Benjamin, Jr., *retired lawyer, retired law educator, former judge*
Warner, Theodore Kugler, Jr., *lawyer*
Wolf, Robert B. *lawyer*

Pipersville
Sigety, Charles Edward *lawyer, family business consultant*

Pittsburgh
Brand, Ronald Alvah *lawyer*
Hill, John Howard *lawyer*
McCartney, Robert Charles *retired lawyer*
Randolph, Robert DeWitt *lawyer*

Solebury
Cross, Robert William *lawyer, venture capital executive*

Springfield
Maclay, Donald Merle *retired lawyer*

Wayne
Wilson, Bruce Brighton *retired transportation executive, lawyer*

Wilkes Barre
Morgan, Dennis Keith *lawyer*

RHODE ISLAND

Little Compton
Caron, Wilfred Rene *retired lawyer*

Providence
Fogarty, Edward Michael *lawyer*
Kean, John Vaughan *retired lawyer*
Kersh, DeWitte Talmadge, Jr., *lawyer*
Long, Beverly Glenn *retired lawyer*

Wakefield
Rothschild, Donald Phillip *lawyer, arbitrator*

Westerly
Matarese, Lauren A. *police officer, lawyer*

SOUTH CAROLINA

Clemson
Cox, Headley Morris, Jr., *lawyer, educator*

Columbia
Day, Richard Earl *lawyer, educator*

Spartanburg
Wise, Steven Lanier *lawyer, clergyman*

SOUTH DAKOTA

Pierre
Johnson, Julie Marie *lawyer, lobbyist*

Sioux Falls
Haas, Joseph Alan *court administrator, lawyer*

TENNESSEE

Brentwood
Brown, Bobby Wayne *lawyer, educator, accountant*

Collierville
Springfield, James Francis *retired lawyer, banker*

Nashville
Conner, Lewis Homer, Jr., *lawyer*
Madu, Leonard Ekwugha *lawyer, human rights officer, newspaper columnist, politician, business executive*

TEXAS

Abilene
Wilson, Stanley Patterson *retired lawyer*

Austin
Dougherty, John Chrysostom, III, *retired lawyer*
Schwartz, Aaron Robert *lawyer, former state legislator*
Stephen, John Erle *lawyer, consultant*

Carrollton
Riggs, Arthur Jordy *retired lawyer*

Dallas
Bolton, Terrell *protective services official*
Burke, William Temple, Jr., *lawyer*
Kinnebrew, Jackson Metcalfe *lawyer*
Thomson, Basil Henry, Jr., *lawyer, university general counsel*

Fort Worth
Quinn, Francis Xavier *arbitrator, mediator, author, lecturer*

Fredericksburg
Benedict, Mark J. *government analyst, marketing executive, lawyer, real estate investment consultant*

Heath
Kolodey, Fred James *lawyer*

Highland Village
Lawrence, William Clarence *business executive, lawyer, mediator, politician*

Houston
Anderson, Thomas Dunaway *retired lawyer*
Caddy, Michael Douglas *lawyer*
Couch, J. O. Terrell *lawyer, former oil company executive*
Farenthold, Frances Tarlton *lawyer*
Heinrich, Randall Wayne *lawyer*
Sales, James Bohus *lawyer*

Huntsville
Stowe, Charles Robinson Beecher *management consultant, educator, lawyer*

Richardson
Sowers, Wesley Hoyt *lawyer, management consultant*

San Antonio
Liesenfeld, Vincent Joseph *lawyer*
Ortiz, Albert *protective services official*

Wimberley
Brinsmade, Lyon Louis *retired lawyer*

UTAH

North Salt Lake
Barden, Robert Christopher *lawyer, psychologist, educator, legislative analyst, speaker, writer*

Salt Lake City
Kimball, Spencer Levan *lawyer, educator*
Roberts, Jack Earl *lawyer, ski resort operator, wood products company executive, real estate developer*

VERMONT

Burlington
Dinse, John Merrell *lawyer*
Wick, Hilton Addison *lawyer*

Montpelier
Guild, Alden *retired lawyer*

Shelburne
Canfield, Andrew Trotter *lawyer, writer*

VIRGINIA

Abingdon
Taylor, Janet Droke *legal secretary*

Alexandria
Hawkins, Edward J. *retired lawyer*
Huckabee, Harlow Maxwell *lawyer, writer*
Kopp, Eugene Paul *lawyer*
Montague, Robert Latane, III, *lawyer*
Pyle, Howard *lawyer, consultant*
Sturtevant, Brereton *retired lawyer, former government official*
Walkup, Charlotte Lloyd *lawyer*

Arlington
Drayton, William *social entrepreneur, lawyer, management consultant*
Hansen, Kenneth D. *lawyer, ophthalmologist*
Metz, Craig Huseman *business executive*

Buckingham
Kensington, Andrew Justus *litigation consultant, practitioner, property manager, small business owner*

Segel, Karen Lynn Joseph *lawyer, taxation specialist*
Shapiro, Sander Wolf *retired lawyer*
Sheldon, Terry Edwin *lawyer, business consultant, advisor*
Smith, Carole Dianne *retired lawyer, editor, writer, product developer*
Smith, Edward Reaugh *retired lawyer, retired funeral director, consultant*
Strutin, Kennard Regan *lawyer, educator, legal information consultant*
Thomajan, Robert *lawyer, management consultant*
Voorhees, James Dayton, Jr., *lawyer*
Walker, Richard Henry *lawyer*
Weston, Michael C. *retired lawyer*
Zagorin, Janet Susan *legal firm administrator, marketing professional*

PARAPROFESSIONAL

UNITED STATES

CALIFORNIA

Long Beach
Boccia Rosado, Ann Marie *paralegal*

Los Angeles
Arbit, Beryl Ellen *legal assistant*
Arnkra, Joe *legal administrator, writer*
Wilson, Mable Jean *paralegal*

Sacramento
Willis, Dawn Louise *legal assistant, small business owner*

COLORADO

Boulder
LaVelle, Betty Sullivan Dougherty *legal professional*

DISTRICT OF COLUMBIA

Washington
Townsend, Brian Douglas *paralegal*

GEORGIA

Atlanta
Banks, Linda T. *legal assistant, massage therapist*

ILLINOIS

East Alton
Clark, Mark Jeffrey *paralegal, researcher*

INDIANA

Highland
Forsythe, Randall Newman *paralegal, educator*

Indianapolis
Kennedy, Emily Kathryn *paralegal*

KANSAS

Leawood
Johnston, Jocelyn Stanwell *paralegal*

LOUISIANA

Baton Rouge
Rasmussen, Ann C. *paralegal*

MISSOURI

Union
Schmelz, Brenda Lea *legal assistant*

MONTANA

Great Falls
Speer, John Elmer *paralegal, reporter, counselor*

NEW YORK

Garden City
Caputo, Kathryn Mary *paralegal*

Syracuse
Gilman, Karen Frenzel *legal assistant*

OHIO

Cleveland
Foster, Dennis James *legal recruiting services executive*

Columbus
Larzelere, Kathy Lynn Heckler *paralegal*

OKLAHOMA

Oklahoma City
Brooks, Norma Newton *legal assistant*

PENNSYLVANIA

Hershey
Kaylor, Gay L. *paralegal, food company administrator*

Pittsburgh
Chipman, Debra Decker *paralegal*

SOUTH CAROLINA

Columbia
Wilson, Karen Wilkerson *paralegal*

Johns Island
Carter, Mary Andrews *paralegal*

TENNESSEE

Knoxville
Davidson, Whitney L. *paralegal*

TEXAS

Dallas
Flood, Joan Moore *paralegal*

Grand Prairie
Avery, Reigh Kessen *legal assistant*

San Antonio
Schuk, Linda Lee *legal assistant, business educator*

UTAH

Manti
Petersen, Benton Lauritz *paralegal*

WASHINGTON

Seattle
Tessier, Dennis Medward *paralegal, lecturer, legal advisor, consultant, cartoonist*

WEST VIRGINIA

Wellsburg
Viderman, Linda Jean *paralegal, corporate executive*

WISCONSIN

Madison
Barnick, Helen *retired judicial clerk*

Ripon
Prissel, Barbara Ann *paralegal, law educator*

ITALY

Milan
Todică, Bianca Nicoleta *legal assistant*

ADDRESS UNPUBLISHED

Edwards, Priscilla Ann *paralegal, business owner*
Hulzebos, Leah Katherine *paralegal*
Rowe, Audrey *paralegal*
Rubinstein, Esta *paralegal*